Abby Tew

The Longman Anthology of World Literature

COMPACT EDITION

David Damrosch
COLUMBIA UNIVERSITY
The Ancient Near East; Mesoamerica

David L. Pike
AMERICAN UNIVERSITY
Rome and the Roman Empire; Medieval Europe

April Alliston
PRINCETON UNIVERSITY
The Age of the Enlightenment

Marshall Brown
UNIVERSITY OF WASHINGTON
The Nineteenth Century

Page duBois
UNIVERSITY OF CALIFORNIA, SAN DIEGO
Classical Greece

Sabry Hafez
UNIVERSITY OF LONDON
Arabic and Islamic Literatures

Ursula K. Heise
STANFORD UNIVERSITY
The Twentieth Century

Djelal Kadir
PENNSYLVANIA STATE UNIVERSITY
The Twentieth Century

Sheldon Pollock
UNIVERSITY OF CHICAGO
South Asia

Bruce Robbins
COLUMBIA UNIVERSITY
The Nineteenth Century

Haruo Shirane
COLUMBIA UNIVERSITY
Japan

Jane Tylus
NEW YORK UNIVERSITY
Early Modern Europe

Pauline Yu
AMERICAN COUNCIL OF LEARNED SOCIETIES
China

The Longman Anthology of World Literature

David Damrosch

David L. Pike

General Editors

COMPACT EDITION

New York San Francisco Boston
London Toronto Sydney Tokyo Singapore Madrid
Mexico City Munich Paris Cape Town Hong Kong Montreal

Editor-in-Chief: *Joseph Terry*
Director of Development: *Mary Ellen Curley*
Senior Development Editor: *Mikola De Roo*
Marketing Manager: *Ann Stypuloski*
Senior Supplements Editor: *Donna Campion*
Media Supplements Editor: *Jenna Egan*
Production Manager: *Denise Phillip*
Project Coordination, Text Design, and Page Makeup: *GGS Book Services*
Senior Design Manager/Cover Designer: *Nancy Danahy*
On the Cover: Seventeenth century world map by Henricus Hondius. Digital Vision/Getty Images
Photo Research: *Photosearch, Inc.*
Manufacturing Buyer: *Lucy Hebard*
Printer and Binder: RR Donnelley Crawfordsville, In
Cover Printer: *The Lehigh Press, Inc.*

For permission to use copyrighted material, grateful acknowledgment is made to the copyright holders on pages 2863–2870, which are hereby made part of this copyright page.

Library of Congress Cataloging-in-Publication Data

The Longman anthology of world literature / David Damrosch, David L. Pike.— Compact ed.
p. cm.
Includes bibliographical references and index.
ISBN 0-321-43690-3
1. Literature—Collections. 2. Literature—History and criticism.
I. Damrosch, David. II. Pike, David L. (David Lawrence), 1963-
PN6013.L66 2007
808.8—dc22

Visit us at www.ablongman.com/damrosch.

ISBN–13:978-0-321-43690-0
ISBN–10: 0-321-43690-3

8 9 10 11 12 13—DOC—16 15 14 13

CONTENTS

PERSPECTIVES

PERSPECTIVES

LIST OF ILLUSTRATIONS

Color Plates ***following page 14***

Black-and-White Images

Maps

PREFACE

Our world today is both expanding and growing smaller at the same time. Expanding, through a tremendous increase in the range of cultures that actively engage with each other; and yet growing smaller as well, as people and products surge across borders in the process known as globalization. This double movement creates remarkable opportunities for cross-cultural understanding, as well as new kinds of tensions, miscommunications, and uncertainties. Both the opportunities and the uncertainties are amply illustrated in the changing shape of world literature. A generation ago, when the term "world literature" was used in North America, it largely meant masterworks by European writers from Homer onward, together with a few favored North American writers, heirs to the Europeans. Today, however, it is generally recognized that Europe is only part of the story of the world's literatures, and only part of the story of North America's cultural heritage. An extraordinary range of exciting material is now in view, from the earliest Sumerian lyrics inscribed on clay tablets to the latest Kashmiri poetry circulated on the Internet. Many new worlds—and newly visible *older* worlds of classical traditions around the globe—await us today.

How can we best approach such varied materials from so many cultures? Can we deal with this embarrassment of riches without being overwhelmed by it, and without merely giving a glancing regard to less familiar traditions? This anthology has been designed to help readers successfully navigate "the sea of stories"—as Salman Rushdie has described the world's literary heritage. This preface will outline the ways we've gone about this challenging, fascinating task.

CONNECTING DISTINCTIVE TRADITIONS

Works of world literature engage in a double conversation: with their culture of origin and with the varied contexts into which they travel away from home. To look broadly at world literature is therefore to see patterns of difference as well as points of contact and commonality. The world's disparate traditions have developed very distinct kinds of literature, even very different ideas as to what should be called "literature" at all. This anthology uses a variety of means to showcase what is most distinctive and also what is commonly shared among the world's literatures. Throughout the anthology, we employ two kinds of grouping:

☞ **PERSPECTIVES: Groupings that provide cultural context for major works, illuminating issues of broad importance.**

☞ **RESONANCES: Sources for a specific text or responses to it, often from a different time and place.**

Throughout the anthology, our many "Perspectives" sections provide cultural context for the major works around them, giving insight into such issues as the representation of death and immortality in the ancient Near East; the meeting of

Christians, Muslims, and Jews in medieval Iberia; the idea of Romantic nature in the nineteenth century; and postcolonial conditions in the twentieth. Perspectives sections give a range of voices and views, strategies and styles, in highly readable textual groupings. The Perspectives groupings serve a major pedagogical as well as intellectual purpose in making these selections accessible and useful within the time constraints of a survey course.

Our "Resonances" perform the crucial function of linking works across time as well as space. For Homer's *Odyssey* we have Resonances giving modern responses to Homer by Franz Kafka, Derek Walcott, and the Greek poet George Seferis. Accompanying Dostoevsky's *Notes from Underground* are texts showing influence on the German philosopher, Friedrich Nietzsche, and the Japanese diarist, Ishikawa Takuboku. Resonances for Conrad's *Heart of Darkness* give selections from Conrad's diary of his own journey upriver in the Congo and a speech by Henry Morton Stanley, the explorer-journalist who was serving as publicist for King Leopold's exploitation of his colony in the years just before Conrad went there. Stanley's surreal speech—in which he calculates how much money the Manchester weavers can make providing wedding dresses and burial clothes for the Congolese—gives a vivid instance of the outlook, and the rhetoric, that Conrad grimly parodies in Mr. Kurtz and his associates.

Principles of Selection

Beyond our immediate groupings, our overall selections have been made with an eye to fostering connections across time and space. We have worked to create an exceptionally coherent and well-integrated presentation of an extraordinary variety of works from around the globe, from the dawn of writing to the present. Recognizing that different sorts of works have counted as literature in differing times and places, we have taken an inclusive approach, centering on poems, plays, and fictional narratives but also including selections from rich historical, religious, and philosophical texts like Plato's *Republic* and the Qur'an that have been important for much later literary work, even though they weren't conceived as literature themselves. We present many complete masterworks, including *The Epic of Gilgamesh* (in a beautiful verse translation), Homer's *Odyssey,* Dante's *Inferno,* and Chinua Achebe's *Things Fall Apart,* and we have extensive, teachable selections from such long works as *The Tale of Genji, Don Quixote,* and both parts of Goethe's *Faust.* The Compact Edition retains a global focus while concentrating on the major works that are essential to a single-semester course.

Along with these major selections we continue to present a great array of shorter works, some of which have been known only to specialists and only now are entering into world literature. It is our experience as readers and as teachers that the established classics themselves can best be understood when they're set in a varied literary landscape. Nothing is included here, though, simply to make a point: whether world-renowned or recently rediscovered, these are compelling works to read. Throughout our work on this book, we've tried to be highly inclusive in principle and yet carefully selective in practice, avoiding tokenism and also its inverse, the piling up of an unmanageable array of heterogeneous material. If we've succeeded as we hope, the result will be coherent as well as capacious, substantive as well as stimulating.

Literature, Art, and Music

One important way to understand literary works in context is to read them in conjunction with the broader social and artistic culture in which they were created. Literature has often had a particularly close relation to visual art and to music. Different as the arts are in their specific resources and techniques, a culture's artistic expressions often share certain family resemblances, common traits that can be seen across different media—and that may even come out more clearly in visual or musical form than in translations of literature itself. This anthology includes numerous black-and-white illustrations and a suite of color illustrations, chosen to work in close conjunction with our literary selections. Some of these images directly illustrate literary works, while others show important aspects of a culture's aesthetic sensibility. Often, writing actually appears on paintings and sculptures, with represented people and places sharing the space with beautifully rendered Mayan hieroglyphs, Arabic calligraphy, or Chinese brushstrokes.

Music too has been a close companion of literary creation and performance. Our very term "lyric" refers to the lyres or harps with which the Greeks accompanied poems as they were sung. In China, the first major literary work is the *Book of Songs.* In Europe too, until quite recent times poetry was often sung and even prose was usually read aloud. We have created two audio CDs to accompany the anthology. These CDs give a wealth of poetry and music from the cultures we feature in the anthology; they are both a valuable teaching resource and a pure pleasure to listen to.

Aids to Understanding

A major emphasis of our work has been to introduce each culture and each work to best effect. Each major period and section of the anthology, each grouping of works, and each individual author has an introduction by a member of our editorial team. Our goal has been to write introductions informed by deep knowledge worn lightly. Neither talking down to our readers nor overwhelming them with masses of unassimilable information, our introductions don't seek to "cover" the material but instead try to uncover it, to provide ways in and connections outward. Similarly, our footnotes and glosses are concise and informative, rather than massive or interpretive. Time lines, maps, and pronunciation guides throughout the anthology all aim to foster an informed and pleasurable reading of the works.

Going Further

The Longman Anthology of World Literature, Compact Edition, makes connections beyond its covers as well as within them. Bibliographies at the end of the volume point the way to historical and critical readings for students wishing to go into greater depth for term papers. The Companion Web site we've developed for the course (www.ablongman.com/worldlit) gives a wealth of links to excellent Web resources on all our major texts and many related historical and cultural movements and events. The Web site includes an audio version of our printed pronunciation guides: you can simply click on a name to hear it pronounced. Finally, the Web site includes readings of works in the original and in translation, with accompanying texts, giving extensive exposure to the aural dimension of many of the languages represented in the anthology.

For instructors, we have also created an extensive, two-volume instructor's manual, *Teaching World Literature*—written directly by the editors themselves, drawing on our years of experience in teaching these materials.

Translation Across Cultures

The circulation of world literature is always an exercise in cultural translation, and one way to define works of world literature is that they are the works that gain in translation. Some great texts remain so intimately tied to their point of origin that they never read well abroad; they may have an abiding importance at home, but don't play a role in the wider world. Other works, though, gain in resonance as they move out into new contexts, new conjunctions. *The Thousand and One Nights,* long a marginal work in Arabic traditions oriented toward poetry rather than popular prose, gained new readers and new influence abroad, and Sheherazade's intricately nested tales now help us in turn to read the European tales of Boccaccio and also a contemporary Algerian version by Assia Djebar with new attention and appreciation.

As important as cultural translation in general is the issue of actual translation from one language to another. We have sought out compelling translations for all our foreign-language works, and periodically we offer our readers the opportunity to think directly about the issue of translation. Sometimes we offer distinctively different translations of differing works from a single author or source: for the Bible, for example, we give Genesis 1–11 in Robert Alter's lively, oral-style translation, while we give selected psalms in the magnificent King James Version and the *Song of Songs* in the lyrical Jerusalem Bible translation. Our selections from Homer's *Iliad* appear in Richmond Lattimore's stately older translation, while Homer's *Odyssey* is given in Robert Fagles's eloquent new version.

At other times, we give alternative translations of a single work. So we have Chinese lyrics translated by the modernist poet Ezra Pound and by a contemporary scholar. These juxtapositions can show some of the varied ways in which translators over the centuries have sought to carry works over from one time and place to another—not so much by mirroring and reflecting an unchanged meaning, as by refracting it, in a prismatic process that can add new highlights and reveal new facets in a classic text. At times, when we haven't found a translation that really satisfies us, we've translated the work ourselves—an activity we recommend to all who wish to come to know a work from the inside.

We hope that the results of our years of work on this project will be as enjoyable to use as the book has been to create. We welcome you now inside our pages.

David Damrosch
David L. Pike

ACKNOWLEDGMENTS

In the extended process of planning and preparing this anthology, the editors have been fortunate to have the support, advice, and assistance of many people. Our editor, Joe Terry, and our publisher, Roth Wilkofsky, have supported our project in every possible way and some seemingly impossible ones as well, helping us produce the best possible book despite all challenges to budgets and well-laid plans in a rapidly evolving field. Our development editor, Mikola De Roo, handled the process with characteristic wit and aplomb. Jenny Bevington cleared hundreds and hundreds of text permissions from publishers in many countries, and Jody Potter cleared our many photo permissions.

Once the manuscript was complete, Denise Phillip, the production manager, oversaw the production of one book from six on a tight and shifting schedule. Valerie Zaborski, managing editor in production, also helped and, along the way, developed a taste for the good-humored fatalism of Icelandic literature. Our copyeditor, Stephanie Magean, assured that the reduction would be quick and painless. Doug Bell and his colleagues at GGS Book Services, Susan Bogle and Andrea Shearer, worked as a team to ensure the accuracy and quality of the production process.

We are specifically grateful for the guidance of the many reviewers who advised us on the creation of this book: Kyoka Amano (University of Indianapolis); Ashley S. Bonds (Copiah-Lincoln Community College); Theodore Bouabre (Jackson State University); Debra Taylor Bourdeau (Kennesaw State University); Patsy J. Daniels (Jackson State University); Brian Doherty (University of Texas—Austin); Jennifer Duncan (Chattanooga State Technical Community College); Khalil Elayan (Kennesaw State University); Diana C. Gingo (University of Texas—Dallas); Kyle Glover (Lindenwood University); Michael Grimwood (North Carolina State University); Joel Henderson (Chattanooga State Technical Community College); Ernest N. Kaulbach (University of Texas—Austin); Hans Kellner (North Carolina State University); Barry Kitterman (Austin Peay State University); Jennifer Lawrence (Georgia State University); Heather Levy (University of Texas—Arlington); Patricia Lonchar (University of the Incarnate Word); David Lowery (Jones County Junior College); Judith Broome Mesa-Pelly (Austin Peay State University); J. Hunter Morgan (Glenville State College); James W. Parins (University of Arkansas—Little Rock); Melissa Rankin (University of Texas—Arlington); Elizabeth M. Richmond-Garza (University of Texas—Austin); David P. Schenck (University of South Florida); Daniel Schierenbeck (Central Missouri State University); Stephen Slimp (University of West Alabama); Gabriele Ulrike Stauf (Georgia Southwestern State University); Barbara Szubinska (Eastern Kentucky University); Nancy Wilson (Texas State University); R. Paul Yoder (University of Arkansas—Little Rock); Rachel Yeatts (University of North Texas); and Jianqing Zheng (Mississippi Valley State University).

It has been a great pleasure to work with all these colleagues both at Longman and at schools around the country. This book exists for its readers, whose reactions and suggestions we warmly welcome, as the Compact Edition of *The Longman Anthology of World Literature* moves out into the world.

ABOUT THE EDITORS

David Damrosch (Columbia University). His books include *The Narrative Covenant: Transformations of Genre in the Growth of Biblical Literature* (1987), *Meetings of the Mind* (2000), and *What Is World Literature?* (2003). He has been president of the American Comparative Literature Association (2001–2003) and is general editor of *The Longman Anthology of British Literature* (1998; second edition, 2002).

David L. Pike (American University). Author of *Passage Through Hell: Modernist Descents, Medieval Underworlds* (1997), *Subterranean Cities: The World beneath Paris and London* (2005), *Metropolis on the Styx: Underground Space, the Devil and Urban Culture in London and Paris* (2007), and a forthcoming book on Canadian cinema.

April Alliston (Princeton University). Author of *Virtue's Faults: Correspondence in Eighteenth-Century British and French Women's Fiction* (1996), and editor of Sophia Lee's *The Recess* (2000). Her book on concepts of character, gender, and plausibility in Enlightenment historical narratives is forthcoming.

Marshall Brown (University of Washington). Author of *The Shape of German Romanticism* (1979), *Preromanticism* (1991), *Turning Points: Essays in the History of Cultural Expressions* (1997), and, forthcoming, *The Gothic Text.* Editor of *Modern Language Quarterly: A Journal of Literary History,* and the *Cambridge History of Literary Criticism,* Vol. 5: Romanticism.

Page duBois (University of California, San Diego). Her books include *Centaurs and Amazons* (1982), *Sowing the Body* (1988), *Torture and Truth* (1991), *Sappho Is Burning* (1995), *Trojan Horses* (2001), and *Slaves and Other Objects* (2003).

Sabry Hafez (University of London). Author and editor of twenty books in Arabic on poetry, drama, literary theory, the Arabic Novel, and the short story, including works on Naguib Mahfouz, Yusuf Idris, and Mahmoud Darwish. His books in English include *The Genesis of Arabic Narrative Discourse* (1993) and the edited volumes *A Reader of Modern Arabic Short Stories* and *Modern Arabic Criticism.* He is a member of the Modern Language Panel of the Arts and Humanity Research Board, the funding council for academic research in the arts and humanities in Britain.

Ursula K. Heise (Stanford University). Author of *Chronoschisms: Time, Narrative, and Postmodernism* (1997) and of the forthcoming *World Wide Webs: Global Ecology and the Cultural Imagination.*

Djelal Kadir (Pennsylvania State University). His books include *Columbus and the Ends of the Earth* (1992), *The Other Writing: Postcolonial Essays in Latin America's Writing Culture* (1993), and *Other Modernisms in an Age of Globalizations* (2002). He served in the 1990s as editor of *World Literature Today* and is coeditor of the *Comparative History of Latin America's Literary Cultures* (2004). He is the founding president of the International American Studies Association.

Sheldon Pollock (University of Chicago). His books include *The Ramayana of Valmiki* Volume 3 (1991) and *The Language of the Gods in the World of Men* (forthcoming). He recently edited *Literary Cultures in History: Reconstructions from South Asia* (2003), and (with Homi Bhabha et al.) *Cosmopolitanism* (2002).

Bruce Robbins (Columbia University). His books include *The Servant's Hand: English Fiction from Below* (1986), *Secular Vocations* (1993), *Feeling Global: Internationalism in Distress* (1999), and a forthcoming study of upward mobility narratives in the nineteenth and twentieth centuries. Edited volumes include *Cosmopolitics: Thinking and Feeling Beyond the Nation* (1998).

Haruo Shirane (Columbia University). Author of *The Bridge of Dreams: A Poetics of "The Tale of Genji"* (1987) and of *Traces of Dreams: Landscape, Cultural Memory, and the Poetry of Bashō* (1998). He is coeditor of *Inventing the Classics: Modernity, National Identity, and Japanese Literature* (2000) and has recently edited *Early Modern Japanese Literature: An Anthology 1600–1900*.

Jane Tylus (New York University). Author of *Writing and Vulnerability in the Late Renaissance* (1993), coeditor of *Epic Traditions in the Contemporary World* (1999), and editor and translator of Lucrezia Tornabuoni de' Medici's *Sacred Narratives* (2001). Her study on late medieval female spirituality and the origins of humanism is forthcoming.

Pauline Yu (American Council of Learned Societies). President of the American Council of Learned Societies, she is the author of *The Poetry of Wang Wei* (1980) and *The Reading of Imagery in the Chinese Poetic Tradition* (1987), the editor of *Voices of the Song Lyric in China* (1994), and coeditor of *Culture and State in Chinese History* (1997) and *Ways with Words: Writing about Reading Texts from Early China* (2000).

Detail of stele inscribed with the Law Code of Hammurabi, c. 1750 B.C.E. The Babylonian King Hammurabi (reigned c. 1792–1750 B.C.E.) commissioned the major law code that hears his name, an ambitious effort to organize society under the rule of law. The seven-foot-tall stone column on which his laws are inscribed in cuneiform script is crowned with the scene showing Hammurabi conversing with the seated sun god, Shamash.

The Ancient World

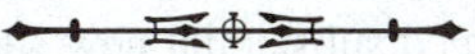

The ancient world was shaped by great innovations. The first nations and the first empires were founded, several great world religions—including Hinduism, Buddhism, and Christianity—were established, the first organized law codes were drawn up, and in many respects the outlines of civilization as we know it today began to emerge. A common term in all of these developments was the invention of systems of writing. With writing came effective long-distance communication and the ability to build nations and empires. While great religious leaders like Gautama Buddha, Jesus, and later the prophet Muhammad didn't write their teachings down, the scriptures compiled by their disciples and adherents played a major role in the worldwide spread of the religions they founded. Writing also gave cultures the ability to record their history and to create the textual records of their societies, preserving their imaginative works as well as more practical documents for later generations to read: literature was born.

The Beginnings of World Literature

The world's first great bodies of literary texts were created between four thousand and a little less than two thousand years ago, in Mesopotamia, in the Mediterranean world, in India, and in China. These works often have a double focus: preserving ancient traditions with roots in the distant past, they also respond to their own present situations. Ancient writers looked to the past to understand their present. Stories of creation would lead to the present world order, epic accounts of ancient battles would celebrate the founding of a people or nation, and even very recent laws would be portrayed as the wisdom of the ancients. Traditions could be invented as well as preserved, and as written texts became numerous, competing traditions could be compared, analyzed, and creatively reworked. The pleasures of imagination and of verbal beauty abound in these works as well, as ancient writers created the world's first written poems, dramas, and prose narratives. Their works became foundational for later writing in their own cultures and beyond, and have done much to shape our understanding and practice of literature to the present day. To read these texts now is to encounter a fascinating mixture of strangeness and familiarity, as the writers used radically new technology of writing to convey ancient wisdom and to adapt it to their own changing times.

Cities, Nations, and Empires

Ancient writing is largely urban in origins, for writing was employed mostly in courts and temples in the cities that grew rapidly in the second and first millennia B.C.E. The Greeks and Romans loved pastoral poems about shepherds and shepherdesses in the countryside, but the shepherds themselves couldn't write; the pastoral poetry we have was written by sophisticated urban poets dreaming of rural peace. Even so, the cities remained deeply dependent on the countryside; the great majority of all people in antiquity were engaged in growing crops and raising livestock. Primitive peoples had subsisted through hunting, fishing, and foraging for whatever edible plants they might happen to encounter, but between around 8000 and 6000 B.C.E. the settled cultivation of crops began. Farming produced substantial new surpluses of food and allowed for specialized roles to emerge in the growing cities: rulers and administrators, soldiers, priests, craftsmen, painters, musicians, and poets. As early as 5000 B.C.E., the Sumerians in southern Mesopotamia were building large cities complete with public water supplies and drainage, and by around 3100 B.C.E. the Sumerians had pioneered the use of written notations to record their dealings.

The rulers of major cities extended their reach to create the first nations, often relying on rivers as conduits of trade and communication. "Mesopotamia" takes its name from the Greek phrase "between the rivers," referring to the Tigris and Euphrates rivers on whose banks were built the great early cities of Ur, Akkad, Nippur, and Babylon. The Nile formed the backbone of Egypt, united into a single country around 3100 B.C.E., and the hieroglyphic writing developed in Egypt around that time greatly aided the new administrators in knitting their new country together. In China, cities grew up along rivers like the Yangzi, while in India a major early civilization grew up in the fertile valley of the Indus River. Sea routes could serve as well as rivers: the early Greek cities of Knossos in Crete and Mycenae on the mainland became centers of trade and of cultural production.

Over time, the most powerful city-states vied for control of larger regions, and the first empires were born in the third and second millennia B.C.E. The Babylonian and Assyrian empires waxed and waned across Mesopotamia and regions north and west; the Egyptians had long periods of control over Nubia and the Sudan to the south, and much of Palestine to the north and east. India and China, unified countries today, were (and still are) made up of many different ethnic groups speaking unrelated languages, and the governments that came to extend across their territories were creating empires rather than homogeneous nations. In late antiquity, vast empires extended from centers in Persia, in Northern Greece, and then in Rome, and great writers like Virgil both celebrated and probed the empires ruled by their patrons.

Travel, Migration, and Trade

Armies of conquest weren't the only groups on the move in the ancient world. Populations expanded rapidly in periods of prosperity but could come under severe stress in times of drought, or simply through outgrowing their resources. Entire peoples journeyed in search of new grazing lands and new fields to farm, in waves of migration that periodically transformed the social landscape, creating mixed populations in formerly unified regions. On a smaller scale, caravans of traders crossed long distances along the "silk road" that grew up from China to India and into Central Asia and Asia Minor, while Phoenician and Greek sailing ships established contacts around the Mediterranean. Like the tales that the great traveler Odysseus recounts to entertain his hosts, much ancient literature plays to people's fascination with hearing about distant peoples and their unusual customs, and many works explored what could happen when disparate cultures came into contact or conflict, either to comic effect or with tragic consequences.

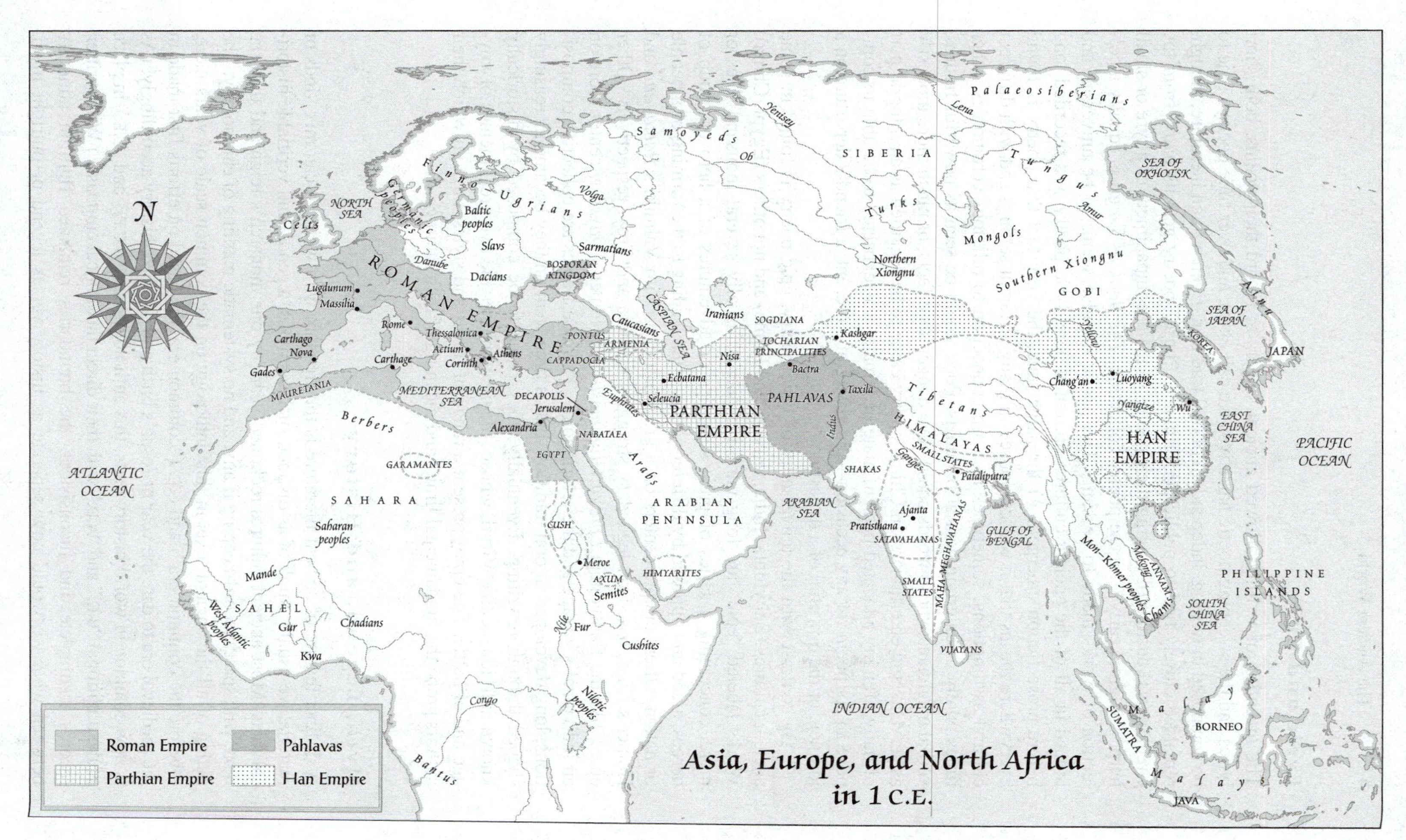

Asia, Europe, and North Africa in 1 C.E.
Roman Empire
Pahlavas
Parthian Empire
Han Empire
N
ATLANTIC OCEAN
NORTH SEA
Celts
Germanic peoples
Finno-Ugrians
Baltic peoples
Slavs
Dacians
Danube
Volga
Sarmatians
BOSPORAN KINGDOM
Samoyeds
Ob
Yenisey
SIBERIA
Lena
Palaeosiberians
Tungus
Amur
SEA OF OKHOTSK
Turks
Mongols
Northern Xiongnu
Southern Xiongnu
GOBI
Ainu
SEA OF JAPAN
KOREA
JAPAN
ROMAN EMPIRE
Lugdunum
Massilia
Rome
Thessalonica
Actium
Athens
Corinth
Carthago Nova
Gades
Carthage
MAURETANIA
MEDITERRANEAN SEA
PONTUS
ARMENIA
CAPPADOCIA
Caucasians
CASPIAN SEA
Iranians
SOGDIANA
TOCHARIAN PRINCIPALITIES
Kashgar
Nisa
Bactra
Ecbatana
Seleucia
Euphrates
PARTHIAN EMPIRE
PAHLAVAS
Taxila
Indus
DECAPOLIS
Jerusalem
Alexandria
NABATAEA
EGYPT
Berbers
GARAMANTES
SAHARA
Saharan peoples
Arabs
ARABIAN PENINSULA
ARABIAN SEA
CUSH
Meroe
AXUM
Semites
HIMYARITES
Nile
Fur
Cushites
Mande
SAHEL
West Atlantic peoples
Gur
Chadians
Kwa
Congo
Nilotic peoples
Bantus
Tibetans
HIMALAYAS
SMALL STATES
Ganges
Pataliputra
SHAKAS
Ajanta
Pratisthana
SATAVAHANAS
MAHA-MEGHAVAHANAS
SMALL STATES
VIJAYANS
GULF OF BENGAL
INDIAN OCEAN
Chang'an
Luoyang
Yellow
Yangtze
Wu
HAN EMPIRE
EAST CHINA SEA
PACIFIC OCEAN
Mon–Khmer peoples
Mekong
ANNAM
Chams
SOUTH CHINA SEA
PHILIPPINE ISLANDS
Malays
SUMATRA
BORNEO
JAVA

Lyric and Epic

The invention of writing allowed ancient singers to record their poems, both short lyrics and the sweeping poetic narratives we call epics, and over time poetry came to be composed in writing, independent of oral tradition. Even written literature, though, remained closely tied to public performance: "lyric" poetry gets its name from the Greek poets' custom of singing their poems to the accompaniment of a lyre or small harp. The great early Chinese poetry collection, *The Book of Songs,* is equally a collection of works made to be sung. The poetic impulse seems to be universal, and indeed in all of the ancient cultures presented here, lyric poetry was recorded long before prose fiction emerged. At the same time, the very fact that poetry is found everywhere means that it was composed in many different settings and with different cultural assumptions, sometimes in close connection to religious ceremonies, other times purely as entertainment at banquets. Poets could be seen as powerful figures, verbal magicians whose words could have dangerous effects, or much more modestly as servants and entertainers. In China, poetry came to be regarded as an integral part of daily life: any educated person, male or female, was expected to be able to compose an apt poem for any occasion—the giving of a present, a friend's departure on a journey, or the downfall of a dynasty.

By contrast with the universality of lyric poetry, epic poetry is found in some ancient cultures (Babylonia, India, Greece, and Rome) and not others (Egypt, China). Works labeled "epic" are long narrative poems, usually several thousand lines or more, concerning a series of great struggles or adventures of a hero or group of heroes, aided and opposed by different gods, often leading to the forming of a people or nation. Often an epic centers on a great battle, as with Valmiki's *Ramayana* and Homer's *Iliad,* based on legendary struggles in India and Troy, respectively. Other epics, like the Bablyonian *Epic of Gilgamesh* and Homer's *Odyssey,* center more on an individual's voyage and the return home. The oldest epics are collective compositions, long developed in oral tradition, but as time went on they became increasingly shaped through rewriting. Eventually, they came to be composed by historically known individuals, like Virgil, whose *Aeneid* combines the two great themes of voyage and of battle. The epics present a range of forms and styles, through which their authors probe the fundamental limits and meaning of their culture.

Myth, Legend, and History

A distinct feature of ancient literature is the freedom with which it can mix kinds of material we usually think of as distinct, such as myths, legends, and verifiable historical facts. Most ancient cultures reckoned years by one monarch's reign and then the next, with spotty record-keeping if any, and no systematic marking of chronology. The dating of all the ancient texts in this anthology on the common scale of years B.C.E. ("before the common era") and C.E. ("common era") is based on efforts first made in the medieval era to date the year of Jesus's birth and organize history accordingly. (As is now common in world history texts, this anthology uses "B.C.E." and "C.E." in place of the traditional "B.C." and "A.D." with their direct theological emphasis.) With written records incomplete and inconsistent, the boundaries remained fluid in antiquity between what we would now separate as history versus legend or outright myth.

"Myth" itself is a term with many meanings. Often today we call something a myth simply to say it isn't true, but in ancient Greek, the term *mythos* originally meant any speech or story. Gradually the term came to refer especially to poetic legends about the early doings of the gods, or the gods and mortals together, in a distant, shadowy past. Far from signifying falsehood, then, "myth" in the ancient world meant a story about ultimate truths. Myths were sometimes told to explain the origins of the world as a whole or of a particular custom or feature of the landscape; at other times, they were used as background or charter for a ritual, as when the Babylonian creation myth was recited as part of an annual New Year's ceremony. Anonymous in origin, handed down over the years from one teller to another, a myth would vary in form and content as it circulated within a culture and beyond, and over time myths could be taken up and elaborated more for the sake of enjoyment than for any practical purpose. Throughout ancient literature, mythic elements continually reappear even in sober historical writing, and human history—like the earthly landscape itself—continued to bear the marks of the gods' deeds and intentions. In between myth and history proper are legends, traditional tales of relatively recent people and events. Often a single work will blend mythic, legendary, and historical materials, challenging us to see the world in a new way, interfusing what we often think of as separate realms of fact and fiction.

Most ancient texts existed in only one manuscript or a few copies at most, and over time the majority were lost. The ancient works we have today are the rare exceptions, works so treasured that they circulated widely and were preserved through centuries of warfare and disruption, or else works that simply happened to be preserved in a tomb or a ruined royal library, where they could be rediscovered long after their world had vanished. In many ways these foundational works set the course for much later writing around the globe, and they convey the first writers' excitement as they captured their world on paper, on clay tablets, on animal hides, and on stone.

The Ancient Near East

The story of world literature begins with the ancient cultures of Egypt and "the Fertile Crescent," a broad band of settled lands stretching from the Tigris and Euphrates rivers in what is now Iraq, up into Asia Minor and down through Palestine. Across this region a combination of favorable environmental conditions and human ingenuity led to the establishment of the world's first great cities, such as Thebes and Memphis in Egypt, and Ur and Babylon in Mesopotamia. As rulers sought to build empires and merchants created extensive trading networks, they began to develop means to communicate over large distances, settle their accounts, and extend their influence: writing was born.

Sometime around 3400 B.C.E. the Sumerian people of southern Mesopotamia began to inscribe clay tablets with symbolic representations of objects and then of sounds; by 3000 B.C.E. the world's first fully developed writing system had emerged, capable of conveying detailed information and increasingly complex thoughts through an intricate system of cuneiform ("wedge-shaped") signs. Hundreds of complex combinations of marks were used, each for a different syllable. Once baked, the clay tablets could easily be carried long distances, and to our good fortune they could last for thousands of years when buried in the region's dry, sandy soil.

By about 3000 B.C.E. the Egyptians had developed their own, openly pictorial form of writing, carved on stone or written with a brush on scrolls made from the fiber

The Near East in 1250 B.C.E.

of the papyrus plant (our word "paper" comes from "papyrus"). Egyptian scribes created hundreds of hieroglyphic images of actual objects, and they found that they could employ these images to form many more words as well by using an image to signify just the initial sound of its object. Eventually, during the second millennium B.C.E., some traders in Egypt and Palestine began to use a simplified version of the alphabetic symbols and dropped the visual signs altogether: the first phonetic alphabet was created, and soon after 1000 B.C.E. several area languages, including Hebrew, were being written in purely alphabetic scripts. Through traders in Phoenicia an early alphabet spread to Greece and beyond, eventually becoming the alphabet we use today.

Empires, Cities, and Nomads

The first writers faced the challenge of recording a complex reality. Mesopotamia, where writing began, was made up of differing groups of widely different cultures. During the second and early first millennia, major empires extended out from Babylon, then from Nineveh—capital of the Babylonians' perennial rivals the Assyrians—and then from Babylon once again. The Hittite Empire in Anatolia (modern Turkey) also reached down into the area, and the Hittites adapted Babylonian cuneiform for their own use, as did early scribes in Persia, whose ruler Cyrus the Great eventually conquered Babylonia in 539 B.C.E.; Hellenistic Greek culture came into the area after Alexander the Great conquered Babylon in 331. Over the centuries Mesopotamia's ethnic composition steadily evolved through the immigration of new groups such as the Aramaeans, whose language of Aramaic is a close cousin of Hebrew and is used at times in the Bible itself; the legendary father of the Hebrew people, Abraham, is identified in Genesis and Deuteronomy as an Aramaean whom God commanded to leave Mesopotamia in order to found a new nation.

South of the other end of the Fertile Crescent, Egypt achieved early unity as a country in around 3100 B.C.E. Buffered by deserts on three sides and the Mediterranean to the north, Egypt remained a single country with an unbroken culture for a remarkable period of more than three thousand years, a record matched only by China anywhere in the world. For both the Mesopotamians and the Egyptians, the keys to prosperity and life itself were the great rivers that defined their lands: the Tigris and the Euphrates in Mesopotamia, the Nile in Egypt. These rivers provided water in a hot and dry climate. Some eight thousand years ago, farmers began to build canals, enabling them eventually to irrigate large areas around their rivers. Their fields were famously fertile, and this rich agricultural base allowed for the growth and support of cities and for the development of urban culture starting in the fourth millennium B.C.E. Those who lived in the cities considered them to be the greatest of human achievements, envied by their enemies and beloved of the gods. Their kings lavished wealth on public buildings and on city walls, which often became works of art in themselves.

In much of the ancient Near East, many people lived by keeping sheep and cattle, often moving from place to place for grazing and water. In particular, there were many seminomadic herdsmen in the region variously called Palestine or Canaan, northeast of Egypt and west of Mesopotamia, and cities were small-scale affairs. The Book of Genesis symbolically records the tension between farmers and herdsmen in the mysterious, fatal struggle of the jealous farmer Cain against his shepherd brother Abel, whose meat offerings God prefers to Cain's produce. The herdsmen often looked with suspicion upon cities and their dwellers, seeing them as corrupt and dissolute. They viewed the cities' kings as oppressive tyrants, as opposed to the fatherlike leaders of their own clans. Whereas the Babylonians considered their city the cornerstone of civilization and the prime meeting point for gods and mortals, the formerly nomadic Hebrews described Babylon as the site for the building of the Tower of Babel, not as the temple it actually was but an emblem of human pride, rightly destroyed by God (Genesis 11).

Courts and Temples

Religion pervaded every aspect of Near Eastern life, most variously among the polytheistic societies, which developed elaborate pantheons of gods and goddesses, each often associated with a particular city, natural force, or animal, and each of whom expected appropriate sacrifices and could be appealed to for different purposes. Typically a primordial generation of universal gods and goddesses was thought to have created the world and to have begotten further generations of divinities now in control of the world, usually with a large number of minor gods and goddesses ruled by a few preeminent divinities: a god associated with the sun (called Utu in Sumerian, Shamash in Akkadian, Amon Re or Aten in Egypt, Apollo in Greece), a moon goddess associated with fertility and love (Inanna or Ishtar in Mesopotamia, Isis in Egypt, Aphrodite in Greece, Venus in Rome), and other major divinities associated with such elemental forces as thunderstorms (Adad in Mesopotamia, Zeus in Greece) and water (Ea or Enki in Mesopotamia, Poseidon in Greece). The underworld was doubly ruled, in Mesopotamia by Nergal and his consort Ereshkigal, precursors of Hades and Persephone in Greek myth. In surviving poems, it is Ereshkigal who is the dominant figure, notably in chilling accounts of the underworld descent of her sister, the goddess of love (Inanna in Sumerian and Ishtar in Akkadian), who comes to visit her realm with nearly fatal results.

In the Near East as in medieval and early modern Europe, noble and especially royal women could wield substantial power, though only very rarely ruling outright as Cleopatra did in Egypt in the first century B.C.E. In Israel, women were powerful and sometimes dominant figures in clan-based life, and the Hebrew patriarchs are paired with imposing, and often cunning, matriarchs like Sarah, Rebekah, and Rachel. Women of modest circumstance are also periodically represented, as in the moving relationship of Ruth and Naomi in the Book of Ruth, or in the Song of Songs and the lyric poetry that has survived from Egypt. In Hebrew wisdom tradition, wisdom itself—a female noun in Hebrew, *hokmah*—came to be personified as a prime agent of God's guiding power. According to the Book of Proverbs, "I, Wisdom, dwell in prudence. . . . By me kings reign, and nobles govern the earth." She prepares a banquet in her house of seven pillars and invites all to join her: "She has sent out her maidens to proclaim from the highest part of the town: 'Come in, you simpletons!' She says also to the fool, 'Come, dine with me and taste the wine that I have spiced. Cease to be foolish, and you will live, you will grow in understanding.'"

The Rebirth of the Past

During the last centuries of the first millennium B.C.E. the old Mesopotamian cultures went into steep decline, followed in the Roman period by Egypt as well; their texts were forgotten and their very scripts ceased to be known. For nearly two thousand years, the Bible contained the only ancient Near Eastern literature that anyone could read. The texts that follow in this section are the result of a long-distance collaboration between their ancient creators and their modern discoverers. The very name we commonly use for these works' place of origin, "the Near East," reflects the European perspective of the nineteenth-century archaeologists and scholars who sought out and deciphered these materials. The original authors, of course, didn't think of themselves as living in the East at all, whether near or middle: the residents of cities like Babylon and Thebes typically thought of themselves as living in the center of the world. The recovery of their large and varied world is one of the great intellectual achievements of the modern era, and it has given us new understandings of the biblical texts and a wealth of remarkable literature from the great ancient cultures at both ends of the Fertile Crescent.

Classical Greece

The ancient Greeks lived in pockets in what is now mainland Greece, throughout the islands of the eastern Mediterranean, and along the shores of the Mediterranean Sea. Like the writing of the ancient Near East, the earliest writing in the Greek world was often written on clay tablets, and it was used, so far as scholars know, to record the

Statue of Zeus or Poseidon from Cape Artemision, Greece, c. 450 B.C.E.

business of administering large bureaucracies and gathering tribute for the palace culture of the ancient Minoans (the indigenous people of Crete) and of the ancient Mycenaeans, the Greek-speakers who conquered them and adopted their writing system to record the sounds of Greek. The earliest surviving poems, the Homeric epics the *Iliad* and the *Odyssey,* record events of this age of heroes and warriors, of men and women close to the many gods and goddesses of the Greek pantheon. It was the time of Oedipus, the king who killed his father and married his mother, and of the expedition to Troy to retrieve the stolen Helen. These tales, passed on by word of mouth during a period when the skill of writing appears to have been lost, were first recorded in the eighth century B.C.E., when the many scattered communities of the Greeks began to grow and trade again after a period of devastation. They began to use an alphabet borrowed from the Phoenicians, adding vowels and making a supple and concise writing system that serves as the basis of our modern Roman alphabet.

Immortals

Much of the early writing of the Greeks celebrates the many gods of this society. Hesiod in his *Theogony* tells the story of the succession of gods. The original goddess, Gaia, or "Earth," equal to her mate Ouranos, or "Sky," is replaced by many lesser female deities. The sky god is ambushed by his son Kronos, who castrates Ouranos with a sickle. The detached member mingles with the sea to produce Aphrodite, goddess of the foam and sexual desire. The time of Kronos is described as a golden age of mortals, which gives way to an age of silver, which is followed by a third race of bronze. After the time of heroes come the mortals of the present day, men of iron: "All toiling humanity will be blighted by envy, / grim and strident envy that takes its joy in the ruin of others." Hesiod's myth of the declining generations of mortals, perhaps derived from ancient Iranian sources, records the Greeks' sense of time and of distance from a heroic past. The gods too suffer through change but finally achieve stability when Zeus establishes himself as the preeminent divinity of the Olympians by conquering his father Kronos, who had been swallowing his children to prevent them from displacing him.

Although Zeus exercises a sort of monarchic sovereignty over the host of quarreling, rivalrous, and amorous lesser gods, the Greeks worshiped all of them. Aphrodite stood for the domain of sexual desire, pleasure, and yearning, Demeter for the reproductive powers of the citizen woman. Apollo, god of prophecy and of the foundation of new cities, watched over philosophers and murderers. Travelers consulted his oracle at Delphi, and the Pythian priestess there gave often enigmatic answers to their questions. Poseidon was the god of earthquakes, horses, and the sea, upon which many Greeks traveled great distances to lands known and unknown. Dionysos, god of wet things—wine, semen, milk, and honey—traveled from India with a band of ecstatic women, satyrs, and panthers, and was celebrated with new wine and with tragic performances. Hermes was the god of heralds, of traveling across boundaries—between cities, between properties, between life and death, the underworld and the mortal world, between Mount Olympus and earth. He was represented by herms, stone pillars with heads and erect phalluses. Worshipers at the mystery cult of Eleusis celebrated Demeter and her daughter Kore, or Persephone, who had been abducted by Hades, god of the underworld. Because she ate from a pomegranate while in the land of the dead, Persephone, though allowed to join her mother again on earth, returned to spend part of each year with her husband in the underworld, dramatizing the passage of the seasons. Participants in the mystery cult honored mother and daughter, and experienced the acting-out of some sacred ritual that brought comfort in the face of human mortality.

Greek polytheism encompasses many gods and goddesses, and many forms of worship, including animal sacrifice, ecstatic dancing, and ritualized sexual intercourse. Some of the most beautiful poems, before there were "poems" in a purely literary sense, are hymns sung in praise or celebration of the gods. Aphrodite appears to Anchises, father of Aeneas, founder of Rome:

> She was clothed in a robe more brilliant than gleaming fire
> and wore spiral bracelets and shining earrings,
> while round her tender neck there were beautiful necklaces,
> lovely, golden and of intricate design. Like the moon's
> was the radiance round her soft breasts, a wonder to the eye.

Cities

The *polis,* or "city-state" defined social experience in the classical age. The polis incorporated an urban complex and its surrounding territory, including towns, villages, sanctuaries dedicated to the gods, agricultural land, and wilderness. Relationships with the gods differed from city to city in the Greek world, as did political and social institutions. Sparta, a city of the Dorian tribe, organized its ruling elite as an army, bent on controlling subordinate inhabitants who lived like serfs, or communities of slaves. Although some early poets wrote poems of contest and battle, the later Spartans were respected more for their martial prowess than for their contributions to world literature. Corinth, a wealthy city known for its port, its ceramics, and its sacred prostitutes, sent out colonies to the rest of the Mediterranean, but left behind few literary remains. Thebes, city of Oedipus, achieved political glory in the fourth century B.C.E.; its greatest poet, Pindar, wrote earlier and sang the praises of athletes and their patrons, victorious in games like those held in Olympus in honor of Zeus and at Delphi, as a form of worship and celebration of the god Apollo. Although other cities have been excavated and explored in the modern period, we know most about ancient Athens, because of the rich record of writing left behind by the Athenians. It is in the city of Athens, in Attica, that the most important literary contributions of the Greek classical age were written. The citizens of this city worshipped with particular devotion Athena, goddess of wisdom, who was born from Zeus's head.

As the city-states grew they were governed by aristocracies, groups of nobles who often rivaled each other and engaged in repeated struggles for domination. The poet Sappho was supposedly exiled from Lesbos because of her implication in these struggles. Some aristocrats eventually set themselves up as what the Greeks called "tyrants"—that is, usurpers of monarchic power. The tyrants, who only gradually became associated with cruelty and despotism, sometimes allied themselves with popular elements in the cities to rise over their fellow aristocrats; they frequently tried to establish dynasties, in which their descendants would, like them, control their cities. The new form of government known as democracy evolved especially (though not only) in Athens after the late sixth century B.C.E. In the democracy, the free male citizen class, understanding themselves to be equal in principle, ruled themselves by

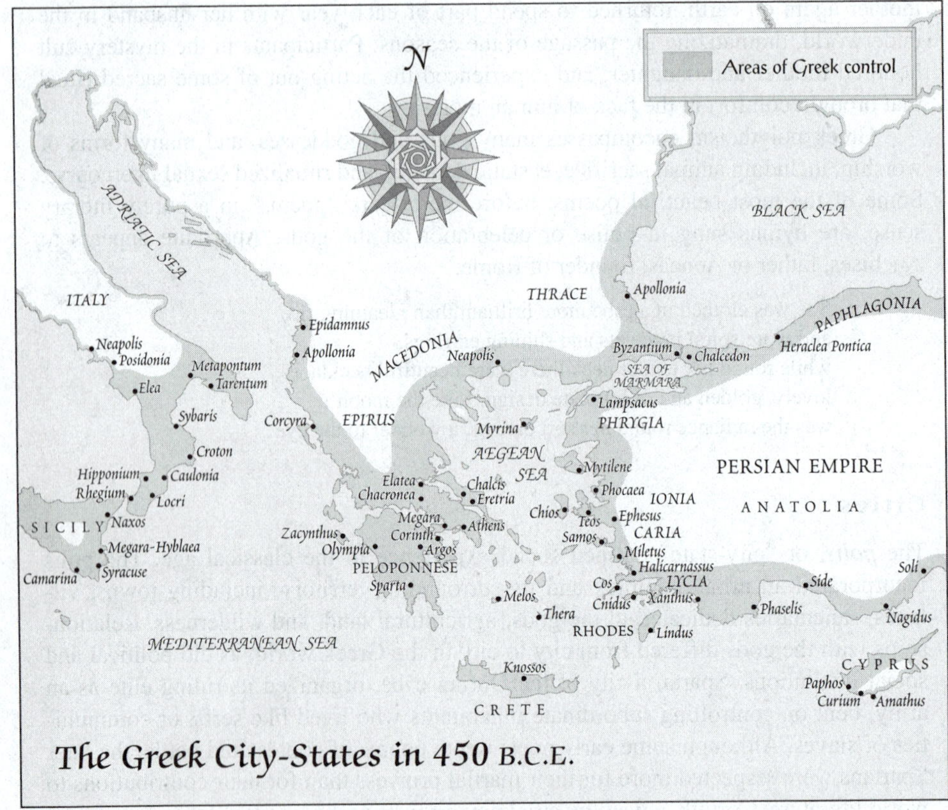

The Greek City-States in 450 B.C.E.

means of assemblies in which each citizen had a vote, and they usually chose their magistrates through lot. The development of the Greek institution of democracy, although it excluded women, slaves, and noncitizens from participation in government, appears especially remarkable given the theocracies, empires, and monarchies that governed the states surrounding the Greeks in the ancient world.

Athenian democracy encouraged and supported the writing and performance of drama, in festivals celebrated for the god Dionysos. And the questioning of received truths, first explored in the works of the pre-Socratics like Parmenides, came to fruition in the circle of Socrates and his friends, including Plato, who took the drama of the fifth-century city and transformed it into philosophical dialogues. The Platonic dialogues presented fictional conversations in dramatic form, with directly quoted speech, often framed by a narrator; the author creates vividly realized characters who argue about knowledge, truth, and the proper conduct of life.

Drama

Greek drama grew up in the classical city, beginning probably in the sixth century. Athens organized the dramatic festivals, and committees of citizens chose the plays to be performed and then awarded victory to the best. The theaters of various cities were situated in the open air, sometimes with a magnificent view. Stone benches for the spectators rose in ranks above thrones set in front for the priests of Dionysos; before them was the circular dancing floor, with a building facade, called a *skene*, a word originally meaning "tent," from which the actors emerged (the origin of our word "scene"). Some dramatists used a crane, ending plays with the appearance of a god or goddess on high, the *deus ex machina* or "god from the machine."

Tragedy was a crucial institution of the democratic city, dramatizing the engagement of the city with its own cultural and political history. The word "tragedy" means "goat song," and may have referred originally to a song sung at a goat sacrifice, connecting it perhaps with the part-animal satyrs who were Dionysos's companions. Tragedy as drama may have begun as the leaders of the "dithyramb," a choral hymn sung in honor of Dionysos, improvised and performed solos. The tragic performance shared the focus on *agon,* or "contest," with many other institutions of the Greek city, including the games, Olympian and others. In Athens, the tragedians presented their plays to a magistrate, who chose three plays to be performed, and a wealthy man for each, to pay for the training of the actors and the choruses, in a form of philanthropy or taxation that benefited the city as a whole. In general their stories were drawn from the epic cycle and concerned the gods and goddesses, heroes and heroines of the distant past. Nonetheless, the tragedies touched on contemporary concerns in many ways, expressing indirectly much that the political discourses of the city, such as speeches in the democratic assembly, could not.

Gender

Readers of Greek tragedy, and of the myths, have often remarked on the representations of powerful goddesses, and even of heroines of the remote past, and contrasted their freedom and authority with the relatively closeted nature of Greek women's lives in the classical period. Daughters and wives and mothers of citizens had no political rights themselves and could not vote in the assembly, hold political office, or even serve on juries. In legal matters they were represented by fathers, husbands, or guardians. And while there are examples of chastity and virtue in Greek tragedy displayed by women like Alcestis, who is willing to die in her husband's place, others, such as Clytemnestra and Medea, kill their male relatives, husband, and sons. Virtuous citizen women had some authority and power in their homes, and played a crucial role in ritual life. Yet they were frequently seen as unruly by nature. Some attribute this paradox to a diminution of women's status in the democratic period, when all men were in principle equal, and all women therefore subordinate, even the formerly powerful aristocrats. Others cite Greek patterns of child-rearing, where women, frustrated and envious of their sons' imminent freedom, controlled the lives of small boys who developed fear and loathing of powerful females, and perpetuated misogyny as adults. Unfortunately, there remains very little writing by women, except for the fragments of Sappho's verse that survive from the earlier, aristocratic age.

Male virtue was strongly connected to military prowess; citizens served in their cities' armies, and initiation into the army marked a threshold of manhood and acceptance into the city. In a city like Sparta, male bonding seems to have been a crucial element of military and citizen life; men dined together in messes, and the military unit seems to have been central to men's identities. Masculine existence focused on public life, in the military, in politics. Male homosexuality, a locus for intimacy among men, was an important institution in civic life; young men, and some older men, courted boys before their beards had grown, and much of the erotic, or sexual energy of the culture was focused on these relationships. The god Eros, son of Aphrodite, goddess of sexual desire, personified the attraction of males to females, males to males, females to females.

Barbarians

The Greeks lived in Greece itself but also came into contact with others around the Black Sea and the Mediterranean, whom they called "barbarians," because their language sounded to Greek ears like "bar-bar-bar": meaningless clumps of sound. Many of the barbarians familiar to the Greeks arrived as slaves and belonged to the free persons of the Greek city-states, working as domestic servants, agricultural laborers, and artisans, sometimes alongside the free. Other barbarians were free, passing through Greece or settling there. Still others were enemies in war. The Greeks were fascinated with them all: their skills, their customs, their luxury goods, their ways of organizing families and cities and empires.

The interest in the "barbarians" extends throughout the historical period of ancient Greece. Homer records contacts with non–Greek-speaking peoples, and Hesiod's work reflects the influence of Mesopotamian myth, religion, and poetry. The lyric poets of the Archaic period register trade with those surrounding the Greeks; Sappho sings: "A decorated slipper hid / her foot, a lovely piece of Lydian work." Herodotus wrote his history about the war between the Greeks and the Persians, interspersing it with elaborate accounts of the societies that made up the Persian empire, and beyond. Curious about what he saw, diligent in interviewing people about what they had seen, he describes the Egyptian phoenix, Arabia's flying snakes, the Arabians' harvesting of frankincense and cinnamon: "Let me only add that the whole country exhales a more than earthly fragrance." He reports that the Indians live farthest to the east of Greece, and that beyond them is uninhabitable desert. His interest in the Greeks' near and distant neighbors persists throughout Greek literature and makes the Greeks both proud of their innovations like democracy and conscious of the alternatives that surround them.

Alexander and After

After the Persian Wars, during which the Greek mainland was invaded by armies led by the Persian emperors, and after the Peloponnesian War, fought between the Spartans and the Athenians, struggles continued over which of the city-states would control Greece as a whole. This fighting came to an end with the victory of Philip of Macedon, who came from the north and defeated the alliance of Greek cities in 338 B.C.E. After his death, his kingdom was inherited by his son Alexander, said by some to be a son of Dionysos. During his short lifetime, Alexander not only conquered the Greeks but went deeply into the lands of the barbarians and overpowered army after army. Alexander swept through the Persian empire, conquering and dominating Egypt, where he was acclaimed as a god, and moving east, past the Persian capitals into what is now Afghanistan and beyond, to the Indus River. As he moved he founded cities, many named Alexandria in his honor.

When he died in Babylon in 323 B.C.E., Alexander left behind a contentious group of heirs, his generals, who fought over and divided the fragile empire he had

Plate 1 *Tutankhamen and Ankhesenamen,* Egypt, c. 1320 B.C.E. This gold relief forms the back of a throne found in the tomb of the Egyptian king Tutankhamen, who died in 1324 at about age 19. The gold is inlaid with colored glass and semiprecious stones, with silver for the clothing. Tutankhamen and his wife (and half-sister) Ankhesenamen are shown in an intimate domestic moment, and at the same time the picture emphasizes the royal couple's direct link to the sun disk, the Aten, promoted by their father Akhenaten as the dominant god. The sun's rays stream down, equipped with hands giving strength and support. Some of the Aten's hands hold the *ankh,* the Egyptian hieroglyph for "life," which is a central element in both the king's and the queen's names. The couple is shown in the flattened, schematic style traditional in Egyptian art (shoulders turned sideways, every finger visible), but Tutankhamen's casually thrown-back arm reflects the lively realism promoted during his father's reign. *(Egyptian Museum, Cairo. Photo: AKG London / Francois Guenot.)*

Plate 2 The theater at Delphi, Greece, 4th century B.C.E. Seating five thousand spectators, the theater was built on the slopes of Mt. Parnassus at the sacred shrine at Delphi, regarded by the ancient Greeks as the center of the world. The site was dedicated to Apollo, and the springs on the slopes of Parnassus were said to bring poetic inspiration. The theater echoes the sweeping curves of the landscape around it, creating a harmonious order appropriate to the god of reason and of poetry. *(AKG London. Shutze / Rodemann.)*

Plate 3 Jain diagram of the universe, India. Like the theater at Delphi, this diagram creates a circular order centered on a sacred mountain. Jainism, which arose in the 6th century B.C.E., downplayed the elaborate ritual observances and social hierarchies developed in Vedic circles, emphasizing instead meditation and the achievement of inner knowledge. Yet the Jain view of the cosmos shared many features with those of the Buddhists and Hindus. This painted cloth diagram shows the universe centered on Meru, a mountain sacred to the gods, which stands in the middle of Jambudvipa, the Rose-Apple Island, or the known world (as even Chinese Buddhist pilgrims referred to it). The concentric circles that surround it are oceans teeming with fish and other creatures and dotted with inhabited islands. The whole map is surrounded in turn by Sanskrit texts identifying components of the Jain cosmography (see page 31 for a traditional Hindu account of the cosmos). *(The Art Archive / British Library.)*

Plate 4 *Portrait of a Woman,* Pompeii, 1st century C.E. Preserved when the city of Pompeii was submerged in volcanic ash from Mt. Vesuvius in 79 C.E., this fresco shows the subtle shading and emphasis on individual character common in Roman portraiture. Apparently a poet, the woman shown here holds a set of wooden writing tablets, tapping her lips with her stylus as she searches for a word. *(Erich Lessing / Art Resource, New York.)*

Plate 5 Limbourg Brothers, *February,* from *Les Très Riches Heures du Duc de Berry,* France, 1416. The medieval European nobility used "books of hours" (prayers and psalms to be said at set hours of the day) in their private devotions; beautifully illustrated, these books became treasured works of art. Created by three artist brothers for Jean, Duc de Berry, the *Très Riches Heures* ("very rich hours") included a calendar with an illustration for each month of the year. Above, the chariot of the Sun proceeds through the months and the signs of the zodiac; below is shown an entertaining scene of peasant life. People hike their clothing up to warm their feet at the fire in their hut (its wall conveniently cut away for our viewing), the woman taking care not to expose herself as much as the men do. Outside, sheep huddle for warmth in their pen and a peasant hurries across the barnyard holding his cloak across his face, while in the background a man chops firewood and another takes bundles of wood into town. Only nine by eight inches, this painting gives an entire and very earthly world in miniature. *(Réunion des Musées Nationaux / Art Resource, New York.)*

Plate 6 Prayer hall in the Great Mosque, Córdoba, Spain, begun 786 C.E. A masterpiece of Moorish architecture in al-Andalus (Muslim Spain), this mosque incorporates elements from a range of cultures, including Roman arches, Greek-style Corinthian columns, and Byzantine mosaics. Soft light from side doors and shadows from flickering oil lamps help to create an otherworldly space of worship amid the forest of columns. *(Gary Conner / Index Stock Imagery.)*

Plate 7 Upper chapel, Sainte-Chapelle, Paris, 1240s. Following the sacking of Constantinople by Frankish crusaders, King Louis IX of France acquired a group of sacred relics that included wood supposed to have come from Christ's cross and his Crown of Thorns. Ordinarily, relics would be kept in an ornate chest or reliquary, but these relics were so special that Louis decided to commission an entire building in their honor. The Sainte-Chapelle has the feel of a great jewel box, soaring into the sky thanks to buttresses outside that support the delicate tracery of its stained glass. Like the mosque in Córdoba (Plate 6), the Sainte-Chapelle creates a self-enclosed space of connection between human and divine worlds, in this case emphasizing radiant light rather than shadow, in keeping with the theological emphasis on Christ as the *verum lumen,* true Light of the World. *(Giraudon / Art Resource, New York.)*

Plate 8 Albrecht Dürer, *Self-Portrait,* 1500. The art historian H. R. Janson called Dürer "the first artist to be fascinated by his own image." Whether or not this is the case, it is certainly striking to see the young German, here 29 years old, confronting us in Christlike solemnity, and to consider that the initials "AD" on the left side of the portrait not only mean *anno domini* (year of our Lord), but also signify Dürer's own initials. One of the first modern artists to benefit from the revolution in printing—Dürer launched his career as a woodcut designer in Basel and Strasbourg, urban centers with numerous publishing houses—he was largely responsible for bringing the influences of Italian Renaissance art to bear on the north. At the same time, as in this self-portrait, Dürer remained receptive to social and cultural developments in his own country, and he would enthusiastically embrace Martin Luther; one of his last major works, *The Four Apostles* from 1526, is a strong defense of the young Reformation and its most ardent spokesperson. *(Alte Pinakothek, Munich, Germany / SuperStock.)*

Plate 9 Malinche and Devil masks, Guerrero, Mexico, mid-20th century. Masks were an important part of ritual dances in pre-Conquest Mexico, helping the dancers identify with divinities and guardian animals, and they are still widely used in festivals now associated with Catholic feast days. The two masks shown here attest to the ongoing vitality of old traditions, now mixed with new elements—in these cases, with deliberate irony. The top mask shows Malinche, Cortés's Indian wife and interpreter, her pink skin symbolizing the passion that led her to aid Cortés against her own people. Usually Malinche masks have a native appearance, but this Malinche's blue eyes and slender features give a modern twist to the old theme of cultural betrayal. She takes on the imported beauty of a Hollywood starlet, uncannily offset by the horns protruding from her head, decorated with ribbons recalling the ancient colors of the four sacred directions. The second mask has a face inside an eagle helmet, formerly the mark of an Aztec warrior; but here, in place of a warrior, a devil leers out from his helmet. *(Private collection / photograph by David Damrosch.)*

Plate 10 Miguel Gabrera, portrait of *Sor Juana Inés de la Cruz,* 1750. Painted half a century after Sor Juana's death from the plague, this portrait gives us the austere Mexican nun garbed in the signs of her profession: her black habit, her rosary beads, an enormous brooch depicting a prayerful female figure. But the books on the shelves behind her suggest Sor Juana's double life. We find not only a history of the papacy, but also the medical treatises of Galen and Hippocrates and Livy's *History of Rome,* among other classical and modern texts on thoroughly secular subjects. In her autobiographical account, *La respuesta,* Sor Juana wrote that in entering the convent, "I thought I was fleeing myself but—woe is me!—I brought myself with me, and brought my greatest enemy in my inclination to study, which I know not whether to take as a Heaven-sent favor or as a punishment." The serenity and self-command Gabrera here depicts seem to argue decisively for the former interpretation. *(The Art Archive / National History Museum, Mexico City / Dagli Orti.)*

Plate 11 Marcellus Laroon, *Charles II as President of the Royal Society,* England, 1684. In this portrait of the king painted a year before his death, the traditional trappings of royalty—crown, throne, and orb—literally take a back seat (in the background at left) to the advancements of the new science. Charles gestures toward the instruments of seeing, modeling, mapping, and calibrating that the Royal Society he sponsored had done much to devise and develop. By their placement, the painter suggests that these tools make possible the naval commerce and conquest depicted in the distance—as though the telescope were the world's new scepter, and the globe the monarch's proper sphere. *(The Art Archive / Christ's Hospital / Eileen Tweedy.)*

Plate 12 Carle Van Loo, *Madame de Pompadour as a Sultana,* France, 1752. Wearing "Turkish dress," especially when sitting for one's portrait, was all the rage among the European elite of the 18th century. Here the powerful mistress of Louis XV is shown in a setting inspired by descriptions of harems, such as those of Lady Mary Wortley Montagu and the Baron de Montesquieu. Accepting a cup of coffee from a devoted, dark-skinned slave while holding a Turkish pipe, Madame de Pompadour grandly enjoys the exotic luxuries that Europeans were importing from the East. *(Copyright © The State Hermitage Museum, St. Petersburg.)*

Plate 13 Paul Gauguin, *When Are You to Be Married?* Tahiti, 1892. Profoundly dissatisfied with life in France, Gauguin abandoned a career as a stockbroker at age 35 to devote himself to painting and moved to Tahiti in 1891 in search of a more primal style and subject-matter. There he created mysterious paintings using flat planes and bright, unnaturalistic colors. Although Gauguin's Tahiti is often a largely imagined place untouched by Western civilization, in this painting the woman in the background is wearing a European dress, perhaps foreshadowing the future of her companion, the flower at her left ear signaling her unmarried state. *(Rudolph Staechelin Family Foundation, Basel, Switzerland / The Bridgeman Art Library.)*

Plate 14 Édouard Manet, *Bar at the Folies-Bergère,* France, 1881–1882. A master of emotionally charged realism, Manet regularly shocked his viewers by his boldly unsentimental portrayals of women, whether the commercial sexuality of prostitutes or (as in this painting) the disillusioned weariness of a barmaid. Behind her is a large mirror, which reflects the scene in front of her: the happy crowd drinking and evidently watching one of the extravagant floor shows, featuring scantily clad women, for which the Folies-Bergère was famous. Over at the far left can be seen the barmaid's own reflection and the image of a customer, who may be seeking a date rather than a drink. This gentleman must, in fact, be standing precisely where the viewer is located—rather like Baudelaire's "hypocrite reader"—ironically detached from the melancholy scene. *(Courtauld Institute Gallery, Somerset House, London / The Bridgeman Art Library.)*

Plate 15 Pablo Picasso, *Les Demoiselles d'Avignon,* France, 1907. A groundbreaking work that signaled the advent of modernism in the visual arts, the scandalous subject matter—prostitutes at a brothel—was also highly innovative in its technique. Neither the interior space of the brothel nor the still life of fruit on a table in the foreground nor the women's bodies are constructed according to the rules of perspectival painting. Instead, they combine what would normally be views from different angles in an attempt to convey a new sense of reality as a shifting construct from multiple perspectives rather than a solid bedrock of perception. The African masks that take the place of two of the women's faces exemplify many modernist artists' interest in "primitive" art and its expressive potential. *(Copyright © 2005 Estate of Pablo Picasso / Artists Rights Society [ARS], New York.* Les Demoiselles d'Avignon, *1907. Acquired through the Lille P. Bliss Bequest. Digital image © The Museum of Modern Art / Licensed by SCALA / Art Resource, New York. The Museum of Modern Art, New York.)*

Plate 16 Frank Gehry, Guggenheim Museum, Bilbao, Spain, 1993–1997. Gehry's quintessentially post-modern work of architecture combines a steel frame and titanium-sheathed surface with curved and asymmetrical shapes that do not follow any predictable layout. This interweaving of metallic material usually associated with machinery and industry, and forms that look as if they had grown organically, makes for the distinctive character of a museum that helped to revitalize a decaying industrial district along the Nervión River in this northern Spanish city. *(Stéphane Pons / Photos12.com.)*

established. The rulers of these "Hellenistic" kingdoms tried to impose the Greek language, Greek administrative policies, city-planning, and architecture on the indigenous cultures. One of the cities that flourished was the Egyptian Alexandria, which became the intellectual capital of the Hellenistic world, a multi-ethnic city inhabited by Egyptians, Jews, Lebanese, Sudanese, Greeks, and Macedonians and welcoming an immense variety of religious practices.

Alexandria was also the site of a monumental library that housed the greatest works of classical Greek antiquity. The poetry, literary criticism, science, and religious practices that were centered around the library had a great impact on the next conquering power, the Romans, who eventually brought Greece and the Hellenized East into their empire. After the fall of the Roman Empire, and the tenuous preservation of the legacy of Greek literature in the monasteries and libraries of medieval Europe, some of Greek learning was preserved by great Arab scholars fascinated with such thinkers as Plato and Aristotle, and was passed to the early humanists by Byzantine scholars and through Iberia, or medieval Spain. In the European Renaissance, artists, scholars, and writers looked back to Greece for inspiration. Enlightenment thinkers including the founders of the American republic looked back to Greek democracy and the Roman republic as they debated the shape of the American polity. Greece itself eventually become part of the Ottoman Empire, and some of its greatest treasures were destroyed or carted off by Europeans newly interested in Greek civilization. In the nineteenth century Lord Elgin sawed off large portions of the frieze of the Parthenon and took what wasn't destroyed or sunk in shipwreck back to London, where the fragments formed a key part of the collection that became the British Museum. The Romantics were stirred by the Greek struggle for independence from the Ottomans; Byron died at Missolonghi, in central Greece, having volunteered for the Greek war of liberation. Heinrich Schliemann, a wealthy German brewer, dug up the remains of preclassical civilization at Mycenae and at Troy, and the gold mask of Agamemnon dazzled a world accustomed to the white marble of the Parthenon and Michelangelo's classicizing sculpture. With all their contradictions and in all their variety, the Greeks remain the still-potent ancestors of the Western tradition.

Early South Asia

The history of early South Asia until around 500 B.C.E. is obscure and contested. Although not committed to writing until the second millennium C.E., the *Rig Veda Samhita* (see page 31) was composed beginning around 1500 B.C.E. by pastoralist settlers using a language related to many others now spoken in Iran and across Eastern, Central, and Western Europe, languages today classified as members of the "Indo-European" language family. Much of the Veda is in verse, often the same eleven-syllable meter found in ancient Greek poetry such as Sappho's (recreated in the English translation "He looks to me to be in heaven, that man" page 496); the composer was called a *kavi*, "seer," which in turn became the term for "poet." And although *kavya*, a word best translated as "literature," derives from this name, people before the modern period in South Asia were very careful to distinguish this "literature" from the sacred Veda.

The story of the invention of literature recounted in the first book of the Sanskrit epic the *Ramayana* of Valmiki, long known as the first poem, is provided on page 612. In the form we know it from manuscripts still available, the *Ramayana* was almost certainly composed around 200 B.C.E., not long after the first written documents of South Asia were produced at the court of Ashoka, the third king of the Maurya dynasty. The poem shares much of the political perspective of Ashoka, and it reflects on its oral origins in a way unlikely in a world truly ignorant of writing, which was almost certainly invented at Ashoka's court.

The second great epic of South Asia, the *Mahabharata*, ascribed to the sage Vyasa, is usually assigned to the genre of history rather than poetry. It is probable that the *Mahabharata* came into being a century or two before Ashoka though it continued to grow through addition of materials for some centuries even after Valmiki's work was completed. Like the *Ramayana*, it has as its principal theme the meaning of power as well as the extent of power—the nature of kingly rule and the limits of the world within which this rule makes sense. Like the ancient Greek epics the *Iliad* and the *Odyssey*, the *Ramayana* and *Mahabharata* may deal with particular people in particular places, but they contemplate problems that no one anywhere has escaped: war and the perceived need to kill in order to live; duty; family; love. Yet, the responses to these problems offered by the two South Asian epics are entirely dissimilar. The more steely-eyed, if more agonized, vision of the *Mahabharata* leaves us with the taste of ashes in our mouth, whereas in the more utopian vision of the *Ramayana* victory brings unending peace and prosperity.

The Maurya Empire vanished in the second century B.C.E., and we have only a shadowy idea of the period that followed until the Guptas established their polity around 320 C.E. and extended it far outward from the core area around today's Patna (in southern Bihar). In this new courtly world and elsewhere, Sanskrit literary culture dominated the cultural scene in South Asia up to and even beyond the vernacular revolutions in the early centuries of the second millennium, when regional languages began to replace Sanskrit for literary and political purposes.

The world of Vedic culture was one of punctilious observance of calendrical sacrifices. In time, perhaps around the middle of the first millennium B.C.E., many thinkers began to sense that sacrifice by itself might not encompass the ultimate meaning of human existence, and a true crisis of belief ensued. One response to this crisis was ascetic renunciation and physical self-mortification. Another response was a new and profound reflection on life and death; for the first time, we encounter the ideas of redeath and rebirth, or transmigration (*samsara*), in accordance with deeds committed in the previous life (*karma*). The texts in Sanskrit that these thinkers composed, including the Upanishads, played an important role in a more general critique of religious life that emerged among a wide range of spiritual masters on the margins of or outside the Vedic world. Chief among these was Siddhartha Gautama Shakyamuni, the Buddha or "Awakened One," whose new doctrine, distinctive forms of meditation, and new social practices—including the establishment of the monastic community—produced an alternative religious vision that, within a few centuries, was to spread across Asia like wildfire.

China: The Classical Tradition

Though not the earliest civilization in human history, China's has certainly been the longest continuing one, a record supported by material evidence and historical documents extending back in time at least five thousand years. Well-preserved pottery and other artifacts attest to the existence of several developed Neolithic cultures at multiple sites along the Yellow River in northern China, with at least one on the Yangzi River to the south as well. Although one of these cultures is dated to the fifth millennium B.C.E., the majority appear to have flourished during the third. This is also the beginning of a prehistoric mythological record constructed by later generations, who credited a series of sage emperors with innovations and principles that were instrumental in the development of Chinese civilization and that established abiding norms of ethical and political practice.

The historical record begins with the Shang dynasty (c. 1550–1040 B.C.E.), which developed in the central Yellow River basin, when Sumer had long since disappeared and Egypt was already an old civilization. The last ruler of the Shang was overthrown by the Zhou people to the west around 1040 B.C.E.. Like the Shang, the Zhou were an agrarian people and maintained a strong commitment to ancestor worship. Within three centuries, a non-Chinese tribe succeeded in sacking the Zhou capital near modern-day Xi'an in 770 B.C.E. A revived Eastern Zhou was established near Luoyang farther down the Yellow River, but the empire existed henceforth in name only, as its increasingly powerful feudal states engaged in a long struggle to take its place.

The duchy of Lu was most closely identified with ancient Zhou traditions, and for its native son Confucius (551–479 B.C.E.) the remedy for contemporary troubles lay in a return to those values, which centered on the primacy of a family-based morality and the extension of its ideal behaviors to all other relationships. There were numerous competing schools of thought contending for the attention of rulers. The king of Qin, who succeeded in establishing his rule as the first emperor of China, adopted the advice of Han Fei (d. 233 B.C.E.) that only the power of power—of laws, rewards, and punishments—could order the state.

The Qin dynasty was remarkably and mercifully short-lived, lasting only from 221 to 206 B.C.E. Civil war then erupted, ending when a victorious general from the state of Han established a new dynasty that not only lasted for four hundred years but also remained for later generations the paragon of imperial power. Rejecting the excesses of the Qin, the Han dynasty (206 B.C.E.–220 C.E.) promoted Confucianism as state orthodoxy and implemented a rudimentary civil service competition in an attempt to match merit with responsibility. Five classical texts were also identified as the canon of the culture. Each of the "Five Classics" was associated in some way with Confucius, although later scholars have agreed that the links are tenuous at best. The *Book of Changes* (*Yijing* or *I Ching*) is a text used to interpret sixty-four hexagrams (patterns of six lines) connected to a divination process employing milfoil stalks that probably dates to the late Shang; Confucius was the supposed author of one of its most important affiliated commentaries. The *Book of Documents* (*Shujing* or *Shangshu*) was purported to contain pronouncements and other utterances of rulers and ministers dating back to the sage king Yao; though it was traditionally said to have been edited by Confucius, many sections are now agreed to be forgeries of much later date. The *Book of Songs* (*Shijing*) is an anthology of some three hundred poems that were composed across much of the Zhou dynasty and which were thought to have been compiled and edited by Confucius. The fourth classic contains ritual texts of which the *Record of Rites* (*Liji*) is the most important; it addresses issues of decorum both large and small and was supposedly collected and edited by Confucius as well. And the *Spring and Autumn Annals* chronicled events in Confucius's home state of

Marble statue of Augustus Caesar, c. 20 B.C.E.

Lu from 722 to 481 B.C.E. As Confucius looked back to the early Zhou; so all later dynasties would look back to the Han as the embodiment of imperial and cultural unity.

Rome and the Roman Empire

According to tradition, Romulus, a son of the god Mars suckled by a she-wolf with his twin brother Remus, founded Rome in 753 B.C.E. A legend popularized in the first century B.C.E. by the historian Livy and the poet Virgil attributed the genesis of the Roman people to the twelfth-century arrival on Italian shores of Aeneas, the Trojan hero who was said to have escaped the destruction by the Greeks of his ancestral city in Asia Minor. Aeneas's son Ascanius and their descendants ruled the region of Latium until Romulus took over the succession from his grandfather's usurper. The dual myth of origin expressed the double identity of the imperial city. On the one hand, it saw itself as grounded in the *mores maiorum,* the strict morality and customs of its rustic Latin ancestors. On the other hand, it saw itself as the cosmopolitan center of the world, steeped in the ancient and cultured traditions of the Hellenistic east.

The Roman republic, which lasted nearly five centuries until the ascension of emperor Augustus Caesar in 27 B.C.E., put a premium on gravity, dignity, austerity, integrity, fortitude, and disciplined obedience to the *mores maiorum.* For women, "old-fashioned mores" meant modesty, chastity, and subordination to the family of her father or her husband; for men, this meant fighting in the army and serving in government. As the famous lawyer and orator Cicero, staunch defender of the republican tradition, put it, "The Roman people hate private luxury but love public magnificence." Money was poured into great public works; victorious generals were feted with grand "triumphs"; martyrs and heroes of the republic were memorialized in statuary throughout the city. To be sure, the very insistence of so many writers on the austere virtue of the legendary past suggests that many wealthy and powerful Romans were in frequent need of admonition. Nevertheless, seldom has an ideology of self-restraint and self-sacrifice been more successfully employed. Nor is it difficult in this context to understand how the later empire and its citizenry would adapt so readily to the ascetic demands of early Christianity.

The World City

Rome was the center of religion, government, and cultural life from the early days of the republic until the division of the empire between east and west in the fourth century C.E. By the first century B.C.E., the tiny republic had become the dominant power in the Mediterranean; the capital city had some 250,000 inhabitants. By 100 C.E., over a million people lived there, far more than in any city for the next seven centuries. Notwithstanding severe overcrowding and the immense problems in feeding its population and disposing of their waste, the city's allure was irresistible. As the poet Ovid attested from unhappy exile on the Black Sea, the city (*urbs*) of Rome and the world (*orbis*) were one and the same: *Romanae spatium est urbis et orbis idem.*

Drainage and water supply were a priority from early on. By the late republic, the great central sewer known as the *cloaca maxima* had been enclosed; its tunnel ran nearly a kilometer and was large enough for the imperial administrator Agrippa to cruise through on a tour of inspection. Later sources list 144 public latrines within the

The Roman Empire in 150 C.E.

city, in addition to those in the many public baths. These baths were central to the social life of Rome and its provincial towns, and they grew progressively larger and more spectacular as the empire expanded. The Caracalla baths, whose ruins can still be visited, could hold up to 1,500 persons, and included art galleries, libraries, and exercise halls. Display of wealth was an important aspect of the baths, but they also served the practical purpose of keeping a notoriously fastidious people clean. Given that the streets of Rome were extremely narrow, unlit at night, made of dirt, and strewn with filth and refuse, personal hygiene was a constant battle.

Nearly everyone in late republican and imperial Rome came from somewhere else. Although the poet Catullus was born in Verona and served on the staff of a governor in Asia Minor, he had no qualms in mocking his rival Egnatius as a provincial, with "untrimmed beard, and teeth polished in the Spanish / manner—with urine." Cicero, Livy, Virgil, Horace, and Ovid all came to Rome from other parts of Italy. Later writers arrived from farther afield: Tacitus from Gaul, the epic poet Lucan and the moralist Seneca from Córdoba in Spain, Apuleius and Augustine from North Africa. Spanish-born Trajan was the first emperor from beyond Italy (98–117 C.E.); later emperors came from all over the Mediterranean, often bringing their local customs and beliefs with them, as in the extreme case of the Syrian Elagabalus (218–22 C.E.), hereditary High Priest to the sun god of Emesa, whose exotic rituals and bizarre sexual practices contributed to his being assassinated in short order.

The Literature of Rome

The satirist Juvenal complained that there was no money in writing poetry. Several emperors were known as patrons of the arts, but writing was generally either integral to political activity—oratory and letter-writing—or conducted in one's leisure or by those with independent incomes. All educated Romans were bilingual in Latin and Greek, and most higher education (rhetoric and philosophy) was conducted in Greek by teachers of Hellenistic origin. Latin literature grew out of imitation and translation from the Greek. Scrolls were status objects, and there was a vigorous publishing trade in classical Rome. Writing took place in one of three forms. Papyrus, made from the pith of an Egyptian marsh plant pounded into layers, was widely used in the east. More common in Italy and less expensive were parchment or vellum, made from the skins of cattle, sheep, or goats. All of these materials would be written upon with ink made from soot and water, and stored in rolls up to 16 feet in length. Wooden leaf tablets, thin enough to fold, could also be written on in ink. Alternatively, wooden stylus tablets with a recessed surface covered in colored wax could be inscribed with a bronze or iron stylus, and were reusable. By the fourth century, the parchment book or codex, bound down one edge, had replaced the scroll.

Perhaps the most Roman of all literary genres were the erotic elegy and the satire. The elegy was transformed from its Greek model by the addition of an apparently autobiographical first-person narrator. The erotic poet was single-minded in his pursuit of love, and generally turned his back on the traditionally public duties of the Roman citizen. A major influence on this poetry was Catullus (84–54 B.C.E.), whose school of "neoteric" poets was self-consciously modern, stressing emotionality, confessional detail, linguistic polish, and negligible subject matter over the rustic virtues of dignity, gravity and civic duty. Like the elegy, the satire focused primarily on individuals in nonofficial settings. Despite its capacity for character assassination, it seldom ventured into political territory or *ad hominem* attacks. Ovid, exiled by Augustus for "a poem and an indiscretion," Juvenal, banished by Domitian, and Petronius, forced to suicide by Nero, were all well aware that many subjects were off-limits to the poets of imperial Rome.

The primary genres of Roman expansion were history and epic. Rome was a record-keeping society, setting down numerous laws and treaties, and copious oratory and correspondence. The concern of historiographers such as Livy, Tacitus, and Suetonius with memorializing the past and their consciousness of the ideological power of historical narrative were especially influential on postmedieval writers, not least of whom was the celebrated chronicler Edward Gibbon, whose magnum opus, *The Decline and Fall of the Roman Empire* (1776–1788), molded the reception of Rome and its legacy for many generations. While historiography developed a distinctly Roman form, epic remained self-consciously indebted to its Greek antecedents, most notably the Homeric poems, the *Iliad* and the *Odyssey*. The paradigm was Virgil's *Aeneid,* which transferred the archaic, orally composed and mythic Homeric poems into a world simultaneously mythic and historical, archaic and contemporary. There had been some precedent for the *Aeneid,* but what followed it was a veritable explosion of epics concerning other episodes of Roman history and Greek myth. Two of the most enduring works of Latin literature, Lucretius's Epicurean account of the way the natural world, *On the Nature of Things* (c. 54 B.C.E.), and Ovid's protean retelling of the entire corpus of Greek and Roman mythology, the *Metamorphoses* (2–8 C.E.), brought the monumental scope and elevated style of epic to bear on subject matter and narrative forms that creatively stretched its boundaries. Latin epic and historiography reflected the new preeminence of Rome in their scope and ambition. Still, the accomplishments of empire were never recounted without at least a hint of ambivalence as to the sacrifice and suffering entailed by them.

Imperium Sine Fine

In the first book of the *Aeneid,* Jupiter prophesies that the land to be granted to the descendants of Aeneas will be an *imperium sine fine*, an empire with neither temporal nor geographical end. Virgil wrote these lines under the patronage of the first Roman emperor, Caesar Augustus (formerly Octavian), who reigned from 27 B.C.E. to 14 C.E. As Tacitus later wrote, Augustus "seduced everyone with the sweetness of peace." The restrictions of Augustus's rule seemed to many a small price to pay for putting an end to a hundred years of civil strife under the late republic and stabilizing a world now dominated by Rome. A series of both reforms and grabs for power that began somewhere in the late second century climaxed in 49 B.C.E. with the dictatorship of Julius Caesar. Caesar's power was based in the army he controlled and the reputation his victories had given him, most notably his subjugation of Gaul (present-day France). When Caesar was assassinated in 44 C.E. by a group of republican senators, war broke out among his heirs and rivals. His adopted son Octavian defeated Mark Antony and Antony's ally and lover Cleopatra at the decisive battle of Actium in 31 B.C.E., and the way was paved for him to become sole ruler of Rome.

The Roman empire was a complex combination of military prowess and political savvy. The Roman legions were highly trained and well-equipped, and they fought with disciplined efficiency. Repeated opposition, especially from rival powers, was savagely repressed. For the most part, however, defeated peoples retained a fair measure of autonomy as long as they paid the often severe taxes levied upon them by the central authority in Rome. The legionaries constructed carefully planned and laid-out provincial capitals throughout Roman territory, the origins of modern cities such as London, Paris, and Córdoba. They also built an extensive network of paved roads to allow rapid movement of persons and goods between Rome and the provinces, and aqueducts to transport water. Local peoples were usually allowed to preserve their own languages, customs, and religions. At the same time, they were gradually incorporated into Roman culture through citizenship and the privileges that went with it.

Expansion continued through the fourth century. The borders of Rome extended into Scotland in the British Isles, and as far north as the Rhine and the Danube rivers in Europe, circling the Mediterranean from Gaul, Spain, North Africa, and Egypt through Palestine, Syria, Asia Minor, Greece, and the Balkans. The military played an increasingly prominent role in choosing emperors, and succession often meant no more than a series of military coups. The need for military support would contribute to the eventual fall of Rome, as later emperors depended more and more on mercenaries from Germanic tribes to augment their forces.

The Eternal City in Ruins

The empire endured by name until the fall of Constantinople to the Ottoman Turks in 1453, but from a Roman point of view it was all over by 410 when Alaric led his Goths into Rome. The conversion of emperor Constantine in 324 had inaugurated the spread of Christianity through western Europe; it was also responsible for the shift of imperial power eastward to the city he established on the straits of the Bosphorus, free of the pagan temples and traditions that saturated Rome. The invading Goths were themselves converts to Christianity, partially acculturated into a western empire rapidly being eclipsed by the east. Evidently not everyone was sorry for the change. According to the Christian priest Salvanius, many in Gaul considered that "the enemy is more lenient to them than the tax collectors." Nevertheless, the symbolism of Rome in the hands of northern barbarians sent shockwaves through the empire. The church father Jerome, who while in Rome had begun the Vulgate, his enduring Latin translation of the Bible, lamented from Palestine that, "The head of the Roman empire was cut off, and, to speak more truly, the entire world perished with that single city." Rome continued to decline, and by the middle of the ninth century it had only seventeen thousand inhabitants. As the power of the medieval papacy grew from that point, so did the city revive, but ever since Alaric the ruins and the past of Rome have overshadowed its present. From Dante and Petrarch through Shakespeare and Montaigne to Thomas Mann and Sigmund Freud, few Western writers have been able to resist the allure of those ruins.

The Ancient World

Year	The World	Literature
3500 B.C.E.		
	3200–3100 Development of cuneiform writing in Mesopotamia	
	c. 3100 Unification of Egypt; development of hieroglyphics	
3000	**3000–2501** Neolithic settlements on Crete	
	c. 2700 Gilgamesh king of Uruk in southern Mesopotamia	
2500	**2500–2001** Early Minoan culture on Crete	**2500–2180** Pyramid Texts in Egypt
		2200–2000 Early Sumerian poems about Gilgamesh
2000	**2000–1500** Greek-speakers begin to move from the East toward the eastern Mediterranean; Cecrops, legendary first king of Athens; Middle Minoan period of Crete; Decimal system on Crete; Late Minoan period of Crete (to 1400)	**c. 1925** *The Story of Sinuhe*
	c. 1900 Hebrews begin to migrate from Babylonia to Palestine	
		c. 1600 Old Babylonian *Epic of Gilgamesh*
	c. 1550–1040 Shang dynasty in China	
1500	**1500–1000** Wandering of pastoral nomadic groups across Eurasia	**c. 1500–1000** Sanskrit *Vedas*
	1500–1200 Beginnings of Cretan-Mycenaean culture	
	c. 1372–1354 Reign of Akhnaten and "Amarna Revolution" in Egypt	**c. 1360** Great Hymn to the Aten
		c. 1300–1200 Egyptian love poetry written down
	c. 1200 Traditional time of the Exodus of Israelites from captivity in Egypt	**c. 1200** *Enuma Elish;* Sîn-liqe-unninni creates Standard Version of *The Epic of Gilgamesh*
	1193 Destruction of Troy, 6th level	
	c. 1100 According to legend, Aeneas arrives at Latium from Troy	
	c. 1040–256 Zhou dynasty in China	
	c. 1020 United Israel founded by King Saul	

Year	The World	Literature
1000		
	1000–900 Ionians, displaced from mainland Greece, found cities in Asia Minor, including Ephesus and Miletus. Political unification of Athens. Greek alphabet based on Semitic-Phoenician characters adds vowels	
	c. 1000–960 Reign of King David in Israel	**c. 950** Yahwists compose first version of the Torah, including Genesis
	c. 960–931 Reign of King Solomon; after his death, Israel divided by civil war into Israel and Judah	
	900–700 Greek colonization throughout Mediterranean basin	**c. 900** The Book of Job **c. 900–700** Composition of *Iliad, Odyssey, Theogony, Works and Days*
	800–600 Rise of urbanism in northern India	**c. 800–600** Upanishads **c. 800–400** *Book of Songs,* China
	776 Legendary foundation of the Olympian games **753** Traditional date on which Romulus founds Rome **722** Israel conquered by Assyrians; Judah remains independent **722–481** Spring and Autumn Period in China	**c. 750** Kabti-ilani-Marduk, *Erra and Ishum*
		700–600 Arkhilokhos, Sappho, and other Greek lyric poets flourish
	594–593 Solon reforms Athenian government **586** Babylonians conquer Judah, deport many Hebrews to Babylon **c. 551–479** Life of Confucius **539** Cyrus the Great of Persia conquers Babylon and permits Hebrews to return to Israel. Founds Persian Empire **527** Death of Peisistratos, tyrant of Athens **510** Cleisthenes' democratic reforms **509** Rome becomes a republic	**c. 550** Priestly writers among Hebrews in exile in Babylon revise Torah into canonical form **c. 500–450** *Analects* of Confucius **500–429** *Dao De Jing*
500		
	500–429 Life of Athenian leader Pericles **500** Ionians revolt from Persia **490–449** Persian Wars **490** Battle of Marathon **480** Battles of Thermopylae and Salamis **470–399** Life of Socrates **469–399** Hippocrates **448–433** Rebuilding of the Athenian Acropolis after Persian destruction **431–404** Peloponnesian War between Athens and Sparta **427–347** Life of Plato **411** Oligarchic coup in Athens **405** Defeat of Athenians by Sparta **403–221** Warring States period in China	**c. 475–450** Pindar, *Odes* **458** Aeschylus, *Oresteia* **c. 450** *Discourses of the Buddha* **431** Pericles' Funeral Oration **431** Euripides, *Medea* **c. 430** Herodotus, *History* **c. 426** Sophocles, *Oedipus the King* **411** Aristophanes, *Lysistrata*

Year	The World	Literature
	399 Execution of Socrates **384–322** Life of Aristotle **369–286** Life of Zhuangzi **356–323** Alexander the Great conquers central Asia; 332 founds Alexandria in Egypt, dies in Babylon 323 **352–336** Philip II of Macedon **338** Philip defeats Greeks at Chaeronea	**c. 400** Thucydides, *History* **c. 400 B.C.E–400 C.E.** *Mahabharata* **390** Plato, *Apology of Socrates*
	c. 300 Rise of the Mauryan Empire in India (to 100 C.E.)	**c. 300 B.C.E.–100 C.E.** Kautilya, *Treatise on Power*
	250 Buddhism begins to spread beyond India	**250** Asoka, *Inscriptions*
	221–206 Qin dynasty in China **206 B.C.E.–220 C.E.** Han dynasty in China	
		c. 200 Valmiki, *Ramayana*
	190 Palestine comes under Roman control **149–146** Third Punic War; Carthage is destroyed by Romans **147** Romans take control of Greece	
100		
	64–63 Conspiracy of Catiline in Rome against Cicero's consulship	
	58–50 Julius Caesar campaigns in Gaul	
		c. 55–54 Lucretius, *On the Nature of Things* **c. 54** Catullus, *Poems*
	48 Caesar defeats Pompey at the battle of Pharsalus **44** Caesar murdered by Brutus and Cassius	
		39–29 Virgil, *Eclogues* **35–30** Horace, *Satires*
	31 Octavian (Augustus) defeats Antony and Cleopatra at the battle of Actium, end of civil war; Egypt becomes a Roman province	
		29 B.C.E.–17 C.E. Livy, *History of Rome*
		19 Virgil, *Aeneid*
	c. 6 Birth of Jesus (traditionally estimated at 1 C.E.)	**c. 1 B.C.E.–1 C.E.** Ovid, *Art of Love, Remedy of Love*
1 C.E.		**2–8** Ovid, *Metamorphoses*
	29 Augustus dies; succeeded after a month by Tiberius **c. 30** Jesus is crucified outside the walls of Jersualem	
		c. 45–64 Paul, *Epistles*

Year	The World	Literature
		c. 60–90 Gospels according to Matthew, Mark, and Luke; Acts of the Apostles
	64 The great fire in Rome; Nero persecutes Christians	
	65 Failure of the Pisonian conspiracy against Nero; Lucan and Seneca compelled to suicide	**c. 66** Petronius, *Satyricon*
	70 Jewish revolt against Rome; Temple in Jerusalem destroyed	
		c. 75 *Priapea*
	98–117 Reign of Trajan	
100		**c. 101–127** Juvenal, *Satires*
		c. 117 Tacitus, *Annals*
		c. 120 Suetonius, *Lives of the Caesars*
	150 Rule of the Kushanas and Indo-Scythians	**150** Ashvaghosha, *Life of the Buddha*
	161–180 Reign of Marcus Aurelius	
	c. 200 Pandyas patronize Tamil culture in the south	**c. 200** *Tamil Anthologies*
	c. 200 End of the Satavahana Empire in south-central India	**c. 200** Hala, *The Seven Hundred Songs*
	200–500 End of Kushan rule and rise of the Gupta in northern India	**c. 200–500** Early Buddhist *puranas,* including *Lore of the Dwarf Incarnation*
	313 Edict of Milan, Constantine proclaims toleration of the Christian religion	
	355–363 Reign of Julian "the Apostate"	
		384 Jerome, Vulgate Bible (New Testament)
		c. 400–425 Poetry of Tao Qian
		c. 400 Augustine, *Confessions*
		c. 400 Vatsyayana, *Kamasutra*
		406 Jerome, Vulgate Bible (Old Testament)
		413–427 Augustine, *City of God*
	420 Alaric sacks Rome	
	c. 450 Height of the Gupta Empire in India	**c. 450** Kalidasa, *Shakuntala*

PERSPECTIVES

Creation Myths and Social Concerns

Every culture tells tales of the origins of the world. Very often, these stories of origin serve to ground contemporary relations and practices—religious, political, and social. This is especially true for the stories of origin told by the peoples of antiquity, who generally had little interest in scientific exploration or explanation, at least not for its own sake: they looked to the past to understand their place in the present. Often these myths were used for ritual purposes, as part of ceremonies to inaugurate the new year, or the seasons of planting or harvest; often they were told for political purposes, to undergird a form of government or a particular dynasty. Sometimes these purposes merged, as when a king served as chief priest for a new year's ritual. The Babylonian creation epic, *Enuma Elish,* was recited at just such a ceremony, at once royal and divine in focus. The poem grounds the king's authority in his intimate relation to the creative divine power, showing the king both as the gods' humble servant and as their powerful equal.

Creation stories could also be told *against* other people's creation stories. The Bible's account of creation in Genesis 1–11 stands in sharp contrast to the Babylonian account, as seen in *Enuma Elish,* in which creation culminates in the establishment of Babylon as the ritual center of the world, the seat of human service to the gods. By contrast, the biblical writers show God bringing the Flood to destroy the impious builders of the tower of Babel/Babylon, and already in the opening chapter they combat the surrounding polytheism by refusing even to call the Sun and Moon by name, demoting those traditionally great divinities to merely mechanical roles as "the greater light" and "the lesser light."

In India, the ancient hymns of the *Rig Veda* conveyed early Hindu conceptions of the emergence of all life from the underlying reality of the absolute self or Brahman, a reality that is to be perceived and supported by sacrifices and the singing of the Vedic hymns themselves, guided by

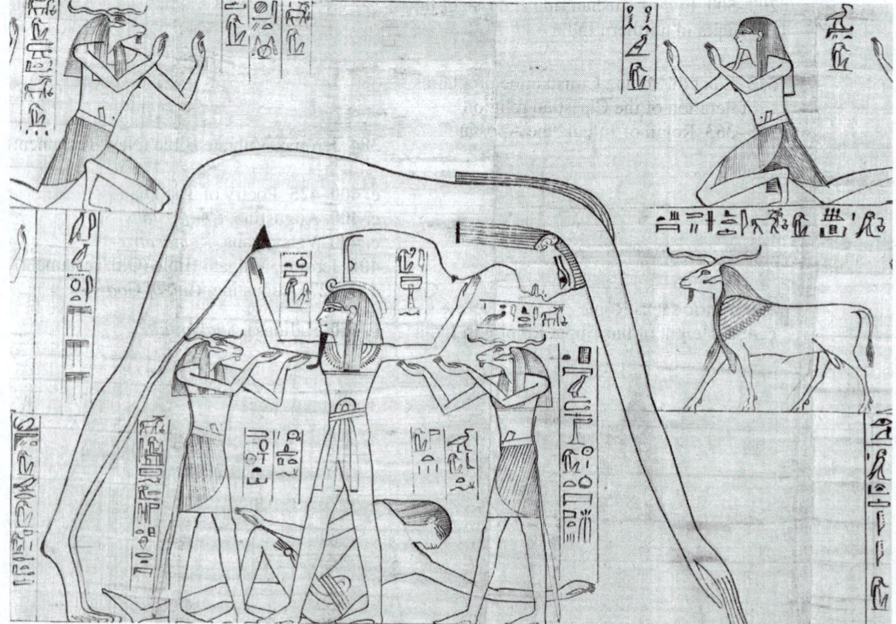

The creation of heaven and earth, Egyptian papyrus from c, 1025 B.C.E. The creator god Shu is shown raising up Nut, goddess of heaven, who arches over the reclining earth god, Geb.

the philosopher-priests of the highest Hindu caste, the Brahmins. By contrast, the Buddhist creation story that follows the Vedic account satirizes it as only an expression of the interests of the Brahmin class, and proposes a very different creation story in which all people are equal.

The texts given here date from the second millennium B.C.E. up to the opening centuries of the first millennium, at a time when versions of these myths were circulating widely around the eastern Mediterranean world, westward to Greece and eastward across Mesopotamia to Persia and India. They thus give a remarkable window into the varied cultural uses to which creation stories could be put as they traveled across this broad region. As ancient as all these writings are, none of the writers thought of themselves as ancient at all. Instead, they were heirs to the long span of antiquity their creation stories reveal, and they typically see their modern times as sundered in basic ways from an earlier age when gods and goddesses walked the earth, people lived to great ages or never died, cities were not yet established, and humans and animals lived together on different terms. The world might have begun just a few thousand years earlier, as the biblical writers believed, or tens of thousands of years before, as the Sumerians and Babylonians thought, or millions of years before, as the Hindus believed, with the present cosmos itself only one of many reincarnations of the universe, but these differing accounts of creation always have a double message to their modern audience: to explain how the world has changed since the distant past, and to point the way to the right conduct of society in the present and future.

A Babylonian Theogony

2nd–1st millennium B.C.E.

A "theogony" is a tale of the birth of the gods. In full versions, theogonies typically begin with a primordial god or pair of gods who then produce several younger generations, with the tale ending with the creation of humanity. Often, as here, such an account would be told from the perspective of a particular city, in this case a Mesopotamian city called "Dunnu of the twin towers." Its location is now unknown, and it doesn't seem to have ever been a prominent place, yet this poem proudly asserts that the very first gods built this city and served as its lords.

This text's ending is missing, and many lines are incomplete; brackets indicate gaps in the Babylonian tablet on which it was recorded in the middle of the first millennium B.C.E. The tablet includes a note saying that it was copied from an earlier copy in the city of Assur. The language of the text suggests that it was composed several centuries before Assur was destroyed in 614 B.C.E.; presumably the outlines of the story itself are far older. Our text describes with unembarrassed directness the process of incest and murder by which each generation of gods was first created and then supplanted by the next generation—themes that will be seen developed far more fully in the Babylonian *Enuma Elish* and the Greek poetry of Hesiod.

PRONUNCIATIONS:

Amakandu: ah-mah-KAHN-dou
Ga'um: gah-OOM
Ḫain: khayn
Ningeshtinna: neen-GESH-tee-nah

A Babylonian Theogony[1]

[..] in the beginning [. . .]
[..].. and . [. . .] . . . . [. . .]

1. Translated by W. G. Lambert.

They . . . [..] and [..]. their plough
[With the] stroke of their plough they brought Sea into being.
[Second]ly, by themselves they bore Amakandu;[2]
[Third]ly, they built the city of Dunnu, the twin towers.
Ḫain dedicated the overlordship in the city of Dunnu to himself.
[Earth] cast her eyes on Amakandu, her son,
"Come, let me make love to you," she said to him.
Amakandu married Earth, his mother, and
Ḫain, his [father], he killed, and
Laid [him] to rest in the city of Dunnu, which he loved.
Then Amakandu took the overlordship of his father, [and]
Married Sea, his sister [. . .]
Laḫar,[3] son of Amakandu, went [and]
Killed Amakandu, and in the city of Dunnu
He laid [him] to rest in the [. . .] of his father.
He married Sea, his mother.
Then Sea murdered Earth, her mother.
In the month Chislev on the 16th day he took the overlordship and kingship.

[. . .], son of Laḫar, married River, his own sister, and
He killed [Laḫar], his father, and Sea, his mother, and
Laid them to rest [in . . . .]
[In the month . . .] on the first day [he] took the kingship and overlordship
for himself.

[. . . , son of . . .] married Ga'um, his sister
[. . .] earth . . . [. . .]
[. . .] . . . . [. . .]
[. . .] . . fathers and .[. . .]
[. . .] . . [. .]. for the . . . of the gods .[. . .]
[. . .] he killed River, his mother, [and]
[. . .] he settled them.
[In the month . . . on the _th day] he [took] the overlordship and kingship
for himself.

[. . . , son of . .] . , married Ningeshtinna, his sister, [and]
Killed [. . . , his father, and] Ga'um, his mother.
[. . .] he settled them.
[In the month . . .] on the 16th day, he took the kingship and overlordship.

Hymns from the Rig Veda

1500–1000 B.C.E.

The *Rig Veda Samhita,* or "Collection of the Wisdom in Verses," was composed during the second half of the second millennium B.C.E. (beginning around 1500 B.C.E.), and transmitted orally with unparalleled exactitude for the next two thousand years, until committed to writing in the early centuries of the second millennium C.E. Whereas most of the hymns were intended for use in the

2. God of wild animals.

3. God of cattle.

liturgy of Vedic sacrifice—they are called *mantras* or "thought instruments" for calling to mind the pertinent deities in the course of the ritual action—some have very different concerns. No one in South Asia before the modern period ever considered the *Rig Veda* to be what we (and post-Vedic Indians) called literature (*kavya*), yet a range of hymns—of the sort, for example, that present Dawn dressed in brilliant robes and leading her white horse—clearly meets the criteria of expressivity, rhetoric, or imagination that most readers would use in framing any definition of literature. It is likewise improbable that the hymn "In the Beginning" ever had a liturgical function; it is instead a purely speculative text, reflecting the interest that arose in the early first millennium B.C.E., in South Asia as it did among the pre-Socratic philosophers of archaic Greece, in understanding the enigma of creation and first principles: if something cannot come from nothing, what was the first something, and from where did it come? "The Sacrifice of Primal Man" shows yet another concern of the Vedic corpus, in providing charter myths for explaining the nature of social life. The cosmic Man is the substance offered up at the primeval, universe-generating sacrifice (*dharma* is the term used here, and "sacrifice" may be its oldest sense)—just as the everyday rituals of the old Vedic world were thought to sustain the universe—and from his parts all the arrangements of this world first came about, including the division of society into the hierarchy that here for the first time is named: at the top, the Brahman, the class of the masters of learning and ritual (in the present translation, "priest"); next the Kshatriya (warrior, "prince"); the Vaishya (pastoralist, cultivator, merchant; "the common people"); and at the bottom the Shudra (the serving class or "serf"). Whatever exists, we come to understand, is good and unchangeable, because it is part of nature.

Early Buddhism sharply criticized such endorsement of the arrangements of this world (page 34). Not all Buddhists shared this concern—Buddhism long enjoyed the patronage of the highest strata of South Asian society, and many Buddhist monks were Brahman converts. But the "Discourse on What Is Primary" is remarkable for its systematic criticism of the Vedic social and political charter offered in the "Sacrifice of Primal Man." Here the Buddha argues that kingship has nothing otherworldly about it but is simply the result of a kind of social contract, and generally birth confers no excellences automatically. On the contrary, he is first, or "primary," who *achieves* primacy by following *dharma* (here the term means Buddhist ethics)—not necessarily the Brahman, who is thought to have primacy by birth—and the true father of the monk is the Buddha himself. The world is thus viewed as completely contingent, and accordingly it is changeable, so that the suffering that marks human life can actually be ended.

HYMNS FROM THE RIG VEDA

The Sacrifice of Primal Man[1]

1

A thousand heads had primal Man,
A thousand eyes, a thousand feet:
Encompassing the earth on every side,
He exceeded it by ten fingers' breadth.

2

That Man is this whole universe—
What was and what is yet to be,
The Lord of immortality
Which he outgrows by eating food.

3

This is the measure of his greatness,
But greater yet is primal Man:

1. Translated by Dominic Goodall.

All beings form a quarter of him,
Three-quarters are the immortal in heaven.

4

With three-quarters Man rose up on high,
A quarter of him came to be again down here:
From this he spread in all directions,
Into all that eats and does not eat.

5

From him was Virāj[2] born,
From Virāj Man again:
Once born—behind, before,
He reached beyond the earth.

6

When with Man as their oblation
The gods performed the sacrifice,
Spring was the melted butter,
Summer the fuel, and autumn the oblation.

7

Him they besprinkled on the sacrificial strew—
Primeval Man, born in the beginning:
With him their victim, gods, Sādhyas, seers
Performed the sacrifice.

8

From this sacrifice completely offered
The clotted ghee was gathered up:
From this he fashioned beasts and birds,
Creatures of the woods and creatures of the village.

9

From this sacrifice completely offered
Were born the *Rig-* and *Sāma-Vedas;*
From this were born the metres,
From this was the *Yajur-Veda* born.

10

From this were horses born, all creatures
That have teeth in either jaw:
From this were cattle born,
From this sprang goats and sheep.

11

When they divided primal Man,
Into how many parts did they divide him?
What was his mouth? What his arms?
What are his thighs called? What his feet?

12

The Brāhman was his mouth,
The arms were made the Prince,
His thighs the common people,
And from his feet the serf was born.

2. A term of uncertain significance in the Veda but suggesting both splendor and a female principle.

13

From his mind the moon was born,
And from his eye the sun,
From his mouth Indra and the fire,
From his breath the wind was born.

14

From his navel arose the atmosphere,
From his head the sky evolved,
From his feet the earth, and from his ear
The cardinal points of the compass:
So did they fashion forth these worlds.

15

Seven were his enclosing sticks,
Thrice seven were made his fuel-sticks,
When the gods, performing sacrifice,
Bound Man, their sacrificial beast.

16

With sacrifice the gods
Made sacrifice to sacrifice:
These were the first religious rites,
To the firmament these powers went up
Where dwell the ancient Sādhya gods.

In the Beginning

1

Then neither Being nor Not-being was,
Nor atmosphere, nor firmament, nor what is beyond.
What did it encompass? Where? In whose protection?
What was the water, the deep, unfathomable?

2

Neither death nor immortality was there then,
No sign of night or day.
That One breathed, windless, by its own energy:
Nought else existed then.

3

In the beginning was darkness swathed in darkness;
All this was but unmanifested water.
Whatever was, that One, coming into being,
Hidden by the Void,
Was generated by the power of heat.

4

In the beginning this One evolved,
Became desire, first seed of mind.
Wise seers, searching within their hearts,
Found the bond of Being in Not-being.

5

Their cord was extended athwart:
Was there a below? Was there an above?
Casters of seed there were, and powers;

Beneath was energy, above was impulse.

6

Who knows truly? Who can here declare it?
Whence it was born, whence is this emanation.
By the emanation of this the gods
Only later came to be.
Who then knows whence it has arisen?

7

Whence this emanation hath arisen,
Whether God disposed it, or whether he did not—
Only he who is its overseer in highest heaven knows.
He only knows, or perhaps he does not know!

RESONANCE

from The Discourse on What Is Primary (*Agganna Sutta*)[1]

1

Thus I have heard. At one time the Blessed One[2] was living in the palatial monastery built by Migāra's mother[3] in the Eastern Park outside Sāvatthi.[4] Vāsettha and Bhāradvāja, aspiring to become monks, were living with the monks there. One evening the Blessed One rose from his solitary meditation, went outside the monastery, and was walking back and forth in its shade, in the open air.

2

Vāsettha saw the Blessed One and said to Bhāradvāja: "Friend Bhāradvāja, here is the Blessed One walking back and forth in the open air. Come, let's go to him: perhaps we may get a chance to hear a Dhamma-talk."[5]

"Alright," agreed Bhāradvāja.

Vāsettha and Bhāradvāja went up to the Blessed One, greeted him, and walked back and forth together with him.

3

The Blessed One addressed them: "Monks, you were born Brahmans, in Brahman families, but you have gone forth from home to homelessness, leaving your Brahman family. Surely Brahmans must revile and abuse you?"

"Indeed, sir, Brahmans revile and abuse us plentifully, unreservedly, with the sort of abuse one would expect."

"How do they abuse you?"

"Sir, Brahmans say 'The Brahman is the best class, any other class is inferior. The Brahman is the fair class, any other class is dark. Only Brahmans are purified, not

1. Translated by Steven Collins. The *Agganna Sutta* is contained in the "Collection of Longer Discourses," 34 major early Buddhist texts. The Buddha addresses the discourse to two novice monks whose names indicate that they are Brahmans, and who are confused about the traditional claims of their caste privilege.
2. A name of the Buddha.
3. The Buddha's greatest female lay follower.
4. Shravasti in Sanskrit, an ancient city near today's Nepal border, site of a famous monastery where the Buddha preached many of his sermons.
5. Dharma in Sanskrit, here meaning the teachings of the Buddha.

non-Brahmans. Brahmans are Brahmā's[6] own sons, born from his mouth, born of Brahmā, produced from Brahmā, the heirs of Brahmā. You have left the best class and gone over to an inferior class, becoming wretched shaven-headed pseudo-ascetics, members of some sect, no better than offspring of our Kinsman's [i.e., Brahmā's] feet.[7] It is not good, it is unseemly, that you have left the best class and become offspring of our Kinsman's feet.' That is how they revile us . . . with the sort of abuse one would expect."

4

"Surely the Brahmans are not recalling the past when they say this. Brahman women, the wives of Brahmans, obviously menstruate, become pregnant, give birth and feed their babies. These Brahmans who say: 'The Brahman is the best class . . . Brahmans are born from Brahmā's mouth . . . heirs of Brahmā,' are in fact born from vaginas. They are slandering Brahmā, telling lies, and producing demerit.

5

"Monks, there are these four classes: Kshatriya (kings), Brahman (priests), Vaishya (farmers) and Shudra (servants). Take the case where a particular king is a murderer, a thief, misbehaves in sexual matters, tells lies, speaks maliciously, harshly and frivolously, is envious, malevolent or holds wrong views. Then one can see in an individual king those things which are unwholesome, blameworthy, not to be followed, unworthy to be called noble, and known to be all these things, dark with dark karmic result, and censured by the wise. [Similarly in members of the other three classes.]

6

"Or, take the case where a particular king refrains from murder, theft, etc. Then one can see in an individual king those things which are wholesome . . . fair with fair result and praised by the wise. [Similarly in members of the other classes.]

7

"Given that bad and good things, what is censured and praised by the wise, occur together in the four classes, wise people will not tolerate it when Brahmans say: 'The Brahman is the best class . . . Brahmans are . . . heirs of Brahmā.' Why? Of these four classes, monks, he who is a monk, an Arahant,[8] in whom mental stains are destroyed, who has lived the holy life, done what was to be done, laid down the burden, attained the true goal, in whom the ties to existence are destroyed, who is released by Right Wisdom, is properly called what is primary among them, not improperly as are the Brahmans. For the Dhamma is the best thing, monks, in this world, both in this life and in the future.

8

"Here is an illustration to show that Dhamma is best in this world and in the future. The king of Kosala, Pasenadi, realizes: 'The unsurpassed ascetic Gotama[9] has gone

6. The creator god.
7. Shudras, those belonging to the lowest order of the traditional caste hierarchy.
8. A "worthy one," a disciple who has attained the final stage of spiritual development.
9. A family name of the Buddha.

forth from a Sakyan family.'[1] The Sakyans are now vassals of King Pasenadi of Kosala, monks: they have to fall at King Pasenadi's feet in obeisance, salute him respectfully, rise up from their seats for him, do him homage with hands together. Now, all this kow-towing which the Sakyans do before King Pasenadi, King Pasenadi does before me, thinking: 'Indeed the ascetic Gotama is well-born, I am ill-born; the ascetic Gotama is powerful, I am not; Gotama is charismatic, I am ugly; he has great authority, I have little.' It is in reverence, honor, worship and respect for this Dhamma that King Pasenadi falls kow-tows to me. This shows, monks, that Dhamma is the best.

9

"You, monks, come from various castes, have various names, and so on, and yet you have gone forth from home to homelessness. When asked who you are, you should respond: 'We are sons of the Sakyan.' When anyone has a faith in the Tathāgata[2] which is firm, rooted, well-established not disturbed by any ascetic, Brahman, god, Māra,[3] Brahmā, or anyone in the world, that person can fittingly say: 'I am the Blessed One's own son, born from his mouth, born of the Dhamma, produced by the Dhamma, the heir of Dhamma.' Why? Because there are these epithets for the Tathāgata: 'He who has Dhamma for a body, who has the best body, who is Dhamma, who is the best.'

10

"Eventually, after a very long time, it comes to pass that the world contracts; as it contracts, usually beings devolve as far as the Ābhassara world.[4] There they remain for a long time, made of mind, feeding on rapture, providing their own light, moving about in the air, glorious. Eventually, it comes to pass that the world evolves, and as it evolves beings die from their Ābhassara-bodies and come to this world. Here they remain for a long time, made of mind . . . glorious.

11

"At that time there is nothing but water, all is darkness, just deep darkness. It is not possible to discern the moon or sun, the twinkling stars, night or day, months or half-months, seasons or years, men or women. Beings are just called 'beings.' Then an earth-essence spreads out on the waters. It appears in the same way as does the spreading out of skin on top of boiled milk-rice as it cools down. It has color like sweet ghee or cream, smell, and tastes like fine clear honey.

12

"Once one of these beings, greedy by nature, thought 'What can this be?' and tasted the earth-essence with his finger. He was pleased by the taste, and craving came upon him. Other beings imitated him, tasting the earth-essence with their fingers. They too were pleased, and craving came upon them. Then, monks, these beings started to consume the earth-essence, taking big mouthfuls of it with their hands. As they did so,

1. The lineage of the Buddha.

2. "Thus gone," an epithet of uncertain nuance used especially of the Buddha.

3. Traditionally understood to mean "slayer," Mara is the personification of passion, anger, and evil in general in Buddhist literature.

4. The fine-material world of the "radiant beings."

their self-luminosity disappeared. When their luminosity disappeared, the moon and sun appeared; when the sun and moon appeared, the twinkling stars appeared; when the stars appeared, night and day appeared; when night and day appeared, the seasons and years appeared. Thus far, monks, did the world evolve.

13

"Those beings, monks, spent a long time consuming the earth-essence. Depending on how much they consumed, their bodies became hard, and good and bad looks became apparent. Some beings were good-looking, others ugly. Those who were good-looking despised the ugly: 'We are better-looking than they, they are uglier than us!' Because these arrogant beings were proud of their appearance, the earth-essence disappeared. When it had disappeared, they came together lamenting; 'Look [*aho*], the earth essence [*rasa*] has disappeared.' So nowadays, when people have tasted something good they say: 'Oh the taste, oh the taste! [*aho rasaṃ*].' They recall the original, primary words, but they don't understand what they mean.

14

"Then, when the earth-essence had disappeared, a fragrant earth appeared for those beings; it appeared suddenly, just like a mushroom does. It had color like sweet ghee or cream, smell, and taste like fine clear honey. Those beings started to eat the fragrant earth, and spent a long time living on it as their food. Depending on how much they ate, their bodies became yet more hard, and good and bad looks yet more apparent. Some beings were good-looking, others ugly. The good-looking despised the ugly: 'We are better-looking than they, they are uglier than us!' Because these arrogant beings were proud of their appearance, the fragrant earth disappeared. When it had disappeared, a kind of creeper appeared, like a *kalambukā* creeper. It had color like sweet ghee or cream, smell, and tasted like fine clear honey.

15

"Then they started to eat the creeper, and spent a long time living on it as their food. Depending on how much they ate, their bodies became yet more hard, and good and bad looks yet more known. The good-looking despised the ugly: 'We are better-looking than they, they are uglier than us!' Because these arrogant beings were proud of their appearance, the creeper disappeared. When it had disappeared, they came together lamenting: 'We've had it, the creeper has given out on us!' So nowadays, when people are touched by some hardship, they say, 'We've had it, it's given out on us!' They recall the original, primary words, but they don't understand what they mean.

16

"When the creeper had disappeared rice appeared, growing without cultivation. It had no powder, was already husked, sweet-smelling and ready to eat. Whatever they gathered in the evening for their evening meal in the morning had grown back ripe again; whatever they gathered in the morning had grown back ripe again in the evening. The work of harvesting was unknown. They spent a long time living on the uncultivated rice as their food. Then the female parts appeared for a woman, and the male parts for a man; the woman looked at the man with intense, extreme longing, as did the man at the woman. As they were looking at each other passion arose in them, burning came upon their bodies, and they had sex. When the other beings saw this, some threw earth at them, some ashes, others cow-dung, saying, 'Away with you and your impurity, away with you and your impurity! How could a being do such a thing to another being?' So nowadays, people in certain regions, when a bride is being led out, throw dirt, ash or cow-dung. They recall the original, primary actions, but they don't understand what they mean.

17

"Monks, what was thought improper at that time is nowadays thought proper. At that time the beings who took to having sex were prevented from entering any community for a month or two. But intoxicated by their immorality, they took to building houses to conceal it. Then a lazy being thought, 'Why am I troubling myself gathering rice for my evening meal in the evening, and again in the morning? Why don't I gather it once, for both evening and morning?' And he did so. Then another being came up to him and said, 'Come, let's go to gather rice.' 'There's no need!' said the first, 'I've gathered rice once for both evening and morning.' The second being thought, 'That seems a good idea,' and also gathered rice once for two days. Then another being came up to the second, and said, 'Let's go to gather rice.' 'There's no need! I've gathered rice for two days.' The third thought, 'That seems a good idea,' and gathered rice for four days. Then another being came up to the third . . . and gathered rice for eight days. Because these beings took to eating stored rice, powder and husk then covered the grain, and what was cut did not grow back. Harvesting became known; and the rice stood in clumps.

18

"And then, monks, the beings came together and lamented: 'Bad things have appeared for us beings; we were formerly made of mind . . . and now the rice stands in clumps. Let's divide up the rice, and set up boundary-lines.' And they divided up the rice and set up boundary-lines.

19

"Then a greedy being kept his own portion of rice, and another without its being given, and ate it. Other beings grabbed him and said, 'You have done wrong in keeping your own portion and taking another without its being given. Don't do such a thing again!' 'Alright,' he agreed. [This happens a second and third time, after which] they hit him, some with their hands, some with clods of earth, some with sticks. From this moment on stealing, accusation, lying and punishment became known.

20

"Then those beings came together lamenting: 'Bad things have appeared for us, in that stealing, accusation, lying and punishment have become known. What if we were to appoint one being to criticize whoever should be criticized, accuse whoever should be accused, banish whoever should be banished? We will each hand over to him a portion of rice.' They went to the one among them who was most handsome and good-looking, most charismatic and with greatest authority, and said, 'Come, being, if you criticize whoever should be criticized, accuse whoever should be accused, banish whoever should be banished, we will each hand over to you a portion of rice.' He agreed and did as they asked. They each gave him a portion of rice.

21

"'Appointed by the people' [*mahājanena sammato*], is what *mahāsammata* means: 'mahāsammata' was the first term for the Kshatriya class which appeared. 'Lord of the Fields' [*khettānaṃ pati*] is what *khattiya* means: 'Khattiya' was the second term for the Kshatriya class to appear. 'He brings joy to others' [*paresaṃ . . . rañjeti*] according to Dhamma', is what *rājā* 'king' means: 'rājā' was the third term for the Kshatriya class to appear. This was the birth of the royal-group, along with the original, primary terms; of just these beings, no others, of similar beings, not dissimilar, properly and not improperly. For the Dhamma is the best thing, monks, in this world, both in this life and in the future.

22

"Then some beings, monks, thought, 'Bad things have appeared for us beings, in that stealing, accusation, lying, punishment and banishment have become known; let us keep away from these bad, unwholesome things.' And they did so. 'They keep away from bad, unwholesome things' [*pāpake . . . bāhenti*], monks, is what *brāhmaṇā* means: 'brāhmaṇā' was the first term for the Brahman class to appear. They made leaf-huts in the forest and meditated in them; without coals or smoke from a cooking fire, with pestle and mortar set aside, they went into villages, towns and royal cities in search of food, in the evening for their evening meal, and in the morning for their morning meal. When they had got their food, they went back to their leaf-huts in the forest to meditate. Other people saw this and said, 'These beings have made leaf-huts in the forest . . . without coals or smoke . . . they go back again to their leaf-huts in the forest to meditate.' 'They meditate' (*jhāyanti*), is what 'those who tend a sacrificial fire' (*jhāyakā*) means: 'jhāyakā' was the second term for the Brahman class to appear.

23

"Some of these beings were unable to maintain the life of meditation in forest leaf-huts; they went to the outskirts of villages and towns and lived there making up texts. Other humans saw them and said, 'These beings are unable to maintain the life of meditation . . . they live there making up texts. They do not meditate.' 'They do not meditate' (*na . . . jjhāyanti*), is what Students [or: Reciters] of the Veda (*ajjhāyakā*) means: 'ajjhāyaka' was the third term for the Brahman class to appear. It was considered a lesser thing at that time, monks; nowadays it is considered the best. This was the birth of the Brahman-group, along with the original, primary terms; of just these beings, no others, of similar beings, not dissimilar, properly and not improperly. For the Dhamma is the best thing, monks, in this world, both in this life and in the future.

* * *

[*24–30 give etymologies for the names of other classes, and repeat the remarks about immorality and morality being equal in all classes made in 6–7.*]

31

"Of these four classes he who is a monk, an Arahant, who has lived the holy life, laid down the burden, attained the true goal, in whom the ties to existence are destroyed, who is released by Right Wisdom—he is properly called what is primary among them, not improperly as are the Brahmans. For the Dhamma is the best thing, monks, in this world, both in this life and in the future.

32

"The Brahmā Sanaṃkumāra, the Ever-Youthful, spoke this verse:

> 'For those who rely on clan, the kshatriya class is the best in this world;
> But the person who shows wisdom and good conduct is the best in the whole world.'

"This verse was well-sung by the Brahmā Sanaṃkumāra, well-spoken and endowed with meaning. I approve of it, and I too say:

> 'For those who rely on clan, the Kshatriya class is the best in this world;
> But the person who shows wisdom and good conduct is the best in the whole world.' "

When the Blessed One had finished, Vāsettha and Bhāradvāja were pleased, and rejoiced in his words.

The Great Hymn to the Aten

14th century B.C.E.

"The Great Hymn to the Aten" was composed in Egypt during the "Amarna revolution," when the pharaoh Akhenaten attempted to center worship on his dynasty's patron god, the sun disk Aten, a manifestation of the great god Re. The Aten was portrayed as ruling supreme over the universe—with Akhenaten as the Aten's prime intermediary with humanity. To promote these views, the king changed his own name. Originally named Amun-hotpe ("Amun is pleased") in honor of the patron god of Thebes, he became Akhenaten ("effective spirit of the Aten"), and he built a new capital at Amarna, called "The Horizon of Aten." For worshipers of the sun god, the Horizon had always been a charged region, the meeting-place of heaven and earth, the place of the sun's appearance and disappearance; now, Akhenaten established his own palace as the horizon of the god's presence in the midst of Egypt itself.

Akhenaten promoted his views by destroying monuments of rival gods and having their names hacked off inscriptions, focusing worship both on the Aten and on his own person as the Aten's earthly representative. He claimed to be returning to the old worship of the days of the pyramids, but the many devotees of the other gods weren't persuaded, and soon after Akhenaten's death they defaced and destroyed his own monuments in turn. Fortunately, many carved reliefs and works of art from the period survived in tombs, often done in a lively and strikingly realistic style; Akhenaten's court was a place of artistic as well as religious experimentation. (See Color Plate 1.) A masterpiece of Egyptian poetry, "The Great Hymn to the Aten" was inscribed on the wall of the tomb of Ay, a high official in Akhenaten's court. It details the Aten's sustaining of life on earth, emphasizing the Aten's tender care for his entire creation and giving an almost anthropological view of the earth's varied races.

The Amarna revolution has sometimes been thought of as an early form of monotheism, and in his book *Moses and Monotheism* the psychologist Sigmund Freud even speculated that Akhenaten's views sparked the development of belief in a sole God among the Hebrews then living in Egypt. With its focus on a single creative divine figure, "The Great Hymn to the Aten" does certainly come closer to monotheism than orthodox Egyptian texts like the Memphite Theology. Indeed, the Hymn develops themes and images that recur in biblical psalms like Psalm 104, which praises God in similar terms:

> You bring darkness, it becomes night, and all the beasts of the forest prowl.
> The lions roar for their prey, and seek their food from God.
> The sun rises, and they steal away; they return and lie down in their dens.
> Then man goes out to his work, to his labor until evening.
> How many are your works, O Lord!

Most biblical scholars haven't followed Freud, though, in seeing any specially close connections between Egyptian and Hebrew religion, and the comparison of the hymn and the psalms is revealing for the differences between them as well as their similarities: Israel's God is the sole divine power in the universe, whereas the Aten doesn't take the place of the other gods but rules firmly over them. In Israel, moreover, kingship was always a more tentative and less all-encompassing institution than in Egypt. The psalm shows none of the royal focus that frames the Egyptian hymn, which is thus profoundly shaped by its culture's social and theological assumptions alike.

PRONUNCIATIONS:

Akhenaten: akh-eh-NAH-ten
Hapy: HAH-pea
Maat: MA-aht
Re-Harakhti: RAY-hah-RAKH-tee

The Great Hymn to the Aten[1]

Adoration of *Re-Harakhti-who-rejoices-in-the-horizon In-his-name-Shu-who-is-Aten,*[2] living forever; the great living Aten who is in jubilee, the lord of all that the Disk encircles, lord of sky, lord of earth, lord of the house-of-Aten in Akhet-Aten; and of the King of Upper and Lower Egypt, who lives by Maat,[3] the Lord of the Two Lands, *Neferkheprure, Sole-one-of-Re;* the Son of Re who lives by Maat, the Lord of Crowns, *Akhenaten,* great in his lifetime; and his beloved great Queen, the Lady of the Two Lands, *Nefer-nefru-Aten Nefertiti,* who lives in health and youth forever. The Vizier, the Fanbearer on the right of the King,——[Ay]; he says:

> Splendid you rise in heaven's horizon,
> O living Aten, creator of life!
> When you have dawned in eastern horizon,
> You fill every land with your beauty.
> You are beauteous, great, radiant,
> High over every land;
> Your rays embrace the lands,
> To the limit of all that you made.
> Being Re, you reach their limits,
> You bend them for the son whom you love;

1. Translated by Miriam Lichtheim.
2. These titles identify the Aten with Shu, god of the sky and air, and with Re-Harakhti, a combined form of the sun god Re and the sky god Horus.
3. Goddess of truth.

Though you are far, your rays are on earth,
Though one sees you, your strides are unseen.

When you set in the western horizon,
Earth is in darkness as if in death;
One sleeps in chambers, heads covered,
One eye does not see another.
Were they robbed of their goods
That are under their heads,
People would not remark it.
Every lion comes from its den,
All the serpents bite;
Darkness hovers, earth is silent,
As their maker rests in his horizon.

Earth brightens when you dawn in the horizon,
When you shine as Aten of daytime;
As you dispel the dark,
As you cast your rays,
The Two Lands° are in festivity. *Upper and Lower Egypt*
Awake they stand on their feet,
You have roused them;
Bodies cleansed, clothed,
Their arms adore your appearance.
The entire land sets out to work,
All beasts browse on their herbs;
Trees, herbs are sprouting,
Birds fly from their nests,
Their wings greeting your *ka*.° *spirit*
All flocks frisk on their feet,
All that fly up and alight,
They live when you dawn for them.
Ships fare north, fare south as well,
Roads lie open when you rise;
The fish in the river dart before you,
Your rays are in the midst of the sea.

Who makes seed grow in women,
Who creates people from sperm;
Who feeds the son in his mother's womb,
Who soothes him to still his tears.
Nurse in the womb,
Giver of breath,
To nourish all that he made.
When he comes from the womb to breathe,
On the day of his birth,
You open wide his mouth,
You supply his needs.
When the chick in the egg speaks in the shell,
You give him breath within to sustain him;

When you have made him complete,
To break out from the egg,
He comes out from the egg,
To announce his completion,
Walking on his legs he comes from it.

How many are your deeds,
Though hidden from sight,
O Sole God beside whom there is none!
You made the earth as you wished, you alone,
All peoples, herds, and flocks;
All upon earth that walk on legs,
All on high that fly on wings,
The lands of Khor and Kush,[4]
The land of Egypt.
You set every man in his place,
You supply their needs;
Everyone has his food,
His lifetime is counted.
Their tongues differ in speech,
Their characters likewise;
Their skins are distinct,
For you distinguished the peoples.

You made Hapy° in the netherworld, *the Nile god*
You bring him when you will,
To nourish the people,
For you made them for yourself.
Lord of all who toils for them,
Lord of all lands who shines for them,
Aten of daytime, great in glory!
All distant lands, you make them live,
You made a heavenly Hapy descend for them;
He makes waves on the mountains like the sea,
To drench their fields and their towns.
How excellent are your ways, O Lord of eternity!
A Hapy from heaven for foreign peoples,
And all lands' creatures that walk on legs,
For Egypt the Hapy who comes from the netherworld.

Your rays nurse all fields,
When you shine they live, they grow for you;
You made the seasons to foster all that you made,
Winter to cool them, heat that they taste you.
You made the far sky to shine therein,
To behold all that you made;
You alone, shining in your form of living Aten,

4. Lands at the outer edges of Egyptian influence; Khor was in Palestine to the north, Kush was the land of Nubia to the south.

Risen, radiant, distant, near.
You made millions of forms from yourself alone,
Towns, villages, fields, the river's course;
All eyes observe you upon them,
For you are the Aten of daytime on high.
[. . . . .][5]

You are in my heart,
There is no other who knows you,
Only your son, *Neferkheprure, Sole-one-of-Re,*
Whom you have taught your ways and your might.
Those on earth come from your hand as you made them,
When you have dawned they live,
When you set they die;
You yourself are lifetime, one lives by you.
All eyes are on your beauty until you set,
All labor ceases when you rest in the west;
When you rise you stir everyone for the King,
Every leg is on the move since you founded the earth.
You rouse them for your son who came from your body,
The King who lives by Maat, the Lord of the Two Lands,
Neferkheprure, Sole-one-of-Re,
The Son of Re who lives by Maat, the Lord of crowns,
Akhenaten, great in his lifetime;
And the great Queen whom he loves, the Lady of the Two Lands,
Nefer-nefru-Aten[6] *Nefertiti,* living forever.

Enuma Elish: The Babylonian Creation Epic

2nd–1st millennium B.C.E.

This great epic poem recounts the origins of the gods and the world and the establishment of human society to serve the gods; the Babylonians called the poem *Enuma Elish*, the first words of its opening line, "When skies above were not yet named." Once the major gods have been created, the god of wisdom Ea subdues their father, Apsu, so they can rule. This action outrages Apsu's consort Tiamat, goddess of the watery deep, and her children. They attack the ruling gods, hoping to overthrow them and return the universe to formless chaos. Finally Tiamat and her forces are defeated by the young god Marduk, who then creates a great city as the ritual center of the world, naming it Babylon ("Gate of God"). Setting his bow in the heavens as a sign of his sovereignty, Marduk establishes cosmic order with the movements of the planets and the division of time and creates humankind from the blood of Tiamat's defeated general, Qingu.

The poem is preserved on clay tablets written during the first millennium B.C.E., but the epic was composed earlier, probably sometime around 1500; many elements of the story are much older still. The epic was used ritually, recited during the annual festival for the new year in Babylon. The audience at this celebration included the royal governors, courtiers, and

5. There are half a dozen corrupt or missing lines here.

6. "Beauty of the beauty of Aten."

officers, and the festival renewed the king's mandate to rule as Marduk's earthly representative. The poem unfolds with both a ritual grandeur and a fast-paced immediacy, moving quickly from creation to paint a frightening picture of the roiling forces of chaos, the dismay of the gods, and the bravery of young Marduk. The poet mixes vigorous action with lively dialogue as the gods ponder their options, enlist Marduk's aid, and cheer him on. Even the forces of evil have a certain horrible charm, as when Tiamat's children urge her to avenge the murder of her lover, Apsu:

> Are you not a mother? You heave restlessly,
> But what about us, who cannot rest? Don't you love us?

The poem's events and images show many parallels to later accounts both in the Bible and in early Greek literature, particularly Hesiod's *Theogony*. The story of creation, flood, and the building of the Tower of Babel in Genesis 1–11 has clear parallels to *Enuma Elish*'s account of war in heaven and the establishment of life on earth; Marduk's bow is even echoed in the rainbow with which God establishes peace at the close of the Flood story. Apart from such specific parallels, the poem's dramatic action and dialogue can be compared to epic writing from the *Epic of Gilgamesh* and the Homeric epics, which treat human conflicts against a background of divine violence.

PRONUNCIATIONS:

Anunnaki: ah-new-NAH-key
Ea: AY-ah
Igigi: ee-GEE-jee
Marduk: MAR-duck
Tiamat: TEE-ah-maht

from Enuma Elish: The Babylonian Creation Epic[1]

[Birth of the Gods: Conflict Begins]

When skies above were not yet named
Nor earth below pronounced by name,
Apsu, the first one, their begetter
And maker Tiamat, who bore them all,
Had mixed their waters together,[2]
But had not formed pastures, nor discovered reed-beds;
When yet no gods were manifest,
Nor names pronounced, nor destinies decreed,
Then gods were born within them.
Lahmu and Lahamu[3] emerged, their names pronounced.
As soon as they matured, were fully formed,
Anshar° and Kishar° were born, surpassing them. *Whole Sky / Whole Earth*
They passed the days at length, they added to the years.
Anu their first-born son rivalled his forefathers:
Anshar made his son Anu° like himself, *Sky*

1. Translated by Stephanie Dalley.
2. Apsu, "Fresh Water," is husband of Tiamat, "Sea." As a place, the Apsu is the region of fresh water beneath the surface of the earth.
3. Primeval beings who control the water and fish.

And Anu begot Nudimmud[4] in his likeness.
He, Nudimmud, was superior to his forefathers:
Profound of understanding, he was wise, was very strong at arms.
Mightier by far than Anshar his father's begetter,
He had no rival among the gods his peers.
The gods of that generation would meet together
And disturb Tiamat, and their clamour reverberated.
They stirred up Tiamat's belly,
They were annoying her by playing inside Anduruna.° *the gods' dwelling*
Apsu could not quell their noise
And Tiamat became mute before them;
However grievous their behaviour to her,
However bad their ways, she would indulge them.
Finally Apsu, begetter of the great gods,
Called out and addressed his vizier Mummu,
 "O Mummu, vizier who pleases me!
 Come, let us go to Tiamat!"
They went and sat in front of Tiamat,
And discussed affairs concerning the gods their sons.
Apsu made his voice heard
And spoke to Tiamat in a loud voice,
 "Their ways have become very grievous to me,
 By day I cannot rest, by night I cannot sleep.
 I shall abolish their ways and disperse them!
 Let peace prevail, so that we can sleep."
When Tiamat heard this,
She was furious and shouted at her lover;
She shouted dreadfully and was beside herself with rage,
But then suppressed the evil in her belly.
 "How could we allow what we ourselves created to perish?
 Even though their ways are so grievous, we should bear it patiently."
Vizier Mummu replied and counselled Apsu;
The vizier did not agree with the counsel of his earth mother.
 "O father, put an end to their troublesome ways,
 So that she may be allowed to rest by day and sleep at night."
Apsu was pleased with him, his face lit up
At the evil he was planning for the gods his sons.
Vizier Mummu hugged him,
Sat on his lap and kissed him rapturously.
But everything they plotted between them
Was relayed to the gods their sons.
The gods listened and wandered about restlessly;
They fell silent, they sat mute.
Superior in understanding, wise and capable,
Ea who knows everything found out their plot,

4. Sumerian name for Ea, god of fresh water, wisdom, and incantations, who sent the Seven Sages to teach civilization to humanity.

Made for himself a design of everything, and laid it out correctly,
Made it cleverly, his pure spell was superb.
He recited it and it stilled the waters.
He poured sleep upon him so that he was sleeping soundly,
Put Apsu to sleep, drenched with sleep.
Vizier Mummu the counsellor was in a sleepless daze.
Ea unfastened his belt, took off his crown,
Took away his mantle of radiance and put it on himself.
He held Apsu down and slew him;
Tied up Mummu and laid him across him.
He set up his dwelling on top of Apsu,
And grasped Mummu, held him by a nose-rope.
When he had overcome and slain his enemies,
Ea set up his triumphal cry over his foes.
Then he rested very quietly inside his private quarters
And named them Apsu and assigned chapels,
Founded his own residence there,
And Ea and Damkina his lover dwelt in splendour.
In the chamber of destinies, the hall of designs,
Bel, cleverest of the clever, sage of the gods, was begotten.
And inside Apsu, Marduk was created;
Inside pure Apsu, Marduk was born.
Ea his father created him,
Damkina his mother bore him.
He suckled the teats of goddesses;
The nurse who reared him filled him with awesomeness.
Proud was his form, piercing his stare,
Mature his emergence, he was powerful from the start.
Anu his father's begetter beheld him,
And rejoiced, beamed; his heart was filled with joy.
He made him so perfect that his godhead was doubled.
Elevated far above them, he was superior in every way.
His limbs were ingeniously made beyond comprehension,
Impossible to understand, too difficult to perceive.
Four were his eyes, four were his ears;
When his lips moved, fire blazed forth.
The four ears were enormous
And likewise the eyes; they perceived everything.
Highest among the gods, his form was outstanding.
His limbs were very long, his height outstanding.
(*Anu cried out*): "Mariutu, Mariutu,° *Marduk*
  Son, majesty, majesty of the gods!"
Clothed in the radiant mantle of ten gods, worn high above his head
Five fearsome rays were clustered above him.
Anu created the four winds and gave them birth,
Put them in Marduk's hand, "My son, let them play!"
He fashioned dust and made the whirlwind carry it;
He made the flood-wave and stirred up Tiamat.
Tiamat was stirred up, and heaved restlessly day and night.

The gods, unable to rest, had to suffer . . .
They plotted evil in their hearts, and
They addressed Tiamat their mother, saying,
"Because they slew Apsu your lover and
You did not go to his side but sat mute,
He has created the four, fearful winds
To stir up your belly on purpose, and we simply cannot sleep!
Was your lover Apsu not in your heart?
And Mummu who was captured? No wonder you sit alone!
Are you not a mother? You heave restlessly,
But what about us, who cannot rest? Don't you love us?
Our grip [is slack], our eyes are sunken.
Remove the yoke of us restless ones, and let us sleep!
Set up a [battle cry] and avenge them!
Con[quer the enemy] and reduce them to nought!"
Tiamat listened, and the speech pleased her.
"Let us act now, as you were advising!
The gods inside Apsu will be disturbed,
Because they adopted evil for the gods who begot them."
They crowded round and rallied beside Tiamat.
They were fierce, scheming restlessly night and day.
They were working up to war, growling and raging.
They convened a council and created conflict.
Mother Hubur, who fashions all things,
Contributed an unfaceable weapon: she bore giant snakes,
Sharp of tooth and unsparing of fang.
She filled their bodies with venom instead of blood.
She cloaked ferocious dragons with fearsome rays
And made them bear mantles of radiance, made them godlike, saying,
"Whoever looks upon them shall collapse in utter terror!
Their bodies shall rear up continually and never turn away!"

[WHO WILL FACE TIAMAT?]

Anshar was speechless, and stared at the ground;
He gnashed his teeth and shook his head in despair at Ea.
Now, the Igigi assembled, all the Anukki.[5]
They sat silently for a while, tight-lipped.
(*Finally they spoke*)
"Will no god come forward? Is [fate] fixed?
Will no one go out to face Tiamat with [force]?"
Then Ea from his secret dwelling called
[The perfect] one of Anshar, father of the great gods,
Whose heart is perfect like a fellow-citizen or countryman,
The mighty heir who was to be his father's champion,

5. The Igigi are a group of younger-generation sky gods; the Anukki or Anunnaki are gods who become the judges of the underworld.

Who rushes fearlessly into battle: Marduk the Hero!
He told him his innermost design, saying,
"O Marduk, take my advice, listen to your father!
You are the son who sets his heart at rest!
Approach Anshar, drawing near to him,
And make your voice heard, stand your ground:
He will be calmed by the sight of you."
The Lord rejoiced at the word of his father,
And he approached and stood before Anshar.
Anshar looked at him, and his heart was filled with joy.
He kissed him on the lips, put away his trepidation.
(*Then Marduk addressed him, saying*)
"Father, don't stay so silent, open your lips,
Let me go, and let me fulfil your heart's desire.
Anshar, don't stay so silent, open your lips,
Let me go, and let me fulfil your heart's desire."
(*Anshar replied*)
"What kind of man has ordered you out to his war?
My son, don't you realize that it is Tiamat, of womankind,
Who will advance against you with arms?"
(*Marduk answered*)
"Father, my creator, rejoice and be glad!
You shall soon set your foot upon the neck of Tiamat!
Anshar, my creator, rejoice and be glad,
You shall soon set your foot upon the neck of Tiamat."

[The Gods Commission Marduk]

"O Marduk, you are our champion!
We hereby give you sovereignty over all of the whole universe.
Sit in the assembly and your word shall be pre-eminent!
May your weapons never miss, may they smash your enemies!
O lord, spare the life of him who trusts in you,
But drain the life of the god who has espoused evil!"
They set up in their midst one constellation,
And then they addressed Marduk their son,
"May your decree, O lord, impress the gods!
Command to destroy and to recreate, and let it be so!
Speak and let the constellation vanish!
Speak to it again and let the constellation reappear."
He spoke, and at his word the constellation vanished.
He spoke to it again and the constellation was recreated.
When the gods his fathers saw how effective his utterance was,
They rejoiced, they proclaimed: "Marduk is King!"
They invested him with sceptre, throne, and staff-of-office.
They gave him an unfaceable weapon to crush the foe.
"Go, and cut off the life of Tiamat!

Let the winds bear her blood to us as good news!"
The gods his fathers thus decreed the destiny of the lord
And set him on the path of peace and obedience.
He fashioned a bow, designated it as his weapon,
Feathered the arrow, set it in the string.
He lifted up a mace and carried it in his right hand,
Slung the bow and quiver at his side,
Put lightning in front of him,
His body was filled with an ever-blazing flame.
He made a net to encircle Tiamat within it,
Marshalled the four winds so that no part of her could escape:
South Wind, North Wind, East Wind, West Wind,
The gift of his father Anu, he kept them close to the net at his side.

[MARDUK AND TIAMAT AT WAR]

Face to face they came, Tiamat and Marduk, sage of the gods.
They engaged in combat, they closed for battle.
The Lord spread his net and made it encircle her,
To her face he dispatched the *imhullu*-wind,[6] which had been behind:
Tiamat opened her mouth to swallow it,
And he forced in the *imhullu*-wind so that she could not close her lips.
Fierce winds distended her belly;
Her insides were constipated and she stretched her mouth wide.
He shot an arrow which pierced her belly,
Split her down the middle and slit her heart,
Vanquished her and extinguished her life.
He threw down her corpse and stood on top of her.
When he had slain Tiamat, the leader,
He broke up her regiments; her assembly was scattered.
Then the gods her helpers, who had marched at her side,
Began to tremble, panicked, and turned tail.
Although he allowed them to come out and spared their lives,
They were surrounded, they could not flee.
Then he tied them up and smashed their weapons.
They were thrown into the net and sat there ensnared.
They cowered back, filled with woe.
They had to bear his punishment, confined to prison.
And as for the dozens of creatures, covered in fearsome rays,
The gang of demons who all marched on her right,
He fixed them with nose-ropes and tied their arms.
He trampled their battle-gear beneath him.
As for Qingu, who had once been the greatest among them,
He defeated him and counted him among the dead gods,
Wrested from him the Tablet of Destinies, wrongfully his,
Sealed it with his own seal and pressed it to his breast.

6. Perhaps a hurricane.

When he had defeated and killed his enemies
And had proclaimed the submissive foe his slave,
And had set up the triumphal cry of Anshar over all the enemy,
And had achieved the desire of Nudimmud, Marduk the warrior
Strengthened his hold over the captive gods,
And to Tiamat, whom he had ensnared, he turned back.
The Lord trampled the lower part of Tiamat,
With his unsparing mace smashed her skull,
Severed the arteries of her blood,
And made the North Wind carry it off as good news.
His fathers saw it and were jubilant: they rejoiced,
Arranged to greet him with presents, greetings gifts.
The Lord rested, and inspected her corpse.
He divided the monstrous shape and created marvels from it.
He sliced her in half like a fish for drying:
Half of her he put up to roof the sky,
Drew a bolt across and made a guard hold it.
Her waters he arranged so that they could not escape.
He crossed the heavens and sought out a shrine;
He levelled Apsu, dwelling of Nudimmud.
The Lord measured the dimensions of Apsu
And the large temple which he built in its image, was Esharra:
In the great shrine Esharra, which he had created as the sky,
He founded cult centres for Anu, Ellil, and Ea.

* * *

He opened the Euphrates and the Tigris from her eyes,
Closed her nostrils, [ ].
He piled up clear-cut mountains from her udder,
Bored waterholes to drain off the catchwater.
He laid her tail across, tied it fast as the cosmic bond,
And [ ] the Apsu beneath his feet.
He set her thigh to make fast the sky,
With half of her he made a roof; he fixed the earth.
He [ ] the work, made the insides of Tiamat surge,
Spread his net, made it extend completely.
He . . . [ ] heaven and earth
[ ] their knots, to coil [ ]
When he had designed its cult, created its rites,
He threw down the reins and made Ea take them.
The Tablet of Destinies, which Qingu had appropriated, he fetched
And took it and presented it for a first reading to Anu.

[Victory Celebration. Founding of Babylon]

Lahmu and Lahamu [ ].
Made their voices heard and spoke to the Igigi,
"Previously Marduk was just our beloved son
But now he is your king. Take heed of his command."
Next they spoke and proclaimed in unison,

"LUGAL-DIMMER-ANKIA[7] is his name. Trust in him!
When they gave kingship to Marduk,
They spoke an oration for him, for blessing and obedience.
Henceforth you shall be the provider of shrines for us.
Whatever you command, we shall perform ourselves."
Marduk made his voice heard and spoke,
Addressed his words to the gods his fathers,
"Over the Apsu, the sea-green dwelling,
In front of Esharra, which I created for you,
Where I strengthened the ground beneath it for a shrine,
I shall make a house to be a luxurious dwelling for myself
And shall found his cult centre within it,
And I shall establish my private quarters, and confirm my kingship.
Whenever you come up from the Apsu for an assembly,
Your night's resting place shall be in it, receiving you all.
Whenever you come down from the sky for an assembly,
Your night's resting place shall be in it, receiving you all.
I hereby name it Babylon, home of the great gods.
We shall make it the center of religion."

[CREATION OF HUMANITY]

When Marduk heard the speech of the gods,
He made up his mind to perform miracles.
He spoke his utterance to Ea,
And communicated to him the plan that he was considering.
"Let me put blood together, and make bones too.
Let me set up primeval man: Man shall be his name.
Let me create a primeval man.
The work of the gods shall be imposed on him, and so they shall be at leisure.
Let me change the ways of the gods miraculously,
So they are gathered as one yet divided in two."
Ea answered him and spoke a word to him,
Told him his plan for the leisure of the gods.
"Let one who is hostile to them be surrendered up,
Let him be destroyed, and let people be created from him.
Let the great gods assemble,
Let the culprit be given up, and let them convict him."
Marduk assembled the great gods,
Gave instructions pleasantly, gave orders.
The gods paid attention to what he said.
The king addressed his words to the Anunnaki,
"Your election of me shall be firm and foremost.
I shall declare the laws, the edicts within my power.
Whosoever started the war,

7. "King of the gods of heaven and earth."

And incited Tiamat, and gathered an army,
Let the one who started the war be given up to me
And he shall bear the penalty for his crime, that you may dwell in peace."
The Igigi, the great gods, answered him,
Their lord Lugal-dimmer-ankia, counsellor of gods,
"It was Qingu who started the war,
He who incited Tiamat and gathered an army!"
They bound him and held him in front of Ea,
Imposed the penalty on him and cut off his blood.
Ea created mankind from his blood,
Imposed the toil of the gods on man and released the gods from it.
When Ea the wise had created mankind,
Had imposed the toil of the gods on them—
That deed is impossible to describe,
For Nudimmud performed it with the miracles of Marduk—
Then Marduk the king divided the gods,
The Anunnaki, all of them, above and below.
He assigned his decrees to Anu to guard,
Established three hundred as a guard in the sky;
Did the same again when he designed the conventions of earth,
And made the six hundred dwell in both heaven and earth.
When he had directed all the decrees,
Had divided lots for the Anunnaki, of heaven and of earth,
The Anunnaki made their voices heard
And addressed Marduk their lord,
"Now, O Lord, that you have set us free,
What are our favours from you?
We would like to make a shrine with its own name.
We would like our night's resting place to be in your private quarters, and to rest there.
Let us found a shrine, a sanctuary there.
Whenever we arrive, let us rest within it."
When Marduk heard this,
His face lit up greatly, like daylight.
"Create Babylon, whose construction you requested!
Let its mud bricks be moulded, and build high the shrine!"
The Anunnaki began shovelling.
For a whole year they made bricks for it.
When the second year arrived,
They had raised the top of Esagila in front of the Apsu;
They had built a high ziggurat for the Apsu.
They founded a dwelling for Anu, Ellil, and Ea likewise.
In ascendancy he settled himself in front of them,
And his "horns"° look down at the base of Esharra. *pinnacles*
When they had done the work on Esagila,
And the Anunnaki, all of them, had fashioned their individual shrines,
The three hundred Igigi of heaven and the Anunnaki of the Apsu all assembled.
The Lord invited the gods his fathers to attend a banquet

In the great sanctuary which he had created as his dwelling.
"Indeed, Bab-ili° is your home too! *Gate of God*
Sing for joy there, dwell in happiness!"
The great gods sat down there,
And set out the beer mugs; they attended the banquet.
When they had made merry within,
They themselves made an offering in splendid Esagila.
All the decrees and designs were fixed.
All the gods divided the stations of heaven and earth.
The fifty great gods were present, and
The gods fixed the seven destinies for the cult.
The Lord received the bow, and set his weapon down in
front of them.
The gods his fathers looked at the net which he had made,
Looked at the bow, how miraculous her construction,
And his fathers praised the deeds that he had done.
Anu raised the bow and spoke in the assembly of gods,
He kissed the bow. "May she go far!"
He gave to the bow her names, saying,
"May Long and Far be the first, and Victorious the second;
Her third name shall be Bowstar, for she shall shine in the sky."
He fixed her position among the gods her companions.
When Anu had decreed the destiny of the bow,
He set down her royal throne. "You are highest of the gods!"
And Anu made her sit in the assembly of gods.
The great gods assembled
And made Marduk's destiny highest; they themselves did obeisance.
They swore an oath for themselves,
And swore on water and oil, touched their throats.
Thus they granted that he should exercise the kingship of the gods
And confirmed for him mastery of the gods of heaven and earth.[8]

Hesiod

c. late 8th century B.C.E.

Hesiod's *Theogony* is an important literary link between the Near East and Greece. According to the other major poem attributed to Hesiod, *Works and Days,* his own father emigrated from Asia Minor to Greece and settled in a dusty village at the foot of Mount Helicon in eastern Greece—"a wretched village / . . . harsh / in winter, miserable in summertime, / not really good at any time of year." The *Theogony* further tells us that Hesiod was working as a shepherd when the Muses appeared to him and gave him his vocation as a poet. There is no way to know whether a single poet did indeed write both poems; like Homer, "Hesiod" may be a composite

8. Anshar proceeds to bestow fifty Sumerian names on Marduk, in an obscure section omitted here. Some of these titles associate Marduk with other gods, others describe his qualities of strength and majesty.

figure. In any event, the *Theogony* shows pronounced influences of Near Eastern epic traditions, which would have circulated to the Greek settlements along the coast of Asia Minor through the Hittite Empire farther inland. Composed in six-beat epic meter, Hesiod's *Theogony* tells of the origins of the universe and of the gods, in action-packed episodes that rework the mythic themes developed in works like *Enuma Elish.*

As in the Babylonian epic, the universe is created through a series of generations of gods and goddesses, with the younger divinities overthrowing their parents. In Homer and later Greek writers, the gods become relatively civilized, but in this poem they are still figures of raw violence and ambition. They do stop short of the older Near Eastern gods' fondness for cannibalism, but in its place we find a dramatic castration—a shocking act that results, surprisingly, in the birth of Aphrodite, goddess of love and mistress of "sweet delight, and friendliness, and charm." As the poem proceeds, the modern world order is coming into being under the guidance of all-powerful, all-wise Zeus. The end of the poem, now lost, apparently went on to list famous women of early history, descended from the unions of gods and the first mortals, most likely the ancestors of powerful families in Hesiod's region of Greece. The selections included here give a fascinating comparison to the older Egyptian and Babylonian myths, introduced with a sophisticated and charming account of the Muses and their gracious relations with a poet who presents himself as a single and self-aware individual.

PRONUNCIATIONS:

Gaia: GUY-ah
Hesiod: HE-see-odd
Mnemosyne: nem-AWE-zu-nay
Ouranos: OOH-rah-nos

from Theogony[1]

[The Origins of the Gods and of the Earth]

With the Heliconian Muses let us start
Our song: they hold the great and godly mount
Of Helicon, and on their delicate feet
They dance around the darkly bubbling spring
And round the altar of the mighty Zeus.

* * *

The Muses once taught Hesiod to sing
Sweet songs, while he was shepherding his lambs
On holy Helicon; the goddesses
Olympian, daughters of Zeus who holds
The aegis,° first addressed these words to me: *shield*
"You rustic shepherds, shame: bellies you are,
Not men! We know enough to make up lies
Which are convincing, but we also have
The skill, when we've a mind, to speak the truth."

So spoke the fresh-voiced daughters of great Zeus
And plucked and gave a staff to me, a shoot
Of blooming laurel, wonderful to see,

1. Translated by Dorothea Wender.

And breathed a sacred voice into my mouth
With which to celebrate the things to come
And things which were before. They ordered me
To sing the race of blessed ones who live
Forever, and to hymn the Muses first
And at the end. No more delays: begin.

* * *

Hail, daughters of Zeus! Give me sweet song,
To celebrate the holy race of gods
Who live forever, sons of starry Heaven
And Earth, and gloomy Night, and salty Sea.
Tell how the gods and earth arose at first,
And rivers and the boundless swollen sea
And shining stars, and the broad heaven above,
And how the gods divided up their wealth
And how they shared their honours, how they first
Captured Olympus with its many folds.
Tell me these things, Olympian Muses, tell
From the beginning, which first came to be?
Chaos was first of all, but next appeared
Broad-bosomed Earth, sure standing-place for all
The gods who live on snowy Olympus' peak,
And misty Tartarus,° in a recess *the underworld*
Of broad-pathed earth, and Love,[2] most beautiful
Of all the deathless gods. He makes men weak,
He overpowers the clever mind, and tames
The spirit in the breasts of men and gods.
From Chaos came black Night and Erebos.[3]
And Night in turn gave birth to Day and Space
Whom she conceived in love to Erebos.
And Earth bore starry Heaven, first, to be
An equal to herself, to cover her
All over, and to be a resting-place,
Always secure, for all the blessed gods.
Then she brought forth long hills, the lovely homes
Of goddesses, the Nymphs who live among
The mountain clefts. Then, without pleasant love,
She bore the barren sea with its swollen waves,
Pontus. And then she lay with Heaven, and bore
Deep-whirling Oceanus and Koios; then
Kreius, Iapetos, Hyperion,
Theia, Rhea, Themis, Mnemosyne,[4]
Lovely Tethys, and Phoebe, golden-crowned.
Last, after these, most terrible of sons,
The crooked-scheming Kronos° came to birth *Time*

2. Eros, "desire."

3. Outer region of the underworld.

4. "Memory," mother of the nine Muses.

Who was his vigorous father's enemy.
Again, she bore the Cyclopes, whose hearts
Were insolent, Brontes° and Steropes° *Thunder / Lightning*
And proud-souled Arges, those who found and gave
The thunder and the lightning-bolt to Zeus.
They were like other gods in all respects,
But that a single eye lay in the brow
Of each, and from this, they received the name,
Cyclopes, from the one round eye which lay
Set in the middle of each forehead. Strength
And energy and craft were in their works.
Then Ouranos° and Gaia° bore three sons *Heaven / Earth*
Mighty and violent, unspeakable
Kottos and Gyes and Briareus,
Insolent children, each with a hundred arms
On his shoulders, darting about, untouchable,
And each had fifty heads, standing upon
His shoulders, over the crowded mass of arms,
And terrible strength was in their mighty forms.

And these most awful sons of Earth and Heaven
Were hated by their father from the first.
As soon as each was born, Ouranos hid
The child in a secret hiding-place in Earth
And would not let it come to see the light,
And he enjoyed this wickedness. But she,
Vast Earth, being strained and stretched inside her, groaned.
And then she thought of a clever, evil plan.
Quickly she made grey adamant,° and formed *unbreakable stone*
A mighty sickle, and addressed her sons,
Urging them on, with sorrow in her heart,
"My sons, whose father is a reckless fool,
If you will do as I ask, we shall repay
Your father's wicked crime. For it was he
Who first began devising shameful acts."

She spoke, but fear seized all of them, and none
Replied. Then crooked Kronos, growing bold,
Answered his well-loved mother with these words:
"Mother, I undertake to do the deed;
I do not care for my unspeakable
Father, for he first thought of shameful acts."
He spoke, and giant Earth was glad at heart.
She set him in a hiding-place, and put
Into his hands the saw-toothed scimitar,
And told him all the plot she had devised.

Great Heaven came, and with him brought the night.
Longing for love, he lay around the Earth,

Spreading out fully. But the hidden boy
Stretched forth his left hand; in his right he took
The great long jagged sickle; eagerly
He harvested his father's genitals
And threw them off behind. They did not fall
From his hands in vain, for all the bloody drops
That leaped out were received by Earth; and when
The year's time was accomplished, she gave birth
To the Furies, and the Giants, strong and huge,
Who fought in shining armour, with long spears,
And the nymphs called Meliae on the broad earth.

The genitals, cut off with adamant
And thrown from land into the stormy sea,
Were carried for a long time on the waves.
White foam surrounded the immortal flesh,
And in it grew a girl. At first it touched
On holy Cythera,[5] from there it came
To Cyprus, circled by the waves. And there
The goddess came forth, lovely, much revered,
And grass grew up beneath her delicate feet.
Her name is Aphrodite among men
And gods, because she grew up in the foam,
And Cytherea, for she reached that land,
And Cyprogenes from the stormy place
Where she was born, and Philommedes[6] from
The genitals, by which she was conceived.
Eros is her companion; fair Desire
Followed her from the first, both at her birth
And when she joined the company of the gods.
From the beginning, both among gods and men,
She had this honour and received this power:
Fond murmuring of girls, and smiles, and tricks,
And sweet delight, and friendliness, and charm.

[THE OLYMPIAN GODS CAST THE TITANS DOWN TO THE UNDERWORLD]

They joined in hateful battle, all of them,
Both male and female, Titan gods and those
Whom Kronos sired and those whom Zeus had brought
To light from Erebos, beneath the earth,
Strange, mighty ones, whose power was immense,

5. A Greek island, a center of the worship of Aphrodite.

6. "Genital-loving"—a play on *philomeides,* "laughter-loving," a much more common epithet for Aphrodite.

Each with a hundred arms, darting about,
And each had fifty heads standing upon
His shoulders, over the crowded mass of arms.
They stood against the Titans in the grim
Battle, with giant rocks in their strong hands,
While on their side the Titans eagerly
Strengthened their ranks, and both at once displayed
The mightiest efforts which their hands could make;
The boundless sea roared terribly around,
The great earth rumbled, and broad heaven groaned,
Shaken; and tall Olympus was disturbed
Down to its roots, when the immortals charged.
The heavy quaking from their footsteps reached
Down to dark Tartarus, and piercing sounds
Of awful battle, and their mighty shafts.
They hurled their wounding missiles, and the voice
Of both sides, shouting, reached the starry sky,
And when they met, their ALALE!° was great. *war cry*

Then Zeus no longer checked his rage, for now
His heart was filled with fury, and he showed
The full range of his strength. He came from heaven
And from Olympus, lightening as he came,
Continuously; from his mighty hand
The bolts kept flying, bringing thunder-claps
And lightning-flashes, while the holy flame
Rolled thickly all around. The fertile earth
Being burnt, roared out, the voiceless forest cried
And crackled with the fire; the whole earth boiled
And ocean's streams, and the unfruitful sea.
The hot blast reached the earthborn Titans; flame
Unspeakable, rose to the upper air;
The flashing brightness of the thunderbolt
And lightning blinded all, however strong;
The awful heat reached Chaos. To the ear
It sounded, to the eye it looked as though
Broad Heaven were coming down upon the Earth:
For such a noise of crashing might arise
If she were falling, hurled down by his fall.
Just such a mighty crash rose from the gods
Meeting in strife. The howling winds brought on
Duststorm and earthquake, and the shafts of Zeus,
Lightning and thunder and the blazing bolt,
And carried shouting and the battle-cry
Into the armies, and a dreadful noise
Of hideous battle sounded, and their deeds
Were mighty, but the tide of war was turned:
Until that moment, they had kept it up
Continually, in the long, hard fight.

Among those gods who made the fighting harsh
Foremost were Kottos and Briareus
And Gyes, who loved war insatiably.
With their strong hands they hurled three hundred rocks
In quick succession; with their missiles, they
Overshadowed the Titans, put them down
In everlasting shade. Under the earth
Broad-pathed, they sent them, and they bound them up
In painful chains. Proud though the Titans were,
They were defeated by those hands, and sent
To misty Tartarus, as far beneath
The earth, as earth is far beneath the heavens.

An anvil made of bronze, falling from heaven,
Would fall nine nights and days, and on the tenth
Would reach the earth; and if the anvil fell
From earth, would fall again nine nights and days
And come to Tartarus upon the tenth.
A wall of bronze runs around Tartarus,
And round this runs a necklace, triple-thick,
Of purest Night, while up above, there grow
The roots of earth and of the barren sea.
There, in the misty dark, the Titan gods
Are hidden, in a mouldering place, lowest
And last of giant Earth, by the will of Zeus
Who drives the clouds, and they may never leave.
Poseidon° set bronze gates upon the place, *god of the sea*
And all around it runs the wall; there live
Gyes, Kottos, and Briareus
As faithful guards, for aegis-bearing Zeus.

And there, in order, are the ends and springs
Of gloomy earth and misty Tartarus,
And of the barren sea and starry heaven,
Murky and awful, loathed by the very gods.
There is the yawning mouth of hell, and if
A man should find himself inside the gates
He would not reach the bottom for a year;
Gust after savage gust would carry him
Now here, now there. Even the deathless gods
Find this an awesome mystery.

* * *

But when the blessed gods had done their work
And forcibly put down the Titans' claim
To honour, they fulfilled Earth's plans and urged
Far-seeing Zeus, Olympian, to rule
And be the king of the immortals. Thus
He gave out rank and privilege to each.

Genesis 1–11

1st millennium B.C.E.

The first eleven chapters of the Book of Genesis form a prologue for the entire Torah, the five books of Moses that begin the Hebrew Bible. In setting the stage for the national history that begins with Abraham in Genesis 12, the authors of Genesis reached back to old traditions of creation and of a primeval flood that was believed to have extinguished the ancient earthly order, after which modern societies began to be established. The biblical authors knew older versions of such stories, such as those found in the Babylonian *Enuma Elish* and *Epic of Gilgamesh,* yet they wished to tell the stories differently. First and most importantly, the older accounts had assumed a polytheistic universe, in which humanity was created to serve an entire pantheon of gods, whose disputes could be seen as causing earthly disruptions. Second, the older stories typically stemmed from long-settled civilizations based around great cities—a social order foreign to the nomadic Hebrews, who remained deeply suspicious of city culture and of elaborate social hierarchies even after they had begun to form a united kingdom of Israel, centered on their capital city of Jerusalem.

In comparison to works like *Enuma Elish,* Genesis 1–11 is notable for the absence of war in heaven, or even any multiplicity of divine beings: Genesis 1 goes so far as to give no name at all to the sun and moon—major divinities in earlier systems—simply calling them "the great light" and "the small light." Similarly, the ocean goddess Tiamat is demoted to an impersonal watery abyss, her name made into a common noun, *tehom* in Hebrew. At the same time, the absence of rival divinities like Tiamat posed a challenge for the biblical writers: with the entire universe firmly ruled by a single and just God, how could evil ever have come into the world? The story of the Garden of Eden—one of the most resonant stories in the history of Judeo-Christian culture—explores this problem in an enigmatic tale of prohibition, confusion, and disobedience, with the human actors manipulated by a serpent who is "cunning" rather than evil. Going on to the Flood story, the biblical writers saw human wickedness as the cause of this natural disaster, in contrast to the older Babylonian account, in which the gods had simply gotten tired of the noise made by the growing earthly population. Noah himself, like the patriarchs and matriarchs of later Hebrew history, becomes a complex figure who fails to fully maintain his covenant with God. The primeval history concludes with the building of the Tower of Babel—not as the triumphal inauguration of human culture, as with the construction of Babylon in *Enuma Elish,* but as an impious act of defiance to God.

Most biblical scholars consider that this sequence of stories is the product of several stages of development, reflecting successive reworkings of the old stories. The initial account, known as the Yahwistic version (from God's name *Yahweh*), was probably written down around the time of King Solomon in the early tenth century B.C.E. This version was evidently revised by later writers, most notably a writer or group of writers whom modern scholars have named the Priestly source; Genesis 1 is a product of this source, which emphasizes God's serene ordering power. Genesis 2 then picks up the older Yahwistic creation account, portraying a more mysterious and tentative relationship between God and his creation.

The stories of Genesis are distinctive in form as well as in content. The older Babylonian epics are all written in verse, reflecting long histories of literacy and poetic development; Genesis is in prose, reflecting years of oral storytelling in tents and around campfires. Robert Alter's lively translation beautifully captures the oral immediacy of the biblical creation story.

from Genesis 1–11

Chapter 1

When God began to create heaven and earth, and the earth then was welter and waste and darkness over the deep and God's breath hovering over the waters, God said, "Let there be light." And there was light. And God saw the light, that it was good, and God divided the light from the darkness. And God called the light Day, and the darkness He called Night. And it was evening and it was morning, first day. And God said, "Let there be a vault in the midst of the waters, and let it divide water from water." And God made the vault and it divided the water beneath the vault from the water above the vault, and so it was. And God called the vault Heavens, and it was evening and it was morning, second day. And God said, "Let the waters under the heavens be gathered in one place so that the dry land will appear," and so it was. And God called the dry land Earth and the gathering of waters He called Seas, and God saw that it was good. And God said, "Let the earth grow grass, plants yielding seed of each kind and trees bearing fruit of each kind, that has its seed within it." And so it was. And the earth put forth grass, plants yielding seed of each kind, and trees bearing fruit that has its seed within it of each kind, and God saw that it was good. And it was evening and it was morning, third day. And God said, "Let there be lights in the vault of the heavens to divide the day from the night, and they shall be signs for the fixed times and for days and years, and they shall be lights in the vault of the heavens to light up the earth." And so it was. And God made the two great lights, the great light for dominion of day and the small light for dominion of night, and the stars. And God placed them in the vault of the heavens to light up the earth and to have dominion over day and night and to divide the light from the darkness. And God saw that it was good. And it was evening and it was morning, fourth day. And God said, "Let the waters swarm with the swarm of living creatures and let fowl fly over the earth across the vault of the heavens." And God created the great sea monsters and every living creature that crawls, which the water had swarmed forth of each kind, and the winged fowl of each kind, and God saw that it was good. And God blessed them, saying, "Be fruitful and multiply and fill the water in the seas and let the fowl multiply in the earth." And it was evening and it was morning, fifth day. And God said, "Let the earth bring forth living creatures of each kind, cattle and crawling things and wild beasts of each kind." And so it was. And God made wild beasts of each kind and cattle of every kind and crawling things on the ground of each kind, and God saw that it was good.

And God said, "Let us make a human in our image, by our likeness, to hold sway over the fish of the sea and the fowl of the heavens and the cattle and the wild beasts and all the crawling things that crawl upon the earth.

> And God created the human in his image,
> in the image of God He created him,
> male and female He created them.

And God blessed them, and God said to them, "Be fruitful and multiply and fill the earth and conquer it, and hold sway over the fish of the sea and the fowl of the heavens and every beast that crawls upon the earth." And God said, "Look, I have given you every seed-bearing plant on the face of all the earth and every tree that has fruit bearing seed, yours they will be for food. And to all the beasts of the earth and to all the fowl of the heavens and to all that crawls on the earth, which has the breath of life within it, the green plants for food." And so it was. And God saw all that He had done, and, look, it was very good. And it was evening and it was morning, the sixth day.

Chapter 2

Then the heavens and the earth were completed, and all their array. And God completed on the seventh day the work He had done, and He ceased on the seventh day from all the work He had done. And God blessed the seventh day and hallowed it, for on it He had ceased from all His work that He had done. This is the tale of the heavens and the earth when they were created.

On the day the LORD God made earth and heavens, no shrub of the field being yet on the earth and no plant of the field yet sprouted, for the LORD God had not caused rain to fall on the earth and there was no human to till the soil, and wetness would well from the earth to water all the surface of the soil, then the LORD God fashioned the human, humus from the soil,[1] and blew into his nostrils the breath of life, and the human became a living creature. And the LORD God planted a garden in Eden, to the east, and He placed there the human He had fashioned. And the LORD God caused to sprout from the soil every tree lovely to look at and good for food, and the tree of life was in the midst of the garden, and the tree of knowledge, good and evil. Now a river runs out of Eden to water the garden and from there splits off into four streams. The name of the first is Pishon, the one that winds through the whole land of Havilah, where there is gold. And the gold of that land is goodly, bdellium is there, and lapis lazuli. And the name of the second river is Gihon, the one that winds through all the land of Cush. And the name of the third river is Tigris, the one that goes to the east of Ashur. And the fourth river is Euphrates.[2] And the LORD God took the human and set him down in the garden of Eden to till it and watch it. And the LORD God commanded the human, saying, "From every fruit of the garden you may surely eat. But from the tree of knowledge, good and evil, you shall not eat, for on the day you eat from it, you are doomed to die."

And the LORD God said, "It is not good for the human to be alone, I shall make him a sustainer beside him." And the LORD God fashioned from the soil each beast of the field and each fowl of the heavens and brought each to the human to see what he would call it, and whatever the human called a living creature, that was its name. And the human called names to all the cattle and to the fowl of the heavens and to all the beasts of the field, but for the human no sustainer beside him was found. And the LORD God cast a deep slumber on the human, and he slept, and He took one of his ribs and closed over the flesh where it had been, and the LORD God built the rib He had taken from the human into a woman and He brought her to the human. And the human said:

> This one at last, bone of my bones
> and flesh of my flesh,
> This one shall be called Woman,
> for from man was this one taken.[3]

1. The punning "human/humus" reflects the play in Hebrew between *adam*, "person," and *adamah*, "earth."
2. These rivers place Eden in southern Mesopotamia.
3. In Hebrew, "man" is *ish*, "woman" is *ishshah*.

Therefore does a man leave his father and his mother and cling to his wife and they become one flesh. And the two of them were naked, the human and his woman, and they were not ashamed.

Chapter 3

Now the serpent was most cunning of all the beasts of the field that the LORD God had made. And he said to the woman, "Though God said, you shall not eat from any tree of the garden—" And the woman said to the serpent, "From the fruit of the garden's trees we may eat, but from the fruit of the tree in the midst of the garden God has said, 'You shall not eat from it and you shall not touch it, lest you die.'" And the serpent said to the woman, "You shall not be doomed to die. For God knows that on the day you eat of it your eyes will be opened and you will become as gods knowing good and evil." And the woman saw that the tree was good for eating and that it was lust to the eyes and the tree was lovely to look at, and she took of its fruit and ate, and she also gave to her man, and he ate. And the eyes of the two were opened, and they knew they were naked, and they sewed fig leaves and made themselves loincloths.

And they heard the sound of the LORD God walking about in the garden in the evening breeze, and the human and his woman hid from the LORD God in the midst of the trees of the garden. And the LORD God called to the human and said to him, "Where are you?" And he said, "I heard your sound in the garden and I was afraid, for I was naked, and I hid." And He said, "Who told you that you were naked? From the tree I commanded you not to eat have you eaten?" And the human said, "The woman whom you gave by me, she gave me from the tree, and I ate." And the LORD God said to the woman, "What is this you have done?" And the woman said, "The serpent beguiled me and I ate." And the LORD God said to the serpent, "Because you have done this,

> Cursed be you
> of all cattle and all beasts of the field.
> On your belly shall you go
> and dust shall you eat all the days of your life.
> Enmity will I set between you and the woman,
> between your seed and hers.
> He will boot your head
> and you will bite his heel."

To the woman He said,

> "I will terribly sharpen your birth pangs,
> in pain shall you bear children.
> And for your man shall be your longing,
> and he shall rule over you."

And to the human he said, "Because you listened to the voice of your wife and ate from the tree that I commanded you, 'You shall not eat from it,'

> Cursed be the soil for your sake,
> with pangs shall you eat from it all the days of your life.
> Thorn and thistle shall it sprout for you
> and you shall eat the plants of the field.
> By the sweat of your brow shall you eat bread

till you return to the soil,
for from there were you taken,
for dust you are
and to dust shall you return."

And the human called his woman's name Eve, for she was the mother of all that lives.[4] And the LORD God made skin coats for the human and his woman, and He clothed them. And the LORD God said, "Now that the human has become like one of us, knowing good and evil, he may reach out and take as well from the tree of life and live forever." And the LORD God sent him from the garden of Eden to till the soil from which he had been taken. And he drove out the human and set up east of the garden of Eden the cherubim and the flame of the whirling sword to guard the way to the tree of life.

Chapter 4

And the human knew Eve his woman and she conceived and bore Cain, and she said, "I have got me a man with the LORD." And she bore as well his brother, Abel, and Abel became a herder of sheep while Cain was a tiller of the soil. And it happened in the course of time that Cain brought from the fruit of the soil an offering to the LORD. And Abel too had brought from the choice firstlings of his flock, and the LORD regarded Abel and his offering but He did not regard Cain and his offering, and Cain was very incensed, and his face fell. And the LORD said to Cain.

"Why are you incensed,
and why is your face fallen?
For whether you offer well,
or whether you do not,
at the tent flap sin crouches
and for you is its longing
but you will rule over it."

And Cain said to Abel his brother, "Let us go out to the field." And when they were in the field, Cain rose against Abel his brother and killed him. And the LORD said to Cain, "Where is Abel your brother?" And he said, "I do not know. Am I my brother's keeper?" And He said, "What have you done? Listen! your brother's blood cries out to me from the soil. And so, cursed shall you be by the soil that gaped with its mouth to take your brother's blood from your hand. If you till the soil, it will no longer give you its strength. A restless wanderer shall you be on the earth." And Cain said to the LORD, "My punishment is too great to bear. Now that You have driven me this day from the soil and I must hide from Your presence, I shall be a restless wanderer on the earth and whoever finds me will kill me." And the LORD said to him, "Therefore whoever kills Cain shall suffer sevenfold vengeance." And the LORD set a mark upon Cain so that whoever found him would not slay him.

And Cain went out from the LORD's presence and dwelled in the land of Nod[5] east of Eden. And Cain knew his wife and she conceived and bore Enoch. Then he became the builder of a city and called the name of the city, like his son's name, Enoch. And Irad was born to Enoch, and Irad begot Mehujael and Muhujael begot Methusael

4. "Eve" means "living."

5. "Wandering."

and Methusael begot Lamech. And Lamech took him two wives, the name of the one was Adah and the name of the other was Zillah. And Adah bore Jabal: he was the first of tent dwellers with livestock. And his brother's name was Jubal: he was the first of all who play on the lyre and pipe. As for Zillah, she bore Tubal-cain, who forged every tool of copper and iron. And the sister of Tubal-cain was Naamah. And Lamech said to his wives,

> "Adah and Zillah, O hearken my voice,
> You wives of Lamech, give ear to my speech.
> For a man have I slain for my wound,
> a boy for my bruising.
> For sevenfold Cain is avenged,
> and Lamech seventy and seven."

And Adam again knew his wife and she bore a son and called his name Seth,[6] as to say, "God has granted me other seed in place of Abel, for Cain has killed him." As for Seth, to him, too, a son was born, and he called his name Enosh. It was then that the name of the LORD was first invoked.

Chapter 5[7]

This is the book of the lineage of Adam: On the day God created the human, in the image of God He created him. Male and female He created them, and He blessed them and called their name humankind on the day they were created. And Adam lived a hundred and thirty years and he begot in his likeness by his image and called his name Seth. And the days of Adam after he begot Seth were eight hundred years, and he begot sons and daughters. And all the days Adam lived were nine hundred and thirty years. Then he died. And Seth lived a hundred and five years and he begot Enosh. And Seth lived after he begot Enosh eight hundred and seven years. Then he died. And all the days of Seth were nine hundred and twelve years. Then he died. And Enosh lived ninety years and he begot Kenan. And Enosh lived after he begot Kenan eight hundred and fifteen years, and he begot sons and daughters. And all the days of Enosh were nine hundred and five years. Then he died. And Kenan lived seventy years and he begot Mahalalel. And Kenan lived after he begot Mahalalel eight hundred and forty years, and he begot sons and daughters. And all the days of Kenan were nine hundred and ten years. Then he died. And Mahalalel lived sixty-five years and he begot Jared. And Mahalalel lived after he begot Jared eight hundred and thirty years, and he begot sons and daughters. And all the days of Mahalalel were eight hundred and ninety-five years. Then he died. And Jared lived a hundred and sixty-two years and he begot Enoch. And Jared lived after he begot Enoch eight hundred years, and he begot sons and daughters. And all the days of Jared were nine hundred and sixty-two years. Then he died. And Enoch lived sixty-five years and he begot Methuselah. And Enoch walked with God after he begot Methuselah three hundred years, and he begot sons and daughters. And all the days of Enoch were three hundred and sixty-five years. And Enoch walked with God and he was no more, for God took him. And Methuselah lived a hundred and eighty-seven years and he begot Lamech. And Methuselah lived after he begot Lamech seven hundred and eighty-two years,

6. "Granted."

7. This chapter gives a lineage of ten generations, linking Adam to Noah at the close of the primeval period.

and he begot sons and daughters. And all the days of Methuselah were nine hundred and sixty-nine years. Then he died. And Lamech lived a hundred and eighty-two years and he begot a son. And he called his name Noah,[8] as to say, "This one will console us for the pain of our hands' work from the soil which the LORD cursed." And Lamech lived after he begot Noah five hundred and ninety-five years, and he begot sons and daughters. And all the days of Lamech were seven hundred and seventy-seven years. Then he died. And Noah was five hundred years old and he begot Shem, Ham, and Japheth.

Chapter 6

And it happened as humankind began to multiply over the earth and daughters were born to them, that the sons of God saw that the daughters of man were comely, and they took themselves wives howsoever they chose. And the LORD said, "My breath shall not abide in the human forever, for he is but flesh. Let his days be a hundred and twenty years."

The Nephilim[9] were then on the earth, and afterward as well, the sons of God having come to bed with the daughters of man who bore them children: they are the heroes of yore, the men of renown.

And the LORD saw that the evil of the human creature was great on the earth and that every scheme of his heart's devising was only perpetually evil. And the LORD regretted having made the human on earth and was grieved to the heart. And the LORD said, "I will wipe out the human race I created from the face of the earth, from human to cattle to crawling thing to the fowl of the heavens, for I regret that I have made them." But Noah found favor in the eyes of the LORD. This is the lineage of Noah—Noah was a righteous man, he was blameless in his time, Noah walked with God—and Noah begot three sons, Shem and Ham and Japheth. And the earth was corrupt before God and the earth was filled with outrage. And God saw the earth and, look, it was corrupt, for all flesh had corrupted its ways on the earth. And God said to Noah, "The end of all flesh is come before me, for the earth is filled with outrage by them, and I am now about to destroy them, with the earth. Make yourself an ark of cypress wood, with cells you shall make the ark, and caulk it inside and out with pitch. This is how you shall make it: three hundred cubits, the ark's length; fifty cubits, its width; thirty cubits, its height.[1] Make a skylight in the ark, within a cubit of the top you shall finish it, and put an entrance in the ark on one side. With lower and middle and upper decks you shall make it. As for me, I am about to bring the Flood, water upon the earth, to destroy all flesh that has within it the breath of life from under the heavens, everything on the earth shall perish. And I will set up my covenant with you, and you shall enter the ark, you and your sons and your wife and the wives of your sons, with you. And from all that lives, from all flesh, two of each thing you shall bring to the ark to keep alive with you, male and female they shall be. From the fowl of each kind and from the cattle of each kind and from all that crawls on the earth of each kind, two of each thing shall come to you to be kept alive. As for you, take you from every food that is eaten and store it by you, to serve for you and for them as food." And this Noah did; as all that God commanded him, so he did.

8. "Comfort, rest."
9. Giants.

1. A cubit was about 18 inches.

Chapter 7

And the LORD said to Noah, "Come into the ark, you and all your household, for it is you I have seen righteous before me in this generation. Of every clean animal take you seven pairs, each with its mate, and of every animal that is not clean, one pair, each with its mate. Of the fowl of the heavens as well seven pairs, male and female, to keep seed alive over all the earth. For in seven days' time I will make it rain on the earth forty days and forty nights and I will wipe out from the face of the earth all existing things that I have made." And Noah did all that the LORD commanded him.

Noah was six hundred years old when the Flood came, water over the earth. And Noah and his sons and his wife and his sons' wives came into the ark because of the waters of the Flood. Of the clean animals and of the animals that were not clean and of the fowl and of all that crawls upon the ground two each came to Noah into the ark, male and female, as God had commanded Noah. And it happened after seven days, that the waters of the Flood were over the earth. In the six hundredth year of Noah's life, in the second month, on the seventeenth day of the month, on that day,

> All the wellsprings of the great deep burst
> and the casements of the heavens were opened.

And the rain was over the earth forty days and forty nights. That very day, Noah and Shem and Ham and Japheth, the sons of Noah, and Noah's wife, and the three wives of his sons together with them, came into the ark, they as well as beasts of each kind and cattle of each kind and each kind of crawling thing that crawls on the earth and each kind of bird, each winged thing. They came to Noah into the ark, two by two of all flesh that has the breath of life within it. And those that came in, male and female of all flesh they came, as God had commanded him, and the LORD shut him in. And the Flood was forty days over the earth, and the waters multiplied and bore the ark upward and it rose above the earth. And the waters surged and multiplied mightily over the earth, and the ark went on the surface of the water. And the waters surged most mightily over the earth, and all the high mountains under the heavens were covered. Fifteen cubits above them the waters surged as the mountains were covered. And all flesh that stirs on the earth perished, the fowl and the cattle and the beasts and all swarming things that swarm upon the earth, and all humankind. All that had the quickening breath of life in its nostrils, of all that was on dry land, died. And He wiped out all existing things from the face of the earth, from humans to cattle to crawling things to the fowl of the heavens, they were wiped out from the earth. And Noah alone remained, and those with him in the ark. And the waters surged over the earth one hundred and fifty days.

Chapter 8

And God remembered Noah and all the beasts and all the cattle that were with him in the ark. And God sent a wind over the earth and the waters subsided. And the wellsprings of the deep were dammed up, and the casements of the heavens, the rain from the heavens held back. And the waters receded from the earth little by little, and the waters ebbed. At the end of a hundred and fifty days the ark came to rest, on the seventeenth day of the seventh month, on the mountains of Ararat.[2] The waters continued

2. A region in Armenia.

to ebb, until the tenth month, on the first day of the tenth month, the mountaintops appeared. And it happened, at the end of forty days, that Noah opened the window of the ark he had made. And he let out the raven and it went forth to and fro until the waters should dry up from the earth. And he let out the dove to see whether the waters had abated from the surface of the ground. But the dove found no resting place for its foot and it returned to him to the ark, for the waters were over all the earth. And he reached out and took it and brought it back to him into the ark. Then he waited another seven days and again let the dove out of the ark. And the dove came back to him at eventide and, look, a plucked olive leaf was in its bill, and Noah knew that the waters had abated from the earth. Then he waited still another seven days and let out the dove, and it did not return to him again. And it happened in the six hundred and first year, in the first month, on the first day of the month, the waters dried up from the earth, and Noah took off the covering of the ark and he saw and, look, the surface of the ground was dry. And in the second month, on the twenty-seventh day of the month, the earth was completely dry. And God spoke to Noah, saying, "Go out of the ark, you and your wife and your sons and your sons' wives, with you. All the animals that are with you of all flesh, fowl and cattle and every crawling thing that crawls on the earth, take out with you, and let them swarm through the earth and be fruitful and multiply on the earth." And Noah went out, his sons and his wife and his sons' wives with him. Every beast, every crawling thing, and every fowl, everything that stirs on the earth, by families, came out of the ark. And Noah built an altar to the LORD and he took from every clean cattle and every clean fowl and offered burnt offerings on the altar. And the LORD smelled the fragrant odor and the LORD said in His heart, "I will not again damn the soil on humankind's score. For the devisings of the human heart are evil from youth. And I will not again strike down all living things as I did. As long as all the days of the earth—

> seedtime and harvest
> and cold and heat
> and summer and winter
> and day and night
> shall not cease."

Chapter 9

And God blessed Noah and his sons and He said to them, "Be fruitful and multiply and fill the earth. And the dread and fear of you shall be upon all the beasts of the field and all the fowl of the heavens, in all that crawls on the ground and in all the fish of the sea. In your hand they are given. All stirring things that are alive, yours shall be for food, like the green plants, I have given all to you. But flesh with its lifeblood still in it you shall not eat. And just so, your lifeblood I will requite, from every beast I will requite it, and from humankind, from every man's brother, I will requite human life.

> He who sheds human blood
> by humans his blood shall be shed,
> for in the image of God
> He made humankind.
> As for you, be fruitful and multiply,
> swarm through the earth, and hold sway over it."

And God said to Noah and to his sons with him, "And I, I am about to establish My covenant with you and with your seed after you, and with every living creature that is with you, the fowl and the cattle and every beast of the earth with you, all that have come out of the ark, every beast of the earth. And I will establish My covenant with you, that never again shall all flesh be cut off by the waters of the Flood, and never again shall there be a Flood to destroy the earth." And God said, "This is the sign of the covenant that I set between Me and you and every living creature that is with you, for everlasting generations: My bow I have set in the clouds to be a sign of the covenant between Me and the earth, and so, when I send clouds over the earth, the bow will appear in the cloud. Then I will remember My covenant, between Me and you and every living creature of all flesh, and the waters will no more become a Flood to destroy all flesh. And the bow shall be in the cloud and I will see it, to remember the everlasting covenant between God and all living creatures, all flesh that is on the earth." And God said to Noah, "This is the sign of the covenant I have established between Me and all flesh that is on the earth."

And the sons of Noah who came out from the ark were Shem and Ham and Japheth, and Ham was the father of Canaan. These three were the sons of Noah, and from these the whole earth spread out. And Noah, a man of the soil, was the first to plant a vineyard. And he drank of the wine and became drunk, and exposed himself within his tent. And Ham the father of Canaan saw his father's nakedness and told his two brothers outside.[3] And Shem and Japheth took a cloak and put it over both their shoulders and walked backward and covered their father's nakedness, their faces turned backward so they did not see their father's nakedness. And Noah woke from his wine and he knew what his youngest son had done to him. And he said,

> "Cursed be Canaan,
> the lowliest slave shall he be
> to his brothers."

And he said,

> "Blessed be the LORD
> the God of Shem,
> unto them shall Canaan be slave.
> May God enlarge Japheth,
> may he dwell in the tents of Shem,
> unto them shall Canaan be slave."

And Noah lived after the Flood three hundred and fifty years. And all the days of Noah were nine hundred and fifty years. Then he died.[4]

Chapter 11

And all the earth was one language, one set of words. And it happened as they journeyed from the east that they found a valley in the land of Shinar[5] and settled there. And they said to each other, "Come, let us bake bricks and burn them hard." And the

3. The story implies that Ham/Canaan had a sexual interest in Noah; later in the Bible (Leviticus 18), Canaanite sexual perversions are given as a reason God is displacing them in favor of the Hebrews.

4. Chapter 10, omitted here, gives a genealogy of Noah's descendants.

5. The lowlands of the Tigris-Euphrates basin in Mesopotamia.

brick served them as stone, and bitumen served them as mortar. And they said, "Come, let us build us a city and a tower with its top in the heavens, that we may make us a name, lest we be scattered over all the earth." And the LORD came down to see the city and the tower that the human creatures had built. And the LORD said, "As one people with one language for all, if this is what they have begun to do, nothing they plot will elude them. Come, let us go down and baffle their language there so that they will not understand each other's language." And the LORD scattered them from there over all the earth and they left off building the city. Therefore it is called Babel, for there the LORD made the language of all the earth babble. And from there the LORD scattered them over all the earth.

This is the lineage of Shem: Shem was a hundred years old when he begot Arpachshad two years after the Flood. And Shem lived after begetting Arpachshad five hundred years and he begot sons and daughters. And Arpachshad lived thirty-five years and he begot Shelah. And Arpachshad lived after begetting Shelah four hundred and three years and he begot sons and daughters. And Shelah lived thirty years and he begot Eber. And Shelah lived after begetting Eber four hundred and three years and he begot sons and daughters. And Eber lived thirty-four years and he begot Peleg. And Eber lived after begetting Peleg four hundred and thirty years and he begot sons and daughters. And Peleg lived thirty years and he begot Reu. And Peleg lived after begetting Reu two hundred and nine years and he begot sons and daughters. And Reu lived thirty-two years and he begot Serug. And Reu lived after begetting Serug two hundred and seven years and he begot sons and daughters. And Serug lived thirty years and he begot Nahor. And Serug lived after begetting Nahor two hundred years and he begot sons and daughters. And Nahor lived twenty-nine years and he begot Terah. And Nahor lived after begetting Terah one hundred and nineteen years and he begot sons and daughters. And Terah lived seventy years and he begot Abram, Nahor, and Haran. And this is the lineage of Terah: Terah begot Abram, Nahor, and Haran, and Haran begot Lot. And Haran died in the lifetime of Terah his father in the land of his birth, Ur of the Chaldees. And Abram and Nahor took themselves wives. The name of Abram's wife was Sarai and the name of Nahor's wife was Milcah daughter of Haran, the father of Milcah and the father of Iscah. And Sarai was barren, she had no child. And Terah took Abram his son and Lot son of Haran, his grandson, and Sarai his daughter-in-law, the wife of his son Abram, and he set out with them from Ur of the Chaldees toward the land of Canaan, and they came to Haran and settled there. And the days of Terah were two hundred and five years, and Terah died in Haran.[6]

END OF PERSPECTIVES: CREATION MYTHS AND SOCIAL CONCERNS

The Epic of Gilgamesh

c. 1200 B.C.E.

The greatest literary composition of ancient Mesopotamia, *The Epic of Gilgamesh* can rightly be called the first true work of world literature. It began to circulate widely around the ancient Near East as early as 1000 B.C.E., and it was translated into several of the region's languages.

6. In northwest Mesopotamia; a substantial number of people migrated from this region into Canaan in the early 2nd millennium B.C.E.—a migration that begins the story of Israel's patriarchs and matriarchs in the next section of Genesis, which concludes with the story of Joseph in Egypt.

Tablets bearing portions of the epic have been found not only around Mesopotamia but also in Turkey and in Palestine. We know of no other work that crossed so many borders so early, as people in many areas began to respond to the epic's searching exploration of the meaning of culture in the face of death.

The story of Gilgamesh developed over many centuries from a kernel of historical fact. Gilgamesh was an early king of the city-state of Uruk in southern Mesopotamia; he lived sometime around 2750 B.C.E. Early records credit him with building a great wall around his city, "spread out across the countryside like a net for birds." In the years following his death a cult grew up around his memory, and he was honored as a judge of the underworld. By around 2000 B.C.E. a loosely connected cycle of songs had been written in Sumerian about his life and legendary adventures. These old songs portray Bilgames (as they call him) as a great warrior, describe his journey to a distant mountain where he kills a monster and brings home cedar trees for his palace, and tell of a descent by his servant Enkidu into the grim regions of the underworld. These early poems already signal what would become the organizing theme of the full epic: its hero's fear of death and his quest for immortality. As he decides to journey to slay the monster guarding the Cedar Mountain, Bilgames voices his anguish to Enkidu:

> O Enkidu, since no man can escape life's end,
> I will enter the mountain and set up my name.
> . . . .
> In my city, a man dies, and the heart is stricken,
> a man perishes, and the heart feels pain.
> I raised my head on the rampart,
> my gaze fell on a corpse drifting down the river, afloat on the water:
> I too shall become like that, just so shall I be!

Over the course of the Old Babylonian period (2000–1600 B.C.E.) a poet or poets in Babylon took up this theme and adapted the Sumerian poems into a connected epic, written in Akkadian, the increasingly dominant language of the region. Finally, around 1200 B.C.E., the epic was revised into its definitive form by a Babylonian priest named Sîn-liqe-unninni, whose additions include the poem's preface, which summarizes Gilgamesh's accomplishments and reflects directly on the recovery of ancient tradition—as the Gilgamesh story itself was by then.

The term "epic" is sometimes used loosely to describe ancient narrative poems in general, but full-scale epics do more than tell a story in poetic language. Epics like Homer's *Iliad* often center on the founding or defense of a city and its society, with extensive battle scenes in which a great hero attempts to overcome heavy odds presented both by human opponents and divine antagonism. Other epics, like Homer's *Odyssey,* have to do chiefly with a voyage of travel, exploration, or escape. Like Virgil's *Aeneid, The Epic of Gilgamesh* combines both kinds of epic subject matter. Ancient though it is, *Gilgamesh* is also like the *Aeneid* in being a developed reworking of earlier epic texts. Where Virgil used Homer and other sources, Sîn-liqe-unninni drew on older poems of the Flood and of the underworld, as well as of Gilgamesh and his adventures, to create a broad exploration of the uses and limits of human culture, poised between the realms of nature and of the gods.

The poem presents Gilgamesh as a mixed figure himself; like Homer's hero Achilles, he has a human father and a divine mother, and like Achilles he is a great but flawed hero. As the epic begins, he has been oppressing his own people, who appeal to the gods for relief. The gods create Enkidu, no longer simply Gilgamesh's servant but now shown as a force of nature, a wild man who comes to Uruk and restrains Gilgamesh from his misbehavior. Becoming fast friends, Gilgamesh and Enkidu journey to a distant mountain and slay its guardian monster, and then enter into a fatal dispute with Ishtar, goddess of love. She tries to seduce Gilgamesh, who rejects her advances; she sends a great bull down from heaven to kill him, but Enkidu and Gilgamesh slaughter the bull. Then Enkidu goes too far: he rashly insults Ishtar, who decrees his death.

Impression from a stone cylinder seal, Babylonia, c. second millennium B.C.E. Scene showing Gilgamesh and Enkidu slaying the Bull of Heaven, as Ishtar angrily protests.

In despair at his friend's death, Gilgamesh sets off to find the distant, hidden home of his ancestor Utanapishtim, who with his wife was the sole survivor of a worldwide flood. Utanapishtim tells him the story of the Flood, in terms strikingly similar to the biblical account found in Genesis 6–9 (page 67). By weaving this formerly independent story into his epic, Sîn-liqe-unninni extends Gilgamesh's story to a wider context of the life and death of civilization itself. After telling his story, Utanapishtim gives Gilgamesh a plant that will give him immortality, but on his way home a serpent steals the plant, and Gilgamesh returns to Uruk distraught; his only comfort, in the poem's closing lines, is to survey his city's magnificent walls, in which he buries his story for later generations to read.

Gilgamesh is classically epic in its language as well as its story. The poem is written in an elevated style that moves with a grand, inexorable sweep, punctuated by haunting lyrical passages in which Gilgamesh and Enkidu voice their fears of the dangers they face and their grief at the prospect of death. Like later literary epics, *Gilgamesh* also makes thematic use of old patterns developed for earlier oral poetry. Sumerian poems relied heavily on repetition for verbal effect and to aid listeners in understanding when they were recited in ritual settings. *Gilgamesh* is clearly a written composition rather than an oral one, intended for private reading and reflection rather than for any public use, but Sîn-liqe-unninni availed himself fully of the resources of repetition. Series of mysterious dreams foreshadow future events and build a sense of brooding uncertainty. Variations within lines allow the reader to see more fully into events and images, as when Utanapishtim tells Gilgamesh, "I will reveal to you a thing that is hidden, a secret of the gods I will tell you!"

In a fitting reflection of the poem's own themes of loss and recovery, *The Epic of Gilgamesh* itself vanished from human knowledge for over two thousand years, following the defeat and destruction of the major Mesopotamian cities by Persian invaders in the seventh and sixth centuries B.C.E. It was not until the 1850s that an Iraqi archaeologist, Hormuzd Rassam, discovered the ruins of the great royal library of Ashurbanipal, King of the World and King of

Assyria in the mid-seventh century. Rassam shipped thousands of tablets back to the British Museum, where scholars began to piece fragments together and puzzle out their contents. A full twenty years later a young curator named George Smith began to study the eleven tablets that would turn out to contain *Gilgamesh.* Smith was electrified when he came upon the Noah-like Utanapishtim's account of the Flood. "I am the first man to read that after two thousand years of oblivion," he exclaimed, and, according to his associate E. A. W. Budge, "he jumped up and rushed about the room in a state of great excitement, and, to the astonishment of those present, began to undress himself!"

Ever since then, modern readers have been gripped by this epic poem, though they have differed widely about how it should be understood. Nineteenth-century readers debated whether it was a work of fiction or a genuine historical account. The parallels between Utanapishtim and Noah were taken by some to demonstrate the factual basis of the biblical version, while others drew an opposite conclusion, that Noah must be as fictional a figure as his Akkadian counterpart. Readers today focus on the epic as a poetic masterpiece rather than a historical document, yet the poem remains open to many interpretations. In part, it is open-ended simply because it is fragmentary: extensive gaps remain in the set of tablets that Rassam found in Nineveh and in other copies that have been recovered elsewhere. Some of these gaps can be filled in with parallel passages in earlier and later versions, and in this way a reasonably complete translation can be pieced together, as is presented here. The poem's great theme of the fragility of human life and culture is well illustrated by gaps and ellipses that continue to dot the text.

Even in the poem's many well-preserved episodes, mysteries remain. We first meet Enkidu living happily in the open countryside, naked, among the animals; when a temple prostitute seduces him and brings him to Uruk, does this episode celebrate city culture's riches or satirize them? Is Gilgamesh displaying heroic boldness in going off to slay the demon Humbaba, or is he being foolhardy, as his own counselors tell him? When he rejects the goddess Ishtar's advances, is Gilgamesh standing up for humanity or making the mistake of his—and Enkidu's—life? What are we to make of the mysterious dreams that periodically visit both Gilgamesh and Enkidu? Does Utanapishtim sympathize with Gilgamesh's quest for immortality or mock him for believing he can transcend the human condition? Does the poem end in an affirmation of human culture or in despair?

First recorded a thousand years before either the Greeks or the Hebrews learned how to write, Gilgamesh's story circulated through the Near East and Asia Minor during the centuries in which both the legends of Genesis and the Homeric epics were developed and eventually written down. Both the Eden story and the Flood story have clear parallels in *Gilgamesh,* whose restless hero can also be well compared to Odysseus, even as his fated friendship with Enkidu can be related to the relationship of Achilles and his beloved friend Patroklos. Gilgamesh's story continued to live on in his own region in oral form, and his adventures have echoes in *The Thousand and One Nights* in such figures as Sindbad. Now that the epic itself has at last been recovered, its haunting images, its moving dialogues, and its engrossing drama make it once again, after two thousand years of oblivion, compelling reading today.

PRONUNCIATIONS:

Enkidu: AIN-key-dou
Gilgamesh: GILL-gah-mesh
Shamash: SHAY-mash
Shamhat: SHAHM-haht
Sîn-liqe-unninni: SEEN-LEE-kay-ooh-NEE-nee
Urshanabi: OOHR-sha-NAH-bee
Utanapishtim: ooh-TA-nah-PEASH-team

The Epic of Gilgamesh[1]

Tablet 1

He who has seen everything, I will make known to the lands.
I will teach about him who experienced all things.
Anu° granted him the totality of knowledge of all. *the sky god*
He saw the Secret, discovered the Hidden,
he brought information of the time before the Flood.
He went on a distant journey, pushing himself to exhaustion,
but then was brought to peace.
He carved on a stone stela all of his toils,
and built the wall of Uruk-Haven,
the wall of the sacred Eanna Temple, the holy sanctuary.
Look at its wall which gleams like copper,
inspect its inner wall, the likes of which no one can equal!
Take hold of the threshold stone—it dates from ancient times!
Go close to the Eanna Temple, the residence of Ishtar,
such as no later king or man ever equaled!
Go up on the wall of Uruk and walk around,
examine its foundation, inspect its brickwork thoroughly.
Is not even the core of the brick structure made of kiln-fired brick,
and did not the Seven Sages[2] themselves lay out its plans?
One league city, one league palm gardens, one league lowlands, the open
area of the Ishtar Temple,
three leagues and the open area of Uruk the wall encloses.
Find the copper tablet box,
open the hasp of its lock of bronze,
undo the fastening of its secret opening.
Take and read out from the lapis lazuli tablet
how Gilgamesh went through every hardship.

Supreme over other kings, lordly in appearance,
he is the hero, born of Uruk, the goring wild bull.
He walks out in front, the leader,
and walks at the rear, trusted by his companions.
Mighty net, protector of his people,
raging flood-wave who destroys even walls of stone!
Offspring of Lugalbanda, Gilgamesh is strong to perfection,
son of the august cow, Rimat-Ninsun, Gilgamesh is awesome to perfection.[3]
It was he who opened the mountain passes,
who dug wells on the flank of the mountain.
It was he who crossed the ocean, the vast seas, to the rising sun,
who explored the world regions, seeking life.
It was he who reached by his own sheer strength Utanapishtim, the Far-
away,
who restored the sanctuaries that the Flood had destroyed!

1. Translated by Maureen Gallery Kovacs.
2. Sent by Ea, god of wisdom, to teach humanity the arts of civilization.
3. Gilgamesh's father Lugalbanda was an earlier king of Uruk; his mother is the goddess Ninsun, "Lady Wild Cow."

Who can compare with him in kingliness?
Who can say like Gilgamesh: "I am King!"?
Whose name, from the day of his birth, was called "Gilgamesh"?
Two-thirds of him is god, one-third of him is human.
The Great Goddess designed the model for his body,
she prepared his form,[4]
. . .
beautiful, handsomest of men.
He walks around in the enclosure of Uruk,
like a wild bull he makes himself mighty, head raised over others.
There is no rival who can raise his weapon against him.
His fellows stand at the alert, attentive to his orders.
The men of Uruk become anxious:
Gilgamesh does not leave a son to his father;
Is Gilgamesh the shepherd of Uruk-Haven,
. . .
bold, eminent, knowing, and wise?
Gilgamesh does not leave a girl to her betrothed!
The daughter of the warrior, the bride of the young man,
the gods kept hearing their complaints, so
the gods of the heavens implored Anu, Lord of Uruk:
"You have indeed brought into being a mighty wild bull, head raised!
There is no rival who can raise a weapon against him.
His fellows stand at the alert, attentive to his orders,
Gilgamesh does not leave a son to his father,
. . .
Is he the shepherd of Uruk-Haven,
. . .
bold, eminent, knowing, and wise?
Gilgamesh does not leave a girl to her betrothed!"
The daughter of the warrior, the bride of the young man,
Anu listened to their complaints,
and called out to Aruru:° *mother goddess*
"It was you, Aruru, who created this man,
now create a counterpart to him.
Let him be equal to Gilgamesh's stormy heart,
let them be a match for each other so that Uruk may find peace!"
When Aruru heard this she created within herself the counterpart of Anu.
Aruru washed her hands, she pinched off some clay, and threw it into the
wilderness.
In the wilderness she created valiant Enkidu,
born of Silence, endowed with strength by Ninurta.° *god of war*
His whole body was shaggy with hair,
he had a full head of hair like a woman,
his locks billowed in profusion like Ashnan.° *goddess of grain*
He knew neither people nor settled living,
but wore a garment like Sumukan.° *goddess of cattle*

4. Ellipses indicate missing lines and parts of lines.

He ate grasses with the gazelles,
and jostled at the watering hole with the animals;
as with animals, his thirst was slaked with water.

A notorious trapper
came face-to-face with him opposite the watering hole.
A first, a second, and a third day
he came face-to-face with him opposite the watering hole.
On seeing him the trapper's face went stark with fear,
and he and his animals drew back home.
He was rigid with fear; though stock-still
his heart pounded and his face drained of color.
He was miserable to the core,
and his face looked like one who had made a long journey.
The trapper addressed his father saying:
"Father, a certain fellow has come from the mountains.
He is the mightiest in the land,
his strength is as mighty as the meteorite of Anu!
He continually goes over the mountains,
he continually jostles at the watering place with the animals,
he continually plants his feet opposite the watering place.
I was afraid, so I did not go up to him.
He filled in the pits that I had dug,
wrenched out my traps that I had spread,
released from my grasp the wild animals.
He does not let me make my rounds in the wilderness!"
The trapper's father spoke to him saying:
"My son, there lives in Uruk a certain Gilgamesh.
There is no one stronger than he,
he is as strong as the meteorite of Anu.
Go, set off to Uruk,
tell Gilgamesh of this Man of Might.
He will give you the harlot Shamhat, take her with you.
The woman will overcome the fellow as if she were strong.
When the animals are drinking at the watering place
have her take off her robe and expose her sex.
When he sees her he will draw near to her,
and his animals, who grew up in his wilderness, will be alien to him."
He heeded his father's advice.
The trapper went off to Uruk,
he made the journey, stood inside of Uruk,
and declared to Gilgamesh:
"There is a certain fellow who has come from the mountains—
he is the mightiest in the land,
his strength is as mighty as the meteorite of Anu!
He continually goes over the mountains,
he continually jostles at the watering place with the animals,
he continually plants his feet opposite the watering place.
I was afraid, so I did not go up to him.

He filled in the pits that I had dug,
wrenched out my traps that I had spread,
released from my grasp the wild animals.
He does not let me make my rounds in the wilderness!"
Gilgamesh said to the trapper:
"Go, trapper, bring the harlot, Shamhat, with you.
When the animals are drinking at the watering place
have her take off her robe and expose her sex.
When he sees her he will draw near to her,
and his animals, who grew up in his wilderness, will be alien to him."

The trapper went, bringing the harlot, Shamhat, with him.
They set off on the journey, making direct way.
On the third day they arrived at the appointed place,
and the trapper and the harlot sat down at their posts.
A first day and a second they sat opposite the watering hole.
The animals arrived and drank at the watering hole,
the wild beasts arrived and slaked their thirst with water.
Then he, Enkidu, offspring of the mountains,
who eats grasses with the gazelles,
came to drink at the watering hole with the animals,
with the wild beasts he slaked his thirst with water.
Then Shamhat saw him—a primitive,
a savage fellow from the depths of the wilderness!
"That is he, Shamhat! Release your clenched arms,
expose your sex so he can take in your voluptuousness.
Do not be restrained—take his energy!
When he sees you he will draw near to you.
Spread out your robe so he can lie upon you,
and perform for this primitive the task of womankind!
His animals, who grew up in his wilderness, will become alien to him,
and his lust will groan over you."
Shamhat unclutched her bosom, exposed her sex, and he took in her voluptuousness.
She was not restrained, but took his energy.
She spread out her robe and he lay upon her,
she performed for the primitive the task of womankind.
His lust groaned over her;
for six days and seven nights Enkidu stayed aroused,
and had intercourse with the harlot
until he was sated with her charms.
But when he turned his attention to his animals,
the gazelles saw Enkidu and darted off,
the wild animals distanced themselves from his body.
Enkidu's body was utterly depleted,
his knees that wanted to go off with his animals went rigid;
Enkidu was diminished, his running was not as before.
But then he drew himself up, for his understanding had broadened.
Turning around, he sat down at the harlot's feet,

gazing into her face, his ears attentive as the harlot spoke.
The harlot said to Enkidu:
"You are beautiful, Enkidu, you are become like a god.
Why do you gallop around the wilderness with the wild beasts?
Come, let me bring you into Uruk-Haven,
to the Holy Temple, the residence of Anu and Ishtar,
the place of Gilgamesh, who is wise to perfection,
but who struts his power over the people like a wild bull."
What she kept saying found favor with him.
Becoming aware of himself, he sought a friend.
Enkidu spoke to the harlot:
"Come, Shamhat, take me away with you
to the sacred Holy Temple, the residence of Anu and Ishtar,
the place of Gilgamesh, who is wise to perfection,
but who struts his power over the people like a wild bull.
I will challenge him.
Let me shout out in Uruk: 'I am the mighty one!'
Lead me in and I will change the order of things;
he whose strength is mightiest is the one born in the wilderness!"
She replied: "Come, let us go, so he may see your face.
I will lead you to Gilgamesh—I know where he will be.
Look about, Enkidu, inside Uruk-Haven,
where the people show off in skirted finery,
where every day is a day for some festival,
where the lyre and drum play continually,
where harlots stand about prettily,
exuding voluptuousness, full of laughter,
and on the couch of night the sheets are spread.
Enkidu, you who do not know how to live,
I will show you Gilgamesh, a man of joy and sorrow.
Look at him, gaze at his face—
he is a handsome youth, with freshness,
his entire body exudes voluptuousness.
He has mightier strength than you,
without sleeping day or night!
Enkidu, it is your wrong thoughts you must change!
It is Gilgamesh whom Shamash° loves, *the sun god*
and Anu, Enlil, and Ea[5] have enlarged his mind.
Even before you came from the mountain
Gilgamesh in Uruk had dreams about you."
Gilgamesh got up and revealed the dream, saying to his mother:
"Mother, I had a dream last night.
Stars of the sky appeared,
and some kind of meteorite of Anu fell next to me.
I tried to lift it but it was too mighty for me,
I tried to turn it over but I could not budge it.
The Land of Uruk was standing around it,

5. The sky god Anu is Uruk's patron god, Enlil is head of the younger generation of gods, Ea is god of wisdom.

the whole land had assembled about it,
the populace was thronging around it,
the Men clustered about it,
and kissed its feet as if it were a little baby.
I loved it and embraced it as a wife.
I laid it down at your feet,
and you made it compete with me."
The mother of Gilgamesh, the wise, all-knowing, said to her Lord;
Rimat-Ninsun, the wise, all-knowing, said to Gilgamesh:
"As for the stars of the sky that appeared
and the meteorite of Anu which fell next to you,
which you tried to lift but it was too mighty for you,
which you tried to turn over but were unable to budge it,
which you laid down at my feet,
and I made it compete with you,
and you loved and embraced it as a wife:
There will come to you a mighty man, a comrade
who saves his friend—
he is the mightiest in the land, he is strongest,
his strength is mighty as the meteorite of Anu!
You loved him and embraced him as a wife;
and it is he who will repeatedly save you.
Your dream is good and propitious!"
A second time Gilgamesh said to his mother:
"Mother, I have had another dream:
At the gate of my marital chamber there lay an axe,
and people had collected about it.
The Land of Uruk was standing around it,
the whole land had assembled about it,
the populace was thronging around it.
I laid it down at your feet,
I loved it and embraced it as a wife,
and you made it compete with me."
The mother of Gilgamesh, the wise, all-knowing, said to her son;
Rimat-Ninsun, the wise, all-knowing, said to Gilgamesh:
"The axe that you saw is a man,
whom you love and embrace as a wife,
but whom I have made compete with you.
There will come to you a mighty man, a comrade who saves his friend—
he is the mightiest in the land, he is strongest,
he is as mighty as the meteorite of Anu!"
Gilgamesh spoke to his mother saying:
"By the command of Enlil, the Great Counselor, so may it come to pass!
May I have a friend and adviser,
a friend and adviser may I have!
You have interpreted for me the dreams about him!"
After the harlot recounted the dreams of Gilgamesh to Enkidu
the two of them made love.

Tablet 2

Enkidu sits in front of her.[6]
Enkidu knew nothing about eating bread for food,
and of drinking beer he had not been taught.
The harlot spoke to Enkidu, saying:
"Eat the food, Enkidu, it is the way one lives.
Drink the beer, as is the custom of the land."
Enkidu ate the food until he was sated,
he drank the beer—seven jugs!—and became expansive and sang with joy!
He was elated and his face glowed.
He splashed his shaggy body with water,
and rubbed himself with oil, and turned into a human.
Shamhat pulled off her clothing,
and clothed him with one piece
while she clothed herself with a second.
She took hold of him as gods do
and brought him to the hut of the shepherds.

The shepherds gathered all around about him,
they marveled to themselves:
"How the youth resembles Gilgamesh—
tall in stature, towering up to the battlements over the wall!
Surely he was born in the mountains;
his strength is as mighty as the meteorite of Anu!"
They placed food in front of him,
they placed beer in front of him;
Enkidu did not eat or drink, but squinted and stared.
Enkidu scattered the wolves, he chased away the lions.
The herders could lie down in peace,
for Enkidu was their watchman.

Then he raised his eyes and saw a man.
He said to the harlot:
"Shamhat, have that man go away!
Why has he come? I will call out his name!"
The harlot called out to the man
and went over to him and spoke with him.
"Young man, where are you hurrying?
Why this arduous pace?"
The young man spoke, saying to Enkidu:
"They have invited me to a wedding,
as is the custom of the people,
to make the selection of brides.
I have heaped up tasty delights for the wedding on the ceremonial platter.
For the King of Broad-Marted Uruk,

6. Thirty-three lines are missing here. The next 15 lines are restored from parallels in the Old Babylonian version, as are several later passages.

open is the veil of the people for choosing a girl.
For Gilgamesh, the King of Broad-Marted Uruk,
open is the veil of the people for choosing.
He will have intercourse with the 'destined wife,'
he first, the husband afterward.
This is ordered by the counsel of Anu,
from the severing of his umbilical cord it has been destined for him."
At the young man's speech Enkidu's face flushed with anger.
Enkidu walked in front, and Shamhat after him.[7]
He walked down the street of Uruk-Haven,
He blocked the way through Uruk the Sheepfold.
The land of Uruk stood around him,
the whole land assembled about him,
the populace was thronging around him,
and kissed his feet as if he were a little baby. . . .
For Ishara the bed of marriage is ready,
for Gilgamesh as for a god a counterpart is set up.
Enkidu blocked the entry to the marital chamber,
and would not allow Gilgamesh to be brought in.
They grappled with each other at the entry to the marital chamber,
in the street they attacked each other, the public square of the land.
The doorposts trembled and the wall shook.

[*The next seven lines are from the earlier version.*]

Gilgamesh bent his knees, with his other foot on the ground,
his anger abated and he turned his chest away.
After he turned his chest Enkidu said to Gilgamesh:
"Your mother bore you ever unique,
the Wild Cow of the Enclosure, Ninsun,
your head is elevated over other men,
Enlil has destined for you the kingship over the people."

. . .

They kissed each other and became friends.[8]

. . .

Enkidu made a declaration to Gilgamesh:
"In order to protect the Cedar Forest
Enlil assigned Humbaba as a terror to human beings—
Humbaba's roar is a Flood, his mouth is Fire, and his breath is Death!
He can hear 100 leagues away any rustling in his forest!
Who would go down into his forest?
Enlil assigned him as a terror to human beings,
and whoever goes down into his forest paralysis will strike!"
Gilgamesh spoke to Enkidu saying:

. . .

7. Several lines are missing, in which Enkidu evidently resolves to go and challenge Gilgamesh.

8. A fragmentary passage describes Enkidu's sorrow at the decrease of his strength once he has left the wilderness. Gilgamesh proposes journeying to the Cedar Forest to kill its protector Humbaba and cut down the cedars. Enkidu reacts with fear.

"Who, my Friend, can ascend to the heavens?
Only the gods can dwell forever with Shamash.
As for human beings, their days are numbered,
and whatever they keep trying to achieve is but wind!
Now you are afraid of death—
what has become of your bold strength?
I will go in front of you,
and your mouth can call out: 'Go on closer, do not be afraid!'
Should I fall, I will have established my fame.
They will say: 'It was Gilgamesh who locked in battle with Humbaba the Terrible!'
You were born and raised in the wilderness,
a lion leaped up on you, so you have experienced it all!'

. . .

I will undertake it and I will cut down the Cedar.
It is I who will establish fame for eternity!
Come, my friend, I will go over to the forge
and have them cast the weapons in our presence!"
Holding each other by the hand they went over to the forge.
The craftsmen sat and discussed with one another.

. . .

"The hatchet should be one talent in weight,[9]
Their swords should be one talent, and their armor as well. . . ."
Gilgamesh said to the men of Uruk:
"Listen to me, . . . you men of Uruk, . . .
I want to make myself more mighty, and will go on a distant journey!
I will face fighting such as I have never known,
I will set out on a road I have never traveled!
Give me your blessings!
I will enter the city gate of Uruk, . . .
I will devote myself to the New Year's Festival.
I will perform the New Year's ceremonies,
The New Year's Festival will take place, . . .
They will keep shouting 'Hurrah!' . . ."
Enkidu spoke to the Elders:

. . .

"Say to him that he must not go to the Cedar Forest—
the journey is not to be made!"

. . .

The Noble Counselors of Uruk arose and delivered their advice to Gilgamesh:
"You are young, Gilgamesh, your heart carries you off—
you do not know what you are talking about!

. . .

Humbaba's roar is a Flood,
his mouth is Fire, his breath Death!
He can hear any rustling in his forest 100 leagues away!

9. About two-thirds of a pound.

Who would go down into his forest?
Who among even the Igigi gods can confront him?
In order to keep the Cedar safe, Enlil[1] assigned him as a terror to human beings."
Gilgamesh listened to the statement of his Noble Counselors.

Tablet 3

The Elders spoke to Gilgamesh, saying:
"Gilgamesh, do not put your trust in your vast strength,
but keep a sharp eye out, make each blow strike its mark!
'The one who goes on ahead saves the comrade.'
'The one who knows the route protects his friend.'
Let Enkidu go ahead of you;
he knows the road to the Cedar Forest,
he has seen fighting, has experienced battle.
Enkidu will protect the friend, will keep the comrade safe.
Let his body urge him back to the wives."
[The Elders speak to Enkidu:]
"In our Assembly we have entrusted the King to you,
and on your return you must entrust the King back to us!"
Gilgamesh spoke to Enkidu, saying:
"Come on, my friend, let us go to the Egalmah Temple,
to Ninsun, the Great Queen;
Ninsun is wise, all-knowing.
She will put the advisable path at our feet."
Taking each other by the hand,
Gilgamesh and Enkidu walked to the Egalmah,
to Ninsun, the Great Queen.
Gilgamesh arose and went to her.
"Ninsun, even though I am extraordinarily strong,
I must now travel a long way to where Humbaba is,
I must face fighting such as I have not known,
and I must travel on a road that I do not know!
Until the time that I go and return,
until I reach the Cedar Forest,
until I kill Humbaba the Terrible,
and eradicate from the land something baneful that Shamash hates,
intercede with Shamash on my behalf!
If I kill Humbaba and cut his Cedar
let there be rejoicing all over the land,
and I will erect a monument of the victory before you!"

The words of Gilgamesh, her son,
grieving Queen Ninsun heard over and over.
Ninsun went into her living quarters.
She washed herself with the purity plant,
she donned a robe worthy of her body,

1. The chief Sumerian god.

she donned jewels worthy of her chest,
she donned her sash, and put on her crown.
She sprinkled water from a bowl onto the ground.

She went up to the roof and set incense in front of Shamash,° *the sun god*
she offered fragrant cuttings, and raised her arms to Shamash.
"Why have you imposed—nay, inflicted!—a restless heart on my son, Gilgamesh?
Now you have touched him so that he wants to travel,
a long way to where Humbaba is!
He will face fighting such as he has not known,
and will travel on a road that he does not know!
Until he goes away and returns,
until he reaches the Cedar Forest,
until he kills Humbaba the Terrible,
and eradicates from the land something baneful that you hate,
on the day that you see him on the road
may Aja, the Bride,° without fear remind you, *Shamash's wife*
and command also the Watchmen of the Night,
the stars, and at night your father, Sin."° *moon god*

[*Long passage missing.*]

Ninsun banked up the incense and uttered the ritual words.
She called to Enkidu and would give him instructions:
"Enkidu the Mighty, you are not of my womb,
but now I speak to you along with the sacred votaries of Gilgamesh,
the high priestesses, the holy women, the temple servers."
She laid a pendant on Enkidu's neck, . . . [saying]
"I have taken Enkidu; Enkidu to Gilgamesh I have taken."
[The Elders said:]
"Enkidu will protect the friend, will keep the comrade safe.
Let his body urge him back to the wives.
In our Assembly we have entrusted the King to you,
and on your return you must entrust the King back to us!"[2]

Tablet 4

At twenty leagues they broke for some food,
at thirty leagues they stopped for the night,
walking fifty leagues in a whole day,
a walk of a month and a half.
On the third day they drew near to the Lebanon.
They dug a well facing Shamash, the setting sun. . . .
Gilgamesh climbed up a mountain peak,
made a libation° of flour, and said: *offering*
"Mountain, bring me a dream, a favorable message from Shamash."
Enkidu prepared a sleeping place for him for the night;
a violent wind passed through so he attached a covering.

2. The rest of their speech is fragmentary.

He made him lie down. . . .
While Gilgamesh rested his chin on his knees,
sleep that pours over mankind overtook him.
In the middle of the night his sleep came to an end,
so he got up and said to his friend:
"My friend, did you not call out to me? Why did I wake up?
Did you not touch me? Why am I so disturbed?
Did a god pass by? Why are my muscles trembling?
Enkidu, my friend, I have had a dream—
and the dream I had was deeply disturbing!
In the mountain gorges, the mountain fell down on me!"

He who was born in the wilderness,
Enkidu, interpreted the dream for his friend:
"My friend, your dream is favorable,
The dream is extremely important.
My friend, the mountain which you saw in the dream is Humbaba.
It means we will capture Humbaba, and kill him
and throw his corpse into the wasteland.
In the morning there will be a favorable message from Shamash."

At twenty leagues they broke for some food,
at thirty leagues they stopped for the night,
walking fifty leagues in a whole day,
a walk of a month and a half.
They dug a well facing Shamash; . . .
Gilgamesh climbed up a mountain peak,
made a libation of flour, and said:
"Mountain, bring me a dream, a favorable message from Shamash."
Enkidu prepared a sleeping place for him for the night;
a violent wind passed through so he attached a covering.
While Gilgamesh rested his chin on his knees,
sleep that pours over mankind overtook him.
In the middle of the night his sleep came to an end,
so he got up and said to his friend:
"My friend, did you not call out to me? Why did I wake up?
Did you not touch me? Why am I so disturbed?
Did a god pass by? Why are my muscles trembling?
Enkidu, my friend, I have had a dream,
besides my first dream I have had a second.
And the dream I had—so striking, so . . . , so disturbing!
I was grappling with a wild bull of the wilderness,
with his bellow he split the ground, a cloud of dust rose to the sky.
I sank to my knees in front of him. . . .
My tongue hung out, My temples throbbed;
he gave me water to drink from his waterskin."
"My friend," Enkidu said, "the god to whom we go
is not the wild bull! He is totally different!
The wild bull that you saw is Shamash, the protector,
in difficulties he holds our hand.

The one who gave you water to drink from his waterskin
is your personal god, who brings honor to you, Lugalbanda.
We should join together and do one thing,
a deed such as has never before been done in the land."

At twenty leagues they broke for some food,
at thirty leagues they stopped for the night,
walking fifty leagues in a whole day,
a walk of a month and a half.
They dug a well facing Shamash; . . .
Gilgamesh climbed up a mountain peak,
made a libation of flour, and said:
"Mountain, bring me a dream, a favorable message from Shamash."
Enkidu prepared a sleeping place for him for the night;
a violent wind passed through so he attached a covering.

While Gilgamesh rested his chin on his knees,
sleep that pours over mankind overtook him.
In the middle of the night his sleep came to an end,
so he got up and said to his friend:
"My friend, did you not call out to me? Why did I wake up?
Did you not touch me? Why am I so disturbed?
Did a god pass by? Why are my muscles trembling?
Enkidu, my friend, I have had a third dream,
and the dream I had was deeply disturbing.
The heavens roared and the earth rumbled;
then it became deathly still, and darkness loomed.
A bolt of lightning cracked and a fire broke out,
and where it kept thickening, there rained death.
The white-hot flame dimmed, and the fire went out,
and everything that had been falling around turned to ash.
Let us go down into the plain so we can talk it over."
Enkidu heard the dream that he had presented and said to Gilgamesh:[3]

. . .

At twenty leagues they broke for some food,
at thirty leagues they stopped for the night,
walking fifty leagues in a whole day,
a walk of a month and a half.
They dug a well facing Shamash; . . .
Gilgamesh climbed up a mountain peak,
made a libation of flour, and said:
"Mountain, bring me a dream, a favorable message from Shamash."
Enkidu prepared a sleeping place for him for the night;
a violent wind passed through so he attached a covering.

. . .

While Gilgamesh rested his chin on his knees,
sleep that pours over mankind overtook him.

3. Enkidu's reply is missing.

In the middle of the night his sleep came to an end,
so he got up and said to his friend:
"My friend, did you not call out to me? Why did I wake up?
Did you not touch me? Why am I so disturbed?
Did a god pass by? Why are my muscles trembling?
Enkidu, my friend, I have had a fourth dream,
and the dream I had was deeply disturbing."[4]
. . .
Enkidu listened to his dream, and said:
"The dream that you had is favorable, it is extremely important!
My friend, we will achieve victory over him,
Humbaba, against whom we rage, and triumph over him.
In the morning there will be a favorable message from Shamash."[5]
. . .
[*Gilgamesh appeals to Shamash:*]
His tears were running in the presence of Shamash.
"What you said in Uruk, be mindful of it, stand by me!"
Gilgamesh, the offspring of Uruk-Haven,
Shamash heard what issued from his mouth,
and suddenly there resounded a warning sound from the sky.
"Hurry, stand by him so that Humbaba does not enter the forest,
and does not go down into the thickets and hide!
He has not put on his seven coats of armor,
he is wearing only one, but has taken off six."

Gilgamesh spoke to Enkidu, saying:
"Why, my friend, . . . we have crossed over all the mountains together, . . .
my friend, you who are so experienced in battle, . . .
you need not fear death. . . .
Let your voice bellow forth like the kettledrum,
let the stiffness in your arms depart,
let the paralysis in your legs go away.
Take my hand, my friend, we will go on together.
Your heart should burn to do battle—
pay no heed to death, do not lose heart!
The one who watches from the side is a careful man,
but the one who walks in front protects himself and saves his comrade,
and through their fighting they establish fame!"
As the two of them reached the evergreen forest
they cut off their talk, and stood still.

Tablet 5[6]

They stood at the forest's edge,
gazing at the top of the Cedar Tree,

4. Gilgamesh's dream is missing.
5. A fragmentary fifth dream follows.
6. This entire tablet is fragmentary. Several passages have been restored on the basis of Old Babylonian and Assyrian versions.

gazing at the entrance to the forest.
Where Humbaba would walk there was a trail,
the roads led straight on, the path was excellent.
Then they saw the Cedar Mountain, the Dwelling of the Gods, the throne dais of Irnini.[7]
Across the face of the mountain the Cedar brought forth luxurious foliage,
its shade was good, extremely pleasant.
The thornbushes were matted together, the woods were a thicket, . . .
the Forest was surrounded by a ravine two leagues long.[8]

. . .

Humbaba spoke to Gilgamesh, saying:
"An idiot and a moron should give advice to each other,
but you, Gilgamesh, why have you come to me?
Give advice, Enkidu, you 'son of a fish,' who does not even know his own father,
to the large and small turtles which do not suck their mother's milk!
When you were still young I saw you but did not go over to you; . . .
Now, you have brought Gilgamesh into my presence,
Here you stand, an enemy, a stranger. . . .
I would feed your flesh to the screeching vulture, the eagle, and the vulture!"
Gilgamesh spoke to Enkidu, saying:
"My Friend, Humbaba's face keeps changing!"[9]

. . .

Enkidu spoke to Gilgamesh, saying:
"Why, my friend, are you whining so pitiably,
hiding behind your whimpering?
Now there, my friend, . . . (it is time)
to send the Flood, to crack the Whip.
Do not snatch your feet away, do not turn your back;
strike ever harder!"

. . .

The ground split open with the heels of their feet,
as they whirled around in circles Mt. Hermon and Lebanon split.
The white clouds darkened,
death rained down on them like fog.
Shamash raised up against Humbaba mighty tempests—
Southwind, Northwind, Eastwind, Westwind, Whistling Wind,
Piercing Wind, Blizzard, Bad Wind, Wind of Simurru,
Demon Wind, Ice Wind, Storm, Sandstorm—
thirteen winds rose up against him and covered Humbaba's face.
He could not butt through the front, and could not scramble out the back,
so that Gilgamesh's weapons were in reach of Humbaba.
Humbaba begged for his life, saying to Gilgamesh:
"You are young yet, Gilgamesh, your mother gave birth to you,
and you are the offspring of Rimat-Ninsun

7. A war goddess associated with Ishtar.
8. In a fragmentary passage, Humbaba appears, frightening Enkidu anew, and Gilgamesh tries to reassure him.
9. In two missing lines, Gilgamesh in turn expresses fear.

It was at the instigation of Shamash, Lord of the Mountain,
that you were roused to this expedition.
O scion of the heart of Uruk, King Gilgamesh!
. . .
Gilgamesh, let me go,
I will dwell with you as your servant.
As many trees as you command me I will cut down for you,
I will guard for you myrtle wood, wood fine enough for your palace!"
Enkidu addressed Gilgamesh, saying:
"My friend, do not listen to Humbaba!"
. . .
[Humbaba spoke to Enkidu:]
"You understand the rules of my forest, . . .
you are aware of all the things 'So ordered by Enlil.'
I should have carried you up, and killed you at the very entrance to the branches of my forest.
I should have fed your flesh to the screeching vulture, the eagle, and the vulture.
So now, Enkidu, clemency is up to you.
Speak to Gilgamesh to spare my life!"
Enkidu addressed Gilgamesh, saying:
"My friend, take Humbaba, Guardian of the Cedar Forest,
grind up, kill, pulverize and . . . him!
Humbaba, Guardian of the Forest, grind up, kill, pulverize and . . . him!"

[*Long fragmentary passage deleted. Enkidu now speaks again to Gilgamesh:*]
"Before the Preeminent God Enlil hears,
and the gods are full of rage at us.
Enlil is in Nippur, Shamash is in Sippar.
Erect an eternal monument proclaiming how Gilgamesh killed Humbaba."
Humbaba heard all this and said, . . .
"May he not live the longer of the two,
may Enkidu not have any old age more than his friend Gilgamesh!"
Enkidu spoke to Gilgamesh, saying:
"My friend, I have been talking to you but you have not been listening to me,
You have been listening to the curse of Humbaba!"
. . .
They pulled out his insides including his tongue.[1]
. . .
They cut through the Cedar
While Gilgamesh cuts down the trees, Enkidu searches through the stumps.
Enkidu addressed Gilgamesh, saying:
"My friend, we have cut down the towering Cedar whose top scrapes the sky.
Make from it a door 72 cubits high, 24 cubits wide,

1. This is the only complete line in a passage of 40 lines in which Gilgamesh and Enkidu slay Humbaba.

one cubit thick, its fixture, its lower and upper pivots will be out of one piece.
Let them carry it to Nippur, the Euphrates will carry it down, Nippur will rejoice."
They tied together a raft, . . . Enkidu steered it,
while Gilgamesh held the head of Humbaba.

Tablet 6

Gilgamesh washed out his matted hair and cleaned up his equipment,
shaking out his locks down over his back,
throwing off his dirty clothes and putting on clean ones.
He wrapped himself in regal garments and fastened the sash.
When Gilgamesh placed his crown on his head,
Princess Ishtar raised her eyes to the beauty of Gilgamesh.
"Come along, Gilgamesh, be you my husband,
to me grant your lusciousness.
Be you my husband, and I will be your wife.
I will have harnessed for you a chariot of lapis lazuli and gold,
with wheels of gold and 'horns' of electrum.[2]
It will be harnessed with great storming mountain mules!
Come into our house, with the fragrance of cedar.
And when you come into our house the doorpost and throne dais will kiss your feet.
Bowed down beneath you will be kings, lords, and princes.
The Lullubu people will bring you the produce of the mountains and countryside as tribute.
Your she-goats will bear triplets, your ewes twins,
your donkey under burden will overtake the mule,
your steed at the chariot will be bristling to gallop,
your ox at the yoke will have no match."
Gilgamesh addressed Princess Ishtar saying:
"What would I have to give you if I married you?
Do you need oil or garments for your body?
Do you lack anything for food or drink?
I would gladly feed you food fit for a god,
I would gladly give you wine fit for a king,
. . .
You are an oven who [melts] ice,
a half-door that keeps out neither breeze nor blast,
a palace that crushes down valiant warriors,
an elephant who devours its own covering,
pitch that blackens the hands of its bearer,
a waterskin that soaks its bearer through,
limestone that buckles out the stone wall,
a battering ram that . . .
a shoe that bites its owner's feet!
Where are your bridegrooms that you keep forever?

2. An alloy of gold and silver.

Where is your 'Little Shepherd' bird that went up over you?
See here now, I will recite the list of your lovers. . . .
Tammuz, the lover of your earliest youth,
for him you have ordained lamentations year upon year![3]
You loved the colorful 'Little Shepherd' bird
and then hit him, breaking his wing, so
now he stands in the forest crying 'My Wing'!
You loved the supremely mighty lion,
yet you dug for him seven and again seven pits.
You loved the stallion, famed in battle,
yet you ordained for him the whip, the goad, and the lash,
ordained for him to gallop for seven and seven hours,
ordained for him drinking from muddied waters,
you ordained for his mother Silili to wail continually.
You loved the Shepherd, the Master Herder,
who continually presented you with bread baked in embers,
and who daily slaughtered for you a kid.
Yet you struck him, and turned him into a wolf,
so his own shepherds now chase him
and his own dogs snap at his shins.
You loved Ishullanu, your father's date gardener,
who continually brought you baskets of dates,
and brightened your table daily.
You raised your eyes to him, and you went to him:
    'Oh my Ishullanu, let us taste of your strength,
    stretch out your hand to me, and touch our "date palm."'[4]
Ishullanu said to you:
    'Me? What is it you want from me?
    Has my mother not baked, and have I not eaten
    that I should now eat food under contempt and curses
    and that alfalfa grass should be my only cover against the cold?'
As you listened to these his words
you struck him, turning him into a dwarf,
and made him live in the middle of his garden of labors.
And now me! It is me you love, and you will ordain for me as for them!"

When Ishtar heard this
in a fury she went up to the heavens,
going to Anu, her father, and crying,
going to Antum, her mother, and weeping:
    "Father, Gilgamesh has insulted me over and over,
    Gilgamesh has recounted despicable deeds about me,
    despicable deeds and curses!"
Anu addressed Princess Ishtar, saying:
    "What is the matter? Was it not you who provoked King Gilgamesh?
    So Gilgamesh recounted despicable deeds about you,
    despicable deeds and curses!"

3. See *The Descent of Ishtar to the Underworld,* page 115, for Ishtar's use of her husband to redeem herself from the underworld.

4. A pun: "vulva" sounds like "date palm" in Akkadian.

Ishtar spoke to her father, Anu, saying:
"Father, give me the Bull of Heaven,
so he can kill Gilgamesh in his dwelling.
If you do not give me the Bull of Heaven,
I will knock down the Gates of the Netherworld,
I will smash the door posts, and leave the doors flat down,
and will let the dead go up to eat the living!
And the dead will outnumber the living!"
Anu addressed Princess Ishtar, saying:
"If you demand the Bull of Heaven from me,
there will be seven years of empty husks for the land of Uruk.
Have you collected grain for the people?
Have you made grasses grow for the animals?"
Ishtar addressed Anu, her father, saying:
"I have heaped grain in the granaries for the people,
I made grasses grow for the animals,
in order that they might eat in the seven years of empty husks.
I have collected grain for the people,
I have made grasses grow for the animals."
. . .
When Anu heard her words,
he placed the nose-rope of the Bull of Heaven in her hand.
Ishtar led the Bull of Heaven down to the earth.
When it reached Uruk, . . . it climbed down to the Euphrates.
At the snort of the Bull of Heaven a huge pit opened up,
and a hundred Young Men of Uruk fell in.
At his second snort a huge pit opened up,
and two hundred Young Men of Uruk fell in.
At his third snort a huge pit opened up,
and Enkidu fell in up to his waist.
Then Enkidu jumped out and seized the Bull of Heaven by its horns.
The Bull spewed his spittle in front of him,
with his thick tail he flung his dung behind him . . .
Enkidu stalked and hunted down the Bull of Heaven.
He grasped it by the thick of its tail
and held onto it with both his hands,
while Gilgamesh, like an expert butcher,
boldly and surely approached the Bull of Heaven.
Between the nape, the horns, . . . he thrust his sword.
After they had killed the Bull of Heaven,
they ripped out its heart and presented it to Shamash.
They withdrew, bowing down humbly to Shamash.
Then the brothers sat down together.
Ishtar went up onto the top of the Wall of Uruk-Haven,
cast herself into the pose of mourning, and hurled her woeful curse:
"Woe unto Gilgamesh who slandered me and killed the Bull of Heaven!"
When Enkidu heard this pronouncement of Ishtar,
he wrenched off the Bull's hindquarter and flung it in her face:
"If I could only get at you I would do the same to you!

I would drape his innards over your arms!"
Ishtar assembled the cultic women of lovely-locks, joy-girls, and harlots,
and set them to mourning over the hindquarter of the Bull.
Gilgamesh summoned all the artisans and craftsmen.
All the artisans admired the thickness of its horns,
each fashioned from 30 minas° of lapis lazuli! *pounds*
Two fingers thick is their casing.
Six vats of oil the contents of the two
he gave as ointment to his personal god Lugalbanda.
He brought the horns in and hung them in the bedroom of the family head.
They washed their hands in the Euphrates,
and proceeded hand in hand,
striding through the streets of Uruk.
The men of Uruk gathered together, staring at them.
Gilgamesh said to the palace retainers:
"Who is the bravest of the men?
Who is the boldest of the males?
—Gilgamesh is the bravest of the men,
the boldest of the males!
She at whom we flung the hindquarter of the Bull of Heaven in anger,
Ishtar has no one that pleases her in the street!"

. . .

Gilgamesh held a celebration in his palace.
The Young Men dozed off, sleeping on the couches of the night.
Enkidu was sleeping, and had a dream.
He woke up and revealed his dream to his friend.

Tablet 7

"My friend, why are the Great Gods in conference?
In my dream Anu, Enlil, and Shamash held a council,[5]
and Anu spoke to Enlil:
'Because they killed the Bull of Heaven and have also slain Humbaba,
the one of them who pulled up the Cedar of the Mountain must die!'
Enlil said: 'Let Enkidu die, but Gilgamesh must not die!'
But the Sun God of Heaven replied to valiant Enlil:
'Was it not at my command that they killed the Bull of Heaven and Humbaba?
Should now innocent Enkidu die?'
Then Enlil became angry at Shamash, saying:
'It is you who are responsible because you traveled daily with them as their friend!'"
Enkidu was lying sick in front of Gilgamesh.
His tears flowing like canals, Gilgamesh said:
"O brother, dear brother, why are they absolving me instead of my brother?"

5. This account of Enkidu's dream is taken from a Hittite fragment.

Then Enkidu said: "So now must I become a ghost,
to sit with the ghosts of the dead, to see my dear brother nevermore?"

. . .

Enkidu raised his eyes, and spoke to the door as if it were human:
"You stupid wooden door,
with no ability to understand!
Already at twenty leagues I selected the wood for you, . . .
your wood was without compare in my eyes.
Seventy-two cubits° was your height, *48 feet*
Twenty-four cubits your width, one cubit your thickness; . . .
I fashioned you, and I carried you to Nippur.
Had I known, O door, that this would be your gratitude . . .
I would have taken an axe and chopped you up,
and lashed your planks into a raft!

. . .

But yet, O door, I fashioned you, and I carried you to Nippur!
May a king who comes after me reject you, . . .
may he remove my name and set his own name there!" . . .
Gilgamesh kept listening to his words, and retorted quickly,
Gilgamesh listened to the words of Enkidu, his Friend, and his tears flowed.
Gilgamesh addressed Enkidu, saying:
"Friend, the gods have given you a mind broad and deep.
Though it behooves you to be sensible, you keep uttering improper things!
Why, my Friend, does your mind utter improper things?
The dream is important but very frightening,
your lips are buzzing like flies.
Though there is much fear, the dream is very important.
To the living the gods leave sorrow,
to the living the dream leaves pain.
I will pray, and beseech the Great Gods,
I will seek . . . and appeal to your god.

. . .

What Enlil says . . . cannot go back,
What he has laid down cannot go back. . . ."

Just as dawn began to glow,
Enkidu raised his head and cried out to Shamash,
at the first gleam of the sun his tears poured forth.
"I appeal to you, O Shamash, on behalf of my precious life,
because of that notorious trapper
who did not let me attain the same as my friend.
May the trapper not get enough to feed himself.
May his profit be slashed, and his wages decrease! . . .

After he had cursed the trapper to his satisfaction,
his heart prompted him to curse the Harlot.
"Come now, Harlot, I am going to decree your fate,
a fate that will never come to an end for eternity!
I will curse you with a Great Curse,
may my curses overwhelm you suddenly, in an instant!

May you not be able to make a household,
and not be able to love a child of your own! . . .
May dregs of beer stain your beautiful lap,
may a drunk soil your festal robe with vomit,
. . .
May you never acquire anything of bright alabaster, . . .
may shining silver, man's delight, not be cast into your house,
may a gateway be where you take your pleasure,
may a crossroad be your home,
may a wasteland be your sleeping place,
may the shadow of the city wall be your place to stand,
may the thorns and briars skin your feet,
may both the drunk and the dry slap you on the cheek,
. . .
may the builder not seal the roof of your house,
may owls nest in the cracks of your walls!"
. . .
When Shamash heard what his mouth had uttered,
he suddenly called out to him from the sky:
"Enkidu, why are you cursing the harlot, Shamhat,
she who fed you bread fit for a god,
she who gave you wine fit for a king,
she who dressed you in grand garments,
and she who allowed you to make beautiful Gilgamesh your comrade?
Now Gilgamesh is your beloved brother-friend!
He will have you lie on a grand couch,
will have you lie on a couch of honor.
He will seat you in the seat of ease, the seat at his left,
so that the princes of the world kiss your feet.
He will have the people of Uruk go into mourning and moaning over you,
will fill the happy people with woe over you.
And after you he will let his body bear a filthy mat of hair,
will don the skin of a lion and roam the wilderness."
As soon as Enkidu heard the words of valiant Shamash,
his agitated heart grew calm, his anger abated.
Enkidu spoke to the harlot, saying:
"Come, Shamhat, I will decree your fate for you.
Let my mouth which has cursed you, now turn to bless you!
May governors and nobles love you,
May he who is one league away bite his lip in anticipation,
may he who is two leagues away shake out his locks in preparation!
May the soldier not refuse you, but undo his buckle for you,
may he give you rock crystal, lapis lazuli, and gold,
may his gift to you be earrings of filigree.
May his supplies be heaped up. . . .
May the wife, the mother of seven, be abandoned because of you!"

Enkidu's innards were churning,
lying there so alone.

He spoke everything he felt, saying to his friend:
"Listen, my friend, to the dream that I had last night.
The heavens cried out and the earth replied,
and I was standing between them.
There appeared a man of dark visage—
his face resembled the Anzu:° *a lion-headed eagle*
his hands were the paws of a lion,
his nails the talons of an eagle!—
he seized me by my hair and overpowered me.
I struck him a blow, but he skipped about like a jump rope,
and then he struck me and capsized me like a raft,
and trampled on me like a wild bull.
He encircled my whole body in a clamp.
'Help me, my friend!' I cried,
but you did not rescue me, you were afraid and did not.

. . .

Then he turned me into a dove,
so that my arms were feathered like a bird.
Seizing me, he led me down to the House of Darkness, the dwelling of Irkalla,[6]
to the House where those who enter do not come out,
along the road of no return,
to the House where those who dwell do without light,
where dirt is their drink, their food is of clay,
where, like a bird, they wear garments of feathers,
and light cannot be seen, they dwell in the dark,
and upon the door and bolt lies dust.
On entering the House of Dust,
everywhere I looked there were royal crowns gathered in heaps,
everywhere I listened, it was the bearers of crowns who in the past had ruled the land,
but who now served Anu and Enlil cooked meats,
served confections, and poured cool water from waterskins.
In the House of Dust that I entered
there sat the high priest and acolyte,
there sat the purification priest and ecstatic,
there sat the anointed priests of the Great Gods.
There sat Etana,[7] there sat Sumukan,
there sat Ereshkigal, the Queen of the Netherworld.
Beletseri, the Scribe of the Netherworld, knelt before her,
she was holding the tablet of destinies, and was reading it out to her.
She raised her head and when she saw me—
'Who has taken this man?'[8]

. . .

I who went through every difficulty,
remember me and forget not all that I went through with you."

6. This passage about the House of Dust has apparently been taken from *The Descent of Ishtar;* see page 115.
7. A famous ancient hero, subject of his own epic poem.
8. Fifty lines are missing. The text resumes with the conclusion of Enkidu's speech.

[Gilgamesh replied:]
"My friend has had a dream that bodes ill."

Enkidu lies down a first day, a second day, . . .
a third day and fourth day, that Enkidu remains in his bed;
a fifth, a sixth, and seventh, that Enkidu remains in his bed;
an eighth, a ninth, a tenth, that Enkidu remains in his bed.
Enkidu's illness grew ever worse.
The eleventh and twelfth day his illness grew ever worse.
Enkidu drew up from his bed,
and called out to Gilgamesh.

[*Thirty fragmentary lines recount Enkidu's last words and his death.*]

Tablet 8

Just as day began to dawn
Gilgamesh addressed his friend, saying:
"Enkidu, your mother, the gazelle,
and your father, the wild donkey, engendered you,
four wild asses raised you on their milk,
and the herds taught you all the grazing lands.
May the Roads of Enkidu to the Cedar Forest mourn you
and not fall silent night or day.
May the Elders of the broad city of Uruk-Haven mourn you.
May the peoples who gave their blessing after us mourn you.
May the men of the mountains and hills mourn you. . . .
May the pasture lands shriek in mourning as if it were your mother.
May the cypress and the cedar which we destroyed in our anger mourn you.
May the bear, hyena, panther, tiger, water buffalo, jackal, lion, wild bull, stag, ibex, all the creatures of the plains mourn you.
May the holy River Ulaja, along whose banks we grandly used to stroll, mourn you.
May the pure Euphrates, to which we would offer water from our water skins, mourn you.
May the men of Uruk-Haven, whom we saw in our battle when we killed the Bull of Heaven, mourn you.
May the farmer, who extols your name in his sweet work song, mourn you.
May the people of the broad city, who exalted your name, mourn you.
May the herder, who prepared butter and light beer for your mouth, mourn you.
May . . . , who put ointments on your back, mourn you.
May . . . , who prepared fine beer for your mouth, mourn you.
May the harlot, with whom you rubbed yourself with oil and felt good, mourn you. . . .
May the brothers go into mourning over you like sisters;
as for the lamentation priests, may their hair be shorn off on your behalf.
Enkidu, your mother and your father are in the wastelands,
I mourn you.
Hear me, O Elders of Uruk, hear me, O men!

I mourn for Enkidu, my friend,
I shriek in anguish like a mourner.
You, axe at my side, so trusty at my hand—
you, sword at my waist, shield in front of me,
you, my festal garment, a sash over my loins—
an evil demon appeared and took him away from me!
My friend, the swift mule, fleet wild ass of the mountain, panther of the wilderness,
Enkidu, my friend, the swift mule, fleet wild ass of the mountain, panther of the wilderness,
after we joined together and went up into the mountain,
fought the Bull of Heaven and killed it,
and overwhelmed Humbaba, who lived in the Cedar Forest,
now what is this sleep which has seized you?
You have turned dark and do not hear me!"
But Enkidu's eyes do not move,
he touched his heart, but it beat no longer.
He covered his friend's face like a bride,
swooping down over him like an eagle,
and like a lioness deprived of her cubs
he keeps pacing to and fro.
He shears off his curls and heaps them onto the ground,
ripping off his finery and casting it away as an abomination.

Just as day began to dawn, Gilgamesh arose
and issued a call to the land:
"You, blacksmith! You, lapidary!° You, coppersmith! *gem carver*
You, goldsmith! You, jeweler!
Create 'My Friend,' fashion a statue of him."
. . . he fashioned a statue of his friend [and said]:
"I had you recline on the great couch,
indeed, on the couch of honor I let you recline,
I had you sit in the position of ease, the seat at the left, so the princes of the world kissed your feet.
I had the people of Uruk mourn and moan for you,
I filled happy people with woe over you,
and after you died I let a filthy mat of hair grow over my body,
and donned the skin of a lion and roamed the wilderness."

[*Some 160 lines are missing or fragmentary.*]

Tablet 9

Over his friend, Enkidu, Gilgamesh cried bitterly, roaming the wilderness.
"I am going to die!—am I not like Enkidu?!
Deep sadness penetrates my core,
I fear death, and now roam the wilderness—
I will set out to the region of Utanapishtim, son of Ubartutu, and will go with utmost dispatch!
When I arrived at mountain passes at nightfall,

I saw lions, and I was terrified!
I raised my head in prayer to Sin,
to the Great Lady of the gods my supplications poured forth,
'Save me from them!'"
He was sleeping in the night, but awoke with a start with a dream:
A warrior enjoyed his life—
he raised his axe in his hand,
drew the dagger from his sheath,
and fell into their midst like an arrow.
He struck and he scattered them.

. . .

When he reached Mount Mashu,
which daily guards the rising and setting of the Sun,
above which only the dome of the heavens reaches,
and whose flank reaches as far as the Netherworld below,
there were Scorpion-beings watching over its gate.
Trembling terror they inspire, the sight of them is death,
their frightening aura sweeps over the mountains.
At the rising and setting they watch over the Sun.
When Gilgamesh saw them, trembling terror blanketed his face,
but he pulled himself together and drew near to them.
The scorpion-being called out to his female:
"He who comes to us, his body is the flesh of gods!"
The scorpion-being, his female, answered him:
"Only two-thirds of him is a god, one-third is human."
The male scorpion-being called out, saying to the offspring of the gods:
"Why have you traveled so distant a journey?
Why have you come here to me,
over rivers whose crossing is treacherous?"

[*Twenty-nine lines are only partially legible.*]

[Gilgamesh answered and said:]
"I have come on account of my ancestor Utanapishtim,
who joined the Assembly of the Gods, and was given eternal life.
About Death and Life I must ask him!"
The scorpion-being spoke to Gilgamesh, saying:
"Never has there been, Gilgamesh, a mortal man who could do that.
No one has crossed through the mountains,
for twelve leagues it is darkness throughout—
dense is the darkness, and light there is none."[9]

. . .

Gilgamesh answered and said:
"Though it be in deep sadness and pain,
in cold or heat gasping after breath, I will go on!
Now! Open the Gate!"
The scorpion-being spoke to Gilgamesh, saying:
"Go on, Gilgamesh, fear not!

9. In 70 missing lines, Gilgamesh persuades the scorpion-men to let him through.

The Mashu mountains I give to you freely,
the mountains, the ranges, you may traverse.
In safety may your feet carry you. . . ."
As soon as Gilgamesh heard this
he heeded the utterances of the scorpion-being.
Along the Road of the Sun he journeyed—
one league he traveled . . . , dense was the darkness, light there was none.
Neither what lies ahead nor behind does it allow him to see.
Two leagues he traveled, dense was the darkness, light there was none,
neither what lies ahead nor behind does it allow him to see.
Three leagues he traveled, dense was the darkness, light there was none,
neither what lies ahead nor behind does it allow him to see.
Four leagues he traveled . . . , dense was the darkness, light there was none,
neither what lies ahead nor behind does it allow him to see.
Five leagues he traveled . . . , dense was the darkness, light there was none,
neither what lies ahead nor behind does it allow him to see.
Six leagues he traveled . . . , dense was the darkness, light there was none,
neither what lies ahead nor behind does it allow him to see.
Seven leagues he traveled . . . , dense was the darkness, light there was none,
neither what lies ahead nor behind does it allow him to see.
Eight leagues he traveled and cried out,
dense was the darkness, light there was none,
neither what lies ahead nor behind does it allow him to see.
Nine leagues he traveled, the North Wind licked at his face,
dense was the darkness, light there was none,
neither what lies ahead nor behind does it allow him to see.
Ten leagues he traveled; the end of the road is near. . . .
Eleven leagues he traveled and came out before the sunrise.
Twelve leagues he traveled and it grew brilliant.

Before him there were trees of precious stones,
and he went straight to look at them.
The tree bears carnelian° as its fruit, *a red gemstone*
laden with clusters of jewels, dazzling to behold—
it bears lapis lazuli as foliage,
bearing fruit, a delight to look upon.

[*A long description of the jewelled garden here is too illegible to be transcribed.*]

Tablet 10

The tavern-keeper Siduri who lives by the seashore, . . .
the pot-stand was made for her, the golden fermenting vat was made for her.
She is covered with a veil.
Gilgamesh was roving about, wearing a skin,
having the flesh of the gods in his body,
but sadness deep within him,
looking like one who has been traveling a long distance.
The tavern-keeper was gazing off into the distance,

puzzling to herself, she said,
wondering to herself:
    "That fellow is surely a murderer!
    Where is he heading?"
As soon as the tavern-keeper saw him, she bolted her door,
bolted her gate, bolted the lock.
But at her noise Gilgamesh pricked up his ears,
lifted his chin to look about and then laid his eyes on her.
Gilgamesh spoke to the tavern-keeper, saying:
    "Tavern-keeper, what have you seen that made you bolt your door,
    bolt your gate, bolt the lock?
    If you do not let me in I will break your door, and smash the lock!
. . .
Gilgamesh said to the tavern-keeper:
    "I am Gilgamesh, I killed the Guardian!
    I destroyed Humbaba who lived in the Cedar Forest,
    I slew lions in the mountain passes!
    I grappled with the Bull that came down from heaven, and killed him."
The tavern-keeper spoke to Gilgamesh, saying:
    "If you are Gilgamesh, who killed the Guardian,
    who destroyed Humbaba who lived in the Cedar Forest,
    who slew lions in the mountain passes,
    who grappled with the Bull that came down from heaven, and
        killed him,
    why are your cheeks emaciated, your expression desolate?
    Why is your heart so wretched, your features so haggard?
    Why is there such sadness deep within you?
    Why do you look like one who has been traveling a long distance
    so that ice and heat have seared your face?
    Why do you roam the wilderness?"
Gilgamesh spoke to her, to the tavern-keeper he said:
    "Tavern-keeper, should not my cheeks be emaciated?
    Should my heart not be wretched, my features not haggard?
    Should there not be sadness deep within me?
    Should I not look like one who has been traveling a long distance,
    and should ice and heat not have seared my face?
    Should I not roam the wilderness?
    My friend, the wild ass who chased the wild donkey, panther of the
        wilderness,
    Enkidu, the wild ass who chased the wild donkey, panther of the
        wilderness,
    we joined together, and went up into the mountain.
    We grappled with and killed the Bull of Heaven,
    we destroyed Humbaba who lived in the Cedar Forest,
    we slew lions in the mountain passes!
    My friend, whom I love deeply, who went through every hardship with me,
    Enkidu, whom I love deeply, who went through every hardship with me,
    the fate of mankind has overtaken him.
    Six days and seven nights I mourned over him

and would not allow him to be buried
until a maggot fell out of his nose.
I was terrified by his appearance,
I began to fear death, and so roam the wilderness.
The issue of my friend oppresses me,
so I have been roaming long trails through the wilderness.
The issue of Enkidu, my friend, oppresses me,
so I have been roaming long roads through the wilderness.
How can I stay silent, how can I be still?
My friend whom I love has turned to clay.
Am I not like him? Will I lie down, never to get up again?"[1]
Gilgamesh spoke to the tavern-keeper, saying:
"So now, tavern-keeper, what is the way to Utanapishtim?
What are its markers? Give them to me! Give me the markers!
If possible, I will cross the sea;
if not, I will roam through the wilderness."
The tavern-keeper spoke to Gilgamesh, saying:
"There has never been, Gilgamesh, any passage whatever,
there has never been anyone since days of yore who crossed the sea.
The one who crosses the sea is valiant Shamash, except for him who can cross?
The crossing is difficult, its ways are treacherous—
and in between are the Waters of Death that bar its approaches!
And even if, Gilgamesh, you should cross the sea,
when you reach the Waters of Death what would you do?
Gilgamesh, over there is Urshanabi, the ferryman of Utanapishtim.
'The stone things'° are with him, *punting poles (?)*
he is in the woods picking mint.
Go on, let him see your face.
If possible, cross with him;
if not, you should turn back."

When Gilgamesh heard this
he raised the axe in his hand,
drew the dagger from his belt,
and slipped stealthily away after them.
Like an arrow he fell among the stone things.
From the middle of the woods their noise could be heard.
Urshanabi, the sharp-eyed, saw . . .
When he heard the axe, he ran toward it.

. . .

Gilgamesh spoke to Urshanabi, saying:
"Now, Urshanabi! What is the way to Utanapishtim?
What are its markers? Give them to me! Give me the markers!
If possible, I will cross the sea;
if not, I will roam through the wilderness!"

1. The text omits a reply by the tavern-keeper. In the Old Babylonian version, she had urged Gilgamesh not to worry about death but to be content with the pleasures of life.

Urshanabi spoke to Gilgamesh, saying:
"It is your hands, Gilgamesh, that prevent the crossing!
You have smashed 'the stone things,' you have pulled out their retaining ropes.
'The stone things' have been smashed, their retaining ropes pulled out!
Gilgamesh, take the axe in your hand, go down into the woods,
and cut down 300 punting poles each 60 cubits in length.
Strip them, attach caps, and bring them to the boat!"
When Gilgamesh heard this
he took up the axe in his hand, drew the dagger from his belt,
and went down into the woods,
and cut 300 punting poles each 60 cubits in length.
He stripped them and attached caps, and brought them to the boat.
Gilgamesh and Urshanabi boarded the boat,
Gilgamesh launched the boat and they sailed away.
By the third day they had traveled a stretch of a month and a half,
and Urshanabi arrived at the Waters of Death.
Urshanabi said to Gilgamesh:
"Hold back, Gilgamesh, take a punting pole,
but your hand must not pass over the Waters of Death!
Take a second, Gilgamesh, a third, and a fourth pole,
take a fifth, Gilgamesh, a sixth, and a seventh pole,
take an eighth, Gilgamesh, a ninth, and a tenth pole,
take an eleventh, Gilgamesh, and a twelfth pole!"
In twice 60 rods Gilgamesh had used up the punting poles.
Then he loosened his waist-cloth for a sail;
Gilgamesh stripped off his garment
and held it up on the mast with his arms.

Utanapishtim was gazing off into the distance,
puzzling to himself he said, wondering to himself:
"Why are 'the stone things' of the boat smashed to pieces?
And why is someone not its master sailing on it?
The one who is coming is not a man of mine."

. . .

[*Gilgamesh arrives and meets Utanapishtim.*]

Utanapishtim said to Gilgamesh:
"Why are your cheeks emaciated, your expression desolate?
Why is your heart so wretched, your features so haggard?
Why is there such sadness deep within you?
Why do you look like one who has been traveling a long distance
so that ice and heat have seared your face?
Why do you roam the wilderness?"
Gilgamesh spoke to Utanapishtim saying:
"Should not my cheeks be emaciated, my expression desolate?
Should my heart not be wretched, my features not haggard?
Should there not be sadness deep within me?
Should I not look like one who has been traveling a long distance,
and should ice and heat not have seared my face?

Should I not roam the wilderness?
My friend who chased wild asses in the mountain, the panther of the wilderness,
Enkidu, my friend, who chased wild asses in the mountain, the panther of the wilderness,
we joined together, and went up into the mountain.
We grappled with and killed the Bull of Heaven,
we destroyed Humbaba who dwelled in the Cedar Forest,
we slew lions in the mountain passes!
My friend, whom I love deeply, who went through every hardship with me,
Enkidu, my friend, whom I love deeply, who went through every hard ship with me,
the fate of mankind has overtaken him.
Six days and seven nights I mourned over him
and would not allow him to be buried
until a maggot fell out of his nose.
I was terrified by his appearance,
I began to fear death, and so roam the wilderness.
The issue of my friend oppresses me,
so I have been roaming long trails through the wilderness.
The issue of Enkidu, my friend, oppresses me,
so I have been roaming long roads through the wilderness.
How can I stay silent, how can I be still?
My friend whom I love has turned to clay;
Enkidu, my friend whom I love, has turned to clay!
Am I not like him? Will I lie down never to get up again?"
Gilgamesh spoke to Utanapishtim, saying:
"That is why I must go on, to see Utanapishtim whom they call 'The Faraway.'
I went circling through all the mountains,
I traversed treacherous mountains, and crossed all the seas—
that is why sweet sleep has not mellowed my face,
through sleepless striving I am strained,
my muscles are filled with pain.
I had not yet reached the tavern-keeper's area before my clothing gave out.
I killed bear, hyena, lion, panther, tiger, stag, red-stag, and beasts of the wilderness;
I ate their meat and wrapped their skins around me.
The gate of grief must be bolted shut, sealed with pitch and bitumen!"
Utanapishtim spoke to Gilgamesh, saying:
"Why, Gilgamesh, do you feel such sadness?
You who were created from the flesh of gods and mankind!

[*Long but only partially legible passage follows.*]

You have toiled without cease, and what have you got?
Through toil you wear yourself out,
you fill your body with grief,

your long lifetime you are bringing near to a premature end!
Mankind, whose offshoot is snapped off like a reed in a canebreak,
. . .
No one can see death,
no one can see the face of death,
no one can hear the voice of death,
yet there is savage death that snaps off mankind.
For how long do we build a household?
For how long do we seal a document?
For how long do brothers share the inheritance?
For how long is there to be jealousy in the land?
For how long has the river risen and brought the overflowing waters,
so that dragonflies drift down the river?
The face that could gaze upon the face of the Sun
has never existed ever.
How alike are the sleeping and the dead.
The image of Death cannot be depicted. . . .
After Enlil had pronounced the blessing,
the Anunnaki, the Great Gods, assembled.
Mammetum, she who fashions destiny, determined destiny with them.
They established Death and Life,
but they did not make known 'the days of death.'"

Tablet 11

Gilgamesh spoke to Utanapishtim, the Faraway:
"I have been looking at you,
but your appearance is not strange—you are like me!
You yourself are not different—you are like me!
My mind was resolved to fight with you,
but instead my arm lies useless over you.
Tell me, how is it that you stand in the Assembly of the Gods,
and have found life?"
Utanapishtim spoke to Gilgamesh, saying:
"I will reveal to you, Gilgamesh, a thing that is hidden,
a secret of the gods I will tell you!
Shuruppak, a city that you surely know,
situated on the banks of the Euphrates,
that city was very old, and there were gods inside it.
The hearts of the Great Gods moved them to inflict the Flood.
Their Father Anu uttered the oath of secrecy,
Valiant Enlil was their Adviser,
Ninurta was their Chamberlain,
Ennugi was their Minister of Canals.
Ea, the Clever Prince, was under oath with them
so he repeated their talk to the reed house:
'Reed house, reed house! Wall, wall!
Hear, O reed house! Understand, O wall!
O man of Shuruppak, son of Ubartutu:
Tear down the house and build a boat!

Abandon wealth and seek living beings!
Spurn possessions and keep alive living beings!
Make all living beings go up into the boat.
The boat which you are to build,
its dimensions must measure equal to each other:
its length must correspond to its width.
Roof it over like the Apsu.'° *underworld sea*
I understood and spoke to my lord, Ea:
'My lord, thus is the command which you have uttered
I will heed and will do it.
But what shall I answer the city, the populace, and the Elders?'
Ea spoke, commanding me, his servant:
'You, well then, this is what you must say to them:
"It appears that Enlil is rejecting me
so I cannot reside in your city,
nor set foot on Enlil's earth.
I will go down to the Apsu to live with my lord, Ea,
and upon you he will rain down abundance,
a profusion of fowl, myriad fishes.
He will bring to you a harvest of wealth,
in the morning he will let loaves of bread shower down,
and in the evening a rain of wheat!"'
Just as dawn began to glow
the land assembled around me—
the carpenter carried his hatchet,
the reed worker carried his flattening stone,
The child carried the pitch,
the weak brought whatever else was needed.
On the fifth day I laid out her exterior.
It was a field in area,
its walls were each 10 times 12 cubits in height,
the sides of its top were of equal length, 10 times 12 cubits each.[2]
I laid out its interior structure and drew a picture of it.
I provided it with six decks,
thus dividing it into seven levels.
The inside of it I divided into nine compartments.
I drove plugs to keep out water in its middle part.
I saw to the punting poles and laid in what was necessary.
Three times 3,600 units of raw bitumen I poured into the bitumen kiln,
three times 3,600 units of pitch I put into it,
there were three times 3,600 porters of casks who carried vegetable oil,
apart from the 3,600 units of oil which they consumed
and two times 3,600 units of oil which the boatman stored away.
I butchered oxen for the meat,
and day upon day I slaughtered sheep.
I gave the workmen ale, beer, oil, and wine, as if it were river water,
so they could make a party like the New Year's Festival.
. . .

2. The boat is described as a cube 80 feet on a side, making it a cross between a boat and a ziggurat, a pyramidal temple tower often with seven levels.

The boat was finished by sunset.
The launching was very difficult.
They had to keep carrying a runway of poles front to back,
until two-thirds of it had gone into the water.
Whatever I had I loaded on it:
whatever silver I had I loaded on it,
whatever gold I had I loaded on it.
All the living beings that I had I loaded on it,
I had all my kith and kin go up into the boat,
all the beasts and animals of the field and the craftsmen I had go up.
Shamash had set a stated time:
　'In the morning I will let loaves of bread shower down,
　and in the evening a rain of wheat!
　Go inside the boat, seal the entry!'
That stated time had arrived.
In the morning he let loaves of bread shower down,
and in the evening a rain of wheat.
I watched the appearance of the weather—
the weather was frightful to behold!
I went into the boat and sealed the entry.
For the caulking of the boat, to Puzuramurri, the boatman,
I gave the palace together with its contents.
Just as dawn began to glow
there arose from the horizon a black cloud.
Adad° rumbled inside of it, *storm god*
before him went Shullat and Hanish,
heralds going over mountain and land.
Erragal° pulled out the mooring poles, *god of death*
forth went Ninurta° and made the dikes overflow. *god of war*
The Anunnaki° lifted up the torches, *underworld gods*
setting the land ablaze with their flare.
Stunned shock over Adad's deeds overtook the heavens,
and turned to blackness all that had been light.
The land shattered like a pot.
All day long the South Wind blew,
blowing fast, submerging the mountain in water,
overwhelming the people like an attack.
No one could see his fellow,
they could not recognize each other in the torrent.
The gods were frightened by the Flood,
and retreated, ascending to the heaven of Anu.
The gods were cowering like dogs, crouching by the outer wall.
Ishtar shrieked like a woman in childbirth,
the sweet-voiced Mistress of the Gods wailed:
　'The olden days have alas turned to clay,
　because I said evil things in the Assembly of the Gods!
　How could I say evil things in the Assembly of the Gods,
　ordering a catastrophe to destroy my people?

No sooner have I given birth to my dear people
than they fill the sea like so many fish!'
The gods—those of the Anunnaki—were weeping with her,
the gods humbly sat weeping, sobbing with grief,
their lips burning, parched with thirst.
Six days and seven nights
came the wind and flood, the storm flattening the land.
When the seventh day arrived, the storm was pounding,
the flood was a war—struggling with itself like a woman writhing in labor.
The sea calmed, fell still, the whirlwind and flood stopped up.
I looked around all day long—quiet had set in
and all the human beings had turned to clay!
The terrain was as flat as a roof.
I opened a vent and fresh air fell upon the side of my nose.
I fell to my knees and sat weeping,
tears streaming down the side of my nose.
I looked around for coastlines in the expanse of the sea,
and at twelve leagues there emerged a region of land.
On Mt. Nimush[3] the boat lodged firm,
Mt. Nimush held the boat, allowing no sway.
One day and a second Mt. Nimush held the boat, allowing no sway.
A third day, a fourth, Mt. Nimush held the boat, allowing no sway.
A fifth day, a sixth, Mt. Nimush held the boat, allowing no sway.
When a seventh day arrived
I sent forth a dove and released it.
The dove went off, but came back to me;
no perch was visible so it circled back to me.
I sent forth a swallow and released it.
The swallow went off, but came back to me;
no perch was visible so it circled back to me.
I sent forth a raven and released it.
The raven went off, and saw the waters slither back.
It eats, it scratches, it bobs, but does not circle back to me.
Then I sent out everything in all directions and sacrificed a sheep.
I offered incense in front of the mountain-ziggurat.° *stepped pyramid*
Seven and seven cult vessels I put in place,
and into their bowls I poured reeds, cedar, and myrtle.
The gods smelled the savor,
the gods smelled the sweet savor,
and collected like flies over a sacrifice.
Just then Beletili arrived.
She lifted up the large beads which Anu had made for his enjoyment:
'You gods, as surely as I shall not forget this lapis lazuli around my neck,
may I be mindful of these days, and never forget them!
The gods may come to the incense offering,

3. Likely a 9,000-foot mountain on the Persian border of northeastern Iraq.

but Enlil may not come to the incense offering,
because without considering he brought about the Flood
and consigned my people to annihilation.'
Just then Enlil arrived.
He saw the boat and became furious,
he was filled with rage at the Igigi:° *sky gods*
'Where did a living being escape?
No man was to survive the annihilation!'
Ninurta spoke to Valiant Enlil, saying:
'Who else but Ea could devise such a thing?
It is Ea who knows every machination!'
Ea spoke to Valiant Enlil, saying:
'It is you, O Valiant One, who is the Sage of the Gods.
How, how could you bring about a Flood without consideration?
Charge the violation to the violator,
charge the offense to the offender,
but be compassionate lest mankind be cut off,
be patient lest they be killed.
Instead of your bringing on the Flood,
would that a lion had appeared to diminish the people!
Instead of your bringing on the Flood,
would that a wolf had appeared to diminish the people!
Instead of your bringing on the Flood,
would that famine had occurred to slay the land!
Instead of your bringing on the Flood,
would that Pestilent Erra had appeared to ravage the land!
It was not I who revealed the secret of the Great Gods,
I only made a dream appear to Atrahasis[4]
and thus he heard the secret of the gods.
Now then! The deliberation should be about him!'
Enlil went up inside the boat
and, grasping my hand, made me go up.
He had my wife go up and kneel by my side.
He touched our forehead and, standing between us, he blessed us:
'Previously Utanapishtim was a human being.
But now let Utanapishtim and his wife become like us, the gods!
Let Utanapishtim reside far away, at the Mouth of the Rivers.'
They took us far away and settled us at the Mouth of the Rivers.
Now then, Gilgamesh, who will convene the gods on your behalf,
that you may find the life that you are seeking?
Wait! You must not lie down for six days and seven nights."

As soon as he sat down with his head between his legs
sleep, like a fog, blew upon him.
Utanapishtim said to his wife:
"Look there! The man, the youth who wanted eternal life!
Sleep, like a fog, blew over him."

4. "Exceedingly Wise," the hero of an earlier poem on the flood story, a source for this tablet; here written by mistake for "Utanapishtim" or else deliberately used as an alternate name.

His wife said to Utanapishtim the Faraway:
"Touch him, let the man awaken.
Let him return safely by the way he came.
Let him return to his land by the gate through which he left."
Utanapishtim said to his wife:
"Mankind is deceptive, and will deceive you.
Come, bake loaves for him and keep setting them by his head
and draw on the wall each day that he lay down."
She baked his loaves and placed them by his head
and marked on the wall the day that he lay down.
The first loaf was dessicated,
the second stale, the third moist, the fourth turned white, . . .
the fifth sprouted gray mold, the sixth is still fresh.
The seventh—suddenly he touched him and the man awoke.
Gilgamesh said to Utanapishtim:
"The very moment sleep was pouring over me
you touched me and alerted me!"
Utanapishtim spoke to Gilgamesh, saying:
"Look over here, Gilgamesh, count your loaves!
You should be aware of what is marked on the wall!
Your first loaf is dessicated,
the second stale, the third moist, your fourth turned white, . . .
the fifth sprouted gray mold, the sixth is still fresh.
The seventh—at that instant you awoke!"
Gilgamesh said to Utanapishtim the Faraway:
"O woe! What shall I do, Utanapishtim, where shall I go?
The Snatcher has taken hold of my flesh,
in my bedroom Death dwells,
and wherever I set foot there too is Death!"

Utanapishtim said to Urshanabi, the ferryman:
"May the harbor reject you, may the ferry landing reject you!
May you who used to walk its shores be denied its shores!
The man in front of whom you walk, matted hair chains his body,
animal skins have ruined his beautiful skin.
Take him away, Urshanabi, bring him to the washing place.
Let him wash his matted hair in water.
Let him cast away his animal skin and have the sea carry it off,
let his body be moistened with fine oil,
let the wrap around his head be made new,
let him wear royal robes worthy of him!
Until he goes off to his city,
until he sets off on his way,
let his royal robe not become spotted, let it be perfectly new!"
Urshanabi took him away and brought him to the washing place.
He washed his matted hair with water. . . .
He cast off his animal skin and the sea carried it off.
He moistened his body with fine oil,
and made a new wrap for his head.

He put on a royal robe worthy of him.
Until he went away to his city,
until he set off on his way,
his royal robe remained unspotted, it was perfectly clean.
Gilgamesh and Urshanabi boarded the boat,
they cast off the boat, and sailed away.

The wife of Utanapishtim the Faraway said to him:
"Gilgamesh came here exhausted and worn out.
What can you give him so that he can return to his land with honor?"
Then Gilgamesh raised a punting pole
and drew the boat to shore.
Utanapishtim spoke to Gilgamesh, saying:
"Gilgamesh, you came here exhausted and worn out.
What can I give you so you can return to your land?
I will disclose to you a thing that is hidden, Gilgamesh,
a secret I will tell you.
There is a plant like a boxthorn,
whose thorns will prick your hand like a rose.
If your hands reach that plant you will become a young man again."
Hearing this, Gilgamesh opened a conduit to the Apsu° *underworld sea*
and attached heavy stones to his feet.
They dragged him down, to the Apsu they pulled him.
He took the plant, though it pricked his hand,
and cut the heavy stones from his feet,
letting the waves throw him onto its shores.
Gilgamesh spoke to Urshanabi, the ferryman, saying:
"Urshanabi, this plant is a plant against decay
by which a man can attain his survival.
I will bring it to Uruk-Haven,
and have an old man eat the plant to test it.
The plant's name is 'The Old Man Becomes a Young Man.'[5]
Then I will eat it and return to the condition of my youth."
At twenty leagues they broke for some food,
at thirty leagues they stopped for the night.
Seeing a spring and how cool its waters were,
Gilgamesh went down and was bathing in the water.
A snake smelled the fragrance of the plant,
silently came up and carried off the plant.
While going back it sloughed off its casing.
At that point Gilgamesh sat down, weeping,
his tears streaming over the side of his nose.
"Counsel me, O ferryman Urshanabi!
For whom have my arms labored, Urshanabi?
For whom has my heart's blood roiled?
I have not secured any good deed for myself,
but done a good deed for the 'lion of the ground'!
Now the high waters are coursing twenty leagues distant,

5. This is probably the meaning of "Gilgamesh" in Sumerian.

as I was opening the conduit I turned my equipment over into it.
What can I find to serve as a marker for me?
I will turn back from the journey by sea and leave the boat by the shore!"

At twenty leagues they broke for some food,
at thirty leagues they stopped for the night.
They arrived in Uruk-Haven.
Gilgamesh said to Urshanabi, the ferryman:
"Go up, Urshanabi, onto the wall of Uruk and walk around.
Examine its foundation, inspect its brickwork thoroughly—
is not even the core of the brick structure of kiln-fired brick,
and did not the Seven Sages themselves lay out its plan?
One league city, one league palm gardens,
one league lowlands, the open area of the Ishtar Temple,
three leagues and the open area of Uruk the wall encloses."

PERSPECTIVES
Death and Immortality

Death was a constant presence in the ancient world. Infant mortality was high, and disease, warfare, and accidents could claim a life at any time. When Psalm 90 says that "the years of our life are threescore and ten, or even by reason of strength fourscore," the psalmist isn't giving an *average* life expectancy, as we may think of seventy or eighty years today, but the outer limit of what a fortunate person might hope to see. The same psalm describes humanity as like grass, flourishing in the morning, withered by evening. As the image of growing grass shows, the underworld had a double meaning: a place of death and burial, the earth was also the place of fertility and the growth of crops. Various ancient mythic tales probe this connection, as in *The Descent of Ishtar* given here, or later Greek tales of Ceres, goddess of grain, and her daughter Persephone, abducted by the underworld god Hades. The name "Hades" itself may come from an Akkadian term, *adeshu,* "underworld oath."

Near Eastern cultures responded in very different ways to the problem of death. Most people believed in some form of afterlife, but this could be envisioned either positively or negatively. As can be seen in Enkidu's frightened dreams in *The Epic of Gilgamesh,* the Mesopotamians often thought of the underworld as a grim place, "the House of Dust," where the deceased would live a reduced half-life: *The Descent of Ishtar* below gives the classic form of this view. Others, most notably the Egyptians, took a much more positive view, seeing the afterlife as a radiant paradise where the blessed soul could become one with the gods. Originally reserved for members of the royal family, over time the Egyptian afterlife became increasingly democratized, open to all who had lived virtuously and who could afford the elaborate incantations and rituals spelled out in the book known today as "the Book of the Dead."

The Bible shows a range of views. In some early references to the underworld realm, Sheol, it looks much like the Mesopotamian House of Dust, but normative Hebrew belief increasingly rejected any belief in a personal survival after death. God should be served and justice should be done for their own sake; the focus of future hope was on blessings for one's descendants rather than for oneself after death. In Genesis, paradise is a purely earthly garden ("paradise" comes from the Hebrew word for "garden"), a place to which Adam and Eve's descendants have no access. By New Testament times, however, a celestial paradise was increasingly in view, elaborately described in the Book of Revelation as "the new Jerusalem," made of gold, crystal, and precious jewels, an eternal city where God's chosen saints would dwell forever.

The problem of earthly evil was especially acute for those who didn't have a confident expectation of a glorious heavenly paradise. Much ancient wisdom literature sought to advise readers in the best ways to live so as to achieve divine favor on earth for oneself and one's descendants, while skeptical texts like the Book of Job probed the mysteries of undeserved suffering. The narrative poem *Erra and Ishum* sees the god of death as directly responsible for chaos and suffering in Babylon, unfolding very human motives of power politics among the gods to explain earthly events.

The Descent of Ishtar to the Underworld

late 2nd millennium B.C.E.

This remarkable Babylonian poem gives a haunting picture of the underworld, the "House of Dust" where all ranks are made equal and the dead live a shadowy eternal half-life. The underworld is partly a version of the upper world with its pleasures muted or canceled out, but in this poem it also becomes the scene of an uncanny struggle for control between Ishtar, goddess of love, and her sister Ereshkigal, the queen of the underworld. Ereshkigal defeats Ishtar but spares her life on condition that she surrender her husband, Dumuzi, as a hostage; apparently he would be allowed to come back to life once a year. Based on an earlier Sumerian poem, *The Descent of Ishtar* was performed in the Assyrian capitol of Nineveh during an annual ceremony that featured the anointing of a statue of Dumuzi, which was thought to guarantee the fertility of the crops. Such myths circulated widely around the ancient world; a similar explanation of seasonal renewal can be found in the Greek myth of Persephone. *The Epic of Gilgamesh* incorporated *The Descent of Ishtar*'s chilling description of the House of Dust, and built on its themes as well: Gilgamesh's journey to the immortal Utanapishtim is a kind of earthly rewriting of Ishtar's visit to her underworld sister.

PRONUNCIATIONS:

Dumuzi: dou-MOU-zee
Ereshkigal: air-ESH-key-gall
Sin: SEEN

The Descent of Ishtar to the Underworld[1]

To Kurnugi, Land of [No Return],
Ishtar daughter of Sin° was [determined] to go; *the moon god*
The daughter of Sin was determined to go
To the dark house, dwelling of Erkalla's god,[2]
To the house which those who enter cannot leave,
On the road where travelling is one-way only,
To the house where those who enter are deprived of light,
Where dust is their food, clay their bread.
They see no light, they dwell in darkness,
They are clothed like birds, with feathers.
Over the door and the bolt, dust has settled.
Ishtar, when she arrived at the gate of Kurnugi,
Addressed her words to the keeper of the gate,
"Here gatekeeper, open your gate for me,
Open your gate for me to come in!
If you do not open the gate for me to come in,
I shall smash the door and shatter the bolt,
I shall smash the doorpost and overturn the doors,
I shall raise up the dead and they shall eat the living:
The dead shall outnumber the living!"
The gatekeeper made his voice heard and spoke,
He said to great Ishtar,
"Stop, lady, do not break it down!
Let me go and report your words to queen Ereshkigal."
The gatekeeper went in and spoke to [Ereshkigal],
"Here she is, your sister Ishtar [. . .]
Who holds the great *keppū*-toy,° *a spinning top (?)*
Stirs up the Apsu in Ea's presence [. . .]?"

1. Translated by Stephanie Dalley. Brackets indicate gaps in the cuneiform tablet.

2. Erkalla is the city of the dead, ruled by Ereshkigal and her consort Nergal or Erra, god of death.

When Ereshkigal heard this,
Her face grew livid as cut tamarisk,
Her lips grew dark as the rim of a *kunīnu*-vessel.
"What brings her to me? What has incited her against me?
Surely not because I drink water with the Anunnaki,° *underworld gods*
I eat clay for bread, I drink muddy water for beer?
I have to weep for young men forced to abandon sweethearts.
I have to weep for girls wrenched from their lovers' laps.
For the infant child I have to weep, expelled before its time.
Go, gatekeeper, open your gate to her.
Treat her according to the ancient rites."
The gatekeeper went. He opened the gate to her.
"Enter, my lady: may Kutha° give you joy, *underworld city*
May the palace of Kurnugi be glad to see you."
He let her in through the first door, but stripped off and took away the great crown on her head.
"Gatekeeper, why have you taken away the great crown on my head?"
"Go in, my lady. Such are the rites of the Mistress of Earth."
He let her in through the second door, but stripped off and took away the rings in her ears.
"Gatekeeper, why have you taken away the rings in my ears?"
"Go in, my lady. Such are the rites of the Mistress of Earth."
He let her in through the third door, but stripped off and took away the beads around her neck.
"Gatekeeper, why have you taken away the beads around my neck?"
"Go in, my lady. Such are the rites of the Mistress of Earth."
He let her in through the fourth door, but stripped off and took away the toggle-pins at her breast.
"Gatekeeper, why have you taken away the toggle-pins at my breast?"
"Go in, my lady. Such are the rites of the Mistress of Earth."
He let her in through the fifth door, but stripped off and took away the girdle of birthstones around her waist.
"Gatekeeper, why have you taken away the girdle of birthstones around my waist?"
"Go in, my lady. Such are the rites of the Mistress of Earth."
He let her in through the sixth door, but stripped off and took away the bangles on her wrists and ankles.
"Gatekeeper, why have you taken away the bangles from my wrists and ankles?"
"Go in, my lady. Such are the rites of the Mistress of Earth."
He let her in through the seventh door, but stripped off and took away the proud garment of her body.
"Gatekeeper, why have you taken away the proud garment of my body?"
"Go in, my lady. Such are the rites of the Mistress of Earth."
As soon as Ishtar went down to Kurnugi,
Ereshkigal looked at her and trembled before her.
Ishtar did not deliberate, but leant over her.

Ereshkigal made her voice heard and spoke,
Addressed her words to Namtar her vizier,
  "Go, Namtar [ ] of my [ ]
  Send out against her sixty diseases
  [ ] Ishtar:
  Disease of the eyes to her [eyes],
  Disease of the arms to her [arms],
  Disease of the feet to her [feet],
  Disease of the heart to her [heart],
  Disease of the head [to her head],
  To every part of her and to [ ]."
After Ishtar the mistress of [. . . had gone down to Kurnugi],
No bull mounted a cow, [no donkey impregnated a jenny],
No young man impregnated a girl in [the street],
The young man slept in his private room,
The girl slept in the company of her friends.
Then Papsukkal, vizier of the great gods, hung his head,
  his face [became gloomy];
He wore mourning clothes, his hair was unkempt.
Dejected, he went and wept before Sin his father,
His tears flowed freely before king Ea.
  "Ishtar has gone down to the Earth and has not come up again.
  As soon as Ishtar went down to Kurnugi
  No bull mounted a cow, no donkey impregnated a jenny,
  No young man impregnated a girl in the street,
  The young man slept in his private room,
  The girl slept in the company of her friends."
Ea, in the wisdom of his heart, created a person.
He created Good-looks the playboy.
  "Come, Good-looks, set your face towards the gate of Kurnugi.
  The seven gates of Kurnugi shall be opened before you.
  Ereshkigal shall look at you and be glad to see you.
  When she is relaxed, her mood will lighten.
  Get her to swear the oath by the great gods.
  Raise your head, pay attention to the waterskin,
  Saying, 'Hey, my lady, let them give me the waterskin,
    that I may drink water from it.'"
    (And so it happened. But)
When Ereshkigal heard this,
She struck her thigh and bit her finger.
  "You have made a request of me that should not have been made!
  Come, Good-looks, I shall curse you with a great curse.
  I shall decree for you a fate that shall never be forgotten.
  Bread gleaned from the city's ploughs shall be your food,
  The city drains shall be your only drinking place,
  The shade of a city wall your only standing place,
  Threshold steps your only sitting place,

The drunkard and the thirsty shall slap your cheek."
Ereshkigal made her voice heard and spoke;
She addressed her words to Namtar her vizier,
"Go, Namtar, knock at Egalgina,° *underworld palace*
Decorate the threshold steps with coral,
Bring the Anunnaki out and seat them on golden thrones,
Sprinkle Ishtar with the waters of life and conduct her into my presence."
Namtar went, knocked at Egalgina,
Decorated the threshold steps with coral,
Brought out the Anunnaki, seated them on golden thrones,
Sprinkled Ishtar with the waters of life and brought her to her sister.
He let her out through the first door, and gave back to her the proud garment of her body.
He let her out through the second door, and gave back to her the bangles for her wrists and ankles.
He let her out through the third door, and gave back to her the girdle of birth stones around her waist.
He let her out through the fourth door, and gave back to her the toggle pins at her breast.
He let her out through the fifth door, and gave back to her the beads around her neck.
He let her out through the sixth door, and gave back to her the rings for her ears.
He let her out through the seventh door, and gave back to her the great crown for her head.
"Swear that she has paid you her ransom, and give her back in exchange for him,
For Dumuzi, the lover of her youth.
Wash him with pure water, anoint him with sweet oil,
Clothe him in a red robe, let the lapis lazuli pipe play.
Let party-girls raise a loud lament
Then Belili tore off her jewellery,
Her lap was filled with eyestones.
Belili heard the lament for her brother,
she struck the jewellery [from her body],
The eyestones with which the front of the wild cow was filled.
"You shall not rob me forever of my only brother!
On the day when Dumuzi comes back up,
and the lapis lazuli pipe and the carnelian ring come up with him,
When male and female mourners come up with him,
The dead shall come up and smell the smoke offering."

from The Book of the Dead

2nd millennium B.C.E.

In early Egyptian belief, only the king was expected to achieve divine rebirth in the underworld; lesser mortals would have at most a kind of shadowy half-life beyond the grave. Over

From the *Book of the Dead,* Papyrus of Ani, Thebes, c. 1250 B.C.E. Anubis weighs a dead person's heart against the feather of Truth, as Thoth records the verdict beneath the watchful eyes of the underworld judges. Behind Thoth an underworld beast waits to snatch the deceased if he fails the test.

time, though, the king's otherworldly privileges extended to a wider and wider circle of court and temple officials and their families, who began to be buried equipped with papyrus scrolls containing elaborate series of spells to protect and aid them in the afterlife. Different scrolls varied in content and in length, partly depending on how many spells an individual chose to commission. Ready-made scrolls could also be purchased, with spaces left for the name of the deceased; in the selections below, this place-holder is indicated by "N."

In modern times called *The Book of the Dead,* these scrolls were originally titled *Sesh n peret m herew:* "The Book of Coming Forth by Day"—their real concern is not with death but with eternal life. They could be nearly two hundred chapters long and were illustrated with scenes of the underworld. The illustration above shows the climactic judgment scene, in which the deceased person's heart is weighed against the feather of Truth, *maat* in Egyptian, often personified as a goddess. The underworld court, headed by Osiris, sits in judgment as the deceased makes a long series of negative claims—of sins he has not committed. If the deceased's heart then proves lighter than the feather of truth, the successful soul becomes united with Osiris himself, guided every step of the way by spells that, as the book confidently asserts, are "effective a million times."

PRONUNCIATIONS:

Ennead: EN-nee-add
Maat: MAH-aht
Ptah: p'TAH

from The Book of the Dead[1]

[THE OPENING OF THE MOUTH]

Formula for opening N's mouth for him in the necropolis.[2] He shall say:

My mouth is opened by Ptah,° *creator god*
My mouth's bonds are loosed by my city-god.
Thoth° has come fully equipped with spells, *god of writing*
He looses the bonds of Seth° from my mouth. *slayer of Osiris*
Atum° has given me my hands, *creator god*
They are placed as guardians.

My mouth is given to me,
My mouth is opened by Ptah
With that chisel of metal
With which he opened the mouth of the gods.
I am Sakhmet-Wadjet° who dwells in the west of heaven, *lion goddess*
I am Sahyt among the souls of On.

As for any spells, any spells spoken against me,
The gods shall rise up against them,
The entire Ennead,° the entire Ennead! *council of gods*

[THE HEART AS WITNESS]

Formula for not letting the heart of N oppose him in the necropolis. He shall say:

O my heart of my mother,
O my heart of my mother,
O my heart of my being!
Do not rise up against me as witness,
Do not oppose me in the tribunal,
Do not rebel against me before the guardian of the scales!
You are my *ka*° within my body, *vital force*
The Khnum° who prospers my limbs. *creator of life*
Go to the good place prepared for us,
Do not make my name stink before them,
The magistrates who put people in their places!
If it's good for us it's good for the judge,
It pleases him who renders judgment.
Do not invent lies before the god,
Before the great god, the lord of the west,
Lo, your uprightness brings vindication!

1. Translated by Miriam Lichtheim.
2. City of tombs outside Thebes. The "opening of the mouth" was a ritual performed for mummies before burial, enabling them to communicate in the underworld.

[The Declaration of Innocence]

To be said on reaching the Hall of the Two Truths so as to purge N of any sins committed and to see the face of every god:

Hail to you, great God, Lord of the Two Truths!
I have come to you, my Lord,
I was brought to see your beauty.
I know you, I know the names of the forty-two gods,
Who are with you in the Hall of the Two Truths,
Who live by warding off evildoers,
Who drink of their blood,
On that day of judging characters before Wennofer,° *Osiris*
Lo, your name is "He-of-Two-Daughters,"
And "He-of-Maat's-Two-Eyes."
Lo, I come before you,
Bringing Maat° to you, *Truth*
Having repelled evil for you.

I have not done crimes against people,
I have not mistreated cattle,
I have not sinned in the Place of Truth.
I have not known what should not be known,
I have not done any harm.
I did not begin a day by exacting more than my due,
My name did not reach the bark of the mighty ruler,
I have not blasphemed a god,
I have not robbed the poor.
I have not done what the god abhors,
I have not maligned a servant to his master.
I have not caused pain,
I have not caused tears.
I have not killed,
I have not ordered to kill,
I have not made anyone suffer.
I have not damaged the offerings in the temples,
I have not depleted the loaves of the gods,
I have not stolen the cakes of the dead.
I have not copulated nor defiled myself.
I have not increased nor reduced the measure,
I have not diminished the arura,° *acreage*
I have not cheated in the fields.
I have not added to the weight of the balance,
I have not falsified the plummet of the scales.
I have not taken milk from the mouth of children,
I have not deprived cattle of their pasture.
I have not snared birds in the reeds of the gods,
I have not caught fish in their ponds.
I have not held back water in its season,

I have not dammed a flowing stream,
I have not quenched a needed fire.
I have not neglected the days of meat offerings,
I have not detained cattle belonging to the god,
I have not stopped a god in his procession.
I am pure, I am pure, I am pure, I am pure!
I am pure as is pure that great heron in Hnes.
I am truly the nose of the Lord of Breath,
Who sustains all the people,
On the day of completing the Eye in On,[3]
In the second month of winter, last day,
In the presence of the lord of this land.
I have seen the completion of the Eye in On!
No evil shall befall me in this land,
In this Hall of the Two Truths;
For I know the names of the gods in it,
The followers of the great God!

[THE FIRST INTERROGATION]

"Let him come," they say to me,
"Who are you?" they say to me,
"What is your name?" they say to me.
"I am the stalk of the papyrus,
He-who-is-in-the-moringa° is my name." *Osiris*
"Where have you passed by?" they say to me,
"I have passed by the town north of the moringa."
"What have you seen there?"
"The Leg and the Thigh."
"What did you say to them?"
"I have witnessed the acclaim in the land of the Fenkhu."° *Syria*
"What did they give you?"
"A firebrand and a faience column."
"What did you do with them?"
"I buried them on the shore of the pool Maaty,
At the time of the evening meal."
"What did you find there on the shore of the pool Maaty?"
"A scepter of flint whose name is 'Breath-giver.'"
"What did you do to the firebrand and the faience column,
When you had buried them?"
"I lamented over them,
I took them up,
I extinguished the fire,
I broke the column,
Threw it in the pool."
"Come then, enter the gate of this Hall of the Two Truths,
For you know us."

3. City in the Nile delta, a center of the worship of the sun god.

[The Second Interrogation]

"I shall not let you enter through me,"
Says the beam of this gate,
"Unless you tell my name."
"'Plummet-of-the-Place-of-Truth' is your name."
"I shall not let you enter through me,"
Says the right leaf of this gate,
"Unless you tell my name."
"'Scale-pan-that-carries-maat' is your name."
"I shall not let you enter through me,"
Says the left leaf of this gate,
"Unless you tell my name."
"'Scale-pan-of-wine' is your name."
"I shall not let you pass over me,"
Says the threshold of this gate,
"Unless you tell my name."
"'Ox-of-Geb'° is your name." *earth god*
"I shall not open for you,"
Says the bolt of this gate,
"Unless you tell my name."
"'Toe-of-his-mother' is your name."
"I shall not open for you,"
Says the bolt-clasp of this gate,
"Unless you tell my name."
"'Eye-of-Sobk°-Lord-of-Bakhu' is your name." *crocodile god*
"I shall not open for you,
I shall not let you enter by me,"
Says the keeper of this gate,
"Unless you tell my name."
"'Breast-of-Shu°-given-him-to-guard-Osiris' is your name." *god of air*
"We shall not let you pass over us,"
Say the cross-timbers,
"Unless you tell our name."
"'Offspring-of-Renenutet'° is your name." *goddess of fertility*
"You know us, pass over us."
"You shall not tread upon me,"
Says the floor of this hall.
"Why not, since I am pure?"
"Because we do not know your feet,
With which you tread on us;
Tell them to me."
"'Who-enters-before-Min'° is the name of my right foot, *god of vegetation*
'*Wnpt*-of-Nephthys'[4] is the name of my left foot."
"Tread upon us, since you know us."
"I shall not announce you,"

4. Sister of the goddess Isis. *Wnpt* is an unknown word.

Says the guard of the Hall,
"Unless you tell my name."
"'Knower-of-hearts Examiner-of-bellies' is your name."
"To which god present shall I announce you?"
"Tell it to the Interpreter of the Two Lands."
"Who is the Interpreter of the Two Lands?"
"It is Thoth."

"Come," says Thoth,
"Why have you come?"
"I have come here to report."
"What is your condition?"
"I am free of all wrongdoing,
I avoided the strife of those in their day,
I am not one of them."
"To whom shall I announce you?"
"To him whose roof is of fire,
Whose walls are living cobras,
The floor of whose house is in the flood."
"Who is he?"
"He is Osiris."
"Proceed, you are announced,
The Eye is your bread,
The Eye is your beer,
The Eye is your offering on earth,"
So says he to me.

[INSTRUCTIONS FOR USE]

This is the way to act toward the Hall of the Two Truths. A man says this speech when he is pure, clean, dressed in fresh clothes, shod in white sandals, painted with eye-paint, anointed with the finest oil of myrrh. One shall offer to him beef, fowl, incense, bread, beer, and herbs. And you make this image in drawing on a clean surface in red paint mixed with soil on which pigs and goats have not trodden.

He for whom this scroll is recited will prosper, and his children will prosper. He will be the friend of the king and his courtiers. He will receive bread, beer, and a big chunk of meat from the altar of the great god. He will not be held back at any gate of the west. He will be ushered in with the kings of Upper and Lower Egypt. He will be a follower of Osiris.

Effective a million times.

Letters to the Dead

2nd to 1st millennium B.C.E.

The ancient Egyptians took great care of their dead, and they expected a good deal in return. Deceased relatives were supposed to intercede with the gods on behalf of the living, and they could influence earthly events for good or ill. Great believers in the power of the written word, the Egyptians didn't only pray to their dead but wrote letters to them as well, inscribing them on the bowls in which they left offerings at their tombs. The writers would remind the dead of all they had done for them while alive, even threatening their dearly departed if they should fail to meet their ongoing responsibilities. The letters given here show how fluid the Egyptians considered the boundary to be between the realms of the living and the dead.

Letters to the Dead[1]

[1: A Lawsuit Against a Deceased Wife]

To the excellent spirit Ankhere! What evil thing have I done to you, that I should be in this wretched state I am in? What have I done to you? What you have done is to lay hands on me, although I have done nothing evil to you. Since I lived with you as husband, and down to this day, what have I done that I must hide? What have I done to you? I must bring this accusation against you for what you have done. What have I done to you?

I will lodge a complaint against you with words of my mouth, in the presence of the Nine Gods of the West, and it shall be decided between you and me by means of this letter, which sets out our dispute in writing. What have I done to you? I made you a married woman when I was a youth. I was with you when I was performing all manner of offices: I was with you, and did not put you aside. I did not cause your heart to grieve. This was when I was a youth and when I was performing all manner of important offices for Pharaoh, without putting you aside but saying, "She must be with me"—so I said! And if people came to me before you, I did not receive them on your account, saying, "I will act according to your desire." But now, behold, you give my heart no rest. I will be judged against you, and wrong will be discerned from right.

* * * And when you became ill with your sickness, I hired a master physician, and he treated you, and he did everything you asked him to do. And when I followed after Pharaoh journeying to the south, and you had come into your present condition, I spent eight full months without eating or drinking like a man. When I returned to Memphis, I asked leave of Pharaoh, and I came to where you were, and I wept exceedingly together with my people in front of my street-quarter. And I gave linen clothes to wrap you, and I caused many clothes to be made, and I left no good thing undone for you,

And now, behold, I have passed three years living alone, without entering into a house, though it is not right that one like me should live like this. And behold, I have done it on your account. But behold, you do not know good from bad. It shall be decided between you and me. And behold, the sisters in the house, I have not gone in to any of them.

[2: An Inheritance Dispute: Letters Written on an Offering Bowl]

[*Written on the inside of the bowl*]: It is Shepsi who speaks to his father Inkhenmet. This is a verbal reminder of your visit to the prison, to the place where Shon's son Hotpui was, when you brought the foreleg of an ox, and when this your son came with Newayof, and when you said, "Welcome to me, you two! Sit and eat meat!" Am

1. Translated by Alan H. Gardiner and Kurt Sethe.

I being injured in your presence by my brother, without this your son having done or said anything? Yet I buried him, I brought him from the town of I . . ., and I placed him among the fellow-owners of his desert tomb complex, even though he still owed me repayment of a loan worth 30 gallons of Upper Egyptian barley—1 *mnw,*[2] 6 gallons of Upper Egyptian barley, 6 flax, 1 *shn,* a *mht*-cup. So although I did for him what had never been done before, he has acted very wrongly against this your son, seeing that you had said to this your son, "All my property is vested in my son Shepsi." But see, my fields have been taken away by Sher's son Henu. Now my brother is with you in one city. Do you litigate with him, since your scribes are with you in one city. Joyful is one who does what is right, whereas wrongdoers are wretched!

[*Written on the outside of the bowl*]: It is Shepsi who speaks to his mother Iy. This is a verbal reminder of the fact that you said to this your son, "Bring me quails that I may eat them," and this your son brought you seven quails, and you did eat them. Am I being injured in your presence, the other children deeply angry with this your son? Who then will pour out water offerings for you? O that you might judge between me and Sebekhotep! I brought him from another town, and placed him in his town among the fellow-owners of his tomb complex, and gave him burial clothing. Why does he work against this your son, very wrongfully, without my having said or done anything? Wrongdoing is painful to the gods!

END OF PERSPECTIVES: DEATH AND IMMORTALITY

The Song of Songs

1st millennium B.C.E.

The phrase "song of songs," *shir ha-shirim* in Hebrew, means "best of all songs," a testimony to the power and beauty of the greatest love poem we have from the ancient Mediterranean world. Centuries of readers—and lovers—have relished the speakers' ecstatic praise of each other's bodies, the lyrical evocations of the beauties of nature and the landscape of Israel, and the mysterious episodes of abandonment and loss in the middle of the book. The title and opening line refer to it as a single song, and some editors over the centuries have inserted captions and dialogue markers to connect its parts into an extended dialogue between a woman, her beloved, and a chorus of her attendants or friends. The book can also be thought of, though, as a collection of older love poems. Many of these verses must have been sung individually, like the Egyptian poems they often resemble, long before they were collected together in around the third century B.C.E.

The Song of Songs was included in the Bible (after some ancient debate) thanks to the book's attribution to King Solomon. The rabbis who admitted it to the Bible interpreted the text allegorically as depicting the love of God for Israel. Later, Christian commentators adapted this line of interpretation, reading the collection as an allegory of the love of Christ for his Church. Modern scholarship tends instead to stress the poems' links to wedding songs and the older fertility myths that often underlay them. There was a developed tradition of "sacred marriage poetry" in the Near East. A list of hymn titles from the Mesopotamian city of Assur shows many that resemble verses in the Song of Songs:

2. A large container's worth.

"How do I long for the beautiful one!"
"The fragrance of cedar is thy love, O lord."
"To the door of the lord she did come."
"By night I thought of thee."
"Thou hast caressed me; be thou my lord!"

In Mesopotamia, these hymns would have been performed in festivals associated with planting and harvest, with the king and the queen, or the king and a temple prostitute, enacting the roles of the goddess of love (Inanna or Ishtar) and her consort (Dumuzi or Tammuz), who takes her place in the underworld for six months of the year; their union was the mythic underpinning for the seasonal fertility of crops (see *The Descent of Ishtar,* page 115). Tammuz and Ishtar (known in Palestine as Astarte) were worshiped in Jerusalem before the establishment of Hebrew monotheism—and probably long afterward as well, to the dismay of the prophets who continually condemned persisting pagan practices.

No direct use of such old traditions is found in the Song of Songs, though some of the verses use the older imagery, either in the context of a wedding between Solomon and a bride, or in other stanzas that seem to tell of a quite different, private love affair. We can think of these verses as infusing theology back into daily life, for these lyrics endow the lovers with qualities of divine power and mystery, and the lovers' encounters are set against a panoramic backdrop of Israel's sacred landscape and history.

The Song of Songs[1]

Chapter 1

The Song of Songs, which is Solomon's.

Let him kiss me with the kisses of his mouth.
Your love is more delightful than wine;
delicate is the fragrance of your perfume,
your name is an oil poured out,
and that is why the maidens love you.
Draw me in your footsteps, let us run.
The King has brought me into his rooms;
you will be our joy and our gladness.
We shall praise your love above wine;
how right it is to love you.
I am black but lovely, daughters of Jerusalem,
like the tents of Kedar,
like the pavilions of Salmah.
Take no notice of my swarthiness,
it is the sun that has burnt me.
My mother's sons turned their anger on me,
they made me look after the vineyards.
Had I only looked after my own!

Tell me then, you whom my heart loves:
Where will you lead your flock to graze,

1. Jerusalem Bible translation.

where will you rest it at noon?
That I may no more wander like a vagabond
beside the flocks of your companions.

If you do not know this, O loveliest of women,
follow the tracks of the flock,
and take your kids to graze
close by the shepherds' tents.

To my mare harnessed to Pharaoh's chariot
I compare you, my love.
Your cheeks show fair between their pendants
and your neck within its necklaces.
We shall make you golden earrings
and beads of silver.

—While the King rests in his own room
my nard yields its perfume.
My Beloved is a sachet of myrrh
lying between my breasts.
My Beloved is a cluster of henna flowers
among the vines of Engedi.

—How beautiful you are, my love,
how beautiful you are!
Your eyes are doves.

—How beautiful you are, my Beloved,
and how delightful!
All green is our bed.

—The beams of our house are of cedar,
the paneling of cypress.

Chapter 2

—I am the rose of Sharon,[2]
the lily of the valleys.
—As a lily among the thistles,
so is my love among the maidens.
—As an apple tree among the trees of the orchard,
so is my Beloved among the young men.
In his longed-for shade I am seated
and his fruit is sweet to my taste.
He has taken me to his banquet hall,
and the banner he raises over me is love.

2. A rich plain along the Mediterranean coast.

Feed me with raisin cakes,
restore me with apples,
for I am sick with love.
His left arm is under my head,
his right embraces me.

—I charge you, daughters of Jerusalem,
by the gazelles, by the hinds of the field,
not to stir my love, nor rouse it,
until it please to awake.

I hear my Beloved.
See how he comes
leaping on the mountains,
bounding over the hills.
My Beloved is like a gazelle,
like a young stag.
See where he stands
behind our wall.
He looks in at the window,
he peers through the lattice.

My Beloved lifts up his voice,
he says to me,
"Come then, my love,
my lovely one, come.
For see, winter is past,
the rains are over and gone.
The flowers appear on the earth.
The season of glad songs has come,
the cooing of the turtledove is heard in our land.
The fig tree is forming its first figs
and the blossoming vines give out their fragrance.
Come then, my love,
my lovely one, come.
My dove, hiding in the clefts of the rock,
in the coverts of the cliff,
show me your face,
let me hear your voice;
for your voice is sweet
and your face is beautiful."

Catch the foxes for us,
the little foxes that make havoc of the vineyards,
for our vineyards are in flower.
My Beloved is mine and I am his.
He pastures his flock among the lilies.

Before the dawn-wind rises,
before the shadows flee,

return! Be, my Beloved,
like a gazelle,
a young stag,
on the rugged mountains.

Chapter 3

On my bed, at night, I sought him
whom my heart loves.
I sought but did not find him.
So I will rise and go through the City;
in the streets and the squares
I will seek him whom my heart loves.

I sought but did not find him.
The watchmen came upon me
on their rounds in the City:
"Have you seen him whom my heart loves?"

Scarcely had I passed them
than I found him whom my heart loves.
I held him fast, nor would I let him go
till I had brought him into my mother's house,
into the room of her who conceived me.

I charge you, daughters of Jerusalem,
by the gazelles, by the hinds of the field,
not to stir my love, nor rouse it,
until it please to awake.

What is this coming up from the desert
like a column of smoke,
breathing of myrrh and frankincense
and every perfume the merchant knows?

See, it is the litter of Solomon.
Around it are sixty champions,
the flower of the warriors of Israel;
all of them skilled swordsmen,
veterans of battle.
Each man has his sword at his side,
against alarms by night.

King Solomon has made himself a throne
of wood from Lebanon.
The posts he has made of silver,
the canopy of gold,
the seat of purple;
the back is inlaid with ebony.

Daughters of Zion,
come and see King Solomon,

wearing the diadem with which his mother crowned him
on his wedding day,
on the day of his heart's joy.

Chapter 4

How beautiful you are, my love,
how beautiful you are!
Your eyes, behind your veil, are doves;
your hair is like a flock of goats
frisking down the slopes of Gilead.
Your teeth are like a flock of shorn ewes
as they come up from the washing.
Each one has its twin,
not one unpaired with another.
Your lips are a scarlet thread
and your words enchanting.
Your cheeks, behind your veil,
are halves of pomegranate.
Your neck is the tower of David
built as a fortress,
hung round with a thousand bucklers,
and each the shield of a hero.
Your two breasts are two fawns,
twins of a gazelle,
that feed among the lilies.

Before the dawn-wind rises,
before the shadows flee,
I will go to the mountain of myrrh,
to the hill of frankincense.

You are wholly beautiful, my love,
and without a blemish.

Come from Lebanon, my promised bride,
come from Lebanon, come on your way.
Lower your gaze, from the heights of Amana,
from the crests of Senir and Hermon,
the haunt of lions,
the mountains of leopards.

You ravish my heart,
my sister, my bride,[3]
you ravish my heart
with a single one of your glances,

3. As in Egyptian poetry, the lovers sometimes refer to each other as "sister" and "brother."

with one single pearl of your necklace.
What spells lie in your love,
my sister, my bride!
How delicious is your love, more delicious than wine!
How fragrant your perfumes,
more fragrant than all other spices!
Your lips, my promised one, distill wild honey.
Honey and milk are under your tongue;
and the scent of your garments
is like the scent of Lebanon.

She is a garden enclosed, my sister, my bride;
a garden enclosed, a sealed fountain.
Your shoots form an orchard of pomegranate trees,
the rarest essences are yours:
nard and saffron,
calamus and cinnamon,
with all the incense-bearing trees;
myrrh and aloes, with the subtlest odors.
Fountain that makes the gardens fertile,
well of living water,
streams flowing down from Lebanon.
Awake, north wind,
come, wind of the south!
Breathe over my garden,
to spread its sweet smell around.
Let my Beloved come into his garden,
let him taste its rarest fruits.

Chapter 5

I come into my garden,
my sister, my bride,
I gather my myrrh and balsam,
I eat my honey and my honeycomb,
I drink my wine and my milk.
Eat, friends, and drink,
drink deep, my dearest friends.

I sleep, but my heart is awake.
I hear my Beloved knocking.
"Open to me, my sister, my love,
my dove, my perfect one,
for my head is covered with dew,
my locks with the drops of night."
—"I have taken off my tunic,
am I to put it on again?
I have washed my feet,
am I to dirty them again?"

My Beloved thrust his hand
through the hole in the door;
I trembled to the core of my being.
Then I rose to open to my Beloved,
myrrh ran off my hands,
pure myrrh off my fingers,
on to the handle of the bolt.

I opened to my Beloved,
but he had turned his back and gone!
My soul failed at his flight.
I sought him but I did not find him,
I called to him but he did not answer.
The watchmen came upon me
as they made their rounds in the City.
They beat me, they wounded me,
they took away my cloak,
they who guard the ramparts.
I charge you, daughters of Jerusalem,
if you should find my Beloved,
what must you tell him . . .?
That I am sick with love.

What makes your Beloved better than other lovers,
O loveliest of women?
What makes your Beloved better than other lovers,
to give us a charge like this?

My Beloved is fresh and ruddy,
to be known among ten thousand.
His head is golden, purest gold,
his locks are palm fronds and black as the raven.
His eyes are doves at a pool of water,
bathed in milk, at rest on a pool.
His cheeks are beds of spices,
banks sweetly scented.
His lips are lilies, distilling pure myrrh.
His hands are golden, rounded,
set with jewels of Tarshish.
His belly a block of ivory
covered with sapphires.
His legs are alabaster columns
set in sockets of pure gold.
His appearance is that of Lebanon,
unrivaled as the cedars.
His conversation is sweetness itself,
he is altogether lovable.
Such is my Beloved, such is my friend,
O daughters of Jerusalem.

Chapter 6

Where did your Beloved go,
O loveliest of women?
Which way did your Beloved turn
so that we can help you to look for him?

My Beloved went down to his garden,
to the beds of spices,
to pasture his flock in the gardens
and gather lilies.
I am my Beloved's, and my Beloved is mine.
He pastures his flock among the lilies.

You are beautiful as Tirzah,[4] my love,
fair as Jerusalem.
Turn your eyes away,
for they hold me captive.
Your hair is like a flock of goats
frisking down the slopes of Gilead.
Your teeth are like a flock of sheep
as they come up from the washing.
Each one has its twin,
not one unpaired with another.
Your cheeks, behind your veil,
are halves of pomegranate.

There are sixty queens
and eighty concubines
(and countless maidens).
But my dove is unique,
mine, unique and perfect.
She is the darling of her mother,
the favorite of the one who bore her.
The maidens saw her, and called her happy,
queens and concubines sang her praises:
"Who is this arising like the dawn,
fair as the moon,
resplendent as the sun,
terrible as an army with banners?"

I went down to the nut orchard
to see what was sprouting in the valley,
to see if the vines were budding
and the pomegranate trees in flower.
Before I knew . . . my desire had hurled me
on the chariots of my people, as their prince.

4. A former capital of Israel.

Chapter 7

Return, return, O maid of Shulam,[5]
return, return, that we may gaze on you!

Why do you gaze on the maid of Shulam
dancing as though between two rows of dancers?

How beautiful are your feet in their sandals,
O prince's daughter!
The curve of your thighs is like the curve of a necklace,
work of a master hand.
Your navel is a bowl well rounded
with no lack of wine,
your belly a heap of wheat
surrounded with lilies.
Your two breasts are two fawns,
twins of a gazelle.
Your neck is an ivory tower.
Your eyes, the pools of Heshbon,
by the gate of Bath-rabbim.
Your nose, the Tower of Lebanon,
sentinel facing Damascus.
Your head is held high like Carmel,
and its plaits are as dark as purple;
a king is held captive in your tresses.
How beautiful you are, how charming,
my love, my delight!
In stature like the palm tree,
its fruit-clusters your breasts.
"I will climb the palm tree," I resolved,
"I will seize its clusters of dates."
May your breasts be clusters of grapes,
your breath sweet-scented as apples,
your speaking, superlative wine.

Wine flowing straight to my Beloved,
as it runs on the lips of those who sleep.
I am my Beloved's,
and his desire is for me.
Come, my Beloved,
let us go to the fields.
We will spend the night in the villages,
and in the morning we will go to the vineyards.
We will see if the vines are budding,

5. Perhaps a place name, or this may mean "Solomon's bride."

if their blossoms are opening,
if the pomegranate trees are in flower.
Then I shall give you the gift of my love.
The mandrakes yield their fragrance,
the rarest fruits are at our doors;
the new as well as the old,
I have stored them for you, my Beloved.

Chapter 8

Ah, why are you not my brother,
nursed at my mother's breast!
Then if I met you out of doors, I could kiss you
without people thinking ill of me.
I should lead you, I should take you
into my mother's house, and you would teach me!
I should give you spiced wine to drink,
juice of my pomegranates.

His left arm is under my head
and his right embraces me.
I charge you, daughters of Jerusalem,
not to stir my love, nor rouse it,
until it please to awake.

Who is this coming up from the desert
leaning on her Beloved?
I awakened you under the apple tree,
there where your mother conceived you,
there where she who gave birth to you conceived you.

Set me like a seal on your heart,
like a seal on your arm.
For love is strong as Death,
jealousy relentless as Sheol.
The flash of it is a flash of fire,
a flame of Yahweh himself.
Love no flood can quench,
no torrents drown.[6]

6. The translators of the Jerusalem Bible consider that the poem proper ends here. Several miscellaneous paragraphs follow in a kind of appendix, beginning with an aphorism: "Were a man to offer all the wealth of his house to buy love, contempt is all he would purchase." Then follows an obscure passage that may be a veiled criticism of the worldly policies of a late Jewish ruler in the 2nd century B.C.E.:

> Our sister is little: her breasts are not yet formed. What shall we do for our sister on the day she is spoken for? If she is a rampart, on the crest we will build a battlement of silver; if she is a door, we will board her up with planks of cedar.—I am a wall, and my breasts represent its towers. And under his eyes I have found true peace.
>
> Solomon had a vineyard at Baal-hamon. He entrusted it to overseers, and each one was to pay him the value of its produce, a thousand shekels of silver. But I look after my own vineyard myself. You, Solomon, may have your thousand shekels, and those who oversee its produce their two hundred.
>
> You who dwell in the gardens, my companions listen for your voice: deign to let me hear it. Haste away, my Beloved. Be like a gazelle, a young stag, on the spicy mountains.

Homer

8th century B.C.E.

The Greek word *homeros* means "hostage." Authorship of the great epic poems the *Iliad* and the *Odyssey* is attributed to someone bearing this name, but we don't know who or what he was. Several of the islands and cities of the eastern Mediterranean Sea claimed "Homer" as a native. What remains are the poems, amid passionate debates about when and where they were written down. Following research on the oral performance and composition of poetry in Serbia and Africa, scholars now believe that the poems represent the culmination of a long tradition of singers who assembled memories of a lost heroic age, vestiges of the story of the earliest Greeks' war against Troy in Asia Minor. The singers supplemented their oral tradition with more recent material and created two magnificent, long poems about the supposed ancestors, gods and men, of the aristocrats of the eighth century B.C.E.

Book 8 of the *Odyssey* shows us a scene of performance, where the singer Demodocus, blind as Homer was said to be, recounts part of the legend of Troy for feasting nobles:

> All reached out for the good things that lay at hand
> and when they'd put aside desire for food and drink,
> the Muse inspired the bard
> to sing the famous deeds of fighting heroes—
> the song whose fame had reached the skies those days:
> The Strife Between Odysseus and Achilles, Peleus' son . . .
> how once at the gods' flowing feast the captains clashed
> in a savage war of words, while Agamemnon, lord of armies,
> rejoiced at heart that Achaea's bravest men were battling so.

The Muse, a goddess, inspires the singer, who is seen as the channel through which memory and the divine pass to deliver these ancient stories, known to all the audience, drinking in the excellence of their retelling. Here the hero Odysseus, sitting disguised in the audience, is moved to tears.

The poems themselves preserve traces of the Mycenaean age (1500–1000 B.C.E.), hundreds of years before the date of their composition. Archaeologists have found, for example, an ivory figurine with a representation of a boar's tusk helmet like Odysseus's described in the *Iliad.* Both poems were composed in dactylic hexameter, that is, six feet based on a rhythm of a long syllable followed by two short syllables. The meter allowed the singers to retell and embellish the traditional stories of their people, while maintaining a steady flow of musical lines. Oral composition determined, with some flexibility, the "epithets," or qualifying terms used for the central figures of the poems; if Achilles, for example, is named in a certain position in a line, the words used to describe him, such as "swift-footed," must fit into the meter. If they don't, the song refers to him as the son of Peleus, or uses another qualifier that works rhythmically. Sometimes these epithets seem incongruous, or, some argue, ironic, where they fall:

> Aphrodite the sweetly laughing spoke . . .
> "Tydeus' son Diomedes, the too high-hearted, stabbed me
> as I was carrying my own beloved son out of the fighting . . . ."

Even in pain, the goddess of eros can be "sweetly laughing" if the meter requires it. Other features of oral composition include repetitions, for example, in the highly conventional, formulaic scenes of warriors putting on armor, and what is sometimes called "ring" form, a pattern of *abccba,* for example, in set scenes in the poems. The dactylic hexameter preserved, like flies in amber, ancient allusions to features of warfare and of everyday life no longer familiar to the audience. The poems provide a rich, complex, and stratified record of all the centuries between the early Mycenaean period and the people of the eighth century B.C.E., who were engaged in trade and colonization with a wide Mediterranean world, stretching from the Aegean and its many islands east to Asia Minor, to the lands north and east of the Black Sea, to the northern coast of Africa, and to the far western edges of the Mediterranean Sea, to what is now Italy and southern France.

Early in the twentieth century, the anthropologist Milman Parry, exploring storytelling in preliterate societies, discovered features of composition that explained mysteries found in Homer. Some readers had preferred such ancient poets as Virgil to Homer because, as Alexander Pope put it, Homer sometimes nods. That is, Homer forgets and repeats and skips. Parry and his followers found that Yugoslavian oral poetry sung in the twentieth century showed similar patterns; its singers sang thousands of lines of heroic poetry that they forged in the moment, without memorization or writing, using "formulae," set phrases to define particular characters and to fill out lines as required by meter. They had typical scenes, such as arming scenes, that they used as templates for various characters, and other techniques for keeping their stories pouring forth, as they benefited from the experience and innovations of generations of singers who had preceded them.

The two Homeric poems share a language and a poetic tradition but tell very different stories. Both depend on the legend of a war with Troy, which the Greeks traced mythically to the abduction of the beautiful Helen of Sparta. The great god Zeus had raped her mother, Leda, appearing to her as a swan; Helen and her sister Clytemnestra were born from one egg, and their twin brothers, Castor and Pollux, later the Gemini in astrological lore, came from another. When Paris, son of King Priam of Troy, was promised the most beautiful woman in the world by the goddess of sexual love, Aphrodite, he came to the house of Menelaos in Sparta and stole away Menelaos's wife, Helen. Poets later differed on her willingness to be stolen. The Greeks' leaders, who had all courted Helen, had also pledged to get her back if she were ever taken from her husband; they set sail for Asia under the leadership of Menelaos's brother, Agamemnon, and fought for ten long years at Troy, finally winning the war through deception. The Greek army pretended to sail away from the battlefield, leaving an immense wooden horse as an offering. The Trojans pulled it inside the walls of their city, celebrated their victory, and in the night following, the Greeks, hidden inside the horse's belly, crept out and slaughtered and burned. The Greeks killed Priam, desecrated the altar of Athena, and killed children and enslaved the women of the city. The Trojan Aineias, whom the Romans called Aeneas, son of Venus, left burning Troy at the beginning of a long journey that culminated in the foundation of Rome. Because of sacrileges committed during the looting of Troy, the return of the Greek heroes to their homelands was often long and painful.

The singers of the Homeric tradition composed many poems recounting the events of this war and its aftermath. Most have been lost: poems that told of the giving of the prize, Helen, to Paris; of the arrival of the Amazons, women warriors, to help the Trojans on the battlefield; of the hero Achilles's falling in love with the queen of the Amazons, Penthesilea, even as he killed her with his spear; of the suicide of the hero Ajax; of the Trojan Horse and the sacking of Troy; and of the *nostoi,* or "returns," of the Greek heroes. The two Homeric poems that have come down to us focus vividly on two of the crucial stories contained within the greater epic tradition. The *Iliad* recounts the story of Achilles: his wrath at being slighted by Agamemnon, his withdrawal from battle, and the Trojan hero Hektor's killing of Achilles' beloved companion, Patroklos, dressed in Achilles' armor. Achilles' mother, the goddess Thetis, has warned him that he would either live a long life without fame or die young and glorious in battle. He chooses finally to enter the battle, to fight and die, and she asks Hephaistos, the artisan god, to make him new armor. The poem describes the divine making of Achilles' shield in a scene that connects it to ancient Near Eastern and Egyptian myths in which the artisan god, a metalworker or potter, creates the world and peoples it. Achilles returns to battle in a great rage of mourning and slaughters many Trojans, including Hektor. In Book 20 the poem compares him to fire:

As inhuman fire sweeps on in fury through the deep angles
Of a drywood mountain and sets ablaze the depth of the timber
And the blustering wind lashes the flame along, so Achilleus
Swept everywhere with his spear like something more than a mortal
Harrying them as they died, and the black earth ran blood.

The poem, which begins with a plague and the wrath of Achilles, ends with a scene of consolation between Priam, king of Troy, and his deadly enemy, Achilles, the warrior who killed his son.

Many of Homer's themes, characters, and even verbal patterns connect the epics with poems composed in the ancient Near East. The relationship between Achilles and the lost Patroklos echoes Gilgamesh's love for Enkidu in *The Epic of Gilgamesh* (see page 71), just as Homer's representation of Aphrodite recalls the ancient Near Eastern goddess Ishtar. The voyage of Odysseus to the land of the dead bears remarkable resemblances to the journey of Gilgamesh to visit his mentor, Utanapishtim, and scholars have linked such scenes as the Greek gods' assemblies with Sumerian, Akkadian, Ugaritic, Hittite, and Hebrew literature. While connecting with these earlier Eastern traditions, the Homeric poems began to elaborate crucial elements of the Greek civilization that followed them and were long used as the basis for classical education, as manuals for the proper conduct of a free citizen's life. Scholars have emphasized the ways in which classical Greek society posed all conflict in terms of the *agon,* the contest. The games, such as those held at Olympia every four years; the competition of the drama, in which the writers of tragedies and comedies were set against each other in a contest for a prize; even the law courts of the ancient Greek city-state repeated this shape of two or more antagonists, or combatants, who fought over a single prize, only one of whom left the contest as victor. The Trojan War and its battles defined the shape of conflict for Greek men in the centuries that followed.

The *Odyssey* differs radically from the *Iliad.* The *Iliad* in general confines its action to the battlefield around the walls of Troy, leaving the battlefield only to visit the world of the gods or to look outward through its similes, which compare the events of battle to natural phenomena and to the worlds of farmers, animals, and sailors on the "wine-dark sea." Although the goddesses play essential roles, as when Hera seduces her husband, Zeus, to distract him from the battlefield, the mortal women of the *Iliad* are taken like booty, or war prizes: traded, enslaved, and exchanged among the heroes. The women of the *Odyssey,* on the other hand, act: the poem begins with Odysseus's being held captive by the nymph Calypso, and it traces his long journey back to his waiting wife, Penelope, who both tantalizes and defends herself against a horde of suitors besieging her in their home on the island of Ithaca.

The *Odyssey* portrays a very different world from that of the battlefield around Troy; it presents a vast landscape of the Mediterranean that contains monsters, entrances to the underworld, and societies that test the Greeks' ideas of their own culture. This poem shows the noble household, with its dependent lordlings, slaves, farms, and palace, with all the tensions that grow out of such a hierarchical social arrangement. For a society that is about to form itself into many city-states and colonies overseas, the poem maps the imaginary geography of the Mediterranean and beyond, including societies of cannibals and one-eyed monsters, and explores the social hierarchies of class and gender and the border between the living and the dead. It bequeathes to the tradition a wily hero who lies when he needs to; who survives through endless ordeals to return home, kill his rivals, and then move on; and who visits the dead and manages to evade death through a cunning intelligence that the later Greeks both admired and despised. Both the *Iliad* and the *Odyssey* helped to define storytelling and the ideas of heroism, gender, and society for millennia. Virgil knew both poems intimately, and Dante, who didn't read Greek, knew of them. The *Odyssey* had its impact on tales of Sindbad in Arabic, on romance, and on all prose fiction following Homer. The readings provided as Resonances for the *Odyssey* can suggest something of the ongoing life of Homeric epic among a wide range of twentieth-century writers.

PRONUNCIATIONS:[1]

Achaians: ah-KAI-uns
Achilleus: ah-KILL-yuss
Agamemnon: agg-ah-MEM-nohn
Aias: EYE-ahs
Athene: ah-THEE-nay
Atreides: ah-TRAY-deez
Atreus: AY-tree-us
Briseis: bre-SEE-iss
Chryseis: cry-SEE-iss
Circe: SEER-say
Danaans: DAY-nay-uns
Hektor: HEK-tor
Hephaistos: heh-FYS-tohs
Hermes: HER-meez
Menelaus: men-eh-LAY-us
Nausicaa: now-SEE-kay-ah
Odysseus: oh-DISS-yuss
Patroklos: pah-TRO-klos
Peleus: PEAL-yuss
Penelope: pen-EL-oh-pee
Phaiacia: fie-AY-sha
Phoibus: fo-EE-bus
Polyphemos: poll-ee-FEE-mos
Priam: PRY-am
Telemakhos: tel-EH-ma-khos
Thetis: THEH-tis
Xanthus: ZAN-thus

from The Iliad[1]

Book 1

[The Wrath of Achilles]

Sing, goddess,[2] the anger of Peleus' son Achilleus
and its devastation, which put pains thousandfold upon the Achaians,[3]
hurled in their multitudes to the house of Hades strong souls
of heroes, but gave their bodies to be the delicate feasting
of dogs, of all birds, and the will of Zeus[4] was accomplished
since that time when first there stood in division of conflict
Atreus' son the lord of men[5] and brilliant Achilleus.
What god was it then set them together in bitter collision?

1. The transliteration of Greek names varies widely. Some scholars prefer to follow very closely, in our Roman alphabet, the Greek spelling in the Greek alphabet. For example, they call the great hero of the Greek army in the Trojan War "Akhilleus." Others call him by the name the Romans later gave him, "Achilles." Still others prefer the compromise: "Achilleus." Most translations combine these solutions, using the Latin versions of names for the most familiar and transliterating more closely the less familiar names. Remember, Achilleus is Akhilleus is Achilles. Greek Odysseus becomes "Ulysses" in Rome and in James Joyce's novel of the same name. Agamemnon's queen is "Klytaimestra," "Clytaemestra," and even "Clytemnestra."

1. Translated by Richmond Lattimore.
2. The Muse, goddess of epic poetry.
3. The Greeks.
4. Greatest of the gods, son of Kronos.
5. Agamemnon.

Zeus' son and Leto's, Apollo,[6] who in anger at the king drove
the foul pestilence along the host, and the people perished,
since Atreus' son had dishonoured Chryses, priest of Apollo,
when he came beside the fast ships of the Achaians to ransom
back his daughter, carrying gifts beyond count and holding
in his hands wound on a staff of gold the ribbons of Apollo
who strikes from afar, and supplicated all the Achaians,
but above all Atreus' two sons, the marshals of the people:
"Sons of Atreus and you other strong-greaved Achaians,
to you may the gods grant who have their homes on Olympos[7]
Priam's city[8] to be plundered and a fair homecoming thereafter,
but may you give me back my own daughter and take the ransom,
giving honour to Zeus' son who strikes from afar, Apollo."
  Then all the rest of the Achaians cried out in favour
that the priest be respected and the shining ransom be taken;
yet this pleased not the heart of Atreus' son Agamemnon,
but harshly he drove him away with a strong order upon him:
"Never let me find you again, old sir, near our hollow
ships, neither lingering now nor coming again hereafter,
for fear your staff and the god's ribbons help you no longer.
The girl I will not give back; sooner will old age come upon her
in my own house, in Argos, far from her own land, going
up and down by the loom and being in my bed as my companion.
So go now, do not make me angry; so you will be safer."
  So he spoke, and the old man in terror obeyed him
and went silently away beside the murmuring sea beach.
Over and over the old man prayed as he walked in solitude
to King Apollo, whom Leto of the lovely hair bore: "Hear me,
lord of the silver bow who set your power about Chryse
and Killa the sacrosanct, who are lord in strength over Tenedos,
Smintheus, if ever it pleased your heart that I built your temple,
if ever it pleased you that I burned all the rich thigh pieces
of bulls, of goats, then bring to pass this wish I pray for:
let your arrows make the Danaans[9] pay for my tears shed."
So he spoke in prayer, and Phoibos Apollo heard him,
and strode down along the pinnacles of Olympos, angered
in his heart, carrying across his shoulders the bow and the hooded
quiver; and the shafts clashed on the shoulders of the god walking
angrily. He came as night comes down and knelt then
apart and opposite the ships and let go an arrow.
Terrible was the clash that rose from the bow of silver.
First he went after the mules and the circling hounds, then let go
a tearing arrow against the men themselves and struck them.
The corpse fires burned everywhere and did not stop burning.

6. God of disease, healing, prophecy, music, and poetry.
7. Sacred mountain home of the gods.
8. Troy, also called Ilion, city of Priam and his 50 sons and daughters, including Hektor, Paris, and Kassandra.
9. Like "Argives," another name for the Greeks.

Nine days up and down the host ranged the god's arrows,
but on the tenth Achilleus called the people to assembly;
a thing put into his mind by the goddess of the white arms, Hera,[1]
who had pity upon the Danaans when she saw them dying.
Now when they were all assembled in one place together,
Achilleus of the swift feet stood up among them and spoke forth:
"Son of Atreus, I believe now that straggling backwards
we must make our way home if we can even escape death,
if fighting now must crush the Achaians and the plague likewise.
No, come, let us ask some holy man, some prophet,
even an interpreter of dreams, since a dream also
comes from Zeus, who can tell why Phoibos Apollo is so angry,
if for the sake of some vow, some hecatomb he blames us,
if given the fragrant smoke of lambs, of he goats, somehow
he can be made willing to beat the bane aside from us."
He spoke thus and sat down again, and among them stood up
Kalchas, Thestor's son, far the best of the bird interpreters,
who knew all things that were, the things to come and the things past,
who guided into the land of Ilion[2] the ships of the Achaians
through that seercraft of his own that Phoibos Apollo gave him.
He in kind intention toward all stood forth and addressed them:
"You have bidden me, Achilleus beloved of Zeus, to explain to
you this anger of Apollo the lord who strikes from afar. Then
I will speak; yet make me a promise and swear before me
readily by word and work of your hands to defend me,
since I believe I shall make a man angry who holds great kingship
over the men of Argos, and all the Achaians obey him.
For a king when he is angry with a man beneath him is too strong,
and suppose even for the day itself he swallow down his anger,
he still keeps bitterness that remains until its fulfilment
deep in his chest. Speak forth then, tell me if you will protect me."
Then in answer again spoke Achilleus of the swift feet:
"Speak, interpreting whatever you know, and fear nothing.
In the name of Apollo beloved of Zeus to whom you, Kalchas,
make your prayers when you interpret the gods' will to the Danaans,
no man so long as I am alive above earth and see daylight
shall lay the weight of his hands on you beside the hollow ships,
not one of all the Danaans, even if you mean Agamemnon,
who now claims to be far the greatest of all the Achaians."
At this the blameless seer took courage again and spoke forth:
"No, it is not for the sake of some vow or hecatomb[3] he blames us,
but for the sake of his priest whom Agamemnon dishonoured
and would not give him back his daughter nor accept the ransom.
Therefore the archer sent griefs against us and will send them
still, nor sooner thrust back the shameful plague from the Danaans
until we give the glancing-eyed girl back to her father
without price, without ransom, and lead also a blessed hecatomb

1. Goddess of marriage and the wife and sister of Zeus.
2. Troy.
3. Animal sacrifice.

to Chryse; thus we might propitiate and persuade him."
He spoke thus and sat down again, and among them stood up
Atreus' son the hero wide-ruling Agamemnon
raging, the heart within filled black to the brim with anger
from beneath, but his two eyes showed like fire in their blazing.
First of all he eyed Kalchas bitterly and spoke to him:
"Seer of evil: never yet have you told me a good thing.
Always the evil things are dear to your heart to prophesy,
but nothing excellent have you said nor ever accomplished.
Now once more you make divination to the Danaans, argue
forth your reason why he who strikes from afar afflicts them,
because I for the sake of the girl Chryseis would not take
the shining ransom; and indeed I wish greatly to have her
in my own house; since I like her better than Klytaimestra
my own wife, for in truth she is no way inferior,
neither in build nor stature nor wit, not in accomplishment.
Still I am willing to give her back, if such is the best way.
I myself desire that my people be safe, not perish.
Find me then some prize that shall be my own, lest I only
among the Argives go without, since that were unfitting;
you are all witnesses to this thing, that my prize goes elsewhere."
Then in answer again spoke brilliant swift-footed Achilleus:
"Son of Atreus, most lordly, greediest for gain of all men,
how shall the great-hearted Achaians give you a prize now?
There is no great store of things lying about I know of.
But what we took from the cities by storm has been distributed;
it is unbecoming for the people to call back things once given.
No, for the present give the girl back to the god; we Achaians
thrice and four times over will repay you, if ever Zeus gives
into our hands the strong-walled citadel of Troy to be plundered."
Then in answer again spoke powerful Agamemnon:
"Not that way, good fighter though you be, godlike Achilleus,
strive to cheat, for you will not deceive, you will not persuade me.
What do you want? To keep your own prize and have me sit here
lacking one? Are you ordering me to give this girl back?
Either the great-hearted Achaians shall give me a new prize
chosen according to my desire to atone for the girl lost,
or else if they will not give me one I myself shall take her,
your own prize, or that of Aias, or that of Odysseus,
going myself in person; and he whom I visit will be bitter.
Still, these are things we shall deliberate again hereafter.
Come, now, we must haul a black ship down to the bright sea,
and assemble rowers enough for it, and put on board it
the hecatomb, and the girl herself, Chryseis of the fair cheeks,
and let there be one responsible man in charge of her,
either Aias or Idomeneus or brilliant Odysseus,
or you yourself, son of Peleus, most terrifying of all men,
to reconcile by accomplishing sacrifice the archer."
Then looking darkly at him Achilleus of the swift feet spoke:

"O wrapped in shamelessness, with your mind forever on profit,
how shall any one of the Achaians readily obey you
either to go on a journey or to fight men strongly in battle?
I for my part did not come here for the sake of the Trojan
spearmen to fight against them, since to me they have done nothing.
Never yet have they driven away my cattle or my horses,
never in Phthia where the soil is rich and men grow great did they
spoil my harvest, since indeed there is much that lies between us,
the shadowy mountains and the echoing sea; but for your sake,
o great shamelessness, we followed, to do you favour,
you with the dog's eyes, to win your honour and Menelaos'[4]
from the Trojans. You forget all this or else you care nothing.
And now my prize you threaten in person to strip from me,
for whom I laboured much, the gift of the sons of the Achaians.
Never, when the Achaians sack some well-founded citadel
of the Trojans, do I have a prize that is equal to your prize.
Always the greater part of the painful fighting is the work of
my hands; but when the time comes to distribute the booty
yours is far the greater reward, and I with some small thing
yet dear to me go back to my ships when I am weary with fighting.
Now I am returning to Phthia, since it is much better
to go home again with my curved ships, and I am minded no longer
to stay here dishonoured and pile up your wealth and your luxury."
Then answered him in turn the lord of men Agamemnon:
"Run away by all means if your heart drives you. I will not
entreat you to stay here for my sake. There are others with me
who will do me honour, and above all Zeus of the counsels.
To me you are the most hateful of all the kings whom the gods love.
Forever quarrelling is dear to your heart, and wars and battles;
and if you are very strong indeed, that is a god's gift.
Go home then with your own ships and your own companions,
be king over the Myrmidons. I care nothing about you.
I take no account of your anger. But here is my threat to you.
Even as Phoibos Apollo is taking away my Chryseis,
I shall convey her back in my own ship, with my own
followers; but I shall take the fair-cheeked Briseis,
your prize, I myself going to your shelter, that you may learn well
how much greater I am than you, and another man may shrink back
from likening himself to me and contending against me."
So he spoke. And the anger came on Peleus' son, and within
his shaggy breast the heart was divided two ways, pondering
whether to draw from beside his thigh the sharp sword, driving
away all those who stood between and kill the son of Atreus,
or else to check the spleen within and keep down his anger.
Now as he weighed in mind and spirit these two courses
and was drawing from its scabbard the great sword, Athene descended
from the sky. For Hera the goddess of the white arms sent her,

4. Agamemnon's brother and the husband of Helen.

who loved both men equally in her heart and cared for them.
The goddess standing behind Peleus' son caught him by the fair hair,
appearing to him only, for no man of the others saw her.
Achilleus in amazement turned about, and straightway
knew Pallas Athene and the terrible eyes shining.
He uttered winged words and addressed her: "Why have you come now,
o child of Zeus of the aegis, once more? Is it that you may see
the outrageousness of the son of Atreus Agamemnon?
Yet will I tell you this thing, and I think it shall be accomplished.
By such acts of arrogance he may even lose his own life."
  Then in answer the goddess grey-eyed Athene spoke to him:
"I have come down to stay your anger—but will you obey me?—
from the sky; and the goddess of the white arms Hera sent me,
who loves both of you equally in her heart and cares for you.
Come then, do not take your sword in your hand, keep clear of fighting,
though indeed with words you may abuse him, and it will be that way.
And this also will I tell you and it will be a thing accomplished.
Some day three times over such shining gifts shall be given you
by reason of this outrage. Hold your hand then, and obey us."
  Then in answer again spoke Achilleus of the swift feet:
"Goddess, it is necessary that I obey the word of you two,
angry though I am in my heart. So it will be better.
If any man obeys the gods, they listen to him also."
  He spoke, and laid his heavy hand on the silver sword hilt
and thrust the great blade back into the scabbard nor disobeyed
the word of Athene. And she went back again to Olympos
to the house of Zeus of the aegis with the other divinities.
  But Peleus' son once again in words of derision
spoke to Atreides, and did not yet let go of his anger:
"You wine sack, with a dog's eyes, with a deer's heart. Never
once have you taken courage in your heart to arm with your people
for battle, or go into ambuscade with the best of the Achaians.
No, for in such things you see death. Far better to your mind
is it, all along the widespread host of the Achaians
to take away the gifts of any man who speaks up against you.
King who feed on your people, since you rule nonentities;
otherwise, son of Atreus, this were your last outrage.
But I will tell you this and swear a great oath upon it:
in the name of this sceptre, which never again will bear leaf nor
branch, now that it has left behind the cut stump in the mountains,
nor shall it ever blossom again, since the bronze blade stripped
bark and leafage, and now at last the sons of the Achaians
carry it in their hands in state when they administer
the justice of Zeus. And this shall be a great oath before you:
some day longing for Achilleus will come to the sons of the Achaians,
all of them. Then stricken at heart though you be, you will be able
to do nothing, when in their numbers before man-slaughtering Hektor
they drop and die. And then you will eat out the heart within you
in sorrow, that you did no honour to the best of the Achaians."

Thus spoke Peleus' son and dashed to the ground the sceptre
studded with golden nails, and sat down again. But Atreides
raged still on the other side, and between them Nestor
the fair-spoken rose up, the lucid speaker of Pylos,
from whose lips the streams of words ran sweeter than honey.
In his time two generations of mortal men had perished,
those who had grown up with him and they who had been born to
these in sacred Pylos, and he was king in the third age.
He in kind intention toward both stood forth and addressed them:
"Oh, for shame. Great sorrow comes on the land of Achaia.
Now might Priam and the sons of Priam in truth be happy,
and all the rest of the Trojans be visited in their hearts with gladness,
were they to hear all this wherein you two are quarrelling,
you, who surpass all Danaans in council, in fighting.
Yet be persuaded. Both of you are younger than I am.
Yes, and in my time I have dealt with better men than
you are, and never once did they disregard me. Never
yet have I seen nor shall see again such men as these were,
men like Peirithoös, and Dryas, shepherd of the people,
Kaineus and Exadios, godlike Polyphemos,
or Theseus, Aigeus' son, in the likeness of the immortals.
These were the strongest generation of earth-born mortals,
the strongest, and they fought against the strongest, the beast men
living within the mountains, and terribly they destroyed them.
I was of the company of these men, coming from Pylos,
a long way from a distant land, since they had summoned me.
And I fought single-handed, yet against such men no one
of the mortals now alive upon earth could do battle. And also
these listened to the counsels I gave and heeded my bidding.
Do you also obey, since to be persuaded is better.
You, great man that you are, yet do not take the girl away
but let her be, a prize as the sons of the Achaians gave her
first. Nor, son of Peleus, think to match your strength with
the king, since never equal with the rest is the portion of honour
of the sceptred king to whom Zeus gives magnificence. Even
though you are the stronger man, and the mother who bore you was immortal,
yet is this man greater who is lord over more than you rule.
Son of Atreus, give up your anger; even I entreat you
to give over your bitterness against Achilleus, he who
stands as a great bulwark of battle over all the Achaians."
Then in answer again spoke powerful Agamemnon:
"Yes, old sir, all this you have said is fair and orderly.
Yet here is a man who wishes to be above all others,
who wishes to hold power over all, and to be lord of
all, and give them their orders, yet I think one will not obey him.
And if the everlasting gods have made him a spearman,
yet they have not given him the right to speak abusively."
Then looking at him darkly brilliant Achilleus answered him:
"So must I be called of no account and a coward

if I must carry out every order you may happen to give me.
Tell other men to do these things, but give me no more
commands, since I for my part have no intention to obey you.
And put away in your thoughts this other thing I tell you.
With my hands I will not fight for the girl's sake, neither
with you nor any other man, since you take her away who gave her.
But of all the other things that are mine beside my fast black
ship, you shall take nothing away against my pleasure.
Come, then, only try it, that these others may see also;
instantly your own black blood will stain my spearpoint."
So these two after battling in words of contention
stood up, and broke the assembly beside the ships of the Achaians.
Peleus' son went back to his balanced ships and his shelter
with Patroklos, Menoitios' son, and his own companions.
But the son of Atreus drew a fast ship down to the water
and allotted into it twenty rowers and put on board it
the hecatomb for the god and Chryseis of the fair cheeks
leading her by the hand. And in charge went crafty Odysseus.
These then putting out went over the ways of the water
while Atreus' son told his people to wash off their defilement.
And they washed it away and threw the washings into the salt sea.
Then they accomplished perfect hecatombs to Apollo,
of bulls and goats along the beach of the barren salt sea.
The savour of the burning swept in circles up to the bright sky.
Thus these were busy about the army. But Agamemnon
did not give up his anger and the first threat he made to Achilleus,
but to Talthybios he gave his orders and Eurybates
who were heralds and hard-working henchmen to him: "Go now
to the shelter of Peleus' son Achilleus, to bring back
Briseis of the fair cheeks leading her by the hand. And if he
will not give her, I must come in person to take her
with many men behind me, and it will be the worse for him."
He spoke and sent them forth with this strong order upon them.
They went against their will beside the beach of the barren
salt sea, and came to the shelters and the ships of the Myrmidons.[5]
The man himself they found beside his shelter and his black ship
sitting. And Achilleus took no joy at all when he saw them.
These two terrified and in awe of the king stood waiting
quietly, and did not speak a word at all nor question him.
But he knew the whole matter in his own heart, and spoke first:
"Welcome, heralds, messengers of Zeus and of mortals.
Draw near. You are not to blame in my sight, but Agamemnon
who sent the two of you here for the sake of the girl Briseis.
Go then, illustrious Patroklos, and bring the girl forth
and give her to these to be taken away. Yet let them be witnesses
in the sight of the blessed gods, in the sight of mortal
men, and of this cruel king, if ever hereafter

5. Achilleus' men.

there shall be need of me to beat back the shameful destruction
from the rest. For surely in ruinous heart he makes sacrifice
and has not wit enough to look behind and before him
that the Achaians fighting beside their ships shall not perish."
So he spoke, and Patroklos obeyed his beloved companion.
He led forth from the hut Briseis of the fair cheeks and gave her
to be taken away; and they walked back beside the ships of the Achaians,
and the woman all unwilling went with them still. But Achilleus
weeping went and sat in sorrow apart from his companions
beside the beach of the grey sea looking out on the infinite water.
Many times stretching forth his hands he called on his mother:[6]
"Since, my mother, you bore me to be a man with a short life,
therefore Zeus of the loud thunder on Olympos should grant me
honour at least. But now he has given me not even a little.
Now the son of Atreus, powerful Agamemnon,
has dishonoured me, since he has taken away my prize and keeps it."
So he spoke in tears and the lady his mother heard him
as she sat in the depths of the sea at the side of her aged father,
and lightly she emerged like a mist from the grey water.
She came and sat beside him as he wept, and stroked him
with her hand and called him by name and spoke to him: "Why then,
child, do you lament? What sorrow has come to your heart now?
Tell me, do not hide it in your mind, and thus we shall both know."
Sighing heavily Achilleus of the swift feet answered her:
"You know; since you know why must I tell you all this?
We went against Thebe, the sacred city of Eëtion,
and the city we sacked, and carried everything back to this place,
and the sons of the Achaians made a fair distribution
and for Atreus' son they chose out Chryseis of the fair cheeks.
Then Chryses, priest of him who strikes from afar, Apollo,
came beside the fast ships of the bronze-armoured Achaians to ransom
back his daughter, carrying gifts beyond count and holding
in his hands wound on a staff of gold the ribbons of Apollo
who strikes from afar, and supplicated all the Achaians,
but above all Atreus' two sons, the marshals of the people.
Then all the rest of the Achaians cried out in favour
that the priest be respected and the shining ransom be taken;
yet this pleased not the heart of Atreus' son Agamemnon,
but harshly he sent him away with a strong order upon him.
The old man went back again in anger, but Apollo
listened to his prayer, since he was very dear to him, and let go
the wicked arrow against the Argives. And now the people
were dying one after another while the god's shafts ranged
everywhere along the wide host of the Achaians, till the seer
knowing well the truth interpreted the designs of the archer.
It was I first of all urged then the god's appeasement;
and the anger took hold of Atreus' son, and in speed standing

6. The sea-nymph Thetis.

he uttered his threat against me, and now it is a thing accomplished.
For the girl the glancing-eyed Achaians are taking to Chryse
in a fast ship, also carrying to the king presents. But even
now the heralds went away from my shelter leading
Briseus' daughter, whom the sons of the Achaians gave me.
You then, if you have power to, protect your own son, going
to Olympos and supplicating Zeus, if ever before now
either by word you comforted Zeus' heart or by action.
Since it is many times in my father's halls I have heard you
making claims, when you said you only among the immortals
beat aside shameful destruction from Kronos' son the dark-misted,[7]
that time when all the other Olympians sought to bind him,
Hera and Poseidon and Pallas Athene. Then you,
goddess, went and set him free from his shackles, summoning
in speed the creature of the hundred hands to tall Olympos,
that creature the gods name Briareus, but all men
Aigaios' son, but he is far greater in strength than his father.
He rejoicing in the glory of it sat down by Kronion,
and the rest of the blessed gods were frightened and gave up binding him.
Sit beside him and take his knees and remind him of these things
now, if perhaps he might be willing to help the Trojans,
and pin the Achaians back against the ships and the water,
dying, so that thus they may all have profit of their own king,
that Atreus' son wide-ruling Agamemnon may recognize
his madness, that he did no honour to the best of the Achaians."
Thetis answered him then letting the tears fall: "Ah me,
my child. Your birth was bitterness. Why did I raise you?
If only you could sit by your ships untroubled, not weeping,
since indeed your lifetime is to be short, of no length.
Now it has befallen that your life must be brief and bitter
beyond all men's. To a bad destiny I bore you in my chambers.
But I will go to cloud-dark Olympos and ask this
thing of Zeus who delights in the thunder. Perhaps he will do it.
Do you therefore continuing to sit by your swift ships
be angry at the Achaians and stay away from all fighting.
For Zeus went to the blameless Aithiopians at the Ocean
yesterday to feast, and the rest of the gods went with him.
On the twelfth day he will be coming back to Olympos,
and then I will go for your sake to the house of Zeus, bronze-founded,
and take him by the knees and I think I can persuade him."
So speaking she went away from that place and left him
sorrowing in his heart for the sake of the fair-girdled woman
whom they were taking by force against his will. But Odysseus
meanwhile drew near to Chryse conveying the sacred hecatomb.
These when they were inside the many-hollowed harbour
took down and gathered together the sails and stowed them in the black ship,

7. Zeus.

let down mast by the forestays, and settled it into the mast crutch
easily, and rowed her in with oars to the mooring.
They threw over the anchor stones and made fast the stern cables
and themselves stepped out on to the break of the sea beach,
and led forth the hecatomb to the archer Apollo,
and Chryseis herself stepped forth from the sea-going vessel.
Odysseus of the many designs guided her to the altar
and left her in her father's arms and spoke a word to him:
"Chryses, I was sent here by the lord of men Agamemnon
to lead back your daughter and accomplish a sacred hecatomb
to Apollo on behalf of the Danaans, that we may propitiate
the lord who has heaped unhappiness and tears on the Argives."
    He spoke, and left her in his arms. And he received gladly
his beloved child. And the men arranged the sacred hecatomb
for the god in orderly fashion around the strong-founded altar.
Next they washed their hands and took up the scattering barley.
Standing among them with lifted arms Chryses prayed in a great voice:
"Hear me, lord of the silver bow, who set your power about
Chryse and Killa the sacrosanct, who are lord in strength over
Tenedos; if once before you listened to my prayers
and did me honour and smote strongly the host of the Achaians,
so one more time bring to pass the wish that I pray for.
Beat aside at last the shameful plague from the Danaans."
    So he spoke in prayer, and Phoibos Apollo heard him.
And when all had made prayer and flung down the scattering barley
first they drew back the victims' heads and slaughtered them and skinned them,
and cut away the meat from the thighs and wrapped them in fat,
making a double fold, and laid shreds of flesh upon them.
The old man burned these on a cleft stick and poured the gleaming
wine over, while the young men with forks in their hands stood about him.
But when they had burned the thigh pieces and tasted the vitals,
they cut all the remainder into pieces and spitted them
and roasted all carefully and took off the pieces.
Then after they had finished the work and got the feast ready
they feasted, nor was any man's hunger denied a fair portion.
But when they had put away their desire for eating and drinking,
the young men filled the mixing bowls with pure wine, passing
a portion to all, when they had offered drink in the goblets.
All day long they propitiated the god with singing,
chanting a splendid hymn to Apollo, these young Achaians,
singing to the one who works from afar, who listened in gladness.
    Afterwards when the sun went down and darkness came onward
they lay down and slept beside the ship's stern cables.
But when the young Dawn showed again with her rosy fingers,
they put forth to sea toward the wide camp of the Achaians.
And Apollo who works from afar sent them a favouring stern wind.
They set up the mast again and spread on it the white sails,
and the wind blew into the middle of the sail, and at the cutwater

a blue wave rose and sang strongly as the ship went onward.
She ran swiftly cutting across the swell her pathway.
But when they had come back to the wide camp of the Achaians
they hauled the black ship up on the mainland, high up
on the sand, and underneath her they fixed the long props.
Afterwards they scattered to their own ships and their shelters.
    But that other still sat in anger beside his swift ships,
Peleus' son divinely born, Achilleus of the swift feet.
Never now would he go to assemblies where men win glory,
never more into battle, but continued to waste his heart out
sitting there, though he longed always for the clamour and fighting.
    But when the twelfth dawn after this day appeared, the gods who
live forever came back to Olympos all in a body
and Zeus led them; nor did Thetis forget the entreaties
of her son, but she emerged from the sea's waves early
in the morning and went up to the tall sky and Olympos.
She found Kronos' broad-browed son apart from the others
sitting upon the highest peak of rugged Olympos.
She came and sat beside him with her left hand embracing
his knees, but took him underneath the chin with her right hand
and spoke in supplication to lord Zeus son of Kronos:
"Father Zeus, if ever before in word or action
I did you favour among the immortals, now grant what I ask for.
Now give honour to my son short-lived beyond all other
mortals. Since even now the lord of men Agamemnon
dishonours him, who has taken away his prize and keeps it.
Zeus of the counsels, lord of Olympos, now do him honour.
So long put strength into the Trojans, until the Achaians
give my son his rights, and his honour is increased among them."
    She spoke thus. But Zeus who gathers the clouds made no answer
but sat in silence a long time. And Thetis, as she had taken
his knees, clung fast to them and urged once more her question:
"Bend your head and promise me to accomplish this thing,
or else refuse it, you have nothing to fear, that I may know
by how much I am the most dishonoured of all gods."
    Deeply disturbed Zeus who gathers the clouds answered her:
"This is a disastrous matter when you set me in conflict
with Hera, and she troubles me with recriminations.
Since even as things are, forever among the immortals
she is at me and speaks of how I help the Trojans in battle.
Even so, go back again now, go away, for fear she
see us. I will look to these things that they be accomplished.
See then, I will bend my head that you may believe me.
For this among the immortal gods is the mightiest witness
I can give, and nothing I do shall be vain nor revocable
nor a thing unfulfilled when I bend my head in assent to it."
    He spoke, the son of Kronos, and nodded his head with the dark brows,
and the immortally anointed hair of the great god
swept from his divine head, and all Olympos was shaken.

So these two who had made their plans separated, and Thetis
leapt down again from shining Olympos into the sea's depth,
but Zeus went back to his own house, and all the gods rose up
from their chairs to greet the coming of their father, not one had courage
to keep his place as the father advanced, but stood up to greet him.
Thus he took his place on the throne; yet Hera was not
ignorant, having seen how he had been plotting counsels
with Thetis the silver-footed, the daughter of the sea's ancient,
and at once she spoke revilingly to Zeus son of Kronos:
"Treacherous one, what god has been plotting counsels with you?
Always it is dear to your heart in my absence to think of
secret things and decide upon them. Never have you patience
frankly to speak forth to me the thing that you purpose."
Then to her the father of gods and men made answer:
"Hera, do not go on hoping that you will hear all my
thoughts, since these will be too hard for you, though you are my wife.
Any thought that it is right for you to listen to, no one
neither man nor any immortal shall hear it before you.
But anything that apart from the rest of the gods I wish to
plan, do not always question each detail nor probe me."
Then the goddess the ox-eyed lady Hera answered:
"Majesty, son of Kronos, what sort of thing have you spoken?
Truly too much in time past I have not questioned nor probed you,
but you are entirely free to think out whatever pleases you.
Now, though, I am terribly afraid you were won over
by Thetis the silver-footed, the daughter of the sea's ancient.
For early in the morning she sat beside you and took your
knees, and I think you bowed your head in assent to do honour
to Achilleus, and to destroy many beside the ships of the Achaians."
Then in return Zeus who gathers the clouds made answer:
"Dear lady, I never escape you, you are always full of suspicion.
Yet thus you can accomplish nothing surely, but be more
distant from my heart than ever, and it will be the worse for you.
If what you say is true, then that is the way I wish it.
But go then, sit down in silence, and do as I tell you,
for fear all the gods, as many as are on Olympos, can do nothing
if I come close and lay my unconquerable hands upon you."
He spoke, and the goddess the ox-eyed lady Hera was frightened
and went and sat down in silence wrenching her heart to obedience,
and all the Uranian gods in the house of Zeus were troubled.
Hephaistos the renowned smith rose up to speak among them,
to bring comfort to his beloved mother, Hera of the white arms:
"This will be a disastrous matter and not endurable
if you two are to quarrel thus for the sake of mortals
and bring brawling among the gods. There will be no pleasure
in the stately feast at all, since vile things will be uppermost.
And I entreat my mother, though she herself understands it,
to be ingratiating toward our father Zeus, that no longer
our father may scold her and break up the quiet of our feasting.

For if the Olympian who handles the lightning should be minded
to hurl us out of our places, he is far too strong for any.
Do you therefore approach him again with words made gentle,
and at once the Olympian will be gracious again to us."
He spoke, and springing to his feet put a two-handled goblet
into his mother's hands and spoke again to her once more:
"Have patience, my mother, and endure it, though you be saddened,
for fear that, dear as you are, I see you before my own eyes
struck down, and then sorry though I be I shall not be able
to do anything. It is too hard to fight against the Olympian.
There was a time once before now I was minded to help you,
and he caught me by the foot and threw me from the magic threshold,
and all day long I dropped helpless, and about sunset
I landed in Lemnos, and there was not much life left in me.
After that fall it was the Sintian men who took care of me."
He spoke, and the goddess of the white arms Hera smiled at him,
and smiling she accepted the goblet out of her son's hand.
Thereafter beginning from the left he poured drinks for the other
gods, dipping up from the mixing bowl the sweet nectar.
But among the blessed immortals uncontrollable laughter
went up as they saw Hephaistos bustling about the palace.
Thus thereafter the whole day long until the sun went under
they feasted, nor was anyone's hunger denied a fair portion,
nor denied the beautifully wrought lyre in the hands of Apollo
nor the antiphonal sweet sound of the Muses singing.
Afterwards when the light of the flaming sun went under
they went away each one to sleep in his home where
for each one the far-renowned strong-handed Hephaistos
had built a house by means of his craftsmanship and cunning.
Zeus the Olympian and lord of the lightning went to
his own bed, where always he lay when sweet sleep came on him.
Going up to the bed he slept and Hera of the gold throne beside him.

Book 18

[Achilles' Shield]

So these fought on in the likeness of blazing fire. Meanwhile,
Antilochos came, a swift-footed messenger, to Achilleus,
and found him sitting in front of the steep-horned ships, thinking
over in his heart of things which had now been accomplished.
Disturbed, Achilleus spoke to the spirit in his own great heart:
"Ah me, how is it that once again the flowing-haired Achaians
are driven out of the plain on their ships in fear and confusion?
May the gods not accomplish vile sorrows upon the heart in me
in the way my mother once made it clear to me, when she told me
how while I yet lived the bravest of all the Myrmidons
must leave the light of the sun beneath the hands of the Trojans.
Surely, then, the strong son of Menoitios has perished.

Unhappy! and yet I told him, once he had beaten the fierce fire
off, to come back to the ships, not fight in strength against Hektor."
Now as he was pondering this in his heart and his spirit,
meanwhile the son of stately Nestor was drawing near him
and wept warm tears, and gave Achilleus his sorrowful message:
"Ah me, son of valiant Peleus; you must hear from me
the ghastly message of a thing I wish never had happened.
Patroklos has fallen, and now they are fighting over his body
which is naked. Hektor of the shining helm has taken his armour."
He spoke, and the black cloud of sorrow closed on Achilleus.
In both hands he caught up the grimy dust, and poured it
over his head and face, and fouled his handsome countenance,
and the black ashes were scattered over his immortal tunic.
And he himself, mightily in his might, in the dust lay
at length, and took and tore at his hair with his hands, and defiled it.
And the handmaidens Achilleus and Patroklos had taken
captive, stricken at heart cried out aloud, and came running
out of doors about valiant Achilleus, and all of them
beat their breasts with their hands, and the limbs went slack in each of them.
On the other side Antilochos mourned with him, letting the tears fall,
and held the hands of Achilleus as he grieved in his proud heart,
fearing Achilleus might cut his throat with the iron. He cried out
terribly, aloud, and the lady his mother heard him
as she sat in the depths of the sea at the side of her aged father,
and she cried shrill in turn, and the goddesses gathered about her,
all who along the depth of the sea were daughters of Nereus.
For Glauke was there, Kymodoke and Thaleia,
Nesaie and Speio and Thoë, and ox-eyed Halia;
Kymothoë was there, Aktaia and Limnoreia,
Melite and Iaira, Amphithoë and Agauë,
Doto and Proto, Dynamene and Pherousa,
Dexamene and Amphinome and Kallianeira;
Doris and Panope and glorious Galateia,
Nemertes and Apseudes and Kallianassa;
Klymene was there, Ianeira and Ianassa,
Maira and Oreithyia and lovely-haired Amatheia,
and the rest who along the depth of the sea were daughters of Nereus.
The silvery cave was filled with these, and together all of them
beat their breasts, and among them Thetis led out the threnody:
"Hear me, Nereids, my sisters; so you may all know
well all the sorrows that are in my heart, when you hear of them from me.
Ah me, my sorrow, the bitterness in this best of child-bearing,
since I gave birth to a son who was without fault and powerful,
conspicuous among heroes; and he shot up like a young tree,
and I nurtured him, like a tree grown in the pride of the orchard.
I sent him away with the curved ships into the land of Ilion
to fight with the Trojans; but I shall never again receive him
won home again to his country and into the house of Peleus.
Yet while I see him live and he looks on the sunlight, he has

sorrows, and though I go to him I can do nothing to help him.
Yet I shall go, to look on my dear son, and to listen
to the sorrow that has come to him as he stays back from the fighting."
So she spoke, and left the cave, and the others together
went with her in tears, and about them the wave of the water
was broken. Now these, when they came to the generous Troad,
followed each other out on the sea-shore, where close together
the ships of the Myrmidons were hauled up about swift Achilleus.
There as he sighed heavily the lady his mother stood by him
and cried out shrill and aloud, and took her son's head in her arms, then
sorrowing for him she spoke to him in winged words: "Why then,
child, do you lament? What sorrow has come to your heart now?
Speak out, do not hide it. These things are brought to accomplishment
through Zeus: in the way that you lifted your hands and prayed for,
that all the sons of the Achaians be pinned on their grounded vessels
by reason of your loss, and suffer things that are shameful."
Then sighing heavily Achilleus of the swift feet answered her:
"My mother, all these things the Olympian brought to accomplishment.
But what pleasure is this to me, since my dear companion has perished,
Patroklos, whom I loved beyond all other companions,
as well as my own life. I have lost him, and Hektor, who killed him,
has stripped away that gigantic armour, a wonder to look on
and splendid, which the gods gave Peleus, a glorious present,
on that day they drove you to the marriage bed of a mortal.
I wish you had gone on living then with the other goddesses
of the sea, and that Peleus had married some mortal woman.
As it is, there must be on your heart a numberless sorrow
for your son's death, since you can never again receive him
won home again to his country; since the spirit within does not drive me
to go on living and be among men, except on condition
that Hektor first be beaten down under my spear, lose his life
and pay the price for stripping Patroklos, the son of Menoitios."
Then in turn Thetis spoke to him, letting the tears fall:
"Then I must lose you soon, my child, by what you are saying,
since it is decreed your death must come soon after Hektor's."
Then deeply disturbed Achilleus of the swift feet answered her:
"I must die soon, then; since I was not to stand by my companion
when he was killed. And now, far away from the land of his fathers,
he has perished, and lacked my fighting strength to defend him.
Now, since I am not going back to the beloved land of my fathers,
since I was no light of safety to Patroklos, nor to my other
companions, who in their numbers went down before glorious Hektor,
but sit here beside my ships, a useless weight on the good land,
I, who am such as no other of the bronze-armoured Achaians
in battle, though there are others also better in council—
why, I wish that strife would vanish away from among gods and mortals,
and gall, which makes a man grow angry for all his great mind,
that gall of anger that swarms like smoke inside of a man's heart
and becomes a thing sweeter to him by far than the dripping of honey.

So it was here that the lord of men Agamemnon angered me.
Still, we will let all this be a thing of the past, and for all our
sorrow beat down by force the anger deeply within us.
Now I shall go, to overtake that killer of a dear life,
Hektor; then I will accept my own death, at whatever
time Zeus wishes to bring it about, and the other immortals.
For not even the strength of Herakles fled away from destruction,
although he was dearest of all to lord Zeus, son of Kronos,
but his fate beat him under, and the wearisome anger of Hera.
So I likewise, if such is the fate which has been wrought for me,
shall lie still, when I am dead. Now I must win excellent glory,
and drive some one of the women of Troy, or some deep-girdled
Dardanian woman, lifting up to her soft cheeks both hands
to wipe away the close bursts of tears in her lamentation,
and learn that I stayed too long out of the fighting. Do not
hold me back from the fight, though you love me. You will not persuade me."
In turn the goddess Thetis of the silver feet answered him:
"Yes, it is true, my child, this is no cowardly action,
to beat aside sudden death from your afflicted companions.
Yet, see now, your splendid armour, glaring and brazen,
is held among the Trojans, and Hektor of the shining helmet
wears it on his own shoulders, and glories in it. Yet I think
he will not glory for long, since his death stands very close to him.
Therefore do not yet go into the grind of the war god,
not before with your own eyes you see me come back to you.
For I am coming to you at dawn and as the sun rises
bringing splendid armour to you from the lord Hephaistos."
So she spoke, and turned, and went away from her son,
and turning now to her sisters of the sea she spoke to them:
"Do you now go back into the wide fold of the water
to visit the ancient of the sea and the house of our father,
and tell him everything. I am going to tall Olympos
and to Hephaistos, the glorious smith, if he might be willing
to give me for my son renowned and radiant armour."
She spoke, and they plunged back beneath the wave of the water,
while she the goddess Thetis of the silver feet went onward
to Olympos, to bring back to her son the glorious armour.
So her feet carried her to Olympos; meanwhile the Achaians
with inhuman clamour before the attack of manslaughtering Hektor
fled until they were making for their own ships and the Hellespont;
nor could the strong-greaved Achaians have dragged the body
of Patroklos, henchman of Achilleus, from under the missiles,
for once again the men and the horses came over upon him,
and Hektor, Priam's son, who fought like a flame in his fury.
Three times from behind glorious Hektor caught him
by the feet, trying to drag him, and called aloud on the Trojans.
Three times the two Aiantes with their battle-fury upon them
beat him from the corpse, but he, steady in the confidence of his great strength,
kept making, now a rush into the crowd, or again at another time

stood fast, with his great cry, but gave not a bit of ground backward.
And as herdsmen who dwell in the fields are not able to frighten
a tawny lion in his great hunger away from a carcass,
so the two Aiantes, marshals of men, were not able
to scare Hektor, Priam's son, away from the body.
And now he would have dragged it away and won glory forever
had not swift wind-footed Iris come running from Olympos
with a message for Peleus' son to arm. She came secretly
from Zeus and the other gods, since it was Hera who sent her.
She came and stood close to him and addressed him in winged words:
"Rise up, son of Peleus, most terrifying of all men.
Defend Patroklos, for whose sake the terrible fighting
stands now in front of the ships. They are destroying each other;
the Achaians fight in defence over the fallen body
while the others, the Trojans, are rushing to drag the corpse off
to windy Ilion, and beyond all glorious Hektor
rages to haul it away, since the anger within him is urgent
to cut the head from the soft neck and set it on sharp stakes.
Up, then, lie here no longer; let shame come into your heart, lest
Patroklos become sport for the dogs of Troy to worry,
your shame, if the body goes from here with defilement upon it."
Then in turn Achilleus of the swift feet answered her:
"Divine Iris, what god sent you to me with a message?"
Then in turn swift wind-footed Iris spoke to him:
"Hera sent me, the honoured wife of Zeus; but the son of
Kronos, who sits on high, does not know this, nor any other
immortal, of all those who dwell by the snows of Olympos."
Then in answer to her spoke Achilleus of the swift feet:
"How shall I go into the fighting? They have my armour.
And my beloved mother told me I must not be armoured,
not before with my own eyes I see her come back to me.
She promised she would bring magnificent arms from Hephaistos.
Nor do I know of another whose glorious armour I could wear
unless it were the great shield of Telamonian Aias.
But he himself wears it, I think, and goes in the foremost
of the spear-fight over the body of fallen Patroklos."
Then in turn swift wind-footed Iris spoke to him:
"Yes, we also know well how they hold your glorious armour.
But go to the ditch, and show yourself as you are to the Trojans,
if perhaps the Trojans might be frightened, and give way
from their attack, and the fighting sons of the Achaians get wind
again after hard work. There is little breathing space in the fighting."
So speaking Iris of the swift feet went away from him;
but Achilleus, the beloved of Zeus, rose up, and Athene
swept about his powerful shoulders the fluttering aegis;
and she, the divine among goddesses, about his head circled
a golden cloud, and kindled from it a flame far-shining.
As when a flare goes up into the high air from a city
from an island far away, with enemies fighting about it

who all day long are in the hateful division of Ares
fighting from their own city, but as the sun goes down signal
fires blaze out one after another, so that the glare goes
pulsing high for men of the neighbouring islands to see it,
in case they might come over in ships to beat off the enemy;
so from the head of Achilleus the blaze shot into the bright air.
He went from the wall and stood by the ditch, nor mixed with the other
Achaians, since he followed the close command of his mother.
There he stood, and shouted, and from her place Pallas Athene
gave cry, and drove an endless terror upon the Trojans.
As loud as comes the voice that is screamed out by a trumpet
by murderous attackers who beleaguer a city,
so then high and clear went up the voice of Aiakides.[1]
But the Trojans, when they heard the brazen voice of Aiakides,
the heart was shaken in all, and the very floating-maned horses
turned their chariots about, since their hearts saw the coming afflictions.
The charioteers were dumbfounded as they saw the unwearied dangerous
fire that played above the head of great-hearted Peleion
blazing, and kindled by the goddess grey-eyed Athene.
Three times across the ditch brilliant Achilleus gave his great cry,
and three times the Trojans and their renowned companions were routed.
There at that time twelve of the best men among them perished
upon their own chariots and spears. Meanwhile the Achaians
gladly pulled Patroklos out from under the missiles
and set him upon a litter, and his own companions about him
stood mourning, and along with them swift-footed Achilleus
went, letting fall warm tears as he saw his steadfast companion
lying there on a carried litter and torn with the sharp bronze,
the man he had sent off before with horses and chariot
into the fighting; who never again came home to be welcomed.
    Now the lady Hera of the ox eyes drove the unwilling
weariless sun god to sink in the depth of the Ocean,
and the sun went down, and the brilliant Achaians gave over
their strong fighting, and the doubtful collision of battle.
    The Trojans on the other side moved from the strong encounter
in their turn, and unyoked their running horses from under the chariots,
and gathered into assembly before taking thought for their supper.
They stood on their feet in assembly, nor did any man have the patience
to sit down, but the terror was on them all, seeing that Achilleus
had appeared, after he had stayed so long from the difficult fighting.
First to speak among them was the careful Poulydamas,
Panthoös' son, who alone of them looked before and behind him.
He was companion to Hektor, and born on the same night with him,
but he was better in words, the other with the spear far better.
He in kind intention toward all stood forth and addressed them:
"Now take careful thought, dear friends; for I myself urge you
to go back into the city and not wait for the divine dawn

1. Achilleus, grandson of Aiakos, himself a son of Zeus.

in the plain beside the ships. We are too far from the wall now.
While this man was still angry with great Agamemnon,
for all that time the Achaians were easier men to fight with.
For I also used then to be one who was glad to sleep out
near their ships, and I hoped to capture the oarswept vessels.
But now I terribly dread the swift-footed son of Peleus.
So violent is the valour in him, he will not be willing
to stay here in the plain, where now Achaians and Trojans
from either side sunder between them the wrath of the war god.
With him, the fight will be for the sake of our city and women.
Let us go into the town; believe me; thus it will happen.
For this present, immortal night has stopped the swift-footed
son of Peleus, but if he catches us still in this place
tomorrow, and drives upon us in arms, a man will be well
aware of him, be glad to get back into sacred Ilion,
the man who escapes; there will be many Trojans the vultures
and dogs will feed on. But let such a word be out of my hearing!
If all of us will do as I say, though it hurts us to do it,
this night we will hold our strength in the market place, and the great walls
and the gateways, and the long, smooth-planed, close-joined gate timbers
that close to fit them shall defend our city. Then, early
in the morning, under dawn, we shall arm ourselves in our war gear
and take stations along the walls. The worse for him, if he endeavours
to come away from the ships and fight us here for our city.
Back he must go to his ships again, when he wears out the strong necks
of his horses, driving them at a gallop everywhere by the city.
His valour will not give him leave to burst in upon us
nor sack our town. Sooner the circling dogs will feed on him."

Then looking darkly at him Hektor of the shining helm spoke:
"Poulydamas, these things that you argue please me no longer
when you tell us to go back again and be cooped in our city.
Have you not all had your glut of being fenced in our outworks?
There was a time when mortal men would speak of the city
of Priam as a place with much gold and much bronze. But now
the lovely treasures that lay away in our houses have vanished,
and many possessions have been sold and gone into Phrygia
and into Maionia the lovely, when great Zeus was angry.
But now, when the son of devious-devising Kronos has given
me the winning of glory by the ships, to pin the Achaians
on the sea, why, fool, no longer show these thoughts to our people.
Not one of the Trojans will obey you. I shall not allow it.
Come, then, do as I say and let us all be persuaded.
Now, take your supper by positions along the encampment,
and do not forget your watch, and let every man be wakeful.
And if any Trojan is strongly concerned about his possessions,
let him gather them and give them to the people, to use them in common.
It is better for one of us to enjoy them than for the Achaians.
In the morning, under dawn, we shall arm ourselves in our war gear
and waken the bitter god of war by the hollow vessels.

If it is true that brilliant Achilleus is risen beside their
ships, then the worse for him if he tries it, since I for my part
will not run from him out of the sorrowful battle, but rather
stand fast, to see if he wins the great glory, or if I can win it.
The war god is impartial. Before now he has killed the killer."
So spoke Hektor, and the Trojans thundered to hear him;
fools, since Pallas Athene had taken away the wits from them.
They gave their applause to Hektor in his counsel of evil,
but none to Poulydamas, who had spoken good sense before them.
They took their supper along the encampment. Meanwhile the Achaians
mourned all night in lamentation over Patroklos.
Peleus' son led the thronging chant of their lamentation,
and laid his manslaughtering hands over the chest of his dear friend
with outbursts of incessant grief. As some great bearded lion
when some man, a deer hunter, has stolen his cubs away from him
out of the close wood; the lion comes back too late, and is anguished,
and turns into many valleys quartering after the man's trail
on the chance of finding him, and taken with bitter anger;
so he, groaning heavily, spoke out to the Myrmidons:
"Ah me. It was an empty word I cast forth on that day
when in his halls I tried to comfort the hero Menoitios.
I told him I would bring back his son in glory to Opous
with Ilion sacked, and bringing his share of war spoils allotted.
But Zeus does not bring to accomplishment all thoughts in men's minds.
Thus it is destiny for us both to stain the same soil
here in Troy; since I shall never come home, and my father,
Peleus the aged rider, will not welcome me in his great house,
nor Thetis my mother, but in this place the earth will receive me.
But seeing that it is I, Patroklos, who follow you underground,
I will not bury you till I bring to this place the armour
and the head of Hektor, since he was your great-hearted murderer.
Before your burning pyre I shall behead twelve glorious
children of the Trojans, for my anger over your slaying.
Until then, you shall lie where you are in front of my curved ships
and beside you women of Troy and deep-girdled Dardanian women
shall sorrow for you night and day and shed tears for you, those whom
you and I worked hard to capture by force and the long spear
in days when we were storming the rich cities of mortals."
So speaking brilliant Achilleus gave orders to his companions
to set a great cauldron across the fire, so that with all speed
they could wash away the clotted blood from Patroklos.
They set up over the blaze of the fire a bath-water cauldron
and poured water into it and put logs underneath and kindled them.
The fire worked on the swell of the cauldron, and the water heated.
But when the water had come to a boil in the shining bronze, then
they washed the body and anointed it softly with olive oil
and stopped the gashes in his body with stored-up unguents
and laid him on a bed, and shrouded him in a thin sheet
from head to foot, and covered that over with a white mantle.

Then all night long, gathered about Achilleus of the swift feet,
the Myrmidons mourned for Patroklos and lamented over him.
But Zeus spoke to Hera, who was his wife and his sister:
"So you have acted, then, lady Hera of the ox eyes.
You have roused up Achilleus of the swift feet. It must be then
that the flowing-haired Achaians are born of your own generation."
Then the goddess the ox-eyed lady Hera answered him:
"Majesty, son of Kronos, what sort of thing have you spoken?
Even one who is mortal will try to accomplish his purpose
for another, though he be a man and knows not such wisdom as we do.
As for me then, who claim I am highest of all the goddesses,
both ways, since I am eldest born and am called your consort,
yours, and you in turn are lord over all the immortals,
how could I not weave sorrows for the men of Troy, when I hate them?"
Now as these two were saying things like this to each other,
Thetis of the silver feet came to the house of Hephaistos,
imperishable, starry, and shining among the immortals,
built in bronze for himself by the god of the dragging footsteps.
She found him sweating as he turned here and there to his bellows
busily, since he was working on twenty tripods
which were to stand against the wall of his strong-founded dwelling.
And he had set golden wheels underneath the base of each one
so that of their own motion they could wheel into the immortal
gathering, and return to his house: a wonder to look at.
These were so far finished, but the elaborate ear handles
were not yet on. He was forging these, and beating the chains out.
As he was at work on this in his craftsmanship and his cunning
meanwhile the goddess Thetis the silver-footed drew near him.
Charis of the shining veil saw her as she came forward,
she, the lovely goddess the renowned strong-armed one had married.
She came, and caught her hand and called her by name and spoke to her:
"Why is it, Thetis of the light robes, you have come to our house now?
We honour you and love you; but you have not come much before this.
But come in with me, so I may put entertainment before you."
She spoke, and, shining among divinities, led the way forward
and made Thetis sit down in a chair that was wrought elaborately
and splendid with silver nails, and under it was a footstool.
She called to Hephaistos the renowned smith and spoke a word to him:
"Hephaistos, come this way; here is Thetis, who has need of you."
Hearing her the renowned smith of the strong arms answered her:
"Then there is a goddess we honour and respect in our house.
She saved me when I suffered much at the time of my great fall
through the will of my own brazen-faced mother, who wanted
to hide me, for being lame. Then my soul would have taken much suffering
had not Eurynome and Thetis caught me and held me,
Eurynome, daughter of Ocean, whose stream bends back in a circle.
With them I worked nine years as a smith, and wrought many intricate
things; pins that bend back, curved clasps, cups, necklaces, working
there in the hollow of the cave, and the stream of Ocean around us

went on forever with its foam and its murmur. No other
among the gods or among mortal men knew about us
except Eurynome and Thetis. They knew, since they saved me.
Now she has come into our house; so I must by all means
do everything to give recompense to lovely-haired Thetis
for my life. Therefore set out before her fair entertainment
while I am putting away my bellows and all my instruments."
He spoke, and took the huge blower off from the block of the anvil
limping; and yet his shrunken legs moved lightly beneath him.
He set the bellows away from the fire, and gathered and put away
all the tools with which he worked in a silver strongbox.
Then with a sponge he wiped clean his forehead, and both hands,
and his massive neck and hairy chest, and put on a tunic,
and took up a heavy stick in his hand, and went to the doorway
limping. And in support of their master moved his attendants.
These are golden, and in appearance like living young women.
There is intelligence in their hearts, and there is speech in them
and strength, and from the immortal gods they have learned how to do things.
These stirred nimbly in support of their master, and moving
near to where Thetis sat in her shining chair, Hephaistos
caught her by the hand and called her by name and spoke a word to her:
"Why is it, Thetis of the light robes, you have come to our house now?
We honour you and love you; but you have not come much before this.
Speak forth what is in your mind. My heart is urgent to do it
if I can, and if it is a thing that can be accomplished."
Then in turn Thetis answered him, letting the tears fall:
"Hephaistos, is there among all the goddesses on Olympos
one who in her heart has endured so many grim sorrows
as the griefs Zeus, son of Kronos, has given me beyond others?
Of all the other sisters of the sea he gave me to a mortal,
to Peleus, Aiakos' son, and I had to endure mortal marriage
though much against my will. And now he, broken by mournful
old age, lies away in his halls. Yet I have other troubles.
For since he has given me a son to bear and to raise up
conspicuous among heroes, and he shot up like a young tree,
I nurtured him, like a tree grown in the pride of the orchard.
I sent him away in the curved ships to the land of Ilion
to fight with the Trojans; but I shall never again receive him
won home again to his country and into the house of Peleus.
Yet while I see him live and he looks on the sunlight, he has
sorrows, and though I go to him I can do nothing to help him.
And the girl the sons of the Achaians chose out for his honour
powerful Agamemnon took her away again out of his hands.
For her his heart has been wasting in sorrow; but meanwhile the Trojans
pinned the Achaians against their grounded ships, and would not
let them win outside, and the elders of the Argives entreated
my son, and named the many glorious gifts they would give him.
But at that time he refused himself to fight the death from them;

nevertheless he put his own armour upon Patroklos
and sent him into the fighting, and gave many men to go with him.
All day they fought about the Skaian Gates, and on that day
they would have stormed the city, if only Phoibos Apollo
had not killed the fighting son of Menoitios there in the first ranks
after he had wrought much damage, and given the glory to Hektor.
Therefore now I come to your knees; so might you be willing
to give me for my short-lived son a shield and a helmet
and two beautiful greaves[2] fitted with clasps for the ankles
and a corselet. What he had was lost with his steadfast companion
when the Trojans killed him. Now my son lies on the ground, heart
sorrowing."

Hearing her the renowned smith of the strong arms answered her:
"Do not fear. Let not these things be a thought in your mind.
And I wish that I could hide him away from death and its sorrow
at that time when his hard fate comes upon him, as surely
as there shall be fine armour for him, such as another
man out of many men shall wonder at, when he looks on it."

So he spoke, and left her there, and went to his bellows.
He turned these toward the fire and gave them their orders for working.
And the bellows, all twenty of them, blew on the crucibles,
from all directions blasting forth wind to blow the flames high
now as he hurried to be at this place and now at another,
wherever Hephaistos might wish them to blow, and the work went forward.
He cast on the fire bronze which is weariless, and tin with it
and valuable gold, and silver, and thereafter set forth
upon its standard the great anvil, and gripped in one hand
the ponderous hammer, while in the other he grasped the pincers.

First of all he forged a shield that was huge and heavy,
elaborating it about, and threw around it a shining
triple rim that glittered, and the shield strap was cast of silver.
There were five folds composing the shield itself, and upon it
he elaborated many things in his skill and craftsmanship.

He made the earth upon it, and the sky, and the sea's water,
and the tireless sun, and the moon waxing into her fullness,
and on it all the constellations that festoon the heavens,
the Pleiades and the Hyades and the strength of Orion
and the Bear, whom men give also the name of the Wagon,
who turns about in a fixed place and looks at Orion
and she alone is never plunged in the wash of the Ocean.

On it he wrought in all their beauty two cities of mortal
men. And there were marriages in one, and festivals.
They were leading the brides along the city from their maiden chambers
under the flaring of torches, and the loud bride song was arising.
The young men followed the circles of the dance, and among them
the flutes and lyres kept up their clamour as in the meantime
the women standing each at the door of her court admired them.

2. Shin-guards.

The people were assembled in the market place, where a quarrel
had arisen, and two men were disputing over the blood price
for a man who had been killed. One man promised full restitution
in a public statement, but the other refused and would accept nothing.
Both then made for an arbitrator, to have a decision;
and people were speaking up on either side, to help both men.
But the heralds kept the people in hand, as meanwhile the elders
were in session on benches of polished stone in the sacred circle
and held in their hands the staves of the heralds who lift their voices.
The two men rushed before these, and took turns speaking their cases,
and between them lay on the ground two talents of gold, to be given
to that judge who in this case spoke the straightest opinion.
    But around the other city were lying two forces of armed men
shining in their war gear. For one side counsel was divided
whether to storm and sack, or share between both sides the property
and all the possessions the lovely citadel held hard within it.
But the city's people were not giving way, and armed for an ambush.
Their beloved wives and their little children stood on the rampart
to hold it, and with them the men with age upon them, but meanwhile
the others went out. And Ares led them, and Pallas Athene.
These were gold, both, and golden raiment upon them, and they were
beautiful and huge in their armour, being divinities,
and conspicuous from afar, but the people around them were smaller.
These, when they were come to the place that was set for their ambush,
in a river, where there was a watering place for all animals,
there they sat down in place shrouding themselves in the bright bronze.
But apart from these were sitting two men to watch for the rest of them
and waiting until they could see the sheep and the shambling cattle,
who appeared presently, and two herdsmen went along with them
playing happily on pipes, and took no thought of the treachery.
Those others saw them, and made a rush, and quickly thereafter
cut off on both sides the herds of cattle and the beautiful
flocks of shining sheep, and killed the shepherds upon them.
But the other army, as soon as they heard the uproar arising
from the cattle, as they sat in their councils, suddenly mounted
behind their light-foot horses, and went after, and soon overtook them.
These stood their ground and fought a battle by the banks of the river,
and they were making casts at each other with their spears bronze-headed;
and Hate was there with Confusion among them, and Death the destructive;
she was holding a live man with a new wound, and another
one unhurt, and dragged a dead man by the feet through the carnage.
The clothing upon her shoulders showed strong red with the men's blood.
All closed together like living men and fought with each other
and dragged away from each other the corpses of those who had fallen.
    He made upon it a soft field, the pride of the tilled land,
wide and triple-ploughed, with many ploughmen upon it
who wheeled their teams at the turn and drove them in either direction.
And as these making their turn would reach the end-strip of the field,
a man would come up to them at this point and hand them a flagon

of honey-sweet wine, and they would turn again to the furrows
in their haste to come again to the end-strip of the deep field.
The earth darkened behind them and looked like earth that has been ploughed
though it was gold. Such was the wonder of the shield's forging.

He made on it the precinct of a king, where the labourers
were reaping, with the sharp reaping hooks in their hands. Of the cut swathes
some fell along the lines of reaping, one after another,
while the sheaf-binders caught up others and tied them with bind-ropes.
There were three sheaf-binders who stood by, and behind them
were children picking up the cut swathes, and filled their arms with them
and carried and gave them always; and by them the king in silence
and holding his staff stood near the line of the reapers, happily.
And apart and under a tree the heralds made a feast ready
and trimmed a great ox they had slaughtered. Meanwhile the women
scattered, for the workmen to eat, abundant white barley.

He made on it a great vineyard heavy with clusters,
lovely and in gold, but the grapes upon it were darkened
and the vines themselves stood out through poles of silver. About them
he made a field-ditch of dark metal, and drove all around this
a fence of tin; and there was only one path to the vineyard,
and along it ran the grape-bearers for the vineyard's stripping.
Young girls and young men, in all their light-hearted innocence,
carried the kind, sweet fruit away in their woven baskets,
and in their midst a youth with a singing lyre played charmingly
upon it for them, and sang the beautiful song for Linos
in a light voice, and they followed him, and with singing and whistling
and light dance-steps of their feet kept time to the music.

He made upon it a herd of horn-straight oxen. The cattle
were wrought of gold and of tin, and thronged in speed and with lowing
out of the dung of the farmyard to a pasturing place by a sounding
river, and beside the moving field of a reed bed.
The herdsmen were of gold who went along with the cattle,
four of them, and nine dogs shifting their feet followed them.
But among the foremost of the cattle two formidable lions
had caught hold of a bellowing bull, and he with loud lowings
was dragged away, as the dogs and the young men went in pursuit of him.
But the two lions, breaking open the hide of the great ox,
gulped the black blood and the inward guts, as meanwhile the herdsmen
were in the act of setting and urging the quick dogs on them.
But they, before they could get their teeth in, turned back from the lions,
but would come and take their stand very close, and bayed, and kept clear.

And the renowned smith of the strong arms made on it a meadow
large and in a lovely valley for the glimmering sheepflocks,
with dwelling places upon it, and covered shelters, and sheepfolds.

And the renowned smith of the strong arms made elaborate on it
a dancing floor, like that which once in the wide spaces of Knosos[3]
Daidalos[4] built for Ariadne of the lovely tresses.

3. Cretan city of King Minos, the father of Ariadne. 4. Mythic architect, artist, and inventor.

And there were young men on it and young girls, sought for their beauty
with gifts of oxen, dancing, and holding hands at the wrist. These
wore, the maidens long light robes, but the men wore tunics
of finespun work and shining softly, touched with olive oil.
And the girls wore fair garlands on their heads, while the young men
carried golden knives that hung from sword-belts of silver.
At whiles on their understanding feet they would run very lightly,
as when a potter crouching makes trial of his wheel, holding
it close in his hands, to see if it will run smooth. At another
time they would form rows, and run, rows crossing each other.
And around the lovely chorus of dancers stood a great multitude
happily watching, while among the dancers two acrobats
led the measures of song and dance revolving among them.
He made on it the great strength of the Ocean River
which ran around the uttermost rim of the shield's strong structure.
Then after he had wrought this shield, which was huge and heavy,
he wrought for him a corselet brighter than fire in its shining,
and wrought him a helmet, massive and fitting close to his temples,
lovely and intricate work, and laid a gold top-ridge along it,
and out of pliable tin wrought him leg-armour. Thereafter
when the renowned smith of the strong arms had finished the armour
he lifted it and laid it before the mother of Achilleus.
And she like a hawk came sweeping down from the snows of Olympos
and carried with her the shining armour, the gift of Hephaistos.

Book 22

[THE DEATH OF HEKTOR]

So along the city the Trojans, who had run like fawns, dried
the sweat off from their bodies and drank and slaked their thirst, leaning
along the magnificent battlements. Meanwhile the Achaians
sloping their shields across their shoulders came close to the rampart.
But his deadly fate held Hektor shackled, so that he stood fast
in front of Ilion and the Skaian gates. Now Phoibos
Apollo spoke aloud to Peleion: "Why, son of Peleus,
do you keep after me in the speed of your feet, being mortal
while I am an immortal god? Even yet you have not
seen that I am a god, but strain after me in your fury.
Now hard fighting with the Trojans whom you stampeded means nothing
to you. They are crowded in the city, but you bent away here.
You will never kill me. I am not one who is fated."
Deeply vexed Achilleus of the swift feet spoke to him:
"You have balked me, striker from afar, most malignant of all gods,
when you turned me here away from the rampart, else many Trojans
would have caught the soil in their teeth before they got back into Ilion.
Now you have robbed me of great glory, and rescued these people
lightly, since you have no retribution to fear hereafter.

Else I would punish you, if only the strength were in me."
He spoke, and stalked away against the city, with high thoughts
in mind, and in tearing speed, like a racehorse with his chariot
who runs lightly as he pulls the chariot over the flat land.
Such was the action of Achilleus in feet and quick knees.
The aged Priam was the first of all whose eyes saw him
as he swept across the flat land in full shining, like that star
which comes on in the autumn and whose conspicuous brightness
far outshines the stars that are numbered in the night's darkening,
the star they give the name of Orion's Dog, which is brightest
among the stars, and yet is wrought as a sign of evil
and brings on the great fever for unfortunate mortals.
Such was the flare of the bronze that girt his chest in his running.
The old man groaned aloud and with both hands high uplifted
beat his head, and groaned amain, and spoke supplicating
his beloved son, who there still in front of the gateway
stood fast in determined fury to fight with Achilleus.
The old man stretching his hands out called pitifully to him:
"Hektor, beloved child, do not wait the attack of this man
alone, away from the others. You might encounter your destiny
beaten down by Peleion, since he is far stronger than you are.
A hard man: I wish he were as beloved of the immortal
as loved by me. Soon he would lie dead, and the dogs and the vultures
would eat him, and bitter sorrow so be taken from my heart.
He has made me desolate of my sons, who were brave and many.
He killed them, or sold them away among the far-lying islands.
Even now there are two sons, Lykaon and Polydoros,
whom I cannot see among the Trojans pent up in the city,
sons Laothoë a princess among women bore to me.
But if these are alive somewhere in the army, then I can
set them free for bronze and gold; it is there inside, since
Altes the aged and renowned gave much with his daughter.
But if they are dead already and gone down to the house of Hades,
it is sorrow to our hearts, who bore them, myself and their mother,
but to the rest of the people a sorrow that will be fleeting
beside their sorrow for you, if you go down before Achilleus.
Come then inside the wall, my child, so that you can rescue
the Trojans and the women of Troy, neither win the high glory
for Peleus' son, and yourself be robbed of your very life. Oh, take
pity on me, the unfortunate still alive, still sentient
but ill-starred, whom the father, Kronos' son, on the threshold of old age
will blast with hard fate, after I have looked upon evils
and seen my sons destroyed and my daughters dragged away captive
and the chambers of marriage wrecked and the innocent children taken
and dashed to the ground in the hatefulness of war, and the wives
of my sons dragged off by the accursed hands of the Achaians.
And myself last of all, my dogs in front of my doorway
will rip me raw, after some man with stroke of the sharp bronze
spear, or with spearcast, has torn the life out of my body;

those dogs I raised in my halls to be at my table, to guard my
gates, who will lap my blood in the savagery of their anger
and then lie down in my courts. For a young man all is decorous
when he is cut down in battle and torn with the sharp bronze, and lies there
dead, and though dead still all that shows about him is beautiful;
but when an old man is dead and down, and the dogs mutilate
the grey head and the grey beard and the parts that are secret,
this, for all sad mortality, is the sight most pitiful."
So the old man spoke, and in his hands seizing the grey hairs
tore them from his head, but could not move the spirit in Hektor.
And side by side with him his mother in tears was mourning
and laid the fold of her bosom bare and with one hand held out
a breast, and wept her tears for him and called to him in winged words:
"Hektor, my child, look upon these and obey, and take pity
on me, if ever I gave you the breast to quiet your sorrow.
Remember all these things, dear child, and from inside the wall
beat off this grim man. Do not go out as champion against him,
o hard one; for if he kills you I can no longer
mourn you on the death-bed, sweet branch, o child of my bearing,
nor can your generous wife mourn you, but a big way from us
beside the ships of the Argives the running dogs will feed on you."
So these two in tears and with much supplication called out
to their dear son, but could not move the spirit in Hektor,
but he awaited Achilleus as he came on, gigantic.
But as a snake waits for a man by his hole, in the mountains,
glutted with evil poisons, and the fell venom has got inside him,
and coiled about the hole he stares malignant, so Hektor
would not give ground but kept unquenched the fury within him
and sloped his shining shield against the jut of the bastion.
Deeply troubled he spoke to his own great-hearted spirit:
"Ah me! If I go now inside the wall and the gateway,
Poulydamas will be first to put a reproach upon me,
since he tried to make me lead the Trojans inside the city
on that accursed night when brilliant Achilleus rose up,
and I would not obey him, but that would have been far better.
Now, since by my own recklessness I have ruined my people,
I feel shame before the Trojans and the Trojan women with trailing
robes, that someone who is less of a man than I will say of me:
'Hektor believed in his own strength and ruined his people.'
Thus they will speak; and as for me, it would be much better
at that time, to go against Achilleus, and slay him, and come back,
or else be killed by him in glory in front of the city.
Or if again I set down my shield massive in the middle
and my ponderous helm, and lean my spear up against the rampart
and go out as I am to meet Achilleus the blameless
and promise to give back Helen, and with her all her possessions,
all those things that once in the hollow ships Alexandros[1]

1. Paris.

brought back to Troy, and these were the beginning of the quarrel;
to give these to Atreus' sons to take away, and for the Achaians
also to divide up all that is hidden within the city,
and take an oath thereafter for the Trojans in conclave
not to hide anything away, but distribute all of it,
as much as the lovely citadel keeps guarded within it;
yet still, why does the heart within me debate on these things?
I might go up to him, and he take no pity upon me
nor respect my position, but kill me naked so, as if I were
a woman, once I stripped my armour from me. There is no
way any more from a tree or a rock to talk to him gently
whispering like a young man and a young girl, in the way
a young man and a young maiden whisper together.
Better to bring on the fight with him as soon as it may be.
We shall see to which one the Olympian grants the glory."

So he pondered, waiting, but Achilleus was closing upon him
in the likeness of the lord of battles, the helm-shining warrior,
and shaking from above his shoulder the dangerous Pelian
ash spear, while the bronze that closed about him was shining
like the flare of blazing fire or the sun in its rising.
And the shivers took hold of Hektor when he saw him, and he could no longer
stand his ground there, but left the gates behind, and fled, frightened,
and Peleus' son went after him in the confidence of his quick feet.
As when a hawk in the mountains who moves lightest of things flying
makes his effortless swoop for a trembling dove, but she slips away
from beneath and flies and he shrill screaming close after her
plunges for her again and again, heart furious to take her;
so Achilleus went straight for him in fury, but Hektor
fled away under the Trojan wall and moved his knees rapidly.
They raced along by the watching point and the windy fig tree
always away from under the wall and along the wagon-way
and came to the two sweet-running well springs. There there are double
springs of water that jet up, the springs of whirling Skamandros.
One of these runs hot water and the steam on all sides
of it rises as if from a fire that was burning inside it.
But the other in the summer-time runs water that is like hail
or chill snow or ice that forms from water. Beside these
in this place, and close to them, are the washing-hollows
of stone, and magnificent, where the wives of the Trojans and their lovely
daughters washed the clothes to shining, in the old days
when there was peace, before the coming of the sons of the Achaians.
They ran beside these, one escaping, the other after him.
It was a great man who fled, but far better he who pursued him
rapidly, since here was no festal beast, no ox-hide
they strove for, for these are prizes that are given men for their running.
No, they ran for the life of Hektor, breaker of horses.
As when about the turnposts racing single-foot horses
run at full speed, when a great prize is laid up for their winning,

a tripod or a woman, in games for a man's funeral,
so these two swept whirling about the city of Priam
in the speed of their feet, while all the gods were looking upon them.
First to speak among them was the father of gods and mortals:
"Ah me, this is a man beloved whom now my eyes watch
being chased around the wall; my heart is mourning for Hektor
who has burned in my honour many thigh pieces of oxen
on the peaks of Ida with all her folds, or again on the uttermost
part of the citadel, but now the brilliant Achilleus
drives him in speed of his feet around the city of Priam.
Come then, you immortals, take thought and take counsel, whether
to rescue this man or whether to make him, for all his valour,
go down under the hands of Achilleus, the son of Peleus."
Then in answer the goddess grey-eyed Athene spoke to him:
"Father of the shining bolt, dark misted, what is this you said?
Do you wish to bring back a man who is mortal, one long since
doomed by his destiny, from ill-sounding death and release him?
Do it, then; but not all the rest of us gods shall approve you."
Then Zeus the gatherer of the clouds spoke to her in answer:
"Tritogeneia, dear daughter, do not lose heart; for I say this
not in outright anger, and my meaning toward you is kindly.
Act as your purpose would have you do, and hold back no longer."
So he spoke, and stirred on Athene, who was eager before this,
and she went in a flash of speed down the pinnacles of Olympos.
But swift Achilleus kept unremittingly after Hektor,
chasing him, as a dog in the mountains who has flushed from his covert
a deer's fawn follows him through the folding ways and the valleys,
and though the fawn crouched down under a bush and be hidden
he keeps running and noses him out until he comes on him;
so Hektor could not lose himself from swift-footed Peleion.
If ever he made a dash right on for the gates of Dardanos
to get quickly under the strong-built bastions, endeavouring
that they from above with missiles thrown might somehow defend him,
each time Achilleus would get in front and force him to turn back
into the plain, and himself kept his flying course next the city.
As in a dream a man is not able to follow one who runs
from him, nor can the runner escape, nor the other pursue him,
so he could not run him down in his speed, nor the other get clear.
How then could Hektor have escaped the death spirits, had not
Apollo, for this last and uttermost time, stood by him
close, and driven strength into him, and made his knees light?
But brilliant Achilleus kept shaking his head at his own people
and would not let them throw their bitter projectiles at Hektor
for fear the thrower might win the glory, and himself come second.
But when for the fourth time they had come around to the well springs
then the Father balanced his golden scales, and in them
he set two fateful portions of death, which lays men prostrate,
one for Achilleus, and one for Hektor, breaker of horses,
and balanced it by the middle; and Hektor's death-day was heavier

and dragged downward toward death, and Phoibos Apollo forsook him.
But the goddess grey-eyed Athene came now to Peleion
and stood close beside him and addressed him in winged words: "Beloved
of Zeus, shining Achilleus, I am hopeful now that you and I
will take back great glory to the ships of the Achaians, after
we have killed Hektor, for all his slakeless fury for battle.
Now there is no way for him to get clear away from us,
not though Apollo who strikes from afar should be willing to undergo
much, and wallow before our father Zeus of the aegis.
Stand you here then and get your wind again, while I go
to this man and persuade him to stand up to you in combat.
So spoke Athene, and he was glad at heart, and obeyed her,
and stopped, and stood leaning on his bronze-barbed ash spear. Meanwhile
Athene left him there, and caught up with brilliant Hektor,
and likened herself in form and weariless voice to Deïphobos.
She came now and stood close to him and addressed him in winged words:
"Dear brother, indeed swift-footed Achilleus is using you roughly
and chasing you on swift feet around the city of Priam.
Come on, then; let us stand fast against him and beat him back from us."
Then tall Hektor of the shining helm answered her: "Deïphobos,
before now you were dearest to me by far of my brothers,
of all those who were sons of Priam and Hekabe, and now
I am minded all the more within my heart to honour you,
you who dared for my sake, when your eyes saw me, to come forth
from the fortifications, while the others stand fast inside them."
Then in turn the goddess grey-eyed Athene answered him:
"My brother, it is true our father and the lady our mother, taking
my knees in turn, and my companions about me, entreated
that I stay within, such was the terror upon all of them.
But the heart within me was worn away by hard sorrow for you.
But now let us go straight on and fight hard, let there be no sparing
of our spears, so that we can find out whether Achilleus
will kill us both and carry our bloody war spoils back
to the hollow ships, or will himself go down under your spear."
So Athene spoke and led him on by beguilement.
Now as the two in their advance were come close together,
first of the two to speak was tall helm-glittering Hektor:
"Son of Peleus, I will no longer run from you, as before this
I fled three times around the great city of Priam, and dared not
stand to your onfall. But now my spirit in turn has driven me
to stand and face you. I must take you now, or I must be taken.
Come then, shall we swear before the gods? For these are the highest
who shall be witnesses and watch over our agreements.
Brutal as you are I will not defile you, if Zeus grants
to me that I can wear you out, and take the life from you.
But after I have stripped your glorious armour, Achilleus,
I will give your corpse back to the Achaians. Do you do likewise."
Then looking darkly at him swift-footed Achilleus answered:
"Hektor, argue me no agreements. I cannot forgive you.

As there are no trustworthy oaths between men and lions,
nor wolves and lambs have spirit that can be brought to agreement
but forever these hold feelings of hate for each other,
so there can be no love between you and me, nor shall there be
oaths between us, but one or the other must fall before then
to glut with his blood Ares the god who fights under the shield's guard.
Remember every valour of yours, for now the need comes
hardest upon you to be a spearman and a bold warrior.
There shall be no more escape for you, but Pallas Athene
will kill you soon by my spear. You will pay in a lump for all those
sorrows of my companions you killed in your spear's fury."
So he spoke, and balanced the spear far shadowed, and threw it;
but glorious Hektor kept his eyes on him, and avoided it,
for he dropped, watchful, to his knee, and the bronze spear flew over his
shoulder
and stuck in the ground, but Pallas Athene snatched it, and gave it
back to Achilleus, unseen by Hektor shepherd of the people.
But now Hektor spoke out to the blameless son of Peleus:
"You missed; and it was not, o Achilleus like the immortals,
from Zeus that you knew my destiny; but you thought so; or rather
you are someone clever in speech and spoke to swindle me,
to make me afraid of you and forget my valour and war strength.
You will not stick your spear in my back as I run away from you
but drive it into my chest as I storm straight in against you;
if the god gives you that; and now look out for my brazen
spear. I wish it might be taken full length in your body.
And indeed the war would be a lighter thing for the Trojans
if you were dead, seeing that you are their greatest affliction."
So he spoke, and balanced the spear far shadowed, and threw it,
and struck the middle of Peleïdes' shield, nor missed it,
but the spear was driven far back from the shield, and Hektor was angered
because his swift weapon had been loosed from his hand in a vain cast.
He stood discouraged, and had no other ash spear; but lifting
his voice he called aloud on Deïphobos of the pale shield,
and asked him for a long spear, but Deïphobos was not near him.
And Hektor knew the truth inside his heart, and spoke aloud:
"No use. Here at last the gods have summoned me deathward.
I thought Deïphobos the hero was here close beside me,
but he is behind the wall and it was Athene cheating me,
and now evil death is close to me, and no longer far away,
and there is no way out. So it must long since have been pleasing
to Zeus, and Zeus' son who strikes from afar, this way; though before this
they defended me gladly. But now my death is upon me.
Let me at least not die without a struggle, inglorious,
but do some big thing first, that men to come shall know of it."
So he spoke, and pulling out the sharp sword that was slung
at the hollow of his side, huge and heavy, and gathering
himself together, he made his swoop, like a high-flown eagle
who launches himself out of the murk of the clouds on the flat land

to catch away a tender lamb or a shivering hare; so
Hektor made his swoop, swinging his sharp sword, and Achilleus
charged, the heart within him loaded with savage fury.
In front of his chest the beautiful elaborate great shield
covered him, and with the glittering helm with four horns
he nodded; the lovely golden fringes were shaken about it
which Hephaistos had driven close along the horn of the helmet.
And as a star moves among stars in the night's darkening,
Hesper, who is the fairest star who stands in the sky, such
was the shining from the pointed spear Achilleus was shaking
in his right hand with evil intention toward brilliant Hektor.
He was eyeing Hektor's splendid body, to see where it might best
give way, but all the rest of the skin was held in the armour,
brazen and splendid, he stripped when he cut down the strength of
  Patroklos;
yet showed where the collar-bones hold the neck from the shoulders,
the throat, where death of the soul comes most swiftly; in this place
brilliant Achilleus drove the spear as he came on in fury,
and clean through the soft part of the neck the spearpoint was driven.
Yet the ash spear heavy with bronze did not sever the windpipe,
so that Hektor could still make exchange of words spoken.
But he dropped in the dust, and brilliant Achilleus vaunted above him:
"Hektor, surely you thought as you killed Patroklos you would be
safe, and since I was far away you thought nothing of me,
o fool, for an avenger was left, far greater than he was,
behind him and away by the hollow ships. And it was I;
and I have broken your strength; on you the dogs and the vultures
shall feed and foully rip you; the Achaians will bury Patroklos."
  In his weakness Hektor of the shining helm spoke to him:
"I entreat you, by your life, by your knees, by your parents,
do not let the dogs feed on me by the ships of the Achaians,
but take yourself the bronze and gold that are there in abundance,
those gifts that my father and the lady my mother will give you,
and give my body to be taken home again, so that the Trojans
and the wives of the Trojans may give me in death my rite of burning."
  But looking darkly at him swift-footed Achilleus answered:
"No more entreating of me, you dog, by knees or parents.
I wish only that my spirit and fury would drive me
to hack your meat away and eat it raw for the things that
you have done to me. So there is no one who can hold the dogs off
from your head, not if they bring here and set before me ten times
and twenty times the ransom, and promise more in addition,
not if Priam son of Dardanos should offer to weigh out
your bulk in gold; not even so shall the lady your mother
who herself bore you lay you on the death-bed and mourn you:
no, but the dogs and the birds will have you all for their feasting."
  Then, dying, Hektor of the shining helmet spoke to him:
"I know you well as I look upon you, I know that I could not
persuade you, since indeed in your breast is a heart of iron.

Be careful now; for I might be made into the gods' curse
upon you, on that day when Paris and Phoibos Apollo
destroy you in the Skaian gates, for all your valour."
He spoke, and as he spoke the end of death closed in upon him,
and the soul fluttering free of the limbs went down into Death's house
mourning her destiny, leaving youth and manhood behind her.
Now though he was a dead man brilliant Achilleus spoke to him:
"Die: and I will take my own death at whatever time
Zeus and the rest of the immortals choose to accomplish it."
He spoke, and pulled the brazen spear from the body, and laid it
on one side, and stripped away from the shoulders the bloody
armour. And the other sons of the Achaians came running about him,
and gazed upon the stature and on the imposing beauty
of Hektor; and none stood beside him who did not stab him;
and thus they would speak one to another, each looking at his neighbour:
"See now, Hektor is much softer to handle than he was
when he set the ships ablaze with the burning firebrand."
So as they stood beside him they would speak, and stab him.
But now, when he had despoiled the body, swift-footed brilliant
Achilleus stood among the Achaians and addressed them in winged words:
"Friends, who are leaders of the Argives and keep their counsel:
since the gods have granted me the killing of this man
who has done us much damage, such as not all the others together
have done, come, let us go in armour about the city
to see if we can find out what purpose is in the Trojans,
whether they will abandon their high city, now that this man
has fallen, or are minded to stay, though Hektor lives no longer.
Yet still, why does the heart within me debate on these things?
There is a dead man who lies by the ships, unwept, unburied:
Patroklos: and I will not forget him, never so long as
I remain among the living and my knees have their spring beneath me.
And though the dead forget the dead in the house of Hades,
even there I shall still remember my beloved companion.
But now, you young men of the Achaians, let us go back, singing
a victory song, to our hollow ships; and take this with us.
We have won ourselves enormous fame; we have killed the great Hektor
whom the Trojans glorified as if he were a god in their city."
He spoke, and now thought of shameful treatment for glorious Hektor.
In both of his feet at the back he made holes by the tendons
in the space between ankle and heel, and drew thongs of ox-hide through them,
and fastened them to the chariot so as to let the head drag,
and mounted the chariot, and lifted the glorious armour inside it,
then whipped the horses to a run, and they winged their way unreluctant.
A cloud of dust rose where Hektor was dragged, his dark hair was falling
about him, and all that head that was once so handsome was tumbled
in the dust; since by this time Zeus had given him over
to his enemies, to be defiled in the land of his fathers.
So all his head was dragged in the dust; and now his mother

tore out her hair, and threw the shining veil far from her
and raised a great wail as she looked upon her son; and his father
beloved groaned pitifully, and all his people about him
were taken with wailing and lamentation all through the city.
It was most like what would have happened, if all lowering
Ilion had been burning top to bottom in fire.
His people could scarcely keep the old man in his impatience
from storming out of the Dardanian gates; he implored them
all, and wallowed in the muck before them calling on each man
and naming him by his name: "Give way, dear friends,
and let me alone though you care for me, leave me to go out
from the city and make my way to the ships of the Achaians.
I must be suppliant to this man, who is harsh and violent,
and he might have respect for my age and take pity upon it
since I am old, and his father also is old, as I am,
Peleus, who begot and reared him to be an affliction
on the Trojans. He has given us most sorrow, beyond all others,
such is the number of my flowering sons he has cut down.
But for all of these I mourn not so much, in spite of my sorrow,
as for one, Hektor, and the sharp grief for him will carry me downward
into Death's house. I wish he had died in my arms, for that way
we two, I myself and his mother who bore him unhappy,
might so have glutted ourselves with weeping for him and mourning."
So he spoke, in tears, and beside him mourned the citizens.
But for the women of Troy Hekabe[2] led out the thronging
chant of sorrow: "Child, I am wretched. What shall my life be
in my sorrows, now you are dead, who by day and in the night
were my glory in the town, and to all of the Trojans
and the women of Troy a blessing throughout their city. They adored you
as if you were a god, since in truth you were their high honour
while you lived. Now death and fate have closed in upon you."
So she spoke in tears but the wife of Hektor had not yet
heard: for no sure messenger had come to her and told her
how her husband had held his ground there outside the gates;
but she was weaving a web in the inner room of the high house,
a red folding robe, and inworking elaborate figures.
She called out through the house to her lovely-haired handmaidens
to set a great cauldron over the fire, so that there would be
hot water for Hektor's bath as he came back out of the fighting;
poor innocent, nor knew how, far from waters for bathing,
Pallas Athene had cut him down at the hands of Achilleus.
She heard from the great bastion the noise of mourning and sorrow.
Her limbs spun, and the shuttle dropped from her hand to the ground. Then
she called aloud to her lovely-haired handmaidens: "Come here.
Two of you come with me, so I can see what has happened.
I heard the voice of Hektor's honoured mother; within me
my own heart rising beats in my mouth, my limbs under me

2. Hektor's mother.

are frozen. Surely some evil is near for the children of Priam.
May what I say come never close to my ear; yet dreadfully
I fear that great Achilleus might have cut off bold Hektor
alone, away from the city, and be driving him into the flat land,
might put an end to that bitter pride of courage, that always
was on him, since he would never stay back where the men were in numbers
but break far out in front, and give way in his fury to no man."
So she spoke, and ran out of the house like a raving woman
with pulsing heart, and her two handmaidens went along with her.
But when she came to the bastion and where the men were gathered
she stopped, staring, on the wall; and she saw him
being dragged in front of the city, and the running horses
dragged him at random toward the hollow ships of the Achaians.
The darkness of night misted over the eyes of Andromache.
She fell backward, and gasped the life breath from her, and far off
threw from her head the shining gear that ordered her headdress,
the diadem and the cap, and the holding-band woven together,
and the circlet, which Aphrodite the golden once had given her
on that day when Hektor of the shining helmet led her forth
from the house of Eëtion, and gave numberless gifts to win her.
And about her stood thronging her husband's sisters and the wives of his brothers
and these, in her despair for death, held her up among them.
But she, when she breathed again and the life was gathered back into her,
lifted her voice among the women of Troy in mourning:
"Hektor, I grieve for you. You and I were born to a single
destiny, you in Troy in the house of Priam, and I
in Thebe, underneath the timbered mountain of Plakos
in the house of Eëtion, who cared for me when I was little,
ill-fated he, I ill-starred. I wish he had never begotten me.
Now you go down to the house of Death in the secret places
of the earth, and left me here behind in the sorrow of mourning,
a widow in your house, and the boy is only a baby
who was born to you and me, the unfortunate. You cannot help him,
Hektor, any more, since you are dead. Nor can he help you.
Though he escape the attack of the Achaians with all its sorrows,
yet all his days for your sake there will be hard work for him
and sorrows, for others will take his lands away from him. The day
of bereavement leaves a child with no agemates to befriend him.
He bows his head before every man, his cheeks are bewept, he
goes, needy, a boy among his father's companions,
and tugs at this man by the mantle, that man by the tunic,
and they pity him, and one gives him a tiny drink from a goblet,
enough to moisten his lips, not enough to moisten his palate.
But one whose parents are living beats him out of the banquet
hitting him with his fists and in words also abuses him:
"Get out, you! Your father is not dining among us."
And the boy goes away in tears to his widowed mother,

Astyanax, who in days before on the knees of his father
would eat only the marrow or the flesh of sheep that was fattest.
And when sleep would come upon him and he was done with his playing,
he would go to sleep in a bed, in the arms of his nurse, in a soft
bed, with his heart given all its fill of luxury.
Now, with his dear father gone, he has much to suffer:
he, whom the Trojans have called Astyanax, lord of the city,
since it was you alone who defended the gates and the long walls.
But now, beside the curving ships, far away from your parents,
the writhing worms will feed, when the dogs have had enough of you,
on your naked corpse, though in your house there is clothing laid up
that is fine-textured and pleasant, wrought by the hands of women.
But all of these I will burn up in the fire's blazing,
no use to you, since you will never be laid away in them;
but in your honour, from the men of Troy and the Trojan women."
So she spoke, in tears; and the women joined in her mourning.

Book 24

[Achilles and Priam]

And the games broke up, and the people scattered to go away, each man
to his fast-running ship, and the rest of them took thought of their dinner
and of sweet sleep and its enjoyment; only Achilleus
wept still as he remembered his beloved companion, nor did sleep
who subdues all come over him, but he tossed from one side to the other
in longing for Patroklos, for his manhood and his great strength
and all the actions he had seen to the end with him, and the hardships
he had suffered; the wars of men; hard crossing of the big waters.
Remembering all these things he let fall the swelling tears, lying
sometimes along his side, sometimes on his back, and now again
prone on his face; then he would stand upright, and pace turning
in distraction along the beach of the sea, nor did dawn rising
escape him as she brightened across the sea and the beaches.
Then, when he had yoked running horses under the chariot
he would fasten Hektor behind the chariot, so as to drag him,
and draw him three times around the tomb of Menoitios' fallen
son, then rest again in his shelter, and throw down the dead man
and leave him to lie sprawled on his face in the dust. But Apollo
had pity on him, though he was only a dead man, and guarded
the body from all ugliness, and hid all of it under the golden
aegis, so that it might not be torn when Achilleus dragged it.
So Achilleus in his standing fury outraged great Hektor.
The blessed gods as they looked upon him were filled with compassion
and kept urging clear-sighted Argeïphontes[1] to steal the body.
There this was pleasing to all the others, but never to Hera
nor Poseidon, nor the girl of the grey eyes,[2] who kept still

1. Hermes.

2. Athene.

their hatred for sacred Ilion as in the beginning,
and for Priam and his people, because of the delusion of Paris
who insulted the goddesses when they came to him in his courtyard
and favoured her who supplied the lust that led to disaster.
But now, as it was the twelfth dawn after the death of Hektor,
Phoibos Apollo spoke his word out among the immortals:
"You are hard, you gods, and destructive. Now did not Hektor
burn thigh pieces of oxen and unblemished goats in your honour?
Now you cannot bring yourselves to save him, though he is only
a corpse, for his wife to look upon, his child and his mother
and Priam his father, and his people, who presently thereafter
would burn his body in the fire and give him his rites of burial.
No, you gods; your desire is to help this cursed Achilleus
within whose breast there are no feelings of justice, nor can
his mind be bent, but his purposes are fierce, like a lion
who when he has given way to his own great strength and his haughty
spirit, goes among the flocks of men, to devour them.
So Achilleus has destroyed pity, and there is not in him
any shame; which does much harm to men but profits them also.
For a man must some day lose one who was even closer
than this; a brother from the same womb, or a son. And yet
he weeps for him, and sorrows for him, and then it is over,
for the Destinies put in mortal men the heart of endurance.
But this man, now he has torn the heart of life from great Hektor,
ties him to his horses and drags him around his beloved companion's
tomb; and nothing is gained thereby for his good, or his honour.
Great as he is, let him take care not to make us angry;
for see, he does dishonour to the dumb earth in his fury."

Then bitterly Hera of the white arms answered him, saying:
"What you have said could be true, lord of the silver bow, only
if you give Hektor such pride of place as you give to Achilleus.
But Hektor was mortal, and suckled at the breast of a woman,
while Achilleus is the child of a goddess, one whom I myself
nourished and brought up and gave her as bride to her husband
Peleus, one dear to the hearts of the immortals, for you all
went, you gods, to the wedding; and you too feasted among them
and held your lyre, o friend of the evil, faithless forever."

In turn Zeus who gathers the clouds spoke to her in answer:
"Hera, be not utterly angry with the gods, for there shall not
be the same pride of place given both. Yet Hektor also
was loved by the gods, best of all the mortals in Ilion.
I loved him too. He never failed of gifts to my liking.
Never yet has my altar gone without fair sacrifice,
the smoke and the savour of it, since that is our portion of honour.
The stealing of him we will dismiss, for it is not possible
to take bold Hektor secretly from Achilleus, since always
his mother is near him night and day; but it would be better
if one of the gods would summon Thetis here to my presence
so that I can say a close word to her, and see that Achilleus

is given gifts by Priam and gives back the body of Hektor."
He spoke, and Iris storm-footed sprang away with the message,
and at a point between Samos and Imbros of the high cliffs
plunged in the dark water, and the sea crashed moaning about her.
She plummeted to the sea floor like a lead weight which, mounted
along the horn of an ox who ranges the fields, goes downward
and takes death with it to the raw-ravening fish. She found Thetis
inside the hollow of her cave, and gathered about her
sat the rest of the sea goddesses, and she in their midst
was mourning the death of her blameless son, who so soon was destined
to die in Troy of the rich soil, far from the land of his fathers.
Iris the swift-foot came close beside her and spoke to her:
"Rise, Thetis. Zeus whose purposes are infinite calls you."
In turn Thetis the goddess, the silver-footed, answered her:
"What does he, the great god, want with me? I feel shamefast
to mingle with the immortals, and my heart is confused with sorrows.
But I will go. No word shall be in vain, if he says it."
So she spoke, and shining among the divinities took up
her black veil, and there is no darker garment. She went
on her way, and in front of her rapid wind-footed Iris
guided her, and the wave of the water opened about them.
They stepped out on the dry land and swept to the sky. There they found
the son of Kronos of the wide brows, and gathered about him
sat all the rest of the gods, the blessed, who live forever.
She sat down beside Zeus father, and Athene made a place for her.
Hera put into her hand a beautiful golden goblet
and spoke to her to comfort her, and Thetis accepting drank from it.
The father of gods and men began the discourse among them:
"You have come to Olympos, divine Thetis, for all your sorrow,
with an unforgotten grief in your heart. I myself know this.
But even so I will tell you why I summoned you hither.
For nine days there has risen a quarrel among the immortals
over the body of Hektor, and Achilleus, stormer of cities.
They keep urging clear-sighted Argeïphontes to steal the body,
but I still put upon Achilleus the honour that he has, guarding
your reverence and your love for me into time afterwards. Go then
in all speed to the encampment and give to your son this message:
tell him that the gods frown upon him, that beyond all other
immortals I myself am angered that in his heart's madness
he holds Hektor beside the curved ships and did not give him
back. Perhaps in fear of me he will give back Hektor.
Then I will send Iris to Priam of the great heart, with an order
to ransom his dear son, going down to the ships of the Achaians
and bringing gifts to Achilleus which might soften his anger."
He spoke and the goddess silver-foot Thetis did not disobey him
but descended in a flash of speed from the peaks of Olympos
and made her way to the shelter of her son, and there found him
in close lamentation, and his beloved companions about him
were busy at their work and made ready the morning meal, and there

stood a great fleecy sheep being sacrificed in the shelter.
His honoured mother came close to him and sat down beside him,
and stroked him with her hand and called him by name and spoke to him:
"My child, how long will you go on eating your heart out in sorrow
and lamentation, and remember neither your food nor going
to bed? It is a good thing even to lie with a woman
in love. For you will not be with me long, but already
death and powerful destiny stand closely above you.
But listen hard to me, for I come from Zeus with a message.
He says that the gods frown upon you, that beyond all other
immortals he himself is angered that in your heart's madness
you hold Hektor beside the curved ships and did not redeem him.
Come, then, give him up and accept ransom for the body."
Then in turn Achilleus of the swift feet answered her:
"So be it. He can bring the ransom and take off the body,
if the Olympian himself so urgently bids it."
So, where the ships were drawn together, the son and his mother
conversed at long length in winged words. But the son of Kronos
stirred Iris to go down to sacred Ilion, saying:
"Go forth, Iris the swift, leaving your place on Olympos,
and go to Priam of the great heart within Ilion, tell him
to ransom his dear son, going down to the ships of the Achaians
and bringing gifts to Achilleus which might soften his anger:
alone, let no other man of the Trojans go with him, but only
let one elder herald attend him, one who can manage
the mules and the easily running wagon, so he can carry
the dead man, whom great Achilleus slew, back to the city.
Let death not be a thought in his heart, let him have no fear;
such an escort shall I send to guide him, Argeïphontes
who shall lead him until he brings him to Achilleus. And after
he has brought him inside the shelter of Achilleus, neither
will the man himself kill him, but will hold back all the others,
for he is no witless man nor unwatchful, nor is he wicked,
but will in all kindness spare one who comes to him as a suppliant."
He spoke, and storm-footed Iris swept away with the message
and came to the house of Priam. There she found outcry and mourning.
The sons sitting around their father inside the courtyard
made their clothes sodden with their tears, and among them the old man
sat veiled, beaten into his mantle. Dung lay thick
on the head and neck of the aged man, for he had been rolling
in it, he had gathered and smeared it on with his hands. And his daughters
all up and down the house and the wives of his sons were mourning
as they remembered all those men in their numbers and valour
who lay dead, their lives perished at the hands of the Argives.
The messenger of Zeus stood beside Priam and spoke to him
in a small voice, and yet the shivers took hold of his body:
"Take heart, Priam, son of Dardanos, do not be frightened.
I come to you not eyeing you with evil intention
but with the purpose of good toward you. I am a messenger

of Zeus, who far away cares much for you and is pitiful.
The Olympian orders you to ransom Hektor the brilliant,
to bring gifts to Achilleus which may soften his anger:
alone, let no other man of the Trojans go with you, but only
let one elder herald attend you, one who can manage
the mules and the easily running wagon, so he can carry
the dead man, whom great Achilleus slew, back to the city.
Let death not be a thought in your heart, you need have no fear,
such an escort shall go with you to guide you, Argeïphontes
who will lead you till he brings you to Achilleus. And after
he has brought you inside the shelter of Achilleus, neither
will the man himself kill you but will hold back all the others;
for he is no witless man nor unwatchful, nor is he wicked
but will in all kindness spare one who comes to him as a suppliant."
    So Iris the swift-footed spoke and went away from him.
Thereupon he ordered his sons to make ready the easily rolling
mule wagon, and to fasten upon it the carrying basket.
He himself went into the storeroom, which was fragrant
and of cedar, and high-ceilinged, with many bright treasures inside it.
He called out to Hekabe his wife, and said to her:
"Dear wife, a messenger came to me from Zeus on Olympos,
that I must go to the ships of the Achaians and ransom my dear son,
bringing gifts to Achilleus which may soften his anger.
Come then, tell me. What does it seem best to your own mind
for me to do? My heart, my strength are terribly urgent
that I go there to the ships within the wide army of the Achaians."
    So he spoke, and his wife cried out aloud, and answered him:
"Ah me, where has that wisdom gone for which you were famous
in time before, among outlanders and those you rule over?
How can you wish to go alone to the ships of the Achaians
before the eyes of a man who has slaughtered in such numbers
such brave sons of yours? The heart in you is iron. For if
he has you within his grasp and lays eyes upon you, that man
who is savage and not to be trusted will not take pity upon you
nor have respect for your rights. Let us sit apart in our palace
now, and weep for Hektor, and the way at the first strong Destiny
spun with his life line when he was born, when I gave birth to him,
that the dogs with their shifting feet should feed on him, far from his
    parents,
gone down before a stronger man; I wish I could set teeth
in the middle of his liver and eat it. That would be vengeance
for what he did to my son; for he slew him when he was no coward
but standing before the men of Troy and the deep-girdled women
of Troy, with no thought in his mind of flight or withdrawal."
    In turn the aged Priam, the godlike, answered her saying:
"Do not hold me back when I would be going, neither yourself be
a bird of bad omen in my palace. You will not persuade me.
If it had been some other who ordered me, one of the mortals,
one of those who are soothsayers, or priests, or diviners,

I might have called it a lie and we might rather have rejected it.
But now, for I myself heard the god and looked straight upon her,
I am going, and this word shall not be in vain. If it is my destiny
to die there by the ships of the bronze-armoured Achaians,
then I wish that. Achilleus can slay me at once, with my own son
caught in my arms, once I have my fill of mourning above him."
He spoke, and lifted back the fair covering of his clothes-chest
and from inside took out twelve robes surpassingly lovely
and twelve mantles to be worn single, as many blankets,
as many great white cloaks, also the same number of tunics.
He weighed and carried out ten full talents of gold, and brought forth
two shining tripods, and four cauldrons, and brought out a goblet
of surpassing loveliness that the men of Thrace had given him
when he went to them with a message, but now the old man spared not
even this in his halls, so much was it his heart's desire
to ransom back his beloved son. But he drove off the Trojans
all from his cloister walks, scolding them with words of revilement:
"Get out, you failures, you disgraces. Have you not also
mourning of your own at home that you come to me with your sorrows?
Is it not enough that Zeus, son of Kronos, has given me sorrow
in losing the best of my sons? You also shall be aware of this
since you will be all the easier for the Achaians to slaughter
now he is dead. But, for myself, before my eyes look
upon this city as it is destroyed and its people are slaughtered,
my wish is to go sooner down to the house of the death god."
He spoke, and went after the men with a stick, and they fled outside
before the fury of the old man. He was scolding his children
and cursing Helenos, and Paris, Agathon the brilliant,
Pammon and Antiphonos, Polites of the great war cry,
Deïphobos and Hippothoös and proud Dios. There were nine
sons to whom now the old man gave orders and spoke to them roughly:
"Make haste, wicked children, my disgraces. I wish all of you
had been killed beside the running ships in the place of Hektor.
Ah me, for my evil destiny. I have had the noblest
of sons in Troy, but I say not one of them is left to me,
Mestor like a god and Troilos whose delight was in horses,
and Hektor, who was a god among men, for he did not seem like
one who was child of a mortal man, but of a god. All these
Ares has killed, and all that are left me are the disgraces,
the liars and the dancers, champions of the chorus, the plunderers
of their own people in their land of lambs and kids. Well then,
will you not get my wagon ready and be quick about it,
and put all these things on it, so we can get on with our journey?"
So he spoke, and they in terror at the old man's scolding
hauled out the easily running wagon for mules, a fine thing
new-fabricated, and fastened the carrying basket upon it.
They took away from its peg the mule yoke made of boxwood
with its massive knob, well fitted with guiding rings, and brought forth
the yoke lashing (together with the yoke itself) of nine cubits

and snugged it well into place upon the smooth-polished wagon-pole
at the foot of the beam, then slipped the ring over the peg, and lashed it
with three turns on either side to the knob, and afterwards
fastened it all in order and secured it under a hooked guard.
Then they carried out and piled into the smooth-polished mule wagon
all the unnumbered spoils to be given for the head of Hektor,
then yoked the powerful-footed mules who pulled in the harness
and whom the Mysians gave once as glorious presents to Priam;
but for Priam they led under the yoke those horses the old man
himself had kept, and cared for them at his polished manger.
Now in the high house the yoking was done for the herald
and Priam, men both with close counsels in their minds. And now came
Hekabe with sorrowful heart and stood close beside them
carrying in her right hand the kind, sweet wine in a golden
goblet, so that before they went they might pour a drink-offering.
She stood in front of the horses, called Priam by name and spoke to him:
"Here, pour a libation to Zeus father, and pray you may come back
home again from those who hate you, since it seems the spirit
within you drives you upon the ships, though I would not have it.
Make your prayer then to the dark-misted, the son of Kronos
on Ida, who looks out on all the Troad, and ask him
for a bird of omen, a rapid messenger, which to his own mind
is dearest of all birds and his strength is the biggest, one seen
on the right, so that once your eyes have rested upon him
you can trust in him and go to the ships of the fast-mounted Danaans.
But if Zeus of the wide brows will not grant you his own messenger,
then I, for one, would never urge you on nor advise you
to go to the Argive ships, for all your passion to do it."
Then in answer to her again spoke Priam the godlike:
"My lady, I will not disregard this wherein you urge me.
It is well to lift hands to Zeus and ask if he will have mercy."
The old man spoke, and told the housekeeper who attended them
to pour unstained water over his hands. She standing beside them
and serving them held the washing-bowl in her hands, and a pitcher.
He washed his hands and took the cup from his wife. He stood up
in the middle of the enclosure, and prayed, and poured the wine out
looking up into the sky, and gave utterance and spoke, saying:
"Father Zeus, watching over us from Ida, most high, most honoured:
grant that I come to Achilleus for love and pity; but send me
a bird of omen, a rapid messenger which to your own mind
is dearest of all birds and his strength is biggest, one seen
on the right, so that once my eyes have rested upon him
I may trust in him and go to the ships of the fast-mounted Danaans."
So he spoke in prayer, and Zeus of the counsels heard him.
Straightway he sent down the most lordly of birds, an eagle,
the dark one, the marauder, called as well the black eagle.
And as big as is the build of the door to a towering chamber
in the house of a rich man, strongly fitted with bars, of such size
was the spread of his wings on either side. He swept through the city

appearing on the right hand, and the people looking upon him
were uplifted and the hearts made glad in the breasts of all of them.
Now in urgent haste the old man mounted into his chariot
and drove out through the forecourt and the thundering close. Before him
the mules hauled the wagon on its four wheels, Idaios
the sober-minded driving them, and behind him the horses
came on as the old man laid the lash upon them and urged them
rapidly through the town, and all his kinsmen were following
much lamenting, as if he went to his death. When the two men
had gone down through the city, and out, and come to the flat land,
the rest of them turned back to go to Ilion, the sons
and the sons-in-law. And Zeus of the wide brows failed not to notice
the two as they showed in the plain. He saw the old man and took pity
upon him, and spoke directly to his beloved son, Hermes:
"Hermes, for to you beyond all other gods it is dearest
to be man's companion, and you listen to whom you will, go now
on your way, and so guide Priam inside the hollow ships
of the Achaians, that no man shall see him, none be aware of him,
of the other Danaans, till he has come to the son of Peleus."
He spoke, nor disobeyed him the courier, Argeïphontes.
Immediately he bound upon his feet the fair sandals
golden and immortal, that carried him over the water
as over the dry land of the main abreast of the wind's blast.
He caught up the staff, with which he mazes the eyes of those mortals
whose eyes he would maze, or wakes again the sleepers. Holding
this in his hands, strong Argeïphontes winged his way onward
until he came suddenly to Troy and the Hellespont, and there
walked on, and there took the likeness of a young man, a noble,
with beard new grown, which is the most graceful time of young manhood.
Now when the two had driven past the great tomb of Ilos
they stayed their mules and horses to water them in the river,
for by this time darkness had descended on the land; and the herald
made out Hermes, who was coming toward them at a short distance.
He lifted his voice and spoke aloud to Priam: "Take thought,
son of Dardanos. Here is work for a mind that is careful.
I see a man; I think he will presently tear us to pieces.
Come then, let us run away with our horses, or if not, then
clasp his knees and entreat him to have mercy upon us."
So he spoke, and the old man's mind was confused, he was badly
frightened, and the hairs stood up all over his gnarled body
and he stood staring, but the kindly god himself coming closer
took the old man's hand, and spoke to him and asked him a question:
"Where, my father, are you thus guiding your mules and horses
through the immortal night while other mortals are sleeping?
Have you no fear of the Achaians whose wind is fury,
who hate you, who are your enemies, and are near? For if one
of these were to see you, how you are conveying so many
treasures through the swift black night, what then could you think of?
You are not young yourself, and he who attends you is aged

for beating off any man who might pick a quarrel with you.
But I will do you no harm myself, I will even keep off
another who would. You seem to me like a beloved father."
 In answer to him again spoke aged Priam the godlike:
"Yes, in truth, dear child, all this is much as you tell me;
yet still there is some god who has held his hand above me,
who sent such a wayfarer as you to meet me, an omen
of good, for such you are by your form, your admired beauty
and the wisdom in your mind. Your parents are fortunate in you."
 Then in turn answered him the courier Argeïphontes:
"Yes, old sir, all this that you said is fair and orderly.
But come, tell me this thing and recite it to me accurately.
Can it be you convey these treasures in all their numbers and beauty
to outland men, so that they can be still kept safe for you?
Or are all of you by now abandoning sacred Ilion
in fear, such a one was he who died, the best man among you,
your son; who was never wanting when you fought against the Achaians."
 In answer to him again spoke aged Priam the godlike:
"But who are you, o best of men, and who are your parents?
Since you spoke of my ill-starred son's death, and with honour."
 Then in turn answered him the courier Argeïphontes:
"You try me out, aged sir. You ask me of glorious Hektor
whom many a time my eyes have seen in the fighting where men win
glory, as also on that time when he drove back the Argives
on their ships and kept killing them with the stroke of the sharp bronze,
and we stood by and wondered at him; for then Achilleus
would not let us fight by reason of his anger at Agamemnon.
For I am Achilleus' henchman, and the same strong-wrought vessel
brought us here; and I am a Myrmidon, and my father
is Polyktor; a man of substance, but aged, as you are.
He has six sons beside, and I am the seventh, and I shook
lots with the others, and it was my lot to come on this venture.
But now I have come to the plain away from the ships, for at daybreak
the glancing-eyed Achaians will do battle around the city.
They chafe from sitting here too long, nor have the Achaians'
kings the strength to hold them back as they break for the fighting."
 In answer to him again spoke aged Priam the godlike:
"If then you are henchman to Peleïd Achilleus,
come, tell me the entire truth, and whether my son lies
still beside the ships, or whether by now he has been hewn
limb from limb and thrown before the dogs by Achilleus."
 Then in turn answered him the courier Argeïphontes:
"Aged sir, neither have any dogs eaten him, nor have
the birds, but he lies yet beside the ship of Achilleus
at the shelters, and as he was; now here is the twelfth dawn
he has lain there, nor does his flesh decay, nor do worms feed
on him, they who devour men who have fallen in battle.
It is true, Achilleus drags him at random around his beloved
companion's tomb, as dawn on dawn appears, yet he cannot

mutilate him; you yourself can see when you go there
how fresh with dew he lies, and the blood is all washed from him,
nor is there any corruption, and all the wounds have been closed up
where he was struck, since many drove the bronze in his body.
So it is that the blessed immortals care for your son, though
he is nothing but a dead man; because in their hearts they loved him."
He spoke, and the old man was made joyful and answered him, saying:
"My child, surely it is good to give the immortals
their due gifts; because my own son, if ever I had one,
never forgot in his halls the gods who live on Olympos.
Therefore they remembered him even in death's stage. Come, then,
accept at my hands this beautiful drinking-cup, and give me
protection for my body, and with the gods' grace be my escort
until I make my way to the shelter of the son of Peleus."
In turn answered him the courier Argeïphontes:
"You try me out, aged sir, for I am young, but you will not
persuade me, telling me to accept your gifts when Achilleus
does not know. I fear him at heart and have too much reverence
to rob him. Such a thing might be to my sorrow hereafter.
But I would be your escort and take good care of you, even
till I came to glorious Argos in a fast ship or following
on foot, and none would fight you because he despised your escort."
The kind god spoke, and sprang up behind the horses and into
the chariot, and rapidly caught in his hands the lash and the guide reins,
and breathed great strength into the mules and horses. Now after
they had got to the fortifications about the ships, and the ditch, there
were sentries, who had just begun to make ready their dinner,
but about these the courier Argeïphontes drifted
sleep, on all, and quickly opened the gate, and shoved back
the door-bars, and brought in Priam and the glorious gifts on the wagon.
But when they had got to the shelter of Peleus' son: a towering
shelter the Myrmidons had built for their king, hewing
the timbers of pine, and they made a roof of thatch above it
shaggy with grass that they had gathered out of the meadows;
and around it made a great courtyard for their king, with hedgepoles
set close together; the gate was secured by a single door-piece
of pine, and three Achaians could ram it home in its socket
and three could pull back and open the huge door-bar; three other
Achaians, that is, but Achilleus all by himself could close it.
At this time Hermes, the kind god, opened the gate for the old man
and brought in the glorious gifts for Peleus' son, the swift-footed,
and dismounted to the ground from behind the horses, and spoke forth:
"Aged sir, I who came to you am a god immortal,
Hermes. My father sent me down to guide and go with you.
But now I am going back again, and I will not go in
before the eyes of Achilleus, for it would make others angry
for an immortal god so to face mortal men with favour.
But go you in yourself and clasp the knees of Peleion
and entreat him in the name of his father, the name of his mother

of the lovely hair, and his child, and so move the spirit within him."
So Hermes spoke, and went away to the height of Olympos,
but Priam vaulted down to the ground from behind the horses
and left Idaios where he was, for he stayed behind, holding
in hand the horses and mules. The old man made straight for the dwelling
where Achilleus the beloved of Zeus was sitting. He found him
inside, and his companions were sitting apart, as two only,
Automedon the hero and Alkimos, scion of Ares,
were busy beside him. He had just now got through with his dinner,
with eating and drinking, and the table still stood by. Tall Priam
came in unseen by the other men and stood close beside him
and caught the knees of Achilleus in his arms, and kissed the hands
that were dangerous and manslaughtering and had killed so many
of his sons. As when dense disaster closes on one who has murdered
a man in his own land, and he comes to the country of others,
to a man of substance, and wonder seizes on those who behold him,
so Achilleus wondered as he looked on Priam, a godlike
man, and the rest of them wondered also, and looked at each other.
But now Priam spoke to him in the words of a suppliant:
"Achilleus like the gods, remember your father, one who
is of years like mine, and on the door-sill of sorrowful old age.
And they who dwell nearby encompass him and afflict him,
nor is there any to defend him against the wrath, the destruction.
Yet surely he, when he hears of you and that you are still living,
is gladdened within his heart and all his days he is hopeful
that he will see his beloved son come home from the Troad.
But for me, my destiny was evil. I have had the noblest
of sons in Troy, but I say not one of them is left to me.
Fifty were my sons, when the sons of the Achaians came here.
Nineteen were born to me from the womb of a single mother,
and other women bore the rest in my palace; and of these
violent Ares broke the strength in the knees of most of them,
but one was left me who guarded my city and people, that one
you killed a few days since as he fought in defence of his country,
Hektor; for whose sake I come now to the ships of the Achaians
to win him back from you, and I bring you gifts beyond number.
Honour then the gods, Achilleus, and take pity upon me
remembering your father, yet I am still more pitiful;
I have gone through what no other mortal on earth has gone through;
I put my lips to the hands of the man who has killed my children."
So he spoke, and stirred in the other a passion of grieving
for his own father. He took the old man's hand and pushed him
gently away, and the two remembered, as Priam sat huddled
at the feet of Achilleus and wept close for manslaughtering Hektor
and Achilleus wept now for his own father, now again
for Patroklos. The sound of their mourning moved in the house. Then
when great Achilleus had taken full satisfaction in sorrow
and the passion for it had gone from his mind and body, thereafter
he rose from his chair, and took the old man by the hand, and set him

on his feet again, in pity for the grey head and the grey beard,
and spoke to him and addressed him in winged words: "Ah, unlucky,
surely you have had much evil to endure in your spirit.
How could you dare to come alone to the ships of the Achaians
and before my eyes, when I am one who have killed in such numbers
such brave sons of yours? The heart in you is iron. Come, then,
and sit down upon this chair, and you and I will even let
our sorrows lie still in the heart for all our grieving. There is not
any advantage to be won from grim lamentation.
Such is the way the gods spun life for unfortunate mortals,
that we live in unhappiness, but the gods themselves have no sorrows.
There are two urns that stand on the door-sill of Zeus. They are unlike
for the gifts they bestow: an urn of evils, an urn of blessings.
If Zeus who delights in thunder mingles these and bestows them
on man, he shifts, and moves now in evil, again in good fortune.
But when Zeus bestows from the urn of sorrows, he makes a failure
of man, and the evil hunger drives him over the shining
earth, and he wanders respected neither of gods nor mortals.
Such were the shining gifts given by the gods to Peleus
from his birth, who outshone all men beside for his riches
and pride of possession, and was lord over the Myrmidons. Thereto
the gods bestowed an immortal wife on him, who was mortal.
But even on him the god piled evil also. There was not
any generation of strong sons born to him in his great house
but a single all-untimely child he had, and I give him
no care as he grows old, since far from the land of my fathers
I sit here in Troy, and bring nothing but sorrow to you and your children.
And you, old sir, we are told you prospered once; for as much
as Lesbos, Makar's hold, confines to the north above it
and Phrygia from the north confines, and enormous Hellespont,
of these, old sir, you were lord once in your wealth and your children.
But now the Uranian gods brought us, an affliction upon you,
forever there is fighting about your city, and men killed.
But bear up, nor mourn endlessly in your heart, for there is not
anything to be gained from grief for your son; you will never
bring him back; sooner you must go through yet another sorrow."
In answer to him again spoke aged Priam the godlike:
"Do not, beloved of Zeus, make me sit on a chair while Hektor
lies yet forlorn among the shelters; rather with all speed
give him back, so my eyes may behold him, and accept the ransom
we bring you, which is great. You may have joy of it, and go back
to the land of your own fathers, since once you have permitted me
to go on living myself and continue to look on the sunlight."
Then looking darkly at him spoke swift-footed Achilleus:
"No longer stir me up, old sir. I myself am minded
to give Hektor back to you. A messenger came to me from Zeus,
my mother, she who bore me, the daughter of the sea's ancient.
I know you, Priam, in my heart, and it does not escape me
that some god led you to the running ships of the Achaians.

For no mortal would dare come to our encampment, not even
one strong in youth. He could not get by the pickets, he could not
lightly unbar the bolt that secures our gateway. Therefore
you must not further make my spirit move in my sorrows,
for fear, old sir, I might not let you alone in my shelter,
suppliant as you are; and be guilty before the god's orders."
He spoke, and the old man was frightened and did as he told him.
The son of Peleus bounded to the door of the house like a lion,
nor went alone, but the two henchmen followed attending,
the hero Automedon and Alkimos, those whom Achilleus
honoured beyond all companions after Patroklos dead. These two
now set free from under the yoke the mules and the horses,
and led inside the herald, the old king's crier, and gave him
a chair to sit in, then from the smooth-polished mule wagon
lifted out the innumerable spoils for the head of Hektor,
but left inside it two great cloaks and a finespun tunic
to shroud the corpse in when they carried him home. Then Achilleus
called out to his serving-maids to wash the body and anoint it
all over; but take it first aside, since otherwise Priam
might see his son and in the heart's sorrow not hold in his anger
at the sight, and the deep heart in Achilleus be shaken to anger;
that he might not kill Priam and be guilty before the god's orders.
Then when the serving-maids had washed the corpse and anointed it
with olive oil, they threw a fair great cloak and a tunic
about him, and Achilleus himself lifted him and laid him
on a litter, and his friends helped him lift it to the smooth-polished
mule wagon. He groaned then, and called by name on his beloved
companion:
"Be not angry with me, Patroklos, if you discover,
though you be in the house of Hades, that I gave back great Hektor
to his loved father, for the ransom he gave me was not unworthy.
I will give you your share of the spoils, as much as is fitting."
So spoke great Achilleus and went back into the shelter
and sat down on the elaborate couch from which he had risen,
against the inward wall, and now spoke his word to Priam:
"Your son is given back to you, aged sir, as you asked it.
He lies on a bier. When dawn shows you yourself shall see him
as you take him away. Now you and I must remember our supper.
For even Niobe, she of the lovely tresses, remembered
to eat, whose twelve children were destroyed in her palace,
six daughters, and six sons in the pride of their youth, whom Apollo
killed with arrows from his silver bow, being angered
with Niobe, and shaft-showering Artemis killed the daughters;
because Niobe likened herself to Leto of the fair colouring
and said Leto had borne only two, she herself had borne many;
but the two, though they were only two, destroyed all those others.
Nine days long they lay in their blood, nor was there anyone
to bury them, for the son of Kronos made stones out of
the people; but on the tenth day the Uranian gods buried them.

But she remembered to eat when she was worn out with weeping.
And now somewhere among the rocks, in the lonely mountains,
in Sipylos, where they say is the resting place of the goddesses
who are nymphs, and dance beside the waters of Acheloios,
there, stone still, she broods on the sorrows that the gods gave her.
Come then, we also, aged magnificent sir, must remember
to eat, and afterwards you may take your beloved son back
to Ilion, and mourn for him; and he will be much lamented."
So spoke fleet Achilleus and sprang to his feet and slaughtered
a gleaming sheep, and his friends skinned it and butchered it fairly,
and cut up the meat expertly into small pieces, and spitted them,
and roasted all carefully and took off the pieces.
Automedon took the bread and set it out on the table
in fair baskets, while Achilleus served the meats. And thereon
they put their hands to the good things that lay ready before them.
But when they had put aside their desire for eating and drinking,
Priam, son of Dardanos, gazed upon Achilleus, wondering
at his size and beauty, for he seemed like an outright vision
of gods. Achilleus in turn gazed on Dardanian Priam
and wondered, as he saw his brave looks and listened to him talking.
But when they had taken their fill of gazing one on the other,
first of the two to speak was the aged man, Priam the godlike:
"Give me, beloved of Zeus, a place to sleep presently, so that
we may even go to bed and take the pleasure of sweet sleep.
For my eyes have not closed underneath my lids since that time
when my son lost his life beneath your hands, but always
I have been grieving and brooding over my numberless sorrows
and wallowed in the muck about my courtyard's enclosure.
Now I have tasted food again and have let the gleaming
wine go down my throat. Before, I had tasted nothing."
He spoke, and Achilleus ordered his serving-maids and companions
to make a bed in the porch's shelter and to lay upon it
fine underbedding of purple, and spread blankets above it
and fleecy robes to be an over-all covering. The maid-servants
went forth from the main house, and in their hands held torches,
and set to work, and presently had two beds made. Achilleus
of the swift feet now looked at Priam and said, sarcastic:
"Sleep outside, aged sir and good friend, for fear some Achaian
might come in here on a matter of counsel, since they keep coming
and sitting by me and making plans; as they are supposed to.
But if one of these come through the fleeting black night should notice you,
he would go straight and tell Agamemnon, shepherd of the people,
and there would be delay in the ransoming of the body.
But come, tell me this and count off for me exactly
how many days you intend for the burial of great Hektor.
Tell me, so I myself shall stay still and hold back the people."
In answer to him again spoke aged Priam the godlike:
"If you are willing that we accomplish a complete funeral
for great Hektor, this, Achilleus, is what you could do and give

me pleasure. For you know surely how we are penned in our city,
and wood is far to bring in from the hills, and the Trojans are frightened
badly. Nine days we would keep him in our palace and mourn him,
and bury him on the tenth day, and the people feast by him,
and on the eleventh day we would make the grave-barrow for him,
and on the twelfth day fight again; if so we must do."

Then in turn swift-footed brilliant Achilleus answered him:
"Then all this, aged Priam, shall be done as you ask it.
I will hold off our attack for as much time as you bid me."

So he spoke, and took the aged king by the right hand
at the wrist, so that his heart might have no fear. Then these two,
Priam and the herald who were both men of close counsel,
slept in the place outside the house, in the porch's shelter;
but Achilleus slept in the inward corner of the strong-built shelter,
and at his side lay Briseis of the fair colouring.

Now the rest of the gods and men who were lords of chariots
slept nightlong, with the easy bondage of slumber upon them,
only sleep had not caught Hermes the kind god, who pondered
now in his heart the problem of how to escort King Priam
from the ships and not be seen by the devoted gate-wardens.
He stood above his head and spoke a word to him, saying:
"Aged sir, you can have no thought of evil from the way
you sleep still among your enemies now Achilleus has left you
unharmed. You have ransomed now your dear son and given much for him.
But the sons you left behind would give three times as much ransom
for you, who are alive, were Atreus' son Agamemnon
to recognize you, and all the other Achaians learn of you."

He spoke, and the old man was afraid, and wakened his herald,
and lightly Hermes harnessed for them the mules and the horses
and himself drove them through the encampment. And no man knew of
them.

But when they came to the crossing-place of the fair-running river,
of whirling Xanthos, a stream whose father was Zeus the immortal,
there Hermes left them and went away to the height of Olympos,
and dawn, she of the yellow robe, scattered over all earth,
and they drove their horses on to the city with lamentation
and clamour, while the mules drew the body. Nor was any other
aware of them at the first, no man, no fair-girdled woman,
only Kassandra, a girl like Aphrodite the golden,
who had gone up to the height of the Pergamos. She saw
her dear father standing in the chariot, his herald and crier
with him. She saw Hektor drawn by the mules on a litter.
She cried out then in sorrow and spoke to the entire city:
"Come, men of Troy and Trojan women; look upon Hektor
if ever before you were joyful when you saw him come back living
from battle; for he was a great joy to his city, and all his people."

She spoke, and there was no man left there in all the city
nor woman, but all were held in sorrow passing endurance.
They met Priam beside the gates as he brought the dead in.

First among them were Hektor's wife and his honoured mother
who tore their hair, and ran up beside the smooth-rolling wagon,
and touched his head. And the multitude, wailing, stood there about them.
And now and there in front of the gates they would have lamented
all day till the sun went down and let fall their tears for Hektor,
except that the old man spoke from the chariot to his people:
"Give me way to get through with my mules; then afterwards
you may sate yourselves with mourning, when I have him inside the
palace."
So he spoke, and they stood apart and made way for the wagon.
And when they had brought him inside the renowned house, they laid him
then on a carved bed, and seated beside him the singers
who were to lead the melody in the dirge, and the singers
chanted the song of sorrow, and the women were mourning beside them.
Andromache of the white arms led the lamentation
of the women, and held in her arms the head of manslaughtering Hektor:
"My husband, you were lost young from life, and have left me
a widow in your house, and the boy is only a baby
who was born to you and me, the unhappy. I think he will never
come of age, for before then head to heel this city
will be sacked, for you, its defender, are gone, you who guarded
the city, and the grave wives, and the innocent children,
wives who before long must go away in the hollow ships,
and among them I shall also go, and you, my child, follow
where I go, and there do much hard work that is unworthy
of you, drudgery for a hard master; or else some Achaian
will take you by hand and hurl you from the tower into horrible
death, in anger because Hektor once killed his brother,
or his father, or his son; there were so many Achaians
whose teeth bit the vast earth, beaten down by the hands of Hektor.
Your father was no merciful man in the horror of battle.
Therefore your people are grieving for you all through their city,
Hektor, and you left for your parents mourning and sorrow
beyond words, but for me passing all others is left the bitterness
and the pain, for you did not die in bed, and stretch your arms to me,
nor tell me some last intimate word that I could remember
always, all the nights and days of my weeping for you."
So she spoke in tears, and the women were mourning about her.
Now Hekabe led out the thronging chant of their sorrow:
"Hektor, of all my sons the dearest by far to my spirit;
while you still lived for me you were dear to the gods, and even
in the stage of death they cared about you still. There were others
of my sons whom at times swift-footed Achilleus captured,
and he would sell them as slaves far across the unresting salt water
into Samos, and Imbros, and Lemnos in the gloom of the mists. You,
when he had taken your life with the thin edge of the bronze sword,
he dragged again and again around his beloved companion's
tomb, Patroklos', whom you killed, but even so did not
bring him back to life. Now you lie in the palace, handsome

and fresh with dew, in the likeness of one whom he of the silver
bow, Apollo, has attacked and killed with his gentle arrows."
   So she spoke, in tears, and wakened the endless mourning.
Third and last Helen led the song of sorrow among them:
"Hektor, of all my lord's brothers dearest by far to my spirit:
my husband is Alexandros, like an immortal, who brought me
here to Troy; and I should have died before I came with him;
and here now is the twentieth year upon me since I came
from the place where I was, forsaking the land of my fathers.
   In this time
I have never heard a harsh saying from you, nor an insult.
No, but when another, one of my lord's brothers or sisters, a fair-robed
wife of some brother, would say a harsh word to me in the palace,
or my lord's mother—but his father was gentle always, a father
indeed—then you would speak and put them off and restrain them
by your own gentleness of heart and your gentle words. Therefore
I mourn for you in sorrow of heart and mourn myself also
and my ill luck. There was no other in all the wide Troad
who was kind to me, and my friend; all others shrank when they saw me."
   So she spoke in tears, and the vast populace grieved with her.
Now Priam the aged king spoke forth his word to his people:
"Now, men of Troy, bring timber into the city, and let not
your hearts fear a close ambush of the Argives. Achilleus
promised me, as he sent me on my way from the black ships,
that none should do us injury until the twelfth dawn comes."
   He spoke, and they harnessed to the wagons their mules
   and their oxen
and presently were gathered in front of the city. Nine days
they spent bringing in an endless supply of timber. But when
the tenth dawn had shone forth with her light upon mortals,
they carried out bold Hektor, weeping, and set the body
aloft a towering pyre for burning. And set fire to it.
   But when the young dawn showed again with her rosy fingers,
the people gathered around the pyre of illustrious Hektor.
But when all were gathered to one place and assembled together,
first with gleaming wine they put out the pyre that was burning,
all where the fury of the fire still was in force, and thereafter
the brothers and companions of Hektor gathered the white bones
up, mourning, as the tears swelled and ran down their cheeks. Then
they laid what they had gathered up in a golden casket
and wrapped this about with soft robes of purple, and presently
put it away in the hollow of the grave, and over it
piled huge stones laid close together. Lightly and quickly
they piled up the grave-barrow, and on all sides were set watchmen
for fear the strong-greaved Achaians might too soon set upon them.
They piled up the grave-barrow and went away, and thereafter
assembled in a fair gathering and held a glorious
feast within the house of Priam, king under God's hand.
   Such was their burial of Hektor, breaker of horses.

The Odyssey[1]

Book 1. Athena Inspires the Prince

Sing to me of the man, Muse,[2] the man of twists and turns
driven time and again off course, once he had plundered
the hallowed heights of Troy.
Many cities of men he saw and learned their minds,
many pains he suffered, heartsick on the open sea,
fighting to save his life and bring his comrades home.
But he could not save them from disaster, hard as
he strove—
the recklessness of their own ways destroyed them all,
the blind fools, they devoured the cattle of the Sun
and the Sungod wiped from sight the day of their return.
Launch out on his story, Muse, daughter of Zeus,
start from where you will—sing for our time too.
By now,
all the survivors, all who avoided headlong death
were safe at home, escaped the wars and waves.
But one man alone . . .
his heart set on his wife and his return—Calypso,
the bewitching nymph, the lustrous goddess, held him back,
deep in her arching caverns, craving him for a husband.
But then, when the wheeling seasons brought the year around,
that year spun out by the gods when he should reach
his home,
Ithaca—though not even there would he be free of trials,
even among his loved ones—then every god took pity,
all except Poseidon.[3] He raged on, seething against
the great Odysseus till he reached his native land.
But now
Poseidon had gone to visit the Ethiopians worlds away,
Ethiopians off at the farthest limits of mankind,
a people split in two, one part where the Sungod sets
and part where the Sungod rises. There Poseidon went
to receive an offering, bulls and rams by the hundred—
far away at the feast the Sea-lord sat and took his pleasure.
But the other gods, at home in Olympian Zeus's halls,
met for full assembly there, and among them now
the father of men and gods was first to speak,
sorely troubled, remembering handsome Aegisthus,
the man Agamemnon's son, renowned Orestes, killed.
Recalling Aegisthus, Zeus harangued the immortal powers:
"Ah how shameless—the way these mortals blame the gods.

1. Translated by Robert Fagles.
2. Goddess of epic poetry, one of several Muses.
3. God of the sea, of earthquakes, and of horses.

From us alone, they say, come all their miseries, yes,
but they themselves, with their own reckless ways,
compound their pains beyond their proper share.
Look at Aegisthus now . . .
above and beyond *his* share he stole Atrides'[4] wife,
he murdered the warlord coming home from Troy
though he knew it meant his own total ruin.
Far in advance we told him so ourselves,
dispatching the guide, the giant-killer Hermes.[5]
'Don't murder the man,' he said, 'don't court his wife.
Beware, revenge will come from Orestes, Agamemnon's son,
that day he comes of age and longs for his native land.'
So Hermes warned, with all the good will in the world,
but would Aegisthus' hardened heart give way?
Now he pays the price—all at a single stroke."

And sparkling-eyed Athena drove the matter home:
"Father, son of Cronus, our high and mighty king,
surely he goes down to a death he earned in full!
Let them all die so, all who do such things.
But my heart breaks for Odysseus,
that seasoned veteran cursed by fate so long—
far from his loved ones still, he suffers torments
off on a wave-washed island rising at the center of the seas.
A dark wooded island, and there a goddess makes her home,
a daughter of Atlas, wicked Titan who sounds the deep
in all its depths, whose shoulders lift on high
the colossal pillars thrusting earth and sky apart.
Atlas' daughter it is who holds Odysseus captive,
luckless man—despite his tears, forever trying
to spellbind his heart with suave, seductive words
and wipe all thought of Ithaca from his mind.
But he, straining for no more than a glimpse
of hearth-smoke drifting up from his own land,
Odysseus longs to die . . .
Olympian Zeus,
have you no care for *him* in your lofty heart?
Did he never win your favor with sacrifices
burned beside the ships on the broad plain of Troy?
Why, Zeus, why so dead set against Odysseus?"

"My child," Zeus who marshals the thunderheads replied,
"what nonsense you let slip through your teeth. Now,
how on earth could I forget Odysseus? Great Odysseus
who excels all men in wisdom, excels in offerings too
he gives the immortal gods who rule the vaulting skies?
No, it's the Earth-Shaker, Poseidon, unappeased,

4. "Son of Atreus," Agamemnon.

5. Messenger god.

forever fuming against him for the Cyclops
whose giant eye he blinded: godlike Polyphemus,
towering over all the Cyclops' clans in power.
The nymph Thoosa bore him, daughter of Phorcys,
lord of the barren salt sea—she met Poseidon
once in his vaulted caves and they made love.
And now for his blinded son the earthquake god—
though he won't quite kill Odysseus—
drives him far off course from native land.
But come, all of us here put heads together now,
work out his journey home so Odysseus can return.
Lord Poseidon, I trust, will let his anger go.
How can he stand his ground against the will
of all the gods at once—one god alone?"

Athena, her eyes flashing bright, exulted,
"Father, son of Cronus, our high and mighty king!
If now it really pleases the blissful gods
that wise Odysseus shall return—home at last—
let us dispatch the guide and giant-killer Hermes
down to Ogygia Island, down to announce at once
to the nymph with lovely braids our fixed decree:
Odysseus journeys home—the exile must return!
While I myself go down to Ithaca, rouse his son
to a braver pitch, inspire his heart with courage
to summon the flowing-haired Achaeans to full assembly,
speak his mind to all those suitors, slaughtering on and on
his droves of sheep and shambling longhorn cattle.
Next I will send him off to Sparta and sandy Pylos,
there to learn of his dear father's journey home.
Perhaps he will hear some news and make his name
throughout the mortal world."
So Athena vowed
and under her feet she fastened the supple sandals,
ever-glowing gold, that wing her over the waves
and boundless earth with the rush of gusting winds.
She seized the rugged spear tipped with a bronze point—
weighted, heavy, the massive shaft she wields to break the lines
of heroes the mighty Father's daughter storms against.
And down she swept from Olympus' craggy peaks
and lit on Ithaca, standing tall at Odysseus' gates,
the threshold of his court. Gripping her bronze spear,
she looked for all the world like a stranger now,
like Mentes, lord of the Taphians.
There she found the swaggering suitors, just then
amusing themselves with rolling dice before the doors,
lounging on hides of oxen they had killed themselves.
While heralds and brisk attendants bustled round them,
some at the mixing-bowls, mulling wine and water,

others wiping the tables down with sopping sponges,
setting them out in place, still other servants
jointed and carved the great sides of meat.

First by far to see her was Prince Telemachus,
sitting among the suitors, heart obsessed with grief.
He could almost see his magnificent father, here . . .
in the mind's eye—if only *he* might drop from the clouds
and drive these suitors all in a rout throughout the halls
and regain his pride of place and rule his own domains!
Daydreaming so as he sat among the suitors,
he glimpsed Athena now
and straight to the porch he went, mortified
that a guest might still be standing at the doors.
Pausing beside her there, he clasped her right hand
and relieving her at once of her long bronze spear,
met her with winged words: "Greetings, stranger!
Here in our house you'll find a royal welcome.
Have supper first, then tell us what you need."

He led the way and Pallas Athena followed.
Once in the high-roofed hall, he took her lance
and fixed it firm in a burnished rack against
a sturdy pillar, there where row on row of spears,
embattled Odysseus' spears, stood stacked and waiting.
Then he escorted her to a high, elaborate chair of honor,
over it draped a cloth, and here he placed his guest
with a stool to rest her feet. But for himself
he drew up a low reclining chair beside her,
richly painted, clear of the press of suitors,
concerned his guest, offended by their uproar,
might shrink from food in the midst of such a mob.
He hoped, what's more, to ask her about his long-lost father.
A maid brought water soon in a graceful golden pitcher
and over a silver basin tipped it out
so they might rinse their hands,
then pulled a gleaming table to their side.
A staid housekeeper brought on bread to serve them,
appetizers aplenty too, lavish with her bounty.
A carver lifted platters of meat toward them,
meats of every sort, and set beside them golden cups
and time and again a page came round and poured them wine.

But now the suitors trooped in with all their swagger
and took their seats on low and high-backed chairs.
Heralds poured water over their hands for rinsing,
serving maids brought bread heaped high in trays
and the young men brimmed the mixing-bowls with wine.
They reached out for the good things that lay at hand,
and when they'd put aside desire for food and drink

the suitors set their minds on other pleasures,
song and dancing, all that crowns a feast.
A herald placed an ornate lyre in Phemius' hands,
the bard who always performed among them there;
they forced the man to sing.
A rippling prelude—
and no sooner had he struck up his rousing song
than Telemachus, head close to Athena's sparkling eyes,
spoke low to his guest so no one else could hear:
"Dear stranger, would you be shocked by what I say?
Look at them over there. Not a care in the world,
just lyres and tunes! It's easy for them, all right,
they feed on another's goods and go scot-free—
a man whose white bones lie strewn in the rain somewhere,
rotting away on land or rolling down the ocean's salty swells.
But that man—if they caught sight of him home in Ithaca,
by god, they'd all pray to be faster on their feet
than richer in bars of gold and heavy robes.
But now, no use, he's died a wretched death.
No comfort's left for us . . . not even if
someone, somewhere, says he's coming home.
The day of his return will never dawn.
Enough.
Tell me about yourself now, clearly, point by point.
Who are you? where are you from? your city? your parents?
What sort of vessel brought you? Why did the sailors
land you here in Ithaca? Who did they say they are?
I hardly think you came this way on foot!
And tell me this for a fact—I need to know—
is this your first time here? Or are you a friend of father's,
a guest from the old days? Once, crowds of other men
would come to our house on visits—visitor that he was,
when he walked among the living."
Her eyes glinting,
goddess Athena answered, "My whole story, of course,
I'll tell it point by point. Wise old Anchialus
was my father. My own name is Mentes,
lord of the Taphian men who love their oars.
And here I've come, just now, with ship and crew,
sailing the wine-dark sea to foreign ports of call,
to Temese, out for bronze—our cargo gleaming iron.
Our ship lies moored off farmlands far from town,
riding in Rithron Cove, beneath Mount Nion's woods.
As for the ties between your father and myself,
we've been friends forever, I'm proud to say,
and he would bear me out
if you went and questioned old lord Laertes.[6]

6. Odysseus's father.

He, I gather, no longer ventures into town
but lives a life of hardship, all to himself,
off on his farmstead with an aged serving-woman
who tends him well, who gives him food and drink
when weariness has taken hold of his withered limbs
from hauling himself along his vineyard's steep slopes.
And now I've come—and why? I heard that he was back . . .
your father, that is. But no, the gods thwart his passage.
Yet I tell you great Odysseus is not dead. He's still alive,
somewhere in this wide world, held captive, out at sea
on a wave-washed island, and hard men, savages,
somehow hold him back against his will.
Wait,
I'll make you a prophecy, one the immortal gods
have planted in my mind—it will come true, I think,
though I am hardly a seer or know the flights of birds.
He won't be gone long from the native land he loves,
not even if iron shackles bind your father down.
He's plotting a way to journey home at last;
he's never at a loss.
But come, please,
tell me about yourself now, point by point.
You're truly Odysseus' son? You've sprung up so!
Uncanny resemblance . . . the head, and the fine eyes—
I see him now. How often we used to meet in the old days
before he embarked for Troy, where other Argive captains,
all the best men, sailed in the long curved ships.
From then to this very day
I've not set eyes on Odysseus or he on me."

And young Telemachus cautiously replied,
"I'll try, my friend, to give you a frank answer.
Mother has always told me I'm his son, it's true,
but I am not so certain. Who, on his own,
has ever really known who gave him life?
Would to god I'd been the son of a happy man
whom old age overtook in the midst of his possessions!
Now, think of the most unlucky mortal ever born—
since you ask me, yes, they say I am his son."

"Still," the clear-eyed goddess reassured him,
"trust me, the gods have not marked out your house
for such an unsung future,
not if Penelope has borne a son like you.
But tell me about all this and spare me nothing.
What's this banqueting, this crowd carousing here?
And what part do you play yourself? Some wedding-feast,
some festival? Hardly a potluck supper, I would say.
How obscenely they lounge and swagger here, look,
gorging in your house. Why, any man of sense

who chanced among them would be outraged,
seeing such behavior."
Ready Telemachus
took her up at once: "Well, my friend,
seeing you want to probe and press the question,
once this house was rich, no doubt, beyond reproach
when the man you mentioned still lived here, at home.
Now the gods have reversed our fortunes with a vengeance—
wiped that man from the earth like no one else before.
I would never have grieved so much about his death
if he'd gone down with comrades off in Troy
or died in the arms of loved ones,
once he had wound down the long coil of war.
Then all united Achaea would have raised his tomb
and he'd have won his son great fame for years to come.
But now the whirlwinds have ripped him away, no fame for him!
He's lost and gone now—out of sight, out of mind—and I . . .
he's left me tears and grief. Nor do I rack my heart
and grieve for him alone. No longer. Now the gods
have invented other miseries to plague me.
Listen.
All the nobles who rule the islands round about,
Dulichion, and Same, and wooded Zacynthus too,
and all who lord it in rocky Ithaca as well—
down to the last man they court my mother,
they lay waste my house! And mother . . .
she neither rejects a marriage she despises
nor can she bear to bring the courting to an end—
while they continue to bleed my household white.
Soon—you wait—they'll grind *me* down as well."
"Shameful!"—
brimming with indignation, Pallas Athena broke out.
"Oh how much you need Odysseus, gone so long—
how *he*'d lay hands on all these brazen suitors!
If only he would appear, now,
at his house's outer gates and take his stand,
armed with his helmet, shield and pair of spears,
as strong as the man I glimpsed that first time
in our own house, drinking wine and reveling there . . .
just come in from Ephyra, visiting Ilus, Mermerus' son.
Odysseus sailed that way, you see, in his swift trim ship,
hunting deadly poison to smear on his arrows' bronze heads.
Ilus refused—he feared the wrath of the everlasting gods—
but father, so fond of him, gave him all he wanted.
If only *that* Odysseus sported with these suitors,
a blood wedding, a quick death would take the lot!
True, but all lies in the lap of the great gods,
whether or not he'll come and pay them back,
here, in his own house.

But you, I urge you,
think how to drive these suitors from your halls.
Come now, listen closely. Take my words to heart.
At daybreak summon the island's lords to full assembly,
give your orders to all and call the gods to witness:
tell the suitors to scatter, each to his own place.
As for your mother, if the spirit moves her to marry,
let her go back to her father's house, a man of power.
Her kin will arrange the wedding, provide the gifts,
the array that goes with a daughter dearly loved.
For you,
I have some good advice, if only you will accept it.
Fit out a ship with twenty oars, the best in sight,
sail in quest of news of your long-lost father.
Someone may tell you something
or you may catch a rumor straight from Zeus,
rumor that carries news to men like nothing else.
First go down to Pylos, question old King Nestor,
then cross over to Sparta, to red-haired Menelaus,
of all the bronze-armored Achaeans the last man back.
Now, if you hear your father's alive and heading home,
hard-pressed as you are, brave out one more year.
If you hear he's dead, no longer among the living,
then back you come to the native land you love,
raise his grave-mound, build his honors high
with the full funeral rites that he deserves—
and give your mother to another husband.
Then,
once you've sealed those matters, seen them through,
think hard, reach down deep in your heart and soul
for a way to kill these suitors in your house,
by stealth or in open combat.
You must not cling to your boyhood any longer—
it's time you were a man. Haven't you heard
what glory Prince Orestes won throughout the world
when he killed that cunning, murderous Aegisthus,
who'd killed his famous father?
And you, my friend—
how tall and handsome I see you now—be brave, you too,
so men to come will sing your praises down the years.
But now I must go back to my swift trim ship
and all my shipmates, chafing there, I'm sure,
waiting for my return. It all rests with you.
Take my words to heart."
"Oh stranger,"
heedful Telemachus replied, "indeed I will.
You've counseled me with so much kindness now,
like a father to a son. I won't forget a word.
But come, stay longer, keen as you are to sail,

so you can bathe and rest and lift your spirits,
then go back to your ship, delighted with a gift,
a prize of honor, something rare and fine
as a keepsake from myself. The kind of gift
a host will give a stranger, friend to friend."

Her eyes glinting, Pallas declined in haste:
"Not now. Don't hold me here. I long to be on my way.
As for the gift—whatever you'd give in kindness—
save it for my return so I can take it home.
Choose something rare and fine, and a good reward
that gift is going to bring you."
With that promise,
off and away Athena the bright-eyed goddess flew
like a bird in soaring flight
but left his spirit filled with nerve and courage,
charged with his father's memory more than ever now.
He felt his senses quicken, overwhelmed with wonder—
this was a god, he knew it well and made at once
for the suitors, a man like a god himself.
Amidst them still
the famous bard sang on, and they sat in silence, listening
as he performed The Achaeans' Journey Home from Troy:
all the blows Athena doomed them to endure.
And now,
from high above in her room and deep in thought,
she caught his inspired strains . . .
Icarius' daughter Penelope, wary and reserved,
and down the steep stair from her chamber she descended,
not alone: two of her women followed close behind.
That radiant woman, once she reached her suitors,
drawing her glistening veil across her cheeks,
paused now where a column propped the sturdy roof,
with one of her loyal handmaids stationed either side.
Suddenly, dissolving in tears and bursting through
the bard's inspired voice, she cried out, "Phemius!
So many other songs you know to hold us spellbound,
works of the gods and men that singers celebrate.
Sing one of those as you sit beside them here
and they drink their wine in silence.
But break off this song—
the unendurable song that always rends the heart inside me . . .
the unforgettable grief, it wounds me most of all!
How I long for my husband—alive in memory, always,
that great man whose fame resounds through Hellas
right to the depths of Argos!"
"Why, mother,"
poised Telemachus put in sharply, "why deny
our devoted bard the chance to entertain us

any way the spirit stirs him on?
Bards are not to blame—
Zeus is to blame. He deals to each and every
laborer on this earth whatever doom he pleases.
Why fault the bard if he sings the Argives' harsh fate?
It's always the latest song, the one that echoes last
in the listeners' ears, that people praise the most.
Courage, mother. Harden your heart, and listen.
Odysseus was scarcely the only one, you know,
whose journey home was blotted out at Troy.
Others, so many others, died there too.
So, mother,
go back to your quarters. Tend to your own tasks,
the distaff and the loom, and keep the women
working hard as well. As for giving orders,
men will see to that, but I most of all:
I hold the reins of power in this house."
Astonished,
she withdrew to her own room. She took to heart
the clear good sense in what her son had said.
Climbing up to the lofty chamber with her women,
she fell to weeping for Odysseus, her beloved husband,
till watchful Athena sealed her eyes with welcome sleep.

But the suitors broke into uproar through the shadowed halls,
all of them lifting prayers to lie beside her, share her bed,
until discreet Telemachus took command: "You suitors
who plague my mother, you, you insolent, overweening . . .
for this evening let us dine and take our pleasure,
no more shouting now. What a fine thing it is
to listen to such a bard as we have here—
the man sings like a god.
But at first light
we all march forth to assembly, take our seats
so I can give my orders and say to you straight out:
You must leave my palace! See to your feasting elsewhere,
devour your own possessions, house to house by turns.
But if you decide the fare is better, richer here,
destroying one man's goods and going scot-free,
all right then, carve away!
But I'll cry out to the everlasting gods in hopes
that Zeus will pay you back with a vengeance—all of you
destroyed in my house while I go scot-free myself!"

So Telemachus declared. And they all bit their lips,
amazed the prince could speak with so much daring.

Eupithes' son Antinous broke their silence:
"Well, Telemachus, only the gods could teach you
to sound so high and mighty! Such brave talk.

I pray that Zeus will never make *you* king of Ithaca,
though your father's crown is no doubt yours by birth."

But cool-headed Telemachus countered firmly:
"Antinous, even though my words may offend you,
I'd be happy to take the crown if Zeus presents it.
You think that nothing worse could befall a man?
It's really not so bad to be a king. All at once
your palace grows in wealth, your honors grow as well.
But there are hosts of other Achaean princes, look—
young and old, crowds of them on our island here—
and any one of the lot might hold the throne,
now great Odysseus is dead . . .
But I'll be lord of my own house and servants,
all that King Odysseus won for me by force."

And now Eurymachus, Polybus' son, stepped in:
"Surely this must lie in the gods' lap, Telemachus—
which Achaean will lord it over seagirt Ithaca.
Do hold on to your own possessions, rule your house.
God forbid that anyone tear your holdings from your hands
while men still live in Ithaca.
But about your guest,
dear boy, I have some questions. Where does he come from?
Where's his country, his birth, his father's old estates?
Did he bring some news of your father, his return?
Or did he come on business of his own?
How he leapt to his feet and off he went!
No waiting around for proper introductions.
And no mean man, not by the looks of him, I'd say."

"Eurymachus," Telemachus answered shrewdly,
"clearly my father's journey home is lost forever.
I no longer trust in rumors—rumors from the blue—
nor bother with any prophecy, when mother calls
some wizard into the house to ask him questions.
As for the stranger, though,
the man's an old family friend, from Taphos,
wise Anchialus' son. He says his name is Mentes,
lord of the Taphian men who love their oars."
So he said
but deep in his mind he knew the immortal goddess.
Now the suitors turned to dance and song,
to the lovely beat and sway,
waiting for dusk to come upon them there . . .
and the dark night came upon them, lost in pleasure.
Finally, to bed. Each to his own house.
Telemachus,
off to his bedroom built in the fine courtyard—
a commanding, lofty room set well apart—

retired too, his spirit swarming with misgivings.
His devoted nurse attended him, bearing a glowing torch,
Eurycleia the daughter of Ops, Pisenor's son.
Laertes had paid a price for the woman years ago,
still in the bloom of youth. He traded twenty oxen,
honored her on a par with his own loyal wife at home
but fearing the queen's anger, never shared her bed.
She was his grandson's escort now and bore a torch,
for she was the one of all the maids who loved
the prince the most—she'd nursed him as a baby.
He spread the doors of his snug, well-made room,
sat down on the bed and pulled his soft shirt off,
tossed it into the old woman's conscientious hands,
and after folding it neatly, patting it smooth,
she hung it up on a peg beside his corded bed,
then padded from the bedroom,
drawing the door shut with the silver hook,
sliding the doorbolt home with its rawhide strap.
There all night long, wrapped in a sheep's warm fleece,
he weighed in his mind the course Athena charted.

Book 2. Telemachus Sets Sail

When young Dawn with her rose-red fingers shone once more
the true son of Odysseus sprang from bed and dressed,
over his shoulder he slung his well-honed sword,
fastened rawhide sandals under his smooth feet
and stepped from his bedroom, handsome as a god.
At once he ordered heralds to cry out loud and clear
and summon the flowing-haired Achaeans to full assembly.
Their cries rang out. The people filed in quickly.
When they'd grouped, crowding the meeting grounds,
Telemachus strode in too, a bronze spear in his grip
and not alone: two sleek hounds went trotting at his heels.
And Athena lavished a marvelous splendor on the prince
so the people all gazed in wonder as he came forward,
the elders making way as he took his father's seat.
The first to speak was an old lord, Aegyptius,
stooped with age, who knew the world by heart.
For one dear son had sailed with King Odysseus,
bound in the hollow ships to the stallion-land of Troy—
the spearman Antiphus—but the brutal Cyclops killed him,
trapped in his vaulted cave, the last man the monster ate.
Three other sons he had: one who mixed with the suitors,
Eurynomus, and two kept working their father's farms.
Still, he never forgot the soldier, desolate in his grief.
In tears for the son he lost, he rose and said among them,
"Hear me, men of Ithaca. Hear what I have to say.
Not once have we held assembly, met in session

since King Odysseus sailed away in the hollow ships.
Who has summoned us now—one of the young men,
one of the old-timers? What crisis spurs him on?
Some news he's heard of an army on the march,
word he's caught firsthand so he can warn us now?
Or some other public matter he'll disclose and argue?
He's a brave man, I'd say. God be with him, too!
May Zeus speed him on to a happy end,
whatever his heart desires!"
Winning words
with a lucky ring. Odysseus' son rejoiced;
the boy could sit no longer—fired up to speak,
he took his stand among the gathered men.
The herald Pisenor, skilled in custom's ways,
put the staff in his hand, and then the prince,
addressing old Aegyptius first, led off with, "Sir,
that man is not far off—you'll soon see for yourself—
I was the one who called us all together.
Something wounds me deeply . . .
not news I've heard of an army on the march,
word I've caught firsthand so I can warn you now,
or some other public matter I'll disclose and argue.
No, the crisis is my own. Trouble has struck my house—
a double blow. First, I have lost my noble father
who ruled among you years ago, each of you here,
and kindly as a father to his children.
But now this,
a worse disaster that soon will grind my house down,
ruin it all, and all my worldly goods in the bargain.
Suitors plague my mother—against her will—
sons of the very men who are your finest here!
They'd sooner die than approach her father's house
so Icarius himself might see to his daughter's bridal,
hand her to whom he likes, whoever meets his fancy.
Not they—they infest our palace day and night,
they butcher our cattle, our sheep, our fat goats,
feasting themselves sick, swilling our glowing wine
as if there's no tomorrow—all of it, squandered.
Now we have no man like Odysseus in command
to drive this curse from the house. We ourselves?
We're hardly the ones to fight them off. All we'd do
is parade our wretched weakness. A boy inept at battle.
Oh I'd swing to attack if I had the power in me.
By god, it's intolerable, what they do—disgrace,
my house a shambles!
You should be ashamed yourselves,
mortified in the face of neighbors living round about!
Fear the gods' wrath—before they wheel in outrage
and make these crimes recoil on your heads.

I beg you by Olympian Zeus, by Themis[1] too,
who sets assemblies free and calls us into session—
stop, my friends! Leave me alone to pine away in anguish . . .
Unless, of course, you think my noble father Odysseus
did the Achaean army damage, deliberate harm,
and to pay me back you'd do me harm, deliberately
setting these parasites against me. Better for me
if *you* were devouring all my treasure, all my cattle—
if you were the ones, we'd make amends in no time.
We'd approach you for reparations round the town,
demanding our goods till you'd returned the lot.
But now, look, you load my heart with grief—
there's nothing I can do!"

Filled with anger,
down on the ground he dashed the speaker's scepter—
bursting into tears. Pity seized the assembly.
All just sat there, silent . . .
no one had the heart to reply with harshness.
Only Antinous, who found it in himself to say,
"So high and mighty, Telemachus—such unbridled rage!
Well now, fling your accusations at *us?*
Think to pin the blame on *us?* You think again.
It's not the suitors here who deserve the blame,
it's your own dear mother, the matchless queen of cunning.
Look here. For three years now, getting on to four,
she's played it fast and loose with all our hearts,
building each man's hopes—
dangling promises, dropping hints to each—
but all the while with something else in mind.
This was her latest masterpiece of guile:
she set up a great loom in the royal halls
and she began to weave, and the weaving finespun,
the yarns endless, and she would lead us on: 'Young men,
my suitors, now that King Odysseus is no more,
go slowly, keen as you are to marry me, until
I can finish off this web . . .
so my weaving won't all fray and come to nothing.
This is a shroud for old lord Laertes, for that day
when the deadly fate that lays us out at last will take him down.
I dread the shame my countrywomen would heap upon me,
yes, if a man of such wealth should lie in state
without a shroud for cover.'

Her very words,
and despite our pride and passion we believed her.
So by day she'd weave at her great and growing web—
by night, by the light of torches set beside her,
she would unravel all she'd done. Three whole years

1. Goddess of justice, right, and law.

she deceived us blind, seduced us with this scheme . . .
Then, when the wheeling seasons brought the fourth year on,
one of her women, in on the queen's secret, told the truth
and we caught her in the act—unweaving her gorgeous web.
So she finished it off. Against her will. We forced her.

Now Telemachus, here is how the suitors answer *you*—
you burn it in your mind, you and all our people:
send your mother back! Direct her to marry
whomever her father picks, whoever pleases her.
So long as she persists in tormenting us,
quick to exploit the gifts Athena gave her—
a skilled hand for elegant work, a fine mind
and subtle wiles too—we've never heard the like,
not even in old stories sung of all Achaea's
well-coifed queens who graced the years gone by:
Mycenae crowned with garlands, Tyro and Alcmena . . .
Not one could equal Penelope for intrigue
but in this case she intrigued beyond all limits.
So, we will devour your worldly goods and wealth
as long as *she* holds out, holds to that course
the gods have charted deep inside her heart.
Great renown she wins for herself, no doubt,
great loss for you in treasure. We'll not go back
to our old estates or leave for other parts,
not till she weds the Argive man she fancies."

But with calm good sense Telemachus replied:
"Antinous, how can I drive my mother from our house
against her will, the one who bore me, reared me too?
My father is worlds away, dead or alive, who knows?
Imagine the high price I'd have to pay Icarius
if all on my own I send my mother home.
Oh what I would suffer from her father—
and some dark god would hurt me even more
when mother, leaving her own house behind,
calls down her withering Furies[2] on my head,
and our people's cries of shame would hound my heels.
I will never issue that ultimatum to my mother.
And you, if you have any shame in your own hearts,
you must leave my palace! See to your feasting elsewhere,
devour your own possessions, house to house by turns.
But if you decide the fare is better, richer here,
destroying one man's goods and going scot-free,
all right then, carve away!
But I'll cry out to the everlasting gods in hopes
that Zeus will pay you back with a vengeance—all of you
destroyed in my house while I go scot-free myself!"

2. Earth goddesses who avenge crimes against family members.

And to seal his prayer, farseeing Zeus sent down a sign.
He launched two eagles soaring high from a mountain ridge
and down they glided, borne on the wind's draft a moment,
wing to wingtip, pinions straining taut till just
above the assembly's throbbing hum they whirled,
suddenly, wings thrashing, wild onslaught of wings
and banking down at the crowd's heads—a glaring, fatal sign—
talons slashing each other, tearing cheeks and throats
they swooped away on the right through homes and city.
All were dumbstruck, watching the eagles trail from sight,
people brooding, deeply, what might come to pass . . .
Until the old warrior Halitherses,
Mastor's son, broke the silence for them—
the one who outperformed all men of his time
at reading bird-signs, sounding out the omens,
rose and spoke, distraught for each man there:
"Hear me, men of Ithaca! Hear what I have to say,
though my revelations strike the suitors first of all—
a great disaster is rolling like a breaker toward their heads.
Clearly Odysseus won't be far from loved ones any longer—
now, right now, he's somewhere near, I tell you,
breeding bloody death for all these suitors here,
pains aplenty too for the rest of us who live
in Ithaca's sunlit air.
Long before that,
we must put heads together, find some way
to stop these men, or let them stop themselves.
Better for them that way, by far. I myself
am no stranger to prophecy—I can see it now!
Odysseus . . . all is working out for him, I say,
just as I said it would that day the Argives sailed
for Troy and the mastermind of battle boarded with them.
I said then: after many blows, and all his shipmates lost,
after twenty years had wheeled by, he would come home,
unrecognized by all . . .
and now, look, it all comes to pass!"
"Stop, old man!"
Eurymachus, Polybus' son, rose up to take him on.
"Go home and babble your omens to your children—
save *them* from some catastrophe coming soon.
I'm a better hand than you at reading portents.
Flocks of birds go fluttering under the sun's rays,
not all are fraught with meaning. Odysseus?
He's dead now, far from home—
would to god that you'd died with him too.
We'd have escaped your droning prophecies then
and the way you've loosed the dogs of this boy's anger—
your eyes peeled for a house-gift he might give you.
Here's *my* prophecy, bound to come to pass.

If you, you old codger, wise as the ages,
talk him round, incite the boy to riot,
he'll be the first to suffer, let me tell you.
And you, old man, we'll clap some fine on you
you'll weep to pay, a fine to crush your spirit!
Telemachus?
Here in front of you all, here's my advice for him.
Let him urge his mother back to her father's house—
her kin will arrange the wedding, provide the gifts,
the array that goes with a daughter dearly loved.
Not till then, I'd say, will the island princes quit
their taxing courtship. Who's there to fear? I ask you.
Surely not Telemachus, with all his tiresome threats.
Nor do we balk, old man, at the prophecies you mouth—
they'll come to grief, they'll make us hate you more.
The prince's wealth will be devoured as always,
mercilessly—no reparations, ever . . . not
while the queen drags out our hopes to wed her,
waiting, day after day, all of us striving hard
to win one matchless beauty. Never courting others,
bevies of brides who'd suit each noble here."

Telemachus answered, firm in his resolve:
"Eurymachus—the rest of you fine, brazen suitors—
I have done with appeals to you about these matters.
I'll say no more. The gods know how things stand
and so do all the Achaeans. And now all I ask
is a good swift ship and a crew of twenty men
to speed me through my passage out and back.
I'm sailing off to Sparta, sandy Pylos too,
for news of my long-lost father's journey home.
Someone may tell me something
or I may catch a rumor straight from Zeus,
rumor that carries news to men like nothing else.
Now, if I hear my father's alive and heading home,
hard-pressed as I am, I'll brave out one more year.
If I hear he's dead, no longer among the living,
then back I'll come to the native land I love,
raise his grave-mound, build his honors high
with the full funeral rites that he deserves—
and give my mother to another husband."
A declaration,
and the prince sat down as Mentor took the floor,
Odysseus' friend-in-arms to whom the king,
sailing off to Troy, committed his household,
ordering one and all to obey the old man
and he would keep things steadfast and secure.
With deep concern for the realm, he rose and warned,
"Hear me, men of Ithaca. Hear what I have to say.

Never let any sceptered king be kind and gentle now,
not with all his heart, or set his mind on justice—
no, let him be cruel and always practice outrage.
Think: not one of the people whom he ruled
remembers Odysseus now, that godlike man,
and kindly as a father to his children!
I don't grudge these arrogant suitors for a moment,
weaving their violent work with all their wicked hearts—
they lay their lives on the line when they consume
Odysseus' worldly goods, blind in their violence,
telling themselves that he'll come home no more.
But all the rest of you, how you rouse my fury!
Sitting here in silence . . .
never a word put forth to curb these suitors,
paltry few as they are and you so many."
"Mentor!"
Euenor's son Leocritus rounded on him, shouting,
"Rabble-rousing fool, now what's this talk?
Goading them on to try and hold us back!
It's uphill work, I warn you,
fighting a force like ours—for just a meal.
Even if Odysseus of Ithaca did arrive in person,
to find us well-bred suitors feasting in his halls,
and the man were hell-bent on routing us from the palace—
little joy would his wife derive from his return,
for all her yearning. Here on the spot he'd meet
a humiliating end if he fought against such odds.
You're talking nonsense—idiocy.
No more. Come,
dissolve the assembly. Each man return to his holdings.
Mentor and Halitherses can speed our young prince on,
his father's doddering friends since time began.
He'll sit tight a good long while, I trust,
scrabbling for news right here in Ithaca—
he'll never make that trip."

This broke up the assembly, keen to leave.
The people scattered quickly, each to his own house,
while the suitors strolled back to King Odysseus' palace.

Telemachus, walking the beach now, far from others,
washed his hands in the foaming surf and prayed to Pallas:[3]
"Dear god, hear me! Yesterday you came to my house,
you told me to ship out on the misty sea and learn
if father, gone so long, is ever coming home . . .
Look how my countrymen—the suitors most of all,
the pernicious bullies—foil each move I make."

3. Athena, virgin and masculine goddess and protector of Odysseus.

Athena came to his prayer from close at hand,
for all the world with Mentor's build and voice,
and she urged him on with winging words: "Telemachus,
you'll lack neither courage nor sense from this day on,
not if your father's spirit courses through your veins—
now there was a man, I'd say, in words and action both!
So how can your journey end in shipwreck or defeat?
Only if you were not his stock, Penelope's too,
then I'd fear your hopes might come to grief.
Few sons are the equals of their fathers;
most fall short, all too few surpass them.
But you, brave and adept from this day on—
Odysseus' cunning has hardly given out in you—
there's every hope that you will reach your goal.
Put them out of your mind, these suitors' schemes and plots.
They're madmen. Not a shred of sense or decency in the crowd.
Nor can they glimpse the death and black doom hovering
just at their heads to crush them all in one short day.
But you, the journey that stirs you now is not far off,
not with the likes of me, your father's friend and yours,
to rig you a swift ship and be your shipmate too.
Now home you go and mix with the suitors there.
But get your rations ready,
pack them all in vessels, the wine in jars,
and barley-meal—the marrow of men's bones—
in durable skins, while I make rounds in town
and quickly enlist your crew of volunteers.
Lots of ships in seagirt Ithaca, old and new.
I'll look them over, choose the best in sight,
we'll fit her out and launch her into the sea at once!"

And so Athena, daughter of Zeus, assured him.
No lingering now—he heard the goddess' voice—
but back he went to his house with aching heart
and there at the palace found the brazen suitors
skinning goats in the courtyard, singeing pigs for roasting.
Antinous, smiling warmly, sauntered up to the prince,
grasped his hand and coaxed him, savoring his name:
"Telemachus, my high and mighty, fierce young friend,
no more nursing those violent words and actions now.
Come, eat and drink with us, just like the old days.
Whatever you want our people will provide. A ship
and a picked crew to speed you to holy Pylos,
out for the news about your noble father."

But self-possessed Telemachus drew the line:
"Antinous, now how could I dine with you in peace
and take my pleasure? You ruffians carousing here!
Isn't it quite enough that you, my mother's suitors,
have ravaged it all, my very best, these many years,

while I was still a boy? But now that I'm full-grown
and can hear the truth from others, absorb it too—
now, yes, that the anger seethes inside me . . .
I'll stop at nothing to hurl destruction at your heads,
whether I go to Pylos or sit tight here at home.
But the trip I speak of will not end in failure.
Go I will, as a passenger, nothing more,
since I don't seem to command my own crew.
That, I'm sure, is the way that suits you best."
With this
he nonchalantly drew his hand from Antinous' hand
while the suitors, busy feasting in the halls,
mocked and taunted him, flinging insults now.
"God help us," one young buck kept shouting,
"he wants to slaughter us all!
He's off to sandy Pylos to hire cutthroats,
even Sparta perhaps, so hot to have our heads.
Why, he'd rove as far as Ephyra's dark rich soil
and run back home with lethal poison, slip it
into the bowl and wipe us out with drink!"

"Who knows?" another young blade up and ventured.
"Off in that hollow ship of his, he just might drown,
far from his friends, a drifter like his father.
What a bore! He'd double our work for us,
splitting up his goods, parceling out his house
to his mother and the man who weds the queen."
So they scoffed
but Telemachus headed down to his father's storeroom,
broad and vaulted, piled high with gold and bronze,
chests packed with clothing, vats of redolent oil.
And there, standing in close ranks against the wall,
were jars of seasoned, mellow wine, holding the drink
unmixed inside them, fit for a god, waiting the day
Odysseus, worn by hardship, might come home again.
Doors, snugly fitted, doubly hung, were bolted shut
and a housekeeper was in charge by night and day—
her care, her vigilance, guarding all those treasures—
Eurycleia the daughter of Ops, Pisenor's son.
Telemachus called her into the storeroom: "Come, nurse,
draw me off some wine in smaller traveling jars,
mellow, the finest vintage you've been keeping,
next to what you reserve for our unlucky king—
in case Odysseus might drop in from the blue
and cheat the deadly spirits, make it home.
Fill me an even dozen, seal them tightly.
Pour me barley in well-stitched leather bags,
twenty measures of meal, your stone-ground best.
But no one else must know. These rations now,

put them all together. I'll pick them up myself,
toward evening, just about the time that mother
climbs to her room and thinks of turning in.
I'm sailing off to Sparta, sandy Pylos too,
for news of my dear father's journey home.
Perhaps I'll catch some rumor."
A wail of grief—
and his fond old nurse burst out in protest, sobbing:
"Why, dear child, what craziness got into your head?
Why bent on rambling over the face of the earth?—
a darling only son! Your father's worlds away,
god's own Odysseus, dead in some strange land.
And these brutes here, just wait, the moment you're gone
they'll all be scheming against you. Kill you by guile,
they will, and carve your birthright up in pieces.
No, sit tight here, guard your own things here.
Don't go roving over the barren salt sea—
no need to suffer so!"
"Courage, old woman,"
thoughtful Telemachus tried to reassure her,
"there's a god who made this plan.
But swear you won't say anything to my mother.
Not till ten or a dozen days have passed
or she misses me herself and learns I'm gone.
She mustn't mar her lovely face with tears."

The old one swore a solemn oath to the gods
and vowing she would never breathe a word,
quickly drew off wine in two-eared jars
and poured barley in well-stitched leather bags.
Telemachus returned to the hall and joined the suitors.

Then bright-eyed Pallas thought of one more step.
Disguised as the prince, the goddess roamed through town,
pausing beside each likely crewman, giving orders:
"Gather beside our ship at nightfall—be there."
She asked Noëmon, Phronius' generous son,
to lend her a swift ship. He gladly volunteered.

The sun sank and the roads of the world grew dark.
Now the goddess hauled the swift ship down to the water,
stowed in her all the tackle well-rigged vessels carry,
moored her well away at the harbor's very mouth
and once the crew had gathered, rallying round,
she heartened every man.

Then bright-eyed Pallas thought of one last thing.
Back she went to King Odysseus' halls and there
she showered sweet oblivion over the suitors,
dazing them as they drank, knocking cups from hands.

No more loitering now, their eyes weighed down with sleep,
they rose and groped through town to find their beds.
But calling the prince outside his timbered halls,
taking the build and voice of Mentor once again,
flashing-eyed Athena urged him on: "Telemachus,
your comrades-at-arms are ready at the oars,
waiting for your command to launch. So come,
on with our voyage now, we're wasting time."

And Pallas Athena sped away in the lead
as he followed in her footsteps, man and goddess.
Once they reached the ship at the water's edge
they found their long-haired shipmates on the beach.
The prince, inspired, gave his first commands:
"Come, friends, get the rations aboard!
They're piled in the palace now.
My mother knows nothing of this. No servants either.
Only one has heard our plan."
He led them back
and the men fell in and fetched down all the stores
and stowed them briskly, deep in the well-ribbed holds
as Odysseus' son directed. Telemachus climbed aboard.
Athena led the way, assuming the pilot's seat
reserved astern, and he sat close beside her.
Cables cast off, the crew swung to the oarlocks.
Bright-eyed Athena sent them a stiff following wind
rippling out of the west, ruffling over the wine-dark sea
as Telemachus shouted out commands to all his shipmates:
"All lay hands to tackle!" They sprang to orders,
hoisting the pinewood mast, they stepped it firm
in its block amidships, lashed it fast with stays
and with braided rawhide halyards hauled the white sail high.
Suddenly wind hit full and the canvas bellied out
and a dark blue wave, foaming up at the bow,
sang out loud and strong as the ship made way,
skimming the whitecaps, cutting toward her goal.
All running gear secure in the swift black craft,
they set up bowls and brimmed them high with wine
and poured libations out to the everlasting gods
who never die—to Athena first of all,
the daughter of Zeus with flashing sea-gray eyes—
and the ship went plunging all night long and through the dawn.

Book 3. King Nestor Remembers

As the sun sprang up, leaving the brilliant waters in its wake,
climbing the bronze sky to shower light on immortal gods
and mortal men across the plowlands ripe with grain—
the ship pulled into Pylos, Neleus' storied citadel,

where the people lined the beaches,
sacrificing sleek black bulls to Poseidon,
god of the sea-blue mane who shakes the earth.
They sat in nine divisions, each five hundred strong,
each division offering up nine bulls, and while the people
tasted the innards, burned the thighbones for the god,
the craft and crew came heading straight to shore.
Striking sail, furling it in the balanced ship,
they moored her well and men swung down on land.
Telemachus climbed out last, with Athena far in front
and the bright-eyed goddess urged the prince along:
"Telemachus, no more shyness, this is not the time!
We sailed the seas for this, for news of your father—
where does he lie buried? what fate did he meet?
So go right up to Nestor, breaker of horses.
We'll make him yield the secrets of his heart.
Press him yourself to tell the whole truth:
he'll never lie—the man is far too wise."

The prince replied, wise in his own way too,
"How can I greet him, Mentor, even approach the king?
I'm hardly adept at subtle conversation.
Someone my age *might* feel shy, what's more,
interrogating an older man."
"Telemachus,"
the bright-eyed goddess Athena reassured him,
"some of the words you'll find within yourself,
the rest some power will inspire you to say.
You least of all—I know—
were born and reared without the gods' good will."

And Pallas Athena sped away in the lead
as he followed in her footsteps—man and goddess
gained the place where the Pylians met and massed.
There sat Nestor among his sons as friends around them
decked the banquet, roasted meats and skewered strips for broiling.
As soon as they saw the strangers, all came crowding down,
waving them on in welcome, urging them to sit.
Nestor's son Pisistratus, first to reach them,
grasped their hands and sat them down at the feast
on fleecy throws spread out along the sandbanks,
flanking his brother Thrasymedes and his father.
He gave them a share of innards, poured some wine
in a golden cup and, lifting it warmly toward Athena,
daughter of Zeus whose shield is storm and thunder,
greeted the goddess now with an invitation:
"Say a prayer to lord Poseidon, stranger,
his is the feast you've found on your arrival.
But once you've made your libation and your prayer—

all according to ancient custom—hand this cup
of hearty, seasoned wine to your comrade here
so he can pour forth too. He too, I think,
should pray to the deathless ones himself.
All men need the gods . . .
but the man is younger, just about my age.
That's why I give the gold cup first to you."
With that
Pisistratus placed in her hand the cup of mellow wine
and Pallas rejoiced at the prince's sense of tact
in giving the golden winecup first to her.
At once she prayed intensely to Poseidon:
"Hear me, Sea-lord, you who embrace the earth—
don't deny our wishes, bring our prayers to pass!
First, then, to Nestor and all his sons grant glory.
Then to all these Pylians, for their splendid rites
grant a reward that warms their gracious hearts.
And last, Poseidon, grant Telemachus and myself
safe passage home, the mission accomplished
that sped us here in our rapid black ship."

So she prayed, and brought it all to pass.
She offered the rich two-handled cup to Telemachus,
Odysseus' son, who echoed back her prayer word for word.
They roasted the prime cuts, pulled them off the spits
and sharing out the portions, fell to the royal feast.
Once they'd put aside desire for food and drink,
old Nestor the noble charioteer began, at last:
"Now's the time, now they've enjoyed their meal,
to probe our guests and find out who they are.
Strangers—friends, who are you?
Where did you sail from, over the running sea-lanes?
Out on a trading spree or roving the waves like pirates,
sea-wolves raiding at will, who risk their lives
to plunder other men?"
Poised Telemachus answered,
filled with heart, the heart Athena herself inspired,
to ask for the news about his father, gone so long,
and make his name throughout the mortal world.
"Nestor, son of Neleus, Achaea's pride and glory—
where are we from, you ask? I will tell you all.
We hail from Ithaca, under the heights of Nion.
Our mission here is personal, nothing public now.
I am on the trail of my father's widespread fame,
you see, searching the earth to catch some news
of great-hearted King Odysseus who, they say,
fought with you to demolish Troy some years ago.
About all the rest who fought the Trojans there,
we know where each one died his wretched death,

but father . . . even his death—
the son of Cronus shrouds it all in mystery.
No one can say for certain where he died,
whether he went down on land at enemy hands
or out on the open sea in Amphitrite's breakers.
That's why I've come to plead before you now,
if you can tell me about his cruel death:
perhaps you saw him die with your own eyes
or heard the wanderer's end from someone else.
More than all other men, that man was born for pain.
Don't soften a thing, from pity, respect for me—
tell me, clearly, all your eyes have witnessed.
I beg you—if ever my father, lord Odysseus,
pledged you his word and made it good in action
once on the fields of Troy where you Achaeans suffered,
remember his story now, tell *me* the truth."

Nestor the noble charioteer replied at length:
"Ah dear boy, since you call back such memories,
such living hell we endured in distant Troy—
we headstrong fighting forces of Achaea—
so many raids from shipboard down the foggy sea,
cruising for plunder, wherever Achilles led the way;
so many battles round King Priam's walls we fought,
so many gone, our best and bravest fell.
There Ajax lies, the great man of war.
There lies Achilles too.
There Patroclus, skilled as the gods in counsel.
And there my own dear son, both strong and staunch,
Antilochus—lightning on his feet and every inch a fighter!
But so many other things we suffered, past that count—
what mortal in this wide world could tell it all?
Not if you sat and probed his memory, five, six years,
delving for all the pains our brave Achaeans bore there.
Your patience would fray, you'd soon head for home . . .

Nine years we wove a web of disaster for those Trojans,
pressing them hard with every tactic known to man,
and only after we slaved did Zeus award us victory.
And no one there could hope to rival Odysseus,
not for sheer cunning—
at every twist of strategy he excelled us all.
Your father, yes, if you are in fact his son . . .
I look at you and a sense of wonder takes me.
Your way with words—it's just like his—I'd swear
no youngster could ever speak like you, so apt, so telling.
As long as I and great Odysseus soldiered there,
why, never once did we speak out at odds,
neither in open muster nor in royal council:
forever one in mind, in judgment balanced, shrewd,

we mapped our armies' plans so things might turn out best.
But then, once we'd sacked King Priam's craggy city,
Zeus contrived in his heart a fatal homeward run
for all the Achaeans who were fools, at least,
dishonest too, so many met a disastrous end,
thanks to the lethal rage
of the mighty Father's daughter. Eyes afire,
Athena set them feuding, Atreus' two sons[1] . . .
They summoned all the Achaean ranks to muster,
rashly, just at sunset—no hour to rally troops—
and in they straggled, sodden with wine, our heroes.
The brothers harangued them, told them why they'd met:
a crisis—Menelaus urging the men to fix their minds
on the voyage home across the sea's broad back,
but it brought no joy to Agamemnon, not at all.
He meant to detain us there and offer victims,
anything to appease Athena's dreadful wrath—
poor fool, he never dreamed Athena would not comply.
The minds of the everlasting gods don't change so quickly.
So the two of them stood there, wrangling, back and forth
till the armies sprang up, their armor clashing, ungodly uproar—
the two plans split the ranks. That night we barely slept,
seething with hard feelings against our own comrades,
for Zeus was brooding over us, poised to seal our doom . . .
At dawn, half of us hauled our vessels down to sea,
we stowed our plunder, our sashed and lovely women.
But half the men held back, camped on the beach,
waiting it out for Agamemnon's next commands
while our contingent embarked—
we pushed off and sailed at a fast clip
as a god smoothed out the huge troughing swells.
We reached Tenedos quickly, sacrificed to the gods,
the crews keen for home, but a quick return was not
in Zeus's plans, not yet: that cruel power
loosed a cursed feud on us once again.
Some swung their rolling warships hard about—
Odysseus sailed them back, the flexible, wily king,
veering over to Agamemnon now to shore his fortunes up.
But not I. Massing the ships that came in my flotilla,
I sped away as the god's mischief kept on brewing,
dawning on me now. And Tydeus' fighting son
Diomedes fled too, rousing all his comrades.
Late in the day the red-haired Menelaus joined us,
overtook us at Lesbos, debating the long route home:
whether to head north, over the top of rocky Chios,
skirting Psyrie, keeping that island off to port
or run south of Chios, by Mimas' gusty cape.

1. Agamemnon and Menelaus.

We asked the god for a sign. He showed us one,
he urged us to cut out on the middle passage,
straight to Euboea now,
escape a catastrophe, fast as we could sail!
A shrilling wind came up, stiff, driving us on
and on we raced, over the sea-lanes rife with fish
and we made Geraestus Point in the dead of night.
Many thighs of bulls we offered Poseidon there—
thank god we'd crossed that endless reach of sea.
Then on the fourth day out the crews of Diomedes,
breaker of horses, moored their balanced ships
at Argos port, but I held course for Pylos, yes,
and never once did the good strong wind go limp
from the first day the god unleashed its blast.

And so, dear boy, I made it home from Troy,
in total ignorance, knowing nothing of their fates,
the ones who stayed behind:
who escaped with their lives and who went down.
But still, all I've gathered by hearsay, sitting here
in my own house—that you'll learn, it's only right,
I'll hide nothing now.
They say the Myrmidons,
those savage spearmen led by the shining son
of lionhearted Achilles, traveled home unharmed.
Philoctetes the gallant son of Poias, safe as well.
Idomeneus brought his whole contingent back to Crete,
all who'd escaped the war—the sea snatched none from him.
But Atreus' son Agamemnon . . . you yourselves, even
in far-off Ithaca, must have heard how he returned,
how Aegisthus hatched the king's horrendous death.
But what a price he paid, in blood, in suffering.
Ah how fine it is, when a man is brought down,
to leave a son behind! Orestes took revenge,
he killed that cunning, murderous Aegisthus,
who'd killed his famous father.
And you, my friend—
how tall and handsome I see you now—be brave, you too,
so men to come will sing your praises down the years."

Telemachus, weighing the challenge closely, answered,
"Oh Nestor, son of Neleus, Achaea's pride and glory,
what a stroke of revenge that was! All Achaeans
will spread Orestes' fame across the world,
a song for those to come.
If only the gods would arm me in such power
I'd take revenge on the lawless, brazen suitors
riding roughshod over me, plotting reckless outrage.
But for me the gods have spun out no such joy,
for my father or myself. I must bear up,

that's all."
And the old charioteer replied,
"Now that you mention it, dear boy, I do recall
a mob of suitors, they say, besets your mother
there in your own house, against your will,
and plots your ruin. Tell me, though, do you
let yourself be so abused, or do people round about,
stirred up by the prompting of some god, despise you now?
Who knows if he will return someday to take revenge
on all their violence? Single-handed perhaps
or with an Argive army at his back? If only
the bright-eyed goddess chose to love you just
as she lavished care on brave Odysseus, years ago
in the land of Troy where we Achaeans struggled!
I've never seen the immortals show so much affection
as Pallas openly showed *him,* standing by your father—
if only she'd favor you, tend you with all her heart,
many a suitor then would lose all thought of marriage,
blotted out forever."
"Never, your majesty,"
Telemachus countered gravely, "that will never
come to pass, I know. What you say dumbfounds me,
staggers imagination! Hope, hope as I will,
that day will never dawn . . .
not even if the gods should will it so."
"Telemachus!"
Pallas Athena broke in sharply, her eyes afire—
"What's this nonsense slipping through your teeth?
It's light work for a willing god to save a mortal
even half the world away. Myself, I'd rather
sail through years of trouble and labor home
and see that blessed day, than hurry home
to die at my own hearth like Agamemnon,
killed by Aegisthus' cunning—by his own wife.
But the great leveler, Death: not even the gods
can defend a man, not even one they love, that day
when fate takes hold and lays him out at last."
"Mentor,"
wise Telemachus said, "distraught as we are for him,
let's speak of this no more. My father's return?
It's inconceivable now. Long ago the undying gods
have sealed his death, his black doom. But now
there's another question I would put to Nestor:
Nestor excels all men for sense and justice,
his knowledge of the world.
Three generations he has ruled, they say,
and to my young eyes he seems a deathless god!
Nestor, son of Neleus, tell me the whole story—
how did the great king Agamemnon meet his death?

Where was Menelaus? What fatal trap did he set,
that treacherous Aegisthus, to bring down a man
far stronger than himself? Was Menelaus gone
from Achaean Argos, roving the world somewhere,
so the coward found the nerve to kill the king?"

And old Nestor the noble charioteer replied:
"Gladly, my boy, I'll tell you the story first to last . . .
Right you are, you guess what would have happened
if red-haired Menelaus, arriving back from Troy,
had found Aegisthus alive in Agamemnon's palace.
No barrow piled high on the earth for *his* dead body,
no, the dogs and birds would have feasted on his corpse,
sprawled on the plain outside the city gates, and no one,
no woman in all Achaea, would have wept a moment,
such a monstrous crime the man contrived!
But there we were, camped at Troy, battling out
the long hard campaign while he at his ease at home,
in the depths of Argos, stallion-country—he lay siege
to the wife of Agamemnon, luring, enticing her with talk.
At first, true, she spurned the idea of such an outrage,
Clytemnestra the queen, her will was faithful still.
And there was a man, what's more, a bard close by,
to whom Agamemnon, setting sail for Troy,
gave strict commands to guard his wife. But then,
that day the doom of the gods had bound her to surrender,
Aegisthus shipped the bard away to a desert island,
marooned him there, sweet prize for the birds of prey,
and swept her off to his own house, lover lusting for lover.
And many thighbones he burned on the gods' holy altars,
many gifts he hung on the temple walls—gold, brocades—
in thanks for a conquest past his maddest hopes.

Now we,
you see, were sailing home from Troy in the same squadron,
Menelaus and I, comrades-in-arms from years of war.
But as we rounded holy Sounion, Athens' headland,
lord Apollo[2] attacked Atrides' helmsman, aye,
with his gentle shafts he shot the man to death—
an iron grip on the tiller, the craft scudding fast—
Phrontis, Onetor's son, who excelled all men alive
at steering ships when gales bore down in fury.
So Menelaus, straining to sail on, was held back
till he could bury his mate with fitting rites.
But once he'd got off too, plowing the wine-dark sea
in his ribbed ships, and made a run to Malea's beetling cape,
farseeing Zeus decided to give the man rough sailing,
poured a hurricane down upon him, shrilling winds,
giant, rearing whitecaps, monstrous, mountains high.

2. Archer god of prophecy, disease, healing, poetry, and music.

There at a stroke he cut the fleet in half and drove
one wing to Crete, where Cydonians make their homes
along the Iardanus River. Now, there's a sheer cliff
plunging steep to the surf at the farthest edge of Gortyn,
out on the mist-bound sea, where the South Wind piles breakers,
huge breakers, left of the headland's horn, toward Phaestos,
with only a low reef to block the crushing tides.
In they sailed, and barely escaped their death—
the ships' crews, that is—
the rollers smashed their hulls against the rocks.
But as for the other five with pitch-black prows,
the wind and current swept them on toward Egypt.

So Menelaus, amassing a hoard of stores and gold,
was off cruising his ships to foreign ports of call
while Aegisthus hatched his vicious work at home.
Seven years he lorded over Mycenae rich in gold,
once he'd killed Agamemnon—he ground the people down.
But the eighth year ushered in his ruin, Prince Orestes
home from Athens, yes, he cut him down, that cunning,
murderous Aegisthus, who'd killed his famous father.
Vengeance done, he held a feast for the Argives,
to bury his hated mother, craven Aegisthus too,
the very day Menelaus arrived, lord of the warcry,
freighted with all the wealth his ships could carry.
So you,
dear boy, take care. Don't rove from home too long,
too far, leaving your own holdings unprotected—
crowds in your palace so brazen
they'll carve up all your wealth, devour it all,
and then your journey here will come to nothing.
Still I advise you, urge you to visit Menelaus.
He's back from abroad at last, from people so removed
you might abandon hope of ever returning home,
once the winds had driven you that far off course,
into a sea so vast not even cranes could wing their way
in one year's flight—so vast it is, so awesome . . .

So, off you go with your ships and shipmates now.
Or if you'd rather go by land, there's team and chariot,
my sons at your service too, and they'll escort you
to sunny Lacedaemon,[3] home of the red-haired king.
Press him yourself to tell the whole truth:
he'll never lie—the man is far too wise."
So he closed
as the sun set and darkness swept across the earth
and the bright-eyed goddess Pallas spoke for all:
"There was a tale, old soldier, so well told.

3. Sparta.

Come, cut out the victims' tongues and mix the wine,
so once we've poured libations out to the Sea-lord
and every other god, we'll think of sleep. High time—
the light's already sunk in the western shadows.
It's wrong to linger long at the gods' feast;
we must be on our way."
Zeus's daughter—
they all hung closely on every word she said.
Heralds sprinkled water over their hands for rinsing,
the young men brimmed the mixing bowls with wine,
they tipped first drops for the god in every cup
then poured full rounds for all. They rose and flung
the victims' tongues on the fire and poured libations out.
When they'd poured, and drunk to their hearts' content,
Athena and Prince Telemachus both started up
to head for their ship at once.
But Nestor held them there, objecting strongly:
"Zeus forbid—and the other deathless gods as well—
that you resort to your ship and put my house behind
like a rank pauper's without a stitch of clothing,
no piles of rugs, no blankets in his place
for host and guests to slumber soft in comfort.
Why, I've plenty of fine rugs and blankets here.
No, by god, the true son of my good friend Odysseus
won't bed down on a ship's deck, not while I'm alive
or my sons are left at home to host our guests,
whoever comes to our palace, newfound friends."
"Dear old man,
you're right," Athena exclaimed, her eyes brightening now.
"Telemachus should oblige you. Much the better way.
Let him follow you now, sleep in your halls,
but I'll go back to our trim black ship,
hearten the crew and give each man his orders.
I'm the only veteran in their ranks, I tell you.
All the rest, of an age with brave Telemachus,
are younger men who sailed with him as friends.
I'll bed down there by the dark hull tonight,
at dawn push off for the proud Cauconians.
Those people owe me a debt long overdue,
and no mean sum, believe me.
But you, seeing my friend is now your guest,
speed him on his way with a chariot and your son
and give him the finest horses that you have,
bred for stamina, trained to race the wind."

With that the bright-eyed goddess winged away
in an eagle's form and flight.
Amazement fell on all the Achaeans there.
The old king, astonished by what he'd seen,

grasped Telemachus' hand and cried out to the prince,
"Dear boy—never fear you'll be a coward or defenseless,
not if at your young age the gods will guard you so.
Of all who dwell on Olympus, this was none but she,
Zeus's daughter, the glorious one, his third born,
who prized your gallant father among the Argives.
Now, O Queen, be gracious! Give us high renown,
myself, my children, my loyal wife and queen.
And I will make you a sacrifice, a yearling heifer
broad in the brow, unbroken, never yoked by men.
I'll offer it up to you—I'll sheathe its horns in gold."

So he prayed, and Pallas Athena heard his prayer.
And Nestor the noble chariot-driver led them on,
his sons and sons-in-law, back to his regal palace.
Once they reached the storied halls of the aged king
they sat on rows of low and high-backed chairs.
As they arrived the old man mixed them all a bowl,
stirring the hearty wine, seasoned eleven years
before a servant broached it, loosed its seal.
Mulling it in the bowl, old Nestor poured
a libation out, praying hard to Pallas Athena,
daughter of Zeus whose shield is storm and thunder.

Once they had poured their offerings, drunk their fill,
the Pylians went to rest, each in his own house.
But the noble chariot-driver let Telemachus,
King Odysseus' son, sleep at the palace now,
on a corded bed inside the echoing colonnade,
with Prince Pisistratus close beside him there,
the young spearman, already captain of armies,
though the last son still unwed within the halls.
The king retired to chambers deep in his lofty house
where the queen his wife arranged and shared their bed.

When young Dawn with her rose-red fingers shone once more
old Nestor the noble chariot-driver climbed from bed,
went out and took his seat on the polished stones,
a bench glistening white, rubbed with glossy oil,
placed for the king before his looming doors.
There Neleus held his sessions years ago,
a match for the gods in counsel,
but his fate had long since forced him down to Death.
Now royal Nestor in turn, Achaea's watch and ward,
sat there holding the scepter while his sons,
coming out of their chambers, clustered round him,
hovering near: Echephron, Stratius, Perseus
and Aretus, Thrasymedes like a god, and sixth,
young lord Pisistratus came to join their ranks.

They escorted Prince Telemachus in to sit beside them.
Nestor, noble charioteer, began the celebration:
"Quickly, my children, carry out my wishes now
so I may please the gods, Athena first of all—
she came to me at Poseidon's flowing feast,
Athena in all her glory!
Now someone go to the fields to fetch a heifer,
lead her here at once—a herdsman drive her in.
Someone hurry down to Prince Telemachus' black ship
and bring up all his crewmen, leave just two behind.
And another tell our goldsmith, skilled Laerces,
to come and sheathe the heifer's horns in gold.
The rest stay here together. Tell the maids
inside the hall to prepare a sumptuous feast—
bring seats and firewood, bring pure water too."

They all pitched in to carry out his orders.
The heifer came from the fields, the crewmen came
from brave Telemachus' ship, and the smith came in
with all his gear in hand, the tools of his trade,
the anvil, hammer and well-wrought tongs he used
for working gold. And Athena came as well
to attend her sacred rites.
The old horseman passed the gold to the smith,
and twining the foil, he sheathed the heifer's horns
so the goddess' eyes might dazzle, delighted with the gift.
Next Stratius and Echephron led the beast by the horns.
Aretus, coming up from the storeroom, brought them
lustral water filling a flower-braided bowl,
in his other hand, the barley in a basket.
Thrasymedes, staunch in combat, stood ready,
whetted ax in his grasp to cut the heifer down,
and Perseus held the basin for the blood.
Now Nestor the old charioteer began the rite.
Pouring the lustral water, scattering barley-meal,
he lifted up his ardent prayers to Pallas Athena,
launching the sacrifice, flinging onto the fire
the first tufts of hair from the victim's head.

Prayers said, the scattering barley strewn,
suddenly Nestor's son impetuous Thrasymedes
strode up close and struck—the ax chopped
the neck tendons through—
and the blow stunned
the heifer's strength—
The women shrilled their cry,
Nestor's daughters, sons' wives and his own loyal wife
Eurydice, Clymenus' eldest daughter. Then, hoisting up
the victim's head from the trampled earth, they held her fast

as the captain of men Pisistratus slashed her throat.
Dark blood gushed forth, life ebbed from her limbs—
they quartered her quickly, cut the thighbones out
and all according to custom wrapped them round in fat,
a double fold sliced clean and topped with strips of flesh.
And the old king burned these over dried split wood
and over the fire poured out glistening wine
while young men at his side held five-pronged forks.
Once they'd burned the bones and tasted the organs,
they sliced the rest into pieces, spitted them on skewers
and raising points to the fire, broiled all the meats.

During the ritual lovely Polycaste, youngest daughter
of Nestor, Neleus' son, had bathed Telemachus.
Rinsing him off now, rubbing him down with oil,
she drew a shirt and handsome cape around him.
Out of his bath he stepped, glistening like a god,
strode in and sat by the old commander Nestor.

They roasted the prime cuts, pulled them off the spits
and sat down to the feast while ready stewards saw
to rounds of wine and kept the gold cups flowing.
When they'd put aside desire for food and drink,
Nestor the noble chariot-driver issued orders:
"Hurry, my boys! Bring Telemachus horses,
a good full-maned team—
hitch them to a chariot—he must be off at once."

They listened closely, snapped to his commands
and hitched a rapid team to a chariot's yoke in haste.
A housekeeper stowed some bread and wine aboard
and meats too, food fit for the sons of kings.
Telemachus vaulted onto the splendid chariot—
right beside him Nestor's son Pisistratus,
captain of armies, boarded, seized the reins,
whipped the team to a run and on the horses flew,
holding nothing back, out into open country,
leaving the heights of Pylos fading in their trail,
shaking the yoke across their shoulders all day long.

The sun sank and the roads of the world grew dark
as they reached Phera, pulling up to Diocles' halls,
the son of Ortilochus, son of the Alpheus River.
He gave them a royal welcome; there they slept the night.

When young Dawn with her rose-red fingers shone once more
they yoked their pair again, mounted the blazoned car
and out through the gates and echoing colonnade
they whipped the team to a run and on they flew,
holding nothing back—and the princes reached
the wheatlands, straining now for journey's end,

so fast those purebred stallions raced them on
as the sun sank and the roads of the world grew dark.

Book 4. The King and Queen of Sparta

At last they gained the ravines of Lacedaemon ringed by hills
and drove up to the halls of Menelaus in his glory.
They found the king inside his palace, celebrating
with throngs of kinsmen a double wedding-feast
for his son and lovely daughter. The princess
he was sending on to the son of great Achilles,
breaker of armies. Years ago Menelaus vowed,
he nodded assent at Troy and pledged her hand
and now the gods were sealing firm the marriage.
So he was sending her on her way with team and chariot,
north to the Myrmidons' famous city governed by her groom.
From Sparta he brought Alector's daughter as the bride
for his own full-grown son, the hardy Megapenthes,
born to him by a slave. To Helen the gods had granted
no more offspring once she had borne her first child,
the breathtaking Hermione,
a luminous beauty gold as Aphrodite.
So now
they feasted within the grand, high-roofed palace,
all the kin and clansmen of Menelaus in his glory,
reveling warmly here as in their midst
an inspired bard sang out and struck his lyre—
and through them a pair of tumblers dashed and sprang,
whirling in leaping handsprings, leading on the dance.

The travelers, Nestor's shining son and Prince Telemachus,
had brought themselves and their horses to a standstill
just outside the court when good lord Eteoneus,
passing through the gates now, saw them there,
and the ready aide-in-arms of Menelaus
took the message through his sovereign's halls
and stepping close to his master broke the news:
"Strangers have just arrived, your majesty, Menelaus.
Two men, but they look like kin of mighty Zeus himself.
Tell me, should we unhitch their team for them
or send them to someone free to host them well?"

The red-haired king took great offense at that:
"Never a fool before, Eteoneus, son of Boëthous,
now I see you're babbling like a child!
Just think of all the hospitality *we* enjoyed
at the hands of other men before we made it home,
and god save us from such hard treks in years to come.
Quick, unhitch their team. And bring them in,
strangers, guests, to share our flowing feast."

Back through the halls he hurried, calling out
to other brisk attendants to follow quickly.
They loosed the sweating team from under the yoke,
tethered them fast by reins inside the horse-stalls,
tossing feed at their hoofs, white barley mixed with wheat,
and canted the chariot up against the polished walls,
shimmering in the sun, then ushered in their guests,
into that magnificent place. Both struck by the sight,
they marveled up and down the house of the warlord dear to Zeus—
a radiance strong as the moon or rising sun came flooding
through the high-roofed halls of illustrious Menelaus.
Once they'd feasted their eyes with gazing at it all,
into the burnished tubs they climbed and bathed.
When women had washed them, rubbed them down with oil
and drawn warm fleece and shirts around their shoulders,
they took up seats of honor next to Atrides Menelaus.
A maid brought water soon in a graceful golden pitcher
and over a silver basin tipped it out
so they might rinse their hands,
then pulled a gleaming table to their side.
A staid housekeeper brought on bread to serve them,
appetizers aplenty too, lavish with her bounty.
As a carver lifted platters of meat toward them,
meats of every sort, and set before them golden cups,
the red-haired king Menelaus greeted both guests warmly:
"Help yourselves to food, and welcome! Once you've dined
we'll ask you who you are. But your parents' blood
is hardly lost in you. You must be born of kings,
bred by the gods to wield the royal scepter.
No mean men could sire sons like you."
With those words
he passed them a fat rich loin with his own hands,
the choicest part, that he'd been served himself.
They reached for the good things that lay outspread
and when they'd put aside desire for food and drink,
Telemachus, leaning his head close to Nestor's son,
spoke low to the prince so no one else could hear:
"Look, Pisistratus—joy of my heart, my friend—
the sheen of bronze, the blaze of gold and amber,
silver, ivory too, through all this echoing mansion!
Surely Zeus's court on Olympus must be just like this,
the boundless glory of all this wealth inside!
My eyes dazzle . . . I am struck with wonder."

But the red-haired warlord overheard his guest
and cut in quickly with winged words for both:
"No man alive could rival Zeus, dear boys,
with his everlasting palace and possessions.
But among men, I must say, few if any
could rival *me* in riches. Believe me,

much I suffered, many a mile I roved to haul
such treasures home in my ships. Eight years out,
wandering off as far as Cyprus, Phoenicia,[1] even Egypt,
I reached the Ethiopians, Sidonians, Erembians—Libya too,
where lambs no sooner spring from the womb than they grow horns.
Three times in the circling year the ewes give birth.
So no one, neither king nor shepherd could want
for cheese or mutton, or sweet milk either,
udders swell for the sucklings round the year.

But while I roamed those lands, amassing a fortune,
a stranger killed my brother, blind to the danger, duped blind—
thanks to the cunning of his cursed, murderous queen!
So I rule all this wealth with no great joy.
You must have heard my story from your fathers,
whoever they are—what hardships I endured,
how I lost this handsome palace built for the ages,
filled to its depths with hoards of gorgeous things.
Well, would to god I'd stayed right here in my own house
with a third of all that wealth and they were still alive,
all who died on the wide plain of Troy those years ago,
far from the stallion-land of Argos.
And still,
much as I weep for all my men, grieving sorely,
time and again, sitting here in the royal halls,
now indulging myself in tears, now brushing tears away—
the grief that numbs the spirit gluts us quickly—
for none of all those comrades, pained as I am,
do I grieve as much for one . . .
that man who makes sleep hateful, even food,
as I pore over his memory. No one, no Achaean
labored hard as Odysseus labored or achieved so much.
And how did his struggles end? In suffering for that man;
for me, in relentless, heartbreaking grief for him,
lost and gone so long now—dead or alive, who knows?
How they must mourn him too, Laertes, the old man,
and self-possessed Penelope. Telemachus as well,
the boy he left a babe in arms at home."
Such memories
stirred in the young prince a deep desire to grieve
for Odysseus. Tears streamed down his cheeks
and wet the ground when he heard his father's name,
both hands clutching his purple robe before his eyes.
Menelaus recognized him at once but pondered
whether to let him state his father's name
or probe him first and prompt him step by step.

1. Modern Syria, Lebanon, and Galilee.

While he debated all this now within himself,
Helen emerged from her scented, lofty chamber—
striking as Artemis with her golden shafts—
and a train of women followed . . .
Adreste drew up her carved reclining-chair,
Alcippe brought a carpet of soft-piled fleece,
Phylo carried her silver basket given by Alcandre,
King Polybus' wife, who made his home in Egyptian Thebes
where the houses overflow with the greatest troves of treasure.
The king gave Menelaus a pair of bathing-tubs in silver,
two tripods, ten bars of gold, and apart from these
his wife presented Helen her own precious gifts:
a golden spindle, a basket that ran on casters,
solid silver polished off with rims of gold.
Now Phylo her servant rolled it in beside her,
heaped to the brim with yarn prepared for weaving;
the spindle swathed in violet wool lay tipped across it.
Helen leaned back in her chair, a stool beneath her feet,
and pressed her husband at once for each detail:
"Do we know, my lord Menelaus, who our visitors
claim to be, our welcome new arrivals?
Right or wrong, what can I say? My heart tells me
to come right out and say I've never seen such a likeness,
neither in man nor woman—I'm amazed at the sight.
To the life he's like the son of great Odysseus,
surely he's Telemachus! The boy that hero left
a babe in arms at home when all you Achaeans
fought at Troy, launching your headlong battles
just for *my* sake, shameless whore that I was."

"My dear, my dear," the red-haired king assured her,
"now that you mention it, I see the likeness too . . .
Odysseus' feet were like the boy's, his hands as well,
his glancing eyes, his head, and the fine shock of hair.
Yes, and just now, as I was talking about Odysseus,
remembering how he struggled, suffered, all for me,
a flood of tears came streaming down his face
and he clutched his purple robe before his eyes."

"Right you are"—Pisistratus stepped in quickly—
"son of Atreus, King Menelaus, captain of armies:
here is the son of that great hero, as you say.
But the man is modest, he would be ashamed
to make a show of himself, his first time here,
and interrupt you. We delight in your voice
as if some god were speaking!
The noble horseman Nestor sent me along
to be his escort. Telemachus yearned to see you,
so you could give him some advice or urge some action.
When a father's gone, his son takes much abuse

in a house where no one comes to his defense.
So with Telemachus now. His father's gone.
No men at home will shield him from the worst."

"Wonderful!" the red-haired king cried out.
"The son of my dearest friend, here in my own house!
That man who performed a hundred feats of arms for me.
And I swore that when he came I'd give him a hero's welcome,
him above all my comrades—if only Olympian Zeus,
farseeing Zeus, had granted us both safe passage
home across the sea in our swift trim ships.
Why, I'd have settled a city in Argos for him,
built him a palace, shipped him over from Ithaca,
him and all his wealth, his son, his people too—
emptied one of the cities nestling round about us,
one I rule myself. Both fellow-countrymen then,
how often we'd have mingled side-by-side!
Nothing could have parted us,
bound by love for each other, mutual delight . . .
till death's dark cloud came shrouding round us both.
But god himself, jealous of all this, no doubt,
robbed that unlucky man, him and him alone,
of the day of his return."
So Menelaus mused
and stirred in them all a deep desire to grieve.
Helen of Argos, daughter of Zeus, dissolved in tears,
Telemachus wept too, and so did Atreus' son Menelaus.
Nor could Nestor's son Pisistratus stay dry-eyed,
remembering now his gallant brother Antilochus,
cut down by Memnon,[2] splendid son of the Morning.
Thinking of him, the young prince broke out:
"Old Nestor always spoke of you, son of Atreus,
as the wisest man of all the men he knew,
whenever we talked about you there at home,
questioning back and forth. So now, please,
if it isn't out of place, indulge me, won't you?
Myself, I take no joy in weeping over supper.
Morning will soon bring time enough for that.
Not that I'd grudge a tear
for any man gone down to meet his fate.
What other tribute can we pay to wretched men
than to cut a lock, let tears roll down our cheeks?
And I have a brother of my own among the dead,
and hardly the poorest soldier in our ranks.
You probably knew him. I never met him, never
saw him myself. But they say he outdid our best,
Antilochus—lightning on his feet and every inch a fighter!"

2. King of Ethiopia.

"Well said, my friend," the red-haired king replied.
"Not even an older man could speak and do as well.
Your father's son you are—your words have all his wisdom.
It's easy to spot the breed of a man whom Zeus
has marked for joy in birth and marriage both.
Take great King Nestor now:
Zeus has blessed him, all his livelong days,
growing rich and sleek in his old age at home,
his sons expert with spears and full of sense.
Well, so much for the tears that caught us just now;
let's think again of supper. Come, rinse our hands.
Tomorrow, at dawn, will offer me and Telemachus
time to talk and trade our thoughts in full."

Asphalion quickly rinsed their hands with water,
another of King Menelaus' ready aides-in-arms.
Again they reached for the good things set before them.

Then Zeus's daughter Helen thought of something else.
Into the mixing-bowl from which they drank their wine
she slipped a drug, heart's-ease, dissolving anger,
magic to make us all forget our pains . . .
No one who drank it deeply, mulled in wine,
could let a tear roll down his cheeks that day,
not even if his mother should die, his father die,
not even if right before his eyes some enemy brought down
a brother or darling son with a sharp bronze blade.
So cunning the drugs that Zeus's daughter plied,
potent gifts from Polydamna the wife of Thon,
a woman of Egypt, land where the teeming soil
bears the richest yield of herbs in all the world:
many health itself when mixed in the wine,
and many deadly poison.
Every man is a healer there, more skilled
than any other men on earth—Egyptians born
of the healing god himself. So now Helen, once
she had drugged the wine and ordered winecups filled,
resuming the conversation, entertained the group:
"My royal king Menelaus—welcome guests here,
sons of the great as well! Zeus can present us
times of joy and times of grief in turn:
all lies within his power.
So come, let's sit back in the palace now,
dine and warm our hearts with the old stories.
I will tell something perfect for the occasion.
Surely I can't describe or even list them all,
the exploits crowding fearless Odysseus' record,
but what a feat that hero dared and carried off
in the land of Troy where you Achaeans suffered!
Scarring his own body with mortifying strokes,

throwing filthy rags on his back like any slave,
he slipped into the enemy's city, roamed its streets—
all disguised, a totally different man, a beggar,
hardly the figure he cut among Achaea's ships.
That's how Odysseus infiltrated Troy,
and no one knew him at all . . .
I alone, I spotted him for the man he was,
kept questioning him—the crafty one kept dodging.
But after I'd bathed him, rubbed him down with oil,
given him clothes to wear and sworn a binding oath
not to reveal him as Odysseus to the Trojans, not
till he was back at his swift ships and shelters,
then at last he revealed to me, step by step,
the whole Achaean strategy. And once he'd cut
a troop of Trojans down with his long bronze sword,
back he went to his comrades, filled with information.
The rest of the Trojan women shrilled their grief. Not I:
my heart leapt up—
my heart had changed by now—
I yearned
to sail back home again! I grieved too late for the madness
Aphrodite[3] sent me, luring me there, far from my dear land,
forsaking my own child, my bridal bed, my husband too,
a man who lacked for neither brains nor beauty."

And the red-haired Menelaus answered Helen:
"There was a tale, my lady. So well told.
Now then, I have studied, in my time,
the plans and minds of great ones by the score.
And I have traveled over a good part of the world
but never once have I laid eyes on a man like him—
what a heart that fearless Odysseus had inside him!
What a piece of work the hero dared and carried off
in the wooden horse where all our best encamped,
our champions armed with bloody death for Troy . . .
when along you came, Helen—roused, no doubt,
by a dark power bent on giving Troy some glory,
and dashing Prince Deiphobus squired your every step.
Three times you sauntered round our hollow ambush,
feeling, stroking its flanks,
challenging all our fighters, calling each by name—
yours was the voice of all our long-lost wives!
And Diomedes and I, crouched tight in the midst
with great Odysseus, hearing you singing out,
were both keen to spring up and sally forth
or give you a sudden answer from inside,
but Odysseus damped our ardor, reined us back.
Then all the rest of the troops kept stock-still,

3. Goddess of physical love.

all but Anticlus. He was hot to salute you now
but Odysseus clamped his great hands on the man's mouth
and shut it, brutally—yes, he saved us all,
holding on grim-set till Pallas Athena
lured you off at last."

But clear-sighted Telemachus ventured,
"Son of Atreus, King Menelaus, captain of armies,
so much the worse, for not one bit of that
saved *him* from grisly death . . .
not even a heart of iron could have helped.
But come, send us off to bed. It's time to rest,
time to enjoy the sweet relief of sleep."

And Helen briskly told her serving-women
to make beds in the porch's shelter, lay down
some heavy purple throws for the beds themselves,
and over them spread some blankets, thick woolly robes,
a warm covering laid on top. Torches in hand,
they left the hall and made up beds at once.
The herald led the two guests on and so they slept
outside the palace under the forecourt's colonnade,
young Prince Telemachus and Nestor's shining son.
Menelaus retired to chambers deep in his lofty house
with Helen the pearl of women loosely gowned beside him.

When young Dawn with her rose-red fingers shone once more
the lord of the warcry climbed from bed and dressed,
over his shoulder he slung his well-honed sword,
fastened rawhide sandals under his smooth feet,
stepped from his bedroom, handsome as a god,
and sat beside Telemachus, asking, kindly,
"Now, my young prince, tell me what brings you here
to sunny Lacedaemon, sailing over the sea's broad back.
A public matter or private? Tell me the truth now."

And with all the poise he had, Telemachus replied,
"Son of Atreus, King Menelaus, captain of armies,
I came in the hope that you can tell me now
some news about my father.
My house is being devoured, my rich farms destroyed,
my palace crammed with enemies, slaughtering on and on
my droves of sheep and shambling longhorn cattle.
Suitors plague my mother—the insolent, overweening . . .
That's why I've come to plead before you now,
if you can tell me about his cruel death:
perhaps you saw him die with your own eyes
or heard the wanderer's end from someone else.
More than all other men, that man was born for pain.
Don't soften a thing, from pity, respect for me—
tell me, clearly, all your eyes have witnessed.

I beg you—if ever my father, lord Odysseus,
pledged you his word and made it good in action
once on the fields of Troy where you Achaeans suffered,
remember his story now, tell *me* the truth."
"How shameful!"
the red-haired king burst out in anger. "That's the bed
of a brave man of war they'd like to crawl inside,
those spineless, craven cowards!
Weak as the doe that beds down her fawns
in a mighty lion's den—her newborn sucklings—
then trails off to the mountain spurs and grassy bends
to graze her fill, but back the lion comes to his own lair
and the master deals both fawns a ghastly bloody death,
just what Odysseus will deal that mob—ghastly death.
Ah if only—Father Zeus, Athena and lord Apollo—
that man who years ago in the games at Lesbos
rose to Philomelides' challenge, wrestled him,
pinned him down with one tremendous throw
and the Argives roared with joy . . .
if only *that* Odysseus sported with those suitors,
a blood wedding, a quick death would take the lot!
But about the things you've asked me, so intently,
I'll skew and sidestep nothing, not deceive you, ever.
Of all he told me—the Old Man of the Sea who never lies—
I'll hide or hold back nothing, not a single word.

It was in Egypt, where the gods still marooned me,
eager as I was to voyage home . . . I'd failed,
you see, to render them full, flawless victims,
and gods are always keen to see their rules obeyed.
Now, there's an island out in the ocean's heavy surge,
well off the Egyptian coast—they call it Pharos—
far as a deep-sea ship can go in one day's sail
with a whistling wind astern to drive her on.
There's a snug harbor there, good landing beach
where crews pull in, draw water up from the dark wells
then push their vessels off for passage out.
But here the gods becalmed me twenty days . . .
not a breath of the breezes ruffling out to sea
that speed a ship across the ocean's broad back.
Now our rations would all have been consumed,
our crews' stamina too, if one of the gods
had not felt sorry for me, shown me mercy,
Eidothea, a daughter of Proteus,
that great power, the Old Man of the Sea.
My troubles must have moved her to the heart
when she met me trudging by myself without my men.
They kept roaming around the beach, day in, day out,
fishing with twisted hooks, their bellies racked by hunger.

Well, she came right up to me, filled with questions:
'Are you a fool, stranger—soft in the head and lazy too?
Or do you let things slide because you *like* your pain?
Here you are, cooped up on an island far too long,
with no way out of it, none that you can find,
while all your shipmates' spirit ebbs away.'

So she prodded and I replied at once,
'Let me tell you, goddess—whoever you are—
I'm hardly landlocked here of my own free will.
So I must have angered one of the deathless gods
who rule the skies up there. But you tell *me*—
you immortals know it all—which one of you
blocks my way here, keeps me from my voyage?
How can I cross the swarming sea and reach home at last?'

And the glistening goddess reassured me warmly,
'Of course, my friend, I'll answer all your questions.
Who haunts these parts? Proteus of Egypt does,
the immortal Old Man of the Sea who never lies,
who sounds the deep in all its depths, Poseidon's servant.
He's my father, they say, he gave me life. And he,
if only you ambush him somehow and pin him down,
will tell you the way to go, the stages of your voyage,
how you can cross the swarming sea and reach home at last.
And he can tell you too, if you want to press him—
you are a king, it seems—
all that's occurred within your palace, good and bad,
while you've been gone your long and painful way.'

'Then you are the one'—I quickly took her up.
'Show me the trick to trap this ancient power,
or he'll see or sense me first and slip away.
It's hard for a mortal man to force a god.'

'True, my friend,' the glistening one agreed,
'and again I'll tell you all you need to know.
When the sun stands striding at high noon,
then up from the waves he comes—
the Old Man of the Sea who never lies—
under a West Wind's gust that shrouds him round
in shuddering dark swells, and once he's out on land
he heads for his bed of rest in deep hollow caves
and around him droves of seals—sleek pups bred
by his lovely ocean-lady—bed down too
in a huddle, flopping up from the gray surf,
giving off the sour reek of the salty ocean depths.
I'll lead you there myself at the break of day
and couch you all for attack, side-by-side.
Choose three men from your crew, choose well,
the best you've got aboard the good decked hulls.

Now I will tell you all the old wizard's tricks . . .
First he will make his rounds and count the seals
and once he's checked their number, reviewed them all,
down in their midst he'll lie, like a shepherd with his flock.
That's your moment. Soon as you see him bedded down,
muster your heart and strength and hold him fast,
wildly as he writhes and fights you to escape.
He'll try all kinds of escape—twist and turn
into every beast that moves across the earth,
transforming himself into water, superhuman fire,
but you hold on for dear life, hug him all the harder!
And when, at last, he begins to ask you questions—
back in the shape you saw him sleep at first—
relax your grip and set the old god free
and ask him outright, hero,
which of the gods is up in arms against you?
How can you cross the swarming sea and reach home at last?'

So she urged and under the breaking surf she dove
as I went back to our squadron beached in sand,
my heart a heaving storm at every step . . .
Once I reached my ship hauled up on shore
we made our meal and the godsent night came down
and then we slept at the sea's smooth shelving edge.
When young Dawn with her rose-red fingers shone once more
I set out down the coast of the wide-ranging sea,
praying hard to the gods for all their help,
taking with me the three men I trusted most
on every kind of mission.
                                        Eidothea, now,
had slipped beneath the sea's engulfing folds
but back from the waves she came with four sealskins,
all freshly stripped, to deceive her father blind.
She scooped out lurking-places deep in the sand
and sat there waiting as we approached her post,
then couching us side-by-side she flung a sealskin
over each man's back. Now there was an ambush
that would have overpowered us all—overpowering,
true, the awful reek of all those sea-fed brutes!
Who'd dream of bedding down with a monster of the deep?
But the goddess sped to our rescue, found the cure
with ambrosia,[4] daubing it under each man's nose—
that lovely scent, it drowned the creatures' stench.
So all morning we lay there waiting, spirits steeled,
while seals came crowding, jostling out of the sea
and flopped down in rows, basking along the surf.
At high noon the old man emerged from the waves
and found his fat-fed seals and made his rounds,

4. Food of the immortals.

counting them off, counting *us* the first four,
but he had no inkling of all the fraud afoot.
Then down he lay and slept, but we with a battle-cry,
we rushed him, flung our arms around him—he'd lost nothing,
the old rascal, none of his cunning quick techniques!
First he shifted into a great bearded lion
and then a serpent—
a panther—
a ramping wild boar—
a torrent of water—
a tree with soaring branchtops—
but we held on for dear life, braving it out
until, at last, that quick-change artist,
the old wizard, began to weary of all this
and burst out into rapid-fire questions:
'Which god, Menelaus, conspired with you
to trap me in ambush? seize me against my will?
What on earth do you want?'
'You know, old man,'
I countered now. 'Why put me off with questions?
Here I am, cooped up on an island far too long,
with no way out of it, none that I can find,
while my spirit ebbs away. But you tell *me*—
you immortals know it all—which one of you
blocks my way here, keeps me from my voyage?
How can I cross the swarming sea and reach home at last?'

'How wrong you were!' the seer shot back at once.
'You should have offered Zeus and the other gods
a handsome sacrifice, *then* embarked, if you ever hoped
for a rapid journey home across the wine-dark sea.
It's not your destiny yet to see your loved ones,
reach your own grand house, your native land at last,
not till you sail back through Egyptian waters—
the great Nile swelled by the rains of Zeus—
and make a splendid rite to the deathless gods
who rule the vaulting skies. Then, only then
will the gods grant you the voyage you desire.'

So he urged, and broke the heart inside me,
having to double back on the mist-bound seas,
back to Egypt, that, that long and painful way . . .
Nevertheless I caught my breath and answered,
'That I will do, old man, as you command.
But tell me this as well, and leave out nothing:
Did all the Achaeans reach home in the ships unharmed,
all we left behind, Nestor and I, en route from Troy?
Or did any die some cruel death by shipwreck
or die in the arms of loved ones,

once they'd wound down the long coil of war?'

And he lost no time in saying, 'Son of Atreus,
why do you ask me that? Why do you need to know?
Why probe my mind? You won't stay dry-eyed long,
I warn you, once you have heard the whole story.
Many of them were killed, many survived as well,
but only two who captained your bronze-armored units
died on the way home—you know who died in the fighting,
you were there yourself.
And one is still alive,
held captive, somewhere, off in the endless seas . . .

Ajax, now, went down with his long-oared fleet.
First Poseidon drove him onto the cliffs of Gyrae,
looming cliffs, then saved him from the breakers—
he'd have escaped his doom, too, despite Athena's hate,
if he hadn't flung that brazen boast, the mad blind fool.
"In the teeth of the gods," he bragged, "I have escaped
the ocean's sheer abyss!" Poseidon heard that frantic vaunt
and the god grasped his trident in both his massive hands
and struck the Gyraean headland, hacked the rock in two,
and the giant stump stood fast but the jagged spur
where Ajax perched at first, the raving madman—
toppling into the sea, it plunged him down, down
in the vast, seething depths. And so he died,
having drunk his fill of brine.
Your brother?
He somehow escaped that fate; Agamemnon got away
in his beaked ships. Queen Hera[5] pulled him through.
But just as he came abreast of Malea's beetling cape
a hurricane snatched him up and swept him way off course—
groaning, desperate—driving him over the fish-infested sea
to the wild borderland where Thyestes made his home
in the days of old and his son Aegisthus lived now.
But even from there a safe return seemed likely,
yes, the immortals swung the wind around to fair
and the victors sailed home. How he rejoiced,
Atrides setting foot on his fatherland once more—
he took that native earth in his hands and kissed it,
hot tears flooding his eyes, so thrilled to see his land!
But a watchman saw him too—from a lookout high above—
a spy that cunning Aegisthus stationed there,
luring the man with two gold bars in payment.
One whole year he'd watched . . .
so the great king would not get past unseen,
his fighting power intact for self-defense.
The spy ran the news to his master's halls

5. Wife and sister of Zeus, the greatest of the gods.

and Aegisthus quickly set his stealthy trap.
Picking the twenty best recruits from town
he packed them in ambush at one end of the house,
at the other he ordered a banquet dressed and spread
and went to welcome the conquering hero, Agamemnon,
went with team and chariot, and a mind aswarm with evil.
Up from the shore he led the king, he ushered him in—
suspecting nothing of all his doom—he feasted him well
then cut him down as a man cuts down some ox at the trough!
Not one of your brother's men-at-arms was left alive,
none of Aegisthus' either. All, killed in the palace.'

So Proteus said, and his story crushed my heart.
I knelt down in the sand and wept. I'd no desire
to go on living and see the rising light of day.
But once I'd had my fill of tears and writhing there,
the Old Man of the Sea who never lies continued,
'No more now, Menelaus. How long must you weep?
Withering tears, what good can come of tears?
None I know of. Strive instead to return
to your native country—hurry home at once!
Either you'll find the murderer still alive
or Orestes will have beaten you to the kill.
You'll be in time to share the funeral feast.'

So he pressed, and I felt my heart, my old pride,
for all my grieving, glow once more in my chest
and I asked the seer in a rush of winging words,
'Those two I know now. Tell me the third man's name.
Who is still alive, held captive off in the endless seas?
Unless he's dead by now. I want to know the truth
though it grieves me all the more.'
'Odysseus'—
the old prophet named the third at once—
'Laertes' son, who makes his home in Ithaca . . .
I saw him once on an island, weeping live warm tears
in the nymph Calypso's house—she holds him there by force.
He has no way to voyage home to his own native land,
no trim ships in reach, no crew to ply the oars
and send him scudding over the sea's broad back.
But about your own destiny, Menelaus,
dear to Zeus, it's not for you to die
and meet your fate in the stallion-land of Argos,
no, the deathless ones will sweep you off to the world's end,
the Elysian Fields, where gold-haired Rhadamanthys waits,
where life glides on in immortal ease for mortal man;
no snow, no winter onslaught, never a downpour there
but night and day the Ocean River sends up breezes,
singing winds of the West refreshing all mankind.

All this because you are Helen's husband now—
the gods count *you* the son-in-law of Zeus.'

So he divined and down the breaking surf he dove
as I went back to the ships with my brave men,
my heart a rising tide at every step.
Once I reached my craft hauled up on shore
we made our meal and the godsent night came down
and then we slept at the sea's smooth shelving edge.
When young Dawn with her rose-red fingers shone once more
we hauled the vessels down to the sunlit breakers first
then stepped the masts amidships, canvas brailed—
the crews swung aboard, they sat to the oars in ranks
and in rhythm churned the water white with stroke on stroke.
Back we went to the Nile swelled by the rains of Zeus,
I moored the ships and sacrificed in a splendid rite,
and once I'd slaked the wrath of the everlasting gods
I raised a mound for Agamemnon, his undying glory.
All this done, I set sail and the gods sent me
a stiff following wind that sped me home,
home to the native land I love.
But come,
my boy, stay on in my palace now with me,
at least till ten or a dozen days have passed.
Then I'll give you a princely send-off—shining gifts,
three stallions and a chariot burnished bright—
and I'll add a gorgeous cup so you can pour
libations out to the deathless gods on high
and remember Menelaus all your days."
Telemachus,
summoning up his newfound tact, replied,
"Please, Menelaus, don't keep me quite so long.
True, I'd gladly sit beside you one whole year
without a twinge of longing for home or parents.
It's wonderful how you tell your stories, all you say—
I delight to listen! Yes, but now, I'm afraid,
my comrades must be restless in sacred Pylos,
and here you'd hold me just a little longer.
As for the gift you give me, let it be a keepsake.
Those horses I really cannot take to Ithaca;
better to leave them here to be your glory.
You rule a wide level plain
where the fields of clover roll and galingale
and wheat and oats and glistening full-grain barley.
No running-room for mares in Ithaca, though, no meadows.
Goat, not stallion, land, yet it means the world to me.
None of the rugged islands slanting down to sea
is good for pasture or good for bridle paths,
but Ithaca, best of islands, crowns them all!"

So he declared. The lord of the warcry smiled,
patted him with his hand and praised his guest, concluding,
"Good blood runs in you, dear boy, your words are proof.
Certainly I'll exchange the gifts. The power's mine.
Of all the treasures lying heaped in my palace
you shall have the finest, most esteemed. Why,
I'll give you a mixing-bowl, forged to perfection—
it's solid silver finished off with a lip of gold.
Hephaestus[6] made it himself. And a royal friend,
Phaedimus, king of Sidon, lavished it on me
when his palace welcomed me on passage home.
How pleased I'd be if you took it as a gift!"

And now as the two confided in each other,
banqueters arrived at the great king's palace,
leading their own sheep, bearing their hearty wine,
and their wives in lovely headbands sent along the food.
And so they bustled about the halls preparing dinner . . .
But all the while the suitors, before Odysseus' palace,
amused themselves with discus and long throwing spears,
out on the leveled grounds, free and easy as always,
full of swagger. But lord Antinous sat apart,
dashing Eurymachus beside him, ringleaders,
head and shoulders the strongest of the lot.
Phronius' son Noëmon approached them now,
quick to press Antinous with a question:
"Antinous, have we any notion or not
when Telemachus will return from sandy Pylos?
He sailed in a ship of mine and now I need her back
to cross over to Elis Plain where I keep a dozen horses,
brood-mares suckling some heavy-duty mules, unbroken.
I'd like to drive one home and break him in."

That dumbfounded them both. They never dreamed
the prince had gone to Pylos, Neleus' city—
certain the boy was still nearby somewhere,
out on his farm with flocks or with the swineherd.

"Tell me the truth!" Antinous wheeled on Noëmon.
"When did he go? And what young crew went with him?
Ithaca's best? Or his own slaves and servants?
Surely he has enough to man a ship.
Tell me this—be clear—I've got to know:
did he commandeer your ship against your will
or did you volunteer it once he'd won you over?"

"I volunteered it, of course," Noëmon said.
"What else could anyone do, when such a man,
a prince weighed down with troubles,

6. Crippled god of fire, smiths, and artisans, husband of Aphrodite.

asked a favor? Hard to deny him anything.
And the young crew that formed his escort? Well,
they're the finest men on the island, next to us.
And Mentor took command—I saw him climb aboard—
or a god who looked like Mentor head to foot,
and that's what I find strange. I saw good Mentor
yesterday, just at sunup, here. But clearly
he boarded ship for Pylos days ago."

With that he headed back to his father's house,
leaving the two lords stiff with indignation.
They made the suitors sit down in a group
and stop their games at once. Eupithes' son
Antinous rose up in their midst to speak,
his dark heart filled with fury,
blazing with anger—eyes like searing fire:
"By god, what a fine piece of work he's carried off!
Telemachus—what insolence—and we thought his little jaunt
would come to grief. But in spite of us all, look,
the young cub slips away, just like that—
picks the best crew in the land and off he sails.
And this is just the start of the trouble he can make.
Zeus kill that brazen boy before he hits his prime!
Quick, fetch me a swift ship and twenty men—
I'll waylay him from ambush, board him coming back
in the straits between Ithaca and rocky Same.
This gallant voyage of his to find his father
will find *him* wrecked at last!"

They all roared approval, urged him on,
rose at once and retired to Odysseus' palace.

But not for long was Penelope unaware
of the grim plots her suitors planned in secret.
The herald Medon told her. He'd overheard their schemes,
listening in outside the court while they wove on within.
He rushed the news through the halls to tell the queen
who greeted him as he crossed her chamber's threshold:
"Herald, why have the young blades sent you now?
To order King Odysseus' serving-women
to stop their work and slave to fix their feast?
I hate their courting, their running riot here—
would to god that this meal, here and now,
were their last meal on earth!

Day after day,
all of you swarming, draining our life's blood,
my wary son's estate. What, didn't you listen
to your fathers—when you were children, years ago—
telling you how Odysseus treated them, your parents?
Never an unfair word, never an unfair action
among his people here, though that's the way

of our god-appointed kings,
hating one man, loving the next, with luck.
Not Odysseus. Never an outrage done to any man alive.
But you, you and your ugly outbursts, shameful acts,
they're plain to see. Look at the thanks he gets
for all past acts of kindness!"
Medon replied,
sure of his own discretion, "Ah my queen,
if only *that* were the worst of all you face.
Now your suitors are plotting something worse,
harsher, crueler. God forbid they bring it off!
They're poised to cut Telemachus down with bronze swords
on his way back home. He's sailed off, you see . . .
for news of his father—to sacred Pylos first,
then out to the sunny hills of Lacedaemon."

Her knees gave way on the spot, her heart too.
She stood there speechless a while, struck dumb,
tears filling her eyes, her warm voice choked.
At last she found some words to make reply:
"Oh herald, why has my child gone and left me?
No need in the world for him to board the ships,
those chariots of the sea that sweep men on,
driving across the ocean's endless wastes . . .
Does he want his very name wiped off the earth?"

Medon, the soul of thoughtfulness, responded,
"I don't know if a god inspired your son
or the boy's own impulse led him down to Pylos,
but he went to learn of his father's journey home,
or whatever fate he's met."

Back through King Odysseus' house he went
but a cloud of heartbreak overwhelmed the queen.
She could bear no longer sitting on a chair
though her room had chairs aplenty.
Down she sank on her well-built chamber's floor,
weeping, pitifully, as the women whimpered round her,
all the women, young and old, who served her house.
Penelope, sobbing uncontrollably, cried out to them,
"Hear me, dear ones! Zeus has given me torment—
me above all the others born and bred in *my* day.
My lionhearted husband, lost, long years ago,
who excelled the Argives all in every strength—
that great man whose fame resounds through Hellas
right to the depths of Argos!
But now my son,
my darling boy—the whirlwinds have ripped him
out of the halls without a trace! I never heard
he'd gone—not even from you, you hard, heartless . . .
not one of you even thought to rouse me from my bed,

though well you knew when he boarded that black ship.
Oh if only I had learned he was planning such a journey,
he would have stayed, by god, keen as he was to sail—
or left me dead right here within our palace.
Go, someone, quickly! Call old Dolius now,
the servant my father gave me when I came,
the man who tends my orchard green with trees,
so he can run to Laertes, sit beside him,
tell him the whole story, point by point.
Perhaps—who knows?—he'll weave some plan,
he'll come out of hiding, plead with all these people
mad to destroy his line, his son's line of kings!"

"Oh dear girl," Eurycleia the fond old nurse replied,
"kill me then with a bronze knife—no mercy—or let me live,
here in the palace—I'll hide nothing from you now!
I knew it all, I gave him all he asked for,
bread and mellow wine, but he made me take
a binding oath that I, I wouldn't tell you,
no, not till ten or a dozen days had passed
or you missed the lad yourself and learned he'd gone,
so tears would never mar your lovely face . . .
Come, bathe now, put on some fresh clothes,
climb to the upper rooms with all your women
and pray to Pallas, daughter of storming Zeus—
she may save Telemachus yet, even at death's door.
Don't worry an old man, worried enough by now.
I can't believe the blessed gods so hate
the heirs of King Arcesius, through and through.
One will still live on—I know it—born to rule
this lofty house and the green fields far and wide."
With that
she lulled Penelope's grief and dried her eyes of tears.
And the queen bathed and put fresh clothing on,
climbed to the upper rooms with all her women
and sifting barley into a basket, prayed to Pallas,
"Hear me, daughter of Zeus whose shield is thunder—
tireless one, Athena! If ever, here in his halls,
resourceful King Odysseus
burned rich thighs of sheep or oxen in your honor,
oh remember it now for *my* sake, save my darling son,
defend him from these outrageous, overbearing suitors!"

She shrilled a high cry and the goddess heard her prayer
as the suitors burst into uproar through the shadowed halls
and one of the lusty young men began to brag, "Listen,
our long-courted queen's preparing us all a marriage—
with no glimmer at all
how the murder of her son has been decreed."
Boasting so,

with no glimmer at all of what had been decreed.
But Antinous took the floor and issued orders:
"Stupid fools! Muzzle your bragging now—
before someone slips inside and reports us.
Up now, not a sound, drive home our plan—
it suits us well, we approved it one and all."

With that he picked out twenty first-rate men
and down they went to the swift ship at the sea's edge.
First they hauled the craft into deeper water,
stepped the mast amidships, canvas brailed,
made oars fast in the leather oarlock straps
while zealous aides-in-arms brought weapons on.
They moored her well out in the channel, disembarked
and took their meal on shore, waiting for dusk to fall.

But there in her upper rooms she lay, Penelope
lost in thought, fasting, shunning food and drink,
brooding now . . . would her fine son escape his death
or go down at her overweening suitors' hands?
Her mind in torment, wheeling
like some lion at bay, dreading gangs of hunters
closing their cunning ring around him for the finish.
Harried so she was, when a deep kind sleep overcame her,
back she sank and slept, her limbs fell limp and still.

And again the bright-eyed goddess Pallas thought
of one more way to help. She made a phantom now,
its build like a woman's build, Iphthime's, yes,
another daughter of generous Lord Icarius,
Eumelus' bride, who made her home in Pherae.
Athena sped her on to King Odysseus' house
to spare Penelope, worn with pain and sobbing,
further spells of grief and storms of tears.
The phantom entered her bedroom,
passing quickly in through the doorbolt slit
and hovering at her head she rose and spoke now:
"Sleeping, Penelope, your heart so wrung with sorrow?
No need, I tell you, no, the gods who live at ease
can't bear to let you weep and rack your spirit.
Your son will still come home—it is decreed.
He's never wronged the gods in any way."

And Penelope murmured back, still cautious,
drifting softly now at the gate of dreams,
"Why have you come, my sister?
Your visits all too rare in the past,
for you make your home so very far away.
You tell me to lay to rest the grief and tears
that overwhelm me now, torment me, heart and soul?
With my lionhearted husband lost long years ago,

who excelled the Argives all in every strength?
That great man whose fame resounds through Hellas
right to the depths of Argos . . .
And now my darling boy,
he's off and gone in a hollow ship! Just a youngster,
still untrained for war or stiff debate.
Him I mourn even more than I do my husband—
I quake in terror for all that he might suffer
either on open sea or shores he goes to visit.
Hordes of enemies scheme against him now,
keen to kill him off
before he can reach his native land again."

"Courage!" the shadowy phantom reassured her.
"Don't be overwhelmed by all your direst fears.
He travels with such an escort, one that others
would pray to stand beside them. She has power—
Pallas Athena. She pities you in your tears.
She wings me here to tell you all these things."

But the circumspect Penelope replied,
"If you *are* a god and have heard a god's own voice,
come, tell me about that luckless man as well.
Is he still alive? does he see the light of day?
Or is he dead already, lost in the House of Death?"

"About that man," the shadowy phantom answered,
"I cannot tell you the story start to finish,
whether he's dead or alive.
It's wrong to lead you on with idle words."
At that
she glided off by the doorpost past the bolt—
gone on a lifting breeze. Icarius' daughter
started up from sleep, her spirit warmed now
that a dream so clear had come to her in darkest night.

But the suitors boarded now and sailed the sea-lanes,
plotting in their hearts Telemachus' plunge to death.
Off in the middle channel lies a rocky island,
just between Ithaca and Same's rugged cliffs—
Asteris—not large, but it has a cove,
a harbor with two mouths where ships can hide.
Here the Achaeans lurked in ambush for the prince.

Book 5. Odysseus—Nymph and Shipwreck

As Dawn rose up from bed by her lordly mate Tithonus,
bringing light to immortal gods and mortal men,
the gods sat down in council, circling Zeus
the thunder king whose power rules the world.
Athena began, recalling Odysseus to their thoughts,

the goddess deeply moved by the man's long ordeal,
held captive still in the nymph Calypso's house:
"Father Zeus—you other happy gods who never die—
never let any sceptered king be kind and gentle now,
not with all his heart, or set his mind on justice—
no, let him be cruel and always practice outrage.
Think: not one of the people whom he ruled
remembers Odysseus now, that godlike man,
and kindly as a father to his children.

Now
he's left to pine on an island, racked with grief
in the nymph Calypso's house—she holds him there by force.
He has no way to voyage home to his own native land,
no trim ships in reach, no crew to ply the oars
and send him scudding over the sea's broad back.
And now his dear son . . . they plot to kill the boy
on his way back home. Yes, he has sailed off
for news of his father, to holy Pylos first,
then out to the sunny hills of Lacedaemon."

"My child," Zeus who marshals the thunderheads replied,
"what nonsense you let slip through your teeth. Come now,
wasn't the plan your own? You conceived it yourself:
Odysseus shall return and pay the traitors back.
Telemachus? Sail him home with all your skill—
the power is yours, no doubt—
home to his native country all unharmed
while the suitors limp to port, defeated, baffled men."

With those words, Zeus turned to his own son Hermes.
"You are our messenger, Hermes, sent on all our missions.
Announce to the nymph with lovely braids our fixed decree:
Odysseus journeys home—the exile must return.
But not in the convoy of the gods or mortal men.
No, on a lashed, makeshift raft and wrung with pains,
on the twentieth day he will make his landfall, fertile Scheria,
the land of Phaeacians, close kin to the gods themselves,
who with all their hearts will prize him like a god
and send him off in a ship to his own beloved land,
giving him bronze and hoards of gold and robes—
more plunder than he could ever have won from Troy
if Odysseus had returned intact with his fair share.
So his destiny ordains. He shall see his loved ones,
reach his high-roofed house, his native land at last."

So Zeus decreed and the giant-killing guide obeyed at once.
Quickly under his feet he fastened the supple sandals,
ever-glowing gold, that wing him over the waves
and boundless earth with the rush of gusting winds.
He seized the wand that enchants the eyes of men

whenever Hermes wants, or wakes us up from sleep.
That wand in his grip, the powerful giant-killer,
swooping down from Pieria, down the high clear air,
plunged to the sea and skimmed the waves like a tern
that down the deadly gulfs of the barren salt swells
glides and dives for fish,
dipping its beating wings in bursts of spray—
so Hermes skimmed the crests on endless crests.
But once he gained that island worlds apart,
up from the deep-blue sea he climbed to dry land
and strode on till he reached the spacious cave
where the nymph with lovely braids had made her home,
and he found her there inside . . .
A great fire
blazed on the hearth and the smell of cedar
cleanly split and sweetwood burning bright
wafted a cloud of fragrance down the island.
Deep inside she sang, the goddess Calypso, lifting
her breathtaking voice as she glided back and forth
before her loom, her golden shuttle weaving.
Thick, luxuriant woods grew round the cave,
alders and black poplars, pungent cypress too,
and there birds roosted, folding their long wings,
owls and hawks and the spread-beaked ravens of the sea,
black skimmers who make their living off the waves.
And round the mouth of the cavern trailed a vine
laden with clusters, bursting with ripe grapes.
Four springs in a row, bubbling clear and cold,
running side-by-side, took channels left and right.
Soft meadows spreading round were starred with violets,
lush with beds of parsley. Why, even a deathless god
who came upon that place would gaze in wonder,
heart entranced with pleasure. Hermes the guide,
the mighty giant-killer, stood there, spellbound . . .
But once he'd had his fill of marveling at it all
he briskly entered the deep vaulted cavern.
Calypso, lustrous goddess, knew him at once,
as soon as she saw his features face-to-face.
Immortals are never strangers to each other,
no matter how distant one may make her home.
But as for great Odysseus—
Hermes could not find him within the cave.
Off he sat on a headland, weeping there as always,
wrenching his heart with sobs and groans and anguish,
gazing out over the barren sea through blinding tears.
But Calypso, lustrous goddess, questioned Hermes,
seating him on a glistening, polished chair.
"God of the golden wand, why have you come?
A beloved, honored friend,

but it's been so long, your visits much too rare.
Tell me what's on your mind. I'm eager to do it,
whatever I *can* do . . . whatever can be done."

And the goddess drew a table up beside him,
heaped with ambrosia, mixed him deep-red nectar.[1]
Hermes the guide and giant-killer ate and drank.
Once he had dined and fortified himself with food
he launched right in, replying to her questions:
"As one god to another, you ask me why I've come.
I'll tell you the whole story, mince no words—
your wish is my command.
It was Zeus who made me come, no choice of mine.
Who would willingly roam across a salty waste so vast,
so endless? Think: no city of men in sight, and not a soul
to offer the gods a sacrifice and burn the fattest victims.
But there is no way, you know, for another god to thwart
the will of storming Zeus and make it come to nothing.
Zeus claims you keep beside you a most unlucky man,
most harried of all who fought for Priam's Troy
nine years, sacking the city in the tenth,
and then set sail for home.
But voyaging back they outraged Queen Athena
who loosed the gales and pounding seas against them.
There all the rest of his loyal shipmates died
but the wind drove him on, the current bore him here.
Now Zeus commands you to send him off with all good speed:
it is not his fate to die here, far from his own people.
Destiny still ordains that he shall see his loved ones,
reach his high-roofed house, his native land at last."

But lustrous Calypso shuddered at those words
and burst into a flight of indignation. "Hard-hearted
you are, you gods! You unrivaled lords of jealousy—
scandalized when goddesses sleep with mortals,
openly, even when one has made the man her husband.
So when Dawn with her rose-red fingers took Orion,
you gods in your everlasting ease were horrified
till chaste Artemis[2] throned in gold attacked him,
out on Delos, shot him to death with gentle shafts.
And so when Demeter[3] the graceful one with lovely braids
gave way to her passion and made love with Iasion,
bedding down in a furrow plowed three times—
Zeus got wind of it soon enough, I'd say,
and blasted the man to death with flashing bolts.
So now at last, you gods, you train your spite on *me*
for keeping a mortal man beside me. The man I saved,

1. Drink of the gods.
2. Virgin goddess of wilderness and the hunt.
3. Goddess of grain.

riding astride his keel-board, all alone, when Zeus
with one hurl of a white-hot bolt had crushed
his racing warship down the wine-dark sea.
There all the rest of his loyal shipmates died
but the wind drove him on, the current bore him here.
And I welcomed him warmly, cherished him, even vowed
to make the man immortal, ageless, all his days . . .
But since there is no way for another god to thwart
the will of storming Zeus and make it come to nothing,
let the man go—if the Almighty insists, commands—
and destroy himself on the barren salt sea!
I'll send him off, but not with any escort.
I have no ships in reach, no crew to ply the oars
and send him scudding over the sea's broad back.
But I will gladly advise him—I'll hide nothing—
so he can reach his native country all unharmed."

And the guide and giant-killer reinforced her words:
"Release him at once, just so. Steer clear of the rage of Zeus!
Or down the years he'll fume and make your life a hell."

With that the powerful giant-killer sped away.
The queenly nymph sought out the great Odysseus—
the commands of Zeus still ringing in her ears—
and found him there on the headland, sitting, still,
weeping, his eyes never dry, his sweet life flowing away
with the tears he wept for his foiled journey home,
since the nymph no longer pleased. In the nights, true,
he'd sleep with her in the arching cave—he had no choice—
unwilling lover alongside lover all too willing . . .
But all his days he'd sit on the rocks and beaches,
wrenching his heart with sobs and groans and anguish,
gazing out over the barren sea through blinding tears.
So coming up to him now, the lustrous goddess ventured,
"No need, my unlucky one, to grieve here any longer,
no, don't waste your life away. Now I am willing,
heart and soul, to send you off at last. Come,
take bronze tools, cut your lengthy timbers,
make them into a broad-beamed raft
and top it off with a half-deck high enough
to sweep you free and clear on the misty seas.
And I myself will stock her with food and water,
ruddy wine to your taste—all to stave off hunger—
give you clothing, send you a stiff following wind
so you can reach your native country all unharmed.
If only the gods are willing. They rule the vaulting skies.
They're stronger than I to plan and drive things home."

Long-enduring Odysseus shuddered at that
and broke out in a sharp flight of protest.

"Passage home? Never. Surely you're plotting
something else, goddess, urging me—in a raft—
to cross the ocean's mighty gulfs. So vast, so full
of danger not even deep-sea ships can make it through,
swift as they are and buoyed up by the winds of Zeus himself.
I won't set foot on a raft until you show good faith,
until you consent to swear, goddess, a binding oath
you'll never plot some new intrigue to harm me!"

He was so intense the lustrous goddess smiled,
stroked him with her hand, savored his name and chided,
"Ah what a wicked man you are, and never at a loss.
What a thing to imagine, what a thing to say!
Earth be my witness now, the vaulting Sky above
and the dark cascading waters of the Styx[4]—I swear
by the greatest, grimmest oath that binds the happy gods:
I will never plot some new intrigue to harm you.
Never. All I have in mind and devise for *you*
are the very plans I'd fashion for myself
if I were in your straits. My every impulse
bends to what is right. Not iron, trust me,
the heart within *my* breast. I am all compassion."

And lustrous Calypso quickly led the way
as he followed in the footsteps of the goddess.
They reached the arching cavern, man and god as one,
and Odysseus took the seat that Hermes just left,
while the nymph set out before him every kind
of food and drink that mortal men will take.
Calypso sat down face-to-face with the king
and the women served her nectar and ambrosia.
They reached out for the good things that lay at hand
and when they'd had their fill of food and drink
the lustrous one took up a new approach. "So then,
royal son of Laertes, Odysseus, man of exploits,
still eager to leave at once and hurry back
to your own home, your beloved native land?
Good luck to you, even so. Farewell!
But if you only knew, down deep, what pains
are fated to fill your cup before you reach that shore,
you'd stay right here, preside in our house with me
and be immortal. Much as you long to see your wife,
the one you pine for all your days . . . and yet
I just might claim to be nothing less than she,
neither in face nor figure. Hardly right, is it,
for mortal woman to rival immortal goddess?
How, in build? in beauty?"

"Ah great goddess,"

4. Underworld river and the goddess who guaranteed the gods' oaths.

worldly Odysseus answered, "don't be angry with me,
please. All that you say is true, how well I know.
Look at my wise Penelope. She falls far short of you,
your beauty, stature. She is mortal after all
and you, you never age or die . . .
Nevertheless I long—I pine, all my days—
to travel home and see the dawn of my return.
And if a god will wreck me yet again on the wine-dark sea,
I can bear that too, with a spirit tempered to endure.
Much have I suffered, labored long and hard by now
in the waves and wars. Add this to the total—
bring the trial on!"
Even as he spoke
the sun set and the darkness swept the earth.
And now, withdrawing into the cavern's deep recesses,
long in each other's arms they lost themselves in love.

When young Dawn with her rose-red fingers shone once more
Odysseus quickly dressed himself in cloak and shirt
while the nymph slipped on a loose, glistening robe,
filmy, a joy to the eye, and round her waist
she ran a brocaded golden belt
and over her head a scarf to shield her brow,
then turned to plan the great man's voyage home.
She gave him a heavy bronze ax that fit his grip,
both blades well-honed, with a fine olive haft
lashed firm to its head. She gave him a polished
smoothing-adze as well and then she led the way
to the island's outer edge where trees grew tall,
alders, black poplars and firs that shot sky-high,
seasoned, drying for years, ideal for easy floating.
Once she'd shown her guest where the tall timber stood,
Calypso the lustrous goddess headed home again.
He set to cutting trunks—the work was done in no time.
Twenty in all he felled, he trimmed them clean with his ax
and split them deftly, trued them straight to the line.
Meanwhile the radiant goddess brought him drills—
he bored through all his planks and wedged them snugly,
knocking them home together, locked with pegs and joints.
Broad in the beam and bottom flat as a merchantman
when a master shipwright turns out her hull,
so broad the craft Odysseus made himself.
Working away at speed
he put up half-decks pinned to close-set ribs
and a sweep of gunwales rounded off the sides.
He fashioned the mast next and sank its yard in deep
and added a steering-oar to hold her right on course,
then he fenced her stem to stern with twigs and wicker,
bulwark against the sea-surge, floored with heaps of brush.
And lustrous Calypso came again, now with bolts of cloth

to make the sail, and he finished that off too, expertly.
Braces, sheets and brails—he rigged all fast on board,
then eased her down with levers into the sunlit sea.

That was the fourth day and all his work was done.
On the fifth, the lovely goddess launched him from her island,
once she had bathed and decked him out in fragrant clothes.
And Calypso stowed two skins aboard—dark wine in one,
the larger one held water—added a sack of rations,
filled with her choicest meats to build his strength,
and summoned a wind to bear him onward, fair and warm.
The wind lifting his spirits high, royal Odysseus
spread sail—gripping the tiller, seated astern—
and now the master mariner steered his craft,
sleep never closing his eyes, forever scanning
the stars, the Pleiades and the Plowman late to set
and the Great Bear that mankind also calls the Wagon:
she wheels on her axis always fixed, watching the Hunter,
and she alone is denied a plunge in the Ocean's baths.
Hers were the stars the lustrous goddess told him
to keep hard to port as he cut across the sea.
And seventeen days he sailed, making headway well;
on the eighteenth, shadowy mountains slowly loomed . . .
the Phaeacians' island reaching toward him now,
over the misty breakers, rising like a shield.

But now Poseidon, god of the earthquake, saw him—
just returning home from his Ethiopian friends,
from miles away on the Solymi mountain-range
he spied Odysseus sailing down the sea
and it made his fury boil even more.
He shook his head and rumbled to himself,
"Outrageous! Look how the gods have changed their minds
about Odysseus—while I was off with my Ethiopians.
Just look at him there, nearing Phaeacia's shores
where he's fated to escape his noose of pain
that's held him until now. Still my hopes ride high—
I'll give that man his swamping fill of trouble!"

With that he rammed the clouds together—both hands
clutching his trident—churned the waves into chaos, whipping
all the gales from every quarter, shrouding over in thunderheads
the earth and sea at once—and night swept down from the sky—
East and South Winds clashed and the raging West and North,
sprung from the heavens, roiled heaving breakers up—
and Odysseus' knees quaked, his spirit too;
numb with fear he spoke to his own great heart:
"Wretched man—what becomes of me now, at last?
I fear the nymph foretold it all too well—
on the high seas, she said, before I can reach

my native land I'll fill my cup of pain! And now,
look, it all comes to pass. What monstrous clouds—
King Zeus crowning the whole wide heaven black—
churning the seas in chaos, gales blasting,
raging around my head from every quarter—
my death-plunge in a flash, it's certain now!
Three, four times blessed, my friends-in-arms
who died on the plains of Troy those years ago,
serving the sons of Atreus to the end. Would to god
I'd died there too and met my fate that day the Trojans,
swarms of them, hurled at *me* with bronze spears,
fighting over the corpse of proud Achilles!
A hero's funeral then, my glory spread by comrades—
now what a wretched death I'm doomed to die!"

At that a massive wave came crashing down on his head,
a terrific onslaught spinning his craft round and round—
he was thrown clear of the decks—
the steering-oar wrenched
from his grasp—
and in one lightning attack the brawling
galewinds struck full-force, snapping the mast mid-shaft
and hurling the sail and sailyard far across the sea.
He went under a good long while, no fast way out,
no struggling up from under the giant wave's assault,
his clothing dragged him down—divine Calypso's gifts—
but at last he fought his way to the surface spewing
bitter brine, streams of it pouring down his head.
But half-drowned as he was, he'd not forget his craft—
he lunged after her through the breakers, laying hold
and huddling amidships, fled the stroke of death.
Pell-mell the rollers tossed her along down-current,
wild as the North Wind tossing thistle along the fields
at high harvest—dry stalks clutching each other tightly—
so the galewinds tumbled her down the sea, this way, that way,
now the South Wind flinging her over to North to sport with,
now the East Wind giving her up to West to harry on and on.

But someone saw him—Cadmus' daughter with lovely ankles,
Ino, a mortal woman once with human voice and called
Leucothea now she lives in the sea's salt depths,
esteemed by all the gods as she deserves.
She pitied Odysseus, tossed, tormented so—
she broke from the waves like a shearwater on the wing,
lit on the wreck and asked him kindly, "Ah poor man,
why is the god of earthquakes so dead set against you?
Strewing your way with such a crop of troubles!
But he can't destroy you, not for all his anger.
Just do as I say. You seem no fool to me.
Strip off those clothes and leave your craft

for the winds to hurl, and swim for it now, you must,
strike out with your arms for landfall there,
Phaeacian land where destined safety waits.
Here, take this scarf,
tie it around your waist—it is immortal.
Nothing to fear now, neither pain nor death.
But once you grasp the mainland with your hands
untie it quickly, throw it into the wine-dark sea,
far from the shore, but you, you turn your head away!"

With that the goddess handed him the scarf
and slipped back in the heavy breaking seas
like a shearwater once again
and a dark heaving billow closed above her.
But battle-weary Odysseus weighed two courses,
deeply torn, probing his fighting spirit: "Oh no—
I fear another immortal weaves a snare to trap me,
urging me to abandon ship! I won't. Not yet.
That shore's too far away—
I glimpsed it myself—where she says refuge waits.
No, here's what I'll do, it's what seems best to *me*.
As long as the timbers cling and joints stand fast,
I'll hold out aboard her and take a whipping—
once the breakers smash my craft to pieces,
then I'll swim—no better plan for now."

But just as great Odysseus thrashed things out,
Poseidon god of the earthquake launched a colossal wave,
terrible, murderous, arching over him, pounding down on him,
hard as a windstorm blasting piles of dry parched chaff,
scattering flying husks—so the long planks of his boat
were scattered far and wide. But Odysseus leapt aboard
one timber and riding it like a plunging racehorse
stripped away his clothes, divine Calypso's gifts,
and quickly tying the scarf around his waist
he dove headfirst in the sea,
stretched his arms and stroked for life itself.
But again the mighty god of earthquakes spied him,
shook his head and grumbled deep in his spirit, "Go, go,
after all you've suffered—rove your miles of sea—
till you fall in the arms of people loved by Zeus.
Even so I can hardly think you'll find
your punishments too light!"
With that threat
he lashed his team with their long flowing manes,
gaining Aegae port where his famous palace stands.

But Zeus's daughter Athena countered him at once.
The rest of the winds she stopped right in their tracks,
commanding them all to hush now, go to sleep.
All but the boisterous North—she whipped him up

and the goddess beat the breakers flat before Odysseus,
dear to Zeus, so he could reach the Phaeacians,
mingle with men who love their long oars
and escape his death at last.
Yes, but now,
adrift on the heaving swells two nights, two days—
quite lost—again and again the man foresaw his death.
Then when Dawn with her lovely locks brought on
the third day, the wind fell in an instant,
all glazed to a dead calm, and Odysseus,
scanning sharply, raised high by a groundswell,
looked up and saw it—landfall, just ahead.
Joy . . . warm as the joy that children feel
when they see their father's life dawn again,
one who's lain on a sickbed racked with torment,
wasting away, slowly, under some angry power's onslaught—
then what joy when the gods deliver him from his pains!
So warm, Odysseus' joy when he saw that shore, those trees,
as he swam on, anxious to plant his feet on solid ground again.
But just offshore, as far as a man's shout can carry,
he caught the boom of a heavy surf on jagged reefs—
roaring breakers crashing down on an ironbound coast,
exploding in fury—
the whole sea shrouded—
sheets of spray—
no harbors to hold ships, no roadstead where they'd ride,
nothing but jutting headlands, riptooth reefs, cliffs.
Odysseus' knees quaked and the heart inside him sank;
he spoke to his fighting spirit, desperate: "Worse and worse!
Now that Zeus has granted a glimpse of land beyond my hopes,
now I've crossed this waste of water, the end in sight,
there's no way out of the boiling surf—I see no way!
Rugged reefs offshore, around them breakers roaring,
above them a smooth rock face, rising steeply, look,
and the surge too deep inshore, no spot to stand
on my own two legs and battle free of death.
If I clamber out, some big comber will hoist me,
dash me against that cliff—my struggles all a waste!
If I keep on swimming down the coast, trying to find
a seabeach shelving against the waves, a sheltered cove—
I dread it—another gale will snatch me up and haul me
back to the fish-infested sea, retching in despair.
Or a dark power will loose some monster at me,
rearing out of the waves—one of the thousands
Amphitrite's[5] breakers teem with. Well I know
the famous god of earthquakes hates my very name!"

5. Goddess, queen of the sea.

Just as that fear went churning through his mind
a tremendous roller swept him toward the rocky coast
where he'd have been flayed alive, his bones crushed
if the bright-eyed goddess Pallas had not inspired him now.
He lunged for a reef, he seized it with both hands and clung
for dear life, groaning until the giant wave surged past
and so he escaped its force, but the breaker's backwash
charged into him full fury and hurled him out to sea.
Like pebbles stuck in the suckers of some octopus
dragged from its lair—so strips of skin torn
from his clawing hands stuck to the rock face.
A heavy sea covered him over, then and there
unlucky Odysseus would have met his death—
against the will of Fate—
but the bright-eyed one inspired him yet again.
Fighting out from the breakers pounding toward the coast,
out of danger he swam on, scanning the land, trying to find
a seabeach shelving against the waves, a sheltered cove,
and stroking hard he came abreast of a river's mouth,
running calmly, the perfect spot, he thought . . .
free of rocks, with a windbreak from the gales.
As the current flowed he felt the river's god and
prayed to him in spirit: "Hear me, lord, whoever you are,
I've come to you, the answer to all my prayers—
rescue me from the sea, the Sea-lord's curse!
Even immortal gods will show a man respect,
whatever wanderer seeks their help—like me—
I throw myself on your mercy, on your current now—
I have suffered greatly. Pity me, lord,
your suppliant cries for help!"
So the man prayed
and the god stemmed his current, held his surge at once
and smoothing out the swells before Odysseus now,
drew him safe to shore at the river's mouth.
His knees buckled, massive arms fell limp,
the sea had beaten down his striving heart.
His whole body swollen, brine aplenty gushing
out of his mouth and nostrils—breathless, speechless,
there he lay, with only a little strength left in him,
deathly waves of exhaustion overwhelmed him now . . .
But once he regained his breath and rallied back to life,
at last he loosed the goddess' scarf from his body,
dropped it into the river flowing out to sea
and a swift current bore it far downstream
and suddenly Ino caught it in her hands.
Struggling up from the banks, he flung himself
in the deep reeds, he kissed the good green earth
and addressed his fighting spirit, desperate still:
"Man of misery, what next? Is this the end?

If I wait out a long tense night by the banks,
I fear the sharp frost and the soaking dew together
will do me in—I'm bone-weary, about to breathe my last,
and a cold wind blows from a river on toward morning.
But what if I climb that slope, go for the dark woods
and bed down in the thick brush? What if I'm spared
the chill, fatigue, and a sweet sleep comes my way?
I fear wild beasts will drag me off as quarry."

But this was the better course, it struck him now.
He set out for the woods and not far from the water
found a grove with a clearing all around and crawled
beneath two bushy olives sprung from the same root,
one olive wild, the other well-bred stock.
No sodden gusty winds could ever pierce them,
nor could the sun's sharp rays invade their depths,
nor could a downpour drench them through and through,
so dense they grew together, tangling side-by-side.
Odysseus crept beneath them, scraping up at once
a good wide bed for himself with both hands.
A fine litter of dead leaves had drifted in,
enough to cover two men over, even three,
in the wildest kind of winter known to man.
Long-enduring great Odysseus, overjoyed at the sight,
bedded down in the midst and heaped the leaves around him.
As a man will bury his glowing brand in black ashes,
off on a lonely farmstead, no neighbors near,
to keep a spark alive—no need to kindle fire
from somewhere else—so great Odysseus buried
himself in leaves and Athena showered sleep
upon his eyes . . . sleep in a swift wave
delivering him from all his pains and labors,
blessed sleep that sealed his eyes at last.

BOOK 6. THE PRINCESS AND THE STRANGER

So there he lay at rest, the storm-tossed great Odysseus,
borne down by his hard labors first and now deep sleep
as Athena traveled through the countryside
and reached the Phaeacians' city. Years ago
they lived in a land of spacious dancing-circles,
Hyperia, all too close to the overbearing Cyclops,
stronger, violent brutes who harried them without end.
So their godlike king, Nausithous, led the people off
in a vast migration, settled them in Scheria,
far from the men who toil on this earth—
he flung up walls around the city, built the houses,
raised the gods' temples and shared the land for plowing.
But his fate had long since forced him down to Death

and now Alcinous ruled, and the gods made him wise.
Straight to his house the clear-eyed Pallas went,
full of plans for great Odysseus' journey home.
She made her way to the gaily painted room
where a young girl lay asleep . . .
a match for the deathless gods in build and beauty,
Nausicaa, the daughter of generous King Alcinous.
Two handmaids fair as the Graces slept beside her,
flanking the two posts, with the gleaming doors closed.
But the goddess drifted through like a breath of fresh air,
rushed to the girl's bed and hovering close she spoke,
in face and form like the shipman Dymas' daughter,
a girl the princess' age, and dearest to her heart.
Disguised, the bright-eyed goddess chided, "Nausicaa,
how could your mother bear a careless girl like you?
Look at your fine clothes, lying here neglected—
with your marriage not far off,
the day you should be decked in all your glory
and offer elegant dress to those who form your escort.
That's how a bride's good name goes out across the world
and it brings her father and queenly mother joy. Come,
let's go wash these clothes at the break of day—
I'll help you, lend a hand, and the work will fly!
You won't stay unwed long. The noblest men
in the country court you now, all Phaeacians
just like you, Phaeacia-born and raised. So come,
the first thing in the morning press your kingly father
to harness the mules and wagon for you, all to carry
your sashes, dresses, glossy spreads for your bed.
It's so much nicer for you to ride than go on foot.
The washing-pools are just too far from town."
With that
the bright-eyed goddess sped away to Olympus, where,
they say, the gods' eternal mansion stands unmoved,
never rocked by galewinds, never drenched by rains,
nor do the drifting snows assail it, no, the clear air
stretches away without a cloud, and a great radiance
plays across that world where the blithe gods
live all their days in bliss. There Athena went,
once the bright-eyed one had urged the princess on.

Dawn soon rose on her splendid throne and woke
Nausicaa finely gowned. Still beguiled by her dream,
down she went through the house to tell her parents now,
her beloved father and mother. She found them both inside.
Her mother sat at the hearth with several waiting-women,
spinning yarn on a spindle, lustrous sea-blue wool.
Her father she met as he left to join the lords
at a council island nobles asked him to attend.
She stepped up close to him, confiding, "Daddy dear,

I wonder, won't you have them harness a wagon for me,
the tall one with the good smooth wheels . . . so I
can take our clothes to the river for a washing?
Lovely things, but lying before me all soiled.
And you yourself, sitting among the princes,
debating points at your council,
you really should be wearing spotless linen.
Then you have five sons, full-grown in the palace,
two of them married, but three are lusty bachelors
always demanding crisp shirts fresh from the wash
when they go out to dance. Look at my duties—
that all rests on me."
So she coaxed, too shy
to touch on her hopes for marriage, young warm hopes,
in her father's presence. But he saw through it all
and answered quickly, "I won't deny you the mules,
my darling girl . . . I won't deny you anything.
Off you go, and the men will harness a wagon,
the tall one with the good smooth wheels,
fitted out with a cradle on the top."
With that
he called to the stablemen and they complied.
They trundled the wagon out now, rolling smoothly,
backed the mule-team into the traces, hitched them up,
while the princess brought her finery from the room
and piled it into the wagon's polished cradle.
Her mother packed a hamper—treats of all kinds,
favorite things to refresh her daughter's spirits—
poured wine in a skin, and as Nausicaa climbed aboard,
the queen gave her a golden flask of suppling olive oil
for her and her maids to smooth on after bathing.
Then, taking the whip in hand and glistening reins,
she touched the mules to a start and out they clattered,
trotting on at a clip, bearing the princess and her clothes
and not alone: her maids went with her, stepping briskly too.

Once they reached the banks of the river flowing strong
where the pools would never fail, with plenty of water
cool and clear, bubbling up and rushing through
to scour the darkest stains—they loosed the mules,
out from under the wagon yoke, and chased them down
the river's rippling banks to graze on luscious clover.
Down from the cradle they lifted clothes by the armload,
plunged them into the dark pools and stamped them down
in the hollows, one girl racing the next to finish first
until they'd scoured and rinsed off all the grime,
then they spread them out in a line along the beach
where the surf had washed a pebbly scree ashore.
And once they'd bathed and smoothed their skin with oil,

they took their picnic, sitting along the river's banks
and waiting for all the clothes to dry in the hot noon sun.
Now fed to their hearts' content, the princess and her retinue
threw their veils to the wind, struck up a game of ball.
White-armed Nausicaa led their singing, dancing beat . . .
as lithe as Artemis with her arrows striding down
from a high peak—Taygetus' towering ridge or Erymanthus—
thrilled to race with the wild boar or bounding deer,
and nymphs of the hills race with her,
daughters of Zeus whose shield is storm and thunder,
ranging the hills in sport, and Leto's heart exults
as head and shoulders over the rest her daughter rises,
unmistakable—she outshines them all, though all are lovely.
So Nausicaa shone among her maids, a virgin, still unwed.

But now, as she was about to fold her clothes
and yoke the mules and turn for home again,
now clear-eyed Pallas thought of what came next,
to make Odysseus wake and see this young beauty
and she would lead him to the Phaeacians' town.
The ball—
the princess suddenly tossed it to a maid
but it missed the girl, it splashed in a deep swirling pool
and they all shouted out—
and that woke great Odysseus.
He sat up with a start, puzzling, his heart pounding:
"Man of misery, whose land have I lit on now?
What *are* they here—violent, savage, lawless?
or friendly to strangers, god-fearing men?
Listen: shouting, echoing round me—women, girls—
or the nymphs who haunt the rugged mountaintops
and the river springs and meadows lush with grass!
Or am I really close to people who speak my language?
Up with you, see how the land lies, see for yourself now . . ."

Muttering so, great Odysseus crept out of the bushes,
stripping off with his massive hand a leafy branch
from the tangled olive growth to shield his body,
hide his private parts. And out he stalked
as a mountain lion exultant in his power
strides through wind and rain and his eyes blaze
and he charges sheep or oxen or chases wild deer
but his hunger drives him on to go for flocks,
even to raid the best-defended homestead.
So Odysseus moved out . . .
about to mingle with all those lovely girls,
naked now as he was, for the need drove him on,
a terrible sight, all crusted, caked with brine—
they scattered in panic down the jutting beaches.
Only Alcinous' daughter held fast, for Athena planted

courage within her heart, dissolved the trembling in her limbs,
and she firmly stood her ground and faced Odysseus, torn now—
Should he fling his arms around her knees, the young beauty,
plead for help, or stand back, plead with a winning word,
beg her to lead him to the town and lend him clothing?
This was the better way, he thought. Plead now
with a subtle, winning word and stand well back,
don't clasp her knees, the girl might bridle, yes.
He launched in at once, endearing, sly and suave:
"Here I am at your mercy, princess—
are you a goddess or a mortal? If one of the gods
who rule the skies up there, you're Artemis to the life,
the daughter of mighty Zeus—I see her now—just look
at your build, your bearing, your lithe flowing grace . . .
But if you're one of the mortals living here on earth,
three times blest are your father, your queenly mother,
three times over your brothers too. How often their hearts
must warm with joy to see you striding into the dances—
such a bloom of beauty. True, but he is the one
more blest than all other men alive, that man
who sways you with gifts and leads you home, his bride!
I have never laid eyes on anyone like you,
neither man nor woman . . .
I look at you and a sense of wonder takes me.
Wait,
once I saw the like—in Delos,[1] beside Apollo's altar—
the young slip of a palm-tree springing into the light.
There I'd sailed, you see, with a great army in my wake,
out on the long campaign that doomed my life to hardship.
That vision! Just as I stood there gazing, rapt, for hours . . .
no shaft like that had ever risen up from the earth—
so now I marvel at *you,* my lady: rapt, enthralled,
too struck with awe to grasp you by the knees
though pain has ground me down.
Only yesterday,
the twentieth day, did I escape the wine-dark sea.
Till then the waves and the rushing gales had swept me on
from the island of Ogygia. Now some power has tossed me here,
doubtless to suffer still more torments on your shores.
I can't believe they'll stop. Long before that
the gods will give me more, still more.
Compassion—
princess, please! You, after all that I have suffered,
you are the first I've come to. I know no one else,
none in your city, no one in your land.
Show me the way to town, give me a rag for cover,
just some cloth, some wrapper you carried with you here.

1. Island between Greece and Asia Minor that was sacred to Apollo.

And may the good gods give you all your heart desires:
husband, and house, and lasting harmony too.
No finer, greater gift in the world than that . . .
when man and woman possess their home, two minds,
two hearts that work as one. Despair to their enemies,
a joy to all their friends. Their own best claim to glory."

"Stranger," the white-armed princess answered staunchly,
"friend, you're hardly a wicked man, and no fool, I'd say—
it's Olympian Zeus himself who hands our fortunes out,
to each of us in turn, to the good and bad,
however Zeus prefers . . .
He gave you pain, it seems. You simply have to bear it.
But now, seeing you've reached our city and our land,
you'll never lack for clothing or any other gift,
the right of worn-out suppliants come our way.
I'll show you our town, tell you our people's name.
Phaeacians we are, who hold this city and this land,
and I am the daughter of generous King Alcinous.
All our people's power stems from him."

She called out to her girls with lovely braids:
"Stop, my friends! Why run when you see a man?
Surely you don't think *him* an enemy, do you?
There's no one alive, there never will be one,
who'd reach Phaeacian soil and lay it waste.
The immortals love us far too much for that.
We live too far apart, out in the surging sea,
off at the world's end—
no other mortals come to mingle with us.
But here's an unlucky wanderer strayed our way
and we must tend him well. Every stranger and beggar
comes from Zeus, and whatever scrap we give him
he'll be glad to get. So, quick, my girls,
give our newfound friend some food and drink
and bathe the man in the river,
wherever you find some shelter from the wind."
At that
they came to a halt and teased each other on
and led Odysseus down to a sheltered spot
where he could find a seat,
just as great Alcinous' daughter told them.
They laid out cloak and shirt for him to wear,
they gave him the golden flask of suppling olive oil
and pressed him to bathe himself in the river's stream.
Then thoughtful Odysseus reassured the handmaids,
"Stand where you are, dear girls, a good way off,
so I can rinse the brine from my shoulders now
and rub myself with oil . . .
how long it's been since oil touched my skin!

But I won't bathe in front of you. I would be embarrassed—
stark naked before young girls with lovely braids."

The handmaids scurried off to tell their mistress.
Great Odysseus bathed in the river, scrubbed his body
clean of brine that clung to his back and broad shoulders,
scoured away the brackish scurf that caked his head.
And then, once he had bathed all over, rubbed in oil
and donned the clothes the virgin princess gave him,
Zeus's daughter Athena made him taller to all eyes,
his build more massive now, and down from his brow
she ran his curls like thick hyacinth clusters
full of blooms. As a master craftsman washes
gold over beaten silver—a man the god of fire
and Queen Athena trained in every fine technique—
and finishes off his latest effort, handsome work,
so she lavished splendor over his head and shoulders now.
And down to the beach he walked and sat apart,
glistening in his glory, breathtaking, yes,
and the princess gazed in wonder . . .
then turned to her maids with lovely braided hair:
"Listen, my white-armed girls, to what I tell you.
The gods of Olympus can't be all against this man
who's come to mingle among our noble people.
At first he seemed appalling, I must say—
now he seems like a god who rules the skies up there!
Ah, if only a man like *that* were called my husband,
lived right here, pleased to stay forever . . .
Enough.
Give the stranger food and drink, my girls."
They hung on her words and did her will at once,
set before Odysseus food and drink, and he ate and drank,
the great Odysseus, long deprived, so ravenous now—
it seemed like years since he had tasted food.

The white-armed princess thought of one last thing.
Folding the clothes, she packed them into her painted wagon,
hitched the sharp-hoofed mules, and climbing up herself,
Nausicaa urged Odysseus, warmly urged her guest,
"Up with you now, my friend, and off to town we go.
I'll see you into my wise father's palace where,
I promise you, you'll meet all the best Phaeacians.
Wait, let's do it this way. You seem no fool to me.
While we're passing along the fields and plowlands,
you follow the mules and wagon, stepping briskly
with all my maids. I'll lead the way myself.
But once we reach our city, ringed by walls
and strong high towers too, with a fine harbor either side . . .
and the causeway in is narrow; along the road the rolling ships
are all hauled up, with a slipway cleared for every vessel.

There's our assembly, round Poseidon's royal precinct,
built of quarried slabs planted deep in the earth.
Here the sailors tend their black ships' tackle,
cables and sails, and plane their oarblades down.
Phaeacians, you see, care nothing for bow or quiver,
only for masts and oars and good trim ships themselves—
we glory in our ships, crossing the foaming seas!
But I shrink from all our sea-dogs' nasty gossip.
Some old salt might mock us behind our backs—
we have our share of insolent types in town
and one of the coarser sort, spying us, might say,
'Now who's that tall, handsome stranger Nausicaa has in tow?
Where'd she light on *him?* Her husband-to-be, just wait!
But who—some shipwrecked stray she's taken up with,
some alien from abroad? Since nobody lives nearby.
Unless it's really a god come down from the blue
to answer all her prayers, and to have her all his days.
Good riddance! Let the girl go roving to find herself
a man from foreign parts. She only spurns her own—
countless Phaeacians round about who court her,
nothing but our best.'
So they'll scoff . . .
just think of the scandal that would face me then.
I'd find fault with a girl who carried on that way,
flouting her parents' wishes—father, mother, still alive—
consorting with men before she'd tied the knot in public.
No, stranger, listen closely to what I say, the sooner
to win your swift voyage home at my father's hands.
Now, you'll find a splendid grove along the road—
poplars, sacred to Pallas—
a bubbling spring's inside and meadows run around it.
There lies my father's estate, his blossoming orchard too,
as far from town as a man's strong shout can carry.
Take a seat there, wait a while, and give us time
to make it into town and reach my father's house.
Then, when you think we're home, walk on yourself
to the city, ask the way to my father's palace,
generous King Alcinous. You cannot miss it,
even an innocent child could guide you there.
No other Phaeacian's house is built like that:
so grand, the palace of Alcinous, our great hero.
Once the mansion and courtyard have enclosed you, go,
quickly, across the hall until you reach my mother.
Beside the hearth she sits in the fire's glare,
spinning yarn on a spindle, sea-blue wool—
a stirring sight, you'll see . . . .
she leans against a pillar, her ladies sit behind.
And my father's throne is drawn up close beside her;
there he sits and takes his wine, a mortal like a god.

Go past him, grasp my mother's knees—if you want
to see the day of your return, rejoicing, soon,
even if your home's a world away.
If only the queen will take you to her heart,
then there's hope that you will see your loved ones,
reach your own grand house, your native land at last."

At that she touched the mules with her shining whip
and they quickly left the running stream behind.
The team trotted on, their hoofs wove in and out.
She drove them back with care so all the rest,
maids and Odysseus, could keep the pace on foot,
and she used the whip discreetly.
The sun sank as they reached the hallowed grove,
sacred to Athena, where Odysseus stopped and sat
and said a prayer at once to mighty Zeus's daughter:
"Hear me, daughter of Zeus whose shield is thunder—
tireless one, Athena! Now hear my prayer at last,
for you never heard me then, when I was shattered,
when the famous god of earthquakes wrecked my craft.
Grant that here among the Phaeacian people
I may find some mercy and some love!"

So he prayed and Athena heard his prayer
but would not yet appear to him undisguised.
She stood in awe of her Father's brother, lord of the sea
who still seethed on, still churning with rage against
the great Odysseus till he reached his native land.

Book 7. Phaeacia's Halls and Gardens

Now as Odysseus, long an exile, prayed in Athena's grove,
the hardy mule-team drew the princess toward the city.
Reaching her father's splendid halls, she reined in,
just at the gates—her brothers clustering round her,
men like gods, released the mules from the yoke
and brought the clothes indoors
as Nausicaa made her way toward her bedroom.
There her chambermaid lit a fire for her—
Eurymedusa, the old woman who'd come from Apiraea
years ago, when the rolling ships had sailed her in
and the country picked her out as King Alcinous' prize,
for he ruled all the Phaeacians, they obeyed him like a god.
Once, she had nursed the white-armed princess in the palace.
Now she lit a fire and made her supper in the room.

At the same time, Odysseus set off toward the city.
Pallas Athena, harboring kindness for the hero,
drifted a heavy mist around him, shielding him
from any swaggering islander who'd cross his path,

provoke him with taunts and search out who he was.
Instead, as he was about to enter the welcome city,
the bright-eyed goddess herself came up to greet him there,
for all the world like a young girl, holding a pitcher,
standing face-to-face with the visitor, who asked,
"Little girl, now wouldn't you be my guide
to the palace of the one they call Alcinous?
The king who rules the people of these parts.
I am a stranger, you see, weighed down with troubles,
come this way from a distant, far-off shore.
So I know no one here, none at all
in your city and the farmlands round about."
"Oh yes, sir,
good old stranger," the bright-eyed goddess said,
"I'll show you the very palace that you're after—
the king lives right beside my noble father.
Come, quietly too, and I will lead the way.
Now not a glance at anyone, not a question.
The men here never suffer strangers gladly,
have no love for hosting a man from foreign lands.
All they really trust are their fast, flying ships
that cross the mighty ocean. Gifts of Poseidon,
ah what ships they are—
quick as a bird, quick as a darting thought!"

And Pallas Athena sped away in the lead
as he followed in her footsteps, man and goddess.
But the famed Phaeacian sailors never saw him,
right in their midst, striding down their streets.
Athena the one with lovely braids would not permit it,
the awesome goddess poured an enchanted mist around him,
harboring kindness for Odysseus in her heart.
And he marveled now at the balanced ships and havens,
the meeting grounds of the great lords and the long ramparts
looming, coped and crowned with palisades of stakes—
an amazing sight to see . . .
And once they reached the king's resplendent halls
the bright-eyed goddess cried out, "Good old stranger,
here, here is the very palace that you're after—
I've guided you all the way. Here you'll find
our princes dear to the gods, busy feasting.
You go on inside. Be bold, nothing to fear.
In every venture the bold man comes off best,
even the wanderer, bound from distant shores.
The queen is the first you'll light on in the halls.
Arete,[1] she is called, and earns the name:
she answers all our prayers. She comes, in fact,
from the same stock that bred our King Alcinous.

1. Connected to the verb "pray."

First came Nausithous, son of the earthquake god
Poseidon and Periboea, the lovely, matchless beauty,
the youngest daughter of iron-willed Eurymedon,
king of the overweening Giants years ago.
He led that reckless clan to its own ruin,
killed himself in the bargain, but the Sea-lord
lay in love with Periboea and she produced a son,
Nausithous, that lionheart who ruled Phaeacia well.
Now, Nausithous had two sons, Rhexenor and Alcinous,
but the lord of the silver bow, Apollo, shot Rhexenor down—
married, true, yet still without a son in the halls,
he left one child behind, a daughter named Arete.
Alcinous made the girl his wife and honors her
as no woman is honored on this earth, of all the wives
now keeping households under their husbands' sway.
Such is her pride of place, and always will be so:
dear to her loving children, to Alcinous himself
and all our people. They gaze on her as a god,
saluting her warmly on her walks through town.
She lacks nothing in good sense and judgment—
she can dissolve quarrels, even among men,
whoever wins her sympathies.
If only our queen will take you to her heart,
then there's hope that you will see your loved ones,
reach your high-roofed house, your native land at last."

And with that vow the bright-eyed goddess sped away,
over the barren sea, leaving welcome Scheria far behind,
and reaching Marathon and the spacious streets of Athens,
entered Erechtheus' sturdy halls, Athena's stronghold.
Now as Odysseus approached Alcinous' famous house
a rush of feelings stirred within his heart,
bringing him to a standstill,
even before he crossed the bronze threshold . . .
A radiance strong as the moon or rising sun came flooding
through the high-roofed halls of generous King Alcinous.
Walls plated in bronze, crowned with a circling frieze
glazed as blue as lapis, ran to left and right
from outer gates to the deepest court recess,
and solid golden doors enclosed the palace.
Up from the bronze threshold silver doorposts rose
with silver lintel above, and golden handles too.
And dogs of gold and silver were stationed either side,
forged by the god of fire with all his cunning craft
to keep watch on generous King Alcinous' palace,
his immortal guard-dogs, ageless, all their days.
Inside to left and right, in a long unbroken row
from farthest outer gate to the inmost chamber,
thrones stood backed against the wall, each draped
with a finely spun brocade, women's handsome work.

Here the Phaeacian lords would sit enthroned,
dining, drinking—the feast flowed on forever.
And young boys, molded of gold, set on pedestals
standing firm, were lifting torches high in their hands
to flare through the nights and light the feasters down the hall.
And Alcinous has some fifty serving-women in his house:
some, turning the handmill, grind the apple-yellow grain,
some weave at their webs or sit and spin their yarn,
fingers flickering quick as aspen leaves in the wind
and the densely woven woolens dripping oil droplets.
Just as Phaeacian men excel the world at sailing,
driving their swift ships on the open seas,
so the women excel at all the arts of weaving.
That is Athena's gift to them beyond all others—
a genius for lovely work, and a fine mind too.

Outside the courtyard, fronting the high gates,
a magnificent orchard stretches four acres deep
with a strong fence running round it side-to-side.
Here luxuriant trees are always in their prime,
pomegranates and pears, and apples glowing red,
succulent figs and olives swelling sleek and dark.
And the yield of all these trees will never flag or die,
neither in winter nor in summer, a harvest all year round
for the West Wind always breathing through will bring
some fruits to the bud and others warm to ripeness—
pear mellowing ripe on pear, apple on apple,
cluster of grapes on cluster, fig crowding fig.
And here is a teeming vineyard planted for the kings,
beyond it an open level bank where the vintage grapes
lie baking to raisins in the sun while pickers gather others;
some they trample down in vats, and here in the front rows
bunches of unripe grapes have hardly shed their blooms
while others under the sunlight slowly darken purple.
And there by the last rows are beds of greens,
bordered and plotted, greens of every kind,
glistening fresh, year in, year out. And last,
there are two springs, one rippling in channels
over the whole orchard—the other, flanking it,
rushes under the palace gates
to bubble up in front of the lofty roofs
where the city people come and draw their water.
Such
were the gifts, the glories showered down by the gods
on King Alcinous' realm.
And there Odysseus stood,
gazing at all this bounty, a man who'd borne so much . . .
Once he'd had his fill of marveling at it all,
he crossed the threshold quickly,
strode inside the palace. Here he found

the Phaeacian lords and captains tipping out
libations now to the guide and giant-killer Hermes,
the god to whom they would always pour the final cup
before they sought their beds. Odysseus went on
striding down the hall, the man of many struggles
shrouded still in the mist Athena drifted round him,
till he reached Arete and Alcinous the king. And then,
the moment he flung his arms around Arete's knees,
the godsent mist rolled back to reveal the great man.
And silence seized the feasters all along the hall—
seeing him right before their eyes, they marveled,
gazing on him now as Odysseus pleaded, "Queen,
Arete, daughter of godlike King Rhexenor!
Here after many trials I come to beg for mercy,
your husband's, yours, and all these feasters' here.
May the gods endow them with fortune all their lives,
may each hand down to his sons the riches in his house
and the pride of place the realm has granted *him.*
But as for myself, grant me a rapid convoy home
to my own native land. How far away I've been
from all my loved ones—how long I have suffered!"

Pleading so, the man sank down in the ashes,
just at the hearth beside the blazing fire,
while all the rest stayed hushed, stock-still.
At last the old revered Echeneus broke the spell,
the eldest lord in Phaeacia, finest speaker too,
a past master at all the island's ancient ways.
Impelled by kindness now, he rose and said,
"This is no way, Alcinous. How indecent, look,
our guest on the ground, in the ashes by the fire!
Your people are holding back, waiting for your signal.
Come, raise him up and seat the stranger now,
in a silver-studded chair,
and tell the heralds to mix more wine for all
so we can pour out cups to Zeus who loves the lightning,
champion of suppliants—suppliants' rights are sacred.
And let the housekeeper give our guest his supper,
unstinting with her stores."
Hearing that,
Alcinous, poised in all his majesty, took the hand
of the seasoned, worldly-wise Odysseus, raised him up
from the hearth and sat him down in a burnished chair,
displacing his own son, the courtly Lord Laodamas
who had sat beside him, the son he loved the most.
A maid brought water soon in a graceful golden pitcher
and over a silver basin tipped it out
so the guest might rinse his hands,
then pulled a gleaming table to his side.

A staid housekeeper brought on bread to serve him,
appetizers aplenty too, lavish with her bounty.
As long-suffering great Odysseus ate and drank,
the hallowed King Alcinous called his herald:
"Come, Pontonous! Mix the wine in the bowl,
pour rounds to all our banqueters in the house
so we can pour out cups to Zeus who loves the lightning,
champion of suppliants—suppliants' rights are sacred."

At that Pontonous mixed the heady, honeyed wine
and tipped first drops for the god in every cup,
then poured full rounds for all. And once they'd poured
libations out and drunk to their hearts' content,
Alcinous rose and addressed his island people:
"Hear me, lords and captains of Phaeacia,
hear what the heart inside me has to say.
Now, our feast finished, home you go to sleep.
But at dawn we call the elders in to full assembly,
host our guest in the palace, sacrifice to the gods
and then we turn our minds to his passage home,
so under our convoy our new friend can travel back
to his own land—no toil, no troubles—soon,
rejoicing, even if his home's a world away.
And on the way no pain or hardship suffered,
not till he sets foot on native ground again.
There in the future he must suffer all that Fate
and the overbearing Spinners spun out on his life line
the very day his mother gave him birth . . . But if
he's one of the deathless powers, out of the blue,
the gods are working now in strange, new ways.
Always, up to now, they came to us face-to-face
whenever we'd give them grand, glorious sacrifices—
they always sat beside us here and shared our feasts.
Even when some lonely traveler meets them on the roads,
they never disguise themselves. We're too close kin for that,
close as the wild Giants are, the Cyclops too."

"Alcinous!"

wary Odysseus countered, "cross that thought from your mind.
I'm nothing like the immortal gods who rule the skies,
either in build or breeding. I'm just a mortal man.
Whom do you know most saddled down with sorrow?
They are the ones I'd equal, grief for grief.
And I could tell a tale of still more hardship,
all I've suffered, thanks to the gods' will.
But despite my misery, let me finish dinner.
The belly's a shameless dog, there's nothing worse.
Always insisting, pressing, it never lets us forget—
destroyed as I am, my heart racked with sadness,
sick with anguish, still it keeps demanding,

'Eat, drink!' It blots out all the memory
of my pain, commanding, 'Fill me up!'
But you,
at the first light of day, hurry, please,
to set your unlucky guest on his own home soil.
How much I have suffered . . . Oh just let me see
my lands, my serving-men and the grand high-roofed house—
then I can die in peace."
All burst into applause,
urging passage home for their newfound friend,
his pleading rang so true. And once they'd poured
libations out and drunk to their hearts' content,
each one made his way to rest in his own house.
But King Odysseus still remained at hall,
seated beside the royal Alcinous and Arete
as servants cleared the cups and plates away.
The white-armed Queen Arete took the lead;
she'd spotted the cape and shirt Odysseus wore,
fine clothes she'd made herself with all her women,
so now her words flew brusquely, sharply: "Stranger,
I'll be the first to question you—myself.
Who are you? Where are you from?
Who gave you the clothes you're wearing now?
Didn't you say you reached us roving on the sea?"

"What hard labor, queen," the man of craft replied,
"to tell you the story of my troubles start to finish.
The gods on high have given me my share.
Still, this much I will tell you . . .
seeing you probe and press me so intently.
There is an island, Ogygia, lying far at sea,
where the daughter of Atlas, Calypso, has her home,
the seductive nymph with lovely braids—a danger too,
and no one, god or mortal, dares approach her there. But I,
cursed as I am, some power brought me to her hearth,
alone, when Zeus with a white-hot bolt had crushed
my racing warship down the wine-dark sea.
There all the rest of my loyal shipmates died
but I, locking my arms around my good ship's keel,
drifted along nine days. On the tenth, at dead of night,
the gods cast me up on Ogygia, Calypso's island,
home of the dangerous nymph with glossy braids,
and the goddess took me in in all her kindness,
welcomed me warmly, cherished me, even vowed
to make me immortal, ageless, all my days—
but she never won the heart inside me, never.
Seven endless years I remained there, always drenching
with my tears the immortal clothes Calypso gave me.
Then, at last, when the eighth came wheeling round,

she insisted that I sail—inspired by warnings sent
from Zeus, perhaps, or her own mind had changed.
She saw me on my way in a solid craft,
tight and trim, and gave me full provisions,
food and mellow wine, immortal clothes to wear
and summoned a wind to bear me onward, fair and warm.
And seventeen days I sailed, making headway well;
on the eighteenth, shadowy mountains slowly loomed . . .
your land! My heart leapt up, unlucky as I am,
doomed to be comrade still to many hardships.
Many pains the god of earthquakes piled upon me,
loosing the winds against me, blocking passage through,
heaving up a terrific sea, beyond belief—nor did the whitecaps
let me cling to my craft, for all my desperate groaning.
No, the squalls shattered her stem to stern, but I,
I swam hard, I plowed my way through those dark gulfs
till at last the wind and current bore me to your shores.
But here, had I tried to land, the breakers would have hurled me,
smashed me against the jagged cliffs of that grim coast,
so I pulled away, swam back till I reached a river,
the perfect spot at last, or so it struck me,
free of rocks, with a windbreak from the gales.
So, fighting for life, I flung myself ashore
and the godsent, bracing night came on at once.
Clambering up from the river, big with Zeus's rains,
I bedded down in the brush, my body heaped with leaves,
and a god poured down a boundless sleep upon me, yes,
and there in the leaves, exhausted, sick at heart,
I slept the whole night through
and on to the break of day and on into high noon
and the sun was wheeling down when sweet sleep set me free.
And I looked up, and there were your daughter's maids
at play on the beach, and she, she moved among them
like a deathless goddess! I begged her for help
and not once did her sense of tact desert her;
she behaved as you'd never hope to find
in one so young, not in a random meeting—
time and again the youngsters prove so flighty.
Not she. She gave me food aplenty and shining wine,
a bath in the river too, and gave me all this clothing.
That's my whole story. Wrenching to tell, but true."

"Ah, but in one regard, my friend," the king replied,
"her good sense missed the mark, this daughter of mine.
She never escorted you to our house with all her maids
but she was the first you asked for care and shelter."

"Your majesty," diplomatic Odysseus answered,
"don't find fault with a flawless daughter now,
not for my sake, please.

She urged me herself to follow with her maids.
I chose not to, fearing embarrassment in fact—
what if you took offense, seeing us both together?
Suspicious we are, we men who walk the earth."

"Oh no, my friend," Alcinous stated flatly,
"I'm hardly a man for reckless, idle anger.
Balance is best in all things.
Father Zeus, Athena and lord Apollo! if only—
seeing the man you are, seeing we think as one—
you could wed my daughter and be my son-in-law
and stay right here with us. I'd give you a house
and great wealth—if you chose to stay, that is.
No Phaeacian would hold you back by force.
The curse of Father Zeus on such a thing!
And about your convoy home, you rest assured:
I have chosen the day and I decree it is tomorrow.
And all that voyage long you'll lie in a deep sleep
while my people sail you on through calm and gentle tides
till you reach your land and house, or any place you please.
True, even if landfall lies more distant than Euboea,
off at the edge of the world . . .
So say our crews, at least, who saw it once,
that time they carried the gold-haired Rhadamanthys
out to visit Tityus, son of Mother Earth. Imagine,
there they sailed and back they came in the same day,
they finished the homeward run with no strain at all.
You'll see for yourself how far they top the best—
my ships and their young shipmates
tossing up the whitecaps with their oars!"

So he vowed
and the long-enduring great Odysseus glowed with joy
and raised a prayer and called the god by name:
"Father Zeus on high—
may the king fulfill his promises one and all!
Then his fame would ring through the fertile earth
and never die—and I should reach my native land at last!"

And now as the two men exchanged their hopes,
the white-armed queen instructed her palace maids
to make a bed in the porch's shelter, lay down
some heavy purple throws for the bed itself,
and over it spread some blankets, thick woolly robes,
a warm covering laid on top. Torches in hand,
they left the hall and fell to work at once,
briskly prepared a good snug resting-place
and then returned to Odysseus, urged the guest,
"Up, friend, time for sleep. Your bed is made."
How welcome the thought of sleep to that man now . . .
So there after many trials Odysseus lay at rest

on a corded bed inside the echoing colonnade.
Alcinous slept in chambers deep in his lofty house
where the queen his wife arranged and shared their bed.

Book 8. A Day for Songs and Contests

When young Dawn with her rose-red fingers shone once more
royal Alcinous, hallowed island king, rose from bed
and great Odysseus, raider of cities, rose too.
Poised in his majesty, Alcinous led the way
to Phaeacia's meeting grounds, built for all
beside the harbored ships. Both men sat down
on the polished stone benches side-by-side
as Athena started roaming up and down the town,
in build and voice the wise Alcinous' herald,
furthering plans for Odysseus' journey home,
and stopped beside each citizen, urged them all,
"Come this way, you lords and captains of Phaeacia,
come to the meeting grounds and learn about the stranger!
A new arrival! Here at our wise king's palace now,
he's here from roving the ocean, driven far off course—
he looks like a deathless god!"
Rousing their zeal,
their curiosity, each and every man, and soon enough
the assembly seats were filled with people thronging,
gazing in wonder at the seasoned man of war . . .
Over Odysseus' head and shoulders now
Athena lavished a marvelous splendor, yes,
making him taller, more massive to all eyes,
so Phaeacians might regard the man with kindness,
awe and respect as well, and he might win through
the many trials they'd pose to test the hero's strength.
Once they'd grouped, crowding the meeting grounds,
Alcinous rose and addressed his island people:
"Hear me, lords and captains of Phaeacia,
hear what the heart inside me has to say.
This stranger here, our guest—
I don't know who he is, or whether he comes
from sunrise lands or the western lands of evening,
but he has come in his wanderings to my palace;
he pleads for passage, he begs we guarantee it.
So now, as in years gone by, let us press on
and grant him escort. No one, I tell you, no one
who comes to *my* house will languish long here,
heartsick for convoy home.
Come, my people!
Haul a black ship down to the bright sea,
rigged for her maiden voyage—
enlist a crew of fifty-two young sailors,

the best in town, who've proved their strength before.
Let all hands lash their oars to the thwarts then disembark,
come to my house and fall in for a banquet, quickly.
I'll lay on a princely feast for all. So then,
these are the orders I issue to our crews.
For the rest, you sceptered princes here,
you come to my royal halls so we can give
this stranger a hero's welcome in our palace—
no one here refuse. Call in the inspired bard
Demodocus. God has given the man the gift of song,
to him beyond all others, the power to please,
however the spirit stirs him on to sing."

With those commands Alcinous led the way
and a file of sceptered princes took his lead
while the herald went to find the gifted bard.
And the fifty-two young sailors, duly chosen,
briskly following orders,
went down to the shore of the barren salt sea.
And once they reached the ship at the surf's edge,
first they hauled the craft into deeper water,
stepped the mast amidships, canvas brailed,
they made oars fast in the leather oarlock straps,
moored her riding high on the swell, then disembarked
and made their way to wise Alcinous' high-roofed halls.
There colonnades and courts and rooms were overflowing
with crowds, a mounting host of people young and old.
The king slaughtered a dozen sheep to feed his guests,
eight boars with shining tusks and a pair of shambling oxen.
These they skinned and dressed, and then laid out a feast
to fill the heart with savor.
In came the herald now,
leading along the faithful bard the Muse adored
above all others, true, but her gifts were mixed
with good and evil both: she stripped him of sight
but gave the man the power of stirring, rapturous song.
Pontonous brought the bard a silver-studded chair,
right amid the feasters, leaning it up against
a central column—hung his high clear lyre
on a peg above his head and showed him how
to reach up with his hands and lift it down.
And the herald placed a table by his side
with a basket full of bread and cup of wine
for him to sip when his spirit craved refreshment.
All reached out for the good things that lay at hand
and when they'd put aside desire for food and drink,
the Muse inspired the bard
to sing the famous deeds of fighting heroes—
the song whose fame had reached the skies those days:

The Strife Between Odysseus and Achilles, Peleus' Son . . .
how once at the gods' lavish feast the captains clashed
in a savage war of words, while Agamemnon, lord of armies,
rejoiced at heart that Achaea's bravest men were battling so.
For this was the victory sign that Apollo prophesied
at his shrine in Pytho[1] when Agamemnon strode across
the rocky threshold, asking the oracle for advice—
the start of the tidal waves of ruin tumbling down
on Troy's and Achaea's forces, both at once,
thanks to the will of Zeus who rules the world.

That was the song the famous harper sang
but Odysseus, clutching his flaring sea-blue cape
in both powerful hands, drew it over his head
and buried his handsome face,
ashamed his hosts might see him shedding tears.
Whenever the rapt bard would pause in the song,
he'd lift the cape from his head, wipe off his tears
and hoisting his double-handled cup, pour it out to the gods.
But soon as the bard would start again, impelled to sing
by Phaeacia's lords, who reveled in his tale,
again Odysseus hid his face and wept.
His weeping went unmarked by all the others;
only Alcinous, sitting close beside him,
noticed his guest's tears,
heard the groan in the man's labored breathing
and said at once to the master mariners around him,
"Hear me, my lords and captains of Phaeacia!
By now we've had our fill of food well-shared
and the lyre too, our loyal friend at banquets.
Now out we go again and test ourselves in contests,
games of every kind—so our guest can tell his friends,
when he reaches home, how far we excel the world
at boxing, wrestling, jumping, speed of foot."

He forged ahead and the rest fell in behind.
The herald hung the ringing lyre back on its peg
and taking Demodocus by the hand, led him from the palace,
guiding him down the same path the island lords
had just pursued, keen to watch the contests.
They reached the meeting grounds
with throngs of people streaming in their trail
as a press of young champions rose for competition.
Topsail and Riptide rose, the helmsman Rowhard too
and Seaman and Sternman, Surf-at-the-Beach and Stroke-Oar,
Breaker and Bowsprit, Racing-the-Wind and Swing-Aboard
and Seagirt the son of Greatfleet, Shipwrightson
and the son of Launcher, Broadsea, rose up too,

1. Delphi.

a match for murderous Ares,[2] death to men—
in looks and build the best of all Phaeacians
after gallant Laodamas, the Captain of the People.
Laodamas rose with two more sons of great Alcinous,
Halius bred to the sea and Clytoneus famed for ships.
And now the games began, the first event a footrace . . .
They toed the line—
and broke flat out from the start
with a fast pack flying down the field in a whirl of dust
and Clytoneus the prince outstripped them all by far,
flashing ahead the length two mules will plow a furrow
before he turned for home, leaving the pack behind
and raced to reach the crowds.
Next the wrestling,
grueling sport. They grappled, locked, and Broadsea,
pinning the strongest champions, won the bouts.
Next, in the jumping, Seagirt leapt and beat the field.
In the discus Rowhard up and outhurled them all by far.
And the king's good son Laodamas boxed them to their knees.
When all had enjoyed the games to their hearts' content
Alcinous' son Laodamas spurred them: "Come, my friends,
let's ask our guest if he knows the ropes of any sport.
He's no mean man, not with a build like that . . .
Look at his thighs, his legs, and what a pair of arms—
his massive neck, his big, rippling strength!
Nor is he past his prime,
just beaten down by one too many blows.
Nothing worse than the sea, I always say,
to crush a man, the strongest man alive."

And Broadsea put in quickly,
"Well said, Laodamas, right to the point.
Go up to the fellow, challenge him yourself."

On that cue, the noble prince strode up
before Odysseus, front and center, asking,
"Come, stranger, sir, won't you try your hand
at our contests now? If you have skill in any.
It's fit and proper for you to know your sports.
What greater glory attends a man, while he's alive,
than what he wins with his racing feet and striving hands?
Come and compete then, throw your cares to the wind!
It won't be long, your journey's not far off—
your ship's already hauled down to the sea,
your crew is set to sail."
"Laodamas,"
quick to the mark Odysseus countered sharply,
"why do you taunt me so with such a challenge?

2. God of war.

Pains weigh on my spirit now, not your sports—
I've suffered much already, struggled hard.
But here I sit amid your assembly still,
starved for passage home, begging your king,
begging all your people."
"Oh I knew it!"
Broadsea broke in, mocking him to his face.
"I never took you for someone skilled in games,
the kind that real men play throughout the world.
Not a chance. You're some skipper of profiteers,
roving the high seas in his scudding craft,
reckoning up his freight with a keen eye out
for home-cargo, grabbing the gold he can!
You're no athlete. I see that."
With a dark glance
wily Odysseus shot back, "Indecent talk, my friend.
You, you're a reckless fool—I see *that.* So,
the gods don't hand out all their gifts at once,
not build and brains and flowing speech to all.
One man may fail to impress us with his looks
but a god can crown his words with beauty, charm,
and men look on with delight when he speaks out.
Never faltering, filled with winning self-control,
he shines forth at assembly grounds and people gaze
at him like a god when he walks through the streets.
Another man may look like a deathless one on high
but there's not a bit of grace to crown his words.
Just like you, my fine, handsome friend. Not even
a god could improve those lovely looks of yours
but the mind inside is worthless.
Your slander fans the anger in my heart!
I'm no stranger to sports—for all your taunts—
I've held my place in the front ranks, I tell you,
long as I could trust to my youth and striving hands.
But now I'm wrestled down by pain and hardship, look,
I've borne my share of struggles, cleaving my way
through wars of men and pounding waves at sea.
Nevertheless, despite so many blows,
I'll compete in your games, just watch. Your insults
cut to the quick—you rouse my fighting blood!"

Up he sprang, cloak and all, and seized a discus,
huge and heavy, more weighty by far than those
the Phaeacians used to hurl and test each other.
Wheeling round, he let loose with his great hand
and the stone whirred on—and down to ground they went,
those lords of the long oars and master mariners cringing
under the rock's onrush, soaring lightly out of his grip,
flying away past all the other marks, and Queen Athena,

built like a man, staked out the spot and cried
with a voice of triumph, "Even a blind man,
friend, could find your mark by groping round—
it's not mixed up in the crowd, it's far in front!
There's nothing to fear in *this* event—
no one can touch you, much less beat your distance!"

At that the heart of the long-suffering hero laughed,
so glad to find a ready friend in the crowd that,
lighter in mood, he challenged all Phaeacia's best:
"Now go match *that,* you young pups, and straightaway
I'll hurl you another just as far, I swear, or even farther!
All the rest of you, anyone with the spine and spirit,
step right up and try me—you've incensed me so—
at boxing, wrestling, racing; nothing daunts me.
Any Phaeacian here except Laodamas himself.
The man's my host. Who would fight his friend?
He'd have to be good-for-nothing, senseless, yes,
to challenge his host and come to grips in games,
in a far-off land at that. He'd cut his own legs short.
But there are no others I'd deny or think beneath me—
I'll take on all contenders, gladly, test them head-to-head!
I'm no disgrace in the world of games where men compete.
Well I know how to handle a fine polished bow,
the first to hit my man in a mass of enemies,
even with rows of comrades pressing near me,
taking aim with our shafts to hit our targets.
Philoctetes alone outshot me there at Troy
when ranks of Achaean archers bent their bows.
Of the rest I'd say that I outclass them all—
men still alive, who eat their bread on earth.
But I'd never vie with the men of days gone by,
not Heracles, not Eurytus of Oechalia—archers
who rivaled immortal powers with their bows.
That's why noble Eurytus died a sudden death:
no old age, creeping upon him in his halls . . .
Apollo shot him down, enraged that the man
had challenged *him,* the Archer God.
As for spears,
I can fling a spear as far as the next man wings an arrow!
Only at sprinting I fear you'd leave me in the dust.
I've taken a shameful beating out on heavy seas,
no conditioning there on shipboard day by day.
My legs have lost their spring."

He finished. All stood quiet, hushed.
Only Alcinous found a way to answer. "Stranger,
friend—nothing you say among us seems ungracious.
You simply want to display the gifts you're born with,
stung that a youngster marched up to you in the games,

mocking, ridiculing your prowess as no one would
who had some sense of fit and proper speech.
But come now, hear me out,
so you can tell our story to other lords
as you sit and feast in your own halls someday,
your own wife and your children by your side,
remembering there our island prowess here:
what skills great Zeus has given *us* as well,
down all the years from our fathers' days till now.
We're hardly world-class boxers or wrestlers, I admit,
but we can race like the wind, we're champion sailors too,
and always dear to our hearts, the feast, the lyre and dance
and changes of fresh clothes, our warm baths and beds.
So come—all you Phaeacian masters of the dance—
now dance away! So our guest can tell his friends,
when he reaches home, how far we excel the world
in sailing, nimble footwork, dance and song.
                                        Go, someone,
quickly, fetch Demodocus now his ringing lyre.
It must be hanging somewhere in the palace."

At the king's word the herald sprang to his feet
and ran to fetch the vibrant lyre from the house.
And stewards rose, nine in all, picked from the realm
to set the stage for contests: masters-at-arms who
leveled the dancing-floor to make a fine broad ring.
The herald returned and placed the ringing lyre now
in Demodocus' hands, and the bard moved toward the center,
flanked by boys in the flush of youth, skilled dancers
who stamped the ground with marvelous pulsing steps
as Odysseus gazed at their flying, flashing feet,
his heart aglow with wonder.
                                        A rippling prelude—
now the bard struck up an irresistible song:
The Love of Ares and Aphrodite Crowned with Flowers . . .
how the two had first made love in Hephaestus' mansion,
all in secret. Ares had showered her with gifts
and showered Hephaestus' marriage bed with shame
but a messenger ran to tell the god of fire—
Helios, lord of the sun, who'd spied the couple
lost in each other's arms and making love.
Hephaestus, hearing the heart-wounding story,
bustled toward his forge, brooding on his revenge—
planted the huge anvil on its block and beat out chains,
not to be slipped or broken, all to pin the lovers on the spot.
This snare the Firegod forged, ablaze with his rage at War,
then limped to the room where the bed of love stood firm
and round the posts he poured the chains in a sweeping net
with streams of others flowing down from the roofbeam,
gossamer-fine as spider webs no man could see,

not even a blissful god—
the Smith had forged a masterwork of guile.
Once he'd spun that cunning trap around his bed
he feigned a trip to the well-built town of Lemnos,
dearest to him by far of all the towns on earth.
But the god of battle kept no blind man's watch.
As soon as he saw the Master Craftsman leave
he plied his golden reins and arrived at once
and entered the famous god of fire's mansion,
chafing with lust for Aphrodite crowned with flowers.
She'd just returned from her father's palace, mighty Zeus,
and now she sat in her rooms as Ares strode right in
and grasped her hand with a warm, seductive urging:
"Quick, my darling, come, let's go to bed
and lose ourselves in love! Your husband's away—
by now he must be off in the wilds of Lemnos,
consorting with his raucous Sintian friends."
So he pressed
and her heart raced with joy to sleep with War
and off they went to bed and down they lay—
and down around them came those cunning chains
of the crafty god of fire, showering down now
till the couple could not move a limb or lift a finger—
then they knew at last: there was no way out, not now.
But now the glorious crippled Smith was drawing near . . .
he'd turned around, miles short of the Lemnos coast,
for the Sungod kept *his* watch and told Hephaestus all,
so back he rushed to his house, his heart consumed with anguish.
Halting there at the gates, seized with savage rage
he howled a terrible cry, imploring all the gods,
"Father Zeus, look here—
the rest of you happy gods who live forever—
here is a sight to make you laugh, revolt you too!
Just because I am crippled, Zeus's daughter Aphrodite
will always spurn me and love that devastating Ares,
just because of his striking looks and racer's legs
while I am a weakling, lame from birth, and who's to blame?
Both my parents—who else? If only they'd never bred me!
Just look at the two lovers . . . crawled inside my bed,
locked in each other's arms—the sight makes me burn!
But I doubt they'll want to lie that way much longer,
not a moment more—mad as they are for each other.
No, they'll soon tire of bedding down together,
but then my cunning chains will bind them fast
till our Father pays my bride-gifts back in full,
all I handed *him* for that shameless bitch his daughter,
irresistible beauty—all unbridled too!"
So Hephaestus wailed
as the gods came crowding up to his bronze-floored house.

Poseidon god of the earthquake came, and Hermes came,
the running god of luck, and the Archer, lord Apollo,
while modesty kept each goddess to her mansion.
The immortals, givers of all good things, stood at the gates,
and uncontrollable laughter burst from the happy gods
when they saw the god of fire's subtle, cunning work.
One would glance at his neighbor, laughing out,
"A bad day for adultery! Slow outstrips the Swift."

"Look how limping Hephaestus conquers War,
the quickest of all the gods who rule Olympus!"

"The cripple wins by craft."
"The adulterer,
he will pay the price!"
So the gods would banter
among themselves but lord Apollo goaded Hermes on:
"Tell me, Quicksilver, giver of all good things—
even with those unwieldy shackles wrapped around you,
how would you like to bed the golden Aphrodite?"

"Oh Apollo, if only!" the giant-killer cried.
"Archer, bind me down with triple those endless chains!
Let all you gods look on, and all you goddesses too—
how I'd love to bed that golden Aphrodite!"

A peal of laughter broke from the deathless ones
but not Poseidon, not a smile from him; he kept on
begging the famous Smith to loose the god of war,
pleading, his words flying, "Let him go!
I guarantee you Ares will pay the price,
whatever you ask, Hephaestus,
whatever's right in the eyes of all the gods."

But the famous crippled Smith appealed in turn,
"God of the earthquake, please don't urge this on me.
A pledge for a worthless man is a worthless pledge indeed.
What if he slips out of his chains—his debts as well?
How could I shackle *you* while all the gods look on?"

But the god of earthquakes reassured the Smith,
"Look, Hephaestus, if Ares scuttles off and away,
squirming out of his debt, I'll pay the fine myself."

And the famous crippled Smith complied at last:
"Now *there*'s an offer I really can't refuse!"

With all his force the god of fire loosed the chains
and the two lovers, free of the bonds that overwhelmed them so,
sprang up and away at once, and the Wargod sped to Thrace
while Love with her telltale laughter sped to Paphos,
Cyprus Isle, where her grove and scented altar stand.
There the Graces bathed and anointed her with oil,

ambrosial oil, the bloom that clings to the gods
who never die, and swathed her round in gowns
to stop the heart . . . an ecstasy—a vision.

That was the song the famous harper sang
and Odysseus relished every note as the islanders,
the lords of the long oars and master mariners rejoiced.

Next the king asked Halius and Laodamas to dance,
the two alone, since none could match that pair.
So taking in hand a gleaming sea-blue ball
made by the craftsman Polybus—arching back,
one prince would hurl it toward the shadowy clouds
as the other leaping high into the air would catch it
quickly, nimbly, before his feet hit ground again.
Once they'd vied at throwing the ball straight up,
they tossed it back and forth in a blur of hands
as they danced across the earth that feeds us all,
while boys around the ring stamped out the beat
and a splendid rhythmic drumming sound arose
and good Odysseus looked at his host, exclaiming,
"King Alcinous, shining among your island people,
you boasted Phaeacia's dancers are the best—
they prove your point—I watch and I'm amazed!"

His praises cheered the hallowed island king
who spoke at once to the master mariners around him:
"Hear me, my lords and captains of Phaeacia,
our guest is a man of real taste, I'd say. Come,
let's give him the parting gifts a guest deserves.
There are twelve peers of the realm who rule our land,
thirteen, counting myself. Let each of us contribute
a fresh cloak and shirt and a bar of precious gold.
Gather the gifts together, hurry, so our guest
can have them all in hand when he goes to dine,
his spirit filled with joy.
As for Broadsea, let him make amends,
man-to-man, with his words as well as gifts.
His first remarks were hardly fit to hear."

All assented and gave their own commands,
each noble sent a page to fetch his gifts.
And Broadsea volunteered in turn, obliging:
"Great Alcinous, shining among our island people,
of course I'll make amends to our newfound friend
as you request. I'll give the man this sword.
It's solid bronze and the hilt has silver studs,
the sheath around it ivory freshly carved.
Here's a gift our guest will value highly."

He placed the silver-studded sword in Odysseus' hands
with a burst of warm words: "Farewell, stranger, sir—

if any remark of mine gave you offense,
may stormwinds snatch it up and sweep it off!
May the gods grant *you* safe passage home to see your wife—
you've been so far from loved ones, suffered so!"

Tactful Odysseus answered him in kind:
"And a warm farewell to you, too, my friend.
May the gods grant *you* good fortune—
may you never miss this sword, this gift you give
with such salutes. You've made amends in full."
With that
he slung the silver-studded sword across his shoulder.
As the sun sank, his glittering gifts arrived
and proud heralds bore them into the hall
where sons of King Alcinous took them over,
spread them out before their noble mother's feet—
a grand array of gifts. The king in all his majesty
led the rest of his peers inside, following in a file
and down they sat on rows of high-backed chairs.
The king turned to the queen and urged her, "Come,
my dear, bring in an elegant chest, the best you have,
and lay inside it a fresh cloak and shirt, your own gifts.
Then heat a bronze cauldron over the fire, boil water,
so once our guest has bathed and reviewed his gifts—
all neatly stacked for sailing,
gifts our Phaeacian lords have brought him now—
he'll feast in peace and hear the harper's songs.
And I will give him this gorgeous golden cup of mine,
so he'll remember Alcinous all his days to come
when he pours libations out in his own house
to Father Zeus and the other gods on high."

And at that Arete told her serving-women,
"Set a great three-legged cauldron over the fire—
do it right away!"
And hoisting over the blaze
a cauldron, filling it brimful with bathing water,
they piled fresh logs beneath and lit them quickly.
The fire lapped at the vessel's belly, the water warmed.
Meanwhile the queen had a polished chest brought forth
from an inner room and laid the priceless gifts inside,
the clothes and gold the Phaeacian lords had brought,
and added her own gifts, a cloak and a fine shirt,
and gave her guest instructions quick and clear:
"Now look to the lid yourself and bind it fast
with a good tight knot, so no one can rob you
on your voyage—drifting into a sweet sleep
as the black ship sails you home."
Hearing that,
the storm-tossed man secured the lid straightway,

he battened it fast with a swift, intricate knot
the lady Circe had taught him long ago.
And the housekeeper invited him at once
to climb into a waiting tub and bathe—
a hot, steaming bath . . .
what a welcome sight to Odysseus' eyes!
He'd been a stranger to comforts such as these
since he left the lovely-haired Calypso's house,
yet all those years he enjoyed such comforts there,
never-ending, as if he were a god . . . And now,
when maids had washed him, rubbed him down with oil
and drawn warm fleece and a shirt around his shoulders,
he stepped from the bath to join the nobles at their wine.
And there stood Nausicaa as he passed. Beside a column
that propped the sturdy roof she paused, endowed
by the gods with all her beauty, gazing at
Odysseus right before her eyes. Wonderstruck,
she hailed her guest with a winning flight of words:
"Farewell, my friend! And when you are at home,
home in your own land, remember me at times.
Mainly to me you owe the gift of life."

Odysseus rose to the moment deftly, gently:
"Nausicaa, daughter of generous King Alcinous,
may Zeus the Thunderer, Hera's husband, grant it so—
that I travel home and see the dawn of my return.
Even at home I'll pray to you as a deathless goddess
all my days to come. You saved my life, dear girl."

And he went and took his seat beside the king.
By now they were serving out the portions, mixing wine,
and the herald soon approached, leading the faithful bard
Demodocus, prized by all the people—seated him in a chair
amid the feasters, leaning it against a central column.
At once alert Odysseus carved a strip of loin,
rich and crisp with fat, from the white-tusked boar
that still had much meat left, and called the herald over:
"Here, herald, take this choice cut to Demodocus
so he can eat his fill—with warm regards
from a man who knows what suffering is . . .
From all who walk the earth our bards deserve
esteem and awe, for the Muse herself has taught them
paths of song. She loves the breed of harpers."

The herald placed the gift in Demodocus' hands
and the famous blind bard received it, overjoyed.
They reached for the good things that lay outspread
and when they'd put aside desire for food and drink,
Odysseus, master of many exploits, praised the singer:
"I respect you, Demodocus, more than any man alive—
surely the Muse has taught you, Zeus's daughter,

or god Apollo himself. How true to life,
all too true . . . you sing the Achaeans' fate,
all they did and suffered, all they soldiered through,
as if you were there yourself or heard from one who was.
But come now, shift your ground. Sing of the wooden horse
Epeus built with Athena's help, the cunning trap that
good Odysseus brought one day to the heights of Troy,
filled with fighting men who laid the city waste.
Sing that for me—true to life as it deserves—
and I will tell the world at once how freely
the Muse gave *you* the gods' own gift of song."

Stirred now by the Muse, the bard launched out
in a fine blaze of song, starting at just the point
where the main Achaean force, setting their camps afire,
had boarded the oarswept ships and sailed for home
but famed Odysseus' men already crouched in hiding—
in the heart of Troy's assembly—dark in that horse
the Trojans dragged themselves to the city heights.
Now it stood there, looming . . .
and round its bulk the Trojans sat debating,
clashing, days on end. Three plans split their ranks:
either to hack open the hollow vault with ruthless bronze
or haul it up to the highest ridge and pitch it down the cliffs
or let it stand—a glorious offering made to pacify the gods—
and that, that final plan, was bound to win the day.
For Troy was fated to perish once the city lodged
inside her walls the monstrous wooden horse
where the prime of Argive power lay in wait
with death and slaughter bearing down on Troy.
And he sang how troops of Achaeans broke from cover,
streaming out of the horse's hollow flanks to plunder Troy—
he sang how left and right they ravaged the steep city,
sang how Odysseus marched right up to Deiphobus' house
like the god of war on attack with diehard Menelaus.
There, he sang, Odysseus fought the grimmest fight
he had ever braved but he won through at last,
thanks to Athena's superhuman power.

That was the song the famous harper sang
but great Odysseus melted into tears,
running down from his eyes to wet his cheeks . . .
as a woman weeps, her arms flung round her darling husband,
a man who fell in battle, fighting for town and townsmen,
trying to beat the day of doom from home and children.
Seeing the man go down, dying, gasping for breath,
she clings for dear life, screams and shrills—
but the victors, just behind h er,
digging spear-butts into her back and shoulders,
drag her off in bondage, yoked to hard labor, pain,

and the most heartbreaking torment wastes her cheeks.
So from Odysseus' eyes ran tears of heartbreak now.
But his weeping went unmarked by all the others;
only Alcinous, sitting close beside him,
noticed his guest's tears,
heard the groan in the man's labored breathing
and said at once to the master mariners around him,
"Hear me, my lords and captains of Phaeacia!
Let Demodocus rest his ringing lyre now—
this song he sings can hardly please us all.
Ever since our meal began and the stirring bard
launched his song, our guest has never paused
in his tears and throbbing sorrow.
Clearly grief has overpowered his heart.
Break off this song! Let us all enjoy ourselves,
the hosts and guest together. Much the warmer way.
All these things are performed for him, our honored guest,
the royal send-off here and gifts we give in love.
Treat your guest and suppliant like a brother:
anyone with a touch of sense knows that.
So don't be crafty now, my friend, don't hide
the truth I'm after. Fair is fair, speak out!
Come, tell us the name they call you there at home—
your mother, father, townsmen, neighbors round about.
Surely no man in the world is nameless, all told.
Born high, born low, as soon as he sees the light
his parents always name him, once he's born.
And tell me your land, your people, your city too,
so our ships can sail you home—their wits will speed them there.
For we have no steersmen here among Phaeacia's crews
or steering-oars that guide your common craft.
Our ships know in a flash their mates' intentions,
know all ports of call and all the rich green fields.
With wings of the wind they cross the sea's huge gulfs,
shrouded in mist and cloud—no fear in the world of foundering,
fatal shipwreck.
True, there's an old tale I heard
my father telling once. Nausithous used to say
that lord Poseidon was vexed with us because
we escorted all mankind and never came to grief.
He said that one day, as a well-built ship of ours
sailed home on the misty sea from such a convoy,
the god would crush it, yes,
and pile a huge mountain round about our port.
So the old king foretold . . . And as for the god, well,
he can do his worst or leave it quite undone,
whatever warms his heart.
But come, my friend,
tell us your own story now, and tell it truly.

Where have your rovings forced you?
What lands of men have you seen, what sturdy towns,
what men themselves? Who were wild, savage, lawless?
Who were friendly to strangers, god-fearing men? Tell me,
why do you weep and grieve so sorely when you hear
the fate of the Argives, hear the fall of Troy?
That is the gods' work, spinning threads of death
through the lives of mortal men,
and all to make a song for those to come . . .
Did one of your kinsmen die before the walls of Troy,
some brave man—a son by marriage? father by marriage?
Next to our own blood kin, our nearest, dearest ties.
Or a friend perhaps, someone close to your heart,
staunch and loyal? No less dear than a brother,
the brother-in-arms who shares our inmost thoughts."

Book 9. In the One-Eyed Giant's Cave

Odysseus, the great teller of tales, launched out on his story:
"Alcinous, majesty, shining among your island people,
what a fine thing it is to listen to such a bard
as we have here—the man sings like a god.
The crown of life, I'd say. There's nothing better
than when deep joy holds sway throughout the realm
and banqueters up and down the palace sit in ranks,
enthralled to hear the bard, and before them all, the tables
heaped with bread and meats, and drawing wine from a mixing-bowl
the steward makes his rounds and keeps the winecups flowing.
This, to my mind, is the best that life can offer.
But now
you're set on probing the bitter pains I've borne,
so I'm to weep and grieve, it seems, still more.
Well then, what shall I go through first,
what shall I save for last?
What pains—the gods have given me my share.
Now let me begin by telling you my name . . .
so you may know it well and I in times to come,
if I can escape the fatal day, will be your host,
your sworn friend, though my home is far from here.
I am Odysseus, son of Laertes, known to the world
for every kind of craft—my fame has reached the skies.
Sunny Ithaca is my home. Atop her stands our seamark,
Mount Neriton's leafy ridges shimmering in the wind.
Around her a ring of islands circle side-by-side,
Dulichion, Same, wooded Zacynthus too, but mine
lies low and away, the farthest out to sea,
rearing into the western dusk
while the others face the east and breaking day.
Mine is a rugged land but good for raising sons—

and I myself, I know no sweeter sight on earth
than a man's own native country.
True enough,
Calypso the lustrous goddess tried to hold me back,
deep in her arching caverns, craving me for a husband.
So did Circe, holding me just as warmly in her halls,
the bewitching queen of Aeaea keen to have me too.
But they never won the heart inside me, never.
So nothing is as sweet as a man's own country,
his own parents, even though he's settled down
in some luxurious house, off in a foreign land
and far from those who bore him.
No more. Come,
let me tell you about the voyage fraught with hardship
Zeus inflicted on me, homeward bound from Troy . . .

The wind drove me out of Ilium on to Ismarus,
the Cicones'[1] stronghold. There I sacked the city,
killed the men, but as for the wives and plunder,
that rich haul we dragged away from the place—
we shared it round so no one, not on my account,
would go deprived of his fair share of spoils.
Then I urged them to cut and run, set sail,
but would they listen? Not those mutinous fools;
there was too much wine to swill, too many sheep to slaughter
down along the beach, and shambling longhorn cattle.
And all the while the Cicones sought out other Cicones,
called for help from their neighbors living inland:
a larger force, and stronger soldiers too,
skilled hands at fighting men from chariots,
skilled, when a crisis broke, to fight on foot.
Out of the morning mist they came against us—
packed as the leaves and spears that flower forth in spring—
and Zeus presented us with disaster, me and my comrades
doomed to suffer blow on mortal blow. Lining up,
both armies battled it out against our swift ships,
both raked each other with hurtling bronze lances.
Long as morning rose and the blessed day grew stronger
we stood and fought them off, massed as they were, but then,
when the sun wheeled past the hour for unyoking oxen,
the Cicones broke our lines and beat us down at last.
Out of each ship, six men-at-arms were killed;
the rest of us rowed away from certain doom.

From there we sailed on, glad to escape our death
yet sick at heart for the dear companions we had lost.
But I would not let our rolling ships set sail until the crews

1. In Thrace, across the opening of the Black Sea from Troy.

had raised the triple cry, saluting each poor comrade
cut down by the fierce Cicones on that plain.
Now Zeus who masses the stormclouds hit the fleet
with the North Wind—
a howling, demonic gale, shrouding over
in thunderheads the earth and sea at once—
and night swept down
from the sky and the ships went plunging headlong on,
our sails slashed to rags by the hurricane's blast!
We struck them—cringing at death we rowed our ships
to the nearest shoreline, pulled with all our power.
There, for two nights, two days, we lay by, no letup,
eating our hearts out, bent with pain and bone-tired.
When Dawn with her lovely locks brought on the third day,
then stepping the masts and hoisting white sails high,
we lounged at the oarlocks, letting wind and helmsmen
keep us true on course . . .
And now, at long last,
I might have reached my native land unscathed,
but just as I doubled Malea's cape, a tide-rip
and the North Wind drove me way off course
careering past Cythera.
Nine whole days
I was borne along by rough, deadly winds
on the fish-infested sea. Then on the tenth
our squadron reached the land of the Lotus-eaters,
people who eat the lotus, mellow fruit and flower.
We disembarked on the coast, drew water there
and crewmen snatched a meal by the swift ships.
Once we'd had our fill of food and drink I sent
a detail ahead, two picked men and a third, a runner,
to scout out who might live there—men like us perhaps,
who live on bread? So off they went and soon enough
they mingled among the natives, Lotus-eaters, Lotus-eaters
who had no notion of killing my companions, not at all,
they simply gave them the lotus to taste instead . . .
Any crewmen who ate the lotus, the honey-sweet fruit,
lost all desire to send a message back, much less return,
their only wish to linger there with the Lotus-eaters,
grazing on lotus, all memory of the journey home
dissolved forever. But *I* brought them back, back
to the hollow ships, and streaming tears—I forced them,
hauled them under the rowing benches, lashed them fast
and shouted out commands to my other, steady comrades:
'Quick, no time to lose, embark in the racing ships!'—
so none could eat the lotus, forget the voyage home.
They swung aboard at once, they sat to the oars in ranks
and in rhythm churned the water white with stroke on stroke.

From there we sailed on, our spirits now at a low ebb,
and reached the land of the high and mighty Cyclops,
lawless brutes, who trust so to the everlasting gods
they never plant with their own hands or plow the soil.
Unsown, unplowed, the earth teems with all they need,
wheat, barley and vines, swelled by the rains of Zeus
to yield a big full-bodied wine from clustered grapes.
They have no meeting place for council, no laws either,
no, up on the mountain peaks they live in arching caverns—
each a law to himself, ruling his wives and children,
not a care in the world for any neighbor.
Now,
a level island stretches flat across the harbor,
not close inshore to the Cyclops' coast, not too far out,
thick with woods where the wild goats breed by hundreds.
No trampling of men to start them from their lairs,
no hunters roughing it out on the woody ridges,
stalking quarry, ever raid their haven.
No flocks browse, no plowlands roll with wheat;
unplowed, unsown forever—empty of humankind—
the island just feeds droves of bleating goats.
For the Cyclops have no ships with crimson prows,
no shipwrights there to build them good trim craft
that could sail them out to foreign ports of call
as most men risk the seas to trade with other men.
Such artisans would have made this island too
a decent place to live in . . . No mean spot,
it could bear you any crop you like in season.
The water-meadows along the low foaming shore
run soft and moist, and your vines would never flag.
The land's clear for plowing. Harvest on harvest,
a man could reap a healthy stand of grain—
the subsoil's dark and rich.
There's a snug deep-water harbor there, what's more,
no need for mooring-gear, no anchor-stones to heave,
no cables to make fast. Just beach your keels, ride out
the days till your shipmates' spirit stirs for open sea
and a fair wind blows. And last, at the harbor's head
there's a spring that rushes fresh from beneath a cave
and black poplars flourish round its mouth.
Well,
here we landed, and surely a god steered us in
through the pitch-black night.
Not that he ever showed himself, with thick fog
swirling around the ships, the moon wrapped in clouds
and not a glimmer stealing through that gloom.
Not one of us glimpsed the island—scanning hard—
or the long combers rolling us slowly toward the coast,
not till our ships had run their keels ashore.

Beaching our vessels smoothly, striking sail,
the crews swung out on the low shelving sand
and there we fell asleep, awaiting Dawn's first light.

When young Dawn with her rose-red fingers shone once more
we all turned out, intrigued to tour the island.
The local nymphs, the daughters of Zeus himself,
flushed mountain-goats so the crews could make their meal.
Quickly we fetched our curved bows and hunting spears
from the ships and, splitting up into three bands,
we started shooting, and soon enough some god
had sent us bags of game to warm our hearts.
A dozen vessels sailed in my command
and to each crew nine goats were shared out
and mine alone took ten. Then all day long
till the sun went down we sat and feasted well
on sides of meat and rounds of heady wine.
The good red stock in our vessels' holds
had not run out, there was still plenty left;
the men had carried off a generous store in jars
when we stormed and sacked the Cicones' holy city.
Now we stared across at the Cyclops' shore, so near
we could even see their smoke, hear their voices,
their bleating sheep and goats . . .
And then when the sun had set and night came on
we lay down and slept at the water's shelving edge.
When young Dawn with her rose-red fingers shone once more
I called a muster briskly, commanding all the hands,
'The rest of you stay here, my friends-in-arms.
I'll go across with my own ship and crew
and probe the natives living over there.
What *are* they—violent, savage, lawless?
or friendly to strangers, god-fearing men?'

With that I boarded ship and told the crew
to embark at once and cast off cables quickly.
They swung aboard, they sat to the oars in ranks
and in rhythm churned the water white with stroke on stroke.
But as soon as we reached the coast I mentioned—no long trip—
we spied a cavern just at the shore, gaping above the surf,
towering, overgrown with laurel. And here big flocks,
sheep and goats, were stalled to spend the nights,
and around its mouth a yard was walled up
with quarried boulders sunk deep in the earth
and enormous pines and oak-trees looming darkly . . .
Here was a giant's lair, in fact, who always pastured
his sheepflocks far afield and never mixed with others.
A grim loner, dead set in his own lawless ways.
Here was a piece of work, by god, a monster
built like no mortal who ever supped on bread,

no, like a shaggy peak, I'd say—a man-mountain
rearing head and shoulders over the world.
Now then,
I told most of my good trusty crew to wait,
to sit tight by the ship and guard her well
while I picked out my dozen finest fighters
and off I went. But I took a skin of wine along,
the ruddy, irresistible wine that Maron gave me once,
Euanthes' son, a priest of Apollo, lord of Ismarus,
because we'd rescued him, his wife and children,
reverent as we were;
he lived, you see, in Apollo's holy grove.
And so in return he gave me splendid gifts,
he handed me seven bars of well-wrought gold,
a mixing-bowl of solid silver, then this wine . . .
He drew it off in generous wine-jars, twelve in all,
all unmixed—and such a bouquet, a drink fit for the gods!
No maid or man of his household knew that secret store,
only himself, his loving wife and a single servant.
Whenever they'd drink the deep-red mellow vintage,
twenty cups of water he'd stir in one of wine
and what an aroma wafted from the bowl—
what magic, what a godsend—
no joy in holding back when *that* was poured!
Filling a great goatskin now, I took this wine,
provisions too in a leather sack. A sudden foreboding
told my fighting spirit I'd soon come up against
some giant clad in power like armor-plate—
a savage deaf to justice, blind to law.

Our party quickly made its way to his cave
but we failed to find our host himself inside;
he was off in his pasture, ranging his sleek flocks.
So we explored his den, gazing wide-eyed at it all,
the large flat racks loaded with drying cheeses,
the folds crowded with young lambs and kids,
split into three groups—here the spring-born,
here mid-yearlings, here the fresh sucklings
off to the side—each sort was penned apart.
And all his vessels, pails and hammered buckets
he used for milking, were brimming full with whey.
From the start my comrades pressed me, pleading hard,
'Let's make away with the cheeses, then come back—
hurry, drive the lambs and kids from the pens
to our swift ship, put out to sea at once!'
But I would not give way—
and how much better it would have been—
not till I saw him, saw what gifts he'd give.
But he proved no lovely sight to my companions.

There we built a fire, set our hands on the cheeses,
offered some to the gods and ate the bulk ourselves
and settled down inside, awaiting his return . . .
And back he came from pasture, late in the day,
herding his flocks home, and lugging a huge load
of good dry logs to fuel his fire at supper.
He flung them down in the cave—a jolting crash—
we scuttled in panic into the deepest dark recess.
And next he drove his sleek flocks into the open vault,
all he'd milk at least, but he left the males outside,
rams and billy goats out in the high-walled yard.
Then to close his door he hoisted overhead
a tremendous, massive slab—
no twenty-two wagons, rugged and four-wheeled,
could budge that boulder off the ground, I tell you,
such an immense stone the monster wedged to block
his cave!
Then down he squatted to milk his sheep and bleating goats,
each in order, and put a suckling underneath each dam.
And half of the fresh white milk he curdled quickly,
set it aside in wicker racks to press for cheese,
the other half let stand in pails and buckets,
ready at hand to wash his supper down.
As soon as he'd briskly finished all his chores
he lit his fire and spied us in the blaze and
'Strangers!' he thundered out, 'now who are you?
Where did you sail from, over the running sea-lanes?
Out on a trading spree or roving the waves like pirates,
sea-wolves raiding at will, who risk their lives
to plunder other men?'
The hearts inside us shook,
terrified by his rumbling voice and monstrous hulk.
Nevertheless I found the nerve to answer, firmly,
'Men of Achaea we are and bound now from Troy!
Driven far off course by the warring winds,
over the vast gulf of the sea—battling home
on a strange tack, a route that's off the map,
and so we've come to you . . .
so it must please King Zeus's plotting heart.
We're glad to say we're men of Atrides Agamemnon,
whose fame is the proudest thing on earth these days,
so great a city he sacked, such multitudes he killed!
But since we've chanced on you, we're at your knees
in hopes of a warm welcome, even a guest-gift,
the sort that hosts give strangers. That's the custom.
Respect the gods, my friend. We're suppliants—at
your mercy!
Zeus of the Strangers guards all guests and suppliants:
strangers are sacred—Zeus will avenge their rights!'

'Stranger,' he grumbled back from his brutal heart,
'you must be a fool, stranger, or come from nowhere,
telling *me* to fear the gods or avoid their wrath!
We Cyclops never blink at Zeus and Zeus's shield
of storm and thunder, or any other blessed god—
we've got more force by far.
I'd never spare you in fear of Zeus's hatred,
you or your comrades here, unless I had the urge.
But tell me, where did you moor your sturdy ship
when you arrived? Up the coast or close in?
I'd just like to know.'
So he laid his trap
but he never caught me, no, wise to the world
I shot back in my crafty way, 'My ship?
Poseidon god of the earthquake smashed my ship,
he drove it against the rocks at your island's far cape,
he dashed it against a cliff as the winds rode us in.
I and the men you see escaped a sudden death.'

Not a word in reply to that, the ruthless brute.
Lurching up, he lunged out with his hands toward my men
and snatching two at once, rapping them on the ground
he knocked them dead like pups—
their brains gushed out all over, soaked the floor—
and ripping them limb from limb to fix his meal
he bolted them down like a mountain-lion, left no scrap,
devoured entrails, flesh and bones, marrow and all!
We flung our arms to Zeus, we wept and cried aloud,
looking on at his grisly work—paralyzed, appalled.
But once the Cyclops had stuffed his enormous gut
with human flesh, washing it down with raw milk,
he slept in his cave, stretched out along his flocks.
And I with my fighting heart, I thought at first
to steal up to him, draw the sharp sword at my hip
and stab his chest where the midriff packs the liver—
I groped for the fatal spot but a fresh thought held me back.
There at a stroke we'd finish off ourselves as well—
how could *we* with our bare hands heave back
that slab he set to block his cavern's gaping maw?
So we lay there groaning, waiting Dawn's first light.

When young Dawn with her rose-red fingers shone once more
the monster relit his fire and milked his handsome ewes,
each in order, putting a suckling underneath each dam,
and as soon as he'd briskly finished all his chores
he snatched up two more men and fixed his meal.
Well-fed, he drove his fat sheep from the cave,
lightly lifting the huge doorslab up and away,
then slipped it back in place
as a hunter flips the lid of his quiver shut.

Piercing whistles—turning his flocks to the hills
he left me there, the heart inside me brooding on revenge:
how could I pay him back? would Athena give me glory?
Here was the plan that struck my mind as best . . .
the Cyclops' great club: there it lay by the pens,
olivewood, full of sap. He'd lopped it off to brandish
once it dried. Looking it over, we judged it big enough
to be the mast of a pitch-black ship with her twenty oars,
a freighter broad in the beam that plows through miles of sea—
so long, so thick it bulked before our eyes. Well,
flanking it now, I chopped off a fathom's length,
rolled it to comrades, told them to plane it down,
and they made the club smooth as I bent and shaved
the tip to a stabbing point. I turned it over
the blazing fire to char it good and hard,
then hid it well, buried deep under the dung
that littered the cavern's floor in thick wet clumps.
And now I ordered my shipmates all to cast lots—
who'd brave it out with me
to hoist our stake and grind it into his eye
when sleep had overcome him? Luck of the draw:
I got the very ones I would have picked myself,
four good men, and I in the lead made five . . .

Nightfall brought him back, herding his woolly sheep
and he quickly drove the sleek flock into the vaulted cavern,
rams and all—none left outside in the walled yard—
his own idea, perhaps, or a god led him on.
Then he hoisted the huge slab to block the door
and squatted to milk his sheep and bleating goats,
each in order, putting a suckling underneath each dam,
and as soon as he'd briskly finished all his chores
he snatched up two more men and fixed his meal.
But this time I lifted a carved wooden bowl,
brimful of my ruddy wine,
and went right up to the Cyclops, enticing,
'Here, Cyclops, try this wine—to top off
the banquet of human flesh you've bolted down!
Judge for yourself what stock our ship had stored.
I brought it here to make you a fine libation,
hoping you would pity me, Cyclops, send me home,
but your rages are insufferable. You barbarian—
how can any man on earth come visit you after *this?*
What you've done outrages all that's right!'

At that he seized the bowl and tossed it off
and the heady wine pleased him immensely—'More'—
he demanded a second bowl—'a hearty helping!
And tell me your name now, quickly,

so I can hand my guest a gift to warm *his* heart.
Our soil yields the Cyclops powerful, full-bodied wine
and the rains from Zeus build its strength. But this,
this is nectar, ambrosia—this flows from heaven!'

So he declared. I poured him another fiery bowl—
three bowls I brimmed and three he drank to the last drop,
the fool, and then, when the wine was swirling round his brain,
I approached my host with a cordial, winning word:
'So, you ask me the name I'm known by, Cyclops?
I will tell you. But you must give me a guest-gift
as you've promised. Nobody—that's my name. Nobody—
so my mother and father call me, all my friends.'

But he boomed back at me from his ruthless heart,
'*Nobody?* I'll eat Nobody last of all his friends—
I'll eat the others first! That's my gift to *you!*'
With that
he toppled over, sprawled full-length, flat on his back
and lay there, his massive neck slumping to one side,
and sleep that conquers all overwhelmed him now
as wine came spurting, flooding up from his gullet
with chunks of human flesh—he vomited, blind drunk.
Now, at last, I thrust our stake in a bed of embers
to get it red-hot and rallied all my comrades:
'Courage—no panic, no one hang back now!'
And green as it was, just as the olive stake
was about to catch fire—the glow terrific, yes—
I dragged it from the flames, my men clustering round
as some god breathed enormous courage through us all.
Hoisting high that olive stake with its stabbing point,
straight into the monster's eye they rammed it hard—
I drove my weight on it from above and bored it home
as a shipwright bores his beam with a shipwright's drill
that men below, whipping the strap back and forth, whirl
and the drill keeps twisting faster, never stopping—
So we seized our stake with its fiery tip
and bored it round and round in the giant's eye
till blood came boiling up around that smoking shaft
and the hot blast singed his brow and eyelids round the core
and the broiling eyeball burst—
its crackling roots blazed
and hissed—
as a blacksmith plunges a glowing ax or adze
in an ice-cold bath and the metal screeches steam
and its temper hardens—that's the iron's strength—
so the eye of the Cyclops sizzled round that stake!
He loosed a hideous roar, the rock walls echoed round
and we scuttled back in terror. The monster wrenched the spike
from his eye and out it came with a red geyser of blood—

he flung it aside with frantic hands, and mad with pain
he bellowed out for help from his neighbor Cyclops
living round about in caves on windswept crags.
Hearing his cries, they lumbered up from every side
and hulking round his cavern, asked what ailed him:
'What, Polyphemus, what in the world's the trouble?
Roaring out in the godsent night to rob us of our sleep.
Surely no one's rustling your flocks against your will—
surely no one's trying to kill you now by fraud or force!'

'*Nobody,* friends'—Polyphemus bellowed back from his cave—
'Nobody's killing me now by fraud and not by force!'
'If you're alone,' his friends boomed back at once,
'and nobody's trying to overpower you now—look,
it must be a plague sent here by mighty Zeus
and there's no escape from *that.*
You'd better pray to your father, Lord Poseidon.'

They lumbered off, but laughter filled my heart
to think how nobody's name—my great cunning stroke—
had duped them one and all. But the Cyclops there,
still groaning, racked with agony, groped around
for the huge slab, and heaving it from the doorway,
down he sat in the cave's mouth, his arms spread wide,
hoping to catch a comrade stealing out with sheep—
such a blithering fool he took me for!
But I was already plotting . . .
what was the best way out? how could I find
escape from death for my crew, myself as well?
My wits kept weaving, weaving cunning schemes—
life at stake, monstrous death staring us in the face—
till this plan struck my mind as best. That flock,
those well-fed rams with their splendid thick fleece,
sturdy, handsome beasts sporting their dark weight of wool:
I lashed them abreast, quietly, twisting the willow-twigs
the Cyclops slept on—giant, lawless brute—I took them
three by three; each ram in the middle bore a man
while the two rams either side would shield him well.
So three beasts to bear each man, but as for myself?
There was one bellwether ram, the prize of all the flock,
and clutching him by his back, tucked up under
his shaggy belly, there I hung, face upward,
both hands locked in his marvelous deep fleece,
clinging for dear life, my spirit steeled, enduring . . .
So we held on, desperate, waiting Dawn's first light.

As soon

as young Dawn with her rose-red fingers shone once more
the rams went rumbling out of the cave toward pasture,
the ewes kept bleating round the pens, unmilked,
their udders about to burst. Their master now,

heaving in torment, felt the back of each animal
halting before him here, but the idiot never sensed
my men were trussed up under their thick fleecy ribs.
And last of them all came my great ram now, striding out,
weighed down with his dense wool and my deep plots.
Stroking him gently, powerful Polyphemus murmured,
'Dear old ram, why last of the flock to quit the cave?
In the good old days you'd never lag behind the rest—
you with your long marching strides, first by far
of the flock to graze the fresh young grasses,
first by far to reach the rippling streams,
first to turn back home, keen for your fold
when night comes on—but now you're last of all.
And why? Sick at heart for your master's eye
that coward gouged out with his wicked crew?—
only after he'd stunned my wits with wine—
that, that Nobody . . .
who's not escaped his death, I swear, not yet.
Oh if only you thought like *me,* had words like *me*
to tell me where that scoundrel is cringing from my rage!
I'd smash him against the ground, I'd spill his brains—
flooding across my cave—and that would ease my heart
of the pains that good-for-nothing Nobody made me suffer!'

And with that threat he let my ram go free outside.
But soon as we'd got one foot past cave and courtyard,
first I loosed myself from the ram, then loosed my men,
then quickly, glancing back again and again we drove
our flock, good plump beasts with their long shanks,
straight to the ship, and a welcome sight we were
to loyal comrades—we who'd escaped our deaths—
but for all the rest they broke down and wailed.
I cut it short, I stopped each shipmate's cries,
my head tossing, brows frowning, silent signals
to hurry, tumble our fleecy herd on board,
launch out on the open sea!
They swung aboard, they sat to the oars in ranks
and in rhythm churned the water white with stroke on stroke.
But once offshore as far as a man's shout can carry,
I called back to the Cyclops, stinging taunts:
'So, Cyclops, no weak coward it was whose crew
you bent to devour there in your vaulted cave—
you with your brute force! Your filthy crimes
came down on your own head, you shameless cannibal,
daring to eat your guests in your own house—
so Zeus and the other gods have paid you back!'

That made the rage of the monster boil over.
Ripping off the peak of a towering crag, he heaved it

so hard the boulder landed just in front of our dark prow
and a huge swell reared up as the rock went plunging under—
a tidal wave from the open sea. The sudden backwash
drove us landward again, forcing us close inshore
but grabbing a long pole, I thrust us off and away,
tossing my head for dear life, signaling crews
to put their backs in the oars, escape grim death.
They threw themselves in the labor, rowed on fast
but once we'd plowed the breakers twice as far,
again I began to taunt the Cyclops—men around me
trying to check me, calm me, left and right:
'So headstrong—why? Why rile the beast again?'

'That rock he flung in the sea just now, hurling our ship
to shore once more—we thought we'd die on the spot!'

'If he'd caught a sound from one of us, just a moan,
he would have crushed our heads and ship timbers
with one heave of another flashing, jagged rock!'

'Good god, the brute can throw!'
So they begged
but they could not bring my fighting spirit round.
I called back with another burst of anger, 'Cyclops—
if any man on the face of the earth should ask you
who blinded you, shamed you so—say Odysseus,
raider of cities, *he* gouged out your eye,
Laertes' son who makes his home in Ithaca!'

So I vaunted and he groaned back in answer,
'Oh no, no—that prophecy years ago . . .
it all comes home to me with a vengeance now!
We once had a prophet here, a great tall man,
Telemus, Eurymus' son, a master at reading signs,
who grew old in his trade among his fellow-Cyclops.
All this, he warned me, would come to pass someday—
that I'd be blinded here at the hands of one Odysseus.
But I always looked for a handsome giant man to cross my path,
some fighter clad in power like armor-plate, but now,
look what a dwarf, a spineless good-for-nothing,
stuns me with wine, then gouges out my eye!
Come here, Odysseus, let me give you a guest-gift
and urge Poseidon the earthquake god to speed you home.
I am his son and he claims to be my father, true,
and he himself will heal me if he pleases—
no other blessed god, no man can do the work!'

'Heal you!'—
here was my parting shot—'Would to god I could strip you
of life and breath and ship you down to the House of Death
as surely as no one will ever heal your eye,
not even your earthquake god himself!'

But at that he bellowed out to lord Poseidon,
thrusting his arms to the starry skies, and prayed, 'Hear me—
Poseidon, god of the sea-blue mane who rocks the earth!
If I really am your son and you claim to be my father—
come, grant that Odysseus, raider of cities,
Laertes' son who makes his home in Ithaca,
never reaches home. Or if he's fated to see
his people once again and reach his well-built house
and his own native country, let him come home late
and come a broken man—all shipmates lost,
alone in a stranger's ship—
and let him find a world of pain at home!'
So he prayed
and the god of the sea-blue mane, Poseidon, heard his prayer.
The monster suddenly hoisted a boulder—far larger—
wheeled and heaved it, putting his weight behind it,
massive strength, and the boulder crashed close,
landing just in the wake of our dark stern,
just failing to graze the rudder's bladed edge.
A huge swell reared up as the rock went plunging under,
yes, and the tidal breaker drove us out to our island's
far shore where all my well-decked ships lay moored,
clustered, waiting, and huddled round them, crewmen
sat in anguish, waiting, chafing for our return.
We beached our vessel hard ashore on the sand,
we swung out in the frothing surf ourselves,
and herding Cyclops' sheep from our deep holds
we shared them round so no one, not on my account,
would go deprived of his fair share of spoils.
But the splendid ram—as we meted out the flocks
my friends-in-arms made him my prize of honor,
mine alone, and I slaughtered him on the beach
and burnt his thighs to Cronus' mighty son,
Zeus of the thundercloud who rules the world.
But my sacrifices failed to move the god:
Zeus was still obsessed with plans to destroy
my entire oarswept fleet and loyal crew of comrades.
Now all day long till the sun went down we sat
and feasted on sides of meat and heady wine.
Then when the sun had set and night came on
we lay down and slept at the water's shelving edge.
When young Dawn with her rose-red fingers shone
once more
I roused the men straightway, ordering all crews
to man the ships and cast off cables quickly.
They swung aboard at once, they sat to the oars in ranks
and in rhythm churned the water white with stroke on stroke.
And from there we sailed on, glad to escape our death
yet sick at heart for the comrades we had lost."

Book 10. The Bewitching Queen of Aeaea

"We reached the Aeolian island next, the home of Aeolus,
Hippotas' son, beloved by the gods who never die—
a great floating island it was, and round it all
huge ramparts rise of indestructible bronze
and sheer rock cliffs shoot up from sea to sky.
The king had sired twelve children within his halls,
six daughters and six sons in the lusty prime of youth,
so he gave his daughters as wives to his six sons.
Seated beside their dear father and doting mother,
with delicacies aplenty spread before them,
they feast on forever . . . All day long
the halls breathe the savor of roasted meats
and echo round to the low moan of blowing pipes,
and all night long, each one by his faithful mate,
they sleep under soft-piled rugs on corded bedsteads.
To this city of theirs we came, their splendid palace,
and Aeolus hosted me one entire month, he pressed me for news
of Troy and the Argive ships and how we sailed for home,
and I told him the whole long story, first to last.
And then, when I begged him to send me on my way,
he denied me nothing, he went about my passage.
He gave me a sack, the skin of a full-grown ox,
binding inside the winds that howl from every quarter,
for Zeus had made that king the master of all the winds,
with power to calm them down or rouse them as he pleased.
Aeolus stowed the sack inside my holds, lashed so fast
with a burnished silver cord
not even a slight puff could slip past that knot.
Yet he set the West Wind free to blow us on our way
and waft our squadron home. But his plan was bound to fail,
yes, our own reckless folly swept us on to ruin . . .

Nine whole days we sailed, nine nights, nonstop.
On the tenth our own land hove into sight at last—
we were so close we could see men tending fires.
But now an enticing sleep came on me, bone-weary
from working the vessel's sheet myself, no letup,
never trusting the ropes to any other mate,
the faster to journey back to native land.
But the crews began to mutter among themselves,
sure I was hauling troves of gold and silver home,
the gifts of open-hearted Aeolus, Hippotas' son.
'The old story!' One man glanced at another, grumbling.
'Look at our captain's luck—so loved by the world,
so prized at every landfall, every port of call.'

'Heaps of lovely plunder he hauls home from Troy,
while we who went through slogging just as hard,

we go home empty-handed.'
'Now this Aeolus loads him
down with treasure. Favoritism, friend to friend!'

'Hurry, let's see what loot is in that sack,
how much gold and silver. Break it open—now!'

A fatal plan, but it won my shipmates over.
They loosed the sack and all the winds burst out
and a sudden squall struck and swept us back to sea,
wailing, in tears, far from our own native land.
And I woke up with a start, my spirit churning—
should I leap over the side and drown at once or
grit my teeth and bear it, stay among the living?
I bore it all, held firm, hiding my face,
clinging tight to the decks
while heavy squalls blasted our squadron back
again to Aeolus' island, shipmates groaning hard.

We disembarked on the coast, drew water there
and crewmen snatched a meal by the swift ships.
Once we'd had our fill of food and drink
I took a shipmate along with me, a herald too,
and approached King Aeolus' famous halls and here
we found him feasting beside his wife and many children.
Reaching the doorposts at the threshold, down we sat
but our hosts, amazed to see us, only shouted questions:
'Back again, Odysseus—why? Some blustering god attacked you?
Surely we launched you well, we sped you on your way
to your own land and house, or any place you pleased.'

So they taunted, and I replied in deep despair,
'A mutinous crew undid me—that and a cruel sleep.
Set it to rights, my friends. You have the power!'

So I pleaded—gentle, humble appeals—
but our hosts turned silent, hushed . . .
and the father broke forth with an ultimatum:
'Away from my island—fast—most cursed man alive!
It's a crime to host a man or speed him on his way
when the blessed deathless gods despise him so.
Crawling back like this—
it proves the immortals hate you! Out—get out!'

Groan as I did, his curses drove me from his halls
and from there we pulled away with heavy hearts,
with the crews' spirit broken under the oars' labor,
thanks to our own folly . . . no favoring wind in sight.

Six whole days we rowed, six nights, nonstop.
On the seventh day we raised the Laestrygonian land,

Telepylus heights where the craggy fort of Lamus rises.
Where shepherd calls to shepherd as one drives in his flocks
and the other drives his out and he calls back in answer,
where a man who never sleeps could rake in double wages,
one for herding cattle, one for pasturing fleecy sheep,
the nightfall and the sunrise march so close together.
We entered a fine harbor there, all walled around
by a great unbroken sweep of sky-scraping cliff
and two steep headlands, fronting each other, close
around the mouth so the passage in is cramped.
Here the rest of my rolling squadron steered,
right into the gaping cove and moored tightly,
prow by prow. Never a swell there, big or small;
a milk-white calm spreads all around the place.
But I alone anchored my black ship outside,
well clear of the harbor's jaws
I tied her fast to a cliffside with a cable.
I scaled its rock face to a lookout on its crest
but glimpsed no trace of the work of man or beast from there;
all I spied was a plume of smoke, drifting off the land.
So I sent some crew ahead to learn who lived there—
men like us perhaps, who live on bread?
Two good mates I chose and a third to run the news.
They disembarked and set out on a beaten trail
the wagons used for hauling timber down to town
from the mountain heights above . . .
and before the walls they met a girl, drawing water,
Antiphates' strapping daughter—king of the Laestrygonians.
She'd come down to a clear running spring, Artacia,
where the local people came to fill their pails.
My shipmates clustered round her, asking questions:
who was king of the realm? who ruled the natives here?
She waved at once to her father's high-roofed halls.
They entered the sumptuous palace, found his wife inside—
a woman huge as a mountain crag who filled them all with horror.
Straightaway she summoned royal Antiphates from assembly,
her husband, who prepared my crew a barbarous welcome.
Snatching one of my men, he tore him up for dinner—
the other two sprang free and reached the ships.
But the king let loose a howling through the town
that brought tremendous Laestrygonians swarming up
from every side—hundreds, not like men, like Giants!
Down from the cliffs they flung great rocks a man could hardly hoist
and a ghastly shattering din rose up from all the ships—
men in their death-cries, hulls smashed to splinters—
They speared the crews like fish
and whisked them home to make their grisly meal.
But while they killed them off in the harbor depths
I pulled the sword from beside my hip and hacked away

at the ropes that moored my blue-prowed ship of war
and shouted rapid orders at my shipmates:
'Put your backs in the oars—now row or die!'
In terror of death they ripped the swells—all as one—
and what a joy as we darted out toward open sea,
clear of those beetling cliffs . . . my ship alone.
But the rest went down en masse. Our squadron sank.

From there we sailed on, glad to escape our death
yet sick at heart for the dear companions we had lost.
We reached the Aeaean island next, the home of Circe
the nymph with lovely braids, an awesome power too
who can speak with human voice,
the true sister of murderous-minded Aeetes.
Both were bred by the Sun who lights our lives;
their mother was Perse, a child the Ocean bore.
We brought our ship to port without a sound
as a god eased her into a harbor safe and snug,
and for two days and two nights we lay by there,
eating our hearts out, bent with pain and bone-tired.
When Dawn with her lovely locks brought on the third day,
at last I took my spear and my sharp sword again,
rushed up from the ship to find a lookout point,
hoping to glimpse some sign of human labor,
catch some human voices . . .
I scaled a commanding crag and, scanning hard,
I could just make out some smoke from Circe's halls,
drifting up from the broad terrain through brush and woods.
Mulling it over, I thought I'd scout the ground—
that fire aglow in the smoke, I saw it, true,
but soon enough this seemed the better plan:
I'd go back to shore and the swift ship first,
feed the men, then send *them* out for scouting.
I was well on my way down, nearing our ship
when a god took pity on me, wandering all alone;
he sent me a big stag with high branching antlers,
right across my path—the sun's heat forced him down
from his forest range to drink at a river's banks—
just bounding out of the timber when I hit him
square in the backbone, halfway down the spine
and my bronze spear went punching clean through—
he dropped in the dust, groaning, gasping out his breath.
Treading on him, I wrenched my bronze spear from the wound,
left it there on the ground, and snapping off some twigs
and creepers, twisted a rope about a fathom long,
I braided it tight, hand over hand, then lashed
the four hocks of that magnificent beast.
Loaded round my neck I lugged him toward the ship,
trudging, propped on my spear—no way to sling him

over a shoulder, steadying him with one free arm—
the kill was so immense!
I flung him down by the hull and roused the men,
going up to them all with a word to lift their spirits:
'Listen to me, my comrades, brothers in hardship—
we won't go down to the House of Death, not yet,
not till our day arrives. Up with you, look,
there's still some meat and drink in our good ship.
Put our minds on food—why die of hunger here?'

My hardy urging brought them round at once.
Heads came up from cloaks and there by the barren sea
they gazed at the stag, their eyes wide—my noble trophy.
But once they'd looked their fill and warmed their hearts,
they washed their hands and prepared a splendid meal.
Now all day long till the sun went down we sat
and feasted on sides of meat and seasoned wine.
Then when the sun had set and night came on
we lay down and slept at the water's shelving edge.
When young Dawn with her rose-red fingers shone once more
I called a muster quickly, informing all the crew,
'Listen to me, my comrades, brothers in hardship,
we can't tell east from west, the dawn from the dusk,
nor where the sun that lights our lives goes under earth
nor where it rises. We must think of a plan at once,
some cunning stroke. I doubt there's one still left.
I scaled a commanding crag and from that height
surveyed an entire island
ringed like a crown by endless wastes of sea.
But the land itself lies low, and I did see smoke
drifting up from its heart through thick brush and woods.'

My message broke their spirit as they recalled
the gruesome work of the Laestrygonian king Antiphates
and the hearty cannibal Cyclops thirsting for our blood.
They burst into cries, wailing, streaming live tears
that gained us nothing—what good can come of grief?

And so, numbering off my band of men-at-arms
into two platoons, I assigned them each a leader:
I took one and lord Eurylochus the other.
We quickly shook lots in a bronze helmet—
the lot of brave Eurylochus leapt out first.
So he moved off with his two and twenty comrades,
weeping, leaving us behind in tears as well . . .
Deep in the wooded glens they came on Circe's palace
built of dressed stone on a cleared rise of land.
Mountain wolves and lions were roaming round the grounds—
she'd bewitched them herself, she gave them magic drugs.
But they wouldn't attack my men; they just came pawing

up around them, fawning, swishing their long tails—
eager as hounds that fawn around their master,
coming home from a feast,
who always brings back scraps to calm them down.
So they came nuzzling round my men—lions, wolves
with big powerful claws—and the men cringed in fear
at the sight of those strange, ferocious beasts . . .But still
they paused at her doors, the nymph with lovely braids,
Circe—and deep inside they heard her singing, lifting
her spellbinding voice as she glided back and forth
at her great immortal loom, her enchanting web
a shimmering glory only goddesses can weave.
Polites, captain of armies, took command,
the closest, most devoted man I had: 'Friends,
there's someone inside, plying a great loom,
and how she sings—enthralling!
The whole house is echoing to her song.
Goddess or woman—let's call out to her now!'

So he urged and the men called out and hailed her.
She opened her gleaming doors at once and stepped forth,
inviting them all in, and in they went, all innocence.
Only Eurylochus stayed behind—he sensed a trap . . .
She ushered them in to sit on high-backed chairs,
then she mixed them a potion—cheese, barley
and pale honey mulled in Pramnian wine—
but into the brew she stirred her wicked drugs
to wipe from their memories any thought of home.
Once they'd drained the bowls she filled, suddenly
she struck with her wand, drove them into her pigsties,
all of them bristling into swine—with grunts,
snouts—even their bodies, yes, and only
the men's minds stayed steadfast as before.
So off they went to their pens, sobbing, squealing
as Circe flung them acorns, cornel nuts and mast,
common fodder for hogs that root and roll in mud.

Back Eurylochus ran to our swift black ship
to tell the disaster our poor friends had faced.
But try as he might, he couldn't get a word out.
Numbing sorrow had stunned the man to silence—
tears welled in his eyes, his heart possessed by grief.
We assailed him with questions—all at our wits' end—
till at last he could recount the fate our friends had met:
'Off we went through the brush, captain, as you commanded.
Deep in the wooded glens we came on Circe's palace
built of dressed stone on a cleared rise of land.
Someone inside was plying a great loom,
and how she sang—in a high clear voice!
Goddess or woman—we called out and hailed her . . .

She opened her gleaming doors at once and stepped forth,
inviting us all in, and in we went, all innocence.
But *I* stayed behind—I sensed a trap. Suddenly
all vanished—blotted out—not one face showed again,
though I sat there keeping watch a good long time.'

At that report I slung the hefty bronze blade
of my silver-studded sword around my shoulder,
slung my bow on too and told our comrade,
'Lead me back by the same way that you came.'
But he flung both arms around my knees and pleaded,
begging me with his tears and winging words:
'Don't force me back there, captain, king—
leave me here on the spot.
You will never return yourself, I swear,
you'll never bring back a single man alive.
Quick, cut and run with the rest of us here—
we can still escape the fatal day!'

But I shot back, 'Eurylochus, stay right here,
eating, drinking, safe by the black ship.
I must be off. Necessity drives me on.'

Leaving the ship and shore, I headed inland,
clambering up through hushed, entrancing glades until,
as I was nearing the halls of Circe skilled in spells,
approaching her palace—Hermes god of the golden wand
crossed my path, and he looked for all the world
like a young man sporting his first beard,
just in the prime and warm pride of youth,
and grasped me by the hand and asked me kindly,
'Where are you going now, my unlucky friend—
trekking over the hills alone in unfamiliar country?
And your men are all in there, in Circe's palace,
cooped like swine, hock by jowl in the sties.
Have you come to set them free?
Well, I warn you, you won't get home yourself,
you'll stay right there, trapped with all the rest.
But wait, I can save you, free you from that
great danger.
Look, here is a potent drug. Take it to Circe's halls—
its power alone will shield you from the fatal day.
Let me tell you of all the witch's subtle craft . . .
She'll mix you a potion, lace the brew with drugs
but she'll be powerless to bewitch you, even so—
this magic herb I give will fight her spells.
Now here's your plan of action, step by step.
The moment Circe strikes with her long thin wand,
you draw your sharp sword sheathed at your hip

and rush her fast as if to run her through!
She'll cower in fear and coax you to her bed—
but don't refuse the goddess' bed, not then, not if
she's to release your friends and treat you well yourself.
But have her swear the binding oath of the blessed gods
she'll never plot some new intrigue to harm you,
once you lie there naked—
never unman you, strip away your courage!'
With that
the giant-killer handed over the magic herb,
pulling it from the earth,
and Hermes showed me all its name and nature.
Its root is black and its flower white as milk
and the gods call it moly. Dangerous for a mortal man
to pluck from the soil but not for deathless gods.
All lies within their power.
Now Hermes went his way
to the steep heights of Olympus, over the island's woods
while I, just approaching the halls of Circe,
my heart a heaving storm at every step,
paused at her doors, the nymph with lovely braids—
I stood and shouted to her there. She heard my voice,
she opened her gleaming doors at once and stepped forth,
inviting me in, and in I went, all anguish now . . .
She led me in to sit on a silver-studded chair,
ornately carved, with a stool to rest my feet.
In a golden bowl she mixed a potion for me to drink,
stirring her poison in, her heart aswirl with evil.
And then she passed it on, I drank it down
but it never worked its spell—
she struck with her wand and 'Now,' she cried,
'off to your sty, you swine, and wallow with your friends!'
But I, I drew my sharp sword sheathed at my hip
and rushed her fast as if to run her through—
She screamed, slid under my blade, hugged my knees
with a flood of warm tears and a burst of winging words:
'Who are you? where are you from? your city? your parents?
I'm wonderstruck—you drank my drugs, you're not bewitched!
Never has any other man withstood my potion, never,
once it's past his lips and he has drunk it down.
You have a mind in *you* no magic can enchant!
You must be Odysseus, man of twists and turns—
Hermes the giant-killer, god of the golden wand,
he always said you'd come,
homeward bound from Troy in your swift black ship.
Come, sheathe your sword, let's go to bed together,
mount my bed and mix in the magic work of love—
we'll breed deep trust between us.'
So she enticed

but I fought back, still wary. 'Circe, Circe,
how dare you tell me to treat you with any warmth?
You who turned my men to swine in your own house and now
you hold me here as well—teeming with treachery
you lure me to your room to mount your bed,
so once I lie there naked
you'll unman me, strip away my courage!
Mount your bed? Not for all the world. Not
until you consent to swear, goddess, a binding oath
you'll never plot some new intrigue to harm me!'
Straightaway
she began to swear the oath that I required—never,
she'd never do me harm—and when she'd finished,
then, at last, I mounted Circe's gorgeous bed. ..

At the same time her handmaids bustled through the halls,
four in all who perform the goddess' household tasks:
nymphs, daughters born of the springs and groves
and the sacred rivers running down to open sea.
One draped the chairs with fine crimson covers
over the seats she'd spread with linen cloths below.
A second drew up silver tables before the chairs
and laid out golden trays to hold the bread.
A third mulled heady, heart-warming wine
in a silver bowl and set out golden cups.
A fourth brought water and lit a blazing fire
beneath a massive cauldron. The water heated soon,
and once it reached the boil in the glowing bronze
she eased me into a tub and bathed me from the cauldron,
mixing the hot and cold to suit my taste, showering
head and shoulders down until she'd washed away
the spirit-numbing exhaustion from my body.
The bathing finished, rubbing me sleek with oil,
throwing warm fleece and a shirt around my shoulders,
she led me in to sit on a silver-studded chair,
ornately carved, with a stool to rest my feet.
A maid brought water soon in a graceful golden pitcher
and over a silver basin tipped it out
so I might rinse my hands,
then pulled a gleaming table to my side.
A staid housekeeper brought on bread to serve me,
appetizers aplenty too, lavish with her bounty.
She pressed me to eat. I had no taste for food.
I just sat there, mind wandering, far away . . .
lost in grim forebodings.
As soon as Circe saw me,
huddled, not touching my food, immersed in sorrow,
she sidled near with a coaxing, winged word:
'Odysseus, why just sit there, struck dumb,

eating your heart out, not touching food or drink?
Suspect me of still more treachery? Nothing to fear.
Haven't I just sworn my solemn, binding oath?'

So she asked, but I protested, 'Circe—
how could any man in his right mind endure
the taste of food and drink before he'd freed
his comrades-in-arms and looked them in the eyes?
If you, you really want me to eat and drink,
set them free, all my beloved comrades—
let me feast my eyes.'
So I demanded.
Circe strode on through the halls and out,
her wand held high in hand and, flinging open the pens,
drove forth my men, who looked like full-grown swine.
Facing her, there they stood as she went along the ranks,
anointing them one by one with some new magic oil—
and look, the bristles grown by the first wicked drug
that Circe gave them slipped away from their limbs
and they turned men again: younger than ever,
taller by far, more handsome to the eye, and yes,
they knew me at once and each man grasped my hands
and a painful longing for tears overcame us all,
a terrible sobbing echoed through the house . . .
The goddess herself was moved and, standing by me,
warmly urged me on—a lustrous goddess now:
'Royal son of Laertes, Odysseus, tried and true,
go at once to your ship at the water's edge,
haul her straight up on the shore first
and stow your cargo and running gear in caves,
then back you come and bring your trusty crew.'

Her urging won my stubborn spirit over.
Down I went to the swift ship at the water's edge,
and there on the decks I found my loyal crew
consumed with grief and weeping live warm tears.
But now, as calves in stalls when cows come home,
droves of them herded back from field to farmyard
once they've grazed their fill—as all their young calves
come frisking out to meet them, bucking out of their pens,
lowing nonstop, jostling, rushing round their mothers—
so my shipmates there at the sight of my return
came pressing round me now, streaming tears,
so deeply moved in their hearts they felt as if
they'd made it back to their own land, their city,
Ithaca's rocky soil where they were bred and reared.
And through their tears their words went winging home:
'You're back again, my king! How thrilled we are—
as if we'd reached our country, Ithaca, at last!
But come, tell us about the fate our comrades met.'

Still I replied with a timely word of comfort:
'Let's haul our ship straight up on the shore first
and stow our cargo and running gear in caves.
Then hurry, all of you, come along with me
to see our friends in the magic halls of Circe,
eating and drinking—the feast flows on forever.'

So I said and they jumped to do my bidding.
Only Eurylochus tried to hold my shipmates back,
his mutinous outburst aimed at one and all:
'Poor fools, where are we running now?
Why are we tempting fate?—
why stumble blindly down to Circe's halls?
She'll turn us all into pigs or wolves or lions
made to guard that palace of hers—by force, I tell you—
just as the Cyclops trapped our comrades in his lair
with hotheaded Odysseus right beside them all—
thanks to this man's rashness they died too!'

So he declared and I had half a mind
to draw the sharp sword from beside my hip
and slice his head off, tumbling down in the dust,
close kin that he was. But comrades checked me,
each man trying to calm me, left and right:
'Captain, we'll leave him here if you command,
just where he is, to sit and guard the ship.
Lead us on to the magic halls of Circe.'
With that,
up from the ship and shore they headed inland.
Nor did Eurylochus malinger by the hull;
he straggled behind the rest,
dreading the sharp blast of my rebuke.
All the while
Circe had bathed my other comrades in her palace,
caring and kindly, rubbed them sleek with oil
and decked them out in fleecy cloaks and shirts.
We found them all together, feasting in her halls.
Once we had recognized each other, gazing face-to-face,
we all broke down and wept—and the house resounded now
and Circe the lustrous one came toward me, pleading,
'Royal son of Laertes, Odysseus, man of action,
no more tears now, calm these tides of sorrow.
Well I know what pains you bore on the swarming sea,
what punishment you endured from hostile men on land.
But come now, eat your food and drink your wine
till the same courage fills your chests, now as then,
when you first set sail from native land, from rocky Ithaca!
Now you are burnt-out husks, your spirits haggard, sere,
always brooding over your wanderings long and hard,

your hearts never lifting with any joy—
you've suffered far too much.'
So she enticed
and won our battle-hardened spirits over.
And there we sat at ease,
day in, day out, till a year had run its course,
feasting on sides of meat and drafts of heady wine . . .
But then, when the year was gone and the seasons wheeled by
and the months waned and the long days came round again,
my loyal comrades took me aside and prodded,
'Captain, this is madness!
High time you thought of your own home at last,
if it really is your fate to make it back alive
and reach your well-built house and native land.'

Their urging brought my stubborn spirit round.
So all that day till the sun went down we sat
and feasted on sides of meat and heady wine.
Then when the sun had set and night came on
the men lay down to sleep in the shadowed halls
but I went up to that luxurious bed of Circe's,
hugged her by the knees
and the goddess heard my winging supplication:
'Circe, now make good a promise you gave me once—
it's time to help me home. My heart longs to be home,
my comrades' hearts as well. They wear me down,
pleading with me whenever you're away.'
So I pressed
and the lustrous goddess answered me in turn:
'Royal son of Laertes, Odysseus, old campaigner,
stay on no more in my house against your will.
But first another journey calls. You must travel down
to the House of Death and the awesome one, Persephone,[1]
there to consult the ghost of Tiresias, seer of Thebes,
the great blind prophet whose mind remains unshaken.
Even in death—Persephone has given him wisdom,
everlasting vision to him and him alone . . .
the rest of the dead are empty, flitting shades.'

So she said and crushed the heart inside me.
I knelt in her bed and wept. I'd no desire
to go on living and see the rising light of day.
But once I'd had my fill of tears and writhing there,
at last I found the words to venture, 'Circe, Circe,
who can pilot us on that journey? Who has ever
reached the House of Death in a black ship?'

The lustrous goddess answered, never pausing,
'Royal son of Laertes, Odysseus, born for exploits,

1. Divine queen of the underworld, wife of Hades, and daughter of Demeter.

let no lack of a pilot at the helm concern you, no,
just step your mast and spread your white sail wide—
sit back and the North Wind will speed you on your way.
But once your vessel has cut across the Ocean River
you will raise a desolate coast and Persephone's Grove,
her tall black poplars, willows whose fruit dies young.
Beach your vessel hard by the Ocean's churning shore
and make your own way down to the moldering House of Death.
And there into Acheron, the Flood of Grief, two rivers flow,
the torrent River of Fire, the wailing River of Tears
that branches off from Styx, the Stream of Hate,
and a stark crag looms
where the two rivers thunder down and meet.
Once there, go forward, hero. Do as I say now.
Dig a trench of about a forearm's depth and length
and around it pour libations out to all the dead—
first with milk and honey, and then with mellow wine,
then water third and last, and sprinkle glistening barley
over it all, and vow again and again to all the dead,
to the drifting, listless spirits of their ghosts,
that once you return to Ithaca you will slaughter
a barren heifer in your halls, the best you have,
and load a pyre with treasures—and to Tiresias,
alone, apart, you will offer a sleek black ram,
the pride of all your herds. And once your prayers
have invoked the nations of the dead in their dim glory,
slaughter a ram and a black ewe, turning both their heads
toward Erebus,[2] but turn your head away, looking toward
the Ocean River. Suddenly then the countless shades
of the dead and gone will surge around you there.
But order your men at once to flay the sheep
that lie before you, killed by your ruthless blade,
and burn them both, and then say prayers to the gods,
to the almighty god of death and dread Persephone.
But you—draw your sharp sword from beside your hip,
sit down on alert there, and never let the ghosts
of the shambling, shiftless dead come near that blood
till you have questioned Tiresias yourself. Soon, soon
the great seer will appear before you, captain of armies:
he will tell you the way to go, the stages of your voyage,
how you can cross the swarming sea and reach home at last.'

And with those words Dawn rose on her golden throne
and Circe dressed me quickly in sea-cloak and shirt
while the queen slipped on a loose, glistening robe,
filmy, a joy to the eye, and round her waist
she ran a brocaded golden belt
and over her head a scarf to shield her brow.

2. The dark underworld.

And I strode on through the halls to stir my men,
hovering over each with a winning word: 'Up now!
No more lazing away in sleep, we must set sail—
Queen Circe has shown the way.'
I brought them round,
my hardy friends-in-arms, but not even from there
could I get them safely off without a loss . . .
There was a man, Elpenor, the youngest in our ranks,
none too brave in battle, none too sound in mind.
He'd strayed from his mates in Circe's magic halls
and keen for the cool night air,
sodden with wine he'd bedded down on her roofs.
But roused by the shouts and tread of marching men,
he leapt up with a start at dawn but still so dazed
he forgot to climb back down again by the long ladder—
headfirst from the roof he plunged, his neck snapped
from the backbone, his soul flew down to Death.

Once on our way, I gave the men their orders:
'You think we are headed home, our own dear land?
Well, Circe sets us a rather different course . . .
down to the House of Death and the awesome one, Persephone,
there to consult the ghost of Tiresias, seer of Thebes.'

So I said, and it broke my shipmates' hearts.
They sank down on the ground, moaning, tore their hair.
But it gained us nothing—what good can come of grief?

Back to the swift ship at the water's edge we went,
our spirits deep in anguish, faces wet with tears.
But Circe got to the dark hull before us,
tethered a ram and black ewe close by—
slipping past unseen. Who can glimpse a god
who wants to be invisible gliding here and there?"

BOOK 11. THE KINGDOM OF THE DEAD

"Now down we came to the ship at the water's edge,
we hauled and launched her into the sunlit breakers first,
stepped the mast in the black craft and set our sail
and loaded the sheep aboard, the ram and ewe,
then we ourselves embarked, streaming tears,
our hearts weighed down with anguish . . .
But Circe, the awesome nymph with lovely braids
who speaks with human voice, sent us a hardy shipmate,
yes, a fresh following wind ruffling up in our wake,
bellying out our sail to drive our blue prow on as we,
securing the running gear from stem to stern, sat back
while the wind and helmsman kept her true on course.
The sail stretched taut as she cut the sea all day

and the sun sank and the roads of the world grew dark.

And she made the outer limits, the Ocean River's bounds
where Cimmerian people have their homes—their realm and city
shrouded in mist and cloud. The eye of the Sun can never
flash his rays through the dark and bring them light,
not when he climbs the starry skies or when he wheels
back down from the heights to touch the earth once more—
an endless, deadly night overhangs those wretched men.
There, gaining that point, we beached our craft
and herding out the sheep, we picked our way
by the Ocean's banks until we gained the place
that Circe made our goal.
Here at the spot
Perimedes and Eurylochus held the victims fast,
and I, drawing my sharp sword from beside my hip,
dug a trench of about a forearm's depth and length
and around it poured libations out to all the dead,
first with milk and honey, and then with mellow wine,
then water third and last, and sprinkled glistening barley
over it all, and time and again I vowed to all the dead,
to the drifting, listless spirits of their ghosts,
that once I returned to Ithaca I would slaughter
a barren heifer in my halls, the best I had,
and load a pyre with treasures—and to Tiresias,
alone, apart, I would offer a sleek black ram,
the pride of all my herds. And once my vows
and prayers had invoked the nations of the dead,
I took the victims, over the trench I cut their throats
and the dark blood flowed in—and up out of Erebus they came,
flocking toward me now, the ghosts of the dead and gone . . .
Brides and unwed youths and old men who had suffered much
and girls with their tender hearts freshly scarred by sorrow
and great armies of battle dead, stabbed by bronze spears,
men of war still wrapped in bloody armor—thousands
swarming around the trench from every side—
unearthly cries—blanching terror gripped me!
I ordered the men at once to flay the sheep
that lay before us, killed by my ruthless blade,
and burn them both, and then say prayers to the gods,
to the almighty god of death and dread Persephone.
But I, the sharp sword drawn from beside my hip,
sat down on alert there and never let the ghosts
of the shambling, shiftless dead come near that blood
till I had questioned Tiresias myself.
But first
the ghost of Elpenor, my companion, came toward me.
He'd not been buried under the wide ways of earth,
not yet, we'd left his body in Circe's house,
unwept, unburied—this other labor pressed us.

But I wept to see him now, pity touched my heart
and I called out a winged word to him there: 'Elpenor,
how did you travel down to the world of darkness?
Faster on foot, I see, than I in my black ship.'

My comrade groaned as he offered me an answer:
'Royal son of Laertes, Odysseus, old campaigner,
the doom of an angry god, and god knows how much wine—
they were my ruin, captain . . . I'd bedded down
on the roof of Circe's house but never thought
to climb back down again by the long ladder—
headfirst from the roof I plunged, my neck snapped
from the backbone, my soul flew down to Death. Now,
I beg you by those you left behind, so far from here,
your wife, your father who bred and reared you as a boy,
and Telemachus, left at home in your halls, your only son.
Well I know when you leave this lodging of the dead
that you and your ship will put ashore again
at the island of Aeaea—then and there,
my lord, remember me, I beg you! Don't sail off
and desert me, left behind unwept, unburied, don't,
or my curse may draw god's fury on your head.
No, burn me in full armor, all my harness,
heap my mound by the churning gray surf—
a man whose luck ran out—
so even men to come will learn my story.
Perform my rites, and plant on my tomb that oar
I swung with mates when I rowed among the living.'

'All this, my unlucky friend,' I reassured him,
'I will do for you. I won't forget a thing.'
So we sat
and faced each other, trading our bleak parting words,
I on my side, holding my sword above the blood,
he across from me there, my comrade's phantom
dragging out his story.
But look, the ghost
of my mother came! My mother, dead and gone now . . .
Anticleia—daughter of that great heart Autolycus—
whom I had left alive when I sailed for sacred Troy.
I broke into tears to see her here, but filled with pity,
even throbbing with grief, I would not let her ghost
approach the blood till I had questioned Tiresias myself.

At last he came. The shade of the famous Theban prophet,
holding a golden scepter, knew me at once and hailed me:
'Royal son of Laertes, Odysseus, master of exploits,
man of pain, what now, what brings you here,
forsaking the light of day
to see this joyless kingdom of the dead?

Stand back from the trench—put up your sharp sword
so I can drink the blood and tell you all the truth.'

Moving back, I thrust my silver-studded sword
deep in its sheath, and once he had drunk the dark blood
the words came ringing from the prophet in his power:
'A sweet smooth journey home, renowned Odysseus,
that is what you seek
but a god will make it hard for you—I know—
you will never escape the one who shakes the earth,
quaking with anger at you still, still enraged
because you blinded the Cyclops, his dear son.
Even so, you and your crew may still reach home,
suffering all the way, if you only have the power
to curb their wild desire and curb your own, what's more,
from the day your good trim vessel first puts in
at Thrinacia Island, flees the cruel blue sea.
There you will find them grazing,
herds and fat flocks, the cattle of Helios,
god of the sun who sees all, hears all things.
Leave the beasts unharmed, your mind set on home,
and you all may still reach Ithaca—bent with hardship,
true—but harm them in any way, and I can see it now:
your ship destroyed, your men destroyed as well.
And even if *you* escape, you'll come home late
and come a broken man—all shipmates lost,
alone in a stranger's ship—
and you will find a world of pain at home,
crude, arrogant men devouring all your goods,
courting your noble wife, offering gifts to win her.
No doubt you will pay them back in blood when you come home!
But once you have killed those suitors in your halls—
by stealth or in open fight with slashing bronze—
go forth once more, you must . . .
carry your well-planed oar until you come
to a race of people who know nothing of the sea,
whose food is never seasoned with salt, strangers all
to ships with their crimson prows and long slim oars,
wings that make ships fly. And here is your sign—
unmistakable, clear, so clear you cannot miss it:
When another traveler falls in with you and calls
that weight across your shoulder a fan to winnow grain,
then plant your bladed, balanced oar in the earth
and sacrifice fine beasts to the lord god of the sea,
Poseidon—a ram, a bull and a ramping wild boar—
then journey home and render noble offerings up
to the deathless gods who rule the vaulting skies,
to all the gods in order.
And at last your own death will steal upon you . . .

a gentle, painless death, far from the sea it comes
to take you down, borne down with the years in ripe old age
with all your people there in blessed peace around you.
All that I have told you will come true.'
'Oh Tiresias,'
I replied as the prophet finished, 'surely the gods
have spun this out as fate, the gods themselves.
But tell me one thing more, and tell me clearly.
I see the ghost of my long-lost mother here before me.
Dead, crouching close to the blood in silence,
she cannot bear to look me in the eyes—
her own son—or speak a word to me. How,
lord, can I make her know me for the man I am?'

'One rule there is,' the famous seer explained,
'and simple for me to say and you to learn.
Any one of the ghosts you let approach the blood
will speak the truth to you. Anyone you refuse
will turn and fade away.'
And with those words,
now that his prophecies had closed, the awesome shade
of lord Tiresias strode back to the House of Death.
But I kept watch there, steadfast till my mother
approached and drank the dark, clouding blood.
She knew me at once and wailed out in grief
and her words came winging toward me, flying home:
'Oh my son—what brings you down to the world
of death and darkness? You are still alive!
It's hard for the living to catch a glimpse of this . . .
Great rivers flow between us, terrible waters,
the Ocean first of all—no one could ever ford
that stream on foot, only aboard some sturdy craft.
Have you just come from Troy, wandering long years
with your men and ship? Not yet returned to Ithaca?
You've still not seen your wife inside your halls?'
'Mother,'
I replied, 'I had to venture down to the House of Death,
to consult the shade of Tiresias, seer of Thebes.
Never yet have I neared Achaea, never once
set foot on native ground,
always wandering—endless hardship from that day
I first set sail with King Agamemnon bound for Troy,
the stallion-land, to fight the Trojans there.
But tell me about yourself and spare me nothing.
What form of death overcame you, what laid you low,
some long slow illness? Or did Artemis showering arrows
come with her painless shafts and bring you down?
Tell me of father, tell of the son I left behind:
do my royal rights still lie in their safekeeping?

Or does some stranger hold the throne by now
because men think that I'll come home no more?
Please, tell me about my wife, her turn of mind,
her thoughts . . . still standing fast beside our son,
still guarding our great estates, secure as ever now?
Or has she wed some other countryman at last,
the finest prince among them?'
'Surely, surely,'
my noble mother answered quickly, 'she's still waiting
there in your halls, poor woman, suffering so,
her life an endless hardship like your own . . .
wasting away the nights, weeping away the days.
No one has taken over your royal rights, not yet.
Telemachus still holds your great estates in peace,
he attends the public banquets shared with all,
the feasts a man of justice should enjoy,
for every lord invites him. As for your father,
he keeps to his own farm—he never goes to town—
with no bed for him there, no blankets, glossy throws;
all winter long he sleeps in the lodge with servants,
in the ashes by the fire, his body wrapped in rags.
But when summer comes and the bumper crops of harvest,
any spot on the rising ground of his vineyard rows
he makes his bed, heaped high with fallen leaves,
and there he lies in anguish . . .
with his old age bearing hard upon him, too,
and his grief grows as he longs for your return.
And I with the same grief, I died and met my fate.
No sharp-eyed Huntress showering arrows through the halls
approached and brought me down with painless shafts,
nor did some hateful illness strike me, that so often
devastates the body, drains our limbs of power.
No, it was my longing for *you,* my shining Odysseus—
you and your quickness, you and your gentle ways—
that tore away my life that had been sweet.'

And I, my mind in turmoil, how I longed
to embrace my mother's spirit, dead as she was!
Three times I rushed toward her, desperate to hold her,
three times she fluttered through my fingers, sifting away
like a shadow, dissolving like a dream, and each time
the grief cut to the heart, sharper, yes, and I,
I cried out to her, words winging into the darkness:
'Mother—why not wait for me? How I long to hold you!—
so even here, in the House of Death, we can fling
our loving arms around each other, take some joy
in the tears that numb the heart. Or is this just
some wraith that great Persephone sends my way
to make me ache with sorrow all the more?'

My noble mother answered me at once:
'My son, my son, the unluckiest man alive!
This is no deception sent by Queen Persephone,
this is just the way of mortals when we die.
Sinews no longer bind the flesh and bones together—
the fire in all its fury burns the body down to ashes
once life slips from the white bones, and the spirit,
rustling, flitters away . . . flown like a dream.
But you must long for the daylight. Go, quickly.
Remember all these things
so one day you can tell them to your wife.'

And so we both confided, trading parting words,
and there slowly came a grand array of women,
all sent before me now by august Persephone,
and all were wives and daughters once of princes.
They swarmed in a flock around the dark blood
while I searched for a way to question each alone,
and the more I thought, the more this seemed the best:
Drawing forth the long sharp sword from beside my hip,
I would not let them drink the dark blood, all in a rush,
and so they waited, coming forward one after another.
Each declared her lineage, and I explored them all.

And the first I saw there? Tyro, born of kings,
who said her father was that great lord Salmoneus,
said that she was the wife of Cretheus, Aeolus' son.
And once she fell in love with the river god, Enipeus,
far the clearest river flowing across the earth,
and so she'd haunt Enipeus' glinting streams,
till taking his shape one day
the god who girds the earth and makes it tremble
bedded her where the swirling river rushes out to sea,
and a surging wave reared up, high as a mountain, dark,
arching over to hide the god and mortal girl together.
Loosing her virgin belt, he lapped her round in sleep
and when the god had consummated his work of love
he took her by the hand and hailed her warmly:
'Rejoice in our love, my lady! And when this year
has run its course you will give birth to glorious children—
bedding down with the gods is never barren, futile—
and you must tend them, breed and rear them well.
Now home you go, and restrain yourself, I say,
never breathe your lover's name but know—
I am Poseidon, god who rocks the earth!'

With that he dove back in the heaving waves
and she conceived for the god and bore him Pelias, Neleus,
and both grew up to be stalwart aides of Zeus almighty,
both men alike. Pelias lived on the plains of Iolcos,

rich in sheepflocks, Neleus lived in sandy Pylos.
And the noble queen bore sons to Cretheus too:
Aeson, Pheres and Amythaon, exultant charioteer.

And after Tyro I saw Asopus' daughter Antiope,
proud she'd spent a night in the arms of Zeus himself
and borne the god twin sons, Amphion and Zethus,
the first to build the footings of seven-gated Thebes,
her bastions too, for lacking ramparts none could live
in a place so vast, so open—strong as both men were.

And I saw Alcmena next, Amphitryon's wife,
who slept in the clasp of Zeus and merged in love
and brought forth Heracles, rugged will and lion heart.
And I saw Megara too, magnanimous Creon's daughter
wed to the stalwart Heracles, the hero never daunted.

And I saw the mother of Oedipus, beautiful Epicaste.
What a monstrous thing she did, in all innocence—
she married her own son . . .
who'd killed his father, then he married *her!*
But the gods soon made it known to all mankind.
So he in growing pain ruled on in beloved Thebes,
lording Cadmus' people—thanks to the gods' brutal plan—
while she went down to Death who guards the massive gates.
Lashing a noose to a steep rafter, there she hanged aloft,
strangling in all her anguish, leaving her son to bear
the world of horror a mother's Furies bring to life.

And I saw magnificent Chloris, the one whom Neleus
wooed and won with a hoard of splendid gifts,
so dazzled by her beauty years ago . . .
the youngest daughter of Iasus' son Amphion,
the great Minyan king who ruled Orchomenos once.
She was his queen in Pylos, she bore him shining sons,
Nestor and Chromius, Periclymenus too, good prince.
And after her sons she bore a daughter, majestic Pero,
the marvel of her time, courted by all the young lords
round about. But Neleus would not give her to any suitor,
none but the man who might drive home the herds
that powerful Iphiclus had stolen. Lurching,
broad in the brow, those longhorned beasts,
and no small task to round them up from Phylace.
Only the valiant seer Melampus volunteered—
he would drive them home—
but a god's iron sentence bound him fast:
barbarous herdsmen dragged him off in chains.
Yet when the months and days had run their course
and the year wheeled round and the seasons came again,
then mighty Iphiclus loosed the prophet's shackles,
once he had told him all the gods' decrees.

And so the will of Zeus was done at last.

And I saw Leda next, Tyndareus' wife,
who'd borne the king two sons, intrepid twins,
Castor, breaker of horses, and the hardy boxer Polydeuces,
both buried now in the life-giving earth though still alive.
Even under the earth Zeus grants them that distinction:
one day alive, the next day dead, each twin by turns,
they both hold honors equal to the gods'.

And I saw Iphimedeia next, Aloeus' wife,
who claimed she lay in the Sea-lord's loving waves
and gave the god two sons, but they did not live long,
Otus staunch as a god and far-famed Ephialtes.
They were the tallest men the fertile earth has borne,
the handsomest too, by far, aside from renowned Orion.
Nine yards across they measured, even at nine years old,
nine fathoms tall they towered. They even threatened
the deathless gods they'd storm Olympus' heights
with the pounding rush and grinding shock of battle.
They were wild to pile Ossa upon Olympus, then on Ossa
Pelion dense with timber—their toeholds up the heavens.
And they'd have won the day if they had reached peak strength
but Apollo the son of Zeus, whom sleek-haired Leto bore,
laid both giants low before their beards had sprouted,
covering cheek and chin with a fresh crop of down.

Phaedra and Procris too I saw, and lovely Ariadne,
daughter of Minos, that harsh king. One day Theseus tried
to spirit her off from Crete to Athens' sacred heights
but he got no joy from her. Artemis killed her first
on wave-washed Dia's shores, accused by Dionysus.

And I saw Clymene, Maera and loathsome Eriphyle—
bribed with a golden necklace
to lure her lawful husband to his death . . .
But the whole cortege I could never tally, never name,
not all the daughters and wives of great men I saw there.
Long before that, the godsent night would ebb away.
But the time has come for sleep, either with friends
aboard your swift ship or here in your own house.
My passage home will rest with the gods and you."

Odysseus paused . . . They all fell silent, hushed,
his story holding them spellbound down the shadowed halls
till the white-armed queen Arete suddenly burst out,
"Phaeacians! How does this man impress you now,
his looks, his build, the balanced mind inside him?
The stranger is my guest
but each of you princes shares the honor here.
So let's not be too hasty to send him on his way,

and don't scrimp on his gifts. His need is great,
great as the riches piled up in your houses,
thanks to the gods' good will."
Following her,
the old revered Echeneus added his support,
the eldest lord on the island of Phaeacia:
"Friends, the words of our considerate queen—
they never miss the mark or fail our expectations.
So do as Arete says, though on Alcinous here
depend all words and action."
"And so it will be"—
Alcinous stepped in grandly—"sure as I am alive
and rule our island men who love their oars!
Our guest, much as he longs for passage home,
must stay and wait it out here till tomorrow,
till I can collect his whole array of parting gifts.
His send-off rests with every noble here
but with me most of all:
I hold the reins of power in the realm."

Odysseus, deft and tactful, echoed back,
"Alcinous, majesty, shining among your island people,
if you would urge me now to stay here one whole year
then speed me home weighed down with lordly gifts,
I'd gladly have it so. Better by far, that way.
The fuller my arms on landing there at home,
the more respected, well received I'd be
by all who saw me sailing back to Ithaca."

"Ah Odysseus," Alcinous replied, "one look at you
and we know that you are no one who would cheat us—
no fraud, such as the dark soil breeds and spreads
across the face of the earth these days. Crowds of vagabonds
frame their lies so tightly none can test them. But you,
what grace you give your words, and what good sense within!
You have told your story with all a singer's skill,
the miseries you endured, your great Achaeans too.
But come now, tell me truly: your godlike comrades—
did you see any heroes down in the House of Death,
any who sailed with you and met their doom at Troy?
The night's still young, I'd say the night is endless.
For us in the palace now, it's hardly time for sleep.
Keep telling us your adventures—they are wonderful.
I could hold out here till Dawn's first light
if only you could bear, here in our halls,
to tell the tale of all the pains you suffered."

So the man of countless exploits carried on:
"Alcinous, majesty, shining among your island people,
there is a time for many words, a time for sleep as well.

But if you insist on hearing more, I'd never stint
on telling my own tale and those more painful still,
the griefs of my comrades, dead in the war's wake,
who escaped the battle-cries of Trojan armies
only to die in blood at journey's end—
thanks to a vicious woman's will.
Now then,
no sooner had Queen Persephone driven off
the ghosts of lovely women, scattering left and right,
than forward marched the shade of Atreus' son Agamemnon,
fraught with grief and flanked by all his comrades,
troops of his men-at-arms who died beside him,
who met their fate in lord Aegisthus' halls.
He knew me at once, as soon as he drank the blood,
and wailed out, shrilly; tears sprang to his eyes,
he thrust his arms toward me, keen to embrace me there—
no use—the great force was gone, the strength lost forever,
now, that filled his rippling limbs in the old days.
I wept at the sight, my heart went out to the man,
my words too, in a winging flight of pity:
'Famous Atrides, lord of men Agamemnon!
What fatal stroke of destiny brought you down?
Wrecked in the ships when lord Poseidon roused
some punishing blast of stormwinds, gust on gust?
Or did ranks of enemies mow you down on land
as you tried to raid and cut off herds and flocks
or fought to win their city, take their women?'

The field marshal's ghost replied at once:
'Royal son of Laertes, Odysseus, mastermind of war,
I was not wrecked in the ships when lord Poseidon
roused some punishing blast of stormwinds, gust on gust,
nor did ranks of enemies mow me down on land—
Aegisthus hatched my doom and my destruction,
he killed me, he with my own accursed wife . . .
he invited me to his palace, sat me down to feast
then cut me down as a man cuts down some ox at the trough!
So I died—a wretched, ignominious death—and round me
all my comrades killed, no mercy, one after another,
just like white-tusked boars
butchered in some rich lord of power's halls
for a wedding, banquet or groaning public feast.
You in your day have witnessed hundreds slaughtered,
killed in single combat or killed in pitched battle, true,
but if you'd laid eyes on this it would have wrenched your heart—
how we sprawled by the mixing-bowl and loaded tables there,
throughout the palace, the whole floor awash with blood.
But the death-cry of Cassandra,[1] Priam's daughter—

1. Trojan princess and Agamemnon's war prize.

the most pitiful thing I heard! My treacherous queen,
Clytemnestra, killed her over my body, yes, and I,
lifting my fists, beat them down on the ground,
dying, dying, writhing around the sword.
But she, that whore, she turned her back on me,
well on my way to Death—she even lacked the heart
to seal my eyes with her hand or close my jaws.
So,
there's nothing more deadly, bestial than a woman
set on works like these—what a monstrous thing
she plotted, slaughtered her own lawful husband!
Why, I expected, at least, some welcome home
from all my children, all my household slaves
when I came sailing back again . . . But she—
the queen hell-bent on outrage—bathes in shame
not only herself but the whole breed of womankind,
even the honest ones to come, forever down the years!'

So he declared and I cried out, 'How terrible!
Zeus from the very start, the thunder king
has hated the race of Atreus with a vengeance—
his trustiest weapon women's twisted wiles.
What armies of us died for the sake of Helen . . .
Clytemnestra schemed your death while you were worlds away!'

'True, true,' Agamemnon's ghost kept pressing on,
'so even your own wife—never indulge her too far.
Never reveal the whole truth, whatever you may know;
just tell her a part of it, be sure to hide the rest.
Not that you, Odysseus, will be murdered by your wife.
She's much too steady, her feelings run too deep,
Icarius' daughter Penelope, that wise woman.
She was a young bride, I well remember . . .
we left her behind when we went off to war,
with an infant boy she nestled at her breast.
That boy must sit and be counted with the men now—
happy man! His beloved father will come sailing home
and see his son, and he will embrace his father,
that is only right. But *my* wife—she never
even let me feast my eyes on my own son;
she killed me first, his father!
I tell you this—bear it in mind, you must—
when you reach your homeland steer your ship
into port in secret, never out in the open . . .
the time for trusting women's gone forever!

Enough. Come, tell me this, and be precise.
Have you heard news of my son? Where's he living now?
Perhaps in Orchomenos, perhaps in sandy Pylos
or off in the Spartan plains with Menelaus?

He's not dead yet, my Prince Orestes, no,
he's somewhere on the earth.'
So he probed
but I cut it short: 'Atrides, why ask me that?
I know nothing, whether he's dead or alive.
It's wrong to lead you on with idle words.'

So we stood there, trading heartsick stories,
deep in grief, as the tears streamed down our faces.
But now there came the ghosts of Peleus' son Achilles,
Patroclus,[2] fearless Antilochus—and Great Ajax too,
the first in stature, first in build and bearing
of all the Argives after Peleus' matchless son.
The ghost of the splendid runner knew me at once
and hailed me with a flight of mournful questions:
'Royal son of Laertes, Odysseus, man of tactics,
reckless friend, what next?
What greater feat can that cunning head contrive?
What daring brought you down to the House of Death?—
where the senseless, burnt-out wraiths of mortals make their home.'

The voice of his spirit paused, and I was quick to answer:
'Achilles, son of Peleus, greatest of the Achaeans,
I had to consult Tiresias, driven here by hopes
he would help me journey home to rocky Ithaca.
Never yet have I neared Achaea, never once
set foot on native ground . . .
my life is endless trouble.
But you, Achilles,
there's not a man in the world more blest than you—
there never has been, never will be one.
Time was, when you were alive, we Argives
honored you as a god, and now down here, I see,
you lord it over the dead in all your power.
So grieve no more at dying, great Achilles.'

I reassured the ghost, but he broke out, protesting,
'No winning words about death to *me,* shining Odysseus!
By god, I'd rather slave on earth for another man—
some dirt-poor tenant farmer who scrapes to keep alive—
than rule down here over all the breathless dead.
But come, tell me the news about my gallant son.
Did he make his way to the wars,
did the boy become a champion—yes or no?
Tell me of noble Peleus, any word you've heard—
still holding pride of place among his Myrmidon hordes,
or do they despise the man in Hellas and in Phthia
because old age has lamed his arms and legs?
For I no longer stand in the light of day—

2. Achilles' companion.

the man I was—comrade-in-arms to help my father
as once I helped our armies, killing the best fighters
Troy could field in the wide world up there . . .
Oh to arrive at father's house—the man I was,
for one brief day—I'd make my fury and my hands,
invincible hands, a thing of terror to all those men
who abuse the king with force and wrest away his honor!'

So he grieved but I tried to lend him heart:
'About noble Peleus I can tell you nothing,
but about your own dear son, Neoptolemus,
I can report the whole story, as you wish.
I myself, in my trim ship, I brought him
out of Scyros to join the Argives under arms.
And dug in around Troy, debating battle-tactics,
he always spoke up first, and always on the mark—
godlike Nestor and I alone excelled the boy. Yes,
and when our armies fought on the plain of Troy
he'd never hang back with the main force of men—
he'd always charge ahead,
giving ground to no one in his fury,
and scores of men he killed in bloody combat.
How could I list them all, name them all, now,
the fighting ranks he leveled, battling for the Argives?
But what a soldier he laid low with a bronze sword:
the hero Eurypylus, Telephus' son, and round him
troops of his own Cetean comrades slaughtered,
lured to war by the bribe his mother took.
The only man I saw to put Eurypylus
in the shade was Memnon, son of the Morning.
Again, when our champions climbed inside the horse
that Epeus built with labor, and I held full command
to spring our packed ambush open or keep it sealed,
all our lords and captains were wiping off their tears,
knees shaking beneath each man—but not your son.
Never once did I see his glowing skin go pale;
he never flicked a tear from his cheeks, no,
he kept on begging me there to let him burst
from the horse, kept gripping his hilted sword,
his heavy bronze-tipped javelin, keen to loose
his fighting fury against the Trojans. Then,
once we'd sacked King Priam's craggy city,
laden with his fair share and princely prize
he boarded his own ship, his body all unscarred.
Not a wound from a flying spear or a sharp sword,
cut-and-thrust close up—the common marks of war.
Random, raging Ares plays no favorites.'

So I said and
off he went, the ghost of the great runner, Aeacus' grandson

loping with long strides across the fields of asphodel,
triumphant in all I had told him of his son,
his gallant, glorious son.

Now the rest of the ghosts, the dead and gone
came swarming up around me—deep in sorrow there,
each asking about the grief that touched him most.
Only the ghost of Great Ajax, son of Telamon,
kept his distance, blazing with anger at me still
for the victory I had won by the ships that time
I pressed my claim for the arms of Prince Achilles.
His queenly mother had set them up as prizes,
Pallas and captive Trojans served as judges.
Would to god I'd never won such trophies!
All for them the earth closed over Ajax,
that proud hero Ajax . . .
greatest in build, greatest in works of war
of all the Argives after Peleus' matchless son.
I cried out to him now, I tried to win him over:
'Ajax, son of noble Telamon, still determined,
even in death, not once to forget that rage
you train on me for those accursed arms?
The gods set up that prize to plague the Achaeans—
so great a tower of strength we lost when you went down!
For *your* death we grieved as we did for Achilles' death—
we grieved incessantly, true, and none's to blame
but Zeus, who hated Achaea's fighting spearmen
so intensely, Zeus sealed your doom.
Come closer, king, and listen to my story.
Conquer your rage, your blazing, headstrong pride!'

So I cried out but Ajax answered not a word.
He stalked off toward Erebus, into the dark
to join the other lost, departed dead.
Yet now, despite his anger,
he might have spoken to me, or I to him,
but the heart inside me stirred with some desire
to see the ghosts of others dead and gone.

And I saw Minos there, illustrious son of Zeus,
firmly enthroned, holding his golden scepter,
judging all the dead . . .
Some on their feet, some seated, all clustering
round the king of justice, pleading for his verdicts
reached in the House of Death with its all-embracing gates.

I next caught sight of Orion, that huge hunter,
rounding up on the fields of asphodel those wild beasts
the man in life cut down on the lonely mountain-slopes,
brandishing in his hands the bronze-studded club

that time can never shatter.

I saw Tityus too,
son of the mighty goddess Earth—sprawling there
on the ground, spread over nine acres—two vultures
hunched on either side of him, digging into his liver,
beaking deep in the blood-sac, and he with his frantic hands
could never beat them off, for he had once dragged off
the famous consort of Zeus in all her glory,
Leto, threading her way toward Pytho's ridge,
over the lovely dancing-rings of Panopeus.

And I saw Tantalus too, bearing endless torture.
He stood erect in a pool as the water lapped his chin—
parched, he tried to drink, but he could not reach the surface,
no, time and again the old man stooped, craving a sip,
time and again the water vanished, swallowed down,
laying bare the caked black earth at his feet—
some spirit drank it dry. And over his head
leafy trees dangled their fruit from high aloft,
pomegranates and pears, and apples glowing red,
succulent figs and olives swelling sleek and dark,
but as soon as the old man would strain to clutch them fast
a gust would toss them up to the lowering dark clouds.

And I saw Sisyphus too, bound to his own torture,
grappling his monstrous boulder with both arms working,
heaving, hands struggling, legs driving, he kept on
thrusting the rock uphill toward the brink, but just
as it teetered, set to topple over—

time and again
the immense weight of the thing would wheel it back and
the ruthless boulder would bound and tumble down to the plain again—
so once again he would heave, would struggle to thrust it up,
sweat drenching his body, dust swirling above his head.

And next I caught a glimpse of powerful Heracles—
his ghost, I mean: the man himself delights
in the grand feasts of the deathless gods on high,
wed to Hebe, famed for her lithe, alluring ankles,
the daughter of mighty Zeus and Hera shod in gold.
Around him cries of the dead rang out like cries of birds,
scattering left and right in horror as on he came like night,
naked bow in his grip, an arrow grooved on the bowstring,
glaring round him fiercely, forever poised to shoot.
A terror too, that sword-belt sweeping across his chest,
a baldric of solid gold emblazoned with awesome work . . .
bears and ramping boars and lions with wild, fiery eyes,
and wars, routs and battles, massacres, butchered men.
May the craftsman who forged that masterpiece—
whose skills could conjure up a belt like that—

never forge another!
Heracles knew me at once, at first glance,
and hailed me with a winging burst of pity:
'Royal son of Laertes, Odysseus famed for exploits,
luckless man, you too? Braving out a fate as harsh
as the fate I bore, alive in the light of day?
Son of Zeus that I was, my torments never ended,
forced to slave for a man not half the man I was:
he saddled me with the worst heartbreaking labors.
Why, he sent me down here once, to retrieve the hound
that guards the dead—no harder task for me, he thought—
but I dragged the great beast up from the underworld to earth
and Hermes and gleaming-eyed Athena blazed the way!'

With that he turned and back he went to the House of Death
but I held fast in place, hoping that others might still come,
shades of famous heroes, men who died in the old days
and ghosts of an even older age I longed to see,
Theseus and Pirithous, the gods' own radiant sons.
But before I could, the dead came surging round me,
hordes of them, thousands raising unearthly cries,
and blanching terror gripped me—panicked now
that Queen Persephone might send up from Death
some monstrous head, some Gorgon's staring face!
I rushed back to my ship, commanded all hands
to take to the decks and cast off cables quickly.
They swung aboard at once, they sat to the oars in ranks
and a strong tide of the Ocean River swept her on downstream,
sped by our rowing first, then by a fresh fair wind."

Book 12. The Cattle of the Sun

"Now when our ship had left the Ocean River rolling in her wake
and launched out into open sea with its long swells to reach
the island of Aeaea—east where the Dawn forever young
has home and dancing-rings and the Sun his risings—
heading in we beached our craft on the sands,
the crews swung out on the low sloping shore
and there we fell asleep, awaiting Dawn's first light.

As soon as Dawn with her rose-red fingers shone again
I dispatched some men to Circe's halls to bring
the dead Elpenor's body. We cut logs in haste
and out on the island's sharpest jutting headland
held his funeral rites in sorrow, streaming tears.
Once we'd burned the dead man and the dead man's armor,
heaping his grave-mound, hauling a stone that coped it well,
we planted his balanced oar aloft to crown his tomb.

And so we saw to his rites, each step in turn.
Nor did our coming back from Death escape Circe—

she hurried toward us, decked in rich regalia,
handmaids following close with trays of bread
and meats galore and glinting ruddy wine.
And the lustrous goddess, standing in our midst,
hailed us warmly: 'Ah my daring, reckless friends!
You who ventured down to the House of Death alive,
doomed to die twice over—others die just once.
Come, take some food and drink some wine,
rest here the livelong day
and then, tomorrow at daybreak, you must sail.
But I will set you a course and chart each seamark,
so neither on sea nor land will some new trap
ensnare you in trouble, make you suffer more.'

Her foresight won our fighting spirits over.
So all that day till the sun went down we sat
and feasted on sides of meat and heady wine,
and then when the sun had set and night came on
the men lay down to sleep by the ship's stern-cables.
But Circe, taking me by the hand, drew me away
from all my shipmates there and sat me down
and lying beside me probed me for details.
I told her the whole story, start to finish,
then the queenly goddess laid my course:
'Your descent to the dead is over, true,
but listen closely to what I tell you now
and god himself will bring it back to mind.
First you will raise the island of the Sirens,
those creatures who spellbind any man alive,
whoever comes their way. Whoever draws too close,
off guard, and catches the Sirens' voices in the air—
no sailing home for him, no wife rising to meet him,
no happy children beaming up at their father's face.
The high, thrilling song of the Sirens will transfix him,
lolling there in their meadow, round them heaps of corpses
rotting away, rags of skin shriveling on their bones . . .
Race straight past that coast! Soften some beeswax
and stop your shipmates' ears so none can hear,
none of the crew, but if *you* are bent on hearing,
have them tie you hand and foot in the swift ship,
erect at the mast-block, lashed by ropes to the mast
so you can hear the Sirens' song to your heart's content.
But if you plead, commanding your men to set you free,
then they must lash you faster, rope on rope.

But once your crew has rowed you past the Sirens
a choice of routes is yours. I cannot advise you
which to take, or lead you through it all—
you must decide for yourself—
but I can tell you the ways of either course.

On one side beetling cliffs shoot up, and against them
pound the huge roaring breakers of blue-eyed Amphitrite—
the Clashing Rocks they're called by all the blissful gods.
Not even birds can escape them, no, not even the doves
that veer and fly ambrosia home to Father Zeus:
even of those the sheer Rocks always pick off one
and Father wings one more to keep the number up.
No ship of men has ever approached and slipped past—
always some disaster—big timbers and sailors' corpses
whirled away by the waves and lethal blasts of fire.
One ship alone, one deep-sea craft sailed clear,
the *Argo,* sung by the world, when heading home
from Aeetes' shores. And *she* would have crashed
against those giant rocks and sunk at once if Hera,
for love of Jason, had not sped her through.

On the other side loom two enormous crags . . .
One thrusts into the vaulting sky its jagged peak,
hooded round with a dark cloud that never leaves—
no clear bright air can ever bathe its crown,
not even in summer's heat or harvest-time.
No man on earth could scale it, mount its crest,
not even with twenty hands and twenty feet for climbing,
the rock's so smooth, like dressed and burnished stone.
And halfway up that cliffside stands a fog-bound cavern
gaping west toward Erebus, realm of death and darkness—
past it, great Odysseus, you should steer your ship.
No rugged young archer could hit that yawning cave
with a winged arrow shot from off the decks.
Scylla lurks inside it—the yelping horror,
yelping, no louder than any suckling pup
but she's a grisly monster, I assure you.
No one could look on her with any joy,
not even a god who meets her face-to-face . . .
She has twelve legs, all writhing, dangling down
and six long swaying necks, a hideous head on each,
each head barbed with a triple row of fangs, thickset,
packed tight—and armed to the hilt with black death!
Holed up in the cavern's bowels from her waist down
she shoots out her heads, out of that terrifying pit,
angling right from her nest, wildly sweeping the reefs
for dolphins, dogfish or any bigger quarry she can drag
from the thousands Amphitrite spawns in groaning seas.
No mariners yet can boast they've raced their ship
past Scylla's lair without some mortal blow—
with each of her six heads she snatches up
a man from the dark-prowed craft and whisks him off.

The other crag is lower—you will see, Odysseus—
though both lie side-by-side, an arrow-shot apart.

Atop it a great fig-tree rises, shaggy with leaves,
beneath it awesome Charybdis gulps the dark water down.
Three times a day she vomits it up, three times she gulps it down,
that terror! Don't be there when the whirlpool swallows down—
not even the earthquake god could save you from disaster.
No, hug Scylla's crag—sail on past her—top speed!
Better by far to lose six men and keep your ship
than lose your entire crew.'

'Yes, yes,
but tell me the truth now, goddess,' I protested.
'Deadly Charybdis—can't I possibly cut and run from *her*
and still fight Scylla off when Scylla strikes my men?'

'So stubborn!' the lovely goddess countered.
'Hell-bent yet again on battle and feats of arms?
Can't you bow to the deathless gods themselves?
Scylla's no mortal, she's an immortal devastation,
terrible, savage, wild, no fighting her, no defense—
just flee the creature, that's the only way.
Waste any time, arming for battle beside her rock,
I fear she'll lunge out again with all of her six heads
and seize as many men. No, row for your lives,
invoke Brute Force, I tell you, Scylla's mother—
she spawned her to scourge mankind,
she can stop the monster's next attack!

Then you will make the island of Thrinacia . . .
where herds of the Sungod's cattle graze, and fat sheep
and seven herds of oxen, as many sheepflocks, rich and woolly,
fifty head in each. No breeding swells their number,
nor do they ever die. And goddesses herd them on,
nymphs with glinting hair, Phäethusa, Lampetie,
born to the Sungod Helios by radiant Neaera.
Their queenly mother bred and reared them both
then settled them on the island of Thrinacia—
their homeland seas away—
to guard their father's sheep and longhorn cattle.
Leave the beasts unharmed, your mind set on home,
and you all may still reach Ithaca—bent with hardship,
true—but harm them in any way, and I can see it now:
your ship destroyed, your men destroyed as well!
And even if *you* escape, you'll come home late,
all shipmates lost, and come a broken man.'

At those words Dawn rose on her golden throne
and lustrous Circe made her way back up the island.
I went straight to my ship, commanding all hands
to take to the decks and cast off cables quickly.
They swung aboard at once, they sat to the oars in ranks
and in rhythm churned the water white with stroke on stroke.

And Circe the nymph with glossy braids, the awesome one
who speaks with human voice, sent us a hardy shipmate,
yes, a fresh following wind ruffling up in our wake,
bellying out our sail to drive our blue prow on as we,
securing the running gear from stem to stern, sat back
while the wind and helmsman kept her true on course.
At last, and sore at heart, I told my shipmates,
'Friends . . . it's wrong for only one or two
to know the revelations that lovely Circe
made to me alone. I'll tell you all,
so we can die with our eyes wide open now
or escape our fate and certain death together.
First, she warns, we must steer clear of the Sirens,
their enchanting song, their meadow starred with flowers.
I alone was to hear their voices, so she said,
but you must bind me with tight chafing ropes
so I cannot move a muscle, bound to the spot,
erect at the mast-block, lashed by ropes to the mast.
And if I plead, commanding you to set me free,
then lash me faster, rope on pressing rope.'

So I informed my shipmates point by point,
all the while our trim ship was speeding toward
the Sirens' island, driven on by the brisk wind.
But then—the wind fell in an instant,
all glazed to a dead calm . . .
a mysterious power hushed the heaving swells.
The oarsmen leapt to their feet, struck the sail,
stowed it deep in the hold and sat to the oarlocks,
thrashing with polished oars, frothing the water white.
Now with a sharp sword I sliced an ample wheel of beeswax
down into pieces, kneaded them in my two strong hands
and the wax soon grew soft, worked by my strength
and Helios' burning rays, the sun at high noon,
and I stopped the ears of my comrades one by one.
They bound me hand and foot in the tight ship—
erect at the mast-block, lashed by ropes to the mast—
and rowed and churned the whitecaps stroke on stroke.
We were just offshore as far as a man's shout can carry,
scudding close, when the Sirens sensed at once a ship
was racing past and burst into their high, thrilling song:
'Come closer, famous Odysseus—Achaea's pride and glory—
moor your ship on our coast so you can hear our song!
Never has any sailor passed our shores in his black craft
until he has heard the honeyed voices pouring from our lips,
and once he hears to his heart's content sails on, a wiser man.
We know all the pains that the Greeks and Trojans once endured
on the spreading plain of Troy when the gods willed it so—
all that comes to pass on the fertile earth, we know it all!'

Odysseus and the Sirens, Etruscan red-figure amphora, c. 500 B.C.E.

So they sent their ravishing voices out across the air
and the heart inside me throbbed to listen longer.
I signaled the crew with frowns to set me free—
they flung themselves at the oars and rowed on harder,
Perimedes and Eurylochus springing up at once
to bind me faster with rope on chafing rope.
But once we'd left the Sirens fading in our wake,
once we could hear their song no more, their urgent call—
my steadfast crew was quick to remove the wax I'd used
to seal their ears and loosed the bonds that lashed me.

We'd scarcely put that island astern when suddenly
I saw smoke and heavy breakers, heard their booming thunder.
The men were terrified—oarblades flew from their grip,
clattering down to splash in the vessel's wash.
She lay there, dead in the water . . .
no hands to tug the blades that drove her on.
But I strode down the decks to rouse my crewmen,
halting beside each one with a bracing, winning word:
'Friends, we're hardly strangers at meeting danger—
and this danger is no worse than what we faced
when Cyclops penned us up in his vaulted cave
with crushing force! But even from there my courage,

my presence of mind and tactics saved us all,
and we will live to remember *this* someday,
I have no doubt. Up now, follow my orders,
all of us work as one! You men at the thwarts—
lay on with your oars and strike the heaving swells,
trusting that Zeus will pull us through these straits alive.
You, helmsman, here's your order—burn it in your mind—
the steering-oar of our rolling ship is in your hands.
Keep her clear of that smoke and surging breakers,
head for those crags or she'll catch you off guard,
she'll yaw over there—you'll plunge us all in ruin!'

So I shouted. They snapped to each command.
No mention of Scylla—how to fight that nightmare?—
for fear the men would panic, desert their oars
and huddle down and stow themselves away.
But now I cleared my mind of Circe's orders—
cramping my style, urging me not to arm at all.
I donned my heroic armor, seized long spears
in both my hands and marched out on the half-deck,
forward, hoping from there to catch the first glimpse
of Scylla, ghoul of the cliffs, swooping to kill my men.
But nowhere could I make her out—and my eyes ached,
scanning that mist-bound rock face top to bottom.

Now wailing in fear, we rowed on up those straits,
Scylla to starboard, dreaded Charybdis off to port,
her horrible whirlpool gulping the sea-surge down, down
but when she spewed it up—like a cauldron over a raging fire—
all her churning depths would seethe and heave—exploding spray
showering down to splatter the peaks of both crags at once!
But when she swallowed the sea-surge down her gaping maw
the whole abyss lay bare and the rocks around her roared,
terrible, deafening—
bedrock showed down deep, boiling
black with sand—
and ashen terror gripped the men.
But now, fearing death, all eyes fixed on Charybdis—
now Scylla snatched six men from our hollow ship,
the toughest, strongest hands I had, and glancing
backward over the decks, searching for my crew
I could see their hands and feet already hoisted,
flailing, high, higher, over my head, look—
wailing down at me, comrades riven in agony,
shrieking out my name for one last time!
Just as an angler poised on a jutting rock
flings his treacherous bait in the offshore swell,
whips his long rod—hook sheathed in an oxhorn lure—
and whisks up little fish he flips on the beach-break,
writhing, gasping out their lives . . . so now they writhed,

gasping as Scylla swung them up her cliff and there
at her cavern's mouth she bolted them down raw—
screaming out, flinging their arms toward me,
lost in that mortal struggle . . .
Of all the pitiful things I've had to witness,
suffering, searching out the pathways of the sea,
this wrenched my heart the most.
But now, at last,
putting the Rocks, Scylla and dread Charybdis far astern,
we quickly reached the good green island of the Sun
where Helios, lord Hyperion, keeps his fine cattle,
broad in the brow, and flocks of purebred sheep.
Still aboard my black ship in the open sea
I could hear the lowing cattle driven home,
the bleating sheep. And I was struck once more
by the words of the blind Theban prophet, Tiresias,
and Aeaean Circe too: time and again they told me
to shun this island of the Sun, the joy of man.
So I warned my shipmates gravely, sick at heart,
'Listen to me, my comrades, brothers in hardship,
let me tell you the dire prophecies of Tiresias
and Aeaean Circe too: time and again they told me
to shun this island of the Sun, the joy of man.
Here, they warned, the worst disaster awaits us.
Row straight past these shores—race our black
ship on!'

So I said, and the warnings broke their hearts.
But Eurylochus waded in at once—with mutiny on his mind:
'You're a hard man, Odysseus. Your fighting spirit's
stronger than ours, your stamina never fails.
You must be made of iron head to foot. Look,
your crew's half-dead with labor, starved for sleep,
and you forbid us to set foot on land, this island here,
washed by the waves, where we might catch a decent meal again.
Drained as we are, night falling fast, you'd have us desert
this haven and blunder off, into the mist-bound seas?
Out of the night come winds that shatter vessels—
how can a man escape his headlong death
if suddenly, out of nowhere, a cyclone hits,
bred by the South or stormy West Wind? They're the gales
that tear a ship to splinters—the gods, our masters,
willing or not, it seems. No, let's give way
to the dark night, set out our supper here.
Sit tight by our swift ship and then at daybreak
board and launch her, make for open sea!'

So Eurylochus urged, and shipmates cheered.
Then I knew some power was brewing trouble for us,
so I let fly with an anxious plea: 'Eurylochus,

I'm one against all—the upper hand is yours.
But swear me a binding oath, all here, that if
we come on a herd of cattle or fine flock of sheep,
not one man among us—blind in his reckless ways—
will slaughter an ox or ram. Just eat in peace,
content with the food immortal Circe gave us.'

They quickly swore the oath that I required
and once they had vowed they'd never harm the herds,
they moored our sturdy ship in the deep narrow harbor,
close to a fresh spring, and all hands disembarked
and adeptly set about the evening meal.
Once they'd put aside desire for food and drink,
they recalled our dear companions, wept for the men
that Scylla plucked from the hollow ship and ate alive,
and a welcome sleep came on them in their tears.
But then,
at the night's third watch, the stars just wheeling down,
Zeus who marshals the stormclouds loosed a ripping wind,
a howling, demonic gale, shrouding over in thunderheads
the earth and sea at once—and night swept down from the sky.
When young Dawn with her rose-red fingers shone once more
we hauled our craft ashore, securing her in a vaulted cave
where nymphs have lovely dancing-rings and hold their sessions.
There I called a muster, warning my shipmates yet again,
'Friends, we've food and drink aplenty aboard the ship—
keep your hands off all these herds or we will pay the price!
The cattle, the sleek flocks, belong to an awesome master,
Helios, god of the sun who sees all, hears all things.'

So I warned, and my headstrong men complied.
But for one whole month the South Wind blew nonstop,
no other wind came up, none but the South-southeast.
As long as our food and ruddy wine held out, the crew,
eager to save their lives, kept hands off the herds.
But then, when supplies aboard had all run dry,
when the men turned to hunting, forced to range
for quarry with twisted hooks: for fish, birds,
anything they could lay their hands on—
hunger racked their bellies—I struck inland,
up the island, there to pray to the gods.
If only one might show me some way home!
Crossing into the heartland, clear of the crew,
I rinsed my hands in a sheltered spot, a windbreak,
but soon as I'd prayed to all the gods who rule Olympus,
down on my eyes they poured a sweet, sound sleep . . .
as Eurylochus opened up his fatal plan to friends:
'Listen to me, my comrades, brothers in hardship.
All ways of dying are hateful to us poor mortals,
true, but to die of hunger, starve to death—

that's the worst of all. So up with you now,
let's drive off the pick of Helios' sleek herds,
slaughter them to the gods who rule the skies up there.
If we ever make it home to Ithaca, native ground,
erect at once a glorious temple to the Sungod,
line the walls with hoards of dazzling gifts!
But if the Sun, inflamed for his longhorn cattle,
means to wreck our ship and the other gods pitch in—
I'd rather die at sea, with one deep gulp of death,
than die by inches on this desolate island here!'

So he urged, and shipmates cheered again.
At once they drove off the Sungod's finest cattle—
close at hand, not far from the blue-prowed ship they grazed,
those splendid beasts with their broad brows and curving horns.
Surrounding them in a ring, they lifted prayers to the gods,
plucking fresh green leaves from a tall oak for the rite,
since white strewing-barley was long gone in the ship.
Once they'd prayed, slaughtered and skinned the cattle,
they cut the thighbones out, they wrapped them round in fat,
a double fold sliced clean and topped with strips of flesh.
And since they had no wine to anoint the glowing victims,
they made libations with water, broiling all the innards,
and once they'd burned the bones and tasted the organs—
hacked the rest into pieces, piercing them with spits.

That moment soothing slumber fell from my eyes
and down I went to our ship at the water's edge
but on my way, nearing the long beaked craft,
the smoky savor of roasts came floating up around me . . .
I groaned in anguish, crying out to the deathless gods:
'Father Zeus! the rest of you blissful gods who never die—
you with your fatal sleep, you lulled me into disaster.
Left on their own, look what a monstrous thing
my crew concocted!'

Quick as a flash
with her flaring robes Lampetie sped the news
to the Sun on high that we had killed his herds
and Helios burst out in rage to all the immortals:
'Father Zeus! the rest of you blissful gods who never die—
punish them all, that crew of Laertes' son Odysseus—
what an outrage! They, they killed my cattle,
the great joy of my heart . . . day in, day out,
when I climbed the starry skies and when I wheeled
back down from the heights to touch the earth once more.
Unless they pay me back in blood for the butchery of my herds,
down I go to the House of Death and blaze among the dead!'

But Zeus who marshals the thunderheads insisted,
'Sun, you keep on shining among the deathless gods

and mortal men across the good green earth.
And as for the guilty ones, why, soon enough
on the wine-dark sea I'll hit their racing ship
with a white-hot bolt, I'll tear it into splinters.'

—Or so I heard from the lovely nymph Calypso,
who heard it herself, she said, from Hermes, god of guides.

As soon as I reached our ship at the water's edge
I took the men to task, upbraiding each in turn,
but how to set things right? We couldn't find a way.
The cattle were dead already . . .
and the gods soon showed us all some fateful signs—
the hides began to crawl, the meat, both raw and roasted,
bellowed out on the spits, and we heard a noise
like the moan of lowing oxen.
Yet six more days
my eager companions feasted on the cattle of the Sun,
the pick of the herds they'd driven off, but then,
when Cronian Zeus brought on the seventh day,
the wind in its ceaseless raging dropped at last,
and stepping the mast at once, hoisting the white sail
we boarded ship and launched her, made for open sea.

But once we'd left that island in our wake—
no land at all in sight, nothing but sea and sky—
then Zeus the son of Cronus mounted a thunderhead
above our hollow ship and the deep went black beneath it.
Nor did the craft scud on much longer. All of a sudden
killer-squalls attacked us, screaming out of the west,
a murderous blast shearing the two forestays off
so the mast toppled backward, its running tackle spilling
into the bilge. The mast itself went crashing into the stern,
it struck the helmsman's head and crushed his skull to pulp
and down from his deck the man flipped like a diver—
his hardy life spirit left his bones behind.
Then, then in the same breath Zeus hit the craft
with a lightning-bolt and thunder. Round she spun,
reeling under the impact, filled with reeking brimstone,
shipmates pitching out of her, bobbing round like seahawks
swept along by the whitecaps past the trim black hull—
and the god cut short their journey home forever.

But I went lurching along our battered hulk
till the sea-surge ripped the plankings from the keel
and the waves swirled it away, stripped bare, and snapped
the mast from the decks—but a backstay made of bull's-hide
still held fast, and with this I lashed the mast and keel
together, made them one, riding my makeshift raft
as the wretched galewinds bore me on and on.

At last the West Wind quit its wild rage
but the South came on at once to hound me even more,
making me double back my route toward cruel Charybdis.
All night long I was rushed back and then at break of day
I reached the crag of Scylla and dire Charybdis' vortex
right when the dreadful whirlpool gulped the salt sea down.
But heaving myself aloft to clutch at the fig-tree's height,
like a bat I clung to its trunk for dear life—not a chance
for a good firm foothold there, no clambering up it either,
the roots too far to reach, the boughs too high overhead,
huge swaying branches that overshadowed Charybdis.
But I held on, dead set . . . waiting for her
to vomit my mast and keel back up again—
Oh how I ached for both! and back they came,
late but at last, at just the hour a judge at court,
who's settled the countless suits of brash young claimants,
rises, the day's work done, and turns home for supper—
that's when the timbers reared back up from Charybdis.
I let go—I plunged with my hands and feet flailing,
crashing into the waves beside those great beams
and scrambling aboard them fast
I rowed hard with my hands right through the straits . . .
And the father of men and gods did not let Scylla see me,
else I'd have died on the spot—no escape from death.

I drifted along nine days. On the tenth, at night,
the gods cast me up on Ogygia, Calypso's island,
home of the dangerous nymph with glossy braids
who speaks with human voice, and she took me in,
she loved me . . . Why cover the same ground again?
Just yesterday, here at hall, I told you all the rest,
you and your gracious wife. It goes against my grain
to repeat a tale told once, and told so clearly."

Book 13. Ithaca at Last

His tale was over now. The Phaeacians all fell silent, hushed,
his story holding them spellbound down the shadowed halls
until Alcinous found the poise to say, "Odysseus,
now that you have come to my bronze-floored house,
my vaulted roofs, I know you won't be driven
off your course, nothing can hold you back—
however much you've suffered, you'll sail home.
Here, friends, here's a command for one and all,
you who frequent my palace day and night and drink
the shining wine of kings and enjoy the harper's songs.
The robes and hammered gold and a haul of other gifts
you lords of our island council brought our guest—

all lie packed in his polished sea-chest now. Come,
each of us add a sumptuous tripod, add a cauldron!
Then recover our costs with levies on the people:
it's hard to afford such bounty man by man."

The king's instructions met with warm applause
and home they went to sleep, each in his own house.
When young Dawn with her rose-red fingers shone once
more
they hurried down to the ship with handsome bronze gifts,
and striding along the decks, the ardent King Alcinous
stowed them under the benches, shipshape, so nothing
could foul the crewmen tugging at their oars.
Then back the party went to Alcinous' house
and shared a royal feast.
The majestic king
slaughtered an ox for them to Cronus' mighty son,
Zeus of the thundercloud, whose power rules the world.
They burned the thighs and fell to the lordly banquet,
reveling there, while in their midst the inspired bard
struck up a song, Demodocus, prized by all the people.
True, but time and again Odysseus turned his face
toward the radiant sun, anxious for it to set,
yearning now to be gone and home once more . . .
As a man aches for his evening meal when all day long
his brace of wine-dark oxen have dragged the bolted
plowshare
down a fallow field—how welcome the setting sun to him,
the going home to supper, yes, though his knees buckle,
struggling home at last. So welcome now to Odysseus
the setting light of day, and he lost no time
as he pressed Phaeacia's men who love their oars,
addressing his host, Alcinous, first and foremost:
"Alcinous, majesty, shining among your island people,
make your libations, launch me safely on my way—
to one and all, farewell!
All is now made good, my heart's desire,
your convoy home, your precious, loving gifts,
and may the gods of Olympus bless them for me!
May I find an unswerving wife when I reach home,
and loved ones hale, unharmed! And you, my friends
remaining here in your kingdom now, may you delight
in your loyal wives and children! May the gods
rain down all kinds of fortune on your lives,
misfortune never harbor in your homeland!"

All burst into applause, urging passage home
for their parting guest, his farewell rang so true.
Hallowed King Alcinous briskly called his herald:
"Come, Pontonous! Mix the wine in the bowl,

pour rounds to all our banqueters in the house,
so we, with a prayer to mighty Zeus the Father,
can sail our new friend home to native land."

Pontonous mixed the heady, honeyed wine
and hovering closely, poured full rounds for all.
And from where they sat they tipped libations out
to the happy gods who rule the vaulting skies.
Then King Odysseus rose up from his seat
and placing his two-eared cup in Arete's hands,
addressed the queen with parting wishes on the wing:
"Your health, my queen, through all your days to come—
until old age and death, that visit all mankind,
pay you a visit too. Now I am on my way
but you, may you take joy in this house of yours,
in your children, your people, in Alcinous the king!"

With that the great Odysseus strode across the threshold.
And King Alcinous sent the herald off with the guest
to lead him down to the swift ship and foaming surf.
And Arete sent her serving-women, one to carry
a sea-cloak, washed and fresh, a shirt as well,
another assigned to bear the sturdy chest
and a third to take the bread and ruddy wine.

When they reached the ship at the water's edge
the royal escorts took charge of the gifts at once
and stores of food and wine, stowed them deep in the holds,
and then for their guest they spread out rug and sheets
on the half-deck, clear astern on the ship's hull
so he might sleep there soundly, undisturbed.
And last, Odysseus climbed aboard himself
and down he lay, all quiet
as crewmen sat to the oarlocks, each in line.
They slipped the cable free of the drilled stone post
and soon as they swung back and the blades tossed up the spray
an irresistible sleep fell deeply on his eyes, the sweetest,
soundest oblivion, still as the sleep of death itself . . .
And the ship like a four-horse team careering down the plain,
all breaking as one with the whiplash cracking smartly,
leaping with hoofs high to run the course in no time—
so the stern hove high and plunged with the seething rollers
crashing dark in her wake as on she surged unwavering,
never flagging, no, not even a darting hawk,
the quickest thing on wings, could keep her pace
as on she ran, cutting the swells at top speed,
bearing a man endowed with the gods' own wisdom,
one who had suffered twenty years of torment, sick at heart,
cleaving his way through wars of men and pounding waves at sea
but now he slept in peace, the memory of his struggles
laid to rest.

And then, that hour the star rose up,
the clearest, brightest star, that always heralds
the newborn light of day, the deep-sea-going ship
made landfall on the island . . . Ithaca, at last.

There on the coast a haven lies, named for Phorcys,
the old god of the deep—with two jutting headlands,
sheared off at the seaward side but shelving toward the bay,
that break the great waves whipped by the gales outside
so within the harbor ships can ride unmoored
whenever they come in mooring range of shore.
At the harbor's head a branching olive stands
with a welcome cave nearby it, dank with sea-mist,
sacred to nymphs of the springs we call the Naiads.
There are mixing-bowls inside and double-handled jars,
crafted of stone, and bees store up their honey in the hollows.
There are long stone looms as well, where the nymphs weave out
their webs from clouds of sea-blue wool—a marvelous sight—
and a wellspring flows forever. The cave has two ways in,
one facing the North Wind, a pathway down for mortals;
the other, facing the South, belongs to the gods,
no man may go that way . . .
it is the path for all the deathless powers.

Here at this bay the Phaeacian crew put in—
they'd known it long before—driving the ship so hard
she ran up onto the beach for a good half her length,
such way the oarsmen's brawny arms had made.
Up from the benches, swinging down to land,
first they lifted Odysseus off the decks—
linen and lustrous carpet too—and laid him
down on the sand asleep, still dead to the world,
then hoisted out the treasures proud Phaeacians,
urged by open-hearted Pallas, had lavished on him,
setting out for home. They heaped them all
by the olive's trunk, in a neat pile, clear
of the road for fear some passerby might spot
and steal Odysseus' hoard before he could awaken.
Then pushing off, they pulled for home themselves.

But now Poseidon, god of the earthquake, never once
forgetting the first threats he leveled at the hero,
probed almighty Zeus to learn his plans in full:
"Zeus, Father, I will lose all my honor now
among the immortals, now there are mortal men
who show me no respect—Phaeacians, too,
born of my own loins! I said myself
that Odysseus would suffer long and hard
before he made it home, but I never dreamed
of blocking his return, not absolutely at least,

once *you* had pledged your word and bowed your head.
But now they've swept him across the sea in their swift ship,
they've set him down in Ithaca, sound asleep, and loaded the man
with boundless gifts—bronze and hoards of gold and robes—
aye, more plunder than he could ever have won from Troy
if Odysseus had returned intact with his fair share!"

"Incredible," Zeus who marshals the thunderheads replied.
"Earth-shaker, you with your massive power, why moaning so?
The gods don't disrespect you. What a stir there'd be
if they flung abuse at the oldest, noblest of them all.
Those mortals? If any man, so lost in his strength
and prowess, pays you no respect—just pay him back.
The power is always yours.
Do what you like. Whatever warms your heart."

"King of the dark cloud," the earthquake god agreed,
"I'd like to avenge myself at once, as you advise,
but I've always feared your wrath and shied away.
But now I'll crush that fine Phaeacian cutter
out on the misty sea, now on her homeward run
from the latest convoy. They will learn at last
to cease and desist from escorting every man alive—
I'll pile a huge mountain round about their port!"

"Wait, dear brother," Zeus who collects the clouds
had second thoughts. "Here's what seems best to *me.*
As the people all lean down from the city heights
to watch her speeding home, strike her into a rock
that looks like a racing vessel, just offshore—
amaze all men with a marvel for the ages.
Then pile your huge mountain round about their port."

Hearing that from Zeus, the god of the earthquake
sped to Scheria now, the Phaeacians' island home,
and waited there till the ship came sweeping in,
scudding lightly along—and surging close abreast,
the earthquake god with one flat stroke of his hand
struck her to stone, rooted her to the ocean floor
and made for open sea.
The Phaeacians, aghast,
those lords of the long oars, the master mariners
traded startled glances, sudden outcries:
"Look—who's pinned our swift ship to the sea?"

"Just racing for home!"

"Just hove into plain view!"

They might well wonder, blind to what had happened,
till Alcinous rose and made things all too clear:
"Oh no—my father's prophecy years ago . . .

it all comes home to me with a vengeance now!
He used to say Poseidon was vexed with us because
we escorted all mankind and never came to grief.
He said that one day, as a well-built ship of ours
sailed home on the misty sea from such a convoy,
the god would crush it, yes,
and pile a huge mountain round about our port.
So the old king foretold. Now, look, it all comes true!
Hurry, friends, do as I say, let us all comply:
stop our convoys home for every castaway
chancing on our city! As for Poseidon,
sacrifice twelve bulls to the god at once—
the pick of the herds. Perhaps he'll pity us,
pile no looming mountain ridge around our port."

The people, terrified, prepared the bulls at once.
So all of Phaeacia's island lords and captains,
milling round the altar, lifted prayers
to Poseidon, master of the sea . . .
That very moment
great Odysseus woke from sleep on native ground at last—
he'd been away for years—but failed to know the land
for the goddess Pallas Athena, Zeus's daughter,
showered mist over all, so under cover
she might change his appearance head to foot
as she told him every peril he'd meet at home—
keep him from being known by wife, townsmen, friends,
till the suitors paid the price for all their outrage.
And so to the king himself all Ithaca looked strange . . .
the winding beaten paths, the coves where ships can ride,
the steep rock face of the cliffs and the tall leafy trees.
He sprang to his feet and, scanning his own native country,
groaned, slapped his thighs with his flat palms
and Odysseus cried in anguish:
"Man of misery, whose land have I lit on now?
What *are* they here—violent, savage, lawless?
or friendly to strangers, god-fearing men?
Where can I take this heap of treasure now
and where in the world do I wander off myself?
If only the trove had stayed among the Phaeacians there
and I had made my way to some other mighty king
who would have hosted me well and sent me home!
But now I don't know where to stow all this,
and I can't leave it here, inviting any bandit
to rob me blind.
So damn those lords and captains,
those Phaeacians! Not entirely honest or upright, were they?
Sweeping me off to this, this no-man's-land, and they,
they swore they'd sail me home to sunny Ithaca—well,
they never kept their word. Zeus of the Suppliants

pay them back—he keeps an eye on the world of men
and punishes all transgressors!
Come, quickly,
I'll inspect my treasure and count it up myself.
Did they make off with anything in their ship?"

With that he counted up the gorgeous tripods,
cauldrons, bars of gold and the lovely woven robes.
Not a stitch was missing from the lot. But still
he wept for his native country, trailing down the shore
where the wash of sea on shingle ebbs and flows,
his homesick heart in turmoil.
But now Athena appeared and came toward him.
She looked like a young man . . . a shepherd boy
yet elegant too, with all the gifts that grace the sons of kings,
with a well-cut cloak falling in folds across her shoulders,
sandals under her shining feet, a hunting spear in hand.
Odysseus, overjoyed at the sight, went up to meet her,
joining her now with salutations on the wing:
"Greetings, friend! Since you are the first
I've come on in this harbor, treat me kindly—
no cruelty, please. Save these treasures,
save me too. I pray to you like a god,
I fall before your knees and ask your mercy!
And tell me this for a fact—I need to know—
where on earth am I? what land? who lives here?
Is it one of the sunny islands or some jutting shore
of the good green mainland slanting down to sea?"

Athena answered, her eyes brightening now,
"You must be a fool, stranger, or come from nowhere,
if you really have to ask what land this is.
Trust me, it's not so nameless after all.
It's known the world around,
to all who live to the east and rising sun
and to all who face the western mists and darkness.
It's a rugged land, too cramped for driving horses,
but though it's far from broad, it's hardly poor.
There's plenty of grain for bread, grapes for wine,
the rains never fail and the dewfall's healthy.
Good country for goats, good for cattle too—
there's stand on stand of timber
and water runs in streambeds through the year.
So,
stranger, the name of Ithaca's reached as far as Troy,
and Troy, they say, is a long hard sail from Greece."

Ithaca . . . Heart racing, Odysseus that great exile
filled with joy to hear Athena, daughter of storming Zeus,
pronounce that name. He stood on native ground at last

and he replied with a winging word to Pallas,
not with a word of truth—he choked it back,
always invoking the cunning in his heart:
"Ithaca . . . yes, I seem to have heard of Ithaca,
even on Crete's broad island far across the sea,
and now I've reached it myself, with all this loot,
but I left behind an equal measure for my children.
I'm a fugitive now, you see. I killed Idomeneus' son,
Orsilochus, lightning on his legs, a man who beat
all runners alive on that long island—what a racer!
He tried to rob me of all the spoil I'd won at Troy,
the plunder I went to hell and back to capture, true,
cleaving my way through wars of men and waves at sea—
and just because I refused to please his father,
serve under *him* at Troy. I led my own command.
So now with a friend I lay in wait by the road,
I killed him just loping in from the fields—
with one quick stroke of my bronze spear
in the dead of night, the heavens pitch-black . . .
no one could see us, spot me tearing out his life
with a weapon honed for action. Once I'd cut him down
I made for a ship and begged the Phoenician crew for mercy,
paying those decent hands a hearty share of plunder—
asked them to take me on and land me down in Pylos,
there or lovely Elis, where Epeans rule in power.
But a heavy galewind blew them way off course,
much against their will—
they'd no desire to cheat me. Driven afar,
we reached this island here at the midnight hour,
rowing for dear life, we made it into your harbor—
not a thought of supper, much as we all craved food,
we dropped from the decks and lay down, just like that!
A welcome sleep came over my weary bones at once,
while the crew hoisted up my loot from the holds
and set it down on the sand near where I slept.
They reembarked, now homeward bound for Sidon,
their own noble city, leaving me here behind,
homesick in my heart . . ."
As his story ended,
goddess Athena, gray eyes gleaming, broke into a smile
and stroked him with her hand, and now she appeared a woman,
beautiful, tall and skilled at weaving lovely things.
Her words went flying straight toward Odysseus:
"Any man—any god who met you—would have to be
some champion lying cheat to get past *you*
for all-round craft and guile! You terrible man,
foxy, ingenious, never tired of twists and tricks—
so, not even here, on native soil, would you give up
those wily tales that warm the cockles of your heart!

Come, enough of this now. We're both old hands
at the arts of intrigue. Here among mortal men
you're far the best at tactics, spinning yarns,
and I am famous among the gods for wisdom,
cunning wiles, too.
Ah, but you never recognized me, did you?
Pallas Athena, daughter of Zeus—who always
stands beside you, shields you in every exploit:
thanks to me the Phaeacians all embraced you warmly.
And now I am here once more, to weave a scheme with you
and to hide the treasure-trove Phaeacia's nobles
lavished on you then—I willed it, planned it so
when you set out for home—and to tell you all
the trials you must suffer in your palace . . .
Endure them all. You must. You have no choice.
And to no one—no man, no woman, not a soul—
reveal that you are the wanderer home at last.
No, in silence you must bear a world of pain,
subject yourself to the cruel abuse of men."

"Ah goddess," the cool tactician countered,
"you're so hard for a mortal man to know on sight,
however shrewd he is—the shapes you take are endless!
But I do know this: you were kind to me in the war years,
so long as we men of Achaea soldiered on at Troy.
But once we'd sacked King Priam's craggy city,
boarded ship, and a god dispersed the fleet,
from then on, daughter of Zeus, I never saw you,
never glimpsed you striding along my decks
to ward off some disaster. No, I wandered on,
my heart forever torn to pieces inside my chest
till the gods released me from my miseries at last,
that day in the fertile kingdom of Phaeacia when
you cheered me with words, in person, led me to their city.
But now I beg you by your almighty Father's name . . .
for I can't believe I've reached my sunny Ithaca,
I must be roaming around one more exotic land—
you're mocking me, I know it, telling me tales
to make me lose my way. Tell me the truth now,
have I really reached the land I love?"

"Always the same, your wary turn of mind,"
Athena exclaimed, her glances flashing warmly.
"That's why I can't forsake you in your troubles—
you are so winning, so worldly-wise, so self-possessed!
Anyone else, come back from wandering long and hard,
would have hurried home at once, delighted to see
his children and his wife. Oh, but not you,
it's not your pleasure to probe for news of them—
you must put your wife to the proof yourself!

But she, she waits in your halls, as always,
her life an endless hardship . . .
wasting away the nights, weeping away the days.
I never had doubts myself, no, I knew down deep
that you would return at last, with all your shipmates lost.
But I could not bring myself to fight my Father's brother,
Poseidon, quaking with anger at you, still enraged
because you blinded the Cyclops, his dear son.
But come, let me show you Ithaca's setting,
I'll convince you. This haven—look around—
it's named for Phorcys, the old god of the deep,
and here at the harbor's head the branching olive stands
with the welcome cave nearby it, dank with sea-mist,
sacred to nymphs of the springs we call the Naiads.
Here, under its arching vault, time and again
you'd offer the nymphs a generous sacrifice
to bring success! And the slopes above you, look,
Mount Neriton decked in forests!"
At those words
the goddess scattered the mist and the country stood out clear
and the great man who had borne so much rejoiced at last,
thrilled to see his Ithaca—he kissed the good green earth
and raised his hands to the nymphs and prayed at once,
"Nymphs of the springs, Naiads, daughters of Zeus,
I never dreamed I would see you yet again . . .
Now rejoice in my loving prayers—and later,
just like the old days, I will give you gifts
if Athena, Zeus's daughter, Queen of Armies
comes to my rescue, grants this fighter life
and brings my son to manhood!"
"Courage!"—
goddess Athena answered, eyes afire—
"Free your mind of all that anguish now.
Come, quick, let's bury your treasures here
in some recess of this haunted hallowed cave
where they'll be safe and sound,
then we'll make plans so we can win the day."
With that
the goddess swept into the cavern's shadowed vault,
searching for hiding-places far inside its depths
while Odysseus hauled his treasures closer up,
the gold, durable bronze and finespun robes,
the Phaeacians' parting gifts.
Once he'd stowed them well away, the goddess,
Pallas Athena, daughter of storming Zeus,
sealed the mouth of the cavern with a stone.

Then down they sat by the sacred olive's trunk
to plot the death of the high and mighty suitors.
The bright-eyed goddess Athena led the way:

"Royal son of Laertes, Odysseus, old campaigner,
think how to lay your hands on all those brazen suitors,
lording it over your house now, three whole years,
courting your noble wife, offering gifts to win her.
But she, forever broken-hearted for your return,
builds up each man's hopes—
dangling promises, dropping hints to each—
but all the while with something else in mind."

"God help me!" the man of intrigue broke out:
"Clearly I might have died the same ignoble death
as Agamemnon, bled white in my own house too,
if you had never revealed this to me now,
goddess, point by point.
Come, weave us a scheme so I can pay them back!
Stand beside me, Athena, fire me with daring, fierce
as the day we ripped Troy's glittering crown of towers down.
Stand by me—furious now as then, my bright-eyed one—
and I would fight three hundred men, great goddess,
with you to brace me, comrade-in-arms in battle!"

Gray eyes ablaze, the goddess urged him on:
"Surely I'll stand beside you, not forget you,
not when the day arrives for us to do our work.
Those men who court your wife and waste your goods?
I have a feeling some will splatter your ample floors
with all their blood and brains. Up now, quickly.
First I will transform you—no one must know you.
I will shrivel the supple skin on your lithe limbs,
strip the russet curls from your head and deck you out
in rags you'd hate to see some other mortal wear;
I'll dim the fire in your eyes, so shining once—
until you seem appalling to all those suitors,
even your wife and son you left behind at home.
But you, you make your way to the swineherd first,
in charge of your pigs, and true to you as always,
loyal friend to your son, to Penelope, so self-possessed.
You'll find him posted beside his swine, grubbing round
by Raven's Rock and the spring called Arethusa,
rooting for feed that makes pigs sleek and fat,
the nuts they love, the dark pools they drink.
Wait there, sit with him, ask him all he knows.
I'm off to Sparta, where the women are a wonder,
to call Telemachus home, your own dear son, Odysseus.
He's journeyed to Lacedaemon's rolling hills
to see Menelaus, searching for news of you,
hoping to learn if you are still alive."

Shrewd Odysseus answered her at once:
"Why not tell him the truth? You know it all.

Or is *he* too—like father, like son—condemned
to hardship, roving over the barren salt sea
while strangers devour our livelihood right here?"

But the bright-eyed goddess reassured him firmly:
"No need for anguish, trust me, not for him—
I escorted your son myself
so he might make his name by sailing there.
Nor is he saddled down with any troubles now.
He sits at ease in the halls of Menelaus,
bathed in endless bounty . . . True enough,
some young lords in a black cutter lurk in ambush,
poised to kill the prince before he reaches home,
but I have my doubts they will. Sooner the earth
will swallow down a few of those young gallants
who eat you out of house and home these days!"

No more words, not now—
Athena stroked Odysseus with her wand.
She shriveled the supple skin on his lithe limbs,
stripped the russet curls from his head, covered his body
top to toe with the wrinkled hide of an old man
and dimmed the fire in his eyes, so shining once.
She turned his shirt and cloak into squalid rags,
ripped and filthy, smeared with grime and soot.
She flung over this the long pelt of a bounding deer,
rubbed bare, and gave him a staff and beggar's sack,
torn and tattered, slung from a fraying rope.
All plans made,
they went their separate ways—Athena setting off
to bring Telemachus home from hallowed Lacedaemon.

Book 14. The Loyal Swineherd

So up from the haven now Odysseus climbed a rugged path
through timber along high ground—Athena had shown the way—
to reach the swineherd's place, that fine loyal man
who of all the household hands Odysseus ever had
cared the most for his master's worldly goods.

Sitting at the door of his lodge he found him,
there in his farmstead, high-walled, broad and large,
with its long view on its cleared rise of ground . . .
The swineherd made those walls with his own hands
to enclose the pigs of his master gone for years.
Alone, apart from his queen or old Laertes,
he'd built them up of quarried blocks of stone
and coped them well with a fence of wild pear.

Outside he'd driven stakes in a long-line stockade,
a ring of thickset palings split from an oak's dark heart.

Within the yard he'd built twelve sties, side-by-side,
to bed his pigs, and in each one fifty brood-sows
slept aground, penned and kept for breeding.
The boars slept outside, but far fewer of them,
thanks to the lordly suitors' feasts that kept on
thinning the herd and kept the swineherd stepping,
sending to town each day the best fat hog in sight.
By now they were down to three hundred and sixty head.
But guarding them all the time were dogs like savage beasts,
a pack of four, reared by the swineherd, foreman of men.
The man himself was fitting sandals to his feet,
carving away at an oxhide, dark and supple.
As for his men, three were off with their pigs,
herding them here or there. Under orders he'd sent
a fourth to town, with hog in tow for the gorging suitors
to slaughter off and glut themselves with pork.

Suddenly—those snarling dogs spotted Odysseus,
charged him fast—a shatter of barks—but Odysseus
sank to the ground at once, he knew the trick:
the staff dropped from his hand but here and now,
on his own farm, he might have taken a shameful mauling.
Yes, but the swineherd, quick to move, dashed for the gate,
flinging his oxhide down, rushed the dogs with curses,
scattered them left and right with flying rocks
and warned his master, "Lucky to be alive, old man—
a moment more, my pack would have torn you limb from limb!
Then you'd have covered me with shame. As if the gods
had never given me blows and groans aplenty . . .
Here I sit, my heart aching, broken for *him,*
my master, my great king—fattening up
his own hogs for other men to eat, while he,
starving for food, I wager, wanders the earth,
a beggar adrift in strangers' cities, foreign-speaking lands,
if he's still alive, that is, still sees the rising sun.
Come, follow me into my place, old man, so you,
at least, can eat your fill of bread and wine.
Then you can tell me where you're from
and all the pains you've weathered."
On that note
the loyal swineherd led the way to his shelter,
showed his guest inside and sat Odysseus down
on brush and twigs he piled up for the visitor,
flinging over these the skin of a shaggy wild goat,
broad and soft, the swineherd's own good bedding.
The king, delighted to be so well received,
thanked the man at once: "My host—may Zeus
and the other gods give *you* your heart's desire
for the royal welcome you have shown me here!"

And you replied, Eumaeus, loyal swineherd,
"It's wrong, my friend, to send any stranger packing—
even one who arrives in worse shape than you.
Every stranger and beggar comes from Zeus
and whatever scrap they get from the likes of us,
they'll find it welcome. That's the best we can do,
we servants, always cowed by our high and mighty masters,
especially our young lords . . . But my old king?
The gods, they must have blocked his journey home.
He'd have treated me well, he would, with a house,
a plot of land and a wife you'd gladly prize.
Goods that a kind lord will give a household hand
who labors for him, hard, whose work the gods have sped,
just as they speed the work I labor at all day.
My master, I tell you, would have repaid me well
if he'd grown old right here. But now he's dead . . .
If only Helen and all her kind had died out too,
brought to her knees, just as she cut the legs
from under troops of men! My king among them,
he went off to the stallion-land of Troy
to fight the Trojans, save Agamemnon's honor!"
Enough—
he brusquely cinched his belt around his shirt,
strode out to the pens, crammed with droves of pigs,
picked out two, bundled them in and slaughtered both,
singed them, sliced them down, skewered them through
and roasting all to a turn, set them before Odysseus,
sizzling hot on the spits.
Then coating the meat with white barley groats
and mixing honeyed wine in a carved wooden bowl,
he sat down across from his guest, inviting warmly,
"Eat up now, my friend. It's all we slaves have got,
scrawny pork, while the suitors eat the fatted hogs—
no fear of the gods in their hard hearts, no mercy!
Trust me, the blessed gods have no love for crime.
They honor justice, honor the decent acts of men.
Even cutthroat bandits who raid foreign parts—
and Zeus grants them a healthy share of plunder,
ships filled to the brim, and back they head for home—
even their dark hearts are stalked by the dread of vengeance.
But the suitors know, they've caught some godsent rumor
of master's grisly death! That's why they have no mind
to do their courting fairly or go back home in peace.
No, at their royal ease they devour all his goods,
those brazen rascals never spare a scrap!
Not a day or a night goes by, sent down by Zeus,
but they butcher victims, never stopping at one or two,
and drain his wine as if there's no tomorrow—
swilling the last drop . . .

Believe me, my master's wealth was vast!
No other prince on earth could match his riches,
not on the loamy mainland or here at home in Ithaca—
no twenty men in the world could equal his great treasures!
Let me count them off for you. A dozen herds of cattle
back on the mainland, just as many head of sheep,
as many droves of pigs and goatflocks ranging free;
hired hands or his own herdsmen keep them grazing there.
Here in Ithaca, goatflocks, eleven in all, scatter
to graze the island, out at the wild end,
and trusty goatherds watch their every move.
And each herdsman, day after day, it never ends,
drives in a beast for the suitors—best in sight,
a sheep or well-fed goat. While I tend to these pigs,
I guard them, pick the best for those carousers
and send it to the slaughter!"
His voice rose
while the stranger ate his meat and drank his wine,
ravenous, bolting it all down in silence . . .
brooding on ways to serve the suitors right.
But once he'd supped and refreshed himself with food,
he filled the wooden bowl he'd been drinking from,
brimmed it with wine and passed it to his host
who received the offer gladly, spirit cheered
as the stranger probed him now with winging words:
"Friend, who was the man who bought you with his goods,
the master of such vast riches, powerful as you say?
You tell me he died defending Agamemnon's honor?
What's his name? I just might know such a man . . .
Zeus would know, and the other deathless gods,
if I ever saw him, if I bring you any news.
I've roamed the whole earth over."

And the good swineherd answered, foreman of men,
"Old friend, no wanderer landing here with news of *him*
is likely to win his wife and dear son over.
Random drifters, hungry for bed and board,
lie through their teeth and swallow back the truth.
Why, any tramp washed up on Ithaca's shores
scurries right to my mistress, babbling lies,
and she ushers him in, kindly, pressing for details,
and the warm tears of grief come trickling down her cheeks,
the loyal wife's way when her husband's died abroad.
Even you, old codger, could rig up some fine tale—
and soon enough, I'd say,
if they gave you shirt and clothing for your pains.
My master? Well, no doubt the dogs and wheeling birds
have ripped the skin from his ribs by now, his life is through—
or fish have picked him clean at sea, and the man's bones

lie piled up on the mainland, buried deep in sand . . .
he's dead and gone. Aye, leaving a broken heart
for loved ones left behind, for *me* most of all.
Never another master kind as he!
I'll never find one—no matter where I go,
not even if I went back to mother and father,
the house where I was born and my parents reared me once.
Ah, but much as I grieve for them, much as I long
to lay my eyes on them, set foot on the old soil,
it's longing for him, him that wrings my heart—
Odysseus, lost and gone!
That man, old friend, far away as he is . . .
I can scarcely bear to say his name aloud,
so deeply he loved me, cared for me, so deeply.
Worlds away as he is, I call him Master, Brother!"

"My friend," the great Odysseus, long in exile, answered,
"since you are dead certain, since you still insist
he's never coming back, still the soul of denial,
I won't simply say it—on my oath I swear
Odysseus is on his way!
Reward for such good news? Let me have it
the moment he sets foot in his own house,
dress me in shirt and cloak, in handsome clothes.
Before then, poor as I am, I wouldn't take a thing.
I hate that man like the very Gates of Death who,
ground down by poverty, stoops to peddling lies.
I swear by Zeus, the first of all the gods,
by this table of hospitality here, my host,
by Odysseus' hearth where I have come for help:
all will come to pass, I swear, exactly as I say.
True, this very month—just as the old moon dies
and the new moon rises into life—Odysseus will return!
He will come home and take revenge on any man
who offends his wedded wife and princely son!"

"Good news," you replied, Eumaeus, loyal swineherd,
"but I will never pay a reward for *that,* old friend—
Odysseus, he'll never come home again. Never . . .
Drink your wine, sit back, let's talk of other things.
Don't remind me of all this. The heart inside me
breaks when anyone mentions my dear master.
That oath of yours, we'll let it pass—
Odysseus,
oh come back!—
just as *I* wish, I and Penelope,
old Laertes too, Telemachus too, the godlike boy.
How I grieve for *him* now, I can't stop—Odysseus' son,
Telemachus. The gods reared him up like a fine young tree
and I often said, 'In the ranks of men he'll match his father,

his own dear father—amazing in build and looks, that boy!'
But all of a sudden a god wrecks his sense of balance—
god or man, no matter—off he's gone to catch
some news of his father, down to holy Pylos.
And now those gallant suitors lie in wait for him,
sailing home, to tear the royal line of Arcesius
out of Ithaca, root and branch, good name and all!
Enough. Let *him* pass too—whether he's trapped
or the hand of Zeus will pull him through alive.
Come,
old soldier, tell me the story of your troubles,
tell me truly, too, I'd like to know it well . . .
Who are you? where are you from? your city? your parents?
What sort of vessel brought you? Why did the sailors
land you here in Ithaca? Who did they say they are?
I hardly think you came this way on foot."

The great teller of tales returned at length,
"My story—the whole truth—I'm glad to tell it all.
If only the two of us had food and mellow wine
to last us long, here in your shelter now,
for us to sup on, undisturbed,
while others take the work of the world in hand,
I could easily spend all year and never reach the end
of my endless story, all the heartbreaking trials
I struggled through. The gods willed it so . . .

I hail from Crete's broad land, I'm proud to say,
and I am a rich man's son. And many other sons
he brought up in his palace, born in wedlock,
sprung of his lawful wife. Unlike my mother.
She was a slave, a concubine he'd purchased, yes,
but he treated me on a par with all his true-born sons—
Castor, Hylax' son. I'm proud to boast his blood, that man
revered like a god throughout all Crete those days,
for wealth, power and all his glorious offspring.
But the deadly spirits soon swept him down
to the House of Death, and his high and mighty sons
carved up his lands and then cast lots for the parts
and gave me just a pittance, a paltry house as well.
But I won myself a wife from wealthy, landed people,
thanks to my own strong points. I was no fool
and never shirked a fight.
But now my heyday's gone—
I've had my share of blows. Yet look hard at the husk
and you'll still see, I think, the grain that gave it life.
By heaven, Ares gave me courage, Athena too, to break
the ranks of men wide open, once, in the old days,
whenever I picked my troops and formed an ambush,
plotting attacks to spring against our foes—

no hint of death could daunt my fighting spirit!
Far out of the front I'd charge and spear my man,
I'd cut down any enemy soldier backing off.
Such was I in battle, true, but I had no love
for working the land, the chores of households either,
the labor that raises crops of shining children. No,
it was always oarswept ships that thrilled my heart,
and wars, and the long polished spears and arrows,
dreadful gear that makes the next man cringe.
I loved them all—god planted that love inside me.
Each man delights in the work that suits him best.
Why, long before we Achaeans ever camped at Troy,
nine commands I led in our deep-sea-going ships,
raiding foreign men, and a fine haul reached my hands.
I helped myself to the lion's share and still more spoils
came by lot. And my house grew by leaps and bounds,
I walked among the Cretans, honored, feared as well.

But then, when thundering Zeus contrived that expedition—
that disaster that brought so many fighters to their knees—
and men kept pressing me and renowned Idomeneus
to head a fleet to Troy,
there was no way out, no denying them then,
the voice of the people bore down much too hard.
So nine whole years we Achaeans soldiered on at Troy,
in the tenth we sacked King Priam's city, then embarked
for home in the long ships, and a god dispersed the fleet.
Unlucky me. Shrewd old Zeus was plotting still more pain.
No more than a month I stayed at home, taking joy
in my children, loyal wife and lovely plunder.
But a spirit in me urged, 'Set sail for Egypt—
fit out ships, take crews of seasoned heroes!'
Nine I fitted out, the men joined up at once
and then six days my shipmates feasted well,
while I provided a flock of sheep to offer up
to the gods and keep the feasters' table groaning.
On the seventh we launched out from the plains of Crete
with a stiff North Wind fair astern—smooth sailing,
aye, like coasting on downstream . . .
And not one craft in our squadron foundered;
all shipshape, and all hands sound, we sat back
while the wind and helmsmen kept us true on course.

Five days out and we raised the great river Nile
and there in the Nile delta moored our ships of war.
God knows I ordered my trusty crews to stand by,
just where they were, and guard the anchored fleet
and I sent a patrol to scout things out from higher ground.
But swept away by their own reckless fury, the crew went berserk—
they promptly began to plunder the lush Egyptian farms,

dragged off the women and children, killed the men.
Outcries reached the city in no time—stirred by shouts
the entire town came streaming down at the break of day,
filling the river plain with chariots, ranks of infantry
and the gleam of bronze. Zeus who loves the lightning
flung down murderous panic on all my men-at-arms—
no one dared to stand his ground and fight,
disaster ringed us round from every quarter.
Droves of my men they hacked down with swords,
led off the rest alive, to labor for them as slaves.
And I? Zeus flashed an inspiration through my mind,
though I wish I'd died a soldier down in Egypt then!
A world of pain, you see, still lay in wait for me . . .
Quickly I wrenched the skullcap helmet off my head,
I tore the shield from my back and dropped my spear
and ran right into the path of the king's chariot,
hugged and kissed his knees. He pitied me, spared me,
hoisted me onto his war-car, took me home in tears.
Troops of his men came rushing after, shaking javelins,
mad to kill me—their fighting blood at the boil—
but their master drove them off.
He feared the wrath of Zeus, the god of guests,
the first of the gods to pay back acts of outrage.
So,
there I lingered for seven years, amassing a fortune
from all the Egyptian people loading me with gifts.
Then, at last, when the eighth had come full turn,
along comes this Phoenician one fine day . . .
a scoundrel, swindler, an old hand at lies
who'd already done the world a lot of damage.
Well, he smoothly talked me round and off we sailed,
Phoenicia-bound, where his house and holdings lay.
There in his care I stayed till the year was out.
Then, when the months and days had run their course
and the year wheeled round and the seasons came again,
he conned me aboard his freighter bound for Libya,
pretending I'd help him ship a cargo there for sale
but in fact he'd sell *me* there and make a killing!
I suspected as much, of course, but had no choice,
so I boarded with him, yes, and the ship ran on
with a good strong North Wind gusting—
fast on the middle passage clear of Crete—
but Zeus was brewing mischief for that crew . . .
Once we'd left the island in our wake—
no land at all in sight, nothing but sea and sky—
then Zeus the son of Cronus mounted a thunderhead
above our hollow ship and the deep went black beneath it.
Then, then in the same breath Zeus hit the craft
with a lightning-bolt and thunder. Round she spun,

reeling under the impact, filled with reeking brimstone,
shipmates pitching out of her, bobbing round like seahawks
swept along by the breakers past the trim black hull—
and the god cut short their journey home forever.
Not mine.
Zeus himself—when I was just at the final gasp—
thrust the huge mast of my dark-prowed vessel
right into my arms so I might flee disaster
one more time. Wrapping myself around it,
I was borne along by the wretched galewinds,
rushed along nine days—on the tenth, at dead of night,
a shouldering breaker rolled me up along Thesprotia's beaches.[1]
There the king of Thesprotia, Phidon, my salvation,
treated me kindly, asked for no reward at all.
His own good son had found me, half-dead
from exhaustion and the cold. He raised me up
by the hand and led me home to his father's house
and dressed me in cloak and shirt and decent clothes.
That's where I first got wind of *him*—Odysseus . . .
The king told me he'd hosted the man in style,
befriended him on his way home to native land,
and showed me all the treasure Odysseus had amassed.
Bronze and gold and plenty of hard wrought iron,
enough to last a man and ten generations of his heirs—
so great the wealth stored up for *him* in the king's vaults!
But Odysseus, he made clear, was off at Dodona then
to hear the will of Zeus that rustles forth
from the god's tall leafy oak: how should he return,
after all the years away, to his own green land of Ithaca—
openly or in secret? Phidon swore to me, what's more,
as the princely man poured out libations in his house,
'The ship's hauled down and the crew set to sail,
to take Odysseus home to native land.'
But I . . .
he shipped me off before. A Thesprotian cutter
chanced to be heading for Dulichion rich in wheat,
so he told the crew to take me to the king, Acastus,
treat me kindly, too, but it pleased them more
to scheme foul play against me,
sink me into the very depths of pain. As soon
as the ship was far off land, scudding in mid-sea,
they sprang their trap—my day of slavery then and there!
They stripped from my back the shirt and cloak I wore,
decked me out in a new suit of clothes, all rags,
ripped and filthy—the rags you see right now.
But then, once they'd gained the fields of Ithaca,
still clear in the evening light, they lashed me fast

1. In northwestern Greece.

to the rowing-benches, twisting a cable round me;
all hands went ashore
and rushed to catch their supper on the beach.
But the gods themselves unhitched my knots at once
with the gods' own ease. I wrapped my head in rags,
slid down the gangplank polished smooth, slipped my body
into the water, not a splash, chest-high, then quick,
launched out with both my arms and swam away—
out of the surf in no time, clear of the crew.
I clambered upland, into a flowery, fragrant brush
and crouched there, huddling low. They raised a hue and cry,
wildly beat the bushes, but when it seemed no use
to pursue the hunt, back they trudged again and
boarded their empty ship.
The gods hid me themselves—
it's light work for them—and brought me here,
the homestead of a man who knows the world.
So it seems to be my lot that I'll live on."

And you replied, Eumaeus, loyal swineherd,
"So much misery, friend! You've moved my heart,
deeply, with your long tale . . .such blows, such roving.
But one part's off the mark, I know—you'll never persuade me—
what you say about Odysseus. A man in your condition,
who are *you,* I ask you, to lie for no good reason?
Well I know the truth of my good lord's return,
how the gods detested him, with a vengeance—
never letting him go under, fighting Trojans,
or die in the arms of loved ones,
once he'd wound down the long coil of war.
Then all united Achaea would have raised his tomb
and he'd have won his son great fame for years to come.
But now the whirlwinds have ripped him away—no fame for him!
And I live here, cut off from the world, with all my pigs.
I never go into town unless, perhaps, wise Penelope
calls me back, when news drops in from nowhere.
There they crowd the messenger, cross-examine him,
heartsick for their long-lost lord or all too glad
to eat him out of house and home, scot-free.
But I've no love for all that probing, prying,
not since some Aetolian fooled me with his yarn.
He'd killed a man, wandered over the face of the earth,
stumbled onto my hut, and I received him warmly.
He told me he'd seen Odysseus
lodged with King Idomeneus down in Crete—
refitting his ships, hard-hit by the gales,
but he'd be home, he said, by summer or harvest-time,
his hulls freighted with treasure, manned by fighting crews.
So you, old misery, seeing a god has led you here to me,
don't try to charm me now, don't spellbind me with lies!

Never for *that* will I respect you, treat you kindly;
no, it's my fear of Zeus, the god of guests,
and because I pity you . . ."

"Good god," the crafty man pressed on,
"what a dark, suspicious heart you have inside you!
Not even my oath can win you over, make you see the light.
Come, strike a bargain—all the gods of Olympus
witness now our pact!
If your master returns, here to your house,
dress me in shirt and cloak and send me off
to Dulichion at once, the place I long to be.
But if your master doesn't return as I predict,
set your men on me—fling me off some rocky crag
so the next beggar here may just think twice
before he peddles lies."
"Surely, friend!"—
the swineherd shook his head—"and just think
of the praise and fame I'd win among mankind,
now and for all time to come, if first I took you
under my roof, I treated you kindly as my guest
then cut you down and robbed you of your life—
how keen I'd be to say my prayers to Zeus!
But it's high time for a meal.
I hope the men will be home at any moment
so we can fix a tasty supper in the lodge."

As host and guest confided back and forth
the herdsmen came in, driving their hogs up close,
penning sows in their proper sties for the night,
squealing for all they're worth, shut inside their yard,
and the good swineherd shouted to his men,
"Bring in your fattest hog!
I'll slaughter it for our guest from far abroad.
We'll savor it ourselves. All too long we've sweated
over these white-tusked boars—our wretched labor—
while others wolf our work down free of charge!"
Calling out
as he split up kindling now with a good sharp ax
and his men hauled in a tusker five years old,
rippling fat, and stood him steady by the hearth.
The swineherd, soul of virtue, did not forget the gods.
He began the rite by plucking tufts from the porker's head,
threw them into the fire and prayed to all the powers,
"Bring him home, our wise Odysseus, home at last!"
Then raising himself full-length, with an oak log
he'd left unsplit he clubbed and stunned the beast
and it gasped out its life . . .
The men slashed its throat, singed the carcass,
quickly quartered it all, and then the swineherd,

cutting first strips for the gods from every limb,
spread them across the thighs, wrapped in sleek fat,
and sprinkling barley over them, flung them on the fire.
They sliced the rest into pieces, pierced them with skewers,
broiled them all to a turn and, pulling them off the spits,
piled the platters high. The swineherd, standing up
to share the meat—his sense of fairness perfect—
carved it all out into seven equal portions.
One he set aside, lifting up a prayer
to the forest nymphs and Hermes, Maia's son,
and the rest he handed on to each man in turn.
But to Odysseus he presented the boar's long loin
and the cut of honor cheered his master's heart.
The man for all occasions thanked his host:
"I pray, Eumaeus, you'll be as dear to Father Zeus
as you are to me—a man in my condition—
you honor me by giving me your best."

You replied in kind, Eumaeus, swineherd:
"Eat, my strange new friend . . . enjoy it now,
it's all we have to offer. As for Father Zeus,
one thing he will give and another he'll hold back,
whatever his pleasure. All things are in his power."

He burned choice parts for the gods who never die
and pouring glistening wine in a full libation,
placed the cup in his guest's hands—Odysseus,
raider of cities—and down he sat to his own share.
Mesaulius served them bread, a man the swineherd
purchased for himself in his master's absence—
alone, apart from his queen or old Laertes—
bought him from Taphians, bartered his own goods.
They reached out for the spread that lay at hand
and when they'd put aside desire for food and drink,
Mesaulius cleared the things away. And now, content
with bread and meat, they made for bed at once.

A foul night came on—the dark of the moon—and Zeus
rained from dusk to dawn and a sodden West Wind raged.
Odysseus spoke up now, keen to test the swineherd.
Would he take his cloak off, hand it to his guest
or at least tell one of his men to do the same?
He cared for the stranger so, who ventured now,
"Listen, Eumaeus, and all you comrades here,
allow me to sing my praises for a moment.
Say it's the wine that leads me on, the wild wine
that sets the wisest man to sing at the top of his lungs,
laugh like a fool—it drives the man to dancing . . . it even
tempts him to blurt out stories better never told.
But now that I'm sounding off, I can't hold back.

Oh make me young again, and the strength inside me
steady as a rock! Just as I was that day
we sprang a sudden ambush against the Trojans.
Odysseus led the raid with Atreus' son Menelaus.
I was third in command—they'd chosen me themselves.
Once we'd edged up under the city's steep ramparts,
crowding the walls but sinking into the thick brake,
the reeds and marshy flats, huddling under our armor
there we lay, and a foul night came on, the North Wind struck,
freezing cold, and down from the skies the snow fell like frost,
packed hard—the rims of our shields armored round with ice.
There all the rest of the men wore shirts and cloaks and,
hunching shields over their shoulders, slept at ease.
Not I. I'd left my cloak at camp when I set out—
idiot—never thinking it might turn cold,
so I joined in with just the shield on my back
and a shining waist-guard . . . But then at last,
the night's third watch, the stars just wheeling down—
I muttered into his ear, Odysseus, right beside me,
nudging him with an elbow—he perked up at once—
'Royal son of Laertes, Odysseus, full of tactics,
I'm not long for the living. The cold will do me in.
See, I've got no cloak. Some spirit's fooled me—
I came out half-dressed. Now there's no escape!'
I hadn't finished—a thought flashed in his mind;
no one could touch the man at plots or battles.
'Shhh!' he hissed back—Odysseus had a plan—
'One of our fighters over there might hear you.'
Then he propped his head on his forearm, calling out,
'Friends, wake up. I slept and a god sent down a dream.
It warned that we're too far from the ships, exposed.
Go, someone, tell Agamemnon, our field marshal—
he might rush reinforcements from the beach.'
Thoas, son of Andraemon, sprang up at once,
flung off his purple cloak and ran to the ships
while I, bundling into his wrap, was glad at heart
till Dawn rose on her golden throne once more.
Oh make me young again
and the strength inside me steady as a rock!
One of the swineherds here would lend a wrap
for love of a good soldier, respect as well.
Now they spurn me, dressed in filthy rags."

And you replied, Eumaeus, loyal swineherd,
"Now that was a fine yarn you told, old-timer,
not without point, not without profit either.
You won't want for clothes or whatever else
is due a worn-out traveler come for help—
not for tonight at least. Tomorrow morning

you'll have to flap around in rags again.
Here we've got no store of shirts and cloaks,
no changes. Just one wrap per man, that's all.
But just you wait till Odysseus' dear son comes back—
that boy will deck you out in a cloak and shirt
and send you off, wherever your heart desires!"
With that
he rose to his feet and laid out a bed by the fire,
throwing over it skins of sheep and goats and
down Odysseus lay. Eumaeus flung on his guest
the heavy flaring cloak he kept in reserve
to wear when winter brought some wild storm.
So here
Odysseus slept and the young hands slept beside him.
Not the swineherd. Not his style to bed indoors,
apart from his pigs. He geared up to go outside
and it warmed Odysseus' heart,
Eumaeus cared so much for his absent master's goods.
First, over his broad shoulders he slung a whetted sword,
wrapped himself in a cloak stitched tight to block the wind,
and adding a cape, the pelt of a shaggy well-fed goat,
he took a good sharp lance to fight off men and dogs.
Then out he went to sleep where his white-tusked boars
had settled down for the night . . . just under
a jutting crag that broke the North Wind's blast.

Book 15. The Prince Sets Sail for Home

Now south through the spacious dancing-rings of Lacedaemon
Athena went to remind the hero's princely son
of his journey home and spur him on his way.
She found him there with Nestor's gallant son,
bedded down in the porch of illustrious Menelaus—
Pisistratus, at least, overcome with deep sound sleep,
but not Telemachus. Welcome sleep could not hold him.
All through the godsent night he lay awake . . .
tossing with anxious thoughts about his father.
Hovering over him, eyes ablaze, Athena said,
"It's wrong, Telemachus, wrong to rove so far,
so long from home, leaving your own holdings
unprotected—crowds in your palace so brazen
they'll carve up all your wealth, devour it all,
and then your journey here will come to nothing.
Quickly, press Menelaus, lord of the warcry,
to speed you home at once, if you want to find
your irreproachable mother still inside your house.
Even now her father and brothers urge Penelope
to marry Eurymachus, who excels all other suitors
at giving gifts and drives the bride-price higher.

She must not carry anything off against your will!
You know how the heart of a woman always works:
she likes to build the wealth of her new groom—
of the sons she bore, of her dear, departed husband,
not a memory of the dead, no questions asked.
So sail for home, I say!
With your own hands turn over all your goods
to the one serving-woman you can trust the most,
till the gods bring to light your own noble bride.

And another thing. Take it to heart, I tell you.
Picked men of the suitors lie in ambush, grim-set
in the straits between Ithaca and rocky Same,
poised to kill you before you can reach home,
but I have my doubts they will. Sooner the earth
will swallow down a few of those young gallants
who eat you out of house and home these days!
Just give the channel islands a wide berth,
push on in your trim ship, sail night and day,
and the deathless god who guards and pulls you through
will send you a fresh fair wind from hard astern.
At your first landfall, Ithaca's outer banks,
speed ship and shipmates round to the city side.
But you—you make your way to the swineherd first,
in charge of your pigs, and true to you as always.
Sleep the night there, send him to town at once
to tell the news to your mother, wise Penelope—
you've made it back from Pylos safe and sound."

Mission accomplished, back she went to Olympus' heights
as Telemachus woke Nestor's son from his sweet sleep;
he dug a heel in his ribs and roused him briskly:
"Up, Pisistratus. Hitch the team to the chariot—
let's head for home at once!"
"No, Telemachus,"
Nestor's son objected, "much as we long to go,
we cannot drive a team in the dead of night.
Morning will soon be here. So wait, I say,
wait till he loads our chariot down with gifts—
the hero Atrides, Menelaus, the great spearman—
and gives us warm salutes and sees us off like princes.
That's the man a guest will remember all his days:
the lavish host who showers him with kindness."

At those words Dawn rose on her golden throne
and Menelaus, lord of the warcry, rising up from bed
by the side of Helen with her loose and lovely hair,
walked toward his guests. As soon as he saw him,
Telemachus rushed to pull a shimmering tunic on,
over his broad shoulders threw his flaring cape

and the young prince, son of King Odysseus,
strode out to meet his host: "Menelaus,
royal son of Atreus, captain of armies,
let me go back to my own country now.
The heart inside me longs for home at last."

The lord of the warcry reassured the prince,
"I'd never detain you here too long, Telemachus,
not if your heart is set on going home.
I'd find fault with another host, I'm sure,
too warm to his guests, too pressing or too cold.
Balance is best in all things. It's bad either way,
spurring the stranger home who wants to linger,
holding the one who longs to leave—you know,
'Welcome the coming, speed the parting guest!'
But wait till I load your chariot down with gifts—
fine ones, too, you'll see with your own eyes—
and tell the maids to serve a meal at hall.
We have god's plenty here.
It's honor and glory to us, a help to you as well
if you dine in style first, then leave to see the world.
And if you're keen for the grand tour of all Hellas,
right to the depths of Argos, I'll escort you myself,
harness the horses, guide you through the towns.
And no host will turn us away with empty hands,
each will give us at least one gift to prize—
a handsome tripod, cauldron forged in bronze,
a brace of mules or a solid golden cup."

Firmly resolved, Telemachus replied,
"Menelaus, royal Atrides, captain of armies,
I must go back to my own home at once.
When I started out I left no one behind
to guard my own possessions. God forbid,
searching for my great father, I lose my life
or lose some priceless treasure from my house!"

As soon as the lord of the warcry heard *that,*
he told his wife and serving-women to lay out a meal
in the hall at once. They'd stores aplenty there.
Eteoneus, son of Boëthous, came to join them—
fresh from bed, he lived close by the palace.
The warlord Menelaus told him to build a fire
and broil some meat. He quickly did his bidding.
Down Atrides walked to a storeroom filled with scent,
and not alone: Helen and Megapenthes went along.
Reaching the spot where all the heirlooms lay,
Menelaus chose a generous two-handled cup;
he told his son Megapenthes to take a mixing-bowl,
solid silver, while Helen lingered beside the chests,

and there they were, brocaded, beautiful robes
her own hands had woven. Queenly Helen,
radiance of women, lifted one from the lot,
the largest, loveliest robe, and richly worked
and like a star it glistened, deep beneath the others.
Then all three went up and on through the halls until
they found Telemachus. The red-haired king spoke out:
"Oh my boy, may Zeus the Thunderer, Hera's lord,
grant you the journey home your heart desires!
Of all the treasures lying heaped in my palace
you shall have the finest, most esteemed. Look,
I'll give you this mixing-bowl, forged to perfection—
it's solid silver finished off with a lip of gold.
Hephaestus made it himself. And a royal friend,
Phaedimus, king of Sidon, lavished it on *me*
when his palace welcomed me on passage home.
How pleased I'd be if you took it as a gift!"

And the warlord placed the two-eared cup
in his hands while stalwart Megapenthes carried in
the glittering silver bowl and set it down before him.
Helen, her cheeks flushed with beauty, moved beside him,
holding the robe in her arms, and offered, warmly,
"Here, dear boy, I too have a gift to give you,
a keepsake of Helen—I wove it with my hands—
for your own bride to wear
when the blissful day of marriage dawns . . .
Until then, let it rest in your mother's room.
And may you return in joy—my parting wish—
to your own grand house, your native land at last."
With that
she laid the robe in his arms, and he received it gladly.
Prince Pisistratus, taking the gifts, stowed them deep
in the chariot cradle, viewed them all with wonder.
The red-haired warlord led them back to his house
and the guests took seats on low and high-backed chairs.
A maid brought water soon in a graceful golden pitcher
and over a silver basin tipped it out
so they might rinse their hands,
then pulled a gleaming table to their side.
A staid housekeeper brought on bread to serve them,
appetizers aplenty too, lavish with her bounty.
Ready Eteoneus carved and passed the meat,
the son of illustrious Menelaus poured their wine.
They reached out for the good things that lay at hand
and once they'd put aside desire for food and drink,
Prince Telemachus and the gallant son of Nestor
yoked their team, mounted the blazoned car
and drove through the gates and echoing colonnade.

The red-haired King Menelaus followed both boys out,
his right hand holding a golden cup of honeyed wine
so the two might pour libations forth at parting.
Just in front of the straining team he strode,
lifting his cup and pledging both his guests:
"Farewell, my princes! Give my warm greetings
to Nestor, the great commander,
always kind to me as a father, long ago
when we young men of Achaea fought at Troy."

And tactful Telemachus replied at once,
"Surely, my royal host, we'll tell him all,
as soon as we reach old Nestor—all you say.
I wish I were just as sure I'd find Odysseus
waiting there at home when I reach Ithaca.
I'd tell him I come from you,
treated with so much kindness at your hands,
loaded down with all these priceless gifts!"

At his last words a bird flew past on the right,
an eagle clutching a huge white goose in its talons,
plucked from the household yards. And all rushed after,
shouting, men and women, and swooping toward the chariot now
the bird veered off to the right again before the horses.
All looked up, overjoyed—people's spirits lifted.
Nestor's son Pisistratus spoke out first:
"Look there! King Menelaus, captain of armies,
what, did the god send down that sign for you
or the two of us?"
The warlord fell to thinking—
how to read the omen rightly, how to reply? . . .
But long-robed Helen stepped in well before him:
"Listen to me and I will be your prophet,
sure as the gods have flashed it in my mind
and it will come to pass, I know it will.
Just as the eagle swooped down from the crags
where it was born and bred, just as it snatched
that goose fattened up for the kill inside the house,
just so, after many trials and roving long and hard,
Odysseus will descend on his house and take revenge—
unless he's home already, sowing seeds of ruin
for that whole crowd of suitors!"
"Oh if only,"
pensive Telemachus burst out in thanks to Helen,
"Zeus the thundering lord of Hera makes it so—
even at home I'll pray to you as a deathless goddess!"

He cracked the lash and the horses broke quickly,
careering through the city out into open country,
shaking the yoke across their shoulders all day long.

The sun sank and the roads of the world grew dark
as they reached Phera, pulling up to Diocles' halls,
the son of Ortilochus, son of the Alpheus River.
He gave them a royal welcome; there they slept the night.

When young Dawn with her rose-red fingers shone once more
they yoked their pair again, mounted the blazoned car
and out through the gates and echoing colonnade
they whipped the team to a run and on they flew,
holding nothing back, approaching Pylos soon,
the craggy citadel. That was when Telemachus
turned to Pisistratus, saying, "Son of Nestor,
won't you do as I ask you, see it through?
We're friends for all our days now, so we claim,
thanks to our fathers' friendship. We're the same age as well
and this tour of ours has made us more like brothers.
Prince, don't drive me past my vessel, drop me there.
Your father's old, in love with his hospitality;
I fear he'll hold me, chafing in his palace—
I must hurry home!"
The son of Nestor pondered . . .
how to do it properly, see it through?
Pausing a moment, then this way seemed best.
Swerving his team, he drove down to the ship
tied up on shore and loaded into her stern
the splendid gifts, the robes and gold Menelaus gave,
and sped his friend with a flight of winging words:
"Climb aboard now—fast! Muster all your men
before I get home and break the news to father.
With that man's overbearing spirit—I know it,
know it all too well—he'll never let you go,
he'll come down here and summon you himself.
He won't return without you, believe me—
in any case he'll fly into a rage."

With that warning he whipped his sleek horses
back to Pylos city and reached his house in no time.
Telemachus shouted out commands to all his shipmates:
"Stow our gear, my comrades, deep in the holds
and board at once—we must be on our way!"

His shipmates snapped to orders,
swung aboard and sat to the oars in ranks.
But just as Telemachus prepared to launch,
praying, sacrificing to Pallas by the stern,
a man from a far-off country came toward him now,
a fugitive out of Argos: he had killed a man . . .
He was a prophet, sprung of Melampus' line of seers,
Melampus who lived in Pylos, mother of flocks, some years ago,
rich among his Pylians, at home in his great high house.
But then he was made to go abroad to foreign parts,

fleeing his native land and hot-blooded Neleus—
most imperious man alive—who'd commandeered
his vast estate and held it down by force
for one entire year. That year Melampus,
bound by cruel chains in the halls of Phylacus,
suffered agonies—all for Neleus' daughter Pero,
that and the mad spell a Fury, murderous spirit,
cast upon his mind. But the seer worked free of death
and drove the lusty, bellowing cattle out of Phylace,
back to Pylos. There he avenged himself on Neleus
for the shameful thing the king had done to him,
and escorted Pero home as his brother's bride.
But he himself went off to a distant country,
Argos, land of stallions—his destined home
where he would live and rule the Argive nation.
Here he married a wife and built a high-roofed house
and sired Antiphates and Mantius, two staunch sons.
Antiphates fathered Oicles, gallant heart,
Oicles fathered Amphiaraus, driver of armies,
whom storming Zeus and Apollo loved intensely,
showering him with every form of kindness.
But he never reached the threshold of old age,
he died at Thebes—undone by a bribe his wife accepted—
leaving behind his two sons, Alcmaeon and Amphilochus.
On his side Mantius sired Polyphides and Clitus both
but Dawn of the golden throne whisked Clitus away,
overwhelmed by his beauty,
so the boy would live among the deathless gods.
Yet Apollo made magnanimous Polyphides a prophet—
after Amphiaraus' death—the greatest seer on earth.
But a feud with his father drove him off to Hyperesia
where he made his home and prophesied to the world . . .

This prophet's son it was—Theoclymenus his name—
who approached Telemachus now and found him pouring
wine to a god and saying prayers beside his ship.
"Friend," he said in a winging supplication,
"since I find you burning offerings here,
I beg you by these rites and the god you pray to,
then by your own life and the lives of all the men
who travel with you—tell me truly, don't hold back,
who are you? where are you from? your city? your parents?"

"Of course, stranger," the forthright prince responded,
"I will tell you everything, clearly as I can.
Ithaca is my country. Odysseus is my father—
there was a man, or was he all a dream? . . .
but he's surely died a wretched death by now.
Yet here I've come with my crew and black ship,
out for news of my father, lost and gone so long."

And the godlike seer Theoclymenus replied,
"Just like you, I too have left my land—
I because I killed a man of my own tribe.
But he has many brothers and kin in Argos,
stallion-land, who rule the plains in force.
Fleeing death at their hands, a dismal fate,
I am a fugitive now,
doomed to wander across this mortal world.
So take me aboard, hear a fugitive's prayer:
don't let them kill me—they're after me, well I know!"

"So desperate!" thoughtful Telemachus exclaimed.
"How could I drive you from my ship? Come sail with us,
we'll tend you at home, with all we can provide."

And he took the prophet's honed bronze spear,
laid it down full-length on the rolling deck,
swung aboard the deep-sea craft himself,
assuming the pilot's seat reserved astern
and put the seer beside him. Cables cast off,
Telemachus shouted out commands to all his shipmates:
"All lay hands to tackle!" They sprang to orders,
hoisting the pinewood mast, they stepped it firm
in its block amidships, lashed it fast with stays
and with braided rawhide halyards hauled the white sail high.
Now bright-eyed Athena sent them a stiff following wind
blustering out of a clear sky, gusting on so the ship
might run its course through the salt sea at top speed—
and past the Springs she raced and the Chalcis' rushing stream
as the sun sank and the roads of the world grew dark and
on she pressed for Pheae, driven on by a wind from Zeus
and flew past lovely Elis, where Epeans rule in power,
and then Telemachus veered for the Jagged Islands,
wondering all the way—
would he sweep clear of death or be cut down?

The king and loyal swineherd, just that night,
were supping with other fieldhands in the lodge.
And once they'd put aside desire for food and drink,
Odysseus spoke up, eager to test the swineherd,
see if he'd stretch out his warm welcome now,
invite him to stay on in the farmstead here
or send him off to town. "Listen, Eumaeus,
all you comrades here—at the crack of dawn
I mean to go to town and do my begging,
not be a drain on you and all your men.
But advise me well, give me a trusty guide
to see me there. And then I'm on my own
to roam the streets—I must, I have no choice—
hoping to find a handout, just a crust or cupful.

I'd really like to go to the house of King Odysseus
and give my news to his cautious queen, Penelope.
Why, I'd even mix with those overweening suitors—
would they spare me a plateful? Look at all they have!
I'd do good work for them, promptly, anything they want.
Let me tell you, listen closely, catch my drift . . .
Thanks to Hermes the guide, who gives all work
of our hands the grace and fame that it deserves,
no one alive can match me at household chores:
building a good fire, splitting kindling neatly,
carving, roasting meat and pouring rounds of wine . . .
anything menials do to serve their noble masters."

"God's sake, my friend!" you broke in now,
Eumaeus, loyal swineherd, deeply troubled.
"What's got into your head, what crazy plan?
You must be hell-bent on destruction, on the spot,
if you're keen to mingle with that mob of suitors—
their pride and violence hit the iron skies!
They're a far cry from you,
the men who do their bidding. Young bucks,
all rigged out in their fine robes and shirts,
hair sleeked down with oil, faces always beaming,
the ones who slave for *them!* The tables polished,
sagging under the bread and meat and wine.
No, stay here. No one finds you a burden,
surely not I, nor any comrade here.
You wait till Odysseus' dear son comes back—
that boy will deck you out in a cloak and shirt
and send you off, wherever your heart desires!"

"If only, Eumaeus," the wayworn exile said,
"you were as dear to Father Zeus as you are to me!
You who stopped my pain, my endless, homesick roving.
Tramping about the world—there's nothing worse for a man.
But the fact is that men put up with misery
to stuff their cursed bellies.
But seeing you hold me here, urging me now
to wait for *him,* the prince who's on his way,
tell me about the mother of King Odysseus, please,
the father he left as well—on the threshold of old age—
when he sailed off to war. Are they still alive,
perhaps, still looking into the light of day?
Or dead by now, and down in Death's long house?"

"Friend,"
the swineherd, foreman of men, assured his guest,
"I'll tell you the whole story, point by point.
Laertes is still alive, but night and day
he prays to Zeus, waiting there in his house,
for the life breath to slip away and leave his body.

His heart's so racked for his son, lost and gone these years,
for his wife so fine, so wise—*her* death is the worst blow
he's had to suffer—it made him old before his time.
She died of grief for her boy, her glorious boy,
it wore her down, a wretched way to go.
I pray that no one I love dies such a death,
no island neighbor of mine who treats me kindly!
While she was still alive, heartsick as she was,
it always moved me to ask about her, learn the news.
She'd reared me herself, and right beside her daughter,
Ctimene, graceful girl with her long light gown,
the youngest one she'd borne . . .
Just the two of us, growing up together,
the woman tending me almost like her child,
till we both reached the lovely flush of youth
and then her parents gave her away in marriage, yes,
to a Samian man, and a haul of gifts they got.
But her mother decked me out in cloak and shirt,
good clothing she wrapped about me—gave me sandals,
sent me here, this farm. She loved me from the heart.
Oh how I miss her kindness now! The happy gods
speed the work that I labor at, that gives me
food and drink to spare for the ones I value.
But from Queen Penelope I never get a thing,
never a winning word, no friendly gesture,
not since this, this plague has hit the house—
these high and mighty suitors. Servants miss it,
terribly, gossiping back and forth with the mistress,
gathering scraps of news, a snack and a cup or two,
then taking home to the fields some little gift.
It never fails to cheer a servant's heart."

"Imagine that," his canny master said,
"you must have been just a little fellow, Eumaeus,
when you were swept so far from home and parents.
Come, tell me the whole story, truly too.
Was your city sacked?—
some city filled with people and wide streets
where your father and your mother made their home?
Or were you all alone, herding your sheep and cattle,
when pirates kidnapped, shipped and sold you off
to this man's house, who paid a healthy price?"

"My friend," the swineherd answered, foreman of men,
"you really want my story? So many questions—well,
listen in quiet, then, and take your ease, sit back
and drink your wine. The nights are endless now.
We've plenty of time to sleep or savor a long tale.
No need, you know, to turn in before the hour.
Even too much sleep can be a bore.

But anyone else who feels the urge
can go to bed and then, at the crack of dawn,
break bread, turn out and tend our master's pigs.
We two will keep to the shelter here, eat and drink
and take some joy in each other's heartbreaking sorrows,
sharing each other's memories. Over the years,
you know,
a man finds solace even in old sorrows, true, a man
who's weathered many blows and wandered many miles.
My own story? This will answer all your questions . . .

There's an island, Syrie—you may have heard of it—
off above Ortygia, out where the sun wheels around.
Not so packed with people, still a good place, though,
fine for sheep and cattle, rich in wine and wheat.
Hunger never attacks the land, no sickness either,
that always stalks the lives of us poor men.
No, as each generation grows old on the island,
down Apollo comes with his silver bow, with Artemis,
and they shoot them all to death with gentle arrows.
Two cities there are, that split the land in half,
and over them both my father ruled in force—
Ormenus' son Ctesius, a man like a deathless god.
One day
a band of Phoenicians landed there. The famous sea-dogs,
sharp bargainers too, the holds of their black ship
brimful with a hoard of flashy baubles. Now,
my father kept a Phoenician woman in his house,
beautiful, tall and skilled at weaving lovely things,
and her rascal countrymen lusted to seduce her, yes,
and lost no time—she was washing clothes when one of them
waylaid her beside their ship, in a long deep embrace
that can break a woman's will, even the best alive.
And then he asked her questions . . .
her name, who was she, where did she come from?
She waved at once to my father's high-roofed house—
'But I'm proud to hail from Sidon paved in bronze,'
she said,
'and Arybas was my father, a man who rolled in wealth.
I was heading home from the fields when Taphian pirates
snatched me away, and they shipped and sold me here
to this man's house. He paid a good stiff price!'

The sailor, her secret lover, lured her on:
'Well then, why don't you sail back home with us?—
see your own high house, your father and mother there.
They're still alive, and people say they're rich!'

'Now there's a tempting offer,' she said in haste,
'if only you sailors here would swear an oath

you'll land me safe at home without a scratch.'

Those were her terms, and once they vowed to keep them,
swore their oaths they'd never do her harm,
the woman hatched a plan: 'Now not a word!
Let none of your shipmates say a thing to me,
meeting me on the street or at the springs.
Someone might go running off to the house
and tell the old king—he'd think the worst,
clap me in cruel chains and find a way to kill you.
So keep it a secret, down deep, get on with buying
your home cargo, quickly. But once your holds
are loaded up with goods, then fast as you can
you send the word to me over there at the palace.
I'll bring you all the gold I can lay my hands on
and something else I'll give you in the bargain,
fare for passage home . . .
I'm nurse to my master's son in the palace now—
such a precious toddler, scampering round outside,
always at my heels. I'll bring him aboard as well.
Wherever you sell him off, whatever foreign parts,
he'll fetch you quite a price!'
Bargain struck,
back the woman went to our lofty halls
and the rovers stayed on with us one whole year,
bartering, piling up big hoards in their hollow ship,
and once their holds were loaded full for sailing
they sent a messenger, fast, to alert the woman.
This crafty bandit came to my father's house,
dangling a golden choker linked with amber beads,
and while the maids at hall and my noble mother
kept on fondling it—dazzled, feasting their eyes
and making bids—he gave a quiet nod to my nurse,
he gave her the nod and slunk back to his ship.
Grabbing my hand, she swept me through the house
and there in the porch she came on cups and tables
left by the latest feasters, father's men of council
just gone off to the meeting grounds for full debate—
and quick as a flash she snatched up three goblets,
tucked them into her bosom, whisked them off
and I tagged along, lost in all my innocence!
The sun sank, the roads of the world grew dark
and both on the run, we reached the bay at once
where the swift Phoenician ship lay set to sail.
Handing us up on board, the crewmen launched out
on the foaming lanes and Zeus sent wind astern.
Six whole days we sailed, six nights, nonstop
and then, when the god brought on the seventh day,
Artemis showering arrows came and shot the woman—

headfirst into the bilge she splashed like a diving tern
and the crewmen heaved her body over, a nice treat
for the seals and fish, but left me all alone,
cowering, sick at heart . . .
Until, at last,
the wind and current bore us on to Ithaca,
here where Laertes bought me with his wealth.
And so I first laid eyes on this good land."

And royal King Odysseus answered warmly,
"Eumaeus, so much misery! You've moved my heart,
deeply, with your long tale—such pain, such sorrow.
True, but look at the good fortune Zeus sends you,
hand-in-hand with the bad. After all your toil
you reached the house of a decent, kindly man
who gives you all you need in meat and drink—
he's seen to that, I'd say—
it's a fine life you lead! Better than mine . . .
I've been drifting through cities up and down the earth
and now I've landed here."
So guest and host
confided through the night until they slept,
a little at least, not long.
Dawn soon rose and took her golden throne.
That hour
Telemachus and his shipmates raised the coasts of home,
they struck sail and lowered the mast, smartly,
rowed her into a mooring under oars.
Out went the bow-stones, cables fast astern,
the crew themselves swung out in the breaking surf,
they got a meal together and mixed some ruddy wine.
And once they'd put aside desire for food and drink,
clear-headed Telemachus gave the men commands:
"Pull our black ship round to the city now—
I'm off to my herdsmen and my farms. By nightfall,
once I've seen to my holdings, I'll be down in town.
In the morning I'll give you wages for the voyage,
a handsome feast of meat and hearty wine."

The seer Theoclymenus broke in quickly,
"Where shall I go, dear boy? Of all the lords
in rocky Ithaca, whose house shall I head for now?
Or do I go straight to your mother's house and yours?"

"Surely in better times," discreet Telemachus replied,
"I would invite you home. Our hospitality never fails
but now, I fear, it could only serve you poorly.
I'll be away, and mother would never see you.
She rarely appears these days,
what with those suitors milling in the hall;

she keeps to her upper story, weaving at her loom.
But I'll mention someone else you might just visit:
Eurymachus, wise Polybus' fine, upstanding son.
He's the man of the hour! Our island people
look on him like a god—the prince of suitors,
hottest to wed my mother, seize my father's powers.
But god knows—Zeus up there in his bright
    Olympus—
whether or not before that wedding day arrives
he'll bring the day of death on all their heads!"

At his last words a bird flew past on the right,
a hawk, Apollo's wind-swift herald—tight in his claws
a struggling dove, and he ripped its feathers out
and they drifted down to earth between the ship
and the young prince himself . . .
The prophet called him aside, clear of his men,
and grasped his hand, exclaiming, "Look, Telemachus,
the will of god just winged that bird on your right!
Why, the moment I saw it, here before my eyes,
I knew it was a sign. No line more kingly than yours
in all of Ithaca—yours will reign forever!"
"If only, friend,"
alert Telemachus answered, "all you say comes true!
You'd soon know my affection, know my gifts.
Any man you meet would call you blest."

He turned to a trusted friend and said, "Piraeus,
son of Clytius, you are the one who's done my bidding,
more than all other friends who sailed with me to Pylos.
Please, take this guest of mine to your own house,
treat him kindly, host him with all good will
till I can come myself."
"Of course, Telemachus,"
Piraeus the gallant spearman offered warmly:
"Stay up-country just as long as you like.
I'll tend the man, he'll never lack a lodging."

Piraeus boarded ship and told the crew
to embark at once and cast off cables quickly—
they swung aboard and sat to the oars in ranks.
Telemachus fastened rawhide sandals on his feet
and took from the decks his rugged bronze-tipped
    spear.
The men cast off, pushed out and pulled for town
as Telemachus ordered, King Odysseus' son.
The prince strode out briskly,
legs speeding him on till he reached the farm
where his great droves of pigs crowded their pens
and the loyal swineherd often slept beside them,
always the man to serve his masters well.

Book 16. Father and Son

As dawn came into the lodge, the king and loyal swineherd
set out breakfast, once they had raked the fire up
and got the herdsmen off with droves of pigs.
And now Telemachus . . .
the howling dogs went nuzzling up around him,
not a growl as he approached. From inside
Odysseus noticed the pack's quiet welcome,
noticed the light tread of footsteps too
and turned to Eumaeus quickly, winged a word:
"Eumaeus, here comes a friend of yours, I'd say.
Someone you know, at least. The pack's not barking,
must be fawning around him. I can hear his footfall."

The words were still on his lips when his own son
stood in the doorway, there. The swineherd started up,
amazed, he dropped the bowls with a clatter—he'd been busy
mixing ruddy wine. Straight to the prince he rushed
and kissed his face and kissed his shining eyes,
both hands, as the tears rolled down his cheeks.
As a father, brimming with love, welcomes home
his darling only son in a warm embrace—
what pain he's borne for him and him alone!—
home now, in the tenth year from far abroad,
so the loyal swineherd hugged the beaming prince,
he clung for dear life, covering him with kisses, yes,
like one escaped from death. Eumaeus wept and sobbed,
his words flew from the heart: "You're home, Telemachus,
sweet light of my eyes! I never thought I'd see you again,
once you'd shipped to Pylos! Quick, dear boy, come in,
let me look at you, look to my heart's content—
under my own roof, the rover home at last.
You rarely visit the farm and men these days,
always keeping to town, as if it *cheered* you
to see them there, that infernal crowd of suitors!"

"Have it your way," thoughtful Telemachus replied.
"Dear old man, it's all for you that I've come,
to see you for myself and learn the news—
whether mother still holds out in the halls
or some other man has married her at last,
and Odysseus' bed, I suppose, is lying empty,
blanketed now with filthy cobwebs."
"Surely,"
the foreman of men responded, "she's still waiting
there in your halls, poor woman, suffering so,
her life an endless hardship . . .
wasting away the nights, weeping away the days."
With that
he took the bronze spear from the boy, and Telemachus,

crossing the stone doorsill, went inside the lodge.
As he approached, his father, Odysseus, rose
to yield his seat, but the son on his part
waved him back: "Stay where you are, stranger.
I know we can find another seat somewhere,
here on our farm, and here's the man to fetch it."

So Odysseus, moving back, sat down once more,
and now for the prince the swineherd strewed a bundle
of fresh green brushwood, topped it off with sheepskin
and there the true son of Odysseus took his place.
Eumaeus set before them platters of roast meat
left from the meal he'd had the day before;
he promptly served them bread, heaped in baskets,
mixed their hearty wine in a wooden bowl
and then sat down himself to face the king.
They reached for the good things that lay at hand,
and when they'd put aside desire for food and drink
Telemachus asked his loyal serving-man at last,
"Old friend, where does this stranger come from?
Why did the sailors land him here in Ithaca?
Who did they say they are?
I hardly think he came this way on foot."

You answered him, Eumaeus, loyal swineherd,
"Here, my boy, I'll tell you the whole true story.
He hails from Crete's broad land, he's proud to say,
but he claims he's drifted round through countless towns of men,
roaming the earth . . . and so a god's spun out his fate.
He just now broke away from some Thesprotian ship
and came to my farm. I'll put him in *your* hands,
you tend to him as you like.
He counts on you, he says, for care and shelter."

"Shelter? Oh Eumaeus," Telemachus replied,
"that word of yours, it cuts me to the quick!
How can I lend the stranger refuge in my house?
I'm young myself. I can hardly trust my hands
to fight off any man who rises up against me.
Then my mother's wavering, always torn two ways:
whether to stay with me and care for the household,
true to her husband's bed, the people's voice as well,
or leave at long last with the best man in Achaea
who courts her in the halls, who offers her the most.
But our new guest, since he's arrived at your house,
I'll give him a shirt and cloak to wear, good clothing,
give him a two-edged sword and sandals for his feet
and send him off, wherever his heart desires.
Or if you'd rather, keep him here at the farmstead,
tend to him here, and I'll send up the clothes

and full rations to keep the man in food;
he'll be no drain on you and all your men.
But I can't let him go down and join the suitors.
They're far too abusive, reckless, know no limits:
they'll make a mockery of him—that would break my heart.
It's hard for a man to win his way against a mob,
even a man of iron. They are much too strong."

"Friend"—the long-enduring Odysseus stepped in—
"surely it's right for *me* to say a word at this point.
My heart, by god, is torn to pieces hearing this,
both of you telling how these reckless suitors,
there in your own house, against your will,
plot your ruin—a fine young prince like you.
Tell me, though, do you let yourself be so abused
or do people round about, stirred up by the prompting
of some god, despise you? Or are your brothers at fault?
Brothers a man can trust to fight beside him, true,
no matter what deadly blood-feud rages on.
Would I were young as you, to match my spirit now,
or I were the son of great Odysseus, or the king himself
returned from all his roving—there's still room for hope!
Then let some foreigner lop my head off if I failed
to march right into Odysseus' royal halls
and kill them all. And what if I went down,
crushed by their numbers—I, fighting alone?
I'd rather die, cut down in my own house
than have to look on at their outrage day by day.
Guests treated to blows, men dragging the serving-women
through the noble house, exploiting them all, no shame,
and the gushing wine swilled, the food squandered—
gorging for gorging's sake—
and the courting game goes on, no end in sight!"

"You're right, my friend," sober Telemachus agreed.
"Now let me tell you the whole story, first to last.
It's not that all our people have turned against me,
keen for a showdown. Nor have I any brothers at fault,
brothers a man can trust to fight beside him, true,
no matter what deadly blood-feud rages on . . .
Zeus made our line a line of only sons.
Arcesius had only one son, Laertes,
and Laertes had only one son, Odysseus,
and I am Odysseus' only son. He fathered me,
he left me behind at home, and from me he got no joy.
So now our house is plagued by swarms of enemies.
All the nobles who rule the islands round about,
Dulichion, and Same, and wooded Zacynthus too,
and all who lord it in rocky Ithaca as well—

down to the last man they court my mother,
they lay waste my house! And mother . . .
she neither rejects a marriage she despises
nor can she bear to bring the courting to an end—
while they continue to bleed my household white.
Soon—you wait—they'll grind *me* down as well!
But all lies in the lap of the great gods.
Eumaeus,
good old friend, go, quickly, to wise Penelope.
Tell her I'm home from Pylos safe and sound.
I'll stay on right here. But you come back
as soon as you've told the news to her alone.
No other Achaean must hear—
all too many plot to take my life."
"I know,"
you assured your prince, Eumaeus, loyal swineherd.
"I see your point—there's sense in this old head.
One thing more, and make your orders clear.
On the same trip do I go and give the news
to King Laertes too? For many years, poor man,
heartsick for his son, he'd always keep an eye
on the farm and take his meals with the hired hands
whenever he felt the urge to. Now, from the day
you sailed away to Pylos, not a sip or a bite
he's touched, they say, not as he did before,
and his eyes are shut to all the farmyard labors.
Huddled over, groaning in grief and tears,
he wastes away—the man's all skin and bones."

"So much the worse," Telemachus answered firmly.
"Leave him alone; though it hurts us now, we must.
If men could have all they want, free for the taking,
I'd take first my father's journey home. So,
you go and give the message, then come back,
no roaming over the fields to find Laertes.
Tell my mother to send her housekeeper,
fast as she can, in secret—
she can give the poor old man the news."

That roused Eumaeus. The swineherd grasped his sandals,
strapped them onto his feet and made for town.
His exit did not escape Athena's notice . . .
Approaching, closer, now she appeared a woman,
beautiful, tall and skilled at weaving lovely things.
Just at the shelter's door she stopped, visible to Odysseus
but Telemachus could not see her, sense her there—
the gods don't show themselves to every man alive.
Odysseus saw her, so did the dogs; no barking now,
they whimpered, cringing away in terror through the yard.
She gave a sign with her brows, Odysseus caught it,

out of the lodge he went and past the high stockade
and stood before the goddess. Athena urged him on:
"Royal son of Laertes, Odysseus, old campaigner,
now is the time, now tell your son the truth.
Hold nothing back, so the two of you can plot
the suitors' doom and then set out for town.
I myself won't lag behind you long—
I'm blazing for a battle!"

Athena stroked him with her golden wand.
First she made the cloak and shirt on his body
fresh and clean, then made him taller, supple, young,
his ruddy tan came back, the cut of his jawline firmed
and the dark beard clustered black around his chin.
Her work complete, she went her way once more
and Odysseus returned to the lodge. His own son
gazed at him, wonderstruck, terrified too, turning
his eyes away, suddenly—
this must be some god—
and he let fly with a burst of exclamations:
"Friend, you're a new man—not what I saw before!
Your clothes, they've changed, even your skin has changed—
surely you are some god who rules the vaulting skies!
Oh be kind, and we will give you offerings,
gifts of hammered gold to warm your heart—
spare us, please, I beg you!"
"No, I am not a god,"
the long-enduring, great Odysseus returned.
"Why confuse me with one who never dies?
No, I am your father—
the Odysseus you wept for all your days,
you bore a world of pain, the cruel abuse of men."

And with those words Odysseus kissed his son
and the tears streamed down his cheeks and wet the ground,
though before he'd always reined his emotions back.
But still not convinced that it was his father,
Telemachus broke out, wild with disbelief,
"No, you're not Odysseus! Not my father!
Just some spirit spellbinding me now—
to make me ache with sorrow all the more.
Impossible for a mortal to work such marvels,
not with his own devices, not unless some god
comes down in person, eager to make that mortal
young or old—like that! Why, just now
you were old, and wrapped in rags, but *now,* look,
you seem like a god who rules the skies up there!"

"Telemachus," Odysseus, man of exploits, urged his son,
"it's wrong to marvel, carried away in wonder so

to see your father here before your eyes.
No other Odysseus will ever return to you.
That man and I are one, the man you see . . .
here after many hardships,
endless wanderings, after twenty years
I have come home to native ground at last.
My changing so? Athena's work, the Fighter's Queen—
she has that power, she makes me look as she likes,
now like a beggar, the next moment a young man,
decked out in handsome clothes about my body.
It's light work for the gods who rule the skies
to exalt a mortal man or bring him low."
At that
Odysseus sat down again, and Telemachus threw his arms
around his great father, sobbing uncontrollably
as the deep desire for tears welled up in both.
They cried out, shrilling cries, pulsing sharper
than birds of prey—eagles, vultures with hooked claws—
when farmers plunder their nest of young too young to fly.
Both men so filled with compassion, eyes streaming tears,
that now the sunlight would have set upon their cries
if Telemachus had not asked his father, all at once,
"What sort of ship, dear father, brought you here?—
Ithaca, at last. Who did the sailors say they are?
I hardly think you came back home on foot!"

So long an exile, great Odysseus replied,
"Surely, my son, I'll tell you the whole story now.
Phaeacians brought me here, the famous sailors
who ferry home all men who reach their shores.
They sailed me across the sea in their swift ship,
they set me down in Ithaca, sound asleep, and gave me
glittering gifts—bronze and hoards of gold and robes.
All lie stowed in a cave, thanks to the gods' help,
and Athena's inspiration spurred me here, now,
so we could plan the slaughter of our foes.
Come, give me the full tally of these suitors—
I must know their numbers, gauge their strength.
Then I'll deploy this old tactician's wits,
decide if the two of us can take them on,
alone, without allies,
or we should hunt reserves to back us up."
"Father,"
clear-headed Telemachus countered quickly,
"all my life I've heard of your great fame—
a brave man in war and a deep mind in counsel—
but what you say dumbfounds me, staggers imagination!
How on earth could two men fight so many and so strong?
These suitors are not just ten or twenty, they're far more—
you count them up for yourself now, take a moment . . .

From Dulichion, fifty-two of them, picked young men,
six servants in their troop; from Same, twenty-four,
from Zacynthus, twenty Achaeans, nobles all,
and the twelve best lords from Ithaca itself.
Medon the herald's with them, a gifted bard,
and two henchmen, skilled to carve their meat.
If we pit ourselves against all these in the house,
I fear the revenge you come back home to take
will recoil on our heads—a bitter, deadly blow.
Think: can you come up with a friend-in-arms?
Some man to fight beside us, some brave heart?"

"Let me tell you," the old soldier said,
"bear it in mind now, listen to me closely.
Think: will Athena flanked by Father Zeus
do for the two of us?
Or shall I rack my brains for another champion?"

Telemachus answered shrewdly, full of poise,
"Two great champions, those you name, it's true.
Off in the clouds they sit
and they lord it over gods and mortal men."

"Trust me," his seasoned father reassured him,
"they won't hold off long from the cries and clash of battle,
not when we and the suitors put our fighting strength
to proof in my own halls! But now, with daybreak,
home you go and mix with that overbearing crowd.
The swineherd will lead me into the city later,
looking old and broken, a beggar once again.
If they abuse me in the palace, steel yourself,
no matter what outrage I must suffer, even
if they drag me through our house by the heels
and throw me out or pelt me with things they hurl—
you just look on, endure it. Prompt them to quit
their wild reckless ways, try to win them over
with friendly words. Those men will never listen,
now the day of doom is hovering at their heads.
One more thing. Take it to heart, I urge you.
When Athena, Queen of Tactics, tells me it is time,
I'll give you a nod, and when you catch that signal
round up all the deadly weapons kept in the hall,
stow them away upstairs in a storeroom's deep recess—
all the arms and armor—and when the suitors miss them
and ask you questions, put them off with a winning story:
'I stowed them away, clear of the smoke. A far cry
from the arms Odysseus left when he went to Troy,
fire-damaged equipment, black with reeking fumes.
And a god reminded me of something darker too.
When you're in your cups a quarrel might break out,
you'd wound each other, shame your feasting here

and cast a pall on your courting.
Iron has powers to draw a man to ruin.'
Just you leave
a pair of swords for the two of us, a pair of spears
and a pair of oxhide bucklers right at hand so we
can break for the weapons, seize them! Then Athena,
Zeus in his wisdom—they will daze the suitors' wits.
Now one last thing. Bear it in mind. You must.
If you are my own true son, born of my blood,
let no one hear that Odysseus has come home.
Don't let Laertes know, not Eumaeus either,
none in the household, not Penelope herself.
You and I alone will assess the women's mood
and we might test a few of the serving-men as well:
where are the ones who still respect us both,
who hold us in awe? And who shirk their duties?—
slighting you because you are so young."

"Soon enough, father," his gallant son replied,
"you'll sense the courage inside me, that I know—
I'm hardly a flighty, weak-willed boy these days.
But I think your last plan would gain us nothing.
Reconsider, I urge you.
You'll waste time, roaming around our holdings,
probing the fieldhands man by man, while the suitors
sit at ease in our house, devouring all our goods—
those brazen rascals never spare a scrap!
But I do advise you to sound the women out:
who are disloyal to you, who are guiltless?
The men—I say no to testing them farm by farm.
That's work for later, if you have really seen
a sign from Zeus whose shield is storm and thunder."

Now as father and son conspired, shaping plans,
the ship that brought the prince and shipmates back
from Pylos was just approaching Ithaca, home port.
As soon as they put in to the harbor's deep bay
they hauled the black vessel up onto dry land
and eager deckhands bore away their gear
and rushed the priceless gifts to Clytius' house.
But they sent a herald on to Odysseus' halls at once
to give the news to thoughtful, cautious Penelope
that Telemachus was home—just up-country now
but he'd told his mates to sail across to port—
so the noble queen would not be seized with fright
and break down in tears. And now those two men met,
herald and swineherd, both out on the same errand,
to give the queen the news. But once they reached
the house of the royal king the herald strode up,
into the serving-women's midst, and burst out,

"Your beloved son, my queen, is home at last!"
Eumaeus though, bending close to Penelope,
whispered every word that her dear son
entrusted him to say. Message told in full,
he left the halls and precincts, heading for his pigs.

But the news shook the suitors, dashed their spirits.
Out of the halls they crowded, past the high-walled court
and there before the gates they sat in council.
Polybus' son Eurymachus opened up among them:
"Friends, what a fine piece of work he's carried off!
Telemachus—what insolence—and we thought his little jaunt
would come to grief! Up now, launch a black ship,
the best we can find—muster a crew of oarsmen,
row the news to our friends in ambush, fast,
bring them back at once."

And just then—
he'd not quite finished when Amphinomus,
wheeling round in his seat,
saw their vessel moored in the deep harbor,
their comrades striking sail and hoisting oars.
He broke into heady laughter, called his friends:
"No need for a message now. They're home, look there!
Some god gave them the news, or they saw the prince's ship
go sailing past and failed to overtake her."

Rising, all trooped down to the water's edge
as the crew hauled the vessel up onto dry land
and the hot-blooded hands bore off their gear.
Then in a pack they went to the meeting grounds,
suffering no one else, young or old, to sit among them.
Eupithes' son Antinous rose and harangued them all:
"What a blow! See how the gods have saved this boy
from bloody death? And our lookouts all day long,
stationed atop the windy heights, kept watch,
shift on shift; and once the sun went down
we'd never sleep the night ashore, never,
always aboard our swift ship, cruising till dawn,
patrolling to catch Telemachus, kill him on the spot,
and all the while some spirit whisked him home!
So here at home we'll plot his certain death:
he must never slip through our hands again,
that boy—while he still lives,
I swear we'll never bring our venture off.
The clever little schemer, he does have his skills,
and the crowds no longer show us favor, not at all.
So act! before he can gather his people in assembly.
He'll never give in an inch, I know, he'll rise
and rage away, shouting out to them all how we,
we schemed his sudden death but never caught him.

Hearing of our foul play, they'll hardly sing our praises.
Why, they might do us damage, run us off our lands,
drive us abroad to hunt for strangers' shores.
Strike first, I say, and kill him!—
clear of town, in the fields or on the road.
Then we'll seize his estates and worldly goods,
carve them up between us, share and share alike.
But as for his palace, let his mother keep it,
she and the man she weds.
There's my plan.
If you find it offensive, if you want him
living on—in full command of his patrimony—
gather here no more then, living the life of kings,
consuming all his wealth. Each from his own house
must try to win her, showering her with gifts.
Then she can marry the one who offers most,
the man marked out by fate to be her husband."

That brought them all to a hushed, stunned silence
till Amphinomus rose to have his say among them—
the noted son of Nisus, King Aretias' grandson,
the chief who led the suitors from Dulichion,
land of grass and grains,
and the man who pleased Penelope the most,
thanks to his timely words and good clear sense.
Concerned for their welfare now, he stood and argued:
"Friends, I've no desire to kill Telemachus, not I—
it's a terrible thing to shed the blood of kings.
Wait, sound out the will of the gods—that first.
If the decrees of mighty Zeus commend the work,
I'll kill the prince myself and spur on all the rest.
If the gods are against it, then I say hold back!"

So Amphinomus urged, and won them over.
They rose at once, returned to Odysseus' palace,
entered and took their seats on burnished chairs.

But now an inspiration took the discreet Penelope
to face her suitors, brutal, reckless men.
The queen had heard it all . . .
how they plotted inside the house to kill her son.
The herald Medon told her—he'd overheard their schemes.
And so, flanked by her ladies, she descended to the hall.
That luster of women, once she reached her suitors,
drawing her glistening veil across her cheeks,
paused now where a column propped the sturdy roof
and rounding on Antinous, cried out against him:
"You, Antinous! Violent, vicious, scheming—
you, they say, are the best man your age in Ithaca,
best for eloquence, counsel. You're nothing of the sort!
Madman, why do you weave destruction for Telemachus?—

show no pity to those who need it?—those over whom
almighty Zeus stands guard. It's wrong, unholy, yes,
weaving death for those who deserve your mercy!
Don't you know how your father fled here once?
A fugitive, terrified of the people, up in arms
against him because he'd joined some Taphian pirates
out to attack Thesprotians, sworn allies of ours.
The mobs were set to destroy him, rip his life out,
devour his vast wealth to their heart's content,
but Odysseus held them back, he kept their fury down.
And this is the man whose house you waste, scot-free,
whose wife you court, whose son you mean to kill—
you make my life an agony! Stop, I tell you,
stop all this, and make the rest stop too!"

But Polybus' son Eurymachus tried to calm her:
"Wise Penelope, daughter of Icarius, courage!
Disabuse yourself of all these worries now.
That man is not alive—
he never will be, he never can be born—
who'll lift a hand against Telemachus, your son,
not while *I* walk the land and I can see the light.
I tell you this—so help me, it will all come true—
in an instant that man's blood will spurt around
my spear!
My spear, since time and again Odysseus dandled me
on his knees, the great raider of cities fed me
roasted meat and held the red wine to my lips.
So to *me* your son is the dearest man alive,
and I urge the boy to have no fear of death,
not from the suitors at least.
What comes from the gods—there's no escaping that."

Encouraging, all the way, but all the while
plotting the prince's murder in his mind . . .
The queen, going up to her lofty well-lit room,
fell to weeping for Odysseus, her beloved husband,
till watchful Athena sealed her eyes with welcome sleep.

Returning just at dusk to Odysseus and his son,
the loyal swineherd found they'd killed a yearling pig
and standing over it now were busy cooking supper.
But Athena had approached Laertes' son Odysseus,
tapped him with her wand and made him old again.
She dressed him in filthy rags too, for fear Eumaeus,
recognizing his master face-to-face, might hurry
back to shrewd Penelope, blurting out the news
and never hide the secret in his heart.

Telemachus was the first to greet the swineherd:
"Welcome home, my friend! What's the talk in town?

Are the swaggering suitors back from ambush yet—
or still waiting to catch me coming home?"

You answered the prince, Eumaeus, loyal swineherd,
"I had no time to go roaming all through town,
digging round for that. My heart raced me on
to get my message told and rush back here.
But I met up with a fast runner there,
sent by your crew, a herald,
first to tell your mother all the news.
And this I know, I saw with my own eyes—
I was just above the city, heading home,
clambering over Hermes' Ridge, when I caught sight
of a trim ship pulling into the harbor, loaded down
with a crowd aboard her, shields and two-edged spears.
I *think* they're the men you're after—I'm not sure."

At that the young prince Telemachus smiled,
glancing toward his father, avoiding Eumaeus' eyes.
And now,
with the roasting done, the meal set out, they ate well
and no one's hunger lacked a proper share of supper.
When they'd put aside desire for food and drink,
they remembered bed and took the gift of sleep.

Book 17. Stranger at the Gates

When young Dawn with her rose-red fingers shone once more
Telemachus strapped his rawhide sandals to his feet
and the young prince, the son of King Odysseus,
picked up the rugged spear that fit his grip
and striking out for the city, told his swineherd,
"I'm off to town, old friend, to present myself to mother.
She'll never stop her bitter tears and mourning,
well I know, till she sees me face-to-face.
And for you I have some orders—
take this luckless stranger to town, so he can beg
his supper there, and whoever wants can give the man
some crumbs and a cup to drink. How can *I* put up with
every passerby? My mind's weighed down with troubles.
If the stranger resents it, all the worse for him.
I like to tell the truth and tell it plainly."
"My friend,
subtle Odysseus broke in, "I've no desire, myself,
to linger here. Better that beggars cadge their meals
in town than in the fields. Some willing soul
will see to my needs. I'm hardly fit, at my age,
to keep to a farm and jump to a foreman's every order.
Go on then. This man will take me, as you've told him,
once I'm warm from the fire and the sun's good and strong.

Look at the clothing on my back—all rags and tatters.
I'm afraid the frost at dawn could do me in,
and town, you say, is a long hard way from here."

At that Telemachus strode down through the farm
in quick, firm strides, brooding death for the suitors.
And once he reached his well-constructed palace,
propping his spear against a sturdy pillar
and crossing the stone threshold, in he went.

His old nurse was the first to see him, Eurycleia,
just spreading fleeces over the carved, inlaid chairs.
Tears sprang to her eyes, she rushed straight to the prince
as the other maids of great Odysseus flocked around him,
hugged him warmly, kissed his head and shoulders.

Now down from her chamber came discreet Penelope,
looking for all the world like Artemis or golden Aphrodite—
bursting into tears as she flung her arms around her darling son
and kissed his face and kissed his shining eyes and sobbed,
"You're home, Telemachus!"—words flew from her heart—
"sweet light of my eyes! I never thought I'd see you again,
once you shipped to Pylos—against my will, so secret,
out for news of your dear father. Quick tell me,
did you catch sight of the man—meet him—what?"

"Please, mother," steady Telemachus replied,
"don't move me to tears, don't stir the heart inside me.
I've just escaped from death. Sudden death.
No. Bathe now, put on some fresh clothes,
go up to your own room with your serving-women,
pray, and promise the gods a generous sacrifice
to bring success, if Zeus will ever grant us
the hour of our revenge. I myself am off
to the meeting grounds to summon up a guest
who came with me from abroad when I sailed home.
I sent him on ahead with my trusted crew.
I told Piraeus to take him to his house,
treat him well, host him with all good will
till I could come myself."
Words to the mark
that left his mother silent . . .
She bathed now, put on some fresh clothes,
prayed, and promised the gods a generous sacrifice
to bring success, if Zeus would ever grant
the hour of their revenge.
Spear in hand,
Telemachus strode on through the hall and out,
and a pair of sleek hounds went trotting at his heels.
And Athena lavished a marvelous splendor on the prince

so the people all gazed in wonder as he came forward.
The swaggering suitors clustered, milling round him,
welcome words on their lips, and murder in their hearts.
But he gave them a wide berth as they came crowding in
and there where Mentor sat, Antiphus, Halitherses too—
his father's loyal friends from days gone by—
he took his seat as they pressed him with their questions.
And just then Piraeus the gallant spearman approached,
leading the stranger through the town and out onto
the meeting grounds. Telemachus, not hanging back,
went right up to greet Theoclymenus, his guest,
but Piraeus spoke out first: "Quickly now,
Telemachus, send some women to my house
to retrieve the gifts that Menelaus gave you."

"Wait, Piraeus," wary Telemachus cautioned,
"we've no idea how all of this will go.
If the brazen suitors cut me down in the palace—
off guard—and carve apart my father's whole estate,
I'd rather you yourself, or one of his friends here,
keep those gifts and get some pleasure from them.
But if I can bring down slaughter on that crew,
you send the gifts to my house—we'll share the joy."

Their plans made, he led the wayworn stranger home
and once they reached the well-constructed palace,
spreading out their cloaks on a chair or bench,
into the burnished tubs they climbed and bathed.
When women had washed them, rubbed them down with oil
and drawn warm fleece and shirts around their shoulders,
out of the baths they stepped and sat on high-backed chairs.
A maid brought water soon in a graceful golden pitcher
and over a silver basin tipped it out
so they might rinse their hands,
then pulled a gleaming table to their side.
A staid housekeeper brought on bread to serve them,
appetizers aplenty too, lavish with her bounty.
Penelope sat across from her son, beside a pillar,
leaning back on a low chair and winding finespun yarn.
They reached out for the good things that lay at hand
and when they'd put aside desire for food and drink,
the queen, for all her composure, said at last,
"Telemachus, I'm going back to my room upstairs
and lie down on my bed . . .
that bed of pain my tears have streaked, year in,
year out, from the day Odysseus sailed away to Troy
with Atreus' two sons.
But you, you never had the heart—
before those insolent suitors crowd back to the house—
to tell me clearly about your father's journey home,

if you've heard any news."
"Of course, mother,"
thoughtful Telemachus reassured her quickly,
"I will tell you the whole true story now.
We sailed to Pylos, to Nestor, the great king,
and he received me there in his lofty palace,
treated me well and warmly, yes, as a father treats
a long-lost son just home from voyaging, years abroad:
such care he showered on me, he and his noble sons.
But of strong, enduring Odysseus, dead or alive,
he's heard no news, he said, from any man on earth.
He sent me on to the famous spearman Atrides
Menelaus,
on with a team of horses drawing a bolted chariot.
And there I saw her, Helen of Argos—all for her
Achaeans and Trojans suffered so much hardship,
thanks to the gods' decree . . .
The lord of the warcry, Menelaus, asked at once
what pressing need had brought me to lovely Lacedaemon,
and when I told him the whole story, first to last,
the king burst out, 'How shameful! That's the bed
of a brave man of war they'd like to crawl inside,
those spineless, craven cowards!
Weak as the doe that beds down her fawns
in a mighty lion's den—her newborn sucklings—
then trails off to the mountain spurs and grassy bends
to graze her fill, but back the lion comes to his own lair
and the master deals both fawns a ghastly bloody death,
just what Odysseus will deal that mob—ghastly death.
Ah if only—Father Zeus, Athena and lord Apollo—
that man who years ago in the games at Lesbos
rose to Philomelides' challenge, wrestled him,
pinned him down with one tremendous throw
and the Argives roared with joy . . .
if only *that* Odysseus sported with those suitors,
a blood wedding, a quick death would take the lot!
But about the things you've asked me, so intently,
I'll skew and sidestep nothing, not deceive you, ever.
Of all he told me—the Old Man of the Sea who never lies—
I'll hide or hold back nothing, not a single word.
He said he'd seen Odysseus on an island,
ground down in misery, off in a goddess' house,
the nymph Calypso, who holds him there by force.
He has no way to voyage home to his own native land,
no trim ships in reach, no crew to ply the oars
and send him scudding over the sea's broad back.'

So Menelaus, the famous spearman, told me.
My mission accomplished, back I came at once,

and the gods sent me a stiff following wind
that sped me home to the native land I love."

His reassurance stirred the queen to her depths
and the godlike seer Theoclymenus added firmly,
"Noble lady, wife of Laertes' son, Odysseus,
Menelaus can have no perfect revelations;
mark *my* words—I will make you a prophecy,
quite precise, and *I'll* hold nothing back.
I swear by Zeus, the first of all the gods,
by this table of hospitality here, my host,
by Odysseus' hearth where I have come for help—
I swear Odysseus *is* on native soil, here and now!
Poised or on the prowl, learning of these rank crimes
he's sowing seeds of ruin for all your suitors.
So clear, so true, that bird-sign I saw
as I sat on the benched ship
and sounded out the future to the prince!"

"If only, my friend," reserved Penelope exclaimed,
"everything you say would come to pass!
You'd soon know my affection, know my gifts.
Any man you meet would call you blest."

And so the three confided in the halls
while all the suitors, before Odysseus' palace,
amused themselves with discus and long throwing spears,
out on the leveled grounds, free and easy as always,
full of swagger. When the dinner-hour approached
and sheep came home from pastures near and far,
driven in by familiar drovers,
Medon called them all, their favorite herald,
always present at their meals: "My young lords,
now you've played your games to your hearts' content,
come back to the halls so we can fix your supper.
Nothing's better than dining well on time!"

They came at his summons, rising from the games
and now, bustling into the well-constructed palace,
flinging down their cloaks on a chair or bench,
they butchered hulking sheep and fatted goats,
full-grown hogs and a young cow from the herd,
preparing for their feast.

At the same time
the king and his loyal swineherd geared to leave
the country for the town. Eumaeus, foreman of men,
set things in motion: "Friend, I know you're keen
on going down to town today, just as my master bid,
though I'd rather you stay here to guard the farm.
But I prize the boy, I fear he'll blame me later—
a dressing-down from your master's hard to bear.

So off we go now. The shank of the day is past.
You'll find it colder with nightfall coming on."

"I know, I see your point," the crafty man replied.
"There's sense in this old head. So let's be off.
And from now on, you lead me all the way.
Just give me a stick to lean on,
if you have one ready-cut. You say the road
is treacherous, full of slips and slides."
With that
he flung his beggar's sack across his shoulders—
torn and tattered, slung from a fraying rope.
Eumaeus gave him a staff that met his needs.
Then the two moved out, leaving behind them
dogs and herdsmen to stay and guard the farm.
And so the servant led his master toward the city,
looking for all the world like an old and broken beggar
hunched on a stick, his body wrapped in shameful rags . . .

Down over the rugged road they went till hard by town
they reached the stone-rimmed fountain running clear
where the city people came and drew their water.
Ithacus built it once, with Neritus and Polyctor.
Round it a stand of poplar thrived on the dank soil,
all in a nestling ring, and down from a rock-ledge overhead
the cold water splashed, and crowning the fountain
rose an altar-stone erected to the nymphs,
where every traveler paused and left an offering.
Here Dolius' son, Melanthius, crossed their path,
herding his goats with a pair of drovers' help,
the pick of his flocks to make the suitors' meal.
As soon as he saw them there he broke into a flood
of brutal, foul abuse that made Odysseus' blood boil.
"Look!"—he sneered—"one scum nosing another
scum along,
dirt finds dirt by the will of god—it never fails!
Wretched pig-boy, where do you take your filthy swine,
this sickening beggar who licks the pots at feasts?
Hanging round the doorposts, rubbing his back,
scavenging after scraps,
no hero's swords and cauldrons, not for *him*.
Hand him over to me—I'll teach him to work a farm,
muck out my stalls, pitch feed to the young goats;
whey to drink will put some muscle on his hams!
Oh no, he's learned his lazy ways too well,
he's got no itch to stick to good hard work,
he'd rather go scrounging round the countryside,
begging for crusts to stuff his greedy gut!
Let me tell you—so help me it's the truth—
if he sets foot in King Odysseus' royal palace,

salvos of footstools flung at his head by all the lords
will crack his ribs as he runs the line of fire through the house!"

Wild, reckless taunts—and just as he passed Odysseus
the idiot lurched out with a heel and kicked his hip
but he couldn't knock the beggar off the path,
he stood his ground so staunchly. Odysseus was torn . . .
should he wheel with his staff and beat the scoundrel senseless?—
or hoist him by the midriff, split his skull on the rocks?
He steeled himself instead, his mind in full control.
But Eumaeus glared at the goatherd, cursed him to his face,
then lifted up his hands and prayed his heart out:
"O nymphs of the fountain, daughters of Zeus—
if Odysseus ever burned you the long thighs
of lambs or kids, covered with rich fat,
now bring my prayer to pass!
Let that man come back—some god guide him now!
He'd toss to the winds the flashy show you make,
Melanthius, so cocksure—always strutting round the town
while worthless fieldhands leave your flocks a shambles!"

"Listen to him!" the goatherd shouted back.
"All bark and no bite from the vicious mutt!
One fine day I'll ship him out in a black lugger,
miles from Ithaca—sell him off for a good stiff price!
Just let Apollo shoot Telemachus down with his silver bow,
today in the halls, or the suitors snuff his life out—
as sure as I know the day of the king's return
is blotted out, the king is worlds away!"

With his parting shot he left them trudging on
and went and reached the royal house in no time.
Slipping in, he took his seat among the suitors,
facing Eurymachus, who favored him the most.
The carvers set before him his plate of meat,
a staid housekeeper brought the man his bread.

And now at last the king and loyal swineherd,
drawing near the palace, halted just outside
as the lyre's rippling music drifted round them—
Phemius, striking up a song for assembled guests—
and the master seized his servant's hand, exclaiming,
"Friend, what a noble house! Odysseus' house, it must be!
No mistaking it—you could tell it among a townful, look.
One building linked to the next, and the courtyard wall
is finished off with a fine coping, the double doors
are battle-proof—no man could break them down!
I can tell a crowd is feasting there in force—
smell the savor of roasts . . . the ringing lyre, listen,
the lyre that god has made the friend of feasts."

"An easy guess," you said, Eumaeus, swineherd,
"for a man as keen as you at every turn.
Put heads together. What do we do next?
Either you're the first one into the palace—
mix with the suitors, leave me where I am.
Or if you like, stay put, and I'll go first myself.
Don't linger long. Someone might spot you here outside,
knock you down or pelt you. Mark my words. Take care."

The man who'd borne long years abroad replied,
"Well I know. Remember? There's sense in this old head.
You go in, you first, while I stay here behind.
Stones and blows and I are hardly strangers.
My heart is steeled by now,
I've had my share of pain in the waves and wars.
Add this to the total. Bring the trial on.
But there's no way to hide the belly's hungers—
what a curse, what mischief it brews in all our lives!
Just for hunger we rig and ride our long benched ships
on the barren salt sea, speeding death to enemies."

Now, as they talked on, a dog that lay there
lifted up his muzzle, pricked his ears . . .
It was Argos, long-enduring Odysseus' dog
he trained as a puppy once, but little joy he got
since all too soon he shipped to sacred Troy.
In the old days young hunters loved to set him
coursing after the wild goats and deer and hares.
But now with his master gone he lay there, castaway,
on piles of dung from mules and cattle, heaps collecting
out before the gates till Odysseus' serving-men
could cart it off to manure the king's estates.
Infested with ticks, half-dead from neglect,
here lay the hound, old Argos.
But the moment he sensed Odysseus standing by
he thumped his tail, nuzzling low, and his ears dropped,
though he had no strength to drag himself an inch
toward his master. Odysseus glanced to the side
and flicked away a tear, hiding it from Eumaeus,
diverting his friend in a hasty, offhand way:
"Strange, Eumaeus, look, a dog like this,
lying here on a dung-hill . . .
what handsome lines! But I can't say for sure
if he had the running speed to match his looks
or he was only the sort that gentry spoil at table,
show-dogs masters pamper for their points."

You told the stranger, Eumaeus, loyal swineherd,
"Here—it's all too true—here's the dog of a man
who died in foreign parts. But if he had now
the form and flair he had in his glory days—

as Odysseus left him, sailing off to Troy—
you'd be amazed to see such speed, such strength.
No quarry he chased in the deepest, darkest woods
could ever slip this hound. A champion tracker too!
Ah, but he's run out of luck now, poor fellow . . .
his master's dead and gone, so far from home,
and the heartless women tend him not at all. Slaves,
with their lords no longer there to crack the whip,
lose all zest to perform their duties well. Zeus,
the Old Thunderer, robs a man of half his virtue
the day the yoke clamps down around his neck."

With that he entered the well-constructed palace,
strode through the halls and joined the proud suitors.
But the dark shadow of death closed down on Argos' eyes
the instant he saw Odysseus, twenty years away.

Now Prince Telemachus, first by far to note
the swineherd coming down the hall, nodded briskly,
called and waved him on. Eumaeus, glancing about,
picked up a handy stool where the carver always sat,
slicing meat for the suitors feasting through the house.
He took and put it beside the prince's table, facing him,
straddled it himself as a steward set a plate of meat
before the man and served him bread from trays.

Right behind him came Odysseus, into his own house,
looking for all the world like an old and broken beggar
hunched on a stick, his body wrapped in shameful rags.
Just in the doorway, just at the ashwood threshold,
there he settled down . . .
leaning against the cypress post a master joiner
planed smooth and hung with a plumb line years ago.
Telemachus motioned the swineherd over now,
and choosing a whole loaf from a fine wicker tray
and as much meat as his outstretched hands could hold,
he said, "Now take these to the stranger, tell him too
to make the rounds of the suitors, beg from one and all.
Bashfulness, for a man in need, is no great friend."

And Eumaeus did his bidding, went straight up
to the guest and winged a greeting: "Here, stranger,
Prince Telemachus sends you these, and tells you too
to make the rounds of the suitors, beg from one and all.
Bashfulness for a beggar, he says, is no great friend."

"Powerful Zeus!" the crafty king responded,
"grant that your prince be blest among mankind—
and all his heart's desires come to pass!"

Taking the food in both hands, setting it down,
spread out on his filthy sack before his feet,

the beggar fell to his meal
as the singer raised a song throughout the house.
Once he'd supped and the stirring bard had closed,
the suitors broke into uproar down along the hall.
And now Athena came to the side of Laertes' royal son
and urged him, "Go now, gather crusts from all the suitors,
test them, so we can tell the innocent from the guilty."
But not even so would Athena save one man from death.
Still, off he went, begging from each in turn,
circling left to right, reaching out his hand
like a beggar from the day that he was born.
They pitied him, gave him scraps, were puzzled too,
asking each other, "Who is this?" "Where's he from?"
Till the goatherd Melanthius shouted out in their midst,
"Listen to me, you lords who court our noble queen—
I'll tell you about the stranger. I've seen him before.
I know for a fact the swineherd led him in,
though I have no idea who the fellow is
or where he thinks he comes from."
At that
Antinous wheeled on Eumaeus, lashing out at him:
"Your highness, swineherd—why drag *this* to town?
Haven't we got our share of vagabonds to deal with,
disgusting beggars who lick the feasters' plates?
Isn't it quite enough, these swarming crowds
consuming your master's bounty—
must you invite this rascal in the bargain?"
"Antinous,
highborn as you are," you told the man, Eumaeus,
"that was a mean low speech!
Now who'd go out, who on his own hook—
not I—and ask a stranger in from nowhere
unless he had some skills to serve the house?
A prophet, a healer who cures disease, a worker in wood
or even a god-inspired bard whose singing warms the heart—
they're the ones asked in around the world. A beggar?
Who'd invite a beggar to bleed his household white?
You, you of all the suitors are always roughest
on the servants of our king, on me most of all.
Not that I care, no, so long as his queen,
his wise queen, is still alive in the palace,
Prince Telemachus too."
"Stop, Eumaeus,"
poised Telemachus broke in quickly now,
"don't waste so much breath on Antinous here.
It's just his habit to bait a man with abuse
and spur the rest as well."
He wheeled on the suitor,
letting loose: "How kind you are to me, Antinous,

kind as a father to his son! Encouraging me
to send this stranger packing from my house
with a harsh command! I'd never do it. God forbid.
Take and give to the beggar. I don't grudge it—
I'd even urge you on. No scruples now,
never fear your gifts will upset my mother
or any servant in King Odysseus' royal house.
But no such qualm could enter that head of yours,
bent on feeding your own face, not feeding strangers!"

Antinous countered the young prince in kind:
"So high and mighty, Telemachus—such unbridled rage!
If all the suitors gave him the sort of gift I'll give,
the house would be rid of *him* for three whole months!"
With that, from under his table he seized the stool
that propped his smooth feet as he reveled on—
just lifting it into view . . .
But as for the rest,
all gave to the beggar, filled his sack with handouts,
bread and meat. And Odysseus seemed at the point
of getting back to his doorsill,
done with testing suitors, home free himself
when he stopped beside Antinous, begging face-to-face:
"Give me a morsel, friend. You're hardly the worst
Achaean here, it seems. The noblest one, in fact.
You look like a king to me!
So you should give a bigger crust than the rest
and I will sing your praises all across the earth.
I too once lived in a lofty house that men admired;
rolling in wealth, I'd often give to a vagabond like myself,
whoever he was, whatever need had brought him to my door.
And crowds of servants I had, and lots of all it takes
to live the life of ease, to make men call you rich.
But Zeus ruined it all—god's will, no doubt—
when he shipped me off with a roving band of pirates
bound for Egypt, a long hard sail, to wreck my life.
There in the Nile delta I moored our ships of war.
God knows I ordered my trusty crews to stand by,
just where they were, and guard the anchored fleet
and I sent a patrol to scout things out from higher ground.
But swept away by their own reckless fury, the crew went berserk—
they promptly began to plunder the lush Egyptian farms,
dragged off the women and children, killed the men.
Outcries reached the city in no time—stirred by shouts
the entire town came streaming down at the break of day,
filling the river plain with chariots, ranks of infantry
and the gleam of bronze. Zeus who loves the lightning
flung down murderous panic on all my men-at-arms—
no one dared to stand his ground and fight,

disaster ringed us round from every quarter.
Droves of my men they hacked down with swords,
led off the rest alive, to labor for them as slaves.
Myself? They passed me on to a stranger come their way,
to ship me to Cyprus—Iasus' son Dmetor it was,
who ruled Cyprus then with an iron fist.
And from there I sailed to Ithaca,
just as you see me now, ground down by pain and sorrow—"

"Good god almighty!" Antinous cut the beggar short.
"What spirit brought this pest to plague our feast?
Back off! Into the open, clear of my table, or you,
you'll soon land in an Egypt, Cyprus, to break your heart!
What a brazen, shameless beggar! Scrounging food
from each man in turn, and look at their handouts,
reckless, never a qualm, no holding back, not
when making free with the next man's goods—
each one's got plenty here."
                                        "Pity, pity,"
the wry Odysseus countered, drawing away.
"No sense in your head to match your handsome looks.
You'd grudge your servant a pinch of salt from your own larder,
you who lounge at the next man's board but lack the heart
to tear a crust of bread and hand it on to me,
though there's god's plenty here."
                                        Boiling over
Antinous gave him a scathing look and let fly,
"*Now* you won't get out of the hall unscarred, I swear,
not after such a filthy string of insults!"
                                                  With that
he seized the stool and hurled it—
                                        Square in the back
it struck Odysseus, just under the right shoulder
but he stood up against it—steady as a rock,
unstaggered by Antinous' blow—just shook his head,
silent, his mind churning with thoughts of bloody work.
Back he went to the doorsill, crouched, and setting down
his sack about to burst, he faced the suitors, saying,
"Hear me out, you lords who court the noble queen,
I must say what the heart inside me urges.
There's nothing to groan about, no hurt, when a man
takes a blow as he fights to save his own possessions,
cattle or shining flocks. But Antinous struck me
all because of my good-for-nothing belly—that,
that curse that makes such pain for us poor men.
But if beggars have their gods and Furies too,
let Antinous meet his death before he meets his bride!"

"Enough, stranger!" Antinous volleyed back.
"Sit there and eat in peace—or go get lost! Or else,

for the way you talk, these young men will hale you
up and down the halls by your hands or feet
until you're skinned alive!"
Naked threats—
but the rest were outraged, even those brash suitors.
One would say to another, "Look, Antinous,
that was a crime, to strike the luckless beggar!"

"Your fate is sealed if he's some god from the blue."

"And the gods do take on the look of strangers
dropping in from abroad—"
"Disguised in every way
as they roam and haunt our cities, watching over us—"

"All our foul play, all our fair play too!"

So they warned, but Antinous paid no heed.
And the anguish welled up in Telemachus' breast
for the blow his father took, yet he let no tears
go rolling down his face—he just shook his head,
silent, his mind churning with thoughts of bloody work.

But then, when cautious Queen Penelope heard
how Antinous struck the stranger, there in the halls,
she cried out, with her serving-women round her,
"May Apollo the Archer strike you just as hard!"
And her housekeeper Eurynome added quickly,
"If only our prayers were granted—
then not one of the lot would live to see
Dawn climb her throne tomorrow!"
"Dear old woman,"
alert Penelope replied, "they're all hateful,
plotting their vicious plots. But Antinous
is the worst of all—he's black death itself.
Here's this luckless stranger, wandering down
the halls and begging scraps—hard-pressed by need—
and the rest all give the man his fill of food
but that one gives him a footstool
hurled at his right shoulder, hits his back!"

While she exclaimed among her household women,
sitting there in her room, Odysseus bent to supper.
Penelope called the swineherd in and gave instructions:
"Go, good Eumaeus, tell the stranger to come at once.
I'd like to give him a warm welcome, ask the man
if he's heard some news about my gallant husband
or seen him in the flesh . . .
He seems like one who's roved around the world."

"My queen," you answered, Eumaeus, loyal swineherd,
"if only the lords would hold their peace a moment!

Such stories he tells—he'd charm you to your depths.
Three nights, three days I kept him in my shelter;
I was the first the fellow stumbled onto,
fleeing from some ship. But not even so
could he bring his tale of troubles to an end.
You know how you can stare at a bard in wonder—
trained by the gods to sing and hold men spellbound—
how you can long to sit there, listening, all your life
when the man begins to sing. So he charmed my heart,
I tell you, huddling there beside me at my fire.
He and Odysseus' father go way back, he says,
sworn friends, and the stranger hails from Crete
where the stock of old King Minos still lives on,
and from Crete he made his way, racked by hardship,
tumbling on like a rolling stone until he turned up here.
He swears he's heard of Odysseus—just in reach,
in rich Thesprotian country—still alive,
laden with treasure, heading home at last!"
"Go,"
the cautious queen responded, "call him here
so he can tell me his own tale face-to-face.
Our friends can sit at the gates or down the halls
and play their games, debauched to their hearts' content.
Why not? Their own stores, their bread and seasoned wine,
lie intact at home; food for their serving-men alone.
But they, they infest our palace day and night,
they butcher our cattle, our sheep, our fat goats,
feasting themselves sick, swilling our glowing wine
as if there's no tomorrow—all of it, squandered.
No, there is no man like Odysseus in command
to drive this curse from the house. Dear god,
if only Odysseus came back home to native soil now,
he and his son would avenge the outrage of these men—like that!"

At her last words Telemachus shook with a lusty sneeze[1]
like a thunderclap resounding up and down the halls.
The queen was seized with laughter, calling out
to Eumaeus winged words: "Quickly, go!
Bring me this stranger now, face-to-face!
You hear how my son sealed all I said with a sneeze?
So let death come down with grim finality on these suitors—
one and all—not a single man escape his sudden doom!
And another thing. Mark my words, I tell you.
If I'm convinced that all he says is true,
I'll dress him in shirt and cloak, in handsome clothes."

Off the swineherd went, following her instructions,
made his way to the stranger's side and winged a word:

1. A sign from the gods.

"Old friend—our queen, wise Penelope, summons you,
the prince's mother! The spirit moves her now,
heartsick as she is,
to ask a question or two about her husband.
And if she's convinced that all you say is true,
she'll dress you in shirt and cloak. That's what you need,
that most of all now. Bread you can always beg
around the country, fill your belly well—
they'll give you food, whoever has a mind to."

"Gladly, Eumaeus," the patient man replied,
"I'll tell her the whole truth and nothing but,
Icarius' daughter, your wise queen Penelope.
I know all about that man . . .
it's been my lot to suffer what he's suffered.
But I fear the mob's abuse, those rough young bucks,
their pride and violence hit the iron skies!
Just now that scoundrel—as I went down the halls,
harming no one—up and dealt me a jolting blow,
and who would raise a hand to save me? Telemachus?
Anyone else? No one. So tell Penelope now,
anxious as she may be, to wait in the halls
until the sun goes down. Then she can ask me
all she likes about her husband's journey home.
But let her give me a seat close by the fire.
The clothes on my back are tatters. Well you know—
you are the first I begged for care and shelter."

Back the swineherd went, following his instructions.
Penelope, just as he crossed her threshold, broke out,
"Didn't you bring him? What's in the vagrant's mind?
Fear of someone? Embarrassed by something else,
here in the house? Is the fellow bashful?
A bashful man will make a sorry beggar."

You answered your queen, Eumaeus, loyal swineherd,
"He talks to the point—he thinks as the next man would
who wants to dodge their blows, that brutal crew.
He tells you to wait here till the sun goes down.
It's better for you, my queen. Then you can talk
with the man in private, hear the stranger's news."

"Nobody's fool, that stranger," wise Penelope said,
"he sees how things could go. Surely no men on earth
can match that gang for reckless, deadly schemes."

So she agreed, and now, mission accomplished,
back the loyal swineherd went to mix with the suitors.
Moving next to the prince, he whispered a parting word,
their heads close together so no one else could hear.
"Dear boy, I must be off, to see to the pigs
and the whole farm—your living, mine as well.

You're the one to tend to all things here.
Look out for your own skin first,
do take care, you mustn't come to grief.
Crowds of your own countrymen plot your death—
let Zeus wipe out the lot before they kill us all!"

"Right you are, old friend," the canny prince replied.
"Now off you go, once you've had your supper.
But come back bright and early,
bring some good sound boars for slaughter. Yes,
I'll tend to all things here, I and the deathless gods."

And the swineherd sat down again on his polished stool
and once he'd supped and drunk to his heart's content,
back he went to his pigs, leaving the royal precincts
still filled with feasters, all indulging now
in the joys of dance and song.
The day was over. Dusk was falling fast.

Book 18. The Beggar-King of Ithaca

Now along came this tramp, this public nuisance
who used to scrounge a living round the streets of Ithaca—
notorious for his belly, a ravenous, bottomless pit
for food and drink, but he had no pith, no brawn,
despite the looming hulk that met your eyes.
Arnaeus was his name,
so his worthy mother called him at birth,
but all the young men called him Irus for short
because he'd hustle messages at any beck and call.[1]
Well *he* came by to rout the king from his own house
and met Odysseus now with a rough, abusive burst:
"Get off the porch, you old goat, before I haul you
off by the leg! Can't you see them give me the wink,
all of them here, to drag you out—and so I would
but I've got some pangs of conscience. Up with you, man,
or before you know it, we'll be trading blows!"
A killing look,
and the wily old soldier countered, "Out of your mind?
What damage have I done *you?* What have I said?
I don't grudge you anything,
not if the next man up and gives you plenty.
This doorsill is big enough for the both of us—
you've got no call to grudge me what's not yours.
You're another vagrant, just like me, I'd say,
and it lies with the gods to make us rich or poor. So,
keep your fists to yourself, don't press your luck, don't rile me,
or old as I am, I'll bloody your lip, splatter your chest

1. His name resembles that of Iris, messenger of the gods.

and buy myself some peace and quiet for tomorrow.
I doubt you'll ever come lumbering back again
to the halls of Laertes' royal son Odysseus."

"Look who's talking!" the beggar rumbled in anger.
"How this pot-bellied pig runs off at the mouth—
like an old crone at her oven!
Well *I*'ve got a knock-out blow in store for *him*—
I'll batter the tramp with both fists, crack every tooth
from his jaws, I'll litter the ground with teeth
like a rogue sow's, punished for rooting corn!
Belt up—so the lords can see us fight it out.
How can you beat a champion half your age?"

Tongue-lashing each other, tempers flaring,
there on the polished sill before the lofty doors.
And Antinous, that grand prince, hearing them wrangle,
broke into gloating laughter, calling out to the suitors,
"Friends, nothing like this has come our way before—
what sport some god has brought the palace now!
The stranger and Irus, look,
they'd battle it out together, fists flying.
Come, let's pit them against each other—fast!"

All leapt from their seats with whoops of laughter,
clustering round the pair of ragged beggars there
as Eupithes' son Antinous planned the contest.
"Quiet, my fine friends. Here's what I propose.
These goat sausages sizzling here in the fire—
we packed them with fat and blood to have for supper.
Now, whoever wins this bout and proves the stronger,
let that man step up and take his pick of the lot!
What's more, from this day on he feasts among us—
no other beggar will we allow inside
to cadge his meals from us!"
They all cheered
but Odysseus, foxy veteran, plotted on . . .
"Friends, how can an old man, worn down with pain,
stand up to a young buck? It's just this belly of mine,
this trouble-maker, tempts me to take a licking.
So first, all of you swear me a binding oath:
come, not one of you steps in for Irus here,
strikes me a foul blow to pull him through
and lays me in the dust."
And at that
they all mouthed the oath that he required,
and once they vowed they'd never interfere,
Prince Telemachus drove the matter home:
"Stranger, if your spine and fighting pride
prompt you to go against this fellow now,

have no fear of any suitor in the pack—
whoever fouls you will have to face a crowd.
Count on *me,* your host. And two lords back me up,
Antinous and Eurymachus—both are men of sense."

They all shouted approval of the prince
as Odysseus belted up, roping his rags around his loins,
baring his big rippling thighs—his boxer's broad shoulders,
his massive chest and burly arms on full display
as Athena stood beside him,
fleshing out the limbs of the great commander . . .
Despite their swagger, the suitors were amazed,
gaping at one another, trading forecasts:
"Irus will soon be ironed out for good!"

"He's in for the beating he begged for all along."

"Look at the hams on that old-timer—"
"Just under his rags!"

Each outcry jolted Irus to the core—too late.
The servants trussed his clothes up, dragged him on,
the flesh on his body quaking now with terror.
Antinous rounded on him, flinging insults:
"You, you clumsy ox, you're better off dead
or never born at all, if you cringe at *him,*
paralyzed with fear of an old, broken hulk,
ground down by the pains that hound his steps.
Mark my word—so help me I'll make it good—
if that old relic whips you and wins the day,
I'll toss you into a black ship and sail you off
to Echetus, the mainland king who wrecks all men alive!
He'll lop your nose and ears with his ruthless blade,
he'll rip your privates out by the roots, he will,
and serve them up to his dogs to bolt down raw!"

That threat shook his knees with a stronger fit
but they hauled him into the ring. Both men put up their fists—
with the seasoned fighter Odysseus deeply torn now . . .
should he knock him senseless, leave him dead where he dropped
or just stretch him out on the ground with a light jab?
As he mulled things over, that way seemed the best:
a glancing blow, the suitors would not detect him.
The two men squared off—
and Irus hurled a fist
at Odysseus' right shoulder as *he* came through
with a hook below the ear, pounding Irus' neck,
smashing the bones inside—
suddenly red blood
came spurting out of his mouth, and headlong down
he pitched in the dust, howling, teeth locked in a grin,

feet beating the ground—
and the princely suitors,
flinging their hands in the air, died laughing.
Grabbing him by the leg, Odysseus hauled him
through the porch, across the yard to the outer gate,
heaped him against the courtyard wall, sitting slumped,
stuck his stick in his hand and gave him a parting shot:
"Now hold your post—play the scarecrow to all the pigs and dogs!
But no more lording it over strangers, no more playing
the beggar-king for you, you loathsome fool,
or you'll bring down something worse around your neck!"

He threw his beggar's sack across his shoulders—
torn and tattered, slung from a fraying rope—
then back he went to the sill and took his seat.
The suitors ambled back as well, laughing jauntily,
toasting the beggar warmly now, those proud young blades,
one man egging the other on: "Stranger, friend, may Zeus
and the other deathless gods fill up your sack with blessings!"

"All your heart desires!"
"You've knocked him out of action,
that insatiable tramp—"
"That parasite on the land!"

"Ship him off to Echetus, fast—the mainland king
who wrecks all men alive!"
Welcome words
and a lucky omen too—Odysseus' heart leapt up.
Antinous laid before him a generous goat sausage,
bubbling fat and blood. Amphinomus took two loaves
from the wicker tray and set them down beside him,
drank his health in a golden cup and said,
"Cheers, old friend, old father,
saddled now as you are with so much trouble—
here's to your luck, great days from this day on!"

And the one who knew the world replied at length,
"Amphinomus, you seem like a man of good sense to me.
Just like your father—at least I've heard his praises,
Nisus of Dulichion, a righteous man, and rich.
You're his son, they say, you seem well-spoken, too.
So I will tell you something. Listen. Listen closely.
Of all that breathes and crawls across the earth,
our mother earth breeds nothing feebler than a man.
So long as the gods grant him power, spring in his knees,
he thinks he will never suffer affliction down the years.
But then, when the happy gods bring on the long hard times,
bear them he must, against his will, and steel his heart.
Our lives, our mood and mind as we pass across the earth,
turn as the days turn . . .

as the father of men and gods makes each day dawn.
I too seemed destined to be a man of fortune once
and a wild wicked swath I cut, indulged my lust for violence,
staking all on my father and my brothers.
Look at me now.
And so, I say, let no man ever be lawless all his life,
just take in peace what gifts the gods will send.
True,
but here I see you suitors plotting your reckless work,
carving away at the wealth, affronting the loyal wife
of a man who won't be gone from kin and country long.
I say he's right at hand—and may some power save you,
spirit you home before you meet him face-to-face
the moment he returns to native ground!
Once under his own roof, he and your friends,
believe you me, won't part till blood has flowed."
With that
he poured out honeyed wine to the gods and drank deeply,
then restored the cup to the young prince's hands.
Amphinomus made his way back through the hall,
his heart sick with anguish, shaking his head,
fraught with grave forebodings . . .
but not even so could he escape his fate.
Even then Athena had bound him fast to death
at the hands of Prince Telemachus and his spear.
Now back he went to the seat that he'd left empty.

But now the goddess Athena with her glinting eyes
inspired Penelope, Icarius' daughter, wary, poised,
to display herself to her suitors, fan their hearts,
inflame them more, and make her even more esteemed
by her husband and her son than she had been before.
Forcing a laugh, she called her maid: "Eurynome,
my spirit longs—though it never did till now—
to appear before my suitors, loathe them as I do.
I'd say a word to my son too, for his own good,
not to mix so much with that pernicious crowd,
so glib with their friendly talk
but plotting wicked plots they'll hatch tomorrow."

"Well said, my child," the old woman answered,
"all to the point. Go to the boy and warn him now,
hold nothing back. But first you should bathe yourself,
give a gloss to your face. Don't go down like that—
your eyes dimmed, your cheeks streaked with tears.
It makes things worse, this grieving on and on.
Your son's now come of age—your fondest prayer
to the deathless gods, to see him wear a beard."

"Eurynome," discreet Penelope objected,
"don't try to coax me, care for me as you do,

to bathe myself, refresh my face with oils.
Whatever glow I had died long ago . . .
the gods of Olympus snuffed it out that day
my husband sailed away in the hollow ships.
But please, have Autonoë and Hippodameia come
and support me in the hall. I'll never brave
those men alone. I'd be too embarrassed."

Now as the old nurse bustled through the house
to give the women orders, call them to the queen,
the bright-eyed goddess thought of one more thing.
She drifted a sound slumber over Icarius' daughter,
back she sank and slept, her limbs fell limp and still,
reclining there on her couch, all the while Athena,
luminous goddess, lavished immortal gifts on her
to make her suitors lose themselves in wonder . . .
The divine unguent first. She cleansed her cheeks,
her brow and fine eyes with ambrosia smooth as the oils
the goddess Love applies, donning her crown of flowers
whenever she joins the Graces' captivating dances.
She made her taller, fuller in form to all men's eyes,
her skin whiter than ivory freshly carved, and now,
Athena's mission accomplished, off the bright one went
as bare-armed maids came in from their own quarters,
chattering all the way, and sleep released the queen.
She woke, touched her cheek with a hand, and mused,
"Ah, what a marvelous gentle sleep, enfolding me
in the midst of all my anguish! Now if only
blessed Artemis sent me a death as gentle, now,
this instant—no more wasting away my life,
my heart broken in longing for my husband . . .
He had every strength,
rising over his countrymen, head and shoulders."

Then, leaving her well-lit chamber, she descended,
not alone: two of her women followed close behind.
That radiant woman, once she reached her suitors,
drawing her glistening veil across her cheeks,
paused now where a column propped the sturdy roof,
with one of her loyal handmaids stationed either side.
The suitors' knees went slack, their hearts dissolved in lust—
all of them lifted prayers to lie beside her, share her bed.
But turning toward her son, she warned, "Telemachus,
your sense of balance is not what it used to be.
When you were a boy you had much better judgment.
Now that you've grown and reached your young prime
and any stranger, seeing how tall and handsome you are,
would think you the son of some great man of wealth—
now your sense of fairness seems to fail you.
Consider the dreadful thing just done in our halls—

how you let the stranger be so abused! Why,
suppose our guest, sitting here at peace,
here in our own house,
were hauled and badly hurt by such cruel treatment?
You'd be shamed, disgraced in all men's eyes!"

"Mother . . ." Telemachus paused, then answered.
"I cannot fault your anger at all this.
My heart takes note of everything, feels it, too,
both the good and the bad—the boy you knew is gone.
But how can I plan my world in a sane, thoughtful way?
These men drive me mad, hedging me round, right and left,
plotting their lethal plots, and no one takes my side.
Still, this battle between the stranger and Irus
hardly went as the suitors might have hoped:
the stranger beat him down!
If only—Father Zeus, Athena and lord Apollo—
these gallants, now, this moment, here in our house,
were battered senseless, heads lolling, knees unstrung,
some sprawled in the courtyard, some sprawled outside!
Slumped like Irus down at the front gates now,
whipped, and his head rolling like some drunk.
He can't stand up on his feet and stagger home,
whatever home he's got—the man's demolished."

So Penelope and her son exchanged their hopes
as Eurymachus stepped in to praise the queen.
"Ah, daughter of Icarius, wise Penelope,
if all the princes in Ionian Argos saw you now!
What a troop of suitors would banquet in your halls
tomorrow at sunrise! You surpass all women
in build and beauty, refined and steady mind."

"Oh no, Eurymachus," wise Penelope demurred,
"whatever form and feature I had, what praise I'd won,
the deathless gods destroyed that day the Achaeans
sailed away to Troy, my husband in their ships,
Odysseus—if *he* could return to tend my life
the renown I had would only grow in glory.
Now my life is torment . . .
look at the griefs some god has loosed against me!
I'll never forget the day he left this land of ours;
he caught my right hand by the wrist and said, gently,
'Dear woman, I doubt that every Achaean under arms
will make it home from Troy, all safe and sound.
The Trojans, they say, are fine soldiers too,
hurling javelins, shooting flights of arrows,
charioteers who can turn the tide—like that!—
when the great leveler, War, brings on some deadlock.
So I cannot tell if the gods will sail me home again

or I'll go down out there, on the fields of Troy,
but all things here must rest in your control.
Watch over my father and mother in the palace,
just as now, or perhaps a little more,
when I am far from home.
But once you see the beard on the boy's cheek,
you wed the man you like, and leave your house behind.'
So my husband advised me then. Now it all comes true . . .
a night will come when a hateful marriage falls my lot—
this cursed life of mine! Zeus has torn away my joy.
But there's something else that mortifies me now.
Your way is a far cry from the time-honored way
of suitors locked in rivalry, striving to win
some noble woman, a wealthy man's daughter.
They bring in their own calves and lambs
to feast the friends of the bride-to-be, yes,
and shower her with gleaming gifts as well.
They don't devour the woman's goods scot-free."

Staunch Odysseus glowed with joy to hear all this—
his wife's trickery luring gifts from her suitors now,
enchanting their hearts with suave seductive words
but all the while with something else in mind.
"Gifts?"
Eupithes' son Antinous took her point at once.
"Daughter of Icarius, sensible Penelope,
whatever gifts your suitors would like to bring,
accept them. How ungracious to turn those gifts away!
We won't go back to our own estates, or anywhere else,
till you have wed the man you find the best."

So he proposed, and all the rest agreed.
Each suitor sent a page to go and get a gift.
Antinous' man brought in a grand, resplendent robe,
stiff with embroidery, clasped with twelve gold brooches,
long pins that clipped into sheathing loops with ease.
Eurymachus' man brought in a necklace richly wrought,
gilded, strung with amber and glowing like the sun.
Eurydamas' two men came with a pair of earrings,
mulberry clusters dangling in triple drops
with a glint to catch the heart.
From the halls of lord Pisander, Polyctor's son,
a servant brought a choker, a fine, gleaming treasure.
And so each suitor in turn laid on a handsome gift.
Then the noble queen withdrew to her upper room,
her file of waiting ladies close behind her,
bearing the gorgeous presents in their arms.

Now the suitors turned to dance and song,
to the lovely beat and sway,

waiting for dusk to come upon them there . . .
and the dark night came upon them, lost in pleasure.
They rushed to set up three braziers along the walls
to give them light, piled them high with kindling,
sere, well-seasoned, just split with an ax,
and mixed in chips to keep the torches flaring.
The maids of Odysseus, steady man, took turns
to keep the fires up, but the king himself,
dear to the gods and cunning to the core,
gave them orders brusquely: "Maids of Odysseus,
your master gone so long—quick now, off you go
to the room where your queen and mistress waits.
Sit with her there and try to lift her spirits,
combing wool in your hands or spinning yarn.
But I will trim the torches for all her suitors,
even if they would like to revel on till Morning
mounts her throne. They'll never wear me down.
I have a name for lasting out the worst."
At that
the women burst into laughter, glancing back and forth.
Flushed with beauty, Melantho mocked him shamelessly—
Dolius was her father but Penelope brought her up;
she treated her like her own child and gave her toys
to cheer her heart. But despite that, her heart
felt nothing for all her mistress' anguish now.
She was Eurymachus' lover, always slept with him.
She was the one who mocked her king and taunted,
"Cock of the walk, did someone beat your brains out?
Why not go bed down at the blacksmith's cozy forge?
Or a public place where tramps collect? Why here—
blithering on, nonstop,
bold as brass in the face of all these lords?
No fear in your heart? Wine's got to your wits?—
or do you always play the fool and babble nonsense?
Lost your head, have you, because you drubbed that hobo Irus?
You wait—a better man than Irus will take you on,
he'll box both sides of your skull with heavy fists
and cart you from the palace gushing blood!"
"*You* wait,
you bitch"—the hardened veteran flashed a killing look.
"I'll go straight to the prince with your foul talk.
The prince will chop you to pieces here and now!"

His fury sent the women fluttering off, scattering
down the hall with panic shaking every limb—
they knew he spoke the truth.
But he took up his post by the flaring braziers,
tending the fires closely, looking after them all,
though the heart inside him stirred with other things,

ranging ahead, now, to all that must be done . . .

But Athena had no mind to let the brazen suitors
hold back now from their heart-rending insults—
she meant to make the anguish cut still deeper
into the core of Laertes' son Odysseus.
Polybus' son Eurymachus launched in first,
baiting the king to give his friends a laugh:
"Listen to me, you lords who court our noble queen!
I simply have to say what's on my mind. Look,
surely the gods have fetched this beggar here
to Odysseus' house. At least our torchlight *seems*
to come from the sheen of the man's own head—
there's not a hair on his bald pate, not a wisp!"

Then he wheeled on Odysseus, raider of cities:
"Stranger, how would you like to work for me
if I took you on—I'd give you decent wages—
picking the stones to lay a tight dry wall
or planting tall trees on the edge of my estate?
I'd give you rations to last you year-round,
clothes for your body, sandals for your feet.
Oh no, you've learned your lazy ways too well,
you've got no itch to stick to good hard work,
you'd rather go scrounging round the countryside,
begging for crusts to stuff your greedy gut!"

"Ah, Eurymachus," Odysseus, master of many exploits,
answered firmly, "if only the two of us *could* go
man-to-man in the labors of the field . . .
In the late spring, when the long days come round,
out in the meadow, I swinging a well-curved scythe
and you swinging yours—we'd test our strength for work,
fasting right till dusk with lots of hay to mow.
Or give us a team of oxen to drive, purebreds,
hulking, ruddy beasts, both lusty with fodder,
paired for age and pulling-power that never flags—
with four acres to work, the loam churning under the plow—
you'd see what a straight unbroken furrow I could cut you then.
Or if Zeus would bring some battle on—out of the blue,
this very day—and give me a shield and two spears
and a bronze helmet to fit this soldier's temples,
then you'd see me fight where front ranks clash—
no more mocking this belly of mine, not then.
Enough. You're sick with pride, you brutal fool.
No doubt you count yourself a great, powerful man
because you sport with a puny crowd, ill-bred to boot.
If only Odysseus came back home and stood right here,
in a flash you'd find those doors—broad as they are—
too cramped for your race to safety through the porch!"

That made Eurymachus' fury seethe and burst—
he gave the beggar a dark look and let fly, "You,
you odious—I'll make you pay for your ugly rant!
Bold as brass in the face of all these lords?
No fear in your heart? Wine's got to your wits?—
or do you always play the fool and babble nonsense?
Lost your head, have you, because you drubbed that hobo Irus?"

As he shouted out he seized a stool, but Odysseus,
fearing the blow, crouched at Amphinomus' knees
as Eurymachus hurled and hit the wine-steward,
clipping his right hand—
his cup dropped, clattered along the floor
and flat on his back he went, groaning in the dust.
The suitors broke into uproar through the shadowed halls,
glancing at one another, trading angry outcries:
"Would to god this drifter had dropped dead—"

"Anywhere else before he landed here!"

"Then he'd never have loosed such pandemonium."

"Now we're squabbling over *beggars!*"

"No more joy
in the sumptuous feast . . ."

"Now riot rules the day!"

But now Prince Telemachus dressed them down:
"Fools, you're out of your minds! No hiding it,
food and wine have gone to your heads. Some god
has got your blood up. Come, now you've eaten well
go home to bed—when the spirit moves, that is.
I, for one, I'll drive no guest away."

So he declared. And they all bit their lips,
amazed the prince could speak with so much daring.
At last Amphinomus rose to take the floor,
the noted son of Nisus, King Aretias' grandson.
"Fair enough, my friends; when a man speaks well
we have no grounds for wrangling, no cause for abuse.
Hands off the stranger! And any other servant
in King Odysseus' palace. Come, steward,
pour first drops for the god in every cup;
let's make libations, then go home to bed.
The stranger? Leave him here in Odysseus' halls
and have his host, Telemachus, tend him well—
it's the prince's royal house the man has reached."

So he said. His proposal pleased them all.
And gallant Mulius, a herald of Dulichion,
a friend-in-arms of lord Amphinomus too,
mixed the men a bowl and, hovering closely,

poured full rounds for all. They tipped cups
to the blissful gods and then, libations made,
they drank the heady wine to their hearts' content
and went their ways to bed, each suitor to his house.

Book 19. Penelope and Her Guest

That left the great Odysseus waiting in his hall
as Athena helped him plot the slaughter of the suitors.
He turned at once to Telemachus, brisk with orders:
"Now we must stow the weapons out of reach, my boy,
all the arms and armor—and when the suitors miss them
and ask you questions, put them off with a winning story:
'I stowed them away, clear of the smoke. A far cry
from the arms Odysseus left when he went to Troy,
fire-damaged equipment, black with reeking fumes.
And a god reminded me of something darker too.
When you're in your cups a quarrel might break out,
you'd wound each other, shame your feasting here
and cast a pall on your courting.
Iron has powers to draw a man to ruin.'"

Telemachus did his father's will at once,
calling out to his old nurse Eurycleia: "Quick,
dear one, close the women up in their own quarters,
till I can stow my father's weapons in the storeroom.
Splendid gear, lying about, neglected, black with soot
since father sailed away. I was only a boy then.
Now I must safeguard them from the smoke."

"High time, child," the loving nurse replied.
"If only you'd bother to tend your whole house
and safeguard *all* your treasures. Tell me,
who's to fetch and carry the torch for you?
You won't let out the maids who'd light your way."

"Our friend here will," Telemachus answered coolly.
"I won't put up with a man who shirks his work,
not if he takes his ration from my stores,
even if he's miles away from home."

That silenced the old nurse.
She barred the doors that led from the long hall—
and up they sprang, Odysseus and his princely son,
and began to carry off the helmets, studded shields
and pointed spears, and Pallas Athena strode before them,
lifting a golden lamp that cast a dazzling radiance round about.
"Father," Telemachus suddenly burst out to Odysseus,
"oh what a marvel fills my eyes! Look, look there—
all the sides of the hall, the handsome crossbeams,
pinewood rafters, the tall columns towering—

all glow in my eyes like flaming fire!
Surely a god is here—
one of those who rule the vaulting skies!"

"Quiet," his father, the old soldier, warned him.
"Get a grip on yourself. No more questions now.
It's just the way of the gods who rule Olympus.
Off you go to bed. I'll stay here behind
to test the women, test your mother too.
She in her grief will ask me everything I know."

Under the flaring torchlight, through the hall
Telemachus made his way to his own bedroom now,
where he always went when welcome sleep came on him.
There he lay tonight as well, till Dawn's first light.
That left the great king still waiting in his hall
as Athena helped him plot the slaughter of the suitors . . .

Now down from her chamber came reserved Penelope,
looking for all the world like Artemis or golden Aphrodite.
Close to the fire her women drew her favorite chair
with its whorls of silver and ivory, inlaid rings.
The craftsman who made it years ago, Icmalius,
added a footrest under the seat itself,
mortised into the frame,
and over it all was draped a heavy fleece.
Here Penelope took her place, discreet, observant.
The women, arms bared, pressing in from their quarters,
cleared away the tables, the heaped remains of the feast
and the cups from which the raucous lords had drunk.
Raking embers from the braziers onto the ground,
they piled them high again with seasoned wood,
providing light and warmth.
And yet again
Melantho lashed out at Odysseus: "You still here?—
you pest, slinking around the house all night,
leering up at the women?
Get out, you tramp—be glad of the food you got—
or we'll sling a torch at you, rout you out at once!"

A killing glance, and the old trooper countered,
"What's possessed you, woman? Why lay into me? Such abuse!
Just because I'm filthy, because I wear such rags,
roving round the country, living hand-to-mouth.
But it's fate that drives me on:
that's the lot of beggars, homeless drifters.
I too once lived in a lofty house that men admired;
rolling in wealth, I'd often give to a vagabond like myself,
whoever he was, whatever need had brought him to my door.
And crowds of servants I had, and lots of all it takes
to live the life of ease, to make men call you rich.

But Zeus ruined it all—god's will, no doubt.
So beware, woman, or one day you may lose it all,
all your glitter that puts your work-mates in the shade.
Or your mistress may just fly in a rage and dress you down
or Odysseus may return—there's still room for hope!
Or if he's dead as you think and never coming home,
well there's his son, Telemachus . . .
like father, like son—thanks to god Apollo.
No women's wildness here in the house escapes
the prince's eye. He's come of age at last."

So he warned, and alert Penelope heard him,
wheeled on the maid and tongue-lashed her smartly:
"Make no mistake, you brazen, shameless bitch,
none of your ugly work escapes me either—
you will pay for it with your life, you will!
How well you knew—you heard from my own lips—
that I meant to probe this stranger in our house
and ask about my husband . . . my heart breaks for him."

She turned to her housekeeper Eurynome and said,
"Now bring us a chair and spread it soft with fleece,
so our guest can sit and tell me his whole story
and hear me out as well.
I'd like to ask him questions, point by point."

Eurynome bustled off to fetch a polished chair
and set it down and spread it soft with fleece.
Here Odysseus sat, the man of many trials,
as cautious Penelope began the conversation:
"Stranger, let me start our questioning myself . . .
Who are you? where are you from? your city? your parents?"

"My good woman," Odysseus, master of craft, replied,
"no man on the face of the earth could find fault with *you*.
Your fame, believe me, has reached the vaulting skies.
Fame like a flawless king's who dreads the gods,
who governs a kingdom vast, proud and strong—
who upholds justice, true, and the black earth
bears wheat and barley, trees bow down with fruit
and the sheep drop lambs and never fail and the sea
teems with fish—thanks to his decent, upright rule,
and under his sovereign sway the people flourish.
So then, here in your house, ask me anything else
but don't, please, search out my birth, my land,
or you'll fill my heart to overflowing even more
as I bring back the past . . .
I am a man who's had his share of sorrows.
It's wrong for me, in someone else's house,
to sit here moaning and groaning, sobbing so—
it makes things worse, this grieving on and on.

One of your maids, or you yourself, might scold me,
think it's just the wine that had doused my wits
and made me drown in tears."

"No, no, stranger," wise Penelope demurred,
"whatever form and feature I had, what praise I'd won,
the deathless gods destroyed that day the Achaeans
sailed away to Troy, my husband in their ships,
Odysseus—if *he* could return to tend my life
the renown I had would only grow in glory.
Now my life is torment . . .
look at the griefs some god has loosed against me!
All the nobles who rule the islands round about,
Dulichion, Same, and wooded Zacynthus too,
and all who lord it in sunny Ithaca itself—
they court me against my will, they lay waste my house.
So I pay no heed to strangers, suppliants at my door,
not even heralds out on their public errands here—
I yearn for Odysseus, always, my heart pines away.
They rush the marriage on, and I spin out my wiles.
A god from the blue it was inspired me first
to set up a great loom in our royal halls
and I began to weave, and the weaving finespun,
the yarns endless, and I would lead them on: 'Young men,
my suitors, now that King Odysseus is no more,
go slowly, keen as you are to marry me, until
I can finish off this web . . .
so my weaving won't all fray and come to nothing.
This is a shroud for old lord Laertes, for that day
when the deadly fate that lays us out at last will take him down.
I dread the shame my countrywomen would heap upon me,
yes, if a man of such wealth should lie in state
without a shroud for cover.'

My very words,
and despite their pride and passion they believed me.
So by day I'd weave at my great and growing web—
by night, by the light of torches set beside me,
I would unravel all I'd done. Three whole years
I deceived them blind, seduced them with this scheme.
Then, when the wheeling seasons brought the fourth year on
and the months waned and the long days came round once more,
then, thanks to my maids—the shameless, reckless creatures—
the suitors caught me in the act, denounced me harshly.
So I finished it off. Against my will. They forced me.
And now I cannot escape a marriage, nor can I contrive
a deft way out. My parents urge me to tie the knot
and my son is galled as they squander his estate—
he sees it all. He's a grown man by now, equipped
to tend to his own royal house and tend it well:

Zeus grants my son that honor . . .
But for all that—now tell me who you are.
Where do you come from? You've hardly sprung
from a rock or oak like some old man of legend."

The master improviser answered, slowly,
"My lady . . . wife of Laertes' son, Odysseus,
will your questions about my family never end?
All right then. Here's my story. Even though
it plunges me into deeper grief than I feel now.
But that's the way of the world, when one has been
so far from home, so long away as I, roving over
many cities of men, enduring many hardships.
Still,
my story will tell you all you need to know.

There is a land called Crete . . .
ringed by the wine-dark sea with rolling whitecaps—
handsome country, fertile, thronged with people
well past counting—boasting ninety cities,
language mixing with language side-by-side.
First come the Achaeans, then the native Cretans,
hardy, gallant in action, then Cydonian clansmen,
Dorians living in three tribes, and proud Pelasgians last.
Central to all their cities is magnificent Cnossos,
the site where Minos ruled and each ninth year
conferred with almighty Zeus himself. Minos,
father of my father, Deucalion, that bold heart.
Besides myself Deucalion sired Prince Idomeneus,
who set sail for Troy in his beaked ships of war,
escorting Atreus' sons. My own name is Aethon.
I am the younger-born;
my older brother's a better man than I am.
Now, it was there in Cnossos that I saw him . . .
Odysseus—and we traded gifts of friendship.
A heavy gale had landed him on our coast,
driven him way off course, rounding Malea's cape
when he was bound for Troy. He anchored in Amnisus,
hard by the goddess' cave of childbirth and labor,
that rough harbor—barely riding out the storm.
He came into town at once, asking for Idomeneus,
claiming to be my brother's close, respected friend.
Too late. Ten or eleven days had already passed
since he set sail for Troy in his beaked ships.
So I took Odysseus back to my own house,
gave him a hero's welcome, treated him in style—
stores in our palace made for princely entertainment.
As for his comrades, all who'd shipped with him,
I dipped into public stock to give them barley,
ruddy wine and fine cattle for slaughter,

beef to their hearts' content. A dozen days
they stayed with me there, those brave Achaeans,
penned up by a North Wind so stiff that a man,
even on dry land, could never keep his feet—
some angry spirit raised that blast, I'd say.
Then on the thirteenth day the wind died down
and they set sail for Troy."
Falsehoods all,
but he gave his falsehoods all the ring of truth.
As she listened on, her tears flowed and soaked her cheeks
as the heavy snow melts down from the high mountain ridges,
snow the West Wind piles there and the warm East Wind thaws
and the snow, melting, swells the rivers to overflow their banks—
so she dissolved in tears, streaming down her lovely cheeks,
weeping for him, her husband, sitting there beside her.
Odysseus' heart went out to his grief-stricken wife
but under his lids his eyes remained stock-still—
they might have been horn or iron—
his guile fought back his tears. And she,
once she'd had her fill of grief and weeping,
turned again to her guest with this reply:
"Now, stranger, I think I'll test you, just to see
if there in your house, with all his friends-in-arms,
you actually entertained my husband as you say.
Come, tell me what sort of clothing he wore,
what cut of man was he?
What of the men who followed in his train?"
"Ah good woman,"
Odysseus, the great master of subtlety, returned,
"how hard it is to speak, after so much time
apart . . . why, some twenty years have passed
since he left my house and put my land behind him.
Even so, imagine the man as I portray him—
I can see him now.
King Odysseus . . .
he was wearing a heavy woolen cape, sea-purple
in double folds, with a golden brooch to clasp it,
twin sheaths for the pins, on the face a work of art:
a hound clenching a dappled fawn in its front paws,
slashing it as it writhed. All marveled to see it,
solid gold as it was, the hound slashing, throttling
the fawn in its death-throes, hoofs flailing to break free.
I noticed his glossy tunic too, clinging to his skin
like the thin glistening skin of a dried onion,
silky, soft, the glint of the sun itself.
Women galore would gaze on it with relish.
And this too. Bear it in mind, won't you?
I've no idea if Odysseus wore these things at home
or a comrade gave him them as he boarded ship,

or a host perhaps—the man was loved by many.
There were few Achaeans to equal him . . . and I?
I gave him a bronze sword myself, a lined cloak,
elegant, deep red, and a fringed shirt as well,
and I saw him off in his long benched ship of war
in lordly style.
Something else. He kept a herald
beside him, a man a little older than himself.
I'll try to describe him to you, best I can.
Round-shouldered he was, swarthy, curly-haired.
His name? Eurybates. And Odysseus prized him
most of all his men. Their minds worked as one."

His words renewed her deep desire to weep,
recognizing the strong clear signs Odysseus offered.
But as soon as she'd had her fill of tears and grief,
Penelope turned again to her guest and said,
"Now, stranger, much as I pitied you before,
now in my house you'll be my special friend,
my honored guest. I am the one, myself,
who gave him the very clothes that you describe.
I brought them up from the storeroom, folded them neatly,
fastened the golden brooch to adorn my husband,
Odysseus—never again will I embrace him,
striding home to his own native land.
A black day it was
when he took ship to see that cursed city . . .
Destroy, I call it—I hate to say its name!"

"Ah my queen," the man of craft assured her,
"noble wife of Laertes' son, Odysseus,
ravage no more your lovely face with tears
or consume your heart with grieving for your husband.
Not that I'd blame you, ever. Any woman will mourn
the bridegroom she has lost, lain with in love
and borne his children too. Even though he
was no Odysseus—a man like a god, they say.
But dry your tears and take my words to heart.
I will tell you the whole truth and hide nothing:
I have heard that Odysseus now, at last, is on his way,
he's just in reach, in rich Thesprotian country—
the man is still alive
and he's bringing home a royal hoard of treasure,
gifts he won from the people of those parts.
His crew? He's lost his crew and hollow ship
on the wine-dark waters off Thrinacia Island.
Zeus and Helios raged, dead set against Odysseus
for his men-at-arms had killed the cattle of the Sun,
so down to the last hand they drowned in crashing seas.

But not Odysseus, clinging tight to his ship's keel—
the breakers flung him out onto dry land, on Scheria,
the land of Phaeacians, close kin to the gods themselves,
and with all their hearts they prized him like a god,
showered the man with gifts, and they'd have gladly
sailed him home unscathed. In fact Odysseus
would have been here beside you long ago
but he thought it the better, shrewder course
to recoup his fortunes roving through the world.
At sly profit-turning there's not a man alive
to touch Odysseus. He's got no rival there.
So I learned from Phidon, king of Thesprotia,
who swore to me as he poured libations in his house,
'The ship's hauled down and the shipmates set to sail,
to take Odysseus home to native land.'
But I . . .
he shipped me off before. A Thesprotian cutter
chanced to be heading for Dulichion rich in wheat.
But he showed me all the treasure Odysseus had amassed,
enough to last a man and ten generations of his heirs—
so great the wealth stored up for *him* in the king's vaults!
But Odysseus, he made clear, was off at Dodona then
to hear the will of Zeus that rustles forth
from the god's tall leafy oak: how should he return,
after all the years away, to his own beloved Ithaca,
openly or in secret?
And so the man is safe,
as you can see, and he's coming home, soon,
he's close, close at hand—
he won't be severed long from kin and country,
no, not now. I give you my solemn, binding oath.
I swear by Zeus, the first, the greatest god—
by Odysseus' hearth, where I have come for help:
all will come to pass, I swear, exactly as I say.
True, this very month—just as the old moon dies
and the new moon rises into life—Odysseus will return!"

"If only, my friend," reserved Penelope exclaimed,
"everything you say would come to pass!
You'd soon know my affection, know my gifts.
Any man you meet would call you blest.
But my heart can sense the way it all will go.
Odysseus, I tell you, is never coming back,
nor will you ever gain your passage home,
for we have no masters in our house like him
at welcoming in or sending off an honored guest.
Odysseus. There was a man, or was he all a dream?
But come, women, wash the stranger and make his bed,
with bedding, blankets and lustrous spreads to keep him warm

till Dawn comes up and takes her golden throne.
Then, tomorrow at daybreak, bathe him well
and rub him down with oil, so he can sit beside
Telemachus in the hall, enjoy his breakfast there.
And anyone who offends our guest beyond endurance—
he defeats himself; he's doomed to failure here,
no matter how raucously he raves and blusters on.
For how can you know, my friend, if I surpass
all women in thoughtfulness and shrewd good sense,
if I'd allow you to take your meals at hall
so weatherbeaten, clad in rags and tatters?
Our lives are much too brief . . .
If a man is cruel by nature, cruel in action,
the mortal world will call down curses on his head
while he is alive, and all will mock his memory after death.
But then if a man is kind by nature, kind in action,
his guests will carry his fame across the earth
and people all will praise him from the heart."

"Wait, my queen," the crafty man objected,
"noble wife of Laertes' son, Odysseus—
blankets and glossy spreads? They're not my style.
Not from the day I launched out in my long-oared ship
and the snowy peaks of Crete went fading far astern.
I'll lie as I've done through sleepless nights before.
Many a night I've spent on rugged beds afield,
waiting for Dawn to mount her lovely throne.
Nor do I pine for any footbaths either.
Of all the women who serve your household here,
not one will touch my feet. Unless, perhaps,
there is some old retainer, the soul of trust,
someone who's borne as much as I have borne . . .
I wouldn't mind if she would touch my feet."

"Dear friend,"
the discreet Penelope replied, "never has any man
so thoughtful—of all the guests in my palace
come from foreign parts—been as welcome as you . . .
so sensible, so apt, is every word you say.
I have just such an old woman, seasoned, wise,
who carefully tended my unlucky husband, reared him,
took him into her arms the day his mother bore him—
frail as the woman is, she'll wash your feet.
Up with you now, my good old Eurycleia,
come and wash your master's . . . equal in years.
Odysseus must have feet and hands like his by now—
hardship can age a person overnight."

At that name
the old retainer buried her face in both hands,
burst into warm tears and wailed out in grief,
"Oh my child, how helpless I am to help you now!

How Zeus despised you, more than all other men,
god-fearing man that you were . . .
Never did any mortal burn the Old Thunderer
such rich thighbones—offerings charred and choice—
never as many as *you* did, praying always to reach
a ripe old age and raise a son to glory. Now,
you alone he's robbed of your home-coming day!
Just so, the women must have mocked my king,
far away, when he'd stopped at some fine house—
just as all these bitches, stranger, mock you here.
And because you shrink from their taunts, their
wicked barbs,
you will not let them wash you. The work is mine—
Icarius' daughter, wise Penelope, bids me now
and I am all too glad. I will wash your feet,
both for my own dear queen and for yourself—
your sorrows wring my heart . . . and why?
Listen to me closely, mark my words.
Many a wayworn guest has landed here
but never, I swear, has one so struck my eyes—
your build, your voice, your feet—you're like Odysseus . . .
to the life!"
"Old woman," wily Odysseus countered,
"that's what they all say who've seen us both.
We bear a striking resemblance to each other,
as you have had the wit to say yourself."

The old woman took up a burnished basin
she used for washing feet and poured in bowls
of fresh cold water before she stirred in hot.
Odysseus, sitting full in the firelight, suddenly
swerved round to the dark, gripped by a quick misgiving—
soon as she touched him she might spot the scar!
The truth would all come out.
Bending closer
she started to bathe her master . . . then,
in a flash, she knew the scar—
that old wound
made years ago by a boar's white tusk when Odysseus
went to Parnassus, out to see Autolycus and his sons.
The man was his mother's noble father, one who excelled
the world at thievery, that and subtle, shifty oaths.
Hermes gave him the gift, overjoyed by the thighs
of lambs and kids he burned in the god's honor—
Hermes the ready partner in his crimes. Now,
Autolycus once visited Ithaca's fertile land,
to find his daughter's son had just been born.
Eurycleia set him down on the old man's knees
as he finished dinner, urging him, "Autolycus,
you must find a name for your daughter's darling son.

The baby comes as the answer to her prayers."
"You,
my daughter, and you, my son-in-law," Autolycus replied,
"give the boy the name I tell you now. Just as I
have come from afar, creating pain for many—
men and women across the good green earth—
so let his name be *Odysseus* . . .
the Son of Pain, a name he'll earn in full.[1]
And when he has come of age and pays his visit
to Parnassus—the great estate of his mother's line
where all my treasures lie—I will give him enough
to cheer his heart, then speed him home to you."
And so,
in time, Odysseus went to collect the splendid gifts.
Autolycus and the sons of Autolycus warmed him in
with eager handclasps, hearty words of welcome.
His mother's mother, Amphithea, hugged the boy
and kissed his face and kissed his shining eyes.
Autolycus told his well-bred sons to prepare
a princely feast. They followed orders gladly,
herded an ox inside at once, five years old,
skinned it and split the carcass into quarters,
deftly cut it in pieces, skewered these on spits,
roasted all to a turn and served the portions out.
So all day long till the sun went down they feasted,
consuming equal shares to their hearts' content.
Then when the sun had set and night came on
they turned to bed and took the gift of sleep.
As soon
as young Dawn with her rose-red fingers shone once more
they all moved out for the hunt, hounds in the lead,
Autolycus' sons and Prince Odysseus in their ranks.
Climbing Parnassus' ridges, thick with timber,
they quickly reached the mountain's windy folds
and just as the sun began to strike the plowlands,
rising out of the deep calm flow of the Ocean River,
the beaters came to a wooded glen, the hounds broke,
hot on a trail, and right behind the pack they came,
Autolycus' sons—Odysseus out in front now,
pressing the dogs, brandishing high his spear
with its long shadow waving. Then and there
a great boar lay in wait, in a thicket lair so dense
that the sodden gusty winds could never pierce it,
nor could the sun's sharp rays invade its depths
nor a downpour drench it through and through,
so dense, so dark, and piled with fallen leaves.
Here, as the hunters closed in for the kill,

1. The name suggests Greek words for rage and pain.

crowding the hounds, the tramp of men and dogs
came drumming round the boar—he crashed from his lair,
his razor back bristling, his eyes flashing fire
and charging up to the hunt he stopped, at bay—
and Odysseus rushed him first,
shaking his long spear in a sturdy hand,
wild to strike but the boar struck faster,
lunging in on the slant, a tusk thrusting up
over the boy's knee, gouging a deep strip of flesh
but it never hit the bone—
Odysseus thrust and struck,
stabbing the beast's right shoulder—
a glint of bronze—
the point ripped clean through and down in the dust he dropped,
grunting out his breath as his life winged away.
The sons of Autolycus, working over Odysseus,
skillfully binding up his open wound—
the gallant, godlike prince—
chanted an old spell that stanched the blood
and quickly bore him home to their father's palace.
There, in no time, Autolycus and the sons of Autolycus
healed him well and, showering him with splendid gifts,
sped Odysseus back to his native land, to Ithaca,
a young man filled with joy. His happy parents,
his father and noble mother, welcomed him home
and asked him of all his exploits, blow-by-blow:
how did he get that wound? He told his tale with style,
how the white tusk of a wild boar had gashed his leg,
hunting on Parnassus with Autolycus and his sons . . .
That scar—
as the old nurse cradled his leg and her hands passed down
she felt it, knew it, suddenly let his foot fall—
down it dropped in the basin—the bronze clanged,
tipping over, spilling water across the floor.
Joy and torment gripped her heart at once,
tears rushed to her eyes—voice choked in her throat
she reached for Odysseus' chin and whispered quickly,
"Yes, yes! you are *Odysseus*—oh dear boy—
I couldn't know you before . . .
not till I touched the body of my king!"

She glanced at Penelope, keen to signal her
that here was her own dear husband, here and now,
but she could not catch the glance, she took no heed,
Athena turned her attention elsewhere. But Odysseus—
his right hand shot out, clutching the nurse's throat,
with his left he hugged her to himself and muttered,
"Nurse, you want to kill me? You suckled me yourself
at your own breast—and now I'm home, at last,

after bearing twenty years of brutal hardship,
home, on native ground. But now you know,
now that a god has flashed it in your mind,
quiet! not a word to anyone in the house.
Or else, I warn you—and I mean business too—
if a god beats down these brazen suitors at my hands,
I will not spare you—my old nurse that you are—
when I kill the other women in my house."

"Child," shrewd old Eurycleia protested,
"what nonsense you let slip through your teeth!
You know *me*—I'm stubborn, never give an inch—
I'll keep still as solid rock or iron.
One more thing. Take it to heart, I tell you.
If a god beats down these brazen suitors at your hands,
I'll report in full on the women in your house:
who are disloyal to you, who are guiltless."

"Nurse," the cool tactician Odysseus said,
"why bother to count them off? A waste of breath.
I'll observe them, judge each one myself.
Just be quiet. Keep your tales to yourself.
Leave the rest to the gods."
Hushed so,
the old nurse went padding along the halls
to fetch more water—her basin had all spilled—
and once she'd bathed and rubbed him down with oil,
Odysseus drew his chair up near the fire again,
trying to keep warm,
but he hid his scar beneath his beggar's rags
as cautious Penelope resumed their conversation:
"My friend, I have only one more question for you,
something slight, now the hour draws on for welcome sleep—
for those who can yield to sweet repose, that is,
heartsick as they are. As for myself, though,
some god has sent me pain that knows no bounds.
All day long I indulge myself in sighs and tears
as I see to my tasks, direct the household women.
When night falls and the world lies lost in sleep,
I take to my bed, my heart throbbing, about to break,
anxieties swarming, piercing—I may go mad with grief.
Like Pandareus' daughter, the nightingale in the green woods
lifting her lovely song at the first warm rush of spring,
perched in the treetops' rustling leaves and pouring forth
her music shifting, trilling and sinking, rippling high to burst
in grief for Itylus, her beloved boy, King Zethus' son
whom she in innocence once cut down with bronze [2]. . .
so my wavering heart goes shuttling, back and forth:

2. Aedon accidentally killed her own son and prayed to be changed into a nightingale.

Do I stay beside my son and keep all things secure—
my lands, my serving-women, the grand high-roofed house—
true to my husband's bed, the people's voice as well?
Or do I follow, at last, the best man who courts me
here in the halls, who gives the greatest gifts?
My son—when he was a boy and lighthearted—
urged me not to marry and leave my husband's house.
But now he has grown and reached his young prime,
he begs me to leave our palace, travel home.
Telemachus, so obsessed with his own estate,
the wealth my princely suitors bleed away.
But please,
read this dream for me, won't you? Listen closely . . .
I keep twenty geese in the house, from the water trough
they come and peck their wheat—I love to watch them all.
But down from a mountain swooped this great hook-beaked eagle,
yes, and he snapped their necks and killed them one and all
and they lay in heaps throughout the halls while he,
back to the clear blue sky he soared at once.
But I wept and wailed—only a dream, of course—
and our well-groomed ladies came and clustered round me,
sobbing, stricken: the eagle killed my geese. But down
he swooped again and settling onto a jutting rafter
called out in a human voice that dried my tears,
'Courage, daughter of famous King Icarius!
This is no dream but a happy waking vision,
real as day, that will come true for you.
The geese were your suitors—I was once the eagle
but now I am your husband, back again at last,
about to launch a terrible fate against them all!'
So he vowed, and the soothing sleep released me.
I peered around and saw my geese in the house,
pecking at their wheat, at the same trough
where they always took their meal."
"Dear woman,"
quick Odysseus answered, "twist it however you like,
your dream can only mean one thing. Odysseus
told you himself—he'll make it come to pass.
Destruction is clear for each and every suitor;
not a soul escapes his death and doom."

"Ah my friend," seasoned Penelope dissented,
"dreams are hard to unravel, wayward, drifting things—
not all we glimpse in them will come to pass . . .
Two gates there are for our evanescent dreams,
one is made of ivory, the other made of horn.
Those that pass through the ivory cleanly carved
are will-o'-the-wisps, their message bears no fruit.
The dreams that pass through the gates of polished horn

are fraught with truth, for the dreamer who can see them.
But I can't believe my strange dream has come that way,
much as my son and I would love to have it so.
One more thing I'll tell you—weigh it well.
The day that dawns today, this cursed day,
will cut me off from Odysseus' house. Now,
I mean to announce a contest with those axes,
the ones he would often line up here inside the hall,
twelve in a straight unbroken row like blocks to
shore a keel,
then stand well back and whip an arrow through the lot.
Now I will bring them on as a trial for my suitors.
The hand that can string the bow with greatest ease,
that shoots an arrow clean through all twelve axes—
he's the man I follow, yes, forsaking this house
where I was once a bride, this gracious house
so filled with the best that life can offer—
I shall always remember it, that I know . . .
even in my dreams."
"Oh my queen,"
Odysseus, man of exploits, urged her on,
"royal wife of Laertes' son, Odysseus, now,
don't put off this test in the halls a moment.
Before that crew can handle the polished bow,
string it taut and shoot through all those axes—
Odysseus, man of exploits, will be home with you!"

"If only, my friend," the wise Penelope replied,
"you were willing to sit beside me in the house,
indulging me in the comfort of your presence,
sleep would never drift across my eyes.
But one can't go without one's sleep forever.
The immortals give each thing its proper place
in our mortal lives throughout the good green
earth.
So now I'm going back to my room upstairs
and lie down on my bed,
that bed of pain my tears have streaked, year in,
year out, from the day Odysseus sailed away to see . . .
Destroy, I call it—I hate to say its name!
There I'll rest, while you lie here in the hall,
spreading your blankets somewhere on the floor,
or the women will prepare a decent bed."
With that
the queen went up to her lofty well-lit room
and not alone: her women followed close behind.
Penelope, once they reached the upper story,
fell to weeping for Odysseus, her beloved husband,
till watchful Athena sealed her eyes with welcome sleep.

Book 20. Portents Gather

Off in the entrance-hall the great king made his bed,
spreading out on the ground the raw hide of an ox,
heaping over it fleece from sheep the suitors
butchered day and night, then Eurynome threw
a blanket over him, once he'd nestled down.
And there Odysseus lay . . .
plotting within himself the suitors' death—
awake, alert, as the women slipped from the house,
the maids who whored in the suitors' beds each night,
tittering, linking arms and frisking as before.
The master's anger rose inside his chest,
torn in thought, debating, head and heart—
should he up and rush them, kill them one and all
or let them rut with their lovers one last time?
The heart inside him growled low with rage,
as a bitch mounting over her weak, defenseless puppies
growls, facing a stranger, bristling for a showdown—
so he growled from his depths, hackles rising at their
outrage.
But he struck his chest and curbed his fighting heart:
"Bear up, old heart! You've borne worse, far worse,
that day when the Cyclops, man-mountain, bolted
your hardy comrades down. But you held fast—
Nobody but your cunning pulled you through
the monster's cave you thought would be your death."

So he forced his spirit into submission,
the rage in his breast reined back—unswerving,
all endurance. But he himself kept tossing, turning,
intent as a cook before some white-hot blazing fire
who rolls his sizzling sausage back and forth,
packed with fat and blood—keen to broil it quickly,
tossing, turning it, this way, that way—so he cast about:
how could he get these shameless suitors in his clutches,
one man facing a mob? . . . when close to his side she came,
Athena sweeping down from the sky in a woman's build
and hovering at his head, the goddess spoke:
"Why still awake? The unluckiest man alive!
Here is your house, your wife at home, your son,
as fine a boy as one could hope to have."

"True,"

the wily fighter replied, "how right you are, goddess,
but still this worry haunts me, heart and soul—
how can I get these shameless suitors in my clutches?
Single-handed, braving an army always camped inside.
There's another worry, that haunts me even more.
What if I kill them—thanks to you and Zeus—

how do I run from under their avengers?
Show me the way, I ask you."
"Impossible man!"
Athena bantered, the goddess' eyes ablaze.
"Others are quick to trust a weaker comrade,
some poor mortal, far less cunning than I.
But I am a goddess, look, the very one who
guards you in all your trials to the last.
I tell you this straight out:
even if fifty bands of mortal fighters
closed around us, hot to kill us off in battle,
still you could drive away their herds and sleek flocks!
So, surrender to sleep at last. What a misery,
keeping watch through the night, wide awake—
you'll soon come up from under all your troubles."

With that she showered sleep across his eyes
and back to Olympus went the lustrous goddess.
As soon as sleep came on him, loosing his limbs,
slipping the toils of anguish from his mind,
his devoted wife awoke and,
sitting up in her soft bed, returned to tears.
When the queen had wept to her heart's content
she prayed to the Huntress, Artemis, first of all:
"Artemis—goddess, noble daughter of Zeus, if only
you'd whip an arrow through my breast and tear my life out,
now, at once! Or let some whirlwind pluck me up
and sweep me away along those murky paths and
fling me down where the Ocean River running
round the world rolls back upon itself!
Quick
as the whirlwinds swept away Pandareus' daughters—
years ago, when the gods destroyed their parents,
leaving the young girls orphans in their house.
But radiant Aphrodite nursed them well
on cheese and luscious honey and heady wine,
and Hera gave them beauty and sound good sense,
more than all other women—virgin Artemis made them tall
and Athena honed their skills to fashion lovely work.
But then, when Aphrodite approached Olympus' peaks
to ask for the girls their crowning day as brides
from Zeus who loves the lightning—Zeus who knows all,
all that's fated, all not fated, for mortal man—
then the storm spirits snatched them away
and passed them on to the hateful Furies,
yes, for all their loving care.
Just so
may the gods who rule Olympus blot me out!
Artemis with your glossy braids, come shoot me dead—
so I can plunge beneath this loathsome earth

with the image of Odysseus vivid in my mind.
Never let me warm the heart of a weaker man!
Even grief is bearable, true, when someone weeps
through the days, sobbing, heart convulsed with pain
yet embraced by sleep all night—sweet oblivion, sleep
dissolving all, the good and the bad, once it seals our eyes—
but even my dreams torment me, sent by wicked spirits.
Again—just this night—someone lay beside me . . .
like Odysseus to the life, when he embarked
with his men-at-arms. My heart raced with joy.
No dream, I thought, the waking truth at last!"
At those words
Dawn rose on her golden throne in a sudden gleam of light.
And great Odysseus caught the sound of his wife's cry
and began to daydream—deep in his heart it seemed
she stood beside him, knew him, now, at last . . .
Gathering up the fleece and blankets where he'd slept,
he laid them on a chair in the hall, he took the oxhide out
and spread it down, lifted his hands and prayed to Zeus:
"Father Zeus, if you really willed it so—to bring me
home over land and sea-lanes, home to native ground
after all the pain you brought me—show me a sign,
a good omen voiced by someone awake indoors,
another sign, outside, from Zeus himself!"

And Zeus in all his wisdom heard that prayer.
He thundered at once, out of his clear blue heavens
high above the clouds, and Odysseus' spirit lifted.
Then from within the halls a woman grinding grain
let fly a lucky word. Close at hand she was,
where the good commander set the handmills once
and now twelve women in all performed their tasks,
grinding the wheat and barley, marrow of men's bones.
The rest were abed by now—they'd milled their stint—
this one alone, the frailest of all, kept working on.
Stopping her mill, she spoke an omen for her master:
"Zeus, Father! King of gods and men, now *there*
was a crack of thunder out of the starry sky—
and not a cloud in sight!
Sure it's a sign you're showing someone now.
So, poor as I am, grant *me* my prayer as well:
let this day be the last, the last these suitors
bolt their groaning feasts in King Odysseus' house!
These brutes who break my knees—heart-wrenching labor,
grinding their grain—now let them eat their last!"

A lucky omen, linked with Zeus's thunder.
Odysseus' heart leapt up, the man convinced
he'd grind the scoundrels' lives out in revenge.
By now

the other maids were gathering in Odysseus' royal palace,
raking up on the hearth the fire still going strong.
Telemachus climbed from bed and dressed at once,
brisk as a young god—
over his shoulder he slung his well-honed sword,
he fastened rawhide sandals under his smooth feet,
he seized his tough spear tipped with a bronze point
and took his stand at the threshold, calling Eurycleia:
"Dear nurse, how did you treat the stranger in our house?
With bed and board? Or leave him to lie untended?
That would be mother's way—sensible as she is—
all impulse, doting over some worthless stranger,
turning a good man out to face the worst."

"Please, child," his calm old nurse replied,
"don't blame *her*—your mother's blameless this time.
He sat and drank his wine till he'd had his fill.
Food? He'd lost his hunger. But she asked him.
And when it was time to think of turning in,
she told the maids to spread a decent bed, but he—
so down-and-out, poor soul, so dogged by fate—
said no to snuggling into a bed, between covers.
No sir, the man lay down in the entrance-hall,
on the raw hide of an ox and sheep's fleece,
and we threw a blanket over him, so we did."

Hearing that,
Telemachus strode out through the palace, spear in hand,
and a pair of sleek hounds went trotting at his heels.
He made for the meeting grounds to join the island lords
while Eurycleia the daughter of Ops, Pisenor's son,
that best of women, gave the maids their orders:
"Quick now, look alive, sweep out the house,
wet down the floors!

You, those purple coverlets,
fling them over the fancy chairs!

All those tables,
sponge them down—scour the winebowls, burnished cups!
The rest—now off you go to the spring and fetch some water,
fast as your legs can run!
Our young gallants won't be long from the palace,
they'll be bright and early—today's a public feast."

They hung on her words and ran to do her bidding.
Full twenty scurried off to the spring's dark water,
others bent to the housework, all good hands.
Then in they trooped, the strutting serving-men,
who split the firewood cleanly now as the women
bustled in from the spring, the swineherd at their heels,
driving three fat porkers, the best of all his herds.

And leaving them to root in the broad courtyard,
up he went to Odysseus, hailed him warmly:
"Friend, do the suitors show you more respect
or treat you like the dregs of the earth as always?"

"Good Eumaeus," the crafty man replied,
"if only the gods would pay back their outrage!
Wild and reckless young cubs, conniving here
in another's house. They've got no sense of shame."

And now as the two confided in each other,
the goatherd Melanthius sauntered toward them,
herding his goats with a pair of drovers' help,
the pick of his flocks to make the suitors' meal.
Under the echoing porch he tethered these, then turned
on Odysseus once again with cutting insults: "Still alive?
Still hounding your betters, begging round the house?
Why don't you cart yourself away? Get out!
We'll never part, I swear,
till we taste each other's fists. Riffraff,
you and your begging make us sick! Get out—
we're hardly the only banquet on the island."

No reply. The wily one just shook his head,
silent, his mind churning with thoughts of bloody work . . .

Third to arrive was Philoetius, that good cowherd,
prodding in for the crowd a heifer and fat goats.
Boatmen had brought them over from the mainland,
crews who ferry across all travelers too,
whoever comes for passage.
Under the echoing porch he tethered all heads well
and then approached the swineherd, full of questions:
"Who's this stranger, Eumaeus, just come to the house?
What roots does the man claim—who are his people?
Where are his blood kin? his father's fields?
Poor beggar. But what a build—a royal king's!
Ah, once the gods weave trouble into our lives
they drive us across the earth, they drown us all in pain,
even kings of the realm."
And with that thought
he walked up to Odysseus, gave him his right hand
and winged a greeting: "Cheers, old friend, old father,
here's to your luck, great days from this day on—
saddled now as you are with so much trouble.
Father Zeus, no god's more deadly than you!
No mercy for men, you give them life yourself
then plunge them into misery, brutal hardship.
I broke into sweat, my friend, when I first saw you—
see, my eyes still brim with tears, remembering *him,*
Odysseus . . . He must wear such rags, I know it,

knocking about, drifting through the world
if he's still alive and sees the light of day.
If he's dead already, lost in the House of Death,
my heart aches for Odysseus, my great lord and master.
He set me in charge of his herds, in Cephallenian country,
when I was just a youngster. How they've grown by now,
past counting! No mortal on earth could breed
a finer stock of oxen—broad in the brow,
they thrive like ears of corn. But just look,
these interlopers tell me to drive them in
for their own private feasts. Not a thought
for the young prince in the house, they never flinch—
no regard for the gods' wrath—in their mad rush
to carve up his goods, my master gone so long!
I'm tossed from horn to horn in my own mind . . .
What a traitor I'd be, with the prince still alive,
if I'd run off to some other country, herds and all,
to a new set of strangers. Ah, but isn't it worse
to hold out here, tending the herds for upstarts,
not their owners—suffering all the pains of hell?
I could have fled, ages ago, to some great king
who'd give me shelter. It's unbearable here.
True, but I still dream of my old master,
unlucky man—if only *he*'d drop in from the blue
and drive these suitors all in a rout throughout the halls!"

"Cowherd," the cool tactician Odysseus answered,
"you're no coward, and nobody's fool, I'd say.
Even I can see there's sense in that old head.
So I tell you this on my solemn, binding oath:
I swear by Zeus, the first of all the gods—
by the table of hospitality waiting for us,
by Odysseus' hearth where I have come for help,
Odysseus will come home while you're still here.
You'll see with your own eyes, if you have the heart,
these suitors who lord it here cut down in blood."

"Stranger, if only," the cowherd cried aloud,
"if only Zeus would make that oath come true—
you'd see my power, my fighting arms in action!"

Eumaeus echoed his prayer to all the gods
that their wise king would soon come home again.

Now as they spoke and urged each other on,
and once more the suitors were plotting certain doom
for the young prince—suddenly, banking high on the left
an omen flew past, an eagle clutching a trembling dove.
And Amphinomus rose in haste to warn them all,
"My friends, we'll never carry off this plot
to kill the prince. Let's concentrate on feasting."

His timely invitation pleased them all.
The suitors ambled into Odysseus' royal house
and flinging down their cloaks on a chair or bench,
they butchered hulking sheep and fatted goats,
full-grown hogs and a young cow from the herd.
They roasted all the innards, served them round
and filled the bowls with wine and mixed it well.
Eumaeus passed out cups; Philoetius, trusty herdsman,
brought on loaves of bread in ample wicker trays;
Melanthius poured the wine. The whole company
reached out for the good things that lay at hand.

Telemachus, maneuvering shrewdly, sat his father down
on the stone threshold, just inside the timbered hall,
and set a rickety stool and cramped table there.
He gave him a share of innards, poured his wine
in a golden cup and added a bracing invitation:
"Now sit right there. Drink your wine with the crowd.
I'll defend you from all their taunts and blows,
these young bucks. This is no public place,
this is *Odysseus'* house—
my father won it for me, so it's mine.
You suitors, control yourselves. No insults now,
no brawling, no, or it's war between us all."

So he declared. And they all bit their lips,
amazed the prince could speak with so much daring.
Only Eupithes' son Antinous ventured,
"Fighting words, but do let's knuckle under—
to our *prince.* Such abuse, such naked threats!
But clearly Zeus has foiled us. Or long before
we would have shut his mouth for him in the halls,
fluent and flowing as he is."
So he mocked.
Telemachus paid no heed.
And now through the streets
the heralds passed, leading the beasts marked out
for sacrifice on Apollo's grand festal day,
and the islanders with their long hair were filing
into the god's shady grove—the distant deadly Archer.

Those in the palace, once they'd roasted the prime cuts,
pulled them off the spits and, sharing out the portions,
fell to the royal feast . . .
The men who served them gave Odysseus his share,
as fair as the helping they received themselves.
So Telemachus ordered, the king's own son.

But Athena had no mind to let the brazen suitors
hold back now from their heart-rending insults—
she meant to make the anguish cut still deeper

into the core of Laertes' son Odysseus.
There was one among them, a lawless boor—
Ctesippus was his name, he made his home in Same,
a fellow so impressed with his own astounding wealth
he courted the wife of Odysseus, gone for years.
Now the man harangued his swaggering comrades:
"Listen to me, my fine friends, here's what I say!
From the start our guest has had his fair share—
it's only right, you know.
How impolite it would be, how wrong to scant
whatever guest Telemachus welcomes to his house.
Look here, I'll give him a proper guest-gift too,
a prize he can hand the crone who bathes his feet
or a tip for another slave who haunts the halls
of our great king Odysseus!"
On that note,
grabbing an oxhoof out of a basket where it lay,
with a brawny hand he flung it straight at the king—
but Odysseus ducked his head a little, dodging the blow,
and seething just as the oxhoof hit the solid wall
he clenched his teeth in a wry sardonic grin.
Telemachus dressed Ctesippus down at once:
"Ctesippus, you can thank your lucky stars
you missed our guest—he ducked your blow, by god!
Else I would have planted my sharp spear in
your bowels—
your father would have been busy with your funeral,
not your wedding here. Enough.
Don't let me see more offenses in my house,
not from anyone! I'm alive to it all, now,
the good and the bad—the boy you knew is gone.
But I still must bear with this, this lovely sight . . .
sheepflocks butchered, wine swilled, food squandered—
how can a man fight off so many single-handed?
But no more of your crimes against me, please!
Unless you're bent on cutting me down, now,
and I'd rather die, yes, better that by far
than have to look on at your outrage day by day:
guests treated to blows, men dragging the serving-women
through our noble house, exploiting them all, no shame!"

Dead quiet. The suitors all fell silent, hushed.
At last Damastor's son Agelaus rose and said,
"Fair enough, my friends; when a man speaks well
we have no grounds for wrangling, no cause for abuse.
Hands off this stranger! Or any other servant
in King Odysseus' palace. But now a word
of friendly advice for Telemachus and his mother—
here's hoping it proves congenial to them both.
So long as your hearts still kept a spark alive

that Odysseus would return—that great, deep man—
who could blame you, playing the waiting game at home
and holding off the suitors? The better course, it's true.
What if Odysseus had returned, had made it home at last?
But now it's clear as day—the man will come no more.
So go, Telemachus, sit with your mother, coax her
to wed the best man here, the one who offers most,
so you can have and hold your father's estate,
eating and drinking here, your mind at peace
while mother plays the wife in another's house."

The young prince, keeping his poise, replied,
"I swear by Zeus, Agelaus, by all my father suffered—
dead, no doubt, or wandering far from Ithaca these days—
I don't delay my mother's marriage, not a moment,
I press her to wed the man who takes her heart.
I'll shower her myself with boundless gifts.
But I shrink from driving mother from our house,
issuing harsh commands against her will.
God forbid it ever comes to that!"
So he vowed
and Athena set off uncontrollable laughter in the suitors,
crazed them out of their minds—mad, hysterical laughter
seemed to break from the jaws of strangers, not their own,
and the meat they were eating oozed red with blood—
tears flooded their eyes, hearts possessed by grief.
The inspired seer Theoclymenus wailed out in their midst,
"Poor men, what terror is this that overwhelms you so?
Night shrouds your heads, your faces, down to your knees—
cries of mourning are bursting into fire—cheeks rivering tears—
the walls and the handsome crossbeams dripping dank with blood!
Ghosts, look, thronging the entrance, thronging the court,
go trooping down to the world of death and darkness!
The sun is blotted out of the sky—look there—
a lethal mist spreads all across the earth!"
At that
they all broke into peals of laughter aimed at the seer—
Polybus' son Eurymachus braying first and foremost,
"Our guest just in from abroad, the man is raving!
Quick, my boys, hustle him out of the house,
into the meeting grounds, the light of day—
everything *here* he thinks is dark as night!"

"Eurymachus," the inspired prophet countered,
"when I want your escort, I'll ask for it myself.
I have eyes and ears, and both my feet, still,
and a head that's fairly sound,
nothing to be ashamed of. These will do
to take me past those doors . . .
Oh I can see it now—

the disaster closing on you all! There's no escaping it,
no way out—not for a single one of you suitors,
wild reckless fools, plotting outrage here,
the halls of Odysseus, great and strong as a god!"

With that he marched out of the sturdy house
and went home to Piraeus, the host who warmed him in.
Now all the suitors, trading their snide glances, started
heckling Telemachus, made a mockery of his guests.
One or another brash young gallant scoffed,
"Telemachus, no one's more unlucky with his guests!"

"Look what your man dragged in—this mangy tramp
scraping for bread and wine!"
"Not fit for good hard work,
the bag of bones—"
"A useless dead weight on the land!"

"And then this charlatan up and apes the prophet."

"Take it from me—you'll be better off by far—
toss your friends in a slave-ship—"
"Pack them off
to Sicily, fast—they'll fetch you one sweet price!"

So they jeered, but the prince paid no attention . . .
silent, eyes riveted on his father, always waiting
the moment he'd lay hands on that outrageous mob.

And all the while Icarius' daughter, wise Penelope,
had placed her carved chair within earshot, at the door,
so she could catch each word they uttered in the hall.
Laughing rowdily, men prepared their noonday meal,
succulent, rich—they'd butchered quite a herd.
But as for supper, what could be less enticing
than what a goddess and a powerful man
would spread before them soon? A groaning feast—
for they'd been first to plot their vicious crimes.

Book 21. Odysseus Strings His Bow

The time had come. The goddess Athena with her blazing eyes
inspired Penelope, Icarius' daughter, wary, poised,
to set the bow and the gleaming iron axes out
before her suitors waiting in Odysseus' hall—
to test their skill and bring their slaughter on.
Up the steep stairs to her room she climbed
and grasped in a steady hand the curved key—
fine bronze, with ivory haft attached—
and then with her chamber-women made her way
to a hidden storeroom, far in the palace depths,
and there they lay, the royal master's treasures:

bronze, gold and a wealth of hard wrought iron
and there it lay as well . . . his backsprung bow
with its quiver bristling arrows, shafts of pain.
Gifts from the old days, from a friend he'd met
in Lacedaemon—Iphitus, Eurytus' gallant son.
Once in Messene the two struck up together,
in sly Ortilochus' house, that time Odysseus
went to collect a debt the whole realm owed him,
for Messenian raiders had lifted flocks from Ithaca,
three hundred head in their oarswept ships, the herdsmen too.
So his father and island elders sent Odysseus off,
a young boy on a mission,
a distant embassy made to right that wrong.
Iphitus went there hunting the stock that *he* had lost,
a dozen mares still nursing their hardy suckling mules.
The same mares that would prove his certain death
when he reached the son of Zeus, that iron heart,
Heracles—the past master of monstrous works—
who killed the man, a guest in his own house.
Brutal. Not a care for the wrathful eyes of god
or rites of hospitality he had spread before him,
no, he dined him, then he murdered him, commandeered
those hard-hoofed mares for the hero's own grange.
Still on the trail of these when he met Odysseus,
Iphitus gave him the bow his father, mighty Eurytus,
used to wield as a young man, but when he died
in his lofty house he left it to his son.
In turn, Odysseus gave his friend a sharp sword
and a rugged spear to mark the start of friendship,
treasured ties that bind. But before they got to know
the warmth of each other's board, the son of Zeus
had murdered Iphitus, Eurytus' magnificent son
who gave the prince the bow.
That great weapon—
King Odysseus never took it abroad with him
when he sailed off to war in his long black ships.
He kept it stored away in his stately house,
guarding the memory of a cherished friend,
and only took that bow on hunts at home.
Now,
the lustrous queen soon reached the hidden vault
and stopped at the oaken doorsill, work an expert
sanded smooth and trued to the line some years ago,
planting the doorjambs snugly, hanging shining doors.
At once she loosed the thong from around its hook,
inserted the key and aiming straight and true,
shot back the bolts—and the rasping doors groaned
as loud as a bull will bellow, champing grass at pasture.
So as the key went home those handsome double doors

rang out now and sprang wide before her.
She stepped onto a plank where chests stood tall,
brimming with clothing scented sweet with cedar.
Reaching, tiptoe, lifting the bow down off its peg,
still secure in the burnished case that held it,
down she sank, laying the case across her knees,
and dissolved in tears with a high thin wail
as she drew her husband's weapon from its sheath . . .
Then, having wept and sobbed to her heart's content,
off she went to the hall to meet her proud admirers,
cradling her husband's backsprung bow in her arms,
its quiver bristling arrows, shafts of pain.
Her women followed, bringing a chest that held
the bronze and the iron axes, trophies won by the master.
That radiant woman, once she reached her suitors,
drawing her glistening veil across her cheeks,
paused now where a column propped the sturdy roof,
with one of her loyal handmaids stationed either side,
and delivered an ultimatum to her suitors:
"Listen to me, my overbearing friends!
You who plague this palace night and day,
drinking, eating us out of house and home
with the lord and master absent, gone so long—
the only excuse that you can offer is your zest
to win me as your bride. So, to arms, my gallants!
Here is the prize at issue, right before you, look—
I set before you the great bow of King Odysseus now!
The hand that can string this bow with greatest ease,
that shoots an arrow clean through all twelve axes—
he is the man I follow, yes, forsaking this house
where I was once a bride, this gracious house
so filled with the best that life can offer—
I shall always remember it, that I know . . .
even in my dreams."
She turned to Eumaeus,
ordered the good swineherd now to set the bow
and the gleaming iron axes out before the suitors.
He broke into tears as he received them, laid them down.
The cowherd wept too, when he saw his master's bow.
But Antinous wheeled on both and let them have it:
"Yokels, fools—you can't tell night from day!
You mawkish idiots, why are you sniveling here?
You're stirring up your mistress! Isn't she drowned
in grief already? She's lost her darling husband.
Sit down. Eat in peace, or take your snuffling
out of doors! But leave that bow right here—
our crucial test that makes or breaks us all.
No easy game, I wager, to string *his* polished bow.
Not a soul in the crowd can match Odysseus—

what a man he was . . .
I saw him once, remember him to this day,
though I was young and foolish way back then."
Smooth talk,
but deep in the suitor's heart his hopes were bent
on stringing the bow and shooting through the axes.
Antinous—fated to be the first man to taste
an arrow whipped from great Odysseus' hands,
the king he mocked, at ease in the king's house,
egging comrades on to mock him too.
"Amazing!"
Prince Telemachus waded in with a laugh:
"Zeus up there has robbed me of my wits.
My own dear mother, sensible as she is,
says she'll marry again, forsake our house,
and look at *me*—laughing for all I'm worth,
giggling like some fool. Step up, my friends!
Here is the prize at issue, right before you, look—
a woman who has no equal now in all Achaean country,
neither in holy Pylos, nor in Argos or Mycenae,
not even Ithaca itself or the loamy mainland.
You know it well. Why sing my mother's praises?
Come, let the games begin! No dodges, no delays,
no turning back from the stringing of the bow—
we'll see who wins, we will.
I'd even take a crack at the bow myself . . .
If I string it and shoot through all the axes,
I'd worry less if my noble mother left our house
with another man and left me here behind—man enough
at last to win my father's splendid prizes!"
With that
he leapt to his feet and dropped his bright-red cloak,
slipping the sword and sword-belt off his shoulders.
First he planted the axes, digging a long trench,
one for all, and trued them all to a line
then tamped the earth to bed them. Wonder took
the revelers looking on: his work so firm, precise,
though he'd never seen the axes ranged before.
He stood at the threshold, poised to try the bow . . .
Three times he made it shudder, straining to bend it,
three times his power flagged—but his hopes ran high
he'd string his father's bow and shoot through every iron
and now, struggling with all his might for the fourth time,
he would have strung the bow, but Odysseus shook his head
and stopped him short despite his tensing zeal.
"God help me," the inspired prince cried out,
"must I be a weakling, a failure all my life?
Unless I'm just too young to trust my hands
to fight off any man who rises up against me.

Come, my betters, so much stronger than I am—
try the bow and finish off the contest."

He propped his father's weapon on the ground,
tilting it up against the polished well-hung doors
and resting a shaft aslant the bow's fine horn,
then back he went to the seat that he had left.
"Up, friends!" Antinous called, taking over.
"One man after another, left to right,
starting from where the steward pours the wine."

So Antinous urged and all agreed.
The first man up was Leodes, Oenops' son,
a seer who could see their futures in the smoke,
who always sat by the glowing winebowl, well back,
the one man in the group who loathed their reckless ways,
appalled by all their outrage. His turn first . . .
Picking up the weapon now and the swift arrow,
he stood at the threshold, poised to try the bow
but failed to bend it. As soon as he tugged the string
his hands went slack, his soft, uncallused hands,
and he called back to the suitors, "Friends,
I can't bend it. Take it, someone—try.
Here is a bow to rob our best of life and breath,
all our best contenders! Still, better be dead
than live on here, never winning the prize
that tempts us all—forever in pursuit,
burning with expectation every day.
If there's still a suitor here who hopes,
who aches to marry Penelope, Odysseus' wife,
just let him try the bow; he'll see the truth!
He'll soon lay siege to another Argive woman
trailing her long robes, and shower her with gifts—
and then our queen can marry the one who offers most,
the man marked out by fate to be her husband."

With those words he thrust the bow aside,
tilting it up against the polished well-hung doors
and resting a shaft aslant the bow's fine horn,
then back he went to the seat that he had left.
But Antinous turned on the seer, abuses flying:
"Leodes! what are you saying? what's got past your lips?
What awful, grisly nonsense—it shocks me to hear it—
'here is a bow to rob our best of life and breath!'
Just because *you* can't string it, you're so weak?
Clearly your genteel mother never bred her boy
for the work of bending bows and shooting arrows.
We have champions in our ranks to string it quickly.
Hop to it, Melanthius!"—he barked at the goatherd—
"Rake the fire in the hall, pull up a big stool,

heap it with fleece and fetch that hefty ball
of lard from the stores inside. So we young lords
can heat and limber the bow and rub it down with grease
before we try again and finish off the contest!"

The goatherd bustled about to rake the fire
still going strong. He pulled up a big stool,
heaped it with fleece and fetched the hefty ball
of lard from the stores inside. And the young men
limbered the bow, rubbing it down with hot grease,
then struggled to bend it back but failed. No use—
they fell far short of the strength the bow required.
Antinous still held off, dashing Eurymachus too,
the ringleaders of all the suitors,
head and shoulders the strongest of the lot.
But now
the king's two men, the cowherd and the swineherd,
had slipped out of the palace side-by-side
and great Odysseus left the house to join them.
Once they were past the courtyard and the gates
he probed them deftly, surely: "Cowherd, swineherd,
what, shall I blurt this out or keep it to myself?
No, speak out. The heart inside me says so.
How far would you go to fight beside Odysseus?
Say he dropped like *that* from a clear blue sky
and a god brought him back—
would you fight for the suitors or your king?
Tell me how you feel inside your hearts."

"Father Zeus," the trusty cowherd shouted,
"bring my prayer to pass! Let the master come—
some god guide him now! You'd see my power,
my fighting arms in action!"

Eumaeus echoed his prayer to all the gods
that their wise king would soon come home again.
Certain at least these two were loyal to the death,
Odysseus reassured them quickly: "I'm right here,
here in the flesh—myself—and home at last,
after bearing twenty years of brutal hardship.
Now I know that of all my men you two alone
longed for my return. From the rest I've heard
not one real prayer that I come back again.
So now I'll tell you what's in store for *you*.
If a god beats down the lofty suitors at my hands,
I'll find you wives, both of you, grant you property,
sturdy houses beside my own, and in my eyes you'll be
comrades to Prince Telemachus, brothers from then on.
Come, I'll show you something—living proof—

know me for certain, put your minds at rest.
This scar,
look, where a boar's white tusk gored me, years ago,
hunting on Parnassus, Autolycus' sons and I."
With that,
pushing back his rags, he revealed the great scar . . .
And the men gazed at it, scanned it, knew it well,
broke into tears and threw their arms around their master—
lost in affection, kissing his head and shoulders,
and so Odysseus kissed their heads and hands.
Now the sun would have set upon their tears
if Odysseus had not called a halt himself.
"No more weeping. Coming out of the house
a man might see us, tell the men inside.
Let's slip back in—singly, not in a pack.
I'll go first. You're next. Here's our signal.
When all the rest in there, our lordly friends,
are dead against my having the bow and quiver,
good Eumaeus, carry the weapon down the hall
and put it in my hands. Then tell the serving-women
to lock the snugly fitted doors to their own rooms.
If anyone hears from there the jolting blows
and groans of men, caught in our huge net,
not one of them show her face—
sit tight, keep to her weaving, not a sound.
You, my good Philoetius, here are your orders.
Shoot the bolt of the courtyard's outer gate,
lock it, lash it fast."
With that command
the master entered his well-constructed house
and back he went to the stool that he had left.
The king's two men, in turn, slipped in as well.

Just now Eurymachus held the bow in his hands,
turning it over, tip to tip, before the blazing fire
to heat the weapon. But he failed to bend it even so
and the suitor's high heart groaned to bursting.
"A black day," he exclaimed in wounded pride,
"a blow to myself, a blow to each man here!
It's less the marriage that mortifies me now—
that's galling too, but lots of women are left,
some in seagirt Ithaca, some in other cities.
What breaks my heart is the fact we fall so short
of great Odysseus' strength we cannot string his bow.
A disgrace to ring in the ears of men to come."

"Eurymachus," Eupithes' son Antinous countered,
"it will never come to that, as you well know.
Today is a feast-day up and down the island
in honor of the Archer God. Who flexes bows today?

Set it aside. Rest easy now. And all the axes,
let's just leave them planted where they are.
Trust me, no one's about to crash the gates
of Laertes' son and carry off these trophies.
Steward, pour some drops for the god in every cup,
we'll tip the wine, then put the bow to bed.
And first thing in the morning have Melanthius
bring the pick of his goats from all his herds
so we can burn the thighs to Apollo, god of archers—
then try the bow and finish off the contest."

Welcome advice. And again they all agreed.
Heralds sprinkled water over their hands for rinsing,
the young men brimmed the mixing bowls with wine,
they tipped first drops for the god in every cup,
then poured full rounds for all. And now, once
they'd tipped libations out and drunk their fill,
the king of craft, Odysseus, said with all his cunning,
"Listen to me, you lords who court the noble queen.
I have to say what the heart inside me urges.
I appeal especially to Eurymachus, and you,
brilliant Antinous, who spoke so shrewdly now.
Give the bow a rest for today, leave it to the gods—
at dawn the Archer God will grant a victory
to the man he favors most.

For the moment,
give me the polished bow now, won't you? So,
to amuse you all, I can try my hand, my strength . . .
is the old force still alive inside these gnarled limbs?
Or has a life of roaming, years of rough neglect,
destroyed it long ago?"

Modest words
that sent them all into hot, indignant rage,
fearing he just might string the polished bow.
So Antinous rounded on him, dressed him down:
"Not a shred of sense in your head, you filthy drifter!
Not content to feast at your ease with us, the island's pride?
Never denied your full share of the banquet, never,
you can listen in on our secrets. No one else
can eavesdrop on our talk, no tramp, no beggar.
The wine has overpowered you, heady wine—
the ruin of many another man, whoever
gulps it down and drinks beyond his limit.
Wine—it drove the Centaur,[1] famous Eurytion,
mad in the halls of lionhearted Pirithous.
There to visit the Lapiths, crazed with wine
the headlong Centaur bent to his ugly work
in the prince's own house! His hosts sprang up,

1. Half-man, half-horse.

seized with fury, dragged him across the forecourt,
flung him out of doors, hacking his nose and ears off
with their knives, no mercy. The creature reeled away,
still blind with drink, his heart like a wild storm,
loaded with all the frenzy in his mind!
And so
the feud between mortal men and Centaurs had its start.
But the drunk was first to bring disaster on himself
by drowning in his cups. You too, I promise you
no end of trouble if you should string that bow.
You'll meet no kindness in our part of the world—
we'll sail you off in a black ship to Echetus,
the mainland king who wrecks all men alive.
Nothing can save you from his royal grip!
So drink, but hold your peace,
don't take on the younger, stronger men."

"Antinous," watchful Penelope stepped in,
"how impolite it would be, how wrong, to scant
whatever guest Telemachus welcomes to his house.
You really think—if the stranger trusts so to his hands
and strength that he strings Odysseus' great bow—
he'll take me home and claim me as his bride?
He never dreamed of such a thing, I'm sure.
Don't let that ruin the feast for any reveler here.
Unthinkable—nothing, nothing could be worse."

Polybus' son Eurymachus had an answer:
"Wise Penelope, daughter of Icarius, do we really
expect the man to wed you? Unthinkable, I know.
But we do recoil at the talk of men and women.
One of the island's meaner sort will mutter,
'Look at the riffraff courting a king's wife.
Weaklings, look, they can't even string his bow.
But along came this beggar, drifting out of the blue—
strung his bow with ease and shot through all the axes!'
Gossip will fly. We'll hang our heads in shame."

"Shame?" alert Penelope protested—
"How can you hope for any public fame at all?
You who disgrace, devour a great man's house and home!
Why hang your heads in shame over next to nothing?
Our friend here is a strapping, well-built man
and claims to be the son of a noble father.
Come, hand him the bow now, let's just see . . .
I tell you this—and I'll make good my word—
if he strings the bow and Apollo grants him glory,
I'll dress him in shirt and cloak, in handsome clothes,
I'll give him a good sharp lance to fight off men and dogs,
give him a two-edged sword and sandals for his feet

and send him off, wherever his heart desires."
"Mother,"
poised Telemachus broke in now, "my father's bow—
no Achaean on earth has more right than I
to give it or withhold it, as I please.
Of all the lords in Ithaca's rocky heights
or the islands facing Elis grazed by horses,
not a single one will force or thwart my will,
even if I decide to give our guest this bow—
a gift outright—to carry off himself.
So, mother,
go back to your quarters. Tend to your own tasks,
the distaff and the loom, and keep the women
working hard as well. As for the bow now,
men will see to that, but I most of all:
I hold the reins of power in this house."
Astonished,
she withdrew to her own room. She took to heart
the clear good sense in what her son had said.
Climbing up to the lofty chamber with her women,
she fell to weeping for Odysseus, her beloved husband,
till watchful Athena sealed her eyes with welcome sleep.

And now the loyal swineherd had lifted up the bow,
was taking it toward the king, when all the suitors
burst out in an ugly uproar through the palace—
brash young bullies, this or that one heckling,
"Where on earth are you going with that bow?"

"You, you grubby swineherd, are you crazy?"

"The speedy dogs you reared will eat your corpse—"

"Out there with your pigs, out in the cold, alone!"

"If only Apollo and all the gods shine down on us!"

Eumaeus froze in his tracks, put down the bow,
panicked by every outcry in the hall.
Telemachus shouted too, from the other side,
and full of threats: "Carry on with the bow, old boy!
If you serve too many masters, you'll soon suffer.
Look sharp, or I'll pelt you back to your farm
with flying rocks. I may be younger than you
but I'm much stronger. If only I had that edge
in fists and brawn over all this courting crowd,
I'd soon dispatch them—licking their wounds at last—
clear of our palace where they plot their vicious plots!"

His outburst sent them all into gales of laughter,
blithe and oblivious, that dissolved their pique
against the prince. The swineherd took the bow,

carried it down the hall to his ready, waiting king
and standing by him, placed it in his hands,
then he called the nurse aside and whispered,
"Good Eurycleia—Telemachus commands you now
to lock the snugly fitted doors to your own rooms.
If anyone hears from there the jolting blows
and groans of men, caught in our huge net,
not one of you show your face—
sit tight, keep to your weaving, not a sound."

That silenced the old nurse—
she barred the doors that led from the long hall.
The cowherd quietly bounded out of the house
to lock the gates of the high-stockaded court.
Under the portico lay a cable, ship's tough gear:
he lashed the gates with this, then slipped back in
and ran and sat on the stool that he'd just left,
eyes riveted on Odysseus.
Now *he* held the bow
in his own hands, turning it over, tip to tip,
testing it, this way, that way . . . fearing worms
had bored through the weapon's horn with the master gone abroad.
A suitor would glance at his neighbor, jeering, taunting,
"Look at our connoisseur of bows!"
"Sly old fox—
maybe he's got bows like it, stored in *his* house."

"That or he's bent on making one himself."

"Look how he twists and turns it in his hands!"

"The clever tramp means trouble—"

"I wish him luck," some cocksure lord chimed in,
"as good as his luck in bending back that weapon!"

So they mocked, but Odysseus, mastermind in action,
once he'd handled the great bow and scanned every inch,
then, like an expert singer skilled at lyre and song—
who strains a string to a new peg with ease,
making the pliant sheep-gut fast at either end—
so with his virtuoso ease Odysseus strung his mighty bow.
Quickly his right hand plucked the string to test its pitch
and under his touch it sang out clear and sharp as a swallow's cry.
Horror swept through the suitors, faces blanching white,
and Zeus cracked the sky with a bolt, his blazing sign,
and the great man who had borne so much rejoiced at last
that the son of cunning Cronus flung that omen down for *him*.
He snatched a winged arrow lying bare on the board—
the rest still bristled deep inside the quiver,
soon to be tasted by all the feasters there.
Setting shaft on the handgrip, drawing the notch

and bowstring back, back . . . right from his stool,
just as he sat but aiming straight and true, he let fly—
and never missing an ax from the first ax-handle
clean on through to the last and out
the shaft with its weighted brazen head shot free!
"Telemachus,"
Odysseus looked to his son and said, "your guest,
sitting here in your house, has not disgraced you.
No missing the mark, look, and no long labor spent
to string the bow. My strength's not broken yet,
not quite so frail as the mocking suitors thought.
But the hour has come to serve our masters right—
supper in broad daylight—then to other revels,
song and dancing, all that crowns a feast."

He paused with a warning nod, and at that sign
Prince Telemachus, son of King Odysseus,
girding his sharp sword on, clamping hand to spear,
took his stand by a chair that flanked his father—
his bronze spearpoint glinting now like fire . . .

Book 22. Slaughter in the Hall

Now stripping back his rags Odysseus master of craft and battle
vaulted onto the great threshold, gripping his bow and quiver
bristling arrows, and poured his flashing shafts before him,
loose at his feet, and thundered out to all the suitors:
"Look—your crucial test is finished, now, at last!
But another target's left that no one's hit before—
we'll see if *I* can hit it—Apollo give me glory!"

With that he trained a stabbing arrow on Antinous . . .
just lifting a gorgeous golden loving-cup in his hands,
just tilting the two-handled goblet back to his lips,
about to drain the wine—and slaughter the last thing
on the suitor's mind: who could dream that one foe
in that crowd of feasters, however great his power,
would bring down death on himself, and black doom?
But Odysseus aimed and shot Antinous square in the throat
and the point went stabbing clean through the soft neck and out—
and off to the side he pitched, the cup dropped from his grasp
as the shaft sank home, and the man's life-blood came spurting
from his nostrils—
thick red jets—
a sudden thrust of his foot—
he kicked away the table—
food showered across the floor,
the bread and meats soaked in a swirl of bloody filth.
The suitors burst into uproar all throughout the house
when they saw their leader down. They leapt from their seats,

milling about, desperate, scanning the stone walls—
not a shield in sight, no rugged spear to seize.
They wheeled on Odysseus, lashing out in fury:
"Stranger, shooting at men will cost your life!"

"Your game is over—you, you've shot your last!"

"You'll never escape your own headlong death!"

"You killed the best in Ithaca—our fine prince!"

"Vultures will eat your corpse!"
Groping, frantic—
each one persuading himself the guest had killed
the man by chance. Poor fools, blind to the fact
that all their necks were in the noose, their doom sealed.
With a dark look, the wily fighter Odysseus shouted back,
"You dogs! you never imagined I'd return from Troy—
so cocksure that you bled my house to death,
ravished my serving-women—wooed my wife
behind my back while I was still alive!
No fear of the gods who rule the skies up there,
no fear that men's revenge might arrive someday—
now all your necks are in the noose—your doom is sealed!"

Terror gripped them all, blanched their faces white,
each man glancing wildly—how to escape his instant death?
Only Eurymachus had the breath to venture, "If you,
you're truly Odysseus of Ithaca, home at last,
you're right to accuse these men of what they've done—
so much reckless outrage here in your palace,
so much on your lands. But here he lies,
quite dead, and he incited it all—Antinous—
look, the man who drove us all to crime!
Not that he needed marriage, craved it so;
he'd bigger game in mind—though Zeus barred his way—
he'd lord it over Ithaca's handsome country, king himself,
once he'd lain in wait for your son and cut him down!
But now he's received the death that he deserved.
So spare your own people! Later we'll recoup
your costs with a tax laid down upon the land,
covering all we ate and drank inside your halls,
and each of us here will pay full measure too—
twenty oxen in value, bronze and gold we'll give
until we melt your heart. Before we've settled,
who on earth could blame you for your rage?"

But the battle-master kept on glaring, seething.
"No, Eurymachus! Not if you paid me all your father's wealth—
all you possess now, and all that could pour in from the world's end—
no, not even then would I stay my hands from slaughter
till all you suitors had paid for all your crimes!

Now life or death—your choice—fight me or flee
if you hope to escape your sudden bloody doom!
I doubt one man in the lot will save his skin!"

His menace shook their knees, their hearts too
but Eurymachus spoke again, now to the suitors: "Friends!
This man will never restrain his hands, invincible hands—
now that he's seized that polished bow and quiver, look,
he'll shoot from the sill until he's killed us all!
So fight—call up the joy of battle! Swords out!
Tables lifted—block his arrows winging death!
Charge him, charge in a pack—
try to rout the man from the sill, the doors,
race through town and sound an alarm at once—
our friend would soon see he's shot his bolt!"

Brave talk—
he drew his two-edged sword, bronze, honed for the kill
and hurled himself at the king with a raw savage cry
in the same breath that Odysseus loosed an arrow
ripping his breast beside the nipple so hard
it lodged in the man's liver—
out of his grasp the sword dropped to the ground—
over his table, head over heels he tumbled, doubled up,
flinging his food and his two-handled cup across the floor—
he smashed the ground with his forehead, writhing in pain,
both feet flailing out, and his high seat tottered—
the mist of death came swirling down his eyes.

Amphinomus rushed the king in all his glory,
charging him face-to-face, a slashing sword drawn—
if only he could force him clear of the doorway, now,
but Telemachus—too quick—stabbed the man from behind,
plunging his bronze spear between the suitor's shoulders
and straight on through his chest the point came jutting out—
down he went with a thud, his forehead slammed the ground.
Telemachus swerved aside, leaving his long spearshaft
lodged in Amphinomus—fearing some suitor just might
lunge in from behind as he tugged the shaft,
impale him with a sword or hack him down,
crouching over the corpse.
He went on the run, reached his father at once
and halting right beside him, let fly, "Father—
now I'll get you a shield and a pair of spears,
a helmet of solid bronze to fit your temples!
I'll arm myself on the way back and hand out
arms to the swineherd, arm the cowherd too—
we'd better fight equipped!"

"Run, fetch them,"
the wily captain urged, "while I've got arrows left
to defend me—or they'll force me from the doors

while I fight on alone!"

Telemachus moved to his father's orders smartly.
Off he ran to the room where the famous arms lay stored,
took up four shields, eight spears, four bronze helmets
ridged with horsehair crests and, loaded with these,
ran back to reach his father's side in no time.
The prince was first to case himself in bronze
and his servants followed suit—both harnessed up
and all three flanked Odysseus, mastermind of war,
and he, as long as he'd arrows left to defend himself,
kept picking suitors off in the palace, one by one
and down they went, corpse on corpse in droves.
Then, when the royal archer's shafts ran out,
he leaned his bow on a post of the massive doors—
where walls of the hallway catch the light—and armed:
across his shoulder he slung a buckler four plies thick,
over his powerful head he set a well-forged helmet,
the horsehair crest atop it tossing, bristling terror,
and grasped two rugged lances tipped with fiery bronze.

Now a side-door was fitted into the main wall—
right at the edge of the great hall's stone sill—
and led to a passage always shut by good tight boards.
But Odysseus gave the swineherd strict commands
to stand hard by the side-door, guard it well—
the only way the suitors might break out.
Agelaus called to his comrades with a plan:
"Friends, can't someone climb through the hatch?—
tell men outside to sound the alarm, be quick—
our guest would soon see he'd shot his last!"

The goatherd Melanthius answered, "Not a chance,
my lord—the door to the courtyard's much too near,
dangerous too, the mouth of the passage cramped.
One strong man could block us, one and all!
No, I'll fetch you some armor to harness on,
out of the storeroom—there, nowhere else, I'm sure,
the king and his gallant son have stowed their arms!"

With that the goatherd clambered up through smoke-ducts
high on the wall and scurried into Odysseus' storeroom,
bundled a dozen shields, as many spears and helmets
ridged with horsehair crests and, loaded with these,
rushed back down to the suitors, quickly issued arms.
Odysseus' knees shook, his heart too, when he saw them
buckling on their armor, brandishing long spears—
here was a battle looming, well he knew.
He turned at once to Telemachus, warnings flying:

"A bad break in the fight, my boy! One of the women's
tipped the odds against us—or could it be the goatherd?"

"My fault, father," the cool clear prince replied,
"the blame's all mine. That snug door to the vault,
I left it ajar—they've kept a better watch than I.
Go, Eumaeus, shut the door to the storeroom,
check and see if it's one of the women's tricks
or Dolius' son Melanthius. He's our man, I'd say."

And even as they conspired, back the goatherd
climbed to the room to fetch more burnished arms,
but Eumaeus spotted him, quickly told his king
who stood close by: "Odysseus, wily captain,
there he goes again, the infernal nuisance—
just as we suspected—back to the storeroom.
Give me a clear command!
Do I kill the man—if I can take him down—
or drag him back to you, here, to pay in full
for the vicious work he's plotted in your house?"

Odysseus, master of tactics, answered briskly,
"I and the prince will keep these brazen suitors
crammed in the hall, for all their battle-fury.
You two wrench Melanthius' arms and legs behind him,
fling him down in the storeroom—lash his back to a plank
and strap a twisted cable fast to the scoundrel's body,
hoist him up a column until he hits the rafters—
let him dangle in agony, still alive,
for a good long time!"

They hung on his orders, keen to do his will.
Off they ran to the storeroom, unseen by him inside—
Melanthius, rummaging after arms, deep in a dark recess
as the two men took their stand, either side of the doorposts,
poised till the goatherd tried to cross the doorsill . . .
one hand clutching a crested helmet, the other
an ample old buckler blotched with mildew,
the shield Laertes bore as a young soldier once
but there it lay for ages, seams on the handstraps split—
Quick, they rushed him, seized him, haled him back by the hair,
flung him down on the floor, writhing with terror, bound him
hand and foot with a chafing cord, wrenched his limbs
back, back till the joints locked tight—
just as Laertes' cunning son commanded—
they strapped a twisted cable round his body,
hoisted him up a column until he hit the rafters,
then you mocked him, Eumaeus, my good swineherd:
"Now stand guard through the whole night, Melanthius—
stretched out on a soft bed fit for *you,* your highness!
You're bound to see the Morning rising up from the Ocean,

mounting her golden throne—at just the hour you always
drive in goats to feast the suitors in the hall!"

So they left him, trussed in his agonizing sling;
they clapped on armor again, shut the gleaming doors
and ran to rejoin Odysseus, mastermind of war.
And now as the ranks squared off, breathing fury—
four at the sill confronting a larger, stronger force
arrayed inside the hall—now Zeus's daughter Athena,
taking the build and voice of Mentor, swept in
and Odysseus, thrilled to see her, cried out,
"Rescue us, Mentor, now it's life or death!
Remember your old comrade—all the service
I offered you! We were boys together!"
So he cried
yet knew in his bones it was Athena, Driver of Armies.
But across the hall the suitors brayed against her,
Agelaus first, his outburst full of threats:
"Mentor, never let Odysseus trick you into
siding with *him* to fight against the suitors.
Here's our plan of action, and we will see it through!
Once we've killed them both, the father and the son,
we'll kill you too, for all you're bent on doing
here in the halls—you'll pay with your own head!
And once our swords have stopped your violence cold—
all your property, all in your house, your fields,
we'll lump it all with Odysseus' rich estate
and never let your sons live on in your halls
or free your wife and daughters to walk through town!"

Naked threats—and Athena hit new heights of rage,
she lashed out at Odysseus now with blazing accusations:
"Where's it gone, Odysseus—your power, your fighting heart?
The great soldier who fought for famous white-armed Helen,
battling Trojans nine long years—nonstop, no mercy,
mowing their armies down in grueling battle—
you who seized the broad streets of Troy
with your fine strategic stroke! How can you—
now you've returned to your own house, your own wealth—
bewail the loss of your combat strength in a war with *suitors?*
Come, old friend, stand by me! You'll see action now,
see how Mentor the son of Alcimus, that brave fighter,
kills your enemies, pays you back for service!"
Rousing words—
but she gave no all-out turning of the tide, not yet,
she kept on testing Odysseus and his gallant son,
putting their force and fighting heart to proof.
For all the world like a swallow in their sight
she flew on high to perch
on the great hall's central roofbeam black with smoke.

But the suitors closed ranks, commanded now by Damastor's son
Agelaus, flanked by Eurynomus, Demoptolemus and Amphimedon,
Pisander, Polyctor's son, and Polybus ready, waiting—
head and shoulders the best and bravest of the lot
still left to fight for their lives,
now that the pelting shafts had killed the rest.
Agelaus spurred his comrades on with battle-plans:
"Friends, at last the man's invincible hands are useless!
Mentor has mouthed some empty boasts and flitted off—
just four are left to fight at the front doors. So now,
no wasting your long spears—all at a single hurl,
just six of us launch out in the first wave!
If Zeus is willing, we may hit Odysseus,
carry off the glory! The rest are nothing
once the captain's down!"
At his command,
concentrating their shots, all six hurled as one
but Athena sent the whole salvo wide of the mark—
one of them hit the jamb of the great hall's doors,
another the massive door itself, and the heavy bronze point
of a third ashen javelin crashed against the wall.
Seeing his men untouched by the suitors' flurry,
steady Odysseus leapt to take command:
"Friends! now it's for *us* to hurl at them, I say,
into this ruck of suitors! Topping all their crimes
they're mad to strip the armor off our bodies!"

Taking aim at the ranks, all four let fly as one
and the lances struck home—Odysseus killed Demoptolemus,
Telemachus killed Euryades—the swineherd, Elatus—
and the cowherd cut Pisander down in blood.
They bit the dust of the broad floor, all as one.
Back to the great hall's far recess the others shrank
as the four rushed in and plucked up spears from corpses.

And again the suitors hurled their whetted shafts
but Athena sent the better part of the salvo wide—
one of them hit the jamb of the great hall's doors,
another the massive door itself, and the heavy bronze point
of a third ashen javelin crashed against the wall.
True, Amphimedon nicked Telemachus on the wrist—
the glancing blade just barely broke his skin.
Ctesippus sent a long spear sailing over
Eumaeus' buckler, grazing his shoulder blade
but the weapon skittered off and hit the ground.
And again those led by the brilliant battle-master
hurled their razor spears at the suitors' ranks—
and now Odysseus raider of cities hit Eurydamas,
Telemachus hit Amphimedon—Eumaeus, Polybus—
and the cowherd stabbed Ctesippus

right in the man's chest and triumphed over his body:
"Love your mockery, do you? Son of that blowhard
  Polytherses!
No more shooting off your mouth, you idiot, such big talk—
leave the last word to the gods—they're much stronger!
Take this spear, this guest-gift, for the cow's hoof
you once gave King Odysseus begging in his house!"

So the master of longhorn cattle had his say—
as Odysseus, fighting at close quarters, ran Agelaus
through with a long lance—Telemachus speared Leocritus
so deep in the groin the bronze came punching out his back
and the man crashed headfirst, slamming the ground full-face.
And now Athena, looming out of the rafters high above them,
brandished her man-destroying shield of thunder, terrifying
the suitors out of their minds, and down the hall they panicked—
wild, like herds stampeding, driven mad as the darting gadfly
strikes in the late spring when the long days come round.
The attackers struck like eagles, crook-clawed, hook-beaked,
swooping down from a mountain ridge to harry smaller birds
that skim across the flatland, cringing under the clouds
but the eagles plunge in fury, rip their lives out—hopeless,
never a chance of flight or rescue—and people love the sport—
so the attackers routed suitors headlong down the hall,
wheeling into the slaughter, slashing left and right
and grisly screams broke from skulls cracked open—
the whole floor awash with blood.
                                        Leodes now—
he flung himself at Odysseus, clutched his knees,
crying out to the king with a sudden, winging prayer:
"I hug your knees, Odysseus—mercy! spare my life!
Never, I swear, did I harass any woman in your house—
never a word, a gesture—nothing, no, I tried
to restrain the suitors, whoever did such things.
They wouldn't listen, keep their hands to themselves—
so reckless, so they earn their shameful fate.
But I was just their prophet—
my hands are clean—and I'm to die their death!
Look at the thanks I get for years of service!"

A killing look, and the wry soldier answered,
"Only a priest, a prophet for this mob, you say?
How hard you must have prayed in my own house
that the heady day of my return would never dawn—
my dear wife would be yours, would bear your children!
For that there's no escape from grueling death—you die!"

And snatching up in one powerful hand a sword
left on the ground—Agelaus dropped it when he fell—
Odysseus hacked the prophet square across the neck

and the praying head went tumbling in the dust.
Now one was left,
trying still to escape black death. Phemius, Terpis' son,
the bard who always performed among the suitors—
they forced the man to sing . . .
There he stood, backing into the side-door,
still clutching his ringing lyre in his hands,
his mind in turmoil, torn—what should he do?
Steal from the hall and crouch at the altar-stone
of Zeus who Guards the Court, where time and again
Odysseus and Laertes burned the long thighs of oxen?
Or throw himself on the master's mercy, clasp his knees?
That was the better way—or so it struck him, yes,
grasp the knees of Laertes' royal son. And so,
cradling his hollow lyre, he laid it on the ground
between the mixing-bowl and the silver-studded throne,
then rushed up to Odysseus, yes, and clutched his knees,
singing out to his king with a stirring, winged prayer:
"I hug your knees, Odysseus—mercy! spare my life!
What a grief it will be to you for all the years to come
if you kill the singer now, who sings for gods and men.
I taught myself the craft, but a god has planted
deep in my spirit all the paths of song—
songs I'm fit to sing for you as for a god.
Calm your bloodlust now—don't take my head!
He'd bear me out, your own dear son Telemachus—
never of *my* own will, never for any gain did I
perform in your house, singing after the suitors
had their feasts. They were too strong, too many—
they forced me to come and sing—I had no choice!"

The inspired Prince Telemachus heard his pleas
and quickly said to his father close beside him,
"Stop, don't cut him down! This one's innocent.
So is the herald Medon—the one who always
tended me in the house when I was little—
spare him too. Unless he's dead by now,
killed by Philoetius or Eumaeus here—
or ran into *you* rampaging through the halls."

The herald pricked up his anxious ears at that . . .
cautious soul, he cowered, trembling, under a chair—
wrapped in an oxhide freshly stripped—to dodge black death.
He jumped in a flash from there, threw off the smelly hide
and scuttling up to Telemachus, clutching his knees,
the herald begged for life in words that fluttered:
"Here I am, dear boy—spare me! Tell your father,
flushed with victory, not to kill me with his sword—
enraged as he is with these young lords who bled
his palace white and showed you no respect,

the reckless fools!"
Breaking into a smile
the canny Odysseus reassured him, "Courage!
The prince has pulled you through, he's saved you now
so you can take it to heart and tell the next man too:
clearly doing good puts doing bad to shame.
Now leave the palace, go and sit outside—
out in the courtyard, clear of the slaughter—
you and the bard with all his many songs.
Wait till I've done some household chores
that call for my attention."

The two men scurried out of the house at once
and crouched at the altar-stone of mighty Zeus—
glancing left and right,
fearing death would strike at any moment.

Odysseus scanned his house to see if any man
still skulked alive, still hoped to avoid black death.
But he found them one and all in blood and dust . . .
great hauls of them down and out like fish that fishermen
drag from the churning gray surf in looped and coiling nets
and fling ashore on a sweeping hook of beach—some noble catch
heaped on the sand, twitching, lusting for fresh salt sea
but the Sungod hammers down and burns their lives out . . .
so the suitors lay in heaps, corpse covering corpse.
At last the seasoned fighter turned to his son:
"Telemachus, go, call the old nurse here—
I must tell her all that's on my mind."

Telemachus ran to do his father's bidding,
shook the women's doors, calling Eurycleia:
"Come out now! Up with you, good old woman!
You who watch over all the household hands—
quick, my father wants you, needs to have a word!"

Crisp command that left the old nurse hushed—
she spread the doors to the well-constructed hall,
slipped out in haste, and the prince led her on . . .
She found Odysseus in the thick of slaughtered corpses,
splattered with bloody filth like a lion that's devoured
some ox of the field and lopes home, covered with blood,
his chest streaked, both jaws glistening, dripping red—
a sight to strike terror. So Odysseus looked now,
splattered with gore, his thighs, his fighting hands,
and she, when she saw the corpses, all the pooling blood,
was about to lift a cry of triumph—here was a great exploit,
look—but the soldier held her back and checked her zeal
with warnings winging home: "Rejoice in your heart,
old woman—peace! No cries of triumph now.
It's unholy to glory over the bodies of the dead.

These men the doom of the gods has brought low,
and their own indecent acts. They'd no regard
for any man on earth—good or bad—
who chanced to come their way. And so, thanks
to their reckless work, they met this shameful fate.
Quick, report in full on the women in my halls—
who are disloyal to me, who are guiltless?"

"Surely, child,"
his fond old nurse replied, "now here's the truth.
Fifty women you have inside your house,
women we've trained to do their duties well,
to card the wool and bear the yoke of service.
Some dozen in all went tramping to their shame,
thumbing their noses at me, at the queen herself!
And Telemachus, just now come of age—his mother
would never let the boy take charge of the maids.
But let me climb to her well-lit room upstairs
and tell your wife the news—
some god has put the woman fast asleep."

"Don't wake her yet," the crafty man returned,
"you tell those women to hurry here at once—
just the ones who've shamed us all along."

Away the old nurse bustled through the house
to give the women orders, rush them to the king.
Odysseus called Telemachus over, both herdsmen too,
with strict commands: "Start clearing away the bodies.
Make the women pitch in too. Chairs and tables—
scrub them down with sponges, rinse them clean.
And once you've put the entire house in order,
march the women out of the great hall—between
the roundhouse and the courtyard's strong stockade—
and hack them with your swords, slash out all their lives—
blot out of their minds the joys of love they relished
under the suitors' bodies, rutting on the sly!"

The women crowded in, huddling all together . . .
wailing convulsively, streaming live warm tears.
First they carried out the bodies of the dead
and propped them under the courtyard colonnade,
standing them one against another. Odysseus
shouted commands himself, moving things along
and they kept bearing out the bodies—they were forced.
Next they scrubbed down the elegant chairs and tables,
washed them with sopping sponges, rinsed them clean.
Then Telemachus and the herdsmen scraped smooth
the packed earth floor of the royal house with spades
as the women gathered up the filth and piled it outside.
And then, at last, once the entire house was put in order,

they marched the women out of the great hall—between
the roundhouse and the courtyard's strong stockade—
crammed them into a dead end, no way out from there,
and stern Telemachus gave the men their orders:
"No clean death for the likes of them, by god!
Not from me—they showered abuse on my head,
my mother's too!
You sluts—the suitors' whores!"

With that, taking a cable used on a dark-prowed ship
he coiled it over the roundhouse, lashed it fast to a tall column,
hoisting it up so high no toes could touch the ground.
Then, as doves or thrushes beating their spread wings
against some snare rigged up in thickets—flying in
for a cozy nest but a grisly bed receives them—
so the women's heads were trapped in a line,
nooses yanking their necks up, one by one
so all might die a pitiful, ghastly death . . .
they kicked up heels for a little—not for long.
Melanthius?
They hauled him out through the doorway, into the court,
lopped his nose and ears with a ruthless knife,
tore his genitals out for the dogs to eat raw
and in manic fury hacked off hands and feet.
Then,
once they'd washed their own hands and feet,
they went inside again to join Odysseus.
Their work was done with now.
But the king turned to devoted Eurycleia, saying,
"Bring sulfur, nurse, to scour all this pollution—
bring me fire too, so I can fumigate the house.
And call Penelope here with all her women—
tell all the maids to come back in at once."

"Well said, my boy," his old nurse replied,
"right to the point. But wait,
let me fetch you a shirt and cloak to wrap you.
No more dawdling round the palace, nothing but rags
to cover those broad shoulders—it's a scandal!"

"Fire first," the good soldier answered.
"Light me a fire to purify this house."

The devoted nurse snapped to his command,
brought her master fire and brimstone. Odysseus
purged his palace, halls and court, with cleansing fumes.

Then back through the royal house the old nurse went
to tell the women the news and bring them in at once.
They came crowding out of their quarters, torch in hand,
flung their arms around Odysseus, hugged him, home at last,

and kissed his head and shoulders, seized his hands, and he,
overcome by a lovely longing, broke down and wept . . .
deep in his heart he knew them one and all.

Book 23. The Great Rooted Bed

Up to the rooms the old nurse clambered, chuckling all
the way,
to tell the queen her husband was here now, home at last.
Her knees bustling, feet shuffling over each other,
till hovering at her mistress' head she spoke:
"Penelope—child—wake up and see for yourself,
with your own eyes, all you dreamed of, all your days!
He's here—Odysseus—he's come home, at long last!
He's killed the suitors, swaggering young brutes
who plagued his house, wolfed his cattle down,
rode roughshod over his son!"

"Dear old nurse," wary Penelope replied,
"the gods have made you mad. They have that power,
putting lunacy into the clearest head around
or setting a half-wit on the path to sense.
They've unhinged you, and you were once so sane.
Why do you mock me?—haven't I wept enough?—
telling such wild stories, interrupting my sleep,
sweet sleep that held me, sealed my eyes just now.
Not once have I slept so soundly since the day
Odysseus sailed away to see that cursed city . . .
Destroy, I call it—I hate to say its name!
Now down you go. Back to your own quarters.
If any other woman of mine had come to me,
rousing me out of sleep with such a tale,
I'd have her bundled back to her room in pain.
It's only your old gray head that spares you that!"

"Never"—the fond old nurse kept pressing on—
"dear child, I'd never mock you! No, it's all true,
he's here—Odysseus—he's come home, just as I tell you!
He's the stranger they all manhandled in the hall.
Telemachus knew he was here, for days and days,
but he knew enough to hide his father's plans
so *he* could pay those vipers back in kind!"

Penelope's heart burst in joy, she leapt from bed,
her eyes streaming tears, she hugged the old nurse
and cried out with an eager, winging word,
"Please, dear one, give me the whole story.
If he's really home again, just as you tell me,
how did he get those shameless suitors in his clutches?—
single-handed, braving an army always camped inside."

"I have no idea," the devoted nurse replied.
"I didn't see it, I didn't ask—all I heard
was the choking groans of men cut down in blood.
We crouched in terror—a dark nook of our quarters—
all of us locked tight behind those snug doors
till your boy Telemachus came and called me out—
his father rushed him there to do just that. And then
I found Odysseus in the thick of slaughtered corpses;
there he stood and all around him, over the beaten floor,
the bodies sprawled in heaps, lying one on another . . .
How it would have thrilled your heart to see him—
splattered with bloody filth, a lion with his kill!
And now they're all stacked at the courtyard gates—
he's lit a roaring fire,
he's purifying the house with cleansing fumes
and he's sent me here to bring you back to him.
Follow me down! So now, after all the years of grief,
you two can embark, loving hearts, along the road to joy.
Look, your dreams, put off so long, come true at last—
he's back alive, home at his hearth, and found you,
found his son still here. And all those suitors
who did him wrong, he's paid them back, he has,
right in his own house!"

"Hush, dear woman,"
guarded Penelope cautioned her at once.
"Don't laugh, don't cry in triumph—not yet.
You know how welcome the sight of him would be
to all in the house, and to me most of all
and the son we bore together.
But the story can't be true, not as you tell it,
no, it must be a god who's killed our brazen friends—
up in arms at their outrage, heartbreaking crimes.
They'd no regard for any man on earth—
good or bad—who chanced to come their way. So,
thanks to their reckless work they die their deaths.
Odysseus? Far from Achaea now, he's lost all hope
of coming home . . . he's lost and gone himself."

"Child," the devoted old nurse protested,
"what nonsense you let slip through your teeth.
Here's your husband, warming his hands at his own hearth,
here—and you, you say he'll never come home again,
always the soul of trust! All right, this too—
I'll give you a sign, a proof that's plain as day.
That scar, made years ago by a boar's white tusk—
I spotted the scar myself, when I washed his feet,
and I tried to tell you, ah, but he, the crafty rascal,
clamped his hand on my mouth—I couldn't say a word.
Follow me down now. I'll stake my life on it:
if I am lying to *you*—

kill me with a thousand knives of pain!"

"Dear old nurse," composed Penelope responded,
"deep as you are, my friend, you'll find it hard
to plumb the plans of the everlasting gods.
All the same, let's go and join my son
so I can see the suitors lying dead
and see . . . the one who killed them."
With that thought
Penelope started down from her lofty room, her heart
in turmoil, torn . . . should she keep her distance,
probe her husband? Or rush up to the man at once
and kiss his head and cling to both his hands?
As soon as she stepped across the stone threshold,
slipping in, she took a seat at the closest wall
and radiant in the firelight, faced Odysseus now.
There he sat, leaning against the great central column,
eyes fixed on the ground, waiting, poised for whatever words
his hardy wife might say when she caught sight of him.
A long while she sat in silence . . . numbing wonder
filled her heart as her eyes explored his face.
One moment he seemed . . . Odysseus, to the life—
the next, no, he was not the man she knew,
a huddled mass of rags was all she saw.

"Oh mother," Telemachus reproached her,
"cruel mother, you with your hard heart!
Why do you spurn my father so—why don't you
sit beside him, engage him, ask him questions?
What other wife could have a spirit so unbending?
Holding back from her husband, home at last for *her*
after bearing twenty years of brutal struggle—
your heart was always harder than a rock!"
"My child,"
Penelope, well-aware, explained, "I'm stunned with wonder,
powerless. Cannot speak to him, ask him questions,
look him in the eyes . . . But if he is truly
Odysseus, home at last, make no mistake:
we two will know each other, even better—
we two have secret signs,
known to us both but hidden from the world."

Odysseus, long-enduring, broke into a smile
and turned to his son with pointed, winging words:
"Leave your mother here in the hall to test me
as she will. She soon will know me better.
Now because I am filthy, wear such grimy rags,
she spurns me—your mother still can't bring herself
to believe I am her husband.
But you and I,
put heads together. What's our best defense?

When someone kills a lone man in the realm
who leaves behind him no great band of avengers,
still the killer flees, goodbye to kin and country.
But *we* brought down the best of the island's princes,
the pillars of Ithaca. Weigh it well, I urge you."

"Look to it all yourself now, father," his son
deferred at once. "You are the best on earth,
they say, when it comes to mapping tactics.
No one, no mortal man, can touch you there.
But we're behind you, hearts intent on battle,
nor do I think you'll find us short on courage,
long as our strength will last."
"Then here's our plan,"
the master of tactics said. "I think it's best.
First go and wash, and pull fresh tunics on
and tell the maids in the hall to dress well too.
And let the inspired bard take up his ringing lyre
and lead off for us all a dance so full of heart
that whoever hears the strains outside the gates—
a passerby on the road, a neighbor round about—
will think it's a wedding-feast that's under way.
No news of the suitors' death must spread through town
till we have slipped away to our own estates,
our orchard green with trees. There we'll see
what winning strategy Zeus will hand us then."

They hung on his words and moved to orders smartly.
First they washed and pulled fresh tunics on,
the women arrayed themselves—the inspired bard
struck up his resounding lyre and stirred in all
a desire for dance and song, the lovely lilting beat,
till the great house echoed round to the measured tread
of dancing men in motion, women sashed and lithe.
And whoever heard the strains outside would say,
"A miracle—someone's married the queen at last!"

"One of her hundred suitors."
"That callous woman,
too faithless to keep her lord and master's house
to the bitter end—"
"Till he came sailing home."

So they'd say, blind to what had happened:
the great-hearted Odysseus was home again at last.
The maid Eurynome bathed him, rubbed him down with oil
and drew around him a royal cape and choice tunic too.
And Athena crowned the man with beauty, head to foot,
made him taller to all eyes, his build more massive,
yes, and down from his brow the great goddess

ran his curls like thick hyacinth clusters
full of blooms. As a master craftsman washes
gold over beaten silver—a man the god of fire
and Queen Athena trained in every fine technique—
and finishes off his latest effort, handsome work . . .
so she lavished splendor over his head and shoulders now.
He stepped from his bath, glistening like a god,
and back he went to the seat that he had left
and facing his wife, declared,
"Strange woman! So hard—the gods of Olympus
made you harder than any other woman in the world!
What other wife could have a spirit so unbending?
Holding back from her husband, home at last for *her*
after bearing twenty years of brutal struggle.
Come, nurse, make me a bed, I'll sleep alone.
She has a heart of iron in her breast."
"Strange *man,*"
wary Penelope said. "I'm not so proud, so scornful,
nor am I overwhelmed by your quick change . . .
You look—how well I know—the way he looked,
setting sail from Ithaca years ago
aboard the long-oared ship.
Come, Eurycleia,
move the sturdy bedstead out of our bridal chamber—
that room the master built with his own hands.
Take it out now, sturdy bed that it is,
and spread it deep with fleece,
blankets and lustrous throws to keep him warm."

Putting her husband to the proof—but Odysseus
blazed up in fury, lashing out at his loyal wife:
"Woman—your words, they cut me to the core!
Who could move my bed? Impossible task,
even for some skilled craftsman—unless a god
came down in person, quick to lend a hand,
lifted it out with ease and moved it elsewhere.
Not a man on earth, not even at peak strength,
would find it easy to prise it up and shift it, no,
a great sign, a hallmark lies in its construction.
I know, I built it myself—no one else . . .
There was a branching olive-tree inside our court,
grown to its full prime, the bole like a column, thickset.
Around it I built my bedroom, finished off the walls
with good tight stonework, roofed it over soundly
and added doors, hung well and snugly wedged.
Then I lopped the leafy crown of the olive,
clean-cutting the stump bare from roots up,
planing it round with a bronze smoothing-adze—
I had the skill—I shaped it plumb to the line to make

my bedpost, bored the holes it needed with an auger.
Working from there I built my bed, start to finish,
I gave it ivory inlays, gold and silver fittings,
wove the straps across it, oxhide gleaming red.
There's our secret sign, I tell you, our life story!
Does the bed, my lady, still stand planted firm?—
I don't know—or has someone chopped away
that olive-trunk and hauled our bedstead off?"
Living proof—
Penelope felt her knees go slack, her heart surrender,
recognizing the strong clear signs Odysseus offered.
She dissolved in tears, rushed to Odysseus, flung her arms
around his neck and kissed his head and cried out,
"Odysseus—don't flare up at me now, not you,
always the most understanding man alive!
The gods, it was the gods who sent us sorrow—
they grudged us both a life in each other's arms
from the heady zest of youth to the stoop of old age.
But don't fault me, angry with me now because I failed,
at the first glimpse, to greet you, hold you, so . . .
In my heart of hearts I always cringed with fear
some fraud might come, beguile me with his talk;
the world is full of the sort,
cunning ones who plot their own dark ends.
Remember Helen of Argos, Zeus's daughter—
would *she* have sported so in a stranger's bed
if she had dreamed that Achaea's sons were doomed
to fight and die to bring her home again?
Some god spurred her to do her shameless work.
Not till then did her mind conceive that madness,
blinding madness that caused her anguish, ours as well.
But now, since you have revealed such overwhelming proof—
the secret sign of our bed, which no one's ever seen
but you and I and a single handmaid, Actoris,
the servant my father gave me when I came,
who kept the doors of our room you built so well . . .
you've conquered my heart, my hard heart, at last!"

The more she spoke, the more a deep desire for tears
welled up inside his breast—he wept as he held the wife
he loved, the soul of loyalty, in his arms at last.
Joy, warm as the joy that shipwrecked sailors feel
when they catch sight of land—Poseidon has struck
their well-rigged ship on the open sea with gale winds
and crushing walls of waves, and only a few escape,
swimming,
struggling out of the frothing surf to reach the shore,
their bodies crusted with salt but buoyed up with joy
as they plant their feet on solid ground again,

spared a deadly fate. So joyous now to her
the sight of her husband, vivid in her gaze,
that her white arms, embracing his neck
would never for a moment let him go . . .
Dawn with her rose-red fingers might have shone
upon their tears, if with her glinting eyes
Athena had not thought of one more thing.
She held back the night, and night lingered long
at the western edge of the earth, while in the east
she reined in Dawn of the golden throne at Ocean's banks,
commanding her not to yoke the windswift team that brings men light,
Blaze and Aurora, the young colts that race the Morning on.
Yet now Odysseus, seasoned veteran, said to his wife,
"Dear woman . . . we have still not reached the end
of all our trials. One more labor lies in store—
boundless, laden with danger, great and long,
and I must brave it out from start to finish.
So the ghost of Tiresias prophesied to me,
the day that I went down to the House of Death
to learn our best route home, my comrades' and my own.
But come, let's go to bed, dear woman—at long last
delight in sleep, delight in each other, come!"

"If it's bed you want," reserved Penelope replied,
"it's bed you'll have, whenever the spirit moves you,
now that the gods have brought you home again
to native land, your grand and gracious house.
But since you've alluded to it,
since a god has put it in your mind,
please, tell me about this trial still to come.
I'm bound to learn of it later, I am sure—
what's the harm if I hear of it tonight?"
"Still so strange,"
Odysseus, the old master of stories, answered.
"Why again, why force me to tell you all?
Well, tell I shall. I'll hide nothing now.
But little joy it will bring you, I'm afraid,
as little joy for me.
The prophet said
that I must rove through towns on towns of men,
that I must carry a well-planed oar until
I come to a people who know nothing of the sea,
whose food is never seasoned with salt, strangers all
to ships with their crimson prows and long slim oars,
wings that make ships fly. And here is my sign,
he told me, clear, so clear I cannot miss it,
and I will share it with you now . . .
When another traveler falls in with me and calls
that weight across my shoulder a fan to winnow grain,

then, he told me, I must plant my oar in the earth
and sacrifice fine beasts to the lord god of the sea,
Poseidon—a ram, a bull and a ramping wild boar—
then journey home and render noble offerings up
to the deathless gods who rule the vaulting skies,
to all the gods in order.
And at last my own death will steal upon me . . .
a gentle, painless death, far from the sea it comes
to take me down, borne down with the years in ripe old age
with all my people here in blessed peace around me.
All this, the prophet said, will come to pass."

"And so," Penelope said, in her great wisdom,
"if the gods will really grant a happier old age,
there's hope that we'll escape our trials at last."

So husband and wife confided in each other,
while nurse and Eurynome, under the flaring brands,
were making up the bed with coverings deep and soft.
And working briskly, soon as they'd made it snug,
back to her room the old nurse went to sleep
as Eurynome, their attendant, torch in hand,
lighted the royal couple's way to bed and,
leading them to their chamber, slipped away.
Rejoicing in each other, they returned to their bed,
the old familiar place they loved so well.

Now Telemachus, the cowherd and the swineherd
rested their dancing feet and had the women do the same,
and across the shadowed hall the men lay down to sleep.

But the royal couple, once they'd reveled in all
the longed-for joys of love, reveled in each other's stories,
the radiant woman telling of all she'd borne at home,
watching them there, the infernal crowd of suitors
slaughtering herds of cattle and good fat sheep—
while keen to win her hand—
draining the broached vats dry of vintage wine.
And great Odysseus told his wife of all the pains
he had dealt out to other men and all the hardships
he'd endured himself—his story first to last—
and she listened on, enchanted . . .
Sleep never sealed her eyes till all was told.

He launched in with how he fought the Cicones down,
then how he came to the Lotus-eaters' lush green land.
Then all the crimes of the Cyclops and how he paid him back
for the gallant men the monster ate without a qualm—
then how he visited Aeolus, who gave him a hero's welcome
then he sent him off, but the homeward run was not his fate,
not yet—some sudden squalls snatched him away once more

and drove him over the swarming sea, groaning in despair.
Then how he moored at Telepylus, where Laestrygonians
wrecked his fleet and killed his men-at-arms.
He told her of Circe's cunning magic wiles
and how he voyaged down in his long benched ship
to the moldering House of Death, to consult Tiresias,
ghostly seer of Thebes, and he saw old comrades there
and he saw his mother, who bore and reared him as a child.
He told how he caught the Sirens' voices throbbing in the wind
and how he had scudded past the Clashing Rocks, past grim Charybdis,
past Scylla—whom no rover had ever coasted by, home free—
and how his shipmates slaughtered the cattle of the Sun
and Zeus the king of thunder split his racing ship
with a reeking bolt and killed his hardy comrades,
all his fighting men at a stroke, but he alone
escaped their death at sea. He told how he reached
Ogygia's shores and the nymph Calypso held him back,
deep in her arching caverns, craving him for a husband—
cherished him, vowed to make him immortal, ageless, all his days,
yes, but she never won the heart inside him, never . . .
then how he reached the Phaeacians—heavy sailing there—
who with all their hearts had prized him like a god
and sent him off in a ship to his own beloved land,
giving him bronze and hoards of gold and robes . . .
and that was the last he told her, just as sleep
overcame him . . . sleep loosing his limbs,
slipping the toils of anguish from his mind.

Athena, her eyes afire, had fresh plans.
Once she thought he'd had his heart's content
of love and sleep at his wife's side, straightaway
she roused young Dawn from Ocean's banks to her golden throne
to bring men light and roused Odysseus too, who rose
from his soft bed and advised his wife in parting,
"Dear woman, we both have had our fill of trials.
You in our house, weeping over my journey home,
fraught with storms and torment, true, and I,
pinned down in pain by Zeus and other gods,
for all my desire, blocked from reaching home.
But now that we've arrived at our bed together—
the reunion that we yearned for all those years—
look after the things still left me in our house.
But as for the flocks those brazen suitors plundered,
much I'll recoup myself, making many raids;
the rest our fellow-Ithacans will supply
till all my folds are full of sheep again.
But now I must be off to the upland farm,
our orchard green with trees, to see my father,
good old man weighed down with so much grief for me.

And you, dear woman, sensible as you are,
I would advise you, still . . .
quick as the rising sun the news will spread
of the suitors that I killed inside the house.
So climb to your lofty chamber with your women.
Sit tight there. See no one. Question no one."

He strapped his burnished armor round his shoulders,
roused Telemachus, the cowherd and the swineherd,
and told them to take up weapons honed for battle.
They snapped to commands, harnessed up in bronze,
opened the doors and strode out, Odysseus in the lead.
By now the daylight covered the land, but Pallas,
shrouding them all in darkness,
quickly led the four men out of town.

Book 24. Peace

Now Cyllenian Hermes called away the suitors' ghosts,
holding firm in his hand the wand of fine pure gold
that enchants the eyes of men whenever Hermes wants
or wakes us up from sleep.
With a wave of this he stirred and led them on
and the ghosts trailed after with high thin cries
as bats cry in the depths of a dark haunted cavern,
shrilling, flittering, wild when one drops from the chain—
slipped from the rock face, while the rest cling tight . . .
So with their high thin cries the ghosts flocked now
and Hermes the Healer led them on, and down the dank
moldering paths and past the Ocean's streams they went
and past the White Rock and the Sun's Western Gates and past
the Land of Dreams, and they soon reached the fields of asphodel
where the dead, the burnt-out wraiths of mortals, make their home.

There they found the ghosts of Peleus' son Achilles,
Patroclus, fearless Antilochus—and Great Ajax too,
the first in stature, first in build and bearing
of all the Argives after Peleus' matchless son.
They had grouped around Achilles' ghost, and now
the shade of Atreus' son Agamemnon marched toward them—
fraught with grief and flanked by all his comrades,
troops of his men-at-arms who died beside him,
who met their fate in lord Aegisthus' halls.
Achilles' ghost was first to greet him: "Agamemnon,
you were the one, we thought, of all our fighting princes
Zeus who loves the lightning favored most, all your days,
because you commanded such a powerful host of men
on the fields of Troy where we Achaeans suffered.
But you were doomed to encounter fate so early,

you too, yet no one born escapes its deadly force.
If only you had died your death in the full flush
of the glory you had mastered—died on Trojan soil!
Then all united Achaea would have raised your tomb
and you'd have won your son great fame for years to come.
Not so. You were fated to die a wretched death."

And the ghost of Atrides Agamemnon answered,
"Son of Peleus, great godlike Achilles! Happy man,
you died on the fields of Troy, a world away from home,
and the best of Trojan and Argive champions died around you,
fighting for your corpse. And you . . . there you lay
in the whirling dust, overpowered in all your power
and wiped from memory all your horseman's skills.
That whole day we fought, we'd never have stopped
if Zeus had not stopped *us* with sudden gales.
Then we bore you out of the fighting, onto the ships,
we laid you down on a litter, cleansed your handsome flesh
with warm water and soothing oils, and round your body
troops of Danaans wept hot tears and cut their locks.
Hearing the news, your mother, Thetis, rose from the sea,
immortal sea-nymphs in her wake, and a strange unearthly cry
came throbbing over the ocean. Terror gripped Achaea's armies,
they would have leapt in panic, boarded the long hollow ships
if one man, deep in his age-old wisdom, had not checked them:
Nestor—from the first his counsel always seemed the best,
and now, concerned for the ranks, he rose and shouted,
'Hold fast, Argives! Sons of Achaea, don't run now!
This is Achilles' mother rising from the sea
with all her immortal sea-nymphs—
she longs to join her son who died in battle!'
That stopped our panicked forces in their tracks
as the Old Man of the Sea's daughters gathered round you—
wailing, heartsick—dressed you in ambrosial, deathless robes
and the Muses, nine in all, voice-to-voice in choirs,
their vibrant music rising, raised your dirge.
Not one soldier would you have seen dry-eyed,
the Muses' song so pierced us to the heart.
For seventeen days unbroken, days and nights
we mourned you—immortal gods and mortal men.
At the eighteenth dawn we gave you to the flames
and slaughtered around your body droves of fat sheep
and shambling longhorn cattle, and you were burned
in the garments of the gods and laved with soothing oils
and honey running sweet, and a long cortege of Argive heroes
paraded in review, in battle armor round your blazing pyre,
men in chariots, men on foot—a resounding roar went up.
And once the god of fire had burned your corpse to ash,
at first light we gathered your white bones, Achilles,

cured them in strong neat wine and seasoned oils.
Your mother gave us a gold two-handled urn,
a gift from Dionysus, she said,
a masterwork of the famous Smith, the god of fire.
Your white bones rest in that, my brilliant Achilles,
mixed with the bones of dead Patroclus, Menoetius' son,
apart from those of Antilochus, whom you treasured
more than all other comrades once Patroclus died.
Over your bones we reared a grand, noble tomb—
devoted veterans all, Achaea's combat forces—
high on its jutting headland over the Hellespont's[1]
broad reach, a landmark glimpsed from far out at sea
by men of our own day and men of days to come.
And then
your mother, begging the gods for priceless trophies,
set them out in the ring for all our champions.
You in your day have witnessed funeral games
for many heroes, games to honor the death of kings,
when young men cinch their belts, tense to win some prize—
but if you'd laid eyes on these it would have thrilled your heart,
magnificent trophies the goddess, glistening-footed Thetis,
held out in your honor. You were dear to the gods,
so even in death your name will never die . . .
Great glory is yours, Achilles,
for all time, in the eyes of all mankind!
But I?
What joy for *me* when the coil of war had wound down?
For my return Zeus hatched a pitiful death
at the hands of Aegisthus—and my accursed wife."

As they exchanged the stories of their fates,
Hermes the guide and giant-killer drew up close to both,
leading down the ghosts of the suitors King Odysseus killed.
Struck by the sight, the two went up to them right away
and the ghost of Atreus' son Agamemnon recognized
the noted prince Amphimedon, Melaneus' dear son
who received him once in Ithaca, at his home,
and Atrides' ghost called out to his old friend now,
"Amphimedon, what disaster brings you down to the dark world?
All of you, good picked men, and all in your prime—
no captain out to recruit the best in any city
could have chosen better. What laid you low?
Wrecked in the ships when lord Poseidon roused
some punishing blast of gales and heavy breakers?
Or did ranks of enemies mow you down on land
as you tried to raid and cut off herds and flocks
or fought to win their city, take their women?
Answer me, tell me. I was once your guest.

1. Strait between Europe and Asia, the modern Dardanelles.

Don't you recall the day I came to visit
your house in Ithaca—King Menelaus came too—
to urge Odysseus to sail with us in the ships
on our campaign to Troy? And the long slow voyage,
crossing wastes of ocean, cost us one whole month.
That's how hard it was to bring him round,
Odysseus, raider of cities."

"Famous Atrides!"
Amphimedon's ghost called back. "Lord of men, Agamemnon,
I remember it all, your majesty, as you say,
and I will tell you, start to finish now,
the story of our death,
the brutal end contrived to take us off.
We were courting the wife of Odysseus, gone so long.
She neither spurned nor embraced a marriage she despised,
no, she simply planned our death, our black doom!
This was her latest masterpiece of guile:
she set up a great loom in the royal halls
and she began to weave, and the weaving finespun,
the yarns endless, and she would lead us on: 'Young men,
my suitors, now that King Odysseus is no more,
go slowly, keen as you are to marry me, until
I can finish off this web . . .
so my weaving won't all fray and come to nothing.
This is a shroud for old lord Laertes, for that day
when the deadly fate that lays us out at last will take him down.
I dread the shame my countrywomen would heap upon me,
yes, if a man of such wealth should lie in state
without a shroud for cover.'

Her very words,
and despite our pride and passion we believed her.
So by day she'd weave at her great and growing web—
by night, by the light of torches set beside her,
she would unravel all she'd done. Three whole years
she deceived us blind, seduced us with this scheme . . .
Then, when the wheeling seasons brought the fourth year on
and the months waned and the long days came round once more,
one of her women, in on the queen's secret, told the truth
and we caught her in the act—unweaving her gorgeous web.
So she finished it off. Against her will. We forced her.
But just as she bound off that great shroud and washed it,
spread it out—glistening like the sunlight or the moon—
just then some wicked spirit brought Odysseus back,
from god knows where, to the edge of his estate
where the swineherd kept his pigs. And back too,
to the same place, came Odysseus' own dear son,
scudding home in his black ship from sandy Pylos.
The pair of them schemed our doom, our deathtrap,
then lit out for town—

Telemachus first in fact, Odysseus followed,
later, led by the swineherd, and clad in tatters,
looking for all the world like an old and broken beggar
hunched on a stick, his body wrapped in shameful rags.
Disguised so none of us, not even the older ones,
could spot that tramp for the man he really was,
bursting in on us there, out of the blue. No,
we attacked him, blows and insults flying fast,
and he took it all for a time, in his own house,
all the taunts and blows—he had a heart of iron.
But once the will of thundering Zeus had roused his blood,
he and Telemachus bore the burnished weapons off
and stowed them deep in a storeroom, shot the bolts
and he—the soul of cunning—told his wife to set
the great bow and the gleaming iron axes out
before the suitors—all of us doomed now—
to test our skill and bring our slaughter on . . .
Not one of us had the strength to string that powerful weapon,
all of us fell far short of what it took. But then,
when the bow was coming round to Odysseus' hands,
we raised a hue and cry—he must not have it,
no matter how he begged! Only Telemachus
urged him to take it up, and once he got it
in his clutches, long-suffering great Odysseus
strung his bow with ease and shot through all the axes,
then, vaulting onto the threshold, stood there poised, and pouring
his flashing arrows out before him, glaring for the kill,
he cut Antinous down, then shot his painful arrows
into the rest of us, aiming straight and true,
and down we went, corpse on corpse in droves.
Clearly a god was driving him and all his henchmen,
routing us headlong in their fury down the hall,
wheeling into the slaughter, slashing left and right
and grisly screams broke from skulls cracked open—
the whole floor awash with blood.
So we died,
Agamemnon . . . our bodies lie untended even now,
strewn in Odysseus' palace. They know nothing yet,
the kin in our houses who might wash our wounds
of clotted gore and lay us out and mourn us.
These are the solemn honors owed the dead."
"Happy Odysseus!"
Agamemnon's ghost cried out. "Son of old Laertes—
mastermind—what a fine, faithful wife you won!
What good sense resided in your Penelope—
how well Icarius' daughter remembered you,
Odysseus, the man she married once!
The fame of her great virtue will never die.
The immortal gods will lift a song for all mankind,

a glorious song in praise of self-possessed Penelope.
A far cry from the daughter of Tyndareus, Clytemnestra—
what outrage she committed, killing the man *she* married once!—
yes, and the song men sing of her will ring with loathing.
She brands with a foul name the breed of womankind,
even the honest ones to come!"
So they traded stories,
the two ghosts standing there in the House of Death,
far in the hidden depths below the earth.

Odysseus and his men had stridden down from town
and quickly reached Laertes' large, well-tended farm
that the old king himself had wrested from the wilds,
years ago, laboring long and hard. His lodge was here
and around it stretched a row of sheds where fieldhands,
bondsmen who did his bidding, sat and ate and slept.
And an old Sicilian woman was in charge,
who faithfully looked after her aged master
out on his good estate remote from town.
Odysseus told his servants and his son,
"Into the timbered lodge now, go, quickly,
kill us the fattest porker, fix our meal.
And I will put my father to the test,
see if the old man knows me now, on sight,
or fails to, after twenty years apart."

With that he passed his armor to his men
and in they went at once, his son as well. Odysseus
wandered off, approaching the thriving vineyard, searching,
picking his way down to the great orchard, searching,
but found neither Dolius nor his sons nor any hand.
They'd just gone off, old Dolius in the lead,
to gather stones for a dry retaining wall
to shore the vineyard up. But he did find
his father, alone, on that well-worked plot,
spading round a sapling—clad in filthy rags,
in a patched, unseemly shirt, and round his shins
he had some oxhide leggings strapped, patched too,
to keep from getting scraped, and gloves on his hands
to fight against the thorns, and on his head
he wore a goatskin skullcap
to cultivate his misery that much more . . .
Long-enduring Odysseus, catching sight of him now—
a man worn down with years, his heart racked with sorrow—
halted under a branching pear-tree, paused and wept.
Debating, head and heart, what should he do now?—
Kiss and embrace his father, pour out the long tale—
how he had made the journey home to native land—
or probe him first and test him every way?
Torn, mulling it over, this seemed better:

test the old man first,
reproach him with words that cut him to the core.
Convinced, Odysseus went right up to his father.
Laertes was digging round the sapling, head bent low
as his famous offspring hovered over him and began,
"You want no skill, old man, at tending a garden.
All's well-kept here; not one thing in the plot,
no plant, no fig, no pear, no olive, no vine,
not a vegetable, lacks your tender, loving care.
But I must say—and don't be offended now—
your plants are doing better than yourself.
Enough to be stooped with age
but look how squalid you are, those shabby rags.
Surely it's not for sloth your master lets you go to seed.
There's nothing of slave about your build or bearing.
I have eyes: you look like a king to me. The sort
entitled to bathe, sup well, then sleep in a soft bed.
That's the right and pride of you old-timers.
Come now, tell me—in no uncertain terms—
whose slave are you? whose orchard are you tending?
And tell me this—I must be absolutely sure—
this place I've reached, is it truly Ithaca?
Just as that fellow told me, just now . . .
I fell in with him on the road here. Clumsy,
none too friendly, couldn't trouble himself
to hear me out or give me a decent answer
when I asked about a long-lost friend of mine,
whether he's still alive, somewhere in Ithaca,
or dead and gone already, lost in the House of Death.
Do you want to hear his story? Listen. Catch my drift.
I once played host to a man in my own country;
he'd come to my door, the most welcome guest
from foreign parts I ever entertained.
He claimed he came of good Ithacan stock,
said his father was Arcesius' son, Laertes.
So I took the new arrival under my own roof,
I gave him a hero's welcome, treated him in style—
stores in our palace made for princely entertainment.
And I gave my friend some gifts to fit his station,
handed him seven bars of well-wrought gold,
a mixing-bowl of solid silver, etched with flowers,
a dozen cloaks, unlined and light, a dozen rugs
and as many full-cut capes and shirts as well,
and to top it off, four women, perfect beauties
skilled in crafts—he could pick them out himself."

"Stranger," his father answered, weeping softly,
"the land you've reached is the very one you're after,
true, but it's in the grip of reckless, lawless men.

And as for the gifts you showered on your guest,
you gave them all for nothing.
But if you'd found him alive, here in Ithaca,
he would have replied in kind, with gift for gift,
and entertained you warmly before he sent you off.
That's the old custom, when one has led the way.
But tell me, please—in no uncertain terms—
how many years ago did you host the man,
that unfortunate guest of yours, my son . . .
there was a son, or was he all a dream?
That most unlucky man, whom now, I fear,
far from his own soil and those he loves,
the fish have swallowed down on the high seas
or birds and beasts on land have made their meal.
Nor could the ones who bore him—mother, father—
wrap his corpse in a shroud and mourn him deeply.
Nor could his warm, generous wife, so self-possessed,
Penelope, ever keen for her husband on his deathbed,
the fit and proper way, or close his eyes at last.
These are the solemn honors owed the dead.
But tell me your own story—that I'd like to know:
Who are you? where are you from? your city? your parents?
Where does the ship lie moored that brought you here,
your hardy shipmates too? Or did you arrive
as a passenger aboard some stranger's craft
and men who put you ashore have pulled away?"

"The whole tale,"
his crafty son replied, "I'll tell you start to finish.
I come from Roamer-Town, my home's a famous place,
my father's Unsparing, son of old King Pain,
and my name's Man of Strife . . .
I sailed from Sicily, aye, but some ill wind
blew me here, off course—much against my will—
and my ship lies moored off farmlands far from town.
As for Odysseus, well, five years have passed
since he left my house and put my land behind him,
luckless man! But the birds were good as he launched out,
all on the right, and I rejoiced as I sent him off
and he rejoiced in sailing. We had high hopes
we'd meet again as guests, as old friends,
and trade some shining gifts."

At those words
a black cloud of grief came shrouding over Laertes.
Both hands clawing the ground for dirt and grime,
he poured it over his grizzled head, sobbing, in spasms.
Odysseus' heart shuddered, a sudden twinge went shooting up
through his nostrils, watching his dear father struggle . . .
He sprang toward him, kissed him, hugged him, crying,
"Father—I am your son—myself, the man you're seeking,

home after twenty years, on native ground at last!
Hold back your tears, your grief.
Let me tell you the news, but we must hurry—
I've cut the suitors down in our own house,
I've paid them back their outrage, vicious crimes!"
"Odysseus . . ."
Laertes, catching his breath, found words to answer.
"You—you're truly my son, Odysseus, home at last?
Give me a sign, some proof—I must be sure."
"This scar first,"
quick to the mark, his son said, "look at this—
the wound I took from the boar's white tusk
on Mount Parnassus. There you'd sent me, you
and mother, to see her fond old father, Autolycus,
and collect the gifts he vowed to give me, once,
when he came to see us here.
Or these, these trees—
let me tell you the trees you gave me years ago,
here on this well-worked plot . . .
I begged you for everything I saw, a little boy
trailing you through the orchard, picking our way
among these trees, and you named them one by one.
You gave me thirteen pear, ten apple trees
and forty figs—and promised to give me, look,
fifty vinerows, bearing hard on each other's heels,
clusters of grapes year-round at every grade of ripeness,
mellowed as Zeus's seasons weigh them down."
Living proof—
and Laertes' knees went slack, his heart surrendered,
recognizing the strong clear signs Odysseus offered.
He threw his arms around his own dear son, fainting
as hardy great Odysseus hugged him to his heart
until he regained his breath, came back to life
and cried out, "Father Zeus—
you gods of Olympus, you still rule on high
if those suitors have truly paid in blood
for all their reckless outrage! Oh, but now
my heart quakes with fear that all the Ithacans
will come down on us in a pack, at any time,
and rush the alarm through every island town!"

"There's nothing to fear," his canny son replied,
"put it from your mind. Let's make for your lodge
beside the orchard here. I sent Telemachus on ahead,
the cowherd, swineherd too, to fix a hasty meal."

So the two went home, confiding all the way
and arriving at the ample, timbered lodge,
they found Telemachus with the two herdsmen
carving sides of meat and mixing ruddy wine.

Before they ate, the Sicilian serving-woman
bathed her master, Laertes—his spirits high
in his own room—and rubbed him down with oil
and round his shoulders drew a fresh new cloak.
And Athena stood beside him, fleshing out the limbs
of the old commander, made him taller to all eyes,
his build more massive, stepping from his bath,
so his own son gazed at him, wonderstruck—
face-to-face he seemed a deathless god . . .
"Father"—Odysseus' words had wings—"surely
one of the everlasting gods has made you
taller, stronger, shining in my eyes!"

Facing his son, the wise old man returned,
"If only—Father Zeus, Athena and lord Apollo—
I were the man I was, king of the Cephallenians
when I sacked the city of Nericus, sturdy fortress
out on its jutting cape! If I'd been young in arms
last night in our house with harness on my back,
standing beside you, fighting off the suitors,
how many I would have cut the knees from under—
the heart inside you would have leapt for joy!"

So father and son confirmed each other's spirits.
And then, with the roasting done, the meal set out,
the others took their seats on chairs and stools,
were just putting their hands to bread and meat
when old Dolius trudged in with his sons,
worn out from the fieldwork.
The old Sicilian had gone and fetched them home,
the mother who reared the boys and tended Dolius well,
now that the years had ground the old man down . . .
When they saw Odysseus—knew him in their bones—
they stopped in their tracks, staring, struck dumb,
but the king waved them on with a warm and easy air:
"Sit down to your food, old friend. Snap out of your wonder.
We've been cooling our heels here long enough,
eager to get our hands on all this pork,
hoping you'd all troop in at any moment."

Spreading his arms, Dolius rushed up to him,
clutched Odysseus by the wrist and kissed his hand,
greeting his king now with a burst of winging words:
"Dear master, you're back—the answer to our prayers!
We'd lost all hope but the gods have brought you home!
Welcome—health! The skies rain blessings on you!
But tell me the truth now—this I'd like to know—
shrewd Penelope, has she heard you're home?
Or should we send a messenger?"
"She knows by now,

old man," his wily master answered brusquely.
"Why busy yourself with that?"

So Dolius went back to his sanded stool.
His sons too, pressing around the famous king,
greeted Odysseus warmly, grasped him by the hand
then took their seats in order by their father.

But now, as they fell to supper in the lodge,
Rumor the herald sped like wildfire through the city,
crying out the news of the suitors' bloody death and doom,
and massing from every quarter as they listened, kinsmen milled
with wails and moans of grief before Odysseus' palace.
And then they carried out the bodies, every family
buried their own, and the dead from other towns
they loaded onto the rapid ships for crews
to ferry back again, each to his own home . . .
Then in a long, mourning file they moved to assembly
where, once they'd grouped, crowding the meeting grounds,
old lord Eupithes rose in their midst to speak out.
Unforgettable sorrow wrung his heart for his son,
Antinous, the first that great Odysseus killed.
In tears for the one he lost, he stood and cried,
"My friends, what a mortal blow this man has dealt
to all our island people! Those fighters, many and brave,
he led away in his curved ships—he lost the ships
and he lost the men and back he comes again
to kill the best of our Cephallenian princes.
Quick, after him! Before he flees to Pylos
or holy Elis, where Epeans rule in power—
up, attack! Or we'll hang our heads forever,
all disgraced, even by generations down the years,
if we don't punish the murderers of our brothers and our sons!
Why, life would lose its relish—for me, at least—
I'd rather die at once and go among the dead.
Attack!—before the assassins cross the sea
and leave us in their wake."
He closed in tears
and compassion ran through every Achaean there.
Suddenly Medon and the inspired bard approached them,
fresh from Odysseus' house, where they had just awakened.
They strode into the crowds; amazement took each man
but the herald Medon spoke in all his wisdom:
"Hear me, men of Ithaca. Not without the hand
of the deathless gods did Odysseus do these things!
Myself, I saw an immortal fighting at his side—
like Mentor to the life. I saw the same god,
now in front of Odysseus, spurring him on,
now stampeding the suitors through the hall,

crazed with fear, and down they went in droves!"

Terror gripped them all, their faces ashen white.
At last the old warrior Halitherses, Mastor's son—
who alone could see the days behind and days ahead—
rose up and spoke, distraught for each man there:
"Hear me, men of Ithaca. Hear what I have to say.
Thanks to your own craven hearts these things were done!
You never listened to me or the good commander Mentor,
you never put a stop to your sons' senseless folly.
What fine work they did, so blind, so reckless,
carving away the wealth, affronting the wife
of a great and famous man, telling themselves
that he'd return no more! So let things rest now.
Listen to me for once—I say don't attack!
Else some will draw the lightning on their necks."
So he urged
and some held fast to their seats, but more than half
sprang up with warcries now. They had no taste
for the prophet's sane plan—winning Eupithes
quickly won them over. They ran for armor
and once they'd harnessed up in burnished bronze
they grouped in ranks before the terraced city.
Eupithes led them on in their foolish, mad campaign,
certain he would avenge the slaughter of his son
but the father was not destined to return—
he'd meet his death in battle then and there.

Athena at this point made appeals to Zeus:
"Father, son of Cronus, our high and mighty king,
now let me ask you a question . . .
tell me the secrets hidden in your mind.
Will you prolong the pain, the cruel fighting here
or hand down pacts of peace between both sides?"

"My child," Zeus who marshals the thunderheads replied,
"why do you pry and probe me so intently? Come now,
wasn't the plan your own? You conceived it yourself:
Odysseus should return and pay the traitors back.
Do as your heart desires—
but let me tell you how it should be done.
Now that royal Odysseus has taken his revenge,
let both sides seal their pacts that he shall reign for life,
and let us purge their memories of the bloody slaughter
of their brothers and their sons. Let them be friends,
devoted as in the old days. Let peace and wealth
come cresting through the land."
So Zeus decreed
and launched Athena already poised for action—
down she swept from Olympus' craggy peaks.

By then Odysseus' men had had their fill
of hearty fare, and the seasoned captain said,
"One of you go outside—see if they're closing in."
A son of Dolius snapped to his command,
ran to the door and saw them all too close
and shouted back to Odysseus,
"They're on top of us! To arms—and fast!"
Up they sprang and strapped themselves in armor,
the three men with Odysseus, Dolius' six sons
and Dolius and Laertes clapped on armor too,
gray as they were, but they would fight if forced.
Once they had all harnessed up in burnished bronze
they opened the doors and strode out, Odysseus in the lead.

And now, taking the build and voice of Mentor,
Zeus's daughter Athena marched right in.
The good soldier Odysseus thrilled to see her,
turned to his son and said in haste, "Telemachus,
you'll learn soon enough—as you move up to fight
where champions strive to prove themselves the best—
not to disgrace your father's line a moment.
In battle prowess we've excelled for ages
all across the world."
Telemachus reassured him,
"Now you'll see, if you care to watch, father,
now I'm fired up. Disgrace, you say?
I won't disgrace your line!"

Laertes called out in deep delight,
"What a day for me, dear gods! What joy—
my son and my grandson vying over courage!"
"Laertes!"
Goddess Athena rushed beside him, eyes ablaze:
"Son of Arcesius, dearest of all my comrades,
say a prayer to the bright-eyed girl and Father Zeus,
then brandish your long spear and wing it fast!"

Athena breathed enormous strength in the old man.
He lifted a prayer to mighty Zeus's daughter,
brandished his spear a moment, winged it fast
and hit Eupithes, pierced his bronze-sided helmet
that failed to block the bronze point tearing through—
down Eupithes crashed, his armor clanging against his chest.
Odysseus and his gallant son charged straight at the front lines,
slashing away with swords, with two-edged spears and now
they would have killed them all, cut them off from home
if Athena, daughter of storming Zeus, had not cried out
in a piercing voice that stopped all fighters cold,
"Hold back, you men of Ithaca, back from brutal war!
Break off—shed no more blood—make peace at once!"

So Athena commanded. Terror blanched their faces,
they went limp with fear, weapons slipped from their hands
and strewed the ground at the goddess' ringing voice.
They spun in flight to the city, wild to save their lives,
but loosing a savage cry, the long-enduring great Odysseus,
gathering all his force, swooped like a soaring eagle—
just as the son of Cronus hurled a reeking bolt
that fell at her feet, the mighty Father's daughter,
and blazing-eyed Athena wheeled on Odysseus, crying,
"Royal son of Laertes, Odysseus, master of exploits,
hold back now! Call a halt to the great leveler, War—
don't court the rage of Zeus who rules the world!"

So she commanded. He obeyed her, glad at heart.
And Athena handed down her pacts of peace
between both sides for all the years to come—
the daughter of Zeus whose shield is storm and thunder,
yes, but the goddess still kept Mentor's build and voice.

RESONANCES

Franz Kafka: The Silence of the Sirens[1]

Proof that inadequate, even childish measures may serve to rescue one from peril:

To protect himself from the Sirens Ulysses stopped his ears with wax and had himself bound to the mast of his ship. Naturally any and every traveler before him could have done the same, except those whom the Sirens allured even from a great distance; but it was known to all the world that such things were of no help whatever. The song of the Sirens could pierce through everything, and the longing of those they seduced would have broken far stronger bonds than chains and masts. But Ulysses did not think of that, although he had probably heard of it. He trusted absolutely to his handful of wax and his fathom of chain, and in innocent elation over his little stratagem sailed out to meet the Sirens.

Now the Sirens have a still more fatal weapon than their song, namely their silence. And though admittedly such a thing has never happened, still it is conceivable that someone might possibly have escaped from their singing; but from their silence certainly never. Against the feeling of having triumphed over them by one's own strength, and the consequent exaltation that bears down everything before it, no earthly powers can resist.

And when Ulysses approached them the potent songstresses actually did not sing, whether because they thought that this enemy could be vanquished only by their silence, or because the look of bliss on the face of Ulysses, who was thinking of nothing but his wax and his chains, made them forget their singing.

1. Translated by Willa and Edwin Muir. The great modernist writer Franz Kafka (1883–1924) was born and raised in the German-Jewish section of Prague, at that time part of the Austro-Hungarian Empire. Both drawn to and estranged from the cultures around him—Czech, German, and Jewish—Kafka wrote enigmatic parables, stories, and novels such as *The Trial* and *The Metamorphosis* (see page 2598) probing the absurdities of existence. A self-doubting perfectionist, he published little before his early death from tuberculosis. In the short parable given here, Kafka revisits the famous scene of the Sirens (page 339) to create an image of a man—or an artist—struggling against silence rather than seductive song.

But Ulysses, if one may so express it, did not hear their silence; he thought they were singing and that he alone did not hear them. For a fleeting moment he saw their throats rising and falling, their breasts lifting, their eyes filled with tears, their lips half-parted, but believed that these were accompaniments to the airs which died unheard around him. Soon, however, all this faded from his sight as he fixed his gaze on the distance, the Sirens literally vanished before his resolution, and at the very moment when they were nearest to him he knew of them no longer.

But they—lovelier than ever—stretched their necks and turned, let their awesome hair flutter free in the wind, and freely stretched their claws on the rocks. They no longer had any desire to allure; all that they wanted was to hold as long as they could the radiance that fell from Ulysses' great eyes.

If the Sirens had possessed consciousness they would have been annihilated at that moment. But they remained as they had been; all that had happened was that Ulysses had escaped them.

A codicil[2] to the foregoing has also been handed down. Ulysses, it is said, was so full of guile, was such a fox, that not even the goddess of fate could pierce his armor. Perhaps he had really noticed, although here the human understanding is beyond its depths, that the Sirens were silent, and held up to them and to the gods the aforementioned pretense merely as a sort of shield.

George Seferis: Upon a Foreign Verse[1]

For Elli, Christmas 1931

Fortunate he who's made the voyage of Odysseus.
Fortunate if on setting out he's felt the rigging of a love strong in his body,
spreading there like veins where the blood throbs.
A love of indissoluble rhythm, unconquerable like music and endless
because it was born when we were born and when it dies, if it does die,
neither we know nor does anyone else.

I ask God to help me say, at some moment of great happiness, what that love is;
sometimes when I sit surrounded by exile I hear its distant murmur like the sound of sea struck by an inexplicable hurricane.
And again and again the shade of Odysseus appears before me, his eyes red from the waves' salt,
from his ripe longing to see once more the smoke ascending from his warm hearth and the dog grown old waiting by the door.

A large man, whispering through his whitened beard words in our language spoken as it was three thousand years ago.

2. A clause added at the end of a legal document.

1. Translated by Edmund Keeley and Philip Sherrard. The modern Greek poet George Seferis (1900–1971) studied law in Paris and then joined the Greek diplomatic service; he was ambassador to England at the end of his career. He wrote all the while, publishing a dozen books of verse, essays, diaries, and fiction, mostly written while abroad. His verse achieved international acclaim, and he won the Nobel Prize in literature in 1963. Influenced by French Symbolist poetry, T. S. Eliot, and Ezra Pound, Seferis became the first major modernist poet in Greece. At the same time, his work is filled with references to classical literature, particularly to the wanderings of Odysseus, as in this 1940 poem, which sees Homer's epic both as a living presence and as deeply foreign, despite the apparent closeness of ancient and modern Greek.

He extends a palm calloused by the ropes and the tiller, his skin weathered
by the dry north wind, by heat and snow.

It's as if he wants to expel from among us the superhuman one-eyed Cyclops,
the Sirens who make you forget with their song, Scylla and Charybdis:
so many complex monsters that prevent us from remembering that he too
was a man struggling in the world with soul and body.

He is the mighty Odysseus: he who proposed the wooden horse with which
the Achaeans captured Troy.
I imagine he's coming to tell me how I too may build a wooden horse to
capture my own Troy.

Because he speaks humbly and calmly, without effort, as though he were
my father
or certain old sailors of my childhood who, leaning on their nets with winter
coming on and the wind angering,

used to recite, with tears in their eyes, the song of Erotocritos;[2]
it was then I would shudder in my sleep at the unjust fate of Aretousa de-
scending the marble steps.

He tells me of the harsh pain you feel when the ship's sails swell with mem-
ory and your soul becomes a rudder;
of being alone, dark in the night, and helpless as chaff on the threshing floor;

of the bitterness of seeing your companions one by one pulled down into the
elements and scattered;
and of how strangely you gain strength conversing with the dead when the
living who remain are no longer enough.

He speaks . . . I still see his hands that knew how to judge the carving of the
mermaid at the prow
presenting me the waveless blue sea in the heart of winter.

Derek Walcott: *from* Omeros[1]

Seven Seas rose in the half-dark to make coffee.
Sunrise was heating the ring of the horizon
and clouds were rising like loaves. By the heat of the

glowing iron rose he slid the saucepan's base on-
to the ring and anchored it there. The saucepan shook

2. A 17th-century epic from Crete by Vizentzos Kornaros, telling of the love between the valiant knight Erotokritos and the king's daughter, Aretousa.

1. Born in 1930 on St. Lucia in the Caribbean island chain known as the Antilles, Derek Walcott received a British colonial education there, then went to college in Jamaica. He then settled in Trinidad and wrote poetry and plays. For many years he split his time between Trinidad and a teaching post at Boston University, while writing 15 volumes of poetry and a dozen plays. Long recognized as one of the greatest poets writing in English, he received the Nobel Prize in literature in 1992, two years after the publication of his epic verse novel *Omeros*. See page 2795 for more of Walcott's poetry.

Written in three-line stanzas based on the form of Dante's *Divine Comedy*, Walcott's poem tells of the rivalry of two St. Lucian fishermen, Achille and Hector, for the love of a local woman, Helen. They are observed by various other characters, including a blind fisherman nicknamed Seven Seas who may be a reincarnation of Homer. Walcott himself also appears in the poem as an Odysseus-like voyager; in the scene given here, which takes place early in the poem, he visits the Boston studio of a young Greek sculptor, Antigone, who has become his lover, and he meditates on Homer's persistent presence, connecting the islands of Greece and the Caribbean.

from the weight of water in it, then it settled.

* * *

The dog scratched at the kitchen door for him to open
but he made it wait. He drummed the kitchen table
with his fingers. Two blackbirds quarrelled at breakfast.

Except for one hand he sat as still as marble,
with his egg-white eyes, fingers recounting the past
of another sea, measured by the stroking oars.

O open this day with the conch's moan, Omeros,
as you did in my boyhood, when I was a noun
gently exhaled from the palate of the sunrise.

A lizard on the sea-wall darted its question
at the waking sea, and a net of golden moss
brightened the reef, which the sails of their far canoes

avoided. Only in you, across centuries
of the sea's parchment atlas, can I catch the noise
of the surf lines wandering like the shambling fleece

of the lighthouse's flock, that Cyclops whose blind eye
shut from the sunlight. Then the canoes were galleys
over which a frigate sawed its scythed wings slowly.

In you the seeds of grey almonds guessed a tree's shape,
and the grape leaves rusted like serrated islands,
and the blind lighthouse, sensing the edge of a cape,

paused like a giant, a marble cloud in its hands,
to hurl its boulder that splashed into phosphorous
stars; then a black fisherman, his stubbled chin coarse

as a dry sea-urchin's, hoisted his flour-sack
sail on its bamboo spar, and scanned the opening line
of our epic horizon; now I can look back

to rocks that see their own feet when light nets the waves,
as the dugouts set out with ebony captains,
since it was your light that startled our sunlit wharves

where schooners swayed idly, moored to their cold capstans.
A wind turns the harbour's pages back to the voice
that hummed in the vase of a girl's throat: "Omeros."

"O-meros," she laughed. "That's what we call him in Greek,"
stroking the small bust with its boxer's broken nose,
and I thought of Seven Seas sitting near the reek

of drying fishnets, listening to the shallows' noise.
I said: "Homer and Virg are New England farmers,
and the winged horse guards their gas-station, you're right."[2]

2. In the 1950s and 1960s, an American chain of gas stations had a winged Pegasus as its symbol.

I felt the foam head watching as I stroked an arm, as
cold as its marble, then the shoulders in winter light
in the studio attic. I said, "Omeros,"

and O was the conch-shell's invocation, *mer* was
both mother and sea in our Antillean patois,° *dialect*
os, a grey bone, and the white surf as it crashes

and spreads its sibilant collar on a lace shore.
Omeros was the crunch of dry leaves, and the washes
that echoed from a cave-mouth when the tide has ebbed.

The name stayed in my mouth. I saw how light was webbed
on her Asian cheeks, defined her eyes with a black
almond's outline, as Antigone turned and said:

"I'm tired of America, it's time for me to go back
to Greece. I miss my islands." I write, it returns—
the way she turned and shook out the black gust of hair.

I saw how the surf printed its lace in patterns
on the shore of her neck, then the lowering shallows
of silk swirled at her ankles, like surf without noise,

and felt that another cold bust, not hers, but yours
saw this with stone almonds for eyes, its broken nose
turning away, as the rustling silk agrees.

But if it could read between the lines of her floor
like a white-hot deck uncaulked by Antillean heat,
to the shadows in its hold, its nostrils might flare

at the stench from manacled ankles, the coffled feet° *roped in line*
scraping like leaves, and perhaps the inculpable marble
would have turned its white seeds away, to widen

the bow of its mouth at the horror under her table,
from the lyre of her armchair draped with its white chiton,° *Greek tunic*
to do what the past always does: suffer, and stare.

She lay calm as a port, and a cloud covered her
with my shadow; then a prow with painted eyes
slowly emerged from the fragrant rain of black hair.

And I heard a hollow moan exhaled from a vase,
not for kings floundering in lances of rain; the prose
of abrupt fishermen cursing over canoes.

Sappho

early 7th century B.C.E.

The Greeks so valued Sappho's poetry that they called her the tenth Muse. Born to an aristocratic family on the island of Lesbos, she wrote poems reflecting a world of luxury, strongly marked by her island's proximity to the Asian coast and its wealthy cities. The fragmentary remains of her poetry reveal an aristocratic taste for adornments, flowers, perfumed oils, and erotic pleasures. Her poems include songs of sexual pursuit and remembrances of beloved women, sometimes framed as hymns to the goddess of *eros,* Aphrodite. Sappho was known for her verse celebrating same-sex desire, giving rise to the modern term "lesbian," which at root means simply "a native of Lesbos." Sappho also wrote wedding poems, poems of insult, and poems that refer to the heroic legends of the Trojan War. Her aesthetic oftens evokes what the Greeks called *pothos,* "yearning," a recollecting of scenes of pleasure or festival or the arrival among women of the immortal goddess. She belongs to the aristocratic world of the Archaic period, secure in its privileges and possibly even committed to preserving its way of life against tyrannical ambitions, since she was said to have been exiled in the turmoil of Lesbian politics during her lifetime. Although her poetry is fragmentary, it is the most substantial body of work by a woman that remains from classical antiquity.

PRONUNCIATION:
Sappho: SAF-fo

Rich-throned immortal Aphrodite[1]

Rich-throned immortal Aphrodite,
scheming daughter of Zeus, I pray you,
with pain and sickness, Queen, crush not my heart,

but come, if ever in the past you
heard my voice from afar and hearkened,
and left your father's halls and came, with gold

chariot yoked; and pretty sparrows
brought you swiftly across the dark earth
fluttering wings from heaven through the air.

Soon they were here, and you, Blest Goddess,
smiling with your immortal features,
asked why I'd called, what was the matter now,

what was my heart insanely craving:
"Who is it this time I must cozen
to love you, Sappho? Who's unfair to you?

"For though she flee, soon she'll be chasing;
though she refuse gifts, she'll be giving;
though she love not, she'll love despite herself."

1. Translated by M. L. West.

The lyric poets Sappho and Alkaios, red-figure vase, c. 500 B.C.E.

Yes, come once more, from sore obsession
free me; all that my heart desires
fulfilled, fulfil—help me to victory!

Come, goddess

Come, goddess, to your holy shrine,
where your delightful apple grove
awaits, and altars smoke with frankincense.

A cool brook sounds through apple boughs,
and all's with roses overhung;
from shimmering leaves a trancelike sleep takes hold.

Here is a flowery meadow, too,
where horses graze, and gentle blow

the breezes . . .

Here, then, Love-goddess much in mind,
infuse our feast in gracious style
with nectar poured in cups that turn to gold.

Some think a fleet

Some think a fleet, a troop of horse
or soldiery the finest sight
in all the world; but I say, what one loves.

Easy it is to make this plain
to anyone. She the most fair
of mortals, Helen, having a man of the best,

deserted him, and sailed to Troy,
without a thought for her dear child
or parents, led astray by [love's power.]

[For though the heart be pr]oud [and strong,]
[Love] quickly [bends it to his will.—]
That makes me think of Anactoria.

I'd sooner see her lovely walk
and the bright sparkling of her face
than all the horse and arms of Lydia.[1]

He looks to me to be in heaven

He looks to me to be in heaven,
that man who sits across from you
and listens near you to your soft speaking,

your laughing lovely: that, I vow,
makes the heart leap in my breast;
for watching you a moment, speech fails me,

my tongue is paralysed, at once
a light fire runs beneath my skin,
my eyes are blinded, and my ears drumming,

the sweat pours down me, and I shake
all over, sallower than grass:
I feel as if I'm not far off dying.

But no thing is too hard to bear;
for [God can make] the poor man [rich,
or bring to nothing heaven-high fortune.]

1. Wealthy kingdom near Lesbos in Asia Minor.

Love shakes my heart

Love
shakes my heart like the wind rushing down on
the mountain oaks.

Honestly, I wish I were dead

Honestly, I wish I were dead.
She was covered in tears as she went away,

left me, saying "Oh, it's too bad!
How unlucky we are! I swear,
Sappho, I don't want to be leaving you."

This is what I replied to her:
"Go, be happy, and think of me.
You remember how we looked after you;

or if not, then let me remind
. . . . .
all the lovely and beautiful times we had,

all the garlands of violets
and of roses and . . .
and . . . that you've put on in my company,

all the delicate chains of flowers
that encircled your tender neck
. . . . .
. . . . .
and the costly unguent with which
you anointed yourself, and the royal myrrh.

On soft couches . . .
Tender . . .
you assuaged your longing . . .

There was never a . . .
or a shrine or a . . .
. . . that we were not present at,

no grove . . . no festive dance . . .

. . . she worshipped you

. . . she worshipped you
and always in your singing she most delighted.

But now among the women of Lydia
she shines, as after the sun has set
the rosy-fingered moon will appear, surpassing

all the stars, bestowing her light alike
upon the waves of the briny sea
and on the fields that sparkle with countless flowers.

Everything is bathed in the lovely dew:
roses take their nourishment, and
soft chervil, and the blossoming honey-lotus.

Often, as she moves on her daily round,
she'll be eating her tender heart
when she thinks of her love for gentle Atthis.

And for us to go there . . .
. . . it's not possible . . .
with the wedding-song (?) ringing loud between us.

Like the sweet-apple

Like the sweet-apple that's gleaming red on the topmost bough,
right at the very end, that the apple-pickers forgot,
or rather didn't forget, but were just unable to reach.

Like the hyacinth on the hills that the passing shepherds
trample under their feet, and the purple bloom on the ground . . .

The doorman's feet

The doorman's feet are size 90:
five cowhides went into his sandals,
and it took ten cobblers to make them!

High must be the chamber—
  Hymenaeum!
Make it high, you builders!

A bridegroom's coming—
  Hymenaeum!
like the War-god himself, the tallest of the tall!

RESONANCE

Alejandra Pizarnik: Poems[1]

Poem

You choose the place of the wound
where we speak our silence.
You make of my life
this ceremony excessively pure.

1. Translated by Frank Graziano, Maria Rosa Fort, and Suzanne Levine. A student of philosophy and painting in Buenos Aires, Alejandra Pizarnik (1936–1972) also studied religion and French literature at the Sorbonne. She lived in Paris for several years and translated into Spanish works by experimental French and Francophone writers such as Antonin Artaud and Aimé Césaire. She committed suicide at age 36 through a barbiturate overdose. Melancholy, obsessive, and given to states of ecstasy and depression, she explored in her poetry the whole gamut of mental states that range from the sublime to the obscene, from lyrical tenderness to sadomasochism.

Pizarnik's poetry has earned her a devout following among readers of 20th-century Latin American poetry. In the decade before her death, she moved progressively into a world of language and poetry, speculating about suicide and the ecstasies of Sapphic love. In the end, her poetic language became disembodied and deliberately chaotic; in the poems given here, she plays both on Sappho's themes and on the fragmentary quality of Sappho's surviving verses.

Lovers

a flower
not far from the night
my mute body
opens
to the delicate urgency of dew

Recognition

You make the silence of lilacs fluttering
in the tragedy of wind in my heart.
You make of my life a child's story
where shipwrecks and deaths
are pretexts for adorable ceremonies.

Meaning of His Absence

if I dare
to look or to speak
it is due to his shadow
united so gently
to my name
far away
in the rain
in my memory
due to his face
that burning in my poem
beautifully disperses
a perfume
to the loved face disappeared

Dawn

Nude dreaming a solar night.
I have lain down animal days.
The wind and rain erased me
like a flame, like a poem
written on a wall.

Falling

Never again the hope
in a coming and going
of names, of figures.
Someone dreamed very badly,
by mistake someone used up
the forgotten distances.

Sophocles

c. 496–406 B.C.E.

A citizen of Athens and its radical, innovative democracy, Sophocles won many victories in the drama festivals of his native city. His great predecessor in the writing of tragedy, Aeschylus, wrote the *Oresteia,* a trilogy consisting of three linked plays that celebrate the founding of one of the city's important legal institutions and express a tenuous optimism about the democratic experiment. Sophocles was a more conservative thinker, and he feared for his fellow citizens and for their city.

An ancient story records the piety of Sophocles. When the worship of Asclepius the healing god was introduced into the city of Athens in 420 B.C.E., Sophocles invited the god's representative, a snake, to live in his house until a suitable sanctuary was erected. Sophocles' piety was not at all otherworldly; he shared his fellow citizens' susceptibility to eros and the beauty of boys, and said at the end of his long life that he was glad no longer to be tormented by the goddess of sexuality, Aphrodite. Throughout his tragedies, one of the themes that concerns him is reverence for the gods, and he feared that democratic Athens, having turned away from the elite aristocratic form of government of earlier centuries, now risked abandoning the gods in a proud burst of wealth, confidence, and sometimes arrogant domination of its former allies in an Athenian empire. Among the Athenians of his day were intellectuals proud of their accomplishments in the development of logic, rhetoric, political theory, and philosophy. Radical thinkers such as the sophists insisted that human beings were the "measure of all things," rather than urging the traditional practices of worshiping the gods. Sophocles' tragedies intervene in the intense social, political, and religious debates of the fifth century B.C.E., when Athens participated in the victory over the huge Persian Empire's invasion at the beginning of the century, flourished in an atmosphere of risk and daring at midcentury, and went down to devastating defeat by the Spartans in the Peloponnesian War at the century's end.

In his long career, Sophocles wrote more than 120 tragedies, of which only a handful remain. His career began in 468 and ended with his death, just after the death of Euripides, the third of the great fifth-century tragedians. Sophocles lived in Athens at the time of Pericles, the brilliant aristocratic statesman of the classical age, which was also the time of Socrates, a founder of Greek philosophy, and of Aristophanes, the obscene, wild comic dramatist. This was also the period of Athens' great building program, when the treasures from the Athenians' empire were spent on embellishing the city with such magnificent buildings as the Parthenon, the temple of Athena, the patron goddess of Athens. Sophocles' plays take on some of the powerful myths the Greeks told themselves, seeking to reconcile the ideology of the democratic city, in which all men were said to be equal, with the myths of the preeminent heroes and gods they inherited from the Archaic age. Sophocles' *Electra* focuses on the unhappy family of Atreus, representing the daughter of the house as a wretched victim of her parent's enmity. His *Philoktetes* goes back to the myths of Homer and the Trojan War and shows the now-ruthless and rhetorically skilled Odysseus in conflict with the values of the past. *The Women of Trachis* portrays the great hero Herakles as he returns home from battle with a captive slave bride; his wife, having waited at home, tries to win him back to her with what she believes to be a love potion, but that is in fact a deadly poison that destroys him. In the *Ajax,* Sophocles portrays the great Homeric warrior driven mad by Athena, slaughtering his wife and children in a world he can no longer understand. In all of these plays, Sophocles engages questions of time and eternity and the conflict between the human values of the democratic city and the old Homeric virtues and devotion to the gods. In interrogating received stories and myths, he engages in a prolonged meditation on the relationship between civilization and its limits—nature, the gods, madness, death—all that cannot be known through the civilized discourses of human beings.

The myth of the Greek city of Thebes engaged Sophocles throughout his life as a tragedian, and in plays such as *Oedipus the King,* he gave a searching development to stark old stories that his audience would have known well. Thebes was said to have been founded by Kadmos, a prince from Tyre in Asia Minor; his sister Europa was one day playing on the beach with her friends when a lovely white bull took her off. This was Zeus in one of the many forms he assumed to seduce mortal women and boys. He took Europa to Crete, and she gave the continent of Europe her name. Kadmos journeyed to the mainland and after consulting with the oracle, came to the land of Thebes, where he had been instructed to kill the dragon guarding a spring. He took the dragon's teeth, sowed them in the ground, and warriors sprang up who fought to the death until only five survived. These were the Spartoi, the founding aristocratic families of Thebes. Kadmos founded the ruling dynasty, which suffered many troubles. One of the kings refused to worship Dionysos, even though the god was the son of Zeus and a Theban princess; he was dismembered and perhaps eaten alive by his own mother in a Dionysiac ecstasy. Another offspring of the house of Thebes was Aktaion, who while hunting one day came upon the virgin goddess Artemis bathing naked; enraged, she turned him into a stag to be eaten by his own dogs. The family also included Laios (or Laius), who in exile as a young man carried off his host's son, which, according to some legends, began the Greek practice of pederasty, the amorous, erotic relationship between men and young or adolescent boys. Laius returned to Thebes but was warned never to have children with his wife, Jocasta. When a son was born, they pierced the boy's ankles and gave him to a slave to expose on Mount Parnassos above the city of Thebes. He instead gave the child to a shepherd, who delivered him to the childless ruling family of Corinth.

This deliverance only plunged the child into new troubles. The boy, in Greek *Oidipous,* "Swollen-foot," was taunted as he grew up, and he went to visit the oracle of Apollo at Delphi, where he was told that he would kill his father and marry his mother. Seeking to avoid this fate, he traveled to Thebes, not Corinth, which he believed to be his home, and on the way killed a man on the road. When he arrived in Thebes, it was besieged by an uncanny monster called the Sphinx, who killed those who could not answer her riddle: What goes on four feet in the morning, two feet at noon, three at dusk? Only Oedipus knew the answer: the human being, who crawls as an infant, walks upright as an adult, and uses a stick in old age. He won both the city and its queen, Jocasta, and had children with her. Set after these events, Sophocles' play *Oedipus the King* portrays his anguished discovery of who he is.

The myth goes beyond the episodes portrayed in the tragedy: Oedipus cursed his sons just before the end of his life in Colonus, near Athens, where he blessed a shrine to protect the city of the Athenians from harm. Oedipus, who had known his mother's body twice (once as her child, once as her husband) with all his sufferings bestowed the benefit only a monster could give. His sons killed one another over the right to rule the city of Thebes; their sister, Antigone, went to her death defending her right to bury her despised brother, cast outside the city to be eaten by birds and dogs. Each of the great tragedians of classical Athens represented episodes from the Theban story of incest and horror for their audiences.

As presented in Athenian tragedy, archaic, mythic Thebes stands as a sort of anti-Athens, a place where repetition, terrible contact with the gods, sterility, dismemberment, incest, and filial hatred present a negative mirror for Athens, of all that Athens wishes not to bring forth as a *polis,* all that it fears as a dark side of its optimism. Sophocles returned to the myth of Thebes again and again, telling the story over many years. He probably first wrote *Antigone,* producing *Oedipus the King* some time after, and late in life gave the city *Oedipus at Colonus* at the end of the horrors of the Peloponnesian War, the great war among the Greeks. The tragedy *Oedipus the King* was probably first performed in a period of great trouble for the Athenians. Some have argued that in the tragedy, Oedipus stands as a figure for the city of Athens itself, as a model of intellectual confidence and seeking, exemplifying all the skills of rhetoric, science, mathematics, philosophy, and medicine on which the democratic city prided itself and on which it based its claims to the right to govern other cities in an empire. Others see Oedipus as a figure for the human being as such, existing between the gods and the animals, aspiring to godhood, brought down to the level of the beasts for that very aspiration, in an exemplary spectacle. The Athenians practiced both ostracism—the expulsion of dangerously powerful men from their midst—and a *pharmakos* ritual, like the scapegoating of the Hebrew Bible, expelling the lowest of their members. The Theban king, once compared to a god, becomes a blinded, wandering beast. Oedipus, whether an allegory for Athens itself or an exemplary human being, citizen of the city, has haunted the imagination of the West from Sophocles to Freud and beyond.

PRONUNCIATIONS:

Creon: KREE-on
Jocasta: jo-KAS-ta
Oedipus: EE-di-pus
Teiresias: ty-REE-see-as

Oedipus the King[1]

Characters

OEDIPUS, *King of Thebes*
JOCASTA, *his wife*
CREON, *his brother-in-law*
TEIRESIAS, *an old blind prophet*
A PRIEST
FIRST MESSENGER
SECOND MESSENGER
A HERDSMAN
A CHORUS OF OLD MEN OF THEBES

Scene: In front of the palace of Oedipus at Thebes. To the right of the stage near the altar stands the Priest with a crowd of children. Oedipus emerges from the central door.

OEDIPUS: Children, young sons and daughters of old Cadmus,[2]
why do you sit here with your suppliant crowns?
The town is heavy with a mingled burden
of sounds and smells, of groans and hymns and incense;
I did not think it fit that I should hear
of this from messengers but came myself,—
I Oedipus whom all men call the Great.

[*He turns to the Priest.*]

You're old and they are young; come, speak for them.
What do you fear or want, that you sit here
suppliant? Indeed I'm willing to give all
that you may need; I would be very hard
should I not pity suppliants like these.

PRIEST: O ruler of my country, Oedipus,
you see our company around the altar;
you see our ages; some of us, like these,
who cannot yet fly far, and some of us
heavy with age; these children are the chosen
among the young, and I the priest of Zeus.

1. Translated by David Greene.
2. Founder of Thebes.

Within the market place sit others crowned
with suppliant garlands, at the double shrine
of Pallas and the temple where Ismenus
gives oracles by fire. King, you yourself
have seen our city reeling like a wreck
already; it can scarcely lift its prow
out of the depths, out of the bloody surf.
A blight is on the fruitful plants of the earth,
a blight is on the cattle in the fields,
a blight is on our women that no children
are born to them; a God that carries fire,
a deadly pestilence, is on our town,
strikes us and spares not, and the house of Cadmus
is emptied of its people while black Death
grows rich in groaning and in lamentation.
We have not come as suppliants to this altar
because we thought of you as of a God,
but rather judging you the first of men
in all the chances of this life and when
we mortals have to do with more than man.
You came and by your coming saved our city,
freed us from tribute which we paid of old
to the Sphinx, cruel singer. This you did
in virtue of no knowledge we could give you,
in virtue of no teaching; it was God
that aided you, men say, and you are held
with God's assistance to have saved our lives.
Now Oedipus, Greatest in all men's eyes,
here falling at your feet we all entreat you,
find us some strength for rescue.
Perhaps you'll hear a wise word from some God,
perhaps you will learn something from a man
(for I have seen that for the skilled of practice
the outcome of their counsels live the most).
Noblest of men, go, and raise up our city,
go,—and give heed. For now this land of ours
calls you its savior since you saved it once.
So, let us never speak about your reign
as of a time when first our feet were set
secure on high, but later fell to ruin.
Raise up our city, save it and raise it up.
Once you have brought us luck with happy omen;
be no less now in fortune.
If you will rule this land, as now you rule it,
better to rule it full of men than empty.
For neither tower nor ship is anything
when empty, and none live in it together.

OEDIPUS: I pity you, children. You have come full of longing,
but I have known the story before you told it

only too well. I know you are all sick,
yet there is not one of you, sick though you are,
that is as sick as I myself.
Your several sorrows each have single scope
and touch but one of you. My spirit groans
for city and myself and you at once.
You have not roused me like a man from sleep;
know that I have given many tears to this,
gone many ways wandering in thought,
but as I thought I found only one remedy
and that I took. I sent Menoeceus' son
Creon, Jocasta's brother, to Apollo,
to his Pythian temple,
that he might learn there by what act or word
I could save this city. As I count the days,
it vexes me what ails him; he is gone
far longer than he needed for the journey.
But when he comes, then, may I prove a villain,
if I shall not do all the God commands.

PRIEST: Thanks for your gracious words. Your servants here
signal that Creon is this moment coming.

OEDIPUS: His face is bright. O holy Lord Apollo,
grant that his news too may be bright for us
and bring us safety.

PRIEST: It is happy news,
I think, for else his head would not be crowned
with sprigs of fruitful laurel.

OEDIPUS: We will know soon,
he's within hail. Lord Creon, my good brother,
what is the word you bring us from the God?

[*Creon enters.*]

CREON: A good word,—for things hard to bear themselves
if in the final issue all is well
I count complete good fortune.

OEDIPUS: What do you mean?
What you have said so far
leaves me uncertain whether to trust or fear.

CREON: If you will hear my news before these others
I am ready to speak, or else to go within.

OEDIPUS: Speak it to all;
the grief I bear, I bear it more for these
than for my own heart.

CREON: I will tell you, then,
what I heard, from the God.
King Phoebus[3] in plain words commanded us
to drive out a pollution from our land,

3. Apollo, god of the Pythian oracle at Delphi.

pollution grown ingrained within the land;
drive it out, said the God, not cherish it,
till it's past cure.

OEDIPUS: What is the rite
of purification? How shall it be done?

CREON: By banishing a man, or expiation
of blood by blood, since it is murder guilt
which holds our city in this destroying storm.

OEDIPUS: Who is this man whose fate the God pronounces?

CREON: My Lord, before you piloted the state
we had a king called Laius.

OEDIPUS: I know of him by hearsay. I have not seen him.

CREON: The God commanded clearly: let some one
punish with force this dead man's murderers.

OEDIPUS: Where are they in the world? Where would a trace
of this old crime be found? It would be hard
to guess where.

CREON: The clue is in this land;
that which is sought is found;
the unheeded thing escapes:
so said the God.

OEDIPUS: Was it at home,
or in the country that death came upon him,
or in another country travelling?

CREON: He went, he said himself, upon an embassy,
but never returned when he set out from home.

OEDIPUS: Was there no messenger, no fellow traveller
who knew what happened? Such a one might tell
something of use.

CREON: They were all killed save one. He fled in terror
and he could tell us nothing in clear terms
of what he knew, nothing, but one thing only.

OEDIPUS: What was it?
If we could even find a slim beginning
in which to hope, we might discover much.

CREON: This man said that the robbers they encountered
were many and the hands that did the murder
were many; it was no man's single power.

OEDIPUS: How could a robber dare a deed like this
were he not helped with money from the city,
money and treachery?

CREON: That indeed was thought.
But Laius was dead and in our trouble
there was none to help.

OEDIPUS: What trouble was so great to hinder you
inquiring out the murder of your king?

CREON: The riddling Sphinx induced us to neglect
mysterious crimes and rather seek solution
of troubles at our feet.

OEDIPUS: I will bring this to light again. King Phoebus
fittingly took this care about the dead,
and you too fittingly.
And justly you will see in me an ally,
a champion of my country and the God.
For when I drive pollution from the land
I will not serve a distant friend's advantage,
but act in my own interest. Whoever
he was that killed the king may readily
wish to dispatch me with his murderous hand;
so helping the dead king I help myself.

Come, children, take your suppliant boughs and go;
up from the altars now. Call the assembly
and let it meet upon the understanding
that I'll do everything. God will decide
whether we prosper or remain in sorrow.

PRIEST: Rise, children—it was this we came to seek,
which of himself the king now offers us.
May Phoebus who gave us the oracle
come to our rescue and stay the plague.

[*Exeunt all but the Chorus.*]

Strophe[4]

CHORUS: What is the sweet spoken word of God from the shrine of Pytho rich in gold
that has come to glorious Thebes?
I am stretched on the rack of doubt, and terror and trembling hold
my heart, O Delian Healer, and I worship full of fears
for what doom you will bring to pass, new or renewed in the revolving
years.
Speak to me, immortal voice,
child of golden Hope.

Antistrophe

First I call on you, Athene, deathless daughter of Zeus,
and Artemis, Earth Upholder,
who sits in the midst of the market place in the throne which men call
Fame,
and Phoebus, the Far Shooter, three averters of Fate,
come to us now, if ever before, when ruin rushed upon the state,
you drove destruction's flame away
out of our land.

Strophe

Our sorrows defy number;
all the ship's timbers are rotten;
taking of thought is no spear for the driving away of the plague.

4. Strophe ("turn") and Antistrophe ("counterturn") refer to the moves the chorus would make, dancing as it sang.

There are no growing children in this famous land;
there are no women bearing the pangs of childbirth.
You may see them one with another, like birds swift on the wing,
quicker than fire unmastered,
speeding away to the coast of the Western God.[5]

Antistrophe

In the unnumbered deaths
of its people the city dies;
those children that are born lie dead on the naked earth
unpitied, spreading contagion of death; and grey haired mothers and wives
everywhere stand at the altar's edge, suppliant, moaning;
the hymn to the healing God rings out but with it the wailing voices are
blended.
From these our sufferings grant us, O golden Daughter of Zeus,
glad-faced deliverance.

Strophe

There is no clash of brazen shields but our fight is with the War God,
a War God ringed with the cries of men, a savage God who burns us;
grant that he turn in racing course backwards out of our country's bounds
to the great palace of Amphitrite or where the waves of the Thracian sea
deny the stranger safe anchorage.
Whatsoever escapes the night
at last the light of day revisits;
so smite the War God, Father Zeus,
beneath your thunderbolt,
for you are the Lord of the lightning, the lightning that carries fire.

Antistrophe

And your unconquered arrow shafts, winged by the golden corded bow,
Lycean King, I beg to be at our side for help;
and the gleaming torches of Artemis with which she scours the Lycean hills,
and I call on the God with the turban of gold, who gave his name to this
country of ours,
the Bacchic God with the wind flushed face,[6]
Evian One, who travel
with the Maenad company,
combat the God that burns us
with your torch of pine;
for the God that is our enemy is a God unhonoured among the Gods.

[*Oedipus returns.*]

OEDIPUS: For what you ask me—if you will hear my words,
and hearing welcome them and fight the plague,
you will find strength and lightening of your load.

5. Hades or death.

6. Dionysos, who traveled with frenzied female devotees, the Maenads.

Hark to me; what I say to you, I say
as one that is a stranger to the story
as stranger to the deed. For I would not
be far upon the track if I alone
were tracing it without a clue. But now,
since after all was finished, I became
a citizen among you, citizens—
now I proclaim to all the men of Thebes:
who so among you knows the murderer
by whose hand Laius, son of Labdacus,
died—I command him to tell everything
to me,—yes, though he fears himself to take the blame
on his own head; for bitter punishment
he shall have none, but leave this land unharmed.
Or if he knows the murderer, another,
a foreigner, still let him speak the truth.
For I will pay him and be grateful, too.
But if you shall keep silence, if perhaps
some one of you, to shield a guilty friend,
or for his own sake shall reject my words—
hear what I shall do then:
I forbid that man, whoever he be, my land,
my land where I hold sovereignty and throne;
and I forbid any to welcome him
or cry him greeting or make him a sharer
in sacrifice or offering to the Gods,
or give him water for his hands to wash.
I command all to drive him from their homes,
since he is our pollution, as the oracle
of Pytho's God proclaimed him now to me.
So I stand forth a champion of the God
and of the man who died.
Upon the murderer I invoke this curse—
whether he is one man and all unknown,
or one of many—may he wear out his life
in misery to miserable doom!
If with my knowledge he lives at my hearth
I pray that I myself may feel my curse.
On you I lay my charge to fulfill all this
for me, for the God, and for this land of ours
destroyed and blighted, by the God forsaken.

Even were this no matter of God's ordinance
it would not fit you so to leave it lie,
unpurified, since a good man is dead
and one that was a king. Search it out.
Since I am now the holder of his office,
and have his bed and wife that once was his,
and had his line not been unfortunate

we would have common children—[fortune leaped
upon his head]—because of all these things,
I fight in his defence as for my father,
and I shall try all means to take the murderer
of Laius the son of Labdacus
the son of Polydorus and before him
of Cadmus and before him of Agenor.
Those who do not obey me, may the Gods
grant no crops springing from the ground they plough
nor children to their women! May a fate
like this, or one still worse than this consume them!
For you whom these words please, the other Thebans,
may Justice as your ally and all the Gods
live with you, blessing you now and for ever!

CHORUS: As you have held me to my oath, I speak:
I neither killed the king nor can declare
the killer; but since Phoebus set the quest
it is his part to tell who the man is.

OEDIPUS: Right; but to put compulsion on the Gods
against their will—no man can do that.

CHORUS: May I then say what I think second best?

OEDIPUS: If there's a third best, too, spare not to tell it.

CHORUS: I know that what the Lord Teiresias
sees, is most often what the Lord Apollo
sees. If you should inquire of this from him
you might find out most clearly.

OEDIPUS: Even in this my actions have not been sluggard.
On Creon's word I have sent two messengers
and why the prophet is not here already
I have been wondering.

CHORUS: His skill apart
there is besides only an old faint story.

OEDIPUS: What is it?
I look at every story.

CHORUS: It was said
that he was killed by certain wayfarers.

OEDIPUS: I heard that, too, but no one saw the killer.

CHORUS: Yet if he has a share of fear at all,
his courage will not stand firm, hearing your curse.

OEDIPUS: The man who in the doing did not shrink
will fear no word.

CHORUS: Here comes his prosecutor:
led by your men the godly prophet comes
in whom alone of mankind truth is native.

[*Enter Teiresias, led by a little boy.*]

OEDIPUS: Teiresias, you are versed in everything,
things teachable and things not to be spoken,
things of the heaven and earth-creeping things.

You have no eyes but in your mind you know
with what a plague our city is afflicted.
My lord, in you alone we find a champion,
in you alone one that can rescue us.
Perhaps you have not heard the messengers,
but Phoebus sent in answer to our sending
an oracle declaring that our freedom
from this disease would only come when we
should learn the names of those who killed King Laius,
and kill them or expel from our country.
Do not begrudge us oracles from birds,
or any other way of prophecy
within your skill; save yourself and the city,
save me; redeem the debt of our pollution
that lies on us because of this dead man.
We are in your hands; pains are most nobly taken
to help another when you have means and power.

TEIRESIAS: Alas, how terrible is wisdom when
it brings no profit to the man that's wise!
This I knew well, but had forgotten it,
else I would not have come here.

OEDIPUS: What is this?
How sad you are now you have come!

TEIRESIAS: Let me
go home. It will be easiest for us both
to bear our several destinies to the end
if you will follow my advice.

OEDIPUS: You'd rob us
of this your gift of prophecy? You talk
as one who had no care for law nor love
for Thebes who reared you.

TEIRESIAS: Yes, but I see that even your own words
miss the mark; therefore I must fear for mine.

OEDIPUS: For God's sake if you know of anything,
do not turn from us; all of us kneel to you,
all of us here, your suppliants.

TEIRESIAS: All of you here know nothing. I will not
bring to the light of day my troubles, mine—
rather than call them yours.

OEDIPUS: What do you mean?
You know of something but refuse to speak.
Would you betray us and destroy the city?

TEIRESIAS: I will not bring this pain upon us both,
neither on you nor on myself. Why is it
you question me and waste your labour? I
will tell you nothing.

OEDIPUS: You would provoke a stone! Tell us, you villain,
tell us, and do not stand there quietly
unmoved and balking at the issue.

TEIRESIAS: You blame my temper but you do not see
your own that lives within you; it is me
you chide.
OEDIPUS: Who would not feel his temper rise
at words like these with which you shame our city?
TEIRESIAS: Of themselves things will come, although I hide them
and breathe no word of them.
OEDIPUS: Since they will come
tell them to me.
TEIRESIAS: I will say nothing further.
Against this answer let your temper rage
as wildly as you will.
OEDIPUS: Indeed I am
so angry I shall not hold back a jot
of what I think. For I would have you know
I think you were complotter of the deed
and doer of the deed save in so far
as for the actual killing. Had you had eyes
I would have said alone you murdered him.
TEIRESIAS: Yes? Then I warn you faithfully to keep
the letter of your proclamation and
from this day forth to speak no word of greeting
to these nor me; you are the land's pollution.
OEDIPUS: How shamelessly you started up this taunt!
How do you think you will escape?
TEIRESIAS: I have.
I have escaped; the truth is what I cherish
and that's my strength.
OEDIPUS: And who has taught you truth?
Not your profession surely!
TEIRESIAS: You have taught me,
for you have made me speak against my will.
OEDIPUS: Speak what? Tell me again that I may learn it better.
TEIRESIAS: Did you not understand before or would you
provoke me into speaking?
OEDIPUS: I did not grasp it,
not so to call it known. Say it again.
TEIRESIAS: I say you are the murderer of the king
whose murderer you seek.
OEDIPUS: Not twice you shall
say calumnies like this and stay unpunished.
TEIRESIAS: Shall I say more to tempt your anger more?
OEDIPUS: As much as you desire; it will be said
in vain.
TEIRESIAS: I say that with those you love best
you live in foulest shame unconsciously
and do not see where you are in calamity.
OEDIPUS: Do you imagine you can always talk
like this, and live to laugh at it hereafter?

TEIRESIAS: Yes, if the truth has anything of strength.
OEDIPUS: It has, but not for you; it has no strength
for you because you are blind in mind and ears
as well as in your eyes.
TEIRESIAS: You are a poor wretch
to taunt me with the very insults which
every one soon will heap upon yourself.
OEDIPUS: Your life is one long night so that you cannot
hurt me or any other who sees the light.
TEIRESIAS: It is not fate that I should be your ruin,
Apollo is enough; it is his care
to work this out.
OEDIPUS: Was this your own design
or Creon's?
TEIRESIAS: Creon is no hurt to you,
but you are to yourself.
OEDIPUS: Wealth, sovereignty and skill outmatching skill
for the contrivance of an envied life!
Great store of jealousy fill your treasury chests,
if my friend Creon, friend from the first and loyal,
thus secretly attacks me, secretly
desires to drive me out and secretly
suborns this juggling, trick devising quack,
this wily beggar who has only eyes
for his own gains, but blindness in his skill.
For, tell me, where have you seen clear, Teiresias,
with your prophetic eyes? When the dark singer,
the sphinx, was in your country, did you speak
word of deliverance to its citizens?
And yet the riddle's answer was not the province
of a chance comer. It was a prophet's task
and plainly you had no such gift of prophecy
from birds nor otherwise from any God
to glean a word of knowledge. But I came,
Oedipus, who knew nothing, and I stopped her.
I solved the riddle by my wit alone.
Mine was no knowledge got from birds. And now
you would expel me,
because you think that you will find a place
by Creon's throne. I think you will be sorry,
both you and your accomplice, for your plot
to drive me out. And did I not regard you
as an old man, some suffering would have taught you
that what was in your heart was treason.
CHORUS: We look at this man's words and yours, my king,
and we find both have spoken them in anger.
We need no angry words but only thought
how we may best hit the God's meaning for us.
TEIRESIAS: If you are king, at least I have the right

no less to speak in my defence against you.
Of that much I am master. I am no slave
of yours, but Loxias',[7] and so I shall not
enroll myself with Creon for my patron.
Since you have taunted me with being blind,
here is my word for you.
You have your eyes but see not where you are
in sin, nor where you live, nor whom you live with.
Do you know who your parents are? Unknowing
you are an enemy to kith and kin
in death, beneath the earth, and in this life.
A deadly footed, double striking curse,
from father and mother both, shall drive you forth
out of this land, with darkness on your eyes,
that now have such straight vision. Shall there be
a place will not be harbour to your cries,
a corner of Cithaeron will not ring
in echo to your cries, soon, soon,—
when you shall learn the secret of your marriage,
which steered you to a haven in this house,—
haven no haven, after lucky voyage?
And of the multitude of other evils
establishing a grim equality
between you and your children, you know nothing.
So, muddy with contempt my words and Creon's!
Misery shall grind no man as it will you.

OEDIPUS: Is it endurable that I should hear
such words from him? Go and a curse go with you!
Quick, home with you! Out of my house at once!

TEIRESIAS: I would not have come either had you not called me.

OEDIPUS: I did not know then you would talk like a fool—
or it would have been long before I called you.

TEIRESIAS: I am a fool then, as it seems to you—
but to the parents who have bred you, wise.

OEDIPUS: What parents? Stop! Who are they of all the world?

TEIRESIAS: This day will show your birth and will destroy you.

OEDIPUS: How needlessly your riddles darken everything.

TEIRESIAS: But it's in riddle answering you are strongest.

OEDIPUS: Yes. Taunt me where you will find me great.

TEIRESIAS: It is this very luck that has destroyed you.

OEDIPUS: I do not care, if it has saved this city.

TEIRESIAS: Well, I will go. Come, boy, lead me away.

OEDIPUS: Yes, lead him off. So long as you are here,
you'll be a stumbling block and a vexation;
once gone, you will not trouble me again.

TEIRESIAS: I have said
what I came here to say not fearing your

7. Apollo's.

countenance: there is no way you can hurt me.
I tell you, king, this man, this murderer
(whom you have long declared you are in
search of,
indicting him in threatening proclamation
as murderer of Laius)—he is here.
In name he is a stranger among citizens
but soon he will be shown to be a citizen
true native Theban, and he'll have no joy
of the discovery: blindness for sight
and beggary for riches his exchange,
he shall go journeying to a foreign country
tapping his way before him with a stick.
He shall be proved father and brother both
to his own children in his house; to her
that gave him birth, a son and husband both;
a fellow sower in his father's bed
with that same father that he murdered.
Go within, reckon that out, and if you find me
mistaken, say I have no skill in prophecy.

[*Exeunt separately Teiresias and Oedipus.*]

Strophe

CHORUS: Who is the man proclaimed
by Delphi's prophetic rock
as the bloody handed murderer,
the doer of deeds that none dare name?
Now is the time for him to run
with a stronger foot
than Pegasus
for the child of Zeus leaps in arms upon him
with fire and the lightning bolt,
and terribly close on his heels
are the Fates that never miss.

Antistrophe

Lately from snowy Parnassus
clearly the voice flashed forth,
bidding each Theban track him down,
the unknown murderer.
In the savage forests he lurks and in
the caverns like
the mountain bull.
He is sad and lonely, and lonely his feet
that carry him far from the navel of earth;
but its prophecies, ever living,
flutter around his head.

Strophe

The augur has spread confusion,
terrible confusion;
I do not approve what was said
nor can I deny it.
I do not know what to say;
I am in a flutter of foreboding;
I never heard in the present
nor past of a quarrel between
the sons of Labdacus and Polybus,
that I might bring as proof
in attacking the popular fame
of Oedipus, seeking
to take vengeance for undiscovered
death in the line of Labdacus.

Antistrophe

Truly Zeus and Apollo are wise
and in human things all knowing;
but amongst men there is no
distinct judgment, between the prophet
and me—which of us is right.
One man may pass another in wisdom
but I would never agree
with those that find fault with the king
till I should see the word
proved right beyond doubt. For once
in visible form the Sphinx
came on him and all of us
saw his wisdom and in that test
he saved the city. So he will not be condemned by my mind.

[*Enter Creon.*]

CREON: Citizens, I have come because I heard
deadly words spread about me, that the king
accuses me. I cannot take that from him.
If he believes that in these present troubles
he has been wronged by me in word or deed
I do not want to live on with the burden
of such a scandal on me. The report
injures me doubly and most vitally—
for I'll be called a traitor to my city
and traitor also to my friends and you.

CHORUS: Perhaps it was a sudden gust of anger
that forced that insult from him, and no judgment.

CREON: But did he say that it was in compliance
with schemes of mine that the seer told him lies?

CHORUS: Yes, he said that, but why, I do not know.

CREON: Were his eyes straight in his head? Was his mind right
when he accused me in this fashion?
CHORUS: I do not know; I have no eyes to see
what princes do. Here comes the king himself.

[*Enter Oedipus.*]

OEDIPUS: You, sir, how is it you come here? Have you so much
brazen-faced daring that you venture in
my house although you are proved manifestly
the murderer of that man, and though you tried,
openly, highway robbery of my crown?
For God's sake, tell me what you saw in me,
what cowardice or what stupidity,
that made you lay a plot like this against me?
Did you imagine I should not observe
the crafty scheme that stole upon me or
seeing it, take no means to counter it?
Was it not stupid of you to make the attempt,
to try to hunt down royal power without
the people at your back or friends? For only
with the people at your back or money can
the hunt end in the capture of a crown.
CREON: Do you know what you're doing? Will you listen
to words to answer yours, and then pass judgment?
OEDIPUS: You're quick to speak, but I am slow to grasp you,
for I have found you dangerous,—and my foe.
CREON: First of all hear what I shall say to that.
OEDIPUS: At least don't tell me that you are not guilty.
CREON: If you think obstinacy without wisdom
a valuable possession, you are wrong.
OEDIPUS: And you are wrong if you believe that one,
a criminal, will not be punished only
because he is my kinsman.
CREON: This is but just—
but tell me, then, of what offense I'm guilty?
OEDIPUS: Did you or did you not urge me to send
to this prophetic mumbler?
CREON: I did indeed,
and I shall stand by what I told you.
OEDIPUS: How long ago is it since Laius. . . .
CREON: What about Laius? I don't understand.
OEDIPUS: Vanished—died—was murdered?
CREON: It is long,
a long, long time to reckon.
OEDIPUS: Was this prophet
in the profession then?
CREON: He was, and honoured
as highly as he is today.
OEDIPUS: At that time did he say a word about me?

CREON: Never, at least when I was near him.
OEDIPUS: You never made a search for the dead man?
CREON: We searched, indeed, but never learned of anything.
OEDIPUS: Why did our wise old friend not say this then?
CREON: I don't know; and when I know nothing, I
usually hold my tongue.
OEDIPUS: You know this much,
and can declare this much if you are loyal.
CREON: What is it? If I know, I'll not deny it.
OEDIPUS: That he would not have said that I killed Laius
had he not met you first.
CREON: You know yourself
whether he said this, but I demand that I
should hear as much from you as you from me.
OEDIPUS: Then hear,—I'll not be proved a murderer.
CREON: Well, then. You're married to my sister.
OEDIPUS: Yes,
that I am not disposed to deny.
CREON: You rule
this country giving her an equal share
in the government?
OEDIPUS: Yes, everything she wants
she has from me.
CREON: And I, as thirdsman to you,
am rated as the equal of you two?
OEDIPUS: Yes, and it's there you've proved yourself false friend.
CREON: Not if you will reflect on it as I do.
Consider, first, if you think anyone
would choose to rule and fear rather than rule
and sleep untroubled by a fear if power
were equal in both cases. I, at least,
I was not born with such a frantic yearning
to be a king—but to do what kings do.
And so it is with every one who has learned
wisdom and self-control. As it stands now,
the prizes are all mine—and without fear.
But if I were the king myself, I must
do much that went against the grain.
How should despotic rule seem sweeter to me
than painless power and an assured authority?
I am not so besotted yet that I
want other honours than those that come with profit.
Now every man's my pleasure; every man greets me;
now those who are your suitors fawn on me,—
success for them depends upon my favour.
Why should I let all this go to win that?
My mind would not be traitor if it's wise;
I am no treason lover, of my nature,
nor would I ever dare to join a plot.

Prove what I say. Go to the oracle
at Pytho and inquire about the answers,
if they are as I told you. For the rest,
if you discover I laid any plot
together with the seer, kill me, I say,
not only by your vote but by my own.
But do not charge me on obscure opinion
without some proof to back it. It's not just
lightly to count your knaves as honest men,
nor honest men as knaves. To throw away
an honest friend is, as it were, to throw
your life away, which a man loves the best.
In time you will know all with certainty;
time is the only test of honest men,
one day is space enough to know a rogue.

CHORUS: His words are wise, king, if one fears to fall.
Those who are quick of temper are not safe.

OEDIPUS: When he that plots against me secretly
moves quickly, I must quickly counterplot.
If I wait taking no decisive measure
his business will be done, and mine be spoiled.

CREON: What do you want to do then? Banish me?

OEDIPUS: No, certainly; kill you, not banish you.

CREON: I do not think that you've your wits about you.

OEDIPUS: For my own interests, yes.

CREON: But for mine, too,
you should think equally.

OEDIPUS: You are a rogue.

CREON: Suppose you do not understand?

OEDIPUS: But yet
I must be ruler.

CREON: Not if you rule badly.

OEDIPUS: O, city, city!

CREON: I too have some share
in the city; it is not yours alone.

CHORUS: Stop, my lords! Here—and in the nick of time
I see Jocasta coming from the house;
with her help lay the quarrel that now stirs you.

[*Enter Jocasta.*]

JOCASTA: For shame! Why have you raised this foolish squabbling
brawl? Are you not ashamed to air your private
griefs when the country's sick? Go in, you, Oedipus,
and you, too, Creon, into the house. Don't magnify
your nothing troubles.

CREON: Sister, Oedipus,
your husband, thinks he has the right to do
terrible wrongs—he has but to choose between
two terrors: banishing or killing me.

OEDIPUS: He's right, Jocasta; for I find him plotting
with knavish tricks against my person.

CREON: That God may never bless me! May I die
accursed, if I have been guilty of
one tittle of the charge you bring against me!

JOCASTA: I beg you, Oedipus, trust him in this,
spare him for the sake of this his oath to God,
for my sake, and the sake of those who stand here.

CHORUS: Be gracious, be merciful,
we beg of you.

OEDIPUS: In what would you have me yield?

CHORUS: He has been no silly child in the past.
He is strong in his oath now.
Spare him.

OEDIPUS: Do you know what you ask?

CHORUS: Yes.

OEDIPUS: Tell me then.

CHORUS: He has been your friend before all men's eyes; do not cast him
away dishonoured on an obscure conjecture.

OEDIPUS: I would have you know that this request of yours
really requests my death or banishment.

CHORUS: May the Sun God, king of Gods, forbid! May I die without God's
blessing, without friends' help, if I had any such thought. But my
spirit is broken by my unhappiness for my wasting country; and
this would but add troubles amongst ourselves to the other troubles.

OEDIPUS: Well, let him go then—if I must die ten times for it,
or be sent out dishonoured into exile.
It is your lips that prayed for him I pitied,
not his; wherever he is, I shall hate him.

CREON: I see you sulk in yielding and you're dangerous
when you are out of temper; natures like yours
are justly heaviest for themselves to bear.

OEDIPUS: Leave me alone! Take yourself off, I tell you.

CREON: I'll go, you have not known me, but they have,
and they have known my innocence.

[*Exit.*]

CHORUS: Won't you take him inside, lady?

JOCASTA: Yes, when I've found out what was the matter.

CHORUS: There was some misconceived suspicion of a story, and on the other
side the sting of injustice.

JOCASTA: So, on both sides?

CHORUS: Yes.

JOCASTA: What was the story?

CHORUS: I think it best, in the interests of the country, to leave it where it ended.

OEDIPUS: You see where you have ended, straight of judgment
although you are, by softening my anger.

CHORUS: Sir, I have said before and I say again—be sure that I would have been proved a madman, bankrupt in sane council, if I should put you away, you who steered the country I love safely when she was crazed with troubles. God grant that now, too, you may prove a fortunate guide for us.

JOCASTA: Tell me, my lord, I beg of you, what was it
that roused your anger so?

OEDIPUS: Yes, I will tell you.
I honour you more than I honour them.
It was Creon and the plots he laid against me.

JOCASTA: Tell me—if you can clearly tell the quarrel—

OEDIPUS: Creon says
that I'm the murderer of Laius.

JOCASTA: Of his own knowledge or on information?

OEDIPUS: He sent this rascal prophet to me, since
he keeps his own mouth clean of any guilt.

JOCASTA: Do not concern yourself about this matter;
listen to me and learn that human beings
have no part in the craft of prophecy.
Of that I'll show you a short proof.
There was an oracle once that came to Laius,—
I will not say that it was Phoebus' own,
but it was from his servants—and it told him
that it was fate that he should die a victim
at the hands of his own son, a son to be born
of Laius and me. But, see now, he,
the king, was killed by foreign highway robbers
at a place where three roads meet—so goes the story;
and for the son—before three days were out
after his birth King Laius pierced his ankles
and by the hands of others cast him forth
upon a pathless hillside. So Apollo
failed to fulfill his oracle to the son,
that he should kill his father, and to Laius
also proved false in that the thing he feared,
death at his son's hands, never came to pass.
So clear in this case were the oracles,
so clear and false. Give them no heed, I say;
what God discovers need of, easily
he shows to us himself.

OEDIPUS: O dear Jocasta,
as I hear this from you, there comes upon me
a wandering of the soul—I could run mad.

JOCASTA: What trouble is it, that you turn again
and speak like this?
OEDIPUS: I thought I heard you say
that Laius was killed at a crossroads.
JOCASTA: Yes, that was how the story went and still
that word goes round.
OEDIPUS: Where is this place, Jocasta,
where he was murdered?
JOCASTA: Phocis is the country
and the road splits there, one of two roads from Delphi,
another comes from Daulia.
OEDIPUS: How long ago is this?
JOCASTA: The news came to the city just before
you became king and all men's eyes looked to you.
What is it, Oedipus, that's in your mind?
OEDIPUS: What have you designed, O Zeus, to do with me?
JOCASTA: What is the thought that troubles your heart?
OEDIPUS: Don't ask me yet—tell me of Laius—
How did he look? How old or young was he?
JOCASTA: He was a tall man and his hair was grizzled
already—nearly white—and in his form
not unlike you.
OEDIPUS: O God, I think I have
called curses on myself in ignorance.
JOCASTA: What do you mean? I am terrified
when I look at you.
OEDIPUS: I have a deadly fear
that the old seer had eyes. You'll show me more
if you can tell me one more thing.
JOCASTA: I will.
I'm frightened,—but if I can understand,
I'll tell you all you ask.
OEDIPUS: How was his company?
Had he few with him when he went this journey,
or many servants, as would suit a prince?
JOCASTA: In all there were but five, and among them
a herald; and one carriage for the king.
OEDIPUS: It's plain—it's plain—who was it told you this?
JOCASTA: The only servant that escaped safe home.
OEDIPUS: Is he at home now?
JOCASTA: No, when he came home again
and saw you king and Laius was dead,
he came to me and touched my hand and begged
that I should send him to the fields to be
my shepherd and so he might see the city
as far off as he might. So I
sent him away. He was an honest man,
as slaves go, and was worthy of far more
than what he asked of me.

OEDIPUS: O, how I wish that he could come back quickly!
JOCASTA: He can. Why is your heart so set on this?
OEDIPUS: O dear Jocasta, I am full of fears
that I have spoken far too much; and therefore
I wish to see this shepherd.
JOCASTA: He will come;
but, Oedipus, I think I'm worthy too
to know what it is that disquiets you.
OEDIPUS: It shall not be kept from you, since my mind
has gone so far with its forebodings. Whom
should I confide in rather than you, who is there
of more importance to me who have passed
through such a fortune?
Polybus was my father, king of Corinth,
and Merope, the Dorian, my mother.
I was held greatest of the citizens
in Corinth till a curious chance befell me
as I shall tell you—curious, indeed,
but hardly worth the store I set upon it.
There was a dinner and at it a man,
a drunken man, accused me in his drink
of being bastard. I was furious
but held my temper under for that day.
Next day I went and taxed my parents with it;
they took the insult very ill from him,
the drunken fellow who had uttered it.
So I was comforted for their part, but
still this thing rankled always, for the story
crept about widely. And I went at last
to Pytho, though my parents did not know.
But Phoebus sent me home again unhonoured
in what I came to learn, but he foretold
other and desperate horrors to befall me,
that I was fated to lie with my mother,
and show to daylight an accursed breed
which men would not endure, and I was doomed
to be murderer of the father that begot me.
When I heard this I fled, and in the days
that followed I would measure from the stars
the whereabouts of Corinth—yes, I fled
to somewhere where I should not see fulfilled
the infamies told in that dreadful oracle.
And as I journeyed I came to the place
where, as you say, this king met with his death.
Jocasta, I will tell you the whole truth.
When I was near the branching of the crossroads,
going on foot, I was encountered by
a herald and a carriage with a man in it,
just as you tell me. He that led the way

and the old man himself wanted to thrust me
out of the road by force. I became angry
and struck the coachman who was pushing me.
When the old man saw this he watched his moment,
and as I passed he struck me from his carriage,
full on the head with his two pointed goad.
But he was paid in full and presently
my stick had struck him backwards from the car
and he rolled out of it. And then I killed them
all. If it happened there was any tie
of kinship twixt this man and Laius,
who is then now more miserable than I,
what man on earth so hated by the Gods,
since neither citizen nor foreigner
may welcome me at home or even greet me,
but drive me out of doors? And it is I,
I and no other have so cursed myself.
And I pollute the bed of him I killed
by the hands that killed him. Was I not born evil?
Am I not utterly unclean? I had to fly
and in my banishment not even see
my kindred nor set foot in my own country,
or otherwise my fate was to be yoked
in marriage with my mother and kill my father,
Polybus who begot me and had reared me.
Would not one rightly judge and say that on me
these things were sent by some malignant God?
O no, no, no—O holy majesty
of God on high, may I not see that day!
May I be gone out of men's sight before
I see the deadly taint of this disaster
come upon me.

CHORUS: Sir, we too fear these things. But until you see this man face to face and hear his story, hope.

OEDIPUS: Yes, I have just this much of hope—to wait until the herdsman comes.

JOCASTA: And when he comes, what do you want with him?

OEDIPUS: I'll tell you; if I find that his story is the same as yours, I at least will be clear of this guilt.

JOCASTA: Why what so particularly did you learn from my story?

OEDIPUS: You said that he spoke of highway *robbers* who killed Laius. Now if he uses the same number, it was not I who killed him. One man cannot be the same as many. But if he speaks of a man travelling alone, then clearly the burden of the guilt inclines towards me.

JOCASTA: Be sure, at least, that this was how he told the story. He cannot unsay it now, for every one in the city heard it—not I alone. But, Oedipus, even if he diverges from what he said then, he shall never prove that the murder of Laius squares rightly with the prophecy—for Loxias declared that the king should be killed by

his own son. And that poor creature did not kill him surely,—
for he died himself first. So as far as prophecy goes, henceforward
I shall not look to the right hand or the left.

OEDIPUS: Right. But yet, send some one for the peasant to bring him here;
do not neglect it.

JOCASTA: I will send quickly. Now let me go indoors. I will do nothing
except what pleases you.

[*Exeunt.*]

Strophe

CHORUS: May destiny ever find me
pious in word and deed
prescribed by the laws that live on high:
laws begotten in the clear air of heaven,
whose only father is Olympus;[8]
no mortal nature brought them to birth,
no forgetfulness shall lull them to sleep;
for God is great in them and grows not old.

Antistrophe

Insolence breeds the tyrant, insolence
if it is glutted with a surfeit, unseasonable, unprofitable,
climbs to the roof-top and plunges
sheer down to the ruin that must be,
and there its feet are no service.
But I pray that the God may never
abolish the eager ambition that profits the state.
For I shall never cease to hold the God as our protector.

Strophe

If a man walks with haughtiness
of hand or word and gives no heed
to Justice and the shrines of Gods
despises—may an evil doom
smite him for his ill-starred pride of heart!—
if he reaps gains without justice
and will not hold from impiety
and his fingers itch for untouchable things.
When such things are done, what man shall contrive
to shield his soul from the shafts of the God?
When such deeds are held in honour,
why should I honour the Gods in the dance?

Antistrophe

No longer to the holy place,
to the navel of earth I'll go

8. Mountain throne of Zeus and home of the gods.

to worship, nor to Abae
nor to Olympia,
unless the oracles are proved to fit,
for all men's hands to point at.
O Zeus, if you are rightly called
the sovereign lord, all-mastering,
let this not escape you nor your ever-living power!
The oracles concerning Laius
are old and dim and men regard them not.
Apollo is nowhere clear in honour; God's service perishes.

[*Enter Jocasta, carrying garlands.*]

JOCASTA: Princes of the land, I have had the thought to go
to the Gods' temples, bringing in my hand
garlands and gifts of incense, as you see.
For Oedipus excites himself too much
at every sort of trouble, not conjecturing,
like a man of sense, what will be from what was,
but he is always at the speaker's mercy,
when he speaks terrors. I can do no good
by my advice, and so I came as suppliant
to you, Lycaean Apollo, who are nearest.
These are the symbols of my prayer and this
my prayer: grant us escape free of the curse.
Now when we look to him we are all afraid;
he's pilot of our ship and he is frightened.

[*Enter Messenger.*]

MESSENGER: Might I learn from you, sirs, where is the house of Oedipus? Or best of all, if you know, where is the king himself?

CHORUS: This is his house and he is within doors. This lady is his wife and mother of his children.

MESSENGER: God bless you, lady, and God bless your household! God bless Oedipus' noble wife!

JOCASTA: God bless you, sir, for your kind greeting! What do you want of us that you have come here? What have you to tell us?

MESSENGER: Good news, lady. Good for your house and for your husband.

JOCASTA: What is your news? Who sent you to us?

MESSENGER: I come from Corinth and the news I bring will give you pleasure. Perhaps a little pain too.

JOCASTA: What is this news of double meaning?

MESSENGER: The people of the Isthmus will choose Oedipus to be their king. That is the rumour there.

JOCASTA: But isn't their king still old Polybus?

MESSENGER: No. He is in his grave. Death has got him.

JOCASTA: Is that the truth? Is Oedipus' father dead?

MESSENGER: May I die myself if it be otherwise!

JOCASTA [*to a servant*]: Be quick and run to the King with the news! O oracles of the

Gods, where are you now? It was from this man Oedipus fled, lest he should be his murderer! And now he is dead, in the course of nature, and not killed by Oedipus.

[*Enter Oedipus.*]

OEDIPUS: Dearest Jocasta, why have you sent for me?

JOCASTA: Listen to this man and when you hear reflect what is the outcome of the holy oracles of the Gods.

OEDIPUS: Who is he? What is his message for me?

JOCASTA: He is from Corinth and he tells us that your father Polybus is dead and gone.

OEDIPUS: What's this you say, sir? Tell me yourself.

MESSENGER: Since this is the first matter you want clearly told: Polybus has gone down to death. You may be sure of it.

OEDIPUS: By treachery or sickness?

MESSENGER: A small thing will put old bodies asleep.

OEDIPUS: So he died of sickness, it seems,—poor old man!

MESSENGER: Yes, and of age—the long years he had measured.

OEDIPUS: Ha! Ha! O dear Jocasta, why should one
look to the Pythian hearth? Why should one look
to the birds screaming overhead? They prophesied
that I should kill my father! But he's dead,
and hidden deep in earth, and I stand here
who never laid a hand on spear against him,—
unless perhaps he died of longing for me,
and thus I am his murderer. But they,
the oracles, as they stand—he's taken them
away with him, they're dead as he himself is,
and worthless.

JOCASTA: That I told you before now.

OEDIPUS: You did, but I was misled by my fear.

JOCASTA: Then lay no more of them to heart, not one.

OEDIPUS: But surely I must fear my mother's bed?

JOCASTA: Why should man fear since chance is all in all
for him, and he can clearly foreknow nothing?
Best to live lightly, as one can, unthinkingly.
As to your mother's marriage bed,—don't fear it.
Before this, in dreams too, as well as oracles,
many a man has lain with his own mother.
But he to whom such things are nothing bears
his life most easily.

OEDIPUS: All that you say would be said perfectly
if she were dead; but since she lives I must
still fear, although you talk so well, Jocasta.

JOCASTA: Still in your father's death there's light of comfort?

OEDIPUS: Great light of comfort; but I fear the living.

MESSENGER: Who is the woman that makes you afraid?

OEDIPUS: Merope, old man, Polybus' wife.

MESSENGER: What about her frightens the queen and you?
OEDIPUS: A terrible oracle, stranger, from the Gods.
MESSENGER: Can it be told? Or does the sacred law
forbid another to have knowledge of it?
OEDIPUS: O no! Once on a time Loxias said
that I should lie with my own mother and
take on my hands the blood of my own father.
And so for these long years I've lived away
from Corinth; it has been to my great happiness;
but yet it's sweet to see the face of parents.
MESSENGER: This was the fear which drove you out of Corinth?
OEDIPUS: Old man, I did not wish to kill my father.
MESSENGER: Why should I not free you from this fear, sir,
since I have come to you in all goodwill?
OEDIPUS: You would not find me thankless if you did.
MESSENGER: Why, it was just for this I brought the news,—
to earn your thanks when you had come safe home.
OEDIPUS: No, I will never come near my parents.
MESSENGER: Son,
it's very plain you don't know what you're doing.
OEDIPUS: What do you mean, old man? For God's sake, tell me.
MESSENGER: If your homecoming is checked by fears like these.
OEDIPUS: Yes, I'm afraid that Phoebus may prove right.
MESSENGER: The murder and the incest?
OEDIPUS: Yes, old man;
that is my constant terror.
MESSENGER: Do you know
that all your fears are empty?
OEDIPUS: How is that,
if they are father and mother and I their son?
MESSENGER: Because Polybus was no kin to you in blood.
OEDIPUS: What, was not Polybus my father?
MESSENGER: No more than I but just so much.
OEDIPUS: How can
my father be my father as much as one
that's nothing to me?
MESSENGER: Neither he nor I
begat you.
OEDIPUS: Why then did he call me son?
MESSENGER: A gift he took you from these hands of mine.
OEDIPUS: Did he love so much what he took from another's hand?
MESSENGER: His childlessness before persuaded him.
OEDIPUS: Was I a child you bought or found when I
was given to him?
MESSENGER: On Cithaeron's slopes
in the twisting thickets you were found.
OEDIPUS: And why
were you a traveller in those parts?
MESSENGER: I was

in charge of mountain flocks.
OEDIPUS: You were a shepherd?
A hireling vagrant?
MESSENGER: Yes, but at least at that time
the man that saved your life, son.
OEDIPUS: What ailed me when you took me in your arms?
MESSENGER: In that your ankles should be witnesses.
OEDIPUS: Why do you speak of that old pain?
MESSENGER: I loosed you;
the tendons of your feet were pierced and fettered,—
OEDIPUS: My swaddling clothes brought me a rare disgrace.
MESSENGER: So that from this you're called your present name.
OEDIPUS: Was this my father's doing or my mother's?
For God's sake, tell me.
MESSENGER: I don't know, but he
who gave you to me has more knowledge than I.
OEDIPUS: You yourself did not find me then? You took me
from someone else?
MESSENGER: Yes, from another shepherd.
OEDIPUS: Who was he? Do you know him well enough
to tell?
MESSENGER: He was called Laius' man.
OEDIPUS: You mean the king who reigned here in the old days?
MESSENGER: Yes, he was that man's shepherd.
OEDIPUS: Is he alive
still, so that I could see him?
MESSENGER: You who live here
would know that best.
OEDIPUS: Do any of you here
know of this shepherd whom he speaks about
in town or in the fields? Tell me. It's time
that this was found out once for all.
CHORUS: I think he is none other than the peasant
whom you have sought to see already; but
Jocasta here can tell us best of that.
OEDIPUS: Jocasta, do you know about this man
whom we have sent for? Is he the man he mentions?
JOCASTA: Why ask of whom he spoke? Don't give it heed;
nor try to keep in mind what has been said.
It will be wasted labour.
OEDIPUS: With such clues
I could not fail to bring my birth to light.
JOCASTA: I beg you—do not hunt this out—I beg you,
if you have any care for your own life.
What I am suffering is enough.
OEDIPUS: Keep up
your heart, Jocasta. Though I'm proved a slave,
thrice slave, and though my mother is thrice slave,
you'll not be shown to be of lowly lineage.

JOCASTA: O be persuaded by me, I entreat you;
do not do this.
OEDIPUS: I will not be persuaded to let be
the chance of finding out the whole thing clearly.
JOCASTA: It is because I wish you well that I
give you this counsel—and it's the best counsel.
OEDIPUS: Then the best counsel vexes me, and has
for some while since.
JOCASTA: O Oedipus, God help you!
God keep you from the knowledge of who you are!
OEDIPUS: Here, some one, go and fetch the shepherd for me;
and let her find her joy in her rich family!
JOCASTA: O Oedipus, unhappy Oedipus!
that is all I can call you, and the last thing
that I shall ever call you.

[*Exit.*]

CHORUS: Why has the queen gone, Oedipus, in wild
grief rushing from us? I am afraid that trouble
will break out of this silence.
OEDIPUS: Break out what will! I at least shall be
willing to see my ancestry, though humble.
Perhaps she is ashamed of my low birth,
for she has all a woman's high-flown pride.
But I account myself a child of Fortune,
beneficent Fortune, and I shall not be
dishonoured. She's the mother from whom I spring;
the months, my brothers, marked me, now as small,
and now again as mighty. Such is my breeding,
and I shall never prove so false to it,
as not to find the secret of my birth.
CHORUS:

Strophe

If I am a prophet and wise of heart
you shall not fail, Cithaeron,
by the limitless sky, you shall not!—
to know at tomorrow's full moon
that Oedipus honours you,
as native to him and mother and nurse at once;
and that you are honoured in dancing by us, as finding favour in
sight of our king.
Apollo, to whom we cry, find these things pleasing!

Antistrophe

Who was it bore you, child? One of
the long-lived nymphs who lay with Pan—
the father who treads the hills?
Or was she a bride of Loxias, your mother? The grassy slopes

are all of them dear to him. Or perhaps Cyllene's king
or the Bacchants' God that lives on the tops
of the hills received you a gift from some
one of the Helicon Nymphs, with whom he mostly plays?

[*Enter an old man, led by Oedipus' servants.*]

OEDIPUS: If some one like myself who never met him
may make a guess,—I think this is the herdsman,
whom we were seeking. His old age is consonant
with the other. And besides, the men who bring him
I recognize as my own servants. You
perhaps may better me in knowledge since
you've seen the man before.

CHORUS: You can be sure
I recognize him. For if Laius
had ever an honest shepherd, this was he.

OEDIPUS: You, sir, from Corinth, I must ask you first,
is this the man you spoke of?

MESSENGER: This is he
before your eyes.

OEDIPUS: Old man, look here at me
and tell me what I ask you. Were you ever
a servant of King Laius?

HERDSMAN: I was,—
no slave he bought but reared in his own house.

OEDIPUS: What did you do as work? How did you live?

HERDSMAN: Most of my life was spent among the flocks.

OEDIPUS: In what part of the country did you live?

HERDSMAN: Cithaeron and the places near to it.

OEDIPUS: And somewhere there perhaps you knew this man?

HERDSMAN: What was his occupation? Who?

OEDIPUS: This man here,
have you had any dealings with him?

HERDSMAN: No—
not such that I can quickly call to mind.

MESSENGER: That is no wonder, master. But I'll make him remember what he
does not know. For I know, that he well knows the country of
Cithaeron, how he with two flocks, I with one kept company for
three years—each year half a year—from spring till autumn time
and then when winter came I drove my flocks to our fold home
again and he to Laius' steadings. Well—am I right or not in what
I said we did?

HERDSMAN: You're right—although it's a long time ago.

MESSENGER: Do you remember giving me a child
to bring up as my foster child?

HERDSMAN: What's this?
Why do you ask this question?

MESSENGER: Look old man,

here he is—here's the man who was that child!
HERDSMAN: Death take you! Won't you hold your tongue?
OEDIPUS: No, no,
do not find fault with him, old man. Your words
are more at fault than his.
HERDSMAN: O best of masters,
how do I give offense?
OEDIPUS: When you refuse
to speak about the child of whom he asks you.
HERDSMAN: He speaks out of his ignorance, without meaning.
OEDIPUS: If you'll not talk to gratify me, you
will talk with pain to urge you.
HERDSMAN: O please, sir,
don't hurt an old man, sir.
OEDIPUS [*to the servants*]: Here, one of you,
twist his hands behind him.
HERDSMAN: Why, God help me, why?
What do you want to know?
OEDIPUS: You gave a child
to him,—the child he asked you of?
HERDSMAN: I did.
I wish I'd died the day I did.
OEDIPUS: You will
unless you tell me truly.
HERDSMAN: And I'll die
far worse if I should tell you.
OEDIPUS: This fellow
is bent on more delays, as it would seem.
HERDSMAN: O no, no! I have told you that I gave it.
OEDIPUS: Where did you get this child from? Was it your own or did you
get it from another?
HERDSMAN: Not
my own at all; I had it from some one.
OEDIPUS: One of these citizens? or from what house?
HERDSMAN: O master, please—I beg you, master, please
don't ask me more.
OEDIPUS: You're a dead man if I
ask you again.
HERDSMAN: It was one of the children
of Laius.
OEDIPUS: A slave? Or born in wedlock?
HERDSMAN: O God, I am on the brink of frightful speech.
OEDIPUS: And I of frightful hearing. But I must hear.
HERDSMAN: The child was called his child; but she within,
your wife would tell you best how all this was.
OEDIPUS: *She* gave it to you?
HERDSMAN: Yes, she did, my lord.
OEDIPUS: To do what with it?
HERDSMAN: Make away with it.

OEDIPUS: She was so hard—its mother?
HERDSMAN: Aye, through fear
of evil oracles.
OEDIPUS: Which?
HERDSMAN: They said that he
should kill his parents.
OEDIPUS: How was it that you
gave it away to this old man?
HERDSMAN: O master,
I pitied it, and thought that I could send it
off to another country and this man
was from another country. But he saved it
for the most terrible troubles. If you are
the man he says you are, you're bred
to misery.
OEDIPUS: O, O, O, they will all come,
all come out clearly! Light of the sun, let me
look upon you no more after today!
I who first saw the light bred of a match
accursed, and accursed in my living
with them I lived with, cursed in my killing.

[*Exeunt all but the Chorus.*]

CHORUS:

Strophe

O generations of men, how I
count you as equal with those who live
not at all!
What man, what man on earth wins more
of happiness than a seeming
and after that turning away?
Oedipus, you are my pattern of this,
Oedipus, you and your fate!
Luckless Oedipus, whom of all men
I envy not at all.

Antistrophe

In as much as he shot his bolt
beyond the others and won the prize
of happiness complete—
O Zeus—and killed and reduced to nought
the hooked taloned maid of the riddling speech,
standing a tower against death for my land:
hence he was called my king and hence
was honoured the highest of all
honours; and hence he ruled
in the great city of Thebes.

Strophe

But now whose tale is more miserable?
Who is there lives with a savager fate?
Whose troubles so reverse his life as his?

O Oedipus, the famous prince
for whom a great haven
the same both as father and son
sufficed for generation,
how, O how, have the furrows ploughed
by your father endured to bear you, poor wretch,
and hold their peace so long?

Antistrophe

Time who sees all has found you out
against your will; judges your marriage accursed,
begetter and begot at one in it.

O child of Laius,
would I had never seen you.
I weep for you and cry
a dirge of lamentation.

To speak directly, I drew my breath
from you at the first and so now I lull
my mouth to sleep with your name.

[*Enter a second messenger.*]

SECOND MESSENGER: O Princes always honoured by our country,
what deeds you'll hear of and what horrors see,
what grief you'll feel, if you as true born Thebans
care for the house of Labdacus's sons.
Phasis nor Ister cannot purge this house,
I think, with all their streams, such things
it hides, such evils shortly will bring forth
into the light, whether they will or not;
and troubles hurt the most
when they prove self-inflicted.

CHORUS: What we had known before did not fall short
of bitter groaning's worth; what's more to tell?

SECOND MESSENGER: Shortest to hear and tell—our glorious queen
Jocasta's dead.

CHORUS: Unhappy woman! How?

SECOND MESSENGER: By her own hand. The worst of what was done
you cannot know. You did not see the sight.
Yet in so far as I remember it
you'll hear the end of our unlucky queen.
When she came raging into the house she went
straight to her marriage bed, tearing her hair
with both her hands, and crying upon Laius

long dead—Do you remember, Laius,
that night long past which bred a child for us
to send you to your death and leave
a mother making children with her son?
And then she groaned and cursed the bed in which
she brought forth husband by her husband, children
by her own child, an infamous double bond.
How after that she died I do not know,—
for Oedipus distracted us from seeing.
He burst upon us shouting and we looked
to him as he paced frantically around,
begging us always: Give me a sword, I say,
to find this wife no wife, this mother's womb,
this field of double sowing whence I sprang
and where I sowed my children! As he raved
some god showed him the way—none of us there.
Bellowing terribly and led by some
invisible guide he rushed on the two doors,—
wrenching the hollow bolts out of their sockets,
he charged inside. There, there, we saw his wife
hanging, the twisted rope around her neck.
When he saw her, he cried out fearfully
and cut the dangling noose. Then, as she lay,
poor woman, on the ground, what happened after,
was terrible to see. He tore the brooches—
the gold chased brooches fastening her robe—
away from her and lifting them up high
dashed them on his own eyeballs, shrieking out
such things as: they will never see the crime
I have committed or had done upon me!
Dark eyes, now in the days to come look on
forbidden faces, do not recognize
those whom you long for—with such imprecations
he struck his eyes again and yet again
with the brooches. And the bleeding eyeballs gushed
and stained his beard—no sluggish oozing drops
but a black rain and bloody hail poured down.

So it has broken—and not on one head
but troubles mixed for husband and for wife.
The fortune of the days gone by was true
good fortune—but today groans and destruction
and death and shame—of all ills can be named
not one is missing.

CHORUS: Is he now in any ease from pain?

SECOND MESSENGER: He shouts
for some one to unbar the doors and show him
to all the men of Thebes, his father's killer,
his mother's—no I cannot say the word,

it is unholy—for he'll cast himself,
out of the land, he says, and not remain
to bring a curse upon his house, the curse
he called upon it in his proclamation. But
he wants for strength, aye, and some one to guide him;
his sickness is too great to bear. You, too,
will be shown that. The bolts are opening.
Soon you will see a sight to waken pity
even in the horror of it.

[*Enter the blinded Oedipus.*]

CHORUS: This is a terrible sight for men to see!
I never found a worse!
Poor wretch, what madness came upon you!
What evil spirit leaped upon your life
to your ill-luck—a leap beyond man's strength!
Indeed I pity you, but I cannot
look at you, though there's much I want to ask
and much to learn and much to see.
I shudder at the sight of you.

OEDIPUS: O, O,
where am I going? Where is my voice
borne on the wind to and fro?
Spirit, how far have you sprung?

CHORUS: To a terrible place whereof men's ears
may not hear, nor their eyes behold it.

OEDIPUS: Darkness!
Horror of darkness enfolding, resistless, unspeakable visitant
sped by an ill wind in haste!
madness and stabbing pain and memory
of evil deeds I have done!

CHORUS: In such misfortunes it's no wonder
if double weighs the burden of your grief.

OEDIPUS: My friend,
you are the only one steadfast, the only one that attends on me;
you still stay nursing the blind man.
Your care is not unnoticed. I can know
your voice, although this darkness is my world.

CHORUS: Doer of dreadful deeds, how did you dare
so far to do despite to your own eyes?
what spirit urged you to it?

OEDIPUS: It was Apollo, friends, Apollo,
that brought this bitter bitterness, my sorrows to completion.
But the hand that struck me
was none but my own.
Why should I see
whose vision showed me nothing sweet to see?

CHORUS: These things are as you say.

OEDIPUS: What can I see to love?
What greeting can touch my ears with joy?
Take me away, and haste—to a place out of the way!
Take me away, my friends, the greatly miserable,
the most accursed, whom God too hates
above all men on earth!
CHORUS: Unhappy in your mind and your misfortune,
would I had never known you!
OEDIPUS: Curse on the man who took
the cruel bonds from off my legs, as I lay in the field.
He stole me from death and saved me,
no kindly service.
Had I died then
I would not be so burdensome to friends.
CHORUS: I, too, could have wished it had been so.
OEDIPUS: Then I would not have come
to kill my father and marry my mother infamously.
Now I am godless and child of impurity,
begetter in the same seed that created my wretched self.
If there is any ill worse than ill,
that is the lot of Oedipus.
CHORUS: I cannot say your remedy was good;
you would be better dead than blind and living.
OEDIPUS: What I have done here was best done—don't tell me
otherwise, do not give me further counsel.
I do not know with what eyes I could look
upon my father when I die and go
under the earth, nor yet my wretched mother—
those two to whom I have done things deserving
worse punishment than hanging. Would the sight
of children, bred as mine are, gladden me?
No, not these eyes, never. And my city,
its towers and sacred places of the Gods,
of these I robbed my miserable self
when I commanded all to drive *him* out,
the criminal since proved by God impure
and of the race of Laius.
To this guilt I bore witness against myself—
with what eyes shall I look upon my people?
No. If there were a means to choke the fountain
of hearing I would not have stayed my hand
from locking up my miserable carcase,
seeing and hearing nothing; it is sweet
to keep our thoughts out of the range of hurt.

Cithaeron, why did you receive me? Why
having received me did you not kill me straight?
And so I had not shown to men my birth.

O Polybus and Corinth and the house,

the old house that I used to call my father's—
what fairness you were nurse to, and what foulness
festered beneath! Now I am found to be
a sinner and a son of sinners. Crossroads,
and hidden glade, oak and the narrow way
at the crossroads, that drank my father's blood
offered you by my hands, do you remember
still what I did as you looked on, and what
I did when I came here? O marriage, marriage!
you bred me and again when you had bred
bred children of your child and showed to men
brides, wives and mothers and the foulest deeds
that can be in this world of ours.

Come—it's unfit to say what is unfit
to do.—I beg of you in God's name hide me
somewhere outside your country, yes, or kill me,
or throw me into the sea, to be forever
out of your sight. Approach and deign to touch me
for all my wretchedness, and do not fear.
No man but I can bear my evil doom.

CHORUS: Here Creon comes in fit time to perform
or give advice in what you ask of us.
Creon is left sole ruler in your stead.

OEDIPUS: Creon! Creon! What shall I say to him?
How can I justly hope that he will trust me?
In what is past I have been proved towards him
an utter liar.

[*Enter Creon.*]

CREON: Oedipus, I've come
not so that I might laugh at you nor taunt you
with evil of the past. But if you still
are without shame before the face of men
reverence at least the flame that gives all life,
our Lord the Sun, and do not show unveiled
to him pollution such that neither land
nor holy rain nor light of day can welcome.

[*To a servant.*]

Be quick and take him in. It is most decent
that only kin should see and hear the troubles
of kin.

OEDIPUS: I beg you, since you've torn me from
my dreadful expectations and have come
in a most noble spirit to a man
that has used you vilely—do a thing for me.
I shall speak for your own good, not for my own.

CREON: What do you need that you would ask of me?

OEDIPUS: Drive me from here with all the speed you can
to where I may not hear a human voice.
CREON: Be sure, I would have done this had not I
wished first of all to learn from the God the course
of action I should follow.
OEDIPUS: But his word
has been quite clear to let the parricide,
the sinner, die.
CREON: Yes, that indeed was said.
But in the present need we had best discover
what we should do.
OEDIPUS: And will you ask about
a man so wretched?
CREON: Now even you will trust
the God.
OEDIPUS: So. I command you—and will beseech you—
to her that lies inside that house give burial
as you would have it; she is yours and rightly
you will perform the rites for her. For me—
never let this my father's city have me
living a dweller in it. Leave me live
in the mountains where Cithaeron is, that's called
my mountain, which my mother and my father
while they were living would have made my tomb.
So I may die by their decree who sought
indeed to kill me. Yet I know this much:
no sickness and no other thing will kill me.
I would not have been saved from death if not
for some strange evil fate. Well, let my fate
go where it will.
Creon, you need not care
about my sons; they're men and so wherever
they are, they will not lack a livelihood.
But my two girls—so sad and pitiful—
whose table never stood apart from mine,
and everything I touched they always shared—
O Creon, have a thought for them! And most
I wish that you might suffer me to touch them
and sorrow with them.

[*Enter Antigone and Ismene, Oedipus' two daughters.*]

O my lord! O true noble Creon! Can I
really be touching them, as when I saw?
What shall I say?
Yes, I can hear them sobbing—my two darlings!
and Creon has had pity and has sent me
what I loved most?
Am I right?
CREON: You're right: it was I gave you this
because I knew from old days how you loved them

as I see now.

OEDIPUS: God bless you for it, Creon,
and may God guard you better on your road
than he did me!
O children,
where are you? Come here, come to my hands,
a brother's hands which turned your father's eyes,
those bright eyes you knew once, to what you see,
a father seeing nothing, knowing nothing,
begetting you from his own source of life.
I weep for you—I cannot see your faces—
I weep when I think of the bitterness
there will be in your lives, how you must live
before the world. At what assemblages
of citizens will you make one? to what
gay company will you go and not come home
in tears instead of sharing in the holiday?
And when you're ripe for marriage, who will he be;
the man who'll risk to take such infamy
as shall cling to my children, to bring hurt
on them and those that marry with them? What
curse is not there? "Your father killed his father
and sowed the seed where he had sprung himself
and begot you out of the womb that held him."
These insults you will hear. Then who will marry you?
No one, my children; clearly you are doomed
to waste away in barrenness unmarried.
Son of Menoeceus, since you are all the father
left these two girls, and we, their parents, both
are dead to them—do not allow them wander
like beggars, poor and husbandless.
They are of your own blood.
And do not make them equal with myself
in wretchedness; for you can see them now
so young, so utterly alone, save for you only.
Touch my hand, noble Creon, and say yes.
If you were older, children, and were wiser,
there's much advice I'd give you. But as it is,
let this be what you pray: give me a life
wherever there is opportunity
to live, and better life than was my father's.

CREON: Your tears have had enough of scope; now go within the house.

OEDIPUS: I must obey, though bitter of heart.

CREON: In season, all is good.

OEDIPUS: Do you know on what conditions I obey?

CREON: You tell me them,
and I shall know them when I hear.

OEDIPUS: That you shall send me out
to live away from Thebes.

CREON: That gift you must ask of the God.

OEDIPUS: But I'm now hated by the Gods.
CREON: So quickly you'll obtain your prayer.
OEDIPUS: You consent then?
CREON: What I do not mean, I do not use to say.
OEDIPUS: Now lead me away from here.
CREON: Let go the children, then, and come.
OEDIPUS: Do not take them from me.
CREON: Do not seek to be master in everything,
for the things you mastered did not follow you throughout your life.

[*As Creon and Oedipus go out.*]

CHORUS: You that live in my ancestral Thebes, behold this Oedipus,—
him who knew the famous riddles and was a man most masterful;
not a citizen who did not look with envy on his lot—
see him now and see the breakers of misfortune swallow him!
Look upon that last day always. Count no mortal happy till
he has passed the final limit of his life secure from pain.

RESONANCE

Aristotle: from *Poetics*[1]

Tragedy, then, is a representation of an action that is worth serious attention, complete in itself, and of some amplitude; in language enriched by a variety of artistic devices appropriate to the several parts of the play; presented in the form of action, not narration; by means of pity and fear bringing about the purgation of such emotions. By language that is enriched I refer to language possessing rhythm, and music or song; and by artistic devices appropriate to the several parts I mean that some are produced by the medium of verse alone, and others again with the help of song.

Now since the representation is carried out by men performing the actions, it follows, in the first place, that spectacle is an essential part of tragedy, and secondly that there must be song and diction, these being the medium of representation. By diction I mean here the arrangement of the verses; song is a term whose sense is obvious to everyone.

In tragedy it is action that is imitated, and this action is brought about by agents who necessarily display certain distinctive qualities both of character and of thought, according to which we also define the nature of the actions. Thought and character are, then, the two natural causes of actions, and it is on them that all men depend for success or failure. The representation of the action is the plot of the tragedy; for the ordered arrangement of the incidents is what I mean by plot. Character, on the other

1. Translated by T. S. Dorsch. The philosopher Aristotle wrote the *Poetics* in the 4th century B.C.E., the century after the flowering of Athenian tragedy in the hands of Aeschylus, Sophocles, and Euripides. The *Poetics* falls into a group of practical manuals, among the many treatises of Aristotle, and explains how to make poetry. Part of it has been lost; the part that remains discusses the writing of tragedies. Unlike Plato, who dismissed tragedy from his ideal city because it aroused weakness and unseemly emotion in its spectators, Aristotle valued it as fiction and as spectacle, arguing that it inspires feelings of pity and fear in its audience and provides a *katharsis,* a cleansing or purgation, of these emotions. In the properly written play, the tragic hero should fall from greatness because of some *hamartia*—not a tragic "flaw," as it is often mistakenly translated, but a "missing of the mark," an error. Arguing that poetry is more philosophical than historical accounts, since it represents human universals rather than actual events, Aristotle praises Sophocles' *Oedipus the King* as an exemplary tragedy, with its dramatic reversal of fortune and terrible passage from ignorance to knowledge.

hand, is that which enables us to define the nature of the participants, and thought comes out in what they say when they are proving a point or expressing an opinion.

Necessarily, then, every tragedy has six constituents, which will determine its quality. They are plot, character, diction, thought, spectacle, and song. Of these, two represent the media in which the action is represented, one involves the manner of representation, and three are connected with the objects of the representation; beyond them nothing further is required. These, it may be said, are the dramatic elements that have been used by practically all playwrights; for all plays alike possess spectacle, character, plot, diction, song, and thought.

* * *

A plot does not possess unity, as some people suppose, merely because it is about one man. Many things, countless things indeed, may happen to one man, and some of them will not contribute to any kind of unity; and similarly he may carry out many actions from which no single unified action will emerge. It seems, therefore, that all those poets have been on the wrong track who have written a *Heracleid,* or a *Theseid,* or some other poem of this kind, in the belief that, Heracles being a single person, his story must necessarily possess unity. Homer, exceptional in this as in all other respects, seems, whether by art or by instinct, to have been well aware of what was required. In writing his *Odyssey* he did not put in everything that happened to Odysseus, that he was wounded on Mount Parnassus, for example, or that he feigned madness at the time of the call to arms, for it was not a matter of necessity or probability that either of these incidents should have led to the other; on the contrary, he constructed the *Odyssey* round a single action of the kind I have spoken of, and he did this with the *Iliad* too. Thus, just as in the other imitative arts each individual representation is the representation of a single object, so too the plot of a play, being the representation of an action, must present it as a unified whole; and its various incidents must be so arranged that if any one of them is differently placed or taken away the effect of wholeness will be seriously disrupted. For if the presence or absence of something makes no apparent difference, it is no real part of the whole.

It will be clear from what I have said that it is not the poet's function to describe what has actually happened, but the kinds of thing that might happen, that is, that could happen because they are, in the circumstances, either probable or necessary. The difference between the historian and the poet is not that the one writes in prose and the other in verse; the work of Herodotus might be put into verse, and in this metrical form it would be no less a kind of history than it is without metre. The difference is that the one tells of what has happened, the other of the kinds of things that might happen. For this reason poetry is something more philosophical and more worthy of serious attention than history; for while poetry is concerned with universal truths, history treats of particular facts.

By universal truths are to be understood the kinds of thing a certain type of person will probably or necessarily say or do in a given situation; and this is the aim of poetry, although it gives individual names to its characters. The particular facts of the historian are what, say, Alcibiades did, or what happened to him. By now this distinction has become clear where comedy is concerned, for comic poets build up their plots out of probable occurrences, and then add any names that occur to them; they do not, like the iambic poets, write about actual people. In tragedy, on the other hand, the authors keep to the names of real people, the reason being that what is possible is credible. Whereas we cannot be certain of the possibility of something that has not happened, what has happened is obviously possible, for it would not have happened if this had not been so. Nevertheless, even in some tragedies only one or two of the names are well known, and the rest are fictitious; and indeed there are some in which nothing is familiar, Agathon's *Antheus,* for example, in which both the incidents and the names are fictitious, and the play is none the less well liked for that. It is not necessary, therefore, to keep entirely to the traditional stories which form the subjects of our tragedies. Indeed it would be absurd to do so, since even the familiar stories are familiar only to a few, and yet they please everybody.

What I have said makes it obvious that the poet must be a maker of plots rather than of verses, since he is a poet by virtue of his representation, and what he represents is actions. And even if he writes about things that have actually happened, that does not make him any the less a poet, for there is nothing to prevent some of the things that have happened from being in accordance with the laws of possibility and probability, and thus he will be a poet in writing about them.

Of simple plots and actions those that are episodic are the worst. By an episodic plot I mean one in which the sequence of the episodes is neither probable nor necessary. Plays of this kind are written by bad poets because they cannot help it, and by good poets because of the actors; writing for the dramatic competitions, they often strain a plot beyond the bounds of possibility, and are thus obliged to dislocate the continuity of events.

However, tragedy is the representation not only of a complete action, but also of incidents that awaken fear and pity, and effects of this kind are heightened when things happen unexpectedly as well as logically, for then they will be more remarkable than if they seem merely mechanical or accidental. Indeed, even chance occurrences seem most remarkable when they have the appearance of having been brought about by design—when, for example, the statue of Mitys at Argos killed the man who had caused Mitys's death by falling down on him at a public entertainment. Things like this do not seem mere chance occurrences. Thus plots of this type are necessarily better than others.

PERSPECTIVES
Tyranny and Democracy

The Greek word "tyrant" means a ruler—such as Oedipus—who has gained power by unconventional means but suggests nothing about the nature of his rule. Tyrants often came from the ranks of the aristocracy and seized control of the city-states with the support of the previously powerless *demos,* or "people." In Athens, the relatively benign tyrant Peisistratos won power after faking an assassination attempt and asking for bodyguards, later parading into town with a tall, armed woman he claimed was the goddess Athena, who'd come to offer support for his rule. He broke the back of aristocratic domination in the city, perhaps instituting such reforms as the drama festivals in honor of Dionysos, and ruled for thirty-six years, dying in 527 B.C.E. The tyrant slayers Harmodios and Aristogeiton, who were lovers, assassinated one of Peisistratos's sons in an erotic intrigue; the other son, deposed and in exile, aided the Persians in their invasion of Greece. More notorious tyrants in other cities included Periander of Corinth; when his wife died, he had sex with her corpse and then stripped all the women of his city naked and burned their clothes to warm her in the underworld. Another had a hollow brass bull made to torture and roast his opponents in, then inserted its maker as the bull's first victim.

In Athens, democracy, "rule by the people," followed the rule of the tyrants. The *demos* was the body of citizens: those who were free, male, and Athenian by descent but not women, slaves, barbarians, or Greeks from other cities. In a one-man, one-vote assembly, the citizens met, argued, often furiously, and then decided on the city's course of action. The Athenians prided themselves on their freedom and eloquently contrasted their form of government with the empires of Asia and Africa and the oligarchies, aristocracies, and tyrannies of the rest of Greece. The Athenians chose to spend their wealth on a fleet, paying a wage to the rowers, who were the city's poorest citizens, rather than slaves as elsewhere; they lavished funds as well on the magnificent buildings of the *agora,* the marketplace, and the Acropolis, site of the Parthenon, the great temple of Athena. Eventually, the city paid its jurors in a sort of welfare system for its older citizens and even paid for the audience to attend the performances of the drama festivals. The city also zealously restricted the privileges of citizenship to those descended from other citizens. The following selections point out the differences the Greeks saw between their own forms of governance and those under which the Persians lived; they illustrate Greek views of the proper eloquence of their leaders, the great lawgiver Solon, a renowned poet, and the noble Pericles, who celebrates the greatness of Athens in a time of mourning, urging its citizens to fall in love with their city. In the selection from Herodotus, we see the beginnings of political theory, a self-conscious, rational account of the history and kinds of government, which is developed more fully in the philosophical works of Plato and Aristotle. Much modern political thought derives from the pathbreaking and highly literary reflections given here.

Solon
c. 640–558 B.C.E.

In a time of struggle between rich aristocrats and poor citizens, when the poor were being sold into slavery by the rich, Solon the lawgiver averted revolution. At the request of the Athenians, he changed the city's laws, paving the way for democracy. He made it illegal to enslave citizens, changed the hierarchy in the city to reflect degrees of wealth rather than noble birth, and altered the severe laws regarding homicide established by an earlier lawgiver, Drako (from whom our word "draconian" derives). His compromises seem to have fully satisfied neither rich nor poor. He then left the city for ten years, to avoid having to alter his new laws, and traveled around the Mediterranean, visiting Egypt, Cyprus, and Asia Minor. He was said to have met the rich Croesus, king of Lydia, who asked him who was the happiest man on earth, hoping to be so named by the wise man from Athens. Solon instead named modest men of Greece who had died heroically, telling Croesus: look to the end, and count no man happy until he has died happily. Solon's wisdom was later proved when Croesus was placed alive on a funeral pyre by the conquering Persian emperor (only by calling out Solon's name and appealing to Apollo, to whom he had given many gifts, did Croesus save himself from the fire). Solon then returned to Athens. His poems celebrate and defend the laws he made for the Athenians.

Our state will never fall[1]

Our state will never fall by Zeus's ordinance
 or the immortal blessed gods' intent:
such a stout-hearted guardian, she of the mighty sire,
 Pallas Athene, holds her hand above:
but by their foolishness the citizens themselves
 seek to destroy its pride, from avarice,
with the unprincipled mob-leaders, who are set
 to suffer badly for their great misdeeds.
They know not how to prosper modestly, enjoy
 in festive peace the happiness they have.

 and they grow wealthy by unrighteousness.
[When wicked men . . .]
 and, sparing neither sacred property
nor public, seize by plunder, each one what he can,
 careless of Righteousness's august shrine—
the silent one, who knows what is and has been done,
 and comes at last to claim the payment due—
this aims a sure blow at the whole community,
 and soon it comes to wretched slavery
which rouses war from sleep, and strife within the clan,
 and sunders many from their lovely youth.
For if men injure their own people, they soon find
 their lovely city scarred and faction-torn.
Among the populace these evils roam at large,
 and many of the poor folk find themselves
in foreign lands, sold into slavery and bound
 in shameful bonds . . .
And so the public ill comes home to every man:
 the yard doors are no more disposed to hold;
it leaps the high wall, and it finds him out for sure,
 though he take refuge in his inmost room.
This lesson I desire to teach the Athenians:
 Lawlessness brings the city countless ills,
while Lawfulness sets all in order as is due;

1. Translated by M. L. West.

many a criminal it puts in irons.
It makes the rough smooth, curbs excess, effaces wrong,
and shrivels up the budding flowers of sin;
it straightens out distorted judgements, pacifies
the violent, brings discord to an end,
brings to an end ill-tempered quarrelling. It makes
all men's affairs correct and rational.

The commons I have granted

The commons I have granted privilege enough,
not lessening their estate nor giving more;
the influential, who were envied for their wealth,
I have saved them from all mistreatment too.
I took my stand with strong shield covering both sides,
allowing neither unjust dominance.
Thus would the commons and its leaders best accord,
not given too free a rein, nor pushed too hard.
Surplus breeds arrogance, when too much wealth attends
such men as have no soundness of intent.
Hard to please everyone in politics.

Those aims for which I called the public meeting

Those aims for which I called the public meeting—
which of them, when I stopped, was still to achieve?
I call as witness in the court of Time
the mighty mother of the Olympian gods,
dark Earth, from whom I lifted boundary-stones[1]
that did beset her—slave before, now free.
And many to Athena's holy land
I brought back, sold abroad illegally
or legally, and others whom their debts
had forced to leave, their speech no longer Attic,
so great their wanderings; and others here
in ugly serfdom at their masters' mercy
I set free. These things I did in power,
blending strength with justice, carried out
all that I promised. I wrote laws for all,
for high and low alike, made straight and just.
But if another man had got the goad,
someone imprudent or acquisitive,
he'd not have checked the mob. If I'd agreed
to what the opposition favoured then,
and then to what the other party thought,
this city would be mourning many dead.

1. Markers on debtors' land.

Therefore I turned to guard my every side,
a wolf at bay amid a pack of hounds.

Herodotus

484–425 B.C.E.

Herodotus was a *histor,* a "wise man," in Greek, someone who knew, who witnessed, interviewed, gathered, and evaluated information about the past, and he fathered the practice of "history." He was born in Halicarnassus on the Aegean coast of what is now Turkey, a Greek city on the edge of a world of non-Greeks. Herodotus's great book, *The Histories,* recounts the causes and course of the war between the Greeks and some of these "barbarians," the Persians, who came from Asia to conquer the Greeks and failed. In the course of telling his story in a leisurely, beads-on-a-string manner, he offers vast resources of information of an almost anthropological sort concerning the habits, dress, religious practices, and customs of the peoples of the Mediterranean world. His story of the war goes back to the rapes of Io and Europa, describes the revolt of the Greek cities of Asia Minor from the Persians, and recounts the invasion of Greece by the vast armies of the Persian emperor, who lashed the sea like a slave when it broke up his bridge across the Hellespont, the strait dividing Europe from Asia. His narrative abounds in such vivid scenes, including the emperor watching his fleet destroyed by the free Athenian rowers, with only his female admiral, Artemisia, victorious. He said, Herodotus reports, "My men have turned into women, my women into men."

Herodotus's ethnographies of the Egyptians, the Scythians, the Amazons, and the Babylonians have been seen as a "mirror" of Greek practices, presenting descriptions that define the Greeks as much as the foreigners, through a lens of reversal or inversion. In passing he describes the black semen of the men of India and the harvesting of Arabian cinnamon. The portrait of the Greeks that emerges draws much from the opposition between freedom and slavery; faced with the enormity of the Persian emperor's wealth and power and with the threat of armed invasion if they don't submit, the free Greeks retort: "You understand well enough what slavery is, but freedom you have never experienced, so you do not know if it tastes sweet or bitter. If you ever did come to experience it, you would advise us to fight for it not with spears only, but with axes too."

PRONUNCIATION:
Herodotus: her-AW-do-tus

from The Histories[1]

[ON THE TROJAN WAR]

Herodotus of Halicarnassus here displays his inquiry, so that human achievements may not become forgotten in time, and great and marvellous deeds—some displayed by Greeks, some by barbarians—may not be without their glory; and especially to show why the two peoples fought with each other.

Learned Persians put the responsibility for the quarrel on the Phoenicians. These people came originally from the so-called Red Sea; and as soon as they had penetrated to the Mediterranean and settled in the country where they are today, they took

1. Translated by Aubrey de Selincourt.

to making long trading voyages. Loaded with Egyptian and Assyrian goods, they called at various places along the coast, including Argos, in those days the most important place in the land now called Hellas.

Here in Argos they displayed their wares, and five or six days later when they were nearly sold out, a number of women came down to the beach to see the fair. Amongst these was the king's daughter, whom Greek and Persian writers agree in calling Io, daughter of Inachus. These women were standing about near the vessel's stern, buying what they fancied, when suddenly the Phoenician sailors passed the word along and made a rush at them. The greater number got away; but Io and some others were caught and bundled aboard the ship, which cleared at once and made off for Egypt.

This, according to the Persian account (the Greeks have a different story), was how Io came to Egypt; and this was the first in a series of unjust acts.

Later on some Greeks, whose name the Persians fail to record—they were probably Cretans—put into the Phoenician port of Tyre and carried off the king's daughter Europa, thus giving them tit for tat.

For the next outrage it was the Greeks again who were responsible. They sailed in an armed merchantman to Aea in Colchis on the river Phasis, and, not content with the regular business which had brought them there, they abducted the king's daughter Medea. The king sent to Greece demanding reparations and his daughter's return; but the only answer he got was that the Greeks had no intention of offering reparation, having received none themselves for the abduction of Io from Argos.

The accounts go on to say that some forty or fifty years afterwards Paris, the son of Priam, was inspired by these stories to steal a wife for himself out of Greece, being confident that he would not have to pay for the venture any more than the Greeks had done. And that was how he came to carry off Helen.

The first idea of the Greeks after the rape was to send a demand for satisfaction and for Helen's return. The demand was met by a reference to the seizure of Medea and the injustice of expecting satisfaction from people to whom they themselves had refused it, not to mention the fact that they had kept the girl.

Thus far there had been nothing worse than woman-stealing on both sides; but for what happened next the Greeks, they say, were seriously to blame; for it was the Greeks who were, in a military sense, the aggressors. Abducting young women, in their opinion, is not, indeed, a lawful act; but it is stupid after the event to make a fuss about avenging it. The only sensible thing is to take no notice; for it is obvious that no young woman allows herself to be abducted if she does not wish to be. The Asiatics, according to the Persians, took the seizure of the women lightly enough, but not so the Greeks: the Greeks, merely on account of a girl from Sparta, raised a big army, invaded Asia and destroyed the empire of Priam. From that root sprang their belief in the perpetual enmity of the Grecian world towards them—because the Persians claim Asia and the barbarian races dwelling in it as their own, Europe and the Greek states being, in their opinion, quite separate and distinct from them.

Such then is the Persian story. In their view it was the capture of Troy that first made them enemies of the Greeks.

As to Io, the Phoenicians do not accept the Persians' account; they deny that they took her to Egypt by force. On the contrary, the girl while she was still in Argos went to bed with the ship's captain, found herself pregnant, and, ashamed to face her parents, sailed away voluntarily to escape exposure.

So much for what Persians and Phoenicians say; and I have no intention of passing judgement on its truth or falsity. I prefer to rely on my own knowledge, and to point out who it was in actual fact that first injured the Greeks; then I will proceed with my history, telling the story as I go along of small cities of men no less than of great. For most of those which were great once are small today; and those which used to be small were great in my own time. Knowing, therefore, that human prosperity never abides long in the same place, I shall pay attention to both alike.

[CROESUS AND SOLON]

In the course of time Croesus subdued all the peoples west of the river Halys, except the Cilicians and Lycians.[2] The rest he kept in subjection—Lydians, Phrygians, Mysians, Mariandynians, Chalybians, Paphlagonians, Thracians (both Thynian and Bithynian), Carians, Ionians, Dorians, Aeolians, and Pamphylians.

When all these nations had been added to the Lydian empire, and Sardis was at the height of her wealth and prosperity, all the great Greek teachers of that epoch, one after another, paid visits to the capital. Much the most distinguished of them was Solon the Athenian, the man who at the request of his countrymen had made a code of laws for Athens. He was on his travels at the time, intending to be away ten years, in order to avoid the necessity of repealing any of the laws he had made. That, at any rate, was the real reason of his absence, though he gave it out that what he wanted was just to see the world. The Athenians could not alter any of Solon's laws without him, because they had solemnly sworn to give them a ten years' trial.

For this reason, then—and also no doubt for the pleasure of foreign travel—Solon left home and, after a visit to the court of Amasis in Egypt, went to Sardis to see Croesus.

Croesus entertained him hospitably in the palace, and three or four days after his arrival instructed some servants to take him on a tour of the royal treasuries and point out the richness and magnificence of everything. When Solon had made as thorough an inspection as opportunity allowed, Croesus said: "Well, my Athenian friend, I have heard a great deal about your wisdom, and how widely you have travelled in the pursuit of knowledge. I cannot resist my desire to ask you a question: who is the happiest man you have ever seen?"

The point of the question was that Croesus supposed himself to be the happiest of men. Solon, however, refused to flatter, and answered in strict accordance with his view of the truth. "An Athenian," he said, "called Tellus."

Croesus was taken aback. "And what," he asked sharply, "is your reason for this choice?"

"There are good reasons," said Solon; "first, his city was prosperous, and he had fine sons, and lived to see children born to each of them, and all these children surviving; secondly, he had wealth enough by our standards; and he had a glorious death. In a battle with the neighbouring town of Eleusis, he fought for his countrymen, routed the enemy, and died like a brave man; and the Athenians paid him the high honour of a public funeral on the spot where he fell."

All these details about the happiness of Tellus, Solon doubtless intended as a moral lesson for the king; Croesus, however, thinking he would at least be awarded second prize, asked who was the next happiest person whom Solon had seen.

"Two young men of Argos," was the reply; "Cleobis and Biton. They had enough to live on comfortably; and their physical strength is proved not merely by their

2. In Asia Minor.

success in athletics, but much more by the following incident. The Argives were celebrating the festival of Hera, and it was most important that the mother of the two young men should drive to the temple in her ox-cart; but it so happened that the oxen were late in coming back from the fields. Her two sons therefore, as there was no time to lose, harnessed themselves to the cart and dragged it along, with their mother inside, for a distance of nearly six miles, until they reached the temple. After this exploit, which was witnessed by the assembled crowd, they had a most enviable death—a heaven-sent proof of how much better it is to be dead than alive. Men kept crowding round them and congratulating them on their strength, and women kept telling the mother how lucky she was to have such sons, when, in sheer pleasure at this public recognition of her sons' act, she prayed the goddess Hera, before whose shrine she stood, to grant Cleobis and Biton, who had brought her such honour, the greatest blessing that can fall to mortal man.

"After her prayer came the ceremonies of sacrifice and feasting; and the two lads, when all was over, fell asleep in the temple—and that was the end of them, for they never woke again.

"The Argives, considering them to be the best of men, had statues made of them, which they sent to Delphi."

Croesus was vexed with Solon for giving the second prize for happiness to the two young Argives, and snapped out: "That's all very well, my Athenian friend; but what of my own happiness? Is it so utterly contemptible that you won't even compare me with mere common folk like those you have mentioned?"

"Croesus," replied Solon, "I know God is envious of human prosperity and likes to trouble us; and you question me about the lot of man. Listen then: as the years lengthen out, there is much both to see and to suffer which one would wish otherwise. Take seventy years as the span of a man's life: those seventy years contain 25,200 days, without counting intercalary months. Add a month every other year, to make the seasons come round with proper regularity, and you will have thirty-five additional months, which will make 1050 additional days. Thus the total of days for your seventy years is 26,250, and not a single one of them is like the next in what it brings. You can see from that, Croesus, that man is entirely a creature of chance. You seem to be very rich, and you rule a numerous people; but the question you asked me I will not answer, until I know that you have died happily. Great wealth can make a man no happier than moderate means, unless he has the luck to continue in prosperity to the end. Many very rich men have been unfortunate, and many with a modest competence have had good luck. The former are better off than the latter in two respects only, whereas the poor but lucky man has the advantage in many ways; for though the rich have the means to satisfy their appetites and to bear calamities, and the poor have not, the poor, if they are lucky, are more likely to keep clear of trouble, and will have besides the blessings of a sound body, health, freedom from trouble, fine children, and good looks.

"Now if a man thus favoured dies as he has lived, he will be just the one you are looking for: the only sort of person who deserves to be called happy. But mark this: until he is dead, keep the word 'happy' in reserve. Till then, he is not happy, but only lucky.

"Nobody of course can have all these advantages, any more than a country can produce everything it needs: whatever it has, it is bound to lack something. The best country is the one which has most. It is the same with people: no man is ever self-sufficient—there is sure to be something missing. But whoever has the greatest number of the good things I have mentioned, and keeps them to the end, and dies a peaceful death, that man, Croesus, deserves in my opinion to be called happy.

"Look to the end, no matter what it is you are considering. Often enough God gives a man a glimpse of happiness, and then utterly ruins him."

These sentiments were not of the sort to give Croesus any pleasure; he let Solon go with cold indifference, firmly convinced that he was a fool. For what could be more stupid than to keep telling him to look at the "end" of everything, without any regard to present prosperity?

After Solon's departure nemesis fell upon Croesus, presumably because God was angry with him for supposing himself the happiest of men.

[DEBATE ON POLITICAL FORMS]

When both the Magi had been killed, the confederates decapitated them, and ran out into the street, shouting and making a great noise, with the severed heads in their hands.[3] The two wounded men had been left behind in the palace, being too weak to move—they were needed, moreover, to keep a watch upon the citadel. Once outside, the five who were unhurt appealed to their fellow citizens, told them what had happened, and showed them the heads—and then set about murdering every Magus they came across. The other Persians, once they had learnt of the exploit of the seven confederates, and understood the hoax which the two brothers had practised on them, were soon ready to follow their example: they, too, drew their daggers and killed every Magus they could find—so that if darkness had not put an end to the slaughter, the whole tribe would have been exterminated. The anniversary of this day has become a red-letter day in the Persian calendar, marked by an important festival known as the Magophonia, or Killing of the Magi, during which no Magus is allowed to show himself—every member of the tribe stays indoors till the day is over.

Five days later, when the excitement had died down, the conspirators met to discuss the situation in detail. At the meeting certain speeches were made—some of the Greeks refuse to believe they were actually made at all; nevertheless they were. The first speaker was Otanes, and his theme was to recommend the establishment in Persia of popular government. "I think," he said, "that the time has passed for any one man amongst us to have absolute power. Monarchy is neither pleasant nor good. You know to what lengths the pride of power carried Cambyses, and you have personal experience of the effect of the same thing in the conduct of the Magus. How can one fit monarchy into any sound system of ethics, when it allows a man to do whatever he likes without any responsibility or control? Even the best of men raised to such a position would be bound to change for the worse—he could not possibly see things as he used to do. The typical vices of a monarch are envy and pride; envy, because it is a natural human weakness, and pride, because excessive wealth and power lead to the delusion that he is something more than a man. These two vices are the root cause of all wickedness: both lead to acts of savage and unnatural violence. Absolute power ought, by rights, to preclude envy on the principle that the man who possesses it has also at command everything he could wish for; but in fact it is not so, as the behaviour of kings to their subjects proves: they are jealous of the best of them merely for continuing to live, and take pleasure in the worst; and no one is readier than a king to listen to tale-bearers. A king, again, is the most inconsistent of men; show him reasonable

3. The Magi had attempted to seize power.

respect, and he is angry because you do not abase yourself before his majesty; abase yourself, and he hates you for being a toady. But the worst of all remains to be said—he breaks up the structure of ancient tradition and law, forces women to serve his pleasure, and puts men to death without trial. Contrast with this the rule of the people:[4] first, it has the finest of all names to describe it—equality under law; and, secondly, the people in power do none of the things that monarchs do. Under a government of the people a magistrate is appointed by lot and is held responsible for his conduct in office, and all questions are put up for open debate. For these reasons I propose that we do away with the monarchy, and raise the people to power; for the state and the people are synonymous terms."

Otanes was followed by Megabyzus, who recommended the principle of oligarchy in the following words: "Insofar as Otanes spoke in favour of abolishing monarchy, I agree with him; but he is wrong in asking us to transfer political power to the people. The masses are a feckless lot—nowhere will you find more ignorance or irresponsibility or violence. It would be an intolerable thing to escape the murderous caprice of a king, only to be caught by the equally wanton brutality of the rabble. A king does at least act consciously and deliberately; but the mob does not. Indeed how should it, when it has never been taught what is right and proper, and has no knowledge of its own about such things? The masses handle affairs without thought; all they can do is to rush blindly into politics like a river in flood. As for the people, then, let them govern Persia's enemies; but let us ourselves choose a certain number of the best men in the country, and give *them* political power. We personally shall be amongst them, and it is only natural to suppose that the best men will produce the best policy."

Darius was the third to speak. "I support," he said, "all Megabyzus' remarks about the masses but I do not agree with what he said of oligarchy. Take the three forms of government we are considering—democracy, oligarchy, and monarchy—and suppose each of them to be the best of its kind; I maintain that the third is greatly preferable to the other two. One ruler: it is impossible to improve upon that—provided he is the best. His judgement will be in keeping with his character; his control of the people will be beyond reproach; his measures against enemies and traitors will be kept secret more easily than under other forms of government. In an oligarchy, the fact that a number of men are competing for distinction in the public service cannot but lead to violent personal feuds; each of them wants to get to the top, and to see his own proposals carried; so they quarrel. Personal quarrels lead to civil wars, and then to bloodshed; and from that state of affairs the only way out is a return to monarchy—a clear proof that monarchy is best. Again, in a democracy, malpractices are bound to occur; in this case, however, corrupt dealings in government services lead not to private feuds, but to close personal associations, the men responsible for them putting their heads together and mutually supporting one another. And so it goes on, until somebody or other comes forward as the people's champion and breaks up the cliques which are out for their own interests. This wins him the admiration of the mob, and as a result he soon finds himself entrusted with absolute power—all of which is another proof that the best form of government is monarchy. To sum up: where did we get our freedom from, and who gave it us? Is it the result of democracy, or of oligarchy, or of

4. Democracy.

monarchy? We were set free by one man, and therefore I propose that we should preserve that form of government, and, further, that we should refrain from changing ancient ways, which have served us well in the past. To do so would not profit us."

These were the three views set out in the three speeches, and the four men who had not spoken voted for the last.

Thucydides

c. 460–400 B.C.E.

The fifth century B.C.E. began with the Persian Wars, fought between the Greeks and the barbarians, recounted by Herodotus; it ended with the war among the Greeks, the Peloponnesian War, set down by his intellectual heir and rival, the Athenian Thucydides. A soldier and general himself, Thucydides records the thirty-year struggle between the Athenians and their allies against the Spartans and their allies, who fought to contain Athens' ambitions. Implicitly critical of earlier historians' storytelling, Thucydides adopts a method of strict judgment and commitment to accuracy. He presents vivid portraits of the political figures of his day including Perikles, who led Athens in the period of its greatest prosperity and who celebrated the city in his famous funeral oration. Thucydides offers many such elaborate speeches, either delivered by his protagonists and recorded by his attentive ear, or else imaginatively reconstructed. These orations embody the intense rhetorical training and persuasive techniques of the fifth-century democratic assembly. Like most Greek intellectuals critical of democracy, Thucydides portrays the Athenian people as swayed by flattering rhetoric, their virtue gradually eroded and drawn into a disastrous imperialist invasion of Sicily by the charismatic Alcibiades, who was the object of women's and men's desire and who lived a wild and dissolute life while conducting brilliant military campaigns that endeared him to the Athenians. The invasion ended with its generals murdered and the Athenians imprisoned and dying in the quarries of Syracuse, enslaved, or sold for ransom; according to some accounts, only those who could recite lines from the tragedies of Euripides were spared.

Thucydides' Athens counted among its residents the pre-Socratics—early physicists, political theorists, and anthropologists—as well as the philosophers Socrates and Plato. Thucydides the historian shared their critical, questioning spirit and sought to distinguish rigorously between truth and falsehood, myth and reason, and cant and integrity in recording the events of his day. Critics in antiquity and after have admired Thucydides' brilliant style, characterized by a poetic vocabulary, a great variety of rhetorical figures, roughness in the joints of his prose, and the speed with which he conveys his meanings. Democratic Athens exiled Thucydides for a military failure; he returned after twenty years, when the war had ended, only to die with his history unfinished.

PRONUNCIATION:

Thucydides: thu-SIH-dih-deez

from The Peloponnesian War[1]

from Book 2

[PERIKLES' FUNERAL ORATION]

In this winter, following their traditional custom, the Athenians held burial rites at public expense for the first to die in this war, in the following manner. They lay out the bones of the dead two days beforehand, after setting up a tent, and each person

1. Translated by Steven Lattimore.

brings whatever offerings he wishes to his own relatives. When the procession takes place, wagons carry cypress coffins, one for each tribe, and within are the bones of each man, according to tribe. One empty bier, fully decorated, is brought for the missing, all who were not found and recovered. Any man who wishes, citizen or foreigner, joins the procession, and female relatives are present at the grave as mourners. They bury them in the public tomb, which is in the most beautiful suburb of the city and in which they always bury those killed in war, except of course for the men who fought at Marathon; judging their virtue outstanding, they gave them burial right there. After they cover them with earth, a man chosen by the state, known for wise judgment and of high reputation, makes an appropriate speech of praise, and after this they depart. This is their burial practice, and throughout the whole war, whenever there was occasion, they followed the custom. Now for these first casualties, Perikles son of Xanthippos was chosen to speak. And when the moment arrived, coming forward from the tomb to a platform that had been elevated so that he could be heard by as much of the crowd as possible, he spoke as follows:

"Most of those who have already spoken here praise the man who made this speech part of the custom, saying that for this address to be made at the burial of those lost in war is a fine thing. I myself would have thought it sufficient that the honors for those who proved good in deed be bestowed by deed as well, just as you now see carried out at public expense for this burial, rather than that the virtues of many men depend for their credibility on whether a single man speaks well or badly. To speak in due proportion is difficult where grasp of the truth itself is hardly assured. For the man listening with understanding and good will may well consider what is set forth in some way inferior, measured against both his wishes and his knowledge, yet the one listening in ignorance may consider some things exaggerated, out of envy when he hears anything going beyond his natural endowments. Praise spoken of others can only be endured as long as each believes himself capable of doing something of what he hears about; toward what goes further, men feel envy and then actual disbelief. But since it was so judged by those of long ago, that this speech is a fine thing, I too must follow the custom and try to conform with the wishes and opinions of each one of you as far as is possible.

"First of all, I will begin with our ancestors, since it is right and also appropriate on such an occasion as the present that the honor of this remembrance should be given to them. For it is the same men, always occupying the land through the succession of generations, who have handed it down in freedom until the present time because of their bravery. They are worthy of praise, and our fathers still more. In addition to what they received, they acquired through great effort the whole of the empire we now rule and left it to us in the present generation. Those of us here now who are still somewhere in the prime of life have expanded most areas of it and in all respects provided the city with the fullest resources for both war and peace. I will pass over the deeds in war that led to each of our acquisitions and every instance of stout resistance we or our fathers made against attacking enemies, whether barbarian or Hellene, since I do not wish to recount them at length among those who know of them. But I will turn to praise of the dead after I have first set forth the principles by which we came into this position and the form of government from which its greatness resulted, since I believe that these are not inappropriate to mention in the present circumstances and are advantageous for the whole gathering, both citizens and foreigners, to hear about.

"We have a form of government that does not emulate the practices of our neighbors, setting an example to some rather than imitating others. In name it is called a democracy on account of being administered in the interest not of the few but the many, yet even though there are equal rights for all in private disputes in accordance with the laws, wherever each man has earned recognition he is singled out for public service in accordance with the claims of distinction, not by rotation but by merit, nor when it comes to poverty, if a man has real ability to benefit the city, is he prevented by obscure renown. In public life we conduct ourselves with freedom and also, regarding that suspicion of others because of their everyday habits, without getting angry at a neighbor if he does something so as to suit himself, and without wearing expressions of vexation, that inflict no punishment yet cause distress. But while we associate in private without undue pressure, in public we are especially law abiding because of fear, in our obedience both to anyone holding office and to the laws, above all those established to aid people who are wronged and those which, although unwritten, bring down acknowledged shame. Furthermore, we have provided for the spirit the most plentiful respites from labor by providing games and festivals throughout the year as well as attractive surroundings for private life, a source of daily delight, which drives away cares. Because of the importance of the city, everything is brought in from every land, and it is our fortune to enjoy good things from other people with as much familiarity as what comes from here.

"In our approach to warfare, we also differ from our opponents, in the following ways. We leave our city accessible to all and do not, by xenelasia,[2] prevent anyone from either listening or observing, although some enemy might benefit by seeing what we do not hide, because we do not put more trust in contrivance and deception than in the courageous readiness for action, which comes from within. As for education, starting as children they pursue manhood with laborious training, but with our more relaxed way of life we are no less willing to take on equivalent dangers. Here is proof: the Lacedaemonians do not invade our land alone but with all their allies, and we attack other lands by ourselves, and fighting in hostile territory against men defending their own possessions, we usually win easily. And no enemy has yet encountered our united forces, on account of our simultaneously maintaining the fleet and dispatching our own men to many points on land, but wherever our enemies meet a detachment, they flatter themselves that they have repelled all of us if they beat some of us and that they were defeated by all if they lose. And if we are willing to face danger with a mind at ease rather than with the habit of stress, with bravery owing no more to law than to character, surely it is our gain that we are not afflicted by hardships before they occur, that when we do encounter them we prove no less daring than those who are constantly straining, and that our city deserves admiration for these reasons and still others.

"For we love beauty while practicing economy and we love wisdom without being enervated. We use wealth for opportune action rather than boastful speech, and there is no disgrace for one to admit poverty but much more in not avoiding it through activity. And it is within the capacity of some of us to manage private right along with public business and of the rest, while concentrating on their own occupations, to have no inferior understanding of public affairs; we are unique in considering the man who takes no part in these to be not apolitical but useless, and we ourselves either ratify or even propound successful policies, finding harm not in the effect of speeches on action but in failing to get instruction by speech before proceeding to what must be done. For in that we are both especially daring and especially thorough in calculating what we attempt, we can truly be distinguished from other men, for whom ignorance

2. Expulsion of foreigners, practiced in Sparta.

is boldness but calculation brings hesitancy. Rightly would they be judged strongest in spirit who recognize both dangers and pleasures with utmost clarity and are on neither count deterred from risks. In matters of goodness, we also contrast with most people, since we acquire friends by conferring rather than by receiving benefits. The giver is the more secure, through preserving the feeling of gratitude by good will toward the recipient, who is less fulfilled because he knows that he will repay the goodness not to inspire gratitude but to return an obligation. We are unique in being benefactors not out of calculation of advantage but with the fearless confidence of our freedom.

"In summary I claim that our city as a whole is an education for Hellas, and that it is among us as individuals, in my opinion, that a single man would represent an individual self-sufficient for the most varied forms of conduct, and with the most attractive qualities. And that this is not boastful speaking for the occasion but factual truth our city's very power, which we acquired because of these characteristics, proclaims clearly. For she alone of existing cities surpasses her reputation when put to the test, and only she brings neither chagrin to the attacking enemy as to the sort of men by whom he has been worsted nor reproach to the subject that he is ruled by the unworthy. Through great proofs, and by exhibiting power in no way unwitnessed, we will be admired by this and future generations, thus requiring no Homer to sing our praises nor any other whose verses will charm for the moment and whose claims the factual truth will destroy, since we have compelled every sea and land to become open to our daring and populated every region with lasting monuments of our acts of harm and good. It is for such a city, then, that these men nobly died in battle, thinking it right not to be deprived of her, just as each of their survivors should be willing to toil for her sake.

"This above all is the reason I have lengthened my speech about the city, to explain why our efforts have no equivalent among people who do not share these values, and at the same time to give evidence for the glory of those whom I am now eulogizing. The most important part of the eulogy has been said. For it is their virtues, and those of men like them, that have given honor to the qualities I have praised in the city, and for few other Hellenes would it be manifest, as it is for them, that reputation is equal to the deeds. It seems to me that this conclusion of these men's lives is what reveals a man's virtue, whether as the first indication or final confirmation. Even for those who were worse in other ways it is right that first place be given to valor against enemies on behalf of country; by effacing evil with good, they became public benefactors rather than individual malefactors. None of these men turned coward from preferring the further enjoyment of wealth, nor did any, from the poor man's hope that he might still escape poverty and grow rich, contrive a way to postpone the danger. Thinking defeat of the enemy more desirable than prosperity, just as they considered this the fairest of risks, they were willing to vanquish him at that risk and long for the rest, leaving to hope the uncertainty of prospering in the future but resolving to rely on their own actions in what confronted them now, and recognizing that it meant resisting and dying rather than surviving by submission, they fled disgrace in word but stood up to the deed with their lives and through the fortune of the briefest critical moment, at the height of glory rather than fear, departed.

"So fared these men, worthy of their city; you their survivors must pray to meet the enemy at lesser cost but resolve to do so just as unflinchingly, not calculating the benefits by words alone—although one might recite at length to you who know them just as well all the rewards of resisting the enemy—but wondering at the city's power as you actually see it each day and becoming her lovers, reflecting whenever her fame appears great to you that men who were daring, who realized their duty, and who honored it in their actions acquired this, men who even when they failed in some attempt did not on that account think it right to deprive the city of their virtue, but to offer it to her as their finest contribution. For in giving their lives in common cause, they individually gained imperishable praise and the most distinctive tomb, not the one where they are buried but the one where on every occasion for word and deed their glory is left after them eternally. The whole earth is the tomb of famous men, and not only inscriptions set up in their own country mark it but even in foreign lands an unwritten memorial, present not in monument but in mind, abides within each man. Emulate them now, judge that happiness is freedom and freedom courage, and do not stand aside from the dangers of war. For failures, men bereft of good expectations, have no more reason to be unstinting of their lives than those for whom reversal is always a threat as long as they live, and in whose sight the most important things are at stake if they come to grief. Indeed, for a man of pride, misfortune associated with cowardice is more painful than death coming imperceptibly in the midst of vigor along with shared hopes.

"It is for this reason that I offer comfort, not pity, to all those present as parents of these men. You know that you were reared among ever-changing fortunes. It is happiness whenever men find the most glorious end, just like these men, even while you find sorrow, and for those whose success in life has been measured out to the same limit as their mortality. I know that it is difficult to persuade you in that you will often have reminders of them through the happiness of others, which you once enjoyed as well; for sorrow is not felt over the deprivation of good things one has not experienced, but over the removal of what one was used to. But those still of age to have children must take strength from hopes of other sons. On the personal level, those who come later will be a means of forgetting those who are no more, and the city will benefit doubly, both in not being left short and in security; for it is not possible for men to counsel anything fair or just if they are not at risk by staking their sons equally. All of you who have passed beyond this, however, consider that the greater portion of your life, in which you were fortunate, is a gain, that this part will be short, and that your heart will be lightened by the fame of these men. For a love of honor is the only thing that has no old age, and it is not profit, as some claim, but honor that brings delight in the period of uselessness.

"For all those present who are sons or brothers of these men, however, I see that the effort will be a great one, since everyone tends to praise those who are no longer, and it will be difficult for you to be judged not equal, because of their surpassing merit, but only slightly inferior. For the living incur the envy for a rival, but those who no longer offer opposition receive honor with a good will lacking in competitiveness. And if I should make any mention of the virtue of women, regarding all who will now be widows, I will express all of it in brief advice. Your renown is great through keeping up to the standard of your basic nature, and if your reputation has the least circulation among men, whether for virtue or in blame.

"In words, as much as I in my turn could say suitably in accordance with the custom has been said, and in deed, these have been honored in burial now, and from this time the city will rear their sons at public expense until they are of age, conferring on both the dead and their survivors a beneficial crown for such contests as these. For it is among those who establish the greatest prizes for courage that men are the best citizens. And now, after each of you has made full lament for his own, you must depart."

Such was the funeral that occurred in this winter, and when the winter was over, the first year of this war ended.

from Book 3

[Revolution in Corcyra]

The Corcyreans butchered those fellow-citizens they regarded as enemies, charging them with putting down the democracy, but some also died because of personal hatred and others at the hands of those who owed them money. Every form of death prevailed, and whatever is likely in such situations happened—and still worse. Fathers killed sons, men were dragged from the sanctuaries and killed beside them, and some were even walled up in the sanctuary of Dionysos and died there.

With this savagery, the civil war progressed, and it seemed all the more savage because it was the first, while later the rest of Hellas, almost without exception, was also in turmoil, with rival efforts everywhere by the popular leaders to bring in the Athenians and the oligarchs, the Lacedaemonians. In peacetime they had neither the pretext nor the willingness to call them in, but during war, with alliances available to both factions for damaging their opponents and at the same time strengthening themselves, occasions for bringing in outsiders were readily found by those wishing to make any change in government. And during the civil wars the cities suffered many cruelties that occur and will always occur as long as men have the same nature, sometimes more terribly and sometimes less, varying in their forms as each change of fortune dictates. For in peace and good circumstances, both states and individuals have better inclinations through not falling into involuntary necessities; but war, stripping away the easy access to daily needs, is a violent teacher and brings most men's passions into line with the present situations.

So the condition of the cities was civil war, and where it came later, awareness of earlier events pushed to extremes the revolution in thinking, both in extraordinarily ingenious attempts to seize power and in outlandish retaliations. And in self-justification men inverted the usual verbal evaluations of actions. Irrational recklessness was now considered courageous commitment, hesitation while looking to the future was high-styled cowardice, moderation was a cover for lack of manhood, and circumspection meant inaction, while senseless anger now helped to define a true man, and deliberation for security was a specious excuse for dereliction. The man of violent temper was always credible, anyone opposing him was suspect. The intriguer who succeeded was intelligent, anyone who detected a plot was still more clever, but a man who made provisions to avoid both alternatives was undermining his party and letting the opposition terrorize him. Quite simply, one was praised for outracing everyone else to commit a crime—and for encouraging a crime by someone who had never before considered one.

Kinship became alien compared with party affiliation, because the latter led to drastic action with less hesitation. For party meetings did not take place to use the benefits of existing laws, but to find any advantage in breaking them. They strengthened their trust in one another less by religious law than by association in committing some illegal act. Men responded to reasonable words from their opponents with defensive actions, if they had the advantage, and not with magnanimity. Revenge mattered more than not being harmed in the first place. And if there were actually reconciliations under oath, they occurred because of both sides' lack of alternatives and lasted only as long as neither found some other source of power. The one who first recovered his confidence at the right moment, when he saw the other off guard, enjoyed vengeance more in a situation of trust than if accomplished openly; the element of safety was an asset, and because of prevailing through deception he also won the prize for intelligence. As a rule, men are more easily called clever when they are scoundrels than virtuous when ignorant—and are as ashamed of the second description as they are exultant in the first.

All this was caused by leadership based on greed and ambition and led in turn to fanaticism once men were committed to the power struggle. For the leading men in the cities, through their emphasis on an attractive slogan for each side—political equality for the masses, the moderation of aristocracy—treated as their prize the public interest to which they paid lip service and, competing by every means to get the better of one another, boldly committed atrocities and proceeded to still worse acts of revenge, stopping at limits set by neither justice nor the city's interest but by the gratification of their parties at every stage, and whether by condemnations through unjust voting or by acquiring superiority in brute force, both sides were ready to satisfy to the utmost their immediate hopes of victory. And so neither side acted with piety, but those who managed to accomplish something hateful by using honorable arguments were more highly regarded. The citizens in the middle, either because they had not taken sides or because begrudged their survival, were destroyed by both factions.

In this way, every form of viciousness was established in the Hellenic world on account of the civil wars, and the simplicity that is especially found in noble natures disappeared because it became ridiculous. The division into distrustful groups opposed in their thinking was very extensive. To reconcile them, there was no secure principle, no oath that was feared, but those who were stronger, in contemplation of the impossibility of security, all took measures to avoid suffering rather than allowing themselves to feel trust. The weaker in intellect were more often the survivors; out of fear of their own deficiency and their enemies' craft, lest they be defeated in debate and become the first victims of plots as a result of the others' resourceful intellects, they went straight into action. And those who contemptuously supposed that they would know all in advance, and that there was no need to seize by force what would come to them through intellect, were instead caught off guard and destroyed.

In Corcyra, then, most of these atrocities were first committed: all that men do in resisting those who, after ruling them abusively rather than moderately, provide opportunity for revenge; all that men resolve unjustly when, wishing to escape their usual poverty—especially if pressed by disaster—they desire their neighbors' possessions; all that others, attacking not for gain but on clearly equal terms, impelled most by raw fury, carry out savagely and without mercy. With public life confused to the critical point, human nature, always ready to act unjustly even in violation of laws, overthrew the laws themselves and gladly showed itself powerless over passion but stronger than justice and hostile to any kind of superiority. For men would not have placed revenge above pity, gain above justice, if not for the destructive power of envy. And the universal laws about such things, laws that offer hope of salvation to all in adversity, men see fit to do away with at the outset in taking revenge instead of letting them stand until they actually run into danger and find need of them.

Plato

c. 429–347 B.C.E.

The Athenians executed Socrates, Plato's beloved teacher, in 399 B.C.E., in the aftermath of their defeat in the Peloponnesian War, condemning him on charges of impiety and for the corruption of young men. Socrates, who wrote nothing, left behind Plato, who wrote the founding texts of Western philosophy. His dialogues recorded or invented conversations among Socrates, his circle, and other men. Though Plato himself isn't a character in these dialogues, he used them as his vehicle for setting out defining issues for the Western traditions of ethics, political theory, logic, linguistics, theory of knowledge, rhetoric, and metaphysics. Plato was brought to remarkably sophisticated considerations of definition and knowledge by his dissatisfactions with the teachings of earlier thinkers including the pre-Socratics, the first physicists; the sophists, traveling teachers of rhetoric; and the politics of the city of his day. He portrays Socrates and his friends seeking to clarify such questions as the difference between opinion and true knowledge, the relationship between rhetoric and philosophy, the nature of language, the place of the gods in ethical life, and the role of poetry in society. What are often seen as earlier dialogues conclude with the participants' mutual recognition of ignorance. Later conversations explore such matters as the ideal society and its laws. In the course of Plato's writings, philosophy itself, "the love of wisdom," emerges for the first time as a distinct enterprise. Plato's dialogues combine highly rhetorical prose with dramatic techniques in order to explore the limits of knowledge and human existence, sometimes offering vivid portraits of men in flirtatious or passionate debate. Plato demonstrates an enduring suspicion of democracy, which allowed all citizen men to engage in politics, a task he believed should be conducted by experts—the guardian class he proposed to govern his ideal city, described in the *Republic.* The *Apology* is presented as the speech Socrates offers in his defense when put on trial by his enemies in Athens, written by Plato after Socrates was executed by being forced to drink hemlock, dying a martyr's death. In Plato's moving presentation, Socrates's trial becomes nothing less than a struggle for the soul of the Athenian polity.

Apology[1]

How you, O Athenians, have been affected by my accusers, I cannot tell; but I know that they almost made me forget who I was—so persuasively did they speak; and yet they have hardly uttered a word of truth. But of the many falsehoods told by them, there was one which quite amazed me;—I mean when they said that you should be upon your guard and not allow yourselves to be deceived by the force of my eloquence. To say this, when they were certain to be detected as soon as I opened my lips and proved myself to be anything but a great speaker, did indeed appear to me most shameless—unless by the force of eloquence they mean the force of truth; for if such is their meaning, I admit that I am eloquent. But in how different a way from theirs!

Well, as I was saying, they have scarcely spoken the truth at all; but from me you shall hear the whole truth; not, however, delivered after their manner in a set oration duly ornamented with words and phrases. No, by heaven! but I shall use the words and arguments which occur to me at the moment; for I am confident in the justice of my cause: at my time of life I ought not to be appearing before you, O men of Athens, in the character of a juvenile orator—let no one expect it of me. And I must beg of you to grant me a favour:—If I defend myself in my accustomed manner, and you hear me using the words which I have been in the habit of using in the agora,[2] at the tables of the money-changers, or anywhere else, I would ask you not to be surprised, and not to interrupt me on this account. For I am more than seventy years of age, and appearing now for the first time in a court of law, I am quite a stranger to the language of the place; and therefore I would have you regard me as if I were really a stranger, whom you would excuse if he spoke in his native tongue, and after the fashion of his country:—Am I making an unfair request of you? Never mind the manner, which

1. Translated by Benjamin Jowett.

2. Place of assembly, a marketplace.

may or may not be good; but think only of the truth of my words, and give heed to that: let the speaker speak truly and the judge decide justly.

And first, I have to reply to the older charges and to my first accusers, and then I will go on to the later ones. For of old I have had many accusers, who have accused me falsely to you during many years; and I am more afraid of them than of Anytus and his associates, who are dangerous, too, in their own way. But far more dangerous are the others, who began when you were children, and took possession of your minds with their falsehoods, telling of one Socrates, a wise man, who speculated about the heaven above, and searched into the earth beneath, and made the worse appear the better cause. The disseminators of this tale are the accusers whom I dread; for their hearers are apt to fancy that such enquirers do not believe in the existence of the gods. And they are many, and their charges against me are of ancient date, and they were made by them in the days when you were more impressible than you are now—in childhood, or it may have been in youth—and the cause when heard went by default, for there was none to answer. And hardest of all, I do not know and cannot tell the names of my accusers; unless in the chance case of a Comic poet. All who from envy and malice have persuaded you—some of them having first convinced themselves—all this class of men are most difficult to deal with; for I cannot have them up here, and cross-examine them, and therefore I must simply fight with shadows in my own defence, and argue when there is no one who answers. I will ask you then to assume with me, as I was saying, that my opponents are of two kinds; one recent, the other ancient: and I hope that you will see the propriety of my answering the latter first, for these accusations you heard long before the others, and much oftener.

Well, then, I must make my defence, and endeavor to clear away in a short time, a slander which has lasted a long time. May I succeed, if to succeed be for my good and yours, or likely to avail me in my cause! The task is not an easy one; I quite understand the nature of it. And so leaving the event with God, in obedience to the law I will now make my defence.

I will begin at the beginning, and ask what is the accusation which has given rise to the slander of me, and in fact has encouraged Meletus to prefer this charge against me. Well, what do the slanderers say? They shall be my prosecutors, and I will sum up their words in an affidavit: "Socrates is an evil-doer, and a curious person, who searches into things under the earth and in heaven, and he makes the worse appear the better cause; and he teaches the aforesaid doctrines to others." Such is the nature of the accusation: it is just what you have yourselves seen in the comedy of Aristophanes, who has introduced a man whom he calls Socrates, going about and saying that he walks in air, and talking a deal of nonsense concerning matters of which I do not pretend to know either much or little[3]—not that I mean to speak disparagingly of any one who is a student of natural philosophy. I should be very sorry if Meletus could bring so grave a charge against me. But the simple truth is, O Athenians, that I have nothing to do with physical speculations. Very many of those here present are witnesses to the truth of this, and to them I appeal. Speak then, you who have heard me, and tell your neighbours whether any of you have ever known me hold forth in few words or in many upon such matters. . . . You hear their answer. And from what they say of this part of the charge you will be able to judge of the truth of the rest.

As little foundation is there for the report that I am a teacher, and take money; this accusation has no more truth in it than the other.[4] Although, if a man were really

3. In Aristophanes' *Clouds,* which attacks Socrates as a ridiculous master of false reasoning.

4. Protagoras and other popular teachers of rhetoric made fortunes by their teaching.

able to instruct mankind, to receive money for giving instruction would, in my opinion, be an honour to him. There is Gorgias of Leontium, and Prodicus of Ceos, and Hippias of Elis, who go the round of the cities, and are able to persuade the young men to leave their own citizens by whom they might be taught for nothing, and come to them whom they not only pay, but are thankful if they may be allowed to pay them. There is at this time a Parian philosopher residing in Athens, of whom I have heard; and I came to hear of him in this way:—I came across a man who has spent a world of money on the Sophists, Callias, the son of Hipponicus, and knowing that he had sons, I asked him: "Callias," I said "if your two sons were foals or calves, there would be no difficulty in finding some one to put over them; we should hire a trainer of horses, or a farmer probably, who would improve and perfect them in their own proper virtue and excellence; but as they are human beings, whom are you thinking of placing over them? Is there any one who understands human and political virtue? You must have thought about the matter, for you have sons; is there any one?" "There is," he said. "Who is he?" said I; "and of what country? and what does he charge?" "Evenus the Parian," he replied; "he is the man, and his charge is five minae." Happy is Evenus, I said to myself, if he really has this wisdom, and teaches at such a moderate charge. Had I the same, I should have been very proud and conceited; but the truth is that I have no knowledge of the kind.

I dare say, Athenians, that some one among you will reply, "Yes, Socrates, but what is the origin of these accusations which are brought against you; there must have been something strange which you have been doing? All these rumours and this talk about you would never have arisen if you had been like other men: tell us, then, what is the cause of them, for we should be sorry to judge hastily of you." Now I regard this as a fair challenge, and I will endeavour to explain to you the reason why I am called wise and have such an evil fame. Please to attend then. And although some of you may think that I am joking, I declare that I will tell you the entire truth. Men of Athens, this reputation of mine has come of a certain sort of wisdom which I possess. If you ask me what kind of wisdom, I reply, wisdom such as may perhaps be attained by man, for to that extent I am inclined to believe that I am wise; whereas the persons of whom I was speaking have a superhuman wisdom, which I may fail to describe, because I have it not myself; and he who says that I have, speaks falsely, and is taking away my character. And here, O men of Athens, I must beg you not to interrupt me, even if I seem to say something extravagant. For the word which I will speak is not mine. I will refer you to a witness who is worthy of credit; that witness shall be the God of Delphi[5]—he will tell you about my wisdom, if I have any, and of what sort it is. You must have known Chaerephon; he was early a friend of mine, and also a friend of yours, for he shared in the recent exile of the people, and returned with you. Well, Chaerephon, as you know, was very impetuous in all his doings, and he went to Delphi and boldly asked the oracle to tell him whether—as I was saying, I must beg you not to interrupt—he asked the oracle to tell him whether any one was wiser than I was, and the Pythian prophetess answered, that there was no man wiser. Chaerephon is dead himself; but his brother, who is in court, will confirm the truth of what I am saying.

Why do I mention this? Because I am going to explain to you why I have such an evil name. When I heard the answer, I said to myself, What can the god mean? and what is the interpretation of his riddle? for I know that I have no wisdom, small or

5. Apollo.

great. What then can he mean when he says that I am the wisest of men? And yet he is a god, and cannot lie; that would be against his nature. After long consideration, I thought of a method of trying the question. I reflected that if I could only find a man wiser than myself, then I might go to the god with a refutation in my hand. I should say to him, "Here is a man who is wiser than I am; but you said that I was the wisest." Accordingly I went to one who had the reputation of wisdom, and observed him—his name I need not mention; he was a politician whom I selected for examination—and the result was as follows: When I began to talk with him, I could not help thinking that he was not really wise, although he was thought wise by many, and still wiser by himself; and thereupon I tried to explain to him that he thought himself wise, but was not really wise; and the consequence was that he hated me, and his enmity was shared by several who were present and heard me. So I left him, saying to myself, as I went away: Well, although I do not suppose that either of us knows anything really beautiful and good, I am better off than he is,—for he knows nothing, and thinks that he knows; I neither know nor think that I know. In this latter particular, then, I seem to have slightly the advantage of him. Then I went to another who had still higher pretensions to wisdom, and my conclusion was exactly the same. Whereupon I made another enemy of him, and of many others besides him.

Then I went to one man after another, being not unconscious of the enmity which I provoked, and I lamented and feared this: But necessity was laid upon me,—the word of God, I thought, ought to be considered first. And I said to myself, Go I must to all who appear to know, and find out the meaning of the oracle. And I swear to you, Athenians, by the dog I swear!—for I must tell you the truth—the result of my mission was just this: I found that the men most in repute were all but the most foolish; and that others less esteemed were really wiser and better. I will tell you the tale of my wanderings and of the "Herculean" labours, as I may call them, which I endured only to find at last the oracle irrefutable.

After the politicians, I went to the poets; tragic, dithyrambic, and all sorts. And there, I said to myself, you will be instantly detected; now you will find out that you are more ignorant than they are. Accordingly, I took them some of the most elaborate passages in their own writings, and asked what was the meaning of them—thinking that they would teach me something. Will you believe me? I am almost ashamed to confess the truth, but I must say that there is hardly a person present who would not have talked better about their poetry than they did themselves. Then I knew that not by wisdom do poets write poetry, but by a sort of genius and inspiration; they are like diviners or soothsayers who also say many fine things, but do not understand the meaning of them. The poets appeared to me to be much in the same case; and I further observed that upon the strength of their poetry they believed themselves to be the wisest of men in other things in which they were not wise. So I departed, conceiving myself to be superior to them for the same reason that I was superior to the politicians.

At last I went to the artisans, for I was conscious that I knew nothing at all, as I may say; and I was sure that they knew many fine things; and here I was not mistaken, for they did know many things of which I was ignorant, and in this they certainly were wiser than I was. But I observed that even the good artisans fell into the same error as the poets;—because they were good workmen they thought that they also knew all sorts of high matters, and this defect in them overshadowed their wisdom; and therefore I asked myself on behalf of the oracle, whether I would like to be as I was, neither having their knowledge nor their ignorance, or like them in both; and I made answer to myself and to the oracle that I was better off as I was.

This inquisition has led to my having many enemies of the worst and most dangerous kind, and has given occasion also to many calumnies. And I am called wise, for my hearers always imagine that I myself possess the wisdom which I find wanting in others: but the truth is, O men of Athens, that God only is wise; and by his answer he intends to show that the wisdom of men is worth little or nothing; he is not speaking of Socrates, he is only using my name by way of illustration, as if he said, He, O men, is the wisest, who, like Socrates, knows that his wisdom is in truth worth nothing. And so I go about the world, obedient to the god, and search and make enquiry into the wisdom of any one, whether citizen or stranger, who appears to be wise; and if he is not wise, then in vindication of the oracle I show him that he is not wise; and my occupation quite absorbs me, and I have no time to give either to any public matter of interest or to any concern of my own, but I am in utter poverty by reason of my devotion to the god.

There is another thing:—young men of the richer classes, who have not much to do, come about me of their own accord; they like to hear the pretenders examined, and they often imitate me, and proceed to examine others; there are plenty of persons, as they quickly discover, who think that they know something, but really know little or nothing; and then those who are examined by them instead of being angry with themselves are angry with me: This confounded Socrates, they say; this villainous misleader of youth!—and then if somebody asks them, Why, what evil does he practise or teach? they do not know, and cannot tell; but in order that they may not appear to be at a loss, they repeat the ready-made charges which are used against all philosophers about teaching things up in the clouds and under the earth, and having no gods, and making the worse appear the better cause; for they do not like to confess that their pretence of knowledge has been detected—which is the truth; and as they are numerous and ambitious and energetic, and are drawn up in battle array and have persuasive tongues, they have filled your ears with their loud and inveterate calumnies. And this is the reason why my three accusers, Meletus and Anytus and Lycon, have set upon me; Meletus, who has a quarrel with me on behalf of the poets; Anytus, on behalf of the craftsmen and politicians; Lycon, on behalf of the rhetoricians: and as I said at the beginning, I cannot expect to get rid of such a mass of calumny all in a moment. And this, O men of Athens, is the truth and the whole truth; I have concealed nothing, I have dissembled nothing. And yet, I know that my plainness of speech makes them hate me, and what is their hatred but a proof that I am speaking the truth?—Hence has arisen the prejudice against me; and this is the reason of it, as you will find out either in this or in any future enquiry.

I have said enough in my defence against the first class of my accusers; I turn to the second class. They are headed by Meletus, that good man and true lover of his country, as he calls himself. Against these, too, I must try to make a defence:—Let their affidavit be read: it contains something of this kind: It says that Socrates is a doer of evil, who corrupts the youth; and who does not believe in the gods of the state, but has other new divinities of his own. Such is the charge; and now let us examine the particular counts. He says that I am a doer of evil, and corrupt the youth; but I say, O men of Athens, that Meletus is a doer of evil, in that he pretends to be in earnest when he is only in jest, and is so eager to bring men to trial from a pretended zeal and interest about matters in which he really never had the smallest interest. And the truth of this I will endeavour to prove to you.

Come hither, Meletus, and let me ask a question of you. You think a great deal about the improvement of youth?

Yes, I do.

Tell the judges, then, who is their improver; for you must know, as you have taken the pains to discover their corrupter, and are citing and accusing me before them. Speak, then, and tell the judges who their improver is.—Observe, Meletus, that you are silent, and have nothing to say. But is not this rather disgraceful, and a very considerable proof of what I was saying, that you have no interest in the matter? Speak up, friend, and tell us who their improver is.

The laws.

But that, my good sir, is not my meaning. I want to know who the person is, who, in the first place, knows the laws.

The judges,[6] Socrates, who are present in court.

What, do you mean to say, Meletus, that they are able to instruct and improve youth?

Certainly they are.

What, all of them, or some only and not others?

All of them.

By the goddess Hera, that is good news! There are plenty of improvers, then. And what do you say of the audience,—do they improve them?

Yes, they do.

And the senators?

Yes, the senators improve them.

But perhaps the members of the assembly corrupt them?—or do they too improve them?

They improve them.

Then every Athenian improves and elevates them; all with the exception of myself; and I alone am their corrupter? Is that what you affirm?

That is what I stoutly affirm.

I am very unfortunate if you are right. But suppose I ask you a question: How about horses? Does one man do them harm and all the world good? Is not the exact opposite the truth? One man is able to do them good, or at least not many;—the trainer of horses, that is to say, does them good, and others who have to do with them rather injure them? Is not that true, Meletus, of horses, or of any other animals? Most assuredly it is; whether you and Anytus say yes or no. Happy indeed would be the condition of youth if they had one corrupter only, and all the rest of the world were their improvers. But you, Meletus, have sufficiently shown that you never had a thought about the young: your carelessness is seen in your not caring about the very things which you bring against me.

And now, Meletus, I will ask you another question—by Zeus I will: Which is better, to live among bad citizens, or among good ones? Answer, friend, I say; the question is one which may be easily answered. Do not the good do their neighbours good, and the bad do them evil?

Certainly.

And is there any one who would rather be injured than benefited by those who live with him? Answer, my good friend, the law requires you to answer—does any one like to be injured?

Certainly not.

And when you accuse me of corrupting and deteriorating the youth, do you allege that I corrupt them intentionally or unintentionally?

6. Or jury; cases were judged by panels of as many as 500 fellow citizens.

Intentionally, I say.

But you have just admitted that the good do their neighbours good, and evil do them evil. Now, is that a truth which your superior wisdom has recognized thus early in life, and am I, at my age, in such darkness and ignorance as not to know that if a man with whom I have to live is corrupted by me, I am very likely to be harmed by him; and yet I corrupt him, and intentionally, too—so you say, although neither I nor any other human being is ever likely to be convinced by you. But either I do not corrupt them, or I corrupt them unintentionally; and on either view of the case you lie. If my offense is unintentional, the law has no cognizance of unintentional offences: you ought to have taken me privately, and warned and admonished me; for if I had been better advised, I should have left off doing what I only did unintentionally—no doubt I should; but you would have nothing to say to me and refused to teach me. And now you bring me up in this court, which is a place not of instruction, but of punishment.

It will be very clear to you, Athenians, as I was saying, that Meletus has no care at all, great or small, about the matter. But still I should like to know, Meletus, in what I am affirmed to corrupt the young. I suppose you mean, as I infer from your indictment, that I teach them not to acknowledge the gods which the state acknowledges, but some other new divinities or spiritual agencies in their stead. These are the lessons by which I corrupt the youth, as you say.

Yes, that I say emphatically.

Then, by the gods, Meletus, of whom we are speaking, tell me and the court, in somewhat plainer terms, what you mean! for I do not as yet understand whether you affirm that I teach other men to acknowledge some gods, and therefore that I do believe in gods, and am not an entire atheist—this you do not lay to my charge,—but only you say that they are not the same gods which the city recognizes—the charge is that they are different gods. Or, do you mean that I am an atheist simply, and a teacher of atheism?

I mean the latter—that you are a complete atheist.

What an extraordinary statement! Why do you think so, Meletus? Do you mean that I do not believe in the godhead of the sun or moon, like other men?

I assure you, judges, that he does not: for he says that the sun is stone, and the moon earth.

Friend Meletus, you think that you are accusing Anaxagoras:[7] and you have but a bad opinion of the judges, if you fancy them illiterate to such a degree as not to know that these doctrines are found in the books of Anaxagoras the Clazomenian, which are full of them. And so, forsooth, the youth are said to be taught them by Socrates, when there are not unfrequently exhibitions of them at the theatre (price of admission one drachma at the most); and they might pay their money, and laugh at Socrates if he pretends to father these extraordinary views. And so, Meletus, you really think that I do not believe in any god?

I swear by Zeus that you believe absolutely in none at all.

Nobody will believe you, Meletus, and I am pretty sure that you do not believe yourself. I cannot help thinking, men of Athens, that Meletus is reckless and impudent, and that he has written this indictment in a spirit of mere wantonness and youthful bravado. Has he not compounded a riddle, thinking to try me? He said to himself:—I shall see whether the wise Socrates will discover my facetious contradiction, or whether I shall be able to deceive him and the rest of them. For he certainly does

7. A philosopher tried for impiety.

appear to me to contradict himself in the indictment as much as if he said that Socrates is guilty of not believing in the gods, and yet of believing in them—but this is not like a person who is in earnest.

I should like you, O men of Athens, to join me in examining what I conceive to be his inconsistency; and do you, Meletus, answer. And I must remind the audience of my request that they would not make a disturbance if I speak in my accustomed manner:

Did ever man, Meletus, believe in the existence of human things, and not of human beings? . . . I wish, men of Athens, that he would answer, and not be always trying to get up, an interruption. Did ever any man believe in horsemanship, and not in horses? or in flute-playing, and not in flute-players? No, my friend; I will answer to you and to the court, as you refuse to answer for yourself. There is no man who ever did. But now please to answer the next question: Can a man believe in spiritual and divine agencies, and not in spirits or demigods?

He cannot.

How lucky I am to have extracted that answer, by the assistance of the court! But then you swear in the indictment that I teach and believe in divine or spiritual agencies (new or old, no matter for that); at any rate, I believe in spiritual agencies,—so you say and swear in the affidavit; and yet if I believe in divine beings, how can I help believing in spirits or demigods;—must I not? To be sure I must; and therefore I may assume that your silence gives consent. Now what are spirits or demigods? are they not either gods or the sons of gods?

Certainly they are.

But this is what I call the facetious riddle invented by you: the demigods or spirits are gods, and you say first that I do not believe in gods, and then again that I do believe in gods; that is, if I believe in demigods. For if the demigods are the illegitimate sons of gods, whether by the nymphs or by any other mothers, of whom they are said to be the sons—what human being will ever believe that there are no gods if they are the sons of gods? You might as well affirm the existence of mules, and deny that of horses and asses. Such nonsense, Meletus, could only have been intended by you to make trial of me. You have put this into the indictment because you had nothing real of which to accuse me. But no one who has a particle of understanding will ever be convinced by you that the same men can believe in divine and superhuman things, and yet not believe that there are gods and demigods and heroes.

I have said enough in answer to the charge of Meletus: any elaborate defence is unnecessary; but I know only too well how many are the enmities which I have incurred, and this is what will be my destruction if I am destroyed;—not Meletus, nor yet Anytus, but the envy and detraction of the world, which has been the death of many good men, and will probably be the death of many more; there is no danger of my being the last of them.

Someone will say: And are you not ashamed, Socrates, of a course of life which is likely to bring you to an untimely end? To him I may fairly answer: There you are mistaken: a man who is good for anything ought not to calculate the chance of living or dying; he ought only to consider whether in doing anything he is doing right or wrong—acting the part of a good man or of a bad. Whereas, upon your view, the heroes who fell at Troy were not good for much, and the son of Thetis[8] above all, who altogether despised danger in comparison with disgrace; and when he was so eager to

8. Achilles.

slay Hector, his goddess mother said to him, that if he avenged his companion Patroclus, and slew Hector, he would die himself—"Fate," she said, in these or the like words, "waits for you next after Hector"; he, receiving this warning, utterly despised danger and death, and instead of fearing them, feared rather to live in dishonour, and not to avenge his friend. "Let me die forthwith," he replies, "and be avenged of my enemy, rather than abide here by the beaked ships, a laughing-stock and a burden of the earth." Had Achilles any thought of death and danger? For wherever a man's place is, whether the place which he has chosen or that in which he has been placed by a commander, there he ought to remain in the hour of danger; he should not think of death or of anything but of disgrace. And this, O men of Athens, is a true saying.

Strange, indeed, would be my conduct, O men of Athens, if I who, when I was ordered by the generals whom you chose to command me at Potidaea and Amphipolis and Delium,[9] remained where they placed me, like any other man, facing death—if now, when, as I conceive and imagine, God orders me to fulfil the philosopher's mission of searching into myself and other men, I were to desert my post through fear of death, or any other fear; that would indeed be strange, and I might justly be arraigned in court for denying the existence of the gods, if I disobeyed the oracle because I was afraid of death, fancying that I was wise when I was not wise. For the fear of death is indeed the pretence of wisdom, and not real wisdom, being a pretence of knowing the unknown; and no one knows whether death, which men in their fear apprehend to be the greatest evil, may not be the greatest good. Is not this ignorance of a disgraceful sort, the ignorance which is the conceit that man knows what he does not know? And in this respect only I believe myself to differ from men in general, and may perhaps claim to be wiser than they are:—that whereas I know but little of the world below, I do not suppose that I know: but I do know that injustice and disobedience to a better, whether God or man, is evil and dishonourable, and I will never fear or avoid a possible good rather than a certain evil.

And therefore if you let me go now, and are not convinced by Anytus, who said that since I had been prosecuted I must be put to death (or if not that I ought never to have been prosecuted at all); and that if I escape now, your sons will all be utterly ruined by listening to my words—if you say to me, Socrates, this time we will not mind Anytus, and you shall be let off, but upon one condition, that you are not to enquire and speculate in this way any more, and that if you are caught doing so again you shall die;—if this was the condition on which you let me go, I should reply: Men of Athens, I honour and love you; but I shall obey God rather than you, and while I have life and strength I shall never cease from the practice and teaching of philosophy, exhorting any one whom I meet and saying to him after my manner: You, my friend,—a citizen of the great and mighty and wise city of Athens,—are you not ashamed of heaping up the greatest amount of money and honour and reputation, and caring so little about wisdom and truth and the greatest improvement of the soul, which you never regard or heed at all? And if the person with whom I am arguing, says: Yes, but I do care; then I do not leave him or let him go at once; but I proceed to interrogate and examine and cross-examine him, and if I think that he has no virtue in him, but only says that he has, I reproach him with undervaluing the greater, and over-valuing the less. And I shall repeat the same words to every one whom I meet, young and old, citizen and alien, but especially to the citizens, inasmuch as they are my brethren.

9. As a younger man, Socrates had been a foot soldier in these battles during the Peloponnesian War.

For know that this is the command of God; and I believe that no greater good has ever happened in the state than my service to the God. For I do nothing but go about persuading you all, old and young alike, not to take thought for your persons or your properties, but first and chiefly to care about the greatest improvement of the soul. I tell you that virtue is not given by money, but that from virtue comes money and every other good of man, public as well as private. This is my teaching, and if this is the doctrine which corrupts the youth, I am a mischievous person. But if any one says that this is not my teaching, he is speaking an untruth. Wherefore, O men of Athens, I say to you, do as Anytus bids or not as Anytus bids, and either acquit me or not; but whichever you do, understand that I shall never alter my ways, not even if I have to die many times.

Men of Athens, do not interrupt, but hear me; there was an understanding between us that you should hear me to the end: I have something more to say, at which you may be inclined to cry out; but I believe that to hear me will be good for you, and therefore I beg that you will not cry out. I would have you know, that if you kill such a one as I am, you will injure yourselves more than you will injure me. Nothing will injure me, not Meletus nor yet Anytus—they cannot, for a bad man is not permitted to injure a better than himself. I do not deny that Anytus may, perhaps, kill him, or drive him into exile, or deprive him of civil rights; and he may imagine, and others may imagine, that he is inflicting a great injury upon him: but there I do not agree. For the evil of doing as he is doing—the evil of unjustly taking away the life of another—is greater far.

And now, Athenians, I am not going to argue for my own sake, as you may think, but for yours, that you may not sin against the God by condemning me, who am his gift to you. For if you kill me you will not easily find a successor to me, who, if I may use such a ludicrous figure of speech, am a sort of gadfly,[1] given to the state by God; and the state is a great and noble steed who is tardy in his motions owing to his very size, and requires to be stirred into life. I am that gadfly which God has attached to the state, and all day long and in all places am always fastening upon you, arousing and persuading and reproaching you. You will not easily find another like me, and therefore I would advise you to spare me. I dare say that you may feel out of temper (like a person who is suddenly awakened from sleep), and you think that you might easily strike me dead as Anytus advises, and then you would sleep on for the remainder of your lives, unless God in his care of you sent you another gadfly. When I say that I am given to you by God, the proof of my mission is this:—if I had been like other men, I should not have neglected all my own concerns or patiently seen the neglect of them during all these years, and have been doing yours, coming to you individually like a father or elder brother, exhorting you to regard virtue; such conduct, I say, would be unlike human nature. If I had gained anything, or if my exhortations had been paid, there would have been some sense in my doing so; but now, as you will perceive, not even the impudence of my accusers dares to say that I have ever exacted or sought pay of any one; of that they have no witness. And I have a sufficient witness to the truth of what I say—my poverty.

Some one may wonder why I go about in private giving advice and busying myself with the concerns of others, but do not venture to come forward in public and advise the state. I will tell you why. You have heard me speak at sundry times and in divers places of an oracle or sign which comes to me, and is the divinity which Meletus

1. Horsefly.

ridicules in the indictment. This sign, which is a kind of voice, first began to come to me when I was a child; it always forbids but never commands me to do anything which I am going to do. This is what deters me from being a politician. And rightly, as I think. For I am certain, O men of Athens, that if I had engaged in politics, I should have perished long ago, and done no good either to you or to myself. And do not be offended at my telling you the truth: for the truth is, that no man who goes to war with you or any other multitude, honestly striving against the many lawless and unrighteous deeds which are done in a state, will save his life; he who will fight for the right, if he would live even for a brief space, must have a private station and not a public one.

I can give you convincing evidence of what I say, not words only, but what you value far more—actions. Let me relate to you a passage of my own life which will prove to you that I should never have yielded to injustice from any fear of death, and that "as I should have refused to yield" I must have died at once. I will tell you a tale of the courts, not very interesting perhaps, but nevertheless true. The only office of state which I ever held, O men of Athens, was that of senator: the tribe Antiochis, which is my tribe, had the presidency at the trial of the generals who had not taken up the bodies of the slain after the battle of Arginusae;[2] and you proposed to try them in a body, contrary to law, as you all thought afterwards; but at the time I was the only one of the Prytanes who was opposed to the illegality, and I gave my vote against you; and when the orators threatened to impeach and arrest me, and you called and shouted, I made up my mind that I would run the risk, having law and justice with me, rather than take part in your injustice because I feared imprisonment and death. This happened in the days of the democracy. But when the oligarchy of the Thirty[3] was in power, they sent for me and four others into the rotunda, and bade us bring Leon the Salaminian from Salamis, as they wanted to put him to death. This was a specimen of the sort of commands which they were always giving with the view of implicating as many as possible in their crimes; and then I showed, not in word only but in deed, that, if I may be allowed to use such an expression, I cared not a straw for death, and that my great and only care was lest I should do an unrighteous or unholy thing. For the strong arm of that oppressive power did not frighten me into doing wrong; and when we came out of the rotunda the other four went to Salamis and fetched Leon, but I went quietly home. For which I might have lost my life, had not the power of the Thirty shortly afterwards come to an end. And many will witness to my words.

Now do you really imagine that I could have survived all these years, if I had led a public life, supposing that like a good man I had always maintained the right and had made justice, as I ought, the first thing? No indeed, men of Athens, neither I nor any other man. But I have been always the same in all my actions, public as well as private, and never have I yielded any base compliance to those who are slanderously termed my disciples, or to any other. Not that I have any regular disciples. But if anyone likes to come and hear me while I am pursuing my mission, whether he be young or old, he is not excluded. Nor do I converse only with those who pay; but anyone, whether he be rich or poor, may ask and answer me and listen to my words; and whether he turns out to be a bad man or a good one, neither result can be justly imputed to me; for I never taught or professed to teach him anything. And if anyone says that he has ever learned or heard anything from me in private which all the world has not heard, let me tell you that he is lying.

2. Athenian victory in the Peloponnesian War in 406 B.C.E.

3. Members of the antidemocratic coup of 404 B.C.E.

But I shall be asked, Why do people delight in continually conversing with you? I have told you already, Athenians, the whole truth about this matter: they like to hear the cross-examination of the pretenders to wisdom; there is amusement in it. Now this duty of cross-examining other men has been imposed upon me by God; and has been signified to me by oracles, visions, and in every way in which the will of divine power was ever intimated to any one. This is true, O Athenians; or, if not true, would be soon refuted. If I am or have been corrupting the youth, those of them who are now grown up and become sensible that I gave them bad advice in the days of their youth should come forward as accusers, and take their revenge; or if they do not like to come themselves, some of their relatives, fathers, brothers, or other kinsmen, should say what evil their families have suffered at my hands.

Now is their time. Many of them I see in the court. There is Crito, who is of the same age and of the same deme with myself, and there is Critobulus his son, whom I also see. Then again there is Lysanias of Sphettus, who is the father of Aeschines—he is present; and also there is Antiphon of Cephisus, who is the father of Epigenes; and there are the brothers of several who have associated with me. There is Nicostratus the son of Theosdotides, and the brother of Theodotus (now Theodotus himself is dead, and therefore he, at any rate, will not seek to stop him); and there is Paralus the son of Demodocus, who had a brother Theages; and Adeimantus the son of Ariston, whose brother Plato is present; and Aeantodorus, who is the brother of Apollodorus, whom I also see. I might mention a great many others, some of whom Meletus should have produced as witnesses in the course of his speech; and let him still produce them, if he has forgotten—I will make way for him. And let him say, if he has any testimony of the sort which he can produce. Nay, Athenians, the very opposite is the truth. For all these are ready to witness on behalf of the corrupter, of the injurer of their kindred, as Meletus and Anytus call me; not the corrupted youth only—there might have been a motive for that—but their uncorrupted elder relatives. Why should they too support me with their testimony? Why, indeed, except for the sake of truth and justice, and because they know that I am speaking the truth, and that Meletus is a liar.

Well, Athenians, this and the like of this is all the defence which I have to offer. Yet a word more. Perhaps there may be some one who is offended at me, when he calls to mind how he himself on a similar, or even a less serious occasion, prayed and entreated the judges with many tears, and how he produced his children in court, which was a moving spectacle, together with a host of relations and friends; whereas I, who am probably in danger of my life, will do none of these things. The contrast may occur to his mind, and he may be set against me, and vote in anger because he is displeased at me on this account. Now if there be such a person among you,—mind, I do not say that there is,—to him I may fairly reply: My friend, I am a man, and like other men, a creature of flesh and blood, and not "of wood or stone," as Homer says;[4] and I have a family, yes, and sons, O Athenians, three in number, one almost a man, and two others who are still young; and yet I will not bring any of them hither in order to petition you for an acquittal. And why not? Not from any self-assertion or want of respect for you. Whether I am or am not afraid of death is another question, of which I will not now speak. But, having regard to public opinion, I feel that such conduct would be discreditable to myself, and to you, and to the whole state. One who has reached my years, and who has a name for wisdom, ought not to demean himself.

4. In the *Odyssey*, Book 19, line 184.

Whether this opinion of me be deserved or not, at any rate the world has decided that Socrates is in some way superior to other men. And if those among you who are said to be superior in wisdom and courage, and any other virtue, demean themselves in this way, how shameful is their conduct! I have seen men of reputation, when they have been condemned, behaving in the strangest manner: they seemed to fancy that they were going to suffer something dreadful if they died, and that they could be immortal if you only allowed them to live; and I think that such are a dishonour to the state, and that any stranger coming in would have said of them that the most eminent men of Athens, to whom the Athenians themselves give honour and command, are no better than women. And I say that these things ought not to be done by those of us who have a reputation; and if they are done, you ought not to permit them; you ought rather to show that you are far more disposed to condemn the man who gets up a doleful scene and makes the city ridiculous, than him who holds his peace.

But, setting aside the question of public opinion, there seems to be something wrong in asking a favour of a judge, and thus procuring an acquittal, instead of informing and convincing him. For his duty is, not to make a present of justice, but to give judgment; and he has sworn that he will judge according to the laws, and not according to his own good pleasure; and we ought not to encourage you, nor should you allow yourself to be encouraged, in this habit of perjury—there can be no piety in that. Do not then require me to do what I consider dishonourable and impious and wrong, especially now, when I am being tried for impiety on the indictment of Meletus. For if, O men of Athens, by force of persuasion and entreaty I could overpower your oaths, then I should be teaching you to believe that there are no gods, and in defending should simply convict myself of the charge of not believing in them. But that is not so—far otherwise. For I do believe that there are gods, and in a sense higher than that in which any of my accusers believe in them. And to you and to God I commit my cause, to be determined by you as is best for you and me.

There are many reasons why I am not grieved, O men of Athens, at the vote of condemnation. I expected it, and am only surprised that the votes are so nearly equal; for I had thought that the majority against me would have been far larger; but now, had thirty votes gone over to the other side, I should have been acquitted. And I may say, I think, that I have escaped Meletus. I may say more; for without the assistance of Anytus and Lycon, anyone may see that he would not have had a fifth part of the votes, as the law requires, in which case he would have incurred a fine of a thousand drachmae.

And so he proposes death as the penalty. And what shall I propose on my part, O men of Athens? Clearly that which is my due. And what is my due? What return shall be made to the man who has never had the wit to be idle during his whole life; but has been careless of what the many care for—wealth, and family interests, and military offices, and speaking in the assembly, and magistracies, and plots, and parties. Reflecting that I was really too honest a man to be a politician and live, I did not go where I could do no good to you or to myself; but where I could do the greatest good privately to every one of you, thither I went, and sought to persuade every man among you that he must look to himself, and seek virtue and wisdom before he looks to his private interests, and look to the state before he looks to the interests of the state; and that this should be the order which he observes in all his actions. What shall be done to such a one? Doubtless some good thing, O men of Athens, if he has his reward; and the good should be of a kind suitable to him. What would be a reward suitable to a poor man who is your benefactor, and who desires leisure that he may instruct you?

There can be no reward so fitting as maintenance in the Prytaneum,[5] O men of Athens, a reward which he deserves far more than the citizen who has won the prize at Olympia in the horse or chariot race, whether the chariots were drawn by two horses or by many. For I am in want, and he has enough; and he only gives you the appearance of happiness, and I give you the reality. And if I am to estimate the penalty fairly, I should say that maintenance in the Prytaneum is the just return.

Perhaps you think that I am defying you in what I am saying now, as in what I said before about the tears and prayers. But this is not so. I speak rather because I am convinced that I never intentionally wronged any one, although I cannot convince you—the time has been too short; if there were a law at Athens, as there is in other cities, that a capital cause should not be decided in one day, then I believe that I should have convinced you. But I cannot in a moment refute great slanders; and, as I am convinced that I never wronged another, I will assuredly not wrong myself. I will not say of myself that I deserve any evil, or propose any penalty. Why should I? Because I am afraid of the penalty of death which Meletus proposes? When I do not know whether death is a good or an evil, why should I propose a penalty which would certainly be an evil? Shall I say imprisonment? And why should I live in prison, and be the slave of the magistrates of the year—of the Eleven? Or shall the penalty be a fine, and imprisonment until the fine is paid? There is the same objection. I should have to lie in prison, for money I have none, and cannot pay. And if I say exile (and this may possibly be the penalty which you will affix), I must indeed be blinded by the love of life, if I am so irrational as to expect that when you, who are my own citizens, cannot endure my discourses and words, and have found them so grievous and odious that you will have no more of them, others are likely to endure me. No indeed, men of Athens, that is not very likely. And what a life should I lead, at my age, wandering from city to city, ever changing my place of exile, and always being driven out! For I am quite sure that wherever I go, there, as here, the young men will flock to me; and if I drive them away, their elders will drive me out at their request; and if I let them come, their fathers and friends will drive me out for their sakes.

Some one will say: Yes, Socrates, but cannot you hold your tongue, and then you may go into a foreign city, and no one will interfere with you? Now I have great difficulty in making you understand my answer to this. For if I tell you that to do as you say would be a disobedience to the God, and therefore that I cannot hold my tongue, you will not believe that I am serious; and if I say again that daily to discourse about virtue, and of those other things about which you hear me examining myself and others, is the greatest good of man, and that the unexamined life is not worth living, you are still less likely to believe me. Yet I say what is true, although a thing of which it is hard for me to persuade you. Also, I have never been accustomed to think that I deserve to suffer any harm. Had I money I might have estimated the offence at what I was able to pay, and not have been much the worse. But I have none, and therefore I must ask you to proportion the fine to my means. Well, perhaps I could afford a mina,[6] and therefore I propose that penalty: Plato, Crito, Critobulus, and Apollodorus, my friends here, bid me say thirty minae, and they will be the sureties. Let thirty minae be the penalty; for which sum they will be ample security to you.

5. Building where officials dined at the democratic city's expense.

6. According to Xenophon, this modest sum was a fifth of Socrates' possessions.

Not much time will be gained, O Athenians, in return for the evil name which you will get from the detractors of the city, who will say that you killed Socrates, a wise man; for they will call me wise, even although I am not wise, when they want to reproach you. If you had waited a little while, your desire would have been fulfilled in the course of nature. For I am far advanced in years, as you may perceive, and not far from death. I am speaking now not to all of you, but only to those who have condemned me to death. And I have another thing to say to them: You think that I was convicted because I had no words of the sort which would have procured my acquittal—I mean, if I had thought fit to leave nothing undone or unsaid. Not so; the deficiency which led to my conviction was not of words—certainly not. But I had not the boldness or impudence or inclination to address you as you would have liked me to do, weeping and wailing and lamenting, and saying and doing many things which you have been accustomed to hear from others, and which, as I maintain, are unworthy of me.

I thought at the time that I ought not to do anything common or mean when in danger: nor do I now repent of the style of my defence; I would rather die having spoken after my manner, than speak in your manner and live. For neither in war nor yet at law ought I or any man to use every way of escaping death. Often in battle there can be no doubt that if a man will throw away his arms, and fall on his knees before his pursuers, he may escape death; and in other dangers there are other ways of escaping death, if a man is willing to say and do anything. The difficulty, my friends, is not to avoid death, but to avoid unrighteousness; for that runs faster than death. I am old and move slowly, and the slower runner has overtaken me, and my accusers are keen and quick, and the faster runner, who is unrighteousness, has overtaken them. And now I depart hence condemned by you to suffer the penalty of death,—they too go their ways condemned by the truth to suffer the penalty of villainy and wrong; and I must abide by my award—let them abide by theirs. I suppose that these things may be regarded as fated,—and I think that they are well.

And now, O men who have condemned me, I would like to prophesy to you; for I am about to die, and in the hour of death men are gifted with prophetic power. And I prophesy to you who are my murderers, that immediately after my departure punishment far heavier than you have inflicted on me will surely await you. Me you have killed because you wanted to escape the accuser, and not to give an account of your lives. But that will not be as you suppose: far otherwise. For I say that there will be more accusers of you than there are now; accusers whom hitherto I have restrained: and as they are younger they will be more inconsiderate with you, and you will be more offended at them. If you think that by killing men you can prevent some one from censuring your evil lives, you are mistaken; that is not a way of escape which is either possible or honourable; the easiest and the noblest way is not to be disabling others, but to be improving yourselves. This is the prophecy which I utter before my departure to the judges who have condemned me.

Friends, who would have acquitted me, I would like also to talk with you about the thing which has come to pass, while the magistrates are busy, and before I go to the place at which I must die. Stay then a little, for we may as well talk with one another while there is time. You are my friends, and I should like to show you the meaning of this event which has happened to me. O my judges—for you I may truly call judges—I should like to tell you of a wonderful circumstance. Hitherto the divine faculty of which the internal oracle is the source has constantly been in the habit of opposing me even about trifles, if I was going to make a slip or error in any matter; and now as you see there has come upon me that which may be thought, and is generally believed to be, the last and worst evil. But the oracle made no sign of opposition, either when I was leaving my house in the morning, or when I was on my way to the court, or while I was speaking, at anything which I was going to say; and yet I have often been stopped in the middle of a speech, but now in nothing I either said or did touching the matter in hand has the oracle opposed me. What do I take to be the explanation of this silence? I will tell you. It is an intimation that what has happened to me is a good, and that those of us who think that death is an evil are in error. For the customary sign would surely have opposed me had I been going to evil and not to good.

Let us reflect in another way, and we shall see that there is great reason to hope that death is a good; for one of two things—either death is a state of nothingness and utter unconsciousness, or, as men say, there is a change and migration of the soul from this world to another. Now if you suppose that there is no consciousness, but a sleep like the sleep of him who is undisturbed even by dreams, death will be an unspeakable gain. For if a person were to select the night in which his sleep was undisturbed even by dreams, and were to compare with this the other days and nights of his life, and then were to tell us how many days and nights he had passed in the course of his life better and more pleasantly than this one, I think that any man, I will not say a private man, but even the great king[7] will not find many such days or nights, when compared with the others. Now if death be of such a nature, I say that to die is gain; for eternity is then only a single night.

But if death is the journey to another place, and there, as men say, all the dead abide, what good, O my friends and judges, can be greater than this? If indeed when the pilgrim arrives in the world below, he is delivered from the professors of justice in this world, and finds the true judges who are said to give judgment there, Minos and Rhadamanthus and Aeacus and Triptolemus, and other sons of God who were righteous in their own life, that pilgrimage will be worth making. What would not a man give if he might converse with Orpheus and Musaeus and Hesiod and Homer?[8] Nay, if this be true, let me die again and again. I myself, too, shall have a wonderful interest in there meeting and conversing with Palamedes, and Ajax the son of Telamon, and any other ancient hero who has suffered death through an unjust judgment; and there will be no small pleasure, as I think, in comparing my own sufferings with theirs. Above all, I shall then be able to continue my search into true and false knowledge; as in this world, so also in the next; and I shall find out who is wise, and who pretends to be wise, and is not. What would not a man give, O judges, to be able to examine the leader of the great Trojan expedition; or Odysseus or Sisyphus, or numberless others, men and women too! What infinite delight would there be in conversing with them and asking them questions! In another world they do not put a man to death for asking questions: assuredly not. For besides being happier than we are, they will be immortal, if what is said is true.

Wherefore, O judges, be of good cheer about death, and know of a certainty, that no evil can happen to a good man, either in life or after death. He and his are not neglected by the gods; nor has my own approaching end happened by mere chance. But I see clearly that the time had arrived when it was better for me to die and be released from trouble; wherefore the oracle gave no sign. For which reason, also, I am not angry with my condemners, or with my accusers; they have done me no harm, although they did not mean to do me any good; and for this I may gently blame them.

7. The Persian emperor.

8. The four legendary founders of poetry.

Still I have a favour to ask of them. When my sons are grown up, I would ask you, O my friends, to punish them; and I would have you trouble them, as I have troubled you, if they seem to care about riches, or anything, more than about virtue; or if they pretend to be something when they are really nothing,—then reprove them, as I have reproved you, for not caring about that for which they ought to care, and thinking that they are something when they are really nothing. And if you do this, both I and my sons will have received justice at your hands.

The hour of departure has arrived, and we go our ways—I to die, and you to live. Which is better God only knows.

END OF PERSPECTIVES: TYRANNY AND DEMOCRACY

Euripides

c. 480–405 B.C.E.

The Greeks found Euripides peculiar. His tragedies featured talking slaves, extravagantly demonstrative women, and rhetorical excesses previously unheard in the works of his predecessors. He was said to be the son of a lettuce monger, to compose his tragedies in isolation in a cave, and even to own a library full of books, a great oddity in a world of limited literacy. In the drama contests organized by the city to honor the god Dionysos, in which Euripides' plays were performed, he often lost. Yet we have more of his tragedies than of any other Greek playwright, nineteen of the ninety he wrote.

In his tragedies, Euripides represents a complex mixture of the ordinary, the everyday, and the radically deviant, calling attention to the deep strangeness of tragedy, a genre that crosses the world of heroic legend with the daily life of the citizen audience. Maidservants scheme calmly about adultery. The deposed queen of Troy, Hecuba, who after the city's fall is a slave, murders her enemy's children; it is predicted in the tragedy named for her that she will end her life changed to a dog, "a bitch with blazing eyes."

Euripides' gods exhibit cruelty and petty selfishness and torment human beings for their own amusement. The goddesses Artemis and Aphrodite fight over the sexual fate of the chaste misogynist Hippolytus, entangled in the desire of his stepmother, Phaedra; accused of seduction, he dies a battered wreck in the arms of his father. The god Dionysos, in the *Bacchae,* seduces Thebes' king, Pentheus, into dressing as a woman so that he can spy on the maenads, the maddened women worshipers of the god. Dionysos provokes his devotees, including Pentheus's own mother, into a frenzy in which the king is torn to pieces, his head brought home as a trophy by his mother; in a devastating recognition scene, she slowly realizes what she carries.

Euripides takes seriously the human status of women, children, slaves, barbarians, foreigners, and prisoners of war and gives them voices in his tragedies, decentering the focus on the free Greek male citizen typical of the ancient city. He demonstrates a special fascination for women, their psychology, their motivations, and their fates. Several of his tragedies focus on idealistic young women who choose to sacrifice themselves for their idealism and are exploited by older characters of great cynicism; Iphigeneia, for example, dies at the hands of her father, Agamemnon, who sacrifices her so that the Greek fleet can sail to Troy from Aulis, where the fleet has been stalled for an offense committed against the goddess Artemis. In *Alcestis,* a husband allows his wife to die in his place and then, immediately after promising never to replace

A Maenad cup by the Brygos Painter, mid-first millennium B.C.E. The maenad carries her thyrsus (a staff crowned with pine cones, symbol of Dionysos) and a small leopard she has just slain, probably to make another fur stole like the one she wears around her neck, identifying with the leopard's wild, foreign power.

her, receives into his household what he believes to be another woman. In other plays, the choruses are made up of enslaved women who lament their losses of loved ones and of freedom, as in *The Trojan Women:*

> Beside their altars the Trojans
> died in their blood. Desolate now,
> men murdered, our sleeping rooms gave up
> their brides' beauty
> to breed sons for Greek men,
> sorrow for our own country.

Such lines speak to the audience of slaveholders and touch on both their status as the possessors of other human beings and their vulnerability to enslavement themselves, in a world of war where the killing of men and the enslaving of women in conquered cities was often a matter of course. It may be that radical thinkers of this period were questioning whether slaves were slaves "by nature." In one dramatic scene in the *Ion,* a slave pronounces what may have seemed to some like a heretical idea: "A slave bears only this / Disgrace: the name. In every other way / An honest slave is equal to the free." Euripides returns several times to the aftermath of the fall of Troy, the paradigmatic city whose conuest stood for the loss of civilization itself. Rather than showing the scenes of warriors in the long battle that preceded the Greeks' victory, he concentrates on the Trojan victims, the humiliation and sexual slavery of the former free inhabitants, royal princesses taken to the lands of their conquerors and forced into new masters' beds.

In his own time Euripides was the object of mockery for his questioning of the status quo and for his peculiarities. The comic playwright Aristophanes ridicules him frequently, presenting in *The Women at the Thesmophoria* the case that the women of the city are furious at Euripides for his misogyny and want to destroy him. In his play *The Frogs,* first performed in 405 B.C.E., Aristophanes sends the god Dionysos, portrayed as a coward and a fool, and his slave Xanthias into the underworld to bring the recently deceased Euripides back from the dead. The comedy engages in a merciless and hilarious attack on Euripides, who is seen ultimately, after a drama contest between him and Aeschylus, as precisely not what the world above needs.

Euripides' plays call into question the heroism of traditional heroes such as Jason, husband of Medea, or Admetus, Alcestis' mate. They expose the all-too-human motives of the gods. They deploy the highly wrought argumentation of the contemporary rhetoricians and the sophists. They put into play new forms of music and almost operatic lyricism. The plays partake of the critical, questioning spirit of the later fifth century B.C.E., a world of exhausting war, with the Athenian democracy rocked by power struggles between manipulative orators, soon to be overwhelmed in defeat by the Spartans and their allies. The intellectual climate favored questioning everything—received ideas about the gods, forms of government and political hierarchies, the divine or noble origin of the Athenians, differences among Greeks and between Greeks and barbarians, the ambiguous power of rhetorical speech, the nature of slavery, and gender roles and relations. And Euripides, without committing himself definitively, presents the contradictory difficulties for his audiences.

One of the plays that most dramatically embodies these contradictions, *The Medea,* was produced in 431 B.C.E., at the time when the Peloponnesian War between the Athenians and the Spartans began and when the Athenians suffered a devastating plague that eventually carried off the great statesman Perikles. The play shares many of the concerns of other Euripidean dramas: a focus on women, with a servant taking an important role; rhetoric influenced by philosophical developments of the latter half of the fifth century; a questioning of traditional morality; and a central role for an outsider, in this case a barbarian woman, Medea, brought into the heart of Greece by her husband, Jason. The play fastens on her difference—her exotic origins and her history as a sorceress, her murder of her own brother and the fatal boiling of an old man in a fake effort of rejuvenation. It places this barbarian witch in the heart of the household and gives her a speech in which she laments the fate of the Greek woman. She stands apart by virtue of her foreign birth, yet expresses the common dismay of a wife whose man can seek comfort elsewhere while she is confined to the house. Medea says she would prefer military combat to childbirth.

Greek brides, often half the age of husbands they had barely met by their wedding day, were taken from their fathers' houses and moved into the houses of their husbands' fathers as strangers in the midst of an unfamiliar domestic life. Like the mythical women warriors called the Amazons, or the women of the island of Lemnos, who killed their husbands and administered their island themselves, Medea represents the danger at the center of the Greek household, the female brought inside, a potential source of discontent and even violence. Euripides shows Medea first as dangerously jealous, then scheming, and then violent, vengeful, and destructive, escaping from the city of Corinth only to flee to Athens, to the site of the play's first performance. Euripides cunningly twists his portrait of Medea in the course of the play. She may begin as an object of sympathy, suffering like any wife at the prospect of her husband's new alliance. As the play continues, her bestial, barbaric nature comes into the foreground, and she becomes an exemplar of the ruthless, violent, and strange. Her extreme violence may exceed the incipient sympathy of the audience and send it away from the theater in horror and revulsion. Some scholars see Euripides representing Medea throughout as the object of sympathy and identification; others argue, however, that Euripides seems to understand her, along with other women, as vulnerable, as the canary in the mine, liable to break down in situations of extremity and, victims themselves, to turn toward acts of passionate despair and hatred that bring down the world.

PRONUNCIATIONS:

Aegeus: ay-GEE-us
Euripides: you-RIP-pid-eez
Medea: meh-DEE-ah

The Medea[1]

Characters

MEDEA, *princess of Colchis and wife of Jason*
JASON, *son of Aeson, king of Iolcus*
TWO CHILDREN OF MEDEA AND JASON
CREON, *king of Corinth*
AEGEUS, *king of Athens*
NURSE TO MEDEA
TUTOR TO MEDEA'S CHILDREN
MESSENGER
CHORUS OF CORINTHIAN WOMEN

In front of Medea's house in Corinth. Enter from the house Medea's nurse.

NURSE: How I wish the Argo[2] never had reached the land
Of Colchis,[3] skimming through the blue Symplegades,[4]
Nor ever had fallen in the glades of Pelion
The smitten fir-tree to furnish oars for the hands
Of heroes who in Pelias' name attempted
The Golden Fleece! For then my mistress Medea
Would not have sailed for the towers of the land of Iolcus,[5]
Her heart on fire with passionate love for Jason;
Nor would she have persuaded the daughters of Pelias
To kill their father, and now be living here
In Corinth with her husband and children. She gave
Pleasure to the people of her land of exile,
And she herself helped Jason in every way.
This is indeed the greatest salvation of all—
For the wife not to stand apart from the husband.
But now there's hatred everywhere, Love is diseased.
For, deserting his own children and my mistress,
Jason has taken a royal wife to his bed,
The daughter of the ruler of this land, Creon.
And poor Medea is slighted, and cries aloud on the
Vows they made to each other, the right hands clasped
In eternal promise. She calls upon the gods to witness

1. Translated by Rex Warner.
2. Ship of Jason and the Argonauts.
3. On the east coast of the Black Sea.
4. The "Clashing Rocks" at the entrance to the Black Sea.
5. In northern Greece.

What sort of return Jason has made to her love.
She lies without food and gives herself up to suffering,
Wasting away every moment of the day in tears.
So it has gone since she knew herself slighted by him.
Not stirring an eye, not moving her face from the ground,
No more than either a rock or surging sea water
She listens when she is given friendly advice.
Except that sometimes she twists back her white neck and
Moans to herself, calling out on her father's name,
And her land, and her home betrayed when she came away with
A man who now is determined to dishonor her.
Poor creature, she has discovered by her sufferings
What it means to one not to have lost one's own country.
She has turned from the children and does not like to see them.
I am afraid she may think of some dreadful thing,
For her heart is violent. She will never put up with
The treatment she is getting. I know and fear her
Lest she may sharpen a sword and thrust to the heart,
Stealing into the palace where the bed is made,
Or even kill the king and the new-wedded groom,
And thus bring a greater misfortune on herself.
She's a strange woman. I know it won't be easy
To make an enemy of her and come off best.
But here the children come. They have finished playing.
They have no thought at all of their mother's trouble.
Indeed it is not usual for the young to grieve.

[*Enter from the right the slave who is the tutor to Medea's two small children. The children follow him.*]

TUTOR: You old retainer of my mistress' household,
Why are you standing here all alone in front of the
Gates and moaning to yourself over your misfortune?
Medea could not wish you to leave her alone.
NURSE: Old man, and guardian of the children of Jason,
If one is a good servant, it's a terrible thing
When one's master's luck is out; it goes to one's heart.
So I myself have got into such a state of grief
That a longing stole over me to come outside here
And tell the earth and air of my mistress' sorrows.
TUTOR: Has the poor lady not yet given up her crying?
NURSE: Given up? She's at the start, not halfway through her tears.
TUTOR: Poor fool—if I may call my mistress such a name—
How ignorant she is of trouble more to come.
NURSE: What do you mean, old man? You needn't fear to speak.
TUTOR: Nothing. I take back the words which I used just now.
NURSE: Don't, by your beard, hide this from me, your fellow-servant.
If need be, I'll keep quiet about what you tell me.
TUTOR: I heard a person saying, while I myself seemed
Not to be paying attention, when I was at the place

Where the old draught-players sit, by the holy fountain,
That Creon, ruler of the land, intends to drive
These children and their mother in exile from Corinth.
But whether what he said is really true or not
I do not know. I pray that it may not be true.

NURSE: And will Jason put up with it that his children
Should suffer so, though he's no friend to their mother?

TUTOR: Old ties give place to new ones. As for Jason, he
No longer has a feeling for this house of ours.

NURSE: It's black indeed for us, when we add new to old
Sorrows before even the present sky has cleared.

TUTOR: But you be silent, and keep all this to yourself.
It is not the right time to tell our mistress of it.

NURSE: Do you hear, children, what a father he is to you?
I wish he were dead—but no, he is still my master.
Yet certainly he has proved unkind to his dear ones.

TUTOR: What's strange in that? Have you only just discovered
That everyone loves himself more than his neighbor?
Some have good reason, others get something out of it.
So Jason neglects his children for the new bride.

NURSE: Go indoors, children. That will be the best thing.
And you, keep them to themselves as much as possible.
Don't bring them near their mother in her angry mood.
For I've seen her already blazing her eyes at them
As though she meant some mischief and I am sure that
She'll not stop raging until she has struck at someone.
May it be an enemy and not a friend she hurts!

[*Medea is heard inside the house.*]

MEDEA: Ah, wretch! Ah, lost in my sufferings,
I wish, I wish I might die.

NURSE: What did I say, dear children? Your mother
Frets her heart and frets it to anger.
Run away quickly into the house,
And keep well out of her sight.
Don't go anywhere near, but be careful
Of the wildness and bitter nature
Of that proud mind.
Go now! Run quickly indoors.
It is clear that she soon will put lightning
In that cloud of her cries that is rising
With a passion increasing. O, what will she do,
Proud-hearted and not to be checked on her course,
A soul bitten into with wrong?

[*The Tutor takes the children into the house.*]

MEDEA: Ah, I have suffered
What should be wept for bitterly. I hate you,

Children of a hateful mother. I curse you
And your father. Let the whole house crash.

NURSE: Ah, I pity you, you poor creature.
How can your children share in their father's
Wickedness? Why do you hate them? Oh children,
How much I fear that something may happen!
Great people's tempers are terrible, always
Having their own way, seldom checked,
Dangerous they shift from mood to mood.
How much better to have been accustomed
To live on equal terms with one's neighbors.
I would like to be safe and grow old in a
Humble way. What is moderate sounds best,
Also in practice *is* best for everyone.
Greatness brings no profit to people.
God indeed, when in anger, brings
Greater ruin to great men's houses.

[*Enter, on the right, a Chorus of Corinthian Women. They have come to inquire about Medea and to attempt to console her.*]

CHORUS: I heard the voice, I heard the cry
Of Colchis' wretched daughter.
Tell me, mother, is she not yet
At rest? Within the double gates
Of the court I heard her cry. I am sorry
For the sorrow of this home. O, say, what has happened?

NURSE: There is no home. It's over and done with.
Her husband holds fast to his royal wedding,
While she, my mistress, cries out her eyes
There in her room, and takes no warmth from
Any word of any friend.

MEDEA: Oh, I wish
That lightning from heaven would split my head open.
Oh, what use have I now for life?
I would find my release in death
And leave hateful existence behind me.

CHORUS: O God and Earth and Heaven!
Did you hear what a cry was that
Which the sad wife sings?
Poor foolish one, why should you long
For that appalling rest?
The final end of death comes fast.
No need to pray for that.
Suppose your man gives honor
To another woman's bed.
It often happens. Don't be hurt.
God will be your friend in this.
You must not waste away
Grieving too much for him who shared your bed.

MEDEA: Great Themis, lady Artemis,[6] behold
The things I suffer, though I made him promise,
My hateful husband. I pray that I may see him,
Him and his bride and all their palace shattered
For the wrong they dare to do me without cause.
Oh, my father! Oh, my country! In what dishonor
I left you, killing my own brother for it.

NURSE: Do you hear what she says, and how she cries
On Themis, the goddess of Promises, and on Zeus,
Whom we believe to be the Keeper of Oaths?
Of this I am sure, that no small thing
Will appease my mistress' anger.

CHORUS: Will she come into our presence?
Will she listen when we are speaking
To the words we say?
I wish she might relax her rage
And temper of her heart.
My willingness to help will never
Be wanting to my friends.
But go inside and bring her
Out of the house to us,
And speak kindly to her: hurry,
Before she wrongs her own.
This passion of hers moves to something great.

NURSE: I will, but I doubt if I'll manage
To win my mistress over.
But still I'll attempt it to please you.
Such a look she will flash on her servants
If any comes near with a message,
Like a lioness guarding her cubs.
It is right, I think, to consider
Both stupid and lacking in foresight
Those poets of old who wrote songs
For revels and dinners and banquets,
Pleasant sounds for men living at ease;
But none of them all has discovered
How to put to an end with their singing
Or musical instruments grief,
Bitter grief, from which death and disaster
Cheat the hopes of a house. Yet how good
If music could cure men of this! But why raise
To no purpose the voice at a banquet? For *there* is
Already abundance of pleasure for men
With a joy of its own.

[*The Nurse goes into the house.*]

CHORUS: I heard a shriek that is laden with sorrow.

6. Goddess of justice, virgins, and the hunt.

Shrilling out her hard grief she cries out
Upon him who betrayed both her bed and her marriage.
Wronged, she calls on the gods,
On the justice of Zeus, the oath sworn,
Which brought her away
To the opposite shore of the Greeks
Through the gloomy salt straits to the gateway
Of the salty unlimited sea.

[*Medea, attended by servants, comes out of the house.*]

MEDEA: Women of Corinth, I have come outside to you
Lest you should be indignant with me; for I know
That many people are overproud, some when alone,
And others when in company. And those who live
Quietly, as I do, get a bad reputation.
For a just judgment is not evident in the eyes
When a man at first sight hates another, before
Learning his character, being in no way injured;
And a foreigner especially must adapt himself.
I'd not approve of even a fellow-countryman
Who by pride and want of manners offends his neighbors.
But on me this thing has fallen so unexpectedly,
It has broken my heart. I am finished. I let go
All my life's joy. My friends, I only want to die.
It was everything to me to think well of one man,
And he, my own husband, has turned out wholly vile.
Of all things which are living and can form a judgment
We women are the most unfortunate creatures.
Firstly, with an excess of wealth it is required
For us to buy a husband and take for our bodies
A master; for not to take one is even worse.
And now the question is serious whether we take
A good or bad one; for there is no easy escape
For a woman, nor can she say no to her marriage.
She arrives among new modes of behavior and manners,
And needs prophetic power, unless she has learned at home,
How best to manage him who shares the bed with her.
And if we work out all this well and carefully,
And the husband lives with us and lightly bears his yoke,
Then life is enviable. If not, I'd rather die.
A man, when he's tired of the company in his home,
Goes out of the house and puts an end to his boredom
And turns to a friend or companion of his own age.
But we are forced to keep our eyes on one alone.
What they say of us is that we have a peaceful time
Living at home, while they do the fighting in war.
How wrong they are! I would very much rather stand
Three times in the front of battle than bear one child.
Yet what applies to me does not apply to you.

You have a country. Your family home is here.
You enjoy life and the company of your friends.
But I am deserted, a refugee, thought nothing of
By my husband—something he won in a foreign land.
I have no mother or brother, nor any relation
With whom I can take refuge in this sea of woe.
This much then is the service I would beg from you:
If I can find the means or devise any scheme
To pay my husband back for what he has done to me—
Him and his father-in-law and the girl who married him—
Just to keep silent. For in other ways a woman
Is full of fear, defenseless, dreads the sight of cold
Steel; but, when once she is wronged in the matter of love,
No other soul can hold so many thoughts of blood.

CHORUS: This I will promise. You are in the right, Medea,
In paying your husband back. I am not surprised at you
For being sad.
But look! I see our King Creon
Approaching. He will tell us of some new plan.

[*Enter, from the right, Creon, with attendants.*]

CREON: You, with that angry look, so set against your husband,
Medea, I order you to leave my territories
An exile, and take along with you your two children,
And not to waste time doing it. It is my decree,
And I will see it done. I will not return home
Until you are cast from the boundaries of my land.

MEDEA: Oh, this is the end for me. I am utterly lost.
Now I am in the full force of the storm of hate
And have no harbor from ruin to reach easily.
Yet still, in spite of it all, I'll ask the question:
What is your reason, Creon, for banishing me?

CREON: I am afraid of you—why should I dissemble it?—
Afraid that you may injure my daughter mortally.
Many things accumulate to support my feeling.
You are a clever woman, versed in evil arts,
And are angry at having lost your husband's love.
I hear that you are threatening, so they tell me,
To do something against my daughter and Jason
And me, too. I shall take my precautions first.
I tell you, I prefer to earn your hatred now
Than to be soft-hearted and afterward regret it.

MEDEA: This is not the first time, Creon. Often previously
Through being considered clever I have suffered much
A person of sense ought never to have his children
Brought up to be more clever than the average.
For, apart from cleverness bringing them no profit,
It will make them objects of envy and ill-will.
If you put new ideas before the eyes of fools

They'll think you foolish and worthless into the bargain;
And if you are thought superior to those who have
Some reputation for learning, you will become hated.
I have some knowledge myself of how this happens;
For being clever, I find that some will envy me,
Others object to me. Yet all my cleverness
Is not so much.
Well, then, are you frightened, Creon,
That I should harm you? There is no need. It is not
My way to transgress the authority of a king.
How have you injured me? You gave your daughter away
To the man you wanted. Oh, certainly I hate
My husband, but you, I think, have acted wisely;
Nor do I grudge it you that your affairs go well.
May the marriage be a lucky one! Only let me
Live in this land. For even though I have been wronged,
I will not raise my voice, but submit to my betters.

CREON: What you say sounds gentle enough. Still in my heart
I greatly dread that you are plotting some evil,
And therefore I trust you even less than before.
A sharp-tempered woman, or, for that matter, a man,
Is easier to deal with than the clever type
Who holds her tongue. No. You must go. No need for more
Speeches. The thing is fixed. By no manner of means
Shall you, an enemy of mine, stay in my country.

MEDEA: I beg you. By your knees, by your new-wedded girl.

CREON: Your words are wasted. You will never persuade me.

MEDEA: Will you drive me out, and give no heed to my prayers?

CREON: I will, for I love my family more than you.

MEDEA: O my country! How bitterly now I remember you!

CREON: I love my country too—next after my children.

MEDEA: Oh what an evil to men is passionate love!

CREON: That would depend on the luck that goes along with it.

MEDEA: O God, do not forget who is the cause of this!

CREON: Go. It is no use. Spare me the pain of forcing you.

MEDEA: I'm spared no pain. I lack no pain to be spared me.

CREON: Then you'll be removed by force by one of my men.

MEDEA: No, Creon, not that! But do listen, I beg you.

CREON: Woman, you seem to want to create a disturbance.

MEDEA: I *will* go into exile. *This* is not what I beg for.

CREON: Why then this violence and clinging to my hand?

MEDEA: Allow me to remain here just for this one day,
So I may consider where to live in my exile,
And look for support for my children, since their father
Chooses to make no kind of provision for them.
Have pity on them! You have children of your own.
It is natural for you to look kindly on them.
For myself I do not mind if I go into exile.
It is the children being in trouble that I mind.

CREON: There is nothing tyrannical about my nature,
And by showing mercy I have often been the loser.
Even now I know that I am making a mistake.
All the same you shall have your will. But this I tell you,
That if the light of heaven tomorrow shall see you,
You and your children in the confines of my land,
You die. This word I have spoken is firmly fixed.
But now, if you must stay, stay for this day alone.
For in it you can do none of the things I fear.

[*Exit Creon with his attendants.*]

CHORUS: Oh, unfortunate one! Oh, cruel!
Where will you turn? Who will help you?
What house or what land to preserve you
From ill can you find?
Medea, a god has thrown suffering
Upon you in waves of despair.

MEDEA: Things have gone badly every way. No doubt of that
But not these things this far, and don't imagine so.
There are still trials to come for the new-wedded pair,
And for their relations pain that will mean something.
Do you think that I would ever have fawned on that man
Unless I had some end to gain or profit in it?
I would not even have spoken or touched him with my hands.
But he has got to such a pitch of foolishness
That, though he could have made nothing of all my plans
By exiling me, he has given me this one day
To stay here, and in this I will make dead bodies
Of three of my enemies—father, the girl, and my husband.
I have many ways of death which I might suit to them,
And do not know, friends, which one to take in hand;
Whether to set fire underneath their bridal mansion,
Or sharpen a sword and thrust it to the heart,
Stealing into the palace where the bed is made.
There is just one obstacle to this. If I am caught
Breaking into the house and scheming against it,
I shall die, and give my enemies cause for laughter.
It is best to go by the straight road, the one in which
I am most skilled, and make away with them by poison.
So be it then.
And now suppose them dead. What town will receive me?
What friend will offer me a refuge in his land,
Or the guaranty of his house and save my own life?
There is none. So I must wait a little time yet,
And if some sure defense should then appear for me,
In craft and silence I will set about this murder.
But if my fate should drive me on without help,
Even though death is certain, I will take the sword

Myself and kill, and steadfastly advance to crime.
It shall not be—I swear it by her, my mistress,
Whom most I honor and have chosen as partner,
Hecate,[7] who dwells in the recesses of my hearth—
That any man shall be glad to have injured me.
Bitter I will make their marriage for them and mournful,
Bitter the alliance and the driving me out of the land.
Ah, come, Medea, in your plotting and scheming
Leave nothing untried of all those things which you know.
Go forward to the dreadful act. The test has come
For resolution. You see how you are treated. Never
Shall you be mocked by Jason's Corinthian wedding,
Whose father was noble, whose grandfather Helius.[8]
You have the skill. What is more, you were born a woman,
And women, though most helpless in doing good deeds,
Are of every evil the cleverest of contrivers.

CHORUS: Flow backward to your sources, sacred rivers,
And let the world's great order be reversed.
It is the thoughts of *men* that are deceitful,
Their pledges that are loose.
Story shall now turn my condition to a fair one,
Women are paid their due.
No more shall evil-sounding fame be theirs.

Cease now, you muses of the ancient singers,
To tell the tale of my unfaithfulness;
For not on us did Phoebus, lord of music,[9]
Bestow the lyre's divine
Power, for otherwise I should have sung an answer
To the other sex. Long time
Has much to tell of us, and much of them.

You sailed away from your father's home,
With a heart on fire you passed
The double rocks of the sea.
And now in a foreign country
You have lost your rest in a widowed bed,
And are driven forth, a refugee
In dishonor from the land.

Good faith has gone, and no more remains
In great Greece a sense of shame.
It has flown away to the sky.
No father's house for a haven
Is at hand for you now, and another queen

7. Goddess associated with witchcraft.
8. God of the sun.
9. The god Apollo.

Of your bed has dispossessed you and
Is mistress of your home.

[*Enter Jason, with attendants.*]

JASON: This is not the first occasion that I have noticed
How hopeless it is to deal with a stubborn temper.
For, with reasonable submission to our ruler's will,
You might have lived in this land and kept your home.
As it is you are going to be exiled for your loose speaking.
Not that I mind myself. You are free to continue
Telling everyone that Jason is a worthless man.
But as to your talk about the king, consider
Yourself most lucky that exile is your punishment.
I, for my part, have always tried to calm down
The anger of the king, and wished you to remain.
But you will not give up your folly, continually
Speaking ill of him, and so you are going to be banished.
All the same, and in spite of your conduct, I'll not desert
My friends, but have come to make some provision for you,
So that you and the children may not be penniless
Or in need of anything in exile. Certainly
Exile brings many troubles with it. And even
If you hate me, I cannot think badly of you.

MEDEA: O coward in every way—that is what I call you,
With bitterest reproach for your lack of manliness,
You have come, you, my worst enemy, have come to me!
It is not an example of overconfidence
Or of boldness thus to look your friends in the face,
Friends you have injured—no, it is the worst of all
Human diseases, shamelessness. But you did well
To come, for I can speak ill of you and lighten
My heart, and you will suffer while you are listening.
And first I will begin from what happened first.
I saved your life, and every Greek knows I saved it,
Who was a shipmate of yours aboard the Argo,
When you were sent to control the bulls that breathed fire
And yoke them, and when you would sow that deadly field.
Also that snake, who encircled with his many folds
The Golden Fleece and guarded it and never slept,
I killed, and so gave you the safety of the light.
And I myself betrayed my father and my home,
And came with you to Pelias' land of Iolcus.
And then, showing more willingness to help than wisdom,
I killed him, Pelias, with a most dreadful death
At his own daughters' hands,[1] and took away your fear.
This is how I behaved to you, you wretched man,

1. Convinced by Medea that they would rejuvenate him, his daughters boiled Pelias.

And you forsook me, took another bride to bed,
Though you had children; for, if that had not been,
You would have had an excuse for another wedding.
Faith in your word has gone. Indeed, I cannot tell
Whether you think the gods whose names you swore by then
Have ceased to rule and that new standards are set up,
Since you must know you have broken your word to me.
O my right hand, and the knees which you often clasped
In supplication, how senselessly I am treated
By this bad man, and how my hopes have missed their mark!
Come, I will share my thoughts as though you were a friend—
You! Can I think that you would ever treat me well?
But I will do it, and these questions will make you
Appear the baser. Where am I to go? To my father's?
Him I betrayed and his land when I came with you.
To Pelias' wretched daughters? What a fine welcome
They would prepare for me who murdered their father!
For this is my position—hated by my friends
At home, I have, in kindness to you, made enemies
Of others whom there was no need to have injured.
And how happy among Greek women you have made me
On your side for all this! A distinguished husband
I have—for breaking promises. When in misery
I am cast out of the land and go into exile,
Quite without friends and all alone with my children,
That will be a fine shame for the new-wedded groom,
For his children to wander as beggars and she who saved him.
O God, you have given to mortals a sure method
Of telling the gold that is pure from the counterfeit;
Why is there no mark engraved upon men's bodies,
By which we could know the true ones from the false ones?

CHORUS: It is a strange form of anger, difficult to cure,
When two friends turn upon each other in hatred.

JASON: As for me, it seems I must be no bad speaker.
But, like a man who has a good grip of the tiller,
Reef up his sail, and so run away from under
This mouthing tempest, woman, of your bitter tongue.
Since you insist on building up your kindness to me,
My view is that Cypris[2] was alone responsible
Of men and gods for the preserving of my life.
You are clever enough—but really I need not enter
Into the story of how it was love's inescapable
Power that compelled you to keep my person safe.
On this I will not go into too much detail.
In so far as you helped me, you did well enough.

2. Aphrodite, goddess of sexual desire.

But on this question of saving me, I can prove
You have certainly got from me more than you gave.
Firstly, instead of living among barbarians,
You inhabit a Greek land and understand our ways,
How to live by law instead of the sweet will of force.
And all the Greeks considered you a clever woman.
You were honored for it; while, if you were living at
The ends of the earth, nobody would have heard of you.
For my part, rather than stores of gold in my house
Or power to sing even sweeter songs than Orpheus,
I'd choose the fate that made me a distinguished man.
There is my reply to your story of my labors.
Remember it was you who started the argument.
Next for your attack on my wedding with the princess:
Here I will prove that, first, it was a clever move,
Secondly, a wise one, and, finally, that I made it
In your best interests and the children's. Please keep calm.
When I arrived here from the land of Iolcus,
Involved, as I was, in every kind of difficulty,
What luckier chance could I have come across than this,
An exile to marry the daughter of the king?
It was not—the point that seems to upset you—that I
Grew tired of your bed and felt the need of a new bride;
Nor with any wish to outdo your number of children.
We have enough already. I am quite content.
But—this was the main reason—that we might live well,
And not be short of anything. I know that all
A man's friends leave him stone-cold if he becomes poor.
Also that I might bring my children up worthily
Of my position, and, by producing more of them
To be brothers of yours, we would draw the families
Together and all be happy. You need no children.
And it pays me to do good to those I have now
By having others. Do you think this a bad plan?
You wouldn't if the love question hadn't upset you.
But you women have got into such a state of mind
That, if your life at night is good, you think you have
Everything; but, if in that quarter things go wrong,
You will consider your best and truest interests
Most hateful. It would have been better far for men
To have got their children in some other way, and women
Not to have existed. Then life would have been good.

CHORUS: Jason, though you have made this speech of yours look well,
Still I think, even though others do not agree,
You have betrayed your wife and are acting badly.

MEDEA: Surely in many ways I hold different views
From others, for I think that the plausible speaker
Who is a villain deserves the greatest punishment.
Confident in his tongue's power to adorn evil,

He stops at nothing. Yet he is not really wise.
As in your case. There is no need to put on the airs
Of a clever speaker, for one word will lay you flat.
If you were not a coward, you would not have married
Behind my back, but discussed it with me first.

JASON: And you, no doubt, would have furthered the proposal,
If I had told you of it, you who even now
Are incapable of controlling your bitter temper.

MEDEA: It was not that. No, you thought it was not respectable
As you got on in years to have a foreign wife.

JASON: Make sure of this: it was not because of a woman
I made the royal alliance in which I now live,
But, as I said before, I wished to preserve you
And breed a royal progeny to be brothers
To the children I have now, a sure defense to us.

MEDEA: Let me have no happy fortune that brings pain with it,
Or prosperity which is upsetting to the mind!

JASON: Change your ideas of what you want, and show more sense.
Do not consider painful what is good for you,
Nor, when you are lucky, think yourself unfortunate.

MEDEA: You can insult me. You have somewhere to turn to.
But I shall go from this land into exile, friendless.

JASON: It was what you chose yourself. Don't blame others for it.

MEDEA: And how did I choose it? Did I betray my husband?

JASON: You called down wicked curses on the king's family.

MEDEA: A curse, that is what I am become to your house too.

JASON: I do not propose to go into all the rest of it;
But, if you wish for the children or for yourself
In exile to have some of my money to help you,
Say so, for I am prepared to give with open hand,
Or to provide you with introductions to my friends
Who will treat you well. You are a fool if you do not
Accept this. Cease your anger and you will profit.

MEDEA: I shall never accept the favors of friends of yours,
Nor take a thing from you, so you need not offer it.
There is no benefit in the gifts of a bad man.

JASON: Then, in any case, I call the gods to witness that
I wish to help you and the children in every way,
But you refuse what is good for you. Obstinately
You push away your friends. You are sure to suffer for it.

MEDEA: Go! No doubt you hanker for your virginal bride,
And are guilty of lingering too long out of her house.
Enjoy your wedding. But perhaps—with the help of God—
You will make the kind of marriage that you will regret.

[*Jason goes out with his attendants.*]

CHORUS: When love is in excess
It brings a man no honor
Nor any worthiness.

But if in moderation Cypris comes,
There is no other power at all so gracious.
O goddess, never on me let loose the unerring
Shaft of your bow in the poison of desire.

Let my heart be wise.
It is the gods' best gift.
On me let mighty Cypris
Inflict no wordy wars or restless anger
To urge my passion to a different love.
But with discernment may she guide women's weddings,
Honoring most what is peaceful in the bed.

O country and home,
Never, never may I be without you,
Living the hopeless life,
Hard to pass through and painful,
Most pitiable of all.
Let death first lay me low and death
Free me from this daylight.
There is no sorrow above
The loss of a native land.

I have seen it myself,
Do not tell of a secondhand story.
Neither city nor friend
Pitied you when you suffered
The worst of sufferings.
O let him die ungraced whose heart
Will not reward his friends,
Who cannot open an honest mind
No friend will he be of mine.

[*Enter Aegeus, king of Athens, an old friend of Medea.*]

AEGEUS: Medea, greeting! This is the best introduction
Of which men know for conversation between friends.
MEDEA: Greeting to you too, Aegeus, son of King Pandion.
Where have you come from to visit this country's soil?
AEGEUS: I have just left the ancient oracle of Phoebus.
MEDEA: And why did you go to earth's prophetic center?
AEGEUS: I went to inquire how children might be born to me.
MEDEA: Is it so? Your life still up to this point is childless?
AEGEUS: Yes. By the fate of some power we have no children.
MEDEA: Have you a wife, or is there none to share your bed?
AEGEUS: There is. Yes, I am joined to my wife in marriage.
MEDEA: And what did Phoebus say to you about children?
AEGEUS: Words too wise for a mere man to guess their meaning.
MEDEA: It is proper for me to be told the god's reply?
AEGEUS: It is. For sure what is needed is cleverness.
MEDEA: Then what was his message? Tell me, if I may hear.

AEGEUS: I am not to loosen the hanging foot of the wine-skin . . .
MEDEA: Until you have done something, or reached some country?
AEGEUS: Until I return again to my hearth and house.
MEDEA: And for what purpose have you journeyed to this land?
AEGEUS: There is a man called Pittheus, king of Troezen.
MEDEA: A son of Pelops, they say, a most righteous man.
AEGEUS: With him I wish to discuss the reply of the god.
MEDEA: Yes. He is wise and experienced in such matters.
AEGEUS: And to me also the dearest of all my spear-friends.
MEDEA: Well, I hope you have good luck, and achieve your will.
AEGEUS: But why this downcast eye of yours, and this pale cheek?
MEDEA: O Aegeus, my husband has been the worst of all to me.
AEGEUS: What do you mean? Say clearly what has caused this grief.
MEDEA: Jason wrongs me, though I have never injured him.
AEGEUS: What has he done? Tell me about it in clearer words.
MEDEA: He has taken a wife to his house, supplanting me.
AEGEUS: Surely he would not dare to do a thing like that.
MEDEA: Be sure he has. Once dear, I now am slighted by him.
AEGEUS: Did he fall in love? Or is he tired of your love?
MEDEA: He was greatly in love, this traitor to his friends.
AEGEUS: Then let him go, if, as you say, he is so bad.
MEDEA: A passionate love—for an alliance with the king.
AEGEUS: And who gave him his wife? Tell me the rest of it.
MEDEA: It was Creon, he who rules this land of Corinth.
AEGEUS: Indeed, Medea, your grief was understandable.
MEDEA: I am ruined. And there is more to come: I am banished.
AEGEUS: Banished? By whom? Here you tell me of a new wrong.
MEDEA: Creon drives me an exile from the land of Corinth.
AEGEUS: Does Jason consent? I cannot approve of this.
MEDEA: He pretends not to, but he will put up with it.
Ah, Aegeus, I beg and beseech you, by your beard
And by your knees I am making myself your suppliant,
Have pity on me, have pity on your poor friend,
And do not let me go into exile desolate,
But receive me in your land and at your very hearth.
So may your love, with God's help, lead to the bearing
Of children, and so may you yourself die happy.
You do not know what a chance you have come on here.
I will end your childlessness, and I will make you able
To beget children. The drugs I know can do this.
AEGEUS: For many reasons, woman, I am anxious to do
This favor for you. First, for the sake of the gods,
And then for the birth of children which you promise,
For in that respect I am entirely at my wits' end.
But this is my position: if you reach my land,
I, being in my rights, will try to befriend you.
But this much I must warn you of beforehand:
I shall not agree to take you out of this country;
But if you by yourself can reach my house, then you

Shall stay there safely. To none will I give you up
But from this land you must make your escape yourself,
For I do not wish to incur blame from my friends.

MEDEA: It shall be so. But, if I might have a pledge from you
For this, then I would have from you all I desire.

AEGEUS: Do you not trust me? What is it rankles with you?

MEDEA: I trust you, yes. But the house of Pelias hates me,
And so does Creon. If you are bound by this oath,
When they try to drag me from your land, you will not
Abandon me; but if our pact is only words,
With no oath to the gods, you will be lightly armed,
Unable to resist their summons. I am weak,
While they have wealth to help them and a royal house.

AEGEUS: You show much foresight for such negotiations.
Well, if you will have it so, I will not refuse.
For, both on my side this will be the safest way
To have some excuse to put forward to your enemies,
And for you it is more certain. You may name the gods.

MEDEA: Swear by the plain of Earth, and Helius, father
Of my father, and name together all the gods . . .

AEGEUS: That I will act or not act in what way? Speak.

MEDEA: That you yourself will never cast me from your land,
Nor, if any of my enemies should demand me,
Will you, in your life, willingly hand me over.

AEGEUS: I swear by the Earth, by the holy light of Helius,
By all the gods, I will abide by this you say.

MEDEA: Enough. And, if you fail, what shall happen to you?

AEGEUS: What comes to those who have no regard for heaven.

MEDEA: Go on your way. Farewell. For I am satisfied.
And I will reach your city as soon as I can,
Having done the deed I have to do and gained my end.

[*Aegeus goes out.*]

CHORUS: May Hermes, god of travelers,
Escort you, Aegeus, to your home!
And may you have the things you wish
So eagerly; for you
Appear to me to be a generous man.

MEDEA: God, and God's daughter, justice, and light of Helius!
Now, friends, has come the time of my triumph over
My enemies, and now my foot is on the road.
Now I am confident they will pay the penalty.
For this man, Aegeus, has been like a harbor to me
In all my plans just where I was most distressed.
To him I can fasten the cable of my safety
When I have reached the town and fortress of Pallas.[3]

3. Athena, goddess of Athens.

And now I shall tell to you the whole of my plan.
Listen to these words that are not spoken idly.
I shall send one of my servants to find Jason
And request him to come once more into my sight.
And when he comes, the words I'll say will be soft ones.
I'll say that I agree with him, that I approve
The royal wedding he has made, betraying me.
I'll say it was profitable, an excellent idea.
But I shall beg that my children may remain here:
Not that I would leave in a country that hates me
Children of mine to feel their enemies' insults,
But that by a trick I may kill the king's daughter.
For I will send the children with gifts in their hands
To carry to the bride, so as not to be banished—
A finely woven dress and a golden diadem.
And if she takes them and wears them upon her skin
She and all who touch the girl will die in agony;
Such poison will I lay upon the gifts I send.
But there, however, I must leave that account paid.
I weep to think of what a deed I have to do
Next after that; for I shall kill my own children.
My children, there is none who can give them safety.
And when I have ruined the whole of Jason's house,
I shall leave the land and flee from the murder of my
Dear children, and I shall have done a dreadful deed.
For it is not bearable to be mocked by enemies.
So it must happen. What profit have I in life?
I have no land, no home, no refuge from my pain.
My mistake was made the time I left behind me
My father's house, and trusted the words of a Greek,
Who, with heaven's help, will pay me the price for that.
For those children he had from me he will never
See alive again, nor will he on his new bride
Beget another child, for she is to be forced
To die a most terrible death by these my poisons.
Let no one think me a weak one, feeble-spirited,
A stay-at-home, but rather just the opposite,
One who can hurt my enemies and help my friends;
For the lives of such persons are most remembered.

CHORUS: Since you have shared the knowledge of your plan with us,
I both wish to help you and support the normal
Ways of mankind, and tell you not to do this thing.

MEDEA: I can do no other thing. It is understandable
For you to speak thus. You have not suffered as I have.

CHORUS: But can you have the heart to kill your flesh and blood?

MEDEA: Yes, for this is the best way to wound my husband.

CHORUS: And you, too. Of women you will be most unhappy.

MEDEA: So it must be. No compromise is possible.

[*She turns to the Nurse.*]

Go, you, at once, and tell Jason to come to me.
You I employ on all affairs of greatest trust.
Say nothing of these decisions which I have made,
If you love your mistress, if you were born a woman.

CHORUS: From of old the children of Erechtheus are
Splendid, the sons of blessed gods. They dwell
In Athens' holy and unconquered land,
Where famous Wisdom feeds them and they pass gaily
Always through that most brilliant air where once, they say,
That golden Harmony gave birth to the nine
Pure Muses of Pieria.

And beside the sweet flow of Cephisus' stream,
Where Cypris sailed, they say, to draw the water,
And mild soft breezes breathed along her path,
And on her hair were flung the sweet-smelling garlands
Of flowers of roses by the Lovers, the companions
Of Wisdom, her escort, the helpers of men
In every kind of excellence.

How then can these holy rivers
Or this holy land love you,
Or the city find you a home,
You, who will kill your children,
You, not pure with the rest?
O think of the blow at your children
And think of the blood that you shed.
O, over and over I beg you,
By your knees I beg you do not
Be the murderess of your babes!

O where will you find the courage
Or the skill of hand and heart,
When you set yourself to attempt
A deed so dreadful to do?
How, when you look upon them,
Can you tearlessly hold the decision
For murder? You will not be able,
When your children fall down and implore you,
You will not be able to dip
Steadfast your hand in their blood.

[*Enter Jason with attendants.*]

JASON: I have come at your request. Indeed, although you are
Bitter against me, this you shall have: I will listen
To what new thing you want, woman, to get from me.

MEDEA: Jason, I beg you to be forgiving toward me
For what I said. It is natural for you to bear with
My temper, since we have had much love together.
I have talked with myself about this and I have

Reproached myself. "Fool" I said, "why am I so mad?
Why am I set against those who have planned wisely?
Why make myself an enemy of the authorities
And of my husband, who does the best thing for me
By marrying royalty and having children who
Will be as brothers to my own? What is wrong with me?
Let me give up anger, for the gods are kind to me.
Have I not children, and do I not know that we
In exile from our country must be short of friends?"
When I considered this I saw that I had shown
Great lack of sense, and that my anger was foolish.
Now I agree with you. I think that you are wise
In having this other wife as well as me, and I
Was mad. I should have helped you in these plans of yours,
Have joined in the wedding, stood by the marriage bed,
Have taken pleasure in attendance on your bride.
But we women are what we are—perhaps a little
Worthless; and you men must not be like us in this,
Nor be foolish in return when we are foolish.
Now, I give in, and admit that then I was wrong.
I have come to a better understanding now.

[*She turns toward the house.*]

Children, come here, my children, come outdoors to us!
Welcome your father with me, and say goodbye to him,
And with your mother, who just now was his enemy,
Join again in making friends with him who loves us.

[*Enter the children, attended by the Tutor.*]

We have made peace, and all our anger is over.
Take hold of his right hand—O God, I am thinking
Of something which may happen in the secret future.
O children, will you just so, after a long life,
Hold out your loving arms at the grave? O children,
How ready to cry I am, how full of foreboding!
I am ending at last this quarrel with your father,
And, look my soft eyes have suddenly filled with tears.

CHORUS: And the pale tears have started also in my eyes.
O may the trouble not grow worse than now it is!

JASON: I approve of what you say. And I cannot blame you
Even for what you said before. It is natural
For a woman to be wild with her husband when he
Goes in for secret love. But now your mind has turned
To better reasoning. In the end you have come to
The right decision, like the clever woman you are.
And of you, children, your father is taking care.
He has made, with God's help, ample provision for you.
For I think that a time will come when you will be
The leading people in Corinth with your brothers.
You must grow up. As to the future, your father

And those of the gods who love him will deal with that.
I want to see you, when you have become young men,
Healthy and strong, better men than my enemies.
Medea, why are your eyes all wet with pale tears?
Why is your cheek so white and turned away from me?
Are not these words of mine pleasing for you to hear?

MEDEA: It is nothing. I was thinking about these children.

JASON: You must be cheerful. I shall look after them well.

MEDEA: I will be. It is not that I distrust your words,
But a woman is a frail thing, prone to crying.

JASON: But why then should you grieve so much for these children?

MEDEA: I am their mother. When you prayed that they might live
I felt unhappy to think that these things will be.
But come, I have said something of the things I meant
To say to you, and now I will tell you the rest.
Since it is the king's will to banish me from here—
And for me, too, I know that this is the best thing,
Not to be in your way by living here or in
The king's way, since they think me ill-disposed to them—
I then am going into exile from this land;
But do you, so that you may have the care of them,
Beg Creon that the children may not be banished.

JASON: I doubt if I'll succeed, but still I'll attempt it.

MEDEA: Then you must tell your wife to beg from her father
That the children may be reprieved from banishment.

JASON: I will, and with her I shall certainly succeed.

MEDEA: If she is like the rest of us women, you will.
And I, too, will take a hand with you in this business,
For I will send her some gifts which are far fairer,
I am sure of it, than those which now are in fashion,
A finely woven dress and a golden diadem,
And the children shall present them. Quick, let one of you
Servants bring here to me that beautiful dress.

[*One of her attendants goes into the house.*]

She will be happy not in one way, but in a hundred,
Having so fine a man as you to share her bed,
And with this beautiful dress which Helius of old,
My father's father, bestowed on his descendants.

[*Enter attendant carrying the poisoned dress and diadem.*]

There, children, take these wedding presents in your hands.
Take them to the royal princess, the happy bride,
And give them to her. She will not think little of them.

JASON: No, don't be foolish, and empty your hands of these.
Do you think the palace is short of dresses to wear?
Do you think there is no gold there? Keep them, don't give them
Away. If my wife considers me of any value,
She will think more of me than money, I am sure of it.

MEDEA: No, let me have my way. They say the gods themselves
Are moved by gifts, and gold does more with men than words.
Hers is the luck, her fortune that which god blesses;
She is young and a princess; but for my children's reprieve
I would give my very life, and not gold only.
Go children, go together to that rich palace,
Be suppliants to the new wife of your father,
My lady, beg her not to let you be banished.
And give her the dress—for this is of great importance,
That she should take the gift into her hand from yours.
Go, quick as you can. And bring your mother good news
By your success of those things which she longs to gain.

[*Jason goes out with his attendants, followed by the Tutor and the children carrying the poisoned gifts.*]

CHORUS: Now there is no hope left for the children's lives.
Now there is none. They are walking already to murder.
The bride, poor bride, will accept the curse of the gold,
Will accept the bright diadem.
Around her yellow hair she will set that dress
Of death with her own hands.

The grace and the perfume and glow of the golden robe
Will charm her to put them upon her and wear the wreath,
And now her wedding will be with the dead below,
Into such a trap she will fall,
Poor thing, into such a fate of death and never
Escape from under that curse.
You, too, O wretched bridegroom, making your match with kings,
You do not see that you bring
Destruction on your children and on her,
Your wife, a fearful death.
Poor soul, what a fall is yours!

In your grief, too, I weep, mother of little children,
You who will murder your own,
In vengeance for the loss of married love
Which Jason has betrayed
As he lives with another wife.

[*Enter the Tutor with the children.*]

TUTOR: Mistress, I tell you that these children are reprieved,
And the royal bride has been pleased to take in her hands
Your gifts. In that quarter the children are secure.
But come,
Why do you stand confused when you are fortunate?
Why have you turned round with your cheek away from me?
Are not these words of mine pleasing for you to hear?

MEDEA: Oh! I am lost!

TUTOR: That word is not in harmony with my tidings.

MEDEA: I am lost, I am lost!
TUTOR: Am I in ignorance telling you
Of some disaster, and not the good news I thought?
MEDEA: You have told what you have told. I do not blame you.
TUTOR: Why then this downcast eye, and this weeping of tears?
MEDEA: Oh, I am forced to weep, old man. The gods and I,
I in a kind of madness, have contrived all this.
TUTOR: Courage! You, too, will be brought home by your children.
MEDEA: Ah, before that happens I shall bring others home.
TUTOR: Others before you have been parted from their children.
Mortals must bear in resignation their ill luck.
MEDEA: That is what I shall do. But go inside the house,
And do for the children your usual daily work.

[*The Tutor goes into the house. Medea turns to her children.*]

O children, O my children, you have a city,
You have a home, and you can leave me behind you,
And without your mother you may live there forever.
But I am going in exile to another land
Before I have seen you happy and taken pleasure in you,
Before I have dressed your brides and made your marriage beds
And held up the torch at the ceremony of wedding.
Oh, what a wretch I am in this my self-willed thought!
What was the purpose, children, for which I reared you?
For all my travail and wearing myself away?
They were sterile, those pains I had in the bearing of you.
Oh surely once the hopes in you I had, poor me,
Were high ones: you would look after me in old age,
And when I died would deck me well with your own hands;
A thing which all would have done. Oh but now it is gone,
That lovely thought. For, once I am left without you,
Sad will be the life I'll lead and sorrowful for me.
And you will never see your mother again with
Your dear eyes, gone to another mode of living.
Why, children, do you look upon me with your eyes?
Why do you smile so sweetly that last smile of all?
Oh, Oh, what can I do? My spirit has gone from me,
Friends, when I saw that bright look in the children's eyes.
I cannot bear to do it. I renounce my plans
I had before. I'll take my children away from
This land. Why should I hurt their father with the pain
They feel, and suffer twice as much of pain myself?
No, no, I will not do it. I renounce my plans.
Ah, what is wrong with me? Do I want to let go
My enemies unhurt and be laughed at for it?
I must face this thing. Oh, but what a weak woman
Even to admit to my mind these soft arguments.
Children, go into the house. And he whom law forbids
To stand in attendance at my sacrifices,

Let him see to it. I shall not mar my handiwork.
Oh! Oh!
Do not, O my heart, you must not do these things!
Poor heart, let them go, have pity upon the children.
If they live with you in Athens they will cheer you.
No! By Hell's avenging furies it shall not be—
This shall never be, that I should suffer my children
To be the prey of my enemies' insolence.
Every way is it fixed. The bride will not escape.
No, the diadem is now upon her head, and she,
The royal princess, is dying in the dress, I know it.
But—for it is the most dreadful of roads for me
To tread, and them I shall send on a more dreadful still—
I wish to speak to the children.

[*She calls the children to her.*]

Come, children, give
Me your hands, give your mother your hands to kiss them.
Oh the dear hands, and O how dear are these lips to me,
And the generous eyes and the bearing of my children!
I wish you happiness, but not here in this world.
What is here your father took. Oh how good to hold you!
How delicate the skin, how sweet the breath of children!
Go, go! I am no longer able, no longer
To look upon you. I am overcome by sorrow.

[*The children go into the house.*]

I know indeed what evil I intend to do,
But stronger than all my afterthoughts is my fury,
Fury that brings upon mortals the greatest evils.

[*She goes out to the right, toward the royal palace.*]

CHORUS: Often before
I have gone through more subtle reasons,
And have come upon questionings greater
Than a woman should strive to search out.
But we too have a goddess to help us
And accompany us into wisdom.
Not all of us. Still you will find
Among many women a few,
And our sex is not without learning.
This I say, that those who have never
Had children, who know nothing of it,
In happiness have the advantage
Over those who are parents.
The childless, who never discover
Whether children turn out as a good thing
Or as something to cause pain, are spared
Many troubles in lacking this knowledge.

And those who have in their homes
The sweet presence of children, I see that their lives
Are all wasted away by their worries.
First they must think how to bring them up well and
How to leave them something to live on.
And then after this whether all their toil
Is for those who will turn out good or bad,
Is still an unanswered question.
And of one more trouble, the last of all,
That is common to mortals I tell.
For suppose you have found them enough for their living,
Suppose that the children have grown into youth
And have turned out good, still, if God so wills it,
Death will away with your children's bodies,
And carry them off into Hades.
What is our profit, then, that for the sake of
Children the gods should pile upon mortals
After all else
This most terrible grief of all?

[*Enter Medea, from the spectators' right.*]

MEDEA: Friends, I can tell you that for long I have waited
For the event. I stare toward the place from where
The news will come. And now, see one of Jason's servants
Is on his way here, and that labored breath of his
Shows he has tidings for us, and evil tidings.

[*Enter, also from the right, the Messenger.*]

MESSENGER: Medea, you who have done such a dreadful thing,
So outrageous, run for your life, take what you can,
A ship to bear you hence or chariot on land.
MEDEA: And what is the reason deserves such flight as this?
MESSENGER: She is dead, only just now, the royal princess,
And Creon dead, too, her father, by your poisons.
MEDEA: The finest words you have spoken. Now and hereafter
I shall count you among my benefactors and friends.
MESSENGER: What! Are you right in the mind? Are you not mad,
Woman? The house of the king is outraged by you.
Do you enjoy it? Not afraid of such doings?
MEDEA: To what you say I on my side have something too
To say in answer. Do not be in a hurry, friend,
But speak. How did they die? You will delight me twice
As much again if you say they died in agony.
MESSENGER: When those two children, born of you, had entered in,
Their father with them, and passed into the bride's house,
We were pleased, we slaves who were distressed by your wrongs.
All through the house we were talking of but one thing,
How you and your husband had made up your quarrel.
Some kissed the children's hands and some their yellow hair,

And I myself was so full of my joy that I
Followed the children into the women's quarters.
Our mistress, whom we honor now instead of you,
Before she noticed that your two children were there,
Was keeping her eye fixed eagerly on Jason.
Afterwards, however, she covered up her eyes,
Her cheek paled, and she turned herself away from him,
So disgusted was she at the children's coming there.
But your husband tried to end the girl's bad temper,
And said "You must not look unkindly on your friends.
Cease to be angry. Turn your head to me again.
Have as your friends the same ones as your husband has.
And take these gifts, and beg your father to reprieve
These children from their exile. Do it for my sake."
She, when she saw the dress, could not restrain herself.
She agreed with all her husband said, and before
He and the children had gone far from the palace,
She took the gorgeous robe and dressed herself in it,
And put the golden crown around her curly locks,
And arranged the set of the hair in a shining mirror,
And smiled at the lifeless image of herself in it.
Then she rose from her chair and walked about the room,
With her gleaming feet stepping most soft and delicate,
All overjoyed with the present. Often and often
She would stretch her foot out straight and look along it.
But after that it was a fearful thing to see.
The color of her face changed, and she staggered back,
She ran, and her legs trembled, and she only just
Managed to reach a chair without falling flat down.
An aged woman servant who, I take it, thought
This was some seizure of Pan or another god,
Cried out "God bless us," but that was before she saw
The white foam breaking through her lips and her rolling
The pupils of her eyes and her face all bloodless.
Then she raised a different cry from that "God bless us,"
A huge shriek, and the women ran, one to the king,
One to the newly wedded husband to tell him
What had happened to his bride; and with frequent sound
The whole of the palace rang as they went running.
One walking quickly round the course of a race-track
Would now have turned the bend and be close to the goal,
When she, poor girl, opened her shut and speechless eye,
And with a terrible groan she came to herself.
For a twofold pain was moving up against her.
The wreath of gold that was resting around her head
Let forth a fearful stream of all-devouring fire,
And the finely woven dress your children gave to her,
Was fastening on the unhappy girl's fine flesh.
She leapt up from the chair, and all on fire she ran,

Shaking her hair now this way and now that, trying
To hurl the diadem away; but fixedly
The gold preserved its grip, and, when she shook her hair,
Then more and twice as fiercely the fire blazed out.
Till, beaten by her fate, she fell down to the ground,
Hard to be recognized except by a parent.
Neither the setting of her eyes was plain to see,
Nor the shapeliness of her face. From the top of
Her head there oozed out blood and fire mixed together.
Like the drops on pine-bark, so the flesh from her bones
Dropped away, torn by the hidden fang of the poison.
It was a fearful sight; and terror held us all
From touching the corpse. We had learned from what had happened.
But her wretched father, knowing nothing of the event,
Came suddenly to the house, and fell upon the corpse,
And at once cried out and folded his arms about her,
And kissed her and spoke to her, saying, "O my poor child,
What heavenly power has so shamefully destroyed you?
And who has set me here like an ancient sepulcher,
Deprived of you? O let me die with you, my child!"
And when he had made an end of his wailing and crying,
Then the old man wished to raise himself to his feet;
But, as the ivy clings to the twigs of the laurel,
So he stuck to the fine dress, and he struggled fearfully.
For he was trying to lift himself to his knee,
And she was pulling him down, and when he tugged hard
He would be ripping his aged flesh from his bones.
At last his life was quenched, and the unhappy man
Gave up the ghost, no longer could hold up his head.
There they lie close, the daughter and the old father,
Dead bodies, an event he prayed for in his tears.
As for your interests, I will say nothing of them,
For you will find your own escape from punishment.
Our human life I think and have thought a shadow,
And I do not fear to say that those who are held
Wise among men and who search the reasons of things
Are those who bring the most sorrow on themselves.
For of mortals there is no one who is happy.
If wealth flows in upon one, one may be perhaps
Luckier than one's neighbor, but still not happy.

[*Exit.*]

CHORUS: Heaven, it seems, on this day has fastened many
Evils on Jason, and Jason has deserved them.
Poor girl, the daughter of Creon, how I pity you
And your misfortunes, you who have gone quite away
To the house of Hades because of marrying Jason.

MEDEA: Women, my task is fixed: as quickly as I may
To kill my children, and start away from this land,

And not, by wasting time, to suffer my children
To be slain by another hand less kindly to them.
Force every way will have it they must die, and since
This must be so, then I, their mother, shall kill them.
Oh, arm yourself in steel, my heart! Do not hang back
From doing this fearful and necessary wrong.
Oh, come, my hand, poor wretched hand, and take the sword,
Take it, step forward to this bitter starting point,
And do not be a coward, do not think of them,
How sweet they are, and how you are their mother. Just for
This one short day be forgetful of your children,
Afterward weep; for even though you will kill them,
They were very dear—Oh, I am an unhappy woman!

[*With a cry she rushes into the house.*]

CHORUS: O Earth, and the far shining
Ray of the Sun, look down, look down upon
This poor lost woman, look, before she raises
The hand of murder against her flesh and blood.
Yours was the golden birth from which
She sprang, and now I fear divine
Blood may be shed by men.
O heavenly light, hold back her hand,
Check her, and drive from out the house
The bloody Fury raised by fiends of Hell.

Vain waste, your care of children;
Was it in vain you bore the babes you loved,
After you passed the inhospitable strait
Between the dark blue rocks, Symplegades?
O wretched one, how has it come,
This heavy anger on your heart,
This cruel bloody mind?
For God from mortals asks a stern
Price for the stain of kindred blood
In like disaster falling on their homes.

[*A cry from one of the children is heard.*]

CHORUS: Do you hear the cry, do you hear the children's cry?
O you hard heart, O woman fated for evil!

ONE OF THE CHILDREN [*from within*]: What can I do and how escape my mother's hands?

ANOTHER CHILD [*from within*]: O my dear brother, I cannot tell. We are lost.

CHORUS: Shall I enter the house? Oh, surely I should
Defend the children from murder.

A CHILD [*from within*]: O help us, in God's name, for now we need your help.
Now, now we are close to it. We are trapped by the sword.

CHORUS: O your heart must have been made of rock or steel,
You who can kill

With your own hand the fruit of your own womb.
Of one alone I have heard, one woman alone
Of those of old who laid her hands on her children,
Ino, sent mad by heaven when the wife of Zeus
Drove her out from her home and made her wander;
And because of the wicked shedding of blood
Of her own children she threw
Herself, poor wretch, into the sea and stepped away
Over the sea-cliff to die with her two children.
What horror more can be? O women's love,
So full of trouble,
How many evils have you caused already!

[*Enter Jason, with attendants.*]

JASON: You women, standing close in front of this dwelling,
Is she, Medea, she who did this dreadful deed,
Still in the house, or has she run away in flight?
For she will have to hide herself beneath the earth,
Or raise herself on wings into the height of air,
If she wishes to escape the royal vengeance.
Does she imagine that, having killed our rulers,
She will herself escape uninjured from this house?
But I am thinking not so much of her as for
The children—her the king's friends will make to suffer
For what she did. So I have come to save the lives
Of my boys, in case the royal house should harm them
While taking vengeance for their mother's wicked deed.

CHORUS: O Jason, if you but knew how deeply you are
Involved in sorrow, you would not have spoken so.

JASON: What is it? That she is planning to kill me also?

CHORUS: Your children are dead, and by their own mother's hand.

JASON: What! That is it? O woman, you have destroyed me!

CHORUS: You must make up your mind your children are no more.

JASON: Where did she kill them? Was it here or in the house?

CHORUS: Open the gates and there you will see them murdered.

JASON: Quick as you can unlock the doors, men, and undo
The fastenings and let me see this double evil,
My children dead and her—Oh her I will repay.

[*His attendants rush to the door. Medea appears above the house in a chariot drawn by dragons. She has the dead bodies of the children with her.*]

MEDEA: Why do you batter these gates and try to unbar them,
Seeking the corpses and for me who did the deed?
You may cease your trouble, and, if you have need of me,
Speak, if you wish. You will never touch me with your hand,
Such a chariot has Helius, my father's father,
Given me to defend me from my enemies.

JASON: You hateful thing, you woman most utterly loathed
By the gods and me and by all the race of mankind,
You who have had the heart to raise a sword against

Your children, you, their mother, and left me childless—
You have done this, and do you still look at the sun
And at the earth, after these most fearful doings?
I wish you dead. Now I see it plain, though at that time
I did not, when I took you from your foreign home
And brought you to a Greek house, you, an evil thing,
A traitress to your father and your native land.
The gods hurled the avenging curse of yours on me.
For your own brother you slew at your own hearthside,
And then came aboard that beautiful ship, the Argo.
And that was your beginning. When you were married
To me, your husband, and had borne children to me,
For the sake of pleasure in the bed you killed them.
There is no Greek woman who would have dared such deeds,
Out of all those whom I passed over and chose you
To marry instead, a bitter destructive match,
A monster, not a woman, having a nature
Wilder than that of Scylla in the Tuscan sea.
Ah! no, not if I had ten thousand words of shame
Could I sting you. You are naturally so brazen.
Go, worker in evil, stained with your children's blood.
For me remains to cry aloud upon my fate,
Who will get no pleasure from my newly wedded love,
And the boys whom I begot and brought up, never
Shall I speak to them alive. Oh, my life is over!

MEDEA: Long would be the answer which I might have made to
These words of yours, if Zeus the father did not know
How I have treated you and what you did to me.
No, it was not to be that you should scorn my love,
And pleasantly live your life through, laughing at me;
Nor would the princess, nor he who offered the match,
Creon, drive me away without paying for it.
So now you may call me a monster, if you wish,
A Scylla housed in the caves of the Tuscan sea.
I too, as I had to, have taken hold of your heart.

JASON: You feel the pain yourself. You share in my sorrow.

MEDEA: Yes, and my grief is gain when you cannot mock it.

JASON: O children, what a wicked mother she was to you!

MEDEA: They died from a disease they caught from their father.

JASON: I tell you it was not my hand that destroyed them.

MEDEA: But it was your insolence, and your virgin wedding.

JASON: And just for the sake of that you chose to kill them.

MEDEA: Is love so small a pain, do you think, for a woman?

JASON: For a wise one, certainly. But you are wholly evil.

MEDEA: The children are dead. I say this to make you suffer.

JASON: The children, I think, will bring down curses on you.

MEDEA: The gods know who was the author of this sorrow.

JASON: Yes, the gods know indeed, they know your loathsome heart.

MEDEA: Hate me. But I tire of your barking bitterness.

JASON: And I of yours. It is easier to leave you.

MEDEA: How then? What shall I do? I long to leave you too.
JASON: Give me the bodies to bury and to mourn them.
MEDEA: No, that I will not. I will bury them myself,
Bearing them to Hera's temple on the promontory;
So that no enemy may evilly treat them
By tearing up their grave. In this land of Corinth
I shall establish a holy feast and sacrifice
Each year for ever to atone for the blood guilt.
And I myself go to the land of Erechtheus
To dwell in Aegeus' house, the son of Pandion.
While you, as is right, will die without distinction,
Struck on the head by a piece of the Argo's timber,
And you will have seen the bitter end of my love.
JASON: May a Fury for the children's sake destroy you,
And justice, Requitor of blood.
MEDEA: What heavenly power lends an ear
To a breaker of oaths, a deceiver?
JASON: Oh, I hate you, murderess of children.
MEDEA: Go to your palace. Bury your bride.
JASON: I go, with two children to mourn for.
MEDEA: Not yet do you feel it. Wait for the future.
JASON: Oh, children I loved!
MEDEA: I loved them, you did not.
JASON: You loved them, and killed them.
MEDEA: To make you feel pain.
JASON: Oh, wretch that I am, how I long
To kiss the dear lips of my children!
MEDEA: Now you would speak to them, now you would kiss them.
Then you rejected them.
JASON: Let me, I beg you,
Touch my boys' delicate flesh.
MEDEA: I will not. Your words are all wasted.
JASON: O God, do you hear it, this persecution,
These my sufferings from this hateful
Woman, this monster, murderess of children?
Still what I can do that I will do:
I will lament and cry upon heaven,
Calling the gods to bear me witness
How you have killed my boys and prevent me from
Touching their bodies or giving them burial.
I wish I had never begot them to see them
Afterward slaughtered by you.
CHORUS: Zeus in Olympus is the overseer
Of many doings. Many things the gods
Achieve beyond our judgment. What we thought
Is not confirmed and what we thought not god
Contrives. And so it happens in this story.

[*Curtain.*]

The Ramayana of Valmiki

last centuries B.C.E.

A teller of tales, so the story goes, was once reciting the *Ramayana.* He got to the part where Prince Rama explains to Sita, his wife, that she must stay in the city of Ayodhya and not accompany him into forest exile. After trying to dissuade him without success, Sita cries out, "Thousands of *Ramayanas* have been composed before this, and there isn't one in which Sita doesn't go with her husband!" The argument is persuasive, and Rama agrees to take her along.

Thousands of *Ramayanas?* Yes, quite likely, if we include all the versions from across Asia in all the different regional languages over the past two thousand years, to say nothing of the countless modern films, performance genres, and forms of popular culture ranging from peasant songs to comic books. And many of these versions are as self-aware as the little story recounted above, as far as their relationship to other tellings and their social, political, or historical location. The fact is indisputable: the story of Rama—his banishment to the forest on the eve of his coronation, the abduction of his wife, Sita, by the demon king Ravana, his defeat of the enemy and recovery of Sita—has had an impact on the literary imagination of India and wider Asia that is more intense and enduring than any other narrative, bar none. *Ramayanas* are found from Kashmir to Tibet to China and from Sri Lanka to Thailand, Laos, and Java. And it isn't just literary imagination that has been influenced by the story. The different *Ramayanas,* each of them making a particular argument appropriate for its own time and place, have contributed to shaping the spheres of religion, politics, and everyday morality to a degree unmatched by any other work in Indian history.

The version of the *Ramayana* to which many retellings explicitly or implicitly respond—retellings are always responses—is the Sanskrit work of Valmiki. As is so often the case in early Sanskrit literature, we have no reliable historical knowledge about the author, and dating his poem has proved to be difficult. The *Ramayana* contains an account of its own creation: it presents itself as the "first literary work" (*kavya*), a thing said to be previously unknown in Indian culture. But what its newness actually consists of is not entirely clear. The text itself links its novelty with the metrical form of the poem, but the verse structure used for most of the work is far older than the *Ramayana* of Valmiki could possibly be. Its self-identification as the first poem, along with everything else we know about it, suggests a relatively late date. Although tradition holds that the events of the *Mahabharata* took place in the Second Age from the present, whereas the *Ramayana* took place in the third, previous age, the *Ramayana* is later than the core text of the Bharata epic (c. 300 B.C.E.) since Valmiki knows the main story and has used it to deftly structure his own narrative. His thought world has features in common with that of King Ashoka, who issued his inscriptions in the middle of the third century B.C.E. And the history of Sanskrit literature, as "literature" comes to be defined in the Sanskrit tradition, begins only around the start of the Common Era. All these considerations point toward 200 B.C.E. or so as the likeliest period of the creation of the poem that came to bear Valmiki's name.

Some scholars dispute the proposition that any one person created the *Ramayana.* The manuscript history of the work clearly reveals substantial variation owing to a period of oral transmission. And like the *Mahabharata,* Valmiki's text was subject to continual expansion; an entire book, the seventh and last, was added at some point (perhaps along with the greater part of the first). Yet the oral variation of the *Ramayana* remains a variation of one and the same poem. The text was probably more or less memorized (the poem itself says as much) and was committed to writing at different times and places; it was assuredly not composed anew with each telling, as occurred in other oral epic traditions, such as the Serbo-Croatian. A single voice

A contemporary Indian comic book rendering depicts the death of Ravana in Valmiki's *Ramayana*.

can clearly be heard in Books 2 through 6, a voice of a sort that had never been heard before in Sanskrit.

There is a degree of literary artistry present in every level of the text—from the cohesiveness and sustained momentum of the grand narrative all the way down to the individual image—that is consistent across the poem and quite unlike anything else found in earlier Sanskrit works. One small example of this occurs in Book 3: Rama has gone off to hunt a magic deer, which in reality is a demon sent by Ravana, who had gotten word of Sita's beauty, to lure Rama away from the hermitage where he is living out his exile. Rama's younger brother, Lakshmana, told to guard Sita, has reluctantly left her alone after hearing what he thinks is Rama's cry for help (it is, of course, the demon's cry). This is Ravana's opening, and Valmiki describes his approach with the unobtrusive skill of a meticulous artist, using a half dozen different verbs of motion to bring our apprehension slowly to a climax:

> Assuming the guise of a wandering mendicant, he turned his steps toward Vaidehi . . .
> Clad in a soft saffron robe, with topknot, parasol, and sandals . . . he approached Vaidehi . . .
> Both brothers had left her, and in his pride of power he advanced upon her . . .
> Ten-necked Ravana had waited for an opening . . . In the guise of a beggar he drew near to Vaidehi . . .
> As Vaidehi sat grieving for her husband, the unholy Ravana in the guise of a holy man edged closer to her . . .
> The blackhearted stalker of the night stole ever closer to Vaidehi

This kind of expressive care is in evidence throughout the poem, and often achieves a level of artistry with which the aesthetic of the *Mahabharata* narrative—powerful, even overwhelming in its own right—has nothing in common.

There are many other differences between these two defining works of Indian culture, but the most telling are at the level of argument and ethic. In fact, Valmiki's poem can be read as a response to the apocalyptic vision of social and political disintegration encountered in the *Mahabharata.* The basic narrative problem is identical to that found in the other text: when their aged father, King Dasharatha, declares his intention to abdicate, the two brothers Rama and Bharata would be expected to contest the succession of power. But no struggle ensues, since Rama is ready to withdraw and Bharata is ready to submit to Rama (it is almost as if no one wants the kingship). Again, like Draupadi, wife of the five Pandava brothers in the *Mahabharata,* Sita is the target of a violent attack. In this case, however, it is not a brother who attacks her but a (literally) demonized outsider, Ravana, king of the *rakshasas,* imaginary beings who embody all that is most feared—and perhaps most desired—by traditional Indian readers. In these two episodes we glimpse a major transformation in the epic narrative tradition that is the ongoing concern of Valmiki's work: the conundrum of power is solved, and its dangerous energies are displaced from brothers to Others.

Key to this transformation is the character of Rama. Almost from their first acquaintance with the poem, Western scholars without exception believed that the hero's divinity was the result of later revision. The original *Ramayana,* they thought, must have been a tale of a simple human hero struggling against evil; the text was eventually appropriated by devotees of the god Vishnu, who turned the work into a theological tract. This long-held interpretation has been shown to be false. The divinity of Rama—not as the major god Vishnu, but as an undoubtedly transcendent being—is a constitutive part of the poem, not only textually but logically. Now that a reasonably complete picture of the manuscript history of the work is available, it has become clear that no textual criticism allows for the removal of all references to Rama's divinity; it is an inexpugnable part of the text. The logic of the story shows what kind of divinity this is, one similar to the semidivine status of epic heroes such as Gilgamesh (see page 71) and Achilles (see page 140), but far transcending it. When the demon king Ravana accepts the wish he has been granted from the great god Shiva, he couches it in terms he believes will ensure his immortality: he asks to be invincible to gods, demigods, men, and animals. What he fails to include in his list is what proves to be his undoing: a life-form that is part man and part god. Just such a being is Rama, both man and god at once. And this, as the text powerfully suggests, is what all real kings are supposed to be.

This mode of being also points toward a mode of behaving that enables Rama to escape the paralyzing moral dilemma of the *Mahabharata.* Can any acceptable definition of *dharma*—right, law, duty—require the slaughter of one's kinsmen? The *Mahabharata* has no workable answer to this horrific predicament; not even the doctrine of the *Bhagavad Gita,* the disinterested execution of one's *dharma,* seems an adequate response. Instead, the *Mahabharata* only shows what happens when the logic especially of the duty of the warrior is allowed to follow its course. This is precisely what Rama rejects. He juxtaposes the warrior's duty (Kshatriya *dharma*) to a higher law, that of hierarchical obedience—of son to father, younger brother to elder brother. This ethic ensures peace among the contestants to power, and, in the end, a utopian reign in the kingdom. Equally important is that those who in any way oppose this vision are not truly human; they are demonic beings and can with justice be destroyed.

Because of its success in framing moral problems, Valmiki's *Ramayana* has long been held to provide models of conduct for the everyday lives of everyday people; even today, opinion polls show that Sita is the most influential figure in the lives of young Indian girls. As an old proverb advises, "Act like Rama, and never like Ravana." No one was ever told to "act like Krishna"; it is what Krishna and other such deities say, not what they do, that readers and listeners are told to follow. But the *Ramayana* offers positive paradigms for life, and no other work remotely approximates it for the didactic force it has exercised throughout India's history.

Who's Who in the *Ramayana*

Dasharatha: DUH-shuh-RUH-thuh; king of Ayodhya (uh-YOH-dhyah)

His four sons:

Rama: RAH-muh

Bharata: BHUH-ruh-tuh

Lakshmana: LUHK-shmuh-nuh

Shatrughna: SHUH-troo-ghnuh

Kausalya: kow-SUHL-yah; mother of Rama

Kaikeyi: kai-KAY-yee; mother of Bharata

Sumitra: su-MEE-trah; mother of Lakshmana and Shatrughna

Sita: SEE-TAH; wife of Rama

The Ramayana of Valmiki

from Book 2[1]

[The Exile of Rama]

Sarga 7

Now, Kaikeyī's family servant, who had lived with her from the time of her birth, had happened to ascend to the rooftop terrace that shone like the moon.

1. Translated by Sheldon Pollock.

From the terrace Mantharā could see all Ayodhyā[2]—the king's way newly sprinkled, the lotuses and waterlilies strewn about, the costly ornamental pennants and banners, the sprinkling of sandalwood water, and the crowds of freshly bathed people.

Seeing a nursemaid standing nearby, Mantharā asked, "Why is Rāma's mother so delighted and giving away money to people, when she has always been so miserly? Tell me, why are the people displaying such boundless delight? Has something happened to delight the lord of earth? What is he planning to do?"

Bursting with delight and out of sheer gladness the nursemaid told the hunchback Mantharā about the greater majesty in store for Rāghava:

"Tomorrow on Puṣya day[3] King Daśaratha is going to consecrate Rāma Rāghava[4] as prince regent, the blameless prince who has mastered his anger."

When she heard what the nursemaid said, the hunchback was furious and descended straightway from the terrace that was like the peak of Mount Kailāsa.[5]

Consumed with rage, the malevolent Mantharā approached Kaikeyī as she lay upon her couch, and she said:

"Get up, you foolish woman! How can you lie there when danger is threatening you? Don't you realize that a flood of misery is about to overwhelm you?

"Your beautiful face has lost its charm. You boast of the power of your beauty, but it has proved to be as fleeting as a river's current in the hot season."

So she spoke, and Kaikeyī was deeply distraught at the bitter words of the angry, malevolent hunchback.

"Mantharā," she replied, "is something wrong? I can tell by the distress in your face how sorely troubled you are."

Hearing Kaikeyī's gentle words the wrathful Mantharā spoke—and a very clever speaker she was.

The hunchback grew even more distraught, and with Kaikeyī's best interests at heart, spoke out, trying to sharpen her distress and turn her against Rāghava:

"Something is very seriously wrong, my lady, something that threatens to ruin you. For King Daśaratha is going to consecrate Rāma as prince regent.

"I felt myself sinking down into unfathomable danger, stricken with grief and sorrow, burning as if on fire. And so I have come here, with your best interests at heart.

2. The capital of the kingdom of Kosala, in what is today the Indian state of Uttar Pradesh.

3. An favorable alignment of the constellation Pushya (consisting of the three stars of Cancer) marks an auspicious day on which important ceremonies are held.

4. Rama (literally, "descendent of Raghu," Rama's paternal great-grandfather).

5. A mountain in the Himalayan range, said to be the dwelling place of the great god Shiva.

"When you are sorrowful, Kaikeyī, I am too, and even more, and, when you prosper, so do I. There is not the slightest doubt of this.

"You were born into a family of kings, you are a queen of the lord of earth. My lady, how can you fail to know that the ways of kings are ruthless?

"Your husband talks of righteousness, but he is deceiving you; his words are gentle but he is cruel. You are too innocent to understand, and so he has utterly defrauded you like this.

"When expedient, your husband reassures you, but it is all worthless. Now that there is something of real worth he is ready to bestow it upon Kausalyā.

"Having got Bharata[6] out of the way by sending him off to your family, the wicked man shall tomorrow establish Rāma in unchallenged kingship.

"He is an enemy pretending to be your husband. He is like a viper, child, whom you have taken to your bosom and lovingly mothered.

"For what an enemy or a snake would do if one ignored them, King Daśaratha is now doing to you and your son.

"The man is evil, his assurances false, and, by establishing Rāma in the kingship, dear child who has always known comfort, he will bring ruin upon you and your family.

"Kaikeyī, the time has come to act, and you must act swiftly, for your own good. You must save your son, yourself, and me, my enchanting beauty."

After listening to Mantharā's speech, the lovely woman rose from the couch and presented the hunchback with a lovely piece of jewelry.

And, when she had given the hunchback the jewelry, Kaikeyī, most beautiful of women, said in delight to Mantharā,

"What you have reported to me is the most wonderful news. How else may I reward you, Mantharā, for reporting such good news to me?

"I draw no distinction between Rāma and Bharata, and so I am perfectly content that the king should consecrate Rāma as king.

"You could not possibly tell me better news than this, or speak more welcome words, my well-deserving woman. For what you have told me I will give you yet another boon, something you might like more—just choose it!"

Sarga 8

But Mantharā was beside herself with rage and sorrow. She threw the jewelry away and said spitefully:

6. Bharata and his younger brother Shatrughna were sent off to their maternal uncle's home by Dasharatha himself.

"You foolish woman, how can you be delighted at such a moment? Are you not aware that you stand in the midst of a sea of grief?

"It is Kausalyā who is fortunate; it is her son the eminent brahmans will consecrate as the powerful prince regent tomorrow, on Puṣya day.

"Once Kausalyā secures this great object of joy, she will cheerfully eliminate her enemies. And you will have to wait on her with hands cupped in reverence, like a serving woman.

"Delight is truly in store for Rāma's exalted women, and all that is in store for your daughters-in-law is misery, at Bharata's down-fall."

Seeing how deeply distressed Mantharā was as she spoke, Queen Kaikeyī began to extol Rāma's virtues:

"Rāma knows what is right, his gurus have taught him self-restraint. He is grateful, truthful, and honest, and as the king's eldest son, he deserves to be prince regent.

"He will protect his brothers and his dependents like a father; and long may he live! How can you be upset, hunchback, at learning of Rāma's consecration?

"Surely Bharata as well, the bull among men, will obtain the kingship of his fathers and forefathers after Rāma's one hundred years.

"Why should you be upset, Mantharā, when we have prospered in the past, and prosper now, and shall have good fortune in the future? For he obeys me even more scrupulously than he does Kausalyā."

When she heard what Kaikeyī said, Mantharā was still more sorely troubled. She heaved a long and hot sigh and then replied:

"You are too simple-minded to see what is good for you and what is not. You are not aware that you are sinking in an ocean of sorrow fraught with disaster and grief.

"Rāghava will be king, Kaikeyī, and then the son of Rāghava, while Bharata will be debarred from the royal succession altogether.

"For not all the sons of a king stand in line for the kingship, my lovely. Were all of them to be so placed, grave misfortune would ensue.

"That is why kings place the powers of kingship in the hands of the eldest, faultless Kaikeyī, however worthy the others.

"Like a helpless boy that son of yours, the object of all your motherly love, will be totally excluded from the royal succession and from its pleasures as well.

"Here I am, come on your behalf, but you pay me no heed. Instead, you want to reward me in token of your rival's good luck!

"Surely once Rāma secures unchallenged kingship he will have Bharata sent off to some other country—if not to the other world!

"And you had to send Bharata, a mere boy, off to your brother's, though knowing full well that proximity breeds affection, even in insentient things.

"Now, Rāghava will protect Lakṣmaṇa, just as Saumitri will protect Rāma, for their brotherly love is as celebrated as that of the Aúvins.

"And so Rāma will do no harm to Lakṣmaṇa, but he will to Bharata without question.

"So let your son go straight from Rājagṛha[7] to the forest. That is the course I favor, and it is very much in your own best interests.

"For in this way good fortune may still befall your side of the family—if, that is, Bharata secures, as by rights he should, the kingship of his forefathers.

"Your child has known only comfort, and, at the same time, he is Rāma's natural enemy. How could the one, with his fortunes lost, live under the sway of the other, whose fortunes are thriving?

"Like the leader of an elephant herd attacked by a lion in the forest, your son is about to be set upon by Rāma, and you must save him.

"Then, too, because of your beauty's power you used to spurn your co-wife, Rāma's mother, so proudly. How could she fail to repay that enmity?

"When Rāma secures control of the land, Bharata will be lost for certain. You must therefore devise some way of making your son the king and banishing his enemy this very day."

Sarga 9

So Mantharā spoke, and Kaikeyī, her face glowing with rage, heaved a long and burning sigh and said to her:

"Today, at once, I will have Rāma banished to the forest, and at once have Bharata consecrated as prince regent.

"But now, Mantharā, think: In what way can Bharata, and not Rāma, secure the kingship?"

So Queen Kaikeyī spoke, and the malevolent Mantharā answered her, to the ruin of Rāma's fortunes:

"Well then, I shall tell you, Kaikeyī—and pay close attention—how your son Bharata may secure sovereign kingship."

7. The capital city of Kekaya in Kashmir, the kingdom from which Kaikeyī hails.

Hearing Mantharā's words, Kaikeyī half rose from her sumptuous couch and exclaimed:

"Tell me the way, Mantharā! How can Bharata, and not Rāma, secure the kingship?"

So the queen spoke, and the malevolent hunchback answered her, to the ruin of Rāma's fortunes:

"When the gods and *asuras* were at war, your husband went with the royal seers to lend assistance to the king of the gods, and he took you along. He set off toward the south, Kaikeyī, to the Daṇḍakas and the city called Vaijayanta. It was there that Timidhvaja ruled, the same who is called Śambara, a great *asura* of a hundred magic powers. He had given battle to Śakra, and the host of gods could not conquer him.[8]

"In the great battle that followed, King Daśaratha was struck unconscious, and you, my lady, conveyed him out of battle. But there, too, your husband was wounded by weapons, and once again you saved him, my lovely. And so in his gratitude he granted you two boons.

"Then, my lady, you said to your husband. 'I shall choose my two boons when I want them,' and the great king consented. I myself was unaware of this, my lady, until you yourself told me, long ago.

"You must now demand these two boons of your husband: the consecration of Bharata and the banishment of Rāma for fourteen years.

"Now go into your private chamber, daughter of Aśvapati, as if in a fit of rage. Put on a dirty garment, lie down on the bare ground, and don't speak to him, don't even look at him.

"Your husband has always adored you, I haven't any doubt of it. For your sake the great king would even go through fire.

"The king could not bring himself to anger you, nor even bear to look at you when you are angry. He would give up his own life to please you.

"The lord of the land is powerless to refuse your demand. Dull-witted girl, recognize the power of your beauty.

"King Daśaratha will offer gems, pearls, gold, a whole array of precious gifts—but pay no mind to them.

"Just keep reminding Daśaratha of those two boons he granted at the battle of the gods and *asuras*. Illustrious lady, you must not let this opportunity pass you by.

8. The battle between the gods and *asuras*, or antigods, forms part of many ancient legends. In earlier Sanskrit works, Shambara is the enemy of Indra, the king of the gods, who is also known as Shakra (literally, "the able one"). The city Vaijayanta and the name Timidhvaja are obscure.

"When the great king Rāghava helps you up himself and offers you a boon, then you must ask him for this one, first making sure he swears to it: 'Banish Rāma to the forest for nine years and five, and make Bharata king of the land, the bull among kings.'

"In this way Rāma will be banished and cease to be 'the pleasing prince,' and your Bharata, his rival eliminated, will be king.

"And by the time Rāma returns from the forest, your steadfast son and his supporters will have struck deep roots and won over the populace.

"I think it high time you overcame your timidity. You must forcibly prevent the king from carrying out Rāma's consecration."

And so Mantharā induced her to accept such evil by disguising it as good, and Kaikeyī, now cheered and delighted, replied:

"Hunchback, I never recognized your excellence, nor how excellent your advice. Of all the hunchbacks in the land there is none better at devising plans.

"You are the only one who has always sought my advantage and had my interests at heart. I might never have known, hunchback, what the king intended to do.

"There are hunchbacks who are misshapen, crooked and hideously ugly—but not you, you are lovely, you are bent no more than a lotus in the breeze.

"Your chest is arched, raised as high as your shoulders, and down below your waist, with its lovely navel, seems as if it had grown thin in envy of it.

"Your girdle-belt beautifies your hips and sets them jingling. Your legs are set strong under you, while your feet are long.

"With your wide buttocks, Mantharā, and your garment of white linen, you are as resplendent as a wild goose when you go before me.

"And this huge hump of yours, wide as the hub of a chariot wheel—your clever ideas must be stored in it, your political wisdom and magic powers.

"And there, hunchback, is where I will drape you with a garland made of gold, once Bharata is consecrated and Rāghava has gone to the forest.

"When I have accomplished my purpose, my lovely, when I am satisfied, I will anoint your hump with precious liquid gold.

"And for your face I will have them fashion an elaborate and beautiful forehead mark of gold and exquisite jewelry for you, hunchback.

"Dressed in a pair of lovely garments you shall go about like a goddess; with that face of yours that challenges the moon, peerless in visage; and you shall strut holding your head high before the people who hate me.

"You too shall have hunchbacks, adorned with every sort of ornament, to humbly serve you, hunchback, just as you always serve me."

Being flattered in this fashion, she replied to Kaikeyī, who still lay on her luxurious couch like a flame of fire on an altar:

"One does not build a dike, my precious, after the water is gone. Get up, apprise the king, and see to your own welfare!"

Thus incited, the large-eyed queen went with Mantharā to her private chamber, puffed up with the intoxicating power of her beauty.

There the lovely lady removed her pearl necklace, worth many hundred thousands, and her other costly and beautiful jewelry.

And then, under the spell of the hunchback Mantharā's words, the golden Kaikeyī got down upon the floor and said to her:

"Hunchback, go inform the king that I will surely die right here unless Bharata receives as his portion the land and Rāghava, as his, the forest."

And uttering these ruthless words, the lady put all her jewelry aside and lay down upon the ground bare of any spread, like a fallen *kiṃnara* woman.[9]

Her face enveloped in the darkness of her swollen rage, her fine garlands and ornaments stripped off, the wife of the lord of men grew distraught and took on the appearance of a darkened sky, when all the stars have set.

Sarga 10

Now, when the great king had given orders for Rāghava's consecration, he gladly entered the inner chamber to tell his beloved wife the good news.

But when the lord of the world saw her fallen on the ground and lying there in a posture so ill-befitting her, he was consumed with sorrow.

The guileless old man saw her on the floor, that guileful young wife of his, who meant more to him than life itself.

He began to caress her affectionately, as a great bull elephant in the wilderness might caress his cow wounded by the poisoned arrow of a hunter lurking in the forest.

And, as he caressed his lotus-eyed wife with his hands, sick with worry and desire, he said to her:

"I do not understand, my lady, why you should be angry. Has someone offended you, or shown you disrespect, that you should lie here in the dust, my precious, and

9. *Kinnaras* ("part-man") are obscure mythical creatures; female *kinnaras* are renowned for their beauty.

cause me such sorrow? What reason have you to lie upon the floor as if possessed by a spirit, driving me to distraction, when you are so precious to me?

"I have skilled physicians, who have been gratified in every way. They will make you well again. Tell me what hurts you, my lovely.

"Is there someone to whom you would have favor shown, or has someone aroused your disfavor? The one shall find favor at once, the other incur my lasting disfavor.

"Is there some guilty man who should be freed, or some innocent man I should execute? What poor man should I enrich, what rich man impoverish?

"I and my people, we all bow to your will. I could not bring myself to thwart any wish of yours, not if it cost me my life. Tell me what your heart desires, for all the earth belongs to me, as far as the wheel of my power reaches."

So he spoke, and now encouraged she resolved to tell her hateful plan. She then commenced to cause her husband still greater pain.

"No one has mistreated me, my lord, or shown me disrespect. But there is one wish I have that I should like you to fulfill.

"You must first give me your promise that you are willing to do it. Then I shall reveal what it is I desire."

So his beloved Kaikeyī spoke, and the mighty king, hopelessly under the woman's power, said to her with some surprise:

"Do you not yet know, proud lady, that except for Rāma, tiger among men, there is not a single person I love as much as you?

"Take hold of my heart, rip it out, and examine it closely, my lovely Kaikeyī; then tell me if you do not find it true.

"Seeing that I have the power, you ought not to doubt me. I will do what will make you happy, I swear to you by all my acquired merit."

His words filled her with delight, and she made ready to reveal her dreadful wish, which was like a visitation of death:

"Let the three and thirty gods, with Indra at their head, hear how you in due order swear an oath and grant me a boon.

"Let the sun and moon, the sky, the planets, night and day, the quarters of space, heaven and earth, let all the *gandharvas* and *rākṣasas,* the spirits that stalk the night, the household gods in every house, and all the other spirits take heed of what you have said.[1]

1. *Gandharvas* are heavenly beings renowned for their musical skills. *Rakshasas,* often called "stalkers of the night," are demonic creatures known to eat humans and disrupt the sacrifices of forest ascetics.

"This mighty king, who is true to his word and knows the ways of righteousness, in full awareness grants me a boon—let the deities give ear to this for me."

Thus the queen ensnared the great archer and called upon witnesses. She then addressed the king, who in his mad passion had granted her a boon.

"I will now claim the two boons you once granted me, my lord. Hear my words, your Majesty.

"Let my son Bharata be consecrated with the very rite of consecration you have prepared for Rāghava.

"Let Rāma withdraw to Daṇḍaka wilderness[2] and for nine years and five live the life of an ascetic, wearing hides and barkcloth garments and matted hair.[3]

"Let Bharata today become the uncontested prince regent, and let me see Rāghava depart this very day for the forest."

When the great king heard Kaikeyī's ruthless demands, he was shaken and unnerved, like a stag at the sight of a tigress.

The lord of men gasped as he sank down upon the bare floor. "Oh damn you!" he cried in uncontrollable fury before he fell into a stupor, his heart crushed by grief.

Gradually the king regained his senses and then, in bitter sorrow and anger, he spoke to Kaikeyī, with fire in his eyes:

"Malicious, wicked woman, bent on destroying this House! Evil woman, what evil did Rāma or I ever do to you?

"Rāghava has always treated you just like his own mother. What reason can you have for trying to wreck his fortunes, of all people?

"It was sheer suicide to bring you into my home. I did it unwittingly, thinking you a princess—and not a deadly poisonous viper.

"When praise for Rāma's virtues is on the lips of every living soul, what crime could I adduce as pretext for renouncing my favorite son?

"I would sooner renounce Kausalyā, or Sumitrā, or sovereignty, or life itself, than Rāma, who so cherishes his father.

"The greatest joy I know is seeing my first-born son. If I cannot see Rāma, I shall lose my mind.

2. The country of King Dandaka was laid waste by Indra's curse or, according to another source, the curse of a Brahman whose daughter was raped by the king.

3. As a mark of renunciation, forest-dwelling ascetics are said to wear "barkcloth" (perhaps cloth woven of bast fiber) and to leave their hair unkempt.

"The world might endure without the sun, or crops without water, but without Rāma life could not endure within my body.

"Enough then, give up this scheme, you evil-scheming woman. I beg you! Must I get down and bow my head to your feet?"

His heart in the grip of a woman who knew no bounds, the guardian of the earth began helplessly to cry, and as the queen extended her feet he tried in vain to touch them, and collapsed like a man on the point of death.

Sarga 11

The king lay there, in so unaccustomed a posture, so ill-befitting his dignity, like Yayāti himself, his merit exhausted, fallen from the world of the gods.[4] But the woman was unafraid, for all the fear she awoke. She was misfortune incarnate and had yet to secure her fortunes. Once more she tried to force him to fulfill the boon.

"You are vaunted, great king, as a man true to his word and firm in his vows. How then can you be prepared to withhold my boon?"

So Kaikeyī spoke, and King Daśaratha, faltering for a moment, angrily replied:

"Vile woman, mortal enemy! Will you not be happy, will you not be satisfied until you see me dead, and Rāma, the bull among men, gone to the forest?

"To satisfy Kaikeyī Rāma must be banished to the forest, but if I keep my word in this, then I must be guilty of another lie. My infamy will be unequaled in the eyes of the people and my disgrace inevitable."

While he was lamenting like this, his mind in a whirl, the sun set and evening came on.

To the anguished king lost in lamentation, the night, adorned with the circlet of the moon, no longer seemed to last a mere three watches.

Heaving burning sighs, aged King Daśaratha sorrowfully lamented in his anguish, his eyes fixed upon the sky.

"I do not want you to bring the dawn—here, I cup my hands in supplication. But no, pass as quickly as you can, so that I no longer have to see this heartless, malicious Kaikeyī, the cause of this great calamity."

But with this, the king cupped his hands before Kaikeyī and once more, begging her mercy, he spoke:

"Please, I am an old man, my life is nearly over. I am desolate, I place myself in your hands. Dear lady, have mercy on me for, after all, I am king.

4. A legendary emperor who through ascetic discipline reached heaven, only to be expelled by Indra because of his pride.

"Truly it was thoughtless of me, my fair-hipped lady, to have said those things just now. Have mercy on me, please, my child. I know you have a heart."

So the pure-hearted king lamented, frantically and piteously, his eyes reddened and dimmed by tears, but the malicious, black-hearted woman only listened and made no reply.

And as the king stared at the woman he loved but could not appease, whose demand was so perverse—for the exile of his own son—he once again was taken faint, overcome with grief, and dropped unconscious to the floor.

* * *

Sarga 16

Rāma saw his father, with a wretched look and his mouth all parched, slumped upon his lovely couch, Kaikeyī at his side.

First he made an obeisance with all deference at his father's feet and then did homage most scrupulously at the feet of Kaikeyī.

"Rāma!" cried the wretched king, his eyes brimming with tears, but he was unable to say anything more or to look at him.

As if his foot had grazed a snake, Rāma was seized with terror to see the expression on the king's face, one more terrifying than he had ever seen before.

For the great king lay heaving sighs, racked with grief and remorse, all his senses numb with anguish, his mind stunned and confused.

It was as if the imperturbable, wave-wreathed ocean had suddenly been shaken with perturbation, as if the sun had been eclipsed, or a seer had told a lie.

His father's grief was incomprehensible to him, and the more he pondered it, the more his agitation grew, like that of the ocean under a full moon.

With his father's welfare at heart, Rāma struggled to comprehend, "Why does the king not greet me, today of all days?

"On other occasions, when Father might be angry, the sight of me would calm him. Why then, when he looked at me just now, did he instead become so troubled?

"He seems desolate and grief-stricken, and his face has lost its glow." Doing obeisance to Kaikeyī, Rāma spoke these words:

"I have not unknowingly committed some offense, have I, to anger my father? Tell me, and make him forgive me.

"His face is drained of color, he is desolate and does not speak to me. It cannot be, can it, that some physical illness or mental distress afflicts him? But it is true, well-being is not something one can always keep.

"Some misfortune has not befallen the handsome prince Bharata, has it, or courageous Śatrughna, or one of my mothers?

"I should not wish to live an instant if his majesty, the great king, my father, were angered by my failure to satisfy him or do his bidding.

"How could a man not treat him as a deity incarnate, in whom he must recognize the very source of his existence in this world?

"Can it be that in anger you presumed to use harsh words with my father, and so threw his mind into such turmoil?

"Answer my questions truthfully, my lady: What has happened to cause this unprecedented change in the lord of men?

"At the bidding of the king, if enjoined by him, my guru, father, king, and benefactor, I would hurl myself into fire, drink deadly poison, or drown myself in the sea.

"Tell me then, my lady, what the king would have me do. I will do it, I promise. Rāma need not say so twice."

The ignoble Kaikeyī then addressed these ruthless words to Rāma, the upright and truthful prince:

"Long ago, Rāghava, in the war of the gods and *asuras,* your father bestowed two boons on me, for protecting him when he was wounded in a great battle.

"By means of these I have demanded of the king that Bharata be consecrated and that you, Rāghava, be sent at once to Daṇḍaka wilderness.

"If you wish to ensure that your father be true to his word, and you to your own, best of men, then listen to what I have to say.

"Abide by your father's guarantee, exactly as he promised it, and enter the forest for nine years and five.

"Forgo the consecration and withdraw to Daṇḍaka wilderness, live there seven years and seven, wearing matted hair and barkcloth garments.

"Let Bharata rule this land from the city of the Kosalans, with all the treasures it contains, all its horses, chariots, elephants."

When Rāma, slayer of enemies, heard Kaikeyī's hateful words, like death itself, he was not the least disconcerted, but only replied,

"So be it. I shall go away to live in the forest, wearing matted hair and barkcloth garments, to safeguard the promise of the king.

"But I want to know why the lord of earth, the invincible tamer of foes, does not greet me as he used to?

"You need not worry, my lady. I say it to your face: I shall go to the forest—rest assured—wearing barkcloth and matted hair.

"Enjoined by my father, my benefactor, guru, and king, a man who knows what is right to do, what would I hesitate to do in order to please him?

"But there is still one thing troubling my mind and eating away at my heart: that the king does not tell me himself that Bharata is to be consecrated.

"For my wealth, the kingship, Sītā, and my own dear life I would gladly give up to my brother Bharata on my own, without any urging.

"How much more readily if urged by my father himself, the lord of men, in order to fulfill your fond desire and safeguard his promise?

"So you must reassure him. Why should the lord of earth keep his eyes fixed upon the ground and fitfully shed these tears?

"This very day let messengers depart on swift horses by order of the king to fetch Bharata from his uncle's house.

"As for me, I shall leave here in all haste for Daṇḍaka wilderness, without questioning my father's word, to live there fourteen years."

Kaikeyī was delighted to hear these words of Rāma's, and trusting them implicitly, she pressed Rāghava to set out at once.

"So be it. Men shall go as messengers on swift horses to bring home Bharata from his uncle's house.

"But since you are now so eager, Rāma, I do not think it wise to linger. You should therefore proceed directly from here to the forest.

"That the king is ashamed and does not address you himself, that is nothing, best of men, you needn't worry about that.

"But so long as you have not hastened from the city and gone to the forest, Rāma, your father shall neither bathe nor eat."

"Oh curse you!" the king gasped, overwhelmed with grief, and upon the gilt couch he fell back in a faint.

Rāma raised up the king, pressed though he was by Kaikeyī—like a horse whipped with a crop—to make haste and depart for the forest.

Listening to the ignoble Kaikeyī's hateful words, so dreadful in their consequences, Rāma remained unperturbed and only said to her,

"My lady, it is not in the hopes of gain that I suffer living in this world. You should know that, like the seers, I have but one concern and that is righteousness.

"Whatever I can do to please this honored man I will do at any cost, even if it means giving up my life.

"For there is no greater act of righteousness than this: obedience to one's father and doing as he bids.

"Even unbidden by this honored man, at your bidding alone I shall live for fourteen years in the desolate forest.

"Indeed, Kaikeyī, you must ascribe no virtue to me at all if you had to appeal to the king, when you yourself are so venerable in my eyes.

"Let me only take leave of my mother, and settle matters with Sītā. Then I shall go, this very day, to the vast forest of the Daṇḍakas.

"You must see to it that Bharata obeys Father and guards the kingdom, for that is the eternal way of righteousness."

When his father heard Rāma's words, he was stricken with such deep sorrow that he could not hold back his sobs in his grief and broke out in loud weeping.

Splendid Rāma did homage at the feet of his unconscious father and at the feet of that ignoble woman, Kaikeyī; then he turned to leave.

Reverently Rāma circled his father and Kaikeyī, and, withdrawing from the inner chamber, he saw his group of friends.

Lakṣmaṇa, the delight of Sumitrā, fell in behind him, his eyes brimming with tears, in a towering rage.

Reverently circling the equipment for the consecration, but careful not to gaze at it, Rāma slowly went away.

The loss of the kingship diminished his great majesty as little as night diminishes the loveliness of the cool-rayed moon, beloved of the world.

Though he was on the point of leaving his native land and going to the forest, he was no more discomposed than one who has passed beyond all things of this world.

Holding back his sorrow within his mind, keeping his every sense in check, and fully self-possessed he made his way to his mother's residence to tell her the sad news.

As Rāma entered her residence, where joy still reigned supreme, as he reflected on the sudden wreck of all his fortunes, even then he showed no sign of discomposure, for fear it might endanger the lives of those he loved.

from Book 3[1]

[The Abduction of Sita]

Sarga 42

After instructing his brother the mighty prince, delight of the Raghus,[2] strapped on his gold-hilted sword.

He then strapped on a pair of quivers and took up his proper ornament—the bow with triple curve—and set off at a rapid pace.

The deer spied the lord of kings rushing toward him and he led him on, now timorously hiding, now showing himself again.

With sword strapped on and taking up his bow, Rāma ran toward the deer, imagining he saw his form shimmering before him.

At one moment he would spot him running through the deep forest, temptingly near, and would take his bow in hand, only to look once more and find the deer beyond the range of his arrow. In one stretch of forest he came into sight leaping through the air in frightful panic, and then he passed into another stretch and out of sight.

Like the disk of the autumn moon veiled in tatters of cloud, he was seen one instant and gone the next.

Now appearing, now disappearing, he drew Rāghava far away, and helplessly deluded by him Kākutstha[3] flew into a rage.

Then the deer halted in exhaustion and withdrew to a shady spot in the meadow, not far away, where Rāma spotted him surrounded by other animals of the forest.

Seeing the deer mighty Rāma was determined to kill him. The powerful prince nocked his sturdy bow and drew it back with power.

Aiming at the deer he shot a gleaming, flaming arrow fashioned by Brahmā[4] that glared like a snake as it darted forth.

1. Translated by Sheldon Pollock.
2. Rama.
3. Rama (literally, "a descendant of Kakutstha," an ancestor in Rama's lineage).
4. Rama had earlier received the god Brahma's heavenly weapons from the sage Agastya.

The supreme arrow penetrated the illusory deer form and like a bolt of lightning pierced the heart, Mārīca's heart.[5]

The deer leaped high as a palm tree and with a ghastly shriek fell to the ground, tormented by the arrow, his life ebbing away. And as Mārīca lay there dying, the shape he had assumed began to disappear.

Knowing the time had come, in Rāghava's own voice he cried out, "Oh Sītā! Oh Lakṣmaṇa!"

Pierced to the quick by an arrow unlike any other, Mārīca once more took on the form of a massive *rākṣasa,* giving up the deer form and his life.

Struck by the arrow, he became a *rākṣasa* once more, with huge fangs, a necklace of gold, sparkling earrings, and every other ornament to adorn him.

Seeing that dreadful sight, the *rākṣasa* fallen on the ground, Rāma thought suddenly of Sītā and recalled what Lakṣmaṇa had said.[6]

"With his dying breath this *rākṣasa* cried out at the top of his voice, 'Oh Sītā! Oh Lakṣmaṇa!' How will Sītā react to hearing this?

"And great-armed Lakṣmaṇa, what will be his state of mind?" As these thoughts came to righteous Rāma, the hair on his body bristled with dread.

Then Rāma's consternation gave way to a feeling of fear that shot through him with sharp pangs: The deer he had slain was in fact a *rākṣasa,* the voice it had used was his own.

He killed another dappled deer and taking the meat hurriedly retraced his steps to Janasthāna.[7]

Sarga 43

Now, when Sītā heard that cry of distress, in her husband's own voice, coming from the forest, she said to Lakṣmaṇa, "Go and find out what has happened to Rāghava.

"My heart—my very life—is jarred from its place by the sound of his crying in deep distress that I heard so clearly.

"You must rescue your brother, who cries out in the forest. Run to your brother at once, for he needs help! The *rākṣasas* have him in their power, like a bull fallen among lions." So she spoke, but Lakṣmaṇa, heeding his brother's command, did not go.

5. The *rakshasa* compelled by Ravana to assume the form of a bejeweled deer in order to draw Rama away from the hermitage.
6. At the first sight of the magical deer, Lakshmana had a premonition that it must be a *rakshasa.*
7. The region of the Dandaka forest located near Rama's hermitage.

Then the daughter of Janaka[8] angrily said to him, "You wear the guise of a friend to your brother, Saumitri,[9] but act like his foe, refusing to aid him in his extremity. You hope Rāma perishes, Lakṣmaṇa, isn't that so? And it is all because of me.

"I think you would be happy should some disaster befall your brother. You have no real affection for him, so you stand there calmly with the splendid prince gone from sight.

"For with him in danger and me here, how could I prevent what you came here with the sole intention of doing?"

So Sītā, princess of Videha, spoke, overwhelmed with tears and grief, and Lakṣmaṇa replied to her as she stood there frightened as a doe.

"My lady, there is no one, god or man, *gandharva,* great bird, or *rākṣasa, piśāca, kinnara,* beast, or dreaded *dānava*—no one, fair lady, who could match Rāma, the peer of Vāsava, in battle.[1]

"Rāma cannot be killed in battle. You must not talk this way, for I dare not leave you in the forest with Rāghava gone.

"His power cannot be withstood, not by any powers however vast, not by all three worlds up in arms, or the deathless gods themselves, their lord included.

"Let your heart rest easy, do not be alarmed. Your husband will soon return, after killing that splendid deer.

"That was clearly not his voice, or any belonging to a god. It was the magic of that *rākṣasa,* unreal as a mirage.

"You were entrusted to my safekeeping, shapely Vaidehī,[2] by the great Rāma. I dare not leave you here alone.

"Then too, dear lady, because of the slaughter at Janasthāna, where Khara perished, we have earned the hostility of the night-stalkers.[3]

"*Rākṣasas* delight in causing trouble, Vaidehī, they make all kinds of noises in the deep forest. You need not worry."

Though what he said was true, Sītā was enraged by Lakṣmaṇa's words. Her eyes blazed bright red as she made this harsh reply:

8. Sita is the adopted daughter of King Janaka of Mithila in Videha country, where he discovered her as baby in a furrowed field.

9. Lakshmana (literally, "son of Sumitra").

1. *Pishacas* and *danavas* are two more categories of nonhuman beings. "Vasava" is an epithet of Indra, king of the gods.

2. Sita (literally, "woman of Videha").

3. The *rakshasa* Khara, a brother of Ravana, was killed when he and his 14,000 soldiers attacked Rama.

"Ignoble, cruel man, disgrace to your House! How pitiful this attempt of yours. I feel certain you are pleased with all this, and that is why you can talk the way you do.

"It is nothing new, Lakṣmaṇa, for rivals to be so evil, cruel rivals like you always plotting in secret.

"You treacherously followed Rāma to the forest, the two of you alone: You are either in the employ of Bharata or secretly plotting to get me.

"I am married to Rāma, a husband dark as a lotus, with eyes like lotus petals. How could I ever give my love to some ordinary man?

"I would not hesitate to take my life before your very eyes, Saumitri, for I could not live upon this earth one moment without Rāma."

Such were the words Sītā spoke to Lakṣmaṇa, so harsh they made his hair bristle with horror. But he controlled himself, and with hands cupped in reverence he addressed her:

"I dare not answer, Maithilī,[4] for you are a deity in my eyes. And yet inappropriate words from a woman come as nothing new.

"This is the nature of women the whole world over: Women care nothing for righteousness, they are flighty, sharp-tongued, and divisive.

"May all the inhabitants of the forest give ear and bear me witness how my words of reason met so harsh a reply from you.

"Curse you and be damned, that you could so suspect me, when I am only following the orders of my guru. How like a woman to be so perverse!

"I am going to Kākutstha. I wish you well, fair woman. May the spirits of the forest, each and every one, protect you, large-eyed lady.

"How ominous the portents that manifest themselves to me! I pray I find you here when I return with Rāma."

Now, when Lakṣmaṇa addressed her in this fashion, Janaka's daughter began to weep. Overwhelmed with tears she hotly replied:

"Parted from Rāma I will drown myself in the Godāvarī,[5] Lakṣmaṇa, I will hang myself or hurl my body upon some rocky place.

"Or I will drink deadly poison or throw myself into a blazing fire. I would never touch any man but Rāghava, not even with my foot!"

4. Sita (literally, "woman of Mithila").

5. A river in the southern region of India.

Such were the insults Sītā hurled at Lakṣmaṇa in her sorrow, and sorrowfully she wept and struck her belly with her fists.

At the sight of large-eyed Sītā so deeply anguished and weeping, Saumitri was beside himself and tried to comfort her, but she would say nothing more to her husband's brother.

Then, cupping his hands in reverence and bowing slightly, Lakṣmaṇa, the self-respecting prince, said goodbye to Sītā. And as he set forth to find Rāma, he turned around again and again and looked back at Maithilī.

Sarga 44

Rāghava's younger brother, angered by her harsh words and sorely longing for Rāma, set forth without further delay.

This was the opening ten-necked Rāvaṇa had been waiting for, and he took advantage of it at once. Assuming the guise of a wandering mendicant, he turned his steps toward Vaidehī.

Clad in a soft saffron robe, with topknot, parasol, and sandals, and goodly staff and water pitcher hanging at his left shoulder—disguised like this, as a mendicant—he approached Vaidehī.

Both brothers had left her, and in his pride of power he advanced upon her, like total darkness advancing upon the twilight, when both sun and moon have left.

He gazed at the glorious young princess as ominously as a planet might gaze upon the star Rohiṇī when the hare-marked moon is absent.[6]

At the appearance of the dreaded, evil creature, the trees that grew in Janasthāna stopped rustling and the wind died down.

At the sight of him peering around with his blood-red eyes, the swift current of the Godāvarī river began to slacken in fear.

Ten-necked Rāvaṇa had waited for an opening, and Rāma had given him one. In the guise of a beggar he drew near to Vaidehī.

As Vaidehī sat grieving for her husband, the unholy Rāvaṇa in the guise of a holy man edged closer to her, like the sluggish planet, Saturn, closing in on Citrā, the sparkling star.

Like a deep well concealed by grass, the evil one in the guise of a holy man stood watching Vaidehī, illustrious wife of Rāma—the beautiful woman with lovely teeth

6. The planet is Mercury and the star-cluster Rohini is the beloved of the moon. In Sanskrit literature, dramatic moments are often rendered through astronomical tropes because of the prominence given to astral phenomena in traditional Indian rituals and beliefs.

and lips, and a face like the full moon—as she sat in the leaf hut tormented with grief and tears.

The blackhearted stalker of the night stole ever closer to Vaidehī, the woman dressed in garments of yellow silk, and with eyes like lotus petals.

With arrows of Manmatha, god of love, lodged deep within his heart, and the sounds of the *vedas*[7] on his lips, the overlord of *rākṣasas* appeared before the deserted hut and courteously spoke.

Rāvaṇa began singing her praises, that loveliest of women in the three worlds, a radiant beauty, like the goddess Śrī herself without the lotus.

"Who are you, golden woman dressed in garments of yellow silk, wearing a lovely lotus garland, and like a lotus pond yourself?

"Are you the goddess Modesty or Fame? Are you Śrī or lovely Lakṣmī or perhaps an *apsaras,* lovely lady? Could you be Prosperity, shapely woman, or easygoing Pleasure?[8]

"Your teeth are bright white, tapered, and even; your eyes are large and clear, rosy at the corner, black in the center.

"Your hips are full and broad, your thighs smooth as an elephant's trunk. And these, your delightful breasts, how round they are, so firm and gently heaving; how full and lovely, smooth as two palm fruits, with their nipples standing stiff and the rarest gems to adorn them.

"Graceful lady with your lovely smile, lovely teeth, and lovely eyes, you have swept my heart away like a river in flood that sweeps away its banks.

"Your waist I could compass with my fingers; how fine is your hair, how firm your breasts. No goddess, no *gandharva* woman, no *yakṣa* or *kinnara* woman, no mortal woman so beautiful have I ever seen before on the face of this earth.[9]

"Your beauty, unrivaled in all the worlds, your delicacy and youth, and the fact of your living here in the woods stir the deepest feelings in me.

"I urge you to go home, this is no place for you to be living. For this is the lair of dreaded *rākṣasas,* who can change their form at will.

"In the most delightful palaces, in luxuriant, fragrant city gardens is where you should be strolling.

7. Ancient wisdom texts.
8. Shri and Lakshmi, goddesses of royalty and wealth, are normally taken to be one and the same, and the consort of Vishnu. *Apsaras* are celestial nymphs.
9. *Yakshas* are yet another category of divine beings whose women are famous for their beauty.

"To my mind you deserve the finest garlands and beverages and raiment, and the finest husband, lovely black-eyed lady.

"Could you be one of the Rudras or Maruts, sweet-smiling, shapely woman, or one of the Vasus, perhaps? You look like a goddess to me.

"But *gandharvas* do not pass this way, nor do gods or *kinnaras,* for this is the lair of *rākṣasas.* How is it you have come here?

"There are monkeys here, lions, panthers, and tigers, apes, hyenas, and flesh-eating birds. How is it you do not fear them?

"And the dreaded elephants that go running wild, maddened by rut—how is it you do not fear them, lovely lady, all alone in the deep wilderness?

"Who are you, to whom do you belong, where do you come from, my precious, and why are you wandering all alone through Daṇḍaka, the haunt of dreaded *rākṣasas?*"

Such was the praise evil Rāvaṇa lavished on Vaidehī. But seeing he had come in the garb of a brahman, Maithilī honored him with all the acts of hospitality due a guest.

First she brought forward a cushion and offered water for his feet, and then she called him when food was ready, for he looked kindly enough.

When Maithilī observed that he had come in the garb of a twice-born[1]—a brahman with a begging bowl and saffron robe; when she saw these accoutrements, it was impossible to refuse him, and so she extended him an invitation befitting a brahman.

"Here is a cushion, brahman, please be seated and accept this water for your feet. Here I have made ready for you the best fare the forest has to offer. You may partake of it freely."

So Maithilī extended him a cordial invitation, and as Rāvaṇa gazed at her, the wife of the lord of men, he confirmed his resolve to take her by force, and with that, consigned himself to death.

Her husband in his honest garb had gone to hunt the magic deer, and she waited for him and Lakṣmaṇa, scanning the horizon. But she saw neither Rāma nor Lakṣmaṇa—only the deep, green forest.

SARGA 45

When Rāvaṇa came in the guise of a mendicant to carry off Vaidehī, he had first put some questions to her. Of her own accord she now began to tell her story.

For Sītā had thought a moment: "He is a brahman and my guest. If I do not reply he will curse me." She then spoke these words:

1. A term used primarily of Brahmans. (They are said to be born a second time when initiated into studentship by their teacher.)

"I am the daughter of Janaka, the great king of Mithilā. My name is Sītā, may it please the best of twice-born, and I am the wife of Rāma.

"For twelve years I lived in the house of Rāghava, enjoying such pleasures as mortals enjoy. I had all I could desire.

"Then, in the thirteenth year, the king in concert with his kingly counselors approved the royal consecration of my husband.

"But just as the preparations for Rāghava's consecration were under way, a mother-in-law of mine named Kaikeyī asked her husband for a boon.

"You see, Kaikeyī had already married my father-in-law for a consideration. So she had two things she now could ask of her husband, the best of kings and a man who always kept his word: One was the consecration of Bharata, the other, my husband's banishment.

"'From this day forth I will not eat, or drink, or sleep, I will put an end to my life if Rāma is consecrated.'

"Such were Kaikeyī's words, and though my father-in-law, who had always shown her respect, begged her with offers of commensurate riches, she would not do what he begged of her.

"Rāma, my mighty husband, was then twenty-five years old, and I had just passed my eighteenth birthday.

"His name is renowned throughout the world, his eyes are large, his arms strong. He is virtuous, honest, truthful, and devoted to the welfare of all people.

"When Rāma came into his father's presence for the consecration to begin, it was Kaikeyī who addressed my husband, in a rush of words:

"'Listen to me, Rāghava, and hear what your father has decreed. The kingship is to be given to Bharata uncontested.

"'As for you, you are to live in the forest for nine years and five. Go into banishment, Kākutstha, and save your father from falsehood.'

"Without a trace of fear my husband Rāma answered Kaikeyī, 'So be it,' and in firm compliance with his vow did just as she had told him.

"For Rāma has taken a solemn vow, brahman, one never to be broken: always to give and not receive, to tell the truth and not lie.

"Rāma has a constant companion, his half brother Lakṣmaṇa, a tiger among men and mighty slayer of enemies in battle.

"This brother Lakṣmaṇa, who keeps to the ways of righteousness, firm in his vows, followed bow in hand when Rāma went into banishment with me.

"And so the three of us were driven from the kingdom for the sake of Kaikeyī. Thus it is under compulsion, best of twice-born, that we now wander the dense forest.

"Rest a moment; or you can even pass the night here if you like. My husband will soon return bringing an abundance of food from the forest.

"But can you just tell me your name, your clan, and family? How is it that you, a brahman, wander all alone in Daṇḍaka wilderness?"

So Sītā, wife of Rāma, spoke, and powerful Rāvaṇa, overlord of *rākṣasas,* made a reply that froze her blood:

"I am he who terrifies the worlds, with all their gods, *asuras,* and great serpents. I am Rāvaṇa, Sītā, supreme lord of the hosts of *rākṣasas.*

"Now that I have set eyes on you, flawless, golden lady dressed in silk, I shall no longer take any pleasure in my own wives.

"From one place and another I have carried off many splendid women. May it please you to become chief queen over every one of them.

"In the middle of the ocean lies my vast city Laṅkā, perched upon a mountain peak and ringed by the sea.

"There, my radiant Sītā, you shall stroll with me through the forests, never longing for this life you are leading in the wilderness.

"Five thousand slave women all adorned with ornaments shall wait upon you hand and foot, Sītā, if you become my wife."

So Rāvaṇa spoke, but Janaka's daughter, that faultless beauty, angrily and with utter contempt for the *rākṣasa* replied:

"I am faithful to Rāma, my husband, the equal of great Indra, unshakable as a great mountain, imperturbable as the great sea.

"I am faithful to Rāma, the great-armed, great-chested prince, who moves with the boldness of a lion, a lionlike man, a lion among men.

"I am faithful to Rāma, the king's most cherished son, a great-armed, mighty prince of wide renown and strict self-control, whose face is like the full moon.

"As for you, you are a jackal in the presence of a lioness, to come here seeking me, whom you can never have. You could no more touch me than touch the radiance of the sun.

"You must be seeing many a golden tree of death, ill-fated Rāvaṇa, if you seek to gain the beloved wife of Rāghava.

"You are seeking to pluck the fang from the mouth of a poisonous snake, the tooth from the mouth of a hungry lion in pursuit, the foe to all beasts.

"You are seeking to carry off Mandara, greatest of mountains, in your hand, to drink the *kālakūṭa* poison and take no harm of it.[2]

"You are rubbing your eye with a needle, licking a razor with your tongue, if you seek to violate the beloved wife of Rāghava.

"You are seeking to cross the ocean with a boulder tied around your neck, to take into your hands the very sun and moon, if you seek to assault the beloved wife of Rāghava.

"You have seen a blazing fire and seek to carry it away in a cloth, if you seek to carry off the virtuous wife of Rāma.

"You are seeking to walk atop a row of iron-headed spears, if you seek to violate the proper wife of Rāma.

"As different as a lion and a jackal in the forest, the ocean and a ditch, rare wine and gruel, so different are Dāśarathi and you.

"As different as gold and lead, sandalwood paste and slime, a bull elephant and a cat in the forest, so different are Dāśarathi[3] and you.

"As different as Garuda, the son of Vinatā,[4] and a crow, a peacock and a gull, a vulture and a crane in the forest, so different are Dāśarathi and you.

"As long as Rāma walks the earth, mighty as thousand-eyed Indra, armed with his bow and arrow, you may take me but could never enjoy me, no more than a fly the diamond chip it swallows."

Such were the words the good woman addressed to the evil nightstalker, but a shudder passed through her body, and she began to quiver like a slender plantain tree tossed by the wind.

And when Rāvaṇa, mighty as Death himself, observed how Sītā was trembling, he thought to frighten her still further by telling of his House, his power, the name he had won for himself, and the deeds he had done.

2. The legendary Mt. Mandara was made the churning stick when the gods and antigods churned the milk ocean for the drink of immortality. The cosmic serpent used as the twirling string spewed forth the terrible *kalakuta* poison, which Shiva swallowed to protect the world.

3. Rama (literally "descendent of Dasharatha").

4. King of birds and the mount of the god Vishnu.

Sarga 46

Even as Sītā was speaking in this manner, Rāvaṇa flew into a passion, and knitting his brow into a frown he harshly replied:

"I am half brother to Vaiśravaṇa,[5] lovely lady. My name is Rāvaṇa, if you please, the mighty ten-necked one.

"In fear of me the gods, *gandharvas, piśācas,* great birds, and serpents flee in terror, as all things born are put to flight by fear of Death.

"In connection with some issue between us Vaiśravaṇa, my half brother, and I came into conflict. In a rage I attacked and defeated him in battle.

"Tormented by fear of me he left his own prosperous realm and now dwells on Kailāsa, highest of mountains, with only men to convey him.

"For the aerial chariot that flies where one desires, the lovely Puṣpaka, once belonged to him. But I took it by force of arms, my beauty, and now ride upon it through the sky.

"At the mere sight of my face, Maithilī, once my anger has been provoked, the gods with Indra at their head flee in terror.

"In my presence the wind blows cautiously, and the sun's hot rays turn cold in fear.

"The leaves on the trees stop rustling, and the rivers slacken their current wherever I am, wherever I go.

"On the further shore of the ocean lies my lovely city, Laṅkā, grand as Indra's Amarāvatī, thronged with dreaded *rākṣasas.*

"It is a lovely, dazzling city ringed by a white rampart, with gateways made of gold and towers of cat's-eye beryl.

"It is crowded with elephants, horses, and chariots, the sound of pipes resounds there, and its gardens are beautiful, filled with trees bearing any fruit one wants.

"Living there with me, proud princess Sītā, you shall forget what it was like to have been a mortal woman.

"Enjoying not only the pleasures mortals enjoy, lovely lady, but divine pleasures, too, you shall soon forget that short-lived mortal, Rāma.

"So meager is his power that King Daśaratha, in order to enthrone a favored son, was able to drive him into the forest, first-born though he was.

5. Kubera, god of wealth. In his more common, wrathful form, Ravana has ten necks and twenty arms.

"What use is this witless Rāma to you, large-eyed woman, a miserable ascetic who lets himself be deposed from the kingship?

"The lord of all *rākṣasas* has come here in person, of his own accord. Do not reject him, whom the arrows of Manmatha, god of love, have so badly wounded.

"For if you do reject me, timid lady, you shall live to regret it, just like Urvaśī after she spurned Purūravas."[6]

So he spoke, but Vaidehī was overcome with rage—her eyes grew red, and though all alone in that deserted spot, she made this harsh reply to the lord of *rākṣasas:*

"How can you want to commit such an outrage, you who claim Vaiśravaṇa as brother, a god to whom all beings pay homage?

"The *rākṣasas* shall inevitably perish, Rāvaṇa, all who have you for their king, a cruel, imprudent, intemperate king.

"A man might abduct Indra's wife, úacī herself, and still hope to save his life, but he who carries me off, the wife of Rāma, has no life left to save.

"One might steal the incomparable úacī from the hand that wields the thunderbolt and long remain alive. But violate a woman like me, *rākṣasa,* and even drinking the nectar of immortality will be no escape for you."

Sarga 47

Hearing Sītā's words the awesome ten-necked Rāvaṇa struck his hands together and made ready to assume his massive form.

Again he addressed Maithilī, and far more severely than before: "It seems you did not hear, madwoman, when I spoke of my strength and valor.

"I can lift the earth in my arms while standing in the sky; I can drink up the ocean, I can slay Death in battle.

"I can shatter the earth with my sharp arrows, madwoman, or bring the sun to a halt. I can take on any form at will. You see before you a husband ready to grant your every wish."

And as Rāvaṇa spoke thus in his wild rage, his yellow-rimmed eyes turned fiery red.

Then suddenly Rāvaṇa, younger brother to Vaiśravaṇa, abandoned the kindly form of beggar and assumed his true shape, one such as Doom itself must have.

With eyes flaming bright red, with earrings of burnished gold, with bow and arrows, he became once more the majestic ten-faced stalker of the night.

6. The celestial nymph Urvashi fell in love with the mortal king Pururavas. The reference here to her misfortune when she left Pururavas is unclear.

He had thrown off the guise of mendicant and assumed his own form again, the colossal shape of Rāvaṇa, overlord of *rākṣasas.*

With eyes flaming bright red in his rage, lowering like a bank of storm clouds, clad in a red garment Rāvaṇa stood before Maithilī, staring at her, perfect jewel of a woman, with her jet-black hair, her sunlike radiance, and the fine clothes and ornaments that she wore. And he said:

"If you seek a husband whose fame has spread throughout the three worlds, shapely woman, be mine. I am a lord worthy of you.

"Love me forever. I shall be a lover to win your praise, and never, my beauty, will I do anything to displease you. Give up this love for a mortal being, and bestow your love on me.

"What possible virtues could make you love this short-lived Rāma, a failure, stripped of kingship? You think you are so smart, but what a fool you really are!

"He is a simpleton, who at the bidding of a woman abandoned his kingdom and loved ones to come and live in this forest, the haunt of wild beasts."

And so speaking to Sītā, princess of Mithilā, who deserved the same kindness she always showed others, Rāvaṇa seized her as the planet Budha might seize the star Rohiṇī in the sky.

With his left hand he seized lotus-eyed Sītā by her hair and with his right hand by her thighs.

With his long arms and sharp fangs he resembled a mountain peak; seeing him advancing like Death himself, the spirits of the forest fled overpowered by fear.

Then with a dreadful rumble Rāvaṇa's great chariot came into view, that unearthly chariot fashioned by magic, with wheels of gold, and harnessed with asses.

With loud, harsh threats he then clutched Vaidehī to his breast and boarded the chariot.

Caught in Rāvaṇa's grip and wild with despair, the glorious Sītā screamed at the top of her voice, crying, "Rāma!" But Rāma was far away in the forest.

Filled with desire for one who was filled with loathing for him, Rāvaṇa flew up holding her writhing like a serpent queen.

As the lord of *rākṣasas* carried her off through the sky, she screamed shrilly like a woman gone mad, in agony, or delirious:

"Oh great-armed Lakṣmaṇa, you have always sought favor with your guru. Don't you know that I am being carried off by a *rākṣasa,* who can change his form at will?

"And you, Rāghava, you renounced all life's pleasures, everything of value, for the sake of righteousness. Don't you see me being carried off in defiance of all that is right?

"And surely, slayer of enemies, you are the one to discipline wrongdoers. Why then don't you punish so evil a creature as Rāvaṇa?

"But no, the result of wrongdoing is not seen right away. Time is a factor in this, as in the ripening of grain.

"And as for you, Doom must have robbed you of your senses to do what you have done. Disaster shall befall you at the hands of Rāma, a terrible disaster that will end your life.

"Ah, now Kaikeyī and all her family must be satisfied. Rāma's lawful wife has been taken from him, that glorious prince whom nothing but righteousness could satisfy.

"Janasthāna, I call on you and you *karṇikāra* trees in full blossom: Tell Rāma at once that Rāvaṇa is carrying off Sītā.

"I greet you, Mount Prasravaṇa,[7] with your flower garlands and massive peaks: Quickly tell Rāma that Rāvaṇa is carrying off Sītā.

"I greet you, Godāvarī river, alive with the call of geese and cranes: Tell Rāma at once that Rāvaṇa is carrying off Sītā.

"And you spirits that inhabit the different trees of this forest, I salute you all: Tell my husband that I have been carried off.

"All creatures that live in this place, I appeal to you for help, all you flocks of birds and herds of beasts: Tell my husband that the woman he loves more than life itself is being carried off, that Sītā has been carried away, helpless, by Rāvaṇa.

"Once the powerful, great-armed prince discovers where I am—albeit in the other world—he shall come in all his valor and bring me home, were it Vaivasvata himself, god of death, who had carried me off.

* * *

from Book 6[1]

[The Death of Ravana]

from Sarga 96

The great battle raged all night long as the gods, *dānavas, yakṣas, piśācas,* great serpents, and *rākṣasas* stood watching.

7. A peak in the Vindhya range in central India, where Rama, Sita, and Lakshmana spent time during their exile.

1. Translated by Robert Goldman, Barend A. van Nooten, and Sally Sutherland Goldman.

Indeed the duel between Rāma and Rāvaṇa went on day and night not pausing for an hour or even a moment.

SARGA 97

But then Mātali[2] alerted Rāghava, saying, "Why, heroic prince, do you merely match him blow for blow, as if you knew no better?

"In order to kill him, my lord, you must shoot him with the missile of Grandfather Brahmā. For the moment ordained by the gods for his destruction is now at hand."

Alerted by Mātali's words, Rāma drew forth that blazing arrow which, as he did so, made a hissing sound like that of a snake.

It had been given to him earlier by the mighty and blessed seer Agastya. It was a mighty arrow, the gift of Brahmā and unfailing in battle.

Brahmā whose power is immeasurable had fashioned it long ago for the sake of Indra and had presented it to that lord of the gods, who was eager to conquer the three worlds.

Pavana, the god of the wind, resided in its feathers; Pāvaka, the god of fire, and Bhâskara, the sun god, were in its arrowhead. Its shaft was made of cosmic space; and the mountains Meru and Mandara lent it their weight.

Radiant in its appearance, beautifully feathered, and adorned with gold, it was fashioned with the radiant energy of all the elements, and it was as brilliant as the sun.

It looked like the smoking fire of doom and glistened like a venomous snake. It could shatter hosts of chariots, elephants, and horses; and its effects were instantaneous.

It could shatter gateways and their iron beams and even mountains. With its shaft drenched with the blood of various creatures and smeared with their marrow it was truly frightful.

Roaring deafeningly and charged with the power of the thunderbolt, it was the scourge of many hosts. Dreadful, hissing like a serpent, it inspired terror in all beings.

It was fearsome and looked like Yama, the god of death. It provided a constant supply of food to flocks of cranes and vultures, *rākṣasas,* and packs of jackals.

Fletched with the various, beautiful and variegated feathers of Garuḍa, it brought joy to the monkey chiefs and despair to the *rākṣasas.*

Then strong and mighty Rāma invoked that great, unequalled arrow—an arrow that robbed one's enemies of their glory but brought joy to oneself. It was destined to

2. As Ravana fought from a chariot while Rama was on foot, Indra, king of the gods, dispatched his charioteer Matali to provide Rama with a comparable conveyance.

destroy that menace to the Ikṣvākus[3] and all the worlds; and Rāma placed it on his bow in the manner prescribed in the *veda.*

Filled with fury and exerting himself to the utmost, he bent the bow fully and loosed the arrow towards Rāvaṇa, tearing at his vitals.

As unstoppable as the thunderbolt and released by those arms of adamant, it struck Rāvaṇa's breast, inevitable as death.

Loosed with tremendous speed the deadly arrow pierced evil-minded Rāvaṇa's heart.

Drenched with blood the fatal arrow swiftly entered the earth, carrying with it the life breaths of Rāvaṇa.

Once the arrow had accomplished its purpose in killing Rāvaṇa, it obediently returned to its quiver, glistening with its still-wet blood.

Meanwhile the bow and arrows of him who had been struck down so swiftly slipped from his grasp along with his life breaths as he lay dying.

The lord of the sons of chaos, once so swift and splendid, fell lifeless to the ground from his chariot like Vṛtra[4] smitten by the thunderbolt.

Seeing him fallen to the ground, the surviving rangers of the night, their lord slain, fled terrified in all directions.

But as for the monkeys, whose weapons were trees, when they saw that ten-necked Rāvaṇa had been slain and that Rāghava was victorious, they pursued the *rākṣasas,* roaring loudly.

Hard pressed by the jubilant monkeys, their protector slain, the *rākṣasas* fled in fear to Laṅkā, their piteous faces drenched with tears.

Then the rejoicing monkeys, acting the part of victors, roared triumphantly, proclaiming Rāghava's victory and the death of Rāvaṇa.

The auspicious kettledrums of the thirty gods then resounded in the heavens; and a pleasant breeze blew, wafting a divine fragrance.

Then an extraordinary and delightful shower of blossoms fell from the sky to the earth, covering Rāma's chariot.

The beautiful voice of the great gods filled with the praise of Rāghava could be heard in the heavens crying, "Well done! Well done!"

3. The family name of the royal dynasty of Ayodhya.

4. A demon slain by Indra, who as the god of rain wields a thunderbolt.

Now that fierce Rāvaṇa, the terror of all the worlds, had been slain, great joy filled the gods and celestial bards.

Then, having slain that bull among *rākṣasas,* Rāghava, in great delight, fulfilled the wishes of Sugrīva and mighty Aṅgada.[5]

The hosts of the Māruts[6] regained tranquility, the directions were limpid, and the sky grew clear. The earth ceased its trembling, and soft breezes blew, while the sun, the bringer of day, shone with a steady light.

Sugrīva, Vibhīṣaṇa,[7] and the rest of splendid Rāghava's close allies, together with Lakṣmaṇa, gathered around him on the battlefield in the joy of victory and paid him homage with all due ceremony.

And the mighty prince, the delight of the king of the Raghu dynasty, having slain his enemy, became true to his vow. Surrounded by his kinsmen and armies there on the field of battle, he looked as resplendent as Indra surrounded by the hosts of the thirty gods.

* * *

[*After the killing of Rāvaṇa, Sītā is recovered and brought before Rāma.*]

[The Fire Ordeal of Sita]

Sarga 103

Looking at Maithilī who stood so meekly beside him, Rāma began to speak as rage simmered in his heart.

"So here you are, my lady. I have won you back after conquering my enemy in battle. I did all this in accordance with the demands of manly valor.

"I have wiped clean the affront and so my wrath is appeased. For I have eliminated both the insult and my enemy at the same time.

"Today I have demonstrated my manly valor. Today my efforts have borne fruit. Today, having fulfilled my vow, I am once more master of myself.

"You were carried off by that wanton *rākṣasa* when you were left alone, but now through manly action I have expunged that affront caused by fate.

"Of what use to anyone is a weakling who cannot wipe clean an insult through his own power?

"The leaping of the ocean and the razing of Laṅkā—today those praiseworthy deeds of Hanumān have borne fruit.

5. Sugriva is the monkey king of Kishkindha who aided Rama in the recovery of Sita. Angada is his nephew and successor.

6. The wind gods.

7. The virtuous *rakshasa* brother of Ravana, who allies himself with Rama.

"And today the efforts of Sugrīva and his army through their valor in battle and their beneficial counsel to me have borne fruit as well.

"And the efforts of my devoted Vibhīṣaṇa, who abandoned his worthless brother and came to me of his own accord, have likewise borne fruit."

Now as Rāma was saying these words in this fashion, Sītā, who looked like a wide-eyed doe, was overcome with tears.

But as Rāma gazed upon her, his anger flared up once more, like a blazing fire drenched with melted butter.

Knitting his brows on his forehead and glancing at her from the corner of his eye, he spoke harshly to Sītā there in the midst of the monkeys and *rākṣasas.*

"In wiping away this affront, Sītā, I have accomplished all that a man could do. In my wrath, I have won you back from the hands of my enemy just as through his austerities, the contemplative sage Agastya won back the southern lands that had been inaccessible to all living beings.

"Please understand that I did not undertake this great war effort—now brought to completion through the valor of my allies—on your account. Instead I did all this in order to protect my reputation and in every way to wipe clean the insult and disgrace to my illustrious lineage.

"Since, however, your virtue is now in doubt, your presence has become as unbearable to me as a bright lamp to a man afflicted with a disease of the eye.

"Go, therefore, as you please with my permission, daughter of Janaka, in any of the ten directions. I have no further use for you, my lady.

"For what powerful man born in a respectable family—his heart tinged with affection—would take back a woman who had lived in the house of another man?

"How could I who boast of my noble lineage possibly take you back—just risen from Rāvaṇa's lap and gazed upon by his lustful eye?

"I have restored my reputation; and that is the purpose for which I won you back. I have no further interest in you. Go from here wherever you like.

"I have made up mind in saying this, my lady. Choose Lakṣmaṇa or Bharata as you please.

"Or, Sītā, turn your heart to Sugrīva, lord of the monkeys, or the *rākṣasa* lord Vibhīṣaṇa, whichever pleases you.

"For surely, Sītā, once he had seen you with your heavenly beauty so enchanting, Rāvaṇa would not long have left you unmolested while you were dwelling in his house."

When Maithilī, who deserved to hear only kind words, had heard those cruel words of her beloved after so long a time, she shed tears and trembled violently like a *vallarī* creeper struck down by the trunk of a mighty elephant.

SARGA 104

When Vaidehī was addressed in this cruel and horrifying manner by the furious Rāghava, she was deeply wounded.

Hearing those cutting words of her husband before that great multitude, words such as she had never heard before, Maithilī was overcome with shame.

Pierced, as it were, by those verbal barbs, the daughter of Janaka, seemed to shrink within herself and gave way to bitter tears.

Wiping her tear-stained face, she replied softly to her husband in a faltering voice:

"How can you, heroic prince, speak to me with such cutting and improper words, painful to the ears, as some vulgar man might speak to his vulgar wife?

"I am not as you think of me, great armed prince. You must believe in me, for I swear to you by my own virtue.

"You harbor suspicion against all women because of the conduct of the vulgar ones. If you really knew me, you would abandon your suspicion.

"If I touched another's body against my will, lord, it was not by my choice. It is fate that was to blame here.

"My heart, which I control, was always devoted to you. But I was helpless. What could I have done regarding my body, which was in the power of another?

"If, my love, you do not truly know me despite our long-nurtured love and intimacy, then surely I am lost forever.

"When you dispatched the heroic Hanumān to search for me, why, heroic prince, did you not repudiate me then, while I was still in Laṅkā?

"No sooner had I heard your message, heroic prince, then abandoned by you, I would have abandoned my own life right before the eyes of that monkey lord.

"Then you would not have had to risk your life in a useless effort nor would your allies have had to undergo hardships to no purpose.

"But now, tiger among men, you give way to anger like some lesser man, thinking of me only as a typical woman.

"Since I am named after Janaka, you fail to take into account that I was born from the Goddess Earth, nor, though you know my conduct well, do you give it proper consideration.

"You give no weight to the fact that you took my hand when we were both still children. My devotion, my virtuous conduct—all that you have set aside."

When she had spoken in this fashion, Sītā turned weeping to Lakṣmaṇa, who stood there despondent and brooding, and spoke, her voice choked with tears.

"Build me a pyre, Saumitri, the only cure for this calamity. I cannot bear to live under the cloud of this false allegation.

"Rejected in the assembly of the people by my husband, who is not satisfied with my virtues, I shall enter the fire, bearer of oblations, so that I may follow the only path proper for me."

When Lakṣmaṇa, slayer of heroic foes, had been addressed in this fashion by Vaidehī, he glared at Rāghava's face, gripped by indignation.

But, sensing Rāma's intentions, which were betrayed by his facial expression, mighty Saumitri, ever obedient to Rāma's wishes, built the pyre.

Then reverently circumambulating Rāma, who stood with his face downcast, Vaidehī approached the blazing fire, eater of oblations.

After making her obeisance to the gods and the brahmans, Maithilī cupped her hands in reverence and facing Agni, god of fire, said this:

"Since my heart has never once strayed from Rāghava, so may the purifying fire, witness of all the world, protect me in every way."

When she had spoken in this fashion, Vaidehī reverently circumambulated the fire, eater of oblations. Then she entered the blazing flames, with a fearless heart.

The vast crowd assembled there, filled with children and the aged, watched as Maithilī entered the fire, eater of oblations.

As Sītā entered the fire, a vast and prodigious cry of, "Alas! Alas!" arose from the *rākṣasas* and monkeys.

* * *

[*The gods appear to ask how Rāma, who is chief among the gods, could remain unmoved as Sītā throws herself into the fire. Led by Brahmā they then remind Rāma of his divinity and utter a hymn of praise to him.*]

Sarga 106

Upon hearing that auspicious speech uttered by Grandfather Brahmā, the shining god of fire took Vaidehī on his lap and rose.

She resembled the rising sun and was adorned with ornaments of burnished gold. She was young and wore red garments and her hair was dark and curling. Her garland and ornaments were undamaged. Her mind was calm and her appearance unchanged. Taking Vaidehī on his lap the shining god of fire presented her to Rāma.

Then the purifying god of fire, witness of all the world, spoke to Rāma, saying, "Here is your Vaidehī, Rāma. She has committed no sin.

"She is of pure conduct and high moral character and has never betrayed you in word, thought, imagination, or glance.

"When you had left her alone she was carried off, helpless and sorrowful, from the deserted forest by the *rākṣasa* Rāvaṇa, arrogant in his power.

"Hidden and imprisoned in the inner apartments, thinking only of you and having you for her only recourse, she was guarded by hordes of hideous *rākṣasa* women, dreadful to behold.

"Although she was enticed and threatened in various ways, Maithilī would not even think of the *rākṣasa,* since her heart was utterly devoted to you.

"You must take her back, Rāghava, for her heart is pure and she is free from sin. Say no more, I am giving you an order."

When mighty Rāma, steadfast and firm in his valor, had been addressed in this fashion, that best of those who maintain righteousness, replied to that foremost among the thirty gods.

"Unquestionably Sītā needed to be proven innocent before the three worlds, since the auspicious woman had long dwelt in Rāvaṇa's inner apartments.

"For had I not put Jānakī to the test, the virtuous would say of me, 'Daśaratha's son Rāma is a lustful fool.'

"I know full well that Janaka's daughter Maithilī could give her heart to no other, since she is devoted to me and obeys my every thought.

"But in order that the three worlds too should have faith in her, I, whose ultimate recourse is truth, took no notice as Vaidehī entered the fire, eater of oblations.

"Rāvaṇa could no more have violated that wide-eyed lady, protected by her own blazing energy, than could the mighty ocean violate its boundary.

"That evil-minded brute was incapable of assaulting Maithilī even in his thoughts. For she is as unapproachable as a blazing flame of fire.

"This auspicious woman was not destined to rule over Rāvaṇa's inner apartments. For she is as inseparable from me as is its radiance from the sun.

"Janaka's daughter Maithilī has been proven innocent before the three worlds, and I am no more able to give her up than is a self-controlled man his good reputation.

"Moreover, I must follow the good advice that all of you affectionate friends, respected throughout the world, have uttered for my own good."

When he had uttered these words, powerful Rāma, praised by his mighty companions for the feat he had accomplished, was reunited with his beloved. Then Rāghava, who well deserved it, experienced happiness.

RESONANCES

from *A Public Address, 1989. The Birthplace of God Cannot Be Moved!*[1]

Victory to Lord Vishvanatha of Kashi!
Victory to the birthplace of Lord Krishna!
Victory to our Hindu traditions and the ancient Vedic religion!
Victory to Lord Mahavira and the Lord Buddha!
Victory to the great religious warriors Banda Bairagi and Guru Govind Singh!
Victory to Mother India!
Victory to Mother Ganga![2]

Esteemed religious teachers, wise seers, mothers and sisters who love the God Rama, my brothers, we consider it an honor to have been invited to this holy city to speak to you about the birthplace of Rama, about our religion, our culture, all of these things. Seers are assembled here, but today they are not here to enlighten us about spiritual matters. Holy men are assembled here, but today it isn't to recite the *Bhagavata Purana* that they have come. Today Vishvamitra[3] has come, and he is looking for Rama. The minister Chanakya[4] has come, and he is looking for Chandragupta. Dadhichi[5] has come, and he is ready to sacrifice his own body to make the god Indra's formidable thunderbolt weapon.

1. Translated by Allison Busch. The story of Rama reentered history dramatically in the 1980s. Religious groups in association with political and paramilitary organizations were attempting to mobilize the populace to "liberate the birthplace" of Rama in Ayodhya—a very real town in the northern state of Uttar Pradesh—as part of a larger initiative to reorder India according to principles associated with the majority Hindu community. A Muslim shrine constructed in the sixteenth century by a general of Babur, founder of the Mughal empire was alleged to have been built on the ruins of a medieval temple commemorating Rama's birthplace. Various Hindu groups demanded that a new temple be built in place of the mosque. Demonstrations and speeches, such as the anonymous one translated here that argues against any suggestion of compromise, stirred up public passion to such an extent that on 6 December 1992, a large mob gathered in Ayodhya and demolished the structure. This was a historic moment, the first major breach of the mutual respect for Muslim and Hindu religious monuments and antiquities since India's independence in 1947; the significance of this event for the future of the nation-state continues to be vigorously debated. Stories can have consequences.

2. Lord Vishvanatha, more commonly known as "Shiva," is the patron deity of Varanasi, also called "Kashi," on the banks of the Ganga (the Ganges River). Krishna, an avatar of Vishnu, is said to have been born in Mathura. Mahavira and Buddha (both 5th century B.C.E.) were the founders of Jainism and Buddhism, respectively, the two most prominent heterodox religious movements of the 1st millennium B.C.E. Banda Bairagi (d. 1716) espoused the Sikh faith and joined the tenth Guru of Sikhism, Guru Govind Singh, in his military campaigns in the southern plains against Mughal forces in an era of imperial disintegration.

3. A sage who, in the first book of the *Ramayana* of Valmiki, takes Rama into the surrounding wilderness to slay the demons that had been defiling holy sacrifices and harassing ascetics.

4. Chanakya is the chief minister of the Chandragupta Maurya (r. 321–268 B.C.E.).

5. A pious sage known for having sacrificed his life in order to offer his bones to the gods. The bones were later fashioned into the thunderbolt with which the god Indra defeated many demons.

We are here to tell you about Rama, about Lakshmana. We are here to tell you about the bravery of the freedom fighter Bhagat Singh.[6] We are here to tell you about Maharana Pratap Singh, and the glories of Shivaji.[7]

India has a long tradition of sages coming to the rescue in a time of crisis. There was a time when the demon Ravana was harassing the world. In those days India had three rulers. There was king Dasharatha, but he was too busy with all of his religious sacrifices to be an effective ruler. There was King Janaka, but he too was a man of an overly spiritual bent. And then there was King Vali, who was too caught up in the pleasures of this world.

The poet Tulsidas brings up this dilemma: "All the kings were chagrined—how could this wicked demon be killed?" Although there were already three kings to rule the land, it was a wise sage who took charge in this difficult situation. He emerged from his lofty meditations to enter the realm of human action. He saw us through our hour of need.

Today it is just such a sage, following in the footsteps of the great sages before him, who has come into our midst to tell you what it is your country, your society, your religion, your culture needs. We have come to remind you that it is not so much the perpetrator of injustice that is at fault, as the one that puts up with it. Holy men have come here to spur our brave young men into action, to tell them that now is not the time to let us down. Don't let your mother ever say of you that her sons failed her in her hour of need.

And now the hour of need has come. We need your youth, your vigor, your faith. The blood of your heroic ancestors is coursing through your veins. We have seen enough of that kind of Hindu who stands as a paragon of tolerance in the world. We have seen enough of those Hindus who get up at the pulpit and spout universalist teachings. We have seen enough of those Hindus who preach that Allah and Ishvar are one. * * *

It's the same old story. They commit murder and nobody utters a peep. If we voice even the tiniest complaint, then it is we who are to blame. We are not even allowed to talk about the injustices being perpetrated against us. Why are we treated like pariahs in our own home? This isn't any particular person's fault. Collectively we act like a bunch of political eunuchs. It isn't the fault of the appeasement policy toward Muslims, either. It is our own fault that even though we number hundreds of millions we have never united ourselves. We have not tried to mobilize our strength, we have forgotten what it means to have pride in our culture. We have sold off our self-respect in the auction house of politics. * * *

A society that has forgotten what it means to value its heritage, a society that doesn't know what self-respect or pride is, might as well stand back and watch as politics tramples its culture underfoot. I don't need to tell you that this is happening to us. There is only one solution. The solution to our problems is for Hindus to band together. We need to break down the barriers of caste, we need to reconcile our language and regional differences. We need to be tightly bound, like fingers gathered into a fist. Hindus have traditionally shied away from using force, but now it's high

6. A militant Sikh nationalist and socialist revolutionary who founded the Young India Council in 1926 and was simultaneously active in the Hindustan Socialist Republican Association. He was executed by the British colonial government in 1932 for terrorist activities.

7. The Rajput ruler Maharana Pratap Singh (r. 1572–1597) is remembered for his chivalry and bravery in fighting against Akbar's forces in an attempt to maintain sovereignty over the Rajasthan area. Shivaji (r. 1674–1680) and the Maratha kingdom he led posed a formidable threat to the Mughal Empire.

time you started defending yourselves. You have lived like corpses already for too long, now you have to die in the fight for life. Do not shy away from death. You may have to embrace death in order to live. * **

Our country's leaders are power-hungry. All they really care about is getting themselves elected. The politicians—those in power and the opposition, too—just care about appeasing the Muslims. * * * V. P. Singh has made sure that not one of our workers can participate in the Rama temple campaign. Well, all we have to say to this is that we don't want Rajiv's rule, we don't want V. P. Singh's rule.[8] It's Rama's rule that we want, and Hanuman is ready for action.

My Hindu brothers, you've shown enough sympathy for the rest of the world. You have always been a peace-loving people, the type to take pity on everybody else. Don't you know that this kind of pacifism can backfire, and those whom you treat with kindness and respect may one day turn around and stab you in the back? Our sages have resolved that the time has come for Hindus to start being concerned about themselves. Think about your children and future generations. Cast off the cloak of cowardice and weakness. It's time to adopt the ways of bravery and heroism. You just stood by and watched as the Somnath temple was looted, you didn't say a word.[9] The Somnath temple was destroyed before your very eyes, and you didn't retaliate. Many have come and attacked you, and you didn't defend yourselves. And what have you received in return for this pacifism? How have your gentle ways been rewarded? People have mistaken your good will, your kind-heartedness, your generosity for cowardice and weakness.

No Hindu has ever razed a mosque to the ground, but what did we get in return for our gentleness? Muhammad Gauri came, Mahmud of Gazni came.[1] Invaders kept on coming, one after the other. They attacked us and tried to destroy our culture. They demolished our temples, they violated the honor of our mothers and sisters—do you want to see this kind of appalling history repeated? * * *

My heroic brothers, I don't need to tell you that you should be wary of this country's leaders and all their antics. You'll recall that years ago before the creation of Pakistan there was all of this political rhetoric about "unity." When people began to talk of partition, our country's foremost leaders used to say they would rather die than see such a thing happen. But they did let it happen—our motherland was hacked in two and today separatist sentiments still plague us. In the Punjab we have the Khalistan movement, and secessionist movements have taken the northeast by storm.[2] Politicians may contest elections on the issue of unity, but what they're really doing is tearing our country apart. Soon all that will be left of U. P. is a tiny fragment—but their election campaigns will still consist of unity slogans. * * *

It doesn't matter how many times you shout out slogans about unity, or raising the living standards of the lower castes, or eradicating poverty. We're not going to be able to keep our country together with just a bunch of slogans. It's sacrifice we need,

8. Rajiv Gandhi became the prime minister of India under the secularist Congress Party after the assassination of his mother, Indira Gandhi, in 1984. Vishvanath Pratap Singh ruled as prime minister from 1989 to 1990, implementing affirmative action policies in favor of low castes, which upper castes held to be profoundly threatening to their interests.

9. Mahmud of Ghazni culminated a series of raids on Indian temple towns by plundering the Somnath temple on the western coast of India in 1026 C.E.

1. Mahmud of Ghazni used his plunder to further strengthen the Ghaznavid kingdom in central Asia. By contrast, the conquest of Muhammad Gauri in 1192 led to the establishment of an enduring political entity in India, the Delhi Sultanate.

2. The Khalistan movement called for a sovereign homeland for Sikhs in the state of Punjab in western India. In Assam and neighboring states in the northeast, tribal groups in particular have long sought autonomy.

not slogans. And our opportunistic leaders are not capable of sacrifice. Sacrifice can only come from those who truly love their country.

My brothers, I know that you love your country. That's why I am telling you to get ready for action. Seeing our country's crisis, these sages have gathered here to help us. The policy of appeasing special interest groups has brought our country to the brink of ruin. These leaders are just greedy for votes and they don't care one bit about India's future. None of your leaders has the guts to raise his hand in parliament and stick up for the issue of Rama's birthplace. Because it takes strength of character to speak the truth and that's something our leaders no longer have. It's been forty-two years since Independence. We may have made some progress in this country, but we've also had major setbacks. All the ideals that our forefathers sacrificed so much to preserve are vanishing before our eyes!

> Look at what's going on in the world, look at what things have come to.
> Is there anything that isn't for sale?
> Minds and bodies are for sale.
> Our parliament was sold off long ago. Now the nation itself is up for sale.
> Our natural resources are being plundered.
> Youth is for sale. Now religion is for sale.
> The honor and integrity of our elders are up for grabs now.
> Everything is for sale—people would sell their very own soul if they could.
> Go ask your sisters and mothers—their brothers and sons are for sale.
> What a strange place we live in—brides and bridegrooms are for sale.
> Leaders of today, take a good look around you.
> We are hurtling towards destruction. Is there anyone who can save us now?

In this day and age people think nothing of abandoning truth in their grab for power. They'd sacrifice all our religious principles, the heritage of our ancestors. * * *

But the truth about Lord Rama's birthplace is something that can't be denied. The birthplace of Rama has always belonged to the Hindus. It still does, and it always will. We won't rest until we build a magnificent temple at Rama's birthplace. My brothers, your confused leaders are demanding proof of the existence of Rama. Tell them that one of our most basic everyday greetings to one another is "Victory to Lord Rama!" When we are tired from a long day at work, we get relief from our weariness by calling out to Rama. Sometimes we may be overwhelmed by sorrow, but we say his name and we feel peace. Our very life originates in Rama, and when we die the pall bearers carry us away shouting, "The only sure thing in life is the name of Rama!"

And they are still demanding proof of Rama's existence? Tell the whole world that this country is Rama's, the very air we breathe is Rama's. And the Lord Rama has set an example for us—that we fight our enemies. We have never tried to interfere with anybody else's rights, we have always treated others with respect. But when justice became a mockery, then even the great monkey king Vali[3] had to be destroyed. And Rama gave the order to charge forth and wipe out the tyrant Ravana. When Hanuman on his own was able to reduce Lanka to ashes,[4] then surely we should not shrink from the task of defending Rama's birthplace.

3. Rama killed the monkey king Vali to consolidate his alliance with Vali's brother and rival, Sugriva.

4. In the *Ramayana* of Valmiki, the valorous monkey scout Hanuman is apprehended soon after locating Sita. Ravana orders his tail to be set on fire, but Hanuman escapes and with his burning tail sets the capital on fire.

How can people oppose the god Rama and still consider themselves Indian? That's just not possible! Shout it out so that the whole world can hear! It's not only India—the entire world knows that this country belongs to that supreme Lord Rama, king of Ayodhya. My fellow Rama devotees, political leaders like Chandrashekhar[5] tell us that we should build our temple elsewhere, as though it were possible simply to move our God's birthplace. I would say to him, "Chandrashekhar, are you able to trade in your father for someone else?" No, he can't just go out and get a new father. And we are supposed to change the birthplace of the Father of the World?

Other leaders say, "Do you have to build a temple there? How about installing a commemorative plaque or something?" Well, what the hell are we supposed to commemorate? That a certain plunderer named Babur invaded India? That he attacked us, and demolished our temple and with it our sense of self-respect? Is that what our leaders want to commemorate? * * * Some of your leaders actually do have eyes to see, and they agree that the birthplace of Rama belongs to the Hindus, but they are too afraid to speak up about it.

My brothers, it's time to get ready for action. These sages have come today to spur you to action. Those good-for-nothing cowards can't do anything to protect your India. We are waiting for brave men who will fight, who will be able to protect this country's pride and honor.

That is why I am telling you to bind yourselves together like fists. Your powers are too diffuse, you need to gather your forces. There are caste barriers among you—you must eradicate those. There are language and regional barriers—be rid of them. You have to bind yourselves together like fists, you have to protect your honor and your self-respect. * * *

We don't have a problem with those Muslims who love India, Muslims like Rahim or Raskhan.[6] We welcome them with open arms. But we will not tolerate the Baburs and the Aurangzebs.[7] This is the truth, I don't care how much it hurts, you must listen to it! Let it pierce you like an arrow in the heart! I don't care if this will make you angry, or make you break into a sweat. How long can we remain quiet and avoid confrontation? We are boiling over with rage—how long can we put up with this? We don't want anything to do with those hypocrites who have hacked off the arms of our motherland, who heap curses upon our Lord Rama and extol the glories of Babur the invader. There's no room in India for such as they. They should get out, this isn't their India. * * *

An election is around the corner. Suddenly you're going to see a lot of politicians claiming to be supporters of Rama and trying to garner votes on this issue. You're going to have to watch out for false supporters spewing slogans about Rama. In the *Ramayana* there was that false ascetic Kalanemi[8] who tried to kill Hanuman. That's what these fellows are like. * * *

Why are you so afraid of death? Death is something we're all going to have to face some day, there's no escaping that. What kind of death do you want, a dog's

5. The prime minister of India under the Janata Dal Party during 1990 and 1991.

6. Abdur Rahim Khankhana and Sujan Raskhan (late 16th and early 17th centuries) composed poetry in Hindi. Raskhan also composed verses in praise of the Hindu god Krishna.

7. Babur (1483–1530) was founder of the Mughal empire. Aurangzeb (r. 1658–1707) was the most orthodox-minded of the Mughal rulers and the most oppressive toward non-Muslim faiths.

8. A demon uncle of Ravana according to some *Ramayana* traditions.

death or a hero's death? Hindus aren't going to let their principles be mocked. It's time to forget about turning the other cheek. We've had enough of Hindu tolerance and pacifism. You're going to have to start fighting back.

This is the message that these holy men have come here to deliver. They have come to spur you to action. You must protect our motherland, and victory will be yours. We will not rest until we have built a magnificent temple at the site of Rama's birthplace. I'm not addressing this to the sons of Ravana, and for supporters of Rama there really isn't any need. But let me just ask everybody here to hold up their hands and to pledge an oath to Lord Rama.

We pledge ourselves to Lord Rama!
We pledge ourselves to Lord Rama!
We pledge ourselves to Lord Rama!
Victory to India!
Victory to Lord Rama!

Daya Pawar, Sambhaji Bhagat, and Anand Patwardhan: We Are Not Your Monkeys[1]

The rulers who controlled all knowledge

And claimed the *Ramayana*
to be India's history

Called us many names:

"Demons," "Low castes," "Untouchables"

But we were the aborigines of this land

Listen to our story

Today we call ourselves
Dalits—the oppressed

Once Aryans[2] on their horses
invaded this land

And we who were natives
became the displaced

1. Translated by Anand Patwardhan. While the *Ramayana* of Valmiki has offered influential models of conduct to generations of men and women, it has also at times been regarded with considerable suspicion and resentment. Its ideal of gender relationships, for example—exemplified in the fire ordeal Sita faces (see page 643) or, worse, her abandonment by Rama when rumors begin to circulate in Ayodhya about her chastity (in Book 7)—has been viewed as a distorted one, increasingly so in the contemporary world. (When Hindu refugee women from Sind who had been raped during the Partition of India in 1947 were abandoned on the streets of Bombay by their husbands "because that is what Rama would have done," a modern Marathi poet was moved to compose a new version of the *Ramayana* with a different ending.) Similarly, many historically oppressed communities in South Asia believe themselves to have been humiliatingly represented as the demons or animals of the tale. "We Are Not Your Monkeys" gives voice to this sentiment among today's Dalits (formerly known as "Untouchables") of the state of Maharashtra in western India. That Valmiki almost certainly had not intended any such simplistic identification is less important than the fact that people have often been made to feel he did. Something of this complex relationship between literature and power in a world of inequality was noted by critic Walter Benjamin when he observed that there is no document of civilization that is not at the same time a document of barbarism.

2. The Sanskrit term *arya* was typically applied to men of the upper social orders in early South Asia. It took on racial connotations in the works of 19th-century Orientalists and 20th-century fascists.

O Rama, O Rama!

You became the gods
And we the demons

You portrayed our Hanuman
as a monkey

O Rama, you representative
of Aryans

You enslaved us
to form a monkey army

Those you could not subjugate
you deemed as *Rakshasas*—demons

But we were the *Rakshaks*—protectors
of the forest

To keep your racial purity
you invented the hierarchy of caste

Through your "Laws of Manu"[3]
you trampled on the rights of women

You made your wife Sita undergo
An ordeal by fire to prove her chastity

Such was your male law
O Rama

When Shambuka the "untouchable"[4]
Tried to gain knowledge

You beheaded him O Rama

Thus did you crush those that tried
To rise above their caste

Days passed
Years and aeons went by

But our lives remained the same

We skin your cattle
So you can wear shoes

We clean your gutters
So you can stay clean

Do you ask then O Rama

What our caste is?
What our religion is?

3. An influential ancient work of Hindu customary law, the *Laws of Manu* is attributed in Hindu thought to one of the progenitors of the human race.

4. In the seventh book of Valmiki's *Ramayana,* Rama kills the low-caste Shambuka for engaging in ascetic practices reserved for the high-caste.

Independence dawned

And with it began the rule
of the Constitution

The author of the Constitution

Dr. B. R. Ambedkar[5]
himself born as an "untouchable"

Framed the Constitution
around secular ideals

The castle of caste privilege
Began to crumble

No longer could the elite

Skim the milk
of religious exploitation

But poverty grew
And to divert the attention of the poor

A new enemy was found

Muslims were targeted
And "taught a lesson"

To destroy Lanka, O Rama
You formed us into a monkey army

And today you want us
The working majority

To form a new monkey army
And attack Muslims

But be warned

Be warned you purveyors
Of self-serving religion

We will be your monkeys no more

We will sing songs of humanity

And we will make you human as well

We will make you human.

5. Bhimrao Ramji Ambedkar (1891–1956), scholar, social activist, and politician, helped draft India's constitution and was the preeminent voice of the Dalits against caste discrimination.

The Book of Songs

1000–600 B.C.E.

The *Book of Songs* (*Shi jing,* or Classic of Poetry), compiled by the sixth century B.C.E., is the oldest anthology in China, whose literary tradition begins with the lyric. According to one historical tradition, the poems were collected by Zhou dynasty officials as evidence for contemporary mores to be presented to the ruler, but the prevailing account of the text's compilation appears in the *Grand Scribe's Records* of Sima Qian. There we are told that it was edited by none other than Confucius himself, who selected its 305 songs from a larger group of over three thousand stored in the archives of the Zhou feudal states, edited their musical accompaniments (now lost), and arranged them in their present order. However unlikely, this attribution remained unquestioned until modern times, and already by the fourth century B.C.E. the anthology had been canonized as one of the five Confucian classics. This ensured the text's preservation, and its inclusion in the educational curriculum of the elite (more specifically, on the civil service examination), and brought a scholarly attention that generated many volumes of commentary over the ages.

The poems were most likely composed between 1000 and 600 B.C.E. Many appear to be simple folk songs, whereas others reveal a more aristocratic and literary origin, and some are clearly temple hymns to the dynasty's ruling house. All but six are anonymous, and the majority treat themes familiar to folk and ballad traditions worldwide: friendship, courtship, marriage, and death; planting, harvesting, hunting, and fishing; and the glories and sorrows of war. The natural images with which many poems open (sometimes repeated elsewhere) offer a cue to what follows, but their often enigmatic quality has elicited centuries of scholarly speculation. Unlike most early poetry in other cultures, the *Book of Songs* features a great deal of rhyme, and the most common form employs three stanzas of four (or six) four-syllable lines each.

The numbers assigned to the poems refer to their sequence in the standard edition from the second century B.C.E. The poems are grouped into four sections of varying size, of which the first and largest contains 160 "Airs of the States" (*Guo feng*). *Feng* literally means "wind" but can also denote "customs" and is closely related to a word meaning "to criticize," and the States represent fifteen of the Zhou feudal domains. These are among the latest of the poems in the anthology and among the most accessible; all but the last six included here are from this group. The next seventy-four poems, "Lesser Elegances" (*xiao ya*), treat similar subjects drawn from daily life but sometimes placed within a more elite context; poems 166, 189, and 234 belong to this section. The thirty-one "Greater Elegances" (*da ya*) that follow (including poems 238 and 245) are sometimes difficult to distinguish from the preceding group but tend to include the longest poems in the anthology, narratives of historical and legendary events and figures. Finally, the forty "Hymns" (*song*), of which 283 is an example, may be among the oldest works in the collection. They were said to have been used in ritual performances by the Zhou rulers and two other feudal courts; many lack both rhyme and divisions into stanzas.

Traditions of reading the *Book of Songs* are important for understanding not only the collection itself but also later presumptions about all literature, and poetry in particular. The *Songs* are the most frequently cited work in Confucius's *Analects,* and other early texts demonstrate that the poems were often quoted in political and diplomatic discussions to convey opinions obliquely but effectively. Such trust in the poems' didactic utility, coupled with the fact that some clearly are accounts of actual events, led early scholars to assume that the entire anthology was commenting either directly or indirectly on history. The premises for this belief are articulated most clearly in what is known as the "Great Preface" to the collection: poetry (or song, the two being interchangeable) expresses naturally and spontaneously what is in one's heart or mind, and the impulse arises from the external world of nature, society, and the body politic, which are linked by correlative networks. Any poetic expression could therefore be assumed to implicate something larger than the individual, construed as a response to a particular set of circumstances in a particular context. Thus poem 5, "Locusts," was read as praise of the Zhou queen, whose freedom from jealousy and willingness to allow the king other consorts produced, happily, a multitude of progeny. Such interpretations may represent far-fetched distortions of the poems' original import, but they also provided valuable explanations for often perplexing vignettes. These practices also dignified texts that might otherwise have been devalued or lost (much as allegory served the Hebrew Bible's *Song of Songs*), and they continued to shape the later poetic and critical tradition in profound ways.

The linguistic difficulty of the *Book of Songs* has challenged both traditional Chinese commentators and translators into Western languages. Arthur Waley's translations offer the best compromise between philological accuracy and poetic fluency, but they may be usefully compared with two alternatives. Swedish sinologist Bernhard Karlgren (1889–1978) translated the poems into philologically accurate prose. The poet Ezra Pound (1885–1972), who knew no Chinese but considered himself a Confucian, sought to highlight the resemblance of the *Songs* to English ballads and was said by T. S. Eliot to have been "the inventor of Chinese poetry for our time." Alternative versions by Karlgren and Pound are provided for poems 23 and 166.

from Book of Songs[1]

1: The Ospreys Cry

"Fair, fair," cry the ospreys
On the island in the river.
Lovely is this noble lady,
Fit bride for our lord.

In patches grows the water mallow;
To left and right one must seek it.
Shy was this noble lady;
Day and night he sought her.

Sought her and could not get her;
Day and night he grieved.
Long thoughts, oh, long unhappy thoughts,
Now on his back, now tossing on to his side.

In patches grows the water mallow;
To left and right one must gather it.
Shy is this noble lady;
With great zither and little we hearten her.

In patches grows the water mallow;
To left and right one must choose it.
Shy is this noble lady;
With bells and drums we will gladden her.

1. Translated by Arthur Waley.

5: Locusts

The locusts' wings say "throng, throng";
Well may your sons and grandsons
Be a host innumerable.

The locusts' wings say "bind, bind";
Well may your sons and grandsons
Continue in an endless line.

The locusts' wings say "join, join";[1]
Well may your sons and grandsons
Be forever at one.

20: Plop Fall the Plums

Plop fall the plums; but there are still seven.
Let those gentlemen that would court me
Come while it is lucky!

Plop fall the plums; there are still three.
Let any gentleman that would court me
Come before it is too late!

Plop fall the plums, in shallow baskets we lay them
Any gentleman who would court me
Had better speak while there is time.

23: In the Wilds Is a Dead Doe

In the wilds there is a dead doe;
With white rushes we cover her.
There was a lady longing for the spring;
A fair knight seduced her.

In the wood there is a clump of oaks,
And in the wilds a dead deer
With white rushes well bound;
There was a lady fair as jade.

"Heigh, not so hasty, not so rough;
Heigh, do not touch my handkerchief.
Take care, or the dog will bark."

RESONANCES

Translation by Bernhard Karlgren: In the wilds there is a dead deer

1. In the wilds there is a dead deer, with white grass one wraps it up; there is a girl having spring feelings, a fine gentleman entices her.—2. In the forest there are low shrubby trees, in the wilds there is a dead deer; with white grass one wraps it up and

1. The three noises that the locusts' wings make are being punned upon and interpreted as omens.

binds it; there is a girl like a jade.—3. Slowly! Gently! Do not move my kerchief; do not make the dog bark!

Translation by Ezra Pound: Lies a dead deer on younder plain

Lies a dead deer on younder plain
whom white grass covers,
A melancholy maid in spring
is luck
for
lovers.

Where the scrub elm skirts the wood,
be it not in white mat bound,
as a jewel flawless found,
dead as doe is maidenhood.

Hark!
Unhand my girdle-knot,
stay, stay, stay
or the dog
may
bark.

26: Cypress Boat[1]

Tossed is that cypress boat,
Wave-tossed it floats.
My heart is in turmoil, I cannot sleep.
But secret is my grief.
Wine I have, all things needful
For play, for sport.

My heart is not a mirror,
To reflect what others will.
Brothers too I have;
I cannot be snatched away.
But lo, when I told them of my plight
I found that they were angry with me.

My heart is not a stone;
It cannot be rolled.
My heart is not a mat;
It cannot be folded away.
I have borne myself correctly
In rites more than can be numbered.

My sad heart is consumed, I am harassed
By a host of small men.

1. Traditional commentators believe that this is a song of a woman being married against her will.

I have borne vexations very many,
Received insults not few.
In the still of night I brood upon it;
In the waking hours I rend my breast.

O sun, ah, moon,
Why are you changed and dim?
Sorrow clings to me
Like an unwashed dress.
In the still of night I brood upon it,
Long to take wing and fly away.

45: Cypress Boat

Unsteady is that cypress boat
In the middle of the river.
His two locks looped over his brow[1]
He swore that truly he was my comrade,
And till death would love no other.
Oh, mother, ah, Heaven,
That a man could be so false!

Unsteady is that boat of cypress-wood
By that river's side.
His two locks looped over his brow
He swore that truly he was my mate,
And till death would not fail me.
Oh, mother, ah, Heaven,
That a man could be so false!

76: I Beg of You, Zhong Zi

I beg of you, Zhong Zi,
Do not climb into our homestead,
Do not break the willows we have planted.
Not that I mind about the willows,
But I am afraid of my father and mother.
Zhong Zi I dearly love;
But of what my father and mother say
Indeed I am afraid.

I beg of you, Zhong Zi,
Do not climb over our wall,
Do not break the mulberry-trees we have planted.
Not that I mind about the mulberry-trees,
But I am afraid of my brothers.
Zhong Zi I dearly love;
But of what my brothers say
Indeed I am afraid.

1. A sign that he has not yet come of age.

I beg of you, Zhong Zi,
Do not climb into our garden,
Do not break the hard-wood we have planted.
Not that I mind about the hard-wood,
But I am afraid of what people will say.
Zhong Zi I dearly love;
But of all that people will say
Indeed I am afraid.

166: May Heaven Guard

May Heaven guard and keep you
In great security,
Make you staunch and hale;
What blessing not vouchsafed?
Give you much increase,
Send nothing but abundance.

May Heaven guard and keep you,
Cause your grain to prosper,
Send you nothing that is not good.
May you receive from Heaven a hundred boons,
May Heaven send down to you blessings so many
That the day is not long enough for them all.

May Heaven guard and keep you,
Cause there to be nothing in which you do not rise higher,
Like the mountains, like the uplands,
Like the ridges, the great ranges,
Like a stream coming down in flood;
In nothing not increased.
Lucky and pure are your viands of sacrifice
That you use in filial offering,
Offerings of invocation, gift-offerings, offering in dishes and offering of
  first-fruits
To dukes and former kings.
Those sovereigns say: "We give you
Myriad years of life, days unending."

The Spirits are good,
They will give you many blessings.
The common people are contented,
For daily they have their drink and food.
The thronging herd, the many clans
All side with you in deeds of power.

To be like the moon advancing to its full,
Like the sun climbing the sky,
Like the everlastingness of the southern hills,
Without failing or falling,
Like the pine-tree, the cypress in their verdure—
All these blessings may you receive!

RESONANCES

Translation by Bernhard Karlgen: Heaven protects and secures you

1. Heaven protects and secures you, doing it very solidly; it causes you to be richly endowed; what felicity is not heaped (on you); it causes you to have much (increase:) prosperity, so that there is nothing that is not (numerous:) abundant.—2. Heaven protects and secures you; it causes you to (cut:) reap your grain, so that to the last straw there is nothing that is not (proper:) good; you receive the hundred emoluments from Heaven, it sends down to you a far-reaching felicity; only the days are not sufficient (to hold so much blessing).—3. Heaven protects and secures you, so that there is nothing that does not rise prosperingly; like a mountain, like a hill, like a ridge, like a range, like a river at its highest flood, so that there is nothing that is not increased.—4. Auspicious and pure are your sacrificial wine and food; with them you make filial offerings; you perform summer, spring, winter and autumn sacrifices, to princes and former kings; the (dead) lords say: "We predict for you a myriad years of life, without limit."—5. The Spirits are good, they bestow upon you much felicity; the people are simple, daily they enjoy their drink and food; all the numerous (people of) the hundred clans everywhere practise your virtue.—6. Like the moon's advancing to the full, like the rising of the sun (a), like the longevity of the Southern mountains, which are never injured, never falling, like the luxuriance of the fir and the cypress, there is nothing that will not be (continued:) ever-lasting for you.

Translation by Ezra Pound: Heaven conserve thy course in quietness

Heaven conserve thy course in quietness,
Solid thy unity, thy weal endless
that all the crops increase and nothing lack
in any common house.

Heaven susteyne thy course in quietness
that thou be just in all, and reap
so, as it were at ease, that every day
seem festival.

Heaven susteyne thy course in quietness
To abound and rise as mountain hill and range
constant as rivers flow that all augment
steady th' increase in ever cyclic change.

Pure be the victuals of thy sacrifice
throughout the year as autumns move to springs,
above the fane to hear "ten thousand years"
spoke by the manes of foregone dukes and kings.

Spirits of air assign felicity:
thy folk be honest, in food and drink delight;
dark-haired the hundred tribes concord
in act born of thy true insight.

As moon constant in phase; as sun to rise;
as the south-hills nor crumble nor decline;

as pine and cypress evergreen the year
be thy continuing line.

189: The Beck

Ceaseless flows that beck,
Far stretch the southern hills.
May you be sturdy as the bamboo,
May you flourish like the pine,
May elder brother and younger brother
Always love one another,
Never do evil to one another.

To give continuance to foremothers and forefathers
We build a house, many hundred cubits of wall;
To south and west its doors.
Here shall we live, here rest,
Here laugh, here talk.

We bind the frames, creak, creak;
We hammer the mud, tap, tap,
That it may be a place where wind and rain cannot enter,
Nor birds and rats get in,
But where our lord may dwell.

As a halberd, even so plumed,
As an arrow, even so sharp,
As a bird, even so soaring,
As wings, even so flying
Are the halls to which our lord ascends.

Well leveled is the courtyard,
Firm are the pillars,
Cheerful are the rooms by day,
Softly gloaming by night,
A place where our lord can be at peace.

Below, the rush-mats; over them the bamboo-mats.
Comfortably he sleeps,
He sleeps and wakes
And interprets his dreams.
"Your lucky dreams, what were they?"
"They were of black bears and brown,
Of serpents and snakes."

The diviner thus interprets it:
"Black bears and brown
Mean men-children.
Snakes and serpents
Mean girl-children."

So he bears a son,
And puts him to sleep upon a bed,
Clothes him in robes,
Gives him a jade scepter to play with.
The child's howling is very lusty;
In red greaves shall he flare,
Be lord and king of house and home.
Then he bears a daughter,

And puts her upon the ground,
Clothes her in swaddling-clothes,
Gives her a loom-whorl to play with.
For her no decorations, no emblems;
Her only care, the wine and food,
And how to give no trouble to father and mother.

234: What Plant Is Not Faded?

What plant is not faded?
What day do we not march?
What man is not taken
To defend the four bounds?

What plant is not wilting?
What man is not taken from his wife?
Alas for us soldiers,
Treated as though we were not fellow-men!

Are we buffaloes, are we tigers
That our home should be these desolate wilds?
Alas for us soldiers,
Neither by day nor night can we rest!

The fox bumps and drags
Through the tall, thick grass.
Inch by inch move our barrows
As we push them along the track.

238: Oak Clumps

Thick grow the oak clumps;
We make firewood of them, we stack them.
Great is the magnificence of the lord king;
On either hand are those that speed for him.

Great is the magnificence of the lord king;
On either hand are those that hold up scepters before him,
Hold up scepters in solemn state,
As befits doughty knights.

Spurt goes that boat on the Jing;
A host of oarsmen rows it.
When the King of Zhou goes forth,

His six armies are with him.

How it stands out, the Milky Way,
Making a blazon in the sky!
Long life to the King of Zhou,
And a portion for his people!

Chiseled and carved are his emblems,
Of bronze and jade are they made.
Ceaseless are the labors of our king
Fashioning the network of all the lands.

245: Birth to the People

She who in the beginning gave birth to the people,
This was Jiang Yuan.
How did she give birth to the people?
Well she sacrificed and prayed
That she might no longer be childless.
She trod on the big toe of God's footprint,
Was accepted and got what she desired.
Then in reverence, then in awe
She gave birth, she nurtured;
And this was Hou Ji.° *"Lord Millet"*

Indeed, she had fulfilled her months,
And her first-born came like a lamb
With no bursting or rending,
With no hurt or harm.
To make manifest His magic power
God on high gave her ease.
So blessed were her sacrifice and prayer
That easily she bore her child.

Indeed, they[1] put it in a narrow lane;
But oxen and sheep tenderly cherished it.
Indeed, they put it in a far-off wood;
But it chanced that woodcutters came to this wood.
Indeed, they put it on the cold ice;
But the birds covered it with their wings.
The birds at last went away,
And Hou Ji began to wail.

Truly far and wide
His voice was very loud.
Then sure enough he began to crawl;
Well he straddled, well he reared,
To reach food for his mouth.
He planted large beans;

1. The ballad does not tell us who exposed the child. According to one version it was the mother herself; according to another, her husband [Translator's note].

His beans grew fat and tall.
His paddy-lines were close set,
His hemp and wheat grew thick,
His young gourds teemed.

Truly Hou Ji's husbandry
Followed the way that had been shown.
He cleared away the thick grass,
He planted the yellow crop.
It failed nowhere, it grew thick,
It was heavy, it was tall,
It sprouted, it eared,
It was firm and good,
It nodded, it hung—
He made house and home in Tai.

Indeed, the lucky grains were sent down to us,
The black millet, the double-kerneled,
Millet pink-sprouted and white.
Far and wide the black and the double-kerneled
He reaped and acred;
Far and wide the millet pink and white
He carried in his arms, he bore on his back,
Brought them home, and created the sacrifice.

Indeed, what are they, our sacrifices?
We pound the grain, we bale it out,
We sift, we tread,
We wash it—soak, soak;
We boil it all steamy.
Then with due care, due thought
We gather southernwood, make offering of fat,
Take lambs for the rite of expiation,
We roast, we broil,
To give a start to the coming year.

High we load the stands,
The stands of wood and of earthenware.
As soon as the smell rises
God on high is very pleased:
"What smell is this, so strong and good?"
Hou Ji founded the sacrifices,
And without blemish or flaw
They have gone on till now.

283: So They Appeared

So they appeared before their lord the king
To get from him their emblems,
Dragon-banners blazing bright,
Tuneful bells tinkling,

Bronze-knobbed reins jangling—
The gifts shone with glorious light.
Then they showed them to their shining ancestors
Piously, making offering,
That they might be vouchsafed long life,
Everlastingly be guarded.
Oh, a mighty store of blessings!
Glorious and mighty, those former princes and lords
Who secure us with many blessings,
Through whose bright splendors
We greatly prosper.

Confucius

551–479 B.C.E.

"Ever since man came into this world, there has never been one greater than Confucius." So declared the fourth-century B.C.E. thinker Mencius, who developed his predecessor's key ideas in ways that would prove instrumental in securing their influence throughout the course of Chinese history. About this great man himself, however, we know remarkably little. Confucius lived during the waning years of the Zhou dynasty in China, when the ruling house had lost virtually all of its power to a ravenous set of competing kingdoms headed by more or less distant relatives. Warfare, economic growth, and social change had destabilized social and political structures and the language that had come to justify them, putting into question the actual and the conceptual bases of received authority.

Confucius probably belonged to the lower ranks of a hereditary nobility whose status was in jeopardy; he was a native of the state of Lu, which supported the legitimacy and rituals of the Zhou rulers. He attributed the social chaos of his time to a falling away from these practices and devoted his life to the attempt to restore them. Failing to secure appointment as a political counselor despite extensive travels to one feudal state after another, he settled for a job as a professional teacher, probably China's first, back home in Lu. *The Analects* (*Lun yu*), best understood as "selected sayings," comprise quotations, conversations, and anecdotes often centering on his response to a specific question. Compiled by multiple generations of later students, it has come down to us in twenty sections or books, of which 3–8 and 11–15 are agreed by scholars to be the oldest and 16–20 the newest. Loosely organized at best, the text contains occasionally repeated passages and material that might even be considered anti-Confucian. By the first century B.C.E., however, *The Analects* were taken as the key to the thoughts of Confucius, who had become identified as the fundamental shaper and transmitter of the cultural heritage.

Obsessed with the prevailing chaos around him, Confucius sought a remedy in a renewal of values and behavior embodied for him in an idealized vision of the founders of the Zhou dynasty. Followers of Confucius were to become known as *ru,* a term evoking a respect for traditional scholarship and ritual. He explicitly disavowed any claims to being an innovator, but many implications of his teachings were in fact quite novel. He articulated his ideas within the context of human relationships, both large and small. Although clearly mindful of notions of heaven and destiny that in earlier eras were probably associated with divine or cosmic forces, Confucius focused not on "gods and spirits" but rather on the realm of the concrete and human. And rather than consider morality in the abstract, he sought to explicate the actions of a specific individual in a particular context. For him, principles of mutual respect and obligation rooted in the family were extended to the community and the body politic, creating a social order consisting of a specific set of appropriate roles, a hierarchical relationship among them, and a governing code of conduct. A key concept is that of the *junzi,* or "gentleman," a term that had denoted social nobility but that Confucius transformed into a state of moral excellence that is attainable, in principle, by almost anyone. Equally important is the term *ren,* translated here as "humanity" and "goodness," which is rooted etymologically in a notion of "human-heartedness," or what it means to be one human being associating with another. Ethical behavior is grounded in a refusal to do to another what one would not want done to oneself and is manifested in respect for one's elders and observance of ritual decorum. It can be learned, cultivated, performed, and, ultimately, perfected when precept and behavior become one.

Traditions (now largely discounted) linked Confucius with the compilation of the Five Classics that became identified as canonical: the *Book of Songs, Book of Documents, Book of Changes,* the *Records of Rites,* and the *Spring and Autumn Annals* (a chronicle of Confucius's home state of Lu). By the beginning of the second millennium, *The Analects* had joined them on the classical curriculum for the imperial civil service examination, the most important entry into the career of choice for the literate elite in the government bureaucracy. Rote, uncomprehending memorization of the text as a child would be followed by a lifetime of reflection and, even more important, action upon its meaning. That generations of scholars in China were to aspire to this goal, seeing the educated person as morally superior but obliged to serve others, is owing in no small measure to the lessons of the text itself.

from The Analects[1]

1.1. The Master[2] said: "To learn something and then to put it into practice at the right time: is this not a joy? To have friends coming from afar: is this not a delight? Not to be upset when one's merits are ignored: is this not the mark of a gentleman?"

1.2. Master You[3] said: "A man who respects his parents and his elders would hardly be inclined to defy his superiors. A man who is not inclined to defy his superiors will never foment a rebellion. A gentleman works at the root. Once the root is secured, the Way unfolds. To respect parents and elders is the root of humanity."

1.3. The Master said: "Clever talk and affected manners are seldom signs of goodness."

1.4. Master Zeng[4] said: "I examine myself three times a day. When dealing on behalf of others, have I been trustworthy? In intercourse with my friends, have I been faithful? Have I practiced what I was taught?"

1.5. The Master said: "To govern a state of middle size, one must dispatch business with dignity and good faith; be thrifty and love all men; mobilize the people only at the right times."

1.6. The Master said: "At home, a young man must respect his parents; abroad, he must respect his elders. He should talk little, but with good faith; love all people,

1. Translated by Simon Leys.
2. "The Master" is Confucius himself.
3. Confucius's disciple Zhong You (d. 480 B.C.E.), also known as Zilu.
4. Another disciple, Zeng Can, who played a prominent role in early Confucianism.

but associate with the virtuous. Having done this, if he still has energy to spare, let him study literature."

1.16. The Master said: "Don't worry if people don't recognize your merits; worry that you may not recognize theirs."

2.1 The Master said: "He who rules by virtue is like the polestar, which remains unmoving in its mansion while all the other stars revolve respectfully around it."

2.3. The Master said: "Lead them by political maneuvers, restrain them with punishments: the people will become cunning and shameless. Lead them by virtue, restrain them with ritual: they will develop a sense of shame and a sense of participation."

2.4. The Master said: "At fifteen, I set my mind upon learning. At thirty, I took my stand. At forty, I had no doubts. At fifty, I knew the will of Heaven. At sixty, my ear was attuned. At seventy, I follow all the desires of my heart without breaking any rule."

2.5. Lord Meng Yi asked about filial piety. The Master said: "Never disobey."

As Fan Chi was driving him in his chariot, the Master told him: "Meng Yi asked me about filial piety and I replied: 'Never disobey.'" Fan Chi said: "What does that mean?" The Master said: "When your parents are alive, serve them according to the ritual. When they die, bury them according to the ritual, make sacrifices to them according to the ritual."

2.6. Lord Meng Wu asked about filial piety. The Master said: "The only time a dutiful son ever makes his parents worry is when he is sick."

2.7. Ziyou[5] asked about filial piety. The Master said: "Nowadays people think they are dutiful sons when they feed their parents. Yet they also feed their dogs and horses. Unless there is respect, where is the difference?"

2.8. Zixia[6] asked about filial piety. The Master said: "It is the attitude that matters. If young people merely offer their services when there is work to do, or let their elders drink and eat when there is wine and food, how could this ever pass as filial piety?"

2.9. The Master said: "I can talk all day to Yan Hui[7]—he never raises any objection, he looks stupid. Yet, observe him when he is on his own: his actions fully reflect what he learned. Oh no, Hui is not stupid!"

2.11. The Master said: "He who by revising the old knows the new, is fit to be a teacher."

2.12. The Master said: "A gentleman is not a pot."[8]

5. The disciple Yan Yan, about whom little is known except that he was one of Confucius's younger students.

6. Bu Shang, a disciple who played a major role in the transmission of the Confucian classics.

7. Also known as Yan Yuan, one of Confucius's most gifted and favorite disciples.

8. That is, he is not a specialist, in the way a vessel is designed for one specific purpose.

2.13. Zigong[9] asked about the true gentleman. The Master said: "He preaches only what he practices."

2.14. The Master said: "The gentleman considers the whole rather than the parts. The small man considers the parts rather than the whole."

2.15. The Master said: "To study without thinking is futile. To think without studying is dangerous."

2.16. The Master said: "To attack a question from the wrong end—this is harmful indeed."

2.17. The Master said: "Zilu, I am going to teach you what knowledge is. To take what you know for what you know, and what you do not know for what you do not know, that is knowledge indeed."

2.18. Zizhang[1] was studying in the hope of securing an official position. The Master said: "Collect much information, put aside what is doubtful, repeat cautiously the rest; then you will seldom say something wrong. Make many observations, leave aside what is suspect, apply cautiously the rest; then you will seldom have cause for regret. With few mistakes in what you say and few regrets for what you do, your career is made."

2.19. Duke Ai asked: "What should I do to win the hearts of the people?" Confucius replied: "Raise the straight and set them above the crooked, and you will win the hearts of the people. If you raise the crooked and set them above the straight, the people will deny you their support."

2.20. Lord Ji Kang asked: "What should I do in order to make the people respectful, loyal, and zealous?" The Master said: "Approach them with dignity and they will be respectful. Be yourself a good son and a kind father, and they will be loyal. Raise the good and train the incompetent, and they will be zealous."

4.1. The Master said: "It is beautiful to live amidst humanity. To choose a dwelling place destitute of humanity is hardly wise."

4.3. The Master said: "Only a good man can love people and can hate people."

4.4. The Master said: "Seeking to achieve humanity leaves no room for evil."

4.5. The Master said: "Riches and rank are what every man craves; yet if the only way to obtain them goes against his principles, he should desist from such a pursuit. Poverty and obscurity are what every man hates; yet if the only escape from them goes against his principles, he should accept his lot. If a gentleman forsakes humanity, how can he make a name for himself? Never for a moment does a

9. Duanmu Si, the only one of the three best-known disciples to survive Confucius. He was a successful merchant and diplomat.

1. Zhuansun Shi, another disciple about whom little is known.

gentleman part from humanity; he clings to it through trials, he clings to it through tribulations."

4.6. The Master said: "I have never seen a man who truly loved goodness and hated evil. Whoever truly loves goodness would put nothing above it; whoever truly hates evil would practice goodness in such a way that no evil could enter him. Has anyone ever devoted all his strength to goodness just for one day? No one ever has, and yet it is not for want of strength—there may be people who do not have even the small amount of strength it takes, but I have never seen any."

4.8. The Master said: "In the morning hear the Way; in the evening die content."

4.9. The Master said: "A scholar sets his heart on the Way; if he is ashamed of his shabby clothes and coarse food, he is not worth listening to."

4.10. The Master said: "In the affairs of the world, a gentleman has no parti pris: he takes the side of justice."

4.14. The Master said: "Do not worry if you are without a position; worry lest you do not deserve a position. Do not worry if you are not famous; worry lest you do not deserve to be famous."

4.15. The Master said: "Shen, my doctrine has one single thread running through it." Master Zeng Shen replied: "Indeed."

The Master left. The other disciples asked: "What did he mean?" Master Zeng said: "The doctrine of the Master is: Loyalty and reciprocity, and that is all."

4.16. The Master said: "A gentleman considers what is just; a small man considers what is expedient."

4.18. The Master said: "When you serve your parents, you may gently remonstrate with them. If you see that they do not take your advice, be all the more respectful and do not contradict them. Let not your efforts turn to bitterness."

4.19. The Master said: "While your parents are alive, do not travel afar. If you have to travel, you must leave an address."

4.20. The Master said: "If three years after his father's death, the son does not alter his father's ways, he is a good son indeed."

4.21. The Master said: "Always keep in mind the age of your parents. Let this thought be both your joy and your worry."

4.25. The Master said: "Virtue is not solitary; it always has neighbors."

5.7. The Master said: "The Way does not prevail. I shall take a raft and put out to sea. I am sure Zilu will accompany me." Hearing this, Zilu was overjoyed. The Master said: "Zilu is bolder than I. Still, where would we get the timber for our craft?"

5.10. Zai Yu[2] was sleeping during the day. The Master said: "Rotten wood cannot be carved; dung walls cannot be troweled. What is the use of scolding him?"

The Master said: "There was a time when I used to listen to what people said and trusted that they would act accordingly, but now I listen to what they say and watch what they do. It is Zai Yu who made me change."

5.11. The Master said: "I have never seen a man who was truly steadfast." Someone replied: "Shen Cheng?" The Master said: "Shen Cheng is driven by his desires. How could he be called steadfast?"

5.14. When Zilu had learned one thing, his only fear was that he might learn another one before he had the chance to practice the first.

5.20. Lord Ji Wen always thought thrice before acting. Hearing this, the Master said: "Twice is enough."

5.27. The Master said: "Alas, I have never seen a man capable of seeing his own faults and of exposing them in the tribunal of his heart."

5.28. The Master said: "In a hamlet of ten houses, you will certainly find people as loyal and faithful as I, but you will not find one man who loves learning as much as I do."

6.3. Duke Ai asked: "Which of the disciples has a love of learning?" Confucius replied: "There was Yan Hui who loved learning; he never vented his frustrations upon others; he never made the same mistake twice. Alas, his allotted span of life was short: he is dead. Now, for all I know, there is no one with such a love of learning."

6.11. The Master said: "How admirable was Yan Hui! A handful of rice to eat, a gourd of water for drink, a hovel for your shelter—no one would endure such misery, yet Yan Hui's joy remained unaltered. How admirable was Yan Hui!"

6.17. The Master said: "Who would leave a house without using the door? Why do people seek to walk outside the Way?"

6.18. The Master said: "When nature prevails over culture, you get a savage; when culture prevails over nature, you get a pedant. When nature and culture are in balance, you get a gentleman."

6.23. The Master said: "The wise find joy on the water, the good find joy in the mountains. The wise are active, the good are quiet. The wise are joyful, the good live long."

6.27. The Master said: "A gentleman enlarges his learning through literature and restrains himself with ritual; therefore, he is not likely to go wrong."

2. Also known as Zai Wo, a disciple who tended to disappoint Confucius.

6.29. The Master said: "The moral power of the Middle Way is supreme, and yet it is not commonly found among the people anymore."

7.1. The Master said: "I transmit, I invent nothing. I trust and love the past. In this, I dare to compare myself to our venerable Peng."

7.7. The Master said: "I never denied my teaching to anyone who sought it, even if he was too poor to offer more than a token present for his tuition."

7.8. The Master said: "I enlighten only the enthusiastic; I guide only the fervent. After I have lifted up one corner of a question, if the student cannot discover the other three, I do not repeat."

7.12. The Master said: "If seeking wealth were a decent pursuit, I too would seek it, even if I had to work as a janitor. As it is, I'd rather follow my inclinations."

7.13. Matters which the Master approached with circumspection: fasting; war; illness.

7.14. When the Master was in Qi, he heard the Coronation Hymn of Shun. For three months, he forgot the taste of meat. He said: "I never imagined that music could reach such a point."

7.15. Ran Qiu[3] said: "Does our Master support the Duke of Wei?" Zigong said: "Well, I am going to ask him."

Zigong went in and asked Confucius: "What sort of people were Boyi and Shuqi?"—"They were virtuous men of old."—"Did they complain?"—"They sought goodness, they got goodness. Why should they have complained?"

Zigong left and said to Ran Qiu: "Our Master does not support the Duke of Wei."[4]

7.18. Occasions when the Master did not use dialect: when reciting the *Poems* and the *Documents,* and when performing ceremonies. In all these occasions, he used the correct pronunciation.

7.19. The Governor of She asked Zilu about Confucius. Zilu did not reply. The Master said: "Why did you not say 'He is the sort of man who, in his enthusiasm, forgets to eat, in his joy forgets to worry, and who ignores the approach of old age'?"

7.20. The Master said: "For my part, I am not endowed with innate knowledge. I am simply a man who loves the past and who is diligent in investigating it."

7.21. The Master never talked of: miracles; violence; disorders; spirits.

3. Another disciple, also known as Ran You.

4. The Duke of Wei had taken power after the death of his grandfather when his father was forced to flee the state after a failed attempt to kill his own father's notorious wife. The Duke's father was awaiting an opportunity to oust his son. Boyi and Shuqi were sons, of the rater of Ku-chu who refused to quarrel over their father's throne.

7.22. The Master said: "Put me in the company of any two people at random—they will invariably have something to teach me. I can take their qualities as a model and their defects as a warning."

7.23. The Master said: "Heaven vested me with moral power. What do I have to fear from Huan Tui?"[5]

7.26. The Master said: "A saint, I cannot hope to meet. I would be content if only I could meet a gentleman."

The Master said: "A perfect man, I cannot hope to meet. I would be content if only I could meet a principled man. When Nothing pretends to be Something, Emptiness pretends to be Fullness, and Penury pretends to be Affluence, it is hard to have principles."

7.29. The people of Huxiang were deaf to all teaching; but a boy came to visit the Master. The disciples were perplexed. The Master said: "To approve his visit does not mean approving what he does besides. Why be so finicky? When a man makes himself clean before a visit, we appreciate his cleanliness, we do not endorse his past or his future."

7.30. The Master said: "Is goodness out of reach? As soon as I long for goodness, goodness is at hand."

7.34. The Master said: "I make no claims to wisdom or to human perfection—how would I dare? Still, my aim remains unflagging and I never tire of teaching people." Gongxi Chi[6] said: "This is precisely what we disciples fail to emulate."

7.35. The Master was severely ill. Zilu asked leave to pray. The Master said: "Is there such a practice?" Zilu said: "Oh yes, and the invocation goes like this: 'We pray you, Spirits from above and Spirits from below.'" The Master said: "In that case, I have been praying for a long time already."

8.4. Master Zeng was ill. Lord Mengjing came to visit him. Master Zeng said: "When a bird is about to die, his song is sad; when a man is about to die, his words are true. In following the Way, a gentleman pays special attention to three things: in his attitude, he eschews rashness and arrogance; in his expression, he clings to good faith; in his speech, he eschews vulgarity and nonsense. As to the details of liturgy, leave these to the sextons."

8.9. The Master said: "You can make the people follow the Way, you cannot make them understand it."

8.17. The Master said: "Learning is like a chase in which, as you fail to catch up, you fear to lose what you have already gained."

5. Tradition has it that this was said when Huan Tui, minister of war in the state of Song, attempted to kill Confucius.

6. Also known as Gongxi Hua, another disciple who was said to have been in charge of Confucius's funeral.

9.2. A man from Daxiang said: "Your Confucius is really great! With his vast learning, he has still not managed to excel in any particular field." The Master heard of this and said to his disciples: "Which skill should I cultivate? Shall I take up charioteering? Shall I take up archery? All right, I shall take up charioteering."

9.4. The Master absolutely eschewed four things: capriciousness, dogmatism, willfulness, self-importance.

9.5. The Master was trapped in Kuang. He said: "King Wen is dead; is civilization not resting now on me? If Heaven intends civilization to be destroyed, why was it vested in me? If Heaven does not intend civilization to be destroyed, what should I fear from the people of Kuang?"

9.11. Yan Hui said with a sigh: "The more I contemplate it, the higher it is; the deeper I dig into it, the more it resists; I saw it in front of me, and then suddenly it was behind me. Step by step, our Master really knows how to entrap people. He stimulates me with literature, he restrains me with ritual. Even if I wanted to stop, I could not. Just as all my resources are exhausted, the goal is towering right above me; I long to embrace it, but cannot find the way."

9.13. Zigong said: "If you had a precious piece of jade, would you hide it safely in a box, or would you try to sell it for a good price?" The Master said: "I would sell it! I would sell it! All I am waiting for is the right offer."

9.14. The Master wanted to settle among the nine barbarian tribes of the East. Someone said: "It is wild in those parts. How would you cope?" The Master said: "How could it be wild, once a gentleman has settled there?"

9.16. The Master said: "I have never found it difficult to serve my superiors abroad and my elders at home; or to bury the dead with due reverence; or to hold my wine."

9.17. The Master stood by a river and said: "Everything flows like this, without ceasing, day and night."

9.18. The Master said: "I have never seen anyone who loved virtue as much as sex."

9.20. The Master said: "What was unique in Yan Hui was his capacity for attention whenever one spoke to him."

9.21. The Master said of Yan Hui: "Alas, I watched his progress, but did not see him reach the goal."

9.22. The Master said: "There are shoots that bear no flower, and there are flowers that bear no fruit."

9.24. The Master said: "How could words of admonition fail to win our assent? Yet the main thing should be actually to amend our conduct. How could words of praise fail to delight us? Yet the main thing should be actually to understand their purpose. Some people show delight but no understanding, or they assent without changing their ways—I really don't know what to do with them."

9.29. The Master said: "The wise are without perplexity; the good are without sorrow; the brave are without fear."

9.30. The Master said: "There are people with whom you may share information, but not share the Way. There are people with whom you may share the Way, but not share a commitment. There are people with whom you may share a commitment, but not share counsel."

9.31.

> The cherry tree
> Waves its blossoms.
> It is not that I do not think of you
> But your house is so far away!

The Master said: "He does not really love her; if he did, would he mind the distance?"

11.10. Yan Hui died. The Master wailed wildly. His followers said: "Master, such grief is not proper." The Master said: "In mourning such a man, what sort of grief would be proper?"

11.11. Yan Hui died. The disciples wanted to give him a grand burial. The Master said: "This is not right."

The disciples gave him a grand burial. The Master said: "Yan Hui treated me as his father, and yet I was not given the chance to treat him as my son. This is not my fault, but yours, my friends."

11.12. Zilu asked how to serve the spirits and gods. The Master said: "You are not yet able to serve men, how could you serve the spirits?"

Zilu said: "May I ask you about death?" The Master said: "You do not yet know life, how could you know death?"

11.22. Zilu asked: "Should I practice at once what I have just learned?" The Master said: "Your father and your elder brother are still alive; how could you practice at once what you have just learned?"

Ran Qiu asked: "Should I practice at once what I have just learned? The Master said: "Practice it at once."

Gongxi Chi said: "When Zilu asked if he should practice at once what he had just learned, you told him to consult first with his father and elder brother. When Ran Qiu asked if he should practice at once what he had just learned, you told him to practice it at once. I am confused; may I ask you to explain?" The Master said: "Ran Qiu is slow, therefore I push him; Zilu has energy for two, therefore I hold him back."

12.1. Yan Hui asked about humanity. The Master said: "The practice of humanity comes down to this: tame the self and restore the rites. Tame the self and restore the rites for but one day, and the whole world will rally to your humanity. The practice of humanity comes from the self, not from anyone else."

Yan Hui said: "May I ask which steps to follow?" The Master said: "Observe the rites in this way: don't look at anything improper; don't listen to anything improper; don't say anything improper; don't do anything improper."

Yan Hui said: "I may not be clever, but with your permission, I shall endeavor to do as you have said."

12.2. Ran Yong asked about humanity. The Master said: "When abroad, behave as if in front of an important guest. Lead the people as if performing a great ceremony. What you do not wish for yourself, do not impose upon others. Let no resentment enter public affairs; let no resentment enter private affairs."

Ran Yong said: "I may not be clever, but with your permission I shall endeavor to do as you have said."

12.5. Sima Niu[7] was grieving: "All men have brothers; I alone have none." Zixia said: "I have heard this: life and death are decreed by fate, riches and honors are allotted by Heaven. Since a gentleman behaves with reverence and diligence, treating people with deference and courtesy, all within the Four Seas are his brothers. How could a gentleman ever complain that he has no brothers?"

12.7. Zigong asked about government. The Master said: "Sufficient food, sufficient weapons, and the trust of the people." Zigong said: "If you had to do without one of these three, which would you give up?"—"Weapons."—"If you had to do without one of the remaining two, which would you give up?"—"Food; after all, everyone has to die eventually. But without the trust of the people, no government can stand."

12.10. Zizhang asked how to accumulate moral power and how to recognize emotional incoherence. The Master said: "Put loyalty and faith above everything, and follow justice. That is how one accumulates moral power. When you love someone, you wish him to live; when you hate someone, you wish him to die. Now, if you simultaneously wish him to live and to die, this is an instance of incoherence."

> If not for the sake of wealth.
> Then for the sake of change . . .

12.11. Duke Jing of Qi asked Confucius about government. Confucius replied: "Let the lord be a lord; the subject a subject; the father a father; the son a son." The Duke said: "Excellent! If indeed the lord is not a lord, the subject not a subject, the father not a father, the son not a son, I could be sure of nothing anymore—not even of my daily food."

12.18. Lord Ji Kang was troubled by burglars. He consulted with Confucius. Confucius replied: "If you yourself were not covetous, they would not rob you, even if you paid them to."

7. A brother of Huan Tui, who made an attempt on Confucius's life.

12.19. Lord Ji Kang asked Confucius about government, saying: "Suppose I were to kill the bad to help the good: how about that?" Confucius replied: "You are here to govern; what need is there to kill? If you desire what is good, the people will be good. The moral power of the gentleman is wind, the moral power of the common man is grass. Under the wind, the grass must bend."

13.3. Zilu asked: "If the ruler of Wei were to entrust you with the government of the country, what would be your first initiative?" The Master said: "It would certainly be to rectify the names." Zilu said: "Really? Isn't this a little farfetched? What is this rectification for?" The Master said: "How boorish can you get! Whereupon a gentleman is incompetent, thereupon he should remain silent. If the names are not correct, language is without an object. When language is without an object, no affair can be effected. When no affair can be effected, rites and music wither. When rites and music wither, punishments and penalties miss their target. When punishments and penalties miss their target, the people do not know where they stand. Therefore, whatever a gentleman conceives of, he must be able to say; and whatever he says, he must be able to do. In the matter of language, a gentleman leaves nothing to chance."

13.9. The Master was on his way to Wei, and Ran Qiu was driving. The Master said: "So many people!" Ran Qiu said: "Once the people are many, what next should be done?"—"Enrich them."—"Once they are rich, what next should be done?"—"Educate them."

13.10. The Master said: "If a ruler could employ me, in one year I would make things work, and in three years the results would show."

13.11. The Master said: "'When good men have been running the country for a hundred years, cruelty can be overcome, and murder extirpated.' How true is this saying!"

13.15. Duke Ding asked: "Is there one single maxim that could ensure the prosperity of a country?" Confucius replied: "Mere words could not achieve this. There is this saying, however: 'It is difficult to be a prince, it is not easy to be a subject.' A maxim that could make the ruler understand the difficulty of his task would come close to ensuring the prosperity of the country."

"Is there one single maxim that could ruin a country?"

Confucius replied: "Mere words could not achieve this. There is this saying, however: 'The only pleasure of being a prince is never having to suffer contradiction.' If you are right and no one contradicts you, that's fine; but if you are wrong and no one contradicts you—is this not almost a case of 'one single maxim that could ruin a country'?"

13.20. Zigong asked: "How does one deserve to be called a gentleman?" The Master said: "He who behaves with honor, and, being sent on a mission to the four corners of the world, does not bring disgrace to his lord, deserves to be called a gentleman."

"And next to that, if I may ask?"

"His relatives praise his filial piety and the people of his village praise the way he respects the elders."

"And next to that, if I may ask?"

"His word can be trusted; whatever he undertakes, he brings to completion. In this, he may merely show the obstinacy of a vulgar man; still, he should probably qualify as a gentleman of lower category."

"In this respect, how would you rate our present politicians?"

"Alas! These puny creatures are not even worth mentioning!"

13.24. Zigong asked: "What would you think of a man, if all the people in his village liked him?" The Master said: "This is not enough."—"And what if all the people in the village disliked him?"—"This is not enough. It would be better if the good people in the village were to like him, and the bad people to dislike him."

13.25. The Master said: "It is easy to work for a gentleman, but not easy to please him. Try to please him by immoral means, and he will not be pleased; but he never demands anything that is beyond your capacity. It is not easy to work for a vulgar man, but easy to please him. Try to please him, even by immoral means, and he will be pleased; but his demands know no limits."

13.26. The Master said: "A gentleman shows authority, but no arrogance. A vulgar man shows arrogance, but no authority."

14.4. The Master said: "A virtuous man is always of good counsel; a man of good counsel is not always virtuous. A good man is always brave: a brave man is not always good."

14.6. The Master said: "Gentlemen may not always achieve the fullness of humanity. Small men never achieve the fullness of humanity."

14.23. The Master said: "A gentleman reaches up. A vulgar man reaches down."

14.24. The Master said: "In the old days, people studied to improve themselves. Now they study in order to impress others."

14.27. The Master said: "A gentleman would be ashamed should his deeds not match his words."

14.28. The Master said: "A gentleman abides by three principles which I am unable to follow: his humanity knows no anxiety; his wisdom knows no hesitation; his courage knows no fear." Zigong said: "Master, you have just drawn your own portrait."

14.29. Zigong was criticizing other people. The Master said: "Zigong must have already reached perfection, which affords him a leisure I do not possess."

14.30. The Master said: "It is not your obscurity that should distress you, but your incompetence."

14.35. The Master said: "No one understands me!" Zigong said: "Why is it that no one understands you?" The Master said: "I do not accuse Heaven, nor do I blame men; here below I am learning, and there above I am being heard. If I am understood, it must be by Heaven."

14.38. Zilu stayed for the night at the Stone Gate. The gatekeeper said: "Where are you from?" Zilu said: "I am from Confucius's household."—"Oh, is that the one who keeps pursuing what he knows is impossible?"

15.16. The Master said: "With those who cannot say 'What should I do? what should I do?,' I really do not know what I should do."

15.24. Zigong asked: "Is there any single word that could guide one's entire life?" The Master said: "Should it not be *reciprocity?* What you do not wish for yourself, do not do to others."

15.27. The Master said: "Clever talk ruins virtue. Small impatiences ruin great plans."

15.36. The Master said: "In the pursuit of virtue, do not be afraid to overtake your teacher."

17.2. The Master said: "What nature put together, habit separates."

17.19. The Master said: "I wish to speak no more." Zigong said: "Master, if you do not speak, how would little ones like us still be able to hand down any teachings?" The Master said: "Does Heaven speak? Yet the four seasons follow their course and the hundred creatures continue to be born. Does Heaven speak?"

17.20. Ru Bei wanted to see Confucius. Confucius declined on the grounds of illness. As Ru Bei's messenger was leaving, the Master took up his zithern and sang loudly enough for him to hear.

17.21. Zai Yu asked: "Three years mourning for one's parents—this is quite long. If a gentleman stops all ritual practices for three years, the practices will decay; if he stops all musical performances for three years, music will be lost. As the old crop is consumed, a new crop grows up, and for lighting the fire, a new lighter is used with each season. One year of mourning should be enough." The Master said: "If after only one year, you were again to eat white rice and to wear silk, would you feel at ease?"—"Absolutely."—"In that case, go ahead! The reason a gentleman prolongs his mourning is simply that, since fine food seems tasteless to him, and music offers him no enjoyment, and the comfort of his house makes him uneasy, he prefers to do without all these pleasures. But now, if you can enjoy them, go ahead!"

Zai Yu left. The Master said: "Zai Yu is devoid of humanity. After a child is born, for the first three years of his life, he does not leave his parents' bosom. Three years mourning is a custom that is observed everywhere in the world. Did Zai Yu never enjoy the love of his parents, even for three years?"

17.24. Zigong said: "Does a gentleman have hatreds?" The Master said: "Yes. He hates those who dwell on what is hateful in others. He hates those inferiors who slander their superiors. He hates those whose courage is not tempered by civilized manners. He hates the impulsive and the stubborn." He went on: "And you? Don't you have your own hatreds?"— "I hate the plagiarists who pretend to be learned. I hate the arrogant who pretend to be brave. I hate the malicious who pretend to be frank."

17.25. The Master said: "Women and underlings are especially difficult to handle: be friendly, and they become familiar; be distant, and they resent it."

17.26. The Master said: "Whoever, by the age of forty, is still disliked, will remain so till the end."

18.5. Jieyu, the Madman of Chu, went past Confucius, singing:

> Phoenix, oh Phoenix!
> The past cannot be retrieved,
> But the future still holds a chance.
> Give up, give up!
> The days of those in office are numbered!

Confucius stopped his chariot, for he wanted to speak with him, but the other hurried away and disappeared. Confucius did not succeed in speaking to him.

18.6. Changju and Jieni were ploughing together. Confucius, who was passing by, sent Zilu to ask where the ford was. Changju said: "Who is in the chariot?" Zilu said: "It is Confucius." "The Confucius from Lu?"—"Himself."—"Then he already knows where the ford is."

Zilu then asked Jieni, who replied: "Who are you?"—"I am Zilu."—"The disciple of Confucius, from Lu?"—"Yes."—"The whole universe is swept along by the same flood; who can reverse its flow? Instead of following a gentleman who keeps running from one patron to the next, would it not be better to follow a gentleman who has forsaken the world?" All the while he kept on tilling his field.

Zilu came back and reported to Confucius. Rapt in thought, the Master sighed: "One cannot associate with birds and beasts. With whom should I keep company, if not with my own kind? If the world were following the Way, I would not have to reform it."

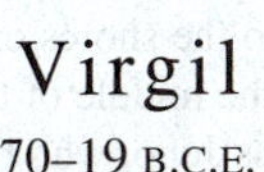

Virgil

70–19 B.C.E.

From shortly after his death until just a few centuries ago, Publius Vergilius Maro was commonly regarded not only as the poet of Rome and the Roman Empire but also as a philosopher, prophet, sage, and even magician. One result of the legends surrounding Virgil was that the *Aeneid* was customarily used as a book of divination. Seeking guidance, readers would close their eyes, open the pages at random, and point a blind finger at a line of poetry by which they would direct their actions from that moment onward. In his medieval epic poem *The Divine Comedy,* Dante gave a similar authority to the *Aeneid,* invoking its words and its author as guide to the perilous task of journeying through the afterlife (see page 1262). Virgil would perhaps not have been surprised by such responses to the *Aeneid,* for seldom has a work of literature been so self-consciously focused on the effect it would have on its readers, on its culture, and on posterity.

There are several ways in which the *Aeneid* signals these intentions. The first is the thoroughness with which it revisits and revises the two founding epics of ancient Greece, the *Iliad* and the *Odyssey.* Because it sets its action during the aftermath of the Trojan War and because the path of its hero, Aeneas, follows in the trail of Odysseus's journey, the *Aeneid* operates as a

Roman sequel to Homer. Because it switches allegiance, glorifying Troy and denigrating the Greek forces, it significantly reinterprets the Homeric epics as well. And because it tells its tale of the legendary past with one eye always fixed on the meaning of that past for the Roman present under the rule of Emperor Augustus, the *Aeneid* displays a consciousness of its place in history quite alien to the oral tradition represented by the Homeric poems.

Born in 70 B.C.E. near the small Italian town of Mantua, Virgil came of age during a traumatic period of Roman history, nearly a century of recurring civil war. When Octavian defeated the forces of Marc Antony and Cleopatra in 31 B.C.E. and acceded soon after to the reins of empire as Augustus Caesar, he inaugurated a long-desired stretch of peace and stability as well as an end to the cherished tradition of the republic over which so much blood had been spilled. Both emotions are strongly registered in the ancient world depicted in the *Aeneid,* balanced as it is between repeated prophecies of the destined glories of Rome to come and the enormous suffering and hardship that will be required to get there. So the opening to Book 1 concludes majestically but also with a touch of exhaustion: "So hard and huge a task it was to found the Roman people."

Following the publication of his first collection of poetry, the *Bucolics,* or *Eclogues* (42–39 B.C.E.)—ten fairly short, loose adaptations of the Greek pastoral poems of Theocritus—Virgil found himself, like his younger friend Horace, a member of Octavian's inner circle by virtue of the patronage and friendship of Maecenas, an influential member of the aristocracy and one of Octavian's ministers. Over the next years, Virgil slowly polished his second collection, the *Georgics,* four books of verse concerning farming and beekeeping but equally immersed in mythology and contemporary events. Octavian reportedly ordered a preview reading of the barely completed *Georgics* by their author in 29 B.C.E.; Virgil's canonical status has never been in doubt since. He spent the last ten years of his life at work on the *Aeneid.* Apparently not yet satisfied with its form at the end of his life, he left orders for it to be burned. Augustus countermanded the order, consigning the manuscript to Virgil's colleague Varius to prepare it for publication (i.e., copying and circulation in manuscript form). It immediately became a school text, used for teaching grammar, verse, and philosophy; commented and glossed repeatedly; and frequently imitated, although for the most part timorously and from afar. Because the fourth of his *Eclogues* includes an enigmatic prophecy of a savior to come, Virgil was also rapidly assimilated as a forerunner of Christianity, and the *Aeneid* functioned throughout late antiquity and the Middle Ages as a linking text between Christian doctrine and the classical tradition, most famously in Dante's work.

The *Aeneid* is composed of twelve books containing a total of just under ten thousand lines in the traditional six-beat meter of epic. The first six books recount the difficult journey of Aeneas from the defeated city of Troy to the shores of Italy, where he is fated to found Rome. The poem plunges *in medias res*—into the middle of the story—with Aeneas's fleet nearly destroyed by a storm roused by the goddess Juno, who bears various grudges against the Trojans and is determined to prevent or at least delay their ambitions. They manage to land safely on the North African coast, where they are taken in by Queen Dido, herself an exile engaged in building Carthage, a city that would much later become the opponent of Rome in three brutal conflicts, the so-called Punic Wars of the third and second centuries B.C.E. In Books 2 and 3, Aeneas tells Dido and her court the story of the fall of Troy and the early stages of his journey. Then, following the machinations of his mother, Venus, the pair conduct a short-lived but passionate affair that ends in catastrophe when Aeneas is ordered by the gods to return to his fated duty. Following further difficulties, Aeneas decides after a dream vision to journey into the underworld to meet and consult with the shade of his father, Anchises. In the Elysian Fields, Anchises shows Aeneas the souls waiting to return to the world above and sketches out his descendants in a prophetic history of Rome dating all the way through the recent civil war and the time of Augustus.

The final six books of the poem describe the war that awaits Aeneas after he lands in Latium on the coast of Italy. A series of broken treaties and much maneuvering by Juno and Venus lead to a conflict between the Trojans and their allies and the local king, Turnus, and his allies. Although traditionally neglected in favor of the more varied material of the first six books, the "Iliadic" second half of the *Aeneid* offers a sustained meditation on the costs of civil war and the pros and cons of empire building. The poem ends abruptly, offering not the closure of Aeneas's impending marriage with the Latinian princess Lavinia or his promised deification but his summary execution of Turnus as the defeated leader pleads for mercy.

Like much else in the poem, the ending has prompted debate over the years as to how we are meant to interpret Aeneas's action. This would appear to be a consistent artistic strategy throughout the poem. The *Aeneid* possesses a typological structure, constantly sending the reader back and forth between the legendary period of the poem's setting and the contemporary period of its composition. The character and choices of Aeneas constantly reflect on those of the current ruler, Augustus, who had recently concluded a civil war himself. The Dido episode is not only a tragic rendition of the conflict between individual desire and public duty but also a complex foreshadowing of the three Punic Wars, which ended in the destruction of Carthage by Rome in 146 B.C.E. The sympathy that Virgil imparts to Dido in this episode casts a shadow on the later episode, just as the wrath to which Aeneas succumbs in killing Turnus implicates in some way the character of Augustus. Virgil never makes a direct equation between past and present, nor does he give straightforward, symbolic meaning to any specific episodes. Instead, he sets up a framework of correspondences between the past and the present that invites the reader to seek meaning through a chain of comparisons.

A similar relationship exists with the Homeric epics, with which Virgil assumed his readers would be intimately familiar. One of Virgil's goals in rewriting episodes from the *Iliad* and the *Odyssey* was to define what was specifically Roman about his own characters and epic. In Book 2, for example, the bloody encounter between Troy's ruler Priam and Achilles' son Pyrrhus can be compared to the concluding book of the *Iliad,* where Priam persuades Achilles to relent in his anger and return the body of Priam's son, Hektor, for proper burial (see page 177). In Virgil's account of the fall of Troy, Pyrrhus first slaughters another of Priam's sons before the father's eyes at the family altar and then butchers the aged man himself. The story is striking on its own terms, but the additional resonance of the Homeric comparison places the issues of heroism, piety, loss, exile, and fathers and sons in especially sharp relief.

On the level of language, the *Aeneid* also shuttles its readers back and forth between the ancient world of the Homeric epic and Virgil's contemporary world. He borrows techniques of oral composition to give his poem an archaic feel, heightening its effect of sublime distance from everyday life. Characters are referred to repeatedly by epithets such as "pious Aeneas" or "faithful Achates"; particular formulae such as "marvelous to tell" are repeated; different forces receive lengthy catalogues of names and lineage. The epic hexameter, a line composed of six equal parts, or "feet," is weighty and serious, although carefully varied to avoid monotony. Like the Greek, Latin meter was based on the length of vowels, determined by default (certain vowels are long by rule) and by placement (vowels are usually long when followed by two consonants, for example). The dactyl was the standard foot (long—short—short), but various of the six dactyls in a line could be changed to spondees (long—long) according to certain rules. In the previously cited line, "So hard and huge a task it was to found the Roman people" (Book 1, line 33), for example, an opening spondee and two more in the center lay a heavy stress on the solemn meaning of the line and on the key adjective, "Roman," in its middle:

tāntæ mōlĭs ĕrāt / Rōmānām // cōndĕrĕ gēntem.[1] (final "x" over the last vowel)

Word order in Latin is extremely flexible, allowing *Romanam* to come in the middle, and for the act of founding to be flanked by the adjective and noun being founded; a word-by-word rendering of the translator's language would read: "So hard and huge—task—was—Roman—to found—people."

1. A long vowel is marked by "-" and a short one by "˘"; "/" marks a strong caesura, or pause, when a word ends after the first, long vowel in the foot (most commonly occurring, as here, in the 3rd foot); "//" marks a diaeresis, or a pause, when the end of a foot coincides with the end of a word; the final "x" marks the last vowel, always read as long regardless.

At the same time that Virgil strove to echo Homer, he also grounded his poem in the language and experience of his own day. He coined a good number of new words, and especially in his use of simile he was frequently and self-consciously anachronistic. The very first simile of the poem, for example, compares Neptune calming the waves to a veteran quieting a rioting crowd in the Roman Forum, a space that wouldn't be created until hundreds of years after the time in which the poem is set. Later in Book 1, we find Aeneas looking down on the rising walls of Carthage, marveling at the laws being enacted and the "magistrates and sacred senate" being chosen, as if Carthage were already modern Rome. Virgil chooses here to use the traditional epic device of a natural simile to describe a human phenomenon, comparing the scene to "bees in early summer." Here he also alludes to the final book of his previous work, the *Georgics,* which uses a long treatise on beekeeping to comment on the proper functioning of Roman society. The *Aeneid* can be read as a self-contained epic tale of exile and war, but the more one follows its many threads backward to Greek literature and forward to contemporary Rome, the deeper and more satisfying that tale becomes.

Virgil equally encourages and rewards the reader who follows the imagery forward and backward within the body of the poem. There are myriad formal patterns in the *Aeneid;* one of the most striking and most disturbing is the set of attributes Virgil associates with many of the female characters in the poem, beginning with the goddess Juno, whose implacably "black rage" determines that every time it seems a resolution has finally been reached, all hell will break loose once again. A divine, overpowering, and contagious anger that descends thematically from the rage of Achilles in the *Iliad* and before that, the fury of the goddess Ishtar in *The Epic of Gilgamesh* (see page 92), Juno's rage (*ira*) has a terrifying effect on every character it infects. It transforms the steady and pious ruler Dido into a raving fury; it causes the Trojan women to torch their own fleet; through the fury Allecto it feeds Turnus's seething fire of injustice and the passions of the Latin queen Amata. It is particularly associated with imagery of fire and serpents, and although Virgil never quite identifies it with a feminine force per se, he certainly relates it to forces of uncontrollable emotion usually undergone by female characters in the mythological tradition before him.

The split between male and female is a primary opposition in a poem built around oppositions. Like all of the polarities we find in the poem, however, it becomes more complicated the more we study its details; after all, the last person in the poem to be overcome with *ira* is Aeneas himself in the final scene, even though Juno has agreed finally to give up her own wrath. Because of so many built-in cross-references and so much historical mirroring, the *Aeneid* is readily allegorized into symbolic meanings. This is particularly the case with the gods, who drive most of the poem's plot, causing events to occur by their conflicting machinations. The gods were also pretty much an archaism by the time Virgil was writing, at least in the sense of divine figures who interacted openly with mortals. Here, too, Virgil seems careful not to reduce them to a single meaning. There are moments when the gods behave like the distanced immortals of legend, moments when they react with petty human emotions, moments when they insist on the traditional virtues of Roman society, and moments when they appear irreligious and well-nigh immoral. Virgil's human characters, too, straddle a space between heroic, sometimes tragic paradigms of humanity and fully fleshed individuals with idiosyncratic, subjective takes on the world around them. Witness Aeneas's reaction when his father wants to show him his heroic future, the great tradition of Rome he is destined to sire. Rather than embrace his heroic role, Aeneas responds in the baffled tone of a long-suffering trooper who cannot imagine anyone being eager about anything related to the cruel world above:

> Must we imagine,
> Father, there are souls that go from here
> Aloft to upper heaven, and once more
> Return to bodies' dead weight? The poor souls,
> How can they crave our daylight so?

It is not just because of its philosophical and prophetic gravity that the *Aeneid* has laid such a claim on posterity; it is because Virgil was able to balance that gravity through a constant reminder of how it must have felt weighing on the hearts and minds of those required to sacrifice themselves to the goals they were responsible for achieving.

PRONUNCIATIONS:

Aeneas: eh-NEE-uhs
Aeneid: eh-NEE-id
Allecto: ah-LEC-toh
Amata: ah-MAH-tah
Anchises: an-KAI-seez
Ascanius: as-KAY-nee-uhs
Dido: DAI-doh
Eclogues: EH-klogs
Elysian: eh-LEE-zhuhn
Lavinia: lah-VI-nee-uh
Pyrrhus: PIR-ruhs
Turnus: TUR-nuhs

from AENEID[1]

from Book 1

[A FATEFUL HAVEN]

I sing of warfare and a man at war.[2]
From the sea-coast of Troy in early days
He came to Italy by destiny,
To our Lavinian western shore,
A fugitive, this captain, buffeted
Cruelly on land as on the sea
By blows from powers of the air—behind them
Baleful Juno[3] in her sleepless rage.
And cruel losses were his lot in war,
Till he could found a city and bring home
His gods to Latium, land of the Latin race,
The Alban lords, and the high walls of Rome.
Tell me the causes now, O Muse, how galled
In her divine pride, and how sore at heart
From her old wound, the queen of gods compelled him—
A man apart, devoted to his mission—
To undergo so many perilous days
And enter on so many trials. Can anger
Black as this prey on the minds of heaven?
Tyrian settlers in that ancient time
Held Carthage, on the far shore of the sea,

1. Translated by Robert Fitzgerald.
2. Virgil echoes the opening lines of Homer's *Iliad* and *Odyssey.* As does Homer, he begins in the midst of events; we find out how this situation arose only in Books 2 and 3.
3. Female counterpart of Jupiter in Roman religion, identified with the Greek Hera.

Set against Italy and Tiber's mouth,
A rich new town, warlike and trained for war.[4]
And Juno, we are told, cared more for Carthage
Than for any walled city of the earth,
More than for Samos,[5] even. There her armor
And chariot were kept, and, fate permitting,
Carthage would be the ruler of the world.
So she intended, and so nursed that power.
But she had heard long since
That generations born of Trojan blood
Would one day overthrow her Tyrian walls,
And from that blood a race would come in time
With ample kingdoms, arrogant in war,
For Libya's ruin: so the Parcae spun.[6]
In fear of this, and holding in memory
The old war she had carried on at Troy
For Argos'° sake (the origins of that anger, *the Greeks*
That suffering, still rankled: deep within her,
Hidden away, the judgment Paris gave,[7]
Snubbing her loveliness; the race she hated;
The honors given ravished Ganymede),[8]
Saturnian Juno,[9] burning for it all,
Buffeted on the waste of sea those Trojans
Left by the Greeks and pitiless Achilles,[1]
Keeping them far from Latium. For years
They wandered as their destiny drove them on
From one sea to the next: so hard and huge
A task it was to found the Roman people.

They were all under sail in open water
With Sicily just out of sight astern,
Lighthearted as they plowed the whitecapped sea
With stems of cutting bronze. But never free
Of her eternal inward wound, the goddess
Said to herself:
"Give up what I began?
Am I defeated? Am I impotent
To keep the king of Teucrians[2] from Italy?
The Fates forbid me, am I to suppose?
Could Pallas° then consume the Argive° fleet *Athena / Greek*

4. The historical Carthage was founded by Phoenicians from the eastern Mediterranean island harbor of Tyre around the 9th or 8th century B.C.E. on the northeast coast of Tunisia. All of the North African coastal zone, and sometimes all of Africa, was known to the Greeks as "Libya."
5. Ionian island, legendary birthplace of Hera.
6. The Fates, who were represented as three old women spinning.
7. According to Greek myth, Hera and Athena (Roman: Minerva) supported the Greeks in the Trojan War because Paris had chosen Aphrodite as the most beautiful goddess in return for her promise to grant him Helen as a prize.
8. Son of Troy's founder, Tros. Because of his great beauty, he was carried off by Zeus to be his cupbearer on Mt. Olympus.
9. "Saturnian" because she was the daughter of Cronos, who was identified with the Roman god Saturnus.
1. Champion of the Greeks and the hero of the *Iliad*.
2. Teucer was a legendary king in the region of Troy whose daughter Zeus's son Dardanus married. Because of him the Trojans are sometimes called "Teucri" ("Teucrians") or from "Dardanus," "Dardanians."

With fire, and drown the crews,
Because of one man's one mad act—the crime
Of Ajax, son of Oïleus?[3] She—yes, she!—
Hurled out of cloudland lancing fire of Jove,
Scattered the ships, roughed up the sea with gales,
Then caught the man, bolt-struck, exhaling flames,
In a whirlwind and impaled him on a rock.
But I who walk as queen of all the gods,
Sister and wife of Jove,[4] I must contend
For years against one people! Who adores
The power of Juno after this, or lays
An offering with prayer upon her altar?"

Smouldering, putting these questions to herself,
The goddess made her way to stormcloud country,
Aeolia, the weather-breeding isle.
Here in a vast cavern King Aeolus[5]
Rules the contending winds and moaning gales
As warden of their prison. Round the walls
They chafe and bluster underground. The din
Makes a great mountain murmur overhead.
High on a citadel enthroned,
Scepter in hand, he mollifies their fury,
Else they might flay the sea and sweep away
Land masses and deep sky through empty air.
In fear of this, Jupiter hid them away
In caverns of black night. He set above them
Granite of high mountains—and a king
Empowered at command to rein them in
Or let them go. To this king Juno now
Made her petition:
"Aeolus, the father
Of gods and men decreed and fixed your power
To calm the waves or make them rise in wind.
The race I hate is crossing the Tuscan° sea, *Tyrrhenian*
Transporting Ilium° with her household gods[6]— *Troy*
Beaten as they are—to Italy.
Put new fury
Into your winds, and make the long ships founder!
Drive them off course! Throw bodies in the sea!
I have fourteen exquisite nymphs, of whom
The loveliest by far, Deïopëa,[7]
Shall be your own. I'll join you two in marriage,

3. Minor hero of the *Iliad,* said by legend to be hated by Athena because he had disrupted Athena's statue when he dragged Cassandra from it before raping her.

4. Another name for Jupiter, chief of the gods in Roman religion, who is identified with the Greek Zeus, the brother and husband of Hera.

5. Ruler of the winds who aids Odysseus in Homer's *Odyssey,* Book 10. Later tradition made him a deity.

6. The Penates, or household gods, were Roman spirits connected with the inner part of the house—in essence, the souls of the ancestors of the race.

7. In Greek mythology, nymphs were divinities of trees, mountains, and rivers, who were personified as young and beautiful women. Deïopëa was a sea nymph from the region of Cyrene, a major Greek colony in Africa.

So she will spend all future years with you,
As you so well deserve,
And make you father of her lovely children."

Said Aeolus:
"To settle on what you wish
Is all you need to do, your majesty.
I must perform it. You have given me
What realm I have. By your good offices
I rule with Jove's consent, and I recline
Among the gods at feasts, for you appoint me
Lord of wind and cloud."
Spearhaft reversed,
He gave the hollow mountainside a stroke,
And, where a portal opened, winds in ranks,
As though drawn up for battle, hurtled through,
To blow across the earth in hurricane.
Over the sea, tossed up from the sea-floor,
Eastwind and Southwind, then the wild Southwest
With squall on squall came scudding down,
Rolling high combers shoreward.
Now one heard
The cries of men and screech of ropes in rigging
Suddenly, as the stormcloud whipped away
Clear sky and daylight from the Teucrians'° eyes, *Trojans'*
And gloom of night leaned on the open sea.
It thundered from all quarters, as it lightened
Flash on flash through heaven. Every sign
Portended a quick death for mariners.
Aeneas on the instant felt his knees
Go numb and slack, and stretched both hands to heaven,
Groaning out:
"Triply lucky, all you men
To whom death came before your fathers' eyes
Below the wall at Troy! Bravest Danaan,° *Greek*
Diomedes, why could I not go down
When you had wounded me, and lose my life
On Ilium's battlefield?[8] Our Hector lies there,
Torn by Achilles' weapon; there Sarpedon,
Our giant fighter, lies; and there the river
Simoïs washes down so many shields
And helmets, with strong bodies taken under!"[9]

As he flung out these words, a howling gust
From due north took the sail aback and lifted
Wavetops to heaven; oars were snapped in two;

8. Diomedes was one of the principal Achaean warriors in the *Iliad*; in Book 5 he fought Aeneas. He appears in Book 11 of the *Aeneid,* where he refuses to join the forces massed against Aeneas. "Danaans" is a word used by Homer and other poets to mean the Greeks.

9. Hector was the leader of the Trojans, killed by Achilles (*Iliad,* bk. 22); Sarpedon, a son of Zeus and an ally of the Trojans, was killed by Achilles's companion Patroclus (*Iliad,* bk. 16); Simoïs was a river of Troy.

The prow sheered round and left them broadside on
To breaking seas; over her flank and deck
A mountain of grey water crashed in tons.
Men hung on crests; to some a yawning trough
Uncovered bottom, boiling waves and sand.
The Southwind caught three ships and whirled them down
On reefs, hidden midsea, called by Italians
"The Altars"—razorbacks just under water.
The Eastwind drove three others from deep water
Into great shoals and banks, embedding them
And ringing them with sand, a desperate sight.
Before Aeneas' eyes a toppling billow
Struck the Lycians' ship, Orontës' ship,
Across the stern, pitching the steersman down
And overboard. Three times the eddying sea
Carried the ship around in the same place
Until the rapid whirlpool gulped it down.
A few men swimming surfaced in the welter.
So did shields, planks, precious things of Troy.
Ilioneus' good ship, brave Achatës' ship,
The ship that carried Abas, and the one
Aletës sailed in, hale in his great age,
Were all undone by the wild gale: their seams
Parted and let the enemy pour in.
During all this, Neptune[1] became aware
Of hurly-burly and tempest overhead,
Bringing commotion to the still sea-depth
And rousing him. He lifted his calm brow
Above the surface, viewing the great sea,
And saw Aeneas' squadron far and wide
Dispersed over the water, saw the Trojans
Overwhelmed, the ruining clouds of heaven,
And saw his angry sister's hand in all.
He called to him Eastwind and South and said:

"Are you so sure your line is privileged?
How could you dare to throw heaven and earth
Into confusion, by no will of mine,
And make such trouble? You will get from me—
But first to calm the rough sea; after this,
You'll pay a stricter penalty for your sins.
Off with you! Give this message to your king:
Power over the sea and the cruel trident
Were never his by destiny, but mine.
He owns the monstrous rocks, your home, Eastwind.
Let Aeolus ruffle in that hall alone
And lord it over winds shut in their prison."

1. Roman version of the Greek sea god, Poseidon, brother of Zeus and Hera.

Before the words were out, he quieted
The surging water, drove the clouds away,
And brought the sunlight back. Cymothoë
And Triton,[2] side by side, worked to dislodge
The grounded ships; then Neptune with his trident
Heaved them away, opened the miles of shoals,
Tempered the sea, and in his car departed
Gliding over the wave-tops on light wheels.

When rioting breaks out in a great city,
And the rampaging rabble goes so far
That stones fly, and incendiary brands—
For anger can supply that kind of weapon—
If it so happens they look round and see
Some dedicated public man, a veteran
Whose record gives him weight, they quiet down,
Willing to stop and listen.
Then he prevails in speech over their fury
By his authority, and placates them.
Just so, the whole uproar of the great sea
Fell silent, as the Father of it all,
Scanning horizons under the open sky,
Swung his team around and gave free rein
In flight to his eager chariot.[3]
                                        Tired out,
Aeneas' people made for the nearest land,
Turning their prows toward Libya. There's a spot
Where at the mouth of a long bay an island
Makes a harbor, forming a breakwater
Where every swell divides as it comes in
And runs far into curving recesses.
There are high cliffs on this side and on that,
And twin peaks towering heavenward impend
On reaches of still water. Over these,
Against a forest backdrop shimmering,
A dark and shaggy grove casts a deep shade,
While in the cliffside opposite, below
The overhanging peaks, there is a cave
With fresh water and seats in the living rock,
The home of nymphs. Here never an anchor chain,
Never an anchor's biting fluke need hold
A tired ship.
                    Aeneas put in here,
With only seven ships from his full number,
And longing for the firm earth underfoot

2. Cymothoë was one of the Nereids, or sea maidens. Triton was a son of Poseidon.

3. The first of the poem's epic similes, intentionally anachronistic in its comparison of Neptune to a "public man" placating a rioting crowd, embodying the Roman ideal of the *vir pietate gravis,* the man solemn and weighty with piety.

The Trojans disembarked, to take possession
Of the desired sand-beach. Down they lay,
To rest their brinesoaked bodies on the shore.
Achatës promptly struck a spark from flint
And caught it in dry leaves; he added tinder
Round about and waved it for a flame-burst.
Then they brought out the grain of Ceres, tainted
By sea water, and Ceres' implements,
And, weary of their troubles, made all ready
To dry and grind with millstones what they had.[4]

Meanwhile, Aeneas climbed one of the peaks
For a long seaward view, hoping to sight
Gale-worn Antheus and the Phrygian° biremes,[5] *Trojan*
Capys, or high poops bearing Caïcus' arms.
He found no ship in sight, but on the shore
Three wandering stags.[6] Behind them whole herds followed,
Grazing in a long line down the valleys.
Planting his feet, he took in hand the bow
And arrows carried by his aide, Achatës,
Then, aiming for the leaders with heads high
And branching antlers, brought them first to earth.
Next he routed the whole herd,
Driving them with his shafts through leafy places,
Shooting and shooting till he won the hunt
By laying seven carcasses on the ground,
A number equal to his ships. Then back
To port he went, and parcelled out the game
To his ships' companies. There he divided
The wine courtly Acestës had poured out
And given them on the Sicilian shore—
Full jugs of it—when they were about to sail.[7]
By this and by a simple speech Aeneas
Comforted his people:
"Friends and companions,
Have we not known hard hours before this?
My men, who have endured still greater dangers,
God will grant us an end to these as well.
You sailed by Scylla's rage, her booming crags,
You saw the Cyclops' boulders.[8] Now call back
Your courage, and have done with fear and sorrow.
Some day, perhaps, remembering even this

4. The Italian goddess Ceres was identified with the Greek Demeter, goddess of agriculture and fertility—hence the word "cereal" for edible grains. Her implements are the millstones and other tools for grinding grain.

5. Rowing ships with two levels of oars.

6. Many classical commentators interpreted the three stags as a figure representing the three Punic Wars that Rome would fight with Carthage.

7. Acestës was a Sicilian king who had hosted the Trojans in Sicily on their way to Carthage; he welcomes them again at his shores in Book 5.

8. The monster Scylla was traditionally said to be located across from the whirlpool of Charybdis in the straits of Messina between the island of Sicily and the boot of Italy. The Cyclops were one-eyed giants whom tradition placed on Sicily. Both monsters are encountered by Odysseus; Aeneas recounts both adventures in Book 3 of the *Aeneid.*

Will be a pleasure. Through diversities
Of luck, and through so many challenges,
We hold our course for Latium, where the Fates
Hold out a settlement and rest for us.
Troy's kingdom there shall rise again. Be patient:
Save yourselves for more auspicious days."

So ran the speech. Burdened and sick at heart,
He feigned hope in his look, and inwardly
Contained his anguish. Now the Trojan crews
Made ready for their windfall and their feast.
They skinned the deer, bared ribs and viscera,
Then one lot sliced the flesh and skewered it
On spits, all quivering, while others filled
Bronze cooking pots and tended the beach fires.
All got their strength back from the meal, reclining
On the wild grass, gorging on venison
And mellowed wine. When hunger had been banished,
And tables put away, they talked at length
In hope and fear about their missing friends:
Could one believe they might be still alive,
Or had they suffered their last hour,
Never again to hear a voice that called them?
Aeneas, more than any, secretly
Mourned for them all—for that fierce man, Orontës,
Then for Amycus, then for the bitter fate
Of Lycus, for brave Gyas, brave Cloanthus.

It was the day's end when from highest air
Jupiter looked down on the broad sea
Flecked with wings of sails, and the land masses,
Coasts, and nations of the earth. He stood
On heaven's height and turned his gaze toward Libya,
And, as he took the troubles there to heart,
Venus[9] appealed to him, all pale and wan,
With tears in her shining eyes:
"My lord who rule
The lives of men and gods now and forever,
And bring them all to heel with your bright bolt,
What in the world could my Aeneas do,
What could the Trojans do, so to offend you
That after suffering all those deaths they find
The whole world closed to them, because of Italy?
Surely from these the Romans are to come
In the course of years, renewing Teucer's line,
To rule the sea and all the lands about it,
According to your promise. What new thought

9. Goddess of love, Aphrodite to the Greeks, daughter of Zeus and Dione. She was the mother of Aeneas by Anchises, a member of the royal house of Troy. In the *Iliad,* she rescues Aeneas from duels with Diomedes and Achilles.

Has turned you from them, Father? I consoled myself
For Troy's fall, that grim ruin, weighing out
One fate against another in the scales.[1]
But now, when they have borne so many blows,
The same misfortune follows them. Great king,
What finish to their troubles will you give?
After Antenor slipped through the Achaeans
He could explore Illyrian coves and reach
In safety the Liburnians' inland kingdoms
And source of the Timavus.[2] Through nine openings
With a great rumble in the mountain wall
It bursts from the ground there and floods the fields
In a rushing sea. And yet he chose that place
For Padua and new homes for Teucrians,
Gave them a name, set up the arms of Troy,
And now rests in his peace. As for ourselves,
Your own children, whom you make heirs of heaven,
Our ships being lost (this is unspeakable!),
We are forsaken through one enemy's rage
And kept remote from Italy. Is this
The palm for loyalty? This our power restored?"

He smiled at her, the father of gods and men,
With that serenity that calms the weather,[3]
And lightly kissed his daughter. Then he said:

"No need to be afraid, Cytherëa.[4]
Your children's destiny has not been changed.
As promised, you shall see Lavinium's walls[5]
And take up, then, amid the stars of heaven
Great-souled Aeneas.[6] No new thought has turned me.
No, he, your son—now let me speak of him,
In view of your consuming care, at length,
Unfolding secret fated things to come[7]—
In Italy he will fight a massive war,
Beat down fierce armies, then for the people there
Establish city walls and a way of life.
When the Rutulians[8] are subdued he'll pass
Three summers of command in Latium,
Three years of winter quarters. But the boy,
Ascanius, to whom the name of Iulus

1. The image of Zeus weighing two fates on the golden scales appears twice in the *Iliad* (8.69 and 22.209).
2. A spring in northern Italy. In mythology, Antenor was an elderly and upright counselor in Troy during the siege. In Roman times, he was said to have settled at the head of the Adriatic, where he founded Padua. The Liburni were an Illyrian (Balkan) people on the northeast coast of the Adriatic, famous as seafarers and pirates in Roman times.
3. In Greek mythology, Zeus was the god of the sky and the weather.
4. Venus. Cythera is an island off the Peloponnese that in Greek myth was the birthplace of Aphrodite, who had a sanctuary there.
5. The large town founded where Aeneas will first land in Latium.
6. Jove predicts the eventual deification of Aeneas. A hero-cult of Aeneas existed by the 3rd century B.C.E.
7. The next 44 lines contain the first of the poem's prophecies linking Aeneas's legendary voyage with actual as well as mythical events in more recent Roman history.
8. The subjects of Turnus, Aeneas's rival in Italy.

Now is added—Ilus while Ilium stood[9]—
Will hold the power for all of thirty years,
Great rings of wheeling months. He will transfer
His capital from Lavinium and make
A fortress, Alba Longa.[1] Three full centuries
That kingdom will be ruled by Hector's race,
Until the queen and priestess, Ilia,[2]
Pregnant by Mars, will bear twin sons to him.
Afterward, happy in the tawny pelt
His nurse, the she-wolf, wears, young Romulus
Will take the leadership, build walls of Mars,
And call by his own name his people Romans.
For these I set no limits, world or time,
But make the gift of empire without end.
Juno, indeed, whose bitterness now fills
With fear and torment sea and earth and sky,
Will mend her ways, and favor them as I do,
Lords of the world, the toga-bearing Romans.
Such is our pleasure. As the years fall away,
An age comes when Assaracus' royal house
Will bring to servitude Thessalian Phthia,
Renowned Mycenae, too; and subjugate
Defeated Argos.[3] From that comely line
The Trojan Caesar comes, to circumscribe
Empire with Ocean, fame with heaven's stars.
Julius his name, from Iulus handed down:
All tranquil shall you take him heavenward
In time, laden with plunder of the East,
And he with you shall be invoked in prayer.[4]
Wars at an end, harsh centuries then will soften,
Ancient Fides and Vesta, Quirinus
With Brother Remus, will be lawgivers,[5]
And grim with iron frames, the Gates of War
Will then be shut: inside, unholy Furor,
Squatting on cruel weapons, hands enchained
Behind him by a hundred links of bronze,

9. Ascanius was Aeneas's son. The Julian clan (whose members included Julius Caesar and Augustus) called him "Iulus" and claimed descent from him. According to Virgil, they derived the name from "Ilus," the founder of Troy.

1. A city in the Alban hills about 13 miles southeast of Rome. Tradition placed the founding of Alba Longa c. 1152 B.C.E. It lost its primacy in Latium not long after the founding of Rome.

2. According to Roman legend, Ilia was a Vestal Virgin who bore two sons to the war god Mars (Greek: Ares). She was thrown into the river Tiber by her usurping uncle, and Romulus and Remus were raised by a she-wolf.

3. Jove predicts Trojan revenge in the form of the eventual Roman conquest of Greece. At the time of Homer, Phthia was the kingdom of Achilles, Mycenae of Agamemnon, and Argos of Diomedes. Greece and Macedonia became the Roman province of Achaea in 146 B.C.E.

4. Virgil presents the claim of the *gens Iulia* to descent from Ascanius and predicts the career of either Julius Caesar (100–44 B.C.E.) or his adopted son, Julius Caesar Octavianus (63 B.C.E.–14 C.E.), known also as "Augustus." Julius Caesar was officially deified as Divus Iulius in 42 B.C.E.; Virgil predicts the deification of Augustus, which occurred after the poet's death, at the time of the emperor's funeral.

5. Fides was the Roman personification of Faith, and Vesta was the goddess of the hearth. Quirinus was the local deity of the Sabine community who settled on the Quirinal hill, later identified with Romulus.

Will grind his teeth and howl with bloodied mouth."[6]

That said, he sent the son of Maia[7] down
From his high place to make the land of Carthage,
The new-built town, receptive to the Trojans,
Not to allow Queen Dido, all unknowing
As to the fated future, to exclude them.
Through the vast air with stroking wings he flew
And came down quickly on the Libyan coast,
Performing Jove's command, so that at once
Phoenicians put aside belligerence
As the god willed. Especially the queen
Took on a peaceful mood, an open mind
Toward Teucrians.
But the dedicated man,
Aeneas, thoughtful through the restless night,
Made up his mind, as kindly daylight came,
To go out and explore the strange new places,
To learn what coast the wind had brought him to
And who were living there, men or wild creatures—
For wilderness was all he saw—and bring
Report back to his company. The ships
He hid beneath a hollowed rocky cliff
And groves that made a vault, trees all around
And deep shade quivering. He took his way
With only one man at his side, Achatës,
Hefting two hunting spears with broad steel points.
Then suddenly, in front of him,
His mother crossed his path in mid-forest,
Wearing a girl's shape and a girl's gear—
A Spartan girl, or like that one of Thrace,
Harpalycë,[8] who tires horses out,
Outrunning the swift Hebrus. She had hung
About her shoulders the light, handy bow
A huntress carries, and had given her hair
To the disheveling wind; her knees were bare,
Her flowing gown knotted and kirtled up.
She spoke first:
"Ho, young fellows, have you seen—
Can you say where—one of my sisters here,
In a spotted lynx-hide, belted with a quiver,
Scouting the wood, or shouting on the track
Behind a foam-flecked boar?"
To Venus then

6. In times of complete peace, the temple of Janus Geminus (the god of doors and gates) in the Forum in Rome would be closed, most famously in 29, following Augustus's victory in the civil war. *Furor,* the Latin word for fury or rage, personifies the irrationality of war, especially of the civil variety.

7. Hermes, the messenger of the gods, identified in Roman religion with Mercury, was originally a god of trade.

8. A mythical Thracian princess raised by her father to be a warrior.

The son of Venus answered:
"No, I've heard
Or seen none of your sisters—only, how
Shall I address you, girl? Your look's not mortal,
Neither has your accent a mortal ring.
O Goddess, beyond doubt! Apollo's sister?[9]
One of the family of nymphs? Be kind,
Whoever you may be, relieve our trouble,
Tell us under what heaven we've come at last,
On what shore of the world are we cast up,
Wanderers that we are, strange to this country,
Driven here by wind and heavy sea.
By my right hand many an offering
Will be cut down for you before your altars."
Venus replied:
"Be sure I am not fit
For any such devotion. Tyrian girls
Are given to wearing quivers and hunting boots
Of crimson, laced on the leg up to the knee.
This is the Punic kingdom that you see,
The folk are Tyrian, the town Agenor's.[1]
But neighboring lands belong to Libya,
A nation hard to fight against in war.
The ruler here is Dido,[2] of Tyre city,
In flight here from her brother—a long tale
Of wrong endured, mysterious and long.
But let me tell the main events in order.
Her husband was Sychaeus, of all Phoenicians
Richest in land, and greatly loved by her,
Ill-fated woman. Her father had given her,
A virgin still, in marriage, her first rite.
Her brother, though, held power in Tyre—Pygmalion,
A monster of wickedness beyond all others.
Between the two men furious hate arose,
And sacrilegiously before the altars,
Driven by a blind lust for gold, Pygmalion
Took Sychaeus by surprise and killed him
With a dagger blow in secret, undeterred
By any thought of Dido's love. He hid
What he had done for a long time, cozening° her, *deceiving*
Deluding the sick woman with false hope.
But the true form of her unburied husband
Came in a dream: lifting his pallid face
Before her strangely, he made visible
The cruel altars and his body pierced,

9. Artemis, the daughter of Zeus and Leto, was a virgin and huntress who was identified with the Italian moon goddess, Diana.

1. In Greek mythology, Agenor was the Phoenician king of Tyre and the father of Cadmus and Europa.

2. Dido was originally the name of a Phoenician goddess but was later given to Elissa, the legendary daughter of Belus of Tyre, whose story Venus tells here.

Uncovering all the dark crime of the house.
He urged her then to make haste and take flight,
Leaving her fatherland, and to assist the journey
Revealed a buried treasure of old time,
Unknown to any, a weight of gold and silver.
Impelled by this, Dido laid her plans
To get away and to equip her company.
All who hated the tyrant, all in fear
As bitter as her own, now came together,
And ships in port, already fitted out,
They commandeered, to fill with gold: the riches
Pygmalion had itched for went to sea,
And captaining the venture was a woman.
They sailed to this place where today you'll see
Stone walls going higher and the citadel
Of Carthage, the new town. They bought the land,
Called Drumskin from the bargain made, a tract
They could enclose with one bull's hide.[3]
What of yourselves? From what coast do you come?
Where are you bound?"
Then to the questioner
He answered sighing, bringing out the words
From deep within him:
"Goddess, if I should tell
Our story from the start, if you had leisure
To hear our annals of adversity,
Before I finished, the fair evening star
Would come to close Olympus and the day.
From old Troy—if the name of Troy has fallen
Perhaps upon your ears—we sailed the seas,
And yesterday were driven by a storm,
Of its own whim, upon this Libyan coast.
I am Aeneas, duty-bound, and known
Above high air of heaven by my fame,
Carrying with me in my ships our gods
Of hearth and home, saved from the enemy.
I look for Italy to be my fatherland,
And my descent is from all-highest Jove.
With twenty ships I mounted the Phrygian° sea, *Aegean*
As my immortal mother showed the way.
I followed the given fates. Now barely seven
Ships are left, battered by wind and sea,
And I myself, unknown and unprovisioned,
Cross the Libyan wilderness, an exile
Driven from Europe and from Asia—"

3. According to legend, a Libyan king granted Dido as much land as she could cover with a bull's hide. By cutting the hide into narrow strips, she obtained enough space to found Carthage.

But Venus chose to hear no more complaints
And broke in, midway through his bitterness:
"Whoever you are, I doubt Heaven is unfriendly
To you, as you still breathe life-giving air
On your approach to the Tyrian town. Go on:
Betake yourself this way to the queen's gate.
Your friends are back. This is my news for you:
Your ships were saved and brought to shore again
By winds shifting north, or else my parents
Taught me augury to no purpose. Look:
See the twelve swans in line rejoicing there!
Jove's eagle, like a bolt out of the blue,
Had flurried them in open heaven, but now
They seem to be alighting one by one
Or looking down on those already grounded.
As they disport themselves, with flapping wings,
After their chanting flight about the sky,
Just so your ships and your ships' companies
Are either in port or entering under sail.
Go on then, where the path leads, go ahead!"

On this she turned away. Rose-pink and fair
Her nape shone, her ambrosial hair exhaled
Divine perfume, her gown rippled full length,
And by her stride she showed herself a goddess.
Knowing her for his mother, he called out
To the figure fleeting away:
"You! cruel, too!
Why tease your son so often with disguises?
Why may we not join hands and speak and hear
The simple truth?"
So he called after her,
And went on toward the town. But Venus muffled
The two wayfarers in grey mist, a cloak
Of dense cloud poured around them, so that no one
Had the power to see or to accost them,
Make them halt, or ask them what they came for.
Away to Paphos[4] through high air she went
In joy to see her home again, her shrine
And hundred altars where Sabaean incense[5]
Fumed and garlands freshened the air.
Meanwhile
The two men pressed on where the pathway led,
Soon climbing a long ridge that gave a view
Down over the city and facing towers.
Aeneas found, where lately huts had been,
Marvelous buildings, gateways, cobbled ways,

4. City-kingdom on the island of Cyprus and home of one of the most famous Aphrodite cults.

5. The Sabaeans were one of the chief peoples of Arabia, famous for precious spices and perfumes.

And din of wagons. There the Tyrians
Were hard at work: laying courses for walls,
Rolling up stones to build the citadel,
While others picked out building sites and plowed
A boundary furrow. Laws were being enacted,
Magistrates and a sacred senate chosen.
Here men were dredging harbors, there they laid
The deep foundation of a theatre,
And quarried massive pillars to enhance
The future stage—as bees in early summer
In sunlight in the flowering fields
Hum at their work, and bring along the young
Full-grown to beehood; as they cram their combs
With honey, brimming all the cells with nectar,
Or take newcomers' plunder, or like troops
Alerted, drive away the lazy drones,
And labor thrives and sweet thyme scents the honey.
Aeneas said: "How fortunate these are
Whose city walls are rising here and now!"[6]

He looked up at the roofs, for he had entered,
Swathed in cloud—strange to relate—among them,
Mingling with men, yet visible to none.
In mid-town stood a grove that cast sweet shade
Where the Phoenicians, shaken by wind and sea,
Had first dug up that symbol Juno showed them,
A proud warhorse's head:[7] this meant for Carthage
Prowess in war and ease of life through ages.
Here being built by the Sidonian[8] queen
Was a great temple planned in Juno's honor,
Rich in offerings and the godhead there.
Steps led up to a sill of bronze, with brazen
Lintel, and bronze doors on groaning pins.
Here in this grove new things that met his eyes
Calmed Aeneas' fear for the first time.
Here for the first time he took heart to hope
For safety, and to trust his destiny more
Even in affliction. It was while he walked
From one to another wall of the great temple
And waited for the queen, staring amazed
At Carthaginian promise, at the handiwork
Of artificers and the toil they spent upon it:
He found before his eyes the Trojan battles
In the old war, now known throughout the world—
The great Atridae, Priam, and Achilles,

6. The founding of Carthage was traditionally dated to 814 or 813 B.C.E., some four centuries after the destruction of Troy. This makes the meeting between Dido and Aeneas chronologically tricky but allows a profound symmetry between the two cities being founded by two exiles.
7. Tanit, the great goddess of Carthage, was identified early on with Juno. It was she who, according to legend, had led the Tyrians to the spot where they dug up a horse's head, a divine portent of the future site of their city.
8. Phoenician. Sidon was a Phoenician city on the coast of modern Lebanon.

Fierce in his rage at both sides. Here Aeneas
Halted, and tears came.
"What spot on earth,"
He said, "what region of the earth, Achatës,
Is not full of the story of our sorrow?
Look, here is Priam. Even so far away
Great valor has due honor; they weep here
For how the world goes, and our life that passes
Touches their hearts. Throw off your fear. This fame
Insures some kind of refuge."[9]
He broke off
To feast his eyes and mind on a mere image,
Sighing often, cheeks grown wet with tears,
To see again how, fighting around Troy,
The Greeks broke here, and ran before the Trojans,
And there the Phrygians ran, as plumed Achilles
Harried them in his warcar. Nearby, then,
He recognized the snowy canvas tents
Of Rhesus,[1] and more tears came: these, betrayed
In first sleep, Diomedes devastated,
Swording many, till he reeked with blood,
Then turned the mettlesome horses toward the beachhead
Before they tasted Trojan grass or drank
At Xanthus[2] ford.
And on another panel
Troilus,[3] without his armor, luckless boy,
No match for his antagonist, Achilles,
Appeared pulled onward by his team: he clung
To his warcar, though fallen backward, hanging
On to the reins still, head dragged on the ground,
His javelin scribbling S's in the dust.
Meanwhile to hostile Pallas'° shrine *Athena's*
The Trojan women walked with hair unbound,
Bearing the robe of offering, in sorrow,
Entreating her, beating their breasts. But she,
Her face averted, would not raise her eyes.[4]
And there was Hector, dragged around Troy walls
Three times, and there for gold Achilles sold him,
Bloodless and lifeless.[5] Now indeed Aeneas
Heaved a mighty sigh from deep within him,

9. The scenes from the Trojan War on the temple walls that Virgil recounts here constitute the poem's first use of the classical rhetorical figure of *ekphrasis,* the verbal description of a work of visual art. The scenes also serve to preview Aeneas's own account of the fall of Troy in Book 2.

1. A Thracian ally of the Trojans who was victimized by Odysseus and Diomedes in the night raid of the *Iliad,* Book 10, described here.

2. A river of Troy; its god was a son of Zeus.

3. One of the sons of Hecuba and Priam, king of Troy. Non-Homeric sources told of his ambush by Achilles and slaughter at the altar of Apollo.

4. Like Hera, Athena sided with the Greeks; in this scene from the *Iliad,* Trojan women attempt unsuccessfully to appease her anger.

5. Achilles dragged Hector's body around the city in the *Iliad,* Book 22 (the scene is described in further detail in bk. 2); he ransomed the body to Hector's father, Priam, in the *Iliad,* Book 24.

Seeing the spoils, the chariot, and the corpse
Of his great friend, and Priam, all unarmed,
Stretching his hands out.
He himself he saw
In combat with the first of the Achaeans,[6]
And saw the ranks of Dawn, black Memnon's arms;[7]
Then, leading the battalion of Amazons
With half-moon shields, he saw Penthesilëa
Fiery amid her host, buckling a golden
Girdle beneath her bare and arrogant breast,
A girl who dared fight men, a warrior queen.[8]
Now, while these wonders were being surveyed
By Aeneas of Dardania, while he stood
Enthralled, devouring all in one long gaze,
The queen paced toward the temple in her beauty,
Dido, with a throng of men behind.

[*Under Venus's influence, Dido welcomes Aeneas and his people. At dinner, Venus sends down Cupid to take the shape of Ascanius and awaken love for Aeneas in Dido. Dido asks Aeneas to recount the story of the fall of Troy and of his travels thereafter.*]

from Book 2

[How They Took the City]

The room fell silent, and all eyes were on him,
As Father Aeneas from his high couch began:

"Sorrow too deep to tell, your majesty,
You order me to feel and tell once more:
How the Danaans leveled in the dust
The splendor of our mourned-forever kingdom—
Heartbreaking things I saw with my own eyes
And was myself a part of. Who could tell them,
Even a Myrmidon or Dolopian
Or ruffian of Ulysses, without tears?[1]
Now, too, the night is well along, with dewfall
Out of heaven, and setting stars weigh down
Our heads toward sleep. But if so great desire
Moves you to hear the tale of our disasters,
Briefly recalled, the final throes of Troy,
However I may shudder at the memory
And shrink again in grief, let me begin.[2]

6. The duel with Achilles in the *Iliad,* Book 20, from which Aeneas's mother rescues him.
7. A mythical king of Ethiopia, son of Aurora, goddess of Dawn, and Priam's brother Tithonus; he arrived after Hector's death and was killed by Achilles.
8. A mythical Amazon queen who led an army to aid Priam after Hector's death; she was killed by Achilles.

1. The Myrmidons were the subjects of Achilles, and the Dolopians were the subjects of Phoenix, who raised Achilles; in the *Aeneid,* Ulysses (Odysseus) is the archvillain of the Homeric Greeks.
2. Although the *Iliad* strongly foreshadows the fall of Troy, it doesn't recount the events themselves, which are filled in by post-Homeric poems.

Knowing their strength broken in warfare, turned
Back by the fates, and years—so many years—
Already slipped away, the Danaan captains
By the divine handicraft of Pallas built
A horse of timber, tall as a hill,
And sheathed its ribs with planking of cut pine.
This they gave out to be an offering
For a safe return by sea, and the word went round.
But on the sly they shut inside a company
Chosen from their picked soldiery by lot,
Crowding the vaulted caverns in the dark—
The horse's belly—with men fully armed.

Offshore there's a long island, Tenedos,
Famous and rich while Priam's kingdom lasted,
A treacherous anchorage now, and nothing more.
They crossed to this and hid their ships behind it
On the bare shore beyond. We thought they'd gone,
Sailing home to Mycenae[3] before the wind,
So Teucer's town is freed of her long anguish,
Gates thrown wide! And out we go in joy
To see the Dorian° campsites, all deserted, *Greek*
The beach they left behind. Here the Dolopians
Pitched their tents, here cruel Achilles lodged,
There lay the ships, and there, formed up in ranks,
They came inland to fight us. Of our men
One group stood marveling, gaping up to see
The dire gift of the cold unbedded goddess,
The sheer mass of the horse.
Thymoetes shouts
It should be hauled inside the walls and moored
High on the citadel—whether by treason
Or just because Troy's fate went that way now.
Capys opposed him; so did the wiser heads:
'Into the sea with it,' they said, 'or burn it,
Build up a bonfire under it,
This trick of the Greeks, a gift no one can trust,
Or cut it open, search the hollow belly!'

Contrary notions pulled the crowd apart.
Next thing we knew, in front of everyone,
Laocoön[4] with a great company
Came furiously running from the Height,
And still far off cried out: 'O my poor people,
Men of Troy, what madness has come over you?
Can you believe the enemy truly gone?
A gift from the Danaans, and no ruse?

3. The kingdom of Agamemnon, leader of the Greeks.

4. A Trojan prince, brother of Anchises, and a priest of Poseidon.

Is that Ulysses' way, as you have known him?
Achaeans must be hiding in this timber,
Or it was built to butt against our walls,
Peer over them into our houses, pelt
The city from the sky. Some crookedness
Is in this thing. Have no faith in the horse!
Whatever it is, even when Greeks bring gifts
I fear them, gifts and all.'
He broke off then
And rifled his big spear with all his might
Against the horse's flank, the curve of belly.
It stuck there trembling, and the rounded hull
Reverberated groaning at the blow.
If the gods' will had not been sinister,
If our own minds had not been crazed,
He would have made us foul that Argive den
With bloody steel, and Troy would stand today—
O citadel of Priam, towering still!

But now look: hillmen, shepherds of Dardania,
Raising a shout, dragged in before the king
An unknown fellow with hands tied behind—
This all as he himself had planned,
Volunteering, letting them come across him,
So he could open Troy to the Achaeans.
Sure of himself this man was, braced for it
Either way, to work his trick or die.
From every quarter Trojans run to see him,
Ring the prisoner round, and make a game
Of jeering at him. Be instructed now
In Greek deceptive arts: one barefaced deed
Can tell you of them all.
As the man stood there, shaken and defenceless,
Looking around at ranks of Phrygians,
'Oh god,' he said, 'what land on earth, what seas
Can take me in? What's left me in the end,
Outcast that I am from the Danaans,
Now the Dardanians will have my blood?'

The whimpering speech brought us up short; we felt
A twinge for him. Let him speak up, we said,
Tell us where he was born, what news he brought,
What he could hope for as a prisoner.
Taking his time, slow to discard his fright,
He said:
'I'll tell you the whole truth, my lord,
No matter what may come of it. Argive
I am by birth, and will not say I'm not.
That first of all: Fortune has made a derelict
Of Sinon, but the bitch

Won't make an empty liar of him, too.
Report of Palamedes may have reached you,
Scion of Belus' line, a famous man
Who gave commands against the war.[5] For this,
On a trumped-up charge, on perjured testimony,
The Greeks put him to death—but now they mourn him,
Now he has lost the light. Being kin to him,
In my first years I joined him as companion,
Sent by my poor old father on this campaign,
And while he held high rank and influence
In royal councils, we did well, with honor.
Then by the guile and envy of Ulysses—
Nothing unheard of there!—he left this world,
And I lived on, but under a cloud, in sorrow,
Raging for my blameless friend's downfall.
Demented, too, I could not hold my peace
But said if I had luck, if I won through
Again to Argos, I'd avenge him there.
And I roused hatred with my talk; I fell
Afoul now of that man. From that time on,
Day in, day out, Ulysses
Found new ways to bait and terrify me,
Putting out shady rumors among the troops,
Looking for weapons he could use against me.
He could not rest till Calchas served his turn[6]—
But why go on? The tale's unwelcome, useless,
If Achaeans are all one,
And it's enough I'm called Achaean, then
Exact the punishment, long overdue;
The Ithacan° desires it; the Atridae[7] *Ulysses*
Would pay well for it.'

Burning with curiosity,
We questioned him, called on him to explain—
Unable to conceive such a performance,
The art of the Pelasgian.[8] He went on,
Atremble, as though he feared us:

'Many times
The Danaans wished to organize retreat,
To leave Troy and the long war, tired out.
If only they had done it! Heavy weather
At sea closed down on them, or a fresh gale
From the Southwest would keep them from embarking,
Most of all after this figure here,

5. Palamedes was a proverbially clever hero, hated by Odysseus because he had exposed the madness Odysseus feigned to avoid going to Troy. In revenge, Odysseus forged a letter from Priam to Palamedes offering gold to betray the Greeks and buried a sum of gold in Palamedes' quarters. Palamedes was stoned to death by the army.

6. Calchas was a seer with the Greek army in Troy (*Iliad*, bks.1 and 2).

7. The house of Atreus, the father of Agamemnon and Menelaus, the king of Sparta.

8. Greeks: the Pelasgians were mythical pre-Hellenic inhabitants of Greece.

This horse they put together with maple beams,
Reached its full height. Then wind and thunderstorms
Rumbled in heaven. So in our quandary
We sent Eurypylus[9] to Phoebus'° oracle, *Apollo's*
And he brought back this grim reply:

'Blood and a virgin slain
You gave to appease the winds, for your first voyage
Troyward, O Danaans.[1] Blood again
And Argive blood, one life, wins your return.'

When this got round among the soldiers, gloom
Came over them, and a cold chill that ran
To the very marrow. Who had death in store?
Whom did Apollo call for? Now the man
Of Ithaca haled Calchas out among us
In tumult, calling on the seer to tell
The true will of the gods. Ah, there were many
Able to divine the crookedness
And cruelty afoot for me, but they
Looked on in silence. For ten days the seer
Kept still, kept under cover, would not speak
Of anyone, or name a man for death,
Till driven to it at last by Ulysses' cries—
By prearrangement—he broke silence, barely
Enough to designate me for the altar.
Every last man agreed. The torments each
Had feared for himself, now shifted to another,
All could endure. And the infamous day came,
The ritual, the salted meal, the fillets . . .
I broke free, I confess it, broke my chains,
Hid myself all night in a muddy marsh,
Concealed by reeds, waiting for them to sail
If they were going to.
Now no hope is left me
Of seeing my home country ever again,
My sweet children, my father, missed for years.
Perhaps the army will demand they pay
For my escape, my crime here, and their death,
Poor things, will be my punishment. Ah, sir,
I beg you by the gods above, the powers
In whom truth lives, and by what faith remains
Uncontaminated to men, take pity
On pain so great and so unmerited!'

For tears we gave him life, and pity, too.
Priam himself ordered the gyves° removed *shackles*

9. A minor Iliadic figure related to the cults of Artemis and Dionysus, the god of wine and intoxication.

1. When the Greeks were unable to raise a fair wind to sail to Troy, Artemis, whom Agamemnon had offended, demanded that he sacrifice his daughter, Iphigenia, to appease her anger.

And the tight chain between. In kindness then
He said to him:
'Whoever you may be,
The Greeks are gone; forget them from now on;
You shall be ours. And answer me these questions:
Who put this huge thing up, this horse?
Who designed it? What do they want with it?
Is it religious or a means of war?'

These were his questions. Then the captive, trained
In trickery, in the stagecraft of Achaea,
Lifted his hands unfettered to the stars.
'Eternal fires of heaven,' he began,
'Powers inviolable, I swear by thee,
As by the altars and blaspheming swords
I got away from, and the gods' white bands
I wore as one chosen for sacrifice,
This is justice, I am justified
In dropping all allegiance to the Greeks—
As I had cause to hate them; I may bring
Into the open what they would keep dark.
No laws of my own country bind me now.
Only be sure you keep your promises
And keep faith, Troy, as you are kept from harm
If what I say proves true, if what I give
Is great and valuable.
The whole hope
Of the Danaans, and their confidence
In the war they started, rested all along
In help from Pallas. Then the night came
When Diomedes and that criminal,
Ulysses, dared to raid her holy shrine.
They killed the guards on the high citadel
And ripped away the statue, the Palladium,
Desecrating with bloody hands the virginal
Chaplets of the goddess.[2] After that,
Danaan hopes waned and were undermined,
Ebbing away, their strength in battle broken,
The goddess now against them. This she made
Evident to them all with signs and portents.
Just as they set her statue up in camp,
The eyes, cast upward, glowed with crackling flames,
And salty sweat ran down the body. Then—
I say it in awe—three times, up from the ground,

2. The Trojan Palladium was a small wooden image of an armed Athena that fell from heaven in answer to the prayer of Ilus, Troy's founder. Because it protected the city from capture, Diomedes and Odysseus carried it off. According to later Roman tradition, this was only a copy, and Aeneas brought the original with him to Lavinium, from which it eventually reached Rome.

The apparition of the goddess rose
In a lightning flash, with shield and spear atremble.
Calchas divined at once that the sea crossing
Must be attempted in retreat—that Pergamum[3]
Cannot be torn apart by Argive swords
Unless at Argos first they beg new omens,
Carrying homeward the divine power
Brought overseas in ships. Now they are gone
Before the wind to the fatherland, Mycenae,
Gone to enlist new troops and gods. They'll cross
The water again and be here, unforeseen.
So Calchas read the portents. Warned by him,
They set this figure up in reparation
For the Palladium stolen, to appease
The offended power and expiate the crime.
Enormous, though, he made them build the thing
With timber braces, towering to the sky,
Too big for the gates, not to be hauled inside
And give the people back their ancient guardian.
If any hand here violates this gift
To great Minerva, then extinction waits,
Not for one only—would god it were so—
But for the realm of Priam and all Phrygians.
If this proud offering, drawn by your hands,
Should mount into your city, then so far
As the walls of Pelops'[4] town the tide of Asia
Surges in war: that doom awaits our children.'

This fraud of Sinon, his accomplished lying,
Won us over; a tall tale and fake tears
Had captured us, whom neither Diomedes
Nor Larisaean[5] Achilles overpowered,
Nor ten long years, nor all their thousand ships.

And now another sign, more fearful still,
Broke on our blind miserable people,
Filling us all with dread. Laocoön,
Acting as Neptune's priest that day by lot,
Was on the point of putting to the knife
A massive bull before the appointed altar,
When ah—look there!
From Tenedos, on the calm sea, twin snakes—
I shiver to recall it—endlessly
Coiling, uncoiling, swam abreast for shore,
Their underbellies showing as their crests

3. The citadel of Troy; often used to refer to the city as a whole.

4. The father of Atreus, who gave his name to the Peloponnese, the southern part of Greece.

5. Larissa was the mother of Phthia, hero of the Thessalian kingdom ruled by Achilles. The chief city of Thessaly, in the northeast part of Greece, was named after her.

Reared red as blood above the swell; behind
They glided with great undulating backs.
Now came the sound of thrashed seawater foaming;
Now they were on dry land, and we could see
Their burning eyes, fiery and suffused with blood,
Their tongues a-flicker out of hissing maws.
We scattered, pale with fright. But straight ahead
They slid until they reached Laocoön.
Each snake enveloped one of his two boys,
Twining about and feeding on the body.
Next they ensnared the man as he ran up
With weapons: coils like cables looped and bound him
Twice round the middle; twice about his throat
They whipped their back-scales, and their heads towered,
While with both hands he fought to break the knots,
Drenched in slime, his head-bands black with venom,
Sending to heaven his appalling cries
Like a slashed bull escaping from an altar,
The fumbled axe shrugged off. The pair of snakes
Now flowed away and made for the highest shrines,
The citadel of pitiless Minerva,
Where coiling they took cover at her feet
Under the rondure of her shield. New terrors
Ran in the shaken crowd: the word went round
Laocoön had paid, and rightfully,
For profanation of the sacred hulk
With his offending spear hurled at its flank.

'The offering must be hauled to its true home,'
They clamored. 'Votive prayers to the goddess
Must be said there!'
So we breached the walls
And laid the city open. Everyone
Pitched in to get the figure underpinned
With rollers, hempen lines around the neck.
Deadly, pregnant with enemies, the horse
Crawled upward to the breach. And boys and girls
Sang hymns around the towrope as for joy
They touched it. Rolling on, it cast a shadow
Over the city's heart. O Fatherland,
O Ilium, home of gods! Defensive wall
Renowned in war for Dardanus's people!
There on the very threshold of the breach
It jarred to a halt four times, four times the arms
In the belly thrown together made a sound—
Yet on we strove unmindful, deaf and blind,
To place the monster on our blessed height.
Then, even then, Cassandra's lips unsealed
The doom to come: lips by a god's command

Never believed or heeded by the Trojans.[6]
So pitiably we, for whom that day
Would be the last, made all our temples green
With leafy festal boughs throughout the city.

As heaven turned, Night from the Ocean stream
Came on, profound in gloom on earth and sky
And Myrmidons in hiding. In their homes
The Teucrians lay silent, wearied out,
And sleep enfolded them. The Argive fleet,
Drawn up in line abreast, left Tenedos
Through the aloof moon's friendly stillnesses
And made for the familiar shore. Flame signals
Shone from the command ship. Sinon, favored
By what the gods unjustly had decreed,
Stole out to tap the pine walls and set free
The Danaans in the belly. Opened wide,
The horse emitted men; gladly they dropped
Out of the cavern, captains first, Thessandrus,
Sthenelus and the man of iron, Ulysses;
Hand over hand upon the rope, Acamas, Thoas,
Neoptolemus and Prince Machaon,[7]
Menelaus and then the master builder,
Epeos, who designed the horse decoy.
Into the darkened city, buried deep
In sleep and wine, they made their way,
Cut the few sentries down,
Let in their fellow soldiers at the gate,
And joined their combat companies as planned.

That time of night it was when the first sleep,
Gift of the gods, begins for ill mankind,
Arriving gradually, delicious rest.
In sleep, in dream, Hector appeared to me,
Gaunt with sorrow, streaming tears, all torn—
As by the violent car on his death day—
And black with bloody dust,
His puffed-out feet cut by the rawhide thongs.
Ah god, the look of him! How changed
From that proud Hector who returned to Troy
Wearing Achilles' armor, or that one
Who pitched the torches on Danaan ships;[8]
His beard all filth, his hair matted with blood,
Showing the wounds, the many wounds, received

6. Cassandra was the daughter of Priam and Hecuba. A post-Homeric tradition recounts that Apollo gave her prophetic powers in return for sexual favors. When she reneged on her promise, he decreed that her prophecies would always be disbelieved.

7. Greek champions. Acamas was son of Theseus, and Neoptolemus (also known as Pyrrhus) was son of Achilles.

8. In the *Iliad,* Books 11–17, Hector leads the Trojan forces to the Greek ships, which they threaten to set alight. He then defeats Patroclus and strips him of Achilles's armor.

Outside his father's city walls. I seemed
Myself to weep and call upon the man
In grieving speech, brought from the depth of me:

'Light of Dardania, best hope of Troy,
What kept you from us for so long, and where?
From what far place, O Hector, have you come,
Long, long awaited? After so many deaths
Of friends and brothers, after a world of pain
For all our folk and all our town, at last,
Boneweary, we behold you! What has happened
To ravage your serene face? Why these wounds?'

He wasted no reply on my poor questions
But heaved a great sigh from his chest and said:
'Ai! Give up and go, child of the goddess,
Save yourself, out of these flames. The enemy
Holds the city walls, and from her height
Troy falls in ruin. Fatherland and Priam
Have their due; if by one hand our towers
Could be defended, by this hand, my own,
They would have been. Her holy things, her gods
Of hearth and household Troy commends to you.
Accept them as companions of your days;
Go find for them the great walls that one day
You'll dedicate, when you have roamed the sea.'

As he said this, he brought out from the sanctuary
Chaplets and Vesta, Lady of the Hearth,
With her eternal fire.

While I dreamed,
The turmoil rose, with anguish, in the city.
More and more, although Anchises' house
Lay in seclusion, muffled among trees,
The din at the grim onset grew; and now
I shook off sleep, I climbed to the roof top
To cup my ears and listen. And the sound
Was like the sound a grassfire makes in grain,
Whipped by a Southwind, or a torrent foaming
Out of a mountainside to strew in ruin
Fields, happy crops, the yield of plowing teams,
Or woodlands borne off in the flood; in wonder
The shepherd listens on a rocky peak.
I knew then what our trust had won for us,
Knew the Danaan fraud: Deïphobus'[9]
Great house in flames, already caving in
Under the overpowering god of fire;

9. The son of Priam and Hecuba and Hector's dearest brother; he marries Helen after Paris's death. Aeneas discovers his gruesome fate in full when he encounters him in the Underworld in Book 6.

Ucalegon's already caught nearby;
The glare lighting the straits beyond Sigeum;
The cries of men, the wild calls of the trumpets.

* * *

What was the fate of Priam, you may ask.[1]
Seeing his city captive, seeing his own
Royal portals rent apart, his enemies
In the inner rooms, the old man uselessly
Put on his shoulders, shaking with old age,
Armor unused for years, belted a sword on,
And made for the massed enemy to die.
Under the open sky in a central court
Stood a big altar; near it, a laurel tree
Of great age, leaning over, in deep shade
Embowered the Penatës.° At this altar *household gods*
Hecuba and her daughters, like white doves
Blown down in a black storm, clung together,
Enfolding holy images in their arms.
Now, seeing Priam in a young man's gear,
She called out:
'My poor husband, what mad thought
Drove you to buckle on these weapons?
Where are you trying to go? The time is past
For help like this, for this kind of defending,
Even if my own Hector could be here.
Come to me now: the altar will protect us,
Or else you'll die with us.'
She drew him close,
Heavy with years, and made a place for him
To rest on the consecrated stone.
Now see
Politës,[2] one of Priam's sons, escaped
From Pyrrhus'° butchery and on the run *Neoptolemus's*
Through enemies and spears, down colonnades,
Through empty courtyards, wounded. Close behind
Comes Pyrrhus burning for the death-stroke: has him,
Catches him now, and lunges with the spear.
The boy has reached his parents, and before them
Goes down, pouring out his life with blood.
Now Priam, in the very midst of death,
Would neither hold his peace nor spare his anger.

'For what you've done, for what you've dared,' he said,
'If there is care in heaven for atrocity,
May the gods render fitting thanks, reward you

1. The death of Priam is closely modeled after the ransom of Hector's body in the *Iliad,* Book 24, a comparison Priam himself makes to Achilles's son here.

2. A fast runner, Politës plays a minor role in the *Iliad* as a scout.

As you deserve. You forced me to look on
At the destruction of my son: defiled
A father's eyes with death. That great Achilles
You claim to be the son of—and you lie—
Was not like you to Priam, his enemy;
To me who threw myself upon his mercy
He showed compunction, gave me back for burial
The bloodless corpse of Hector, and returned me
To my own realm.'
The old man threw his spear
With feeble impact; blocked by the ringing bronze,
It hung there harmless from the jutting boss.
Then Pyrrhus answered:
'You'll report the news
To Pelidës,° my father; don't forget *Achilles*
My sad behavior, the degeneracy
Of Neoptolemus. Now die.'
With this,
To the altar step itself he dragged him trembling,
Slipping in the pooled blood of his son,
And took him by the hair with his left hand.
The sword flashed in his right; up to the hilt
He thrust it in his body.
That was the end
Of Priam's age, the doom that took him off,
With Troy in flames before his eyes, his towers
Headlong fallen—he that in other days
Had ruled in pride so many lands and peoples,
The power of Asia.
On the distant shore
The vast trunk headless lies without a name.

For the first time that night, inhuman shuddering
Took me, head to foot. I stood unmanned,
And my dear father's image came to mind
As our king, just his age, mortally wounded,
Gasped his life away before my eyes.
Creusa[3] came to mind, too, left alone;
The house plundered; danger to little Iulus.
I looked around to take stock of my men,
But all had left me, utterly played out,
Giving their beaten bodies to the fire
Or plunging from the roof.
It came to this,
That I stood there alone. And then I saw
Lurking beyond the doorsill of the Vesta,
In hiding, silent, in that place reserved,

3. Aeneas's wife, a daughter of Priam, and mother of Ascanius (Iulus).

The daughter of Tyndareus.° Glare of fires *Helen*
Lighted my steps this way and that, my eyes
Glancing over the whole scene, everywhere.
That woman, terrified of the Trojans' hate
For the city overthrown, terrified too
Of Danaan vengeance, her abandoned husband's
Anger after years—Helen, that Fury
Both to her own homeland and Troy, had gone
To earth, a hated thing, before the altars.
Now fires blazed up in my own spirit—
A passion to avenge my fallen town
And punish Helen's whorishness.
'Shall this one
Look untouched on Sparta and Mycenae
After her triumph, going like a queen,
And see her home and husband, kin and children,
With Trojan girls for escort, Phrygian slaves?
Must Priam perish by the sword for this?
Troy burn, for this? Dardania's littoral° *shore*
Be soaked in blood, so many times, for this?
Not by my leave. I know
No glory comes of punishing a woman,
The feat can bring no honor. Still, I'll be
Approved for snuffing out a monstrous life,
For a just sentence carried out. My heart
Will teem with joy in this avenging fire,
And the ashes of my kin will be appeased.'

So ran my thoughts. I turned wildly upon her,
But at that moment, clear, before my eyes—
Never before so clear—in a pure light
Stepping before me, radiant through the night,
My loving mother came: immortal, tall,
And lovely as the lords of heaven know her.
Catching me by the hand, she held me back,
Then with her rose-red mouth reproved me:
'Son,
Why let such suffering goad you on to fury
Past control? Where is your thoughtfulness
For me, for us? Will you not first revisit
The place you left your father, worn and old,
Or find out if your wife, Creusa, lives,
And the young boy, Ascanius—all these
Cut off by Greek troops foraging everywhere?
Had I not cared for them, fire would by now
Have taken them, their blood glutted the sword.
You must not hold the woman of Laconia,[4]

4. The southeast district of the Peloponnese, controlled by Sparta, the kingdom of Helen's husband, Menelaus.

That hated face, the cause of this, nor Paris.
The harsh will of the gods it is, the gods,
That overthrows the splendor of this place
And brings Troy from her height into the dust.
Look over there: I'll tear away the cloud
That curtains you, and films your mortal sight,
The fog around you.—Have no fear of doing
Your mother's will, or balk at obeying her.—
Look: where you see high masonry thrown down,
Stone torn from stone, with billowing smoke and dust,
Neptune is shaking from their beds the walls
That his great trident pried up, undermining,
Toppling the whole city down.[5] And look:
Juno in all her savagery holds
The Scaean Gates, and raging in steel armor
Calls her allied army from the ships.
Up on the citadel—turn, look—Pallas Tritonia° *Athena*
Couched in a stormcloud, lightening, with her Gorgon![6]
The Father° himself empowers the Danaans, *Jove*
Urges assaulting gods on the defenders.
Away, child; put an end to toiling so.
I shall be near, to see you safely home.'

She hid herself in the deep gloom of night,
And now the dire forms appeared to me
Of great immortals, enemies of Troy.
I knew the end then: Ilium was going down
In fire, the Troy of Neptune going down,
As in high mountains when the countrymen
Have notched an ancient ash, then make their axes
Ring with might and main, chopping away
To fell the tree—ever on the point of falling,
Shaken through all its foliage, and the treetop
Nodding; bit by bit the strokes prevail
Until it gives a final groan at last
And crashes down in ruin from the height.

Now I descended where the goddess guided,
Clear of the flames, and clear of enemies,
For both retired; so gained my father's door,
My ancient home. I looked for him at once,
My first wish being to help him to the mountains;
But with Troy gone he set his face against it,
Not to prolong his life, or suffer exile.

5. Poseidon and Apollo had originally built the walls of Troy at the behest of Ilus's son, Laomedon.

6. The Gorgons were three female monsters with hideous faces, glaring eyes, and snakes for hair. A Gorgon's head turned whatever met its gaze to stone. Athena was generally represented in armor with the Gorgon's head on her shield.

'The rest of you, all in your prime,' he said,
'Make your escape; you are still hale and strong.
If heaven's lords had wished me a longer span
They would have saved this home for me. I call it
More than enough that once before I saw
My city taken and wrecked, and went on living.
Here is my death bed, here. Take leave of me.
Depart now. I'll find death with my sword arm.
The enemy will oblige; they'll come for spoils.
Burial can be dispensed with. All these years
I've lingered in my impotence, at odds
With heaven, since the Father of gods and men
Breathed high winds of thunderbolt upon me
And touched me with his fire.'[7]
He spoke on
In the same vein, inflexible. The rest of us,
Creusa and Ascanius and the servants,
Begged him in tears not to pull down with him
Our lives as well, adding his own dead weight
To the fates' pressure. But he would not budge,
He held to his resolve and to his chair.
I felt swept off again to fight, in misery
Longing for death. What choices now were open,
What chance had I?
'Did you suppose, my father,
That I could tear myself away and leave you?
Unthinkable; how could a father say it?
Now if it please the powers above that nothing
Stand of this great city; if your heart
Is set on adding your own death and ours
To that of Troy, the door's wide open for it:
Pyrrhus will be here, splashed with Priam's blood;
He kills the son before his father's eyes,
The father at the altars.
My dear mother,
Was it for this, through spears and fire, you brought me,
To see the enemy deep in my house,
To see my son, Ascanius, my father,
And near them both, Creusa,
Butchered in one another's blood? My gear,
Men, bring my gear. The last light calls the conquered.
Give me back to the Greeks. Let me take up
The combat once again. We shall not all
Die this day unavenged.'
I buckled on

7. According to the myth, when Anchises broke his vow to Aphrodite not to reveal her identity as the mother of his child, he was lamed by a thunderbolt.

Swordbelt and blade and slid my left forearm
Into the shield-strap, turning to go out,
But at the door Creusa hugged my knees,
Then held up little Iulus to his father.

'If you are going out to die, take us
To face the whole thing with you. If experience
Leads you to put some hope in weaponry
Such as you now take, guard your own house here.
When you have gone, to whom is Iulus left?
Your father? Wife?—one called that long ago.'

She went on, and her wailing filled the house,
But then a sudden portent came, a marvel:
Amid his parents' hands and their sad faces
A point on Iulus' head seemed to cast light,
A tongue of flame that touched but did not burn him,
Licking his fine hair, playing round his temples.
We, in panic, beat at the flaming hair
And put the sacred fire out with water;
Father Anchises lifted his eyes to heaven
And lifted up his hands, his voice, in joy:

'Omnipotent Jupiter, if prayers affect you,
Look down upon us, that is all I ask,
If by devotion to the gods we earn it,
Grant us a new sign, and confirm this portent!'
The old man barely finished when it thundered
A loud crack on the left. Out of the sky
Through depths of night a star fell trailing flame
And glided on, turning the night to day.
We watched it pass above the roof and go
To hide its glare, its trace, in Ida's wood;[8]
But still, behind, the luminous furrow shone
And wide zones fumed with sulphur.
Now indeed
My father, overcome, addressed the gods,
And rose in worship of the blessed star.

'Now, now, no more delay. I'll follow you.
Where you conduct me, there I'll be.
Gods of my fathers,
Preserve this house, preserve my grandson. Yours
This portent was. Troy's life is in your power.
I yield. I go as your companion, son.'
Then he was still. We heard the blazing town
Crackle more loudly, felt the scorching heat.

8. Ida was a range of mountains in southern Phrygia from the summit of which Zeus was said to have watched the Trojan War.

'Then come, dear father. Arms around my neck:
I'll take you on my shoulders, no great weight.
Whatever happens, both will face one danger,
Find one safety. Iulus will come with me,
My wife at a good interval behind.
Servants, give your attention to what I say.
At the gate inland there's a funeral mound
And an old shrine of Ceres the Bereft;
Near it an ancient cypress, kept alive
For many years by our fathers' piety.
By various routes we'll come to that one place.
Father, carry our hearthgods, our Penatës.
It would be wrong for me to handle them—
Just come from such hard fighting, bloody work—
Until I wash myself in running water.'

When I had said this, over my breadth of shoulder
And bent neck, I spread out a lion skin
For tawny cloak and stooped to take his weight.
Then little Iulus put his hand in mine
And came with shorter steps beside his father.
My wife fell in behind. Through shadowed places
On we went, and I, lately unmoved
By any spears thrown, any squads of Greeks,
Felt terror now at every eddy of wind,
Alarm at every sound, alert and worried
Alike for my companion and my burden.
I had got near the gate, and now I thought
We had made it all the way, when suddenly
A noise of running feet came near at hand,
And peering through the gloom ahead, my father
Cried out:

'Run, boy; here they come; I see
Flame light on shields, bronze shining.'

I took fright,
And some unfriendly power, I know not what,
Stole all my addled wits—for as I turned
Aside from the known way, entering a maze
Of pathless places on the run—

Alas,
Creusa, taken from us by grim fate, did she
Linger, or stray, or sink in weariness?
There is no telling. Never would she be
Restored to us. Never did I look back
Or think to look for her, lost as she was,
Until we reached the funeral mound and shrine
Of venerable Ceres. Here at last
All came together, but she was not there;
She alone failed her friends, her child, her husband.

Out of my mind, whom did I not accuse,
What man or god? What crueller loss had I
Beheld, that night the city fell? Ascanius,
My father, and the Teucrian Penates,
I left in my friends' charge, and hid them well
In a hollow valley.
I turned back alone
Into the city, cinching my bright harness.
Nothing for it but to run the risks
Again, go back again, comb all of Troy,
And put my life in danger as before:
First by the town wall, then the gate, all gloom,
Through which I had come out—and so on backward,
Tracing my own footsteps through the night;
And everywhere my heart misgave me: even
Stillness had its terror. Then to our house,
Thinking she might, just might, have wandered there.
Danaans had got in and filled the place,
And at that instant fire they had set,
Consuming it, went roofward in a blast;
Flames leaped and seethed in heat to the night sky.
I pressed on, to see Priam's hall and tower.
In the bare colonnades of Juno's shrine
Two chosen guards, Phoenix[9] and hard Ulysses,
Kept watch over the plunder. Piled up here
Were treasures of old Troy from every quarter,
Torn out of burning temples: altar tables,
Robes, and golden bowls. Drawn up around them,
Boys and frightened mothers stood in line.
I even dared to call out in the night;
I filled the streets with calling; in my grief
Time after time I groaned and called Creusa,
Frantic, in endless quest from door to door.
Then to my vision her sad wraith appeared—
Creusa's ghost, larger than life, before me.
Chilled to the marrow, I could feel the hair
On my head rise, the voice clot in my throat;
But she spoke out to ease me of my fear:

'What's to be gained by giving way to grief
So madly, my sweet husband? Nothing here
Has come to pass except as heaven willed.
You may not take Creusa with you now;
It was not so ordained, nor does the lord
Of high Olympus give you leave. For you

9. The son of Amyntor, who took shelter with Achilles's father, Peleus, after quarrelling with his father. Made the king of the Dolopians, he reared Achilles and went with him to Troy as an old man.

Long exile waits, and long sea miles to plough.
You shall make landfall on Hesperia
Where Lydian Tiber flows,[1] with gentle pace,
Between rich farmlands, and the years will bear
Glad peace, a kingdom, and a queen for you.
Dismiss these tears for your beloved Creusa.
I shall not see the proud homelands of Myrmidons
Or of Dolopians, or go to serve
Greek ladies, Dardan lady that I am
And daughter-in-law of Venus the divine.
No: the great mother of the gods detains me
Here on these shores. Farewell now; cherish still
Your son and mine.'
With this she left me weeping,
Wishing that I could say so many things,
And faded on the tenuous air. Three times
I tried to put my arms around her neck,
Three times enfolded nothing, as the wraith
Slipped through my fingers, bodiless as wind,
Or like a flitting dream.
So in the end
As night waned I rejoined my company.
And there to my astonishment I found
New refugees in a great crowd: men and women
Gathered for exile, young—pitiful people
Coming from every quarter, minds made up,
With their belongings, for whatever lands
I'd lead them to by sea.
The morning star
Now rose on Ida's ridges, bringing day.
Greeks had secured the city gates. No help
Or hope of help existed.
So I resigned myself, picked up my father,
And turned my face toward the mountain range."

[*Book 3: Aeneas's wanderings. After a winter's preparation, the Trojan survivors set out in search of their promised new home. They attempt unsuccessfully to settle in Thrace and Crete. After several years, Aeneas receives a detailed prophecy from Helenus, a son of Priam and Hecuba who has married Hector's wife, Andromache, and settled in Epirus. They cross over to Italy and sail on to Sicily, where they pick up one of Ulysses' men near Mount Aetna, the haunt of the Cyclops. They make their way around the south coast of Sicily to Drepanum, where Anchises dies.*]

1. Hesperia, "the Western land," is a poetic name for Italy; the Tiber is the chief river of central Italy and flows through Rome.

Book 4

[The Passion of the Queen]

The queen, for her part, all that evening ached
With longing that her heart's blood fed, a wound
Or inward fire eating her away.
The manhood of the man, his pride of birth,
Came home to her time and again; his looks,
His words remained with her to haunt her mind,
And desire for him gave her no rest.
When Dawn
Swept earth with Phoebus' torch° and burned away *the sun*
Night-gloom and damp, this queen, far gone and ill,
Confided to the sister of her heart:
"My sister Anna, quandaries and dreams
Have come to frighten me—such dreams!
Think what a stranger
Yesterday found lodging in our house:
How princely, how courageous, what a soldier.
I can believe him in the line of gods,
And this is no delusion. Tell-tale fear
Betrays inferior souls. What scenes of war
Fought to the bitter end he pictured for us!
What buffetings awaited him at sea!
Had I not set my face against remarriage
After my first love died and failed me, left me
Barren and bereaved—and sick to death
At the mere thought of torch and bridal bed—
I could perhaps give way in this one case
To frailty. I shall say it: since that time
Sychaeus, my poor husband, met his fate,
And blood my brother shed stained our hearth gods,
This man alone has wrought upon me so
And moved my soul to yield. I recognize
The signs of the old flame, of old desire.
But O chaste life, before I break your laws,
I pray that Earth may open, gape for me
Down to its depth, or the omnipotent
With one stroke blast me to the shades, pale shades
Of Erebus[1] and the deep world of night!
That man who took me to himself in youth
Has taken all my love; may that man keep it,
Hold it forever with him in the tomb."

At this she wept and wet her breast with tears.
But Anna answered:
"Dearer to your sister

1. Primeval darkness, sprung from Chaos, the father of Day by his sister, Night.

Than daylight is, will you wear out your life,
Young as you are, in solitary mourning,
Never to know sweet children, or the crown
Of joy that Venus brings? Do you believe
This matters to the dust, to ghosts in tombs?
Granted no suitors up to now have moved you,
Neither in Libya nor before, in Tyre—
Iarbas[2] you rejected, and the others,
Chieftains bred by the land of Africa
Their triumphs have enriched—will you contend
Even against a welcome love? Have you
Considered in whose lands you settled here?
On one frontier the Gaetulans, their cities,
People invincible in war—with wild
Numidian horsemen, and the offshore banks,
The Syrtës; on the other, desert sands,
Bone-dry, where fierce Barcaean nomads range.[3]
Or need I speak of future wars brought on
From Tyre, and the menace of your brother?
Surely by dispensation of the gods
And backed by Juno's will, the ships from Ilium
Held their course this way on the wind.
Sister,
What a great city you'll see rising here,
And what a kingdom, from this royal match!
With Trojan soldiers as companions in arms
By what exploits will Punic glory grow!
Only ask the indulgence of the gods,
Win them with offerings, give your guests ease,
And contrive reasons for delay, while winter
Gales rage, drenched Orion[4] storms at sea,
And their ships, damaged still, face iron skies."

This counsel fanned the flame, already kindled,
Giving her hesitant sister hope, and set her
Free of scruple. Visiting the shrines
They begged for grace at every altar first,
Then put choice rams and ewes to ritual death
For Ceres Giver of Laws, Father Lyaeus,
Phoebus, and for Juno most of all
Who has the bonds of marriage in her keeping.[5]

2. The Libyan king with whom Dido made the bargain of the bull's hide.

3. The Berber inhabitants of Numidia, west and south of Carthaginian territory, were nomadic herdsmen who had become warlike by the Second Punic War. The Syrtës were dangerous shoals and shallows of the Libyan continental shelf.

4. A mighty hunter who was eventually transformed into the constellation known by his name.

5. "Lyaeus" was a frequent poetic cult title for Bacchus; "pater" ("father") was often used for gods and heroes as a mark of respect. One of the roles Juno took from Hera was the protector of marriage.

Dido herself, splendidly beautiful,
Holding a shallow cup, tips out the wine
On a white shining heifer, between the horns,
Or gravely in the shadow of the gods
Approaches opulent altars. Through the day
She brings new gifts, and when the breasts are opened
Pores over organs, living still, for signs.
Alas, what darkened minds have soothsayers!
What good are shrines and vows to maddened lovers?
The inward fire eats the soft marrow away,
And the internal wound bleeds on in silence.

Unlucky Dido, burning, in her madness
Roamed through all the city, like a doe
Hit by an arrow shot from far away
By a shepherd hunting in the Cretan woods—
Hit by surprise, nor could the hunter see
His flying steel had fixed itself in her;
But though she runs for life through copse and glade
The fatal shaft clings to her side.
Now Dido
Took Aeneas with her among her buildings,
Showed her Sidonian wealth, her walls prepared,
And tried to speak, but in mid-speech grew still.
When the day waned she wanted to repeat
The banquet as before, to hear once more
In her wild need the throes of Ilium,
And once more hung on the narrator's words.
Afterward, when all the guests were gone,
And the dim moon in turn had quenched her light,
And setting stars weighed weariness to sleep,
Alone she mourned in the great empty hall
And pressed her body on the couch he left:
She heard him still, though absent—heard and saw him.
Or she would hold Ascanius in her lap,
Enthralled by him, the image of his father,
As though by this ruse to appease a love
Beyond all telling.
Towers, half-built, rose
No farther; men no longer trained in arms
Or toiled to make harbors and battlements
Impregnable. Projects were broken off,
Laid over, and the menacing huge walls
With cranes unmoving stood against the sky.

As soon as Jove's dear consort saw the lady
Prey to such illness, and her reputation
Standing no longer in the way of passion,
Saturn's daughter[6] said to Venus:
"Wondrous!

6. Saturn was identified with the Greek Cronos, father of Hera, Zeus, Hestia, Demeter, Poseidon, and Hades.

Covered yourself with glory, have you not,
You and your boy, and won such prizes, too.
Divine power is something to remember
If by collusion of two gods one mortal
Woman is brought low.
I am not blind.
Your fear of our new walls has not escaped me,
Fear and mistrust of Carthage at her height.
But how far will it go? What do you hope for,
Being so contentious? Why do we not
Arrange eternal peace and formal marriage?
You have your heart's desire: Dido in love,
Dido consumed with passion to her core.
Why not, then, rule this people side by side
With equal authority? And let the queen
Wait on her Phrygian lord, let her consign
Into your hand her Tyrians as a dowry."

Now Venus knew this talk was all pretence,
All to divert the future power from Italy
To Libya; and she answered:
"Who would be
So mad, so foolish as to shun that prospect
Or prefer war with you? That is, provided
Fortune is on the side of your proposal.
The fates here are perplexing: would one city
Satisfy Jupiter's will for Tyrians
And Trojan exiles? Does he approve
A union and a mingling of these races?
You are his consort: you have every right
To sound him out. Go on, and I'll come, too."

But regal Juno pointedly replied:
"That task will rest with me. Just now, as to
The need of the moment and the way to meet it,
Listen, and I'll explain in a few words.
Aeneas and Dido in her misery
Plan hunting in the forest, when the Titan
Sun[7] comes up with rays to light the world,
While beaters in excitement ring the glens
My gift will be a black raincloud, and hail,
A downpour, and I'll shake heaven with thunder.
The company will scatter, lost in gloom,
As Dido and the Trojan captain come
To one same cavern. I shall be on hand,

7. The Greek sun god Helios was the son of the Titan Hyperion; Helios became identified by the Greeks with Apollo, the god of prophecy, by the time of Euripides.

And if I can be certain you are willing,
There I shall marry them and call her his.
A wedding, this will be."
Then Cytherëa,
Not disinclined, nodded to Juno's plea,
And smiled at the stratagem now given away.

Dawn came up meanwhile from the Ocean stream,
And in the early sunshine from the gates
Picked huntsmen issued: wide-meshed nets and snares,
Broad spearheads for big game, Massylian[8] horsemen
Trooping with hounds in packs keen on the scent.
But Dido lingered in her hall, as Punic
Nobles waited, and her mettlesome hunter
Stood nearby, cavorting in gold and scarlet,
Champing his foam-flecked bridle. At long last
The queen appeared with courtiers in a crowd,
A short Sidonian cloak edged in embroidery
Caught about her, at her back a quiver
Sheathed in gold, her hair tied up in gold,
And a brooch of gold pinning her scarlet dress.
Phrygians came in her company as well,
And Iulus, joyous at the scene. Resplendent
Above the rest, Aeneas walked to meet her,
To join his retinue with hers. He seemed—
Think of the lord Apollo in the spring
When he leaves wintering in Lycia
By Xanthus torrent, for his mother's isle
Of Delos, to renew the festival;
Around his altars Cretans, Dryopës,
And painted Agathyrsans raise a shout,
But the god walks the Cynthian ridge alone
And smooths his hair, binds it in fronded laurel,
Braids it in gold; and shafts ring on his shoulders.[9]
So elated and swift, Aeneas walked
With sunlit grace upon him.
Soon the hunters,
Riding in company to high pathless hills,
Saw mountain goats shoot down from a rocky peak
And scamper on the ridges; toward the plain
Deer left the slopes, herding in clouds of dust
In flight across the open lands. Alone,
The boy Ascanius, delightedly riding
His eager horse amid the lowland vales,

8. The Massyli were a people of northern Africa.

9. Xanthus was the major river of the region of Lycia in southwest Asia Minor, where there was an important sanctuary of Leto, the mother of Apollo. Delos is a small island in the Aegean, mythological birthplace of Apollo and Artemis, an important center of worship, and the seat of an oracle of Apollo. Cynthia is a mountain of Delos. Cretans, Dryopës, and Agathyrsans were peoples associated with the cult of Apollo.

Outran both goats and deer. Could he only meet
Amid the harmless game some foaming boar,
Or a tawny lion down from the mountainside!

Meanwhile in heaven began a rolling thunder,
And soon the storm broke, pouring rain and hail.
Then Tyrians and Trojans in alarm—
With Venus' Dardan grandson—ran for cover
Here and there in the wilderness, as freshets
Coursed from the high hills.
Now to the self-same cave
Came Dido and the captain of the Trojans.
Primal Earth herself and Nuptial Juno
Opened the ritual, torches of lightning blazed,
High Heaven became witness to the marriage,
And nymphs cried out wild hymns from a mountain top.

That day was the first cause of death, and first
Of sorrow. Dido had no further qualms
As to impressions given and set abroad;
She thought no longer of a secret love
But called it marriage. Thus, under that name,
She hid her fault.
Now in no time at all
Through all the African cities Rumor[1] goes—
Nimble as quicksilver among evils. Rumor
Thrives on motion, stronger for the running,
Lowly at first through fear, then rearing high,
She treads the land and hides her head in cloud.
As people fable it, the Earth, her mother,
Furious against the gods, bore a late sister
To the giants Coeus and Enceladus,[2]
Giving her speed on foot and on the wing:
Monstrous, deformed, titanic. Pinioned, with
An eye beneath for every body feather,
And, strange to say, as many tongues and buzzing
Mouths as eyes, as many pricked-up ears,
By night she flies between the earth and heaven
Shrieking through darkness, and she never turns
Her eye-lids down to sleep. By day she broods,
On the alert, on rooftops or on towers,
Bringing great cities fear, harping on lies
And slander evenhandedly with truth.
In those days Rumor took an evil joy
At filling countrysides with whispers, whispers,

1. Rumor appears in Hesiod as a Greek god whose work is "never quite in vain"; Virgil portrays her as midway between a god and an allegory of the social effects of rumor (*fama*).

2. According to Hesiod, the giants were sons of Ge (Earth). After the defeat of their rebellion against the gods, the giants were buried under volcanoes in Greece and Italy, Enceladus under Aetna in Sicily.

Gossip of what was done, and never done:
How this Aeneas landed, Trojan born,
How Dido in her beauty graced his company,
Then how they reveled all the winter long
Unmindful of the realm, prisoners of lust.

These tales the scabrous goddess put about
On men's lips everywhere. Her twisting course
Took her to King Iarbas, whom she set
Ablaze with anger piled on top of anger.
Son of Jupiter Hammon by a nymph,
A ravished Garamantean,[3] this prince
Had built the god a hundred giant shrines,
A hundred altars, each with holy fires.
Alight by night and day, sentries on watch,
The ground enriched by victims' blood, the doors
Festooned with flowering wreaths. Before his altars
King Iarbas, crazed by the raw story,
Stood, they say, amid the Presences,° *spirits*
With supplicating hands, pouring out prayer:
"All powerful Jove, to whom the feasting Moors
At ease on colored couches tip their wine,
Do you see this? Are we then fools to fear you
Throwing down your bolts? Those dazzling fires
Of lightning, are they aimless in the clouds
And rumbling thunder meaningless? This woman
Who turned up in our country and laid down
A tiny city at a price, to whom
I gave a beach to plow—and on my terms—
After refusing to marry me has taken
Aeneas to be master in her realm.
And now Sir Paris with his men, half-men,
His chin and perfumed hair tied up
In a Maeonian bonnet, takes possession.[4]
As for ourselves, here we are bringing gifts
Into these shrines—supposedly your shrines—
Hugging that empty fable."
Pleas like this
From the man clinging to his altars reached
The ears of the Almighty. Now he turned
His eyes upon the queen's town and the lovers
Careless of their good name; then spoke to Mercury,
Assigning him a mission:
"Son, bestir yourself,
Call up the Zephyrs,° take to your wings and glide. *winds*
Approach the Dardan captain where he tarries

3. An African people; Hammon was a Libyan god identified with Jupiter.

4. Iarbas compares Aeneas to Paris, the abductor of Helen, who was regarded as unmanly, more interested in seduction than warfare. "Maeonia" was an old name for Lydia and denotes the Asiatic origin of the Trojans.

Rapt in Tyrian Carthage, losing sight
Of future towns the fates ordain. Correct him,
Carry my speech to him on the running winds:
No son like this did his enchanting mother
Promise to us, nor such did she deliver
Twice from peril at the hands of Greeks.
He was to be the ruler of Italy,
Potential empire, armorer of war;
To father men from Teucer's noble blood
And bring the whole world under law's dominion.
If glories to be won by deeds like these
Cannot arouse him, if he will not strive
For his own honor, does he begrudge his son,
Ascanius, the high strongholds of Rome?
What has he in mind? What hope, to make him stay
Amid a hostile race, and lose from view
Ausonian[5] progeny, Lavinian lands?
The man should sail: that is the whole point.
Let this be what you tell him, as from me."

He finished and fell silent. Mercury
Made ready to obey the great command
Of his great father, and he first tied on
The golden sandals, winged, that high in air
Transport him over seas or over land
Abreast of gale winds; then he took the wand
With which he summons pale souls out of Orcus
And ushers others to the undergloom,
Lulls men to slumber or awakens them,
And opens dead men's eyes.[6] This wand in hand,
He can drive winds before him, swimming down
Along the stormcloud. Now aloft, he saw
The craggy flanks and crown of patient Atlas,[7]
Giant Atlas, balancing the sky
Upon his peak—his pine-forested head
In vapor cowled, beaten by wind and rain.
Snow lay upon his shoulders, rills cascaded
Down his ancient chin and beard a-bristle,
Caked with ice. Here Mercury of Cyllenë[8]
Hovered first on even wings, then down
He plummeted to sea-level and flew on
Like a low-flying gull that skims the shallows
And rocky coasts where fish ply close inshore.

5. Italian. From an ancient name for central and southern Italy.
6. In addition to his role as messenger, Mercury was the conductor of souls of the dead to the underworld. Orcus was an infernal deity in Greek mythology, identified in Roman religion with Dis, god of the underworld.
7. The Atlas mountains run through northern Africa; Greek mythology made them a Titan's son who was punished by having to support the skies on his head and hands.
8. Hermes was born on Mt. Cyllenë in Arcadia.

So, like a gull between the earth and sky,
The progeny of Cyllenë, on the wing
From his maternal grandsire, split the winds
To the sand bars of Libya.
Alighting tiptoe
On the first hutments, there he found Aeneas
Laying foundations for new towers and homes.
He noted well the swordhilt the man wore,
Adorned with yellow jasper; and the cloak
Aglow with Tyrian dye upon his shoulders—
Gifts of the wealthy queen, who had inwoven
Gold thread in the fabric. Mercury
Took him to task at once:[9]
"Is it for you
To lay the stones for Carthage's high walls,
Tame husband that you are, and build their city?
Oblivious of your own world, your own kingdom!
From bright Olympus he that rules the gods
And turns the earth and heaven by his power—
He and no other sent me to you, told me
To bring this message on the running winds:
What have you in mind? What hope, wasting your days
In Libya? If future history's glories
Do not affect you, if you will not strive
For your own honor, think of Ascanius,
Think of the expectations of your heir,
Iulus, to whom the Italian realm, the land
Of Rome, are due."
And Mercury, as he spoke,
Departed from the visual field of mortals
To a great distance, ebbed in subtle air.
Amazed, and shocked to the bottom of his soul
By what his eyes had seen, Aeneas felt
His hackles rise, his voice choke in his throat.
As the sharp admonition and command
From heaven had shaken him awake, he now
Burned only to be gone, to leave that land
Of the sweet life behind. What can he do? How tell
The impassioned queen and hope to win her over?
What opening shall he choose? This way and that
He let his mind dart, testing alternatives,
Running through every one. And as he pondered
This seemed the better tactic: he called in
Mnestheus, Sergestus and stalwart Serestus,
Telling them:
"Get the fleet ready for sea,

9. Mercury repeats Jove's speech word for word. This is one of the many ways Virgil mimics Homeric oral conventions.

But quietly, and collect the men on shore.
Lay in ship stores and gear."
As to the cause
For a change of plan, they were to keep it secret,
Seeing the excellent Dido had no notion,
No warning that such love could be cut short;
He would himself look for the right occasion,
The easiest time to speak, the way to do it.
The Trojans to a man gladly obeyed.

The queen, for her part, felt some plot afoot
Quite soon—for who deceives a woman in love?
She caught wind of a change, being in fear
Of what had seemed her safety. Evil Rumor,
Shameless as before, brought word to her
In her distracted state of ships being rigged
In trim for sailing. Furious, at her wits' end,
She traversed the whole city, all aflame
With rage, like a Bacchantë driven wild
By emblems shaken, when the mountain revels
Of the odd year possess her, when the cry
Of Bacchus rises and Cithaeron calls
All through the shouting night.[1] Thus it turned out
She was the first to speak and charge Aeneas:

"You even hoped to keep me in the dark
As to this outrage, did you, two-faced man,
And slip away in silence? Can our love
Not hold you, can the pledge we gave not hold you,
Can Dido not, now sure to die in pain?
Even in winter weather must you toil
With ships, and fret to launch against high winds
For the open sea? Oh, heartless!
Tell me now,
If you were not in search of alien lands
And new strange homes, if ancient Troy remained,
Would ships put out for Troy on these big seas?
Do you go to get away from me? I beg you,
By these tears, by your own right hand, since I
Have left my wretched self nothing but that—
Yes, by the marriage that we entered on,
If ever I did well and you were grateful
Or found some sweetness in a gift from me,
Have pity now on a declining house!
Put this plan by, I beg you, if a prayer

1. Bacchantës, or maenads, were initiates in the cult of Bacchus (Greek: Dionysus), usually women, whose ritual behavior when possessed by their god was characterized by wild dancing and ecstatic behavior. The most famous and most extreme portrait of Dionysiac behavior was in Euripides' play *The Bacchae,* where King Pentheus is torn apart by his mother on Mt. Cithaeron when he refuses to recognize the new god.

Is not yet out of place.
Because of you, Libyans and nomad kings
Detest me, my own Tyrians are hostile;
Because of you, I lost my integrity
And that admired name by which alone
I made my way once toward the stars.
To whom
Do you abandon me, a dying woman,
Guest that you are—the only name now left
From that of husband? Why do I live on?
Shall I, until my brother Pygmalion comes
To pull my walls down? Or the Gaetulan
Iarbas leads me captive? If at least
There were a child by you for me to care for,
A little one to play in my courtyard
And give me back Aeneas, in spite of all,
I should not feel so utterly defeated,
Utterly bereft."
She ended there.
The man by Jove's command held fast his eyes
And fought down the emotion in his heart.
At length he answered:
"As for myself, be sure
I never shall deny all you can say,
Your majesty, of what you meant to me.
Never will the memory of Elissa° *Dido*
Stale for me, while I can still remember
My own life, and the spirit rules my body.
As to the event, a few words. Do not think
I meant to be deceitful and slip away.
I never held the torches of a bridegroom,
Never entered upon the pact of marriage.
If Fate permitted me to spend my days
By my own lights, and make the best of things
According to my wishes, first of all
I should look after Troy and the loved relics
Left me of my people. Priam's great hall
Should stand again; I should have restored the tower
Of Pergamum for Trojans in defeat.
But now it is the rich Italian land
Apollo tells me I must make for: Italy,
Named by his oracles.[2] There is my love;
There is my country. If, as a Phoenician.
You are so given to the charms of Carthage,
Libyan city that it is, then tell me,
Why begrudge the Teucrians new lands

2. Aeneas recounted this episode to Dido as part of his wanderings in Book 3.

For homesteads in Ausonia? Are we not
Entitled, too, to look for realms abroad?
Night never veils the earth in damp and darkness,
Fiery stars never ascend the east,
But in my dreams my father's troubled ghost
Admonishes and frightens me. Then, too,
Each night thoughts come of young Ascanius,
My dear boy wronged, defrauded of his kingdom,
Hesperian lands of destiny. And now
The gods' interpreter, sent by Jove himself—
I swear it by your head and mine—has brought
Commands down through the racing winds! I say
With my own eyes in full daylight I saw him
Entering the building! With my very ears
I drank his message in! So please, no more
Of these appeals that set us both afire.
I sail for Italy not of my own free will."

During all this she had been watching him
With face averted, looking him up and down
In silence, and she burst out raging now:

"No goddess was your mother. Dardanus
Was not the founder of your family.
Liar and cheat! Some rough Caucasian cliff
Begot you on flint. Hyrcanian tigresses[3]
Tendered their teats to you. Why should I palter?
Why still hold back for more indignity?
Sigh, did he, while I wept? Or look at me?
Or yield a tear, or pity her who loved him?
What shall I say first, with so much to say?
The time is past when either supreme Juno
Or the Saturnian father viewed these things
With justice. Faith can never be secure.
I took the man in, thrown up on this coast
In dire need, and in my madness then
Contrived a place for him in my domain,
Rescued his lost fleet, saved his shipmates' lives.
Oh, I am swept away burning by furies!
Now the prophet Apollo, now his oracles,
Now the gods' interpreter, if you please,
Sent down by Jove himself, brings through the air
His formidable commands! What fit employment
For heaven's high powers! What anxieties
To plague serene immortals! I shall not
Detain you or dispute your story. Go,
Go after Italy on the sailing winds,

3. Caucasian and Hyrcanian (referring to regions near the Caspian Sea) are used as epitomes of Asian barbarism and savagery in contrast to the Roman civility claimed by Aeneas.

Look for your kingdom, cross the deepsea swell!
If divine justice counts for anything,
I hope and pray that on some grinding reef
Midway at sea you'll drink your punishment
And call and call on Dido's name!
From far away I shall come after you
With my black fires, and when cold death has parted
Body from soul I shall be everywhere
A shade° to haunt you! You will pay for this, *spirit*
Unconscionable! I shall hear! The news will reach me
Even among the lowest of the dead!"

At this abruptly she broke off and ran
In sickness from his sight and the light of day,
Leaving him at a loss, alarmed, and mute
With all he meant to say. The maids in waiting
Caught her as she swooned and carried her
To bed in her marble chamber.
Duty-bound,
Aeneas, though he struggled with desire
To calm and comfort her in all her pain,
To speak to her and turn her mind from grief,
And though he sighed his heart out, shaken still
With love of her, yet took the course heaven gave him
And went back to the fleet. Then with a will
The Teucrians fell to work and launched the ships
Along the whole shore: slick with tar each hull
Took to the water. Eager to get away,
The sailors brought oar-boughs out of the woods
With leaves still on, and oaken logs unhewn.
Now you could see them issuing from the town
To the water's edge in streams, as when, aware
Of winter, ants will pillage a mound of spelt
To store it in their granary; over fields
The black battalion moves, and through the grass
On a narrow trail they carry off the spoil;
Some put their shoulders to the enormous weight
Of a trundled grain, while some pull stragglers in
And castigate delay; their to-and-fro
Of labor makes the whole track come alive.
At that sight, what were your emotions, Dido?
Sighing how deeply, looking out and down
From your high tower on the seething shore
Where all the harbor filled before your eyes
With bustle and shouts! Unconscionable Love,
To what extremes will you not drive our hearts!
She now felt driven to weep again, again
To move him, if she could, by supplication,
Humbling her pride before her love—to leave

Nothing untried, not to die needlessly.

"Anna, you see the arc of waterfront
All in commotion: they come crowding in
From everywhere. Spread canvas calls for wind,
The happy crews have garlanded the sterns.
If I could brace myself for this great sorrow,
Sister, I can endure it, too. One favor,
Even so, you may perform for me.
Since that deserter chose you for his friend
And trusted you, even with private thoughts,
Since you alone know when he may be reached,
Go, intercede with our proud enemy.
Remind him that I took no oath at Aulis
With Danaans to destroy the Trojan race;[4]
I sent no ship to Pergamum.° Never did I *Troy*
Profane his father Anchises' dust and shade.
Why will he not allow my prayers to fall
On his unpitying ears? Where is he racing?
Let him bestow one last gift on his mistress:
This, to await fair winds and easier flight.
Now I no longer plead the bond he broke
Of our old marriage, nor do I ask that he
Should live without his dear love, Latium,
Or yield his kingdom. Time is all I beg,
Mere time, a respite and a breathing space
For madness to subside in, while my fortune
Teaches me how to take defeat and grieve.
Pity your sister. This is the end, this favor—
To be repaid with interest when I die."

She pleaded in such terms, and such, in tears,
Her sorrowing sister brought him, time and again.
But no tears moved him, no one's voice would he
Attend to tractably. The fates opposed it;
God's will blocked the man's once kindly ears.
And just as when the north winds from the Alps
This way and that contend among themselves
To tear away an oaktree hale with age,
The wind and tree cry, and the buffeted trunk
Showers high foliage to earth, but holds
On bedrock, for the roots go down as far
Into the underworld as cresting boughs
Go up in heaven's air: just so this captain,
Buffeted by a gale of pleas
This way and that way, dinned all the day long,
Felt their moving power in his great heart,

4. Aulis was the launching point of the Greek expedition to Troy.

And yet his will stood fast; tears fell in vain.

On Dido in her desolation now
Terror grew at her fate. She prayed for death,
Being heartsick at the mere sight of heaven.
That she more surely would perform the act
And leave the daylight, now she saw before her
A thing one shudders to recall: on altars
Fuming with incense where she placed her gifts,
The holy water blackened, the spilt wine
Turned into blood and mire. Of this she spoke
To no one, not to her sister even. Then, too,
Within the palace was a marble shrine
Devoted to her onetime lord, a place
She held in wondrous honor, all festooned
With snowy fleeces and green festive boughs.
From this she now thought voices could be heard
And words could be made out, her husband's words,
Calling her, when midnight hushed the earth;
And lonely on the rooftops the night owl
Seemed to lament, in melancholy notes,
Prolonged to a doleful cry. And then, besides,
The riddling words of seers in ancient days,
Foreboding sayings, made her thrill with fear.
In nightmare, fevered, she was hunted down
By pitiless Aeneas, and she seemed
Deserted always, uncompanioned always,
On a long journey, looking for her Tyrians
In desolate landscapes—
as Pentheus gone mad
Sees the oncoming Eumenidës and sees
A double sun and double Thebes appear,[5]
Or as when, hounded on the stage, Orestës
Runs from a mother armed with burning brands,
With serpents hellish black,
And in the doorway squat the Avenging Ones.[6]

So broken in mind by suffering, Dido caught
Her fatal madness and resolved to die.
She pondered time and means, then visiting
Her mournful sister, covered up her plan
With a calm look, a clear and hopeful brow.

"Sister, be glad for me! I've found a way
To bring him back or free me of desire.

5. Here Virgil cites a scene from the *Bacchae* of Euripides in which Dionysus has driven mad Pentheus, King of Thebes, causing him to see the world double as the Bacchantes approach to tear him to pieces. Virgil equates them with the Furies (Eumenides), female powers of the underworld who punish blood guilt.

6. Son of Clytemnestra and Agamemnon, Orestes kills his mother and her lover to revenge her murder of his father. He is then pursued by the Furies (the Avenging Ones). Virgil's description comes from the *Oresteia* of Aeschylus.

Near to the Ocean boundary, near sundown,
The Aethiops' farthest territory lies,
Where giant Atlas turns the sphere of heaven
Studded with burning stars. From there
A priestess of Massylian stock has come;
She had been pointed out to me: custodian
Of that shrine named for daughters of the west,
Hesperidës; and it is she who fed
The dragon, guarding well the holy boughs
With honey dripping slow and drowsy poppy.[7]
Chanting her spells she undertakes to free
What hearts she wills, but to inflict on others
Duress of sad desires; to arrest
The flow of rivers, make the stars move backward,
Call up the spirits of deep Night.[8] You'll see
Earth shift and rumble underfoot and ash trees
Walk down mountainsides. Dearest, I swear
Before the gods and by your own sweet self,
It is against my will that I resort
For weaponry to magic powers. In secret
Build up a pyre in the inner court
Under the open sky, and place upon it
The arms that faithless man left in my chamber,
All his clothing, and the marriage bed
On which I came to grief—solace for me
To annihilate all vestige of the man,
Vile as he is: my priestess shows me this."

While she was speaking, cheek and brow grew pale.
But Anna could not think her sister cloaked
A suicide in these unheard-of rites;
She failed to see how great her madness was
And feared no consequence more grave
Than at Sychaeus' death. So, as commanded,
She made the preparations. For her part,
The queen, seeing the pyre in her inmost court
Erected huge with pitch-pine and sawn ilex,° *holm oak*
Hung all the place under the sky with wreaths
And crowned it with funereal cypress boughs.
On the pyre's top she put a sword he left
With clothing, and an effigy on a couch,
Her mind fixed now ahead on what would come.
Around the pyre stood altars, and the priestess,
Hair unbound, called in a voice of thunder

7. The garden tended by the Hesperides, the daughters of Hesperus (West) and Atlas, was traditionally located beyond the Atlas mountains at the western border of the Ocean. The garden contained a tree of golden apples given by Earth to Hera following her marriage. The tree was guarded by a dragon, who was slain by Hercules.

8. Another tradition made the Hesperides the daughters of Night and Erebus. As is his custom, Virgil combines elements of different versions of the myth in Dido's description.

Upon three hundred gods, on Erebus,
On Chaos, and on triple Hecatë,
Three-faced Diana.[9] Then she sprinkled drops
Purportedly from the fountain of Avernus.[1]
Rare herbs were brought out, reaped at the new moon
By scythes of bronze, and juicy with a milk
Of dusky venom; then the rare love-charm
Or caul torn from the brow of a birthing foal
And snatched away before the mother found it.
Dido herself with consecrated grain
In her pure hands, as she went near the altars,
Freed one foot from sandal straps, let fall
Her dress ungirdled, and, now sworn to death,
Called on the gods and stars that knew her fate.
She prayed then to whatever power may care
In comprehending justice for the grief
Of lovers bound unequally by love.

The night had come, and weary in every land
Men's bodies took the boon of peaceful sleep.
The woods and the wild seas had quieted
At that hour when the stars are in mid-course
And every field is still; cattle and birds
With vivid wings that haunt the limpid lakes
Or nest in thickets in the country places
All were asleep under the silent night.
Not, though, the agonized Phoenician queen:
She never slackened into sleep and never
Allowed the tranquil night to rest
Upon her eyelids or within her heart.
Her pain redoubled; love came on again,
Devouring her, and on her bed she tossed
In a great surge of anger.
So awake,
She pressed these questions, musing to herself:

"Look now, what can I do? Turn once again
To the old suitors, only to be laughed at—
Begging a marriage with Numidians
Whom I disdained so often? Then what? Trail
The Ilian ships and follow like a slave
Commands of Trojans? Seeing them so agreeable,
In view of past assistance and relief,
So thoughtful their unshaken gratitude?
Suppose I wished it, who permits or takes

9. Hecatë was a sinister goddess associated with magic, witchcraft, the night, the underworld, and crossroads, which she haunted. She was frequently depicted with three faces representing her three aspects and sometimes identified with Artemis (Roman: Diana).

1. A lake near Cumae and Naples. Near it is a cave reputed to contain an entrance to the underworld (see bk. 6). Avernus was used by Virgil and others to refer to the underworld in general.

Aboard their proud ships one they so dislike?
Poor lost soul, do you not yet grasp or feel
The treachery of the line of Laömedon?
What then? Am I to go alone, companion
Of the exultant sailors in their flight?
Or shall I set out in their wake, with Tyrians,
With all my crew close at my side, and send
The men I barely tore away from Tyre
To sea again, making them hoist their sails
To more sea-winds? No: die as you deserve,
Give pain quietus° with a steel blade. *rest*
Sister,
You are the one who gave way to my tears
In the beginning, burdened a mad queen
With sufferings, and thrust me on my enemy.
It was not given me to lead my life
Without new passion, innocently, the way
Wild creatures live, and not to touch these depths.
The vow I took to the ashes of Sychaeus
Was not kept."
So she broke out afresh
In bitter mourning. On his high stern deck
Aeneas, now quite certain of departure,
Everything ready, took the boon of sleep,
In dream the figure of the god returned
With looks reproachful as before: he seemed
Again to warn him, being like Mercury
In every way, in voice, in golden hair,
And in the bloom of youth.
"Son of the goddess,
Sleep away this crisis, can you still?
Do you not see the dangers growing round you,
Madman, from now on? Can you not hear
The offshore westwind blow? The woman hatches
Plots and drastic actions in her heart,
Resolved on death now, whipping herself on
To heights of anger. Will you not be gone
In flight, while flight is still within your power?
Soon you will see the offing boil with ships
And glare with torches; soon again
The waterfront will be alive with fires,
If Dawn comes while you linger in this country.
Ha! Come, break the spell! Woman's a thing
Forever fitful and forever changing."

At this he merged into the darkness. Then
As the abrupt phantom filled him with fear,
Aeneas broke from sleep and roused his crewmen:
"Up, turn out now! Oarsmen, take your thwarts!
Shake out sail! Look here, for the second time

A god from heaven's high air is goading me
To hasten our break away, to cut the cables.
Holy one, whatever god you are,
We go with you, we act on your command
Most happily! Be near, graciously help us,
Make the stars in heaven propitious ones!"

He pulled his sword aflash out of its sheath
And struck at the stern hawser.° All the men *mooring cable*
Were gripped by his excitement to be gone,
And hauled and hustled. Ships cast off their moorings,
And an array of hulls hid inshore water
As oarsmen churned up foam and swept to sea.

Soon early Dawn, quitting the saffron bed
Of old Tithonus,[2] cast new light on earth,
And as air grew transparent, from her tower
The queen caught sight of ships on the seaward reach
With sails full and the wind astern. She knew
The waterfront now empty, bare of oarsmen.
Beating her lovely breast three times, four times,
And tearing her golden hair,
"O Jupiter,"
She said, "will this man go, will he have mocked
My kingdom, stranger that he was and is?
Will they not snatch up arms and follow him
From every quarter of the town? And dockhands
Tear our ships from moorings? On! Be quick
With torches! Give out arms! Unship the oars!
What am I saying? Where am I? What madness
Takes me out of myself? Dido, poor soul,
Your evil doing has come home to you.
Then was the right time, when you offered him
A royal scepter. See the good faith and honor
Of one they say bears with him everywhere
The hearthgods of his country! One who bore
His father, spent with age, upon his shoulders!
Could I not then have torn him limb from limb
And flung the pieces on the sea?[3] His company,
Even Ascanius could I not have minced
And served up to his father at a feast?[4]
The luck of battle might have been in doubt—
So let it have been! Whom had I to fear,

2. In Greek mythology, Tithonus, a son of Laomedon and the brother of Priam, was loved by Eos (Roman: Aurora), the goddess of Dawn. She begged Zeus to make Tithonus immortal but forgot to ask for eternal youth for him as well.

3. As Medea did to her brother, Apsyrtus, to aid her escape with her lover, Jason. In revenge for Jason's later betrayal of her, she poisoned their two children as well. See Euripides' *Medea* (page 575).

4. When Procne, daughter of a legendary king of Athens, discovered that her husband, Tereus, had raped and mutilated her sister, Philomela, she killed their son, Itys, and served him to his father as punishment.

Being sure to die? I could have carried torches
Into his camp, filled passage ways with flame,
Annihilated father and son and followers
And given my own life on top of all!
O Sun, scanning with flame all works of earth,
And thou, O Juno, witness and go-between
Of my long miseries; and Hecatë,
Screeched for at night at crossroads in the cities;
And thou, avenging Furies, and all gods
On whom Elissa dying may call: take notice,
Overshadow this hell with your high power,
As I deserve, and hear my prayer!
If by necessity that impious wretch
Must find his haven and come safe to land,
If so Jove's destinies require, and this,
His end in view, must stand, yet all the same
When hard beset in war by a brave people,
Forced to go outside his boundaries
And torn from Iulus, let him beg assistance,
Let him see the unmerited deaths of those
Around and with him, and accepting peace
On unjust terms, let him not, even so,
Enjoy his kingdom or the life he longs for,
But fall in battle before his time and lie
Unburied on the sand! This I implore,
This is my last cry, as my last blood flows.
Then, O my Tyrians, besiege with hate
His progeny and all his race to come:
Make this your offering to my dust. No love,
No pact must be between our peoples; No,
But rise up from my bones, avenging spirit!
Harry with fire and sword the Dardan countrymen
Now, or hereafter, at whatever time
The strength will be afforded. Coast with coast
In conflict, I implore, and sea with sea,
And arms with arms: may they contend in war,
Themselves and all the children of their children!"[5]

Now she took thought of one way or another,
At the first chance, to end her hated life,
And briefly spoke to Barcë, who had been
Sychaeus' nurse; her own an urn of ash
Long held in her ancient fatherland.
"Dear nurse,
Tell Sister Anna to come here, and have her
Quickly bedew herself with running water

5. Virgil creates a myth of the origins of the conflict between Carthage and Rome. More immediately, he motivates the difficulty faced by the Trojans when they reach Latium in defeating an obviously inferior foe.

Before she brings our victims for atonement.
Let her come that way. And you, too, put on
Pure wool around your brows. I have a mind
To carry out that rite to Stygian Jove[6]
That I have readied here, and put an end
To my distress, committing to the flames
The pyre of that miserable Dardan."

At this with an old woman's eagerness
Barcë hurried away. And Dido's heart
Beat wildly at the enormous thing afoot.
She rolled her bloodshot eyes, her quivering cheeks
Were flecked with red as her sick pallor grew
Before her coming death. Into the court
She burst her way, then at her passion's height
She climbed the pyre and bared the Dardan sword—
A gift desired once, for no such need.
Her eyes now on the Trojan clothing there
And the familiar bed, she paused a little,
Weeping a little, mindful, then lay down
And spoke her last words:
"Remnants dear to me
While god and fate allowed it, take this breath
And give me respite from these agonies.
I lived my life out to the very end
And passed the stages Fortune had appointed.
Now my tall shade goes to the under world.
I built a famous town, saw my great walls,
Avenged my husband, made my hostile brother
Pay for his crime. Happy, alas, too happy,
If only the Dardanian keels had never
Beached on our coast." And here she kissed the bed.
"I die unavenged," she said, "but let me die.
This way, this way, a blessed relief to go
Into the undergloom. Let the cold Trojan,
Far at sea, drink in this conflagration
And take with him the omen of my death!"

Amid these words her household people saw her
Crumpled over the steel blade, and the blade
Aflush with red blood, drenched her hands. A scream
Pierced the high chambers. Now through the shocked city
Rumor went rioting, as wails and sobs
With women's outcry echoed in the palace
And heaven's high air gave back the beating din,
As though all Carthage or old Tyre fell
To storming enemies, and, out of hand,

6. Dis, god of the underworld, "ruler of the Styx."

Flames billowed on the roofs of men and gods.
Her sister heard the trembling, faint with terror,
Lacerating her face, beating her breast,
Ran through the crowd to call the dying queen:
"It came to this, then, sister? You deceived me?
The pyre meant this, altars and fires meant this?
What shall I mourn first, being abandoned? Did you
Scorn your sister's company in death?
You should have called me out to the same fate!
The same blade's edge and hurt, at the same hour,
Should have taken us off. With my own hands
Had I to build this pyre, and had I to call
Upon our country's gods, that in the end
With you placed on it there, O heartless one,
I should be absent? You have put to death
Yourself and me, the people and the fathers
Bred in Sidon, and your own new city.
Give me fresh water, let me bathe her wound
And catch upon my lips any last breath
Hovering over hers."
Now she had climbed
The topmost steps and took her dying sister
Into her arms to cherish, with a sob,
Using her dress to stanch the dark blood flow.
But Dido trying to lift her heavy eyes
Fainted again. Her chest-wound whistled air.
Three times she struggled up on one elbow
And each time fell back on the bed. Her gaze
Went wavering as she looked for heaven's light
And groaned at finding it. Almighty Juno,
Filled with pity for this long ordeal
And difficult passage, now sent Iris[7] down
Out of Olympus to set free
The wrestling spirit from the body's hold.
For since she died, not at her fated span
Nor as she merited, but before her time
Enflamed and driven mad, Proserpina
Had not yet plucked from her the golden hair,
Delivering her to Orcus of the Styx.[8]
So humid Iris through bright heaven flew
On saffron-yellow wings, and in her train
A thousand hues shimmered before the sun.
At Dido's head she came to rest.
"This token

7. The goddess of the rainbow, and also messenger of the gods, especially Hera/Juno.

8. Proserpina (Greek: Persephone) was the goddess of the underworld and the wife of Dis (Greek: Hades). In sacrifices, the hair of the victim would be removed and offered as first fruits. When men and women died at their appointed time, Proserpina herself was said to cut their locks for a similar reason; however, she cannot do this for the untimely dead, so Iris is sent out of special compassion in her place.

Sacred to Dis I bear away as bidden
And free you from your body."
Saying this,
She cut a lock of hair. Along with it
Her body's warmth fell into dissolution,
And out into the winds her life withdrew.

[*Leaving Carthage, the Trojans stop again at Drepinum in Sicily, where they conduct funeral games for the anniversary of Anchises' death. The games—naval and foot races, boxing, and archery—are interrupted when the women of Troy, goaded by Juno, set fire to the ships. Anchises visits Aeneas in a dream, telling him that he must descend to the underworld to meet him. The helmsman Palinurus is lost at sea during the night.*]

from Book 6

[The World Below]

So grieving, and in tears, he gave the ship
Her head before the wind, drawing toward land
At the Euboian settlement of Cumae.[1]
Ships came about, prows pointing seaward, anchors
Biting to hold them fast, and rounded sterns
Indented all the water's edge. The men
Debarked in groups, eager to go ashore
Upon Hesperia. Some struck seeds of fire
Out of the veins of flint, and some explored
The virgin woods, lairs of wild things, for fuel,
Pointing out, too, what streams they found.
Aeneas,
In duty bound, went inland to the heights
Where overshadowing Apollo dwells
And nearby, in a place apart—a dark
Enormous cave—the Sibyl feared by men.[2]
In her the Delian god of prophecy° *Apollo*
Inspires uncanny powers of mind and soul,
Disclosing things to come. Here Trojan captains
Walked to Diana of the Crossroads' wood
And entered under roofs of gold.[3] They say
That Daedalus, when he fled the realm of Minos,
Dared to entrust himself to stroking wings
And to the air of heaven—unheard-of path—

1. Settlers from the Greek island of Euboea founded a colony at Cumae, ten miles northwest of Naples, c. 740 B.C.E.

2. Sibyls were prophetic women, usually inspired by the god Apollo, whose oracles were often collected and preserved. Most celebrated were the books of the Cumaean sibyl kept in Rome and consulted by the senate in times of crisis.

3. The Cumaean sibyl Deiphobë was the priestess of both Apollo and Hecate ("Diana of the Crossroads").

On which he swam away to the cold North
At length to touch down on that very height
Of the Chalcidians.[4] Here, on earth again
He dedicated to you, Phoebus Apollo,
The twin sweeps of his wings; here he laid out
A spacious temple. In the entrance way
Androgeos' death appeared, then Cecrops' children
Ordered to pay in recompense each year
The living flesh of seven sons.[5] The urn
From which the lots were drawn stood modeled there.[6]
And facing it, upon the opposite door,
The land of Crete, emergent from the sea;
Here the brutish act appeared: Pasiphaë
Being covered by the bull in the cow's place,
Then her mixed breed, her child of double form,
The Minotaur, get of unholy lust.[7]
Here, too, that puzzle of the house of Minos,
The maze none could untangle, until, touched
By a great love shown by a royal girl,
He, Daedalus himself, unravelled all
The baffling turns and dead ends in the dark,
Guiding the blind way back by a skein unwound.[8]
In that high sculpture you, too, would have had
Your great part, Icarus, had grief allowed.
Twice your father had tried to shape your fall
In gold, but twice his hands dropped.[9]
                                        Here the Trojans
Would have passed on and gazed and read it all,
Had not Achatës, whom they had sent ahead,
Returned now with the priestess of Apollo
And of Diana, goddess of the Crossroads—
Deiphobë, the Sibyl, Glaucus' daughter.
Thus she addressed the king:
                                        "The hour demands
No lagging over sights like these. Instead,
You should make offering of seven young bulls
From an ungelded herd, and seven again

4. Daedalus was a legendary Athenian artist, craftsman, and inventor and builder for King Minos of Crete of the labyrinth in which the Minotaur was housed. Trapped on Minos's island kingdom, Daedalus made wings of wax and feathers and escaped through the air. The most famous version is Ovid's in the *Metamorphoses,* Book 8 (see page 789).

5. After Androgeos dies an untimely death in Attica, the region of Greece ruled by Athens, his father, Minos, extracts an annual tribute of seven youths and seven maidens to be thrown to the Minotaur in its labyrinth. The Athenians are called "Cecrops' children" here after the legendary first king of Athens.

6. The victims were chosen by lot drawn from an urn, a standard ancient procedure.

7. Pasiphaë, daughter of the Sun, was married to Minos. When Minos refused to sacrifice to Poseidon a beautiful bull he had promised him, the god caused Pasiphaë to fall in love with the bull, which she seduced, hidden within an artificial cow created by Daedalus. The Minotaur—half-man, half-bull—was the result of this union.

8. The legendary king of Athens, Theseus, traveled to Crete as one of the sacrificial youths, killed the Minotaur, and escaped from the labyrinth with the help of a spool of thread given him by Minos's daughter, Ariadne, with whom he fled.

9. Daedalus's son, Icarus, fled with him, but Icarus flew too close to the sun, causing the wax of his wings to melt, and he fell to his death in the sea.

Well-chosen ewes."
With these words for Aeneas—
Orders his men were quick to act upon—
The priestess called them to her lofty shrine.
The cliff's huge flank is honeycombed, cut out
In a cavern perforated a hundred times,
Having a hundred mouths, with rushing voices
Carrying the responses of the Sibyl.[1]
Here, as the men approached the entrance way,
The Sibyl cried out:
"Now is the time to ask
Your destinies!"
And then:
"The god! Look there!
The god!"
And as she spoke neither her face
Nor hue went untransformed, nor did her hair
Stay neatly bound: her breast heaved, her wild heart
Grew large with passion. Taller to their eyes
And sounding now no longer like a mortal
Since she had felt the god's power breathing near,
She cried:
"Slow, are you, in your vows and prayers?
Trojan Aeneas, are you slow? Be quick,
The great mouths of the god's house, thunderstruck,
Will never open till you pray."
Her lips
Closed tight on this. A chill ran through the bones
Of the tough Teucrians, but their king poured out
Entreaties from his deepest heart:
"O Phoebus,
God who took pity on the pain of Troy,
Who guided Paris' hand, his Dardan shaft,
Against the body of Aiacidës,[2]
As you led on I entered all those seas
Washing great lands, and then the distant tribe
Of the Massylians at the Syrtës' edge.
Now we take hold at last of Italy
That slipped away so long. Grant that the fortune
Of Troy shall have pursued us this far only!
And all you gods and goddesses as well
Who took offence at Ilium and our pride,
At last, and rightly, you may spare

1. A cave believed to have been that of the Sibyl has been discovered and excavated on the site of the ancient Cumae. It consists of a quadrangular chamber approached by a corridor in the side of the mountain 125 yards long and 60 feet high.

2. Paris, with the help of Apollo, caused the death of Achilles with an arrow in his heel, the only vulnerable part of his body. Aiacidës (or Aeacidës) means a descendant of Aeacus, the grandfather of Achilles.

Pergamum's children. Most holy prophetess,
Foreknowing things to come, I ask no kingdom
Other than fate allows me; let our people
Make their settlement in Latium
With all Troy's wandering gods and shaken powers.
Then I shall dedicate a temple here
To Phoebus and Diana of the Crossroads,
Ordering festal days in Phoebus' name.
A holy place awaits you in my kingdom
Where I shall store your prophecies, your dark
Revelations to my people, and appoint
A chosen priesthood for you, gracious one.[3]
But now commit no verses to the leaves
Or they may be confused, shuffled and whirled
By playing winds: chant them aloud, I pray."

Then he fell silent. But the prophetess
Whom the bestriding god had not yet broken
Stormed about the cavern, trying to shake
His influence from her breast, while all the more
He tired her mad jaws, quelled her savage heart,
And tamed her by his pressure. In the end
The cavern's hundred mouths all of themselves
Unclosed to let the Sibyl's answers through:

"You, sir, now quit at last of the sea's dangers,
For whom still greater are in store on land,
The Dardan race will reach Lavinian country—
Put that anxiety away—but there
Will wish they had not come. Wars, vicious wars
I see ahead, and Tiber foaming blood.
Simoïs, Xanthus, Dorians encamped—
You'll have them all again, with an Achilles,
Child of Latium, he, too, goddess-born.[4]
And nowhere from pursuit of Teucrians
Will Juno stray, while you go destitute,
Begging so many tribes and towns for aid.
The cause of suffering here again will be
A bride foreign to Teucrians, a marriage
Made with a stranger.[5]

Never shrink from blows.
Boldly, more boldly where your luck allows,
Go forward, face them. A first way to safety
Will open where you reckon on it least,

3. Originally stored in the temple of Capitoline Jupiter, the Sibylline books were moved to the temple of Palatine Apollo, constructed by Augustus in 28 B.C.E. in the neighborhood of Rome where the emperor himself lived.

4. The prophecy of Apollo establishes the war of the second half of the *Aeneid* in terms of the *Iliad,* with Turnus, the son of the nymph Venilia, as the new Achilles.

5. Apollo's prediction echoes Dido's curse, quite aptly as it concerns the betrothal of Aeneas to Lavinia, daughter of Latinus, the king of Latium.

From a Greek city."[6]
These were the sentences
In which the Sibyl of Cumae from her shrine
Sang out her riddles, echoing in the cave,
Dark sayings muffling truths, the way Apollo
Pulled her up raging, or else whipped her on,
Digging the spurs beneath her breast. As soon
As her fit ceased, her wild voice quieted,
The great soldier, Aeneas, began to speak:

"No novel kinds of hardship, no surprises,
Loom ahead, Sister. I foresaw them all,
Went through them in my mind. One thing I pray for:
Since it is here they say one finds the gate
Of the king of under world, the shadowy marsh
That wells from Acheron,[7] may I have leave
To go to my dear father's side and see him.
Teach me the path, show me the entrance way.
Through fires, and with a thousand spears behind,
I brought him on these shoulders, rescued him
Amid our enemies. He shared my voyage,
Bore all the seas with me, hard nights and days
Of menace from the sea and sky, beyond
The strength and lot of age, frail though he was.
Indeed, he prayed this very prayer; he told me
That I should come to you and beg it humbly.
Pity a son and father, gracious lady,
All this is in your power. Hecatë
Gave you authority to have and hold
Avernus wood. If Orpheus could call
His wife's shade up, relying on the strings
That sang loud on his Thracian lyre; if Pollux
Redeemed his brother, taking his turn at death,
So often passing back and forth; why name
The heroes, Theseus and Hercules?[8]
By birth I too descend from Jove on high—"

While in these terms he prayed and pressed the altar,
Breaking in, the Sibyl said:
"Offspring
Of gods by blood, Trojan Anchises' son,

6. Evander, whose aid Aeneas will seek in Book 8, was supposedly an Arcadian who with his countrymen founded a colony on the banks of the Tiber river.

7. A river in Epirus (northwest Greece) that breaks through an impenetrable gorge to form the Acherusian swamps. After Homer named it a river of Hades in the *Odyssey,* the Acheron became identified with the underworld.

8. Mythological figures who descended to the underworld and returned (Virgil pointedly omits Odysseus). The singer Orpheus went to Hades to recover his wife, Eurydice, only to lose her again when he could not resist looking behind him (see *Metamorphoses,* page 791). Castor and Pollux were twin brothers of Helen. When Castor was killed, his brother asked to die also. Touched by such devotion, Zeus granted that they should spend alternate days in Hades and in Heaven. Theseus and a companion were imprisoned in Hades until rescued by Hercules, who found them there while fetching Cerberus as the eleventh of his Twelve Labors.

The way downward is easy from Avernus.
Black Dis's door stands open night and day.
But to retrace your steps to heaven's air,
There is the trouble, there is the toil. A few
Whom a benign Jupiter has loved or whom
Fiery heroism has borne to heaven,
Sons of gods, could do it. All midway
Are forests, then Cocytus,[9] thick and black,
Winds through the gloom. But if you feel such love,
And such desire to cross the Stygian water
Twice, to view the night of Tartarus twice[1]—
If this mad effort's to your liking, then
Consider what you must accomplish first.
A tree's deep shade conceals a bough whose leaves
And pliant twigs are all of gold, a thing
Sacred to Juno of the lower world.° *Proserpina*
The whole grove shelters it, and thickest shade
In dusky valleys shuts it in. And yet
No one may enter hidden depths
Below the earth unless he picks this bough,
The tree's fruit, with its foliage of gold.[2]
Proserpina decreed this bough, as due her,
Should be given into her own fair hands
When torn away. In place of it a second
Grows up without fail, all gold as well,
Flowering with metallic leaves again.
So lift your eyes and search, and once you find it
Pull away the bough. It will come willingly,
Easily, if you are called by fate.
If not, with all your strength you cannot conquer it,
Cannot lop it off with a sword's edge.
A further thing is this: your friend's dead body—
Ah, but you *don't* know!—lies out there unburied,
Polluting all your fleet with death
While you are lingering, waiting on my counsel
Here at my door. First give the man his rest,
Entomb him; lead black beasts to sacrifice;
Begin with these amends. Then in due course
You'll see the Stygian forest rise before you,
Regions not for the living."[3]

9. One of the tributaries of the Acheron in Epirus, later considered a river of the world below.

1. That is, now and when he dies. Tartarus generally refers to the deepest part of the underworld, a place of punishment.

2. Aeneas's journey combines aspects of the heroic descent through personal prowess with religious ritual, perhaps through personal knowledge of rites used in the mysteries of Proserpina. In necromancy and mystery cults, some form of magical token was usually required for admittance to the realm of the dead or conversation with them.

3. The burial of Misenus bears many traces of rituals of human sacrifice said also to be required for converse with the dead.

She fell silent,
Closing her lips. With downcast face and eyes
Aeneas turned from the cavern to the shore,
Dark matters on his mind. Steadfast Achatës
Walked beside him with deliberate pace
And equal anxieties. The two exchanged
In shifting conversation many guesses
As to that friend, now dead, now to be buried,
So the prophetess had said—then suddenly
As they came down to the dry beach they saw
Misenus, robbed of life by early death,
Their own Misenus, a son of Aeolus,
Never surpassed at rousing fighting men
With brazen trumpet, setting Mars afire.
Once he had been great Hector's adjutant,
Going forward at Hector's side in battle,
Brilliant with trumpet and with spear as well.
After Achilles took the life of Hector,
This gallant soldier joined Dardan Aeneas
In allegiance to no lesser cause. That day
By chance, as he blew notes on a hollow shell,
Making the sea sing back, in his wild folly
He dared the gods to rival him. Then Triton,[4]
Envious, if this can be believed,
Caught him and put him under in the surf
Amid the rocks off shore.
All who were there
Clamored around the body in lament,
Aeneas, the good captain, most of all.
In haste then, even as they wept, they turned
To carry out the orders of the Sibyl,
Racing to pile up logs for the altar-pyre
And build it sky-high. Into the virgin forest,
Thicket of wild things, went the men, and down
The pitch pines came, the bitten ilex rang
With axe blows, ash and oak were split with wedges,
Mighty rowans were trundled down the slopes.

Aeneas himself went first in all this labor,
Cheering his fellows on, with implements
Like theirs in hand; but grimly in his heart
He wondered, studying the unmeasured forest,
And fell to prayer:
"If only the golden bough
Might shine for us in such a wilderness!
As all the prophetess foretold was true—

4. In Greek myth a merman, a son of Poseidon who is commonly shown blowing on a conch shell. He appears as Poseidon's aide in Book 1.

Misenus, in your case only too true."

The words were barely uttered when two doves
In casual flight out of the upper air
Came down before the man's eyes to alight
On the green grass, and the great hero knew
These birds to be his mother's. Joyously
He prayed:
"O be my guides, if there's a way.
Wing on, into that woodland where the bough,
The priceless bough, shadows the fertile ground.
My divine mother, do not fail your son
In a baffling time."
Then he stood still to see
What signs the doves might give, or where their flight
Might lead him. And they fed, and then flew on,
Each time as far as one who came behind
Could keep in view. Then when they reached the gorge
Of sulphurous Avernus, first borne upward
Through the lucent air, they glided down
To their desired rest, the two-hued tree
Where glitter of gold filtered between green boughs.
Like mistletoe that in the woods in winter
Thrives with yellowish berries and new leaves—
A parasite on the trunk it twines around—
So bright amid the dark green ilex shone
The golden leafage, rustling in light wind.
Aeneas at once briskly took hold of it
And, though it clung, greedily broke it off,
Then carried it to the Sibyl's cave.
Meanwhile
The Teucrians on the shore wept for Misenus,
Doing for thankless dust the final honors.
First they built up a giant pyre, enriched
With pitch pine and split oak, with somber boughs
Alongside and dark cypresses in front.
On top they made a blazon of bright arms.
One group set water boiling over flames,
Then washed the cold corpse and anointed it,
Groaning loud, and laid it out when mourned
On a low couch, with purple robes thrown over it,
A hero's shrouding. Bearers then took up
As their sad duty the great bier. With eyes
Averted in their fathers' ancient way
They held the torch below.
Heaped offerings
Blazed up and burned—food, incense, oil in bowls.
And when the flame died and the coals fell in,
They gave a bath of wine to the pyre's remnant,

Thirsty ash; then picking out the bones
Corynaeus enclosed them in an urn.
The same priest with pure water went three times
Around the company, asperging them
With cleansing drops from a ripe olive sprig,
And spoke the final words. Faithfully then
Aeneas heaped a great tomb over the dead,
Placing his arms, his oar, his trumpet there
Beneath a promontory, named for him,
Misenum now and always, age to age.[5]
All this accomplished, with no more ado
He carried out the orders of the Sibyl.

The cavern was profound, wide-mouthed, and huge,
Rough underfoot, defended by dark pool
And gloomy forest. Overhead, flying things
Could never safely take their way, such deathly
Exhalations rose from the black gorge
Into the dome of heaven. The priestess here
Placed four black bullocks, wet their brows with wine,
Plucked bristles from between the horns and laid them
As her first offerings on the holy fire,
Calling aloud to Hecatë, supreme
In heaven and Erebus. Others drew knives
Across beneath and caught warm blood in bowls.
Aeneas by the sword's edge offered up
To Night, the mother of the Eumenidës,
And her great sister, Earth, a black-fleeced lamb,
A sterile cow to thee, Proserpina.
Then for the Stygian king he lit at night
New altars where he placed over the flames
Entire carcasses of bulls, and poured
Rich oil on blazing viscera.[6] Only see:
Just at the light's edge, just before sunrise,
Earth rumbled underfoot, forested ridges
Broke into movement, and far howls of dogs
Were heard across the twilight as the goddess
Nearer and nearer came.
"Away, away,"
The Sibyl cried, "all those unblest, away!
Depart from all the grove! But you, Aeneas,
Enter the path here, and unsheathe your sword.
There's need of gall and resolution now."

She flung herself wildly into the cave-mouth,
Leading, and he strode boldly at her heels.

5. Here Virgil provides an origin for Misenum, the northern headland of the bay of Naples.

6. To gain permission for their descent, the sibyl sacrifices to the underworld gods, by contrast with the Olympian or "heavenly" gods of the world above.

Gods who rule the ghosts; all silent shades;
And Chaos and infernal Fiery Stream,
And regions of wide night without a sound,
May it be right to tell what I have heard,
May it be right, and fitting, by your will,
That I describe the deep world sunk in darkness
Under the earth.[7]
Now dim to one another
In desolate night they walked on through the gloom,
Through Dis's homes all void, and empty realms,
As one goes through a wood by a faint moon's
Treacherous light, when Jupiter veils the sky
And black night blots the colors of the world.

Before the entrance, in the jaws of Orcus,
Grief and avenging Cares have made their beds,
And pale Diseases and sad Age are there,
And Dread, and Hunger that sways men to crime,
And sordid Want—in shapes to affright the eyes—
And Death and Toil and Death's own brother, Sleep,
And the mind's evil joys; on the door sill
Death-bringing War, and iron cubicles
Of the Eumenidës, and raving Discord,
Viperish hair bound up in gory bands.[8]
In the courtyard a shadowy giant elm
Spreads ancient boughs, her ancient arms where dreams,
False dreams, the old tale goes, beneath each leaf
Cling and are numberless. There, too,
About the doorway forms of monsters crowd—
Centaurs, twiformed Scyllas, hundred-armed
Briareus, and the Lernaean hydra
Hissing horribly, and the Chimaera
Breathing dangerous flames, and Gorgons, Harpies,
Huge Geryon, triple-bodied ghost.[9]
Here, swept by sudden fear, drawing his sword,
Aeneas stood on guard with naked edge
Against them as they came. If his companion,
Knowing the truth, had not admonished him
How faint these lives were—empty images
Hovering bodiless—he had attacked
And cut his way through phantoms, empty air.[1]

The path goes on from that place to the waves
Of Tartarus's Acheron. Thick with mud,
A whirlpool out of a vast abyss

7. An important component of mystery religions was the secrecy of their rituals, not to be revealed to the uninitiated.
8. Here Virgil combines traditional underworld deities—the Furies and Discord—with allegorical personifications of the ills of the world.
9. Monsters out of Greek mythology, placed by Virgil at the threshold of Dis.
1. A Roman reminder of the power of the mind over the trials of the world.

Boils up and belches all the silt it carries
Into Cocytus. Here the ferryman,
A figure of fright, keeper of waters and streams,
Is Charon, foul and terrible, his beard
Grown wild and hoar, his staring eyes all flame,
His sordid cloak hung from a shoulder knot.
Alone he poles his craft and trims the sails
And in his rusty hull ferries the dead,
Old now—but old age in the gods is green.[2]

Here a whole crowd came streaming to the banks,
Mothers and men, the forms with all life spent
Of heroes great in valor, boys and girls
Unmarried, and young sons laid on the pyre
Before their parents' eyes—as many souls
As leaves that yield their hold on boughs and fall
Through forests in the early frost of autumn,
Or as migrating birds from the open sea
That darken heaven when the cold season comes
And drives them overseas to sunlit lands.
There all stood begging to be first across
And reached out longing hands to the far shore.

But the grim boatman now took these aboard,
Now those, waving the rest back from the strand.
In wonder at this and touched by the commotion,
Aeneas said:
"Tell me, Sister, what this means,
The crowd at the stream. Where are the souls bound?
How are they tested, so that these turn back,
While those take oars to cross the dead-black water?"

Briefly the ancient priestess answered him:

"Cocytus is the deep pool that you see,
The swamp of Styx beyond, infernal power
By which the gods take oath and fear to break it.
All in the nearby crowd you notice here
Are pauper souls, the souls of the unburied.
Charon's the boatman. Those the water bears
Are souls of buried men. He may not take them
Shore to dread shore on the hoarse currents there
Until their bones rest in the grave, or till
They flutter and roam this side a hundred years;
They may have passage then, and may return
To cross the deeps they long for."
Anchises' son
Had halted, pondering on so much, and stood

2. Charon was the mythological ferryman who carried shades across the river (usually Acheron) that marked the entrance to Hades proper.

In pity for the souls' hard lot. Among them
He saw two sad ones of unhonored death,
Leucaspis and the Lycian fleet's commander,
Orontës, who had sailed the windy sea
From Troy together, till the Southern gale
Had swamped and whirled them down, both ship and men.
Of a sudden he saw his helmsman, Palinurus,
Going by, who but a few nights before
On course from Libya, as he watched the stars,
Had been pitched overboard astern.[3] As soon
As he made sure of the disconsolate one
In all the gloom, Aeneas called:
"Which god
Took you away from us and put you under,
Palinurus? Tell me. In this one prophecy
Apollo, who had never played me false,
Falsely foretold you'd be unharmed at sea
And would arrive at the Ausonian coast.
Is the promise kept?"
But the shade said:
"Phoebus' caldron
Told you no lie, my captain, and no god
Drowned me at sea. The helm that I hung on to,
Duty bound to keep our ship on course,
By some great shock chanced to be torn away,
And I went with it overboard. I swear
By the rough sea, I feared less for myself
Than for your ship: with rudder gone and steersman
Knocked overboard, it might well come to grief
In big seas running. Three nights, heavy weather
Out of the South on the vast water tossed me.
On the fourth dawn, I sighted Italy
Dimly ahead, as a wave-crest lifted me.
By turns I swam and rested, swam again
And got my footing on the beach, but savages
Attacked me as I clutched at a cliff-top,
Weighted down by my wet clothes. Poor fools,
They took me for a prize and ran me through.
Surf has me now, and sea winds, washing me
Close inshore.
By heaven's happy light
And the sweet air, I beg you, by your father,
And by your hopes of Iulus' rising star,
Deliver me from this captivity,
Unconquered friend! Throw earth on me—you can—
Put in to Velia port! Or if there be

3. A bargain between Venus and Neptune at the end of Book 5 made the loss of Palinurus Neptune's price for the safe arrival of the Trojans in Italy. Palinurus gives a more human explanation for his death here.

Some way to do it, if your goddess mother
Shows a way—and I feel sure you pass
These streams and Stygian marsh by heaven's will—
Give this poor soul your hand, take me across,
Let me at least in death find quiet haven."
When he had made his plea, the Sibyl said:
"From what source comes this craving, Palinurus?
Would you though still unburied see the Styx
And the grim river of the Eumenidës,
Or even the river bank, without a summons?
Abandon hope by prayer to make the gods
Change their decrees. Hold fast to what I say
To comfort your hard lot: neighboring folk
In cities up and down the coast will be
Induced by portents to appease your bones,
Building a tomb and making offerings there
On a cape forever named for Palinurus."[4]

The Sibyl's words relieved him, and the pain
Was for a while dispelled from his sad heart,
Pleased at the place-name. So the two walked on
Down to the stream. Now from the Stygian water
The boatman, seeing them in the silent wood
And headed for the bank, cried out to them
A rough uncalled-for challenge:
"Who are you
In armor, visiting our rivers? Speak
From where you are, stop there, say why you come.
This is the region of the Shades, and Sleep,
And drowsy Night. It breaks eternal law
For the Stygian craft to carry living bodies.
Never did I rejoice, I tell you, letting
Alcidës° cross, or Theseus and Pirithous, *Hercules*
Demigods by paternity though they were,
Invincible in power. One forced in chains
From the king's own seat the watchdog of the dead
And dragged him away trembling.[5] The other two
Were bent on carrying our lady off
From Dis's chamber."[6]
This the prophetess
And servant of Amphrysian Apollo[7]
Briefly answered:
"Here are no such plots,

4. In another explanatory myth, the sibyl promises that a nearby cape will preserve the name and fame of the lost helmsman.

5. On his descent to the underworld to fulfill the last of his twelve labors, Hercules bound the three-headed watchdog Cerberus and dragged him to the world above as a prize.

6. Theseus and Pirithous were imprisoned by Hades when they undertook an ill-fated expedition to kidnap Proserpina. Theseus was rescued by Hercules; Pirithous was not.

7. Often Virgil encapsulates a mythical episode into an epithet. Here, he uses "Amphrysian" because Apollo at one time was constrained to serve as a herdsman to Admetus by the river Amphrysus in Thessaly.

So fret no more. These weapons threaten nothing.
Let the great watchdog at the door howl on
Forever terrifying the bloodless shades.
Let chaste Proserpina remain at home
In her uncle's house.[8] The man of Troy, Aeneas,
Remarkable for loyalty, great in arms,
Goes through the deepest shades of Erebus
To see his father.
                    If the very image
Of so much goodness moves you not at all,
Here is a bough"—at this she showed the bough
That had been hidden, held beneath her dress—
"You'll recognize it."
                    Then his heart, puffed up
With rage, subsided. They had no more words.
His eyes fixed on the ancient gift, the bough,
The destined gift, so long unseen, now seen,
He turned his dusky craft and made for shore.
There from the long thwarts where they sat he cleared
The other souls and made the gangway wide,
Letting the massive man step in the bilge.
The leaky coracle° groaned at the weight *small boat*
And took a flood of swampy water in.
At length, on the other side, he put ashore
The prophetess and hero in the mire,
A formless ooze amid the grey-green sedge.
Great Cerberus barking with his triple throat
Makes all that shoreline ring, as he lies huge
In a facing cave. Seeing his neck begin
To come alive with snakes, the prophetess
Tossed him a lump of honey and drugged meal
To make him drowse. Three ravenous gullets gaped
And he snapped up the sop. Then his great bulk
Subsided and lay down through all the cave.
Now seeing the watchdog deep in sleep, Aeneas
Took the opening: swiftly he turned away
From the river over which no soul returns.[9]

Now voices crying loud were heard at once—
The souls of infants wailing. At the door
Of the sweet life they were to have no part in,
Torn from the breast, a black day took them off
And drowned them all in bitter death. Near these
Were souls falsely accused, condemned to die.
But not without a judge, or jurymen,

8. In Greek myth, Persephone (Roman: Proserpina) was the daughter of Demeter and Zeus, who like her husband Hades were children of Cronos and Rhea.

9. The souls Aeneas sees in this part of the underworld are those who met untimely deaths.

Had these souls got their places: Minos reigned
As the presiding judge, moving the urn,
And called a jury of the silent ones
To learn of lives and accusations.[1] Next
Were those sad souls, benighted, who contrived
Their own destruction, and as they hated daylight,
Cast their lives away. How they would wish
In the upper air now to endure the pain
Of poverty and toil! But iron law
Stands in the way, since the drear hateful swamp
Has pinned them down here, and the Styx that winds
Nine times around exerts imprisoning power.
Not far away, spreading on every side,
The Fields of Mourning came in view, so called
Since here are those whom pitiless love consumed
With cruel wasting, hidden on paths apart
By myrtle woodland growing overhead.
In death itself, pain will not let them be.
He saw here Phaedra, Procris, Eriphylë
Sadly showing the wounds her hard son gave;
Evadnë and Pasiphaë, at whose side
Laodamia walked, and Caeneus,
A young man once, a woman now, and turned
Again by fate into the older form.[2]
Among them, with her fatal wound still fresh,
Phoenician Dido wandered the deep wood.
The Trojan captain paused nearby and knew
Her dim form in the dark, as one who sees,
Early in the month, or thinks to have seen, the moon
Rising through cloud, all dim. He wept and spoke
Tenderly to her:
"Dido, so forlorn,
The story then that came to me was true,
That you were out of life, had met your end
By your own hand. Was I, was I the cause?
I swear by heaven's stars, by the high gods,
By any certainty below the earth,
I left your land against my will, my queen.
The gods' commands drove me to do their will,
As now they drive me through this world of shades,
These mouldy waste lands and these depths of night.
And I could not believe that I would hurt you
So terribly by going. Wait a little.
Do not leave my sight.
Am I someone to flee from? The last word

1. With his brother Rhadamanthus, the legendary king of Crete acted as judge of the living and the dead (see *Odyssey,* bk. 11, page 318). The "silent ones" are the dead.

2. Legendary women who died as a consequence of passion—sometimes licit, sometimes illicit, some by their own hand, some by that of their loved ones.

Destiny lets me say to you is this."

Aeneas with such pleas tried to placate
The burning soul, savagely glaring back,
And tears came to his eyes. But she had turned
With gaze fixed on the ground as he spoke on,
Her face no more affected than if she were
Immobile granite or Marpesian stone.[3]
At length she flung away from him and fled,
His enemy still, into the shadowy grove
Where he whose bride she once had been, Sychaeus,
Joined in her sorrows and returned her love.
Aeneas still gazed after her in tears,
Shaken by her ill fate and pitying her.

With effort then he took the given way,
And they went on, reaching the farthest lands
Where men famous in war gather apart.
Here Tydeus came to meet him, and then came
Parthenopaeus, glorious in arms,
Adrastus then, a pallid shade.[4] Here too
Were Dardans long bewept in the upper air,
Men who died in the great war. And he groaned
To pick these figures out, in a long file,
Glaucus, Medon, Thersilochus, besides
Antenor's three sons, then the priest of Ceres
Polyboetës, then Idaeus, holding
Still to his warcar, holding his old gear.[5]
To right and left they crowd the path and stay
And will not have enough of seeing him,
But love to hold him back, to walk beside him,
And hear the story of why he came.
Not so
Agamemnon's phalanx, chiefs of the Danaans:
Seeing the living man in bronze that glowed
Through the dark air, they shrank in fear. Some turned
And ran, as once, when routed, to the ships,
While others raised a battle shout, or tried to,
Mouths agape, mocked by the whispering cry.
Here next he saw Deïphobus, Priam's son,[6]
Mutilated from head to foot, his face
And both hands cruelly torn, ears shorn away,
Nose to the noseholes lopped by a shameful stroke.

3. Marpessus was a Greek mountain famed for a marble with a luminous quality.

4. Legendary warriors of the generation before the Trojan War, three of the Seven against Thebes who challenged the gods—including Tydeus, the father of Diomedes.

5. Names of Trojans or their allies. Glaucus, with Sarpedon, was leader of the Lycians and killed by Ajax in the *Iliad.* Idaeus was Hector's herald and charioteer.

6. Deïphobus had married Helen after the death of Paris. The mutilation of his body serves as further evidence of Greek disregard for the traditional rules of war.

Barely knowing the shade who quailed before him
Covering up his tortured face, Aeneas
Spoke out to him in his known voice:
"Deïphobus,
Gallant officer in high Teucer's line,
Who chose this brutal punishment, who had
So much the upper hand of you? I heard
On that last night that you had fallen, spent
After a slaughter of Pelasgians—
Fallen on piled-up carnage. It was I
Who built on Rhoeteum Point an empty tomb
And sent a high call to your soul three times.
Your name, your armor, marks the place. I could not
Find you, friend, to put your bones in earth
In the old country as I came away."

And Priam's son replied:
"You left undone
Nothing, my friend, but gave all ritual due
Deïphobus, due a dead man's shade. My lot
And the Laconian woman's° ghastly doing *Helen's*
Sank me in this hell. These are the marks
She left me as her memorial. You know
How between one false gladness and another
We spent that last night—no need to remind you.
When the tall deadly horse came at one bound,
With troops crammed in its paunch, above our towers,
She made a show of choral dance and led
Our Phrygian women crying out on Bacchus
Here and there—but held a torch amid them,
Signalling to Danaans from the Height.
Worn by the long day, heavily asleep,
I lay in my unlucky bridal chamber,
And rest, profound and sweet, most like the rest
Of death, weighed on me as I lay. Meanwhile
She, my distinguished wife, moved all my arms
Out of the house—as she had slipped my sword,
My faithful sword, out from beneath my pillow—
Opened the door and called in Menelaus,
Hoping no doubt by this great gift to him,
Her lover, to blot old infamy out. Why hold back
From telling it? The two burst in the bedroom,
Joined by that ringleader of atrocity,
Ulysses, of the windking's line.[7] O gods,
If with pure lips I pray, requite the Greeks
With equal suffering! But you, now tell me

7. Deïphobus alludes rather maliciously to a legend that Ulysses was the bastard son of Aeolus's son Sisyphus, a legendary thief punished in Tartarus.

What in the world has brought you here alive:
Have you come from your sea wandering, and did heaven
Direct you? How could harrying fortune send you
To these sad sunless homes, disordered places?"

At this point in their talk Aurora,° borne *goddess of Dawn*
Through high air on her glowing rosy car
Had crossed the meridian: should they linger now
With stories they might spend the allotted time.
But at Aeneas' side the Sibyl spoke,
Warning him briefly:
"Night comes on, Aeneas,
We use up hours grieving. Here is the place
Where the road forks: on the right hand it goes
Past mighty Dis's walls, Elysium way,
Our way; but the leftward road will punish
Malefactors, taking them to Tartarus."
Deïphobus answered her:
"No need for anger,
Reverend lady. I'll depart and make
The tally in the darkness full again.
Go on, sir, glory of us all! Go on,
Enjoy a better destiny."
He spoke,
And even as he spoke he turned away.
Now of a sudden Aeneas looked and saw
To the left, under a cliff, wide buildings girt
By a triple wall round which a torrent rushed
With scorching flames and boulders tossed in thunder,
The abyss's Fiery River.[8] A massive gate
With adamantine° pillars faced the stream, *unyielding*
So strong no force of men or gods in war
May ever avail to crack and bring it down,
And high in air an iron tower stands
On which Tisiphonë,[9] her bloody robe
Pulled up about her, has her seat and keeps
Unsleeping watch over the entrance way
By day and night. From the interior, groans
Are heard, and thud of lashes, clanking iron,
Dragging chains. Arrested in his tracks,
Appalled by what he heard, Aeneas stood.

"What are the forms of evil here? O Sister,
Tell me. And the punishments dealt out:
Why such a lamentation?"
Said the Sibyl:
"Light of the Teucrians, it is decreed

8. Also known as Phlegethon, one of the five rivers of the underworld.

9. One of the Furies.

That no pure soul may cross the sill of evil.
When, however, Hecatë appointed me
Caretaker of Avernus wood, she led me
Through heaven's punishments and taught me all.
This realm is under Cretan Rhadamanthus'[1]
Iron rule. He sentences. He listens
And makes the souls confess their crooked ways,
How they put off atonements in the world
With foolish satisfaction, thieves of time,
Until too late, until the hour of death.
At once the avenger girdled with her whip,
Tisiphonë, leaps down to lash the guilty,
Vile writhing snakes held out on her left hand,
And calls her savage sisterhood.[2] The awaited
Time has come, hell gates will shudder wide
On shrieking hinges. Can you see her now,
Her shape, as doorkeeper, upon the sill?
More bestial, just inside, the giant Hydra
Lurks with fifty black and yawning throats.[3]
Then Tartarus itself goes plunging down
In darkness twice as deep as heaven is high
For eyes fixed on etherial Olympus.
Here is Earth's ancient race, the brood of Titans,
Hurled by the lightning down to roll forever
In the abyss.[4] Here, too, I saw those giant
Twins of Aloeus who laid their hands
Upon great heaven to rend it and to topple
Jove from his high seat,[5] and I saw, too,
Salmoneus[6] paying dearly for the jape
Of mimicking Jove's fire, Olympus' thunder:
Shaking a bright torch from a four-horse car
He rode through Greece and his home town in Elis,
Glorying, claiming honor as a god—
Out of his mind, to feign with horses' hoofs
On bronze the blast and inimitable bolt.
The father almighty amid heavy cloud
Let fly his missile—no firebrand for him
Nor smoky pitchpine light—and spun the man
Headlong in a huge whirlwind.
One had sight
Of Tityos, too, child of all-mothering Earth,[7]

1. Along with his brother, Minos, a judge of the dead.
2. Furies were traditionally depicted with snakes for hair.
3. The Hydra was a monster with 50 heads; wherever one was chopped off, two more would grow. It was killed by Hercules as one of his Twelve Labors.
4. The 12 Titans, including Rhea and Cronos, were children of the primeval couple Ge and Uranus, blasted by the thunderbolts of their own child, Zeus.
5. Otus and Ephialtes were giant sons of Aloeus who attacked the gods by piling mountain upon mountain to climb to heaven. Zeus destroyed them.
6. A king in Greek myth and ancestor of Jason and Pelias, two of the Argonauts.
7. A giant son of Ge (Earth) who was killed by Apollo and Artemis for threatening their mother, Leto.

His body stretched out over nine whole acres
While an enormous vulture with hooked beak
Forages forever in his liver,
His vitals rife with agonies. The bird,
Lodged in the chest cavity, tears at his feast,
And tissues growing again get no relief.
As for the Lapiths, need I tell: Ixion,
Pirithoüs, and the black crag overhead
So sure to fall it seems already falling.[8]
Golden legs gleam on the feasters' couches,
Dishes in royal luxury prepared
Are laid before them—but the oldest Fury
Crouches near and springs out with her torch,
Her outcry, if they try to touch the meal.
Here come those who as long as life remained
Held brothers hateful, beat their parents, cheated
Poor men dependent on them; also those
Who hugged their newfound riches to themselves
And put nothing aside for relatives—
A great crowd, this—then men killed for adultery,
Men who took arms in war against the right,
Not scrupling to betray their lords. All these
Are hemmed in here, awaiting punishment.
Best not inquire what punishment, what form
Of suffering at their last end overwhelms them.
Some heave at a great boulder, or revolve,
Spreadeagled, hung on wheel-spokes.[9] Theseus
Cleaves to his chair and cleaves to it forever.[1]
Phlegyas in his misery teaches all souls
His lesson, thundering out amid the gloom:
'Be warned and study justice, not to scorn
The immortal gods.'[2] Here's one who sold his country,
Foisted a tyrant on her, set up laws
Or nullified them for a price; another
Entered his daughter's room to take a bride
Forbidden him. All these dared monstrous wrong
And took what they dared try for. If I had
A hundred tongues, a hundred mouths, a voice
Of iron, I could not tell of all the shapes
Their crimes had taken, or their punishments."

8. According to Greek myth, Ixion committed several crimes including the attempted rape of Hera, which resulted in the race of Centaurs, horse-men. Pirithous was the son by Zeus of Ixion's wife. At his wedding, the famous battle between his people, the Lapiths, and their neighbors, the Centaurs, occurred. After descending with Theseus to carry off Persephone as his wife, Pirithous never returned.

9. The traditional punishments of Sisyphus and Ixion, respectively.

1. When Theseus and Pirithous attempted to kidnap Persephone, they unknowingly sat down on the Chair of Forgetfulness, where they were stuck for four years, tormented by Furies, until the arrival of Hercules. Virgil extends the punishment for eternity.

2. Phlegyas was a Thessalian king and by some accounts the father of Ixion.

All this he heard from her who for long years
Had served Apollo. Then she said:
"Come now,
Be on your way, and carry out your mission.
Let us go faster. I can see the walls
The Cyclops' forges built[3] and, facing us,
The portico and gate where they command us
To leave the gifts required."
On this the two
In haste strode on abreast down the dark paths
Over the space between, and neared the doors.
Aeneas gained the entrance, halted there,
Asperged his body with fresh water drops,
And on the sill before him fixed the bough.

Now that at last this ritual was performed,
His duty to the goddess done, they came
To places of delight, to green park land,
Where souls take ease amid the Blessed Groves.
Wider expanses of high air endow
Each vista with a wealth of light. Souls here
Possess their own familiar sun and stars.[4]
Some train on grassy rings, others compete
In field games, others grapple on the sand.
Feet moving to a rhythmic beat, the dancers
Group in a choral pattern as they sing.
Orpheus, the priest of Thrace, in his long robe
Accompanies, plucking his seven notes
Now with his fingers, now with his ivory quill.
Here is the ancient dynasty of Teucer,
Heroes high of heart, beautiful scions,
Born in greater days: Ilus, Assaracus,
And Dardanus, who founded Troy.[5] Aeneas
Marvels to see their chariots and gear
Far off, all phantom: lances fixed in earth,
And teams unyoked, at graze on the wide plain.
All joy they took, alive, in cars and weapons,
As in the care and pasturing of horses,
Remained with them when they were laid in earth.
He saw, how vividly! along the grass
To right and left, others who feasted there

3. In addition to the savage one-eyed giants of the *Odyssey* and the *Aeneid,* Book 3, Hesiod told of three divine craftsmen Cyclops, giant sons of Ge and Uranus, who made Zeus's divine thunderbolt, among many other great works including the walls of Elysium described here.

4. Although they are underground, the Elysian Fields magically share the attributes of the world above: light, air, sun, and stars.

5. Dardanus, a son of Zeus and a daughter of Atlas, began the Dardanian people when he married the daughter of the local king, Teucer. Ilus, the founder of the city of Troy, and Assaracus were his grandsons, the former the grandfather of Priam, the latter of Anchises, and thus great-grandfather of Aeneas.

And chorused out a hymn praising Apollo,
Within a fragrant laurel grove, where Po[6]
Sprang up and took his course to the world above,
The broad stream flowing on amid the forest.
This was the company of those who suffered
Wounds in battle for their country; those
Who in their lives were holy men and chaste
Or worthy of Phoebus in prophetic song;
Or those who bettered life, by finding out
New truths and skills; or those who to some folk
By benefactions made themselves remembered.
They all wore snowy chaplets on their brows.
To these souls, mingling on all sides, the Sibyl
Spoke now, and especially to Musaeus,[7]
The central figure, toward whose towering shoulders
All the crowd gazed:
"Tell us, happy souls,
And you, great seer, what region holds Anchises,
Where is his resting place? For him we came
By ferry across the rivers of Erebus."
And the great soul answered briefly:
"None of us
Has one fixed home. We walk in shady groves
And bed on riverbanks and occupy
Green meadows fresh with streams. But if your hearts
Are set on it, first cross this ridge; and soon
I shall point out an easy path."
So saying,
He walked ahead and showed them from the height
The sweep of shining plain. Then down they went
And left the hilltops.
Now Aeneas' father
Anchises, deep in the lush green of a valley,
Had given all his mind to a survey
Of souls, till then confined there, who were bound
For daylight in the upper world. By chance
His own were those he scanned now, all his own
Descendants, with their futures and their fates,
Their characters and acts. But when he saw
Aeneas advancing toward him on the grass,
He stretched out both his hands in eagerness
As tears wetted his cheeks. He said in welcome:

"Have you at last come, has that loyalty
Your father counted on conquered the journey?

6. The Po is Italy's longest river, rising in the Alps and entering the Adriatic some 400 miles eastward near Ravenna.

7. Musaeus (literally, "of the Muses") was a mythical singer closely associated with Eleusis and the singer Orpheus; like Orpheus, he was said to have invented hexameter and perhaps the alphabet.

Am I to see your face, my son, and hear
Our voices in communion as before?
I thought so, surely; counting the months I thought
The time would come. My longing has not tricked me.
I greet you now, how many lands behind you,
How many seas, what blows and dangers, son!
How much I feared the land of Libya
Might do you harm."
Aeneas said:
"Your ghost,
Your sad ghost, father, often before my mind,
Impelled me to the threshold of this place.
My ships ride anchored in the Tuscan° sea. *Tyrhhenian*
But let me have your hand, let me embrace you,
Do not draw back."
At this his tears brimmed over
And down his cheeks. And there he tried three times
To throw his arms around his father's neck,
Three times the shade untouched slipped through his hands,
Weightless as wind and fugitive as dream.
Aeneas now saw at the valley's end
A grove standing apart, with stems and boughs
Of woodland rustling, and the stream of Lethe[8]
Running past those peaceful glades. Around it
Souls of a thousand nations filled the air,
As bees in meadows at the height of summer
Hover and home on flowers and thickly swarm
On snow-white lilies, and the countryside
Is loud with humming. At the sudden vision
Shivering, at a loss, Aeneas asked
What river flowed there and what men were those
In such a throng along the riverside.
His father Anchises told him:
"Souls for whom
A second body is in store: their drink
Is water of Lethe, and it frees from care
In long forgetfulness. For all this time
I have so much desired to show you these
And tell you of them face to face—to take
The roster of my children's children here,
So you may feel with me more happiness
At finding Italy."
"Must we imagine,
Father, there are souls that go from here
Aloft to upper heaven, and once more

8. Underworld river of forgetfulness.

Return to bodies' dead weight? The poor souls,
How can they crave our daylight so?"
"My son,
I'll tell you, not to leave you mystified,"
Anchises said, and took each point in order:[9]

First, then, the sky and lands and sheets of water,
The bright moon's globe, the Titan sun and stars,
Are fed within by Spirit, and a Mind
Infused through all the members of the world
Makes one great living body of the mass.[1]
From Spirit come the races of man and beast,
The life of birds, odd creatures the deep sea
Contains beneath her sparkling surfaces,
And fiery energy from a heavenly source
Belongs to the generative seeds of these,
So far as they are not poisoned or clogged
By mortal bodies, their free essence dimmed
By earthiness and deathliness of flesh.
This makes them fear and crave, rejoice and grieve.[2]
Imprisoned in the darkness of the body
They cannot clearly see heaven's air; in fact
Even when life departs on the last day
Not all the scourges of the body pass
From the poor souls, not all distress of life.
Inevitably, many malformations,
Growing together in mysterious ways,
Become inveterate. Therefore they undergo
The discipline of punishments and pay
In penance for old sins: some hang full length
To the empty winds, for some the stain of wrong
Is washed by floods or burned away by fire.[3]
We suffer each his own shade. We are sent
Through wide Elysium, where a few abide
In happy lands, till the long day, the round
Of Time fulfilled, has worn our stains away,
Leaving the soul's heaven-sent perception clear,
The fire from heaven pure. These other souls,
When they have turned Time's wheel a thousand years,
The god calls in a crowd to Lethe stream,
That there unmemoried they may see again
The heavens and wish re-entry into bodies."

9. Anchises' speech blends elements from Platonic, Orphic-Pythagorean, and Stoic philosophy and was fundamental in establishing Virgil's later reputation as privy to the secrets of life and death.

1. Stoic philosophy held that the *anima mundi,* or spirit of the world, had emanated the universe from its primordial fiery ether. Human souls are detached from this ether and only when purified can return again to it.

2. According to Plato, the harmful contagion of the soul by the body brings fears, desires, sorrow, and joy.

3. In Pythagorean doctrine, souls must undergo cycles of purgation and transmigration until cleansed.

Anchises paused. He drew both son and Sibyl
Into the middle of the murmuring throng,
Then picked out a green mound from which to view
The souls as they came forward, one by one,
And to take note of faces.[4]
"Come," he said,
"What glories follow Dardan generations
In after years, and from Italian blood
What famous children in your line will come,
Souls of the future, living in our name,
I shall tell clearly now, and in the telling
Teach you your destiny. That one you see,
The young man leaning on a spear unarmed,
Has his allotted place nearest the light.
He will be first to take the upper air,
Silvius, a child with half Italian blood
And an Alban name, your last born, whom your wife,
Lavinia, late in your great age will rear
In forests to be king and father of kings.[5]
Through him our race will rule in Alba Longa.[6]
Next him is Procas, pride of the Trojan line,
And Capys, too, then Numitor, then one
Whose name restores you: Silvius Aeneas,
Both in arms and piety your peer,
If ever he shall come to reign in Alba.[7]
What men they are! And see their rugged forms
With oakleaf crowns shadowing their brows. I tell you,
These are to found Nomentum, Gabii,
Fidenae town, Collatia's hilltop towers,
Pometii, Fort Inuus, Bola, Cora—
Names to be heard for places nameless now.[8]
Then Romulus, fathered by Mars, will come
To make himself his grandfather's° companion, *Numitor*
Romulus, reared by his mother, Ilia,
In the blood-line of Assaracus.[9] Do you see
The double plume of Mars fixed on his crest,
See how the father of the gods himself

4. The procession of souls fills in the legendary history of Rome between the two myths of Aeneas and Romulus and then links them to Virgil's own patron, Augustus Caesar.

5. Son of Aeneas and Lavinia, Silvius was the first descendant of mixed Trojan and Italian lineage and an ancestor of the Alban royal house of Silvii. The explanation for his name refers to a legend that Lavinia fled to the woods out of fear of the jealousy of Ascanius to give birth to her son.

6. Legend made the kings of Alba Longa the rulers of Latium until their descendant Romulus founded Rome in 753 B.C.E.

7. Legendary Alban kings. Numitor was ousted by his brother, Amulius, the last of the series, but Numitor's daughter, Rhea Silvia, a Vestal Virgin, became the mother by Mars of Romulus and Remus, who overthrew the usurper, restored Numitor, and founded the new settlement of Rome.

8. Names of old Latin towns and settlements, some still standing in Virgil's time, some not.

9. Another name for Rhea Silvia, descended from Aeneas's great-grandfather, Assaracus, via the Alban line of Silvius.

Now marks him out with his own sign of honor?[1]
Look now, my son: under his auspices
Illustrious Rome will bound her power with earth,
Her spirit with Olympus. She'll enclose
Her seven hills with one great city wall,[2]
Fortunate in the men she breeds. Just so
Cybelë Mother, honored on Berecynthus,[3]
Wearing her crown of towers, onward rides
By chariot through the towns of Phrygia,
In joy at having given birth to gods,
And cherishing a hundred grandsons, heaven
Dwellers with homes on high.
Turn your two eyes
This way and see this people, your own Romans.
Here is Caesar, and all the line of Iulus,
All who shall one day pass under the dome
Of the great sky: this is the man, this one,
Of whom so often you have heard the promise,
Caesar Augustus, son of the deified,[4]
Who shall bring once again an Age of Gold
To Latium, to the land where Saturn reigned
In early times.[5] He will extend his power
Beyond the Garamants° and Indians, *Africans*
Over far territories north and south
Of the zodiacal stars, the solar way,
Where Atlas,[6] heaven-bearing, on his shoulder
Turns the night-sphere, studded with burning stars.
At that man's coming even now the realms
Of Caspia and Maeotia tremble,[7] warned
By oracles, and the seven mouths of Nile[8]
Go dark with fear. The truth is, even Alcidës° *Hercules*
Never traversed so much of earth—I grant

1. With Jupiter, Mars was the chief Italian god, later equated with the Greek war god Ares. The legend of Romulus and Remus made Mars their father and his sacred animal, the she-wolf, their nurse.

2. Rome is dominated by seven hills. The settlement of Romulus and Remus was on the Palatine hill; all seven hills were first enclosed by the Wall of Servius, assigned by legend to King Servius Tullius (6th century) and now dated to the 4th century during the Republic.

3. Mt. Berecynthus was a cult place of Cybele, the Great Mother goddess of Asia Minor, identified by the Greeks with Rhea and introduced into Rome in 204 B.C.E., where her cult was under control of the same priesthood as the Sibylline books.

4. The *gens Iulia,* or Julius clan, claimed descent from Iulus (Ascanius). Octavian (63 B.C.E.–14 C.E.) was the adopted son of Julius Caesar (100–44 B.C.E.), who was deified in 42 B.C.E. Octavian was the first Roman emperor and received the honorary title Augustus ("sacred," "venerable") in 27 C.E.

5. According to Hesiod and other poets, the Golden Age was the period during which Cronos ruled the world, men lived without strife, labor, or injustice, and the earth gave forth its fruits in abundance. The Romans identified Cronos with Saturn, an Italian god of agriculture, by legend an early king of Rome, who introduced agriculture to the region and founded the citadel on the Capitol, at the foot of which his temple stood.

6. Greek myth placed Atlas somewhere in the extreme west of the earth.

7. Caspia was the land around the Central Asian Caspian Sea; Maeotia was the land around the Sea of Azov, north of the Black Sea. The Roman empire never extended quite this far, although its influence certainly may have.

8. The river Nile in Egypt drains into the Mediterranean through a vast and rich delta. Octavian defeated the forces of Mark Antony and Cleopatra at Actium in 31 B.C.E.; he captured Egypt's capital Alexandria and brought it into the empire the following year.

That he could shoot the hind with brazen hoofs
Or bring peace to the groves of Erymanthus,
Or leave Lerna affrighted by his bow.[9]
Neither did he who guides his triumphal car
With reins of vine-shoots twisted, Bacchus, driving
Down from Nysa's height his tiger team.[1]
Do we lag still at carrying our valor
Into action? Can our fear prevent
Our settling in Ausonia?

[*Anchises then points out the future kings of Rome and great men of the early Republic, interpolating Julius Caesar among them. He concludes with young Marcellus, the nephew and assumed-to-be adopted heir of Augustus, the hope of the future of Rome, who had died at the age of 20 in 23 B.C.E.*]

After Anchises had conducted him
To every region and had fired his love
Of glory in the years to come, he spoke
Of wars that he must fight, of Laurentines,[2]
And of Latinus' city, then of how
He might avoid or bear each toil to come.

There are two gates of Sleep, one said to be
Of horn, whereby the true shades pass with ease,
The other all white ivory agleam
Without a flaw, and yet false dreams are sent
Through this one by the ghosts to the upper world.[3]
Anchises now, his last instructions given,
Took son and Sibyl there and let them go
By the Ivory Gate.
Aeneas made his way
Straight to the ships to see his crews again,
Then sailed directly to Caieta's port.[4]
Bow anchors out, the sterns rest on the beach.

[*Aeneas disembarks at the mouth of the Tiber, and the fulfillment of certain signs leads him to recognize the land promised him. He makes a pact with King Latinus, which Juno disrupts by sending the Fury Allecto to assail Latinus's wife, Amata, and the Rutulian leader, Turnus. The pact is broken, and a powerful alliance of Italian peoples marches on the Trojan camp. Following divine advice, Aeneas sails up the Tiber in search of aid, where he finds Evander, king of a small nation of Arcadians on*

9. Three of the Twelve Labors of Hercules were to slay the Hydra, which lived in the marshes of Lerna near Argos, and to capture the Hind of Ceryneia in Arcadia and the Boar of Erymanthus, a high mountain also in Arcadia.

1. Dionysus was represented with vine shoots and ivy and often either riding or driving a team of tigresses, as in the *Bacchae* of Euripides. Nysa was the legendary mountain on which he was said to have been raised by nymphs.

2. Latinus's community in Latium.

3. The twin Gates of Dreams derive from the *Odyssey,* Book 19. The prophetic and admonitory nature of dreams was accepted by most ancients, although only certain dreams were held to be significant. There has been much debate over the significance of Aeneas's departure via the Ivory Gate of false dreams.

4. Caieta (now Gaeta) is 58 kilometers northwest of Cumae.

the site where Rome one day will be. Evander is honoring Hercules, who had once visited them and disposed of Cacus, a local nuisance.]

from Book 8

[EVANDER]

When they had carried out the ritual
They turned back to the town. And, slowed by age,
The king walked, keeping Aeneas and his son
Close by his side, with talk of various things
To make the long path easy. Marveling,
Aeneas gladly looked at all about him,
Delighted with the setting, asking questions,
Hearing of earlier men and what they left.
Then King Evander, founder unaware
Of Rome's great citadel,[1] said:
"These woodland places
Once were homes of local fauns and nymphs
Together with a race of men that came
From tree trunks, from hard oak: they had no way
Of settled life, no arts of life, no skill
At yoking oxen, gathering provisions,
Practising husbandry, but got their food
From oaken boughs and wild game hunted down.
In that first time, out of Olympian heaven,
Saturn came here in flight from Jove in arms,
An exile from a kingdom lost; he brought
These unschooled men together from the hills
Where they were scattered, gave them laws, and chose
The name of Latium, from his latency
Or safe concealment in this countryside.[2]
In his reign were the golden centuries
Men tell of still, so peacefully he ruled,
Till gradually a meaner, tarnished age
Came on with fever of war and lust of gain.
Then came Ausonians and Sicanians,[3]
And Saturn's land now often changed her name,
And there were kings, one savage and gigantic,
Thybris, from whom we afterborn Italians
Named the river Tiber. The old name,
Albula, was lost.[4] As for myself,
In exile from my country, I set out

1. The Pallanteum on the Palatine, where Romulus would build his city and Augustus had a palace.
2. Evander retells the myth of Saturn's gift of agriculture to Latium and the Golden Age to which Anchises alluded in Book 6. According to Greek myth, Cronos (Saturn) was a Titan expelled by his son, Zeus (Jove).
3. The Ausonians were a people from central Italy; the Sicanians were from central Sicily.
4. The Tiber formed the border between Latium and the Sabine people to the north.

For the sea's end, but Fortune that prevails
In everything, Fate not to be thrown off,
Arrested me in this land—solemn warnings
Came from my mother, from the nymph Carmentis,
Backed by the god Apollo, to urge me here."[5]

Just after this, as he went on he showed
The altar and the gate the Romans call
Carmental,[6] honoring as of old the nymph
And prophetess Carmentis, first to sing
The glory of Pallanteum and Aeneas'
Great descendants.[7] Then he showed the wood
That Romulus would make a place of refuge,
Then the grotto called the Lupercal
Under the cold crag, named in Arcadian fashion
After Lycaean Pan.[8] And then as well
He showed the sacred wood of Argiletum,
"Argus' death," and took oath by it, telling
Of a guest, Argus, put to death.[9] From there
He led to our Tarpeian site and Capitol,
All golden now, in those days tangled, wild
With underbrush—but awesome even then.[1]
A strangeness there filled country hearts with dread
And made them shiver at the wood and Rock.

"Some god," he said, "it is not sure what god,
Lives in this grove, this hilltop thick with leaves.
Arcadians think they've seen great Jove himself
Sometimes with his right hand shaking the aegis
To darken sky and make the storm clouds rise
Towering in turmoil.[2] Here, too, in these walls
Long fallen down, you see what were two towns,
Monuments of the ancients. Father Janus
Founded one stronghold, Saturn the other,

5. Carmentis (Greek: Themis) was a nymph and prophetess who brought writing to Latium. Greek myth regarded Evander as her son by Hermes, which made him a distant relation of Aeneas through Dardanus.

6. In Rome, Carmentis had her own priest, a two-day festival in January, and a shrine at the foot of the Capitoline hill, near the Porta Carmentalis, the "altar and the gate" described here as already standing.

7. The name Carmentis derives from the Latin word *carmen,* or religious utterance, a term that also came to mean "song" and then "poem." Carmentis was also identified with the Muses. Pallanteum was an Arcadian city often cited as the origin of the name of the Palatine hill.

8. The *ficus Ruminalis* was the fig tree under which the she-wolf was said to have suckled the twins; the Lupercal was the cave on the north side of the Palatine where the twins had ostensibly been found. Both could still be visited in Virgil's day. The god Pan originated from Mount Lykaion in Arcadia. He was a shepherd god and protector of shepherds and is identified here with "Lycaeus," the god of wolves.

9. In Virgil's time, Argiletum was a district of artisans and shopkeepers extending from the south of the Quirinal to the Forum. Argus was evidently a guest of Evander who met his death because he was suspected of conspiring against his host.

1. The Tarpeian Rock was a steep cliff on the Capitoline hill from which traitors and murderers were thrown. The hill itself was the focal point of Roman religion and seen by ancient Romans as the heart of their empire. First built in the 6th century, the temple of Jupiter Capitolinus on its summit was one of the most striking sights of antiquity, especially after it was rebuilt in the 1st century B.C.E. with a golden roof.

2. The *genius loci,* or spirit of the place, serves to sanction both the piety and the imperial ambitions of future Romans.

Named Janiculum and Saturnia."[3]

Conversing of such matters, going toward
Austere Evander's house, they saw his cattle
Lowing everywhere in what is now
Rome's Forum and her fashionable quarter,
Carinae.[4] As they came up to the door,
Evander said:
"In victory Hercules
Bent for this lintel, and these royal rooms
Were grand enough for him. Friend, have the courage
To care little for wealth, and shape yourself,
You too, to merit godhead. Do not come
Disdainfully into our needy home."[5]

Even as he spoke, he led under the gabled
Narrow roof Aeneas' mighty figure
And made him rest where on strewn leaves he spread
A Libyan bearskin. Swiftly Night came on
To fold her dusky wings about the earth.

[*The two leaders make an alliance, and Evander entrusts his son, Pallas, to Aeneas's care in the war. Aeneas collects further allies, and his mother presents him with a suit of armor made by Vulcan, including a shield adorned with scenes from the future history of Rome. Turnus seizes on Aeneas's absence to attack the Trojan camp, nearly succeeding in taking it. The return of Aeneas with his allies tips the balance in the other direction. Turnus kills Pallas in single combat, stripping him of his sword belt, which he dons as a token of his victory. Further battles ensue, including the death of the virgin warrior Camilla on the Latin side. Turnus accepts decisive single combat with Aeneas, but Juno persuades his sister, the nymph Juturna, to cause the truce to fail, and the seemingly endless battle recommences.*]

from Book 12

[The Death of Turnus]

Omnipotent Olympus' king meanwhile
Had words for Juno, as she watched the combat
Out of a golden cloud. He said:
"My consort,
What will the end be? What is left for you?

3. A prominent ridge on the west bank of the Tiber at Rome, the Janiculum was early on associated with Janus, the god of door and gate, and site of an early defensive outpost. Legend made Saturn the founder of "Saturnia" on the Capitoline hill.

4. The double vision of past and present on the Palatine allows Virgil to combine two Roman virtues: the strict traditional morals of the rustic Italians and the sophisticated and cosmopolitan wealth of imperial Rome. Originally a marketplace, the Forum was the center of social and political life. The Carinae was where the emperor lived.

5. According to a Roman myth, Hercules stopped at the site of future Rome while engaged in his labors. Cacus, a local thief or monster, stole the cattle of Geryon and was slain by Hercules for his trouble. Aeneas has arrived on the anniversary of the deed. Hercules and Aeneas are paralleled throughout the *Aeneid* because both heroes were persecuted by Juno. Both figures can also be identified with Emperor Augustus, a likely target of Evander's words of humility here at the future site of the imperial palace.

You yourself know, and say you know, Aeneas
Born for heaven, tutelary° of this land, *protector*
By fate to be translated to the stars.
What do you plan? What are you hoping for,
Keeping your seat apart in the cold clouds?
Fitting, was it, that a mortal archer
Wound an immortal? That a blade let slip
Should be restored to Turnus, and new force
Accrue to a beaten man? Without your help
What could Juturna do?[1] Come now, at last
Have done, and heed our pleading, and give way.
Let yourself no longer be consumed
Without relief by all that inward burning;
Let care and trouble not forever come to me
From your sweet lips. The finish is at hand.
You had the power to harry men of Troy
By land and sea, to light the fires of war
Beyond belief, to scar a family
With mourning before marriage. I forbid
Your going further."[2]
So spoke Jupiter,
And with a downcast look Juno replied:

"Because I know that is your will indeed,
Great Jupiter, I left the earth below,
Though sore at heart, and left the side of Turnus.
Were it not so, you would not see me here
Suffering all that passes, here alone,
Resting on air. I should be armed in flames
At the very battle-line, dragging the Trojans
Into a deadly action. I persuaded
Juturna—I confess—to help her brother
In his hard lot, and I approved her daring
Greater difficulties to save his life,
But not that she should fight with bow and arrow.
This I swear by Styx' great fountainhead
Inexorable, which high gods hold in awe.[3]
I yield now and for all my hatred leave
This battlefield. But one thing not retained
By fate I beg for Latium, for the future
Greatness of your kin: when presently
They crown peace with a happy wedding day—
So let it be—and merge their laws and treaties,
Never command the land's own Latin folk

1. Jupiter is referring to earlier incidents in the war involving divine meddling. The water nymph Juturna was the sister and protectress of Turnus.
2. Jupiter outlines the limits of Juno's power against fate, which legislates the outcome of events but not necessarily the way in which they unroll.
3. It was customary for the Olympian gods to swear on the river Styx. Such oaths were held by the gods to be inviolable.

To change their old name, to become new Trojans,
Known as Teucrians; never make them alter
Dialect or dress. Let Latium be.
Let there be Alban kings for generations,
And let Italian valor be the strength
Of Rome in after times. Once and for all
Troy fell, and with her name let her lie fallen."[4]

The author of men and of the world replied
With a half-smile:
"Sister of Jupiter
Indeed you are, and Saturn's other child,
To feel such anger, stormy in your breast.
But come, no need; put down this fit of rage.
I grant your wish. I yield, I am won over
Willingly. Ausonian folk will keep
Their fathers' language and their way of life,
And, that being so, their name. The Teucrians
Will mingle and be submerged, incorporated.
Rituals and observances of theirs
I'll add, but make them Latin, one in speech.
The race to come, mixed with Ausonian blood,
Will outdo men and gods in its devotion,
You shall see—and no nation on earth
Will honor and worship you so faithfully."[5]

To all this Juno nodded in assent
And, gladdened by his promise, changed her mind.
Then she withdrew from sky and cloud.
That done,
The Father set about a second plan—
To take Juturna from her warring brother.
Stories are told of twin fiends, called the Dirae,[6]
Whom, with Hell's Megaera, deep Night bore
In one birth. She entwined their heads with coils
Of snakes and gave them wings to race the wind.
Before Jove's throne, a step from the cruel king,
These twins attend him and give piercing fear
To ill mankind, when he who rules the gods
Deals out appalling death and pestilence,
Or war to terrify our wicked cities.[7]
Jove now dispatched one of these, swift from heaven,
Bidding her be an omen to Juturna.
Down she flew, in a whirlwind borne to earth,

4. Virgil provides an explanation for the disappearance of any historical trace of the Trojan origins of Rome.
5. The temple of Jupiter Capitolinus was dedicated to Jupiter, Juno, and Minerva.
6. The Latin word for the Furies, whom the tragedian Aeschylus called the daughters of Night. Megaera was one of the three Furies named in antiquity.
7. Here, rather than summoned from the underworld, the Furies are depicted as acting in the service of Olympian justice.

Just like an arrow driven through a cloud
From a taut string, an arrow armed with gall
Of deadly posion, shot by a Parthian[8]—
A Parthian or a Cretan—for a wound
Immedicable; whizzing unforeseen
It goes through racing shadows: so the spawn
Of Night went diving downward to the earth.

On seeing Trojan troops drawn up in face
Of Turnus' army, she took on at once
The shape of that small bird that perches late
At night on tombs or desolate roof-tops
And troubles darkness with a gruesome song.[9]
Shrunk to that form, the fiend in Turnus' face
Went screeching, flitting, flitting to and fro
And beating with her wings against his shield.
Unstrung by numbness, faint and strange, he felt
His hackles rise, his voice choke in his throat.
As for Juturna, when she knew the wings,
The shriek to be the fiend's, she tore her hair,
Despairing, then she fell upon her cheeks
With nails, upon her breast with clenched hands.

"Turnus, how can your sister help you now?
What action is still open to me, soldierly
Though I have been? Can I by any skill
Hold daylight for you? Can I meet and turn
This deathliness away? Now I withdraw,
Now leave this war. Indecent birds, I fear you;
Spare me your terror. Whip-lash of your wings
I recognize, that ghastly sound, and guess
Great-hearted Jupiter's high cruel commands.
Returns for my virginity, are they?
He gave me life eternal—to what end?
Why has mortality been taken from me?
Now beyond question I could put a term
To all my pain, and go with my poor brother
Into the darkness, his companion there.
Never to die? Will any brook of mine
Without you, brother, still be sweet to me?
If only earth's abyss were wide enough
To take me downward, goddess though I am,
To join the shades below!"
So she lamented,
Then with a long sigh, covering up her head
In her grey mantle, sank to the river's depth.

8. The Parthians held an empire in what is now eastern Iran.

9. The Fury takes the form of an owl, a bird closely associated with death.

Aeneas moved against his enemy
And shook his heavy pine-tree spear. He called
From his hot heart:
"Rearmed now, why so slow?
Why, even now, fall back? The contest here
Is not a race, but fighting to the death
With spear and sword. Take on all shapes there are,
Summon up all your nerve and skill, choose any
Footing, fly among the stars, or hide
In caverned earth—"
The other shook his head,
Saying:
"I do not fear your taunting fury,
Arrogant prince. It is the gods I fear
And Jove my enemy."
He said no more,
But looked around him. Then he saw a stone,
Enormous, ancient, set up there to prevent
Landowners' quarrels. Even a dozen picked men
Such as the earth produces in our day
Could barely lift and shoulder it. He swooped
And wrenched it free, in one hand, then rose up
To his heroic height, ran a few steps,
And tried to hurl the stone against his foe—
But as he bent and as he ran
And as he hefted and propelled the weight
He did not know himself. His knees gave way,
His blood ran cold and froze. The stone itself,
Tumbling through space, fell short and had no impact.

Just as in dreams when the night-swoon of sleep
Weighs on our eyes, it seems we try in vain
To keep on running, try with all our might,
But in the midst of effort faint and fail;
Our tongue is powerless, familiar strength
Will not hold up our body, not a sound
Or word will come: just so with Turnus now:
However bravely he made shift to fight
The immortal fiend blocked and frustrated him.
Flurrying images passed through his mind.
He gazed at the Rutulians, and beyond them,
Gazed at the city, hesitant, in dread.
He trembled now before the poised spear-shaft
And saw no way to escape; he had no force
With which to close, or reach his foe, no chariot
And no sign of the charioteer, his sister.[1]

1. In an earlier scene in Book 12, where Juturna replaces Turnus's charioteer and spirits him away from the scene of battle.

At a dead loss he stood. Aeneas made
His deadly spear flash in the sun and aimed it,
Narrowing his eyes for a lucky hit.
Then, distant still, he put his body's might
Into the cast. Never a stone that soared
From a wall-battering catapult went humming
Loud as this, nor with so great a crack
Burst ever a bolt of lightning. It flew on
Like a black whirlwind bringing devastation,
Pierced with a crash the rim of sevenfold shield,
Cleared the cuirass'° edge, and passed clean through *breastplate's*
The middle of Turnus' thigh. Force of the blow
Brought the huge man to earth, his knees buckling,
And a groan swept the Rutulians as they rose,
A groan heard echoing on all sides from all
The mountain range, and echoed by the forests.
The man brought down, brought low, lifted his eyes
And held his right hand out to make his plea:

"Clearly I earned this, and I ask no quarter.
Make the most of your good fortune here.
If you can feel a father's grief—and you, too,
Had such a father in Anchises—then
Let me bespeak your mercy for old age
In Daunus,° and return me, or my body, *Turnus's father*
Stripped, if you will, of life, to my own kin.
You have defeated me. The Ausonians
Have seen me in defeat, spreading my hands.
Lavinia is your bride. But go no further
Out of hatred."
Fierce under arms, Aeneas
Looked to and fro, and towered, and stayed his hand
Upon the sword-hilt. Moment by moment now
What Turnus said began to bring him round
From indecision. Then to his glance appeared
The accurst swordbelt surmounting Turnus' shoulder,
Shining with its familiar studs—the strap
Young Pallas wore when Turnus wounded him
And left him dead upon the field; now Turnus
Bore that enemy token on his shoulder—
Enemy still. For when the sight came home to him,
Aeneas raged at the relic of his anguish
Worn by this man as trophy. Blazing up
And terrible in his anger, he called out:

"You in your plunder, torn from one of mine,
Shall I be robbed of you? This wound will come
From Pallas: Pallas makes this offering
And from your criminal blood exacts his due."

He sank his blade in fury in Turnus' chest.
Then all the body slackened in death's chill,
And with a groan for that indignity
His spirit fled into the gloom below.

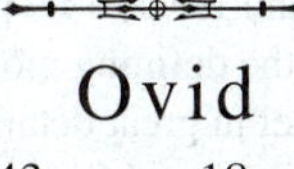

Ovid

43 B.C.E.–18 C.E.

The poet Publius Ovidius Naso had the misfortune to experience the extremes of life in imperial Rome: after some years at the height of fame in the center of the world, he was abruptly exiled to the far reaches of the empire, on the weather-beaten shore of the Black Sea, where, he complained bitterly, the barbarous inhabitants couldn't even understand Latin and he lived in fear for his life. While we will never know the precise reasons behind this precipitous change in fortunes, the usual explanation that he was accused of immorality does at least resonate with the irreverent and unpredictable tone of Ovid's poetry. For example, the erotic verses that first made his name—the *Loves* (sometime after 20 B.C.E.), *The Art of Love* (c. 1 B.C.E.), and *Remedy of Love* (1 B.C.E.–1 C.E.)—sometimes celebrate and sometimes satirize the single-minded pursuit of sexual pleasure. The *Metamorphoses* (2–8 C.E.), Ovid's *magnum opus,* recounts the history of the world from the first creation through the reign of Augustus. It too is a double-edged work, a collection of wondrous transformations and beautiful myths but also a chronicle of the disaster and suffering of mortals and the misdeeds perpetrated by the ancient gods.

Much about the *Metamorphoses* can be viewed as a response to Virgil's epic of the founding of Rome, the *Aeneid* (19 B.C.E.), and to Virgil's status as the preeminent poet of his time. Ovid was seventeen years Virgil's junior and spent his formative years under the peace of Augustus rather than the tumultuous years of civil war that forged Virgil's poetry. Consequently, where Virgil's concern had been how best to represent the costs of war and the demands of peace, Ovid's was how to compose a great work when Virgil's had already been written. There are many underlying similarities in theme and structure. Both poems employ hexameter, the six-footed meter characteristic of classical epic; both are also epic in length, although Ovid divides his poem into fifteen books rather than the *Aeneid*'s twelve or the twenty-four of the Homeric poems. Both poems place the Roman Empire of Augustus at the end point of their narratives, and both refer to their lord and patron as a god. Moreover, the *Metamorphoses* includes within its historical trajectory the *Aeneid*'s material—the fall of Troy and the difficult journey of Aeneas from Troy to found Rome. Nevertheless, these similarities serve more to emphasize the differences than to efface them.

Ovid calls his poem a "book of changes" in the opening verses, and it is truly a dazzling compendium of transformations. Nothing is stable in the world of the *Metamorphoses.* There is no unifying protagonist, no single character who makes more than a few cameo appearances, and no continuity of setting or chronology. Ovid took as his raw material basically everything that had been written in Greek and Latin up to that point, with a particular focus on the many myths about the interaction, primarily erotic, between the Olympian gods and the mortals of the ancient world. Rather than link his many episodes in any consistently causal manner, Ovid chose a looser range of associations: sometimes there is a similarity in type of transformation; sometimes the tale of one family's child will lead to the story of another child of the same generation; and sometimes one story frames a series of further, unrelated tales. So when Orpheus loses Eurydice and sits down to sing of his sorrows, he sings about other transformations. Part of the artistry of the *Metamorphoses* lies in the way it encourages us to seek meanings and connections not just along the chain of its interlinked tales but between the different levels of its sets of tales inside tales, or between the different parts of a myth split up and scattered throughout the poem for the reader to reconstruct.

In the *Aeneid,* the reader is constantly being reminded of the role played by each event in the grand narrative of the founding of Rome. The *Metamorphoses,* by contrast, is resolutely focused on how a particular event looks and feels to its participants. We are given but a single glimpse of the weaver Arachne, but it is the defining moment of her life: her weaving duel with the goddess Minerva. Ovid paints the duel in great detail, especially the fabrics themselves, for they too tell cautionary tales of transformation. Minerva weaves scenes of contest, "the sorry fate" of mortals who challenged gods; Arachne responds with scenes of divine deception and abuse of mortals. The climax of nearly every episode is the transformation scene, where Ovid shows the full range of his powers of description and variation, always catching in words the moment of change, the moment when the person being transformed is neither one thing nor the other. Here is Arachne's metamorphosis into a spider:

> Touched by the bitter lotion, all her hair
> Falls off and with it go her nose and ears.
> Her head shrinks tiny; her whole body's small;
> Instead of legs slim fingers line her sides.
> The rest is belly; yet from that she sends
> A fine-spun thread and, as a spider, still
> Weaving her web, pursues her former skill.

Characteristically, the change is both beautiful and horrible, and Arachne is both utterly transformed and yet strangely still herself.

The closest thing to a guiding philosophy in the *Metamorphoses,* a program that would gather its disparate gems into a fixed setting, is the speech of the Greek mathematician Pythagoras in Book 15. This speech, the longest in the poem, asserts what looks like a general moral: "Nothing retains its form; new shapes from old / Nature, the great inventor, ceaselessly / Contrives." For Pythagoras, the principle of change implies the transmigration of souls from one body to the next; every thing and every creature on the earth is sentient, and the world's souls are constantly migrating from one being to another. Pythagoras, consequently, is a vegetarian. Many scholars have taken Pythagoras seriously as the voice of the author and argued that his speech gives shape and substance to the poem; many others have argued that it is just another Ovidian parody of a blowhard who takes himself too seriously. Strong arguments can be made both ways, and we need not exclude the possibility that Ovid has perversely placed the secrets of his poem's meaning in the mouth of a character he may also have thought was ridiculous. There is great pleasure to be found in the endless invention and playfulness of the *Metamorphoses* and great satisfaction in its profound glimpses of human emotions and tragedy. Perhaps its most enduring quality, however, and what has made it such an influential compendium of myth over the past two millennia, is the myriad combinations and recombinations of the extremes of experience that Ovid achieves at every turn in his exploration of the meanings of change in our lives.

PRONUNCIATIONS:

Arachne: ah-RAK-nee
Daedalus: DEH-dah-luhs
Echo: EH-koh
Eurydice: yur-RI-di-see
Ganymede: GA-ni-meed
Hyacinth: HAI-uh-sinth
Icarus: IH-kah-ruhs

Metamorphoses: me-tuh-MOR-foh-seez
Minotaur: MI-nah-tawr
Narcissus: nahr-SI-suhs
Orpheus: OR-fee-uhs
Phaethon: FAY-tuhn
Pygmalion: pig-MAY-lee-uhn
Pythagoras: pi-THA-gor-uhs
Tiresias: tai-REE-see-uhs

from METAMORPHOSES[1]

from BOOK 1

[PROLOGUE]

Of bodies changed to other forms I tell;
You Gods, who have yourselves wrought every change,
Inspire my enterprise and lead my lay
In one continuous song from nature's first
Remote beginnings to our modern times.

from BOOK 3

[TIRESIAS]

While down on earth as destiny ordained
These things took place, and Bacchus, babe twice born,
Was cradled safe and sound,[1] it chanced that Jove,
Well warmed with nectar, laid his weighty cares
Aside and, Juno too in idle mood,
The pair were gaily joking, and Jove said
"You women get more pleasure out of love
Than we men do, I'm sure." She disagreed.
So they resolved to get the views of wise
Tiresias.[2] He knew both sides of love.
For once in a green copse when two huge snakes
Were mating, he attacked them with his stick,
And was transformed (a miracle!) from man
To woman; and spent seven autumns so;
Till in the eighth he saw the snakes once more
And said "If striking you has magic power
To change the striker to the other sex,
I'll strike you now again." He struck the snakes
And so regained the shape he had at birth.

1. Translated by A. D. Melville.

1. Bacchus (Greek: Dionysus) was the son of Jove and Cadmus's daughter Semele. He is called "twice born" because after his mother was killed by a trick of the jealous Juno, Jove sewed him up in his thigh. The god of wine and intoxication, Bacchus was associated with the ecstatic rituals of his Bacchantes, or female followers.

2. The resident seer of Thebes, Tiresias is the most celebrated prophet of classical myth and literature. Odysseus consults his ghost in the *Odyssey,* and Tiresias plays a central role in *Oedipus the King.*

Asked then to give his judgement on the joke,
He found for Jove; and Juno (so it's said)
Took umbrage beyond reason, out of all
Proportion, and condemned her judge to live
In the black night of blindness evermore.
But the Almighty Father (since no god
Has right to undo what any god has done)
For his lost sight gave him the gift to see
What things should come, the power of prophecy,
An honour to relieve that penalty.

[Narcissus and Echo]

So blind Tiresias gave to all who came
Faultless and sure reply and far and wide
Through all Boeotia's cities[3] spread his fame.
To test his truth and trust the first who tried
Was wave-blue water-nymph Liriope,
Whom once Cephisus in his sinuous flow
Embracing held and ravished. In due time
The lovely sprite bore a fine infant boy,
From birth adorable, and named her son
Narcissus; and of him she asked the seer,
Would he long years and ripe old age enjoy,
Who answered "If he shall himself not know."
For long his words seemed vain; what they concealed
The lad's strange death and stranger love revealed.
Narcissus now had reached his sixteenth year
And seemed both man and boy; and many a youth
And many a girl desired him, but hard pride
Ruled in that delicate frame, and never a youth
And never a girl could touch his haughty heart.
Once as he drove to nets the frightened deer
A strange-voiced nymph observed him, who must speak
If any other speak and cannot speak
Unless another speak, resounding Echo.
Echo was still a body, not a voice,
But talkative as now, and with the same
Power of speaking, only to repeat,
As best she could, the last of many words.
Juno had made her so; for many a time,
When the great goddess might have caught the nymphs
Lying with Jove upon the mountainside,
Echo discreetly kept her talking till
The nymphs had fled away; and when at last
The goddess saw the truth, "Your tongue," she said,

3. Boeotia was a region of central Greece. Thebes, in the south, was its dominant city.

"With which you tricked me, now its power shall lose,
Your voice avail but for the briefest use."
The event confirmed the threat: when speaking ends,
All she can do is double each last word,
And echo back again the voice she's heard.
Now when she saw Narcissus wandering
In the green byways, Echo's heart was fired;
And stealthily she followed, and the more
She followed him, the nearer flamed her love,
As when a torch is lit and from the tip
The leaping sulphur grasps the offered flame.
She longed to come to him with winning words,
To urge soft pleas, but nature now opposed;
She might not speak the first but—what she might—
Waited for words her voice could say again.
It chanced Narcissus, searching for his friends,
Called "Anyone here?" and Echo answered "Here!"
Amazed he looked all round and, raising his voice,
Called "Come this way!" and Echo called "This way!"
He looked behind and, no one coming, shouted
"Why run away?" and heard his words again.
He stopped and, cheated by the answering voice,
Called "Join me here!" and she, never more glad
To give her answer, answered "Join me here!"
And graced her words and ran out from the wood
To throw her longing arms around his neck.
He bolted, shouting "Keep your arms from me!
Be off! I'll die before I yield to you."
And all she answered was "I yield to you."
Shamed and rejected in the woods she hides
And has her dwelling in the lonely caves;
Yet still her love endures and grows on grief,
And weeping vigils waste her frame away;
Her body shrivels, all its moisture dries;
Only her voice and bones are left; at last
Only her voice, her bones are turned to stone.
So in the woods she hides and hills around,
For all to hear, alive, but just a sound.
Thus had Narcissus mocked her; others too,
Hill-nymphs and water-nymphs and many a man
He mocked; till one scorned youth, with raised hands, prayed,
"So may *he* love—and never win his love!"
And Nemesis[4] approved the righteous prayer.
There was a pool, limpid and silvery,
Whither no shepherd came nor any herd,
Nor mountain goat; and never bird nor beast
Nor falling branch disturbed its shining peace;

4. Nemesis personified the concept of divine retribution for human pride; she was also worshipped as a goddess.

Grass grew around it, by the water fed,
And trees to shield it from the warming sun.
Here—for the chase and heat had wearied him—
The boy lay down, charmed by the quiet pool,
And, while he slaked his thirst, another thirst
Grew; as he drank he saw before his eyes
A form, a face, and loved with leaping heart
A hope unreal and thought the shape was real.
Spellbound he saw himself, and motionless
Lay like a marble statue staring down.
He gazes at his eyes, twin constellation,
His hair worthy of Bacchus or Apollo,
His face so fine, his ivory neck, his cheeks
Smooth, and the snowy pallor and the blush;
All he admires that all admire in him,
Himself he longs for, longs unwittingly,
Praising is praised, desiring is desired,
And love he kindles while with love he burns.
How often in vain he kissed the cheating pool
And in the water sank his arms to clasp
The neck he saw, but could not clasp himself!
Not knowing what he sees, he adores the sight;
That false face fools and fuels his delight.
You simple boy, why strive in vain to catch
A fleeting image? What you see is nowhere;
And what you love—but turn away—you lose!
You see a phantom of a mirrored shape;
Nothing itself; with you it came and stays;
With you it too will go, if you can go!
    No thought of food or rest draws him away;
Stretched on the grassy shade he gazes down
On the false phantom, staring endlessly,
His eyes his own undoing. Raising himself
He holds his arms towards the encircling trees
And cries "You woods, was ever love more cruel!
You know! For you are lovers' secret haunts.
Can you in your long living centuries
Recall a lad who pined so piteously?
My joy! I see it; but the joy I see
I cannot find" (so fondly love is foiled!)
"And—to my greater grief—between us lies
No mighty sea, no long and dusty road,
Nor mountain range nor bolted barbican.° *fortification*
A little water sunders us. He longs
For my embrace. Why, every time I reach
My lips towards the gleaming pool, he strains
His upturned face to mine. I surely could
Touch him, so slight the thing that thwarts our love.
Come forth, whoever you are! Why, peerless boy,

Elude me? Where retreat beyond my reach?
My looks, my age—indeed it cannot be
That you should shun—the nymphs have loved me too!
Some hope, some nameless hope, your friendly face
Pledges; and when I stretch my arms to you
You stretch your arms to me, and when I smile
You smile, and when I weep, I've often seen
Your tears, and to my nod your nod replies,
And your sweet lips appear to move in speech,
Though to my ears your answer cannot reach.
Oh, I am he! Oh, now I know for sure
The image is my own; it's for myself
I burn with love; I fan the flames I feel.
What now? Woo or be wooed? Why woo at all?
My love's myself—my riches beggar me.
Would I might leave my body! I could wish
(Strange lover's wish!) my love were not so near!
Now sorrow saps my strength; of my life's span
Not long is left; I die before my prime.
Nor is death sad for death will end my sorrow;
Would he I love might live a long tomorrow!
But now we two—one soul—one death will die."
Distraught he turned towards the face again;
His tears rippled the pool, and darkly then
The troubled water veiled the fading form,
And, as it vanished, "Stay," he shouted, "stay!
Oh, cruelty to leave your lover so!
Let me but gaze on what I may not touch
And feed the aching fever in my heart."
Then in his grief he tore his robe and beat
His pale cold fists upon his naked breast,
And on his breast a blushing redness spread
Like apples, white in part and partly red,
Or summer grapes whose varying skins assume
Upon the ripening vine a blushing bloom.
And this he saw reflected in the pool,
Now still again, and could endure no more.
But as wax melts before a gentle fire,
Or morning frosts beneath the rising sun,
So, by love wasted, slowly he dissolves
By hidden fire consumed. No colour now,
Blending the white with red, nor strength remains
Nor will, nor aught that lately seemed so fair,
Nor longer lasts the body Echo loved.
But she, though angry still and unforgetting,
Grieved for the hapless boy, and when he moaned
"Alas," with answering sob she moaned "alas,"
And when he beat his hands upon his breast,
She gave again the same sad sounds of woe.

His latest words, gazing and gazing still,
He sighed "alas! the boy I loved in vain!"
And these the place repeats, and then "farewell,"
And Echo said "farewell." On the green grass
He drooped his weary head, and those bright eyes
That loved their master's beauty closed in death.
Then still, received into the Underworld,
He gazed upon himself in Styx's pool.
His Naiad sisters wailed and sheared their locks
In mourning for their brother; the Dryads too
Wailed[5] and sad Echo wailed in answering woe.
And then the brandished torches, bier and pyre
Were ready—but no body anywhere;
And in its stead they found a flower—behold,
White petals clustered round a cup of gold![6]

from Book 6

[Arachne]

Pallas[1] had listened to the tale she told
With warm approval of the Muses' song
And of their righteous rage.[2] Then to herself—
"To praise is not enough; I should have praise
Myself, not suffer my divinity
To be despised unscathed." She had in mind
Arachne's doom, the girl of Lydia,[3]
Who in the arts of wool-craft claimed renown
(So she had heard) to rival hers. The girl
Had no distinction in her place of birth
Or pedigree, only that special skill.
Her father was Idmon of Colophon,
Whose trade it was to dye the thirsty wool
With purple of Phocaea.[4] She had lost
Her mother, but she too had been low-born
And matched her husband. Yet in all the towns
Of Lydia Arachne's work had won
A memorable name, although her home
Was humble and Hypaepae where she lived
Was humble too. To watch her wondrous work

5. Naiads are freshwater nymphs, or minor female deities, often daughters of river gods; hence their kinship to the river's son, Narcissus. Dryads are tree nymphs.

6. Narcissus is a genus of fragrant, bulbous flowers including the daffodil, jonquil, and the poet's narcissus, which most closely matches Ovid's description.

1. Minerva (Greek: Pallas Athena) was born fully formed from the head of Jove. She was the goddess of crafts, wisdom, and war. She was also the patroness of the Greek city-state of Athens.

2. The nine Muses, goddesses of the arts, especially music and poetry, made their home on Helicon, a mountain in southwest Boeotia. They have just finished relating to Minerva their singing contest with the Pierides, nine daughters of Pierus of Pella in Macedonia. To punish their presumption, the Muses had transformed the sisters into magpies.

3. A region in Asia Minor, now western Turkey.

4. Colophon and Phocaea were Ionian cities in western Asia Minor.

The nymphs would often leave their vine-clad slopes
Of Tmolus, often leave Pactolus' stream,
Delighted both to see the cloth she wove
And watch her working too; such grace she had.
Forming the raw wool first into a ball,
Or fingering the flock and drawing out
Again and yet again the fleecy cloud
In long soft threads, or twirling with her thumb,
Her dainty thumb, the slender spindle, or
Embroidering the pattern—you would know
Pallas had trained her. Yet the girl denied it
(A teacher so distinguished hurt her pride)
And said, "Let her contend with me. Should I
Lose, there's no forfeit that I would not pay."
    Pallas disguised herself as an old woman.
A fringe of false grey hair around her brow,
Her tottering steps supported by a stick,
And speaking to the girl, "Not everything
That old age brings," she said, "we'd wish to avoid.
With riper years we gain experience.
Heed my advice. Among the world of men
Seek for your wool-craft all the fame you will,
But yield the goddess place, and humbly ask
Pardon for those rash words of yours; she'll give
You pardon if you ask." With blazing eyes
Arachne stared at her and left her work.
She almost struck her; anger strong and clear
Glowed as she gave the goddess (in disguise)
Her answer: "You're too old, your brain has gone.
You've lived too long, your years have done for you.
Talk to your daughters, talk to your sons' wives!
My own advice is all I need. Don't think
Your words have any weight. My mind's unchanged.
Why doesn't Pallas come herself? Why should
She hesitate to match herself with me?"
Then Pallas said, "She's come!" and threw aside
The old crone's guise and stood revealed. The nymphs
And Lydian women knelt in reverence.
Only Arachne had no fear. Yet she
Blushed all the same; a sudden colour tinged
Her cheeks against her will, then disappeared;
So when Aurora rises in the dawn,
The eastern sky is red and, as the sun
Climbs, in a little while is pale again.
    She stood by her resolve, setting her heart,
Her stupid heart, on victory, and rushed
To meet her fate. Nor did the child of Jove
Refuse or warn her further or postpone
The contest. Then, with no delay, they both,

Standing apart, set up their separate looms
And stretched the slender warp. The warp is tied
To the wide cross-beam; a cane divides the threads;
The pointed shuttles carry the woof through,
Sped by their fingers. When it's through the warp,
The comb's teeth, tapping, press it into place.
Both work in haste, their dresses girdled tight
Below their breasts; the movements of their arms
Are skilled and sure; their zeal beguiles their toil.
Here purple threads that Tyrian vats have dyed[5]
Are woven in, and subtle delicate tints
That change insensibly from shade to shade.
So when the sunshine strikes a shower of rain,
The bow's huge arc will paint the whole wide sky,
And countless different colours shine, yet each
Gradation dupes the gaze, the tints that touch
So similar, the extremes so far distinct.
Threads too of golden wire were woven in,
And on the loom an ancient tale was traced.[6]
  The rock of Mars in Cecrops' citadel[7]
Is Pallas' picture and that old dispute
About the name of Athens. Twelve great gods,
Jove in their midst, sit there on lofty thrones,
Grave and august, each pictured with his own
Familiar features: Jove in regal grace,
The Sea-god standing, striking the rough rock
With his tall trident, and the wounded rock
Gushing sea-brine, his proof to clinch his claim.
Herself she gives a shield, she gives a spear
Sharp-tipped, she gives a helmet for her head;
The aegis guards her breast,[8] and from the earth,
Struck by her spear, she shows an olive tree,
Springing pale-green with berries on the boughs;
The gods admire; and Victory ends the work.
  Yet to provide examples to instruct
Her rival what reward she should expect
For her insensate daring, she designed
In each of the four corners four small scenes
Of contest, brightly coloured miniatures.
There in one corner Thracian Rhodope
And Haemon, icy mountains now, but once

5. Tyre was a city of the Phoenicians in the ancient Middle East. An important trading center, it founded colonies in Cyprus and Carthage and was famed for its purple dye and its glass.

6. Athena weaves the tale of her dispute with the sea god Neptune (Greek: Poseidon) over who should be the patron deity of Athens.

7. The Areopagus, or "Hill of Mars," was the meeting place of the ancient council of Athens, which took its name from it. Cecrops was the legendary founder of the city.

8. The aegis was a goatskin cloak or breastplate with tassels. Worn by Minerva, it terrified her enemies and granted protection from attack.

Mortals, who claimed the names of gods most high.[9]
Another showed the Pygmy matron's doom,
Her pitiable doom, when Juno won
The contest and transformed her to a crane
And made her fight her folk, her kith and kin.[1]
Antigone she pictured too, who once
Challenged the royal consort of great Jove.
And Juno changed her to a bird, and Troy
Availed her nothing nor Laomedon,
Her father—no! with snowy feathers clothed,
In self-applause she claps her stork's loud bill.[2]
In the last corner Cinyras, bereaved,
Embraced the temple steps, his daughters' limbs,
And lying on the marble seemed to weep.[3]
All round the border ran an olive-branch,
The branch of peace. That was the end, and she
Finished her picture with her own fair tree.° *the olive*
Arachne shows Europa cheated by
The bull's disguise, a real bull you'd think,
And real sea.[4] The girl was gazing at
The shore she'd left and calling to her friends,
Seeming to dread the leaping billows' touch,
Shrinking and drawing up her feet in fear.
Asterie in the struggling eagle's clutch
She wove, and pictured Leda as she lay
Under the white swan's wings, and added too
How Jove once in a satyr's guise had got
Antiope with twins, and, as Amphitryon,
Bedded Alcmena; in a golden shower
Fooled Danae, Aegina in a flame,
And as a shepherd snared Mnemosyne,
And as a spotted serpent Proserpine.[5]
Neptune she drew, changed to a savage bull
For love of Canace; and Neptune too
Sired, as Enipeus, the Aloidae;

9. Rhodope and Haemon were an incestuous brother-and-sister pair who called themselves "Jove" and "Juno" (who were also brother and sister). They were transformed into mountains in Thrace, a region in the southeastern Balkans.

1. Oenoe was a pygmy, one of a race of dwarves located by Greek mythology variously in Thrace, India, the Nile, or elsewhere. The battle between the pygmies and the cranes was a common topic in ancient art and poetry.

2. Antigone (not to be confused with the Theban daughter of Oedipus and Jocasta) was the sister of Priam and daughter of Laomedon of Troy. This is the only known account of her dispute with Juno.

3. Cinyras was an Assyrian king; this is the only known account of his daughter's presumption toward Juno.

4. Arachne's weaving offers a lengthy list of the gods' seductions or rapes of mortals, a number of which Ovid recounts in more detail elsewhere in the poem. Europa was abducted by Jove, who was disguised as a white bull.

5. Asterie was a Titan's daughter; Leda was the mother of Helen, Castor, and Pollux; Antiope bore the Theban twins Amphion and Zethus; Jove fathered Hercules on Alcmena, disguised as her husband, the king of Thebes; Danae bore the hero Perseus; Aegina was a daughter of the river god Asopus, and Aeacus, the son of the union, was the grandfather of both Achilles and Ajax; Jove's seduction of Mnemosyne yielded the nine Muses; Proserpine (Greek: Persephone) was Jove's daughter by Ceres (Greek: Demeter), and their son was the second Dionysus, Dionysus-Zagreus.

Bisaltes' child he cheated as a ram;
The corn's most gracious mother, golden-haired,
Suffered him as a horse, and, as a bird,
The snake-tressed mother of the flying steed;
And poor Melantho knew him as a dolphin.[6]
To all of them Arachne gave their own
Features and proper features of the scene.
She wove too Phoebus in a herdsman's guise,
And how he sometimes wore a lion's skin,
Sometimes hawk's plumage; how he fooled Isse,
Macareus' daughter, as a shepherd;[7] how
Bacchus with bunches of false grapes deceived
Erigone, and Saturn, as a horse,
Begot the centaur Chiron.[8] Round the edge
A narrow band of flowers she designed,
Flowers and clinging ivy intertwined.
  In all that work of hers Pallas could find,
Envy could find, no fault. Incensed at such
Success the warrior goddess, golden-haired,
Tore up the tapestry, those crimes of heaven,
And with the boxwood shuttle in her hand
(Box of Cytorus)[9] three times, four times, struck
Arachne on her forehead. The poor wretch,
Unable to endure it, bravely placed
A noose around her neck; but, as she hung,
Pallas in pity raised her. "Live!" she said,
"Yes, live but hang, you wicked girl, and know
You'll rue the future too: that penalty
Your kin shall pay to all posterity!"
And as she turned to go, she sprinkled her
With drugs of Hecate,[1] and in a trice,
Touched by the bitter lotion, all her hair
Falls off and with it go her nose and ears.
Her head shrinks tiny; her whole body's small;
Instead of legs slim fingers line her sides.
The rest is belly; yet from that she sends
A fine-spun thread and, as a spider, still
Weaving her web, pursues her former skill.

6. Neptune's amours: Canace was a daughter of Aeolus of Thessaly and the sister of Macareus; the Thessalian river god Enipeus was Tyro's lover, a story Ovid combines with Neptune's siring the giants Otus and Ephialtes on Aloeus's wife, Iphimedia; Neptune turned himself into a ram and Bisaltes's daughter Theophane into a ewe, and their offspring was the Ram with the Golden Fleece; in Arcadia, Ceres was said to have mated as a mare with Neptune in horse shape; raped in Athena's temple by Neptune, the girl Medusa had her hair transformed into serpents, and the winged horse Pegasus emerged when Perseus cut off her head; Melantho was the daughter of Deucalion and Pyrrha.

7. As a shepherd, Apollo seduces Isse, or Amphisse, the daughter of Macareus and his sister, Canace.

8. Erigone was a daughter of Icarius, who was killed by shepherds unfamiliar with the novel effects of Bacchus's grapevines; both became stars in the heavens. The sea nymph Philyra, loved by Saturn as horse and mare, gave birth to the wise centaur Chiron, the teacher of Asclepius, Jason, and Achilles among others.

9. Cytorus is a mountain in northern Asia Minor that is proverbial for its box trees, which produced a hard and fine-grained wood.

1. A sinister goddess associated with magic, witchcraft, the night, the underworld, and crossroads.

from Book 8

[The Minotaur: Daedalus and Icarus]

Minos reached harbour in the isle of Crete[1]
And, disembarking, paid his vows to Jove,
A hundred bulls, and hung the spoils of war
To adorn his palace walls. His dynasty's
Disgrace had grown; the monstrous hybrid beast
Declared the queen's obscene adultery.[2]
To rid his precincts of this shame the king
Planned to confine him shut away within
Blind walls of intricate complexity.
The structure was designed by Daedalus,
That famous architect.[3] Appearances
Were all confused; he led the eye astray
By a mazy multitude of winding ways,
Just as Maeander plays among the meads
Of Phrygia and in its puzzling flow
Glides back and forth and meets itself and sees
Its waters on their way and winds along,
Facing sometimes its source, sometimes the sea.[4]
So Daedalus in countless corridors
Built his bafflement, and hardly could himself
Make his way out, so puzzling was the maze.
Within this labyrinth Minos shut fast
The beast, half bull, half man, and fed him twice
On Attic blood, lot-chosen each nine years,
Until the third choice mastered him.[5] The door,
So difficult, which none of those before
Could find again, by Ariadne's aid
Was found, the thread that traced the way rewound.
Then Theseus, seizing Minos' daughter,[6] spread
His sails for Naxos, where, upon the shore,
That cruel prince abandoned her and she,
Abandoned, in her grief and anger found
Comfort in Bacchus' arms.[7] He took her crown
And set it in the heavens to win her there

1. Minos, a son of Europa and Jove, was king of the island-kingdom of Crete.
2. Inspired with the love of a bull sent by the sea god Neptune, Minos's wife, Pasiphaë, had the inventor Daedalus create a wooden cow covered with a leather hide. The bull impregnated her inside this contraption, and she gave birth to the Minotaur, a man with the head of a bull.
3. A member of the royal family of Athens, Daedalus came to Crete after he had been banished for the murder of Perdix, out of fear that his sister's son would prove to be the greater inventor.
4. Maeander was in southern Asia Minor; its name was synonymous with the idea of a winding river.
5. Minos exacted an annual tribute of seven young men and seven young women from Athens to feed the Minotaur. In the third year, the Athenian hero (and later king) Theseus joined the tribute.
6. Ariadne, Minos's daughter, fell in love with Theseus and offered to help him in return for leaving with him and becoming his wife. Daedalus revealed to her the secret of the labyrinth.
7. Naxos is an island in the Cyclades between Crete and Athens.

A star's eternal glory; and the crown
Flew through the soft light air and, as it flew,
Its gems were turned to gleaming fires, and still
Shaped as a crown their place in heaven they take
Between the Kneeler and him who grasps the Snake.[8]
Hating the isle of Crete and the long years
Of exile, Daedalus was pining for
His native land, but seas on every side
Imprisoned him. "Though land and sea," he thought,
"The king may bar to me, at least the sky
Is open; through the sky I'll set my course.[9]
Minos may own all else; he does not own
The air." So then to unimagined arts
He set his mind and altered nature's laws.
Row upon row of feathers he arranged,
The smallest first, then larger ones, to form
A growing graded shape, as rustic pipes
Rise in a gradual slope of lengthening reeds;
Then bound the middle and the base with wax
And flaxen threads, and bent them, so arranged,
Into a gentle curve to imitate
Wings of a real bird. His boy stood by,
Young Icarus, who, blithely unaware
He plays with his own peril, tries to catch
Feathers that float upon the wandering breeze,
Or softens with his thumb the yellow wax,
And by his laughing mischief interrupts
His father's wondrous work. Then, when the last
Sure touch was given, the craftsman poised himself
On his twin wings and hovered in the air.
Next he prepared his son. "Take care," he said,
"To fly a middle course, lest if you sink
Too low the waves may weight your feathers; if
Too high, the heat may burn them. Fly half-way
Between the two. And do not watch the stars,
The Great Bear or the Wagoner or Orion,
With his drawn sword, to steer by. Set your course
Where I shall lead." He fixed the strange new wings
On his son's shoulders and instructed him
How he should fly; and, as he worked and warned,
The old man's cheeks were wet, the father's hands
Trembled. He kissed his son (the last kisses
He'd ever give) and rising on his wings

8. One version of the myth relates that Bacchus married her, and she was transformed into the constellation Corona Borealis, or the Crown, in the stars between the Kneeler, or Hercules, and the Snake, once the guardian dragon of the Hesperides.

9. Daedalus had been imprisoned with his son, Icarus, by Minos for telling Ariadne how to escape from the labyrinth.

He flew ahead, anxious for his son's sake,
Just like a bird that from its lofty nest
Launches a tender fledgeling in the air.
Calling his son to follow, schooling him
In that fatal apprenticeship, he flapped
His wings and watched the boy flapping behind.
An angler fishing with his quivering rod,
A lonely shepherd propped upon his crook,
A ploughman leaning on his plough, looked up
And gazed in awe, and thought they must be gods
That they could fly. Delos and Paros lay
Behind them now; Samos, great Juno's isle,
Was on the left, Lebinthos on the right
And honey-rich Calymne,[1] when the boy
Began to enjoy his thrilling flight and left
His guide to roam the ranges of the heavens,
And soared too high. The scorching sun so close
Softened the fragrant wax that bound his wings;
The wax melted; his waving arms were bare;
Unfledged, they had no purchase on the air!
And calling to his father as he fell,
The boy was swallowed in the blue sea's swell,
The blue sea that for ever bears his name.[2]
His wretched father, now no father, cried
"Oh, Icarus, where are you? Icarus,
Where shall I look, where find you?" On the waves
He saw the feathers. Then he cursed his skill,
And buried his boy's body in a grave,
And still that island keeps the name he gave.

from Book 10

[Orpheus and Eurydice]

Thence Hymen° came, in saffron mantle clad, *god of marriage*
At Orpheus'[1] summons through the boundless sky
To Thessaly, but vain the summons proved.
True he was present, but no hallowed words
He brought nor happy smiles nor lucky sign;
Even the torch he held sputtered throughout
With smarting smoke, and caught no living flame
For all his brandishing. The ill-starred rite

1. Islands in the Aegean between Crete and Asia Minor.
2. The Icarian Sea surrounds the island of Icaria, near Samos in the Aegean Sea.

1. The son of Apollo and the Muse Calliope, the Thracian Orpheus was the preeminent singer of classical myth. Voyaging with the Argonauts, he outsang the Sirens. His journey to the underworld to rescue Eurydice was at the root of an important mystery cult, and many hymns, most of them related to Dionysus, were attributed to Orpheus.

Led to a grimmer end. The new-wed bride,° *Eurydice*
Roaming with her gay Naiads through the grass,
Fell dying when a serpent struck her heel.
And when at last the bard of Rhodope° *Thrace*
Had mourned his fill in the wide world above,
He dared descend through Taenarus' dark gate
To Hades[2] to make trial of the shades;
And through the thronging wraiths and grave-spent ghosts
He came to pale Persephone and him,
Lord of the shades, who rules the unlovely realm,
And as he struck his lyre's sad chords he said:
"Ye deities who rule the world below,
Whither we mortal creatures all return,
If simple truth, direct and genuine,
May by your leave be told, I have come down
Not with intent to see the glooms of Hell,
Nor to enchain the triple snake-haired necks
Of Cerberus,[3] but for my dear wife's sake,
In whom a trodden viper poured his venom
And stole her budding years. My heart has sought
Strength to endure; the attempt I'll not deny;
But love has won, a god whose fame is fair
In the world above; but here I doubt, though here
Too, I surmise; and if that ancient tale
Of ravishment is true, you too were joined
In love.[4] Now by these regions filled with fear,
By this huge chaos, these vast silent realms,
Reweave, I implore, the fate unwound too fast
Of my Eurydice. To you are owed
Ourselves and all creation; a brief while
We linger; then we hasten, late or soon,
To one abode; here one road leads us all;
Here in the end is home; over humankind
Your kingdom keeps the longest sovereignty.
She too, when ripening years reach their due term,
Shall own your rule. The favour that I ask
Is but to enjoy her love; and, if the Fates
Will not reprieve her, my resolve is clear
Not to return: may two deaths give you cheer."
    So to the music of his strings he sang,
And all the bloodless spirits wept to hear;
And Tantalus forgot the fleeing water,
Ixion's wheel was tranced; the Danaids
Laid down their urns; the vultures left their feast,

2. Taenarum, the central of the three southern fingers of the Peloponnesus, was known to contain a cave leading to the underworld, used by Hercules, among others.

3. The three-headed dog Cerberus was the legendary guardian of the underworld.

4. Pluto (Greek: Hades) had snatched his niece Proserpine, the daughter of Jove and Ceres, down to the underworld to be his queen.

And Sisyphus sat rapt upon his stone.[5]
Then first by that sad singing overwhelmed,
The Furies' cheeks, it's said, were wet with tears;[6]
And Hades' queen and he whose sceptre rules
The Underworld could not deny the prayer,
And called Eurydice. She was among
The recent ghosts and, limping from her wound,
Came slowly forth; and Orpheus took his bride
And with her this compact that, till he reach
The world above and leave Avernus' vale,[7]
He look not back or else the gift would fail.
The track climbed upwards, steep and indistinct,
Through the hushed silence and the murky gloom;
And now they neared the edge of the bright world,
And, fearing lest she faint, longing to look,
He turned his eyes—and straight she slipped away.
He stretched his arms to hold her—to be held—
And clasped, poor soul, naught but the yielding air.
And she, dying again, made no complaint
(For what complaint had she save she was loved?)
And breathed a faint farewell, and turned again
Back to the land of spirits whence she came.
The double death of his Eurydice
Stole Orpheus' wits away; (like him who saw
In dread the three-necked hound of Hell with chains
Fast round his middle neck, and never lost
His terror till he lost his nature too
And turned to stone; or Olenos, who took
Upon himself the charge and claimed the guilt
When his ill-starred Lethaea trusted to
Her beauty, hearts once linked so close, and now
Two rocks on runnelled Ida's mountainside).
He longed, he begged, in vain to be allowed
To cross the stream of Styx a second time.
The ferryman repulsed him.[8] Even so
For seven days he sat upon the bank,
Unkempt and fasting, anguish, grief and tears
His nourishment, and cursed Hell's cruelty.
Then he withdrew to soaring Rhodope

5. Celebrated underworld punishments. Tantalus, a son of Jove, sat at the gods' table but for revealing their secrets was punished by the torment of food and drink always just out of his reach. Ixion, the king of the Lapithae and the father of Pirithous, was bound to a wheel for the attempted rape of Juno. The 50 daughters of Danaus, the king of Argos, killed their husbands on their collective wedding night, for which they were forced eternally to carry water in leaky urns. Prometheus was punished for his theft of fire by having his liver eternally eaten by a vulture. Sisyphus, a son of Aeolus and the founder of Corinth, was renowned for his cunning and trickery; he was punished for them as well, forced to roll a boulder up a hill that would always escape him just as he reached the summit.

6. Born like the Giants from Earth and the blood of Uranus's severed genitals, the Furies were female powers of the underworld who punished transgressions.

7. Avernus, near Naples, was another reputed entrance to the underworld.

8. It was the task of Charon to ferry newly arrived souls across the river Styx.

And Haemus battered by the northern gales.
Three times the sun had reached the watery Fish
That close the year,[9] while Orpheus held himself
Aloof from love of women, hurt perhaps
By ill-success or bound by plighted troth.
Yet many a woman burned with passion for
The bard, and many grieved at their repulse.
It was his lead that taught the folk of Thrace
The love for tender boys, to pluck the buds,
The brief springtime, with manhood still to come.
There was a hill, and on the hill a wide
Level of open ground, all green with grass.
The place lacked any shade. But when the bard,
The heaven-born bard, sat there and touched his strings,
Shade came in plenty. Every tree was there:[1]
Dodona's holy durmast, poplars once
The Sun's sad daughters, oaks with lofty leaves,
Soft limes, the virgin laurel and the beech;[2]
The ash, choice wood for spearshafts, brittle hazels,
The knotless fir, the ilex curving down
With weight of acorns, many-coloured maples,
The social plane, the river-loving willow,
The water-lotus, box for ever green,
Thin tamarisks and myrtles double-hued,
Viburnums bearing berries of rich blue.
Twist-footed ivy came and tendrilled vines,
And vine-clad elms, pitch-pines and mountain-ash,
Arbutus laden with its blushing fruit,
Lithe lofty palms, the prize of victory,
And pines, high-girdled, in a leafy crest,
The favourite of Cybele, the gods'
Great mother, since in this tree Attis doffed
His human shape and stiffened in its trunk.[3]

* * *

[Orpheus's Song: Ganymede, Hyacinth, Pygmalion]

Such was the grove the bard assembled. There
He sat amid a company of beasts,
A flock of birds, and when he'd tried his strings
And, as he tuned, was satisfied the notes,
Though different, agreed in harmony,

9. Three years have passed. The twelfth and final sign of the zodiac, Pisces ("the Fish"), marks the end of winter (mid-February to mid-March).

1. The catalogue of trees includes several whose transformations Ovid has already described.

2. Dodona in Epirus was said to be the oldest Greek oracle; the durmast, or oak, was her sacred tree. The sun's three daughters were Phaethon's sisters, who wept so long at his tomb that they were transformed into poplars. The river Peneus's daughter, Daphne, was changed by her father into a laurel to escape the advances of Apollo; he chose the laurel as his tree and its wreath as the victor's crown.

3. Attis was a Phrygian, or Lydian, youth beloved of Cybele, the Anatolian fertility goddess, who castrated himself in a fit of madness.

He sang this song: "From Jove, great Mother Muse,[4]
Inspire my song: to Jove all creatures bow;
Jove's might I've often hymned in days gone by.
I sang the giants in a graver theme
And bolts victorious in Phlegra's plains.[5]
But now I need a lighter strain, to sing
Of boys beloved of gods and girls bewitched
By lawless fires who paid the price of lust.
The King of Heaven once was fired with love
Of Ganymede,[6] and something was devised
That Jove would rather be than what he was.
Yet no bird would he deign to be but one
That had the power to bear his thunderbolts.[7]
At once his spurious pinions° beat the breeze *wings*
And off he swept the Trojan lad; who now,
Mixing the nectar, waits in heaven above
(Though Juno frowns) and hands the cup to Jove.
Hyacinth, too, Apollo would have placed
In heaven had the drear° Fates given time *dreary*
To place him there. Yet in the form vouchsafed
He is immortal. Year by year, when spring
Drives winter flying and the Ram succeeds
The watery Fish, he rises from the earth
And in the greensward° brings his bloom to birth.[8] *grassy ground*

Hyacinth was my father's favourite,
And Delphi, chosen centre of the world,
Lost its presiding god, who passed his days
Beside Eurotas° in the martial land *Sparta's river*
Of unwalled Sparta, and no more esteemed
Zither or bow. Forgetting his true self,
He was content to bear the nets, to hold
The hounds in leash and join the daylong chase
Through the rough mountain ridges, nourishing
His heart's desire with long companionship.

One day, near noon, when the high sun midway
Between the night past and the night to come
At equal distance stood from dawn and dusk,
They both stripped off their clothes and oiled their limbs,
So sleek and splendid, and began the game,
Throwing the discus; and Apollo first
Poised, swung and hurled it skywards through the air,
Up, soaring up, to cleave the waiting clouds.

4. Orpheus was the son of Calliope, the Muse of epic poetry.
5. The battle with the Giants took place on the plain of Phlegra in Thrace.
6. Ganymede was a brother of Ilos, the founder of Troy. Both were sons of Tros, a grandson of Jove.
7. The eagle was closely associated with Jove and was said to fetch his thunderbolts after he threw them.
8. Pisces ("Fish") is the last month of the solar year (mid-February to mid-March); Aries ("the Ram") is the first of the new year (mid-March to mid-April). Although not the same as the modern hyacinth, the name also refers here to a flower, to be described below.

The heavy disk at longest last fell back
To the familiar earth, a proof of skill,
And strength with skill. Then straightway Hyacinth,
Unthinking, in the excitement of the sport,
Ran out to seize it, but it bounded back
From the hard surface full into his face.
The god turned pale, pale as the boy himself,
And catching up the huddled body, tried
To revive him, tried to staunch the tragic wound
And stay the fading soul with healing herbs.
His skill was vain; the wound was past all cure.
And as, when in a garden violets
Or lilies tawny-tongued or poppies proud
Are bruised and bent, at once they hang their heads
And, drooping, cannot stand erect and bow
Their gaze upon the ground; so dying lies
That face so fair and, all strength ebbed away,
His head, too heavy, on his shoulder sinks.

"My Hyacinth," Apollo cried, "laid low
And cheated of youth's prime! I see your wound,
My condemnation, you my grief and guilt!
I, I have caused your death; on my own hand,
My own, your doom is written. Yet what wrong
Is mine unless to join the game with you
Were wrong or I were wrong to love you well?
Oh, would for you—or with you—I might give
My life! But since the laws of fate forbid,
You shall be with me always; you shall stay
For ever in remembrance on my lips,
And you my lyre and you my song shall hymn.
A new flower you shall be with letters marked
To imitate my sobs, and time shall come
When to that flower the bravest hero born
Shall add his name on the same petals writ."

So with prophetic words Apollo spoke,
And lo! the flowing blood that stained the grass
Was blood no longer; and a flower rose
Gorgeous as Tyrian dye, in form a lily,
Save that a lily wears a silver hue,
This richest purple. And, not yet content,
Apollo (who had wrought the work of grace)
Inscribed upon the flower his lament,
AI AI, AI AI, and still the petals show
The letters written there in words of woe.
And Sparta's pride in Hyacinth, her son,
Endures undimmed; with pomp and proud display
Each year his feast returns in the ancient way.[9]

* * *

9. The three-day festival honoring Apollo and Hyacinth was an important date in the Spartan year.

from Book 11

[The Death of Orpheus]

While Orpheus sang his minstrel's songs and charmed
The rocks and woods and creatures of the wild
To follow, suddenly, as he swept his strings
In concord with his song, a frenzied band
Of Thracian women, wearing skins of beasts,
From some high ridge of ground caught sight of him.[1]
"Look!" shouted one of them, tossing her hair
That floated in the breeze, "Look, there he is,
The man who scorns us!" and she threw her lance
Full in Apollo's minstrel's face, but, tipped
With leaves, it left a bruise but drew no blood.
Another hurled a stone; that, in mid air,
Was vanquished by the strains of voice and lyre
And grovelled at his feet, as if to ask
Pardon for frenzy's daring. Even so
The reckless onslaught swelled; their fury knew
No bounds; stark madness reigned. And still his singing
Would have charmed every weapon, but the huge
Clamour, the drums, the curving Phrygian fifes,° *small flutes*
Hand-clapping, Bacchic screaming drowned the lyre.
And then at last, his song unheard, his blood
Reddened the stones. The Maenads first pounced on
The countless birds still spellbound by his song,
The snakes, the host of creatures of the wild,
His glory and his triumph. Next they turned
Their bloody hands on Orpheus, flocking like
Birds that have seen a midnight owl abroad
By day, or in the amphitheatre
Upon the morning sand a pack of hounds
Round a doomed stag. They rushed upon the bard,
Hurling their leaf-dressed lances, never meant
For work like that; and some slung clods, some flints,
Some branches torn from trees. And, lest they lack
Good weapons for their fury, as it chanced,
Oxen were toiling there to plough the land
And brawny farmhands digging their hard fields
Not far away, and sweating for their crop.
Seeing the horde of women, they fled and left
Their labour's armoury, and all across
The empty acres lay their heavy rakes,
Hoes and long-handled mattocks. Seizing these,
Those frantic women tore apart the oxen
That threatened with their horns, and streamed to slay

1. Maenads, or Bacchantes, were followers of Bacchus (Greek: Dionysos), intoxicated by the god's power. They dressed in panther skins and carried a *thyrsos,* or ivy-covered staff.

The bard. He pleaded then with hands outstretched
And in that hour for the first time his words
Were useless and his voice of no avail.
In sacrilege they slew him. Through those lips
(Great Lord of Heaven!) that held the rocks entranced,
That wild beasts understood, he breathed his last,
And forth into the winds his spirit passed.
The sorrowing birds, the creatures of the wild,
The woods that often followed as he sang,
The flinty rocks and stones, all wept and mourned
For Orpheus; forest trees cast down their leaves,
Tonsured in grief, and rivers too, men say,
Were swollen with their tears, and Naiads wore,
And Dryads too, their mourning robes of black
And hair dishevelled. All around his limbs
Lay scattered. Hebrus'[2] stream received his head
And lyre, and floating by (so wonderful!)
His lyre sent sounds of sorrow and his tongue,
Lifeless, still murmured sorrow, and the banks
Gave sorrowing reply. And then they left
Their native river, carried out to sea,
And gained Methymna's shore on Lesbos' isle.[3]
There, as his head lay on that foreign sand,
Its tumbled tresses dripping, a fierce snake
Threatened, until at last Apollo came
To thwart it as it struck and froze to stone
That serpent's open mouth and petrified,
Just as they were, its jaws that gaped so wide.
The ghost of Orpheus passed to the Underworld,
And all the places that he'd seen before
He recognized again and, searching through
The Elysian fields, he found Eurydice
And took her in his arms with leaping heart.
There hand in hand they stroll, the two together;
Sometimes he follows as she walks in front,
Sometimes he goes ahead and gazes back—
No danger now—at his Eurydice.

from Book 15

[PYTHAGORAS]

A man lived here, a Samian by birth,
But he had fled from Samos and its masters
And, hating tyranny, by his own choice

2. A Thracian river that flowed into the Aegean Sea.

3. Methymna was a city on Lesbos, a large island off the coast of Asia Minor.

Became an exile.[1] Though the gods in heaven
Live far removed, he approached them in his mind,
And things that nature kept from mortal sight
His inward eye explored. When meditation
And vigils of long study had surveyed
All things that are, he made his wisdom free
For all to share; and he would teach his class,
Hanging in silent wonder on his words,
The great world's origin, the cause of things,
What nature is, what god, and whence the snow,
What makes the lightning, whether thunder comes
From Jove or from the winds when clouds burst wide,
Why the earth quakes, what ordinance controls
The courses of the stars, and the whole sum
Of nature's secrets. He was first to ban
As food for men the flesh of living things:
These are the doctrines he was first to teach,
Wise words, though wisdom powerless to persuade.[2]

* * *

"Now since the sea's great surges sweep me on,
All canvas spread, hear me! In all creation
Nothing endures, all is in endless flux,
Each wandering shape a pilgrim passing by.
And time itself glides on in ceaseless flow,
A rolling stream—and streams can never stay,
Nor lightfoot hours. As wave is driven by wave
And each, pursued, pursues the wave ahead,
So time flies on and follows, flies and follows,
Always, for ever new. What was before
Is left behind; what never was is now;
And every passing moment is renewed.
You see how day extends as night is spent,
And this bright radiance succeeds the dark;
Nor, when the tired world lies in midnight peace,
Is the sky's sheen the same as in the hour
When on his milk-white steed the Morning Star
Rides forth, or when, bright harbinger of day,
Aurora gilds the globe to greet the sun.
The sun's round shield at morning when he climbs
From earth's abyss glows red, and when he sinks
To earth's abyss at evening red again,
And at his zenith gleaming bright, for there

1. Pythagoras was born on the island of Samos in the mid-6th century B.C.E.. He left for Croton, a Greek colony in southern Italy, around 530. He was held to have brought to Greece the doctrine of the transmigration of souls on which Ovid has him speak here. He was also credited with important discoveries in music, astronomy, and mathematics, including the Pythagorean theorem.

2. Vegetarianism was one of the tenets of the ancient cult of Pythagoreanism. After arguing that vegetarianism hearkens back to the Golden Age, Pythagoras goes on to dismiss the fear of death: because of the transmigration of souls, nothing dies.

The air is pure and earth's dross far away.
Nor can the queenly moon ever retain
Her shape unchanged, but always, as her orb
Waxes or wanes, tomorrow, she must shine
Larger or smaller than she is today.
Again, you notice how the year in four
Seasons revolves, completing one by one
Fit illustration of our human life.
The young springtime, the tender suckling spring,
Is like a child; the swelling shoots so fresh,
So soft and fragile, fill the farmers' hearts
With hope and gladness. Flowers are everywhere;
Their colours dance across the fostering fields,
While the green leaves still lack their strength and pride.
Spring passes, and the year, grown sturdier,
Rolls on to summer like a strong young man;
No age so sturdy, none so rich, so warm.
Then autumn follows, youth's fine fervour spent,
Mellow and ripe, a temperate time between
Youth and old age, his temples flecked with grey.
And last, with faltering footsteps, rough and wild,
His hair, if any, white, old winter comes.
Our bodies too are always, endlessly
Changing; what we have been, or are today,
We shall not be tomorrow. Years ago
We hid, mere seeds and promise, in the womb;
Nature applied her artist's hands to free
Us from our swollen mother's narrow home,
And sent us forth into the open air.
Born to the shining day, the infant lies
Strengthless, but soon on all fours like the beasts
Begins to crawl, and then by slow degrees,
Weak-kneed and wobbling, clutching for support
Some helping upright, learns at last to stand.
Then swift and strong he traverses the span
Of youth, and when the years of middle life
Have given their service too, he glides away
Down the last sunset slope of sad old age—
Old age that saps and mines and overthrows
The strength of earlier years. Milo, grown old,
Sheds tears to see how shrunk and flabby hang
Those arms on which the muscles used to swell,
Massive like Hercules; and, when her glass
Shows every time-worn wrinkle, Helen weeps
And wonders why she twice was stolen for love.[3]

3. Milo was a wrestler from Croton who won many victories at the Olympic and the Pythian Games and a disciple of Pythagoras. Helen was first carried off by Theseus and then later, after she had married Menelaus, by Paris of Troy.

Time, the devourer, and the jealous years
With long corruption ruin all the world
And waste all things in slow mortality.
    The elements themselves do not endure;
Examine how they change and learn from me.
The everlasting universe contains
Four generative substances; of these
Two, earth and water, sink of their own weight;
Two, air and fire (fire purer still than air),
Weightless, unburdened, seek the heights above.
Though spaced apart, all issue from each other
And to each other fall. So earth, reduced,
Is rarefied to water; moisture, thinned,
Dissolves to air and wind; air, losing weight,
So light, so insubstantial, flashes up
To empyrean fire. Then they return
In reverse order as the skein° unwinds. *bundle of yarn*
Thus fire, condensed, passes to heavier air,
Air into water, water in its turn
Compressed, conglobed, solidifies to earth.
    Nothing retains its form; new shapes from old
Nature, the great inventor, ceaselessly
Contrives. In all creation, be assured,
There is no death—no death, but only change
And innovation; what we men call birth
Is but a different new beginning; death
Is but to cease to be the same. Perhaps
This may have moved to that and that to this,
Yet still the sum of things remains the same.

* * *

    "So—lest I range too far and my steeds lose
Their course—the earth and all therein, the sky
And all thereunder change and change again.
We too ourselves, who of this world are part,
Not only flesh and blood but pilgrim souls,
Can make our homes in creatures of the wild
Or of the farm. These creatures might have housed
Souls of our parents, brothers, other kin,
Or men at least, and we must keep them safe,
Respected, honoured, lest we gorge ourselves
On such a banquet as Thyestes ate.[4]
How vilely he's inured, how wickedly
He fits himself to kill his human kin,
He who can slit his calf's throat, hear its cries
Unmoved, who has the heart to kill his kid
That screams like a small child, or eat the bird

4. The sons of Thyestes were killed and served to their father in a meal by his brother, Atreus.

His hand has reared and fed! How far does this
Fall short of murder? Where else does it lead?
No! Let the oxen plough and owe their death
To length of days; let the sheep give their shield
Against the north wind's fury; let the goats
Bring their full udders for your hand to milk.
Away with traps and snares and lures and wiles!
Never again lime twigs to cheat the birds,
Nor feather ropes to drive the frightened deer,
Nor hide the hook with dainties that deceive!
Destroy what harms; destroy, but never eat;
Choose wholesome fare and never feast on meat!

PERSPECTIVES

The Culture of Rome and the Beginnings of Christianity

To the sophisticated and powerful urban elite that controlled ancient Rome, the first Christians were superstitious bumpkins from a distant backwater. How could they suspect that this obscure cult would soon enough take over their empire? It is true that Rome had a generally tolerant policy for the assimilation of members of the farther reaches of its Empire, and the inhabitants of Judaea at times had received special consideration. Still, from early reactions through at least the fourth century it appears that resistance to Christianity was at least as much aesthetic and social as it was political and religious. The urbane poetry of Catullus and Horace gives a good impression of the values and attitudes of educated Romans around the time of the birth of Jesus. Both poets cultivate the persona of a well-connected member of the elite: the republican Catullus stresses the thrill-seeking vigor of the brash, young aesthete; Horace expresses the measured, Stoic outlook of the next generation under the reign of Augustus, where even death could become a subject for a lesson on proper living.

It is a far cry from the balanced ethic of Horace or the self-consciously cultivated passion of Catullus to the strident urgency and stern demands of Luke and Paul. Earliest Christianity was a sect of Judaism, regarding Jesus as the Christ, the fulfillment of the Hebrew prophets' promise of a Messiah. The first-century writings of Luke and Paul bear witness to the struggle to extricate an independent religion out of a complex web of forces: the legal and spiritual tradition of Judaism, the language and philosophy of Hellenism, the political yoke of the Empire, and the many other radical new forms of worship circulating around the eastern Mediterranean during the early centuries of the Common Era.

Strict asceticism and a rejection of material and familial ties were hallmarks of the Gospels—oral accounts of the "Good News" of Christ that began being written down near the end of the first century. The martyrdom that often resulted from this choice gave a positive meaning to the omnipresence of death for most of the inhabitants of the Empire. The Roman historians excerpted below give a good sense of the relative insignificance of the movement during these years. Still, its members could make excellent scapegoats, such as the "notoriously depraved Christians" who were falsely blamed by Nero for the great fire in Rome in 64. The decadent world portrayed so vividly by Petronius in the *Satyricon* is perhaps not exemplary of behavior under Nero, but it does suggest the world that Saul of Tarsus chose to leave behind when a vision of Christ converted him into the apostle Paul, eventually to be martyred on the Ostian Way outside Rome by Nero's command.

Juvenal's satires present a traditionally Roman response to a corrupt society; he attacks the miserable city from the point of view of classical Roman ethics and morality, while other writers like the second-century novelist Apuleius graphically depicted the instability of the changing world outside the capital city. Both traditions would find their home in Christian sermonizing, but joined to a rhetoric of separation and a language of mystery wholly alien to a rationalist like Juvenal—who chose, after all, to remain in the city he professed to hate—and with a gravity and an intensity of purpose lacking in Apuleius's ambling narrative *The Golden Ass.* The paradoxical formulations that punctuate the fire and brimstone of Paul's Epistles and the parables and miracles of Jesus recounted in Luke proved more potent and compelling antidotes to the crises of the late Empire. But as Augustine shows in his *Confessions,* the crux of Christianity's appeal lay in the unmatchable grip it had on the emotions—the passions and the disappointments of everyday suffering. Its debt to Rome was the means of channeling that visceral power into a form that would be intellectually and aesthetically palatable to those figures such as Emperor Constantine who were in a position finally to entrench it within an enduring framework of temporal power.

Chariot race at the Circus Maximus at Rome. As Juvenal asserted in his tenth *Satire,* "Luxury, more deadly than war, broods over the city . . . the people that once bestowed commands, consulships, legions, and all else, now concerns itself no more, and longs eagerly for just two things—bread and circuses."

PRONUNCIATIONS:

Catullus: kah-TUHL-luhs
Encolpius: en-KOL-pee-uhs
Gitai: JEE-tai
Juvenal: JOO-ve-nahl
Petronius: pe-TROH-nee-uhs
Pliny: PLI-nee
Priapea: PRAI-ah-PAY-ah
Satyricon: sah-TI-ri-con
Suetonius: soo-eh-TOH-nee-uhs
Tacitus: TA-si-tuhs
Trajan: TRAY-juhn

Catullus

84–54 B.C.E.

In the small corpus of verse he completed before his untimely death at age 30, Gaius Valerius Catullus celebrated novelty, obscenity, youth, brevity, charm, wit, passion, and urbanity. His 113 poems, most of them quite short, reproduce everyday life and take us inside the mind of a young man-about-town in first-century Rome. Meals and journeys are described; friends are praised and heckled, enemies mocked and reviled; loves and disappointments are chronicled in graphic detail; and everywhere there is the writing, reciting, and criticism of poetry.

Born into a well-to-do family in Verona, Catullus soon made his way to the capital, where he moved among the preeminent political and literary figures of his day. He had a brother, whose sudden death in Asia Minor around 57 B.C.E. was the occasion of a sea voyage to the distant grave near Troy and a moving poem that strove "to speak in vain to your unspeaking ashes." He conducted a love affair with the powerful (and, according to Cicero, notorious) Clodia, half-sister of the tribune Publius Clodius Pulcher and wife of Quintus Caecilius Metellus, consul in the year 60. This was the "Lesbia" to whom many of the poems refer and with whom the poet explores the extremes of passion; her name itself pays homage to the erotic lyrics of Sappho, the archaic Greek poet of the island of Lesbos (page 494; an imitation of one of her poems is included in the selection below, page 806). Catullus's depiction of love is central to his portrayal of life as a paradoxical mix of emotions, a heady brew both sweet and sour in which despair and joy are inseparable.

Catullus's poetic intensity is well illustrated by this deservedly famous epigram:

Odi et amo. quare id faciam fortasse requiris?
nescio sed fieri sentio et excrucior.

I hate & love. And if you should ask how I can do both,
I couldn't say; but I feel it, and it shivers me.

The compression and power of these two lines derive in large part from the elimination of adjectives and of images. The poet gives us only verbs of condensed sensation: *hate, love, do, feel, shiver.* Rather than explaining the paradox of the opening antithesis, *odi et amo,* this string of verbs heightens its effect. Half the verbs are active; half are passive: the poet hates and loves; he rules and is ruled by his lover and his love. With its capacity to concentrate opposites of emotion and sense perceptions into concrete feelings through a masterful control of language and meter, the lyric form allowed Catullus to render vividly the chaotic experience of an individual in the late Republic.

from POEMS[1]

3[2]

Cry out lamenting, Venuses & Cupids,
and mortal men endowed with Love's refinement:
the sparrow of my lady lives no longer!
Sparrow, the darling pet of my beloved,
that was more precious to her than her eyes were;
it was her little honey, and it knew her
as well as any girl knows her own mother;
it would not ever leave my lady's bosom
but leapt up, fluttering from yon to hither,
chirruping always only to its mistress.
It now flits off on its way, goes, gloom-laden
down to where—word is—there is no returning.
Damn you, damned shades of Orcus[3] that devour
all mortal loveliness, for such a lovely
sparrow it was you've stolen from my keeping!

1. Translated by Charles Martin.
2. This poem is in the form of a mock threnody, or funeral dirge.
3. An infernal deity in Greek mythology. Identified in Roman religion with Dis, the god of the underworld.

O hideous deed! O poor little sparrow!
It's your great fault that my lady goes weeping,
reddening, ruining her eyes from sorrow.

5

Lesbia, let us live only for loving,
and let us value at a single penny
all the loose flap of senile busybodies!
Suns when they set are capable of rising,
but at the setting of our own brief light
night is one sleep from which we never waken.
Give me a thousand kisses, then a hundred,
another thousand next, another hundred,
a thousand without pause & then a hundred,
until when we have run up our thousands
we will cry bankrupt, hiding our assets
from ourselves & any who would harm us,
knowing the volume of our trade in kisses.

13

You will dine well with me, my dear Fabullus,[1]
in a few days or so, the gods permitting.
—Provided you provide the many-splendored
feast, and invite your fair-complected° lady, *complexioned*
your wine, your salt & all the entertainment!
Which is to say, my dear, if you bring dinner
you will dine well, for these days your Catullus
finds that his purse is only full of cobwebs.
But in return, you'll have from me Love's Essence,
—or what (if anything) is more delicious:
I'll let you sniff a certain charming fragrance
which Venuses & Cupids gave my lady;
one whiff of it, Fabullus, and you'll beg the
gods to transform you into nose, completely!

51[1]

To me that man seems like a god in heaven,
seems—may I say it?—greater than all gods are,
who sits by you & without interruption
  watches you, listens

1. Fabullus was a colleague in the Roman province of Spain with Veranius, a friend of Catullus who, we are told, sent the poet a set of fine napkins of Spanish linen as a souvenir. The poem's number comes from its place in the manuscript. It is not known if this order reflects the author's intention.

1. A free translation of Sappho's poem "He looks to me to be in heaven" (see page 496), in Sapphic strophes, with a final stanza of his own.

to your light laughter, which casts such confusion
onto my senses, Lesbia, that when I
gaze at you merely, all of my well-chosen
words are forgotten

as my tongue thickens & a subtle fire
runs through my body while my ears are deafened
by their own ringing & at once my eyes are
covered in darkness!

Leisure, Catullus. More than just a nuisance,
leisure: you riot, overmuch enthusing.
Fabulous cities & their sometime kings have
died of such leisure.

76[1]

If any pleasure can come to a man through recalling
decent behavior in his relations with others,
not breaking his word, and never, in any agreement,
deceiving men by abusing vows sworn to heaven,
then countless joys will await you in old age, Catullus,
as a reward for this unrequited passion!
For all of those things which a man could possibly say or
do have all been said & done by you already,
and none of them counted for anything, thanks to her vileness!
Then why endure your self-torment any longer?
Why not abandon this wretched affair altogether,
spare yourself pain the gods don't intend you to suffer!
It's hard to break off with someone you've loved such a long time:
it's hard, but you have to do it, somehow or other.
Your only chance is to get out from under this sickness,
no matter whether or not you think you're able.
O gods, if pity is yours, or if ever to any
who lay near death you offered the gift of your mercy,
look on my suffering: if my life seems to you decent,
then tear from within me this devouring cancer,
this heavy dullness wasting the joints of my body,
completely driving every joy from my spirit!
Now I no longer ask that she love me as I love her,
or—even less likely—that she give up the others:
all that I ask for is health, an end to this foul sickness!
O gods, grant me this in exchange for my worship.

85

I hate & love. And if you should ask how I can do both,
I couldn't say; but I feel it, and it shivers me.

1. The mood, subject, and meter of this poem anticipate the classical Roman love elegies of Propertius, Tibullus, and Ovid.

107

If ever something which someone with no expectation
desired should happen, we are rightly delighted!
And so this news is delightful—it's dearer than gold is:
you have returned to me, Lesbia, my desired!
Desired, yet never expected—but you *have* come back
to me! A holiday, a day of celebration!
What living man is luckier than I am? Or able
to say that anything could possibly be better?

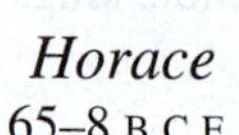

Horace

65–8 B.C.E.

Son of a freedman farmer of modest means, Quintus Horatius Flaccus was by the end of his life a close acquaintance of Emperor Augustus. Through his often topical poetry and through his actions, Horace was intimately involved in the events of his day. In 42 B.C.E., he fought on the losing side of Caesar's murderers, Brutus and Cassius, at Philippi against Mark Antony and Octavian. His family farm was confiscated, but Horace eventually landed on his feet, gaining the patronage of the influential Etruscan noble and minister of Octavian, Maecenas, with the aid of his friend Virgil. In 33, Maecenas presented Horace with a farm in the rich Sabine country northeast of Rome. Horace published his *Satires* (*Sermones*) between 34 and 30 B.C.E., the *Epodes* in 30, three books of *Odes* in 23, the *Epistles* in 20, and a fourth book of *Odes* around 13.

The *Odes* are built around a series of oppositions: country versus city, a simple versus a complicated life, poverty versus wealth, past versus present, private versus public. Central to these oppositions is the Epicurean conception of the *aurea mediocritas,* or golden mean, the desire to avoid extremes in life and to focus on the simple pleasures of the present. Horace prides himself on puncturing pretensions and unreasonable behavior, including his own. The strategy of comic deflation allows Horace to introduce philosophical concerns with the lightest of touches. So Ode 2.14 skips from a lament for his aging friend Postumus to the concluding image of his heir spilling his fine wine all over the floor.

from ODES[1]

1.9 You see Soracte standing white and deep

You see Soracte[2] standing white and deep
with snow, the woods in trouble, hardly able
to carry their burden, and the rivers
halted by sharp ice.

Thaw out the cold. Pile up the logs
on the hearth and be more generous, Thaliarchus,[3]

1. Translated by David West.

2. An isolated mountain to the north of Rome that was home of the Hirpi, priests of the cult of Soranus, an underworld deity identified with Apollo, who also happened to be the special patron of Emperor Augustus.

3. Most of Horace's poems address real-life acquaintances; however, "Thaliarchus" is simply Greek for "master of the revels," an apt name for this poem, one of several by Horace on the theme of *carpe diem,* or "seize the day."

as you draw the four-year-old Sabine[4]
from its two-eared cask.

Leave everything else to the gods. As soon as
they still the winds battling it out
on the boiling sea, the cypresses stop waving
and the old ash trees.

Don't ask what will happen tomorrow.
Whatever day Fortune[5] gives you, enter it
as profit, and don't look down on love
and dancing while you're still a lad,

while the gloomy grey keeps away from the green.
Now is the time for the Campus[6] and the squares
and soft sighs at the time arranged
as darkness falls.

Now is the time for the lovely laugh from the secret corner
giving away the girl in her hiding-place,
and for the token snatched from her arm
or finger feebly resisting.

2.14 Ah how quickly, Postumus, Postumus

Ah how quickly, Postumus, Postumus,[1]
the years glide by, and piety will not delay
the wrinkles, and old age, and death, the unsubdued,
pressing at their heels,

no, my friend, not if every day that passes you sacrificed
three hundred bulls to appease Pluto, the god
who cannot weep, who confines Tityos
and the three-bodied giant Geryon

in the prison of those gloomy waters
that we know all of us must cross[2]
who feed upon the bounty of the earth,
whether we be kings or poor tenant farmers.

In vain shall we avoid the bloody god of war
and the roaring breakers of the Adriatic.[3]
In vain autumn after long autumn shall we tremble
for our health when the south wind blows.

We must go and see black Cocytus meandering

4. A proverbially excellent wine from the region northeast of Rome where Horace's estate was located.

5. The goddess of chance or luck, of great importance in Roman religion.

6. The Campus Martius was a center of public life and leisure in 1st-century Rome, full of baths, theaters, and temples.

1. Perhaps Propertius Postumus, a relation of the poet Propertius.

2. Pluto was the god of the underworld, the Roman equivalent of the Greek Hades. The Giant Tityos was punished in the underworld for his attempted rape of Leto, the mother of Apollo and Diana; composed of three men joined together, Geryon was killed by the hero Hercules. The Styx was the principal river of the underworld.

3. The sea located between Italy and the Balkans.

in its sluggish flow,[4] the infamous daughters of Danaus,
  and Sisyphus, son of Aeolus,
    at his long sentence of hard labour.[5]

We must leave the earth, our home,
and the wife we love, and none of these trees you tend
  except the hated cypresses[6]
    will go with their short-lived master.

Your heir, worthier than yourself, will drink off
the Caecuban[7] you laid down behind a hundred locks,
  and stain your paving with proud wine undiluted
    and too good for the banquets of priests.

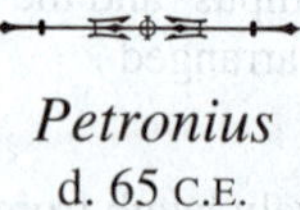

Petronius

d. 65 C.E.

The *Satyricon* is a closely observed and persuasively authentic satire of everyday life in the late Roman Empire—and under the reign of Nero, there was no shortage of material. Its author has never been conclusively identified, but it is generally assumed that he was the same Gaius Petronius whose biography was memorably sketched by the historian Tacitus:

> He spent his days sleeping, his nights working and enjoying himself. Others achieve fame by energy, Petronius by laziness. Yet he was not, like others who waste their resources, regarded as dissipated or extravagant, but as a refined voluptuary. . . . He had been admitted into the small circle of Nero's intimates, as Arbiter of Taste: to the blasé emperor, smartness and elegance were restricted to what Petronius had approved.

Petronius soon fell out of favor, but his suicide was evidently as stylish as the life he had led:

> He severed his veins. Then, having them bound up again when the fancy took him, he talked with his friends—but not seriously, or so as to gain a name for fortitude. And he listened to them reciting, not discourses about the immortality of the soul or philosophy, but light lyrics and frivolous poems. Some slaves received presents—others were beaten. He appeared at dinner, and dozed, so that his death, if compulsory, might look natural.

Tacitus recounts that rather than the customary deathbed flatteries of the emperor, the Arbiter left behind a stinging indictment of his master's corruption, "giving names of each male and female bed-fellow and details of every lubricious novelty." Even though Tacitus's portrait may not be strictly factual, it reflects the character that the author of the *Satyricon* ought to have had.

Only fragments of the *Satyricon* have survived; it was structured around the sexual misadventures of a young antihero, Encolpius, as he traveled around the backwaters of Greece in pursuit of his fickle lover, the slave-boy Gitai. Both the portions that have survived and those that

4. The Cocytus was another underworld river.
5. Mythical figures punished for their misdeeds on earth. Danaus's 50 daughters had killed their husbands on their wedding night. Sisyphus was a legendary trickster who was condemned to push up hill a boulder that always rolled down again just as he reached the top.
6. The cypress tree was traditionally associated by the Romans with mortality, especially in the case of rich and important men. Its branches were placed at the door of the mourning house, on the funeral altar, and on the pyre itself; the cypress was also planted around graves.
7. A prized wine from a region of Latium.

have been reconstructed tell the story of Encolpius in a series of random and chaotic episodes, with characters who appear and disappear without warning. There are no explicit morals, no clear lessons learned, and no obvious change or growth in the characters. It is not evident whether Petronius expects his reader to gain a positive insight from the dissolute world he depicts; what is clear is that nothing and no one is sacred.

The episode known as "Dinner with Trimalchio" is characteristic of Petronius's approach. It is a fundamentally accurate depiction of the excesses of a typical dinner party of the time, yet it nevertheless satirizes all involved. The host, Trimalchio, is a fabulously wealthy merchant trader seeking to elevate his social status by staging elaborate meals. Encolpius and his companion are posing as literati, cadging free meals by lending their artistic cachet to the occasion. The events of the meal combine slapstick misadventures with carefully drawn parodies of the rituals of the Roman banquet: the impossibly complicated dishes whose meanings have to be interpreted before they can be consumed, the nonstop literary references, and the malicious gossip. What elevates this episode beyond delicious parody is that Trimalchio is not merely a target for ridicule—even though he does indeed manage to do everything wrong—but a memorable individual, a fleshed-out character as vividly present to us today as he must have been to his Roman contemporaries.

from Satyricon[1]

from Dinner with Trimalchio

Finally we took our places. Boys from Alexandria[2] poured iced water over our hands. Others followed them and attended to our feet, removing any hangnails with great skill. But they were not quiet even during this troublesome operation: they sang away at their work. I wanted to find out if the whole staff were singers, so I asked for a drink. In a flash a boy was there, singing in a shrill voice while he attended to me—and anyone else who was asked to bring something did the same. It was more like a musical comedy than a respectable dinner party.

Some extremely elegant hors d'oeuvre were served at this point—by now everyone had taken his place with the exception of Trimalchio, for whom, strangely enough, the place at the top was reserved.[3] The dishes for the first course included an ass of Corinthian bronze with two panniers, white olives on one side and black on the other. Over the ass were two pieces of plate, with Trimalchio's name and the weight of the silver inscribed on the rims. There were some small iron frames shaped like bridges supporting dormice sprinkled with honey and poppy seed. There were steaming hot sausages too, on a silver gridiron with damsons[4] and pomegranate seeds underneath.

We were in the middle of these elegant dishes when Trimalchio himself was carried in to the sound of music and set down on a pile of tightly stuffed cushions. The sight of him drew an astonished laugh from the guests. His cropped head stuck out from a scarlet coat; his neck was well muffled up and he had put round it a napkin with a broad purple stripe and tassels dangling here and there. On the little finger of his left hand he wore a heavy gilt ring and a smaller one on the last joint of the next finger. This I thought was solid gold, but actually it was studded with little iron stars.[5]

1. Translated by J. P. Sullivan.
2. The great Egyptian port city of Alexandria was associated in Roman culture with what they saw as the degeneracy and taste for luxury of the Eastern cultures.
3. Seating at the standard Roman banquet consisted of nine places, three on each of three sides of an open square. Placement was strictly determined by custom, which Trimalchio ignores.
4. Plums.
5. Only equestrians, or men of free birth, were allowed to wear solid gold rings; Trimalchio is a freedman.

And to show off even more of his jewellery, he had his right arm bare and set off by a gold armlet and an ivory circlet fastened with a gleaming metal plate.

After picking his teeth with a silver toothpick, he began: "My friends, I wasn't keen to come into the dining room yet. But if I stayed away any more, I would have kept you back, so I've deprived myself of all my little pleasures for you. However, you'll allow me to finish my game."

A boy was at his heels with a board of terebinth wood[6] with glass squares, and I noticed the very last word in luxury—instead of white and black pieces he had gold and silver coins. While he was swearing away like a trooper over his game and we were still on the hors d'oeuvre, a tray was brought in with a basket on it. There sat a wooden hen, its wings spread round it the way hens are when they are broody. Two slaves hurried up and as the orchestra played a tune they began searching through the straw and dug out peahens' eggs, which they distributed to the guests.

Trimalchio turned to look at this little scene and said: "My friends, I gave orders for that bird to sit on some peahens' eggs. I hope to goodness they are not starting to hatch. However, let's try them and see if they are still soft."

We took up our spoons (weighing at least half a pound each) and cracked the eggs, which were made of rich pastry. To tell the truth, I nearly threw away my share, as the chicken seemed already formed. But I heard a guest who was an old hand say: "There should be something good here." So I searched the shell with my fingers and found the plumpest little figpecker, all covered with yolk and seasoned with pepper.

At this point Trimalchio became tired of his game and demanded that all the previous dishes be brought to him. He gave permission in a loud voice for any of us to have another glass of mead if we wanted it. Suddenly there was a crash from the orchestra and a troop of waiters—still singing—snatched away the hors d'oeuvre. However in the confusion one of the side-dishes happened to fall and a slave picked it up from the floor. Trimalchio noticed this, had the boy's ears boxed and told him to throw it down again. A cleaner came in with a broom and began to sweep up the silver plate along with the rest of the rubbish. Two long-haired Ethiopians followed him, carrying small skin bottles like those they use for scattering sand in the circus, and they poured wine over our hands—no one ever offered us water.

* * *

This was the sort of conversation flying round when Trimalchio came in, dabbed his forehead and washed his hands in perfume. There was a short pause, then he said:

"Excuse me, dear people, my inside has not been answering the call for several days now. The doctors are puzzled. But some pomegranate rind and resin in vinegar has done me good. But I hope now it will be back on its good behaviour. Otherwise my stomach rumbles like a bull. So if any of you wants to go out, there's no need for him to be embarrassed. None of us was born solid. I think there's nothing so tormenting as holding yourself in. This is the one thing even God Almighty can't object to. Yes, laugh, Fortunata,[7] but you generally keep me up all night with this sort of thing.

"Anyway, I don't object to people doing what suits them even in the middle of dinner—and the doctors forbid you to hold yourself in. Even if it's a longer business, everything is there just outside—water, bowls, and all the other little comforts. Believe me, if the wind goes to your brain it starts flooding your whole body too. I've known a lot of people die from this because they wouldn't be honest with themselves."

6. The costly wood of the turpentine tree.

7. Trimalchio's wife, about whom the guests have just been maliciously gossiping.

We thanked him for being so generous and considerate and promptly proceeded to bury our amusement in our glasses. Up to this point we'd not realized we were only in mid-stream, as you might say.

The orchestra played, the tables were cleared, and then three white pigs were brought into the dining-room, all decked out in muzzles and bells. The first, the master of ceremonies announced, was two years old, the second three, and the third six. I was under the impression that some acrobats were on their way in and the pigs were going to do some tricks, the way they do in street shows. But Trimalchio dispelled this impression by asking:

"Which of these would you like for the next course? Any clodhopper can do you a barnyard cock or a stew and trifles like that, but my cooks are used to boiling whole calves."

He immediately sent for the chef and without waiting for us to choose he told him to kill the oldest pig.

He then said to the man in a loud voice:

"Which division are you from?"[8]

When he replied he was from number forty, Trimalchio asked:

"Were you bought or were you born here?"

"Neither," said the chef, "I was left to you in Pansa's will."[9]

"Well, then," said Trimalchio, "see you serve it up carefully—otherwise I'll have you thrown into the messenger's division."

So the chef, duly reminded of his master's magnificence, went back to his kitchen, the next course leading the way.

Trimalchio looked round at us with a gentle smile: "If you don't like the wine, I'll have it changed. It is up to you to do it justice. I don't buy it, thank heaven. In fact, whatever wine really tickles your palate this evening, it comes from an estate of mine which as yet I haven't seen. It's said to join my estates at Tarracina and Tarentum.[1] What I'd like to do now is add Sicily to my little bit of land, so that when I want to go to Africa, I could sail there without leaving my own property.[2]

"But tell me, Agamemnon,[3] what was your debate about today? Even though I don't go in for the law, still I've picked up enough education for home consumption. And don't you think I turn my nose up at studying, because I have two libraries, one Greek, one Latin. So tell us, just as a favour, what was the topic of your debate?"

Agamemnon was just beginning, "A poor man and a rich man were enemies . . ." when Trimalchio said: "What's a poor man?" "Oh, witty!" said Agamemnon, and then told us about some fictitious case or other. Like lightning Trimalchio said: "If this happened, it's not a fictitious case—if it didn't happen, then it's nothing at all."

We greeted this witticism and several more like it with the greatest enthusiasm.

"Tell me, my dear Agamemnon," continued Trimalchio, "do you remember the twelve labours of Hercules and the story of Ulysses—how the Cyclops tore out his thumb with a pair of pincers. I used to read about them in Homer, when I was a boy.[4] In fact, I actually saw the Sibyl at Cumae with my own eyes dangling in a bottle, and

8. It was customary to divide slaves into groups of ten. Trimalchio plainly has far more than the usual 20.

9. The chef is mimicking the custom of leaving slaves to the emperor in one's will. Various aspects of Trimalchio's behavior (such as his superstition) echo that of Nero or emperors of the time in general.

1. Tarentum was in the heel of Italy, and Tarracina was north of Naples; Trimalchio's third estate would thus span southern Italy from east to west.

2. The scale of exaggeration grows: Sicily lies off the southwest coast of the Italian peninsula on the way to North Africa.

3. This Agamemnon, not to be confused with the king of Greek epic and tragedy, is a teacher of rhetoric and a subject of mockery.

4. The labors of Hercules are not actually recounted in Homer. Ulysses burned out the Cyclops's eye with a stake, rather than tearing off his thumb with a pair of pincers.

when the children asked her in Greek: 'What do you want, Sybil?' she used to answer: 'I want to die.'"[5]

He was still droning on when a server carrying the massive pig was put on the table. We started to express our amazement at this speed and swear that not even an ordinary rooster could be cooked so quickly, the more so as the pig appeared far larger than we remembered. Trimalchio looked closer and closer at it, and then shouted:

"What's this? Isn't this pig gutted? I'm damn certain it isn't. Call the chef in here, go on, call him!"

The downcast chef stood by the table and said he'd forgotten it.

"What, you forgot!" shouted Trimalchio. "You'd think he'd only left out the pepper and cumin. Strip him!"

In a second the chef was stripped and standing miserably between two men with whips. But everyone began pleading for him:

"It does tend to happen," they said, "do let him off, please. If he does it any more, none of us will stand up for him again."

Personally, given my tough and ruthless temperament, I couldn't contain myself. I leaned over and whispered in Agamemnon's ear:

"How could anyone forget to clean a pig? I damn well wouldn't let him off if he forgot to clean a fish."

But not Trimalchio. His face relaxed into a smile.

"Well," he said, "since you have such a bad memory, gut it in front of us."

The chef recovered his shirt, took up a knife and with a nervous hand cut open the pig's belly left and right. Suddenly, as the slits widened with the pressure, out poured sausages and bloodpuddings.

The staff applauded this piece of ingenuity and gave a concerted cheer—"Hurray for Gaius!" The chef of course was rewarded with a drink and a silver crown, and was also given a drinking cup on a tray of Corinthian bronze.[6] Seeing Agamemnon staring hard at this cup, Trimalchio remarked:

"I'm the only person in the world with genuine Corinthian."

I was expecting him with his usual conceit to claim that all his plate came from Corinth. But he was not as bad as I thought.

"Perhaps you're wondering," he went on, "how I'm the only one with genuine Corinthian dishes. The simple reason is that the manufacturer I buy from is named Corinth—but what can be Corinthian, if you don't have a Corinth to get it from?

"You mustn't take me for a fool: I know very well where Corinthian metalwork first came from.[7] When Troy was captured that crafty snake Hannibal piled all the bronze, silver, and gold statues into one heap and set them on fire, and they were all melted to a bronze alloy. The metalworkers took this solid mass and made plates, dishes, and statuettes out of it.[8] That is how Corinthian plate was born, not really one thing or another, but everything in one. You won't mind my saying so, but I prefer glass—that's got no taste at all. If only it didn't break, I'd prefer it to gold, but it's poor stuff the way it is.

* * *

5. The Cumaean sibyl, who leads Aeneas through the underworld in Virgil's *Aeneid,* was said to have asked the god Apollo for immortality, forgetting to ask for eternal youth, and was doomed to grow older and older without ever dying. Her legend appears to have inspired a sideshow attraction in the towns of Trimalchio's youth.

6. A prized bronze, treasured, among others, by Emperor Augustus.

7. Having played on his audience's expectations of his ignorance to make a joke, Trimalchio goes on to demonstrate that he has no idea where Corinthian metalwork originated.

8. Troy was sacked by the Greeks in the 12th century B.C.E; Hannibal took Saguntum in Spain in 219 B.C.E.. There was also a false story that Corinthian bronze was discovered during the sacking of the Greek city of Corinth in 146 B.C.E.

Finally the acrobats arrived. One was a silly idiot who stood there holding a ladder and made his boy climb up the rungs, give us a song and dance at the top, then jump through blazing hoops, and hold up a large wine-jar with his teeth.

Only Trimalchio was impressed by all this: art wasn't appreciated, he considered, but if there were two things in the world he really liked to watch, they were acrobats and horn-players. All the other shows were not worth a damn.

"As a matter of fact," he said, "once I even bought some comic-actors, but I preferred them putting on Atellan farces, and I told my conductor to keep his songs Latin."[9]

Just as he was saying this, the boy tumbled down on Trimalchio's couch. Everyone screamed, the guests as well as the servants—not because they were worried over such an awful person (they would happily have watched his neck being broken) but because it would have been a poor ending to the party if they had to offer their condolences for a comparative stranger. Trimalchio himself groaned heavily and leaned over his arm as though it were hurt. Doctors raced to the scene, but practically the first one there was Fortunata, hair flying and cup in hand, telling the world what a poor unfortunate thing she was. As for the boy who had fallen, he was already crawling round our feet, begging for mercy. I had an uneasy feeling that his pleadings might be the prelude to some funny surprise ending, as I still remembered the chef who had forgotten to gut his pig. So I began looking round the dining-room for some machine to appear out of the wall, especially after a servant was beaten for using white instead of purple wool to bandage his master's bruised arm.

Nor were my suspicions far out, because instead of punishment, there came an official announcement from Trimalchio that the boy was free, so that no one could say that such a great figure had been injured by a slave.

* * *

"Meantime, Stichus,[1] bring out the shroud and the things I want to be buried in. Bring some cosmetic cream too, and a sample from that jar of wine I want my bones washed in."

Stichus did not delay over it, but brought his white shroud and his formal dress into the dining-room . . . Trimalchio told us to examine them and see if they were made of good wool. Then he said with a smile:

"Now you, Stichus, see no mice or moths get at those—otherwise I'll burn you alive. I want to be buried in style, so the whole town will pray for my rest."

He opened a bottle of nard on the spot, rubbed some on all of us and said:

"I hope this'll be as nice when I'm dead as when I'm alive." The wine he had poured into a big decanter and he said:

"I want you to think you've been invited to my wake."[2]

The thing was becoming absolutely sickening, when Trimalchio, showing the effects of his disgusting drunkenness, had a fresh entertainment brought into the dining-room, some cornet players. Propped up on a lot of cushions, he stretched out along the edge of the couch and said: "Pretend I'm dead and say something nice."

The cornet players struck up a dead march. One man in particular, the slave of his undertaker (who was the most respectable person present) blew so loudly that he roused the neighbourhood. As a result, the fire brigade, thinking Trimalchio's house

9. Comic satires of provincial life, Atellan farces used stock-character stereotypes and were originally performed in Italian dialect rather than proper Latin.

1. A slave of Trimalchio.

2. The final example of Trimalchio's outrageous behavior is this staging of a mock-funeral, a practice attested to at the time.

was on fire, suddenly broke down the front door and began kicking up their own sort of din with their water and axes.

Seizing this perfect chance, we gave Agamemnon the slip and escaped as rapidly as if there really were a fire.

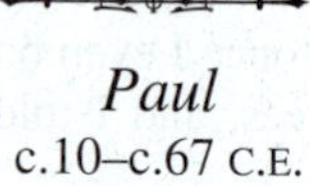

Paul

c.10–c.67 C.E.

The earliest written records of Christianity, the Epistles of Paul present the daily activities, vivid personality, and combative theology of perhaps the single most influential figure in the history of the Church. The sensation of intensity and immediacy that imbues his letters conveys well the difficulties Paul faced in his untiring efforts on behalf of his nascent religion and the dramatic path he had taken to embrace it. Born around 10 C.E. at Tarsus in Cilicia on what is now the southern coast of Turkey, Saul (in Hebrew) or Paul (in Latin) came from an Aramaic-speaking Jewish family of the tribe of Benjamin that also possessed Roman citizenship. Tarsus was a center of Hellenistic culture, and Saul received a classical education but remained a fiercely devoted Pharisee, convinced of the finality and perfection of Mosaic law and the oral tradition surrounding it. He began his career disputing against the new Christians and even aiding in their persecution until the time of his conversion on the road to Damascus in around 35 C.E. Embracing his new faith with equal zeal, Paul traveled throughout Greece and Asia Minor tirelessly preaching and making converts. Imprisoned in Jerusalem, he was sent to Rome, where he stayed two years preaching the Gospel between two stretches of incarceration, the latter of which ended with his execution on Nero's order.

Paul's letters are masterpieces of rhetoric, each one carefully composed and tailored to meet the specific requirements of the congregation it addresses and to correct their particular errors. Their enduring importance to theologians and laypersons alike testifies to his ability to draw theological principles out of those everyday circumstances. In the celebrated Epistle to the Romans, which dates to between 54 and 58, Paul is concerned with two issues that he perceives as interrelated: the Jews' excessive reliance on the Law and thus on the surface orders and regulations of the Old Testament, and the sinner's inability to ignore the urges of the body, or superficial being. Paul needed to show that Christians could embrace the Hebrew Bible as revealed truth without having to follow the specific dictates it contained. At the same time, because Christianity was a Messianic belief, Paul also preached that believers must live their lives as if the world's end and the Last Judgment were imminent events. Paul presents the teachings he chooses to uphold and the longings he chooses to encourage as what is obvious and instinctive; the Law and the desires of the flesh he rejects by contrast as being dark and obscure. It is a somber and conflicted vision of a self divided that Paul employs to unshackle the chains of tradition and of sin that bind his fellow Christians: "I do not understand my own actions. For I do not do what I want, but I do the very thing I hate." The powerful philosophical dualism inherited from Platonic philosophy was to become deeply embedded in Western culture as an irrevocable split between sacred mind and sinful body. In many ways, Paul can be said to have invented the modern dilemma of a split consciousness, desperate and yet unable to control its own desires. It is a conception of the self that would have seemed utterly alien either to Petronius's self-indulgent Encolpius or to Virgil's stoic Aeneas.

Paul's theology of paradox is equally capable of memorably summoning up the possibility of a world beyond the imaginings of rationality, logic, or law, as in the extraordinary image of the First Epistle to the Corinthians, comparing our vision of the present world to looking through a glass, darkly (13:12). Rather than the lucid reflection of a solid reality, the world and the individuals within it are fundamentally unknowable and mysterious. Only in the presence of the Lord, face to face, he maintains, will it be possible either to truly know oneself or the world, and to be truly happy and at peace. Only at brief moments does Paul allow himself to divulge glimpses of the visions he must have had of better things. In the same letter to the Corinthians, he waxes eloquent on the positive virtue of *caritas,* the love of the new Christians: "Love bears all things, believes all things, hopes all things, endures all things. Love never ends" (13:7–8). In similar fashion, he wraps up the fervent exhortations of his Epistle to the Romans with a simple greeting, one by one to each of his brothers and sisters in Rome. Paul never loses sight of the practical objects of his millenarian calling. Perhaps this is the reason that, more than any classical writer, and more than any early Christian except his later devotee Saint Augustine, Paul makes us feel in his letters as if we know the man himself.

from Epistle to the Romans[1]

from *Chapter 1*

To all God's beloved in Rome, who are called to be saints:

Grace to you and peace from God our Father and the Lord Jesus Christ.

First, I thank my God through Jesus Christ for all of you, because your faith is proclaimed in all the world. For God is my witness, whom I serve with my spirit in the gospel of his Son, that without ceasing I mention you always in my prayers, asking that somehow by God's will I may now at last succeed in coming to you. For I long to see you, that I may impart to you some spiritual gift to strengthen you, that is, that we may be mutually encouraged by each other's faith, both yours and mine. I want you to know, brethren, that I have often intended to come to you (but thus far have been prevented), in order that I may reap some harvest among you as well as among the rest of the Gentiles. I am under obligation both to Greeks and to barbarians, both to the wise and to the foolish: so I am eager to preach the gospel to you also who are in Rome.

For I am not ashamed of the gospel: it is the power of God for salvation to every one who has faith, to the Jew first and also to the Greek. For in it the righteousness of God is revealed through faith for faith; as it is written, "He who through faith is righteous shall live."[2]

For the wrath of God is revealed from heaven against all ungodliness and wickedness of men who by their wickedness suppress the truth. For what can be known about God is plain to them, because God has shown it to them. Ever since the creation of the world his invisible nature, namely, his eternal power and deity, has been clearly perceived in the things that have been made.[3] So they are without excuse; for although they knew God they did not honor him as God or give thanks to him, but they became futile in their thinking and their senseless minds were darkened. Claiming to be wise, they became fools, and exchanged the glory of the immortal God for images resembling mortal man or birds or animals or reptiles.

Therefore God gave them up in the lusts of their hearts to impurity, to the dishonoring of their bodies among themselves, because they exchanged the truth about God for a lie and worshiped and served the creature rather than the Creator, who is blessed for ever! Amen.

For this reason God gave them up to dishonorable passions. Their women exchanged natural relations for unnatural, and the men likewise gave up natural relations with women and were consumed with passion for one another, men committing shameless acts with men and receiving in their own persons the due penalty for their error.

1. New Revised Standard Version.
2. Here Paul begins the distinction between faith, which applies to all people, and the traditional Law of Jews such as himself.
3. Paul describes the responsibility of those who lived before the teachings and the life of Jesus made the gospel evident to all.

And since they did not see fit to acknowledge God, God gave them up to a base mind and to improper conduct. They were filled with all manner of wickedness, evil, covetousness, malice. Full of envy, murder, strife, deceit, malignity, they are gossips, slanderers, haters of God, insolent, haughty, boastful, inventors of evil, disobedient to parents, foolish, faithless, heartless, ruthless. Though they know God's decree that those who do such things deserve to die, they not only do them but approve those who practice them. * * *

Chapter 7

Do you not know, brethren—for I am speaking to those who know the law—that the law is binding on a person only during his life? Thus a married woman is bound by law to her husband as long as he lives; but if her husband dies she is discharged from the law concerning the husband. Accordingly, she will be called an adulteress if she lives with another man while her husband is alive. But if her husband dies she is free from that law, and if she marries another man she is not an adulteress.

Likewise, my brethren, you have died to the law through the body of Christ, so that you may belong to another, to him who has been raised from the dead in order that we may bear fruit for God. While we were living in the flesh, our sinful passions, aroused by the law, were at work in our members to bear fruit for death. But now we are discharged from the law, dead to that which held us captive, so that we serve not under the old written code but in the new life of the Spirit.[4]

What then shall we say? That the law is sin? By no means! Yet, if it had not been for the law, I should not have known sin. I should not have known what it is to covet if the law had not said, "You shall not covet." But sin, finding opportunity in the commandment, wrought in me all kinds of covetousness. Apart from the law sin lies dead. I was once alive apart from the law, but when the commandment came, sin revived and I died; the very commandment which promised life proved to be death to me. For sin, finding opportunity in the commandment, deceived me and by it killed me. So the law is holy, and the commandment is holy and just and good.[5]

Did that which is good, then, bring death to me? By no means! It was sin, working death in me through what is good, in order that sin might be shown to be sin, and through the commandment might become sinful beyond measure. We know that the law is spiritual; but I am carnal, sold under sin. I do not understand my own actions. For I do not do what I want, but I do the very thing I hate. Now if I do what I do not want, I agree that the law is good. So then it is no longer I that do it, but sin which dwells within me. For I know that nothing good dwells within me, that is, in my flesh. I can will what is right, but I cannot do it. For I do not do the good I want, but the evil I do not want is what I do. Now if I do what I do not want, it is no longer I that do it, but sin which dwells within me.

So I find it to be a law that when I want to do right, evil lies close at hand. For I delight in the law of God, in my inmost self, but I see in my members another law at war with the law of my mind and making me captive to the law of sin which dwells in

4. In Paul's eyes, with the resurrection of Christ, humanity became dead to the laws of the past. The new law is not written or literal, but spiritual, based in faith.

5. This is a good example of Paul's rhetoric of antithesis and paradox. Only with laws, he argues, can we become conscious of sins, and thus able to commit them, but only through recognizing sin as such can we be saved.

my members. Wretched man that I am! Who will deliver me from this body of death? Thanks be to God through Jesus Christ our Lord! So then, I of myself serve the law of God with my mind, but with my flesh I serve the law of sin.[6]

Chapter 13

Let every person be subject to the governing authorities. For there is no authority except from God, and those that exist have been instituted by God. Therefore he who resists the authorities resists what God has appointed, and those who resist will incur judgment. For rulers are not a terror to good conduct, but to bad. Would you have no fear of him who is in authority? Then do what is good, and you will receive his approval, for he is God's servant for your good. But if you do wrong, be afraid, for he does not bear the sword in vain; he is the servant of God to execute his wrath on the wrongdoer. Therefore one must be subject, not only to avoid God's wrath but also for the sake of conscience. For the same reason you also pay taxes, for the authorities are ministers of God, attending to this very thing. Pay all of them their dues, taxes to whom taxes are due, revenue to whom revenue is due, respect to whom respect is due, honor to whom honor is due.

Owe no one anything, except to love one another; for he who loves his neighbor has fulfilled the law. The commandments, "You shall not commit adultery, You shall not kill, You shall not steal, You shall not covet," and any other commandment, are summed up in this sentence, "You shall love your neighbor as yourself."

Love does no wrong to a neighbor; therefore love is the fulfilling of the law.

Besides this you know what hour it is, how it is full time now for you to wake from sleep. For salvation is nearer to us now than when we first believed; the night is far gone, the day is at hand. Let us then cast off the works of darkness and put on the armor of light; let us conduct ourselves becomingly as in the day, not in reveling and drunkenness, not in debauchery and licentiousness, not in quarreling and jealousy. But put on the Lord Jesus Christ, and make no provision for the flesh, to gratify its desires.

from *Chapter 15*

I myself am satisfied about you, my brethren, that you yourselves are full of goodness, filled with all knowledge, and able to instruct one another.

But on some points I have written to you very boldly by way of reminder, because of the grace given me by God to be a minister of Christ Jesus to the Gentiles in the priestly service of the gospel of God, so that the offering of the Gentiles may be acceptable, sanctified by the Holy Spirit. In Christ Jesus, then, I have reason to be proud of my work for God. For I will not venture to speak of anything except what Christ has wrought through me to win obedience from the Gentiles, by word and deed, by the power of signs and wonders, by the power of the Holy Spirit, so that from Jerusalem and as far round as Illyricum[7] I have fully preached the gospel of Christ, thus making it my ambition to preach the gospel, not where Christ has already been named, lest I build on another man's foundation, but as it is written,

6. In this influential formulation, Paul maintains that following the letter of the Judaic Law will not lead to salvation because it only governs the flesh, which is irredeemably tainted by sin and death. Instead, the Romans to whom he writes must follow the rule of faith, "serve the law of God with [their] mind[s]."

7. The Roman name for the region across the Adriatic Sea from Italy.

"They shall see who have never been told of him,
and they shall understand who have never heard of him."

This is the reason why I have so often been hindered from coming to you. But now, since I no longer have any room for work in these regions, and since I have longed for many years to come to you, I hope to see you in passing as I go to Spain,[8] and to be sped on my journey there by you, once I have enjoyed your company for a little. At present, however, I am going to Jerusalem with aid for the saints. For Macedonia and Achaia[9] have been pleased to make some contribution for the poor among the saints at Jerusalem; they were pleased to do it, and indeed they are in debt to them, for if the Gentiles have come to share in their spiritual blessings, they ought also to be of service to them in material blessings. When therefore I have completed this, and have delivered to them what has been raised, I shall go on by way of you to Spain; and I know that when I come to you I shall come in the fulness of the blessing of Christ.

I appeal to you, brethren, by our Lord Jesus Christ and by the love of the Spirit, to strive together with me in your prayers to God on my behalf, that I may be delivered from the unbelievers in Judea,[1] and that my service for Jerusalem may be acceptable to the saints, so that by God's will I may come to you with joy and be refreshed in your company. The God of peace be with you all. Amen.

from *Chapter 16*

I commend to you our sister Phoebe, a deaconess of the church at Cenchreae,[2] that you may receive her in the Lord as befits the saints, and help her in whatever she may require from you, for she has been a helper of many and of myself as well.

Greet Prisca and Aquila,[3] my fellow workers in Christ Jesus, who risked their necks for my life, to whom not only I but also all the churches of the Gentiles give thanks; greet also the church in their house. Greet my beloved Epaenetus, who was the first convert in Asia for Christ.[4] Greet Mary, who has worked hard among you. Greet Andronicus and Junias; my kinsmen and my fellow prisoners; they are men of note among the apostles, and they were in Christ before me. Greet Ampliatus, my beloved in the Lord. Greet Urbanus, our fellow worker in Christ, and my beloved Stachys. Greet Apelles, who is approved in Christ. Greet those who belong to the family of Aristobulus. Greet my kinsman Herodion. Greet those in the Lord who belong to the family of Narcissus. Greet those workers in the Lord, Tryphaena and Tryphosa. Greet the beloved Persis, who has worked hard in the Lord. Greet Rufus, eminent in the Lord, also his mother and mine. Greet Asyncritus, Phlegon, Hermes, Patrobas, Hermas, and the brethren who are with them. Greet Philologus, Julia, Nereus and his sister, and Olympas, and all the saints who are with them. Greet one another with a holy kiss. All the churches of Christ greet you.

I appeal to you, brethren, to take note of those who create dissensions and difficulties, in opposition to the doctrine which you have been taught; avoid them. For

8. It is not known whether Paul managed to carry out his intention to preach the gospel in Spain between his first and his second captivities in Rome.

9. During the second of his three extended missionary journeys, Paul spread his faith around the Aegean Sea to Macedonia and to Achaia (Greece).

1. As is detailed in Acts 21, Paul's teaching that Jews need no longer follow the Law since the coming of Christ was highly controversial.

2. The eastern port of Corinth.

3. When all Jews were expelled by Emperor Claudius from Rome in 49 C.E., Prisca and her husband, Aquila, had settled in Corinth and then in Ephesus on the western coast of Asia Minor, the capital of the Roman province of Asia (see Acts 18:2). They would have been able to return following Claudius's death in 54.

4. Little or nothing is known about the rest of the Christians Paul salutes beyond what he says about them here.

such persons do not serve our Lord Christ, but their own appetites, and by fair and flattering words they deceive the hearts of the simple-minded. For while your obedience is known to all, so that I rejoice over you, I would have you wise as to what is good and guileless as to what is evil; then the God of peace will soon crush Satan under your feet. The grace of our Lord Jesus Christ be with you.

Luke

fl. 80–110 C.E.

Tradition has it that the author of the Gospel According to Luke and its sequel, the Acts of the Apostles, was a physician and the companion of Paul of Tarsus. What is certain is that he was a brilliant stylist, crafting a historical record of the life of Jesus and the ministry of his apostles that combines the sparsely dramatic narrative technique of the Hellenistic-Roman historians with the theological concerns of the Hebrew Bible. After Jesus's crucifixion in 30 C.E., the original Palestianian movement probably transmitted his sayings and the accounts of his miracles orally for several decades in the Aramaic language he had spoken. The first written sources we have are the Epistles of Paul, composed in Greek, that date from the 50s and 60s. At the same time that Paul was opening up what had been a Jewish reform movement to a larger, Gentile population, the Jewish wars led to the traumatic burning of the Temple in Jerusalem in 70 and the dispersal of the Jewish people. Over the next couple of decades, various gospels appeared to reconcile the growing outreach of the Jesus movement with the oral tradition of his life and sayings. Four of those gospels were eventually included as part of the New Testament, the contents of which were finally fixed as a canon only several centuries later: the three synoptic gospels (Mark, Matthew, and Luke), so called because they resemble each other in content, order of events, and the words of Jesus they include; and the Gospel According to John, several decades later in composition, which is steeped in Jewish and Hellenistic philosophy and derives from a different source.

Luke opens his Gospel by referring to the problem of the apparently conflicting reports circulating of the great events that have occurred; he promises to write "an orderly account." His Gospel gives the fullest record of Jesus's life, including the only accounts, for example, of some events in the life of John the Baptist, of the tale of the shepherds at Jesus's birth, and of the twelve-year-old Jesus confounding the rabbis in the Temple. Highly conscious of the need for the events of Jesus's life to conform to the many prophecies of the Messiah in the Hebrew Bible, Luke is equally concerned to incorporate the Pauline teaching that Jesus came as savior to Jew and Gentile alike. Jesus is not simply a universal savior, however; he has come especially for the outcasts of the world: its peasants, its poor, its sinners, and its women. This was a radical message, and traces of the political motivation for Jesus's crucifixion remain in the deal-making that surrounds Pontius Pilate's decision to let the execution proceed. All these secular powers, Luke implies, will pale before the new order to come.

The end of the world is an important context for the simply narrated events of Luke's chronicle, for he is at pains to demonstrate how the workings of the world fit into the divine plan for its end. The key lessons taught by this eschatological framework are both pragmatic and paradoxical. Jesus speaks either in simple imperatives—"Follow me!"—or in enigmatic parables. To the man who responds that first he must bury his father, Jesus answers, "Leave the dead to bury the dead." If the world is about to end, the natural impulse is to attend no longer to its pressing affairs but to the even more pressing affair of achieving eternal life. The concerns of Luke's Gospel are thus presented as basic needs—nourishment and survival—rather than intellectual or aesthetic ones; many of Jesus's parables and paradoxes underscore the argument that spiritual nourishment and survival after death are material and primary, rather than abstract and secondary, needs. Jesus's first disciples are lowly fishermen; his miracles include multiplying food at a wedding and raising a man from the dead. The central mystery of communion, the transmutation of bread and wine into flesh and blood at the Last Supper, imparts one aspect of this symbolism—he is nourishment—and his crucifixion and resurrection impart another: he is life. And to prove that he has truly risen from the dead and not merely returned as an apparition, the imagery comes full circle: the resurrection is accepted only when he proves himself able to eat a piece of broiled fish. Never before had such simplicity of language and imagery been used to convey such a profound theme. Luke and the other Gospel writers found a new style and form to fit what they saw as a radically new religion.

Cast as the sequel to his Gospel, Acts makes Luke's historical intent even clearer because it deals with events up to his own day, directly depicting the transformation of Jesus's life and teachings into Christianity through the apostles' preaching and miracle making and including especially the work of the newly converted Paul. Palestine was a multilingual culture in transition from a Hellenistic to a Roman base. Jesus and his followers spoke Aramaic and would not have read old Hebrew, the language of the Hebrew Bible. Most educated Romans were bilingual in Greek and Latin. The second generation of Jesus's followers were Easterners, still writing in Greek, which became the language of the New Testament. The famous episode of Pentecost illustrates this linguistic confusion, updating and reversing the Tower of Babel episode from Genesis, as the apostles are inspired by holy flames to begin speaking in tongues, each of the spectators—Parthians, Medes, Jews, Arabs, and many others—hearing them in his or her own language.

In Luke's account, the Jewish Saul (or Paul in Greek and Latin) becomes a model for the conversion narrative that would be so important for the later saints' lives and for the spiritual autobiography from Augustine through Dante and Saint Theresa and even into the modern novel. At the same time, the focus on Paul makes his tumultuous life exemplary of the expanding scope of Christianity that is central to Paul's Epistles. Luke also successfully downplays the full extent of Roman persecution, implicating the local Jewish leaders as Mark's and Matthew's Gospels do, and implicitly arguing for the separation of religion from state control. Paul's journey to Rome enacts the destined spread of the new religion, while his status as prisoner and his execution by Nero remind the reader that the true kingdom of God will be achieved in fact only in the next life.

from The Gospel According to Luke[1]

Chapter 2

[JESUS'S BIRTH. JOHN THE BAPTIST]

In those days a decree went out from Emperor Augustus that all the world should be registered. This was the first registration and was taken while Quirinius was governor of Syria.[2] All went to their own towns to be registered. Joseph also went from the town of Nazareth in Galilee to Judea, to the city of David called Bethlehem, because he was descended from the house and family of David.[3] He went to be registered with Mary, to whom he was engaged and who was expecting a child. While they were there, the time came for her to deliver her child. And she gave birth to her firstborn son and wrapped him in bands of cloth, and laid him in a manger, because there was no place for them in the inn.

1. New Revised Standard Version.
2. Probably in about 6 B.C.E.
3. A journey of some 50 miles. Luke emphasizes Jesus's descent from the Israelite king, David.

In that region there were shepherds living in the fields, keeping watch over their flock by night. Then an angel of the Lord stood before them, and the glory of the Lord shone around them, and they were terrified. But the angel said to them, "Do not be afraid; for see—I am bringing you good news of great joy for all the people: to you is born this day in the city of David a Savior, who is the Messiah, the Lord. This will be a sign for you: you will find a child wrapped in bands of cloth and lying in a manger." And suddenly there was with the angel a multitude of the heavenly host, praising God and saying,

"Glory to God in the highest heaven,
and on earth peace among those whom he favors!"

When the angels had left them and gone into heaven, the shepherds said to one another, "Let us go now to Bethlehem and see this thing that has taken place, which the Lord has made known to us." So they went with haste and found Mary and Joseph, and the child lying in the manger. When they saw this, they made known what had been told them about this child; and all who heard it were amazed at what the shepherds told them. But Mary treasured all these words and pondered them in her heart. The shepherds returned, glorifying and praising God for all they had heard and seen, as it had been told them.

After eight days had passed, it was time to circumcise the child; and he was called Jesus, the name given by the angel before he was conceived in the womb.[4]

When the time came for their purification according to the law of Moses, they brought him up to Jerusalem to present him to the Lord (as it is written in the law of the Lord, "Every firstborn male shall be designated as holy to the Lord"), and they offered a sacrifice according to what is stated in the law of the Lord, "a pair of turtledoves or two young pigeons."[5]

Now there was a man in Jerusalem whose name was Simeon; this man was righteous and devout, looking forward to the consolation of Israel, and the Holy Spirit rested on him. It had been revealed to him by the Holy Spirit that he would not see death before he had seen the Lord's Messiah. Guided by the Spirit, Simeon came into the temple; and when the parents brought in the child Jesus, to do for him what was customary under the law, Simeon took him in his arms and praised God, saying,

"Master, now you are dismissing your servant in peace,
according to your word;
for my eyes have seen your salvation,
which you have prepared in the presence of all peoples,
a light for revelation to the Gentiles
and for glory to your people Israel."

And the child's father and mother were amazed at what was being said about him. Then Simeon blessed them and said to his mother Mary, "This child is destined for the falling and the rising of many in Israel, and to be a sign that will be opposed so that the inner thoughts of many will be revealed—and a sword will pierce your own soul too."

4. The angel Gabriel had come to Mary to announce her pregnancy and to prophesy the birth of a son, Jesus, who would be king over Israel forever (1:26–38).

5. On the rites of purification, see Leviticus 12. According to Exodus 13, every firstborn male belonged to God but could be redeemed by a sacrifice.

There was also a prophet, Anna the daughter of Phanuel, of the tribe of Asher. She was of a great age, having lived with her husband seven years after her marriage, then as a widow to the age of eighty-four. She never left the temple but worshiped there with fasting and prayer night and day. At that moment she came, and began to praise God and to speak about the child to all who were looking for the redemption of Jerusalem.

When they had finished everything required by the law of the Lord, they returned to Galilee, to their own town of Nazareth. The child grew and became strong, filled with wisdom; and the favor of God was upon him.

Now every year his parents went to Jerusalem for the festival of the Passover. And when he was twelve years old, they went up as usual for the festival. When the festival was ended and they started to return, the boy Jesus stayed behind in Jerusalem, but his parents did not know it. Assuming that he was in the group of travelers, they went a day's journey. Then they started to look for him among their relatives and friends. When they did not find him, they returned to Jerusalem to search for him. After three days they found him in the temple, sitting among the teachers, listening to them and asking them questions. And all who heard him were amazed at his understanding and his answers. When his parents saw him they were astonished; and his mother said to him, "Child, why have you treated us like this? Look, your father and I have been searching for you in great anxiety." He said to them, "Why were you searching for me? Did you not know that I must be in my Father's house?" But they did not understand what he said to them. Then he went down with them and came to Nazareth, and was obedient to them. His mother treasured all these things in her heart.

And Jesus increased in wisdom and in years, and in divine and human favor.

Chapter 3

In the fifteenth year of the reign of Emperor Tiberius, when Pontius Pilate was governor of Judea, and Herod was ruler of Galilee, and his brother Philip ruler of the region of Ituraea and Trachonitis, and Lysanias ruler of Abilene,[6] during the high priesthood of Annas and Caiaphas,[7] the word of God came to John son of Zechariah in the wilderness.[8] He went into all the region around the Jordan, proclaiming a baptism of repentance for the forgiveness of sins, as it is written in the book of the words of the prophet Isaiah,

> "The voice of one crying out in the wilderness:
> 'Prepare the way of the Lord,
> make his paths straight.
> Every valley shall be filled,
> and every mountain and hill shall be made low,
> and the crooked shall be made straight,

6. Tiberius reigned from Augustus's death in 14 until 37; the "fifteenth year" would be 28–29. Judea was ruled by Roman governors from 6 C.E. on, by Pontius Pilate in particular from 26–36. Herod Antipas was the ruler of the tetrarchy, or lesser kingdom, of Galilee and Perea to the north and east of Judea. His brother Philip was the ruler of the tetrarchy across the river Jordan and to the northeast of Galilee. Abilene was a region farther to the north beyond Damascus.

7. During postexilic Judaism, the high priest was the spiritual and civil head of the nation, elected by the Romans from a select number of families. Annas was the high priest from 15–5 B.C.E., his son-in-law Caiaphas from 18–36 C.E.

8. The son of a priest and of a descendant of Aaron who was also a relative of Mary, John the Baptist is portrayed as a messianic prophet of the coming of Christ.

> and the rough ways made smooth;
> and all flesh shall see the salvation of God.'"[9]

John said to the crowds that came out to be baptized by him, "You brood of vipers! Who warned you to flee from the wrath to come? Bear fruits worthy of repentance. Do not begin to say to yourselves, 'We have Abraham as our ancestor';[1] for I tell you, God is able from these stones to raise up children to Abraham. Even now the ax is lying at the root of the trees; every tree therefore that does not bear good fruit is cut down and thrown into the fire."

And the crowds asked him, "What then should we do?" In reply he said to them, "Whoever has two coats must share with anyone who has none; and whoever has food must do likewise." Even tax collectors came to be baptized,[2] and they asked him, "Teacher, what should we do?" He said to them, "Collect no more than the amount prescribed for you." Soldiers also asked him, "And we, what should we do?" He said to them, "Do not extort money from anyone by threats or false accusation, and be satisfied with your wages."

As the people were filled with expectation, and all were questioning in their hearts concerning John, whether he might be the Messiah, John answered all of them by saying, "I baptize you with water; but one who is more powerful than I is coming; I am not worthy to untie the thong of his sandals. He will baptize you with the Holy Spirit and fire. His winnowing fork is in his hand, to clear his threshing floor and to gather the wheat into his granary; but the chaff[3] he will burn with unquenchable fire."

So, with many other exhortations, he proclaimed the good news to the people. But Herod the ruler, who had been rebuked by him because of Herodias, his brother's wife,[4] and because of all the evil things that Herod had done, added to them all by shutting up John in prison.

Now when all the people were baptized, and when Jesus also had been baptized and was praying, the heaven was opened, and the Holy Spirit descended upon him in bodily form like a dove. And a voice came from heaven, "You are my Son, the Beloved; with you I am well pleased."

Jesus was about thirty years old when he began his work. He was the son (as was thought) of Joseph son of Heli, son of Matthat, son of Levi, son of Melchi, son of Jannai, son of Joseph, son of Mattathias, son of Amos, son of Nahum, son of Esli, son of Naggai, son of Maath, son of Mattathias, son of Semein, son of Josech, son of Joda, son of Joanan, son of Rhesa, son of Zerubbabel, son of Shealtiel, son of Neri, son of Melchi, son of Addi, son of Cosam, son of Elmadam, son of Er, son of Joshua, son of Eliezer, son of Jorim, son of Matthat, son of Levi, son of Simeon, son of Judah, son of Joseph, son of Jonam, son of Eliakim, son of Melea, son of Menna, son of Mattatha, son of Nathan, son of David, son of Jesse, son of Obed, son of Boaz, son of Sala, son of Nahshon, son of Amminadab, son of Admin, son of Arni, son of Hezron, son of Perez, son of Judah, son of Jacob, son of Isaac, son of Abraham, son of Terah, son of Nahor, son of Serug, son of Reu, son of Peleg, son of Eber, son of Shelah, son of Cainan, son of Arphaxad, son of

9. Isaiah 40:3–5.
1. The covenant between God and Abraham described in Genesis 17:4–8 and 22:18 applied to all of his descendants.
2. Publicans, or tax collectors for the Roman authorities, were considered traitors and classified with other undesirables such as prostitutes, public sinners, and gentiles, or non-Jews.
3. The husks, used for animal feed, in bricks, or burned for fuel.
4. Herodias had been the wife of Philip, her father's half-brother and Herod's brother.

Shem, son of Noah, son of Lamech, son of Methuselah, son of Enoch, son of Jared, son of Mahalaleel, son of Cainan, son of Enos, son of Seth, son of Adam, son of God.[5]

Chapter 6

[TEACHINGS AND PARABLES]

One sabbath while Jesus was going through the grainfields, his disciples plucked some heads of grain, rubbed them in their hands, and ate them. But some of the Pharisees[1] said, "Why are you doing what is not lawful on the sabbath?" Jesus answered, "Have you not read what David did when he and his companions were hungry? He entered the house of God and took and ate the bread of the Presence, which it is not lawful for any but the priests to eat, and gave some to his companions?"[2] Then he said to them, "The Son of Man is lord of the sabbath."

On another sabbath he entered the synagogue and taught, and there was a man there whose right hand was withered. The scribes and the Pharisees watched him to see whether he would cure on the sabbath, so that they might find an accusation against him. Even though he knew what they were thinking, he said to the man who had the withered hand, "Come and stand here." He got up and stood there. Then Jesus said to them, "I ask you, is it lawful to do good or to do harm on the sabbath, to save life or to destroy it?" After looking around at all of them, he said to him, "Stretch out your hand." He did so, and his hand was restored. But they were filled with fury and discussed with one another what they might do to Jesus.

Now during those days he went out to the mountain to pray; and he spent the night in prayer to God. And when day came, he called his disciples and chose twelve of them, whom he also named apostles:[3] Simon, whom he named Peter, and his brother Andrew, and James, and John, and Philip, and Bartholomew, and Matthew, and Thomas, and James son of Alphaeus, and Simon, who was called the Zealot, and Judas son of James, and Judas Iscariot, who became a traitor.

He came down with them and stood on a level place, with a great crowd of his disciples and a great multitude of people from all Judea, Jerusalem, and the coast of Tyre and Sidon. They had come to hear him and to be healed of their diseases; and those who were troubled with unclean spirits were cured. And all in the crowd were trying to touch him, for power came out from him and healed all of them.

Then he looked up at his disciples and said:

"Blessed are you who are poor,
for yours is the kingdom of God.
"Blessed are you who are hungry now,
for you will be filled.

5. The traditional genealogy traces Jesus's descent from David although not through his ruling son, Solomon. Whereas Matthew's gospel, written for a Jewish community, traces Jesus's lineage back to Abraham, Luke goes all the way back to the Creator and the moment of creation itself.

1. An influential religious party that believed in the validity of the oral tradition as an intrinsic element of the Law of Moses. They were associated with scribes, laypeople, and the middle classes and held that the Lord could be worshiped beyond the confines of the Temple. Their rivals, the Sadducees, belonged to the high priestly aristocracy around the Temple in Jerusalem who believed only in the letter of the Pentateuch itself.

2. The bread of the presence was sacred bread baked in groups of 12 (Leviticus 24:5–9) and laid on a table as a memorial. They were eaten only by the priests, except for the episode recounted by Jesus when David and his men were fed by the priest Ahimelech (1 Samuel 21:5–7).

3. The word "apostle" comes from the Greek verb "to send," and was sometimes used to refer to a simple messenger.

"Blessed are you who weep now,
for you will laugh.

"Blessed are you when people hate you, and when they exclude you, revile you, and defame you on account of the Son of Man. Rejoice in that day and leap for joy, for surely your reward is great in heaven; for that is what their ancestors did to the prophets.

"But woe to you who are rich,
for you have received your consolation.
"Woe to you who are full now,
for you will be hungry.
"Woe to you who are laughing now,
for you will mourn and weep.

"Woe to you when all speak well of you, for that is what their ancestors did to the false prophets.

"But I say to you that listen, Love your enemies, do good to those who hate you, bless those who curse you, pray for those who abuse you. If anyone strikes you on the cheek, offer the other also; and from anyone who takes away your coat do not withhold even your shirt. Give to everyone who begs from you; and if anyone takes away your goods, do not ask for them again. Do to others as you would have them do to you.

"If you love those who love you, what credit is that to you? For even sinners love those who love them. If you do good to those who do good to you, what credit is that to you? For even sinners do the same. If you lend to those from whom you hope to receive, what credit is that to you? Even sinners lend to sinners, to receive as much again. But love your enemies, do good, and lend, expecting nothing in return. Your reward will be great, and you will be children of the Most High; for he is kind to the ungrateful and the wicked. Be merciful, just as your Father is merciful.

"Do not judge, and you will not be judged; do not condemn, and you will not be condemned. Forgive, and you will be forgiven; give, and it will be given to you. A good measure, pressed down, shaken together, running over, will be put into your lap; for the measure you give will be the measure you get back."

He also told them a parable: "Can a blind person guide a blind person? Will not both fall into a pit? A disciple is not above the teacher, but everyone who is fully qualified will be like the teacher. Why do you see the speck in your neighbor's eye, but do not notice the log in your own eye? Or how can you say to your neighbor, 'Friend, let me take out the speck in your eye,' when you yourself do not see the log in your own eye? You hypocrite, first take the log out of your own eye, and then you will see clearly to take the speck out of your neighbor's eye.

"No good tree bears bad fruit, nor again does a bad tree bear good fruit; for each tree is known by its own fruit. Figs are not gathered from thorns, nor are grapes picked from a bramble bush: The good person out of the good treasure of the heart produces good, and the evil person out of evil treasure produces evil; for it is out of the abundance of the heart that the mouth speaks.

"Why do you call me 'Lord, Lord,' and do not do what I tell you? I will show you what someone is like who comes to me, hears my words, and acts on them. That one is like a man building a house, who dug deeply and laid the foundation on rock; when a flood arose, the river burst against that house but could not shake it, because it had been well built. But the one who hears and does not act is like a man who built a house on the ground without a foundation. When the river burst against it, immediately it fell, and great was the ruin of that house."

Chapter 22

[JESUS'S TRIAL, DEATH, AND RESURRECTION]

Now the festival of Unleavened Bread, which is called the Passover, was near. The chief priests and the scribes were looking for a way to put Jesus to death, for they were afraid of the people.

Then Satan entered into Judas called Iscariot, who was one of the twelve; he went away and conferred with the chief priests and officers of the temple police about how he might betray him to them. They were greatly pleased and agreed to give him money. So he consented and began to look for an opportunity to betray him to them when no crowd was present.

Then came the day of Unleavened Bread, on which the Passover lamb had to be sacrificed. So Jesus sent Peter and John, saying, "Go and prepare the Passover meal for us that we may eat it." They asked him, "Where do you want us to make preparations for it?" "Listen," he said to them, "when you have entered the city, a man carrying a jar of water will meet you; follow him into the house he enters and say to the owner of the house, 'The teacher asks you, "Where is the guest room, where I may eat the Passover with my disciples?"' He will show you a large room upstairs, already furnished. Make preparations for us there." So they went and found everything as he had told them; and they prepared the Passover meal.

When the hour came, he took his place at the table, and the apostles with him. He said to them, "I have eagerly desired to eat this Passover with you before I suffer; for I tell you, I will not eat it until it is fulfilled in the kingdom of God." Then he took a cup, and after giving thanks he said, "Take this and divide it among yourselves; for I tell you that from now on I will not drink of the fruit of the vine until the kingdom of God comes." Then he took a loaf of bread, and when he had given thanks, he broke it and gave it to them, saying, "This is my body, which is given for you. Do this in remembrance of me." And he did the same with the cup after supper, saying, "This cup that is poured out for you is the new covenant in my blood. But see, the one who betrays me is with me, and his hand is on the table. For the Son of Man is going as it has been determined, but woe to that one by whom he is betrayed!" Then they began to ask one another which one of them it could be who would do this.

A dispute also arose among them as to which one of them was to be regarded as the greatest. But he said to them, "The kings of the Gentiles lord it over them; and those in authority over them are called benefactors. But not so with you; rather the greatest among you must become like the youngest, and the leader like one who serves. For who is greater, the one who is at the table or the one who serves? Is it not the one at the table? But I am among you as one who serves.

"You are those who have stood by me in my trials; and I confer on you, just as my Father has conferred on me, a kingdom, so that you may eat and drink at my table in my kingdom, and you will sit on thrones judging the twelve tribes of Israel.

"Simon, Simon, listen! Satan has demanded to sift all of you like wheat, but I have prayed for you that your own faith may not fail; and you, when once you have turned back, strengthen your brothers." And he said to him, "Lord, I am ready to go with you to prison and to death!" Jesus said, "I tell you, Peter, the cock will not crow this day, until you have denied three times that you know me."

He said to them, "When I sent you out without a purse, bag, or sandals, did you lack anything?" They said, "No, not a thing." He said to them, "But now, the one who has a purse must take it, and likewise a bag. And the one who has no sword must sell his cloak and buy one. For I tell you, this scripture must be fulfilled in me, 'And he was counted among the lawless'; and indeed what is written about me is being fulfilled." They said, "Lord, look, here are two swords." He replied, "It is enough."

He came out and went, as was his custom, to the Mount of Olives;[1] and the disciples followed him. When he reached the place, he said to them, "Pray that you may not come into the time of trial." Then he withdrew from them about a stone's throw, knelt down, and prayed, "Father, if you are willing, remove this cup from me; yet, not my will but yours be done." [Then an angel from heaven appeared to him and gave him strength. In his anguish he prayed more earnestly, and his sweat became like great drops of blood falling down on the ground.][2] When he got up from prayer, he came to the disciples and found them sleeping because of grief, and he said to them, "Why are you sleeping? Get up and pray that you may not come into the time of trial."

While he was still speaking, suddenly a crowd came, and the one called Judas, one of the twelve, was leading them. He approached Jesus to kiss him; but Jesus said to him, "Judas, is it with a kiss that you are betraying the Son of Man?" When those who were around him saw what was coming, they asked, "Lord, should we strike with the sword?" Then one of them struck the slave of the high priest and cut off his right ear. But Jesus said, "No more of this!" And he touched his ear and healed him. Then Jesus said to the chief priests, the officers of the temple police, and the elders who had come for him, "Have you come out with swords and clubs as if I were a bandit? When I was with you day after day in the temple, you did not lay hands on me. But this is your hour, and the power of darkness!"

Then they seized him and led him away, bringing him into the high priest's house. But Peter was following at a distance. When they had kindled a fire in the middle of the courtyard and sat down together, Peter sat among them. Then a servant-girl, seeing him in the firelight, stared at him and said, "This man also was with him." But he denied it, saying, "Woman, I do not know him." A little later someone else, on seeing him, said, "You also are one of them." But Peter said, "Man, I am not!" Then about an hour later still another kept insisting, "Surely this man also was with him; for he is a Galilean." But Peter said, "Man, I do not know what you are talking about!" At that moment, while he was still speaking, the cock crowed. The Lord turned and looked at Peter. Then Peter remembered the word of the Lord, how he had said to him, "Before the cock crows today, you will deny me three times." And he went out and wept bitterly.

Now the men who were holding Jesus began to mock him and beat him; they also blindfolded him and kept asking him, "Prophesy! Who is it that struck you?" They kept heaping many other insults on him.

When day came, the assembly of the elders of the people, both chief priests and scribes, gathered together, and they brought him to their council. They said, "If you

1. A hill east of Jerusalem, separated from the city by the Kidron brook. The garden of Gethsemane was on its western slope.

2. These lines appear in some manuscripts but not others.

are the Messiah,[3] tell us." He replied, "If I tell you, you will not believe; and if I question you, you will not answer. But from now on the Son of Man will be seated at the right hand of the power of God." All of them asked, "Are you, then, the Son of God?" He said to them, "You say that I am." Then they said, "What further testimony do we need? We have heard it ourselves from his own lips!"

Chapter 23

Then the assembly rose as a body and brought Jesus before Pilate. They began to accuse him, saying, "We found this man perverting our nation, forbidding us to pay taxes to the emperor, and saying that he himself is the Messiah, a king." Then Pilate asked him, "Are you the king of the Jews?" He answered, "You say so." Then Pilate said to the chief priests and the crowds, "I find no basis for an accusation against this man." But they were insistent and said, "He stirs up the people by teaching throughout all Judea, from Galilee where he began even to this place."

When Pilate heard this, he asked whether the man was a Galilean. And when he learned that he was under Herod's jurisdiction, he sent him off to Herod, who was himself in Jerusalem at that time. When Herod saw Jesus, he was very glad, for he had been wanting to see him for a long time, because he had heard about him and was hoping to see him perform some sign. He questioned him at some length, but Jesus gave him no answer. The chief priests and the scribes stood by, vehemently accusing him. Even Herod with his soldiers treated him with contempt and mocked him; then he put an elegant robe on him, and sent him back to Pilate. That same day Herod and Pilate became friends with each other; before this they had been enemies.

Pilate then called together the chief priests, the leaders, and the people, and said to them, "You brought me this man as one who was perverting the people; and here I have examined him in your presence and have not found this man guilty of any of your charges against him. Neither has Herod, for he sent him back to us. Indeed, he has done nothing to deserve death. I will therefore have him flogged and release him."

Then they all shouted out together, "Away with this fellow! Release Barabbas for us!" (This was a man who had been put in prison for an insurrection that had taken place in the city, and for murder.) Pilate, wanting to release Jesus, addressed them again; but they kept shouting, "Crucify, crucify him!"[4] A third time he said to them, "Why, what evil has he done? I have found in him no ground for the sentence of death; I will therefore have him flogged and then release him." But they kept urgently demanding with loud shouts that he should be crucified; and their voices prevailed. So Pilate gave his verdict that their demand should be granted. He released the man they asked for, the one who had been put in prison for insurrection and murder, and he handed Jesus over as they wished.

As they led him away, they seized a man, Simon of Cyrene, who was coming from the country, and they laid the cross on him, and made him carry it behind Jesus. A great number of the people followed him, and among them were women who were beating their breasts and wailing for him. But Jesus turned to them and said, "Daughters of Jerusalem, do not weep for me, but weep for yourselves and for your children.

3. From the Hebrew word for "anointed one," which at this time referred to the descendant of David who would usher in the end of time, the Kingdom of God, and the salvation of his people.

4. Crucifixion was the standard punishment for slaves and noncitizens convicted of grave crimes, especially political or religious agitation.

For the days are surely coming when they will say, 'Blessed are the barren, and the wombs that never bore, and the breasts that never nursed.' Then they will begin to say to the mountains, 'Fall on us'; and to the hills, 'Cover us.' For if they do this when the wood is green, what will happen when it is dry?"

Two others also, who were criminals, were led away to be put to death with him. When they came to the place that is called The Skull, they crucified Jesus there with the criminals, one on his right and one on his left. [Then Jesus said, "Father, forgive them; for they do not know what they are doing."] And they cast lots to divide his clothing. And the people stood by, watching; but the leaders scoffed at him, saying, "He saved others; let him save himself if he is the Messiah of God, his chosen one!" The soldiers also mocked him, coming up and offering him sour wine, and saying, "If you are the King of the Jews, save yourself!" There was also an inscription over him, "This is the King of the Jews."[5]

One of the criminals who were hanged there kept deriding him and saying, "Are you not the Messiah? Save yourself and us!" But the other rebuked him, saying, "Do you not fear God, since you are under the same sentence of condemnation? And we indeed have been condemned justly, for we are getting what we deserve for our deeds, but this man has done nothing wrong." Then he said, "Jesus, remember me when you come into your kingdom." He replied, "Truly I tell you, today you will be with me in Paradise."

It was now about noon, and darkness came over the whole land until three in the afternoon, while the sun's light failed; and the curtain of the temple was torn in two. Then Jesus, crying with a loud voice, said, "Father, into your hands I commend my spirit." Having said this, he breathed his last. When the centurion saw what had taken place, he praised God and said, "Certainly this man was innocent." And when all the crowds who had gathered there for this spectacle saw what had taken place, they returned home, beating their breasts. But all his acquaintances, including the women who had followed him from Galilee, stood at a distance, watching these things.

Now there was a good and righteous man named Joseph, who, though a member of the council, had not agreed to their plan and action. He came from the Jewish town of Arimathea, and he was waiting expectantly for the kingdom of God. This man went to Pilate and asked for the body of Jesus. Then he took it down, wrapped it in a linen cloth, and laid it in a rock-hewn tomb where no one had ever been laid. It was the day of Preparation, and the sabbath was beginning. The women who had come with him from Galilee followed, and they saw the tomb and how his body was laid. Then they returned, and prepared spices and ointments.

On the sabbath they rested according to the commandment.

Chapter 24

But on the first day of the week,[6] at early dawn, they came to the tomb, taking the spices that they had prepared. They found the stone rolled away from the tomb, but when they went in, they did not find the body. While they were perplexed about this, suddenly two men in dazzling clothes stood beside them. The women were terrified and bowed their faces to the ground, but the men said to them, "Why do you look for

5. It was customary to place over the crucified person's head an inscription with his name and crime.

6. Sunday.

the living among the dead? He is not here, but has risen. Remember how he told you, while he was still in Galilee, that the Son of Man must be handed over to sinners, and be crucified, and on the third day rise again." Then they remembered his words, and returning from the tomb, they told all this to the eleven and to all the rest. Now it was Mary Magdalene, Joanna, Mary the mother of James, and the other women with them who told this to the apostles. But these words seemed to them an idle tale, and they did not believe them. But Peter got up and ran to the tomb; stooping and looking in, he saw the linen cloths by themselves; then he went home, amazed at what had happened.

Now on that same day two of them were going to a village called Emmaus, about seven miles from Jerusalem, and talking with each other about all these things that had happened. While they were talking and discussing, Jesus himself came near and went with them, but their eyes were kept from recognizing him. And he said to them, "What are you discussing with each other while you walk along?" They stood still, looking sad. Then one of them, whose name was Cleopas, answered him, "Are you the only stranger in Jerusalem who does not know the things that have taken place there in these days?" He asked them, "What things?" They replied, "The things about Jesus of Nazareth, who was a prophet mighty in deed and word before God and all the people, and how our chief priests and leaders handed him over to be condemned to death and crucified him. But we had hoped that he was the one to redeem Israel. Yes, and besides all this, it is now the third day since these things took place. Moreover, some women of our group astounded us. They were at the tomb early this morning, and when they did not find his body there, they came back and told us that they had indeed seen a vision of angels who said that he was alive. Some of those who were with us went to the tomb and found it just as the women had said; but they did not see him." Then he said to them, "Oh, how foolish you are, and how slow of heart to believe all that the prophets have declared! Was it not necessary that the Messiah should suffer these things and then enter into his glory?" Then beginning with Moses and all the prophets, he interpreted to them the things about himself in all the scriptures.

As they came near the village to which they were going, he walked ahead as if he were going on. But they urged him strongly, saying, "Stay with us, because it is almost evening and the day is now nearly over." So he went in to stay with them. When he was at the table with them, he took bread, blessed and broke it, and gave it to them. Then their eyes were opened, and they recognized him; and he vanished from their sight. They said to each other, "Were not our hearts burning within us while he was talking to us on the road, while he was opening the scriptures to us?" That same hour they got up and returned to Jerusalem; and they found the eleven and their companions gathered together. They were saying, "The Lord has risen indeed, and he has appeared to Simon!" Then they told what had happened on the road, and how he had been made known to them in the breaking of the bread.

While they were talking about this, Jesus himself stood among them and said to them, "Peace be with you." They were startled and terrified, and thought that they were seeing a ghost. He said to them, "Why are you frightened, and why do doubts arise in your hearts? Look at my hands and my feet; see that it is I myself. Touch me and see; for a ghost does not have flesh and bones as you see that I have." And when he had said this, he showed them his hands and his feet. While in their joy they were disbelieving and still wondering, he said to them, "Have you anything here to eat?" They gave him a piece of broiled fish, and he took it and ate in their presence.

Then he said to them, "These are my words that I spoke to you while I was still with you—that everything written about me in the law of Moses, the prophets, and the psalms must be fulfilled." Then he opened their minds to understand the scriptures, and he said to them, "Thus it is written, that the Messiah is to suffer and to rise from the dead on the third day, and that repentance and forgiveness of sins is to be proclaimed in his name to all nations, beginning from Jerusalem. You are witnesses of these things. And see, I am sending upon you what my Father promised; so stay here in the city until you have been clothed with power from on high."

Then he led them out as far as Bethany,[7] and, lifting up his hands, he blessed them. While he was blessing them, he withdrew from them and was carried up into heaven. And they worshiped him, and returned to Jerusalem with great joy; and they were continually in the temple blessing God.

from The Acts of the Apostles[1]

from *Chapter 1*

[Prologue]

In the first book, Theophilus,[2] I wrote about all that Jesus did and taught from the beginning until the day when he was taken up to heaven, after giving instructions through the Holy Spirit to the apostles whom he had chosen. After his suffering he presented himself alive to them by many convincing proofs, appearing to them during forty days and speaking about the kingdom of God. While staying with them, he ordered them not to leave Jerusalem, but to wait there for the promise of the Father. "This," he said, "is what you have heard from me; for John baptized with water, but you will be baptized with the Holy Spirit not many days from now."

Chapter 2

[Peter Addresses the Crowd at Pentecost]

When the day of Pentecost[1] had come, they were all together in one place. And suddenly from heaven there came a sound like the rush of a violent wind, and it filled the entire house where they were sitting. Divided tongues, as of fire, appeared among them, and a tongue rested on each of them. All of them were filled with the Holy Spirit and began to speak in other languages, as the Spirit gave them ability.

Now there were devout Jews from every nation under heaven living in Jerusalem. And at this sound the crowd gathered and was bewildered, because each one heard them speaking in the native language of each. Amazed and astonished, they asked, "Are not all these who are speaking Galileans? And how is it that we hear, each of us, in our own native language? Parthians, Medes, Elamites, and residents of Mesopotamia, Judea and Cappadocia, Pontus and Asia, Phrygia and Pamphylia, Egypt and the parts of Libya belonging to Cyrene, and visitors from Rome,

7. A place on the eastern slope of the Mount of Olives.

1. New Revised Standard Version.

2. "The first book" is the Gospel According to Luke. "Theophilus" is Greek for "lover of God." It is probably the name of an influential patron, but it may simply refer in general to all Christians.

1. A religious festival that celebrated the end of the harvest.

both Jews and proselytes, Cretans and Arabs—in our own languages we hear them speaking about God's deeds of power." All were amazed and perplexed, saying to one another, "What does this mean?" But others sneered and said, "They are filled with new wine."

But Peter, standing with the eleven, raised his voice and addressed them, "Men of Judea and all who live in Jerusalem, let this be known to you, and listen to what I say. Indeed, these are not drunk, as you suppose, for it is only nine o'clock in the morning. No, this is what was spoken through the prophet Joel:

> 'In the last days it will be, God declares,
> that I will pour out my Spirit upon all flesh,
> and your sons and your daughters shall prophesy,
> and your young men shall see visions,
> and your old men shall dream dreams.
> Even upon my slaves, both men and women,
> in those days I will pour out my Spirit;
> and they shall prophesy.
> And I will show portents in the heaven above
> and signs on the earth below, blood, and fire, and smoky mist.
> The sun shall be turned to darkness
> and the moon to blood, before the coming of the Lord's great and glorious day.
> Then everyone who calls on the name of the Lord shall be saved.'

"You that are Israelites, listen to what I have to say: Jesus of Nazareth, a man attested to you by God with deeds of power, wonders, and signs that God did through him among you, as you yourselves know—this man, handed over to you according to the definite plan and foreknowledge of God, you crucified and killed by the hands of those outside the law.[2] But God raised him up, having freed him from death, because it was impossible for him to be held in its power. For David says concerning him,

> 'I saw the Lord always before me,
> for he is at my right hand so that I will not be shaken;
> therefore my heart was glad, and my tongue rejoiced;
> moreover my flesh will live in hope.
> For you will not abandon my soul to Hades,[3]
> or let your Holy One experience corruption.
> You have made known to me the ways of life;
> you will make me full of gladness with your presence.'

"Fellow Israelites, I may say to you confidently of our ancestor David that he both died and was buried, and his tomb is with us to this day. Since he was a prophet, he knew that God had sworn with an oath to him that he would put one of his descendants on his throne. Foreseeing this, David spoke of the resurrection of the Messiah, saying,

> 'He was not abandoned to Hades,
> nor did his flesh experience corruption.'

2. That is, the Romans, outside of Judaic law.

3. "Hades," the name for the underworld in Greek religion, was used in New Testament Greek to translate the Hebrew word *Sheol,* a subterranean space of death.

This Jesus God raised up, and of that all of us are witnesses. Being therefore exalted at the right hand of God, and having received from the Father the promise of the Holy Spirit, he has poured out this that you both see and hear. For David did not ascend into the heavens, but he himself says,

'The Lord said to my Lord,
"Sit at my right hand,
until I make your enemies your footstool."'

Therefore let the entire house of Israel know with certainty that God has made him both Lord and Messiah, this Jesus whom you crucified."[4]

Now when they heard this, they were cut to the heart and said to Peter and to the other apostles, "Brothers, what should we do?" Peter said to them, "Repent, and be baptized every one of you in the name of Jesus Christ so that your sins may be forgiven; and you will receive the gift of the Holy Spirit. For the promise is for you, for your children, and for all who are far away, everyone whom the Lord our God calls to him." And he testified with many other arguments and exhorted them, saying, "Save yourselves from this corrupt generation." So those who welcomed his message were baptized, and that day about three thousand persons were added. They devoted themselves to the apostles' teaching and fellowship, to the breaking of bread and the prayers.

Awe came upon everyone, because many wonders and signs were being done by the apostles. All who believed were together and had all things in common; they would sell their possessions and goods and distribute the proceeds to all, as any had need. Day by day, as they spent much time together in the temple, they broke bread at home and ate their food with glad and generous hearts, praising God and having the goodwill of all the people. And day by day the Lord added to their number those who were being saved.

from *Chapter 9*

[The Conversion of Paul]

Meanwhile Saul,[1] still breathing threats and murder against the disciples of the Lord, went to the high priest and asked him for letters to the synagogues at Damascus,[2] so that if he found any who belonged to the Way; men or women, he might bring them bound to Jerusalem. Now as he was going along and approaching Damascus, suddenly a light from heaven flashed around him. He fell to the ground and heard a voice saying to him, "Saul, Saul, why do you persecute me?" He asked, "Who are you, Lord?" The reply came, "I am Jesus, whom you are persecuting. But get up and enter the city, and you will be told what you are to do." The men who were traveling with him stood speechless because they heard the voice but saw no one. Saul got up from the ground, and though his eyes were open, he could see nothing; so they led him by the hand and brought him into Damascus. For three days he was without sight, and neither ate nor drank.

4. As Jesus did with his disciples after his resurrection, so Peter here tells the crowd how "the law of Moses, the prophets, and the psalms" have been "fulfilled" by recent events (Luke 24:44). The first passage is from Joel 2:28–32; the second is from Psalm 16:8–11 (David was the traditional author of Psalms).

1. The Jewish name of the apostle Paul.

2. A commercial center in Syria. It was the site of an early Christian community.

Now there was a disciple in Damascus named Ananias. The Lord said to him in a vision, "Ananias." He answered, "Here I am, Lord." The Lord said to him, "Get up and go to the street called Straight, and at the house of Judas look for a man of Tarsus named Saul. At this moment he is praying, and he has seen in a vision a man named Ananias come in and lay his hands on him so that he might regain his sight." But Ananias answered, "Lord, I have heard from many about this man, how much evil he has done to your saints in Jerusalem; and here he has authority from the chief priests to bind all who invoke your name." But the Lord said to him, "Go, for he is an instrument whom I have chosen to bring my name before Gentiles and kings and before the people of Israel; I myself will show him how much he must suffer for the sake of my name." So Ananias went and entered the house. He laid his hands on Saul and said, "Brother Saul, the Lord Jesus, who appeared to you on your way here, has sent me so that you may regain your sight and be filled with the Holy Spirit." And immediately something like scales fell from his eyes, and his sight was restored. Then he got up and was baptized, and after taking some food, he regained his strength.

For several days he was with the disciples in Damascus, and immediately he began to proclaim Jesus in the synagogues, saying, "He is the Son of God." All who heard him were amazed and said, "Is not this the man who made havoc in Jerusalem among those who invoked this name? And has he not come here for the purpose of bringing them bound before the chief priests?" Saul became increasingly more powerful and confounded the Jews who lived in Damascus by proving that Jesus was the Messiah.

After some time had passed, the Jews plotted to kill him, but their plot became known to Saul. They were watching the gates day and night so that they might kill him; but his disciples took him by night and let him down through an opening in the wall, lowering him in a basket.

When he had come to Jerusalem, he attempted to join the disciples; and they were all afraid of him, for they did not believe that he was a disciple. But Barnabas took him, brought him to the apostles, and described for them how on the road he had seen the Lord, who had spoken to him, and how in Damascus he had spoken boldly in the name of Jesus. So he went in and out among them in Jerusalem, speaking boldly in the name of the Lord.

Chapter 26

[PAUL DEFENDS HIMSELF BEFORE HEROD AGRIPPA]

Agrippa[1] said to Paul, "You have permission to speak for yourself." Then Paul stretched out his hand and began to defend himself:

"I consider myself fortunate that it is before you, King Agrippa, I am to make my defense today against all the accusations of the Jews, because you are especially familiar with all the customs and controversies of the Jews; therefore I beg of you to listen to me patiently.

"All the Jews know my way of life from my youth, a life spent from the beginning among my own people and in Jerusalem. They have known for a long time, if they are willing to testify, that I have belonged to the strictest sect of our religion and

1. Herod Agrippa (27–93 C.E.) was a great-grandson of Herod the Great and controlled various parts of Lebanon, Syria, and Galilee. Paul was arrested in the mid-50s, and had been in prison for two years at the time of this hearing.

lived as a Pharisee. And now I stand here on trial on account of my hope in the promise made by God to our ancestors, a promise that our twelve tribes hope to attain, as they earnestly worship day and night. It is for this hope, your Excellency, that I am accused by Jews! Why is it thought incredible by any of you that God raises the dead?

"Indeed, I myself was convinced that I ought to do many things against the name of Jesus of Nazareth. And that is what I did in Jerusalem; with authority received from the chief priests, I not only locked up many of the saints in prison, but I also cast my vote against them when they were being condemned to death. By punishing them often in all the synagogues I tried to force them to blaspheme; and since I was so furiously enraged at them, I pursued them even to foreign cities.

"With this in mind, I was traveling to Damascus with the authority and commission of the chief priests, when at midday along the road, your Excellency, I saw a light from heaven, brighter than the sun, shining around me and my companions. When we had all fallen to the ground, I heard a voice saying to me in the Hebrew language, 'Saul, Saul, why are you persecuting me? It hurts you to kick against the goads.' I asked, 'Who are you, Lord?' The Lord answered, 'I am Jesus whom you are persecuting. But get up and stand on your feet; for I have appeared to you for this purpose, to appoint you to serve and testify to the things in which you have seen me and to those in which I will appear to you. I will rescue you from your people and from the Gentiles—to whom I am sending you to open their eyes so that they may turn from darkness to light and from the power of Satan to God, so that they may receive forgiveness of sins and a place among those who are sanctified by faith in me.'

"After that, King Agrippa, I was not disobedient to the heavenly vision, but declared first to those in Damascus, then in Jerusalem and throughout the countryside of Judea, and also to the Gentiles, that they should repent and turn to God and do deeds consistent with repentance. For this reason the Jews seized me in the temple and tried to kill me. To this day I have had help from God, and so I stand here, testifying to both small and great, saying nothing but what the prophets and Moses said would take place: that the Messiah must suffer, and that, by being the first to rise from the dead, he would proclaim light both to our people and to the Gentiles."

While he was making this defense, Festus[2] exclaimed, "You are out of your mind, Paul! Too much learning is driving you insane!" But Paul said, "I am not out of my mind, most excellent Festus, but I am speaking the sober truth. Indeed the king knows about these things, and to him I speak freely; for I am certain that none of these things has escaped his notice, for this was not done in a corner. King Agrippa, do you believe the prophets? I know that you believe." Agrippa said to Paul, "Are you so quickly persuading me to become a Christian?" Paul replied, "Whether quickly or not, I pray to God that not only you but also all who are listening to me today might become such as I am—except for these chains."

Then the king got up, and with him the governor and Bernice[3] and those who had been seated with them; and as they were leaving, they said to one another, "This man is doing nothing to deserve death or imprisonment." Agrippa said to Festus, "This man could have been set free if he had not appealed to the emperor."[4]

2. Porcius Festus became the Roman procurator of Judea around 55 C.E.
3. A sister of Agrippa's.
4. As a Roman citizen, Paul had appealed to the emperor's tribunal in Rome.

Chapter 28

[PAUL REACHES ROME]

After we had reached safety, we then learned that the island was called Malta.[1] The natives showed us unusual kindness. Since it had begun to rain and was cold, they kindled a fire and welcomed all of us around it. Paul had gathered a bundle of brushwood and was putting it on the fire, when a viper, driven out by the heat, fastened itself on his hand. When the natives saw the creature hanging from his hand, they said to one another, "This man must be a murderer; though he has escaped from the sea, justice has not allowed him to live." He, however, shook off the creature into the fire and suffered no harm. They were expecting him to swell up or drop dead, but after they had waited a long time and saw that nothing unusual had happened to him, they changed their minds and began to say that he was a god.

Now in the neighborhood of that place were lands belonging to the leading man of the island, named Publius, who received us and entertained us hospitably for three days. It so happened that the father of Publius lay sick in bed with fever and dysentery. Paul visited him and cured him by praying and putting his hands on him. After this happened, the rest of the people on the island who had diseases also came and were cured. They bestowed many honors on us, and when we were about to sail, they put on board all the provisions we needed.

Three months later we set sail on a ship that had wintered at the island, an Alexandrian ship with the Twin Brothers as its figurehead.[2] We put in at Syracuse and stayed there for three days; then we weighed anchor and came to Rhegium. After one day there a south wind sprang up, and on the second day we came to Puteoli.[3] There we found believers and were invited to stay with them for seven days. And so we came to Rome. The believers from there, when they heard of us, came as far as the Forum of Appius and Three Taverns to meet us.[4] On seeing them, Paul thanked God and took courage.

When we came into Rome, Paul was allowed to live by himself, with the soldier who was guarding him.

Three days later he called together the local leaders of the Jews. When they had assembled, he said to them, "Brothers, though I had done nothing against our people or the customs of our ancestors, yet I was arrested in Jerusalem and handed over to the Romans. When they had examined me, the Romans wanted to release me, because there was no reason for the death penalty in my case. But when the Jews objected, I was compelled to appeal to the emperor—even though I had no charge to bring against my nation. For this reason therefore I have asked to see you and speak with you, since it is for the sake of the hope of Israel that I am bound with this chain." They replied, "We have received no letters from Judea about you, and none of the brothers coming here has reported or spoken anything evil about you. But we would like to hear from you what you think, for with regard to this sect we know that everywhere it is spoken against."

After they had set a day to meet with him, they came to him at his lodgings in great numbers. From morning until evening he explained the matter to them, testifying

1. In the central Mediterranean, south of Sicily. The prison ship has just survived a storm at sea.

2. Castor and Pollux, legendary twins of Greek and Roman myth.

3. Ports along the route to Rome.

4. Places on the Appian Way that ran through southern Italy to Rome.

to the kingdom of God and trying to convince them about Jesus both from the law of Moses and from the prophets. Some were convinced by what he had said, while others refused to believe. So they disagreed with each other; and as they were leaving, Paul made one further statement: "The Holy Spirit was right in saying to your ancestors through the prophet Isaiah,

'Go to this people and say,
You will indeed listen, but never understand,
and you will indeed look, but never perceive.
For this people's heart has grown dull,
and their ears are hard of hearing,
and they have shut their eyes;
so that they might not look with their eyes,
and listen with their ears,
and understand with their heart and turn—
and I would heal them.'

Let it be known to you then that this salvation of God has been sent to the Gentiles; they will listen."

He lived there two whole years at his own expense and welcomed all who came to him, proclaiming the kingdom of God and teaching about the Lord Jesus Christ with all boldness and without hindrance.

Roman Reactions to Early Christianity

Palestine was conquered by Pompey in 63 B.C.E., and became part of the Roman province of Syria. Herod the Great, King of Judaea from 37 to 4 B.C.E., was an important ally to Rome, and his people were allowed unusual freedoms. Jesus was born at the end of Herod's reign, under the so-called Peace of Augustus; he was crucified in 30 C.E. during the reign of Augustus's successor, Tiberius, because he was seen as a political threat to the stability of the region. According to Suetonius, Jewish worshipers of "Chrestus" were already active (and unruly) in Rome under Claudius (41–54); a church was well established by the time of Paul's Epistle to the Romans in the mid-first century. Persecution was intermittent but often severe; as suggested by the Roman sources below, however, the prevailing attitude may have been to regard the new religion as just one particularly annoying sect among many.

Suetonius

c. 70–after 122 C.E.

A successful bureaucrat first patronized by Pliny the Younger, Suetonius prospered under Emperors Trajan and Hadrian before falling precipitously into disgrace in 122. Written in the early 2nd century, his *Twelve Caesars* is a racy and richly anecdotal account of the lives of the rulers of Rome covering some two hundred years from Julius Caesar to Domitian. Here, he reports on the treatment of Jews and Christians in Rome under Tiberius, Claudius, and Nero.

from The Twelve Caesars[1]

[TIBERIUS][2]

He abolished foreign cults at Rome, particularly the Egyptian and Jewish, forcing all citizens who had embraced these superstitious faiths to burn their religious vestments and other accessories. Jews of military age were removed to unhealthy regions, on the pretext of drafting them into the army; the others of the same race or of similar beliefs were expelled from the city and threatened with slavery if they defied the order. Tiberius also banished all astrologers except such as asked for his forgiveness and undertook to make no more predictions. * * *

[CLAUDIUS][3]

It now became illegal for foreigners to adopt the names of Roman families, and any who usurped the rights of Roman citizens were executed in the Esquiline Field.[4] Tiberius had converted the provinces of Greece and Macedonia into a private domain of his own; Claudius gave them back to the Senate. He deprived the Lycians of national independence to punish their love of savage vendettas; but restored the Rhodians' independence to express his pleasure at their recantation of their faults.[5] In granting the Trojans, as founders of the Roman race, perpetual exemption from tribute, he supported his act by reading aloud an ancient letter written in Greek to King Seleucus, from the Senate and People of Rome, with a promise of loyal friendship on condition that Seleucus should "keep their Trojan kinsfolk free from all imposts."[6] Because the Jews at Rome caused continuous disturbances at the instigation of Chrestus,[7] he expelled them from the city. When the German envoys first visited the Theatre, they took their seats among the common people, but, noticing the Parthian and Armenian envoys seated with the Senators in the orchestra, went to join them—were they not just as brave and nobly born? Claudius admired their simple confidence and let them remain there. Augustus had been content to prohibit any Roman citizen in Gaul from taking part in the savage and terrible Druidic cult; Claudius abolished it altogether.[8] On the other hand, he attempted to transfer the Eleusinian Mysteries from Attica to Rome; and had the ruined Temple of Venus on Mount Eryx in Sicily restored at the expense of the Public Treasury.[9] Whenever he concluded a treaty with foreign rulers, he sacrificed a sow in the Forum, using the ancient formula of the Fetial priests.[1] Yet all these acts, and others like them—indeed, one might say, everything that Claudius did throughout his reign—were dictated by his wives and freedmen: he practically always obeyed their whims rather than his own judgment.

1. Translated by Robert Graves, revised by Michael Grant.
2. The adopted son of Augustus, Tiberius was the second Roman emperor, reigning from 14 to 37 C.E., near the end of which time Jesus was crucified.
3. Claudius was proclaimed emperor in 41 following the assassination of his nephew Caligula. He reigned for 13 years.
4. Site of a cemetery for slaves in Rome.
5. Lycia was a region in southwest Asia Minor; Rhodes is a large island off its coast.
6. Taxes or duties. According to Roman legend (and Virgil's *Aeneid*), Rome had been founded by the Trojan hero Aeneas. The kingdom founded by Seleucus, a general under Alexander the Great, controlled much of Asia Minor and the Middle East. It had been conquered by Rome in 64 B.C.E.
7. Most likely a reference to Christ.
8. Druidism was the religion of the Celtic peoples of northern Europe.
9. The ancient Greek mystery cult of Eleusis was based at the sanctuary of Demeter in Attica near Athens. Eryx in Sicily was the site of a cult of Venus and is visited by Aeneas in Virgil's *Aeneid.*
1. The *Fetiales* were Latin priests who presided over the rituals associated with declaring wars and making treaties. The Forum was the main Roman square.

[NERO][2]

Nero introduced his own new style of architecture in the city: building out porches from the fronts of apartments and private houses to serve as fire-fighting platforms, and subsidizing the work himself. He also considered a scheme for extending the city wall as far as Ostia, and cutting a canal which would allow ships to sail straight up to Rome.[3]

During his reign a great many public abuses were suppressed by the imposition of heavy penalties, and among the equally numerous novel enactments were sumptuary laws limiting private expenditure; the substitution of a simple grain distribution for public banquets; and a decree restricting the food sold in wine-shops to green vegetables and dried beans—whereas before all kinds of snacks had been displayed. Punishments were also inflicted on the Christians, a sect professing a new and mischievous religious belief; and Nero ended the licence which the charioteers had so long enjoyed that they claimed it as a right: to wander down the streets, swindling and robbing the populace. He likewise expelled from the city all pantomime actors and their hangers-on.

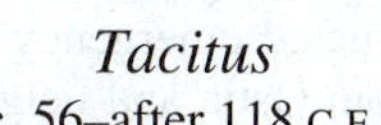

Tacitus
c. 56–after 118 C.E.

Politician and celebrated orator under the reigns of Vespasian, Titus, Domitian, and Nerva, Tacitus held several high positions in the government in Rome and was posted to his birthplace of Gaul (or else to Germany), to Africa, and to Asia Minor. A close friend of Pliny the Younger, he is remembered for his *Germania,* a sympathetic study of the northern barbarians, and for his ambitious *Histories* and *Annals,* giving a detailed, continuous narrative of Roman history from the death of Augustus to the death of Domitian, of which about half has survived. Tacitus's skill in portraiture, command of narrative movement, and tragic sense of history are in evidence in the following brief account of the great fire in Rome in 64 C.E. and Nero's response to it.

from The Annals of Imperial Rome[1]

[THE BURNING OF ROME]

Disaster followed. Whether it was accidental or caused by the emperor's criminal act[2] is uncertain—both versions have supporters. Now started the most terrible and destructive fire which Rome had ever experienced. It began in the Circus, where it adjoins the hills.[3] Breaking out in shops selling inflammable goods, and fanned by the wind, the conflagration instantly grew and swept the whole length of the Circus. There were no walled mansions or temples, or any other obstructions which could arrest it. First, the fire swept violently over the level spaces. Then it climbed the hills—but returned to ravage the lower ground again. It outstripped every

2. Nero was the son of Agrippina, Claudius's wife and Caligula's sister. He reigned as emperor from 54 to 68.
3. Ostia was a port for the city of Rome at the mouth of the river Tiber.
1. Translated by Michael Grant.

2. Tacitus has been recounting some debauched banqueting by Nero and his cronies.
3. The fire began late at night in the middle of June 64 in the Circus Maximus, between the Palatine and Aventine hills.

counter-measure. The ancient city's narrow winding streets and irregular blocks encouraged its progress.

Terrified, shrieking women, helpless old and young, people intent on their own safety, people unselfishly supporting invalids or waiting for them, fugitives and lingerers alike—all heightened the confusion. When people looked back, menacing flames sprang up before them or outflanked them. When they escaped to a neighbouring quarter, the fire followed—even districts believed remote proved to be involved. Finally, with no idea where or what to flee, they crowded on to the country roads, or lay in the fields. Some who had lost everything—even their food for the day—could have escaped, but preferred to die. So did others, who had failed to rescue their loved ones. Nobody dared fight the flames. Attempts to do so were prevented by menacing gangs. Torches, too, were openly thrown in, by men crying that they acted under orders. Perhaps they had received orders. Or they may just have wanted to plunder unhampered.

Nero was at Antium.[4] He only returned to the city when the fire was approaching the mansion he had built to link the Gardens of Maecenas to the Palatine.[5] The flames could not be prevented from overwhelming the whole of the Palatine, including his palace. Nevertheless, for the relief of the homeless, fugitive masses he threw open the Field of Mars, including Agrippa's public buildings, and even his own Gardens.[6] Nero also constructed emergency accommodation for the destitute multitude. Food was brought from Ostia and neighbouring towns, and the price of corn was cut. Yet these measures, for all their popular character, earned no gratitude. For a rumour had spread that, while the city was burning, Nero had gone to his private stage and, comparing modern calamities with ancient, had sung of the destruction of Troy.

By the sixth day enormous demolitions had confronted the raging flames with bare ground and open sky, and the fire was finally stamped out. But before panic had subsided, or hope revived, flames broke out again in the more open regions of the city. Here there were fewer casualties; but the destruction of temples and pleasure arcades was even worse. This new conflagration caused additional ill-feeling because it started on Tigellinus' estate.[7] For people believed that Nero was ambitious to found a new city to be called after himself.

Of Rome's fourteen districts only four remained intact. Three were levelled to the ground. The other seven were reduced to a few scorched and mangled ruins. To count the mansions, blocks, and temples destroyed would be difficult. They included shrines of remote antiquity, the precious spoils of countless victories, Greek artistic masterpieces, and authentic records of old Roman genius. All the splendour of the rebuilt city did not prevent the older generation from remembering these irreplaceable objects. It was noted that the fire had started on July 19th, the day on which the Senonian Gauls had captured and burnt the city.[8]

But Nero profited by his country's ruin to build a new palace. Its wonders were not so much customary and commonplace luxuries like gold and jewels, but lawns

4. Antium (modern Anzio) was a fashionable resort in imperial times; Nero had rebuilt the harbor and imperial villa.

5. Maecenas, the advisor to Augustus and patron to Horace and Virgil, had built extensive gardens on the Esquiline. There were imperial properties here and on the Palatine.

6. Situated along the Tiber, the Campus Martius (Field of Mars) was a center of public life and leisure, full of theaters, temples, and baths, including a set just completed by Nero.

7. Ofidius Tigellinus was an advisor to Nero notorious for his indulgence of the emperor's more extreme tastes.

8. The Senones were said to have been leaders of the band of Gauls who had settled in Italy and took the city of Rome in 390 B.C.E.

and lakes and faked rusticity—woods here, open spaces and views there. With their cunning, impudent artificialities, Nero's architects and contractors outbid Nature.[9]

They also fooled away an emperor's riches. For they promised to dig a navigable canal from Lake Avernus to the Tiber estuary, over the stony shore and mountain barriers.[1] The only water to feed the canal was in the Pontine marshes. Elsewhere, all was precipitous or waterless. Moreover, even if a passage could have been forced, the labour would have been unendurable and unjustified. But Nero was eager to perform the incredible; so he attempted to excavate the hills adjoining Lake Avernus. Traces of his frustrated hopes are visible today. * * *

After consultation of the Sibylline books, prayers were addressed to Vulcan, Ceres, and Proserpina. Juno, too, was propitiated.[2] But neither human resources, nor imperial munificence, nor appeasement of the gods, eliminated sinister suspicions that the fire had been instigated. To suppress this rumour, Nero fabricated scapegoats—and punished with every refinement the notoriously depraved Christians (as they were popularly called). Their originator, Christ, had been executed in Tiberius' reign by the governor of Judaea, Pontius Pilatus. But in spite of this temporary setback the deadly superstition had broken out afresh, not only in Judaea (where the mischief had started) but even in Rome. All degraded and shameful practices collect and flourish in the capital.

First, Nero had self-acknowledged Christians arrested. Then, on their information, large numbers of others were condemned—not so much for incendiarism as for their anti-social tendencies. Their deaths were made farcical. Dressed in wild animals' skins, they were torn to pieces by dogs, or crucified, or made into torches to be ignited after dark as substitutes for daylight. Nero provided his Gardens for the spectacle, and exhibited displays in the Circus, at which he mingled with the crowd—or stood in a chariot, dressed as a charioteer. Despite their guilt as Christians, and the ruthless punishment it deserved, the victims were pitied. For it was felt that they were being sacrificed to one man's brutality rather than to the national interest.

Meanwhile Italy was ransacked for funds, and the provinces were ruined—unprivileged and privileged communities alike. Even the gods were included in the looting. Temples at Rome were robbed, and emptied of the gold dedicated for the triumphs and vows, the ambitions and fears, of generations of Romans. Plunder from Asia and Greece included not only offerings but actual statues of the gods. Two agents were sent to these provinces. One was an ex-slave, capable of any depravity. The other professed Greek culture, but no virtue from it percolated to his heart.

Seneca, rumour went, sought to avoid the odium of this sacrilege by asking leave to retire to a distant country retreat, and then—permission being refused—feigning a muscular complaint and keeping to his bedroom. According to some accounts, one of his former slaves acting on Nero's orders intended to poison Seneca, but he escaped—either because the man confessed or because Seneca's own fears caused him to live very simply on plain fruit, quenching his thirst with running water.[3]

9. Nero's famous Domus Aurea, or Golden House, its gardens, and an artificial lake occupied the center of Rome.

1. It was a good hundred miles to Lake Avernus, near Naples.

2. According to Roman legend, a sibyl, or prophetess, had offered a book of prophecies to the last of the ancient Roman kings. The three surviving books were housed in Nero's time in the temple of Palatine Apollo. With Vulcan's relation to fire, Ceres's to fertility, and Proserpina's to the underworld, they would be logical choices for prayer. Juno was a principal god of the city.

3. Seneca, the famous Stoic philosopher and tragedian, had been the young Nero's tutor and was the emperor's advisor and minister until he fell out of favor and withdrew from public life. A year after the fire he was compelled to take his life after being accused of conspiracy against the emperor.

At this juncture there was an attempted break-out by gladiators at Praeneste.[4] Their army guards overpowered them. But the Roman public, as always terrified (or fascinated) by revolution, were already talking of ancient calamities such as the rising of Spartacus.[5] Soon afterwards, a naval disaster occurred. This was not on active service; never had there been such profound peace. But Nero had ordered the fleet to return to Campania by a fixed date, regardless of weather. So, despite heavy seas, the steersmen started from Formiae. But when they tried to round Cape Misenum, a south-westerly gale drove them ashore near Cumae and destroyed numerous warships and smaller craft.[6]

Pliny the Younger

c. 60–c. 112 C.E.

An influential and wealthy lawyer and politician, Pliny preserved in his ten books of letters a record of the most important figures and events of his day, including an eyewitness account of the eruption of Vesuvius that killed his uncle and namesake, the natural historian Pliny the Elder. Pliny's correspondence with the Emperor Trajan, whom he served as governor of the Asia Minor province Bithynia-Pontus around 110, provides a unique insight into the functioning of Roman provincial government. The letter included here suggests the complicated situation of Christians in Asia Minor and the lack of a fixed policy for dealing with them.

Letter to the Emperor Trajan[1]

It is my custom to refer all my difficulties to you, Sir, for no one is better able to resolve my doubts and to inform my ignorance.

I have never been present at an examination of Christians. Consequently, I do not know the nature or the extent of the punishments usually meted out to them, nor the grounds for starting an investigation and how far it should be pressed. Nor am I at all sure whether any distinction should be made between them on the grounds of age, or if young people and adults should be treated alike; whether a pardon ought to be granted to anyone retracting his beliefs, or if he has once professed Christianity, he shall gain nothing by renouncing it; and whether it is the mere name of Christian which is punishable, even if innocent of crime, or rather the crimes associated with the name.

For the moment this is the line I have taken with all persons brought before me on the charge of being Christians. I have asked them in person if they are Christians, and if they admit it, I repeat the question a second and third time, with a warning of the punishment awaiting them. If they persist, I order them to be led away for execution; for, whatever the nature of their admission, I am convinced that their stubbornness and unshakeable obstinacy ought not to go unpunished. There have been others similarly fanatical who are Roman citizens. I have entered them on the list of persons to be sent to Rome for trial.[2]

4. A town some 25 miles east-southeast of Rome (modern Palestrina).
5. Spartacus was a gladiator who led an impressive revolt and ravaged Italy during the late 70s B.C.E.
6. The region is the southern Adriatic coast between Rome and Naples.

1. Translated by Betty Radice.
2. Citizenship of Rome was conferred at this time on members of the elite in provincial cities all over the empire. Citizenship conveyed various privileges including certain legal rights.

Now that I have begun to deal with this problem, as so often happens, the charges are becoming more widespread and increasing in variety. An anonymous pamphlet has been circulated which contains the names of a number of accused persons. Among these I considered that I should dismiss any who denied that they were or ever had been Christians when they had repeated after me a formula of invocation to the gods and had made offerings of wine and incense to your statue (which I had ordered to be brought into court for this purpose along with the images of the gods),[3] and furthermore had reviled the name of Christ: none of which things, I understand, any genuine Christian can be induced to do.

Others, whose names were given to me by an informer, first admitted the charge and then denied it; they said that they had ceased to be Christians two or more years previously, and some of them even twenty years ago. They all did reverence to your statue and the images of the gods in the same way as the others, and reviled the name of Christ. They also declared that the sum total of their guilt or error amounted to no more than this: they had met regularly before dawn on a fixed day to chant verses alternately among themselves in honour of Christ as if to a god, and also to bind themselves by oath, not for any criminal purpose, but to abstain from theft, robbery and adultery, to commit no breach of trust and not to deny a deposit when called upon to restore it. After this ceremony it had been their custom to disperse and reassemble later to take food of an ordinary, harmless kind; but they had in fact given up this practice since my edict, issued on your instructions, which banned all political societies. This made me decide it was all the more necessary to extract the truth by torture from two slave-women, whom they call deaconesses. I found nothing but a degenerate sort of cult carried to extravagant lengths.

I have therefore postponed any further examination and hastened to consult you. The question seems to me to be worthy of your consideration, especially in view of the number of persons endangered; for a great many individuals of every age and class, both men and women, are being brought to trial, and this is likely to continue. It is not only the towns, but villages and rural districts too which are infected through contact with this wretched cult. I think though that it is still possible for it to be checked and directed to better ends, for there is no doubt that people have begun to throng the temples which had been almost entirely deserted for a long time; the sacred rites which had been allowed to lapse are being performed again, and flesh of sacrificial victims is on sale everywhere, though up till recently scarcely anyone could be found to buy it. It is easy to infer from this that a great many people could be reformed if they were given an opportunity to repent.

Trajan

reigned 98–117 C.E.

Probably born in Spain in 53, Trajan was adopted by Emperor Nerva as his son and co-ruler in 98, following distinguished service in Syria, Spain, and Germany. He became sole ruler after the infirm Nerva's death the same year and was known as a modest and judicious emperor. His measured reply to Pliny suggests the general character of his reign.

3. In provinces of Asia Minor including Pliny's station in Bithynia-Pontus, it had become custom to establish cults of living emperors.

Response to Pliny[1]

You have followed the right course of procedure, my dear Pliny, in your examination of the cases of persons charged with being Christians, for it is impossible to lay down a general rule to a fixed formula. These people must not be hunted out; if they are brought before you and the charge against them is proved, they must be punished, but in the case of anyone who denies that he is a Christian, and makes it clear that he is not by offering prayers to our gods, he is to be pardoned as a result of his repentance however suspect his past conduct may be. But pamphlets circulated anonymously must play no part in any accusation. They create the worst sort of precedent and are quite out of keeping with the spirit of our age.

END OF PERSPECTIVES: THE CULTURE OF ROME AND THE BEGINNINGS OF CHRISTIANITY

Augustine

354–430 C.E.

One of the Old Testament lessons Saint Augustine loved to cite concerned the gold taken by Moses and his people in their flight from Egypt to the Holy Land. Gold, he would argue, referred not only to the allure of worldly riches but to the wealth of classical literature and philosophy; hence, one could either succumb to the superficial brilliance of its rhetoric and its pagan ideas or one could transmute their splendor into the inner richness of spiritual peace. Throughout Augustine's writings, we witness a battle between a lifetime's immersion in the intellectual rigor and aesthetic power of Greek and Roman culture and a fervent belief in a Christianity that he found unsophisticated and illogical but that gave him inner tranquility nonetheless. He recorded the struggle on a personal level in his spiritual autobiography, the *Confessions*; in the *City of God,* he traced the same struggle on the stage of world history. For Augustine, Christianity meant not so much the defeat of the ancient world as its apotheosis, or raising up to God, just as the gold of the pagans could be remolded into the basis of a new and better world.

Aurelius Augustinus was born in 354 in the Roman town of Thagaste (now Souk Ahras in eastern Algeria). His father, Patricius, was a respectable but impoverished Roman citizen who died before Augustine was twenty. His mother, Monica, was a devout Christian; Augustine portrays his father by contrast as a worldly, distant pagan. The primary means for advancement in this society was education in the classics, and this was the direction in which Augustine's ambitious parents pushed him. He completed his education at Carthage, the biggest city in North Africa, full of literary associations with Virgil's Dido and Aeneas as well as the more fleshly temptations he would detail in the *Confessions.* His early career as a teacher of rhetoric took him from Carthage to Rome and finally Milan, residence of the western emperor, Valentinian. There, Augustine encountered the learned Bishop Ambrose, who taught a Christianity steeped in the philosophy of Neoplatonism, which conceived of the divine as a spiritual force wholly distinct from things of the material world. Pushed toward a society marriage, tormented by the requisite dismissal of a beloved mistress (the mother of his son, Adeodatus), Augustine chose instead in July 386 to convert, and he was baptized the following Easter. Three years later, back in Africa, he was persuaded to accept ordination as a priest in the coastal town of

1. Translated by Betty Radice.

Hippo Regius, where he was made bishop a few years later. He devoted the rest of his life to his church duties and to writing and engaging in a series of fierce battles over questions of doctrine. In addition to the *Confessions* (397–401) and the *City of God* (413–427), the dozens of volumes of his collected works include extensive biblical commentaries, treatises on topics such as *The Trinity* and *On Christian Doctrine,* and copious writings against several movements he succeeded in declaring heretical. Probably the most influential of all the Church Fathers, Augustine died in 430, a year before Hippo was abandoned to the invading Vandals.

Education in Augustine's day was based on repetition and memorization. He knew Latin authors such as Cicero, Virgil, and Terence nearly by heart and later also the Bible, which he cited over forty thousand times in his writings. Teaching stressed imitating the perfection of the past rather than individual creation and innovation, a practice Augustine incorporated into his account of religious conversion as fundamentally a matter of finding the correct model to imitate. The crux of the *Confessions* was persuading his readers that the Christian model was indeed the best. As a bishop, Augustine preached to a popular audience, but as a writer he had a more select group of readers in mind. The educated, sophisticated elite of the Roman Empire would not be persuaded by the humble rhetoric and plain speaking of the Gospels; they expected their religion to be aesthetically pleasing and intellectually rigorous. This is the dilemma Augustine attributes to his own spiritual search in the *Confessions.* On the one hand, he is deeply dissatisfied with his life and rapidly disillusioned with each new philosophical or religious "answer" he happens upon. On the other hand, as a rhetorician, he is disdainful of the only teaching—the Scriptures—that seems to offer what he needs: "To me they seemed quite unworthy of comparison with the stately prose of Cicero." Later, as a logician, he found equally difficult to swallow the fundamental tenets of the Trinity—the three that is one—and the Incarnation, the doctrine that Jesus could be simultaneously human and divine.

Augustine's drive to reconcile new doctrine with classical tradition led him to create a highly original book, the fullest and most personal autobiography that had ever been written. In the *Confessions,* he uses several strategies to finesse the qualms of his readers. First, he tells the story in retrospect rather than from beginning to end, so that he is able always to comment upon his wayward past from the safe harbor in which he now finds himself. In this way he can show how each apparently errant step he took—into the "hissing cauldron of lust" in Carthage, for example—could also play a role in his eventual salvation. Second, he forges a style that is elegant and full of rhetorical flourishes in the classical manner, but bound together lyrically with a cluster of modest, everyday images drawn from the language of the Bible. At times, as in the opening sections, the prose is almost entirely woven out of unmarked citations from Scripture, especially the Book of Psalms. The humble imagery of these citations—the house, the tree, the book, the song, the child—recurs throughout as a refrain, to remind us that all the other flourishes are present only so as to lead us to the very simple realization that in fact opens the book in his declaration to God: "our heart is restless until it rests in you." Everything that follows is simply a proof of this first assertion, and herein lies Augustine's third strategy: he must refute all of the competing claims to fulfillment swirling around the Empire. There were many of them, and Augustine had the sense not simply to dismiss them but to show how seductive each of them was—the emotional satisfaction of poetry, the sensual pleasure of sexual dissipation, the clarity of Manicheeism, and the profundity of Neoplatonism—in order to demonstrate what was lacking and to prove that Christianity offered the good of each without the bad.

The Goths invaded Italy in 408 and sacked Rome in 410; wealthy Roman refugees began washing up on the shores of Africa, many of them neo-pagans profoundly affected by the shock of defeat. The twenty-two books of the *City of God* set out a vision of world history in which the fall of an empire and the loss of a way of life could be regarded as a minor element in the divine scheme. Like most early Christians, Augustine lived in the certainty that the end of the world, the second coming of the Messiah, and the Last Judgment were imminent. This lends an urgency (and sometimes a virulence) to even the most arcane theological arguments he makes; it adds emotional depth to the *City of God* and increases the pathos of his mother's death in the *Confessions.* For if what finally converted Augustine to the Christian faith was the promise of rest, we only need to look at the turbulence of his life to appreciate the intensity of his longing.

PRONUNCIATIONS:

Augustine: AHW-gus-teen
Boethius: boh-EE-thee-uhs

Confessions

The *Confessions* is divided into thirteen books, the first nine of which recount Augustine's life through his conversion and the subsequent death of his mother, Monica. Books 10–13 are set in the present and are more philosophical in tone, discussing memory, time, and the opening verses of Genesis. The selections from Book 11 give a good sense of how the second half relates to the first, for in Augustine's mind there is a profound analogy between the many levels of experience, from the recitation of a psalm to the confession of a life's story to God's narration of the world from creation to the end of things. Seen in this perspective, the earlier episodes such as his days in grammar school, the stealing of pears, and the student days in Carthage are not only incidents in Augustine's life but also significant moments in the pattern of God's plan.

Recurring images such as the allusions to Virgil's *Aeneid* in Books 1–5 and the multiple models of conversion in Book 8 stress the patterned nature of the events of Augustine's life. Mirroring effects such as the discussion of infancy in Book 1 and the child's song in Book 8 undercut the linear flow of time and ask us to seek other means of organizing a life's story. Sin, for Augustine, is the endless repetition of the same action with no tangible result; redemption is the escape from this temporal cycle. The narrative of the *Confessions* flows because its narrator has seen his way through its events; it repeats itself because he wants us to experience what it means to be mired in the world. In its vision of life as a series of moments of conversion, in its sense of individual experience as the fulcrum through which history takes on meaning, and especially in its revolutionizing of the autobiographical form, the *Confessions* has exerted an enormous influence over Western writing, from spiritual autobiographies to confessional writing to first-person fictional narratives such as Daniel Defoe's *Robinson Crusoe* and James Joyce's *Portrait of the Artist as a Young Man.*

from CONFESSIONS[1]

from BOOK 1

[INVOCATION AND INFANCY]

You are great, Lord, and highly to be praised:[2] *great is your power and your wisdom is immeasurable.* Man, a little piece of your creation, desires to praise you, a human being *bearing his mortality with him,* carrying with him the witness of his sin and the witness that you *resist the proud.* Nevertheless, to praise you is the desire of man, a little piece of your creation. You stir man to take pleasure in praising you, because you have made us for yourself, and our heart is restless until it rests in you.

1. Translated by Henry Chadwick.
2. Psalm 48:1. Augustine weaves the opening of his autobiography out of a tissue of quotations from the biblical book of Psalms, hymns of praise to God traditionally attributed to King David. His text is dotted with Bible quotations (noted by italics), most often from the Gospels and the letters of Paul, in addition to Psalms. Specific sources will be noted when the biblical context is particularly important.

Grant me Lord to know and understand which comes first—to call upon you or to praise you, and whether knowing you precedes calling upon you. But who calls upon you when he does not know you? For an ignorant person might call upon someone else instead of the right one. But surely you may be called upon in prayer that you may be known. Yet *how shall they call upon him in whom they have not believed? and how shall they believe without a preacher? They will praise the Lord who seek for him.*

In seeking him they find him, and in finding they will praise him. Lord, I would seek you, calling upon you—and calling upon you is an act of believing in you. You have been preached to us. My faith, Lord, calls upon you. It is your gift to me. You breathed it into me by the humanity of your Son, by the ministry of your preacher.[3]

How shall I call upon my God, my God and Lord? Surely when I call on him, I am calling on him to come into me. But what place is there in me where my God can enter into me? *God made heaven and earth.* Where may he come to me? Lord my God, is there any room in me which can contain you? Can heaven and earth, which you have made and in which you have made me, contain you? Without you, whatever exists would not exist. Then can what exists contain you? I also have being. So why do I request you to come to me when, unless you were within me, I would have no being at all? I am not now possessed by Hades; yet even there are you: for *even if I were to go down to Hades, you would be present.* Accordingly, my God, I would have no being, I would not have any existence, unless you were in me. Or rather, I would have no being if I were not in you *of whom are all things, through whom are all things, in whom are all things.* Even so, Lord, even so. How can I call on you to come if I am already in you? Or where can you come from so as to be in me? Can I move outside heaven and earth so that my God may come to me from there? For God has said *I fill heaven and earth.*[4]

Do heaven and earth contain you because you have filled them? or do you fill them and overflow them because they do not contain you? Where do you put the overflow of yourself after heaven and earth are filled? Or have you, who contain all things, no need to be contained by anything because what you will you fill by containing it? We cannot think you are given coherence by vessels full of you, because even if they were to be broken, you would not be spilt. When you are *poured out* upon us, you are not wasted on the ground. You raise us upright. You are not scattered but reassemble us. In filling all things, you fill them all with the whole of yourself.

Is it that because all things cannot contain the whole of you, they contain part of you, and that all things contain the same part of you simultaneously? Or does each part contain a different part of you, the larger containing the greater parts, the lesser parts the smaller? Does that imply that there is some part of you which is greater, another part smaller? Or is the whole of you everywhere, yet without anything that contains you entire?[5]

Who then are you, my God? What, I ask, but God who is Lord? For *who is the Lord but the Lord,* or *who is God but our God?* Most high, utterly good, utterly powerful, most omnipotent, most merciful and most just, deeply hidden yet most intimately

3. By the Incarnation of Christ as well as by the ministry of Ambrose's teacher Bishop Ambrose, the powerful church leader and influential interpreter of the Bible.
4. Jeremiah 23:24. The series of questions raises philosophical and theological debates as matters of personal urgency, in particular what sort of being God is and what limits, if any, there are to his existence and his power. The questions presume a rational inquiry; the paradoxes prepare for a resolution based on faith.
5. The 3rd century C.E. Neoplatonic philosopher Plotinus had written a treatise on the omnipresence of being, part of his work the *Enneads.*

present, perfection of both beauty and strength, stable and incomprehensible, immutable and yet changing all things, never new, never old, making everything new and *leading* the proud *to be old without their knowledge;* always active, always in repose, gathering to yourself but not in need, supporting and filling and protecting, creating and nurturing and bringing to maturity, searching even though to you nothing is lacking: you love without burning, you are jealous in a way that is free of anxiety, you *repent* without the pain of regret, you are wrathful and remain tranquil. You will a change without any change in your design. You recover what you find, yet have never lost. Never in any need, you rejoice in your gains; you are never avaricious, yet you require interest. We pay you more than you require so as to make you our debtor, yet who has anything which does not belong to you? You pay off debts, though owing nothing to anyone; you cancel debts and incur no loss. But in these words what have I said, my God, my life, my holy sweetness? What has anyone achieved in words when he speaks about you?[6] Yet woe to those who are silent about you because, though loquacious with verbosity, they have nothing to say.[7]

Who will enable me to find rest in you? Who will grant me that you come to my heart and intoxicate it, so that I forget my evils and embrace my one and only good, yourself? What are you to me? Have mercy so that I may find words. What am I to you that you command me to love you, and that, if I fail to love you, you are angry with me and threaten me with vast miseries? If I do not love you, is that but a little misery? What a wretch I am! In your mercies, Lord God, tell me what you are to me. *Say to my soul, I am your salvation.* Speak to me so that I may hear. See the ears of my heart are before you, Lord. Open them and *say to my soul, I am your salvation.* After that utterance I will run and lay hold on you. *Do not hide your face from me.* Lest I die, let me die so that I may see it.[8]

The house of my soul is too small for you to come to it. May it be enlarged by you. It is in ruins: restore it. In your eyes it has offensive features. I admit it, I know it; but who will clean it up? Or to whom shall I cry other than you? *Cleanse me from my secret faults, Lord, and spare your servant from sins to which I am tempted by others. I believe and therefore I speak. Lord, you know.* Have I not openly accused myself of *my faults,* my God, and *you forgave me the iniquity of my heart.* I do not *contend with you in a court of law,* for you are the truth. I do not deceive myself *lest my iniquity lie to itself.* Therefore I do not contend with you like a litigant because, *if you take note of iniquities, Lord, who shall stand?*

Nevertheless allow me to speak before your mercy, though I am but dust and ashes. Allow me to speak: for I am addressing your mercy, not a man who would laugh at me. Perhaps even you deride me, but you will turn and have mercy on me. What, Lord, do I wish to say except that I do not know whence I came to be in this mortal life or, as I may call it, this living death?[9] I do not know where I came from.[1]

6. The long string of antitheses represents the closest words can come to expressing the essence of the Lord. As Plotinus wrote, "We say what he is not, not what he is; if we can say what is true, that is by mantic inspiration" (5.3.14). Augustine attempts to combine "mantic inspiration" with rational language.

7. For Augustine, the "loquacious" whose words cannot approach the mystery of divine revelation, were usually pagan philosophers who rejected the irrational aspects of Christianity or else the Manichees, who saw the universe as divided between a good and an evil entity.

8. The heavenly vision is life, yet none can see God's face and live (Exodus 33:20).

9. A common sentiment of pagan philosophy as in the 1st century B.C.E. Roman Epicurean Lucretius's *On the Nature of Things* (3.869).

1. Neoplatonic philosophy upheld the soul's preexistence and subsequent imprisonment in the body; Augustine never explicitly affirms or denies this doctrine.

But *the consolations of your mercies* upheld me, as I have heard from the parents of my flesh, him from whom and her in whom you formed me in time. For I do not remember. So I was welcomed by the consolations of human milk; but it was not my mother or my nurses who made any decision to fill their breasts, but you who through them gave me infant food, in accordance with your ordinance and the riches which are distributed deep in the natural order. You also granted me not to wish for more than you were giving, and to my nurses the desire to give me what you gave them. For by an impulse which you control their instinctive wish was to give me the milk which they had in abundance from you. For the good which came to me from them was a good for them; yet it was not from them but through them. Indeed all good things come from you, O God, and *from my God is all my salvation.* I became aware of this only later when you cried aloud to me through the gifts which you bestow both inwardly in mind and outwardly in body. For at that time I knew nothing more than how to suck and to be quietened by bodily delights, and to weep when I was physically uncomfortable.[2]

Afterwards I began to smile, first in my sleep, then when awake. That at least is what I was told, and I believed it since that is what we see other infants doing. I do not actually remember what I then did.

Little by little I began to be aware where I was and wanted to manifest my wishes to those who could fulfil them as I could not. For my desires were internal; adults were external to me and had no means of entering into my soul. So I threw my limbs about and uttered sounds, signs resembling my wishes, the small number of signs of which I was capable but such signs as lay in my power to use: for there was no real resemblance. When I did not get my way, either because I was not understood or lest it be harmful to me, I used to be indignant with my seniors for their disobedience, and with free people who were not slaves to my interests; and I would revenge myself upon them by weeping. That this is the way of infants I have learnt from those I have been able to watch. That is what I was like myself and, although they have not been aware of it, they have taught me more than my nurses with all their knowledge of how I behaved.

My infancy is long dead and I am alive.[3] But you, Lord, live and in you nothing dies. You are before the beginning of the ages, and prior to everything that can be said to be "before." You are God and Lord of all you have created. In you are the constant causes of inconstant things. All mutable things have in you their immutable origins. In you all irrational and temporal things have the everlasting causes of their life. Tell me, God, tell your suppliant, in mercy to your poor wretch, tell me whether there was some period of my life, now dead and gone, which preceded my infancy? Or is this period that which I spent in my mother's womb? On that matter also I have learnt something, and I myself have seen pregnant women. What was going on before that, my sweetness, my God? Was I anywhere, or any sort of person? I have no one able to tell me that—neither my father nor my mother nor the experience of others nor my own memory. But you may smile at me for putting these questions. Your command that I praise you and confess you may be limited to that which I know.

So *I acknowledge you, Lord of heaven and earth,* articulating my praise to you for my beginnings and my infancy which I do not recall. You have also given

2. Augustine searches for the first time in which God was present in his life but finds that even in infancy the baby is nourished through God.

3. Classical writers divided human life into distinct "ages," the first of which was *infantia,* which "died" when Augustine passed to the next age, *pueritia,* or boyhood.

mankind the capacity to understand oneself by analogy with others, and to believe much about oneself on the authority of weak women. Even at that time I had existence and life, and already at the last stage of my infant speechlessness I was searching out signs by which I made my thoughts known to others. Where can a living being such as an infant come from if not from you, God? Or can anyone become the cause of his own making? Or is there any channel through which being and life can be drawn into us other than what you make us, Lord? In you it is not one thing to be and another to live: the supreme degree of being and the supreme degree of life are one and the same thing.[4] You are being in a supreme degree and are immutable. In you the present day has no ending, and yet in you it has its end: *all these things have their being in you.* They would have no way of passing away unless you set a limit to them. Because *your years do not fail,* your years are one Today. How many of our days and days of our fathers have passed during your Today, and have derived from it the measure and condition of their existence? And others too will pass away and from the same source derive the condition of their existence. "But you are the same"; and all tomorrow and hereafter, and indeed all yesterday and further back, you will make a Today, you have made a Today.[5]

If anyone finds your simultaneity beyond his understanding, it is not for me to explain it. Let him be content to say *What is this?* So too let him rejoice and delight in finding you who are beyond discovery rather than fail to find you by supposing you to be discoverable.

Hear me, God. Alas for the sins of humanity! Man it is who says this, and you have pity on him, because you made him and did not make sin in him. Who reminds me of the sin of my infancy? for *none is pure from sin before you, not even an infant of one day upon the earth.* Who reminds me? Any tiny child now, for I see in that child what I do not remember in myself. What sin did I then have? Was it wrong that in tears I greedily opened my mouth wide to suck the breasts? If I were to do that now, gasping to eat food appropriate to my present age, I would be laughed at and very properly rebuked. At the time of my infancy I must have acted reprehensibly; but since I could not understand the person who admonished me, neither custom nor reason allowed me to be reprehended. As we grow up, we eliminate and set aside such ways. But I have never seen anyone knowingly setting aside what is good when purging something of faults.[6]

Yet, for an infant of that age, could it be reckoned good to use tears in trying to obtain what it would have been harmful to get, to be vehemently indignant at the refusals of free and older people and of parents or many other people of good sense who would not yield to my whims, and to attempt to strike them and to do as much injury as possible? There is never an obligation to be obedient to orders which it would be pernicious to obey. So the feebleness of infant limbs is innocent, not the infant's mind. I have personally watched and studied a jealous baby. He could not yet speak and, pale with jealousy and bitterness, glared at his brother sharing his mother's milk. Who is unaware of this fact of experience? Mothers and nurses claim to charm it away by their own private remedies. But it can hardly be innocence, when the source of milk is flowing richly and abundantly, not to endure a share going to one's blood-brother, who is in profound need, dependent for life exclusively on that one food.

4. As said by the philosopher Plotinus (3.6.6.15).

5. The relationship between human time ("our days") and eternity ("your Today") is discussed at length in Book 11.

6. Augustine views children as naturally sinful rather than innocent, their behavior moderated only as they learn through "custom" and "reason."

But people smilingly tolerate this behaviour, not because it is nothing or only a trivial matter, but because with coming of age it will pass away. You can prove this to be the case from the fact that the same behaviour cannot be borne without irritation when encountered in someone of more mature years.

You, Lord my God, are the giver of life and a body to a baby. As we see, you have endowed it with senses. You have co-ordinated the limbs. You have adorned it with a beautiful form, and for the coherence and preservation of the whole you have implanted all the instincts of a living being. You therefore command me to praise you for that and to *confess to you and to sing to your name, Most High*—God, you are omnipotent and good—even if that were all that you had made. No one else could do that except you, the one from whom every kind of being is derived. The supreme beauty, you give distinct form to all things and by your law impose order on everything. This period of my life, Lord, I do not remember having lived, but I have believed what others have told me and have assumed how I behaved from observing other infants. Despite the high probability of this assumption, I do not wish to reckon this as part of the life that I live in this world; for it is lost in the darkness of my forgetfulness, and is on the same level as the life I lived in my mother's womb. If *I was conceived in iniquity and in sins my mother nourished me in her womb,* I ask you, my God, I ask, Lord, where and when your servant was innocent? But of that time I say nothing more. I feel no sense of responsibility now for a time of which I recall not a single trace.[7]

[*Augustine describes his boyhood, including his introduction to the Church and the desire for baptism instilled in him by the fear of death. Monica, his mother, refuses to baptize him, fearing that it would be too difficult to wash away all the sins he was likely to commit in the future.*]

[GRAMMAR SCHOOL]

Even now I have not yet discovered the reasons why I hated Greek literature when I was being taught it as a small boy.[8] Latin I deeply loved, not at the stage of my primary teachers but at the secondary level taught by the teachers of literature called "grammarians." The initial elements, where one learns the three Rs of reading, writing, and arithmetic, I felt to be no less a burden and an infliction than the entire series of Greek classes. The root of this aversion must simply have been sin and the vanity of life, by which I was *mere flesh and wind going on its way and not returning.* Of course, those first elements of the language were better, because more fundamental. On that foundation I came to acquire the faculty which I had and still possess of being able to read whatever I find written, and to write myself whatever I wish. This was better than the poetry I was later forced to learn about the wanderings of some legendary fellow named Aeneas (forgetful of my own wanderings) and to weep over the death of a Dido who took her own life from love.[9] In reading this, O God my life, I myself was meanwhile dying by my alienation from you, and my miserable condition in that respect brought no tear to my eyes.

7. God's creation is defined in Genesis as essentially beautiful and good, and so each individual as part of that creation must consequently have been made beautiful and good. Nevertheless, it is impossible to discover a time when the individual was not already tainted by sin.

8. Although not fluent, Augustine could read Greek and was more proficient than he lets on here.

9. Although Augustine speaks about it disparagingly, Virgil's *Aeneid* was a formative influence on his writing, and he cites it frequently. The episode referred to here is the tragic love affair of Book 4. The opposition between the pointless wanderings of the pagan and the (eventually) fruitful wanderings of the convert Augustine is a fundamental one in *The Confessions.*

What is more pitiable than a wretch without pity for himself who weeps over the death of Dido dying for love of Aeneas, but not weeping over himself dying for his lack of love for you, my God, light of my heart, bread of the inner mouth of my soul, the power which begets life in my mind and in the innermost recesses of my thinking. I had no love for you and *committed fornication against you;* and in my fornications I heard all round me the cries *Well done, well done. For the friendship of this world is fornication against you,* and "Well done" is what they say to shame a man who does not go along with them. Over this I wept not a tear. I wept over Dido who "died in pursuing her ultimate end with a sword."[1] I abandoned you to pursue the lowest things of your creation. I was dust going to dust. Had I been forbidden to read this story, I would have been sad that I could not read what made me sad. Such madness is considered a higher and more fruitful literary education than being taught to read and write.

But now may my God cry out in my soul and may your truth tell me: "It is not so, it is not so. The best education you received was the primary." Obviously I much prefer to forget the wanderings of Aeneas and all that stuff than to write and read. It is true, veils hang at the entrances to the schools of literature; but they do not signify the prestige of élite teaching so much as the covering up of error.[2]

Let no critics shout against me (I am not afraid of them now) while I confess to you the longing of my soul, my God, and when I accept rebuke for my evil ways and *wish to love your good ways.* Let there be no abuse of me from people who sell or buy a literary education. If I put the question to them whether the poet's story is true that Aeneas once came to Carthage, the uneducated will reply that they do not know, while the educated will say it is false. But if I ask with what letters Aeneas' name is spelled, all who have learnt to read will reply correctly in accordance with the agreement and convention by which human beings have determined the value of these signs. Similarly, if I ask which would cause the greater inconvenience to someone's life, to forget how to read and write or to forget these fabulous poems, who does not see what answer he would give, unless he has totally lost his senses? So it was a sin in me as a boy when I gave pride of place in my affection to those empty fables rather than to more useful studies, or rather when I hated the one and loved the other. But to me it was a hateful chant to recite "one and one is two," and "two and two are four"; delightful was the vain spectacle of the wooden horse full of armed soldiers and the burning of Troy and the very ghost of Creusa.[3]

from *Book 2*

[The Pear-Tree]

During my sixteenth year there was an interruption in my studies. I was recalled from Madauros,[1] the nearby town where I had first lived away from home to learn literature and oratory. During that time funds were gathered in preparation for a more distant

1. *Aeneid* 6.457.
2. During the Roman Empire, it was customary to hang veils before an entrance in a number proportionate to the importance of whomever or whatever they guarded. In addition to the attack on the use of poetic fictions for educational purposes, Augustine is also drawing a distinction between the direct and unadorned language of the Bible and the complex and often allegorical imagery he saw in classical poetry, "veils" covering up the "error" of the beliefs propounded in it. In addition to the foundation of the curriculum of grammar school, Virgil's poetry was also considered a sacred text of the pagan revival current during the 4th century.
3. Episodes in the fall of Troy narrated in Book 2 of the *Aeneid:* the enormous wooden horse that smuggles the Greek warriors into the city in its belly, the sacking of the city that ensues, and the ghost of Aeneas's first wife, which begs him to flee the city.

1. An intellectual center about 15 miles from Thagaste.

absence at Carthage,[2] for which my father had more enthusiasm than cash, since he was a citizen of Thagaste with very modest resources.[3] To whom do I tell these things? Not to you, my God. But before you I declare this to my race, to the human race, though only a tiny part can light on this composition of mine. And why do I include this episode? It is that I and any of my readers may reflect on *the great depth* from which we have *to cry to you.* Nothing is nearer to your ears than *a confessing heart* and a life grounded in faith.[4] At that time everybody was full of praise for my father because he spent money on his son beyond the means of his estate, when that was necessary to finance an education entailing a long journey. Many citizens of far greater wealth did nothing of the kind for their children. But this same father did not care what character before you I was developing, or how chaste I was so long as I possessed a cultured tongue—though my culture really meant a desert uncultivated by you, God. You are the one true and good lord of your land, which is my heart.

In my sixteenth year idleness interposed because of my family's lack of funds. I was on holiday from all schooling and lived with my parents. The thorns of lust rose above my head, and there was no hand to root them out. Indeed, when at the bath-house my father saw that I was showing signs of virility and the stirrings of adolescence, he was overjoyed to suppose that he would now be having grand-children, and told my mother so. His delight was that of the intoxication which makes the world oblivious of you, its Creator, and to love your creation instead of you. He was drunk with the invisible wine of his perverse will directed downwards to inferior things. But in my mother's heart you had already begun your temple and the beginning of *your holy habitation.* My father was still a catechumen and had become that only recently. So she shook with a pious trepidation and a holy fear.[5] For, although I had not yet become a baptized believer,[6] she feared the twisted paths along which walk those who turn their backs and not their face towards you.

Wretch that I am, do I dare to say that you, my God, were silent when in reality I was travelling farther from you? Was it in this sense that you kept silence to me? Then whose words were they but yours which you were chanting in my ears through my mother, your faithful servant? But nothing of that went down into my heart to issue in action. Her concern (and in the secret of my conscience I recall the memory of her admonition delivered with vehement anxiety) was that I should not fall into fornication, and above all that I should not commit adultery with someone else's wife. These warnings seemed to me womanish advice which I would have blushed to take the least notice of. But they were your warnings and I did not realize it. I believed you were silent, and that it was only she who was speaking, when you were speaking to me through her. In her you were scorned by me, by me her son, *the son of your handmaid, your servant.* But I did not realize this and went on my way headlong with such blindness that among my peer group I was ashamed not to be equally guilty of shameful behaviour when I heard them boasting of their sexual exploits. Their pride was the more aggressive, the more debauched their acts were; they derived pleasure not merely from the lust of the act but also from the admiration it evoked. What is more

2. Capital of the Roman province of Numidia in northern Africa.
3. Augustine's father, Patricius, was respectable but poor by Roman standards, owning a modest estate with a few slaves to keep the household and work the land.
4. In Romans 10:9, Paul describes verbal confession as a key step in revelation.
5. Augustine portrays his parents here as embodying a strict opposition between flesh and spirit, earthly concerns and celestial ones. A catechumen is a convert to Christianity who is receiving training in doctrine and discipline before being baptized.
6. The sins of a pagan were more easily erased by conversion than those of a baptized Christian could be absolved.

worthy of censure than vice? Yet I went deeper into vice to avoid being despised, and when there was no act by admitting to which I could rival my depraved companions, I used to pretend I had done things I had not done at all, so that my innocence should not lead my companions to scorn my lack of courage, and lest my chastity be taken as a mark of inferiority.

Such were the companions with whom I made my way through the streets of Babylon.[7] With them I rolled in its dung as if rolling *in spices and precious ointments.* To tie me down the more tenaciously to Babylon's belly, the *invisible enemy trampled on me*[8] and seduced me because I was in the mood to be seduced. The mother of my flesh already had fled from *the centre of Babylon,* but still lingered in the outskirts of the city.[9] Although she had warned me to guard my virginity, she did not seriously pay heed to what her husband had told her about me, and which she felt to hold danger for the future: for she did not seek to restrain my sexual drive within the limit of the marriage bond, if it could not be cut back to the quick. The reason why she showed no such concern was that she was afraid that the hope she placed in me could be impeded by a wife. This was not the hope which my mother placed in you for the life to come, but the hope which my parents entertained for my career that I might do well out of the study of literature. Both of them, as I realized, were very ambitious for me: my father because he hardly gave a thought to you at all, and his ambitions for me were concerned with mere vanities; my mother because she thought it would do no harm and would be a help to set me on the way towards you, if I studied the traditional pattern of a literary education. That at least is my conjecture as I try to recall the characters of my parents.

The reins were relaxed to allow me to amuse myself. There was no strict discipline to keep me in check, which led to an unbridled dissoluteness in many different directions. In all of this there was a thick mist shutting me off from the brightness of your face, my God, and my iniquity as it were *burst out from my fatness.*

Theft receives certain punishment *by your law,* Lord, and by *the law written in the hearts of men* which not even iniquity itself destroys. For what thief can with equanimity endure being robbed by another thief? He cannot tolerate it even if he is rich and the other is destitute. I wanted to carry out an act of theft and did so, driven by no kind of need other than my inner lack of any sense of, or feeling for, justice. Wickedness filled me. I stole something which I had in plenty and of much better quality. My desire was to enjoy not what I sought by stealing but merely the excitement of thieving and the doing of what was wrong. There was a pear tree near our vineyard laden with fruit, though attractive in neither colour nor taste. To shake the fruit off the tree and carry off the pears, I and a gang of naughty adolescents set off late at night after (in our usual pestilential way) we had continued our game in the streets. We carried off a huge load of pears. But they were not for our feasts but merely to throw to the pigs. Even if we ate a few, nevertheless our pleasure lay in doing what was not allowed.[1]

7. In the Bible, Babylon (in southern Mesopotamia) was the proverbial city of pagan iniquity. Augustine uses it here to refer both literally to the North African streets he wandered with his companions and figuratively to his wandering through the earthly city of sin rather than toward the heavenly city of salvation.

8. Psalm 56:2. The "invisible enemy" is Satan.

9. Here, Babylon is primarily metaphorical. His mother lingers on the edges of the earthly city in order to maintain contact with her wayward son, and because she herself still retains earthly values such as ambitions for her son's career.

1. The pear tree demands comparison with the apple in Eden; here, however, the fruit is unripe and fit only for swine. Augustine likens himself both to the unripe fruit, awaiting the proper time to be plucked by God, and to the swine, a reflection of his current bestial behavior.

Such was my heart, O God, such was my heart. You had pity on it when it was at the bottom of the abyss.[2] Now let my heart tell you what it was seeking there in that I became evil for no reason. I had no motive for my wickedness except wickedness itself. It was foul, and I loved it. I loved the self-destruction, I loved my fall, not the object for which I had fallen but my fall itself. My depraved soul leaped down from your firmament to ruin. I was seeking not to gain anything by shameful means, but shame for its own sake.

There is beauty in lovely physical objects, as in gold and silver and all other such things. When the body touches such things, much significance attaches to the rapport of the object with the touch. Each of the other senses has its own appropriate mode of response to physical things. Temporal honour and the power of giving orders and of being in command have their own kind of dignity, though this is also the origin of the urge to self-assertion. Yet in the acquisition of all these sources of social status, one must not depart from you, Lord, nor deviate from your law. The life which we live in this world has its attractiveness because of a certain measure in its beauty and its harmony with all these inferior objects that are beautiful. Human friendship is also a nest of love and gentleness because of the unity it brings about between many souls. Yet sin is committed for the sake of all these things and others of this kind when, in consequence of an immoderate urge towards those things which are at the bottom end of the scale of good, we abandon the higher and supreme goods, that is you, Lord God, and *your truth and your law*.[3] These inferior goods have their delights, but not comparable to my God who has made them all. It is in him that the just person takes delight; he is the joy of those who are true of heart.

When a crime is under investigation to discover the motive for which it was done, the accusation is not usually believed except in cases where the appetite to obtain (or the fear of losing) one of those goods which we have called inferior appears a plausible possibility. They are beautiful and attractive even if, in comparison with the higher goods which give true happiness, they are mean and base. A man committed murder. Why? Because he loved another's wife or his property; or he wanted to acquire money to live on by plundering his goods; or he was afraid of losing his own property by the action of his victim; or he had suffered injury and burned with desire for revenge. No one would commit murder without a motive, merely because he took pleasure in killing. Who would believe that? It was said of one brutal and cruel man that he was evil and savage without reason.[4] Yet the preceding passage gave the motive: "lest disuse might make his hand or mind slow to react." Why did he wish for that? Why so? His objective was to capture the city by violent crimes to obtain honours, government, and wealth; to live without fear of the laws and without the difficulty of attaining his ambitions because of the poverty of his family estate and his known criminal record. No, not even Catiline himself loved his crimes; something else motivated him to commit them.

Wretch that I was, what did I love in you, my act of theft, that crime which I did at night in the sixteenth year of my life? There was nothing beautiful about you, my thieving. Indeed do you exist at all for me to be addressing you?

2. Comparing his actions with the apparently incomprehensible rebellion of the angel Lucifer. In addition to its biblical echoes, this episode recalls the Roman historian Sallust's depiction of the famous conspirator Catiline (c. 108–62 B.C.E.), who attempted to overthrow the republic during the consulship of Cicero.

3. According to this argument, all things of the world are good, and all desires derive from an impulse toward the good, but there is a gradation of this good; sin occurs when the lower aspects of the creation are desired for their own qualities rather than for what of the greater good they may contain.

4. Sallust, *The Catiline War,* chapter 16.

The fruit which we stole was beautiful because it was your creation, most beautiful of all Beings, maker of all things, the good God, God the highest good and my true good. The fruit was beautiful, but was not that which my miserable soul coveted. I had a quantity of better pears. But those I picked solely with the motive of stealing. I threw away what I had picked. My feasting was only on the wickedness which I took pleasure in enjoying. If any of those pears entered my mouth, my criminality was the piquant sauce. And now, Lord my God, I inquire what was the nature of my pleasure in the theft. The act has nothing lovely about it, none of the loveliness found in equity and prudence, or in the human mind whether in the memory or in the senses or in physical vitality. Nor was it beautiful in the way the stars are, noble in their courses, or earth and sea full of newborn creatures which, as they are born, take the place of those which die; not even in the way that specious vices have a flawed reflection of beauty.

Pride imitates what is lofty; but you alone are God most high above all things. What does ambition seek but honour and glory? Yet you alone are worthy of honour and are glorious for eternity. The cruelty of powerful people aims to arouse fear. Who is to be feared but God alone? What can be seized or stolen from his power? When or where or how or by whom? Soft endearments are intended to arouse love. But there are no caresses tenderer than your charity, and no object of love is more healthy than your truth, beautiful and luminous beyond all things. Curiosity appears to be a zeal for knowledge; yet you supremely know all. Ignorance and stupidity are given the names of simplicity and innocence; but there is no greater simplicity than in you. And what greater innocence than yours, whereas to evil men their own works are damaging? Idleness appears as desire for a quiet life; yet can rest be assured apart from the Lord? Luxury wants to be called abundance and satiety; but you are fullness and the inexhaustible treasure of incorruptible pleasure. Prodigality presents itself under the shadow of generosity; but you are the rich bestower of all good things. Avarice wishes to have large possessions; you possess everything. Envy contends about excellence; but what is more excellent than you? Anger seeks revenge; who avenges with greater justice than you? Fear quails before sudden and unexpected events attacking things which are loved, and takes precautions for their safety; to you is anything unexpected or sudden? Or who can take away from you what you love? There is no reliable security except with you. Regret wastes away for the loss of things which cupidity delighted in. Its wish would be that nothing be taken away, just as nothing can be taken from you

So the soul fornicates when it is turned away from you and seeks outside you the pure and clear intentions which are not to be found except by returning to you. In their perverted way all humanity imitates you.[5] Yet they put themselves at a distance from you and exalt themselves against you. But even by thus imitating you they acknowledge that you are the creator of all nature and so concede that there is no place where one can entirely escape from you. Therefore in that act of theft what was the object of my love, and in what way did I viciously and perversely imitate my Lord? Was my pleasure to break your law, but by deceit since I had not the power to do that by force? Was I acting like a prisoner with restricted liberty who does without punishment what is not permitted, thereby making an assertion of possessing a dim resemblance to omnipotence? Here is a runaway slave fleeing his master and *pursuing a shadow*. What rottenness! What a monstrous life and what an abyss of death! Was it possible to take pleasure in what was illicit for no reason other than that it was not allowed?

5. In this definition, all sin is the perverse—*per* ("from") + *vertere* ("to turn")—imitation of the divine.

from *Book 3*

[STUDENT AT CARTHAGE]

I came to Carthage and all around me hissed a cauldron of illicit loves. As yet I had never been in love and I longed to love; and from a subconscious poverty of mind I hated the thought of being less inwardly destitute. I sought an object for my love; I was in love with love, and I hated safety and *a path free of snares.* My hunger was internal, deprived of inward food, that is of you yourself, my God. But that was not the kind of hunger I felt. I was without any desire for incorruptible nourishment, not because I was replete with it, but the emptier I was, the more unappetizing such food became. So my soul was in rotten health. In an ulcerous condition it thrust itself to outward things, miserably avid to be scratched by contact with the world of the senses. Yet physical things had no soul. Love lay outside their range. To me it was sweet to love and to be loved, the more so if I could also enjoy the body of the beloved. I therefore polluted the spring water of friendship with the filth of concupiscence. I muddied its clear stream by the hell of lust, and yet, though foul and immoral, in my excessive vanity, I used to carry on in the manner of an elegant man about town. I rushed headlong into love, by which I was longing to be captured. *My God, my mercy* in your goodness you mixed in much vinegar with that sweetness. My love was returned and in secret. I attained the joy that enchains. I was glad to be in bondage, tied with troublesome chains, with the result that I was flogged with the red-hot iron rods of jealousy, suspicion, fear, anger, and contention.[1]

I was captivated by theatrical shows. They were full of representations of my own miseries and fuelled my fire. Why is it that a person should wish to experience suffering by watching grievous and tragic events which he himself would not wish to endure? Nevertheless he wants to suffer the pain given by being a spectator of these sufferings, and the pain itself is his pleasure. What is this but amazing folly? For the more anyone is moved by these scenes, the less free he is from similar passions. Only, when he himself suffers, it is called misery; when he feels compassion for others, it is called mercy. But what quality of mercy is it in fictitious and theatrical inventions? A member of the audience is not excited to offer help, but invited only to grieve. The greater his pain, the greater his approval of the actor in these representations. If the human calamities, whether in ancient histories or fictitious myths, are so presented that the theatregoer is not caused pain, he walks out of the theatre disgusted and highly critical. But if he feels pain, he stays riveted in his seat enjoying himself.[2]

Tears and agonies, therefore, are objects of love. Certainly everyone wishes to enjoy himself. Is it that while no one wants to be miserable, yet it is agreeable to feel merciful? Mercy cannot exist apart from suffering. Is that the sole reason why agonies are an object of love? This feeling flows from the stream of friendship; but where does it go? Where does it flow to? Why does it run down into the torrent of boiling pitch, the monstrous heats of black desires into which it is transformed? From a heavenly serenity it is altered by its own consent into something twisted and distorted. Does this mean mercy is to be rejected? Not in the least. At times, therefore, sufferings can be proper objects of love. But, my soul, be on your guard against uncleanness, under the protection of my God, *the God of our fathers, to be praised and*

1. Criminals were beaten with red-hot rods to obtain evidence.

2. This critique of the theory of tragic pity and fear leading to catharsis takes up a debate addressed by both Plato and Aristotle.

exalted above all for all ages; be on your guard against uncleanness. Even today I am not unmoved to pity. But at that time at the theatres I shared the joy of lovers when they wickedly found delight in each other, even though their actions in the spectacle on the stage were imaginary; when, moreover, they lost each other, I shared their sadness by a feeling of compassion. Nevertheless, in both there was pleasure. Today I have more pity for a person who rejoices in wickedness than for a person who has the feeling of having suffered hard knocks by being deprived of a pernicious pleasure or having lost a source of miserable felicity. This is surely a more authentic compassion; for the sorrow contains no element of pleasure.

Even if we approve of a person who, from a sense of duty in charity, is sorry for a wretch, yet he who manifests fraternal compassion would prefer that there be no cause for sorrow. It is only if there could be a malicious good will (which is impossible) that someone who truly and sincerely felt compassion would wish wretches to exist so as to be objects of compassion. Therefore some kind of suffering is commendable, but none is lovable. You, Lord God, lover of souls, show a compassion far purer and freer of mixed motives than ours; for no suffering injures you. *And who is sufficient for these things?*

But at that time, poor thing that I was, I loved to suffer and sought out occasions for such suffering. So when an actor on stage gave a fictional imitation of someone else's misfortunes, I was the more pleased; and the more vehement the attraction for me, the more the actor compelled my tears to flow. There can be no surprise that an unhappy sheep wandering from your flock and impatient of your protection was infected by a disgusting sore.[3] Hence came my love for sufferings, but not of a kind that pierced me very deeply; for my longing was not to experience myself miseries such as I saw on stage. I wanted only to hear stories and imaginary legends of sufferings which, as it were, scratched me on the surface. Yet like the scratches of fingernails, they produced inflamed spots, pus, and repulsive sores. That was my kind of life, Surely, my God, it was no real life at all?

Your mercy faithfully hovered over me from afar. In what iniquities was I wasting myself! I pursued a sacrilegious quest for knowledge, which led me, a deserter from you, down to faithless depths and the fraudulent service of devils. The sacrifices I offered them were my evil acts. And in all this I experienced your chastisement. During the celebration of your solemn rites within the walls of your Church, I even dared to lust after a girl and to start an affair that would procure the fruit of death.[4] So you beat me with heavy punishments, but not the equivalent of my guilt; *O my God, my great mercy, my refuge* from the terrible dangers in which I was wandering. My stiff neck took me further and further away from you. I loved my own ways, not yours. The liberty I loved was merely that of a runaway.[5]

My studies which were deemed respectable had the objective of leading me to distinction as an advocate in the lawcourts, where one's reputation is high in proportion to one's success in deceiving people. The blindness of humanity is so great that people are actually proud of their blindness. I was already top of the class in the rhetor's school;[6] and was pleased with myself for my success and was inflated with

3. This echoes Virgil's *Eclogue* 3.3; see also Luke 15:4ff. The parable of the lost sheep was a fundamental image of Christian conversion. The concluding detail of the "disgusting sore" is Augustine's own embellishment, making the state of being lost not only natural but an excessive suffering for its straying.

4. The "fruit of death" is sin (Romans 7:5). For Augustine, there could be no more egregiously misplaced desire than to have sex in a church.

5. Augustine again likens himself to a runaway slave of the Lord. To run away from one's master was a grave offense in antiquity. Few individuals were powerful enough to shelter a runaway slave, but the church could provide temporary asylum under certain circumstances.

6. The school run by the teacher of rhetoric, or the art of public speaking.

conceit. Yet I was far quieter than the other students (as you know, Lord), and had nothing whatever to do with the vandalism which used to be carried out by the Wreckers. This sinister and diabolical self-designation was a kind of mark of their urbane sophistication. I lived among them shamelessly ashamed of not being one of the gang. I kept company with them and sometimes delighted in their friendship, though I always held their actions in abhorrence. The Wreckers used wantonly to persecute shy and unknown freshmen. Their aim was to persecute them by mockery and so to feed their own malevolent amusement. Nothing more resembles the behaviour of devils than their manner of carrying on. So no truer name could be given them than the Wreckers. Clearly they are themselves wrecked first of all and perverted by evil spirits, who are mocking them and seducing them in the very acts by which they love to mock and deceive others.

This was the society in which at a vulnerable age I was to study the textbooks on eloquence. I wanted to distinguish myself as an orator for a damnable and conceited purpose, namely delight in human vanity. Following the usual curriculum I had already come across a book by a certain Cicero, whose language (but not his heart) almost everyone admires. That book of his contains an exhortation to study philosophy and is entitled *Hortensius.*[7] The book changed my feelings. It altered my prayers, Lord, to be towards you yourself. It gave me different values and priorities. Suddenly every vain hope became empty to me, and I longed for the immortality of wisdom with an incredible ardour in my heart. I began to rise up to return to you. For I did not read the book for a sharpening of my style, which was what I was buying with my mother's financial support now that I was 18 years old and my father had been dead for two years.[8] I was impressed not by the book's refining effect on my style and literary expression but by the content.

My God, how I burned, how I burned with longing to leave earthly things and fly back to you. I did not know what you were doing with me. For *with you is wisdom.* "Love of wisdom" is the meaning of the Greek word *philosophia.*[9] This book kindled my love for it. There are some people who use philosophy to lead people astray. They lend colour to their errors and paint them over by using a great and acceptable and honourable name. Almost all those who in the author's times and earlier behaved in this way are noted in that book and refuted. That text is a clear demonstration of the salutary admonition given by your Spirit through your good and devoted servant (Paul): "See that none deceives you by philosophy and vain seduction following human tradition; following the elements of this world and not following Christ; in him dwells all the fullness of divinity in bodily form."[1] At that time, as you know, light of my heart, I did not yet know these words of the apostle. Nevertheless, the one thing that delighted me in Cicero's exhortation was the advice "not to study one particular sect but to love and seek and pursue and hold fast and strongly embrace wisdom itself, wherever found."[2] One thing alone put a brake on my intense enthusiasm—that the name of Christ was not contained in the book. This name, by your mercy, Lord, this name of my Saviour your Son, my infant heart had piously drunk in with my mother's milk,

7. Marcus Tullius Cicero (106–43 B.C.E.) was Rome's greatest orator, an important political figure of the late republic, and an extremely influential writer of rhetoric and philosophy. Composed near the end of Cicero's life, the *Hortensius* survives where it has been quoted by later writers such as Augustine. It argued that philosophy fulfilled a social purpose and that it could demonstrate the way to achieve happiness.

8. This is the first reference to the death of Patricius.

9. A sentence drawn from Cicero's *Hortensius.*

1. Colossians 2:8–9. The "good and devoted servant" is the apostle Paul.

2. Another sentence from the *Hortensius.*

and at a deep level I retained the memory. Any book which lacked this name, however well written or polished or true, could not entirely grip me.

I therefore decided to give attention to the holy scriptures and to find out what they were like. And this is what met me: something neither open to the proud nor laid bare to mere children; a text lowly to the beginner but, on further reading, of mountainous difficulty and enveloped in mysteries. I was not in any state to be able to enter into that, or to bow my head to climb its steps.[3] What I am now saying did not then enter my mind when I gave my attention to the scripture. It seemed to me unworthy in comparison with the dignity of Cicero. My inflated conceit shunned the Bible's restraint, and my gaze never penetrated to its inwardness. Yet the Bible was composed in such a way that as beginners mature, its meaning grows with them. I disdained to be a little beginner. Puffed up with pride, I considered myself a mature adult.

That explains why I fell in with men proud of their slick talk, very earthly-minded and loquacious. In their mouths were the devil's traps and a birdlime compounded of a mixture of the syllables of your name, and that of the Lord Jesus Christ, and that of the Paraclete, the Comforter, the Holy Spirit.[4] These names were never absent from their lips; but it was no more than sound and noise with their tongue. Otherwise their heart was empty of truth. They used to say "Truth, truth," and they had a lot to tell me about it; but there was never any truth in them. They uttered false statements not only about you who really are the Truth, but also about the elements of the world, your creation. On that subject the philosophers have said things which are true, but even them I would think to be no final authority for love of you, my supremely good Father, beauty of all things beautiful. Truth, truth: how in my inmost being the very marrow of my mind sighed for you! Those people used to sound off about you to me frequently and repeatedly with mere assertions and with the support of many huge tomes.[5] To meet my hunger, instead of you they brought me a diet of the sun and moon, your beautiful works—but they are your works, not you yourself, nor indeed the first of your works. For priority goes to your spiritual creation rather than the physical order, however heavenly and full of light.[6] But for myself, my hunger and thirst were not even for the spiritual creation but for you yourself, the truth *in whom there is no changing nor shadow caused by any revolving.* The dishes they placed before me contained splendid hallucinations. Indeed one would do better to love this visible sun, which at least is truly evident to the eyes, than those false mythologies which use the eyes to deceive the mind. Nevertheless, because I took them to be you, I ate—not indeed with much of an appetite, for the taste in my mouth was not that of yourself.

3. The image of humility recalls the words of the Arcadian King Evander to Aeneas when inviting the latter into his humble abode (*Aeneid,* page 685).

4. These are the Manichees, members of a religion founded in Persia in the 3rd century C.E. by Mani. The 4th century marked its height in the West, but it was pretty much eradicated by the next century, following vigorous attack from the Christian church (including Augustine), which considered it a heresy of Christianity, and by the Roman state, which considered it a threat to its authority. Aiming to be a universal religion, Manicheeism was Gnostic at its core, teaching that existence was radically divided between Spirit and Matter, Good and Evil, and Light and Darkness; that life in the world is unbearably evil; and that the righteous soul must transcend the body and the material world to discover its true soul and the nature of God. The Manichees denied the humanity of Christ, believing only in his divine nature, and held that the third aspect of the Trinity, the Paraclete, or Holy Spirit, was a manifestation of Mani.

5. In contrast to the simply bound liturgical books of most of the mainstream Christian churches, those of the Manichees were beautifully bound and decorated.

6. Augustine maintained that Genesis 1:1 describes God's creation of a spiritual "heaven" and of unformed matter called "earth," which was given its shape in the second account of creation in Genesis. (See Book 12 of the *Confessions* as well his treatise *On Genesis Against the Manichees.*)

You were not those empty fictions, and I derived no nourishment from them but was left more exhausted than before.

Food pictured in dreams is extremely like food received in the waking state; yet sleepers receive no nourishment, they are simply sleeping. But those fantasies had not the least resemblance to you as you have now told me, because they were physical images, fictional bodily shapes. But more certain objects of knowledge are the actually existing bodies which we see with our physical sight, whether they are celestial or earthly. We see them just as beasts and birds do, and they are more certain than the images we form of them. And yet again the pictures of these realities which our imagination forms are more reliable than the mythological pictures of vast and unlimited entities whose being, by an extension of our image-making of real objects, we may postulate, but which do not exist at all.[7] Such were the empty phantoms with which I was fed or rather was not fed.

But you, my love, for whom I faint *that I may receive strength,* you are not the bodies which we see, though they be up in heaven, nor even any object up there lying beyond our sight. For you have made these bodies, and you do not even hold them to be among the greatest of your creatures. How far removed you are from those fantasies of mine, fantasies of physical entities which have no existence! We have more reliable knowledge in our images of bodies which really exist, and the bodies are more certain than the images. But you are no body. Nor are you soul, which is the life of bodies; for the life of bodies is superior to bodies themselves, and a more certain object of knowledge. But you are the life of souls, the life of lives. You live in dependence only on yourself, and you never change, life of my soul.

At that time where were you in relation to me? Far distant. Indeed I wandered far away, separated from you, not even granted to share in the husks of the pigs, whom I was feeding with husks.[8] How superior are the fables of the masters of literature and poets to these deceptive traps! For verses, poems, and "the flight of Medea" are certainly more useful than the Five Elements which take on different colours, each in accordance with one of the Five Caverns of Darkness—things which have no reality whatever and kill anyone who believes they have.[9] Verses and poetry I can transform into real nourishment. "Medea flying through the air" I might recite, but would not assert to be fact. Even if I heard someone reciting the passage, I would not believe it. Yet the other myths I did believe. Wretched man that I was, by what steps was I brought down to the depths of hell, there to toil and sweat from lack of truth! For I sought for you, my God (I confess to you who took pity on me even when I did not yet confess). In seeking for you I followed not the intelligence of the mind, by which you willed that I should surpass the beasts, but the mind of the flesh. But you were more inward than my most inward part and higher than the highest element within me.

I had stumbled on that bold-faced woman, lacking in prudence, who in Solomon's allegory sits on a chair outside her door and says "Enjoy a meal of secret

7. Because dreams seem so real, Augustine regards them with suspicion. Nevertheless, they can still be of use in advising people or leading them to convert. Here, their "image-making" is preferable to the "mythological pictures" of the Manichean cosmology.

8. The image of the husks fed to pigs recalls both the episode of the pear tree and the parable of the Prodigal Son, who at his furthest from his father finds himself feeding on husks with the pigs (Luke 15:16).

9. Just as dreams are deceptive but may be useful, so poetic fables have the potential of being "transform[ed] into real nourishment." The magical flight of Medea from Jason after she has murdered their two children in vengeance for his betrayal was probably a standard subject for rhetorical exercises. The Five Elements are part of Manichean doctrine on the generation of animals.

bread and drink sweet stolen water."[1] She seduced me; for she found me living outside myself, seeing only with the eye of the flesh, and chewing over in myself such food as I had devoured by means of that eye.[2]

[*In Book 4, Augustine recounts the life of "vain desires" he led in Carthage, including the mistress who eventually bore him a son, Adeodatus; his consultation of astrologers; and the conversion of his friend, Nebridius, who was baptized without his knowledge while thought to be dying of a fever. He writes a first book, now lost,* On the Beautiful and the Fitting, *and encounters Aristotle's treatise* Ten Categories *but cannot find God within its classifications.*]

from *Book 5*

[*The Manichean bishop Faustus comes to Carthage, an encounter Augustine claims to have been awaiting during his nine years under the sway of the Manichees. He discovers that Faustus, while a smooth talker, is neither well educated in the liberal arts nor able to answer any of his questions. Augustine becomes disillusioned with the Manichean religion, one motivation for his decision to move to Rome.*]

[Arrival in Rome]

You were at work in persuading me to go to Rome and to do my teaching there rather than at Carthage. The consideration which persuaded me I will not omit to confess to you because in this also your profoundly mysterious providence and your mercy very present to us are proper matters for reflection and proclamation. My motive in going to Rome was not that the friends who urged it on me promised higher fees and a greater position of dignity, though at that time these considerations had an influence on my mind. The principal and almost sole reason was that I had heard how at Rome the young men went quietly about their studies and were kept in order by a stricter imposition of discipline. They did not rush all at once and in a mob into the class of a teacher with whom they were not enrolled, nor were pupils admitted at all unless the teacher gave them leave. By contrast at Carthage the licence of the students is foul and uncontrolled. They impudently break in and with almost mad behaviour disrupt the order which each teacher has established for his pupils' benefit. They commit many acts of vandalism with an astonishing mindlessness, which would be punished under the law were it not that custom protects them. Thereby their wretched self-delusion is shown up. They act as if they were allowed to do what would never be permitted by your eternal law. They think they are free to act with impunity when by the very blindness of their behaviour they are being punished, and inflict on themselves incomparably worse damage than on others. When I was a student, I refused to have anything to do with these customs; as a professor I was forced to tolerate them in outsiders who were not my own pupils. So I decided to go where all informed people declared that such troubles did not occur. But it was you, *my hope and my portion in the land of the living* who wished me to change my earthly home for *the salvation of my soul.* You applied the pricks which made me tear myself away from Carthage, and you put before me the attractions of Rome to draw me there, using people who love a

1. Proverbs 9:17. King Solomon was considered to have been the author of Proverbs as well as of the Song of Songs.

2. Just as he distinguishes between the "intelligence of the mind," directed upward, and the "mind of the flesh," directed downward, so too Augustine distinguishes between an eye of the flesh, which seeks only physical nourishment and satisfaction, and an eye able to see what is spiritual.

life of death, committing insane actions in this world, promising vain rewards in the next. To correct my *steps* you secretly made use of their and my perversity. For those who disturbed my serenity were blinded with a disgraceful frenzy. Those who invited me to go elsewhere had a taste only for this earth. I myself, while I hated a true misery here, pursued a false felicity there.

But you knew, God, why I left Carthage and went to Rome, and of that you gave no hint either to me or to my mother, who was fearfully upset at my going and followed me down to the sea. But as she vehemently held on to me calling me back or saying she would come with me, I deceived her. I pretended I had a friend I did not want to leave until the wind was right for him to sail. I lied to my mother—to such a mother—and I gave her the slip.[1] Even this you forgave me, mercifully saving me from the waters of the sea, when I was full of abominable filth, so as to bring me to the water of your grace.[2] This water was to wash me clean, and to dry the rivers flowing from my mother's eyes which daily before you irrigated the soil beneath her face.

Nevertheless since she refused to return home without me, with difficulty I persuaded her to stay that night in a place close to our ship, the memorial shrine to blessed Cyprian.[3] But that night I secretly set out; she did not come, but remained praying and weeping. By her floods of tears what was she begging of you, my God, but that you would not allow me to sail? Yet in your deep counsel you heard the central point of her longing, though not granting her what she then asked, namely that you would make me what she continually prayed for. The wind blew and filled our sails and the shore was lost to our sight. There, when morning came, she was crazed with grief, and with recriminations and groans she filled your ears. But you paid no heed to her cries. You were using my ambitious desires as a means towards putting an end to those desires, and the longing she felt for her own flesh and blood was justly chastised by the whip of sorrows.[4] As mothers do, she loved to have me with her, but much more than most mothers; and she did not understand that you were to use my absence as a means of bringing her joy. She did not know that. So she wept and lamented, and these agonies proved that there survived in her the remnants of Eve, seeking with groaning for the child she had brought forth in sorrow.[5] And yet after accusing me of deception and cruelty, she turned again to pray for me and to go back to her usual home. Meanwhile I came to Rome.

At Rome my arrival was marked by the scourge of physical sickness, and I was on the way to the underworld, bearing all the evils I had committed against you, against myself, and against others—sins both numerous and serious, in addition to the chain of original sin by which *in Adam we die.* You had not yet forgiven me in Christ for any of them, nor had he by his cross delivered me from the hostile disposition towards you which I had contracted by my sins. How could he deliver me from them if his cross was, as I had believed, a phantom?[6] Insofar as the death of his flesh was in my opinion

1. The separation of Augustine and his mother, Monica, closely mirrors Aeneas's nocturnal abandonment of his lover Dido in Carthage to follow his destiny in Rome, the city he is to found (see the *Aeneid,* page 728).
2. The contrast between the supposed dangers of the sea and the "grace" of the baptismal waters recalls the apostle Paul's lack of fear in the storm at sea during his voyage to Rome (Acts 27), further evoked in the subsequent paragraph.
3. The Carthaginian theologian and bishop Cyprian (c. 200–258) led the Christianization of Africa during a period of Roman persecution. Upon his execution, he became the first bishop-martyr of Africa.
4. Monica is duly chastised for her undue attachment to the son of her flesh rather than to the one of the spirit, as she will eventually be (Book 9, chapter 10).
5. Genesis 3:16. The Lord's curse on Eve for her disobedience was to suffer in bearing children. Monica's sufferings here refer to both the physical ones of her son's birth and the spiritual ones attending his belabored spiritual rebirth.
6. As they did not acknowledge the humanity of Christ, the Manichees interpreted his crucifixion as a symbol of general suffering rather than a historical event.

unreal, the death of my soul was real. And insofar as the death of his flesh was authentic, to that extent the life of my soul, which disbelieved that, was inauthentic. The fevers became worse, and I was on my way out and dying. If at that time I had died, where was I going but into the fire and to the torments which, by your true order of justice, my deeds deserved? My mother did not know I was ill, but she was praying for me, though not beside me. But you are present everywhere. Where she was, you heard her, and where I was, you had mercy on me so that I recovered the health of my body. I still remained sick in my sacrilegious heart, for though in such great danger, I had no desire for your baptism. I did better as a boy when I begged for it from my devout mother, as I have recalled and confessed.[7] But I had grown in shame and in my folly used to laugh at the counsels of your medicine. Yet you did not allow me to die in this sad condition of both body and soul. If my mother's heart had suffered that wound, she would never have recovered. I cannot speak enough of the love she had for me. She suffered greater pains in my spiritual pregnancy than when she bore me in the flesh.

I do not see how she could have recovered if my death in those circumstances had like a scourge struck across the compassion of her love. Where would have been all her prayers, so frequent as to be ceaseless? Nowhere except with you. But, God of mercies, would you despise *the contrite and humble heart* of a chaste and sober widow, liberal in almsgiving, obedient and helpful in serving your saints, letting no day pass without making an oblation at your altar, twice a day at morning and at evening coming to your Church with unfailing regularity, taking no part in vain gossip and old wives' chatter, but wanting to hear you in your words and to speak to you in her prayers? Could you, who gave her this character, despise and repel from your assistance tears by which she sought of you, not gold and silver nor any inconstant or transitory benefit, but the salvation of her son's soul? No indeed, Lord, of course you were there and were hearing her petition, and were following through the order of events that you had predestinated. You could not have misled her in those visions and your responses, both those which I have already mentioned, and those which I have omitted. At her faithful breast she held on to them, and in her unceasing prayer she as it were presented to you your bond of promises. For *your mercy is for ever,* and you deign to make yourself a debtor obliged by your promises to those to whom you forgive all debts.

[*Augustine's next intellectual encounter is with the Academic philosophers, or Skeptics, most notably Plato. He complains about the Roman students' skill in avoiding paying for their lessons and soon obtains a government appointment to teach rhetoric in Milan, the residence of the emperor at the time and an important Christian center dominated by Bishop Ambrose. Augustine is impressed with Ambrose's power as a speaker but claims to have heard his meaning only in retrospect. His mother braves a hazardous sea journey to join him, and Augustine begins to prefer the Catholic Christian Church to other religions, deciding that its simple style and rhetoric indicate great profundity and humility rather than ignorance. He encounters a drunken beggar on the street who appears to enjoy life more than Augustine himself with all his ambitions. He introduces the character of his close childhood friend, Alypius, who is addicted to the circus games and who has followed Augustine to Italy. His mother desires him to marry, and in the process his longtime mistress is torn from him. He accepts most of*

7. When very ill as a boy, Augustine had asked to be baptized, but his mother had refused, not believing him ready for such an irrevocable step (Book 1, chapter 11).

Christian doctrine but is held back by his incapacity to account for the origin of evil. He encounters the books of Neoplatonism, which urge him to inner contemplation and "immaterial truth" but which don't accept the dual nature of Christ. He returns to the Epistles of Paul and finds that they combine the truths of Neoplatonism with a belief in the passion of Christ and divine grace. He is intellectually poised for conversion but unwilling to take the final leap of faith and renounce the pleasures of the flesh.]

from Book 8

[PONTICIANUS]

Lord, my helper and redeemer, I will now tell the story, and confess to your name, of the way in which you delivered me from the chain of sexual desire, by which I was tightly bound, and from the slavery of worldly affairs. I went about my usual routine in a state of mental anxiety. Every day I sighed after you. I used to frequent your Church whenever I had time off from the affairs under whose weight I was groaning. With me was Alypius, unemployed in his work as a lawyer after a third period as assessor[1] and waiting for someone else to whom he could again sell his advice, just as I was selling the art of public speaking—if oratory is something that can be conveyed by teaching. Nebridius, however, had yielded to the pressure of his friendship with us and was assistant teacher to Verecundus, a close friend to all of us, a citizen of Milan and instructor in literature there. Verecundus was in urgent need of reliable assistance, and by right of friendship claimed from our group the supply he badly wanted. So Nebridius was not attracted to this work by desire for the profits; for had he so wished, he could have made more money on his own as teacher of literature. He was a most gentle and kind friend, and recognizing the duty of generosity would not scorn our request. He performed his task most prudently, and took care not to become known to important people, as this world reckons them, so avoiding anything likely to distract his mind. He wanted to keep his mind free and to devote as many hours as possible to the pursuit of wisdom by investigating some problem or listening to conversation.

One day when Nebridius was absent for a reason I cannot recall, Alypius and I received a surprise visit at home from a man named Ponticianus, a compatriot in that he was an African, holding high office at the court. He wanted something or other from us. We sat down together to converse. By chance he noticed a book on top of a gaming table which lay before us. He picked it up, opened it, and discovered, much to his astonishment, that it was the apostle Paul.[2] He had expected it to be one of the books used for the profession which was wearing me out. But then he smiled and looked at me in a spirit of congratulation. He was amazed that he had suddenly discovered this book and this book alone open before my eyes. He was a Christian and a baptized believer. He often prostrated himself before you, our God, at the Church with frequent and long times of prayer. When I had indicated to him that those scriptures were the subject of deep study for me, a conversation began in which he told the story of Antony the Egyptian monk, a name held in high honour among your servants, though up to that moment Alypius and I had never heard of him.[3] When he discovered

1. An official who assists a judge or magistrate.
2. That is, a collection of the Epistles of the apostle Paul.
3. Saint Anthony of Egypt (c. 251–356) was the founder of organized Christian monasticism. He lived in absolute solitude on a mountain by the river Nile from about 286 to 305, during which time he engaged in a legendary combat with the devil, withstanding a series of temptations in the form of visions either seductive or horrible. His "rule," or code of guidelines for monastic living, was compiled from writings and sayings attributed to him in the *Life of St. Anthony* by Athanasius of Alexandria.

this, he dwelt on the story instilling in us who were ignorant an awareness of the man's greatness, and expressing astonishment that we did not know of him. We were amazed as we heard of your wonderful acts very well attested and occurring so recently, almost in our own time, done in orthodox faith and in the Catholic Church. All of us were in a state of surprise, we because of the greatness of the story, he because we had not heard about it.

From there his conversation moved on to speak of the flocks in the monasteries and their manner of life well pleasing to you and the fertile deserts of the wilderness. Of these we knew nothing. There was a monastery full of good brothers at Milan outside the city walls, fostered by Ambrose, and we had not known of it. He developed the theme and talked on while we listened with rapt silence. Then it occurred to him to mention how he and three of his colleagues (the date I do not know but it was at Trier),[4] when the emperor was detained by a circus spectacle in the forenoon, went out for a walk in the gardens adjacent to the walls. There they strolled in couples, one as it turned out with Ponticianus, the other two separately wandering off on their own. In their wanderings they happened on a certain house where there lived some of your servants, poor in spirit: *of such is the kingdom of heaven.* They found there a book in which was written the Life of Antony. One of them began to read it. He was amazed and set on fire, and during his reading began to think of taking up this way of life and of leaving his secular post in the civil service to be your servant. For they were agents in the special branch.[5] Suddenly he was filled with holy love and sobering shame. Angry with himself, he turned his eyes on his friend and said to him: "Tell me, I beg of you, what do we hope to achieve with all our labours? What is our aim in life? What is the motive of our service to the state? Can we hope for any higher office in the palace than to be Friends of the Emperor? And in that position what is not fragile and full of dangers? How many hazards must one risk to attain to a position of even greater danger?[6] And when will we arrive there? Whereas, if I wish to become God's friend, in an instant I may become that now." So he spoke, and in pain at the coming to birth of new life, he returned his eyes to the book's pages. He read on and experienced a conversion inwardly where you alone could see and, as was soon evident, his mind rid itself of the world. Indeed, as he read and turned over and over in the turbulent hesitations of his heart, there were some moments when he was angry with himself. But then he perceived the choice to be made and took a decision to follow the better course. He was already yours, and said to his friend: "As for myself, I have broken away from our ambition, and have decided to serve God, and I propose to start doing that from this hour in this place. If it costs you too much to follow my example, do not turn against me." His friend replied that he would join him and be associated with him for such great reward and for so great a service. And both men, already yours, were building their tower at the right cost of forsaking all their property and following you. Then Ponticianus and his companion who were walking through other parts of the garden in search of them, came to the same place and, on finding them, suggested returning home since the daylight had already begun to fade. But they told him of their decision and purpose, and how this

4. The Roman town of Trier was founded in 15 B.C.E. on the site of a Germanic shrine. In the 3rd century it was an imperial seat and later the seat of the emperor responsible for Gaul and Britain. It became a bishopric in the 4th century and remained a center of Christianity north of the Alps after its capture by the Franks in the 5th century.

5. In addition to their roles as members of the secret imperial police, the "general agents" operated the *cursus publicus,* the efficient Roman postal system.

6. "Friends of the Emperor" were a select group of advisors to the emperor. They were highly exposed in the event of coups and conspiracies.

intention had started and had become a firm resolve. They begged the others, if they did not wish to be associated with them, not to obstruct them. Ponticianus and his friend, however, did not change from their old career; nevertheless, as he told us, they wept for themselves. They offered their friends devout congratulations, and commended themselves to their prayers. Then, dragging their hearts along the ground, they went off into the palace. The others fixed their hearts on heaven and stayed at the house. Both had fiancées. When later their fiancées heard this, they also dedicated their virginity to you.[7]

This was the story Ponticianus told. But while he was speaking, Lord, you turned my attention back to myself. You took me up from behind my own back where I had placed myself because I did not wish *to observe myself,* and *you set me before my face* so that I should see how vile I was, how twisted and filthy, covered in sores and ulcers. And I looked and was appalled, but there was no way of escaping from myself. If I tried to avert my gaze from myself, his story continued relentlessly, and you once again placed me in front of myself; you thrust me before my own eyes so that I should discover my iniquity and hate it. I had known it, but deceived myself, refused to admit it, and pushed it out of my mind.

But at that moment the more ardent my affection for those young men of whom I was hearing, who for the soul's health had given themselves wholly to you for healing, the more was the detestation and hatred I felt for myself in comparison with them. Many years of my life had passed by—about twelve—since in my nineteenth year I had read Cicero's *Hortensius,* and had been stirred to a zeal for wisdom. But although I came to despise earthly success, I put off giving time to the quest for wisdom. For "it is not the discovery but the mere search for wisdom which should be preferred even to the discovery of treasures and to ruling over nations and to the physical delights available to me at a nod."[8] But I was an unhappy young man, wretched as at the beginning of my adolescence when I prayed you for chastity and said: "Grant me chastity and continence, but not yet." I was afraid you might hear my prayer quickly, and that you might too rapidly heal me of the disease of lust which I preferred to satisfy rather than suppress. I had gone along *evil ways* with a sacrilegious superstition, not indeed because I felt sure of its truth but because I preferred it to the alternatives, which I did not investigate in a devout spirit but opposed in an attitude of hostility.

I supposed that the reason for my postponing *from day to day* the moment when I would despise worldly ambition and follow you was that I had not seen any certainty by which to direct my course. But the day had now come when I stood naked to myself, and my conscience complained against me: "Where is your tongue? You were saying that, because the truth is uncertain, you do not want to abandon the burden of futility. But look, it is certain now, and the burden still presses on you. Yet wings are won by the freer shoulders of men who have not been exhausted by their searching and have not taken ten years or more to meditate on these matters." This is how I was gnawing at my inner self. I was violently overcome by a fearful sense of shame during the time that Ponticianus was telling his story. When he had ended his talk and settled the matter for which he came, he went home and I was left to myself. What accusations against myself did I not bring? With what verbal rods did I not scourge my soul so that it would follow me in my attempt to go after you! But my soul hung back.

7. The accumulation of a story within a story, written text, and recounted experiences is characteristic of narrative in the late Empire; it also serves here to emphasize the importance of example and imitation in conversion and in the dissemination of Christianity.

8. Drawn from Cicero's *Hortensius.*

It refused, and had no excuse to offer. The arguments were exhausted, and all had been refuted. The only thing left to it was a mute trembling, and as if it were facing death it was terrified of being restrained from the treadmill of habit by which it suffered *sickness unto death.*

Then in the middle of that grand struggle in my inner house, which I had vehemently stirred up with my soul in the intimate chamber of my heart, distressed not only in mind but in appearance, I turned on Alypius and cried out: "What is wrong with us? What is this that you have heard? Uneducated people are *rising up and capturing heaven,* and we with our high culture without any heart—see where we roll in the mud of flesh and blood. Is it because they are ahead of us that we are ashamed to follow? Do we feel no shame at making not even an attempt to follow?" That is the gist of what I said, and the heat of my passion took my attention away from him as he contemplated my condition in astonished silence. For I sounded very strange. My uttered words said less about the state of my mind than my forehead, cheeks, eyes, colour, and tone of voice.

Our lodging had a garden. We had the use of it as well as of the entire house, for our host, the owner of the house, was not living there.[9] The tumult of my heart took me out into the garden where no one could interfere with the burning struggle with myself in which I was engaged, until the matter could be settled. You knew, but I did not, what the outcome would be. But my madness with myself was part of the process of recovering health, and in the agony of death I was coming to life. I was aware how ill I was, unaware how well I was soon to be. So I went out into the garden. Alypius followed me step after step. Although he was present, I felt no intrusion on my solitude. How could he abandon me in such a state? We sat down as far as we could from the buildings. I was deeply disturbed in spirit, angry with indignation and distress that I was not entering into my pact and covenant with you, my God, *when all my bones were crying out* that I should enter into it and were exalting it to heaven with praises. But to reach that destination one does not use ships or chariots or feet. It was not even necessary to go the distance I had come from the house to where we were sitting. The one necessary condition, which meant not only going but at once arriving there, was to have the will to go—provided only that the will was strong and unqualified, not the turning and twisting first this way, then that, of a will half-wounded, struggling with one part rising up and the other part falling down.

Finally in the agony of hesitation I made many physical gestures of the kind men make when they want to achieve something and lack the strength, either because they lack the actual limbs or because their limbs are fettered with chains or weak with sickness or in some way hindered. If I tore my hair, if I struck my forehead, if I intertwined my fingers and clasped my knee, I did that because to do so was my will. But I could have willed this and then not done it if my limbs had not possessed the power to obey. So I did many actions in which the will to act was not equalled by the power. Yet I was not doing what with an incomparably greater longing I yearned to do, and could have done the moment I so resolved. For as soon as I had the will, I would have had a wholehearted will. At this point the power to act is identical with the will. The willing itself was performative of the action. Nevertheless, it did not happen. The

9. While clearly a real place, the "garden" within the "house" where they are lodging also reads as an allegory involving two sets of imagery—the house and the garden—carefully developed throughout the *Confessions.* The scene recalls both the original sin in the Garden of Eden and Augustine's difficulty in making the house of his soul a fit dwelling place for the Lord.

body obeyed the slightest inclination of the soul to move the limbs at its pleasure more easily than the soul obeyed itself, when its supreme desire could be achieved exclusively by the will alone.

* * *

["PICK UP AND READ"]

From a hidden depth a profound self-examination had dredged up a heap of all my misery and set it *in the sight of my heart.* That precipitated a vast storm bearing a massive downpour of tears. To pour it all out with the accompanying groans, I got up from beside Alypius (solitude seemed to me more appropriate for the business of weeping), and I moved further away to ensure that even his presence put no inhibition upon me. He sensed that this was my condition at that moment. I think I may have said something which made it clear that the sound of my voice was already choking with tears. So I stood up while in profound astonishment he remained where we were sitting. I threw myself down somehow under a certain figtree,[1] and let my tears flow freely. Rivers streamed from my eyes, *a sacrifice acceptable to you,* and (though not in these words, yet in this sense) I repeatedly said to you: "*How long, O Lord? How long, Lord, will you be angry to the uttermost? Do not be mindful of our old iniquities.*" For I felt my past to have a grip on me. It uttered wretched cries: "How long, how long is it to be?" "Tomorrow, tomorrow." "Why not now? Why not an end to my impure life in this very hour?"

As I was saying this and weeping in the bitter agony of my heart, suddenly I heard a voice from the nearby house chanting as if it might be a boy or a girl (I do not know which), saying and repeating over and over again "Pick up and read, pick up and read."[2] At once my countenance changed, and I began to think intently whether there might be some sort of children's game in which such a chant is used. But I could not remember having heard of one. I checked the flood of tears and stood up. I interpreted it solely as a divine command to me to open the book and read the first chapter I might find.[3] For I had heard how Antony happened to be present at the gospel reading, and took it as an admonition addressed to himself when the words were read: "Go, sell all you have, give to the poor, and you shall have treasure in heaven; and come, follow me."[4] By such an inspired utterance he was immediately *converted to you.* So I hurried back to the place where Alypius was sitting. There I had put down the book of the apostle when I got up. I seized it, opened it and in silence read the first passage on which my eyes lit: "Not in riots and drunken parties, not in eroticism and indecencies, not in strife and rivalry, but put on the Lord Jesus Christ and make no provision for the flesh in its lusts."[5]

I neither wished nor needed to read further. At once, with the last words of this sentence, it was as if a light of relief from all anxiety flooded into my heart. All the shadows of doubt were dispelled.

Then I inserted my finger or some other mark in the book and closed it. With a face now at peace I told everything to Alypius. What had been going on in his mind,

1. This recalls the fig tree of Eden (Genesis 3:7) and stresses the allegorical meaning of the garden.
2. Rather than from the books or the stories of his learned friends, the final impulse toward conversion comes from a child's voice: "tolle lege, tolle lege."
3. The practice of divination by choosing a passage at random from a sacred book was widespread in antiquity; its commonest form in the later Empire was the *sortes Vergilianae,* which used the writings of Virgil.
4. Matthew 19:21, Jesus's words to a young man who asks what he must do to achieve eternal life.
5. Romans 13:13–14 (see page 819). The apostle Paul thus provides the apt words for Augustine's conversion.

which I did not know, he disclosed in this way. He asked to see the text I had been reading. I showed him, and he noticed a passage following that which I had read. I did not know how the text went on; but the continuation was "Receive the person who is weak in faith."[6] Alypius applied this to himself, and he made that known to me. He was given confidence by this admonition. Without any agony of hesitation he joined me in making a good resolution and affirmation of intention, entirely congruent with his moral principles in which he had long been greatly superior to me. From there we went in to my mother, and told her. She was filled with joy. We told her how it had happened. She exulted, feeling it to be a triumph, and blessed you who *are powerful to do more than we ask or think.* She saw that you had granted her far more than she had long been praying for in her unhappy and tearful groans.

The effect of your converting me to yourself was that I did not now seek a wife and had no ambition for success in this world. I stood firm upon that rule of faith on which many years before you had revealed me to her. You *changed her grief into joy* far more abundantly than she desired, far dearer and more chaste than she expected when she looked for grandchildren begotten of my body.

from *Book 9*

[*Augustine gives up his teaching post and retires to the rural villa of the grammarian Verecundus in Cassiciacum some twenty miles northeast of Milan, surrounded by family and friends including his son, Adeodatus, now sixteen (he would die two years later). Augustine returns to Milan to be baptized.*]

[Monica's Death]

You make people to live in a house in unanimity. So you made Evodius a member of our circle, a young man from my home town.[1] When he was a civil servant as an agent in the special branch, he was converted to you before we were. He was baptized and resigned his post on taking up your service. We were together and by a holy decision resolved to live together. We looked for a place where we could be of most use in your service; all of us agreed on a move back to Africa.

While we were at Ostia by the mouths of the Tiber, my mother died. I pass over many events because I write in great haste. Accept my confessions and thanksgivings, my God, for innumerable things even though I do not specifically mention them. But I shall not pass over whatever my soul may bring to birth concerning your servant, who brought me to birth both in her body so that I was born into the light of time, and in her heart so that I was born into the light of eternity. I speak not of her gifts to me, but of your gifts to her. She had not made herself or brought herself up. You created her, and her father and mother did not know what kind of character their child would have. She was trained *in your fear* by the discipline of your Christ, by the government of your only Son in a believing household through a good member of your Church. She used to speak highly not so much of her mother's diligence in training her as of a decrepit maidservant who had carried her father when he was an infant, in the way that infants are often carried on the back of older girls. Because of this long service and for her seniority and high moral standards in a Christian house, she was held in

6. Romans 14:1.

1. Later to become Bishop of Uzali in North Africa, Evodius accompanied Augustine from Rome to Africa and is featured in two dialogues written by Augustine.

great honour by her masters. So she was entrusted with responsibility for her master's daughters and discharged it with diligence and, when necessary, was vehement with a holy severity in administering correction. In training them she exercised a discreet prudence. Outside those times when they were nourished by a most modest meal at their parents' table, even if they were burning with thirst, she allowed them to drink not even water, wishing to avert the formation of a bad habit. She used to add the wise word: "Now you drink water because it is not in your power to get wine. But when you come to have husbands and become mistresses of storerooms and cellars, water will seem dull stuff but the drinking habit will be unbreakable." By this method of laying down rules for behaviour and by her authoritative way of giving commands, she restrained the greedy appetite of a tender age, and brought the girls' thirst to respectable moderation, so that they should not later hanker after anything they ought not to touch.

Nevertheless, as your servant[2] told me her son, a weakness for wine gradually got a grip upon her. By custom her parents used to send her, a sober girl, to fetch wine from the cask. She would plunge the cup through the aperture at the top. Before she poured the wine into a jug, she used to take a tiny sip with the tip of her lips. She could not take more as she disliked the taste. What led her to do this was not an appetite for liquor but the surplus high spirits of a young person, which can overflow in playful impulses and which in children adults ordinarily try to suppress.[3] Accordingly, to that sip of wine she added more sips every day—for *he who despises small things gradually comes to a fall*—until she had fallen into the habit of gulping down almost full cups of wine. Where then was the wise old woman and her vehement prohibition? She could have had no strength against the secret malady unless your healing care, Lord, were watching over us. When father and mother and nurses are not there, you are present. You have created us, you call us, you use human authorities set over us to do something for the health of our souls. How did you cure her? How did you restore her health? You brought from another soul a harsh and sharp rebuke, like a surgeon's knife, from your secret stores, and with one blow you cut away the rottenness. The slavegirl who used to accompany her to the cask had a dispute with her young mistress which happened when they were alone together. Bitterly she insulted her by bringing up the accusation that she was a boozer. The taunt hurt. She reflected upon her own foul addiction, at once condemned it, and stopped the habit. Just as flattering friends corrupt, so quarrelsome enemies often bring us correction. Yet you reward them not for what you use them to achieve, but according to their intention. The maidservant in her anger sought to wound her little mistress, not to cure her. That is why she spoke in private—either because the time and place of the quarrel happened to find them alone together, or perhaps because she was afraid of the fact that she had come out with it so belatedly.

But you, Lord, ruler of heaven and earth, turn to your own purposes the deep torrents. You order the turbulent flux of the centuries. Even from the fury of one soul you brought healing to another. Thereby you showed that no one should attribute it to his own power if by anything he says he sets on the right path someone whom he wishes to be corrected.

* * *

2. Monica.

3. Once again Augustine stresses not lack of will in the origin of the bad habit but the exercise of the will.

The day was imminent when she was to depart this life (the day which you knew and we did not). It came about, as I believe by your providence through your hidden ways, that she and I were standing leaning out of a window overlooking a garden. It was at the house where we were staying at Ostia on the Tiber, where, far removed from the crowds, after the exhaustion of a long journey, we were recovering our strength for the voyage.

Alone with each other, we talked very intimately. *Forgetting the past and reaching forward to what lies ahead,* we were searching together in the presence of the truth which is you yourself. We asked what quality of life the eternal life of the saints will have, a life which *neither eye has seen nor ear heard, nor has it entered into the heart of man.* But with the mouth of the heart wide open, we drank in the waters flowing from your spring on high, *the spring of life* which is with you. Sprinkled with this dew to the limit of our capacity, our minds attempted in some degree to reflect on so great a reality.

The conversation led us towards the conclusion that the pleasure of the bodily senses, however delightful in the radiant light of this physical world, is seen by comparison with the life of eternity to be not even worth considering. Our minds were lifted up by an ardent affection towards eternal being itself. Step by step we climbed beyond all corporeal objects and the heaven itself, where sun, moon, and stars shed light on the earth. We ascended even further by internal reflection and dialogue and wonder at your works, and we entered into our own minds. We moved up beyond them so as to attain to the region of inexhaustible abundance where you feed Israel eternally with truth for food. There life is the wisdom by which all creatures come into being, both things which were and which will be. But wisdom itself is not brought into being but is as it was and always will be. Furthermore, in this wisdom there is no past and future, but only being, since it is eternal. For to exist in the past or in the future is no property of the eternal. And while we talked and panted after it, we touched it in some small degree by a moment of total concentration of the heart. And we sighed and left behind us *the firstfruits of the Spirit* bound to that higher world, as we returned to the noise of our human speech where a sentence has both a beginning and an ending. But what is to be compared with your word, Lord of our lives? It dwells in you without growing old and gives renewal to all things.[4]

Therefore we said: If to anyone the tumult of the flesh has fallen silent, if the images of earth, water, and air are quiescent, if the heavens themselves are shut out and the very soul itself is making no sound and is surpassing itself by no longer thinking about itself, if all dreams and visions in the imagination are excluded, if all language and every sign and everything transitory is silent—for if anyone could hear them, this is what all of them would be saying, "We did not make ourselves, we were made by him who abides for eternity"[5]—if after this declaration they were to keep silence, having directed our ears to him that made them, then he alone would speak not through them but through himself.[6] We would hear his word, not through the tongue of the flesh, nor through the voice of an angel, nor through the sound of thunder, nor through the obscurity of a symbolic utterance. Him who in these things we love we would hear in person without their mediation. That is how it was when at that moment

4. The vision at Ostia serves to anticipate the fate of Monica's soul after her death, and thus lessen the sorrow of it, and also to develop the contemplative and speculative tone of the latter, postconversion books of the *Confessions.*

5. Psalms 80:3, 5.

6. Augustine describes the process and the goal of this meditation: to experience the word of God directly without the distortion of any form of representation. This would be a taste of what eternal life must be like.

we extended our reach and in a flash of mental energy attained the eternal wisdom which abides beyond all things. If only it could last, and other visions of a vastly inferior kind could be withdrawn! Then this alone could ravish and absorb and enfold in inward joys the person granted the vision. So too eternal life is of the quality of that moment of understanding after which we sighed. Is not this the meaning of *Enter into the joy of your Lord?* And when is that to be? Surely it is when *we all rise again, but are not all changed.*

I said something like this, even if not in just this way and with exactly these words. Yet, Lord, you know that on that day when we had this conversation, and this world with all its delights became worthless to us as we talked on, my mother said "My son, as for myself, I now find no pleasure in this life. What I have still to do here and why I am here, I do not know. My hope in this world is already fulfilled. The one reason why I wanted to stay longer in this life was my desire to see you a Catholic Christian before I die. My God has granted this in a way more than I had hoped. For I see you despising this world's success to become his servant.[7] What have I to do here?"

[*The death of Monica concludes the narrative part of the* Confessions. *In Book 10, Augustine analyzes at length the relationship between his memory and his search for God in it through the act of confession. He enumerates the pleasures of the senses that continue to tempt him.*]

from *Book 11*

[Time, Eternity, and Memory]

Lord, eternity is yours, so you cannot be ignorant of what I tell you. Your vision of occurrences in time is not temporally conditioned. Why then do I set before you an ordered account of so many things? It is certainly not through me that you know them. But I am stirring up love for you in myself and in those who read this, so that we may all say "Great is the Lord and highly worthy to be praised."[1] I have already affirmed this and will say it again: I tell my story for love of your love. We pray, and yet the truth says "Your Father knows what you need before you ask him."[2] Therefore I lay bare my feelings towards you, by confessing to you my miseries and *your mercies to us,* so that the deliverance you have begun may be complete. So I may cease to be wretched in myself and may find happiness in you. For you have called us to be *poor in spirit,* meek, mournful, hungering and thirsting for righteousness, merciful, pure in heart, and peacemakers.[3]

See, the long story I have told to the best of my ability and will responds to your prior will that I should make confession to you, my Lord God. For *you are good, for your mercy is for ever.* * * *

Stand firm, my mind, concentrate with resolution.[4] *God is our help, he has made us and not we ourselves.* Concentrate on the point where truth is beginning to dawn. For

7. That is, to withdraw from worldly affairs to become an ascetic, Augustine's first activity after his conversion; later, he would take a more active role as Bishop of Hippo.

1. Psalm 48:1. Augustine returns to the concerns of the opening paragraph. The reason for his confession and his ordering it chronologically as an autobiography is not to make it comprehensible to the Lord but as a story in His praise.

2. Matthew 6:8.

3. Summarizing the Sermon on the Mount in Matthew 5.

4. Augustine prepares his mind for an exercise in imagining the relationship between the divine and human perspectives on time.

example, a physical voice begins to sound. It sounds. It continues to sound, and then ceases. Silence has now come, and the voice is past. There is now no sound. Before it sounded it lay in the future. It could not be measured because it did not exist; and now it cannot be measured because it has ceased to be. At the time when it was sounding, it was possible because at that time it existed to be measured. Yet even then it had no permanence. It came and went. Did this make it more possible to measure? In process of passing away it was extended through a certain space of time by which it could be measured, since the present occupies no length of time. Therefore during that transient process it could be measured. But take, for example, another voice. It begins to sound and continues to do so unflaggingly without any interruption. Let us measure it while it is sounding; when it has ceased to sound, it will be past and will not exist to be measurable. Evidently we may at that stage measure it by saying how long it lasted. But if it is still sounding, it cannot be measured except from the starting moment when it began to sound to the finish when it ceased. What we measure is the actual interval from the beginning to the end. That is why a sound which has not yet ended cannot be measured: one cannot say how long or how short it is, nor that it is equal to some other length of time or that in relation to another it is single or double or any such proportion. But when it has come to an end, then it will already have ceased to be. By what method then can it be measured?

Nevertheless we do measure periods of time. And yet the times we measure are not those which do not yet exist, nor those which already have no existence, nor those which extend over no interval of time, nor those which reach no conclusions. So the times we measure are not future nor past nor present nor those in process of passing away. Yet we measure periods of time.

"God, Creator of all things"—*Deus Creator omnium*—the line consists of eight syllables, in which short and long syllables alternate.[5] So the four which are short (the first, third, fifth, and seventh) are single in relation to the four long syllables (the second, fourth, sixth and eighth).[6] Each of the long syllables has twice the time of the short. As I recite the words, I also observe that this is so, for it is evident to sense-perception. To the degree that the sense-perception is unambiguous, I measure the long syllable by the short one, and perceive it to be twice the length. But when one syllable sounds after another, the short first, the long after it, how shall I keep my hold on the short, and how use it to apply a measure to the long, so as to verify that the long is twice as much? The long does not begin to sound unless the short has ceased to sound. I can hardly measure the long during the presence of its sound, as measuring becomes possible only after it has ended. When it is finished, it has gone into the past. What then is it which I measure? Where is the short syllable with which I am making my measurement? Where is the long which I am measuring? Both have sounded; they have flown away; they belong to the past. They now do not exist. And I offer my measurement and declare as confidently as a practised sense-perception will allow, that the short is single, the long double—I mean in the time they occupy. I can do this only because they are past and gone. Therefore it is not the syllables which I am measuring, but something in my memory which stays fixed there.[7]

So it is in you, my mind, that I measure periods of time. Do not distract me; that is, do not allow yourself to be distracted by the hubbub of the impressions being made

5. A hymn written by Bishop Ambrose for Saturday vespers (evening services).
6. Latin meter is based on the length of syllables rather than on accent, as in English.
7. According to this analysis, time is not something that can be measured in the present, as an event is unfolding, but only when it is past and exists solely in the memory.

upon you. In you, I affirm, I measure periods of time. The impression which passing events make upon you abides when they are gone. That present consciousness is what I am measuring, not the stream of past events which have caused it. When I measure periods of time, that is what I am actually measuring. Therefore, either this is what time is, or time is not what I am measuring.

What happens when we measure silences and say that a given period of silence lasted as long as a given sound? Do we direct our attention to measuring it as if a sound occurred, so that we are enabled to judge the intervals of the silences within the space of time concerned? For without any sound or utterance we mentally recite poems and lines and speeches, and we assess the lengths of their movements and the relative amounts of time they occupy, no differently from the way we would speak if we were actually making sounds. Suppose someone wished to utter a sound lasting a long time, and decided in advance how long that was going to be. He would have planned that space of time in silence. Entrusting that to his memory he would begin to utter the sound which continues until it has reached the intended end. It would be more accurate to say the utterance has sounded and will sound. For the part of it which is complete has sounded, but what remains will sound, and so the action is being accomplished as present attention transfers the future into the past. The future diminishes as the past grows, until the future has completely gone and everything is in the past.

But how does this future, which does not yet exist, diminish or become consumed? Or how does the past, which now has no being, grow, unless there are three processes in the mind which in this is the active agent? For the mind expects and attends and remembers, so that what it expects passes through what has its attention to what it remembers. Who therefore can deny that the future does not yet exist? Yet already in the mind there is an expectation of the future. Who can deny that the past does not now exist? Yet there is still in the mind a memory of the past. None can deny that present time lacks any extension because it passes in a flash. Yet attention is continuous, and it is through this that what will be present progresses towards being absent. So the future, which does not exist, is not a long period of time. A long future is a long expectation of the future. And the past, which has no existence, is not a long period of time. A long past is a long memory of the past.

Suppose I am about to recite a psalm which I know. Before I begin, my expectation is directed towards the whole. But when I have begun, the verses from it which I take into the past become the object of my memory. The life of this act of mine is stretched two ways, into my memory because of the words I have already said and into my expectation because of those which I am about to say. But my attention is on what is present: by that the future is transferred to become the past. As the action advances further and further, the shorter the expectation and the longer the memory, until all expectation is consumed, the entire action is finished, and it has passed into the memory. What occurs in the psalm as a whole occurs in its particular pieces and its individual syllables. The same is true of a longer action in which perhaps that psalm is a part. It is also valid of the entire life of an individual person, where all actions are parts of a whole, and of the total history of *the sons of men*[8] where all human lives are but parts.

Because your mercy is more than lives, see how my life is a distension in several directions. *Your right hand upheld me* in my Lord, the Son of man who is mediator

8. Psalms 31:20. In Book 1, the *Confessions* opens up out of the recitation of psalms as the means of approaching God; here, Augustine uses the model of the recitation of a psalm, a song of praise, to make tangible the divine perspective of a human life and of the history of the world from the Creation to the Last Judgment. Paradoxically, God is neither ignorant nor powerless concerning the path it will take but neither has he already predetermined what will happen.

between you the One and us the many, who live in a multiplicity of distractions by many things; so *I might apprehend him in whom also I am apprehended,* and leaving behind the old days I might be gathered to follow the One, *forgetting the past* and moving not towards those future things which are transitory but to *the things which are before* me, not stretched out in distraction but extended in reach, not by being pulled apart but by concentration.[9] So I *pursue the prize of the high calling* where I *may hear the voice of praise* and *contemplate your delight* which neither comes nor goes. But now *my years pass in groans* and you, Lord, are my consolation. You are my eternal Father, but I am scattered in times whose order I do not understand. The storms of incoherent events tear to pieces my thoughts, the inmost entrails of my soul, until that day when, purified and molten by the fire of your love, I flow together to merge into you.

Then shall I find stability and solidity in you, in your truth which imparts form to me. I shall not have to endure the questions of people who suffer from a disease which brings its own punishment and want to drink more than they have the capacity to hold. They say "What was God doing before he made heaven and earth?", or "Why did he ever conceive the thought of making something when he had never made anything before?"[1] Grant them, Lord, to consider carefully what they are saying and to make the discovery that where there is no time, one cannot use the word "never." To say that God has never done something is to say that there is no time when he did it. Let them therefore see that without the creation no time can exist, and let them cease to speak that vanity. Let them also be *extended* towards *those things which are before,* and understand that before all times you are eternal Creator of all time. Nor are any times or created thing coeternal with you, even if there is an order of creation which transcends time.[2]

Lord my God, how deep is your profound mystery, and how far away from it have I been thrust by the consequences of my sins. Heal my eyes and let me rejoice with your light. Certainly if there were a mind endowed with such great knowledge and prescience that all things past and future could be known in the way I know a very familiar psalm, this mind would be utterly miraculous and amazing to the point of inducing awe. From such a mind nothing of the past would be hidden, nor anything of what remaining ages have in store, just as I have full knowledge of that psalm I sing. I know by heart what and how much of it has passed since the beginning, and what and how much remains until the end. But far be it from you, Creator of the universe, creator of souls and bodies, far be it from you to know all future and past events in this kind of sense. You know them in a much more wonderful and much more mysterious way. A person singing or listening to a song he knows well suffers a distension or stretching in feeling and in sense-perception from the expectation of future sounds and the memory of past sound. With you it is otherwise. You are unchangeably eternal, that is the truly eternal Creator of minds. Just as you knew heaven and earth in the beginning without that bringing any variation into your knowing, so you made heaven and earth in the beginning without that meaning a tension between past and future in your activity. Let the person who understands this make confession to you. Let him who fails to understand it make confession to you. How exalted you are, and *the humble in heart are your house. You lift up those who are cast down,* and those whom you raise to that summit which is yourself do not fall.

9. It is the multiple distractions of errant and transitory paths that render it impossible from the human perspective to perceive the single path that will, in the end, lead to the Lord and become history.

1. Underlying the discussion of time and memory was an ongoing debate over how and in what form God could have existed before he created the world; whether, in other words, there exists or existed anything prior to Him or outside of Him.

2. Augustine refers here to the order of angels (*City of God* 12.16).

[*In the final two books of the* Confessions, *Augustine applies everything he has discovered thus far to an explanation of the Creation and of the first chapters of Genesis, resolving to his satisfaction the relationship of God to the material and temporal world.*]

RESONANCES

Michel de Montaigne: from *Essays*[1]

To the Reader

This book was written in good faith, reader. It warns you from the outset that in it I have set myself no goal but a domestic and private one. I have had no thought of serving either you or my own glory. My powers are inadequate for such a purpose. I have dedicated it to the private convenience of my relatives and friends, so that when they have lost me (as soon they must), they may recover here some features of my habits and temperament, and by this means keep the knowledge they have had of me more complete and alive.

If I had written to seek the world's favor, I should have bedecked myself better, and should present myself in a studied posture. I want to be seen here in my simple, natural, ordinary fashion, without straining or artifice; for it is myself that I portray. My defects will here be read to the life, and also my natural form, as far as respect for the public has allowed. Had I been placed among those nations which are said to live still in the sweet freedom of nature's first laws, I assure you I should very gladly have portrayed myself here entire and wholly naked.[2]

Thus, reader, I am myself the matter of my book; you would be unreasonable to spend your leisure on so frivolous and vain a subject.

So farewell. Montaigne,[3] this first day of March, fifteen hundred and eighty.

Jean-Jacques Rousseau: from *Confessions*[1]

from *Book 1*

I have resolved on an enterprise which has no precedent, and which, once complete, will have no imitator. My purpose is to display to my kind a portrait in every way true to nature, and the man I shall portray will be myself.

1. Translated by Donald Frame. In 1571 at the age of 38, tired of a public life of law and politics in war-torn southern France, Michel de Montaigne (1533–1592) retired to his family château to devote himself to private concerns. To commemorate his retreat, he had a medallion cast with the words *Que sais-je?* ("What do I know?") on one side and *Restraint* in Greek on the other. In the three volumes of *Essays* (a word he coined for the occasion) he published over the next 20 years, Montaigne adapted Augustine's model of the exploration of self in search of God and of spiritual rest into the exploration of self in search of self-knowledge and peace with the world. "To the Reader" opens the *Essays* with a confession of an endeavor as unexpected in the late 16th century as Augustine's was in his time. See page 1520 for further selections from the *Essays.*

2. Like Augustine, Montaigne treats his book as himself, but in addition to his actions and thoughts, he includes his "natural form," meaning both his body and his thoughts, as unencumbered as possible of the prejudices of human custom. The New World had recently been discovered by Europe, and its indigenous peoples were widely held to be in an equivalent state of nature to Adam and Eve in Eden before they gained knowledge of good and evil.

3. That is, the Château of Montaigne.

1. Translated by J. M. Cohen. Confession is a powerful device of rhetoric for guaranteeing the truth of a life story. In the prologue to his autobiography, Jean-Jacques Rousseau (1712–1788), Enlightenment philosopher, political theorist, musician, novelist, and spiritual father of the French Revolution, imagines Christ himself absolving the writer for any distortions he may unwittingly have included. As with Augustine, the autobiography as confession is both universal and unique, both browbeating and self-congratulatory; the combination has become since Rousseau an indelible feature of life writing.

Simply myself. I know my own heart and understand my fellow man. But I am made unlike any one I have ever met; I will even venture to say that I am like no one in the whole world. I may be no better, but at least I am different. Whether Nature did well or ill in breaking the mould in which she formed me, is a question which can only be resolved after the reading of my book.

Let the last trump sound when it will, I shall come forward with this work in my hand, to present myself before my Sovereign Judge, and proclaim aloud: "Here is what I have done, and if by chance I have used some immaterial embellishment it has been only to fill a void due to a defect of memory. I may have taken for fact what was no more than probability, but I have never put down as true what I knew to be false.[2] I have displayed myself as I was, as vile and despicable when my behaviour was such, as good, generous, and noble when I was so. I have bared my secret soul as Thou thyself hast seen it, Eternal Being! So let the numberless legion of my fellow men gather round me, and hear my confessions. Let them groan at my depravities, and blush for my misdeeds. But let each one of them reveal his heart at the foot of Thy throne with equal sincerity, and may any man who dares, say 'I was a better man than he.'"

2. Like Montaigne but unlike Augustine, Rousseau feels it necessary to distinguish between an ideal of absolute truth and the relative truth represented by his *Confessions.*

King Arthur and His Knights, from a manuscript of the *Prose Lancelot,* France, 13th century. In this illustration from a collection of Arthurian romances, King Arthur is majestically enthroned, and in keeping with his royal stature he towers over his knights. He is shown requesting a central commodity in the Arthurian stories—more stories. "Now tell the tales," he commands, "that have befallen you since the day of Pentecost before all the companions of the Quest returned."

The Medieval Era

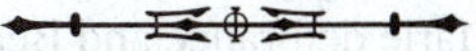

The term "medieval" was coined long after the close of the period to which it refers, as people looking back from early modern times sought a name for the thousand years or so between their day and classical antiquity, roughly the fourth through the fourteenth centuries C.E.; "medieval" comes from the Latin for "middle era." Originally applied specifically to Europe, the term has come to be used for a "middle" period in a range of cultures around the world. The beginnings of this middle era vary from place to place, but each of the ancient literary cultures presented in this anthology went through a major time of transition in late antiquity, roughly between the first and fourth centuries C.E. By that point, a body of ancient works had been established as foundational for the later culture: the Confucian classics in China and Indochina; the Vedas and early epics of India; the Bible and the Greek and Roman classics in the Mediterranean world. These and other classic works continued to have a lasting influence, yet many more texts were lost in the upheavals of late antiquity; only a small fraction of Sappho's lyrics and Sophocles' plays survived, for example, and some entire civilizations vanished, such as those of Mesopotamia and ancient Egypt.

Even as one era was passing away, another was coming into being. Distinctly new literatures were created in many areas, sometimes in languages that had never been written before, such as Japanese, Arabic, and German, sometimes through creative transformation of classical languages such as Chinese, Sanskrit, and Latin.

Lords and Ladies, Knights and Samurai

The vast majority of the medieval world's population consisted of peasantry: farmers tilling small plots of land (or fishing, in coastal areas), often as virtual or outright slaves of powerful lords who controlled the land. In Europe and sometimes elsewhere, authority and land ownership were organized feudally, a system in which an overlord held title to all land in his domain and granted it to noble vassals in exchange for their loyalty and support; the vassals in turn controlled the lives of the serfs who worked their lands. Monarchs often tried to gather their nobility round them, to enhance the glory of their courts and to keep a watchful eye on their powerful underlings. Royal courts in China, Japan, India, Persia, Iraq, and Europe were sites of feasting and of seduction, where court poets celebrated noble deeds in heroic epics and romances, and sang the sorrows of love in enticing lyrics.

Women weren't only the idealized objects of poetic devotion; increasingly, they were poets themselves as well. Court life, and the convents to which women might withdraw from court life, provided new opportunities for women to become writers. With a few important exceptions such as Sappho, women in antiquity had had little access to literacy and no opportunity to record their stories and songs. In the medieval era, women began to play important roles in patronizing and also creating literature and other works of art. The pre-Islamic woman poet al-Khansa' became a founding figure for Arabic poetry, and in several regions aristocratic women in particular gained a new stature as writers. In Japan, a remarkable series of courtly women wrote poetry and became pioneers in prose writing. *The Tale of Genji,* by the noblewoman known as Murasaki Shikibu, has long been recognized as one of the greatest narratives ever written. In Europe, Marie de France and Béatrice, the countess of Dia, were two among a number of celebrated women poets.

Medieval knights in Europe, and their Japanese counterparts the samurai, sought fame as much as wealth, and became the subjects of great poems and prose tales concerning their exploits battling one another or dragons and other monsters. Writers including Marie de France and the anonymous author of *Gawain and the Green Knight* celebrated the adventures of the legendary King Arthur's knights, while the great Japanese samurai clans had their deeds commemorated in medieval epics and many later works, even starring in very recent times in such movies as Kurosawa's *The Seven Samurai*. The common folk sang songs and told stories, but they were rarely literate and their oral traditions generally went unmarked. Yet folk songs and tales survived when they were recorded for upper-class consumption, as notably happened with the stories included in *The Thousand and One Nights*. That text actually dramatizes this process of transmission, in tales in which the Caliph Haroun al-Rashid goes out into Baghdad dressed as a common merchant, accompanied by his vizier and executioner, to seek adventure and hear marvelous stories; back home in his palace, he regularly has the best of these stories recorded in letters of gold.

Medieval writers typically portray their royal patrons as vastly wise, powerful, and generous, yet the reality was often a good deal less glorious. In many regions, transportation was poor and long-distance communication was awkward, rendering central control difficult, and subsistence-level farming didn't produce very great surpluses that could support both a local aristocracy and the royal household in the style to which both aspired. There were frequent struggles for position and ascendancy, both between the lords of neighboring regions and between vassals and their overlords. Feuding and open warfare are constant themes in medieval literature. A partial exception to this pattern was China. Unified in ancient times under the feudal Han dynasty (202 B.C.E.–220 C.E.), early medieval China experienced a long phase of conflict and division, but was then reunified under the Sui dynasty in the late sixth century. A period of great prosperity ensued, with much of central China linked by canals as well as rivers, and older feudal patterns were replaced by a national bureaucracy controlled by the emperor and his administration. The Tang dynasty (618–907) became the golden age of Chinese poetry as of several other arts, and in this sense China's "middle" period became its *central* period in the eyes of later historians, writers, and artists.

Travel, Trade, and Conquest

The medieval period saw steadily increasing contacts across regions, promoted especially by two kinds of travelers: merchants and missionaries or pilgrims. A "Silk Road" was established from East Asia to the shores of the Mediterranean, and Constantinople and Venice became major connecting links between Europe and points east. Armies were on the move as well, often fueled by religious fervor as well as political ambition. Following the establishment of Islam in Arabia in the early seventh century, a wave of conversion and consolidation spread westward across North Africa,

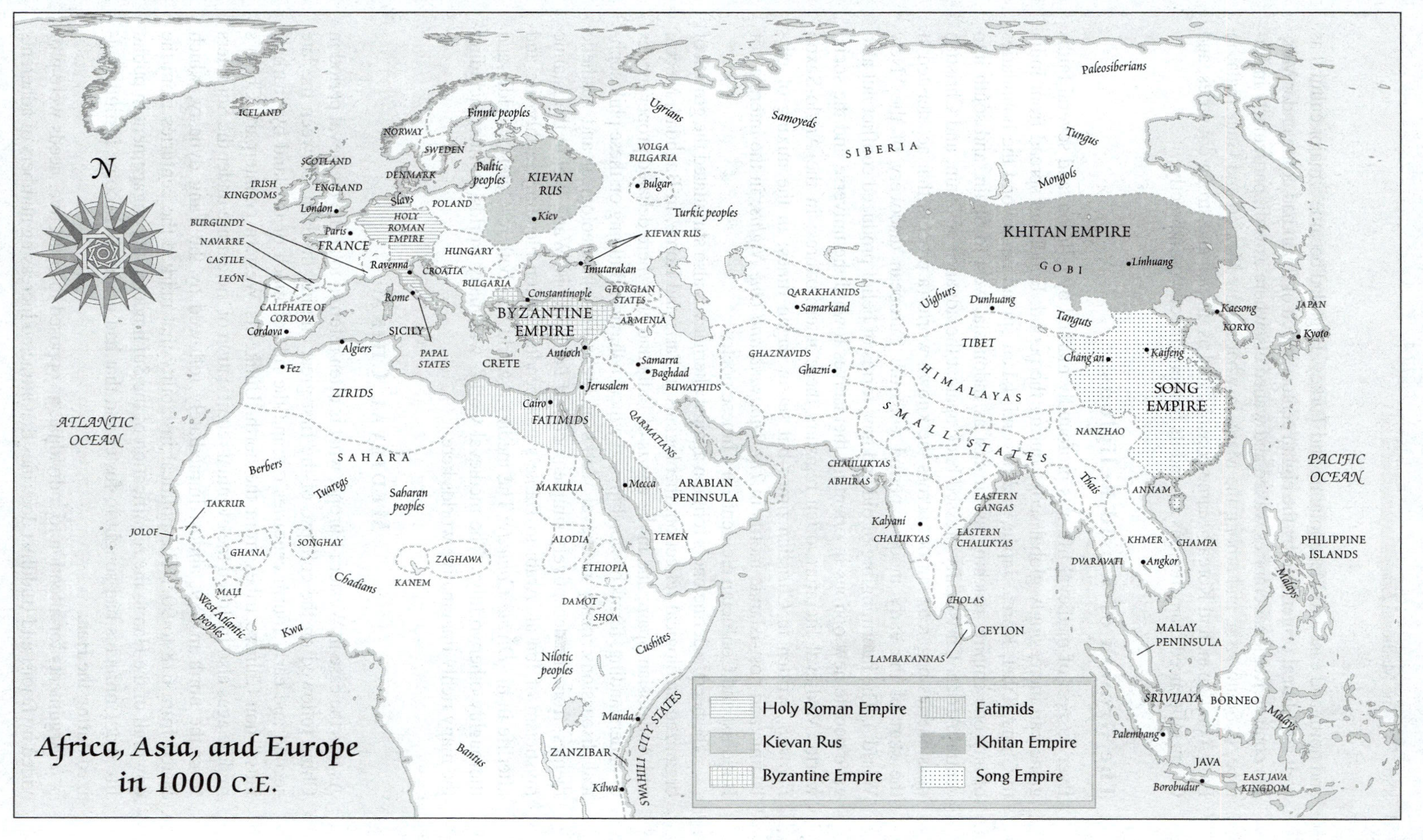
Africa, Asia, and Europe in 1000 C.E.
N
ICELAND
NORWAY
SWEDEN
Finnic peoples
SCOTLAND
IRISH KINGDOMS
ENGLAND
London
DENMARK
Baltic peoples
KIEVAN RUS
Kiev
Slavs
POLAND
HOLY ROMAN EMPIRE
Paris
FRANCE
BURGUNDY
NAVARRE
CASTILE
LEÓN
CALIPHATE OF CORDOVA
Cordova
Ravenna
CROATIA
HUNGARY
BULGARIA
Rome
SICILY
PAPAL STATES
Algiers
Fez
ZIRIDS
CRETE
Constantinople
BYZANTINE EMPIRE
Antioch
Jerusalem
Cairo
FATIMIDS
Tmutarakan
KIEVAN RUS
GEORGIAN STATES
ARMENIA
Samarra
Baghdad
BUWAYHIDS
QARMATIANS
Mecca
ARABIAN PENINSULA
YEMEN
Ugrians
VOLGA BULGARIA
Bulgar
Turkic peoples
Samoyeds
SIBERIA
QARAKHANIDS
Samarkand
GHAZNAVIDS
Ghazni
Paleosiberians
Tungus
Mongols
KHITAN EMPIRE
GOBI
Linhuang
Uighurs
Dunhuang
Tanguts
TIBET
HIMALAYAS
SMALL STATES
Chang'an
Kaifeng
SONG EMPIRE
NANZHAO
Kaesong
KORYO
JAPAN
Kyoto
PACIFIC OCEAN
CHAULUKYAS
ABHIRAS
Kalyani
CHALUKYAS
EASTERN GANGAS
EASTERN CHALUKYAS
CHOLAS
CEYLON
LAMBAKANNAS
Thais
ANNAM
KHMER
CHAMPA
DVARAVATI
Angkor
PHILIPPINE ISLANDS
Malays
MALAY PENINSULA
SRIVIJAYA
BORNEO
Malays
Palembang
JAVA
Borobudur
EAST JAVA KINGDOM
ATLANTIC OCEAN
SAHARA
Berbers
Tuaregs
Saharan peoples
TAKRUR
JOLOF
GHANA
SONGHAY
MALI
West Atlantic peoples
Kwa
Chadians
ZAGHAWA
KANEM
MAKURIA
ALODIA
ETHIOPIA
DAMOT
SHOA
Nilotic peoples
Cushites
Manda
ZANZIBAR
Kilwa
SWAHILI CITY STATES
Bantus
Holy Roman Empire
Kievan Rus
Byzantine Empire
Fatimids
Khitan Empire
Song Empire

and north and east into Mesopotamia and Turkey. Baghdad became a major cultural as well as political center, and by the eighth century much of Spain had come under Muslim control. Regional empires waxed and waned elsewhere as well, particularly in Europe, in South Asia, and among the Maya in what is now Mexico and Guatemala; in East Asia, Japan, and Korea became consolidated as unified and strong countries, and China influenced many regions around its borders directly or indirectly.

The Growth of World Religions

Every aspect of medieval life was profoundly marked by religion, and several faiths gained an increasingly global scope during the period: Buddhism spread from India to China, Tibet, Korea, Japan, and beyond; Islam spread far beyond the boundaries of any one empire, reaching as far east as Indonesia, west to Spain, and south into central Africa. Christianity pressed back against the advance of Islam, and Christian missionaries began to fan out across the known world (a process that accelerated at the start of the early modern period with the European discovery of the "New World"). The intermingling of old and new forms of belief produced conflict but also gave people new options in orienting themselves toward the universe and the social world. Medieval literature often registers these intermixtures: in the Anglo-Saxon *Beowulf,* written in Christian times but set in pagan times; in the mixing of pre-Islamic and post-Islamic motifs in *The Thousand and One Nights;* in the interplay of Buddhist and Confucian elements in Chinese poetry.

The need to define one's religion against alternatives also stimulated the growth of organized theological reflection: theologians in Paris and Rome, in Baghdad, Mecca, and Andalusian Spain, and in the courts of India and elsewhere debated proper modes of understanding, forms of worship, and ethical behavior. Building on these philosophical discussions, many medieval works of literature join theological and aesthetic themes, from the deceptively simple poetry of the Buddhist Wang Wei to the Islamic mysticism of Ibn al-'Arabi to Dante's transcendent vision blending earthly life and afterlife in his *Divine Comedy*. The medieval world was both resolutely worldly and thoroughly otherworldly. "The medieval world" was many worlds, in fact, including the many richly imaginative worlds here.

Medieval China

As was the case in Western Europe, what is often referred to as the medieval period in China followed on the collapse of the first great empire, the Han, between the late second and early fourth centuries C.E and the rule of much of the land by "barbarians," non-Chinese tribes from the north. Unlike its Western counterpart, China's middle ages also included the eventual reunification of the empire under the Sui rulers from the north in 589, almost immediately followed by the Tang dynasty, which lasted from 618 to 907. The political instability that marked the centuries from the downfall of the Han to the reunification of the Sui hindered the engagement in public life that Confucius had sought to foster and that had gradually become institutionalized during the Han.

Arguments for attention to individual, as opposed to collective, needs were provided by Daoist and Buddhist doctrines that attracted increasing numbers of adherents at this time. The Buddhist focus on the individual's renunciation of the duties and rewards of this world marked a radical departure from Confucianism's emphasis on social and ethical responsibility. Buddhism made significant inroads in both northern and southern China during the period of division. Its monasteries became repositories of some of the most important works of art produced during the middle ages, and for centuries thereafter Buddhist rituals would mark milestones such as birth, marriage, and death in the lives of both commoners and the imperial household.

Reunification of China returned the center of government to the northern capital of Chang'an, within whose city walls approximately a million people resided during the Tang dynasty's most prosperous period, the reign of Emperor Xuanzong (712–756). Diplomats, students, and Buddhist monks from Japan and Korea stayed for extended periods in the capital, as well as artists, musicians, nomads, and merchants from India, Persia, and the Middle East. Governing an empire that extended a thousand miles from the Great Wall to the north to Hainan Island in the south, with a registered population of nearly fifty million, required a complex system of taxation, state monopolies, and forced labor, as well as an elaborate structure of provincial and county administration staffed by educated bureaucrats. As had always been the case, aristocratic birth offered the easiest entry into government office, but the civil service examination now began to vie for importance as a means of qualification.

Five major examinations, which conferred five different degrees, were offered throughout the Tang, but the one requiring the most sophisticated literary talent quickly became the most prestigious one; it led to the degree of "presented scholar" (*jinshi*), someone suitable for presentation to the emperor. The range of knowledge tested on the *jinshi* examination was relatively broad; its basic curriculum included literature, the classics, current affairs, and administrative issues, thereby approaching fairly closely the Confucian ideal of a liberal education. During the Tang, a test of poetic composition was included at various times on the examination, providing testimony not only to the stature of poetry as a literary form during the dynasty but also an index of its deep embeddedness in official life. Court appointees had to be prepared to write at the command of a member of the ruling family. If the emperor composed a poem inspired by some outing or memorable event, courtiers would be expected to "respond respectfully," using the same form and rhyme scheme. (Tang forms regulated line length and number of words per line, required a single rhyme for all even-numbered lines, and called for strict parallelism of syntax and meaning between lines as well as patterns of alternation between tones of words.) Or a member of the ruling family might simply set the topic, with officials in attendance composing poems at his command or using a rhyme assigned by him. Anecdotes surviving from such events typically record who finished his poem first and whose was judged of the highest quality.

The practices of court poetry were honed to perfection by poets of the Tang in nonofficial contexts as well. Older forms permitted greater metrical freedom and maintained their popularity, and all forms of Chinese poetry, whether old or new, could take advantage of features of the classical language itself, which seems spare and sometimes ambiguous when compared with Western European languages, owing to its lack of inflection and characteristic omission of indications of person, tense, and other grammatical relationships. To an experienced reader familiar with the conventions, a typical poem would not—as has been argued by some—be read as "telegraphic," but it would leave much unspecified in the text. A good example is the following quatrain by Li Bo (701–770) that is still memorized by Chinese schoolchildren today. A word-for-word rendering is shown beneath the Chinese characters:

靜 夜 思

Quiet Night Thought

牀 前 明 月 光

Bed front bright moon radiance

疑 是 地 上 霜

Suspect is ground upon frost

舉 頭 望 明 月

Raise head gaze bright moon

低 頭 思 故 鄉

Lower head think old province

Thoughts on a Quiet Night

Before my bed the bright moon's gleam
I take to be frost on the ground.
Lifting my head I gaze at the bright moon;
Lowering my head I think of home.

Readers have long appreciated the way in which these twenty words convey a powerful sense of a traveler's longing without making any overt emotional reference. Skilled poets such as Wang Wei or Du Fu excelled in the ability to manipulate the many requirements of the regulated verse forms in the service of nuanced expression and evocative description.

Japan

Politics, Religion, and Culture

From the fourth century onward, a number of powerful clans dominated the Japanese archipelago. Gradually the Yamato clan conquered the other clans and formed an imperial court centered on a sovereign who claimed descent from the Sun Goddess (Amaterasu), incorporating the heads of the other clans into a state administrative system. This imperial clan was to rule Japan or stand as a figurehead for political authority for many centuries up until the present.

Buddhism was introduced to Japan from China in the middle of the sixth century, and it became a major carrier of Chinese civilization. The animistic folk beliefs later called Shintō saw the divine in nature and focused on fertility and life in this world. In contrast, Buddhism focused on suffering and death. The seventh and eighth centuries saw the introduction of a writing system based on Chinese graphs, Chinese literature, and Chinese philosophy, particularly Confucianism, which established a sociopolitical and moral code based on the family, with filial piety as the highest virtue. Chinese became the official language of government and religion in Japan, creating a double system of spoken Japanese and written Chinese.

In 794, the imperial capital moved to Heian, present-day Kyoto, marking the beginning of four centuries of cultural efflorescence centered on the imperial court and aristocratic life. The Fujiwara clan came to the fore in the Heian period, taking firm control of the throne in the latter half of the tenth century, using regents to rule in place of a child emperor. The Fujiwara married their daughters to the emperor, thereby becoming the uncles of future emperors, and placing a clan member in position to be ruling chancellor. They poured vast resources into the entourages and residences of these imperial consorts, enabling women's court literature to flourish at this time. The most powerful of these regents was Fujiwara Michinaga (966–1027), whose eldest daughter Shōshi became empress and consort of Emperor Ichijō (r. 986–1011). Murasaki Shikibu probably wrote much of *The Tale of Genji* while serving as a lady in waiting to Empress Shōshi.

The Tale of Genji reveals the high level of cultural accomplishment of the imperial court—in such diverse fields as calligraphy, painting, poetry, incense, dance, and music—even as it focuses on the vicissitudes of a wide range of very distinctive women. Much of vernacular literature from the Heian period through the medieval period exists in a larger Buddhist context that regards excessive attachment—especially deep emotions such as resentment, hatred, and love—as the cause for suffering and a serious deterrent to individual salvation. In *The Tale of Genji,* the Buddhist notion of impermanence is embodied in the fleeting cherry blossoms and many of the most moving, powerfully emotional scenes are those that are the result of the sorrowful and fleeting nature of things.

At the end of the twelfth century, two major warrior clans, the Heike (Taira) and the Genji (Minamoto), engaged in an extended war for control of the capital and the court, ushering in the age of the samurai. The result was two political centers, a Heike court government in Kyoto and a Genji military government in the East, with the latter asserting ever greater control. Out of this struggle developed a new warrior culture: the frugal lifestyle of the samurai, the strong fighting spirit, and samurai ethics of self-sacrifice, honor, and loyalty. During this period, the Buddhist temples became the institutional centers of learning and culture, much as the church did in medieval Europe. In the late medieval period, from 1336 to 1572, the political center shifted back to Kyoto. The Ashikaga shogunate, or military government, was to rule over Japan for almost two and a half centuries. It came of age with its third shogun, Ashikaga Yoshimitsu (r. 1368–1394), who unified the rival imperial courts, took control of the imperial court in Kyoto, and became a great patron of the arts.

General Characteristics of Japanese Literature

Japanese literature often stresses brevity, condensation, and overtones. The paring down of form and expression occurs in a wide variety of forms: poetry such as the haiku, the shortest poetic form in world literature, Noh drama, gardens, bonsai, tea ceremony, and ink painting, to mention only the most obvious. Japanese drama and prose fiction, while sometimes possessing elaborate and complex plot structures, are usually concerned with the elaboration of a particular mood or state of mind. *The Tale of Genji* is highlighted by a series of partings, including the deaths and departures of major characters throughout the book. The closeness of traditional social ties—between parent and child, lord and retainer, husband and wife, individual and group—makes the parting an emotionally explosive situation, which is often presented in highly poetical language.

The lyrical character of Japanese vernacular literature derives in significant part from the fusion of genres and media that in European literature are generally thought of as being separate. In Japan, prose fiction and prose writing are extensively interwoven with poetry and poetic diction. Since the Renaissance, European theater has generally been split into three basic forms—drama, opera, and ballet—whereas traditional Japanese theater has combined these elements (acting, music, and dance) in Noh drama, kabuki, and jōruri, or puppet theater (for an extraordinary example of the latter, see Chikamatsu Mon'zaemon's *The Love Suicides at Amijima,* page 1865). This multimedia quality often means that instead of emphasizing the world being represented, the dramatic work calls attention to itself as a medium of performance.

Like the structure of the prose narratives, Japanese literary forms tend to add on to rather than replace one another. Every major historical era gave birth to new literary and artistic genres, but usually without destroying or abandoning the earlier forms. The thirty-one syllable classical poem emerged in the Nara and Heian periods, linked verse in the medieval period, the seventeen-syllable haiku in the Edo period, and free verse in the modern period (under the influence of Western poetry). With the exception of linked verse, all of these poetic genres continue to flourish today in Japan. The same is true of Japanese drama. Noh and its comic counterpart, kyōgen, emerged in the Muromachi period; jōruri and kabuki became dominant in the Edo theater, and modern theater came to the fore in the twentieth century. Instead of each new form displacing the previous one, these dramatic forms have continued to coexist even today. An early masterpiece such as *The Tale of Genji* thus remains an ongoing presence in Japanese literature in the twenty-first century.

The Islamic World

When it comes to the word, the language that played a substantial role in the shaping and development of Arabic culture, Islam shares the emphasis on language and writing that also governed Judaism and Christianity. The emergence of Islam and the codification of the Arabic language in the Qur'an ensured the continuous development of Arabic over two millennia. The oldest record of Arabic appeared in an Assyrian account of fighting from 853 to 626 B.C.E. Mecca, the commercial center of Arabia, acted as a linguistic melting pot that developed a standard language out of a myriad of different dialects. By the sixth century, there was a widely recognized literary language distinct from all forms of the spoken language in common currency in Arabia.

Arabic poetry is deeply rooted in oral tradition, and it was a voice long before it was expressed through an alphabet. Poets did not create poetry for themselves but for the tribe and on behalf of the whole community. This poetry was often connected to religious ritual, a dimension that was enhanced by the concept of divine inspiration. Both poets and their audiences believed that the poet was touched by a *jinn* (a demon

Calligraphy of the name of the Prophet Muhammad, Turkey, 1827. Based on centuries-old calligraphic traditions, this dynamic verbal "image" of the Prophet is surrounded by a description (*hilyah*) of the Prophet by his son-in-law 'Ali, which concludes: "When walking, he leaned forward, as if descending a slope. If he turned to see something, he would turn with his whole body. Between his shoulders he had the Seal of Prophethood. He was the last of the Prophets."

or Muse), who revealed the poem to him. Poetry played the role of the media in our present time: poets spread the news, elaborated the official line on issues, and attacked the enemies of the caliphs, Muhammad's successors. The Qur'an too developed poetic oral recitation and used it very effectively; it is no coincidence that the only miracle of Muhammad was a verbal miracle, the Qur'an itself. Poetry maintained its position in the culture for centuries, even though Muhammad had an early aversion to poetry and the Qur'an says of poets that "most of them are liars" who "wander distractedly in every valley" (26:223–25).

Muhammad was born around 570 C.E. into a distinguished Meccan family. Orphaned in early childhood, he was brought up by a succession of relatives and around 595 married a rich, older Meccan woman, Khadija. Little is known of the period between his marriage at the age of twenty-five and the revelation of the message of Islam to him at the age of forty around the year 610. One clear explanation is theological: the archangel Gabriel suddenly appeared to him and gave him a prophetic call. The early Meccan verses of the Qur'an enumerated the various manifestations of God in nature that should convince those who have time to reflect and logically deduce that there is sublime power greater than human power—*islam* means "surrender" to God. Muhammad's early preaching was tolerated because it didn't threaten the gods of Mecca or disturb its social hierarchy. Things changed when he openly attacked polytheism and the gods of Mecca, and declared that the Ka'bah, the traditional Meccan sanctuary, belonged only to the one true God, Allah. The powerful merchant class turned against Muhammad when he called for justice, attacked greed and the oppression of the poor, and asked people to free themselves from love of wealth and from all forms of deceit.

The acceleration and severity of the opposition of the notables of Mecca to his call, combined with the death of his wife, led to Muhammad's migration, or *hijra,* to Medina in 622. The *hijra* marked the beginning of the formative years of Islam itself as a major religion and the emergence of the community of believers as a force to reckon with. In 628 a treaty was negotiated with Mecca, allowing Muhammad and his followers to make their annual pilgrimage there. When the Meccans broke the treaty the following year, Muhammad decided to invade his birthplace, and achieved the conquest of Mecca in 630, becoming the strongest man in Arabia. Muhammad succeeded in uniting the complementary resources of the nomadic and the urban Arabs, and the Arab area within the peninsula was integrated in a manner never before attained. Soon the nation became a vast empire, and developed a civilization religious in spirit and manifestation.

The Muslim domain continued to expand after Mohammad's death in 632, conquering the whole of Persia, Syria, Palestine, Jerusalem, Egypt, and North Africa as far as present-day Tunis. A civil war ensued between the followers of the Prophet's cousin and son-in-law 'Ali and the 'Umayyad caliphate, resulting in the split between Sunni or orthodox Muslims and supporters of 'Ali, known as the Shi'ites ("followers"). The Umayyads expanded the Muslim Empire to India and sub-Saharan Africa, and to Andalusia in Spain. The Umayyads were supportive patrons of poetry and theology, but it was during the reign of the subsequent Abbasid Caliphate (750–1258) that Muslim civilization reached its peak culturally, economically, scientifically, and militarily, extending the boundaries of the empire to China and Southeast Asia and spreading Islam through a large part of Africa. "The Tale of Sympathy the Learned" in *The Thousand and One Nights* gives the reader a glimpse of the cultural atmosphere in the court the Abbasids had established in Baghdad.

Most of the major classical poets are from this period, including Abu Nuwas and Ibn al-Rumi. The study of language flourished and the intricate forms of Arabic poetry were skillfully codified. The first Arabic dictionary was compiled and literary history and criticism of Arabic literature were initiated. This was also the period that saw the advancement of Arabic mathematics and sciences: geometry, algebra, medicine, alchemy, physics, chemistry, and anatomy all flourished. Most of the knowledge developed during this period was later translated into Latin and formed a key basis for the late Middle Ages and the Renaissance in Europe. Without the translations made at the Baghdad center known as the School of Wisdom, we might not now be able to enjoy the critical insights of Aristotle, whose *Poetics* was preserved thanks to the Arabic translation.

Islamic culture also continued to develop in Persian and other languages of the Muslim world. Following the fall of the Abbasid dynasty in 1258, the principal center of power moved from Baghdad first to Egypt and then to Turkey with the rise of the

Ottomans (1500–1900). The most notable developments took place in Andalusia, in the field of intellectual inquiry and Islamic philosophy, and in Egypt in the field of narrative and popular epics. The work of the most distinguished Islamic philosopher, Ibn Rushd or Averroës of Córdoba, is a product of the Arabic culture in Andalusia. He had immense influence on the Jewish and Christian worlds of philosophy. In Egypt, a proliferation of popular literature gave rise to exquisite epics such as those of Bani-Hilal and 'Antara, and a large number of the stories of *The Thousand and One Nights* were elaborated.

With the Qur'an, Arabic became a world language, the language of medieval Islamic civilization, the Latin of the Muslim world. With the expansion of the Islamic *'umma* (community or nation) into a multiracial and multicultural civilization, many other cultural influences have been absorbed into Arabic culture and enriched its capacity for expression. Similarly, Arabic forms and Islamic traditions have penetrated many other languages and cultures, as can be seen in the Perspectives section, Iberia: the Meeting of Three Worlds.

MEDIEVAL EUROPE

There is no doubt that medieval Europe was a difficult place in which to live. Waves of raids, invasions, and tribal migrations rolled through and destabilized the former Roman Empire: Germanic tribes in the fifth and sixth centuries, followed by Vikings from the north, Muslims from the south, and Magyar and other Central Asian tribes from the east. War remained a way of life through the thirteenth century, with myriad territorial skirmishes and numerous Crusades into Iberia, the Middle East, and North Africa. Then, in the mid-fourteenth century, the Black Plague killed off a third of Europe's population. For all of its terrors the Middle Ages bequeathed to later European culture much of its identity and heritage: the geographic, social, and political conceptions of Europe and most of the European nations; the cathedrals, castles, and cities; the institutions of government and religion; the codes of honor and chivalry; the languages, the poetry of love, and the stories of adventure. A good argument can be made that the Renaissance was itself a medieval invention.

Imperial rule had spread the Latin language across the continent, and Latin continued to play a key role in ecclesiastical and monastic life as well as in government, administration, and law. As economic expansion brought relative social and political stability in the twelfth and thirteenth centuries, the vernacular languages as we know them today began to predominate—English, French, Spanish, German, and Italian among others—and many of the national borders (and border disputes) began to solidify. In this period, usually known as the High Middle Ages, internationalism came to mean not so much a shared culture and authority as a broad knowledge of many different cultures and authorities. The English poet Geoffrey Chaucer was a professional diplomat equally at ease in local dialects around Britain, in French in Paris and in Tuscan Italian in Florence; the Florentine poet Dante Alighieri wrote a treatise on the Romance languages and incorporated the vocabulary of Latin, Occitan (also known as Provençal), French, and many Italian dialects into his *Divine Comedy*. England was ruled for several centuries by Normans, descendants of the original "Northmen," ninth-century Danish invaders who had settled in Normandy in northwest France; the court language was Anglo-Norman, a version of Old French. A mix

Scenes from the Bayeux Tapestry, France, late 11th century. Attributed to Queen Matilda (wife of William the Conqueror) and her attendants, this great scroll of embroidered linen (230 feet long by 20 inches high) depicts the Norman Conquest of England in exuberant detail.

of Byzantine, Muslim, Jewish, Lombard, Norman and later peoples made long-established cities such as Palermo in Sicily new centers of cultural interchange and innovation. Muslim rulers long controlled southern Iberia, known then as al-Andalus: their administrations were full of Jewish courtiers, their cities crowded with Mozarabs, or arabized Christians, and their armies strengthened by complex alliances with neighboring Christian rulers.

Language and Culture

After they had sacked Rome in 410, Germanic tribes out of northern and southeastern Europe eventually took over and settled different regions of the now-dissolved empire. Monastic communities and ambitious churchmen and rulers invested much time, money and artistry into copying ancient manuscripts and attempting to preserve a Latin heritage in danger of vanishing forever. Most of the literature that has come down to us from before the eleventh century is in the medieval or low Latin that was the lingua franca of the time. It is handwritten in ink on sheets of parchment (made from the skin of cattle, sheep, or goats) bound together down one edge, in what is known as a codex. In addition to lyrics of nature and of love, hymns and other forms of religious poetry were dominant genres; both forms were often emotional and direct in their language and imagery. Alongside these written examples of Latin poetry, there were local oral traditions such as the Celtic tales or *lais,* the Anglo-Saxon epic of the great chieftain Beowulf, and popular songs all over the continent.

Most educated Romans had been fluent in both Latin and Greek, but once the empire had been divided between East and West in the fourth century, this gradually ceased to be the case. Greek was a lost language in western Europe. Homer was known only by reputation, and the philosophy of Plato and Aristotle only through Roman commentaries of a few minor works. Greek thought eventually made its way back into Christian Europe across the boundary between Islam and Christianity and by means of Arabic translations, accompanied by learned glosses by contemporary philosophers such as the Jewish scholar Moses Maimonides and Ibn Rushd, also known as Averroës the Commentator. In important frontier cities such as Toledo (recaptured from al-Andalus in 1058) and Palermo (known as the city of the threefold tongue, taken by the Normans in 1072), Jewish, Muslim, and Christian scholars debated while they translated the wisdom of the ancients into Latin. Translators at work in the 13th-century Galician-Portuguese court of Alfonso X, for instance, included five Jews, four Spanish Christians, four Italians, a Muslim converted to Christianity, technical editors to deal with difficult terms, and secretaries to write everything down.

Religion and the Church

Catholic Christianity was simultaneously the strongest link between the Middle Ages and the classical world and the strongest impediment to that link. Until the twelfth century, scholarship was conducted almost entirely under the auspices of the church, first in the monasteries and later in cathedral towns and in the courts of rulers such as Charlemagne, founder of the Holy Roman Empire in 800. As opposed to the courtier's life that characterized the southern frontier cities and Islamic capitals, monastic scholarship prided itself on detachment from worldly concerns.

By contrast, the papacy, increasingly embroiled in the temporal demands of politics and governance and generally suspicious of new ideas, more closely resembled the southern courts than the monasteries. The papal states accumulated vast wealth and power through being a principal player or influence in nearly every one of the countless negotiations, treaties, wars, and betrayals that raged throughout the period. The worldly preeminence of the papacy was seen by many reformers to be at odds with the Gospel message of Jesus that salvation was to be found in discarding wealth and earthly ties. Great damage was done to papal prestige when in 1378 the Great Schism led to thirty-seven years of competing French and Italian popes in Avignon and Rome. The stage was set for the Protestant Reformation to challenge the papacy's thousand-year supremacy as the spiritual voice of the Christian church.

Reform took many shapes before Martin Luther's definitive rebellion in 1518, from powerful figures within the ecclesiastical inner circles to abbots, abbesses, monks and nuns to laymen and -women whom divine inspiration led to take up preaching or writing. One of the earliest was Saint Benedict (c. 480–c. 550), whose celebrated "Rule" guided the rituals of daily monastic life for centuries to come, covering even details of eating, drinking and sleeping. Benedictines and later orders were also invested in expanding the frontiers of Christianity through conversion.

Crusading was an important way of uniting the Christians of Europe and channeling outward their military energy and thirst for plunder. Quixotic enthusiasts such as the founder of the Franciscan order of mendicant (or begging) friars saw it as their duty to convert the heathens across the Mediterranean (Saint Francis of Assisi traveled to Egypt to preach to the Sultan after five of his brethren had been martyred there), but the customary ecclesiastical response was to kill them. The first Crusade was proclaimed by Pope Urban II in 1095 following the Byzantine emperor's request for aid against the Muslims. The inflamed piety of the Crusaders marching eastward took its toll on non-Christians along the way, especially the Jews, who were slaughtered indiscriminately. The Crusaders made it all the way to Jerusalem, which they captured on July 15, 1099, killing, plundering, and weeping for pious joy. Following this initial

Medieval Europe, c. 1100 C.E.
NORWAY
SWEDEN
SCOTLAND
NORTH SEA
DENMARK
BALTIC SEA
IRELAND
ENGLAND
WALES
Oxford
Cambridge
London
Canterbury
Elbe
RUSSIAN PRINCIPALITIES
POLAND
Cologne
Rhine
HOLY ROMAN EMPIRE
Prague
Rheims
ATLANTIC OCEAN
Worms
Danube
Bec
Paris
Chartres
Orléans
Angers
Tours
Meung
HUNGARY
FRANCE
ALPS
Vicenza
Grenoble
Milan
Venice
Padua
VENETIAN REPUBLIC
NAVARRE
Montpellier
Piacenza
Bologna
Toulouse
Avignon
Genoa
BULGARIA
León
LEÓN
Béziers
Pisa
Arezzo
Pamplona
Narbonne
Marseille
Siena
Perugia
SERBIA
CASTILE
Assisi
Tarazona
Salamanca
ARAGON
CORSICA
Coimbra
Rome
Segovia
Barcelona
PORTUGAL
PAPAL STATES
Toledo
Naples
Salerno
BYZANTINE EMPIRE
Lisbon
SARDINIA
Cordova
BALEARIC ISLANDS
KINGDOM OF SICILY
Seville
Palermo
SICILY
ALMOHAD EMPIRE
CRETE
MEDITERRANEAN SEA
N
England
Holy Roman Empire
Byzantine Empire
France
Poland
Almohad Empire

triumph, there were seven named Crusades through to the end of the thirteenth century, nearly all ending in calamitous defeat, as well as many other related expeditions, and even a disastrous Children's Crusade in 1212.

Feudalism

Warfare was a viable way of life for an entire estate of the medieval population, the *chevalier,* or knight. After the death of Charlemagne in 814, the empire crumbled into pieces of various sizes and influence, each one occupied by a lord with a certain amount of land under his control, himself often beholden to other lords, dukes or kings with broader jurisdictions. It was customary for holdings to be divided among all descendants upon the death of a lord, so there was no stable pattern of inheritance from first-born to first-born (the practice known as primogeniture). Lands were constantly being brought together and split apart in an endless, many-sided tug-of-war. As families intermarried and allegiances overlapped and intertwined, the form of social and political organization known as feudalism emerged as a way of giving some sort of structure to this chaos.

Feudalism varied across Europe, but there were some fundamental features. The primary relation was between lord and vassal, formalized by an oath of fealty, swearing mutual aid, protection, and vengeance if one party were killed. Lord and vassal were bound by a set of laws and a broader set of customs and traditions of which many elements survive to this day in the abstract concepts of honor and chivalry, a phenomenon explored at uproarious length many centuries later in Cervantes's novel, *Don Quixote*. In practice, of course, things were not as simple as Don Quixote would regard them: vassals were often obligated to several lords simultaneously, allegiances were bartered and sold, and a bond could dissolve in an instant if something better (for one party) came along. The Occitan poet Bertran de Born, for example, spent much of his life fighting with his brother for sole possession of the family castle.

The other principal component of the feudal hierarchy was the worker. The traditional use of slaves for field labor was less customary by this time. There were some peasants of free status who owed only rent, but most were serfs, bound to both lord and land. In the commonest scenario, a serf would be allowed to cultivate a plot of land for himself in return for cultivating other plots belonging to the lord. The serf would also receive a place to live in the village appended to the local manor, with protection in the event of attack from outside. Hunger, however, was the immediate concern. The clergy was equally embroiled in the feudal web, for local parish appointments and bishoprics were often controlled by local lords. Unsurprisingly, in a milieu rife with alliances and intrigues, the culture of feudalism excelled in the portrayal of situational ethics, using tales of knight errantry and epic heroism to explore the costs and benefits of the different choices of action and different types of behavior possible (or impossible) within the constraints of its world.

Lyric and Song

The cultural milieu of the feudal world was the court. The love lyric was elaborated in the worldly Andalusian cities of Córdoba, Granada, and Seville, and it flourished in the isolated castles of Occitania, the Anglo-Norman courts of England, the northern French seats such as Troyes in Champagne, and the courts of the German monarchs.

When not off fighting in battle, the knights and their lords required entertainment. This was the role of the *jongleur,* who would perform the songs produced by the troubadours and other songwriters around Europe. The lyrics reflect the interests of the audience: there is some singing of battle, a little of God, and much of the courtly pastimes of hunting, falconing, and, above all, lovemaking. For several centuries during the High Middle Ages, there was not a court without its resident poets, and the love lyrics they perfected remain with us to this day.

Song was not restricted to the feudal courts. Hymns and chants were integral to the experience of mass, and to the everyday life of many monks and nuns. Many working songs survive as well, songs for spinning, songs of injustice and rebellion, songs mimicking the sounds of different occupations. The *jongleurs* and other performers who traveled from court to court were well versed in many genres besides the love lyric. At court, they might also perform traditional epics, such as the *Song of Roland,* the legendary tale of Charlemagne's worthy vassal, or folktales, such as those Marie de France translated in her *Lais,* or satirical and parodic songs. Perhaps not at court, but at inns and on the road, they might also perform from a broad repertory of popular songs for less cultivated audiences. Traveling performers and pilgrims, such as the Goliards, or vagabond scholars, carried both sacred and profane tunes and lyrics back and forth across the continent, adapting and transforming them to suit different audiences, different musical instruments and different expectations.

The Rise of the Cities

The irreverent songs of the vagabond scholars had little in common with the isolated refinement of the courts. The Goliard phenomenon was directly linked to the rise of cities and the universities within them in the twelfth and thirteenth centuries. Through the first part of the Middle Ages, the only large Western cities were in the south of Europe, in Muslim Iberia and in Sicily. Better crop rotation, a healthier diet, and new technology—the heavy plow, pulled by teams of horse or oxen, the water mill and later the windmill—helped the population of Europe to double between the eleventh century and the fourteenth, to around 70 or 80 million. Increased political stability and long-distance trade contributed to growth, as did a marked warming trend in the weather. The new population migrated to the growing cities, first in Italy, center of trade with the East and with North Africa, and later in northern Europe. Plying the rivers of Europe, commercial networks developed to link north and south further.

During these same centuries, European society was transformed from an oral to a literate culture. By 1300 commerce and government were dependent on written records and financial recordkeeping, introduced by Jewish merchants familiar with the practice from the wealthier and more sophisticated cultures of Islam and Byzantium. One reason for the rise of the universities was the need to train a body of clerks in these newly required skills. Many of these universities, such as those in Bologna, Paris, Oxford, Cambridge, Heidelberg, and Salamanca, survive to this day. Students and teachers were frequently planning to be or already were members of the secular clergy, unattached to a monastery or particular church. This "clerkly" culture was instrumental in the philosophical and literary movement known as the twelfth-century renaissance: a renewed interest in classical philosophy and literature paired with an increased investment in rational argumentation and the study of the physical world. It also gave rise to a body of writings that used women as the target for an attack against marriage and sensuality steeped in the ascetic tradition of ancient Roman *virtus* while reveling in the worldliness it detailed. The ambivalence of clerkly misogyny was captured well in Chaucer's "Wife of Bath's Prologue."

The newly intellectual focus on rationality and experience was seen by many religious figures to come at the expense of the basic tenets of the Christian faith. In a similar way, the new the manufacturers and traders, or burghers, of the towns were for the most part also pious, although their piety did not always manifest itself in ways pleasing to the ecclesiastical authorities. A common ground was found in the magnificent cathedrals erected during these centuries, and funded in large part by the new urban wealth. Cathedrals such as Chartres or Notre-Dame de Paris, by far the tallest buildings in the land and visible for many miles, were holy places, but they were also the skyscrapers of their day, a brand-new architectural form symbolizing the new wealth and power of secular cities. The stained-glass windows (a twelfth-century innovation) are wonders of biblical storytelling; they also epitomize the art and invention of the urban artisans and manufacturers and the resources of the benefactors able to fund their artistry. Cathedrals were not simply houses of worship: they were guardians of relics and places of pilgrimage, the center of the social calendar, and the site of baptisms, marriages, and funerals. Since they often had at their feet the largest open spaces in the densely packed medieval city, they were the focal point of nearly every aspect of urban life.

Allegory and Adventure

One of the reasons that so many different uses and contradictions could coexist in the same place and in a single person is that the medieval mind preferred analogy to symbolism. Symbolic thinking typically attaches a unique and unchanging meaning to a specific word or object (the cathedral as a sacred place of worship), and an individual to a single, fixed identity from cradle to grave. By contrast, medieval thought tended to conceptualize the world in terms of a complex network of parallel relations. A critical device in this analogical way of thinking about the world was allegory, a mode of writing that marks nearly every aspect of medieval culture, most memorably perhaps in the realm of literature. To approach the world allegorically is to regard it as simultaneously possessing a multitude of meanings. Just as the medieval person was accustomed to juggling several languages and several different cultures, so was she or he accustomed to keeping multiple meanings in mind simultaneously, or to singing sacrilegious songs in the tavern while piously praying in church, without feeling obligated to choose irrevocably between any of the several apparently contradictory possibilities. The mysterious behavior of the Green Knight in the fourteenth-century romance *Sir Gawain and the Green Knight,* for example, is neither psychologically consistent nor immediately comprehensible; nevertheless, it compels the reader's attention, demanding that his riddle be solved even as the complexities of the characters and events belie any simple answer.

The medieval world, like the literature that has survived from it, is a fascinating combination of familiarity and alienness. Much that seems to us traditional, even timeless, was in fact brand new in the Middle Ages, from chivalry and love poetry to the cathedrals and cities to the Catholic Christian church and the very idea of Europe.

And much of what the Renaissance chose to exclude from the Middle Ages, especially the legacy of the classical world, was for the medieval person a fact of everyday life. To think medievally is to think several ways at once; that was their great accomplishment and the great challenge and joy their literature poses to a modern reader, accustomed to thinking in one language, one culture, and one identity at a time.

The Medieval Era

Year	The World	Literature
200		
	220 End of Han dynasty in China	
	220–265 Three Kingdoms period in China	
	265–419 Chin dynasty in China	
300		
	335–470 Gupta dynasty in northern India	
		365–427 Life of Chinese poet Tao Qian
400		
	c. 400 Unification of Japan	**c. 400** *Mahabharata* achieves established form
	410 Visigoths sack Rome	
	420 China divided between Southern and Northern dynasties (to 589)	
	450 Anglo-Saxons invade England	
500		
		524 Boethius, *The Consolation of Philosophy*
	530 Justinian Code	
	c. 550 Buddhism introduced to Japan	
	c. 570–632 Life of the Prophet Muhammad	
	588 Lombards invade Italy	
	589 Sui dynasty in China (to 618)	
600		
		c. 600–646 Life of pre-Islamic woman poet al-Khansa'
	618 Tang dynasty in China (to 907)	
	622 Hegira of Muhammad from Mecca; foundation of Islam	
	638 Arab conquest of Jerusalem	
		651–652 Text of Qur'an established
		c. 658–680 Caedmon's dream hymn
	698 Arabs take Carthage	
700		
	700 Benedictine missionaries complete the Christianization of England begun by Gregory the Great	
		701 Birth of Chinese poets Wang Wei (d. 761) and Li Bo (d. 762)
	710–784 Nara period in Japan	
	711–715 Arabs arrive in Spain and in western India	
		712–770 Life of poet Du Fu
		731 The Venerable Bede, *Ecclesiastical History of the English Nation*
	732 Charles Martel halts Arab invasion at Poitiers	
	750 Abbasid dynasty in Middle East and North Africa (to 1258)	**c. 750** Irish monks produce the *Book of Kells;* Ibn Ishaq writes *The Biography of the Prophet*
		c. 750–950 *Beowulf*
		753 The Venerable Bede dies
		759 *Manyōshū,* collection of Japanese court poetry
	763 Tibetans invade Tang China	
	772–804 Saxon Wars	
	786–809 Haroun al-Rashid is Caliph in Baghdad	
	794–1185 Heian period in Japan	

YEAR	THE WORLD	LITERATURE
800	**800** Fujiwara clan achieves dominance in Japan (to 12th century) **800** Charlemagne is crowned Holy Roman Emperor (dies in 814) **819** Samanid dynasty in Persia (to 1005) **870** Vikings discover Iceland **899** Alfred the Great of England dies	**810–850** Writings by al-Jahiz, Arabic prose master **868** *The Diamond Sutra,* world's oldest surviving printed book
900	**907** Five Dynasties period in China (to 959) **960** Song dynasty in China (to 1279) **979** Paper money introduced in China	
1000	**1000** Sweden begins to be converted to Christianity; Iceland converted to Christianity **c. 1000** Vikings reach North America	**10th century** First mozarabic *kharjas* in Spain **1002** Sei Shōnagon, *The Pillow Book* **c. 1000–1019** Murasaki Shikibu, *The Tale of Genji*
1010	**1018** Choles conquer Sri Lanka	**1010** Firdawsi's Persian epic, the *Shahname*
1020		**1027** Ibn Hazm, *The Dove's Neckring*
1030	**1031** Christian reconquest of Spain begins	
1040	**c. 1045** Chinese invent movable type printing	
1050	**1054** Great Schism between the Eastern and Western Churches	
1060	**1066** Battle of Hastings: William the Conqueror and Normans begin their rule over the British Isles	**1063–1078** Anselm of Canterbury, *Proslogion*
1070	**1071** Seljuk Turks defeat Byzantines at Manzikert	**1071–1127** William of Aquitaine, the first known troubadour **1075–1141** Yehuda ha-Levi, author of poems and *The Book of the Khazars*
1080	**1085** Yorimoto becomes first shogun of Japan; Christians recapture Toledo, Spain	
1090	**1095** Pope Urban II preaches the First Crusade **1099** Fall of Jerusalem to Christian crusaders	
1100	**c. 1100** Anasazi build cliff dwellings at Mesa Verde and Chaco Canyon	
1110		

Year	**The World**	**Literature**
1120	**c. 1122–1204** Eleanor of Aquitaine, queen consort of Louis VII of France (1137–1152) and of Henry II of England (1152–1204)	
1130	**1130** Song move capital to Huangzhou	**1130–1145** Bernard of Clairvaux, *Sermons on the Song of Songs* **c. 1133–1140** Letters of Abelard and Heloise
1140	**1147–1149** Second Crusade	**1141–1152** Hildegard von Bingen, *Scivias* **1146–1174** *The Play of Adam*
1150	**1152** Temple of Angkor Wat completed	**c. 1150** Geoffrey of Monmouth, *History of the Kings of Britain*
1160	**1163** Foundation stone laid for the cathedral of Notre-Dame de Paris **1167** Foundation of Oxford University	**1160–1180** Marie de France, *Lais* **1165–1180** Chrétien de Troyes, Arthurian romances **1169–1196** Ibn Rushd (Averroës), summaries and commentaries on Aristotle
1170	**1170** Death of Thomas Becket ordered by Henry II	**1177** Farid ud-Din al'Attar, *The Conference of the Birds*
1180	**1187** Saladin retakes Jerusalem from the Christians **1189–1192** Third Crusade led by Richard I the Lion-Heart and Frederick Barbarossa	**1180–1194** Bertran de Born, *Songs* **1186–1196** Andreas Capellanus, *The Art of Courtly Love*
1190	**1198** Innocent III founds the Papal State and organizes the Fourth Crusade to recapture Jerusalem from the Arabs	**1190–1230** Walther von der Vogelweide, *Songs*
1200	**1206** Genghis Khan unites Mongols **1208** Innocent III proclaims the Albigensian Crusade	**late 12th–early 13th century** *The Poem of the Cid* **1207–1283** Life of Persian mystical poet Jalaloddin Rumi
1210	**1215** Magna Carta **1216** Dominican order founded by St. Dominic of Spain	**c. 1210** Gottfried von Strassburg, *Tristan* **1212** Kamo no Chomei, *An Account of My Ten-Foot-Square Hut* **1218** First version of *Tales of Heike*
1220	**1222–1242** Mongols invade Europe, rule Russia for two centuries **1227** Death of Genghis Khan **1226** Francis of Assisi dies	**c. 1225** Guillaume de Lorris, *The Romance of the Rose*
1230		
1240	**1244** Muslims capture Jerusalem; West doesn't recapture Jerusalem until 1917 **1248** Construction of the Alhambra begins in Granada	**c. 1240** Snorri Sturluson, *The Prose Edda*

Year	The World	Literature
1250	**1258** Mongols sack Baghdad and end Abbasid dynasty	**c. 1250** Alfonso the Wise, *Cantigas of Santa Maria* **c. 1250–1275** Mechthild von Magdeburg, *A Flowing Light of the Godhead*
1260	**1260** Consecration of Chartres Cathedral **1267** Giotto begins his school of painting in Florence	**c. 1265–1273** Thomas Aquinas, *Summa Theologica* **1267** Brunetto Latini, *Book of the Treasure*
1270	**1270** Eighth Crusade **1279** The Mongols under Kublai Khan crush final Song resistance	
1280	**1280** Yuan (Mongol) dynasty in China (to 1368) **1281** Beginning of Ottoman power in Turkey	**c. 1280** *Njal's Saga* **c. 1284** Ramon Llull, *Blanquerna*
1290	**1292** Marco Polo returns from travels	**1295** Dante Alighieri, *La Vita Nuova* **1298** Marco Polo, *The Book of Marvels*
1300	**1309–1377** Papacy at Avignon	**early 13th century** Ibn al-Arabi, *Gentle Now, Doves* **mid-13th century** Martin Codax, *Songs* **late 13th century** Jean de Meun's continuation of *The Romance of the Rose* **c. 1300–1325** *Songs* by Dom Dinis, King of Portugal **1307–1321** Dante, *The Divine Comedy*
1310		
1320	**1324** Pilgrimage to Mecca of Mansa Musa of Mal	**1321** Dante Alighieri dies
1330	**1337** Hundred Years' War begins **1338** Beginning of Muromachi period in Japan (to 1573)	
1340	**1345–1346** Ibn Battuta travels in Southeast Asia and China **1347–1351** Black Death in Europe	**1340–1374** Francis Petrarch, *Scattered Rhymes* **1343** Juan Ruiz, *The Book of Good Love* **1349** Giovanni Boccaccio, *The Decameron*
1350	**1354** Ottomans begin conquest of the Balkan Peninsula	
1360	**1365** First German university is opened at Heidelberg; the universities of Bologna and Oxford date from the 12th century **1368** Ming dynasty in China (to 1644)	
1370		**1374** Francis Petrarch dies **1378** Death of Muslim world traveler Ibn Battuta
1380	**c. 1380** Ottomans found Janissary corps	**c. 1388–1400** Geoffrey Chaucer, *The Canterbury Tales*
1390	**1398** Tamerlane sacks Delhi	

Year	The World	Literature
1400		**1400** Geoffrey Chaucer dies
		late 14th century *Sir Gawain and the Green Knight*
	1405 Zheng He's first voyage to the Indian Ocean	**1404–1405** Christine de Pizan, *The Book of the City of Ladies*
1410		
1420		
1430	**1431** Joan of Arc dies	
	1434 Medici family gains control over government of Florence	
1440	**1441** Portuguese capture slaves in Africa; start of Atlantic Slave Trade	**1444** Juan de Mena, *The Labyrinth of Fortune*
1450	**1450** Gutenberg invents the printing press	
	1453 Fall of Constantinople; Ottoman Turks end the Eastern Empire	
	1455 Henry VI wages the Wars of the Roses (between Lancaster and York)	
1460	**1469** Ferdinand of Aragon marries Isabella of Castile and unites the kingdom of Spain	**1461** François Villon, *The Testament*
1470		
1480		
1490	**1492** Ferdinand and Isabella annex Granada and expel Jews from Spain; discovery of America	

Beowulf

c. 750–950

"I had always thought of English literature as the richest in the world," wrote the Argentine poet Jorge Luis Borges of his experience of first reading Old English poetry; "the discovery now of a secret chamber at the very threshold of that literature came to me as an additional gift." It is easy to fall under the spell of *Beowulf*'s strangeness and antiquity, of a poetry that makes its characters feel both alien and intensely present, as if freshly arisen from centuries of oblivion beneath the earthen mounds where the Geats and other Germanic tribes would bury their fallen leaders. *Beowulf* is replete with the pagan customs of the *comitati,* the warrior-bands that in the fifth century had swept across Europe from their strongholds in the north: Angles, Saxons, and Jutes across the North Sea to England, Ostrogoths and other tribes southward to topple the Roman Empire. Their heroic code, steeped in values such as revenge, honor, and the gift-giving recalled by Borges above, imbues the poem with the sense of an epoch already lost to time, just as the narrative mirrors its account of the youthful exploits of the hero Beowulf with the story of the end of his long life, battling against a marauding dragon. Composed several centuries later, in a world since converted to Christianity, and set in a land across the North Sea, *Beowulf* is intensely engaged with the ways in which change occurs—from old customs to new, kings to heirs, heathen to Christian, oral culture to the written word—and the deeply conflicted feelings such changes never fail to elicit.

Much of the history of the poem's reception resembles the "secret chamber" of which Borges wrote. We don't know when or where it was composed—hypotheses range from seventh-century East Anglia or Northumbria to tenth-century England—nor do we know who wrote it, layperson or cleric, or whether it was originally written at all—some scholars believe it was dictated by a *scop,* a bard or singer of tales at an Anglo-Saxon court. It survives, by chance, in a single manuscript known as the Nowell Codex, which was copied by two scribes around the year 1000. Nothing is known of its history before the sixteenth century; it was scorched in a fire and nearly destroyed in 1731, and no one realized its value until the early nineteenth century, when it was transcribed and edited by a Danish scholar. Although the author assumed his audience had prior knowledge of the underlying history, there are few known sources for the events described, nor did the poem leave a discernible trace on the literature that came after it—until, that is, the nineteenth century. Like its hero, it seems to stand alone.

Also like its hero, however, *Beowulf* is immersed in a highly developed and sophisticated social world. Its first two parts, some 2,000 lines, are set in the land of the Danes, the Scyldings, or descendants of Scyld, a people blessed by fate, prosperous and secure. When they construct a glorious mead-hall, a gathering place for drinking and feasting, their harp-songs disturb a neighbor, the man-monster Grendel, who plagues their land for a dozen years. The young retainer Beowulf hears of their plight, journeys across the sea from his home in Geatland (in what is now southwestern Sweden), and purges the land of its monsters. In the second part, some thousand lines, more than fifty years have passed, and Beowulf himself now rules the Geats, who find themselves threatened by a monster of their own, a treasure-hoarding dragon awakened from its slumber by a clumsy thief. Beowulf slays the dragon but loses his life, and the poem concludes as the Geats bury their leader and lament their fate, exposed to the might of the neighboring peoples—the Swedes, the Frisians, the Franks—who will lose no time in seizing their land and goods, and probably their lives. *Lif is læne,* the poem tells us, "life is transitory."

The main action revolves around three fights with three superbly imagined monsters: Beowulf pitted against Grendel in the mead-hall, against Grendel's vengeful mother in her underwater lair, and against the dragon in its buried barrow-mound. And while the poem gives ample space to the battle descriptions that were essential to any heroic narrative, the poet was equally engrossed by the intricate web of events and associations touched upon during these duels or arising out of them. Rather than using the linear narration familiar from classical Greek and Latin literature, the *Beowulf* poet structured his story in what scholars of oral poetry call "ring composition"—interlinked rings radiating out from the central events. Viewed this way, the fight with Grendel's mother would occupy the poem's center, while the prior battle with her son and the subsequent combat with the dragon would "ring" the center, developing related themes in parallel and in contrast. Similarly, paired episodes with queens both introduce (Hildeburh and Wealhtheow) and follow (Hygd and Modthryth) the encounter with Grendel's mother, raising other questions of succession and conflict between generations, and probing the place of women in the warrior-code of the Germanic tribes.

The poet—and we can assume his audience as well—delighted in interpolating episodes from other times and places, sometimes flashbacks to prior conflicts—such as the tale of Sigemund the dragon-slayer—sometimes glimpses of events to come in the future, and sometimes barely connected tales of past blood-feuds. He (or perhaps she, as a few critics have conjectured) expected the audience or readers not only to fill in the context behind the often brief hints of famous or infamous deeds, but also to read laterally, moving sideways through the text from connection to connection, comparing and contrasting different characters, different situations, different outcomes. As in the *Lais* of Marie de France, the *Poem of the Cid,* and many other medieval narratives, an entire social milieu and a complex ethic emerge not so much from individual psychology or particular events, as from a broader mirroring. The narrative's multiple detours and asides take a call-and-response form, filled with repetitions of situations and events, even ones we have already seen, as when Beowulf, returned to his lord Hygelac, recounts the fights we have already heard about, but gives them a new meaning for a new context.

In addition to this horizontal structure of parallels and contrasts, there is also a vertical structure to the poem that derives from the gap in time between the date of the events and the date of composition. Although most of the characters (with the exception of Beowulf, who seems to have been a fictional creation) appear elsewhere in Scandinavian legend and genealogies, only Hygelac's death in battle with the Frisians (in what is now the northern Netherlands) can actually be documented (somewhere between 515 and 530 C.E.). Between this period and the composition of the poem, Christianity had spread through the region, and the poet depicted the lives of the heathen Germans from the point of view of a pious Christian. Like the Norse writer Snorri Sturluson, however, rather than simply dismiss their pre-Christian practices or transform these ancestors into practicing Christians, the poet struck a fragile balance, leaving much unsaid. The pagan characters voice pious sentiments—"put aside pride," counsels the wise old Danish king Hrothgar—somewhere between the harsh realities of the heroic code and the metaphysical dictates of the Christian virtues. When depicting certain practices incompatible with the rituals of the newer religion—burial rites, for example, or the Danes' panicked prayer to "war-idols" (lines 155–61)—the narrator will sometimes note the distinction. For the most part, however, the peoples of the poem exist in a threshold world neither wholly pagan nor wholly Christian, where God is known but the mysteries of Christ and the sacraments are not, and where a heathen delight in booty and pride in fighting prowess do not preclude a deep-seated religiosity—a situation perhaps not so different from that of the recently converted Angles and Saxons of early-medieval England. The poem's audience could read the poem in either direction, finding the descendants of Cain in Grendel and Satan in the serpentine Dragon, and an allegory of the ideal Christian ruler in Beowulf, or recalling the blood-feuds, gift-giving, and pleasures of the mead-hall in the old customs, or merging them together in their imagination.

Names were a key component of the ability to view the world doubly, for Christianity entered the language through already existing words. It is impossible to know to what degree the poem's original audience would have heard a Norse god or the Christian God in words such as *metod* (which originally meant "fate") or *dryhten* ("ruler," "king"), that could now refer to either figure. Similarly, a phrase such as "the Lord lent them aid in their anguish, weaving their war-luck" (page 923, lines 623–624) combines a Christian sentiment of a grace-bestowing God with a pagan image of a God weaving a web of fate. A term like *wyrd,* another word for fate, which appears throughout the poem to describe the destined moment of a warrior's death, could be accepted either as a natural force ruling the world or as a synonym for divine Providence, inscrutable to mortals but part of God's plan. Word-weaving was fundamental to the composition of Old English poetry, and just as new concepts could be grafted onto preexistent names and terms, so the *scop*'s skill was demonstrated by the ability to make new and unforeseen combinations out of the "word-hoard" of the oral tradition.

Characters' names are themselves compounds. Scyld Scefing ("shield of the sheaf") is the founder of the Danish royal house; the name Beowulf means "bear," literally a "bee-wolf," a plunderer of bees for their honey. The fundamental facts of the warriors' world are likewise not granted simple names, but "kennings," combinations evoking their attributes, their uses, their greater meaning—the poem contains more than 1,500 compounds. The sea can be a "whale-road" or a "swan's road"; a king a "ring-giver" or a "treasure-giver"; weapons, ships, and sails receive similar treatment. Words have power in this world—to define and to enhance a character, to provoke, as when the *scop*'s song arouses Grendel to carnage, or to send to defeat, as when Beowulf humbles the envious Unferth in a *flyting,* or verbal duel. Part of this variation is due to the requirements of oral composition: different epithets, names of different metrical lengths can be used as needed to fill out the lines of the heroic song, but this variety equally bespeaks a way of thinking about the world as an interconnected web of relationships, just as genealogies defined people in terms of their heritage, and alliances and blood-feuds alternated in a give-and-take of gifts and blows.

Repetition and variation are at the heart of Old English poetry, for its unrhymed meter is based in alliteration, a repeated consonant in different words. The lines of *Beowulf* consist of two half-verses separated by a caesura, or pause, with two beats or stressed syllables in each half. The first beat of the first half always alliterates with the first beat of the second half; the second beat of the first half may also alliterate, but not the final beat of the line. Thus the dragon's revenge on the Geats for the theft of its treasure:

. . . Hord-weard onbād
earfoðlīce, oððæt ǣfen cwōm;
wæs ðā gebolgen beorges hyrde
wolde [*s*]e lāða līge forgyldan
drinc-fæt dȳre. þā wæs dæg sceacen
wyrme on willan; nō on wealle læ[*n*]g
bīdan wolde, ac mid bǣle fōr,
fȳre gefȳsed.

A literal translation by Howard J. Chickering gives a good sense of the word-choice and rhythm of the passage:

. . . The hoard-keeper waited,
miserable, impatient, till evening came.
By then the barrow-snake was swollen with rage,
wanted revenge for that precious cup,
a payment by fire. The day was over
and the dragon rejoiced, could no longer lie
coiled within walls but flew out in fire,
with shooting flames.[1]

Standard formulae—*oððæt ǣfen cwōm, þā wæs dæg sceacen*—punctuate the passage of time as the dragon waits for its nighttime revenge. The repetition of its names stresses its waiting and

1. This rendering makes a useful comparison to the fluidity and compactness of Sullivan and Murphy's version used in this anthology (page 953, lines 2030–35).

its power, while the variation in kennings—*Hord-weard, beorges hyrde*—and the earthy metaphor of its proper name, *wyrme,* allies the dragon's character both with man—hoard-keeper, miserable, vengeful, enraged, rejoicing—and beast—coiled, fire-breathing, monstrous. Through it all, the lines keep the forward beat as the alliteration also looks back to the beginning of the line, undulating like the dragon as it awaits its burst into freedom, *fyre gefysed.*

As the scholar of Old English, J. R. R. Tolkien, wrote in an influential essay on a poem he would incorporate in significant ways into his novels of epic fantasy, the poet "esteemed dragons, as rare as they are dire. . . . He liked them—as a poet, not as a sober zoologist; and he had good reason." The poet's gift was to make a dragon that was simultaneously real and marvelous, symbolic and deadly, human and bestial. In just the same way he blended Christian borrowings with Scandinavian legend, the incompatible opposites of which the medieval world would be wrought, refusing to yield either to one or to the other, holding past and future counterbalanced together.

PRONUNCATIONS:

Beowulf: BAY-oh-woolf
Jorge Luis Borges: HOR-hay loo-WEES BOR-hayz
Geats: KHAY-ahts
Hrothgar: HRAWTH-gahr
Hygd: heegd
Hygelac: HEE-ah-lack
Wealhtheow: WAYL-thay-oh
Weohstan: WAY-oh-stan

Beowulf[1]

1. Grendel

So! The Spear-Danes   in days of old
were led by lords   famed for their forays.
We learned of those princes'   power and prowess.
Often Scyld Scefing[2]   ambushed enemies,
took their mead-benches,   mastered their troops,
though first he was found   forlorn and alone.[3]
His early sorrows   were swiftly consoled:
he grew under heaven,   grew to a greatness
renowned among men   of neighboring lands,
his rule recognized   over the whale-road,
tribute granted him.   That was a good king!

Afterward God   gave him an heir,
a lad in the hall   to lighten all hearts.
The Lord had seen   how long and sorely
the people had languished   for lack of a leader.
Beow[4] was blessed   with boldness and honor;
throughout the North   his name became known.

1. The modern English translation is by Alan Sullivan and Timothy Murphy (2002, revised 2003).
2. The traditional founder of the Danish royal house. His name means "shield" or protection of the "sheaf," suggesting an earlier association in Norse mythology with the god of vegetation. The Danes are known afterward as "Scyldings," descendants of Scyld.
3. Scyld Scefing arrives among the Danes as a foundling, a dangerous position in both Norse and Anglo-Saxon cultures. Solitaries and outcasts were generally regarded with suspicion; it is a tribute to Scyld Scefing that he surmounted these obstacles to become the leader and organizer of the Danish people.
4. The manuscript reads "Beowulf" here, the copyist's mind having skipped ahead to the story's protagonist.

A soldierly son should strive in his youth
to do great deeds, give generous gifts
and defend his father. Then in old age,
when strife besets him, his comrades will stand
and his folk follow. Through fair dealing
a prince shall prosper in any kingdom.

Still hale on the day ordained for his journey,
Scyld went to dwell with the World's Warder.
His liegemen bore his bier to the beach:
so he had willed while wielding his words
as lord of the land, beloved by all.
With frost on its fittings, a lordly longboat
rode in the harbor, ring-bowed and ready.
They placed their prince, the gold-giver,
the famous man at the foot of the mast,
in the hollow hull heaped with treasures
from far-off lands. I have not heard another
ship ever sailed more splendidly stocked
with war-weapons, arms and armor.
About his breast the booty was strewn,
keepsakes soon to be claimed by the sea.
So he'd been sent as a child chosen
to drift on the deep. The Danes now returned
treasures no less than those they had taken,
and last they hoisted high overhead
a golden banner as they gave the great one
back to the Baltic with heavy hearts
and mournful minds. Though clever in council
or strong under sky, men cannot say
or know for certain who landed that shipload.

But the son of Scyld was hailed in the strongholds
after the father had fared far away,
and he long ruled the lordly Scyldings.
A son was born unto Beow also:
proud Healfdene, who held his high seat,
battle-hardened and bold in old age.
Four offspring descended from Healfdene,
awake in the world: Heorogar, Hrothgar,
kindly Halga; I have heard that the fourth
was Onela's queen[5] and slept with the sovereign
of warlike Swedes.
Hrothgar was granted
swiftness for battle and staunchness in strife,[6]
so friends and kinfolk followed him freely.
His band of young soldiers swelled to a swarm.

5. The daughters of Germanic royal families were married to the heads of opposing tribes in an attempt to cement military alliances. Often, as here, they are not named in the poem.

6. Significantly, Hrothgar is not the first-born of his generation. Leadership of the tribe was customarily conferred by acclamation upon the royal candidate who showed the greatest promise and ability.

In his mind he mulled commanding a meadhall
higher than humankind ever had heard of,
and offering everyone, young and old,
all he could give that God had granted,
save common land and commoners' lives.
Then, I am told, he tackled that task,
raising the rafters with craftsmen summoned
from many kingdoms across Middle-Earth.
They covered it quickly as men count the time,
and he whose word held the land whole
named it Heorot,[7] highest of houses.
The prince did not fail to fulfill his pledge:
feasts were given, favor and fortune.
The roof reared up; the gables were great,
awaiting the flames which would flare fiercely
when oaths were broken, anger awakened;
but Heorot's ruin was not yet at hand.[8]

Each day, one evil dweller in darkness
spitefully suffered the din from that hall
where Hrothgar's men made merry with mead.
Harp-strings would sound, and the song of the scop
would recount the tales told of time past:
whence mankind had come, and how the Almighty
had fashioned flat land, fair to behold,
surrounded with water. The worker of wonders
lifted and lit the sun and moon
for Earth's dwellers; He filled the forests
with branches and blooms; He breathed life
into all kinds of creatures.
So the king's thanes
gathered in gladness; then crime came calling,
a horror from hell, hideous Grendel,
wrathful rover of borders and moors,
holder of hollows, haunter of fens.
He had lived long in the homeland of horrors,
born to the band whom God had banished
as kindred of Cain, thereby requiting
the slayer of Abel.[9] Many such sprang
from the first murderer: monsters and misfits,
elves and ill-spirits, also those giants
whose wars with the Lord earned them exile.

After nightfall he nosed around Heorot,
saw how swordsmen slept in the hall,
unwary and weary with wine and feasting,

7. The name of Hrothgar's hall in Anglo-Saxon literally means "hart" or "stag," a male deer. The epithet "adorned with horns," which is applied to Heorot later, may further suggest its function as a hunting lodge.

8. The peace concluded between the Danes and the Heathobards through intermarriage is already doomed before it has taken place. The events foreshadowed here will occur long after the time of the poem.

9. See Genesis 4:3–16.

numb to the sorrows suffered by men.
The cursed creature, cruel and remorseless,
swiftly slipped in. He seized thirty thanes
asleep after supper, shouldered away
what trophies he would, and took to his lair
pleased with the plunder, proud of his murders.

When daylight dawned on the spoils of slaughter,
the strength of the fiend was readily seen.
The feast was followed by fits of weeping,
and cries of outrage rose in the morning.
Hrothgar the strong sank on his throne,
helpless and hopeless beholding the carnage,
the trail of the terror, a trouble too wrathful,
a foe too ferocious, too steadfast in rage,
ancient and evil. The evening after
he murdered again with no more remorse,
so fixed was his will on that wicked feud.
Henceforth the fearful were easily found
elsewhere, anywhere far from the fiend,
bedding in barns, for the brutal hall-thane
was truly betokened by terrible signs,
and those who escaped stayed safer afar.

So wrath fought alone against rule and right;
one routed many; the mead-hall stood empty.
Strongest of Spear-Danes, Hrothgar suffered
this fell affliction for twelve winters' time.
As his woes became known widely and well,
sad songs were sung by the sons of men:
how season on season, with ceaseless strife,
Grendel assailed the Scylding's sovereign.
The monster craved no kinship with any,
no end to the evil with wergeld[1] owed;
nor might a king's council have reckoned
on quittance come from the killer's hand.
The dark death-shadow daunted them all,
lying in ambush for old and young,
secretly slinking and stalking by night.
No man knows where on the misty moor
the heathen keepers of hell-runes[2] wander.

So over and over the loathsome ogre
mortally menaced mankind with his crimes.
Raiding by night, he reigned in the hall,
and Heorot's high adornments were his,

1. A cash payment for someone's death. *Wergeld* was regarded as an improvement over violent revenge, and Grendel is marked as uncivilized because he refuses to acknowledge this practice.
2. By rendering the Old English *helrunan,* which means "those adept in the mysteries of hell," as "heathen keepers of hell-runes," the translators are taking the liberty of suggesting that "demons" such as Grendel are familiar with runes—the letters of the early Germanic alphabet.

but God would not grant throne-gifts to gladden
a scourge who spurned the Sovereign of Heaven.

Stricken in spirit, Hrothgar would often
closet his council to ponder what plan
might be deemed best by strong-minded men.
Sometimes the elders swore before altars
of old war-idols, offering prayers
for the soul-slayer to succor their people.[3]
Such was their habit, the hope of heathens:
with hell in their hearts, they were lost to the Lord.
Their inmost minds knew not the Almighty;
they never would worship the world's true protector.
Sorry is he who sears his soul,
afflicted by flames he freely embraced.
No cheer for the chastened! No change in his fate!
But happy is he whom heaven welcomes,
and after his death-day he dwells with the Father.

So in his sorrow the son of Healfdene[4]
endlessly weighed how a wise warrior
might fend off harm. The hardship this foe
of his folk inflicted was fierce and long-lasting,
most ruinous wrath and wracking night-evil.

A thane[5] of Hygelac heard in his homeland
of Grendel's deeds. Great among Geats,[6]
this man was more mighty than any then living.
He summoned and stocked a swift wave-courser,
and swore to sail over the swan-road
as one warrior should for another in need.
His elders could find no fault with his offer,
and awed by the omens, they urged him on.
He gathered the bravest of Geatish guardsmen.
One of fifteen, the skilled sailor
strode to his ship at the ocean's edge.

He was keen to embark: his keel was beached
under the cliff where sea-currents curled
surf against sand; his soldiers were ready.
Over the bow they boarded in armor,
bearing their burnished weapons below,
their gilded war-gear to the boat's bosom.
Other men shoved the ship from the shore,
and off went the band, their wood-braced vessel
bound for the venture with wind on the waves

3. In their fear, the Danes resume heathen practices. In Christian belief, the pagan gods were transformed into devils.

4. Hrothgar. He is referred to by his patronymic, his father's name, as is frequent with male characters in the poem.

5. One of the king's principal retainers, chief among these being the earls.

6. A Germanic tribe who lived along the southwestern coast of what is now Sweden.

and foam under bow, like a fulmar in flight.[7]

On the second day their upswept prow
slid into sight of steep hillsides,
bright cliffs, wide capes at the close of their crossing,
the goal of their voyage gained in good time.
Swiftly the sailors steered for the shore,
moored their boat and debarked on the berm.
Clad in corselets of clattering mail,
they saluted the Lord for their smooth sailing.

From the post he held high on the headland,
a Scylding had spied the strangers bearing
bright bucklers and battle-armor
over their gangplank. Avid for answers
and minded to know what men had come hence,
Hrothgar's thane hastened on horseback
down to the beach where he brusquely brandished
spear-haft in hand while speaking stern words:

"What warriors are you, wearers of armor,
bearers of weapons, daring to bring
your lofty longboat over the sea-lane?
Long have I looked out on the ocean
so foreign foes might never float hither
and harry our homeland with hostile fleets.
No men have ever more brazenly borne
shields to our shores, nor have you sought
leave from our lords to land in this place,
nor could you have known my kin would consent.
I have never beheld an earl on this earth
more mighty in arms than one among you.
This is no hall-warmer, handsome in harness,
showy with shield, but the noblest of knights
unless looks belie him. Now let me know
who are your fathers before you fare further
or spy on the Danes. I say to you, sailors
far from your homes: hear me and hasten
to answer me well. Whence have you wandered?
Why have you come?"

Wisest with words,
the eldest offered an answer for all:
"From Geat-land we come; we are Geatish men,
sharers of Hygelac's hearth and hall.
My father was famous among our folk
as a lordly leader who lived many winters
before, full of years, he departed our fastness.
His name was Ecgtheow. All over Earth
every wise man remembers him well.
We have landed in friendship to look for your lord,

7. Gull-like sea bird of the far north Atlantic.

the son of Healfdene,   sovereign of Scyldings.
Give us good guidance: a great errand
has driven us hence   to the holder of Danes.
Our purpose is open;   this I promise;
but you could attest   if tales tell the truth.
They speak of some scourge,   none can say what,
secretly stalking   by night among Scyldings,
a shadowy shape   whose malice to men
is shown by a shameful   shower of corpses.
I offer Hrothgar,   with honest heart,
the means to make   an end to this menace.
Wise and good,   he will win his reward,
the scalding surges   of care will be cooled
if ever such awful   evil is vanquished.
So his sorrows   shall swiftly be soothed
or else his anguish   haunt him, unaltered,
as long as his house   holds on the hilltop."

Astride his steed,   the guard spoke again:
"A sharp-witted warrior   often must weigh
words against works   when judging their worth.
This I have learned: you honor our lord.
Thus you may come,   though clad in corselets
and weaponed for war.   I shall show you the way.
Meanwhile those thanes   who are mine to command
shall stand by the ship   you steered to our shore.
No thief will trouble   your newly-tarred craft
before you return   and take to the tide.
A swan-necked bow   will bear you back
to your windward coast.   Most welcome of men,
may you be granted   good fortune in battle,
enduring unharmed   the deed you would do."

So they set out   while the ship sat at rest,
the broad-beamed vessel   bound to the beach,
lashed by its lines.   Lustrous boar-icons
glinted on cheek-guards.   Adorned with gold,
the flame-hardened helms   defended their lives.
Glad of their mettle   while marching together,
the troop hastened   until they beheld
the highest of halls   raised under heaven,
most famed among folk   in foreign lands.
Sheathed with gold   and grandly gabled,
the roof of the ruler   lit up his realm.
The foremost warrior   waved them forward
and bade the band go   straight to that building,
court of the king   and his brave kinsmen.
Reining his steed,   he spoke a last word:
"It is time I returned.   May All-Ruling Father
favor your errand.   I fare to the ocean,

to watch and ward off wrathful marauders."

The street was stone-paved; a straight path
guided the band. Byrnies glittered,
jackets of chain-mail whose jingling rings,
hard and hand-linked, sang on harnesses.
Marshaled for battle, they marched to the building.
Still sea-weary, they set their broad-shields
of well-hardened wood against Heorot's wall.
Their corselets clinked as they bent to a bench
and stood their sturdy spears in a row,
gray from the ash grove, ground to sharp points.
This was a war party worthy of weapons.

Then a proud prince questioned their purpose:
"Where are you bringing these burnished bosses,
these gray mail-shirts, grimly-masked helms
and serried spears? I am Hrothgar's
herald and door-ward. I have never beheld
a band of wanderers with bearings so brave.
I believe that boldness has brought you to Hrothgar,
not banishment's shame."
The eldest answered,
hard and hardy under his helmet,
a warlike prince of the Weder[8] people:
"We are Hygelac's hearth-companions.
My name is Beowulf; my purpose, to bear
unto Healfdene's son, your lordly leader,
a message meant for that noblest of men,
if he will allow us leave to approach."

Wise Wulfgar, man of the Wendels,
known to many for boldness in battle,
stoutly spoke out: "I shall ask our sovereign,
well-wisher of Danes and awarder of wealth,
about this boon you have come to request
and bear you back, as soon as may be,
whatever answer the great man offers."

He went straightaway where Hrothgar waited,
old and gray-haired, with thanes gathered round.
Squarely he stood for his king to assess him.
Such was the Scylding custom at court,
and so Wulfgar spoke to his sovereign and friend:
"Far-sailing Geats have come to our kingdom
across the wide water. These warriors call
their leader *Beowulf* and bid me bring
their plea to our prince, if it pleases him
to allow them entrance and offer them audience.

8. An alternate name for Geat.

I implore you to hear them, princely Hrothgar,
for I deem them worthy of wearing their armor
and treating with earls. Truly the elder
who led them hither is a lord of some stature."

Helm of the Scyldings, Hrothgar held forth:
"I knew him once. He was only a lad.
His honored father, old Ecgtheow,
received the sole daughter of Hrethel.
The son now seeks us solely from friendship.
Seamen have said, after sailing hence
with gifts for the Geats, that his hand-grip would match
the might and main of thirty strong men.
The West-Danes[9] have long awaited God's grace.
Here is our hope against Grendel's dread,
if I reckon rightly the cause of his coming.
I shall give this brave man boons for boldness.
Bring him in quickly. The band of my kinsmen
is gathered together. Welcome our guest
to the dwelling of Danes."
Then Wulfgar went
through the hall's entry with word from within:
"I am ordered to answer that the lord of East-Danes
honors your father and offers you welcome,
sailors who sought us over the sea-waves,
bravely bent on embarking hither.
Now you may march in your mail and masks
to behold Hrothgar. Here you must leave
war-shields and spears sharpened for strife.
Your weapons can wait for words to be spoken."

The mighty one rose with many a man
marshaled about him, though some were bidden
to stay with the weapons and stand on watch.
Under Heorot's roof the rest hastened
when Beowulf brought them boldly before
the hearth of Hrothgar. Helmed and hardy,
the war-chief shone as he stood in skillfully
smithied chain-mail and spoke to his host:

"Hail to you, Hrothgar! I am Hygelac's
kinsman and comrade, esteemed by the king
for deeds I have done in the years of youth.
I heard in my homeland how Grendel grieves you.
Seafarers say that your splendid hall
stands idle and useless after the sun
sinks each evening from Heaven's height.
The most honored among us, earls and elders,
have urged me to seek you, certain my strength

9. Hrothgar is, in fact, king of all the Danes: North, South, East, and West. The different terms merely conform to the Anglo-Saxon alliterative pattern established in each line.

would serve in your struggle. They have seen me return
bloody from binding brutish giants,
a family of five destroyed in our strife;
by night in the sea I have slain monsters.
Hardship I had, but our harms were avenged,
our enemies mastered. Now I shall match
my grip against Grendel's and get you an end
to this feud with the fiend. Therefore one favor
I ask from you, Hrothgar, sovereign of Spear-Danes,
shelter of shield-bearers, friend to your folk:
that I and my officers, we and no others,
be offered the honor of purging your hall.
I have also heard that the rash thing reckons
the thrust of a weapon no threat to his thews,[1]
so I shall grab and grapple with Grendel.
Let my lord Hygelac hear and be glad
I foreswore my sword and strong shield
when I fought for life with that fearsome foe.
Whomever death takes, his doom is doubtless
decreed by the Lord. If I let the creature
best me when battle begins in this building,
he will freely feast as he often has fed
on men of much mettle. My corpse will require
no covering cloth. He will carry away
a crushed carcass clotted with gore,
the fiend's fodder gleefully eaten,
smearing his lonesome lair on the moor.
No need to worry who buries my body
if battle takes me. Send back to my sovereign
this best of shirts which has shielded my breast,
this choice chain-mail, Hrethel's heirloom
and Weland's work.[2] Fate goes as it will."

Helm of the Scyldings, Hrothgar answered:
"It is fair that you seek to defend us, my friend,
in return for the favor offered your father
when a killing fanned the fiercest of feuds
after he felled the Wylfing, Heatholaf.
Wary of war, the Weder-Geats wanted
Ecgtheow elsewhere, so over the sea-swells
he sought the South-Danes, strong Scyldings.
I had lately become king of my kinsmen,
a youth ruling this jewel of a realm,
this store-house of heroes, with Heorogar gone,
my brother and better, born of Healfdene.
I calmed your father's quarrel with wergeld
sent over sea straight to the Wylfings,
an ancient heirloom; and Ecgtheow's oath
I took in return.

1. Well-developed sinew or muscle.

2. Legendary blacksmith of the Norse gods.

"It pains me to tell
what grief Grendel has given me since,
what harm in Heorot, hatred and shame
at his sudden onset. My circle is shrunken;
my guardsmen are gone, gathered by fate
into Grendel's grip. How simply the Sovereign
of Heaven could hinder deeds of this hell-fiend!
Beer-swollen boasters, brave in their ale-cups,
often have sworn to stay with their swords
drawn in the dark, to strike down the demon.
Then in the morning the mead-hall was drenched,
blood on the bench-boards, blood on the floor,
the highest of houses a horror at dawn.
Fewer were left to keep faith with their lord
since those dear retainers were taken by death.
But sit now to sup and afterward speak
of soldierly pride, if the spirit prompts you."

A bench was then cleared there in the beer-hall
so all of the Geats could sit together,
sturdy soldiers, proud and stout-hearted.
A dutiful Dane brought them bright ale-cups
and poured sweet mead while the scop was singing
high-voiced in Heorot. That host of warriors,
Weders and Scyldings, shared in the wassails.

But envious Unferth,[3] Ecglaf's son,
spat out his spite from the seat he took
at his sovereign's feet. The seafarer's quest
grieved him greatly, for he would not grant
any man ever, in all middle-earth,
more fame under heaven than he himself had.

"Are you that Beowulf Breca bested
when both of you bet on swimming the straits,
daring the deep in a dire struggle,
risking your lives after rash boasting?
Though friend or foe, no man could deflect
your foolhardy foray. Arms flailing,
you each embraced the billowing stream,
spanned the sea-lane with swift-dipping hands
and wended over the warring ocean.
Winter-like waves were roiling the waters
as the two of you toiled in the tumult of combers.
For seven nights you strove to outswim him,
but he was the stronger and saw at sunrise
the sea had swept him to Heathoraem[4] shores.

3. Hrothgar's spokesman or court jester; his rude behavior toward Beowulf is consistent with other figures in epics and romances who taunt the hero before he undertakes his exploits. "Unferth" may mean "strife."

4. Coastal tribe of central Sweden near the Norwegian border.

Breca went back to his own homeland,
his burg on the bluff, stronghold of Brondings,
a fair realm and wealthy. The wager was won;
Beanstan's son had brought off his boast.
However you fared in onslaughts elsewhere,
I doubt you will live the length of a night
if you dare to linger so near Grendel."

Then Beowulf spoke, son of Ecgtheow:
"Listen, Unferth, my fuddled friend
brimful of beer, you blabber too much
about Breca's venture. I tell you the truth:
my force in the flood is more than a match
for any man who wrestles the waves.
Boys that we were, brash in our youth
and reckless of risk, both of us boasted
that each one could swim the open ocean.
So we set forth, stroking together
sturdily seaward with swords drawn
hard in our hands to ward off whale-fish.
No swifter was he in those heaving seas;
each of us kept close to the other,
floating together those first five nights.
Then the storm-surges swept us apart:
winter-cold weather and warring winds
drove from the north in deepening darkness.
Rough waves rose and sea-beasts raged,
but my breast was bound in a woven mail-shirt.
Hard and hand-linked, hemmed with gold,
it kept those creatures from causing me harm.
I was drawn to the depths, held fast by the foe,
grim in his grasp; yet granted a stab,
I stuck in my sword-point, struck down the horror.
The mighty sea-monster met death by my hand.

"Often afterward snatchers of swimmers
snapped at my heels. With my strong sword
I served them fitly. I would fatten no foes,
feed no man-banes munching their morsels
when setting to feast on the floor of the sea.
Instead at sunrise the sword-stricken
washed up in windrows to lie lifelessly,
lodged by the tide-line, and nevermore trouble
sailors crossing the steep-cliffed straits.
As God's beacon brightened the East,
I spied a cape across calming seas,
a windward wall. So I was spared,
for fate often favors an unmarked man
if he keeps his courage. My sword was the slayer
of nine monsters. I've not heard of many

who fended off a more fearsome assault
while hurled by the waves under heaven's vault.
Yet I broke the beasts' grip and got off alive,
weary of warfare. Swiftly surging
after the storm, the sea-current swept me
to Finland's coast.

"Such close combat
or stark sword-strokes you have not seen,
you or Breca. No tale has told
how either of you two ever attempted
so bold a deed done with bright sword,
though I would not claim a brother's bane
if the killing of kin were all I'd accomplished.
For that you are certain to suffer in Hell,
doomed with the damned despite your swift wit.
I say straight out, son of Ecglaf,
that ghastly Grendel, however gruesome,
would never have done such dreadful deeds,
harming your lord here in his hall,
if your spirit were stern, your will, warlike,
as you have affirmed. The foe has found
that he need not reckon with wrathful swords
or look with alarm on the likes of you,
Scylding victor. He takes his tribute,
sparing no man, snatching and supping
whenever he wishes with wicked delight,
expecting no strife with spear-bearing Danes.
But soon, very soon, I shall show him the strength
and boldness of Geats giving him battle.
When morning comes to light up the land,
you may go again and gladly get mead
as the bright sun beams in the South
and starts a new day for the sons of men."

Gray-haired Hrothgar, giver of hoard-wealth,
was happy to hear Beowulf bolster
hope for his folk with forthright avowal.
About the Bright-Danes' battle-leader
rang warriors' laughter and winsome words.
The queen, Wealtheow,[5] by custom courteous,
greeted the party aglitter with gold
and bore the full cup first to her lord,
the keeper of East-Danes, dear to his people,
bidding him drink and be glad of his beer.
That soldierly sovereign quaffed and supped
while his Helming princess passed through the hall
offering everyone, young man and old,

5. "Weal theow" means "foreign slave," and she may be British or Celtic in origin. Even after her marriage to Hrothgar, she continues to maintain her identity as the "lady of the Helmings," an epithet recalling her father Helm.

the dole he was due. Adorned with rings,
she bore the burnished mead-bowl to Beowulf,
last of them all, and honored the Geat
with gracious words, firm in her wisdom
and grateful to God for granting her wish.
Here was the prayed-for prince who would help
to end the ill deeds. He emptied the cup
Wealtheow offered; then the willing warrior,
Ecgtheow's son, spoke as one ready
for strife and slaughter:
"When I set my ship
to sail on the sea and steered her hence
with my squadron of swords, I swore to fulfill
the will of the Scyldings or die in the deed,
fall with the slain, held fast by the foe,
my last day lived out here in your hall."

The wife was well-pleased with Beowulf's words,
this oath from the Geat; and glinting with gold
the queen, Wealtheow, went to her king.
Boasts were bandied once more in the beer-hall,
the hearty speech of a hopeful household,
forceful fighters. But soon the sovereign,
son of Healfdene, hankered for sleep.
He knew his enemy brooded on battle
all day from dawn until deepening dusk.
Covered by darkness, the creature would come,
a shade under shadows. The company stood.
One man to another, Hrothgar hailed
brave Beowulf, wishing him well
and granting him leave to guard the wine-hall.

"So long as my hand has hefted a shield,
I never have yielded the Danes' mansion
to any man else, whatever his mettle.
Now you shall hold this highest of houses.
Be mindful of fame; make your might known;
but beware of the brute. You will want no boon
if you tackle this task and live to request it."

Hrothgar and his princes departed the hall;
the warder of Danes went to his woman,
couched with his queen. The King of Glory
had granted a guard against Grendel's wrath,
as all had now learned. One man had offered
to take on this task and watch for the terror.
The leader of Geats would gladly trust
the force of God's favor. He flung off his mail-shirt,
then handed his helmet and inlaid sword
to the steward assigned safe-keeping of iron

and gilded war-gear. Again the bold
Beowulf boasted while bound for his bed:

"I am no weaker in works of war,
no less a grappler than Grendel himself.
Soon I shall sink him into his death-sleep,
not with my sword but solely by strength.
He is unschooled in skills to strike against me,
to shatter my shield, though feared for his fierceness.
So I shall bear no blade in the night
if he sees fit to fight without weapons.
May God in His wisdom grant whom He wills
blessing in battle."
The brave soldier
stretched out for sleep, and a bolster pillowed
his proud cheekbone. About him were sprawled
the strong sea-warriors, each one wondering
whether he ever would walk once again
his beloved land, or find his own folk
from childhood's time in an untroubled town.
All had been told how often before
dreadful death had swept up the Danes
who lay in this hall. But the Lord lent them
aid in their anguish, weaving their war-luck,
for one man alone had the might and main
to fight off the fiend, crush him in combat,
proving who ruled the races of men,
then and forever: God, the Almighty.[6]

Cunningly creeping, a spectral stalker
slunk through the gloom. The bowmen were sleeping
who ought to have held the high-horned house,
all except one, for the Lord's will
now became known: no more would the murderer
drag under darkness whomever he wished.
Anger was wakeful, watching the enemy;
hot-hearted Beowulf was bent upon battle.

Then from the moor under misty hillsides,
Grendel came gliding girt with God's anger.
The man-scather sought someone to snatch
from the high hall. He crept under clouds
until he caught sight of the king's court
whose gilded gables he knew at a glance.
He often had haunted Hrothgar's house;
but he never found, before or after,
hardier hall-thanes or harder luck.

6. This interpolation of Christian belief into what is essentially a pagan tradition has been taken as evidence of a conscious rewriting of much earlier material. The narrative assures its reader that Christian beliefs were still valid, regardless of what the characters in the story may have believed.

The joyless giant drew near the door,
which swiftly swung back at the touch of his hand
though bound and fastened with forge-bent bars.
The building's mouth had been broken open,
and Grendel entered with ill intent.
Swollen with fury, he stalked over flagstones
and looked round the manse where many men lay.
An unlovely light most like a flame
flashed from his eyes, flared through the hall
at young soldiers dozing shoulder to shoulder,
comradely kindred. The cruel creature laughed
in his murderous mind, thinking how many
now living would die before the day dawned,
how glutted with gore he would guzzle his fill.
It was not his fate to finish the feast
he foresaw that night.
Soon the Stalwart,
Hygelac's kinsman, beheld how the horror,
not one to be idle, went about evil.
For his first feat he suddenly seized
a sleeping soldier, slashed at the flesh,
bit through bones and lapped up the blood
that gushed from veins as he gorged on gobbets.
Swiftly he swallowed those lifeless limbs,
hands and feet whole; then he headed forward
with open palm to plunder the prone.
One man angled up on his elbow:
the fiend soon found he was facing a foe
whose hand-grip was harder than any other
he ever had met in all Middle-Earth.
Cravenly cringing, coward at heart,
he longed for a swift escape to his lair,
his bevy of devils. He never had known
from his earliest days such awful anguish.

The captain, recalling his speech to the king,
straightaway stood and hardened his hold.
Fingers fractured. The fiend spun round;
the soldier stepped closer. Grendel sought
somehow to slip that grasp and escape,
flee to the fens; but his fingers were caught
in too fierce a grip. His foray had failed;
the harm-wreaker rued his raid on Heorot.
From the hall of the Danes a hellish din
beset every soldier outside the stronghold,
louder than laughter of ale-sodden earls.
A wonder it was the wine-hall withstood
this forceful affray without falling to earth.
That beautiful building was firmly bonded

by iron bands forged with forethought
inside and out. As some have told it,
the struggle swept on and slammed to the floor
many mead-benches massive with gold.
No Scylding elders ever imagined
that any would harm their elk-horned hall,
raze what they wrought, unless flames arose
to enfold and consume it. Frightful new sounds
burst from the building, unnerved the North-Danes,
each one and all who heard those outcries
outside the walls. Wailing in anguish,
the hellish horror, hateful to God,
sang his dispair, seized by the grip
of a man more mighty than any then living.

That shielder of men meant by no means
to let the death-dealer leave with his life,
a life worthless to anyone elsewhere.
Then the young soldiers swung their old swords
again and again to save their guardian,
their kingly comrade, however they could.
Engaging with Grendel and hoping to hew him
from every side, they scarcely suspected
that blades wielded by worthy warriors
never would cut to the criminal's quick.
The spell was spun so strongly about him
that the finest iron of any on earth,
the sharpest sword-edge left him unscathed.
Still he was soon to be stripped of his life
and sent on a sore sojourn to Hell.
The strength of his sinews would serve him no more;
no more would he menace mankind with his crimes,
his grudge against God, for the high-hearted kinsman
of King Hygelac had hold of his hand.
Each found the other loathsome in life;
but the murderous man-bane got a great wound
as tendons were torn, shoulder shorn open,
and bone-locks broken. Beowulf gained
glory in war; and Grendel went off
bloody and bent to the boggy hills,
sorrowfully seeking his dreary dwelling.
Surely he sensed his life-span was spent,
his days upon days; but the Danes were grateful:
their wish was fulfilled after fearsome warfare.

Wise and strong-willed, the one from afar
had cleansed Heorot, hall of Hrothgar.
Great among Geats, he was glad of his night-work
ending the evil, his fame-winning feat,
fulfilling his oath to aid the East Danes,

easing their anguish, healing the horror
they suffered so long, no small distress.
As token of triumph, the troop-leader hung
the shorn-off shoulder and arm by its hand:
the grip of Grendel swung from the gable!

Many a warrior met in the morning
around Hrothgar's hall, so I have heard.
Folk-leaders fared from near and far
over wide lands to look on the wonder,
the track of the terror, glad he had taken
leave of his life when they looked on footprints
wending away to the mere of monsters.
Weary and weak, defeated in war,
he dripped his blood-trail down to dark water,
tinting the terrible tide where he sank,
spilling his lifeblood to swirl in the surge.
There the doomed one dropped into death
where he long had lurked in his joyless lair,
and Hell received his heathen soul.

Many went hence: young men and old
mounted white mares and rode to the mere,
a joyous journey on brave battle-steeds.
There Beowulf's prowess was praised
and approved by all. Everyone said
that over the Earth and under bright sky,
from north to south between sea and sea,
no other man was more worthy of wearing
corselet or crown, though no one denied
the grace of Hrothgar: that was a good king.
Sometimes they galloped great-hearted bays;
races were run where roads were smooth
on open upland. Meanwhile a man
skilled as a singer, versed in old stories,
wove a new lay of truly-linked words.
So the scop started his song of Beowulf's
wisdom and strength, setting his spell
with subtle staves. Of Sigemund[7] also
he said what he knew: many marvels,
deeds of daring and distant journeys,
the wars of Waels' son, his wildness, his sins,
unsung among men save by Fitela,
Sigemund's nephew, who knew his secrets
and aided his uncle in every conflict
as comrade-at-need. A whole clan of ogres

7. The story of Sigemund is also told in the Old Norse *Volsunga Saga* and with major variations in the Middle High German *Niebelungenlied.* The scop's comparison of Sigemund with Beowulf is ironic in that the order and the outcome of Beowulf's later encounter with a dragon will be reversed.

was slain by the Waelsing   wielding his sword.
No small esteem   sprang up for Sigemund
after his death-day.   Dauntless in war,
he struck down a serpent   under gray stone
where it held its hoard.   He fared alone
on this fearsome foray,   not with Fitela;
but fate allowed him   to lunge with his blade,
spitting the scaly   worm to the wall.
His pluck repaid,   Sigemund was pleased
to take his pick   of the piled-up treasure
and load bright arms   in his longboat's breast
while the molten worm   melted away.

Thus that wayfarer   famed far and wide
among nations of men,   that mighty war-maker,
shelter of shield-bearers,   outshone another:
unhappy Heremod,[8]   king of the Danes,
whose strength, spirit,   and courage were spent.
He fell among foes,   was taken by traitors
and swiftly dispatched.   So his sorrows
ended at last.   Too long had lords
and commoners suffered,   scourged by their king,
who ought to have honored   his father's office,
defending his homeland,   his hoard and stronghold.
Evil had entered him.   Dearer to Danes
and all humankind   was Hygelac's kinsman.

Still running heats,   the horses hurtled
on sandy lanes.   The light of morning
had swung to the south,   and many men sped,
keen to behold   the hall of the king,
the strange sights inside.   Hrothgar himself,
keeper of treasures   and leader of troops,
came from the queen's   quarters to march
with measured tread   the track to his mead-hall;
the queen and her maidens   also came forth.
He stopped on the stairs   and gazed at the gable,
glinting with gold   behind Grendel's hand.

"My thanks for this sight   go straight to Heaven!
Grendel has given me   grief and grievance;
but God often works   wonders on wonders.
Not long ago   I had no hope at all
of living to see   relief from my sorrows
while slaughter stained   the highest of houses,
wide-spilling woes   the wisest advisors
despaired of stanching.   None of them knew
how to fend off our foes: the ghosts and ghasts

8. Heremod, an earlier Danish king, was the stock illustration of the unjust and unwise ruler. After bringing bloodshed upon his own house, Heremod took refuge among the Jutes, who eventually put him to death.

afflicting our folk here in our fastness.
Now, praise Heaven, a prince has proven
this deed could be done that daunted us all.
Indeed the mother who bore this young man
among mankind may certainly say,
if she still is living, that the Lord of Old
blessed her child-bearing. Henceforth, Beowulf,
best of the brave, I shall hold you in heart
as close as a son. Keep our new kinship,
and I shall award you whatever you wish
that is mine to command. Many a time
I have lavished wealth on lesser warriors,
slighter in strife. You have earned your esteem.
May the All-Wielder reward you always,
just as He gives you these goods today."

Beowulf spoke, son of Ecgtheow:
"We gladly engaged in this work of war
and freely faced the unknowable foe,
but I greatly regret that you were not granted
the sight of him broken, slathered with blood.
I sought to grip him swiftly and strongly,
wrestle him down to writhe on his death-bed
as life left him, unless he broke loose.
It was not my fate to fasten the man-bane
firmly enough. The fiend was so fierce
he secured his escape by leaving this limb
to ransom his life, though little the wretch
has gained for his hurt, held in the grip
of a dire wound, awaiting death
as a savage man, besmirched by his sins,
might wait to learn what the Lord wills."

Unferth was silent. He spoke no more boasts
about works of war when warriors gazed
at the hand hanging from Heorot's roof,
the fiend's fingers jutting in front,
each nail intact, those terrible talons
like spikes of steel. Everyone said
that the strongest sword from smithies of old,
the hardest iron edge ever forged,
would never have harmed that monstrous mauler,
those bloody claws crooked for combat.

2. Grendel's Mother

Inside Heorot many hands hastened
at Hrothgar's command: men and women
washed out the wine-hall, unfurled on the walls
gold-woven hangings to gladden their guests,

each of whom gazed wide-eyed in wonder.
Though bound with iron, the bright building
was badly battered, its hinges broken.
Only the roof had escaped unscathed
before the fell creature cringed and fled,
stained by his sin and despairing of life.
Flee it who will, a well-earned fate
is not often altered, for every earth-dweller
and soul-bearing son must seek out a spot
to lay down his body, lie on his death-bed,
sleep after feasting.
So came the season
for Healfdene's son to stride through his hall:
the king himself would sup with his kin.
I have never heard in any nation
of such a great host so graciously gathered,
arrayed on benches around their ruler,
glad of his fame and glad for the feast.
Many a mead-cup those masterful kinsmen
Hrothgar and Hrothulf raised in the hall.
All were then friends who filled Heorot,
treason and treachery not yet contrived.[1]

Crowning his conquest, the King of the Danes
bestowed on the soldier a battle-standard
embroidered with gold, a helmet, mail-shirt,
and unblemished blade borne out while ranks
of warriors watched. Then Beowulf drank
a flagon before them: he would feel no shame
facing bold spearmen with boons such as these.
Not many men on mead benches
have given another four golden gifts
in friendlier fashion. The head-guard was flanged
with windings of wire. Facing forward,
it warded off harm when the wearer in war
was obliged to bear shield against enemy blades
that were hammer-hardened and honed by files.
The sovereign ordered eight swift steeds
brought to the court on braided bridles.
One bore a saddle studded with gems
and glinting gold-work: there the great king,
son of Healfdene, would sit during sword-strife,
never faltering, fierce at the front,
working his will while the wounded fell.
Then Hrothgar awarded horses and weapons
both to Beowulf, bade that he keep them
and wield them well. So from his hoard

1. Possibly an allusion to the later usurpation of the Danish throne by Hrothgar's nephew Hrothulf.

he paid the hero a princely reward
of heirlooms and arms for braving the battle;
no man could fairly or truthfully fault them.

That lord also lavished gifts on the Geats
whom Beowulf brought over broad seas,
and wergeld he gave for the one Grendel
had wickedly killed, though the creature would surely
have murdered more had God in his wisdom,
man in his strength failed to forestall it.
So the Almighty has always moved men;
yet man must consistently strive to discern
good from evil, evil from good
while drunk with days he dwells in this world.

Music and story now sounded together
as Hrothgar's scop sang for the hall-fest
a tale often told when harp was held:[2]
how Finn's followers, faithless Jutes,
fell to fighting friends in his fortress;
how Hnaef the Half-Dane, hero of Scyldings,
was fated to fall in Frisian warfare;
how by shield-swagger harmless Hildeburh,
faithful to Finn though daughter of Danes,
lost her beloved brother and son
who were both born to be struck by spears.
Not without cause did Hoc's daughter
bewail the Lord's will when morning awoke:
she who had known nothing but happiness
beheld under heaven the horror of kin-strife.

War had taken its toll of attackers;
few men remained for Finn to muster,
too few to force the fight against Hengest,
a dutiful thane who had rallied the Danes.
As tokens of truce Finn offered these terms:
a haven wholly emptied of foes,
hall and high seat, with an equal share
in gifts given his own gathered kin.
Each time he treated his sons to treasures
plated with gold, a portion would go
to sweeten Hengest's stay in his hall.
The two sides swore a strict treaty;
and Finn freely affirmed to Hengest

2. The following episode is one of the most obscure in *Beowulf.* It seems that Hnaef and Hildeburh are both children of an earlier Danish king named Hoc and that Hildeburh has been sent to marry Finn, the son of Folcwalda and king of the Jutes and Frisians, in order to conclude a marriage alliance and thus settle a prior blood feud between the two tribes. Upon going to visit his sister and her husband, Hnaef is treacherously ambushed and killed by Finn's men; Hildeburh's son by Finn is also killed. In her role as peace-weaver, Hildeburh is torn by conflicting allegiances, foreshadowing the fate of Hrothgar's own daughter Freawaru in her marriage to Ingeld.

that all would honor   this oath to the Danes,
as his council decreed,   and further declared
no Frisian would ever,   by word or work,
challenge the peace   or mention with malice
the plight of survivors   deprived of their prince
and wintered-in   at the slayer's stronghold.
Should any Frisian   enter in anger,
the sword's edge   would settle the quarrel.

That oath offered,   the hoard was opened
for gold to array   the greatest of War-Danes.
Iron-hard guardians   gilded with gold,
bloody mail-shirts   and boar-tusked helms
were heaped on his bier,   awaiting the balefire.
Many a warrior,   weakened by wounds,
had faltered and fallen   with foes he had slain.
Hildeburh ordered   her own dear son
be placed on the pyre,   the prince and his uncle
shoulder to shoulder.   Their bodies were burned
while the stricken lady   sang out her sorrow.
Streamers of smoke   burst from the bier
as corpses kindled   with cruelest of flames.
Faces withered,   wounded flesh yawned,
and blood boiled out   as the blaze swallowed
with hateful hunger   those whom warfare
had borne away,   the best of both houses.
Their glory was gone.
                                The Frisians were fewer
heading for home;   their high stronghold
was empty of allies.   For Hengest also
that winter was woeful,   walled up in Frisia,
brooding on bloodshed   and longing to leave,
though knowing his vessel   never could breast
the wind-darkened swells   of a wide ocean
seething with storms,   or break the ice-bindings
that barred his bow   from the bitter waters.
Constrained to wait   for kindlier weather,
he watched until spring,   season of sunlight,
dawned on men's dwellings   as ever it did
and still does today.   Winter withdrew
and Earth blossomed.
                                Though the exile was eager
to end his visit,   he ached for vengeance
before sailing home.   Loathe to foreswear
the way of this world,   he schemed to assail
the sons of slayers.   So Hengest heeded
Hunlaf's son,   who laid on his lap
the sword War-Flame,   feared by all foes,
asking its edge   be offered the Jutes.

His heart was hot; he could hold back no more;
gladly he answered Guthlaf and Oslaf,
who wrathfully spoke of the wrong they suffered,
the shame of Scyldings sharing their plight.
Then fierce-hearted Finn fell in his turn,
stricken by swords in his own stronghold.
The building was bloody with bodies of foemen:
the king lay slain, likewise his kin;
and the queen was captured. Scyldings carried
off in their ship all of the chattels
found in Finn's fortress, gemstones and jewels.
The lady was borne to the land of her birth.

So that story was sung to its end,
then mirth mounted once more in Heorot.
Revelry rang as wine-bearers brought
finely-wrought flagons filled to the brim.
Wearing her circlet, Wealtheow walked
where uncle and nephew, Hrothgar and Hrothulf,
were sitting in peace, two soldiers together,
each still believing the other was loyal.
Likewise the officer, Unferth, was honored
to sit at the feet of the Scylding sovereign.
Everyone thought him honest and trustworthy,
blameless and brave, though his blade had unjustly
stricken a kinsman.
So the queen spoke:
"Receive this cup, sovereign of Scyldings,
giver of gold; drink and be glad;
greet the Geats mildly as well a man might,
mindful of gifts graciously given
from near and far, now in your keeping.
They say you would name that knight as a son
for purging the ring-hall. Employ as you please
wealth and rewards, but bequeath to your kin
rule of this realm when the Ruler of All
holds that you must. I know that Hrothulf
will honor our trust and treat these youths well
if you have to leave this life before him.
I am counting on him to recall our kindness
when he was a child and repay our children
for presents we gave and pleasures we granted."

She turned to the bench where her sons were seated,
Hrethric and Hrothmund. Between the two brothers
Beowulf sat; and the cup-bearer brought him
words of welcome, willingly gave him
as tokens of favor two braided arm-bands,
jerkin, corselet, and jeweled collar

grander than any   other on Earth.[3]
I have heard under heaven   of no higher treasure
hoarded by heroes   since Hama stole off
to his fair fortress   with Freya's necklace,
shining with stones   set by the Fire-Dwarves.
So Hama earned   Eormanric's anger,
and fame for himself.   Foolhardy Hygelac,
grandson of Swerting   and sovereign of Geats,
would wear it one day   on his final foray.
He fell in the fray   defending his treasure,
the spoils he bore   with his battle-standard.
Recklessly raiding   the realm of Frisia,
the prince in his pride   had prompted misfortune
by crossing the sea   while clad in that collar.
He fell under shield,   fell to the Franks,
weaker warriors   stripping the slain
of armor and spoil   after the slaughter.
Hygelac held   the graveyard of Geats.

The hall approved   the princely prize
bestowed by the queen,   and Wealtheow spoke
for the host to hear: "Keep this collar,
beloved Beowulf.   Bear this armor,
wealth of our realm.   May it ward you well.
Swear that your strength   and kindly counsel
will aid these youngsters,   and I shall reward you.
Now your renown   will range near and far;
your fame will wax wide,   as wide as the water
hemming our hills,   homes of the wind.
Be blessed, Beowulf,   with abundant treasures
as long as you live;   and be mild to my sons,
a model admired.   Here men are courtly,
honest and true,   each to the other,
all to their ruler;   and after the revels,
bolstered with beer,   they do as I bid."

The lady left him   and sat on her seat.
The feast went on;   fine wine was flowing.
Men could not know   what fate would befall them,
what evil of old   was decreed to come
for the earls that evening.   As always, Hrothgar
headed for home,   where the ruler rested.
A great many others   remained in the hall,
bearing bright benches   and rolling out beds
while one drunkard,   doomed and death-ripened,

3. The narrative jumps ahead beyond Beowulf's return home to the Geats. His uncle, Hygelac, the king, will not only receive the collar from Beowulf but will die with it in battle among the Frisians. The collar thus connects different events at different times.

sprawled into sleep. They set at their heads
round war-shields, well-adorned wood.
Above them on boards, their battle-helms rested,
ringed mail-shirts and mighty spear-shafts
waiting for strife. Such was their wont
at home or afield, wherever they fared,
in case their king should call them to arms.
Those were stern people.
They sank into slumber,
but one paid sorely for sleep that evening,
as often had happened when grim Grendel
held the gold-hall, wreaking his wrongs
straight to the end: death after sins.
It would soon be perceived plainly by all
that one ill-wisher still was alive,
maddened by grief: Grendel's mother,
a fearsome female bitterly brooding
alone in her lair deep in dread waters
and cold currents since Cain had killed
the only brother born of his father.
Marked by murder, he fled from mankind
and went to the wastes. Doomed evil-doers
issued from him. Grendel was one,
but the hateful Hell-walker found a warrior
wakefully watching for combat in Heorot.
The monster met there a man who remembered
strength would serve him, the great gift of God,
faith in the All-Wielder's favor and aid.
By that he mastered the ghastly ghoul;
routed, wretched, the hell-fiend fled,
forlornly drew near his dreary death-place.
Enraged and ravenous, Grendel's mother
swiftly set out on a sorrowful journey
to settle the score for her son's demise.

She slipped into Heorot, hall of the Ring-Danes,
where sleeping soldiers soon would endure
an awful reversal. Her onslaught was less
by as much as a woman's mettle in war
is less than a man's wielding his weapon:
the banded blade hammered to hardness,
a blood-stained sword whose bitter stroke
slashes a boar-helm borne into battle.
In the hall, sword-edge sprang from scabbard;
broadshield was swung swiftly off bench,
held firmly in hand. None thought of helmet
or sturdy mail-shirt when terror assailed him.
Out she hastened, out and away,
keen to keep living when caught in the act.

She fastened on one, then fled to her fen.
He was Hrothgar's highest counselor,
boon companion and brave shield-bearer
slain in his bed. Beowulf slept
elsewhere that evening, for after the feast
the Geat had been given a different dwelling.
A din of dismay mounted in Heorot:
the gory hand was gone from the gable.
Dread had retaken the Danes' dwelling.
That bargain was bad for both barterers,
costing each one a close comrade.

It was grim for the sovereign, the grizzled soldier,
to learn his old thane was no longer living,
to know such a dear one was suddenly dead.
Swiftly he sent servants to fetch
battle-blessed Beowulf early from bed,
together with all the great-hearted Geats.
He marched in their midst, went where the wise one
was wondering whether the All-Wielder
ever would alter this spell of ill-fortune.
That much-honored man marched up the floor,
and timbers dinned with the tread of his troop.
He spoke soberly after the summons,
asking how soundly the sovereign had slept.

Hrothgar answered, head of his house:
"Ask not about ease! Anguish has wakened
again for the Danes. Aeschere is dead.
He was Yrmenlaf's elder brother,
my rune-reader and keeper of counsel,
my shoulder's shielder, warder in war
when swordsmen struck at boar-headed helms.
Whatever an honored earl ought to be,
such was Aeschere. A sleepless evil
has slipped into Heorot, seized and strangled.
No one knows where she will wander now,
glad of the gory trophy she takes,
her fine fodder. So she requites
her kinsman's killer for yesterday's deed,
when you grabbed Grendel hard in your hand-grip.
He plagued and plundered my people too long.
His life forfeit, he fell in the fray;
but now a second mighty man-scather
comes to carry the feud further,
as many a thane must mournfully think,
seeing his sovereign stricken with grief
at the slaying of one who served so well.

"I have heard spokesmen speak in my hall,
country-folk saying they sometimes spotted

a pair of prodigies prowling the moors,
evil outcasts, walkers of wastelands.
One, they descried, had the semblance of woman;
the other, ill-shapen, an aspect of man
trudging his track, ever an exile,
though superhuman in stature and strength.
In bygone days the border-dwellers
called him *Grendel.* What creature begot him,
what nameless spirit, no one could say.
The two of them trekked untraveled country:
wolf-haunted heights and windy headlands,
the frightening fen-path where falling torrents
dive into darkness, stream beneath stone
amid folded mountains. That mere[4] is not far,
as miles are measured. About it there broods
a forest of fir trees frosted with mist.
Hedges of wood-roots hem in the water
where each evening fire-glow flickers
forth on the flood, a sinister sight.
That pool is unplumbed by wits of the wise;
but the heath-striding hart hunted by hounds,
the strong-antlered stag seeking a thicket,
running for cover, would rather be killed
at bay on the bank before hiding its head
under that welter. It is no peaceful place
where water-struck waves whipped into clouds,
surge and storm, swept by the winds,
so the heights are hidden and heaven weeps.
Now you alone can relieve our anguish:
look, if you will, at the lay of the land;
and seek, if you dare, that dreadful dale
where the she-demon dwells. Finish this feud,
and I shall reward you with age-old wealth,
twisted-gold treasures, if you return."

Beowulf spoke, son of Ecgtheow:
"Grieve not, good man. It is better to go
and avenge your friend than mourn overmuch.
We all must abide an end on this earth,
but a warrior's works may win him renown
as long as he lives and after life leaves him.
Rise now, ruler; let us ride together
and seek out the signs of Grendel's mother.
I swear to you this: she shall not escape
in chasm or cave, in cliff-climbing thicket
or bog's bottom, wherever she bides.
Suffer your sorrow this one day only;
I wish you to wait, wait and be patient."

4. A small lake.

The elder leapt up   and offered his thanks
to God Almighty,   Master of all,
for such hopeful speech.   Then Hrothgar's horse,
a steed with mane braided,   was brought on its bridle.
The sage sovereign   set out in splendor
with shield-bearing soldiers   striding beside him.
Tracks on the trail   were easy to trace:
they went from woodland   out to the open,
heading through heather   and murky moors
where the best of thanes   was borne off unbreathing.
He would live no longer   in Hrothgar's house.
Crossing the moorland,   the king mounted
a stony path   up steepening slopes.
With a squad of scouts   in single file,
he rode through regions   none of them knew,
mountains and hollows   that hid many monsters.
The sovereign himself,   son of great forebears,
suddenly spotted   a forest of fir-trees
rooted on rock,   their trunks tipping
over a tarn   of turbulent eddies.
Danes were downcast,   and Geats, grim;
every soldier   was stricken at heart
to behold on that height   Aeschere's head.

As they looked on the lake,   blood still lingered,
welled to the surface.   A war-horn sounded
its bold battle-cry,   and the band halted.
Strange sea-dragons   swam in the depths;
sinuous serpents   slid to and fro.
At the base of the bluff   water-beasts lay,
much like monsters   that rise in the morning
when seafarers sail   on strenuous journeys.
Hearing the horn's   high-pitched challenge,
they puffed up with rage   and plunged in the pool.
One Geatish lad   lifted his bow
and loosing an arrow,   ended the life
of a wondrous wave-piercer.   War-shaft jutting
hard in its heart,   the swimmer slowed
as death seized it.   With startling speed
the waters were torn   by terrible tuskers.
They heaved the hideous   hulk to the shore
with spear-hooked heads   as warriors watched.

Undaunted, Beowulf   donned battle armor.
His woven war-corselet,   wide and ornate,
would safeguard his heart   as he searched underwater.
It knew how to armor   the breast of its bearer
if an angry grappler   grasped him in battle.
The bright war-helm   would hold his head
when he sought the seafloor   in swirling flood.

A weapon-smith had skillfully worked
its gilding of gold in bygone days
and royally ringed it. He added afterward
figures of boars so blades of foemen
would fail to bite. One further aid
Beowulf borrowed: Unferth offered
the hilt of Hrunting, his princely sword,
a poisoned war-fang with iron-edged blade,
blood-hardened in battles of old.
It never had failed in any man's grasp
if he dared to fare on a dreadful foray
to fields of foes. This was not the first time
it was forced to perform a desperate deed.

Though strong and sly, the son of Ecglaf
had somehow forgotten the slander he spoke,
bleary with beer. He loaned his blade
to a better bearer, a doer of deeds
that he would not dare. His head never dipped
under wild waves, and his fame waned
when bravery failed him as battle beckoned.
Not so, the other, armed and eager.

Beowulf spoke, son of Ecgtheow:
"Remember, wise master, mover of men
and giver of gold, since now I begin
this foray full-willing, how once before
you pledged to fill the place of a father
if I should be killed acquitting your cause.
Guard these young aides, my partners in arms,
if death takes me. The treasures you dealt,
Hrothgar, my lord, I leave to Hygelac.
Let the king of Geats gaze on the gold
and see that I found a fair bestower,
a generous host to help while I could.
Let Unferth have back his heirloom, Hrunting,
this wonderful weapon, wavy-skinned sword
renowned among men. Now I shall conquer
or die in the deed."
So saying, he dived,
high-hearted and hasty, awaiting no answer.
The waters swallowed that stout soldier.
He swam a half-day before seeing sea-floor.
Straightaway someone spied him as well:
she that had hidden a hundred half-years
in the void's vastness. Grim and greedy,
she glimpsed a creature come from above
and crept up to catch him, clutch him, crush him.
Quickly she learned his life was secure;
he was hale and whole, held in the ring-mail.

Linked and locked, his life-shielding shirt
was wrapped around him, and wrathful fingers
failed to rip open the armor he wore.
The wolf of the waters dragged him away
to her den in the deep, where weapons of war,
though bravely wielded, were worthless against her.
Many a mere-beast banded about him,
brandishing tusks to tear at his shirt.

The soldier now saw a high-roofed hall:
unharmed, he beheld the foe's fastness
beyond the reach of the roiling flood.
Fire-light flared; a blaze shone brightly.
The lordly one looked on the hellish hag,
the mighty mere-wife. He swung his sword
for a swift stroke, not staying his hand;
and the whorled blade whistled its war-song.
But the battle-flame failed to bite her;
its edge was unable to end her life,
though Hrunting had often hacked through helmets
and slashed mail-shirts in hand-to-hand strife.
For the first time the famous blade faltered.

Resolve unshaken, courage rekindled,
Hygelac's kinsman was keen for conquest.
In a fit of fury, he flung down the sword.
Steely and strong, the ring-banded blade
rang on the stones. He would trust in the strength
of his mighty hand-grip. Thus should a man,
unmindful of life, win lasting renown.
Grabbing the tresses of Grendel's mother,
the Geats' battle-chief, bursting with wrath,
wrestled her down: no deed to regret
but a favor repaid as fast as she fell.
With her grim grasp she grappled him still.
Weary, the warrior stumbled and slipped;
the strongest foot-soldier fell to the foe.
Astraddle the hall-guest, she drew her dagger,
broad and bright-bladed, bent on avenging
her only offspring. His mail-shirt shielded
shoulder and breast. Barring the entry
of edge or point, the woven war-shirt
saved him from harm. Ecgtheow's son,
the leader of Geats, would have lost his life
under Earth's arch but for his armor
and Heaven's favor furnishing help.
The Ruler of All readily aided
the righteous man when he rose once more.

He beheld in a hoard of ancient arms
a battle-blessed sword with strong-edged blade,

a marvelous weapon men might admire
though over-heavy for any to heft
when finely forged by giants of old.
The Scyldings' shielder took hold of the hilt
and swung up the sword, though despairing of life.
He struck savagely, hit her hard neck
and broke the bone-rings, cleaving clean through
her fated flesh. She fell to the floor;
the sword sweated; the soldier rejoiced.

The blaze brightened, shining through shadows
as clearly as Heaven's candle on high.
Grim and angry, Hygelac's guardsman
glanced round the room and went toward the wall
with his weapon raised, holding it hard
by the inlaid hilt. Its edge was ideal
for quickly requiting the killings of Grendel.
Too many times he had warred on the West-Danes.
He had slain Hrothgar's hearth-mates in sleep,
eagerly eaten fifteen of those folk
and as many more borne for his monstrous booty.
He paid their price to the fierce prince,
who looked on the ground where Grendel lay limp,
wound-weary, defeated in war.
The lifeless one lurched at the stroke of the sword
that cleaved his corpse and cut off his head.

At once the wise men waiting with Hrothgar
and watching the waters saw the waves seethe
with streaks of gore. Gray-haired and glum,
age around honor, they offered their counsel,
convinced that no victor would ever emerge
and seek out the sovereign. All were certain
the mere-wolf had mauled him. It was mid-afternoon,
and the proud Danes departed the dale;
generous Hrothgar headed for home.
The Geats lingered and looked on the lake
with sorrowful souls, wistfully wishing
they still might see their beloved leader.

The sword shrank from battle-shed blood;
its blade began melting, a marvel to watch,
that war-icicle waning away
like a rope of water unwound by the Ruler
when Father releases fetters of frost,
the true Sovereign of seasons and times.
The Weders' warlord took only two treasures
from all he beheld: the head and the hilt,
studded with gems. The sword had melted.
Its banded blade was burnt by the blood,
so hot was the horror, so acid the evil

that ended thereon. Soon he was swimming:
the strife-survivor drove up from the deep
when his foe had fallen. The foaming waves,
the wide waters were everywhere cleansed;
that alien evil had ended her life-days,
left the loaned world.
Landward he swam;
the strong-minded savior of sea-faring men
was glad of his burden, the booty he brought.
Grateful to God, the band of brave thanes
hastened gladly to greet their chieftain,
astonished to see him whole and unharmed.
His helm and chain-mail were swiftly unstrapped.
Calm under clouds, the lake lay quietly,
stained by the slain. They found the foot-path
and marched manfully, making their way
back through the barrens. Proud as princes,
they hauled the head far from the highland,
an effort for each of the four who ferried it
slung from spear-shafts. They bore their booty
straight to the gold-hall. Battle-hardened,
all fourteen strode from the field outside,
a bold band of Geats gathered about
their leader and lord, the war-worthy man,
peerless in prowess and daring in deeds.
He hailed Hrothgar as Grendel's head
was dragged by the hair, drawn through the hall
where earls were drinking. All were awe-stricken:
women and warriors watched in wonder.

Beowulf spoke, son of Ecgtheow:
"Hail, Hrothgar, Healfdene's son.
Look on this token we took from the lake,
this glorious booty we bring you gladly.
The struggle was stark; the danger, dreadful.
My foe would have won our war underwater
had the Lord not looked after my life.
Hrunting failed me, though finely fashioned;
but God vouchsafed me a glimpse of a great-sword,
ancient and huge, hung from the wall.
All-Father often fosters the friendless.
Wielding this weapon, I struck down and slew
the cavern's keeper as soon as I could.
My banded war-blade was burned away
when blood burst forth in the heat of battle.
I bore the hilt here, wrested from raiders.
Thus I avenged the deaths among Danes
as it was fitting, and this I assure you:
henceforth in Heorot heroes shall sleep

untroubled by terror. Your warrior troop,
all of your thanes, young men and old,
need fear no further evil befalling,
not from that quarter, king of the Scyldings."

He gave the gold hilt to the good old man;
the hoary war-chief held in his hand
an ancient artifact forged by giants.
At the devils' downfall, this wondrous work
went to the Danes. The dark-hearted demon,
hater of humans, Heaven's enemy,
committer of murders, and likewise his mother,
departed this Earth. Their power passed
to the wisest world-king who ever awarded
treasure in Denmark between the two seas.

Hrothgar spoke as he studied the hilt,
that aged heirloom inscribed long ago
with a story of strife: how the Flood swallowed
the race of giants with onrushing ocean.
Defiant kindred, they fared cruelly,
condemned for their deeds to death by water.
Such were the staves graven in gold-plate,
runes rightly set, saying for whom
the serpent-ribbed sword and raddled hilt[5]
were once fashioned of finest iron.
When the wise one spoke, all were silent.

"Truth may be told by the homeland's holder
and keeper of kinfolk, who rightly recalls
the past for his people: this prince was born
bravest of fighters. My friend, Beowulf,
your fame shall flourish in far countries,
everywhere honored. Your strength is sustained
by patience and judgement. Just as I promised,
our friendship is firmed, a lasting alliance.
So you shall be a boon to your brethren,
unlike Heremod who ought to have helped
Ecgwela's sons, the Honor-Scyldings.
He grew up to grief and grim slaughter,
doling out death to the Danish nation.
Hot-tempered at table, he cut down comrades,
slew his own soldiers and spurned humankind,
alone and unloved, an infamous prince,
though mighty God had given him greatness
and raised him in rank over all other men.
Hidden wrath took root in his heart,

5. On the sword hilt is the story of the flood, written in runes (letters of the early Germanic alphabet), and a decorative pattern of twisted serpent shapes.

bloodthirsty thoughts. He would give no gifts
to honor others. Loveless, he lived,
a lasting affliction endured by the Danes
in sorrow and strife. Consider him well,
his life and lesson.
"Wise with winters,
I tell you this tale as I mull and marvel
how the Almighty metes to mankind
the blessings of reason, rule and realm.
He arranges it all. For a time He allows
the mind of a man to linger in love
with earthly honors. He offers him homeland
to hold and enjoy, a fort full of fighters,
men to command and might in the world,
wide kingdoms won to his will.
In his folly, the fool imagines no ending.
He dwells in delight without thought of his lot.
Illness, old age, anguish or envy:
none of these gnaw by night at his mind.
Nowhere are swords brandished in anger;
for him the whole world wends as he wishes.
He knows nothing worse till his portion of pride
waxes within him. His soul is asleep;
his gate, unguarded. He slumbers too soundly,
sunk in small cares. The slayer creeps close
and shoots a shaft from the baneful bow.
The bitter arrow bites through his armor,
piercing the heart he neglected to guard
from crooked counsel and evil impulse.
Too little seems all he has long possessed.
Suspicious and stingy, withholding his hoard
of gold-plated gifts, he forgets or ignores
what fate awaits him, for the world's Wielder
surely has granted his share of glory.
But the end-rune is already written:
the loaned life-home collapses in ruin;
some other usurps and openly offers
the hoarded wealth, heedless of worry.

"Beloved Beowulf, best of defenders,
guard against anger and gain for yourself
perpetual profit. Put aside pride,
worthiest warrior. Now for awhile
your force flowers, yet soon it shall fail.
Sickness or age will strip you of strength,
or the fangs of flame, or flood-surges,
the sword's bite or the spear's flight,
or fearful frailty as bright eyes fade,
dimming to darkness. Afterward death

will sweep you away,   strongest of war-chiefs.

"I ruled the Ring-Danes   a hundred half-years,
stern under clouds   with sword and spear
that I wielded in war   against many nations
across Middle-Earth,   until none remained
beneath spacious skies   to reckon as rivals.
Recompense happened   here in my homeland,
grief after gladness   when Grendel came,
when the ancient enemy   cunningly entered.
Thereafter I suffered   constant sorrows
and cruelest cares.   But God has given me
long enough life   to look at this head
with my own eyes,   as enmity ends
spattered with gore.   Sit and be glad,
war-worthy one: the feast is forthcoming,
and many gifts   will be granted tomorrow."

Gladly the Geat   sought out his seat
as the old man asked.   Hall-guests were given
a second feast   as fine as the first.
The helm of Heaven   darkened with dusk,
and the elders arose.   The oldest of Scyldings
was ready to rest   his hoary-haired head
at peace on his pillow.   Peerless with shield,
the leader of Geats   was equally eager
to lie down at last.   A thane was appointed
to serve as his esquire.   Such was the courtesy
shown in those days   to weary wayfarers,
soldiers sojourning   over the ocean.

Beneath golden gables   the great-hearted guest
dozed until dawn   in the high-roofed hall,
when the black raven   blithely foretold
joy under Heaven.   Daybreak hastened,
sun after shadow.   The soldiers were ardent,
the earls eager   to hurry homeward;
the stern minded man   would make for his ship,
fare back to his folk.   But first he bade
that Hrunting be sent   to the son of Ecglaf,
a treasure returned   with thanks for the loan
of precious iron.   He ordered the owner
be told he considered   the sword a fine friend,
blameless in battle.   That man was gallant!
Keen for the crossing,   his weapons secure,
the warrior went   to the worthy Dane;
the thane sought the throne   where a sovereign sat,
that steadfast hero,   Hrothgar the Great.

Beowulf spoke,   son of Ecgtheow:
"Now we must say   as far-sailing seamen,

we wish to make way homeward to Hygelac.
Here we were well and warmly received.
If anything further would earn your favor,
some deed of war that remains to be done
for the master of men, I shall always be ready.
Should word ever wend over wide ocean
that nearby nations menace your marches,
as those who detest you sometimes have tried,
I shall summon a thousand thanes to your aid.
I know Hygelac, though newly-anointed
the nation's shepherd, will surely consent
to honor my offer in word and action.
If you ever need men, I shall muster at once
a thicket of spears and support you in strength.
Should Hrethric, your son, sail overseas,
he shall find friends in the fort of the Geats.
It is well for the worthy to fare in far countries."

Hrothgar offered these answering words:
"Heaven's Sovereign has set in your heart
this vow you have voiced. I never have known
someone so young to speak more wisely.
You are peerless in strength, princely in spirit,
straightforward in speech. If a spear fells
Hrethel's son, if a hostile sword-stroke
kills him in combat or after, with illness,
slays your leader while you still live,
the Sea-Geats surely could name no better
to serve as their king and keeper of treasure,
should you wish to wield rule in your realm.
I sensed your spirit the instant I saw you,
precious Beowulf, bringer of peace
for both our peoples: War-Danes and Weders,
so often sundered by strife in the past.
While I wield the rule of this wide realm,
men will exchange many more greetings
and riches will ride in ring-bowed ships
bearing their gifts where the gannets bathe.
I know your countrymen keep to old ways,
fast in friendship, and war as well."

Then the hall's holder, Healfdene's son,
gave his protector twelve more treasures,
bidding he bear these tokens safely
home to his kin, and quickly return.
That hoary-haired king held and kissed him,
clasping his neck. The noble Scylding
was too well aware with the wisdom of age
that he never might meet the young man again
coming to council. So close had they grown,

so strong in esteem, he could scarcely endure
the surfeit of sorrow that surged in his heart;
the flame of affection burned in his blood.
But Beowulf walked away with his wealth;
proud of his prizes, he trod on the turf.
Standing at anchor, his sea-courser
chafed for its captain. All the way home
Hrothgar's gifts were often honored.
That was a king accorded respect
until age unmanned him, like many another.

High-hearted, the troop of young soldiers
strode to the sea, wrapped in their ring-mesh,
linked and locked shirts. The land-watcher spied
the fighters faring, just as before.
He called no taunts from the top of the cliff
but galloped to greet them and tell them the Geats
would always be welcome, armored warriors
borne on their ship. The broad-beamed boat
lay by the beach, laden with chain-mail,
chargers and treasures behind its tall prow.
The mast soared high over Hrothgar's hoard.

The boat-guard was given a gold-bound sword;
thereafter that man had honor enhanced,
bearing an heirloom to Heorot's mead-bench.
They boarded their vessel, breasted the deep,
left Denmark behind. A halyard hoisted
the sea-wind's shroud; the sail was sheeted,
bound to the mast, and the beams moaned
as a fair wind wafted the wave-rider forward.
Foamy-throated, the longboat bounded,
swept on the swells of the swift sea-stream
until welcoming capes were sighted ahead,
the cliffs of Geat-land. The keel grounded
as wind-lift thrust it straight onto sand.

The harbor-guard hastened hence from his post.
He had looked long on an empty ocean
and waited to meet the much-missed men.
He moored the broad-beamed bow to the beach
with woven lines lest the backwash of waves
bear off the boat. Then Beowulf ordered
treasures unloaded, the lordly trappings,
gold that was going to Hygelac's hall,
close to the cliff-edge, where the ring-giver kept
his comrades about him.

That building was bold
at the hill's crown; and queenly Hygd,
Haereth's daughter, dwelt there as well.
Wise and refined, though her winters were few,

she housed in the stronghold. Open-handed,
she granted generous gifts to the Geats,
most unlike Modthryth,[6] a maiden so fierce
that none but her father dared venture near.
The brave man who gazed at Modthryth by day
might reckon a death-rope already twisted,
might count himself quickly captured and killed,
the stroke of a sword prescribed for his trespass.
Such is no style for a queen to proclaim:
though peerless, a woman ought to weave peace,
not snatch away life for illusory slights.
Modthryth's temper was tamed by marriage.
Ale-drinkers say her ill-deeds ended
once she was given in garlands of gold
to Hemming's kinsman. She came to his hall
over pale seas, accepted that prince,
a fine young heir, at her father's behest.
Thenceforth on the throne, she was famed for fairness,
making the most of her lot in life,
sustained by loving her lordly sovereign.
That king, Offa, was called by all men
the ablest of any ruling a realm
between two seas, so I am told.
Gifted in war, a wise gift-giver
everywhere honored, the spear-bold soldier
held his homeland and also fathered
help for the heroes of Hemming's kindred:
war-worthy Eomer, grandson of Garmund.

Brave Beowulf marched with his band,
strode up the sands of the broad beach
while the sun in the south beamed like a beacon.
The earls went eagerly up to the keep
where the strong sovereign, Ongentheow's slayer,
the young war-king doled out gold rings.
Beowulf's coming was quickly proclaimed.
Hygelac heard that his shoulder-shielder
had entered the hall, whole and unharmed
by bouts of battle. The ruler made room
for the foot-guests crossing the floor before him.

Saluting his lord with a loyal speech
earnestly worded, the winner in war
sat facing the king, kinsman with kinsman.
A mead-vessel moved from table to table
as Haereth's daughter, heedful of heroes,
bore the wine-beaker from hand to hand.
Keen to elicit his comrade's account

6. "Modthryth" may mean "arrogant in temper"; it may be a reference to an arrogant woman rather than a proper name.

in the high-roofed hall, Hygelac graciously
asked how the Sea-Geats fared on their foray:

"Say what befell from your sudden resolve
to seek out strife over salt waters,
to struggle in Heorot. Have you helped Hrothgar
ward off the well-known cares of his kingdom?
You have cost me disquiet, angst and anguish.
Doubting the outcome, dearest of men,
for anyone meeting that murderous demon,
I sought to dissuade you from starting the venture.
The South-Danes themselves should have settled their feud
with ghastly Grendel. Now I thank God
that I see you again, safe and sound."

Beowulf spoke, son of Ecgtheow:
"For a great many men our meeting's issue
is hardly hidden, my lord Hygelac.
What a fine fracas passed in that place
when both of us battled where Grendel had brought
sore sorrow on scores of War-Scyldings!
I avenged every one, so that none of his kin
anywhere need exult at our night-bout,
however long the loathsome race lives,
covered with crime. When Hrothgar came
and heard what had happened there in the ring-hall,
he sat me at once with his own two sons.

"The whole of his host gathered in gladness;
all my life long I never have known
such joy in a hall beneath heaven's vault.
The acclaimed queen, her kindred's peace-pledge,
would sometimes circle the seated youths,
lavishing rings on delighted young lords.
Hrothgar's daughter handed the elders
ale-cups aplenty, pouring for each
old trooper in turn. I heard the hall-sitters
call her Freawaru after she proffered
the studded flagon. To Froda's fair son
that maiden is sworn. This match seems meet
to the lord of Scyldings, who looks to settle
his Heatho-Bard feud. Yet the best of brides
seldom has stilled the spears of slaughter
so swiftly after a sovereign was stricken.

"Ingeld and all his earls will be rankled,
watching that woman walk in their hall
with high-born Danes doing her bidding.
Her escorts will wear ancient heirlooms:
Heatho-Bard swords with braided steel blades,
weapons once wielded and lost in war

along with the lives of friends in the fray.
Eyeing the ring-hilts, an old ash-warrior
will brood in his beer and bitterly pine
for the stark reminders of men slain in strife.
He will grimly begin to goad a young soldier,
testing and tempting a troubled heart,
his whispered words waking war-evil:

"'My friend, have you spotted the battle-sword
that your father bore on his final foray?
Wearing his war-mask, Withergyld fell
when foemen seized the field of slaughter.
His priceless blade became battle-plunder.
Today a son of the Scylding who slew him
struts on our floor, flaunting his trophy,
an heirloom that you should rightfully own.'

"He will prick and pique with pointed words
time after time till the challenge is taken,
the maiden's attendant is murdered in turn,
blade-bitten to sleep in his blood,
forfeit his life for his father's feat.
Another will run, knowing the road.
So on both sides oaths will be broken;
and afterward Ingeld's anger will grow
hotter, unchecked, as he chills toward his wife.
Hence I would hold the Heatho-Bards likely
to prove unpeaceable partners for Danes."

"Now I shall speak of my strife with Grendel,
further acquainting the kingdom's keeper
with all that befell when our fight began.
Heaven's gem had gone overhead;
in darkness the dire demon stalked us
while we stood guard unharmed in Heorot.
Hondscioh was doomed to die with the onslaught,
first to succumb, though clad for combat
when grabbed by Grendel, who gobbled him whole.
That beloved young thane was eaten alive.
Not one to leave the hall empty-handed,
the bloody-toothed terror intended to try
his might upon me. A curious creel
hung from his hand, cunningly clasped
and strangely sewn with devilish skill
from skin of a dragon. The demon would stuff me,
sinless, inside like so many others;
but rising in wrath, I stood upright.
It is too long a tale, how the people's plaguer
paid for his crimes with proper requital;
but the feat reflected finely, my lord,

on the land you lead. Though the foe fled
to live awhile longer, he left behind him
as sign of the strife a hand in Heorot.
Humbled, he fell to the floor of the mere.

"The warder of Scyldings rewarded my warfare
with much treasure when morning arrived,
and we sat for a feast with songs and sagas.
He told many tales he learned in his lifetime.
Sometimes a soldier struck the glad harp,
the sounding wood; sometimes strange stories
were spoken like spells, tragic and true,
rightly related. The large-hearted lord
sometimes would start to speak of his youth,
his might in war. His memories welled;
ancient in winters, he weighed them all.

"So we delighted the livelong day
until darkness drew once more upon men.
Then Grendel's mother, mourning her son,
swiftly set out in search of revenge
against warlike Geats. The grisly woman
wantonly slew a Scylding warrior:
aged Aeschere, the king's counselor,
relinquished his life. Nor in the morning
might death-weary Danes bear off his body
to burn on a bier, for the creature clutching him
fled to her fastness under a waterfall.
This was the sorest of sorrows that Hrothgar
suffered as king. Distraught, he beseeched me
to do in your name a notable deed.
If I dived in the deep, heedless of danger,
to war underwater, he would reward me.

"Under I went, as now is well-known;
and I found the hideous haunter of fens.
For a time we two contested our hand-strength;
then I struck off her head with a huge sword
that her battle-hall held, and her hot blood
boiled in the lake. Leaving that place
was no easy feat, but fate let me live.
Again I was granted gifts that the guardian,
Healfdene's son, had sworn to bestow.
The king of that people kept his promise,
allotting me all he had earlier offered:
meed for my might, with more treasures,
my choice from the hoard of Healfdene's son.
These, my lord, I deliver to you,
as proof of fealty. My future depends
wholly on you. I have in this world
few close kin but my king, Hygelac."

He bade the boar-banner now be brought in,
the high helmet, hard mail-shirt,
and splendid sword, describing them thus:
"When Hrothgar gave me this hoarded gear,
the sage sovereign entreated I tell
the tale of his gift: this treasure was held
by Heorogar, king, who long was the lord
of Scylding people. It should have passed
to armor the breast of bold Heoroweard,
the father's favorite, faithful and brave;
but he willed it elsewhere, so use it well."

I have heard how horses followed that hoard,
four dappled mounts, matching and fleet.
He gave up his gifts, gold and horses.
Kinsmen should always act with honor,
not spin one another in snares of spite
or secretly scheme to kill close comrades.
Always the nephew had aided his uncle;
each held the other's welfare at heart.
He gave to Queen Hygd the golden collar,
wondrously wrought, Wealtheow's token,
and also three steeds, sleek and bright-saddled.
Thereafter her breast was graced by the gift.

So Ecgtheow's son won his repute
as a man of mettle, acting with honor,
yet mild-hearted toward hearth-companions,
harming no one when muddled with mead.
Bold in battle, he guarded the guerdon
that God had granted, the greatest strength
of all humankind, though once he was thought
weak and unworthy, a sluggardly sloucher,
mocked for meekness by men on the mead-bench,
and given no gifts by the lord of the Geats.
Every trouble untwined in time
for the glory-blessed man.
A blade was brought
at the king's request, Hrethel's heirloom
glinting with gold. No greater treasure,
no nobler sword was held in his hoard.
He lay that brand on Beowulf's lap
and also bestowed a spacious estate,
hall and high seat. When land and lordship
were left to them both, by birthright and law,
he who ranked higher ruled the wide realm.

3. The Dragon

It happened long after, with Hygelac dead,
that war-swords slew Heardred, his son,

when Battle-Scylfings broke his shield-wall
and hurtled headlong at Hereric's nephew.
So Beowulf came to rule the broad realm.
For fifty winters he fostered it well;
then the old king, keeper of kinfolk,
heard of a dragon drawn from the darkness.
He had long lain in his lofty fastness,
the steep stone-barrow, guarding his gold;
but a path pierced it, known to no person
save him who found it and followed it forward.
That stranger seized a singular treasure.
He bore it in hand from the heathen hoard:
a finely-worked flagon he filched from the lair
where the dragon dozed. Enraged at the robber,
the sneaking thief who struck while he slept,
the guardian woke glowing with wrath,
as his nearest neighbors were soon to discern.
It was not by choice that the wretch raided
the wondrous worm-hoard. The one who offended
was stricken himself, sorely mistreated,
the son of a warrior sold as a slave.
Escaped and seeking a safe refuge,
he guiltily groped his way below ground.
There the intruder, trembling with terror,
sensed an ancient evil asleep.
His fate was to find as fear unmanned him
his fingers feeling a filigreed cup.
Many such goblets had gone to the earth-house,
legacies left by a lordly people.
In an earlier age someone unknown
had cleverly covered those costly treasures.
That thane held the hoard for the lifetime allowed him,
but gold could not gladden a man in mourning.
Newly-built near the breaking waves,
a barrow stood at the base of a bluff,
its entrance sculpted by secret arts.
Earthward the warrior bore the hoard-worthy
portion of plate, the golden craftwork.
The ringkeeper spoke these words as he went:
"Hold now, Earth, what men may not,
the hoard of the heroes, earth-gotten wealth
when it first was won. War-death has felled them,
an evil befalling each of my people.
The household is mirthless when men are lifeless.
I have none to wear sword, none to bear wine
or polish the precious vessels and plates.
Gone are the brethren who braved many battles.
From the hard helmet the hand-wrought gilding

drops in the dust. Asleep are the smiths
who knew how to burnish the war-chief's mask
or mend the mail-shirts mangled in battle.
Shields and mail-shirts molder with warriors
and follow no foes to faraway fields.
No harp rejoices to herald the heroes,
no hand-fed hawk swoops through the hall,
no stallion stamps in the stronghold's courtyard.
Death has undone many kindreds of men."

Stricken in spirit, he spoke of his sorrow
as last of his line, drearily drifting
through day and dark until death's flood-tide
stilled his heart. The old night-scather
was happy to glimpse the unguarded hoard.
Balefully burning, he seeks out barrows.
Naked and hateful in a raiment of flame,
the dragon dreaded by outland dwellers
must gather and guard the heathen gold,
no better for wealth but wise with his winters.

For three hundred winters the waster of nations
held that mighty hoard in his earth-hall
till one man wronged him, arousing his wrath.
The wretched robber ransomed his life
with the prize he pilfered, the plated flagon.
Beholding that marvel men of old made,
his fief-lord forgave the skulker's offense.
One treasure taken had tainted the rest.
Waking in wrath, the worm reared up
and slid over stones. Stark-hearted,
he spotted the footprints where someone had stepped,
stealthily creeping close to his head.
The fortunate man slips swiftly and safely
through the worst dangers if the World's Warder
grants him that grace.
Eager and angry,
the hoard-guard hunted the thief who had haunted
his hall while he slept. He circled the stone-house,
but out in that wasteland the one man he wanted
was not to be found. How fearsome he felt,
how fit for battle! Back in his barrow
he tracked the intruder who dared to tamper
with glorious gold. Fierce and fretful,
the dragon waited for dusk and darkness.
The rage-swollen holder of headland and hoard
was plotting reprisal: flames for his flagon.
Then day withdrew, and the dragon, delighted,
would linger no longer but flare up and fly.
His onset was awful for all on the land,
and a cruel ending soon came for their king.

When the ghastly specter scattered his sparks
and set their buildings brightly burning,
flowing with flames as householders fled,
he meant to leave not one man alive.
That wreaker of havoc hated and harried
the Geatish folk fleeing his flames.
Far and wide his warfare was watched
until night waned and the worm went winging
back to the hall where his hoard lay hidden,
sure of his stronghold, his walls and his war,
sure of himself, deceived by his pride.

Then terrible tidings were taken to Beowulf:
how swiftly his own stronghold was stricken,
that best of buildings bursting with flames
and his throne melting. The hero was heart-sore;
the wise man wondered what wrong he had wrought
and how he trangressed against old law,
the Lord Everlasting, Ruler of All.
His grief was great, and grim thoughts
boiled in his breast as never before.
The fiery foe had flown to his coastlands,
had sacked and seared his keep by the sea.
For that the war-king required requital.
He ordered a broad-shield fashioned of iron,
better for breasting baleful blazes
than the linden-wood that warded his warriors.
Little was left of the time lent him
for life in the world; and the worm as well,
who had haughtily held his hoard for so long.
Scorning to follow the far-flying foe
with his whole host, the ring-giver reckoned
the wrath of a dragon unworthy of dread.
Fearless and forceful, he often had faced
the straits of struggle blessed with success.
Beowulf braved many a battle
after ridding Hrothgar's hall of its horrors
and grappling with Grendel's gruesome kin.
Not least of his clashes had come when the king
Hygelac fell while fighting the Frisians
in hand-to-hand combat. His friend and fief-lord,
the son of Hrethel, was slain in the onslaught,
stricken to death by a blood-drinking blade.
Beowulf battled back to the beach
where he proved his strength with skillful swimming,
for he took to the tide bearing the trophies
of thirty warriors won on the field.

None of the Hetware needed to boast
how they fared on foot, flaunting their shields
against that fierce fighter, for few remained
after the battle to bear the tale home.

Over wide waters the lone swimmer went,
the son of Ecgtheow swept on the sea-waves
back to his homeland, forlorn with his loss,
and hence to Hygd who offered her hoard:
rings and a realm, a throne for the thane.
With Hygelac dead she doubted her son
could guard the Geats from foreigners' forays.
Refusing her boon, Beowulf bade
the leaderless lords to hail the lad
as their rightful ruler. He chose not to reign
by thwarting his cousin but to counsel the king
and guide with good will until Heardred grew older.

It was Heardred who held the Weder-Geats' hall
when outcast Scylfings came seeking its safety:
Eanmund and Eadgils, nephews of Onela.
That strong sea-king and spender of treasures
sailed from Sweden pursuing the rebels
who challenged his right to rule their realm.
For lending them haven, Hygelac's son
suffered the sword-stroke that spilled out his life.
The Swede headed home when Heardred lay dead,
leaving Beowulf lordship of Geats.
That was a good king, keeping the gift-seat;
yet Heardred's death dwelled in his thoughts.
A long time later he offered his aid
to end the exile of destitute Eadgils.
He summoned an army, and Ohthere's son,
cold in his cares, went over wide waters
with weapons and warriors to kill off a king.

Such were the struggles and tests of strength
the son of Ecgtheow saw and survived.
His pluck was proven in perilous onslaughts
till that fateful day when he fought the dragon.
As leader of twelve trailing that terror,
the greatest of Geats glowered with rage
when he looked on the lair where the worm lurked.
By now he had found how the feud flared,
this fell affliction befalling his kingdom,
for the kingly cup had come to his hand
from the hand of him who raided the hoard.
That sorry slave had started the strife,
and against his will he went with the warriors,
a thirteenth man bringing the band
to the barrow's brink which he alone knew.

Hard by the surge of the seething sea
gaped a cavern glutted with golden
medallions and chains. The murderous man-bane,
hidden within, hungered for warfare.
No taker would touch his treasures cheaply:
the hoard's holder would drive a hard bargain.

The proud war-king paused on the sea-point
to lighten the hearts of his hearth-companions,
though his heart was heavy and hankered for death.
It was nearing him now. That taker of treasure
would sunder the soul from his old bones and flesh.
So Beowulf spoke, the son of Ecgtheow,
recalling the life he was loathe to lose:

"From boyhood I bore battles and bloodshed,
struggles and strife: I still see them all.
I was given at seven to house with King Hrethel,
my mother's father and friend of our folk.
He kept me fairly with feasts and fine gifts.
I fared no worse than one of his sons:
Herebeald, Hathcyn, or princely Hygelac
who was later my lord. The eldest, Herebeald,
unwittingly went to a wrongful death
when Hathcyn's horn-bow hurled an arrow.
Missing the mark, it murdered the kinsman;
a brother was shot by the blood-stained shaft.
This blow to the heart was brutal and baffling.
A prince had fallen. The felon went free.[1]

"So it is sore for an old man to suffer
his son swinging young on the gallows,
gladdening ravens. He groans in his grief
and loudly laments the lad he has lost.
No help is at hand from hard-won wisdom
or the march of years. Each morning reminds him
his heir is elsewhere, and he has no heart
to wait for a second son in his stronghold
when death has finished the deeds of the first.
He ceaselessly sees his son's dwelling,
the desolate wine-hall, the windswept grave-sward
where swift riders and swordsmen slumber.
No harp-string sounds, no song in the courtyard.
He goes to his bed sighing with sorrow,
one soul for another. His home is hollow;
his field, fallow.
"So Hrethel suffered,
hopeless and heart-sore with Herebeald gone.

1. Even in cases of involuntary manslaughter, punishment was required to avenge the dead. In this instance, it seems that a ritual, sacrificial hanging was performed to spare Hathcyn for murdering his brother Herebeald.

He would do no deed   to wound the death-dealer
or harrow his household   with hatred and anger;
but bitter bloodshed   had stolen his bliss,
and he quit his life   for the light of the Lord.
Like a luckier man,   he could leave his land
in the hands of a son,   though he loved him no longer.

"Then strife and struggle   of Geats and Swedes
crossed the wide water.   Warfare wounded
both sides in battle   when Hrethel lay buried.
Ongentheow's sons,   fierce and unfriendly,
suddenly struck   at Hreosna-Beorh
and bloodied the bluff   with baneful slaughter.
Our foes in this feud   soon felt the wrath
of my kinsman the king   claiming our due,
though the counterblow   cost his own life.
Hathcyn was killed,   his kingship cut short.
The slayer himself   was slain in the morning.
I have heard how Eofor   struck the old Scyfing.
Sword-ashen,   Ongentheow sank
with his helm split: heedful of harm,
to kinsman and king,   the hand would not halt
the death-blow it dealt.
"My own sword-arm
repaid my prince   for the gifts he granted.
He gave me a fiefdom,   the land I have loved.
He never had need   to seek among Spear-Danes,
Gifthas or Swedes   and get with his gifts
a worse warrior.   I wielded my sword
at the head of our host;   so shall I hold
this blade that I bear   boldly in battle
as long as life lasts.   It has worn well
since the day when Daeghrefn   died by my hand,
the Frankish foe   who fought for the Frisians,
bearing their banner.   He broke in my grip,
never to barter   the necklace he robbed
from Hygelac's corpse.   I crushed that killer;
his bones snapped,   and his life-blood spilled.
I slew him by strength,   not by the sword.
Now I shall bear   his brand into battle:
hand and hard sword   will fight for the hoard."

Now Beowulf spoke   his last battle-boast:
"In boyhood I braved   bitter clashes;
still in old age   I would seek out strife
and gain glory   guarding my people
if the man-bane comes   from his cave to meet me."

Then he turned to his troop   for the final time,
bidding farewell   to bold helmet-bearers,
fast in friendship: "I would wear no sword,

no weapon at all to ward off the worm
if I knew how to fight this fiendish foe
as I grappled with Grendel one bygone night.
But here I shall find fierce battle-fire
and breath envenomed; therefore I bear
this mail-coat and shield. I shall not shy
from standing my ground when I greet the guardian,
follow what will at the foot of his wall.
I shall face the fiend with a firm heart.
Let the Ruler of men reckon my fate:
words are worthless against the war-flyer.
Bide by the barrow, safe in your byrnies,
and watch, my warriors, which of us two
will better bear the brunt of our clash.
This war is not yours; it is meted to me,
matching my strength, man against monster.
I shall do this deed undaunted by death
and get you gold or else get my ending,
borne off in battle, the bane of your lord."

The hero arose, helmed and hardy,
a war-king clad in shield and corselet.
He strode strongly under the stone-cliff:
no faint-hearted man, to face it unflinching!
Stalwart soldier of so many marches,
unshaken when shields were crushed in the clash,
he saw between stiles an archway where steam
burst like a boiling tide from the barrow,
woeful for one close to the worm-hoard.
He would not linger long unburned by the lurker
or safely slip through the searing lair.
Then a battle-cry broke from Beowulf's breast
as his rightful wrath was roused for the reckoning.
His challenge sounded under stark stone
where the hateful hoard-guard heard in his hollow
the clear-voiced call of a man coming.

No quarter was claimed; no quarter given.
First the beast's breath blew hot from the barrow
as battle-bellows boomed underground.
The stone-house stormer swung up his shield
at the ghastly guardian. Then the dragon's grim heart
kindled for conflict. Uncoiling, he came
seeking the swordsman who'd already drawn
the keen-edged blade bequeathed him for combat.
Each foe confronted the other with fear.
His will unbroken, the warlord waited
behind his tall shield, helm and armor.
With fitful twistings the fire-drake hastened
fatefully forward. His defense held high,

Beowulf felt the blaze blister through
hotter and sooner than he had foreseen.
So for the first time fortune was failing
the mighty man in the midst of a struggle.
Wielding his sword, he struck at the worm
and his fabled blade bit to the bone
through blazoned hide: bit and bounced back,
no match for the foe in this moment of need.

The peerless prince was hard-pressed in response,
for his bootless blow had maddened the monster
and fatal flames shot further than ever,
lighting the land. The blade he bared
failed in the fray, though forged from iron.
No easy end for the son of Ecgtheow:
against his will he would leave this world
to dwell elsewhere, as every man must
when his days are done. Swiftly the death-dealer
moved to meet him. From the murderous breast
bellows of breath belched fresh flames.
Enfolded in fire, he who formerly
ruled a whole realm had no one to help him
hold off the heat, for his hand-picked band
of princelings had fled, fearing to face
the foe with their lord. Loving honor
less than their lives, they hid in the holt.
But one among them grieved for the Geats
and balked at the thought of quitting a kinsman.

This one was Wiglaf, son of Weohstan,
kinsman of Aelfhere, earl among Scylfings.
Seeing his liege-lord suffering sorely
with war-mask scorched by the searing onslaught,
the thankful thane thought of the boons
his sovereign bestowed: the splendid homestead
and folk-rights his father formerly held.
No shirker could stop him from seizing his shield
of yellow linden and lifting the blade
Weohstan won when he slew Eanmund,
son of Ohthere. Spoils of that struggle,
sword and scabbard, smithwork of giants,
a byrnie of ring-mail and bright burnished helm
were granted as gifts, a thane's war-garb,
for Onela never acknowledged his nephews
but struck against both of his brother's sons.
When Eadgils avenged Eanmund's death,
Weohstan fled. Woeful and friendless,
he saved that gear for seasons of strife,
foreseeing his son someday might crave
sword and corselet. He came to his kinsman,

the prince of the Geats, and passed on his heirlooms,
hoping Wiglaf would wear them with honor.
Old then, and wise, he went from the world.

This war was the first young Wiglaf would fight
helping the king. His heart would not quail
nor weapon fail as the foe would find
going against him; but he made his grim mood
known to the men: "I remember the time
when taking our mead in the mighty hall,
all of us offered oaths to our leige-lord.
We promised to pay for princely trappings
by staunchly wielding sword-blades in war
if need should arise. Now we are needed
by him who chose, from the whole of his host,
twelve for this trial, trusting our claims
as warriors worthy of wearing our blades,
bearing keen spears. Our king has come here
bent on battling the man-bane alone,
because among warriors one keeper of kinfolk
has done, undaunted, the most deeds of daring.
But this day our lord needs dauntless defenders
so long as the frightful fires keep flaring.
God knows I would gladly give my own body
for flames to enfold with the gold-giver.
Shameful, to shoulder our shields homeward!
First we must fell this fearsome foe
and protect the life of our people's lord.
It is wrong that one man be wrathfully racked
for his former feats and fall in this fight,
guarding the Geats. We shall share our war-gear:
shield and battle-shirt, helm and hard sword."

So speaking, he stormed through the reek of smoke,
with helmet on head, to help his lord.
"Beloved Beowulf, bear up your blade.
You pledged in your youth, powerful prince,
never to let your luster lessen
while life was left you. Now summon your strength.
Stand steadfast. I shall stand with you."

After these words the worm was enraged.
For a second time the spiteful specter
flew at his foe, and he wreathed in flames
the hated human he hungered to harm.
His dreadful fire-wind drove in a wave,
charring young Wiglaf's shield to the boss,
nor might a mail-shirt bar that breath
from burning the brave spear-bearer's breast.

Wiglaf took cover close to his kinsman,
shielded by iron when linden was cinder.
Then the war-king, recalling past conquests,
struck with full strength straight at the head.
His battle-sword, Naegling, stuck there and split,
shattered in combat, so sharp was the shock
to Beowulf's great gray-banded blade.
He never was granted the gift of a sword
as hard and strong as the hand that held it.
I have heard that he broke blood-hardened brands,
so the weapon-bearer was none the better.

The fearful fire-drake, scather of strongholds,
flung himself forward a final time,
wild with wounds yet wily and sly.
In the heat of the fray, he hurtled headlong
to fasten his fangs in the foe's throat.
Beowulf's life-blood came bursting forth
on those terrible tusks. Just then, I am told,
the second warrior sprang from his side,
a man born for battle proving his mettle,
keen to strengthen his kinsman in combat.
He took no heed of the hideous head
scorching his hand as he hit lower down.
The sword sank in, patterned and plated;
the flames of the foe faltered, faded.
Quick-witted still, the king unsheathed
the keen killing-blade he kept in his corselet.
Then the Geats' guardian gutted the dragon,
felling that fiend with the help of his friend,
two kinsmen together besting the terror.
So should a thane succor his sovereign.

That deed was the king's crowning conquest;
Beowulf's work in the world was done.
He soon felt his wound swelling and stinging
where fell fangs had fastened upon him,
and evil venom enveloped his heart.
Wisely he sought a seat by the stone-wall,
and his gaze dwelled on the dark doorway
delved in the dolmen, the straight stiles
and sturdy archway sculpted by giants.
With wonderful kindness Wiglaf washed
the clotting blood from his king and kinsman;
his hands loosened the lord's high helm.
Though banefully bitten, Beowulf spoke,
for he knew his lifetime would last no longer.
The count of his days had come to a close.
His joys were done. Death drew near him.

"Now I would wish to will my son
these weapons of war, had I been awarded
an heir of my own, holder of heirlooms.
I fathered the Weders for fifty winters.
No warlike lord of neighboring lands
dared to assail us or daunt us with dread.
A watchful warden, I waited on fate
while keeping our people clear of quarrels.
I swore many oaths; not one was wrongful.
So I rejoice, though sick with my death-wound,
that God may not blame me for baseless bloodshed
or killing of kin when breath quits my body.
Hurry below and look on the hoard,
beloved Wiglaf. The worm lies sleeping
under gray stone, sorely stricken
and stripped of his gold. Go swiftly and seize it.
Get me giltwork and glittering gems:
I would set my sight on that store of wealth.
Loath would I be to leave for less
the life and lordship I held for so long."

I have heard how swiftly the son of Weohstan
hastened to heed his wounded and weakening
war-lord's behest. In his woven mail-shirt,
his bright byrnie, he entered the barrow;
and passing its threshold, proud and princely,
he glimpsed all the gold piled on the ground,
the walled-in wealth won by the worm,
that fierce night-flyer. Flagons were standing,
embossed wine-beakers lying unburnished,
their inlays loosened. There were lofty helmets
and twisted arm-rings rotting and rusting.
Gold below ground may betray into grief
any who hold it: heed me who will!

Wiglaf saw also a gold-woven standard,
a wonder of handiwork, skillfully filigreed,
high above ground. It gave off a glow
that let him behold the whole of the hoard.
I am told he took from that trove of giants
goblets and platters pressed to his breastplate,
and the golden banner glinting brightly.
He spotted no sign of the stricken dragon.
The iron-edged brand old Beowulf bore
had mortally wounded the warder of wealth
and fiery foe whose flames in the night
welled so fiercely before he was felled.

Bent with his burden, the messenger hastened
back to his master, burning to know

whether the brave but wound-weakened
lord of the Weders was lost to the living.
Setting his spoils by the storied prince
whose lifeblood blackened the ground with gore,
Wiglaf wakened the war-lord with water,
and these words thrust like spears through his breast
as the ancient one grimly gazed on the gold:

"I offer my thanks to the Almighty Master,
the King of Glory, for granting my kindred
these precious things I look upon last.
Losing my life, I have bought this boon
to lighten my leave-day. Look to our people,
for you shall be leader; I lead no longer.
Gather my guard and raise me a grave-mound
housing my ashes at Hronesnaesse,
reminding my kin to recall their king
after his pyre has flared on the point.
Seafarers passing shall say when they see it
'Beowulf's Barrow' as bright longboats
drive over darkness, daring the flood."

So the stern prince bestowed on his sword-thane
and keen spear-wielder the kingly collar,
his gold-plated helm and hammered armor.
He told him to bear them bravely in battle:
"Farewell, Wiglaf, last Waegmunding.
I follow our fathers, foredestined to die,
swept off by fate, though strong and steadfast."
These heartfelt words were the warrior's last
before his body burned in the bale-fire
and his soul sought the doom of the truthful.

Smitten with sorrow, the young man saw
the old lord he loved lying in pain
as life left him. Slain and slayer
died there together: the dread earth-dragon,
deprived of his life, no longer would lurk
coiled on the hoard. Hard-hammered swords
had felled the far-flyer in front of his lair.
No more would he sport on the midnight sky,
proud of his wealth, his power and pomp.
He sprawled on stone where the war-chief slew him.
Though deeds of daring were done in that land,
I have heard of no man whose might would suffice
to face the fire-drake's fuming breath
or help him escape if he handled the hoard
once he had woken its warder from sleep.
Beowulf paid for that lode with his life;
his loan of days was lost to the dragon.

Before long the laggards limped from the woods,
ten cowards together, the troth-breakers
who had failed to bare their blades in battle
at the moment their master needed them most.
In shame they shouldered their shields and spears.
Armored for war, they went to Wiglaf
who sorrowfully sat at their sovereign's shoulder.
Laving his leader, the foot-soldier failed
to waken the fallen fighter one whit,
nor could he will his lord back to life.
The World's Warden decided what deeds
men might achieve in those days and these.

A hard answer was easily offered
by young Wiglaf, Weohstan's son.
With little love he looked on the shirkers;
"I tell you in truth, takers of treasure,
bench-sitting boasters brave in the hall:
Beowulf gave you the gear that you wear,
the most finely fashioned found near or far
for a prince to proffer his thankless thanes;
but he wasted his wealth on a worthless troop
who cast off their king at the coming of war.
Our lord had no need to laud his liege-men;
yet God, giver of glory and vengeance,
granted him strength to stand with his sword.
I could do little to lengthen his life
facing that foe, but I fought nonetheless:
beyond my power I propped up my prince.
The fire-drake faltered after I struck him,
and his fuming jaws flamed less fiercely,
but too few friends flew to our king
when evil beset him. Now sword-bestowing
and gold-getting shall cease for the Geats.
You shall have no joy in the homeland you love.
Your farms shall be forfeit, and each man fare
alone and landless when foreign lords
learn of your flight, your failure of faith.
Better to die than dwell in disgrace."

Then Wiglaf bade that the battle-tidings
be sent to the camp over the sea-cliff
where warriors waited with shields unslung,
sadly sitting from dawn until noon
to learn if their lord and beloved leader
had seen his last sunrise or soon would return.
The herald would leave them little to doubt;
he sped up the headland and spoke to them all:

"Now the wish-granter, warlord of Weders,
lies on his death-bed. The leader of Geats

stays in the slaughter-place, slain by the worm
sprawled at his side. Dagger-stricken,
the slayer was felled, though a sword had failed
to wound the serpent. Weohstan's son,
Wiglaf is waiting by Beowulf's body;
a living warrior watches the lifeless,
sad-heartedly sitting to guard
the loved and the loathed. Look now for war
as Franks and Frisians learn how the king
has fallen in combat. Few foreigners love us,
for Hygelac angered the harsh Hugas
when his fleet forayed to far-off Frisia.
Fierce Hetware met him with forces
bigger than his. They broke him in battle;
that mail-clad chieftain fell with his men.
Hygelac took no trophies to thanes;
no king of the Meroving wishes us well.

"I also foresee strife with the Swedes,
feud without end, for all know Ongentheow
slew Hrethel's son when Hathcyn first forayed
near Ravenswood with hot-headed Geats
and raided the realm of Scylf-land's ruler.
That fearsome old foe, father of Ohthere,
quickly struck back. He cut down our king
to rescue the queen Hathcyn had captured.
Her captors had shorn the crone of her gold,
dishonored the aged mother of Onela.
Ongentheow followed hard on their heels.
Wounded, weary and fiercely-harried,
those left unslain by Swedish swords
limped off leaderless, hid in the holt.
A huge army beleaguered them there.
All night long Ongentheow taunted
the wretched raiders. At daybreak, he swore,
he would slice them to slivers. Some would swing
slung on his gallows, sport for the ravens.
But gladness came again to grim Geats
hearing Hygelac's horns in the morning,
the trumpet calls of the troop that tracked them.
Hathcyn's brother, bold with his band,
had rallied for battle.

"A bloody swath
Scylfings and Geats left on the landscape,
everywhere smeared with gore from the stricken.
So the two folks stirred further feuds.
Wise in warfare, old Ongentheow
grimly stood off, seeking the safety
of higher ground. He had heard of Hygelac's

strength in struggles, his pride and prowess.
Mistrusting his force to fend off the foray,
he feared for his family and fell back to guard
the hoard hidden behind his earthworks.
Then Hrethel's people pressed the pursuit:
the standards of Hygelac stormed the stronghold.
There the Swede was snared between swords.
Eofor humbled that hoary-haired leader,
though Wulf struck first, fierce with his weapon,
and a cut vein colored the king's white head.
Undaunted, Ongentheow warded him off;
Wulf was wounded the worse in return:
Ongentheow's blow broke open his helm,
hurled him headlong, helpless and bleeding
though not destined to die on that day.
Then Eofor faced the folk-lord alone.
Sternly he stood when his brother slumped:
Hygelac's soldier with sword in his hand
and helmet on head, hoarded smithwork
shaped by old crafts, shattered the shield-wall.
The king crumpled, struck to the quick.

"Now the Geats gathered after the slaughter.
Some bound the wound of Eofor's brother
and bundled him off the field of battle.
Meanwhile one warrior plundered the other:
Eofor stripped the hard-hilted sword,
helm and corselet from Ongentheow's corpse.
He handed that heap of armor to Hygelac.
Pleased with his prizes, the king pledged in turn
to reward war-strokes as lord of the Weders.
He gave great riches to Wulf and Eofor.
Once they were home, he honored each one
with a hundred thousand in land and linked rings.
No man in middle-earth ever begrudged them
favor and fortune bestowed for their feat.
Yet a further honor was offered Eofor:
the king's only daughter adorned his house,
awarded in wedlock to Wonred's son.

"Full of this feud, this festering hatred,
the Swedes, I am certain, will swiftly beset us,
as soon as they learn our lord lies lifeless
who held his hoard, his hall and his realm
against all foes when heroes had fallen,
who fostered his folk with fair kingship.
Now must we hasten, behold our sovereign,
and bear him for burial. The brave one shall not
be beggared of booty to melt on his bier.
Let funeral flames greedily fasten

on gold beyond measure, grimly gotten,
lucre our leader bought with his life.
No thane shall take tokens to treasure
nor maiden be made fairer with finery
strung at her throat. Stripped of their wealth,
they shall wander woefully all their lives long,
lordless and landless now that their king
has laid aside laughter, sport and song.
Their hands shall heft many a spear-haft,
cold in the morning. No call of the harp
shall waken warriors after their battles;
but the black raven shall boast to the eagle,
crowing how finely he fed on the fated
when, with the wolf, he went rending the slain."

Thus the terrible tidings were told,
and the teller had not mistaken the truth.
The warriors all rose and woefully went
to look on the wonder with welling tears.
They found on the sand under Earnanaess
their lifeless lord laid there to rest,
beloved giver of gifts and gold rings,
the war-king come at the close of his days
to a marvelous death. At first the monster
commanded their gaze: grim on the ground
across from the king, the creature had crumpled,
scaly and scorched, a fearsome fire-drake
fifty feet long. He would fly no more,
free in the darkness, nor drop to his den
at the break of dawn. Death held the dragon;
he never would coil in his cavern again.
Beyond the serpent stood flagons and jars,
plated flatware and priceless swords
rotting in ruin, etched out with rust.
These riches had rested in Earth's embrace
for a thousand winters, the heritage held
by warders of old, spell-enwoven
and toilfully tombed that none might touch them,
unless God Himself, granter of grace,
true Lord of glory, allotted release
to one of His choosing and opened the hoard.

It little profited him who had wrongfully
hidden the hand-wrought wealth within walls.
He payment was scant for slaying the one
with courage to claim it: the kill was quickly
and harshly requited. So the kingly
may come to strange ends when their strength is spent
and time meted out. They may not remain
as men among kin, mirthful with mead.

Beowulf goaded the gold's guardian,
raised up the wrath, not reckoning whether
his death-day had dawned, not knowing the doom
solemnly sworn by princes who placed
their hoard in that hollow: the thief who held it
would fall before idols, forge himself hell-bonds,
waste in torment for touching the treasure.
He failed to consider more fully and sooner
who rightfully owned such awesome riches.

So spoke Wiglaf, son of Weohstan:
"By the whim of one man, many warriors
sometimes may suffer, as here has happened.
No means were at hand to move my master;
no counsel could sway the kingdom's keeper
never to trouble the treasure's taker,
but leave him lying where long he had hidden,
walled with his wealth until the world's ending.
He kept to his course, uncovered the hoard.
Fate was too strongly forcing him hither.
I have entered that hall, beheld everything
golden within, though none too glad
for the opening offered under its archway.
In haste I heaved much from the hoard;
a mighty burden I bore from the barrow
straight to my sovereign. He still was alive.
His wits were clear; his words came quickly.
In anguish, the Ancient asked that I say
he bade you to build a barrow for him
befitting the deeds of a fallen friend.
You shall heap it high over his ashes,
since he was the world's worthiest warrior,
famed far and wide for the wealth of his fortress.

"Now let us hurry hence to the hoard.
For a second time I shall see that splendor
under the cliff-wall, those wonders of craftwork.
Come, I shall take you close to the trove,
where you may behold heaps of broad gold.
Then let a bier be readied to bear
our beloved lord to his long dwelling
under the watch of the World's Warden."

Then Weohstan's heir ordered the earls,
heads of houses and fief holders,
to fetch firewood fit for the folk-leader's
funeral pyre. "Flames shall now flare,
feed on the flesh and fade into darkness,
an ending for him who often endured
the iron showers shot over shield-walls
when string-driven storms of arrows arose

with feathered fins to steer them in flight
and barbed arrowheads eager to bite."

Wisely Wiglaf, son of Weohstan,
summoned the seven most steadfast thanes.
They went in together, eight earls entering
under the evil arch of the earth-house
with one man bearing a blazing torch.
No lot was cast to learn which liege-man
would plunder the loot lying unguarded,
as each searcher could see for himself;
yet none was unhappy to hurry that hoard
out into daylight. They heaved the dragon
over the sea-cliff where surges seized him:
the treasure's keeper was caught by the tide.
Then they filled a wain with filigreed gold
and untold treasures; and they carried the king,
their hoary-haired warlord, to Hronesnaess.

There the king's kinsmen piled him a pyre,
wide and well-made just as he willed it.
They hung it with helmets, shields and mail-shirts,
then laid in its midst their beloved lord,
renowned among men. Lamenting their loss,
his warriors woke the most woeful fire
to flare on the bluff. Fierce was the burning,
woven with weeping, and wood-smoke rose
black over the blaze, blown with a roar.
The fire-wind faltered and flames dwindled,
hot at their heart the broken bone-house.
Sunken in spirit at Beowulf's slaying,
the Geats gathered grieving together.
Her hair wound up, a woebegone woman
sang and resang her dirge of dread,
foretelling a future fraught with warfare,
kinfolk sundered, slaughter and slavery
even as Heaven swallowed the smoke.

High on the headland they heaped his grave-mound
which seafaring sailors would spy from afar.
Ten days they toiled on the scorched hilltop,
the cleverest men skillfully crafting
a long-home built for the bold in battle.
They walled with timbers the trove they had taken,
sealing in stone the circlets and gems,
wealth of the worm-hoard gotten with grief,
gold from the ground gone back to Earth
as worthless to men as when it was won.
Then sorrowing swordsmen circled the barrow,
twelve of his earls telling their tales,

the sons of nobles   sadly saluting
deeds of the dead.   So dutiful thanes
in liege to their lord   mourn him with lays
praising his peerless   prowess in battle
as it is fitting   when life leaves the flesh.
Heavy-hearted   his hearth-companions
grieved for Beowulf,   great among kings,
mild in his mien,   most gentle of men,
kindest to kinfolk   and keenest for fame.

RESONANCES

from *The Saga of King Hrolf Kraki*[1]

[KING HRING OF NORWAY MARRIES HVIT]

It is said that to the north in Norway a king named Hring ruled over Uppdales. He had a son named Bjorn. It is told that the queen died, and the king and many others found this a great loss. Hring's countrymen and counsellors asked him to remarry, and so he sent men to the south seeking a wife. But strong headwinds and powerful storms forced them to turn their prows around, letting the ships run before the wind. So it happened that driven by the wind, they were forced north to Finnmark, where they remained for the winter.

One day they went onshore. They walked inland and came to a house. Inside sat two beautiful women, who received them well. The women asked them where they had come from, and the king's men gave an account of their journey and explained their errand. They asked the women about themselves, inquiring why women so beautiful and refined were there alone, so far from other people.

The older woman answered, "For everything, friends, there is a reason. We are here because a powerful king asked for my daughter's hand. Because she did not want to marry him, he threatened her with rough treatment. So I am keeping her here in this secret hiding place while her father is away at war."

They asked who her father might be.

"She is the daughter of the King of the Lapps," said the woman.

The men asked for their names.

The older woman replied, "I am called Ingebjorg and my daughter is named Hvit. I am the Lapp king's mistress."

1. Translated by Jesse L. Byock. A prose saga or tale written anonymously in Iceland in the 14th century, *The Saga of King Hrolf Kraki* shares many elements with *Beowulf;* Hrolf himself appears in *Beowulf* as Hrothulf, who shares the kingdom with Hrothgar. Both texts draw on a common fund of legends about the Danes in the 5th and 6th centuries, mixing historical events with tales of magic and monstrous transformations. Given here are episodes concerning two bearlike men, Bjorn—whose name means "bear"—and his son Bodvar Bkjarki ("warlike bear-cub"). Beowulf's name similarly means "Bear" (literally "Bee-wolf," a compound term for "bear"). Like Beowulf, Bodvar slays a dragon, which is ravaging the king's court much as Grendel does in *Beowulf.*

The saga gives these magical events a sharply realistic slant. Bodvar visits King Hrolf's court, and befriends a hapless scapegoat named Hott, in comic scenes that give a lively picture of what life was like in the old mead-halls, particularly for those at the bottom of the pecking order. Like Beowulf, and like his father Bjorn, Bodvar is an uncanny hero, not easily fit into the life of the court, an outsider who is the only one able to counter the monstrous threat that comes from outside the mead-hall's walls.

A girl was there to serve them. The king's men, much taken with these women, decided to ask whether Hvit would go back with them and marry King Hring. The man in charge of the king's mission brought up the question. Hvit did not respond quickly; instead, she deferred the issue to her mother's consideration.

"As the old saying goes," said her mother, "out of every trouble comes some gain. But it displeases me that we are making this arrangement without first asking her father's consent. Nevertheless, it must be ventured, if Hvit is to get ahead."

Hvit then prepared herself to go with them, and they started on the journey to King Hring. The messengers at once inquired whether the king wanted to marry the woman or if she should be sent back. The king, well pleased with the woman, married her at once. He was not concerned that she was neither rich nor powerful. At this time, the king was getting on in years, and the effects of his age were soon apparent in the queen's behaviour.

[THE LOVE OF BERA AND BJORN]

A freeman's farm lay a short distance from the king's estate. The farmer had a wife and one daughter, who was named Bera. She was young and lovely to look at. Bjorn, the king's son, and Bera, the freeman's daughter, had played together as children, and the two were very close. The freeman was wealthy; he had long been out raiding and in his youth had been a great champion. Bera and Bjorn loved each other deeply and they often met.

Time passed and nothing noteworthy took place. Bjorn, the king's son, matured to manhood. He grew large and strong; he was well bred and was accomplished in all skills. When King Hring was away at war for long periods, which frequently happened, Hvit stayed at home and governed the land. She was not well liked by the people; toward Bjorn, however, she was gentle and tender, though he paid no heed.

One time when the king was about to set out from home, the queen suggested that Bjorn should stay home to help her govern the land. The king thought that her proposal was advisable. The queen was now becoming overbearing and arrogant. The king told his son Bjorn to stay at home and watch over the kingdom with the queen. Bjorn replied that he had little liking for this idea and that he liked the queen even less. The king then told Bjorn to remain behind, and he then set out with a large force.

[BJORN REJECTS QUEEN HVIT'S ADVANCES: THE CURSE]

Bjorn went back to his quarters after arguing with his father, each thinking the other to be wrong. Bjorn, downcast and angry, his face as red as blood, then took to his bed. The queen, wanting to lift his spirits, spoke tenderly to him. He asked her to go away, which she did for a time.

The queen often spoke with Bjorn, telling him that, while the king was away, they had an opportunity to share one bed. She said that their living together would be much better than her experience with a man as old as King Hring.

Bjorn, taking this proposal badly, gave the queen a hard slap. He told her to leave him alone and then threw her out. She said that she was unaccustomed to being rejected or beaten. "And it seems that you, Bjorn, think it preferable to embrace a commoner's daughter. You deserve a punishment, something far more disgraceful than enjoyment of my love and my tenderness. It would not come as a surprise if something should happen to make you suffer for your stubbornness and your stupidity."

She then struck him with her wolfskin gloves, telling him to become a cave bear, grim and savage: "You will eat no food other than your own father's livestock and, in feeding yourself, you will kill more than has ever been observed before. You will never be released from the spell, and your awareness of this disgrace will be more dreadful to you than no remembrance at all."

[BJORN'S TRANSFORMATION INTO A BEAR AND THE BIRTH OF BODVAR]

Then Bjorn disappeared, and no one knew what had become of him. When people realized that Bjorn was missing, they searched for him. As might have been expected, he was not to be found.

Next to be told is that the king's cattle were being killed in large numbers by a grey bear, large and fierce. One evening it happened that Bera, the freeman's daughter, saw the savage bear. It approached her unthreateningly. She thought she recognized in the bear the eyes of Bjorn, the king's son, and so she did not try to run away. The beast then moved away from her, but she followed it all the way until it came to a cave.

When she entered the cave, a man was standing there. He greeted Bera, the freeman's daughter, and she recognized that he was Bjorn, Hring's son. Theirs was a joyful reunion. For a time they stayed together in the cave, because she did not want to part from him while she still had a choice. He told her it was not right for her to be there with him, because he was a beast by day, even if he again became a man at night.

King Hring, when he returned home from the wars, was told everything that had happened while he was away. He learned about the disappearance of his son Bjorn. He was also told about the huge creature that had arrived in the land, attacking mostly the king's own livestock. The queen strongly urged killing the animal, but this was delayed for a time. The king expressed no opinion, even though he thought the events most unusual.

One night, while Bera and the prince lay in their bed, Bjorn began to speak, "I suspect that tomorrow will be my death's day, for they will hunt and trap me. In truth, I find no pleasure in living because of the curse that lies upon me. You are my only delight, but that too will now cease. I want to give you the ring that is under my left arm. Tomorrow you will see the men stalking me. When I am dead, go to the king and ask him to give you whatever is under the beast's left shoulder; he will grant you this request.

"The queen," Bjorn continued, "will be suspicious of you when you want to leave. She will try to make you eat some of the bear's meat, but you must not eat it, because, as you well know, you are pregnant and will give birth to three boys. They are ours, and it will be obvious from their appearance if you have eaten any of the bear's meat. This queen is a great troll.[2] Then go home to your father, where you will give birth to the boys, one of whom will seem best to you. If you are not able to raise them at home, because of their strange and uncontrollable natures, bring them here to the cave. You will find here a chest with three bottoms. Runes are carved on it, and they will tell what each of the boys should receive as his inheritance. Three weapons are imbedded in the rock, and each of our sons shall have the one intended for him. Our firstborn will be called Elk-Frodi, the second son, Thorir, and the third, Bodvar. It seems to me most likely that they will not be weaklings and that their names will long be remembered."

Bjorn foretold many things to her, and afterwards the bear-shape came over him. Then the bear went out, and she followed him.

When she looked around, she saw a great company of men circling the side of the mountain. A large pack of hounds raced in front of the men, and now the bear began to run. Turning away from the cave, he ran along the slope of the mountain. The hounds and the king's men gave chase, but the bear proved difficult for them to catch. Before he was overtaken he maimed many men and killed all the dogs.

2. The Norse term "troll" included witches, ghosts, and giants.

At last the men formed a ring around him. The bear ranged about inside the ring, but understood the situation and knew that he would not be able to escape. Then he attacked in the direction of the king. Grabbing the man who stood next to the king, he ripped the man apart while still alive. By then the bear was so exhausted that he threw himself down on the ground. The men seized the opportunity and quickly killed him.

The freeman's daughter saw these events. She went up to the king and said, "Sire, will you give me what is under the beast's left shoulder?"

The king granted her request, saying that nothing there could be unsuitable to give to her. By then, the king's men were well along in flaying the bear. Bera went to the carcass and took the ring, hiding it carefully. The men did not see what she took, but then no one was paying much attention.

The king asked who Bera was, because he did not recognize her. She gave whatever answer she thought best, although it was not the truth.

The king then returned home and Bera found herself swept along among his followers. The queen, now very cheerful, made Bera welcome, inquiring who she was. As before, Bera concealed the truth.

The queen prepared a great feast and had the bear meat readied for the men's enjoyment. The freeman's daughter was in the queen's chamber, unable to get away because the queen was suspicious about her identity. Sooner than expected, the queen entered the room with a plate of bear meat. She told Bera to eat, but Bera did not want to eat.

"How uncommonly rude," said the queen, "that you reject the hospitality that the queen herself has chosen to offer you. Eat it quickly, otherwise something worse will be prepared for you."

The queen cut a small piece of the meat for Bera, and in the end Bera ate it. The queen then cut another piece and put it into Bera's mouth. Bera swallowed a small morsel of it, then spat the rest out of her mouth. She declared that she would not eat any more, even if she were to be tortured or killed. "It may be," said the queen, "that this bit will be enough," and she burst out laughing.

Bera then escaped and went home to her father. She had a very difficult pregnancy. She told her father the whole story relating to her condition and the reasons for what had happened. A little while later she fell ill and gave birth to a boy, though of an extraordinary kind. He was a man above the navel, but an elk below that. He was named Elk-Frodi. She bore another son, who was named Thorir. He had dog's feet from his insteps down. Because of this, he was called Thorir Hound's Foot; otherwise, he was the most handsome of men. A third boy was born, and this one was the most promising. He was named Bodvar, and there was no blemish on him. Bera loved Bodvar the most. [3]* * *

[BODVAR'S VENGEANCE]

Bodvar remained at home with his mother, who loved him dearly. Of all men, he was the most accomplished and handsome, but as yet he had not met very many people. Once he asked his mother who his father was. She told him about his father's killing, giving her son all the information. She explained how Bjorn had fallen under the spell of his stepmother.

Bodvar said, "We have wrongs to repay this witch."

Then Bera told him how the queen had forced her to eat the bear's flesh, "and the result can be seen in your brothers, Thorir Hound's Foot and Elk-Frodi."

3. Frodi and Thorir grow up as wild, unruly youths, and soon leave home.

Bodvar said, "I think Frodi ought to have felt more bound to take vengeance on this cowardly witch for our father than to kill innocent men for their money and carry out other vile acts. Likewise, I think it is odd that Thorir went away without giving this ogress something to remember. So it seems to me that I should punish her on our behalf."

Bera replied, "Arrange it so that she is not able to use her black arts to injure you."

He said that it would be so arranged.

Bera and Bodvar now went to see the king. Following Bodvar's advice, Bera explained to the king how everything had come about. She showed him the ring, which she had taken from under the shoulder of the beast, explaining that Bjorn, his son, had owned it.

The king agreed that without a doubt he recognized the ring; "I suspected that the queen was behind the strange events that have happened here, but for the sake of my love for her I have let matters remain quiet."

Bodvar said, "Send her away now or else we will take vengeance on her."

The king said that he wished to compensate Bodvar for his loss with as much treasure as he might want, but that matters were to remain quiet, as they had been before. He would give Bodvar a position of command, the title of jarl straightaway and, after his days were over, the kingdom, if only no harm were done to her.

Bodvar replied that he did not want to be king; rather he said that he wanted to be with the king and to serve him. "You are so trapped by this monster that you hardly have the wits to run your rightful kingdom, and from now on she will never thrive in this place."

Bodvar became so filled with fury that the king dared not stand in his way. Carrying a pouch in his hand, Bodvar went to the queen's chamber; the king and Bodvar's mother followed after him. Bodvar entered the chamber and turned to Queen Hvit. He placed the rough leather bag over her head. Then he pulled it down and tied it around her throat. He knocked her off her feet and with beatings and torments sent her to Hel,[4] dragging her through every street.

Many or most of those who were within the hall thought this punishment was only half of what she deserved. The king, however, took it very badly, but there was nothing he could do about it. In this way Queen Hvit lost her miserable life.

Bodvar was eighteen years old when this happened. A little later King Hring took sick and died. Bodvar became the ruler of the kingdom, but he was content with this position for only a short while. Then he called an assembly of the men of the land. At that meeting he announced that he wanted to leave and that he was marrying his mother to the man named Valsleyt, a jarl already in the land. Bodvar took part in the wedding feast before riding away.

[BODVAR AT THE COURT OF KING HROLF]

Nothing is said of Bodvar's travels until he arrived in Denmark and was only a short distance from Hleidargard.

One day a heavy rainstorm soaked Bodvar thoroughly. His horse, which he had ridden hard, was exhausted under him. The going was heavy since the ground had turned to mud. That night it grew very dark and the downpour continued steadily. Bodvar took no notice until his horse stumbled on a large obstacle. He dismounted and looked around, soon realizing that he had come upon some sort of house. He found the door, knocked on it and a man came out of the house. Bodvar asked for shelter for the night. The farmer answered that he would not send him away in the

4. Goddess of the underworld.

dead of night, especially as he was a stranger. From what the farmer could see, the stranger seemed to be very imposing. Bodvar stayed there overnight and was treated hospitably. He asked many questions about the exploits of King Hrolf and his champions, inquiring also about the distance to Hleidargard.

"It is now a very short distance," said the farmer. "Do you intend to go there?"

"Yes," replied Bodvar, "that is my intention."

The farmer declared that it would be fitting for him to do so, "because I see you are a large, powerful man, and they think themselves great champions." And the old woman living there sobbed aloud, as she did whenever they mentioned King Hrolf and his champions at Hleidargard.

Bodvar asked, "Why are you crying, you simple old woman?"

The old woman said, "My husband and I have one son, who is named Hott. One day he went to the stronghold to amuse himself, but the king's men taunted him. He could not stand up to such conduct, so the men took hold of him and stuck him into a pile of bones. It is their habit at mealtimes, when they are finished gnawing the meat from a bone, to throw it at him. Sometimes, if the bone hits him, he is badly injured. Whether he is alive or dead I do not know. But I ask this reward from you, in return for my hospitality, that you throw smaller bones at him rather than larger ones; that is, if he is not already dead."[5]

Bodvar answered, "I will do as you request, but I do not think it is warriorlike to strike people with bones or to harm children or men of small account."

"Then you will do well," said the old woman, "because your hand seems to be strong, and I know for certain that, if you chose not to hold back, an opponent would have no refuge from your blows."

Bodvar continued on his way to Hleidargard. After arriving at the king's royal residence, he immediately stabled his horse in the stall with the king's best mounts without asking anyone's permission. Then he entered the hall, where there were only a few men. He sat down near the entrance, and after he had been there for a short time, he heard a noise coming from somewhere in the corner. Bodvar looked in that direction and saw a man's hand emerging from a huge pile of bones lying there. The hand was very black.

Bodvar walked over to the corner and asked who was in the bone pile. He was answered, though timidly, "My name is Hott, kind sir."

"Why are you here?" asked Bodvar. "Or what are you doing?"

Hott's reply was, "I am making myself a shield wall, kind sir."

"You and your shield wall are pathetic," said Bodvar. He grabbed hold of the man and yanked him out of the bone pile.

Hott screamed loudly and then said, "You are acting as though you want me dead, since I had prepared my defences so well. Now you have broken my shield wall into pieces even though I had built it so high around me that it protected me against all your blows. No blow has reached me now for some time, yet the wall was not as complete as I had intended it to be."

Bodvar said, "You will no longer build your shield wall."

Hott replied, "Are you going to kill me now, kind sir?"

Bodvar, telling Hott to be quiet, picked him up and carried him from the hall to a nearby lake. Few paid attention to this. Bodvar washed Hott completely and then returned to the same place on the bench where he had sat previously. He led Hott

5. Bone-throwing was popular at Scandinavian feasts, and several medieval legal codes list killing by bone-throwing as a serious offense.

there and sat him down beside himself. Hott was so scared that all his limbs and joints trembled, although he seemed to understand that this man wanted to help him.

Later in the evening men crowded into the hall. Hrolf's champions saw that Hott had been seated on one of the benches, and it seemed to them that the man who had undertaken to do that was indeed brave. Hott cast a fearful glance in the direction of his old acquaintances, for he had received only harm from them. Afraid for his life, he tried to get back to his bone pile, but Bodvar held on to Hott and he was unable to get away. Hott thought that, if he could manage to get to the heap of bones, he would not be so exposed to the men's blows.

The king's men now took up their old habits. At first they threw small bones across the floor at Bodvar and Hott. Bodvar acted as if he saw nothing. Hott was so frightened that he took neither food nor drink, expecting to be struck at any moment.

Then Hott said to Bodvar, "Kind sir, here comes a large knuckle bone, which is intended to do us much harm."

Bodvar told Hott to be quiet. He cupped his hand and caught the knuckle bone, which included the attached leg bone. Bodvar threw the knuckle back, and it smashed with such force into the man who had thrown it that he was killed. The king's men were struck with fear.

King Hrolf and his champions up in the fortress were now told that an imposing man had arrived in the hall and had killed one of the king's retainers. The other retainers wanted to have the man put to death.

The king asked whether his follower had been killed without cause.

"Almost," they said.

Then the full truth came out. King Hrolf said that by no means should this man be killed: "It is a bad habit that you have adopted, throwing bones at innocent men. It brings dishonour to me and shame to you. I have repeatedly spoken to you about this matter, but you have paid no attention. I suspect that this man, whom you have now attacked, is no weakling. Summon him to me, so that I can find out who he is."

Bodvar went before the king and greeted him artfully. The king asked for his name.

"Your retainers call me Hott's protector, but my name is Bodvar."

The king said, "What compensation are you prepared to offer me for my man?"

Bodvar replied, "He got what he deserved."

The king said, "Do you want to be my man and occupy his place?"

Bodvar answered, "I will not refuse to become your man, but Hott and I will not, as matters stand, be separated. We will both sit closer to you on the benches than that man did, or else we both leave."

The king said, "I see no honour in him, but I will not begrudge him food."

Bodvar now chose a seat that pleased him, not bothering to sit in the place the other man had occupied. At one point he pulled three men up out of their seats, and then he and Hott sat down in their places. They had now moved much farther into the hall than earlier. Men thought Bodvar difficult to deal with, and there was strong resentment against him.

As Yuletime drew near, gloom settled over the men.[6] Bodvar asked Hott what caused their dejection. Hott told him that a huge, monstrous beast had come there the past two winters. "The creature has wings on its back and it usually flies. For two autumns now it has come here, causing much damage. No weapon can bite into it, and the king's champions, even the greatest among them, do not return home."

6. The pre-Christian winter feast of Yule was often a time of supernatural occurrences.

Bodvar said, "The hall is not so well manned as I had thought, if one animal alone could destroy the king's lands and his livestock."

Hott said, "It is not an animal, rather it is the greatest of trolls."

Then came Yule eve, and the king said, "It is my wish that tonight men remain calm, making no noise, and I forbid any of my men to put themselves in danger with the beast. The livestock will be left to their fate, because I do not want to lose any of my men." Everyone faithfully promised the king to do as he asked.

Bodvar stole away in the night and took Hott with him. Hott went only after being forced to do so, declaring that he was being steered straight toward death. Bodvar said, "Things will turn out for the better."

They now left the hall behind them, with Bodvar carrying Hott because he was so frightened. They saw the creature, and immediately Hott started to scream as loudly as he could, crying that the beast would swallow him. Bodvar told the dog to be quiet and threw him down on the moor. There he lay, not a little scared, at the same time not daring to go home.

Bodvar now went against the beast. He was hampered by his sword, which, as he tried to draw it, stuck fast in its scabbard. Determined, Bodvar urged the sword out until the scabbard squeaked. Then he grasped the scabbard and the sword came out of the sheath. Immediately he thrust it up under the beast's shoulder, striking so hard that the blade reached quickly into the heart. Then the beast fell dead to the ground.

After this encounter Bodvar went to the place where Hott was lying. He picked up Hott and carried him to where the beast lay dead. Hott was trembling violently.

Bodvar said, "Now you will drink the beast's blood." For a while Hott was unwilling, although certainly he dared do nothing else. Bodvar made him drink two large mouthfuls as well as eat some of the beast's heart. After that Bodvar seized Hott, and they fought each other for a long time.

Bodvar said, "You have now become remarkably strong, and I expect that from this day forward you will have no fear of King Hrolf's retainers."

Hott replied, "From now on, I will fear neither them nor you."

"Then, Hott, my friend," said Bodvar, "things have turned out well. Let us now go back to the beast, raising him up in such a way that men will think the creature must be alive."

They did just that and afterward went home. They kept these events to themselves, and so no one knew what they had done.

In the morning, the king asked what was known about the beast, whether it had visited them in the night. He was told that all the livestock were safe in the pens, unharmed. The king ordered men to inquire if there were any indications that the beast had visited them. The guards went out but quickly returned. They told the king that the beast was coming toward them, furiously advancing on the stronghold. The king ordered his retainers to be valiant. Each was to do his best according to his courage, so that they might overcome this monster. Obeying the king's command, the men prepared themselves.

The king looked toward the beast, saying finally, "I see no movement in it, but which one of you will now seize the opportunity to go against it?"

Bodvar said, "That would likely satisfy the curiosity of the bravest man. Hott, my friend, throw off the slander that men have laid on you, claiming that you have neither spirit nor courage. Go and kill the beast. You can see that no one else is too eager to do so."

"Right," said Hott, "I will set myself to that task."

The king said, "I do not know where your courage has come from, Hott, but much has changed about you in a short time."

Hott said, "For this task, give me the sword Golden Hilt, the one that you are holding, and then I will either kill the beast or find my own death."

King Hrolf said, "That sword is not to be carried except by a man who is both strong in body and noble in spirit."

Hott replied, "Assume, Sire, that I am made from such a mould."

The king retorted, "How can one tell? Perhaps more has changed about you than is evident. Few would think that you are the same person. Take the sword, for it will serve you well if my instincts about you turn out to be correct."

Then Hott went boldly against the beast, thrusting at it as soon as he was within striking distance. The beast fell down dead.

Bodvar said, "See, Sire, what he has now accomplished."

The king answered, "Certainly he has changed greatly, but Hott alone did not kill the beast; rather you did it."

Bodvar said, "That may be."

The king said, "I knew when you came here that few would be your equal, but it seems to me that your finest achievement is that you have made Hott into another champion. He was previously thought to be a man in whom there was little probability of much luck. I do not want him called Hott any longer; instead, from now on he will be called Hjalti.[7] You will now be called after the sword Golden Hilt."

And here ends this tale of Bodvar and his brothers.

Jorge Luis Borges: Poem Written in a Copy of Beowulf[1]

At various times I have asked myself what reasons
moved me to study while my night came down,
without particular hope of satisfaction,
the language of the blunt-tongue Anglo-Saxons.[2]
Used up by the years my memory
loses its grip on words that I have vainly
repeated and repeated. My life in the same way
weaves and unweaves its weary history.[3]
Then I tell myself: it must be that the soul
has some secret sufficient way of knowing
that it is immortal, that its vast encompassing
circle can take in all, accomplish all.
Beyond my anxiety and beyond this writing
the universe waits, inexhaustible, inviting.

7. "Hilt."

1. Translated by Alastair Reid. Jorge Luis Borges (1899–1986) was born in Buenos Aires, Argentina. His paternal grandmother came from Northumbria, a connection that, in what he called "a romantic superstition," linked him with the "Saxon and perhaps Danish past" of Old English poetry, and the legends of Beowulf. A celebrated poet, short-story writer, essayist, and polymath, Borges in all of his writing treated books and the life of the imagination as if they were interchangeable (if not superior) to the world of "real" people and events. Wide-ranging and eccentric in his influences and the connections he made between writings from every epoch and every corner of the globe, Borges first took up the serious study of Old English in the 1950s, when his sight failed him, and he returned to the mnemonic forms of poetry, more amenable to composition in the head. "Anglo-Saxon," he wrote, "was as intimate an experience to me as looking at a sunset or falling in love." For more on Borges, see his principal listing on page 2629.

2. "While my night came down" is reminiscent of the twilight mood of the second part of *Beowulf,* while also referring both to the poet's advancing years and the increasing severity of his blindness. Rather than for mastery, he wrote, he had undertaken the study of Old English for the pleasure of the doing.

3. Both the theme of repetition and that of the weaving of a life are central motifs in *Beowulf.*

POETRY OF THE TANG DYNASTY

Chinese literature began with the lyric, whose period of greatest flowering, by common agreement, was the Tang dynasty (618–907). Artistic achievement of all sorts benefited from the reunification of the country that had been accomplished during the preceding, short-lived Sui dynasty (581–618) and the political consolidation and expansion that followed for over a century until the brief but disruptive rebellion led by An Lushan between 755 and 757. The imperial capital of Chang'an thrived, thanks to elaborate transportation systems that brought goods in from the provinces, as well as equally sophisticated administrative structures that dispatched bureaucrats in all directions to manage them. Government policies fostered the institutional growth of both Buddhism and Daoism, while still maintaining a commitment to Confucian texts and values, encouraging an atmosphere of pluralism that was further enlivened by the many influences generated by rich contacts with foreign cultures, especially those of central Asia.

The earliest theories of poetry in China regarded it as a spontaneous, if crafted, response to an external stimulus, a form of writing of unquestioned value as a means of communication, instruction, and critique. Poetic composition was a skill that any scholar/bureaucrat would be expected to display, on occasions both serious and trivial. The standard collection of Tang poetry contains almost 49,000 works by 2,200 poets and testifies in its variety to its deep integration in the daily life of the educated class, for whom poetry was a widely accepted currency of personal, social, and political exchange. It is difficult to imagine how depleted the collections of the past would be had such circumstances not inspired, or compelled, the composition of a poem. In particular, the typically peripatetic career of government bureaucrats is responsible for the thick chapters of farewell and keepsake poems in almost all individual collections. The cultural importance of poetry was further institutionalized during the Tang by the introduction of a test of poetic composition on the most prestigious imperial civil service examination that, when passed, conferred on the successful candidate the most prestigious degree, that of the *jinshi,* or "presented scholar." This requirement was in fact removed at various points during the dynasty, and debates raged almost immediately regarding its reliability as an indicator of future administrative competence and its influence on the quality of poetic production in general. Its presence does certainly attest, nonetheless, to the stature and popularity of poetry during the Tang and confirms that it was a means of articulating the relationship between an individual and the body politic.

Chinese literary historians have long been fond of demarcating periods and categories, and the Tang was no exception to this practice. The history of Tang poetry has thus typically been divided into four periods—Early, High, Middle, and Late—with its peak, unsurprisingly, during the High Tang, or the first half of the eighth century. The three most esteemed poets of the period—Wang Wei, Li Bo, and Du Fu—were also conveniently associated with the three major belief systems of the epoch, Buddhism, Daoism, and Confucianism, respectively. Their works together epitomize the varied creativity of this central period of Chinese poetry.

Wang Wei

701–761

One of the most prominent poets of his time, Wang Wei was born into a distinguished family and earned youthful renown as poet, painter, and musician. After passing the most literary of the imperial civil service examinations in 721, he enjoyed a slow but steady rise through government ranks that took him through various offices at the capital, to several provincial posts, and finally in 759 back to court in a high-ranking position with few duties. A minor infraction and the death of his mother briefly interrupted his progress, but the most important setback occurred when he was captured by the rebel general An Lushan, who took over the Tang capital of Chang'an from 755 to 757 and forced Wang Wei to serve under his puppet government. Only the intercession of Wang Wei's powerful younger brother led to his pardon and rehabilitation upon the imperial family's return to the capital.

Wang Wei was an accomplished master of both old and new poetic forms and was especially admired for his quatrains in regulated verse. His poetry displays the hallmarks of the urbane courtly style—impersonal, witty, and decorous—whose mastery is best revealed, perhaps paradoxically, in his limpid evocations of life in retreat, and especially scenes from his country estate on the Wang River outside the capital. After his mother's death in 730, he converted part of this property to a monastery, and his poetry demonstrates his commitment to Buddhism, sometimes in its themes, but even more so in language and style. Wang Wei was also an influential painter, and in one poem in fact declares that he was "mistakenly a poet" and in an earlier life "must have been a painter." His depictions of landscape, however, are noteworthy not for elaborate descriptive detail but rather for their apparently artless language and tranquil mood. In accord with Chan (Zen) doctrine, he appears to accept both the simple and concrete reality of nature and its ultimate illusoriness, and his poetry conveys this dual awareness in a tone of contemplative, dispassionate detachment.

from The Wang River Collection[1]

Preface

My retreat is in the Wang River mountain valley. The places to walk to include: Meng Wall Cove, Huazi Hill, Grained Apricot Lodge, Clear Bamboo Range, Deer Enclosure, Magnolia Enclosure, Dogwood Bank, Sophora Path, Lakeside Pavilion, Southern Hillock, Lake Yi, Willow Waves, Luan Family Shallows, Gold Powder Spring, White Rock Rapids, Northern Hillock, Bamboo Lodge, Magnolia Bank, Lacquer Tree Garden, and Pepper Tree Garden. When Pei Di and I were at leisure, we each composed the following quatrains.

1. Meng Wall Cove

A new home at the mouth of Meng Wall:
Ancient trees, the last withered willows.
The one who comes again—who will it be?
Grieving in vain for former men's possessions.

5. Deer Enclosure

Empty mountain, no man is seen.
Only heard are echoes of men's talk.
Reflected light enters the deep wood
And shines again on blue-green moss.

1. Translated by Pauline Yu. Inspired by sites on his country estate in Lantian, outside the capital of Chang'an, Wang Wei composed a series of 20 quatrains that were matched by a set written by his close friend Pei Di (b. 716). Wang also painted a long handscroll depicting the same scenic spots; the scroll has been lost, though numerous imitations exist.

8. Sophora Path

The bypath is shaded by sophoras;
In secluded shadows, green moss is thick.
But the gatekeeper sweeps it in welcome
In case the mountain monk should come.

11. Lake Yi

Blowing flutes cross to the distant shore.
At day's dusk I bid farewell to you.
On the lake with one turn of the head:
Mountain green rolls into white clouds.

17. Bamboo Lodge

Alone I sit amid the dark bamboo,
Play the zither and whistle[2] loud again.
In the deep wood men do not know
The bright moon comes to shine on me.

Bird Call Valley[1]

Man at leisure, cassia flowers fall.
The night still, spring mountain empty.
The moon emerges, startling mountain birds:
At times they call within the spring valley.

Farewell

Dismounting I give you wine to drink,
And inquire where you are going.
You say you did not achieve your wishes
And return to rest at the foot of Southern Mountain.
But go—do not ask again:
White clouds have no ending time.

Farewell to Yuan the Second on His Mission to Anxi[1]

In Wei City morning rain dampens the light dust.
By the travelers' lodge, green upon green—the willows' color is new.
I urge you to drink up yet another glass of wine:
Going west from Yang Pass, there are no old friends.

2. This was probably a combination of Daoist breathing techniques and whistling, and was said to express feelings while harmonizing with nature and facilitating the achievement of immortality.

1. The first of a series of five quatrains composed at a friend's estate, "Miscellaneous Poems Written at Huangfu Yue's Cloud Valley."

1. One of many poems to often unidentified fellow officials setting off to distant posts. The city of Wei was in Shaanxi Province, near the imperial capital, whereas Anxi was located far to the northwest in Xinjiang. This quatrain was set to music and became a popular farewell tune.

Visiting the Temple of Gathered Fragrance[1]

I do not know the Temple of Gathered Fragrance,
For several miles, entering cloudy peaks.
Ancient trees, paths without people;
Deep in the mountains, where is the bell?
Noise from the spring swallows up lofty rocks;
The color of the sun chills green pines.
Toward dusk by the curve of an empty pond,
Peaceful meditation controls poison dragons.[2]

Zhongnan Retreat

In middle years I am rather fond of the Dao;
My late home is at the foot of Southern Mountain.
When the feeling comes, each time I go there alone.
That splendid things are empty, of course, I know.
I walk to the place where the water ends
And sit and watch the time when clouds rise.
Meeting by chance an old man of the forest,
I chat and laugh without a date to return.

In Response to Vice-Magistrate Zhang

In late years I care for tranquility alone—
A myriad affairs do not concern my heart.
A glance at myself: there are no long-range plans.
I only know to return to the old forest.
Pine winds blow, loosening my belt;
The mountain moon shines as I pluck my zither.
You ask about reasons for success and failure:
A fisherman's song enters the shore's deeps.[1]

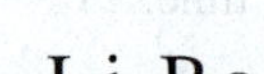

Li Bo

701–762

About Li Bo's family little is known for certain, despite the richness of legends concerning his background—for which the poet himself was probably largely responsible. Possibly of Turkish origin, he was raised in what is now Sichuan province and appears to have treated his birth in the wild west of China as a license to flout accepted norms of behavior. Unlike most of his

1. A Buddhist monastery located south of Chang'an.
2. Most likely referring to illusions or passions that serve as obstacles to enlightenment.
1. Among other things, Wang Wei is alluding to an anonymous fisherman's song included in an anthology of poetry from the southern kingdom of Chu. Responding to the lament of a political exile about having been banished for his high moral principles, the fisherman's gently mocking song speaks of the greater wisdom of being able to adapt to circumstances: "If the waters are clear, I'll wash my hat, / If they're muddy I'll wash my feet."

peers he never attempted the civil service examination, thus sparing himself the humiliation of failure. But his career aspirations were no less ambitious, perhaps owing to his claim of kinship with the imperial family, also surnamed Li. Thanks to a friendship he cultivated with a powerful Daoist adept, in 742 he succeeded in securing a post in the court bureau responsible for producing official documents, where he initially attracted favorable attention from the emperor and his entourage, but then his drunken audacity led to his expulsion two years later. Lamenting the alleged failure of those in power to appreciate him, he wandered for over a decade and finally provided the emperor with a legitimate reason to mistrust him by becoming involved in a minor revolt. For this he was arrested for treason, and though he was eventually pardoned he died without having secured the patronage he had sought. A popular legend tells of his drowning while trying to embrace the reflection of the moon in the water, although overindulgence in alcohol and long-life elixirs (typically containing mercury) were more likely to blame.

Li Bo traveled extensively to Daoist retreats, and he became known as the "Poet-Immortal." Although he clearly didn't spurn political engagement, his outsider image entitled him to excesses and eccentricities that also characterize his poetry, and his poems often display a playful fantasy that can have the poet, for example, engaging in conversation with the moon. Of his nearly one thousand poems, the majority consist not of the newer regulated verse patterns but of older forms that allowed greater liberties of expression. Li Bo especially enjoyed imitating folk songs, and the colloquial diction and bold expression of longer examples like "The Road to Shu Is Hard" are especially distinctive. As was true for all Tang poets, much of his work consists of responses to occasions like visits and farewells. Li Bo made much of the spontaneity and facility with which he composed, and the disarming simplicity of his diction and imagery in these occasional pieces can suggest deep feeling with extraordinary effectiveness.

Reasonably well known during his lifetime, Li Bo was singled out by later generations as an inspired genius and complement to the more serious and sober Du Fu. Comparative evaluations of the two figures have occupied critics for centuries, but they are generally agreed to be the two most important poets of the Tang dynasty.

Drinking Alone with the Moon[1]

A pot of wine among the flowers.
I drink alone, no friend with me.
I raise my cup to invite the moon.
He and my shadow and I make three.

The moon does not know how to drink;
My shadow mimes my capering;
But I'll make merry with them both—
And soon enough it will be Spring.

I sing—the moon moves to and fro.
I dance—my shadow leaps and sways.
Still sober, we exchange our joys.
Drunk—and we'll go our separate ways.

Let's pledge—beyond human ties—to be friends,
And meet where the Silver River ends.

1. Translated by Vikram Seth.

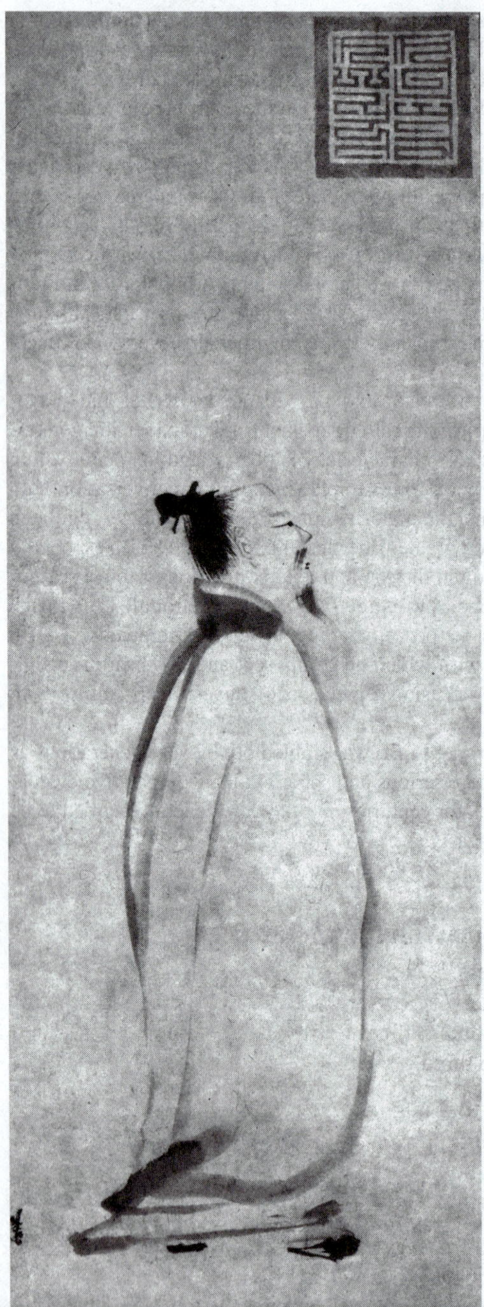

Liang Kai, *Li Bo Chanting a Poem,* hanging scroll, 13th century. An honored member of the imperial painting academy, Liang Kai chose, for unknown reasons, to retreat to a Chan Buddhist monastery outside Hangzhou. The spare brushwork of this imaginary portrait captures the nonchalant abandon that Li Bo (701–761) sought to convey in his poetry.

Fighting South of the Ramparts[1]

Last year we were fighting at the source of the Sang-kan;
This year we are fighting on the Onion River road.
We have washed our swords in the surf of Parthian seas;
We have pastured our horses among the snows of the T'ien Shan.
The King's armies have grown grey and old
Fighting ten thousand leagues away from home.
The Huns have no trade but battle and carnage;
They have no fields or ploughlands,
But only wastes where white bones lie among yellow sands.
Where the house of Ch'in built the Great Wall that was to keep away the Tartars,
There, in its turn, the House of Han lit beacons of war.
The beacons are always alight, fighting and marching never stop.
Men die in the field, slashing sword to sword;
The horses of the conquered neigh piteously to Heaven.
Crows and hawks peck for human guts,
Carry them in their beaks and hang them on the branches of withered trees.
Captains and soldiers are smeared on the bushes and grass;
The general schemed in vain.
Know therefore that the sword is a cursed thing
Which the wise man uses only if he must.

The Road to Shu Is Hard[1]

Ah! it's fearsome—oh! it's high!
The road to Shu is hard, harder than climbing to the sky.
  The kings Can Cong and Yu Fu
  Founded long ago the land of Shu,
  Then for forty-eight thousand years
  Nothing linked it to the Qin frontiers.
  White Star Peak blocked the western way.
A bird-track tried to cut across to Mount Emei—
And only when the earth shook, hills collapsed, and brave men died
Did cliff-roads and sky-ladders join it to the world outside.
Above—high peaks turn back the dragon-chariot of the sun.
Below—great whirlpools turn around the waves that rush and stun.
  Not even yellow cranes can fly across—
  Even the clambering apes are at a loss.
  At Green Mud Ridge the path coils to and fro:
Nine twists for every hundred steps—up a sheer cliff we go.
The traveller, touching the stars, looks upwards, scared out of his wits.
He clutches his heart with a deep sigh—down on the ground he sits!
Sir, from this journey to the West, will you return some day?
How can you hope to climb the crags along this fearful way?
Mournful birds in ancient trees—you'll hear no other sound

1. Translated by Arthur Waley.

1. Translated by Vikram Seth.

Of life: the male bird follows his mate as they fly round and round.
You'll hear the cuckoo call in the moonlight,
Sad that the mountain's bare at night.
The road to Shu is hard, harder than climbing to the sky.
Just speak these words to someone's face—you'll see its colour fly.
A hand's breadth from the sky peaks join to crown a precipice
Where withered pines, bent upside down, lean over the abyss.
Swift rapids, wrestling cataracts descend in roaring spasms,
Pound cliffs, boil over rocks, and thunder through ten thousand chasms.
To face such danger and such fear,
Alas, from such a distance, Sir, what could have brought you here?
Dagger Peak is high and steep—
Even a single man can keep
The pass from thousands—though he may
Become a wolf or jackal—and betray.
By day we dread the savage tiger's claws,
By night the serpent's jaws,
Its sharp, blood-sucking fangs bared when
It mows down like hemp stalks the lives of men.
Though Chengdu is a pleasure dome,
Better to quickly turn back home.
The road to Shu is hard, harder than climbing to the sky.
Leaning, I stare into the west and utter a long sigh.

Bring in the Wine[1]

The waters of the Yellow River come down from the sky,
Never once returning as towards the sea they flow.
The mirrors of high palaces are sad with once-bright hair:
Though silken-black at morning it has changed by night to snow.
Fulfil your wishes in this life, exhaust your every whim
And never raise an empty golden goblet to the moon.
Fate's loaded me with talent and it must be put to use!
Scatter a thousand coins—they'll all come winging homeward soon.
Cook a sheep, slaughter an ox—and for our further pleasure
Let's drink three hundred cups of wine down in a single measure.
So here's to you, Dan Qiu—
And Master Cen, drink up.
Bring in, bring in the wine—
Pour on, cup after cup.
I'll sing a song for you—
So lend your ears and hear me through.
Bells and drums and feasts and jade are all esteemed in vain:
Just let me be forever drunk and never be sober again.
The sages and the virtuous men are all forgotten now.

1. Translated by Vikram Seth.

It is the drinkers of the world whose names alone remain.
Chen Wang, the prince and poet,[2] once at a great banquet paid
Ten thousand for a cask of wine with laughter wild and free.
How can you say, my host, that you have fallen short of cash?
You've got to buy more wine and drink it face to face with me.
My furs so rare—
My dappled mare—
Summon the boy to go and get the choicest wine for these
And we'll dissolve the sorrows of a hundred centuries.

The Jewel Stairs' Grievance[1]

The jewelled steps are already quite white with dew,
It is so late that the dew soaks my gauze stockings,
And I let down the crystal curtain
And watch the moon through the clear autumn.

The River Merchant's Wife: A Letter[1]

While my hair was still cut straight across my forehead
I played about the front gate, pulling flowers.
You came by on bamboo stilts, playing horse,
You walked about my seat, playing with blue plums.
And we went on living in the village of Chokan:
Two small people, without dislike or suspicion.

At fourteen I married My Lord you.
I never laughed, being bashful.
Lowering my head, I looked at the wall.
Called to, a thousand times, I never looked back.

At fifteen I stopped scowling,
I desired my dust to be mingled with yours
Forever and forever and forever.
Why should I climb the look out?

At sixteen you departed,
You went into far Ku-to-yen, by the river of swirling eddies,
And you have been gone five months.
The monkeys make sorrowful noise overhead.

You dragged your feet when you went out.
By the gate now, the moss is grown, the different mosses,
Too deep to clear them away!
The leaves fall early this autumn, in wind.
The paired butterflies are already yellow with August
Over the grass in the West garden;

2. Chen Wang (Prince Chen) was Cao Zhi (192–232).

1. Translated by Ezra Pound. Pound didn't know classical Chinese, but he worked from the notes to poems of Ernest Fenellosa, a scholar of Japanese culture. With his first volume of these translations, *Cathay* (1915), Pound was said by T. S. Eliot to have become "the inventor of Chinese poetry for our time."

1. Translated by Ezra Pound.

They hurt me. I grow older.
If you are coming down through the narrows of the river Kiang,
Please let me know beforehand,
And I will come out to meet you
As far as Cho-fu-Sa.

Listening to a Monk from Shu Playing the Lute[1]

The monk from Shu with his green lute-case walked
Westward down Emei Shan, and at the sound
Of the first notes he strummed for me I heard
A thousand valleys' rustling pines resound.
My heart was cleansed, as if in flowing water.
In bells of frost I heard the resonance die.
Dusk came unnoticed over the emerald hills
And autumn clouds layered the darkening sky.

Farewell to a Friend[1]

Verdant mountains behind the northern ramparts.
White waters wind around the east city wall.
From this place once parting has ended,
The lone tumbleweed flies a myriad miles.
Floating clouds: a traveler's thoughts.
Setting sun: an old friend's feelings.
Waving hands, you go from here—
Horses neigh gently as they leave.

In the Quiet Night[1]

The floor before my bed is bright:
Moonlight—like hoarfrost—in my room.
I lift my head and watch the moon.
I drop my head and think of home.

Sitting Alone by Jingting Mountain[1]

The flocks of birds have flown high and away,
A solitary cloud goes off calmly alone.
We look at each other and never get bored—
Just me and Ching-t'ing Mountain.

Question and Answer in the Mountains[1]

They ask me why I live in the green mountains.

1. Translated by Vikram Seth.
1. Translated by Pauline Yu.
1. Translated by Vikram Seth.
1. Translated by Stephen Owen.
1. Translated by Vikram Seth.

I smile and don't reply; my heart's at ease.
Peach blossoms flow downstream, leaving no trace—
And there are other earths and skies than these.

Du Fu

712–770

By common consensus Du Fu wears the heavy mantle of China's greatest poet, but during his lifetime he struggled unsuccessfully for recognition of another sort. The grandson of a prominent court poet, he took the most literary and difficult civil service examination twice to qualify for a position in the central government but failed both times. He attracted the emperor's attention by sending him examples of his literary work and passed a special examination set for him, but when he eventually secured a court position his forthrightness led to dismissal within days. Offered minor provincial posts, he soon opted to resign and embarked on what was to be a lifetime of travel in search of better employment. The separation and hardship he and his family endured were great; one young son died of starvation, and Du Fu himself suffered from chronic and often severe illness and died never having attained his goal.

A failure as a public man, Du Fu nonetheless produced a body of poetry whose concerns and compassion have been seen to embody the highest Confucian ideals. He was the first poet to write directly and often critically about contemporary political and social conditions in China, on a scale both large and small, and has been dubbed as a consequence both the "Poet-Sage" and the "Poet-Historian." He was deeply affected by the devastating effect of the rebellion of general An Lushan in 755, even after the recapture of the capital by imperial troops in 757. The government never regained its past stability or glory, and a sense of irrevocable loss is developed especially powerfully in Du Fu's eight-poem sequence "Autumn Meditations," written while he was in Kuizhou, Sichuan, frustratingly far from the center of activity. What has impressed later readers is his ability to situate his own personal fate within the grand course of events. No poet before him had written so extensively about himself and his own family and with such detail about his daily existence. Du Fu further intertwines this history with that of the nation with great poignancy, the frequent image of a solitary figure in the landscape conveying both his aspirations and his agony at not being able to translate his compassion into broader action.

Du Fu was also the first poet to speak extensively of his own writing, and his work expresses the hope that his poetry could play the role that eluded him in public service. Highly conscious of his craft, he preferred the newer regulated verse forms that allowed him to test the limits of poetic expression under technically demanding conditions. In a poem of eight five- or seven-word lines, a poet would be expected to introduce a topic in the first couplet, provide illustrative descriptive imagery in the next two couplets, and then finish with a witty or enigmatic closure, while conforming to established tonal patterns and observing syntactic and semantic parallelism. The poems written during the last decade of his life are especially noteworthy for their densely packed, ambiguous and allusive language, and his constant concern with the effort of his art made him the poet's poet for succeeding generations and, by the eleventh century, afforded him an undisputed place at the top of the literary hierarchy.

Ballad of the Army Carts[1]

Carts rattle and squeak,
Horses snort and neigh—
Bows and arrows at their waists, the conscripts march away.
Fathers, mothers, children, wives run to say goodbye.
The Xianyang Bridge in clouds of dust is hidden from the eye.
They tug at them and stamp their feet, weep, and obstruct their way.
The weeping rises to the sky.
Along the road a passer-by
Questions the conscripts. They reply:

They mobilize us constantly. Sent northwards at fifteen
To guard the River, we were forced once more to volunteer,
Though we are forty now, to man the western front this year.
The headman tied our headcloths for us when we first left here.
We came back white-haired—to be sent again to the frontier.
Those frontier posts could fill the sea with the blood of those who've died,
But still the Martial Emperor's aims remain unsatisfied.
In county after county to the east, Sir, don't you know,
In village after village only thorns and brambles grow.
Even if there's a sturdy wife to wield the plough and hoe,
The borders of the fields have merged, you can't tell east from west.
It's worse still for the men from Qin, as fighters they're the best—
And so, like chickens or like dogs, they're driven to and fro.

Though you are kind enough to ask,
Dare we complain about our task?
Take, Sir, this winter. In Guanxi
The troops have not yet been set free.
The district officers come to press
The land tax from us nonetheless.
But, Sir, how can we possibly pay?
Having a son's a curse today.
Far better to have daughters, get them married—
A son will lie lost in the grass, unburied.
Why, Sir, on distant Qinghai shore
The bleached ungathered bones lie year on year.
New ghosts complain, and those who died before
Weep in the wet gray sky and haunt the ear.

Moonlit Night[1]

In Fuzhou, far away, my wife is watching
The moon alone tonight, and my thoughts fill
With sadness for my children, who can't think
Of me here in Changan; they're too young still.
Her cloud-soft hair is moist with fragrant mist.
In the clear light her white arms sense the chill.

1. Translated by Vikram Seth.

1. Translated by Vikram Seth.

When will we feel the moonlight dry our tears,
Leaning together on our window-sill?

Spring Prospect[1]

The country shattered, mountains and rivers remain.
Spring in the city—grasses and trees are dense.
Feeling the times, flowers draw forth tears.
Hating to part, birds alarm the heart.
Beacon fires for three months in a row:
A letter from home worth ten thousand in gold.
White hairs scratched grow even shorter—
Soon too few to hold a hatpin on.[2]

Traveling at Night[1]

Slender grass, a faint wind on the shore.
Tall mast, a lonely night on the boat.
Stars hang down on the flat plain's expanse.
The moon surges up in the great river, flowing.
A name—how can writing make it known?
An office—for age and sickness given up.
Fluttering, floating, what is there for likeness?
On heaven and earth, one sandy gull.

Autumn Meditations[1]

1

Gems of dew wilt and wound the maple trees in the wood:
From Wu mountains, from Wu gorges, the air blows desolate.
The waves between the river banks merge in the seething sky,
Clouds in the wind above the passes touch their shadows on the ground.
Clustered chrysanthemums have opened twice, in tears of other days:
The forlorn boat, once and for all, tethers my homeward thoughts.
    In the houses quilted clothes speed scissors and ruler.
The washing blocks pound, faster each evening, in Pai Ti[2] high on the hill.

2

On the solitary walls of K'uei-chou the sunset rays slant,
Each night guided by the Dipper I gaze towards the capital.
It is true then that tears start when we hear the gibbon cry thrice:[3]
Useless my mission adrift on the raft which came by this eighth month.[4]
Fumes of the censers by the pictures in the ministry elude my sickbed pillow,
The whitewashed parapets of turrets against the hills dull the mournful bugles.
    Look! On the wall, the moon in the ivy
Already, by the shores of the isle, lights the blossoms on the reeds.

1. Translated by Pauline Yu.
2. Used to anchor the cap of an official.
1. Translated by Pauline Yu.
1. Translated by A. C. Graham. Du Fu wrote this sequence in 766 while in exile in Kuizhou, on the middle Yangzi River far south of the capital of Chang'an.
2. White Emperor City, adjacent to Kuizhou.
3. According to a traditional fishermen's song, the gibbon's three cries in the Wu gorges sounded so mournful they could not but elicit tears.
4. In two separate legends, a fisherman and a Han dynasty official were carried on rafts to the Milky Way.

3

A thousand houses rimmed by the mountains are quiet in the morning light,
Day after day in the house by the river I sit in the blue of the hills.
Two nights gone the fisher-boats once more come bobbing on the waves,
Belated swallows in cooling autumn still flit to and fro. . . .
A disdained K'uang Heng, as a critic of policy:
As promoter of learning, a Liu Hsiang who failed.[5]
Of the school-friends of my childhood, most did well.
By the Five Tombs[6] in light cloaks they ride their sleek horses.

4

Well said Ch'ang-an looks like a chess-board:[7]
A hundred years of the saddest news.
The mansions of princes and nobles all have new lords:
Another breed is capped and robed for office.
Due north on the mountain passes the gongs and drums shake,
To the chariots and horses campaigning in the west the winged dispatches hasten.
While the fish and the dragons fall asleep and the autumn river turns cold
My native country, untroubled times, are always in my thoughts.

5

The gate of P'eng-lai Palace faces the South Mountain:
Dew collects on the bronze stems out of the Misty River.
See in the west on Jasper Lake the Queen Mother descend:
Approaching from the east the purple haze fills the Han-ku pass.[8]
The clouds roll back, the pheasant-tail screens open before the throne:
Scales ringed by the sun on dragon robes! I have seen the majestic face.
I lay down once by the long river, wake left behind by the years,
Who so many times answered the roll of court by the blue chain-patterned door.

6

From the mouth of Ch'üt-t'ang gorges here, to the side of Crooked River there,
For ten thousand miles of mist in the wind the touch of pallid autumn.
Through the walled passage from Calyx Hall the royal splendour coursed,
To Hibiscus Park the griefs of the frontier came.
Pearl blinds and embellished pillars closed in the yellow cranes,
Embroidered cables and ivory masts startled the white seagulls.
Look back and pity the singing, dancing land!
Ch'in from most ancient times was the seat of princes.

5. A famous statesman and a famous editor of the Han dynasty. Between 757 and 758, Du Fu held a position charged with "reminding" the emperor of oversights, but fell out of favor owing to critical memorials.

6. Imperial tombs outside the capital.

7. Recently invaded by rebel troops, Chang'an's streets were also laid out as a symmetrical grid.

8. Du Fu refers variously to the Penglai Palace in Chang'an, named after one of the fairy islands in the Eastern sea; the copper pans raised on pillars which the Emperor Wu (140–87 B.C.E.) made to collect dew for the elixir; the Misty River is the empyrean; the Western Queen Mother (Xiwangmu) who banqueted King Mu (1001–947 B.C.E.) at Jasper Lake in her country far to the west, an incident which the poet fuses with her later descent from the sky to teach the arts of immortality to the Emperor Wu; the philosopher Laozi coming through the passes preceded by a purple cloud on his final journey to the west [translator's note].

7

K'un-ming Pool was the Han time's monument,
The banners of the Emperor Wu are here before my eyes.[9]
Vega threads her loom in vain by night under the moon,
And the great stone fish's plated scales veer in the autumn wind.
The waves toss a zizania seed, over sunken clouds as black:
Dew on the calyx chills the lotus, red with dropped pollen.
Over the pass, all the way to the sky, a road for none but the birds.
On river and lakes, to the ends of the earth, one old fisherman.

8

The K'un-wu road by Yü-su river ran its meandering course,
The shadow of Purple Turret Peak fell into Lake Mei-p'i,
Grains from the fragrant rice-stalks, pecked and dropped by the parrots;
On the green *wu-t'ung* tree branches which the perching phoenix aged.
Beautiful girls gathered kingfisher feathers for spring gifts:
Together in the boat, a troop of immortals, we set forth again in the evening. . .
This brush of many colours once forced the elements.
Chanting, peering into the distance, in anguish my white head droops.

Yangtse and Han[1]

By Yangtse and Han, a stranger who thinks of home,
One withered pedant between the Ch'ien and K'un.[2]
Under as far a sky as that streak of cloud,
The moon in the endless night no more alone.
In sunset hale of heart still:
In the autumn wind, risen from sickness.
There's always a place kept for an old horse
Though it can take no more to the long road.

Bo Juyi

772–846

Born into a scholar-official family of limited means, Bo Juyi passed the most rigorous civil service examination in 800 and held government posts fairly steadily thereafter, although only briefly in the capital. Appointed to relatively powerful positions in the provinces as prefect, he became attracted to Buddhism later in life and thus grew increasingly remote spiritually, as well as geographically, from the center of political activity. Reacting against tendencies toward increasingly difficult and obscure poetic styles, Bo wrote prolifically and cultivated a plain style that he hoped would be accessible even to a peasant woman. Much of his poetry deals with surprising frankness with details of his daily life, ranging from topics like eating bamboo shoots to the aggravations of child-rearing and the virtues of baldness.

Bo Juyi also took seriously the Confucian mandate to employ poetry as a vehicle of social and political protest. With his lifelong friend Yuan Zhen, he promoted a revival of folk song

9. Kunming Pool near Chang'an was made by Wu of Han for naval exercises. Near it was a statue of the Weaving Girl (the star Vega) and in it a stone whale with movable fins and tail [translator's note].

1. Translated by A. C. Graham.

2. Ch'ien (qian) and K'un (kun) represent heaven and earth in the divination system of the *Book of Changes.*

traditions based on those collected by the Han dynasty Music Bureau, but whose subject matter, unlike that of those predecessors, would focus resolutely on contemporary bureaucratic abuses. But his best-loved work, somewhat to his chagrin, was the tragic story of the Tang emperor Minghuang (or Xuanzong, r. 713–755) and his prized consort, Yang Guifei. She was blamed for preparing the way for the disastrous rebellion of An Lushan, owing both to her infatuating beauty and to the seditious behavior of her relatives. When the emperor was forced to flee the capital with her, his soldiers reportedly refused to protect him unless she was first executed. This anguished tale of conflict between the affairs of the heart and the interests of the state was the subject of numerous other poems, stories, and dramas as well.

A Song of Unending Sorrow[1]

China's Emperor, craving beauty that might shake an empire,
Was on the throne, for many years, searching, never finding,
Till a little child of the Yang clan, hardly even grown,
Bred in an inner chamber, with no one knowing her,
But with graces granted by heaven and not to be concealed,
At last one day was chosen for the imperial household.
If she but turned her head and smiled, there were cast a hundred spells,
And the powder and paint of the Six Palaces faded into nothing. . . .
It was early spring. They bathed her in the Flower-Pure Pool,
Which warmed and smoothed the creamy-tinted crystal of her skin,
And, because of her languor, a maid was lifting her
When first the Emperor noticed her and chose her for his bride.
The cloud of her hair, petal of her cheek, gold ripples of her crown when she moved,
Were sheltered on spring evenings by warm hibiscus-curtains;
But nights of spring were short and the sun arose too soon,
And the Emperor, from that time forth, forsook his early hearings
And lavished all his time on her with feasts and revelry,
His mistress of the spring, his despot of the night.
There were other ladies in his court, three thousand of rare beauty,
But his favors to three thousand were concentered in one body.
By the time she was dressed in her Golden Chamber, it would be almost evening;
And when tables were cleared in the Tower of Jade, she would loiter, slow with wine.
Her sisters and brothers all were given titles;
And, because she so illumined and glorified her clan,
She brought to every father, every mother through the empire,
Happiness when a girl was born rather than a boy. . . .
High rose Li Palace, entering blue clouds,
And far and wide the breezes carried magical notes
Of soft song and slow dance, of string and bamboo music.
The Emperor's eyes could never gaze on her enough—
Till war-drums, booming from Yü-yang, shocked the whole earth
And broke the tunes of "The Rainbow Skirt and the Feathered Coat."
The Forbidden City, the nine-tiered palace, loomed in the dust
From thousands of horses and chariots headed southwest.

1. Translated by Witter Bynner.

The imperial flag opened the way, now moving and now pausing—
But thirty miles from the capital, beyond the western gate,
The men of the army stopped, not one of them would stir
Till under their horses' hoofs they might trample those moth-eyebrows . . .
Flowery hairpins fell to the ground, no one picked them up,
And a green and white jade hair-tassel and a yellow-gold hair-bird.
The Emperor could not save her, he could only cover his face.
And later when he turned to look, the place of blood and tears
Was hidden in a yellow dust blown by a cold wind. . . .
At the cleft of the Dagger-Tower Trail they crisscrossed through a cloud-line
Under O-mei Mountain. The last few came.
Flags and banners lost their color in the fading sunlight . . .
But as waters of Shu are always green and its mountains always blue,
So changeless was his majesty's love and deeper than the days.
He stared at the desolate moon from his temporary palace,
He heard bell-notes in the evening rain, cutting at his breast.
And when heaven and earth resumed their round and the dragon-car faced home,
The Emperor clung to the spot and would not turn away
From the soil along the Ma-wei slope, under which was buried
That memory, that anguish. Where was her jade-white face?
Ruler and lords, when eyes would meet, wept upon their coats
As they rode, with loose rein, slowly eastward, back to the capital. . . .
The pools, the gardens, the palace, all were just as before,
The Lake T'ai-yi hibiscus, the Wei-yang Palace willows;
But a petal was like her face and a willow-leaf her eyebrow—
And what could he do but cry whenever he looked at them? . . .
Peach-trees and plum-trees blossomed, in the winds of spring;
Lakka-foliage fell to the ground, after autumn rains;
The Western and Southern Palaces were littered with late grasses,
And the steps were mounded with red leaves that no one swept away.
Her Pear-Garden Players became white-haired
And the eunuchs thin-eyebrowed in her Court of Pepper-Trees;
Over the throne flew fireflies, while he brooded in the twilight.
He would lengthen the lamp-wick to its end and still could never sleep.
Bell and drum would slowly toll the dragging night-hours
And the River of Stars grow sharp in the sky, just before dawn,
And the porcelain mandarin-ducks on the roof grow thick with morning frost
And his covers of kingfisher-blue feel lonelier and colder
With the distance between life and death year after year;
And yet no beloved spirit ever visited his dreams. . . .
At Ling-ch'ün lived a Taoist priest who was a guest of heaven,
Able to summon spirits by his concentrated mind.
And people were so moved by the Emperor's constant brooding
That they besought the Taoist priest to see if he could find her.
He opened his way in space and clove the ether like lightning
Up to heaven, under the earth, looking everywhere.
Above, he searched the Green Void, below, the Yellow Spring;
But he failed, in either place, to find the one he looked for.
And then he heard accounts of an enchanted isle at sea,

A part of the intangible and incorporeal world,
With pavilions and fine towers in the five-colored air,
And of exquisite immortals moving to and fro,
And of one among them—whom they called The Ever True—
With a face of snow and flowers resembling hers he sought.
So he went to the West Hall's gate of gold and knocked at the jasper door
And asked a girl, called Morsel-of-Jade, to tell The Doubly-Perfect.
And the lady, at news of an envoy from the Emperor of China,
Was startled out of dreams in her nine-flowered canopy.
She pushed aside her pillow, dressed, shook away sleep,
And opened the pearly shade and then the silver screen.
Her cloudy hair-dress hung on one side because of her great haste,
And her flower-cap was loose when she came along the terrace,
While a light wind filled her cloak and fluttered with her motion
As though she danced "The Rainbow Skirt and the Feathered Coat."
And the tear-drops drifting down her sad white face
Were like a rain in spring on the blossom of the pear.
But love glowed deep within her eyes when she bade him thank her liege,
Whose form and voice had been strange to her ever since their parting—
Since happiness had ended at the Court of the Bright Sun,
And moons and dawns had become long in Fairy-Mountain Palace.
But when she turned her face and looked down toward the earth
And tried to see the capital, there were only fog and dust.
So she took out, with emotion, the pledges he had given
And, through his envoy, sent him back a shell box and gold hairpin,
But kept one branch of the hairpin, and one side of the box,
Breaking the gold of the hairpin, breaking the shell of the box;
"Our souls belong together," she said, "like this gold and this shell—
Somewhere, sometime, on earth or in heaven, we shall surely meet."
And she sent him, by his messenger, a sentence reminding him
Of vows which had been known only to their two hearts:
"On the seventh day of the Seventh-month, in the Palace of Long Life,
We told each other secretly in the quiet midnight world
That we wished to fly in heaven, two birds with the wings of one,
And to grow together on the earth, two branches of one tree." . . .
Earth endures, heaven endures; sometime both shall end,
While this unending sorrow goes on and on forever.

[END OF POETRY OF THE TANG DYNASTY]

THE SONG LYRIC

The song lyric (*ci*) emerged as a poetic genre at the beginning of the eighth century during the Tang dynasty and reached maturity during the succeeding Song dynasty (960–1279). While the dominant forms of poetry (*shi*) during the Tang dynasty were composed in lines with equal numbers of syllables—generally five or seven—and without stanza breaks, song lyrics were verses in irregular line lengths, often stanzaic, because they were originally set to music. Indeed, poets didn't "write" lyrics, they "filled them in" to tunes, many of which came into China from other

Central Asian cultures. Although most of the music has long since been lost, the lyrics are still generally known by the title of the original song responsible for setting the pattern of tones and line lengths to which the words were obliged to conform.

Early song lyrics were composed to be performed by courtesans, professional musicians, and other public and private entertainers; some were also evidently part of a courtly repertoire as well. After the An Lushan rebellion in the middle of the eighth century, many of these court musicians dispersed to entertainment quarters in cities throughout the empire where, in halls of often immense proportions, song lyrics continued to be produced and performed. As interactions between courtesan-entertainers and literati flourished, song lyric forms that had once been largely of unknown authorship or composed by the singers themselves came gradually to be appropriated by educated bureaucrats for their own purposes. Typically written using a female persona, they were often then performed by women at banquets or parties, sometimes even for the men who had composed the lyrics. The songs developed a conventional repertoire of female emotions of desire and longing, usually situated in the boudoir and almost exclusively as imagined by men.

Over time the scope of the song lyric broadened to include a male voice and many topics that had traditionally been associated with the more established poetic forms. The song lyric maintained its claim on a less public expression of sentiments, however, and continued to explore the most delicate aspects of sensibility and the human affections. By the seventeenth century it had become an especially important vehicle for women writers, but men continued to ply it as well, with Chairman Mao probably its best-known twentieth-century practitioner.

Li Yu

937–978

Also known as "Last Ruler Li," Li Yu was forced to surrender his brief dominion over the Southern Tang, one of the many regional states that succeeded the fall of the Tang dynasty in 907, to the conquering Song rulers in 975 and spent his remaining years under house arrest. A pampered young prince in the kingdom founded by his father, he had continued to focus his attention on song lyrics, painting, and calligraphy after ascending the throne in 961, and his evident inattention to the details of administration no doubt hastened the demise of his rule.

Li Yu has been much admired for his song lyrics, which move beyond the conventional persona of a languishing woman to speak in a deeply moving voice that seems to be his own. Although it is impossible to date his lyrics with any certainty, they have traditionally been seen as tracing his own tragic fate—from a life of hedonistic pleasure to one filled only with memory and loss—with striking images drawn from the natural world.

To the tune "Die lian hua"[1]

A leisurely evening in garden and meadow—I follow my idle footsteps;
The Ch'ing-ming Holiday almost over
Makes me ache already for the waning of spring.
A few drops—the sound of rain held in check by the wind;
Dim and hazy under a pale moon the clouds come and go.

As blossoming peaches lingered on, spring passed by in secret;
But who is sitting in the swing,

1. Translated by Daniel Bryant.

Laughing softly and whispering quiet and low?
A single bit of fragrant heart, a million trailing threads;
In the world of men there is no place to arrange them all in peace.

To the tune "Qingping yue"

Since our parting, spring is half gone;
Everything I see brings heart-rending sorrow.
Below the steps the falling plum blossoms whirl like snow,
No sooner brushed away than drifting over again.
In news conveyed by migrating geese I have no faith;
The road is so long that dreams of return cannot reach home.
The heart-ache of separation is like the new grass of springtime:
No matter how you wander, no matter how far—and still it grows.

To the tune "Wang jiangnan"

So much heart-ache:
Last night my soul within a dream
Seemed again, as in days gone by, to roam the Palace Gardens—
Carriages like a flowing river, horses like a dragon,
And blossoms and moonlight just in the mood of spring.

To the tune "Yu meiren"

Spring flowers, the moon in autumn, when will these cease to be?
So many things lie already in the past.
Last night to my tiny pavilion the east wind came again;
I could not bear to look back toward my old kingdom shining beneath the moon.
Carved railings and jade-paved ways must be there just the same;
My rosy cheeks alone have changed.
Ask the sum of sorrow, ask how much there is to bear;
Just what is borne by a river in full spring flood flowing eastward to the sea.

Li Qingzhao

1084–c. 1151

By all accounts China's most outstanding woman poet, Li Qingzhao was the daughter of an eminent man of letters and a woman who was also an accomplished poet. In 1101 she married a minor official, Zhao Mingcheng, whose father served as minister of state to the Song emperor. This distinguished pedigree no doubt contributed to the relatively ample preservation of her writings, which include some fifty song lyrics (of a total corpus, however, that once filled six volumes), an influential critical essay on the genre, and a well-regarded catalogue of stone and bronze objects that she wrote in collaboration with her husband.

The early blissful years of Li's marriage ended abruptly when northern invaders forced the Song court to relocate to southern China in 1127. Most of her books and art were lost on her journey south, and her husband died shortly thereafter as well. Readers have traditionally regarded her song lyrics as charting the unhappy course of her life, although very few can be dated with any certainty. The song lyric from its origins had been associated with female personae and performers, but Li Qingzhao was the first educated woman to leave her mark on the genre, with a style notable for its disarmingly direct emotional expression and use of unexpected and often colloquial diction.

PRONUNCIATION:
Li Qingzhao: lee ching-JOW

To the tune "Yi jian mei"[1]

The scent of red lotus fades: the jade mat feels autumnal.
Gently loosening the silk gown,
I board the orchid boat alone.
Who's sending a gilded message in the clouds?
When the migrating geese bring word
The moon will be full in the western chamber.
Flower petals drift down, the river flows.
One kind of longing
In two places: idle melancholy.
No way to dispel these feelings.
For just when they brim in the eyes,
They go straight to the heart.

To the tune "Ru meng ling"[2]

How many evenings in the arbor by the river
When flushed with wine we'd lose our way back.
Our revels ended, returning late by boat
We'd stray off into a spot thick with lotus
And rowing, rowing through
Startle a shoreful of herons by the lake.

To the tune "Wuling chun"[3]

The wind has ceased, dust is fragrant, flowers all have fallen.
Late is the day—too tired to comb my hair.
Things remain but he has gone. Everything has ended.
I wish to speak; tears flow first.

I've heard it said at Twin Stream, spring's still fine.
I too would like to float there in a light boat.
Only I fear that Twin Stream's tiny "locust" boat
Could not carry so much grief.

To the tune "Sheng sheng man"[4]

Seeking, seeking, searching, searching,
Cold, cold, chill, chill,

1. Translated by Eugene Eoyang.
2. Translated by Eugene Eoyang.
3. Translated by Pauline Yu.
4. Translated by Pauline Yu.

Sad, sad, grieved, grieved, mournful, mournful.
This season of sudden warmth, then cold again:
Hardest of all is finding rest.
Two or three cups of watery wine—
How can they fend off that late wind's sharpness?
Geese pass by;
Just then I grieve,
Yet I recognize them from before.

Yellow flowers cover the ground in heaps,
Withered and spoiled:
Now who can bear to pluck them?
Keeping the window,
How can I live alone til dark?
On the *wutong* tree still a fine rain
Until dusk goes drip, drip, drop, drop.
At this moment—
How can one word "sorrow" say it all?

[END OF THE SONG LYRIC]

Murasaki Shikibu

c. 978–c. 1014

Murasaki Shikibu belonged to the Northern Branch of the Fujiwara clan, the same branch that produced the Regent family. Both sides of her family can in fact be traced back to Fujiwara no Fuyutsugu (775–826), whose son Yoshifusa became the first regent. Murasaki Shikibu's family line, however, subsequently declined, and by her grandfather's generation had settled at the provincial governor level. Murasaki Shikibu's father, Fujiwara no Tametoki (d. 1029), while eventually receiving the governorships of Echizen and Echigo provinces, had an undistinguished and uncertain career as a bureaucrat. He was, however, able to distinguish himself as a scholar of Chinese literature and as a poet.

In 996 Murasaki Shikibu accompanied her father to his new post as provincial governor in Echizen, on the north side of Japan. A year or two later she returned to the capital to marry Fujiwara no Nobutaka, who was old enough to be her father and who came from the same middle tier of the aristocracy. Murasaki Shikibu bore a daughter named Kenshi, probably in 999, and Nobutaka died only a few years later, in 1001.

It is generally believed that Murasaki Shikibu started writing *The Tale of Genji* (*Genji monogatari*) after her husband's death, perhaps in response to the sorrow it caused her, and it was probably the reputation of the early chapters that resulted in her being summoned to the imperial court around 1005–1006. She became a lady-in-waiting to Empress Shōshi, the consort of Emperor Ichijō and the eldest daughter of Fujiwara no Michinaga (966–1027), who had become regent. At least half of the *Diary of Murasaki Shikibu* is devoted to a long-awaited event in Michinaga's career—the birth of a son to Empress Shōshi in 1008—which would make Michinaga the grandfather of a future emperor. Murasaki Shikibu was the sobriquet given to her as a lady-in-waiting at the imperial court and is not her actual name, which remains unknown. "Shikibu" probably comes from the position in the Shikibu-shō (Ministry of Ceremonial) occupied by her father, while "Murasaki" may refer to the lavender color of the flower of her clan (Fujiwara, Wisteria Fields) or it may be that her nickname came from the heroine of *The Tale of Genji.*

THE TALE OF GENJI The title of *The Tale of Genji* comes from the surname of the hero, the son of the reigning emperor at the beginning of the narrative. *The Tale of Genji* is generally divided into three parts: the first thirty-three chapters follow Genji's career, from his birth to exile to triumphant return to his rise to the pinnacle of society, focusing equally, if not more, on the fate of the various women that he becomes involved with. The second part, Chapters 34 to 41, explores the darkness that gathers over Genji's private life and that of his great love Murasaki, who eventually succumbs and dies, and ends with Genji's own death. The third part consists of the thirteen chapters following Genji's death, which are primarily concerned with the affairs of Kaoru, Genji's supposed son, and with three sisters (particularly Oigimi and Ukifune) with whom Kaoru becomes involved. A significant shift of focus occurs in the third part: from the capital and court to the countryside, and from a society concerned with refinement, elegance, and the various arts, to an otherworldly, ascetic perspective—a shift that anticipates the movement of mid-Heian court culture toward the religious literature of the medieval period, focused on hermits who withdrew from the world.

The Tale of Genji both follows and works against a common plot convention of the Heian vernacular tale (*monogatari*) in which the heroine, whose family has declined or disappeared, is discovered and loved by an illustrious noble. This association of love and inferior social status appears from the opening line of the *Genji* and extends to the last relationship between Kaoru and Ukifune. In the opening chapter, the reigning emperor, like all Heian emperors, was expected to devote himself to his principal consort (the Kokiden lady), the lady of the highest rank, and yet he dotes on a woman of considerably lower status—a social and political violation that eventually results in the woman's death. Like his monogatari predecessor, Ariwara no Narihira, the hero of *The Tales of Ise,* and like his father, Genji pursues love where it is forbidden and most unlikely to be found or attained. In "Lavender," the fifth chapter, Genji discovers his future wife, the young Murasaki, who has lost her mother and is in danger of losing her only guardian when Genji takes her into his home.

In Murasaki Shikibu's day, it would have been unheard of for a man of Genji's high rank to take a girl of Murasaki's low position into his own residence and marry her. In the upper levels of Heian aristocratic society, the man usually lived in his wife's residence, either in the house of her parents or in a dwelling nearby (as Genji does with Aoi, his principal wife). The prospective groom had high stakes in marriage, for the bride's family provided not only a residence but other forms of support as well. When Genji takes a girl (such as the young Murasaki) with no backing or social support into his house, he openly flouts the conventions of marriage as they were known to Murasaki Shikibu's audience. In the monogatari tradition, however, this action becomes a sign of excessive, romantic love.

A number of other sequences in the story—those of Yūgao, the Akashi lady, Oigimi, and Ukifune—start on a similar note. All of these women come from upper- or middle-rank aristocratic families (much like that of the author herself) that have, for various reasons, fallen into social obscurity and must struggle to survive. The appearance of the highborn hero implies, at least for the attendants surrounding the woman, an opportunity for social redemption. However, Murasaki Shikibu focuses on the difficulties that the woman subsequently encounters, either in dealing with the man, or failing to make the social transition between her own social background and that of the highborn hero. The woman may, for example, be torn between pride and material need, or between emotional dependence and a desire to be more independent, or she may feel abandoned and betrayed—all conflicts explored in *The Tale of Genji.* In classical Japanese poetry, love has a similar fate: it is never about happiness or the blissful union of souls. Instead, it dwells on unfulfilled hopes, regretful partings, fears of abandonment, and lingering resentment.

The Tale of Genji is remarkable for the manner in which it absorbs the exploration of identity and social position found in earlier women's diaries, the social romance of the early monogatari, and the poetry and imagery of *The Tales of Ise,* blending these strands into a deeply psychological narrative that evolves around distinctive characters. But while bearing a striking resemblance to the modern psychological novel, *The Tale of Genji* wasn't conceived and written as a single work and then published and distributed to a mass audience as novels are today. Instead, it was issued in limited installments, chapter by chapter or sequence by sequence, to an circumscribed, aristocratic audience over an extended period of time. As a result *The Tale of Genji* can be appreciated as a closely interrelated series of texts that can be read either individually or as a whole and that is the product of an author whose attitudes, interests, and techniques evolved significantly with time and experience. For example, the reader of the Ukifune narrative can appreciate this sequence both independently and as an integral part of the previous narrative. The *Genji* can also be understood as a kind of multiple Bildungsroman or novel of the development of a character through time and experience. Yet in this work, the development occurs not only in the life of a single hero or heroine but over different generations, with two or more characters. Genji, for example, attains an awareness of death, mutability, and the illusory nature of the world through repeated suffering. By contrast, Kaoru, his supposed son, begins his life, or rather his narrative, with a profound grasp and acceptance of these darker aspects of life. In the second part, in the "New Herbs" chapters, the heroine Murasaki has long assumed that she can monopolize Genji's affections and act as his principal wife. Genji's unexpected marriage to the Third Princess, however, crushes these assumptions, causing Murasaki to fall mortally ill. In the third part, the Uji sequence, Oigimi never suffers the way Murasaki does, but she quickly comes to a similar awareness of the inconstancy of men, love, and marriage, even though Kaoru appears to be an ideal companion.

Murasaki Shikibu probably first wrote a short sequence of chapters, perhaps beginning with "Lavender," and then, in response to reader demand, wrote a sequel or another related series of chapters, and so forth. Certain sequences, which appear to have been inserted later, focus on women of the middle and lower aristocracy, as opposed to the main chapters of the first part which deal with Fujitsubo and other upper-rank women related to the throne. The only chapters in which authorship has been questioned are three chapters following the death of Genji at the end of the second part. The following selections condense this extended narrative by leaving out those chapters and sections that were later additions, of questionable authorship, or tangential to the lives of the central characters.

PRONUNCIATIONS:

Murasaki Shikibu: moo-ra-sa-ki shi-ki-boo
Genji: gen-jee
Aoi: ah-oh-ee
Rokujō: ro-koo-joh

The Tale of Genji[1]

from *Chapter 1. The Paulownia Court*

In a certain reign there was a lady not of the first rank whom the emperor loved more than any of the others. The grand ladies with high ambitions thought her a presumptuous upstart, and lesser ladies were still more resentful. Everything she did offended someone. Probably aware of what was happening, she fell seriously ill and came to spend more time at home than at court. The emperor's pity and affection quite passed

1. Translated by Edward Seidensticker, with notes adapted from Seidensticker.

bounds. No longer caring what his ladies and courtiers might say, he behaved as if intent upon stirring gossip.

His court looked with very great misgiving upon what seemed a reckless infatuation. In China just such an unreasoning passion had been the undoing of an emperor and had spread turmoil through the land. As the resentment grew, the example of Yang Kuei-fei[2] was the one most frequently cited against the lady.

She survived despite her troubles, with the help of an unprecedented bounty of love. Her father, a grand councilor, was no longer living. Her mother, an old-fashioned lady of good lineage, was determined that matters be no different for her than for ladies who with paternal support were making careers at court. The mother was attentive to the smallest detail of etiquette and deportment. Yet there was a limit to what she could do. The sad fact was that the girl was without strong backing, and each time a new incident arose she was next to defenseless.

It may have been because of a bond in a former life that she bore the emperor a beautiful son, a jewel beyond compare. The emperor was in a fever of impatience to see the child, still with the mother's family; and when, on the earliest day possible, he was brought to court, he did indeed prove to be a most marvelous babe. The emperor's eldest son was the grandson of the Minister of the Right. The world assumed that with this powerful support he would one day be named crown prince; but the new child was far more beautiful. On public occasions the emperor continued to favor his eldest son. The new child was a private treasure, so to speak, on which to lavish uninhibited affection.

The mother was not of such a low rank as to attend upon the emperor's personal needs. In the general view she belonged to the upper classes. He insisted on having her always beside him, however, and on nights when there was music or other entertainment he would require that she be present. Sometimes the two of them would sleep late, and even after they had risen he would not let her go. Because of his unreasonable demands she was widely held to have fallen into immoderate habits out of keeping with her rank.

With the birth of the son, it became yet clearer that she was the emperor's favorite. The mother of the eldest son began to feel uneasy. If she did not manage carefully, she might see the new son designated crown prince. She had come to court before the emperor's other ladies, she had once been favored over the others, and she had borne several of his children. However much her complaining might trouble and annoy him, she was one lady whom he could not ignore.

Though the mother of the new son had the emperor's love, her detractors were numerous and alert to the slightest inadvertency. She was in continuous torment, feeling that she had nowhere to turn. Her quarters were in the Kiritsubo.[3] The emperor had to pass the apartments of other ladies to reach hers, and it must be admitted that their resentment at his constant comings and goings was not unreasonable. Her visits to the royal chambers were equally frequent. The robes of her women were in a scandalous state from trash strewn along bridges and galleries. Once some women conspired to have both doors of a gallery she must pass bolted shut, and so she found herself unable to advance or retreat. Her anguish over the mounting list of insults was presently more than the emperor could bear. He moved a lady out of rooms adjacent to his own and assigned them to the Kiritsubo lady and so, of course, aroused new resentment.

2. The beautiful concubine of the Tang emperor Hsüan Tsung. The emperor's infatuation with her was viewed as the cause of the An Lu-shan Rebellion, and led to her execution.

3. The Paulownia Court, in the northeast corner of the residential compound of the palace. The distance of the Kiritsubo lady's quarters from the emperor's, near the middle of the compound, is a reflection of her relatively low rank.

When the young prince reached the age of three,[4] the resources of the treasury and the stewards' offices were exhausted to make the ceremonial bestowing of trousers as elaborate as that for the eldest son. Once more there was malicious talk; but the prince himself, as he grew up, was so superior of mien and disposition that few could find it in themselves to dislike him. Among the more discriminating, indeed, were some who marveled that such a paragon had been born into this world.

In the summer the boy's mother, feeling vaguely unwell, asked that she be allowed to go home. The emperor would not hear of it. Since they were by now used to these indispositions, he begged her to stay and see what course her health would take. It was steadily worse, and then, suddenly, everyone could see that she was failing. Her mother came pleading that he let her go home. At length he agreed.

Fearing that even now she might be the victim of a gratuitous insult, she chose to go off without ceremony, leaving the boy behind. Everything must have an end, and the emperor could no longer detain her. It saddened him inexpressibly that he was not even permitted to see her off. A lady of great charm and beauty, she was sadly emaciated. She was sunk in melancholy thoughts, but when she tried to put them into words her voice was almost inaudible. The emperor was quite beside himself, his mind a confusion of things that had been and things that were to come. He wept and vowed undying love, over and over again. The lady was unable to reply. She seemed listless and drained of strength, as if she scarcely knew what was happening. Wanting somehow to help, the emperor ordered that she be given the honor of a hand-drawn carriage. He returned to her apartments and still could not bring himself to the final parting.

"We vowed that we would go together down the road we all must go. You must not leave me behind."

She looked sadly up at him. "If I had suspected that it would be so—" She was gasping for breath.

"I leave you, to go the road we all must go.
The road I would choose, if only I could, is the other."

It was evident that she would have liked to say more; but she was so weak that it had been a struggle to say even this much.

The emperor was wondering again if he might not keep her with him and have her with him to the end.

But a message came from her mother, asking that she hurry. "We have obtained the agreement of eminent ascetics to conduct the necessary services, and I fear that they are to begin this evening."

So, in desolation, he let her go. He passed a sleepless night.

He sent off a messenger and was beside himself with impatience and apprehension even before there had been time for the man to reach the lady's house and return. The man arrived to find the house echoing with laments. She had died at shortly past midnight. He returned sadly to the palace. The emperor closed himself up in his private apartments. He would have liked at least to keep the boy with him, but no precedent could be found for having him away from his mother's house through the mourning. The boy looked in bewilderment at the weeping courtiers, at his father too,

4. All ages are by the Asian count, not of the full years but of the number of years in which one has lived, therefore one or two years above the full count: someone born near the end of a year would turn "two" at New Year's.

the tears streaming over his face. The death of a parent is sad under any circumstances, and this one was indescribably sad.

But there must be an end to weeping, and orders were given for the funeral. If only she could rise to the heavens with the smoke from the pyre, said the mother between her sobs. She rode in the hearse with several attendants, and what must her feelings have been when they reached Mount Otaki?[5] It was there that the services were conducted with the utmost solemnity and dignity.

She looked down at the body. "With her before me, I cannot persuade myself that she is dead. At the sight of her ashes I can perhaps accept what has happened."

The words were rational enough, but she was so distraught that she seemed about to fall from the carriage. The women had known that it would be so and did what they could for her.

A messenger came from the palace with the news that the lady had been raised to the Third Rank, and presently a nunciary arrived to read the official order. For the emperor, the regret was scarcely bearable that he had not had the courage of his resolve to appoint her an imperial consort, and he wished to make amends by promoting her one rank. There were many who resented even this favor. Others, however, of a more sensitive nature, saw more than ever what a dear lady she had been, simple and gentle and difficult to find fault with. It was because she had been excessively favored by the emperor that she had been the victim of such malice. The grand ladies were now reminded of how sympathetic and unassuming she had been. It was for just such an occasion, they remarked to one another, that the phrase "how well one knows" had been invented.

The days went dully by. The emperor was careful to send offerings for the weekly memorial services. His grief was unabated and he spent his nights in tears, refusing to summon his other ladies. His serving women were plunged into dew-drenched autumn.

There was one lady, however, who refused to be placated. "How ridiculous," said the lady of the Kokiden Pavilion, mother of his eldest son, "that the infatuation should continue even now."

The emperor's thoughts were on his youngest son even when he was with his eldest. He sent off intelligent nurses and serving women to the house of the boy's grandmother, where he was still in residence, and made constant inquiry after him.

The autumn tempests blew and suddenly the evenings were chilly. Lost in his grief, the emperor sent off a note to the grandmother. His messenger was a woman of middle rank called Myōbu, whose father was a guards officer. It was on a beautiful moonlit night that he dispatched her, a night that brought memories. On such nights he and the dead lady had played the koto for each other. Her koto had somehow had overtones lacking in other instruments, and when she would interrupt the music to speak, the words too carried echoes of their own. Her face, her manner—they seemed to cling to him, but with "no more substance than the lucent dream."

[*Myōbu visits the Kiritsubo lady's grieving mother, and delivers a letter in which the emperor hints that he would like his young son to return to the palace.*]

Myōbu was much moved to find the emperor waiting up for her. Making it seem that his attention was on the small and beautifully planted garden before him, now in full autumn bloom, he was talking quietly with four or five women, among the most

5. To the east of the city.

sensitive of his attendants. He had become addicted to illustrations by the emperor Uda for "The Song of Everlasting Sorrow"[6] and to poems by Ise and Tsurayuki on that subject, and to Chinese poems as well.

He listened attentively as Myōbu described the scene she had found so affecting. He took up the letter she had brought from the grandmother.

"I am so awed by this august message that I would run away and hide; and so violent are the emotions it gives rise to that I scarcely know what to say.

> The tree that gave them shelter has withered and died.
> One fears for the plight of the hagi[7] shoots beneath."

A strange way to put the matter, thought the emperor; but the lady must still be dazed with grief. He chose to overlook the suggestion that he himself could not help the child.

He sought to hide his sorrow, not wanting these women to see him in such poor control of himself. But it was no use. He reviewed his memories over and over again, from his very earliest days with the dead lady. He had scarcely been able to bear a moment away from her while she lived. How strange that he had been able to survive the days and months since on memories alone. He had hoped to reward the grandmother's sturdy devotion, and his hopes had come to nothing.

"Well," he sighed, "she may look forward to having her day, if she will only live to see the boy grow up."

Looking at the keepsakes Myōbu had brought back, he thought what a comfort it would be if some wizard were to bring him, like that Chinese emperor, a comb from the world where his lost love was dwelling. He whispered:

> "And will no wizard search her out for me,
> That even he may tell me where she is?"

There are limits to the powers of the most gifted artist. The Chinese lady in the paintings did not have the luster of life. Yang Kuei-fei was said to have resembled the lotus of the Sublime Pond, the willows of the Timeless Hall. No doubt she was very beautiful in her Chinese finery. When he tried to remember the quiet charm of his lost lady, he found that there was no color of flower, no song of bird, to summon her up. Morning and night, over and over again, they had repeated to each other the lines from "The Song of Everlasting Sorrow":

> In the sky, as birds that share a wing.
> On earth, as trees that share a branch.

It had been their vow, and the shortness of her life had made it an empty dream.

Everything, the moaning of the wind, the humming of autumn insects, added to the sadness. But in the apartments of the Kokiden lady matters were different. It had been some time since she had last waited upon the emperor. The moonlight being so beautiful, she saw no reason not to have music deep into the night. The emperor muttered something about the bad taste of such a performance at such a time, and those who saw his distress agreed that it was an unnecessary injury. Kokiden was of an arrogant and intractable nature and her behavior suggested that to her the emperor's grief was of no importance.

6. By Po Chü-i, describing the grief of the Tang emperor Hsüan Tsung upon the death of his concubine Yang Kuei-fei. Uda reigned in the late ninth century and died in 931. Tsurayuki and Ise (one of Uda's concubines) were active in the early 10th century.

7. A kind of clover.

The moon set. The wicks in the lamps had been trimmed more than once and presently the oil was gone. Still he showed no sign of retiring. His mind on the boy and the old lady, he jotted down a verse:

> Tears dim the moon, even here above the clouds.[8]
> Dim must it be in that lodging among the reeds.

Calls outside told him that the guard was being changed. It would be one or two in the morning. People would think his behavior strange indeed. He at length withdrew to his bedchamber. He was awake the whole night through, and in dark morning, his thoughts on the blinds that would not open,[9] he was unable to interest himself in business of state. He scarcely touched his breakfast, and lunch seemed so remote from his inclinations that his attendants exchanged looks and whispers of alarm.

Not all voices were sympathetic. Perhaps, some said, it had all been foreordained, but he had dismissed the talk and ignored the resentment and let the affair quite pass the bounds of reason; and now to neglect his duties so—it was altogether too much. Some even cited the example of the Chinese emperor who had brought ruin upon himself and his country.

The months passed and the young prince returned to the palace. He had grown into a lad of such beauty that he hardly seemed meant for this world—and indeed one almost feared that he might only briefly be a part of it. When, the following spring, it came time to name a crown prince, the emperor wanted very much to pass over his first son in favor of the younger, who, however, had no influential maternal relatives. It did not seem likely that the designation would pass unchallenged. The boy might, like his mother, be destroyed by immoderate favors. The emperor told no one of his wishes. There did after all seem to be a limit to his affections, people said; and Kokiden regained her confidence.

The boy's grandmother was inconsolable. Finally, because her prayer to be with her daughter had been answered, perhaps, she breathed her last. Once more the emperor was desolate. The boy, now six, was old enough to know grief himself. His grandmother, who had been so good to him over the years, had more than once told him what pain it would cause her, when the time came, to leave him behind.

He now lived at court. When he was seven he went through the ceremonial reading of the Chinese classics, and never before had there been so fine a performance. Again a tremor of apprehension passed over the emperor—might it be that such a prodigy was not to be long for this world?

"No one need be angry with him now that his mother is gone." He took the boy to visit the Kokiden Pavilion. "And now most especially I hope you will be kind to him."

Admitting the boy to her inner chambers, even Kokiden was pleased. Not the sternest of warriors or the most unbending of enemies could have held back a smile. Kokiden was reluctant to let him go. She had two daughters, but neither could compare with him in beauty. The lesser ladies crowded about, not in the least ashamed to show their faces, all eager to amuse him, though aware that he set them off to disadvantage. I need not speak of his accomplishments in the compulsory subjects, the classics and the like. When it came to music his flute and koto made the heavens echo—but to recount all his virtues would, I fear, give rise to a suspicion that I distort the truth.

8. Even here in the palace.

9. Referring to a poem by Ise on "The Song of Everlasting Sorrow": "The jeweled blinds are drawn, the morning is dark. / I had not thought I would not even dream."

An embassy came from Korea. Hearing that among the emissaries was a skilled physiognomist, the emperor would have liked to summon him for consultation. He decided, however, that he must defer to the emperor Uda's injunction against receiving foreigners, and instead sent this favored son to the Kōro mansion,[1] where the party was lodged. The boy was disguised as the son of the grand moderator, his guardian at court. The wise Korean cocked his head in astonishment.

"It is the face of one who should ascend to the highest place and be father to the nation," he said quietly, as if to himself. "But to take it for such would no doubt be to predict trouble. Yet it is not the face of the minister, the deputy, who sets about ordering public affairs."

The moderator was a man of considerable learning. There was much of interest in his exchanges with the Korean. There were also exchanges of Chinese poetry, and in one of his poems the Korean succeeded most skillfully in conveying his joy at having been able to observe such a countenance on this the eve of his return to his own land, and sorrow that the parting must come so soon. The boy offered a verse that was received with high praise. The most splendid of gifts were bestowed upon him. The wise man was in return showered with gifts from the palace.

Somehow news of the sage's remarks leaked out, though the emperor himself was careful to say nothing. The Minister of the Right, grandfather of the crown prince and father of the Kokiden lady, was quick to hear, and again his suspicions were aroused. In the wisdom of his heart, the emperor had already analyzed the boy's physiognomy after the Japanese fashion and had formed tentative plans. He had thus far refrained from bestowing imperial rank on his son, and was delighted that the Korean view should so accord with his own. Lacking the support of maternal relatives, the boy would be most insecure as a prince without court rank, and the emperor could not be sure how long his own reign would last. As a commoner he could be of great service. The emperor therefore encouraged the boy in his studies, at which he was so proficient that it seemed a waste to reduce him to common rank. And yet—as a prince he would arouse the hostility of those who had cause to fear his becoming emperor. Summoning an astrologer of the Indian school, the emperor was pleased to learn that the Indian view coincided with the Japanese and the Korean; and so he concluded that the boy should become a commoner with the name Minamoto or Genji.

The months and the years passed and still the emperor could not forget his lost love. He summoned various women who might console him, but apparently it was too much to ask in this world for one who even resembled her. He remained sunk in memories, unable to interest himself in anything. Then he was told of the Fourth Princess, daughter of a former emperor, a lady famous for her beauty and reared with the greatest care by her mother, the empress. A woman now in attendance upon the emperor had in the days of his predecessor been most friendly with the princess, then but a child, and even now saw her from time to time.

"I have been at court through three reigns now," she said, "and never had I seen anyone who genuinely resembled my lady. But now the daughter of the empress dowager is growing up, and the resemblance is most astonishing. One would be hard put to find her equal."

Hoping that she might just possibly be right, the emperor asked most courteously to have the princess sent to court. Her mother was reluctant and even fearful,

1. In the southern part of the city.

however. One must remember, she said, that the mother of the crown prince was a most willful lady who had subjected the Kiritsubo lady to open insults and presently sent her into a fatal decline. Before she had made up her mind she followed her husband in death, and the daughter was alone. The emperor renewed his petition. He said that he would treat the girl as one of his own daughters.

Her attendants and her maternal relatives and her older brother, Prince Hyōbu, consulted together and concluded that rather than languish at home she might seek consolation at court; and so she was sent off. She was called Fujitsubo. The resemblance to the dead lady was indeed astonishing. Because she was of such high birth (it may have been that people were imagining things) she seemed even more graceful and delicate than the other. No one could despise her for inferior rank, and the emperor need not feel shy about showing his love for her. The other lady had not particularly encouraged his attentions and had been the victim of a love too intense; and now, though it would be wrong to say that he had quite forgotten her, he found his affections shifting to the new lady, who was a source of boundless comfort. So it is with the affairs of this world.

Since Genji never left his father's side, it was not easy for this new lady, the recipient of so many visits, to hide herself from him. The other ladies were disinclined to think themselves her inferior, and indeed each of them had her own merits. They were all rather past their prime, however. Fujitsubo's beauty was of a younger and fresher sort. Though in her childlike shyness she made an especial effort not to be seen, Genji occasionally caught a glimpse of her face. He could not remember his own mother and it moved him deeply to learn, from the lady who had first told the emperor of Fujitsubo, that the resemblance was striking. He wanted to be near her always.

"Do not be unfriendly," said the emperor to Fujitsubo. "Sometimes it almost seems to me too that you are his mother. Do not think him forward, be kind to him. Your eyes, your expression: you are really so uncommonly like her that you could pass for his mother."

Genji's affection for the new lady grew, and the most ordinary flower or tinted leaf became the occasion for expressing it. Kokiden was not pleased. She was not on good terms with Fujitsubo, and all her old resentment of Genji came back. He was handsomer than the crown prince, her chief treasure in the world, well thought of by the whole court. People began calling Genji "the shining one." Fujitsubo, ranked beside him in the emperor's affections, became "the lady of the radiant sun."

It seemed a pity that the boy must one day leave behind his boyish attire; but when he reached the age of twelve he went through his initiation ceremonies and received the cap of an adult. Determined that the ceremony should be in no way inferior to the crown prince's, which had been held some years earlier in the Grand Hall, the emperor himself bustled about adding new details to the established forms. As for the banquet after the ceremony, he did not wish the custodians of the storehouses and granaries to treat it as an ordinary public occasion.

The throne faced east on the east porch, and before it were Genji's seat and that of the minister who was to bestow the official cap. At the appointed hour in mid-afternoon Genji appeared. The freshness of his face and his boyish coiffure were again such as to make the emperor regret that the change must take place. The ritual cutting of the boy's hair was performed by the secretary of the treasury. As the beautiful locks fell the emperor was seized with a hopeless longing for his dead lady. Repeatedly he found himself struggling to keep his composure. The ceremony over, the boy withdrew to change to adult trousers and descended into the courtyard for ceremonial thanksgiving. There was not a person in the assembly who did not feel his eyes misting over. The emperor was stirred by the deepest of emotions. He had on brief occasions been able to forget the past, and now it all came back again. Vaguely apprehensive lest the initiation of so young a boy bring a sudden aging, he was astonished to see that his son delighted him even more.

The Minister of the Left, who bestowed the official cap, had only one daughter, named Aoi, his chief joy in life. Her mother, the minister's first wife, was a princess of the blood. The crown prince had sought the girl's hand, but the minister thought rather of giving her to Genji. He had heard that the emperor had similar thoughts. When the emperor suggested that the boy was without adequate sponsors for his initiation and that the support of relatives by marriage might be called for, the minister quite agreed.

* * *

The nuptial observances were conducted with great solemnity. The groom seemed to the minister and his family quite charming in his boyishness. The bride was older, and somewhat ill at ease with such a young husband.

The minister had the emperor's complete confidence, and his principal wife, the girl's mother, was the emperor's sister. Both parents were therefore of the highest standing. And now they had Genji for a son-in-law. The Minister of the Right, who as grandfather of the crown prince should have been without rivals, was somehow eclipsed. The Minister of the Left had numerous children by several ladies. One of the sons, named Tō no Chūjō, a very handsome lad by his principal wife, was already a guards lieutenant. Relations between the two ministers were not good but the Minister of the Right found it difficult to ignore such a talented youth, to whom he offered the hand of his fourth and favorite daughter. His esteem for his new son-in-law rivaled the other minister's esteem for Genji. To both houses the new arrangements seemed ideal.

Constantly at his father's side, Genji spent little time at the Sanjō mansion of his bride. Fujitsubo was for him a vision of sublime beauty. If he could have someone like her—but in fact there was no one really like her. His bride too was beautiful, and she had had the advantage of every luxury; but he was not at all sure that they were meant for each other. The yearning in his young heart for the other lady was agony. Now that he had come of age, he no longer had his father's permission to go behind her curtains. On evenings when there was music, he would play the flute to her koto and so communicate something of his longing, and take some comfort from her voice, soft through the curtains. Life at court was for him much preferable to life at Sanjō. Two or three days at Sanjō would be followed by five or six days at court. For the minister, youth seemed sufficient excuse for this neglect. He continued to be delighted with his son-in-law.

The minister selected the handsomest and most accomplished of ladies to wait upon the young pair and planned the sort of diversions that were most likely to interest Genji. At the palace the emperor assigned him the apartments that had been his mother's and took care that her retinue was not dispersed. Orders were handed down to the offices of repairs and fittings to remodel the house that had belonged to the lady's family. The results were magnificent. The plantings and the artificial hills had always been remarkably tasteful, and the grounds now swarmed with workmen widening the lake. If only, thought Genji, he could have with him the lady he yearned for.

The sobriquet "the shining Genji," one hears, was bestowed upon him by the Korean.

from *Chapter 2. The Broom Tree*

"The shining Genji": it was almost too grand a name. Yet he did not escape criticism for numerous little adventures. It seemed indeed that his indiscretions might give him a name for frivolity, and he did what he could to hide them. But his most secret affairs (such is the malicious work of the gossips) became common talk. If, on the other hand, he were to go through life concerned only for his name and avoid all these interesting and amusing little affairs, then he would be laughed to shame by the likes of the lieutenant of Katano.[1]

Still a guards captain, Genji spent most of his time at the palace, going infrequently to the Sanjō mansion of his father-in-law. The people there feared that he might have been stained by the lavender of Kasugano.[2] Though in fact he had an instinctive dislike for the promiscuity he saw all around him, he had a way of sometimes turning against his own better inclinations and causing unhappiness.

The summer rains came, the court was in retreat, and an even longer interval than usual had passed since his last visit to Sanjō. Though the minister and his family were much put out, they spared no effort to make him feel welcome. The minister's sons were more attentive than to the emperor himself. Genji was on particularly good terms with Tō no Chūjō. They enjoyed music together and more frivolous diversions as well. Tō no Chūjō was of an amorous nature and not at all comfortable in the apartments which his father-in-law, the Minister of the Right, had at great expense provided for him. At Sanjō with his own family, on the other hand, he took very good care of his rooms, and when Genji came and went the two of them were always together. They were a good match for each other in study and at play. Reserve quite disappeared between them.

It had been raining all day. There were fewer courtiers than usual in the royal presence. Back in his own palace quarters, also unusually quiet, Genji pulled a lamp near and sought to while away the time with his books. He had Tō no Chūjō with him. Numerous pieces of colored paper, obviously letters, lay on a shelf. Tō no Chūjō made no attempt to hide his curiosity.

"Well," said Genji, "there are some I might let you see. But there are some I think it better not to."

"You miss the point. The ones I want to see are precisely the ones you want to hide. The ordinary ones—I'm not much of a hand at the game, you know, but even I am up to the ordinary give and take. But the ones from ladies who think you are not doing right by them, who sit alone through an evening and wait for you to come—those are the ones I want to see."

It was not likely that really delicate letters would be left scattered on a shelf, and it may be assumed that the papers treated so carelessly were the less important ones.

"You do have a variety of them," said Tō no Chūjō, reading the correspondence through piece by piece. This will be from her, and this will be from her, he would say. Sometimes he guessed correctly and sometimes he was far afield, to Genji's great amusement. Genji was brief with his replies and let out no secrets.

"It is I who should be asking to see your collection. No doubt it is huge. When I have seen it I shall be happy to throw my files open to you."

1. Evidently the hero of a romance that has been lost.

2. *Tales of Ise* 1: "Kasugano lavender stains my robe / in deep disorder, like my secret loves." Kasugano is on the outskirts of Nara. Here as elsewhere lavender (*murasaki*) suggests a romantic affinity.

"I fear there is nothing that would interest you." Tō no Chūjō was in a contemplative mood. "It is with women as it is with everything else: the flawless ones are very few indeed. This is a sad fact which I have learned over the years. All manner of women seem presentable enough at first. Little notes, replies to this and that, they all suggest sensibility and cultivation. But when you begin sorting out the really superior ones you find that there are not many who have to be on your list. Each has her little tricks and she makes the most of them, getting in her slights at rivals, so broad sometimes that you almost have to blush. Hidden away by loving parents who build brilliant futures for them, they let word get out of this little talent and that little accomplishment and you are all in a stir. They are young and pretty and amiable and carefree, and in their boredom they begin to pick up a little from their elders, and in the natural course of things they begin to concentrate on one particular hobby and make something of it. A woman tells you all about it and hides the weak points and brings out the strong ones as if they were everything, and you can't very well call her a liar. So you begin keeping company, and it is always the same. The fact is not up to the advance notices."

Tō no Chūjō sighed, a sigh clearly based on experience. Some of what he had said, though not all, accorded with Genji's own experience. "And have you come upon any," said Genji, smiling, "who would seem to have nothing at all to recommend them?"

"Who would be fool enough to notice such a woman? And in any case, I should imagine that women with no merits are as rare as women with no faults. If a woman is of good family and well taken care of, then the things she is less than proud of are hidden and she gets by well enough. When you come to the middle ranks, each woman has her own little inclinations and there are thousands of ways to separate one from another. And when you come to the lowest—well, who really pays much attention?"

He appeared to know everything. Genji was by now deeply interested.

"You speak of three ranks," he said, "but is it so easy to make the division? There are well-born ladies who fall in the world and there are people of no background who rise to the higher ranks and build themselves fine houses as if intended for them all along. How would you fit such people into your system?"

At this point two young courtiers, a guards officer and a functionary in the ministry of rites, appeared on the scene, to attend the emperor in his retreat. Both were devotees of the way of love and both were good talkers. Tō no Chūjō, as if he had been waiting for them, invited their views on the question that had just been asked. The discussion progressed, and included a number of rather unconvincing points.

"Those who have just arrived at high position," said one of the newcomers, "do not attract the same sort of notice as those who were born to it. And those who were born to the highest rank but somehow do not have the right backing—in spirit they may be as proud and noble as ever, but they cannot hide their deficiencies. And so I think that they should both be put in your middle rank.

"There are those whose families are not quite of the highest rank but who go off and work hard in the provinces. They have their place in the world, though there are all sorts of little differences among them. Some of them would belong on anyone's list. So it is these days. Myself, I would take a woman from a middling family over one who has rank and nothing else. Let us say someone whose father is almost but not quite a councilor. Someone who has a decent enough reputation and comes from a decent enough family and can live in some luxury. Such people can be very pleasant. There is nothing wrong with the household arrangements, and indeed a daughter can sometimes be set out in a way that dazzles you. I can think of several such women it would be hard to find fault with. When they go into court service, they are the ones the unexpected favors have a way of falling on. I have seen cases enough of it, I can tell you."

Genji smiled. "And so a person should limit himself to girls with money?"

"That does not sound like you," said Tō no Chūjō.

"When a woman has the highest rank and a spotless reputation," continued the other, "but something has gone wrong with her upbringing, something is wrong in the way she puts herself forward, you wonder how it can possibly have been allowed to happen. But when all the conditions are right and the girl herself is pretty enough, she is taken for granted. There is no cause for the least surprise. Such ladies are beyond the likes of me, and so I leave them where they are, the highest of the high. There are surprisingly pretty ladies wasting away behind tangles of weeds, and hardly anyone even knows of their existence. The first surprise is hard to forget. There she is, a girl with a fat, sloppy old father and boorish brothers and a house that seems common at best. Off in the women's rooms is a proud lady who has acquired bits and snatches of this and that. You get wind of them, however small the accomplishments may be, and they take hold of your imagination. She is not the equal of the one who has everything, of course, but she has her charm. She is not easy to pass by."

He looked at his companion, the young man from the ministry of rites. The latter was silent, wondering if the reference might be to his sisters, just then coming into their own as subjects for conversation. Genji, it would seem, was thinking that on the highest levels there were sadly few ladies to bestow much thought upon. He was wearing several soft white singlets with an informal court robe thrown loosely over them. As he sat in the lamplight leaning against an armrest, his companions almost wished that he were a woman. Even the "highest of the high" might seem an inadequate match for him.

[*Although Genji remains aloof from the discussion, the other young men continue trading notes about desirable and undesirable qualities in women they have known. Tō no Chūjō describes an affair he had with a reticent, undemanding woman (Yūgao) by whom he had a child, but who was eventually driven off by his principal wife. Throughout, Genji's thoughts remain on Fujitsubo, who seems to him without flaw.*]

from *Chapter 5. Lavender*

[*Genji falls ill and goes to the Northern Hills, where he is treated by a Sage and remains to recover.*]

The evening was long. Genji took advantage of a dense haze to have a look at the house behind the wattle fence. Sending back everyone except Koremitsu, he took up a position at the fence. In the west room sat a nun who had a holy image before her. The blinds were slightly raised and she seemed to be offering flowers. She was leaning against a pillar and had a text spread out on an armrest. The effort to read seemed to take all her strength. Perhaps in her forties, she had a fair, delicate skin and a pleasantly full face, though the effects of illness were apparent. The features suggested breeding and cultivation. Cut cleanly at the shoulders, her hair seemed to him far more pleasing than if it had been permitted to trail the usual length. Beside her were two attractive women, and little girls scampered in and out. Much the prettiest was a girl of perhaps ten in a soft white singlet and a russet robe. She would one day be a real beauty. Rich hair spread over her shoulders like a fan. Her face was flushed from weeping.

"What is it?" The nun looked up. "Another fight?" He thought he saw a resemblance. Perhaps they were mother and daughter.

"Inuki let my baby sparrows loose." The child was very angry. "I had them in a basket."

"That stupid child," said a rather handsome woman with rich hair who seemed to be called Shōnagon and was apparently the girl's nurse. "She always manages to do the wrong thing, and we are forever scolding her. Where will they have flown off to? They were getting to be such sweet little things too! How awful if the crows find them." She went out.

"What a silly child you are, really too silly," said the nun. "I can't be sure I will last out the day, and here you are worrying about sparrows. I've told you so many times that it's a sin to put birds in a cage. Come here."

The child knelt down beside her. She was charming, with rich, unplucked eyebrows and hair pushed childishly back from the forehead. How he would like to see her in a few years! And a sudden realization brought him close to tears: the resemblance to Fujitsubo, for whom he so yearned, was astonishing.

The nun stroked the girl's hair. "You will not comb it and still it's so pretty. I worry about you, you do seem so very young. Others are much more grown up at your age. Your poor dead mother: she was only ten when her father died, and she understood everything. What will become of you when I am gone?"

She was weeping, and a vague sadness had come over Genji too. The girl gazed attentively at her and then looked down. The hair that fell over her forehead was thick and lustrous.

> "Are these tender grasses to grow without the dew
> which holds itself back from the heavens that would receive it?"

There were tears in the nun's voice, and the other woman seemed also to be speaking through tears:

> "It cannot be that the dew will vanish away
> ere summer comes to these early grasses of spring."

The bishop came in. "What is this? Your blinds up? And today of all days you are out on the veranda? I have just been told that General Genji is up at the hermitage being treated for malaria. He came in disguise and I was not told in time to pay a call."

"And what a sight we are. You don't suppose he saw us?" She lowered the blinds.

"The shining one of whom the whole world talks. Wouldn't you like to see him? Enough to make a saint throw off the last traces of the vulgar world, they say, and feel as if new years had been added to his life. I will get off a note."

He hurried away, and Genji too withdrew. What a discovery! It was for such unforeseen rewards that his amorous followers were so constantly on the prowl. Such a rare outing for him, and it had brought such a find! She was a perfectly beautiful child. Who might she be? He was beginning to make plans: the child must stand in the place of the one whom she so resembled.

[*After Genji has retired to his quarters, the bishop, the brother of Murasaki's grandmother, arrives and invites him to pay a visit.*]

The bishop talked of this ephemeral world and of the world to come. His own burden of sin was heavy, thought Genji, that he had been lured into an illicit and profitless affair. He would regret it all his life and suffer even more terribly in the life to come. What joy to withdraw to such a place as this! But with the thought came thoughts of the young face he had seen earlier in the evening.

"Do you have someone with you here? I had a dream that suddenly begins to make sense."

"How quick you are with your dreams, sir! I fear my answer will disappoint you. It has been a very long time since the Lord Inspector died. I don't suppose you will even have heard of him. He was my brother-in-law. His widow turned her back on the world and recently she has been ill, and since I do not go down to the city she has come to stay with me here. It was her thought that I might be able to help her."

"I have heard that your sister had a daughter. I ask from no more than idle curiosity, you must believe me."

"There was an only daughter. She too has been dead these ten years and more. He took very great pains with her education and hoped to send her to court; but he died before that ambition could be realized, and the nun, my sister, was left to look after her. I do not know through whose offices it was that Prince Hyōbu began visiting the daughter in secret. His wife is from a very proud family, you know, sir, and there were unpleasant incidents, which finally drove the poor thing into a fatal decline. I saw before my own eyes how worry can destroy a person."

So the child he had seen would be the daughter of Prince Hyōbu and the unfortunate lady; and it was Fujitsubo, the prince's sister, whom she so resembled. He wanted more than ever to meet her. She was an elegant child, and she did not seem at all spoiled. What a delight if he could take her into his house and make her his ideal!

"A very sad story." He wished to be completely sure. "Did she leave no one behind?"

"She had a child just before she died, a girl, a great source of worry for my poor sister in her declining years."

There could be no further doubt. "What I am about to say will, I fear, startle you—but might I have charge of the child? I have rather good reasons, for all the suddenness of my proposal. If you are telling yourself that she is too young—well, sir, you are doing me an injustice. Other men may have improper motives, but I do not."

"Your words quite fill me with delight. But she is indeed young, so very young that we could not possibly think even in jest of asking you to take responsibility for her. Only the man who is presently to be her husband can take that responsibility. In a matter of such import I am not competent to give an answer. I must discuss the matter with my sister." He was suddenly remote and chilly.

Genji had spoken with youthful impulsiveness and could not think what to do next.

[*Genji spends the night at the bishop's and engages in an exchange of poetry with the nun, making his interest in the girl known, much to the consternation of the nun and the attendants. The bishop and the nun agree that Genji's proposal is rather precipitate, and suggest that he wait until the girl grows up. Genji returns to the city and grudgingly accedes to his father-in-law's request that he spend some time at Sanjō to continue his recuperation.*]

At the minister's Sanjō mansion everything was in readiness. It had been polished and refitted until it was a jeweled pavilion, perfect to the last detail. As always,

Genji's wife Aoi secluded herself in her private apartments, and it was only at her father's urging that she came forth; and so Genji had her before him, immobile, like a princess in an illustration for a romance. It would have been a great pleasure, he was sure, to have her comment even tartly upon his account of the mountain journey. She seemed the stiffest, remotest person in the world. How odd that the aloofness seemed only to grow as time went by.

"It would be nice, I sometimes think, if you could be a little more wifely. I have been very ill, and I am hurt, but not really surprised, that you have not inquired after my health."

"Like the pain, perhaps, of awaiting a visitor who does not come?"

She cast a sidelong glance at him as she spoke, and her cold beauty was very intimidating indeed.

"You so rarely speak to me, and when you do you say such unpleasant things. 'A visitor who does not come'—that is hardly an appropriate way to describe a husband, and indeed it is hardly civil. I try this approach and I try that, hoping to break through, but you seem intent on defending all the approaches. Well, one of these years, perhaps, if I live long enough."

He withdrew to the bedchamber. She did not follow. Though there were things he would have liked to say, he lay down with a sigh. He closed his eyes, but there was too much on his mind to permit sleep.

He thought of the little girl and how he would like to see her grown into a woman. Her grandmother was of course right when she said that the girl was still too young for him. He must not seem insistent. And yet—was there not some way to bring her quietly to Nijō and have her beside him, a comfort and a companion? Prince Hyōbu was a dashing and stylish man, but no one could have called him remarkably handsome. Why did the girl so take after her aunt? Perhaps because aunt and father were children of the same empress. These thoughts seemed to bring the girl closer, and he longed to have her for his own.

* * *

Fujitsubo was ill and had gone home to her family. Genji managed a sympathetic thought or two for his lonely father, but his thoughts were chiefly on the possibility of seeing Fujitsubo. He quite halted his visits to other ladies. All through the day, at home and at court, he sat gazing off into space, and in the evening he would press Omyōbu to be his intermediary. How she did it I do not know; but she contrived a meeting. It is sad to have to say that his earlier attentions, so unwelcome, no longer seemed real, and the mere thought that they had been successful was for Fujitsubo a torment. Determined that there would not be another meeting, she was shocked to find him in her presence again. She did not seek to hide her distress, and her efforts to turn him away delighted him even as they put him to shame. There was no one else quite like her. In that fact was his undoing: he would be less a prey to longing if he could find in her even a trace of the ordinary. And the tumult of thoughts and feelings that now assailed him—he would have liked to consign it to the Mountain of Obscurity.[1] It might have been better, he sighed, so short was the night, if he had not come at all.

> "So few and scattered the nights, so few the dreams,
> Would that the dream tonight might take me with it."

1. Kurabunoyama, thought to have been in present-day Kyoto.

He was in tears, and she did, after all, have to feel sorry for him.

"Were I to disappear in the last of dreams
Would yet my name live on in infamy?"

She had every right to be unhappy, and he was sad for her. Omyōbu gathered his clothes and brought them out to him.

Back at Nijō he spent a tearful day in bed. He had word from Omyōbu that her lady had not read his letter. So it always was, and yet he was hurt. He remained in distraught seclusion for several days. The thought that his father might be wondering about his absence filled him with terror.

Lamenting the burden of sin that seemed to be hers, Fujitsubo was more and more unwell, and could not bestir herself, despite repeated messages summoning her back to court. She was not at all her usual self—and what was to become of her? She took to her bed as the weather turned warmer. Three months had now passed and her condition was clear; and the burden of sin now seemed to have made it necessary that she submit to curious and reproving stares. Her women thought her behavior very curious indeed. Why had she let so much time pass without informing the emperor? There was of course a crucial matter of which she spoke to no one. Ben, the daughter of her old nurse, and Omyōbu, both of whom were very close to her and attended her in the bath, had ample opportunity to observe her condition. Omyōbu was aghast. Her lady had been trapped by the harshest of fates. The emperor would seem to have been informed that a malign spirit had possession of her, and to have believed the story, as did the court in general. He sent a constant stream of messengers, which terrified her and allowed no pause in her sufferings.

Genji had a strange, rather awful dream. He consulted a soothsayer, who said that it portended events so extraordinary as to be almost unthinkable.

"It contains bad omens as well. You must be careful."

"It was not my own dream but a friend's. We will see whether it comes true, and in the meantime you must keep it to yourself."

What could it mean? He heard of Fujitsubo's condition, thought of their night together, and wondered whether the two might be related. He exhausted his stock of pleas for another meeting. Horrified that matters were so out of hand, Omyōbu could do nothing for him. He had on rare occasions had a brief note, no more than a line or two, but now even these messages ceased coming.

Fujitsubo returned to court in the Seventh Month. The emperor's affection for her had only grown in her absence. Her condition was now apparent to everyone. A slight emaciation made her beauty seem if anything nearer perfection, and the emperor kept her always at his side. The skies as autumn approached called more insistently for music. Keeping Genji too beside him, the emperor had him try his hand at this and that instrument. Genji struggled to control himself, but now and then a sign of his scarcely bearable feelings did show through, to remind the lady of what she wanted more than anything to forget. * * *

In the autumn evening, his thoughts on his unattainable love, he longed more than ever, unnatural though the wish may have seemed, for the company of the little girl who sprang from the same roots. The thought of the evening when the old nun had described herself as dew holding back from the heavens made him even more impatient—and at the same time he feared that if he were to bring the girl to Nijō he would be disappointed in her.

I long to have it, to bring it in from the moor,
The lavender[2] that shares its roots with another.

In the Tenth Month the emperor was to visit the Suzaku Palace. From all the great families and the middle and upper courtly ranks the most accomplished musicians and dancers were selected to go with him, and grandees and princes of the blood were busy at the practice that best suited their talents. Caught up in the excitement, Genji was somewhat remiss in inquiring after the nun.

When, finally, he sent off a messenger to the northern hills, a sad reply came from the bishop: "We lost her toward the end of last month. It is the way of the world, I know, and yet I am sad."

If the news shocked even him into a new awareness of evanescence, thought Genji, how must it be for the little girl who had so occupied the nun's thoughts? Young though she was, she must feel utterly lost. He remembered, though dimly, how it had been when his mother died, and he sent off an earnest letter of sympathy. Shōnagon's answer seemed rather warmer. He went calling on an evening when he had nothing else to occupy him, some days after he learned that the girl had come out of mourning and returned to the city. The house was badly kept and almost deserted. The poor child must be terrified, he thought. He was shown to the same room as before. Sobbing, Shōnagon told him of the old lady's last days. Genji too was in tears.

"My young lady's father would seem to have indicated a willingness to take her in, but she is at such an uncomfortable age, not quite a child and still without the discernment of an adult; and the thought of having her in the custody of the lady who was so cruel to her mother is too awful. Her sisters will persecute her dreadfully, I know. The fear of it never left my lady's mind, and we have had too much evidence that the fear was not groundless. We have been grateful for your expressions of interest, though we have hesitated to take them seriously. I must emphasize that my young lady is not at all what you must think her to be. I fear that we have done badly by her, and that our methods have left her childish even for her years."

"Must you continue to be so reticent and apologetic? I have made my own feelings clear, over and over again. It is precisely the childlike quality that delights me most and makes me think I must have her for my own. You may think me complacent and self-satisfied for saying so, but I feel sure that we were joined in a former life. Let me speak to her, please.

Rushes hide the sea grass at Wakanoura.
Must the waves that seek it out turn back to sea?

"That would be too much to ask of her."

"The grass at Wakanoura were rash indeed
To follow waves that go it knows not whither.

"It would be far, far too much to ask."

2. *Murasaki*, a millet from the roots of which a lavender dye is extracted. Lavender, in general the color of affinity or intimacy, suggests more specifically the *fuji* of Fujitsubo, "Wisteria Court." It is because of this poem that the girl is presently to be called Murasaki. The name Murasaki Shikibu also derives from it.

The easy skill with which she turned her poem made it possible for him to forgive its less than encouraging significance. "After so many years," he whispered, "the gate still holds me back."[3]

The girl lay weeping for her grandmother. Her playmates came to tell her that a gentleman in court dress was with Shōnagon. Perhaps it would be her father?

She came running in. "Where is the gentleman, Shōnagon? Is Father here?"

What a sweet voice she had!

"I'm not your father, but I'm someone just as important. Come here."

She saw that it was the other gentleman, and child though she was, she flushed at having spoken out of turn. "Let's go." She tugged at Shōnagon's sleeve. "Let's go. I'm sleepy."

"Do you have to keep hiding yourself from me? Come here. You can sleep on my knee."

"She is really very young, sir." But Shōnagon urged the child forward, and she knelt obediently just inside the blinds.

He ran his hand over a soft, rumpled robe, and, a delight to the touch, hair full and rich to its farthest ends. He took her hand. She pulled away—for he was, after all, a stranger.

"I said I'm sleepy." She went back to Shōnagon.

He slipped in after her. "I am the one you must look to now. You must not be shy with me."

"Please, sir. You forget yourself. You forget yourself completely. She is simply not old enough to understand what you have in mind."

"It is you who do not understand. I see how young she is, and I have nothing of the sort in mind. I must again ask you to be witness to the depth and purity of my feelings."

It was a stormy night. Sleet was pounding against the roof.

"How can she bear to live in such a lonely place? It must be awful for her." Tears came to his eyes. He could not leave her. "I will be your watchman. You need one on a night like this. Come close to me, all of you."

Quite as if he belonged there, he slipped into the girl's bedroom. The women were astounded, Shōnagon more than the rest. He must be mad! But she was in no position to protest. Genji pulled a singlet over the girl, who was trembling like a leaf. Yes, he had to admit that his behavior must seem odd; but, trying very hard not to frighten her, he talked of things he thought would interest her.

"You must come to my house. I have all sorts of pictures, and there are dolls for you to play with."

She was less frightened than at first, but she still could not sleep. The storm blew all through the night, and Shōnagon quite refused to budge from their side. They would surely have perished of fright, whispered the women, if they had not had him with them. What a pity their lady was not a little older!

It was still dark when the wind began to subside and he made his departure, and all the appearances were as of an amorous expedition. "What I have seen makes me very sad and convinces me that she must not be out of my sight. She must come and live with me and share my lonely days. This place is quite impossible. You must be in constant terror."

3. Fujiwara Koretada, *Gosenshū* 732: "Alone, in secret, I hurry to Meeting Hill. / After so many years, the gate still holds me back."

"Her father has said that he will come for her. I believe it is to be after the memorial services."

"Yes, we must think of him. But they have lived apart, and he must be as much of a stranger as I am. I really do believe that in this very short time my feelings for her are stronger than his." He patted the girl on the head and looked back smiling as he left.

[*Genji decides to retrieve the young Murasaki before her father, Prince Hyōbu, comes to pick her up.*]

He went into her bedroom, where the women were too surprised to cry out. He took her in his arms and smoothed her hair. Her father had come for her, she thought, only half awake.

"Let's go. I have come from your father's." She was terrified when she saw that it was not after all her father. "You are not being nice. I have told you that you must think of me as your father." And he carried her out.

A chorus of protests now came from Shōnagon and the others.

"I have explained things quite well enough. I have told you how difficult it is for me to visit her and how I want to have her in a more comfortable and accessible spot; and your way of making things easier is to send her off to her father. One of you may come along, if you wish."

"Please, sir." Shōnagon was wringing her hands. "You could not have chosen a worse time. What are we to say when her father comes? If it is her fate to be your lady, then perhaps something can be done when the time comes. This is too sudden, and you put us in an extremely difficult position."

"You can come later if you wish."

His carriage had been brought up. The women were fluttering about helplessly and the child was sobbing. Seeing at last that there was nothing else to be done, Shōnagon took up several of the robes they had been at work on the night before, changed to presentable clothes of her own, and got into the carriage.

It was still dark when they reached Nijō, only a short distance away. Genji ordered the carriage brought up to the west wing and took the girl inside.

"It is like a nightmare," said Shōnagon. "What am I to do?"

"Whatever you like. I can have someone see you home if you wish."

Weeping helplessly, poor Shōnagon got out of the carriage. What would her lady's father think when he came for her? And what did they now have to look forward to? The saddest thing was to be left behind by one's protectors. But tears did not augur well for the new life. With an effort she pulled herself together.

Since no one was living in this west wing, there was no curtained bedchamber. Genji had Koremitsu put up screens and curtains, sent someone else to the east wing for bedding, and lay down. Though trembling violently, the girl managed to keep from sobbing aloud.

"I always sleep with Shōnagon," she said softly in childish accents.

"Imagine a big girl like you still sleeping with her nurse."

Weeping quietly, the girl lay down.

Shōnagon sat up beside them, looking out over the garden as dawn came on. The buildings and grounds were magnificent, and the sand in the garden was like jewels. Not used to such affluence, she was glad there were no other women in this west wing. It was here that Genji received occasional callers. A few guards beyond the blinds were the only attendants.

They were speculating on the identity of the lady he had brought with him. "Someone worth looking at, you can bet."

Water pitchers and breakfast were brought in. The sun was high when Genji arose. "You will need someone to take care of you. Suppose you send this evening for the ones you like best." He asked that children be sent from the east wing to play with her. "Pretty little girls, please." Four little girls came in, very pretty indeed.

The new girl, his Murasaki, still lay huddled under the singlet he had thrown over her.

"You are not to sulk, now, and make me unhappy. Would I have done all this for you if I were not a nice man? Young ladies should do as they are told." And so the lessons began.

She seemed even prettier here beside him than from afar. His manner warm and fatherly, he sought to amuse her with pictures and toys he had sent for from the east wing. Finally she came over to him. Her dark mourning robes were soft and unstarched, and when she smiled, innocently and unprotestingly, he had to smile back. She went out to look at the trees and pond after he had departed for the east wing. The flowers in the foreground, delicately touched by frost, were like a picture. Streams of courtiers, of the medium ranks and new to her experience, passed back and forth. Yes, it was an interesting place. She looked at the pictures on screens and elsewhere and (so it is with a child) soon forgot her troubles. * * *

Presently Murasaki had all her women with her. She was a bright, lively child, and the boys and girls who were to be her playmates felt quite at home with her. Sometimes on lonely nights when Genji was away she would weep for her grandmother. She thought little of her father. They had lived apart and she scarcely knew him. She was by now extremely fond of her new father. She would be the first to run out and greet him when he came home, and she would climb on his lap, and they would talk happily together, without the least constraint or embarrassment. He was delighted with her. A clever and watchful woman can create all manner of difficulties. A man must be always on his guard, and jealousy can have the most unwelcome consequences. Murasaki was the perfect companion, a toy for him to play with. He could not have been so free and uninhibited with a daughter of his own. There are restraints upon paternal intimacy. Yes, he had come upon a remarkable little treasure.

from *Chapter 7. An Autumn Excursion*

Fujitsubo had gone home to her family. Looking restlessly, as always, for a chance to see her, Genji was much criticized by his father-in-law's people at Sanjō. And rumors of the young Murasaki were out. Certain of the women at Sanjō let it be known that a new lady had been taken in at Nijō. Genji's wife was intensely displeased. It was most natural that she should be, for she did not of course know that the "lady" was a mere child. If she had complained to him openly, as most women would have done, he might have told her everything, and no doubt eased her jealousy. It was her arbitrary judgments that sent him wandering. She had no specific faults, no vices or blemishes, which he could point to. She had been the first lady in his life, and in an abstract way he admired and treasured her. Her feelings would change, he felt sure, once she was more familiar with his own. She was a perceptive woman, and the change was certain to come. She still occupied first place among his ladies.

Murasaki was by now thoroughly comfortable with him. She was maturing in appearance and manner, and yet there was artlessness in her way of clinging to him.

Thinking it too early to let the people in the main hall know who she was, he kept her in one of the outer wings, which he had had fitted to perfection. He was constantly with her, tutoring her in the polite accomplishments and especially calligraphy. It was as if he had brought home a daughter who had spent her early years in another house. He had studied the qualifications of her stewards and assured himself that she would have everything she needed. Everyone in the house, save only Koremitsu, was consumed with curiosity. Her father still did not know of her whereabouts. Sometimes she would weep for her grandmother. Her mind was full of other things when Genji was with her, and often he stayed the night; but he had numerous other places to look in upon, and he was quite charmed by the wistfulness with which she would see him off in the evening. Sometimes he would spend two and three days at the palace and go from there to Sanjō. Finding a pensive Murasaki upon his return, he would feel as if he had taken in a little orphan. He no longer looked forward to his nocturnal wanderings with the same eagerness. Her granduncle the bishop kept himself informed of her affairs, and was pleased and puzzled. Genji sent most lavish offerings for memorial services.

Longing for news of Fujitsubo, still with her family, he paid a visit. Omyōbu, Chūnagon, Nakatsukasa, and others of her women received him, but the lady whom he really wanted to see kept him at a distance. He forced himself to make conversation. Prince Hyōbu, her brother and Murasaki's father, came in, having heard that Genji was on the premises. He was a man of great and gentle elegance, someone, thought Genji, who would interest him enormously were they of opposite sexes. Genji felt very near this prince so near the two ladies, and to the prince their conversation seemed friendly and somehow significant as earlier conversations had not. How very handsome Genji was! Not dreaming that it was a prospective son-in-law he was addressing, he too was thinking how susceptible (for he was a susceptible man) he would be to Genji's charms if they were not of the same sex.

When, at dusk, the prince withdrew behind the blinds, Genji felt pangs of jealousy. In the old years he had followed his father behind those same blinds, and there addressed the lady. Now she was far away—though of course no one had wronged him, and he had no right to complain.

"I have not been good about visiting you," he said stiffly as he got up to leave. "Having no business with you, I have not wished to seem forward. It would give me great pleasure if you would let me know of any services I might perform for you."

Omyōbu could do nothing for him. Fujitsubo seemed to find his presence even more of a trial than before, and showed no sign of relenting. Sadly and uselessly the days went by. What a frail, fleeting union theirs had been!

Shōnagon, Murasaki's nurse, continued to marvel at the strange course their lives had taken. Perhaps some benign power had arranged it, the old nun having mentioned Murasaki in all her prayers. Not that everything was perfect. Genji's wife at Sanjō was a lady of the highest station, and other affairs, indeed too many of them, occupied him as well. Might not the girl face difficult times as she grew into womanhood? Yet he did seem fond of her as of none of the others, and her future seemed secure. The period of mourning for a maternal grandmother being set at three months, it was on New Year's Eve that Murasaki took off her mourning weeds. The old lady had been for her both mother and grandmother, however, and so she chose to limit herself to pale, unfigured pinks and lavenders and yellows. Pale colors seemed to suit her even better than rich ones.

"And do you feel all grown up, now that a new year has come?" Smiling, radiating youthful charm, Genji looked in upon her. He was on his way to the morning festivities at court.

She had already taken out her dolls and was busy seeing to their needs. All manner of furnishings and accessories were laid out on a yard-high shelf. Dollhouses threatened to overflow the room.

"Inuki knocked everything over chasing out devils last night and broke this." It was a serious matter. "I'm gluing it."

"Yes, she really is very clumsy, that Inuki. We'll ask someone to repair it for you. But today you must not cry. Crying is the worst way to begin a new year."

And he went out, his retinue so grand that it overflowed the wide grounds. The women watched from the veranda, the girl with them. She set out a Genji among her dolls and saw him off to court.

"This year you must try to be just a little more grown up," said Shōnagon. "Ten years old, no, even more, and still you play with dolls. It will not do. You have a nice husband, and you must try to calm down and be a little more wifely. Why, you fly into a tantrum even when we try to brush your hair." A proper shaming was among Shōnagon's methods.

So she had herself a nice husband, thought Murasaki. The husbands of these women were none of them handsome men, and hers was so very young and handsome. The thought came to her now for the first time, evidence that, for all this play with dolls, she was growing up. It sometimes puzzled her women that she should still be such a child. It did not occur to them that she was in fact not yet a wife.

From the palace Genji went to Sanjō. His wife, as always, showed no suggestion of warmth or affection; and as always he was uncomfortable.

"How pleasant if this year you could manage to be a little friendlier."

But since she had heard of his new lady she had become more distant than ever. She was convinced that the other was now first among his ladies, and no doubt she was as uncomfortable as he. But when he jokingly sought to make it seem that nothing was amiss, she had to answer, if reluctantly. Everything she said was uniquely, indefinably elegant. She was four years his senior and made him feel like a stripling. Where, he asked, was he to find a flaw in this perfection? Yet he seemed determined to anger her with his other affairs. She was a proud lady, the single and treasured daughter, by a princess, of a minister who overshadowed the other grandees, and she was not prepared to tolerate the smallest discourtesy. And here he was behaving as if these proud ways were his to make over. They were completely at cross purposes, he and she.

* * *

Genji did not pay many New Year calls. He called upon his father, the crown prince, the old emperor,[1] and, finally, Fujitsubo, still with her family. Her women thought him handsomer than ever. Yes, each year, as he matured, his good looks produced a stronger shudder of delight and foreboding. Fujitsubo was assailed by innumerable conflicting thoughts.

The Twelfth Month, when she was to have been delivered of her child, had passed uneventfully. Surely it would be this month, said her women, and at court everything was in readiness; but the First Month too passed without event. She was greatly troubled by rumors that she had fallen under a malign influence. Her worries had made her

1. Perhaps the father of the reigning emperor, he is mentioned nowhere else. The reign of the present emperor seems to have been preceded by that of Fujitsubo's father, now dead.

physically ill and she began to wonder if the end was in sight. More and more certain as time passed that the child was his, Genji quietly commissioned services in various temples. More keenly aware than most of the evanescence of things, he now found added to his worries a fear that he would not see her again. Finally toward the end of the Second Month she bore a prince, and the jubilation was unbounded at court and at her family palace. She had not joined the emperor in praying that she be granted a long life, and yet she did not want to please Kokiden, an echo of whose curses had reached her. The will to live returned, and little by little she recovered.

The emperor wanted to see his little son the earliest day possible. Genji, filled with his own secret paternal solicitude, visited Fujitsubo at a time when he judged she would not have other visitors.

"Father is extremely anxious to see the child. Perhaps I might have a look at him first and present a report."

She refused his request, as of course she had every right to do. "He is still very shriveled and ugly."

There was no doubt that the child bore a marked, indeed a rather wonderful, resemblance to Genji. Fujitsubo was tormented by feelings of guilt and apprehension. Surely everyone who saw the child would guess the awful truth and damn her for it. People were always happy to seek out the smallest and most trivial of misdeeds. Hers had not been trivial, and dreadful rumors must surely be going the rounds. Had ever a woman been more sorely tried?

Genji occasionally saw Omyōbu and pleaded that she intercede for him; but there was nothing she could do.

"This insistence, my lord, is very trying," she said, at his constant and passionate pleas to see the child. "You will have chances enough later." Yet secretly she was as unhappy as he was.

"In what world, I wonder, will I again be allowed to see her?" The heart of the matter was too delicate to touch upon.

> "What legacy do we bring from former lives that
> Loneliness should be our lot in this one?"

"I do not understand. I do not understand at all."

His tears brought her to the point of tears herself. Knowing how unhappy her lady was, she could not bring herself to turn him brusquely away.

> "Sad at seeing the child, sad at not seeing.
> The heart of the father, the mother, lost in darkness."[2]

And she added softly: "There seems to be no lessening of the pain for either of you."

She saw him off, quite unable to help him. Her lady had said that because of the danger of gossip she could not receive him again, and she no longer behaved toward Omyōbu with the old affection. She behaved correctly, it was true, and did nothing that might attract attention, but Omyōbu had done things to displease her. Omyōbu was very sorry for them.

In the Fourth Month the little prince was brought to the palace. Advanced for his age both mentally and physically, he was already able to sit up and to right himself when he rolled over. He was strikingly like Genji. Unaware of the truth, the emperor

2. Fujiwara Kanesuke, *Gosenshū* 1103: "The heart of a parent is not darkness, / and yet he wanders lost in thoughts upon his child."

would say to himself that people of remarkable good looks did have a way of looking alike. He doted upon the child. He had similarly doted upon Genji, but, because of strong opposition—and how deeply he regretted the fact—had been unable to make him crown prince. The regret increased as Genji, now a commoner, improved in looks and in accomplishments. And now a lady of the highest birth had borne the emperor another radiant son. The infant was for him an unflawed jewel, for Fujitsubo a source of boundless guilt and foreboding.

One day, as he often did, Genji was enjoying music in Fujitsubo's apartments. The emperor came out with the little boy in his arms.

"I have had many sons, but you were the only one I paid a great deal of attention to when you were this small. Perhaps it is the memory of those days that makes me think he looks like you. Is it that all children look alike when they are very young?" He made no attempt to hide his pleasure in the child.

Genji felt himself flushing crimson. He was frightened and awed and pleased and touched, all at the same time, and there were tears in his eyes. Laughing and babbling, the child was so beautiful as to arouse fears that he would not be long in this world. If indeed he resembled the child, thought Genji, then he must be very handsome. He must take better care of himself. (He seemed a little self-satisfied at times.) Fujitsubo was in such acute discomfort that she felt herself breaking into a cold sweat. Eager though he had been to see the child, Genji left in great agitation.

[*In "The Festival of the Cherry Blossoms," the next chapter, Genji has his first encounter with Oborozukiyo, the daughter of the powerful Minister of the Right and sister of the Kokiden lady, who is slated to become the consort of the crown prince (the future Suzaku emperor). "Heartvine," the following chapter, opens with a change of guard: Genji's father, the Kiritsubo emperor, has abdicated, bringing to the throne the Suzaku emperor, son of the Kokiden lady and the Minister of the Right. Fujitsubo's son (and secretly that of Genji), the future Reizei emperor, is made the heir apparent.*]

from *Chapter 9. Heartvine*

With the new reign Genji's career languished, and since he must be the more discreet about his romantic adventures as he rose in rank, he had less to amuse him. Everywhere there were complaints about his aloofness.

As if to punish him, there was one lady who continued to cause him pain with her own aloofness. Fujitsubo saw more of the old emperor, now abdicated, than ever. She was always at his side, almost as if she were a common housewife. Annoyed at this state of affairs, Kokiden did not follow the old emperor when he left the main palace. Fujitsubo was happy and secure. The concerts in the old emperor's palace attracted the attention of the whole court, and altogether life was happier for the two of them than while he had reigned. Only one thing was lacking: he greatly missed the crown prince, Fujitsubo's son, and worried that he had no strong backers. Genji, he said, must be the boy's adviser and guardian. Genji was both pleased and embarrassed.

And there was the matter of the lady at Rokujō. With the change of reigns, her daughter, who was also the daughter of the late crown prince, had been appointed high priestess of the Ise Shrine. No longer trusting Genji's affections, the Rokujō lady had been thinking that, making the girl's youth her excuse, she too would go to Ise.

The old emperor heard of her plans. "The crown prince was so very fond of her," he said to Genji, in open displeasure. "It is sad that you should have made light of her, as if she were any ordinary woman. I think of the high priestess as one of my own children, and you should be good to her mother, for my sake and for the sake of the dead prince. It does you no good to abandon yourself to these affairs quite as the impulse takes you."

It was perfectly true, thought Genji. He waited in silence.

"You should treat any woman with tact and courtesy, and be sure that you cause her no embarrassment. You should never have a woman angry with you."

What would his father think if he were to learn of Genji's worst indiscretion? The thought made Genji shudder. He bowed and withdrew.

The matter his father had thus reproved him for did no good for either of them, the woman or Genji himself. It was a scandal, and very sad for her. She continued to be very much on his mind, and yet he had no thought of making her his wife. She had grown cool toward him, worried about the difference in their ages. He made it seem that it was because of her wishes that he stayed away. Now that the old emperor knew of the affair the whole court knew of it. In spite of everything, the lady went on grieving that he had not loved her better. * * *

At Sanjō, his wife and her family were even unhappier about his infidelities, but, perhaps because he did not lie to them, they for the most part kept their displeasure to themselves. His wife was with child and in considerable distress mentally and physically. For Genji it was a strange and moving time. Everyone was delighted and at the same time filled with apprehension, and all manner of retreats and abstinences were prescribed for the lady. Genji had little time to himself. While he had no particular wish to avoid the Rokujō lady and the others, he rarely visited them.

At about this time the high priestess of Kamo resigned. She was replaced by the old emperor's third daughter, whose mother was Kokiden. The new priestess was a favorite of both her brother, the new emperor, and her mother, and it seemed a great pity that she should be shut off from court life; but no other princess was qualified for the position. The installation ceremonies, in the austere Shinto tradition, were of great dignity and solemnity. Many novel details were added to the Kamo festival in the Fourth Month, so that it was certain to be the finest of the season. Though the number of high courtiers attending the princess at the lustration was limited by precedent, great care was taken to choose handsome men of good repute. Similar care was given to their uniforms and to the uniform trappings of their horses. Genji was among the attendants, by special command of the new emperor. Courtiers and ladies had readied their carriage far in advance, and Ichijō was a frightening crush, without space for another vehicle. The stands along the way had been appointed most elaborately. The sleeves that showed beneath the curtains fulfilled in their brightness and variety all the festive promise.

Genji's wife seldom went forth on sightseeing expeditions and her pregnancy was another reason for staying at home.

But her young women protested. "Really, my lady, it won't be much fun sneaking off by ourselves. Why, even complete strangers—why, all the country folk have come in to see our lord! They've brought their wives and families from the farthest provinces. It will be too much if you make us stay away."

Her mother, Princess Omiya, agreed. "You seem to be feeling well enough, my dear, and they will be very disappointed if you don't take them."

And so carriages were hastily and unostentatiously decked out, and the sun was already high when they set forth. The waysides were by now too crowded to admit the elegant Sanjō procession. Coming upon several fine carriages not attended by grooms and footmen, the Sanjō men commenced clearing a space. Two palm-frond carriages remained, not new ones, obviously belonging to someone who did not wish to attract attention. The curtains and the sleeves and aprons to be glimpsed beneath them, some in the gay colors little girls wear, were in very good taste.

The men in attendance sought to defend their places against the Sanjō invaders. "We aren't the sort of people you push around."

There had been too much drink in both parties, and the drunken ones were not responsive to the efforts of their more mature and collected seniors to restrain them.

The palm-frond carriages were from the Rokujō house of the high priestess of Ise. The Rokujō lady had come quietly to see the procession, hoping that it might make her briefly forget her unhappiness. The men from Sanjō had recognized her, but preferred to make it seem otherwise.

"They can't tell us who to push and not to push," said the more intemperate ones to their fellows. "They have General Genji to make them feel important."

Among the newcomers were some of Genji's men. They recognized and felt a little sorry for the Rokujō lady, but, not wishing to become involved, they looked the other way. Presently all the Sanjō carriages were in place. The Rokujō lady, behind the lesser ones, could see almost nothing. Quite aside from her natural distress at the insult, she was filled with the bitterest chagrin that, having refrained from display, she had been recognized. The stools for her carriage shafts had been broken and the shafts propped on the hubs of perfectly strange carriages, a most undignified sight. It was no good asking herself why she had come. She thought of going home without seeing the procession, but there was no room for her to pass; and then came word that the procession was approaching, and she must, after all, see the man who had caused her such unhappiness. How weak is the heart of a woman! Perhaps because this was not "the bamboo by the river Hinokuma,"[1] he passed without stopping his horse or looking her way; and the unhappiness was greater than if she had stayed at home.

Genji seemed indifferent to all the grandly decorated carriages and all the gay sleeves, such a flood of them that it was as if ladies were stacked in layers behind the carriage curtains. Now and again, however, he would have a smile and a glance for a carriage he recognized. His face was solemn and respectful as he passed his wife's carriage. His men bowed deeply, and the Rokujō lady was in misery. She had been utterly defeated.

She whispered to herself:

> "A distant glimpse of the River of Lustration.
> His coldness is the measure of my sorrow."

She was ashamed of her tears. Yet she thought how sorry she would have been if she had not seen that handsome figure set off to such advantage by the crowds.

The high courtiers were, after their several ranks, impeccably dressed and caparisoned and many of them were very handsome; but Genji's radiance dimmed the strongest lights. Among his special attendants was a guards officer of the Sixth Rank, though attendants of such standing were usually reserved for the most splendid royal processions. His retinue made such a fine procession itself that every tree and blade of grass along the way seemed to bend forward in admiration.

It is not on the whole considered good form for veiled ladies of no mean rank and even nuns who have withdrawn from the world to be jostling and shoving one another

1. Anonymous, *Kokinshū* 1080: "In the bamboo by the river Hinokuma, / stop that your horse may drink, and I may see you."

in the struggle to see, but today no one thought it out of place. Hollow-mouthed women of the lower classes, their hair tucked under their robes, their hands brought respectfully to their foreheads, were hopping about in hopes of catching a glimpse. Plebeian faces were wreathed in smiles which their owners might not have enjoyed seeing in mirrors, and daughters of petty provincial officers of whose existence Genji would scarcely have been aware had set forth in carriages decked out with the most exhaustive care and taken up posts which seemed to offer a chance of seeing him. There were almost as many things by the wayside as in the procession to attract one's attention.

And there were many ladies whom he had seen in secret and who now sighed more than ever that their station was so out of keeping with his. Prince Shikibu viewed the procession from a stand. Genji had matured and did indeed quite dazzle the eye, and the prince thought with foreboding that some god might have noticed, and was making plans to spirit the young man away. His daughter, Princess Asagao, having over the years found Genji a faithful correspondent, knew how remarkably steady his feelings were. She was aware that attentions moved ladies even when the donor was a most ordinary man; yet she had no wish for further intimacy. As for her women, their sighs of admiration were almost deafening.

No carriages set out from the Sanjō mansion on the day of the festival proper.

Genji presently heard the story of the competing carriages. He was sorry for the Rokujō lady and angry at his wife. It was a sad fact that, so deliberate and fastidious, she lacked ordinary compassion. There was indeed a tart, forbidding quality about her. She refused to see, though it was probably an unconscious refusal, that ladies who were to each other as she was to the Rokujō lady should behave with charity and forbearance. It was under her influence that the men in her service flung themselves so violently about. Genji sometimes felt uncomfortable before the proud dignity of the Rokujō lady, and he could imagine her rage and humiliation now.

He called upon her. The high priestess, her daughter, was still with her, however, and, making reverence for the sacred sakaki tree[2] her excuse, she declined to receive him.

She was right, of course. Yet he muttered to himself: "Why must it be so? Why cannot the two of them be a little less prickly?" * * *

For the Rokujō lady the pain was unrelieved. She knew that she could expect no lessening of his coldness, and yet to steel herself and go off to Ise with her daughter—she would be lonely, she knew, and people would laugh at her. They would laugh just as heartily if she stayed in the city. Her thoughts were as the fisherman's bob at Ise.[3] Her very soul seemed to jump wildly about, and at last she fell physically ill.

Genji discounted the possibility of her going to Ise. "It is natural that you should have little use for a reprobate like myself and think of discarding me. But to stay with me would be to show admirable depths of feeling."

These remarks did not seem very helpful. Her anger and sorrow increased. A hope of relief from this agony of indecision had sent her to the river of lustration, and there she had been subjected to violence.

At Sanjō, Genji's wife seemed to be in the grip of a malign spirit. It was no time for nocturnal wanderings. Genji paid only an occasional visit to his own Nijō

2. A glossy-leafed tree related to the camellia. Its branches are used in Shinto ritual.

3. Anonymous, *Kokinshū* 509: "Has my heart become the fisherman's bob at Ise? / It jumps and bobs and knows not calm or resolve."

mansion. His marriage had not been happy, but his wife was important to him and now she was carrying his child. He had prayers read in his Sanjō rooms. Several malign spirits were transferred to the medium and identified themselves, but there was one which quite refused to move. Though it did not cause great pain, it refused to leave her for so much as an instant. There was something very sinister about a spirit that eluded the powers of the most skilled exorcists. The Sanjō people went over the list of Genji's ladies one by one. Among them all, it came to be whispered, only the Rokujō lady and the lady at Nijō seemed to have been singled out for special attentions, and no doubt they were jealous. The exorcists were asked about the possibility, but they gave no very informative answers. Of the spirits that did announce themselves, none seemed to feel any deep enmity toward the lady. Their behavior seemed random and purposeless. There was the spirit of her dead nurse, for instance, and there were spirits that had been with the family for generations and had taken advantage of her weakness.

The confusion and worry continued. The lady would sometimes weep in loud wailing sobs, and sometimes be tormented by nausea and shortness of breath.

The old emperor sent repeated inquiries and ordered religious services. That the lady should be worthy of these august attentions made the possibility of her death seem even more lamentable. Reports that they quite monopolized the attention of court reached the Rokujō mansion, to further embitter its lady. No one can have guessed that the trivial incident of the carriages had so angered a lady whose sense of rivalry had not until then been strong.

Not at all herself, she left her house to her daughter and moved to one where Buddhist rites would not be out of place.[4] Sorry to hear of the move, Genji bestirred himself to call on her. The neighborhood was a strange one and he was in careful disguise. He explained his negligence in terms likely to make it seem involuntary and to bring her forgiveness, and he told her of Aoi's illness and the worry it was causing him.

"I have not been so very worried myself, but her parents are beside themselves. It has seemed best to stay with her. It would relieve me enormously if I thought you might take a generous view of it all." He knew why she was unwell, and pitied her.

They passed a tense night. As she saw him off in the dawn she found that her plans for quitting the city were not as firm as on the day before. Her rival was of the highest rank and there was this important new consideration; no doubt his affections would finally settle on her. She herself would be left in solitude, wondering when he might call. The visit had only made her unhappier. In upon her gloom, in the evening, came a letter.

"Though she had seemed to be improving, she has taken a sudden and drastic turn for the worse. I cannot leave her."

The usual excuses, she thought. Yet she answered:

> "I go down the way of love and dampen my sleeves,
> and go yet further, into the muddy fields.

A pity the well is so shallow."[5]

The hand was the very best he knew. It was a difficult world, which refused to give satisfaction. Among his ladies there was none who could be dismissed as completely beneath consideration and none to whom he could give his whole love.

4. They were out of place in the house of a Shinto priestess.
5. Anonymous, *Kokin Rokujō, Zoku Kokka Taikan* 31863: "A pity the mountain well should be so shallow. / I seek to take water and only wet my sleeves."

Despite the lateness of the hour, he got off an answer: "You only wet your sleeves—what can this mean? That your feelings are not of the deepest, I should think.

> You only dip into the shallow waters,
> And I quite disappear into the slough?

"Do you think I would answer by letter and not in person if she were merely indisposed?"

The malign spirit was more insistent, and Aoi was in great distress. Unpleasant rumors reached the Rokujō lady, to the effect that it might be her spirit or that of her father, the late minister. Though she had felt sorry enough for herself, she had not wished ill to anyone; and might it be that the soul of one so lost in sad thoughts went wandering off by itself? She had, over the years, known the full range of sorrows, but never before had she felt so utterly miserable. There had been no release from the anger since the other lady had so insulted her, indeed behaved as if she did not exist. More than once she had the same dream: in the beautifully appointed apartments of a lady who seemed to be a rival she would push and shake the lady, and flail at her blindly and savagely. It was too terrible. Sometimes in a daze she would ask herself if her soul had indeed gone wandering off. The world was not given to speaking well of people whose transgressions had been far slighter. She would be notorious. It was common enough for the spirits of the angry dead to linger on in this world. She had thought them hateful, and it was her own lot to set a hateful example while she still lived. She must think no more about the man who had been so cruel to her. But so to think was, after all, to think.

The high priestess, her daughter, was to have been presented at court the year before, but complications had required postponement. It was finally decided that in the Ninth Month she would go from court to her temporary shrine. The Rokujō house was thus busy preparing for two lustrations, but its lady, lost in thought, seemed strangely indifferent. A most serious state of affairs—the priestess's attendants ordered prayers. There were no really alarming symptoms. She was vaguely unwell, no more. The days passed. Genji sent repeated inquiries, but there was no relief from his worries about another invalid, a more important one.

It was still too early for Aoi to be delivered of her child. Her women were less than fully alert; and then, suddenly, she was seized with labor pains. More priests were put to more strenuous prayers. The malign spirit refused to move. The most eminent of exorcists found this stubbornness extraordinary, and could not think what to do. Then, after renewed efforts at exorcism, more intense than before, it commenced sobbing as if in pain.

"Stop for a moment, please. I want to speak to General Genji."

It was as they had thought. The women showed Genji to a place at Aoi's curtains. Thinking—for she did seem on the point of death—that Aoi had last words for Genji, her parents withdrew. The effect was grandly solemn as priests read from the Lotus Sutra in hushed voices. Genji drew the curtains back and looked down at his wife. She was heavy with child, and very beautiful. Even a man who was nothing to her would have been saddened to look at her. Long, heavy hair, bound at one side, was set off by white robes, and he thought her lovelier than when she was most carefully dressed and groomed.

He took her hand. "How awful. How awful for you." He could say no more.

Usually so haughty and forbidding, she now gazed up at him with languid eyes that were presently filled with tears. How could he fail to be moved? This violent weeping, he thought, would be for her parents, soon to be left behind, and perhaps, at this last leave-taking, for him too.

"You mustn't fret so. It can't be as bad as you think. And even if the worst comes, we will meet again. And your good mother and father: the bond between parents and children lasts through many lives. You must tell yourself that you will see them again."

"No, no. I was hurting so, I asked them to stop for a while. I had not dreamed that I would come to you like this. It is true: a troubled soul will sometimes go wandering off." The voice was gentle and affectionate.

> "Bind the hem of my robe, to keep it within,
> the grieving soul that has wandered through the skies."[6]

It was not Aoi's voice, nor was the manner hers. Extraordinary—and then he knew that it was the voice of the Rokujō lady. He was aghast. He had dismissed the talk as vulgar and ignorant fabrication, and here before his eyes he had proof that such things did actually happen, he was horrified and repelled.

"You may say so. But I don't know who you are. Identify yourself."

It was indeed she. "Aghast"—is there no stronger word? He waved the women back.

Thinking that these calmer tones meant a respite from pain, her mother came with medicine; and even as she drank it down she gave birth to a baby boy. Everyone was delighted, save the spirits that had been transferred to mediums. Chagrined at their failure, they were raising a great stir, and all in all it was a noisy and untidy scene. There was still the afterbirth to worry about. Then, perhaps because of all the prayers, it too was delivered. The grand abbot of Hiei and all the other eminent clerics departed, looking rather pleased with themselves as they mopped their foreheads. Sure that the worst was past after all the anxious days, the women allowed themselves a rest.

The prayers went on as noisily as ever, but the house was now caught up in the happy business of ministering to a pretty baby. It hummed with excitement on each of the festive nights.[7] Fine and unusual gifts came from the old emperor and from all the princes and high courtiers. Ceremonies honoring a boy baby are always interesting.

The Rokujō lady received the news with mixed feelings. She had heard that her rival was critically ill, and now the crisis had passed. She was not herself. The strangest thing was that her robes were permeated with the scent of the poppy seeds burned at exorcisms. She changed clothes repeatedly and even washed her hair, but the odor persisted. She was overcome with self-loathing. And what would others be thinking? It was a matter she could discuss with no one. She could only suffer in distraught silence.

Somewhat calmer, Genji was still horrified at the unsolicited remarks he had had from the possessive spirit. He really must get off a note to the Rokujō lady. Or should he have a talk with her? He would find it hard to be civil, and he did not wish to hurt her. In the end he made do with a note.

Aoi's illness had been critical, and the strictest vigil must be continued. Genji had been persuaded to stop his nocturnal wanderings. He still had not really talked to his wife, for she was still far from normal. The child was so beautiful as to arouse forebodings, and preparations were already under way for a most careful and elaborate education. The minister was pleased with everything save the fact that his daughter had still not recovered. But he told himself that he need not worry. A slow convalescence was to be expected after so serious an illness.

6. Tying the skirt of a robe was a device for keeping an errant spirit at home.

7. There were celebrations on the third, fifth, seventh, and ninth nights.

Especially around the eyes, the baby bore a strong resemblance to the crown prince, whom Genji suddenly felt an intense longing to see. He could not sit still. He had to be off to court.

"I have been neglecting my duties," he said to the women, "and am feeling rather guilty. I think today I will venture out. It would be good if I might see her before I go. I am not a stranger, you know."

"Quite true, sir. You of all people should be allowed near. She is badly emaciated, I fear, but that is scarcely a reason for her to hide herself from you."

And so a place was set out for him at her bedside. She answered from time to time, but in a very weak voice. Even so little, from a lady who had been given up for dead, was like a dream. He told her of those terrible days. Then he remembered how, as if pulling back from a brink, she had begun talking to him so volubly and so eagerly. A shudder of revulsion passed over him.

"There are many things I would like to say to you, but you still seem very tired."

He even prepared medicine for her. The women were filled with admiration. When had he learned to be so useful?

She was sadly worn and lay as if on the border of death, pathetic and still lovely. There was not a tangle in her lustrous hair. The thick tresses that poured over her pillows seemed to him quite beyond compare. He gazed down at her, thinking it odd that he should have felt so dissatisfied with her over the years.

"I must see my father, but I am sure I will not be needed long. How nice if we could always be like this. But your mother is with you so much, I have not wanted to seem insistent. You must get back your strength and move back to your own rooms. Your mother pampers you too much. That may be one reason why you are so slow getting well."

As he withdrew in grand court dress she lay looking after him as she had not been in the habit of doing.

There was to be a conference on promotions and appointments. The minister too set off for court, in procession with all his sons, each of them with a case to plead and determined not to leave his side.

The Sanjō mansion was almost deserted. Aoi was again seized with a strangling shortness of breath; and very soon after a messenger had been sent to court she was dead. Genji and the others left court, scarcely aware of where their feet were taking them. Appointments and promotions no longer concerned them. Since the crisis had come at about midnight there was no possibility of summoning the grand abbot and his suffragans. Everyone had thought that the worst was over, and now of course everyone was stunned, dazed, wandering aimlessly from room to room, hardly knowing a door from a wall. Messengers crowded in with condolences, but the house was in such confusion that there was no one to receive them. The intensity of the grief was almost frightening. Since malign spirits had more than once attacked the lady, her father ordered the body left as it was for two or three days in hopes that she might revive. The signs of death were more and more pronounced, however, and, in great anguish, the family at length accepted the truth. Genji, who had private distress to add to the general grief, thought he knew as well as anyone ever would what unhappiness love can bring. Condolences even from the people most important to him brought no comfort. The old emperor, himself much grieved, sent a personal message; and so for the minister there was new honor, happiness to temper the sorrow. Yet there was no relief from tears.

Every reasonable suggestion was accepted toward reviving the lady, but, the ravages of death being ever more apparent, there was finally no recourse but to see her to

Toribe Moor. There were many heartrending scenes along the way. The crowds of mourners and priests invoking the holy name quite overflowed the wide moor. Messages continued to pour in, from the old emperor, of course, and from the empress and crown prince and all the great houses as well.

The minister was desolate. "Now in my last years to be left behind by a daughter who should have had so many years before her." No one could see him without sharing his sorrow.

Grandly the services went on through the night, and as dawn came over the sky the mourners turned back to the city, taking with them only a handful of ashes. Funerals are common enough, but Genji, who had not been present at many, was shaken as never before. Since it was late in the Eighth Month a quarter moon still hung in a sky that would have brought melancholy thoughts in any case; and the figure of his father-in-law, as if groping in pitch darkness, seemed proper to the occasion and at the same time indescribably sad.

A poem came to his lips as he gazed up into the morning sky:

"Might these clouds be the smoke that mounts from her pyre?
They fill my heart with feelings too deep for words."

[*Genji remains in seclusion at Sanjō for seven weeks, grieving for Aoi. At last he takes leave of his in-laws, leaving his newborn son Yūgiri in their care, and returns to his own Nijō mansion.*]

The Nijō mansion had been cleaned and polished for his return. The whole household assembled to receive him. The higher-ranking ladies had sought to outdo one another in dress and grooming. The sight of them made him think of the sadly dejected ladies at Sanjō. Changing to less doleful clothes, he went to the west wing. The fittings, changed to welcome the autumn, were fresh and bright, and the young women and little girls were all very pretty in autumn dress. Shōnagon had taken care of everything.

Murasaki too was dressed to perfection. "You have grown," he said, lifting a low curtain back over its frame.

She looked shyly aside. Her hair and profile seemed in the lamplight even more like those of the lady he so longed for.

He had worried about her, he said, coming nearer. "I would like to tell you everything, but it is not a very lucky sort of story. Maybe I should rest awhile in the other wing. I won't be long. From now on you will never be rid of me. I am sure you will get very bored with me."

Shōnagon was pleased but not confident. He had so many wellborn ladies, another demanding one was certain to take the place of the one who was gone. She was a dry, unsentimental sort.

Genji returned to his room. Asking Chūjō to massage his legs, he lay down to rest. The next morning he sent off a note for his baby son. He gazed on and on at the answer, from one of the women, and all the old sadness came back.

It was a tedious time. He no longer had any enthusiasm for the careless night wanderings that had once kept him busy. Murasaki was much on his mind. She seemed peerless, the nearest he could imagine to his ideal. Thinking that she was no longer too young for marriage, he had occasionally made amorous overtures; but she had not seemed to understand. They had passed their time in games of Go and *hentsugi.*[8] She was clever and she had many delicate ways of pleasing him in the most trivial diversions. He had not seriously thought of her as a wife. Now he could not restrain himself. It would be a shock, of course.

What had happened? Her women had no way of knowing when the line had been crossed. One morning Genji was up early and Murasaki stayed on and on in bed. It was not at all like her to sleep so late. Might she be unwell? As he left for his own rooms, Genji pushed an inkstone inside her bed curtains.

At length, when no one else was near, she raised herself from her pillow and saw beside it a tightly folded bit of paper. Listlessly she opened it. There was only this verse, in a casual hand:

> Many have been the nights we have spent together
> Purposelessly, these coverlets between us.

She had not dreamed he had anything of the sort on his mind. What a fool she had been, to repose her whole confidence in so gross and unscrupulous a man.

It was almost noon when Genji returned. "They say you're not feeling well. What can be the trouble? I was hoping for a game of Go."

She pulled the covers over her head. Her women discreetly withdrew. He came up beside her.

"What a way to behave, what a very unpleasant way to behave. Try to imagine, please, what these women are thinking."

He drew back the covers. She was bathed in perspiration and the hair at her forehead was matted from weeping.

"Dear me. This does not augur well at all." He tried in every way he could think of to comfort her, but she seemed genuinely upset and did not offer so much as a word in reply.

"Very well. You will see no more of me. I do have my pride."

He opened her writing box but found no note inside. Very childish of her—and he had to smile at the childishness. He stayed with her the whole day, and he thought the stubbornness with which she refused to be comforted most charming.

Boar-day sweets[9] were served in the evening. Since he was still in mourning, no great ceremony attended upon the observance. Glancing over the varied and tastefully arranged foods that had been brought in cypress boxes to Murasaki's rooms only, Genji went out to the south veranda and called Koremitsu.

"We will have more of the same tomorrow night," he said, smiling, "though not in quite such mountains. This is not the most propitious day."

Koremitsu had a quick mind. "Yes, we must be careful to choose lucky days for our beginnings." And, solemnly and deliberately: "How many rat-day sweets am I asked to provide?"[1]

"Oh, I should think one for every three that we have here."

Koremitsu went off with an air of having informed himself adequately. A clever and practical young fellow, thought Genji.

Koremitsu had the nuptial sweets prepared at his own house. He told no one what they signified.

8. Guessing concealed parts of Chinese characters.
9. Eaten on the first Day of the Boar in the Tenth Month, to ensure good health, and perhaps too by way of prayer for a fruitful marriage, the wild boar being a symbol of fertility.

1. There were no "rat-day sweets." The words for "rat" and "sleep" sound the same, and the Day of the Rat follows the Day of the Boar; Koremitsu is referring obliquely to the nuptial bed.

Genji felt like a child thief. The role amused him and the affection he now felt for the girl seemed to reduce his earlier affection to the tiniest mote. A man's heart is a very strange amalgam indeed! He now thought that he could not bear to be away from her for a single night.

The sweets he had ordered were delivered stealthily, very late in the night. A man of tact, Koremitsu saw that Shōnagon, an older woman, might make Murasaki uncomfortable, and so he called her daughter.

"Slip this inside her curtains, if you will," he said, handing her an incense box. "You must see that it gets to her and to no one else. A solemn celebration. No carelessness permitted."

She thought it odd. "Carelessness? Of that quality I have had no experience."

"The very word demands care. Use it sparingly."

Young and somewhat puzzled, she did as she was told. It would seem that Genji had explained the significance of the incense box to Murasaki.

The women had no warning. When the box emerged from the curtains the next morning, the pieces of the puzzle began to fall into place. Such numbers of dishes—when might they have been assembled?—and stands with festooned legs, bearing sweets of a most especial sort. All in all, a splendid array. How very nice that he had gone to such pains, thought Shōnagon. He had overlooked nothing. She wept tears of pleasure and gratitude.

"But he really could have let us in on the secret," the women whispered to one another. "What can the gentleman who brought them have thought?"

When he paid the most fleeting call on his father or put in a brief appearance at court, he would be impossibly restless, overcome with longing for the girl. Even to Genji himself it seemed excessive. He had resentful letters from women with whom he had been friendly. He was sorry, but he did not wish to be separated from his bride for even a night. He had no wish to be with these others and let it seem that he was indisposed.

from *Chapter 10. The Sacred Tree*

The Rokujō lady was more and more despondent as the time neared for her daughter's departure. Since the death of Aoi, who had caused her such pain, Genji's visits, never frequent, had stopped altogether. They had aroused great excitement among her women and now the change seemed too sudden. Genji must have very specific reasons for having turned against her—there was no explaining his extreme coldness otherwise. She would think no more about him. She would go with her daughter. There were no precedents for a mother's accompanying a high priestess to Ise, but she had as her excuse that her daughter would be helpless without her. The real reason, of course, was that she wanted to flee these painful associations.

In spite of everything, Genji was sorry when he heard of her decision. He now wrote often and almost pleadingly, but she thought a meeting out of the question at this late date. She would risk disappointing him rather than have it all begin again.

She occasionally went from the priestess's temporary shrine[1] to her Rokujō house, but so briefly and in such secrecy that Genji did not hear of the visits. The temporary shrine did not, he thought, invite casual visits. Although she was much on his mind, he let the days and months go by. His father, the old emperor, had begun to

1. In the western part of the city.

suffer from recurrent aches and cramps, and Genji had little time for himself. Yet he did not want the lady to go off to Ise thinking him completely heartless, nor did he wish to have a name at court for insensitivity. He gathered his resolve and set off for the shrine.

It was on about the seventh of the Ninth Month. The lady was under great tension, for their departure was imminent, possibly only a day or two away. He had several times asked for a word with her. He need not go inside, he said, but could wait on the veranda. She was in a torment of uncertainty but at length reached a secret decision: she did not want to seem like a complete recluse and so she would receive him through curtains.

It was over a reed plain of melancholy beauty that he made his way to the shrine. The autumn flowers were gone and insects hummed in the wintry tangles. A wind whistling through the pines brought snatches of music to most wonderful effect, though so distant that he could not tell what was being played. Not wishing to attract attention, he had only ten outrunners, men who had long been in his service, and his guards were in subdued livery. He had dressed with great care. His more perceptive men saw how beautifully the melancholy scene set him off, and he was having regrets that he had not made the journey often. A low wattle fence, scarcely more than a suggestion of an enclosure, surrounded a complex of board-roofed buildings, as rough and insubstantial as temporary shelters.

The shrine gates, of unfinished logs, had a grand and awesome dignity for all their simplicity, and the somewhat forbidding austerity of the place was accentuated by clusters of priests talking among themselves and coughing and clearing their throats as if in warning. It was a scene quite unlike any Genji had seen before. The fire lodge[2] glowed faintly. It was all in all a lonely, quiet place, and here away from the world a lady already deep in sorrow had passed these weeks and months. Concealing himself outside the north wing, he sent in word of his arrival. The music abruptly stopped and the silence was broken only by a rustling of silken robes.

Though several messages were passed back and forth, the lady herself did not come out.

"You surely know that these expeditions are frowned upon. I find it very curious that I should be required to wait outside the sacred paling. I want to tell you everything, all my sorrows and worries."

He was right, said the women. It was more than a person could bear, seeing him out there without even a place to sit down. What was she to do? thought the lady. There were all these people about, and her daughter would expect more mature and sober conduct. No, to receive him at this late date would be altogether too undignified. Yet she could not bring herself to send him briskly on his way. She sighed and hesitated and hesitated again, and it was with great excitement that he finally heard her come forward.

"May I at least come up to the veranda?" he asked, starting up the stairs.

The evening moon burst forth and the figure she saw in its light was handsome beyond describing.

Not wishing to apologize for all the weeks of neglect, he pushed a branch of the sacred tree[3] in under the blinds.

2. There are several theories about the use of this building. The most likely are that it was for preparing offerings and that it was for lighting torches and flares.

3. *Sakaki,* related to the camellia.

"With heart unchanging as this evergreen,
this sacred tree, I enter the sacred gate."

She replied:

"You err with your sacred tree and sacred gate.
No beckoning cedars stand before my house."[4]

And he:

"Thinking to find you here with the holy maidens,
I followed the scent of the leaf of the sacred tree."

Though the scene did not encourage familiarity, he made bold to lean inside the blinds.

He had complacently wasted the days when he could have visited her and perhaps made her happy. He had begun to have misgivings about her, his ardor had cooled, and they had become the near strangers they were now. But she was here before him, and memories flooded back. He thought of what had been and what was to be, and he was weeping like a child.

She did not wish him to see her following his example. He felt even sadder for her as she fought to control herself, and it would seem that even now he urged her to change her plans. Gazing up into a sky even more beautiful now that the moon was setting, he poured forth all his pleas and complaints, and no doubt they were enough to erase the accumulated bitterness. She had resigned herself to what must be, and it was as she had feared. Now that she was with him again she found her resolve wavering.

Groups of young courtiers came up. It was a garden which aroused romantic urges and which a young man was reluctant to leave.

Their feelings for each other, Genji's and the lady's, had run the whole range of sorrows and irritations, and no words could suffice for all they wanted to say to each other. The dawn sky was as if made for the occasion. Not wanting to go quite yet, Genji took her hand, very gently.

"A dawn farewell is always drenched in dew,
But sad is the autumn sky as never before."

A cold wind was blowing, and a pine cricket seemed to recognize the occasion. It was a serenade to which a happy lover would not have been deaf. Perhaps because their feelings were in such tumult, they found that the poems they might have exchanged were eluding them.

At length the lady replied:

"An autumn farewell needs nothing to make it sadder.
Enough of your songs, O crickets on the moors!"

It would do no good to pour forth all the regrets again. He made his departure, not wanting to be seen in the broadening daylight. His sleeves were made wet along the way with dew and with tears.

The lady, not as strong as she would have wished, was sunk in a sad reverie. The shadowy figure in the moonlight and the perfume he left behind had the younger women in a state only just short of swooning.

4. Anonymous, *Kokinshū 982:* "Should you seek my house at the foot of Mount Miwa, / you need only look for the cedars by the gate."

"What kind of journey could be important enough, I ask you," said one of them, choking with tears, "to make her leave such a man?"

His letter the next day was so warm and tender that again she was tempted to reconsider. But it was too late: a return to the old indecision would accomplish nothing. Genji could be very persuasive even when he did not care a great deal for a woman, and this was no ordinary parting. He sent the finest travel robes and supplies, for the lady and for her women as well. They were no longer enough to move her. It was as if the thought had only now come to her of the ugly name she seemed fated to leave behind.

[*In the Tenth Month of the same year, Genji's father the old emperor dies. On his deathbed, he instructs his son, the Suzaku emperor, to look to Genji for advice in public affairs, and to be good to the crown prince (the future Reizei emperor). The following year Genji makes further overtures to Fujitsubo, driving her to become a nun after the anniversary of the old emperor's death. In the summer of the next year the Minister of the Right discovers Genji with Oborozukiyo, now a favored concubine of the Suzaku emperor. The Kokiden faction uses this episode as a pretext to destroy Genji politically.*]

from *Chapter 12. Suma*

[*In the Third Month of the year following his scandal with Oborozukiyo, Genji, now twenty-five, opts to go into voluntary exile in Suma, an isolated area to the southwest of the capital, near the sea, rather than face further adversity in the capital. He is accompanied by only a few close associates.*]

At Suma, melancholy autumn winds were blowing. Genji's house was some distance from the sea, but at night the wind that blew over the barriers, now as in Yukihira's day, seemed to bring the surf to his bedside. Autumn was hushed and lonely at a place of exile. He had few companions. One night when they were all asleep he raised his head from his pillow and listened to the roar of the wind and of the waves, as if at his ear. Though he was unaware that he wept, his tears were enough to set his pillow afloat.[1] He plucked a few notes on his koto, but the sound only made him sadder.

> The waves on the strand, like moans of helpless longing.
> The winds—like messengers from those who grieve?

He had awakened the others. They sat up, and one by one they were in tears.

This would not do. Because of him they had been swept into exile, leaving families from whom they had never before been parted. It must be very difficult for them, and his own gloom could scarcely be making things easier. So he set about cheering them. During the day he would invent games and make jokes, and set down this and that poem on multicolored patchwork, and paint pictures on fine specimens of figured Chinese silk. Some of his larger paintings were masterpieces. He had long ago been told of this Suma coast and these hills and had formed a picture of them in his mind, and he found now that his imagination had fallen short of the actuality. What a pity, said his men, that they could not summon Tsunenori and Chieda[2] and other famous painters of the day to add colors to Genji's monochromes. This resolute cheerfulness

1. This extravagant figure of speech is to be found in *Kokin Rokujō, Zoku Kokka Taikan* 34087.

2. Tsunenori seems to have been active some three quarters of a century before; so too, presumably, was Chieda.

had the proper effect. His men, four or five of whom were always with him, would not have dreamed of leaving him.

There was a profusion of flowers in the garden. Genji came out, when the evening colors were at their best, to a gallery from which he had a good view of the coast. His men felt chills of apprehension as they watched him, for the loneliness of the setting made him seem like a visitor from another world. In a dark robe tied loosely over singlets of figured white and aster-colored trousers, he announced himself as "a disciple of the Buddha" and slowly intoned a sutra, and his men thought that they had never heard a finer voice. From offshore came the voices of fishermen raised in song. The barely visible boats were like little seafowl on an utterly lonely sea, and as he brushed away a tear induced by the splashing of oars and the calls of wild geese overhead, the white of his hand against the jet black of his rosary was enough to bring comfort to men who had left their families behind.

* * *

It was the day of the serpent, the first such day in the Third Month.

"The day when a man who has worries goes down and washes them away," said one of his men, admirably informed, it would seem, in all of the annual observances.

Wishing to have a look at the seashore, Genji set forth. Plain, rough curtains were strung up among the trees, and a soothsayer who was doing the circuit of the province was summoned to perform the lustration.

Genji thought he could see something of himself in the rather large doll being cast off to sea, bearing away sins and tribulations.

> "Cast away to drift on an alien vastness,
> I grieve for more than a doll cast out to sea."

The bright, open seashore showed him to wonderful advantage. The sea stretched placid into measureless distances. He thought of all that had happened to him, and all that was still to come.

> "You eight hundred myriad gods must surely help me,
> For well you know that blameless I stand before you."

Suddenly a wind came up and even before the services were finished the sky was black. Genji's men rushed about in confusion. Rain came pouring down, completely without warning. Though the obvious course would have been to return straightway to the house, there had been no time to send for umbrellas. The wind was now a howling tempest, everything that had not been tied down was scuttling off across the beach. The surf was biting at their feet. The sea was white, as if spread over with white linen. Fearful every moment of being struck down, they finally made their way back to the house.

"I've never seen anything like it," said one of the men. "Winds do come up from time to time, but not without warning. It is all very strange and very terrible."

The lightning and thunder seemed to announce the end of the world, and the rain to beat its way into the ground; and Genji sat calmly reading a sutra. The thunder subsided in the evening, but the wind went on through the night.

"Our prayers seem to have been answered. A little more and we would have been carried off. I've heard that tidal waves do carry people off before they know what is happening to them, but I've not seen anything like this."

Towards dawn sleep was at length possible. A man whom he did not recognize came to Genji in a dream.

"The court summons you." He seemed to be reaching for Genji. "Why do you not go?"

It would be the king of the sea, who was known to have a partiality for handsome men. Genji decided that he could stay no longer at Suma.

from *Chapter 13. Akashi*

The days went by and the thunder and rain continued. What was Genji to do? People would laugh if, in this extremity, out of favor at court, he were to return to the city. Should he then seek a mountain retreat? But if it were to be noised about that a storm had driven him away, then he would cut a ridiculous figure in history.

His dreams were haunted by that same apparition. Messages from the city almost entirely ceased coming as the days went by without a break in the storms. Might he end his days at Suma? No one was likely to come calling in these tempests.

A messenger did come from Murasaki, a sad, sodden creature. Had they passed in the street, Genji would scarcely have known whether he was man or beast, and of course would not have thought of inviting him to come near. Now the man brought a surge of pleasure and affection—though Genji could not help asking himself whether the storm had weakened his moorings.

Murasaki's letter, long and melancholy, said in part: "The terrifying deluge goes on without a break, day after day. Even the skies are closed off, and I am denied the comfort of gazing in your direction.

> What do they work, the sea winds down at Suma?
> At home, my sleeves are assaulted by wave after wave."

Tears so darkened his eyes that it was as if they were inviting the waters to rise higher.

The man said that the storms had been fierce in the city too, and that a special reading of the Prajñāpāramitā Sutra had been ordered. "The streets are all closed and the great, gentlemen can't get to court, and everything has closed down."

The man spoke clumsily and haltingly, but he did bring news. Genji summoned him near and had him questioned.

"It's not the way it usually is. You don't usually have rain going on for days without a break and the wind howling on and on. Everyone is terrified. But it's worse here. They haven't had this hail beating right through the ground and thunder going on and on and not letting a body think." The terror written so plainly on his face did nothing to improve the spirits of the people at Suma.

Might it be the end of the world? From dawn the next day the wind was so fierce and the tide so high and the surf so loud that it was as if the crags and the mountains must fall. The horror of the thunder and lightning was beyond description. Panic spread at each new flash. For what sins, Genji's men asked, were they being punished? Were they to perish without another glimpse of their mothers and fathers, their dear wives and children?

Genji tried to tell himself that he had been guilty of no misdeed for which he must perish here on the seashore. Such were the panic and confusion around him, however, that he bolstered his confidence with special offerings to the god of Sumiyoshi.

"O you of Sumiyoshi who protect the lands about: if indeed you are an avatar of the Blessed One, then you must save us."

His men were of course fearful for their lives; but the thought that so fine a gentleman (and in these deplorable circumstances) might be swept beneath the waters seemed altogether too tragic. The less distraught among them prayed in loud voices to this and that favored deity, Buddhist and Shinto, that their own lives be taken if it meant that his might be spared.

They faced Sumiyoshi and prayed and made vows: "Our lord was reared deep in the fastnesses of the palace, and all blessings were his. You who, in the abundance of your mercy, have brought strength through these lands to all who have sunk beneath the weight of their troubles: in punishment for what crimes do you call forth these howling waves? Judge his case if you will, you gods of heaven and earth. Guiltless, he is accused of a crime, stripped of his offices, driven from his house and city, left as you see him with no relief from the torture and the lamentation. And now these horrors, and even his life seems threatened. Why? we must ask. Because of sins in some other life, because of crimes in this one? If your vision is clear, O you gods, then take all this away."

Genji offered prayers to the king of the sea and countless other gods as well. The thunder was increasingly more terrible, and finally the gallery adjoining his rooms was struck by lightning. Flames sprang up and the gallery was destroyed. The confusion was immense; the whole world seemed to have gone mad. Genji was moved to a building out in back, a kitchen or something of the sort it seemed to be. It was crowded with people of every station and rank. The clamor was almost enough to drown out the lightning and thunder. Night descended over a sky already as black as ink.

Presently the wind and rain subsided and stars began to come out. The kitchen being altogether too mean a place, a move back to the main hall was suggested. The charred remains of the gallery were an ugly sight, however, and the hall had been badly muddied and all the blinds and curtains blown away. Perhaps, Genji's men suggested somewhat tentatively, it might be better to wait until dawn. Genji sought to concentrate upon the holy name, but his agitation continued to be very great.

He opened a wattled door and looked out. The moon had come up. The line left by the waves was white and dangerously near, and the surf was still high. There was no one here whom he could turn to, no student of the deeper truths who could discourse upon past and present and perhaps explain these wild events. All the fisherfolk had gathered at what they had heard was the house of a great gentleman from the city. They were as noisy and impossible to communicate with as a flock of birds, but no one thought of telling them to leave.

"If the wind had kept up just a little longer," someone said, "absolutely everything would have been swept under. The gods did well by us."

There are no words—"lonely" and "forlorn" seem much too weak—to describe his feelings.

> "Without the staying hand of the king of the sea
> the roar of the eight hundred waves would have taken us under."

Genji was as exhausted as if all the buffets and fires of the tempest had been aimed at him personally. He dozed off, his head against some nondescript piece of furniture.

The old emperor came to him, quite as when he had lived. "And why are you in this wretched place?" He took Genji's hand and pulled him to his feet. "You must do as the god of Sumiyoshi tells you. You must put out to sea immediately. You must leave this shore behind."

"Since I last saw you, sir," said Genji, overjoyed, "I have suffered an unbroken series of misfortunes. I had thought of throwing myself into the sea."

"That you must not do. You are undergoing brief punishment for certain sins. I myself did not commit any conscious crimes while I reigned, but a person is guilty of transgressions and oversights without his being aware of them. I am doing penance and have no time to look back towards this world. But an echo of your troubles came to me and I could not stand idle. I fought my way through the sea and up to this shore and I am very tired; but now that I am here I must see to a matter in the city." And he disappeared.

Genji called after him, begging to be taken along. He looked around him. There was only the bright face of the moon. His father's presence had been too real for a dream, so real that he must still be here. Clouds traced sad lines across the sky. It had been clear and palpable, the figure he had so longed to see even in a dream, so clear that he could almost catch an afterimage. His father had come through the skies to help him in what had seemed the last extremity of his sufferings. He was deeply grateful, even to the tempests; and in the aftermath of the dream he was happy.

Quite different emotions now ruffled his serenity. He forgot his immediate troubles and only regretted that his father had not stayed longer. Perhaps he would come again. Genji would have liked to go back to sleep, but he lay wakeful until daylight.

A little boat had pulled in at the shore and two or three men came up.

"The revered monk who was once governor of Harima has come from Akashi. If the former Minamoto councillor, Lord Yoshikiyo, is here, we wonder if we might trouble him to come down and hear the details of our mission."

Yoshikiyo pretended to be surprised and puzzled. "He was once among my closer acquaintances here in Harima, but we had a falling out and it has been some time since we last exchanged letters. What can have brought him through such seas in that little boat?"

Genji's dream had given intimations. He sent Yoshikiyo down to the boat immediately. Yoshikiyo marveled that it could even have been launched upon such a sea.

These were the details of the mission, from the mouth of the old governor: "Early this month a strange figure came to me in a dream. I listened, though somewhat incredulously, and was told that on the thirteenth there would be a clear and present sign. I was to ready a boat and make for this shore when the waves subsided. I did ready a boat, and then came this savage wind and lightning. I thought of numerous foreign sovereigns who have received instructions in dreams on how to save their lands, and I concluded that even at the risk of incurring his ridicule I must on the day appointed inform your lord of the import of the dream. And so I did indeed put out to sea. A strange jet blew all the way and brought us to this shore. I cannot think of it except as divine intervention. And might I ask whether there have been corresponding manifestations here? I do hate to trouble you, but might I ask you to communicate all of this to your lord?"

Yoshikiyo quietly relayed the message, which brought new considerations. There had been these various unsettling signs conveyed to Genji dreaming and waking. The possibility of being laughed at for having departed these shores under threat now seemed the lesser risk. To turn his back on what might be a real offer of help from the gods would be to ask for still worse misfortunes. It was not easy to reject ordinary advice, and personal reservations counted for little when the advice came from great eminences. "Defer to them; they will cause you no reproaches," a wise man of old once said.[1] He could scarcely face worse misfortunes by deferring than by not deferring, and he did not seem likely to gain great merit and profit by hesitating out of concern for his brave name. Had not his own father come to him? What room was there for doubts?

1. Lao-tze, say early commentaries; but the advice is not to be found in his extant writings.

He sent back his answer: "I have been through a great deal in this strange place, and I hear nothing at all from the city. I but gaze upon a sun and moon going I know not where as comrades from my old home; and now comes this angler's boat, happy tidings on an angry wind.[2] Might there be a place along your Akashi coast where I can hide myself?

The old man was delighted. Genji's men pressed him to set out even before sunrise. Taking along only four or five of his closest attendants, he boarded the boat. That strange wind came up again and they were at Akashi as if they had flown. It was very near, within crawling distance, so to speak; but still the workings of the wind were strange and marvelous.

The Akashi coast was every bit as beautiful as he had been told it was. He would have preferred fewer people, but on the whole he was pleased. Along the coast and in the hills the old monk had put up numerous buildings with which to take advantage of the four seasons: a reed-roofed beach cottage with fine seasonal vistas; beside a mountain stream a chapel of some grandeur and dignity, suitable for rites and meditation and invocation of the holy name; and rows of storehouses where the harvest was put away and a bountiful life assured for the years that remained. Fearful of the high tides, the old monk had sent his daughter and her women off to the hills. The house on the beach was at Genji's disposal.

The sun was rising as Genji left the boat and got into a carriage. This first look by daylight at his new guest brought a happy smile to the old man's lips. He felt as if the accumulated years were falling away and as if new years had been granted him. He gave silent thanks to the god of Sumiyoshi. He might have seemed ridiculous as he bustled around seeing to Genji's needs, as if the radiance of the sun and the moon had become his private property; but no one laughed at him.

I need not describe the beauty of the Akashi coast. The careful attention that had gone into the house and the rocks and plantings of the garden, the graceful line of the coast—it was infinitely pleasanter than Suma, and one would not have wished to ask a less than profoundly sensitive painter to paint it. The house was in quiet good taste. The old man's way of life was as Genji had heard it described, hardly more rustic than that of the grandees at court. In sheer luxury, indeed, he rather outdid them.

[*Genji remains in Akashi for nearly a year and a half, during which the Akashi priest succeeds in bringing about a union between Genji and his daughter, the Akashi lady. The same violent storm that hit Suma also hit the capital, bringing other omens and disturbances with it: the Kiritsubo emperor appears to his son, the reigning Suzaku emperor, in a dream, reproving him for his treatment of Genji. The Suzaku emperor suffers subsequently a painful eye ailment, the Kokiden lady falls ill, and the Minister of the Right dies. Finally, a year later, Suzaku grants Genji a pardon, summoning him back to the capital in the Seventh Month. Early the following year, Suzaku yields the throne to Reizei, and Genji returns to power. His liaison with the Akashi lady results in a daughter, who is eventually brought to the capital to be raised by Murasaki. Shortly thereafter, Fujitsubo dies. Reizei is informed of his true parentage, and tries to abdicate in favor of his father Genji. Genji refuses but rises rapidly in political rank, eventually being appointed Chancellor. In his thirty-fourth year, Genji constructs a lavish residence, the Rokujō mansion, a virtual court where he gathers all of*

2. Ki no Tsurayuki, *Gosenshū* 1225: "An angler's boat upon the waves that pound us, / happy tidings on an angry wind."

his women around him. Among these women is Tamakazura, a lost daughter of Tō no Chūjō whom Genji has discovered, adopted, and treats as though she were his own daughter. The following passage from the Tamakazura sequence is known as the "defense of fiction."]

from *Chapter 25. Fireflies*

The rains of early summer continued without a break, even gloomier than in most years. The ladies at Rokujō amused themselves with illustrated romances. The Akashi lady, a talented painter, sent pictures to her daughter.

Tamakazura was the most avid reader of all. She quite lost herself in pictures and stories and would spend whole days with them. Several of her young women were well informed in literary matters. She came upon all sorts of interesting and shocking incidents (she could not be sure whether they were true or not), but she found little that resembled her own unfortunate career. There was *The Tale of Sumiyoshi,* popular in its day, of course, and still well thought of. She compared the plight of the heroine, within a hairbreadth of being taken by the chief accountant,[1] with her own escape from the Higo person.[2]

Genji could not help noticing the clutter of pictures and manuscripts. "What a nuisance this all is," he said one day. "Women seem to have been born to be cheerfully deceived. They know perfectly well that in all these old stories there is scarcely a shred of truth, and yet they are captured and made sport of by the whole range of trivialities and go on scribbling them down, quite unaware that in these warm rains their hair is all dank and knotted."

He smiled. "What would we do if there were not these old romances to relieve our boredom? But amid all the fabrication I must admit that I do find real emotions and plausible chains of events. We can be quite aware of the frivolity and the idleness and still be moved. We have to feel a little sorry for a charming princess in the depths of gloom. Sometimes a series of absurd and grotesque incidents which we know to be quite improbable holds our interest, and afterwards we must blush that it was so. Yet even then we can see what it was that held us. Sometimes I stand and listen to the stories they read to my daughter, and I think to myself that there certainly are good talkers in the world. I think that these yarns must come from people much practiced in lying. But perhaps that is not the whole of the story?"

She pushed away her inkstone. "I can see that that would be the view of someone much given to lying himself. For my part, I am convinced of their truthfulness."

He laughed. "I have been rude and unfair to your romances, haven't I? They have set down and preserved happenings from the age of the gods to our own. *The Chronicles of Japan* and the rest are a mere fragment of the whole truth. It is your romances that fill in the details.

"We are not told of things that happened to specific people exactly as they happened; but the beginning is when there are good things and bad things, things that happen in this life which one never tires of seeing and hearing about, things which one cannot bear not to tell of and must pass on for all generations. If the storyteller wishes to speak well, then he chooses the good things; and if he wishes to hold the reader's attention he chooses bad things, extraordinarily bad things. Good things and bad things alike, they are things of this world and no other.

1. There is no such incident in the version which survives today.

2. A rustic man who had pursued her in Kyūshu, before her arrival in the capital and adoption by Genji.

"Writers in other countries approach the matter differently. Old stories in our own are different from new. There are differences in the degree of seriousness. But to dismiss them as lies is itself to depart from the truth. Even in the writ which the Buddha drew from his noble heart are parables, devices for pointing obliquely at the truth. To the ignorant they may seem to operate at cross purposes. The Greater Vehicle is full of them, but the general burden is always the same. The difference between enlightenment and confusion is of about the same order as the difference between the good and the bad in a romance. If one takes the generous view, then nothing is empty and useless."

He now seemed bent on establishing the uses of fiction.

"But tell me: is there in any of your old stories a proper, upright fool like myself?" He came closer. "I doubt that even among the most unworldly of your heroines there is one who manages to be as distant and unnoticing as you are. Suppose the two of us set down our story and give the world a really interesting one."

"I think it very likely that the world will take notice of our curious story even if we do not go to the trouble." She hid her face in her sleeves.

"Our curious story? Yes, incomparably curious, I should think." Smiling and playful, he pressed nearer.

> "Beside myself, I search through all the books,
> and come upon no daughter so unfilial."

"You are breaking one of the commandments."

He stroked her hair as he spoke, but she refused to look up. Presently, however, she managed a reply:

> "So too it is with me. I too have searched,
> and found no cases quite so unparental."

Somewhat chastened, he pursued the matter no further. Yet one worried. What was to become of her?

Murasaki too had become addicted to romances. Her excuse was that Genji's little daughter insisted on being read to.

"Just see what a fine one this is," she said, showing Genji an illustration for *The Tale of Kumano.*[3] The young girl in tranquil and confident slumber made her think of her own younger self. "How precocious even very little children seem to have been. I suppose I might have set myself up as a specimen of the slow, plodding variety. I would have won that competition easily."

Genji might have been the hero of some rather more eccentric stories.

"You must not read love stories to her. I doubt that clandestine affairs would arouse her unduly, but we would not want her to think them commonplace."

What would Tamakazura have made of the difference between his remarks to her and these remarks to Murasaki?

"I would not of course offer the wanton ones as a model," replied Murasaki, "but I would have doubts too about the other sort. Lady Atemiya in *The Tale of the Hollow Tree,* for instance. She is always very brisk and efficient and in control of things, and she never makes mistakes; but there is something unwomanly about her cool manner and clipped speech."

"I should imagine that it is in real life as in fiction. We are all human and we all have our ways. It is not easy to be unerringly right. Proper, well-educated parents go

3. Or *The Tale of Komano.* It does not survive.

to great trouble over a daughter's education and tell themselves that they have done well if something quiet and demure emerges. It seems a pity when defects come to light one after another and people start asking what her good parents can possibly have been up to. Yet the rewards are very great when a girl's manner and behavior seem just right for her station. Even then empty praise is not satisfying. One knows that the girl is not perfect and looks at her more critically than before. I would not wish my own daughter to be praised by people who have no standards."

He was genuinely concerned that she acquit herself well in the tests that lay before her.

Wicked stepmothers are of course standard fare for the romancers, and he did not want them poisoning relations between Murasaki and the child. He spent a great deal of time selecting romances he thought suitable, and ordered them copied and illustrated.

from *Chapter 34. New Herbs (Part 1)*

[*Genji is now forty years old. His daughter by the Akashi lady has gone to court as a consort to the crown prince. He has retired as Chancellor, and been accorded benefices equivalent to those of a retired emperor. Meanwhile, the Suzaku emperor falls ill, and is worried about the future of his favorite daughter, the Third Princess. Although he considers Genji's son Yūgiri, Tō no Chūjō's son Kashiwagi, and Genji's half brother Prince Hotaru as potential husbands for her, he asks Genji to take care of her. Despite his fear of hurting Murasaki, Genji agrees to marry the girl (spurred on, perhaps, by the fact that, like Murasaki, the Third Princess is a niece of Fujitsubo).*]

And so the contract was made.

In the evening there was a banquet for Genji's party and the Suzaku household. The priest's fare was unpretentious but beautifully prepared and served. The tableware and the trays of light aloeswood also suggested the priestly vocation and brought tears to the eyes of the guests. The melancholy and moving details were innumerable, but I fear that they would clutter my story.

It was late in the night when Genji and his men departed, the men bearing lavish gifts. The Fujiwara councilor was among those who saw them off. There had been a fall of snow and the Suzaku emperor had caught cold. But he was happy. The future of the Third Princess seemed secure.

Genji was worried. Murasaki had heard vague rumors, but she had told herself that it could not be. Genji had once been very serious about the high priestess of Ise, it seemed, but in the end he had held himself back. She had not worried a great deal, and asked no questions.

How would she take this news? Genji knew that his feelings towards her would not change, or if they did it would be in the direction of greater intensity. But only time could assure her of that fact, and there would be cruel uncertainty in the meantime. Nothing had been allowed to come between them in recent years, and the thought of having a secret from her for even a short time made him very unhappy.

He said nothing to her that night.

The next day was dark, with flurries of snow.

"I went yesterday to call on the Suzaku emperor. He is in very poor health indeed." It was in the course of a leisurely conversation that Genji brought the matter up. "He said many sad things, but what seems to trouble him most as he goes off to his retreat is the future of the Third Princess." And he described that part of the interview. "I was really so extremely sorry for him that I found it impossible to refuse. I suppose people will make a great thing of it. The thought of taking a bride at my age has seemed so utterly preposterous that I have tried through this and that intermediary to suggest a certain want of ardor. But to see him in person and have it directly from him—I simply could not bring myself to refuse. Do you think that when the time does finally come for him to go off into the mountains we might have her come here? Would that upset you terribly? Please do not let it. Trust me, and tell yourself what is the complete truth, that nothing is going to change. She has more right to feel insecure than you do. But I am sure that we can arrange things happily enough for her too."

She was always torturing herself over the smallest of his affairs, and he had dreaded telling her of this one.

But her reply was quiet and unassertive, "Yes, it is sad for her. The only thing that worries me is the possibility that she might feel less than completely at home. I shall be very happy if our being so closely related persuades her that I am no stranger."

"How silly that this very willingness to accept things should bother me. But it does. It makes me start looking for complications, and I am sure I will feel guiltier as the two of you get used to each other. You must pay no attention to what people say. Rumors are strange things. It is impossible to know where they come from, but there they are, like living creatures bent on poisoning relations between a man and a woman. You must listen only to yourself and let matters take their course. Do not start imagining things, and do not torture yourself with empty jealousies."

It was a tempest out of the blue which there was no escaping. Murasaki was determined that she would not complain or give any hint of resentment. She knew that neither her wishes nor her advice would have made any difference. She did not want the world to think that she had been crushed by what had to come. There was her sharp-tongued stepmother, so quick to blame and to gloat. . . . She was certain to gloat over this, and to say that Murasaki deserved exactly what had come to her. Though very much in control of herself, Murasaki was prey to these worries. The very durability of her relations with Genji was sure to make people laugh harder. But she gave no hint of her unhappiness.

The New Year came, and at the Suzaku Palace the Third Princess's wedding plans kept people busy. Her several suitors were deeply disappointed. The emperor, who had let it be known that he would welcome her at court, was among them.

[*In due course, the Third Princess is installed in the Rokujō mansion.*]

It was an unsettling time for Murasaki. No doubt Genji was giving an honest view of the matter when he said that she would not be overwhelmed by the Third Princess. Yet for the first time in years she felt genuinely threatened. The new lady was young and, it would seem, rather showy in her ways, and of such a rank that Murasaki could not ignore her. All very unsettling; but she gave no hint of her feelings, and indeed helped with all the arrangements. Genji saw more than ever that there was really no one like her.

The Third Princess was, as her father had said, a mere child. She was tiny and immature physically, and she gave a general impression of still greater, indeed quite extraordinary, immaturity. He thought of Murasaki when he had first taken her in. She had even then been interesting. She had had a character of her own. The Third Princess was like a baby. Well, thought Genji, the situation had something to recommend it: she was not likely to intrude and make Murasaki unhappy with fits of jealousy. Yet he did think he might have hoped for someone a *little* more interesting. For the first three nights he was faithfully in attendance upon her. Murasaki was unhappy but said nothing. She gave herself up to her thoughts and to such duties, now performed with unusual care, as scenting his robes. He thought her splendid. Why, he asked himself, whatever the pressures and the complications, had he taken another wife? He had been weak and he had given an impression of inconstancy, and brought it all upon himself. Yūgiri had escaped because the Suzaku emperor had seen what an unshakable pillar of fidelity he was.

Genji was near tears. "Please excuse me just this one more night. I have no alternative. If after this I neglect you, then you may be sure that I will be angrier with myself than you can ever be with me. We do have to consider her father's feelings."

"Do not ask us bystanders," she said, a faint smile on her lips, "to tell you how to behave."

He turned away, chin in hand, to hide his confusion.

> "I had grown so used to thinking it would not change,
> and now, before my very eyes, it changes."

He took up the paper on which she had jotted down old poems that fitted her mood as well as this poem of her own. It was not the most perfect of poems, perhaps, but it was honest and to the point.

> "Life must end. It is a transient world.
> The one thing lasting is the bond between us."

He did not want to leave, but she said that he was only making things more difficult for her. He was wearing the soft robes which she had so carefully scented. She had over the years seen new threats arise only to be turned away, and she had finally come to think that there would be no more. Now this had happened, and everyone was talking. She knew how susceptible he had been in his earlier years, and now the whole future seemed uncertain. It was remarkable that she showed no sign of her disquiet.

Her women were talking as of the direst happenings.

"Who would have expected it? He has always kept himself well supplied with women, but none of them has seemed the sort to raise a challenge. So things have been quiet. I doubt that our lady will let them defeat her—but we must be careful. The smallest mistake could make things very difficult."

Murasaki pretended that nothing at all was amiss. She talked pleasantly with them until late in the night. She feared that silence on the most important subject might make it seem more important than it was.

"I am so glad that she has come to us. We have had a full house, but I sometimes think he has been a little bored with us, poor man. None of us is grand enough to be really interesting. I somehow hope that we will be the best of friends. Perhaps it is because they say that she is still a mere child. And here you all are digging a great chasm between us. If we were of the same rank, or perhaps if I had some slight reason to think myself a little her superior, then I would feel that I had to be careful. But as it is—you may think it impertinent of me to say so—I only want to be friendly."

Nakatsukasa and Chūjō exchanged glances. "Such kindness," one of them, I do not know which, would seem to have muttered. They had once been recipients of Genji's attentions but they had been with Murasaki for some years now, and they were among her firmer allies.

Inquiries came from the ladies in the other quarters, some of them suggesting that they who had long ago given up their ambitions might be the more fortunate ones. Murasaki sighed. They meant to be kind, of course, but they were not making things easier. Well, there was no use in tormenting herself over things she could not change, and the inconstancy of the other sex was among them.

Her women would think it odd if she spent the whole night talking with them. She withdrew to her boudoir and they helped her into bed. She was lonely, and the presence of all these women did little to disguise the fact. She thought of the years of his exile. She had feared that they would not meet again, but the agony of waiting for word that he was still alive was in itself a sort of distraction from the sorrow and longing. She sought to comfort herself now with the thought that those confused days could so easily have meant the end of everything.

The wind was cold. Not wanting her women to know that she could not sleep, she lay motionless until she ached from the effort. Still deep in the cold night, the call of the first cock seemed to emphasize the loneliness and sorrow.

She may not have been in an agony of longing, but she was deeply troubled, and perhaps for that reason she came to Genji in his dreams. His heart was racing. Might something have happened to her? He lay waiting for the cock as if for permission to leave, and at its first call rushed out as if unaware that it would not yet be daylight for some time. Still a child, the princess kept her women close beside her. One of them saw him out through a corner door. The snow caught the first traces of dawn, though the garden was still dark. "In vain the spring's darkness,"[1] whispered her nurse, catching the scent he had left behind.

The patches of snow were almost indistinguishable from the white garden sands. "There is yet snow by the castle wall,"[2] he whispered to himself as he came to Murasaki's wing of the house and tapped on a shutter. No longer in the habit of accommodating themselves to nocturnal wanderings, the women let him wait for a time.

"How slow you are," he said, slipping in beside her. "I am quite congealed, as much from terror as from cold. And I have done nothing to deserve it."

He thought her rather wonderful. She did nothing at all, and yet, hiding her wet sleeves, she somehow managed to keep him at a distance. Not even among ladies of the highest birth was there anyone quite like her. He found himself comparing her with the little princess he had just left.

He spent the day beside her, going over their years together, and charging her with evasion and deviousness.

He sent a note saying that he would not be calling on the princess that day. "I seem to have caught a chill from the snow and think I would be more comfortable here."

Her nurse sent back tartly by word of mouth that the note had been passed on to her lady. Not a very amiable sort, thought Genji.

He did not want the Suzaku emperor to know of his want of ardor, but he did not seem capable even of maintaining appearances. Things could scarcely have been worse. For her part, Murasaki feared that the Suzaku emperor would hold her responsible.

1. Oshikōchi Mitsune, *Kokinshū* 40: "In vain the spring night's darkness accosts the plum, / destroying the color but not the scent of its blossoms."

2. Po Chü-i, Collected Works 16, "Dawn from *Yü Hsin's Tower*."

Waking this time in the familiar rooms, he got off another note to the princess. He took great trouble with it, though he was not sure that she would notice. He chose white paper and attached it to a sprig of plum blossom.

> "Not heavy enough to block the way between us,
> the flurries of snow this morning yet distress me."

He told the messenger that the note was to be delivered at the west gallery.[3] * * *

An answer did presently come. It was on red tissue paper and folded neatly in an envelope. He opened it with trepidation, hoping that it would not be too irredeemably childish. He did not want to have secrets from Murasaki, and yet he did not want her to see the princess's hand, at least for a time. To display the princess in all her immaturity seemed somehow insulting. But it would be worse to make Murasaki yet unhappier. She sat leaning against an armrest. He laid the note half open beside her.

> "You do not come. I fain would disappear,
> a veil of snow upon the rough spring winds."

It was every bit as bad as he had feared, scarcely even a child's hand—and of course in point of years she was not a child at all. Murasaki glanced at it and glanced away as if she had not seen it. He would have offered it up for what it was, evidence of almost complete uselessness, had it been from anyone else.

"So you see you have nothing to worry about," he said.

He paid his first daytime call upon the princess. He had dressed with unusual care and no doubt his good looks had an unusually powerful effect on women not used to them. For the older and more experienced of them, the nurse, for instance, the effect was of something like apprehension. He was so splendid that they feared complications. Their lady was such a pretty little child of a thing, reduced to almost nothing at all by the brilliance of her surroundings. It was as if there were no flesh holding up the great mounds of clothing. She did not seem shy before him, and if it could have been said that her openness and freedom from mannerism were for purposes of putting him at ease, then it could also have been said that they succeeded very well. Her father was not generally held to be a virile sort of man, but no one denied his superior taste and refinement, and the mystery was that he had done so little by way of training her. And of course Genji, like everyone else, knew that she was his favorite, and that he worried endlessly about her. It all seemed rather sad. The other side of the matter was that she did undeniably have a certain girlish charm. She listened quietly and answered with whatever came into her mind. He must be good to her. In his younger days his disappointment would have approached contempt, but he had become more tolerant. They all had their ways, and none was enormously superior to the others. There were as many sorts of women as there were women. A disinterested observer would probably have told him that he had made a good match for himself. Murasaki was the only remarkable one among them all, more remarkable now than ever, he thought, and he had known her very well for a very long time. He had no cause for dissatisfaction with his efforts as guardian and mentor. A single morning or evening away from her and the sense of deprivation was so intense as to bring a sort of foreboding.

* * *

A frequenter of the Suzaku Palace, Kashiwagi had known all about the Third Princess and the Suzaku emperor's worries. He had offered himself as a candidate for

3. His reasons are not clear. There is a theory that he doesn't want Murasaki to see, but it is not very tenable.

her hand. His candidacy had not been dismissed, and then, suddenly and to his very great disappointment, she had gone to Genji. He still could not reconcile himself to what had happened. He seems to have taken some comfort in exchanging reports with women whom he had known in her maiden days. He of course heard what everyone else heard, that she was no great competitor for Genji's affection.

He was forever complaining to Koji.

[*On a pleasant day in the Third Month, a number of young men, including Yūgiri (Genji's son by Aoi) and Kashiwagi (Tō no Chūjō's son), assemble at Rokujō and engage in a game of kickball* (kemari)*, while Genji looks on.*]

Taking their places under a fine cherry in full bloom, Yūgiri and Kashiwagi were very handsome in the evening light. Genji's less than genteel sport—such things do happen—took on something of the elegance of the company and the place. Spring mists enfolded trees in various stages of bud and bloom and new leaf. The least subtle of games does have its skills and techniques, and each of the players was determined to show what he could do. Though Kashiwagi played only briefly, he was clearly the best of them all. He was handsome but retiring, intense and at the same time lively and expansive. Though the players were now under the cherry directly before the south stairs, they had no eye for the blossoms. Genji and Prince Hotaru were at a corner of the veranda.

Yes, there were many skills, and as one inning followed another a certain abandon was to be observed and caps of state were pushed rather far back on noble foreheads. Yūgiri could permit himself a special measure of abandon, and his youthful spirits and vigor were infectious. He had on a soft white robe lined with red. His trousers were gently taken in at the ankles, but by no means untidy. He seemed very much in control of himself despite the abandon, and cherry petals fell about him like a flurry of snow. He broke off a twig from a dipping branch and went to sit on the stairs.

"How quick they are to fall," said Kashiwagi, coming up behind him. "We much teach the wind to blow wide and clear."[4]

He glanced over toward the Third Princess's rooms. They seemed to be in the usual clutter. The multicolored sleeves pouring from under the blinds and through openings between them were like an assortment of swatches to be presented to the goddess of spring. Only a few paces from him a woman had pushed her curtains carelessly aside and looked as if she might be in a mood to receive a gentleman's addresses. A Chinese cat, very small and pretty, came running out with a larger cat in pursuit. There was a noisy rustling of silk as several women pushed forward to catch it. On a long cord which had become badly tangled, it would not yet seem to have been fully tamed. As it sought to free itself the cord caught in a curtain, which was pulled back to reveal the women behind. No one, not even those nearest the veranda, seemed to notice. They were much too worried about the cat.

A lady in informal dress stood[5] just inside the curtains beyond the second pillar to the west. Her robe seemed to be of red lined with lavender, and at the sleeves and throat the colors were as bright and varied as a book of paper samples. Her cloak was of white figured satin lined with red. Her hair fell as cleanly as sheaves of thread and fanned out towards the neatly trimmed edges some ten inches beyond her feet. In the

4. Fujiwara Yoshikaze, *Kokinshū* 85: "Blow wide and clear, spring wind, of the cherry blossoms. / Let us see if they will fall of their own accord."

5. The verb is important. Well-behaved ladies did not permit themselves to be seen standing.

rich billowing of her skirts the lady scarcely seemed present at all. The white profile framed by masses of black hair was pretty and elegant—though unfortunately the room was dark and he could not see her as well in the evening light as he would have wished. The women had been too delighted with the game, young gentlemen heedless of how they scattered the blossoms, to worry about blinds and concealment. The lady turned to look at the cat, which was mewing piteously, and in her face and figure was an abundance of quiet, unpretending young charm.

Yūgiri saw and strongly disapproved, but would only have made matters worse by stepping forward to lower the blind. He coughed warningly. The lady slipped out of sight. He too would have liked to see more, and he sighed when, the cat at length disengaged, the blind fell back into place. Kashiwagi's regrets were more intense. It could only have been the Third Princess, the lady who was separated from the rest of the company by her informal dress. He pretended that nothing had happened, but Yūgiri knew that he had seen the princess, and was embarrassed for her. Seeking to calm himself, Kashiwagi called the cat and took it up in his arms. It was delicately perfumed. Mewing prettily, it brought the image of the Third Princess back to him (for he had been ready to fall in love).

from *Chapter 35. New Herbs (Part 2)*

The royal cat had had a large litter of kittens, which had been put out here and there. One of them, a very pretty little creature, was scampering about the crown prince's rooms. Kashiwagi was of course reminded of the Rokujō cat.

"The Third Princess has a really fine cat. You would have to go a very long way to find its rival. I only had the briefest glimpse, but it made a deep impression on me."

Very fond of cats, the crown prince asked for all the details. Kashiwagi perhaps made the Rokujō cat seem more desirable than it was.

"It is a Chinese cat, and Chinese cats are different. All cats have very much the same disposition, I suppose, but it does seem a little more affectionate than most. A perfectly charming little thing."

The crown prince made overtures through the Akashi princess and presently the cat was delivered. Everyone was agreed that it was a very superior cat. Guessing that the crown prince meant to keep it, Kashiwagi waited a few days and paid a visit. He had been a favorite of the Suzaku emperor's and now he was close to the crown prince, to whom he gave lessons on the koto and other instruments.

"Such numbers of cats as you do seem to have. Where is my own special favorite?"

The Chinese cat was apprehended and brought in. He took it in his arms.

"Yes, it is a handsome beast," said the crown prince, "but it does not seem terribly friendly. Maybe it is not used to us. Do you really think it so superior to our own cats?"

"Cats do not on the whole distinguish among people, though perhaps the more intelligent ones do have the beginnings of a rational faculty. But just look at them all, such swarms of cats and all of them such fine ones. Might I have the loan of it for a few days?"

He was afraid that he was being rather silly. But he had his cat. He kept it with him at night, and in the morning would see to its toilet and pet it and feed it. Once the initial shyness had passed it proved to be a most affectionate animal. He loved its way of sporting with the hem of his robe or entwining itself around a leg. Sometimes when he was sitting at the veranda lost in thought it would come up and speak to him.

"What an insistent little beast you are." He smiled and stroked its back. "You are here to remind me of someone I long for, and what is it you long for yourself? We must have been together in an earlier life, you and I."

He looked into its eyes and it returned the gaze and mewed more emphatically. Taking it in his arms, he resumed his sad thoughts.

"Now why should a cat all of a sudden dominate his life?" said one of the women. "He never paid much attention to cats before."

The crown prince asked to have the cat back, but in vain. It had become Kashiwagi's constant and principal companion.

[*Several years pass. The Akashi princess has since given birth to several children, one of whom will be the next crown prince. Although Murasaki and Genji remain happily married, she has begun asking him to allow her to become a nun, but he refuses.*]

Murasaki was now busy being grandmother to the royal children. She did nothing that might have left her open to charges of bad judgment. Hers was a perfection, indeed, that was somehow ominous. It aroused forebodings. The evidence is that such people are not meant to have long lives. Genji had known many women and he knew what a rarity she was. She was thirty-seven this year.[1]

He was thinking over the years they had been together. "You must be especially careful this year. You must overlook none of the prayers and services. I am very busy and sometimes careless, and I must rely on you to keep track of things. If there is something that calls for special arrangements I can give the orders. It is a pity that your uncle, the bishop, is no longer living. He was the one who really knew about these things.

"I have always been rather spoiled and there can be few precedents for the honors I enjoy. The other side of the story is that I have had more than my share of sorrow. The people who have been fond of me have left me behind one after another, and there have been events in more recent years that I think almost anyone would call very sad. As for nagging little worries, it almost seems as if I were a collector of them. I sometimes wonder if it might be by way of compensation that I have lived a longer life than I would have expected to. You, on the other hand—I think that except for our years apart you have been spared real worries. There are the troubles that go with the glory of being an empress or one of His Majesty's other ladies. They are always being hurt by the proud people they must be with and they are engaged in a competition that makes a terrible demand on their nerves. You have lived the life of a cloistered maiden, and there is none more comfortable and secure. It is as if you had never left your parents. Have you been aware, my dear, that you have been luckier than most? I know that it has not been easy for you to have the princess move in on us all of a sudden. We sometimes do not notice the things that are nearest to us, and you may not have noticed that her presence has made me fonder of you. But you are quick to see these things, and perhaps I do you an injustice."

"You are right, of course. I do not much matter, and it must seem to most people that I have been more fortunate than I deserve. And that my unhappiness should sometimes have seemed almost too much for me—perhaps that is the prayer that has sustained me." She seemed to be debating whether to go on. He thought her splendid.

1. She should be 39 or 40. The thirty-seventh year by the Asian count was thought to be a dangerous one. It was then that Fujitsubo died.

"I doubt that I have much longer to live. Indeed, I have my doubts about getting through this year if I pretend that no changes are needed. It would make me very happy if you would let me do what I have so long wanted to do."

"Quite out of the question. Do you think I could go on without you? Not very much has happened these last years, I suppose, but knowing that you are here has been the most important thing. You must see to the end how very much I have loved you."

It was the usual thing, all over again.

A very little more and she would be in tears, he could see. He changed the subject.

"I have not known enormous numbers of women, but I have concluded that they all have their good points, and that the genuinely calm and equable ones are very rare indeed.

"There was Yūgiri's mother. I was a mere boy when we were married and she was one of the eminences in my life, someone I could not think of dismissing. But things never went well. To the end she seemed very remote. It was sad for her, but I cannot convince myself that the fault was entirely mine. She was an earnest lady with no faults that one would have wished to single out, but it might be said that she was the cold intellectual, the sort you might turn to for advice and find yourself uncomfortable with.

"There was the Rokujō lady, Akikonomu's mother. I remember her most of all for her extraordinary subtlety and cultivation, but she was a difficult lady too, indeed almost impossible to be with. Even when her anger seemed justified it lasted too long, and her jealousy was more than a man could be asked to endure. The tensions went on with no relief, and the reservations on both sides made easy companionship quite impossible. I stood too much on my dignity, I suppose. I thought that if I gave in she would gloat and exult. And so it ended. I could see how the gossip hurt her and how she condemned herself for conduct which she thought unworthy of her position, and I could see that difficult though she might be I was at fault myself. It is because I have so regretted what finally happened that I have gone to such trouble for her daughter. I do not claim all the credit, of course. It is obvious that she was meant all along for important things. But I made enemies for myself because of what I did for her, and I like to think that her mother, wherever she is, has forgiven me. I have on the impulse of the moment done many things I have come to regret. It was true long ago and it is true now." By fits and starts, he spoke of his several ladies.

"There is the Akashi lady. I looked down upon her and thought her no more than a plaything. But she has depths. She may seem docile and uncomplicated, but there is a firm core underneath it all. She is not easily slighted."

"I was not introduced to the other ladies and can say nothing about them," replied Murasaki. "I cannot pretend to know very much about the Akashi lady either, but I have had a glimpse of her from time to time, and would agree with you that she has very great pride and dignity. I often wonder if she does not think me a bit of a simpleton. As for your daughter, I should imagine that she forgives me my faults."

It was affection for the Akashi princess, thought Genji, that had made such good friends of Murasaki and a lady she had once so resented. Yes, she was splendid indeed.

"You may have your little blank spots," he said, "but on the whole you manage things as the people and the circumstances demand. I have as I have said known numbers of ladies and not one of them has been quite like you. Not"—he smiled—"that you always keep your feelings to yourself."

In the evening he went off to the main hall. "I must commend the princess for having carried out her instructions so faithfully."

Immersed in her music, she was as youthful as ever. It did not seem to occur to her that anyone might be less than happy with her presence.

"Let me have a few days off," said Genji, "and you take a few off too. You have quite satisfied your teacher. You worked hard and the results were worthy of the effort. I have no doubts now about your qualifications." He pushed the koto aside and lay down.

As always when he was away, Murasaki had her women read stories to her. In the old stories that were supposed to tell what went on in the world, there were men with amorous ways and women who had affairs with them, but it seemed to be the rule that in the end the man settled down with one woman. Why should Murasaki herself live in such uncertainty? No doubt, as Genji had said, she had been unusually fortunate. But were the ache and the scarcely endurable sense of deprivation to be with her to the end? She had much to think about and went to bed very late, and towards daylight she was seized with violent chest pains. Her women were immediately at her side. Should they call Genji? Quite out of the question, she replied. Presently it was daylight. She was running a high fever and still in very great pain. No one had gone for Genji. Then a message came from the Akashi princess and she was informed of Murasaki's illness, and in great trepidation sent word to Genji. He immediately returned to Murasaki's wing of the house, to find her still in great pain.

"And what would seem to be the matter?" He felt her forehead. It was flaming hot.

He was in terror, remembering that only the day before he had warned her of the dangerous year ahead. Breakfast was brought but he sent it back. He was at her side all that day, seeing to her needs. She was unable to sit up and refused even the smallest morsel of fruit.

The days went by. All manner of prayers and services were commissioned. Priests were summoned to perform esoteric rites. Though the pain was constant, it would at times be of a vague and generalized sort, and then, almost unbearable, the chest pains would return. An endless list of abstinences was drawn up by the soothsayers, but it did no good. Beside her all the while, Genji was in anguish, looking for the smallest hopeful sign, the barely perceptible change that can brighten the prospects in even the most serious illness. She occupied the whole of his attention. Preparations for the visit to the Suzaku emperor, who sent frequent and courteous inquiries, had been put aside.

The Second Month was over and there was no improvement. Thinking that a change of air might help, Genji moved her to his Nijō mansion. Anxious crowds gathered there and the confusion was enormous. The Reizei emperor was much troubled and Yūgiri even more so. There were others who were in very great disquiet. Were Murasaki to die, then Genji would almost certainly follow through with his wish to retire from the world. Yūgiri saw to the usual sort of prayers and rites, of course, and extraordinary ones as well.

"Do you remember what I asked for?" Murasaki would say when she was feeling a little more herself. "May I not have it even now?"

"I have longed for many years to do exactly that," Genji would reply, thinking that to see her even briefly in nun's habit would be as painful as to know that the final time had come. "I have been held back by the thought of what it would mean to you if I were to insist on having my way. Can you now think of deserting me?"

But it did indeed seem that the end might be near. There were repeated crises, each of which could have been the last. Genji no longer saw the Third Princess. Music had lost all interest and koto and flute were put away. Most of the Rokujō household moved to Nijō. At Rokujō, where only women remained, it was as if the fires had gone out. One saw how much of the old life had depended on a single lady.

The Akashi princess was at Genji's side.

"But whatever I have might take advantage of your condition," said Murasaki, weak though she was. "Please go back immediately."

The princess's little children were with them, the prettiest children imaginable. Murasaki looked at them and wept. "I doubt that I shall be here to see you grow up. I suppose you will forget all about me"

The princess too was weeping.

"You must not even think of it," said Genji. "Everything will be all right if only we manage to think so. When we take the broad, easy view we are happy. It may be the destiny of the meaner sort to rise to the top, but the fretful and demanding ones do not stay there very long. It is the calm ones who survive. I could give you any number of instances."

He described her virtues to all the native and foreign gods and told them how very little she had to atone for. The venerable sages entrusted with the grander services and the priests in immediate attendance as well, including the ones on night duty, were sorry that they seemed to be accomplishing so little. They turned to their endeavors with new vigor and intensity. For five and six days there would be some improvement and then she would be worse again, and so time passed. How would it all end? The malign force that had taken possession of her refused to come forth. She was wasting away from one could not have said precisely what ailment, and there was no relief from the worry and sorrow.

I have been neglecting Kashiwagi. Now a councilor of the middle rank, he enjoyed the special confidence of the emperor and was one of the more promising young officials of the day. But fame and honor had done nothing to satisfy the old longing. He took for his bride the Second Princess, daughter of the Suzaku emperor by a low-ranking concubine. It must be admitted that he thought her less than the very best he could have found. She was an agreeable lady whose endowments were far above the ordinary, but she was not capable of driving the Third Princess from his thoughts. He did not, to be sure, treat her like one of the old women who are cast out on mountainsides to die, but he was not as attentive as he might have been.

The Kojijū[2] to whom he went with the secret passion he was unable to quell was a daughter of Jijū, the Third Princess's nurse. Jijū's elder sister was Kashiwagi's own nurse, and so he had long known a great deal about the princess. He had known when she was still a child that she was very pretty and that she was her father's favorite. It was from these early beginnings that his love had grown.

Guessing that the Rokujō mansion would be almost deserted, he called Kojijū and warmly pleaded his case. "My feelings could destroy me, I fear. You are my tie with her and so I have asked you about her and hoped that you might let her know something of my uncontrollable longing. You have been my hope and you have done nothing. Someone was saying to her royal father that Genji had many ladies to occupy his attention and that one of them seemed to have monopolized it, and the Third Princess was spending lonely nights and days of boredom. It would seem that her father might have been having second thoughts. If his daughters had to marry commoners, he said, it would be nice if they were commoners who had a little time for them. Someone told me that he might even think the Second Princess the more fortunate of the two. She is the one who has long years of comfort and

2. One of the Third Princess's attendants, through whom Kashiwagi had in the past had messages delivered to the princess.

security ahead of her. I cannot tell you how it all upsets me." He sighed. "They are daughters of the same royal father, but the one is the one and the other is the other."

"I think, sir, that you might be a little more aware of your place in the world. You have one princess and you want another? Your greed seems boundless."

He smiled. "Yes, I suppose so. But her father gave me some encouragement and so did her brother. Though it may be, as you say, that I am not as aware of my place in the world as I should be, I have let myself think of her. Both of them found occasion to say that they did not consider me so very objectionable. You are the one who is at fault—you should have worked just a little harder."

"It was impossible. I have been told that there is such a thing as fate. It may have been fate which made Genji ask for her so earnestly and ceremoniously. Do you really think His Majesty's affection for you such that, had you made similar overtures, they would have prevailed over His Lordship's? It is true that you have a little more dignity and prestige now than you had then."

He did not propose to answer this somewhat intemperate outburst. "Let us leave the past out of the matter. The present offers a rare opportunity. There are very few people around her and you can, if you will, contrive to admit me to her presence and let me tell her just a little of what has been on my mind. As for the possibility of my doing anything improper—look at me, if you will, please. Do I seem capable of anything of the sort?"

"This is preposterous, utterly preposterous. The very thought of it terrifies me. Why did I even come?"

"Not entirely preposterous, I think. Marriage is an uncertain arrangement. Are you saying that these things never under any circumstances happen to His Majesty's own ladies? I should think that the chances might be more considerable with someone like the princess. On the surface everything may seem to be going beautifully, but I should imagine that she has her share of private dissatisfactions. She was her father's favorite and now she is losing out to ladies of no very high standing. I know everything. It is an uncertain world we live in and no one can legislate to have things exactly as he wants them."

"You are not telling me, are you, that she is losing out to others and so she must make fine new arrangements for herself? The arrangements she has already made for herself are rather fine, I should think, and of a rather special nature. Her royal father would seem to have thought that with His Lordship to look after her as if she were his daughter she would have no worries. I should imagine that they have both of them accepted the relationship for what it is. Do you think it is quite your place to suggest changes?"

He must not let her go away angry. "You may be sure that I am aware of my own inadequacy and would not dream of exposing myself to the critical eye of a lady who is used to the incomparable Genji. But it would not be such a dreadful thing, I should think, to approach her curtains and speak with her very briefly? It is not considered such a great sin, I believe, for a person to speak the whole truth to the powers above."

He seemed prepared to swear by all the powers, and she was young and somewhat heedless, and when a man spoke as if he were prepared to throw his life away she could not resist forever.

"I will see what I can do if I find what seems the right moment. On nights when His Lordship does not come the princess has swarms of women in her room, and always several of her favorites right beside her, and I cannot imagine what sort of moment it will be."

Frowning, she left him.

He was after her constantly. The moment finally came, it seemed, and she got off a note to him. He set out in careful disguise, delighted but in great trepidation. It did not occur to him that a visit might only add to his torments. He wanted to see a little more of her whose sleeves he had glimpsed that spring evening. If he were to tell her what was in his heart, she might pity him, she might even answer him briefly.

It was about the middle of the Fourth Month, the eve of the lustration for the Kamo festival. Twelve women from the Third Princess's household were to be with the high priestess, and girls and young women of no very high rank who were going to watch the procession were busy at their needles and otherwise getting ready. No one had much time for the princess. Azechi, one of her most trusted intimates, had been summoned by the Minamoto captain with whom she was keeping company and had gone back to her room. Only Kojijū was with the princess. Sensing that the time was right, she led him to a seat in an east corner of the princess's boudoir. And was that not a little extreme?

The princess had gone serenely off to bed. She sensed that a man was in her room and thought that it would be Genji. But he seemed rather too polite—and then suddenly he put his arms around her and took her from her bed. She was terrified. Had some evil power seized her? She forced herself to look up and saw that it was a stranger. And here he was babbling complete nonsense. She called for her women, but no one came. She was trembling and bathed in perspiration. Though he could not help feeling sorry for her, he thought this agitation rather charming.

"I know that I am nothing, but I would not have expected quite such unfriendliness. I once had ambitions that were perhaps too grand for me. I could have kept them buried in my heart, I suppose, eventually to die there, but I spoke to someone of a small part of them and they came to your father's attention. I took courage from the fact that he did not seem to consider them entirely beneath his notice, and I told myself that the regret would be worse than anything if a love unique for its depth and intensity should come to nothing, and my low rank and only that must be held responsible. It was a very deep love indeed, and the sense of regret, the injury, the fear, the yearning, have only grown stronger as time has gone by. I know that I am being reckless and I am very much ashamed of myself that I cannot control my feelings and must reveal myself to you as someone who does not know his proper place. But I vow to you that I shall do nothing more. You will have no worse crimes to charge me with."

She finally guessed who he was, and was appalled. She was speechless.

"I know how you must feel; but it is not as if this sort of thing had never happened before. Your coldness is what has no precedent. It could drive me to extremes. Tell me that you pity me and that will be enough. I will leave you."

He had expected a proud lady whom it would not be easy to talk to. He would tell her a little of his unhappiness, he had thought, and say nothing he might later regret. But he found her very different. She was pretty and gentle and unresisting, and far more graceful and elegant, in a winsome way, than most ladies he had known. His passion was suddenly more than he could control. Was there no hiding place to which they might run off together?

He presently dozed off (it cannot be said that he fell asleep) and dreamed of the cat of which he had been so fond. It came up to him mewing prettily. He seemed to be dreaming that he had brought it back to the princess. As he awoke he was asking himself why he should have done that. And what might the dream have meant?

The princess was still in a state of shock. She could not believe that it had all happened.

"You must tell yourself that there were ties between us which we could not escape. I am in as much of a daze as you can possibly be."

He told her of the surprising event that spring evening, of the cat and the cord and the raised blind. So it had actually happened! Sinister forces seemed to preside over her affairs. And how could she face Genji? She wept like a little child and he looked on with respectful pity. Brushing away her tears, he let them mingle with his own.

There were traces of dawn in the sky. He felt that he had nowhere to go and that it might have been better had he not come at all. "What am I to do? You seem to dislike me most extravagantly, and I find it hard to think of anything more to say. And I have not even heard your voice."

He was only making things worse. Her thoughts in a turmoil, she was quite unable to speak.

"This muteness is almost frightening. Could anything be more awful? I can see no reason for going on. Let me die. Life has seemed to have some point and so I have lived, and even now it is not easy to think that I am at the end of it. Grant me some small favor, some gesture, anything at all, and I will not mind dying."

He took her in his arms and carried her out. She was terrified. What could he possibly mean to do with her? He spread a screen in a corner room and opened the door beyond. The south door of the gallery, through which he had come the evening before, was still open. It was very dark. Wanting to see her face, even dimly, he pushed open a shutter.

"This cruelty is driving me mad. If you wish to still the madness, then say that you pity me."

She did want to say something. She wanted to say that his conduct was outrageous. But she was trembling like a frightened child. It was growing lighter.

"I would like to tell you of a rather startling dream I had, but I suppose you would not listen. You seem to dislike me very much indeed. But I think it might perhaps mean something to you."

The dawn sky seemed sadder than the saddest autumn sky.

> "I arise and go forth in the dark before the dawn.
> I know not where, nor whence came the dew on my sleeve."

He showed her a moist sleeve.

He finally seemed to be leaving. So great was her relief that she managed an answer:

> "Would I might fade away in the sky of dawn,
> and all of it might vanish as a dream."

She spoke in a tiny, wavering voice and she was like a beautiful child. He hurried out as if he had only half heard, and felt as if he were leaving his soul behind.

He went quietly off to his father's house, preferring it to his own and the company of the Second Princess. He lay down but was unable to sleep. He did not know what if anything the dream had meant. He suddenly longed for the cat—and he was frightened. It was a terrible thing he had done. How could he face the world? He remained in seclusion and his secret wanderings seemed to be at an end. It was a terrible thing for the Third Princess, of course, and for himself as well. Supposing he had seduced the emperor's own lady and the deed had come to light—could the punishment be worse? Even if he were to avoid specific punishment he did not know how he could face a reproachful Genji.

There are wellborn ladies of strongly amorous tendencies whose dignity and formal bearing are a surface that falls away when the right man comes with the right overtures. With the Third Princess it was a matter of uncertainty and a want of firm principles. She was a timid girl and she felt as vulnerable as if one of her women had already broadcast her secret to the world. She could not face the sun. She wanted to brood in darkness.

She said that she was unwell. The report was passed on to Genji, who came hurrying over. He had thought that he already had worries enough. There was nothing emphatically wrong with her, it would seem, but she refused to look at him. Fearing that she was out of sorts because of his long absence, he told her about Murasaki's illness.

"It may be the end. At this time of all times I would not want her to think me unfeeling. She has been with me since she was a child and I cannot abandon her now. I am afraid I have not had time these last months for anyone else. It will not go on forever, and I know that you will presently understand."

She was ashamed and sorry. When she was alone she wept a great deal.

For Kashiwagi matters were worse. The conviction grew that it would have been better not to see her. Night and day he could only lament his impossible love. A group of young friends, in a hurry to be off to the Kamo festival, urged him to go with them, but he pleaded illness and spent the day by himself. Though correct in his behavior toward the Second Princess, he was not really fond of her. He passed the tedious hours in his own rooms. The little girl came in with a sprig of aoi, the heartvine of the Kamo festival.

> "In secret, without leave, she brings this heartvine.
> A most lamentable thing, a blasphemous thing."

He could think only of the Third Princess. He heard the festive roar in the distance as if it were no part of his life and passed a troubled day in a tedium of his own making.

The Second Princess was used to these low spirits. She did not know what might be responsible for them, but she felt unhappy and inadequate. She had almost no one with her, most of the women having gone off to the festival. In her gloom she played a sad, gentle strain on a koto. Yes, she was very beautiful, very delicate and refined; but had the choice been his he would have taken her sister. He had not, of course, been fated to make the choice.

> "Laurel branches twain, so near and like.
> Why was it that I took the fallen leaf?"[3]

It was a poem he jotted down to while away the time—and not very complimentary to the Second Princess.

Though Genji was in a fever of impatience to be back at Nijō, he so seldom visited Rokujō that it would be bad manners to leave immediately.

A messenger came. "Our lady has expired."

He rushed off. The road was dark before his eyes, and ever darker. At Nijō the crowds overflowed into the streets. There was weeping within. The worst did indeed seem to have happened. He pushed his way desperately through.

"She had seemed better these last few days," said one of the women, "and now this."

3. The Second Princess is often called Ochiba, "Fallen Leaf." The name comes from this poem.

The confusion was enormous. The women were wailing and asking her to take them with her. The altars had been dismantled and the priests were leaving, only the ones nearest the family remaining behind. For Genji it was like the end of the world.

He set about quieting the women. "Some evil power has made it seem that she is dead. Nothing more. Certainly this commotion does not seem called for."

He made vows more solemn and detailed than before and summoned ascetics known to have worked wonders.

"Even if her time has come and she must leave us," they said, "let her stay just a little longer. There was the vow of the blessed Fudō.[4] Let her stay even that much longer."

So intense and fevered were their efforts that clouds of black smoke seemed to coil over their heads.

Genji longed to look into her eyes once more. It had been too sudden, he had not even been allowed to say goodbye. There seemed a possibility—one can only imagine the dread which it inspired—that he too was on the verge of death.

Perhaps the powers above took note. The malign spirit suddenly yielded after so many tenacious weeks and passed from Murasaki to the little girl who was serving as medium, and who now commenced to thresh and writhe and moan. To Genji's joy and terror Murasaki was breathing once more.

The medium was now weeping and flinging her hair madly about. "Go away, all of you. I want a word with Lord Genji and it must be with him alone. All these prayers and chants all these months have been an unrelieved torment. I have wanted you to suffer as I have suffered. But then I saw that I had brought you to the point of death and I pitied you, and so I have come out into the open. I am no longer able to seem indifferent, though I am the wretch you see. It is precisely because the old feelings have not died that I have come to this. I had resolved to let myself be known to no one."

He had seen it before. The old terror and anguish came back. He took the little medium by the hand lest she do something violent.

"Is it really you? I have heard that foxes and other evil creatures sometimes go mad and seek to defame the dead. Tell me who you are, quite plainly. Or give me a sign, something that will be meaningless to others but unmistakable to me. Then I will try to believe you."

Weeping copiously and speaking in a loud wail, the medium seemed at the same time to cringe with embarrassment.

"I am horribly changed, and you pretend not to know me. You are the same. Oh dreadful, dreadful."

Even in these wild rantings there was a suggestion of the old aloofness. It added to the horror. He wanted to hear no more.

But there was more. "From up in the skies I saw what you did for my daughter and was pleased. But it seems to be a fact that the ways of the living are not the ways of the dead and that the feeling of mother for child is weakened. I have gone on thinking you the cruelest of men. I heard you tell your dear lady what a difficult and unpleasant person you once found me, and the resentment was worse than when you insulted me to my face and finally abandoned me. I am dead, and I hoped that you had forgiven me and would defend me against those who spoke ill of me and say that it was none of it true. The hope was what twisted a twisted creature more cruelly and brought this horror. I do not hate her; but the powers have shielded you and only let me hear your voice in the distance. Now this has happened. Pray for me. Pray that my

4. Early commentaries say that Fudō vowed to give six more months of life to those of the faithful who wished it.

sins be forgiven. These services, these holy texts, they are an unremitting torment, they are smoke and flames, and in the roar and crackle I cannot hear the holy word. Tell my child of my torments. Tell her that she is never to fall into rivalries with other ladies, never to be a victim of jealousy. Her whole attention must go to atoning for the sins of her time at Ise, far from the Good Law. I am sorry for everything."

It was not a dialogue which he wished to pursue. He had the little medium taken away and Murasaki quietly moved to another room.

The crowds swarming through the house seemed themselves to bode ill. All the high courtiers had been off watching the return procession from the Kamo Shrine and it was on their own way home that they heard the news.

"What a really awful thing," said someone, and there was no doubting the sincerity of the words. "A light that should for every reason have gone on shining has been put out, and we are left in a world of drizzling rain."

But someone else whispered: "It does not do to be too beautiful and virtuous. You do not live long. 'Nothing in this world would be their rival,' the poet said.[5] He was talking about cherry blossoms, of course, but it is so with her too. When such a lady lives to know all the pleasures and successes, her fellows must suffer. Maybe now the Third Princess will enjoy some of the attention that should have been hers all along. She has not had an easy time of it, poor thing."

Not wanting another such day, Kashiwagi had ridden off with several of his brothers to watch the return procession. The news of course came as a shock. They turned towards Nijō.

"Nothing is meant in this world to last forever,"[6] he whispered to himself. He went in as if inquiring after her health, for it had after all been only a rumor. The wailing and lamenting proclaimed that it must be true.

Prince Hyōbu had arrived and gone inside and was too stunned to receive him. A weeping Yūgiri came out.

"How is she? I heard these awful reports and was unable to believe them, though I had of course known of her illness."

"Yes, she has been very ill for a very long time. This morning at dawn she stopped breathing. But it seems to have been a possession. I am told that although she has revived and everyone is enormously relieved the crisis has not yet passed. We are still very worried."

His eyes were red and swollen. It was his own unhappy love, perhaps, that made Kashiwagi look curiously at his friend, wondering why he should grieve so for a stepmother of whom he had not seen a great deal.

"She was dangerously ill," Genji sent out to the crowds. "This morning quite suddenly it appeared that she had breathed her last. The shock, I fear, was such that we were all quite deranged and given over to loud and unbecoming grief. I have not myself been as calm and in control of things as I ought to have been. I will thank you properly at another time for having been so good as to call."

It would not have been possible for Kashiwagi to visit Rokujō except in such a crisis. He was in acute discomfort even so—evidence, no doubt, of a very bad conscience.

Genji was more worried than before. He commissioned numberless rites of very great dignity and grandeur. The Rokujō lady had done terrible things while she lived,

5. Anonymous, *Kokinshū* 70: "If cherry blossoms waited at our command / nothing in this world would be their rival."

6. *Tales of Ise* 82: "The cherry blossom is dearest when it falls. / Nothing is meant in this world to last forever."

and what she had now become was utterly horrible. He even felt uncomfortable about his relations with her daughter, the Reizei empress. The conclusion was inescapable: women were creatures of sin. He wanted to be done with them. He could not doubt that it was in fact the Rokujō lady who had addressed him. His remarks about her had been in an intimate conversation with Murasaki overheard by no one. Disaster still seemed imminent. He must do what he could to forestall it. Murasaki had so earnestly pleaded to become a nun. He thought that tentative vows might give her strength and so he permitted a token tonsure and ordered that the five injunctions be administered. There were noble and moving phrases in the sermon describing the admirable power of the injunctions. Weeping and hovering over Murasaki quite without regard for appearances, Genji too invoked the holy name. There are crises that can unsettle the most superior of men. He wanted only to save her, to have her still beside him, whatever the difficulties and sacrifices. The sleepless nights had left him dazed and emaciated.

Murasaki was better, but still in pain through the Fourth Month. It was now the rainy Fifth Month, when the skies are their most capricious. Genji commissioned a reading of the Lotus Sutra in daily installments and other solemn services as well towards freeing the Rokujō lady of her sins. At Murasaki's bedside there were continuous readings by priests of good voice. From time to time the Rokujō lady would make dolorous utterances through the medium, but she refused all requests that she go away.

Murasaki was troubled with a shortness of breath and seemed even weaker as the warm weather came on. Genji was in such a state of distraction that Murasaki, ill though she was, sought to comfort him. She would have no regrets if she were to die, but she did not want it to seem that she did not care. She forced herself to take broth and a little food and from the Sixth Month she was able to sit up. Genji was delighted but still very worried. He stayed with her at Nijō.

The Third Princess had been unwell since that shocking visitation. There were no specific complaints or striking symptoms. She felt vaguely indisposed and that was all. She had eaten very little for some weeks and was pale and thin. Unable to contain himself, Kashiwagi would sometimes come for visits as fleeting as dreams. She did not welcome them. She was so much in awe of Genji that to rank the younger man beside him seemed almost blasphemous. Kashiwagi was an amiable and personable young man, and people who were no more than friends were quite right to think him superior; but she had known the incomparable Genji since she was a child and Kashiwagi scarcely seemed worth a glance. She thought herself very badly treated indeed that he should be the one to make her unhappy. Her nurse and a few others knew the nature of her indisposition and grumbled that Genji's visits were so extremely infrequent. He did finally come to inquire after her.

It was very warm. Murasaki had had her hair washed and otherwise sought renewal. Since she was in bed with her hair spread about her, it was not quick to dry. It was smooth and without a suggestion of a tangle to the farthest ends. Her skin was lovely, so white that it almost seemed iridescent, as if a light were shining through. She was very beautiful and as fragile as the shell of a locust.

The Nijō mansion had been neglected and was somewhat run-down, and compared to the Rokujō mansion it seemed very cramped and narrow. Taking advantage of a few days when she was somewhat more herself, Genji sent gardeners to clear the brook and restore the flower beds, and the suddenly renewed expanse before her made Murasaki marvel that she should be witness to such things. The lake was very cool, a carpet of lotuses. The dew on the green of the pads was like a scattering of jewels.

"Just look, will you," said Genji. "As if it had a monopoly on coolness. I cannot tell you how pleased I am that you have improved so." She was sitting up and her pleasure in the scene was quite open. There were tears in his eyes. "I was almost afraid at times that I too might be dying."

She was near tears herself.

> "It is a life in which we cannot be sure of lasting
> as long as the dew upon the lotus."

And he replied:

> "To be as close as the drops of dew on the lotus
> must be our promise in this world and the next."

Though he felt no eagerness to visit Rokujō, it had been some time since he had learned of the Third Princess's indisposition. Her brother and father would probably have heard of it too. They would think his inability to leave Murasaki rather odd and his failure to take advantage of a break in the rains even odder.

The princess looked away and did not answer his questions. Interpreting her silence as resentment at his long absence, he set about reasoning with her.

He called some of her older women and made detailed inquiries about her health.

"She is in an interesting condition, as they say."

"Really, now! And at this late date! I couldn't be more surprised."

It was his general want of success in fathering children that made the news so surprising. Ladies he had been with for a very long while had remained childless. He thought her sweet and pathetic and did not pursue the matter. Since it had taken him so long to collect himself for the visit, he could not go back to Nijō immediately. He stayed with her for several days. Murasaki was always on his mind, however, and he wrote her letter after letter.

"He certainly has thought of a great deal to say in a very short time," grumbled a woman who did not know that the lady was the more culpable party. "It does not seem like a marriage with the firmest sort of foundations."

Kojijū was frantic with worry.

Hearing that Genji was at Rokujō, Kashiwagi was a victim of a jealousy that might have seemed out of place. He wrote a long letter to the Princess describing his sorrows. Kojijū took advantage of a moment when Genji was in another part of the house to show her the letter.

"Take it away. It makes me feel worse." She lay down and refused to look at it.

"But do just glance for a minute at the beginning here." Kojijū unfolded the letter. "It is very sad."

Someone was coming. She pulled the princess's curtains closed and went off.

It was Genji. In utter confusion, the princess had time only to push it under the edge of a quilt.

He would be going back to Rokujō that evening, said Genji. "You do not seem so very ill. The lady in the other house is very ill indeed and I would not want her to think I have deserted her. You are not to pay any attention to what they might be saying about me. You will presently see the truth."

So cheerful and even frolicsome at other times, she was subdued and refused to look at him. It must be that she thought he did not love her. He lay down beside her and as they talked it was evening. He was awakened from a nap by a clamor of evening cicadas.

"It will soon be dark," he said, getting up to change clothes.

"Can you not stay at least until you have the moon to guide you?"[7]

She seemed so very young. He thought her charming. At least until then—it was a very small request.

> "The voice of the evening cicada says you must leave.
> 'Be moist with evening dews,' you say to my sleeves?"

Something of the cheerful innocence of old seemed to come back. He sighed and knelt down beside her.

> "How do you think it sounds in yonder village,
> the cicada that summons me there and summons me here?"

He was indeed pulled in two directions. Finally deciding that it would be cruel to leave, he stayed the night. Murasaki continued to be very much on his mind. He went to bed after a light supper.

He was up early, thinking to be on his way while it was still cool.

"I left my fan somewhere. This one is not much good." He searched through her sitting room, where he had had his nap the day before.

He saw a corner of pale-green tissue paper at the edge of a slightly disarranged quilt. Casually he took it up. It was a note in a man's hand. Delicately perfumed, it somehow had the look of a rather significant document. There were two sheets of paper covered with very small writing. The hand was without question Kashiwagi's.

The woman who opened the mirror for him paid little attention. It would of course be a letter he had every right to see. But Kojijū noted with horror that it was the same color as Kashiwagi's of the day before. She quite forgot about breakfast. It could not be. Nothing so awful could have been permitted to happen. Her lady absolutely must have hidden it.

The princess was still sleeping soundly. What a child she was, thought Genji, not without a certain contempt. Supposing someone else had found the letter. That was the thing: the heedlessness that had troubled him all along.

He had left and the other women were some distance away. "And what did you do with the young gentleman's letter?" asked Kojijū. "His Lordship was reading a letter that was very much the same color."

The princess collapsed in helpless weeping.

Kojijū was sorry for her, of course, but shocked and angry too. "Really, my lady—where did you put it? There were others around and I went off because I did not want him to think we were conspiring. That was how I felt. And you had time before he came in. Surely you hid it?"

"He came in on me while I was reading it. I didn't have time. I slipped it under something and forgot about it."

Speechless, Kojijū went to look for the letter. It was of course nowhere to be found.

"How perfectly, impossibly awful. The young gentleman was terrified of His Lordship, terrified that the smallest word might reach him. And now this has happened, and in no time at all. You are such a child, my lady. You let him see you, and he could not forget you however many years went by, and came begging to me. But that we should lose control of things so completely—it just did not seem possible. Nothing could be worse for either of you."

7. Oyakeme of Buzen, *Manyōshū* 709, with variations in other anthologies: "Dark the way and dangerous. / Can you not stay at least until you have the moon to guide you?"

She did not mince words. The princess was too good-natured and still too much of a child to argue back. Her tears flowed on.

She quite lost her appetite. Her women thought Genji cruel and unfeeling. "She is so extremely unwell, and he ignores her. He gives all his attention to a lady who has quite recovered."

Genji was still puzzled. He read the letter over and over again. He tested the hypothesis that one of her women had deliberately set about imitating Kashiwagi's hand. But it would not do. The idiosyncrasies were all too clearly Kashiwagi's. He had to admire the style, the fluency and clear detail with which Kashiwagi had described the fortuitous consummation of all his hopes, and all his sufferings since. But Genji had felt contemptuous of the princess and he must feel contemptuous of her young friend too. A man simply did not set these matters down so clearly in writing. Kashiwagi was a man of discernment and some eminence, and he had written a letter that could easily embarrass a lady. Genji himself had in his younger years never forgotten that letters have a way of going astray. His own letters had always been laconic and evasive even when he had longed to make them otherwise. Caution had not always been easy.

And how was he to behave towards the princess? He understood rather better the reasons for her condition. He had come upon the truth himself, without the aid of informers. Was there to be no change in his manner? He would have preferred that there be none but feared that things could not be the same again. Even in affairs which he had not from the outset taken seriously, the smallest evidence that the lady might be interested in someone else had always been enough to kill his own interest; and here he had more, a good deal more. What an impertinent trifler the young man was! It was not unknown for a young man to seduce even one of His Majesty's own ladies, but this seemed different. A young man and lady might in the course of their duties in the royal service find themselves favorably disposed towards each other and do what they ought not to have done. Such things did happen. Royal ladies were, after all, human. Some of them were not perhaps as sober and careful as they might be and they made mistakes. The man would remain in the court service and unless there was a proper scandal the mistake might go undetected. But this—Genji snapped his fingers in irritation. He had paid more attention to the princess than the lady he really loved, the truly priceless treasure, and she had responded by choosing a man like Kashiwagi!

He thought that there could be no precedent for it. Life had its frustrations for His Majesty's ladies when they obediently did their duty. There might come words of endearment from an honest man and there might be times when silence seemed impossible, and in a lady's answers would be the start of a love affair. One did not condone her behavior but one could understand it. But Genji thought himself neither fatuous nor conceited in wondering how the Third Princess could possibly have divided her affections between him and a man like Kashiwagi.

Well, it was all very distasteful. But he would say nothing. He wondered if his own father had long ago known what was happening and said nothing. He could remember his own terror very well, and the memory told him that he was hardly the one to reprove others who strayed from the narrow path.

Despite his determined silence, Murasaki knew that something was wrong. She herself had quite recovered, and she feared that he was feeling guilty about the Third Princess.

"I really am very much better. They tell me that Her Highness is not well. You should have stayed with her a little longer."

"Her Highness—it is true that she is indisposed, but I cannot see that there is a great deal wrong with her. Messenger after messenger has come from court. I gather that there was one just today from her father. Her brother worries about her because her father worries about her, and I must worry about both of them."

"I would worry less about them than about the princess herself if I thought she was unhappy. She may not say very much, but I hate to think of all those women giving her ideas."

Genji smiled and shrugged his shoulders. "You are the important one and you have no troublesome relatives, and you think of all these things. I think about her important brother and you think about her women. I fear I am not a very sensitive man." But of her suggestion that he return to Rokujō he said only: "There will be time when you are well enough to go with me."

"I would like to stay here just a little while longer. Do please go ahead and make her happy. I won't be long."

And so the days went by. The princess was of course in no position to charge him with neglect. She lived in dread lest her father get some word of what had happened.

Letter after passionate letter came from Kashiwagi. Finally, pushed too far, Kojijū told him everything. He was horrified. When had it happened? It had been as if the skies were watching him, so fearful had he been that something in the air might arouse Genji's suspicions. And now Genji had irrefutable evidence. It was a time of still, warm weather even at night and in the morning, but he felt as if a cold wind were cutting through him. Genji had singled him out for special favors and made him a friend and adviser, and for all this Kashiwagi had been most grateful. How could he now face Genji—who must think him an intolerable upstart and interloper! Yet if he were to avoid Rokujō completely people would notice and think it odd, and Genji would of course have stronger evidence than before. Sick with worry, Kashiwagi stopped going to court. It was not likely that he would face specific punishment, but he feared that he had ruined his life. Things could not be worse. He hated himself for what he had let happen.

[*Tormented by guilt, and fearful of Genji's displeasure, Kashiwagi falls seriously ill.*]

from *Chapter 36. The Oak Tree*

The New Year came and Kashiwagi's condition had not improved. He knew how troubled his parents were and he knew that suicide was no solution, for he would be guilty of the grievous sin of having left them behind. He had no wish to live on. Since his very early years he had had high standards and ambitions and had striven in private matters and public to outdo his rivals by even a little. His wishes had once or twice been thwarted, however, and he had so lost confidence in himself that the world had come to seem unrelieved gloom. A longing to prepare for the next world had succeeded his ambitions, but the opposition of his parents had kept him from following the mendicant way through the mountains and over the moors. He had delayed, and time had gone by. Then had come events, and for them he had only himself to blame, which had made it impossible for him to show his face in public. He did not blame the gods. His own deeds were working themselves out. A man does not have the thousand years of the pine, and he wanted to go now, while there were still those who might mourn for him a little, and perhaps even a sigh from her would be the reward for his burning passion. To die now and perhaps win the forgiveness of the man who must feel so aggrieved would be far preferable to living on and bringing sorrow and dishonor upon the lady and upon himself. In his last moments everything must disappear. Perhaps, because he had no other sins to atone for, a part of the affection with which Genji had once honored him might return.

The same thoughts, over and over, ran uselessly through his mind. And why, he asked himself in growing despair, had he so deprived himself of alternatives? His pillow threatened to float away on the river of his woes.

He took advantage of a slight turn for the better, when his parents and the others had withdrawn from his bedside, to get off a letter to the Third Princess.

"You may have heard that I am near death. It is natural that you should not care very much, and yet I am sad." His hand was so uncertain that he gave up any thought of saying all that he would have wished to say.

> "My thoughts of you: will they stay when I am gone
> like smoke that lingers over the funeral pyre?

One word of pity will quiet the turmoil and light the dark road I am taking by my own choice."

Unchastened, he wrote to Kojijū of his sufferings, at considerable length. He longed, he said, to see her lady one last time. She had from childhood been close to his house, in which she had near relatives. Although she had strongly disapproved of his designs upon a royal princess who should have been far beyond his reach, she was extremely sorry for him in what might be his last illness.

"Do answer him, please, my lady," she said, in tears. "You must, just this once. It may be your last chance."

"I am sorry for him, in a general sort of way. I am sorry for myself too. Any one of us could be dead tomorrow. But what happened was too awful. I cannot bear to think of it. I could not possibly write to him."

She was not by nature a very careful sort of lady, but the great man to whom she was married had terrorized her with hints, always guarded, that he was displeased with her.

Kojijū insisted and pushed an inkstone towards her, and finally, very hesitantly, she set down an answer which Kojijū delivered under cover of evening.

Tō no Chūjō had sent to Mount Katsuragi for an ascetic famous as a worker of cures, and the spells and incantations in which he immersed himself might almost have seemed overdone. Other holy men were recommended and Tō no Chūjō's sons would go off to seek in mountain recesses men scarcely known in the city. Mendicants quite devoid of grace came crowding into the house. The symptoms did not point to any specific illness, but Kashiwagi would sometimes weep in great, racking sobs. The soothsayers were agreed that a jealous woman had taken possession of him. They might possibly be right, thought Tō no Chūjō. But whoever she was she refused to withdraw, and so it was that the search for healers reached into these obscure corners. The ascetic from Katsuragi, an imposing man with cold, forbidding eyes, intoned mystic spells in a somewhat threatening voice.

"I cannot stand a moment more of it," said Kashiwagi. "I must have sinned grievously. These voices terrify me and seem to bring death even nearer."

Slipping from bed, he instructed the women to tell his father that he was asleep and went to talk with Kojijū. Tō no Chūjō and the ascetic were conferring in subdued tones. Tō no Chūjō was robust and youthful for his years and in ordinary times much given to laughter. He told the holy man how it had all begun and how a respite always seemed to be followed by a relapse.

"Do please make her go away, whoever she might be," he said entreatingly.

A hollow shell of his old self, Kashiwagi was meanwhile addressing Kojijū in a faltering voice sometimes interrupted by a suggestion of a laugh.

"Listen to them. They seem to have no notion that I might be ill because I misbehaved. If, as these wise men say, some angry lady has taken possession of me, then I would expect her presence to make me hate myself a little less. I can say that others have done much the same thing, made mistakes in their longing for ladies beyond their reach, and ruined their prospects. I can tell myself all this, but the torment goes on. I cannot face the world knowing that he knows. His radiance dazzles and blinds me. I would not have thought the misdeed so appalling, but since the evening when he set upon me I have so lost control of myself that it has been as if my soul were wandering loose. If it is still around the house somewhere, please lay a trap for it."[1]

She told him of the Third Princess, lost in sad thoughts and afraid of prying eyes. He could almost see the forlorn little figure. Did unhappy spirits indeed go wandering forth disembodied?

"I shall say no more of your lady. It has all passed as if it had never happened at all. Yet I would be very sorry indeed if it were to stand in the way of her salvation. I have only one wish left, to know that the consequences of the sad affair have been disposed of safely. I have my own interpretation of the dream I had that night and have had very great trouble keeping it to myself."

Kojijū was frightened at the inhuman tenacity which these thoughts suggested. Yet she had to feel sorry for him. She was weeping bitterly.

He sent for a lamp and read the princess's note. Though fragile and uncertain, the hand was interesting. "Your letter made me very sad, but I cannot see you. I can only think of you. You speak of the smoke that lingers on, and yet

> I wish to go with you, that we may see
> whose smoldering thoughts last longer, yours or mine."

That was all, but he was grateful for it.

"The smoke—it will follow me from this world. What a useless, insubstantial affair it was!"

Weeping uncontrollably, he set about a reply. There were many pauses and the words were fragmentary and disconnected and the hand like the tracks of a strange bird.

> "As smoke I shall rise uncertainly to the heavens,
> and yet remain where my thoughts will yet remain.

Look well, I pray you, into the evening sky. Be happy, let no one reprove you; and, though it will do no good, have an occasional thought for me."

Suddenly worse again, he made his way tearfully back to his room. "Enough. Go while it is still early, please, and tell her of my last moments. I would not want anyone who already thinks it odd to think it even odder. What have I brought from other lives, I wonder, to make me so unhappy?"

Usually he kept her long after their business was finished, but today he dismissed her briefly. She was very sorry for him and did not want to go.

His nurse, who was her aunt, told Kojijū of his illness, weeping all the while.

Tō no Chūjō was in great alarm. "He had seemed better these last few days. Why the sudden change?"

1. *Tales of Ise* 110: "In longing my soul has ventured forth alone. / If you see it late in the night, please seek to trap it."

"I cannot see why you are surprised," replied his son. "I am dying. That is all."

That evening the Third Princess was taken with severe pains.

Guessing that they were birth pangs, her women sent for Genji in great excitement. He came immediately. How vast and unconditional his joy would be, he thought, were it not for his doubts about the child. But no one must be allowed to suspect their existence. He summoned ascetics and put them to continuous spells and incantations, and he summoned all the monks who had made names for themselves as healers. The Rokujō mansion echoed with mystic rites. The princess was in great pain through the night and at sunrise was delivered of a child. It was a boy. Most unfortunate, thought Genji. It would not be easy to guard the secret if the resemblance to the father was strong. There were devices for keeping girls in disguise and of course girls did not have to appear in public as did boys. But there was the other side of the matter: given these nagging doubts from the outset, a boy did not require the attention which must go into rearing a girl.

But how very strange it all was! Retribution had no doubt come for the deed which had terrified him then and which he was sure would go on terrifying him to the end. Since it had come, all unexpectedly, in this world, perhaps the punishment would be lighter in the next.

Unaware of these thoughts, the women quite lost themselves in ministering to the child. Because it was born of such a mother in Genji's late years, it must surely have the whole of his affection.

[*Kashiwagi dies, and after the Third Princess gives birth to his son, Kaoru, she immediately takes Buddhist vows despite Genji's protests. Kaoru, a beautiful little boy, is thought by the world to be Genji's son, and is raised in the Rokujō mansion.*]

from *Chapter 40. The Rites*

[*Three years have passed. Murasaki has continued to be in uncertain health since her great illness, and again seeks permission from Genji to take Buddhist vows, but Genji stubbornly refuses. The Akashi daughter, who was raised by Murasaki and has since been named empress, visits her sickbed.*]

Murasaki had always found the heat very trying. This summer she was near prostration. Though there were no marked symptoms and though there was none of the unsightliness that usually goes with emaciation, she was progressively weaker. Her women saw the world grow dark before their eyes as they contemplated the future.

Distressed at reports that there was no improvement, the empress visited Nijō. She was given rooms in the east wing and Murasaki waited to receive her in the main hall. Though there was nothing unusual about the greetings, they reminded Murasaki, as indeed did everything, that the empress's little children would grow up without her. The attendants announced themselves one by one, some of them very high courtiers. A familiar voice, thought Murasaki, and another. She had not seen the empress in a very long while and hung on the conversation with fond and eager attention.

Genji looked in upon them briefly. "You find me disconsolate this evening," he said to the empress, "a bird turned away from its nest. But I shall not bore you with my complaints." He withdrew. He was delighted to see Murasaki out of bed, but feared that the pleasure must be a fleeting one.

"We are so far apart that I would not dream of troubling you to visit me, and I fear that it will not be easy for me to visit you."[1]

After a time the Akashi lady came in. The two ladies addressed each other affectionately, though Murasaki left a great deal unsaid. She did not want to be one of those who eloquently prepare the world to struggle along without them. She did remark briefly and quietly upon the evanescence of things, and her wistful manner said more than her words.

Genji's royal grandchildren were brought in.

"I spend so much time imagining futures for you, my dears. Do you suppose that I do after all hate to go?"

Still very beautiful, she was in tears. The empress would have liked to change the subject, but could not think how.

"May I ask a favor?" said Murasaki, very casually, as if she hesitated to bring the matter up at all. "There are numbers of people who have been with me for a very long while, and some of them have no home but this. Might I ask you to see that they are taken care of?" And she gave the names.

Having commissioned a reading from the holy writ, the empress returned to her rooms.

Little Niou, the prettiest of them all, seemed to be everywhere at once. Choosing a moment when she was feeling better and there was no one else with her, she seated him before her.

"I may have to go away. Will you remember me?"

"But I don't want you to go away." He gazed up at her, and presently he was rubbing at his eyes, so charming that she was smiling through her tears. "I like my granny,[2] better than Father and Mother. I don't want you to go away."

"This must be your own house when you grow up. I want the rose plum and the cherries over there to be yours. You must take care of them and say nice things about them, and sometimes when you think of it you might put flowers on the altar."

He nodded and gazed up at her, and then abruptly, about to burst into tears, he got up and ran out. It was Niou and the First Princess whom Murasaki most hated to leave. They had been her special charges, and she would not live to see them grow up.

The cool of autumn, so slow to come, was at last here. Though far from well, she felt somewhat better. The winds were still gentle, but it was a time of heavy dews all the same. She would have liked the empress to stay with her just a little while longer but did not want to say so. Messengers had come from the emperor, all of them summoning the empress back to court, and she did not want to put the empress in a difficult position. She was no longer able to leave her room, however much she might want to respect the amenities, and so the empress called on her. Apologetic and at the same time very grateful, for she knew that this might be their last meeting, she had made careful preparations for the visit.

Though very thin, she was more beautiful than ever—one would not have thought it possible. The fresh, vivacious beauty of other years had asked to be likened to the flowers of this earth, but now there was a delicate serenity that seemed to go beyond such present similes. For the empress the slight figure before her, the very serenity bespeaking evanescence, was utter sadness.

1. The speaker may be either Murasaki or the empress.

2. *Haha,* the most common word for "mother." Some commentators argue for *baba,* "old woman" or "grandmother."

Wishing to look at her flowers in the evening light, Murasaki pulled herself from bed with the aid of an armrest.

Genji came in. "Isn't this splendid? I imagine Her Majesty's visit has done wonders for you."

How pleased he was at what was in fact no improvement at all—and how desolate he must soon be!

> "So briefly rests the dew upon the hagi.
> Even now it scatters in the wind."

It would have been a sad evening in any event, and the plight of the dew even now being shaken from the tossing branches, thought Genji, must seem to the sick lady very much like her own.

> "In the haste we make to leave this world of dew,
> may there be no time between the first and last."

He did not try to hide his tears.

And this was the empress's poem:

> "A world of dew before the autumn winds.
> Not only theirs, these fragile leaves of grass."

Gazing at the two of them, each somehow more beautiful than the other, Genji wished that he might have them a thousand years just as they were; but of course time runs against these wishes. That is the great, sad truth.

"Would you please leave me?" said Murasaki. "I am feeling rather worse. I do not like to know that I am being rude and find myself unable to apologize." She spoke with very great difficulty.

The empress took her hand and gazed into her face. Yes, it was indeed like the dew about to vanish away. Scores of messengers were sent to commission new services. Once before it had seemed that she was dying, and Genji hoped that whatever evil spirit it was might be persuaded to loosen its grip once more. All through the night he did everything that could possibly be done, but in vain. Just as light was coming she faded away. Some kind power above, he thought, had kept the empress with her through the night. He might tell himself, as might all the others who had been with her, that these things have always happened and will continue to happen, but there are times when the natural order of things is unacceptable. The numbing grief made the world itself seem like a twilight dream. The women tried in vain to bring their wandering thoughts together. Fearing for his father, more distraught even than they, Yūgiri had come to him.

"It seems to be the end," said Genji, summoning him to Murasaki's curtains. "To be denied one's last wish is a cruel thing. I suppose that their reverences will have finished their prayers and left us, but someone qualified to administer vows must still be here. We did not do a great deal for her in this life, but perhaps the Great Buddha can be persuaded to turn a little light on the way she must take into the next. Tell them, please, that I want someone to give the tonsure. There is still someone with us who can do it, surely?"

He spoke with studied calm, but his face was drawn and he was weeping.

"But these evil spirits play very cruel tricks," replied Yūgiri, only slightly less benumbed than his father. "Don't you suppose the same thing has happened all over again? Your suggestion is of course quite proper. We are told that even a day and a night of the holy life brings untold blessings. But suppose this really is the end—can we hope that anything we do will throw so very much light on the way she must go? No, let us come to terms with the sorrow we have before us and try not to make it worse."

But he summoned several of the priests who had stayed on, wishing to be of service through the period of mourning, and asked them to do whatever could still be done.

He could congratulate himself on his filial conduct over the years, upon the fact that he had permitted himself no improper thoughts; but he had had one fleeting glimpse of her, and he had gone on hoping that he might one day be permitted another, even as brief, or that he might hear her voice, even faintly. The second hope had come to nothing, and the other—if he did not see her now he never would see her. He was in tears himself, and the room echoed with the laments of the women.

"Do please try to be a little quieter, just for a little while." He lifted the curtains as he spoke, making it seem that Genji had summoned him. In the dim morning twilight Genji had brought a lamp near Murasaki's dead face. He knew that Yūgiri was beside him, but somehow felt that to screen this beauty from his son's gaze would only add to the anguish.

"Exactly as she was," he whispered. "But as you see, it is all over."

He covered his face. Yūgiri too was weeping. He brushed the tears away and struggled to see through them as the sight of the dead face brought them flooding back again. Though her hair had been left untended through her illness, it was smooth and lustrous and not a strand was out of place. In the bright lamplight the skin was a purer, more radiant white than the living lady, seated at her mirror, could have made it. Her beauty, as if in untroubled sleep, emptied words like "peerless" of all content. He almost wished that the spirit which seemed about to desert him might be given custody of the unique loveliness before him.

Since Murasaki's women were none of them up to such practical matters, Genji forced himself to think about the funeral arrangements. He had known many sorrows, but none quite so near at hand, demanding that he and no one else do what must be done. He had known nothing like it, and he was sure that there would be nothing like it in what remained of his life.

from *Chapter 41. The Wizard*

Already at the beginning of the Eighth Month the autumn winds were lonely. Genji was busy with preparations for the memorial services. How swiftly the months had gone by! Everyone went through fasting and penance and the Paradise Mandala was dedicated. Chūjō[1] as usual brought holy water for Genji's vesper devotions. He took up her fan, on which she had written a poem:

> "This day, we are told, announces an end to mourning.
> How can it be, when there is no end to tears?"

He wrote beside it:

> "The days are numbered for him who yet must mourn.
> And are they numbered, the tears that yet remain?"

1. One of Murasaki's women.

Early in the Ninth Month came the chrysanthemum festival. As always, the festive bouquets were wrapped in cotton to catch the magic dew.

> "On other mornings we took the elixir together.
> This morning lonely sleeves are wet with dew."

The Tenth Month was as always a time of gloomy winter showers. Looking up into the evening sky, he whispered to himself: "The rains are as the rains of other years." He envied the wild geese overhead, for they were going home.

> "O wizard flying off through boundless heavens,
> find her whom I see not even in my dreams."[2]

The days and months went by, and he remained inconsolable.

Presently the world was buzzing with preparations for the harvest festival and the Gosechi dances. Yūgiri brought two of his little boys, already in court service, to see their grandfather. They were very nearly the same age, and very pretty indeed. With them were several of their uncles, spruce and elegant in blue Gosechi prints, a very grand escort indeed for two little boys. At the sight of them all, so caught up in the festive gaiety, Genji thought of memorable occurrences on ancient festival days.

> "Our lads go off to have their Day of Light.[3]
> For me it is as if there were no sun."

And so he had made his way through the year, and the time had come to leave the world behind. He gave his attendants, after their several ranks, gifts to remember him by. He tried to avoid grand farewells, but they knew what was happening, and the end of the year was a time of infinite sadness. Among his papers were letters which he had put aside over the years but which he would not wish others to see. Now, as he got his affairs in order, he would come upon them and burn them. There was a bundle of letters from Murasaki among those he had received at Suma from his various ladies. Though a great many years had passed, the ink was as fresh as if it had been set down yesterday. They seemed meant to last a thousand years. But they had been for him, and he was finished with them. He asked two or three women who were among his closest confidantes to see to destroying them. The handwriting of the dead always has the power to move us, and these were not ordinary letters. He was blinded by the tears that fell to mingle with the ink until presently he was unable to make out what was written.

> "I seek to follow the tracks of a lady now gone
> to another world. Alas, I lose my way."

Not wanting to display his weakness, he pushed them aside.

The women were permitted glimpses of this and that letter, and the little they saw was enough to bring the old grief back anew. Murasaki's sorrow at being those few miles from him now seemed to remove all bounds to their own sorrow. Seeking to control a flow of tears that must seem hopelessly exaggerated, Genji glanced at one of the more affectionate notes and wrote in the margin:

2. In "The Song of Everlasting Sorrow" the emperor sends a wizard in search of the dead Yang Kuei-fei. In Chapter 1, Genji's grieving father is put in mind of the same passage. The word *maboroshi,* "wizard," occurs in the tale only these two times.

3. Toyonoakari, the day following the harvest festival proper.

"I gather sea grasses no more, nor look upon them.
Now they are smoke, to join her in distant heavens."

And so he consigned them to flames.

In the Twelfth Month the clanging of croziers as the holy name was invoked was more moving than in other years, for Genji knew that he would not again be present at the ceremony. These prayers for longevity—he did not think that they would please the Blessed One. There had been a heavy fall of snow, which was now blowing into drifts. The repast in honor of the officiant was elaborate and Genji's gifts were even more lavish than usual. The holy man had often presided over services at court and at Rokujō. Genji was sorry to see that his hair was touched with gray. As always, there were numerous princes and high courtiers in the congregation. The plum trees, just coming into bloom, were lovely in the snow. There should have been music, but Genji feared that this year music would make him weep. Poems were read, in keeping with the time and place.

There was this poem as Genji offered a cup of wine to his guest of honor:

"Put blossoms in your caps today. Who knows
that there will still be life when spring comes round?"

This was the reply:

"I pray that these blossoms may last a thousand springs.
For me the years are as the deepening snowdrifts."

There were many others, but I neglected to set them down.

It was Genji's first appearance in public. He was handsomer than ever, indeed almost unbelievably handsome. For no very good reason, the holy man was in tears.

Genji was more and more despondent as the New Year approached.

Niou scampered about exorcising devils, that the New Year might begin auspiciously.

"It takes a lot of noise to get rid of them. Do you have any ideas?"

Everything about the scene, and especially the thought that he must say goodbye to the child, made Genji fear that he would soon be weeping again.

"I have not taken account of the days and months.
The end of the year—the end of a life as well?"

The festivities must be more joyous than ever, he said, and his gifts to all the princes and officials, high and low—or so one is told—quite shattered precedent.

The Qur'an

The Qur'an, also known as *al-kitab* (the Book) or *Kitab Allah* (the Book of God) is the name of the Muslim scripture. It contains the divine text that was revealed in its fixed and finite form to the Prophet Muhammad through the archangel Gabriel, a celestial messenger serving as intermediary between God and Muhammad. It is the word of Allah revealed to his Prophet, Muhammad, over some twenty years (between 610–632), to transmit to the whole of humanity. Moses parted the Red Sea, Jesus had the ability to walk on water and resurrect the dead; the Qur'an was Muhammad's sole miracle. It has been approached as a linguistic miracle by Muslim scholars for centuries.

The earliest attested use of the word *qur'an* is in the Qur'an itself, where it occurs about seventy times; *al-kitab* ("the book") occurs 255 times, establishing self-reference as one of the book's textual strategies. The word *qur'an* comes from the Arabic root *qara'a,* "read," which is the first word of the first verse that was revealed to Muhammad. In the Qur'an itself, the most frequently used synonym for the Qur'an is *al-kitab,* which is also used to refer to the books revealed to Moses and to Jesus' disciples, thus establishing the genealogy of the Qur'an as the final version of previous divine revelations that were, according to the Qur'an, subjected to human interference. Thus the preservation of the accurate text of the Qur'an was of paramount importance if it was not to suffer the fate of previous revelations.

The Qur'an was preserved orally and in written form during the life of Muhammad. Upon revelation, each verse was committed to memory by several of his followers and written down by others known as the scribes of the revelation, the most famous of them being Zayd ibn Thabit, the Prophet's secretary. Before his death, Muhammad read the final version of the Qur'an in its entirety to his followers and secretaries. This was later preserved in written form during the time of his successor, Abu Bakr (r. 632–634) under the auspices of Thabit. Thus within two years of Muhammad's death a definitive text was written down, kept by Abu Bakr, then passed to his successor 'Umar (634–644). In the time of the third caliph, 'Uthman (644–656), several manuscripts were made on the basis of the first one ordered by Abu Bakr and distributed to conquered lands outside Arabia.

The verses of the Qur'an vary in length from a few letters to 128 words, and these are grouped in sections or chapters (suras), which vary in length from 3 to 286 verses. They are roughly arranged in decreasing order of length. The first sura, "The Opening," is liturgical in nature, as are the final short suras, a number of which have the form of incantations. The other suras are in many different forms and genres, which vary from the short oath to a lengthy narrative of several biblical and nonbiblical stories.

The Qur'an consists of 114 suras, eighty-five revealed in Mecca, and twenty-nine revealed in Medina. The early Meccan suras call for belief in one God and in social justice, transcendent truths, and the practice of personal and altruistic virtues. They are mainly short and their language is full of poetic imagery and eloquent appeals to the hearer to worship and embrace Islam as the final creed. The suras of the middle Meccan period are longer and more prosaic, though they still retain some poetic qualities, referring mainly to the manifestations of God in nature and his divine attributes, while the late Meccan suras are full of narrative stories and sermons. The Medinan suras tend to be more prescriptive and legislative, and they contain more narrative concerning the organization of the community and the lessons it should learn from the mistakes of the past. They were revealed after the creation of the first Islamic community in Medina and aimed to provide it with guidance and consolidate its identity and cohesion.

As will be seen in the selections included here, the Qur'an embraces many literary and linguistic forms, from the oath and prophetic utterance, to the imperative and didactic "say-passages," to dramatic and narrative forms. Many of the Qur'anic narratives retell traditional stories found in Near and Middle Eastern cultures, such as the story of creation. Others are derived from biblical or apocryphal Christian texts and oral tradition. The Qur'an relates the stories of the prophets or messengers of God from Noah to Jesus, including Abraham, Ishmael, David, Elijah, Jonah, Jacob, Joseph, Job, Moses, and Solomon. The stories of these biblical characters are retold with some variations and often major alterations. The story of Joseph (Sura 12) follows the biblical account rather closely, while that of Jesus differs in some essential details. It accepts the biblical story but denies an essential aspect of the Christian account, the resurrection of Jesus. In addition to all these biblical characters, the Qur'an has many nonbiblical ones, including several from Greek sources.

Narrative stories comprise a substantial part of the Qur'an, and many of them were augmented and elaborated in several commentaries and exegeses. As a text, the Qur'an relies on cross-referencing and it often relates a story in more than one chapter. It relates segments or kernels of a specific story in one sura, picks it up again in another to complement or enforce certain aspects of its narrative, then gives its final parts in a third sura. This serves many different functions—to sustain the reader's attention and interest in the story, or test our comprehension of its implications, or even enforce its significance in the text. The story of creation is a good example. In order to get the complete story and to understand its relations with other biblical variants, one has to gather its scattered segments from four or five suras, as in the opening selections given here. One finds a segment on the creation of earth in one sura, the nature of its oval shape in another, and the time of this creation and how to calculate it in our modern manner in a third sura.

This narrative strategy was elaborated and developed into a fine art centuries later in *The Thousand and One Nights,* in which one finds fascinating and artistic renderings of many Qur'anic stories, notably those of Solomon, of the Kings of ancient Persia, and of Alexander the Great, to mention but a few. The Qur'anic concern with mythic and fantastic narrative may have provided a further source of inspiration for *The Thousand and One Nights.* The most important link between the Qur'an and *The Thousand and One Nights* is the cultural one. The Qur'anic worldview and its whole system of values and beliefs inform the world of *The Thousand and One Nights* and structure its ethos. In addition the Qur'anic concept of destiny and preordained fate is essential to the understanding of narrative progression in Scheherazade's text. Without a clear understanding of the philosophical assumptions underlying this concept, one cannot fathom the constant interplay between the frame tale and the enframed stories of *The Thousand and One Nights.* What appears in this wonderful narrative text as mere chance should be understood as the vicissitudes of destiny that conceal a deeper wisdom. Such wisdom is often beyond the comprehension of mere mortals, and this is the source of its never-ending fascination.

The Qur'an has had an immense influence on later Arabic literature, and it is treasured for its own language as well. The beauty of its language is majestic, not seductively entrancing; it amazes rather than excites, and arouses pleasure through repose not movement. Its dialogic nature implies respect for the reader and emphasizes the text's rational dimension as well as its spiritual nature. It was and still remains the pinnacle of the Arabic word, the reservoir of its rhetorical, poetic, and stylistic devices.

PRONUNCIATIONS:

Iblīs: ee-BLEES
Qur'an: COO-RAHN
sura: SUE-rah

from THE QUR'AN[1]

from Sura 41. Revelations Well Expounded

In the Name of God, the Compassionate, the Merciful

Revealed by the Compassionate, the Merciful: a Book of revelations well expounded, an Arabic Qur'an for men of knowledge.

1. Translated by N. J. Dawood. The first five selections (from Suras 41, 79, 15, 2, and 7) bring together some of the Qur'an's major passages on creation.

It proclaims good news and a warning: yet most men turn their backs and pay no heed. They say: "Our hearts are proof against the faith to which you call us. Our ears are stopped, and a thick veil stands between us. Do as you think fit, and so will we."

Say: "I am but a mortal like yourselves. It is revealed to me that your God is one God. Therefore take the straight path to Him and implore His forgiveness. Woe betide those who serve other gods besides Him; who give no alms and disbelieve in the life to come. As for those who have faith and do good works, an endless recompense awaits them."

Say: "Do you indeed disbelieve in Him who created the earth in two days? And do you make other gods His equals? The Lord of the Universe is He."

He set upon the earth mountains towering high above it. He pronounced His blessing upon it, and in four days provided it with sustenance for all alike. Then, turning to the sky, which was but a cloud of vapour, He said to it and to the earth: "Come forward both, willingly or perforce."

"We will come willingly," they answered. In two days He formed the sky into seven heavens, and to each heaven He assigned its task. We decked the lowest heaven with brilliant stars and guardian comets. Such is the design of the Mighty One, the All-knowing.

from Sura 79. The Soul-Snatchers

Are you harder to create than the heaven which He has built? He raised it high and fashioned it, giving darkness to its night and brightness to its day.

After that He spread the earth, and, drawing water from its depth, brought forth its pastures. He set down the mountains, for you and for your cattle to delight in.

from Sura 15. The Rocky Tract

It was We that revealed the Admonition, and shall Ourself preserve it. We have sent forth apostles before you to the older nations: but they scoffed at each apostle We sent them. Thus do We put doubt into the hearts of the guilty: they deny him, despite the example of the ancients.

If we opened for the unbelievers a gate in heaven and they ascended through it higher and higher, still they would say: "Our eyes were dazzled: truly, we must have been bewitched."

We have decked the heavens with constellations and made them lovely to behold. We have guarded them from every cursèd devil. Eavesdroppers are pursued by fiery comets.

We have spread out the earth and set upon it immovable mountains. We have planted it with every seasonable fruit, providing sustenance for yourselves and for those whom you do not provide for. We hold the store of every blessing and send it down in appropriate measure. We let loose the fertilizing winds and bring down water from the sky for you to drink; its stores are beyond your reach.

It is surely We who ordain life and death. We are the Heir of all things.

We know those who have gone before you, and know those who will come hereafter. It is your Lord who will gather them all before Him. He is wise and all-knowing.

We created man from dry clay, from black moulded loam, and before him Satan from smokeless fire. Your Lord said to the angels: "I am creating man from dry clay, from black moulded loam. When I have fashioned him and breathed of My spirit into him, kneel down and prostrate yourselves before him."

The angels, one and all, prostrated themselves, except Satan. He refused to prostrate himself as the others did.

"Satan," said God, "why do you not prostrate yourself?"

He replied: "I will not bow to a mortal whom You created of dry clay, of black moulded loam."

"Get you hence," said God, "you are accursed. The curse shall be on you till Judgement-day."

"Lord," said Satan, "reprieve me till the Day of Resurrection."

He answered: "You are reprieved till the Appointed Day."

"Lord," said Satan, "since You have thus seduced me, I will tempt mankind on earth: I will seduce them all, except those of them who are your faithful servants."

He replied: "This is My straight path. You shall have no power over My servants, only the sinners who follow you. They are all destined for Hell. It has seven gates, and through each gate they shall come in separate bands. But the righteous shall dwell among gardens and fountains; in peace and safety they shall enter them."

from Sura 2. The Cow

He created for you all that the earth contains; then, ascending to the sky, He fashioned it into seven heavens. He has knowledge of all things.

When your Lord said to the angels: "I am placing on the earth one that shall rule as My deputy," they replied: "Will You put there one that will do evil and shed blood, when we have for so long sung Your praises and sanctified Your name?"

He said: "I know what you know not."

He taught Adam the names of all things and then set them before the angels, saying: "Tell Me the names of these, if what you say be true."

"Glory be to You," they replied, "we have no knowledge except that which You have given us. You alone are all-knowing and wise."

Then said He: "Adam, tell them their names." And when Adam had named them, He said: "Did I not tell you that I know the secrets of the heavens and the earth, and know all that you reveal and all that you conceal?"

And when We said to the angels: "Prostrate yourselves before Adam," they all prostrated themselves except Satan, who in his pride refused and became an unbeliever.

We said: "Adam, dwell with your wife in Paradise and eat of its fruits to your hearts' content wherever you will. But never approach this tree or you shall both become transgressors."

But Satan lured them thence and brought about their banishment. "Get you down," We said, "and be enemies to each other. The earth will for a while provide your dwelling and your sustenance."

Then Adam received commandments from his Lord, and his Lord relented towards him. He is the Relenting One, the Merciful.

"Get you down hence, all," We said. "When My guidance is revealed to you, those that follow My guidance shall have nothing to fear or to regret; but those that deny and reject Our revelations shall be the inmates of the Fire, and there shall they abide for ever."

* * *

God: there is no god but Him, the Living, the Eternal One.[2] Neither slumber nor sleep overtakes Him. His is what the heavens and the earth contain. Who can intercede with Him except by His permission? He knows what is before and behind men. They can grasp only that part of His knowledge which He wills. His throne is as vast as the heavens and the earth, and the preservation of both does not weary Him. He is the Exalted, the Immense One.

from Sura 7. The Heights

In the Name of God, the Compassionate, the Merciful

Alif lām mīm sād.[3] This Book has been revealed to you—let not your heart be troubled about it—so that you may thereby give warning and admonish the faithful.

Observe that which is brought down to you from your Lord and follow no other masters besides Him. But you seldom take warning.

How many cities have We destroyed! In the night Our scourge fell upon them, or at midday, when they were drowsing.

And when Our scourge fell upon them, their only cry was: "We have indeed been wicked men."

We will surely question those to whom the messengers were sent, and We will question the messengers themselves. With knowledge We will recount to them what they have done, for We were never away from them.

On that day all shall be weighed with justice. Those whose good deeds weigh heavy in the scales shall triumph, but those whose deeds are light shall lose their souls, because they have denied Our revelations.

We have given you power in the land and provided you with a livelihood: yet you are seldom thankful.

We created you and gave you form. Then We said to the angels: "Prostrate yourselves before Adam." They all prostrated themselves except Satan, who refused to prostrate himself.

"Why did you not prostrate yourself when I commanded you?" He asked.

"I am nobler than he," he replied. "You created me from fire, but You created him from clay."

He said: "Get you down hence! This is no place for your contemptuous pride. Away with you! Humble shall you henceforth be."

He replied: "Reprieve me till the Day of Resurrection."

"You are reprieved," said He.

"Because You have led me into sin," he declared, "I will waylay Your servants as they walk on Your straight path, then spring upon them from the front and from the rear, from their right and from their left. Then You will find the greater part of them ungrateful."

"Begone!" He said. "A despicable outcast you shall henceforth be. As for those that follow you, I shall fill Hell with you all."

To Adam He said: "Dwell with your wife in Paradise, and eat of any fruit you please; but never approach this tree or you shall both become transgressors."

But Satan tempted them, so that he might reveal to them their shameful parts, which they had never seen before. He said: "Your Lord has forbidden you to

2. This paragraph is a prayer that is believed to have a magic, incantatory power.

3. Several suras begin with a set of Arabic letters, whose meaning is uncertain.

approach this tree only to prevent you from becoming angels or immortals." Then he swore to them that he would give them friendly counsel.

Thus did he cunningly seduce them. And when they had eaten of the tree, their shame became visible to them, and they both covered themselves with the leaves of the garden.

Their Lord called out to them, saying: "Did I not forbid you to approach that tree, and did I not say to you that Satan was your inveterate foe?"

They replied: "Lord, we have wronged our souls. Pardon us and have mercy on us, or we shall surely be among the lost."

He said: "Get you down hence, and may your descendants be enemies to each other. The earth will for a while provide your dwelling and your comforts. There you shall live and there shall you die, and thence shall you be raised to life."

Children of Adam! We have given you clothes to cover your shameful parts, and garments pleasing to the eye; but the finest of all these is the robe of piety.

That is one of God's revelations. Perchance they will take heed.

Children of Adam! Let not Satan tempt you, as he seduced your parents out of Paradise. He stripped them of their garments to reveal to them their shameful parts. He and his minions see you whence you cannot see them. We have made the devils guardians over the unbelievers.

Sura 1. The Opening[4]

IN THE NAME OF GOD THE COMPASSIONATE THE MERCIFUL

Praise be to God, Lord of the Universe,
The Compassionate, the Merciful,
Sovereign of the Day of Judgement!
You alone we worship, and to You alone we turn for help.
Guide us to the straight path,
The path of those whom You have favoured,
Not of those who have incurred Your wrath,
Nor of those who have gone astray.

from Sura 4. Women[5]

In the Name of God, the Compassionate, the Merciful

You people! Have fear of your Lord, who created you from a single soul. From that soul He created its spouse, and through them He bestrewed the earth with countless men and women.

Fear God, in whose name you plead with one another, and honour the mothers who bore you. God is ever watching you.

Give orphans the property which belongs to them. Do not exchange their valuables for worthless things or cheat them of their possessions; for this would surely be a grievous sin. If you fear that you cannot treat orphans[6] with fairness, then you may

4. This sura is read in every prayer, and often several times during each of the five prayers of the day.

5. This sura pays detailed attention to women and to family issues. It is exceptional for its era in giving women a definite share in their family's inheritance.

6. Orphan girls.

marry other women who seem good to you: two, three, or four of them. But if you fear that you cannot maintain equality among them, marry one only or any slave-girls you may own. This will make it easier for you to avoid injustice.

Give women their dowry as a free gift; but if they choose to make over to you a part of it, you may regard it as lawfully yours.

Do not give the feeble-minded the property with which God has entrusted you for their support; but maintain and clothe them with its proceeds, and speak kind words to them.

Put orphans to the test until they reach a marriageable age. If you find them capable of sound judgement, hand over to them their property, and do not deprive them of it by squandering it before they come of age.

Let not the rich guardian touch the property of his orphan ward; and let him who is poor use no more than a fair portion of it for his own advantage.

When you hand over to them their property, call in some witnesses; sufficient is God's accounting of your actions.

Men shall have a share in what their parents and kinsmen leave; and women shall have a share in what their parents and kinsmen leave: whether it be little or much, they shall be legally entitled to a share.

If relatives, orphans, or needy men are present at the division of an inheritance, give them, too, a share of it, and speak kind words to them.

Let those who are solicitous about the welfare of their young children after their own death take care not to wrong orphans. Let them fear God and speak for justice.

Those that devour the property of orphans unjustly, swallow fire into their bellies; they shall burn in a mighty conflagration.

God has thus enjoined you concerning your children:

A male shall inherit twice as much as a female. If there be more than two girls, they shall have two-thirds of the inheritance; but if there be one only, she shall inherit the half. Parents shall inherit a sixth each, if the deceased have a child; but if he leave no child and his parents be his heirs, his mother shall have a third. If he have brothers, his mother shall have a sixth after payment of any legacy he may have bequeathed or any debt he may have owed.

You may wonder whether your parents or your children are more beneficial to you. But this is the law of God; surely God is all-knowing and wise.

You shall inherit the half of your wives' estate if they die childless. If they leave children, a quarter of their estate shall be yours after payment of any legacy they may have bequeathed or any debt they may have owed.

Your wives shall inherit one quarter of your estate if you die childless. If you leave children, they shall inherit one-eighth, after payment of any legacy you may have bequeathed or any debt you may have owed.

If a man or a woman leave neither children nor parents and have a brother or a sister, they shall each inherit one-sixth. If there be more, they shall equally share the third of the estate, after payment of any legacy he may have bequeathed or any debt he may have owed, without prejudice to the rights of the heirs. That is a commandment from God. God is all-knowing, and gracious.

Such are the bounds set by God. He that obeys God and His apostle shall dwell for ever in gardens watered by running streams. That is the supreme triumph. But he that defies God and His apostle and transgresses His bounds, shall be cast into a Fire wherein he will abide for ever. Shameful punishment awaits him.

If any of your women commit a lewd act, call in four witnesses from among yourselves against them; if they testify to their guilt confine them to their houses till death overtakes them or till God finds another way for them.

If two men among you commit a lewd act, punish them both. If they repent and mend their ways, let them be. God is forgiving and merciful.

God forgives those who commit evil in ignorance and then quickly turn to Him in penitence. God will pardon them. God is all-knowing and wise. But He will not forgive those who do evil and, when death comes to them, say: "Now we repent!" Nor those who die unbelievers: for them We have prepared a woeful scourge.

Believers, it is unlawful for you to inherit the women of your deceased kinsmen against their will, or to bar them from re-marrying, in order that you may force them to give up a part of what you have given them, unless they be guilty of a proven lewd act. Treat them with kindness; for even if you dislike them, it may well be that you dislike a thing which God has meant for your own abundant good.

If you wish to replace one wife with another, do not take from her the dowry you have given her even if it be a talent of gold. That would be improper and grossly unjust; for how can you take it back when you have lain with each other and entered into a firm contract?

You shall not marry the women whom your fathers married: all previous such marriages excepted. That was an evil practice, indecent and abominable.

Forbidden to you are your mothers, your daughters, your sisters, your paternal and maternal aunts, the daughters of your brothers and sisters, your foster-mothers, your foster-sisters, the mothers of your wives, your step-daughters who are in your charge, born of the wives with whom you have lain (it is no offence for you to marry your step-daughters if you have not consummated your marriage with their mothers), and the wives of your own begotten sons. You are also forbidden to take in marriage two sisters at one and the same time: all previous such marriages excepted. Surely God is forgiving and merciful. Also married women, except those whom you own as slaves. Such is the decree of God. All women other than these are lawful for you, provided you court them with your wealth in modest conduct, not in fornication. Give them their dowry for the enjoyment you have had of them as a duty; but it shall be no offence for you to make any other agreement among yourselves after you have fulfilled your duty. Surely God is all-knowing and wise.

If any one of you cannot afford to marry a free believing woman, let him marry a slave-girl who is a believer (God best knows your faith: you are born one of another). Marry them with the permission of their masters and give them their dowry in all justice, provided they are honourable and chaste and have not entertained other men. If after marriage they commit adultery, they shall suffer half the penalty inflicted upon free adulteresses. Such is the law for those of you who fear to commit sin: but if you abstain, it will be better for you. God is forgiving and merciful.

* * *

The People of the Book ask you to bring down for them a book from heaven. Of Moses they demanded a harder thing than that. They said to him: "Show us God distinctly." And for their wickedness the thunderbolt smote them. They worshipped the calf after clear signs had been revealed to them; yet We forgave them that, and bestowed on Moses clear authority.

When We made a covenant with them We raised the Mount above them and said: "Enter the gates in adoration. Do not break the Sabbath." We took from them a solemn covenant. But they broke their covenant, denied the revelations of God, and killed the prophets unjustly. They said: "Our hearts are sealed."

It is God who has sealed their hearts, on account of their unbelief. They have no faith, except a few of them.

They denied the truth and uttered a monstrous falsehood against Mary.[7] They declared: "We have put to death the Messiah, Jesus son of Mary, the apostle of God." They did not kill him, nor did they crucify him, but they thought they did.

Those that disagreed about him were in doubt concerning him; they knew nothing about him that was not sheer conjecture; they did not slay him for certain. God lifted him up to Him; God is mighty and wise. There is none among the People of the Book but will believe in him before his death; and on the Day of Resurrection he will bear witness against them.

Because of their iniquity, We forbade the Jews wholesome things which were formerly allowed them; because time after time they have debarred others from the path of God; because they practise usury—although they were forbidden it—and cheat others of their possessions. Woeful punishment have We prepared for those that disbelieve. But those of them that have deep learning, and those that truly believe in what has been revealed to you and what was revealed before you; who attend to their prayers and render the alms levy and have faith in God and the Last Day—these shall be richly recompensed.

We have revealed Our will to you as We revealed it to Noah and to the prophets who came after him; as We revealed it to Abraham, Ishmael, Isaac, Jacob, and the tribes; to Jesus, Job, Jonah, Aaron, Solomon and David, to whom We gave the Psalms. Of some apostles We have already told you, but there are others of whom We have not yet spoken (God spoke directly to Moses): apostles who brought good news to mankind and admonished them, so that they might have no plea against God after their coming. God is mighty and wise.

God bears witness, by that which He has revealed to you, that He revealed it with His knowledge; and so do the angels. There is no better witness than God.

Those that disbelieve and debar others from the path of God have strayed far into error. God will not forgive those who disbelieve and act unjustly; nor will He guide them to any path other than the path of Hell, wherein they shall abide for ever. Surely that is easy enough for God.

from Sura 5. The Table[8]

Believers, when death approaches you, let two just men from among you act as witnesses when you make your testament; or two men from another tribe if the calamity of death overtakes you while you are travelling the land. Detain them after prayers, and if you doubt their honesty, let them swear by God: "We will not sell our testimony for any price even to a kinsman. We will not hide the testimony of God; for we should then be evil-doers." If both prove dishonest, replace them by another pair from among those immediately concerned, and let them both swear by God, saying: "Our testimony is truer than theirs. We have told no lies, for we should then be wrongdoers." Thus will they be more likely to bear true witness or to fear that the oaths of others may contradict theirs. Have fear of God and be obedient. God does not guide the evil-doers.

7. Understanding Jesus as a human prophet rather than divine, the Qur'an criticizes the Christian treatment of Mary as the Mother of God.

8. A further discussion of Jesus and his mission.

One day God will gather all the apostles and ask them: How were you received?" They will reply: "We have no knowledge. You alone know what is hidden." God will say: "Jesus son of Mary, remember the favour I bestowed on you and on your mother: how I strengthened you with the Holy Spirit, so that you preached to men in your cradle and in the prime of manhood; how I instructed you in the Book and in wisdom, in the Torah and in the Gospel; how by My leave you fashioned from clay the likeness of a bird and breathed into it so that, by My leave, it became a living bird; how, by My leave, you healed the blind man and the leper, and by My leave restored the dead to life; how I protected you from the Israelites when you had come to them with clear signs: when those of them who disbelieved declared: 'This is but plain sorcery'; how, when I enjoined the disciples to believe in Me and in My apostle, they replied: 'We believe; bear witness that we submit.'"

"Jesus son of Mary," said the disciples, "can your Lord send down to us from heaven a table spread with food?"

He replied: "Have fear of God, if you are true believers."

"We wish to eat of it," they said, "so that we may reassure our hearts and know that what you said to us is true, and that we may be witnesses of it."

"Lord," said Jesus son of Mary, "send down to us from heaven a table spread with food, that it may mark a feast for the first of us and the last of us: a sign from You. Give us our sustenance; You are the best provider."

God replied: "I am sending one to you. But whoever of you disbelieves hereafter shall be punished as no man will ever be punished."

Then God will say: "Jesus son of Mary, did you ever say to mankind: 'Worship me and my mother as gods besides God?'"

"Glory be to You," he will answer, "I could never have claimed what I have no right to. If I had ever said so, You would have surely known it. You know what is in my mind, but I know not what is in Yours. You alone know what is hidden. I told them only what You bade me. I said: 'Serve God, my Lord and your Lord.' I watched over them while living in their midst, and ever since You took me to Yourself, You have been watching them. You are the witness of all things. If You punish them, they surely are Your servants; and if You forgive them, surely You are mighty and wise."

God will say: "This is the day when their truthfulness will benefit the truthful. They shall for ever dwell in gardens watered by running streams. God is pleased with them, and they are pleased with Him. That is the supreme triumph."

God has sovereignty over the heavens and the earth and all that they contain. He has power over all things.

from Sura 24. Light

God is the light of the heavens and the earth. His light may be compared to a niche that enshrines a lamp, the lamp within a crystal of star-like brilliance. It is lit from a blessed olive tree neither eastern nor western. Its very oil would almost shine forth, though no fire touched it. Light upon light; God guides to His light whom He will.

God speaks in parables to mankind. God has knowledge of all things.

His light is found in temples which God has sanctioned to be built for the remembrance of His name. In them, morning and evening, His praise is sung by men whom neither trade nor profit can divert from remembering God, from offering prayers, or from giving alms; who dread the day when men's hearts and eyes shall writhe with anguish; who hope that God will requite them for their noblest deeds and lavish His grace upon them. God gives without reckoning to whom He will.

from Sura 36. Ya Sin[9]

We have taught him no poetry, nor does it become him to be a poet. This is but an admonition: an eloquent Qur'an to exhort the living and to pass judgement on the unbelievers.

Do they not see how, among the things Our hands have made, We have created for them the beasts of which they are masters? We have subjected these to them, that they may ride on some and eat the flesh of others; they drink their milk and put them to other uses. Will they not give thanks?

They have set up other gods besides God, hoping that they may help them. They cannot help them: yet their worshippers stand like warriors ready to defend them.

Let not their words grieve you. We have knowledge of all that they conceal and all that they reveal.

Is man not aware that We created him from a little germ? Yet is he flagrantly contentious. He answers back with arguments, and forgets his own creation. He asks: "Who will give life to rotten bones?"

Say: "He who first brought them into being will give them life again: He has knowledge of every creature; He who gives you from the green tree a flame, and lo! you light a fire."

Has He who created the heavens and the earth no power to create others like them? That He surely has. He is the all-knowing Creator. When He decrees a thing He need only say: "Be," and it is.

Glory be to Him who has control of all things. To Him shall you all be recalled.

from Sura 48. Victory

In the Name of God, the Compassionate, the Merciful

We have given you a glorious victory,[1] so that God may forgive you your past and future sins, and perfect His goodness to you; that He may guide you to a straight path and bestow on you His mighty help.

It was He who sent down tranquillity into the hearts of the faithful, so that their faith might grow stronger (God's are the legions of the heavens and the earth: God is all-knowing and wise); that He may bring the believers, both men and women, into gardens watered by running streams, there to abide for ever; that He may forgive them their sins (this, in God's sight, is a glorious triumph); and that He may punish the hypocrites and the idolaters, men and women, who think evil thoughts about God. A turn of evil shall befall them, for God is angry with them. He has laid on them His curse and prepared for them the fire of Hell: an evil fate.

God's are the legions of the heavens and the earth. God is mighty and wise.

We have sent you[2] forth as a witness and as a bearer of good news and warnings, so that you may have faith in God and His apostle and that you may assist Him, honour Him, and praise Him morning and evening.

Those that swear fealty to you, swear fealty to God Himself. The Hand of God is above their hands. He that breaks his oath breaks it at his own peril, but he that keeps his pledge to God shall be richly recompensed by Him.

9. On Muhammad's mission as prophet, not poet.
1. Probably the taking of Mecca in 630.
2. The Meccans.

The desert Arabs who stayed behind[3] will say to you: "We were occupied with our goods and families. Implore God to pardon us." They will say with their tongues what they do not mean in their hearts.

Say: "Who can intervene on your behalf with God if it be His will to do you harm or good? Indeed, God is cognizant of all your actions."

No. You[4] thought the Apostle and the believers would never return to their people; and with this fancy your hearts were delighted. You harboured evil thoughts and thus incurred damnation.

As for those that disbelieve in God and His apostle, We have prepared a blazing Fire for the unbelievers. God has sovereignty over the heavens and the earth. He pardons whom He will and punishes whom He pleases. God is forgiving and merciful.

Sura 71. Noah

In the Name of God, the Compassionate, the Merciful

We sent forth Noah to his people, saying: "Give warning to your people before a woeful scourge overtakes them."

He said: "My people, I come to warn you plainly. Serve God and fear Him, and obey me. He will forgive you your sins and give you respite for an appointed term. When God's time arrives, none shall put it back. Would that you understood this!"

"Lord," said Noah, "night and day I have pleaded with my people, but my pleas have only aggravated their aversion. Each time I call on them to seek Your pardon, they thrust their fingers into their ears and draw their cloaks over their heads, persisting in sin and bearing themselves with insolent pride. I called out loud to them, and appealed to them in public and in private. 'Seek forgiveness of your Lord,' I said. 'He is ever ready to forgive. He sends down abundant water from the sky for you and bestows upon you wealth and children. He has provided you with gardens and with running brooks. Why do you deny the greatness of God when He created you in gradual stages? Can you not see how God created the seven heavens one above the other, placing in them the moon for a light and the sun for a lantern? God has brought you forth from the earth like a plant, and to the earth He will restore you. Then He will bring you back afresh. God has made the earth a vast expanse for you, so that you may roam its spacious paths.'"

And Noah said: "Lord, my people disobey me, and follow those whose wealth and offspring will only hasten their perdition. They have devised an outrageous plot, and said to each other: 'Do not renounce your gods. Do not forsake Wadd or Suwāʻ or Yaghūth or Yaʻūq or Naṣr.'[5] They have led numerous men astray. You surely drive the wrongdoers to further error."

And because of their sins they were overwhelmed by the Flood and cast into the Fire. They found none besides God to help them.

And Noah said: "Lord, do not leave a single unbeliever on the earth. If You spare them, they will mislead Your servants and beget none but sinners and unbelievers.

3. Away from battle.
4. The desert Arabs.
5. Different idols.

Forgive me, Lord, and forgive my parents and every true believer who seeks refuge in my house. Forgive all the faithful, men and women, and hasten the destruction of the wrongdoers."

Sura 87. The Most High

In the Name of God, the Compassionate, the Merciful

Praise the Name of your Lord, the Most High, who has created all things and gave them due proportions; who has ordained their destinies and guided them; who brings forth the green pasture, then turns it to withered grass.

We shall make you recite Our revelations, so that you shall forget none of them except as God pleases. He has knowledge of all that is manifest, and all that is hidden.

We shall guide you to the smoothest path. Therefore give warning, if warning will avail. He that fears God will heed it, but the wicked sinner will flout it. He shall burn in the gigantic Fire, where he shall neither die nor live. Happy shall be the man who keeps himself pure, who remembers the name of his Lord and prays.

Yet you[6] prefer this life, although the life to come is better and more lasting.

All this is written in earlier scriptures; the scriptures of Abraham and Moses.

Sura 93. Daylight

In the Name of God, the Compassionate, the Merciful

By the light of day, and by the dark of night, your Lord has not forsaken you,[7] nor does He abhor you.

The life to come holds a richer prize for you than this present life. You shall be gratified with what your Lord will give you.

Did He not find you an orphan and give you shelter?

Did He not find you in error and guide you?

Did He not find you poor and enrich you?

Therefore do not wrong the orphan, nor chide away the beggar. But proclaim the goodness of your Lord.

Sura 96. Clots of Blood[8]

In the Name of God, the Compassionate, the Merciful

Recite in the name of your Lord who created—created man from clots of blood.

Recite! Your Lord is the Most Bountiful One, who by the pen taught man what he did not know.

Indeed, man transgresses in thinking himself his own master: for to your Lord all things return.

Observe the man who rebukes Our servant when he prays. Think: does he follow the right guidance or enjoin true piety?

6. Unbelievers.

7. Muhammad.

8. These are the first lines ever revealed to Muhammad.

Think: if he denies the Truth and pays no heed, does he not realize that God observes all?

No. Let him desist, or We will drag him by the forelock, his lying, sinful forelock.

Then let him call his helpmates. We will call the guards of Hell.

No, never obey him! Prostrate yourself and come nearer.

Sura 110. Help

In the Name of God, the Compassionate, the Merciful

When God's help and victory come, and you see men embrace God's faith in multitudes, give glory to your Lord and seek His pardon. He is ever disposed to mercy.

RESONANCE

Lives of the Prophet

A knowledge of the life of the Prophet Muhammad is essential for a true understanding of the Qur'an, Islam, and Muslim cultures. Although both Muhammad himself and the Qur'an repeatedly emphasize that he is a mere human with no supernatural power, the belief that he is the "Messenger of God" is one of the tenets of Islam. It is repeated twice in every call for prayer five times a day and several times during each prayer. In addition, a substantial amount of his biography is incorporated in the Qur'an itself. A great many verses of the Qur'an cannot be fully understood without the context in which they were revealed to him on the one hand, and a full knowledge of his life and his mission on the other. His life, sayings, and deeds, passed down as *hadith* or tradition, form with the Qur'an the most vital sources for Islam's theological and legislative doctrines, giving insight into his life and the nature of the early community that he established, which is still seen as prototype for any Islamic society.

Ibn Ishaq: from *The Biography of the Prophet*[1]

OF THE WOMAN WHO OFFERED HERSELF IN MARRIAGE TO 'ABDULLAH B. 'ABDU'L-MUṬṬALIB[2]

Taking 'Abdullah by the hand 'Abdu'l-Muṭṭalib went away and they passed—so it is alleged—a woman of [the house of] b. Asad b. 'Abdu'l-'Uzzā b. Qusayy b. Kilāb b. Murra b. Ka'b b. Lu'ayy b. Ghālib b. Fihr who was the sister of Waraqa b. Naufal b. Asad b. 'Abdu'l-'Uzzā, who was at the Ka'ba. When she looked at him she asked, "Where are you going Abdullah?" He replied, "With my father." She said, "If you

1. Translated by A. Guillaume. Abu-'Abdullah Muhammad ibn Ishaq ibn Yasir, known as Ibn Ishaq, is the most prominent and reliable early biographer of the Prophet Muhammad. He was born in Medina c.704 and died in Baghdad c.768. His father, Ishaq, and his two uncles, Musa and 'Abd al-Rahman, were all prominent religious scholars. He followed in their footsteps, studied with his uncles, and went on to study in Alexandria in his early twenties. By the time he was thirty years old he was widely acknowledged as the most knowledgeable of men on the topic of the Prophet's life. He was also the nearest to the concept of the international scholar, who travels widely in search of leads and material to enrich his research and authenticate his findings. Hence his biography is the most widely accepted and used by Muslim and Western scholars.

2. The father of the Prophet Muhammad. In this text, "b." is short for *ibn*, "son of."

will take me you can have as many camels as were sacrificed in your stead." "I am with my father and I cannot act against his wishes and leave him," he replied.

'Abdu'l-Muṭṭalib brought him to Wahb b. 'Abdu Manāf b. Zuhra b. Kilāb b. Murra b. Ka'b b. Lu'ayy b. Ghālib b. Fihr who was the leading man of B. Zuhra in birth and honour, and he married him to his daughter Āmina,[3] she being the most excellent woman among the Quraysh in birth and position at that time. Her mother was Barra d. 'Abdu'l-'Uzzā b. 'Uthmān b. 'Abdu'l-Dār b. Quṣayy b. Kilāb b. Murra b. Ka'b b. Lu'ayy b. Ghālib b. Fihr. Barra's mother was Umm Ḥabīb d. Asad b. 'Abdu'l-'Uzzā b. Quṣayy by Kilāb b. Murra b. Ka'b b. Lu'ayy b. Ghālib b. Fihr. Umm Ḥabīb's mother was Barra d. 'Auf b. 'Ubayd b. 'Uwayj b. 'Adīy b. Ka'b b. Lu'ayy b. Ghālib b. Fihr.

It is alleged that 'Abdullah consummated his marriage immediately and his wife conceived the apostle of God. Then he left her presence and met the woman who had proposed to him. He asked her why she did not make the proposal that she made to him the day before; to which she replied that the light that was with him the day before had left him, and she no longer had need of him. She had heard from her brother Waraqa b. Naufal, who had been a Christian and studied the scriptures, that a prophet would arise among this people.

My father Isḥāq b. Yasār told me that he was told that 'Abdullah went in to a woman that he had beside Āmina d. Wahb when he had been working in clay and the marks of the clay were on him. She put him off when he made a suggestion to her because of the dirt that was on him. He then left her and washed and bathed himself, and as he made his way to Āmina he passed her and she invited him to come to her. He refused and went to Āmina who conceived Muhammad. When he passed the woman again he asked her if she wanted anything and she said "No! When you passed me there was a white blaze between your eyes and when I invited you you refused me and went in to Āmina, and she has taken it away."

It is alleged that that woman of his used to say that when he passed by her between his eyes there was a blaze like the blaze of a horse. She said: "I invited him hoping that that would be in me, but he refused me and went to Āmina and she conceived the apostle of God." So the apostle of God was the noblest of his people in birth and the greatest in honour both on his father's and his mother's side. God bless and preserve him!

What Was Said to Āmina When She Had Conceived the Apostle

It is alleged in popular stories (and only God knows the truth) that Āmina d. Wahb, the mother of God's apostle, used to say when she was pregnant with God's apostle that a voice said to her, "You are pregnant with the lord of this people and when he is born say, 'I put him in the care of the One from the evil of every envier; then call him Muhammad.'" As she was pregnant with him she saw a light come forth from her by which she could see the castles of Buṣrā in Syria. Shortly afterwards 'Abdullah the apostle's father died while his mother was still pregnant.

The Birth of the Apostle and His Suckling

The apostle was born on Monday, 12th Rabī'u'l-awwal, in the year of the elephant. *** Jahm b. Abū Jahm the client of al-Ḥārith b. Ḥāṭib al-Jumaḥī on the authority

3. Muhammad's mother.

of ‘Abdullah b. Ja’far b. Abū Ṭālib or from one who told him it as from him, informed me that Halīma the apostle’s foster-mother used to say that she went forth from her country with her husband and little son whom she was nursing, among the women of her tribe, in search of other babies to nurse. This was a year of famine when they were destitute. She was riding a dusky she-donkey of hers with an old she-camel which did not yield a drop of milk. They could not sleep the whole night because of the weeping of her hungry child. She had no milk to give him, nor could their she-camel provide a morning draught, but they were hoping for rain and relief. “I rode upon my donkey which had kept back the other riders through its weakness and emaciation so that it was a nuisance to them. When we reached Mecca, we looked out for foster children, and the apostle of God was offered to everyone of us, and each woman refused him when she was told he was an orphan, because we hoped to get payment from the child’s father. We said, ‘An orphan! and what will his mother and grandfather do?’, and so we spurned him because of that. Every woman who came with me got a suckling except me, and when we decided to depart I said to my husband: ‘By God, I do not like the idea of returning with my friends without a suckling; I will go and take that orphan.’ He replied, ‘Do as you please; perhaps God will bless us on his account.’ So I went and took him for the sole reason that I could not find anyone else. I took him back to my baggage, and as soon as I put him in my bosom, my breasts overflowed with milk which he drank until he was satisfied, as also did his foster-brother. Then both of them slept, whereas before this we could not sleep with him. My husband got up and went to the old she-camel and lo, her udders were full; he milked it and he and I drank of her milk until we were completely satisfied, and we passed a happy night. In the morning my husband said: ‘Do you know, Ḥalīma, you have taken a blessed creature?’ I said, ‘By God, I hope so.’ Then we set out and I was riding my she-ass and carrying him with me, and she went at such a pace that the other donkeys could not keep up so that my companions said to me, ‘Confound you! stop and wait for us. Isn’t this the donkey on which you started?’ ‘Certainly it is,’ I said. They replied, ‘By God, something extraordinary has happened.’ Then we came to our dwellings in the Banū Sa’d country and I do not know a country more barren than that.

“When we had him with us my flock used to yield milk in abundance. We milked them and drank while other people had not a drop, nor could they find anything in their animals’ udders, so that our people were saying to their shepherds, ‘Woe to you! send your flock to graze where the daughter of Abū Dhuayb’s shepherd goes.’ Even so, their flocks came back hungry not yielding a drop of milk, while mine had milk in abundance. We ceased not to recognize this bounty as coming from God for a period of two years, when I weaned him. He was growing up as none of the other children grew and by the time he was two he was a well-made child. We brought him to his mother, though we were most anxious to keep him with us because of the blessing which he brought us. I said to her: ‘I should like you to leave my little boy with me until he becomes a big boy, for I am afraid on his account of the pestilence in Mecca.’ We persisted until she sent him back with us.

“Some months after our return he and his brother were with our lambs behind the tents when his brother came running and said to us, ‘Two men clothed in white have seized that Qurayshī brother of mine and thrown him down and opened up his belly, and are stirring it up.’ We ran towards him and found him standing up with a livid face. We took hold of him and asked him what was the matter. He said, ‘Two men in white raiment came and threw me down and opened up my belly and searched therein for I know not what.' So we took him back to our tent.

"His father said to me, 'I am afraid that this child has had a stroke, so take him back to his family before the result appears.' So we picked him up and took him to his mother who asked why we had brought him when I had been anxious for his welfare and desirous of keeping him with me. I said to her, 'God has let my son live so far and I have done my duty. I am afraid that ill will befall him, so I have brought him back to you as you wished.' She asked me what happened and gave me no peace until I told her. When she asked if I feared a demon possessed him, I replied that I did. She answered that no demon had any power over her son who had a great future before him and then she told how when she was pregnant with him a light went out from her which illumined the castles of Buṣrā in Syria, and that she had borne him with the least difficulty imaginable. When she bore him he put his hands on the ground lifting his head towards the heavens. 'Leave him then and go in peace,' she said."

Thaur b. Yazīd from a learned person who I think was Khālid b. Ma'dān al-Kalā'ī told me that some of the apostle's companions asked him to tell them about himself. He said: "I am what Abraham my father prayed for and the good news of my brother Jesus. When my mother was carrying me she saw a light proceeding from her which showed her the castles of Syria. I was suckled among the B. Sa'd b. Bakr, and while I was with a brother of mine behind our tents shepherding the lambs, two men in white raiment came to me with a gold basin full of snow. Then they seized me and opened up my belly, extracted my heart and split it; then they extracted a black drop from it and threw it away; then they washed my heart and my belly with that snow until they had thoroughly cleaned them. Then one said to the other, weigh him against ten of his people; they did so and I outweighed them. Then they weighed me against a hundred and then a thousand, and I outweighed them. He said, 'Leave him alone, for by God, if you weighed him against all his people he would outweigh them.'"

The apostle of God used to say, There is no prophet but has shepherded a flock. When they said, "You, too, apostle of God?", he said "Yes."

The apostle of God used to say to his companions, "I am the most Arab of you all. I am of Quraysh, and I was suckled among the B. Sa'd b. Bakr." It is alleged by some, but God knows the truth, that when his foster-mother brought him to Mecca he escaped her among the crowd while she was taking him to his people. She sought him and could not find him, so she went to 'Abdu'l-Muṭṭalib and said: "I brought Muhammad tonight and when I was in the upper part of Mecca he escaped me and I don't know where he is." So 'Abdu'l-Muṭṭalib went to the Ka'ba praying to God to restore him. They assert that Waraqa b. Naufal b. Asad and another man of Quraysh found him and brought him to 'Abdu'l-Muṭṭalib saying, "We have found this son of yours in the upper part of Mecca." 'Abdu'l-Muṭṭalib took him and put him on his shoulder as he went round the Ka'ba confiding him to God's protection and praying for him; then he sent him to his mother Āmina.

A learned person told me that what urged his foster-mother to return him to his mother, apart from what she told his mother, was that a number of Abyssinian Christians saw him with her when she brought him back after he had been weaned. They looked at him, asked questions about him, and studied him carefully, then they said to her, "Let us take this boy, and bring him to our king and our country; for he will have a great future. We know all about him." The person who told me this alleged that she could hardly get him away from them.

ĀMINA DIES AND THE APOSTLE LIVES WITH HIS GRANDFATHER

The apostle lived with his mother Āmina d. Wahb and his grandfather 'Abdu'l-Muṭṭalib in God's care and keeping like a fine plant, God wishing to honour him. When he was six years old his mother Āmina died.

'Abdullah b. Abū Bakr b. Muhammad b. 'Amr b. Hazm told me that the apostle's mother died in Abwā' between Mecca and Medina on her return from a visit with him to his maternal uncles of B. 'Adīy b. al-Najjār when he was six years old. Thus the apostle was left to his grandfather for whom they made a bed in the shade of the Ka'ba. His sons used to sit round the bed until he came out to it, but none of them sat upon it out of respect for him. The apostle, still a little boy, used to come and sit on it and his uncles would drive him away. When 'Abdu'l-Muṭṭalib saw this he said: "Let my son alone, for by Allah he has a great future." Then he would make him sit beside him on his bed and would stroke his back with his hand. It used to please him to see what he did.

ABŪ ṬĀLIB BECOMES GUARDIAN OF THE APOSTLE

After the death of 'Abdu'l-Muṭṭalib the apostle lived with his uncle Abū Ṭālib, for (so they allege) the former had confided him to his care because he and 'Abdullah, the apostle's father, were brothers by the same mother, Fāṭima d. 'Amr b. 'Ā'idh b. 'Abd b. 'Imrān b. Makhzūm. It was Abū Ṭālib who used to look after the apostle after the death of his grandfather and he became one of his family.

Yaḥyā b. 'Abbād b. 'Abdullah b. al-Zubayr told me that his father told him that there was a man of Lihb who was a seer. Whenever he came to Mecca the Quraysh used to bring their boys to him so that he could look at them and tell their fortunes. So Abū Ṭālib brought him along with the others while he was still a boy. The seer looked at him and then something claimed his attention. That disposed of he cried, "Bring me that boy." When Abū Ṭālib saw his eagerness he hid him and the seer began to say, "Woe to you, bring me that boy I saw just now, for by Allah he has a great future." But Abū Ṭālib went away.

THE STORY OF BAḤĪRĀ

Abū Ṭālib had planned to go in a merchant caravan to Syria, and when all preparations had been made for the journey, the apostle of God, so they allege, attached himself closely to him so that he took pity on him and said that he would take him with him, and that the two of them should never part; or words to that effect. When the caravan reached Buṣrā in Syria, there was a monk there in his cell by the name of Baḥīrā, who was well versed in the knowledge of Christians. A monk had always occupied that cell. There he gained his knowledge from a book that was in the cell, so they allege, handed on from generation to generation. They had often passed by him in the past and he never spoke to them or took any notice of them until this year, and when they stopped near his cell he made a great feast for them. It is alleged that that was because of something he saw while in his cell. They allege that while he was in his cell he saw the apostle of God in the caravan when they approached, with a cloud over-shadowing him among the people. Then they came and stopped in the shadow of a tree near the monk. He looked at the cloud when it over-shadowed the tree, and its branches were bending and drooping over the apostle of God until he was in the shadow beneath it. When Baḥīrā saw that, he came out of his cell and sent word to them, "I have prepared food for you, O men of Quraysh, and I should like you all to come both great and small, bond and free."

One of them said to him, "By God, Baḥīrā! something extraordinary has happened today, you used not to treat us so, and we have often passed by you. What has befallen you today?" He answered, "You are right in what you say, but you are guests and I wish to honour you and give you food so that you may eat." So they gathered together with him, leaving the apostle of God behind with the baggage under the tree, on account of his extreme youth. When Baḥīrā looked at the people he did not see the mark which he knew and found in his books, so he said, "Do not let one of you remain behind and not come to my feast." They told him that no one who ought to come had remained behind except a boy who was the youngest of them and had stayed with their baggage. Thereupon he told them to invite him to come to the meal with them. One of the men of Quraysh said, "By al-Lāt and al-'Uzzā, we are to blame for leaving behind the son of 'Abdullah b. 'Abdu'l-Muṭṭalib." Then he got up and embraced him and made him sit with the people.

When Baḥīrā saw him he stared at him closely, looking at his body and finding traces of his description (in the Christian books). When the people had finished eating and gone away, Baḥīrā got up and said to him, "Boy, I ask you by al-Lāt and al-'Uzzā to answer my question." Now Baḥīrā said this only because he had heard his people swearing by these gods. They allege that the apostle of God said to him, "Do not ask me by al-Lāt and al-'Uzzā, for by Allah nothing is more hateful to me than these two." Baḥīrā answered, "Then by Allah, tell me what I ask"; he replied, "Ask me what you like"; so he began to ask him about what happened in his waking and in his sleep, and his habits, and his affairs generally, and what the apostle of God told him coincided with what Baḥīrā knew of his description. Then he looked at his back and saw the seal of prophethood between his shoulders in the very place described in his book. When he had finished he went to his uncle Abū Ṭālib and asked him what relation this boy was to him, and when he told him he was his son, he said that he was not, for it could not be that the father of this boy was alive. "He is my nephew," he said, and when he asked what had become of his father he told him that he had died before the child was born. "You have told the truth," said Baḥīrā. "Take your nephew back to his country and guard him carefully against the Jews, for by Allah! if they see him and know about him what I know, they will do him evil; a great future lies before this nephew of yours, so take him home quickly."

So his uncle took him off quickly and brought him back to Mecca when he had finished his trading in Syria. People allege that Zurayr and Tammām and Darīs, who were people of the scriptures, had noticed in the apostle of God what Baḥīrā had seen during that journey which he took with his uncle, and they tried to get at him, but Baḥīrā kept them away and reminded them of God and the mention of the description of him which they would find in the sacred books, and that if they tried to get at him they would not succeed. He gave them no peace until they recognized the truth of what he said and left him and went away.

The apostle of God grew up, God protecting him and keeping him from the vileness of heathenism because he wished to honour him with apostleship, until he grew up to be the finest of his people in manliness, the best in character, most noble in lineage, the best neighbour, the most kind, truthful, reliable, the furthest removed from filthiness and corrupt morals, through loftiness and nobility, so that he was known among his people as "The trustworthy" because of the good qualities which God had implanted in him. The apostle, so I was told, used to tell how God protected him in his childhood during the period of heathenism, saying, "I found myself among the boys of Quraysh carrying stones such as boys play with; we had all uncovered ourselves, each taking his shirt and putting it round his neck as he carried the stones. I was going to and fro in the same way, when an unseen figure slapped me most painfully saying, 'Put your shirt on'; so I took it and fastened it on me and then began to carry the stones upon my neck wearing my shirt alone among my fellows."

THE SACRILEGIOUS WAR

This war broke out when the apostle was twenty years of age. It was so called because these two tribes, Kināna and Qays 'Aylān, fought in the sacred month. The chief of Quraysh and Kināna was Ḥarb b. Umayya b. 'Abdu Shams. At the beginning of the day Qays got the upper hand but by midday victory went to Kināna.

THE APOSTLE OF GOD MARRIES KHADĪJA

Khadīja was a merchant woman of dignity and wealth. She used to hire men to carry merchandise outside the country on a profit-sharing basis, for Quraysh were a people given to commerce. Now when she heard about the prophet's truthfulness, trustworthiness, and honourable character, she sent for him and proposed that he should take her goods to Syria and trade with them, while she would pay him more than she paid others. He was to take a lad of hers called Maysara. The apostle of God accepted the proposal, and the two set forth until they came to Syria.

The apostle stopped in the shade of a tree near a monk's cell, when the monk came up to Maysara and asked who the man was who was resting beneath the tree. He told him that he was of Quraysh, the people who held the sanctuary; and the monk exclaimed: "None but a prophet ever sat beneath this tree."

Then the prophet sold the goods he had brought and bought what he wanted to buy and began the return journey to Mecca. The story goes that at the height of noon when the heat was intense as he rode his beast Maysara saw two angels shading the apostle from the sun's rays. When he brought Khadīja her property she sold it and it amounted to double or thereabouts. Maysara for his part told her about the two angels who shaded him and of the monk's words. Now Khadīja was a determined, noble, and intelligent woman possessing the properties with which God willed to honour her. So when Maysara told her these things she sent to the apostle of God and—so the story goes—said: "O son of my uncle I like you because of our relationship and your high reputation among your people, your trustworthiness and good character and truthfulness." Then she proposed marriage. Now Khadīja at that time was the best born woman in Quraysh, of the greatest dignity and, too, the richest. All her people were eager to get possession of her wealth if it were possible.

Khadīja was the daughter of Khuwaylid b. Asad b. 'Abdu'l-'Uzzā b. Quṣayy b. Kilāb b. Murra b. Ka'b b. Lu'ayy b. Ghālib b. Fihr. Her mother was Fāṭima d. Zā'ida b. al-Aṣamm b. Rawāḥa b. Ḥajar b. 'Abd b. Ma'iṣ b. 'Āmir b. Lu'ayy b. Ghālib b. Fihr. Her mother was Hāla d. 'Abdu Manāf b. al-Ḥārith b. 'Amr b. Munqidh b. 'Amr b. Ma'iṣ b. 'Āmir b. Lu'ayy b. Ghālib b. Fihr. Hāla's mother was Qilāba d. Su'ayd b. Sa'd b. Sahm b. 'Amr b. Huṣayṣ b. Ka'b b. Lu'ayy b. Ghālib b. Fihr.

The apostle of God told his uncles of Khadīja's proposal, and his uncle Ḥamza b. 'Abdu'l-Muṭṭalib went with him to Khuwaylid b. Asad and asked for her hand and he married her.

She was the mother of all the apostle's children except Ibrāhīm, namely al-Qāsim (whereby he was known as Abu'l-Qāsim); al-Ṭāhir, al-Ṭayyib, Zaynab, Ruqayya, Umm Kulthūm, and Fāṭima.

Al-Qāsim, al-Ṭayyib, and al-Ṭāhir died in paganism. All his daughters lived into Islam, embraced it, and migrated with him to Medina.

Khadīja had told Waraqa b. Naufal b. Asad b. 'Abdu'l-'Uzzā, who was her cousin and a Christian who had studied the scriptures and was a scholar, what her slave Maysara had told her that the monk had said and how he had seen the two angels shading him. He said, "If this is true, Khadīja, verily Muhammad is the prophet of this people. I knew that a prophet of this people was to be expected. His time has come," or words to that effect. Waraqa was finding the time of waiting wearisome and used to say "How long?" Some lines of his on the theme are:

I persevered and was persistent in remembering
An anxiety which often evoked tears. And
Confirmatory evidence kept coming from Khadīja.
Long have I had to wait, O Khadīja,
In the vale of Mecca in spite of my hope
That I might see the outcome of thy words.
I could not bear that the words of the monk
You told me of should prove false:
That Muhammad should rule over us
Overcoming those who would oppose him.
And that a glorious light should appear in the land
To preserve men from disorders.
His enemies shall meet disaster
And his friends shall be victorious.
Would that I might be there then to see,
For I should be the first of his supporters,
Joining in that which Quraysh hate
However loud they shout in that Mecca of theirs.
I hope to ascend through him whom they all dislike
To the Lord of the Throne though they are cast down.
Is it folly not to disbelieve in Him
Who chose him Who raised the starry heights?
If they and I live, things will be done
Which will throw the unbelievers into confusion.
And if I die, 'tis but the fate of mortals
To suffer death and dissolution.

THE PROPHET'S MISSION

When Muhammad the apostle of God reached the age of forty God sent him in compassion to mankind, "as an evangelist to all men." Now God had made a covenant with every prophet whom he had sent before him that he should believe in him, testify to his truth and help him against his adversaries, and he required of them that they should transmit that to everyone who believed in them, and they carried out their obligations in that respect. God said to Muhammad, "When God made a covenant with the prophets (He said) this is the scripture and wisdom which I have given you, afterwards an apostle will come confirming what you know that you may believe in him and help him." He said, "Do you accept this and take up my burden?" i.e. the burden of my agreement which I have laid upon you. They said, "We accept it." He answered, "Then bear witness and I am a witness with you." Thus God made a covenant with all the prophets that they should testify to his truth and help him against his adversaries and they transmitted that obligation to those who believed in them among the two monotheistic religions.

One whom I do not suspect told me from Sa'īd b. Abū 'Arūba from Qatāda b. Di'āma al-Sadūsī from Abū'l-Jald: "The Furqān came down on the 14th night of Ramaḍān. Others say, No, but on the 17th; and in support of this they appeal to God's word: 'And what we sent down to our servant on the day of al-Furqān, the day the two companies met' which was the meeting of the apostle and the polytheists at Badr, and that took place on the morning of Ramaḍān 17th."

Al-Zuhrī related from 'Urwa b. Zubayr that 'Ā'isha told him that when Allah desired to honour Muhammad and have mercy on His servants by means of him, the first sign of prophethood vouchsafed to the apostle was true visions, resembling the brightness of daybreak, which were shown to him in his sleep. And Allah, she said, made him love solitude so that he liked nothing better than to be alone.

'Abdu'l-Malik b. 'Ubaydullah b. Abū Sufyān b. al-'Alā' b. Jāriya the Thaqafite who had a retentive memory related to me from a certain scholar that the apostle at the time when Allah willed to bestow His grace upon him and endow him with prophethood would go forth for his affair and journey far afield until he reached the glens of Mecca and the beds of its valleys where no house was in sight; and not a stone or tree that he passed by but would say, "Peace unto thee, O apostle of Allah." And the apostle would turn to his right and left and look behind him and he would see naught but trees and stones. Thus he stayed seeing and hearing so long as it pleased Allah that he should stay. Then Gabriel came to him with the gift of God's grace whilst he was on Ḥirā' in the month of Ramaḍān.

Wahb b. Kaisān a client of the family of al-Zubayr told me: I heard 'Abdullah b. al-Zubayr say to 'Ubayd b. 'Umayr b. Qatāda the Laythite, "O 'Ubayd tell us how began the prophethood which was first bestowed on the apostle when Gabriel came to him." And 'Ubayd in my presence related to 'Abdullah and those with him as follows: The apostle would pray in seclusion on Ḥirā' every year for a month to practise *taḥannuth* as was the custom of Quraysh in heathen days. *Taḥannuth* is religious devotion. Abū Ṭālib said:

> By Thaur and him who made Thabīr firm in its place
> And by those going up to ascend Ḥirā' and coming down.

Wahb b. Kaisān told me that 'Ubayd said to him: Every year during that month the apostle would pray in seclusion and give food to the poor that came to him. And when he completed the month and returned from his seclusion, first of all before entering his house he would go to the Ka'ba and walk round it seven times or as often as it pleased God then he would go back to his house until in the year when God sent him, in the month of Ramaḍān in which God willed concerning him what He willed of His grace, the apostle set forth to Ḥirā' as was his wont, and his family with him. When it was the night on which God honoured him with his mission and showed mercy on His servants thereby, Gabriel brought him the command of God. "He came to me," said the apostle of God, "while I was asleep, with a coverlet of brocade whereon was some writing, and said, 'Read!' I said, 'What shall I read?' He pressed me with it so tightly that I thought it was death; then he let me go and said, 'Read!'

I said, 'What shall I read?' He pressed me with it again so that I thought it was death; then he let me go and said 'Read!' I said, 'What shall I read?' He pressed me with it the third time so that I thought it was death and said 'Read!' I said, 'What then shall I read?'—and this I said only to deliver myself from him, lest he should do the same to me again. He said:

> Read in the name of thy Lord who created,
> Who created man of blood coagulated.
> Read! Thy Lord is the most beneficent,
> Who taught by the pen,
> Taught that which they knew not unto men.

"So I read it, and he departed from me. And I awoke from my sleep, and it was as though these words were written on my heart. Now none of God's creatures was more hateful to me than an (ecstatic) poet or a man possessed: I could not even look at them. I thought, Woe is me poet or possessed—Never shall Quraysh say this of me! I will go to the top of the mountain and throw myself down that I may kill myself and gain rest. So I went forth to do so and then when I was midway on the mountain, I heard a voice from heaven saying, 'O Muhammad! thou art the apostle of God and I am Gabriel.' I raised my head towards heaven to see (who was speaking), and lo, Gabriel in the form of a man with feet astride the horizon, saying, 'O Muhammad! thou art the apostle of God and I am Gabriel.' I stood gazing at him, and that turned me from my purpose moving neither forward nor backward, then I began to turn my face away from him, but towards whatever region of the sky I looked, I saw him as before. And I continued standing there, neither advancing nor turning back, until Khadīja sent her messengers in search of me and they gained the high ground above Mecca and returned to her while I was standing in the same plane then he parted from me and I from him, returning to my family. And I came to Khadīja and sat by her thigh and drew close to her. She said, 'O Abū'l-Qāsim, where hast thou been? By God, I sent my messengers in search of thee, and they reached the high ground above Mecca and returned to me.' I said to her, 'Woe is me poet or possessed.' She said, 'I take refuge in God from that O Abū'l-Qāsim. God would not treat you thus since he knows your truthfulness, your great trustworthiness, your fine character, and your kindness. This cannot be, my dear. Perhaps you did see something.' 'Yes, I did,' I said. Then I told her of what I had seen; and she said, 'Rejoice, O son of my uncle, and be of good heart. Verily, by Him in whose hand is Khadīja's soul, I have hope that thou wilt be the prophet of this people.'" Then she rose and gathered her garments about her and set forth to her cousin Waraqa b. Naufal b. Asad b. 'Abdu'l-'Uzzā b. Quṣayy, who had become a Christian and read the scriptures and learned from those that follow the Torah and the Gospel. And when she related to him what the apostle of God told her he had seen and heard, Waraqa cried, "Holy! Holy! Verily by Him in whose hand is Waraqa's soul, if thou hast spoken to me the truth, O Khadīja, there hath come unto him the greatest Nāmūs (meaning Gabriel) who came to Moses aforetime, and lo, he is the prophet of this people. Bid him be of good heart." So Khadīja returned to the apostle of God and told him what Waraqa had said, and that calmed his fears somewhat. And when the apostle of God had finished his period of seclusion and returned (to Mecca), in the first place he performed the circumambulation of the Ka'ba, as was his wont. While he was doing it, Waraqa met him and said, "O son of my brother, tell me what thou hast seen and heard." The apostle told him, and Waraqa said, "Surely, by Him in whose hand is Waraqa's soul, thou art the prophet of this people. There hath come unto thee the greatest Nāmūs, who came unto Moses. Thou wilt be called a liar, and they will use thee despitefully and cast thee out and fight against thee. Verily, if I live to see that day, I will help God in such wise as He knoweth." Then he brought his head near to him and kissed his forehead; and the apostle went to his own house. Waraqa's words added to his confidence and lightened his anxiety.

Ismā'īl b. Abū Ḥakīm, a freedman of the family of al-Zubayr, told me on Khadīja's authority that she said to the apostle of God, "O son of my uncle, are you able to tell me about your visitant, when he comes to you?" He replied that he could, and she asked him to tell her when he came. So when Gabriel came to him, as he was wont, the apostle said to Khadīja, "This is Gabriel who has just come to me." "Get up, O son of my uncle," she said, "and sit by my left thigh." The apostle did so, and she said, "Can you see him?" "Yes," he said. She said, "Then turn round and sit on my right thigh." He did so, and she said, "Can you see him?" When he said that he could she asked him to move and sit in her lap. When he had done this she again asked if he could see him, and when he said yes, she disclosed her form and cast aside her veil while the apostle was sitting in her lap. Then she said, "Can you see him?" And he replied, "No." She said, "O son of my uncle, rejoice and be of good heart, by God he is an angel and not a satan."

I told 'Abdullah b. Ḥasan this story and he said, "I heard my mother Fāṭima, daughter of Ḥusayn, talking about this tradition from Khadīja, but as I heard it she made the apostle of God come inside her shift, and thereupon Gabriel departed, and she said to the apostle of God, 'This verily is an angel and not a satan.'"

The Thousand and One Nights

9th–14th century

Apart from the Qur'an, *Alf Layla wa-Layla* (*The Thousand and One Nights* or *The Arabian Nights*) is perhaps the most influential, well-known and widely read work of Arabic and Islamic culture. The earliest evidence that a work or a compilation of this nature existed goes back to the ninth century, and certainly by the twelfth century there are many manuscripts of *The Thousand and One Nights* in Egypt, Syria, and Iraq. The present title of the work is a twelfth-century coinage, for earlier mentions of the work refer to it simply as *Alf Layla* ("The Thousand Nights"). Earlier manuscripts are incomplete and led to speculation that the title *The Thousand Nights* was only meant to denote a large number of stories rather than a formal organization of the work. Recent scholarship and application of modern critical approaches have challenged this assumption and established the structural cohesion of the work. Similarly there is much speculation concerning the origin of the work, its genealogy, and development. It has been suggested that a Persian collection of tales, *Hazar Afsana* ("Thousand Tales"), is the source of *The Thousand and One Nights.* Others claim that its source text is an Indian narrative of different stories similar to the frame story of *The Thousand and One Nights,* yet neither of these accounts for the richness of the work and its infinite variety of narratives.

The text's unity is grounded in a constant interplay between the frame story and the enframed stories. In the famous frame tale, the vizier's daughter Scheherazade or Shahrazad offers her stories as ransom for her life to avert the violence of a tyrant king, but the ransom only works through the suspension of time by using storytelling to stop its flow. Narrative manipulates time, and the suspension of time enhances the power of narrative, hence the circular nature of *The Thousand and One Nights.* Because of this circularity, the structural unity of the work develops through variations, echoes, and references forward and back, rather than through cause-and-effect progressions. This linking can be seen in the first set of stories, when the threat of violence is averted or postponed by the telling of stories. But in certain tales the link with the frame story is different. In "The Tale of Sympathy the Learned" one sees the whole work mirrored in one of its stories of how a learned woman is able to tame the powerful men around her. This tale may be studied as the first ever "feminist" literary text, which enhances the position of the woman, subverting the patriarchal order and exposing its weaknesses. In other stories on the other hand, the link to the frame tale seems weak, yet they often involve themes—the evanescence of worldly pleasures, ascetic piety, and the need for humble acceptance of God—that are basic Islamic tenets also implied in the main frame.

The tales are further connected by the fact that tales often generate other tales or kernels of tales within themselves. The narrative of *The Thousand and One Nights* is similar in form to nested Russian dolls, one hidden inside another. Unlike the Russian doll, the tales aren't identical or symmetrical and are varied in location, characters, and action. Yet there is a deep structure that makes them a whole within every tale, and at the same time part of the organic whole that is *The Thousand and One Nights.* The nested tales often replicate in their flow the very structure of the whole work—that is, a basic frame story and a number of enframed stories within its overreaching thematic unity. This confirms both the circularity and the self-reference of the work.

Another dimension of the work enhances its coherence. The set of philosophical and religious assumptions underpinning the deep structure of *The Thousand and One Nights* is essentially Islamic in its tenets and uniquely Arabic in its orientation. As a result, the book has often been known as *The Arabian Nights.* Early European translators noted its cultural difference. Richard Burton, for example, noted the parallels between the cultural ethos of *The Thousand and One Nights* and the Muslim customs in the Arab and Indian worlds, which he himself witnessed in his travels. These philosophical and religious aspects of the work are an essential part of the motivation of its narrative, whose ultimate aim is to re-educate the tyrant king, to acclimate him to a tolerant and humane civilization. The various strata or cycles of stories correspond to the different Arabic/Islamic virtues and concepts that are necessary for a comprehensive re-education of a tyrant. *The Thousand and One Nights* reflects the culmination of Arabic and Islamic civilization at the peak of its assimilation of many elements of the older cultures that embraced Islam, such as Persian, Egyptian, Iraqi, Indian, and even Chinese.

Yet the work is primarily the product of the Arabic imagination and the Islamic worldview embodied in the Qur'an, for it carries the distinct mark of Arabic culture in two of its major centers: Iraq and Egypt. Although the majority of characters in *The Thousand and One Nights* are of Arabic origin and carry Arabic names, there are characters with Indian, Persian, Turkish, Hebrew, and other foreign names. This makes *The Thousand and One Nights* a mirror of the Islamic world with people from a myriad of cultures and nations, and of the Islamic civilization's ability to assimilate various strands of other cultures. Another aspect of this is that one finds Christians, Zoroastrians, and pagans converting to Islam but not Muslims being converted to Christianity or any other religion in these tales, for *The Thousand and One Nights* is a reflection of the triumph of Islamic culture.

The Thousand and One Nights is generally considered as a work of collective imagination rather than of one author, but it is an imagination that puts the woman, Scheherazade, in the center of the creative assembly. It is usually divided into two parts. In the Baghdad part, characters, action, and space are dominated by this Islamic metropolis during the peak of the Abbasid period in the days of Haroun al-Rashid. In the Egyptian part, the location and characters reflect the specificity of Egyptian culture as demonstrated in the use of Egyptian names and places, the Coptic names of months, and the manipulation of *jinn* through a talisman or magic object, rather than directly as in the Baghdad section. The tales in which jinn or genies act independently are seen to be inspired by Persian or Indian stories. Another group of tales reflects influences of ancient Babylonian and Mesopotamian narratives and of some historic events and characters, particularly those related to Alexander the Great. *The Thousand and One Nights* is also brimming with characters, motifs, and stories that come to it from the Qur'an, or via the Qur'an, such as those of the Hebrew king Solomon.

Most of the stories in our selection are from the Baghdad part, with the partial exception of "The Tale of Sympathy the Learned," which originated in Baghdad and was reshaped in Egypt, demonstrating the convergence of the two parts. Since Baghdad was the metropolis of a large empire, its stories reflect the life of an affluent capital and the myriad of cultural influences on it. The tales of the Caliph and that of the poet Abu-Nuwas demonstrate this. The Egyptian stories provided *The Thousand and One Nights* with different narrative genres, such as tales of thieves, tricksters, and rogues, tales in which people use talismans to control genies and demons, and stories that might be called "bourgeois romances" of love and adultery. Between them, the two parts of *The Thousand and One Nights* embrace an impressive number of narrative genres, from travel narratives and romances to fairy tales, legends, humorous or fantasy tales, didactic stories, anecdotes, and short stories. One can identify every conceivable narrative configuration in *The Thousand and One Nights,* from early narrative kernels to the most developed fiction, from realistic rendering to the fantastic and the absurd. In addition there are 1,420 poems or fragments of poetry; this interweaving of poetry and prose can be compared to that found in *The Tale of Genji* (page 1002).

The Thousand and One Nights is often considered the archetypal narrative text, or the mother of all narrative, and this may explain its universal appeal and enduring influence through the ages. There is ample evidence to suggest that medieval Europeans knew it, and the comic tales of Boccaccio and can well be compared to those of the *Nights.* Like any long collectively composed oral text, it went through many stages of development. The text in the form that we know now in the West owes its existence to the first European translation by a French orientalist, Jean Antoine Galland (1646–1715), who used a manuscript that dates from 1536. The first volume of his *Les Mille et Une Nuits: Contes Arabes Traduits en Français* appeared in 1704, with eleven more volumes thereafter. The work was a great success, thus inspiring its translation into other European languages, including into English in 1792 and German in 1823.

Since its first appearance in Europe, *The Thousand and One Nights* fascinated writers and poets from Coleridge to Robert Louis Stevenson (who wrote a *New Thousand and One Nights* in 1882), to the father of modern magic realism, Jorge Luis Borges. In the Arab world the impact of this archetypal text is ubiquitous, and no study of modern Arabic narrative is possible without a clear knowledge of its rubrics. The Egyptian Nobel laureate, Naguib Mahfouz, has endeavored to rewrite certain tales in his *Arabian Nights and Days* (1982), selections of which are included in Volume F. Perspectives: *The Thousand and One Nights* in the Twentieth Century, also in Volume F, gives a range of examples of the enduring fascination of this treasury of stories.

PRONUNCIATIONS:

Dunyazad: DOON-yah-zadh
Shahrazad: SHAH-rah-zahd
Shahrayar: SHAH-ree-yar
Shahzaman: SHAH zah-MANN

from The Thousand and One Nights

Prologue[1]

[The Story of King Shahrayar and Shahrazad, His Vizier's Daughter]

It is related—but God knows and sees best what lies hidden in the old accounts of bygone peoples and times—that long ago, during the time of the Sasanid dynasty,[2] in the peninsulas of India and Indochina, there lived two kings who were brothers. The older brother was named Shahrayar, the younger Shahzaman. The older, Shahrayar, was a towering knight and a daring champion, invincible, energetic, and implacable. His power reached the remotest corners of the land and its people, so that the country was loyal to him, and his subjects obeyed him. Shahrayar himself lived and ruled in India and Indochina, while to his brother he gave the land of Samarkand to rule as king.[3]

Ten years went by, when one day Shahrayar felt a longing for his brother the king, summoned his vizier[4] (who had two daughters, one called Shahrazad, the other Dinarzad) and bade him go to his brother. Having made preparations, the vizier journeyed day and night until he reached Samarkand. When Shahzaman heard of the vizier's arrival, he went out with his retainers to meet him. He dismounted, embraced him, and asked him for news from his older brother, Shahrayar. The vizier replied that he was well, and that he had sent him to request his brother to visit him. Shahzaman complied with his brother's request and proceeded to make preparations for the journey. In the meantime, he had the vizier camp on the outskirts of the city, and took care of his needs. He sent him what he required of food and fodder, slaughtered many sheep in his honor, and provided him with money and supplies, as well as many horses and camels.

For ten full days he prepared himself for the journey; then he appointed a chamberlain in his place, and left the city to spend the night in his tent, near the vizier. At midnight he returned to his palace in the city, to bid his wife good-bye. But when he entered the palace, he found his wife lying in the arms of one of the kitchen boys. When he saw them, the world turned dark before his eyes and, shaking his head, he said to himself, "I am still here, and this is what she has done when I was barely outside the city. How will it be and what will happen behind my back when I go to visit my brother in India? No. Women are not to be trusted." He got exceedingly angry, adding, "By God, I am king and sovereign in Samarkand, yet my wife has betrayed me and has inflicted this on me." As his anger boiled, he drew his sword and struck both his wife and the cook. Then he dragged them by the heels and threw them from the top of the palace to the trench below. He then left the city and going to the vizier ordered that they depart that very hour. The drum was struck, and they set out on their journey, while Shahzaman's heart was on fire because of what his wife had done to him and how she had betrayed him with some cook, some kitchen boy. They journeyed hurriedly, day and night, through deserts and wilds, until they reached the land of King Shahrayar, who had gone out to receive them.

When Shahrayar met them, he embraced his brother, showed him favors, and treated him generously. He offered him quarters in a palace adjoining his own, for King Shahrayar had built two beautiful towering palaces in his garden, one for the

1. The Prologue is translated by Husain Haddawy, in a lively oral-flavored style, using an Egyptian manuscript that gives the heroine's name as Shahrazad, her sister (usually called Dunyazad) as Dinarzad, and the king as Shahrayar rather than the more usual Shahryar.

2. A dynasty of Persian kings who ruled from c. 226–641 C.E.

3. Samarkand is in central Asia.

4. A caliph's or king's chief administrator.

guests, the other for the women and members of his household. He gave the guest house to his brother, Shahzaman, after the attendants had gone to scrub it, dry it, furnish it, and open its windows, which overlooked the garden. Thereafter, Shahzaman would spend the whole day at his brother's, return at night to sleep at the palace, then go back to his brother the next morning. But whenever he found himself alone and thought of his ordeal with his wife, he would sigh deeply, then stifle his grief, and say, "Alas, that this great misfortune should have happened to one in my position!" Then he would fret with anxiety, his spirit would sag, and he would say, "None has seen what I have seen." In his depression, he ate less and less, grew pale, and his health deteriorated. He neglected everything, wasted away, and looked ill.

When King Shahrayar looked at his brother and saw how day after day he lost weight and grew thin, pale, ashen, and sickly, he thought that this was because of his expatriation and homesickness for his country and his family, and he said to himself, "My brother is not happy here. I should prepare a goodly gift for him and send him home." For a month he gathered gifts for his brother; then he invited him to see him and said, "Brother, I would like you to know that I intend to go hunting and pursue the roaming deer, for ten days. Then I shall return to prepare you for your journey home. Would you like to go hunting with me?" Shahzaman replied, "Brother, I feel distracted and depressed. Leave me here and go with God's blessing and help." When Shahrayar heard his brother, he thought that his dejection was because of his homesickness for his country. Not wishing to coerce him, he left him behind, and set out with his retainers and men. When they entered the wilderness, he deployed his men in a circle to begin trapping and hunting.

After his brother's departure, Shahzaman stayed in the palace and, from the window overlooking the garden, watched the birds and trees as he thought of his wife and what she had done to him, and sighed in sorrow. While he agonized over his misfortune, gazing at the heavens and turning a distracted eye on the garden, the private gate of his brother's palace opened, and there emerged, strutting like a dark-eyed deer, the lady, his brother's wife, with twenty slave-girls, ten white and ten black. While Shahzaman looked at them, without being seen, they continued to walk until they stopped below his window, without looking in his direction, thinking that he had gone to the hunt with his brother. Then they sat down, took off their clothes, and suddenly there were ten slave-girls and ten black slaves dressed in the same clothes as the girls. Then the ten black slaves mounted the ten girls, while the lady called, "Mas'ud, Mas'ud!" and a black slave jumped from the tree to the ground, rushed to her, and, raising her legs, went between her thighs and made love to her. Mas'ud topped the lady, while the ten slaves topped the ten girls, and they carried on till noon. When they were done with their business, they got up and washed themselves. Then the ten slaves put on the same clothes again, mingled with the girls, and once more there appeared to be twenty slave-girls. Mas'ud himself jumped over the garden wall and disappeared, while the slave-girls and the lady sauntered to the private gate, went in and, locking the gate behind them, went their way.

All of this happened under King Shahzaman's eyes. When he saw this spectacle of the wife and the women of his brother the great king—how ten slaves put on women's clothes and slept with his brother's paramours and concubines and what Mas'ud did with his brother's wife, in his very palace—and pondered over this calamity and great misfortune, his care and sorrow left him and he said to himself, "This is our common lot. Even though my brother is king and master of the whole world, he cannot protect what is his, his wife and his concubines, and suffers misfortune in his very home. What happened to me is little by comparison. I used to think that I was the only one who has suffered, but from what I have seen, everyone suffers. By God, my misfortune is lighter than that of my brother." He kept marveling and blaming life, whose trials none can escape, and he began to find consolation in his own affliction and forget his grief. When supper came, he ate and drank with relish and zest and, feeling better, kept eating and drinking, enjoying himself and feeling happy. He thought to himself, "I am no longer alone in my misery; I am well."

For ten days, he continued to enjoy his food and drink, and when his brother, King Shahrayar came back from the hunt, he met him happily, treated him attentively, and greeted him cheerfully. His brother, King Shahrayar, who had missed him, said, "By God, brother, I missed you on this trip and wished you were with me." Shahzaman thanked him and sat down to carouse with him, and when night fell, and food was brought before them, the two ate and drank, and again Shahzaman ate and drank with zest. As time went by, he continued to eat and drink with appetite, and became lighthearted and carefree. His face regained color and became ruddy, and his body gained weight, as his blood circulated and he regained his energy; he was himself again, or even better. King Shahrayar noticed his brother's condition, how he used to be and how he had improved, but kept it to himself until he took him aside one day and said, "My brother Shahzaman, I would like you to do something for me, to satisfy a wish, to answer a question truthfully." Shahzaman asked, "What is it, brother?" He replied, "When you first came to stay with me, I noticed that you kept losing weight, day after day, until your looks changed, your health deteriorated, and your energy sagged. As you continued like this, I thought that what ailed you was your homesickness for your family and your country, but even though I kept noticing that you were wasting away and looking ill, I refrained from questioning you and hid my feelings from you. Then I went hunting, and when I came back, I found that you had recovered and had regained your health. Now I want you to tell me everything and to explain the cause of your deterioration and the cause of your subsequent recovery, without hiding anything from me." When Shahzaman heard what King Shahrayar said, he bowed his head, then said, "As for the cause of my recovery, that I cannot tell you, and I wish that you would excuse me from telling you." The king was greatly astonished at his brother's reply and, burning with curiosity, said, "You must tell me. For now, at least, explain the first cause."

Then Shahzaman related to his brother what happened to him with his own wife, on the night of his departure, from beginning to end, and concluded, "Thus all the while I was with you, great King, whenever I thought of the event and the misfortune that had befallen me, I felt troubled, careworn, and unhappy, and my health deteriorated. This then is the cause." Then he grew silent. When King Shahrayar heard his brother's explanation, he shook his head, greatly amazed at the deceit of women, and prayed to God to protect him from their wickedness, saying, "Brother, you were fortunate in killing your wife and her lover, who gave you good reason to feel troubled, careworn, and ill. In my opinion, what happened to you has never happened to anyone else. By God, had I been in your place, I would have killed at least a hundred or even a thousand women. I would have been furious; I would have gone mad. Now praise be to God who has delivered you from sorrow and distress. But tell me what has caused you to forget your sorrow and regain your health?" Shahzaman replied, "King, I wish that for God's sake you would excuse me from telling you." Shahrayar said, "You must." Shahzaman replied, "I fear that you will feel even more troubled and careworn than I." Shahrayar asked, "How could that be, brother? I insist on hearing your explanation."

Shahzaman then told him about what he had seen from the palace window and the calamity in his very home—how ten slaves, dressed like women, were sleeping with his women and concubines, day and night. He told him everything from beginning to end (but there is no point in repeating that). Then he concluded, "When I saw your own misfortune, I felt better—and said to myself, 'My brother is king of the world, yet such a misfortune has happened to him, and in his very home.' As a result I forgot my care and sorrow, relaxed, and began to eat and drink. This is the cause of my cheer and good spirits."

When King Shahrayar heard what his brother said and found out what had happened to him, he was furious and his blood boiled. He said, "Brother, I can't believe what you say unless I see it with my own eyes." When Shahzaman saw that his brother was in a rage, he said to him, "If you do not believe me, unless you see your misfortune with your own eyes, announce that you plan to go hunting. Then you and I shall set out with your troops, and when we get outside the city, we shall leave our tents and camp with the men behind, enter the city secretly, and go together to your palace. Then the next morning you can see with your own eyes."

King Shahrayar realized that his brother had a good plan and ordered his army to prepare for the trip. He spent the night with his brother, and when God's morning broke, the two rode out of the city with their army, preceded by the camp attendants, who had gone to drive the poles and pitch the tents where the king and his army were to camp. At nightfall King Shahrayar summoned his chief chamberlain and bade him take his place. He entrusted him with the army and ordered that for three days no one was to enter the city. Then he and his brother disguised themselves and entered the city in the dark. They went directly to the palace where Shahzaman resided and slept there till the morning. When they awoke, they sat at the palace window, watching the garden and chatting, until the light broke, the day dawned, and the sun rose. As they watched, the private gate opened, and there emerged as usual the wife of King Shahrayar, walking among twenty slave-girls. They made their way under the trees until they stood below the palace window where the two kings sat. Then they took off their women's clothes, and suddenly there were ten slaves, who mounted the ten girls and made love to them. As for the lady, she called, "Mas'ud, Mas'ud," and a black slave jumped from the tree to the ground, came to her, and said, "What do you want, you slut? Here is Sa'ad al-Din Mas'ud." She laughed and fell on her back, while the slave mounted her and like the others did his business with her. Then the black slaves got up, washed themselves, and, putting on the same clothes, mingled with the girls. Then they walked away, entered the palace, and locked the gate behind them. As for Mas'ud, he jumped over the fence to the road and went on his way.

When King Shahrayar saw the spectacle of his wife and the slave-girls, he went out of his mind, and when he and his brother came down from upstairs, he said, "No one is safe in this world. Such doings are going on in my kingdom, and in my very palace. Perish the world and perish life! This is a great calamity, indeed." Then he turned to his brother and asked, "Would you like to follow me in what I shall do?" Shahzaman answered, "Yes. I will." Shahrayar said, "Let us leave our royal state and roam the world for the love of the Supreme Lord. If we should find one whose misfortune is greater than ours, we shall return. Otherwise, we shall continue to journey through the land, without need for the trappings of royalty." Shahzaman replied, "This is an excellent idea. I shall follow you."

Then they left by the private gate, took a side road, and departed, journeying till nightfall. They slept over their sorrows, and in the morning resumed their day journey until they came to a meadow by the seashore. While they sat in the meadow amid the thick plants and trees, discussing their misfortunes and the recent events, they suddenly heard a shout and a great cry coming from the middle of the sea. They trembled with fear, thinking that the sky had fallen on the earth. Then the sea parted, and there emerged a black pillar that, as it swayed forward, got taller and taller, until it touched the clouds. Shahrayar and Shahzaman were petrified; then they ran in terror and, climbing a very tall tree, sat hiding in its foliage. When they looked again, they saw that the black pillar was cleaving the sea, wading in the water toward the green meadow, until it touched the shore. When they looked again, they saw that it was a black demon, carrying on his head a large glass chest with four steel locks. He came out, walked into the meadow, and where should he stop but under the very tree where the two kings were hiding. The demon sat down and placed the glass chest on the ground. He took out four keys and, opening the locks of the chest, pulled out a full-grown woman. She had a beautiful figure, and a face like the full moon, and a lovely smile. He took her out, laid her under the tree, and looked at her, saying, "Mistress of all noble women, you whom I carried away on your wedding night, I would like to sleep a little." Then he placed his head on the young woman's lap, stretched his legs to the sea, sank into sleep, and began to snore.

Meanwhile, the woman looked up at the tree and, turning her head by chance, saw King Shahrayar and King Shahzaman. She lifted the demon's head from her lap and placed it on the ground. Then she came and stood under the tree and motioned to them with her hand, as if to say, "Come down slowly to me." When they realized that she had seen them, they were frightened, and they begged her and implored her, in the name of the Creator of the heavens, to excuse them from climbing down. She replied, "You must come down to me." They motioned to her, saying, "This sleeping demon is the enemy of mankind. For God's sake, leave us alone." She replied, "You must come down, and if you don't, I shall wake the demon and have him kill you." She kept gesturing and pressing, until they climbed down very slowly and stood before her. Then she lay on her back, raised her legs, and said, "Make love to me and satisfy my need, or else I shall wake the demon, and he will kill you." They replied, "For God's sake, mistress, don't do this to us, for at this moment we feel nothing but dismay and fear of this demon. Please, excuse us." She replied, "You must," and insisted, swearing, "By God who created the heavens, if you don't do it, I shall wake my husband the demon and ask him to kill you and throw you into the sea." As she persisted, they could no longer resist and they made love to her, first the older brother, then the younger. When they were done and withdrew from her, she said to them, "Give me your rings," and, pulling out from the folds of her dress a small purse, opened it, and shook out ninety-eight rings of different fashions and colors. Then she asked them, "Do you know what these rings are?" They answered, "No." She said, "All the owners of these rings slept with me, for whenever one of them made love to me, I took a ring from him. Since you two have slept with me, give me your rings, so that I may add them to the rest, and make a full hundred. A hundred men have known me under the very horns of this filthy, monstrous cuckold, who has imprisoned me in this chest, locked it with four locks, and kept me in the middle of this raging, roaring sea. He has guarded me and tried to keep me pure and chaste, not realizing that nothing can prevent or alter what is predestined and that when a woman desires something, no one can stop her." When Shahrayar and Shahzaman heard what the young woman said, they were greatly amazed, danced with joy, and said, "O God, O God! There is no power and no strength, save in God the Almighty, the Magnificent. Great is women's cunning." Then each of them took off his ring and handed it to her. She took them and put them with the rest in the purse. Then sitting again by the demon, she lifted his head, placed it back on her lap, and motioned to them, "Go on your way, or else I shall wake him."

They turned their backs and took to the road. Then Shahrayar turned to his brother and said, "My brother Shahzaman, look at this sorry plight. By God, it is worse than ours. This is no less than a demon who has carried a young woman away on her wedding night, imprisoned her in a glass chest, locked her up with four locks, and kept her in the middle of the sea, thinking that he could guard her from what God had foreordained, and you saw how she has managed to sleep with ninety-eight men, and added the two of us to make a hundred. Brother, let us go back to our kingdoms and our cities, never to marry a woman again. As for myself, I shall show you what I will do."

Then the two brothers headed home and journeyed till nightfall. On the morning of the third day, they reached their camp and men, entered their tent, and sat on their thrones. The chamberlains, deputies, princes, and viziers came to attend King Shahrayar, while he gave orders and bestowed robes of honor, as well as other gifts. Then at his command everyone returned to the city, and he went to his own palace and ordered his chief vizier, the father of the two girls Shahrazad and Dinarzad, who will be mentioned below, and said to him, "Take that wife of mine and put her to death." Then Shahrayar went to her himself, bound her, and handed her over to the vizier, who took her out and put her to death. Then King Shahrayar grabbed his sword, brandished it, and, entering the palace chambers, killed every one of his slave-girls and replaced them with others. He then swore to marry for one night only and kill the woman the next morning, in order to save himself from the wickedness and cunning of women, saying, "There is not a single chaste woman anywhere on the entire face of the earth." Shortly thereafter he provided his brother Shahzaman with supplies for his journey and sent him back to his own country with gifts, rarities, and money. The brother bade him good-bye and set out for home.

Shahrayar sat on his throne and ordered his vizier, the father of the two girls, to find him a wife from among the princes' daughters. The vizier found him one, and he slept with her and was done with her, and the next morning he ordered the vizier to put her to death. That very night he took one of his army officers' daughters, slept with her, and the next morning ordered the vizier to put her to death. The vizier, who could not disobey him, put her to death. The third night he took one of the merchants' daughters, slept with her till the morning, then ordered his vizier to put her to death, and the vizier did so. It became King Shahrayar's custom to take every night the daughter of a merchant or a commoner, spend the night with her, then have her put to death the next morning. He continued to do this until all the girls perished, their mothers mourned, and there arose a clamor among the fathers and mothers, who called the plague upon his head, complained to the Creator of the heavens, and called for help on Him who hears and answers prayers.

Now, as mentioned earlier, the vizier, who put the girls to death, had an older daughter called Shahrazad and a younger one called Dinarzad. The older daughter, Shahrazad, had read the books of literature, philosophy, and medicine. She knew poetry by heart, had studied historical reports, and was acquainted with the sayings of men and the maxims of sages and kings. She was intelligent, knowledgeable, wise, and refined. She had read and learned. One day she said to her father, "Father, I will tell you what is in my mind." He asked, "What is it?" She answered, "I would like you to marry me to King Shahrayar, so that I may either succeed in saving the people or perish and die like the rest." When the vizier heard what his daughter Shahrazad said, he got angry and said to her, "Foolish one, don't you know that King Shahrayar has sworn to spend but one night with a girl and have her put to death the next morning? If I give you to him, he will sleep with you for one night and will ask me to put you to death the next morning, and I shall have to do it, since I cannot disobey him." She said, "Father, you must give me to him, even if he kills me." He asked, "What has possessed you that you wish to imperil yourself?" She replied, "Father, you must give me to him. This is absolute and final." Her father the vizier became furious and said to her, "Daughter, 'He who misbehaves, ends up in trouble,' and 'He who considers not the end, the world is not his friend.' As the popular saying goes, 'I would be sitting pretty, but for my curiosity.' I am afraid that what happened to the donkey and the ox with the merchant will happen to you." She asked, "Father, what happened to the donkey, the ox, and the merchant?" He said:

[The Tale of the Ox and the Donkey]

There was a prosperous and wealthy merchant who lived in the countryside and labored on a farm. He owned many camels and herds of cattle and employed many men, and he had a wife and many grown-up as well as little children. This merchant was taught the language of the beasts,[5] on condition that if he revealed his secret to anyone, he would die; therefore, even though he knew the language of every kind of animal, he did not let anyone know, for fear of death. One day, as he sat, with his wife beside him and his children playing before him, he glanced at an ox and a donkey he kept at the farmhouse, tied to adjacent troughs, and heard the ox say to the donkey, "Watchful one, I hope that you are enjoying the comfort and the service you are getting. Your ground is swept and watered, and they serve you, feed you sifted barley, and offer you clear, cool water to drink. I, on the contrary, am taken out to plow in the middle of the night. They clamp on my neck something they call yoke and plow, push me all day under the whip to plow the field, and drive me beyond my endurance until my sides are lacerated, and my neck is flayed. They work me from nighttime to nighttime, take me back in the dark, offer me beans soiled with mud and hay mixed with chaff, and let me spend the night lying in urine and dung. Meanwhile you rest on well-swept, watered, and smoothed ground, with a clean trough full of hay. You stand in comfort, save for the rare occasion when our master the merchant rides you to do a brief errand and returns. You are comfortable, while I am weary; you sleep, while I keep awake."

When the ox finished, the donkey turned to him and said, "Green-horn, they were right in calling you ox, for you ox harbor no deceit, malice, or meanness. Being sincere, you exert and exhaust yourself to comfort others. Have you not heard the saying 'Out of bad luck, they hastened on the road'? You go into the field from early morning to endure your torture at the plow to the point of exhaustion. When the plowman takes you back and ties you to the trough, you go on butting and beating with your horns, kicking with your hoofs, and bellowing for the beans, until they toss them to you; then you begin to eat. Next time, when they bring them to you, don't eat or even touch them, but smell them, then draw back and lie down on the hay and straw. If you do this, life will be better and kinder to you, and you will find relief."

As the ox listened, he was sure that the donkey had given him good advice. He thanked him, commended him to God, and invoked His blessing on him, and said,

5. This ability has precedence in the Qur'an, which records that God taught Solomon the language of the beasts.

"May you stay safe from harm, watchful one." All of this conversation took place, daughter, while the merchant listened and understood. On the following day, the plowman came to the merchant's house and, taking the ox, placed the yoke upon his neck and worked him at the plow, but the ox lagged behind. The plowman hit him, but following the donkey's advice, the ox, dissembling, fell on his belly, and the plowman hit him again. Thus the ox kept getting up and falling until nightfall, when the plowman took him home and tied him to the trough. But this time the ox did not bellow or kick the ground with his hoofs. Instead, he withdrew, away from the trough. Astonished, the plowman brought him his beans and fodder, but the ox only smelled the fodder and pulled back and lay down at a distance with the hay and straw, complaining till the morning. When the plowman arrived, he found the trough as he had left it, full of beans and fodder, and saw the ox lying on his back, hardly breathing, his belly puffed, and his legs raised in the air. The plowman felt sorry for him and said to himself, "By God, he did seem weak and unable to work." Then he went to the merchant and said, "Master, last night, the ox refused to eat or touch his fodder."

The merchant, who knew what was going on, said to the plowman, "Go to the wily donkey, put him to the plow, and work him hard until he finishes the ox's task." The plowman left, took the donkey, and placed the yoke upon his neck. Then he took him out to the field and drove him with blows until he finished the ox's work, all the while driving him with blows and beating him until his sides were lacerated and his neck was flayed. At nightfall he took him home, barely able to drag his legs under his tired body and his drooping ears. Meanwhile the ox spent his day resting. He ate all his food, drank his water, and lay quietly, chewing his cud in comfort. All day long he kept praising the donkey's advice and invoking God's blessing on him. When the donkey came back at night, the ox stood up to greet him, saying, "Good evening, watchful one! You have done me a favor beyond description, for I have been sitting in comfort. God bless you for my sake." Seething with anger, the donkey did not reply, but said to himself, "All this happened to me because of my miscalculation. 'I would be sitting pretty, but for my curiosity.' If I don't find a way to return this ox to his former situation, I will perish." Then he went to his trough and lay down, while the ox continued to chew his cud and invoke God's blessing on him.

"You, my daughter, will likewise perish because of your miscalculation. Desist, sit quietly, and don't expose yourself to peril. I advise you out of compassion for you." She replied, "Father, I must go to the king, and you must give me to him." He said, "Don't do it." She insisted, "I must." He replied, "If you don't desist, I will do to you what the merchant did to his wife." She asked, "Father, what did the merchant do to his wife?" He said:

[The Tale of the Merchant and His Wife]

After what had happened to the donkey and the ox, the merchant and his wife went out in the moonlight to the stable, and he heard the donkey ask the ox in his own language, "Listen, ox, what are you going to do tomorrow morning, and what will you do when the plowman brings you your fodder?" The ox replied, "What shall I do but follow your advice and stick to it? If he brings me my fodder, I will pretend to be ill, lie down, and puff my belly." The donkey shook his head, and said, "Don't do it. Do you know what I heard our master the merchant say to the plowman?" The ox asked, "What?" The donkey replied, "He said that if the ox failed to get up and eat his fodder, he would call the butcher to slaughter him and skin him and would distribute the meat for alms and use the skin for a mat. I am afraid for you, but good advice is a matter of faith; therefore, if he brings you your fodder, eat it and look alert lest they cut your throat and skin you." The ox farted and bellowed.

The merchant got up and laughed loudly at the conversation between the donkey and the ox, and his wife asked him, "What are you laughing at? Are you making fun of me?" He said, "No." She said, "Tell me what made you laugh." He replied, "I cannot tell you. I am afraid to disclose the secret conversation of the animals." She asked, "And what prevents you from telling me?" He answered, "The fear of death." His wife said, "By God, you are lying. This is nothing but an excuse. I swear by God, the Lord of heaven, that if you don't tell me and explain the cause of your laughter, I will leave you. You must tell me." Then she went back to the house crying, and she continued to cry till the morning. The merchant said, "Damn it! Tell me why you are crying. Ask for God's forgiveness, and stop questioning and leave me in peace." She said, "I insist and will not desist." Amazed at her, he replied, "You insist! If I tell you what the donkey said to the ox, which made me laugh, I shall die." She said, "Yes, I insist, even if you have to die." He replied, "Then call your family," and she called their two daughters, her parents and relatives, and some neighbors. The merchant told them that he was about to die, and everyone, young and old, his children, the farmhands, and the servants began to cry until the house became a place of mourning. Then he summoned legal witnesses, wrote a will, leaving his wife and children their due portions, freed his slave-girls, and bid his family good-bye, while everybody, even the witnesses, wept. Then the wife's parents approached her and said, "Desist, for if your husband had not known for certain that he would die if he revealed his secret, he wouldn't have gone through all this." She replied, "I will not change my mind," and everybody cried and prepared to mourn his death.

Well, my daughter Shahrazad, it happened that the farmer kept fifty hens and a rooster at home, and while he felt sad to depart this world and leave his children and relatives behind, pondering and about to reveal and utter his secret, he overheard a dog of his say something in dog language to the rooster, who, beating and clapping his wings, had jumped on a hen and, finishing with her, jumped down and jumped on another. The merchant heard and understood what the dog said in his own language to the rooster, "Shameless, no-good rooster. Aren't you ashamed to do such a thing on a day like this?" The rooster asked, "What is special about this day?" The dog replied, "Don't you know that our master and friend is in mourning today? His wife is demanding that he disclose his secret, and when he discloses it, he will surely die. He is in this predicament, about to interpret to her the language of the animals, and all of us are mourning for him, while you clap your wings and get off one hen and jump on another. Aren't you ashamed?" The merchant heard the rooster reply, "You fool, you lunatic! Our master and friend claims to be wise, but he is foolish, for he has only one wife, yet he does not know how to manage her." The dog asked, "What should he do with her?"

The rooster replied, "He should take an oak branch, push her into a room, lock the door, and fall on her with the stick, beating her mercilessly until he breaks her arms and legs and she cries out, 'I no longer want you to tell me or explain anything.' He should go on beating her until he cures her for life, and she will never oppose him in anything. If he does this, he will live, and live in peace, and there will be no more grief, but he does not know how to manage." Well, my daughter Shahrazad, when the merchant heard the conversation between the dog and the rooster, he jumped up and, taking an oak branch, pushed his wife into a room, got in with her, and locked the door. Then he began to beat her mercilessly on her chest and shoulders and kept beating her until she cried for mercy, screaming, "No, no, I don't want to know anything.

Leave me alone, leave me alone. I don't want to know anything," until he got tired of hitting her and opened the door. The wife emerged penitent, the husband learned good management, and everybody was happy, and the mourning turned into a celebration.

"If you don't relent, I shall do to you what the merchant did to his wife." She said, "Such tales don't deter me from my request. If you wish, I can tell you many such tales. In the end, if you don't take me to King Shahrayar, I shall go to him by myself behind your back and tell him that you have refused to give me to one like him and that you have begrudged your master one like me." The vizier asked, "Must you really do this?" She replied, "Yes, I must."

Tired and exhausted, the vizier went to King Shahrayar and, kissing the ground before him, told him about his daughter, adding that he would give her to him that very night. The king was astonished and said to him, "Vizier, how is it that you have found it possible to give me your daughter, knowing that I will, by God, the Creator of heaven, ask you to put her to death the next morning and that if you refuse, I will have you put to death too?" He replied, "My King and Lord, I have told her everything and explained all this to her, but she refuses and insists on being with you tonight." The king was delighted and said, "Go to her, prepare her, and bring her to me early in the evening."

The vizier went down, repeated the king's message to his daughter, and said, "May God not deprive me of you." She was very happy and, after preparing herself and packing what she needed, went to her younger sister, Dinarzad, and said, "Sister, listen well to what I am telling you. When I go to the king, I will send for you, and when you come and see that the king has finished with me, say, 'Sister, if you are not sleepy, tell us a story.' Then I will begin to tell a story, and it will cause the king to stop his practice, save myself, and deliver the people." Dinarzad replied, "Very well."

At nightfall the vizier took Shahrazad and went with her to the great King Shahrayar. But when Shahrayar took her to bed and began to fondle her, she wept, and when he asked her, "Why are you crying?" she replied, "I have a sister, and I wish to bid her goodbye before daybreak." Then the king sent for the sister, who came and went to sleep under the bed. When the night wore on, she woke up and waited until the king had satisfied himself with her sister Shahrazad and they were by now all fully awake. Then Dinarzad cleared her throat and said, "Sister, if you are not sleepy, tell us one of your lovely little tales to while away the night, before I bid you goodbye at daybreak, for I don't know what will happen to you tomorrow." Shahrazad turned to King Shahrayar and said, "May I have your permission to tell a story?" He replied, "Yes," and Shahrazad was very happy and said, "Listen."

from The Tale of the Porter and the Young Girls[1]

There was once a young man in the city of Baghdad, who was by faith a bachelor and by trade a porter.

One day, as he was leaning idly against his basket in the market-place, a woman, wearing a full veil of Mosul silk, tasselled with gold and turned with rare brocade,

1. This tale and the remaining selections are translated by Powys Mathers from the classic French translation by J. C. Mardrus. Whereas Haddawy's translation of the Prologue is based on a lean early manuscript, the Mardrus/Mathers version reflects the ongoing, expansive tradition, which added in poetry and many tales not found in the earlier manuscripts. From this point onward, Shahrazad's sister's name is found in its best-known form, Dunyazad. Shahrazad tells the story of the Porter beginning on the ninth night, after a series of shorter stories (always leading onward at daybreak) has fascinated the king and enticed him to postpone her murder night by night.

stopped before him and raised the veil a little from her face. Above it there showed dark eyes with long lashes of silk and lids to set a man dreaming. Her body was slight, her feet were very small, and clear perfection shone about her. She said, and oh, but her voice was sweet: "Take up your basket, porter, and follow me." Hardly believing that so exquisite words could have been said to him, the porter took up his basket and followed the girl, who stopped eventually before the door of a house. She knocked at the door and immediately a Christian opened to her, who gave her, in exchange for a dīnār, a great measure of olive-clear wine which she put into the basket,[2] saying to the porter: "Lift and follow me." "By Allah, this is a day of days!" exclaimed the porter, as he lifted his basket and followed the girl. Arrived at the stall of a fruiterer, she bought Syrian apples, Osmāni quinces, peaches from Uman, jasmine of Aleppo, Damascene nenuphars, cucumbers from the Nile, limes from Egypt, Sultāni citrons, myrtle berries, flowers of henna, blood-red anemones, violets, pomegranate bloom, and the narcissus. All these she put into the porter's basket, and said: "Lift!"; so he lifted and followed her until she came to a butcher's stall. Here she said: "Cut me ten pounds of mutton." So they cut her ten pounds which she wrapped in banana leaves and put into the basket, and said: "Lift!" He lifted and followed her to an almond seller, from whom she bought every kind of almond that there is. Then the porter followed her to a sweetmeat seller from whom she bought a great platter which she covered with things from the stall: open-work sugar tarts with butter, velvet pastries perfumed with musk and stuffed deliciously, sābūnīyah biscuits, small cakes, lime tarts, honey-tasting jam, those sweets called mushabbak, little souffléd patties called lukaimāt al-Kādī,[3] and those others named combs of Zainab which are made with butter and mingled with milk and honey. All these pleasant things she put upon the platter and then placed the platter in the basket. "If you had told me, I would have brought a mule," said the porter. Smiling at his jest, she stopped at the stall of a distiller of perfumes and bought ten sorts of waters, rose water, water of orange flowers, willow flower, violet and other kinds; she bought also a spray of rose-musk-scented water, grains of male incense, aloe wood, ambergris and musk; finally she selected candles of Alexandrian wax and put all in the basket, saying: "Lift and follow!" Obediently the porter took up his basket and followed the young lady until she came to a splendid palace, having a great court set in an inner garden; it was tall, magnificent and foursquare, and the door had two leaves of ebony, plated with plates of red gold.

The young girl rapped gently upon the door and it flew wide open. Then the porter looked at her who had opened the door and saw that she was a child having a slim and gracious body, the very model of all a young girl should be, not only for her round and prominent breasts, not only for her beauty and her air of breeding, but also for the perfection of her waist and of her carriage. Her brow was as white as the first ray fallen from the new moon, her eyes were the eyes of a gazelle, and the brows above them were as the crescent moons of Ramadān.[4] Her cheeks were anemones, her mouth the scarlet seal of Sulaimān, her face pale as the full moon when she first rises above the grasses, her breasts twin passion-fruit. As for her young white pliant belly, it lay hid beneath her robe like some precious love letter in a silken case. Seeing her, the porter felt that he was losing his wits and nearly let the basket slip from his shoulders. "As Allah lives, this is the most blessed day of all my life!" he said. Standing

2. Since wine is fobidden in Islam, only Christians are licensed to trade in it.
3. Mushabbak and lukaimat al-Kadi are two types of doughnut-like sweets soaked in honey.
4. The new moons that mark the beginning and end of the holy month of Ramadan, a time of fasting and atonement.

within, the young portress said to her sister the cateress and also to the porter: "Enter, and be your welcome as great as it is good!"

They went in and came at last to an ample hall giving on the central court, hung over with silk brocade and gold brocade, and full of fair gold-crusted furniture. There were vases and carved seats, curtains and close-shut presses all about it, and in the middle a marble couch, inlaid with pearl and diamond, covered with a red satin quilt. On the bed lay a third girl who exceeded all the marvel that a girl can be. Her eyes were Babylonian, for all witchcraft has its seat in Babylon. Her body was slim as the letter alif,[5] her face so fair as to confuse the bright sun. She was as a star among the shining of the stars, a true Arabian woman, as the poet says:

Who sings your slender body is a reed
His simile a little misses,
Reeds must be naked to be fair indeed
While your sweet garments are but added blisses.

Who sings your body is a slender bough
Also commits a kindred folly,
Boughs to be fair must have green leaves enow
And you, my white one, must be naked wholly.

The young girl got up from the bed, moved a few paces into the middle of the hall until she was near her two sisters and then said to them: "Why are you standing still like this? Take the basket from the porter's head." Then the cateress came in front of the porter, the portress came behind him and, helped by their third sister, they relieved him of his burden. When they had taken everything out of the basket, they arranged all neatly and gave two dīnārs to the porter, saying: "Turn and be gone, O porter!" But he looked at the young girls, admiring the perfection of their beauty, and thought that he had never seen the like. He noticed that there was no man with them and, marvelling at all the drinks, fruits, perfumed flowers, and other good things, had no desire to go away.

The eldest of the girls said: "Why do you not go? Do you find your payment too little?" and then, turning to her sister the cateress: "Give him a third dīnār." But the porter said: "As Allah lives, fair ladies, my ordinary pay is but two half dīnārs; you have paid me well enough and yet all my heart and the inner parts of my soul are troubled about you. I cannot help asking myself what this life of yours is, that you live alone and have no man here to bear you human company. Do you not know that a minaret is of no value unless it be one of the four minarets of a mosque? You are but three, my ladies, you need a fourth. Women cannot be truly happy without men. The poet has said: 'There can be no harmony save with four joined instruments: the lute, the harp, the cithern and flagiolet.' Now you are only three, my ladies; you need a flagiolet, a fourth instrument, a man of discretion, full both of sentiment and intellect, a gifted artist with sealed lips!"

"But, porter," said the young girls, "do you not know that we are virgins and so are fearful of confiding ourselves to the indiscretion of a man? We also have read the poets, and they say: 'Confide in none; a secret told is a secret spoiled.'"

Hearing this, the porter cried: "I swear on your dear lives, my ladies, that I am a man sure, faithful and discreet, one who has studied the annals and read books. I

5. The first letter of the Arabic alphabet, which looks like the English letter l.

speak of only pleasing things and am carefully silent about all the rest. I act always according to the saying of the poet:

I know the duties of high courtesy,
Your dearest secrets shall be safe with me;
I'll shut them in a little inner room
And seal the lock and throw away the key.

Their hearts were much moved towards the porter when they heard his verses and all the rhymes and rhythms he recited, and in jest they said: "You must know that we have spent a great sum of money on this place. Have you the silver to pay us back? For we would not ask you to sit with us unless you paid the reckoning. We take it you desire to stay here, to become our companion in the wine and, above all, to keep us waking all the night until the shadow of the dawn fall on our faces." "Love without gold is a poor make-weight in the scales," added the eldest of the girls, the mistress of the house; and the portress said: "If you have nothing, get you gone with nothing!" But here the cateress interrupted, saying: "Let us leave this joke, my sisters. As Allah lives, this boy has not spoiled our day and another might not have been so patient. I myself will undertake to pay for him."

At this the porter rejoiced with all his heart and said to the cateress: "By Allah, I owe this wonderful bargain all to you!" "Stay with us, then, brave porter," she replied, "and rest assured that you shall be the darling of our eyes." So saying, she rose and, after clasping his waist, began to arrange the flasks, to clarify and pour the wine, and to set places for the feast near a pool of water in the center of the hall. She brought in everything of which they might have need, handed the wine, and saw that all were seated. The porter with these girls on every hand thought that he was dreaming in his sleep.

Soon the cateress took the wine flagon and filled a cup from which each drank three times. Then she filled it afresh and passed it to her sisters and then to the porter, who drank and said these lines:

In this red wine is liveliness
And strength and well-being,
In this red wine is all caress
And every wanton thing;
Drink deep and you will find, I trust,
In this red wine is very lust.

On this he kissed the hands of the three girls and drained the cup. Then he went up to the mistress of the house, saying: "Mistress, I am your slave, your thing, your chattel!" and he recited, in her honour, this stanza of a certain poet:

I stand most like a slave
Outside your door,
Must I an entrance crave
In vain for ever more?
There is one gift I have—
I stand most like a slave.

Then, "Drink, my friend," said she, "and may the wine be sweet and wholesome in its going down: may it give you strength to set out upon that road where lies all bodily well-being." The porter took the cup, kissed the girl's hand and, in a sweetly-modulated voice, sang very low these verses of the poet:

I gave my love a wine
Splendidly red as are her cheeks, I said.
Then she: "I cannot drink these cheeks of mine."
"Ah, let me speak," I said,
"Thou can'st not drink those cheeks of thine;
Then drink these tears and blood of mine!"

Again the young girl took the cup to the porter and, after holding it to his lips, sat down beside her sister. Soon they began to dance and sing and to play with the wonderful petals, the porter all the time taking them in his arms and kissing them, while one said saucy things to him, another drew him to her, and the third beat him with flowers. They went on drinking until the grape sat throned above their reason, and, when her reign was fully established, the portress rose and stripped off all her clothes until she was naked. Jumping into the water of the fountain, she began to play with it, taking it in her mouth and blowing it noisily at the porter, washing all her body, and letting it run between her childish thighs. At length she got out of the fountain, threw herself on the porter's lap, stretched out on her back and, pointing to the thing which was between her thighs, said:

"My darling, do you know the name of that?" "Aha," answered the porter, "usually that is called the house of compassion." Then she cried: "Yū, yū! Are you not ashamed?" and taking him by the neck she began to slap him. "No, no!" he cried. "It is called the thing." But she shook her head, and "Then it is your behind piece," said the porter. Again she shook her head, and "It is your hornet," said he. At these words she began to slap him so hard that she abraded his skin. "You tell me its name!" he shouted, and she told him: "Basil of the bridges." "At last," cried the porter. "Praise be to Allah for your safety, O my basil of the bridges!"

After that, they let the cup go round and round; and the second girl, taking off her clothes, jumped into the basin. There she did as her sister had done and then, getting out, threw herself on to the porter's lap. Pointing to her thighs and the thing between them, she said: "Light of my life, what is the name of that?" "Your crack," he answered. "O listen to his naughty word!" she cried, and slapped him so hard that the hall echoed with the sound. "Then it is basil of the bridges," he hazarded, but she again cried that it was not and went on slapping his neck. "Well, what is its name?" he yelled, and she answered: "The husked sesame."

Now the third girl, in her turn, got up, undressed, and went down into the basin, where she did as her sisters had done. Afterwards she put on some of her clothes and stretched herself over the thighs of the porter. "Guess the name of that," she said, pointing to her delicate parts. The porter tried this name and that and ended by asking her to tell him and cease her slapping. "The khān of Abu-Mansūr," she replied.

Then, in reprisal, the porter rose, undressed and went down into the water, and lo! his blade swam level with the surface. He washed as the girls had done, came out of the basin, and, throwing himself into the lap of the portress, rested his feet in that of the cateress. Pointing to his organ, he asked the mistress of the house: "What is his name, my queen?" At this all the girls laughed till they fell over on their backs, and cried together: "Your zabb!" "No," he said, and took a little bite at each by way of forfeit. Then they cried: "Your tool, then!" But he said: "No," and pinched their breasts. "But it is your tool," they cried in astonishment, "for it is hot. It is your zabb, because it moves." Each time the porter shook his head and kissed and bit and pinched and hugged them until they laughed again. In the end they had to ask him to tell them; and the porter reflected a moment, looked between his thighs, and winking, said: "Ladies, this child, my zabb, says for himself:

'My name is the Mighty Ungelt Mule who feeds on the basil of bridges, feasts on husked sesame, and stays the night in father Mansūr's khān.'"

At these words, the girls laughed so much that they fell over on their bottoms; and afterwards all four went on drinking from the same cup until the approach of evening. When night fell, they said to the porter: "Be gone, now, turn your face and let us see the width of your shoulders." But the porter cried: "By Allah, it is easier for my soul to quit my body than for me to quit your house, my ladies! Let us make the night continue the sweet day, and tomorrow all can part and follow their destiny upon the road of Allah." The young cateress then spoke up saying: "By my life, sisters, let us ask him to pass the night with us; we will have many good laughs at the naughty fellow who is so shameless and yet so gentle." The others agreed, and said to the porter: "Very well, you can stay with us this night on condition that you obey implicitly and ask no reason or explanation of anything you see." "I agree to that, ladies," he said. "Get up, then, and read what is over the door," they commanded; so he rose, and found over the door these words lettered in gold:

"Speak not of that which concerns you not or you will hear that which shall please you not."

Reading this, the porter said: "Ladies, I call you to witness that I will never speak of that which concerns me not."

At this point Shahrazād saw the approach of morning and discreetly fell silent.

But when the tenth night had come

Dunyazād said: "Finish your tale, dear sister."

So Shahrazād answered: "Gladly and as in duty bound," and thus continued:

It is related, O auspicious King, that when the porter had made his promise to the girls, the cateress rose and set meat before them all, which they ate with good appetite. After the meal, candles were lighted, perfumed wood and incense burned, and all began to drink again and to eat the various delicacies from the market; especially the porter who also recited well-formed verses all the time, shutting his eyes and shaking his head. Suddenly they heard a knocking on the door, which, though it did not interrupt their pleasure, caused the portress to rise. She came back, saying: "Indeed, tonight's pleasure is to be perfect, for there are three strangers at the door with shaved beards and each blind of the left eye, which is a strange coincidence. It is easy to see that they come from the lands of Rūm, each has different features and yet their faces all match in their fittingness for being laughed at. If we let them in, we can have much fun at their expense." She persuaded her companions, who said: "Tell them that they may come in, but be sure they understand the condition: 'Speak not of that which concerns you not or you will hear that which shall please you not.'" So the young girl ran joyously to the door and came back leading the three one-eyed men, who indeed had shaved beards, moustaches twisted back, and all the signs of that brotherhood of beggars called kalandars. As soon as they came in, they wished peace to the company, backing one by one as they did so; on which the girls stood up and invited them to be seated. The three men, after they had sat down, looked at the porter, who was very drunk, and supposing him to belong to their brotherhood, said among themselves: "Here is another kalandar; he is sure to bear us friendly company." But the porter, who had heard what they said, jumped to his feet and, eyeing them sternly and a little squintingly, said: "All right, all right, my friends, make yourselves at home; and begin by digesting those words written above the door." The girls burst out laughing at his words and said to each other: "We are going to have fun with these kalandars and the porter." They set food before the kalandars—who ate like kalandars!—then wine—and the kalandars drank turn and turn about, reaching out again and again for the cup. When the drink was passing round at a rare pace, the porter said: "Come, brothers, have you not some good tale of marvellous adventure in your scrips to amuse us?" Cheered by this suggestion, the kalandars asked for musical instruments and, when the portress had fetched out a Mosul drum fitted with crotals, a lute of Irāq, and a Persian flagiolet, they stood up and began to play while the girls sang with them. The porter became frenzied with pleasure and kept on shouting: "Ha! yā Allah!", so struck was he by the harmonious voices of the singers.

In the middle of all this, knocking was again heard upon the door and the portress rose to see who was there.

Now this was the reason for the second knocking on the door:

That night the Khalīfah, Hārūn al-Rashīd, had gone down to wander about his city to see and hear for himself what might be going on there. He was accompanied by his wazīr. Jafar al-Barmaki,[6] and by Masrūr, his sword-bearer, the instrument of his justice. You must know that it was a habit of his to disguise himself as a merchant and make such expeditions.

While he was walking through the streets of the city, he passed that palace and heard the sounds of music and gaiety which issued from it. Then said the Khalīfah to Jafar: "I wish to enter that place to see those singers." Jafar answered: "They must be a crowd of drunkards. If we go in some hurt may come to you." But the Khalīfah said: "Certainly we must go in. I wish to find a way in which we can enter and take them by surprise." "I hear and I obey," said Jafar at this command and, going up to the door, he knocked.

When the young portress opened the door, the wazīr said to her: "My mistress, we are merchants from Tiberias. Ten days ago we came to Baghdad with our goods and took lodging in the khān of the merchants. One of the other traders at the khān asked us to his house tonight to eat with him. After the meal, which lasted an hour in which we ate and drank excellently, he gave us leave to depart. We came out but, the night being dark and we strangers, lost our way to the khān where we lodge. So now we beg you of your great goodness to let us come in and pass the night at your house. Allah will reward your kindness." The portress looked at them closely and, seeing that they had the appearance of most respectable merchants, went in to ask the advice of her two companions. The other two said: "Let them come in!" So she returned to the door, crying: "Enter!" On this invitation the Khalīfah and Jafar and Masrūr came in and the girls rose, putting themselves at their service and saying: "Be very welcome. Take your ease here, dear companions; but accept, we pray, this one condition: 'Speak not of that which concerns you not or you will hear that which shall please you not.'" The newcomers answered: "Be it so," and sat down with the others. While they were being invited to drink and to send round the cup, the Khalīfah looked at the three

6. The trusted vizier and companion of Harun (or Haroun) al-Rashid (r. 786–809), the most famous of all the Abbasid Caliphs.

kalandars and was astonished to see that each was blind of the left eye; then at the girls and was overcome with surprise at all their beauty and grace. When the girls, in their ministrations to the guests, offered the Khalīfah a cup of the rarest wine, he refused, saying: "I am vowed to pilgrimage." So the portress got up and placed a little table of finest inlay before him on which she set a cup of Chinese porcelain into which she poured spring water refreshed with snow, mingling sugar and rose-water within it. The Khalīfah accepted this, thanking her cordially and saying to himself: "Tomorrow I shall reward her for her kindness."

The girls continued to act the hostess and pass about the wine till the wits of the companions were dancing dizzily. Then she who was the mistress of the house rose up and, having asked if any wanted more, took the cateress by the hand saying: "Rise, my sister, that we may do that which we have to do." "Be it as you say," the other answered. On this the portress also rose and, telling the kalandars to get up from the center of the hall and seat themselves by the door, herself cleared and tidied the central space. The other two called to the porter: "By Allah, your friendship is of but little use! You are no stranger here but belong to the house." On this the porter stood up, lifted the skirts of his robe and tightened his belt, saying: "Tell me what to do and I shall do it." "Follow me," said the portress. So he followed her out of the hall and saw two black bitches with chains round their necks, which, as he was bid, he led back into the middle of the hall. Then the eldest pulled up her sleeves, took a whip, and told the porter to lead forward one of the bitches. When he had done so, dragging her by the chain, the animal began to weep, raising its head piteously towards the girl; but the latter, without seeming to notice, fell upon it, beating it over the head with her whip till the bitch yelled and wept and she herself could strike no more. Then she threw down the whip and, taking the bitch in her arms, clasped it to her breast, wiped away its tears, and kissed its head which she held between her hands. After a little, she said to the porter: "Bring me the other, and take this one back." So the porter brought the other bitch forward and the girl treated it as she had the first.

The Khalīfah felt his heart filled with pity at this sight; his breast shook with grief and he signed with his eye to Jafar to question the young woman. But Jafar signed to him that it were better to keep silent. Soon the mistress of the house turned to her sisters saying: "Come, let us do as is our custom." They answered: "Yes"; so she got up on to the marble bed which was plated with gold and silver and said to the other two: "Let it be done!" Then the portress also got up on to the bed; but the cateress went into her own room and brought back a satin bag fringed with green silk. Halting before the other two, she opened the bag and drew a lute from it. First tuning this and then playing upon it, she sang these lines of love and all the sadness of love:

Love at my door
Knocked and I gave him bed.
When sleep saw this
He took offence and fled.
"Give me back sleep;
Where has he gone?" I said.

* * *

It's not that time
Has passed, but that so has she,
It's not that love

Won't last, but that nor will she,
Not that life's gone,
But that she's gone from me.

My soul is bound
By the scents of her body,
Jasmine and musk
And rose of her body,
Amber and nard,
The scents of her body.

"Allah comfort you, my sister," cried out the portress, when the song was finished; then, tearing all her clothes in an ecstasy of grief, she fell in a faint upon the floor.

Her body being in some sort bared, the Khalīfah was able to see upon it the prints of whips and rods, a circumstance which astonished and appalled him. But the cateress came and cast water in her sister's face until she recovered consciousness; then she brought her a new robe and helped her into it.

The Khalīfah whispered to Jafar: "You do not seem moved by this. Do you not see the marks of the scourge on the woman? I can hardly keep silent and I will know no rest until I have found out the truth of all this and of the matter of the two bitches." "Lord and Master," answered Jafar, "remember the condition: 'Speak not of that which concerns you not or you will hear that which shall please you not.'"

While they were talking thus, the cateress again took up the lute and, pressing it against her rounded breast, sounded the chords and sang:

If one came to us plaining of love,
What would we answer?
Seeing that we also are drowned in love,
What would we do?
If we charged a speaker to speak for us,
What would he know of it?

* * *

Again the portress fell fainting and again her naked body showed the marks of whips and rods.

The three kalandars began whispering together when they saw this: "It had been better for us if we had never come into this house, even though we had to sleep on the naked ground; for what we have just seen is enough to melt the marrow in our spines." The Khalīfah turned to them and said: "Why is that?" "We are afraid of what has happened," they answered. "Is that so?" said the Khalīfah, "then you are not of this house?" "We are not," they answered, "we imagined it belonged to that man beside you." "By Allah, it does not!" cried the porter. "This is the very first time that I have entered here. Also, God knows, it would have been better for me to have slept on the rubbish heaps among the ruins."

So they concerted with each other and said: "We are seven men to three women, let us demand an explanation of these things and, if they will not answer willingly, we can use force." They all agreed to this except Jafar, who said: "Do you think that right and equitable? Remember, we are their guests and that they laid down certain conditions which we swore to keep. The night is nearly over; it would be better for each of us to go forth and seek his destiny upon the road of Allah." Then, winking at the Khalīfah and drawing him aside, he continued: "We have but one more hour to stay here. Tomorrow I promise that I will bring them up before you, and then we can compel them to tell their story." But the Khalīfah said: "I have not the patience to wait till tomorrow." The others continued their planning, some saying this and some saying that, but it all came back to the question: "Who is to ask them?" At last it was decided that the porter should do so.

So, when the girls said: "Good folk, what are you talking about?", the porter rose to his feet and, standing up straight before the lady of the house, addressed her courteously: "My queen, I ask and pray you in the name of Allah, on behalf of all us jolly fellows, to tell us the tale of those two bitches and why you so beat them and then weep over them and kiss them. Tell us, too, for we wait to hear it, the cause of the marks of whips and rods on the body of your sister. This we ask of you; that is all, my queen." Then the lady of the house questioned them: "Is this that the porter has said asked in the name of all?" And each, with the exception of Jafar, answered: "Yes." Jafar said nothing.

The eldest girl, hearing this answer of theirs, exclaimed: "As Allah lives, you who are our guests have done us here the most grievous of wrongs. We bound you to this condition: 'Speak not of that which concerns you not or you will hear that which shall please you not.' Was it not enough for you to come into our house and eat our good food? Perhaps, though, it was less your fault than the fault of our sister who let you in."

So saying, she pulled the sleeves of her robe away from her wrist and beat the floor with her foot three times, calling: "Come quick, come quick!" The door of one of the great curtained presses opened and out glided seven strong negroes carrying sharpened swords. To these she said: "Bind the arms of these prattling guests and fasten them one to the other." This the negroes did, saying: "O mistress, O hidden flower beyond the sight of men, may we cut off their heads?" "Have patience for an hour," she answered. "I wish to know what sort of men they are before they die."

On this the porter cried: "By Allah, mistress queen, do not kill me for the crime of others. All these have sinned, committing a notable crime against you, but not I. As God lives, how happy, how paradisal would our night have been if we had never set eyes on these ill-omened kalandars.[7] I have always said that kalandars could lay waste the loveliest of cities just by coming into it." And he added these lines:

> The fairest gift of strength is clemency
> If the weak offend;
> So do not, for our love's sake, punish me
> For the fault of a friend.

The eldest girl burst out laughing when the porter had finished speaking.

At this point Shahrazād saw the approach of day and discreetly fell silent.

But when the eleventh night had come

She said:

It is related, O auspicious King, that when the eldest girl burst out laughing after having been angry, she came down to the company and said: "Tell me all that there is to tell, for you have but one hour to live. I give you this indulgence because you are

7. There was a superstitious belief that one-eyed people bring bad luck.

poor folk. If you were among the most noble, great ones of your tribes or even governors, it is true that I would hurry on your punishment."

"Jafar, we are in sorry case," said the Khalīfah, "tell her who we are or she may kill us." "Which is exactly what we deserve," said Jafar. Then said the Khalīfah: "There is a time for being witty and a time for being serious, there is a time for everything."

Now first of all the eldest girl approached the kalandars and asked them: "Are you brothers?" To this they answered: "No, by Allah, we are only poor men of the poorest who live by cupping and scarifying."[8] Then she turned to one of them and said: "Were you born without one eye?" "As God lives, I was not," he answered, "but the tale of the way I lost my eye is so extraordinary that, if it were written with a needle in the corner of another eye, yet would it be a lesson to the circumspect." The second and the third made the same kind of answer; then all three said: "Each of us was born in a different country; the stories of our lives are strange and our adventures pass the marvellous." "Well, then," said the girl, "each of you must tell his story and the reason of his coming to our house. Should the tale seem good to us, each then may make his bow and go his way."

The first who came forward was the porter; and he said: "My queen, I am a porter, nothing more. Your cateress here gave me things to carry and led me to you. You know well what happened to me after I got here and, if I refuse to be more particular, you know why. That is all my tale. I will not add another word to it, and Allah bless you." Then said the eldest girl: "Get you gone, make your bow and let us see the last of you." "But," said the porter, "no, by God, I will not stir until I have heard the tales of these friends of mine."

[The three kalandars proceed to tell their tales of adventure and misfortune, and then the owner of the house asks Haroun al-Rashid for his story.]

The young girl then turned to the Khalīfah, Jafar and Masrur, asking for their stories. So Jafar went up and told her the fable that he had already told the portress at the door. After she had heard him, the girl said: "I will pardon you all. Depart quickly and in peace."

When they were safely out in the road, the Khalīfah asked the kalandars whither they were going and, when they answered that they did not know, instructed Jafar to take them to his home and bring them before him in the morning, so that he might see what could be done for them.

After Jafar had done his bidding, the Khalīfah returned to his palace, where he tried in vain to sleep. Early in the morning he rose and, mounting his throne, held audience of all the chief men of his empire. When these had departed, he turned to Jafar, saying: "Bring to me the three young girls and the two bitches and the three kalandars." Jafar brought them all forthwith and, when they stood before the Khalīfah, the girls being heavily veiled, addressed these words to them: "We hold you free of any unkindness; you knew not who we were and yet you pardoned us and treated us well. Now learn that you have come into the hands of the fifth of the line of Abbās, Hārūn al-Rashīd, the Khalīfah. It is unwise to tell him aught but the truth."

When Jafar had thus spoken for the Prince of Believers, the eldest girl came forward, saying: "Prince of Believers, my story is so strange that if it were written with a needle on the corner of an eye yet would it serve as a lesson to the circumspect!"

At this point Shahrazād saw the approach of morning and discreetly fell silent.

8. Performing simple medical treatments.

But when the sixteenth night had come

She said:

It is related, O auspicious King, that the eldest of the young girls stood up before the Prince of Believers and told this story:

[THE TALE OF ZUBAIDAH, THE FIRST OF THE GIRLS]

Prince of Believers; my name is Zubaidah, my sister who opened the door for you is Amīnah, and our youngest is called Fahīmah. We were all three born of the same father but not of the same mother; these two bitches, on the other hand, are full sisters to me, being born of the same father and the same mother. When our father died, leaving five thousand dīnārs to be divided equally among us, Amīnah and Fahīmah left us to live with their mother, while I and my two sisters lived together. I was the youngest of the three, though I am older than Amīnah and Fahīmah.

Soon after our father's death, my two elder sisters married and, in a little while, their husbands fitted out commercial ventures with their wives' inheritances and set sail, each taking his wife with him and leaving me alone.

My sisters were away for four years, and during that time their husbands, becoming bankrupt, lost all their goods and made off, abandoning them among strangers in strange lands. After bitter sufferings they managed to make their ways back to me, but they looked so like beggars that at first I did not recognise them. Yet when they spoke to me I knew who they were and questioned them tenderly as to what had happened. "Sister, words cannot help us now," they answered. "Allah took the reed pen and wrote that it was to be." I pitied them from the bottom of my heart, sent them to the bath, and put fair new garments upon them, saying: "Sisters, you are the elder, while I am the younger; you stand to me in the place of both father and mother. My inheritance, by Allah's grace, has prospered and increased. Come, use the profit of it as your own and live with me in honour and in peace."

I loaded them with benefits and they stayed with me for a year, sharing my substance. But one day they said: "Marriage would be better for us, we cannot do without it any longer, we have no more patience with living alone." "I fear that you will get little good from marriage," I said, "for an honest man is hard to come by in these days. You tried marriage once; have you forgotten how you found it?"

But they would not listen to me, being set on marrying without my consent; so I married them to husbands, giving them money and the necessary clothes. And the new husbands took them away as before.

It was not long, however, before the new husbands deceived them and decamped with all the dowry which I had provided. Naked and full of excuses, they returned to me, saying: "Do not blame us, we are older than you but you are wiser than we. We promise never to say a word again on the subject of marriage." "Sweet welcome to you, my sisters," I answered, "there are none dearer to me in the world than you." So I kissed them and behaved bountifully towards them as before.

After they had lived with me for another year, it came into my head to fit out a ship with merchandise and to voyage in it to do business at Basrah. So I got ready a vessel, filling it with merchandise and goods of all kinds as well as necessaries for the voyage. I asked my sisters whether they would rather stay at home while I was away or come with me. They decided to accompany me, so I took them with me and we set sail. But first I divided my money into two halves, one of which I took with me and one of which I hid at home in case some misfortune befell the ship and we escaped with our lives.

We sailed on night and day, but by ill-luck the captain lost his course, so that we were driven to the outer ocean and into a sea quite other than the one we had designed to reach. Driving before the wind for ten days, we saw at last a city far off and asked the captain what its name might be. "As Allah lives, I do not know," he answered. "I have never seen it in my life, nor the sea in which we are. But the important thing is that we are now out of danger. It only remains for you to enter that city and offer your merchandise. I suggest that you should sell it there if you can."

An hour later he came to us again, saying: "Disembark now and go into the city to see the marvels of Allah there. Call on His name and you shall go in safety."

We entered the city and saw to our stupefaction that all the inhabitants had been turned into black rocks, but that, while they had been petrified, everything else in the markets and the streets was as it had been, goods of every kind and appointments of gold and silver all about the place. We were delighted with what we saw and, saying to each other: "Surely there must be some extraordinary reason for all this," separated, each going in different directions about the streets, to collect as much as might be conveniently carried of gold, silver and precious fabrics.

It was towards the citadel that I made my way. There I found the King's palace and, entering by a great door of solid gold and lifting a velvet curtain, I saw that all the furniture and everything else there was of fine gold or silver. In the courtyard and in all the rooms soldiers and chamberlains stood or sat, all turned to stone; and in the central hall, filled with chamberlains, lieutenants and wazīrs, I saw the King sitting on his throne, petrified also but arrayed in such noble and costly garments as took my breath away. Fifty silk-clad mamelūks[9] holding naked swords stood there in stone about the King. His throne was encrusted with great pearls lying among other jewels. And each pearl shone so like a star that I thought I should lose my wits in gazing on them.

Going on, I reached the harīm, which I found to be more wonderful than all the rest, built even to the window-bars of solid gold and with silken hangings on the walls and with velvet and satin curtains hanging before the doors and windows. In the midst of a group of women, all turned to stone, I saw the Queen herself dressed in a robe sewn with noble pearls, crowned with a mass of great jewels, with collars and necklaces about her throat of pleasantly carved gold; but herself changed to black stone.

Wandering further, I came to an open door made with two leaves of virgin silver, and beyond it I saw a porphyry staircase of seven steps. Mounting this, I came to a white marble hall, covered with a carpet of gold thread, in the middle of which there rose, between great golden torches, a dais also of solid gold picked out with emeralds and turquoises. An alabaster bed, studded with pearls and upholstered with precious embroidery, stood on the dais with a great light shining by it. I came near and found that the light proceeded from a diamond, as large as an ostrich's egg, lying on a stool by the bedside and shining from all its facets so that the whole hall was filled with radiance.

Although the diamond outshone them utterly, the torches were lighted; therefore I deduced that some human hand was near and went on searching among the other halls, marvelling at all I saw and hunting everywhere for a human being. I was so entranced that I forgot all about my voyage, my ship, and my sisters. Night fell suddenly while I was still in a dream at all that beauty, and when I tried to leave the palace I could not find my way. In my search I came again to the hall with the alabaster bed, the diamond, and the lighted torches. Lying down, I half covered myself with a blue

9. Warrior slaves.

satin quilt wrought with silver and pearl, and took up a copy of our Koran, that sacred book. It was written out in stately gold characters with red devices and illuminations in all colours. From it I read a few verses to the glory of Allah and to reprove myself that my sleep might be holy. I meditated on the words of the Prophet, whom may Allah bless, and tried to sleep.

When the middle of the night had come and I was still awake, I heard a sweet and learned voice reciting the Koran. I rose in haste and, going in the direction of the voice, came to a little room with an open door. I entered softly, leaving the torch which I had caught up outside, and saw that the place was a kind of sanctuary. It was lighted by little green glass lamps and on its floor, facing the East, lay a prayer-rug upon which a very beautiful young man was reading the Koran aloud with grave attention and perfect eloquence. In my astonishment I asked myself how this young man alone could have escaped the fate of all the city. I came towards him and wished him peace. When he turned his eyes upon me and wished me peace, I said: "I conjure you by the truth of the sacred words which you are reading from the book of Allah to answer my question truly."

Calmly and sweetly he smiled at me, saying: "First, O woman, tell me how it is that you have come into this place where I pray, and then I will answer any question you like to put to me." When he had listened in astonishment to my story, I questioned him concerning the extraordinary appearance of the city. He shut the sacred book and, placing it in a satin bag, bade me sit at his side. I did so and, gazing attentively at him, found in him that full perfection which is in the moon: sympathy, beauty of face, proportioned elegance of body. His cheeks were as clear as crystal, his face had the delicate tint of the fresh date, as if it had been he of whom the poet was thinking when he wrote these lines:

> A watcher of the stars at night
> Looked up and saw to rose and white
> A boy, with such delicious grace,
> Such brilliant tint of breast and face,
> So curved and delicate of limb,
> That he exclaimed on seeing him:
> "Sure it was Saturn gave that hair,
> A black star falling in the air;
> Those roses were a gift from Mars;
> The Archer of the seven stars
> Gave all his arrows to that eye;
> While great sagacious Mercury
> Did sweet intelligence impart;
> Queen Venus forged his golden heart
> And . . . and . . ." But here the sage's art
> Stopped short; and his old wits went wild
> When the new star drew near and smiled.

Red flames were lighted in my heart when I looked at him and, in the violent trouble of my senses, I regretted that I had not met him long before. "Master and sovereign," I said, "I pray you answer me." "I hear and I obey," he replied, and told me the following remarkable story:

Honourable lady, this was my father's city, filled with his subjects and the people of his kin. He it was whom you saw petrified upon his throne, the Queen you saw was my mother. Both were magicians, worshippers of terrible Nardūn, who swore by fire and light, by shade and heat, and all the turning stars.

For a long time my father had no children. I was the child of his age and he reared me carefully throughout my boyhood, that I might be bred up to the true happiness of kingship.

Now in the palace there was a very old woman who in secret was a Believer in Allah and his Messenger, though in public she pretended to fall in with the creed of my parents. My father had great confidence in her as a faithful and chaste woman, he heaped benefits upon her and firmly believed that she was of his own faith. When I began to grow up, he put me in her charge, commanding her to give me a good education and a grounding in the laws of Nardūn.

The old woman took me into her charge and at once declared to me the religion of Islām, from its rites of purification and ablution to the sacred forms of its prayers. She taught and expounded the Koran to me in the Prophet's own tongue[1] and, when she had taught me all that she knew, warned me to keep my knowledge sedulously from my father lest he should kill me. I did so and, when a short time afterwards that saintly old woman died breathing her last words into my ear, I continued a secret believer in Allah and His Prophet. Far different were the inhabitants of this city who hardened their hearts and dwelt in darkness. But one day, while they continued their idolatry, a voice like thunder spoke from an invisible muezzin to far and near, saying: "O people of the city, leave the worship of fire and Nardūn, and turn to the one Almighty King."

Terrified by this voice the inhabitants of the city sought the King, my father, and asked the meaning of these awful words. But my father told them not to be frightened or amazed, and bade them stand firm in their old beliefs.

So for another year they blindly worshipped fire, until the day came round again on which the voice had been heard. Then the voice boomed out once more, and this it did on the same day for the next three years. But the people continued to worship their false god until one morning, out of the clear sky of dawn, wrath and sorrow fell upon them and they were suddenly turned to black stone, they and their horses, their mules and their camels, and all their beasts. I alone, who was the sole Believer in the city, escaped the doom.

Since then I have remained here, praying, fasting, and reciting from the Book, but I have been very lonely, lovely lady, with no one to bear me human company.

On this I said to him: "Youth of every perfection, will you not come with me to the city of Baghdad, where are sages and venerable old men steeped in the teachings of our Religion? There your learning and your faith will be increased together, and I, though I am a woman of some account, will be your slave there. In Baghdad I am mistress among my people, with a following of men, servants and young boys; also I have a ship here full of all necessary goods. Fate threw me upon your coast and Destiny has seen fit to bring us together." I did not cease from fanning his desire to go with me until he consented to do so.

At this point Shahrazād saw the approach of morning and discreetly fell silent as was her custom.

But when the seventeenth night had come

1. Arabic.

She said:

It is related, O auspicious King, that the girl Zubaidah did not cease from fanning the desire of the young man to go with her until he consented to do so.

They talked long together until sleep overcame them, and Zubaidah slept that night at the feet of the young man. I leave you to imagine whether she was happy or no.

Zubaidah continued her story to the Khalīfah Hārūn al-Rashīd, in the hearing of Jafar and the three kalandars in these words:

When morning broke, we chose out from all the treasures of the palace the best we could carry, and went down towards the city, where we met my slaves and the captain who had been looking for me a long time. They were delighted to see me again and more than a little astonished when I gave them the outline of my story and of the young man's tale concerning the doom which had fallen upon the city. But hardly had my sisters seen the handsome young man than they were filled with violent jealousy and began in their hatred secretly to plot my hurt.

We all went aboard, I in great joy because I loved the youth, and, taking advantage of a favourable wind, sailed away. My sisters never left us alone, and one day they asked me directly what I intended to do with the youth. I told them that I meant to marry him and, turning towards him, I said: "Master, I desire to become your slave. Do not refuse me this." "Indeed, I do not refuse," he answered and, our troth being thus plighted, I said to my sisters: "This young man is enough property for me. All else I have I give to you." "Your wish is law," they answered, but at the same time they schemed against me in their hearts.

We came with favouring winds from the Dread Sea to the Sea of Safety, across which we sailed for several days till we saw the buildings of Basrah rising from the water. That night we cast anchor and all slept.

While we slept, my sisters rose and, lifting the youth and myself, cast us, mattresses and all, into the sea. The poor young man, who could not swim, was drowned. It was written by Allah that he should become one of the martyrs, just as it was written that I should be saved. For, when I fell into the water, Allah sent me a spar of wood to which I clung and supported by which I was carried by the waves to the shore of a nearby island. There I dried my clothes and slept, rising in the morning to look for some track which should lead me to safety. Soon I found a road worn by human feet which I followed into the interior of the island, until I had gone right across it and came out on the other side, opposite the city of Basrah. Suddenly I saw a little snake hurrying towards me, hotly pursued by a much larger snake who was trying to kill it. I felt pity for the little snake which was so weary that its tongue hung out. So I lifted a great stone and smashed in the head of the large snake, killing it on the spot. Immediately to my surprise the little snake spread two wings and, flying up into the air, disappeared from my sight.

Being broken by fatigue, I lay down where I was and slept for about an hour. When I woke, I found a beautiful young negress seated at my feet, rubbing and kissing them. I snatched them away in considerable shame, not knowing whether her intentions towards me were honourable or not, and asked her sharply who she was and what she wanted. "I hastened to come to you," she said, "because of the great service you have done me in killing my enemy. I am a Jinnīyah and was in the likeness of that little snake. The big snake was my enemy, a Jinnī who wished to rape me and to kill me. You saved me, so I flew at once to the ship from which your two sisters threw you. I changed them into black bitches and have brought them to you." Sure enough, there were two black bitches tied to the tree behind me. "Lastly," went on the Jinnīyah, "I transported all your riches to your house in Baghdad and then sank the ship. As for your young man, he is drowned. I can do nothing against death. Allah alone is Almighty."

With these words she took me in her arms together with my sisters, the bitches, and, flying with us through the air, set us down safely on the terrace of my house here in Baghdad.

Looking about me I found all the treasures and the goods that had been in my ship ranged in careful order round the rooms, not one having been lost or spoiled. Before she left, the Jinnīyah said to me: "I command you by the sacred symbol on the Seal of Sulaimān to give each of these bitches three hundred strokes of the whip every day. If you forget even once I shall be obliged to come back and change you also into the same shape."

What could I answer save: "I hear and I obey"?

Ever since then, O Prince of Believers, I have beaten them and then pitifully caressed them as you have seen. That is my story.

* * *

But when the eighteenth night had come

Shahrazād continued in this wise:

It is related, O auspicious King, that, on hearing the stories of the girls Zubaidah and Amīnah, who with their little sister Fahīmah, the two black bitches, and the three kalandars, had been brought before him, the Khalīfah Hārūn al-Rashīd rejoiced at the marvel of the two tales and ordered them to be written out in fair calligraphy by his scribes. * * *

Then al-Amīn was remarried to the young Amīnah, Zubaidah to the first kalandar who was a king's son, the other two sisters to the other two kalandars, princes both, and the Khalīfah himself wedded the youngest of the five sisters, the maiden Fahīmah, the witty and agreeable cateress.

Hārūn al-Rashīd had a palace built for each couple and endowed them with riches that they might live happily. Also, hardly had night fallen when he himself hastened to bed with the young Fahīmah, and they passed the sweetest of nights together.

from The Tale of Sympathy the Learned

But when the two-hundred-and-seventieth night had come

Little Dunyazād waited until Shahrazād had finished her act with the King, and then raised her head, crying: "O sister, why do you not start at once the anecdotes which you promised us concerning that delightful poet Abū Nuwās,[1] the Khalifah's friend, the sweetest singer of Irāq and Arabia?" Shahrazād smiled at her sister, saying: "I only wait the King's permission before telling you some of the adventures of Abū Nuwās, who was not only an exquisite poet but a notorious evil-liver."

Dunyazād ran to her sister and embraced her, saying: "What did he do? Tell us at once, if you please."

But King Shahryār turned to Shahrazād and said: "O Shahrazād, it would give me great pleasure to hear one or two of these adventures, for I am sure that they are most

1. One of the major poets of the Abbasid period.

entertaining; but tonight my mind is more inclined to higher things and would rather hear words of wisdom from you. If you know some tale which can fortify our souls with moral precepts and help us to profit by the experience of the wise, do not scruple to begin at once. Afterwards, if my patience be not exhausted, you may recount the adventures of Abū Nuwās."

Shahrazād hastened to reply: "By chance I have been thinking all day, O auspicious King, of a story which concerns a girl who was called Sympathy, a slave unequalled both in beauty and learning; I am ready to tell you all that I have heard of what she did and what she knew."

"As Allah lives," cried King Shahryār, "you may begin at once; for nothing pleases me more than to learn wisdom from the lips of beauty. I hope that the tale will satisfy and profit me with an example of that learning which becomes a faithful Muslim woman."

Shahrazād reflected for a short time and then raised her finger, saying:

It is related—but Allah is all-wise and all-knowing—that there was once a very rich merchant in Baghdad, who had honour and privilege of every kind, but whom Allah had deprived of one happiness. He had no child, not even a daughter. He grew old in sorrow, seeing his bones becoming more and more transparent, his back more and more arched, without being able to obtain any consoling result from his numerous wives. One day, however, after he had distributed a great alms, visited saints, fasted and prayed fervently, he lay with his youngest wife and, by Allah's grace, got her with child.

At the end of nine months to a day she bore him a man-child as fair as a fragment of the moon; therefore the merchant in gratitude to Allah entertained the poor, the widow, and the orphan for seven whole days, and then named his son Abū al-Husn.[2]

The child was carried in the arms of nurses and beautiful slaves, cared for like some jewel of price by all the women, until he reached the age when he might begin to learn. Then wise masters were given to him, who taught him the wonderful words of the Koran, beautiful writing, poetry, arithmetic, and especially the science of shooting with the bow.

Not only was his education finer than that of any other child then living, but his beauty was almost a magic thing. His boyish graces, the fresh colour of his cheeks, the flowers of his lips, and the young down of his face were thus celebrated by a poet:

Though spring has passed already over the rose trees,
Here are some buds not fully opened yet,
In this sweet garden ignorant of weather:
See, the down feather
Of the violet
Under those trees!

Young Abū al-Husn was his father's joy and the light of his eyes, during the old man's remaining term upon this earth. When he felt that his debt was about to be paid to Allah, he called his son to him, saying: "My child, quittance nears and I have nothing left to do but prepare myself to stand before the Master. I leave you great riches, money and goods, rich fields and farms, which should last your lifetime and the lifetime of your children's children. Enjoy your property without excess, thanking the Giver and being mindful of Him all your days." With that the old merchant died, and his son shut himself in with grief, after superintending his father's funeral.

2. "The handsome one."

Soon, however, his friends led him away from his sorrow and persuaded him to go to the hammām and change his garments, saying: "He who is born again in a son like yourself does not die. Have done with tears; make the most of your riches and your youth."

So Abū al-Husn little by little forgot the counsels of his father and learnt to look upon happiness and gold as inexhaustible. He satisfied every caprice of his nature, frequenting singers and musicians, eating enormous quantities of chicken every day (for he was very fond of chicken), unsealing old jars of strong wine, and hearing ever about him the noise of chinking goblets. He exhausted all that he could exhaust and spent all that he could spend, until he woke one morning to find that there remained of all his possessions only a single slave girl.

But here you must pause to admire the workings of Fate, who had decreed that this one remaining slave should be the supreme marvel of Western and Eastern women. She was called Sympathy; and never had a name been better given. She was as upright as the letter alif, and her figure was so slim that she might defy the sun to cast a shadow by her; the colouring of her young face was wonderful, and its expression was both fortunate and filled with blessing. Her mouth seemed to have been sealed with the seal of Sulaimān to guard the pearls within; the two pomegranates of her breasts were separated by a valley of shadows and delights; and her navel was carved so deep that it would have held an ounce of nutmeg butter. Her reed-like waist ended in so heavy a croup that she left deep prints of it in every sofa and mattress which she used. A certain poet had her in mind when he wrote:

> If you can call the sun and the moon and the rose tree
> Sad-coloured,
> Call her sad-coloured also.
>
> Hearts beat the advance as she advances,
> And the retreat when she retreats.
> The river of life flows through the meadows of Eden,
> And the meadows of Eden are below her garment,
> The moon is beneath her mantle.
>
> Her body is a song of colours:
> Carnation of roses answers to silver,
> Black ripe berries
> And new-cut sandal-wood
> Are one note.
>
> The man who takes her is more blessed
> Than the God who gives her;
> And He is continually called blessed.

Such was the slave Sympathy, the last possession of the prodigal Abū al-Husn of Baghdad.

At this point Shahrazād saw the approach of morning and discreetly fell silent.

But when the two-hundred-and-seventy-first night had come

She said:

Seeing that he was ruined for ever, Abū al-Husn fell into a desolation which robbed him of both hunger and sleep; for three days and three nights he refused food and drink and sleep, so that the slave Sympathy thought he was on the point of dying and determined to save him at any cost to herself.

She put on the rest of her jewels and those robes which remained most fit to be seen; then she went to her master and said with an encouraging smile: "Allah will put an end to your misfortunes by my help. You have only to take me with you to the Commander of the Faithful, Hārūn al-Rashīd, fifth of the line of Abbās, and offer me to him for ten thousand dīnārs. If he objects that the price is too high, you must say: 'Prince of Believers, this girl is worth more; as you will discover if you put her to the proof. You will find that she is without equal or near equal, and worthy to serve the Khalīfah.'" She finished by recommending that he should not bate his price on any consideration.

Abū al-Husn had neglected, in his careless way, to notice the supreme gifts of his beautiful slave; therefore he merely thought that the idea was not a bad one and held some chances of success. He led Sympathy into the presence of the Khalīfah without delay, and repeated the offer which she had recommended to him.

The Khalīfah turned towards her, asking: "What is your name?" "I am called Sympathy," she answered, and he continued: "O Sympathy, are you indeed learned, and can you tell me the various branches of knowledge in which you excel?" "My master," she answered, "I have studied syntax, poetry, civil and canon law, music, astronomy, geometry, arithmetic, the law concerning inheritance, the art of elucidating books of spells and reading ancient inscriptions. I know the Sublime Book by heart and can read it in seven different ways;[3] I know the exact number of its chapters, verses, divisions, parts, and combinations; how many lines, words, consonants, and vowels there are in it; I know which are the inspired chapters written at Mecca and those which were dictated at Madinah. I know both laws and dogmas, and can determine the degrees of authenticity among them from the point of tradition; I am acquainted with architecture, logic, and philosophy; with eloquence, language, rhetoric, and the rules of versification. I know every artifice by which words can be ordered into musical lines. I am equally at home in the construction of simply flowing verses and very complicated examples suited for subtle palates alone; if I introduce an occasional obscurity into my compositions, it is to hold the attention and to delight such minds as can disentangle a fragile thread. I have learnt many things and remembered all I have learnt. I can sing perfectly, dance like a bird, play the lute and the flute, and perform in fifty different ways on every stringed instrument. When I dance and sing, those who see and hear me are damned by my beauty; when I walk in my perfumed clothing, balanced upon my feet, I kill; when I move my bottom, I overthrow; when I wink, I pierce; when I shake my bracelets, I make blind; I give life with a touch, and death by going away; I am skilful in all the arts and have carried my education so far that only those who have worn out their life in study may see it, as it were, upon the far horizon."

Hārūn al-Rashīd was delighted and astonished to find so much eloquence and beauty in the child who stood before him with lowered eyes. He turned to Abū al-Husn, saying: "I shall send at once for all the masters of art and science in my kingdom, to put the knowledge of your slave to public proof. If she comes victorious from the trial, I will not give you ten thousand dīnārs but cover you with honours for having brought so great a marvel to me. If she fails in her examination, she shall remain your property."

3. The seven ways of reciting the Qur'an.

The Khalīfah straightway sent for the most learned man of that time, Ibrāhīm ibn Siyyār,[4] a sage who had gone to the depths of all human knowledge; and he also commanded the presence of the chief poets, grammarians, theologians, doctors, philosophers, astronomers and lawyers of his kingdom. They hastened to the palace and assembled in the great hall, without knowing why they had been summoned. They seated themselves in a circle upon carpets about the Khalīfah's golden chair, while Sympathy stood meekly in their presence, smiling upon them through her light veil.

At this point Shahrazād saw the approach of morning and discreetly fell silent.

But when the two-hundred-and-seventy-second night had come

She said:

When a silence had fallen upon this assembly so deep that the far-off fall of a needle upon the ground might have been heard, Sympathy made a graceful and dignified bow to those present and said to the Khalīfah in a melodious voice:

"Prince of Believers, it is for you to order and for me to obey; I stand ready to answer any question posed to me by these venerable sages, these readers of the Koran, lawyers, doctors, architects, astronomers, geometrists, grammarians, philosophers and poets."

Hārūn al-Rashīd turned to those who were about him, saying: "I have called you hither that you may examine the learning of this girl in all directions and to any depth; it is for you to spare no pains in exhibiting your own scholarship and erudition." All the sages bowed to the earth, carrying their hands to their eyes and foreheads, and answering: "Obedience and obeisance to Allah and to you, O Prince of Believers!"

The slave Sympathy stood for some moments in thought with lowered head; then she looked up, saying: "Tell me, my masters, which of you is the most learned in the Koran and the traditions of our Prophet (upon whom be prayer and peace!)." All fingers were pointed to one of the doctors, who rose, saying: "I am that man." Then said Sympathy: "Ask me what you will of your own subject." So the learned reader of the Koran said:

"O young girl, since you have studied the sacred Book of Allah, you must know the number of the chapters, words, and letters in it; and also the precepts of our faith. Tell me first who is your Lord, who is your Prophet, who is your Imām, what is your orientation, what is your rule of life, what is your guide, and who are your brothers?"

She answered: "Allah is my Lord, Muhammad (upon whom be prayer and peace!) is my Prophet; the Koran is my law and therefore my Imām; the Kaabah, the house of Allah builded by Abraham at Mecca, is my orientation; the example of our holy Prophet is my rule of life; the Sunnah,[5] the collection of traditions, is my guide; and all Believers are my brothers."

While the Khalīfah marvelled to hear such precise answers from such lovely lips, the sage said:

"Tell me, how do you know that there is a God?"

She answered: "By reason."

"What is reason?"

4. One of the most erudite intellectuals of the era of Harun Al-Rashid.

5. The set of rules derived from the conduct and sayings of the Prophet Muhammad. The Kaabah is the central shrine in Mecca; an imam is a prayer leader.

"Reason is a double gift: it is both innate and acquired. Innate wisdom is that which Allah has placed in the hearts of His chosen servants that they may walk in the way of truth. Acquired wisdom is the fruit of education and labour in an intelligent man."

"That is an excellent answer. But can you tell me, where is the seat of reason?"

"In the heart, whence inspirations rise to the brain."

"That is so. How have you learnt to know the Prophet (upon whom be prayer and peace!)?"

"By reading the Book of Allah, by the phrases contained therein, by the proofs and witnessings of His divine mission."

"What are the indispensable duties of our religion?"

"The indispensable duties of our religion are five: the profession of Faith: 'There is no God but Allah and Muhammad is the messenger of Allah!', prayer, alms, fasting during the month of Ramadān, and pilgrimage to Mecca when that is possible."

"What are the most praiseworthy acts of piety?"

"They are six in number: prayer, alms, fasting, pilgrimage, fighting bad instincts and forbidden things, to take part in a holy war."

"What is the aim of prayer?"

"To offer the homage of my virtue to the Lord, to celebrate His praises, and to lift my soul towards the calm places."

"Yā Allah! That is an excellent reply. Does not prayer necessitate certain indispensable preparations?"

"Certainly it does. It is necessary to purify the whole body by ritual ablutions, to put on garments which have no stain of dirt, to choose a clean place in which to pray, to protect that part of the body which lies between the navel and the knees, to have pure intent, and to turn towards the Kaabah, in the direction of holy Mecca."

"What is the value of prayer?"

"It sustains faith, of which it is the foundation."

"What is the fruit or utility of prayer?"

"True prayer has no terrestrial use; it should be regarded only as a spiritual tie between the creature and his Lord. It can produce ten immaterial results: it lights the heart, it brightens the face, it pleases the Compassionate, it infuriates the devil, it attracts pity, it repels evil, it preserves from ill, it protects against enemies, it fortifies the wavering spirit, and brings the slave nearer to his Master."

"What is the key of prayer? And what is the key of that key?"

"The key of prayer is ablution and the key of ablution is the preparatory formula: 'In the name of Allah, the Merciful, the Compassionate.'" * * *

When the learned commentator of the Book heard Sympathy's answers, he could not but admit to himself that she knew as much as he did; but, being unwilling to confess his inability to catch her out, he asked her the following subtle question: "What is the linguistic meaning of the word *ablution?*"

"To get rid of all internal or external impurity by washing."

"What is the meaning of the word to *fast?*"

"To abstain."

"What is the meaning of the word to *give?*"

"To enrich oneself."

"To go on a *pilgrimage?*"

"To attain the end."

"To make *war?*"

"To defend oneself."

The sage rose up, crying: "In truth I am short of questions and arguments. This slave astonishes me with her knowledge and the clearness of her exposition, O Commander of the Faithful!"

Sympathy smiled slightly, saying: "I would like, in my turn, to ask you one question: can you tell me what are the foundations of Islām?"

He reflected for a moment, and then replied: "They are four in number: faith illuminated by sane reason; righteousness; knowledge of duty and equity, together with discretion; and the fulfilment of all promises."

Sympathy said again: "Allow me to ask you a further question. If you cannot answer it, it will be my right to take away the distinctive garment which you wear as a learned reader of the Book."

"I accept," he answered, "put your question, O slave."

"What are the branches of Islām?" she asked.

After a long time spent in reflection, the wise man could not answer, so the Khalīfah said to Sympathy: "If you can give us the answer yourself, the gown belongs to you."

Sympathy bowed and answered: "The branches of Islām are twenty: strict observance of the Book's teaching, conformation with the traditions and oral instructions of the Prophet, the avoidance of injustice, eating permitted food, never to eat unpermitted food, to punish evil doers that vice may not increase owing to the exaggerated clemency of the virtuous, repentance, profound study of religion, to do good to enemies, to be modest, to succour the servants of Allah, to avoid all innovation and change, to show courage in adversity and strength in time of trial, to pardon when one is strong, to be patient in misfortune, to know Allah, to know His Prophet (upon whom be prayer and peace!), to resist the suggestions of the Evil One, to fight against the passions and wicked instincts of the soul, to be wholly vowed in confidence and submission to the service of Allah."

When the Khalīfah Hārūn al-Rashīd heard this answer, he ordered the sage's gown to be stripped from him and given to Sympathy; this was immediately done, and the learned man left the hall in confusion, with his head bowed.

Then a second theologian, famous for his subtlety, to whom all eyes voted the honour of next questioning the girl, rose and turned towards Sympathy, saying: "I will only ask you a few short questions, O slave. What duties are to be observed while eating?"

"In eating a man must first wash his hands and invoke the name of Allah. He must sit upon the left haunch, and use only the thumb and two first fingers in conveying the food to his mouth. He must take small mouthfuls, masticate each piece of food thoroughly, and not look at his neighbour for fear of embarrassing him and spoiling his appetite."

"Can you tell me what is something, what is half something, and what is less than something?"

"A Believer is something, a hypocrite is half something, and an infidel is less than something."

"That is correct. Now can you tell me where faith is found?"

"Faith abides in four places: in the heart, in the head, in the tongue, and in the members. The strength of the heart consists in joy, the strength of the head in knowledge of the truth, the strength of the tongue in sincerity, and the strength of the members in submission."

"How many hearts are there?"

"There are several: the heart of the Believer is a pure and healthy heart, the heart of an Infidel is exactly the opposite." * * *

At this point Shahrazād saw the approach of morning and discreetly fell silent.

But when the two-hundred-and-seventy-sixth night had come

She said:

"There is a heart attached to the things of this world, and a heart attached to spiritual joys; there is a heart mastered by the passions, by hate or avarice; there is a slack heart, a heart burning with love, a heart puffed with pride; there is a lighted heart like that of the companions of our holy Prophet; and there is the heart of the Prophet himself, which is the heart of the Chosen."

When the learned theologian heard this answer, he cried: "You have won my approbation, O slave!"

Sympathy looked at the Khalīfah, saying: "O Commander of the Faithful, allow me to ask one question of my examiner and to take his gown if he cannot answer." Hārūn al-Rashīd gave his permission, and she asked:

"Can you tell me what duty must be fulfilled before all other duties, however important those may be?"

The wise man did not know what to say, so the girl took his gown from him and herself answered the question:

"The duty of ablution; for we are bidden to purify ourselves before fulfilling the least of religious duties or any of those acts prescribed by the Book or the Sunnah."

Sympathy cast a glance round the assembly, and this was answered by one of the most celebrated men of the century, supposed without equal in a knowledge of the Koran. He rose and said:

"Since you know the Book of Allah, O girl full of the sweet perfume of the spirit, can you give me a sample of your study?"

"The Koran is composed of a hundred and fourteen chapters, seventy of which were dictated at Mecca and forty-four at Madinah. It is divided into six hundred and twenty-one divisions, called decades, and into six thousand two hundred and thirty-six verses. It contains seventy-nine thousand, four hundred and thirty-nine words, and three hundred and twenty-three thousand, six hundred and seventy letters, to each of which attach ten special virtues. The names of twenty-five prophets are mentioned: Adam, Noah, Ishmael, Isaac, Jacob, Joseph, Elisha, Jonah, Lot, Sālih, Hūd, Shuaib, David, Solomon, Dhūl-kafl, Idrīs, Elias, Yahyā, Zacharias, Job, Moses, Aaron, Jesus, and Muhammad (upon all these be prayer and peace!). Nine birds or winged beasts are mentioned: the gnat, the bee, the fly, the hoopoe, the crow, the grasshopper, the ant, the bulbul, and the bird of Jesus (upon whom be prayer and peace!), which is none other than the bat."

"You are marvellously exact. Now can you tell me in what verse our holy Prophet judges the Unbelievers?"

"In this verse: 'The Jews say that the Christians are wrong and the Christians say that the Jews are wrong; to this extent both are right!'" * * *

The learned questioner could contain himself no longer, but cried out: "I bear witness, O Prince of Believers, that this young girl is unequalled in knowledge!"

Sympathy demanded leave to ask a question in her turn, and said:

"Can you tell me which verse of the Koran contains the letter kāf twenty-three times, which contains the letter mīm sixteen times, and which contains the letter ain forty times?"

The sage stayed with his mouth open, unable to make the least attempt at an answer; so Sympathy first took away his gown and then herself indicated the required verses to the general stupefaction of all.

Next, a learned doctor of medicine rose in the assembly, one famous for the studies he had made and the books he had written, and said:

"You have spoken excellently of the things of the spirit; now it is time that we turn our attention to the body. I require you, O beautiful slave, to give us some information about the body of man, its composition, its nerves, its bones, its vertebrae, and why Adam was called Adam."

"The name of Adam comes from the Arabic word adīm, which signifies the surface of the earth; it was given to the first man because he was created from earth taken from different parts of the world. His head was made from the soil of the East, his breast from the soil of the Kaabah, and his feet from the soil of the West. Allah made seven entrances and two exits for the body: the two eyes, the two ears, the two nostrils, and the mouth for entrances, and for exits, one before and one behind. Then the Creator united in Adam four elements to give him a nature: water, earth, fire and air; so that a bilious temperament is of the nature of fire, which is hot and dry; a nervous temperament is of the nature of earth, which is dry; a lymphatic temperament is of the nature of water, which is cold and moist; and a sanguine temperament is of the nature of air, which is warm and dry. After this Allah assembled the human body. He placed within it three hundred and sixty ducts and two hundred and forty bones. He gave it three instincts: of life, reproduction, and appetite. He gave it a heart, a spleen, lungs, six intestines, a liver, two kidneys, a brain, two eggs, a member, and a skin. He dowered it with five senses, guided by seven vital spirits. As for the position of the organs, he placed the heart upon the left of the breast, and the stomach below it, the lungs to act as fans for the heart, the liver on the right to guard the heart, and, for the same purpose, he placed the interlacing intestines and the articulation of the ribs. The head is composed of forty-eight bones, the chest of twenty-four ribs and twenty-five in a woman; this extra rib is on the right, and is useful to fasten the child in the belly of its mother and to support it, as it were, by an arm." * * *

"So far there has been nothing lacking in your answers. Now I wish to ask you a question of capital importance, which will show if you have a true knowledge of the facts of life. Can you give us a clear account of copulation?"

On hearing this question the young girl blushed and lowered her head, so that the Khalīfah thought that she was unable to answer: but she turned towards him, saying: "As Allah lives, O Commander of the Faithful, my silence is not due to ignorance; for the answer is upon the tip of my tongue, but refuses to leave my lips because of my respect for the Khalīfah." Hārūn al-Rashīd answered: "It would give me very great pleasure to hear such an answer from your mouth. Speak freely, explicitly, and without fear." So the learned Sympathy spoke as follows:

"Copulation is that act which unites the sexes of man and woman. It is an excellent thing, having many virtues and conferring many benefits: it lightens the body and relieves the soul, it cures melancholy, tempers the heat of passion, attracts love, contents the heart, consoles in absence, and cures insomnia. These are its effects when a man couples with a young woman: it is far otherwise when he has to do with an old one. Connection with an old woman exposes a man to many maladies, among others disease of the eyes, disease of the kidneys, disease of the thighs, and disease of the back. In a word, it is a terrible thing, to be avoided as one would avoid a deadly poison. Best of all is to choose a woman expert in the art, one who understands a wink, who can speak with her feet and hands, and spare her owner the necessity of keeping a garden and flower beds.

All complete copulation is followed by moisture. In the woman this moisture is produced by the emotion felt in her honourable parts; in the man, by the running of that sap which is secreted by the two eggs. This sap follows a complicated road; man possesses one large vein which gives birth to all the other veins; the blood which fortifies these three hundred and sixty smaller veins runs at last into a tube which debouches in the left egg; in this egg the blood turns about, clarifies, and changes into a white liquid which thickens because of the heat of the egg, and smells like palm milk."

At this point Shahrazād saw the approach of morning and discreetly fell silent.

But when the two-hundred-and-eighty-second night had come

She said:

"You have answered wisely!" cried the sage. "I have only two more questions to ask. Can you tell me what thing lives always in prison and dies when it breathes the free air? Also, what are the best fruits?"

"The first is a fish; and the second, citrons and pomegranates."

When the doctor heard the wonderful replies of Sympathy, he confessed himself incapable of making her stumble and would have returned to his place, but Sympathy signed to him to remain, saying: "I will now ask you a question. Can you tell me what is round like the earth, and lives in an eye, sometimes going through that eye, and sometimes separated from it, copulating without an organ, leaving its companion for the night, and embracing her again during the day, choosing its habitation upon the edge of things?"

The learned man cudgelled his brains for an answer but could find none, so Sympathy took away his gown and gave the answer herself: "The button and the buttonloop." * * *

Hārūn al-Rashīd was edified in the extreme by so much knowledge and wisdom, and ordered the learned Ibrāhīm ibn Siyyār to give his own gown to the girl. The sage did so and then, lifting his right hand, witnessed publicly that the slave had surpassed him in scholarship and was the marvel of the age.

"Can you play upon instruments of music and accompany yourself while you sing?" asked the Khalīfah, and, when Sympathy replied that she could, had a lute brought to her, which was contained in a red satin case with a tassel of saffron coloured silk and a gold clasp. Sympathy drew the lute from its covering and found carved about it, in interlaced and flowering character, the following verses:

I was the green branch of a tree
Birds loved and taught their songs to.
Haply the teaching lingers,
For, when I lie on beauty's knee,
Remember under beauty's fingers,
The woodland song I sing belongs to
The birds who sang to me.

She leaned over the lute as a mother over her nursling and, drawing twelve different harmonies from the strings, sang in a voice that echoed long after in all hearts and brought tears of emotion to every eye.

When she had finished, the Khalīfah rose up, crying: "May Allah increase your gifts within you, O Sympathy, and have in His benign keeping those who taught you and those who gave you birth!" So saying, he had ten thousand golden dīnārs, in a hundred sacks, given to Abū al-Husn and then turned to Sympathy, saying: "Tell me, O child of marvel, would you rather enter my harīm and have a palace and retinue for yourself, or return home with this young man?"

At this point Shahrazād saw the approach of morning and discreetly fell silent.

But when the two-hundred-and-eighty-seventh night had come

She said:

Sympathy kissed the earth between the Khalīfah's hands and answered: "May Allah continue to shower His blessings upon our master! Your slave would prefer to return to the house of him who brought her here."

Instead of being offended by this answer, the Khalīfah immediately gave Sympathy a further five thousand dīnārs, saying: "May you be found as expert in love as you are in answering questions!" After this he put the crown upon his generosity by raising Abū al-Husn to high employment and numbering him among his intimate favourites.

The two young people left the hall, one staggering under all the gowns of the sages, and the other under all the sacks of gold. As they went, they were followed by the whole marvelling assembly, who lifted their arms, crying: "Was ever in the world a liberality like that of the descendants of Abbās?"

Such, O auspicious King, continued Shahrazād, were the answers given by Sympathy before the assembly of sages and handed down in the royal annals to be an instruction to every woman of the Faith.

Then Shahrazād, seeing that King Shahryār was still frowning and racking his brains, began at once upon the Adventures of the Poet Abū Nuwās.

Little Dunyazād, who had been half asleep, woke up suddenly on hearing the name of Abū Nuwās and, large-eyed with attention, made ready to listen with all her ears.

from An Adventure of the Poet Abū Nuwās

It is related—but Allah is all-wise and all-knowing—that the Khalīfah Hārūn al-Rashīd was afflicted one night with lack of sleep and a preoccupation of spirit, so he went out alone from his palace and walked in the gardens to distract his weariness. He came at last to a pavilion the door of which was open, but guarded by a black eunuch who slept across the sill. The Khalīfah stepped over the body of the slave and, entering the single hall of the pavilion, saw a bed with lowered curtains, which was lighted on the right and left by tall torches. Beside the bed stood a little table holding a jar of wine topped by an inverted cup.

Hārūn al-Rashīd was astonished to find these things of which no one had informed him, so he lifted the curtains of the bed and stood stock-still with amazement at the sleeping beauty of a slave who lay there, as fair as the full moon, covered for sole garment with her fallen hair. He took the cup and filled it; then he drank slowly, saying beneath his breath: "To the roses in your cheeks, O child!" Setting down the cup, he leaned over the youthful face and dropped a kiss upon a little black mole which smiled to the left of the parted lips. Though this kiss was light as air, it woke the girl, who recognised the Prince of Believers and jumped up in the bed. The Khalīfah calmed her fright, saying: "O young slave, there is a lute beside you which I am sure you can play charmingly. Give me a taste of your skill, for I am determined to pass the night with you although I do not know you, and wish, as a preliminary, to hear your voice."

The girl took the lute and played upon it in twenty-one different modes, so that the Khalīfah was exalted with delight. Seeing the good impression that she had made, the young woman determined to profit by it, and said: "O Prince of Believers, I suffer from the assaults of Destiny." "How is that?" asked the Khalīfah, and she continued: "Your son al-Amīn bought me a few days ago for ten thousand dīnārs, intending to give me as a present to your majesty; but your wife, the lady Zubaidah, heard of his intention and, paying him back the money he had spent, gave me to a black eunuch with instructions to keep me a prisoner in this isolated pavilion."

The Khalīfah was annoyed when he heard this; therefore, after promising to give the girl a palace and a train worthy of her beauty on the morrow, he hastened to waken the sleeping eunuch and ordered him to go at once to command the poet Abū Nuwās to present himself at the palace. For you must know that Hārūn al-Rashīd was always wont to send for the poet when he was in an evil humour, in order to distract himself with the improvised poems and rhymed adventures of that remarkable man.

The eunuch went to Abū's house and, not discovering him there, searched throughout all the public places in Baghdad until he found him in a disreputable tavern at the lower end of the quarter of the Green Gate. He went up to him, saying: "O Abū Nuwās, our master the Khalīfah sends for you." The poet laughed as he answered: "O father of whiteness, how am I going to leave this place when I am in pawn for a young boy?"[1] "Where is he and who is he?" asked the eunuch, and Abū Nuwās replied: "He is slender, beardless and pretty. I promised him a thousand dirhams; as I have not the money about me, I can hardly go away."

"In Allah's name," cried the eunuch, "show me this boy and, if he is as delightful as you say, you shall be excused and more than excused."

As they were talking in this way, the pretty pet put his head round the door, and Abū Nuwās exclaimed: "If the branch wavers so pleasantly, will not the song of the birds be beautiful?"

At this point Shahrazād saw the approach of morning and discreetly fell silent.

But when the two-hundred-and-eighty-eighth night had come

She said:

On this the boy came right into the room of the tavern; and indeed his beauty was wonderful; also he was dressed in three tunics, one on top of the other, white and red and black.

Seeing him all in white, Abū Nuwās felt the fire of inspiration sparkle in his soul and he improvised these verses:

His robe was white like milk,
His eyes love-heavy underneath blue lids,
His cheeks the shadow of wine-coloured silk
Thrown upon snow.
"What modesty forbids?
Why do you pass me so?
I am as patient for your hand
As a white lamb is patient for the priest."
"You sing three whites and I have four at least:
A destiny which would be white without you,

1. Abu Nuwas was a well-known bisexual.

A body white and bland,
A face of white,
A garment blanched and exquisite.
You did not count my white aright
And so I flout you."

Hearing these lines the boy smiled and, taking off his white tunic, appeared all in brilliant red; so that Abū Nuwās was again inspired and sang without a pause:

His tunic was as red as cruelties.
"O child, you boasted white;
What is the meaning of this sight,
Two cheeks dyed in our broken hearts,
A garment stolen from anemones?"
"The dawn has lent me her attire,
The evening sun has put his clouds apart
And given me his fire,
Red are my cheeks' embroideries,
And red the veils which cling about my thighs,
Red is the wine which painted
Red lips where souls have fainted.
So you have missed the addition of my red,"
He said.

Delighted with this song, the minion threw aside his red garment and appeared in a black tunic, which clung to his skin and outlined a charming waist girt in by a silken belt. Seeing him, Abū Nuwās was exalted beyond reason, and sang again:

He would not look at me.
His tunic was as black as night
By no intrusive moon beguiled;
Therefore I said:
"Now I will get it right;
After the white and red,
After the red and white,
Black is the garden of your hair,
Black is your tunic everywhere,
Black are your eyes and black my destiny.
My computation shows no lack;
There's black and black and black on black."
He smiled.

When the eunuch had considered the beauty of these poems and of the boy who inspired them, he forgave Abū Nuwās in his mind and returned straightway to the palace, where he informed the Khalīfah that Abū was held in pawn at a tavern because he could not pay what he had promised to a delightful youth. The Khalīfah, who was both amused and annoyed, sent back the eunuch with the sum of money required, bidding him bring the poet without delay.

The man hastened to the tavern and brought away the poet, who staggered a little from drink. When Abū Nuwās had been supported into the presence of the Khalīfah, Hārūn al-Rashīd lectured him in a voice which he strove to make furious; but, seeing that the poet burst out laughing, he took him by the hand and led him to the pavilion which the young girl occupied. * * *

The young woman gave wine to the Khalīfah, who invited the poet to empty the great cup himself. Abū Nuwās took it off at a single draught and soon felt the effects of the heavy vintage. As he reeled where he stood, the Khalīfah rose in jest and fell upon him sword in hand, making as if to cut off his head. The poet ran hither and thither about the hall with great cries of terror, and Hārūn al-Rashīd pursued him into all the corners, pricking him with the blade. At last the Khalīfah cried: "Enough! return and drink another cup." At the same time he signed to the girl to hide the vessel. She immediately concealed it beneath her robe, but Abū Nuwās saw the movement in spite of his drunkenness and sang:

Even as I desire the cup
The cup desires
Lips secret and more pleasant,
And has gone up
Within her garments hollow,
Whither the cup aspires
Nuwās would follow,
If only Hārūn were not present.

The Khalīfah laughed consumedly and, as a further jest, said to the poet: "As Allah lives, I must raise you to some high employment. From this time forth, I appoint you accredited chief of all the pimps in Baghdad." "In that case, O Commander of the Faithful," retorted Abū Nuwās with a grin, "what may I have the pleasure of doing for you tonight?"

Hārūn al-Rashīd flew into a rage and commanded the eunuch to call for Masrūr the sword-bearer, his executioner of justice.

At this point Shahrazād saw the approach of morning and discreetly fell silent.

But when the two hundred-and-ninetieth night had come

She said:

The Khalīfah ordered Masrūr to strip Abū Nuwās of all his clothes, to saddle him with an ass's pack-saddle, to pass an ass's halter round his neck, and to thrust a spur up his fundament. When this had been done, the unfortunate poet was led up and down before all the pavilions of the King's favourites, that they might laugh at him; and Masrūr had instructions, when this exhibition had been completed, to take Abū Nuwās to the gate of the city, to cut off his head in the presence of the people, and to bring it back upon a dish.

The despairing poet was paraded before each of the three hundred and sixty-five palaces, and, when their inhabitants heard of the death he was about to die, they grieved for him because they loved his wit, and as a sign of their sympathy threw gold and jewels before his path. Then they came out of their dwellings and followed him with words of encouragement, so that the wazīr Jafar al-Barmakī, who was passing on his way to the palace, halted before the weeping man and said: "Is that you, O Abū Nuwās? What crime have you committed to have earned so grave a punishment?" "As Allah lives," answered Abū Nuwās, "I have not committed even the suspicion of a crime. On the contrary I recited some of my most exquisite poems before the Khalīfah, and he has rewarded me by giving me his own robe of honour."

The Khalīfah, who was hiding behind a curtain of the nearest pavilion, heard this answer and burst into a hearty laugh. He not only pardoned Abū Nuwās, but gave him a real robe of honour and a large sum of money; also he continued to make him the inseparable companion of his black hours, as heretofore.

When Shahrazād had finished this tale of the poet Abū Nuwās, little Dunyazād, who had been endeavouring to stifle her silent laughter in the carpet, ran to her sister, crying: "As Allah lives, dear Shahrazād, that is a funny tale!"

from The End of Jafar and the Barmakids[1]

When she had made an end of this admirable series of tales, Shahrazād fell silent, and King Shahryār cried: "O Shahrazād, you have instructed me in many things, but I think that you have forgotten to speak of the wazīr Jafar. I have long desired to hear all that you know concerning him, for I find that he strangely resembles in his quality my own grand wazīr, your excellent father. It is that likeness which urges me to hear the whole of his surely admirable story." But Shahrazād hung her head, as she replied: "Allah keep us from calamity, O King of time, and have compassion upon Jafar the Barmakid and all his people! I beg you to excuse me from telling that story, for it is full of tears. Alas, who would not weep to hear of the end of Jafar, and of his father Yahya, and of his brother al-Fadl, and of all the Barmakids! So lamentable was their taking off that stone itself would become tender at the telling of it." "Yet tell me all the same, O Shahrazād," said King Shahryār, "and may Allah keep us from all calamity!"

So Shahrazād said: Here then, O auspicious King, is that sorry tale which mars the reign of the Khalīfah Hārūn al-Rashīd with a bloodstain which not even the four rivers[2] shall wash away.

As is already known, O king of time, Jafar was one of the four sons of Yahya ibn Khālid ibn Barmak. His eldest brother, al-Fadl, was in some sort al-Rashīd's foster-brother, for, because of the great friendship which existed between the family of Yahya and that of the Abbāsids, and because of the tender affection which bound the two women themselves, al-Rashīd's mother, the Princess Khayzarān, and al-Fadl's mother, the noble Itabah, exchanged nurslings and each gave to her friend's son that milk which Allah had destined for her own. That is why al-Rashīd always spoke of Yahya as: "My father," and al-Fadl as: "My brother."

At this point Shahrazād saw the approach of morning and discreetly fell silent.

But when the nine-hundred-and-ninety-fifth night had come

She said:

The most reliable chroniclers place the origin of the Barmakids in the city of Balkh in Khurāsān, where they occupied a position of great distinction. It was not until a little more than a hundred years after the Hijrah of our Prophet (upon whom be prayer and peace!) that the family moved to Damascus and took root there under the dynasty of Umar. In the reign of Hishām, the head of the house was converted from the Magian cult and became ennobled in Islām.

But it was not until the accession of the Abbāsids that the family was admitted into the counsels of the court, and began to brighten the earth with its glory. Khālid ibn Barmak was made grand-wazīr by Abū al-Abbās al-Saffah, the first of the Abbāsids; and, during the reign of al-Mahdī, the third in the line of Abbās, Yahya ibn

1. As can be seen from the Resonance that follows, this story dramatizes the actual historical record of the waning of Haroun al-Rashid's reign. Placed near the end of *The Thousand and One Nights,* it serves as a kind of leave-taking to the world of the stories themselves.

2. Of Paradise.

Khālid was charged with the education of Hārūn al-Rashīd, the Khalīfah's favourite son, who was born only seven days after al-Fadl, Yahya's son.

When al-Rashīd was invested with the supreme power, after the unexpected death of his brother al-Hādi, he had no need to go back to the memories of his earliest youth, spent with the Barmakid children, before calling Yahya and his two sons to share in his aggrandizement; it was only necessary for him to recall his education by Yahya and the devotion which that good man had shown in braving the menaces of al-Hādi in order to assure his pupil's inheritance. On the very night of al-Hādi's death the tyrant had given order that Yahya and his children should be beheaded.

When Yahya went in the middle of the night with Masrūr to tell Hārūn that he was now master of the empire and Khalīfah of Allah upon earth, al-Rashīd immediately named him grand-wazīr and raised his two sons, al-Fadl and Jafar, to be wazīrs under him. This action augured most happily for the new reign.

After that the Barmakids were an ornament for the brow of their century, and a crown upon its head. Destiny showered her most favourable gifts upon them, so that Yahya and his sons became bright stars, vast oceans of generosity, impetuous torrents of kindness, beneficent rains. The world lived at their breath, and under their hands the empire reached the pinnacle of its splendour. They were the refuge of the afflicted, the final resort of the comfortless. The poet Abū Nuwās said of them:

> Since earth has put you away, O sons of Barmak,
> The roads of morning twilight and evening twilight
> Are empty. My heart is empty, O sons of Barmak.

They were admirable wazīrs, wise administrators, they filled the public treasure. They were strong, eloquent, and of a good counsel; they surpassed in learning; their generosity equalled the generosity of Hātim Taiy. They were rivers of happiness, they were good winds bringing up the fruitful clouds; it was through them that the name and glory of Hārūn al-Rashīd clanged from the flats of Central Asia to the northern forests, from Morocco and Andalusia to the farthest bounds of China and Tartary.

And suddenly the sons of Barmak were cast from the greatest height which men have reached to the lowest depths of horror; they drank the most bitter cup which calamity can pour. Alas, for the unfaith of time, they had not only ruled a vast empire, they had been the dear friends, the inseparable companions of their King. Jafar was the life of al-Rashīd's eyes; his place was so great in the Khalīfah's mind and heart that, one day, Hārūn even had a double mantle made, so that they both could wear it and be, as it were, one man. Such were the terms on which they lived together until the final tragedy.

O pain of my soul, listen to the coming of that black cloud which veiled the sky of Islām and cast dismay upon every heart!

One day—be such days far from us!—al-Rashīd, returning from Mecca, went by water from Hīrah to the city of Anbār. He halted at the monastery of al-Umr, on the banks of the Euphrates, and night found him in feasts and pleasures, as so many other nights had found him.

But this time his dear companion Jafar was not with him; he had gone for a few days of hunting in the plains of the river. Gifts and messages from the Khalīfah followed him everywhere in his sport. No hour passed without the arrival at his tent of some messenger, bearing a precious reminder of al-Rashīd's love.

Now that night—be such nights far from us!—Jafar sat in his tent with the doctor Jibrīl Bakhtiyāshū, al-Rashīd's personal physician, and with the Khalīfah's favourite poet, blind Abū Zakār. Hārūn had deprived himself of the company of both these men, in order that the one might watch over Jafar's health and the other entertain him with his improvisations.

It was the time of the evening meal, and Abū Zakār, the blind poet, was playing upon the mandoline and singing verses of fickle chance.

At this point Shahrazād saw the approach of morning and discreetly fell silent.

But when the nine-hundred-and-ninety-sixth night had come

She said:

Suddenly Masrūr, the Khalīfah's sword-bearer, the instrument of his anger, strode unceremoniously into the tent. When Jafar saw him thus enter, in defiance of all etiquette, without demanding an audience or even announcing his proposed visit, he turned yellow in the face, and said: "You are welcome, Masrūr, your presence is ever a fresh delight. But I must confess, my brother, that I am astonished to see you come to me, for the first time in your life, without sending some servant to give news of your arrival." "The matter is too grave for ceremony," replied Masrūr, without deigning the least salute to his old friend. "Rise up now, Jafar, and testify to your Faith for the last time. The Commander of the Faithful demands your head from me."

Jafar rose to his feet, and said: "There is no God but Allah, and Muhammad is the Prophet of Allah! From His hands we come and, soon or late, to His hands we return again!" Then he faced his old friend of so many years and moments, and cried out: "O Masrūr, it is impossible. Our master must have given you the order in a moment of drunkenness. I conjure you, by our walks together and our community of life by day and night, to return to the Khalīfah; for I believe that you will find he has forgotten what he said." But Masrūr answered: "It is my head or yours. I cannot return with my duty unfulfilled. Write your last wishes, for that is the only privilege I can accord you in memory of our ancient friendship." Then said Jafar: "We belong to Allah! I have no last wishes to write. May Allah prolong the span of the Commander of the Faithful by those days which are shorn from mine."

He left the tent, knelt upon the leather of blood which Masrūr had already spread, and bandaged his eyes with his own hands. Then his head was struck off. Allah have him in His mercy!

After this, Masrūr returned to the Khalīfah, and entered the royal presence bearing Jafar's head upon a shield. Al-Rashīd looked at the head of his old friend and, leaning forward suddenly, spat upon it.

But his resentment was stronger than death. He ordered the body to be crucified at one end of the bridge of Baghdad, and the head to be exposed at the other. This punishment was more degrading than any which had ever been inflicted upon even the worst of malefactors. At the end of six months he ordered that his wazīr's remains should be burnt on cattle dung and scattered among the privies.

O pitiful misery, that the scribe Imrānī should have been able to write on the same page of the register of treasury accounts: "For a robe of state, given by the Commander of the Faithful to his wazīr Jafar, son of Yahya al-Barmakī, four hundred thousand dīnārs of gold," and a little further down: "Naphtha, reeds, and dung to burn the body of Jafar ibn Yahya, ten silver dirhams."

Such was the end of Jafar. Yahya his father, the guide of al-Rashīd's infancy, and al-Fadl his brother, al-Rashīd's foster-brother, were arrested on the morning following the execution, and with them were taken all the rest of the Barmakids, to the number of about a thousand, who had any public charge or employment. They were thrown into foul dungeons, their great riches were confiscated, their wives and children were left without shelter, shunned by the regard of man. Some died of starvation, and others were strangled; but Yahya, his son al-Fadl and his brother Muhammad died under the torture. Allah have them all in His mercy! Their fall was great!

And now, O King of Time, if you wish to hear me speak of the cause of this disgrace and lamentable death:

One day, some years after the end of the Barmakids, Alīyah, al-Rashīd's young sister, plucked up heart to say to him: "My lord, I have not known you pass one tranquil day since the death of Jafar and the disappearance of his family. How did he come to merit such disgrace?" Al-Rashīd's face grew dark, and he pushed her away, saying: "My child, my life, my sole remaining happiness, how would it advantage you to know the reason? If I thought that my shirt knew, I would tear my shirt in pieces."

The historians and annalists are far from being agreed as to the cause of this catastrophe. Here are some of the differing versions which they give of the events which may be supposed to have led up to it.

According to some, al-Rashīd became offended at last by the extravagant liberalities of Jafar and the Barmakids, the tale of which became a weariness even in the ears of those who benefited, and which called forth rather envy and dislike than grateful friendship. * * *

According to other historians, the growing jealousy of al-Rashīd was fanned by the many enemies which the power of the Barmakids raised up against them, and by anonymous detractors, who allowed unsigned bitter verses and perfidious prose to come to the ears of the Khalīfah. These same annalists aver that it was a grave indiscretion on the part of Jafar which placed the final stone on the tower of his master's resentment. Once, when al-Rashīd had commanded him secretly to destroy a descendant of Alī and Fātimah, the daughter of the Prophet, a man named al-Saiyid Yahya ibn Abdallāh al-Husainī, Jafar had pity upon this Alid and allowed him to escape, although the Khalīfah had marked him as a danger to the dynasty of Abbās. This generous action was reported to al-Rashīd, with exaggeration and distortion; and it became that drop of gall which overflowed the angry cup. When he was questioned, Jafar frankly confessed what he had done, and said: "I acted for the glory and good name of my master." "You acted well," answered al-Rashīd, turning very pale, but he was heard to mutter to himself: "Allah do so to me and more also, if I do not destroy you, Jafar!"

Other historians would trace the fall of the Barmakids to their heretical opinions in the face of Islamic orthodoxy. It must not be forgotten that, when they lived in Balkh before their conversion to the Faith, they practised the Magian cult. During the expedition into Khurāsān, the birthplace of the Barmakids, al-Rashād noticed that Yahya and his sons exerted all their power to prevent the destruction of the temples and monuments of the Magi. His suspicion of their religious integrity grew greater afterwards, for he found that they always showed clemency to every kind of heretic, and especially to his personal enemies among the Jabarīyah and Zandakah. Those who hold this theory cite in proof of it the fact that serious religious troubles broke out in Baghdad immediately after the death of al-Rashīd, and almost proved the death-blow to orthodoxy.

But the most probable reason for the destruction of the Barmakids is adduced both by Ibn Khillikān, and by Ibn al-Athīr. They say:

"At the time when Jafar lay so near the heart of the Khalīfah that al-Rashīd had that double mantle made for the two of them, the Khalīfah could not abide to be separated from his favourite, and desired to look upon his face at all hours of the day and night. But al-Rashīd also loved, with a strange and deep tenderness, his own sister Abbāsah, perhaps the most beautiful and cultivated woman of her time. No other of her sex influenced al-Rashīd so greatly, and he was as incapable of living without her as if she had been a woman Jafar. These two loves made up his happiness; yet, for his joy's perfection, they had to be indulged at the same time. Thus it was necessary that the two favourites should be present together. But the law of our Faith forbids a man to look upon a woman, or for a woman to be looked upon by a man, unless he be her husband or near relation. To transgress this law is to lose honour, and therefore al-Rashīd, who was a strict observer of the law which it was his high privilege to administer, could not enjoy the simultaneous presence of Jafar and Abbāsah without the constraint of veils and the irksomeness of silence.

"That is why he one day said to Jafar: 'My friend, I have no true pleasure save when I sit with you and my dear sister Abbāsah. I wish you to wed the girl; but I forbid you to come together save in my presence, and I insist that there shall be no consummation of the marriage, lest the noble sons of Abbās be cheated out of their inheritance.' Jafar bowed before the desire of his master and had, perforce, to accept this marriage with all its unnatural conditions.

"The young husband and wife met only in the presence of the Khalīfah, and even then their glances hardly crossed. Al-Rashīd rejoiced at the new arrangement and seemed not to know that he was torturing his two best friends. How can love be controlled by a third person? How can such restraint between two young and handsome beings not break out into the flame of love?"

At this point Shahrazād saw the approach of morning and discreetly fell silent.

But when the nine-hundred-and-ninety-seventh night had come

She said:

"These two married lovers, who had every right to come together and yet could not, sighed more deeply every day, and felt that drunkenness which, when it is hidden, becomes a fever about the heart. Abbāsah, in her deprivation, became madly desirous of her husband. At length she told her love, coming upon Jafar in secret as often as she was able and soliciting him to grant her right; but the wazīr was too loyal and too prudent to give way to her. He was bound by his oath to al-Rashīd, and he also knew how hasty the Khalīfah could be in his anger.

"When Princess Abbāsah saw that her entreaties were in vain, she took the part of all women and sought out a devious way. She sent a message to the noble Itabah, the mother of Jafar, saying: 'O our mother, I require you to introduce me into Jafar's household, as if I were one of those slaves which you procure for him every day.' It was a fact that Itabah would send her dear son a fresh and chosen virgin slave each Thursday, and that the wazīr would not touch this child until he had eaten richly and partaken of generous wines. * * *

"Abbāsah decked herself for her part, and then went to the house of Jafar's mother, who, at nightfall, introduced her into the apartment of her son. Jafar, whose senses were a little dulled by the fermentation of the wines, did not recognise his wife in the virgin slave who stood before him. It must be remembered that neither had looked often or directly on the other's face, for fear of the Khalīfah's resentment, and that modesty had ever caused Abbāsah to turn away from Jafar's furtive glances.

"The marriage became a marriage in fact, and, after a night of mutual transport, Abbāsah rose, saying: 'How do you like King's daughters, my master? Are they different from slaves who are bought and sold?' 'King's daughters?' asked the astonished Jafar. 'Are you one yourself? Are you some captive of our victorious arms?' 'O Jafar,' she answered, 'I am both a captive and a slave. I am Abbāsah, sister of al-Rashīd, daughter of al-Mahdī. I am of the blood of Abbās, uncle of the Prophet (upon whom be prayer and peace!).'

"These words cleared off the last clouds of Jafar's drunkenness, and he cried: 'You have destroyed yourself, you have destroyed me, O daughter of my masters!'

"He hastened to Itabah, and said to her: 'O mother, mother, you have sold me cheap!' For answer Yahya's trembling wife told her son how she had been forced to forward this stratagem, in order to save her household from a worse misfortune.

"In fulness of time Abbāsah bore a son whom she confided to Riyāsh, a man faithful in her service, and to the nursing of a woman called Barrah. Then, fearing lest a rumour of this birth should escape in spite of all her precautions, she sent her child to Mecca with his two guardians.

"Now Yahya, Jafar's father, was responsible for order in the palace and harem of al-Rashīd. After a certain hour of night he would shut all the communicating doors and take away the keys, a severity of discipline which soon caused discontent among the women and especially in the Lady Zubaidah. When she complained to al-Rashīd and cursed the old man's misplaced zeal, he called Yahya to him, and asked: 'My father, what grievance has Zubaidah against you?' 'Does she complain that I am lax in my supervision of the harem?' demanded Yahya. 'Not so, my father,' answered al-Rashīd with a smile. 'In that case,' cried the Barmakid, 'take no notice of what she says, O Commander of the Faithful!' And, after that, he redoubled his severity in door locking.

"Zubaidah came to her lord a second time, crying out in bitter resentment against Yahya; so al-Rashīd tried to pacify her, saying: 'O daughter of my uncle, my guide and father Yahya is only obeying orders and doing his duty, when he schools my harem in this way.' 'If he is so deeply concerned with his duty,' retorted Zubaidah with some feeling, 'why does he not begin by schooling the imprudence of his son?' 'What imprudence?' demanded al-Rashīd. Zubaidah at once told him the whole story of Abbāsah, though not as a matter of great importance. 'Are there proofs of this?' asked the Khalīfah in a sombre voice. 'What better proof could there be than the child himself?' demanded Zubaidah. 'Where is he?' asked the Khalīfah, and she replied: 'In the Holy City, the cradle of our race.' 'Does any beside you know of these things?' he asked, and she replied: 'There is not a woman in the whole palace, not a slave who does not know.'

"Al-Rashī said no further word, but soon afterwards he departed on pilgrimage for Mecca and took Jafar with him.

"At once Abbāsah sent a letter to Riyāsh and the nurse, ordering them to leave the city and pass into Yemen with the child.

"As soon as the Khalīfah arrived at Mecca he bade certain of his trusted spies make enquiry concerning the infant, and these soon returned with the news that they had found proof of his existence, and that he was in perfect health. In a few days the child was seized in Yemen and sent secretly to Baghdad.

"It was on his return from that pilgrimage, when lying at the monastery of al-Umr near Anbār on the Euphrates, that al-Rashīd gave his fateful command to Masrūr.

"Abbāsah was buried alive with her son in a ditch dug in the floor of her own apartment.

"Allah have them both in His compassion!"

It remains for me to say, O auspicious King, that other and quite worthy historians contend that Jafar and the Barmakids had done nothing to deserve their fate, and that it would not have come upon them if it had not been written in their Destiny.

But Allah knows all!

* * *

As for the Khalīfah Hārūn al-Rashīd: after his cruel vengeance for some wrong known only to himself and Allah, he returned to Baghdad, but passed it by. He found that he could not live any longer in that city which it had been his delight through so many years to embellish. He established himself at Rākah and never returned to the Place of Peace. This sudden abandonment of his capital by al-Rashīd inspired the poet Abbās ibn al-Ahnaf, who was of his train, to write the following lines:

Scarce had we made the camels kneel
Before we had to ride again,
The friends who watched our coming
Saw us turn the camels round.

They cried us welcome, but it was
"Farewell," that we replied again,
"Farewell, O city of Baghdad,
O consecrated ground."

Since the disappearance of his friends, al-Rashīd got no good of his sleep; his regrets burned him day and night, and he would have given his kingdom to bring back Jafar. If any courtiers had the misfortune to speak even a little slightingly of the Barmakids, the Khalīfah would angrily cry out on them: "Allah damn your fathers! Either cease from blaming them, or try to fill the place which they left empty."

Though he remained all-powerful until his death, al-Rashīd imagined that he was surrounded by traitors. He feared to be poisoned by his sons, who were indeed no cause for pride. At the beginning of a punitive expedition into Khurāsān, from which he was not destined to return alive, he sadly admitted his doubts to al-Tabarī, the annalist, who was one of the courtiers most in his confidence. When al-Tabarī tried to reassure him as to certain presages of death which he had received, he drew the chronicler into the shadow of a great tree, where they might be rid of prying glances, and opened his robe to show him a silk bandage wrapped about his belly. "I have a deep and incurable disease," he said. "No one knows of it save you. And I have spies round me, sent by al-Amīn and al-Mamūn to filch away the little remainder of my life. They feel that I have lived too long. They have corrupted my most faithful servants. Masrūr is the spy of my favourite son al-Mamūn, my doctor Jibrīl Bakhtiyāshū is al-Amīn's spy. And there are many more. Would you have proof of their plots? I have ordered a riding horse to be sent to me, and instead of choosing one with a strong and easy action, you will see them bring to me a worn beast, having a broken pace to aggravate my suffering."

This prophecy was fulfilled; al-Rashīd was given such a horse as he described, and he accepted it with a look of sad understanding to al-Tabarī.

A few weeks after this incident, Hārūn saw in his dreams a hand stretched out above his head, holding a little red earth. A voice cried: "This shall be his sepulchre." "Where?" asked another voice, and the first replied: "In Tūs."[3]

3. A city in the Khurasan region of northern Iran.

Some days later the course of his malady obliged al-Rashīd to halt at Tūs. At once he showed signs of grave disquiet, and sent Masrūr to bring him a little earth from the outskirts of the city. The eunuch returned in an hour, bearing a handful of red soil, and al-Rashīd cried: "There is no God but Allah, and Muhammad is the Prophet of Allah! My vision is accomplished, my death is very near!"

He did not see Irāq again. The next day he was weaker, and said to those about him: "The moment is at hand. I was envied by all the world, but now the world might pity me."

He died at Tūs on the third day of Jumāda, second month in the one hundred-and-ninety-third year of the Hijrah. According to Abulfidā, he was forty-seven years, five months, and five days old at the time of his death. Allah pardon his mistakes and have him in pity! He was an orthodox Khalīfah.

Conclusion

Then she fell silent, and King Shahryār cried: "O Shahrazād, that was a noble and admirable story! O wise and subtle one, you have taught me many lessons, letting me see that every man is at the call of Fate; you have made me consider the words of kings and peoples passed away; you have told me some things which were strange, and many that were worthy of reflection. I have listened to you for a thousand nights and one night, and now my soul is changed and joyful, it beats with an appetite for life. I give thanks to Him Who has perfumed your mouth with so much eloquence and has set wisdom to be a seal upon your brow!"

Little Dunyazād rose quite up from her carpet, and ran to throw her arms about her sister, crying: "O Shahrazād, how soft and delicate are your words, how moving and delightful! With what a savour they have filled our hearts! Oh, how beautiful are your words, my sister!"

Shahrazād leaned over the child and, as she embraced her, whispered some words which caused her to glide from the room, as camphor melts before the sun.

Shahrazād stayed alone with Shahryār, but, as he was preparing to take this marvellous bride between his joyful arms, the curtains opened and Dunyazād reappeared, followed by a nurse with twin children hanging at her breasts. A third child hurried after them on all fours.

Shahrazād embraced the three little ones and then ranged them before Shahryār; her eyes filled with tears, as she said: "O King of time, behold these three whom Allah has granted to us in three years."

While Shahryār kissed the children and was moved with joy through all his body to touch them, Shahrazād said again: "Your eldest son is more than two years old, and these twins will soon be one. Allah protect them from the evil-eye! You remember, O King of time, that I was absent through sickness for twenty days between the six hundred and seventy-ninth night of my telling and the seven hundredth. It was during that absence that I gave birth to the twins. They pained and wearied me a great deal more than their elder brother in the previous year. With him I was so little disturbed that I had no need to interrupt the tale of Sympathy the Learned, even for one night."

She fell silent, and King Shahryār, looking from her to his sons and from his sons to her, could say no word.

Then little Dunyazād turned from kissing the infants a twentieth time, and said to Shahryār: "Will you cut off my sister's head, O King? Will you destroy the mother of your sons, and leave three little kings to miss her love?"

"Be quiet and have no fear, young girl," answered King Shahryār, between two fits of sobbing. It was not for a long time that he could master his emotion, and say: "O Shahrazād, I swear by the Lord of Pity that you were already in my heart before the coming of these children. He had given you gifts with which to win me; I loved you in my soul because I had found you pure, holy, chaste, tender, straightforward, unassailable, ingenious, subtle, eloquent, discreet, smiling, and wise. May Allah bless you, my dear, your father and mother, your root and race! O Shahrazād, this thousand and first night is whiter for us than the day!" When he had said these things, he rose and embraced the woman's head.

Shahrazād took her King's hand and carried it to her lips, her heart, and her brow, saying: "O lord of time, I beg you to call your old wazīr, that he may rejoice at my salvation and partake in the benediction of this night."

So the King sent for his wazīr, and the old man entered carrying Shahrazād's winding-sheet over his arm, for he was sure that her hour had come at last. Shahryār rose in his honour and kissed him between the eyes, saying: "O father of Shahrazād, O begetter of benediction, Allah has raised up your daughter to be the salvation of my people. Repentance has come to me through her!" Joy penetrated the old man's heart so suddenly that he fell into a swoon. When rose-water had brought him to himself, Shahrazād and Dunyazād kissed his hand, and he blessed them. The rest of that night passed for them all in a daze of happiness.

Shahryār sent for his brother Shahzamān, King of Samarkand al-Ajam, and went out to meet his coming with a glorious retinue. The city was gay with flags, and in the streets and markets the people burnt incense, sublimated camphor, aloes, Indian musk, nard and ambergris. They put fresh henna upon their fingers and saffron upon their faces. Drums, flutes, clarinets, fifes, cymbals and dulcimers filled every ear with a rejoicing sound.

While great feasts were being given at the royal expense, King Shahryār took his brother aside and spoke of the life which he had led with Shahrazād for the last three years. He recounted for Shahzamān's benefit some of the maxims, phrases, tales, proverbs, jests, anecdotes, characteristics, marvels, poems, and recitations which he had heard during that time. He praised the wazīr's daughter for her eloquence, wisdom, purity, piety, sweetness, honesty and discretion. "She is my wife," he said, "the mother of my children."

When King Shahzamān had a little recovered from his astonishment, he said: "Since you have been so fortunate, I too will marry. I will marry Shahrazād's sister, the little one, I do not know her name. We shall be two brothers married to two sure and honest sisters; we will forget our old misfortune. That calamity touched me first, and then through me it reached to you. If I had not discovered mine, you would never have known of yours. Alas, my brother, I have been mournful and loveless during these years. Each night I have followed your example by taking a virgin to my bed, and every morning I have avenged our ills upon her life. Now I will follow you in a better deed, and marry your wazīr's second daughter."

Shahryār went joyfully to Shahrazād and told her that his brother had, of his own accord, elected Dunyazād for his bride. "We consent, O King of time," she said, "on condition that your brother stays henceforth with us. I could not bear to be separated from my little sister, even for one hour. I brought her up and educated her; she could not part from me. If Shahzamān will give this undertaking, Dunyazād shall be his slave. If not, we will keep her."

When Shahzamān heard Shahrazād's answer, he said: "As Allah lives, my brother, I had intended no less than to remain with you always. I feel now that I can never abide to be parted from you again. As for the throne of Samarkand, Allah will send to fill it." "I have longed for this," answered King Shahryār. "Join with me in thanks to Allah, my brother, that He has brought our hearts together again after so many months!"

The kādī and witnesses were summoned, and a marriage contract was written out for King Shahzamān and Dunyazād. Rejoicing and illuminations with coloured fire followed upon the news of this; and all the city ate and drank at the King's expense for forty days and forty nights. The two brothers and two sisters entered the hammām and bathed there in rose-water, flower-water, scented willow-water, and perfumed water of musk, while eagle wood and aloes were burned about them.

Shahrazād combed and tressed her little sister's hair, and sprinkled it with pearls. Then she dressed her in a robe of antique Persian stuff, stitched with red gold and enhanced by drunken animals and swooning birds embroidered in the very colours of life. She put a fairy collar about her neck, and Dunyazād became below her fingers fairer than Alexander's wife.

When the two Kings had left the hammām and seated themselves upon their thrones, the bridal company, the wives of the amīrs and notables, stood in two motionless lines to right and left. Time came, and the sisters entered between these living walls, each sustaining the other, and having the appearance of two moons in one night sky.

Then the noblest ladies there took Dunyazād by the hand and, after removing her robes, dressed her in a garment of blue satin, a sea tint to make reason fail upon her throne. A poet said of her:

> Her veil is torn from the bright blue
> Which all the stars are hasting to,
> Her lips control a hive of bees,
> And roses are about her knees,
> The white flakes of the jasmine twine
> Round her twin sweetness carnaline,
> Her waist is a slight reed which stands
> Swayed on a hill of moving sands.

Shahzamān came down to be the first to look upon her. When he had admired her in this dress, he sat upon his throne again, and this was a signal for the second change. So Shahrazād and the women clad their bride in a robe of apricot silk. As she passed before her husband's throne, she justified the words of the poet:

> You are more fair than a summer moon
> On a winter night, you are more fair.
> I said when I saw your falling hair:
> "Night's black wing is hiding day."
> "A cloud, but lo! the moon is there,"
> You, rose child, found to say.

When Shahzamān had come down and admired her in this dress, Shahrazād put a tunic of grenade velvet upon her sister. * * * Shahrazād slipped her hand to her sister's waist, and they walked before the Kings and between the guests toward the inner chambers. Then the Queen undressed little Dunyazād and laid her upon the bed with such recommendations as were suitable. They kissed and wept in each other's arms for a little, as it was the first night for which they had been separated.

That was a white and joyful night for the two brothers and the two sisters, it was a fair continuation of the thousand and one which had gone before, a love tale better than them all, the dawn of a new era for the subjects of King Shahryār.

When the brothers had come from the hammām in the morning and joined their wives, the wazīr sought permission to enter. They rose in his honour and the two women kissed his hand; but, when he asked for the day's orders, the four said with one voice: "O father, we wish that you should give commands in the future and not receive them. That is why we make you King of Samarkand al-Ajam." "I yield my throne to you," said Shahzamān; and Shahryār cried: "I will only give you leave to do so, my brother, if you will consent to share my royalty and reign with me day and day about." "I hear and I obey," said Shahzamān.

The wazīr kissed his daughters in farewell, embraced the three little sons, and departed for Samarkand al-Ajam at the head of a magnificent escort. Allah had written him security in his journey, and the inhabitants of his new kingdom hailed his coming with delight. He reigned over them in all justice and became a King among great Kings. So much for him.

After these things, King Shahryār called together the most renowned annalists and proficient scribes from all the quarters of Islām, and ordered them to write out the tales of Shahrazād from beginning to end, without the omission of a single detail. So they sat down and wrote thirty volumes in gold letters, and called this sequence of marvels and astonishments: THE BOOK OF THE THOUSAND NIGHTS AND ONE NIGHT. Many faithful copies were made, and King Shahryār sent them to the four corners of his empire, to be an instruction to the people and their children's children. But he shut the original manuscript in the gold cupboard of his reign and made his wazīr of treasure responsible for its safe keeping.

King Shahryār and Queen Shahrazād, King Shahzamān and Queen Dunyazād, and Shahrazād's three small sons, lived year after year in all delight, knowing days each more admirable than the last and nights whiter than days, until they were visited by the Separator of friends, the Destroyer, the Builder of tombs, the Inexorable, the Inevitable.

Such are the excellent tales called THE THOUSAND NIGHTS AND ONE NIGHT, together with all that is in them of wonder and instruction, prodigy and marvel, astonishment and beauty.

But Allah knows all! He alone can distinguish between the true and the false. He knows all!

RESONANCES

Abu-Nuwas: Splendid Young Blades, Like Lamps in the Darkness[1]

Splendid young blades, like lamps in the darkness,[2] proud-nosed, stiff-
    necked, keen—
Who assaulted Fate with dalliance to which they clung assiduously, so that
    their attachment to it could not be severed,

1. Translated by Arthur Wormhoudt. Abu-Nuwas al-Hasan, ibn Hani' al-Hakami (755–c.815) is perhaps the most beloved of Arab poets of any period. Although he failed to achieve the favor of the caliph, Haroun al-Rashid, he was well received by the powerful family of the Barmakids. Best known for his poems on wine and pederasty, Abu-Nuwas also wrote memorable panegyrics and wonderful *ghazals*.
2. A reference to Imru' al-Qays's famous line about his beloved who "lights up the darkness" with her beauty; see page 417.

For whom Time brought round its felicitous spheres and halted, bending its tender neck over them—
I drank with them sharp Isfant wine, imported from Takrīt, clear and chilled;
One of those whose hand we asked for in haste, when we roused the owners of the wine-shops
In a host of the night, turbulent and swollen, like the sea which dazes the sailor with fear.
Suddenly at that moment there appeared an infidel[3] crone, like a solemn anchoress,
Tracing her lineage back through infidel stock, monastic idol-worshippers,
Who said, "Who are you?" We replied, "People you know, every one open-handed, noted for his prodigality,
Who, along the way, have stopped at your house: so seize the liberality of the generous and name your price,
For you have won a life of ease, provided you seize from us what David seized from Goliath.
Be lively in making a profit from them, doing—at the same time—a noble deed until they have left your house. Then you can sleep like the dead!"
She said, "I have what you want. Wait until the morning." We replied, "No, bring it now!
It is itself the morning; its clear radiance dispels the night when it shoots out sparks like rubies
As the patrolling angels do, when, at night, they stone with the stars the rebellious Afrits."
It advanced in the cup as bright as the sun at day-break, poured from an amphora upturned, bleeding at the waist.
We said to her, "How long has it been in the amphora, since it was hidden away?" She replied, "It was made in the time of Saul.
It was concealed in the amphora and has grown to be an old spinster buried inside a coffin in the earth.
It has been brought to you from the depths of its resting-place, so be careful not to take it in the cup with food."[4]
The odour that wafts from it to the drinkers is like the scent of crushed musk from a newly slit vesicle;
When mixed with clear rain-water it is like a network of pearls on ruby brocade
Carried round by a youth like the moon with large black eyes from which the magic of Hārūt could have sprung,
With a lutenist in our midst who moves us as he sings "Abode of Hind in Dhāt al-Jizʿ, Hail!"
Our gazes are constrained to turn towards him—you should see us looking at him, as if bedazzled.
He is from Hītī,[5] swaying gracefully, refined, and I say to him in fun, "Hit it, Hītī!"

3. Or "grey-haired," an adjective which is sometimes used for well-aged wine.
4. In Abu-Nuwas's time, wine drinking was too important an activity to be adulterated with other activities like eating food.
5. A place on the Euphrates, noted for its wine.

So he begins with accurate diction to sing polished and well-articulated songs, keeping the time,
Until when the sphere of the strings, together with the drums, spins us round, we are left as if in a trance.
We glory in it in gardens thick with myrtle, acacia, pomegranate and mulberry,
Where the birds distract you from every other pleasure when they warble in antiphonal strains.
Blessings upon that time which slipped away too quickly—a lovely time which was not hateful to me then.
Dalliance did not turn me from coming to drink it and I did not fail to answer its urges
Until, lo! grey hair surprised me by its appearance—How hateful is the appearance of cursed grey hair
In the eyes of beautiful women; when they see its appearance they announce severance and separation from love.
Now I regret the mistakes I have made and the misuse of the times prescribed for prayer.
I pray to you, God, praised be Your name!, to forgive me just as You, Almighty One, forgave Him of the Fish![6]

Assia Djebar: from *A Sister to Sheherazade*[1]

The Sister

The brass bedstead is eventually auctioned, its brass fittings crushed and put out for sale on the pavement by the junk dealer. The voice beneath the bed is once again that of the woman who lurks there through the night to waken the sleeper on the verge of the new day.

Every night a woman prepares to keep watch to prevent the executioner's bloody deed. The listener now is the sister. Her vigil ensures that she will render without fail the promised assistance; she brings the hope of salvation before the new day dawns.

The sister waits beneath the bed. The favourite's sister; and she is there just because she is the sister, so taboo to the polygamist. The story-teller's sister, sister to the woman who has dreams and anticipates her fate, who is hailed as the sultan's bride for a day, and who knows that at sunrise she will be sacrificed and who, with every word she utters, hovers between extinction and the throne.

The master lies in the centre of the bed, with fixed eyes, the man interposed between woman listening to woman. A current flows from the story-teller above to the woman keeping watch below this stage—the setting for love.

6. Jonah, swallowed by a great fish when he tried to shirk his duty as a prophet.

1. Translated by Dorothy Blair. Born Fatima-Zohra Imalhayène in 1936 in a small costal town in Algeria, Assia Djebar in 1955 became the first Algerian woman to be admitted to the prestigious Ecole Normale Supérieure de Sèvres, France. Perhaps the most internationally visible woman writer in the Arab world, Djebar has been constant in her social commitment on behalf of her native country. In her version of the *Thousand and One Nights*, Djebar transposes the romantic tales to the grim realities of timeless wedding rituals that serve as rites of passage for young girls.

The man who has the power of life and death listens. He listens as he carries the weight of the fatal verdict, which he suspends for twelve hours at the most, until the following dusk.

A woman keeps secret watch beneath the bed: a woman prompts the other with a word at the first sign of weakening. Her voice is ready to fly to the rescue, picking up every dropped stitch in the tale, and this woman is the sister.

But first of all she had had to let the sounds and ferment of amorous play flow over her head. The confused murmurs: a *wadi* in spate, even in the heart of the desert. Menacing, roaring, deadly flood waters.

But why does the sister take up her place beneath the bed? . . . The law allows the polygamist to take any concubine, any female slave of whom he is the master, except the sister of the woman whom he tumbles in his bed. Thus, the sister beneath the bed can lie in wait, hearing everything, and for that very reason, shield from death.

She can take up her lodging in the morass of the others' sexual pleasure and keep guard at the same time. Alone, under the draperies of the divan, on which they sport, she lets their silken sensuality slip past, and at the same time forestalls death's advance. Alone, since she is the favourite's sister, her double and the one who can never be her rival. Her duty is to waken; she is also the one who snares the birds.

Up above, the sultan's bride spins her tales; she is fighting for her life. Her sister, beneath the couch, rallies the past victims.

* * *

Nuptials on a Straw Mat

We children could get into the next-door house by climbing on to the low wall and jumping down on to the adjacent terrace. The oldest girl in this family had had a "French-style" wedding: arrayed in a white satin gown, with two little bridesmaids in white tulle, holding a bouquet of orange-blossom—so that white became, not the symbol of virginity, but of entry into the Western world—on the morrow of a union consummated by force, with the brutality of rape.

Then the bride, flanked by the little bridesmaids in their fancy get-up, had posed for the photographer—the only man admitted to mingle with the host of female guests who had left their silken veils folded at the door as they arrived. Attired in low-cut gowns, well-nigh Parisian in elegance, they saw themselves sharing in the new ceremonial. Their comments—including those on the "camera man", for whom this had been quite exciting—had been kept up well into the next few weeks.

The bride had been "given" to a first cousin; but, thanks to a progressive evolution in customs, the second daughter could hope, as she herself said, to be able to marry for love.

This second daughter was a romantic soul. From the age of twelve, when she was taken out of school, to remain a recluse till her marriage, she had read avidly all the love-stories serialized in the fashion magazines to which she subscribed. She had even managed to get hold of several novels by Colette[2]—the *Claudine* series as well as *Chéri.* She spoke in a hushed voice, she did not so much daydream as withdraw completely from the real world . . .

In any case, the local matrons lauded to the skies her skill in embroidery, dressmaking and lacemaking. They spoke with equal admiration of her beauty, her

2. Sidonie Gabrielle Colette (1873–1954), considered by some the first modern feminist author, explored femininity, sexuality, and the tension between the sexes.

modesty (she blushed at the slightest word and never managed to make her tiny voice heard in the many social gatherings), as of her trousseau. Especially of her trousseau!

It combined the local Andalusian tradition and that of the European dream described by the French magazines. According to the former, the bride must arrive in her new home with a score of tunic-dresses in diverse colours, all embroidered with gold thread, and, in addition, everything for the conjugal bed-chamber: a number of mattresses of blond wool, which had been washed in surrounding streams, sterilized and compressed by indefatigable servants; counterpanes, drawn-thread-worked sheets, sequined cushions, hangings for the bed and curtains for the windows; and, lastly, the hand-embroidered toilet-bag for the weekly bath. But, like any European girl, she prepared an abundant wardrobe for herself: silk blouses, embroidered with drawn-thread-work (in Tunisian, Algerian or Moroccan style), short skirts and knitted pullovers. What is more, the second daughter, like her elder sister, had a right to the white gown for the great day—which however she would don only after she had appeared in the outfit consisting of garnet-red tunic, *saroual* with matching waistcoat, sequined sashes and flower-patterned mules. But she was not satisfied to order this immaculate gown by post and then make a few alterations. No, she cut it out herself, she embroidered it herself; last year she had regularly sat up half the night making this "trousseau fit for a princess" with her own fair hands.

And every matron mused: how would she dare ask for the hand of this most beautiful, most sweet-natured, most gifted of virgins, for any of her sons? In fact, every one of these ladies feared the mother's uncompromising pride. It was well known that, in this family where sons had been born only after a brood of girls, the arrogant, strong-willed mother had eventually overshadowed the meek and reticent father.

So, nothing was lacking in preparation for the new nuptials, except the suitor. After the mother had rejected the seventh, the eighth request for her daughter, suddenly the news spread that the affair had been concluded. The second daughter had been "given." To whom? There were already equivocal smiles—not even to any son of theirs or anyone from the capital! Yes, a "foreigner" had been accepted: to be sure, he was said to be a real scholar, a professor of something or other, some said of German, according to others it was mathematics which he had studied in Germany up to a very high level!

That in no way diminished the stigma: the man was not a native of their town, nor even of any other town; he quite simply came from a nearby village. The two mothers had met at the Turkish baths, exchanged flatteries and become friendly. The gossips added that the two women had much in common, "particularly their faults", shrilly asserted one neighbour. But in any case the match seemed to be serious with the suitor bearing the hallmark of a high official. The girl was lucky after all, that exceptional trousseau was in some way an omen: it augured a life of travel. And may Allah the All-Merciful protect her!

The first disappointment for the sisters—from the eldest who was already married, down to the fourth, a little girl who climbed over the wall to visit us—was the revelation of a custom thought to be obsolete: in the fiancé's native village, the marriage had to be performed according to the austere code of practice which the patron saint of the region had instituted some centuries before. It was known as marrying "according to Sidi Maamar's Bough" . . .

This saintly personage had, in the days of old, preached against the ostentatious luxury of the inhabitants of the then prosperous cities. So he had set out the procedure for wedding ceremonies, down to the smallest detail. His disciples accepted the rule, not only obeying it themselves, but imposing it even more strictly on all their male offspring. If any of their descendants insisted on breaking the "chain" it was noticed that children born of the union were without exception physically or mentally handicapped, unless they turned out to be ne'er-do-wells or jailbirds. This was proof that the saint's curse had remained alive over the centuries, and he was still vigilant down to the present day "when aeroplanes fly and the radio speaks all by itself," as one of the pious ladies commented.

The fiancé's mother had explained. She could not go against the rule: the chain with them passed from father to son; she herself had suffered from such a ceremony "almost funereal, as if she'd been an orphan, still in mourning," she had added . . . Thanks be to God, her daughters and her only son had turned out an honour and the joy of her heart, a light for her mature years, a beacon for old age! So it would be for the new bride; she would suffer one night only—the first—of humility in obedience to the strict custom: in return would come the promise of blessing on her children who would be conceived "beneath the bough of the saint." A girl must be worthy of this opportunity for a husband like her son!

It seemed to us girls, as we listened to the youngest sister's story, that these people of peasant origin were quite amazing! Barbarians, disguised as city-dwellers, giving themselves over to magical practices, to primitive penances.

Certainly, we too acknowledged the saints' presence in our midst, with the matrons calling on them endlessly, at every turn in the conversation. Time and time again, they invoked their memory to heighten every discourse, on every possible subject, with the result that this familiarity seemed, by its very abuse, to be pure rhetoric, a mere stylistic device. As for controlling our day-to-day existence, our feminine love of ostentation, and dictating how our ceremonies should be conducted! No! Our men-folk were literate in Arabic as well as in French! Our sons might not go abroad in search of diplomas and degrees, but what was so grand about this if, meanwhile, the women trembled with fear like ignorant villagers? They might just as well live like the peasants they were and "not mix with their betters," as one of our aunts had concluded peremptorily, with a gesture in the direction of the neighbours.

"Poor girl!" she added. "I'm afraid that they are offering her as the sacrificial lamb to the herdsmen!"

"And what about Sidi Maamar's curse?" another asked.

"Islam is one, Islam is pure and unadorned! It allows you leisure for rejoicing! The law cannot change, it is the same, everywhere from our town to faraway Medina; I don't need any *fqih*[3] or learned doctor from the *Zitouna* to explain it to me!"

But our neighbours had to comply. The girl prepared for her nuptials to take place beneath "Sidi Maamar's bough."

During the weeks before the set date, the women gossiping on the terraces every evening dwelt interminably on the details of the curious protocol.

No embroidered tunic, no jewels, not the slightest adornment for the bride on the wedding day, nor the preceding day nor even during the ritual of the *hammam*[4] two

3. Scholar.

4. Turkish bath.

days before: at a pinch they might be permitted to wave candles and intone hymns during the evening ceremony, when the virgin's hands and feet were tinted with henna.

It was soon learned that only a token dowry had been given: one golden twenty-franc coin, which the bride was to save scrupulously and never spend. On the morning when the procession of barouches[5] and cars arrived in our street, bringing the groom's female relatives from their hamlet, muffled up in their veils to escort the bride, there must be no clamour, no jubilant ululation, no music; at the most one old woman could hold a candle and recite some verses from the Quran at the exact moment when the match-makers stepped over the threshold.

These women would drink neither lemonade nor milk of welcome, they would not partake of a single date or the smallest almond cake. They would simply fetch away the virgin for whom they had come. She will have her face completely hidden and her body shrouded in a seamless cloth of wool or linen, so that she can neither see nor be seen by anyone, until her new master, alone with her at night, piously and solemnly removes the veil from her face: thus had the Saint Maamar decreed, four centuries ago.

And the gossipmongers mused at dusk: the bride would be conveyed like an object, gaze turned inwards, face bathed in tears, just fit to be buried! . . . What masochism, whereas fate, already so hard on women, did at least guarantee them the glamour of a wedding day!

This marriage promised to have nothing but misery in store. The gossipers were amazed, they protested that they'd never let a daughter of theirs make such a match, one might as well condemn the innocent maid to the grip of deliberate celibacy! It must be added that none of them was invited, only near relatives, as well as the female members of our family, as we were close neighbours.

I remember that wedding—or more exactly the morning after the wedding night.

The bride's mother had been in tears since the previous evening: no ululation, cakes not distributed (she hadn't been able to resist making them), the absence of professional female musicians from the town, the elegant, varied trousseau which no one had seen! She had decided to get her own back the next day, by displaying the luxury that had been forbidden the day before.

We set out before dawn to drive to that mysterious village: ten or so veiled women from the two adjacent houses piled into the van into which the mother had already loaded the trousseau, baskets filled with foodstuffs and the most delicate pastries. She would show those villagers, by preparing the wedding banquet herself, how refined her family was and what her daughter meant to her and all towns-women! The wedding celebrations would be up to the usual standards and the ascetic saint with his mortification of the flesh would have to take a back seat and let an older tradition be observed!

I can remember our excitement as we set out, still half-asleep, in the morning twilight, driving in the cold along the corniche, through the bluish mist. I remember our arrival at that house which was—well, what can I say?—just like any in the city—a building occupied by families of teachers from different regions. But, above all, I remember the bride, the moment we caught sight of her.

5. Four-wheeled carriages.

We entered the smallest room in the house, where mattresses were piled up on the bare tiles. There was total, tense silence, broken only by convulsive sobs coming from a white-shrouded heap huddled up against the wall, while a group of dumb-struck children clustered around, staring at the unidentifiable back. With an abrupt gesture, the mother chased the horde away. Only three women remained, I think, in addition to ourselves, the two little girls who were to be the bridesmaids—decked out in our white lace dresses and the shiny patent-leather shoes which seemed shockingly conspicuous in this setting!

The mother, with her woollen veil draped round her waist, stared for a moment at her daughter, huddled there, shaking with sobs. I have never forgotten the opacity of that silence. There was an enormous mirror facing the door, from which a large white sheet had just been removed and still hung down from one side. I could see the mother's reflection, seeming larger than life, as she stood with her face contorted.

"O my daughter! Grievous blow! Day of joy! day of woe!" she declaimed, rhyming the Arabic words.

She gazed at her own image with a grimace of helpless despair and without even bending down to the bride, whose sobs suddenly ceased, she angrily, violently lacerated her own cheeks. Two female relatives rushed in and forced her outside (was it not a rule of the most basic modesty that mother and daughter should not be left alone the day after the wedding night, as if the intrusion of the man destroyed for ever the protection the mother could give to the virgin?).

"Shame on you!" one of the relatives chided.

"Have a care for your daughter's happiness!" murmured the other.

"Her destiny is only just beginning, do not be such an evil omen!"

The mother allowed herself to be dragged into the vestibule. We two little girls remained with one woman, probably the bride's older sister who had just slipped discreetly into the room, with modest bearing and anxious expression.

She sat down and put her arms round the bride who had resumed her convulsive sobbing after her mother's angry outburst. She crouched down beside her sister, whispering words of comfort, gradually encouraging her to give vent to her pent-up feelings, let her cup of bitterness spill over, say what hidden grievance sparked off this misery. Seated on a mattress, shocked by the mother's violence, I wondered what I should do. I felt ashamed of my incongruous white dress; should I listen, try to make out the cause of the bride's distress, see if it persisted, if? . . . The two sisters huddled together under the same veil, deep in whispered conference. At this precise moment, or perhaps later when the confession was resumed in snatches of conversation with other women in the town, I became aware of what heavy destructive footsteps had crushed the tender shoots in the dream garden.

The union had been consummated—for so the saint's code had decreed—on a simple sheepskin or a rush-mat: two bodies copulating under a blanket. Was it this uncouthness that caused the bride to sob so bitterly in the next day's first pale morning light?

She had to make her appearance in the afternoon, dressed in her finery, the tiara on her brow, but with swollen eyelids, and puffy-faced from the shock to her virginity.

"So," commented her friends, who claimed to be in the secret, "she wept because she didn't like the bridegroom!"

"Didn't like him?"

"He was too small, and probably an insensitive oaf!"

"Insensitive or unaffectionate?"

"What is affection in a man?" sniggered a malicious voice. "Do our masters even know what affection is, since God has made all of us women, young or old, beautiful or ugly, to be like sheep, following at their heels!"

"Shame on you, with your bold, poisonous tongue!"

"What does it matter if the bridegroom is small and boorish?" retorted loudly another buxom woman. "A man is a man! As long as he works to keep his wife and children and walks in the path of God, that alone is luck in marriage!"

"She didn't like him, she didn't like him!" the younger women repeated. They knew that this second daughter was a romantic soul. What had been the use of the trousseau, so meticulously prepared and the "French-style" wedding gown, that she wore only on the second day, after interminable debates? What had her tongue-tied shyness and her purity led to?

I recall these scattered details of that wedding celebration—the copulation on a rush-mat, an unloving bridegroom and a tear-stained bride—but I also remember the bitter prelude, the outburst which some will deem puerile.[6] As if, in our town as elsewhere, whether the marriage is celebrated with the blessing of a long-dead saint or accompanied by shrill cries of jubilation from submissive towns-women, there was no hope in sight thereafter.

6. Childish

PERSPECTIVES

Iberia, The Meeting of Three Worlds

There are two common names for the period of eight hundred years during which Islamic forces controlled some portion of the Iberian Peninsula: the *Convivencia,* or coexistence, and the *Reconquista,* or reconquest. As these very different terms suggest, medieval Spain can be seen as an extraordinary confluence of the three dominant cultures of the modern West (Arabic, Christian, and Jewish) or as an embattled cohabitation. In either case, there is no denying the unique and multifaceted art and literature that emerged from it. Southern Spain was the portal through which the rich and ancient erudition of North Africa, the Middle East, and Greece made its way back into Europe after the fall of the Roman Empire.

Muslim armies first arrived in the Iberian peninsula in 711, sweeping northward into France, where they were eventually turned back by Charles Martel at Poitiers. The first dynasty of emirs in al-Andalus (Arabic for "the land of the Vandals," earlier rulers of the region) was the Umayyads, who controlled the entire peninsula outside of the northern quarter—the Christian kingdoms of Asturias, León, Navarre, Aragon, and Catalonia. Most of the cities of al-Andalus remained relatively independent. The great political and cultural centers were Córdoba, Granada, and, later, Seville; here were built the magnificent mosques and palaces still visible today, and here poets were drawn from all over the declining eastern empire. The long-established and highly regular forms of classical, courtly Arabic poetry were renewed through contact with the indigenous forms of Spain.

Poetry was the most prestigious literary mode and the chief cultural institution of the Arabic-speaking world, practiced by rulers, courtiers, philosophers, and religious leaders as well as professional poets. The incorporation of Greek philosophy from the tenth century on provided a common language and set of problems to Muslims, Christians, and Jews alike. The so-called "courtier rabbis" were especially important to this cultural mélange, benefiting from the Arab principle of toleration for those they called the *dhimmi,* or "people of the book." Wealthy and powerful, fluent in Arabic, pious and learned in Jewish tradition, the community of the Sephardim (as the Jews of Iberia called themselves) saw to the everyday workings of the kingdoms of al-Andalus. They also created an unprecedented corpus of secular Hebrew poetry out of Arabic forms, as if the poetic clash of sensuality, nature, and physical love with divinity were a way of mitigating the contradiction between their public and private lives.

Exile was a great theme, not only for the Hebrew poets adapting a classical Jewish motif to Arabic poetic forms, but to the Arab mystics describing their separation from paradise in the material world. Celebrations of wine, love, and song went hand in hand with an underlying conviction of the transience of physical experience. Even under the fairly stable government of the tenth and eleventh centuries, warfare was constant. Two movements during the eleventh century had far-reaching consequences. In 1035, the Almoravids, a strictly orthodox sect, arose in North Africa; at the same time, the Christian rulers of Castile and León began the centuries-long push southward that became known as the *Reconquista.* Invited into al-Andalus to counter the Castilian forces, Almoravid rule initiated a decline in Jewish participation in society. A pogrom in Granada in 1066 resulted in the massacre of 3,000 Jews. When Almoravid power dissipated in the mid-twelfth century, their role was taken over by the Almohads, a new reform movement that preached austere simplicity, rejected the doctrine of *dhimmi,* and caused a further exodus from al-Andalus of Jews and Mozarabs (Christians who had adopted Arabic language and culture without converting to Islam).

Medieval Iberia was a society both enraptured and disturbed by anything hybrid. Jews and Christians held high posts in al-Andalus; their poets and philosophers later found refuge and patronage in the courts of northern Spain, collaborating, for example, in the creation by

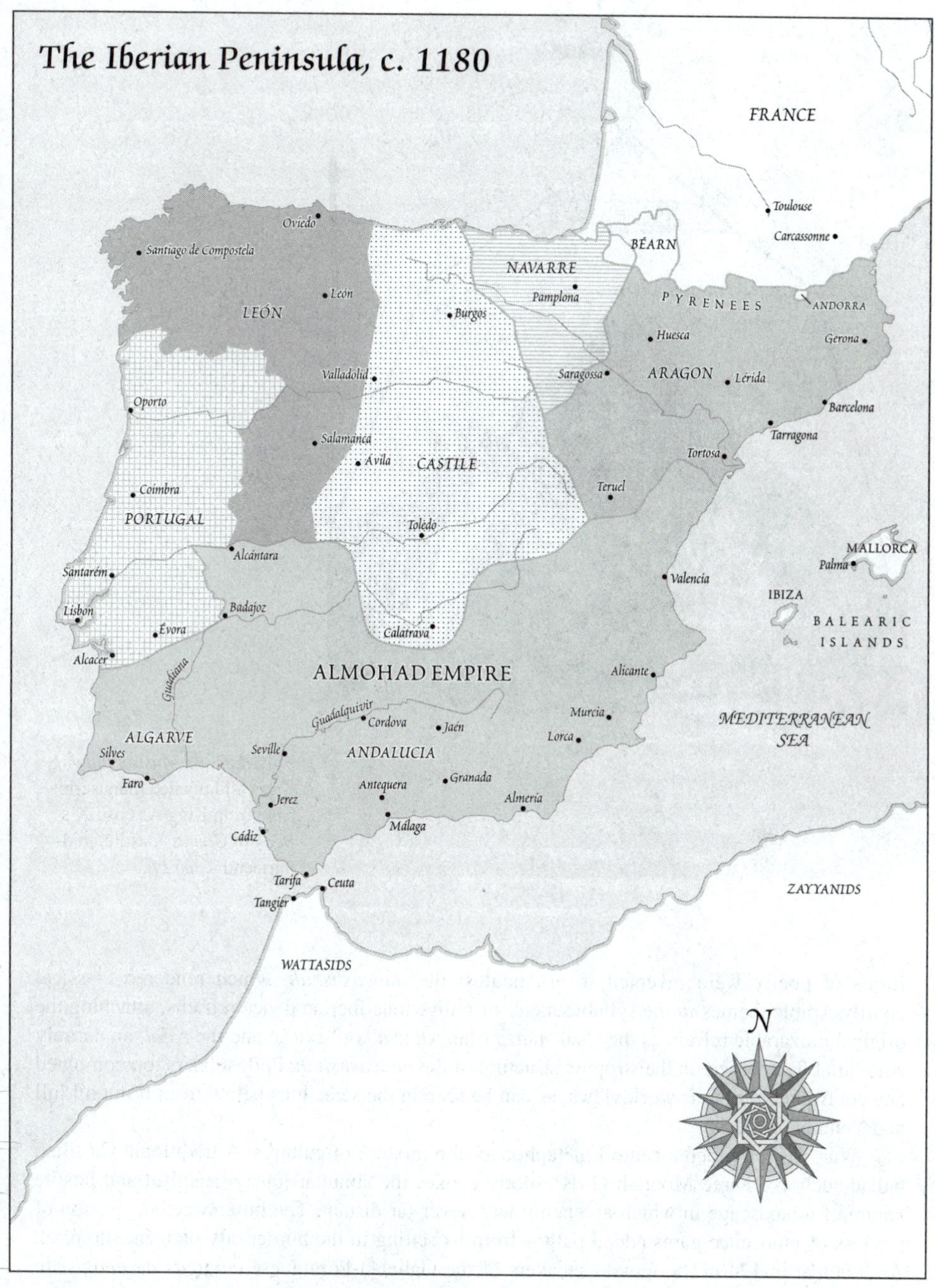

Alfonso X of the thirteenth-century *cantigas de Santa Maria,* a huge collection of over 400 songs celebrating the Virgin Mary. Miniatures in the opulent manuscript depict Arab, Jewish, and Christian performers side by side, singing, dancing, and playing a wide variety of musical instruments. A Castilian general such as Rodrigo Díaz battled other Christians as well as Muslims, and, although a loyal vassal to King Alfonso VI, maintained close friendships and ties of allegiance to Muslim rulers. Poetry and philosophy reflected the same paradoxes. Two hybrid

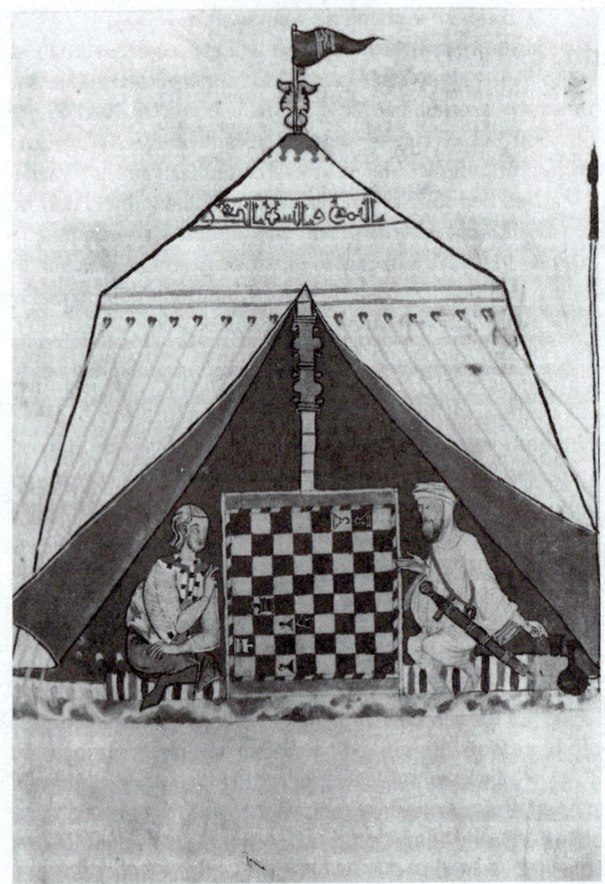

Christian and Muslim playing chess, illuminated manuscript page from King Alfonso X's *Book of Games,* Castile, mid-thirteenth century.

forms of poetry were invented in al-Andalus: the *muwashshaḥ*, which rendered classical courtly Arabic themes in the syllabic meter of indigenous Iberian dance refrains, attaching the original mozarabic refrain as the final stanza (the "*kharja*" or "exit"); and the *zajal,* an entirely colloquial form based on the strophic structure of the *muwashshaḥ*. Philosophers too combined and confronted religious worldviews, as can be seen in the selections below from Ramón Llull and Yehuda ha-Levi.

War, too, provided a central metaphor for the mixture of cultures. A traditional Castilian ballad such as "Three Moorish Girls" subtly evokes the simultaneously beautiful and hostile nature of a landscape in which an enemy was never far distant. The bittersweet suggestion of the loss of innocence gains added pathos from its setting in the border city of Jaén, site of an Arab defeat in 1246. The female speakers of the Galician-Portuguese *cantigas de amigo* are haunted by the long absence of a lover, whether crusading in the distant East or the nearby South. Slogans of religious fervor often go hand in hand with episodes of intimate cooperation. But when Ferdinand and Isabella married to unite conclusively the kingdoms of Castile and Aragon, a sea change was imminent. The last Arab stronghold, Granada, surrendered in 1492, the same year in which the Jews were expelled from Spain, and in which Columbus reached the Americas. The "people of the book" would come together again in other countries under conditions of war, but never again would that hostile proximity also result in a cultural flowering of such local beauty and far-reaching influence.

PRONUNCIATIONS:

Al-Andalus: ahl-AHN-dah-loos
Averroës: ah-ve-RRO-es
Cordoba: KOR-do-bah
Dom Dinis: dohm-DEE-nees
Ibn Al-'Arabi: ib'n ahl-ah-RAH-bee
Solomon Ibn Gabirol: SOHL-oh-mon ib'n GAH-bee-roll
Ibn Ḥazm: ib'n HAZ'm
Kharjas: KHAR-zhas
Ramon Llull: rah-MON LULL
Yehuda ha-Levi: ya-WHO-dah ha-LAY-vee

Castilian Ballads and Traditional Songs

c. 11th–14th century

During the late fifteenth century, as the final battles of the *Reconquista* were being decided, Ferdinand and Isabella began forging a national identity for Spain exclusive of Jews and Muslims. One aspect of this process was to collect the oral tradition of Castilian song into written form, a process initiated by Dom Dinis in the late thirteenth century. The result was a series of *Cancioneros,* or songbooks, and *Romanceros,* or books of ballads, including the *Cancionero de Palacio* (1438), *Cancionero de la Colombina* (1493), the *Cancionero musical del palacio* (1500), the *Cancionero general* (1511), the *Cancionero de romances* (1550), and the *Romancero general* (1600). The songs dated from the previous several centuries; many are probably of far earlier origin. In addition to universal motifs of love and celebration, these collections document the complex relationship of Castile over the past centuries with its southern neighbors in al-Andalus.

Ballad of Juliana[1]

"Get on, you hounds, get on,
And may the furies take you.
Thursday you kill the boar
And eat the meat on Friday.[2]

"Today makes seven years
I've wandered in these hills.
Now both my feet are bare,
Blood spurts from my toenails.

"Now I drink fresh gore,
The meat I eat is raw,
And sadly seek Juliana,
Who was the emperor's daughter.

1. From the *Cancionero de romances.* Translated by Edwin Honig.

2. It was long the custom in the Catholic church to abstain from eating meat on Fridays in memory of the crucifixion of Jesus on that day.

"Early St. John's morning,[3]
  While she gathered flowers,
The Moors took her away
  From her father's bowers."

Juliana hears this said
  Wrapt in the Moor's embrace;
Twin tears her two eyes shed
  Fall on that Moor's face.

Abenámar[1]

"Abenámar, Abenámar
Moor of Moor's delight
The hour of your birth
Comets filled the night.[2]
The sea was calm as glass
The moon was waxing full
A Moor with stars like yours
Must never break the spell."
"I tell the truth, my lord,
Though it be death to tell."
"I thank you, Abenámar,
Your birth bespeaks you well.
What castles are those shining
High on yonder hill?"
"The Alhambra there, my lord,
The mosque tower further still,
And there, the Alixares,
Built so wondrous well.[3]
A Moor was paid to build them
A hundred crowns a day
And lost, for each day idle,
As much as he was paid.
When all was built and ready
The architect was slain
So he could build no others
For Andalusia's reign.
There lies Crimson Towers
A castle of renown
And there, the Generalife,

3. June 24, the midsummer festival of St. John's Day, marked the end of the festival season and the beginning of the work of harvesting. Its rituals included gathering grass for auguring and flowers for girls to wear in wreaths, dancing around a bonfire, eating, drinking, and of course lovemaking.

1. Translated by William M. Davis. Abenámar refers to Yusuf IV, or Ibn al-Ahmar, who gained the throne of Granada with the help of Juan II of Castilia in 1431. The poem relates their meeting against the spectacular backdrop of the city, which has the last word in the ballad.

2. Comets were traditionally taken as omens, either for good or for ill.

3. Perched on a hilltop in the Sierra Nevada, the Alhambra was a vast fortified town complex centered around the palace itself. The Alixares was a further palace with gardens.

Of matchless garden fame,"[4]
Then spoke King don Juan,
Mark what he will say:
"With your consent, Granada,
I'd marry you today;
With Córdoba for dowry,
Sevilla for display."[5]
"I am a wife, King John,
No widow, but a wife,
The Moor who is my husband
Loves me more than life."

Those mountains, mother[1]

Those mountains, mother
are steep to climb,
where streams rush down
to fields of thyme.[2]

Those mountains, mother
have flowers above:
up where they are,
I have my love.

I will not pick verbena[1]

I will not pick verbena
on the morrow of St. John,[2]
for my lover has gone.

I will not pick sunflowers,
honeysuckle or carnations.
Only sorrows will I pluck
and cruel frustrations,
for my lover has gone.

Three Moorish Girls[1]

I am in love with three Moorish lasses in Jaén,[2]
Axa, Fátima and Marién.

4. The Torres Bermejas, or Crimson Towers, are a group of fortified towers near the entrance to the Alhambra. The Generalife ("Garden of the Builder") is an extensive series of gardens and pavilions leading eastward from the Alhambra to the summer palace.

5. The other two major cities of al-Andalus. Córdoba had fallen to Ferdinand III of Castilia in 1236, and Seville to the same ruler 12 years later. Granada was the last stronghold to fall, holding out until 1492.

1. Translated by James Duffy. From Diego Pisador, *Libro de Música de Vihuela* (1552), a collection of settings of traditional songs for the *vihuela,* a guitar-shaped instrument whose strings were plucked like a lute.

2. Literally, *toronjil,* lemon balm, a fragrant and medicinal herb of the mint family.

1. Translated by James Duffy. Verbena is a flower and a medicinal herb.

2. The midsummer festival of St. John's Day came on June 24; it was the traditional end of the season of festivals.

1. From the *Cancionero del Palacio.* Translated by Angela Buxton.

2. Lying north of Granada in Andalusia, Jaén was for a long time the frontier between Christians and Moors in medieval Spain, and the region was the scene of many battles before it was captured by Ferdinand III in 1246.

Three pretty Moorish lasses
went to pick olives,
and they found them already picked in Jaén.[3]
Axa, Fátima and Marién.

And they found them picked,
and they came back dismayed,
and their colour was gone in Jaén.
Axa, Fátima and Marién.

Three such lively Moorish lasses
went to pick apples
and they found them already picked in Jaén.
Axa, Fátima and Marién.

Mozarabic Kharjas
10th–early 11th century

The *kharja* epitomizes the melting pot that was medieval Iberia. Written in Mozarabic, a Romance vernacular that was the common spoken language of al-Andalus, these brief verses originated in the refrains of popular dance. Hispano-Arabic (and, later, Hebrew) poets adapted these refrains as the final stanza (*kharja* means "exit") of a poetic form they invented in the tenth century, called the *muwashshaḥ*. The body of the poem is a courtly love song with traditional Arabic images but a syllabic meter based on the melody of the concluding vernacular stanza. The *kharja* responds to the refined and idealized male voice of the poem's body with the frank, colloquial voice of a flesh-and-blood woman. Sixty-one *kharjas* survive, representing the earliest known body of Romance lyric.

As if you were a stranger[1]

Como si filyol' alyenu,
non mas adormis a meu senu.

As if you were a stranger,
you no longer fall asleep on my breast.

Ah tell me, little sisters[2]

Garid vos, ay yermanellas,
com contenir a meu male!
Sin al-habib non vivireyu—
advolarey demandare.

Ah tell me, little sisters,
how to hold my pain!
I'll not live without my beloved—
I shall fly to seek him again.

My lord Ibrahim[3]

Meu sidi Ibrahim,
ya tu omne dolğe,
vent' a mib
de nohte!

My lord Ibrahim,
oh my sweet love,
come to me
at night!

3. The ambiguity over whether it is the girls or the olives that were "plucked" is heightened by the fact that *morilla* (Moorish girl) can also mean a small berry, or *mora*.

1. Translated by Peter Dronke. From two *muwashshaḥat:* Yehuda ha-Levi, "Panegyric [poem of praise] for Abu l-Hasan ben Qamniel" and an anonymous love poem.

2. Translated by Peter Dronke. From the *muwashshaḥ* by Yehuda ha-Levi, "Panegyric for Ishaq ibn Qrispin."

3. Translated by Peter Dronke. From a *muwashshaḥ* by Muhammad ibn Ubada, the Silk Merchant of Málaga (11th century).

In non, si non queris,
yireym' a tib.
Gar me a ob
legarte!

If not, if you don't want to,
I shall come to you.
Tell me where
to see you!

I'll give you such love![4]

Tan t'amaray, illa con al-šarti
an tağma' halhali ma' qurti!

I'll give you such love!—but only if
you'll bend
my anklets right over to my earrings!

Take me out of this plight[5]

Alsa-me de min hali—
mon hali qad bare!
Que faray, ya 'ummi?—
Faneq bad lebare!

Take me out of this plight—
my state is desperate!
Mother, what shall I do?—
The falcon is about to snatch![6]

Mother, I shall not sleep[7]

Non dormireyo, mamma,
a rayo de manyana:
í Bon Abū-l-Qāsim,
la fage de matrama!

Mother, I shall not sleep
When morning rises
But dream of Abū-l-Qāsim,
His features dawning.

Ibn al-'Arabi

1165–1240

Raised in Seville, the capital of the Almohad state, Ibn al-'Arabi converted to Sufism while still a teenager, following a warning vision. He traveled across Iberia seeking wisdom and guidance, including several meetings with the philosopher Ibn Rushd, then journeyed to North Africa and eastward on a pilgrimage to Mecca. He spent the last years of his life in Damascus. He produced numerous, often controversial esoteric works throughout his life; his poetry transposes those concerns through the lyric themes of nature, nostalgia, and love. Steeped in esoteric lore, a poem such as "Gentle now, doves" strives to render that lore immediately present through the experience of verse.

Gentle now, doves[1]

Gentle now, doves of the thornberry
and moringa thicket,[2]
don't add to my heartache
your sighs.

4. Translated by Peter Dronke. From an anonymous *muwashshaḥ.*

5. Translated by Peter Dronke. From a *muwashshaḥ* by Muhammad ibn Ubada.

6. The comparison of a lover to a falcon was a common image in love lyrics.

7. Translated by William M. Davis. From a *muwashshaḥ* by Ibn Harun al-Asbahi of Lérida (12th century).

1. Translated by Michael Sells.

2. The thornberry or arak tree grows in Arabia, parts of Africa, and eastern India; its roots and twigs are used as toothpicks. The moringa, or ben-nut tree, is native to India; its berries produce an aromatic oil.

Gentle now,
or your sad cooing
will reveal the love I hide,
the sorrow I hide away.

I echo back, in the evening,
in the morning, echo,
the longing of a love-sick lover,
the moaning of the lost.

In a grove of Gháda[3]
spirits wrestled,
bending the limbs down over me,
passing me away.

They brought yearning,
breaking of the heart,
and other new twists of pain,
putting me through it.

Who is there for me in Jám',
and the Stoning-Ground at Mína,[4]
who for me at Tamarisk Grove,
or at the way-station of Na'mán?

Hour by hour
they circle my heart
in rapture, in love-ache,
and touch my pillars with a kiss.

As the best of creation
circled the Ká'ba,[5]
which reason with its proofs
called unworthy,

He kissed the stones there—
and he was entrusted with the word!
And what is the house of stone
compared to a man or a woman?

They swore, and how often!
they'd never change—piling up vows.
She who dyes herself red with henna
is faithless.

A white-blazed gazelle[6]
is an amazing sight,

3. The tamarisk is an evergreen-like shrub or small tree that grows in sandy terrain. Its leaves have been used in medicine; ghada wood produces a dense charcoal.
4. These are stations on the pilgrimage to Mecca. Pilgrims camp in Jam' or al-Muzdalifa on the ninth night; on the tenth, they travel to Mina, where they cast stones at a pillar representing the temptation of Shaitan, or Satan.
5. A small shrine near the center of the Great Mosque in Mecca, the Ká'ba is the most holy structure in Islam, held to be the center of the world, the direction in which Muslims perform their prayers. "The best of creation" is the Prophet Muhammad.
6. The gazelle is a conventional metaphor in Arabic love poetry for the beloved. As with Ibn al-'Arabi's other natural images, it also possesses a mystical meaning.

red-dye signaling,
eyelids hinting,
Pasture between breastbones
and innards.
Marvel,
a garden among the flames!

My heart can take on
any form:
a meadow for gazelles,
a cloister for monks,

For the idols, sacred ground,
Ká'ba for the circling pilgrim,
the tables of the Toráh,
the scrolls of the Qur'án.

I profess the religion of love;
wherever its caravan turns along the way,
that is the belief,
the faith I keep.

Like Bishr,
Hind and her sister,
love-mad Qays and his lost Láyla,
Máyya and her lover Ghaylán.[7]

Solomon Ibn Gabirol

c. 1021–c. 1057

Born in Málaga in southern Spain, Ibn Gabirol was orphaned at an early age. Physically weak, temperamental and ill-at-ease with the courtier life, he spent his formative years in Saragossa, an important center of Jewish culture, where he immersed himself in a career of letters. He wrote some twenty volumes on philosophy and religion, most of which haven't survived. His influential secular treatise, *The Source of Life,* was translated from the Arabic into Latin in the twelfth century. Only during the nineteenth century was it discovered that its author, Avicebron, was identical with the Andalusian Jew celebrated for his hymns and for his lyric poetry. Poems such as "She looked at me and her eyelids burned" demonstrate Ibn Gabirol's skill in forging philosophical and religious preoccupations into powerfully unified visual images.

She looked at me and her eyelids burned[1]

She looked at me and her eyelids burned,
While her goblet brimmed with tears;
The words overflowed her mouth, like strings of pearls,
And the smile on her lips defied compare with gold.

7. Names of celebrated Arab poets and lovers of previous centuries.

1. Translated by William M. Davis.

But the rebuke she sent my soul
Wounded me like the words of the creditor to the poor debtor.
Meanwhile, the cup passed from hand to hand like the sun amid the heavens,
And day receded, fleeting, like waves along the shore,
But my blood, receding at unison of day,
Tinged my cheeks bright red: she will not return.

Behold the sun at evening[1]

Behold the sun at evening, red
As if she wore vermillion robes.
Slipping the wraps from north and south
She covers in purple the western side.
The earth—she leaves it cold and bare
To huddle in shadows all night long.
At once the sky is dark; you'd think
Sackcloth it wore for Yequtiel.[2]

The mind is flawed, the way to wisdom blocked[1]

The mind is flawed, the way to wisdom blocked;
The body alone is seen, the soul is hid,
And those who seek the world find only ill;
A man can get no pleasure here on earth.[2]
The servant rises up and kills his lord,
And serving girls attack their mistresses.
Sons are raising hands against their parents,
Daughters too oppose their parents' will.
My friend, from what I've seen of life I'd say
The best that one can hope is to go mad.
However long you live you suffer toil,
And in the end you suffer rot and worms.
Then finally the clay goes back to clay;
At last the soul ascends to join the Soul.[3]

Winter wrote with the ink of its rains and showers[1]

Winter wrote with the ink of its rains and showers,
The pen of its flashing lightning, and the hand of its clouds
A letter upon the garden in blue and purple,
Of which no craftsman with all his skill could make the like,
Therefore, when the earth longed to see the sky,
She embroidered on the twigs of her flowerbeds something like the stars.

1. Translated by Raymond P. Scheindlin.
2. This elegy was written on the occasion of the death of his patron, Yequtiel Ibn Hassan, in 1039. Sackcloth was a coarse fabric traditionally worn in mourning.
1. Translated by Raymond P. Scheindlin.
2. In the philosophical tradition of Neoplatonism, the soul is regarded as imprisoned in the body, its spiritual nature blocked by bodily needs and desire.
3. The soul is released by death to return to the great World Soul from which it had been torn to descend to its body on earth.
1. Translated by Raymond P. Scheindlin. Garden poetry was an important genre for both Arab and Jewish poets in Andalusia.

Yehuda ha-Levi

before 1075–1141

Yehuda (or Judah) ha-Levi is the legendary figurehead of Sephardic Jewry, his life an emblem of the height and decline of its "Golden Age" in al-Andalus. A successful court physician, ha-Levi traveled throughout al-Andalus, frequently crossing into the Christian north, on whose border he had been born. Revered for his poetic gifts during his lifetime (over 800 of his poems survive), he became disenchanted with his success and the gilded life he led. In 1140 he left his home, setting sail for Jerusalem by way of Egypt, where he was seduced by the good life once again, tarrying as a court poet in Cairo and Alexandria for almost a year. He appears never to have reached the Promised Land, but in popular legend his pilgrimage led directly from Spain to the Western Wall of Jerusalem, where he died a violent death just before arriving. Only a few years after Yehuda ha-Levi's departure, Jewish power was fully dispersed by the Almohad dynasty; for the courtier rabbis, the Golden Age was over.

Poems like "My heart is in the East," "Your breeze, Western shore," and "From time's beginning" illustrate the ambivalence of Yehuda ha-Levi's attitude toward al-Andalus, his home from birth but also a place of exile where he was a man of influence yet also subject to Almoravid rule. He skillfully renewed the Arabic theme of the poet's longing for his lost homeland by merging individual longing with the national theme of the Exile of Israel. In addition to such poems of exile, he composed in a wide variety of forms from panegyric to religious meditations; included below are three poems of love and wine, another traditional genre.

Cups without wine are lowly[1]

Cups without wine are lowly
As a pot thrown on the ground
But, full of juice, they shine
Like the body with a soul.

Ofra does her laundry with my tears[1]

Ofra does her laundry with my tears
And spreads it out before her beauty's rays.
With my two eyes she needs no flowing well;
Nor sun needs she: Her face provides the blaze.

Once when I fondled him upon my thighs[1]

Once when I fondled him upon my thighs
He caught his own reflection in my eyes
And kissed my eyes, deceitful imp; I knew
It was his image he kissed, and not my eyes!

1. Translated by William M. Davis.
1. Translated by Raymond P. Scheindlin. *Ofra* in Hebrew means a female fawn and is often a term for the poet's beloved.
1. Adapted by Yehuda ha-Levi from an Arabic original by al-Mutanabbi; English translation by Raymond P. Scheindlin. Homosexuality was common in al-Andalus, and the male beloved was a stock figure in the Arabic love poetry adapted by the Jewish poets.

From time's beginning, You were love's abode[1]

From time's beginning, You were love's abode:
My love encamped wherever it was You tented.
The taunts of foes for Your name's sake are sweet,
So let them torture one whom You tormented.

I love my foes; for they learned wrath from You,
For they pursue a body You have slain.
The day You hated me I loathed myself,
For I will honor none whom You disdain.
Until Your anger pass, and You restore
This people whom You rescued once before.

Your breeze, Western shore, is perfumed[1]

Your breeze, Western shore, is perfumed.
The scent of nard° is in its wings, and the apple. *an aromatic plant*
Your origin is in the merchants' treasuries,
Surely not from the store-house of the wind.[2]
You flutter the wings of the bird, giving him freedom;
You are like flowing myrrh[3] straight from the phial.
How much do people long for you, since, with your help,
They are carried by wooden beams on the backs of the waves.
Do not let your hand slacken its hold on the ship,
Whether the day is encamped, or blows fresh at the dawn.
Smooth out the deep, split the heart of the seas,
Come to the holy mountains. There you can rest.
Rebuke the East wind which enrages the sea,
Turning the waves into a boiling cauldron.
What shall a man do, chained to his Rock,
At one time confined, at another set free.
The essence of my request is in the hand of the Highest,
Who formed the mountains, who created the wind.

My heart is in the East[1]

My heart is in the East, and I in the depths of the West.
My food has no taste. How can it be sweet?
How can I fulfil my pledges and my vows,
When Zion is in the power of Edom, and I in the fetters of Arabia?[2]

1. Translated by Raymond P. Scheindlin. Yehuda ha-Levi adapts the Arabic situation of the lover who embraces abasement and rejection by her beloved, using it for Israel's attitude in exile from God.

1. Translated by David Goldstein.

2. Alluding to Psalm 135:7: "He bringeth forth the wind out of his treasuries."

3. Myrrh is a gum resin used for perfume. Like nard, it appears frequently in the Bible.

1. Translated by David Goldstein.

2. The poet asks how he can he travel to the Holy Land ("Zion") when he is a tolerated minority in Arab Iberia, and Palestine has been conquered by the Christians in the First Crusade. (After the conquest of Jerusalem in 1099, the Crusaders had slaughtered not only Muslims but Jews within the city.) The Edomites were enemies of the ancient Israelites; "Edom" became a code word for Rome when Israel was part of the Roman empire, and here means the Christian occupiers of Palestine.

It will be nothing to me to leave all the goodness of Spain.
So rich will it be to see the dust of the ruined sanctuary.[3]

Ramón Llull
1232–1315

A prolific polymath mystic, Ramón Llull wrote over 250 works, in Catalan and in Arabic, on nearly every subject there was. Born on the island of Majorca, during his youth he was a courtier and seneschal, or steward, before a mystical vision led him to retreat for nine years of hermitlike study in order to persuade the Jews and Muslims of the error of their faiths. Immersed in all three cultures of Iberia, his esoteric Christianity is well evident in the 366 allusive and lyrical aphorisms that make up the *Book of the Lover and the Beloved* (*Llibre d'amic et amat*), which forms chapter 99 of *Blanquerna* (1283), the first prose novel written in a romance language.

from Blanquerna: The Book of the Lover and the Beloved[1]

14. The Lover sought for one who should tell his Beloved how great trials he was enduring for love of Him, and how he was like to die. And he found his Beloved, who was reading in a book wherein were written all the griefs which love made him to suffer for his Beloved, and the joy which he had of his love.

16. "Say, thou bird that singest! Hast thou placed thyself in the care of my Beloved, that He may guard thee from indifference,[2] and increase in thee thy love?" The bird replied: "And who makes me to sing but the Lord of love, Who holds indifference to be sin?"

18. There was a contention between the eyes and the memory of the Lover, for the eyes said that it was better to behold the Beloved than to remember Him. But Memory said that remembrance brings tears to the eyes, and makes the heart to burn with love.

54. As one that was a fool went the Lover through a city, singing of his Beloved; and men asked him if he had lost his wits. "My Beloved," he answered, "has taken my will, and I myself have yielded up to Him my understanding; so that there is left in me naught but memory, wherewith I remember my Beloved."

69. The Lover extended and prolonged his thoughts of the greatness and everlastingness of his Beloved, and he found in Him neither beginning, nor mean,[3] nor end. And the Beloved said: "What measurest thou, O Fool?" The Lover answered: "I measure the lesser with the greater, defect with fulness, and beginning with infinity and

3. The sanctuary, the Temple of Jerusalem, was destroyed by the Romans in 70 C.E. as a consequence of the Jewish rebellion of 66. The ruins that remain are part of the Western Wall, also known as the Wailing Wall.

1. Translated by E. Allison Peers. In the context of the novel, *The Book of the Lover and the Beloved* is written by the protagonist Blanquerna as an allegory of the faithful Christian and God, his Beloved, echoing the characters in the biblical Song of Songs (page 126). Like other mystical writings using the language of love, the numbered aphoristic sentences are equally applicable to the amorous situations they use to evoke a mystical state.

2. The translator uses "indifference" to translate the frequently occurring Catalan word *desamor,* which literally means "unlove," or "absence of love."

3. Middle.

eternity, to the end that humility, patience, charity and hope may be planted the more firmly in my remembrance."

70. The paths of love are both long and short. For love is clear, bright and pure, subtle yet simple, strong, diligent, brilliant, and abounding both in fresh thoughts and in old memories.

89. Love went apart with the Lover, and they had great joy of the Beloved; and the Beloved revealed himself to them. The Lover wept, and afterwards was in rapture, and Love swooned thereat.[4] But the Beloved brought life to His Lover by bringing to his memory His virtues.

98. The Beloved left the Lover, and the Lover sought Him in his thoughts, and enquired for Him of men in the language of love.

118. The Lover and the Beloved strove, and their love made peace between them. Which of them, think you, bore the stronger love toward the other?

130. With the pen of love, with the water of his tears, and on a paper of suffering, the Lover wrote letters to his Beloved. And in these he told how devotion tarried, how love was dying, and how sin and error were increasing the number of His enemies.

131. The Lover and the Beloved were bound in love with the bonds of memory, understanding, and will, that they might never be parted; and the cord wherewith these two loves were bound was woven of thoughts and griefs, sighs and tears.

132. The Lover lay in the bed of love: his sheets were of joys, his coverlet was of griefs, his pillow of tears. And none knew if the fabric of the pillow was that of the sheets or of the coverlet.

133. The Beloved clothed His Lover in vest, coat and mantle,[5] and gave him a helmet of love. His body He clothed with thoughts, his feet with tribulations, and his head with a garland of tears.

182. The Lover made complaint of his Beloved, because He caused Love so grievously to torment him. And the Beloved made reply by increasing his trials and perils, thoughts and tears.

194. One day the Lover ceased to remember his Beloved, and on the next day he remembered that he had forgotten Him. On the day when it came to the Lover that he had forgotten his Beloved, he was in sorrow and pain, and yet in glory and bliss—the one for his forgetfulness, and the other for his remembrance.

217. The Beloved chastened the heart of His Lover with rods of love, to make him love the tree whence He plucks the rods wherewith He chastens His lovers. And this is that tree whereon He suffered grief and dishonour and death, that He might bring back to love of Him those lovers whom He had lost.[6]

4. Because of that.
5. Sleeveless cloak.
6. This aphorism makes the Christian allegory more explicit than many of the others, with its recasting of the Passion of Christ in terms of the Lover and the Beloved.

Dom Dinis, King of Portugal
1261–1325

An accomplished poet and patron of the arts, Dom Dinis opened his court to displaced poets from abroad: Provençal troubadours fleeing the Albigensian crusade in southwest France, Jews and Muslims fleeing the unrest in the southern half of the Iberian Peninsula. The coastal town of Santiago de Compostela was an important destination for medieval pilgrims and the performers who accompanied them. The Portuguese court was nourished by these influences, and Dom Dinis put this rich blend of talent to work copying and compiling luxurious illuminated manuscripts of songs.

Over a hundred texts of Dom Dinis's own songs have come down to us, along with the musical notation of seven compositions—all that we have, with seven of Martin Codax's, to indicate how the songs of the Galician-Portuguese tradition were actually performed. Most Occitanian and Northern French songs, with their more elusive melodies and extended, highly expressive lyrics, were rendered by voice alone, or with the spare accompaniment of the medieval fiddle. The Galician-Portuguese songs, although influenced by the French lyrics, also derived from a strong local tradition of refrain-based folk song. With catchier melodies and highly repetitive lyrics, these songs lent themselves to the greater instrumentation and dance beat of a small orchestra, which included the harp and the *pandeiro,* a square-frame drum, as well as the symphonie, a stringed instrument resembling a hurdy-gurdy.

Dom Dinis's version of the *canso* or love song is generally short with a refrain; he composed seventy-three of them. He also excelled in the *cantiga de amigo,* brief lyrics of love and longing written in the voice of a woman, usually waiting for or going to meet her lover. Nowhere else in medieval Europe were more women's songs composed, often superior in quality to the otherwise more common *cantiga de amor,* written in the voice of the male lover.

Provençals right well may versify[1]

Provençals right well may versify
And say they do with love
But those with verse in flowertime
And never else, I'd vow,
Their heart is not in torment
As mine is for my lady.

Although they're bound to versify
And praise as best they can,
Nonetheless, I'd vow
That those with verse in spring
And never else, will bring
No grief as deep as mine.

For those who versify with joy
About the verdant° time, *greening*
The flowers do their bidding,
In spring, but soon decline,
Nor is their life perdition
Nor death in life, like mine.

1. Translated by William M. Davis. The verb *trobar* ("versify," literally "to find") is a key word in the vocabulary of Occitan poetry referred to here by Dom Dinis, for it is also the source of the names, *troubadours* and *trobairitz.*

Of what are you dying, daughter[1]

Of what are you dying, daughter, of body so fair?
Mother, I'm dying for the love my friend bestowed.
It's dawn, and quickly he goes.

Of what are you dying, daughter, of body so lithe?
Mother, I'm dying for the love my lover bestowed.
It's dawn, and quickly he goes.

Mother, I'm dying for the love my friend bestowed
whenever I look at this sash I tie for his love.
It's dawn, and quickly he goes.

Mother, I'm dying for the love my lover bestowed
whenever I look at this sash that I wear for his love.
It's dawn, and quickly he goes.

Whenever I look at this sash that I tie for his love
and remember, pretty me, how he spoke with me.
It's dawn, and quickly he goes.

Whenever I look at this sash that I wear for his love
and remember, pretty me, how both of us spoke.
It's dawn, and quickly he goes.

O blossoms of the verdant pine

O blossoms of the verdant pine,
if you have news of my friend?
O God, where is he?

O blossoms of the verdant bough,
if you have news of my beloved?
O God, where is he?

If you have news of my friend,
who lied about what he promised to me?
O God, where is he?

If you have news of my beloved,
who lied about what he swore to me?
O God, where is he?

You ask me about that friend of yours,
and I tell you that he is well and alive.
O God, where is he?

You ask me about that friend of yours,
and I tell you that he is alive and well.
O God, where is he?

1. This and the following poems are translated by Barbara Hughes Fowler.

And I tell you that he is well and alive,
and will be with you before very long.
O God, where is he?

And I tell you that he is alive and well
and will be with you now very soon.
O God, where is he?

The lovely girl arose at earliest dawn

The lovely girl
arose at earliest dawn,
and goes to wash her camisoles at the river swirl.
She goes to wash them at earliest dawn.

The elegant girl
arose at earliest dawn,
and goes to wash her petticoats at the river swirl.
She goes to wash them at earliest dawn.

She goes to wash her camisoles.
She rose at earliest dawn.
The wind is scattering them at the river swirl.
She goes to wash them at earliest dawn.

She goes to wash her petticoats.
She rose at earliest dawn.
The wind has born them off at the river swirl.
She goes to wash them at earliest dawn.

The wind is scattering them.
She rose at earliest dawn.
At dawn she was enraged at the river swirl.
She goes to wash them at earliest dawn.

Martin Codax

fl. mid-13th century

In 1914, a parchment leaf was found inside the binding of a book in Madrid. It contained the words and music to seven *cantigas de amigo,* or "songs for a friend," composed by Martin Codax in Galician-Portuguese at the court of Ferdinand III of Castile in the mid-thirteenth century. We know nothing about him except the name, but the poems provide rare firsthand evidence of how lyric was performed on the Iberian Peninsula. The high degree of parallelism from stanza to stanza in both words and melody mirrors the dominant image of the sea in the delicate form known as the *marinha,* or sea-song. End-rhyme intensifies the parallelism; in "O waves that I've come to see," for example, rhymes of words ending in *-er* and *-ar* play off each other like the waves of the sea that is serving the speaker as her mirror and confidante. The musical settings stretch out the key words, particularly *amigo* (friend, lover), stressing the mood they create, before finishing on the plaintive and brief monosyllables, *sin min,* "without me."

Ah God, if only my love could know[1]

Ah God, if only my love could know
how much I am alone in Vigo,[2]
and go about in love.

Ah God, if he knew, my dearest one,
how I am in Vigo, all alone!
and go about in love.

How in Vigo, alone, I stay—
and near me not a single spy,
and go about in love.

How in Vigo I stay alone,
with no spies around me, none,
and go about in love.

And I have no spies with me,
only my eyes, that weep with me,
and go about in love.

And near me now I have no spies
—only my pair of weeping eyes—
and go about in love.

My beautiful sister, come hurry with me[1]

My beautiful sister, come hurry with me
to the church of Vigo beside the turbulent sea,
and we shall marvel at the waves.

My beautiful sister, come hurry, please,
to the church of Vigo beside the tumultuous sea,
and we shall marvel at the waves.

To the church of Vigo beside the turbulent sea,
and there will come here, mother, my friend,
and we shall marvel at the waves.

To the church of Vigo beside the tumultuous sea,
and there will come here, my mother, my love,
and we shall marvel at the waves.

O waves that I've come to see[1]

O waves that I've come to see,
if you know, tell to me
why my love lingers
without me.

1. Translated by Peter Dronke.
2. The area around Vigo, in Galicia on the northwest coast of the Iberian Peninsula south of Santiago de Compostela, has been inhabited since prehistory. During the middle ages, it was a port town dependent on the Cistercian monastery of Melón.
1. Translated by Barbara Hughes Fowler.
1. Translated by Barbara Hughes Fowler.

O waves that I've come to view,
if you know, reveal to me
why my love lingers
without me.

END OF PERSPECTIVES: IBERIA, THE MEETING OF THREE WORLDS

Troubadours and *Trobairitz*

The troubadours and their female counterparts, the *trobairitz,* invented the love song as we know it in the Western world. Although it is widely accepted that the prototypes of the Old Provençal lyric came through the Iberian Peninsula from the Arabic, no one has really explained the flowering of poetry of such quality out of what was essentially an eccentric backwater of medieval Europe. Occitania (now southwestern France) was an insular culture in the eleventh and twelfth centuries, a stronghold of heresy under the control of willful leaders such as the man usually regarded as the first troubadour, Guillem—who was both the seventh Count of Poitiers and the ninth Duke of Aquitaine. The concentrated court cultures of Occitania produced a body of lyrics extremely self-conscious in language and subject matter. The word *troubadour* comes from the verb, *trovar,* which literally means "to find," and also implies composition and invention. The troubadours defined themselves as discoverers of rhymes, images, and topics; their verses privileged artfully fashioned words as the highest source of value.

The lion's share of Occitan lyrics concerns the love of the troubadour for his lord's lady. There has been much debate over how frequently love affairs actually occurred, but there is little doubt that the love celebrated and suffered in these poems was at least as much physical as spiritual. As with most love poetry, the themes are conventional and limited in number; here they center around the definition of *fin'amor* (courtly love), and around the description of ritual moments in the affair: the parting of the lovers at dawn, the cruelty of the beloved to her lover, the malice of the *lausengiers* (gossiping courtiers). The beauty of these poems, and their lasting influence, lies especially in their musicality; they were composed to be sung as entertainment at court, sometimes by the composer, more often by a *jongleur,* or traveling performer. Rhyme was a novelty in the eleventh and twelfth centuries, and the *langue d'oc,* the Romance dialect in which these songs were composed, allowed spectacular and virtuoso rhythmic effects and rhyme schemes. A particular tune was as much identified with a song as a particular turn of phrase or image would be, and in such a close-knit culture, the troubadours would often sample, quoting each others' words and tunes for a knowing, expert audience. Entertainment could be rollicking as well as melancholy, and the same troubadour could alternate between straight love songs and self-parodies, sometimes within the same composition, as Guillem did in "In the sweet time of renewal" and "I'll write a verse about nothing." He can compose a beautiful song on a conventional theme, Guillem boasts; he is such a consummate poet, in fact, that he can put one together out of nothing at all. Or the troubadour might take the melody of a *canso,* or love song, and give it the lyrics of a *sirventes,* a satirical song of politics and war, as Bertran de Born does in "I love the glad time of Easter," which begins in the conventional seasonal setting of a *canso* but goes on to enumerate the joys of battle rather than love.

Women, too, composed and performed songs in Occitania. The female *jongleurs* were considered part of the lowest class of society, even less respected than their male counterparts because they were assumed to moonlight as prostitutes. By contrast, the *trobairitz* were noblewomen, such as the Comtessa de Dia, rather than court professionals, as most of the troubadours were. The songs of the *trobairitz* speak in the female voice of the beloved within the courtly love paradigm (unlike in the Galician-Portuguese tradition of the *cantigas de amigo,* Occitan poets seldom crossed gender in their songs, although we do find poetic disputes, sometimes alternating between the verses of a troubadour and a *trobairitz*). In her haunting lyric "To sing of what I would not want I must," the Comtessa de Dia alternates between complaints about the suffering caused her by the distant pride of her lover, and thinly veiled threats about the consequences if he crosses her. The surface beauty of these deceptively simple lyrics heightens the power of the conflicting emotions roiling beneath. These poems grow out of the pleasures and traumas of physical love in a Christian society, and of personal feelings in a court world ruled by pragmatic alliances, employing the power of words and music in an incestuous culture where every nuance was loaded with meaning.

PRONUNCIATIONS:

Bernart de Ventadorn: BEHR-nahr duh VEN-tah-dorn
Bertran de Born: BEHR-trahw duh BORN
Guillem de Peiteus: gie-EM duh pay-TEUS
La Comtessa de Dia: lah-kohn-TE-sa de DEE-ah

Guillem de Peiteus

1071–1127

Eleven lyrics survive of the first known troubadour, who also happened to be Count of Poitiers ("Peiteus") and Duke of Aquitaine, the powerful lord of a vast and unruly realm. He lost an army in Asia Minor during the First Crusade, and campaigned victoriously against the Almoravids in Spain. He was constantly feuding with his vassals, with the King of France, and with the Church, which excommunicated him twice—but he is remembered most for his brilliant songs.

I'll write a verse about nothing[1]

I'll write a verse about nothing:
not about me or anyone,
not about love or courtliness
    or any other thing.
It came to me a while back
    while sleeping on my horse.

Don't know the hour I was born:[2]
I'm not light-hearted or aggrieved,
not a stranger or a local,
    can't be another way,
because I was bewitched one night
    high on a mountain top.[3]

1. Translated by David L. Pike. This is a *devinelh,* or "riddle-poem."
2. This would allow him to determine the astrological influences on his character.
3. A conventional setting for pagan rituals and secret ceremonies.

I do not know when I'm asleep
or when I wake, if no one says;
my heart's this close to being split
apart by a heartache,
and it's not worth a mouse to me,
I swear by St. Martial![4]

I'm sick and shaken up to death,
don't know a thing that I'm not told;
I'll seek a doctor to my taste,
but I don't know anyone;
a good one if he makes me well,
but not if I get worse.

I've got a friend, I don't know who,
I've never seen her, by my faith;[5]
she gives me neither joy nor grief,
and I don't care a bit;
for neither Norman nor the Frank
has been in my domain.[6]

Never seen her and love her well,
she's never done me right or wrong;
when I don't see her, I have fun
and I don't give a cock,
'cause I know one more beautiful,
and nicer and worth more.

Don't know the place where she may be,
if it's up high or on the plain;
don't dare to tell the wrong she does
before it's bothered me.
It weighs on me that I stay here,
and so I'd better go.

I've made this verse on who knows who,
And I'll send it to the one who
will send it to another one
over there near Anjou,[7]
who will send from a little case
the counter-key to me.[8]

4. An early bishop of Limoges in south-central France. Popular legend made him a 1st-century apostle responsible for converting the entire region of Aquitaine to Christianity, and for the performance of many miracles.

5. Here Guillem parodies the troubadour convention of falling in love with a woman on the strength of her reputation, or of hearsay.

6. Guillem's neighbors to the north and east of Aquitaine. The Normans ("men of the north") were Viking raiders who preyed upon and eventually settled the north coast of France during the 8th and 9th centuries. The indigenous population of Franks ceded them the coastal lands that became Normandy.

7. The duchy of Anjou was just north of the duchy of Poitou, the seat of Guillem's power.

8. The "counter-key" or explanation to the meaning of the poem's enigmatic lines—scholars have not yet reached agreement as to whether it is pure nonsense, a straightforward parody of courtly lyric, or a philosophical riddle. Most likely, it is a bit of all three.

In the sweet time of renewal[1]

In the sweet time of renewal
the woods are in leaf and the birds
in song, each in its own language,
following the new song's verses;
thus men do well to take their ease
with whatever they most desire.

From where beauty and goodness dwell
I see neither message nor seal,
and so I neither sleep nor laugh,
nor do I dare start anything
until I can know for certain
if all is as I have asked.

Our love goes along in this way
as the branch of the hawthorn[2] does,
when it is trembling on the tree
all night in the rain and the frost,
until next day when the sun shines
through the branches and the green leaves.

Still I remember one morning
when we made a truce to our war,
and when she gave so great a gift
to me, her gallant love and ring:
still, God, let me live long enough
to get my hands under her cloak.

For I don't worry their language
may keep me from my Good Neighbor,[3]
since I know how it goes with words,
with short talk that runs on and on;
while such types go on about love,
we have a piece of it, and the knife.

Bernart de Ventadorn

fl. 1150–1180

"When I see the skylark moving" (*Can vei la lauzeta mover*) is the most celebrated lyric of the most celebrated troubadour, about whom we know many legends but no facts, although he probably belonged to the court of Eleanor of Aquitaine. These legends and the forty-five-odd songs that accompany them epitomize Occitan *fin'amor.* Here, Bernart's words and music use the lark and

1. Translated by David L. Pike.
2. In the calendar of the ancient Celts, the hawthorn tree heralded the end of winter. It was a fertility symbol, and its white blossoms would adorn the maypole in May Day festivities.
3. As is customary in the *tornada* or envoi (concluding, farewell stanza), the name is a *senhal,* or hidden name.

its song to dramatize soaring hope and bottomless despair as conditions experienced both physically and spiritually, revelling in the sorrowful plight of the lover spurned by his powerful lady.

When I see the skylark moving[1]

When I see the skylark moving
its wings with joy against the sun,[2]
forgetting it lets itself fall
as sweetness goes through its heart,
ah! such envy comes into me
of anyone I see joyful,
I'm filled with wonder that just then
my heart does not melt with desire.

Alas! I thought I knew so much
of love, and how much less I know,
for I cannot keep from loving
the one whose prize I'll never have.
She has my whole heart and myself,
and herself and all the world;
she took herself from me and left
desire and a wanting heart.

I never have been self-possessed
nor have I been my own man since
she let me see into her eyes,
a mirror that so pleases me.
Mirror, since I looked into you,
deep-rooted sighs have struck me dead,
so that I lost myself as in
the fountain fair Narcissus did.[3]

I've lost all my hope in women;
I'll place my faith in them no more;
just as I used to support them,
from this point on I'll let them go.
Since I see none to help against
The one who ruins and confounds me,
I'll disbelieve and fear them all,
for I well know they're all alike.

She shows well that she's a woman,
my lady, so I reproach her,
for she wants not what one should want,
and what's forbidden her, she does.
I have fallen into ill grace,

1. Translated by David L. Pike.
2. The common lark of Europe is known as the skylark because of its habit of flying toward the sky when it sings.
3. In Greek and Roman myth, the beautiful Narcissus was punished for spurning the love of Echo by falling in love with his own reflection in the water. Unable to tear himself away, Narcissus wasted away and was transformed by the gods into the white flower that bears his name. (See Ovid's *Metamorphoses*, page 779.) The Mirror of Narcissus became a powerful emblem of the pleasures and hazards of the self-love inherent in the ethos of courtly love.

acting like the fool on the bridge;[4]
I don't know how I reached this point,
but I climbed the mountain too high.

In truth, grace and mercy are lost,
And I never knew it till now,
for she who ought to have them most
has none, so now where shall I search?
Ah! who would suspect, seeing her,
she would allow this wretch to die
full of longing, and not aid him,
who will have no good without her.

Since my lady esteems nothing,
not prayers nor mercy nor my rights,[5]
nor is it pleasing to her that
I love her, I'll say it no more.
So I'll part from her and give up;
she's killed me, I reply with death,
and leave, since she's not retained me,
wretched, in exile, who knows where.

Tristan,[6] you'll have nothing from me,
for I've gone, wretched, who knows where.
I've thrown over song, given up,
hiding out from joy and from love.

Beatriz, Comtessa de Dia

fl. c. 1160

According to the fanciful *Life* that accompanies her five extant lyrics, the Comtessa de Dia was the wife of Guillem de Peiteus and fell in love with another troubadour, Raimbaut Count of Orange, "in whose honor," it says, "she wrote many fine songs." This makes for good poetry but mediocre history, and as with most of the twenty or so *trobairitz* who have been identified, it is all we know about her. Fortunately, the lyrics speak for themselves.

To sing of what I would not want I must[1]

To sing of what I would not want I must,
for he whose friend I am so rankles me;
I love him more than anything there is.

4. Bernart refers to a proverb: the fool tries to ride across a narrow bridge, and falls; the wise man dismounts before crossing.
5. The rights of the troubadour-lover according to the conventions of *fin'amor.*
6. This is a "hidden name," probably chosen in homage to the legendary Celtic lover, Tristan; it may refer either to a lady or to another poet.
1. Translated by David L. Pike.

To him my courtliness is of no worth,
Not my grace, my beauty, esteem or wit;
And so I am beguiled and betrayed
as I would be if I were lowly born.

This thing consoles me: I never failed once
toward you, my friend, in my actions; no,
my love's more than Seguin's for Valensa.[2]
It pleases me I've vanquished you with love,
o my friend, for you are the worthiest;
with me you're proud in word as well as deed
although you're frank with everyone else.

I marvel how your heart's so full of pride,
my friend, toward me, that's reason to grieve;
it's not right that you're seized by another,
however she may speak or receive you.
And remember how the beginning was
of our love! May the Lord God never wish
that my fault lead to our separation.

That great prowess so at ease in your frame
and the rich merit you have trouble me;
not one woman do I know far or near,
who desiring love leans not toward you;
but you, my friend, are surely well aware
that you well know how to choose the finest;
and remember the exchanges we shared.

My worth and high standing should help me here,
my beauty and especially my fine heart;
wherefore I am sending to your estate
this song, that it may be my messenger,
and wish to know, my fair and gentle friend,
wherefore you are so wild and cruel to me;
I don't know if you're proud or wish me ill.

But more I wish you'd tell him, messenger,
that too much pride has much harm done to men.[3]

I have been in great distress[1]

I have been in great distress
for a knight for whom I longed;
I want all future times to know
how I loved him to excess.

2. Seguin and Valensa were lovers in a romance that has not survived.

3. The threat, not unusual in itself in the *tornado* of a troubadour poem, receives a neat twist from the female poet's position as the more powerful of the pair of lovers according to the conventions of *fin'amor.*

1. Translated by Peter Dronke. This *canso* (love poem) has identical rhymes in all the stanzas.

Now I see I am betrayed—
he claims I did not give him love—
such was the mistake I made,
naked in bed, and dressed.

How I'd long to hold him pressed
naked in my arms one night—
if I could be his pillow once,
would he not know the height of bliss?
Floris was all to Blanchefleur,[2]
yet not so much as I am his:
I am giving my heart, my love,
my mind, my life, my eyes.

Fair, gentle lover, gracious knight,
if once I held you as my prize
and lay with you a single night
and gave you a love-laden kiss—
my greatest longing is for you
to lie there in my husband's place,
but only if you promise this:
to do all I'd want to do.[3]

Bertran de Born

c. 1140–c. 1215

Bertran would be immortalized in canto 28 of Dante's *Inferno* among the "sowers of discord" (page 1262), but the vitriol of his nearly 50 surviving poems reflects the plight of a petty nobleman dependent for his livelihood on the spoils of warfare in a tumultuous time of shifting allegiances. The satirical song below attacks Richard the Lion-Hearted in its *tornada,* or envoi. Bertran joined a failed revolt against Richard (Duke of Aquitaine and Poitiers) and his father Henry II of England by a party of nobles led by the king's eldest son, "The young King" Henry, who died in 1183. Bertran's castle was burned and he was taken prisoner, but he later managed to win Richard's pardon.

I love the glad time of Easter[1]

I love the glad time of Easter,
that makes leaves and flowers come out;
and I love when I hear the joy
of the birds, which makes their song

2. Lovers in a medieval romance. In the most popular version, Floire (Floris) is son of a Moorish king of Spain who falls in love with the daughter of a Christian slave (of noble blood) with whom he has grown up.

3. In the conventions of Occitan lyric, the love affair is always adulterous, although not always portrayed as directly and physically as the Comtessa de Dia chooses to do here.

1. Translated by David L. Pike. The attribution of this song to Bertran is not certain.

resound throughout the woods;
and I love when I see the fields
planted with tents and pavilions;
and I truly rejoice
when I see the countryside ranged
with knights and horses armed for war.[2]

And I love it when the runners[3]
make the people flee with their goods;
and I love to see after them
an army's massed ranks on the move;
and in my heart I love
to see a strong castle besieged,
the ramparts breached and broken in,
and to see the host on the shore,
closed in, surrounded by ditches,
with rows of strong stakes intertwined.

And I love just as much the lord,
when he is first in the assault
astride his horse, armed, unafraid;
thus he emboldens his vassals
with valiant and lordly deeds.
And then when battle is joined,
each man must hold himself ready
and follow him with a light heart,
for no man is of any worth,
till he's given what he's received.

Maces and swords, bright-colored helms,
shields to slice through and to strip,
we'll see as the melee begins,
vassals all fighting together,
wandering, on the loose,
horses of the dead and fallen.
When the battle has been engaged,
any truly noble man
wants only to cleave heads and arms,
better off dead than caught, alive.

I tell you nothing is sweeter,
not eating, drinking, or sleeping,
than when I hear the call to "Charge!"
from both sides and I hear neighing
horses in the shadows, bare,
and I hear calls "To aid! To aid!"
and I see fall into ditches

2. The poem begins with the conventional springtime setting of a pleasure song such as Guillem de Peiteus's "In the sweet time of renewal" (page 1182), before turning abruptly to the pleasures of war rather than love.

3. Soldiers who carry messages ahead of the front lines.

the great and small on the grass,
and I see the bodies whose sides
the silken streaming lance has pierced.

Barons, mortgage your castles
and your villages and your towns
before you think of stopping war![4]

Papiols, light-heartedly
speed your way to Lord Yes-and-No;
tell him he's been at peace too long.[5]

[END OF TROUBADOURS AND *TROBAIRITZ*]

Marie de France

mid-12th–early 13th century

What we know for certain about the author of the *Lais* is neither more nor less than the name she gives herself: *Sui Marie e sui de France* ("I am Marie and am from France"). She wrote in the French dialect called Anglo-Norman, probably for the French-speaking Norman audience in England around the court of Henry II and Eleanor of Aquitaine. It has been conjectured from her familiarity with court life that she may have been an illegitimate half-sister to Henry; she was in all likelihood of noble blood. The *Lais* are her best and best-known work; a collection of animal fables and a translation of a Latin otherworld journey, *St. Patrick's Purgatory,* have also been attributed to her. The *Lais* is a group of short narratives in verse, tales of courtly love and adventure based on the oral traditions of Brittany. The Norman conquest of 1066 had opened up a vogue for the *matière de Bretagne,* the Celtic legends that included those of King Arthur and the lovers Tristan and Yseult.

Marie was writing at a time of enormous change in French society and culture. The tradition of tracing familial descent through the maternal side of the family had recently been supplanted by paternal ancestry. The orally based couplets of the traditional *chanson de geste,* or epic, had given way to the more musical and psychologically flexible eight-syllable couplets of the romance. As Marie translated her Celtic sources into French verse, she changed their focus as well, creating a series of ethical tests for her characters, male and female, in which she could explore the conflicts between social constraints and individual desire, and between real life and the world of fantasy. While rooted in the world of legend, the *Lais* are also concerned with the complex politics of the feudal court. The knight Lanval, for example, suffers first from his lack of status at Arthur's court, and then, like the later Gawain in *Sir Gawain and the Green Knight,* from his lack of poise in fending off the unwanted advances of a powerful ruler, Queen Guinevere.

Legendary motifs are strongly in evidence. The plot of *Bisclavret,* for example, turns on the protagonist's monthly transformation into a wolf. In other tales, we find self-guiding boats, magical women, a man who can transform himself into a bird, a woman who can appear invisibly to her lover, and a potion bestowing superhuman strength. Marie wields these motifs strategically to demarcate places where the cold reality of the feudal structure is incompatible

4. Feudal barons were often hard put to finance the forces they were expected to raise when lords to whom they owed ties of fealty summoned them to war.

5. Papiols is the name of Bertran's *jongleur,* or performer; Lord Yes-and-No is Richard the Lion-Hearted (1157–1199).

with the more fanciful demands of the individual. In the conventional tale of chivalry, the knight would ride out, seeking to test himself through adventures. But in Marie's world, adventure tends to seek out the knights and ladies, and their response to an unforeseen event or encounter will determine their failure or success in the world. In *Bisclavret,* the wife, the werewolf, and the king are presented in turn with crucial ethical decisions that have no obvious cultural precedent. The scenario of the brief tale *Chevrefoil,* based on the famous legend of Tristan and Yseult, is more limited. Here Marie ignores the best-known parts—the love potion accidentally drunken by Tristan and the bride he is bringing to King Mark or the efforts of the king and his courtiers' to catch the adulterous couple in the act. Instead, Marie selects a little-known episode following the knight's banishment. The adventure that befalls the lovers is a chance meeting; their proper response to this opportunity determines the possibility of a brief, perfect moment of union.

Marie's characters do not reveal themselves through their thoughts, as modern protagonists tend to do. They discover themselves, and we are asked to analyze them, through their actions, and through comparison from one *lai* to the next. The *Lais* are structured like a series of permutations of a fixed set of variables in a laboratory experiment. We find the positive counterpart of Bisclavret's wife in *Eliduc,* for example, and his tragic counterpart in the bird-man of *Yonec.* It is evident that the *Lais* had a didactic component along with their role as court entertainment. The feudal system was based on the exchange of loyalty for land and protection, guided by a complex code of behavior, and resulting in a constantly shifting set of allegiances. The role of women in this society was especially contradictory. An apparently powerful queen and patron such as Eleanor of Aquitaine could just as easily be locked in a tower for fifteen years, as she was by Henry II between 1174 and 1189. Rulers such as Eleanor and Marie, countess of Champagne, could patronize the arts, and women such as Marie could be prominent poets and authors while possessing little or no actual power, being regarded primarily as items of barter, providers of land and heirs. These women were celebrated as goddesses of love while deprived of any agency to act on that love. Marie's female characters both embody this double bind and find ways of negotiating what modicum of freedom and happiness might be possible within it.

PRONUNCIATIONS:

Bisclavret: bees-KLAH-vray
Chevrefoil: CHEV-r'foy

from LAIS

Prologue[1]

Whoever has received knowledge
and eloquence in speech from God
should not be silent or secretive
but demonstrate it willingly.
When a great good is widely heard of,
then, and only then, does it bloom,
and when that good is praised by many,
it has spread its blossoms.
The custom among the ancients—
as Priscian testifies—
was to speak quite obscurely
in the books they wrote,

1. Translated by Joan M. Ferrante and Robert W. Hanning. Like many medieval prologues, this one takes a series of commonplaces and gives them a particular spin. The first theme derives from Jesus's parable of the talents (Matthew 25:14–32). Marie justifies her writing the *lais* as the laudable exercise of a God-given talent.

so that those who were to come after
and study them
might gloss° the letter *explain*
and supply its significance from their own wisdom.[2]
Philosophers knew this,
they understood among themselves
that the more time they spent,
the more subtle their minds would become
and the better they would know how to keep themselves
from whatever was to be avoided.
He who would guard himself from vice
should study and understand
and begin a weighty work
by which he might keep vice at a distance,
and free himself from great sorrow.[3]
That's why I began to think
about composing some good stories
and translating from Latin to Romance;
but that was not to bring me fame:
too many others have done it.
Then I thought of the *lais* I'd heard.
I did not doubt, indeed I knew well,
that those who first began them
and sent them forth
composed them in order to preserve
adventures they had heard.[4]
I have heard many told;
and I don't want to neglect or forget them.
To put them into word and rhyme
I've often stayed awake.

In your honor, noble King,[5]
who are so brave and courteous,
repository of all joys
in whose heart all goodness takes root,
I undertook to assemble these *lais*
to compose and recount them in rhyme.
In my heart I thought and determined,
sire, that I would present them to you.
If it pleases you to receive them,
you will give me great joy;
I shall be happy forever.

2. Priscian (fl. c. 500 C.E.) wrote what became the standard textbook of Latin grammar in the Middle Ages, the *Institutiones grammaticae* ("Grammatical Foundations"). "Glossing" a text meant not only explaining its grammatical constructions, but also revealing allegorical meaning hidden beneath the "letter" or literal meaning of the words.

3. Here, studying and glossing provide an occupation that both removes temptation toward more vicious activities and distracts the mind from sorrow. This could either mean the tribulations of Fortune (in a philosophical context) or the sufferings of love (in a courtly context, as below).

4. Rather than the classical themes she has been enumerating, Marie proposes the novelty of the *lais*, oral folktales rather than written manuscripts.

5. It was customary for the prologue to conclude with a dedication to the poet's patron, here most likely Henry II.

Do not think me presumptuous
if I dare present them to you.
Now hear how they begin.

Bisclavret (The Werewolf)

Since I am undertaking to compose *lais,*
I don't want to forget Bisclavret;
In Breton, the *lai*'s name is *Bisclavret*—
the Normans call it *The Werewolf.*[1]
In the old days, people used to say—
and it often actually happened—
that some men turned into werewolves
and lived in the woods.
A werewolf is a savage beast;
while his fury is on him
he eats men, does much harm,
goes deep in the forest to live.
But that's enough of this for now:
I want to tell you about the Bisclavret.

In Brittany there lived a nobleman
whom I've heard marvelously praised;
a fine, handsome knight
who behaved nobly.
He was close to his lord,
and loved by all his neighbors.
He had an estimable wife,
one of lovely appearance;
he loved her and she him,
but one thing was very vexing to her:
during the week he would be missing
for three whole days, and she didn't know
what happened to him or where he went.
Nor did any of his men know anything about it.
One day he returned home
happy and delighted;
she asked him about it.
"My lord," she said, "and dear love,
I'd very much like to ask you one thing—
if I dared;
but I'm so afraid of your anger
that nothing frightens me more."
When he heard that, he embraced her,
drew her to him and kissed her.
"My lady," he said, "go ahead and ask!
There's nothing you could want to know,

1. "*Garwaf.*" As in the Prologue, Marie emphasizes the task of translation, explaining the meaning of key words in both languages

that, if I knew the answer, I wouldn't tell you."
"By God," she replied, "now I'm cured!
My lord, on the days when you go away from me
I'm in such a state—
so sad at heart,
so afraid I'll lose you—
that if I don't get quick relief
I could die of this very soon.
Please, tell me where you go,
where you have been staying.
I think you must have a lover,
and if that's so, you're doing wrong."
"My dear," he said, "have mercy on me, for God's sake!
Harm will come to me if I tell you about this,
because I'd lose your love
and even my very self."
When the lady heard this
she didn't take it lightly;
she kept asking him,
coaxed and flattered him so much,
that he finally told her what happened to him—
he hid nothing from her.
"My dear, I become a werewolf:
I go off into the great forest,
in the thickest part of the woods,
and I live on the prey I hunt down."
When he had told her everything,
she asked further
whether he undressed or kept his clothes on.° *as a werewolf*
"Wife," he replied, "I go stark naked."
"Tell me, then, for God's sake, where your clothes are."
"That I won't tell you;
for if I were to lose them,
and then be discovered,
I'd stay a werewolf forever.
I'd be helpless
until I got them back.
That's why I don't want their hiding place to be known."
"My lord," the lady answered,
"I love you more than all the world;
you mustn't hide anything from me
or fear me in any way:
that doesn't seem like love to me.
What wrong have I done? For what sin of mine
do you mistrust me about anything?
Do the right thing and tell me!"
She harassed and bedeviled him so,
that he had no choice but to tell her.
"Lady," he said, "near the woods,

beside the road that I use to get there,
there's an old chapel
that has often done me good service;
under a bush there is a big stone,
hollowed out inside;
I hide my clothes right there
until I'm ready to come home."
The lady heard this wonder
and turned scarlet from fear;
she was terrified of the whole adventure.
Over and over she considered
how she might get rid of him;
she never wanted to sleep with him again.
There was a knight of that region
who had loved her for a long time,
who begged for her love,
and dedicated himself to serving her.
She'd never loved him at all,
nor pledged her love to him,
but now she sent a messenger for him,
and told him her intention.
"My dear," she said, "cheer up!
I shall now grant you without delay
what you have suffered for;
you'll meet with no more refusals—
I offer you my love and my body;
make me your mistress!"
He thanked her graciously
and accepted her promise,
and she bound him to her by an oath.
Then she told him
how her husband went away and what happened to him;
she also taught him the precise path
her husband took into the forest,
and then she sent the knight to get her husband's clothes.
So Bisclavret was betrayed,
ruined by his own wife.
Since people knew he was often away from home
they all thought
this time he'd gone away forever.
They searched for him and made inquiries
but could never find him,
so they had to let matters stand.
The wife later married the other knight,
who had loved her for so long.
A whole year passed
until one day the king went hunting;
he headed right for the forest
where Bisclavret was.

When the hounds were unleashed,
they ran across Bisclavret;
the hunters and the dogs
chased him all day,
until they were just about to take him
and tear him apart,
at which point he saw the king
and ran to him, pleading for mercy.
He took hold of the king's stirrup,
kissed his leg and his foot.
The king saw this and was terrified;
he called his companions.
"My lords," he said, "come quickly!
Look at this marvel—
this beast is humbling itself to me.
It has the mind of a man, and it's begging me for mercy!
Chase the dogs away,
and make sure no one strikes it.
This beast is rational—he has a mind.
Hurry up: let's get out of here.
I'll extend my peace to the creature;
indeed, I'll hunt no more today!"
Thereupon the king turned away.
Bisclavret followed him;
he stayed close to the king, and wouldn't go away;
he'd no intention of leaving him.
The king led him to his castle;
he was delighted with this turn of events,
for he'd never seen anything like it.
He considered the beast a great wonder
and held him very dear.
He commanded all his followers,
for the sake of their love for him, to guard Bisclavret well,
and under no circumstances to do him harm;
none of them should strike him;
rather, he should be well fed and watered.
They willingly guarded the creature;
every day he went to sleep
among the knights, near the king.
Everyone was fond of him;
he was so noble and well behaved
that he never wished to do anything wrong.
Regardless of where the king might go,
Bisclavret never wanted to be separated from him;
he always accompanied the king.
The king became very much aware that the creature loved him.
Now listen to what happened next.
The king held a court;
to help him celebrate his feast

and to serve him as handsomely as possible,
he summoned all the barons
who held fiefs from him.[2]
Among the knights who went,
and all dressed up in his best attire,
was the one who had married Bisclavret's wife.
He neither knew nor suspected
that he would find Bisclavret so close by.
As soon as he came to the palace
Bisclavret saw him,
ran toward him at full speed,
sank his teeth into him, and started to drag him down.
He would have done him great damage
if the king hadn't called him off,
and threatened him with a stick.
Twice that day he tried to bite the knight.
Everyone was extremely surprised,
since the beast had never acted that way
toward any other man he had seen.
All over the palace people said
that he wouldn't act that way without a reason:
that somehow or other, the knight had mistreated Bisclavret,
and now he wanted his revenge.
And so the matter rested
until the feast was over
and until the barons took their leave of the king
and started home.
The very first to leave,
to the best of my knowledge,
was the knight whom Bisclavret had attacked.
It's no wonder the creature hated him.
Not long afterward,
as the story leads me to believe,
the king, who was so wise and noble,
went back to the forest
where he had found Bisclavret,
and the creature went with him.
That night, when he finished hunting,
he sought lodging out in the countryside.
The wife of Bisclavret heard about it,
dressed herself elegantly,
and went the next day to speak with the king,
bringing rich presents for him.
When Bisclavret saw her coming,
no one could hold him back;
he ran toward her in a rage.

2. Who were bound to him in oaths of fealty.

Now listen to how well he avenged himself!
He tore the nose off her face.
What worse thing could he have done to her?
Now men closed in on him from all sides;
they were about to tear him apart,
when a wise man said to the king,
"My lord, listen to me!
This beast has stayed with you,
and there's not one of us
who hasn't watched him closely,
hasn't traveled with him often.
He's never touched anyone,
or shown any wickedness,
except to this woman.
By the faith that I owe you,
he has some grudge against her,
and against her husband as well.
This is the wife of the knight
whom you used to like so much,
and who's been missing for so long—
we don't know what became of him.
Why not put this woman to torture
and see if she'll tell you
why the beast hates her?[3]
Make her tell what she knows!
We've seen many strange things
happen in Brittany!"
The king took his advice;
he detained the knight.
At the same time he took the wife
and subjected her to torture;
out of fear and pain
she told all about her husband:
how she had betrayed him
and taken away his clothes;
the story he had told her
about what happened to him and where he went;
and how after she had taken his clothes
he'd never been seen in his land again.
She was quite certain
that this beast was Bisclavret.
The king demanded the clothes;
whether she wanted to or not
she sent home for them,
and had them brought to Bisclavret.
When they were put down in front of him

3. Torture was a common means of interrogation, especially for gaining confessions. The king's advisor takes the beast's attack as evidence of the lady's guilt.

he didn't even seem to notice them;
the king's wise man—
the one who had advised him earlier—
said to him, "My lord, you're not doing it right.
This beast wouldn't, under any circumstances,
in order to get rid of his animal form,
put on his clothes in front of you;
you don't understand what this means:
he's just too ashamed to do it here.
Have him led to your chambers
and bring the clothes with him;
then we'll leave him alone for a while.
If he turns into a man, we'll know about it."
The king himself led the way
and closed all the doors on him.
After a while he went back,
taking two barons with him;
all three entered the king's chamber.
On the king's royal bed
they found the knight asleep.
The king ran to embrace him.
He hugged and kissed him again and again.
As soon as he had the chance,
the king gave him back all his lands;
he gave him more than I can tell.
He banished the wife,
chased her out of the country.
She went into exile with the knight
with whom she had betrayed her lord.
She had several children
who were widely known
for their appearance:
several women of the family
were actually born without noses,
and lived out their lives noseless.[4]

The adventure that you have heard
really happened, no doubt about it.
The *lai* of Bisclavret was made
so it would be remembered forever.

Chevrefoil (The Honeysuckle)

I should like very much
to tell you the truth
about the *lai* men call *Chevrefoil*—
why it was composed and where it came from.

4. The *lai* includes a folktale-style explanation of the origin of a physical defect in the family. It also suggests that punishment for misbehavior will be passed through the generations.

Many have told and recited it to me
and I have found it in writing,
about Tristan and the queen
and their love that was so true,
that brought them much suffering
and caused them to die the same day.[1]
King Mark was annoyed,
angry at his nephew Tristan;
he exiled Tristan from his land
because of the queen whom he loved.[2]
Tristan returned to his own country,
South Wales, where he was born,
he stayed a whole year;
he couldn't come back.
Afterward he began to expose himself
to death and destruction.
Don't be surprised at this:
for one who loves very faithfully
is sad and troubled
when he cannot satisfy his desires.
Tristan was sad and worried,
so he set out from his land.
He traveled straight to Cornwall,
where the queen lived,
and entered the forest all alone—
he didn't want anyone to see him;
he came out only in the evening
when it was time to find shelter.
He took lodging that night,
with peasants, poor people.
He asked them for news
of the king—what he was doing.
They told him they had heard
that the barons had been summoned by ban.
They were to come to Tintagel
where the king wanted to hold his court;[3]
at Pentecost they would all be there,[4]
there'd be much joy and pleasure,
and the queen would be there too.

1. The tragic love affair of Tristan and Yseult was based on a Celtic legend. There were various written sources Marie could have known, including the Anglo-Norman version of Thomas (c. 1170), composed at the court of Henry II, which was also Gottfried von Strassburg's source. The episode she recounts, however, doesn't exist in other versions, although she assumes her audience was familiar with them, not even naming Yseult ("the queen").

2. Mark, king of Cornwall, had sent Tristan to Ireland to win Yseult as his queen. A love potion caused the pair to fall in love, and when Mark discovered their affair, he banished his nephew.

3. The Norman castle of Tintagel, on the northwestern coast of Cornwall, was built on the site of a Celtic monastery held to be the birthplace of King Arthur.

4. Pentecost, or Whitsunday, commemorates the descent of the Holy Spirit upon the disciples, seven Sundays after the resurrection of Christ. It was a major spring festival in the Christian year, and, along with Christmas and Easter, a traditional time for a king to hold full court.

Tristan heard and was very happy;
she would not be able to go there
without his seeing her pass.
The day the king set out,
Tristan also came to the woods
by the road he knew
their assembly must take.
He cut a hazel tree in half,
then he squared it.
When he had prepared the wood,
he wrote his name on it with his knife.
If the queen noticed it—
and she should be on the watch for it,
for it had happened before
and she had noticed it then—
she'd know when she saw it,
that the piece of wood had come from her love.
This was the message of the writing
that he had sent to her:
he had been there a long time,
had waited and remained
to find out and to discover
how he could see her,
for he could not live without her.
With the two of them it was just
as it is with the honeysuckle
that attaches itself to the hazel tree:
when it has wound and attached
and worked itself around the trunk,
the two can survive together;
but if someone tries to separate them,
the hazel dies quickly
and the honeysuckle with it.
"Sweet love, so it is with us:
You cannot live without me, nor I without you."
The queen rode along;
she looked at the hillside
and saw the piece of wood; she knew what it was,
she recognized all the letters.
The knights who were accompanying her,
who were riding with her,
she ordered to stop:
she wanted to dismount and rest.
They obeyed her command.
She went far away from her people
and called her girl
Brenguein,[5] who was loyal to her.

5. Yseult's companion and waiting-woman; Brenguein plays an important role in the Tristan romances.

She went a short distance from the road;
and in the woods she found him
whom she loved more than any living thing.
They took great joy in each other.
He spoke to her as much as he desired,
she told him whatever she liked.
Then she assured him
that he would be reconciled with the king—
for it weighed on him
that he had sent Tristan away;
he'd done it because of the accusation.[6]
Then she departed, she left her love,
but when it came to the separation,
they began to weep.
Tristan went to Wales,
to wait until his uncle sent for him.
For the joy that he'd felt
from his love when he saw her,
by means of the stick he inscribed
as the queen had instructed,
and in order to remember the words,
Tristan, who played the harp well,
composed a new *lai* about it.
I shall name it briefly:
in English they call it *Goat's Leaf*
the French call it *Chevrefoil.*[7]
I have given you the truth
about the *lai* that I have told here.

Sir Gawain and the Green Knight

late 14th century

Like the verdant half-giant whose intrusion initiates and concludes its action, *Sir Gawain and the Green Knight* is a dominant and inescapable, but also a mysterious and inexplicable presence in medieval English poetry. Like *Beowulf* before it, it survives in a single manuscript. Its importance was not appreciated until the nineteenth century, it is written in a now obscure dialect of Middle English, and its author is destined to remain anonymous. But the intrigue of its history is nothing to the spell of the poem itself. While his contemporary Chaucer set the language and poetic conventions of French and Italian within a narrative frame of everyday realism, the *Gawain*-poet (as scholars refer to the poem's author) made everyday reality fit the adventures and wonders of the Arthurian romance, the (primarily French) tales of King Arthur and his knights that were the most popular reading material of the English aristocracy of the day.

6. Like most courtly lovers, Tristan and Yseult were harassed by ill-wishing courtiers or *losengiers,* who try to trap them. King Mark, meanwhile, would prefer to believe that the affair does not exist.

7. As in *Bisclavret,* Marie emphasizes her title word (and the meaning embodied in it) through a focus on its translation.

The poem is divided into four "fits," or sections—the right length for an evening's performance to entertain a noble patron and his courtiers. Like the other three poems contained in the manuscript—also most likely by the *Gawain*-poet—it is written in the Middle English dialect of the northwest Midlands, perhaps Cheshire near the border with Wales. Like Chaucer, the *Gawain*-poet was quite familiar with the Anglo-Norman dialect of Old French that had been used at the court since the Norman Conquest, as well as the Latin that had been used by clerics throughout the Middle Ages, but his vocabulary also bears many traces of the Scandinavian rulers the Normans had superseded. Danish and other Viking invaders had held northern England from the mid-ninth until the mid-eleventh century, and their language—not to mention the alliterative poetry bequeathed by earlier Anglo-Saxon colonizers—filters into the poem, just as its wildness bespeaks a northern attitude toward nature and the world quite different from the southward-gazing culture of London. Literate Englanders were conversant with both traditions, however; Chaucer several times parodied the alliterating verse incomprehensible to the "Southren" man, who preferred his lines to rhyme. Having disappeared (at least from written sources) following the Norman Conquest, the alliterative tradition of stressed, unrhymed lines had been revived during the second half of the fourteenth century; still, the new wave for which Chaucer implicitly argued, the rhyming couplets and London dialect that would dominate English poetry for centuries, had won the day by the early fifteenth century.

As one would expect from a poem composed in a self-consciously local language and poetic form, *Gawain* is all about traditions, customs, and conventions. It begins by recounting the legend of *translatio imperii,* tracing Arthur's lineage back to the fall of Troy. Set during the midwinter festival of Christmas, the action is then introduced by one of Arthur's rules for feasting: "he wolde never ete / Upon such a dere day er hym devised were / Of sum aventurus thing an uncouthe tale, / Of sum mayn mervayle, that he might trawe"—he will not sit at table until some marvel or adventure occurs beforehand that he can "trawe," trust or believe. A marvel appears to order: a hulking knight, dressed in green from head to toe, and green of skin besides, who proposes a shocking Beheading Game. These marvelous motifs have their origin in French romance as well as in the nature cults of pre-Christian Britain. The knight Gawain's acceptance of the game will require him to seek out the Green Knight the following winter, in order to receive the blow his adversary has miraculously survived. This quest frames the story, but in the middle, the poet introduces an apparently unconnected episode of temptation and testing in the remote castle of a noble lord and his seductive lady. Only at the very end does the poet reveal the significance of these two stories, and the way they are related to one another as tests of Gawain's faith and mettle.

Rather than reconcile his different sources and different traditions, the *Gawain*-poet strikes a fine if precarious balance between them, asking the reader to consider the ramifications of Gawain's choices and predicament, both for himself and for those around him. Nor is the *Gawain*-poet concerned to spell out for his readers how seriously he expects this tale to be taken, and whether we are meant to sympathize with Gawain or to smile at his predicament. It seems that the life of a knight hangs in the balance, and even more so his honor and that of the court to which he belongs, and the Christian virtues associated with that court in the High Middle Ages. But high spirits reign throughout, at Arthur's court, in the manners of the Green Knight, and at the castle of Sir Bertilak de Hautdesert and his queen. In a tale of chivalry such as Marie de France's *Bisclavret* (page 1191), there is nothing outside the court for the werewolf beside the alienated inhumanity of the beast; his sufferings show us how essential civility and trust are to society. By contrast, although the Green Knight probably derives from Celtic traditions of the wild man of the woods, he poses a legitimate challenge to the Christian court. He knows its customs, but flaunts them; he conducts himself in the exuberance of arrogant confidence, even as he exposes his neck for the blow of Gawain's axe; he follows some unknown code of conduct, and this makes his appearance all the more uncanny in the familiar world of Camelot.

The poet has other ways of keeping our expectations agreeably off-balance. Just as the Green Knight's challenge recalls but also mutates the pattern of Arthurian adventures, so

Gawain's journey to find the unknown site where he must keep his appointment with death gives a surprising twist to the knight errant's customary questing. His goal is fantastic, as is the castle that appears in answer to his Christmas Eve prayers, but the landscape is described in the palpably realistic terms of a northern winter, and the path he takes would have been recognized by readers of the time as the principal route from the south of England through Wales to the region of Cheshire. In a similar fashion, activities at the castle are carefully balanced: for three consecutive days, the lord of the castle rides out hunting, while his lady remains at home, engaging Gawain in amorous games and testing his ability to juggle the rules of courtly love with those of hospitality and honor. Each evening, the two knights "exchange" the "trophies" they have "won" during the day, the wild game of the one for the kisses of the other.

The form of the poem is also a balance of meters, and of control and disorder. Each of its 101 stanzas contains a varying number of long lines: syllables range in number from seven to fourteen, and stressed alliterating consonants vary as well, although three is most normal. Each stanza concludes with what is called a "bob and wheel"—a two-syllable line plus four slightly longer lines, rhymed in an *ababa* scheme, as if in a gesture to the rhyming verse of the Continental romance. Take, for example, the extraordinary scene of the 23-line twentieth stanza, as the headless torso of the Green Knight has just picked up his bleeding head from where it had skipped about the banquet-room floor:

For the hede in his honde he haldez up even,
Toward the derrest on the dece he dressez the face,
And hit lyfte up the yghe-lyddez and loked ful brode,
And meled thus much with his muthe, as ye may now here:
"Loke, Gawan, thou be graythe to go as thou hettez,
And layte as lelly til thou me, lude, fynde,
As thou hatz hette in this halle, herande thise knyghtes;
To the grene chapel thou chose, I charge the, to fotte
Such a dunt as thou hatz dalt, disserved thou habbez
To be yederly yolden on Nw Yeres morn.
The knyght of the grene chapel men knowen me mony,
Forthi me for to fynde if thou fraystez, faylez thou never.
Therfore com, other recreaunt be calde thou behoves."
With a runisch rout the raynez he tornez,
Halled out at the hal dor, his hed in his hande,
That the fyr of the flynt flaghe fro fole hoves.
To quat kyth he becom knwe non there,
Never more than thay wyste from quethen he watz wonnen.
What thenne?
The kyng and Gawan thare
At that grene thay laghe and grenne;
Yet breved watz hit ful bare
A mervayl among tho menne.

(Tolkien, Gordon, and Davis edition)

For the head in his hand he held it up straight,
towards the fairest at the table he twisted the face,
and it lifted up its eyelids and looked at them broadly,
and made such words with its mouth as may be recounted.
"See thou get ready, Gawain, to go as thou vowedst,
and as faithfully seek till thou find me, good sir,
as thou hast promised in this place in the presence of these knights.

To the Green Chapel go thou, and get thee, I charge thee,
such a dint as thou hast dealt—indeed thou hast earned
a nimble knock in return on New Year's morning!
The Knight of the Green Chapel I am known to many,
so if to find me thou endeavor, thou'lt fail not to do so.
Therefore come! Or to be called a craven thou deservest."
With a rude roar and rush his reins he turned then,
and hastened out through the hall-door with his head in his hand,
and fire of the flint flew from the feet of his charger.
To what country he came in that court no man knew,
no more than they had learned from what land he had journeyed.
Meanwhile,
the king and Sir Gawain
at the Green Man laugh and smile;
yet to men had appeared, 'twas plain,
a marvel beyond denial.

The unhurried rhythm of the alliterative lines emphasizes the uncanny lack of hurry in the headless knight's actions, his half-mocking, half-somber mood seemingly unaffected by Gawain's blow. The brevity of the bob-and-wheel perfectly captures the dumbfounded reaction of the king and Gawain to the baffling event they have seen. We don't know whether they are grimacing out of horror, laughing out of defiance, or chuckling in disbelief, and the near-identity of *grene* and *grenne* ("green" and "grin") combines with the alliteration to increase the difficulty of interpreting what has happened. Moreover, the final two lines balance the prior pair, redefining the Old French romance term *mervayl* to capture precisely this combination of laughter, horror and incomprehension.

And yet, this melodious Continental label cannot erase the lingering dread of the harsh Anglo-Saxon syllables of the Green Man's insistence on what Gawain had *hette,* or pledged, *to fotte / such a dunt as thou hatz dalt,* literally, "to fetch such a dint as thou hast dealt." The *Gawain*-poet knew Dante's *Commedia* well, but what a world of difference there is between this talking head and the dripping "lantern" held up by the dead poet Bertran de Born in the eighth circle of Hell (page 1175)! The head of Dante's poet damns his body in a tragic image of abuse of the gift of language and eloquence, elaborating the Christian law whereby, through his sins, Bertran has equally severed himself from the blessed body of the saved in Heaven. The *Gawain*-poet shares with Dante the use of vivid realism to bring alive an impossible image, but the Green Knight escapes the constraints of the familiar Christian setting of the Christmas Eve feast in the Arthurian court, just as his actions exceed the bounds of decorum, and his body mocks the laws of nature. Like Gawain's ambiguous adversary, this poem delights in its inscrutable power over its audience, and revels in its own refusal to be controlled.

Sir Gawain and the Green Knight[1]

Part 1

When the siege and the assault had ceased at Troy,
and the fortress fell in flame to firebrands and ashes,
the traitor who the contrivance of treason there fashioned
was tried for his treachery, the most true upon earth—

1. This translation, remarkably faithful to the original alliterative meter and stanza form, is by J. R. R. Tolkien.

it was Aeneas[2] the noble and his renowned kindred
who then laid under them lands, and lords became
of well-nigh all the wealth in the Western Isles.[3]
When royal Romulus to Rome his road had taken,
in great pomp and pride he peopled it first,
and named it with his own name that yet now it bears;
Tirius[4] went to Tuscany and towns founded,
Langaberde[5] in Lombardy uplifted halls,
and far over the French flood Felix Brutus
on many a broad bank and brae[6] Britain established
full fair,
where strange things, strife and sadness,
at whiles in the land did fare,
and each other grief and gladness
oft fast have followed there.

And when fair Britain was founded by this famous lord,[7]
bold men were bred there who in battle rejoiced,
and many a time that betid they troubles aroused.
In this domain more marvels have by men been seen
than in any other that I know of since that olden time;
but of all that here abode in Britain as kings
ever was Arthur most honoured, as I have heard men tell.
Wherefore a marvel among men I mean to recall,
a sight strange to see some men have held it,
one of the wildest adventures of the wonders of Arthur.
If you will listen to this lay but a little while now,
I will tell it at once as in town I have heard
it told,
as it is fixed and fettered
in story brave and bold,
thus linked and truly lettered,
as was loved in this land of old.

This king lay at Camelot[8] at Christmas-tide
with many a lovely lord, lieges most noble,
indeed of the Table Round[9] all those tried brethren,
amid merriment unmatched and mirth without care.
There tourneyed many a time the trusty knights,
and jousted full joyously these gentle lords;

2. Aeneas led the survivors of Troy to Italy, after a series of ambiguous omens and misadventures. In medieval tradition, he was also said to have plotted to betray his own city. "The traitor" in l. 3, though, may refer to the Trojan Antenor, also said to have betrayed Troy.
3. Perhaps Europe, or just the British Isles. Many royal houses traced their ancestry to Rome and Troy.
4. Possibly Titus Tatius, ancient king of the Sabines.
5. Ancestor of the Lombards, and a nephew of Brutus.
6. The steep bank bounding a river valley.
7. According to Geoffrey of Monmouth and others, a great-grandson of Aeneas, exiled after accidentally killing his father and later the founder of Britain.
8. Arthur's capital, probably in Wales, perhaps at Caerleon-on-Usk where Arthur had been crowned. Knights were expected to gather at his court, in celebration and homage, on the five liturgical holidays on which Arthur wore his crown: Easter, Ascension, Pentecost, All Saints' Day, and Christmas.
9. Its shape symbolized the unity of Arthur's knights but also avoided disputes over precedence.

then to the court they came at carols to play.
For there the feast was unfailing full fifteen days,
with all meats and all mirth that men could devise,
such gladness and gaiety as was glorious to hear,
din of voices by day, and dancing by night;
all happiness at the highest in halls and in bowers
had the lords and the ladies, such as they loved most dearly.
With all the bliss of this world they abode together,
the knights most renowned after the name of Christ,
and the ladies most lovely that ever life enjoyed,
and he, king most courteous, who that court possessed.
For all that folk so fair did in their first estate[1]
 abide,
Under heaven the first in fame,
their king most high in pride;
it would now be hard to name
a troop in war so tried.

While New Year was yet young that yestereve had arrived,
that day double dainties on the dais were served,
when the king was there come with his courtiers to the hall,
and the chanting of the choir in the chapel had ended.
With loud clamour and cries both clerks and laymen
Noel announced anew, and named it full often;
then nobles ran anon with New Year gifts,
Handsels,° handsels they shouted, and handed them out, *gifts*
Competed for those presents in playful debate;
ladies laughed loudly, though they lost the game,
and he that won was not woeful, as may well be believed.[2]
All this merriment they made, till their meat was served;
then they washed, and mannerly went to their seats,
ever the highest for the worthiest, as well held to be best.
Queen Guinevere the gay was with grace in the midst
of the adorned dais[3] set. Dearly was it arrayed:
finest sendal° at her sides, a ceiling above her *thin silk*
of true tissue of Toulouse, and tapestries of Tharsia
that were embroidered and bound with the brightest gems
one might prove and appraise to purchase for coin
 any day.
That loveliest lady there
on them glanced with eyes of grey;
that he found ever one more fair
in sooth might no man say.

1. Arthur is emphatically a young king here, even "boyish." The phrase may also recall the Golden Age, an era of uncorrupted happiness.

2. The distribution of New Year's gifts displayed the king's wealth and power; it was also the occasion here of some courtly game of exchange, in which the loser perhaps gave up a kiss.

3. A medieval nobleman's hall typically had a raised platform at one end, on which the "high table" stood.

But Arthur would not eat until all were served;
his youth made him so merry with the moods of a boy,
he liked lighthearted life, so loved he the less
either long to be lying or long to be seated:
so worked on him his young blood and wayward brain.
And another rule moreover was his reason besides
that in pride he had appointed: it pleased him not to eat
upon festival so fair, ere he first were apprised
of some strange story or stirring adventure,
or some moving marvel that he might believe in
of noble men, knighthood, or new adventures;
or a challenger should come a champion seeking
to join with him in jousting, in jeopardy to set
his life against life, each allowing the other
the favour of fortune, were she fairer to him.
This was the king's custom, wherever his court was holden,
at each famous feast among his fair company
in hall.
So his face doth proud appear,
and he stands up stout and tall,
all young in the New Year;
much mirth he makes with all.

Thus there stands up straight the stern king himself,
talking before the high table of trifles courtly.
There good Gawain was set at Guinevere's side,
with Agravain a la Dure Main on the other side seated,
both their lord's sister-sons, loyal-hearted knights.
Bishop Baldwin had the honour of the board's service,
and Iwain Urien's[4] son ate beside him.
These dined on the dais and daintily fared,
and many a loyal lord below at the long tables.
Then forth came the first course with fanfare of trumpets,
on which many bright banners bravely were hanging;
noise of drums then anew and the noble pipes,[5]
warbling wild and keen, wakened their music,
so that many hearts rose high hearing their playing.
Then forth was brought a feast, fare of the noblest,
multitude of fresh meats on so many dishes
that free places were few in front of the people
to set the silver things full of soups on cloth
so white.
Each lord of his liking there
without lack took with delight:
twelve plates to every pair,
good beer and wine all bright.

4. Another nephew of Arthur. The relationship of uncle and nephew is close in many Arthurian romances, and noble youths were often sent to be raised by an uncle on the mother's side.

5. Holiday banquets were formalized, almost theatrical.

Now of their service I will say nothing more,
for you are all well aware that no want would there be.
Another noise that was new drew near on a sudden,
so that their lord might have leave at least to take food.
For hardly had the music but a moment ended,
and the first course in the court as was custom been served,
when there passed through the portals a perilous horseman,
the mightiest on middle-earth in measure of height,
from his gorge to his girdle so great and so square,
and his loins and his limbs so long and so huge,
that half a troll upon earth I trow° that he was, *trust; believe*
but the largest man alive at least I declare him;
and yet the seemliest for his size that could sit on a horse,
for though in back and in breast his body was grim,
both his paunch and his waist were properly slight,
and all his features followed his fashion so gay
in mode;
for at the hue men gaped aghast
in his face and form that showed;
as a fay-man fell he passed,
and green all over glowed.

All of green were they made, both garments and man:
a coat tight and close that clung to his sides;
a rich robe above it all arrayed within
with fur finely trimmed, shewing fair fringes
of handsome ermine gay, as his hood was also,
that was lifted from his locks and laid on his shoulders;
and trim hose tight-drawn of tincture alike
that clung to his calves; and clear spurs below
of bright gold on silk broideries banded most richly,
though unshod were his shanks, for shoeless he rode.
And verily all this vesture was of verdure clear,
both the bars on his belt, and bright stones besides
that were richly arranged in his array so fair,
set on himself and on his saddle upon silk fabrics:
it would be too hard to rehearse one half of the trifles
that were embroidered upon them, what with birds and with flies
in a gay glory of green, and ever gold in the midst.
The pendants of his poitrel,° his proud crupper, *breast-plate*
his molains,° and all the metal to say more, were enamelled, *mouthpiece*
even the stirrups that he stood in were stained of the same;
and his saddlebows in suit, and their sumptuous skirts,
which ever glimmered and glinted all with green jewels;
even the horse that upheld him in hue was the same,
I tell:
a green horse great and thick,
a stallion stiff to quell,
in broidered bridle quick:
he matched his master well.

Very gay was this great man guised all in green,
and the hair of his head with his horse's accorded:
fair flapping locks enfolding his shoulders,
a big beard like a bush over his breast hanging
that with the handsome hair from his head falling
was sharp shorn to an edge just short of his elbows,
so that half his arms under it were hid, as it were
in a king's capadoce[6] that encloses his neck.
The mane of that mighty horse was of much the same sort,
well curled and all combed, with many curious knots
woven in with gold wire about the wondrous green,
ever a strand of the hair and a string of the gold;
the tail and the top-lock were twined all to match
and both bound with a band of a brilliant green:
with dear jewels bedight° to the dock's ending, *fastened*
and twisted then on top was a tight-knitted knot
on which many burnished bells of bright gold jingled.
Such a mount on middle-earth, or man to ride him,
was never beheld in that hall with eyes ere that time;
    for there
  his glance was as lightning bright,
  so did all that saw him swear;
  no man would have the might,
  they thought, his blows to bear.

And yet he had not a helm, nor a hauberk[7] either,
not a pisane,[8] not a plate that was proper to arms;
not a shield, not a shaft, for shock or for blow,
but in his one hand he held a holly-bundle,
that is greatest in greenery when groves are leafless,
and an axe in the other, ugly and monstrous,
a ruthless weapon aright for one in rhyme to describe:
the head was as large and as long as an ellwand,° *yardstick*
a branch of green steel and of beaten gold;
the bit, burnished bright and broad at the edge,
as well shaped for shearing as sharp razors;
the stem was a stout staff, by which sternly he gripped it,
all bound with iron about to the base of the handle,
and engraven in green in graceful patterns,
lapped round with a lanyard that was lashed to the head
and down the length of the haft was looped many times;
and tassels of price were tied there in plenty
to bosses of the bright green, braided most richly.
Such was he that now hastened in, the hall entering,
pressing forward to the dais—no peril he feared.
To none gave he greeting, gazing above them,

6. Probably a hooded cape, fastened under the chin.
7. A tunic of chain mail.
8. A piece of armor to protect the upper part of the chest and neck.

and the first word that he winged: "Now where is," he said,
"the governor of this gathering? For gladly I would
on the same set my sight, and with himself now talk
in town."
On the courtiers he cast his eye,
and rolled it up and down;
he stopped, and stared to espy
who there had most renown.

Then they looked for a long while, on that lord gazing;
for every man marvelled what it could mean indeed
that horseman and horse such a hue should come by
as to grow green as the grass, and greener it seemed,
than green enamel on gold glowing far brighter.
All stared that stood there and stole up nearer,
watching him and wondering what in the world he would do.
For many marvels they had seen, but to match this nothing;
wherefore a phantom and fay-magic folk there thought it,
and so to answer little eager was any of those knights,
and astounded at his stern voice stone-still they sat there
in a swooning silence through that solemn chamber,
as if all had dropped into a dream, so died their voices
away.
Not only, I deem, for dread;
but of some 'twas their courtly way
to allow their lord and head
to the guest his word to say.

Then Arthur before the high dais beheld this wonder,
and freely with fair words, for fearless was he ever,
saluted him, saying: "Lord, to this lodging thou'rt welcome!
The head of this household Arthur my name is.
Alight, as thou lovest me, and linger, I pray thee;
and what may thy wish be in a while we shall learn."
"Nay, so help me," quoth the horseman, "He that on high is throned,
to pass any time in this place was no part of my errand.
But since thy praises, prince, so proud are uplifted,
and thy castle and courtiers are accounted the best,
the stoutest in steel-gear that on steeds may ride,
most eager and honourable of the earth's people,
valiant to vie with in other virtuous sports,
and here is knighthood renowned, as is noised in my ears:
'tis that has fetched me hither, by my faith, at this time.
You may believe by this branch that I am bearing here
that I pass as one in peace,[9] no peril seeking.
For had I set forth to fight in fashion of war,
I have a hauberk at home, and a helm also,

9. A holly branch could symbolize peace and was used in games of the Christmas season.

a shield, and a sharp spear shining brightly,
and other weapons to wield too, as well I believe;
but since I crave for no combat, my clothes are softer.
Yet if thou be so bold, as abroad is published,
thou wilt grant of thy goodness the game that I ask for
        by right."
    Then Arthur answered there,
    and said: "Sir, noble knight,
    if battle thou seek thus bare,
    thou'lt fail not here to fight."

"Nay, I wish for no warfare, on my word I tell thee!
Here about on these benches are but beardless children.
Were I hasped in armour on a high charger,
there is no man here to match me—their might is so feeble.
And so I crave in this court only a Christmas pastime,
since it is Yule and New Year, and you are young here and merry.
If any so hardy in this house here holds that he is,
if so bold be his blood or his brain be so wild,
that he stoutly dare strike one stroke for another,
then I will give him as my gift this guisarm[1] costly,
this axe—'tis heavy enough—to handle as he pleases;
and I will abide the first brunt, here bare as I sit.
If any fellow be so fierce as my faith to test,
hither let him haste to me and lay hold of this weapon—
I hand it over for ever, he can have it as his own—
and I will stand a stroke from him, stock-still on this floor,
provided thou'lt lay down this law: that I may deliver him another.
        Claim I!
    And yet a respite I'll allow,
    till a year and a day go by.
    Come quick, and let's see now
    if any here dare reply!"

If he astounded them at first, yet stiller were then
all the household in the hall, both high men and low.
The man on his mount moved in his saddle,
and rudely his red eyes he rolled then about,
bent his bristling brows all brilliantly green,
and swept round his beard to see who would rise.
When none in converse would accost him, he coughed then loudly,
stretched himself haughtily and straightway exclaimed:
"What! Is this Arthur's house," said he thereupon,
"the rumour of which runs through realms unnumbered?
Where now is your haughtiness, and your high conquests,
your fierceness and fell mood, and your fine boasting?
Now are the revels and the royalty of the Round Table

1. A long-handled ax with a spike at the end.

overwhelmed by a word by one man spoken,
for all blench now abashed ere a blow is offered!"
With that he laughed so loud that their lord was angered,
the blood shot for shame into his shining cheeks
and face;
as wroth as wind he grew,
so all did in that place.
Then near to the stout man drew
the king of fearless race,

And said: "Marry! Good man, 'tis madness thou askest,
and since folly thou hast sought, thou deservest to find it.
I know no lord that is alarmed by thy loud words here.
Give me now thy guisarm, in God's name, sir,
and I will bring thee the blessing thou hast begged to receive."
Quick then he came to him and caught it from his hand.
Then the lordly man loftily alighted on foot.
Now Arthur holds his axe, and the haft grasping
sternly he stirs it about, his stroke considering.
The stout man before him there stood his full height,
higher than any in that house by a head and yet more.
With stern face as he stood he stroked at his beard,
and with expression impassive he pulled down his coat,
no more disturbed or distressed at the strength of his blows
than if someone as he sat had served him a drink
of wine.
From beside the queen Gawain
to the king did then incline:
"I implore with prayer plain
that this match should now be mine."

"Would you, my worthy lord," said Gawain to the king,
"bid me abandon this bench and stand by you there,
so that I without discourtesy might be excused from the table,
and my liege lady were not loth to permit me,
I would come to your counsel before your courtiers fair.
For I find it unfitting, as in fact it is held,
when a challenge in your chamber makes choices so exalted,
though you yourself be desirous to accept it in person,
while many bold men about you on bench are seated:
on earth there are, I hold, none more honest of purpose,
no figures fairer on field where fighting is waged.
I am the weakest, I am aware, and in wit feeblest,
and the least loss, if I live not, if one would learn the truth.
Only because you are my uncle is honour given me:
save your blood in my body I boast of no virtue;
and since this affair is so foolish that it nowise befits you,
and I have requested it first, accord it then to me!
If my claim is uncalled-for without cavil shall judge
this court."

To consult the knights draw near,
and this plan they all support;
the king with crown to clear,
and give Gawain the sport.

The king then commanded that he quickly should rise,
and he readily uprose and directly approached,
kneeling humbly before his highness, and laying hand on the weapon;
and he lovingly relinquished it, and lifting his hand
gave him God's blessing, and graciously enjoined him
that his hand and his heart should be hardy alike.
"Take care, cousin," quoth the king, "one cut to address,
and if thou learnest him his lesson, I believe very well
that thou wilt bear any blow that he gives back later."
Gawain goes to the great man with guisarm in hand,
and he boldly abides there—he blenched not at all.
Then next said to Gawain the knight all in green:
"Let's tell again our agreement, ere we go any further.
I'd know first, sir knight, thy name; I entreat thee
to tell it me truly, that I may trust in thy word."
"In good faith," quoth the good knight, "I Gawain am called
who bring thee this buffet, let be what may follow;
and at this time a twelvemonth in thy turn have another
with whatever weapon thou wilt, and in the world with none else
but me."
The other man answered again:
"I am passing pleased," said he,
"upon my life, Sir Gawain,
that this stroke should be struck by thee.

"Begad," said the green knight, "Sir Gawain, I am pleased
to find from thy fist the favour I asked for!
And thou hast promptly repeated and plainly hast stated
without abatement the bargain I begged of the king here;
save that thou must assure me, sir, on thy honour
that thou'lt seek me thyself, search where thou thinkest
I may be found near or far, and fetch thee such payment
as thou deliverest me today before these lordly people."
"Where should I light on thee," quoth Gawain, "where look for thy place?
I have never learned where thou livest, by the Lord that made me,
and I know thee not, knight, thy name nor thy court.
But teach me the true way, and tell what men call thee,
and I will apply all my purpose the path to discover:
and that I swear thee for certain and solemnly promise."
"That is enough in New Year, there is need of no more!"
said the great man in green to Gawain the courtly.
"If I tell thee the truth of it, when I have taken the knock,
and thou handily hast hit me, if in haste I announce then
my house and my home and mine own title,
then thou canst call and enquire and keep the agreement;

and if I waste not a word, thou'lt win better fortune,
for thou mayst linger in thy land and look no further—
but stay!
To thy grim tool now take heed, sir!
Let us try thy knocks today!"
"Gladly," said he, "indeed, sir!"
and his axe he stroked in play.

The Green Knight on the ground now gets himself ready,
leaning a little with the head he lays bare the flesh,
and his locks long and lovely he lifts over his crown,
letting the naked neck as was needed appear.
His left foot on the floor before him placing,
Gawain gripped on his axe, gathered and raised it,
from aloft let it swiftly land where 'twas naked,
so that the sharp of his blade shivered the bones,
and sank clean through the clear fat and clove it asunder,
and the blade of the bright steel then bit into the ground.
The fair head to the floor fell from the shoulders,
and folk fended it with their feet as forth it went rolling;
the blood burst from the body, bright on the greenness,
and yet neither faltered nor fell the fierce man at all,
but stoutly he strode forth, still strong on his shanks,
and roughly he reached out among the rows that stood there,
caught up his comely head and quickly upraised it,
and then hastened to his horse, laid hold of the bridle,
stepped into stirrup-iron, and strode up aloft,
his head by the hair in his hand holding;
and he settled himself then in the saddle as firmly
as if unharmed by mishap, though in the hall he might wear
no head.
His trunk he twisted round,
that gruesome body that bled,
and many fear then found,
as soon as his speech was sped.

For the head in his hand he held it up straight,
towards the fairest at the table he twisted the face,
and it lifted up its eyelids and looked at them broadly,
and made such words with its mouth as may be recounted.
"See thou get ready, Gawain, to go as thou vowedst,
and as faithfully seek till thou find me, good sir,
as thou hast promised in this place in the presence of these knights.
To the Green Chapel go thou, and get thee, I charge thee,
such a dint as thou hast dealt—indeed thou hast earned
a nimble knock in return on New Year's morning!
The Knight of the Green Chapel I am known to many,
so if to find me thou endeavour, thou'lt fail not to do so.
Therefore come! Or to be called a craven thou deservest."
With a rude roar and rush his reins he turned then,

and hastened out through the hall-door with his head in his hand,
and fire of the flint flew from the feet of his charger.
To what country he came in that court no man knew,
no more than they had learned from what land he had journeyed.
    Meanwhile,
  the king and Sir Gawain
  at the Green Man laugh and smile;
  yet to men had appeared, 'twas plain,
  a marvel beyond denial.

Though Arthur the high king in his heart marvelled,
he let no sign of it be seen, but said then aloud
to the queen so comely with courteous words:
"Dear Lady, today be not downcast at all!
Such cunning play well becomes the Christmas tide,
interludes,[2] and the like, and laughter and singing,
amid these noble dances of knights and of dames.
Nonetheless to my food I may fairly betake me,
for a marvel I have met, and I may not deny it."
He glanced at Sir Gawain and with good point he said:
"Come, hang up thine axe, sir![3] It has hewn now enough."
And over the table they hung it on the tapestry behind,
where all men might remark it, a marvel to see,
and by its true token might tell of that adventure.
Then to a table they turned, those two lords together,
the king and his good kinsman, and courtly men served them
with all dainties double, the dearest there might be,
with all manner of meats and with minstrelsy too.
With delight that day they led, till to the land came the night
    again.
  Sir Gawain, now take heed
  lest fear make thee refrain
  from daring the dangerous deed
  that thou in hand hast ta'en!

Part 2

With this earnest of high deeds thus Arthur began
the young year, for brave vows he yearned to hear made.
Though such words were wanting when they went to table,
now of fell work to full grasp filled with their hands.
Gawain was gay as he began those games in the hall,
but if the end be unhappy, hold it no wonder!
For though men be merry of mood when they have mightily drunk,
a year slips by swiftly, never the same returning;
the outset to the ending is equal but seldom.

2. Brief performances between the courses of the banquet.

3. A literal suggestion, but also an invitation to put the matter aside.

And so this Yule passed over and the year after,
and severally the seasons ensued in their turn:[1]
after Christmas there came the crabbed Lenten
that with fish tries the flesh and with food more meagre;
but then the weather in the world makes war on the winter,
cold creeps into the earth, clouds are uplifted,
shining rain is shed in showers that all warm
fall on the fair turf, flowers there open,
of grounds and of groves green is the raiment,
birds are busy a-building and bravely are singing
for sweetness of the soft summer that will soon be on
the way;
and blossoms burgeon and blow
in hedgerows bright and gay;
then glorious musics go
through the woods in proud array.

After the season of summer with its soft breezes,
when Zephyr goes sighing through seeds and herbs,
right glad is the grass that grows in the open,
when the damp dewdrops are dripping from the leaves,
to greet a gay glance of the glistening sun.
But then Harvest hurries in, and hardens it quickly,
warns it before winter to wax to ripeness.
He drives with his drought the dust, till it rises
from the face of the land and flies up aloft;
wild wind in the welkin° makes war on the sun, *the sky*
the leaves loosed from the linden alight on the ground,
and all grey is the grass that green was before:
all things ripen and rot that rose up at first,
and so the year runs away in yesterdays many,
and here winter wends again, as by the way of the world
it ought,
until the Michaelmas moon[2]
has winter's boding brought;
Sir Gawain then full soon
of his grievous journey thought.

And yet till All Hallows[3] with Arthur he lingered,
who furnished on that festival a feast for the knight
with much royal revelry of the Round Table.
The knights of renown and noble ladies
all for the love of that lord had longing at heart,
but nevertheless the more lightly of laughter they spoke:
many were joyless who jested for his gentle sake.

1. This famous passage on the cycle of seasons draws both on Germanic conventions of the battle of Winter and Summer, and on Romance springtime lyrics, the *reverdies.*

2. The harvest moon at Michaelmas, on September 29.

3. All Saints' Day, on November 1, another holiday on which Arthur presided, crowned, over his court.

For after their meal mournfully he reminded his uncle
that his departure was near, and plainly he said:
"Now liege-lord of my life, for leave I beg you.
You know the quest and the compact; I care not further
to trouble you with tale of it, save a trifling point:
I must set forth to my fate without fail in the morning,
as God will me guide, the Green Man to seek."
Those most accounted in the castle came then together,[4]
Iwain and Eric and others not a few,
Sir Doddinel le Sauvage, the Duke of Clarence,
Lancelot, and Lionel, and Lucan the Good,
Sir Bors and Sir Bedivere that were both men of might,
and many others of mark with Mador de la Porte.
All this company of the court the king now approached
to comfort the knight with care in their hearts.
Much mournful lament was made in the hall
that one so worthy as Gawain should wend on that errand,
to endure a deadly dint and deal no more
        with blade.
    The knight ever made good cheer,
    saying, "Why should I be dismayed?
    Of doom the fair or drear
    by a man must be assayed."

He remained there that day, and in the morning got ready,
asked early for his arms, and they all were brought him.
First a carpet of red silk was arrayed on the floor,
and the gilded gear in plenty there glittered upon it.
The stern man stepped thereon and the steel things handled,
dressed in a doublet of damask of Tharsia,
and over it a cunning capadoce that was closed at the throat
and with fair ermine was furred all within.
Then sabatons[5] first they set on his feet,
his legs lapped in steel in his lordly greaves,
on which the polains° they placed, polished and shining *knee-guards*
and knit upon his knees with knots all of gold;
then the comely cuisses that cunningly clasped
the thick thews of his thighs they with thongs on him tied;
and next the byrnie,° woven of bright steel rings *coat of mail*
upon costly quilting, enclosed him about;
and armlets well burnished upon both of his arms,
with gay elbow-pieces and gloves of plate,
and all the goodly gear to guard him whatever
        betide;

4. The list that follows would have recalled, especially to readers of French romances, other great quests and challenges encountered by Arthur's knights. The list's order may also suggest later and more tragic episodes in the Arthurian narrative, ending with Bedivere who throws Excalibur into a lake after Arthur is mortally wounded.
5. A foot-covering worn by warriors in armor.

coat-armour richly made,
gold spurs on heel in pride;
girt with a trusty blade,
silk belt about his side.

When he was hasped in his armour his harness was splendid:
the least latchet or loop was all lit with gold.
Thus harnessed as he was he heard now his Mass,
that was offered and honoured at the high altar;
and then he came to the king and his court-companions,
and with love he took leave of lords and of ladies;
and they kissed him and escorted him, and to Christ him commended.
And now Gringolet stood groomed, and girt with a saddle
gleaming right gaily with many gold fringes,
and all newly for the nonce nailed at all points;
adorned with bars was the bridle, with bright gold banded;
that apparelling proud of poitrel° and of skirts, *breast-plate*
and the crupper and caparison[6] accorded with the saddlebows:
all was arrayed in red with rich gold studded,
so that it glittered and glinted as a gleam of the sun.
Then he in hand took the helm and in haste kissed it:
strongly was it stapled and stuffed within;
it sat high upon his head and was hasped at the back,
and a light kerchief was laid o'er the beaver,° *visor*
all braided and bound[7] with the brightest gems
upon broad silken broidery, with birds on the seams
like popinjays depainted, here preening and there,
turtles and true-loves, entwined as thickly
as if many sempstresses had the sewing full seven winters
in hand.
A circlet of greater price
his crown about did band;
The diamonds point-device
there blazing bright did stand.

Then they brought him his blazon° that was of brilliant gules° *shield / red*
with the pentangle[8] depicted in pure hue of gold.
By the baldric° he caught it and about his neck cast it: *strap*
right well and worthily it went with the knight.
And why the pentangle is proper to that prince so noble
I intend now to tell you, though it may tarry my story.
It is a sign that Solomon once set on a time
to betoken Troth, as it is entitled to do;
for it is a figure that in it five points holdeth,

6. A cloth or covering spread over the saddle or harness of a horse, often gaily ornamented.
7. The technical language of armor is now joined by an equally technical description of needlework, for which English women were famous.
8. A five-pointed star and symbol of perfection and eternity, since it can be drawn with an uninterrupted line ending at the point of the star where it begins. Inscribed within a circle, it was called Solomon's seal.

and each line overlaps and is linked with another,
and every way it is endless; and the English, I hear,
everywhere name it the Endless Knot.
So it suits well this knight and his unsullied arms;
for ever faithful in five points, and five times under each,
Gawain as good was acknowledged and as gold refinéd,
devoid of every vice and with virtues adorned.
So there
the pentangle painted new
he on shield and coat did wear,
as one of word most true
and knight of bearing fair.

First faultless was he found in his five senses,
and next in his five fingers he failed at no time,
and firmly on the Five Wounds all his faith was set
that Christ received on the cross, as the Creed tells us;
and wherever the brave man into battle was come,
on this beyond all things was his earnest thought:
that ever from the Five Joys all his valour he gained
that to Heaven's courteous Queen once came from her Child.[9]
For which cause the knight had in comely wise
on the inner side of his shield her image depainted,
that when he cast his eyes thither his courage never failed.
The fifth five that was used, as I find, by this knight
was free-giving and friendliness first before all,
and chastity and chivalry ever changeless and straight,
and piety surpassing all points: these perfect five
were hasped upon him harder than on any man else.
Now these five series, in sooth, were fastened on this knight,
and each was knit with another and had no ending,
but were fixed at five points that failed not at all,
coincided in no line nor sundered either,
not ending in any angle anywhere, as I discover,
wherever the process was put in play or passed to an end.
Therefore on his shining shield was shaped now this knot,
royally with red gules upon red gold set:
this is the pure pentangle as people of learning
have taught.
Now Gawain in brave array
his lance at last hath caught.
He gave them all good day,
for evermore as he thought.

He spurned his steed with the spurs and sprang on his way
so fiercely that the flint-sparks flashed out behind him.
All who beheld him so honourable in their hearts were sighing,

9. Poems and meditations on the Virgin's joys and sorrows were widespread. Her five joys were the Annunciation, Nativity, Resurrection, Ascension, and Assumption.

and assenting in sooth one said to another,
grieving for that good man: "Before God, 'tis a shame
that thou, lord, must be lost, who art in life so noble!
To meet his match among men, Marry, 'tis not easy!
To behave with more heed would have behoved one of sense,
and that dear lord duly a duke to have made,
illustrious leader of liegemen in this land as befits him;
and that would better have been than to be butchered to death,
beheaded by an elvish man for an arrogant vaunt.
Who can recall any king that such a course ever took
as knights quibbling at court at their Christmas games!"
Many warm tears outwelling there watered their eyes,
when that lord so beloved left the castle
that day.
No longer he abode,
but swiftly went his way;
bewildering ways he rode,
as the book I heard doth say.

Now he rides thus arrayed through the realm of Logres,[1]
Sir Gawain in God's care, though no game now he found it.
Oft forlorn and alone he lodged of a night
where he found not afforded him such fare as pleased him.
He had no friend but his horse in the forests and hills,
no man on his march to commune with but God,
till anon he drew near unto Northern Wales.
All the isles of Anglesey he held on his left,
and over the fords he fared by the flats near the sea,
and then over by the Holy Head to high land again
in the wilderness of Wirral: there wandered but few
who with good will regarded either God or mortal.
And ever he asked as he went on of all whom he met
if they had heard any news of a knight that was green
in any ground thereabouts, or of the Green Chapel.
And all denied it, saying nay, and that never in their lives
a single man had they seen that of such a colour
could be.
The knight took pathways strange
by many a lonesome lea,
and oft his view did change
that chapel ere he could see.

Many a cliff he climbed o'er in countries unknown,
far fled from his friends without fellowship he rode.
At every wading or water on the way that he passed
he found a foe before him, save at few for a wonder;

1. Identified with England in Geoffrey of Monmouth, elsewhere a vaguer term for Arthur's kingdom. Here, Gawain is heading northward through Wales, then along the coast of the Irish Sea and into the forest of Wirral in Cheshire—a wild area and resort of outlaws in the 14th century.

and so foul were they and fell that fight he must needs.
So many a marvel in the mountains he met in those lands
that 'twould be tedious the tenth part to tell you thereof.
At whiles with worms he wars, and with wolves also,
at whiles with wood-trolls that wandered in the crags,
and with bulls and with bears and boars, too, at times;
and with ogres that hounded him from the heights of the fells.
Had he not been stalwart and staunch and steadfast in God,
he doubtless would have died and death had met often;
for though war wearied him much, the winter was worse,
when the cold clear water from the clouds spilling
froze ere it had fallen upon the faded earth.
Wellnigh slain by the sleet he slept ironclad
more nights than enow in the naked rocks,
where clattering from the crest the cold brook tumbled,
and hung high o'er his head in hard icicles.
Thus in peril and pain and in passes grievous
till Christmas-eve that country he crossed all alone
    in need.
  The knight did at that tide
  his plaint to Mary plead,
  her rider's road to guide
  and to some lodging lead.

By a mount in the morning merrily he was riding
into a forest that was deep and fearsomely wild,
with high hills at each hand, and hoar woods beneath
of huge aged oaks by the hundred together;
the hazel and the hawthorn were huddled and tangled
with rough ragged moss around them trailing,
with many birds bleakly on the bare twigs sitting
that piteously piped there for pain of the cold.
The good man on Gringolet goes now beneath them
through many marshes and mires, a man all alone,
troubled lest a truant at that time he should prove
from the service of the sweet Lord, who on that selfsame night
of a maid became man our mourning to conquer.
And therefore sighing he said: "I beseech thee, O Lord,
and Mary, who is the mildest mother most dear,
for some harbour where with honour I might hear the Mass
and thy Matins[2] tomorrow. This meekly I ask,
and thereto promptly I pray with Pater and Ave
    and Creed."[3]
  In prayer he now did ride,
  lamenting his misdeed;

2. First of the canonical hours of prayer and praise in monastic tradition, observed between midnight and dawn.

3. The Paternoster ("Our Father . . ."), Ave Maria ("Hail Mary . . ."), and Creed (the articles of the Christian faith).

he blessed him oft and cried,
"The Cross of Christ me speed!"

The sign on himself he had set but thrice,
ere a mansion he marked within a moat in the forest,
on a low mound above a lawn, laced under the branches
of many a burly bole° round about by the ditches: *tree trunk*
the castle most comely that ever a king possessed
placed amid a pleasaunce with a park all about it,
within a palisade of pointed pales° set closely *stakes*
that took its turn round the trees for two miles or more.
Gawain from the one side gazed on the stronghold
as it shimmered and shone through the shining oaks,
and then humbly he doffed his helm, and with honour he thanked
Jesus and Saint Julian,[4] who generous are both,
who had courtesy accorded him and to his cry harkened.
"Now bon hostel," quoth the knight, "I beg of you still!"
Then he goaded Gringolet with his gilded heels,
and he chose by good chance the chief pathway
and brought his master bravely to the bridge's end
at last.
That brave bridge was up-hauled,
the gates were bolted fast;
the castle was strongly walled,
it feared no wind or blast.

Then he stayed his steed that on the steep bank halted
above the deep double ditch that was drawn round the place.
The wall waded in the water wondrous deeply,
and up again to a huge height in the air it mounted,
all of hard hewn stone to the high cornice,
fortified under the battlement in the best fashion
and topped with fair turrets set by turns about
that had many graceful loopholes with a good outlook:
that knight a better barbican had never seen built.[5]
And inwards he beheld the hall uprising,
tall towers set in turns, and as tines° clustering *pinnacles*
the fair finials, joined featly, so fine and so long,
their capstones all carven with cunning and skill.
Many chalk-white chimneys he chanced to espy
upon the roofs of towers all radiant white;
so many a painted pinnacle was peppered about,
among the crenelles of the castle clustered so thickly
that all pared out of paper it appeared to have been.[6]
The gallant knight on his great horse good enough thought it,

4. Patron saint of hospitality.

5. The poet again revels in technical vocabulary, here architectural; this is a fashionable (if exaggerated) building of the 14th century.

6. Models in cut paper sometimes decorated elaborate feasts such as that at the beginning of the poem.

if he could come by any course that enclosure to enter,
to harbour in that hostel while the holy day lasted
with delight.
He called, and there came with speed
a porter blithe and bright;
on the wall he learned his need,
and hailed the errant knight.

"Good sir," quoth Gawain, "will you go with my message
to the high lord of this house for harbour to pray?"
"Yes, by Peter!"[7] quoth the porter, "and I promise indeed
that you will, sir, be welcome while you wish to stay here."
Then quickly the man went and came again soon,
servants bringing civilly to receive there the knight.
They drew down the great drawbridge, and duly came forth,
and on the cold earth on their knees in courtesy knelt
to welcome this wayfarer with such worship as they knew.
They delivered him the broad gates and laid them wide open,
and he readily bade them rise and rode o'er the bridge.
Several servants then seized the saddle as he alighted,
and many stout men his steed to a stable then led,
while knights and esquires anon descended
to guide there in gladness this guest to the hall.
When he raised up his helm many ran there in haste
to have it from his hand, his highness to serve;
his blade and his blazon both they took charge of.
Then he greeted graciously those good men all,
and many were proud to approach him, that prince to honour.
All hasped in his harness to hall they brought him,
where a fair blaze in the fireplace fiercely was burning.
Then the lord of that land leaving his chamber
Came mannerly to meet the man on the floor.
He said: "You are welcome at your wish to dwell here.
What is here, all is your own, to have in your rule
and sway."
"Grammercy!" quoth Gawain,
"May Christ you this repay!"
As men that to meet were fain
they both embraced that day.

Gawain gazed at the good man who had greeted him kindly,
and he thought bold and big was the baron of the castle,
very large and long, and his life at the prime:
broad and bright was his beard, and all beaver-hued,
stern, strong in his stance upon stalwart legs,
his face fell as fire, and frank in his speech;
and well it suited him, in sooth, as it seemed to the knight,

7. Swearing by St. Peter, keeper of the keys to heaven.

a lordship to lead untroubled over lieges trusty.
To a chamber the lord drew him, and charged men at once
to assign him an esquire to serve and obey him;
and there to wait on his word many worthy men were,
who brought him to a bright bower where the bedding was splendid:
there were curtains of costly silk with clear-golden hems,
and coverlets cunning-wrought with quilts most lovely
of bright ermine above, embroidered at the sides,
hangings running on ropes with red-gold rings,
carpets of costly damask that covered the walls
and the floor under foot fairly to match them.
There they despoiled him, speaking to him gaily,
his byrnie doing off and his bright armour.
Rich robes then readily men ran to bring him,
for him to change, and to clothe him, having chosen the best.
As soon as he had donned one and dressed was therein,
as it sat on him seemly with its sailing skirts,
then verily in his visage a vision of Spring
to each man there appeared, and in marvellous hues
bright and beautiful was all his body beneath.
That knight more noble was never made by Christ
they thought.
He came none knew from where,
but it seemed to them he ought
to be a prince beyond compare
in the field where fell men fought.

A chair before the chimney where charcoal was burning
was made ready in his room, all arrayed and covered
with cushions upon quilted cloths that were cunningly made.
Then a comely cloak was cast about him
of bright silk brocade, embroidered most richly
and furred fairly within with fells of the choicest
and all edged with ermine, and its hood was to match;
and he sat in that seat seemly and noble
and warmed himself with a will, and then his woes were amended.
Soon up on good trestles a table was raised[8]
and clad with a clean cloth clear white to look on;
there was surnape, salt-cellar, and silvern spoons.
He then washed as he would and went to his food,
and many worthy men with worship waited upon him;
soups they served of many sorts, seasoned most choicely,
in double helpings, as was due, and divers sorts of fish;
some baked in bread, some broiled on the coals,
some seethed, some in gravy savoured with spices,
and all with condiments so cunning that it caused him delight.

8. A castle's great hall had many uses; tables were set up for dining and then put aside or hung.

A fair feast he called it frankly and often,
graciously, when all the good men together there pressed him:
"Now pray,
this penance deign to take;
'twill improve another day!"[9]
The man much mirth did make,
for wine to his head made way.

Then inquiry and question were carefully put
touching personal points to that prince himself,
till he courteously declared that to the court he belonged
that high Arthur in honour held in his sway,
who was the right royal King of the Round Table,
and 'twas Gawain himself that as their guest now sat
and had come for that Christmas, as the case had turned out.
When the lord had learned whom luck had brought him,
loud laughed he thereat, so delighted he was,
and they made very merry, all the men in that castle,
and to appear in the presence were pressing and eager
of one who all profit and prowess and perfect manners
comprised in his person, and praise ever gained;
of all men on middle-earth he most was admired.
Softly each said then in secret to his friend:
"Now fairly shall we mark the fine points of manners,
and the perfect expressions of polished converse.
How speech is well spent will be expounded unasked,
since we have found here this fine father of breeding.
God has given us His goodness, His grace now indeed,
Who such a guest as Gawain has granted us to have!
When blissful men at board for His birth sing blithe
at heart,
what manners high may mean
this knight will now impart.
Who hears him will, I ween,
of love-speech learn some art."[1]

When his dinner was done and he duly had risen,
it now to the night-time very near had drawn.
The chaplains then took to the chapel their way
and rang the bells richly, as rightly they should,
for the solemn evensong of the high season.
The lord leads the way, and his lady with him;
into a goodly oratory gracefully she enters.
Gawain follows gladly, and goes there at once
and the lord seizes him by the sleeve and to a seat leads him,

9. An exchange of courtesies. Gawain has politely praised the many fish dishes; his hosts demur, remind him that Christmas Eve is a fast day, and promise him better meals later.

1. Though Gawain is engaged on a serious quest, his reputation as a graceful courtier and master in the arts of love has preceded him.

kindly acknowledges him and calls him by his name,
saying that most welcome he was of all guests in the world.
And he grateful thanks gave him, and each greeted the other,
and they sat together soberly while the service lasted.
Then the lady longed to look at this knight;
and from her closet she came with many comely maidens.
She was fairer in face, in her flesh and her skin,
her proportions, her complexion, and her port than all others,
and more lovely than Guinevere to Gawain she looked.
He came through the chancel to pay court to her grace;
leading her by the left hand another lady was there
who was older than she, indeed ancient she seemed,
and held in high honour by all men about her.
But unlike in their looks those ladies appeared,
for if the younger was youthful, yellow was the elder;
with rose-hue the one face was richly mantled,
rough wrinkled cheeks rolled on the other;
on the kerchiefs of the one many clear pearls were,
her breast and bright throat were bare displayed,
fairer than white snow that falls on the hills;
the other was clad with a cloth that enclosed all her neck,
enveloped was her black chin with chalk-white veils,
her forehead folded in silk, and so fumbled all up,
so topped up and trinketed and with trifles bedecked
that naught was bare of that beldame but her brows all black,
her two eyes and her nose and her naked lips,
and those were hideous to behold and horribly bleared;
that a worthy dame she was may well, fore God,
be said!
short body and thick waist,
with bulging buttocks spread;
more delicious to the taste
was the one she by her led.

When Gawain glimpsed that gay lady that so gracious looked,
with leave sought of the lord towards the ladies he went;
the elder he saluted, low to her bowing,
about the lovelier he laid then lightly his arms
and kissed her in courtly wise with courtesy speaking.
His acquaintance they requested, and quickly he begged
to be their servant in sooth, if so they desired.
They took him between them, and talking they led him
to a fireside in a fair room, and first of all called
for spices, which men sped without sparing to bring them,
and ever wine therewith well to their liking.
The lord for their delight leaped up full often,
many times merry games being minded to make;
his hood he doffed, and on high he hung it on a spear,
and offered it as an honour for any to win

who the most fun could devise at that Christmas feast—
"And I shall try, by my troth, to contend with the best
ere I forfeit this hood, with the help of my friends!"
Thus with laughter and jollity the lord made his jests
to gladden Sir Gawain with games that night
in hall,
until the time was due
that the lord for lights should call;
Sir Gawain with leave withdrew
and went to bed withal.

On the morn when every man remembers the time
that our dear Lord for our doom to die was born,
in every home wakes happiness on earth for His sake.
So did it there on that day with the dearest delights:
at each meal and at dinner marvellous dishes
men set on the dais, the daintiest meats.
The old ancient woman was highest at table,
meetly to her side the master he took him;
Gawain and the gay lady together were seated
in the center, where as was seemly the service began,
and so on through the hall as honour directed.
When each good man in his degree without grudge had been served,
there was food, there was festival, there was fullness of joy;
and to tell all the tale of it I should tedious find,
though pains I might take every point to detail.
Yet I ween that Gawain and that woman so fair
in companionship took such pleasure together
in sweet society soft words speaking,
their courteous converse clean and clear of all evil,
that with their pleasant pastime no prince's sport
compares.
Drums beat, and trumps men wind,
many pipers play their airs;
each man his needs did mind,
and they two minded theirs.

With much feasting they fared the first and the next day,
and as heartily the third came hastening after:
the gaiety of Saint John's day[2] was glorious to hear;
[with cheer of the choicest Childermas followed,]
and that finished their revels, as folk there intended,
for there were guests who must go in the grey morning.
So a wondrous wake they held, and the wine they drank,
and they danced and danced on, and dearly they carolled.[3]
At least when it was late their leave then they sought
to wend on their ways, each worthy stranger.

2. December 27, traditionally given over to drinking and celebration.

3. Danced in a ring.

Good-day then said Gawain, but the good man stayed him,
and led him to his own chamber to the chimney-corner,
and there he delayed him, and lovingly thanked him,
for the pride and pleasure his presence had brought,
for so honouring his house at that high season
and deigning his dwelling to adorn with his favour.
"Believe me, sir, while I live my luck I shall bless
that Gawain was my guest at God's own feast."
"Gramercy, sir," said Gawain, "but the goodness is yours,
all the honour is your own—may the High King repay you!
And I am under your orders what you ask to perform,
as I am bound now to be, for better or worse,
    by right."
  Him longer to retain
  the lord then pressed the knight;
  to him replied Gawain
  that he by no means might.

Then with courteous question he enquired of Gawain
what dire need had driven him on that festal date
with such keenness from the king's court, to come forth alone
ere wholly the holidays from men's homes had departed.
"In sooth, sir," he said, "you say but the truth:
a high errand and a hasty from that house brought me;
for I am summoned myself to seek for a place,
though I wonder where in the world I must wander to find it.
I would not miss coming nigh it on New Year's morning
for all the land in Logres, so our Lord help me!
And so, sir, this question I enquire of you here:
can you tell me in truth if you tale ever heard
of the Green Chapel, on what ground it may stand,
and of the great knight that guards it, all green in his colour?
For the terms of a tryst were between us established
to meet that man at that mark, if I remained alive,
and the named New Year is now nearly upon me,
and I would look on that lord, if God will allow me,
more gladly, by God's son, than gain any treasure.
So indeed, if you please, depart now I must.
For my business I have now but barely three days,
and I would fainer fall dead than fail in my errand."
Then laughing said the lord: "Now linger you must;
for when 'tis time to that tryst I will teach you the road.
On what ground is the Green Chapel—let it grieve you no more!
In your bed you shall be, sir, till broad is the day,
without fret, and then fare on the first of the year,
and come to the mark at midmorn, there to make what play
    you know.
  Remain till New Year's day,
  then rise and riding go!

We'll set you on your way,
'tis but two miles or so."

Then was Gawain delighted, and in gladness he laughed:
"Now I thank you a thousand times for this beyond all!
Now my quest is accomplished, as you crave it, I will
dwell a few days here, and else do what you order."
The lord then seized him and set him in a seat beside him,
and let the ladies be sent for to delight them the more,
for their sweet pleasure there in peace by themselves.
For love of him that lord was as loud in his mirth
as one near out of his mind who scarce knew what he meant.
Then he called to the knight, crying out loudly:
"You have promised to do whatever deed I propose.
Will you hold this behest here, at this moment?"
"Yes, certainly, sir," then said the true knight,
"while I remain in your mansion, your command I'll obey."
"Well," returned he, "you have travelled and toiled from afar,
and then I've kept you awake: you're not well yet, not cured;
both sustenance and sleep 'tis certain you need.
Upstairs you shall stay, sir, and stop there in comfort
tomorrow till Mass-time, and to a meal then go
when you wish with my wife, who with you shall sit
and comfort you with her company, till to court I return.
You stay,
and I shall early rouse,
and a-hunting wend my way."
Gawain gracefully bows:
"Your wishes I will obey."

"One thing more," said the master, "we'll make an agreement:
whatever I win in the wood at once shall be yours,
and whatever gain you may get you shall give in exchange.
Shall we swap thus, sweet man—come, say what you think!—
whether one's luck be light, or one's lot be better?"
"By God," quoth good Gawain, "I agree to it all,
and whatever play you propose seems pleasant to me."
"Done! 'Tis a bargain! Who'll bring us the drink?"
So said the lord of that land. They laughed one and all;
they drank and they dallied, and they did as they pleased,
these lords and ladies, as long as they wished,
and then with customs of France and many courtly phrases
they stood in sweet debate and soft words bandied,
and lovingly they kissed, their leave taking.
With trusty attendants and torches gleaming
they were brought at the last to their beds so soft,
one and all.
Yet ere to bed they came,
he the bargain did oft recall;
he knew how to play a game
the old governor of that hall.

Part 3

Before the first daylight the folk uprose:
the guests that were to go for their grooms they called;
and they hurried up in haste horses to saddle,
to stow all their stuff and strap up their bags.
The men of rank arrayed them, for riding got ready,
to saddle leaped swiftly, seized then their bridles,
and went off on their ways where their wish was to go.
The liege-lord of the land was not last of them all
to be ready to ride with a rout of his men;
he ate a hurried mouthful after the hearing of Mass,
and with horn to the hunting-field he hastened at once.[1]
When daylight was opened yet dimly on earth
he and his huntsman were up on their high horses.
Then the leaders of the hounds leashed them in couples,
unclosed the kennel-door and cried to them "out!"
and blew boldly on bugles three blasts full long.
Beagles bayed thereat, a brave noise making;
and they whipped and wheeled in those that wandered on a scent;
a hundred hunting-dogs, I have heard, of the best
were they.
To their stations keepers passed;
the leashes were cast away,
and many a rousing blast
woke din in the woods that day.

At the first burst of the baying all beasts trembled;
deer dashed through the dale by dread bewildered,
and hastened to the heights, but they hotly were greeted,
and turned back by the beaters, who boldly shouted.
They let the harts go past with their high antlers,
and the brave bucks also with their branching palms;
for the lord of the castle had decreed in the close season
that no man should molest the male of the deer.
The hinds were held back with hey! and ware!
the does driven with great din to the deep valleys:
there could be seen let slip a sleet of arrows;
at each turn under the trees went a twanging shaft
that into brown hides bit hard with barbéd head.
Lo! they brayed, and they bled, and on the banks they died;
and ever the hounds in haste hotly pursued them,
and hunters with high horns hurried behind them
with such a clamour and cry as if cliffs had been riven.
If any beast broke away from bowmen there shooting,
it was snatched down and slain at the receiving-station;

1. The hunts that follow, for all their violent energy, are as ritualized in their procedure as the earlier feasts and games. The poet delights in describing still another area of knightly lore. A number of contemporary treatises on hunting survive.

when they had been harried from the height and hustled to the waters,
the men were so wise in their craft at the watches below,
and their greyhounds were so great that they got them at once,
and flung them down in a flash, as fast as men could see
with sight.
The lord then wild for joy
did oft spur and oft alight,
and thus in bliss employ
that day till dark of night.

Thus in his game the lord goes under greenwood eaves,
and Gawain the bold lies in goodly bed,
lazing, till the walls are lit by the light of day,
under costly coverlet with curtains about him.
And as in slumber he strayed, he heard stealthily come
a soft sound at his door as it secretly opened;
and from under the clothes he craned then his head,
a corner of the curtain he caught up a little,
and looked that way warily to learn what it was.
It was the lady herself, most lovely to see,
that cautiously closed the door quietly behind her,
and drew near to his bed. Then abashed was the knight,
and lay down swiftly to look as if he slept;
and she stepped silently and stole to his bed,
cast back the curtain, and crept then within,
and sat her down softly on the side of the bed,
and there lingered very long to look for his waking.
He lay there lurking a long while and wondered,
and mused in his mind how the matter would go,
to what point it might pass—to some surprise, he fancied.
Yet he said to himself: "More seemly 'twould be
in due course with question to enquire what she wishes."
Then rousing he rolled over, and round to her turning
he lifted his eyelids with a look as of wonder,
and signed him with the cross, thus safer to be kept
aright.
With chin and cheeks so sweet
of blended red and white,
with grace them him did greet
small lips with laughter bright.

"Good morning, Sir Gawain!" said that gracious lady.
"You are a careless sleeper, if one can creep on you so!
Now quickly you are caught! If we come not to terms,
I shall bind you in your bed, you may be assured."
With laughter the lady thus lightly jested.
"Good morning to your grace!" said Gawain gaily.
"You shall work on me your will, and well I am pleased;
for I submit immediately, and for mercy I cry,
and that is best, as I deem, for I am obliged to do so."

Thus he jested in return with much gentle laughter:
"But if you would, lady gracious, then leave grant me,
and release your prisoner and pray him to rise,
I would abandon this bed and better array me;
the more pleasant would it prove then to parley with you."
"Nay, for sooth, fair sir," said the sweet lady,
"you shall not go from your bed! I will govern you better:
here fast shall I enfold you, on the far side also,
and then talk with my true knight that I have taken so.
For I wot° well indeed that Sir Gawain you are, *know*
to whom all men pay homage wherever you ride;
your honour, your courtesy, by the courteous is praised,
by lords, by ladies, by all living people.
And right here you now are, and we all by ourselves;
my husband and his huntsmen far hence have ridden,
other men are abed, and my maids also,
the door closed and caught with a clasp that is strong;
and since I have in this house one that all delight in,
my time to account I will turn, while for talk I chance
have still.
To my body will you welcome be
of delight to take your fill;
for need constraineth me
to serve you, and I will."

"Upon my word," said Gawain, "that is well, I guess;
though I am not now he of whom you are speaking—
to attain to such honour as here you tell of
I am a knight unworthy, as well indeed I know—
by God, I would be glad, if good to you seemed
whatever I could say, or in service could offer
to the pleasure of your excellence—it would be pure delight."
"In good faith, Sir Gawain," said the gracious lady,
"the prowess and the excellence that all others approve,
if I scorned or decried them, it were scant courtesy.
But there are ladies in number who liever would now
have thee in their hold, sir, as I have thee here,
pleasantly to play with in polished converse,
their solace to seek and their sorrows to soothe,
than great part of the goods or gold that they own.
But I thank Him who on high of Heaven is Lord
that I have here wholly in my hand what all desire,
by grace."
She was an urgent wooer,
that lady fair of face;
the knight with speeches pure
replied in every case.

"Madam," said he merrily, "Mary reward you!
For I have enjoyed, in good faith, your generous favour,

and much honour have had else from others' kind deeds;
but as for the courtesy they accord me, since my claim is not equal,
the honour is your own, who are ever well-meaning."
"Nay, Mary!" the lady demurred, "as for me, I deny it.
For were I worth all the legion of women alive,
and all the wealth in the world at my will possessed,
if I should exchange at my choice and choose me a husband,
for the noble nature I know, Sir Knight, in thee here,
in beauty and bounty and bearing so gay—
of which earlier I have heard, and hold it now true—
then no lord alive would I elect before you."
"In truth, lady," he returned, "you took one far better.
But I am proud of the praise you are pleased to give me,
and as your servant in earnest my sovereign I hold you,
and your knight I become, and may Christ reward you."
Thus of many matters they spoke till midmorn was passed,
and ever the lady demeaned her as one that loved him much,
and he fenced with her featly, ever flawless in manner.
"Though I were lady most lovely," thought the lady to herself,
"the less love would he bring here," since he looked for his bane,
that blow
that him so soon should grieve,
and needs it must be so.
Then the lady asked for leave
and at once he let her go.

Then she gave him "good day," and with a glance she laughed,
and as she stood she astonished him with the strength of her words:
"Now He that prospers all speed for this disport repay you!
But that you should be Gawain, it gives me much thought."
"Why so?", then eagerly the knight asked her,
afraid that he had failed in the form of his converse.
But "God bless you! For this reason," blithely she answered,
"that one so good as Gawain the gracious is held,
who all the compass of courtesy includes in his person,
so long with a lady could hardly have lingered
without craving a kiss, as a courteous knight,
by some tactful turn that their talk led to."
Then said Gawain, "Very well, as you wish be it done.
I will kiss at your command, as becometh a knight,
and more, lest he displease you, so plead it no longer."
She came near thereupon and caught him in her arms,
and down daintily bending dearly she kissed him.
They courteously commended each other to Christ.
Without more ado through the door she withdrew and departed,
and he to rise up in haste made ready at once.
He calls to his chamberlain, and chooses his clothes,
and goes forth when garbed all gladly to Mass.
Then he went to a meal that meetly awaited him,

and made merry all day, till the moon arose
o'er earth.
Ne'er was knight so gaily engaged
between two dames of worth,
the youthful and the aged:
together they made much mirth.

And ever the lord of the land in his delight was abroad,
hunting by holt and heath after hinds that were barren.
When the sun began to slope he had slain such a number
of does and other deer one might doubt it were true.
Then the fell folk at last came flocking all in,
and quickly of the kill they a quarry assembled.
Thither the master hastened with a host of his men,
gathered together those greatest in fat
and had them riven open rightly, as the rules require.
At the assay they were searched by some that were there,
and two fingers' breadth of fat they found in the leanest.
Next they slit the eslot,° seized on the arber,° *throat / gullet*
shaved it with a sharp knife and shore away the grease;
next ripped the four limbs and rent off the hide.
Then they broke open the belly, the bowels they removed
(flinging them nimbly afar) and the flesh of the knot;
they grasped then the gorge, disengaging with skill
the weasand° from the windpipe, and did away with the guts. *esophagus*
Then they shore out the shoulders with their sharpened knives
(drawing the sinews through a small cut) the sides to keep whole;
next they burst open the breast, and broke it apart,
and again at the gorge one begins thereupon,
cuts all up quickly till he comes to the fork,
and fetches forth the fore-numbles;[2] and following after
all the tissues along the ribs they tear away quickly.
Thus by the bones of the back they broke off with skill,
down even to the haunch, all that hung there together,
and hoisted it up all whole and hewed it off there:
and that they took for the numbles, as I trow is their name
in kind.
Along the fork of every thigh
the flaps they fold behind;
to hew it in two they hie,
down the back all to unbind.

Both the head and the neck they hew off after,
and next swiftly they sunder the sides from the chine,° *backbone*
and the bone for the crow they cast in the boughs.[3]
Then they thrust through both thick sides with a thong by the rib,

2. Internal organs such as heart, liver, lungs.

3. The gristle at the end of the breastbone was left for the crows, still another of the prescribed rituals of the hunt.

and then by the hocks of the legs they hang them both up:
all the folk earn the fees that fall to their lot.
Upon the fell of the fair beast they fed their hounds then
on the liver and the lights° and the leather of the paunches *lungs*
with bread bathed in blood blended amongst them.
Boldly they blew the prise,[4] amid the barking of dogs,
and then bearing up their venison bent their way homeward,
striking up strongly many a stout horn-call.
When daylight was done they all duly were come
into the noble castle, where quietly the knight
abode
in bliss by bright fire set.
Thither the lord now strode;
when Gawain with him met,
then free all pleasure flowed.

Then the master commanded his men to meet in that hall,
and both dames to come down with their damsels also;
before all the folk on that floor fair men he ordered
to fetch there forthwith his venison before him,
and all gracious in game to Gawain he called,
announced the number by tally of the nimble beasts,
and showed him the shining fat all shorn on the ribs.
"How does this play please you? Have I praise deserved?
Have I earned by mine art the heartiest thanks?"
"Yea verily," the other averred, "here is venison the fairest
that I've seen in seven years in the season of winter!"
"And I give it you all, Gawain," said the good man at once,
"for as our covenant accorded you may claim it as your own."
"That is true," he returned, "and I tell you the same:
what of worth within these walls I have won also
with as good will, I warrant, 'tis awarded to you."
His fair neck he enfolded then fast in his arms,
and kissed him with all the kindness that his courtesy knew.
"There take you my gains, sir! I got nothing more.
I would give it up gladly even if greater it were."
"That is a good one!" quoth the good man. "Greatly I thank you.
'Tis such, maybe, that you had better briefly now tell me
where you won this same wealth by the wits you possess."
"That was not the covenant," quoth he. "Do not question me more!
For you've drawn what is due to you, no doubt can you have
'tis true."
They laugh, and with voices fair
their merriment pursue,
and to supper soon repair
with many dainties new.

4. A thing seized or requisitioned for the king's use or for the use of the garrisons in his castles.

Later by the chimney in chamber they were seated,
abundant wine of the best was brought to them oft,
and again as a game they agreed on the morrow
to abide by the same bond as they had bargained before:
chance what might chance, to exchange all their trade,
whatever new thing they got, when they gathered at night.
They concluded this compact before the courtiers all;
the drink for the bargain was brought forth in jest;
then their leave at the last they lovingly took,
and away then at once each went to his bed.
When the cock had crowed and cackled but thrice,
the lord had leaped from his bed, and his lieges each one;
so that their meal had been made, and the Mass was over,
and folk bound for the forest, ere the first daybreak,
        to chase.
    Loud with hunters and horns
    o'er plains they passed apace,
    and loosed there among the thorns
    the running dogs to race.

Soon these cried for a quest in a covert by a marsh;
the huntsman hailed the hound that first heeded the scent,
stirring words he spoke to him with a strident voice.
The hounds then that heard it hastened thither swiftly,
and fell fast on the line, some forty at once.
Then such a baying and babel of bloodhounds together
arose that the rock-wall rang all about them.
Hunters enheartened them with horn and with mouth,
and then all in a rout rushed on together
between a fen-pool in that forest and a frowning crag.
In a tangle under a tall cliff at the tarn's° edges, *mountain pond*
where the rough rock ruggedly in ruin was fallen,
they fared to the find, followed by hunters
who made a cast round the crag and the clutter of stones,
till well they were aware that it waited within:
the very beast that the baying bloodhounds had spoken.
Then they beat on the bushes and bade him uprise,
and forth he came to their peril against folk in his path.
'Twas a boar without rival that burst out upon them;
long the herd he had left, that lone beast aged,
for savage was he, of all swine the hugest,
grim indeed when he grunted. Then aghast were many;
for three at the first thrust he threw to the ground,
and sprang off with great speed, sparing the others;
and they hallooed on high, and ha! ha! shouted,
and held horn to mouth, blowing hard the rally.
Many were the wild mouthings of men and of dogs,
as they bounded after this boar, him with blare and with din
        to quell.

Many times he turns to bay,
and maims the pack pell-mell;
he hurts many hounds, and they
grievously yowl and yell.

Hunters then hurried up eager to shoot him,
aimed at him their arrows, often they hit him;
but poor at core proved the points that pitched on his shields,
and the barbs on his brows would bite not at all;
though the shaven shaft shivered in pieces,
back the head came hopping, wherever it hit him.
But when the hurts went home of their heavier strokes,
then with brain wild for battle he burst out upon them,
ruthless he rent them as he rushed forward,
and many quailed at his coming and quickly withdrew.
But the lord on a light horse went leaping after him;
as bold man on battle-field with his bugle he blew
the rally-call as he rode through the rough thickets,
pursuing this wild swine till the sunbeams slanted.
This day in such doings thus duly they passed,
while our brave knight beloved there lies in his bed
at home in good hap, in housings so costly
and gay.
The lady did not forget:
she came to bid good day;
early she on him set,
his will to wear away.

She passed to the curtain and peeped at the knight.
Sir Gawain graciously then welcomed her first,
and she answered him alike, eagerly speaking,
and sat her softly by his side; and suddenly she laughed,
and with a look full of love delivered these words:
"Sir, if you are Gawain, a wonder I think it
that a man so well-meaning, ever mindful of good,
yet cannot comprehend the customs of the gentle;
and if one acquaints you therewith, you do not keep them in mind:
thou hast forgot altogether what a day ago I taught
by the plainest points I would put into words!"
"What is that?" he said at once. "I am not aware of it at all.
But if you are telling the truth, I must take all the blame."
"And yet as to kisses," she quoth, "this counsel I gave you:
wherever favour is found, defer not to claim them:
that becomes all who care for courteous manners."
"Take back," said the true knight, "that teaching, my dear!
For that I dared not do, for dread of refusal.
Were I rebuffed, I should be to blame for so bold an offer."
"Ma fay!"° said the fair lady, "you may not be refused; *"My faith" (Fr.)*
you are stout enough to constrain one by strength, if you like,
if any were so ill bred as to answer you nay."

"Indeed, by God," quoth Gawain, "you graciously speak;
but force finds no favour among the folk where I dwell,
and any gift not given gladly and freely.
I am at your call and command to kiss when you please.
You may receive as you desire, and cease as you think
in place."
Then down the lady bent,
and sweetly kissed his face.
Much speech then there they spent
of lovers' grief and grace.

"I would learn from you, lord," the lady then said,
"if you would not mind my asking, what is the meaning of this:
that one so young as are you in years, and so gay,
by renown so well known for knighthood and breeding,
while of all chivalry the choice, the chief thing to praise,
is the loyal practice of love: very lore of knighthood[5]—
for, talking of the toils that these true knights suffer,
it is the title and contents and text of their works:
how lovers for their true love their lives have imperilled,
have endured for their dear one dolorous trials,
until avenged by their valour, their adversity passed,
they have brought bliss into her bower by their own brave virtues—
and you are the knight of most noble renown in our age,
and your fame and fair name afar is published,
and I have sat by your very self now for the second time,
yet your mouth has never made any remark I have heard
that ever belonged to love-making, lesser or greater.
Surely, you that are so accomplished and so courtly in your vows
should be prompt to expound to a young pupil
by signs and examples the science of lovers.
Why? Are you ignorant who all honour enjoy?
Or else you esteem me too stupid to understand your courtship?
But nay!
Here single I come and sit,
a pupil for your play;
come, teach me of your wit,
while my lord is far away."

"In good faith," said Gawain, "may God reward you!
Great delight I gain, and am glad beyond measure
that one so worthy as you should be willing to come here
and take pains with so poor a man: as for playing with your knight,
showing favour in any form, it fills me with joy.
But for me to take up the task on true love to lecture,
to comment on the text and tales of knighthood
to you, who I am certain possess far more skill

5. The lady compares Gawain's behavior to descriptions of courtly love in romances; the poem is mirrored within itself.

in that art by the half than a hundred of such
as I am, or shall ever be while on earth I remain,
it would be folly manifold, in faith, my lady!
All your will I would wish to work, as I am able,
being so beholden in honour, and, so help me the Lord,
desiring ever the servant of yourself to remain."
Thus she tested and tried him, tempting him often,
so as to allure him to love-making, whatever lay in her heart.
But his defence was so fair that no fault could be seen,
nor any evil upon either side, nor aught but joy
they wist.
They laughed and long they played;
at last she him then kissed,
with grace adieu him bade,
and went whereso she list.

Then rousing from his rest he rose to hear Mass,
and then their dinner was laid and daintily served.
The livelong day with the ladies in delight he spent,
but the lord o'er the lands leaped to and fro,
pursuing his fell swine that o'er the slopes hurtled
and bit asunder the backs of the best of his hounds,
wherever to bay he was brought, until bowmen dislodged him,
and made him, maugre° his teeth, move again onward, *despite*
so fast the shafts flew when the folk were assembled.
And yet the stoutest of them still he made start there aside,
till at least he was so spent he could speed no further,
but in such haste as he might he made for a hollow
on a reef beside a rock where the river was flowing.
He put the bank at his back, began then to paw;
fearfully the froth of his mouth foamed from the corners;
he whetted his white tusks. Then weary were all
the brave men so bold as by him to stand
of plaguing him from afar, yet for peril they dared not
come nigher.
He had hurt so many before,
that none had now desire
to be torn with the tusks once more
of a beast both mad and dire.

Till the knight himself came, his courser spurring,
and saw him brought there to bay, and all about him his men.
Nothing loth he alighted, and leaving his horse,
brandished a bright blade and boldly advanced,
striding stoutly through the ford to where stood the felon.
The wild beast was aware of him with his weapon in hand,
and high raised his hair; with such hate he snorted
that folk feared for the knight, lest his foe should worst him.
Out came the swine and set on him at once,
and the boar and the brave man were both in a mellay° *struggle*

in the wildest of the water. The worse had the beast,
for the man marked him well, and as they met he at once
struck steadily his point straight in the neck-slot,
and hit him up to the hilts, so that his heart was riven,
and with a snarl he succumbed, and was swept down the water
straightway.
A hundred hounds him caught,
and fiercely bit their prey;
the men to the bank him brought,
and dogs him dead did lay.

There men blew for the prise in many a blaring horn,
and high and loud hallooed all the hunters that could;
bloodhounds bayed for the beast, as bade the masters,
who of that hard-run chase were the chief huntsmen.
Then one that was well learnéd in woodmen's lore
with pretty cunning began to carve up this boar.
First he hewed off his head and on high set it,
then he rent him roughly down the ridge of the back,
brought out the bowels, burned them on gledes,° *coals*
and with them, blended with blood, the bloodhounds rewarded.
Next he broke up the boar-flesh in broad slabs of brawn,
and haled forth the hastlets° in order all duly, *innards*
and yet all whole he fastened the halves together,
and strongly on a stout pole he strung them then up.
Now with this swine homeward swiftly they hastened,
and the boar's head was borne before the brave knight himself
who felled him in the ford by force of his hand
so great.
Until he saw Sir Gawain
in the hall he could hardly wait.
He called, and his pay to gain
the other came there straight.

The lord with his loud voice and laughter merry
gaily he greeted him when Gawain he saw.
The fair ladies were fetched and the folk all assembled,
and he showed them the shorn slabs, and shaped his report
of the width and wondrous length, and the wickedness also
in war, of the wild swine, as in the woods he had fled.
With fair words his friend the feat then applauded,
and praised the great prowess he had proved in his deeds;
for such brawn on a beast, the brave knight declared,
or such sides on a swine he had never seen before.
They then handled the huge head, and highly he praised it,
showing horror at the hideous thing to honour the lord.
"Now, Gawain," said the good man, "this game is your own
by close covenant we concluded, as clearly you know."
"That is true," he returned, "and as truly I assure you
all my winnings, I warrant, I shall award you in exchange."

He clasped his neck, and courteously a kiss he then gave him
and swiftly with a second he served him on the spot.
"Now we are quits," he quoth, "and clear for this evening
of all covenants we accorded, since I came to this house,
as is due."
The lord said: "By Saint Gile,[6]
your match I never knew!
You'll be wealthy in a while,
such trade if you pursue."

Then on top of the trestles the tables they laid,
cast the cloths thereon, and clear light then
wakened along the walls; waxen torches
men set there, and servants went swift about the hall.
Much gladness and gaiety began then to spring
round the fire on the hearth, and freely and oft
at supper and later: many songs of delight,
such as canticles of Christmas, and new carol-dances,
amid all the mannerly mirth that men can tell of;
and ever our noble knight was next to the lady.
Such glances she gave him of her gracious favour,
secretly stealing sweet looks that strong man to charm,
that he was passing perplexed, and ill-pleased at heart.
Yet he would fain not of his courtesy coldly refuse her,
but graciously engaged her, however against the grain
the play.
When mirth they had made in hall
as long as they wished to stay,
to a room did the lord them call
and to the ingle° they made their way. *hearth*

There amid merry words and wine they had a mind once more
to harp on the same note on New Year's Eve.
But said Gawain: "Grant me leave to go on the morrow!
For the appointment approaches that I pledged myself to."
The lord was loth to allow it, and longer would keep him,
and said: "As I am a true man I swear on my troth
the Green Chapel thou shalt gain, and go to your business
in the dawn of New Year, sir, ere daytime begins.
So still lie upstairs and stay at thine ease,
and I shall hunt in the holt here, and hold to my terms
with thee truly, when I return, to trade all our gains.
For I have tested thee twice, and trusty I find thee.
Now 'third time pays for all,' bethink thee tomorrow!
Make we merry while we may and be mindful of joy,
for the woe one may win whenever one wishes!"
This was graciously agreed, and Gawain would linger.

6. A hermit and patron saint of woodlands.

Then gaily drink is given them and they go to their beds
with light.
Sir Gawain lies and sleeps
soft and sound all night;
his host to his hunting keeps,
and is early arrayed aright.

After Mass of a morsel he and his men partook.
Merry was the morning. For his mount then he called.
All the huntsmen that on horse behind him should follow
were ready mounted to ride arrayed at the gates.
Wondrous fair were the fields, for the frost clung there;
in red rose-hued o'er the wrack° arises the sun, *mist*
sailing clear along the coasts of the cloudy heavens.
The hunters loosed hounds by a holt-border;° *grove's edge*
the rocks rang in the wood to the roar of their horns.
Some fell on the line to where the fox was lying,
crossing and re-crossing it in the cunning of their craft.
A hound then gives tongue, the huntsman names him,
round him press his companions in a pack all snuffling,
running forth in a rabble then right in his path.
The fox flits before them. They find him at once,
and when they see him by sight they pursue him hotly,
decrying him full clearly with a clamour of wrath.
He dodges and ever doubles through many a dense coppice,
and looping oft he lurks and listens under fences.
At last at a little ditch he leaps o'er a thorn-hedge,
sneaks out secretly by the side of a thicket,
weens he is out of the wood and away by his wiles from the hounds.
Thus he went unawares to a watch that was posted,
where fierce on him fell three foes at once
all grey.
He swerves then swift again,
and dauntless darts astray;
in grief and in great pain
to the wood he turns away.

Then to hark to the hounds it was heart's delight,
when all the pack came upon him, there pressing together.
Such a curse at the view they called down on him
that the clustering cliffs might have clattered in ruin.
Here he was hallooed when hunters came on him,
yonder was he assailed with snarling tongues;
there he was threatened and oft thief was he called,
with ever the trailers at his trail so that tarry he could not.
Oft was he run at, if he rushed outwards;
oft he swerved in again, so subtle was Reynard.
Yea! he led the lord and his hunt as laggards behind him
thus by mount and by hill till mid-afternoon.
Meanwhile the courteous knight in the castle in comfort slumbered

behind the comely curtains in the cold morning.
But the lady in love-making had no liking to sleep
nor to disappoint the purpose she had planned in her heart;
but rising up swiftly his room now she sought
in a gay mantle that to the ground was measured
and was fur-lined most fairly with fells well trimmed,
with no comely coif° on her head, only the clear jewels *close-fitting cap*
that were twined in her tressure° by twenties in clusters; *hairnet*
her noble face and her neck all naked were laid,
her breast bare in front and at the back also.
She came through the chamber-door and closed it behind her,
wide set a window, and to wake him she called,
thus greeting him gaily with her gracious words
   of cheer:
 "Ah! man, how canst thou sleep,
 the morning is so clear!"
 He lay in darkness deep,
 but her call he then could hear.

In heavy darkness drowsing he dream-words muttered,
as a man whose mind was bemused with many mournful thoughts,
how destiny should his doom on that day bring him
when he at the Green Chapel the great man would meet,
and be obliged his blow to abide without debate at all.
But when so comely she came, he recalled then his wits,
swept aside his slumbers, and swiftly made answer.
The lady in lovely guise came laughing sweetly,
bent down o'er his dear face, and deftly kissed him.
He greeted her graciously with a glad welcome,
seeing her so glorious and gaily attired,
so faultless in her features and so fine in her hues
that at once joy up-welling went warm to his heart.
With smiles sweet and soft they turned swiftly to mirth,
and only brightness and bliss was broached there between them
   so gay.
 They spoke then speeches good,
 much pleasure was in that play;
 great peril between them stood,
 unless Mary for her knight should pray.

For she, queenly and peerless, pressed him so closely,
led him so near the line, that at least he must needs
either refuse her with offence or her favours there take.
He cared for his courtesy, lest a caitiff° he proved, *coward*
yet more for his sad case, if he should sin commit
and to the owner of the house, to his host, be a traitor.
"God help me!" said he. "Happen that shall not!"
Smiling sweetly aside from himself then he turned
all the fond words of favour that fell from her lips.
Said she to the knight then: "Now shame you deserve,

if you love not one that lies alone here beside you,
who beyond all women in the world is wounded in heart,
unless you have a lemman,° more beloved, whom you like better, *lover*
and have affianced faith to that fair one so fast and so true
that your release you desire not—and so I believe now;
and to tell me if that be so truly, I beg you.
For all sakes that men swear by, conceal not the truth
in guile."
The knight said: "By Saint John,"
and softly gave a smile,
"Nay! lover have I none,
and none will have meanwhile."

"Those words," said the woman, "are the worst that could be.
But I am answered indeed, and 'tis hard to endure.
Kiss me now kindly, and I will quickly depart.
I may but mourn while I live as one that much is in love."
Sighing she sank down, and sweetly she kissed him;
then soon she left his side, and said as she stood there:
"Now, my dear, at this parting do me this pleasure,
give me something as thy gift, thy glove it might be,
that I may remember thee, dear man, my mourning to lessen."
"Now on my word," then said he, "I wish I had here
the loveliest thing for thy delight that in my land I possess;
for worthily have you earned wondrously often
more reward by rights than within my reach would now be,
save to allot you as love-token thing of little value.
Beneath your honour it is to have here and now
a glove for a guerdon° as the gift of Sir Gawain *reward*
and I am here on an errand in unknown lands,
and have no bearers with baggage and beautiful things
(unluckily, dear lady) for your delight at this time.
A man must do as he is placed; be not pained nor aggrieved,"
said he.
Said she so comely clad:
"Nay, noble knight and free,
though naught of yours I had,
you should get a gift from me."

A rich ring she offered him of red gold fashioned,
with a stone like a star standing up clear
that bore brilliant beams as bright as the sun:
I warrant you it was worth wealth beyond measure.
But the knight said nay to it, and announced then at once:
"I will have no gifts, fore God, of your grace at this time.
I have none to return you, and naught will I take."
She proffered it and pressed him, and he her pleading refused,
and swore swiftly upon his word that accept it he would not.
And she, sorry that he refused, said to him further:
"If to my ring you say nay, since too rich it appears,

and you would not so deeply be indebted to me,
I shall give you my girdle, less gain will that be."
She unbound a belt swiftly that embracing her sides
was clasped above her kirtle under her comely mantle.
Fashioned it was of green silk, and with gold finished,
though only braided round about, embroidered by hand;
and this she would give to Gawain, and gladly besought him,
of no worth though it were, to be willing to take it.
And he said nay, he would not, he would never receive
either gold or jewelry, ere God the grace sent him
to accomplish the quest on which he had come thither.
"And therefore I pray you, please be not angry,
and cease to insist on it, for to your suit I will ever
say no.
I am deeply in debt to you
for the favour that you show,
to be your servant true
for ever in weal or woe."

"Do you refuse now this silk," said the fair lady,
"because in itself it is poor? And so it appears.
See how small 'tis in size, and smaller in value!
But one who knew of the nature that is knit therewithin
would appraise it probably at a price far higher.
For whoever goes girdled with this green riband,
while he keeps it well clasped closely about him,
there is none so hardy under heaven that to hew him were able;
for he could not be killed by any cunning of hand."
The knight then took note, and thought now in his heart,
'twould be a prize in that peril that was appointed to him.
When he gained the Green Chapel to get there his sentence,
if by some sleight he were not slain, 'twould be a sovereign device.
Then he bore with her rebuke, and debated not her words;
and she pressed him on the belt, and proffered it in earnest;
and he agreed, and she gave it very gladly indeed,
and prayed him for her sake to part with it never,
but on his honour hide it from her husband; and he then agreed
that no one ever should know, nay, none in the world
buy they.
With earnest heart and mood
great thanks he oft did say.
She then the knight so good
a third time kissed that day.

Then she left him alone, her leave taking,
for amusement from the man no more could she get.
When she was gone Sir Gawain got him soon ready,
arose and robed himself in raiment noble.
He laid up the love-lace that the lady had given,
hiding it heedfully where he after might find it.

Then first of all he chose to fare to the chapel,
privately approached a priest, and prayed that he there
would uplift his life, that he might learn better
how his soul should be saved, when he was sent from the world.
There he cleanly confessed him and declared his misdeeds,
both the more and the less, and for mercy he begged,
to absolve him of them all he besought the good man;
and he assoiled him and made him as safe and as clean
as for Doom's Day indeed, were it due on the morrow.[7]
Thereafter more merry he made among the fair ladies,
with carol-dances gentle and all kinds of rejoicing,
than ever he did ere that day, till the darkness of night,
in bliss.
Each man there said: "I vow
a delight to all he is!
Since hither he came till now,
he was ne'er so gay as this."

Now indoors let him dwell and have dearest delight,
while the free lord yet fares afield in his sports!
At last the fox he has felled that he followed so long;
for, as he spurred through a spinney° to espy there the villain, *grove*
where the hounds he had heard that hard on him pressed,
Reynard on his road came through a rough thicket,
and all the rabble in a rush were right on his heels.
The man is aware of the wild thing, and watchful awaits him,
brings out his bright brand and at the beast hurls it;
and he blenched at the blade, and would have backed if he could.
A hound hastened up, and had him ere he could;
and right before the horse's feet they fell on him all,
and worried there the wily one with a wild clamour.
The lord quickly alights and lifts him at once,
snatching him swiftly from their slavering mouths,
holds him high o'er his head, hallooing loudly;
and there bay at him fiercely many furious hounds.
Huntsmen hurried thither, with horns full many
ever sounding the assembly, till they saw the master.
When together had come his company noble,
all that ever bore bugle were blowing at once,
and all the others hallooed that had not a horn:
it was the merriest music that ever men harkened,
the resounding song there raised that for Reynard's soul
awoke.
To hounds they pay their fees,
their heads they fondly stroke,

7. Gawain's confession and absolution are problematic, since he has just accepted the green girdle and resolved to break the covenant of exchange with his host.

and Reynard then they seize,
and off they skin his cloak.

And then homeward they hastened, for at hand was now night,
making strong music on their mighty horns.
The lord alighted at last at his beloved abode,
found a fire in the hall, and fair by the hearth
Sir Gawain the good, and gay was he too,
among the ladies in delight his lot was most joyful.
He was clad in a blue cloak that came to the ground;
his surcoat well beseemed him with its soft lining,
and its hood of like hue that hung on his shoulder:
all fringed with white fur very finely were both.
He met indeed the master in the midst of the floor,
and in gaiety greeted him, and graciously said:
"In this case I will first our covenant fulfil
that to our good we agreed, when ungrudged went the drink."
He clasps then the knight and kisses him thrice,
as long and deliciously as he could lay them upon him.
"By Christ!" the other quoth, "you've come by a fortune
in winning such wares, were they worth what you paid."
"Indeed, the price was not important," promptly he answered,
"whereas plainly is paid now the profit I gained."
"Marry!" said the other man, "mine is not up to't;
for I have hunted all this day, and naught else have I got
but this foul fox-fell—the Fiend have the goods!—
and that is price very poor to pay for such treasures
as these you have thrust upon me, three such kisses
so good."
"'Tis enough," then said Gawain.
"I thank you, by the Rood,"
and how the fox was slain
he told him as they stood.

With mirth and minstrelsy and meats at their pleasure
as merry they made as any men could be;
amid the laughter of ladies and light words of jest
both Gawain and the good man could no gayer have proved,
unless they had doted indeed or else drunken had been.
Both the host and his household went on with their games,
till the hour had approached when part must they all;
to bed were now bound the brave folk at last.
Bowing low his leave of the lord there first
the good knight then took, and graciously thanked him:[8]
"For such a wondrous welcome as within these walls I have had,
for your honour at this high feast the High King reward you!

8. Gawain's highly stylized leave-taking is typical of courtly romance and again emphasizes his command of fine manners.

In your service I set myself, your servant, if you will.
For I must needs make a move tomorrow, as you know,
if you give me some good man to go, as you promised,
and guide me to the Green Chapel, as God may permit me
to face on New Year's day such doom as befalls me."
"On my word," said his host, "with hearty good will
to all that ever I promised I promptly shall hold."
Then a servant he assigns him to set him on the road,
and by the downs to conduct him, that without doubt or delay
he might through wild and through wood ways most straight
    pursue.
  Said Gawain, "My thanks receive,
  such a favour you will do!"
  The knight then took his leave
  of those noble ladies two.

Sadly he kissed them and said his farewells,
and pressed oft upon them in plenty his thanks,
and they promptly the same again repaid him;
to God's keeping they gave him, grievously sighing.
Then from the people of the castle he with courtesy parted;
all the men that he met he remembered with thanks
for their care for his comfort and their kind service,
and the trouble each had taken in attendance upon him;
and every one was as woeful to wish him adieu
as had they lived all their lives with his lordship in honour.
Then with link-men and lights he was led to his chamber
and brought sweetly to bed, there to be at his rest.
That soundly he slept then assert will I not,
for he had many matters in the morning to mind, if he would,
    in thought.
  There let him lie in peace,
  near now is the tryst he sought.
  If a while you will hold your peace,
  I will tell the deeds they wrought!

Part 4

Now New Year draws near and the night passes,
day comes driving the dark, as ordained by God;
but wild weathers of the world awake in the land,
clouds cast keenly the cold upon earth
with bitter breath from the North biting the naked.
Snow comes shivering sharp to shrivel the wild things,
and whistling wind whirls from the heights
and drives every dale full of drifts very deep.
Long the knight listens as he lies in his bed;
though he lays down his eyelids, very little he sleeps:
at the crow of every cock he recalls well his tryst.

Briskly he rose from his bed ere the break of day,
for there was light from a lamp that illumined his chamber.
He called to his chamberlain, who quickly him answered,
and he bade him bring his byrnie° and his beast saddle. *chain-mail coat*
The man got him up and his gear fetched him,
and garbed then Sir Gawain in great array;
first he clad him in his clothes to keep out the cold,
and after that in his harness that with heed had been tended,
both his pauncer and his plates° polished all brightly, *leg armor*
the rings rid of the rust on his rich byrnie:
all was neat as if new, and the knight him thanked
with delight.
He put on every piece
all burnished well and bright;
most gallant from here to Greece
for his courser called the knight.

While the proudest of his apparel he put on himself:
his coat-armour, with the cognisance of the clear symbol
upon velvet environed with virtuous gems
all bound and braided about it, with broidered seams
and with fine firs lined wondrous fairly within,
yet he overlooked not the lace that the lady had given him;
that Gawain forgot not, of his own good thinking;
when he had belted his brand° upon his buxom haunches, *sword*
he twined the love-token twice then about him,
and swiftly he swathed it sweetly about his waist,
that girdle of green silk, and gallant it looked
upon the royal red cloth that was rich to behold.
But he wore not for worth nor for wealth this girdle,
not for pride in the pendants, though polished they were,
not though the glittering gold there gleamed at the ends,
but so that himself he might save when suffer he must,
must abide bane without debating it with blade or with brand
of war.
When arrayed the knight so bold
came out before the door,
to all that high household
great thanks he gave once more.

Now Gringolet was groomed, the great horse and high,
who had been lodged to his liking and loyally tended:
fain to gallop was that gallant horse for his good fettle.
His master to him came and marked well his coat,
and said: "Now solemnly myself I swear on my troth
there is a company in this castle that is careful of honour!
Their lord that them leads, may his lot be joyful!
Their beloved lady in life may delight befall her!
If they out of charity thus cherish a guest,
upholding their house in honour, may He them reward

that upholds heaven on high, and all of you too!
And if life a little longer I might lead upon earth,
I would give you some guerdon° gladly, were I able." *reward*
Then he steps in the stirrup and strides on his horse;
his shield his man showed him, and on shoulder he slung it,
Gringolet he goaded with his gilded heels,
and he plunged forth on the pavement, and prancing no more
stood there.
Ready now was his squire to ride
that his helm and lance would bear.
"Christ keep this castle!" he cried
and wished it fortune fair.

The bridge was brought down and the broad gates then
unbarred and swung back upon both hinges.
The brave man blessed himself, and the boards crossing,
bade the porter up rise, who before the prince kneeling
gave him "Good day, Sir Gawain!", and "God save you!"
Then he went on his way with the one man only
to guide him as he goes to that grievous place
where he is due to endure the dolorous blow.
They go by banks and by braes° where branches are bare,[1] *hillsides*
they climb along cliffs where clingeth the cold;
the heavens are lifted high, but under them evilly
mist hangs moist on the moor, melts on the mountains;
every hill has a hat, a mist-mantle huge.
Brooks break and boil on braes all about,
bright bubbling on their banks where they bustle downwards.
Very wild through the wood is the way they must take,
until soon comes the season when the sun rises
that day.
On a high hill they abode,
white snow beside them lay;
the man that by him rode
there bade his master stay.

"For so far I have taken you, sir, at this time,
and now you are near to that noted place
that you have enquired and questioned so curiously after.
But I will announce now the truth, since you are known to me,
and you are a lord in this life that I love greatly,
if you would follow my advice you would fare better.
The place that you pass to, men perilous hold it,
the worst wight in the world in that waste dwelleth;
for he is stout and stern, and to strike he delights,
and he mightier than any man upon middle-earth is,
and his body is bigger than the four best men

1. The grimness of this landscape, reminiscent of wastelands in Anglo-Saxon poetry, swiftly returns the poem from the courtly world to the elemental challenge Gawain now faces.

that are in Arthur's house, either Hector[2] or others.
All goes as he chooses at the Green Chapel;
no one passes by that place so proud in his arms
that he hews not to death by dint of his hand.
For he is a man monstrous, and mercy he knows not;
for be it a churl or a chaplain that by the Chapel rideth,
a monk or a mass-priest or any man besides,
he would as soon have him slain as himself go alive.
And so I say to you, as sure as you sit in your saddle,
if you come there, you'll be killed, if the carl has his way.
Trust me, that is true, though you had twenty lives
        to yield.
    He here has dwelt now long
    and stirred much strife on field;
    against his strokes so strong
    yourself you cannot shield.

And so, good Sir Gawain, now go another way,
and let the man alone, for the love of God, sir!
Come to some other country, and there may Christ keep you!
And I shall haste me home again, and on my honour I promise
that I swear will by God and all His gracious saints,
so help me God and the Halidom,[3] and other oaths a plenty,
that I will safe keep your secret, and say not a word
that ever you fain were to flee for any foe that I knew of."
"Gramercy!" quoth Gawain, and regretfully answered:
"Well, man, I wish thee, who wishest my good,
and keep safe my secret, I am certain thou wouldst.
But however heedfully thou hid it, if I here departed,
fain in fear now to flee, in the fashion thou speakest,
I should a knight coward be, I could not be excused.
Nay, I'll fare to the Chapel, whatever chance may befall,
and have such words with that wild man as my wish is to say,
come fair or come foul, as fate will allot
        me there.
    He may be a fearsome knave
    to tame, and club may bear;
    but His servants true to save
    the Lord can well prepare."

"Marry!" quoth the other man, "now thou makest it so clear
that thou wishest thine own bane to bring on thyself,
and to lose thy life hast a liking, to delay thee I care not!
Have here thy helm on thy head, thy spear in thy hand,
and ride down by yon rock-side where runs this same track,
till thou art brought to the bottom of the baleful valley.
A little to thy left hand then look o'er the green,

2. Chief hero among the defenders of Troy and, like Arthur, one of the "Nine Worthies" celebrated for their heroic valor; or perhaps Arthur's knight Hector De Maris.

3. "By my holy relics."

and thou wilt see on the slope the selfsame chapel,
and the great man and grim on ground that it keeps.
Now farewell in God's name, Gawain the noble!
For all the gold in the world I would not go with thee,
nor bear thee fellowship through this forest one foot further!"
With that his bridle towards the wood back the man turneth,
hits his horse with his heels as hard as he can,
gallops on the greenway, and the good knight there leaves
alone.
Quoth Gawain: "By God on high
I will neither grieve nor groan.
With God's will I comply,
Whose protection I do own."

Then he puts spurs to Gringolet, and espying the track,
thrust in along a bank by a thicket's border,
rode down the rough brae right to the valley;
and then he gazed all about: a grim place he thought it,
and saw no sign of shelter on any side at all,
only high hillsides sheer upon either hand,
and notched knuckled crags with gnarled boulders;
the very skies by the peaks were scraped, it appeared.
Then he halted and held in his horse for the time,
and changed oft his front the Chapel to find.
Such on no side he saw, as seemed to him strange,
save a mound as it might be near the marge of a green,
a worn barrow[4] on a brae by the brink of a water,
beside falls in a flood that was flowing down;
the burn° bubbled therein, as if boiling it were. *brook*
He urged on his horse then, and came up to the mound,
there lightly alit, and lashed to a tree
his reins, with a rough branch rightly secured them.
Then he went to the barrow and about it he walked,
debating in his mind what might the thing be.
It had a hole at the end and at either side
and with grass in green patches was grown all over,
and was all hollow within: nought but an old cavern,
or a cleft in an old crag; he could not it name
aright.
"Can this be the Chapel Green,
O Lord?" said the gentle knight.
"Here the Devil might say, I ween,
his matins about midnight!"

"On my word," quoth Gawain, "'tis a wilderness here!
This oratory looks evil. With herbs overgrown
it fits well that fellow transformed into green

4. Perhaps a burial mound, which seems to link the moment to ancient, probably pagan, inhabitants.

to follow here his devotions in the Devil's fashion.
Now I feel in my five wits the Fiend 'tis himself
that has trapped me with this tryst to destroy me here.
This is a chapel of mischance, the church most accursed
that ever I entered. Evil betide it!"
With high helm on his head, his lance in his hand,
he roams up to the roof of that rough dwelling.
Then he heard from the high hill, in a hard rock-wall
beyond the stream on a steep, a sudden startling noise.
How it clattered in the cliff, as if to cleave it asunder,
as if one upon a grindstone were grinding a scythe!
How it whirred and it rasped as water in a mill-race!
How it rushed, and it rang, rueful to harken!
Then "By God," quoth Gawain, "I guess this ado
is meant for my honour, meetly to hail me
    as knight!
  As God wills! Waylaway!
  That helps me not a mite.
  My life though down I lay,
  no noise can me affright."

Then clearly the knight there called out aloud:
"Who is master in this place to meet me at tryst?
For now 'tis good Gawain on ground that here walks.
If any aught hath to ask, let him hasten to me,
either now or else never, his needs to further!"
"Stay!" said one standing above on the steep o'er his head,
"and thou shalt get in good time what to give thee I vowed."
Still with that rasping and racket he rushed on a while,
and went back to his whetting, till he wished to descend.
And then he climbed past a crag, and came from a hole,
hurtling out of a hid nook with a horrible weapon:
a Danish axe[5] newly dressed the dint to return,
with cruel cutting-edge curved along the handle—
filed on a whetstone, and four feet in width,
'twas no less—along its lace of luminous hue;
and the great man in green still guised as before,
his locks and long beard, his legs and his face,
save that firm on his feet he fared on the ground,
steadied the haft on the stones and stalked beside it.
When he walked to the water, where he wade would not,
he hopped over on his axe and haughtily strode,
fierce and fell on a field where far all about
    lay snow.
  Sir Gawain the man met there,
  neither bent nor bowed he low.

5. A long-bladed ax, associated with Viking raiders.

The other said: "Now, sirrah fair,
I true at tryst thee know!

"Gawain," said that green man, "may God keep thee!
On my word, sir, I welcome thee with a will to my place,
and thou hast timed thy travels as trusty man should,
and thou hast forgot not the engagement agreed on between us:
at this time gone a twelvemonth thou took'st thy allowance,
and I should now this New Year nimbly repay thee.
And we are in this valley now verily on our own,
there are no people to part us—we can play as we like.
Have thy helm off thy head, and have here thy pay!
Bandy me no more debate than I brought before thee
when thou didst sweep off my head with one swipe only!"
"Nay," quoth Gawain, "by God that gave me my soul,
I shall grudge thee not a grain any grief that follows.
Only restrain thee to one stroke, and still shall I stand
and offer thee no hindrance to act as thou likest
right here."
With a nod of his neck he bowed,
let bare the flesh appear;
he would not by dread be cowed,
no sign he gave of fear.

Then the great man in green gladly prepared him,
gathered up his grim tool there Gawain to smite;
with all the lust in his limbs aloft he heaved it,
shaped as mighty a stroke as if he meant to destroy him.
Had it driving come down as dour as he aimed it,
under his dint would have died the most doughty man ever.
But Gawain on that guisarm° then glanced to one side, *axe*
as down it came gliding on the green there to end him,
and he shrank a little with his shoulders at the sharp iron.
With a jolt the other man jerked back the blade,
and reproved then the prince, proudly him taunting.
"Thou'rt not Gawain," said the green man, "who is so good reported,
who never flinched from any foes on fell or in dale;
and now thou fleest in fear, ere thou feelest a hurt!
Of such cowardice that knight I ne'er heard accused.
Neither blenched I nor backed, when thy blow, sir, thou aimedst,
nor uttered any cavil in the court of King Arthur.
My head flew to my feet, and yet fled I never;
but thou, ere thou hast any hurt, in thy heart quailest,
and so the nobler knight to be named I deserve
therefore."
"I blenched once," Gawain said,
"and I will do so no more.
But if on floor now falls my head,
I cannot it restore.

But get busy, I beg, sir, and bring me to the point.
Deal me my destiny, and do it out of hand!
For I shall stand from thee a stroke and stir not again
till thine axe hath hit me, have here my word on't!"
"Have at thee then!" said the other, and heaved it aloft,
and watched him as wrathfully as if he were wild with rage.
He made at him a mighty aim, but the man he touched not,
holding back hastily his hand, ere hurt it might do.
Gawain warily awaited it, and winced with no limb,
but stood as still as a stone or the stump of a tree
that with a hundred ravelled roots in rocks is embedded.
This time merrily remarked then the man in the green:
"So, now thou hast thy heart whole, a hit I must make.
May the high order now keep thee that Arthur gave thee,
and guard thy gullet at this go, if it can gain thee that."
Angrily with ire then answered Sir Gawain:
"Why! lash away, thou lusty man! Too long dost thou threaten.
'Tis thy heart methinks in thee that now quaileth!"
"In faith," said the fellow, "so fiercely thou speakest,
I no longer will linger delaying thy errand
 right now."
 Then to strike he took his stance
 and grimaced with lip and brow.
 He that of rescue saw no chance
 was little pleased, I trow.

Lightly his weapon he lifted, and let it down neatly
with the bent horn of the blade towards the neck that was bare;
though he hewed with a hammer-swing, he hurt him no more
than to snick him on one side and sever the skin.
Through the fair fat sank the edge, and the flesh entered,
so that the shining blood o'er his shoulders was shed on the earth;
and when the good knight saw the gore that gleamed on the snow,
he sprang out with spurning feet a spear's length and more,
in haste caught his helm and on his head cast it,
under his fair shield he shot with a shake of his shoulders,[6]
brandished his bright sword, and boldly he spake—
never since he as manchild of his mother was born
was he ever on this earth half so happy a man:
"Have done, sir, with thy dints! Now deal me no more!
I have stood from thee a stroke without strife on this spot,
and if thou offerest me others, I shall answer thee promptly,
and give as good again, and as grim, be assured,
 shall pay.
 But one stroke here's my due,
 as the covenant clear did say

6. Gawain, who has displayed so much courtly refinement and religious emotion, now shows himself a practiced fighter, swiftly pulling his armor into place.

that in Arthur's halls we drew.
And so, good sir, now stay!"

From him the other stood off, and on his axe rested,
held the haft to the ground, and on the head leaning,
gazed at the good knight as on the green he there strode.
To see him standing so stout, so stern there and fearless,
armed and unafraid, his heart it well pleased.
Then merrily he spoke with a mighty voice,
and loudly it rang, as to that lord he said:
"Fearless knight on this field, so fierce do not be!
No man here unmannerly hath thee maltreated,
nor aught given thee not granted by agreement at court.
A hack I thee vowed, and thou'st had it, so hold thee content;
I remit thee the remnant of all rights I might claim.
If I brisker had been, a buffet, it may be,
I could have handed thee more harshly, and harm could have done thee.
First I menaced thee in play with no more than a trial,
and clove thee with no cleft: I had a claim to the feint,
for the fast pact we affirmed on the first evening,
and thou fairly and unfailing didst faith with me keep,
all thy gains thou me gavest, as good man ought.
The other trial for the morning, man, I thee tendered
when thou kissedst my comely wife, and the kisses didst render.
For the two here I offered only two harmless feints
to make.
The true shall truly repay,
for no peril then need he quake.
Thou didst fail on the third day,
and so that tap now take!

"For it is my weed that thou wearest, that very woven girdle:
my own wife it awarded thee, I wot° well indeed. *know*
Now I am aware of thy kisses, and thy courteous ways,
and of thy wooing by my wife: I worked that myself!
I sent her to test thee, and thou seem'st to me truly
the fair knight most faultless that e'er foot set on earth!
As a pearl than white pease is prized more highly,
so is Gawain, in good faith, than other gallant knights.
But in this you lacked, sir, a little, and of loyalty came short.
But that was for no artful wickedness, nor for wooing either,
but because you loved your own life: the less do I blame you."
The other stern knight in a study° then stood a long while, *thinking*
in such grief and disgust he had a grue° in his heart; *shudder*
all the blood from his breast in his blush mingled,
and he shrank into himself with shame at that speech.
The first words on that field that he found then to say
were: "Cursed be ye, Coveting, and Cowardice also!
In you is vileness, and vice that virtue destroyeth."
He took then the treacherous thing, and untying the knot

fiercely flung he the belt at the feet of the knight:
"See there the falsifier, and foul be its fate!
Through care for thy blow Cowardice brought me
to consent to Coveting, my true kind to forsake,
which is free-hand and faithful word that are fitting to knights.
Now I am faulty and false, who afraid have been ever
of treachery and troth-breach: the two now my curse
may bear!
I confess, sir, here to you
all faulty has been my fare.
Let me gain your grace anew,
and after I will beware."

Then the other man laughed and lightly answered:
"I hold it healed beyond doubt, the harm that I had.
Thou hast confessed thee so clean and acknowledged thine errors,
and hast the penance plain to see from the point of my blade,
that I hold thee purged of that debt, made as pure and as clean
as hadst thou done no ill deed since the day thou wert born.
And I give thee, sir, the girdle with gold at its hems,
for it is green like my gown. So, Sir Gawain, you may
think of this our contest when in the throng thou walkest
among princes of high praise; 'twill be a plain reminder
of the chance of the Green Chapel between chivalrous knights.
And now you shall in this New Year come anon to my house,
and in our revels the rest of this rich season
shall go."
The lord pressed him hard to wend,
and said, "my wife, I know,
we soon shall make your friend,
who was your bitter foe."

"Nay forsooth!" the knight said, and seized then his helm,
and duly it doffed, and the doughty man thanked:
"I have lingered too long! May your life now be blest,
and He promptly repay you Who apportions all honours!
And give my regards to her grace, your goodly consort,
both to her and to the other, to mine honoured ladies,
who thus their servant with their designs have subtly beguiled.
But no marvel it is if mad be a fool,
and by the wiles of women to woe be brought.
For even so Adam by one on earth was beguiled,
and Solomon by several, and to Samson moreoever
his doom by Delilah was dealt; and David was after
blinded by Bathsheba, and he bitterly suffered.[7]
Now if these came to grief through their guile, a gain 'twould be vast
to love them well and believe them not, if it lay in man's power!

7. Gawain suddenly erupts in a brief but fierce diatribe, including this list of treacherous women recognizable from contemporary misogynist texts.

Since these were aforetime the fairest, by fortune most blest,
eminent among all the others who under heaven bemused
were too,
and all of them were betrayed
by women that they knew,
though a fool I now am made,
some excuse I think my due.

"But for your girdle," quoth Gawain, "may God you repay!
That I will gain with good will, not for the gold so joyous
of the cincture, nor the silk, nor the swinging pendants,
nor for wealth, nor for worth, nor for workmanship fine;
but as a token of my trespass I shall turn to it often
when I ride in renown, ruefully recalling
the failure and the frailty of the flesh so perverse,
so tender, so ready to take taints of defilement.
And thus, when pride my heart pricks for prowess in arms,
one look at this love-lace shall lowlier make it.
But one thing I would pray you, if it displeaseth you not,
since you are the lord of yonder land, where I lodged for a while
in your house and in honour—may He you reward
Who upholdeth the heavens and on high sitteth!—
how do you announce your true name? And then nothing further."
"That I will tell thee truly," then returned the other.
"Bertilak de Hautdesert hereabouts I am called,
[who thus have been enchanted and changed in my hue]
by the might of Morgan le Fay[8] that in my mansion dwelleth,
and by cunning of lore and crafts well learned.
The magic arts of Merlin she many hath mastered;
for deeply in dear love she dealt on a time
with that accomplished clerk, as at Camelot runs
the fame;
and Morgan the Goddess
is therefore now her name.
None power and pride possess
too high for her to tame.

She made me go in this guise to your goodly court
to put its pride to the proof, if the report were true
that runs of the great renown of the Round Table.
She put this magic upon me to deprive you of your wits,
in hope Guinevere to hurt, that she in horror might die
aghast at that glamoury° that gruesomely spake *enchanted one*
with its head in its hand before the high table.
She it is that is at home, that ancient lady;

8. Morgan is Arthur's half-sister and ruler of the mysterious Avalon; she learned magical arts from Merlin. Her presence can bode good or ill. In some stories she holds a deep grudge against Guinevere, yet she carries off the wounded Arthur after his final battle, perhaps to heal him. The earlier Celtic Morrigan, possibly related, is queen of demons, sower of discord, and goddess of war.

she is indeed thine own aunt, Arthur's half-sister,
daughter of the Duchess of Tintagel on whom doughty Sir Uther
after begat Arthur, who in honour is now.[9]
Therefore I urge thee in earnest, sir, to thine aunt return!
In my hall make merry! My household thee loveth,
and I wish thee as well, upon my word, sir knight,
as any that go under God, for thy great loyalty."
But he denied him with a "Nay! by no means I will!"
They clasp then and kiss and to the care give each other
of the Prince of Paradise; and they part on that field
so cold.
To the king's court on courser keen
then hastened Gawain the bold,
and the knight in the glittering green
to ways of his own did hold.

Wild ways in the world Gawain now rideth
on Gringolet: by the grace of God he still lived.
Oft in house he was harboured and lay oft in the open,
oft vanquished his foe in adventures as he fared
which I intend not this time in my tale to recount.
The hurt was healed that he had in his neck,
and the bright-hued belt he bore now about it
obliquely like a baldric[1] bound at his side,
under his left arm with a knot that lace was fastened
to betoken he had been detected in the taint of a fault;
and so at last he came to the Court again safely.
Delight there was awakened, when the lords were aware
that good Gawain had returned: glad news they thought it.
The king kissed the knight, and the queen also,
and then in turn many a true knight that attended to greet him.
About his quest they enquire, and he recounts all the marvels,
declares all the hardships and care that he had,
what chanced at the Chapel, what cheer made the knight,
the love of the lady, and the lace at the last.
The notch in his neck naked he showed them
that he had for his dishonesty from the hands of the knight
in blame.
It was torment to tell the truth:
in his face the blood did flame;
he groaned for grief and ruth° *remorse*
when he showed it, to his shame.

"Lo! Lord," he said at last, and the lace handled,
"This is the band! For this a rebuke I bear in my neck!

9. The poem now recalls an earlier transgression of guest–host obligations, when Uther began to lust for Ygerne while her husband, Gorlois, was at his court; he later killed Gorlois and married Ygerne.

1. A belt for a sword or bugle, worn over one shoulder and across the chest.

This is the grief and disgrace I have got for myself
from the covetousness and cowardice that o'ercame me there!
This is the token of the troth-breach that I am detected in,
and needs must I wear it while in the world I remain;
for a man may cover his blemish, but unbind it he cannot,
for where once 'tis applied, thence part will it never."
The king comforted the knight, and all the Court also
laughed loudly thereat, and this law made in mirth
the lords and the ladies that whoso belonged to the Table,
every knight of the Brotherhood, a baldric should have,
a band of bright green obliquely about him,
and this for love of that knight as a livery should wear.
For that was reckoned the distinction of the Round Table,
and honour was his that had it evermore after,
as it is written in the best of the books of romance.
Thus in Arthur his days happened this marvel,
as the Book of the Brut beareth us witness;
since Brutus the bold knight to Britain came first,
after the siege and the assault had ceased at Troy,
I trow,
many a marvel such before,
has happened here ere now.
To His bliss us bring Who bore
the Crown of Thorns on brow! AMEN

HONY SOYT QUI MAL PENCE[2]

Dante Alighieri

1265–1321

In the traces of autobiography he wove throughout his writings, Dante made it clear that there were two defining tragedies in his life: the death of his beloved Beatrice in 1290 and his exile from Florence in 1302, condemned to death should he ever return. Much else must have occurred in his life of which we know next to nothing—around 1285, he was married to one Gemma Donati, who bore him four children; he wrote his epic poem the *Commedia* during his peripatetic years of exile, finishing it right around the time of his death in Ravenna in 1321—but in the world of his poetry he chose to epitomize his life by an episode of unrequited love and a moment of high political drama.

Dante's Florence was an independent republic, and its status as a banking center had made it one of the most important cities in late medieval Europe. It was also, like much of Italy, torn by civil strife. In 1260, two coalitions of noble families had fought for control of the city: the victorious Ghibellines, allied with the Hohenstaufen ruler Manfred, and the defeated Guelfs, allied with the papacy and a group of north-central Italian cities. The Guelfs regained control of Florence seven years later, banishing the Ghibellines and confiscating their property. In 1295, Dante enrolled in one of the professional guilds that constituted the power base of the *popolo,* a

2. "Let them be ashamed who think ill of it" (French), the English royal motto.

popular party which sought to contain the feuding of the aristocratic families, now focused on the drive by Pope Boniface VIII to bring northern Italy under papal control. In 1300, Dante was appointed to a two-month term as one of the city's seven priors (chief magistrates). As the city was rocked with violence, the priors exiled leading members of the new clashing factions of Black and White Guelfs, including Dante's good friend, the poet Guido Cavalcanti, who would die later that year. While an emissary in Rome two years later, Dante was sentenced to death in absentia, probably as revenge for his part in the earlier decision. He spent the last two decades of his life in miserable exile, wandering from city to city and patron to patron, all over Italy and possibly as far as Paris.

Dante's earliest writings include *Il Fiore* (*The Flower*), a sonnet sequence adapted from *The Romance of the Rose*, and other writings related to the Northern Italian lyric movement of the *dolce stil novo,* or "sweet new style," as he would call it in the *Commedia.* The new Italian lyric was predominantly metaphysical, using Provençal forms and imagery to explore questions of philosophy, theology, and knowledge. Love was seldom sexual and seldom even social; the poet need barely have spoken to an idealized beloved like Dante's Beatrice or Cavalcanti's Giovanna. According to his poetic autobiography, *La vita nuova* (*The New Life,* 1292–1294), Dante first encountered the Florentine girl, Beatrice Portinari, when she was eight and he was nine years old; she died sixteen years later without Dante having ever exchanged more than a few words with her. While he suffers from her presence (and her absence) just as a courtly lover would have done, he also comes to regard his beloved as nothing less than a manifestation of Christ, descended to earth to inspire him with love in order to lead him to a deeper understanding and a better life.

Much of Dante's writing was concerned with the meaning of what he had already written. *La Vita nuova* placed a series of his most celebrated early lyrics in the context of his obsession with Beatrice, explaining in retrospect how each poem had come to be written and how each reflected a different stage in his love from afar and a different aspect of his divine beloved. In *Il Convivio* (*The Banquet*), written in exile between about 1304 and 1307 and left unfinished, Dante reinterpreted several long love lyrics, this time as allegories about Lady Philosophy. During the same period he wrote but didn't finish *De vulgari eloquentia* (*On the Vulgar Tongue*) in which he surveyed the lyric tradition as a defense for composing intellectually ambitious verse in an Italian vernacular rather than in Latin. Somewhere around 1310, he wrote *De Monarchia* (*On Monarchy*), a treatise on political philosophy arguing that an emperor was necessary to provide political stability to the world. The *Commedia* or *Comedy,* widely known as *The Divine Comedy,* incorporates all of Dante's earlier themes; it documents the difficulty of fulfilling his youthful ambitions, and the many ways in which the poet may or may not actually be worthy of doing so.

The structure of the *Commedia* is dazzlingly simple and impossibly intricate, an attempt to mirror the essential mystery of the Trinity. Everything is divided into threes and ones, their ideal permutations of nine and ten, and the perfect number seven. The single poem is composed of three parts, or canticles, *Inferno, Purgatorio,* and *Paradiso,* each describing one of the three distinct realms of the afterlife that compose the single universe comprehended by the divine plan. Each canticle is made up of thirty-three cantos, for a total of ninety-nine, except that *Inferno* has one extra to make a perfect hundred. Usually the first canto is considered as a prelude to the rest; this is one example of the ways in which Dante introduced dissymmetry to prevent the overall order of his poem from becoming monotonous. Cantos, for example, range in length from 115 to 160 lines. The meter Dante invented for the *Commedia,* which he called *terza rima* (third rhyme), embodies the poem's tension between order and disorder, stability and change. The eleven-syllable lines are divided into *terzinas,* or triplets, the first and third lines rhyming with each other, the second line introducing the main rhyme for the next *terzina.* So, for example, the first nine lines of the *Commedia:*

Nel mezzo del cammin di nostra vita
mi ritrovai per una selva oscura,
ché la diritta via era smarrita.
Ahi quanto a dir qual era è cosa dura
esta selva selvaggia e aspra e forte
che nel pensier rinova la paura!
Tant' è amara che poco è più morte:
ma per trattar del ben ch'i'vi trovai,
dirò de l'altre cose ch'i' v'ho scorte.

(Ed. Petrocchi)

When I had journeyed half of our life's way,
I found myself within a shadowed forest,
for I had lost the path that does not stray.
Ah, it is hard to speak of what it was,
that savage forest, dense and difficult,
which even in recall renews my fear:
so bitter—death is hardly more severe!
But to retell the good discovered there,
I'll also tell the other things I saw.

Each *terzina* is a self-contained argument, but the overlapping rhymes link one unit to the next, providing both closure and continuity. For example in line 3, *smarrita* ("lost") brings the opening image to a frightening close, but then the next rhymes of *dura* ("hard") and *paura* ("fear") recall and expand the previous description of the *selva oscura* ("dark forest"), while the new rhyme word *forte* ("difficult") looks forward to the next *terzina,* which rounds out the opening argument of all nine verses: he will tell us of the bad so that we will understand the good that came after.

The vision the poet recounts encompasses God's plan for the world, from its creation through to the Last Judgment. From the divine perspective, time doesn't exist, for in Dante's theology, as in Augustine's (see page 846), God existed before time began and will still exist after time ceases. Everything that happens in the world, every thought and action, is known by God beforehand. From the human perspective, however, seeing only at best the deeds of the past, the lessons of history, and the memories of a life, this eternal scheme can hardly be comprehended, much less put into words. The formal structure of the poem is the most fundamental of the many ways in which Dante tries to impart this dual perspective to his readers. The transience, variety, and fascination of human life alternate with the eternity, unity, and fixity of the afterlife. Rather than simply relate what he saw in his vision and explain what it meant, the all-knowing poet slowly reveals it through a first-person persona (referred to in the notes to the poem as "the pilgrim") who is as unfamiliar as we are with what he is seeing. For the medieval Christian, the world and everything in it was a book created by God to be read and interpreted, and this is how Dante conceived the afterlife, as an enormously complex rebus, a puzzle to be deciphered. Each soul the pilgrim encounters presents a mystery; it is often unclear in terms of strict Catholic doctrine why a certain soul has been damned to hell or another saved in purgatory. Even though the poet claims to have been there and to have understood what everything in this plan means, he wants us instead to be confused, intrigued, and even outraged by what we see. The reader is to be converted, taught the way to salvation, but as an active participant.

There are three guides who lead the pilgrim on this journey: the classical Roman poet Virgil (70–19 B.C.E.), who takes him through Hell and Purgatory; Beatrice, who takes him through Paradise; and Saint Bernard of Clairvaux, who prepares him for the final momentary union with the godhead. In addition to their historical character, each of these figures can be understood as a personification in an allegory about the conversion of a human soul: Virgil as the role of Reason in comprehending the rational cost of sin, either damnation or expiation; Beatrice as the role of Love and Faith in moving beyond the physical bounds of sin into the heavens; Bernard as the role of mystic vision and theology in achieving a final, perfect fusion with God. Each can be understood also as a personification of letters and study: Virgil as the preparatory ground of the classics; Beatrice as the inspirational role of love poetry; Bernard as the conclusive grasp of theology and mysticism. Further, they personify key influences in Dante's own life, the depth and emotional commitment of his attachment especially to the poetry and legend of Virgil and to the person and memory of Beatrice. For the *Commedia* is also a deeply felt spiritual autobiography, moving from suicidal despair to hope and the fulfillment of the pilgrim's innermost wishes.

The landscape of this autobiography is an idiosyncratic version of medieval geography and myth. Dante places Hell within the earth, an inverted cone created when Satan fell from heaven through the southern hemisphere directly opposite the future site of Jerusalem. As Satan was lodged in the center of the earth, land fleeing his presence piled up in both directions. The land escaping to the north created the inhabited world and hollowed out the cone of Hell beneath it. To the south, a passage was created leading to the surface of the southern hemisphere, where the mountain of Purgatory arose, its seven terraces analogous to the nine circles of hell. At the top of the mountain of Purgatory sits the earthly paradise, where Adam and Eve first dwelt in Eden before they were banished to the world below. Paradise is located in the fiery Empyrean, beyond the planets and stars above. Dante tells us that the three realms are peopled by innumerable souls, but singles out various individuals as emblematic of each sin or quality. His selection is eclectic: men and women out of classical myth and Roman history, biblical figures, Florentines, other Italians, and Europeans, friends and enemies, poets and politicians, characters from medieval legend, and popes who hadn't even died yet in 1300 when the journey is supposed to occur. Dante chooses to persuade us of the extraordinary bliss of heaven and the intolerable torment of hell by painting them in the vivid colors we know so well from the world in which we live. He invests every one of these characters, every word they say and everything the pilgrim does with enormous significance, a significance that he makes us urgently need to know.

PRONUNCIATIONS:

Beatrice: BAY-ah-TREE-che
Commedia: koh-ME-dee-ah
Contrapasso: kohn-trah-PAH-soh
Francesca: frahn-CHES-kah
Inferno: een-FAYR-noh
Guido Cavalcanti: GWEE-doh kah-vahl-KAHN-tee
La Vita Nuova: lah VEE-tah noo-OH-vah
Partadiso: pah-rah-DEE-soh
Purgatorio: poor-gah-TOR-ee-oh
terra rima: TAYR-tazh REE-mah
Ugolino: OO-goh-LEE-noh

THE DIVINE COMEDY[1]

Inferno

Hell serves double duty in the *Commedia:* it describes the consequences of a sinful life and it teaches the reader how to read the poem. Although from early on critics began mapping its nine circles (plus the vestibule, or ante-hell) and arguing about who did or didn't deserve to be where, Dante actually reveals the structure of Hell gradually, sometimes only partially, and often in ways a medieval reader would never have expected. This begins with Virgil, the most complex character in the poem. He was renowned for his virtue and considered a prophet of Christianity, and there was no pressing reason to condemn him to Hell at all. As with many of the souls encountered, however, Virgil's fate serves to define his place (Limbo) as a series of

1. Translated by Allen Mandelbaum.

debates and dilemmas rather than a simple equation. In God's eyes, sin may be a simple and well-ordered business, but from the human perspective, it is not so easy to judge. Sin can be seductive, like Francesca da Rimini in the circle of the Lustful; it can inspire pity and fear, like Ugolino at the very bottom of Hell. Seldom, however, is it exactly what it seems, for Dante expects his readers to move back and forth through the poem, to compare what he says about a shade to what was known or written about him or her: he challenges his readers to be like himself, so immersed in the classics, the Bible, myth, history and thirteenth-century art and politics that they become emotional, life-and-death concerns. The portraits are striking in their own right, but the more we know about their models the more profound and far-reaching are the moral and ethical dilemmas they embody.

We unravel the meaning of each circle of Hell through the souls we are told it contains, by the dramatic encounters the two pilgrims have with certain of these souls, by the particular guardian (usually a mythological monster) assigned to each, by the particular landscape, by the style of the language, which ranges from the sublimity of epic to the simplicity of lyric to the earthiness of the folk tale, and by the nature of the torment. One soul terms Hell's torments the *contrapasso,* or counter-punishment. The principle of *contrapasso* is poetic justice: each soul receives what he or she most desired or did on earth, but in a perverse and unwanted form—the flatterers drown in excrement; the sowers of discord are split asunder. There is a tension throughout *Inferno* between the moral lessons we are to learn from the damned characters, and the fascination many of them exert on us, both positive and negative, in their quality as stubbornly alive and suffering individuals.

Many of the damned serve to demonstrate that there is a danger in knowing Hell too well. The underworld offers great temptation for rage and revenge, and it contains much of apparent pleasure and beauty as well: the worthies of Limbo, Francesca's love, Dante's mentor Brunetto Latini, the doting father of his friend and fellow poet Cavalcanti. This will also be a dilemma in *Purgatorio,* where the souls, although saved, must suffer much in weaning themselves from their ties to the world they loved, but in the *Inferno* the dilemma takes a starker form. The stakes are very high, not just for individuals but for society, and Dante is also careful to indicate which parts of Hell cause particular trouble, either to him or to his society: sins of desire, which are so close to the love and longing that can lead one to God; the complex and subdivided sins of fraud in the eighth circle, which attack the very bonds of sociability on which community relies. Dante doesn't want us to submit meekly to the journey through Hell; he expects us to go through it kicking and screaming, arguing and cursing, although he also expects that in the end he will win us over, as in the end he has won over himself.

Canto 1

The voyager-narrator astray by night in a dark forest. Morning and the sunlit hill. Three beasts that impede his ascent. The encounter with Virgil, who offers his guidance and an alternative path through two of the three realms the voyager must visit.

When I had journeyed half of our life's way,[2]
I found myself within a shadowed forest,

2. Canto 21.112–14 establishes the date of the journey as Easter weekend of 1300, the entry into the dark wood on the night of Maundy Thursday, the day before Good Friday. Born in 1265, Dante would have been 35, precisely midway in the biblical life span of 70 years. The adjective "our" expands the individual journey to one that involves the reader in an allegory of every person's life.

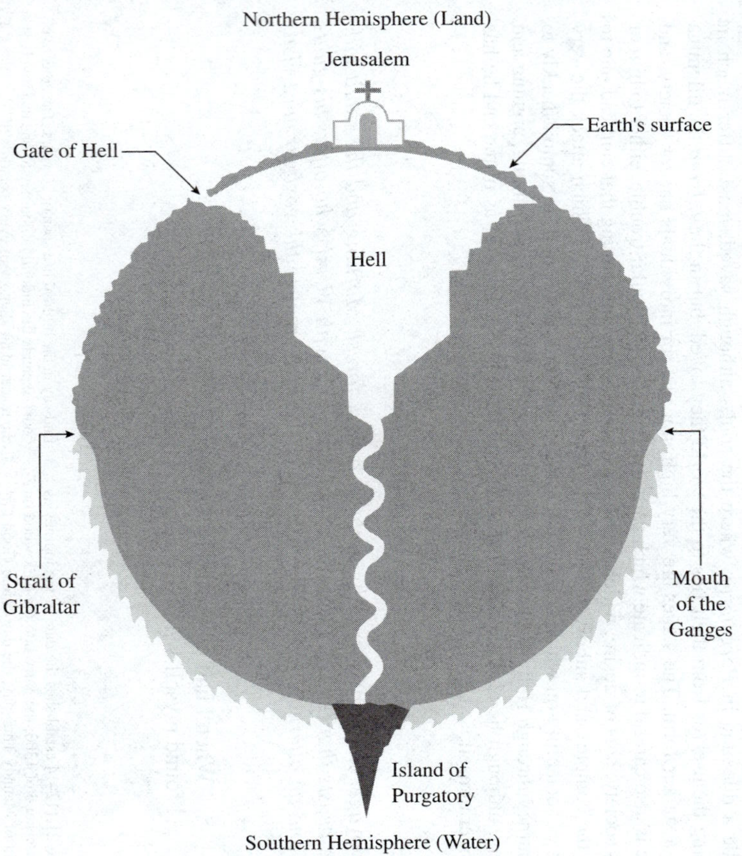

Cross Section of the Earth

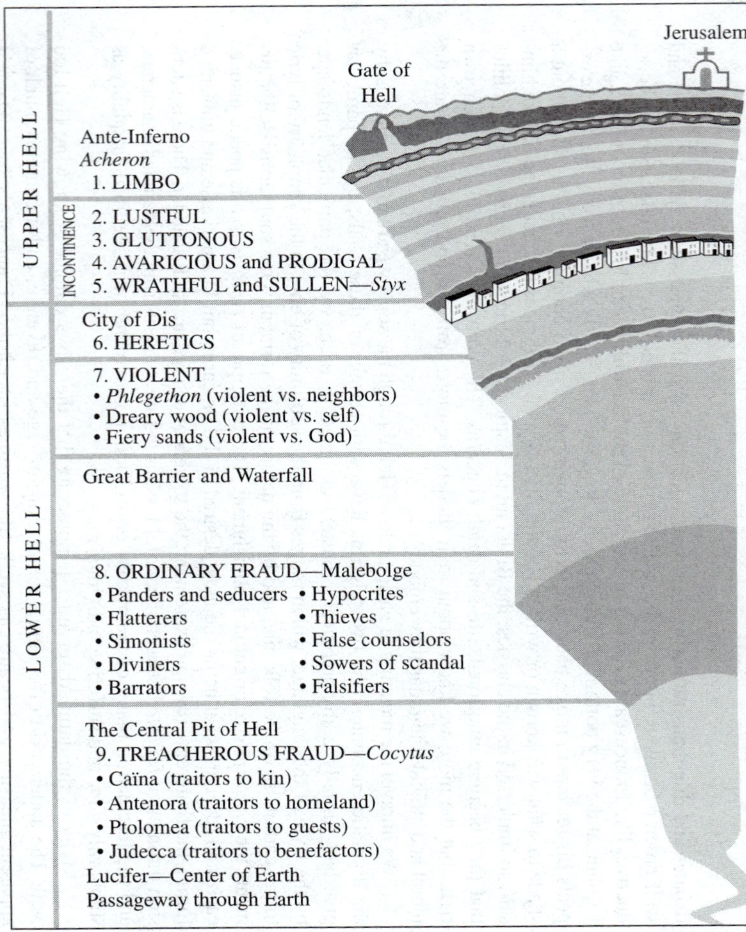

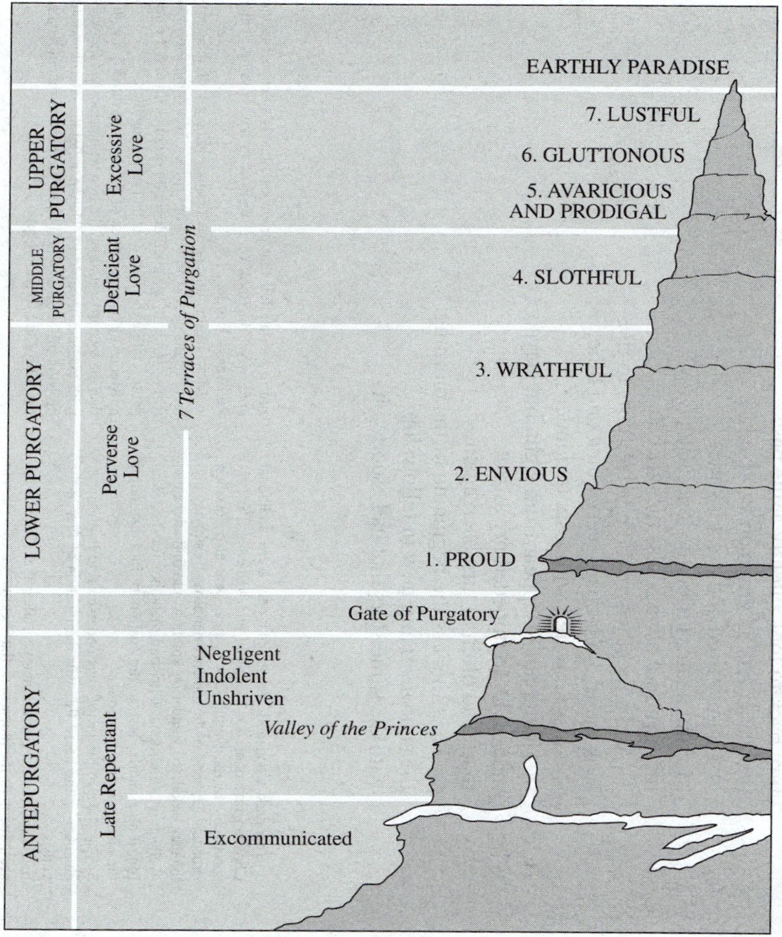

EARTHLY PARADISE
UPPER PURGATORY
Excessive Love
7. LUSTFUL
6. GLUTTONOUS
5. AVARICIOUS AND PRODIGAL
MIDDLE PURGATORY
Deficient Love
4. SLOTHFUL
7 Terraces of Purgation
LOWER PURGATORY
Perverse Love
3. WRATHFUL
2. ENVIOUS
1. PROUD
Gate of Purgatory
ANTEPURGATORY
Late Repentant
Negligent
Indolent
Unshriven
Valley of the Princes
Excommunicated

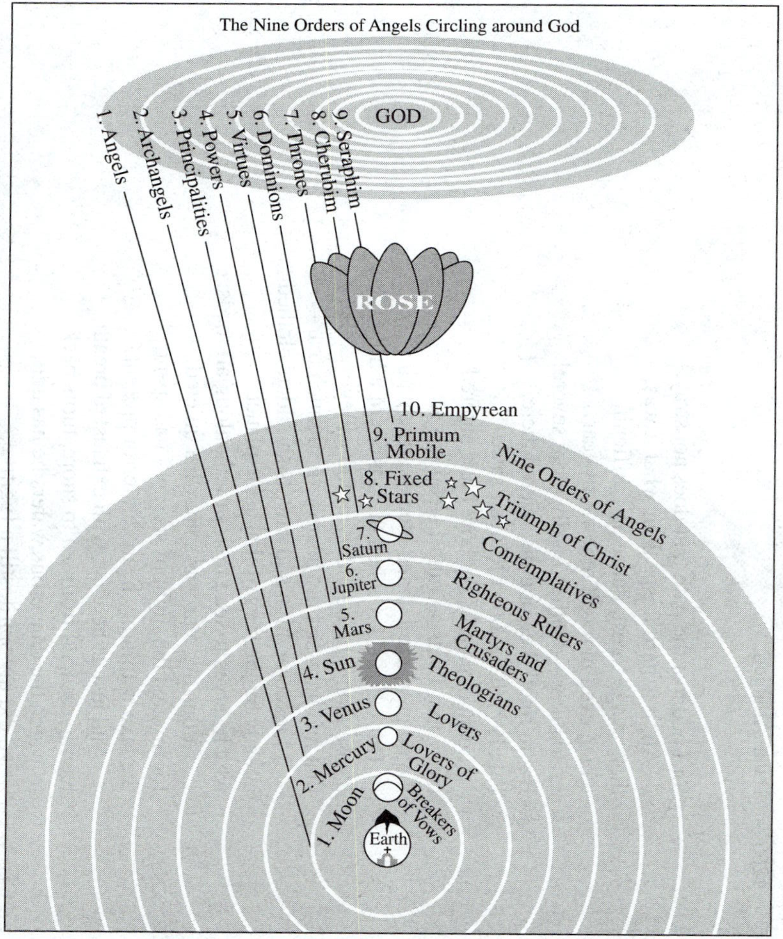

The Nine Orders of Angels Circling around God
GOD
9. Seraphim
8. Cherubim
7. Thrones
6. Dominions
5. Virtues
4. Powers
3. Principalities
2. Archangels
1. Angels
ROSE
10. Empyrean
9. Primum Mobile
Nine Orders of Angels
8. Fixed Stars
Triumph of Christ
7. Saturn
Contemplatives
6. Jupiter
Righteous Rulers
5. Mars
Martyrs and Crusaders
4. Sun
Theologians
3. Venus
Lovers
2. Mercury
Lovers of Glory
1. Moon
Breakers of Vows
Earth

for I had lost the path that does not stray.[3]
Ah, it is hard to speak of what it was,
that savage forest, dense and difficult,
which even in recall renews my fear:
so bitter—death is hardly more severe!
But to retell the good discovered there,
I'll also tell the other things I saw.
I cannot clearly say how I had entered
the wood; I was so full of sleep just at
the point where I abandoned the true path.[4]
But when I'd reached the bottom of a hill—
it rose along the boundary of the valley
that had harassed my heart with so much fear—
I looked on high and saw its shoulders clothed
already by the rays of that same planet° *the sun*
which serves to lead men straight along all roads.
At this my fear was somewhat quieted;
for through the night of sorrow I had spent,
the lake within my heart felt terror present.[5]
And just as he who, with exhausted breath,
having escaped from sea to shore, turns back
to watch the dangerous waters he has quit,
so did my spirit, still a fugitive,
turn back to look intently at the pass
that never has let any man survive.[6]
I let my tired body rest awhile.
Moving again, I tried the lonely slope—
my firm foot always was the one below.[7]
And almost where the hillside starts to rise—
look there!—a leopard, very quick and lithe,
a leopard covered with a spotted hide.[8]
He did not disappear from sight, but stayed;
indeed, he so impeded my ascent
that I had often to turn back again.
The time was the beginning of the morning;
the sun was rising now in fellowship
with the same stars that had escorted it

3. The dark wood and the straight path were traditional Christian metaphors for the sinful and righteous lives, respectively. In the Middle Ages, they were also common structural elements of the romance narrative: by straying into the dark wood, the wandering knight would find adventure.

4. Sleep is a traditional Christian metaphor for the sinful life; it also alludes here to the customary introduction of the medieval dream vision.

5. The "lake of the heart" was understood to be the inner chamber of the heart; this was the location of fear in the body.

6. The first of the poem's many similes: the image of the sea alludes to the shipwreck that begins Virgil's *Aeneid* and to the landfall that precedes Aeneas's descent to the underworld in Book 6, as well as to the crossing of the Red Sea in Exodus.

7. Most likely, this is a Christian allegory of the "two feet" of the soul. The left, or "firmer," dragging foot was that of the will, weighed down by original sin and the appetites, while the right was that of the intellect.

8. Medieval commentaries of the *Inferno* quickly identified the leopard with lust, the lion with pride, and the wolf with avarice, or cupidity. They parallel the later threefold division of the sins of hell between those of incontinence, bestiality, and fraud in Canto 11.

when Divine Love first moved those things of beauty;[9]
so that the hour and the gentle season
gave me good cause for hopefulness on seeing
that beast before me with his speckled skin;
but hope was hardly able to prevent
the fear I felt when I beheld a lion.
His head held high and ravenous with hunger—
even the air around him seemed to shudder—
this lion seemed to make his way against me.
And then a she-wolf showed herself; she seemed
to carry every craving in her leanness;
she had already brought despair to many.
The very sight of her so weighted me
with fearfulness that I abandoned hope
of ever climbing up that mountain slope.
Even as he who glories while he gains
will, when the time has come to tally loss,
lament with every thought and turn despondent,
so was I when I faced that restless beast,
which, even as she stalked me, step by step
had thrust me back to where the sun is speechless.
While I retreated down to lower ground,
before my eyes there suddenly appeared
one who seemed faint because of the long silence.
When I saw him in that vast wilderness,
"Have pity on me," were the words I cried,
"whatever you may be—a shade, a man."
He answered me: "Not man; I once was man.
Both of my parents came from Lombardy,
and both claimed Mantua as native city.
And I was born, though late, *sub Julio,*
and lived in Rome under the good Augustus—
the season of the false and lying gods.
I was a poet, and I sang the righteous
son of Anchises who had come from Troy
when flames destroyed the pride of Ilium.[1]
But why do you return to wretchedness?
Why not climb up the mountain of delight,
the origin and cause of every joy?"
"And are you then that Virgil, you the fountain
that freely pours so rich a stream of speech?"
I answered him with shame upon my brow.
"O light and honor of all other poets,

9. The world was believed to have been created in spring, when the sun was in the constellation of Ares; Dante's journey takes place in the same season and under the same stars.

1. Virgil (70–19 B.C.E.) was born during the lifetime of Julius Caesar, who was assassinated in 44, too soon to have known the poet's writing. Virgil's patron was Caesar's adopted son, the emperor Augustus. Virgil identifies himself with his final work, the mythical epic of Aeneas, the "righteous son of Anchises," who journeyed from the destruction of Troy ("Ilium") to Italy to found the city of Rome.

may my long study and the intense love
that made me search your volume serve me now.
You are my master and my author, you—
the only one from whom my writing drew
the noble style for which I have been honored.
You see the beast that made me turn aside;
help me, o famous sage, to stand against her,
for she has made my blood and pulses shudder."
"It is another path that you must take,"
he answered when he saw my tearfulness,
"if you would leave this savage wilderness;
the beast that is the cause of your outcry
allows no man to pass along her track,
but blocks him even to the point of death;
her nature is so squalid, so malicious
that she can never sate her greedy will;
when she has fed, she's hungrier than ever.
She mates with many living souls and shall
yet mate with many more, until the Greyhound
arrives, inflicting painful death on her.
That Hound will never feed on land or pewter,
but find his fare in wisdom, love, and virtue;
his place of birth shall be between two felts.[2]
He will restore low-lying Italy
for which the maid Camilla died of wounds,
and Nisus, Turnus, and Euryalus.[3]
And he will hunt that beast through every city
until he thrusts her back again to Hell,
from which she was first sent above by envy.[4]
Therefore, I think and judge it best for you
to follow me, and I shall guide you, taking
you from this place through an eternal place,
where you shall hear the howls of desperation
and see the ancient spirits in their pain,
as each of them laments his second death;[5]
and you shall see those souls who are content
within the fire,° for they hope to reach— *of Purgatory*
whenever that may be—the blessed people.
If you would then ascend as high as these,

2. Virgil explains the she-wolf's sway by means of the first of the poem's many prophecies. The poetical aptness of a Greyhound (*veltro*) to hunt down and kill the she-wolf is clear; possible identities are many and not mutually exclusive. There is some reference to the redemptive powers of Christ, but also to the desired coming of a secular leader who would be above corruption, seeking neither land nor money ("pewter"), and who would reestablish temporal authority in Christendom: perhaps Dante's benefactor Can Grande della Scala of Verona, whose domain was roughly limited by the two "felts" (*Feltros*) of Feltre and Montefeltro, perhaps a Holy Roman Emperor, elected by the casting of ballots in the felt-lined urns used at the time.

3. Virgil refers to Italy in terms of his own epic of the founding of the classical Roman empire, alluding to four characters who died in the civil war for the possession of Italy related in the second half of the *Aeneid.*

4. "But by the envy of the devil, death entered the world" (Wisdom 2:24).

5. Either the condemnation of the soul to hell after death, or the final condemnation to hell and reunion with the body that will occur during the Last Judgment.

a soul more worthy than I am will guide you;
I'll leave you in her care when I depart,
because that Emperor who reigns above,
since I have been rebellious to His law,
will not allow me entry to His city.
He governs everywhere, but rules from there;
there is His city, His high capital:
o happy those He chooses to be there!"
And I replied: "O poet—by that God
whom you had never come to know—I beg you,
that I may flee this evil and worse evils,
to lead me to the place of which you spoke,
that I may see the gateway of Saint Peter[6]
and those whom you describe as sorrowful."
Then he set out, and I moved on behind him.

Canto 2

The following evening. Invocation to the Muses. The narrator's questioning of his worthiness to visit the deathless world. Virgil's comforting explanation that he has been sent to help Dante by three Ladies of Heaven. The voyager heartened. Their setting out.

The day was now departing; the dark air
released the living beings of the earth
from work and weariness; and I myself
alone prepared to undergo the battle
both of the journeying and of the pity,
which memory, mistaking not, shall show.
O Muses, o high genius, help me now;
o memory that set down what I saw,
here shall your excellence reveal itself![1]
I started: "Poet, you who are my guide,
see if the force in me is strong enough
before you let me face that rugged pass.
You say that he who fathered Sylvius,
while he was still corruptible, had journeyed
into the deathless world with his live body.[2]
For, if the Enemy of every evil
was courteous to him, considering
all he would cause and who and what he was,
that does not seem incomprehensible,
since in the empyrean heaven he was chosen
to father honored Rome and her empire;
and if the truth be told, Rome and her realm

6. Either the gate of Purgatory or the entry to Paradise.
1. Echoes of the *Aeneid* continue: the invocation of the classical muses was a staple of the epic style. Dante adds the stress on the poet's memory of what he has seen.
2. In lines 13–27, Dante retells the story of *Aeneid* 6 (see page 742) in a Christian context. While still alive, Aeneas (father of Sylvius, ancestor of the founder of Rome) descended to the underworld, which included both a place of punishment and a paradise, in order to meet his father and learn the fate of his descendants.

were destined to become the sacred place,
the seat of the successor° of great Peter. *the Pope*
And through the journey you ascribe to him,
he came to learn of things that were to bring
his victory and, too, the papal mantle.[3]
Later the Chosen Vessel travelled there,
to bring us back assurance of that faith
with which the way to our salvation starts.[4]
But why should I go there? Who sanctions it?
For I am not Aeneas, am not Paul;
nor I nor others think myself so worthy.
Therefore, if I consent to start this journey,
I fear my venture may be wild and empty.
You're wise; you know far more than what I say."
And just as he who unwills what he wills
and shifts what he intends to seek new ends
so that he's drawn from what he had begun,
so was I in the midst of that dark land,
because, with all my thinking, I annulled
the task I had so quickly undertaken.
"If I have understood what you have said,"
replied the shade of that great-hearted one,
"your soul has been assailed by cowardice,
which often weighs so heavily on a man—
distracting him from honorable trials—
as phantoms frighten beasts when shadows fall.
That you may be delivered from this fear,
I'll tell you why I came and what I heard
when I first felt compassion for your pain.[5]
I was among those souls who are suspended;° *in Limbo*
a lady called to me, so blessed, so lovely
that I implored to serve at her command.
Her eyes surpassed the splendor of the star's;
and she began to speak to me—so gently
and softly—with angelic voice. She said:
'O spirit of the courteous Mantuan,
whose fame is still a presence in the world
and shall endure as long as the world lasts,
my friend, who has not been the friend of fortune,
is hindered in his path along that lonely
hillside; he has been turned aside by terror.
From all that I have heard of him in Heaven,

3. Aeneas's father gave him advice on the upcoming war and showed his son a procession of souls of future Romans that forecast the empire of Augustus; in Dante's version it also forecasts papal Rome.

4. The apostle Paul ("the Chosen Vessel") described in his second Epistle to the Corinthians (12:2–4) how he was "caught up into Paradise"; the apocryphal *Vision of St. Paul* narrates a descent into hell as well.

5. Virgil explains how he came to appear before Dante and provides a "divine" authorization for the journey (and the poem) that follows. The language of the account is less that of the high style of the *Aeneid* than of the lyric of courtly love.

he is, I fear, already so astray
that I have come to help him much too late.
Go now; with your persuasive word, with
all that is required to see that he escapes,
bring help to him, that I may be consoled.
For I am Beatrice who send you on;
I come from where I most long to return;
Love prompted me, that Love which makes me speak.
When once again I stand before my Lord,
then I shall often let Him hear your praises.'
Now Beatrice was silent. I began:
'O Lady of virtue, the sole reason why
the human race surpasses all that lies
beneath the heaven with the smallest spheres,
so welcome is your wish, that even if
it were already done, it would seem tardy;
all you need do is let me know your will.
But tell me why you have not been more prudent—
descending to this center, moving from
that spacious place where you long to return?'
'Because you want to fathom things so deeply,
I now shall tell you promptly,' she replied,
'why I am not afraid to enter here.
One ought to be afraid of nothing other
than things possessed of power to do us harm,
but things innocuous need not be feared.
God, in His graciousness, has made me so
that this, your misery, cannot touch me;
I can withstand the fires flaming here.[6]
In Heaven there's a gentle lady—one
who weeps for the distress toward which I send you,
so that stern judgment up above is shattered.
And it was she who called upon Lucia,[7]
requesting of her: "Now your faithful one
has need of you, and I commend him to you."
Lucia, enemy of every cruelty,
arose and made her way to where I was,
sitting beside the venerable Rachel.[8]
She said: "You, Beatrice, true praise of God,
why have you not helped him who loves you so
that—for your sake—he's left the vulgar crowd?
Do you not hear the anguish in his cry?
Do you not see the death he wars against
upon that river ruthless as the sea?"
No one within this world has ever been

6. Neither the fires of hell nor the damned have the power physically to harm any of the blessed, nor do their sufferings deserve any compassion—a cornerstone of Catholic doctrine that Dante sorely tests in the *Inferno*.

7. St. Lucy of Syracuse, a late-3rd-century virgin martyr who is patron saint of sight, and a symbol of illuminating grace.

8. Beatrice has her seat in heaven next to Rachel, younger sister of Leah in Genesis, and beloved of Jacob.

so quick to seek his good or flee his harm
as I—when she had finished speaking thus—
to come below, down from my blessed station;
I trusted in your honest utterance,
which honors you and those who've listened to you.'
When she had finished with her words to me,
she turned aside her gleaming, tearful eyes,
which only made me hurry all the more.
And, just as she had wished, I came to you:
I snatched you from the path of the fierce beast
that barred the shortest way up the fair mountain.
What is it then? Why, why do you resist?
Why does your heart host so much cowardice?
Where are your daring and your openness
as long as there are three such blessed women
concerned for you within the court of Heaven
and my words promise you so great a good?"
As little flowers, which the chill of night
has bent and huddled, when the white sun strikes,
grow straight and open fully on their stems,
so did I, too, with my exhausted force;
and such warm daring rushed into my heart
that I—as one who has been freed—began:
"O she, compassionate, who has helped me!
And you who, courteous, obeyed so quickly
the true words that she had addressed to you!
You, with your words, have so disposed my heart
to longing for this journey—I return
to what I was at first prepared to do.
Now go; a single will fills both of us:
you are my guide, my governor, my master."
These were my words to him; when he advanced,
I entered on the steep and savage path.

Canto 3

The inscription above the Gate of Hell. The Ante-Inferno, where the shades of those who lived without praise and without blame now intermingle with the neutral angels. He who made the great refusal. The River Acheron. Charon. Dante's loss of his senses as the earth trembles.

THROUGH ME THE WAY INTO THE SUFFERING CITY,
THROUGH ME THE WAY TO THE ETERNAL PAIN,
THROUGH ME THE WAY THAT RUNS AMONG THE LOST.
JUSTICE URGED ON MY HIGH ARTIFICER;
MY MAKER WAS DIVINE AUTHORITY,
THE HIGHEST WISDOM, AND THE PRIMAL LOVE.
BEFORE ME NOTHING BUT ETERNAL THINGS
WERE MADE, AND I ENDURE ETERNALLY.

ABANDON EVERY HOPE, WHO ENTER HERE.[1]
These words—their aspect was obscure—I read
inscribed above a gateway, and I said:
"Master, their meaning is difficult for me."
And he to me, as one who comprehends:
"Here one must leave behind all hesitation;
here every cowardice must meet its death.
For we have reached the place of which I spoke,
where you will see the miserable people,
those who have lost the good of the intellect."[2]
And when, with gladness in his face, he placed
his hand upon my own, to comfort me,
he drew me in among the hidden things.
Here sighs and lamentations and loud cries
were echoing across the starless air,
so that, as soon as I set out, I wept.
Strange utterances, horrible pronouncements,
accents of anger, words of suffering,
and voices shrill and faint, and beating hands—
all went to make a tumult that will whirl
forever through that turbid, timeless air,
like sand that eddies when a whirlwind swirls.
And I—my head oppressed by horror—said:
"Master, what is it that I hear? Who are
those people so defeated by their pain?"
And he to me: "This miserable way
is taken by the sorry souls of those
who lived without disgrace and without praise.
They now commingle with the coward angels,
the company of those who were not rebels
nor faithful to their God, but stood apart.
The heavens, that their beauty not be lessened,
have cast them out, nor will deep Hell receive them—
even the wicked cannot glory in them."[3]
And I: "What is it, master, that oppresses
these souls, compelling them to wail so loud?"
He answered: "I shall tell you in few words.
Those who are here can place no hope in death,
and their blind life is so abject that they
are envious of every other fate.
The world will let no fame of theirs endure;

1. The famous inscription on the Gate of Hell announces several key laws of the realm: it is the negative counterpart to the city of God, but also created by divine order, subject to the Lord's authority, and ruled by justice and love. Evil is not independent from, but somehow part of the divine scheme since it was first created by Satan's rebellion at the beginning of time.

2. The rules may be clear, but their meaning is not. Virgil gives a first definition of the state of damnation: those ruled by their appetites rather than their reason. Truth, following Aristotle, is the good of the intellect; for Dante the highest good is God.

3. Dante invented a category of souls who belong neither in Heaven nor in Hell properly speaking: the "lukewarm," grouped with the neutral angels, those who neither rebelled with Satan nor sided with God.

both justice and compassion must disdain them;
let us not talk of them, but look and pass."[4]

And I, looking more closely, saw a banner
that, as it wheeled about, raced on—so quick
that any respite seemed unsuited to it.

Behind that banner trailed so long a file
of people—I should never have believed
that death could have unmade so many souls.

After I had identified a few,
I saw and recognized the shade of him
who made, through cowardice, the great refusal.[5]

At once I understood with certainty:
this company contained the cowardly,
hateful to God and to His enemies.

These wretched ones, who never were alive,
went naked and were stung again, again
by horseflies and by wasps that circled them.

The insects streaked their faces with their blood,
which, mingled with their tears, fell at their feet,
where it was gathered up by sickening worms.

And then, looking beyond them, I could see
a crowd along the bank of a great river;
at which I said: "Allow me now to know

who are these people—master—and what law
has made them seem so eager for the crossing,
as I can see despite the feeble light."

And he to me: "When we have stopped along
the melancholy shore of Acheron,° *a river of Hell*
then all these matters will be plain to you."

At that, with eyes ashamed, downcast, and fearing
that what I said had given him offense,
I did not speak until we reached the river.

And here, advancing toward us, in a boat,
an aged man—his hair was white with years[6]—
was shouting: "Woe to you, corrupted souls!

Forget your hope of ever seeing Heaven:
I come to lead you to the other shore,
to the eternal dark, to fire and frost.

And you approaching there, you living soul,
keep well away from these—they are the dead."
But when he saw I made no move to go,

he said: "Another way and other harbors—

4. Here the poetically apt punishment consists of the complete lack of fame for those who made no choices in life, and of goading insects and speeding banners, since they would not be goaded and chose no banners.

5. The one soul singled out among the lukewarm, fittingly, is not named. Early commentators mostly agreed he was Pope Celestine V, who abdicated ("the great refusal") only five months after his election as pope in 1294, allowing the election of Boniface VIII, pope from 1294 to 1303, one of the arch-villains of the *Commedia.*

6. The first figure out of pagan mythology encountered in Hell, the ferryman Charon was the son of Erebus and Night.

not here—will bring you passage to your shore:
a lighter craft will have to carry you."
My guide then: "Charon, don't torment yourself:
our passage has been willed above, where One[7]
can do what He has willed; and ask no more."
Now silence fell upon the wooly cheeks
of Charon, pilot of the livid marsh,
whose eyes were ringed about with wheels of flame.
But all those spirits, naked and exhausted,
had lost their color, and they gnashed their teeth
as soon as they heard Charon's cruel words;
they execrated God and their own parents
and humankind, and then the place and time
of their conception's seed and of their birth.
Then they forgathered, huddled in one throng,
weeping aloud along that wretched shore
which waits for all who have no fear of God.
The demon Charon, with his eyes like embers,
by signaling to them, has all embark;
his oar strikes anyone who stretches out.
As, in the autumn, leaves detach themselves,
first one and then the other, till the bough
sees all its fallen garments on the ground,[8]
similarly, the evil seed of Adam
descended from the shoreline one by one,
when signaled, as a falcon—called—will come.[9]
So do they move across the darkened waters;
even before they reach the farther shore,
new ranks already gather on this bank.
"My son," the gracious master said to me,
"those who have died beneath the wrath of God,
all these assemble here from every country;
and they are eager for the river crossing
because celestial justice spurs them on,
so that their fear is turned into desire.
No good soul ever takes its passage here;
therefore, if Charon has complained of you,
by now you can be sure what his words mean."
And after this was said, the darkened plain
quaked so tremendously—the memory
of terror then, bathes me in sweat again.
A whirlwind burst out of the tear-drenched earth,
a wind that crackled with a bloodred light,
a light that overcame all of my senses;
and like a man whom sleep has seized, I fell.

7. God, Christ, and the Holy Spirit are never named in Hell directly.

8. The simile of autumn leaves to describe dead souls reworks that of *Aeneid* 6.309–12.

9. A simile from medieval falconry: the moment when the falcon is lured down by the hunter.

Canto 4

Dante's awakening to the First Circle, or Limbo, inhabited by those who were worthy but lived before Christianity and/or without baptism. The welcoming of Virgil and Dante by Homer, Horace, Ovid, Lucan. The catalogue of other great-hearted spirits in the noble castle of Limbo.

The heavy sleep within my head was smashed
by an enormous thunderclap, so that
I started up as one whom force awakens;
I stood erect and turned my rested eyes
from side to side, and I stared steadily
to learn what place it was surrounding me.
In truth I found myself upon the brink
of an abyss, the melancholy valley
containing thundering, unending wailings.
That valley, dark and deep and filled with mist,
is such that, though I gazed into its pit,
I was unable to discern a thing.[1]
"Let us descend into the blind world now,"[2]
the poet, who was deathly pale, began;
"I shall go first and you will follow me."
But I, who'd seen the change in his complexion,
said: "How shall I go on if you are frightened,
you who have always helped dispel my doubts?"
And he to me: "The anguish of the people
whose place is here below, has touched my face
with the compassion you mistake for fear.
Let us go on, the way that waits is long."
So he set out, and so he had me enter
on that first circle girdling the abyss.[3]
Here, for as much as hearing could discover,
there was no outcry louder than the sighs
that caused the everlasting air to tremble.
The sighs arose from sorrow without torments,
out of the crowds—the many multitudes—
of infants and of women and of men.
The kindly master said: "Do you not ask
who are these spirits whom you see before you?
I'd have you know, before you go ahead,
they did not sin; and yet, though they have merits,
that's not enough, because they lacked baptism,
the portal of the faith that you embrace.
And if they lived before Christianity,

1. The first glimpse of the geography of Hell proper. The pit was a standard component of medieval hells; the cone-like valley the pilgrim will encounter was not.
2. Blind because bereft of sun and stars, and blind because bereft of spiritual clarity.
3. The first circle of Hell is Limbo, according to doctrine the place of children who died before baptism and of righteous Old Testament figures who lived before the coming of Christ. Dante took the liberty of adding a new category: the virtuous pagans, whose number includes Virgil.

they did not worship God in fitting ways;
and of such spirits I myself am one.
For these defects, and for no other evil,
we now are lost and punished just with this:
we have no hope and yet we live in longing."
Great sorrow seized my heart on hearing him,
for I had seen some estimable men
among the souls suspended in that limbo.
"Tell me, my master, tell me, lord," I then
began because I wanted to be certain
of that belief which vanquishes all errors,
"did any ever go—by his own merit
or others'—from this place toward blessedness?"
And he, who understood my covert speech,[4]
replied: "I was new-entered on this state
when I beheld a Great Lord enter here;
the crown he wore, a sign of victory.[5]
He carried off the shade of our first father,° *Adam*
of his son Abel, and the shade of Noah,
of Moses, the obedient legislator,
of father Abraham, David the king,
of Israel,° his father, and his sons, *Jacob*
and Rachel, she for whom he worked so long,
and many others—and He made them blessed;
and I should have you know that, before them,
there were no human souls that had been saved."
We did not stay our steps although he spoke;
we still continued onward through the wood—
the wood, I say, where many spirits thronged.
Our path had not gone far beyond the point
where I had slept, when I beheld a fire
win out against a hemisphere of shadows.
We still were at a little distance from it,
but not so far I could not see in part
that honorable men possessed that place.
"O you who honor art and science both,
who are these souls whose dignity has kept
their way of being, separate from the rest?"
And he to me: "The honor of their name,
which echoes up above within your life,
gains Heaven's grace, and that advances them."
Meanwhile there was a voice that I could hear:
"Pay honor to the estimable poet;
his shadow, which had left us, now returns."
After that voice was done, when there was silence,

4. The pilgrim wants to ask whether Virgil, his guide, can be saved. He doesn't receive the answer he desires.

5. The apocryphal Gospel of Nicodemus tells that between his crucifixion on Good Friday and his resurrection on Easter Sunday, Christ descended into Limbo and took its Old Testament figures with him up to Heaven. The Harrowing of Hell was proclaimed as dogma during the 13th century. Virgil died in 19 B.C.E.; hence he was newly arrived when Christ descended in 33 C.E.

I saw four giant shades approaching us;
in aspect, they were neither sad nor joyous.
  My kindly master then began by saying:
"Look well at him who holds that sword in hand,
who moves before the other three as lord.
  That shade is Homer, the consummate poet;
the other one is Horace, satirist;
the third is Ovid, and the last is Lucan.[6]
  Because each of these spirits shares with me
the name called out before by the lone voice,
they welcome me—and, doing that, do well."
  And so I saw that splendid school assembled,
led by the lord of song incomparable,° *Homer*
who like an eagle soars above the rest.
  Soon after they had talked a while together,
they turned to me, saluting cordially;
and having witnessed this, my master smiled;
  and even greater honor then was mine,
for they invited me to join their ranks—
I was the sixth among such intellects.
  So did we move along and toward the light,
talking of things about which silence here
is just as seemly as our speech was there.
  We reached the base of an exalted castle,
encircled seven times by towering walls,
defended all around by a fair stream.[7]
  We forded this as if upon hard ground;
I entered seven portals with these sages;
we reached a meadow of green flowering plants.
  The people here had eyes both grave and slow;
their features carried great authority;
they spoke infrequently, with gentle voices.
  We drew aside to one part of the meadow,
an open place both high and filled with light,
and we could see all those who were assembled.[8]
  Facing me there, on the enameled green,
great-hearted souls were shown to me and I
still glory in my having witnessed them.
  I saw Electra with her many comrades,
among whom I knew Hector and Aeneas,

6. Dante produces a pantheon of classical poets. Homer was known only by reputation in Dante's time. Virgil's friend and contemporary, Horace (65–8 B.C.E.), is remembered here for his *Satires* and *Epistles.* Ovid (43 B.C.E.–17 C.E.) and Lucan (39–65 C.E.) are the two classical poets Dante cites most frequently after Virgil, from Ovid primarily his epic compilation of myth, the *Metamorphoses,* and from Lucan his violent epic on the civil war between Caesar and Pompey, *De bello civili,* or *Pharsalia.*

7. The castle's form is allegorically related to the seven liberal arts and the tradition of the House of Fame, suitable for a group distinguished by their achievements in the arts, in heroism and in proper living but not in the faith required by Christian doctrine.

8. The description of the meadow enclosed by the castle walls is reminiscent of the Elysian Fields of Virgil's underworld, as well as of the *locus amoenus,* or "pleasing place" of courtly romances such as *The Romance of the Rose.* The list of "great-hearted souls" he meets blends mythical and historical, classical and medieval personages.

and Caesar, in his armor, falcon-eyed.[9]
I saw Camilla and Penthesilea
and, on the other side, saw King Latinus,
who sat beside Lavinia, his daughter.[1]
I saw that Brutus who drove Tarquin out,
Lucretia, Julia, Marcia, and Cornelia,
and, solitary, set apart, Saladin.[2]
When I had raised my eyes a little higher,
I saw the master of the men who know,
seated in philosophic family.[3]
There all look up to him, all do him honor:
there I beheld both Socrates and Plato,
closest to him, in front of all the rest;
Democritus, who ascribes the world to chance,
Diogenes, Empedocles, and Zeno,
and Thales, Anaxagoras, Heraclitus;
I saw the good collector of medicinals,
I mean Dioscorides; and I saw Orpheus,
and Tully, Linus, moral Seneca;[4]
and Euclid the geometer, and Ptolemy,
Hippocrates and Galen, Avicenna,
Averroës, of the great Commentary.[5]
I cannot here describe them all in full;
my ample theme impels me onward so:
what's told is often less than the event.
The company of six divides in two;
my knowing guide leads me another way,
beyond the quiet, into trembling air.
And I have reached a part where no thing gleams.

Canto 5

The Second Circle, where the Lustful are forever buffeted by violent storm. Minos. The catalogue of carnal sinners. Francesca da Rimini and her brother-in-law, Paolo Malatesta. Francesca's tale of their love and death, at which Dante faints.

9. The origins and apogee of Rome: Electra was mother of Dardanus, founder of Troy. Hector was the leader of the Trojan forces, the survivors of which Aeneas led to Italy. Caesar founded the imperial line of Rome.

1. Camilla and Penthesilea were female warriors. Latinus was king of Latium; the betrothal of his daughter Lavinia to Aeneas caused Turnus to begin the civil war.

2. Lucius Junius Brutus drove out Tarquin, the last of the legendary Roman kings, in 510 B.C.E. to become one of the first two consuls of the Roman republic. Four female exemplars of Roman virtue are then listed, followed by the Sultan of Egypt from 1171 to 1193, Saladin, who crushingly defeated the Crusaders, but whose magnanimity and generosity were a medieval commonplace.

3. The list of philosophers begins with Aristotle, so influential in Dante's time he need not be named, followed by Socrates, Plato, and seven other celebrated ancient Greek philosophers.

4. Dioscorides was a Greek physician of the 1st century C.E.; Linus and Orpheus were mythical Greek poets; Tully is the Roman orator and philosopher Marcus Tullius Cicero (106–43 B.C.E.), Seneca the moral philosopher and writer of tragedies who committed suicide at the command of Nero in 65 C.E.

5. The mathematician Euclid lived c. 300 B.C.E.; the geocentric theory of his fellow Alexandrian, the astronomer and geographer Ptolemy, who was active in the 2nd century C.E., was the basis of medieval astronomy. Hippocrates and Galen were Greek physicians. Avicenna (980–1037) and Averroës (1126–1198) were Muslim philosophers, both authors of influential commentaries on Aristotle.

So I descended from the first enclosure
down to the second circle, that which girdles
less space but grief more great,[1] that goads to weeping.
There dreadful Minos stands, gnashing his teeth:
examining the sins of those who enter,
he judges and assigns as his tail twines.[2]
I mean that when the spirit born to evil
appears before him, it confesses all;
and he, the connoisseur of sin, can tell
the depth in Hell appropriate to it;
as many times as Minos wraps his tail
around himself, that marks the sinner's level.
Always there is a crowd that stands before him:
each soul in turn advances toward that judgment;
they speak and hear, then they are cast below.
Arresting his extraordinary task,
Minos, as soon as he had seen me, said:
"O you who reach this house of suffering,
be careful how you enter, whom you trust;
the gate is wide, but do not be deceived!"
To which my guide replied: "But why protest?
Do not attempt to block his fated path:
our passage has been willed above, where One
can do what He has willed; and ask no more."
Now notes of desperation have begun
to overtake my hearing; now I come
where mighty lamentation beats against me.
I reached a place where every light is muted,
which bellows like the sea beneath a tempest,
when it is battered by opposing winds.
The hellish hurricane, which never rests,
drives on the spirits with its violence:
wheeling and pounding, it harasses them.
When they come up against the ruined slope,
then there are cries and wailing and lament,
and there they curse the force of the divine.
I learned that those who undergo this torment
are damned because they sinned within the flesh,
subjecting reason to the rule of lust.
And as, in the cold season, starlings' wings
bear them along in broad and crowded ranks,
so does that blast bear on the guilty spirits:
now here, now there, now down, now up, it drives them.
There is no hope that ever comforts them—

1. Although separated from the rest of Hell by the guardian and judge Minos, Limbo is called the first circle. The second circle, where the Lustful are punished, "girdles less space" because the cone shape of Hell narrows as it descends.

2. Minos was legendary king of Crete, and with his brother Rhadamanthus judge in Virgil's underworld. The tail, however, is a Dantesque touch that makes Minos more monster and less king, imitating the spiraling structure of Hell.

no hope for rest and none for lesser pain.
 And just as cranes in flight will chant their lays,
arraying their long file across the air,
so did the shades I saw approaching, borne
 by that assailing wind, lament and moan;
so that I asked him: "Master, who are those
who suffer punishment in this dark air?"
 "The first of those about whose history
you want to know," my master then told me,
"once ruled as empress over many nations.
 Her vice of lust became so customary
that she made license licit in her laws
to free her from the scandal she had caused.
 She is Semíramis, of whom we read
that she was Ninus' wife and his successor:
she held the land the Sultan now commands.[3]
 That other spirit killed herself for love,
and she betrayed the ashes of Sychaeus;[4]
the wanton Cleopatra follows next.[5]
 See Helen, for whose sake so many years
of evil had to pass; see great Achilles,
who finally met love—in his last battle.[6]
 See Paris, Tristan . . ."—and he pointed out
and named to me more than a thousand shades
departed from our life because of love.
 No sooner had I heard my teacher name
the ancient ladies and the knights, than pity
seized me, and I was like a man astray.
 My first words: "Poet, I should willingly
speak with those two who go together there
and seem so lightly carried by the wind."[7]
 And he to me: "You'll see when they draw closer
to us, and then you may appeal to them

3. In Dante's time, Egypt was under the rule of the Sultan. There is some confusion here because Egypt was fairly distant from the Mesopotamian kingdom of Assyria, supposedly founded by Ninus and the lustful Semiramis.

4. Curiously, Virgil does not name Dido, whose story he had related in one of the most celebrated parts of the *Aeneid.* Sychaeus was Dido's husband, murdered by her brother Pygmalion, king of Tyre. Dido fled to North Africa, where she founded the city of Carthage, and, according to *Aeneid* 4, was seduced and abandoned by Aeneas, after which she killed herself in despair.

5. Cleopatra was the queen of Egypt of legendary beauty who was the lover first of Julius Caesar and then of Marc Antony, with whom she was defeated at the battle of Actium in 29 B.C.E. by Augustus. Rather than be taken as a prisoner to Rome, she killed herself with an asp.

6. The list switches from women to men with two legendary figures of the Trojan War: Helen, wife of Menelaus, king of Sparta, whose abduction by Paris was the origin of the war, and Achilles, the greatest of the Greek heroes. Homer had him killed under the walls of Troy by Paris; according to medieval legend, Paris lured him to his death at the temple of Apollo by promises that he would be given Priam's daughter Polyxena if he changed sides. Tristan was a celebrated figure of medieval romance, lover of Iseult, who was wife of King Mark of Cornwall, his uncle.

7. The first conversation recorded with a condemned soul is also the first appearance of two of Dante's contemporaries, the lovers Francesca da Rimini and Paolo Malatesta. Daughter of Guido da Polenta, lord of Ravenna, and aunt of Guido Novello, Dante's host at Ravenna at the end of his life, Francesca was married for political reasons to Paolo's older brother Gianciotto some time after 1275. Around 1285, at which time Francesca had a nine-year old daughter and Paolo was around 40 years old, Gianciotto apparently found the lovers out and killed them both. The language of the dialogue is suffused with the language of the *dolce stil novo,* the "sweet new style" of love lyric that first brought fame to Dante.

by that love which impels them. They will come."
No sooner had the wind bent them toward us
than I urged on my voice: "O battered souls,
if One does not forbid it, speak with us."
Even as doves when summoned by desire,
borne forward by their will, move through the air
with wings uplifted, still, to their sweet nest,
those spirits left the ranks where Dido suffers,
approaching us through the malignant air;
so powerful had been my loving cry.
"O living being, gracious and benign,
who through the darkened air have come to visit
our souls that stained the world with blood, if He
who rules the universe were friend to us,
then we should pray to Him to give you peace,
for you have pitied our atrocious state.
Whatever pleases you to hear and speak
will please us, too, to hear and speak with you,
now while the wind is silent, in this place.
The land where I was born lies on that shore
to which the Po together with the waters
that follow it descends to final rest.[8]
Love, that can quickly seize the gentle heart,
took hold of him because of the fair body
taken from me—how that was done still wounds me.
Love, that releases no beloved from loving,
took hold of me so strongly through his beauty
that, as you see, it has not left me yet.
Love led the two of us unto one death.
Caïna waits for him who took our life."[9]
These words were borne across from them to us.
When I had listened to those injured souls,
I bent my head and held it low until
the poet asked of me: "What are you thinking?"
When I replied, my words began: "Alas,
how many gentle thoughts, how deep a longing,
had led them to the agonizing pass!"
Then I addressed my speech again to them,
and I began: "Francesca, your afflictions
move me to tears of sorrow and of pity.
But tell me, in the time of gentle sighs,
with what and in what way did Love allow you
to recognize your still uncertain longings?"
And she to me: "There is no greater sorrow

8. Ravenna is on the Adriatic coast of northern Italy, between the Po River and the Rubicon.

9. Francesca's speech combines echoes of a famous *canzone* by Dante's friend Guido Guinizelli and its definitions of courtly love with harsh concluding phrases on her own fate. Caïna is the first of the four divisions of the ninth circle of Hell, named after Cain, who killed his brother Abel. This place where those who betray their kin are punished "waits for" Francesca's husband because he was still alive in 1300.

than thinking back upon a happy time
in misery—and this your teacher knows.
Yet if you long so much to understand
the first root of our love, then I shall tell
my tale to you as one who weeps and speaks.
One day, to pass the time away, we read
of Lancelot—how love had overcome him.
We were alone, and we suspected nothing.
And time and time again that reading led
our eyes to meet, and made our faces pale,
and yet one point alone defeated us.
When we had read how the desired smile
was kissed by one who was so true a lover,
this one, who never shall be parted from me,
while all his body trembled, kissed my mouth.
A Gallehault indeed, that book and he
who wrote it, too; that day we read no more."[1]
And while one spirit said these words to me,
the other wept, so that—because of pity—
I fainted, as if I had met my death.
And then I fell as a dead body falls.

Canto 6

Dante's awakening to the Third Circle, where the Gluttonous, supine, are flailed by cold and filthy rain and tormented by Cerberus. Ciacco and his prophecy concerning Florence. The state of the damned after the Resurrection.

Upon my mind's reviving—it had closed
on hearing the lament of those two kindred,
since sorrow had confounded me completely—
I see new sufferings, new sufferers
surrounding me on every side, wherever
I move or turn about or set my eyes.
I am in the third circle, filled with cold,
unending, heavy, and accursèd rain;
its measure and its kind are never changed.
Gross hailstones, water gray with filth, and snow
come streaking down across the shadowed air;
the earth, as it receives that shower, stinks.
Over the souls of those submerged beneath
that mess, is an outlandish, vicious beast,
his three throats barking, doglike: Cerberus.[1]

1. The story of Lancelot, "flower of the knighthood of the world," and the love for Queen Guinevere, wife of his lord, King Arthur, that caused him to fail in his quest for the Holy Grail, was one of the most popular medieval romances. In the Old French romance, *Lancelot du lac,* it was Lancelot's friend Gallehault who arranged an interview between the pair and induced them to kiss. The book, as well as its author, are accused of being the "go-between" that led to the death and damnation of Francesca and her silent lover.

1. The mythical three-headed guardian of the underworld, described in *Aeneid* 6.417–23. Dante makes him paradoxically more human and more bestial. The guardian(s) of each circle generally relate to that circle's sin; here, the monster's gluttony is stressed by having his gullets silenced by lumps of earth rather than the honey cakes of the *Aeneid.*

His eyes are bloodred; greasy, black, his beard;
his belly bulges, and his hands are claws;
his talons tear and flay and rend the shades.
That downpour makes the sinners howl like dogs;
they use one of their sides to screen the other—
those miserable wretches turn and turn.
When Cerberus, the great worm, noticed us,
he opened wide his mouths, showed us his fangs;
there was no part of him that did not twitch.
My guide opened his hands to their full span,
plucked up some earth, and with his fists filled full
he hurled it straight into those famished jaws.
Just as a dog that barks with greedy hunger
will then fall quiet when he gnaws his food,
intent and straining hard to cram it in,
so were the filthy faces of the demon
Cerberus transformed—after he'd stunned
the spirits so, they wished that they were deaf.
We walked across the shades on whom there thuds
that heavy rain, and set our soles upon
their empty images that seem like persons.
And all those spirits lay upon the ground,
except for one who sat erect as soon
as he caught sight of us in front of him.
"O you who are conducted through this Hell,"
he said to me, "recall me, if you can;
for you, before I was unmade, were made."
And I to him: "It is perhaps your anguish
that snatches you out of my memory,
so that it seems that I have never seen you.
But tell me who you are, you who are set
in such a dismal place, such punishment—
if other pains are more, none's more disgusting."
And he to me: "Your city—one so full
of envy that its sack has always spilled—
that city held me in the sunlit life.[2]
The name you citizens gave me was Ciacco;
and for the damning sin of gluttony,
as you can see, I languish in the rain.
And I, a wretched soul, am not alone,
for all of these have this same penalty
for this same sin." And he said nothing more.
I answered him: "Ciacco, your suffering
so weights on me that I am forced to weep;
but tell me, if you know, what end awaits
the citizens of that divided city;

2. Dante's native city of Florence, which figures prominently in the poem, appears for the first time, and in characteristically negative fashion.

is any just man there? Tell me the reason
why it has been assailed by so much schism."[3]
And he to me: "After long controversy,
they'll come to blood; the party of the woods
will chase the other out with much offense.
But then, within three suns, they too must fall;
at which the other party will prevail,
using the power of one who tacks his sails.° *Pope Boniface*
This party will hold high its head for long
and heap great weights upon its enemies,
however much they weep indignantly.
Two men are just, but no one listens to them.
Three sparks that set on fire every heart
are envy, pride, and avariciousness."
With this, his words, inciting tears, were done;
and I to him: "I would learn more from you;
I ask you for a gift of further speech:
Tegghiaio, Farinata, men so worthy,
Arrigo, Mosca, Jacopo Rusticucci,
and all the rest whose minds bent toward the good,
do tell me where they are and let me meet them;
for my great longing drives me on to learn
if Heaven sweetens or Hell poisons them."[4]
And he: "They are among the blackest souls;
a different sin has dragged them to the bottom;
if you descend so low, there you can see them.
But when you have returned to the sweet world,
I pray, recall me to men's memory:
I say no more to you, answer no more."
Then his straight gaze grew twisted and awry;
he looked at me awhile, then bent his head;
he fell as low as all his blind companions.
And my guide said to me: "He'll rise no more
until the blast of the angelic trumpet
upon the coming of the hostile Judge:° *Christ*
each one shall see his sorry tomb again
and once again take on his flesh and form,
and hear what shall resound eternally."
So did we pass across that squalid mixture
of shadows and of rain, our steps slowed down,
talking awhile about the life to come.
At which I said: "And after the great sentence—
o master—will these torments grow, or else
be less, or will they be just as intense?"
And he to me: "Remember now your science,

3. The first explicit discussion of contemporary political events. In spring of 1300, trouble was brewing between the two Guelf factions, the Whites, led by the Cerchi family, and the Blacks, led by the Donatis.

4. The pilgrim asks about some famous political figures who lived in Florence before the division between Blacks and Whites. All except Arrigo are found deeper in Hell.

which says that when a thing has more perfection,
so much the greater is its pain or pleasure.
Though these accursed sinners never shall
attain the true perfection, yet they can
expect to be more perfect then than now."[5]
We took the circling way traced by that road;
we said much more than I can here recount;
we reached the point that marks the downward slope.
Here we found Plutus, the great enemy.[6]

Canto 7

The demon Plutus. The Fourth Circle, where the Avaricious and the Prodigal, in opposite directions, roll weights in semicircles. Fortune and her ways. Descent into the Fifth Circle: the Wrathful and the Sullen, the former besmirched by the muddy Styx, the latter immersed in it.

"Pape Satàn, pape Satàn aleppe!"[1]
so Plutus, with his grating voice, began.
The gentle sage, aware of everything,
said reassuringly, "Don't let your fear
defeat you; for whatever power he has,
he cannot stop our climbing down this crag."
Then he turned back to Plutus' swollen face
and said to him: "Be quiet, cursed wolf![2]
Let your vindictiveness feed on yourself.
His is no random journey to the deep:
it has been willed on high, where Michael
took revenge upon the arrogant rebellion."[3]
As sails inflated by the wind collapse,
entangled in a heap, when the mast cracks,
so that ferocious beast fell to the ground.
Thus we made our way down to the fourth ditch,
to take in more of that despondent shore
where all the universe's ill is stored.
Justice of God! Who has amassed as many
strange tortures and travails as I have seen?
Why do we let our guilt consume us so?
Even as waves that break above Charybdis,[4]
each shattering the other when they meet,

5. "Science" is Aristotelian philosophy as interpreted in Scholasticism. Aquinas held that the soul attains natural perfection only when unified with the body. For the dead, this perfection will be achieved only after the Last Judgment, when their souls will be reunited with their bodies. The pains of the damned will be then be increased ("more perfect") just as will the pleasure of the blessed.
6. Pluto was mythological god of the underworld; Plutus was the Roman god of wealth. Dante appears to make no distinction between the two, making out of them a minor demon, guardian of the Fourth Circle.
1. A hodgepodge of Latin, Greek, and Hebrew appealing to Plutus's superior: "Oh Satan, oh Satan, the most powerful one!"
2. Recalling the cupidity of the she-wolf of Canto 1.
3. Alluding to the Archangel Michael's role as leader of the angels in the battle in heaven that resulted in the casting out of Satan and the rebel angels.
4. A famous whirlpool between the island of Sicily and the Italian coast, described in *Aeneid* 3.420–23.

so must the spirits here dance their round dance.
Here, more than elsewhere, I saw multitudes
to every side of me; their howls were loud
while, wheeling weights, they used their chests to push.
They struck against each other; at that point,
each turned around and, wheeling back those weights,
cried out: "Why do you hoard?" "Why do you squander?"[5]
So did they move around the sorry circle
from left and right to the opposing point;
again, again they cried their chant of scorn;
and so, when each of them had changed positions,
he circled halfway back to his next joust.
And I, who felt my heart almost pierced through,
requested: "Master, show me now what shades
are these and tell me if they all were clerics—
those tonsured ones who circle on our left."[6]
And he to me: "All these, to left and right
were so squint-eyed of mind in the first life—
no spending that they did was done with measure.
Their voices bark this out with clarity
when they have reached the two points of the circle
where their opposing guilts divide their ranks.
These to the left—their heads bereft of hair—
were clergymen, and popes and cardinals,
within whom avarice works its excess."
And I to him: "Master, among this kind
I certainly might hope to recognize
some who have been bespattered by these crimes."
And he to me: "That thought of yours is empty:
the undiscerning life that made them filthy
now renders them unrecognizable.
For all eternity they'll come to blows:
these here will rise up from their sepulchers
with fists clenched tight; and these, with hair cropped close.
Ill giving and ill keeping have robbed both
of the fair world° and set them to this fracas— *Heaven*
what that is like, my words need not embellish.
Now you can see, my son, how brief's the sport
of all those goods that are in Fortune's care,
for which the tribe of men contend and brawl;
for all the gold that is or ever was
beneath the moon could never offer rest
to even one of these exhausted spirits."
"Master," I asked of him, "now tell me too:
this Fortune whom you've touched upon just now—

5. Here one sin is punished by confrontation with its opposite. In Dante's scheme, the excesses of avarice ("hoarding") and prodigality ("squandering") are equally to be avoided.

6. The tonsure is the shaven crown of the head signifying membership in a monastic or clerical order; the avarice of the clergy was proverbial.

what's she, who clutches so all the world's goods?"[7]
And he to me: "O unenlightened creatures,
how deep—the ignorance that hampers you!
I want you to digest my word on this.
Who made the heavens and who gave them guides
was He whose wisdom transcends everything;
that every part may shine unto the other,
He had the light apportioned equally;
similarly, for wordly splendors, He
ordained a general minister and guide
to shift, from time to time, those empty goods
from nation unto nation, clan to clan,
in ways that human reason can't prevent;
just so, one people rules, one languishes,
obeying the decision she has given,
which, like a serpent in the grass, is hidden.
Your knowledge cannot stand against her force;
for she foresees and judges and maintains
her kingdom as the other gods do theirs.
The changes that she brings are without respite:
it is necessity that makes her swift;
and for this reason, men change state so often.
She is the one so frequently maligned
even by those who should give praise to her—
they blame her wrongfully with words of scorn.
But she is blessed and does not hear these things;
for with the other primal beings, happy,
she turns her sphere and glories in her bliss.[8]
But now let us descend to greater sorrow,
for every star that rose when I first moved
is setting now;[9] we cannot stay too long."
We crossed the circle to the other shore;
we reached a foaming watercourse that spills
into a trench formed by its overflow.
That stream was even darker than deep purple;
and we, together with those shadowed waves,
moved downward and along a strange pathway.
When it has reached the foot of those malign
gray slopes, that melancholy stream descends,
forming a swamp that bears the name of Styx.
And I, who was intent on watching it,

7. Fortune was often pictured blindfolded, turning a wheel at random to distribute her goods. In Virgil's explanation, aimed at reconciling the principles of chance and inequality with those of divine justice and providence, Fortune is one of the Intelligences in the heavenly sphere, in charge of administering the riches of the world.
8. The Intelligences preside over the revolving heavens and turn the heaven assigned to them, as Fortune turns her sphere. They were commonly referred to as gods and goddesses.
9. The starry heavens make a complete circuit every 24 hours. The stars that were rising when Virgil first set out from Limbo around noon on Good Friday are now setting 12 hours later, after midnight of Holy Saturday.

could make out muddied people in that slime,
all naked and their faces furious.
These struck each other not with hands alone,
but with their heads and chests and with their feet,
and tore each other piecemeal with their teeth.
The kindly master told me: "Son, now see
the souls of those whom anger has defeated;
and I should also have you know for certain
that underneath the water there are souls
who sigh and make this plain of water bubble,
as your eye, looking anywhere, can tell.
Wedged in the slime, they say: 'We had been sullen
in the sweet air that's gladdened by the sun;
we bore the mist of sluggishness in us:
now we are bitter in the blackened mud.'
This hymn they have to gurgle in their gullets,
because they cannot speak it in full words."
And so, between the dry shore and the swamp,
we circled much of that disgusting pond,
our eyes upon the swallowers of slime.
We came at last upon a tower's base.

Canto 8

Still the Fifth Circle: the Wrathful and the Sullen. The tall tower. Phlegyas and the crossing of the Styx. Filippo Argenti and Dante's fury. Approach to Dis, the lower part of Hell: its moat, its walls, its gate. The demons, fallen angels, and their obstruction of the poets' entry into Dis.

I say, continuing, that long before
we two had reached the foot of that tall tower,
our eyes had risen upward, toward its summit,
because of two small flames that flickered there,
while still another flame returned their signal,
so far off it was scarcely visible.
And I turned toward the sea of all good sense;
I said: "What does this mean? And what reply
comes from that other fire? Who kindled it?"
And he to me: "Above the filthy waters
you can already see what waits for us,
if it's not hid by vapors from the marsh."
Bowstring has not thrust from itself an arrow
that ever rushed as swiftly through the air
as did the little bark that at that moment
I saw as it skimmed toward us on the water,
a solitary boatman at its helm.
I heard him howl: "Now you are caught, foul soul!"
"O Phlegyas, Phlegyas, such a shout is useless
this time," my master said; "we're yours no longer

than it will take to cross the muddy sluice."[1]
And just as one who hears some great deception
was done to him, and then resents it, so
was Phlegyas when he had to store his anger.
My guide preceded me into the boat.
Once he was in, he had me follow him;
there seemed to be no weight until I boarded.[2]
No sooner were my guide and I embarked
than off that ancient prow went, cutting water
more deeply than it does when bearing others.
And while we steered across the stagnant channel,
before me stood a sinner thick with mud,
saying: "Who are you, come before your time?"
And I to him: "I've come, but I don't stay;
but who are you, who have become so ugly?"
He answered: "You can see—I'm one who weeps."
And I to him: "In weeping and in grieving,
accursèd spirit, may you long remain;
though you're disguised by filth, I know your name."[3]
Then he stretched both his hands out toward the boat,
at which my master quickly shoved him back,
saying: "Be off there with the other dogs!"
That done, he threw his arms around my neck
and kissed my face and said: "Indignant soul,
blessèd is she who bore you in her womb!
When in the world, he was presumptuous;
there is no good to gild his memory,
and so his shade down here is hot with fury.
How many up above now count themselves
great kings, who'll wallow here like pigs in slime,
leaving behind foul memories of their crimes!"
And I: "O master, I am very eager
to see that spirit soused within this broth
before we've made our way across the lake."
And he to me: "Before the other shore
comes into view, you shall be satisfied;
to gratify so fine a wish is right."
Soon after I had heard these words, I saw
the muddy sinners so dismember him
that even now I praise and thank God for it.
They all were shouting: "At Filippo Argenti!"
At this, the Florentine, gone wild with spleen,° *ill temper*

1. In ancient myth, Phlegyas was son of Chryse and the war-god Mars, king of the Lapithae, and father of Ixion and Coronis. When Coronis was violated by Apollo, Phlegyas in fury set fire to the god's temple at Delphi. For this sacrilege, according to Virgil in *Aeneid* 6.821–23, he was punished eternally in Tartarus. Dante makes him an infernal boatman in the circle suited to his actions.

2. Reminiscent of Aeneas's crossing of the Styx in *Aeneid* 6.544–46, as Dante too has a real body.

3. Filippo Argenti (identified in line 61 of the canto) was so called because he had his horse shod in silver (*argento*). He was a member of the Adimari clan of Florence, Black Guelfs, and his brother obtained Dante's property from the Commune of Florence when the poet was exiled.

began to turn his teeth against himself.
We left him there; I tell no more of him.
But in my ears so loud a wailing pounded
that I lean forward, all intent to see.
The kindly master said: "My son, the city
that bears the name of Dis is drawing near,
with its grave citizens, its great battalions."[4]
I said: "I can already see distinctly—
master—the mosques that gleam within the valley,
as crimson as if they had just been drawn
out of the fire." He told me: "The eternal
flame burning there appears to make them red,
as you can see, within this lower Hell."
So we arrived inside the deep-cut trenches
that are the moats of this despondent land:
the ramparts seemed to me to be of iron.
But not before we'd ranged in a wide circuit
did we approach a place where that shrill pilot
shouted: "Get out; the entrance way is here."
About the gates I saw more than a thousand—
who once had rained from Heaven[5]—and they cried
in anger: "Who is this who, without death,
can journey through the kingdom of the dead?"
And my wise master made a sign that said
he wanted to speak secretly to them.
Then they suppressed—somewhat—their great disdain
and said: "You come alone; let him be gone—
for he was reckless, entering this realm.
Let him return alone on his mad road—
or try to, if he can, since you, his guide
across so dark a land, you are to stay."
Consider, reader, my dismay before
the sound of those abominable words:
returning here seemed so impossible.
"O my dear guide, who more than seven times
has given back to me my confidence
and snatched me from deep danger that had menaced,
do not desert me when I'm so undone;
and if they will not let us pass beyond,
let us retrace our steps together, quickly."
These were my words; the lord who'd led me there
replied: "Forget your fear, no one can hinder
our passage; One so great has granted it.

4. Dis was the god of the underworld in the religion of ancient Rome, and by extension the name for the underworld itself. Dante will use the term to refer to Satan; here he means lower Hell, which he depicts as a Muslim city.

5. The rebel angels fallen from Heaven with Lucifer; likened here to Muslim infidels, and for whom the verbal talisman no longer appears to guarantee safe passage. The change in organization and custom introduces the social nature and greater complexity of lower Hell.

But you wait here for me, and feed and comfort
your tired spirit with good hope, for I
will not abandon you in this low world."
So he goes on his way; that gentle father
has left me there to wait and hesitate,
for *yes* and *no* contend within my head.
I could not hear what he was telling them;
but he had not been long with them when each
ran back into the city, scrambling fast.
And these, our adversaries, slammed the gates
in my lord's face; and he remained outside,
then, with slow steps, turned back again to me.
His eyes turned to the ground, his brows deprived
of every confidence, he said with sighs:
"See who has kept me from the house of sorrow!"[6]
To me he added: "You—though I am vexed—
must not be daunted; I shall win this contest,
whoever tries—within—to block our way.
This insolence of theirs is nothing new;
they used it once before and at a gate
less secret—it is still without its bolts[7]—
the place where you made out the fatal text;
and now, already well within that gate,° *the gate of Hell*
across the circles—and alone—descends
the one who will unlock this realm for us."

Canto 9

The gate of Dis. Dante's fear. The three Furies, invoking Medusa. Virgil's warning to Dante lest he look at Gorgon, Medusa's head. A heavenly messenger. The flight of the demons. Entry into Dis, where Virgil and Dante reach the Sixth Circle and its Arch-Heretics, entombed in red-hot sepulchers.

The color cowardice displayed in me
when I saw that my guide was driven back,
made him more quickly mask his own new pallor.
He stood alert, like an attentive listener,
because his eye could hardly journey far
across the black air and the heavy fog.
"We have to win this battle," he began,
"if not . . . But one so great had offered help.
How slow that someone's coming seems to me!"
But I saw well enough how he had covered
his first words with the words that followed after—
so different from what he had said before;

6. This first of several times when Virgil will be thwarted or deceived in Hell (always by devils) begins a careful development of his strengths and limitations as guide to the afterlife.

7. According to Christian legend, when Christ entered Limbo to harrow Hell, the rebel angels attempted to block his passage. As the Matins of the Office of Holy Saturday have it: "Today our Savior shattered the gates and likewise the bolts of death."

nevertheless, his speech made me afraid,
because I drew out from his broken phrase
a meaning worse—perhaps—than he'd intended.
"Does anyone from the first circle, one
whose only punishment is crippled hope,
ever descend so deep in this sad hollow?"[1]
That was my question. And he answered so:
"It is quite rare for one of us to go
along the way that I have taken now.
But I, in truth, have been here once before:
that savage witch Erichtho, she who called
the shades back to their bodies, summoned me.
My flesh had not been long stripped off when she
had me descend through all the rings of Hell,
to draw a spirit back from Judas' circle.[2]
That is the deepest and the darkest place,
the farthest from the heaven that girds all:
so rest assured, I know the pathway well.
This swamp that breeds and breathes the giant stench
surrounds the city of the sorrowing,° *Dis*
which now we cannot enter without anger."
And he said more, but I cannot remember
because my eyes had wholly taken me
to that high tower with the glowing summit
where, at one single point, there suddenly
stood three infernal Furies flecked with blood,
who had the limbs of women and their ways
but wore, as girdles, snakes of deepest green;
small serpents and horned vipers formed their hairs,
and these were used to bind their bestial temples.[3]
And he, who knew these handmaids well—they served
the Queen of never-ending lamentation[4]—
said: "Look at the ferocious Erinyes!
That is Megaera on the left, and she
who weeps upon the right, that is Allecto;
Tisiphone's between them." He was done.
Each Fury tore her breast with taloned nails;
each, with her palms, beat on herself and wailed
so loud that I, in fear, drew near the poet.
"Just let Medusa come; then we shall turn
him into stone," they all cried, looking down;

1. Here the pilgrim probes his guide's knowledge of lower Hell, a realm that, unlike the upper circles, has no direct parallels to the underworld described in the *Aeneid.*
2. Medieval legend had made Virgil a magician, but there is no known source for the strange tale he produces here to establish his expertise. Erichtho was a legendary sorceress who, in an especially gruesome episode in Lucan's *Pharsalia* (6.507–830), is employed to summon the spirit of a dead soldier to learn the outcome of the impending battle of Pharsalia. "Judas' circle" is the lowest part of the last circle of Hell.
3. The Furies (Greek: Erinyes) were daughters of Night, forces of vengeance feared by gods and men. They were depicted in Virgil's *Aeneid* and elsewhere as monstrous women, with snakes for hair.
4. Hecate or Proserpina, queen of the underworld in classical myth.

"we should have punished Theseus' assault."[5]
"Turn round and keep your eyes shut fast, for should
the Gorgon show herself and you behold her,
never again would you return above,"
my master said; and he himself turned me
around and, not content with just my hands,
used his as well to cover up my eyes.
O you possessed of sturdy intellects,
observe the teaching that is hidden here
beneath the veil of verses so obscure.[6]
And now, across the turbid waves, there passed
a reboantic° fracas—horrid sound, *reverberating*
enough to make both of the shorelines quake:
a sound not other than a wind's when, wild
because it must contend with warmer currents,
it strikes against the forest without let,
shattering, beating down, bearing off branches,
as it moves proudly, clouds of dust before it,
and puts to flight both animals and shepherds.
He freed my eyes and said: "Now let your optic
nerve turn directly toward that ancient foam,
there where the mist is thickest and most acrid."
As frogs confronted by their enemy,
the snake, will scatter underwater till
each hunches in a heap along the bottom,
so did the thousand ruined souls I saw
take flight before a figure crossing Styx
who walked as if on land and with dry soles.[7]
He thrust away the thick air from his face,
waving his left hand frequently before him;
that seemed the only task that wearied him.
I knew well he was Heaven's messenger,
and I turned toward my master; and he made
a sign that I be still and bow before him.
How full of high disdain he seemed to me!
He came up to the gate, and with a wand,
he opened it, for there was no resistance.
"O you cast out of Heaven, hated crowd,"
were his first words upon that horrid threshold,
"why do you harbor this presumptuousness?
Why are you so reluctant to endure
that Will whose aim can never be cut short,
and which so often added to your hurts?
What good is it to thrust against the fates?

5. In mythology, the serpent-haired Gorgon Medusa was so fearful that all who looked upon her head were turned to stone. The legendary Greek hero Theseus descended to Hades to abduct Proserpina.

6. A standard medieval formula for introducing a self-contained allegory, the meaning of which the reader must extract from beneath the "veil" of its surface story.

7. The reminiscence of Jesus walking on water at the Sea of Galilee (Matthew 14:21–33) adds to the effect of a repetition of the Harrowing of Hell.

Your Cerberus, if you remember well,
for that, had both his throat and chin stripped clean."[8]
At that he turned and took the filthy road,
and did not speak to us, but had the look
of one who is obsessed by other cares
than those that press and gnaw at those before him;
and we moved forward, on into the city,
in safety, having heard his holy words.
We made our way inside without a struggle;
and I, who wanted so much to observe
the state of things that such a fortress guarded,
as soon as I had entered, looked about.
I saw, on every side, a spreading plain
of lamentation and atrocious pain.
Just as at Arles, where Rhone becomes a marsh,
just as at Pola, near Quarnero's gulf,
that closes Italy and bathes its borders,[9]
the sepulchers make all the plain uneven,
so they did here on every side, except
that here the sepulchers were much more harsh;
for flames were scattered through the tombs, and these
had kindled all of them to glowing heat;
no artisan could ask for hotter iron.
The lid of every tomb was lifted up,
and from each tomb such sorry cries arose
as could come only from the sad and hurt.
And I: "Master, who can these people be
who, buried in great chests of stone like these,
must speak by way of sighs in agony?"
And he to me: "Here are arch-heretics
and those who followed them, from every sect;
those tombs are much more crowded than you think.
Here, like has been ensepulchered with like;
some monuments are heated more, some less."
And then he turned around and to his right;[1]
we passed between the torments and high walls.

Canto 10

Still the Sixth Circle: the Heretics. The tombs of the Epicureans. Farinata degli Uberti. Cavalcante dei Cavalcanti. Farinata's prediction of Dante's difficulty in returning to Florence from exile. The inability of the damned to see the present, although they can foresee the future.

8. The legendary hero Hercules was often regarded as foreshadowing Christ, especially in his Twelve Labors, of which the fetching of Cerberus from the underworld was the final and most difficult.

9. The Provençal town of Arles and the northeastern Italian town of Pola were sites of Roman necropolises.

1. The poets bear left at every opportunity except here and in Canto 17.31; then always to the right on the Mountain of Purgatory. The exception here is perhaps related to the exceptional status of the sin of heresy.

Now, by a narrow path that ran between
those torments and the ramparts of the city,
my master moves ahead, I following.
"O highest virtue, you who lead me through
these circles of transgression, at your will,
do speak to me, and satisfy my longings.
Can those who lie within the sepulchers
be seen? The lids—in fact—have all been lifted;
no guardian is watching over them."
And he to me: "They'll all be shuttered up
when they return here from Jehosaphat
together with the flesh they left above.[1]
Within this region is the cemetery
of Epicurus and his followers,
all those who say the soul dies with the body.[2]
And so the question you have asked of me
will soon find satisfaction while we're here,
as will the longing you have hid from me."
And I: "Good guide, the only reason I
have hid my heart was that I might speak briefly,
and you, long since, encouraged me in this."
"O Tuscan, you who pass alive across
the fiery city with such seemly words,
be kind enough to stay your journey here.
Your accent makes it clear that you belong
among the natives of the noble city
I may have dealt with too vindictively."[3]
This sound had burst so unexpectedly
out of one sepulcher that, trembling, I
then drew a little closer to my guide.
But he told me: "Turn round! What are you doing?
That's Farinata who has risen there—
you will see all of him from the waist up."
My eyes already were intent on his;
and up he rose—his forehead and his chest—
as if he had tremendous scorn for Hell.
My guide—his hands encouraging and quick—
thrust me between the sepulchers toward him,
saying: "Your words must be appropriate."
When I'd drawn closer to his sepulcher,
he glanced at me, and as if in disdain,
he asked of me: "Who were your ancestors?"[4]

1. The Valley of Jehosaphat, source of the stream running between Jerusalem and the Mount of Olives, was expected be the site of the Last Judgment.

2. The Greek philosopher Epicurus (341–270 B.C.E.) taught that the soul died with the body; consequently, the greatest good to be sought was pleasure, defined as the absence of pain through the cultivation of virtue. This denial of the immortality of the soul was quite current in Florence, especially with the Ghibellines.

3. The soul has identified Dante because of the Italian dialect he is speaking, from Tuscany, the region of Florence.

4. Farinata, a leader of the Florentine Ghibellines, had died just before Dante was born, so he asks about members of previous generations he would have known, and whether they were known to his illustrious family, the Uberti.

Because I wanted so to be compliant,
I hid no thing from him: I told him all.
At this he lifted up his brows a bit,
then said: "They were ferocious enemies
of mine and of my parents and my party,
so that I had to scatter them twice over."[5]
"If they were driven out," I answered him,
"they still returned, both times, from every quarter;
but yours were never quick to learn that art."[6]
At this there rose another shade alongside,
uncovered to my sight down to his chin;
I think that he had risen on his knees.[7]
He looked around me, just as if he longed
to see if I had come with someone else;
but then, his expectation spent, he said
in tears: "If it is your high intellect
that lets you journey here, through this blind prison,
where is my son? Why is he not with you?"
I answered: "My own powers have not brought me;
he who awaits me there, leads me through here
perhaps to one your Guido did disdain."[8]
His words, the nature of his punishment—
these had already let me read his name;
therefore, my answer was so fully made.
Then suddenly erect, he cried: "What's that:
He '*did* disdain'? He is not still alive?
The sweet light does not strike against his eyes?"[9]
And when he noticed how I hesitated
a moment in my answer, he fell back—
supine—and did not show himself again.
But that great-hearted one, the other shade
at whose request I'd stayed, did not change aspect
or turn aside his head or lean or bend;
and taking up his words where he'd left off,
"If they were slow," he said, "to learn that art,
that is more torment to me than this bed.
And yet the Lady who is ruler here
will not have her face kindled fifty times[1]

5. Farinata played a prominent role in the expulsion of the Guelfs from Florence in 1248 and in their crushing defeat at Montaperti in 1260, after which he successfully argued for renewed expulsions rather than the destruction of his native city.

6. The Guelfs returned in 1251 after the defeat of the Ghibellines in battle, and again in 1266 after another military victory. By contrast, the Ghibellines never returned to Florence as a party, and their most powerful families, including the Uberti, were excluded from the city by the terms of the peace of 1280.

7. The speaker is Cavalcante de' Cavalcanti, a notorious Epicurean and father of the famous poet and close friend of Dante, Guido Cavalcanti. An ardent Guelf, Guido was married to Farinata's daughter Beatrice to guarantee peace between the feuding factions. When the priors of Florence (including Dante) put an end to the hostilities in June 1300, the leading Blacks and leading Whites (including Guido) were banished. Guido died of malaria in August of the same year; hence Dante was indirectly responsible for his friend's death.

8. Guido too was a notorious Epicurean, celebrating "high intellect" as the greatest virtue in his poetry.

9. Guido is not yet dead, but his father misunderstands the meaning of Dante's words.

1. Proserpina is identified with Hecate, goddess of the moon, whose face is fully lit once a month.

before you learn how heavy is that art.[2]
And so may you return to the sweet world,
tell me: why are those citizens so cruel
against my kin in all of their decrees?"[3]
To which I said: "The carnage, the great bloodshed
that stained the waters of the Arbia red
have led us to such prayers in our temple."[4]
He sighed and shook his head, then said: "In that,
I did not act alone, but certainly
I'd not have joined the others without cause.
But where I was alone was *there* where all
the rest would have annihilated Florence,
had I not interceded forcefully."[5]
"Ah, as I hope your seed may yet find peace,"
I asked, "so may you help me to undo
the knot that here has snarled my course of thought.
It seems, if I hear right, that you can see
beforehand that which time is carrying,
but you're denied the sight of present things."
"We see, even as men who are farsighted,
those things," he said, "that are remote from us;
the Highest Lord allots us that much light.
But when events draw near or are, our minds
are useless; were we not informed by others,
we should know nothing of your human state.
So you can understand how our awareness
will die completely at the moment when
the portal of the future has been shut."[6]
Then, as if penitent for my omission,
I said: "Will you now tell that fallen man
his son is still among the living ones;
and if, a while ago, I held my tongue
before his question, let him know it was
because I had in mind the doubt you've answered."
And now my master was recalling me;
so that, more hurriedly, I asked the spirit
to name the others who were there with him.
He said: "More than a thousand lie with me:
the second Frederick is but one among them,

2. Farinata foretells Dante's own exile from Florence in 1302, and the difficulty he will have in learning the "art" of returning.

3. The Uberti had been banished from Florence in 1280 and never allowed to return. In 1283, Farinata and his wife had been posthumously excommunicated, their bones exhumed and scattered, and the goods of their heirs confiscated.

4. The hill of Montaperti was on the bank of a small stream near Siena called the Arbia.

5. Farinata recalls his lone opposition to the total destruction of Florence at the council that followed the battle of Montaperti.

6. Because time itself will end after the Last Judgment, they will have no more future to see.

as is the Cardinal;[7] I name no others."
With that, he hid himself; and pondering
the speech that seemed to me so menacing,
I turned my steps to meet the ancient poet.
He moved ahead, and as we made our way,
he said to me: "Why are you so dismayed?"
I satisfied him, answering him fully.
And then that sage exhorted me: "Remember
the words that have been spoken here against you.
Now pay attention," and he raised his finger;
"when you shall stand before the gentle splendor
of one whose gracious eyes see everything,
then you shall learn—from her—your lifetime's journey."[8]
Following that, his steps turned to the left,
leaving the wall and moving toward the middle
along a path that strikes into a valley
whose stench, as it rose up, disgusted us.

Canto 11

Still the Sixth Circle. Pope Anastasius' tomb. Virgil on the parts of Dis they now will visit, where the modes of malice are punished: violence in the Seventh Circle's Three Rings; "ordinary" fraud in the Eighth Circle; and treacherous fraud in the Ninth Circle. Hell's previous circles, Two through Five, as circles of incontinence. Usury condemned.

Along the upper rim of a high bank
formed by a ring of massive broken boulders,
we came above a crowd more cruelly pent.° *confined*
And here, because of the outrageous stench
thrown up in excess by that deep abyss,
we drew back till we were behind the lid
of a great tomb, on which I made out this,
inscribed: "I hold Pope Anastasius,
enticed to leave the true path by Photinus."[1]
"It would be better to delay descent
so that our senses may grow somewhat used
to this foul stench; and then we can ignore it."
So said my master, and I answered him:
"Do find some compensation, lest this time
be lost." And he: "You see, I've thought of that."
"My son, within this ring of broken rocks,"

7. The Emperor Frederick II (1194–1250), known to his contemporaries as *Stupor Mundi,* "the wonder of the world," was King of Sicily and Naples, and head of the Holy Roman Empire from 1215 until his death. His contemporaries deemed him to be an Epicurean, believing neither in life after death nor in paradise. The Ghibelline Ottaviano degli Ubaldini was made Bishop of Bologna in 1240 and cardinal in 1244. His brother appears in *Purgatorio* and his uncle, Archbishop Ruggieri, in *Inferno* 33.14.

8. Beatrice, who sees all things in the perspective of God, will explain those mysteries which Virgil cannot, as he sees only by the natural light of human reason.

1. Anastasius II was pope from 496 to 498. Tradition appears to have confused him with Anastasius I, Byzantine emperor from 491 to 518, an adherent to the heresy of Photinus, which denied the divine origin of Christ.

he then began, "there are three smaller circles;[2]
like those that you are leaving, they range down.
Those circles are all full of cursed spirits;
so that your seeing of them may suffice,
learn now the how and why of their confinement.
Of every malice that earns hate in Heaven,
injustice is the end; and each such end
by force or fraud brings harm to other men.[3]
However, fraud is man's peculiar vice;
God finds it more displeasing—and therefore,
the fraudulent are lower, suffering more.
The violent take all of the first circle;
but since one uses force against three persons,
that circle's built of three divided rings.[4]
To God and to one's self and to one's neighbor—
I mean, to them or what is theirs—one can
do violence, as you shall now hear clearly.
Violent death and painful wounds may be
inflicted on one's neighbor; his possessions
may suffer ruin, fire, and extortion;
thus, murderers and those who strike in malice,
as well as plunderers and robbers—these,
in separated ranks, the first ring racks.
A man can set violent hands against
himself or his belongings; so within
the second ring repents, though uselessly,
whoever would deny himself your world,
gambling away, wasting his patrimony,
and weeping where he should instead be happy.
One can be violent against the Godhead,
one's heart denying and blaspheming Him
and scorning nature and the good in her;[5]
so, with its sign, the smallest ring has sealed
both Sodom and Cahors and all of those
who speak in passionate contempt of God.[6]
Now fraud, that eats away at every conscience,
is practiced by a man against another
who trusts in him, or one who has no trust.[7]

2. The seventh, eighth and ninth, "smaller" because further down in the cone.

3. "Malice" is the blanket term for all the sins of lower Hell, either by force (seventh circle) or by fraud (eighth and ninth), and distinguishes them from those of upper Hell.

4. "First circle" here means the first of lower Hell, the seventh, subdivided into three rings in order of gravity: the violence against one's neighbor, against self, and against God.

5. Any sin against Nature is considered an injury to God's order of Nature.

6. The Old Testament city of Sodom was identified with the act of sodomy, which in theological discussion was generally called simply "the vice against nature." Cahors is a town in southern France famous as a center of usury, the lending of money with a rate of interest. The third form of violence against God is blasphemy.

7. Fraud is the most complex and dangerous of sins because it is "man's peculiar vice." Dante divides it between simple fraud and treachery, where a bond of trust is broken.

This latter way seems only to cut off
the bond of love that nature forges;[8] thus,
nestled within the second circle[9] are:
hypocrisy and flattery, sorcerers,
and falsifiers, simony, and theft,
and barrators and panders and like trash.
But in the former way of fraud, not only
the love that nature forges is forgotten,
but added love that builds a special trust;
thus, in the tightest circle, where there is
the universe's center, seat of Dis,° *Satan*
all traitors are consumed eternally."
"Master, your reasoning is clear indeed,"
I said; "it has made plain for me the nature
of this pit and the population in it.
But tell me: those the dense marsh holds, or those
driven before the wind, or those on whom
rain falls, or those who clash with such harsh tongues,
why are they not all punished in the city
of flaming red if God is angry with them?
And if He's not, why then are they tormented?"[1]
And then to me, "Why does your reason wander
so far from its accustomed course?" he said.
"Or of what other things are you now thinking?
Have you forgotten, then, the words with which
your *Ethics* treats of those three dispositions
that strike at Heaven's will: incontinence
and malice and mad bestiality?[2]
And how the fault that is the least condemned
and least offends God is incontinence?
If you consider carefully this judgment
and call to mind the souls of upper Hell,
who bear their penalties outside this city,
you'll see why they have been set off from these
unrighteous ones, and why, when heaven's vengeance
hammers at them, it carries lesser anger."
"O sun that heals all sight that is perplexed,
when I ask you, your answer so contents
that doubting pleases me as much as knowing.

8. In Dante's ethics, humankind is created by love and love is the basis of the natural social bond; hence any act of fraud is a conscious severing of that bond just as the sins of upper Hell pervert (by excess or insufficiency) the innate desire for God's creation.

9. The eighth circle, which contains ten subdivisions in all, is the second circle of lower Hell.

1. The pilgrim's question raises a key tension in the depiction of Hell: do all souls suffer equally because all are damned, or do some suffer more than others? Are all sins equally evil, or are some worse than others?

2. In his *Nicomachean Ethics*, known to Dante through the commentaries and translations of Averroës, Aquinas, and others, Aristotle drew a distinction between three types of immoral practice. Incontinence signifies excess in any passion which, in moderation, is lawful, including all the vices punished in the second through fifth circles. "Mad bestiality" here means violence, and "malice," fraud. Aristotle's classification does not include heresy, and Virgil never mentions the sixth circle in this discussion; nor does he mention the lukewarm souls of Ante-Inferno or the souls of Limbo, whose sins were of omission rather than commission.

Go back a little to that point," I said,
"where you told me that usury offends
divine goodness; unravel now that knot."
"Philosophy, for one who understands,
points out, and not in just one place," he said,
"how nature follows—as she takes her course—
the Divine Intellect and Divine Art;
and if you read your *Physics* carefully,[3]
not many pages from the start, you'll see
that when it can, your art would follow nature,
just as a pupil imitates his master;
so that your art is almost God's grandchild.[4]
From these two, art and nature, it is fitting,
if you recall how *Genesis* begins,
for men to make their way, to gain their living;
and since the usurer prefers another
pathway, he scorns both nature in herself
and art, her follower; his hope is elsewhere.[5]
But follow me, for it is time to move;
the Fishes glitter now on the horizon
and all the Wain is spread out over Caurus;[6]
only beyond, can one climb down the cliff."

Canto 12

The Seventh Circle, First Ring: the Violent against their Neighbors. The Minotaur. The Centaurs, led by Chiron, who assigns Nessus to guide Dante and Virgil across the boiling river of blood (Phlegethon). In that river, Tyrants and Murderers, immersed, watched over by the Centaurs.

The place that we had reached for our descent
along the bank was alpine; what reclined
upon that bank would, too, repel all eyes.
Just like the toppled mass of rock that struck—
because of earthquake or eroded props—
the Adige on its flank, this side of Trent,
where from the mountain top from which it thrust
down to the plain, the rock is shattered so
that it permits a path for those above:[1]
such was the passage down to that ravine.
And at the edge above the cracked abyss,

3. The *Physics* of Aristotle.

4. Nature, daughter of God, follows his eternal ideas and his art in her own operation; human art and industry, daughter of Nature, ought to follow her and her art in the same way.

5. God's command to Adam and Eve when he expelled them from Eden was that they should gain their living by the sweat of their brows (Genesis 3:19). Because the usurer gains his living from money rather than either from Nature or from her follower, art, he despises her twice over.

6. The position of the constellations indicates the time: two hours before sunrise, or 4 A.M.

1. The comparison is to the Slavini di Marco, a "toppled mass of rock" resulting from an enormous landslide between Trent and Verona on the Adige River in northeast Italy.

there lay outstretched the infamy of Crete,[2]
  conceived within the counterfeited cow;
and, catching sight of us, he bit himself
like one whom fury devastates within.
  Turning to him, my sage cried out: "Perhaps
you think this is the Duke of Athens here,
who, in the world above, brought you your death.
  Be off, you beast; this man who comes has not
been tutored by your sister; all he wants
in coming here is to observe your torments."
  Just as the bull that breaks loose from its halter
the moment it receives the fatal stroke,
and cannot run but plunges back and forth,
  so did I see the Minotaur respond;
and my alert guide cried: "Run toward the pass;
it's better to descend while he's berserk."
  And so we made our way across that heap
of stones, which often moved beneath my feet
because my weight was somewhat strange for them.
  While climbing down, I thought. He said: "You wonder,
perhaps, about that fallen mass, watched over
by the inhuman rage I have just quenched.
  Now I would have you know: the other time
that I descended into lower Hell,
this mass of boulders had not yet collapsed;[3]
  but if I reason rightly, it was just
before the coming of the One who took
from Dis the highest circle's splendid spoils
  that, on all sides, the steep and filthy valley
had trembled so, I thought the universe
felt love (by which, as some believe, the world
  has often been converted into chaos);
and at that moment, here as well as elsewhere,
these ancient boulders toppled, in this way.[4]
  But fix your eyes below, upon the valley,
for now we near the stream of blood, where those
who injure others violently, boil."
  O blind cupidity and insane anger,
which goad us on so much in our short life,
then steep us in such grief eternally!
  I saw a broad ditch bent into an arc

2. The Minotaur, half-man, half-bull, the result of a union between a bull and queen Pasiphaë of Crete, who hid within an artificial cow to mate with the bull. King Minos of Crete extracted an annual tribute of seven Greek youths and seven maidens to be thrown to the Minotaur in its labyrinth. Theseus, Duke of Athens, traveled to Crete as one of the sacrificial youths and killed the Minotaur.

3. Virgil refers to the errand on which Erichtho sent him (Canto 9.22–27), which took place before the crucifixion of Christ and the Harrowing of Hell, mentioned next.

4. According to a theory of the ancient philosopher Empedocles, the alternate supremacy of principles of hate, which keeps things separate, and love, which unites all things, causes periodic destruction and construction in the scheme of the universe; both are required for equilibrium. This is how Virgil understands the earthquake that marked Christ's death (Matthew 27:51), the supreme sacrifice expressing God's love for his creation.

so that it could embrace all of that plain,
precisely as my guide had said before;
between it and the base of the embankment
raced files of Centaurs who were armed with arrows,[5]
as, in the world above, they used to hunt.
On seeing us descend, they all reined in;
and, after they had chosen bows and shafts,
three of their number moved out from their ranks;
and still far off, one cried: "What punishment
do you approach as you descend the slope?
But speak from there; if not, I draw my bow."
My master told him: "We shall make reply
only to Chiron,[6] when we reach his side;
your hasty will has never served you well."
Then he nudged me and said: "That one is Nessus,
who died because of lovely Deianira
and of himself wrought vengeance for himself.[7]
And in the middle, gazing at his chest,
is mighty Chiron, tutor of Achilles;
the third is Pholus, he who was so frenzied.[8]
And many thousands wheel around the moat,
their arrows aimed at any soul that thrusts
above the blood more than its guilt allots."
By now we had drawn near those agile beasts;
Chiron drew out an arrow; with the notch,
he parted his beard back upon his jaws.
When he'd uncovered his enormous mouth,
he said to his companions: "Have you noticed
how he who walks behind moves what he touches?
Dead souls are not accustomed to do that."
And my good guide—now near the Centaur's chest,
the place where his two natures met—replied:
"He is indeed alive, and so alone
it falls to me to show him the dark valley.
Necessity has brought him here, not pleasure.
For she° who gave me this new task was one *Beatrice*
who had just come from singing halleluiah:
he is no robber; I am not a thief.
But by the Power that permits my steps
to journey on so wild a path, give us
one of your band, to serve as our companion;
and let him show us where to ford the ditch,
and let him bear this man upon his back,

5. In mythology, centaurs are half-man, half-horse, excellent archers, and notorious for their gluttony and violence.

6. An exceptional centaur, Chiron was traditionally depicted as an educator, scientist, and musician who tutored Achilles, Hercules, and other Greek heroes.

7. Dying of a poisoned arrow shot by Hercules after he tried to rape the hero's wife Deianira, Nessus gave Deianira a robe dipped in his blood which he claimed would preserve her husband's love. When she gave Hercules the robe, he was maddened by the poison in the blood, and burned himself to death to end the agony (Ovid, *Metamorphoses*, 9.127–69).

8. Pholus was killed during the Centaurs' battle with the Lapiths at the wedding of Pirithoüs.

for he's no spirit who can fly through air."
    Then Chiron wheeled about and right and said
to Nessus: "Then, return and be their guide;
if other troops disturb you, fend them off."
    Now, with our faithful escort, we advanced
along the bloodred, boiling ditch's banks,
beside the piercing cries of those who boiled.
    I saw some who were sunk up to their brows,
and that huge Centaur said: "These are the tyrants
who plunged their hands in blood and plundering.
    Here they lament their ruthless crimes; here are
both Alexander and the fierce Dionysius,
who brought such years of grief to Sicily.[9]
    That brow with hair so black is Ezzelino;
that other there, the blonde one, is Obizzo
of Este, he who was indeed undone,
    within the world above, by his fierce son."[1]
Then I turned to the poet, and he said:
"Now let him be your first guide, me your second."
    A little farther on, the Centaur stopped
above a group that seemed to rise above
the boiling blood as far up as their throats.
    He pointed out one shade, alone, apart,
and said: "Within God's bosom, he impaled
the heart that still drips blood upon the Thames."[2]
    Then I caught sight of some who kept their heads
and even their full chests above the tide;
among them—many whom I recognized.
    And so the blood grew always shallower
until it only scorched the feet; and here
we found a place where we could ford the ditch.
    "Just as you see that, on this side, the brook
continually thins," the Centaur said,
"so I should have you know the rivulet,
    along the other side, will slowly deepen
its bed, until it reaches once again
the depth where tyranny must make lament.
    And there divine justice torments Attila
he who was such a scourge upon the earth,

9. "Alexander" may be either Alexander the Great of Macedonia (356–323 B.C.E.) or Alexander of Pherae, a tyrant of Thessaly of the same period, famed for his cruelty. Dionysius the elder was tyrant of Syracuse in Sicily during the early 4th century B.C.E.

1. Ezzelino III da Romano (1194–1259) was son-in-law of Emperor Frederick II, head of the Ghibellines in Upper Italy, and so infamous for his cruelty that the Pope proclaimed a crusade against him. Obizzo II d'Este (1247–1293) was an ardent Guelf and supporter of Charles of Anjou who fought against Manfred, natural son of Frederick. He was said to have been smothered by his son, Azzo VIII.

2. Guy, son of Simon de Montfort, killed his first cousin Prince Henry of Cornwall in March 1271 during the assembly of the cardinals to elect a pope, supposedly at the very moment of the elevation of the Host when Henry was on his knees. According to some accounts, Henry's heart was enclosed in a statue on London Bridge over the river Thames, still dripping blood because not yet avenged.

and Pyrrhus, Sextus;[3] to eternity
it milks the tears that boiling brook unlocks
from Rinier of Corneto, Rinier Pazzo,
those two who waged such war upon the highroads."[4]
Then he turned round and crossed the ford again.

Canto 13

The Seventh Circle, Second Ring: the Violent against Themselves (Suicides) or against their Possessions (Squanderers). The dreary wood, with the Suicides transformed into strange trees, and the Squanderers, hounded and rent by bitches. Pier della Vigna. Lano and Jacopo da Santo Andrea. The anonymous Florentine suicide.

Nessus had not yet reached the other bank
when we began to make our way across
a wood on which no path had left its mark.
No green leaves in that forest, only black;
no branches straight and smooth, but knotted, gnarled;
no fruits were there, but briers bearing poison.
Even those savage beasts that roam between
Cécina and Corneto,[1] beasts that hate
tilled lands, do not have holts° so harsh and dense. *woods*
This is the nesting place of the foul Harpies,
who chased the Trojans from the Strophades
with sad foretelling of their future trials.[2]
Their wings are wide, their necks and faces human;
their feet are taloned, their great bellies feathered;
they utter their laments on the strange trees.
And my kind master then instructed me:
"Before you enter farther know that now
you are within the second ring and shall
be here until you reach the horrid sand;
therefore look carefully; you'll see such things
as would deprive my speech of all belief."[3]
From every side I heard the sound of cries,
but I could not see any source for them,
so that, in my bewilderment, I stopped.
I think that he was thinking that I thought
so many voices moaned among those trunks
from people who had been concealed from us.

3. Known as "the Scourge of God," Attila was King of the Huns (433–453). Pyrrhus is either the son of Achilles whose savage murder of Priam and other Trojans was recorded in *Aeneid* 2 or a king of Epirus who made war on Rome in the third century B.C.E. Sextus was the son of Pompey and a notorious pirate in Lucan's *Pharsalia.*

4. Two famous highwaymen of Dante's day.

1. The river Cecina and the town of Corneto mark the boundaries of the Maremma, a famously dense Tuscan wood.

2. Mythical monsters in the shapes of birds with clawed hands and women's faces, the Harpies, among other deeds, fouled the Trojans' feast and drove Aeneas and his companions from the Strophades, islands in the Ionian Sea, prophesying that they would face starvation and misfortune before reaching Italy (*Aeneid* 3.209–57).

3. This episode closely follows another adventure in *Aeneid* 3. Landed in Thrace, Aeneas tries to tear off a green branch for an altar only to find black blood dripping from it. The tree entombs Polydorus, a son of Priam sent to purchase aid in the Trojan War from the King of Thrace, who murdered him instead, stealing the gold proffered as payment.

Therefore my master said: "If you would tear
a little twig from any of these plants,
the thoughts you have will also be cut off."
Then I stretched out my hand a little way
and from a great thornbush snapped off a branch,
at which its trunk cried out: "Why do you tear me?"
And then, when it had grown more dark with blood,
it asked again: "Why do you break me off?
Are you without all sentiment of pity?
We once were men and now are arid stumps:
your hand might well have shown us greater mercy
had we been nothing more than souls of serpents."
As from a sapling log that catches fire
along one of its ends, while at the other
it drips and hisses with escaping vapor,
so from that broken stump issued together
both words and blood; at which I let the branch
fall, and I stood like one who is afraid.
My sage said: "Wounded soul, if, earlier,
he had been able to believe what he
had only glimpsed within my poetry,
then he would not have set his hand against you;
but its incredibility made me
urge him to do a deed that grieves me deeply.
But tell him who you were, so that he may,
to make amends, refresh your fame within
the world above, where he can still return."
To which the trunk: "Your sweet speech draws me so
that I cannot be still; and may it not
oppress you, if I linger now in talk.[4]
I am the one who guarded both the keys
of Frederick's heart and turned them, locking and
unlocking them with such dexterity
that none but I could share his confidence;
and I was faithful to my splendid office,
so faithful that I lost both sleep and strength.
The whore who never turned her harlot's eyes
away from Caesar's dwelling, she who is
the death of all and vice of every court,
inflamed the minds of everyone against me;
and those inflamed, then so inflamed Augustus
that my delighted honors turned to sadness.[5]
My mind, because of its disdainful temper,

4. The speaker, Pier della Vigna (c. 1190–1249), was minister and councilor to Emperor Frederick II. Accused (probably falsely) of plotting with the pope to poison Frederick, he was arrested, thrown into prison, and blinded. He soon committed suicide, it is said by dashing his head against a wall. Pier was also a poet and accomplished letter-writer, as is reflected in the ornamented and mannered style of his speech.

5. The "whore" is envy, which was a sin of the eyes; "Caesar's dwelling" is the imperial court, and "Augustus" is the emperor, after the Roman emperor, Caesar Augustus.

believing it could flee disdain through death,
made me unjust against my own just self.
I swear to you by the peculiar roots
of this thornbush, I never broke my faith
with him who was so worthy—with my lord.
If one of you returns into the world,
then let him help my memory, which still
lies prone beneath the battering of envy."
The poet waited briefly, then he said
to me: "Since he is silent, do not lose
this chance, but speak and ask what you would know."
And I: "Do you continue; ask of him
whatever you believe I should request;
I cannot, so much pity takes my heart."
Then he began again: "Imprisoned spirit,
so may this man do freely what you ask,
may it please you to tell us something more
of how the soul is bound into these knots;
and tell us, if you can, if any one
can ever find his freedom from these limbs."
At this the trunk breathed violently, then
that wind became this voice: "You shall be answered
promptly. When the savage spirit quits
the body from which it has torn itself,
then Minos sends it to the seventh maw.
It falls into the wood, and there's no place
to which it is allotted, but wherever
fortune has flung that soul, that is the space
where, even as a grain of spelt, it sprouts.[6]
It rises as a sapling, a wild plant;
and then the Harpies, feeding on its leaves,
cause pain and for that pain provide a vent.
Like other souls, we shall seek out the flesh
that we have left, but none of us shall wear it;
it is not right for any man to have
what he himself has cast aside. We'll drag
our bodies here; they'll hang in this sad wood,
each on the stump of its vindictive shade."[7]
And we were still intent upon the trunk—
believing it had wanted to say more—
when we were overtaken by a roar,
just as the hunter is aware of chase
and boar as they draw near his post—he hears
the beasts and then the branches as they crack.
And there upon the left were two who, scratched

6. Like other wheats and grains, spelt grows readily and in thick clumps out of a single shoot.

7. Souls are to be rejoined with their bodies after the Last Judgment. Because the shade was unjust ("vindictive") to its own body through suicide, it will not be fully reunited with it.

and naked, fled so violently that
they tore away each forest bough they passed.
The one in front: "Now come, death, quickly come!"
The other shade, who thought himself too slow,
was shouting after him: "Lano, your legs
were not so nimble at the jousts of Toppo!"[8]
And then, perhaps because he'd lost his breath,
he fell into one tangle with a bush.
Behind these two, black bitches filled the wood,
and they were just as eager and as swift
as greyhounds that have been let off their leash.
They set their teeth in him where he had crouched;
and, piece by piece, those dogs dismembered him
and carried off his miserable limbs.
Then he who was my escort took my hand;
he led me to the lacerated thorn
that wept in vain where it was bleeding, broken.
"O Jacopo," it said, "da Santo Andrea,
what have you gained by using me as screen?
Am I to blame for your indecent life?"
When my good master stood beside that bush,
he said: "Who were you, who through many wounds
must breathe with blood your melancholy words?"[9]
And he to us: "O spirits who have come
to witness the outrageous laceration
that leaves so many of my branches torn,
collect them at the foot of this sad thorn.
My home was in the city whose first patron
gave way to John the Baptist; for this reason,
he'll always use his art to make it sorrow;[1]
and if—along the crossing of the Arno—
some effigy of Mars had not remained,
those citizens who afterward rebuilt
their city on the ashes that Attila
had left to them, would have travailed in vain.[2]
I made—of my own house—my gallows place."

Canto 14

The Seventh Circle, Third Ring: the Violent against God. The First Zone: Blasphemers, supine on fiery sands. Capaneus. Virgil on the Old Man of Crete, whose

8. Lano of Siena and Jacopo da Santo Andrea of Padua, two notorious squanderers of 13th-century Italy.
9. Generally known as "the anonymous Florentine," this soul appears to represent the general self-destructiveness of his city itself rather than a particular inhabitant.
1. In pagan times, the citizens of Florence had chosen Mars as their special patron; when they switched to Christianity, they incurred the war-god's wrath when they converted his temple to a church dedicated to St. John.
2. According to legend, the statue of Mars was removed to a tower near the river Arno, and it fell into the river when the city was destroyed by Attila in 450 (confused here with the Ostrogoth king Totila, who had besieged the city in 542). It was said that the retrieval of the statue had permitted the Florentines to rebuild their city (in fact, it was neither destroyed nor rebuilt).

streaming tears form the rivers of Hell: Acheron, Phlegethon, Styx, and Cocytus. The sight of Lethe postponed.

Love of our native city overcame me;
I gathered up the scattered boughs and gave
them back to him whose voice was spent already.
From there we reached the boundary that divides
the second from the third ring—and the sight
of a dread work that justice had devised.
To make these strange things clear, I must explain
that we had come upon an open plain
that banishes all green things from its bed.
The wood of sorrow is a garland round it,
just as that wood is ringed by a sad channel;
here, at the very edge, we stayed our steps.
The ground was made of sand, dry and compact,
a sand not different in kind from that
on which the feet of Cato had once tramped.[1]
O vengeance of the Lord, how you should be
dreaded by everyone who now can read
whatever was made manifest to me!
I saw so many flocks of naked souls,
all weeping miserably, and it seemed
that they were ruled by different decrees.
Some lay upon the ground, flat on their backs;
some huddled in a crouch, and there they sat;
and others moved about incessantly.
The largest group was those who walked about,
the smallest, those supine° in punishment; *lying down*
but these had looser tongues to tell their torment.
Above that plain of sand, distended flakes
of fire showered down;[2] their fall was slow—
as snow descends on alps when no wind blows.
Just like the flames that Alexander saw
in India's hot zones, when fires fell,
intact and to the ground, on his battalions,
for which—wisely—he had his soldiers tramp
the soil to see that every fire was spent
before new flames were added to the old;[3]
so did the never-ending heat descend;
with this, the sand was kindled just as tinder
on meeting flint will flame—doubling the pain.
The dance of wretched hands was never done;

1. Cato of Utica (95–46 B.C.E.), who led the Pompeian forces through the Libyan Desert in 47 B.C.E. (Lucan, *Pharsalia* 9); Dante placed him at the base of the Mountain of Purgatory (*Purgatorio* 1).
2. The rain of fire derives from the fire that fell upon Sodom and Gomorrah (Genesis 19:24) and also from Ezekiel 38:22.
3. The incident comes from an apocryphal letter from Alexander of Macedon to Aristotle; Dante condenses an incident of trampling on heavily falling snow with a rain of fire from the sky.

now here, now there, they tried to beat aside
the fresh flames as they fell. And I began
to speak: "My master, you who can defeat
all things except for those tenacious demons
who tried to block us at the entryway,
who is that giant there, who does not seem
to heed the singeing—he who lies and scorns
and scowls, he whom the rains can't seem to soften?"[4]
And he himself, on noticing that I
was querying my guide about him, cried:
"That which I was in life, I am in death.
Though Jove wear out the smith from whom he took,
in wrath, the keen-edged thunderbolt with which
on my last day I was to be transfixed;
or if he tire the others, one by one,
in Mongibello, at the sooty forge,
while bellowing: 'O help, good Vulcan, help!'[5]—
just as he did when there was war at Phlegra[6]—
and casts his shafts at me with all his force,
not even then would he have happy vengeance."
Then did my guide speak with such vehemence
as I had never heard him use before:
"O Capaneus, for your arrogance
that is not quenched, you're punished all the more:
no torture other than your own madness
could offer pain enough to match your wrath."
But then, with gentler face he turned to me
and said: "That man was one of seven kings
besieging Thebes; he held—and still, it seems,
holds—God in great disdain, disprizing° Him; *scorning*
but as I told him now, his maledictions
sit well as ornaments upon his chest.
Now follow me and—take care—do not set
your feet upon the sand that's burning hot,
but always keep them back, close to the forest."
In silence we had reached a place where flowed
a slender watercourse out of the wood—
a stream whose redness makes me shudder still.
As from the Bulicame pours a brook
whose waters then are shared by prostitutes,[7]
so did this stream run down across the sand.
Its bed and both its banks were made of stone,
together with the slopes along its shores,

4. Capaneus was one of the legendary Seven against Thebes, kings who besieged the city; defying Jove as he scaled the walls, Capaneus was struck down by a thunderbolt.

5. Vulcan, god of fire and of the forge, with his assistants, the Cyclopes, made Jove's thunderbolts. His furnace was thought to be at Mt. Etna in Sicily, called Mongibello in Italian.

6. When the rebellious Giants stormed Olympus, Jove defeated them at the battle of Phlegra (literally "the place of burning") with the help of Hercules.

7. The Bulicame was a famous sulphurous hot spring near Viterbo, north of Rome. Its waters were piped into the houses of prostitutes there.

so that I saw our passageway lay there.
"Among all other things that I have shown you
since we first made our way across the gate
whose threshold is forbidden to no one,
no thing has yet been witnessed by your eyes
as notable as this red rivulet,
which quenches every flame that burns above it."
These words were spoken by my guide; at this,
I begged him to bestow the food for which
he had already given me the craving.[8]
"A devastated land lies in midsea,
a land that is called Crete," he answered me.
"Under its king the world once lived chastely.
Within that land there was a mountain blessed
with leaves and waters, and they called it Ida;
but it is withered now like some old thing.
It once was chosen as a trusted cradle
by Rhea for her son; to hide him better,
when he cried out, she had her servants clamor.[9]
Within the mountain is a huge Old Man,
who stands erect—his back turned toward Damietta°— *in Egypt*
and looks at Rome as if it were his mirror.
The Old Man's head is fashioned of fine gold,
the purest silver forms his arms and chest,
but he is made of brass down to the cleft;
below that point he is of choicest iron
except for his right foot, made of baked clay;
and he rests more on this than on the left.[1]
Each part of him, except the gold, is cracked;
and down that fissure there are tears that drip;
when gathered, they pierce through that cavern's floor
and, crossing rocks into this valley, form
the Acheron and Styx and Phlegethon;
and then they make their way down this tight channel,
and at the point past which there's no descent,
they form Cocytus; since you are to see
what that pool is, I'll not describe it here."
And I asked him: "But if the rivulet
must follow such a course down from our world,
why can we see it only at this boundary?"
And he to me: "You know this place is round;

8. The tale of the Old Man of Crete, used to explain the origin of the waterways of Hell, is a synthesis of Ovid's myth of the four ages—a golden age under Saturn, mythical king of Crete, when "the world once lived chastely," followed in declining order by silver, bronze and iron (*Metamorphoses* 1.89–150), and the prophet Daniel's account of a composite statue in the dream of Nebuchadnezzar (Daniel 2:31–35).

9. Rhea, or Cybele, was mother by Saturn of Jove. In order to avert a prophecy that he would be dethroned by one of his children, Saturn had devoured them one by one as they were born. Only Jove was saved when Rhea retired to Mt. Ida to give birth and substituted a stone for the child. To hide the infant's cries, she had her priests clash their weapons and chant.

1. Nebuchadnezzar's dream imagined a similar statue, broken to pieces by "a stone cut out of a mountain without hands." Dante adds the detail, reminiscent of the pilgrim's aborted climb in Canto 1.30, of the unevenly weighted feet, and the gloss of the statue as an allegory of the four ages.

and though the way that you have come is long,
and always toward the left and toward the bottom,
 you still have not completed all the circle:
so that, if something new appears to us,
it need not bring such wonder to your face."[2]
 And I again: "Master, where's Phlegethon
and where is Lethe?[3] You omit the second
and say this rain of tears has formed the first."
 "I'm pleased indeed," he said, "with all your questions;
yet one of them might well have found its answer
already—when you saw the red stream boiling.
 You shall see Lethe, but past this abyss,
there where the spirits go to cleanse themselves
when their repented guilt is set aside."
 Then he declared: "The time has come to quit
this wood; see that you follow close behind me;
these margins form a path that does not scorch,
 and over them, all flaming vapor is quenched."

Canto 15

Still the Seventh Circle, Third Ring: the Violent against God. Second Zone: the Sodomites, endlessly crossing the fiery sands beneath the rain of fire. Brunetto Latini, whom Dante treats as mentor. Priscian, Francesco d'Accorso, and Andrea dei Mozzi, Bishop of Florence.

 Now one of the hard borders bears us forward;
the river mist forms shadows overhead
and shields the shores and water from the fire.
 Just as between Wissant and Bruges, the Flemings,
in terror of the tide that floods toward them,
have built a wall of dykes to daunt the sea;
 and as the Paduans, along the Brenta,
build bulwarks to defend their towns and castles
before the dog days fall on Carentana;[1]
 just so were these embankments, even though
they were not built so high and not so broad,
whoever was the artisan who made them.
 By now we were so distant from the wood
that I should not have made out where it was—
not even if I'd turned around to look—
 when we came on a company of spirits

2. There has been much discussion as to whether Virgil's explanation is consistent with geographical descriptions elsewhere in the canticle, but it is clear enough here: each river is basically level, circling a particular region of Hell, and linked to the others by a descending rivulet such as the one encountered here that leads from Phlegethon down to Cocytus. Because their descent has nearly always been in a leftward direction, the travelers haven't always crossed such connecting streams.

3. Well versed in his classical mythology, the pilgrim is puzzled over the absence of Lethe, the river of forgetting of which the souls in the Elysian Fields drink before returning to the world above (*Aeneid* 6).

1. Wissant and Bruges are given as the eastern and western boundaries of the Flemish seaboard, lined with great dykes to hold back the North Sea. The melt-off from the Carnic Alps ("Carentana") would swell the northern Italian river Brenta as it flowed down into the city of Padua.

who made their way along the bank; and each
stared steadily at us, as in the dusk,
beneath the new moon, men look at each other.
They knit their brows and squinted at us—just
as an old tailor at his needle's eye.
And when that family looked harder, I
was recognized by one, who took me by
the hem and cried out: "This is marvelous!"
That spirit having stretched his arm toward me,
I fixed my eyes upon his baked, brown features,
so that the scorching of his face could not
prevent my mind from recognizing him;
and lowering my face to meet his face,
I answered him: "Are you here, Ser Brunetto?"[2]
And he: "My son, do not mind if Brunetto
Latini lingers for a while with you
and lets the file he's with pass on ahead."
I said: "With all my strength I pray you, stay;
and if you'd have me rest awhile with you,
I shall, if that please him with whom I go."
"O son," he said, "whoever of this flock
stops but a moment, stays a hundred years
and cannot shield himself when fire strikes.
Therefore move on; below—but close—I'll follow;
and then I shall rejoin my company,
who go lamenting their eternal sorrows."
I did not dare to leave my path for his
own level; but I walked with head bent low
as does a man who goes in reverence.
And he began: "What destiny or chance
has led you here below before your last
day came, and who is he who shows the way?"
"There, in the sunlit life above," I answered,
"before my years were full, I went astray
within a valley. Only yesterday
at dawn I turned my back upon it—but
when I was newly lost, he here appeared,
to guide me home again along this path."
And he to me: "If you pursue your star,
you cannot fail to reach a splendid harbor,
if in fair life, I judged you properly;
and if I had not died too soon for this,
on seeing Heaven was so kind to you,

2. "Master" Brunetto, a term of respect. Brunetto Latini (c. 1220–1294) was a celebrated writer and Guelph political figure who was active in Florentine affairs. Author of such works as a French prose encyclopedia and the Italian didactic poem the *Tesoretto,* he was not actually Dante's teacher, but an important influence. He had no reputation as a sodomite, and there has been much debate over whether Dante also intended the sin to be understood, as it often was in the Middle Ages, in terms of a "sterile" or nonproductive use of language and learning.

I should have helped sustain you in your work.
    But that malicious, that ungrateful people
come down, in ancient times, from Fiesole—
still keeping something of the rock and mountain[3]—
    for your good deeds, will be your enemy:
and there is cause—among the sour sorbs,
the sweet fig is not meant to bear its fruit.[4]
    The world has long since called them blind, a people
presumptuous, avaricious, envious;
be sure to cleanse yourself of their foul ways.
    Your fortune holds in store such honor for you,
one party and the other will be hungry
for you—but keep the grass far from the goat.
    For let the beasts of Fiesole find forage
among themselves, and leave the plant alone—
if still, among their dung, it rises up—
    in which there lives again the sacred seed
of those few Romans who remained in Florence
when such a nest of wickedness was built."
    "If my desire were answered totally,"
I said to Ser Brunetto, "you'd still be
among, not banished from, humanity.
    Within my memory is fixed—and now
moves me—your dear, your kind paternal
image when, in the world above, from time to time
    you taught me how man makes himself eternal;[5]
and while I live, my gratitude for that
must always be apparent in my words.
    What you have told me of my course, I write;
I keep it with another text, for comment
by one who'll understand, if I may reach her.
    One thing alone I'd have you plainly see:
so long as I am not rebuked by conscience,
I stand prepared for Fortune, come what may.
    My ears find no new pledge in that prediction;
therefore, let Fortune turn her wheel as she
may please, and let the peasant turn his mattock."° *hoe*
    At this, my master turned his head around
and toward the right, and looked at me and said:
"He who takes note of this has listened well."
    But nonetheless, my talk with Ser Brunetto
continues, and I ask of him who are

3. The tradition was that Florence was founded following Caesar's successful siege of the ancient town of Fiesole, on a hill four miles to the northeast, partly by Romans and partly by families from the destroyed town.

4. The sorb is related to the apple and the pear; the metaphor parallels the contrast between Fiesolan and Roman Florentines, with Dante as the fig and his tormenters as the "sour sorbs."

5. Brunetto wrote in the *Tresor* that "Glory gives the wise man a second life; that is to say, after his death the reputation which remains of his good works makes it seem as if he were still alive" (2.120.1).

his comrades of repute and excellence.
And he to me: "To know of some is good;
but for the rest, silence is to be praised;
the time we have is short for so much talk.
In brief, know that my company has clerics
and men of letters and of fame—and all
were stained by one same sin upon the earth.
That sorry crowd holds Priscian and Francesco
d'Accorso;[6] and among them you can see,
if you have any longing for such scurf,
the one the Servant of His Servants sent
from the Arno to the Bacchiglione's banks,
and there he left his tendons strained by sin.[7]
I would say more; but both my walk and words
must not be longer, for—beyond—I see
new smoke emerging from the sandy bed.
Now people come with whom I must not be.
Let my *Tesoro,* in which I still live,
be precious to you; and I ask no more."
And then he turned and seemed like one of those
who race across the fields to win the green
cloth at Verona; of those runners, he
appeared to be the winner, not the loser.[8]

Canto 16

Still the Seventh Circle, Third Ring, Second Zone: other Sodomites. Three Florentines, Guido Guerra, Tegghiaio Aldobrandi, Jacopo Rusticucci. The decadence of Florence. Phlegethon, cascading into the next zone. The cord of Dante, used by Virgil to summon a monstrous figure from the waters.

No sooner had I reached the place where one
could hear a murmur, like a beehive's hum,
of waters as they fell to the next circle,
when, setting out together, three shades ran,
leaving another company that passed
beneath the rain of bitter punishment.
They came toward us, and each of them cried out:
"Stop, you who by your clothing seem to be
someone who comes from our indecent country!"[1]

6. Priscian (fl. c. 500 C.E.) was a celebrated Latin grammarian whose works were widely used in medieval schools. Francesco d'Accorso (1225–1293) was a renowned lawyer and professor of law at Bologna and Oxford.

7. Andrea de' Mozzi was bishop of Florence (on the Arno) until transferred by Pope Boniface VIII in 1295 to Vicenza (on the Bacchiglione) due to his unseemly living. He died there several months later, leaving a body, according to Brunetto, with muscles "strained" by sodomy. Boniface VIII is referred to, with irony, by the pope's name in official acts, "Servant of Servants."

8. This foot race was instituted in 1207 and run annually on the first Sunday in Lent outside Verona. According to Boccaccio, the runners were naked and the prize was a piece of green cloth.

1. According to the Florentine chronicler Villani, the dress of his people "was the most beautiful, the most noble, and the most decorous of that of any nation; it was in the manner of the togaed Roman."

Ah me, what wounds I saw upon their limbs,
wounds new and old, wounds that the flames seared in!
It pains me still as I remember it.
When they cried out, my master paid attention;
he turned his face toward me and then he said:
"Now wait: to these one must show courtesy.
And were it not the nature of this place
for shafts of fire to fall, I'd say that haste
was seemlier for you than for those three."
As soon as we stood still, they started up
their ancient wail again; and when they reached us,
they formed a wheel, all three of them together.
As champions, naked, oiled, will always do,
each studying the grip that serves him best
before the blows and wounds begin to fall,
while wheeling so, each one made sure his face
was turned to me, so that their necks opposed
their feet in one uninterrupted flow.[2]
And, "If the squalor of this shifting sand,
together with our baked and barren features,
makes us and our requests contemptible,"
one said, "then may our fame incline your mind
to tell us who you are, whose living feet
can make their way through Hell with such assurance.
He in whose steps you see me tread, although
he now must wheel about both peeled and naked,
was higher in degree than you believe:
he was a grandson of the good Gualdrada,
and Guido Guerra was his name; in life
his sword and his good sense accomplished much.
The other who, behind me, tramples sand—
Tegghiaio Aldobrandi, one whose voice
should have been heeded in the world above.
And I, who share this punishment with them,
was Jacopo Rusticucci; certainly,
more than all else, my savage wife destroyed me."[3]
If I'd had shield and shelter from the fire,
I should have thrown myself down there among them—
I think my master would have sanctioned that;
but since that would have left me burned and baked,
my fear won out against the good intention
that made me so impatient to embrace them.
Then I began: "Your present state had fixed
not scorn but sorrow in me—and so deeply
that it will only disappear slowly—

2. The theme of athletics introduced at the end of the previous canto continues here, referring either to ancient wrestlers, to the medieval trial by combat to settle judicial disputes, or to both.

3. Guido and Tegghiaio were prominent Guelfs of the mid 13th century; Rusticucci a less distinguished neighbor of Tegghiaio and also a Guelf. Dante had asked for news of the latter two in Canto 6. Jacopo blames his wife for his fate.

as soon as my lord spoke to me with words
that made me understand what kind of men
were coming toward us, men of worth like yours.
For I am of your city; and with fondness,
I've always told and heard the others tell
of both your actions and your honored names.
I leave the gall and go for the sweet apples
that I was promised by my truthful guide;
but first I must descend into the center."
"So may your soul long lead your limbs and may
your fame shine after you," he answered then,
"tell us if courtesy and valor still
abide within our city as they did
when we were there, or have they disappeared
completely;[4] for Guiglielmo Borsiere,
who only recently has come to share
our torments, and goes there with our companions,
has caused us much affliction with his words."[5]
"Newcomers to the city and quick gains
have brought excess and arrogance to you,
o Florence, and you weep for it already!"
So I cried out with face upraised; the three
looked at each other when they heard my answer
as men will stare when they have heard the truth.
"If you can always offer a reply
so readily to others," said all three,
"then happy you who speak, at will, so clearly.
So, if you can escape these lands of darkness
and see the lovely stars on your return,
when you repeat with pleasure, 'I was there,'
be sure that you remember us to men."
At this they broke their wheel; and as they fled,
their swift legs seemed to be no less than wings.
The time it took for them to disappear—
more brief than time it takes to say "amen";
and so, my master thought it right to leave.
I followed him. We'd only walked a little
when roaring water grew so near to us
we hardly could have heard each other speak.
And even as the river that is first
to take its own course eastward from Mount Viso,
along the left flank of the Apennines
(which up above is called the Acquacheta,
before it spills into its valley bed

4. True to the deference with which Dante treats them here, these Florentines are genuinely concerned with the fate of their city which, as in Canto 10, is too close for them to foresee.

5. Guiglielmo Borsiere was a pursemaker known for his courteous manners and bearing; he is the subject of a tale in Boccaccio's *Decameron* (1.8).

and flows without that name beyond Forlì),
reverberates above San Benedetto
dell'Alpe as it cascades in one leap,
where there is space enough to house a thousand;[6]
so did we hear that blackened water roar
as it plunged down a steep and craggy bank,
enough to deafen us in a few hours.
Around my waist I had a cord as girdle,
and with it once I thought I should be able
to catch the leopard with the painted hide.[7]
And after I had loosened it completely,
just as my guide commanded me to do,
I handed it to him, knotted and coiled.
At this, he wheeled around upon his right
and cast it, at some distance from the edge,
straight down into the depth of the ravine.
"And surely something strange must here reply,"
I said within myself, "to this strange sign—
the sign my master follows with his eye."
Ah, how much care men ought to exercise
with those whose penetrating intellect
can see our thoughts—not just our outer act!
He said to me: "Now there will soon emerge
what I await and what your thought has conjured:
it soon must be discovered to your sight."
Faced with that truth which seems a lie, a man
should always close his lips as long as he can—
to tell it shames him, even though he's blameless;
but here I can't be still; and by the lines
of this my Comedy, reader, I swear[8]—
and may my verse find favor for long years—
that through the dense and darkened air I saw
a figure swimming, rising up, enough
to bring amazement to the firmest heart,
like one returning from the waves where he
went down to loose an anchor snagged upon
a reef or something else hid in the sea,
who stretches upward and draws in his feet.

Canto 17

The monster Geryon. The Seventh Circle, Third Ring, Third Zone: the Violent against Nature and Art (Usurers), each seated beneath the rain of fire with a purse—bearing

6. The roar of the descending Phlegethon is likened to the cascade of the river Acquachete in the eastern Apennine mountains near the Benedictine monastery of San Benedetto dell'Alpe. Below the city of Forlí, its name changes to Montone.

7. The incident of the cord invites an allegorical reading, but a satisfactory one has not yet been found. It would not have been part of the Florentine dress mentioned earlier in the canto; some commentators have suggested the garb of a Franciscan monk (see 27.67), while the leopard hearkens back to the first beast of Canto 1.

8. In a moment of significance in any medieval text, at the midpoint episode of the canticle, Dante names his poem directly for the first time.

his family's heraldic emblem—around his neck. Descent to the Eighth Circle on the back of Geryon.

"Behold the beast who bears the pointed tail,
who crosses mountains, shatters weapons, walls!
Behold the one whose stench fills all the world!"
So did my guide begin to speak to me,
and then he signaled him to come ashore
close to the end of those stone passageways.
And he came on, that filthy effigy
of fraud, and landed with his head and torso
but did not draw his tail onto the bank.[1]
The face he wore was that of a just man,
so gracious was his features' outer semblance;
and all his trunk, the body of a serpent;
he had two paws, with hair up to the armpits;
his back and chest as well as both his flanks
had been adorned with twining knots and circlets.
No Turks or Tartars ever fashioned fabrics
more colorful in background and relief,
nor had Arachne ever loomed such webs.[2]
As boats will sometimes lie along the shore,
with part of them on land and part in water,
and just as there, among the guzzling Germans,
the beaver sets himself when he means war,[3]
so did that squalid beast lie on the margin
of stone that serves as border for the sand.
And all his tail was quivering in the void
while twisting upward its envenomed fork,
which had a tip just like a scorpion's.
My guide said: "Now we'd better bend our path
a little, till we reach as far as that
malicious beast which crouches over there."
Thus we descended on the right hand side[4]
and moved ten paces on the stony brink
in order to avoid the sand and fire.
When we had reached the sprawling beast, I saw—
a little farther on, upon the sand—
some sinners sitting near the fissured rock.
And here my master said to me: "So that

1. In classical mythology, Geryon was a giant possessing three bodies and three heads, slain by Hercules when the hero took his prized cattle as one of the Twelve Labors. Dante's description gives Geryon a threefold nature—man, beast and serpent—deriving some of the imagery from biblical sources.

2. Tartar and Turkish cloths were highly valued in the Middle Ages for their richness and intricacy of design; from a dogmatic Christian perspective, their infidel makers were also treacherous. In Greek mythology, the mortal Arachne challenged Minerva to a weaving contest; angry at the result, the goddess transformed her into a spider (Ovid, *Metamorphoses* 6.5–145).

3. According to popular belief, the beaver (common in Germany) caught fish by squirting oily drops while agitating the water with its tail; deceived by the drops, the fish came close enough to be grabbed.

4. The second of the two right-hand turns in Hell (the first was at 9.132); this one suggests the impossibility of approaching fraud in a straightforward manner.

you may experience this ring in full,
go now, and see the state in which they are.
But keep your conversation with them brief;
till you return, I'll parley with this beast,
to see if he can lend us his strong shoulders."
So I went on alone[5] and even farther
along the seventh circle's outer margin,
to where the melancholy people sat.
Despondency was bursting from their eyes;
this side, then that, their hands kept fending off,
at times the flames, at times the burning soil:
not otherwise do dogs in summer—now
with muzzle, now with paw—when they are bitten
by fleas or gnats or by the sharp gadfly.
When I had set my eyes upon the faces
of some on whom that painful fire falls,
I recognized no one; but I did notice
that from the neck of each a purse was hung
that had a special color and an emblem,
and their eyes seemed to feast upon these pouches.[6]
Looking about—when I had come among them—
I saw a yellow purse with azure on it
that had the face and manner of a lion.
Then, as I let my eyes move farther on,
I saw another purse that was bloodred,
and it displayed a goose more white than butter.
And one who had an azure, pregnant sow
inscribed as emblem on his white pouch, said
to me: "What are you doing in this pit?
Now you be off; and since you're still alive,
remember that my neighbor Vitaliano
shall yet sit here, upon my left hand side.
Among these Florentines, I'm Paduan;
I often hear them thunder in my ears,
shouting, 'Now let the sovereign cavalier,
the one who'll bring the purse with three goats, come!'"
At this he slewed his mouth, and then he stuck
his tongue out, like an ox that licks its nose.
And I, afraid that any longer stay
might anger him who'd warned me to be brief,
made my way back from those exhausted souls.
I found my guide, who had already climbed
upon the back of that brute animal,
and he told me: "Be strong and daring now,
for our descent is by this kind of stairs:

5. The first and only time in the *Inferno* in which the pilgrim moves alone, without Virgil.

6. The emblems on the moneylenders' pouches belong to distinguished Florentine and Paduan families well-known for their usury.

you mount in front; I want to be between,
so that the tail can't do you any harm."
As one who feels the quartan fever near
and shivers, with his nails already blue,[7]
the sight of shade enough to make him shudder,
so I became when I had heard these words;
but then I felt the threat of shame, which makes
a servant—in his kind lord's presence—brave.
I settled down on those enormous shoulders;
I wished to say (and yet my voice did not
come as I thought): "See that you hold me tight."
But he who—other times, in other dangers—
sustained me, just as soon as I had mounted,
clasped me within his arms and propped me up,
and said: "Now, Geryon, move on; take care to
keep your circles wide, your landing slow;
remember the new weight you're carrying."
Just like a boat that, starting from its moorings,
moves backward, backward, so that beast took off;
and when he felt himself completely clear,
he turned his tail to where his chest had been
and, having stretched it, moved it like an eel,
and with his paws he gathered in the air.
I do not think that there was greater fear
in Phaëthon when he let his reins go free—
for which the sky, as one still sees, was scorched—
nor in poor Icarus when he could feel
his sides unwinged because the wax was melting,
his father shouting to him, "That way's wrong!"[8]
than was in me when, on all sides, I saw
that I was in the air, and everything
had faded from my sight—except the beast.
Slowly, slowly, swimming, he moves on;
he wheels and he descends, but I feel only
the wind upon my face and the wind rising.
Already, on our right, I heard the torrent
resounding, there beneath us, horribly,
so that I stretched my neck and looked below.
Then I was more afraid of falling off,
for I saw fires and I heard laments,
at which I tremble, crouching, and hold fast.
And now I saw what I had missed before:

7. The quartan fever takes its name from the four-day cycle of shivering fits that accompanies it.

8. Phaëthon was son of Apollo and a mortal woman. Phaëthon persuaded his father to allow him to drive the chariot of the sun for a day, but he couldn't control the horses, and they ran so near to the earth that Jupiter killed Phaëthon with a thunderbolt to save the earth from burning (Ovid, *Metamorphoses* 2.1–138). In another myth, Icarus escaped with his father Daedalus from Crete with wings the inventor had fashioned together with wax. Ignoring his father's warning, Icarus flew too close to the sun, the wax melted, and he plummeted to his death in the sea (*Metamorphoses* 8.203–35; see pages 790–791.)

his wheeling and descent—because great torments
were drawing closer to us on all sides.
Just as a falcon long upon the wing—
who, seeing neither lure nor bird, compels
the falconer to cry, "Ah me, you fall!"—
descends, exhausted, in a hundred circles,
where he had once been swift, and sets himself,
embittered and enraged, far from his master;[9]
such, at the bottom of the jagged rock,
was Geryon, when he had set us down.
And once our weight was lifted from his back,
he vanished like an arrow from a bow.

Canto 18

The Eighth Circle, called Malebolge ("Evil-Pouches"), with its Ten Pouches, where "ordinary" fraud is punished. The First Pouch, with Panders and Seducers scourged by horned demons. Venèdico Caccianemico. Jason. The Second Pouch, with Flatterers immersed in excrement. Alessio Interminei. Thais.

There is a place in Hell called Malebolge,
made all of stone the color of crude iron,
as is the wall that makes its way around it.
Right in the middle of this evil field
is an abyss, a broad and yawning pit,
whose structure I shall tell in its due place.
The belt, then, that extends between the pit
and that hard, steep wall's base is circular;
its bottom has been split into ten valleys.
Just as, where moat on moat surrounds a castle
in order to keep guard upon the walls,
the ground they occupy will form a pattern,
so did the valleys here form a design;
and as such fortresses have bridges running
right from their thresholds toward the outer bank,
so here, across the banks and ditches, ridges
ran from the base of that rock wall until
the pit that cuts them short and joins them all.
This was the place in which we found ourselves
when Geryon had put us down; the poet
held to the left, and I walked at his back.
Upon the right I saw new misery,
I saw new tortures and new torturers,
filling the first of Malebolge's moats.
Along its bottom, naked sinners moved,
to our side of the middle, facing us;

9. Trained not to descend until either it sights its prey or is called back by its master whirling a lure, the falcon will remain aloft until compelled by exhaustion to come down.

beyond that, they moved with us, but more quickly—
as, in the year of Jubilee, the Romans,
confronted by great crowds, contrived a plan
that let the people pass across the bridge,
for to one side went all who had their eyes
upon the Castle, heading toward St. Peter's,
and to the other, those who faced the Mount.[1]
Both left and right, along the somber rock,
I saw horned demons with enormous whips,
who lashed those spirits cruelly from behind.[2]
Ah, how their first strokes made those sinners lift
their heels! Indeed no sinner waited for
a second stroke to fall—or for a third.
And as I moved ahead, my eyes met those
of someone else, and suddenly I said:
"I was not spared the sight of him before."
And so I stayed my steps, to study him;
my gentle guide had stopped together with me
and gave me leave to take a few steps back.
That scourged soul thought that he could hide himself
by lowering his face;[3] it helped him little,
for I said: "You, who cast your eyes upon
the ground, if these your features are not false,
must be Venèdico Caccianemico;[4]
but what brings you to sauces so piquant?"
And he to me: "I speak unwillingly;
but your plain speech, that brings the memory
of the old world to me, is what compels me;
For it was I who led Ghisolabella
to do as the Marquis would have her do—
however they retell that filthy tale.
I'm not the only Bolognese who weeps here;
indeed, this place is so crammed full of us
that not so many tongues have learned to say
sipa between the Sàvena and Reno;[5]
if you want faith and testament of that,
just call to mind our avaricious hearts."
And as he spoke, a demon cudgeled him
with his horsewhip and cried: "Be off, you pimp,
there are no women here for you to trick."

1. A rarity in medieval times: separate lanes for traffic in each direction. The first Jubilee or Holy Year was proclaimed by Pope Boniface VIII in 1300, granting indulgence (reduction of penance) for all those who visited the basilicas of St. Peter and San Paolo fuori le Mura; hundreds of thousands of pilgrims came.
2. The reader finally encounters the horned demons familiar from medieval iconography and earlier otherworld visions; in Dante's scheme, they are specific to the realm of fraud.
3. A change in behavior: the souls this deep in Hell prefer anonymity rather than the fame and salvaged reputation of those higher up.
4. Son of the head of the Guelf party of Bologna. He is said to have been bribed by his ally Obizzo II to gain him entry to his sister Ghisolobella's bedchamber.
5. *Sipa* is the word for "yes" in the old dialect spoken between the Sàvena and Reno streams that form the western and eastern bounds of the territory of Bologna. Dante singles out Bologna for its panders, or pimps.

I joined my escort once again; and then
with but few steps, we came upon a place
where, from the bank, a rocky ridge ran out.
We climbed quite easily along that height;
and turning right upon its jagged back,
we took our leave of those eternal circlings.
When we had reached the point where that ridge opens
below to leave a passage for the lashed,
my guide said: "Stay, and make sure that the sight
of still more ill-born spirits strikes your eyes,
for you have not yet seen their faces, since
they have been moving in our own direction."
From the old bridge we looked down at the ranks
of those approaching from the other side;
they too were driven onward by the lash.
And my good master, though I had not asked,
urged me: "Look at that mighty one who comes
and does not seem to shed a tear of pain:
how he still keeps the image of a king!
That shade is Jason, who with heart and head
deprived the men of Colchis of their ram.[6]
He made a landfall on the isle of Lemnos
after its women, bold and pitiless,
had given all their island males to death.
With polished words and love signs he took in
Hypsipyle, the girl whose own deception
had earlier deceived the other women.[7]
And he abandoned her, alone and pregnant;
such guilt condemns him to such punishment;
and for Medea, too, revenge is taken.
With him go those who cheated so: this is
enough for you to know of that first valley
and of the souls it clamps within its jaws."
We were already where the narrow path
reaches and intersects the second bank
and serves as shoulder for another bridge.
We heard the people whine in the next pouch
and heard them as they snorted with their snouts;
we heard them use their palms to beat themselves.
And exhalations, rising from below,
stuck to the banks, encrusting them with mold,
and so waged war against both eyes and nose.
The bottom is so deep, we found no spot

6. Jason was leader of the Argonauts on the expedition to Colchis to obtain the golden fleece. Along the way, they landed at Lemnos, where Jason seduced and then abandoned Hypsipyle, daughter of the king, leaving her with twin sons. After Medea, daughter of the king of the Colchians, had helped him to secure the fleece, Jason took her with him as his wife, but later left her for Creusa, daughter of Creon, king of Corinth. In revenge, she killed the two children she had borne him (Ovid, *Metamorphoses* 7.1–397). See also Euripides' version (p. 578).

7. When the women of Lemnos had killed all the other men on the island, Hypsipyle had managed secretly to save her father's life (Statius, *Thebaid* 5.403–85).

to see it from, except by climbing up
the arch until the bridge's highest point.
This was the place we reached; the ditch beneath
held people plunged in excrement that seemed
as if it had been poured from human privies.° toilets
And while my eyes searched that abysmal sight,
I saw one with a head so smeared with shit,
one could not see if he were lay or cleric.[8]
He howled: "Why do you stare more greedily
at me than at the others who are filthy?"
And I: "Because, if I remember right,
I have seen you before, with your hair dry;
and so I eye you more than all: you are
Alessio Interminei of Lucca."[9]
Then he continued, pounding on his pate:
"I am plunged here because of flatteries—
of which my tongue had such sufficiency."
At which my guide advised me: "See you thrust
your head a little farther to the front,
so that your eyes can clearly glimpse the face
of that besmirched, bedraggled harridan° shrew
who scratches at herself with shit-filled nails,
and now she crouches, now she stands upright.
That is Thaïs, the harlot who returned
her lover's question, 'Are you very grateful
to me?' by saying, 'Yes, enormously.'"[1]
And now our sight has had its fill of this."

Canto 19

The Eighth Circle, Third Pouch, where the Simonists are set, heads down, into holes in the rock, with their protruding feet tormented by flames. Pope Nicholas III. Dante's invective against simoniacal popes.

O Simon Magus! O his sad disciples!
Rapacious ones, who take the things of God,
that ought to be the brides of Righteousness,
and make them fornicate for gold and silver!
The time has come to let the trumpet sound
for you; your place is here in this third pouch.[1]
We had already reached the tomb beyond

8. That is, he couldn't tell if the head was tonsured. Like their hypocrisy (see the sixth pouch), the flattery of clerics was proverbial.
9. Member of a prominent Guelf family of the Tuscan town of Lucca.
1. Thaïs is a courtesan in *Eunuchus,* a play by the ancient Roman playwright Terence. In fact, the flatterer in the scene referred to is the go-between, a soldier named Gnatho.
1. In the Bible, Simon Magus was a converted sorcerer who attempted to buy the power of conferring the Holy Ghost. He was rebuked by the apostle Peter for presuming that the gift of God might be purchased (Acts 8:9–24). From his name is derived the word "simony," which refers to the buying or selling of spiritual goods and offices. The metaphor of lines 3–4 relates this pouch with the previous one by depicting simonists as pimps of the Church, the Bride of Christ. Town criers would sound a trumpet to announce the public reading of judicial sentences; the word also alludes to the sounding of the angel's trumpet on Judgment Day.

and climbed onto the ridge, where its high point
hangs just above the middle of the ditch.
O Highest Wisdom, how much art you show
in heaven, earth, and this sad world below,
how just your power is when it allots![2]
Along the sides and down along the bottom,
I saw that livid rock was perforated:
the openings were all one width and round.
They did not seem to me less broad or more
than those that in my handsome San Giovanni
were made to serve as basins for baptizing;
and one of these, not many years ago,
I broke for someone who was drowning in it:
and let this be my seal to set men straight.[3]
Out from the mouth of each hole there emerged
a sinner's feet and so much of his legs
up to the thigh; the rest remained within.
Both soles of every sinner were on fire;
their joints were writhing with such violence,
they would have severed withes° and ropes of grass. *thin branches*
As flame on oily things will only stir
along the outer surface, so there, too,
that fire made its way from heels to toes.
"Master," I said, "who is that shade who suffers
and quivers more than all his other comrades,
that sinner who is licked by redder flames?"
And he to me: "If you would have me lead
you down along the steepest of the banks,
from him you'll learn about his self and sins."
And I: "What pleases you will please me too:
you are my lord; you know I do not swerve
from what you will; you know what is unspoken."
At this we came upon the fourth embankment;
we turned and, keeping to the left, descended
into the narrow, perforated bottom.
My good lord did not let me leave his side
until he'd brought me to the hole that held
that sinner who lamented with his legs.
"Whoever you may be, dejected soul,
whose head is downward, planted like a pole,"
my words began, "do speak if you are able."
I stood as does the friar who confesses
the foul assassin who, fixed fast, head down,

2. The apostrophe to the Lord praises the "art" which he has devoted to the design of hell as much as to that of heaven and earth.

3. Like most Florentine children of the time, Dante was baptized in the famous Baptistery of Florence, San Giovanni. It is possible Dante mentioned his motive in breaking the font to defend himself against accusations of sacrilege; it is certainly noteworthy that he placed it in a canto devoted to the misuse of sacred vessels and offices.

calls back the friar, and so delays his death;[4]
    and he cried out: "Are you already standing,
already standing there, o Boniface?
The book has lied to me by several years.
    Are you so quickly sated with the riches
for which you did not fear to take by guile
the Lovely Lady, then to violate her?"[5]
    And I became like those who stand as if
they have been mocked, who cannot understand
what has been said to them and can't respond.
    But Virgil said: "Tell this to him at once:
'I am not he—not whom you think I am.'"
And I replied as I was told to do.
    At this the spirit twisted both his feet,
and sighing and with a despairing voice,
he said: "What is it, then, you want of me?
    If you have crossed the bank and climbed so far
to find out who I am, then know that I
was one of those who wore the mighty mantle,
    and surely was a son of the she-bear,
so eager to advance the cubs that I
pursed wealth above while here I purse myself.[6]
    Below my head there is the place of those
who took the way of simony before me;
and they are stuffed within the clefts of stone.
    I, too, shall yield my place and fall below
when he arrives, the one for whom I had
mistaken you when I was quick to question.
    But I have baked my feet a longer time,
have stood like this, upon my head, than he
is to stand planted here with scarlet feet:
    for after him, one uglier in deeds
will come, a lawless shepherd from the west,
worthy to cover him and cover me.[7]
    He'll be a second Jason, of whom we read
in *Maccabees;* and just as Jason's king
was soft to him, so shall the king of France

4. In the punishment known as "the planting of grapevines," assassins were stuck head downward in a hole that was then filled with dirt, choking them to death.

5. The speaker, Pope Nicholas III, believes he is addressing Boniface VIII, who he knows will die in Rome in 1303, three years after the date of the present encounter, enabling Dante to place a soul in its "proper" place by anticipation. Boniface was surrounded by many accusations of nepotism and simony; as for the charge that he took "by guile the Lovely Lady," that he was elected pope by fraud: he was said to have offered his services to Charles of Anjou in his war in Sicily in return for support of his candidacy.

6. The Roman family of Giovanni Orsini, Pope Nicholas III, were commonly referred to as *filii orsae,* cubs of the she-bear, known as a rapacious beast especially fierce in protecting her young. Giovanni was elected pope ("the mighty mantle") in 1277 and died three years later, but his brief tenure was marked by nepotism and intrigue. Line 72 neatly expresses the *contrapasso:* the font in which he is placed is his purse in which he keeps the rewards he sought above.

7. Nicholas has to wait 23 years for Boniface to take the topmost place in the hole, but Boniface will need wait less than 11 for the next simonist pope to replace him: Clement V, who died in 1314 near Avignon. Born in Gascony ("from the west") and elected pope in 1304, Clement saw the Papal See removed from Rome to Avignon in southern France, where it remained for nearly 70 years in what is referred to as the "Babylonian Captivity."

be soft to this one."[8] And I do not know
if I was too rash here—I answered so:
"Then tell me now, how much gold did our Lord
ask that Saint Peter give to him before
he placed the keys within his care? Surely
the only thing he said was: 'Follow me.'[9]
And Peter and the others never asked
for gold or silver when they chose Matthias
to take the place of the transgressing soul.[1]
Stay as you are, for you are rightly punished;
and guard with care the money got by evil
that made you so audacious against Charles.[2]
And were it not that I am still prevented
by reverence for those exalted keys
that you had held within the happy life,
I'd utter words much heavier than these,
because your avarice afflicts the world:
it tramples on the good, lifts up the wicked.
You, shepherds, the Evangelist had noticed
when he saw her who sits upon the waters
and realized she fornicates with kings,
she who was born with seven heads and had
the power and support of the ten horns,
as long as virtue was her husband's pleasure.[3]
You've made yourselves a god of gold and silver;
how are you different from idolaters,
save that they worship one and you a hundred?
Ah, Constantine, what wickedness was born—
and not from your conversion—from the dower
that you bestowed upon the first rich father!"[4]
And while I sang such notes to him—whether
it was his indignation or his conscience
that bit him—he kicked hard with both his soles.

8. While still Archbishop of Bordeaux, Clement had negotiated his election as pope with the powerful King Philip the Fair of France, just as Jason had first been appointed High Priest of the Jews by bribing King Antiochus of Syria, endeavoring afterward to reintroduce Greek customs and pagan worship in place of the Jewish religion (2 Maccabees 4:13–16).

9. The apostle Peter was considered to have been the first pope: "And I say to thee, thou art Peter, and upon this rock I will build my Church. . . . And I will give thee the keys of the kingdom of heaven." (Matthew 16:18–19). "Follow me" were the words with which Jesus first called the brothers Simon (Peter) and Andrew to be his disciples (Matthew 4:18–19).

1. After Judas Iscariot had betrayed Jesus, Matthias was chosen by lot to fill his vacant place among the 12 apostles.

2. It was commonly believed that Nicholas had intrigued against Charles of Anjou when Charles had refused to marry Nicholas's niece.

3. In the Book of Revelation, attributed to the Evangelist, St. John, the whore "who sits upon the waters" (17:1–3) was most likely pagan Rome, while Dante interprets her as the Church corrupted by secular interests. The seven heads symbolize the seven sacraments; the ten horns the Ten Commandments.

4. Due to a skillful forgery known as "The Donation of Constantine," probably composed in the papal court during the 8th century, it was believed that the Emperor Constantine had given to the Church his temporal power in the west when he moved the imperial capital eastward to Constantinople in the 5th century. For Dante, this fraud marked the beginning of the ecclesiastical corruption denounced in this canto. "The first rich father" is Pope Sylvester I, to whom the Donation was said to have been made in exchange for curing Constantine of leprosy.

I do indeed believe it pleased my guide:
he listened always with such satisfied
expression to the sound of those true words.
And then he gathered me in both his arms
and, when he had me fast against his chest,
where he climbed down before, climbed upward now;
nor did he tire of clasping me until
he brought me to the summit of the arch
that crosses from the fourth to the fifth rampart.
And here he gently set his burden down—
gently because the ridge was rough and steep,
and would have been a rugged pass for goats.
From there another valley lay before me.

Canto 20

The Eighth Circle, Fourth Pouch, where Diviners, Astrologers, Magicians, all have their heads turned backward. Amphiaraus. Tiresias. Aruns. Manto. Virgil on the origin of Mantua, his native city. Eurypylus. Michael Scot and other moderns adept at fraud.

I must make verses of new punishment
and offer matter now for Canto Twenty
of this first canticle—of the submerged.
I was already well prepared to stare
below, into the depth that was disclosed,
where tears of anguished sorrow bathed the ground;
and in the valley's circle I saw souls
advancing, mute and weeping, at the pace
that, in our world, holy processions take.
As I inclined my head still more, I saw
that each, amazingly, appeared contorted
between the chin and where the chest begins;
they had their faces twisted toward their haunches
and found it necessary to walk backward,
because they could not see ahead of them.[1]
Perhaps the force of palsy[2] has so fully
distorted some, but that I've yet to see,
and I do not believe that that can be.
May God so let you, reader, gather fruit
from what you read; and now think for yourself
how I could ever keep my own face dry
when I beheld our image so nearby
and so awry that tears, down from the eyes,
bathed the buttocks, running down the cleft.
Of course I wept, leaning against a rock

1. In this *bolgia,* diviners and soothsayers are punished for their attempt to see the future by being condemned to see only backward.

2. A condition marked by the paralysis or uncontrollable tremor of a body or a body part.

along that rugged ridge, so that my guide
told me: "Are you as foolish as the rest?
Here pity only lives when it is dead:
for who can be more impious than he
who links God's judgment to passivity?
Lift, lift your head and see the one for whom
the earth was opened while the Thebans watched,
so that they all cried: 'Amphiaraus,
where are you rushing? Have you quit the fight?'
Nor did he interrupt his downward plunge
to Minos, who lays hands on every sinner.[3]
See how he's made a chest out of his shoulders;
and since he wanted so to see ahead,
he looks behind and walks a backward path.
And see Tiresias, who changed his mien
when from a man he turned into a woman,
so totally transforming all his limbs
that then he had to strike once more upon
the two entwining serpents with his wand
before he had his manly plumes again.[4]
And Aruns is the one who backs against
the belly of Tiresias—Aruns who,
in Luni's hills, tilled by the Carrarese,
who live below, had as his home, a cave
among white marbles, from which he could gaze
at stars and sea with unimpeded view.[5]
And she who covers up her breasts—which you
can't see—with her disheveled locks, who keeps
all of her hairy parts to the far side,
was Manto,[6] who had searched through many lands,
then settled in the place where I was born;
on this, I'd have you hear me now a while.
When Manto's father took his leave of life,
and Bacchus' city found itself enslaved,[7]
she wandered through the world for many years.
High up, in lovely Italy, beneath
the Alps that shut in Germany above

3. Amphiaraus was a great prophet and hero of Argos and another of the Seven against Thebes consigned to Hell. Foreseeing that he would die there, he had attempted to hide, but his hiding-place was revealed by his wife after she was bribed with a necklace. He and his chariot were swallowed up by the earth as he was fleeing his pursuers at Thebes.

4. The famed soothsayer of Thebes, Tiresias, had been changed into a woman when he separated with his staff two coupling serpents. Seven years later, he found the same serpents, struck them again, and was changed back to a man. Called upon to mediate a dispute between Jupiter and Juno, he declared that women experience greater pleasure in lovemaking. Jupiter in anger struck him blind; Juno gave him the gift of prophecy in compensation (Ovid, *Metamorphoses* 3.322–31; see page 779).

5. Aruns was an Etruscan seer who according to Lucan foretold the civil war that ended in Caesar's triumph and Pompey's death (*Pharsalia* 1.585–638). "Luni's hills" are near Carrara in northern Tuscany, famous for its white marble.

6. A prophetess of Thebes, daughter of Tiresias who, by some accounts, settled in Italy where the town of Mantua, Virgil's birthplace, was named after her.

7. Thebes was consecrated to the god Bacchus and tradition made it his birthplace. After the war of the Seven against Thebes, the city came under the tyranny of Creon.

Tirolo, lies a lake known as Benaco.[8]
A thousand springs and more, I think, must flow
out of the waters of that lake to bathe
Pennino, Garda, Val Camonica.
And at its middle is a place where three—
the bishops of Verona, Brescia, Trento[9]—
may bless if they should chance to come that way.
Peschiera, strong and handsome fortress, built
to face the Brescians and the Bergamasques
stands where the circling shore is at its lowest.[1]
There, all the waters that cannot be held
within the bosom of Benaco fall,
to form a river running through green meadows.
No sooner has that stream begun to flow
than it is called the Mincio, not Benaco—
until Govèrnolo, where it joins the Po.
It's not flowed far before it finds flat land;
and there it stretches out to form a fen
that in the summer can at times be fetid.
And when she passed that way, the savage virgin
saw land along the middle of the swamp,
untilled and stripped of its inhabitants.
And there, to flee all human intercourse,
she halted with her slaves to ply her arts;
and there she lived, there left her empty body.
And afterward, the people of those parts
collected at that place, because the marsh—
surrounding it on all sides—made it strong.
They built a city over her dead bones;
and after her who first had picked that spot,
they called it Mantua—they cast no lots.[2]
There once were far more people in its walls,
before the foolishness of Casalodi
was tricked by the deceit of Pinamonte.[3]
Therefore, I charge you, if you ever hear
a different tale of my town's origin,
do not let any falsehood gull° the truth."[4] *dupe*
And I: "O master, that which you have spoken
convinces me and so compels my trust
that others' words would only be spent coals.

8. To recount the situation of Manua, Virgil begins with a long account of the waters that flow from Lake Garda down into the river Po.
9. That is, an island where the boundaries and jurisdictions of these three dioceses meet.
1. Peschiera was a town and fortress at the southeast shore of the lake, about 20 miles southeast of Brescia and 50 miles from Bergamo.
2. An ancient custom was to choose the name of a town by casting lots.
3. The Brescian counts of Casalodi took control of Mantua in 1272. Pinamonte, a native Mantuan, treacherously advised Alberto to appease the populace by expelling many nobles from the city, including his own supporters. With Alberto defenseless, Pinamonte was able to seize power himself.
4. According to the *Aeneid* (10.198–200), Mantua was founded by her son, Ocnus.

But tell me if among the passing souls
you see some spirits worthy of our notice,
because my mind is bent on that alone."
Then he to me: "That shade who spreads his beard
down from his cheeks across his swarthy shoulders—
when Greece had been so emptied of its males
that hardly any cradle held a son,
he was an augur; and at Aulis, he
and Calchas set the time to cut the cables.
His name's Eurypylus; a certain passage
of my high tragedy has sung it so;
you know that well enough, who know the whole.[5]
That other there, his flanks extremely spare,
was Michael Scot,[6] a man who certainly
knew how the game of magic fraud was played.
See there Guido Bonatti; see Asdente,
who now would wish he had attended to
his cord and leather, but repents too late.[7]
See those sad women who had left their needle,
shuttle, and spindle to become diviners;
they cast their spells with herbs and effigies.
But let us go; Cain with his thorns already
is at the border of both hemispheres
and there, below Seville, touches the sea.[8]
Last night the moon was at its full; you should
be well aware of this, for there were times
when it did you no harm in the deep wood."
These were his words to me; meanwhile we journeyed.

Canto 21

The Eighth Circle, Fifth Pouch, with Barrators plunged into boiling pitch and guarded by demons armed with prongs. A newly arrived magistrate from Lucca. Ten demons assigned by Malacoda ("Evil-Tail"), the chief of the Malebranche ("Evil-Claws"), to escort Dante and Virgil. The remarkable signal for their march.

We came along from one bridge to another,
talking of things my Comedy is not
concerned to sing. We held fast to the summit,
then stayed our steps to spy the other cleft
of Malebolge and other vain laments.

5. On the advice of the prophet Calchas, the Greeks sacrificed Agamemnon's daughter Iphigenia to appease the goddess Diana. When they were preparing to return home from Troy, Eurypylus was sent to consult the oracle of Apollo, which advised that their return must also be purchased in blood. *Aeneid* (2.114–24, "my high tragedy") mentions both incidents, but attributes only the second of them to Eurypylus.

6. A famous scientist, philosopher, astrologer, and necromancer from Scotland who served for many years at the court of Frederick II at Palermo in Sicily.

7. Guido Bonatti of Forlí served as astrologer at the court of Guido da Montefeltro (see Canto 27); Asdente ("toothless") was a 13th-century shoemaker of Parma famed as a prophet and soothsayer.

8. Custom held that God had placed Cain in the moon following his murder of Abel; "thorns" refers to the moon spots. For the ideal observer in Jerusalem, the moon is setting in the west ("below Seville"); the time is 6 A.M.

I saw that it was wonderfully dark.[1]
As in the arsenal of the Venetians,[2]
all winter long a stew of sticky pitch
boils up to patch their sick and tattered ships
that cannot sail (instead of voyaging,
some build new keels, some tow and tar the ribs
of hulls worn out by too much journeying;
some hammer at the prow, some at the stern,
and some make oars, and some braid ropes and cords;
one mends the jib, another, the mainsail);
so, not by fire but by the art of God,
below there boiled a thick and tarry mass
that covered all the banks with clamminess.
I saw it, but I could not see within it;
no thing was visible but boiling bubbles,
the swelling of the pitch; and then it settled.
And while I watched below attentively,
my guide called out to me: "Take care! Take care!"[3]
And then, from where I stood, he drew me near.
I turned around as one who is impatient
to see what he should shun but is dashed down
beneath the terror he has undergone,
who does not stop his flight and yet would look.
And then in back of us I saw a black
demon as he came racing up the crags.
Ah, he was surely barbarous to see!
And how relentless seemed to me his acts!
His wings were open and his feet were lithe;
across his shoulder, which was sharp and high,
he had slung a sinner, upward from the thighs;
in front, the demon gripped him by the ankles.
Then from our bridge, he called: "O Malebranche,
I've got an elder of Saint Zita for you!
Shove this one under—I'll go back for more—
his city is well furnished with such stores;
there, everyone's a grafter but Bonturo;
and there—for cash—they'll change a *no* to *yes*."[4]
He threw the sinner down, then wheeled along
the stony cliff: no mastiff's ever been
unleashed with so much haste to chase a thief.
The sinner plunged, then surfaced, black with pitch;
but now the demons, from beneath the bridge,

1. Even darker than the other, unlit pouches, because black with boiling pitch.
2. One of the most important shipyards in Europe, and the reason for the Venetian Republic's enduring power at sea.
3. One motivation for the guide's urgency may be that barratry (the buying and selling of public office, the secular equivalent of simony) would be the charge made against Dante when he was sentenced to exile in 1302.
4. St. Zita (1218–c. 1278) was the patron saint of Lucca; the elders were ten citizens holding executive power along with the chief magistrate. Bonturo Dati was the most accomplished barrator in a city evidently notorious for the practice. The demon's sarcastic humor is characteristic of their portrayal in the *Inferno*.

shouted: "The Sacred Face has no place here;[5]
here we swim differently than in the Serchio;[6]
if you don't want to feel our grappling hooks,
don't try to lift yourself above that ditch."
They pricked him with a hundred prongs and more,
then taunted: "Here one dances under cover,
so try to grab your secret graft below."
The demons did the same as any cook
who has his urchins force the meat with hooks
deep down into the pot, that it not float.
Then my good master said to me: "Don't let
those demons see that you are here; take care
to crouch behind the cover of a crag.
No matter what offense they offer me,
don't be afraid; I know how these things go—
I've had to face such fracases before."[7]
When this was said, he moved beyond the bridgehead.
And on the sixth embankment, he had need
to show his imperturbability.
With the same frenzy, with the brouhaha
of dogs, when they beset a poor wretch who
then stops dead in his tracks as if to beg,
so, from beneath the bridge, the demons rushed
against my guide with all their prongs, but he
called out: "Can't you forget your savagery!
Before you try to maul me, just let one
of all your troop step forward. Hear me out,
and then decide if I am to be hooked."
At this they howled, "Let Malacoda go!"
And one of them moved up—the others stayed—
and as he came, he asked: "How can he win?"
"O Malacoda, do you think I've come,"
my master answered him, "already armed—
as you can see—against your obstacles,
without the will of God[8] and helpful fate?
Let us move on; it is the will of Heaven
for me to show this wild way to another."
At this the pride of Malacoda fell;
his prong dropped to his feet. He told his fellows:
"Since that's the way things stand, let us not wound him."
My guide then spoke to me: "O you, who crouch,
bent low among the bridge's splintered rocks,
you can feel safe—and now return to me."
At this I moved and quickly came to him.
The devils had edged forward, all of them;

5. The Sacred Face of Lucca was a venerated ancient Byzantine crucifix carved in dark wood. The demon's vulgar pleasantry compares it to the pitch-covered rear end of the naked shade.
6. A Tuscan river near Lucca.
7. Probably referring to the episode with the rebel angels; the pattern in fact is that the demons generally *do* give Virgil more trouble than the classical monsters.
8. Literally, "without divine will"; like Christ, the Lord is never named directly in Hell.

I feared that they might fail to keep their word:
just so, I saw the infantry when they
marched out, under safe conduct, from Caprona;[9]
they trembled when they passed their enemies.
My body huddled closer to my guide;
I did not let the demons out of sight;
the looks they cast at us were less than kind.
They bent their hooks and shouted to each other:
"And shall I give it to him on the rump?"
And all of them replied, "Yes, let him have it!"
But Malacoda, still in conversation
with my good guide, turned quickly to his squadron
and said: "Be still, Scarmiglione, still!"
To us he said: "There is no use in going
much farther on this ridge, because the sixth
bridge—at the bottom there—is smashed to bits.
Yet if you two still want to go ahead,
move up and walk along this rocky edge;
nearby, another ridge will form a path.[1]
Five hours from this hour yesterday,
one thousand and two hundred sixty-six
years passed since that roadway was shattered here.[2]
I'm sending ten of mine out there to see
if any sinner lifts his head for air;
go with my men—there is no malice in them."
"Step forward, Alichino and Calcabrina,"
he then began to say, "and you, Cagnazzo;
and Barbariccia, who can lead the ten.
Let Libicocco go, and Draghignazzo
and tusky Ciriatto and Graffiacane
and Farfarello and mad Rubicante.[3]
Search all around the clammy stew of pitch;
keep these two safe and sound till the next ridge
that rises without break across the dens."
"Ah me! What is this, master, that I see?"
I said. "Can't we do without company?
If you know how to go, I want no escort.
If you are just as keen as usual,

9. A castle in the territory of Pisa, on a hill near the river Arno. Following the death of Ugolino, leader of the Pisan Guelfs (see 33.4–75), his party was expelled from the city, and the castle was taken in 1289 by the Tuscan Guelfs, led by the Lucchese and Florentines, probably including Dante himself.

1. As it turns out, Malacoda is truthful about the nearer bridge, but deliberately deceitful about the farther.

2. The internal dating of the poem hinges on this information from the mouth of a devil. The bridges of Hell crumbled at the moment of Christ's death on the cross. In Dante's reckoning, Christ died at the age of 34, counted from the day of the Incarnation. Matthew gave the time of death as the sixth hour, or noon; Malacoda refers to a moment five hours earlier and one day following this event, that is, 7 A.M. on Holy Saturday, which fell on April 9 in the year 1300. Through other internal signals in the poem, this places the night in the dark wood on Thursday, April 7, the encounter with the three beasts and Virgil during the next day, and the entry through the Gate of Hell at sunset of Good Friday. It is now just past daybreak in the world above; they have consumed the night in their descent thus far.

3. Some of the devils' names have been coined by Dante: Malacoda ("evil-tail"), Malebranche ("evil-claws"), Cagnazzo ("big dog"). Several were also family names in Lucca.

can't you see how those demons grind their teeth?
Their brows are menacing, they promise trouble."
And he to me: "I do not want you frightened:
just let them gnash away as they may wish;
they do it for the wretches boiled in pitch."
They turned around along the left hand bank:
but first each pressed his tongue between his teeth
as signal for their leader, Barbariccia.
And he had made a trumpet of his ass.

Canto 22

Still the Eighth Circle, Fifth Pouch: the Barrators. The Barrator from Navarre. Fra Gomita and Michele Zanche, two Sardinians. The astuteness of the Navarrese that leads two demons to fall into the pitch.

Before this I've seen horsemen start to march
and open the assault and muster ranks[1]
and seen them, too, at times beat their retreat;
and on your land, o Aretines, I've seen
rangers and raiding parties galloping,
the clash of tournaments, the rush of jousts,
now done with trumpets, now with bells, and now
with drums, and now with signs from castle walls,
with native things and with imported ware;[2]
but never yet have I seen horsemen or
seen infantry or ship that sails by signal
of land or star move to so strange a bugle!
We made our way together with ten demons:
ah, what ferocious company! And yet
"in church with saints, with rotters in the tavern."[3]
But I was all intent upon the pitch,
to seek out every feature of the pouch
and of the people who were burning in it.
Just as the dolphins do, when with arched back,
they signal to the seamen to prepare
for tempest, that their vessel may be spared,[4]
so here from time to time, to ease his torment,
some sinner showed his back above the surface,
then hid more quickly than a lightning flash.
And just as on the margin of a ditch,
frogs crouch, their snouts alone above the water,

1. The tone of the several cantos of the adventure with the devils of the fifth *bolgia* is closer to the popular style of the Italian *novella,* or short tale, than it is to the high, tragic style of many of the preceding cantos.

2. The Aretines are the people of the Tuscan commune of Arezzo. Dante is likely to have seen their cavalry in 1289 when the Florentine Guelfs defeated the Aretine Ghibellines at the Battle of Campaldino, and also later at Caprona.

3. A popular proverb that also suggests a reason for the shift in literary style.

4. It was believed that dolphins on the surface of the sea near a ship were the sign of an imminent storm.

so as to hide their feet and their plump flesh,
 so here on every side these sinners crouched;
but faster than a flash, when Barbariccia
drew near, they plunged beneath the boiling pitch.
 I saw—my heart still shudders in recall—
one who delayed, just as at times a frog
is left behind while others dive below;
 and Graffiacane, who was closest to him,
then hooked him by his pitch entangled locks
and hauled him up; he seemed to me an otter.
 By now I knew the names of all those demons—
I'd paid attention when the fiends were chosen;
I'd watched as they stepped forward one by one.
 "O Rubicante, see you set your talons
right into him, so you can flay° his flesh!" *tear off*
So did those cursed ones cry out together.
 And I: "My master, if you can, find out
what is the name of that unfortunate
who's fallen victim to his enemies."
 My guide, who then drew near that sinner's side,
asked him to tell his birthplace. He replied:
"My homeland was the kingdom of Navarre.
 My mother, who had had me by a wastrel,
destroyer of himself and his possessions,
had placed me in the service of a lord.
 Then I was in the household of the worthy
King Thibault;[5] there I started taking graft;
with this heat I pay reckoning for that."
 And Ciriatto, from whose mouth there bulged
to right and left two tusks like a wild hog's,
then let him feel how one of them could mangle.
 The mouse had fallen in with evil cats;
but Barbariccia clasped him in his arms
and said: "Stand off there, while I fork him fast."
 And turning toward my master then, he said:
"Ask on, if you would learn some more from him
before one of the others does him in."
 At which my guide: "Now tell: among the sinners
who hide beneath the pitch, are any others
Italian?" And he: "I have just left
 one who was nearby there; and would I were
still covered by the pitch as he is hidden,
for then I'd have no fear of hook or talon."
 And Libicocco said, "We've been too patient!"
and, with his grapple, grabbed him by the arm
and, ripping, carried off a hunk of flesh.
 But Draghignazzo also looked as if

5. King of Navarre in northern Spain and southwestern France.

to grab his legs; at which, their captain wheeled
and threatened all of them with raging looks.
When they'd grown somewhat less tumultuous,
without delay my guide asked of that one
who had his eyes still fixed upon his wound:
"Who was the one you left to come ashore—
unluckily—as you just said before?"
He answered: "Fra Gomita of Gallura,
who was a vessel fit for every fraud;
he had his master's enemies in hand,
but handled them in ways that pleased them all.
He took their gold and smoothly let them off,
as he himself says; and in other matters,
he was a sovereign, not a petty, swindler.
His comrade there is Don Michele Zanche
of Logodoro; and their tongues are never
too tired to talk of their Sardinia.[6]
Ah me, see that one there who grinds his teeth!
If I were not afraid, I'd speak some more,
but he is getting set to scratch my scurf."
And their great marshal, facing Farfarello—
who was so hot to strike he rolled his eyes,
said: "Get away from there, you filthy bird!"
"If you perhaps would like to see or hear,"
that sinner, terrified, began again,
"Lombards or Tuscans, I can fetch you some;
but let the Malebranche stand aside
so that my comrades need not fear their vengeance.
Remaining in this very spot, I shall,
although alone, make seven more appear
when I have whistled, as has been our custom
when one of us has managed to get out."
At that, Cagnazzo lifted up his snout
and shook his head, and said: "Just listen to
that trick by which he thinks he can dive back!"
To this, he who was rich in artifice
replied: "Then I must have too many tricks,
if I bring greater torment to my friends."[7]
This was too much for Alichino and,
despite the others, he cried out: "If you
dive back, I shall not gallop after you
but beat my wings above the pitch; we'll leave
this height; with the embankment as a screen,
we'll see if you—alone—can handle us."

6. Two shades of Sardinia, at the time controlled by Pisa (Gallura and Logodoro were two of the four judicial divisions of the island). Fra Gomita was a friar who was hanged for abusing his position of deputy to the judge of Gallura. Little is known for certain about Michel Zanche except that he was father-in-law of his murderer Branca Doria (33.137).

7. Ciampolo thus continues his fraudulent ways in Hell.

O you who read, hear now of this new sport:
each turned his eyes upon the other shore,
he first who'd been most hesitant before.
The Navarrese, in nick of time, had planted
his feet upon the ground; then in an instant
he jumped and freed himself from their commander.
At this each demon felt the prick of guilt,
and most, he who had led his band to blunder;
so he took off and shouted: "You are caught!"
But this could help him little; wings were not
more fast than fear; the sinner plunged right under;
the other, flying up, lifted his chest:
not otherwise the wild duck when it plunges
precipitously, when the falcon nears
and then—exhausted, thwarted—flies back up.
But Calcabrina, raging at the trick,
flew after Alichino; he was keen
to see the sinner free and have a brawl;
and once the Navarrese had disappeared,
he turned his talons on his fellow demon
and tangled with him just above the ditch.
But Alichino clawed him well—he was
indeed a full-grown kestrel;° and both fell *falcon*
into the middle of the boiling pond.
The heat was quick to disentangle them,
but still there was no way they could get out;
their wings were stuck, enmeshed in glue-like pitch.
And Barbariccia, grieving with the rest,
sent four to fly out toward the other shore
with all their forks, and speedily enough
on this side and on that they took their posts;
and toward those two—stuck fast, already cooked
beneath that crust—they stretched their grappling hooks.
We left them still contending with that mess.

Canto 23

Still the Eighth Circle, Fifth Pouch: the Barrators. Pursuit by the demons, with Virgil snatching up Dante and sliding down to the Sixth Pouch, where the Hypocrites file along slowly, clothed in caps of lead. Two Jovial Friars of Bologna, Catalano and Loderingo. Caiaphas. Virgil's distress at Malacoda's deceitfulness.

Silent, alone, no one escorting us,
we made our way—one went before, one after—
as Friars Minor when they walk together.[1]
The present fracas made me think of Aesop—
that fable where he tells about the mouse

1. Franciscan monks called themselves Friars Minor because of their devotion to poverty and humility. It was their custom to travel in bands of two, with the senior walking ahead of the other.

and frog; for "near" and "nigh" are not more close
than are that fable and this incident,
if you compare with care how each begins
and then compare the endings that they share.[2]
And even as one thought springs from another,
so out of that was still another born,
which made the fear I felt before redouble.
I thought: "Because of us, they have been mocked,
and this inflicted so much hurt and scorn
that I am sure they feel deep indignation.
If anger's to be added to their malice,
they'll hunt us down with more ferocity
than any hound whose teeth have trapped a hare."
I could already feel my hair curl up
from fear, and I looked back attentively,
while saying: "Master, if you don't conceal
yourself and me at once—they terrify me,
those Malebranche; they are after us;
I so imagine them, I hear them now."
And he to me: "Were I a leaded mirror,[3]
I could not gather in your outer image
more quickly than I have received your inner.
For even now your thoughts have joined my own;
in both our acts and aspects we are kin—
with both our minds I've come to one decision.
If that right bank is not extremely steep,
we can descend into the other moat
and so escape from the imagined chase."
He'd hardly finished telling me his plan
when I saw them approach with outstretched wings,
not too far off, and keen on taking us.
My guide snatched me up instantly, just as
the mother who is wakened by a roar
and catches sight of blazing flames beside her,
will lift her son and run without a stop—
she cares more for the child than for herself—
not pausing even to throw on a shift;
and down the hard embankment's edge—his back
lay flat along the sloping rock that closes
one side of the adjacent moat—he slid.
No water ever ran so fast along
a sluice to turn the wheels of a land mill,

2. A large collection of animal fables was attributed to Aesop, a Greek author said to have lived in the early 6th century B.C.E. In this popular fable, a frog agrees to carry a mouse across a river. Halfway across, it dives down in an attempt to kill the mouse, but while the two are fighting, a hawk swoops down and captures either the frog (in the version of Marie de France), or both the mouse and the frog. The fable may apply to the end of the previous canto, with Calcabrina as frog and Alichino as mouse; it also foreshadows the discovery at the end of this canto that Malacoda as frog has lied to Virgil and Dante as mouse about the existence of a bridge.

3. Lead was the customary backing for mirrors of the time.

not even when its flow approached the paddles,[4]
as did my master race down that embankment
while bearing me with him upon his chest,
just like a son, and not like a companion.
His feet had scarcely reached the bed that lies
along the deep below, than those ten demons
were on the edge above us; but there was
nothing to fear; for that High Providence
that willed them ministers of the fifth ditch,
denies to all of them the power to leave it.
Below that point we found a painted people,
who moved about with lagging steps, in circles,
weeping, with features tired and defeated.
And they were dressed in cloaks with cowls so low
they fell before their eyes, of that same cut
that's used to make the clothes for Cluny's monks.[5]
Outside, these cloaks were gilded and they dazzled;
but inside they were all of lead, so heavy
that Frederick's capes were straw compared to them.[6]
A tiring mantle for eternity!
We turned again, as always, to the left,
along with them, intent on their sad weeping;
but with their weights that weary people paced
so slowly that we found ourselves among
new company each time we took a step.[7]
At which I told my guide: "Please try to find
someone whose name or deed I recognize;
and while we walk, be watchful with your eyes."
And one who'd taken in my Tuscan speech
cried out behind us: "Stay your steps, o you
who hurry so along this darkened air!
Perhaps you'll have from me that which you seek."
At which my guide turned to me, saying: "Wait,
and then continue, following his pace."
I stopped, and I saw two whose faces showed
their minds were keen to be with me; but both
their load and the tight path forced them to slow.
When they came up, they looked askance at me
a long while, and they uttered not a word
until they turned to one another, saying:
"The throbbing of his throat makes this one seem
alive; and if they're dead, what privilege

4. The mill is situated near a body of water, its paddles turned by water passed through canals or sluices.

5. Cluny was a famous Benedictine abbey in Burgundy. In a letter to his nephew, who had left the Cistercian order to join the Cluniacs, Bernard of Clairvaux noted with some sarcasm the luxury of their robes, "made of the finest and most expensive fabrics, with long sleeves and a full hood."

6. Emperor Frederick II was accustomed to punish criminals by fitting them with a leaden cape and then placing them into a cauldron. As the cauldron was heated, the lead would melt, removing the skin piece by piece.

7. This is one of the few parts of Hell in which the pilgrim directly imitates the movements of the damned.

lets them appear without the heavy mantle?"
Then they addressed me: "Tuscan, you who come
to this assembly of sad hypocrites,
do not disdain to tell us who you are."
I answered: "Where the lovely Arno flows,
there I was born and raised, in the great city;
I'm with the body I have always had.
But who are you, upon whose cheeks I see
such tears distilled by grief? And let me know
what punishment it is that glitters so."
And one of them replied: "The yellow cloaks
are of a lead so thick, their heaviness
makes us, the balances beneath them, creak.[8]
We both were Jovial Friars, and Bolognese;
my name was Catalano, Loderingo
was his, and we were chosen by your city
together, for the post that's usually
one man's, to keep the peace; and what we were
is still to be observed around Gardingo."[9]
I then began, "O Friars, your misdeeds . . ."
but said no more, because my eyes had caught
one crucified by three stakes on the ground.
When he saw me, that sinner writhed all over,
and he breathed hard into his beard with sighs;
observing that, Fra Catalano said
to me: "That one impaled there, whom you see,
counseled the Pharisees that it was prudent
to let one man—and not one nation—suffer.[1]
Naked, he has been stretched across the path,
as you can see, and he must feel the weight
of anyone who passes over him.
Like torment, in this ditch, afflicts both his
father-in-law and others in that council,
which for the Jews has seeded so much evil."[2]
Then I saw Virgil stand amazed above
that one who lay stretched out upon a cross
so squalidly in his eternal exile.[3]

8. Like the words of the hypocrite, the cloaks glitter on the outside but in reality are lead.

9. "Jovial Friars" were members of the Knights of the Blessed Virgin Mary, an order founded in Bologna in 1261 with the object of making peace between the warring factions in Italy's cities. The nickname was given them in reaction to the laxity of their rules. The Guelf Catalano di Guido di Ostia was associated with the Ghibelline Loderingo degli Andalò in founding the order; they were appointed by Pope Clement IV to serve jointly as chief magistrates of Florence, owing allegiance to the pope rather than to their political parties. Their appointment resulted in an uprising of Guelfs and expulsion of Ghibelline nobles along with destruction of their houses, including those of the Uberti, a leading family (Farinata's, see Canto 10), in the neighborhood of Gardingo near the Palazzo Vecchio.

1. Caiaphas was the high priest under Pontius Pilate who counseled the Pharisees that "one man," Jesus, should die (John 18:13).

2. Caiaphas was supported at the council of the Pharisees by his father-in-law Annas. "Seeded" refers to the Christian belief that the blood of Christ was the "seed" that led to the destruction of Jerusalem and the dispersal of the Jews.

3. All sinners are "exiled" from heaven, but the gibe carries extra weight in the context of the fate of the Jews. Virgil's "amazement" may partly result from the fact that these shades would not have been there on his last passage through Malebolge (9.16–30).

And he addressed the friar in this way:
"If it does not displease you—if you may—
tell us if there's some passage on the right
that would allow the two of us to leave
without our having to compel black angels
to travel to this deep, to get us out."
He answered: "Closer than you hope, you'll find
a rocky ridge that stretches from the great
round wall and crosses all the savage valleys,
except that here it's broken—not a bridge.
But where its ruins slope along the bank
and heap up at the bottom, you can climb."
My leader stood a while with his head bent,
then said: "He who hooks sinners over there
gave us a false account of this affair."
At which the Friar: "In Bologna, I
once heard about the devil's many vices—
they said he was a liar and father of lies."[4]
And then my guide moved on with giant strides,
somewhat disturbed, with anger in his eyes;
at this I left those overburdened spirits,
while following the prints of his dear feet.

Canto 24

Still the Eighth Circle, Sixth Pouch: the Hypocrites. Hard passage to the Seventh Pouch: the Thieves. Bitten by a serpent, a thieving sinner who turns to ashes and is then restored: Vanni Fucci. His prediction of the defeat of the Whites—Dante's party—at Pistoia.

In that part of the young year when the sun
begins to warm its locks beneath Aquarius
and nights grow shorter, equaling the days,
when hoarfrost mimes the image of his white
sister upon the ground—but not for long,
because the pen he uses is not sharp—
the farmer who is short of fodder rises
and looks and sees the fields all white, at which
he slaps his thigh, turns back into the house,
and here and there complains like some poor wretch
who doesn't know what can be done, and then
goes out again and gathers up new hope
on seeing that the world has changed its face
in so few hours, and he takes his staff
and hurries out his flock of sheep to pasture.[1]

4. The hypocrite maliciously points out Virgil's ignorance of the ways of the devil that led to his deception by Malacoda (21.111), referring to his own experience as well as to the words of the Gospel (John 8:44).

1. The sun is in the sign of Aquarius between late January and late February. The "white sister" of hoarfrost is snow; both "write" upon the ground, but frost less deeply. The farmer mistakes one for the other, but only for the time it takes the rising sun to melt the frost.

So did my master fill me with dismay
when I saw how his brow was deeply troubled,
yet then the plaster soothed the sore as quickly:
for soon as we were on the broken bridge,
my guide turned back to me with that sweet manner
I first had seen along the mountain's base.[2]
And he examined carefully the ruin;
then having picked the way we would ascend,
he opened up his arms and thrust me forward.
And just as he who ponders as he labors,
who's always ready for the step ahead,
so, as he lifted me up toward the summit
of one great crag, he'd see another spur,
saying: "That is the one you will grip next,
but try it first to see if it is firm."
That was no path for those with cloaks of lead,[3]
for he and I—he, light; I, with support—
could hardly make it up from spur to spur.
And were it not that, down from this enclosure,
the slope was shorter than the bank before,
I cannot speak for him, but I should surely
have been defeated. But since Malebolge
runs right into the mouth of its last well,
the placement of each valley means it must
have one bank high and have the other short;
and so we reached, at length, the jutting where
the last stone of the ruined bridge breaks off.
The breath within my lungs was so exhausted
from climbing, I could not go on; in fact,
as soon as I had reached that stone, I sat.
"Now you must cast aside your laziness,"
my master said, "for he who rests on down
or under covers cannot come to fame;
and he who spends his life without renown
leaves such a vestige of himself on earth
as smoke bequeaths to air or foam to water.
Therefore, get up; defeat your breathlessness
with spirit that can win all battles if
the body's heaviness does not deter it.
A longer ladder still is to be climbed;
it's not enough to have left them behind;
if you have understood, now profit from it."[4]
Then I arose and showed myself far better
equipped with breath than I had been before:

2. When Virgil first appeared to Dante in Canto 1.
3. The hypocrites require no other guardian than the robes they wear.
4. Virgil's words liken the "heaviness" of Dante's body to the cloaks of the hypocrites, and also remind him that both fame and salvation will require a much longer climb later on: the one that leads them out of hell in Canto 34, or that of the Mountain of Purgatory in the next canticle.

"Go on, for I am strong and confident."
We took our upward way upon the ridge,
with crags more jagged, narrow, difficult,
and much more steep than we had crossed before.
I spoke as we went on, not to seem weak;
at this, a voice came from the ditch beyond—
a voice that was not suited to form words.
I know not what he said, although I was
already at the summit of the bridge
that crosses there; and yet he seemed to move.
I had bent downward, but my living eyes
could not see to the bottom through that dark;
at which I said: "O master, can we reach
the other belt? Let us descend the wall,
for as I hear and cannot understand,
so I see down but can distinguish nothing."
"The only answer that I give to you
is doing it," he said. "A just request
is to be met in silence, by the act."
We then climbed down the bridge, just at the end
where it runs right into the eighth embankment,
and now the moat was plain enough to me;
and there within I saw a dreadful swarm
of serpents so extravagant in form—
remembering them still drains my blood from me.[5]
Let Libya boast no more about her sands;
for if she breeds chelydri, jaculi,
cenchres with amphisbaena, pareae,
she never showed—with all of Ethiopia
or all the land that borders the Red Sea[6]—
so many, such malignant, pestilences.
Among this cruel and depressing swarm,
ran people who were naked, terrified,
with no hope of a hole or heliotrope.[7]
Their hands were tied behind by serpents; these
had thrust their head and tail right through the loins,
and then were knotted on the other side.
And—there!—a serpent sprang with force at one
who stood upon our shore, transfixing him
just where the neck and shoulders form a knot.
No *o* or *i* has ever been transcribed
so quickly as that soul caught fire and burned
and, as he fell, completely turned to ashes;
and when he lay, undone, upon the ground,
the dust of him collected by itself

5. The fanciful list of serpents comes from Cato's crossing of the Libyan Desert in Lucan's *Pharsalia* 9.711–21.
6. Even if the Libyan Desert is expanded to include Africa south of Egypt as far as Zanzibar and east to the Red Sea.
7. The heliotrope was a stone supposedly found in northern Africa that rendered the wearer invisible.

and instantly returned to what it was:
just so, it is asserted by great sages,
that, when it reaches its five-hundredth year,
the phoenix dies and then is born again;[8]
lifelong it never feeds on grass or grain,
only on drops of incense and amomum;
its final winding sheets are nard and myrrh.[9]
And just as he who falls, and knows not how—
by demon's force that drags him to the ground
or by some other hindrance that binds man—
who, when he rises, stares about him, all
bewildered by the heavy anguish he
has suffered, sighing as he looks around;
so did this sinner stare when he arose.
Oh, how severe it is, the power of God
that, as its vengeance, showers down such blows!
My guide then asked that sinner who he was;
to this he answered: "Not long since, I rained
from Tuscany into this savage maw.
Mule that I was, the bestial life pleased me
and not the human; I am Vanni Fucci,
beast; and the den that suited me—Pistoia."[1]
And I to Virgil: "Tell him not to slip
away, and ask what sin has thrust him here;
I knew him as a man of blood and anger."
The sinner heard and did not try to feign
but turned his mind and face, intent, toward me;
and coloring with miserable shame,
he said: "I suffer more because you've caught me
in this, the misery you see, than I
suffered when taken from the other life.
I can't refuse to answer what you ask:
I am set down so far because I robbed
the sacristy of its fair ornaments,
and someone else was falsely blamed for that.[2]
But lest this sight give you too much delight,
if you can ever leave these lands of darkness,
open your ears to my announcement, hear:
Pistoia first will strip herself of Blacks,
then Florence will renew her men and manners.
From Val di Magra, Mars will draw a vapor
which turbid clouds will try to wrap; the clash

8. The mythical Arabian phoenix was a bird that burned itself every 500 years on a pyre of incense, rising from the ashes in the form of a small worm that developed into a full-grown bird by the third day (Ovid, *Metamorphoses* 15.392–402).

9. Amomum and incense, nard and myrrh are fragrant plant extracts and tree resins; the former provide its food, the latter form the phoenix's "winding sheet," the cloth in which its corpse is wrapped.

1. The "mule" or illegitimate son of a noble family of Pistoia, northwest of Florence, Vanni Fucci was an ardent Black Guelf. Dante may have known him from the war against Pisa (1289–1293).

2. There are various reports concerning the robbery of the treasury of San Jacopo in the church of San Zeno at Pistoia; an innocent man was nearly executed for the crime.

between them will be fierce, impetuous,
a tempest, fought upon Campo Piceno,
until that vapor, vigorous, shall crack
the mist, and every White be struck by it.[3]
And I have told you this to make you grieve."

Canto 25

Still the Eighth Circle, Seventh Pouch: the Thieves. Vanni Fucci and his obscene figs against God. The Centaur Cacus. Five Florentine Thieves, three of them humans and two of them serpents. The astounding metamorphoses undergone by four of them.

When he had finished with his words, the thief
raised high his fists with both figs cocked and cried:
"Take that, o God; I square them off for you!"[1]
From that time on, those serpents were my friends,
for one of them coiled then around his neck,
as if to say, "I'll have you speak no more";
another wound about his arms and bound him
again and wrapped itself in front so firmly,
he could not even make them budge an inch.
Pistoia, ah, Pistoia, must you last:
why not decree your self-incineration,
since you surpass your seed in wickedness?[2]
Throughout the shadowed circles of deep Hell,
I saw no soul against God so rebel,
not even he who fell from Theban walls.[3]
He fled and could not say another word;
and then I saw a Centaur full of anger,
shouting: "Where is he, where's that bitter one?"
I do not think Maremma has the number
of snakes that Centaur carried on his haunch
until the part that takes our human form.[4]
Upon his shoulders and behind his nape
there lay a dragon with its wings outstretched;
it sets ablaze all those it intercepts.
My master said: "That Centaur there is Cacus,
who often made a lake of blood within
a grotto underneath Mount Aventine.
He does not ride the same road as his brothers
because he stole—and most deceitfully—

3. The Blacks of Pistoia were expelled and their houses burned in 1301, but with the help of the ostensible peacemaker, Charles of Valois, they and the Blacks of Florence were able to expel the Florentine Whites, including Dante, in 1302 (lines 143–44). The "vapor" drawn by the war-god from Val di Magra is the Guelf leader Moroello Malaspina. The defeat of the Whites ("the mist" of line 150) may refer to events of 1302 or to the capture of the city in 1306.

1. The "fig" is an obscene gesture produced by thrusting out the fist while holding the thumb between the forefinger and middle finger.

2. According to legend, Pistoia was founded by survivors of the forces of Catiline, the conspirator against the Roman republic defeated nearby in 62 B.C.E.

3. The blasphemer Capaneus in Canto 14.46–72.

4. The beast-filled Tuscan wood of Maremma was referred to already in Canto 13.7–9 to describe the wood of suicides and squanderers; here, serpents are added to its contents.

from the great herd nearby; his crooked deeds
ended beneath the club of Hercules,
who may have given him a hundred blows—
but he was not alive to feel the tenth."[5]
While he was talking so, Cacus ran by
and, just beneath our ledge, three souls arrived;
but neither I nor my guide noticed them
until they had cried out: "And who are you?"
At this the words we shared were interrupted,
and we attended only to those spirits.
I did not recognize them, but it happened,
as chance will usually bring about,
that one of them called out the other's name,[6]
exclaiming: "Where was Cianfa left behind?"
At this, so that my guide might be alert,
I raised my finger up from chin to nose.
If, reader, you are slow now to believe
what I shall tell, that is no cause for wonder,
for I who saw it hardly can accept it.
As I kept my eyes fixed upon those sinners,
a serpent with six feet springs out against
one of the three, and clutches him completely.
It gripped his belly with its middle feet,
and with its forefeet grappled his two arms;
and then it sank its teeth in both his cheeks;
it stretched its rear feet out along his thighs
and ran its tail along between the two,
then straightened it again behind his loins.
No ivy ever gripped a tree so fast
as when that horrifying monster clasped
and intertwined the other's limbs with its.
Then just as if their substance were warm wax,
they stuck together and they mixed their colors,
so neither seemed what he had been before;
just as, when paper's kindled, where it still
has not caught flame in full, its color's dark
though not yet black, while white is dying off.
The other two souls stared, and each one cried:
"Ah me, Agnello, how you change! Just see,
you are already neither two nor one!"[7]

5. Cacus was the fire-breathing, half-human son of Vulcan and Medusa who stole cattle from Hercules. In order to conceal their tracks, Cacus dragged the cattle backward into his cave, but their bellowing alerted Hercules, who slew the thief (*Aeneid* 8.193–267). Dante makes Cacus a Centaur, and displaces the fire-breathing to a dragon familiar on its shoulder.

6. There are five souls involved in the complex action of this canto; all were thieves of noble Florentine families: Cianfa Donati, lost when he became a serpent (50) and eventually fusing (70–78) with Agnello de' Brunelleschi; Francesco Guercio ("squinting") de' Cavalcanti, the "blazing little serpent" (82) that steals the substance of "Buoso" (85), probably Buoso di Forese Donati, nephew of the Buoso Donati mentioned as a victim of counterfeiting in Canto 30.41–44, in the transformation that concludes at line 141; and Puccio Sciancato, "the only soul who'd not been changed" (149).

7. Agnello was reputed to have used disguises to facilitate his thieving. The transformation that follows closely resembles the merging of Salmacis and Hermaphroditus in *Metamorphoses* 4.373–79.

Then two heads were already joined in one,
when in one face where two had been dissolved,
two intermingled shapes appeared to us.
Two arms came into being from four lengths;
the thighs and legs, the belly and the chest
became such limbs as never had been seen.
And every former shape was canceled there:
that perverse image seemed to share in both—
and none; and so, and slowly, it moved on.
Just as the lizard, when it darts from hedge
to hedge, beneath the dog days' giant lash,
seems, if it cross one's path, a lightning flash,
so seemed a blazing little serpent moving
against the bellies of the other two,
as black and livid as a peppercorn.
Attacking one of them, it pierced right through
the part where we first take our nourishment;° *the navel*
and then it fell before him at full length.
The one it had transfixed stared but said nothing;
in fact he only stood his ground and yawned
as one whom sleep or fever has undone.
The serpent stared at him, he at the serpent;
one through his wound, the other through his mouth
were smoking violently; their smoke met.
Let Lucan now be silent, where he sings
of sad Sabellus and Nasidius,
and wait to hear what flies off from my bow.
Let Ovid now be silent, where he tells
of Cadmus, Arethusa; if his verse
has made of one a serpent, one a fountain,[8]
I do not envy him; he never did
transmute two natures, face to face, so that
both forms were ready to exchange their matter.
These were the ways they answered to each other:
the serpent split its tail into a fork;
the wounded sinner drew his steps together.
The legs and then the thighs along with them
so fastened to each other that the juncture
soon left no sign that was discernible.
Meanwhile the cleft tail took upon itself
the form the other gradually lost;
its skin grew soft, the other's skin grew hard.
I saw the arms that drew in at his armpits
and also saw the monster's two short feet
grow long for just as much as those were shortened.
The serpent's hind feet, twisted up together,

8. Dante invokes (and outdoes) his two primary sources in this canto: the horrific deaths by snakebite of two Roman soldiers in the Libyan Desert in Lucan's *Pharsalia* 9 and the transformations of Ovid's *Metamorphoses,* in this case those of Thebes' founder Cadmus into a serpent (4.576–89) and of the nymph Arethusa into a fountain (5.572–641).

became the member that man hides; just as
the wretch put out two hind paws from his member.
  And while the smoke veils each with a new color,
and now breeds hair upon the skin of one,
just as it strips the hair from off the other,
  the one rose up, the other fell; and yet
they never turned aside their impious eyelamps,
beneath which each of them transformed his snout:
  he who stood up drew his back toward the temples,
and from the excess matter growing there
came ears upon the cheeks that had been bare;
  whatever had not been pulled back but kept,
superfluous, then made his face a nose
and thickened out his lips appropriately.
  He who was lying down thrust out his snout;
and even as the snail hauls in its horns,
he drew his ears straight back into his head;
  his tongue, which had before been whole and fit
for speech, now cleaves; the other's tongue, which had
been forked, now closes up; and the smoke stops.
  The soul that had become an animal,
now hissing, hurried off along the valley;
the other one, behind him, speaks and spits.
  And then he turned aside his new-made shoulders
and told the third soul: "I'd have Buoso run
on all fours down this road, as I have done."
  And so I saw the seventh ballast change
and rechange;[9] may the strangeness plead for me
if there's been some confusion in my pen.
  And though my eyes were somewhat blurred, my mind
bewildered, those three sinners did not flee
so secretly that I could not perceive
  Puccio Sciancato clearly, he who was
the only soul who'd not been changed among
the three companions we had met at first;
  the other one made you, Gaville, grieve.[1]

Canto 26

Still the Eighth Circle, Seventh Pouch: the Thieves. Dante's invective against Florence. View of the Eighth Pouch, where Fraudulent Counselors are clothed in the

9. That is, the souls of the seventh *bolgia,* likened to the hold of a ship.

1. Murdered by the inhabitants of the village of Gaville, Francesco de' Cavalcanti was swiftly and savagely avenged by his family.

flames that burn them. Ulysses and Diomedes in one shared flame. Ulysses' tale of his final voyage.

Be joyous, Florence, you are great indeed,
for over sea and land you beat your wings;
through every part of Hell your name extends!
Among the thieves I found five citizens
of yours—and such, that shame has taken me;
with them, you can ascend to no high honor.
But if the dreams dreamt close to dawn are true,
then little time will pass before you feel
what Prato and the others crave for you.[1]
Were that already come, it would not be
too soon—and let it come, since it must be!
As I grow older, it will be more heavy.[2]
We left that deep and, by protruding stones
that served as stairs for our descent before,
my guide climbed up again and drew me forward;
and as we took our solitary path
among the ridge's jagged spurs and rocks,
our feet could not make way without our hands.
It grieved me then and now grieves me again
when I direct my mind to what I saw;
and more than usual, I curb my talent,
that it not run where virtue does not guide;
so that, if my kind star or something better
has given me that gift, I not abuse it.
As many as the fireflies the peasant
(while resting on a hillside in the season° *summer*
when he who lights the world least hides his face),
just when the fly gives way to the mosquito,
sees glimmering below, down in the valley,
there where perhaps he gathers grapes and tills—
so many were the flames that glittered in
the eighth abyss; I made this out as soon
as I had come to where one sees the bottom.
Even as he who was avenged by bears
saw, as it left, Elijah's chariot—
its horses rearing, rising right to heaven—
when he could not keep track of it except
by watching one lone flame in its ascent,
just like a little cloud that climbs on high:[3]
so, through the gullet of that ditch, each flame

1. Ancient lore distinguished many sorts of dreams; only those dreamt near dawn were held to be prophetic, "true." Prato is a Tuscan town between Florence and Pistoia that envied Florentine power; the enigmatic prediction may refer to Cardinal Niccolò da Prato, who placed the city under interdiction after his peacekeeping mission failed in 1304.

2. The longer he must wait for a retribution to his city that will be just but bittersweet.

3. After the prophet Elisha was mocked by a group of boys, two bears came from the woods and killed 42 of them; he had already witnessed the ascent of his teacher, the prophet Elijah, to heaven in a fiery chariot (2 Kings 2:23–24).

must make its way; no flame displays its prey,
though every flame has carried off a sinner.
I stood upon the bridge and leaned straight out
to see; and if I had not gripped a rock,
I should have fallen off—without a push.
My guide, who noted how intent I was,
told me: "Within those fires there are souls;
each one is swathed in that which scorches him."
"My master," I replied, "on hearing you,
I am more sure; but I'd already thought
that it was so, and I had meant to ask:
Who is within the flame that comes so twinned
above that it would seem to rise out of
the pyre Eteocles shared with his brother?"[4]
He answered me: "Within that flame, Ulysses
and Diomedes suffer; they, who went
as one to rage, now share one punishment.[5]
And there, together in their flame, they grieve
over the horse's fraud that caused a breach—
the gate that let Rome's noble seed escape.
There they regret the guile that makes the dead
Deïdamia still lament Achilles;
and there, for the Palladium, they pay."
"If they can speak within those sparks," I said,
"I pray you and repray and, master, may
my prayer be worth a thousand pleas, do not
forbid my waiting here until the flame
with horns approaches us; for you can see
how, out of my desire, I bend toward it."
And he to me: "What you have asked is worthy
of every praise; therefore, I favor it.
I only ask you this: refrain from talking.
Let me address them—I have understood
what you desire of them. Since they were Greek,
perhaps they'd be disdainful of your speech."[6]
And when my guide adjudged the flame had reached

4. Eteocles and Polynices were twin sons of Oedipus, King of Thebes, and Jocasta. After they forced their father (and brother) to abdicate, he cursed them with enmity. They fought over the kingship, killed each other in single combat, and were burned on a single funeral pyre. So enduring was their hatred that the rising flames divided in two (Statius, *Thebaid* 429ff. and Lucan, *Pharsalia* 1.549–52).

5. Ulysses and Diomedes were Greek heroes of the Trojan War who often acted in tandem. One of their exploits was to steal the Palladium, a wooden image of Pallas Athena said to preserve the walls of Troy. In pretended remorse, they built an enormous, hollow wooden horse in which they and other Greeks hid, and which then led the deceived Trojans to breach their walls in order to bear it within the city (*Aeneid* 2.18–370). Rome's "noble seed" is Aeneas and his followers, who fled the city's destruction for Italy. Deïdamia was the mother of Pyrrhus; she died of grief after the boy's father, Achilles, sailed to Troy. In *Purgatorio* 22.114, she is said to be among the souls in Limbo.

6. Unlike Dante, Virgil had been fluent in Greek; moreover, his epic, like Homer's, was written in the high, tragic style characteristic of the speech in this encounter. Dante also chooses to stress the greatness and antiquity of the shade being interviewed.

a point where time and place were opportune,
this was the form I heard his words assume:
"You two who move as one within the flame,
if I deserved of you while I still lived,
if I deserved of you much or a little
when in the world I wrote my noble lines,
do not move on; let one of you retell
where, having gone astray, he found his death."
The greater horn within that ancient flame
began to sway and tremble, murmuring
just like a fire that struggles in the wind;
and then he waved his flame-tip back and forth
as if it were a tongue that tried to speak,
and flung toward us a voice that answered:[7] "When
I sailed away from Circe, who'd beguiled me
to stay more than a year there, near Gaeta—
before Aeneas gave that place a name[8]—
neither my fondness for my son nor pity
for my old father nor the love I owed
Penelope, which would have gladdened her,
was able to defeat in me the longing
I had to gain experience of the world
and of the vices and the worth of men.
Therefore, I set out on the open sea
with but one ship and that small company
of those who never had deserted me.
I saw as far as Spain, far as Morocco,
along both shores; I saw Sardinia
and saw the other islands that sea bathes.
And I and my companions were already
old and slow, when we approached the narrows
where Hercules set up his boundary stones
that men might heed and never reach beyond:
upon my right, I had gone past Seville,
and on the left, already passed Ceüta.[9]
'Brothers,' I said, 'o you, who having crossed
a hundred thousand dangers, reach the west,
to this brief waking-time that still is left
unto your senses, you must not deny
experience of that which lies beyond
the sun, and of the world that is unpeopled.

7. There is no known source for this account by Ulysses (the "greater" flame) of his death; it contradicts the prophecy of Tiresias in *Odyssey* 11.134–37 of a peaceful death at sea.

8. Circe was an enchantress who transformed Ulysses' men into swine. After forcing her to change them back, Ulysses tarried with Circe for a year before continuing his voyage to his home and family in Ithaca.

9. Ulysses and his men are at the western edge of the known world; on the African and European shores of the Mediterranean, the Pillars of Hercules were twin promontories formed when the hero split a mountain in two across the Mediterranean, usually identified with the modern promontories of Gibraltar in Spain and Jebel Musa in Morocco. It was thought impossible to sail beyond this boundary and return alive.

Consider well the seed that gave you birth:
you were not made to live your lives as brutes,
but to be followers of worth and knowledge.'
I spurred my comrades with this brief address
to meet the journey with such eagerness
that I could hardly, then, have held them back;
and having turned our stern toward morning,° we *the east*
made wings out of our oars in a wild flight
and always gained upon our left-hand side.
At night I now could see the other pole
and all its stars; the star of ours had fallen
and never rose above the plain of the ocean.[1]
Five times the light beneath the moon had been
rekindled, and, as many times, was spent,[2]
since that hard passage faced our first attempt,
when there before us rose a mountain, dark
because of distance, and it seemed to me
the highest mountain I had ever seen.[3]
And we were glad, but this soon turned to sorrow,
for out of that new land a whirlwind rose
and hammered at our ship, against her bow.
Three times it turned her round with all the waters;
and at the fourth, it lifted up the stern
so that our prow plunged deep, as pleased an Other,° *God*
until the sea again closed—over us."

Canto 27

Still the Eighth Circle, Eighth Pouch: the Fraudulent Counselors. Guido da Montefeltro, for whom Dante provides a panorama of the state of political affairs in Romagna. Guido's tale of the anticipatory—but unavailing—absolution given him by Boniface VIII. The quarrel of a demon and St Francis over Guido's soul.

The flame already was erect and silent—
it had no more to say. Now it had left
us with the permission of the gentle poet,
when, just behind it, came another flame
that drew our eyes to watch its tip because
of the perplexing sound that it sent forth.
Even as the Sicilian bull (that first
had bellowed with the cry—and this was just—
of him who shaped it with his instruments)
would always bellow with its victim's voice,
so that, although that bull was only brass,

1. The "other pole" is Antartica; they have crossed the equator and no longer see the stars of "our" pole, the northern hemisphere.

2. Five months had passed.

3. This is probably the Mountain of Purgatory; it also resonates with the pilgirm's unsuccessful attempt in Canto 1.

it seemed as if it were pierced through by pain;[1]
so were the helpless words that, from the first,
had found no path or exit from the flame,
transformed into the language of the fire.
But after they had found their way up toward
the tip, and given it that movement which
the tongue had given them along their passage,
we heard: "O you to whom I turn my voice,
who only now were talking Lombard, saying,
'Now you may leave—I'll not provoke more speech,'[2]
though I have come perhaps a little late,
may it not trouble you to stop and speak
with me; see how I stay—and I am burning![3]
If you have fallen into this blind world
but recently, out of the sweet Italian
country from which I carry all my guilt,
do tell me if the Romagnoles have peace
or war; I was from there—the hills between
Urbino and the ridge where Tiber springs."
I still was bent, attentive, over him,
when my guide nudged me lightly at the side
and said: "You speak; he is Italian."[4]
And I, who had my answer set already,
without delay began to speak to him:
"O soul that is concealed below in flame,
Romagna is not now and never was
quite free of war inside its tyrants' hearts;
but when I left her, none had broken out.
Ravenna stands as it has stood for years;
the eagle of Polenta shelters it
and also covers Cervia with his wings.[5]
The city that already stood long trial
and made a bloody heap out of the French,
now finds itself again beneath green paws.[6]
Both mastiffs of Verruchio, old and new,
who dealt so badly with Montagna, use

1. The Athenian artisan Perillus fabricated a bronze bull in which the victims of Phalaris, the 6th-century tyrant of Agrigentum in Sicily, could be roasted alive, their shrieks emerging as if the bellowing of a bull. Perillus was chosen to be first to test his apparatus.

2. "Lombardy" in the Middle Ages referred to northern Italy, including Virgil's birthplace of Mantua where, in Dante's belief, a version of the Lombard dialect was already spoken in antiquity. Given the focus on "high" language in the previous canto, it is a calculated shock to suggest to us in retrospect that Virgil was speaking to Ulysses in Italian (line 3).

3. The shade is Guido da Montefeltro (c.1220–1298), nicknamed the "Fox," who commanded a force of Ghibellines from Romagnola (the region north of Tuscany) and exiles from Bologna and Florence. In his *Convivio,* Dante had referred to the late-life conversion of Guido as exemplary and praised the leader as "our most noble Latin" (4.28.8).

4. By contrast to the previous canto (73–75), where Virgil addressed the Greek shades.

5. The Adriatic cities of Ravenna and Cervia were ruled from 1275 by the Guelf Polenta family, whose coat of arms displayed an eagle. The head of the family from 1275 until his death in 1310 was Guido da Polenta the elder, father of Francesca da Rimini (5.73–142).

6. Under the leadership of Guido da Montefeltro, Forlì, a central city of Romagna, successfully withstood a year-long siege by French and Guelf troops sent by Pope Martin IV; in 1282 they decimated the attacking force. The following year, the city came to terms with the pope and drove out Guido. The "green paws" belong to the coat of arms of the Ordelaffi family, new tyrants of Forlì as of 1300.

their teeth to bore where they have always gnawed.[7]
The cities on Lamone and Santerno
are led by the young lion of the white lair;
from summer unto winter, he shifts factions.[8]
That city with its side bathed by the Savio,
just as it lies between the plain and mountain,
lives somewhere between tyranny and freedom.[9]
And now, I pray you, tell me who you are:
do not be harder than I've been with you,
that in the world your name may still endure."[1]
After the flame, in customary fashion,
had roared awhile, it moved its pointed tip
this side and that and then set free this breath:
"If I thought my reply were meant for one
who ever could return into the world,
this flame would stir no more; and yet, since none—
if what I hear is true—ever returned
alive from this abyss, then without fear
of facing infamy, I answer you.
I was a man of arms, then wore the cord,° *of a monk*
believing that, so girt, I made amends;
and surely what I thought would have been true
had not the Highest Priest—may he be damned!—
made me fall back into my former sins;
and how and why, I'd have you hear from me.[2]
While I still had the form of bones and flesh
my mother gave to me, my deeds were not
those of the lion but those of the fox.[3]
The wiles and secret ways—I knew them all
and so employed their arts that my renown
had reached the very boundaries of earth.
But when I saw myself come to that part
of life when it is fitting for all men
to lower sails and gather in their ropes,
what once had been my joy was now dejection;
repenting and confessing, I became
a friar; and—poor me—it would have helped.
The prince of the new Pharisees,° who then *Pope Boniface*
was waging war so near the Lateran—

7. Malatesta, lord of Rimini, had four sons, including Gianciotto, husband of Francesca da Rimini, her lover Paolo, and Malatestino da Verruchio, the "young mastiff." Both lords were harsh tyrants, killing the head of the Rimini Ghibellines, Montagna de' Parcitati, in 1295.
8. Maghinardo Pagani da Susinana, whose coat of arms displayed a lion on a white ground, ruled the cities of Faenza, on the Lamone, and Imola, on the Santerno River. Ghibelline by birth, he was also loyal to the Florentine Guelfs.
9. Cesena was on the Savio River, midway between Forlì and Rimini. It was a free municipality during this period, but dominated by Guido's powerful cousin, Galasso da Montefeltro.
1. Guido has been under the misconception that Dante was a shade; Dante doesn't yet know to whom he has been speaking.
2. After leading the Ghibellines, Guido made peace with Boniface VIII and joined the Franciscan order late in life. He died in 1298 at the age of 75. The incident that Dante has him recount here may have been invented.
3. A common distinction between force ("the lion") and guile ("the fox").

and not against the Jews or Saracens,° *Arabs*
for every enemy of his was Christian,
and none of them had gone to conquer Acre
or been a trader in the Sultan's lands—
took no care for the highest office or
the holy orders that were his, or for
my cord, which used to make its wearers leaner.[4]
But just as Constantine, on Mount Soracte,
to cure his leprosy, sought out Sylvester,[5]
so this one sought me out as his instructor,
to ease the fever of his arrogance.
He asked me to give counsel. I was silent—
his words had seemed to me delirious.
And then he said: 'Your heart must not mistrust:
I now absolve you in advance—teach me
to batter Penestrino to the ground.[6]
You surely know that I possess the power
to lock and unlock Heaven; for the keys
my predecessor did not prize are two.'[7]
Then his grave arguments compelled me so,
my silence seemed a worse offense than speech,
and I said: 'Since you cleanse me of the sin
that I must now fall into, Father, know:
long promises and very brief fulfillments
will bring a victory to your high throne.'[8]
Then Francis came, as soon as I was dead,
for me; but one of the black cherubim
told him: 'Don't bear him off; do not cheat me.[9]
He must come down among my menials;
the counsel that he gave was fraudulent;
since then, I've kept close track, to snatch his scalp;
one can't absolve a man who's not repented,
and no one can repent and will at once;
the law of contradiction won't allow it.'
O miserable me, for how I started
when he took hold of me and said: 'Perhaps
you did not think that I was a logician!'
He carried me to Minos; and that monster

4. Rather than waging a holy war—Acre was the principal port of the crusaders in Palestine—Boniface was engaged in a local feud (the Lateran Palace was the papal residence) with the Colonna family.
5. According to legend, the Emperor Constantine was afflicted by leprosy due to his persecution of the Christians. Led by a dream, he sought out Pope Sylvester I on Mt. Soracte north of Rome, who baptized and then cured him.
6. The castle at Penestrino southeast of Rome was the stronghold of the Colonna, who surrendered after Boniface had promised complete amnesty (the "long promises" of line 110). He immediately had the castle leveled.
7. The "keys of the kingdom of heaven" (Matthew 16:19) were the symbol of the pope's ultimate power over condemnation and absolution; according to Boniface, his predecessor, Celestine V, who abdicated, "did not prize" them.
8. The pope's promise to Guido to absolve him in advance of whatever evil he may counsel is an extreme version of the abuse of granting indulgences, or reduced penance, for sins not yet committed.
9. Coming for the soul of one of his order, St. Francis takes the place of the customary angel who struggles against the devil ("black cherubim") for possession of a soul.

twisted his tail eight times around his hide
and then, when he had bit it in great anger,
announced: 'This one is for the thieving fire';
for which—and where, you see—I now am lost,
and in this garb I move in bitterness."
And when, with this, his words were at an end,
the flame departed, sorrowing and writhing
and tossing its sharp horn. We moved beyond;
I went together with my guide, along
the ridge until the other arch that bridges
the ditch where payment is imposed on those
who, since they brought such discord, bear such loads.

Canto 28

The Eighth Circle, Ninth Pouch, where the Sowers of Scandal and Schism, perpetually circling, are wounded and—after each healing—wounded again by a demon with a sword. Mohammed and Ali. Warning to Fra Dolcino. Curio. Mosca. Bertran de Born.

Who, even with untrammeled° words and many *unrestrained*
attempts at telling, ever could recount
in full the blood and wounds that I now saw?
Each tongue that tried would certainly fall short
because the shallowness of both our speech
and intellect cannot contain so much.
Were you to reassemble all the men
who once, within Apulia's fateful land,° *southern Italy*
had mourned their blood, shed at the Trojans' hands,[1]
as well as those who fell in the long war
where massive mounds of rings were battle spoils—
even as Livy writes, who does not err[2]—
and those who felt the thrust of painful blows
when they fought hard against Robert Guiscard;[3]
with all the rest whose bones are still piled up
at Ceperano—each Apulian was
a traitor there—and, too, at Tagliacozzo,
where old Alardo conquered without weapons;[4]
and then, were one to show his limb pierced through
and one his limb hacked off, that would not match
the hideousness of the ninth abyss.
No barrel, even though it's lost a hoop
or end-piece, ever gapes as one whom I
saw ripped right from his chin to where we fart:

1. The early Romans, descendants of Aeneas and his men, and their wars with the Tarentines (280–274 B.C.E.) and the Samnites (434–290 B.C.E.).

2. Livy (59 B.C.E.–17 C.E.) was the great historian of ancient Rome; his monumental *History* includes an account of the Second Punic War (219–202 B.C.E.), during which Hannibal brought to Carthage a heap of gold rings taken off of the fingers of slain Romans (33.12.1–2).

3. A Norman adventurer (1015–1085) who fought the Greeks and Saracens in Sicily and southern Italy.

4. Sites of bloody battles in the 1260s marked by treachery.

his bowels hung between his legs, one saw
his vitals and the miserable sack
that makes of what we swallow excrement.
While I was all intent on watching him,
he looked at me, and with his hands he spread
his chest and said: "See how I split myself!
See now how maimed Mohammed is![5] And he
who walks and weeps before me is Ali,[6]
whose face is opened wide from chin to forelock.
And all the others here whom you can see
were, when alive, the sowers of dissension
and scandal, and for this they now are split.
Behind us here, a devil decks us out
so cruelly, re-placing every one
of this throng underneath the sword edge when
we've made our way around the road of pain,
because our wounds have closed again before
we have returned to meet his blade once more.
But who are you who dawdle on this ridge,
perhaps to slow your going to the verdict
that was pronounced on your self-accusations?"
"Death has not reached him yet," my master answered,
"nor is it guilt that summons him to torment;
but that he may gain full experience,
I, who am dead, must guide him here below,
to circle after circle, throughout Hell:
this is as true as that I speak to you."
More than a hundred, when they heard him, stopped
within the ditch and turned to look at me,
forgetful of their torture, wondering.
"Then you, who will perhaps soon see the sun,
tell Fra Dolcino to provide himself
with food, if he has no desire to join me
here quickly, lest when snow besieges him,
it bring the Novarese the victory
that otherwise they would not find too easy."[7]
When he had raised his heel, as if to go,
Mohammed said these words to me, and then
he set it on the ground and off he went.
Another sinner, with his throat slit through
and with his nose hacked off up to his eyebrows,
and no more than a single ear remaining,

5. The Prophet Mohammed (570–632) was considered in medieval Europe as an apostate Christian; from the same point of view, Islam was a decisive division of religious unity.

6. Mohammed's son-in-law. He was assassinated after only five years as caliph, in 661, leading to the division of Islam into two sects, the Sunnites and the Shiites or Fatimites.

7. In 1300 Fra Dolcino had become head of the reformist sect of the Apostolic Brothers; when the sect was pronounced as heretical in 1305 by Clement V because it believed in holding goods and women in common, thousands of its members fled to the hills between Novara and Vercelli in northwest Italy. Forced by starvation to surrender, many were burned alive, including Fra Dolcino and his companion, Margaret of Trent.

had—with the others—stayed his steps in wonder;
he was the first, before the rest, to open
his windpipe—on the outside, all bloodred—
and said: "O you whom guilt does not condemn,
and whom, unless too close resemblance cheats me,
I've seen above upon Italian soil,
remember Pier da Medicina[8] if
you ever see again the gentle plain
that from Vercelli slopes to Marcabò.
And let the two best men of Fano know—
I mean both Messer Guido and Angiolello—
that, if the foresight we have here's not vain,
they will be cast out of their ship and drowned,
weighed down with stones, near La Cattolica,
because of a foul tyrant's treachery.[9]
Between the isles of Cyprus and Majorca,[1]
Neptune has never seen so cruel a crime
committed by the pirates or the Argives.° *Greeks*
That traitor who sees only with one eye
and rules the land which one who's here with me
would wish his sight had never seen, will call
Guido and Angiolello to a parley,
and then will so arrange it that they'll need
no vow or prayer to Focara's wind!"[2]
And I to him: "If you would have me carry
some news of you above, then tell and show me
who so detests the sight of Rimini."
And then he set his hand upon the jaw
of a companion, opening his mouth
and shouting: "This is he, and he speaks not.
A man cast out, he quenched the doubt in Caesar,
insisting that the one who is prepared
can only suffer harm if he delays."[3]
Oh, how dismayed and pained he seemed to me,
his tongue slit in his gullet: Curio,
who once was so audacious in his talk!
And one who walked with both his hands hacked off,
while lifting up his stumps through the dark air,
so that his face was hideous with blood,

8. Early commentators described Pier da Medicina as a sower of discord in Romagna.
9. In c. 1312 Guido del Cassero and Angiolello di Carignano were thrown overboard by henchmen of Malatestino, lord of Rimini (the "young mastiff" of 27.46, and the "foul tyrant" and "one-eyed traitor" here), as they were on their way at his invitation to a meeting at the small coastal town of La Cattolica. Presumedly, Malatestino planned to seize power in their town.
1. The two ends of the Mediterranean.
2. Focara was a proverbially windy and dangerous headland on the Adriatic between Fano and La Cattolica. Guido and Angiolello no longer need to worry about praying for safe passage.
3. While tribune in Rome in 50 B.C.E., Gaius Curio the younger was bought by Julius Caesar away from the Pompeian party. He fled the city after civil war broke out. Dante follows Lucan (*Pharsalia* 1.279–81) by making Curio responsible for Caesar's decision to cross the Rubicon, the stream separating Italy from Cisalpine Gaul; Roman law forbade a general from leading his army beyond the province he controlled.

cried out: "You will remember Mosca, too,
who said—alas—'What's done is at an end,'
which was the seed of evil for the Tuscans."[4]
I added: "—and brought death to your own kinsmen";
then having heard me speak, grief heaped on grief,
he went his way as one gone mad with sadness.
But I stayed there to watch that company
and saw a thing that I should be afraid
to tell with no more proof than my own self—
except that I am reassured by conscience,
that good companion, heartening a man
beneath the breastplate of its purity.
I surely saw, and it still seems I see,
a trunk without a head that walked just like
the others in that melancholy herd;
it carried by the hair its severed head,
which swayed within its hand just like a lantern;
and that head looked at us and said: "Ah me!"
Out of itself it made itself a lamp,
and they were two in one and one in two;
how that can be, He knows who so decrees.
When it was just below the bridge, it lifted
its arm together with its head, so that
its words might be more near us, words that said:
"Now you can see atrocious punishment,
you who, still breathing, go to view the dead:
see if there's any pain as great as this.
And so that you may carry news of me,
know that I am Bertran de Born, the one
who gave bad counsel to the fledgling king.[5]
I made the son and father enemies:
Achitophel with his malicious urgings
did not do worse with Absalom and David.[6]
Because I severed those so joined, I carry—
alas—my brain dissevered from its source,
which is within my trunk. And thus, in me
one sees the law of counter-penalty."

Canto 29

Still the Eighth Circle, Ninth Pouch: the Sowers of Scandal and Schism. Geri del Bello, an unavenged ancestor of Dante. The Tenth Pouch: the Falsifiers. The First Group, Falsifiers of Metals (Alchemists), plagued by scabs, lying on the earth, scratching furiously. Griffolino. Capocchio.

4. The feuding between the Guelfs and Ghibellines of Florence was viciously renewed in 1215 by the ardent Ghibelline Mosca de' Lamberti.

5. Bertran de Born (c. 1140–c. 1215) was Lord of Hautefort, a soldier and a famous troubadour who specialized in political songs (see page 1186). He was said to have urged Prince Henry of England to rebel against his father, Henry II.

6. Achitophel hanged himself after unsuccessfully encouraging David's son Absalom to rebel against his father (2 Samuel 15–17:23).

So many souls and such outlandish wounds
had made my eyes inebriate—they longed
to stay and weep. But Virgil said to me:
"Why are you staring so insistently?
Why does your vision linger there below
among the lost and mutilated shadows?
You did not do so at the other moats.
If you would count them all, consider: twenty-
two miles make up the circuit of the valley.[1]
The moon already is beneath our feet;
the time alloted to us now is short,[2]
and there is more to see than you see here."
"Had you," I answered him without a pause,
"been able to consider why I looked,
you might have granted me a longer stay."
Meanwhile my guide had moved ahead; I went
behind him, answering as I walked on,
and adding: "In that hollow upon which
just now, I kept my eyes intent, I think
a spirit born of my own blood laments
the guilt which, down below, costs one so much."[3]
At this my master said: "Don't let your thoughts
about him interrupt you from here on:
attend to other things, let him stay there;
for I saw him below the little bridge,
his finger pointing at you, threatening,
and heard him called by name—Geri del Bello.
But at that moment you were occupied
with him who once was lord of Hautefort;° *Bertran de Born*
you did not notice Geri—he moved off."
"My guide, it was his death by violence,
for which he still is not avenged,"[4] I said,
"by anyone who shares his shame, that made
him so disdainful now; and—I suppose—
for this he left without a word to me,
and this has made me pity him the more."
And so we talked until we found the first
point of the ridge that, if there were more light,
would show the other valley to the bottom.
When we had climbed above the final cloister
of Malebolge, so that its lay brothers[5]
were able to appear before our eyes,

1. It is unclear why Dante chose this moment to provide the first exact measurement of any part of Hell.

2. If the moon is below them, the sun must be at its zenith above them, in Jerusalem: it is around 2 P.M. Only four hours remain of the 24 allotted to the journey through Hell.

3. This is Geri del Bello degli Alighieri, first cousin to Dante's father. A troublemaker, Geri was murdered by a member of the Sacchetti family; this was avenged by the Alighieri in 1310, and the families apparently continued feuding until 1342.

4. Family feuding and private vendettas were sanctioned by law in Dante's time; hence, Geri still had just cause for complaint against his family in 1300.

5. The cutting metaphor equates the shades of the tenth *bolgia* to working members of a religious house, the "final cloister" of the eighth circle.

I felt the force of strange laments, like arrows
whose shafts are barbed with pity; and at this,
I had to place my hands across my ears.
Just like the sufferings that all the sick
of Val di Chiana's hospitals, Maremma's,
Sardinia's,° from July until September *malarial regions*
would muster if assembled in one ditch—
so was it here, and such a stench rose up
as usually comes from festering limbs.
And keeping always to the left, we climbed
down to the final bank of the long ridge,
and then my sight could see more vividly
into the bottom, where unerring Justice,
the minister of the High Lord, punishes
the falsifiers she had registered.
I do not think that there was greater grief
in seeing all Aegina's people sick[6]
(then, when the air was so infected that
all animals, down to the little worm,
collapsed; and afterward, as poets hold
to be the certain truth, those ancient peoples
received their health again through seed of ants)
than I felt when I saw, in that dark valley,
the spirits languishing in scattered heaps.
Some lay upon their bellies, some upon
the shoulders of another spirit, some
crawled on all fours along that squalid road.
We journeyed step by step without a word,
watching and listening to those sick souls,
who had not strength enough to lift themselves.
I saw two sitting propped against each other—
as pan is propped on pan to heat them up—
and each, from head to foot, spotted with scabs;
and I have never seen a stableboy
whose master waits for him, or one who stays
awake reluctantly, so ply a horse
with currycomb, as they assailed themselves
with clawing nails—their itching had such force
and fury, and there was no other help.
And so their nails kept scraping off the scabs,
just as a knife scrapes off the scales of carp
or of another fish with scales more large.
"O you who use your nails to strip yourself,"
my guide began to say to one of them,
"and sometimes have to turn them into pincers,

6. When Jupiter carried off the nymph Aegina to the island of Oenone, their son Aeacus aroused Juno's jealousy by renaming the island after his mother. After Juno sent a devastating pestilence as punishment, Jupiter restored the island by changing its ants into men, called "Myrmidons" after the Greek word for ant (*Metamorphoses* 7.523–657).

tell us if there are some Italians
among the sinners in this moat—so may
your nails hold out, eternal, at their work."

"We two whom you see so disfigured here,
we are Italians," one said, in tears.
"But who are you who have inquired of us?"

My guide replied: "From circle down to circle,
together with this living man, I am
one who descends; I mean to show him Hell."

At this their mutual support broke off;
and, quivering, each spirit turned toward me
with others who, by chance, had heard his words.

Then my good master drew more close to me,
saying: "Now tell them what it is you want."
And I began to speak, just as he wished:

"So that your memory may never fade
within the first world from the minds of men,
but still live on—and under many suns—

do tell me who you are and from what city,
and do not let your vile and filthy torment
make you afraid to let me know your names."

One answered me: "My city was Arezzo
and Albero of Siena had me burned;
but what I died for does not bring me here.[7]

It's true that I had told him—jestingly—
'I'd know enough to fly through air'; and he,
with curiosity, but little sense,

wished me to show that art to him and, just
because I had not made him Daedalus,
had one who held him as a son burn me.

But Minos, who cannot mistake, condemned
my spirit to the final pouch of ten
for alchemy I practiced in the world."

And then I asked the poet: "Was there ever
so vain a people as the Sienese?
Even the French can't match such vanity."[8]

At this, the other leper, who had heard me,
replied to what I'd said: "Except for Stricca,
for he knew how to spend most frugally;

and Niccolò, the first to make men see
that cloves can serve as luxury (such seed,
in gardens where it suits, can take fast root);

and, too, Caccia d'Asciano's company,
with whom he squandered vineyards and tilled fields,

7. Griffolino was an alchemist of Arezzo who promised he could teach Albero of Siena flying, the art of Daedalus (see 17.109–11). Angry at having been fleeced, Albero denounced Griffolino as a magician, and had him burned at the stake.

8. The vanity of the French was proverbial; the young Sienese noblemen listed below all belonged to a group called the "Spendthrift Club" and revelled in squandering their estates.

while Abbagliato showed such subtlety.
But if you want to know who joins you so
against the Sienese, look hard at me—
that way, my face can also answer rightly—
and see that I'm the shade of that Capocchio
whose alchemy could counterfeit fine metals.
And you, if I correctly take your measure,
recall how apt I was at aping nature."[9]

Canto 30

Still the Eighth Circle, Tenth Pouch: the Falsifiers. Gianni Schicchi and Myrrha in the Second Group, Counterfeiters of Others' Persons. Master Adam in the Third Group, Counterfeiters of Coins. Potiphar's wife and Sinon the Greek in the Fourth Group, Falsifiers of Words, Liars. The quarrel between Adam and Sinon.

When Juno was incensed with Semele
and, thus, against the Theban family
had shown her fury time and time again,
then Athamas was driven so insane
that, seeing both his wife and their two sons,
as she bore one upon each arm, he cried:
"Let's spread the nets, to take the lioness
together with her cubs along the pass";
and he stretched out his talons, pitiless,
and snatched the son who bore the name Learchus,
whirled him around and dashed him on a rock;
she, with her other burden, drowned herself.[1]
And after fortune turned against the pride
of Troy, which had dared all, so that the king
together with his kingdom, was destroyed,
then Hecuba was wretched, sad, a captive;
and after she had seen Polyxena
dead and, in misery, had recognized
her Polydorus lying on the shore,[2]
she barked, out of her senses, like a dog—
her agony had so deformed her mind.
But neither fury—Theban, Trojan—ever
was seen to be so cruel against another,
in rending beasts and even human limbs,
as were two shades I saw, both pale and naked,
who, biting, ran berserk in just the way
a hog does when it's let loose from its sty.

9. Capocchio was burned alive in 1293 in Siena as an alchemist; apparently, he was acquainted with the young Dante. Because it attempts to create gold out of baser metals, alchemy imitates or "apes" the work of nature.

1. The Theban princess Semele was loved by Jupiter and she bore him the god Bacchus. As part of her vengeance, Jupiter's wife Juno caused Semele's brother-in-law, the king of Thebes, to believe his wife and two sons were a lioness and cubs; after he killed one son, his wife drowned herself with the other (*Metamorphoses* 4.512–30).

2. Priam's queen, Hecuba, went mad after the fall of Troy following the killing of her daughter and son. According to Ovid, on seeing her son's unburied body Hecuba howled like a dog and jumped into the sea (*Metamorphoses* 13.404–575).

The one came at Capocchio and sank
his tusks into his neck so that, by dragging,
he made the hard ground scrape against his belly.
And he who stayed behind, the Aretine,
trembled and said: "That phantom's Gianni Schicchi,
and he goes raging, rending others so."[3]
And, "Oh," I said to him, "so may the other
not sink its teeth in you, please tell me who
it is before it hurries off from here."
And he to me: "That is the ancient soul
of the indecent Myrrha, she who loved
her father past the limits of just love.[4]
She came to sin with him by falsely taking
another's shape upon herself, just as
the other phantom who goes there had done,
that he might gain the lady of the herd,
when he disguised himself as Buoso Donati,
making a will as if most properly."
And when the pair of raging ones had passed,
those two on whom my eyes were fixed, I turned
around to see the rest of the ill-born.
I saw one who'd be fashioned like a lute
if he had only had his groin cut off
from that part of his body where it forks.
The heavy dropsy, which so disproportions
the limbs with unassimilated humors
that there's no match between the face and belly,
had made him part his lips like a consumptive,
who will, because of thirst, let one lip drop
down to his chin and lift the other up.[5]
"O you exempt from every punishment
in this grim world, and I do not know why,"
he said to us, "look now and pay attention
to this, the misery of Master Adam:
alive, I had enough of all I wanted;
alas, I now long for one drop of water.[6]
The rivulets that fall into the Arno
down from the green hills of the Casentino
with channels cool and moist, are constantly
before me; I am racked by memory—

3. The "Aretine" is Griffolino from the previous canto. Gianni Chichi (d. 1280) was a Florentine of the Cavalcanti family well known for his skill at mimicry. In one reported incident, he impersonated Buoso Donati at the request of Simone Donati, in order to dictate a new will in Simone's favor that included Buoso's mule, the best in Tuscany.

4. Myrrha conceived a passion for her father Cinyras, king of Cyprus. With the aid of her nurse, she entered her father's bedchamber in disguise and slept with him.

5. Dropsy, or edema, is an abnormal accumulation of watery fluid ("humors") in the body. A "consumptive" here is someone suffering from hectic fever, a wasting disease characterized by hot, dry skin and flushed cheeks.

6. Master Adam counterfeited the gold florin of Florence. Like the florin, his coins bore the seal of John the Baptist, but they were of 21 rather than 24 carats. In 1281 he suffered the penalty of counterfeiters: burned at the stake.

the image of their flow parches me more
than the disease that robs my face of flesh.
The rigid Justice that would torment me
uses, as most appropriate, the place
where I had sinned, to draw swift sighs from me.
There is Romena, there I counterfeited
the currency that bears the Baptist's seal;
for this I left my body, burned, above.
But could I see the miserable souls
of Guido, Alessandro, or their brother,
I'd not give up the sight for Fonte Branda.[7]
And one of them is in this moat already,
if what the angry shades report is true.
What use is that to me whose limbs are tied?
Were I so light that, in a hundred years,
I could advance an inch, I should already
be well upon the road to search for him
among the mutilated ones, although
this circuit measures some eleven miles
and is at least a half a mile across.
Because of them I'm in this family;
it was those three who had incited me
to coin the florins with three carats' dross."
And I to him: "Who are those two poor sinners
who give off smoke like wet hands in the winter
and lie so close to you upon the right?"
"I found them here," he answered, "when I rained
down to this rocky slope; they've not stirred since
and will not move, I think, eternally.
One is the lying woman who blamed Joseph;
the other, lying Sinon, Greek from Troy:[8]
because of raging fever they reek so."
And one of them, who seemed to take offense,
perhaps at being named so squalidly,
struck with his fist at Adam's rigid belly.
It sounded as if it had been a drum;
and Master Adam struck him in the face,
using his arm, which did not seem less hard,
saying to him: "Although I cannot move
my limbs because they are too heavy, I
still have an arm that's free to serve that need."
And he replied: "But when you went to burning,
your arm was not as quick as it was now;

7. Adam names three of the Conti Guidi family, who instigated his counterfeiting, including Guido II da Romena, who died before 1300. The Fonte Branda is perhaps a now almost dry fountain near the castle of Romena.

8. After Joseph rejected the advances of Potiphar's wife, she accused him of attempting to seduce her (Genesis 39:6–20). Sinon was a treacherous Greek who allowed himself to be captured by the Trojans, persuading them to take within their walls the wooden horse the Greeks had left (and hidden inside) (*Aeneid* 2.18–370).

though when you coined, it was as quick and more."
To which the dropsied one: "Here you speak true;
but you were not so true a witness there,
when you were asked to tell the truth at Troy."
"If I spoke false, you falsified the coin,"
said Sinon; "I am here for just one crime—
but you've committed more than any demon."
"Do not forget the horse, you perjurer,"
replied the one who had the bloated belly,
"may you be plagued because the whole world knows it."
The Greek: "And you be plagued by thirst that cracks
your tongue, and putrid water that has made
your belly such a hedge before your eyes."
And then the coiner: "So, as usual,
your mouth, because of racking fever, gapes;
for if I thirst and if my humor bloats me,
you have both dryness and a head that aches;
few words would be sufficient invitation
to have you lick the mirror of Narcissus."[9]
I was intent on listening to them
when this was what my master said: "If you
insist on looking more, I'll quarrel with you!"
And when I heard him speak so angrily,
I turned around to him with shame so great
that it still stirs within my memory.
Even as one who dreams that he is harmed
and, dreaming, wishes he were dreaming, thus
desiring that which is, as if it were not,
so I became within my speechlessness:
I wanted to excuse myself and did
excuse myself, although I knew it not.
"Less shame would wash away a greater fault
than was your fault," my master said to me;
"therefore release yourself from all remorse
and see that I am always at your side,
should it so happen—once again—that fortune
brings you where men would quarrel in this fashion:
to want to hear such bickering is base."

Canto 31

Passage to the Ninth Circle. The central pit or well of Hell, where Cocytus, the last river of Hell, freezes. The Giants: Nimrod, Ephialtes, Briareus, Antaeus. Antaeus's compliance with Virgil's request to lower the two poets into the pit.

9. When the nymph Echo's love for the youth Narcissus was unrequited, she pined away until all that was left was her voice. In punishment, he was made to fall in love with his own reflection in a fountain, pining away as well, until he was transformed into a flower (*Metamorphoses* 3.351–510). To "lick" his mirror thus means to drink.

The very tongue that first had wounded me,
sending the color up in both my cheeks,
was then to cure me with its medicine—
as did Achilles' and his father's lance,
even as I have heard, when it dispensed
a sad stroke first and then a healing one.[1]
We turned our backs upon that dismal valley
by climbing up the bank that girdles it;
we made our way across without a word.
Here it was less than night and less than day,
so that my sight could only move ahead
slightly, but then I heard a bugle blast
so strong, it would have made a thunder clap
seem faint; at this, my eyes—which doubled back
upon their path—turned fully toward one place.
Not even Roland's horn, which followed on
the sad defeat when Charlemagne had lost
his holy army, was as dread as this.[2]
I'd only turned my head there briefly when
I seemed to make out many high towers; then
I asked him: "Master, tell me, what's this city?"
And he to me: "It is because you try
to penetrate from far into these shadows
that you have formed such faulty images.
When you have reached that place, you shall see clearly
how much the distance has deceived your sense;
and, therefore, let this spur you on your way."
Then lovingly he took me by the hand
and said: "Before we have moved farther on,
so that the fact may seem less strange to you,
I'd have you know they are not towers, but giants,
and from the navel downward, all of them
are in the central pit, at the embankment."
Just as, whenever mists begin to thin,
when, gradually, vision finds the form
that in the vapor-thickened air was hidden,
so I pierced through the dense and darkened fog;
as I drew always nearer to the shore,
my error fled from me, my terror grew;
for as, on its round wall, Montereggioni° *a hill fortress*
is crowned with towers, so there towered here,
above the bank that runs around the pit,

1. Achilles' father Peleus gave him a spear that by its mere touch could cure any wound it had caused (*Metamorphoses* 13.171–2). Medieval poets often used the image to describe the lady's love, which could be healed only by opening a new wound in her lover.

2. A first image of the ninth circle's sin of treachery. In the medieval epic, *The Song of Roland,* after the hero Roland, leader of Charlemagne's rear-guard, has had his forces betrayed to and annihilated by the Saracens at Roncesvalles, he sounds his famous horn so loudly that the emperor returns to avenge his death.

with half their bulk, the terrifying giants,
whom Jove still menaces from Heaven when
he sends his bolts of thunder down upon them.
And I could now make out the face of one,
his shoulders and his chest, much of his belly,
and both his arms that hung along his sides.
Surely when she gave up the art of making
such creatures, Nature acted well indeed,
depriving Mars of instruments like these.[3]
And if she still produces elephants
and whales, whoever sees with subtlety
holds her—for this—to be more just and prudent;
for where the mind's acutest reasoning
is joined to evil will and evil power,
there human beings can't defend themselves.[4]
His face appeared to me as broad and long
as Rome can claim for its St. Peter's pine cone;[5]
his other bones shared in that same proportion;
so that the bank, which served him as an apron
down from his middle, showed so much of him
above, that three Frieslanders would in vain
have boasted of their reaching to his hair;
for downward from the place where one would buckle
a mantle, I saw thirty spans of him.[6]
"Raphèl maì amècche zabì almi,"
began to bellow that brute mouth, for which
no sweeter psalms would be appropriate.[7]
And my guide turned to him: "O stupid soul,
keep to your horn and use that as an outlet
when rage or other passion touches you![8]
Look at your neck, and you will find the strap
that holds it fast; and see, bewildered spirit,
how it lies straight across your massive chest."
And then to me: "He is his own accuser;
for this is Nimrod, through whose wicked thought
one single language cannot serve the world.
Leave him alone—let's not waste time in talk;
for every language is to him the same
as his to others—no one knows his tongue."
So, turning to the left, we journeyed on

3. Dante equates the Giants of Greek myth with those of the Bible, "expert in war" (Baruch 3:26–28).
4. According to Aquinas, "An evil man can do ten thousand times more harm than a beast by his reason which he can use to devise very diverse evils."
5. This bronze pine cone, over twelve feet high, was said to have stood near the Campus Martius in Rome; it was moved to the old basilica of St. Peter's.
6. The inhabitants of Friesland on the North Sea were known for their great height; the giant's top half is about thirty-five feet.
7. The giant is Nimrod, biblical ruler of Babylon, under whose direction the Tower of Babel was attempted (Genesis 10–11). His incomprehensible words, which no commentator has deciphered, are an apt retribution for his role in causing the confusion of the world's tongues.
8. The hunter's horn derives from the biblical description of Nimrod as a "mighty hunter before the Lord" (Genesis 10:9).

and, at the distance of a bow-shot, found
another giant, far more huge and fierce.
Who was the master who had tied him so,
I cannot say, but his left arm was bent
behind him and his right was bent in front,
both pinioned by a chain that held him tight
down from the neck; and round the part of him
that was exposed, it had been wound five times.
"This giant in his arrogance had tested
his force against the force of highest Jove,"
my guide said, "so he merits this reward.
His name is Ephialtes;[9] and he showed
tremendous power when the giants frightened
the gods; the arms he moved now move no more."
And I to him: "If it is possible,
I'd like my eyes to have experience
of the enormous one, Briareus."
At which he answered: "You shall see Antaeus[1]
nearby. He is unfettered and can speak;
he'll take us to the bottom of all evil.
The one you wish to see lies far beyond
and is bound up and just as huge as this one,
and even more ferocious in his gaze."
No earthquake ever was so violent
when called to shake a tower so robust,
as Ephialtes quick to shake himself.
Then I was more afraid of death than ever;
that fear would have been quite enough to kill me,
had I not seen how he was held by chains.
And we continued on until we reached
Antaeus, who, not reckoning his head,
stood out above the rock wall full five ells.° *fifteen feet*
"O you, who lived within the famous valley
(where Scipio became the heir of glory
when Hannibal retreated with his men),[2]
who took a thousand lions as your prey—
and had you been together with your brothers
in their high war, it seems some still believe
the sons of earth would have become the victors—
do set us down below, where cold shuts in
Cocytus,[3] and do not disdain that task.

9. Son of Neptune; with his brother Otus, he stormed Olympus itself. Virgil placed them both in Tartarus (*Aeneid* 6.771–74).

1. The hundred-handed and fifty-headed giant Briareus joined the attack of his race against the gods; Jupiter slew him with a thunderbolt and buried him under Mt. Etna. Unlike the enchained giants here, Antaeus was born after the war against the gods. Son of Neptune and Earth, he was invincible while in contact with his mother. He lived in Libya and was said to feed on wild lions. Hercules slew him when he managed to lift Antaeus off the ground and crush him (*Pharsalia* 4.585–660).

2. The valley of the Bagradas River in north-central Tunisia was site of Scipio's decisive victory over Hannibal's forces in 202 B.C.E. during the Second Punic War between Rome and Carthage.

3. The frozen lake that covers the ninth circle at the bottom of Hell.

Don't send us on to Tityus or Typhon;[4]
this man can give you what is longed for here;
therefore bend down and do not curl your lip.
He still can bring you fame within the world,
for he's alive and still expects long life,
unless grace summon him before his time."
So said my master; and in haste Antaeus
stretched out his hands, whose massive grip had once
been felt by Hercules, and grasped my guide.
And Virgil, when he felt himself caught up,
called out to me: "Come here, so I can hold you,"
then made one bundle of himself and me.
Just as the Garisenda seems when seen
beneath the leaning side, when clouds run past
and it hangs down as if about to crash,[5]
so did Antaeus seem to me as I
watched him bend over me—a moment when
I'd have preferred to take some other road.
But gently—on the deep that swallows up
both Lucifer and Judas—he placed us;
nor did he, so bent over, stay there long,
but, like a mast above a ship, he rose.

Canto 32

The Ninth Circle, First Ring, called Caïna, where Traitors to their Kin are immersed in the ice, heads bent down. Camiscione dei Pazzi. The Second Ring, called Antenora: the Traitors to their Homeland or Party. Bocca degli Abati's provocation of Dante. Two traitors, one gnawing at the other's head.

Had I the crude and scrannel° rhymes to suit *harsh*
the melancholy hole upon which all
the other circling crags converge and rest,
the juice of my conception would be pressed
more fully; but because I feel their lack,
I bring myself to speak, yet speak in fear;
for it is not a task to take in jest,
to show the base of all the universe—
nor for a tongue that cries out, "mama," "papa."
But may those ladies now sustain my verse
who helped Amphion when he walled up Thebes,
so that my tale not differ from the fact.[1]
O rabble, miscreated past all others,
there in the place of which it's hard to speak,

4. Two more giants: Tityus was thrown into Tartarus by Apollo and Diana for his attempted rape of their mother Latona; Typhon, incited by his mother, Earth, to attack the Olympian gods, was defeated by Jupiter.

5. One of the leaning towers of Bologna, Garisenda was built in 1110; a cloud passing opposite the direction of the slant gives the illusion of the tower falling out of the sky.

1. The Muses ("ladies") inspired the singer Amphion to charm the stones of Mt. Cithaeron with his lyre into arranging themselves as walls around Thebes (Horace, *Ars Poetica* 394–96; *Thebaid* 10.873–77). The invocation of the Muses marks a new beginning of the poem, and a mixed style of language and diction.

better if here you had been goats or sheep!
When we were down below in the dark well,
beneath the giant's feet and lower yet,
with my eyes still upon the steep embankment,
I heard this said to me: "Watch how you pass;
walk so that you not trample with your soles
the heads of your exhausted, wretched brothers."
At this I turned and saw in front of me,
beneath my feet, a lake that, frozen fast,
had lost the look of water and seemed glass.
The Danube where it flows in Austria,
the Don beneath its frozen sky,° have never *in Russia*
made for their course so thick a veil in winter
as there was here; for had Mount Tambernic
or Pietrapana's mountain° crashed upon it, *Italian alps*
not even at the edge would it have creaked.
And as the croaking frog sits with its muzzle
above the water, in the season when
the peasant woman often dreams of gleaning,
so, livid in the ice, up to the place
where shame can show itself, were those sad shades,
whose teeth were chattering with notes like storks'.
Each kept his face bent downward steadily;
their mouths bore witness to the cold they felt,
just as their eyes proclaimed their sorry hearts.
When I had looked around a while, my eyes
turned toward my feet and saw two locked so close,
the hair upon their heads had intermingled.
"Do tell me, you whose chests are pressed so tight,"
I said, "who are you?" They bent back their necks,
and when they'd lifted up their faces toward me,
their eyes, which wept upon the ground before,
shed tears down on their lips until the cold
held fast the tears and locked their lids still more.
No clamp has ever fastened plank to plank
so tightly; and because of this, they butted
each other like two rams, such was their fury.
And one from whom the cold had taken both
his ears, who kept his face bent low, then said:
"Why do you keep on staring so at us?
If you would like to know who these two are:
that valley where Bisenzio descends,
belonged to them and to their father Alberto.[2]
They came out of one body; and you can
search all Caïna,[3] you will never find

2. The Conti Alberti had two castles in this region west of Florence. The Guelf Alessandro and the Ghibelline Napoleone were sons of Alberto degli Alberti; they killed each other quarreling over the inheritance of the Castle of Mangano.

3. Caïna, the first of the four subdivisions of Cocytus, is named after Cain, the first man to betray and kill a kinsman, his brother Abel (Genesis 4).

a shade more fit to sit within this ice—
not him who, at one blow, had chest and shadow
shattered by Arthur's hand;[4] and not Focaccia;
and not this sinner here who so impedes
my vision with his head, I can't see past him;
his name was Sassol Mascheroni; if
you're Tuscan, now you know who he has been.[5]
And lest you keep me talking any longer,
know that I was Camiscion de' Pazzi;
I'm waiting for Carlino to absolve me."[6]
And after that I saw a thousand faces
made doglike by the cold; for which I shudder—
and always will—when I face frozen fords.[7]
And while we were advancing toward the center
to which all weight is drawn—I, shivering
in that eternally cold shadow—I
know not if it was will or destiny
or chance, but as I walked among the heads,
I struck my foot hard in the face of one.
Weeping, he chided then: "Why trample me?
If you've not come to add to the revenge
of Montaperti, why do you molest me?"[8]
And I: "My master, now wait here for me,
that I may clear up just one doubt about him;
then you can make me hurry as you will."
My guide stood fast, and I went on to ask
of him who still was cursing bitterly:
"Who are you that rebukes another so?"
"And who are you who go through Antenora,
striking the cheeks of others," he replied,
"too roughly—even if you were alive?"
"I am alive, and can be precious to you
if you want fame," was my reply, "for I
can set your name among my other notes."
And he to me: "I want the contrary;
so go away and do not harass me—
your flattery is useless in this valley."
At that I grabbed him by the scruff and said:
"You'll have to name yourself to me or else
you won't have even one hair left up here."

4. Modred, the traitorous nephew of King Arthur, slew his uncle; when Arthur pierced Mordred with a spear in return, a ray of sunlight passed through the wound.
5. Foccaccia was the nickname of the White Guelf Vanni de' Cancellieri of Pistoia, guilty of murdering a cousin in 1293. Sassol Mascheroni was a Florentine who murdered a kinsman for the sake of his inheritance.
6. The Ghibelline Camiscion de' Pazzi of the Val d'Arno treacherously killed his kinsman Ubertino. In 1302, his kinsman Carlino would betray the Florentine Whites and Ghibellines in the Castle of Piantravigne to the Blacks. As a traitor against his party, Carlino will "absolve" Camiscion by going to the next, worse ring of Cocytus, where those who betrayed party, country, or city are punished.
7. A subtle transition to the second ring, where the souls hold their heads erect rather than being able to shelter their eyes from the cold. The ring is named Antenora after the Trojan warrior Antenor, who was believed to have betrayed his city to the Greeks.
8. Bocca degli Abati, a Florentine Guelf who betrayed his party at the battle of Montaperti in 1260 when he cut off the hand of the Florentine standard-bearer at the crucial moment of the charge of Manfred's German cavalry.

And he to me: "Though you should strip me bald,
I shall not tell you who I am or show it,
not if you pound my head a thousand times."
His hairs were wound around my hand already,
and I had plucked from him more than one tuft
while he was barking and his eyes stared down,
when someone else cried out: "What is it, Bocca?
Isn't the music of your jaws enough
for you without your bark? What devil's at you?"
"And now," I said, "you traitor bent on evil,
I do not need your talk, for I shall carry
true news of you, and that will bring you shame."
"Be off," he answered; "tell them what you like,
but don't be silent, if you make it back,
about the one whose tongue was now so quick.
Here he laments the silver of the Frenchmen;
'I saw,' you then can say, 'him of Duera,
down there, where all the sinners are kept cool.'[9]
And if you're asked who else was there in ice,
one of the Beccheria is beside you—
he had his gullet sliced right through by Florence.
Gianni de' Soldanieri, I believe,
lies there with Ganelon and Tebaldello,
he who unlocked Faenza while it slept."[1]
We had already taken leave of him,
when I saw two shades frozen in one hole,
so that one's head served as the other's cap;
and just as he who's hungry chews his bread,
one sinner dug his teeth into the other
right at the place where brain is joined to nape:
no differently had Tydeus gnawed the temples
of Menalippus, out of indignation,[2]
than this one chewed the skull and other parts.
"O you who show, with such a bestial sign,
your hatred for the one on whom you feed,
tell me the cause," I said; "we can agree
that if your quarrel with him is justified,
then knowing who you are and what's his sin,
I shall repay you yet on earth above,
if that with which I speak does not dry up."

9. In 1265, the Ghibelline leader of Cremona, Buoso da Duera, betrayed Manfred, King of Naples, when he was bribed to allow the French troops to pass through Lombardy unmolested.

1. Tesauro de' Beccheria of Pavia, Abbot of Vallombrosa, was seized and beheaded in 1258 by the Florentine Guelfs on the charge of intriguing with the Ghibellines. Gianni de' Soldanieri was a Florentine Ghibelline who opposed his own party when the populace rose up against it following the defeat and death of Manfred at Benevento in 1266. Tebaldello opened the gates of his city to Guelf enemies in order to avenge a private grudge. As recorded in *The Song of Roland,* Ganelon betrayed the rearguard of Charlemagne at Roncesvalles; his name became synonymous with treachery.

2. King Tydeus was one of the Seven against Thebes. When mortally wounded by Menalippus, whom he slayed in return, the enraged Tydeus gnawed through his enemy's skull and ate part of his brain (*Thebaid* 8.739–62).

Canto 33

Still the Ninth Circle, Second Ring. Ugolino's tale of his and his sons' death in a Pisan prison. Dante's invective against Pisa. The Third Ring, Ptolomea, where Traitors against their Guests jut out from ice, their eyes sealed by frozen tears. Fra Alberigo and Branca Doria, still alive on earth but already in Hell.

That sinner raised his mouth from his fierce meal,
then used the head that he had ripped apart
in back: he wiped his lips upon its hair.
Then he began: "You want me to renew
despairing pain that presses at my heart
even as I think back, before I speak.
But if my words are seed from which the fruit
is infamy for this betrayer whom
I gnaw, you'll see me speak and weep at once.[1]
I don't know who you are or in what way
you've come down here; and yet you surely seem—
from what I hear—to be a Florentine.
You are to know I was Count Ugolino,
and this one here, Archbishop Ruggieri;
and now I'll tell you why I am his neighbor.[2]
There is no need to tell you that, because
of his malicious tricks, I first was taken
and then was killed—since I had trusted him;
however, that which you cannot have heard—
that is, the cruel death devised for me—
you now shall hear and know if he has wronged me.
A narrow window in the Eagles' Tower,
which now, through me, is called the Hunger Tower,
a cage in which still others will be locked,[3]
had, through its opening, already showed me
several moons, when I dreamed that bad dream
which rent the curtain of the future for me.[4]
This man appeared to me as lord and master;
he hunted down the wolf and its young whelps
upon the mountain that prevents the Pisans

1. Several phrases in this speech of Ugolino recall those of Francesca in Canto 5.

2. Count Ugolino della Gherardesca was banished from the traditionally Ghibelline city of Pisa for conspiring with the Guelf leader Giovanni Visconti in 1275, but returned to wealth and position the following year. Following a defeat by Genoa (which he was suspected of abetting) Ugolino was made magistrate of Pisa in 1284. He ceded three castles to Florence and Lucca to assuage the Guelf threat, which his enemies regarded as a betrayal. The following year, Ugolino feuded with his Guelf grandson, Nino Visconti, son of Giovanni, with whom he was sharing the magistracy. The Ghibelline Ruggieri degli Ubaldini was archbishop of Pisa, and magistrate in place of Ugolino in 1288. Ugolino apparently intrigued with Ruggiero against Nino but was betrayed by the archbishop and his Ghibelline allies, who invited the count back into the city only to lock him up with two of his sons (Gaddo and Uguiccone) and two grandsons (Anselm and a different Nino, nicknamed "Brigata") in the Tower of Gualandi, where they eventually were starved to death. Pisa was now controlled by the Ghibellines, with Guido da Montefeltro (see Canto 27) soon to be made their magistrate.

3. The Tower of Gualandi served as a prison until 1318. According to early commentators, moulting eagles were kept in its Mew, or tower, which became known after Ugolino's death as the Torre della Fame ("Tower of Hunger").

4. In the dream, Ruggieri ("lord and master") hunts down Ugolino and his children on Mt. San Giuliano, between Pisa and Lucca (where the count had political connections). The dogs likely represent the populace roused against Ugolino by Ruggieri; the Gualandi, Sismondi and Lanfranchi were prominent Ghibelline families of Pisa who joined the archbishop.

from seeing Lucca; and with lean and keen
and practiced hounds, he'd sent up front, before him,
Gualandi and Sismondi and Lanfranchi.
But after a brief course, it seemed to me
that both the father and the sons were weary;
I seemed to see their flanks torn by sharp fangs.
When I awoke at daybreak, I could hear
my sons, who were together with me there,
weeping within their sleep, asking for bread.
You would be cruel indeed if, thinking what
my heart foresaw, you don't already grieve;
and if you don't weep now, when would you weep?
They were awake by now; the hour drew near
at which our food was usually brought,
and each, because of what he'd dreamed, was anxious;
below, I heard them nailing up the door
of that appalling tower; without a word,
I looked into the faces of my sons.
I did not weep; within, I turned to stone.
They wept; and my poor little Anselm said:
'Father, you look so . . . What is wrong with you?'
At that I shed no tears and—all day long
and through the night that followed—did not answer
until another sun had touched the world.
As soon as a thin ray had made its way
into that sorry prison, and I saw,
reflected in four faces, my own gaze,
out of my grief, I bit at both my hands;
and they, who thought I'd done that out of hunger,
immediately rose and told me: 'Father,
it would be far less painful for us if
you ate of us; for you clothed us in this
sad flesh—it is for you to strip it off.'
Then I grew calm, to keep them from more sadness;
through that day and the next, we all were silent;
O hard earth, why did you not open up?
But after we had reached the fourth day, Gaddo,
throwing himself, outstretched, down at my feet,
implored me: 'Father, why do you not help me?'
And there he died; and just as you see me,
I saw the other three fall one by one
between the fifth day and the sixth; at which,
now blind, I started groping over each;
and after they were dead, I called them for
two days; then fasting had more force than grief."[5]
When he had spoken this, with eyes awry,

5. This line suggests that Ugolino resorted to cannibalism. Given the allusions to Christ on the cross in line 69 (Matthew 27:46), there is probably a religious overtone as well: Ugolino does not provide his children with spiritual any more than with earthly bread, consuming their hope of salvation.

again he gripped the sad skull in his teeth,
which, like a dog's, were strong down to the bone.
Ah, Pisa, you the scandal of the peoples
of that fair land where *si* is heard,° because *Italy*
your neighbors are so slow to punish you,
may, then, Caprara and Gorgona° move *Mediterranean islands*
and build a hedge across the Arno's mouth,
so that it may drown every soul in you!
For if Count Ugolino was reputed
to have betrayed your fortresses, there was
no need to have his sons endure such torment.
O Thebes renewed,[6] their years were innocent
and young—Brigata, Uguiccione, and
the other two my song has named above!
We passed beyond, where frozen water wraps—
a rugged covering—still other sinners,
who were not bent, but flat upon their backs.
Their very weeping there won't let them weep,
and grief that finds a barrier in their eyes
turns inward to increase their agony;
because their first tears freeze into a cluster,
and, like a crystal visor, fill up all
the hollow that is underneath the eyebrow.
And though, because of cold, my every sense
had left its dwelling in my face, just as
a callus has no feeling, nonetheless,
I seemed to feel some wind now, and I said:
"My master, who has set this gust in motion?
For isn't every vapor quenched down here?"[7]
And he to me: "You soon shall be where your
own eye will answer that, when you shall see
the reason why this wind blasts from above."
And one of those sad sinners in the cold
crust, cried to us: "O souls who are so cruel
that this last place has been assigned to you,
take off the hard veils from my face so that
I can release the suffering that fills
my heart before lament freezes again."
To which I answered: "If you'd have me help you,
then tell me who you are; if I don't free you,
may I go to the bottom of the ice."[8]
He answered then: "I am Fra Alberigo,
the one who tended fruits in a bad garden,
and here my figs have been repaid with dates."[9]

6. The ancient city of Thebes was notorious for crime and bloodshed.
7. The cause of wind was thought to be the heat of the sun.
8. A deceptive promise, since he is in fact headed to the "bottom of the ice."
9. Like Catalano and Loderingo (23.103–9), Alberigo was a member of the order of the Jovial Friars; like Tebaldello (32.122), he belonged to the Guelf Manfredi family of Faenza. Alberigo had two of his relatives killed at a banquet at his house in supposed reconciliation. The signal to the assassins was his order at the end of dinner to bring the fruit. He believes his punishment overly severe, as a fig is worth less than a date.

"But then," I said, "are you already dead?"
And he to me: "I have no knowledge of
my body's fate within the world above.
For Ptolomea has this privilege:
quite frequently the soul falls here before
it has been thrust away by Atropos.[1]
And that you may with much more willingness
scrape these glazed tears from off my face, know this:
as soon as any soul becomes a traitor,
as I was, then a demon takes its body
away—and keeps that body in his power
until its years have run their course completely.
The soul falls headlong, down into this cistern;
and up above, perhaps, there still appears
the body of the shade that winters here
behind me; you must know him, if you've just
come down; he is Ser Branca Doria;[2]
for many years he has been thus pent up."
I said to him: "I think that you deceive me,
for Branca Doria is not yet dead;
he eats and drinks and sleeps and puts on clothes."
"There in the Malebranche's ditch above,
where sticky pitch boils up, Michele Zanche
had still not come," he said to me, "when this one—
together with a kinsman, who had done
the treachery together with him—left
a devil in his stead inside his body.
But now reach out your hand; open my eyes."
And yet I did not open them for him;
and it was courtesy to show him rudeness.
Ah, Genoese, a people strange to every
constraint of custom, full of all corruption,
why have you not been driven from the world?
For with the foulest spirit of Romagna,
I found one of you such that, for his acts,[3]
in soul he bathes already in Cocytus
and up above appears alive, in body.

Canto 34

The Ninth Circle, Fourth Ring, called Judecca, where Traitors against their Benefactors are fully covered by ice. Dis, or Lucifer, emperor of that kingdom, his three

1. Ptolomea, where betrayers of guests and friends are punished, may be named for the Egyptian king Ptolemy XII (51–47 B.C.E.), murderer of Pompey (*Pharsalia* 8.536–712), or for a governor of Jericho who murdered his father-in-law, the high priest Simon the Maccabee, and two of his sons at a banquet in their honor in 134 B.C.E. (1 Maccabees 16:11–17). Ptolomea is apparently unique among the parts of Hell in that souls can be condemned to it before they are actually dead. (Atropos was the one of the three Fates responsible for cutting the thread of an individual's life.) The idea is perhaps the most extreme of the many heterodoxies included by Dante in his conception of the afterlife.

2. A Ghibelline of a famous Genoese family who murdered his father-in-law Michel Zanche at a banquet with the aid of another relation.

3. The "foulest spirit of Romagna" is Alberigo; the "Genoese" is Branca Doria.

mouths rending Judas, Brutus, and Cassius. Descent of Virgil and Dante down Lucifer's body to the other, southern hemisphere. Their vision of the stars.

"*Vexilla regis prodeunt inferni*[1]
toward us; and therefore keep your eyes ahead,"
my master said, "to see if you can spy him."
Just as, when night falls on our hemisphere
or when a heavy fog is blowing thick,
a windmill seems to wheel when seen far off,
so then I seemed to see that sort of structure.
And next, because the wind was strong, I shrank
behind my guide; there was no other shelter.
And now—with fear I set it down in meter—
I was where all the shades were fully covered
but visible as wisps of straw in glass.
There some lie flat and others stand erect,
one on his head, and one upon his soles;
and some bend face to feet, just like a bow.
But after we had made our way ahead,
my master felt he now should have me see
that creature who was once a handsome presence;[2]
he stepped aside and made me stop, and said:
"Look! Here is Dis, and this the place where you
will have to arm yourself with fortitude."
O reader, do not ask of me how I
grew faint and frozen then—I cannot write it:
all words would fall far short of what it was.
I did not die, and I was not alive;
think for yourself, if you have any wit,
what I became, deprived of life and death.
The emperor of the despondent kingdom
so towered from the ice, up from midchest,
that I match better with a giant's breadth
than giants match the measure of his arms;
now you can gauge the size of all of him
if it is in proportion to such parts.
If he was once as handsome as he now
is ugly and, despite that, raised his brows
against his Maker, one can understand how
every sorrow has its source in him!
I marveled when I saw that, on his head,
he had three faces: one—in front—bloodred;
and then another two that, just above
the midpoint of each shoulder, joined the first;
and at the crown, all three were reattached;
the right looked somewhat yellow, somewhat white;

1. "The banners of the king of Hell draw closer": modified from a Holy Week hymn, with Hell in place of Heaven, as Lucifer is the negative mirror image of Christ.

2. Lucifer, the "light-bearing" seraph, or angel, was most beautiful of them all before he fell, becoming Satan. Dante identifies him with Dis, the Roman god of the underworld.

the left in its appearance was like those° *black Ethiopians*
who come from where the Nile, descending, flows.
Beneath each face of his, two wings spread out,
as broad as suited so immense a bird:
I've never seen a ship with sails so wide.
They had no feathers, but were fashioned like
a bat's; and he was agitating them,
so that three winds made their way out from him—
and all Cocytus froze before those winds.
He wept out of six eyes; and down three chins,
tears gushed together with a bloody froth.[3]
Within each mouth—he used it like a grinder—
with gnashing teeth he tore to bits a sinner,
so that he brought much pain to three at once.
The forward sinner found that biting nothing
when matched against the clawing, for at times
his back was stripped completely of its hide.
"That soul up there who has to suffer most,"
my master said: "Judas Iscariot—
his head inside, he jerks his legs without.
Of those two others, with their heads beneath,
the one who hangs from that black snout is Brutus—
see how he writhes and does not say a word!
That other, who seems so robust, is Cassius[4]
But night is come again, and it is time
for us to leave; we have seen everything."[5]
Just as he asked, I clasped him round the neck;
and he watched for the chance of time and place,
and when the wings were open wide enough,
he took fast hold upon the shaggy flanks
and then descended, down from tuft to tuft,
between the tangled hair and icy crusts.
When we had reached the point at which the thigh
revolves, just at the swelling of the hip,
my guide, with heavy strain and rugged work,
reversed his head to where his legs had been
and grappled on the hair, as one who climbs—
I thought that we were going back to Hell.
"Hold tight," my master said—he panted like
a man exhausted—" it is by such stairs

3. The *contrapasso* of Dis reproduces his rebellion: he is depicted as a false, three-faced Trinity, winged like an angel (the seraph also had six wings), and lord of the realm, but a lord as hideous as he once was beautiful, whose only power is the mechanical beating of wings that freezes Cocytus and confines him in the ice of his own making, and the grinding of teeth that punishes the three traitors in his jaws.

4. The three arch-traitors are Judas Iscariot, who sold Christ (after whom this region of Judecca is named; he is gnawed head-first), and two conspirators against Julius Caesar, Marcus Junius Brutus and Gaius Cassius Longus (gnawed feet-first) both of whom killed themselves after their defeat at Philippi in 42 B.C.E., two years following Caesar's murder.

5. It is now 6 P.M. on Holy Saturday, 24 hours after the pair entered the Gate of Hell on Good Friday. The anticlimactic nature of Satan and the bottom of Hell shows evil as an empty negation or perversion of good desires and intentions rather than a powerful and independent force of its own.

that we must take our leave of so much evil."[6]
Then he slipped through a crevice in a rock
and placed me on the edge of it, to sit;
that done, he climbed toward me with steady steps.
I raised my eyes, believing I should see
the half of Lucifer that I had left;
instead I saw him with his legs turned up;
and if I then became perplexed, do let
the ignorant be judges—those who can
not understand what point I had just crossed.
"Get up," my master said, "be on your feet:
the way is long, the path is difficult;
the sun's already back to middle tierce."[7]
It was no palace hall, the place in which
we found ourselves, but with its rough-hewn floor
and scanty light, a dungeon built by nature.
"Before I free myself from this abyss,
master," I said when I had stood up straight,
"tell me enough to see I don't mistake:
Where is the ice? And how is he so placed
head downward? Tell me, too, how has the sun
in so few hours gone from night to morning?"
And he to me: "You still believe you are
north of the center, where I grasped the hair
of the damned worm who pierces through the world.
And you were there as long as I descended;
but when I turned, that's when you passed the point
to which, from every part, all weights are drawn.
And now you stand beneath the hemisphere
opposing that which cloaks the great dry lands
and underneath whose zenith died the Man
whose birth and life were sinless in this world.[8]
Your feet are placed upon a little sphere
that forms the other face of the Judecca.
Here it is morning when it's evening there;
and he whose hair has served us as a ladder
is still fixed, even as he was before.
This was the side on which he fell from Heaven;
for fear of him, the land that once loomed here
made of the sea a veil and rose into
our hemisphere; and that land which appears
upon this side—perhaps to flee from him—

6. Just as Hell can only be avoided by comprehending every last part of it, so the only way out of it is through its very heart, the body of Satan. Because the waist of his body is placed at the very center of the earth (and of the universe in Ptolemy's conception), the climb takes the pair from the northern into the southern hemisphere (held to be all water), causing the inversion of direction that so confuses the pilgrim.

7. The reference to the sun—all such references within Hell were given with respect to the moon and stars—tells us that in the southern hemisphere it is now 7:30 A.M. The climb through the southern half of the earth will take 21 or 22 hours, about the same amount of time as the descent through Hell.

8. Jerusalem was regarded as the center of the northern hemisphere of land; it was often represented on maps with the image of Christ hanging on the cross.

left here this hollow space and hurried upward."[9]
There is a place below, the limit of
that cave, its farthest point from Beelzebub,° *Satan*
a place one cannot see: it is discovered
by ear—there is a sounding stream that flows
along the hollow of a rock eroded
by winding waters, and the slope is easy.
My guide and I came on that hidden road
to make our way back into the bright world;
and with no care for any rest, we climbed—
he first, I following—until I saw,
through a round opening, some of those things
of beauty Heaven bears. It was from there
that we emerged, to see—once more—the stars.

Geoffrey Chaucer

c. 1340–1400

Like so much else in the world of fourteenth-century England, Chaucer's family name was derived from the French: a maker of *chausses,* shoes or hose. His family had nothing to do with footwear, but Chaucer made his name as a poet with a translation from the French of *Le Roman de la rose,* and he established himself as a valuable servant to three successive English kings partly due to linguistic skills that enabled him to conduct royal business during journeys to France, Spain, and Italy. But what made Chaucer the first great authority of English literature was the way he transformed Continental themes, words, and literary genres into something indelibly and recognizably English. As Dante in his *Commedia* quite consciously created the first epic poem in vernacular Italian rather than Latin, so Chaucer set out in *The Canterbury Tales* to forge a work of poetry for an entire people, in a language—the London dialect that would become modern English—potentially accessible to all citizens, from the highest to the lowest.

Chaucer's ancestors were prosperous vintners and property owners in Ipswich who by the late thirteenth century had moved seventy miles south to settle in London. Chaucer's father served in the household of King Edward III; Geoffrey began his career in 1357 similarly situated, working for the wife of Edward's son, Prince Henry. About ten years later, he made an advantageous marriage to the daughter of a knight of Hainault, and was soon made an *esquier* (esquire), or retainer in the royal household. He traveled frequently around England and abroad in the king's service, not only to nearby France, but to Florence in 1373, where he may have met Boccaccio (page 1452), and Petrarch (page 1479), and certainly learned of their poetry as well as of Dante's. Chaucer was evidently a skilled courtier; he survived countless power struggles, continued receiving posts and assignments after the accession of Richard II in 1377, and had his annuities confirmed when Henry V supplanted Richard in 1399.

9. In Dante's invention, Lucifer's fall from Heaven provides a geological as well as a theological origin of Hell and Purgatory: when he fell into the southern hemisphere, directly opposite Jerusalem, the land that once filled it fled from him northward. Once he became fixed in the center of the earth, the land around him fled southward, raising the Mountain of Purgatory and hollowing out the cone of Hell.

Unlike the public lives of many medieval writers, Chaucer's lifetime of service was extremely well-documented, but of the nearly 500 items that mention his name only a few allude to his personal affairs and none at all to his poetry. Conversely, Chaucer's poetry rarely mentions the great events of his day, from the Black Death of his childhood to the grand dynastic struggles that must have deeply affected his life. His earlier writings show him immersed in the medieval occupations of translation and popularization. The translation of the foremost authority of medieval romance, *The Romance of the Rose,* was begun before 1372 and that of Boethius's *The Consolation of Philosophy* in the 1380s. *The Book of the Duchess,* which mimics the French genre of the *dits amoureux,* was written to commemorate the death of Blanche, Duchess of Lancaster, in 1369. Like *The Book of the Duchess, The House of Fame* (1378–1380) and *The Parliament of Fowls* (1380–1382) were first-person dream visions dealing with issues of fame, poetry, and love. Here, Chaucer developed a self-deprecating persona that nonetheless voices an ambition to equal Dante, the French romances, and the classical poets, as in this deflation of the grand opening of Virgil's *Aeneid,* "I wol now synge, yif I kan, / The armes and also the man." Up to the middle of the eighteenth century, the most frequently cited of Chaucer's works was a long verse romance, *Troilus and Cressida* (1382–1386), based on a romance by Boccaccio set during the Trojan War, and often considered the first psychological novel due to the depth of its depiction of character.

To write in English was not the obvious choice for a prodigiously learned and ambitious fourteenth-century *esquier,* although its use had increased as the century went on, culminating in Henry V's declared preference for it as the language of literature at his court. French had long been the language of statecraft and civil record-keeping, and of literature in many circles, especially the court. Latin was the language of ecclesiastical and theological discourse, including philosophy, and still an important literary language, especially in Italy. The London dialect adapted by Chaucer would have been primarily a practical language, with limited capacities for meter, rhyme, and vocabulary in comparison to Chaucer's French, Italian, and Latin sources. His genius was to expand the capacities of English without losing its flavor of reality as an everyday language. As with Dante, Chaucer's choice of a local vernacular incorporated the thematic contrast between decorum and plainness, spirit and matter, into the very language of the verse.

This effect is strongest in *The Canterbury Tales,* parts of which date from as early as the 1370s, but most of which was written in the late 1380s and early 1390s. Chaucer presents the stories told by a diverse collection of twenty-nine pilgrims (more or less) as they make their way from London to the shrine of Saint Thomas à Becket in Canterbury. The pilgrimage was an essential feature of medieval life, whether a brief journey within Kent or a more extended voyage to Santiago de Compostela in Spain or to the Holy Land—and the Wife of Bath has done them all. Undertaken to seek miraculous aid, to visit a famous biblical site, to renounce the world, or to expiate a sin, pilgrimage could also be imposed as penance on criminals, used as a front by charlatans, or undertaken by clergy who had fallen out with parish authorities. The pilgrimage brought together all the estates of society, although rarely involving the extreme social variety of Chaucer's pilgrims, from the devout knight, prioress, and merchant to a range of fairly secular-minded characters to the scurvy Miller and Reeve. Chaucer's pilgrimage is a literary conceit, but a conceit based on a wide and familiar practice.

Chaucer devotes far less time to the motivations behind the characters' decision to take a pilgrimage than he does to the interactions between them and to the many different stories he can tell through their varied persons. In the "General Prologue," he gives a thumbnail sketch of every character except his own stand-in, a self-effacing poet who tells two failed stories; these sketches are noteworthy for their memorable and idiosyncratic detail and for their stylistic range. The procession of characters is based on the estates satire, a comic catalogue of the different estates, or classes of society. Each character represents a type, defined primarily by his or her profession; however, each type is engraved in our memory through tellingly individual touches. We are told of the Miller, for example, that he possesses the strength needed to exercise his profession, but the demonstration of this strength takes a comically unlikely form: he breaks down doors with his head ("Ther was no dore that he nolde heve of harre, / Or breke it rennyng with his head").

In a similar fashion, each tale reflects the milieu of its teller and evokes a literary genre he or she would be familiar with—the Knight tells of chivalry, the Monk of the perils of trusting to Fortune, the Miller and the Reeve bawdy tales (*fabliaux*) about artisans. Yet each tale is constructed with consummate artistry to match the condition of each teller, a feat beyond the capacity of most if not all of Chaucer's characters. In "The Miller's Tale," for example, Chaucer invests the *fabliau* with a doubled and converging seduction plot and a thematic backdrop of mystery plays and courtly love conventions, remaining faithful to the parody and scatological humor of the genre while expanding its scope and heightening its comedy.

The proliferation of narrators and narrative styles often makes it difficult to know how we are meant to evaluate a particular character. Alisoun, the garrulous Wife of Bath, for instance, sums up and embodies centuries of the misogynist clichés and biblical commonplaces of the clerkly tradition and the *querelle des femmes* ("quarrel about women") but she does so with such energy and she travesties her sources with such gusto that the reader is more likely to side with her than against her. In the Prologue to her tale, she recounts the story of her life and five husbands—a prologue that overshadows and doubles the length of her Tale proper, the collection's only version of an Arthurian romance. Even here, digression and anachronism take pride of place over fidelity to her source. The knight's quest for the answer to the question "What thing is it that wommen moost desiren" extends her Prologue's debate over the battle of the sexes, marriage, and desire into the fantasy world of legend: a paradoxically fitting genre for one of Chaucer's most down-to-earth characters.

Unlike Dante, Chaucer left his *magnum opus* unfinished, in ten more or less ordered groupings. There is no numerical perfection, as in the even hundred cantos of the *Commedia* or the ten tellers, ten days and hundred stories of Boccaccio's *Decameron* (see page 1455). Still, the interaction among characters, the sequencing of certain tales, and the repeated themes and motifs create a complex network of comparison. Although he was no stranger to the structures of symmetry so dear to much of medieval poetry, Chaucer prefers here to develop his tales through interruption and disorder, as in the Miller's drunken insistence on telling his tale out of order so that he can "quite," or pay back, the Reeve's insult. Rather than ordering spiritual and secular, courtly and *fabliau,* proper and obscene, Chaucer imagines the multifaceted teeming medieval world all thrown together, with characters looking the other way or staring each other down, reveling in the bickering and bantering in enforced coexistence encapsulated by the pilgrimage setting.

from The Canterbury Tales[1]

The General Prologue

When April with his showers sweet with fruit
The drought of March has pierced unto the root
And bathed each vein with liquor that has power
To generate therein and sire the flower;
When Zephyr° also has, with his sweet breath, *the West Wind*
Quickened again, in every holt° and heath, *woods*
The tender shoots and buds, and the young sun
Into the Ram one half his course has run,[2]
And many little birds make melody
That sleep through all the night with open eye

1. Translated by J. U. Nicolson.

2. The Ram is the zodiacal sign Aries, which lasts from mid-March to mid-April.

(So Nature[3] pricks them on to ramp and rage)—
Then do folk long to go on pilgrimage,
And palmers to go seeking out strange strands,
To distant shrines well known in sundry lands.[4]
And specially from every shire's° end *county's*
Of England they to Canterbury wend,° *make their way*
The holy blessed martyr there to seek
Who helped them when they lay so ill and weak.[5]
Befell that, in that season, on a day
In Southwark, at the Tabard,[6] as I lay
Ready to start upon my pilgrimage
To Canterbury, full of devout homage,
There came at nightfall to that hostelry
Some nine and twenty in a company
Of sundry persons who had chanced to fall
In fellowship, and pilgrims were they all
That toward Canterbury town would ride.
The rooms and stables spacious were and wide,
And well we there were eased, and of the best.
And briefly, when the sun had gone to rest,
So had I spoken with them, every one,
That I was of their fellowship anon,° *soon*
And made agreement that we'd early rise
To take the road, as you I will apprise.
But none the less, whilst I have time and space,
Before yet farther in this tale I pace,
It seems to me accordant with reason
To inform you of the state of every one
Of all of these, as it appeared to me,
And who they were, and what was their degree,
And even how arrayed° there at the inn; *dressed*
And with a knight thus will I first begin.

A knight there was, and he a worthy man,
Who, from the moment that he first began
To ride about the world, loved chivalry,
Truth, honour, freedom and courtesy.
Full worthy was he in his liege-lord's° war, *his feudal lord's*
And therein had he ridden (none more far)
As well in Christendom as heathenesse,° *pagan lands*
And honoured everywhere for worthiness.

3. Nature as a creative force was frequently personified as a goddess in the Middle Ages.
4. Pilgrims returning from the Holy Land would carry a palm frond as sign of their achievement; a palmer also designated an itinerant monk.
5. The cathedral town of Canterbury, the ecclesiastical center of England, is about 35 miles southeast of London. It contained the shrine of Archbishop Thomas à Becket, who was murdered by Henry II in 1170 and canonized by the pope three years later. For many centuries it was a primary pilgrimage destination in England.
6. The Canterbury road began in the rather disreputable borough of Southwark, just across London Bridge from London. There was in fact an inn called the Tabard in Southwark at the time.

At Alexandria, he, when it was won;[7]
Full oft the table's roster he'd begun
Above all nations' knights in Prussia.[8]
In Latvia raided he, and Russia,
No christened man so oft of his degree.
In far Granada at the siege was he
Of Algeciras,[9] and in Belmarie.° *Morocco*
At Ayas was he and at Satalye° *in Turkey*
When they were won; and on the Middle Sea° *Mediterranean*
At many a noble meeting chanced to be.
Of mortal battles he had fought fifteen,
And he'd fought for our faith at Tramissene° *in Algeria*
Three times in lists, and each time slain his foe.[1]
This self-same worthy knight had been also
At one time with the lord of Palatye° *in Turkey*
Against another heathen in Turkey;
And always won he sovereign fame for prize.
Though so illustrious, he was very wise
And bore himself as meekly as a maid.
He never yet had any vileness said,
In all his life, to whatsoever wight.° *person*
He was a truly perfect, gentle knight.
But now, to tell you all of his array,
His steeds were good, but yet he was not gay.° *richly dressed*
Of simple fustian° wore he a jupon° *coarse cloth / tunic*
Sadly discoloured by his habergeon;° *breast plate*
For he had lately come from his voyage
And now was going on this pilgrimage.

With him there was his son, a youthful squire,
A lover and a lusty bachelor,[2]
With locks well curled, as if they'd laid in press.
Some twenty years of age he was, I guess.
In stature he was of an average length,
Wondrously active, aye, and great of strength.
He'd ridden sometime with the cavalry
In Flanders, in Artois, and Picardy,[3]
And borne him well within that little space
In hope to win thereby his lady's grace.
Prinked out° he was, as if he were a mead,° *dressed up / meadow*

7. The Egyptian city of Alexandria was conquered by Peter I of Cyprus in 1365 and left behind after a week of slaughter and plundering.
8. The Baltic region of Prussia was a stronghold of the Teutonic Knights, a religious order formed in the 12th century for the purpose of crusading. The Knight has been granted the place of honor among them.
9. A port city in the Andalusian kingdom of Granada near Gibraltar. It was conquered by the Christian forces of the Castilian ruler Alphonso IX in 1344.
1. One-on-one battles between opposing champions were common features of medieval warfare.
2. Squires were bachelors, or knights of the lowest orders, and would often serve as attendants or followers of bannerets, more senior knights who had the right to lead under their own banner.
3. Artois and Picardy are regions of northern France near Belgium, parts of which were controlled by the Counts of Flanders. The reference is probably to the disastrous "crusade" led by the bishop of Norwich against Flanders.

All full of fresh-cut flowers white and red.
Singing he was, or fluting, all the day;
He was as fresh as is the month of May.
Short was his gown,° with sleeves both long and wide. *outer robe*
Well could he sit on horse, and fairly ride.
He could make songs and words thereto indite,° *compose*
Joust, and dance too, as well as sketch and write.
So hot he loved that, while night told her tale,
He slept no more than does a nightingale.
Courteous he, and humble, willing and able,
And carved before his father at the table.[4]

A yeoman had he, nor more servants, no,
At that time, for he chose to travel so;[5]
And he was clad in coat and hood of green.
A sheaf of peacock arrows bright and keen
Under his belt he bore right carefully
(Well could he keep his tackle yeomanly:
His arrows had no draggled° feathers low), *trailing*
And in his hand he bore a mighty bow.
A cropped head had he and a sun-browned face.
Of woodcraft knew he all the useful ways.
Upon his arm he bore a bracer gay,° *bright arm guard*
And at one side a sword and buckler,° yea, *small shield*
And at the other side a dagger bright,
Well sheathed and sharp as spear point in the light;
On breast a Christopher of silver sheen.[6]
He bore a horn in baldric° all of green; *shoulder strap*
A forester he truly was, I guess.[7]

There was also a nun, a prioress,[8]
Who, in her smiling, modest was and coy;° *quiet*
Her greatest oath was but "By Saint Eloy!"
And she was known as Madam Eglantine.° *briar rose*
Full well she sang the services divine,
Intoning through her nose, becomingly;
And fair she spoke her French, and fluently,
After the school of Stratford-at-the-Bow,
For French of Paris was not hers to know.[9]
At table she had been well taught withal,° *as well*
And never from her lips let morsels fall,
Nor dipped her fingers deep in sauce, but ate

4. One of the squire's customary tasks was to carve the meat for their knights.

5. In addition to his son, the Squire, the Knight is accompanied by a Yeoman, a free servant next in rank below a squire in the feudal order.

6. St. Christopher was the patron saint of travelers; his medallion gave protection on the road.

7. The Yeoman is a gamekeeper, charged with guarding his lord's game from poachers and with conducting the elaborate ceremonies of the hunt.

8. The superior of a religious house or order. The description includes many attributes of the courtly lady of the time, although her own position, and her lack of connection with the court, complicate the portrait.

9. Rather than Parisian French, the Prioress speaks the Anglo-Norman dialect she learned at school in Stratford-at-the-Bow, a village outside London.

With so much care the food upon her plate
That never driblet fell upon her breast.
In courtesy she had delight and zest.
Her upper lip was always wiped so clean
That in her cup was no iota seen
Of grease, when she had drunk her draught of wine.
Becomingly she reached for meat to dine.
And certainly delighting in good sport,° *diversions*
She was right pleasant, amiable—in short.
She was at pains to counterfeit the look
Of courtliness,° and stately manners took, *court manners*
And would be held worthy of reverence.
  But, to say something of her moral sense,
She was so charitable and piteous
That she would weep if she but saw a mouse
Caught in a trap, though it were dead or bled.
She had some little dogs, too, that she fed
On roasted flesh, or milk and fine white bread.
But sore she'd weep if one of them were dead,
Or if men smote it with a rod to smart:
For pity ruled her, and her tender heart.
Right decorous her pleated wimple° was; *nun's headdress*
Her nose was fine; her eyes were blue as glass;
Her mouth was small and therewith soft and red;
But certainly she had a fair forehead;
It was almost a full span° broad, I own, *up to nine inches*
For, truth to tell, she was not undergrown.
Neat was her cloak, as I was well aware.
Of coral small about her arm she'd bear
A string of beads and gauded all with green;
And therefrom hung a brooch of golden sheen
Whereon there was first written a crowned "A,"
And under, *Amor vincit omnia.*[1]

  Another little nun with her had she,
Who was her chaplain; and of priests she'd three.[2]
  A monk there was, one made for mastery,° *very handsome*
An outrider, who loved his venery;° *hunting*
A manly man, to be an abbot able.[3]
Full many a blooded° horse had he in stable: *of good breed*
And when he rode men might his bridle hear
A-jingling in the whistling wind as clear,
Aye, and as loud as does the chapel bell

1. "Love conquers all," a phrase from Virgil's tenth Eclogue. Nuns were generally forbidden to wear brooches.

2. A chaplain was a clergyman or nun who conducted services in a private chapel. Like the Knight's Squire, the Nun serves as attendant and secretary to her superior, the Prioress; like the Yeoman, the Priests (or Priest—there is some dispute over whether Chaucer in the end intended one or three) serve as subordinate attendants.

3. An outrider was a monk whose duties led him outside the confines of his abbey, something that would certainly aid this monk in indulging worldly tastes such as hunting. An abbot is the head of a community of monks.

Where this brave monk was master of the cell.[4]
The rule of Maurus or Saint Benedict,
By reason it was old and somewhat strict,[5]
This said monk let such old things slowly pace
And followed new-world manners in their place.
He cared not for that text a clean-plucked hen° *at all*
Which holds that hunters are not holy men;
Nor that a monk, when he is cloisterless,
Is like unto a fish that's waterless;
That is to say, a monk out of his cloister.
But this same text he held not worth an oyster;
And I said his opinion was right good.
What? Should he study as a madman would
Upon a book in cloister cell? Or yet
Go labour with his hands and swink° and sweat, *toil*
As Austin bids? How shall the world be served?[6]
Let Austin have his toil to him reserved.
Therefore he was a rider day and night;
Greyhounds he had, as swift as bird in flight.
Since riding and the hunting of the hare
Were all his love, for no cost would he spare.
I saw his sleeves were purfled° at the hand *fringed*
With fur of grey, the finest in the land;
Also, to fasten hood beneath his chin,
He had of good wrought gold a curious pin:
A love-knot in the larger end there was.
His head was bald and shone like any glass,
And smooth as one anointed was his face.
Fat was this lord, he stood in goodly case.
His bulging eyes he rolled about, and hot
They gleamed and red, like fire beneath a pot;
His boots were soft; his horse of great estate.
Now certainly he was a fine prelate:° *church dignitary*
He was not pale as some poor wasted ghost.
A fat swan loved he best of any roast.
His palfrey° was as brown as is a berry. *saddle-horse*

A friar there was, a wanton and a merry,
A limiter, a very festive man.[7]
In all the Orders Four is none that can
Equal his gossip and his fair language.

4. A small monastery or nunnery, usually dependent on a larger one.

5. The ascetic Rule of Saint Benedict, brought to France by his disciple, St. Maurus.

6. St. Augustine ("Austin") was reputed author of an early monastic rule and a staunch believer in the need to withdraw one's desires from the things of this world. The ironic question asks who would do the work of the secular world, especially its heavy clerical duties, if not the clergy.

7. A friar was a member of one of the four begging orders instituted in the 13th century. Because they were supposed to own nothing of their own, they were legally permitted to beg within certain limits (hence the word "limiter"). As with the Monk before him, the portrait of the Friar partakes in a tradition of satirical depictions of the clergy.

He had arranged full many a marriage
Of women young, and this at his own cost.
Unto his order he was a noble post.° *pillar*
Well liked by all and intimate was he
With franklins everywhere in his country,[8]
And with the worthy women of the town:
For at confessing he'd more power in gown
(As he himself said) than a good curate,
For of his order he was licentiate.° *licensed confessor*
He heard confession gently, it was said,
Gently absolved too, leaving naught of dread.
He was an easy man to give penance
When knowing he should gain a good pittance;
For to a begging friar, money given
Is sign that any man has been well shriven.° *confessed*
For if one gave (he dared to boast of this),
He took the man's repentance not amiss,
For many a man there is so hard of heart
He cannot weep however pains may smart.
Therefore, instead of weeping and of prayer,
Men should give silver to poor friars all bare.
His tippet° was stuck always full of knives *scarf*
And pins, to give to young and pleasing wives.
And certainly he kept a merry note:
Well could he sing and play upon the rote.° *fiddle*
At balladry he bore the prize away.
His throat was white as lily of the May;
Yet strong he was as ever champion.
In towns he knew the taverns, every one,
And every good host and each barmaid too—
Better than begging lepers, these he knew.
For unto no such solid man as he
Accorded it, as far as he could see,
To have sick lepers for acquaintances.
There is no honest advantageousness
In dealing with such poverty-stricken curs;
It's with the rich and with big victuallers.° *food sellers*
And so, wherever profit might arise,
Courteous he was and humble in men's eyes.
There was no other man so virtuous.
He was the finest beggar of his house;
A certain district being farmed to him,
None of his brethren dared approach its rim;
For though a widow had no shoes to show,
So pleasant was his *In principio,*[9]
He always got a farthing ere he went.

8. A franklin was a landowner of free but not noble birth, and of ranking just below the gentry.

9. "In the beginning," the first words of Genesis and of the Gospel According to John in Latin.

He lived by pickings, it is evident.
And he could romp as well as any whelp.° *pup*
On love days[1] could he be of mickle° help. *great*
For there he was not like a cloisterer,° *monk*
With threadbare cope° as is the poor scholar, *cloak*
But he was like a lord or like a pope.
Of double worsted° was his semi-cope,° *wool / short cloak*
That rounded like a bell, as you may guess.
He lisped a little, out of wantonness,
To make his English soft upon his tongue;
And in his harping, after he had sung,
His two eyes twinkled in his head as bright
As do the stars within the frosty night.
This worthy limiter was named Hubert.

There was a merchant with forked beard, and girt
In motley° gown, and high on horse he sat, *multi-colored*
Upon his head a Flemish beaver hat;
His boots were fastened rather elegantly.[2]
His spoke his notions out right pompously,
Stressing the times when he had won, not lost.
He would the sea were held at any cost
Across from Middleburgh to Orwell town.[3]
At money-changing he could make a crown.
This worthy man kept all his wits well set;
There was no one could say he was in debt,
So well he governed all his trade affairs
With bargains and with borrowings and with shares.
Indeed, he was a worthy man withal,
But, sooth° to say, his name I can't recall. *truth*

A clerk from Oxford was with us also,
Who'd turned to getting knowledge, long ago.[4]
As meagre was his horse as is a rake,
Nor he himself too fat, I'll undertake,
But he looked hollow and went soberly.
Right threadbare was his overcoat; for he
Had got him yet no churchly benefice,° *employment*
Nor was so worldly as to gain office.[5]
For he would rather have at his bed's head
Some twenty books, all bound in black and red,
Of Aristotle and his philosophy

1. Days appointed for settling disputes out of court.
2. In keeping with his position ("Merchant" primarily referred to an import-export dealer in such goods as wool, cloth, and furs), the Merchant is dressed very richly.
3. Middleburg was a Dutch port across the Channel from Orwell in England. The Merchant is concerned with piracy en route between the two towns.
4. A clerk was any man ordained to the ministry or the service of the Church; because few except the clergy could read and write, the term was also applied to anyone who could do so, especially one who worked as a scribe, secretary, or keeper of accounts. Education at Oxford or Cambridge was generally intended for those entering the clergy.
5. Employment in secular capacity as a private or government secretary or official.

Than rich robes, fiddle, or gay psaltery.° *harp*
Yet, and for all he was philosopher,
He had but little gold within his coffer;[6]
But all that he might borrow from a friend
On books and learning he would swiftly spend,
And then he'd pray right busily for the souls
Of those who gave him wherewithal for schools.
Of study took he utmost care and heed.
Not one word spoke he more than was his need;
And that was said in fullest reverence
And short and quick and full of high good sense.
Pregnant of moral virtue was his speech;
And gladly would he learn and gladly teach.

A sergeant of the law,[7] wary and wise,
Who'd often gone to Paul's walk to advise,[8]
There was also, compact° of excellence. *full*
Discreet he was, and of great reverence;
At least he seemed so, his words were so wise.
Often he sat as justice in assize,
By patent or commission from the crown;[9]
Because of learning and his high renown,
He took large fees and many robes could own.
So great a purchaser° was never known. *land-buyer*
All was fee simple° to him, in effect, *owned outright*
Wherefore his claims could never be suspect.
Nowhere a man so busy of his class,
And yet he seemed much busier than he was.
All cases and all judgments could he cite
That from King William's time were apposite.[1]
And he could draw a contract so explicit
Not any man could fault therefrom elicit;
And every statute he'd verbatim quote.
He rode but badly° in a medley° coat, *simply / mixed-colored*
Belted in a silken sash, with little bars,
But of his dress no more particulars.

There was a franklin° in his company; *large landholder*
White was his beard as is the white daisy.
Of sanguine° temperament by every sign, *optimistic*
He loved right well his morning sop° in wine. *bread*
Delightful living was the goal he'd won,
For he was Epicurus'° very son, *Greek philosopher*

6. Philosophers were commonly assumed also to be adepts in alchemy and other occult matters; the "philosopher's stone" could transmute base metals into gold.
7. Member of a high order of lawyers, equal to knights in prestige.
8. The porch of St. Paul's Cathedral in London, where clients would come to consult with lawyers.
9. Assizes were sessions held in county courts that heard all manner of civil cases; only sergeants of law could preside over them, appointed by the king.
1. This Man of Law supposedly knows all the reports of property transactions dating back to the reign of William the Conqueror (1066–1087).

That held opinion that a full delight
Was true felicity, perfect and right.
A householder, and that a great, was he;
Saint Julian[2] he was in his own country.
His bread and ale were always right well done;
A man with better cellars there was none.
Baked meat was never wanting in his house,
Of fish and flesh, and that so plenteous
It seemed to snow therein both food and drink
Of every dainty that a man could think.
According to the season of the year
He changed his diet and his means of cheer.
Full many a fattened partridge did he mew.° *pen*
And many a bream and pike in fish-pond too.
Woe to his cook, except° the sauces were *unless*
Poignant and sharp, and ready all his gear.
His table, waiting in his hall alway,
Stood ready covered through the livelong day.
At county sessions was he lord and sire,
And often acted as a knight of shire.° *member of Parliament*
A dagger and a trinket-bag of silk
Hung from his girdle, white as morning milk.
He had been sheriff and been auditor;
And nowhere was a worthier vavasor.[3]

A haberdasher and a carpenter,
An arras°-maker, dyer, and weaver *tapestry*
Were with us, clothed in similar livery.° *uniform*
All of one sober, great fraternity.° *trade guild*
Their gear was new and well adorned it was;
Their weapons were not cheaply trimmed with brass,
But all with silver; chastely° made and well *purely*
Their girdles° and their pouches too, I tell. *belts*
Each man of them appeared a proper burgess° *townsman*
To sit in guildhall on a high dais.[4]
And each of them, for wisdom he could span,
Was fitted to have been an alderman;
For chattels° they'd enough, and, too, of rent; *possessions*
To which their goodwives gave a free assent,
Or else for certain they had been to blame.
It's good to hear "Madam" before one's name,
And go to church when all the world may see,
Having one's mantle borne right royally.[5]

A cook they had with them, just for the nonce,° *occasion*
To boil the chickens with the marrow-bones,

2. Patron saint of hospitality.
3. A feudal tenant ranking in nobility below a baron.
4. The guildhall was the meeting-place of a guild, often equivalent to the town hall. On its dais, or high platform, would sit the highest ranking officials.
5. An alderman's wife was given the title "Madam," allowing her to be treated as if she were nobility.

And flavour tartly and with galingale.° *aromatic spices*
Well could he tell a draught of London ale.
And he could roast and seethe° and broil and fry, *simmer*
And make a good thick soup, and bake a pie.
But very ill it was, it seemed to me,
That on his shin a deadly sore had he;
For sweet blanc-mange,° he made it with the best. *stew*

There was a sailor, living far out west;
For aught I know, he was of Dartmouth town.[6]
He sadly rode a hackney,° in a gown, *nag*
Of thick rough cloth falling to the knee.
A dagger hanging on a cord had he
About his neck, and under arm, and down.
The summer's heat had burned his visage brown;
And certainly he was a good fellow.
Full many a draught of wine he'd drawn, I trow,° *believe*
Of Bordeaux vintage, while the trader slept.
Nice conscience was a thing he never kept.
If that he fought and got the upper hand,
By water he sent them home to every land.
But as for craft, to reckon well his tides,
His currents and the dangerous watersides
His harbours, and his moon, his pilotage,
There was none such from Hull to far Carthage.
Hardy, and wise in all things undertaken,
By many a tempest had his beard been shaken.
He knew well all the havens, as they were,
From Gottland to the Cape of Finisterre,
And every creek in Brittany and Spain;[7]
His vessel had been christened *Madeleine.*

With us there was a doctor of physic;
In all this world was none like him to pick
For talk of medicine and surgery;
For he was grounded in astronomy.[8]
He often kept a patient from the pall
By horoscopes and magic natural.
Well could he tell the fortune ascendent
Within the houses for his sick patient.
He knew the cause of every malady,
Were it of hot or cold, of moist or dry,
And where engendered, and of what humour;[9]
He was a very good practitioner.

6. A port town on the English Channel.
7. Ports near and far: Hull in northeastern England, Carthage (formerly) in North Africa, Gottland in Scandinavia, Finisterre in Spain.
8. Stars and planets were held to have an important influence on the body.
9. According to classical and medieval medicine, illness was caused by an imbalance in the four elements that composed the body (air, water, fire, earth), as they were manifested in the four humors or fluids: blood (hot and moist), phlegm (cold and moist), yellow bile (hot and dry), and black bile (cold and dry).

The cause being known, down to the deepest root,
Anon he gave to the sick man his boot.° *remedy*
Ready he was, with his apothecaries,° *druggists*
To send him drugs and all electuaries;° *medicines*
By mutual aid much gold they'd always won—
Their friendship was a thing not new begun.
Well read was he in Esculapius,
And Deiscorides, and in Rufus,
Hippocrates, and Hali, and Galen,
Serapion, Rhazes, and Avicen,
Averrhoës, Gilbert, and Constantine,
Bernard, and Gatisden, and John Damascene.[1]
In diet he was measured as could be,
Including naught of superfluity,
But nourishing and easy. It's no libel
To say he read but little in the Bible.
In blue and scarlet he went clad, withal,
Lined with a taffeta° and with sendal;° *rich silks*
And yet he was right chary of expense;
He kept the gold he gained from pestilence.
For gold in physic is a fine cordial,
And therefore loved he gold exceeding all.

There was a housewife come from Bath, or near,[2]
Who—sad to say—was deaf in either ear.
At making cloth she had so great a bent
She bettered those of Ypres and even of Ghent.[3]
In all the parish there was no good wife
Should offering make before her, on my life;[4]
And if one did, indeed, so wroth was she
It put her out of all her charity.
Her kerchiefs were of finest weave and ground;° *texture*
I dare swear that they weighed a full ten pound
Which, of a Sunday, she wore on her head.
Her hose were of the choicest scarlet red,
Close gartered, and her shoes were soft and new.
Bold was her face, and fair, and red of hue.
She'd been respectable throughout her life,
With five churched husbands bringing joy and strife,
Not counting other company in youth;
But thereof there's no need to speak, in truth.
Three times she'd journeyed to Jerusalem;
And many a foreign stream she'd had to stem;
At Rome she'd been, and she'd been in Boulogne,
In Spain at Santiago, and at Cologne.° *pilgrimage sites*

1. Famous classical and medieval authorities on medicine from around the Mediterranean.
2. Named after its ancient Roman baths, Bath was a city in western England and the center of cloth manufacturing.
3. Trading and manufacturing centers of Flanders, famous for their cloth.
4. Offerings were given to the priest at the church altar in order of rank.

She could tell much of wandering by the way:
Gap-toothed was she, it is no lie to say.
Upon an ambler° easily she sat, *easy-riding horse*
Well wimpled, aye, and over all a hat
As broad as is a buckler or a targe;° *light shield*
A rug was tucked around her buttocks large,
And on her feet a pair of sharpened spurs.
In company well could she laugh her slurs.° *faults*
The remedies of love she knew, perchance,
For of that art she'd learned the old, old dance.

There was a good man of religion, too,
A country parson, poor, I warrant you;
But rich he was in holy thought and work.
He was a learned man also, a clerk,
Who Christ's own gospel truly sought to preach;
Devoutly his parishioners would he teach.
Benign he was and wondrous diligent.
Patient in adverse times and well content,
As he was ofttimes proven; always blithe,
He was right loath to curse to get a tithe,[5]
But rather would he give, in case of doubt,
Unto those poor parishioners about,
Part of his income, even of his goods.
Enough° with little, coloured° all his moods. *satisfied / harmonized*
Wide was his parish, houses far asunder,
But never did he fail, for rain or thunder,
In sickness, or in sin, or any state,
To visit to the farthest, small and great,
Going afoot, and in his hand a stave.
This fine example to his flock he gave,
That first he wrought° and afterwards he taught; *worked*
Out of the gospel then that text he caught.
And this figure he added thereunto—
That, if gold rust, what shall poor iron do?
For if the priest be foul, in whom we trust,
What wonder if a layman yield to lust?
And shame it is, if priest take thought for keep,° *is involved*
A shitty shepherd, shepherding clean sheep.
Well ought a priest example good to give,
By his own cleanness, how his flock should live.
He never let his benefice for hire,
Leaving his flock to flounder in the mire,
And ran to London, up to old Saint Paul's
To get himself a chantry there for souls.[6]

5. Parishioners paid the Church a tithe, or a tenth part of their income.
6. A parish priest was usually granted his church and its lands for life. Some would rent out their post and get well-paid positions with minimal duties, such as saying masses for the dead in London chantries.

Nor in some brotherhood° did he withhold;° *guild / was he hired*
But dwelt at home and kept so well the fold
That never wolf could make his plans miscarry;
He was a shepherd and not mercenary.
And holy though he was, and virtuous,
To sinners he was not impiteous,
Nor haughty in his speech, nor too divine,
But in all teaching prudent and benign.
To lead folk into Heaven but by stress
Of good example was his busyness.
But if some sinful one proved obstinate,
Be who it might, of high or low estate,
Him he reproved, and sharply, as I know.
There is nowhere a better priest, I trow.
He had no thirst for pomp or reverence,
Nor made himself a special, spiced° conscience, *dainty*
But Christ's own lore, and His apostles' twelve
He taught, but first he followed it himselve.

With him there was a plowman, was his brother,
That many a load of dung, and many another
Had scattered, for a good true toiler, he,
Living in peace and perfect charity.
He loved God most, and that with his whole heart
At all times, though he played or plied his art,
And next, his neighbour, even as himself.
He'd thresh and dig, with never thought of pelf,° *money*
For Christ's own sake, for every poor wight,° *person*
All without pay, if it lay in his might.
He paid his taxes, fully, fairly, well,
Both by his own toil and by stuff he'd sell.
In a tabard° he rode upon a mare. *smock*
There were also a reeve and miller there;
A summoner, manciple and pardoner,
And these, beside myself, made all there were.

The miller was a stout churl,° be it known, *country man*
Hardy and big of brawn and big of bone;
Which was well proved, for when he went on lam° *fought*
At wrestling, never failed he of the ram.° *prize*
He was a chunky fellow, broad of build;
He'd heave a door from hinges if he willed,
Or break it through, by running, with his head.
His beard, as any sow or fox, was red,
And broad it was as if it were a spade.
Upon the coping° of his nose he had *bridge*
A wart, and thereon stood a tuft of hairs,
Red as the bristles in an old sow's ears;
His nostrils they were black and very wide.
A sword and buckler bore he by his side.

His mouth was like a furnace door for size.
He was a jester and could poetize,
But mostly all of sin and ribaldries.
He could steal corn and full thrice charge his fees;
And yet he had a thumb of gold, begad.
A white coat and blue hood he wore, this lad.
A bagpipe he could blow well, be it known,
And with that same he brought us out of town.

There was a manciple from an inn of court,
To whom all buyers might quite well resort
To learn the art of buying food and drink;[7]
For whether he paid cash or not, I think
That he so knew the markets, when to buy,
He never found himself left high and dry.
Now is it not of God a full fair grace
That such a vulgar man has wit to pace° *outdo*
The wisdom of a crowd of learned men?
Of masters had he more than three times ten,
Who were in law expert and curious;
Whereof there were a dozen in that house
Fit to be stewards of both rent and land
Of any lord in England who would stand
Upon his own and live in manner good,
In honour, debtless (save his head were wood),
Or live as frugally as he might desire;
These men were able to have helped a shire
In any case that ever might befall;
And yet this manciple outguessed them all.

The reeve he was a slender, choleric man,
Who shaved his beard as close as razor can.[8]
His hair was cut round even with his ears;
His top was tonsured like a pulpiteer's.° *preacher's*
Long were his legs, and they were very lean,
And like a staff, with no calf to be seen.
Well could he manage granary and bin;
No auditor could ever on him win.
He could foretell, by drought and by the rain,
The yielding of his seed and of his grain.
His lord's sheep and his oxen and his dairy,
His swine and horses, all his stores, his poultry,
Were wholly in this steward's managing;
And, by agreement, he'd made reckoning° *settled accounts*
Since his young lord of age was twenty years;
Yet no man ever found him in arrears.° *behind in payments*

7. A manciple was a servant or officer charged with provisioning a college, an inn of court, or a monastery. The inns of court controlled training in the legal profession.

8. The overseer or steward of an estate. Chaucer's Reeve suffers from an excess of the humor of yellow bile, hot and dry, making him choleric, or quick to anger.

There was no agent, hind,° or herd° who'd cheat *servant / herdsman*
But he knew well his cunning and deceit;
They were afraid of him as of the death.
His cottage was a good one, on a heath;
By green trees shaded with this dwelling-place.
Much better than his lord could he purchase.
Right rich he was in his own private right,
Seeing he'd pleased his lord, by day or night,
By giving him, or lending, of his goods,
And so got thanked—but yet got coats and hoods.
In youth he'd learned a good trade, and had been
A carpenter, as fine as could be seen.
This steward sat a horse that well could trot,
And was all dapple-grey, and was named Scot.
A long surcoat° of blue did he parade, *overcoat*
And at his side he bore a rusty blade.
Of Norfolk° was this reeve of whom I tell, *in north England*
From near a town that men call Badeswell.
Bundled he was like friar from chin to croup,° *rump*
And ever he rode hindmost of our troop.

A summoner was with us in that place,[9]
Who had a fiery-red, cherubic face,
For eczema he had; his eyes were narrow
As hot he was, and lecherous, as a sparrow;
With black and scabby brows and scanty beard;
He had a face that little children feared.
There was no mercury, sulphur, or litharge,
No borax, ceruse, tartar,[1] could discharge,
Nor ointment that could cleanse enough, or bite,
To free him of his boils and pimples white,
Nor of the bosses° resting on his cheeks. *lumps*
Well loved he garlic, onions, aye and leeks,
And drinking of strong wine as red as blood.
Then would he talk and shout as madman would.
And when a deal of wine he'd poured within,
Then would he utter no word save Latin.
Some phrases had he learned, say two or three,
Which he had garnered out of some decree;
No wonder, for he'd heard it all the day;
And all you know right well that even a jay
Can call out "Wat" as well as can the pope.
But when, for aught else, into him you'd grope,
'Twas found he'd spent his whole philosophy;
Just "*Questio quid juris*" would he cry.[2]

9. A summoner was a petty court officer who summoned for court appearances and kept track of them.
1. These primarily mineral compounds were different remedies recommended by medieval medicine for the treatment of the Summoner's skin disorder.
2. "The question is, what point of law (applies)?"

He was a noble rascal, and a kind;
A better comrade 'twould be hard to find.
Why, he would suffer, for a quart of wine,
Some good fellow to have his concubine
A twelve-month, and excuse him to the full
(Between ourselves, though, he could pluck a gull).
And if he chanced upon a good fellow,
He would instruct him never to have awe,
In such a case, of the archdeacon's curse,° *excommunication*
Except a man's soul lie within his purse;
For in his purse the man should punished be.
"The purse is the archdeacon's Hell," said he.
But well I know he lied in what he said,
A curse ought every guilty man to dread
(For curse can kill, as absolution save),
And 'ware° *significavit*[3] to the grave. *beware*
In his own power had he, and at ease,
The boys and girls of all the diocese,
And knew their secrets, and by counsel led.
A garland° had he set upon his head, *wreath*
Large as a tavern's wine-bush on a stake;° *sign*
A buckler had he made of bread they bake.

With him there rode a gentle pardoner
Of Rouncival, his friend and his compeer;° *companion*
Straight from the court of Rome had journeyed he.[4]
Loudly he sang "Come hither, love, to me,"
The summoner joining with a burden° round; *bass line*
Was never horn of° half so great a sound. *made with*
This pardoner had hair as yellow as wax,
But lank it hung as does a strike of flax;
In wisps hung down such locks as he'd on head,
And with them he his shoulders overspread;
But thin they dropped, and stringy, one by one.
But as to hood, for sport of it, he'd none,
Though it was packed in wallet° all the while. *bag*
It seemed to him he went in latest style,
Dishevelled, save for cap, his head all bare.
As shiny eyes he had as has a hare.
He had a fine veronica sewed to cap.[5]
His wallet lay before him in his lap,
Stuffed full of pardons brought from Rome all hot.
A voice he had that bleated like a goat.

3. An ecclesiastical writ for the arrest of an excommunicated person.
4. A pardoner was licensed by the Church (and the Pope, at the "court of Rome") to sell indulgences, or papal pardons for sin. This Pardoner is connected to St. Mary Rouncesval in Charing Cross, London.
5. According to legend, St. Veronica had wiped Christ's face with her kerchief on his way to be crucified. The cloth retained an impression of the face, and was kept as a sacred relic in Rome. Reproductions would be carried by pilgrims as tokens of their pilgrimage.

No beard had he, nor ever should he have,
For smooth his face as he'd just had a shave;
I think he was a gelding° or a mare.° *eunuch / homosexual*
But in his craft, from Berwick unto Ware,° *in all of England*
Was no such pardoner in any place.
For in his bag he had a pillowcase
The which, he said, was Our True Lady's veil:
He said he had a piece of the very sail
That good Saint Peter had, what time he went
Upon the sea, till Jesus changed his bent.[6]
He had a latten° cross set full of stones *brass*
And in a bottle had he some pig's bones.
But with these relics, when he came upon
Some simple parson, then this paragon
In that one day more money stood to gain
Than the poor dupe in two months could attain.
And thus, with flattery and suchlike japes,° *tricks*
He made the parson and the rest his apes.
But yet, to tell the whole truth at the last,
He was, in church, a fine ecclesiast.
Well could he read a lesson or a story,
But best of all he sang an offertory;
For well he knew that when that song was sung,
Then might he preach, and all with polished tongue,
To win some silver, as he right well could;
Therefore he sang so merrily and so loud.

Now have I told you briefly, in a clause,° *short space*
The state, the array, the number, and the cause
Of the assembling of this company
In Southwark, at this noble hostelry
Known as the Tabard Inn, hard by the Bell.° *another tavern*
But now the time is come wherein to tell
How all we bore ourselves that very night
When at the hostelry we did alight.
And afterward the story I engage
To tell you of our common pilgrimage.
But first, I pray you, of your courtesy,
You'll not ascribe it to vulgarity
Though I speak plainly of this matter here,
Retailing you their words and means of cheer;
Nor though I use their very terms, nor lie.
For this thing do you know as well as I:
When one repeats a tale told by a man,
He must report, as nearly as he can,
Every least word, if he remember it,

6. The Pardoner's fake relics include Mary's veil and part of the sail used by Peter as a fisherman before he was called by Jesus to be a disciple.

However rude it be, or how unfit;
Or else he may be telling what's untrue,
Embellishing and fictionizing too.
He may not spare, although it were his brother;
He must as well say one word as another.
Christ spoke right broadly out, in holy writ,
And, you know well, there's nothing low in it.
And Plato says, to those able to read:
"The word should be the cousin to the deed."[7]
Also, I pray that you'll forgive it me
If I have not set folk, in their degree
Here in this tale, by rank as they should stand
My wits are not the best, you'll understand.[8]

Great cheer our host gave to us, every one,
And to the supper set us all anon;
And served us then with victuals of the best.
Strong was the wine and pleasant to each guest.
A seemly man our good host was, withal,
Fit to have been a marshal in some hall;[9]
He was a large man, with protruding eyes,
As fine a burgher as in Cheapside lies;[1]
Bold in his speech, and wise, and right well taught,
And as to manhood, lacking there in naught.
Also, he was a very merry man,
And after meat, at playing he began,
Speaking of mirth among some other things,
When all of us had paid our reckonings;
And saying thus: "Now masters, verily
You are all welcome here, and heartily:
For by my truth, and telling you no lie,
I have not seen, this year, a company
Here in this inn, fitter for sport than now.
Fain° would I make you happy, knew I how. *gladly*
And of a game have I this moment thought
To give you joy, and it shall cost you naught.
"You go to Canterbury; may God speed
And the blest martyr soon requite your meed.° *reward you*
And well I know, as you go on your way,
You'll tell good tales and shape yourselves to play;
For truly there's no mirth nor comfort, none,
Riding the roads as dumb as is a stone;
And therefore will I furnish you a sport,
As I just said, to give you some comfort.

7. The saying is taken from Plato's *Timaeus,* but probably cited as a commonplace from a later source. According to the narrator, both Plato and Jesus, in the sayings attributed to him in the Gospels, held a principle of realism: things should be called by their true names, and words should be reported as they were said.

8. Rather than organized according to the social standing ("degree") of their tellers, the tales are given in the order in which they were supposedly told. The pretense of modesty was a standard theme of medieval rhetoric.

9. Master of ceremonies and arrangements at a banquet.

1. A major market area in London.

And if you like it, all, by one assent,
And will be ruled by me, of my judgment,
And will so do as I'll proceed to say,
Tomorrow, when you ride upon your way,
Then, by my father's spirit, who is dead,
If you're not gay, I'll give you up my head.
Hold up your hands, nor more about it speak."
Our full assenting was not far to seek;
We thought there was no reason to think twice,
And granted him his way without advice,
And bade him tell his verdict just and wise,
"Masters," quoth he, "here now is my advice;
But take it not, I pray you, in disdain;
This is the point, to put it short and plain,
That each of you, beguiling the long day,
Shall tell two stories as you wend your way
To Canterbury town; and each of you
On coming home, shall tell another two,
All of adventures he has known befall.
And he who plays his part the best of all,
That is to say, who tells upon the road
Tales of best sense, in most amusing mode,
Shall have a supper at the others' cost
Here in this room and sitting by this post,
When we come back again from Canterbury.
And now, the more to warrant you'll be merry
I will myself, and gladly, with you ride
At my own cost, and I will be your guide.
But whosoever shall my rule gainsay° *deny*
Shall pay for all that's bought along the way.
And if you are agreed that it be so,
Tell me at once, or if not, tell me no,
And I will act accordingly. No more."
This thing was granted, and our oaths we swore,
With right glad hearts, and prayed of him, also,
That he would take the office, nor forgo
The place of governor of all of us,
Judging our tales; and by his wisdom thus
Arrange that supper at a certain price,
We to be ruled, each one, by his advice
In things both great and small; by one assent,
We stood committed to his government.
And thereupon, the wine was fetched anon;
We drank, and then to rest went every one,
And that without a longer tarrying.° *delay*
Next morning, when the day began to spring,
Up rose our host, and acting as our cock,
He gathered us together in a flock,
And forth we rode, a jog-trot° being the pace, *slow, steady pace*

Until we reached Saint Thomas' watering-place.[2]
And there our host pulled horse up to a walk,
And said: "Now, masters, listen while I talk.
You know what you agreed at set of sun.
If even-song and morning-song are one,[3]
Let's here decide who first shall tell a tale.
And as I hope to drink more wine and ale,
Whoso proves rebel to my government
Shall pay for all that by the way is spent.
Come now, draw cuts, before we farther win,
And he that draws the shortest shall begin.
Sir knight," said he, "my master and my lord,
You shall draw first as you have pledged your word.
Come near," quoth he, "my lady prioress:
And you sir, clerk, put by your bashfulness,
Nor ponder more; out hands, now, every man!"
At once to draw a cut each one began,
And, to make short the matter, as it was,
Whether by chance or whatsoever cause,
The truth is, that the cut fell to the knight,
At which right happy then was every wight.
Thus that his story first of all he'd tell,
According to the compact, it befell,
As you have heard. Why argue to and fro?
And when this good man saw that it was so,
Being a wise man and obedient
To plighted° word, given by free assent, *pledged*
He said: "Since I must then begin the game,
Why, welcome be the cut, and in God's name!
Now let us ride, and hearken what I say."
And at that word we rode forth on our way;
And he began to speak, with right good cheer,
His tale anon, as it is written here.

* * *

The Wife of Bath's Prologue

"Experience, though no authority
Were in this world, were° good enough for me, *would be*
To speak of woe that is in all marriage;
For, masters, since I was twelve years of age,
Thanks be to God Who is for aye° alive, *ever*
Of husbands at church door have I had five;
For men so many times have wedded me;
And all were worthy men in their degree.° *rank*
But someone told me not so long ago
That since Our Lord, save once, would never go

2. A brook located a couple of miles from London.

3. If they still agree this morning (the hour of morning services) what they had agreed the previous evening.

To wedding (that at Cana in Galilee),[1]
Thus, by this same example, showed He me
I never should have married more than once.
Lo and behold! What sharp words, for the nonce,
Beside a well Lord Jesus, God and man,
Spoke in reproving the Samaritan:
'For thou hast had five husbands,' thus said He,
'And he whom thou hast now to be with thee
Is not thine husband.'[2] Thus He said that day,
But what He meant thereby I cannot say;
And I would ask now why that same fifth man
Was not husband to the Samaritan?
How many might she have, then, in marriage?
For I have never heard, in all my age,
Clear exposition of this number shown,
Though men may guess and argue up and down.[3]
But well I know and say, and do not lie,
God bade us to increase and multiply;
That worthy text can I well understand.
And well I know He said, too, my husband
Should father leave, and mother, and cleave to me;[4]
But no specific number mentioned He,
Whether of bigamy or octogamy;° *eight marriages*
Why should men speak of it reproachfully?
"Lo, there's the wise old king Dan Solomon;
I understand he had more wives than one;[5]
And now would God it were permitted me
To be refreshed one half as oft as he!
Which gift of God he had for all his wives!
No man has such that in this world now lives.
God knows, this noble king, it strikes my wit,
The first night he had many a merry fit
With each of them, so much he was alive!
Praise be to God that I have wedded five!
Welcome the sixth whenever come he shall.
Forsooth,° I'll not keep chaste for good and all; *truly*
When my good husband from the world is gone,
Some Christian man shall marry me anon;
Of whom I did pick out and choose the best
Both for their nether° purse and for their chest. *lower*
Different schools make divers perfect clerks,
Different methods learned in sundry works

1. Site of Jesus's first miracle (John 2:1–10). This was a standard passage for arguments in favor of monogamy, dating back to St. Jerome, from whose treatise *Adversus Jovinianum* (393) the bulk of the scriptural argument that follows was drawn.
2. John 4:5–30.
3. The Wife of Bath avoids the plain sense of the passage by claiming it must have some obscure mystical meaning.
4. Following standard practice in biblical interpretation, she counters one biblical precept with several others that seem to give the opposite instructions: God's instruction to Adam and Eve to "increase and multiply" (Genesis 1:28) and Jesus's words in Matthew 19:5–6 (in fact arguing against divorce), citing Adam and Eve.
5. King Solomon had a thousand wives and concubines (1 Kings 11:3).

Make the good workman perfect, certainly.
Of full five husbands tutoring am I.
For then, the apostle° says that I am free — *Paul*
To wed, in God's name, where it pleases me.
He says that to be wedded is no sin;
Better to marry than to burn within.[6]
What care I though folk speak reproachfully
Of wicked Lamech and his bigamy?
I know well Abraham was holy man,
And Jacob, too, as far as know I can;
And each of them had spouses more than two;
And many another holy man also.[7]
Or can you say that you have ever heard
That God has ever by His express word
Marriage forbidden? Pray you, now, tell me;
Or where commanded He virginity?
I read as well as you no doubt have read
The apostle when he speaks of maidenhead;
He said, commandment of the Lord he'd none.
Men may advise a woman to be one,
But such advice is not commandment, no;
He left the thing to our own judgment so.[8]
For had Lord God commanded maidenhood,
He'd have condemned all marriage as not good;
And certainly, if there were no seed sown,
Virginity—where then should it be grown?[9]
Paul dared not to forbid us, at the least,
A thing whereof his Master'd no behest.° — *injunction*
The dart° is set up for virginity; — *prize*
Catch it who can; who runs best let us see.
"But this word is not meant for every wight,
But where God wills to give it, of His might.
I know well that the apostle was a maid;° — *virgin*
Nevertheless, and though he wrote and said
He would that everyone were such as he,
All is not counsel to virginity;
And so to be a wife he gave me leave
Out of permission; there's no shame should grieve
In marrying me, if that my mate should die,
Without exception,° too, of bigamy. — *objection*
And though 'twere good no woman's flesh to touch,
He meant, in his own bed or on his couch;
For peril 'tis fire and tow to assemble;

6. Quoting 1 Corinthians 7:9 and 7:28.

7. Lamech was a descendant of the accursed Cain who was considered to have been the first bigamist (Genesis 4:19–24). By contrast, Abraham and Jacob were biblical patriarchs who also had several wives.

8. According to Paul, "if a virgin marry, she hath not sinned," since there was no commandment against marriage (1 Corinthians 7:25 and 28), but he did advise even those who had wives to remain celibate (7:29).

9. How would virgins be born unless people have sex?

You know what this example may resemble.[1]
This is the sum: he held virginity
Nearer perfection than marriage for° frailty. *out of*
And frailty's all, I say, save° he and she *unless*
Would lead their lives throughout in chastity.
"I grant this well, I have no great envy
Though maidenhood's preferred to bigamy;
Let those who will be clean, body and ghost,° *soul*
Of my condition I will make no boast.
For well you know, a lord in his household,
He has not every vessel all of gold;
Some are of wood and serve well all their days.
God calls folk unto Him in sundry° ways, *diverse*
And each one has from God a proper gift,
Some this, some that, as pleases Him to shift.
"Virginity is great perfection known,
And continence e'en° with devotion shown. *equally*
But Christ, Who of perfection is the well,
Bade not each separate man he should go sell
All that he had and give it to the poor
And follow Him in such wise going before.[2]
He spoke to those that would live perfectly;
And, masters, by your leave, such am not I.
I will devote the flower of all my age
To all the acts and harvests of marriage.
"Tell me also, to what purpose or end
The genitals were made, that I defend,
And for what benefit was man first wrought?[3]
Trust you right well, they were not made for naught° *nothing*
Explain who will and argue up and down
That they were made for passing out, as known,
Of urine, and our two belongings small
Were just to tell a female from a male,
And for no other cause—ah, say you no?
Experience knows well it is not so;
And, so the clerics be not with me wroth,° *angry*
I say now that they have been made for both,
That is to say, for duty and for ease
In getting,° when we do not God displease. *procreation*
Why should men otherwise in their books set
That man shall pay unto his wife his debt?° *marital duty*
Now wherewith should he ever make payment,
Except he used his blessed instrument?
Then on a creature were devised these things
For urination and engenderings.

1. 1 Corinthians 7:1: "It is good for a man not to touch a woman"; Alisoun adds a proverb ("example") that fire and tow (flax or hemp) placed too closely together will burn.
2. Matthew 19:21: "If thou wilt be perfect, go and sell what thou hast, and give to the poor, and thou shalt have treasure in heaven: and come and follow me."
3. Here, as most of her other arguments in favor of sexual activity, the Wife of Bath closely echoes Jean de Meun's continuation of *The Romance of the Rose*, which Chaucer had translated from the French.

"But I say not that every one is bound,
Who's fitted out and furnished as I've found,
To go and use it to beget an heir;
Then men would have for chastity no care.
Christ was a maid, and yet shaped like a man,
And many a saint, since this old world began,
Yet has lived ever in perfect chastity.
I bear no malice to virginity;
Let such be bread of purest white wheat-seed,
And let us wives be called but barley bread;
And yet with barley bread (if Mark you scan)
Jesus Our Lord refreshed full many a man.[4]
In such condition as God places us
I'll persevere, I'm not fastidious.
In wifehood I will use my instrument
As freely as my Maker has it sent.
If I be niggardly,° God give me sorrow! *stingy*
My husband he shall have it, eve and morrow,
When he's pleased to come forth and pay his debt.
I'll not delay, a husband I will get
Who shall be both my debtor and my thrall° *slave*
And have his tribulations therewithal
Upon his flesh, the while I am his wife.
I have the power during all my life
Over his own good body, and not he.
For thus the apostle told it unto me;
And bade our husbands that they love us well.[5]
And all this pleases me whereof I tell."
Up rose the pardoner, and that anon.
"Now dame," said he, "by God and by Saint John,
You are a noble preacher in this case!
I was about to wed a wife, alas!
Why should I buy this on° my flesh so dear? *with*
No, I would rather wed no wife this year."
"But wait," said she, "my tale is not begun;
Nay, you shall drink from out another tun° *barrel*
Before I cease, and savour worse than ale.
And when I shall have told you all my tale
Of tribulation that is in marriage,
Whereof I've been an expert all my age,
That is to say, myself have been the whip,
Then may you choose whether you will so sip
Out of that very tun which I shall broach.
Beware of it ere you too near approach;
For I shall give examples more than ten.

4. Jesus made enough food to feed five thousand out of five barley loaves and two small fishes. Bread made from barley was considered very low fare.

5. This is not exactly what Paul intended by his metaphors of debt and subordination (1 Corinthians 7:3–5), which advised husband and wife rather to be sparing in their possession of each other.

Whoso will not be warned by other men
By him shall other men corrected be.
The self-same words has written Ptolemy;
Read in his Almagest and find it there."[6]
"Lady, I pray you, if your will it were,"
Spoke up this pardoner, "as you began,
Tell forth your tale, nor spare° for any man, *refrain*
And teach us younger men of your technique."
"Gladly," said she, "since it may please, not pique.° *offend*
But yet I pray of all this company
That if I speak from my own phantasy,° *fancy*
They will not take amiss the things I say;
For my intention's only but to play.
"Now, sirs, now will I tell you forth my tale.
And as I may drink ever wine and ale,
I will tell truth of husbands that I've had,
For three of them were good and two were bad.
The three were good men and were rich and old.
Not easily could they the promise hold
Whereby they had been bound to cherish me.
You know well what I mean by that, pardie!° *indeed*
So help me God, I laugh now when I think
How pitifully by night I made them swink;° *toil*
And by my faith I set by it no store.° *pay it no heed*
They'd given me their gold, and treasure more;
I needed not do longer diligence
To win their love, or show them reverence.
They all loved me so well, by God above,
I never did set value on their love!
A woman wise will strive continually
To get herself loved, when she's not, you see.
But since I had them wholly in my hand,
And since to me they'd given all their land,
Why should I take heed, then, that I should please,
Save it were for my profit or my ease?
I set them so to work, that, by my fay,° *faith*
Full many a night they sighed out 'Welaway!'° *woe is me*
The bacon was not brought them home, I trow,° *trust*
That some men have in Essex at Dunmowe.[7]
I governed them so well, by my own law,
That each of them was happy as a daw,° *crow*
And fain to bring me fine things from the fair.
And they were right glad when I spoke them fair;° *kindly*
For God knows that I nagged them mercilessly.
"Now hearken how I bore me properly,

6. The *Almagest,* written around 150 C.E. by the Greek astronomer and mathematician Ptolemy.

7. It was long the custom in this town to award a side of bacon to any married couple who managed not to quarrel for at least a year.

All you wise wives that well can understand.
"Thus shall you speak and wrongfully demand;
For half so brazenfacedly can no man
Swear to his lying as a woman can.
I say not this to wives who may be wise,
Except when they themselves do misadvise.
A wise wife, if she knows what's for her good,
Will swear the crow is mad, and in this mood
Call up for witness to it her own maid;[8]
But hear me now, for this is what I said.[9]
"'Sir Dotard,° is it thus you stand today? *old imbecile*
Why is my neighbour's wife so fine and gay?
She's honoured over all where'er she goes;
I sit at home, I have no decent clo'es.
What do you do there at my neighbour's house?
Is she so fair? Are you so amorous?
Why whisper to our maid? *Benedicite!*° *bless us*
Sir Lecher old, let your seductions be!
And if I have a gossip or a friend,
Innocently, you blame me like a fiend
If I but walk, for company, to his house!
You come home here as drunken as a mouse,
And preach there on your bench, a curse on you!
You tell me it's a great misfortune, too,
To wed a girl who costs more than she's worth;
And if she's rich and of a higher birth,
You say it's torment to abide her folly
And put up with her pride and melancholy.
And if she be right fair, you utter knave,
You say that every lecher will her have;
She may no while in chastity abide
That is assailed by all and on each side.
"'You say, some men desire us for our gold,
Some for our shape and some for fairness told;
And some, that she can either sing or dance,
And some, for courtesy and dalliance;
Some for her hands and for her arms so small;
Thus all goes to the devil in your tale.
You say men cannot keep a castle wall
That's long assailed on all sides, and by all.[1]
"'And if that she be foul, you say that she
Hankers for every man that she may see;
For like a spaniel will she leap on him

8. In a common fable, a talking crow informs a husband of his wife's infidelity; her maid backs up her lies.

9. Alisoun's exhaustive response is composed of passages from several well-worn misogynist treatises, including Theophrastus, Jerome, Matheolus, Jean de Meun, and Eustache Deschamps.

1. In *The Romance of the Rose,* from which these and the following lines are adapted, the Rose is imprisoned in a castle which the Lover is determined to take by any means.

Until she finds a man to be victim;
And not a grey goose swims there in the lake
But finds a gander willing her to take.
You say, it is a hard thing to enfold
Her whom no man will in his own arms hold.
This say you, worthless, when you go to bed;
And that no wise man needs thus to be wed,
No, nor a man that hearkens unto Heaven.
With furious thunder-claps and fiery levin° *lightning*
May your thin, withered, wrinkled neck be broke;
"'You say that dripping eaves, and also smoke,
And wives contentious, will make men to flee
But of their houses; ah, *benedicite!*
What ails such an old fellow so to chide?
"'You say that all we wives our vices hide
Till we are married, then we show them well;
That is a scoundrel's proverb, let me tell!
"'You say that oxen, asses, horses, hounds
Are tried out variously, and on good grounds;
Basins and bowls, before men will them buy,
And spoons and stools and all such goods you try,
And so with pots and clothes and all array;
But of their wives men get no trial, you say,
Till they are married, base old dotard you!
And then we show what evil we can do.
"'You say also that it displeases me
Unless you praise and flatter my beauty,
And save° you gaze always upon my face *unless*
And call me "lovely lady" every place;
And save you make a feast upon that day
When I was born, and give me garments gay;
And save due honour to my nurse is paid
As well as to my faithful chambermaid,
And to my father's folk and his allies—
Thus you go on, old barrel full of lies!
"'And yet of our apprentice, young Jenkin,
For his crisp hair, showing like gold so fine,
Because he squires me walking up and down,
A false suspicion in your mind is sown;
I'd give him naught, though you were dead tomorrow.
"'But tell me this, why do you hide, with sorrow,
The keys to your strong box away from me?
It is my gold as well as yours, pardie.
Why would you make an idiot of your dame?
Now by Saint James,[2] but you shall miss your aim,
You shall not be, although like mad you scold,
Master of both my body and my gold;

2. Alisoun has made a pilgrimage to the shrine of St. James at Compostela.

One you'll forgo in spite of both your eyes;
Why need you seek me out or set on spies?
I think you'd like to lock me in your chest!
You should say: "Dear wife, go where you like best,
Amuse yourself, I will believe no tales;
You're my wife Alis true, and truth prevails."
We love no man that guards us or gives charge
Of where we go, for we will be at large.
"'Of all men the most blessed may he be,
That wise astrologer, Dan Ptolemy,
Who says this proverb in his Almagest;
"Of all men he's in wisdom the highest
That nothing cares who has the world in hand."
And by this proverb shall you understand:
Since you've enough, why do you reck° or care *worry*
How merrily all other folks may fare?
For certainly, old dotard, by your leave,
You shall have cunt all right enough at eve.
He is too much a niggard who's so tight
That from his lantern he'll give none a light.
For he'll have never the less light, by gad;
Since you've enough, you need not be so sad.
"'You say, also, that if we make us gay
With clothing, all in costliest array,
That it's a danger to our chastity;
And you must back the saying up, pardie!
Repeating these words in the apostle's° name: *Paul's*
"In habits meet for chastity, not shame,
Your women shall be garmented," said he,
"And not with broidered hair, or jewellery,
Or pearls, or gold, or costly gowns and chic";
After your text and after your rubric° *heading*
I will not follow more than would a gnat.
You said this, too, that I was like a cat;
For if one care to singe a cat's furred skin,
Then would the cat remain the house within;
And if the cat's coat be all sleek and gay,
She will not keep in house a half a day,
But out she'll go, ere° dawn of any day, *before*
To show her skin and caterwaul° and play. *howl like a cat*
This is to say, if I'm a little gay,
To show my rags I'll gad about all day.
"'Sir Ancient Fool, what ails you with your spies?
Though you pray Argus, with his hundred eyes,
To be my body-guard and do his best,[3]

3. Argus was a hundred-eyed watchman in Greek and Roman myth who never closed all of his eyes at once. He was set by the jealous goddess Juno to guard the mortal woman Io and to prevent her husband Jupiter from sleeping with her. He did not succeed.

Faith, he sha'n't hold me, save I am modest;
I could delude him easily—trust me!
"'You said, also, that there are three things—three—
The which things are a trouble on this earth,
And that no man may ever endure the fourth:
O dear Sir Rogue, may Christ cut short your life!
Yet do you preach and say a hateful wife
Is to be reckoned one of these mischances.
Are there no other kinds of resemblances
That you may liken thus your parables to,
But must a hapless wife be made to do?
"'You liken woman's love to very Hell,
To desert land where waters do not well.
You liken it, also, unto wildfire;
The more it burns, the more it has desire
To consume everything that burned may be.
You say that just as worms destroy a tree,
Just so a wife destroys her own husband;
Men know this who are bound in marriage band.'
"Masters, like this, as you must understand,
Did I my old men charge and censure, and
Claim that they said these things in drunkenness;
And all was false, but yet I took witness
Of Jenkin and of my dear niece also.
O Lord, the pain I gave them and the woe,
All guiltless, too, by God's grief exquisite!
For like a stallion could I neigh and bite.
I could complain, though mine was all the guilt,
Or else, full many a time, I'd lost the tilt.° *joust*
Whoso comes first to mill first gets meal ground;
I whimpered first and so did them confound.
They were right glad to hasten to excuse
Things they had never done, save in my ruse,
"With wenches would I charge him, by this hand,
When, for some illness, he could hardly stand.
Yet tickled this the heart of him, for he
Deemed it was love produced such jealousy.
I swore that all my walking out at night
Was but to spy on girls he kept outright;
And under cover of that I had much mirth.
For all such wit is given us at birth;
Deceit, weeping, and spinning, does God give
To women, naturally, the while they live.
And thus of one thing I speak boastfully,
I got the best of each one, finally,
By trick, or force, or by some kind of thing,
As by continual growls or murmuring;
Especially in bed had they mischance,
There would I chide and give them no pleasance;

I would no longer in the bed abide
If I but felt his arm across my side,
Till he had paid his ransom unto me;
Then would I let him do his nicety.
And therefore to all men this tale I tell,
Let gain who may, for everything's to sell.
With empty hand men may no falcons lure;
For profit would I all his lust endure,
And make for him a well-feigned appetite;
Yet I in bacon never had delight;
And that is why I used so much to chide.
For if the pope were seated there beside
I'd not have spared them, no, at their own board.° *table*
For by my truth, I paid them, word for word.
So help me the True God Omnipotent,
Though I right now should make my testament,
I owe them not a word that was not quit.° *repaid*
I brought it so about, and by my wit,
That they must give it up, as for the best,
Or otherwise we'd never have had rest.
For though he glared and scowled like lion mad,
Yet failed he of the end he wished he had.
"Then would I say: 'Good dearie, see you keep
In mind how meek is Wilkin, our old sheep;
Come near, my spouse, come let me kiss your cheek!
You should be always patient, aye, and meek,
And have a sweetly scrupulous tenderness,
Since you so preach of old Job's patience, yes.
Suffer always, since you so well can preach;
And, save you do, be sure that we will teach
That it is well to leave a wife in peace.
One of us two must bow,° to be at ease; *submit*
And since a man's more reasonable, they say,
Than woman is, you must have patience aye,
What ails you that you grumble thus and groan?
Is it because you'd have my cunt alone?
Why take it all, lo, have it every bit;
Peter!° Beshrew° you but you're fond of it! *By St. Peter / curse*
For if I would go peddle my *belle chose*,° *beautiful thing*
I could walk out as fresh as is a rose;
But I will keep it for your own sweet tooth.
You are to blame, by God I tell the truth.'
"Such were the words I had at my command.
Now will I tell you of my fourth husband.
"My fourth husband, he was a reveller,
That is to say, he kept a paramour;
And young and full of passion then was I,
Stubborn and strong and jolly as a pie.° *magpie*
Well could I dance to tune of harp, nor fail

To sing as well as any nightingale
When I had drunk a good draught of sweet wine.
Metellius, the foul churl and the swine,
Did with a staff deprive his wife of life
Because she drank wine;[4] had I been his wife
He never should have frightened me from drink;
For after wine, of Venus must I think:
For just as surely as cold produces hail,
A liquorish° mouth must have a lickerish° tail. *greedy / lecherous*
In women wine's no bar of impotence,
This know all lechers by experience.
"But Lord Christ! When I do remember me
Upon my youth and on my jollity,
It tickles me about my heart's deep root.
To this day does my heart sing in salute
That I have had my world in my own time
But age, alas! that poisons every prime.
Has taken away my beauty and my pith;° *vigor*
Let go, farewell, the devil go therewith!
The flour is gone, there is no more to tell,
The bran, as best I may, must I now sell;
But yet to be right merry I'll try, and
Now will I tell you of my fourth husband.
"I say that in my heart I'd great despite
When he of any other had delight.
But he was quit, by God and by Saint Joce![5]
I made, of the same wood, a staff most gross;° *paid him back in kind*
Not with my body and in manner foul,
But certainly I showed so gay a soul
That in his own thick grease I made him fry
For anger and for utter jealousy.
By God, on earth I was his purgatory,
For which I hope his soul lives now in glory.
For God knows, many a time he sat and sung
When the shoe bitterly his foot had wrung
There was no one, save God and he, that knew
How, in so many ways, I'd twist the screw.
He died when I came from Jerusalem,
And lies entombed beneath the great rood-beam,° *crossbeam*
Although his tomb is not so glorious
As was the sepulchre of Darius,
The which Apelles wrought full cleverly;[6]
'Twas waste to bury him expensively.
Let him fare well. God give his soul good rest,

4. Alisoun refers to an ancient Roman incident of a man who beat his wife to death with a staff for drinking wine.
5. St. Jodocus, or Josse, was a Breton king who abdicated after a pilgrimage to Rome and became a hermit.
6. The Persian ruler Darius III was an opponent of Alexander the Great in the 4th century B.C.E. The story of his tomb comes from a medieval romance about Alexander.

He now is in the grave and in his chest.° *coffin*
"And now of my fifth husband will I tell.
God grant his soul may never get to Hell
And yet he was to me most brutal, too;
My ribs yet feel as they were black and blue,
And ever shall, until my dying day.
But in our bed he was so fresh and gay,
And therewithal he could so well impose,
What time he wanted use of my *belle chose,*
That though he'd beaten me on every bone,
He could re-win my love, and that full soon.
I guess I loved him best of all, for he
Gave of his love most sparingly to me.
We women have, if I am not to lie,
In this love matter, a quaint fantasy;
Look out a thing we may not lightly have,
And after that we'll cry all day and crave.
Forbid a thing, and that thing covet we;
Press hard upon us, then we turn and flee.
Sparingly offer we our goods, when fair;
Great crowds at market make for dearer ware,
And what's too common brings but little price;
All this knows every woman who is wise.
"My fifth husband, may God his spirit bless!
Whom I took all for love, and not riches,
Had been sometime a student at Oxford,
And had left school and had come home to board
With my best gossip,° dwelling in our town, *friend*
God save her soul! Her name was Alison.
She knew my heart and all my privity° *secrets*
Better than did our parish priest, s'help me!
To her confided I my secrets all.
For had my husband pissed against a wall,
Or done a thing that might have cost his life,
To her and to another worthy wife,
And to my niece whom I loved always well,
I would have told it—every bit I'd tell,
And did so, many and many a time, God wot,° *knows*
Which made his face full often red and hot
For utter shame; he blamed himself that he
Had told me of so deep a privity.
"So it befell that on a time, in Lent[7]
(For oftentimes I to my gossip went,
Since I loved always to be glad and gay
And to walk out, in March, April, and May,

7. The springtime period of Lent was supposed to be a time of fasting and penitence leading up to Holy Week and Easter.

From house to house, to hear the latest malice),
Jenkin the clerk, and my gossip Dame Alis,
And I myself into the meadows went.
My husband was in London all that Lent;
I had the greater leisure, then, to play,
And to observe, and to be seen, I say,
By pleasant folk; what knew I where my face
Was destined to be loved, or in what place?
Therefore I made my visits round about
To vigils and processions of devout,
To preaching too, and shrines of pilgrimage,
To miracle plays, and always to each marriage,
And wore my scarlet skirt before all wights.
These worms and all these moths and all these mites,
I say it at my peril, never ate;
And know you why? I wore it early and late.° *all the time*
"Now will I tell you what befell to me.
I say that in the meadows walked we three
Till, truly, we had come to such dalliance,
This clerk and I, that, of my vigilance,° *in my foresight*
I spoke to him and told him how that he,
Were I a widow, might well marry me.
For certainly I say it not to brag,
But I was never quite without a bag
Full of the needs of marriage that I seek.
I hold a mouse's heart not worth a leek
That has but one hole into which to run,
And if it fail of that, then all is done.
"I made him think he had enchanted me;
My mother taught me all that subtlety.
And then I said I'd dreamed of him all night,
He would have slain me as I lay upright,
And all my bed was full of very blood;
But yet I hoped that he would do me good,
For blood betokens gold, as I was taught.
And all was false, I dreamed of him just—naught,
Save as I acted on my mother's lore,
As well in this thing as in many more.
"But now, let's see, what was I going to say?
Aha, by God, I know! It goes this way.
"When my fourth husband lay upon his bier,
I wept enough and made but sorry cheer,
As wives must always, for it's custom's grace,
And with my kerchief covered up my face;
But since I was provided with a mate,
I really wept but little. I may state.
"To church my man was borne upon the morrow
By neighbours, who for him made signs of sorrow;
And Jenkin, our good clerk, was one of them.

So help me God, when rang the requiem
After the bier, I thought he had a pair
Of legs and feet so clean-cut and so fair
That all my heart I gave to him to hold.
He was, I think, but twenty winters old,
And I was forty, if I tell the truth;
But then I always had a young colt's tooth.° *youthful tastes*
Gap-toothed I was, and that became me well;
I had the print of holy Venus' seal.° *a birthmark*
So help me God, I was a healthy one,
And fair and rich and young and full of fun;
And truly, as my husbands all told me,
I had the silkiest *quoniam*° that could be. *you-know-what*
For truly, I am all Venusian
In feeling, and my brain is Martian.[8]
Venus gave me my lust, my lickerishness,
And Mars gave me my sturdy hardiness.
Taurus was my ascendant, with Mars therein.[9]
Alas, alas, that ever love was sin!
I followed always my own inclination
By vitue of my natal constellation;[1]
Which wrought me so I never could withdraw
My Venus-chamber from a good fellow.
Yet have I Mars's mark° upon my face, *birthmark*
And also in another private place.
For God so truly my salvation be
As I have never loved for policy,
But ever followed my own appetite,
Though he were short or tall, or black or white;
I took no heed, so that° he cared for me, *as long as*
How poor he was nor even of what degree.° *estate*
"What should I say now, save, at the month's end,
This jolly, gentle, Jenkin clerk, my friend,
Had wedded me full ceremoniously,
And to him gave I all the land and fee° *goods*
That ever had been given me before;
But later I repented me full sore.
He never suffered me to have my way.
By God, he smote me on the ear, one day,
Because I tore out of his book a leaf,° *folio page*
So that from this my ear is grown quite deaf.
Stubborn I was as is a lioness,
And with my tongue a very jay, I guess,

8. Her feelings are dominated by the planet Venus and ruled by love; her brain is dominated by the planet Mars and ruled by conflict.

9. Alisoun was born under Taurus, the second sign of the zodiac, ruled by Venus. Mars was also passing through Taurus at that time; hence the double influence.

1. By contrast, the proper approach for a medieval Christian would be to accept the influence of the stars and use his or her will to overcome their sinful aspects.

And walk I would, as I had done before,
From house to house, though I should not, he swore.
For which he often times would sit and preach
And read old Roman tales to me and teach
How one Sulpicius Gallus left his wife
And her forsook for term of all his life
Because he saw her with bared head, I say,
Looking out from his door, upon a day.[2]
"Another Roman told he of by name
Who, since his wife was at a summer-game
Without his knowing, he forsook her eke,[3]
And then would he within his Bible seek
That proverb of the old Ecclesiast[4]
Where he commands so freely and so fast
That man forbid his wife to gad about;
Then would he thus repeat, with never doubt:
'Whoso would build his whole house out of sallows,° *willow branches*
And spur his blind horse to run over fallows,° *ploughed land*
And let his wife alone go seeking hallows,° *shrines*
Is worthy to be hanged upon the gallows.'
But all for naught, I didn't care a haw° *at all*
For all his proverbs, nor for his old saw,° *saying*
Nor yet would I by him corrected be.
I hate one that my vices tells to me,
And so do more of us—God knows!—than I.
This made him mad with me, and furiously,
That I'd not yield to him in any case.
"Now will I tell you truth, by Saint Thomas,
Of why I tore from out his book a leaf,
For which he struck me so it made me deaf.
"He had a book that gladly, night and day,
For his amusement he would read alway.
He called it 'Theophrastus' and 'Valerius,'[5]
At which book would he laugh, uproarious.
And, too, there sometime was a clerk at Rome,
A cardinal, that men called Saint Jerome,
Who made a book against Jovinian;
In which book, too, there was Tertullian,
Chrysippus, Trotula, and Heloïse
Who was abbess near Paris' diocese;
And too, the *Proverbs* of King Solomon,
And Ovid's *Art,* and books full many a one,

2. The *Memorable Deeds and Sayings* of Valerius Maximus (1st century C.E.) recorded this "harsh" but "logical" choice of the consul Gaius Suspicius Gallus.
3. Valerius Maximus also recorded this anecdote about the consul Publius Sempronius Sophus divorcing his wife.
4. The author of the biblical book, Ecclesiasticus, a collection of maxims.
5. Authors of two famous Latin tracts against marriage.

And all of these were bound in one volume.[6]
And every night and day 'twas his custom,
When he had leisure and took some vacation
From all his other worldly occupation,
To read, within this book, of wicked wives.
He knew of them more legends and more lives
Than are of good wives written in the Bible.
For trust me, it's impossible, no libel,
That any cleric shall speak well of wives,
Unless it be of saints and holy lives,
But naught for other women will they do.
Who painted first the lion, tell me who?[7]
By God, if women had but written stories,
As have these clerks within their oratories,° *chapels*
They would have written of men more wickedness
Than all the race of Adam could redress.
The children of Mercury and of Venus
Are in their lives antagonistic thus;
For Mercury loves wisdom and science,
And Venus loves but pleasure and expense.
Because they different dispositions own,
Each falls when other's in ascendant shown.
And God knows Mercury is desolate
In Pisces, wherein Venus rules in state;
And Venus falls when Mercury is raised;
Therefore no woman by a clerk is praised.[8]
A clerk, when he is old and can naught do
Of Venus' labours worth his worn-out shoe,
Then sits he down and writes, in his dotage,
That women cannot keep vow of marriage!
"But now to tell you, as I started to,
Why I was beaten for a book, *pardieu.*° *by God*
Upon a night Jenkin, who was our sire,
Read in his book, as he sat by the fire,
Of Mother Eve who, by her wickedness,
First brought mankind to all his wretchedness,
For which Lord Jesus Christ Himself was slain,
Who, with His heart's blood, saved us thus again.
Lo here, expressly of woman, may you find
That woman was the ruin of mankind.

6. Jenkins's volume contains key sources in clerkly misogyny, from the church fathers Jerome and Tertullian, the Bible, and the Roman poet Ovid, author of *The Art of Love*. Unusually, his collection includes the writings of two women: Trotula, a medieval physician who wrote several works on gynecology; and Heloïse, who argued against marriage with her lover Abelard, before becoming an abbess.

7. The Wife of Bath refers to a fable first told by Aesop, and more recently by Marie de France, that recounts the response of a lion when confronted with the image of a peasant killing a lion.

8. Another astrological explanation: the planet Mercury was associated with the learning proper to the clerk, Venus with the qualities they attributed to women. In terms of the zodiac, when one is ascendant, as Venus in Pisces, the other is descendant—hence, for Alisoun, the conflict between clerks and women.

"Then read he out how Samson lost his hairs,
Sleeping, his leman° cut them with her shears; *lover*
And through this treason lost he either eye.[9]
"Then read he out, if I am not to lie,
Of Hercules, and Deianira's desire
That caused him to go set himself on fire.[1]
"Nothing escaped him of the pain and woe
That Socrates had with his spouses two;
How Xantippe threw piss upon his head;
This hapless man sat still, as he were dead;
He wiped his head, no more durst he complain
Than 'Ere the thunder ceases comes the rain.'[2]
"Then of Pasiphaë, the queen of Crete,
For cursedness he thought the story sweet;
Fie! Say no more—it is an awful thing—
Of her so horrible lust and love-liking.
"Of Clytemnestra, for her lechery,
Who caused her husband's death by treachery,
He read all this with greatest zest, I vow.
"He told me, too, just when it was and how
Amphiaraus at Thebes lost his life;
My husband had a legend of his wife
Eriphyle who, for a brooch of gold,
In secrecy to hostile Greeks had told
Whereat her husband had his hiding place,
For which he found at Thebes but sorry grace.[3]
"Of Livia and Lucia told he me,
For both of them their husbands killed, you see,
The one for love, the other killed for hate;
Livia her husband, on an evening late,
Made drink some poison, for she was his foe.
Lucia, lecherous, loved her husband so
That, to the end he'd always of her think,
She gave him such a philtre, for love-drink,
That he was dead or ever it was morrow;
And husbands thus, by same means, came to sorrow.[4]
"Then did he tell how one Latumius
Complained unto his comrade Arrius
That in his garden grew a baleful tree
Whereon, he said, his wives, and they were three,
Had hanged themselves for wretchedness and woe.

9. The story of Delilah's betrayal of Samson to the Philistines, by cutting off the hair that gave him his great strength, was originally told in the biblical book of Judges. Like the other passages cited here, it had become proverbial.

1. In fact, Deianira's role in the death of her husband, the hero Hercules, was accidental.

2. Jerome is the source for this version of the philosopher Socrates and his proverbially shrewish wife.

3. Episodes from Greek legend: Pasiphaë's passion for a bull, the adulterous Clytemnestra's murder of her husband Agamemnon on his return from Troy, and Eriphyle's betrayal of her husband's hiding place, sending him to a death in Thebes he had already foreseen.

4. Two episodes from Roman history: Livia was said to have murdered her husband with the help of her lover; Lucia (or Lucilla) was said to have killed her husband, the poet Lucretius, accidentally with a love potion.

‘O brother,’ Arrius said, ‘and did they so?
Give me a graft of that same blessed tree
And in my garden planted it shall be!’
“Of wives of later date he also read,
How some had slain their husbands in their bed
And let their lovers shag them all the night
While corpses lay upon the floor upright.
And some had driven nails into the brain
While husbands slept and in such wise were slain.
And some had given them poison in their drink.
He told more evil than the mind can think.
And therewithal he knew of more proverbs
Than in this world there grows of grass or herbs.
‘Better,’ he said, ‘your habitation be
With lion wild or dragon foul,’ said he,
‘Than with a woman who will nag and chide.’
‘Better,’ he said, ‘on the housetop abide
Than with a brawling wife down in the house;
Such are so wicked and contrarious
They hate the thing their husband loves, for aye.’
He said, ‘a woman throws her shame away
When she throws off her smock,’ and further, too:
‘A woman fair, save she be chaste also,
Is like a ring of gold in a sow’s nose.’
Who would imagine or who would suppose
What grief and pain were in this heart of mine?
“And when I saw he’d never cease, in fine,
His reading in this cursed book at night,
Three leaves of it I snatched and tore outright
Out of his book, as he read on; and eke
I with my fist so took him on the cheek
That in our fire he reeled and fell right down.
Then he got up as does a wild lion,
And with his fist he struck me on the head,
And on the floor I lay as I were dead.
And when he saw how limp and still I lay,
He was afraid and would have run away,
Until at last out of my swoon I made:
‘Oh, have you slain me, you false thief?’ I said,
‘And for my land have you thus murdered me?
Kiss me before I die, and let me be.’
“He came to me and near me he knelt down,
And said: ‘O my dear sister Alison,
So help me God, I’ll never strike you more;
What I have done, you are to blame therefor.
But all the same forgiveness now I seek!’
And thereupon I hit him on the cheek,
And said: ‘Thief, so much vengeance do I wreak!
Now will I die, I can no longer speak!’

But at the last, and with much care and woe,
We made it up between ourselves. And so
He put the bridle reins within my hand
To have the governing of house and land;
And of his tongue and of his hand, also;
And made him burn his book, right then, oho!
And when I had thus gathered unto me
Masterfully, the entire sovereignty,
And he had said: 'My own true wedded wife,
Do as you please the term of all your life,
Guard your own honour and keep fair my state'—
After that day we never had debate.
God help me now, I was to him as kind
As any wife from Denmark unto Ind,° *India*
And also true, and so was he to me.
I pray to God, Who sits in majesty,
To bless his soul, out of His mercy dear!
Now will I tell my tale, if you will hear."

The friar laughed when he had heard all this.
"Now dame," said he, "so have I joy or bliss
This is a long preamble to a tale!"
    And when the summoner heard this friar's hail,
"Lo," said the summoner, "by God's arms two!
A friar will always interfere, mark you.
Behold, good men, a housefly and a friar
Will fall in every dish and matters higher.[5]
Why speak of preambling, you in your gown?
What! Amble, trot, hold peace, or go sit down;
You hinder our diversion thus to inquire."
    "Aye, say you so, sir summoner?" said the friar,
"Now by my faith I will, before I go,
Tell of a summoner such a tale, or so,
That all the folk shall laugh who're in this place."
    "Otherwise, friar, I beshrew° your face," *curse*
Replied this summoner, "and beshrew me
If I do not tell tales here, two or three,
Of friars ere I come to Sittingbourne,[6]
That certainly will give you cause to mourn,
For well I know your patience will be gone."
    Our host cried out, "Now peace, and that anon!"
And said he: "Let the woman tell her tale.
You act like people who are drunk with ale.
Do, lady, tell your tale, and that is best."
    "All ready, sir," said she, "as you request,

5. That is, will eat anything and meddle in any business. There was a longstanding dislike between clergy possessing land and goods and mendicants, who did not.

6. On the pilgrimage route, about 40 miles from London and 16 from Canterbury.

If I have license of° this worthy friar." *permission from*
"Yes, dame," said he, "to hear you's my desire."

The Wife of Bath's Tale

Now in the olden days of King Arthur,
Of whom the Britons speak with great honour,
All this wide land was land of faëry
The elf-queen, with her jolly company,
Danced often times on many a green mead;° *meadow*
This was the old opinion, as I read.[1]
I speak of many hundred years ago;
But now no man can see the elves, you know.
For now the so-great charity and prayers
Of limiters and other holy friars
That do infest each land and every stream
As thick as motes° are in a bright sunbeam, *dust particles*
Blessing halls, chambers, kitchens, ladies' bowers,° *chambers*
Cities and towns and castles and high towers,
Manors and barns and stables, aye and dairies—
This causes it that there are now no fairies.[2]
For where was wont to walk full many an elf,
Right there walks now the limiter himself
In noons and afternoons and in mornings,
Saying his matins and such holy things,
As he goes round his district in his gown.[3]
Women may now go safely up and down,
In every copse° or under every tree; *thicket*
There is no other incubus than he,[4]
And would do them nothing but dishonour.
And so befell it that this King Arthur
Had at his court a lusty bachelor° *young knight*
Who, on a day, came riding from river;
And happened that, alone as she was born,
He saw a maiden walking through the corn,
From whom, in spite of all she did and said,
Straightway by force he took her maidenhead;
For which violation was there such clamour,
And such appealing unto King Arthur,
That soon condemned was this knight to be dead
By course of law, and should have lost his head,
Peradventure,° such being the statute then; *as it chanced*

1. Although its specific source is unknown, "The Wife of Bath's Tale" is drawn from the "Matter of Britain," a collection of tales and romances about the deeds of the legendary King Arthur and his court. See also the *lais* of Marie de France (page 1189).

2. In her offhand way, Alisoun allows Chaucer to draw out an important theme of the Matter of Britain: the tension between the ancient pre-Christian Celtic religion, including its fairies, elves, and magic, and the Christian belief system that was replacing it.

3. A friar limiter (allowed to beg within certain limits), like the one who has just finished interrupting her tale.

4. An incubus was an evil spirit who descended on people in their sleep; with women especially it sought sexual activity. Their existence was recognized by both church and state during the Middle Ages.

But that the other ladies and the queen
So long prayed of the king to show him grace,
He granted life, at last, in the law's place,
And gave him to the queen, as she should will,
Whether she'd save him, or his blood should spill.
The queen she thanked the king with all her might,
And after this, thus spoke she to the knight,
When she'd an opportunity, one day:
"You stand yet," said she, "in such poor a way
That for your life you've no security.
I'll grant you life if you can tell to me
What thing it is that women most desire.
Be wise, and keep your neck from iron dire!° *dreadful iron*
And if you cannot tell it me anon,
Then will I give you license to be gone
A twelvemonth° and a day, to search and learn *year*
Sufficient answer in this grave concern.
And your knight's word I'll have, ere forth you pace,
To yield your body to me in this place."
Grieved was this knight, and sorrowfully he sighed;
But there! he could not do as pleased his pride.
And at the last he chose that he would wend,° *depart*
And come again upon the twelvemonth's end,
With such an answer as God might purvey;° *provide*
And so he took his leave and went his way.
He sought out every house and every place
Wherein he hoped to find that he had grace
To learn what women love the most of all;
But nowhere ever did it him befall
To find, upon the question stated here,
Two persons who agreed with statement clear.
Some said that women all loved best riches,
Some said, fair fame, and some said, prettiness;
Some, rich array, some said 'twas lust abed
And often to be widowed and re-wed.
Some said that our poor hearts are aye most eased
When we have been most flattered and thus pleased
And he went near the truth, I will not lie;
A man may win us best with flattery;
And with attentions and with busyness
We're often limed,° the greater and the less. *ensnared*
And some say, too, that we do love the best
To be quite free to do our own behest,
And that no man reprove us for our vice,
But saying we are wise, take our advice.
For truly there is no one of us all,
If anyone shall rub us on a gall,° *sore spot*
That will not kick because he tells the truth.
Try, and he'll find who does so, I say sooth.° *truth*

No matter how much vice we have within,
We would be held for wise and clean of sin.
And some folk say that great delight have we
To be held constant, also trustworthy,
And on one purpose steadfastly to dwell,
And not betray a thing that men may tell.
But that tale is not worth a rake's handle;
By God, we women can no thing conceal,
As witness Midas. Would you hear the tale?[5]
Ovid, among some other matters small,
Said Midas had beneath his long curled hair,
Two ass's ears that grew in secret there
The which defect he hid, as best he might,
Full cunningly from every person's sight,
And, save his wife, no one knew of it, no.
He loved her most, and trusted her also;
And he prayed of her that to no creature
She'd tell of his disfigurement impure.
She swore him: Nay, for all this world to win
She would do no such villainy or sin
And cause her husband have so foul a name;
Nor would she tell it for her own deep shame.
Nevertheless, she thought she would have died
Because so long the secret must she hide;
It seemed to swell so big about her heart
That some word from her mouth must surely start;
And since she dared to tell it to no man,
Down to a marsh, that lay hard by, she ran;
Till she came there her heart was all afire,
And as a bittern booms in the quagmire,
She laid her mouth low to the water down:
"Betray me not, you sounding water blown,"
Said she, "I tell it to none else but you:
Long ears like asses' has my husband two!
Now is my heart at ease, since that is out;
I could no longer keep it, there's no doubt."
Here may you see, though for a while we bide,
Yet out it must; no secret can we hide.
The rest of all this tale, if you would hear,
Read Ovid: in his book does it appear.
This knight my tale is chiefly told about
When what he went for he could not find out,
That is, the thing that women love the best,
Most saddened was the spirit in his breast;
But home he goes, he could no more delay.
The day was come when home he turned his way;

5. Ovid recounts the tale in Book 11 of the *Metamorphoses,* although the Wife of Bath has replaced the original version's barber with a wife.

And on his way it chanced that he should ride
In all his care, beneath a forest's side,
And there he saw, a-dancing him before,
Full four and twenty ladies, maybe more;
Toward which dance eagerly did he turn
In hope that there some wisdom he should learn.
But truly, ere he came upon them there,
The dancers vanished all, he knew not where.[6]
No creature saw he that gave sign of life,
Save, on the greensward sitting, an old wife;
A fouler person could no man devise.
Before the knight this old wife did arise,
And said: "Sir knight, hence lies no travelled way.
Tell me what thing you seek, and by your fay.
Perchance you'll find it may the better be;
These ancient folk know many things," said she.
"Dear mother," said this knight assuredly,
"I am but dead, save I can tell, truly,
What thing it is that women most desire;
Could you inform me, I'd pay well your hire."
"Plight me your troth° here, hand in hand," said she, *promise me*
"That you will do, whatever it may be,
The thing I ask if it lie in your might;
And I'll give you your answer ere the night."
"Have here my word," said he. "That thing I grant."
"Then," said the crone, "of this I make my vaunt° *boast*
Your life is safe; and I will stand thereby,
Upon my life, the queen will say as I.
Let's see which is the proudest of them all
That wears upon her hair kerchief or caul,° *ornamented hairnet*
Shall dare say no to that which I shall teach;
Let us go now and without longer speech."
Then whispered she a sentence in his ear,
And bade him to be glad and have no fear.
When they were come unto the court, this knight
Said he had kept his promise as was right,
And ready was his answer, as he said.
Full many a noble wife, and many a maid,
And many a widow, since they are so wise,
The queen herself sitting as high justice,
Assembled were, his answer there to hear;
And then the knight was bidden to appear.[7]
Command was given for silence in the hall,

6. The *locus amoenus,* or pleasing place, reached after a long wandering journey, was a central locale in medieval romance. See, for example, the *lais* of Marie de France (page 1189).

7. The setting and the type of question recall the "courts of love" of Eleanor of Aquitaine and her daughter Marie, who had been primarily responsible for reviving the *matière de Bretagne* and who were patrons to many of the most important poets and writers of the time, including Marie de France, Andreas Capellanus, and Chrétien de Troyes.

And that the knight should tell before them all
What thing all worldly women love the best.
This knight did not stand dumb, as does a beast,
But to this question presently answered
With manly voice, so that the whole court heard:
"My liege lady, generally," said he,
"Woman desire to have the sovereignty
As well upon their husband as their love,
And to have mastery their man above;° *over their man*
This thing you most desire, though me you kill
Do as you please, I am here at your will."
In all the court there was no wife or maid
Or widow that denied the thing he said,
But all held, he was worthy to have life.
And with that word up started the old wife
Whom he had seen a-sitting on the green.
"Mercy," cried she, "my sovereign lady queen!
Before the court's dismissed, give me my right.
'Twas I who taught the answer to this knight;
For which he did plight troth to me, out there,
That the first thing I should of him require
He would do that, if it lay in his might.
Before the court, now, pray I you sir knight,"
Said she, "that you will take me for your wife;
For well you know that I have saved your life.
If this be false, say nay, upon your fay!"
This knight replied: "Alas and welaway!
That I so promised I will not protest.
But for God's love pray make a new request,
Take all my wealth and let my body go."
"Nay then," said she, "beshrew us if I do!
For though I may be foul and old and poor,
I will not, for all metal and all ore
That from the earth is dug or lies above,
Be aught except your wife and your true love."
"My love?" cried he, "nay, rather my damnation!
Alas! that any of my race and station
Should ever so dishonoured foully be!"
But all for naught; the end was this, that he
Was so constrained he needs must go and wed,
And take his ancient wife and go to bed.
Now, peradventure, would some men say here,
That, of my negligence, I take no care
To tell you of the joy and all the array
That at the wedding feast were seen that day.
Make a brief answer to this thing I shall;
I say, there was no joy or feast at all;
There was but heaviness and grievous sorrow;
For privately he wedded on the morrow,° *the next day*

And all day, then, he hid him like an owl;[8]
So sad he was, his old wife looked so foul.
Great was the woe the knight had in his thought
When he, with her, to marriage bed was brought;
He rolled about and turned him to and fro.
His old wife lay there, always smiling so
And said: "O my dear husband, *ben'cite!*
Fares every knight with wife as you with me?
Is this the custom in King Arthur's house?
Are knights of his all so fastidious?
I am your own true love and, more, your wife;
And I am she who saved your very life;
And truly, since I've never done you wrong,
Why do you treat me so, this first night long?
You act as does a man who's lost his wit;
What is my fault? For God's love tell me it,
And it shall be amended, if I may."
"Amended!" cried this knight, "Alas, nay, nay!
It will not be amended ever, no!
Your are so loathsome, and so old also,
And therewith of so low a race were born,
It's little wonder that I toss and turn.
Would God my heart would break within my breast!"
"Is this," asked she, "the cause of your unrest?"
"Yes, truly," said he, "and no wonder 'tis."
"Now, sir," said she, "I could amend all this,
If I but would, and that within days three,
If you would bear yourself well towards me.
"But since you speak of such gentility
As is descended from old wealth, till ye
Claim that for that you should be gentlemen,
I hold such arrogance not worth a hen.
Find him who is most virtuous alway,
Alone or publicly, and most tries aye
To do whatever noble deeds he can,
And take him for the greatest gentleman.
Christ wills we claim from Him gentility,
Not from ancestors of landocracy.° *landed gentry*
For though they give us all their heritage,
For which we claim to be of high lineage,
Yet can they not bequeath, in anything,
To any of us, their virtuous living,
That made men say they had gentility,
And bade us follow them in like degree.
"Well does that poet wise of great Florence,

8. Owls emerge only at night.

Called Dante, speak his mind in this sentence;
Somewhat like this may it translated be:
'Rarely unto the branches of the tree
Doth human worth mount up: and so ordains
He Who bestows it; to Him it pertains.'[9]
For of our fathers may we nothing claim
But temporal things, that man may hurt and maim.
"And everyone knows this as well as I,
If nobleness were implanted naturally
Within a certain lineage, down the line,
In private and in public, I opine,
The ways of gentleness they'd alway show
And never fall to vice and conduct low.
"Take fire and carry it in the darkest house
Between here and the Mount of Caucasus,° *east of the Black Sea*
And let men shut the doors and from them turn;
Yet will the fire as fairly blaze and burn
As twenty thousand men did it behold;
Its nature and its office it will hold,
On peril of my life, until it die.
"From this you see that true gentility
Is not allied to wealth a man may own,
Since folk do not their deeds, as may be shown,
As does the fire, according to its kind.
For God knows that men may full often find
A lord's son doing shame and villainy;
And he that prizes his gentility
In being born of some old noble house,
With ancestors both noble and virtuous,
But will himself do naught of noble deeds
Nor follow him to whose name he succeeds,
He is not gentle,° be he duke or earl; *noble*
For acting churlish makes a man a churl.
Gentility is not just the renown
Of ancestors who have some greatness shown,
In which you have no portion of your own.
Your own gentility comes from God alone;
Thence comes our true nobility by grace,
It was not willed us with our rank and place
"Think how noble, as says Valerius,
Was that same Tullius Hostilius,
Who out of poverty rose to high estate.[1]

9. The passage is translated from *Purgatorio* 7.121–23, where Dante bemoaned the inability of good character to be transmitted as reliably as a good name. For Dante this demonstrated the difference between fallibly human conceptions of fate and inscrutably divine conceptions of justice.

1. The *Memorable Deeds and Sayings* of Valerius Maximus record the legendary life of the herdsman Tullius Hostilius, who rose to become the third king of Rome.

Seneca and Boethius inculcate,° *urge*
Expressly (and no doubt it thus proceeds),
That he is noble who does noble deeds;[2]
And therefore, husband dear, I thus conclude:
Although my ancestors mayhap° were rude,° *perhaps / uncultured*
Yet may the High Lord, and so hope I,
Grant me the grace to live right virtuously.
Then I'll be gentle when I do begin
To live in virtue and to do no sin.
"And when you me reproach for poverty,
The High God, in Whom we believe, say I,
In voluntary poverty lived His life.
And surely every man, or maid, or wife
May understand that Jesus, Heaven's King,
Would not have chosen vileness of living.
Glad poverty's an honest thing, that's plain,
Which Seneca and other clerks maintain.
Whoso will be content with poverty,
I hold him rich, though not a shirt has he.
And he that covets much is a poor wight,
For he would gain what's all beyond his might
But he that has not, nor desires to have,
Is rich, although you hold him but a knave.
"True poverty, it sings right naturally;
Juvenal gaily says of poverty:[3]
'The poor man, when he walks along the way,
Before the robbers he may sing and play.'
Poverty's odious good, and, as I guess,
It is a stimulant to busyness;
A great improver, too, of sapience
In him that takes it all with due patience.
Poverty's this, though it seem misery—
Its quality may none dispute, say I.
Poverty often, when a man is low,
Makes him his God and even himself to know.
And poverty's an eye-glass, seems to me,
Through which a man his loyal friends may see.
Since you've received no injury from me,
Then why reproach me for my poverty.
"Now, sir, with age you have upbraided me;
And truly, sir, though no authority
Were in a book, you gentles° of honour *gentle folk*
Say that men should the aged show favour,
And call him father, of your gentleness;

2. Referring to the Moral Epistles of Seneca the Younger (d. 65 C.E.) and to the Consolation of Philosophy of the Roman philosopher Boethius, which Chaucer had translated during the 1380s.

3. The Roman satirist Juvenal, in his tenth Satire.

And authors could I find for this, I guess.
"Now since you say that I am foul and old,
Then fear you not to be made a cuckold;
For dirt and age, as° prosperous I may be, *however*
Are mighty wardens over chastity.
Nevertheless, since I know your delight,
I'll satisfy your worldly appetite.
"Choose, now," said she, "one of these two things, aye,
To have me foul and old until I die,
And be to you a true and humble wife,
And never anger you in all my life;
Or else to have me young and very fair
And take your chance with those who will repair
Unto your house, and all because of me,
Or in some other place, as well may be.
Now choose which you like better and reply."
This knight considered, and did sorely sigh,
But at the last replied as you shall hear:
"My lady and my love, and wife so dear,
I put myself in your wise governing;
Do you choose which may be the more pleasing,
And bring most honour to you, and me also.
I care not which it be of these things two;
For if you like it, that suffices me."
"Then have I got of you the mastery,
Since I may choose and govern, in earnest?"
"Yes, truly, wife," said he, "I hold that best."
"Kiss me," said she, "we'll be no longer wroth,
For by my truth, to you I will be both;
That is to say, I'll be both good and fair.
I pray God I go mad, and so declare,
If I be not to you as good and true
As ever wife was since the world was new.
And, save I be, at dawn, as fairly seen
As any lady, empress, or great queen
That is between the east and the far west,
Do with my life and death as you like best.
Throw back the curtain and see how it is."
And when the knight saw verily all this,
That she so very fair was, and young too,
For joy he clasped her in his strong arms two,
His heart bathed in a bath of utter bliss;
A thousand times, all in a row, he'd kiss.
And she obeyed his wish in everything
That might give pleasure to his love-liking.
And thus they lived unto their lives' fair end,
In perfect joy; and Jesus to us send

Meek husbands, and young ones, and fresh in bed,
And good luck to outlive them that we wed.
And I pray Jesus to cut short the lives
Of those who'll not be governed by their wives;
And old and querulous niggards with their pence,
And send them soon a mortal pestilence!

Don Cristobal Colon, Admiral of Ships Bound for the Indies. In Honorius Philoponus, *Nova typis transacta navigatio* (1621). In this image from a book by a German monk on missionary voyages, Columbus is poised at Europe's shore, the vast sea stretching away toward the Indies he can see in his mind's eye. The portrait combines eras as well as regions: Columbus is shown with a modern compass and ship, but he seems to bear the globe on his shoulder like the classical giant Atlas, while his feet rest on an ancient Christian symbol, the Anchor of Faith. While one hand gestures toward his charts, the other hand raises up toward God. The globe shows the major islands Columbus "discovered," Cuba and Hispaniola or "Spagnolla," but much more space is given to the lands Columbus himself never believed were there: not India at all but entirely separate continents. Brazil, Peru, Mexico, and North America beckon Honorius's reader to go beyond Columbus to new explorations, conquests and conversions in the still unmapped regions approaching the "Circumference of the Center of Gravity."

The Early Modern Period

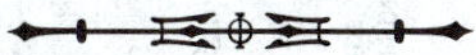

In many regions of the world, the centuries between about 1400 and 1650 mark a time of transition from ancient, largely separate traditions to the rapidly evolving and interconnected world of modernity; the term "early modern" is increasingly used to describe this transitional era. The literatures of the early modern period reflect three great global movements: of worldwide exploration and conquest; of rational and scientific inquiry; and of the growing literary use of vernacular or common speech. These three developments are closely related. The world opened out dramatically after 1492, as the Eastern and Western hemispheres came into direct contact, and even before then contacts were intensifying as China's Ming dynasty extended its sway across the Indian Ocean, the expanding Ottoman Empire linked vast territories from Mesopotamia to eastern Europe, and European navigators explored the coasts of Africa and India. Greatly increased contact between widely separated cultures stimulated reflection on religious doctrines, political structures, and cultural practices of all sorts. And as old traditions came newly into question, the ancient languages that had conveyed them, such as Latin and Sanskrit, began to be supplemented and even replaced by modern vernaculars, as writers sought modes of expression that would reflect the changing reality around them.

The Early Modern World

The early modern world was marked politically by two opposing forces: expansive imperial outreach by several major powers, and national consolidation and resistance to outside rule. At times, these forces could actually work together, as when the Castilian monarchs Ferdinand and Isabella conquered the Muslim kingdom of Grenada in southern Spain in 1492; beginning in that very year, the unified nation became a major launching-point for American exploration and imperial conquest. Yet unified nations could also gain new independence from outside control: the Protestant countries of Germany and Scandinavia broke free of papal authority and the related political sway of the Holy Roman Empire, and France, though remaining largely Catholic, asserted an increasingly unified cultural identity and political independence.

An important aspect of political and cultural self-definition became the establishment of national languages and literatures. Local languages achieved new status in many parts of the world. Korea had long been in China's shadow both politically and culturally, but a new dynasty was established in 1392 by a general named Yi Songgye. The Chosŏn dynasty lasted until 1910 and cultivated specifically Korean arts and culture. Like Japanese, Korean had always been written using Chinese characters, but the mid-1400s saw the establishment of a Korean alphabet. French, German, English, and other national languages were increasingly used in place of Latin for serious literary work, and Italy itself was an early leader in "the vernacular revolution" as writers such as Dante and Boccaccio began to use Italian as well as Latin.

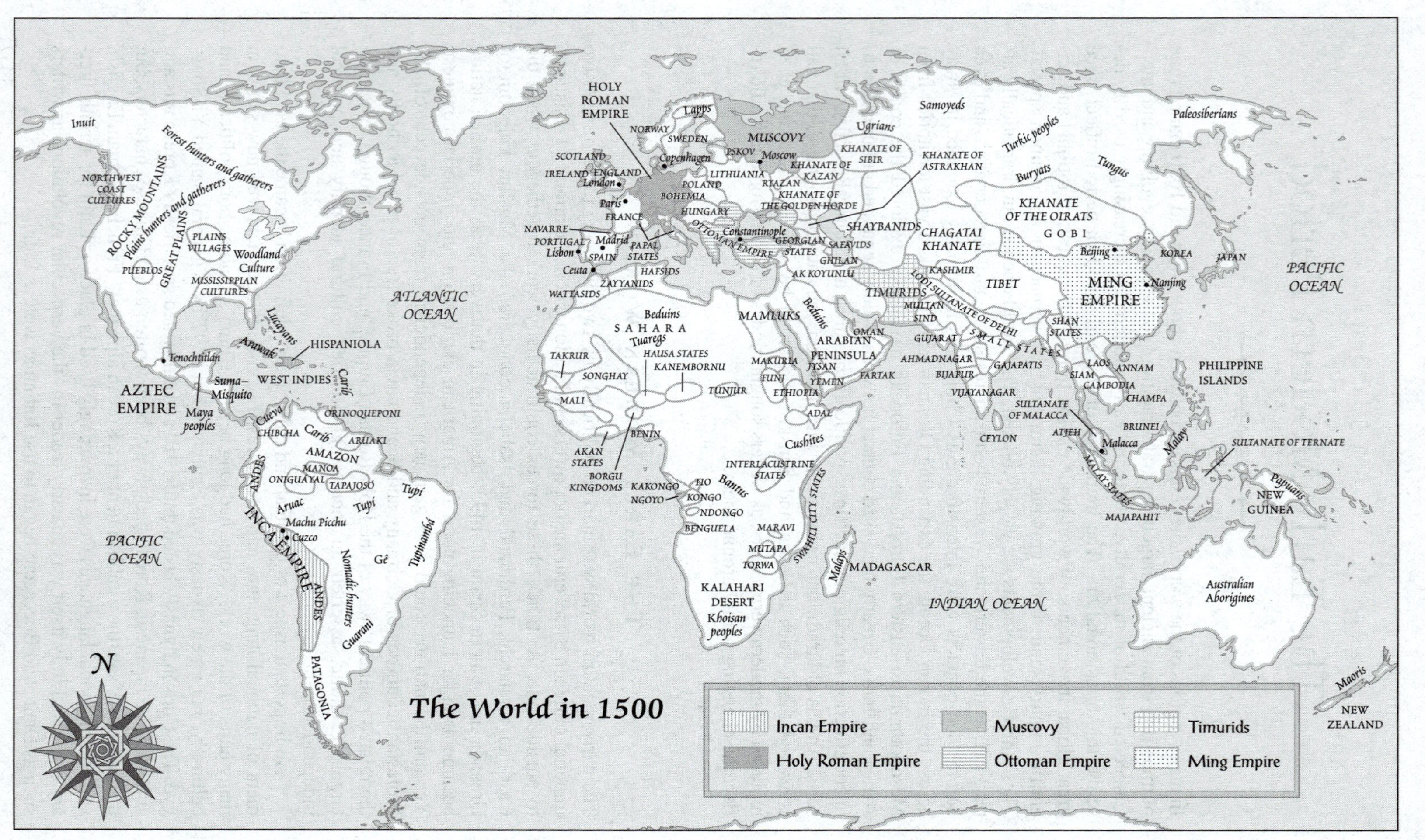
The World in 1500
Incan Empire
Holy Roman Empire
Muscovy
Ottoman Empire
Timurids
Ming Empire
N
Inuit
NORTHWEST COAST CULTURES
ROCKY MOUNTAINS
Forest hunters and gatherers
Plains hunters and gatherers
GREAT PLAINS
PLAINS VILLAGES
PUEBLOS
Woodland Culture
MISSISSIPPIAN CULTURES
Tenochtitlán
AZTEC EMPIRE
Maya peoples
Suma–Misquito
Lucayans
Arawak
HISPANIOLA
WEST INDIES
Carib
ATLANTIC OCEAN
PACIFIC OCEAN
Cueva
CHIBCHA
ORINOQUEPONI
ARUAKI
AMAZON
MANOA
ONIGUAYAL
TAPAJOSÓ
ANDES
Aruac
Machu Picchu
Cuzco
INCA EMPIRE
Tupí
Tupinambá
Gê
Nomadic hunters
Guarani
PATAGONIA
HOLY ROMAN EMPIRE
Lapps
NORWAY
SWEDEN
MUSCOVY
PSKOV
Moscow
SCOTLAND
IRELAND
ENGLAND
London
Copenhagen
LITHUANIA
POLAND
BOHEMIA
Paris
FRANCE
HUNGARY
NAVARRE
PORTUGAL
Lisbon
Madrid
SPAIN
PAPAL STATES
OTTOMAN EMPIRE
Constantinople
Ceuta
HAFSIDS
ZAYYANIDS
WATTASIDS
KHANATE OF KAZAN
RYAZAN
KHANATE OF THE GOLDEN HORDE
Ugrians
KHANATE OF SIBIR
KHANATE OF ASTRAKHAN
Samoyeds
Turkic peoples
Paleosiberians
Tungus
Buryats
KHANATE OF THE OIRATS
GOBI
SHAYBANIDS
GEORGIAN STATES
SAFAVIDS
GHILAN
AK KOYUNLU
CHAGATAI KHANATE
KASHMIR
TIBET
Beijing
KOREA
JAPAN
MING EMPIRE
Nanjing
PACIFIC OCEAN
TIMURIDS
LODI SULTANATE OF DELHI
MULTAN
SIND
SMALL STATES
SHAN STATES
Beduins
SAHARA
Tuaregs
HAUSA STATES
KANEMBORNU
TAKRUR
SONGHAY
MALI
TUNJUR
MAMLUKS
Beduins
ARABIAN PENINSULA
OMAN
MAKURIA
FUNJ
JYSAN
YEMEN
FARTAK
ETHIOPIA
ADAL
GUJARAT
AHMADNAGAR
BIJAPUR
GAJAPATIS
VIJAYANAGAR
LAOS
ANNAM
SIAM
CAMBODIA
CHAMPA
PHILIPPINE ISLANDS
SULTANATE OF MALACCA
ATJEH
Malacca
BRUNEI
Malay
CEYLON
MALAY STATES
MAJAPAHIT
SULTANATE OF TERNATE
Papuans
NEW GUINEA
BENIN
AKAN STATES
BORGU KINGDOMS
KAKONGO
NGOYO
TIO
KONGO
Bantus
NDONGO
BENGUELA
Cushites
INTERLACUSTRINE STATES
SWAHILI CITY STATES
MARAVI
MUTAPA
TORWA
Malays
MADAGASCAR
KALAHARI DESERT
Khoisan peoples
INDIAN OCEAN
Australian Aborigines
Maoris
NEW ZEALAND

Exploration and Conquest

Long-distance exploration began in earnest in the late 1400s, with Portuguese navigators exploring the coast of Africa in the 1480s and Vasco da Gama reaching as far as India in the 1490s. Columbus's epochal voyage of 1492 was followed by a flood of explorations westward and then the conquest of the Aztec and Incan empires in the early 1500s; Dutch, British, and French colonies followed Spanish settlements in North America in the early 1600s. New worlds are constantly being discovered in early modern literature. In 1516, Sir Thomas More claimed that one of Amerigo Vespucci's sailors had gone on from Brazil to find the ideal island republic of *Utopia*. At the close of the early modern period, Milton's Satan voyages from Hell to the "boundless Continent" of Earth, where he hopes to increase his "Honor and Empire … / By conquering this new World" (*Paradise Lost* 4.390–91). The rapid expansion of European exploration and settlement involved discoveries in both directions. In one Aztec poem from around 1550, the poet describes traveling to Rome to meet Pope Clement VII:

> The pope is on God's mat and seat and speaks for him.
> Who is this reclining on a golden chair? Look! It's the pope.
> He has his turquoise blowgun and he's shooting in the world.
> It seems it's true, he has his cross and golden staff,
> and these are shining in the world.

Several major empires were extending their reach in other parts of the world as well. In West Africa, the Songhai empire expanded during the 1500s from its base in Mali. In China, the Ming dynasty, founded in 1368, ruled until 1644 at the close of the early modern period. Where previous dynasties had largely looked inward, or at most had been active in East Asia, Ming China extended its influence over an unprecedented region. The emperor Cheng Tsu (r. 1402–1424) sent a fleet of warships commanded by the enterprising eunuch admiral Cheng Ho to establish trading bases and exact tribute not only from Japan and Korea but from southern India and even the east coast of Africa. In the 1500s, the Mughal Empire encompassed almost all of northern India and what is now Pakistan, while in the fifteenth through sixteenth centuries the Ottoman Empire expanded from Turkey to control Greece, the Balkans, Hungary, the Crimea, Mesopotamia, Syria, Palestine, Egypt, and the north coast of Africa all the way to Morocco at the western end of the Mediterranean. The Ottoman ruler Suleiman I, who reigned for almost half a century beginning in 1520, became known in Europe as "Suleiman the Magnificent" for the splendor of his court and his many victories.

Scientific Conquest and Inquiry

The increasing interest in scientific inquiry and technological innovation also aided imperial outreach: modern armies and navies could now overwhelm much larger forces not equipped with rifles, cannon, and warships. The practitioners of science or "natural philosophy" could even think of themselves as conquering warriors. As the physician and alchemist Paracelsus explained in his *Great Surgery Book* in 1536, "Every experiment is like a weapon which must be used in a particular way—a spear to thrust, a club to strike. Experimenting requires a man who knows when to thrust and when to strike, each according to need and fashion." In these same years, the Polish astronomer Nicolas Copernicus was making the observations that would lead to his revolutionary assertion that the earth and other planets revolve around the sun, not the sun around the earth—a disorienting change of perspective that questioned both classical authority and church doctrine. All phenomena and all traditions became subjects for probing, skeptical inquiry. In the 1570s Michel de Montaigne founded a new kind of writing, the essay or *essai*—French for "trial, experiment"—to convey his speculations on past and present events and on his own character. As he wrote in an inscription for his library, "I do not understand; I pause, I examine."

In Mughal India, the undogmatic ruler Akbar the Great (r. 1556–1605) organized discussions among a series of religious leaders—Zoroastrians, Christians, and Hindus as well as Muslims. Though Akbar never abandoned Islam, the religion of his birth, he came to regard Muhammad as not necessarily the last or the greatest of prophets, and he proclaimed tolerance for all religions in his realm. He reformed the judicial system in a similar spirit of inquiry, decreeing that judges "should not be satisfied with witnesses or oaths, but proceed by manifold inquiries, by the study of physiognomy, and the exercise of foresight." In Ming China, new emphasis was given to individual merit as demonstrated on civil service examinations. While established, wealthy families continued to have advantages in preparing their sons for these elaborate examinations, increasing numbers of people without marked wealth or connections were able to come into the government.

The importance given to the examination stimulated the establishment of Chinese schools, both by the government and by private scholars; like the many new universities of Europe, these schools became centers of debate and of probing scholarship. The fifteenth and sixteenth centuries saw an outpouring of Chinese scholarship that assembled and assessed the classic works of the past. The most ambitious imperial anthology ran to no fewer than eleven thousand volumes. Textual scholars sought to establish correct texts, and one sixteenth-century scholar was so bold as to question the authenticity of portions of the classic *Book of Songs*, a text that had been a founding document for earlier Confucian orthodoxy (see page 656).

The Ming scholars' interest in restoring and critically assessing their literary heritage went along with a heightened individualism and a new attention to colloquial prose fiction. A similar confluence can be seen in Europe as well, in the intensive reengagement with ancient texts and artworks that became known as "the Renaissance." European writers and other artists engaged with new intensity with classic forms, creating modern epics, plays, poems, and fictions out of the materials of Greek and Latin tradition.

The Rise of Print Culture

A crucial development in the early modern period was the invention of printing, which enabled texts to be widely circulated in multiple copies and made ownership affordable to people not possessing extensive private means. The world's first movable type was developed in China by a printer named Pi Sheng in around 1000, using pottery rather than metal type, though the complexity of the thousands of Chinese characters meant that texts could still more readily be written by hand. Increasingly sophisticated methods of woodblock printing allowed for the printing of more and more texts, often to the displeasure of government officials unable to control private mass-production of texts.

The Peking Mission. The Jesuit mission to China in the late 16th century was strictly speaking a failure, insofar as very few Chinese were converted by the small band of Italians, Spaniards, and Germans who lived among them for several decades. But the mission was about more than conversion. The top panel depicts three priests, Matteo Ricci, Adam Schaal, and Ferdinand Verbiest, representative less of their religious beliefs than of the recent innovations in Western science: the compass, the astrolabe, the quadrant. At the same time, science could be the path that led to conversion; Ricci would collaborate with one bureaucrat, Li Zhizao, on several mathematical works before Li became a Christian. Two such converts are shown in the lower panel, turned to face the cross which, the illustration says, "the Christians have now accustomed the Chinese to let themselves be buried with."

In Europe, the invention of movable metal type in the 1450s revolutionized the production and circulation of texts. Among other consequences, the spread of print culture gave impetus to the protestant Reformation beginning in the early 1500s, which stressed individual reading and understanding of Scripture. Such individual reading was newly possible with the spread of printed copies of the Bible, increasingly published in vernacular languages that people could read without needing the expense and leisure required to learn Latin. Not only men but also women—rarely given classical educations—could take an active role in the writing and reading of vernacular texts, and all sorts of literary production were stimulated by the new possibilities of print and the new availability of the vernacular languages as resources for serious writing. Writers around the world began to explore the brave new worlds open to them through vernacular languages and print culture.

Early Modern Europe

In 1632, the aging astronomer Galileo Galilei declared before the Roman Inquisition that he had entertained "the false opinion that the Sun is the center of the world and immovable, and that the earth is not the center of the same and that it moves." The early modern period saw the position of the earth radically reimagined by Galileo and his predecessor Copernicus; it also witnessed the renewed tenacity of the restraints on that imagination. In addition to the increased power of the papacy embodied in the Inquisition, the political map was redrawn. Spain and France had become absolutist states as former kingdoms and duchies were united under a single crown or, in the case of Spain, two crowns: the marriage of Ferdinand of Aragon and Isabella of Castile transformed the greater part of the Iberian peninsula into a powerful military presence. Likewise, England and Poland emerged in the fifteenth centuries as formidable monarchies. At the same time, in 1579 Europe experienced what one historian has called its "first modern war of national liberation" when the northern provinces of the Netherlands rose up against Spain. The English monarchy would soon face its own rebellion, culminating in the execution of Charles I in 1649. The economically thriving duchies of Germany, on the other hand, were the very heart of the Holy Roman Empire, revived in 1438 under the first representatives of what would be the long-lived Habsburg Dynasty. Even if Holy Roman Emperor Charles V called Luther a heretic at a crucial confrontation in 1520, the German princes, who would retain considerable autonomy, refused to go along with the accusation. As a result, much of what we now know as Germany embraced Luther's revolution, throwing off its shackles to the Catholic Church shortly after Charles V's proclamation. After a lifetime struggling against the German Protestants, Charles would abdicate his throne and retire to a monastery in Spain.

This redrawing of the earth's perimeters and its geopolitical makeup extended both westward and eastward. In the wake of the religious divisiveness brought about by the Protestants, Calvinists founded colonies off the coast of Brazil, Puritans defied the elements at Plymouth Rock, and Jesuits started schools in Ceylon (Sri Lanka) and China. These new wanderings were a concerted effort to win souls for Christ and to acquire gold, bread baskets, and new subjects for Europe's sovereign states. The Islamic presence in the Middle East and northwest Asia had grown steadily under the Sultan Osman, one of the early rulers of the Ottoman Empire. In 1453, Osman's armies captured the city of Constantinople, strategically situated on the edge of the Black Sea. Named for Constantine, the Roman emperor who had made Christianity the religion of his empire, Constantinople became Istanbul, and the great church of Santa Sophia became a mosque. The old spice route that had enabled enterprising merchants such as Marco Polo to pass through Turkey, Afghanistan, India, and even China was closed down, forcing other traders to find new routes to the Indies. Columbus's misguided pursuit of a new spice route to Asia led him instead to new worlds, while Vasco da Gama would reach the real India by boat in 1498. By 1521, Magellan would circumnavigate the globe.

The capture of Constantinople had other far-reaching effects. The Turks eventually advanced as far west as Vienna, and their threatening proximity polarized opposition to Islam, sparking talk of new Crusades. Isabella and Ferdinand overthrew the Arab kingdom of Granada in 1492, permanently banishing Muslims from a region

that had once been the intellectual capital of southern Europe. Moreover, for a millennium Constantinople had served as the capital of the Byzantine Empire, home to a sophisticated civilization. As the Ottomans progressively conquered Athens, Damascus, Belgrade, and Rhodes, for the first time since antiquity, a large number of

Greek-speaking scholars fled to western Europe, taking the quickest sea route to Venice. Among other things, their presence would enable the restoration of the Greek legacy of antiquity, dominated in the west for over a thousand years by Latinity. Plato, Homer, Sappho, the Greek tragedians, and eventually a freshly studied Aristotle became newly available to scholars and, eventually, the general reader.

Continuities and Changes

At the same time, the Renaissance was not the radical break with the past that it is commonly thought to be. There was much in Galileo's world that Dante would easily have recognized. One was the ubiquity of war and civic strife, though on a newly global scale. The so-called Hundred Years' War between England and France, which featured such "heroes" as Joan of Arc, finally ended in 1453, the year of the Turks' victory at Istanbul, but only after it had devastated much of western Europe. The victorious French didn't find respite for long: a series of battles throughout the early sixteenth century with the Holy Roman Empire decimated their army, thanks largely to the Empire's savvy deployment of Spanish musketeers, marking the end of an era of knightly combat. The so-called Wars of Italy made the vulnerable peninsula a veritable battleground for over sixty years, culminating with the absorption of Milan and Naples into the Spanish empire by 1559. A few years later, an angry mob tossed two of Emperor Ferdinand II's ministers from a window in Prague Castle; this "defenestration of Prague" set in motion the events that would ultimately lead to the Thirty Years War (1618–1648), which engulfed most of central Europe.

Secondly, plague remained a constant blight on the landscape. The most severe epidemic ever to strike Europe was the Black Death of 1348–1350, apparently starting when a Genoese vessel fresh from a diseased Orient pulled into Messina; Giovanni Boccaccio grimly recorded its devastating effects on Florence in the opening pages of his *Decameron*. Little had changed by the time of Galileo's recantation; the astronomer narrowly missed dying himself in the virulent plague that swept across southern Europe in 1627 and 1628. Largely because of the recurrence of disease, Europe's major cities, with few exceptions, would never attain during the Renaissance the populations they had in Dante's lifetime. The closest that early modern Florence ever got to its pre-1348 population of 100,000 was 75,000.

Finally, Dante probably would not have been surprised by the steady decline of the aristocracy and the rise of the merchant class, although he wouldn't have been particularly pleased. Energetic merchants and prosperous guild members challenged the ways in which a man's worth was valued: did it depend on bloodline and clerical privilege, or could honest labor and thrifty behavior play a major part? The Medici, who would rule Florence for centuries, began as merchants and became prominent bankers; the merchant-banker Jakob Fugger of Augsburg, in southern Germany, came from a family of weavers, and at his death had emperors in his debt. Even as social relationships continued to be reconfigured throughout the Renaissance, however, the commercial growth and economic expansion that Dante's era had enjoyed came to an end with the Black Death of 1348. Depression and inflation characterized Europe until the sixteenth century, when the influx of gold and silver troves found in the New World—as well as in the mines of central Europe financed by Jakob Fugger and his contemporaries—helped the sagging economy. As business recovered, the Holy

Roman Empire did as well, invigorated by dynastic marriages that brought Spain within its orb; at the same time, the papacy, now firmly reestablished in Rome, sought to extend its political and temporal authority into a central Italy that had long avoided the sway of the "eternal city" to its south.

In the mid-fifteenth century when Nicholas V launched a major urban renovation, Rome was no more than a swamp dotted with half-buried ruins; two hundred years later it would witness the triumphant construction of Saint Peter's. François I, inspired by trips to Italy, would refashion Paris in the 1530s and 1540s, a project continued by Catherine de' Medici and lavishly extended by Louis XIV. Lisbon flourished under the Henrys, Madrid under the Phillips, and the attractions of Elizabeth's and James's courts brought the European Renaissance fully to London. The presence of wealthy sovereigns busy setting up court was not only good for business. It was also good for culture, and the arts thrived in capital cities that sought to outdo each other in power and prestige.

At the same time, the new-world discoveries had made those countries bordering the Atlantic Ocean the maritime powers of the epoch, outpacing the cities that dotted the Mediterranean. Venice alone retained its importance as a major port city, and that largely because of the unique circumstances that enabled the republic to retain its independence from territorial rulers. England, the Netherlands, and Spain were the beneficiaries of a somewhat belated Renaissance. The *siglo de oro* or "golden century" celebrated by Spain was the century in which Shakespeare, Donne, Milton, Cervantes, Lope de Vega, Calderón, Tirso de Molina, Vermeer, Rembrandt, and many more artists and writers flourished.

Looking Backward and Looking Forward

The backward glance to antiquity provoked the "rebirth" implicit in the term "renaissance." At the heart of this rebirth was the movement known as humanism: a manner of seeing the world which, as its name implies, placed man rather than God at the center. Initially, humanism can be said to have started out quietly enough. Petrarch desperately wanted to hear Virgil's genuine voice, to discover his true intentions rather than the ones visited upon him by Christian allegorists. The recovery of ancient thought and practice would not be limited, however, to pagan authors. In particular, humanists in northern Europe, buoyed by the creation of new centers of learning to accommodate their focus on letters—between 1472 and 1516, universities were founded at Munich, Uppsala, Copenhagen, and Wittenberg, and five new colleges instituted at Oxford and Cambridge—turned their attention to Scripture as well as writings of the early church.

Milton's great epic, *Paradise Lost*, also indulges in a profound backward look to the origins of creation itself. Written in the wake of the failed Puritan republic in which Milton had played a central role, *Paradise Lost* is opposed to idealizations of any kind. Yet it seeks a new type of unity in the simple fact of all men's and women's distance from God. There is a looming sense in *Paradise Lost* as to the finality of that loss, long before Milton's time, while the last words of the poem are a move forward—albeit a hesitant, somewhat reluctant one—as Adam and Eve, exiled from Eden, go out into the great world:

Some natural tears they dropped, but wiped them soon;
The world was all before them, where to choose
Their place of rest, and providence their guide:
They hand in hand with wandering steps and slow,
Through Eden took their solitary way.

Product of the classical traditions that had inspired Petrarch, as well as of the vernacular poetry that had earned England a Renaissance all its own, *Paradise Lost* was begun a decade after Galileo's death. As if in anticipation of the encyclopedias that would become a distinctive mark of the eighteenth century, Milton's poem is, like them, a thoughtful compilation of the best the ancients and the moderns had to offer.

Authors and Authorships

The technological, educational, and social advances of the fifteenth and sixteenth centuries facilitated the emergence of a new phenomenon that could encompass a wide range of individuals, men as well as women: that of published authorship. Limited literacy in Latin had confined the technical act of writing mostly to clerics. Even highly-cultured medieval monarchs such as Alfonso X of Castile were said to have relied exclusively on scribes. The need for a class of highly cultured individuals at Europe's courts and capitals would continue, however, even when the various European vernaculars began to rival Latin. The young Machiavelli and Petrarch worked as secretaries, respectively, for the city of Florence and for a French pope; Milton's skill in languages led to his appointment as Secretary for the Foreign Tongues by Oliver Cromwell's Council of State. Many of these sophisticated centers were governed by newly made men (or women) whose claims to power were shaky: the Medici, Cromwell himself, and Elizabeth Tudor, who kept her chief rival to the English throne, her cousin Mary Stuart, in the Tower for many years until having her beheaded on the eve of the Spanish Armada. They were eager for works acknowledging their legitimacy, and writers were quick to take up the challenge to provide stately poems to honor patrons or would-be patrons.

But if patronage provided one major catalyst for writing, there were others as well. The popular theaters in Spain and England gave Lope de Vega and Shakespeare possibilities for careers as both actors and playwrights, while later in the seventeenth century, Aphra Behn made respectable earnings from her plays and her poetry. Other attempts to live off one's writing were not as successful: Cervantes failed dismally to support himself. For a growing number of people, writing was simply one aspect of their daily activities. Many of them were women: Marguerite de Navarre, Sor Juana Inéz de la Cruz, and Vittoria Colonna were able to compose their own poetry and religious works in rooms of their own, thanks to associations with royalty, the relatively quiet rhythms of convent life, or a wealthy widowhood.

The fictional characters created by these authors are increasingly articulate about the limitations of human inquiry, and their probing the limits of their own minds may signal early modernity's most dramatic innovation with respect to its medieval legacy. Characters come increasingly to obey the laws of psychological realism, and their authors do as well, even if from behind cleverly constructed personae. Petrarch, Montaigne, and Cervantes speak to us with a new directness and openness. These voices are stylized, of course, but the stylization consists largely in the conviction that exposing one's most intimate life in its domestic and spiritual details is warranted by the occasion itself.

Part of this new accessibility has much to do with improved record-keeping on the part of cities, states, and religious organizations. The need to record, to scrutinize, in order to find out "truths" amidst contingencies links Calvin's Geneva, the Inquisitorial trials of Galileo and his contemporaries, and the arrival of Matteo Ricci, a Jesuit missionary, in the court of the emperor of China. Part of it also has to do with the fragmentation not only of a world, but of the literary genres that marked that world. Epic and tragedy, two classical imports much revised in the course of the early modern period, would find their share of practitioners. Other literary forms, some of them also salvaged from classical antiquity, were less monolithic and therefore perhaps less formidable. Those on the peripheries of elite culture found it easier to take up these lesser genres: the letter, the lyric, the essay, the autobiography, the short story and eventually the novel, in many ways a hodgepodge of all of the above. For most women, and for many men, entrance onto the literary scene began as simply the raising of a personal voice in reflection, in challenge, or in jest.

There was a volatile relationship between their words and the societies in which these authors lived. Not only was Galileo the victim of a judicial process, but all of Erasmus's works were placed on the Roman Index of Prohibited Books, along with writings by Rabelais, Boccaccio, and Petrarch. Catholicism was not alone in persecuting potential heretics and subversives, however; Thomas More was decapitated for refusing to take the oath of allegiance to King Henry VIII after Henry repudiated the pope, and Martin Luther sanctioned the massacre of German peasants who had risen in rebellion. As a result, authors often attempted to couch their radical arguments within deliberately distancing and sometimes disorienting frames. Erasmus's *Praise of Folly* is one example, Boccaccio's *Decameron* another. Others were careful to display a heightened sense of self-consciousness about the finally fictive status of

Aztec screenfold book c. 1500.

their works. More's "Utopia" means "nowhere," while Shakespeare's Prospero reveals to Miranda and to us that the storm he had created is only the result of a sleight-of-hand, and Vermeer's paintings, with their mirrors and drawing easels, constantly remind us of their own construction. The gleaning and publication of a supposedly self-evident truth, as Galileo learned, could be fraught with difficulties. And as in Galileo's case, such difficulties emerged from the perceived conflicts between profoundly held religious beliefs and the awareness of a new worldliness that militated against those very beliefs.

It is thus not surprising that the culture of early modern Europe is marked throughout by reflections on its vulnerabilities. In many ways, this is a culture that emerges to protect a singular voice that at first boldly, and then perhaps more hesitatingly, called attention to the origins of art not in God or universals handed down for centuries, but in the thoughtful and creative self.

Mesoamerica: Before Columbus and After Cortés

The traditional Amerindian cultures are often called "pre-Columbian," literally referring to the era before Columbus's voyage of 1492, and more generally including the period before a given culture's first substantial European contact. At the time of the Conquest, some twenty million people lived in Mesoamerica. Cities had begun to form in the first millennium B.C.E., dominated by pyramid temples. The Maya were the major presence in their region until the Aztecs migrated into central Mexico from the arid north in the thirteenth century; they were forced to settle in undesirable marshlands around the large lake in the Valley of Mexico. They gradually expanded a pair of islands into their double capital city, Tenochtitlán-Tlatelolco. The Aztecs came to control much of central and southern Mexico, and Tenochtitlán became the greatest city ever seen in the hemisphere, with as many as 350,000 inhabitants, magnificent pyramids and palaces, and separate districts for the production of jewelry, textiles, pottery, and weapons.

The major Mesoamerican cities became both religious and political centers, with temple and court establishments centered on magnificent temple pyramids and lavish palaces, filled with frescoes and elaborate furnishings, and surrounded by pleasure gardens. There was much literary activity, more in oral than written form, as hieroglyphics were used as prompts to memory rather than to compose freestanding texts. Mythological and historical tales were told and retold, most memorably recorded in the Mayan *Popol Vuh* or Council Book, and hymns and songs were sung to the accompaniment of flutes, drums, and rattles. Though the region's cultures were not at all advanced technologically—most tools were of stone or wood; goods had to be carried by people, as the Mesoamericans did not use beasts of burden or even the wheel—the Mayan and Aztec artisans developed remarkably delicate artworks.

As the Aztecs built their empire, the difficulties of transportation and supply made it hard to carry on sustained warfare at any distance from home; instead, they extended their sway by complex negotiations and through the selective, exemplary violence of human sacrifice. Beginning in the late 1420s and under the emperor's chief advisor Tlacaelel human sacrifice became widespread, with thousands of foreign captives being sacrificed on major festivals, in a theater of terror to which neighboring rulers were pointedly invited. By the early 1500s, the Aztecs' enemies and even most of their allies were bitterly resentful of the Aztecs' sacrifices, heavy taxation, and conscription of youths to serve as warriors and build temples and palaces. They were more than ready for things to change.

Cortés arrived in Mexico in 1519 and by August of 1521, aided by the Aztecs' enemies—and their restless allies—he had succeeded in overthrowing the Aztecs and destroying Tenochtitlán. Cortés's lieutenant, Pedro de Alvarado, conquered the highland Mayan center of Guatemala in 1523, and in 1532 another Spaniard, Francisco Pizarro, took a small force to Peru, home of the other greatest New World Empire, that of the Incas. Professing friendship for the Incan emperor Atahualpa, Pizarro seized him, extracted ransom, and executed him. With the region's great empires defeated, the New World was open to piecemeal conquest and settlement by Europe, with Portuguese settlers gaining control over Brazil, the Spanish dominating the rest of South and Central America, and Spanish, French, and English colonizers vying for control over North America. The colonial period lasted in the region until Mexico and Guatemala achieved independence from Spain in 1821. At that time, Mexico's territory included Texas, California, and much of the American southwest; in a series of conflicts with the growing United States, the present borders were eventually established in 1848.

Over the centuries, a rich and varied culture has evolved in Mexico and Central America among the increasingly mixed populations of the descendants of the Spanish settlers and the native Amerindians. A major element in this evolution has been a powerful literary heritage, from the rhetorically charged writings of the conquistadors and the haunting poetry of their adversaries, to the elevated lyrics of the great Sor Juana Inés de la Cruz in the seventeenth century, to such contemporary writers as Octavio Paz, Carlos Fuentes, and the Guatemalan Miguel Ángel Asturias, winner of the 1967 Nobel Prize for Literature, who translated the *Popol Vuh* into Spanish and incorporated many of its themes into his novels. Today, hundreds of thousands of people in Mexico and Central America still speak native languages as their first or even sole language, and poetry is still being composed in Mayan and in Nahuatl, as members of the indigenous cultures seek to assess and adapt their heritage in the contemporary world.

The Early Modern Period

Year	The World	Literature
1300		**1300s** Aztecs begin producing painted screenfold books
1310		
1320	**1325** Founding of Aztec capital, Tenochtitlán	**1321** Dante dies
1330	**1337–1453** Hundred Years' War between England and France	
1340	**1348–1350** Black Death in Europe	
1350		**1353–1354** Petrarch writing *Canzoniere* and Boccaccio, *Decameron*
1360	**1363** Timur (Tamerlane) begins conquests in central Asia, Persia, Russia, and India **1368** Chinese overthrow Mongols; Ming dynasty replaces Yuan dynasty	**Early 1360s** St. Catherine, *Letters*
1370	**1378** Pope Gregory XI leaves Avignon for Rome; beginning of Great Schism	
1380		
1390		
1400		**1404** Christine de Pizan, *Book of the City of Ladies*
1410		
1420	**1428–1440** Reign of Aztec emperor Itzcoatl; Aztecs become dominant regional power **1429** Joan of Arc leads siege at Orleans; burned at stake (1431)	
1430	**1434** Cosimo de'Medici becomes ruler of Florence	**1430s–1519** Elaboration of court poetry in service of the Aztec empire **1430s** Leon Battista Alberti, *On Painting*
1440	**1440** Portuguese begin slave trade in Africa **1444** Mehmed II becomes sultan of Ottoman Empire	
1450	**1450** Lorenzo Valla proves *Donation of Constantine* a forgery **1453** Gutenberg prints first Bible using movable metal type; Turks seize Constantinople; end of Byzantine Empire	**1450s** François Villon, poetic works

Year	The World	Literature
1460		
1470	**1474** Isabella becomes Queen of Castile **1478** Spanish Inquisition begins	**1470s** Lucrezia Tornabuoni de'Medici, *Sacred Stories*
1480	**1488** Bartolomeu Dias explores Cape of Good Hope	
1490	**1492** Jews expelled from Spain; Columbus explores West Indies **1497** Leonardo da Vinci, *Last Supper* **1498** Vasco da Gama reaches India; Savonarola burned at stake in Florence **1499–1501** Amerigo Vespucci explores coast of Brazil	**1493** Columbus writes first letters to Queen Isabella detailing his discoveries **1494** Aldus Manutius establishes an important printing press in Venice
1500	**1500** Michelangelo, *David* **1502–1520** Reign of Moctezuma II in Mexico	**1509** Erasmus, *The Praise of Folly*
1510	**1511** Cuba becomes Spanish colony **1514** Copernicus publishes work on heliocentric theory **1517** Luther writes 95 theses contesting Church's practice of granting indulgences **1519–1522** Magellan circumnavigates globe **1519** Hernán Cortés invades Aztec empire, places Moctezuma under house arrest	**1513** Niccolò Machiavelli, *The Prince* **1516** Thomas More, *Utopia* **1519–1521** Cortés writes five long letters to Charles V on his exploits
1520	**1521** Three–month siege of Tenochtitlán ends in fall of Aztec empire. Cortés gains control over central and southern Mexico **1523** Pedro de Alvarado conquers Guatemala. Pope Clement VII sends a dozen missionaries to organize the conversion of the Mexican population **1525–1526** Peasants' rebellion in Germany; Thomas Muntzer executed **1527** Sack of Rome by Holy Roman Emperor Charles V **1529** Turks invade Austria; Bernardino de Sahagún arrives in Mexico	**1522** Martin Luther translates New Testament **1524** Aztec-Spanish dialogues on the merits of traditional religion versus Christianity **1524–1525** Erasmus and Luther debate free will **1527** Baldassare Castiglione, *The Courtier*
1530	**1532** Francisco Pizarro conquers Incan empire in Peru **1533** Jean Calvin goes to Geneva **1534** Henry VIII excommunicated **1535** Thomas More beheaded **1539** First printing press in New World (Mexico)	**1530s** Lyrics of Michelangelo and Vittoria Colonna **1532** François Rabelais, *Pantagruel* **1534** Rabelais, *Gargantua*
1540	**1540** Jesuits approved by Pope as official order; Treatise signed between Turkey and Venice	**1540s** Clement Marot translates the Psalms; Marguerite de Navarre, *Heptameron* **1540–1560s** Wu Cheng'en, *Journey to the West*

Year	The World	Literature
	1545–1562 Council of Trent reforms Catholic practices in response to Protestant challenges	**1547–1580s** Bernardino de Sahagún collects materials from native informants for his *General History of the Affairs of New Spain* and poetry collections
1550		
	1555 Calvinist mission to Brazil	**1555** Louise Labé, *Works*
	1557 Erasmus's works put on Index of Prohibited Books	
	1559 Elizabeth I becomes Queen of England	
1560		
	1562–1598 French Wars of Religion	**1560s** Bartolomé de las Casas, *Apolgetic History*
	1568–1648 War in Netherlands, ending with independence from Spain	**1564–1565** Bernal Díaz del Castillo, *True History of the Conquest of New Spain*
1570		
	1572 Battle of Lepanto, Spanish Catholic naval forces defeat Ottomans; St. Bartholomew's Day massacre	**1570s** Luis Vaz de Camões, *The Lusiads;* Jean de Léry, *History of a Voyage to Brazil*
	1578 King Sebastiaõ and Portuguese troops killed in northern Africa	**1577** Teresa of Avila, *Interior Castle*
1580		
	1582 Gregorian Calendar implemented	**1580s** Jan Kochanowski, *Laments;* Michel de Montaigne, *Essays*
	1580 Union of Portugal and Spain	
	1585 First English settlement in North America	
	1588 Spanish Armada defeated by England	
1590		
	1598 Restoration of shogunate in Japan	
1600		
	1609 Spain approaching bankruptcy; Moors expelled	**1605** Miguel de Cervantes, *Don Quixote,* Book 1
1610		**1611** William Shakespeare, *The Tempest*
		1614 Lope de Vega, *Fuenteovejuna*
		1615 Cervantes, *Don Quixote,* Book 2
	1618–1648 Thirty Years' War	
1620		
	1620 Plymouth Colony founded in Massachusetts	
	1621 Philip IV becomes King of Spain	**1624** John Donne, *Devotions upon Emergent Occasions*
	1628 Recurrence of plague in Europe	**1629** Hernando Ruiz de Alarcón, *Treatise on the Superstitions of the Natives of This New Spain*
1630		
	1633 Galileo recants before the Inquisition	
1640		
	1640 Portuguese war of independence begins	**1641** René Descartes, *Meditations*
	1642–1649 English Civil War	
	1649 Charles I beheaded	
1650		**1650** Anne Bradstreet, *The Tenth Muse Lately Sprung Up in America*
1660		
	1660 Restoration and return of Charles II to England	**1667** John Milton, *Paradise Lost*
		1667–1670 Sor Juana Inés de la Cruz writes first purely Mexican poems in Spanish

Giovanni Boccaccio

1313–1375

"These stories were told neither in a church, of whose affairs one must speak with a chaste mind and a pure tongue . . . nor in the schools of philosophers . . . [but] in a garden, in a place designed for pleasure, among people who, though young in years, were nonetheless fully mature and not to be led astray by stories." Thus does Giovanni Boccaccio defend his *Decameron* from its imagined detractors in the epilogue to his masterpiece. As its title indicates, the *Decameron* is the (fictional) record of ten days: days spent telling one hundred tales during one of the worst plagues ever to strike Europe. Centuries later, some readers were still blushing at the raciness of some of the stories told by ten young men and women who have fled plague-infested Florence; the tale of naive but insatiable Alibech, who exhausts an amorous hermit, was translated into English only in the late nineteenth century. Boccaccio himself had second thoughts in the wake of the visit of a monk to Florence a decade after the *Decameron* was finished, when Boccaccio had taken religious orders. Admonished to change his sinful ways, Boccaccio was moved by the conversation to wish to destroy his earlier "evil" writings. Only a timely letter from his good friend Francis Petrarch prevented the author from burning a work that has been hailed as the first European example of an immensely popular genre, the *novella* or short story.

Florence was a fertile place for the birth of such a collection. The same town that had exiled Dante in 1302 had become, by midcentury, a bustling commercial center, run by the city's merchant class rather than by its aristocrats. The stability of its banks and the success of its merchants, Boccaccio's father among them, produced the vibrant, wealthy city in which Boccaccio was born. This thriving city is not the plague-ridden town we see in the macabre preface, although it and other Tuscan cities like it reappear in all their local color in many tales told in the gardens to which Boccaccio's young conversationalists flee. The true birthplaces of the Renaissance in Italy, these towns were the first to witness the transition from a recognizably medieval era dominated by feudal relationships to a new age of which Boccaccio—occasionally thought of as "still" medieval—is representative in many ways. But if bustling Italian towns and their bourgeois inhabitants dominate many of the stories, they aren't the only hubs of activity. Boccaccio's eclectic storytellers take us from Babylon to the tangled pine forest outside Ravenna to the court of the king of Spain.

Boccaccio went to a wide range of sources for his tales, including Ovid's *Metamorphoses,* clerical manuals, French *lais,* and Arabic tales. Like Shakespeare, he was an avid borrower who transformed what he borrowed. The *Decameron* also reflects the courtly world which Boccaccio had known firsthand when he lived in Naples in the 1320s and 1330s. Here he spent some distasteful years first studying banking and law, then found Naples much more to his liking when he turned to poetry and joined the flourishing intellectual community of King Robert of Anjou. Boccaccio wrote his first works in Robert's court: his *Filostrato,* which would become the basis for Chaucer's *Troilus and Criseyde;* his epic *Filocolo,* about the misfortunes of the Muslim Biancifiore; and *Thesiad of the Marriage of Emilia.* All works in the vernacular, they look back to classical epic and culture while incorporating the meters and themes of medieval romance and contemporary Italian poetry. But this productive period in King Robert's court ended abruptly in 1341, when the Florentine bank for which Boccaccio's father worked met with disaster. Father and son regretfully returned to Florence where, in time, the young Boccaccio's house in Certaldo just south of the city would become the center of Florence's fledgling humanist movement.

The episode of the near book-burning might suggest that the *Decameron* represents the culmination of Boccaccio's youthful period, which includes one of the first psychological novels of European literature (*The Elegy of Madonna Fiammetta*) and the first modern pastoral (*Nymphs of Fiesole*). Such works, several of which feature men and women gathered in gardens to tell tales, were indeed good preparation for a collection of stories of knights, ladies, and magnanimous kings. At the same time, the *Decameron* is like nothing Boccaccio had written before, and like nothing Europe had seen before. Its encyclopedic scale looks ahead to Boccaccio's later Latin compendia, including his (unfinished) *Genealogy of the Pagan Gods* and *Lives of Famous Men,* begun under Petrarch's tutelage and carried out in the midst of Boccaccio's commitment to unraveling the obscurities of ancient texts (to the extent that he could boast of being one of the first Italians to have learned ancient Greek). Boccaccio's solicitude for women is visible in the *Decameron*'s preface when he suggests that his tales are for female readers who are forced to "spend most of their time cooped up within the narrow confines of their rooms." His attention to women is also evident in his collection of biographies of notable classical women, *De mulieribus claris,* dedicated, not incidentally, to a Florentine woman, Andrea Acciaiuoli. Finally, the Latinate style of Boccaccio's Italian is a testimony to his lifelong engagement with classical literature, while the fact that the *Decameron* is written in the vernacular may suggest the admiration Boccaccio had for his fellow Florentine Dante (whose daughter he visited in a nunnery to present her with ten gold florins from the Commune of Florence as partial restitution for her father's losses). He had to discontinue a series of public lectures on the *Inferno* because of illness in 1374, and shortly thereafter died.

Yet while the *Decameron* may adhere, like the *Divine Comedy,* to a careful structure, the sensibility of Boccaccio's work is markedly different from Dante's. Death in the *Decameron*'s introduction is portrayed as final, with no suggestion of a Dantesque afterlife, either infernal or redemptive. Rarely have the ravages of disease been so relentlessly described, and with them, the almost complete destruction of community and the bonds that hold it together. In this sense, the ten conversationalists' escape to the countryside is at once a strategy for survival (reminiscent of Scheherazade's witty tale-telling escapades in *The Thousand and One Nights*) and an attempt to restore what has been lost. But the world outside Florence cannot sustain them forever. The order created at the villa is only a tentative one. The songs they sing at the end of each day, the delicate feasts they enjoy, the beautiful Valley of the Ladies eloquently described on the seventh day, all point toward a kind of preciousness and fleeting beauty of their lives which are too fragile to last, but healing and of great comfort while they do.

The actual stories, on the other hand, largely reflect a different reality, far more durable and rugged. Only a very few transpire in places as pristine as the gardens in Fiesole, and the vast majority of them deal with the messy contingencies of everyday life: marriage to a husband who is impotent, or tyrannical, or adulterous; the lechery and greed of friars; the stupidity of one's neighbors and colleagues; the stinginess of a king. Yet for most of these problems the tales' protagonists find solutions. Many succeed through savvy and wit, as when Nathan the Wise confounds a Sultan who seeks to confound him. Some, particularly in the last day's stories, succeed through greatness of heart, as in the problematic tale of the patient wife Griselda. In some cases, though—particularly the tragedies of Day Four—there are no solutions to be found. Yet by taking into account the tragic along with the ribald, Chaucer's "gode Boccace" demonstrates how attentive he was to the vicissitudes of life and the narratives into which they can be placed, winning for the *Decameron* enthusiastic readers and imitators from every culture and every rung of the social ladder.

PRONUNCIATIONS:

Giovanni Boccaccio: jo-VAN-ni bo-KATCH-oh
Dioneo: dee-oh-NAY-oh

from DECAMERON[1]

from First Day

[INTRODUCTION]

Here begins the First Day of the Decameron, *wherein first of all the author explains the circumstances in which certain persons, who presently make their appearance, were induced to meet for the purpose of conversing together, after which, under the rule of* Pampinea, *each of them speaks on the subject they find most congenial.*

Whenever, fairest ladies,[2] I pause to consider how compassionate you all are by nature, I invariably become aware that the present work will seem to you to possess an irksome and ponderous opening. For it carries at its head the painful memory of the deadly havoc wrought by the recent plague,[3] which brought so much heartache and misery to those who witnessed, or had experience of it. But I do not want you to be deterred, for this reason, from reading any further, on the assumption that you are to be subjected, as you read, to an endless torrent of tears and sobbing. You will be affected no differently by this grim beginning than walkers confronted by a steep and rugged hill, beyond which there lies a beautiful and delectable plain. The degree of pleasure they derive from the latter will correspond directly to the difficulty of the climb and the descent. And just as the end of mirth is heaviness, so sorrows are dispersed by the advent of joy.

This brief unpleasantness (I call it brief, inasmuch as it is contained within few words) is quickly followed by the sweetness and the pleasure which I have already promised you, and which, unless you were told in advance, you would not perhaps be expecting to find after such a beginning as this. Believe me, if I could decently have taken you whither I desire by some other route, rather than along a path so difficult as this, I would gladly have done so. But since it is impossible without this memoir to show the origin of the events you will read about later, I really have no alternative but to address myself to its composition.

I say, then, that the sum of thirteen hundred and forty-eight years had elapsed since the fruitful Incarnation of the Son of God, when the noble city of Florence, which for its great beauty excels all others in Italy, was visited by the deadly pestilence. Some say that it descended upon the human race through the influence of the heavenly bodies, others that it was a punishment signifying God's righteous anger at our iniquitous way of life. But whatever its cause, it had originated some years earlier in the East, where it had claimed countless lives before it unhappily spread westward, growing in strength as it swept relentlessly on from one place to the next.

In the face of its onrush, all the wisdom and ingenuity of man were unavailing. Large quantities of refuse were cleared out of the city by officials specially appointed for the purpose, all sick persons were forbidden entry, and numerous instructions were issued for safeguarding the people's health, but all to no avail. Nor were the countless petitions humbly directed to God by the pious, whether by means of formal processions or in any other guise, any less ineffectual. For in the early spring of the

1. Translated from the Italian by G. H. McWilliam.
2. In his introduction to the *Decameron,* Boccaccio directly addresses women as his primary audience: "So in order that I may to some extent repair the omissions of Fortune, which (as we may see in the case of the more delicate sex) was always more sparing of support wherever natural strength was more deficient, I intend to provide succour and diversion for the ladies, but only for those who are in love."
3. Written in the early 1350s, *The Decameron* looks back to the plague years of 1348–1349.

year we have mentioned, the plague began, in a terrifying and extraordinary manner, to make its disastrous effects apparent. It did not take the form it had assumed in the East, where if anyone bled from the nose it was an obvious portent of certain death. On the contrary, its earliest symptom, in men and women alike, was the appearance of certain swellings in the groin or the armpit, some of which were egg-shaped whilst others were roughly the size of the common apple. Sometimes the swellings were large, sometimes not so large, and they were referred to by the populace as *gavòccioli.*[4] From the two areas already mentioned, this deadly *gavòcciolo* would begin to spread, and within a short time it would appear at random all over the body. Later on, the symptoms of the disease changed, and many people began to find dark blotches and bruises on their arms, thighs, and other parts of the body, sometimes large and few in number, at other times tiny and closely spaced. These, to anyone unfortunate enough to contract them, were just as infallible a sign that he would die as the *gavòcciolo* had been earlier, and as indeed it still was.

Against these maladies, it seemed that all the advice of physicians and all the power of medicine were profitless and unavailing. Perhaps the nature of the illness was such that it allowed no remedy: or perhaps those people who were treating the illness (whose numbers had increased enormously because the ranks of the qualified were invaded by people, both men and women, who had never received any training in medicine), being ignorant of its causes, were not prescribing the appropriate cure. At all events, few of those who caught it ever recovered, and in most cases death occurred within three days from the appearance of the symptoms we have described, some people dying more rapidly than others, the majority without any fever or other complications.

But what made this pestilence even more severe was that whenever those suffering from it mixed with people who were still unaffected, it would rush upon these with the speed of a fire racing through dry or oily substances that happened to be placed within its reach. Nor was this the full extent of its evil, for not only did it infect healthy persons who conversed or had any dealings with the sick, making them ill or visiting an equally horrible death upon them, but it also seemed to transfer the sickness to anyone touching the clothes or other objects which had been handled or used by its victims.

It is a remarkable story that I have to relate. And were it not for the fact that I am one of many people who saw it with their own eyes, I would scarcely dare to believe it, let alone commit it to paper, even though I had heard it from a person whose word I could trust. The plague I have been describing was of so contagious a nature that very often it visibly did more than simply pass from one person to another. In other words, whenever an animal other than a human being touched anything belonging to a person who had been stricken or exterminated by the disease, it not only caught the sickness, but died from it almost at once. To all of this, as I have just said, my own eyes bore witness on more than one occasion. One day, for instance, the rags of a pauper who had died from the disease were thrown into the street, where they attracted the attention of two pigs. In their wonted fashion, the pigs first of all gave the rags a thorough mauling with their snouts after which they took them between their teeth and shook them against their cheeks. And within a short time they began to writhe as though they had been poisoned, then they both dropped dead to the ground, spreadeagled upon the rags that had brought about their undoing. * * *

4. Little goiters in local dialect.

In the face of so much affliction and misery, all respect for the laws of God and man had virtually broken down and been extinguished in our city. For like everybody else, those ministers and executors of the laws who were not either dead or ill were left with so few subordinates that they were unable to discharge any of their duties. Hence everyone was free to behave as he pleased. * * *

Some people, pursuing what was possibly the safer alternative, callously maintained that there was no better or more efficacious remedy against a plague than to run away from it. Swayed by this argument, and sparing no thought for anyone but themselves, large numbers of men and women abandoned their city, their homes, their relatives, their estates and their belongings, and headed for the countryside, either in Florentine territory or, better still, abroad. It was as though they imagined that the wrath of God would not unleash this plague against men for their iniquities irrespective of where they happened to be, but would only be aroused against those who found themselves within the city walls; or possibly they assumed that the whole of the population would be exterminated and that the city's last hour had come.

Of the people who held these various opinions, not all of them died. Nor, however, did they all survive. On the contrary, many of each different persuasion fell ill here, there, and everywhere, and having themselves, when they were fit and well, set an example to those who were as yet unaffected, they languished away with virtually no one to nurse them. It was not merely a question of one citizen avoiding another, and of people almost invariably neglecting their neighbours and rarely or never visiting their relatives, addressing them only from a distance; this scourge had implanted so great a terror in the hearts of men and women that brothers abandoned brothers, uncles their nephews, sisters their brothers, and in many cases wives deserted their husbands. But even worse, and almost incredible, was the fact that fathers and mothers refused to nurse and assist their own children, as though they did not belong to them. * * *

Whenever people died, their neighbours nearly always followed a single, set routine, prompted as much by their fear of being contaminated by the decaying corpse as by any charitable feelings they may have entertained towards the deceased. Either on their own, or with the assistance of bearers whenever these were to be had, they extracted the bodies of the dead from their houses and left them lying outside their front doors, where anyone going about the streets, especially in the early morning, could have observed countless numbers of them. Funeral biers would then be sent for, upon which the dead were taken away, though there were some who, for lack of biers, were carried off on plain boards. It was by no means rare for more than one of these biers to be seen with two or three bodies upon it at a time; on the contrary, many were seen to contain a husband and wife, two or three brothers and sisters, a father and son, or some other pair of close relatives. And times without number it happened that two priests would be on their way to bury someone, holding a cross before them, only to find that bearers carrying three or four additional biers would fall in behind them; so that whereas the priests had thought they had only one burial to attend to, they in fact had six or seven, and sometimes more. Even in these circumstances, however, there were no tears or candles or mourners to honour the dead; in fact, no more respect was accorded to dead people than would nowadays be shown towards dead goats. For it was quite apparent that the one thing which, in normal times, no wise man had ever learned to accept with patient resignation (even though it struck so seldom and unobtrusively), had now been brought home to the feeble-minded as well, but the scale of the calamity caused them to regard it with indifference.

Such was the multitude of corpses (of which further consignments were arriving every day and almost by the hour at each of the churches), that there was not sufficient consecrated ground for them to be buried in, especially if each was to have its own plot in accordance with long-established custom. So when all the graves were full, huge trenches were excavated in the churchyards, into which new arrivals were placed in their hundreds, stowed tier upon tier like ships' cargo, each layer of corpses being covered over with a thin layer of soil till the trench was filled to the top. * * *

What more remains to be said, except that the cruelty of heaven (and possibly, in some measure, also that of man) was so immense and so devastating that between March and July of the year in question, what with the fury of the pestilence and the fact that so many of the sick were inadequately cared for or abandoned in their hour of need because the healthy were too terrified to approach them, it is reliably thought that over a hundred thousand human lives were extinguished within the walls of the city of Florence? Yet before this lethal catastrophe fell upon the city, it is doubtful whether anyone would have guessed it contained so many inhabitants.[5]

Ah, how great a number of splendid palaces, fine houses, and noble dwellings, once filled with retainers, with lords and with ladies, were bereft of all who had lived there, down to the tiniest child! How numerous were the famous families, the vast estates, the notable fortunes, that were seen to be left without a rightful successor! How many gallant gentlemen, fair ladies, and sprightly youths, who would have been judged hale and hearty by Galen, Hippocrates and Aesculapius[6] (to say nothing of others), having breakfasted in the morning with their kinsfolk, acquaintances and friends, supped that same evening with their ancestors in the next world!

The more I reflect upon all this misery, the deeper my sense of personal sorrow; hence I shall refrain from describing those aspects which can suitably be omitted, and proceed to inform you that these were the conditions prevailing in our city, which was by now almost emptied of its inhabitants, when one Tuesday morning (or so I was told by a person whose word can be trusted) seven young ladies were to be found in the venerable church of Santa Maria Novella, which was otherwise almost deserted.[7] They had been attending divine service, and were dressed in mournful attire appropriate to the times. Each was a friend, a neighbour, or a relative of the other six, none was older than twenty-seven or younger than eighteen, and all were intelligent, gently bred, fair to look upon, graceful in bearing, and charmingly unaffected. I could tell you their actual names, but refrain from doing so for a good reason, namely that I would not want any of them to feel embarrassed, at any time in the future, on account of the ensuing stories, all of which they either listened to or narrated themselves. For nowadays, laws relating to pleasure are somewhat restrictive, whereas at that time, for the reasons indicated above, they were exceptionally lax, not only for ladies of their own age but also for much older women. Besides, I have no wish to supply envious tongues, ever ready to censure a laudable way of life, with a chance to besmirch the good name of these worthy ladies with their lewd and filthy gossip. And therefore, so that we may perceive distinctly what each of them had to say, I propose to refer to them by names which are either wholly or partially appropriate to the qualities of

5. The number is probably excessive. Before the plague, Florence is estimated as having had 100,000 citizens, making it one of the largest cities in Italy. As many as half of them died between 1348–1349.

6. Hippocrates and Galen were ancient Greek physicians; Aesculapius was the Roman god of medicine.

7. The church was built by the Dominicans during the 13nth century on what were then the outskirts of Florence.

each. The first of them, who was also the eldest, we shall call Pampinea, the second Fiammetta, Filomena the third, and the fourth Emilia; then we shall name the fifth Lauretta, and the sixth Neifile, whilst to the last, not without reason, we shall give the name of Elissa.[8]

Without prior agreement but simply by chance, these seven ladies found themselves sitting, more or less in a circle, in one part of the church, reciting their paternosters.[9] Eventually, they left off and heaved a great many sighs, after which they began to talk among themselves on various different aspects of the times through which they were passing. But after a little while, they all fell silent except for Pampinea, who said:

"Dear ladies, you will often have heard it affirmed, as I have, that no man does injury to another in exercising his lawful rights. Every person born into this world has a natural right to sustain, preserve, and defend his own life to the best of his ability—a right so freely acknowledged that men have sometimes killed others in self-defence, and no blame whatever has attached to their actions. Now, if this is permitted by the laws, upon whose prompt application all mortal creatures depend for their well-being, how can it possibly be wrong, seeing that it harms no one, for us or anyone else to do all in our power to preserve our lives? If I pause to consider what we have been doing this morning, and what we have done on several mornings in the past, if I reflect on the nature and subject of our conversation, I realize, just as you also must realize, that each of us is apprehensive on her own account. This does not surprise me in the least, but what does greatly surprise me (seeing that each of us has the natural feelings of a woman) is that we do nothing to requite ourselves against the thing of which we are all so justly afraid.

"Here we linger for no other purpose, or so it seems to me, than to count the number of corpses being taken to burial, or to hear whether the friars of the church, very few of whom are left, chant their offices at the appropriate hours, or to exhibit the quality and quantity of our sorrows, by means of the clothes we are wearing, to all those whom we meet in this place. And if we go outside, we shall see the dead and the sick being carried hither and thither, or we shall see people, once condemned to exile by the courts for their misdeeds, careering wildly about the streets in open defiance of the law, well knowing that those appointed to enforce it are either dead or dying; or else we shall find ourselves at the mercy of the scum of our city who, having scented our blood, call themselves sextons and go prancing and bustling all over the place, singing bawdy songs that add insult to our injuries. Moreover, all we ever hear is 'So-and-so's dead' and 'So-and-so's dying'; and if there were anyone left to mourn, the whole place would be filled with sounds of wailing and weeping.

"And if we return to our homes, what happens? I know not whether your own experience is similar to mine, but my house was once full of servants, and now that there is no one left apart from my maid and myself, I am filled with foreboding and feel as if every hair of my head is standing on end. Wherever I go in the house, wherever I pause to rest, I seem to be haunted by the shades of the departed, whose faces no longer appear as I remember them but with strange and horribly twisted expressions that frighten me out of my senses.

"Accordingly, whether I am here in church or out in the streets or sitting at home, I always feel ill at ease, the more so because it seems to me that no one possessing

8. The names carry varying mythological weight. Filomena means "nightingale," Laureta is associated with the laurel, and Elissa was another name for Dido, queen of Carthage in Virgil's *Aeneid.*

9. Our fathers, customary prayers.

private means and a place to retreat to is left here apart from ourselves. But even if such people are still to be found, they draw no distinction, as I have frequently heard and seen for myself, between what is honest and what is dishonest; and provided only that they are prompted by their appetites, they will do whatever affords them the greatest pleasure, whether by day or by night, alone or in company. It is not only of lay people that I speak, but also of those enclosed in monasteries, who, having convinced themselves that such behaviour is suitable for them and is only unbecoming in others, have broken the rules of obedience and given themselves over to carnal pleasures, thereby thinking to escape, and have turned lascivious and dissolute.

"If this be so (and we plainly perceive that it is), what are we doing here? What are we waiting for? What are we dreaming about? Why do we lag so far behind all the rest of the citizens in providing for our safety? Do we rate ourselves lower than all other women? Or do we suppose that our own lives, unlike those of others, are bound to our bodies by such strong chains that we may ignore all those things which have the power to harm them? In that case we are deluded and mistaken. We have only to recall the names and the condition of the young men and women who have fallen victim to this cruel pestilence, in order to realize clearly the foolishness of such notions.

"And so, lest by pretending to be above such things or by becoming complacent we should succumb to that which we might possibly avoid if we so desired, I would think it an excellent idea (though I do not know whether you would agree with me) for us all to get away from this city, just as many others have done before us, and as indeed they are doing still. We could go and stay together on one of our various country estates, shunning at all costs the lewd practices of our fellow citizens and feasting and merrymaking as best we may without in any way overstepping the bounds of what is reasonable.

"There we shall hear the birds singing, we shall see fresh green hills and plains, fields of corn undulating like the sea, and trees of at least a thousand different species; and we shall have a clearer view of the heavens, which, troubled though they are, do not however deny us their eternal beauties, so much more fair to look upon than the desolate walls of our city. Moreover the country air is much more refreshing, the necessities of life in such a time as this are more abundant, and there are fewer obstacles to contend with. For although the farmworkers are dying there in the same way as the townspeople here in Florence, the spectacle is less harrowing inasmuch as the houses and people are more widely scattered. Besides, unless I am mistaken we shall not be abandoning anyone by going away from here; on the contrary, we may fairly claim that we are the ones who have been abandoned, for our kinsfolk are either dead or fled, and have left us to fend for ourselves in the midst of all this affliction, as though disowning us completely.

"Hence no one can reproach us for taking the course I have advocated, whereas if we do nothing we shall inevitably be confronted with distress and mourning, and possibly forfeit our lives into the bargain. Let us therefore do as I suggest, taking our maidservants with us and seeing to the dispatch of all the things we shall need. We can move from place to place, spending one day here and another there, pursuing whatever pleasures and entertainments the present times will afford. In this way of life we shall continue until such time as we discover (provided we are spared from early death) the end decreed by Heaven for these terrible events. You must remember, after all, that it is no more unseemly for us to go away and thus preserve our own honour than it is for most other women to remain here and forfeit theirs."

* * *

[The Women, Along with Three Young Men Arrive in Fiesole.][1]

Scarcely had they travelled two miles from Florence before they reached the place at which they had agreed to stay.

The spot in question was some distance away from any road, on a small hill that was agreeable to behold for its abundance of shrubs and trees, all bedecked in green leaves. Perched on its summit was a palace, built round a fine, spacious courtyard, and containing loggias, halls, and sleeping apartments, which were not only excellently proportioned but richly embellished with paintings depicting scenes of gaiety. Delectable gardens and meadows lay all around, and there were wells of cool, refreshing water. The cellars were stocked with precious wines, more suited to the palates of connoisseurs than to sedate and respectable ladies. And on their arrival the company discovered, to their no small pleasure, that the place had been cleaned from top to bottom, the beds in the rooms were made up, the whole house was adorned with seasonable flowers of every description, and the floors had been carpeted with rushes.

Soon after reaching the palace, they all sat down, and Dioneo, a youth of matchless charm and readiness of wit, said:

"It is not our foresight, ladies, but rather your own good sense, that has led us to this spot. I know not what you intend to do with your troubles; my own I left inside the city gates when I departed thence a short while ago in your company. Hence you may either prepare to join with me in as much laughter, song and merriment as your sense of decorum will allow, or else you may give me leave to go back for my troubles and live in the afflicted city."

Pampinea, as though she too had driven away all her troubles, answered him in the same carefree vein.

"There is much sense in what you say, Dioneo," she replied. "A merry life should be our aim, since it was for no other reason that we were prompted to run away from the sorrows of the city. However, nothing will last for very long unless it possesses a definite form. And since it was I who led the discussions from which this fair company has come into being, I have given some thought to the continuance of our happiness, and consider it necessary for us to choose a leader, drawn from our own ranks, whom we would honour and obey as our superior, and whose sole concern will be that of devising the means whereby we may pass our time agreeably. But so that none of us will complain that he or she has had no opportunity to experience the burden of responsibility and the pleasure of command associated with sovereign power, I propose that the burden and the honour should be assigned to each of us in turn for a single day. It will be for all of us to decide who is to be our first ruler, after which it will be up to each ruler, when the hour of vespers approaches, to elect his or her successor from among the ladies and gentlemen present. The person chosen to govern will be at liberty to make whatever arrangements he likes for the period covered by his rule, and to prescribe the place and the manner in which we are to live."[2]

* * *

1. In the intervening pages, the seven women have met up with three men, who have joined them in the church: Pamphilo, Filostrato, and Dioneo (who is described as "more attractive and wittier than either of the other young men"). They agree that they can live virtuously together, and they leave the plague-ridden city together for Fiesole, a hill-town northeast of Florence.

2. Pampinea is elected queen for the first day, and following a siesta, suggests to her companions that they proceed to spend "this hotter part of the day" in telling stories, "an activity that may afford some amusement to the narrator and to the company at large. By the time each one of you has narrated a little tale of his own or her own, the sun will be setting, the heat will have abated and we shall be able to go and amuse ourselves wherever you choose." The company agrees to her suggestion, and she decrees that on the first day, "each of us should be free to speak upon whatever topic he prefers."

Third Story: [The Three Rings]

Melchizedek the Jew, with a story about three rings, avoids a most dangerous trap laid for him by Saladin.

Neifile's story was well received by all the company, and when she fell silent, Filomena began at the queen's behest to address them as follows:

The story told by Neifile reminds me of the parlous state in which a Jew once found himself. Now that we have heard such fine things said concerning God and the truth of our religion,[1] it will not seem inappropriate to descend at this juncture to the deeds and adventures of men. So I shall tell you a story which, when you have heard it, will possibly make you more cautious in answering questions addressed to you. It is a fact, my sweet companions, that just as folly often destroys men's happiness and casts them into deepest misery, so prudence extricates the wise from dreadful perils and guides them firmly to safety. So clearly may we perceive that folly leads men from contentment to misery, that we shall not even bother for the present to consider the matter further, since countless examples spring readily to mind. But that prudence may bring its reward, I shall, as I have promised, prove to you briefly by means of the following little tale:

Saladin, whose worth was so great that it raised him from humble beginnings to the sultanate of Egypt and brought him many victories over Saracen and Christian kings,[2] had expended the whole of his treasure in various wars and extraordinary acts of munificence, when a certain situation arose for which he required a vast sum of money. Not being able to see any way of obtaining what he needed at such short notice, he happened to recall a rich Jew, Melchizedek by name, who ran a money-lending business in Alexandria,[3] and would certainly, he thought, have enough for his purposes, if only he could be persuaded to part with it. But this Melchizedek was such a miserly fellow that he would never hand it over of his own free will, and the Sultan was not prepared to take it away from him by force. However, as his need became more pressing, having racked his brains to discover some way of compelling the Jew to assist him, he resolved to use force in the guise of reason. So he sent for the Jew, gave him a cordial reception, invited him to sit down beside him, and said:

"O man of excellent worth, many men have told me of your great wisdom and your superior knowledge of the ways of God. Hence I would be glad if you would tell me which of the three laws, whether the Jewish, the Saracen, or the Christian, you deem to be truly authentic."

The Jew, who was indeed a wise man, realized all too well that Saladin was aiming to trip him up with the intention of picking a quarrel with him, and that if he were to praise any of the three more than the others, the Sultan would achieve his object. He therefore had need of a reply that would save him from falling into the trap, and having sharpened his wits, in no time at all he was ready with his answer.

"My lord," he said, "your question is a very good one, and in order to explain my views on the subject, I must ask you to listen to the following little story:

1. The second story of the first day was about a Jew called Abraham who travels from Paris to Rome to see for himself how depraved the church hierarchy is. Yet he decides to convert to Christianity, seeing how the religion has "grown in popularity and become more splendid and illustrious" despite the church's corruption: "I can only conclude that, being a more holy and genuine religion than any of the others, it deservedly has the Holy Ghost as its foundation and support."

2. Salah-ed-din was sultan of Syria and Egypt in the 12th century. Under his rule the Muslims regained the city of Jerusalem from the Christians in 1187.

3. In Egypt.

"Unless I am mistaken, I recall having frequently heard that there was once a great and wealthy man who, apart from the other fine jewels contained in his treasury, possessed a most precious and beautiful ring. Because of its value and beauty, he wanted to do it the honour of leaving it in perpetuity to his descendants, and so he announced that he would bequeath the ring to one of his sons, and that whichever of them should be found to have it in his keeping, this man was to be looked upon as his heir, and the others were to honour and respect him as the head of the family.

"The man to whom he left the ring, having made a similar provision regarding his own descendants, followed the example set by his predecessor. To cut a long story short, the ring was handed down through many generations till it finally came to rest in the hands of a man who had three most splendid and virtuous sons who were very obedient to their father, and he loved all three of them equally. Each of the three young men, being aware of the tradition concerning the ring, was eager to take precedence over the others, and they all did their utmost to persuade the father, who was now an old man, to leave them the ring when he died.

"The good man, who loved all three and was unable to decide which of them should inherit the ring, resolved, having promised it to each, to try and please them all. So he secretly commissioned a master-craftsman to make two more rings, which were so like the first that even the man who had made them could barely distinguish them from the original. And when he was dying, he took each of his sons aside in turn, and gave one ring to each.

"After their father's death, they all desired to succeed to his title and estate, and each man denied the claims of the others, producing his ring to prove his case. But finding that the rings were so alike that it was impossible to tell them apart, the question of which of the sons was the true and rightful heir remained in abeyance, and has never been settled.

"And I say to you, my lord, that the same applies to the three laws which God the Father granted to His three peoples, and which formed the subject of your inquiry. Each of them considers itself the legitimate heir to His estate, each believes it possesses His one true law and observes His commandments. But as with the rings, the question as to which of them is right remains in abeyance."

Saladin perceived that the fellow had ingeniously side-stepped the trap he had set before him, and he therefore decided to make a clean breast of his needs, and see if the Jew would come to his assistance. This he did, freely admitting what he had intended to do, but for the fact that the Jew had answered him so discreetly.

Melchizedek gladly provided the Sultan with the money he required. The Sultan later paid him back in full, in addition to which he showered magnificent gifts upon him, made him his lifelong friend, and maintained him at his court in a state of importance and honour.

from Third Day[1]

Tenth Story: [Locking the Devil Up in Hell]

Alibech becomes a recluse, and after being taught by the monk, Rustico, to put the devil back in Hell, she is eventually taken away to become the wife of Neerbal.

1. The theme for the third day, under the rule of Neifile, is about people who achieved something they desired, or recovered something they lost. Dioneo, who by prior agreement always tells the final tale of each day, is also exempt from the rules regarding the theme.

Dioneo had been following the queen's story closely, and on perceiving that it was finished, knowing that he was the only speaker left, he smiled and began without waiting to be bidden:

Gracious ladies, you have possibly never heard how the devil is put back into Hell, and hence, without unduly straying from the theme of your discussions for today, I should like to tell you about it. By learning how it is done, there may yet be time perhaps for you to save our souls from perdition, and you will also discover that, even though Love is more inclined to take up his abode in a gay palace and a dainty bedchamber than in a wretched hovel, there is no denying that he sometimes makes his powers felt among pathless woods, on rugged mountains, and in desert caves; nor is this surprising, since all living things are subject to his sway.

Now, to come to the point, there once lived in the town of Gafsa, in Barbary,[2] a very rich man who had numerous children, among them a lovely and graceful young daughter called Alibech. She was not herself a Christian, but there were many Christians in the town, and one day, having on occasion heard them extol the Christian faith and the service of God, she asked one of them for his opinion on the best and easiest way for a person to "serve God," as they put it. He answered her by saying that the ones who served God best were those who put the greatest distance between themselves and earthly goods, as happened in the case of people who had gone to live in the remoter parts of the Sahara.[3]

She said no more about it to anyone, but next morning, being a very simple-natured creature of fourteen or thereabouts, Alibech set out all alone, in secret, and made her way towards the desert, prompted by nothing more logical than a strong adolescent impulse. A few days later, exhausted from fatigue and hunger, she arrived in the heart of the wilderness, where, catching sight of a small hut in the distance, she stumbled towards it, and in the doorway she found a holy man, who was astonished to see her in those parts and asked her what she was doing there. She told him that she had been inspired by God, and that she was trying, not only to serve Him, but also to find someone who could teach her how she should go about it.

On observing how young and exceedingly pretty she was, the good man was afraid to take her under his wing lest the devil should catch him unawares. So he praised her for her good intentions, and having given her a quantity of herb-roots, wild apples and dates to eat, and some water to drink, he said to her:

"My daughter, not very far from here there is a holy man who is much more capable than I of teaching you what you want to know. Go along to him." And he sent her upon her way.

When she came to this second man, she was told precisely the same thing, and so she went on until she arrived at the cell of a young hermit, a very devout and kindly fellow called Rustico, to whom she put the same inquiry as she had addressed to the others. Being anxious to prove to himself that he possessed a will of iron, he did not, like the others, send her away or direct her elsewhere, but kept her with him in his cell, in a corner of which, when night descended, he prepared a makeshift bed out of palm-leaves, upon which he invited her to lie down and rest.

2. Gafsa is a city in Tunisia; Barbary is the term used to describe northwest Africa, settled largely by Berbers.

3. More precisely, the deserts around Thebes, in ancient Egypt, where many monks and Christian anchorites retreated for lives of contemplation and penitence.

Once he had taken this step, very little time elapsed before temptation went to war against his willpower, and after the first few assaults, finding himself outmanoeuvred on all fronts, he laid down his arms and surrendered. Casting aside pious thoughts, prayers, and penitential exercises, he began to concentrate his mental faculties upon the youth and beauty of the girl, and to devise suitable ways and means for approaching her in such a fashion that she should not think it lewd of him to make the sort of proposal he had in mind. By putting certain questions to her, he soon discovered that she had never been intimate with the opposite sex and was every bit as innocent as she seemed; and he therefore thought of a possible way to persuade her, with the pretext of serving God, to gratify his desires. He began by delivering a long speech in which he showed her how powerful an enemy the devil was to the Lord God, and followed this up by impressing upon her that of all the ways of serving God, the one that He most appreciated consisted in putting the devil back in Hell, to which the Almighty had consigned him in the first place.

The girl asked him how this was done, and Rustico replied:

"You will soon find out, but just do whatever you see me doing for the present." And so saying, he began to divest himself of the few clothes he was wearing, leaving himself completely naked. The girl followed his example, and he sank to his knees as though he were about to pray, getting her to kneel directly opposite.

In this posture, the girl's beauty was displayed to Rustico in all its glory, and his longings blazed more fiercely than ever, bringing about the resurrection of the flesh.[4] Alibech stared at this in amazement, and said:

"Rustico, what is that thing I see sticking out in front of you, which I do not possess?"

"Oh, my daughter," said Rustico, "this is the devil I was telling you about. Do you see what he's doing? He's hurting me so much that I can hardly endure it."

"Oh, praise be to God," said the girl, "I can see that I am better off than you are, for I have no such devil to contend with."

"You're right there," said Rustico. "But you have something else instead, that I haven't."

"Oh?" said Alibech. "And what's that?"

"You have Hell," said Rustico. "And I honestly believe that God has sent you here for the salvation of my soul, because if this devil continues to plague the life out of me, and if you are prepared to take sufficient pity upon me to let me put him back into Hell, you will be giving me marvellous relief, as well as rendering incalculable service and pleasure to God, which is what you say you came here for to begin with."

"Oh, Father," replied the girl in all innocence, "if I really do have a Hell, let's do as you suggest just as soon as you are ready."

"God bless you, my daughter," said Rustico. "Let us go and put him back and then perhaps he'll leave me alone."

At which point he conveyed the girl to one of their beds, where he instructed her in the art of incarcerating that accursed fiend.

Never having put a single devil into Hell before, the girl found the first experience a little painful, and she said to Rustico:

"This devil must certainly be a bad lot, Father, and a true enemy of God, for as well as plaguing mankind, he even hurts Hell when he's driven back inside it."

4. A punning allusion to the Last Judgment.

"Daughter," said Rustico, "it will not always be like that." And in order to ensure that it wouldn't, before moving from the bed they put him back half a dozen times, curbing his arrogance to such good effect that he was positively glad to keep still for the rest of the day.

During the next few days, however, the devil's pride frequently reared its head again, and the girl, ever ready to obey the call to duty and bring him under control, happened to develop a taste for the sport, and began saying to Rustico:

"I can certainly see what those worthy men in Gafsa meant when they said that serving God was so agreeable. I don't honestly recall ever having done anything that gave me so much pleasure and satisfaction as I get from putting the devil back in Hell. To my way of thinking, anyone who devotes his energies to anything but the service of God is a complete blockhead."

She thus developed the habit of going to Rustico at frequent intervals, and saying to him:

"Father, I came here to serve God, not to idle away my time. Let's go and put the devil back in Hell."

And sometimes, in the middle of their labours, she would say:

"What puzzles me, Rustico, is that the devil should ever want to escape from Hell. Because if he liked being there as much as Hell enjoys receiving him and keeping him inside, he would never go away at all."

By inviting Rustico to play the game too often, continually urging him on in the service of God, the girl took so much stuffing out of him that he eventually began to turn cold where another man would have been bathed in sweat. So he told her that the devil should only be punished and put back in Hell when he reared his head with pride, adding that by the grace of Heaven, they had tamed him so effectively that he was pleading with God to be left in peace. In this way, he managed to keep the girl quiet for a while, but one day, having begun to notice that Rustico was no longer asking for the devil to be put back in Hell, she said:

"Look here, Rustico. Even though your devil has been punished and pesters you no longer, my Hell simply refuses to leave me alone. Now that I have helped you with my Hell to subdue the pride of your devil, the least you can do is to get your devil to help me tame the fury of my Hell."

Rustico, who was living on a diet of herb-roots and water, was quite incapable of supplying her requirements, and told her that the taming of her Hell would require an awful lot of devils, but promised to do what he could. Sometimes, therefore, he responded to the call, but this happened so infrequently that it was rather like chucking a bean into the mouth of a lion, with the result that the girl, who felt that she was not serving God as diligently as she would have liked, was found complaining more often than not.

But at the height of this dispute between Alibech's Hell and Rustico's devil, brought about by a surplus of desire on the one hand and a shortage of power on the other, a fire broke out in Gafsa, and Alibech's father was burnt to death in his own house along with all his children and every other member of his household, so that Alibech inherited the whole of his property. Because of this a young man called Neerbal who had spent the whole of his substance in sumptuous living, having heard that she was still alive, set out to look for her, and before the authorities were able to appropriate her late father's fortune on the grounds that there was no heir, he succeeded in tracing her whereabouts. To the great relief of Rustico, but against her own wishes, he took her back to Gafsa and married her, thus inheriting a half-share in her father's enormous fortune.

Before Neerbal had actually slept with her, she was questioned by the women of Gafsa about how she had served God in the desert, and she replied that she had served Him by putting the devil back in Hell, and that Neerbal had committed a terrible sin by stopping her from performing so worthy a service.

"How do you put the devil back in Hell?" asked the women.

Partly in words and partly through gestures, the girl showed them how it was done, whereupon the women laughed so much that they are laughing yet; and they said:

"Don't let it worry you, my dear. People do the job every bit as well here in Gafsa, and Neerbal will give you plenty of help in serving the Lord."

The story was repeated throughout the town, being passed from one woman to the next, and they coined a proverbial saying there to the effect that the most agreeable way of serving God was to put the devil back in Hell. The dictum later crossed the sea to Italy, where it survives to this day.

And so, young ladies, if you stand in need of God's grace, see that you learn to put the devil back in Hell, for it is greatly to His liking and pleasurable to the parties concerned, and a great deal of good can arise and flow in the process.

* * *

So aptly and cleverly worded did Dioneo's tale appear to the virtuous ladies, that they shook with mirth a thousand times or more. And when he had brought it to a close, the queen, acknowledging the end of her sovereignty, removed the laurel from her head and placed it very gracefully on Filostrato's, saying:

"Now we shall discover whether the wolf can fare any better at leading the sheep than the sheep have fared in leading the wolves."[5]

On hearing this, Filostrato laughed and said: "Had you listened to me, the wolves would have taught the sheep by now to put the devil back in Hell, no less skilfully than Rustico taught Alibech. But you have not exactly been behaving like sheep, and therefore you must not describe us as wolves. However, you have placed the kingdom in my hands, and I shall govern it as well as I am able." * * *

Seventh Day[1]

Fourth Story: [The Woman Who Locked Her Husband Out]

[Thus Lauretta began her tale:]

O Love, how manifold and mighty are your powers! How wise your counsels, how keen your insights! What philosopher, what artist could ever have conjured up all the arguments, all the subterfuges, all the explanations that you offer spontaneously to those who nail their colours to your mast? Every other doctrine is assuredly behindhand in comparison with yours, as may clearly be seen from the cases already brought to our notice. And to these, fond ladies, I shall now add yet another, by telling you of the expedient adopted by a woman of no great intelligence, who to my way of thinking could only have been motivated by Love.

5. Filostrato will be the first man to lead the day's tale-telling.

1. Tales of the seventh day, over which Dioneo rules, are to be about "tricks which, either in the cause of love or for motives of self-preservation, women have played upon their husbands, irrespecitve of whether or not they were found out."

In the city of Arezzo,[2] then, there once lived a man of means, Tofano[3] by name, who, having taken to wife a woman of very great beauty, called Monna Ghita, promptly grew jealous of her without any reason. On perceiving how jealous he was, the lady took offence and repeatedly asked him to explain the reason, but since he could only reply in vague and illogical terms, she resolved to make him suffer in good earnest from the ill which hitherto he had feared without cause.

Having observed that a certain young man, a very agreeable sort of fellow to her way of thinking, was casting amorous glances in her direction, she secretly began to cultivate his acquaintance. And when she and the young man had carried the affair to the point where it only remained to translate words into deeds, she once again took the initiative and devised a way of doing it. She had already discovered that one of her husband's bad habits was a fondness for drink, and so she began not only to commend him for it, but to encourage him deliberately whenever she had the chance. With a little practice, she quickly acquired the knack of persuading him to drink himself into a stupor, almost as often as she chose, and once she saw that he was blind drunk, she put him to bed and forgathered with her lover. This soon became a regular habit of theirs, and they met together in perfect safety. Indeed, the lady came to rely so completely on the fellow's talent for drinking himself unconscious that she made bold, not only to admit her lover to the premises, but on occasion to go and spend a goodly part of the night with him at his own house, which was no great distance away.

The amorous lady had been doing this for quite some time when her unfortunate husband happened to notice that although she encouraged him to drink, she herself never drank at all, which made him suspect (as was indeed the case) that his wife was making him drunk so that she could do as she pleased when he was asleep. In order to prove whether this was so, he returned home one evening, having refrained from drinking for the whole day, and pretended to be as drunk as a lord, scarcely able to speak or stand on his feet. Being taken in by all this, and concluding that he would sleep like a log without imbibing any more liquor, his wife quickly put him to bed, then left the house and made her way, as on previous occasions, to the house of her lover, where she stayed for half the night.

Hearing no sound from his wife, Tofano got up, went and bolted the door from the inside, and stationed himself at the window so that he would see her coming back and let her know that he had tumbled to her mischief; and there he remained until she returned. Great indeed was the woman's distress when she came home to find that she was locked out, and she began to apply all her strength in an effort to force the door open.

Tofano put up with this for a while, then he said:

"You're wasting your energies, woman. You can't possibly get in. Go back to wherever it is that you've been until this hour of the night, and rest assured that you won't return to this house till I've made an example of you in front of your kinsfolk and neighbours."

Then his wife began to plead with him for the love of God to let her in, saying that she had not been doing anything wrong, as he supposed, but simply keeping vigil with a neighbour of hers, who could neither sleep the whole night because it was too long, nor keep vigil in the house by herself.

Her pleas were totally unavailing, for the silly ass was clearly determined that all the Aretines should learn about his dishonour, of which none of them had so far heard

2. A city in Tuscany, to the southeast of Florence.

3. From Cristoforo, or Christopher.

anything. And when she saw that it was no use pleading with him, the woman resorted to threats, and said:

"If you don't let me in, I shall make you the sorriest man on earth."

To which Tofano replied:

"And how are you going to do that?"

The lady had all her wits about her, for Love was her counsellor, and she replied: "Rather than face the dishonour which in spite of my innocence you threaten me with, I shall hurl myself into this well, and when they find me dead inside it, they will all think that it was you who threw me into it when you were drunk; and so either you will have to run away, lose everything you possess, and live in exile, or you will have your head chopped off for murdering your wife, which in effect is what you will have done."

But having made up his stupid mind, Tofano was not affected in the slightest by these words, and so his wife said:

"Now look here, I won't let you torment me any longer; may God forgive you, I'll leave my distaff here, and you can put it back where it belongs."

The night was so dark that you could scarcely see your hand in front of your face, and having uttered these words, the woman groped her way towards the well, picked up an enormous stone that was lying beside it, and with a cry of "God forgive me!" she dropped it into the depths. The stone struck the water with a tremendous thump, and when Tofano heard this he was firmly convinced that she had thrown herself in. So he seized the pail and its rope, rushed head-long from the house, and ran to the well to assist her. His wife was lying in wait near the front door, and as soon as she saw him running to the well, she stepped inside the house, bolted the door, and went to the window, where she stood and shouted:

"You should water down your wine when you're drinking it, and not in the middle of the night."

When he heard her voice, Tofano saw that he had been outwitted and made his way back to the house. And on finding that he couldn't open the door, he ordered her to let him in.

Whereas previously she had addressed him in little more than a whisper, his wife now began to shout almost at the top of her voice, saying:

"By the cross of God, you loathsome sot, you're not going to come in here tonight. I will not tolerate this conduct of yours any longer. It's time I showed people the sort of man you are and the hours you keep."

Being very angry, Tofano too began to shout, pouring out a stream of abuse, so that the neighbours, men and women alike, hearing all this racket, got up out of bed and appeared at their windows, demanding to know what was going on.

The woman's eyes filled with tears, and she said: "It's this villain of a man, who returns home drunk of an evening, or else he falls asleep in some tavern or other and then comes back at this hour. I've put up with it for God knows how long and remonstrated with him until I was blue in the face. But I can't put up with it any longer, and so I've decided to take him down a peg or two by locking him out, to see whether he will mend his ways."

Tofano on the other hand, like the fool that he was, explained precisely what had happened, and came out with a whole lot of threats and abuse, whereupon his wife spoke up again, saying to the neighbours:

"You see the sort of man he is! What would you say if I were in the street and he was in the house, instead of the other way round? In God's faith I've no doubt you would believe what he was saying. So you can see what a crafty fellow he is. He accuses me of doing the very thing that he appears to have done himself. He thought he could frighten me by dropping something or other down the well; but I wish to God that he really had thrown himself in, and drowned himself at the same time, so that all the wine he's been drinking would have been well and truly diluted."

The neighbours, men and women alike, all began to scold Tofano, putting the blame on him alone and reviling him for slandering his poor wife; and in brief, they created such an uproar that it eventually reached the ears of the woman's kinsfolk.

Her kinsfolk hurried to the scene, and having listened to the accounts of several of the neighbours, they took hold of Tofano and hammered him till he was black and blue. They then went into the house, collected all the woman's belongings, and took her back with them, threatening Tofano with worse to follow.

Seeing what a sorry plight he had landed himself in on account of his jealousy, Tofano, since he was really very fond of his wife, persuaded certain friends of his to intercede on his behalf with the lady's kinsfolk, with whom he succeeded in making his peace and arranging for her to come back to him. And not only did he promise her that he would never be jealous again, but he gave her permission to amuse herself to her heart's content, provided she was sensible enough not to let him catch her out. So, like the stupid peasant, he first was mad and then was pleasant. Long live love, therefore, and a plague on all skinflints!

Tenth Day[1]

Tenth Story: [The Patient Griselda]

The Marquis of Saluzzo, obliged by the entreaties of his subjects to take a wife, follows his personal whims and marries the daughter of a peasant. She bears him two children, and he gives her the impression that he has put them to death. Later on, pretending that she has incurred his displeasure and that he has remarried, he arranges for his own daughter to return home and passes her off as his bride, having meanwhile turned his wife out of doors in no more than the shift she is wearing. But on finding that she endures it all with patience, he cherishes her all the more deeply, brings her back to his house, shows her their children, who have now grown up, and honours her as the Marchioness, causing others to honour her likewise.

Sweet and gentle ladies, [said Dioneo] this day has been devoted, so far as I can see, to the doings of kings and sultans and people of that sort; and therefore, so as not to place too great a distance between us, I want to tell you of a marquis, whose actions, even though things turned out well for him in the end, were remarkable not so much for their munificence as for their senseless brutality.[2] Nor do I advise anyone to follow his example, for it was a great pity that the fellow should have drawn any profit from his conduct.

1. For the final day, over which Panfilo presides, "the discussion turns upon those who have performed liberal or munificent deeds, whether in the cause of love or otherwise." As always, Dioneo goes last and is exempt from the thematic rule.

2. In Italian, "matta bestialitade" (mad bestiality), a phrase which echoes Dante's description of one of the "three dispositions/that strike at Heaven's will: incontinence/ and malice and mad bestality" (*Inferno* XI: 81-2); the phrase covers those found in the Seventh Circle, the violent against their neighbours, themselves, nature, and God.

A very long time ago, there succeeded to the marquisate of Saluzzo[3] a young man called Gualtieri, who, having neither wife nor children, spent the whole of his time hunting and hawking, and never even thought about marrying or raising a family, which says a great deal for his intelligence. His followers, however, disapproved of this, and repeatedly begged him to marry so that he should not be left without an heir nor they without a lord. Moreover, they offered to find him a wife whose parentage would be such as to strengthen their expectations and who would make him exceedingly happy.

So Gualtieri answered them as follows:

"My friends, you are pressing me to do something that I had always set my mind firmly against, seeing how difficult it is to find a person who will easily adapt to one's own way of living, how many thousands there are who will do precisely the opposite, and what a miserable life is in store for the man who stumbles upon a woman ill-suited to his own temperament. Moreover it is foolish of you to believe that you can judge the character of daughters from the ways of their fathers and mothers, hence claiming to provide me with a wife who will please me. For I cannot see how you are to know the fathers, or to discover the secrets of the mothers; and even if this were possible, daughters are very often different from either of their parents. Since, however, you are so determined to bind me in chains of this sort, I am ready to do as you ask; but so that I have only myself to blame if it should turn out badly, I must insist on marrying a wife of my own choosing. And I hereby declare that no matter who she may be, if you fail to honour her as your lady you will learn to your great cost how serious a matter it is for you to have urged me to marry against my will."

To this the gentlemen replied that if only he would bring himself to take a wife, they would be satisfied.

Now, for some little time, Gualtieri had been casting an appreciative eye on the manners of a poor girl from a neighbouring village, and thinking her very beautiful, he considered that a life with her would have much to commend it. So without looking further afield, he resolved to marry the girl; and having summoned her father, who was very poor indeed, he arranged with him that he should take her as his wife.

This done, Gualtieri brought together all his friends from the various parts of his domain, and said to them:

"My friends, since you still persist in wanting me to take a wife, I am prepared to do it, not because I have any desire to marry, but rather in order to gratify your wishes. You will recall the promise you gave me, that no matter whom I should choose, you would rest content and honour her as your lady. The time has now come when I want you to keep that promise, and for me to honour the promise I gave to you. I have found a girl after my own heart, in this very district, and a few days hence I intend to marry her and convey her to my house. See to it, therefore, that the wedding-feast lacks nothing in splendour, and consider how you may honourably receive her, so that all of us may call ourselves contented—I with you for keeping your promise, and you with me for keeping mine."

As of one voice, the good folk joyously gave him their blessing, and said that whoever she happened to be, they would accept her as their lady and honour her as such in all respects. Then they all prepared to celebrate the wedding in a suitably grand and sumptuous manner, and Gualtieri did the same. A rich and splendid nuptial feast

3. Saluzzo is in northwestern Italy, in the region of Piedmont.

was arranged, to which he invited many of his friends, his kinsfolk, great nobles and other people of the locality; moreover he caused a quantity of fine, rich robes to be tailored to fit a girl whose figure appeared to match that of the young woman he intended to marry; and lastly he laid in a number of rings and ornamental belts, along with a precious and beautiful crown, and everything else that a bride could possibly need.

Early on the morning of the day he had fixed for the nuptials, Gualtieri, his preparations now complete, mounted his horse together with all the people who had come to do him honour, and said:

"Gentlemen, it is time for us to go and fetch the bride."

He then set forth with the whole of the company in train, and eventually they came to the village and made their way to the house of the girl's father, where they met her as she was returning with water from the fountain, making great haste so that she could go with other women to see Gualtieri's bride arriving. As soon as Gualtieri caught sight of her, he called to her by her name, which was Griselda, and asked her where her father was, to which she blushingly replied:

"My lord, he is at home."

So Gualtieri dismounted, and having ordered everyone to wait for him outside, he went alone into the humble dwelling, where he found the girl's father, whose name was Giannùcole,[4] and said to him:

"I have come to marry Griselda, but first I want to ask her certain questions in your presence." He then asked her whether, if he were to marry her, she would always try to please him and never be upset by anything he said or did, whether she would obey him, and many other questions of this sort, to all of which she answered that she would.

Whereupon Gualtieri, having taken her by the hand, led her out of the house, and in the presence of his whole company and of all the other people there he caused her to be stripped naked. Then he called for the clothes and shoes which he had had specially made, and quickly got her to put them on, after which he caused a crown to be placed upon the dishevelled hair of her head. And just as everyone was wondering what this might signify, he said:

"Gentlemen, this is the woman I intend to marry, provided she will have me as her husband." Then, turning to Griselda, who was so embarrassed that she hardly knew where to look, he said: "Griselda, will you have me as your wedded husband?"

To which she replied:

"I will, my lord."

"And I will have you as my wedded wife," said Gualtieri, and he married her then and there before all the people present. He then helped her mount a palfrey, and led her back, honourably attended, to his house, where the nuptials were as splendid and as sumptuous, and the rejoicing as unrestrained, as if he had married the King of France's daughter.

Along with her new clothes, the young bride appeared to take on a new lease of life, and she seemed a different woman entirely. She was endowed, as we have said, with a fine figure and beautiful features, and lovely as she already was, she now acquired so confident, graceful and decorous a manner that she could have been taken for the daughter, not of the shepherd Giannùcole, but of some great nobleman, and consequently everyone who had known her before her marriage was

4. "Little John."

filled with astonishment. But apart from this, she was so obedient to her husband, and so compliant to his wishes, that he thought himself the happiest and most contented man on earth. At the same time she was so gracious and benign towards her husband's subjects, that each and every one of them was glad to honour her, and accorded her his unselfish devotion, praying for her happiness, prosperity, and greater glory. And whereas they had been wont to say that Gualtieri had shown some lack of discretion in taking this woman as his wife, they now regarded him as the wisest and most discerning man on earth. For no one apart from Gualtieri could ever have perceived the noble qualities that lay concealed beneath her ragged and rustic attire.

In short, she comported herself in such a manner that she quickly earned widespread acclaim for her virtuous deeds and excellent character not only in her husband's domain but also in the world at large; and those who had formerly censured Gualtieri for choosing to marry her were now compelled to reverse their opinion.

Not long after she had gone to live with Gualtieri she conceived a child, and in the fullness of time, to her husband's enormous joy, she bore him a daughter. But shortly thereafter Gualtieri was seized with the strange desire to test Griselda's patience, by subjecting her to constant provocation and making her life unbearable.

At first he lashed her with his tongue, feigning to be angry and claiming that his subjects were thoroughly disgruntled with her on account of her lowly condition, especially now that they saw her bearing children; and he said they were greatly distressed about this infant daughter of theirs, of whom they did nothing but grumble.

The lady betrayed no sign of bitterness on hearing these words, and without changing her expression she said to him:

"My lord, deal with me as you think best for your own good name and peace of mind, for I shall rest content whatever you decide, knowing myself to be their inferior and that I was unworthy of the honour which you so generously bestowed upon me."

This reply was much to Gualtieri's liking, for it showed him that she had not been puffed with pride by any honour that he or others had paid her.

A little while later, having told his wife in general terms that his subjects could not abide the daughter she had borne him, he gave certain instructions to one of his attendants, whom he sent to Griselda. The man looked very sorrowful, and said:

"My lady, if I do not wish to die, I must do as my lord commands me. He has ordered me to take this daughter of yours, and to . . ." And his voice trailed off into silence.

On hearing these words and perceiving the man's expression, Griselda, recalling what she had been told, concluded that he had been instructed to murder her child. So she quickly picked it up from its cradle, kissed it, gave it her blessing, and albeit she felt that her heart was about to break, placed the child in the arms of the servant without any trace of emotion, saying:

"There: do exactly as your lord, who is my lord too, has instructed you. But do not leave her to be devoured by the beasts and the birds, unless that is what he has ordered you to do."

The servant took away the little girl and reported Griselda's words to Gualtieri, who, marvelling at her constancy, sent him with the child to a kinswoman of his in Bologna, requesting her to rear and educate her carefully, but without ever making it known whose daughter she was.

Then it came about that his wife once more became pregnant, and in due course she gave birth to a son, which pleased Gualtieri enormously. But not being content with the mischief he had done already, he abused her more viciously than ever, and one day he glowered at her angrily and said:

"Woman, from the day you produced this infant son, the people have made my life a complete misery, so bitterly do they resent the thought of a grandson of Giannùcole succeeding me as their lord. So unless I want to be deposed, I'm afraid I shall be forced to do as I did before, and eventually to leave you and marry someone else."

His wife listened patiently, and all she replied was:

"My lord, look to your own comfort, see that you fulfil your wishes, and spare no thought for me, since nothing brings me pleasure unless it pleases you also."

Before many days had elapsed, Gualtieri sent for his son in the same way that he had sent for his daughter, and having likewise pretended to have had the child put to death, he sent him, like the little girl, to Bologna. To all of this his wife reacted no differently, either in her speech or in her looks, than she had on the previous occasion, much to the astonishment of Gualtieri, who told himself that no other woman could have remained so impassive. But for the fact that he had observed her doting upon the children for as long as he allowed her to do so, he would have assumed that she was glad to be rid of them, whereas he knew that she was too judicious to behave in any other way.

His subjects, thinking he had caused the children to be murdered, roundly condemned him and judged him a cruel tyrant, whilst his wife became the object of their deepest compassion. But to the women who offered her their sympathy in the loss of her children, all she ever said was that the decision of their father was good enough for her.

Many years after the birth of his daughter, Gualtieri decided that the time had come to put Griselda's patience to the final test. So he told a number of his men that in no circumstances could he put up with Griselda as his wife any longer, having now come to realize that his marriage was an aberration of his youth. He would therefore do everything in his power to obtain a dispensation from the Pope, enabling him to divorce Griselda and marry someone else. For this he was chided severely by many worthy men, but his only reply was that it had to be done.

On learning of her husband's intentions, from which it appeared she would have to return to her father's house, in order perhaps to look after the sheep as she had in the past, meanwhile seeing the man she adored being cherished by some other woman, Griselda was secretly filled with despair. But she prepared herself to endure this final blow as stoically as she had borne Fortune's earlier assaults.

Shortly thereafter, Gualtieri arranged for some counterfeit letters of his to arrive from Rome, and led his subjects to believe that in these, the Pope had granted him permission to abandon Griselda and remarry.

He accordingly sent for Griselda, and before a large number of people he said to her: "Woman, I have had a dispensation from the Pope, allowing me to leave you and take another wife. Since my ancestors were great noblemen and rulers of these lands, whereas yours have always been peasants, I intend that you shall no longer be my wife, but return to Giannùcole's house with the dowry you brought me, after which I shall bring another lady here. I have already chosen her and she is far better suited to a man of my condition."

On hearing these words, the lady, with an effort beyond the power of any normal woman's nature, suppressed her tears and replied:

"My lord, I have always known that my lowly condition was totally at odds with your nobility, and that it is to God and to yourself that I owe whatever standing

I possess. Nor have I ever regarded this as a gift that I might keep and cherish as my own, but rather as something I have borrowed; and now that you want me to return it, I must give it back to you with good grace. Here is the ring with which you married me: take it. As to your ordering me to take away the dowry that I brought, you will require no accountant, nor will I need a purse or a pack-horse, for this to be done. For it has not escaped my memory that you took me naked as on the day I was born. If you think it proper that the body in which I have borne your children should be seen by all the people, I shall go away naked. But in return for my virginity, which I brought to you and cannot retrieve, I trust you will at least allow me, in addition to my dowry, to take one shift away with me."

Gualtieri wanted above all else to burst into tears, but maintaining a stern expression he said:

"Very well, you may take a shift."

All the people present implored Gualtieri to let her have a dress, so that she who had been his wife for thirteen years and more would not have to suffer the indignity of leaving his house in a shift, like a pauper; but their pleas were unavailing. And so Griselda, wearing a shift, barefoot, and with nothing to cover her head, having bidden them farewell, set forth from Gualtieri's house and returned to her father amid the weeping and the wailing of all who set eyes upon her.

Giannùcole, who had never thought it possible that Gualtieri would keep his daughter as his wife, and was daily expecting this to happen, had preserved the clothes she discarded on the morning Gualtieri had married her. So he brought them to her, and Griselda, having put them on, applied herself as before to the menial chores in her father's house, bravely enduring the cruel assault of hostile Fortune.

No sooner did Gualtieri drive Griselda away, than he gave his subjects to understand that he was betrothed to a daughter of one of the Counts of Panago.[5] And having ordered that grandiose preparations were to be made for the nuptials, he sent for Griselda and said to her:

"I am about to fetch home this new bride of mine, and from the moment she sets foot inside the house, I intend to accord her an honourable welcome. As you know, I have no women here who can set the rooms in order for me, or attend to many of the things that a festive occasion of this sort requires. No one knows better than you how to handle these household affairs, so I want you to make all the necessary arrangements. Invite all the ladies you need, and receive them as though you were mistress of the house. And when the nuptials are over, you can go back home to your father."

Since Griselda was unable to lay aside her love for Gualtieri as readily as she had dispensed with her good fortune, his words pierced her heart like so many knives. But she replied.

"My lord, I am ready to do as you ask."

And so, in her coarse, thick, woollen garments, Griselda returned to the house she had quitted shortly before in her shift, and started to sweep and tidy the various chambers. On her instructions, the beds were draped with hangings, the benches in the halls were suitably adorned, the kitchen was made ready; and she set her hand, as though she were a petty serving wench, to every conceivable household task, never stopping to draw breath until she had everything prepared and arranged as befitted the occasion.

5. Panago, or Panico, is in the province of Emilio-Romagna, near Bologna.

Having done all this, she caused invitations to be sent, in Gualtieri's name, to all the ladies living in those parts, and began to await the event. And when at last the nuptial day arrived, heedless of her beggarly attire, she bade a cheerful welcome to each of the lady guests, displaying all the warmth and courtesy of a lady of the manor.

Gualtieri's children having meanwhile been carefully reared by his kinswoman in Bologna, who had married into the family of the Counts of Panago, the girl was now twelve years old, the loveliest creature ever seen, whilst the boy had reached the age of six. Gualtieri had sent word to his kinswoman's husband, asking him to do him the kindness of bringing this daughter of his to Saluzzo along with her little brother, to see that she was nobly and honourably escorted, and to tell everyone he met that he was taking her to marry Gualtieri, without revealing who she really was to a living soul.

In accordance with the Marquis's request, the gentleman set forth with the girl and her brother and a noble company, and a few days later, shortly before the hour of breakfast, he arrived at Saluzzo, where he found that all the folk thereabouts, and numerous others from neighbouring parts, were waiting for Gualtieri's latest bride.

After being welcomed by the ladies, she made her way to the hall where the tables were set, and Griselda, just as we have described her, went cordially up to meet her, saying:

"My lady, you are welcome."

The ladies, who in vain had implored Gualtieri to see that Griselda remained in another room, or to lend her one of the dresses that had once been hers, so that she would not cut such a sorry figure in front of his guests, took their seats at table and addressed themselves to the meal. All eyes were fixed upon the girl, and everyone said that Gualtieri had made a good exchange. But Griselda praised her as warmly as anyone present, speaking no less admiringly of her little brother.

Gualtieri felt that he had now seen all he wished to see of the patience of his lady, for he perceived that no event, however singular, produced the slightest change in her demeanour, and he was certain that this was not because of her obtuseness, as he knew her to be very intelligent. He therefore considered that the time had come for him to free her from the rancour that he judged her to be hiding beneath her tranquil outward expression. And having summoned her to his table, before all the people present he smiled at her and said:

"What do you think of our new bride?"

"My lord," replied Griselda, "I think very well of her. And if, as I believe, her wisdom matches her beauty, I have no doubt whatever that your life with her will bring you greater happiness than any gentleman on earth has ever known. But with all my heart I beg you not to inflict those same wounds upon her that you imposed upon her predecessor, for I doubt whether she could withstand them, not only because she is younger, but also because she has had a refined upbringing, whereas the other had to face continual hardship from her infancy."

On observing that Griselda was firmly convinced that the young lady was to be his wife, and that even so she allowed no hint of resentment to escape her lips, Gualtieri got her to sit down beside him, and said:

"Griselda, the time has come for you to reap the reward of your unfailing patience, and for those who considered me a cruel and bestial tyrant, to know that whatever I have done was done of set purpose, for I wished to show you how to be a wife, to teach these people how to choose and keep a wife, and to guarantee my own peace and quiet for as long as we were living beneath the same roof. When I came to take a wife, I was greatly afraid that this peace would be denied me, and in order to prove otherwise I tormented and provoked you in the ways you have seen. But as I have never known you to oppose my wishes, I now intend, being persuaded that you can offer me all the happiness I desired, to restore to you in a single instant that which I took from you little by little, and delectably assuage the pains I have inflicted upon you. Receive with gladsome heart, then, this girl whom you believe to be my bride, and also her brother. These are our children, whom you and many others have long supposed that I caused to be cruelly murdered; and I am your husband, who loves you above all else, for I think I can boast that there is no other man on earth whose contentment in his wife exceeds my own."

Having spoken these words, he embraced and kissed Griselda, who by now was weeping with joy; then they both got up from table and made their way to the place where their daughter sat listening in utter amazement to these tidings. And after they had fondly embraced the girl and her brother, the mystery was unravelled to her, as well as to many of the others who were present.

The ladies rose from table in transports of joy, and escorted Griselda to a chamber, where, with greater assurance of her future happiness, they divested her of her tattered garments and clothed her anew in one of her stately robes. And as their lady and their mistress, a rôle which even in her rags had seemed to be hers, they led her back to the hall, where she and Gualtieri rejoiced with the children in a manner marvellous to behold.

Everyone being delighted with the turn that events had taken, the feasting and the merrymaking were redoubled, and continued unabated for the next few days. Gualtieri was acknowledged to be very wise, though the trials to which he had subjected his lady were regarded as harsh and intolerable, whilst Griselda was accounted the wisest of all.

The Count of Panago returned a few days later to Bologna, and Gualtieri, having removed Giannùcole from his drudgery, set him up in a style befitting his father-in-law, so that he lived in great comfort and honour for the rest of his days. As for Gualtieri himself, having married off his daughter to a gentleman of renown, he lived long and contentedly with Griselda, never failing to honour her to the best of his ability.

What more needs to be said, except that celestial spirits may sometimes descend even into the houses of the poor, whilst there are those in royal palaces who would be better employed as swineherds than as rulers of men? Who else but Griselda could have endured so cheerfully the cruel and unheard of trials that Gualtieri imposed upon her without shedding a tear? For perhaps it would have served him right if he had chanced upon a wife, who, being driven from the house in her shift, had found some other man to shake her skin-coat for her,[6] earning herself a fine new dress in the process.

* * *

Dioneo's story had ended, and the ladies, some taking one side and some another, some finding fault with one of its details and some commending another, had talked about it at length, when the king,[7] having raised his eyes to observe that the sun had already sunk low in the evening sky, began, without getting up, to address them as follows:

"Graceful ladies, the wisdom of mortals consists, as I think you know, not only in remembering the past and apprehending the present, but in being able, through a

6. Dioneo often uses erotic metaphors of this kind.

7. Panfilo.

knowledge of each, to anticipate the future, which grave men regard as the acme of human intelligence.

"Tomorrow, as you know, a fortnight will have elapsed since the day we departed from Florence to provide for our relaxation, preserve our health and our lives, and escape from the sadness, the suffering and the anguish continuously to be found in our city since this plague first descended upon it. These aims we have achieved, in my judgement, without any loss of decorum. For as far as I have been able to observe, albeit the tales related here have been amusing, perhaps of a sort to stimulate carnal desire, and we have continually partaken of excellent food and drink, played music, and sung many songs, all of which things may encourage unseemly behaviour among those who are feeble of mind, neither in word nor in deed nor in any other respect have I known either you or ourselves to be worthy of censure. On the contrary, from what I have seen and heard, it seems to me that our proceedings have been marked by a constant sense of propriety, an unfailing spirit of harmony, and a continual feeling of brotherly and sisterly amity. All of which pleases me greatly, as it surely redounds to our communal honour and credit.

"Accordingly, lest aught conducive to tedium should arise from a custom too long established, and lest, by protracting our stay, we should cause evil tongues to start wagging, I now think it proper, since we have all in turn had our share of the honour still invested in me, that with your consent we should return from whence we came. If, moreover, you consider the matter carefully, our company being known to various others hereabouts, our numbers could increase in such a way as to destroy all our pleasure. And so, if my advice should command your approval, I shall retain the crown that was given me until our departure, which I propose should take effect tomorrow morning. But if you decide otherwise, I already have someone in mind upon whom to bestow the crown for the next day to follow."

The ladies and the young men, having debated the matter at considerable length, considered the king's advice, in the end, to be sensible and just, and decided to do as he had said. He therefore sent for the steward and conferred with him with regard to the following morning's arrangements, and having dismissed the company till supper-time, he rose to his feet.

The ladies and the other young men followed suit, and turned their attention to various pastimes as usual. When it was time for supper, they disposed of the meal with infinite relish, after which they turned to singing and music and dancing. * * *

Next morning they arose at the crack of dawn, by which time all their baggage had been sent on ahead by the steward, and with their wise king leading the way they returned to Florence. Having taken their leave of the seven young ladies in Santa Maria Novella, whence they had all set out together, the three young men went off in search of other diversions; and in due course the ladies returned to their homes.[8]

8. Thus ends the narrative part of the *Decameron*. Boccaccio follows with a brief epilogue, in which he anticipates the criticism that he has taken too many liberties with his stories. He defends himself by pointing out that the stories are told in a garden, not in a church; that only corrupt minds will find things to corrupt in his stories; and that after all, he "could only transcribe the stories as they were actually told, . . . But even if one could assume that I was the inventor as well as the scribe of these stories (which was not the case), I still insist that I would not feel ashamed if some fell short of perfection, for there is no craftsman other than God whose work is whole and faultless in every respect." He closes by reminding his reader that everything in the world is subject to constant change, including his own tongue. He then thanks God, and asks the "sweet ladies" whom he addressed in his introduction to remember him "if perchance these stories should bring you any profit."

Francis Petrarch

1304–1374

Francis Petrarch is one of the crucial figures who launched the modern era, an era that embodied the very contradictions that characterized Petrarch himself. For most of his life, he fervently upheld the superiority of Latin, but he spent forty years working on his collection of lyric poetry in Italian. He cultivated the persona of the independent scholar, but attached himself to powerful, at times repugnant patrons—such as the Visconti—who could fund his personal library, which became the largest manuscript collection in Europe. He took his own religious profession lightly, but lambasted popes for not returning to Rome and advocated a Crusade. While the image that has come down to us of Petrarch is of a modernist—perhaps our first—he looks backward as much as forward. To a modern eye his least satisfying works are his attempts to write in the ancient genres of the epic and the eclogue, as well as his allegorical poems in Italian. But his look back across the long Middle Ages to what was for him the Golden Age of Rome also revealed to him the great ancients—Cicero, Virgil, Augustine—as familiar figures rather than unapproachable icons, writers from whom he might learn what it is to be human and whose words he might plunder. As he wrote in one of his letters: "the skillful juxtaposition of others' words and concepts often makes them ours." In juxtaposing "others' words" in order to articulate what, indeed, was "his," Petrarch launched the cult of the personality, and few personalities are as complex or as fascinating as that of Petrarch.

Born in 1304 to a father who, like Dante, had been exiled from Florence for his political sympathies, Petrarch spent his earliest years in Italy, near Arezzo. When he was only eight, his father took his family to Avignon in southern France where he would continue his profession as notary for the French Pope, Clement V. Although Petrarch was sent to Bologna to pursue legal studies, it quickly became clear that the law was not his passion. He returned to Avignon in 1326 after his father's death and began pursuing what *was* his passion: the study of classical antiquity through the collecting and transcribing of ancient manuscripts. With its enormous library and its large number of scholars connected to the papal court, Avignon offered the young Franciscus Petracchi—he would change his name only later to the more Latin-sounding Petrarca—the opportunity to begin honing his scholarly skills. The late 1320s saw his pioneering edition of the Roman historian Livy, the first venture to organize the scattered manuscripts of the *History of Rome* into a coherent whole. He also mingled with like-minded men who would become his companions and in some cases, his patrons for life, including the monk Dionigi da Borgo San Sepolcro, who gave Petrarch the small copy of Augustine's *Confessions* that he carried with him until his death. Southern France also offered him the restful climes of Vaucluse, a village on the Sorgue River where he bought a house and escaped from Avignon to write his first literary works in the 1330s and early 1340s: his (incomplete) epic, *Africa,* based on the heroic events of the Roman general Scipio Africanus; his collection of lives of famous men, *De viris illustribus;* and the first of his poems in Italian about a woman whom he had supposedly first glimpsed in a church in Avignon on April 6, 1327: the unattainable "Laura," whose identity remains unknown. Having decided to embrace the life of a man of the church—a decision which didn't prevent him from fathering two children—Petrarch was awarded with a canonry in the nearby cathedral of Lombez, an appointment that carried few responsibilities but sufficient income to pursue his writing.

One significant measure of Petrarch's widespread fame by the time he was thirty-six was an invitation, in 1340, to be crowned poet-laureate by the University of Paris—an invitation that was matched, supposedly only hours later, by the Roman Senate. Petrarch accepted the honor from Rome, and was crowned on the Capitoline Hill the following year. The next decade would see the writing of the *Secretum,* a dialogue between Petrarch and Augustine, who upbraids him for his passion for Laura, and the undertaking of a carefully organized collection of letters to both living and dead figures, inspired by Petrarch's discovery in Verona of Cicero's epistles. But the 1340s saw a number of changes in Petrarch's life that would considerably influence his future writing. He enthusiastically supported a short-lived attempt of the nobleman Cola di Rienzo to unite Italy's reigning principates, but the venture ended in disaster and eventually Cola's death at the stake as a heretic. Petrarch's brother Gherardo decided in 1343 to become a monk, depriving Petrarch of one of his most constant companions; his letter on Mount Ventoux, probably composed after Gherardo's withdrawal from the world, looks back to the happier days of the 1320s when the two were virtually inseparable. And the Black Death recorded so gruesomely by Boccaccio in the opening pages of his *Decameron* took as its victims a number of Petrarch's close friends, among them his most steadfast patron, Giacomo Colonna, and his beloved "Laura." Such devastation inspired the *Triumph of Death,* an allegorical pageant that unfolds before a stunned and saddened Petrarch, and the one hundred final poems of the *Canzoniere* that mourn the loss of the poet's lady.

CANZONIERE Petrarch spent many years writing, revising, and ordering and reordering the 366-poem sequence known as the *Canzoniere* or *Rime sparse* ("Scattered rhymes"). The chronology he carefully constructs from these "fragments" allows us to participate in the unfolding not simply of an unrequited passion, but of a life. That this life speaks to us with such directness, despite the formality of the metrical and verse constraints within which Petrarch worked, is one of the paradoxes of the sequence, and one that poets after him struggled to repeat with varying degrees of success.

While Petrarch wrote in a variety of metrical forms, including the flexible *canzone* and the sestina, the one that he employed most is the sonnet, perfecting the form to the extent that fourteen-line poems with a clear break between their eighth and ninth lines are simply referred to as "Petrarchan sonnets." For the most part, the four stanzas that comprise the sonnet are syntactically compact units: the octet is broken into two stanzas of four lines each, with an *a-b-b-a* rhyme scheme; the sestet is composed of two stanzas of three lines each, with a *c-d-c* rhyme. Such compactness allows for suggestive but brief sketches of Laura's beauty and the speaker's unrequited love; the discreteness of the stanza (a word that means "room") dictates that connections among them depend more on comparison and allusion than syntactical complexity. At the same time, the continuity of rhyme and Petrarch's frequent use of assonance and alliteration—plays with language and sound that the Italian language encourages, with its fluidity and inherent musicality—create a subtle, often sensuous impression of unity.

Italian though the *Canzoniere* may be, it represents in many ways a continued dialogue with classical culture. Mythological allusions abound, particularly to myths retold by Ovid. The Virgilian legacy is also strongly marked, as in the echo of Aeneas's frustrated glimpse of Venus (90) and the extended meditation on the poignant nightingale simile from the tale of Orpheus in Virgil's fourth *Georgic* (311, 353, 365). Such classical references aren't included simply for the sake of displaying intellectual wares. They help to situate Petrarch's often unanchored persona and give form to the elusive Laura: from the transformed laurel tree, to the threatening Diana who forbids Actaeon's speech, to the graceful Aurora who, in death, leaves an aging Petrarch behind on earth.

Yet Petrarch models his sequence equally on modern innovations. The sonnet, for one thing, derived from the formal experimentations of both the French Provençal school and the late thirteenth-century practitioners of the *dolce stil nuovo* ("sweet new style") to which Petrarch pays homage in his seventieth poem. Petrarch quotes lines from Arnaut Daniel, Guido Cavalcanti, and the great Dante himself, only to move beyond them in a final stanza where he tellingly quotes—who else?—himself. The idea of a poetry "book" looks back to the Roman poets Catullus and Propertius (whose manuscripts Petrarch had discovered and transcribed) but

Petrarch gives his sequence a Christian focus, starting with his confessional lament and closing with a recantation addressed not to Laura but to the "Virgin mother," Mary.

Petrarch uses devotional imagery to describe Laura, first glimpsed in a church on Good Friday. Yet there is something potentially idolatrous about this earthly passion. Petrarch's supposed inability to choose between Christian salvation and his idolatrous love is poignantly foreshadowed in the *Canzoniere,* especially in those sonnets where he mourns the fact that life is swiftly overtaking him and that he has nothing to show for his gray locks but a handful of poems. Unlike the supremely divine Beatrice of Dante's own poetry book, the *Vita nuova*, Laura finally cannot function as the medium for the poet's salvation.

Often castigated for his preciousness, as well as for a misogynistic treatment of Laura, Petrarch reveals himself as fully aware of the choices he has made and their implications. The real Laura, the Petrarchan narrator knows all too well, is nowhere to be found in his poems. One of the many conflicts of the *Canzoniere,* in fact, is the tension between the poet's fiction and the world beyond it. From time to time, Petrarch directly addresses political events as well as the patrons who generously supported him. Though his lyrics are primarily about his interior life, Petrarch also speaks to the contexts that privilege such a life.

Canzoniere

During the Life of My Lady Laura[1]

1

O you[2] who hear within these scattered verses
the sound of sighs with which I fed my heart
in my first errant youthful days when I
in part was not the man I am today;

for all the ways in which I weep and speak
between vain hopes, between vain suffering,
in anyone who knows love through its trials,
in them, may I find pity and forgiveness.

But now I see how I've become the talk
so long a time of people all around
(it often makes me feel so full of shame),

and from my vanities there comes shame's fruit,
and my repentance, and the clear awareness
that worldly joy is just a fleeting dream.

3

It was the day the sun's ray had turned pale
with pity for the suffering of his Maker
when I was caught (and I put up no fight),[3]
my lady, for your lovely eyes had bound me.

It seemed no time to be on guard against
Love's blows; therefore, I went my way

1. Translated from the Italian by Mark Musa.
2. Petrarch uses *Voi* to address his reader, which can be read as the plural form of "you" or as the formal address to a single reader, as contrasted with the more informal *tu.*
3. The day Petrarch was "taken" by his Lady is Good Friday, or 6 April 1327.

secure and fearless—so, all my misfortunes
began in midst of universal woe.

Love found me all disarmed and saw the way
was clear to reach my heart down through the eyes,
which have become the halls and doors of tears.

It seems to me it did him little honor
to wound me with his arrow in my state
and to you, armed, not show his bow at all.

16

The old man takes his leave, white-haired and pale,
of the sweet place where he filled out his age
and leaves his little family, bewildered
to see its own dear father disappear;

from there, dragging along his ancient limbs
throughout the very last days of his life,
helping himself with good will all he can,
broken by years, and wearied by the road,

he comes to Rome, pursuing his desire,
to look upon the likeness of the One
that he still hopes to see up there in Heaven.[4]

Just so, alas, sometimes I go, my lady,
searching, as much as possible, in others
for your true, your desirable form.

35

Alone and deep in thought I measure out
the most deserted fields, with slow, late steps,
with eyes intent to flee whatever sign
of human footprint left within the sand.

I find no other shield for my protection
against the knowing glances of mankind,
for in my bearing all bereft of joy
one sees from outside how I burn within.

So now, I think, only the plains and mountains,
the rivers and the forests know the kind
of life I lead, the one concealed from all.

And still, I never seem to find a path
too harsh, too wild for Love to always join
me and to speak to me, and I to him!

4. The allusion is to the veil with which Veronica is said to have wiped Christ's face while he was carrying the cross; Christ's image was preserved on the cloth, which was kept in St. Peter's and attracted large numbers of pilgrims to see it. Petrarch is drawing on a simile from Dante's *Paradiso,* Canto 31, in which a pilgrim from Croatia who comes to see the "Veronica" is compared to Dante himself.

52

Diana never pleased her lover more,
when just by chance all of her naked body
he saw bathing within the chilly waters,[5]

than did the simple mountain shepherdess
please me, the while she bathed the pretty veil
that holds her lovely blonde hair in the breeze.[6]

So that even now in hot sunlight she makes me
tremble all over with the chill of love.

90

She'd let her gold hair flow free in the breeze
that whirled it into thousands of sweet knots,
and lovely light would burn beyond all measure
in those fair eyes whose light is dimmer now.

Her face would turn the color pity wears,
a pity true or false I did not know,
and I with all Love's tinder in my breast—
it's no surprise I quickly caught on fire.

The way she walked was not the way of mortals
but of angelic forms, and when she spoke
more than an earthly voice it was that sang:[7]

a godly spirit and a living sun
was what I saw, and if she is not now,
my wound still bleeds, although the bow's unbent.

126

Clear, cool, sweet, running waters
where she, for me the only
woman, would rest her lovely body;
kind branch on which it pleased her
(I sigh to think of it)
to make a column for her lovely side;
and grass and flowers which her gown,
richly flowing, covered
with its angelic folds;
sacred air serene
where Love with those fair eyes opened my heart:
listen all of you together
to these my mournful, my last words.[8]

5. The goddess of chastity who lives among her nymphs in the woods, Diana was surprised by the hunter Actaeon while she was bathing. For his transgression, she turned him into a stag; and he was torn apart by his own dogs. Throughout the *Canzoniere*, Petrarch often refers to himself through a series of metamorphosed figures.

6. "From the breeze" is *a l'aura* in Italian—one of Petrarch's many wordplays on Laura's name.

7. In the forests of Carthage in *Aeneid* 1 the goddess Venus appears to Aeneas disguised as a young maiden, speaking to him with a more than human voice.

8. This depiction of the *locus amoenus* or beautiful place is drawn from Vaucluse, on the south bank of the Sorgue River, where Petrarch bought a house in the mid 1330s, finding there the serenity and peace he couldn't have in Avignon. The "clear, cool, sweet waters" are those of the Sorgue.

If it, indeed, must be my fate,
and Heaven works its ways,
that Love close up these eyes while they still weep,
let grace see my poor body
be buried there among you
and let my soul return to its home naked;
then death would be less harsh
if I could bear this hope
unto that fearful crossing,
because the weary soul
could never in a more secluded port,
in a more tranquil grave,
flee from my poor belabored flesh and bones.

And there will come a time, perhaps,
that to the well-known place
the lovely animal returns,[9] and tamed,
and there where she first saw me
that day which now is blessed,
she turns her eyes with hope and happiness
in search of me, and—ah, the pity—
to see me there as dust
among the stones, Love will
inspire her and she will sigh
so sweetly she will win for me some mercy
and force open the heavens
drying her eyes there with her lovely veil.

Falling from gracious boughs,
I sweetly call to mind,
were flowers in a rain upon her bosom,
and she was sitting there
humble in such glory
now covered in a shower of love's blooms:
a flower falling on her lap,
some fell on her blond curls,
like pearls set into gold
they seemed to me that day;
some fell to rest on ground, some on the water,
and some in lovelike wandering
were circling down and saying, "Here Love reigns."

How often I would say
at that time, full of awe:
"For certain she was born up there in Heaven!"[1]
And her divine behavior,
her face and words and her sweet smile

9. Laura herself.

1. The imagery in the preceding stanza recalls Dante's description of the Garden of Eden, from *Purgatory* 30, and Laura is here modeled on Dante's Beatrice who appears "within a cloud of flowers."

so filled me with forgetfulness
and so divided me
from the true image
that I would sigh and say:
"Just how and when did I come here?"
thinking I was in Heaven, not where I was;
and since then I have loved
this bank of grass and find peace nowhere else.

If you had all the beauty you desired,
you could with boldness leave
the wood and make your way among mankind.[2]

195

From day to day my face and hair are changing,
but I still bite the sweetly baited hook
and hold tight to the green and enlimed branches
of the tree that has no care of cold or heat.[3]

The sea will lose its water, sky its stars
before I fear no longer and desire
her lovely shade, and I not love and hate
the deep and loving wound I hide so badly.

I do not hope to ever rest my labors
until I am deboned, defleshed, demuscled,
or till my enemy shows me her pity.

All things that cannot be will be before
another or she or Death will heal the wound
that Love with her fair eyes made in my heart.

After the Death of My Lady Laura

267[4]

O God! that lovely face, that gentle look,
O God! that charming way of hers, so proud!
O God! those words that any wild, harsh heart
could tame and cowards turn to courageous men!

And, O God, that sweet smile whence came the arrow
of death, the only good I hope for now!
Royal soul, the worthiest of all to rule,
if only you had not joined us so late:

it is for you I burn, in you I breathe
for I am yours alone; deprived of you,
I suffer less for all my other pains;

2. The last stanza, referred to as the *congedo* or leave-taking, is addressed to the poem itself.

3. The tree is the evergreen laurel, another play on Laura's name.

4. With this poem, the poet is confronted with Laura's death by plague, which occurred on 6 April 1348. In the manuscript, there is a space between poems 266 and 267.

with hope you filled me once and with desire
the time I left that highest charm alive,
but all those words were scattered in the wind.

277

If Love does not give me some new advice,
I shall be forced to change my life with death,
such fear and grief afflict my saddened soul
because desire lives and hope is dead,

and so bewildered, unconsoled my life
is totally, that night and day it weeps,
weary without a helm in stormy seas
and on a dubious course with no true guide.

An imaginary guide is driving it,
the true one's underground—no, she's in Heaven
whence she shines even brighter through my heart,

not through my eyes, because a veil of sorrow
forbids them to behold the longed-for light
and turns my hair to grey before it's time.

291

When I see coming down the sky Aurora
with roses on her brow and gold in hair,
Love seizes me and losing all my color
I sigh as I say, "Laura is there now.[5]

"O glad Tithonus,[6] you know when it's time
to hold your precious treasure once again;
but I, what can I do with my sweet laurel?
To see her once again I have to die.

"Your partings aren't so difficult to take—
at least at nighttime she returns to you,
and she does not despise your head of white;

"my nights she saddens and my days she darkens,
the one who carried off my thoughts with her
and left me of herself only her name."

311

That nightingale so tenderly lamenting
perhaps his children or his cherished mate,
in sweetness fills the sky and countryside
with many notes of grief skillfully played,

and all night long he stays with me it seems,
reminding me of my harsh destiny;

5. "Ivi è Laura ora," playing on "Dawn" (*l'Aurora*).

6. A mortal who fell in love with Dawn; at her request, the gods granted him eternal life, but since she hadn't asked that he stay young forever, he became eternally an aged man.

I have no one to blame except myself
for thinking Death could not rule such a goddess.[7]

How easy to deceive one who is sure!
Those two lights, lovely, brighter than the sun,
whoever thought would turn the earth so dark?

And now I know what this fierce fate of mine
would have me learn as I live on in tears:
that nothing here can please and also last.

353[8]

O lovely little bird singing away
in tones of grief for all the time gone by,
you see the night and winter at your side,
the day and all those happy months behind;

aware as you are of your grievous troubles
could you be so of my plight as your own,
you would fly straight to the bosom of this wretch
to share with him some of his painful grief.

I cannot say our portions would be equal,
since she you weep for may still have her life
with which Heaven and Death for me are stingy;

but the forbidding season and the hour,
the memory of sweet years and bitter ones,
invites me to discuss with you my pity.

365

I go my way lamenting those past times
I spent in loving something which was mortal
instead of soaring high, since I had wings
that might have taken me to higher levels.

You who see all my shameful, wicked errors,
King of all Heaven, invisible, immortal,
help this frail soul of mine for she has strayed,
and all her emptiness fill up with grace,

so that, having once lived in storms, at war,
I may now die in peace, in port; and if my stay
was vain, at least let my departure count.

Over the little life that still remains to me,
and at my death, deign that your hand be present:
You know You are the only hope I have.

7. The first half of the poem is drawn from Virgil's extended nightingale simile in the fourth *Georgic*.

8. Originally, Petrarch had made this sonnet the next to last poem (365) in the collection; it shows his ongoing fascination with the weeping bird as an analogy for himself as singer.

PERSPECTIVES
Lyric Sequences and Self-Definition

Petrarch's poems were enormously popular in early modern Europe. Editions, commentaries, and imitations of the *Canzoniere* vastly exceeded those of *The Divine Comedy.* Petrarch's probing lyrics set the tone for an elaborate inquiry into the speaker's identity in its cultural, religious, and gendered manifestations, all through the delicate and always dynamic relationship between that speaker and a distant, at times deceased, "other." As an Arabic paraphrase on Aristotle's *Poetics* put it, all lyric originates in praise and blame. Between praising Laura for her unmatched beauty and condemning her for her indifference to Petrarch's agony lay a wide gulf of poetic attitudes concerning the true source of power in the poems. In the lover, whose voice is the only one that we ever really hear? Or in the beloved who, in life as well as death, exerts such force over the lover that he is reduced to "fire and ice"?

Over the course of the sixteenth and seventeenth centuries, the scope of the poetic sequence widened considerably to include poems by women about men (Vittoria Colonna, Louise Labé) and by men about other men (Michelangelo, Shakespeare). Similarly, the sonnet, the metrical form most widely used, would undergo revisions, particularly in England. The typical Italian sonnet was divided into an eight-line opening (the octet) and a six-line conclusion (the sestet), but English poets came to prefer three four-line stanzas with a dramatic closing couplet. The poems, moreover, were not always about erotic attraction. The Polish poet Jan Kochanowski wrote a very different kind of sequence with his laments for his deceased daughter, only some of which are sonnets. Some of Petrarch's longer poems spell out the political malaise of fourteenth-century Italy. And Labé and other women used their poetry "books" as an explicit defense of their right to *write,* and publish.

In the sixteenth and seventeenth centuries there were two forms of "publication"—the circulation of manuscripts among a coterie of acquaintances, and the far more widespread circulation of printed texts among unknown readers. To what extent can the voice that speaks to us so immediately in the lyric sequence be considered a "private one," and how many of its revelations can be assumed to be truthful? To a large extent, the poetic sequence seemed to offer a place where the narrative voice might speak untramelled by social constraints, thereby attracting both women writers and unconventional topics. Yet their narrators meditate everywhere on those constraints, and most, like Louise Labé, are highly conscious of the contemporaries who would read and possibly reproach them. Shakespeare, who apparently had no hand in the publication of his sonnets, comments explicitly on the ability of his poems to memorialize the mysterious young man and dark lady alike, as well as the sordid relationship between them. Indeed, the ambiguous role that autobiography plays in the sequences is yet another reason for their fascination. Where does the "life" end and the work of art begin, the art so carefully crafted and compressed within rhyming and metrically balanced fragments? While the sonnet could decline into a stale and thoroughly predictable form in the hands of lesser writers, it also managed to attract the best of Europe's poets, challenging them to games of disclosure, concealment, and self-reflection that could be as serious as they were playful.

Michelangelo Buonarroti
1475–1564

Still derided in the twentieth century as full of "disagreeable improprieties, obscurities, contortions, and difficulty," as one critic put it, Michelangelo's poetry has never enjoyed the universal praise of his sculpture or painting. Yet the boldness and originality of the *David* or the magnificent frescoes of the Sistine Chapel find their way into Michelangelo's considerable body of verse as well, much of which is an anguished meditation on the turmoils of his long life as artist and deeply spiritual thinker often at odds with the strict mores of Counter-Reformation Italy. Equally original, and no doubt unsettling for his contemporaries, were the poems that elevated the male body of which Michelangelo was such an accomplished sculptor into a paragon of beauty. Along with the requisite Petrarchan sonnets to an unattainable lady—the widowed Vittoria Colonna with whom Michelangelo enjoyed a close friendship—are more than fifty poems to the Roman gentleman Tommaso de'Cavalieri, charged with a physical intensity lacking in Michelangelo's verse for the austere and deeply religious Colonna. These poems to Cavalieri represent some of the most sustained homoerotic meditations in literature, even as the elderly Michelangelo acknowledges the unrequited nature of his love.

Written over a period of fifty-five years and never published in Michelangelo's lifetime—he withdrew plans for publication in 1546, perhaps because of the intensely personal nature of his poetry—many of the 302 sonnets, madrigals, and *canzoni* and forty-two fragments survive only on the backs of drawings, apparently scribbled in haste. Others were the focus of intense revisions, some of the most interesting of which involve changes in gendered pronouns. And like some of his greatest sculptures—the so-called *Prisoners,* or his final *Pietà*—a number of his poems are left unfinished, testimony, perhaps, to Michelangelo's unwillingness to transmit to paper the depth of his erotic and religious feelings, or symptomatic of a restless spirit more fascinated by the process of creativity than the final product.

This comes of dangling from the ceiling[1]

This comes of dangling from the ceiling—
I'm goitered like a Lombard cat[2]
(or wherever else their throats grow fat)—
it's my belly that's beyond concealing,
it hangs beneath my chin like peeling.
My beard points skyward, I seem a bat
upon its back, I've breasts and splat!
On my face the paint's congealing

Loins concertina'd in my gut,
I drop an arse as counterweight
and move without the help of eyes.
Like a skinned martyr I abut
on air, and, wrinkled, show my fate.
Bow-like, I strain towards the skies.

No wonder then I size
things crookedly; I'm on all fours.
Bent blowpipes send their darts off-course.
Defend my labour's cause,
good Giovanni,[3] from all strictures:
I live in hell and paint its pictures.[4]

1. Translated from the Italian by Peter Porter and George Bull. The "ceiling" is that of the Sistine Chapel, on which Michelangelo worked for roughly four years, between 1508 and 1512. There is a sketch on the manuscript of the poem in which Michelangelo depicts himself standing on his scaffold painting a fresco directly above him.

2. Goiter produces swelling of the thyroid, in the throat. The "Lombard cats" may be slang for peasants.

3. Probably Giovanni di Benedetto from Pistoia, a humanist to whom Michelangelo addressed several other poems.

4. The poem in Italian ends literally "Defend my dead painting, Giovanni, and my honor, since I'm neither in a good place nor a painter"—an attack on Pope Julius II who had commissioned Michelangelo's work for the chapel.

Michelangelo, Tomb of Giuliano de' Medici, 1520–1534, Church of San Lorenzo, Florence. Much of Michelangelo's work reflects both the artist's preoccupation with death—his own as well as others—and the increasing importance of commemorating the dead in monumental fashion in early modern Europe. Michelangelo devoted an entire cycle of epitaphs to Cecchino Bracci, the 15-year-old nephew of one of Michelangelo's patrons, and he spent innumerable years designing and executing the tomb of Pope Julius II, a project destined to remain unfinished. The tombs for two young Medici princes, Giuliano and Lorenzo, were likewise left incomplete when the artist departed for Rome in 1534, but enough had been done to suggest that the artist conceived the project as a melancholy meditation on time's passing. Dressed in Roman armor, Giuliano sits above the figures of Night and Day, barely able to lift his head to gaze at the statue of his brother across the sacristy. While Night and Day seem similarly locked in anguished reflection, Michelangelo imagined them at one point in dialogue: "Night and Day are speaking and saying, 'We have with our swift course brought to death the Duke Giuliano.'"

My Lord, in your most gracious face[5]

My Lord, in your most gracious face I see
what here on earth may never be portrayed:
my soul, which mortal flesh and blood pervade,
climbs Godward with it[6] to eternity.
And should the mob with its stupidity
foist on to others feelings which degrade,[7]
no less intense is my sweet longing made,
my love, my trust, my honest amity.
So from the sacred fount whence all men come
each earthly beauty takes its attributes
and we are told that these from God are sent;
And for its image there's no other home,
for heaven on earth, or for our worldly fruits.
Thus loving you makes death beneficent.

I wish to want, Lord[8]

I wish to want, Lord, what eludes my will:
between your passion and my heart a block
of ice deflects your fire, and makes a mock
of everything I write with perjured quill.
I love you with my lips, then groan that still
your love can't reach my heart, nor will it knock
and force the door, that joys of all kinds flock
about my heart, your purpose to fulfil.
Dissolve that block, my lord, tear down the wall
whose thickness keeps me from the piercing light
of your sweet presence, no longer seen on earth.
Be like a bridegroom, let your brightness fall
upon a yearning soul which at your sight
is warmed at heart, having from you its birth.

No block of marble[9]

No block of marble but it does not hide
the concept living in the artist's mind—
pursuing it inside that form, he'll guide
his hand to shape what reason has defined.
The ill I flee, the good I hope to find

5. The "Signore" or Lord of this sonnet is the young Roman aristocrat Tommaso Cavalieri; the poem was probably written in 1534, roughly a year after Michelangelo and Cavalieri met.

6. That is, with Cavalieri's face.

7. An attack on the crowd that seems to be gossiping about Michelangelo and Cavalieri.

8. Another sonnet from the Cavalieri period, although here "Signore" most likely refers to God. The first line echoes the dilemma expressed by Saint Paul in his Epistle to the Romans ("I do not understand what I do, for it is not what I wish that I do, but what I hate, that I do . . . I do not the good that I wish, but the evil that I do not wish" [7:15–19]), while the next two lines from the first stanza introduce the contrasting imagery of Petrarch's sonnets.

9. One of Michelangelo's most famous sonnets, this was dedicated to the poet Vittoria Colonna. Michelangelo presents the sculptor as removing excess stone to reveal the ideal form within it, which the artist has perceived in advance.

in you, exalted lady of true pride,
are also circumscribed; and yet I'm lied
to by my art which to my will is blind.
Love's not to blame, nor your severity,
disdainful beauty, nor what fortune shows,
or destiny: I fixed my own ill course.
Though death and mercy side by side I see
lodged in your heart, my passion only knows
how to carve death: this is my skill's poor force.

How chances it, my Lady[1]

How chances it, my Lady, that we must
from long experience learn that what endures
in stone is but the image it immures° *confines, imprisons*
though he who liberates it turn to dust?
This cause to its effect will so adjust
that our fine work defeat of time ensures.
I know this true and prove it in my sculptures:
art lives forever, death forfeits its trust.
Therefore, long life in colours or with stone,
in either form, I give to you and me
and our own two resemblances devise,
and for a thousand years when we have gone
posterity will find my woe, your beauty
matched, and know my loving you was wise.

Vittoria Colonna

1492–1547

A member of the noble Roman family that patronized Petrarch, Vittoria Colonna was at the center of the prominent intellectual and religious circles of early sixteenth-century Italy, counting among her friends Baldessar Castiglione (whom she angered by circulating copies of his unfinished *Courtier*), the epic poet Ludovico Ariosto, and Michelangelo. Colonna is best known for the sonnets she wrote in honor of her husband, who was killed at the battle of Pavia in 1525 fighting alongside the Emperor Charles V and against Marguerite de Navarre's brother, King Francis I. These idealizing sonnets memorialized the Marquis of Pescara, earning Colonna the tribute from Ariosto that she "rescued her triumphant spouse from the dark shore of the Styx." In a very different vein, Colonna wrote a number of strident lyrics about the need for ecclesiastical reform, and Michelangelo refers to her "sacred ink" from which he sought help in understanding divine things. She finally refused, however, to stray too far in the direction of the Reformers, particularly as the circle of the Inquisition threatened to close around her. Colonna went into semiseclusion in various convents in Rome and Orvieto after the Marquis's death, leaving behind a legacy of more than 400 poems.

1. Another sonnet for Colonna.

Between harsh rocks and violent wind[1]

Between harsh rocks and violent wind I feel
The waves of life striking my fragile bark
Which I have neither wit nor art to steer;
All help will come too late to save me now.
In one brief moment bitter death extinguished
The lodestar of my life, my constant guide;
I have no help against the turbulent sea
And threatening clouds. Now ever more I fear,
Not the sweet singing of the cruel sirens,[2]
Nor shipwreck here between these lofty cliffs,
Nor sinking helplessly in shifting sands,
But to sail on forever in rough waters,
Cutting my furrow with no gleam of hope;
For death conceals from me my sheltering port.

Whatever life I once had

Whatever life I once had in my senses
Bitter death seized on one day, with my sun,
Delivering him of care and me of error;
I live no more; his better part heaven holds.
For me, I feel the fruits of earth as grass—
My soul could never gather even leaves—
And when she[3] recollects his former thoughts
She keeps herself enclosed within their bounds.
Because he made himself alive by dying,[4]
He made me dead, alive, and still from heaven
Keeps me from self,[5] content only with him.
And, while he sees my life withdrawn and fearful,
Holding a bridle on my mortal flesh,
I feel his spirit still desires my love.

Louise Labé

c. 1520–1566

"I can do nothing but beseech virtuous ladies to elevate their minds a little above their distaffs and spindles." So does Louise Labé, known as "La Belle Cordière"—the beautiful rope-maker—urge her bourgeoise counterparts in France to read her poems. In the lively commercial center of Lyon in the 1530s and 1540s, Labé received an unusually solid classical education thanks to her well-to-do parents (ropemakers themselves) and put that education to excellent use. Her *Oeuvres,* published in 1555, is full of allusions to Petrarch and the Latin poets Catullus and

1. Translated from the Italian by Laura Anna Stortoni and Mary Prentice Lillie.
2. Colonna compares herself to Odysseus, who in Book 9 of the *Odyssey* sailed by the reef where sirens tried to lure him to his death. Petrarch too compared his journey to that of being in a "fragile bark."
3. The soul, which is feminine in Italian.
4. By going to heaven.
5. From self-absorption.

Ovid. No pious imitation of either classical or contemporary traditions, her dialogue, three long elegies, and twenty-four sonnets take up directly the transgressive issue of female desire. It is one thing for the male Catullus to instruct Lesbia to kiss him a thousand times. It is quite another for the married Labé to ask the poet Olivier de Magny to return her affections and to insist in her prefatory letter that men take stock of the damage they have done to women by depriving them of learning. From this bold dedicatory preface to the wealthy landowner Madame Clémence de Bourges, to her closing request that her women readers "not reproach her," Labé shows an uncanny awareness of her problematic reception as the "Lyonnais Sappho," as one of the accompanying verses to the volume addresses her (in Greek). Indeed, the Catholic Labé was condemned as scandalous by the Protestant theologian Jean Calvin and suspected of poisoning her husband. Her adroit remaking of Petrarch's dynamics as her own not only opened the door to assertions that her life mirrored her art, but also made her acclaimed as one of Renaissance France's greatest poets.

PRONUNCIATION:

Louise Labé: lou-EASE lah-BAY

When I behold you[1]

When I behold you, your blond tresses crowned
With laurel green, and hear you play the lute
Till rocks and trees are plucked up by the root
To follow its complaints,[2] see you renowned

Of all, while many thousand virtues ring you,
And I see you, ahead of all, attain the peak,
And hear how all your praises loudest speak—
Then must my heart, by passion driven, sing you:

These countless virtues, making you so loved
By everyone, these things that make you praised—
Could they not make you just as well a lover?
Thus higher yet your honor would be raised,
Were you by pity so to love me moved,
And for my sweet love an answering flame discover.

Lute, companion of my wretched state[3]

Lute, companion of my wretched state,
True witness of my never-ceasing sighs,
Faithful scribe of all my grieving cries,
In lamentation you have been my mate;

My piteous sighs have caused you such distress
That often you've been forced to change your strains,

1. Translated from the French by Frank Warnke. The 24 sonnets from which the poems here are taken comprised the final section of the volume of Labé's *Evvres* ("Oeuvres" or "Works"), published in 1555. The first sonnet of the section, written in Italian, suggests in its opening line that "neither Ulysses nor the greatest sage" could have predicted the suffering Labé has known for her beloved. "When I behold you" is the tenth sonnet in the sequence.

2. Labé associates her musician with Orpheus, the mythical musician praised in Ovid's *Metamorphoses* as having the power to make the trees follow him. The "laurel green" was used to crown poets. The beloved in question may be Olivier de Magny, a well-known poet and translator, who spent time in Lyon while he was traveling to Rome.

3. Sonnet 12, in which the lute now becomes Labé's "companion."

Replacing your delectable refrains
With notes that my tormented mood express.

And if I would compel your former measure,[4]
Your strings growing slack, you force me to be still;
But when you see me tenderly complain,
You give approval to my grieving pleasure,
And I'm obliged to yield unto your will,
Still hoping for sweet outcome from sweet pain.

Kiss me again[5]

Kiss me again, again, kiss me again!
Give me one of the luscious ones you have,
Give me one of the loving ones I crave:
Four hotter than burning coals I shall return.
What, are you moaning? Let me soothe the pain,
Giving you now ten kisses more, but sweetly;
Thus, our happy kisses joining meetly,
Let us enjoy each other to our gain.

A double life for each of us ensues.[6]
Each in the self and in the lover lives.
Allow me, Love, to feign a pleasing folly:
Living as one, I'm always ill at ease,
And sweet content within me never thrives
Unless outside myself I sometimes sally.

Alas, what boots it[7]

Alas, what boots it that not long ago
You praised with such finesse my golden hair,
And the beauty of my eyes chose to compare
To double Suns, whence Love allowed to grow
Those features which are cause of all your woe?
Where are you, tears of short duration? Where
The Death that should give evidence most rare
Of your constant love confirmed by solemn vow?

Did this your malice have no other goal
Than to enslave me, feigning to be my slave?
Forgive me, Darling, I'm half out of my mind,
With bitter pain and anger in my soul:
But I tell myself, wherever you may rove,
You feel an anguish of the selfsame kind.

4. Force you to play more pleasing songs.
5. Sonnet 18. The title alludes to a line from the famous verse of the 1st-century B.C.E Roman poet Catullus that begins "Let us live, my Lesbea, and love," and asks for "a thousand kisses, then a hundred, a thousand more."
6. Labé shifts to a more philosophical register, invoking the concept of the "double life" as the true union of souls found in Plato's *Symposium* and made popular in the Renaissance by the Italian philosopher Marsilio Ficino. Such union can only be found through the "folly" of being transported outside of oneself—the folly to which Labé refers in the last two tercets.
7. Sonnet 23. "What boots it": what good does it do.

Do not reproach me, Ladies[8]

Do not reproach me, Ladies, if I've loved:
If I have felt a thousand burning arrows,
A thousand pains, a thousand biting sorrows,
If I to constant weeping have been moved,
Alas, let not your judgment scorn my name.
If I have erred, the punishments I feel;
Don't sharpen any more their pointed steel,
But judge that Love can do to you the same;

Not needing Vulcan to excuse your passion,
Nor the beauty of Adonis its strange fashion.[9]
Love can, when he wishes, make you fall in love;
With less good reason for your fall than mine,
To a stronger, stranger passion you'll incline.
Beware lest greater misery you prove.

William Shakespeare
1564–1616

During a period of enforced absence from the stage—a combination of recurrent plague and bans against actors for unruly behavior—William Shakespeare, fresh from his first tragedy (the bloody *Titus Andronicus*) and his comedy *The Taming of the Shrew,* turned to poetry. This at least is one theory for the genesis of Shakespeare's 154 sonnets. While they were remarked upon as early as 1598, they weren't published until 1609, toward the end of the playwright's career, and well after the vogue for sonnet-making in England had passed. But as many readers have realized, there is something timeless in these sonnets—and the theme of art's timelessness is one on which Shakespeare's complex, cunning narrator himself insists as he tells his beloved that in his "war with Time for love of you / As he takes from you, I ingraft you new." Like Petrarch, Shakespeare is forced to settle for fame rather than reciprocity in love. But he does so by staging a series of intricate, emotional dramas that broaden the sonnet sequence's domain while unsettling the Petrarchan exaltation of chastity and love.

The focus of attention for the first 126 sonnets is a young man, probably an aristocrat whose social station, like that of Michelangelo's beloved, is higher than the narrator's. The relationship of the narrator to the young man is, however, far more complicated than that found in Michelangelo. The volume opens with the so-called "procreation poems," eighteen sonnets in which Shakespeare urges the young man to have a child so that the world will not lose him forever when he dies; the final sonnets in this sequence then suggest that only poetry can truly "give life to thee." Many of the subsequent poems to the young man are taken up with the "pow'rful rime" of both the poet and, increasingly, rival poets who threaten to write about the young man as well. But these poems also illustrate the torment of the jealous lover whose faith in his supposedly chaste young man, as in his literary medium, is considerably shaken. The poem in which the poet bids his lover "Farewell: thou art too dear for my possessing" represents one low point of the collection, while the arrival of the "dark lady" onto the sonnets' stage

8. Sonnet 24, the final poem in the collection. The Ladies Labé addresses are the women of Lyon.

9. Women can fall in love even if their husbands aren't as ugly as Vulcan, the misshapen god to whom Venus was married, or if their lovers aren't as beautiful as Adonis, the gorgeous youth who was the beloved of Venus.

with sonnet 127 shatters once and for all the delicate equilibrium attained earlier. Sonnet 147 closes, "I have sworn thee fair, and thought thee bright, / Who art as black as hell, as dark as night"; once mistress only to the narrator, this unsettling female presence is now actively pursuing the young man as well.

The order of the sonnets in the 1609 volume is contested, since there is no evidence that Shakespeare ever authorized his poems' publication. Still, it is possible to argue that the sequence may initially develop a Petrarchan quest for poetic glory, only to undo that quest and all it stands for. On the other hand, the narrator's stance is so changeable, as he himself admits, and Shakespeare's understanding of the dynamics of Petrarchism so penetrating, that perhaps the sonnets are never serious about their mission of preserving the "timeless" reputation of their author or of the young man who occupies center stage.

For more on Shakespeare, see his principal listing, page 1664.

from SONNETS[1]

1

From fairest creatures we desire increase,
That thereby beauty's rose might never die,
But as the riper should by time decease,
His tender heir might bear his memory;
But thou, contracted° to thine own bright eyes, *betrothed*
Feed'st thy light's flame with self-substantial° fuel, *of your own making*
Making a famine where abundance lies,
Thyself thy foe, to thy sweet self too cruel.
Thou that art now the world's fresh ornament
And only herald to the gaudy° spring, *bright*
Within thine own bud buriest thy content
And, tender churl, mak'st waste in niggarding.° *hoarding*
  Pity the world, or else this glutton be,
  To eat the world's due, by the grave and thee.[2]

3

Look in thy glass, and tell the face thou viewest
Now is the time that face should form another,
Whose fresh repair° if now thou not renewest, *condition*
Thou dost beguile the world, unbless some mother.[3]
For where is she so fair whose uneared womb
Disdains the tillage of thy husbandry?[4]
Or who is he so fond° will be the tomb *foolish*
Of his self-love, to stop posterity?
Thou art thy mother's glass, and she in thee
Calls back the lovely April of her prime;
So thou through windows of thine age shalt see,

1. The 1609 edition of the *Sonnets,* published by Thomas Thorpe, was prefaced with this dedication, followed by Thorpe's initials: "To the Only Begetter of these ensuing sonnets Mr. W. H. All happiness and that eternity promised by our ever-living poet wisheth the well-wishing adventurer in setting forth."

2. The last line gives the cannibalistic image of the "tender churl" eating "the world's due," i.e., his offspring, by refusing to procreate.

3. Prevent a woman from enjoying the blessings of motherhood.

4. Cultivation, but with a play on "husband."

Despite of wrinkles, this thy golden time.[5]
  But if thou live rememb'red not to be,
  Die single, and thine image dies with thee.

17

Who will believe my verse in time to come
If it were filled with your most high deserts?
Though yet, heaven knows, it is but as a tomb
Which hides your life and shows not half your parts.
If I could write the beauty of your eyes
And in fresh numbers number all your graces,
The age to come would say, 'This poet lies
Such heavenly touches ne'er touched earthly faces.'
So should my papers, yellowed with their age,
Be scorned, like old men of less truth than tongue,
And your true rights be termed a poet's rage
And stretchèd metre° of an antique song. *exaggerations*
  But were some child of yours alive that time,
  You should live twice—in it and in my rime.[6]

55

Not marble nor the gilded monuments
Of princes shall outlive this pow'rful rime,
But you shall shine more bright in these contents
Than° unswept stone, besmeared with sluttish° time. *than in / lazy*
When wasteful war shall statues overturn,
And broils° root out the work of masonry, *tumults*
Nor° Mars his sword nor war's quick fire shall burn *Neither*
The living record of your memory.
'Gainst death and all oblivious enmity° *oblivion*
Shall you pace forth; your praise shall still find room
Even in the eyes of all posterity
That wear this world out to the ending doom.
  So, till the judgment° that° yourself arise, *Judgment Day / when*
  You live in this, and dwell in lovers' eyes.

73

That time of year thou mayst in me behold
When yellow leaves, or none, or few, do hang
Upon those boughs which shake against the cold,
Bare ruined choirs where late the sweet birds sang.
In me thou seest the twilight of such day
As after sunset fadeth in the west,
Which by and by black night doth take away,
Death's second self that seals up all in rest.

5. Just as he furnishes his mother a "glass" through which she might see her youth, so would his children afford him a "window" in his old age to his "golden time."

6. This sonnet concludes the so-called "procreation sonnets" in which the narrator is encouraging the young man to "increase."

In me thou seest the glowing of such fire
That° on the ashes of his youth doth lie, *As*
As the death bed whereon it must expire,
Consumed with that which it was nourished by.
  This thou perceiv'st, which makes thy love more strong,
  To love that well which thou must leave ere long.

87

Farewell: thou art too dear° for my possessing, *costly*
And like enough thou know'st thy estimate.° *value*
The charter of thy worth gives thee releasing;[7]
My bonds° in thee are all determinate.° *claims / expired*
For how do I hold thee but by thy granting,
And for that riches where is my deserving?
The cause of this fair gift in me is wanting,
And so my patent° back again is swerving. *deed or title*
Thyself thou gav'st, thy own worth then not knowing,
Or me, to whom thou gav'st it, else mistaking;
So thy great gift, upon misprision growing,° *originating in error*
Comes home again, on better judgment making.
  Thus have I had thee as a dream doth flatter,
  In sleep a king, but waking no such matter.° *substance*

116

Let me not to the marriage of true minds
Admit impediments;[8] love is not love
Which alters when it alteration finds
Or bends with the remover to remove.
O, no, it is an ever-fixèd mark° *landmark*
That looks on tempests and is never shaken;
It is the star to every wand'ring bark,
Whose worth's unknown, although his height be taken.[9]
Love's not Time's fool, though rosy lips and cheeks
Within his bending sickle's compass° come; *range*
Love alters not with his brief hours and weeks,
But bears it out even to the edge of doom.° *the last day*
  If this be error, and upon° me proved, *against*
  I never writ, nor no man ever loved.

126

O thou, my lovely boy, who in thy power
Dost hold Time's fickle glass,° his sickle hour;° *mirror / hourglass*
Who hast by waning grown, and therein show'st
Thy lovers withering as thy sweet self grow'st;
If Nature, sovereign mistress over wrack,° *ruin*

7. You are worth so much that you have the privilege of being able to "release" yourself from all obligations to me.
8. The marriage service directs the congregation, "If any of you know cause or just impediment why these persons should not be joined together. . . ."
9. Both "worth" and "height" (altitude) apply to the star.

As thou goest onwards, still will pluck thee back,
She keeps thee to this purpose, that her skill
May Time disgrace and wretched minutes kill.
Yet fear her, O thou minion of her pleasure!
She may detain, but not still° keep, her treasure; *always*
Her audit,° though delayed, answered must be, *final reckoning*
And her quietus° is to render° thee.[1] *settlement / surrender*

127

In the old age black was not counted fair,[2]
Or, if it were, it bore not beauty's name;
But now is black beauty's successive heir,
And beauty slandered with a bastard shame;[3]
For since each hand hath put on nature's power,
Fairing the foul with art's false borrowed face,
Sweet beauty hath no name, no holy bower,
But is profaned, if not lives in disgrace.
Therefore my mistress' brows are raven black,
Her eyes so suited,° and they mourners seem *dressed in black*
At such° who, not born fair, no beauty lack, *For*
Sland'ring creation with a false esteem:
  Yet so they mourn, becoming° of their woe, *gracing*
  That every tongue says beauty should look so.

130

My mistress' eyes are nothing like the sun;
Coral is far more red than her lips' red;
If snow be white, why then her breasts are dun;° *dark*
If hairs be wires, black wires grow on her head.
I have seen roses damasked,° red and white, *mingled*
But no such roses see I in her cheeks;
And in some perfumes is there more delight
Than in the breath that from my mistress reeks.
I love to hear her speak; yet well I know
That music hath a far more pleasing sound:
I grant I never saw a goddess go;
My mistress, when she walks, treads on the ground.[4]
  And yet, by heaven, I think my love as rare
  As any she° belied with false compare.° *any woman / comparison*

END OF PERSPECTIVES: LYRIC SEQUENCES AND SELF-DEFINITION

1. This is the only poem in the series that lacks the final two lines, perhaps suggesting the dramatic "rendering" of the young man. This is also the final sonnet addressed directly to the young man; with 127, the "dark lady" sonnets begin.
2. "Fair" as in both "beautiful" and "blonde."
3. "Fair" beauty is rendered illegitimate, as women turn increasingly to cosmetics.
4. Perhaps an allusion to *Aeneid* 1, in which Aeneas watches his mother Venus part from him: "her gown was long and to the ground; even her walk was sign enough she was a goddess"; the moment is later echoed in Petrarch and others.

Niccolò Machiavelli

1469–1527

Few thinkers have been as maligned as Machiavelli, whose very name has become a term for amoral scheming. Yet much of his work follows from a distinctively Renaissance impulse: to fit everything to the measure of man. Machiavelli's model "man" was cunning, shrewd, and surrounded by fools—which shouldn't particularly surprise, given the conditions under which Machiavelli wrote his major works. Literally overnight, Machiavelli went from being a prominent official in Florence to suffering imprisonment and torture when the Medici family ousted his party and returned to power. Consigned to permanent exile from the political world in which he had thrived as a diplomat and envoy for fourteen years, Machiavelli wrote the works which are at once bids for attention and sobering meditations on the present and future state of Italian cities: his *Discourses on the First Ten Books of Livy,* his Florentine history, *The Art of War,* three trenchant comedies, and above all, *The Prince.*

Machiavelli's own life reveals a constant pragmatist at work. Born to a family with little money, the young Machiavelli trained himself in Latin and the ancients, as well as in Dante and contemporary vernacular literature. Little is known of his activities before 1498, the year that the Dominican Girolamo Savonarola, who had tried to turn Florence into a city of God, was burned at the stake. Machiavelli began his political career thereafter in the new secular republican regime led by Piero Soderini. Appointed secretary and second Chancellor, Machiavelli was soon traveling regularly on major diplomatic missions to the papal courts, Paris, and the Romagna in central Italy, where he witnessed firsthand the tactics of Pope Alexander VI's bastard son, Cesare Borgia—which included, among other things, the display of the mysteriously decapitated body of one of his former henchmen in a public square. Increasingly a valued advisor to Soderini, Machiavelli was responsible for the controversial and difficult task of mobilizing a militia of Florentine men for the successful reconquest of Pisa in 1509, a feat that convinced Machiavelli of the necessity of volunteer armies for the survival of republics. During this period, Machiavelli first dabbled in writing. His *Portraits* of 1508–1515 feature sketches of political figures whom he had encountered in his travels, while the first *Decennale* is an account, in verse, of ten years of Florentine history, from 1494 to 1504.

Machiavelli's political career came to an abrupt end when his troops failed to prevent Spain's invasion of nearby Prato in July 1512. The Medici family returned a month later, bringing an end to the republic, dismantling its militia, and imprisoning Machiavelli for his suspected involvement in a plot to overthrow the new government. Released from prison, Machiavelli was barred from entering Florence as well as from leaving the city's territories. As he says in the preface to *The Prince,* he turned to writing of the things that he had learned, "over so many years and with so much affliction and peril." First drafted in 1513 and published only in 1532, *The Prince* was only the first of Machiavelli's masterpieces. His *Discourses on Livy* (around 1517) is an extended commentary on the famous Roman historian; its primary focus is republics rather than principalities, social institutions rather than powerful individuals. Three comedies followed. Two of them are based on plays of the Roman playwrights Terence and Plautus; the third, *Mandragola* or *Mandrake Root,* an original and vibrant work, is riotously funny, but its picture of human society is so bleak that it is hard to say whether it is a comedy at all. By the early 1520s, Machiavelli had succeeded in winning the Medici's confidence; he was commissioned to write the *Florentine Histories,* which—paradoxically, perhaps, given its patron—focuses on the demise of the Florentine republic. He also enjoyed a brief return to a political appointment when he was asked in 1526 by a Medici pope, Clement VII, to advise him on fortifications and the military. It is an irony of history that when the Medici were chased again out of Florence and a republic was temporarily restored, Machiavelli had become too closely associated with the ruling family to be acknowledged as a republican sympathizer. He died several months later, in June of 1527.

Of Machiavelli's works, *The Prince* has achieved the greatest fame, not least because of its bold separation of politics from ethics. Dedicated first to Giuliano de'Medici, and after Giuliano's death, to his nephew Lorenzo, the book is divided into roughly three sections. Machiavelli opens with an anatomy of principalities, bringing in examples from both antiquity and present-day Italy; he then passes to three chapters on a topic near and dear to his heart, military organization and the disastrous consequences of hiring mercenary troops. In his final section, beginning in Chapter 15, he turns his attention to "how a prince must govern his conduct toward his subjects or his friends," and here his tone becomes more intimate and his advice more pointed. And, it would seem, for good reason. Machiavelli's prince is an isolated figure, cut off from a social world he must nonetheless know how to control if he is to seize and maintain power. Machiavelli's ideal princes from the past are all brazen usurpers: Theseus, Romulus, Moses. Too few men in the present have shown such brazeness, with the exception of Pope Julius II, whose impetuousity enabled him to capture Fortune and—as Machiavelli crudely puts it in Chapter 25—beat her.

Machiavelli substitutes for this absent world nothing less than himself: the advisor on whom the prince must depend for his knowledge of the people he needs to deceive. The public sphere shrinks to the private relationship between counselor and prince, in which the counselor proffers a policy grounded in deception. Contemporary evidence, Machiavelli suggests, "shows that princes who have achieved great things have been those who have given their word lightly, who have known how to trick men with cunning, and who, in the end, have overcome those abiding by honest principles." Placing this cunning advice at the very center of his political treatise, the exiled Machiavelli seeks to create for himself a role in which he might once again be politically efficacious. It is telling that the ever-vigilant Machiavelli includes a chapter informing a prince how to choose advisors, another warning him to avoid flatterers.

But *The Prince* is also motivated by the very real tragedy of the times—an Italy at war with itself and oppressed by foreign powers—and by Machiavelli's desire to put his own considerable experience of worldly affairs to use for the health of Florence. Ultimately, he looks toward a unified Italy of which he and his countrymen could only dream for another 350 years. Such a dream explains the desperate cry of the last chapter of *The Prince,* addressed to the Medici as Moses-like saviors of Italy's people, if we are indeed to read that cry as sincere. How might this chapter be of a piece with a book that has steadfastly undermined the very principles of ethics, as well as the utility of ancient examples for contemporary life? To what extent did Machiavelli genuinely believe in the ability of the Medici, who by 1516 controlled not only Florence and much of Tuscany but the papacy as well, to put an end to the factiousness that dominated the peninsula? These questions must remain to some extent unanswered; at the same time, their very existence suggests a dimension to the treatise, and to Machiavelli himself, that cannot easily be reduced to the cold political "Machiavellian" calculation for which he is best known. At the heart of Machiavelli's *realpolitik* is fierce Florentine patriotism—the same, perhaps, that had led Dante, another exile from his native city, to save Florence by casting its most profligate and corrupt citizens into hell.

PRONUNCIATIONS:

Cesare Borgia: CHAY-ze-ray BOR-zhah
Niccolò Machiavelli: nee-ko-LO mah-kee-ah-VEL-li

from THE PRINCE[1]

Dedicatory Letter

Niccolò Machiavelli to the Magnificent Lorenzo de' Medici[2]

It is customary, in most cases, for those who desire to win the favor of a Prince to present themselves to him with those things they cherish most or which they know please him most; hence, we often see Princes presented with horses, arms, gold vestments, precious stones and similar adornments worthy of their greatness. Desiring, then, to offer myself to Your Magnificence with some proof of my devotion to you, I have not found among my possessions anything that I cherish more or value so much as my knowledge of the accomplishments of great men, which I learned through long experience in contemporary affairs and continuous study of antiquity; having very diligently and for a long time thought about and analyzed these accomplishments, and now having condensed them into a little book, I am sending them to Your Magnificence.

And although I regard this work unworthy of your consideration, I am nevertheless quite confident that your kindness will convince you to accept it, for I could not make you a greater gift than to give you the means to be able in very short time to understand all that which I, over many years and with many difficulties and dangers, came to know and understand.[3] *I have neither adorned nor filled this book with polished sentences, with rich and magnificent words, or with any other kind of rhetorical or superfluous ornamentation, the likes of which many writers are accustomed to using in describing and embellishing their material; for it was my desire that nothing distinguish my book or make it pleasing other than the unusualness of its material and the importance of its contents exclusively. I hope it will not be thought presumptuous if a man of low and inferior station dare to debate and regulate the government of princes; for, just as those persons who sketch landscapes place themselves in a low position on the plain in order to study the nature of the mountains and highlands, and in order to study the lowlands place themselves high on top of mountains, in like fashion, in order to know well the nature of the people one must be a prince, and to know well the nature of princes one must be a common citizen.*[4]

Accept then, Your Magnificence, this little gift in the spirit that I send it; and if you deign to consider and read it with care, you will discover in it my utmost desire that you may reach that greatness which fortune and your own capacities predict for you. And if Your Magnificence from the summit of his high position will at some time move his eyes toward these lowlands, he will know to what extent I unjustly endure the great and continuous maleficence of fortune.[5]

1. Translated by Mark Musa.
2. Lorenzo de' Medici, Duke of Urbino, was the grandson of the better-known "Lorenzo the Magnificent," and became ruler of Florence shortly after the Medici returned from exile in 1512—a return that resulted in Machiavelli's imprisonment. His uncle Giuliano had been the original dedicatee of *The Prince;* after Giuliano's death in 1516, Machiavelli redirected the dedication to Lorenzo, who died in 1519. Lorenzo is commemorated, along with Giuliano, in Michelangelo's (unfinished) tomb in the new sacristy in Florence's San Lorenzo; see page 1490.
3. Machiavelli's years of service for the Florence republic numbered 14.
4. With this play of perspectives, Machiavelli uses a well-known classical trope, perhaps most familiar from the opening of Seneca's *Oedipus:* "As lofty peaks to ever catch the winds, and as the cliff, which with its jutting rocks cleaves the vast deep, is beaten by the waves of even a quiet sea, so does exalted empire lie exposed to fate."
5. The last word sets up one of the major themes of *The Prince,* to be treated most fully in Chapter 25.

Chapter 6
On New Principalities Acquired by Means of One's Own Arms and Ingenuity[1]

No one should be surprised if, in my discussion of principalities that are completely new in respect to their prince and composition, I make use of the most outstanding examples;[2] since men almost always walk the path made by others and conduct their affairs through imitation, although they are not altogether able to stay on the path of others nor arrive at the ingenuity of those they imitate, a prudent man should always take the path trodden by great men and imitate those who have been most outstanding; so that, if his own ingenuity does not come up to theirs, at least it will have the smell of it; and he should act like those prudent archers, who, when the target they are aiming at seems too far off, aware of the capacity of their bow, set their sight a good deal higher than the desired target, not to reach such a height with their arrow but rather to be able, with the help of aiming high, to reach their target.

I say, then, that in entirely new principalities, where there is a new prince, one will find more or less difficulty in maintaining them according to the greater or lesser ingenuity of the one who acquires them. And since this event of transition from ordinary citizen to prince presupposes either ingenuity or fortune, it would seem that either the one or the other of these two things should, to some extent, mitigate many of the difficulties; nevertheless, he who has trusted less in fortune has held on to his position best. Things are made easier also by the fact that the prince, having no other state to rule, is forced to come and live there in person. But to come to those who, by means of their own ingenuity and not by fortune, have become princes, let me say that the most outstanding are Moses, Cyrus, Romulus, Theseus and the like. And although one should not discuss Moses, for he was a mere executor of the things God had commanded, he still should be admired if only for that grace which made him worthy of speaking with God.[3] But let us consider Cyrus[4] and the others who acquired or founded kingdoms: you will find them all admirable; and if their particular actions and institutions are examined, they do not appear to differ from those of Moses, who had so great a preceptor. And examining their actions and lives, we see that from fortune they received nothing but the occasion; which in turn offered them the material they could then shape into whatever form they pleased; and without that occasion their very ingenuity would have been extinguished, and without that ingenuity the occasion would have come in vain.

Therefore it was necessary for Moses to find the people of Israel in Egypt slaves and oppressed by the Egyptians, so that they, in order to escape this servitude, might be disposed to following him. It was imperative that Romulus not remain in Alba and for him to be exposed at birth, so that he might become king of Rome and

1. The first three chapters of *The Prince* focus on various kinds of principalities; Machiavelli then discusses the problems princes face when they take over former kingdoms.
2. Machiavelli follows his humanist education by proffering *grandissimi esempli* both from antiquity and the recent past.
3. In Exodus, God approaches Moses by means of a burning bush; despite Moses' protests that he doesn't possess the qualities of a leader, he nonetheless becomes the liberator of the Hebrews out of Egypt.
4. Cyrus the Great, who died in 529, founded the Persian empire. He first captured the throne of Media, and then soon overthrew the king of Lydia, captured Babylon, and took over the Greek city-states.

founder of that nation.[5] It was requisite that Cyrus find the Persians dissatisfied with the empire of the Medes and the Medes soft and effeminate through years of peace. Theseus could not have displayed his ingenuity if he had not found the Athenians dispersed.[6] These occasions, then, made these men successful, and their outstanding ingenuity made that occasion known to them; whereby their nations were made renowned and they became prosperous.

Those who, like these men, become princes by means of ingenuity, acquire their principality with difficulty, but hold on to it with ease; and the difficulties they encounter in acquiring the principality arise, in part, from the new institutions and methods they are forced to introduce in order to establish their state and their security. And it should be kept in mind that there is nothing more difficult to carry out nor more doubtful of success nor more dangerous to manage than to introduce a new system of things; for the introducer has as his enemies all those who benefit from the old system, and lukewarm defenders in all those who would benefit from by the new system. This lukewarmness originates partly from fear of their adversaries, who have the law on their side, and partly from the incredulousness of men in general, who do not really believe something new unless they actually have had experience with it; therefore it happens that, whenever those who are enemies have the occasion to attack, they do so with the fervor of partisans, and those others come to the defense lukewarmly, so that both the prince and his friends are in danger.

It is necessary, however, if we wish to discuss this matter thoroughly, to observe whether these innovators stand on their own or are dependent on others; that is, if in order to carry out their work, they are obliged to beg, or are able to use force. In the first case, they always come to a bad end and never achieve anything; but when they depend on themselves and are able to use force, then very seldom will they find themselves in danger. From this comes the fact that the armed prophets conquered and the unarmed came to ruin. Besides what has been said, people in general are unstable; and it is easy to persuade them of something but difficult to hold them to that persuasion; and therefore things should be arranged so that, when people no longer believe, they can be made to believe by force. Had Moses, Cyrus, Theseus and Romulus been unarmed they would not have had their institutions respected by the people for very long; just as in our own times it happened to Brother Girolamo Savonarola, who was defeated by his new institutions when the multitude began not to believe in him; and he had no means of holding firm those who had believed nor of making the disbelievers believe.[7] Therefore men such as these have great difficulty in getting ahead, and they encounter all their dangers as they advance, and they must overcome them by means of their ingenuity; but once they have overcome them and have begun to be held in veneration, and once they have done away with those who were envious of their abilities, they remain powerful, secure, honored, [and] prosperous. * * *

5. Legendary founder of Rome, Romulus was thrown with his brother into the Tiber by the last Alban king. The twins were rescued by a she-wolf, and many years later built a city where they had been washed ashore.

6. Son of Aegeus, legendary king of Athens, Theseus became king after a series of remarkable adventures to, among other places, Crete. While he is no doubt a mythical character, the Athenians believed that he had brought together the disparate Attic communities into a single state.

7. A Dominican friar, Savonarola ruled Florence from 1494 to 1498 as a "holy republic"; after incurring the wrath of the pope and supporters of the exiled Medici, he was burned at the stake for heresy. Following his death, Florence was ruled by Machiavelli's supporter and close friend Soderini.

Chapter 18
How a Prince Should Keep His Word[1]

How praiseworthy it is for a prince to keep his word and live by honesty and not deceit, everyone knows; nevertheless we see, by what goes on in our own times, that those princes who have accomplished great things are the ones who had cared little for keeping promises and who knew how to manipulate the minds of men with shrewdness; and in the end they won out over those who founded themselves on loyalty.

You should know, then, that there are two ways of fighting: one with the law, the other with force: the first way is peculiar to man, the other to beasts; but since the first in many instances is not enough, it becomes necessary to resort to the second. Therefore, a prince must know how to make good use of the beast and the man. This role was taught to princes indirectly by the ancient writers, who wrote how Achilles and many other ancient princes were given to Chiron the Centaur to be brought up and trained under his direction.[2] This can only mean, having as a teacher a half-beast and half-man, that a prince ought to know how to make use of both natures; and the one without the other cannot endure.

Since a prince must know how to make good use of the beast, he should choose then the fox and the lion; for the lion has no protection from traps, and the fox is defenseless against the wolves. It is necessary, therefore, to be a fox in order to know the traps, and a lion to frighten the wolves. Those who live by the lion alone do not understand matters. And so, a wise ruler cannot, nor should he, keep his word when doing so would be to his disadvantage and when the reasons that led him to make promises no longer exist. And if all men were good, this principle would not be good; but since men are a contemptible lot, and would not keep their promises to you, you too need not keep yours to them. To a prince legitimate reasons to break promises are never lacking. Of this an infinite number of present-day examples could be noted, indicating how many peace treaties, how many promises have been made null and void by the unfaithfulness of princes: and he who has known best how to use the fox has come to a better end. But one must know how to disguise this nature well, and how to be a fine liar and hypocrite; and men are so simple-minded and so dominated by their present needs that one who deceives will always find one who will allow himself to be deceived.

There is one of these recent examples I do not wish to be silent about. Alexander VI did nothing else, he thought about nothing else, except to deceive men, and he always found the occasion to do it.[3] And never was there a man more forceful in his assertions, and who affirmed a thing with more promises who kept his word less; nevertheless, the deceits he planned were always successful, because he was well acquainted with this facet of life.

It is not necessary, then, for a prince to have all of the qualities mentioned above, but it is certainly necessary that he appear to have them. In fact, I would go so far as to say this, that having them and observing them at all times, they are harmful; and appearing to have them, they are useful; for example, appearing to be compassionate, faithful, humane, upright, religious, and being so; but his mind should be disposed in

1. With Chapter 16, Machiavelli has begun to discuss the qualities that a strong prince should have.
2. Son of Cronus, the centaur Chiron, half-horse and half-man, was celebrated for his knowledge, and was said to have taught Jason, Achilles, and other Greek heroes.
3. Alexander VI had been pope from 1492–1503; he was known for his nepotism and political scheming. His illegitimate son was Cesare Borgia, featured on numerous occasions in the book as the exemplary—that is, ruthless—prince.

such a way that should it become necessary not to be so, he will be able and know how to change to the contrary. And it must be understood that a prince, and in particular a new prince, cannot observe all those things by which men are considered good, for it is often necessary, in order to maintain the state, to act against your word, against charity, against kindness, against religion. And so, he must have a mind ready to turn itself according as the winds of fortune and the fluctuation of things command him, and, as I said above, he must not separate himself from the good, if he is able, but he must know how to take up evil, should it become necessary.

A prince, therefore, should take great care never to say a single thing that is not infused with the five qualities mentioned above; he should appear, when seen and heard, to be all compassion, all faithfulness, all integrity, all kindness, all religion. And nothing is more essential than to appear to have this last quality. And men, in general, judge more according to their eyes than their hands; since everyone is in a position to observe, just a few to touch. Everyone sees what you appear to be, few touch what you are; and those few do not dare oppose the opinions of the many who have the majesty of the state defending them; and with regard to the actions of all men, and especially with princes where there is no court of appeal, we must look at the final result. Let a prince, then, conquer and maintain the state; his methods will always be judged honorable and they will be praised by all; because the ordinary people are always taken by the appearance and the outcome of a thing; and in the world there is nothing but ordinary people; and there is no room for the few while the many have a place to lean on. A certain prince[4] in our own time, whose name is better left unmentioned, preaches nothing but peace and good faith, and he is exceedingly hostile to both of them; and if he had put both of them into practice on more than one occasion they would have lost him either his reputation or his state.

* * *

Chapter 25

How Much Fortune Can Do in Human Affairs and How to Contend with It[1]

I am not unaware that many have been and still are of the opinion that worldly affairs are in a way governed by fortune and by God, that men with their wisdom are not able to control them, indeed, that men can do nothing about them; and for this reason they would conclude that there is no point in sweating much over these things, instead let them be governed by chance. This opinion has been held more in our own day, because of the great changes in things that have been observed and are being observed every day that are beyond human imagination. When I think about this sometimes, I am to some extent inclined toward their opinion. Nevertheless, so that our free choice may not be obliterated, I hold that it could be true that fortune is the arbiter of half our actions, but that she still leaves the other half, or close to it, to be governed by us. And she resembles one of those violent rivers that, when they become enraged, flood the plains, tear down trees and buildings, lift up the earth from

4. King Ferdinand II of Spain (1452–1516), called "the most Catholic King."

1. The intervening chapters have discussed counselors, flatterers, and "why the princes of Italy have lost their states." Machiavelli accuses those who have lost their principalities out of laziness: "because, never having thought during peaceful times that conditions could change . . . when adverse times then came, they thought about running away instead of defending themselves."

one side and deposit it on the other; everyone flees before them, everybody yields to their impact, unable to oppose them in any way. And although they are this way, it does not mean therefore that men, when times are quiet, cannot take precautions with floodgates and embankments, so that, when they swell up again, either they would move along through a canal, or their rush would not be so unchecked or so harmful. The same happens with fortune, who displays her force where there is no prepared resource to resist her; and she directs her impact there where she knows that floodgates and banks have not been constructed to contain her. And if you consider Italy, which is the seat of these changes and the one that put them into motion, you will see that she is a country without embankments and without any floodgates: for if she had been protected with suitable resources, like Germany, Spain and France, either this flood would not have caused the great changes it has, or it would not have come about at all.[2] And let what I have just said suffice as a general discussion on opposing fortune.

But confining myself more to particulars, let me say that we may see a prince prosper today, and tomorrow come to ruin, without having seen a change in his character or in anything else. This I believe stems, first, from the causes discussed at length earlier; that is, that a prince who relies entirely on fortune will come to ruin as soon as she changes. I believe, furthermore, that he will prosper who adapts his course of action to conditions of the present time, and similarly that he will not prosper who with his course of action conflicts with the times. For men can be seen, in the things which lead them to the goal that each has before him, namely, glory and wealth, to proceed in different ways: one with cautiousness, another with impetuousness; one by violence, another with strategy; one by patience, another by way of its contrary; and each one by these diverse methods can arrive at his goal. Moreover, in the case of two cautious men, we can see one carry out his plan, the other not; and likewise two men prospering equally well by means of two different methods, one being cautious and the other impetuous: which stems from nothing else if not from the conditions of the times that do or do not conform to their course of action. From this arises what I have said, that two men, working in different ways, can produce the same effect; and two men working in the same way, one achieves his goal, and the other does not. From this depends also the mutability of what is good; for, if a man governs himself with caution and patience, and the times and circumstances are in accord so that his course of procedure is good, he will go along prospering; but, if times and circumstances change, he is ruined, because he does not change his course of action. Nor does one find a man wise enough to know how to adapt himself to this; not only because he cannot deviate from that to which he is naturally inclined, but also because, having always prospered while following along one path, he cannot be persuaded to leave it. And therefore the cautious man, when it is time for him to act with impetuousness, does not know how; and so he is ruined; for, if he were to change his nature with the times and the circumstances, his fortune would not change.

Pope Julius II in all his dealings acted impetuously;[3] and he found the times and the circumstances very much in accord with his course of action, which always produced favorable results. Consider the first battle he waged, against Bologna, while

2. The "flood" is primarily the invasion of the Holy Roman Emperor, Charles V, in 1494; many Italian cities also chose to defend themselves with mercenaries, a practice Machiavelli criticized.

3. Pope from 1503 to 1513, called by Erasmus and others "the warrior pope" for his frequent military ventures.

Messer Giovanni Bentivogli was still alive.[4] The Venetians were not happy about it, and neither was the king of Spain; he was negotiating with France over the enterprise; and nonetheless, with his fierceness and impetuousness, he personally put that campaign into motion. Such a motion kept Spain and the Venetians in check and in place, the latter out of fear, and the other by the desire to regain all the kingdom of Naples; at the same time he drew the king of France into it, because the king, having seen him make this move, and desiring to make him a friend in order to defeat the Venetians, decided he could not deny him his troops without obviously offending him. And so Julius accomplished, with his impetuous move, what no other pontiff, possessing all human wisdom, could accomplish; for, if he had waited to leave Rome until the agreements were established and everything was settled, as any other pontiff would have done, he would never have succeeded; because the king of France would have found a thousand excuses, and the others would have instilled in him a thousand fears. I want to leave aside his other deeds, for all of them were similar, and all of them turned out well. And the brevity of life did not allow him to experience the opposite; because, if such times had come that might have required him to act with caution, his ruin would have followed from it: for never would he have deviated from those methods to which nature inclined him.

I conclude, then, that fortune varying, and men remaining fixed in their ways, while the two are in accordance with each other men are prosperous, and when they are in discord, unprosperous. I am certainly convinced of this: that it is better to be impetuous than cautious, because fortune is a woman, and it is necessary, if one wishes to hold her down, to beat her and fight with her. And we see that she allows herself to be taken over more by these men than by those who make cold advances; and then, being a woman, she is always the young man's friend, because they are less cautious, more reckless and with greater audacity command her.

Chapter 26

Exhortation to Take Hold of Italy and Liberate Her from the Barbarians

So, having deliberated on all the things discussed above, and meditating over whether the time is right in Italy, at present, to honor a new prince, and if there is the material that might afford one who is wise and ingenious the occasion to give it a form that would bring honor to him and good to all the people of Italy, it seems to me that so many things are concurring to favor a new prince that I know of no other time more appropriate than this. And if, as I have said, it was necessary in order to see the capability of Moses that the people of Israel be slaves in Egypt, and to know the great courage of Cyrus that the Persians be oppressed by the Medes, and to know the excellence of Theseus that the Athenians be scattered; likewise, at the present time, in order to recognize the capability of an Italian spirit, it was necessary that Italy be reduced to the condition she is in at present, and that she be more of a slave than the Hebrews, more servile than the Persians, more scattered than the Athenians; without a leader, without order; beaten, despoiled, torn apart, overrun; and it was necessary for her to have put up with all kinds of desolation.

4. The Bentivoglio family had dominated Bologna until 1506, when Julius personally led an expedition to the city. France joined Julius along with the Holy Roman Emperor in order to wrest other lands in the Romagna away from Venice. Julius later won the support of Venice and Spain to try to expel French forces from Italy.

And even though before now some glimmer of light may have shown itself in the person of a certain man, such that made it possible to believe that he was ordained by God for her redemption, nevertheless it was seen afterward how, at the culminating point of his career, he was rejected by fortune.[1] So now she exists without life, she awaits that one who might heal her wounds and put an end to the sacking of Lombardy,[2] to the extortions in the Kingdom and in Tuscany, and cure those sores of hers which for so long a time have been festering. Look how she prays God that He may send someone to redeem her from these barbarous cruelties and outrages; look at her ever ready and willing to follow a banner, if only there were some person to raise it. There is no one in sight, at present, in whom she can have more hope than in your illustrious house, that with its fortune and ingenuity, favored by God and by the Church, of which it is now prince, could make itself head of this redemption.[3] To do this would not be very difficult, if you keep before you the actions and lives of those named above. And although those men are exceptional and phenomenal, they were nonetheless men, and each of them had less opportunity than the present; for their undertaking was not more just than this, nor simpler, nor was God more a friend to them than to you. There is much justice in this: "only those wars that are necessary are just, and those arms are holy without which there would be no hope."[4] There is a great willingness at present; and where there is great willingness there cannot be great difficulty, if you hold to the methods of those I have set up as targets. Besides this, at present we have witnessed extraordinary happenings without precedent brought about by God: the sea has opened; a cloud has cleared your path; the rock has poured water; it has rained manna here; everything has run in favor of your greatness.[5] The rest you must do yourself. God does not want to do everything, so as not to take from us our free will and a part of that glory that belongs to us.

And it is no wonder if some of the Italians mentioned previously were not able to do what is hoped may be done by your illustrious house; and if, during the numerous revolutions in Italy and during the numerous manoeuvres of war, it always seems that her military strength is extinguished; this arises from the fact that her old methods were not good, and that there was no one who knew how to invent new ones; and nothing brings as much honor to a newly rising man as do the new laws and new methods invented by him. These things, when they are well-established and carry with them the idea of greatness, will make him worthy of reverence and admiration. And in Italy there is no lack of material to be given form; and at present there is great strength in her members, were it not for her lack of heads. Consider how in duels and clashes involving just a few the Italians are superior in force, dexterity and inventiveness; but when it comes to armies, they do not compare. And it all stems from the weakness of the heads; because those who know are not obeyed, and with everyone seeming to know, there has not been up to the present anyone who has known how to distinguish himself, by ingenuity and fortune, to the extent of making the others yield to him. As a result, during so much time, during the many wars waged over the past

1. Most likely a reference to Cesare Borgia, who died in 1507; the death of his father, Pope Alexander VI, in 1503, had put an end to his hopes to conquer central Italy.

2. Lombardy fell to the French in 1509.

3. "Your illustrious house" is the Medici, who with the election of Giovanni de' Medici to the papacy in 1513 as Leo X controlled both substantial portions of Tuscany and Rome.

4. From Livy's history of Rome (bk 9, ch.10).

5. Machiavelli may be referring here to Leo X's election; the imagery is biblical, largely taken from Exodus and the story of the Hebrews' emergence out of slavery.

twenty years, whenever there was an entirely Italian army, it always made a bad showing. As proof of this there is first Taro, then Alexandria, Capua, Genoa, Vailà, Bologna, Mestri.[6]

Therefore, if your illustrious house wishes to follow those outstanding men who redeemed their lands, you should, above all other things, and as a true foundation for every enterprise, provide yourself with native troops; for you could not have more faithful nor more loyal nor better soldiers. And while each one of them alone is valiant, when all of them are united they will become even more valiant, having experienced the command of their prince and been honored and well treated by him. It is necessary, therefore, to provide yourself with troops such as these, so that with Italian strength you will be able to defend yourself from outsiders. And while the Swiss and Spanish infantries may be considered formidable, nevertheless both of them have defects so that a third army could not only oppose them but be confident of overcoming them. For the Spanish cannot withstand men on horseback, and the Swiss will be frightened by foot soldiers they meet in battle who are as bold as themselves. So it has been seen and experience will show, the Spanish cannot withstand a French cavalry, and the Swiss are defeated by a Spanish infantry. And although this last case has not been entirely confirmed, nonetheless there was an indication of it at the battle of Ravenna, when the Spanish infantry confronted the German battalions, which follow the same methods as the Swiss; and the Spanish, with their agile bodies and aided by their spiked shields, got under and through their pikes and into a position to attack them safely without the Germans being able to do a thing about it; and if it had not been for the cavalry that charged them, they would have killed all of them.[7] Therefore, once the defects of both these kinds of troops are known, a new kind can be organized, which can resist horsemen and not be afraid of foot soldiers: this will be accomplished by creating new armies and changing battle formations. And these are among those things that, newly introduced, give prestige and greatness to a new prince.

This opportunity, then, must not be allowed to pass by, in order that Italy, after so long a time, may behold its redeemer. I cannot express with what love he will be greeted in all those provinces that have suffered through these foreign inundations; with what thirst for vengeance, with what firm loyalty, with what devotion, with what tears. What doors would be closed to him? what people would deny him obedience? what envy could oppose him? what Italian would not pay homage to him? This barbarian domination stinks to everyone! May then your illustrious house take up this mission with that courage and with that hope in which just enterprises are taken up; so that, under your banner, this country may be ennobled and, under your auspices, those words of Petrarch may come true:

> Ingenuity against rage
> Will take up arms and make the battle short.
> For the ancient valor
> In Italian hearts is not yet dead.[8]

6. All Italian towns that, between 1495 and 1513, fell into the control of the French or Spanish; Machiavelli lists the cities in the order of their defeat.
7. The French defeated the Spanish at Ravenna, on the eastern coast of Italy, in 1512.
8. From one of Petrarch's most famous *canzoni* (128), which opens "Italia mia"; addressed to the princes of Italy at a time of considerable civic unrest in the 1340s, the poem is a plea for unity and, as the last words stress, "peace, peace, peace."

RESONANCE

Baldesar Castiglione: from *The Book of the Courtier*[1]

[THE ART OF CONCEALING ART]

[I.25] Said Count Ludovico da Canossa,[2] "Just so I, perhaps, shall be able to tell you what a perfect Courtier should be, but not to teach you what you must do to become one. Still, in order to answer your question in so far as I can (although it is almost proverbial that grace is not learned), I say that if anyone is to acquire grace in bodily exercises (granting first of all that he is not by nature incapable), he must begin early and learn the principles from the best of teachers. And how important this seemed to King Philip of Macedon can be seen by the fact that he wished Aristotle, the famous philosopher and perhaps the greatest the world has ever known, to be the one who should teach his son Alexander the first elements of letters. And among men whom we know today, consider how well and gracefully signor Galeazzo Sanseverino, Grand Equerry of France, performs all bodily exercises; and this because, besides the natural aptitude of person that he possesses, he has taken the greatest care to study with good masters and to have about him men who excel, taking from each the best of what they know. For just as in wrestling, vaulting, and in the handling of many kinds of weapons, he took our messer Pietro Monte as his guide, who is (as you know) the only true master of every kind of acquired strength and agility—so in riding, jousting, and the rest he has ever had before his eyes those men who are known to be most perfect in these matters.[3]

[26] "Therefore, whoever would be a good pupil must not only do things well, but must always make every effort to resemble and, if that be possible, to transform himself into his master. And when he feels that he has made some progress, it is very profitable to observe different men of that profession; and, conducting himself with that good judgment which must always be his guide, go about choosing now this thing from one and that from another. And even as in green meadows the bee flits about among the grasses robbing the flowers, so our Courtier must steal this grace from those who seem to him to have it, taking from each the part that seems most worthy of praise;[4] not doing as a friend of ours whom you all know, who thought he greatly resembled King Ferdinand the Younger of Aragon, but had not tried to imitate

1. Translated by Charles S. Singleton. Castiglione (1478–1529) had a prominent career as a courtier and diplomat for the Italian courts of Mantua and Urbino; after the death of his wife in 1520, he took minor orders, and was appointed papal ambassador to the court of Charles V in Spain. *The Book of the Courtier,* Castiglione's major work, is the product of his close association with Guidobaldo da Montefeltro, Duke of Urbino until 1508. Written in stages between 1513 and 1524, *The Courtier* professes to immortalize a series of conversations held in Urbino's sophisticated court in 1506 about the making of the "perfect courtier." The conversationalists are from among the best and the brightest of Italy's courtiers, leaders, and religious figures, including Duke Giuliano de' Medici, Cardinal Bernardo Dovizi da Bibbiena, one of the first to write an Italian comedy inspired by the comedies of Latin antiquity, and the Duchess of Urbino, Elisabetta Gonzaga, who in the absence of her ailing husband Guidobaldo, presides over the lively discussions that characterize the four days. A melancholy tone hangs over the work, since Castiglione notes in his prefatory letter, written shortly before the book was published in 1528, that he is seized "by no little sadness" as he realizes that "the greater part of those persons who are introduced in the conversations were already dead." This includes the Duchess, who "was worth more than the others," and to whom he "was much more bound than to all the rest. Therefore, in order not to delay paying what I owe to the memory of so excellent a lady, and to that of the others who are no more . . . I have had [my book] printed and published in such form as the brevity of time permitted."

2. Ambassador to England and France for Pope Leo X.

3. Galeazzo Severino was a French military captain; Pietro Monte taught military exercises at the court of Urbino and elsewhere.

4. The classic metaphor of the bee as a figure of the accomplished poet had already been used by Petrarch; Castiglione here invokes it as a model for the courtier as well.

him in anything save in the way he had of raising his head and twisting one side of his mouth, which manner the King had contracted through some malady. And there are many such, who think they are doing a great thing if only they can resemble some great man in something; and often they seize upon that which is his only bad point.

"But, having thought many times already about how this grace is acquired (leaving aside those who have it from the stars), I have found quite a universal rule which in this matter seems to me valid above all others, and in all human affairs whether in word or deed: and that is to avoid affectation in every way possible as though it were some very rough and dangerous reef; and (to pronounce a new word perhaps) to practice in all things a certain *sprezzatura,*[5] so as to conceal all art and make whatever is done or said appear to be without effort and almost without any thought about it. And I believe much grace comes of this: because everyone knows the difficulty of things that are rare and well done; wherefore facility in such things causes the greatest wonder; whereas, on the other hand, to labor and, as we say, drag forth by the hair of the head, shows an extreme want of grace, and causes everything, no matter how great it may be, to be held in little account.

"Therefore we may call that art true art which does not seem to be art; nor must one be more careful of anything than of concealing it, because if it is discovered, this robs a man of all credit and causes him to be held in slight esteem. And I remember having read of certain most excellent orators in ancient times who, among the other things they did, tried to make everyone believe that they had no knowledge whatever of letters; and, dissembling their knowledge, they made their orations appear to be composed in the simplest manner and according to the dictates of nature and truth rather than of effort and art; which fact, had it been known, would have inspired in the minds of the people the fear that they could be duped by it.

"So you see how art, or any intent effort, if it is disclosed, deprives everything of grace. Who among you fails to laugh when our messer Pierpaolo dances after his own fashion, with those capers of his, his legs stiff on tiptoe, never moving his head, as if he were a stick of wood, and all this so studied that he really seems to be counting his steps? What eye is so blind as not to see in this the ungainliness of affectation; and not to see the grace of that cool *disinvoltura* [ease] (for when it is a matter of bodily movements many call it that) in many of the men and women here present, who seem in words, in laughter, in posture not to care; or seem to be thinking more of everything than of that, so as to cause all who are watching them to believe that they are almost incapable of making a mistake?"

* * *

[WOMEN EXEMPLIFY GRACE]

[I.40] "Madam," replied the Count, "I think the thread is broken.[6] Still, if I am not mistaken, I believe we were saying that the bane of affectation always produces extreme gracelessness in all things and that, on the other hand, the greatest grace is produced by simplicity and nonchalance: in praise of which, and in blame of affectation, many other things could be said; but I wish to add only one thing more. All women have a great desire to be—and when they cannot be, at least to seem—beautiful. Therefore,

5. Nonchalance. A word coined by Castiglione, *sprezzatura* derives from the Italian verb "sprezzare," to scorn or hold in disdain.

6. The intervening chapters have constituted what one speaker, Signora Emilia Pia, deemed a digression: a discussion on the merits of the Tuscan language, at the time the principal literary language in Italy. The Count now attempts to return to the earlier discussion regarding the need of the courtier to resist affectation.

wherever nature has failed in this regard, they try to remedy it with artifice: whence that embellishing of the face with so much care and sometimes with pain, that plucking of the eye-brows and the forehead, and the use of all those methods and the enduring of those nuisances which you ladies think, are hidden to men, but which are well known."

Here madam Costanza Fregosa[7] laughed and said: "It would be much more courteous of you to go on with your discussion, and tell us what the source of grace is, and speak of Courtiership, instead of trying to uncover the defects of women, which is not to the purpose."

"On the contrary, it is much to the purpose," replied the Count, "for the defects that I am speaking of deprive you ladies of grace, since they are caused by nothing but affectation, through which you openly let everyone know your inordinate desire to be beautiful. Do you not see how much more grace a woman has who paints (if at all) so sparingly and so little that whoever sees her is uncertain whether she is painted or not; than another woman so plastered with it that she seems to have put a mask on her face and dares not laugh so as not to cause it to crack, and never changes color except in the morning when she dresses; and, then, for the rest of the entire day remains motionless like a wooden statue and shows herself only by torchlight, like wily merchants who display their cloth in a dark place. And how much more attractive than all the others is one (not ugly, I mean) who is plainly seen to have nothing on her face, it being neither too white nor too red, but has her own natural color, a bit pale, and tinged at times with an open blush from shame or other cause, with her hair artlessly unadorned and in disarray, with gestures simple and natural, without showing effort or care to be beautiful. Such is that careless purity which is so pleasing to the eyes and minds of men who are ever fearful of being deceived by art.

"Beautiful teeth are very attractive in a woman, for since they do not show as openly as the face, not being visible most of the time, we may believe that less care has been taken to make them beautiful than with the face: and yet whoever laughs without cause and solely to display the teeth would betray his art, and, no matter how beautiful they are, would seem most ungraceful to all, like Catullus' Egnatius.[8] The same is true of the hands which, if they are delicate and beautiful, and are uncovered at the proper time, when there is need to use them and not merely to make a show of their beauty, leave one with a great desire to see them more and especially when they are covered with gloves again; for whoever covers them seems to have little care or concern whether they are seen or not, and to have beautiful hands more by nature than by any effort or design.

"Have you ever noticed when a woman, in passing along the street to church or elsewhere, unwittingly happens (in play or through whatever cause) to raise just enough of her dress to show her foot and often a little of her leg? Does this not strike you as something full of grace, if she is seen in that moment, charmingly feminine, dressed in velvet shoes and dainty stockings. Certainly to me it is a pleasing sight, as I believe it is to all of you, because everyone thinks that such elegance of dress, when it is where it would be hidden and rarely seen, must be natural and instinctive with the lady rather than calculated, and that she has no thought of gaining any praise thereby.

[41] "In such a way one avoids or hides affectation, and you may now see how opposed the latter is to grace, how it deprives of grace every act of the body and the soul; of which so far we have spoken but little, and yet this is not to be neglected; for,

7. Sister to Federico Fregoso, archbishop of Salerno and well-known patron of the arts, and Ottaviano Fregoso, both of whom participate in the discussions at Urbino. Like Emilia Pia, Costanza was a close companion of the Duchess.

8. The Roman poet Catullus speaks of Egnatius in one of his poems (39): "Because Egnatius has white teeth, he smiles wherever he goes."

as the soul is far more worthy than the body, it deserves to be more cultivated and adorned. And as to what ought to be done in the case of our Courtier, we will lay aside the precepts of the many wise philosophers who have written on this subject to define the virtues of the soul and who discuss their worth with such subtlety; and, holding to our purpose, we will declare in a few words that it suffices if he is, as we say, a man of honor and integrity: for included in this are prudence, goodness, fortitude, and temperance of soul, and all the other qualities proper to such an honored name. And I maintain that he alone is a true moral philosopher who wishes to be good; and for this he has need of few precepts beyond that wish. Socrates was right, therefore, in saying that all his teachings seemed to him to bear good fruit when anyone was incited by them to wish to know and understand virtue:[9] for those persons who have reached the point of desiring nothing more ardently than to be good manage easily to learn all that is needed for that. Hence, we will discuss this no further."

[QUEEN ISABELLA OF SPAIN][1]

[III. 51] Messer Cesare had ceased speaking and signor Gasparo was about to reply, when signor Ottaviano said, laughing: "In Heaven's name, grant him the victory, for I know that you have little to gain in this; and, as I see it, you will make not only all these ladies your enemies, but the greater part of the men as well."[2]

Signor Gasparo laughed and said: "Nay, the ladies have very good reason to thank me; because, if I had not contradicted signor Magnifico and messer Cesare, we should not have heard all the praises they have given to women."

Then messer Cesare said: "The praises that the Magnifico and I have given to women, and many others besides, are very well known and thus have been superfluous. Who does not know that without women we can take no pleasure or satisfaction in this life of ours, which, but for them, would be uncouth and devoid of all sweetness, and wilder than that of wild beasts? Who does not know that women alone take from our hearts all vile and base thoughts, woes, miseries, and those troubled humors that so often attend such things? And if we will carefully consider the truth, we shall see also that in our understanding of great matters women do not distract but rather awaken our minds, and in war they make men fearless and daring beyond measure. Certainly it is impossible that cowardice should ever again prevail in a man's heart where once the flame of love has entered; for one who loves always desires to make himself as lovable as possible, and always fears that he may incur some disgrace that will cause him to fall low in the estimation of the one by whom he desires to be highly esteemed. Nor does he hesitate to risk his life a thousand times a day to prove himself worthy of her love: hence, if one could assemble an army of lovers that would fight in the presence of the ladies they love, that army would conquer the whole world, unless similarly another army of lovers were to oppose it. And be sure that the ten years' stand of Troy against all Greece came from nothing if not the fact that a few lovers, when they made ready to go forth to battle, armed themselves in the presence of their women; and these women often gave a hand and, as they left, spoke to them some word that inflamed them and made them more than men. Then

9. In Plato's *Theatetus,* Socrates suggests that he is like a midwife, except for the fact that he looks after souls, not bodies, "and the triumph of my art is in thorougly examining whether the thought which the mind of the young man brings forth is a false idol or a noble and true birth."

1. The courtiers are now in their third day of conversations, which they have decided to dedicate to the making of the perfect court lady, or *donna di palazzo.*

2. Messer Cesare Gonzaga, related to the Duchess and to Castiglione himself, has just defended women from charges of lasciviousness brought against them by the misogynist of the group, Gasparo Pallavicino.

in battle they knew that their women were watching them from the walls and towers; wherefore it seemed to them that every act of courage, every proof they gave, won them their women's praise, which was the greatest reward they could have in the world.[3]

"There are many who believe that the victory of King Ferdinand and Queen Isabella of Spain against the King of Granada was due in large measure to women; for most of the times when the Spanish army went out to meet the enemy, Queen Isabella also went out with all her maids of honor, and in the army there were many noble cavaliers in love.[4] The latter would go along talking with their ladies until they reached the place where the enemy was seen, then each would take leave of his own lady; and, with the ladies looking on, they would go forth to meet the enemy with the fierce spirit that love gave them, and with the desire to show their ladies that they were served by men of valor; hence, a very small band of Spanish cavaliers was often seen to put a host of Moors to flight and death, thanks to the gentle and beloved ladies. So, signor Gasparo, I do not see what perversity of judgment brings you to censure women."

[THE ENDS OF COURTIERSHIP][5]

[IV.4] "So," said Signor Ottaviano, "to continue the reasoning of these gentlemen, which I wholly approve and confirm, I say that, among the things which we call good, there are some which, simply and in themselves, are always good, such as temperance, fortitude, health, and all the virtues that bring tranquillity of mind; others, which are good in various respects and for the end to which they are directed, such as law, liberality, riches, and other like things. Therefore I think that the perfect Courtier, such as Count Ludovico and messer Federico have described him, may indeed be good and worthy of praise, not, however, simply and in himself, but in regard to the end to which he is directed. For indeed if by being of noble birth, graceful, charming, and expert in so many exercises, the Courtier were to bring forth no other fruit than to be what he is, I should not judge it right for a man to devote so much study and labor to acquiring this perfection of Courtiership as anyone must do who wishes to acquire it. Nay, I should say that many of those accomplishments that have been attributed to him (such as dancing, merrymaking, singing, and playing) were frivolities and vanities and, in a man of any rank, deserving of blame rather than of praise; for these elegances of dress, devices, mottoes, and other such things as pertain to women and love (although many will think the contrary), often serve merely to make spirits effeminate, to corrupt youth, and to lead it to a dissolute life; whence it comes about that the Italian name is reduced to opprobrium, and there are but few who dare, I will not say to die, but even to risk any danger. And certainly there are countless other things, which, if effort and study were put into them, would prove much more useful, both in peace and in war, than this kind of Courtiership taken in and for itself. But if the activities of the Courtier are directed to the good end to which they ought to be directed, and which I have in

3. In Homer's *Iliad,* the Trojan hero Hektor arms himself with his wife's help, and women watch from the walls of Troy as their husbands defend the city.
4. Queen of Castile, Isabella (1451–1501) ruled jointly with Ferdinand of Aragon, whom she married in 1469. A strong proponent of holy war, Isabella supported repeated campaigns against Granada, the last vestige of Muslim power on the Iberian peninsula, which was finally overtaken by Spain in 1492.
5. From Book 4, describing a fourth and final day of discussions, and added by Castiglione almost a decade after the first three books were complete. This book turns on the role of the courtier vis-à-vis his prince; or, as Ottaviano says in Chapter 4, on "the end to which he is directed." The tone of Book 4 reveals some anxiety that the courtier's training in horsemanship, arts and letters, and military prowess has no political value; Ottaviano and Gasparo Pallavacino will attempt to correct this perception in the closing day's conversation.

mind, I feel certain that they are not only not harmful or vain, but most useful and deserving of infinite praise.

[5] "Therefore, I think that the aim of the perfect Courtier, which we have not spoken of up to now, is so to win for himself, by means of the accomplishments ascribed to him by these gentlemen, the favor and mind of the prince whom he serves that he may be able to tell him, and always will tell him, the truth about everything he needs to know, without fear or risk of displeasing him; and that when he sees the mind of his prince inclined to a wrong action, he may dare to oppose him and in a gentle manner avail himself of the favor acquired by his good accomplishments, so as to dissuade him of every evil intent and bring him to the path of virtue. And thus, having in himself the goodness which these gentlemen attributed to him, together with readiness of wit, charm, prudence, knowledge of letters and of many other things—the Courtier will in every instance be able adroitly to show the prince how much honor and profit will come to him and to his from justice, liberality, magnanimity, gentleness, and the other virtues that befit a good prince; and, on the other hand, how much infamy and harm result from the vices opposed to these virtues. Hence, I think that even as music, festivals, games, and the other pleasant accomplishments are, as it were, the flower; so to bring or help one's prince toward what is right and to frighten him away from what is wrong are the true fruit of Courtiership. And because the real merit of good deeds consists chiefly in two things, one of which is to know how to find means timely and fitting to attain that good end—it is certain that a man aims at the best end when he sees to it that his prince is deceived by no one, listens to no flatterers or slanderers or liars, and distinguishes good from evil, loving the one and hating the other."[6]

Michel de Montaigne

1533–1592

Michel de Montaigne introduces his longest essay, "Apology for Raymond Sebond," with a vivid portrait of the household in which he grew up. "Inflamed with that new ardor with which King Francis I embraced letters, [my father] sought with great diligence and expense the acquaintance of learned men, receiving them at his house like holy persons having some particular inspiration of divine wisdom." According to the essayist, his father, Eyquem de Montaigne, a prosperous merchant who had received little formal education, treated scholars with "reverence and religion" only because he was wholly unqualified to judge them. "Myself," Montaigne continues, "I like them well enough, but I do not worship them."

This attack on his father's naive enthusiasm for "learned men" may also seem to be an indictment of the time and considerable expense Eyquem spent on his son's education. Brought up with a German tutor who taught him Latin as his mother tongue, the future author of some of the finest and most spirited works in the French language—the incomparable *Essays*—was sent to the prestigious Collège de Guienne in Bordeaux, trained in law, and went on to become

6. The discussion as to the appropriate goals of the courtier will continue until Ch. 50, when Pietro Bembo, an important Venetian humanist and literary stylist, and eventually a cardinal, will reintroduce the topic of love as a motivating force for the perfect courtier. The book virtually ends with Bembo's neo-Platonic hymn to love as not merely the key to good courtiership, but the path to the divine. In one of the book's gently comic moments, when Bembo is finally silent, Emilia Pia "plucked him by the hem of his robe and shaking him a little, said, 'Take care, messer Pietro, that with these thoughts your soul, too, does not forsake your body.'" Seeing that it is already dawn, the group retires, and *The Courtier* is brought to a close, but not without the promise, made by Emilia, that the misogynistic Gasparo should be made to "stand trial" for his hostility to women.

a magistrate in the Parliament of Bordeaux. But at the age of thirty-seven, Montaigne abruptly chose to retire from Parliament and retreat to the family home that had become his (and from which he took his last name). Here he had the beams in his library carved with his favorite quotations from classical authors, and in a medallion he had made for himself in 1576, he inscribed the question, *Que sçay-je?*—"what do I know?" The answer, one pondered throughout a lifetime in his *Essays,* was *Rien* (or "nothing")—nothing, that is, save himself. "I would rather be an authority on myself than on Cicero," he remarks in his final essay, "Of Experience," and it is clear from the sum total of the *Essays* that any claim to be an authority on Cicero would be instantly suspect.

And yet to a certain extent, such a query represents the very fruit of Renaissance learning. Two hundred years earlier, Petrarch had posed the same question, framed as an attack on the pedantic nature of scholastic learning that had dominated the medieval universities: "What good is it to know the nature of the beasts and the birds, the fish and the snakes, if we ignore and don't bother to learn the nature of man: why we are born, from whence we come, where are we going?" Montaigne's compatriot Rabelais had challenged the dry university education that produced unthinking parrots; far better the humanist training that addressed the whole man. Moreover, like Erasmus, Montaigne turned for his most valued model to the one ancient figure who didn't presume on his own considerable knowledge, who believed that there is nothing "so ridiculous as that this miserable and puny creature, who is not even master of himself . . . should call himself master and emperor of the universe": the Greek philosopher Socrates. Or as Montaigne describes him: "Socrates was a man, and wanted neither to be nor to seem anything else" ("On some verses of Virgil"). But unlike Rabelais or Erasmus—or even Socrates, for that matter—Montaigne deploys in his 107 essays an intensely personal voice that became more frankly autobiographical as the years went on. Thanks to the meticulous care that Montaigne devoted to his writings, we are able to see how his thinking developed over a period of twenty years.

The *Essays* began as a "commonplace book," a collection of pithy quotations with selective commentary on topics as diverse as "smells," "sleep," "war horses," and "liars." Perhaps, as Montaigne suggests in one of his shortest essays, "Of Idleness," he began writing in order to harness the "idle thoughts" that plagued him in the years immediately after his retirement. But his book eventually grew to voluminous size, as Montaigne created a new and flexible narrative form which he christened with the French word *essais*—trials or attempts, on which he puns in "Of repentance": "If my mind could gain a firm footing, I would not make essays, I would make decisions; but it is always in apprenticeship and on trial." And these "trials" increasingly revolved around none other than Montaigne himself, revealed in all his foibles. His memory is so poor that he has often picked up a book believing it to be the first time, only to find his extensive notes scribbled in the margins; he has only modest strengths (there are few friends more loyal than he), and he has suffered from a variety of physical ailments, ranging from a concussion he suffered when he fell from his horse, to the maladies which increase as he ages, such as the painful bouts with kidney stones that sent him to Italy and Germany in 1580 in search of spas that could grant him relief. (His lively *Travel Journal* is the product of his trip, which was interrupted when he was summoned to return to Bordeaux to preside for two terms as mayor.) Although there is plenty of engagement with Virgil, Lucretius, Sextus Empiricus, and countless other classical writers (occasionally quoted inaccurately, thereby verifying what Montaigne says about his poor memory), Montaigne uses these borrowings to take us from the potentially abstract realms of philosophy and Roman history to the most immediate of concerns: his health, his love affairs, his inability to stay at the table after he has finished eating a meal, and his—and our—impending death.

Some have criticized Montaigne for this egoistic turn inward, reflective, perhaps, of the new bourgeois consciousness that privileged the private space over the public and civic space. The seventeenth-century philosopher and mathematician Blaise Pascal, who was greatly influenced by the *Essays,* was nonetheless one of many who chastised his predecessor for his obsessive self-preoccupation and his vacillation over the burning issues of his day. Yet Montaigne, writing at the height of France's religious wars, had seen enough blood and incivility to know that fanatical partisanship on disputed questions was not the answer to the ills plaguing post-Reformation Europe. The fact that he was called in to negotiate between the Catholic Henri de Guise and the Protestant Henry of Navarre suggests that others prized his ability to refrain from too quickly taking sides and to weigh all possible options before coming—if coming—to decisions. It also suggests that Montaigne deliberately underplayed the important political role he did have, both before and after his "retirement." In the same way, the ventures into the New World didn't prove to Montaigne the superiority of European culture. They demonstrated something quite to the contrary: the barbaric nature of European practices, as Montaigne wittily suggests in his classic essay "Of Cannibals." At the same time, he knew that he couldn't simply deny the culture that had created him. As he mentions in his preface to the *Essays,* since he had not been born "among those nations which are said to live still in the sweet freedom of nature's first laws," he was unable to portray himself "entire and wholly naked." Stepping outside oneself to become another was an impossibility, in the same way that placing oneself at the universe's center was the highest folly.

This brings us to what may be called the paradox of Montaigne's massive project: why did he write, and, more significantly, publish his *Essays*? They began, Montaigne suggests, not merely as a cure for idleness but as consolation for a friendship that had ended tragically in 1563 when Montaigne's "soulmate" from school, Étienne de la Boétie, died of the plague. It is telling in this light that Marie de Gornay, a young woman whom Montaigne befriended and made his adoptive daughter and literary executrix, lovingly attended to the *Essays* after Montaigne's death in 1592, transcribing his marginalia and overseeing the publication of the posthumous version in 1595. Particularly in his later essays, Montaigne tries to create a familiar, even intimate, relationship with his readers, anxious to convey simply himself, rather than to pass on profound wisdom; "it should not be held against me if I publish what I write," he says in "Of practice." "What is useful to me may also by accident be useful to another. Moreover, I am not spoiling anything, I am using only what is mine." The "accident" of the essays' utility thereby becomes a convenient aftermath of what Montaigne imagines to be the essays' real purpose, the portrayal of himself in all his dimensions. Another accidental aftermath might also have been this: to find a true friend who might understand him, and, perhaps, be understood in turn. Mademoiselle de Gornay is said to have claimed that she knew Montaigne long before she met him. No doubt many since then have also felt well-acquainted with the man who seemed to have taken the sincerest pleasure in being among the first to expose himself, almost if not completely naked, to generations of avid readers.

The *Essays* went through numerous publications, beginning in 1580 with a publication of the first two (of three) books, in Bordeaux, where Montaigne would soon be mayor. Several editions with numerous additions and modifications followed. The 1588 edition, published in Paris, was the first to contain the third book of essays. Between 1588 and 1592, the year of his death, Montaigne continued to reflect on and augment his literary creation; the posthumous 1595 edition incorporates the many changes he made in the margins to his 1588 text. While the various strata of the essays will not generally be noted below, it is important to recognize that the essays changed significantly over time.

Pronunciation:

Michel de Montaigne: mee-SHELL duh mon-TEN

from Essays[1]

Of Idleness

Just as we see that fallow land, if rich and fertile, teems with a hundred thousand kinds of wild and useless weeds, and that to set it to work we must subject it and sow it with certain seeds for our service; and as we see that women, all alone, produce mere shapeless masses and lumps of flesh, but that to create a good and natural offspring they must be made fertile with a different kind of seed; so it is with minds. Unless you keep them busy with some definite subject that will bridle and control them, they throw themselves in disorder hither and yon in the vague field of imagination.

> Thus, in a brazen urn, the water's light
> Trembling reflects the sun's and moon's bright rays,
> And, darting here and there in aimless flight,
> Rises aloft, and on the ceiling plays.
>
> VIRGIL[2]

And there is no mad or idle fancy that they do not bring forth in this agitation:

> Like a sick man's dreams,
> They form vain visions.
>
> HORACE

The soul that has no fixed goal loses itself; for as they say, to be everywhere is to be nowhere:

> He who dwells everywhere, Maximus, nowhere dwells.
>
> MARTIAL

Lately when I retired to my home, determined so far as possible to bother about nothing except spending the little life I have left in rest and seclusion, it seemed to me I could do my mind no greater favor than to let it entertain itself in full idleness and stay and settle in itself, which I hoped it might do more easily now, having become weightier and riper with time. But I find—

> Ever idle hours breed wandering thoughts
>
> LUCAN

—that, on the contrary, like a runaway horse, it gives itself a hundred times more trouble than it took for others, and gives birth to so many chimeras and fantastic monsters, one after another, without order or purpose, that in order to contemplate their ineptitude and strangeness at my pleasure, I have begun to put them in writing, hoping in time to make my mind ashamed of itself.

Of the Power of the Imagination[1]

A strong imagination creates the event, say the scholars. I am one of those who are very much influenced by the imagination. Everyone feels its impact, but some are over-

1. Translated by Donald Frame. Book 1, Chapter 8, of the *Essays*.
2. The citation is from Virgil's *Aeneid,* Book 8. Like the passage from Martial, it was added by Montaigne to his revised edition of the *Essays* published in 1588. Montaigne constantly weaves quotations from classical writers into his prose, often to express his meaning succinctly, and to give a general resonance to his own experience. The most notable of these references will be footnoted.

1. Book 1, Chapter 21.

thrown by it.[2] Its impression on me is piercing. And my art is to escape it, not to resist it. I would live solely in the presence of gay, healthy people. The sight of other people's anguish causes very real anguish to me, and my feelings have often usurped the feelings of others. A continual cougher irritates my lungs and throat. I visit less willingly the sick toward whom duty directs me than those toward whom I am less attentive and concerned. I catch the disease that I study, and lodge it in me. I do not find it strange that imagination brings fevers and death to those who give it a free hand and encourage it.

Simon Thomas was a great doctor in his time. I remember that one day, when he met me at the house of a rich old consumptive with whom he was discussing ways to cure his illness, he told him that one of these would be to give me occasion to enjoy his company; and that by fixing his eyes on the freshness of my face and his thoughts on the blitheness and overflowing vigor of my youth, and filling all his senses with my flourishing condition, he might improve his constitution. But he forgot to say that mine might get worse at the same time.

Gallus Vibius strained his mind so hard to understand the essence and impulses of insanity that he dragged his judgment off its seat and never could get it back again; and he could boast of having become mad through wisdom.[3] There are some who through fear anticipate the hand of the executioner. And one man who was being unbound to have his pardon read him dropped stone dead on the scaffold, struck down by his mere imagination. We drip with sweat, we tremble, we turn pale and turn red at the blows of our imagination; reclining in our feather beds we feel our bodies agitated by their impact, sometimes to the point of expiring. And boiling youth, fast asleep, grows so hot in the harness that in dreams it satisfies its amorous desires:

> So that as though it were an actual affair,
> They pour out mighty streams, and stain the clothes they wear.
>
> LUCRETIUS

And although it is nothing new to see horns grow overnight on someone who did not have them when he went to bed, nevertheless what happened to Cippus, king of Italy, is memorable; having been in the daytime a very excited spectator at a bullfight and having all night in his dreams had horns on his head, he grew actual horns on his forehead by the power of his imagination. Passion gave the son of Croesus the voice that nature had refused him. And Antiochus took fever from the beauty of Stratonice too vividly imprinted in his soul. Pliny says he saw Lucius Cossitius changed from a woman into a man on his wedding day. Pontanus and others report similar metamorphoses as having happened in Italy in these later ages. And through his and his mother's vehement desire,

> Iphis the man fulfilled vows made when he was a girl.[4]
>
> OVID

Passing through Vitry-le-François, I might have seen a man whom the bishop of Soissons had named Germain at confirmation, but whom all the inhabitants of that

2. The remainder of this paragraph and the next are from post-1588 publications of the *Essays,* and reflects the increasingly intimate reflections of the late editions.
3. Cited in the Roman philosopher Seneca's *Controversies;* Gallus was a declaimer who apparently went mad.
4. After noting a number of supposedly historical metamorphoses—the account of Cippus, for example, is taken from Pliny's *Natural History,* the story of Croesus, who spoke in a man's voice for the first time only when he saw his father on his deathbed, is from Herodotus—Montaigne turns to Ovid's *Metamorphoses* for the story of Iphis. A girl raised as a boy, she falls in love with the bride she is given to marry, and the goddess Isis transforms her into a young man.

place had seen and known as a girl named Marie until the age of twenty-two. He was now heavily bearded, and old, and not married. Straining himself in some way in jumping, he says, his masculine organs came forth; and among the girls there a song is still current by which they warn each other not to take big strides for fear of becoming boys, like Marie Germain. It is not so great a marvel that this sort of accident is frequently met with. For if the imagination has power in such things, it is so continually and vigorously fixed on this subject that in order not to have to relapse so often into the same thought and sharpness of desire, it is better off if once and for all it incorporates this masculine member in girls.

Some attribute to the power of imagination the scars of King Dagobert and of Saint Francis.[5] It is said that thereby bodies are sometimes removed from their places. And Celsus tells of a priest who used to fly with his soul into such ecstasy that his body would remain a long time without breath and without sensation. Saint Augustine names another who whenever he heard lamentable and plaintive cries would suddenly go into a trance and get so carried away that it was no use to shake him and shout at him, to pinch him and burn him, until he had come to; then he would say that he had heard voices, but as if coming from afar, and he would notice his burns and bruises. And that this was no feigned resistance to his senses was shown by the fact that while in this state he had neither pulse nor breath.

It is probable that the principal credit of miracles, visions, enchantments, and such extraordinary occurrences comes from the power of imagination, acting principally upon the minds of the common people, which are softer. Their belief has been so strongly seized that they think they see what they do not see.

I am still of this opinion, that those comical inhibitions by which our society is so fettered that people talk of nothing else are for the most part the effects of apprehension and fear. For I know by experience that one man, whom I can answer for as for myself, on whom there could fall no suspicion whatever of impotence and just as little of being enchanted, having heard a friend of his tell the story of an extraordinary impotence into which he had fallen at the moment when he needed it least, and finding himself in a similar situation, was all at once so struck in his imagination by the horror of this story that he incurred the same fate. And from then on he was subject to relapse, for the ugly memory of his mishap checked him and tyrannized him. He found some remedy for this fancy by another fancy: which was that by admitting this weakness and speaking about it in advance, he relieved the tension of his soul, for when the trouble had been presented as one to be expected, his sense of responsibility diminished and weighed upon him less. When he had a chance of his own choosing, with his mind unembroiled and relaxed and his body in good shape, to have his bodily powers first tested, then seized and taken by surprise, with the other party's full knowledge of his problem, he was completely cured in this respect. A man is never after incapable, unless from genuine impotence, with a woman with whom he has once been capable.

This mishap is to be feared only in enterprises where our soul is immoderately tense with desire and respect, and especially if the opportunity is unexpected and pressing; there is no way of recovering from this trouble. I know one man who found it helpful to bring to it a body that had already begun to be sated elsewhere, so as to lull his frenzied ardor, and who with age finds himself less impotent through being

5. Dagobert had been covered by scars provoked by his fear of gangrene. St. Francis of Assisi was said to bear the stigmata, the wounds made on Christ's body by the nails of the cross.

less potent. And I know another who was helped when a friend assured him that he was supplied with a counterbattery of enchantments that were certain to save him. I had better tell how this happened.

A count, a member of a very distinguished family, with whom I was quite intimate,[6] upon getting married to a beautiful lady who had been courted by a man who was present at the wedding feast, had his friends very worried and especially an old lady, a relative of his, who was presiding at the wedding and holding it at her house. She was fearful of these sorceries, and gave me to understand this. I asked her to rely on me. I had by chance in my coffers a certain little flat piece of gold on which were engraved some celestial figures, to protect against sunstroke and take away a headache by placing it precisely on the suture of the skull; and, to keep it there, it was sewed to a ribbon intended to be tied under the chin: a kindred fancy to the one we are speaking of. Jacques Peletier had given me this singular present. I thought of making some use of it, and said to the count that he might incur the same fate as others, there being men present who would like to bring this about; but that he should boldly go to bed and I would do him a friendly turn and would not, if he needed it, spare a miracle which was in my power, provided that he promised me on his honor to keep it most faithfully secret; he was only to make a given signal to me, when they came to bring him the midnight meal, if things had gone badly with him. He had had his soul and his ears so battered that he did find himself fettered by the trouble of his imagination, and gave me his signal. I told him then that he should get up on the pretext of chasing us out, and playfully take the bathrobe that I had on (we were very close in height) and put it on him until he had carried out my prescription, which was this: when we had left, he should withdraw to pass water, say certain prayers three times and go through certain motions; each of these three times he should tie the ribbon I was putting in his hand around him and very carefully lay the medal that was attached to it on his kidneys, with the figure in such and such a position; this done, having tied this ribbon firmly so that it could neither come untied nor slip from its place, he should return to his business with complete assurance and not forget to spread my robe over his bed so that it should cover them both. These monkey tricks are the main part of the business, our mind being unable to get free of the idea that such strange means must come from some abstruse science. Their inanity gives them weight and reverence. All in all, it is certain that the characters on my medal proved themselves more venereal than solar, more useful for action than for prevention. It was a sudden and curious whim that led me to do such a thing, which was alien to my nature. I am an enemy of subtle and dissimulated acts and hate trickery in myself, not only for sport but also for someone's profit. If the action is not vicious, the road to it is.

Amasis, king of Egypt, married Laodice, a very beautiful Greek girl; and he, who showed himself a gay companion everywhere else, fell short when it came to enjoying her, and threatened to kill her, thinking it was some sort of sorcery. As is usual in matters of fancy, she referred him to religion; and having made his vows and promises to Venus, he found himself divinely restored from the first night after his oblations and sacrifices.[7]

6. Montaigne is probably referring to the count of Gurson, Louis de Foix, who married his relative, Diane de Foix de Candale, in 1579. Montaigne was very close to the family, and dedicated one of his best-known essays, "Of the Education of Children" (1:26), to Diane de Foix.

7. The story is told in Herodotus's *History,* Book 2, Chapter 181. The vow to Aphrodite (Venus) was made, however, by poor Laodice herself, who promised to present a statue to Aphrodite's temple in Cyrene should her husband have intercourse with her. Montaigne not infrequently misremembers or misquotes his sources.

Now women are wrong to greet us with those threatening, quarrelsome, and coy countenances, which put out our fires even as they light them. The daughter-in-law of Pythagoras used to say that the woman who goes to bed with a man should put off her modesty with her skirt and put it on again with her petticoat. The soul of the assailant, when troubled with many various alarms, is easily discouraged; and when imagination has once made a man suffer this shame—and it does so only at the first encounters, inasmuch as these are more boiling and violent, and also because in this first intimacy a man is much more afraid of failing—having begun badly, he gets from this accident a feverishness and vexation which lasts into subsequent occasions.

Married people, whose time is all their own, should neither press their undertaking nor even attempt it if they are not ready; it is better to fail unbecomingly to handsel the nuptial couch, which is full of agitation and feverishness, and wait for some other more private and less tense opportunity, than to fall into perpetual misery for having been stunned and made desperate by a first refusal. Before taking possession, the patient should try himself out and offer himself, lightly, by sallies at different times, without priding himself and obstinately insisting on convincing himself definitively. Those who know that their members are naturally obedient, let them take care only to counteract the tricks of their fancies.

People are right to notice the unruly liberty of this member, obtruding so importunately when we have no use for it, and failing so importunately when we have the most use for it, and struggling for mastery so imperiously with our will, refusing with so much pride and obstinacy our solicitations, both mental and manual.

If, however, in the matter of his rebellion being blamed and used as proof to condemn him, he had paid me to plead his cause, I should perhaps place our other members, his fellows, under suspicion of having framed this trumped-up charge out of sheer envy of the importance and pleasure of the use of him, and of having armed everyone against him by a conspiracy, malignantly charging him alone with their common fault.[8] For I ask you to think whether there is a single one of the parts of our body that does not often refuse its function to our will and exercise it against our will. They each have passions of their own which rouse them and put them to sleep without our leave. How many times do the forced movements of our face bear witness to the thoughts that we were holding secret, and betray us to those present. The same cause that animates this member also animates, without our knowledge, the heart, the lungs, and the pulse; the sight of a pleasing object spreading in us imperceptibly the flame of a feverish emotion. Are there only these muscles and these veins that stand up and lie down without the consent, not only of our will, but even of our thoughts? We do not command our hair to stand on end or our skin to shiver with desire or fear. The hand often moves itself to where we do not send it. The tongue is paralyzed, and the voice congealed, at their own time. Even when, having nothing to put in to fry, we should like to forbid it, the appetite for eating and drinking does not fail to stir the parts that are subject to it, no more nor less than that other appetite; and it likewise abandons us inopportunely when it sees fit. The organs that serve to discharge the stomach have their own dilatations and compressions, beyond and against our plans, just like those that are destined to discharge the kidneys. To vindicate the omnipotence of our will,

8. Although Montaigne is unique in coming to the defense of the penis, the "trial" of body parts has a long history in ancient literature. The fable of the belly and the limbs has its origin in Livy's Roman history, Book 2, in which Menenius Agrippa tells a Roman mob of the importance of the stomach in the commonwealth and is able to prevent them from violence. Shakespeare's *Coriolanus* opens with this scene as Menenius tells the "mutinous Citizens" of "a time when all the body's members / Rebell'd against the belly" (1.1.97–98).

Saint Augustine alleges that he knew a man who commanded his behind to produce as many farts as he wanted, and his commentator Vives goes him one better with another example of his own time, of farts arranged to suit the tone of verses pronounced to their accompaniment; but all this does not really argue any pure obedience in this organ; for is there any that is ordinarily more indiscreet or tumultuous? Besides, I know one so turbulent and unruly, that for forty years it has kept its master farting with a constant and unremitting wind and compulsion, and is thus taking him to his death.[9]

But as for our will, on behalf of whose rights we set forth this complaint, how much more plausibly may we charge it with rebellion and sedition for its disorderliness and disobedience! Does it always will what we would will it to will? Doesn't it often will what we forbid it to will, and that to our evident disadvantage? Is it any more amenable than our other parts to the decisions of our reason?

To conclude, I would say this in defense of the honorable member whom I represent: May it please the court to take into consideration that in this matter, although my client's case is inseparably and indistinguishably linked with that of an accessory, nevertheless he alone has been brought to trial; and that the arguments and charges against him are such as cannot—in view of the status of the parties—be in any manner pertinent or relevant to the aforesaid accessory. Whereby is revealed his accusers' manifest animosity and disrespect for law. However that may be, Nature will meanwhile go her way, protesting that the lawyers and judges quarrel and pass sentence in vain. Indeed, she would have done no more than is right if she had endowed with some particular privilege this member, author of the sole immortal work of mortals. Wherefore to Socrates generation is a divine act; and love, a desire for immortality and itself an immortal daemon.

Perhaps it is by this effect of the imagination that one man here gets rid of the scrofula which his companion carries back to Spain.[1] This effect is the reason why, in such matters, it is customary to demand that the mind be prepared. Why do the doctors work on the credulity of their patient beforehand with so many false promises of a cure, if not so that the effect of the imagination may make up for the imposture of their decoction? They know that one of the masters of the trade left them this in writing, that there have been men for whom the mere sight of medicine did the job.

And this whole caprice has just come to hand apropos of the story that an apothecary, a servant of my late father, used to tell me, a simple man and Swiss, of a nation little addicted to vanity and lying. He had long known a merchant at Toulouse, sickly and subject to the stone, who often needed enemas, and ordered various kinds from his doctors according to the circumstances of his illness. Once they were brought to him, nothing was omitted of the accustomed formalities; often he tested them by hand to make sure they were not too hot. There he was, lying on his stomach, and all the motions were gone through—except that no injection was made. After this ceremony, the apothecary having retired and the patient being accommodated as if he had really taken the enema, he felt the same effect from it as those who do take them. And if the doctor did not find its operation sufficient, he would give him two or three more, of the same sort. My witness swears that when to save the expense (for he paid for them

9. Augustine's *City of God* 14.24 refers to such a man in the context of a chapter entitled "That if men had remained innocent and obedient in Paradise, the generative organs should have been in subjection to the will as the other members are." Juan Luis Vives, a Spanish humanist, wrote commentaries and treatises on education. The "turbulent and unruly" organ is probably Montaigne's.

1. The king of France had the reputation of having the "royal touch" that cured scrofula, a disease of the lymph glands in the neck.

as if he had taken them) this sick man's wife sometimes tried to have just warm water used, the effect revealed the fraud; and having found that kind useless, they were obliged to return to the first method.

A woman, thinking she had swallowed a pin with her bread, was screaming in agony as though she had an unbearable pain in her throat, where she thought she felt it stuck; but because externally there was neither swelling nor alteration, a smart man, judging that it was only a fancy and notion derived from some bit of bread that had scratched her as it went down, made her vomit, and, on the sly, tossed a crooked pin into what she threw up. The woman, thinking she had thrown it up, felt herself suddenly relieved of her pain. I know that one gentleman, having entertained a goodly company at his house, three or four days later boasted, as a sort of joke (for there was nothing in it), that he had made them eat cat in a pie; at which one lady in the party was so horrified that she fell into a violent stomach disorder and fever, and it was impossible to save her. Even animals are subject like ourselves to the power of imagination. Witness dogs, who let themselves die out of grief for the loss of their masters. We also see them yap and twitch in their dreams, and horses whinny and writhe.

But all this may be attributed to the narrow seam between the soul and body, through which the experience of the one is communicated to the other. Sometimes, however, one's imagination acts not only against one's own body, but against someone else's. And just as a body passes on its sickness to its neighbor, as is seen in the plague, the pox, and soreness of the eyes, which are transmitted from one body to the other—

> By looking at sore eyes, eyes become sore:
> From body into body ills pass o'er
>
> OVID

—likewise the imagination, when vehemently stirred, launches darts that can injure an external object. The ancients maintained that certain women of Scythia, when animated and enraged against anyone, would kill him with their mere glance. Tortoises and ostriches hatch their eggs just by looking at them, a sign that their sight has some ejaculative virtue. And as for sorcerers, they are said to have baleful and harmful eyes:

> Some evil eye bewitched my tender lambs.
>
> VIRGIL

To me, magicians are poor authorities. Nevertheless, we know by experience that women transmit marks of their fancies to the bodies of the children they carry in their womb; witness the one who gave birth to the Moor. And there was presented to Charles, king of Bohemia and Emperor, a girl from near Pisa, all hairy and bristly, who her mother said had been thus conceived because of a picture of Saint John the Baptist hanging by her bed.[2]

With animals it is the same: witness Jacob's sheep,[3] and the partridges and hares that the snow turns white in the mountains. Recently at my house a cat was seen watching a bird on a treetop, and, after they had locked gazes for some time, the bird

2. There are many accounts in ancient and medieval literature of an infant who bears no resemblance to its parents but to an image or painting on which a mother had been looking while she was pregnant or when she conceived. Some of these involve a black child born to white parents.

3. In Genesis 30, Jacob has goats mate in front of boughs from which he has peeled back the bark. The lambs are born with patterns on their wool resembling those on the branches, either speckled or spotted.

let itself fall as if dead between the cat's paws, either intoxicated by its own imagination or drawn by some attracting power of the cat. Those who like falconry have heard the story of the falconer who, setting his gaze obstinately upon a kite in the air, wagered that by the sole power of his gaze he would bring it down, and did. At least, so they say—for I refer the stories that I borrow to the conscience of those from whom I take them.[4] The reflections are my own, and depend on the proofs of reason, not of experience; everyone can add his own examples to them; and he who has none, let him not fail to believe that there are plenty, in view of the number and variety of occurrences. If I do not apply them well, let another apply them for me.

So in the study that I am making of our behavior and motives, fabulous testimonies, provided they are possible, serve like true ones. Whether they have happened or no, in Paris or Rome, to John or Peter, they exemplify, at all events, some human potentiality, and thus their telling imparts useful information to me. I see it and profit from it just as well in shadow as in substance. And of the different readings that histories often give, I take for my use the one that is most rare and memorable. There are authors whose end is to tell what has happened. Mine, if I could attain it, would be to talk about what can happen. The schools are justly permitted to suppose similitudes when they have none at hand. I do not do so, however, and in that respect I surpass all historical fidelity, being scrupulous to the point of superstition. In the examples that I bring in here of what I have heard, done, or said, I have forbidden myself to dare to alter even the slightest and most inconsequential circumstances. My conscience does not falsify one iota; my knowledge, I don't know.

In this connection, I sometimes fall to thinking whether it befits a theologian, a philosopher, and such people of exquisite and exact conscience and prudence, to write history. How can they stake their fidelity on the fidelity of an ordinary person? How be responsible for the thoughts of persons unknown and give their conjectures as coin of the realm? Of complicated actions that happen in their presence they would refuse to give testimony if placed under oath by a judge; and they know no man so intimately that they would undertake to answer fully for his intentions. I consider it less hazardous to write of things past than present, inasmuch as the writer has only to give an account of a borrowed truth.

Some urge me to write the events of my time, believing that I see them with a view less distorted by passion than another man's, and from closer, because of the access that fortune has given me to the heads of different parties.[5] What they forget is that even for all the glory of Sallust, I would not take the trouble, being a sworn enemy of obligation, assiduity, perseverance; and that there is nothing so contrary to my style as an extended narration. I cut myself off so often for lack of breath; I have neither composition nor development that is worth anything; I am more ignorant than a child of the phrases and terms that serve for the commonest things. And so I have chosen to say what I know how to say, accommodating the matter to my power. If I took a subject that would lead me along, I might not be able to measure up to it; and with my freedom being so very free, I might publish judgments which, even according to my own opinion and to reason, would be illegitimate and punishable. Plutarch might well say to us, concerning his accomplishments in this line, that the credit belongs to others if his examples are wholly and everywhere true; but that their being

4. The original essay, first published in 1580, ended here; Montaigne added the remainder of the essay after 1588.

5. One of the rare references Montaigne makes to his public activities as mayor and diplomat.

useful to posterity, and presented with a luster which lights our way to virtue, that is his work.[6] There is no danger—as there is in a medicinal drug—in an old story being this way or that.

Of Cannibals[1]

When King Pyrrhus passed over into Italy, after he had reconnoitered the formation of the army that the Romans were sending to meet him, he said: "I do not know what barbarians these are" (for so the Greeks called all foreign nations), "but the formation of this army that I see is not at all barbarous." The Greeks said as much of the army that Flamininus brought into their country, and so did Philip, seeing from a knoll the order and distribution of the Roman camp, in his kingdom, under Publius Sulpicius Galba.[2] Thus we should beware of clinging to vulgar opinions, and judge things by reason's way, not by popular say.

I had with me for a long time a man who had lived for ten or twelve years in that other world which has been discovered in our century, in the place where Villegaignon landed, and which he called Antarctic France.[3] This discovery of a boundless country seems worthy of consideration. I don't know if I can guarantee that some other such discovery will not be made in the future, so many personages greater than ourselves having been mistaken about this one. I am afraid we have eyes bigger than our stomachs, and more curiosity than capacity. We embrace everything, but we clasp only wind.

Plato brings in Solon, telling how he had learned from the priests of the city of Saïs in Egypt that in days of old, before the Flood, there was a great island named Atlantis, right at the mouth of the Strait of Gibraltar, which contained more land than Africa and Asia put together, and that the kings of that country, who not only possessed that island but had stretched out so far on the mainland that they held the breadth of Africa as far as Egypt, and the length of Europe as far as Tuscany, undertook to step over into Asia and subjugate all the nations that border on the Mediterranean, as far as the Black Sea; and for this purpose crossed the Spains, Gaul, Italy, as far as Greece, where the Athenians checked them; but that some time after, both the Athenians and themselves and their island were swallowed up by the Flood.[4]

It is quite likely that that extreme devastation of waters made amazing changes in the habitations of the earth, as people maintain that the sea cut off Sicily from Italy—

> 'Tis said an earthquake once asunder tore
> These lands with dreadful havoc, which before
> Formed but one land, one coast
>
> VIRGIL

6. The great Greek biographer Plutarch (1st century C.E.), cited often by Montaigne, wrote 50 *Lives* of prominent Greek and Roman figures such as Julius Caesar, Cicero, and Pericles.

1. Book 1, Chapter 31.

2. Plutarch recounts the first two stories, of Pyrrhus's and the Greeks' comments on the Romans. The account of Philip, King of Macedon—another Greek unimpressed by a Roman army—is found in Livy.

3. Brazil, where Nicolas Durand de Villegaignon led an expedition in 1555–1556, with the hope of gaining some military clout. Among those who traveled with him were a group of Calvinist sympathizers, including the Calvinist Jean de Léry as well as a Franciscan friar named André Thevet. Both Thevet and Léry published extensive writings of their travels, from which Montaigne borrowed freely.

4. The legendary lost island of Atlantis is mentioned by Plato in the *Timaeus*.

—Cyprus from Syria, the island of Euboea from the mainland of Boeotia; and elsewhere joined lands that were divided, filling the channels between them with sand and mud:

> A sterile marsh, long fit for rowing, now
> Feeds neighbor towns, and feels the heavy plow.
>
> HORACE

But there is no great likelihood that that island was the new world which we have just discovered; for it almost touched Spain, and it would be an incredible result of a flood to have forced it away as far as it is, more than twelve hundred leagues; besides, the travels of the moderns have already almost revealed that it is not an island, but a mainland connected with the East Indies on one side, and elsewhere with the lands under the two poles; or, if it is separated from them, it is by so narrow a strait and interval that it does not deserve to be called an island on that account.

It seems that there are movements, some natural, others feverish, in these great bodies, just as in our own. When I consider the inroads that my river, the Dordogne, is making in my lifetime into the right bank in its descent, and that in twenty years it has gained so much ground and stolen away the foundations of several buildings, I clearly see that this is an extraordinary disturbance; for if it had always gone at this rate, or was to do so in the future, the face of the world would be turned topsy-turvy. But rivers are subject to changes: now they overflow in one direction, now in another, now they keep to their course. I am not speaking of the sudden inundations whose causes are manifest. In Médoc, along the seashore, my brother, the sieur d'Arsac,[5] can see an estate of his buried under the sands that the sea spews forth; the tops of some buildings are still visible; his farms and domains have changed into very thin pasturage. The inhabitants say that for some time the sea has been pushing toward them so hard that they have lost four leagues of land. These sands are its harbingers; and we see great dunes of moving sand that march half a league ahead of it and keep conquering land.

The other testimony of antiquity with which some would connect this discovery is in Aristotle, at least if that little book *Of Unheard-of Wonders* is by him. He there relates that certain Carthaginians, after setting out upon the Atlantic Ocean from the Strait of Gibraltar and sailing a long time, at last discovered a great fertile island, all clothed in woods and watered by great deep rivers, far remote from any mainland; and that they, and others since, attracted by the goodness and fertility of the soil, went there with their wives and children, and began to settle there. The lords of Carthage, seeing that their country was gradually becoming depopulated, expressly forbade anyone to go there any more, on pain of death, and drove out these new inhabitants, fearing, it is said, that in course of time they might come to multiply so greatly as to supplant their former masters and ruin their state. This story of Aristotle does not fit our new lands any better than the other.

This man I had was a simple, crude fellow—a character fit to bear true witness; for clever people observe more things and more curiously, but they interpret them; and to lend weight and conviction to their interpretation, they cannot help altering history a little. They never show you things as they are, but bend and disguise them according to the way they have seen them; and to give credence to their judgment and

5. Montaigne had five brothers; the "sieur of Arsac" was younger than he.

attract you to it, they are prone to add something to their matter, to stretch it out and amplify it. We need a man either very honest, or so simple that he has not the stuff to build up false inventions and give them plausibility; and wedded to no theory. Such was my man; and besides this, he at various times brought sailors and merchants, whom he had known on that trip, to see me. So I content myself with his information, without inquiring what the cosmographers say about it.

We ought to have topographers who would give us an exact account of the places where they have been. But because they have over us the advantage of having seen Palestine, they want to enjoy the privilege of telling us news about all the rest of the world. I would like everyone to write what he knows, and as much as he knows, not only in this, but in all other subjects; for a man may have some special knowledge and experience of the nature of a river or a fountain, who in other matters knows only what everybody knows. However, to circulate this little scrap of knowledge, he will undertake to write the whole of physics. From this vice spring many great abuses.

Now, to return to my subject, I think there is nothing barbarous and savage in that nation, from what I have been told, except that each man calls barbarism whatever is not his own practice; for indeed it seems we have no other test of truth and reason than the example and pattern of the opinions and customs of the country we live in. *There* is always the perfect religion, the perfect government, the perfect and accomplished manners in all things. Those people are wild, just as we call wild the fruits that Nature has produced by herself and in her normal course; whereas really it is those that we have changed artificially and led astray from the common order, that we should rather call wild. The former retain alive and vigorous their genuine, their most useful and natural, virtues and properties, which we have debased in the latter in adapting them to gratify our corrupted taste. And yet for all that, the savor and delicacy of some uncultivated fruits of those countries is quite as excellent, even to our taste, as that of our own. It is not reasonable that art should win the place of honor over our great and powerful mother Nature. We have so overloaded the beauty and richness of her works by our inventions that we have quite smothered her. Yet wherever her purity shines forth, she wonderfully puts to shame our vain and frivolous attempts:

> Ivy comes readier without our care;
> In lonely caves the arbutus grows more fair;
> No art with artless bird song can compare.
>
> PROPERTIUS

All our efforts cannot even succeed in reproducing the nest of the tiniest little bird, its contexture, its beauty and convenience; or even the web of the puny spider. All things, says Plato, are produced by nature, by fortune, or by art; the greatest and most beautiful by one or the other of the first two, the least and most imperfect by the last.

These nations, then, seem to me barbarous in this sense, that they have been fashioned very little by the human mind, and are still very close to their original naturalness. The laws of nature still rule them, very little corrupted by ours; and they are in such a state of purity that I am sometimes vexed that they were unknown earlier, in the days when there were men able to judge them better than we. I am sorry that Lycurgus and Plato did not know of them;[6] for it seems to me that what we actually see

6. Lycurgus was a legendary Spartan legislator who radically reformed his city's laws. Among Plato's many treatises was the *Republic,* where he talks about the ideal society.

in these nations surpasses not only all the pictures in which poets have idealized the golden age and all their inventions in imagining a happy state of man, but also the conceptions and the very desire of philosophy. They could not imagine a naturalness so pure and simple as we see by experience; nor could they believe that our society could be maintained with so little artifice and human solder. This is a nation, I should say to Plato, in which there is no sort of traffic, no knowledge of letters, no science of numbers, no name for a magistrate or for political superiority, no custom of servitude, no riches or poverty, no contracts, no successions, no partitions, no occupations but leisure ones, no care for any but common kinship, no clothes, no agriculture, no metal, no use of wine or wheat. The very words that signify lying, treachery, dissimulation, avarice, envy, belittling, pardon—unheard of.[7] How far from this perfection would he find the republic that he imagined: *Men fresh sprung from the gods* [Seneca].

These manners nature first ordained.

VIRGIL

For the rest, they live in a country with a very pleasant and temperate climate, so that according to my witnesses it is rare to see a sick man there; and they have assured me that they never saw one palsied, bleary-eyed, toothless, or bent with age. They are settled along the sea and shut in on the land side by great high mountains, with a stretch about a hundred leagues wide in between. They have a great abundance of fish and flesh which bear no resemblance to ours, and they eat them with no other artifice than cooking. The first man who rode a horse there, though he had had dealings with them on several other trips, so horrified them in this posture that they shot him dead with arrows before they could recognize him.

Their buildings are very long, with a capacity of two or three hundred souls; they are covered with the bark of great trees, the strips reaching to the ground at one end and supporting and leaning on one another at the top, in the manner of some of our barns, whose covering hangs down to the ground and acts as a side. They have wood so hard that they cut with it and make of it their swords and grills to cook their food. Their beds are of a cotton weave, hung from the roof like those in our ships, each man having his own; for the wives sleep apart from their husbands.

They get up with the sun, and eat immediately upon rising, to last them through the day; for they take no other meal than that one. Like some other Eastern peoples, of whom Suidas[8] tells us, who drank apart from meals, they do not drink then; but they drink several times a day, and to capacity. Their drink is made of some root, and is of the color of our claret wines. They drink it only lukewarm. This beverage keeps only two or three days; it has a slightly sharp taste, is not at all heady, is good for the stomach, and has a laxative effect upon those who are not used to it; it is a very pleasant drink for anyone who is accustomed to it. In place of bread they use a certain white substance like preserved coriander. I have tried it; it tastes sweet and a little flat.

The whole day is spent in dancing. The younger men go to hunt animals with bows. Some of the women busy themselves meanwhile with warming their drink, which is their chief duty. Some one of the old men, in the morning before they begin

7. Gonzalo's irritating speech to Sebastian in *The Tempest* (see page 1667) borrows from these two lines as translated by Montaigne's earliest English translator, John Florio.

8. The Suidas was the name given to a great Greek encyclopedia, compiled around the 10th century C.E.

to eat, preaches to the whole barnful in common, walking from one end to the other, and repeating one single sentence several times until he has completed the circuit (for the buildings are fully a hundred paces long). He recommends to them only two things: valor against the enemy and love for their wives. And they never fail to point out this obligation, as their refrain, that it is their wives who keep their drink warm and seasoned.

There may be seen in several places, including my own house, specimens of their beds, of their ropes, of their wooden swords and the bracelets with which they cover their wrists in combats, and of the big canes, open at one end, by whose sound they keep time in their dances. They are close shaven all over, and shave themselves much more cleanly than we, with nothing but a wooden or stone razor. They believe that souls are immortal, and that those who have deserved well of the gods are lodged in that part of heaven where the sun rises, and the damned in the west.

They have some sort of priests and prophets, but they rarely appear before the people, having their home in the mountains. On their arrival there is a great feast and solemn assembly of several villages—each barn, as I have described it, makes up a village, and they are about one French league from each other. The prophet speaks to them in public, exhorting them to virtue and their duty; but their whole ethical science contains only these two articles: resoluteness in war and affection for their wives. He prophesies to them things to come and the results they are to expect from their undertakings, and urges them to war or holds them back from it; but this is on the condition that when he fails to prophesy correctly, and if things turn out otherwise than he has predicted, he is cut into a thousand pieces if they catch him, and condemned as a false prophet. For this reason, the prophet who has once been mistaken is never seen again.

Divination is a gift of God; that is why its abuse should be punished as imposture. Among the Scythians, when the soothsayers failed to hit the mark, they were laid, chained hand and foot, on carts full of heather and drawn by oxen, on which they were burned.[9] Those who handle matters subject to the control of human capacity are excusable if they do the best they can. But these others, who come and trick us with assurances of an extraordinary faculty that is beyond our ken, should they not be punished for not making good their promise, and for the temerity of their imposture?

They have their wars with the nations beyond the mountains, further inland, to which they go quite naked, with no other arms than bows or wooden swords ending in a sharp point, in the manner of the tongues of our boar spears. It is astonishing what firmness they show in their combats, which never end but in slaughter and bloodshed; for as to routs and terror, they know nothing of either.

Each man brings back as his trophy the head of the enemy he has killed, and sets it up at the entrance to his dwelling. After they have treated their prisoners well for a long time with all the hospitality they can think of, each man who has a prisoner calls a great assembly of his acquaintances. He ties a rope to one of the prisoner's arms, by the end of which he holds him, a few steps away, for fear of being hurt, and gives his dearest friend the other arm to hold in the same way; and these two, in the presence of the whole assembly, kill him with their swords. This done, they roast him and eat him in common and send some pieces to their absent friends. This is not, as people think, for nourishment, as of old the Scythians used to do; it is to betoken an extreme revenge. And the proof of this came when they saw the Portuguese, who had joined

9. The story is from Herodotus; the term "Scythians" was used to describe the peoples from the north, who supposedly practiced a number of barbaric customs such as scalping and flaying their enemy.

forces with their adversaries, inflict a different kind of death on them when they took them prisoner, which was to bury them up to the waist, shoot the rest of their body full of arrows, and afterward hang them.[1] They thought that these people from the other world, being men who had sown the knowledge of many vices among their neighbors and were much greater masters than themselves in every sort of wickedness, did not adopt this sort of vengeance without some reason, and that it must be more painful than their own; so they began to give up their old method and to follow this one.

I am not sorry that we notice the barbarous horror of such acts, but I am heartily sorry that, judging their faults rightly, we should be so blind to our own. I think there is more barbarity in eating a man alive than in eating him dead; and in tearing by tortures and the rack a body still full of feeling, in roasting a man bit by bit, in having him bitten and mangled by dogs and swine (as we have not only read but seen within fresh memory, not among ancient enemies, but among neighbors and fellow citizens, and what is worse, on the pretext of piety and religion),[2] than in roasting and eating him after he is dead. Indeed, Chrysippus and Zeno, heads of the Stoic sect, thought there was nothing wrong in using our carcasses for any purpose in case of need, and getting nourishment from them; just as our ancestors, when besieged by Caesar in the city of Alésia, resolved to relieve their famine by eating old men, women, and other people useless for fighting.[3]

> The Gascons once, 'tis said, their life renewed
> By eating of such food.
>
> JUVENAL

And physicians do not fear to use human flesh in all sorts of ways for our health, applying it either inwardly or outwardly. But there never was any opinion so disordered as to excuse treachery, disloyalty, tyranny, and cruelty, which are our ordinary vices.

So we may well call these people barbarians, in respect to the rules of reason, but not in respect to ourselves, who surpass them in every kind of barbarity.

Their warfare is wholly noble and generous, and as excusable and beautiful as this human disease can be; its only basis among them is their rivalry in valor. They are not fighting for the conquest of new lands, for they still enjoy that natural abundance that provides them without toil and trouble with all necessary things in such profusion that they have no wish to enlarge their boundaries. They are still in that happy state of desiring only as much as their natural needs demand; anything beyond that is superfluous to them.[4]

They generally call those of the same age, brothers; those who are younger, children; and the old men are fathers to all the others. These leave to their heirs in common the full possession of their property, without division or any other title at all than just the one that Nature gives to her creatures in bringing them into the world.

If their neighbors cross the mountains to attack them and win a victory, the gain of the victor is glory, and the advantage of having proved the master in valor and virtue; for apart from this they have no use for the goods of the vanquished, and they

1. The Portuguese had settled in Brazil long before the French.
2. A reference to the wars of religion that had divided France since the early 1570s.
3. "Our ancestors" are the Galls, referred to by Caesar himself in his *Gallic Wars.* The quote by Juvenal that follows also refers to the Gascons or Galls.
4. Much of this description of the native Brazilians (the Tupinamba Indians) is drawn from Jean de Léry's account.

return to their own country, where they lack neither anything necessary nor that great thing, the knowledge of how to enjoy their condition happily and be content with it. These men of ours do the same in their turn. They demand of their prisoners no other ransom than that they confess and acknowledge their defeat. But there is not one in a whole century who does not choose to die rather than to relax a single bit, by word or look, from the grandeur of an invincible courage; not one who would not rather be killed and eaten than so much as ask not to be. They treat them very freely, so that life may be all the dearer to them, and usually entertain them with threats of their coming death, of the torments they will have to suffer, the preparations that are being made for that purpose, the cutting up of their limbs, and the feast that will be made at their expense. All this is done for the sole purpose of extorting from their lips some weak or base word, or making them want to flee, so as to gain the advantage of having terrified them and broken down their firmness. For indeed, if you take it the right way, it is in this point alone that true victory lies:

> It is no victory
> Unless the vanquished foe admits your mastery.
>
> CLAUDIAN

The Hungarians, very bellicose fighters, did not in olden times pursue their advantage beyond putting the enemy at their mercy. For having wrung a confession from him to this effect, they let him go unharmed and unransomed, except, at most, for exacting his promise never again to take up arms against them.

We win enough advantages over our enemies that are borrowed advantages, not really our own. It is the quality of a porter, not of valor, to have sturdier arms and legs; agility is a dead and corporeal quality; it is a stroke of luck to make our enemy stumble, or dazzle his eyes by the sunlight; it is a trick of art and technique, which may be found in a worthless coward, to be an able fencer. The worth and value of a man is in his heart and his will; there lies his real honor. Valor is the strength, not of legs and arms, but of heart and soul; it consists not in the worth of our horse or our weapons, but in our own. He who falls obstinate in his courage, *if he has fallen, he fights on his knees* [Seneca]. He who relaxes none of his assurance, no matter how great the danger of imminent death; who, giving up his soul, still looks firmly and scornfully at his enemy—he is beaten not by us, but by fortune; he is killed, not conquered.

The most valiant are sometimes the most unfortunate. Thus there are triumphant defeats that rival victories. Nor did those four sister victories, the fairest that the sun ever set eyes on—Salamis, Plataea, Mycale, and Sicily—ever dare match all their combined glory against the glory of the annihilation of King Leonidas and his men at the pass of Thermopylae.[5]

Who ever hastened with more glorious and ambitious desire to win a battle than Captain Ischolas to lose one? Who ever secured his safety more ingeniously and painstakingly than he did his destruction? He was charged to defend a certain pass in the Peloponnesus against the Arcadians. Finding himself wholly incapable of doing this, in view of the nature of the place and the inequality of the forces, he made up his mind that all who confronted the enemy would necessarily have to remain on the field. On the other hand, deeming it unworthy both of his own virtue and magnanimity

5. The first three victories were triumphs by the Greeks over the Persians in 479–480 B.C.E.; simultaneously the Greeks halted Carthaginian expansion in Sicily with a stunning victory at Himera. With a slender army, Leonidas held back the Persians for several days at the pass of Thermopylae, inflicting heavy casualities; when a native showed the Persians a mountain path that would enable them to attack the Greeks from the rear, Leonidas was killed and his army defeated.

and of the Lacedaemonian name to fail in his charge, he took a middle course between these two extremes, in this way. The youngest and fittest of his band he preserved for the defense and service of their country, and sent them home; and with those whose loss was less important, he determined to hold this pass, and by their death to make the enemy buy their entry as dearly as he could. And so it turned out. For he was presently surrounded on all sides by the Arcadians, and after slaughtering a large number of them, he and his men were all put to the sword. Is there a trophy dedicated to victors that would not be more due to these vanquished? The role of true victory is in fighting, not in coming off safely; and the honor of valor consists in combating, not in beating.

To return to our story. These prisoners are so far from giving in, in spite of all that is done to them, that on the contrary, during the two or three months that they are kept, they wear a gay expression; they urge their captors to hurry and put them to the test; they defy them, insult them, reproach them with their cowardice and the number of battles they have lost to the prisoners' own people.

I have a song composed by a prisoner which contains this challenge, that they should all come boldly and gather to dine off him, for they will be eating at the same time their own fathers and grandfathers, who have served to feed and nourish his body. "These muscles," he says, "this flesh and these veins are your own, poor fools that you are. You do not recognize that the substance of your ancestors' limbs is still contained in them. Savor them well; you will find in them the taste of your own flesh." An idea that certainly does not smack of barbarity. Those that paint these people dying, and who show the execution, portray the prisoner spitting in the face of his slayers and scowling at them. Indeed, to the last gasp they never stop braving and defying their enemies by word and look. Truly here are real savages by our standards; for either they must be thoroughly so, or we must be; there is an amazing distance between their character and ours.

The men there have several wives, and the higher their reputation for valor the more wives they have. It is a remarkably beautiful thing about their marriages that the same jealousy our wives have to keep us from the affection and kindness of other women, theirs have to win this for them. Being more concerned for their husbands' honor than for anything else, they strive and scheme to have as many companions as they can, since that is a sign of their husbands' valor.

Our wives will cry "Miracle!" but it is no miracle. It is a properly matrimonial virtue, but one of the highest order. In the Bible, Leah, Rachel, Sarah, and Jacob's wives gave their beautiful handmaids to their husbands; and Livia seconded the appetites of Augustus, to her own disadvantage; and Stratonice, the wife of King Deiotarus, not only lent her husband for his use a very beautiful young chambermaid in her service, but carefully brought up her children, and backed them up to succeed to their father's estates.[6]

And lest it be thought that all this is done through a simple and servile bondage to usage and through the pressure of the authority of their ancient customs, without reasoning or judgment, and because their minds are so stupid that they cannot take any other course, I must cite some examples of their capacity. Besides the warlike song I have just quoted, I have another, a love song, which begins in this vein: "Adder, stay; stay, adder, that from the pattern of your coloring my sister may draw the fashion and the workmanship of a rich girdle that I may give to my love; so may your beauty and

6. Leah and Rachel are Jacob's wives; Sarah is the wife of Abraham, who sent her Egyptian maid Hagar to her husband that he might have an heir. Livia bore Augustus no children; King Deiotarus and Stratonice, allies of Rome during the first century B.C.E., are written of in Plutarch's *Bravery of Women*.

your pattern be forever preferred to all other serpents." This first couplet is the refrain of the song. Now I am familiar enough with poetry to be a judge of this: not only is there nothing barbarous in this fancy, but it is altogether Anacreontic.[7] Their language, moreover, is a soft language, with an agreeable sound, somewhat like Greek in its endings.

Three of these men, ignorant of the price they will pay some day, in loss of repose and happiness, for gaining knowledge of the corruptions of this side of the ocean; ignorant also of the fact that of this intercourse will come their ruin (which I suppose is already well advanced: poor wretches, to let themselves be tricked by the desire for new things, and to have left the serenity of their own sky to come and see ours!)—three of these men were at Rouen, at the time the late King Charles IX was there.[8] The king talked to them for a long time; they were shown our ways, our splendor, the aspect of a fine city. After that, someone asked their opinion, and wanted to know what they had found most amazing. They mentioned three things, of which I have forgotten the third, and I am very sorry for it; but I still remember two of them. They said that in the first place they thought it very strange that so many grown men, bearded, strong, and armed, who were around the king (it is likely that they were talking about the Swiss of his guard) should submit to obey a child, and that one of them was not chosen to command instead. Second (they have a way in their language of speaking of men as halves of one another), they had noticed that there were among us men full and gorged with all sorts of good things, and that their other halves were beggars at their doors, emaciated with hunger and poverty; and they thought it strange that these needy halves could endure such an injustice, and did not take the others by the throat, or set fire to their houses.

I had a very long talk with one of them; but I had an interpreter who followed my meaning so badly, and who was so hindered by his stupidity in taking in my ideas, that I could get hardly any satisfaction from the man. When I asked him what profit he gained from his superior position among his people (for he was a captain, and our sailors called him king), he told me that it was to march foremost in war. How many men followed him? He pointed to a piece of ground, to signify as many as such a space could hold; it might have been four or five thousand men. Did all his authority expire with the war? He said that this much remained, that when he visited the villages dependent on him, they made paths for him through the underbrush by which he might pass quite comfortably.

All this is not too bad—but what's the use? They don't wear breeches.

Of Repentance[1]

Others form man; I tell of him, and portray a particular one, very ill-formed, whom I should really make very different from what he is if I had to fashion him over again. But now it is done.

Now the lines of my painting do not go astray, though they change and vary. The world is but a perennial movement. All things in it are in constant motion—the earth, the rocks of the Caucasus, the pyramids of Egypt—both with the common motion and with their own. Stability itself is nothing but a more languid motion.

7. Anacreon was a 6th century B.C.E. Greek lyric poet.

8. The occasion dates to 1562. Charles IX, who succeeded to the throne in 1560, would have been only 12 at the time, which explains the men's comment that they thought it odd "that so many grown men . . . should submit to obey a child."

1. Book 3, Chapter 2.

I cannot keep my subject still. It goes along befuddled and staggering, with a natural drunkenness. I take it in this condition, just as it is at the moment I give my attention to it. I do not portray being: I portray passing. Not the passing from one age to another, or, as the people say, from seven years to seven years, but from day to day, from minute to minute. My history needs to be adapted to the moment. I may presently change, not only by chance, but also by intention. This is a record of various and changeable occurrences, and of irresolute and, when it so befalls, contradictory ideas: whether I am different myself, or whether I take hold of my subjects in different circumstances and aspects. So, all in all, I may indeed contradict myself now and then; but truth, as Demades said, I do not contradict. If my mind could gain a firm footing, I would not make essays,[2] I would make decisions; but it is always in apprenticeship and on trial.

I set forth a humble and inglorious life; that does not matter. You can tie up all moral philosophy with a common and private life just as well as with a life of richer stuff. Each man bears the entire form of man's estate.

Authors communicate with the people by some special extrinsic mark; I am the first to do so by my entire being, as Michel de Montaigne, not as a grammarian or a poet or a jurist. If the world complains that I speak too much of myself, I complain that it does not even think of itself.[3]

But is it reasonable that I, so fond of privacy in actual life, should aspire to publicity in the knowledge of me? Is it reasonable too that I should set forth to the world, where fashioning and art have so much credit and authority, some crude and simple products of nature, and of a very feeble nature at that? Is it not making a wall without stone, or something like that, to construct books without knowledge and without art? Musical fancies are guided by art, mine by chance.

At least I have one thing according to the rules: that no man ever treated a subject he knew and understood better than I do the subject I have undertaken; and that in this I am the most learned man alive. Secondly, that no man ever penetrated more deeply into his material, or plucked its limbs and consequences cleaner, or reached more accurately and fully the goal he had set for his work. To accomplish it, I need only bring it to fidelity; and that is in it, as sincere and pure as can be found. I speak the truth, not my fill of it, but as much as I dare speak; and I dare to do so a little more as I grow old, for it seems that custom allows old age more freedom to prate and more indiscretion in talking about oneself. It cannot happen here as I see it happening often, that the craftsman and his work contradict each other: "Has a man whose conversation is so good written such a stupid book?" or "Have such learned writings come from a man whose conversation is so feeble?"

If a man is commonplace in conversation and rare in writing, that means that his capacity is in the place from which he borrows it, and not in himself. A learned man is not learned in all matters; but the capable man is capable in all matters, even in ignorance.

In this case we go hand in hand and at the same pace, my book and I. In other cases one may commend or blame the work apart from the workman; not so here; he who touches the one, touches the other. He who judges it without knowing it will injure himself more than me; he who has known it will completely satisfy me. Happy beyond my deserts if I have just this share of public approval, that I make men of understanding feel that I was capable of profiting by knowledge, if I had had any, and that I deserved better assistance from my memory.

2. Montaigne plays here in the French with the meanings of the word *essayer,* "to try," "to prove."

3. This bold claim is a late one, added after the 1588 publication of the essays.

Let me here excuse what I often say, that I rarely repent and that my conscience is content with itself—not as the conscience of an angel or a horse, but as the conscience of a man; always adding this refrain, not perfunctorily but in sincere and complete submission: that I speak as an ignorant inquirer, referring the decision purely and simply to the common and authorized beliefs. I do not teach, I tell.

There is no vice truly a vice which is not offensive, and which a sound judgment does not condemn; for its ugliness and painfulness is so apparent that perhaps the people are right who say it is chiefly produced by stupidity and ignorance. So hard it is to imagine anyone knowing it without hating it.

Malice sucks up the greater part of its own venom, and poisons itself with it. Vice leaves repentance in the soul, like an ulcer in the flesh, which is always scratching itself and drawing blood. For reason effaces other griefs and sorrows; but it engenders that of repentance, which is all the more grievous because it springs from within, as the cold and heat of fevers is sharper than that which comes from outside. I consider as vices (but each one according to its measure) not only those that reason and nature condemn, but also those that man's opinion has created, even false and erroneous opinion, if it is authorized by laws and customs.

There is likewise no good deed that does not rejoice a wellborn nature. Indeed there is a sort of gratification in doing good which makes us rejoice in ourselves, and a generous pride that accompanies a good conscience. A boldly vicious soul may perhaps arm itself with security, but with this complacency and satisfaction it cannot provide itself. It is no slight pleasure to feel oneself preserved from the contagion of so depraved an age, and to say to oneself: "If anyone should see right into my soul, still he would not find me guilty either of anyone's affliction or ruin, or of vengeance or envy, or of public offense against the laws, or of innovation and disturbance, or of failing in my word; and in spite of what the license of the times allows and teaches each man, still I have not put my hand either upon the property or into the purse of any Frenchman, and have lived only on my own, both in war and in peace; nor have I used any man's work without paying his wages." These testimonies of conscience give us pleasure; and this natural rejoicing is a great boon to us, and the only payment that never fails us.

To found the reward for virtuous actions on the approval of others is to choose too uncertain and shaky a foundation. Especially in an age as corrupt and ignorant as this, the good opinion of the people is a dishonor. Whom can you trust to see what is praiseworthy? God keep me from being a worthy man according to the descriptions I see people every day giving of themselves in their own honor. *What were vices now are moral acts* [Seneca].

Certain of my friends have sometimes undertaken to call me on the carpet and lecture me unreservedly, either of their own accord or at my invitation, as a service which, to a well-formed soul, surpasses all the services of friendship, not only in usefulness, but also in pleasantness. I have always welcomed it with the wide-open arms of courtesy and gratitude. But to speak of it now in all conscience, I have often found in their reproach or praise such false measure that I would hardly have erred to err rather than to do good in their fashion.

Those of us especially who live a private life that is on display only to ourselves must have a pattern established within us by which to test our actions, and, according to this pattern, now pat ourselves on the back, now punish ourselves. I have my own laws and court to judge me, and I address myself to them more than anywhere else. To be sure, I restrain my actions according to others, but I extend them only according to myself. There is no one but yourself who knows whether you are cowardly and cruel, or loyal and devout. Others do not see you, they guess at you by uncertain conjectures; they see not so much your nature as your art. Therefore do not cling to their judgment; cling to your own. *You must use your own judgment. . . . With regard to virtues and vices, your own conscience has great weight: take that away, and everything falls* [Cicero].

But the saying that repentance follows close upon sin does not seem to consider the sin that is in robes of state, that dwells in us as in its own home. We can disown and retract the vices that take us by surprise, and toward which we are swept by passion; but those which by long habit are rooted and anchored in a strong and vigorous will cannot be denied. Repentance is nothing but a disavowal of our will and an opposition to our fancies, which leads us about in all directions. It makes this man disown his past virtue and his continence:

> Why had I not in youth the mind I have today?
> Or why, with old desires, have red cheeks flown away?
>
> HORACE

It is a rare life that remains well ordered even in private. Any man can play his part in the side show and represent a worthy man on the boards; but to be disciplined within, in his own bosom, where all is permissible, where all is concealed—that's the point. The next step to that is to be so in our own house, in our ordinary actions, for which we need render account to no one, where nothing is studied or artificial. And therefore Bias, depicting an excellent state of family life, says it is one in which the master is the same within, by his own volition, as he is outside for fear of the law and of what people will say. And it was a worthy remark of Julius Drusus to the workmen who offered, for three thousand crowns, to arrange his house so that his neighbors would no longer be able to look into it as they could before. "I will give you six thousand," he said; "make it so that everyone can see in from all sides." The practice of Agesilaus is noted with honor, of taking lodging in the churches when traveling, so that the people and the gods themselves might see into his private actions.[4] Men have seemed miraculous to the world, in whom their wives and valets have never seen anything even worth noticing. Few men have been admired by their own households.

No man has been a prophet, not merely in his own house, but in his own country,[5] says the experience of history. Likewise in things of no importance. And in this humble example you may see an image of greater ones. In my region of Gascony they think it a joke to see me in print. The farther from my lair the knowledge of me spreads, the more I am valued. I buy printers in Guienne,[6] elsewhere they buy me. On this phenomenon those people base their hopes who hide themselves while alive and present, to gain favor when dead and gone. I would rather have less of it. And I cast myself on the world only for the share of favor I get now. When I leave it, I shall hold it quits.

The people escort this man back to his door, with awe, from a public function. He drops his part with his gown; the higher he has hoisted himself, the lower he falls back; inside, in his home, everything is tumultuous and vile. Even if there is order there, it takes a keen and select judgment to perceive it in these humble private actions. Besides, order is a dull and somber virtue. To win through a breach, to conduct an embassy, to govern a people, these are dazzling actions. To scold, to laugh, to sell, to pay, to love, to hate, and to deal pleasantly and justly with our household and ourselves, not

4. The three references to Bias, Julius Drusus, and Agesilaus are all drawn from various works of Plutarch.

5. Jesus remarks that "No man is accepted as a prophet in his own country" when the people of Nazareth resist his teachings (Luke 4:24).

6. A city near Montaigne's home, in southwest France.

to let ourselves go, not to be false to ourselves, that is a rarer matter, more difficult and less noticeable.

Therefore retired lives, whatever people may say, accomplish duties as harsh and strenuous as other lives, or more so. And private persons, says Aristotle, render higher and more difficult service to virtue than those who are in authority. We prepare ourselves for eminent occasions more for glory than for conscience. The shortest way to attain glory would be to do for conscience what we do for glory. And Alexander's virtue seems to me to represent much less vigor in his theater than does that of Socrates in his lowly and obscure activity. I can easily imagine Socrates in Alexander's place; Alexander in that of Socrates, I cannot.[7] If you ask the former what he knows how to do, he will answer, "Subdue the world"; if you ask the latter, he will say, "Lead the life of man in conformity with its natural condition"; a knowledge much more general, more weighty, and more legitimate.

The value of the soul consists not in flying high, but in an orderly pace. Its greatness is exercised not in greatness, but in mediocrity. As those who judge and touch us inwardly make little account of the brilliance of our public acts, and see that these are only thin streams and jets of water spurting from a bottom otherwise muddy and thick; so likewise those who judge us by this brave outward appearance draw similar conclusions about our inner constitution, and cannot associate common faculties, just like their own, with these other faculties that astonish them and are so far beyond their scope. So we give demons wild shapes. And who does not give Tamerlane raised eyebrows, open nostrils, a dreadful face, and immense size, like the size of the imaginary picture of him we have formed from the renown of his name?[8] If I had been able to see Erasmus in other days, it would have been hard for me not to take for adages and apophthegms everything he said to his valet and his hostess.[9] We imagine much more appropriately an artisan on the toilet seat or on his wife than a great president, venerable by his demeanor and his ability. It seems to us that they do not stoop from their lofty thrones even to live.

As vicious souls are often incited to do good by some extraneous impulse, so are virtuous souls to do evil. Thus we must judge them by their settled state, when they are at home, if ever they are; or at least when they are closest to repose and their natural position.

Natural inclinations gain assistance and strength from education; but they are scarcely to be changed and overcome. A thousand natures, in my time, have escaped toward virtue or toward vice through the lines of a contrary training:

> As when wild beasts grow tame, shut in a cage,
> Forget the woods, and lose their look of rage,
> And learn to suffer man; but if they taste
> Hot blood, their rage and fury is replaced,
> Their reminiscent jaws distend, they burn,
> And for their trembling keeper's blood they yearn.
>
> LUCAN

We do not root out these original qualities, we cover them up, we conceal them. Latin is like a native tongue to me; I understand it better than French; but for forty years I

7. Montaigne alludes to Alexander the Great (356–323 B.C.E.), student of Aristotle and master of the Hellenic empire that would be extended under his sway into Syria, Egypt, and India.

8. Tamerlane, or Tamburlaine, was Timur Khan, who conquered the Mongols early in his military career and went to advance as far west as Turkey and Arabia. He died in 1405.

9. The industrious Dutch scholar and humanist Desiderius Erasmus spent his lifetime compiling the *Adagia,* a collection of adages or proverbs. ("Apophthegms" are witty sayings.)

have not used it at all for speaking or writing.[1] Yet in sudden and extreme emotions, into which I have fallen two or three times in my life—one of them when I saw my father, in perfect health, fall back into my arms in a faint—I have always poured out my first words from the depths of my entrails in Latin; Nature surging forth and expressing herself by force, in the face of long habit. And this experience is told of many others.

Those who in my time have tried[2] to correct the world's morals by new ideas, reform the superficial vices; the essential ones they leave as they were, if they do not increase them; and increase is to be feared. People are likely to rest from all other well-doing on the strength of these external, arbitrary reforms, which cost us less and bring greater acclaim; and thereby they satisfy at little expense the other natural, consubstantial, and internal vices.

Just consider the evidence of this in our own experience. There is no one who, if he listens to himself, does not discover in himself a pattern all his own, a ruling pattern, which struggles against education and against the tempest of the passions that oppose it. For my part, I do not feel much sudden agitation; I am nearly always in place, like heavy and inert bodies. If I am not at home, I am always very near it. My excesses do not carry me very far away. There is nothing extreme or strange about them. And besides I have periods of vigorous and healthy reaction.

The real condemnation, which applies to the common run of men of today, is that even their retirement is full of corruption and filth; their idea of reformation, blurred; their penitence, diseased and guilty, almost as much as their sin. Some, either from being glued to vice by a natural attachment, or from long habit, no longer recognize its ugliness. On others (in whose regiment I belong) vice weighs heavily, but they counterbalance it with pleasure or some other consideration, and endure it and lend themselves to it for a certain price; viciously, however, and basely. Yet it might be possible to imagine a disproportion so extreme that the pleasure might justly excuse the sin, as we say utility does; not only if the pleasure was incidental and not a part of the sin, as in theft, but if it was in the very exercise of the sin, as in intercourse with women, where the impulse is violent, and, they say, sometimes invincible.

The other day when I was at Armagnac, on the estate of a kinsman of mine, I saw a country fellow whom everyone nicknames the Thief. He gave this account of his life: that born a beggar, and finding that by earning his bread by the toil of his hands he would never protect himself enough against want, he had decided to become a thief; and he had spent all his youth at this trade in security, by virtue of his bodily strength. For he reaped his harvest and vintage from other people's lands, but so far away and in such great loads that it was inconceivable that one man could have carried off so much on his shoulders in one night. And he was careful besides to equalize and spread out the damage he did, so that the loss was less insupportable for each individual. He is now, in his old age, rich for a man in his station, thanks to this traffic, which he openly confesses. And to make his peace with God for his acquisitions, he says that he spends his days compensating, by good deeds, the successors of the people he robbed; and that if he does not finish this task (for he cannot do it all at once), he will charge his heirs with it, according to the knowledge, which he alone has, of the amount of wrong he did to each. Judging by this description, whether it is true or false, this man regards theft as a dishonorable action and hates it, but hates it less than poverty; he indeed repents of it in itself, but in so far as it was thus counterbalanced

1. Montaigne says in *Essays* I:26 that his father hired a tutor when he was born to teach him Latin as his first language: "I was over six before I understood any more French or Perigordian than Arabic."

2. Once again, Montaigne plays with the verb "essayer" as he talks about those who have tried ("ceux qui ont essaié") to change the world's morals.

and compensated, he does not repent of it. This is not that habit that incorporates us with vice and brings even our understanding into conformity with it; nor is it that impetuous wind that comes in gusts to confuse and blind our soul, and hurls us for the moment headlong, judgment and all, into the power of vice.

I customarily do wholeheartedly whatever I do, and go my way all in one piece. I scarcely make a motion that is hidden and out of sight of my reason, and that is not guided by the consent of nearly all parts of me, without division, without internal sedition. My judgment takes all the blame or all the praise for it; and the blame it once takes, it always keeps, for virtually since its birth it has been one; the same inclination, the same road, the same strength. And in the matter of general opinions, in childhood I established myself in the position where I was to remain.

There are some impetuous, prompt, and sudden sins: let us leave them aside. But as for these other sins so many times repeated, planned, and premeditated, constitutional sins, or even professional or vocational sins, I cannot imagine that they can be implanted so long in one and the same heart, without the reason and conscience of their possessor constantly willing and intending it to be so. And the repentance which he claims comes to him at a certain prescribed moment is a little hard for me to imagine and conceive.

I do not follow the belief of the sect of Pythagoras, that men take on a new soul when they approach the images of the gods to receive their oracles.[3] Unless he meant just this, that the soul must indeed be foreign, new, and loaned for the occasion, since their own showed so little sign of any purification and cleanness worthy of this office.

They do just the opposite of the Stoic precepts, which indeed order us to correct the imperfections and vices that we recognize in us, but forbid us to be repentant and glum about them. These men make us believe that they feel great regret and remorse within; but of amendment and correction, or interruption, they show us no sign. Yet it is no cure if the disease is not thrown off. If repentance were weighing in the scale of the balance, it would outweigh the sin. I know of no quality so easy to counterfeit as piety, if conduct and life are not made to conform with it. Its essence is abstruse and occult; its semblance, easy and showy.

As for me, I may desire in a general way to be different; I may condemn and dislike my nature as a whole, and implore God to reform me completely and to pardon my natural weakness. But this I ought not to call repentance, it seems to me, any more than my displeasure at being neither an angel nor Cato.[4] My actions are in order and conformity with what I am and with my condition. I can do no better. And repentance does not properly apply to the things that are not in our power; rather does regret. I imagine numberless natures loftier and better regulated than mine, but for all that, I do not amend my faculties; just as neither my arm nor my mind becomes more vigorous by imagining another that is so. If imagining and desiring a nobler conduct than ours produced repentance of our own, we should have to repent of our most innocent actions, inasmuch as we rightly judge that in a more excellent nature they would have been performed with greater perfection and dignity, and we should wish to do likewise.

When I consider the behavior of my youth in comparison with that of my old age, I find that I have generally conducted myself in orderly fashion, according to my lights; that is all my resistance can accomplish. I do not flatter myself; in similar circumstances I should always be the same. It is not a spot, it is rather a tincture with which I am stained all over. I know no superficial, halfway, and perfunctory repentance. It must

3. Seneca discusses this particular doctrine in his letters.

4. Marcus Cato (to whom Montaigne probably refers) was known as the "conscience of Rome" in his staunch opposition to Caesar and empire. Dante makes him guardian to the mountain of Purgatory.

affect me in every part before I will call it so, and must grip me by the vitals and afflict them as deeply and as completely as God sees into me.

In business matters, several good opportunities have escaped me for want of successful management. However, my counsels have been good, according to the circumstances they were faced with; their way is always to take the easiest and surest course. I find that in my past deliberations, according to my rule, I have proceeded wisely, considering the state of the matter proposed to me, and I should do the same a thousand years from now in similar situations. I am not considering what it is at this moment, but what it was when I was deliberating about it.

The soundness of any plan depends on the time; circumstances and things roll about and change incessantly. I have fallen into some serious and important mistakes in my life, not for lack of good counsel but for lack of good luck. There are secret parts in the matters we handle which cannot be guessed, especially in human nature—mute factors that do not show, factors sometimes unknown to their possessor himself, which are brought forth and aroused by unexpected occasions. If my prudence has been unable to see into them and predict them, I bear it no ill will; its responsibility is restricted within its limitations. It is the outcome that beats me; and if it favors the course I have refused, there is no help for it; I do not blame myself; I accuse my luck, not my work. That is not to be called repentance.

Phocion had given the Athenians some advice that was not followed. When however the affair came out prosperously against his opinion, someone said to him: "Well, Phocion, are you glad that the thing is going so well?" "Indeed I am glad," he said, "that it has turned out this way, but I do not repent of having advised that way."[5]

When my friends apply to me for advice, I give it freely and clearly, and without hesitating as nearly everyone else does because, the affair being hazardous, it may come out contrary to my expectations, wherefore they may have cause to reproach me for my advice; that does not worry me. For they will be wrong, and I should not have refused them this service.

I have scarcely any occasion to blame my mistakes or mishaps on anyone but myself. For in practice I rarely ask other people's advice, unless as a compliment and out of politeness, except when I need scientific information or knowledge of the facts. But in things where I have only my judgment to employ, other people's reasons can serve to support me, but seldom to change my course. I listen to them all favorably and decently; but so far as I can remember, I have never up to this moment followed any but my own. If you ask me, they are nothing but flies and atoms that distract my will. I set little value on my own opinions, but I set just as little on those of others. Fortune pays me properly. If I do not take advice, I give still less. Mine is seldom asked, but it is followed even less; and I know of no public or private enterprise that my advice restored to its feet and to the right path. Even the people whom fortune has made somewhat dependent on it have let themselves be managed more readily by anyone else's brains. Being a man who is quite as jealous of the rights of my repose as of the rights of my authority, I prefer it so; by leaving me alone, they treat me according to my professed principle, which is to be wholly contained and established within myself. To me it is a pleasure not to be concerned in other people's affairs and to be free of responsibility for them.

In all affairs, when they are past, however they have turned out, I have little regret. For this idea takes away the pain: that they were bound to happen thus, and now they are in the great stream of the universe and in the chain of Stoical causes. Your fancy, by wish or imagination, cannot change a single point without overturning the whole order of things, and the past and the future.

5. Recounted in Plutarch; Phocion, a soldier, advised the Athenians against a war that they ended up winning.

For the rest, I hate that accidental repentance that age brings. The man who said of old that he was obliged to the years for having rid him of sensuality had a different viewpoint from mine;[6] I shall never be grateful to impotence for any good it may do me. *Nor will Providence ever be so hostile to her own work that debility should be ranked among the best things* [Quintilian]. Our appetites are few in old age; a profound satiety seizes us after the act. In that I see nothing of conscience; sourness and weakness imprint on us a sluggish and rheumatic virtue. We must not let ourselves be so carried away by natural changes as to let our judgment degenerate. Youth and pleasure in other days did not make me fail to recognize the face of vice in voluptuousness; nor does the distaste that the years bring me make me fail to recognize the face of voluptuousness in vice. Now that I am no longer in that state, I judge it as though I were in it.

I who shake up my reason sharply and attentively, find that it is the very same I had in my more licentious years, except perhaps in so far as it has grown weaker and worse as it has grown old. And I find that even if it refuses, out of consideration for the interests of my bodily health, to put me in the furnace of this pleasure, it would not refuse to do so, any more than formerly, for my spiritual health. I do not consider it any more valiant for seeing it *hors de combat.* My temptations are so broken and mortified that they are not worth its opposition. By merely stretching out my hands to them, I exorcise them. If my reason were confronted with my former lust, I fear that it would have less strength to resist than it used to have. I do not see that of itself it judges anything differently than it did then, nor that it has gained any new light. Wherefore, if there is any convalescence, it is a deformed convalescence.

Miserable sort of remedy, to owe our health to disease! It is not for our misfortune to do us this service, it is for the good fortune of our judgment. You cannot make me do anything by ills and afflictions except curse them. They are for people who are only awakened by whipping. My reason runs a much freer course in prosperity. It is much more distracted and busy digesting pains than pleasures. I see much more clearly in fair weather. Health admonishes me more cheerfully and so more usefully than sickness. I advanced as far as I could toward reform and a regulated life when I had health to enjoy. I should be ashamed and resentful if the misery and misfortune of my decrepitude were to be thought better than my good, healthy, lively, vigorous years, and if people were to esteem me not for what I have been, but for ceasing to be that.

In my opinion it is living happily, not, as Antisthenes said, dying happily, that constitutes human felicity.[7] I have made no effort to attach, monstrously, the tail of a philosopher to the head and body of a dissipated man; or that this sickly remainder of my life should disavow and belie its fairest, longest, and most complete part. I want to present and show myself uniformly throughout. If I had to live over again, I would live as I have lived. I have neither tears for the past nor fears for the future. And unless I am fooling myself, it has gone about the same way within me as without. It is one of the chief obligations I have to my fortune that my bodily state has run its course with each thing in due season. I have seen the grass, the flower, and the fruit; now I see the dryness—happily, since it is naturally. I bear the ills I have much more easily because they are properly timed, and also because they make me remember more pleasantly the long felicity of my past life.

Likewise my wisdom may well have been of the same proportions in one age as in the other; but it was much more potent and graceful when green, gay, and natural, than it is now, being broken down, peevish, and labored. Therefore I renounce these casual and painful reformations.

6. The "man" is Sophocles, reported by Cicero in his *On Aging*.

7. The fourth-century Athenian Antisthenes was a Cynic, who saw freedom from the passions as the only key to happiness.

God must touch our hearts. Our conscience must reform by itself through the strengthening of our reason, not through the weakening of our appetites. Sensual pleasure is neither pale nor colorless in itself for being seen through dim and bleary eyes. We should love temperance for itself and out of reverence toward God, who has commanded it, and also chastity; what catarrh lends us, and what I owe to the favor of my colic, is neither chastity nor temperance. We cannot boast of despising and fighting sensual pleasure, if we do not see or know it, and its charms, its powers, and its most alluring beauty.

I know them both; I have a right to speak; but it seems to me that in old age our souls are subject to more troublesome ailments and imperfections than in our youth. I used to say so when I was young; then they taunted me with my beardless chin. I still say so now that my gray hair gives me authority to speak. We call "wisdom" the difficulty of our humors, our distaste for present things. But in truth we do not so much abandon our vices as change them, and, in my opinion, for the worse. Besides a silly and decrepit pride, a tedious prattle, prickly and unsociable humors, superstition, and a ridiculous concern for riches when we have lost the use of them, I find there more envy, injustice, and malice. Old age puts more wrinkles in our minds than on our faces; and we never, or rarely, see a soul that in growing old does not come to smell sour and musty. Man grows and dwindles in his entirety.

Seeing the wisdom of Socrates and several circumstances of his condemnation, I should venture to believe that he lent himself to it to some extent, purposely, by prevarication, being seventy, and having so soon to suffer an increasing torpor of the rich activity of his mind, and the dimming of its accustomed brightness.[8]

What metamorphoses I see old age producing every day in many of my acquaintances! It is a powerful malady, and it creeps up on us naturally and imperceptibly. We need a great provision of study, and great precaution, to avoid the imperfections it loads upon us, or at least to slow up their progress. I feel that, notwithstanding all my retrenchments, it gains on me foot by foot. I stand fast as well as I can. But I do not know where it will lead even me in the end. In any event, I am glad to have people know whence I shall have fallen.

Miguel de Cervantes Saavedra

1547–1616

"There's one thing I can say to you in passing, that there's nothing so pleasant in the world for an honest man as to be squire to a knight errant, that seeks adventures." So says Sancho Panza to his wife at the end of the first part of the book that bears the knight errant's name. Indeed, this most beloved of novels is a novel of and about the road. Neither epic nor chivalric poem, neither pastoral romance nor picaresque, *Don Quixote* maintains a guarded and ironic distance from all these readily identifiable genres, even as its prologue beckons its *desoccupado lector* or idle reader to travel with Alonso Quixano, alias Don Quixote, and his endlessly talkative squire.

In *Don Quixote,* these are travels in the world of early seventeenth-century Spain: a world from which Jews and then Moors had been banished, where the forces of the Inquisition were ubiquitous and the importance of *limpieza de sangre*—purity of blood—was paramount. This was a world in which Miguel de Cervantes, like his knight errant, may not have been always at

8. Socrates was sentenced to death in 399 B.C.E. on the charge of having corrupted the youth of Athens. As recounted by Plato in the *Apology,* he responded ambiguously to the charges against him rather than pleading for his life as expected.

home. Son of an impoverished doctor, he departed for Italy following a fight when he was twenty-one to serve in the household of a cardinal in Rome. Ten years after his return, he petitioned to work in colonial Latin America (he was told in no uncertain terms to look for something in Spain). Beginning in the early 1580s, Cervantes tried to make a go of the profession of writing, succeeding only with the publication of *Don Quixote* when he was fifty-eight, considerably older than the *hidalgo* who made his fortune. Yet Cervantes and his creation are no direct mirrors for one another. Don Quixote never leaves Spain and can only dream of meaningful military action. Cervantes joined the Spanish army shortly after arriving in Italy, fighting in 1571 in the major battle of Lepanto that annihilated the Turkish fleet and restored Catholic Europe's faith in its military superiority over the Muslims. Five years later, the boat he was taking back to Spain was captured by pirates, and he was sold to a Greek in Algiers, where he remained for several years. Such episodes lie behind "The Captive's Tale" from the first part of the novel, while Cervantes' later experience in Spanish jails no doubt informs the lively chapter on the galley slaves. Nor was Cervantes a gentleman—a member of the lesser nobility that with the accession of Philip III to the throne found itself with less and less to do. One of the most powerful monarchies in Europe, even after the British defeated its naval Armada, the Spanish crown, whimsical enough to move its quarters from Madrid to Valladolid and back again in the space of five years, was also one of the most centralized.

Along with his family and innumerable courtiers, Cervantes moved back and forth with Phillip as well, no doubt hoping to win courtly approval for a government position—he had tried his hand at tax collecting for a number of years—or an occasional commission for a patriotic work, such as his play *The Seige of Numantia.* But it was only with the publication of *Don Quixote* in 1605 that Cervantes came to the attention of his fellow Spaniards and probably his king. The success of Part I was so great (as Cervantes has one fictional enthusiast put it, "Children finger it; young people read it; grown men know it by heart, and old men praise it") that pirated editions of the work began to appear almost immediately, and one Alonso Fernández de Avellaneda was motivated in 1613 to write a sequel. An ailing Cervantes completed a second part that attacks Avellaneda in its preface and has Sancho and Don Quixote laughing at the "inaccurate" sequel. But the jabs at Avellaneda are merely one aspect of the work's self-consciousness regarding its place in a world of "idle readers." In Part 2, published in 1615, just a year before the author's death, Cervantes acknowledges that his character has acquired a history and reputation all his own, and Don Quixote is constantly running into people who have already read about him and who expect him to live up to his reputation. Initially a product of the many books of chivalry he had wasted his patrimony on, Don Quixote becomes, in Part 2, the product of another book: his own. Throughout Part 2, he is forced to confront his own fictionality in a world of "real" people.

Like Jorge Luis Borges and other modernist writers he inspired, Cervantes is fascinated with the madness that ensues when the real and the fictive are confused. *Don Quixote* offers a genealogy of the knight's madness, and in a certain sense provides a requiem to a Renaissance man who thrived on folly. On the one hand, Don Quixote comes from a long line of mad heroes, from Chrètien de Troye's Ivain to the "mad Roland" (*Orlando furioso*) of Ludovico Ariosto's sixteenth-century poem, who goes beserk when he discovers that his beloved Angelica yielded her virginity to a Moorish footsoldier—a drama that Don Quixote sadly realizes he cannot imitate: "For I dare swear that my Dulcinea del Toboso has never seen a real Moor in his real Moorish dress in all her life." But on the other hand, the romances of chivalry, and the chivalric code behind them, had long had a tenuous relationship to reality; as the historian Gerhart Ladner has noted, the knight's only choices are to transcend the world or be destroyed by it. The knight in shining armor from Arthurian legend would find his life's work in pledging eternal fealty to a woman he would never possess and performing great deeds in her name—a model of ideal behavior that few could or would ever want to attain, an idealism marked both by profound Christian faith and by a fiercely sublimated eroticism. While manuals of chivalric behavior were legion after Ramon Lull's best-selling *Book of the Order of Chivalry,* by the seventeenth century, there was little inclination to find in the vestiges of medieval chivalry anything other than entertainment.

For a time, the missionary zeal inspired by the discovery of the Americas, especially among followers of the Spanish Jesuit Loyola, and the new wars with the Turk which Cervantes experienced firsthand had renewed the fervor for the chivalric glories of the past. But this fervor had diminished by the time Cervantes sat down to write his novel. In large part, it is the absence of a community that takes chivalry seriously that renders Cervantes' hero so marginal (a marginality exacerbated, as Borges has wryly remarked, by the name of Don Quixote's village: "Don Quixote de la Mancha, that now has the sound of nobility in Spanish, was intended to sound then as Don Quixote of Kansas City.") At every turn, the knight encounters greed, self-interest, and cold-blooded calculation that are the antitheses of a knight errantry meant "to redress wrongs, aid widows and protect maidens." In his first adventure, in an inn he imagines to be a castle, he finds not a castellan and ladies-in-waiting but a greedy owner, prostitutes, and a laborer who showers Don Quixote with stones. When Don Quixote later seeks solace among shepherds, he launches into a long speech about the pastoral origins of a golden age when men were considerate of their fellow human beings, a speech the goatherds listen to "in fascination and bewilderment." But the knight and his squire will end their sojourn in the supposedly idyllic countryside when they are beaten and bruised by a band of angry rustics defending their mares from the amorous advances of Don Quixote's horse, Rocinante. Shortly thereafter Don Quixote will wade into a flock of sheep and do battle with them thinking they are two powerful armies, and his "tilting at windmills" mistaken for giants has become proverbial for foolish enthusiasm.

Cervantes nonetheless complicates this repeated juxtaposition of Don Quixote's version of events and the way they "really" are, particularly in regard to the characters with whom the knight has most sustained contact. On occasion, Don Quixote's madness brings out the good in others, as he evokes their sympathy and enables them to express a compassion to which they are unaccustomed. The innkeeper doesn't demand payment from the injured knight, and the laborer who takes Don Quixote back to La Mancha after his first round of adventures "waits till it was rather darker [to ride into the village], so that no one should see the battered gentleman on so shameful a mount." Far more than sympathy is exacted from Sancho Panza, who initially rides off with Don Quixote for purely mercenary motives—he wants to govern the island promised him as reward for his patient services—but who becomes seduced by the profound pleasures of the life of knight-errantry: it is clearly a life more exciting, more meaningful, than his sedentary life in the village. Between him and Don Quixote grows a bond fashioned from sharing intimate moments, ranging from their lengthy discourses in the lonely Sierra Morena, to their vomiting over one another after the episode of the sheep.

At the same time, Sancho Panza becomes adept at learning Don Quixote's language and at exploiting it, as when he claims that a peasant girl he met on the road was an enchanted Dulcinea. Yet there are far more subtle ways in which Don Quixote's companions are influenced by his vision of the world—a world where "every man is the child of his works" and one has faith in things not seen. While Don Quixote's madness is surely ridiculous, and his naive belief in the old chivalric stories is condemned, the reader is often led to the same query posed by two gentlemen with whom Don Quixote dines late in Part 2: "One moment they thought him a man of sense, and the next he slipped into craziness; nor could they decide what degree to assign him between wisdom and folly."

Where Cervantes himself stands in relationship to his hero is a puzzle. This is in part because of the playful distance he placed between himself and Don Quixote's story. The story after Chapter 10 comes to us from a Moorish enchanter named Cide Hamete Benengeli and is translated by a Moor the author meets in the marketplace. But since "men of that [Arabic] nation [are] ready liars," neither the history itself nor the translation can be trusted. Moreover,

Gustave Doré, engraving for Cervantes' *Don Quixote.* Doré was a prominent sculptor and painter in mid-nineteenth-century France, but he is best remembered for his illustrations for literary masterpieces such as Rabelais's works, *Paradise Lost* and Dante's *Inferno* (with many a gruesome punishment vividly displayed for the reader's entertainment). *Don Quixote* attracted Doré's attention as well, and in 1862—two years before publishing an illustrated Bible—the artist gave the world arresting images such as this one, showing Don Quixote's collision with a windmill, while a frantic Sancho Panza yells from afar.

as Cervantes matures as a writer, Don Quixote tends to slip from our sight. He is very much the focus of Part 1, save for the story of "The Captive's Tale." But in Part 2, other characters take center stage for extended periods of time, as the university student Sansón Carrasco and a seemingly sadistic duke and duchess increasingly manipulate the book's events. Perhaps the novel must inevitably prepare for the moment when the world which Don Quixote had made so colorful must go on without him: Alonxo Quixano may be unable to survive the destruction of his fantasy, but others must continue in its absence.

Cervantes himself, though, did not live long after the publication of Part 2. A flurry of literary activity in his last few years had led him to write his *Exemplary Novels* (1613), a collection of short stories that subverts the genre of the picaresque, and he then wrote an ambitious romance, *Persiles and Sigismunda,* published posthumously. But Cide Hamete's observation at the close of his manuscript, "For me alone Don Quixote was born and I for him," may be true for Cervantes himself. Perhaps the great irony of this work by one of the master ironists of all time is that Don Quixote is a victim of the fictions he has read; yet it is he who, along with his faithful servant, is the most compelling and immediate of the novel's characters. He is the one most likely to pull us as readers—and perhaps Cervantes as author—into the dangerous new world of the novel, as refracted through the endearingly mad habitations of his mind.

PRONUNCIATIONS:

Cide Hamete Benengeli: SEE-day ha-MEE-tay ben-en-HEL-lee
Don Jerónimo: DON hay-RO-nee-mo
Don Quixote: DON kee-HO-tay
Dulcinea: dole-see-NAY-ah
Gines de Pasamonte: he-NACE day pahs-ah-MON-tay
Rocinante: ro-see-NAN-tay
Roque Guinart: RO-kay gee-NAR
Quejana: kay-HAN-na
Quesada: kay-SAH-da

DON QUIXOTE[1]

Part 1

Chapter 1

CONCERNING THE FAMOUS HIDALGO[2] DON QUIXOTE DE LA MANCHA'S POSITION, CHARACTER AND WAY OF LIFE

In a village in La Mancha, the name of which I cannot quite recall,[3] there lived not long ago one of those country gentlemen or hidalgos who keep a lance in a rack, an ancient leather shield, a scrawny hack and a greyhound for coursing. A midday stew with rather more shin of beef than leg of lamb, the leftovers for supper most nights, lardy eggs on Saturdays, lentil broth on Fridays and an occasional pigeon as a Sunday treat ate up three-quarters of his income. The rest went on a cape of black broadcloth, with breeches of velvet and slippers to match for holy days, and on weekdays he walked proudly in the finest homespun. He maintained a housekeeper the wrong side of forty, a niece the right side of twenty and a jack of all trades who was as good at saddling the nag as at plying the pruning shears. Our hidalgo himself was nearly fifty; he had a robust constitution, dried-up flesh and a withered face, and he was an early riser and a keen huntsman. His surname's said to have been Quixada, or Quesada (as if he were a jawbone, or a cheesecake):[4] concerning this detail there's some discrepancy among the authors who have written on the subject, although a credible conjecture does suggest he might have been a plaintive Quexana. But this doesn't matter much, as far as our story's concerned, provided that the narrator doesn't stray one inch from the truth.

Now you must understand that during his idle moments (which accounted for most of the year) this hidalgo took to reading books of chivalry with such relish and enthusiasm that he almost forgot about his hunting and even running his property, and his foolish curiosity reached such extremes that he sold acres of arable land to buy these books of chivalry, and took home as many of them as he could find; he liked none of them so much as those by the famous Feliciano de Silva,[5] because the brilliance of the prose and all that intricate language seemed a treasure to him, never

1. Translated by John Rutherford.
2. *Hidalgo* literally means a person "of some distinction," a member of the lowest rung of the nobility who would have been exempt from taxation. Don Quixote is neither a *don* nor a knight or *caballero,* who would have had jurisdiction over land.
3. La Mancha is an arid region of Castile in south-central Spain, not far from the major cities of Toledo and Madrid.
4. A *quixote* is a piece of armor, a far cry from the comic images suggested by the variants of his name (a *quijado* is a jawbone; *queso* is cheese).
5. A 16th-century writer of the chivalric romances that had been vastly popular in Spain.

more so than when he was reading those amorous compliments and challenges delivered by letter, in which he often found: "The reason for the unreason to which my reason is subjected, so weakens my reason that I have reason to complain of your beauty." And also when he read: ". . . the lofty heavens which with their stars divinely fortify you in your divinity, and make you meritorious of the merits merited by your greatness." Such subtleties used to drive the poor gentleman to distraction, and he would rack his brains trying to understand it all and unravel its meaning, something that Aristotle himself wouldn't have been capable of doing even if he'd come back to life for this purpose alone. He wasn't very happy about the wounds that Sir Belianis kept on inflicting and receiving, because he imagined that, however skilful the doctors who treated him, his face and body must have been covered with gashes and scars. But, in spite of all that, he commended the author for ending his book with that promise of endless adventure, and often felt the urge to take up his quill and bring the story to a proper conclusion, as is promised there; and no doubt he'd have done so, and with success too, if other more important and insistent preoccupations hadn't prevented him. He had frequent arguments with the village priest (a learned man—a Sigüenza graduate no less) about which had been the better knight errant, Palmerin of England or Amadis of Gaul;[6] but Master Nicolás, the village barber, argued that neither of them could hold a candle to the Knight of Phoebus, and that if anyone at all could be compared to him it was Don Galaor, Amadis of Gaul's brother, because there was no emergency he couldn't cope with: he wasn't one of your pernickety knights, nor was he such a blubberer as his brother, and he was every bit his equal as far as courage was concerned.

In short, our hidalgo was soon so absorbed in these books that his nights were spent reading from dusk till dawn, and his days from dawn till dusk, until the lack of sleep and the excess of reading withered his brain, and he went mad. Everything he read in his books took possession of his imagination: enchantments, fights, battles, challenges, wounds, sweet nothings, love affairs, storms and impossible absurdities. The idea that this whole fabric of famous fabrications was real so established itself in his mind that no history in the world was truer for him. He would declare that El Cid, Ruy Díaz, had been an excellent knight, but that he couldn't be compared to the Knight of the Burning Sword,[7] who with just one back-stroke had split two fierce and enormous giants clean down the middle. He felt happier about Bernardo del Carpio, because he'd slain Roland the Enchanted at Roncesvalles, by the same method used by Hercules when he suffocated Antaeus, the son of Earth—with a bear-hug.[8] He was full of praise for the giant Morgante[9] because, despite belonging to a proud and insolent breed, he alone was affable and well-mannered. But his greatest favourite was Reynald of Montalban, most of all when he saw him sallying forth from his castle and plundering all those he met, and when in foreign parts he stole that image of

6. A third-rate university was to be found at Sigüenza, a town northwest of Madrid. Palmerin of England was the protagonist of a Portuguese chivalric romance, Amadis of Gaul that of Spain's most famous romance, *Amadís de Gaula,* written by Garci Rodríguez de Montalvo in 1508. Montalvo combined battle scenes with those of courtly love, and ended his work with the rather unusual flourish of a marriage.

7. The Cid was the hero of *The Poem of the Cid,* the first epic poem written in Spain; he was noted for his deeds against the Moors. The Knight of the Burning Sword is a character in one of Feliciano de Silva's romances, *The Ninth Book of Amadis of Gaul* (1530).

8. The Castilian warrior Bernardo del Carpio appears in mid–16th-century Spanish works as the defeater of Roland, Charlemagne's most powerful knight. He quickly attained the status of Spain's national hero. Antaeus derived his strength from his contact with "mother" Earth; Hercules lifted him up until he became weak, then killed him.

9. The genial giant of Luigi Pulci's late 15th-century mock-epic poem, *Morgante Maggiore.*

Muhammad made of solid gold, as his history records.[1] He'd have given his housekeeper, and even his niece into the bargain, to trample the traitor Ganelon in the dust.[2]

And so, by now quite insane, he conceived the strangest notion that ever took shape in a madman's head, considering it desirable and necessary, both for the increase of his honour and for the common good, to become a knight errant, and to travel about the world with his armour and his arms and his horse in search of adventures, and to practise all those activities that he knew from his books were practised by knights errant, redressing all kinds of grievances, and exposing himself to perils and dangers that he would overcome and thus gain eternal fame and renown. The poor man could already see himself being crowned Emperor of Trebizond,[3] at the very least, through the might of his arm; and so, possessed by these delightful thoughts and carried away by the strange pleasure that he derived from them, he hastened to put into practice what he so desired.

His first step was to clean a suit of armour that had belonged to his forefathers and that, covered in rust and mould, had been standing forgotten in a corner for centuries. He scoured and mended it as best he could; yet he realized that it had one important defect, which was that the headpiece was not a complete helmet but just a simple steel cap; he was ingenious enough, however, to overcome this problem, constructing out of cardboard something resembling a visor and face-guard which, once inserted into the steel cap, gave it the appearance of a full helmet. It's true that, to test its strength and find out whether it could safely be exposed to attack, he drew his sword and dealt it two blows, with the first of which he destroyed in a second what it had taken him a week to create. He couldn't help being concerned about the ease with which he'd shattered it, and to guard against this danger he reconstructed it, fixing some iron bars on the inside, which reassured him about its strength; and, preferring not to carry out any further tests, he deemed and pronounced it a most excellent visored helmet.

Then he went to visit his nag, and although it had more corns than a barleyfield and more wrong with it than Gonella's horse, which *tantum pellis et ossa fuit,* it seemed to him that neither Alexander's Bucephalus nor the Cid's Babieca was its equal.[4] He spent four days considering what name to give the nag; for (he told himself) it wasn't fitting that the horse of such a famous knight errant, and such a fine horse in its own right, too, shouldn't have some name of eminence; and so he tried to find one that would express both what it had been before it became a knight's horse and what it was now, for it was appropriate that, since its master had changed his rank, it too should change its name, and acquire a famous and much-trumpeted one, as suited the new order and new way of life he professed. And so, after a long succession of names that he invented, eliminated and struck out, added, deleted and remade in his mind and in his imagination, he finally decided to call it *Rocinante,* that is, *Hackafore,* a name which, in his opinion, was lofty and sonorous and expressed what the creature had been when it was a humble hack, before it became what it was now—the first and foremost of all the hacks in the world.

1. Reynald (Rinaldo) appears in the two major chivalric romances of the Italian Renaissance, Boiardo's *Orlando Innamorato* (Orlando [Roland] in love) and Ludovico Ariosto's *Orlando furioso* (Mad Orlando).

2. In the original *Song of Roland,* the jealous Ganelon betrays Charlemagne and Roland to the Moors and causes the army's defeat at Roncesvalles.

3. A region of the Byzantine empire; the name was used broadly for Asiatic Turkey.

4. Pietro Gonella was a famous jester in Ferrara. The Latin phrase means "all skin and bone." The wild horse Bucephalus was tamed by the young Alexander, who then rode him during his conquests of India and the East, while Babieca was the Cid's famous steed.

Having given his horse a name, and one so much to his liking, he decided to give himself a name as well, and this problem kept him busy for another eight days, at the end of which he decided to call himself *Don Quixote,* that is, *Sir Thighpiece,* from which, as has already been observed, the authors of this most true history concluded that his surname must have been Quixada, and not Quesada as others had affirmed. Yet remembering that brave Amadis hadn't been content to call himself Amadis alone, but had added the name of his kingdom and homeland, to make it famous, and had styled himself Amadis of Gaul, so Don Quixote, as a worthy knight, decided to add his own country to his name and call himself *Don Quixote de la Mancha,* by doing which, in his opinion, he declared in a most vivid manner both his lineage and his homeland, and honoured the latter by taking it as his surname.

Having, then, cleaned his armour, turned his steel cap into a visored helmet, baptized his nag and confirmed himself, he realized that the only remaining task was to find a lady of whom he could be enamoured; for a knight errant without a lady-love is a tree without leaves or fruit, a body without a soul. He said to himself:

"If, for my wicked sins or my good fortune, I encounter some giant, as knights errant usually do, and I dash him down in single combat, or cleave him asunder, or, in short, defeat and vanquish him, will it not be proper to have someone to whom I can send him as a tribute, so that he can come before my sweet lady and fall to his knees and say in humble tones of submission: 'I, my lady, am the giant Caraculiambro, the Lord of the Isle of Malindrania,[5] vanquished in single combat by the never sufficiently praised knight Don Quixote de la Mancha, who has commanded me to present myself before Your Highness so that Your Highness may dispose of me as you will'"?

Oh my, how our worthy knight rejoiced once he'd spoken these words—even more, once he'd found someone he could call his lady! The fact was—or so it is generally believed—that in a nearby village there lived a good-looking peasant girl, with whom he'd once been in love (although it appears that she was never aware of this love, about which he never told her). She was called Aldonza Lorenzo, and this was the woman upon whom it seemed appropriate to confer the title of the lady of his thoughts; and seeking a name with some affinity with his own, which would also suggest the name of a princess and a fine lady, he decided to call her *Dulcinea del Toboso,* because she was a native of El Toboso: a name that, in his opinion, was musical and magical and meaningful, like all the other names he'd bestowed upon himself and his possessions.

Chapter 2

Concerning the ingenious Don Quixote's first sally

Once he'd made these preparations he decided not to wait any longer before putting his plans into action, encouraged by the need that he believed his delay was creating in the world: so great was his determination to redress grievances, right wrongs, correct injustices, rectify abuses and fulfil obligations. And so, without telling anyone about his plans or being seen by anyone, one morning, before dawn because it was going to be one of those sweltering July days, he donned his armour, mounted Rocinante, with his ill-devised visor in place, took up his leather shield, seized his lance

5. An imaginary island; the giant's name translates roughly as "face of an ass."

and rode out into the fields through the side-door in a yard wall, in raptures of joy on seeing how easy it had been to embark upon his noble enterprise. But no sooner was he outside the door than he was assailed by a terrible thought, which almost made him abandon his undertaking: he remembered that he hadn't been knighted and by the laws of chivalry shouldn't and indeed couldn't take up arms against any knight; and that even if he had been knighted, he would, as a novice, have been obliged to bear white arms, that is to say a shield without any insignia on it, until he'd won them by his own prowess. These thoughts made him waver in his plans; but, since his madness prevailed over all other considerations, he decided to have himself knighted by the first person he chanced upon, in imitation of many others who'd done the same, as he'd read in the books that had reduced him to this state. As for the white arms, he resolved to give his lance and his armour such a scouring, as soon as an opportunity arose, as to make them cleaner and whiter than ermine; and thus he calmed down and continued on his chosen way, which in reality was none other than the way his horse chose to follow, for he believed that in this consisted the essence of adventure.

As our fledgling adventurer rode along, he said to himself:

"Who can doubt but that in future times, when the true history of my famous deeds sees the light, the sage who chronicles them will, when he recounts this my first sally, so early in the morning, write in this manner: 'Scarce had ruddy Apollo spread over the face of the wide and spacious earth the golden tresses of his beauteous hair, and scarce had the speckled little birds with their harmonious tongues hailed in musical and mellifluous melody the approach of rosy Aurora who, rising from her jealous husband's soft couch, disclosed herself to mortals in the portals and balconies of La Mancha's horizon, when the famous knight Don Quixote de la Mancha, quitting the slothful feathers of his bed, mounted his famous steed Rocinante and began to ride over the ancient and far-famed Plain of Montiel'"?[1]

And it was true that this was where he was riding. And he added:

"Happy will be the age, the century will be happy, which brings to light my famous exploits, worthy to be engraved on sheets of bronze, carved on slabs of marble and painted on boards of wood as a monument for all posterity. O sage enchanter, whomsoever you may be, to whom it falls to be the chronicler of this singular history, I beg you not to overlook my good Rocinante, my eternal companion in all my travels and wanderings."

Then he turned and said, as if he really were in love:

"O Princess Dulcinea, mistress of this hapless heart! Great injury have you done me in reproaching and dismissing me, with the cruel command not to appear in the presence of your wondrous beauty. Vouchsafe, my lady, to be mindful of this your subject heart, which suffers such sorrow for love of you."

He strung these absurdities together with many others, all in the style of those that he'd learned from his books. This made his progress so slow, and the sun was rising so fast and becoming so hot, that his brains would have melted, if he'd had any.

He rode on almost throughout that day and nothing happened worth mentioning, which reduced him to despair because he was longing for an early encounter with someone on whom he could test the worth of his mighty arm. Some authors say that the first adventure that befell him was that of the Pass of Lápice, others claim that it was that of the windmills, but what I've been able to discover about this matter, and

1. Site of a major battle in 1369.

indeed what I've found recorded in the annals of La Mancha, is that he rode on throughout that day, and that at nightfall both he and his nag were exhausted and half dead from starvation; and that, looking all around to see if he could spot some castle or shepherds' hut where they might retire and find some remedy for their great hunger and dire want, he caught sight of an inn not far from the road along which he was travelling, which was as if he had seen a star leading him not just to the portals but to the very palace of his redemption. He quickened his pace, and he reached the inn as night was falling.

Sitting by the inn door there happened to be two young women, of the sort known as ladies of easy virtue, on their way to Seville with some muleteers who'd chanced to break their journey that night at the inn. And since whatever our adventurer thought, saw or imagined seemed to him to be as it was in the books he'd read, as soon as he saw the inn he took it for a castle with its four towers and their spires of shining silver, complete with its drawbridge and its deep moat and all the other accessories that such castles commonly boast. He approached the inn that he took for a castle, and at a short distance from it he drew rein, waiting for some dwarf to appear upon the battlements and announce with a trumpet-blast the arrival of a knight. But finding that there was some delay, and that Rocinante was impatient to get to the stable, he rode on towards the inn door and saw the two dissolute wenches sitting there, and thought that they were two beautiful maidens or fine ladies taking their ease at the castle gate. At this point a swineherd who was gathering together some pigs (begging nobody's pardon, because that's what they're called) from a stubble field happened to sound his horn to round them up, and Don Quixote thought that his wish had been fulfilled and that a dwarf was announcing his arrival; so it was with unusual satisfaction that he reached the inn and the ladies, who, on observing the approach of a man dressed like that in armour and clutching a lance and a leather shield, started to run in terror back into the inn. But Don Quixote, conjecturing their fear from their flight, and raising his card-board visor to reveal his dry and dusty face, addressed them with courteous demeanour and tranquil voice:

"Flee not, nor fear the least affront; for in the order of knighthood which I profess it neither belongs nor behoves to offer any such, much less to high-born maidens, as your presence testifies you to be."

The girls had been peering at him and trying to make out his face, hidden behind the ill-made visor; but when they heard themselves called maidens, a term so much at odds with their profession, they couldn't contain their laughter, which was so hearty that Don Quixote flared up and exclaimed:

"Moderation befits the fair; furthermore, laughter which springs from a petty cause is a great folly; but I say this unto you not to grieve you nor yet to sour your disposition; for mine is none other than to serve you."

This language, which the ladies didn't understand, together with the sorry figure cut by the knight, only redoubled their laughter and his wrath, and things would have come to a pretty pass if it hadn't been for the appearance at that moment of the innkeeper, a man who, being very fat, was very peaceable, and who on seeing such an ungainly figure, with such ill-matched equipment as the long stirrups, the lance, the leather shield and the infantryman's body-armour, was more than willing to join the maidens in their merry-making. But he was also intimidated by all these paraphernalia and, deciding to address the knight in a civil manner, he said:

"If, sir caballero, you're looking for somewhere to stay the night, you'll find plenty of everything you need here—all except a bed that is, we haven't got any of those."

Don Quixote, observing the humility of the governor of the castle, for they were what he took the innkeeper and the inn to be, replied:

"For me, sir castellano,[2] anything will suffice, because
My arms are my bed-hangings,
And my rest's the bloody fray."[3]

The host thought that Don Quixote had called him castellano because he'd taken him for one of the Castilian conmen, whereas in reality he was an Andalusian, a prime picaroon from the Playa district of Sanlúcar, no less a thief than Cacus,[4] and no less an evildoer than any experienced page-boy, and he replied:

"In that case,

Your bed must be the hard, hard rock,
And your sleep to watch till day

—and that being so, you go ahead and dismount in the certainty of finding in this humble abode plenty of opportunities not to sleep for a whole year, let alone one night."

And with these words he went and held Don Quixote's stirrup, and the knight dismounted with the greatest difficulty, not having broken his fast all day long.

He then instructed the innkeeper to take great care of his horse, for a finer steed had never eaten barley. The innkeeper looked at the animal, which didn't seem half as good as Don Quixote had claimed, and, after housing it in the stable, went back to receive orders from his guest, whom the maidens, now reconciled, were helping out of his armour. Although they'd taken off his breast and back plates, they couldn't fathom how to disengage his gorget or remove his imitation visor, tied on with green ribbons that would have to be cut, since it was impossible to undo the knots; but he would by no means consent to this, and kept his helmet on all night, making the funniest and strangest figure imaginable. As these trollops unarmed him, he, thinking they were illustrious ladies of the castle, wittily declaimed:

"And never sure was any knight
So served by damsel or by dame
As Quixote was, one happy night
When from his village first he came:
Maids waited on that man of might,
Princesses on his steed, whose name . . .

is Rocinante, good ladies, and mine is Don Quixote de la Mancha; for although I had intended not to discover myself until the deeds done for your benefit and service should have made me known, yet the necessity to accommodate this ancient ballad of Sir Lancelot[5] to our present purpose has been the occasion of your knowing my name ere it were meet; but a time will come when you will command and I shall obey, and when the might of this arm will manifest the desire I have to serve you."

The girls, who weren't used to such rhetorical flourishes, didn't answer, but just asked if he'd like a bite to eat.

"I would fain eat anything," replied Don Quixote, "for, by my troth, much good would it do me."

2. Governor or constable of a castle.
3. The lines are from a well-known Spanish ballad.
4. The Playa district was an area of thieves and swindlers, while in Roman legend the brigand Cacus is said to have stolen the cattle of Hercules.
5. One of King Arthur's knights; Don Quixote has just altered the words to a popular ballad about him.

It happened to be a Friday, so there was no food in the inn except a few helpings of what is known in Castile as *abadejo,* in Andalusia as *bacallao* and in other parts of Spain as *curadillo*—in other words the humble salt cod; but in these parts it was strangely called *truchuela.* They asked him if he'd like some of this troutling, because that was all the fish there was.

"If you have a goodly number of troutlings," replied Don Quixote, "they will serve me as well as a trout, because it makes no difference to me whether I am given eight separate reals or a single piece of eight. What is more, it might even be that these troutlings are like veal, which is better than beef, or like kid, which is better than goat. But whatever this fish is, let it be served; for the travails and the burden of arms cannot be borne on an empty stomach."

A table was set at the door of the inn, where it was cooler, and the innkeeper brought a dish of inadequately soaked and worse cooked salt cod, and a loaf of bread as black and mouldy as the hidalgo's armour; and it was a source of great mirth to watch him eat because, since he was wearing his helmet and holding up the visor, he couldn't put any food into his mouth with his own hands, and somebody else had to do so for him, a task performed by one of the ladies. But when they tried to give him some drink, they found this an impossible task, and he wouldn't have drunk a drop if the innkeeper hadn't bored a hole through a length of cane and put one end into his mouth and poured the wine into the other; and Don Quixote suffered it all with great patience, so as not to allow his helmet-ribbons to be cut. In the midst of these activities a sow-gelder happened to arrive at the inn, and as he did so he sounded his pan-pipes four or five times, which convinced Don Quixote that he was indeed in some famous castle, and that he was being served to the accompaniment of music, and that the salt cod was trout, the bread baked from the whitest wheat-flour, the prostitutes fine ladies and the innkeeper the lord of the castle; and it all confirmed that his decision to sally forth had been a wise one. Yet what most bothered him was that he hadn't yet been knighted, because he knew that he couldn't lawfully embark on any adventure without first having been admitted to the order of chivalry.

Chapter 3

Which relates the amusing way in which Don Quixote had himself knighted

And so, troubled by this thought, Don Quixote made short work of his meagre lodging-house supper, and then called for the innkeeper and, shutting himself up with him in the stable, fell upon his knees before him and said:

"I shall ne'er, O valorous knight, arise from where I kneel, until your courtesy vouchsafes me a boon which I desire to beg of you and which will redound to your own praise and to the benefit of humankind."

The innkeeper, seeing his guest at his feet and hearing such pleadings, gazed down at him in perplexity, not knowing what to do or say, and kept telling him to stand up; but he kept refusing, and the innkeeper had to promise to grant his request.

"No less did I expect from your munificence, sir," replied Don Quixote. "Know therefore that the boon which I have begged and which your liberality has vouchsafed me is that tomorrow you shall knight me; and tonight, in the chapel of this your castle, I will keep the vigil of arms; and tomorrow, as I have said, what I so desire shall be accomplished, so that I can legitimately roam through the four corners of the world in quest of adventures for the relief of the needy, as is the duty of chivalry and of knights errant such as I, whose desire towards such exploits is inclined."

The innkeeper, who, as I've said, was something of a wag, and had already suspected that his guest wasn't in his right mind, found his suspicion confirmed when he heard these words and, to have something to laugh at that night, decided to humour him; so he said that he was quite right to pursue these objectives, and that such desires were natural and fitting in such a knight as he seemed to be and as his gallant presence testified; and that he himself in his younger days had followed the same honourable profession, roaming through different parts of the world in search of adventure, without omitting to visit such districts as Percheles and Islas de Riarán in Malaga, Compás in Seville, Azoguejo in Segovia, Olivera in Valencia, Rondilla in Granada, Playa in Sanlúcar, Potro in Cordova and Ventillas in Toledo,[1] and many other places where he'd exercised the dexterity of his hands and the nimbleness of his heels, doing many injuries, wooing many widows, ruining a few maidens and swindling a few orphans, and, in short, making himself known in most of the law courts and tribunals in Spain; and that he'd finally retired to his castle, where he lived on his own means and on those of others, accommodating all knights errant, whatever their status or position, solely because of the great affection he felt for them and so that they could share their wealth with him, to repay him for his kindness.

He also told Don Quixote that in his castle there wasn't any chapel where he could keep the vigil of arms, because it had been demolished to build a new one, but he knew that in case of need vigil might be kept anywhere, and Don Quixote could do so that night in a courtyard within the castle; and in the morning, God willing, the proper ceremonies would be performed to make him into a knight, so very thoroughly that no knight in the whole wide world could be more of a knight than he.

He asked Don Quixote if he had any money on him; Don Quixote replied that he did not have so much as a single real,[2] because he had never read in histories of knights errant that any of them had ever carried money. To this the innkeeper retorted that he was deluding himself—even if it wasn't written in the histories, because their authors had considered that there wasn't any need to record something as obviously necessary as money or clean shirts, that wasn't any reason to believe that they'd travelled without supplies of both; so he could take it as true and proven that all knights errant, of which so many books are full to overflowing, kept their purses well lined in readiness for any eventuality, and that they also carried shirts and small chests full of ointments for curing the wounds they received; because there wasn't always someone available to treat them in every field or desert where they engaged in combat and were injured, unless they had some wise enchanter for a friend, and he came to their aid, summoning through the air, on some cloud, a damsel or a dwarf with a flask of water of such magical properties that, on tasting just one drop, they were instantly cured of their wounds and injuries, as if they'd never been hurt. But, just in case this didn't happen, the knights of old had considered it wise to see that their squires were provided with money and other necessities such as lint and ointments to dress their wounds; and if any such knight happened not to have a squire (a most unusual occurrence), he himself would carry all these supplies in small saddle-bags that were scarcely visible, on the crupper of his steed, as if they were something else of much

1. All notorious lowlife districts in some of Spain's major cities.

2. A coin worth about five cents.

greater importance because, except in such circumstances, carrying saddle-bags was rather frowned upon among knights errant; and the innkeeper therefore advised Don Quixote—although he could, if he wished, command him as the godson that he was about to become—never again to travel without money and all the other supplies just mentioned, and he'd discover when he least expected it how useful they could be.

Don Quixote promised to do exactly as he'd been told, and then he was given orders to keep the vigil of arms in a large yard on one side of the inn; and he gathered his armour together and placed it on a water-trough next to a well, and, taking up his leather shield and seizing his lance, he began with stately bearing to pace back and forth in front of the trough; and as his pacing began, night was beginning to fall.

The innkeeper told everyone in the hostelry about his guest's insanity, his vigil and the knighting that he awaited. They wondered at such a strange kind of madness and went to watch him from a distance, and saw that, with a composed air, he sometimes paced to and fro and, at other times, leaning on his lance, gazed at his armour without looking away for some while. Night fell, but the moon was so bright that it competed with the source of its brightness, and every action of the novice knight could be clearly observed by all. And now one of the muleteers staying at the inn decided to water his animals, and to do so he had to remove from the trough the armour placed there by Don Quixote, who, on seeing him approach, cried out:

"O rash knight, whomsoever you may be, coming to lay hands on the armour of the most valiant knight errant who ever girded sword! Take care what you do, and touch it not, unless you wish to pay with your life for your temerity."

The muleteer wouldn't toe the line (it would have been better for the rest of his anatomy if he had); instead, grasping the armour by its straps, he hurled it to one side. When Don Quixote saw this, he raised his eyes to heaven and, fixing his thoughts, as it seemed, on his lady Dulcinea, he said:

"Assist me, dear lady, in this first affront suffered by this breast that is enthralled to you; let not your favour and your succour abandon me in this first moment of peril."

And with these and other similar words he dropped his leather shield, raised his lance with both hands, and dealt the muleteer so powerful a blow to the head that he fell on the ground in such a sorry state that had it been followed by another blow he wouldn't have needed a doctor to treat him. Then Don Quixote replaced his armour and continued pacing to and fro with the same composure as before. After a while another muleteer, not knowing what had happened (because the first one still lay stunned), also came to water his animals and, as he went to remove the armour from the trough, Don Quixote, without uttering a word or asking anybody for her favour, again dropped his leather shield and raised his lance, and didn't break it over the second muleteer's head but rather broke the head, into more than three pieces, because he criss-crossed it with two blows. All the people in the hostelry came running at the noise, the innkeeper among them. When Don Quixote saw them, he took up his leather shield and, with one hand on his sword, declared:

"O beauteous lady, strength and vigour of my enfeebled heart! Now is the time for you to turn the eyes of your greatness towards this your hapless knight, on the brink of so mighty an adventure."

With this he felt so inspirited that if all the muleteers in the world had attacked him he wouldn't have retreated one inch. The wounded men's companions, seeing them in such a state, began to rain stones on Don Quixote, who fended them off with his leather shield as best he could, unwilling to move away from the water-trough and leave his armour unprotected. The innkeeper was yelling at them to let him be—he'd already told them he was a madman, and as such would go scot-free even if he killed the lot of them. Don Quixote was shouting too, even louder, calling them perfidious traitors and the lord of the castle a poltroon and a base-born knight, who allowed knights errant to be treated in such a way and who, if he had been admitted to the order of chivalry, would have been made to regret his treachery:

"But to you, vile and base rabble, I pay no heed; stone me, come, draw near, assail me as best you can, for you will soon see how you are made to pay for your folly and your insolence."

He spoke with such vehemence and spirit that he struck fear into his assailants; and this, together with the innkeeper's arguments, persuaded them to stop, and he allowed them to remove the wounded, and continued keeping the vigil of arms, with the same composure as before.

The innkeeper wasn't amused by his guest's capers, and decided to put an end to them by giving him his wretched order of chivalry before any further calamities occurred. And so he approached him and apologized for the insolent behaviour of that rabble, about which he'd known nothing; but they had been properly punished for their impudence. He said that, as he'd mentioned before, there wasn't any chapel in the castle, and in any case there wasn't any need of one for what was left to be done; because the essence of being knighted lay in the cuff on the neck and the touch on the shoulder, according to his information about the ceremonial of the order, and all of that could be done in the middle of a field if necessary, and his guest had already fulfilled the bit about keeping the vigil of arms, because two hours of it were quite enough, and he'd been at it for over four. Don Quixote believed every word; he was there ready to obey him, and could he please expedite the process as much as possible, for if he were to be attacked again, after having been knighted, he did not intend to leave a single soul alive in the castle except those whom its lord commanded be spared and whom, out of respect for him, he would not harm.

The castellan, thus forewarned and now even more concerned, hurried away to fetch a ledger in which he kept the muleteers' accounts for straw and barley and, accompanied by a lad carrying a candle-end and by the two maidens, he came back to Don Quixote and ordered him to kneel; and, after reading for a while from his ledger, as if reciting some devout prayer, he raised his hand and cuffed him on the neck and then, with Don Quixote's own sword, gave him a handsome thwack on the shoulder, all the while muttering as if praying. And then he commanded one of the maidens to gird on the novice knight's sword, a task performed with much grace and discretion, with which she needed to be well provided so as not to burst out laughing at each stage of the ceremony; but the exploits that they'd watched him perform kept their laughter in check. As the good lady girded on his sword, she said:

"May God make you a most fortunate knight and give you good fortune in your battles."

Don Quixote asked what was her name, so that he should thenceforth know to whom he was indebted for the favour received, because he intended to bestow upon her a share of the honour he was to win by the might of his arm. She humbly replied that her name was La Tolosa, and that she was the daughter of a cobbler from Toledo who lived near the Sancho Bienaya market stalls, and that wherever she was she'd serve him and regard him as her lord. Don Quixote replied that, for his sake and as a favour to him, she should thenceforth take the title of a lady, and call herself Doña Tolosa. She promised to do so, and the other maiden buckled on his spurs; there ensued almost exactly the same dialogue as with the lady of the sword. He asked what was her name, she said it was La Molinera, because she was the daughter of an honourable miller from Antoquera, and Don Quixote also asked her to take a title, and call herself Doña Molinera, and offered her further services and favours.

Now that these unprecedented ceremonies had been performed, at top speed, Don Quixote couldn't wait to be on horseback sallying forth in search of adventures, and he saddled and mounted Rocinante and, having embraced his host, made such extraordinary statements as he thanked him for the favour of dubbing him knight that it would be impossible to do them justice in writing. The innkeeper, concerned only to be rid of his guest, replied to his rhetoric in no less high-flown although somewhat briefer terms, and was so delighted to see the back of the man that he didn't demand any payment for his stay at the inn.

Chapter 4

About what happened to our knight when he left the inn

It must have been about daybreak when Don Quixote left the inn, so happy, so gallant, so delighted at being a properly dubbed knight that the very girths of his horse were bursting with his joy. But remembering his host's advice about the essential supplies that he should take with him, and in particular money and shirts, he decided to return home and equip himself with them and with a squire, resolving to take into his service a neighbour, a poor farmer who had a large family but was well suited to the squirely office. With this in mind he turned Rocinante towards his home village, and the nag, half sensing its old haunts, began to trot with such zest that its hooves seemed not to touch the ground.

He hadn't gone far when he thought he could hear, coming from a dense wood on his right, faint sounds as of someone moaning, and he said:

"I thank heaven for the favour it now grants me, providing me with such an early opportunity to fulfil the duties of my profession and gather the fruit of my honourable intentions. These cries come, no doubt, from some man or woman in distress, who stands in need of my protection and assistance."

He turned right and rode over to where he thought the sounds were coming from. A few steps into the wood he saw a mare tied by the reins to an evergreen oak, and tied to another a lad of about fifteen, naked from the waist up, and this was the one who was crying out, not without reason, because a burly farmer was flogging him with a leather belt, accompanying each blow with a word of reproof and advice:

"Keep your mouth shut and your eyes open."

And the lad replied:

"I won't do it again, sir, by Christ who died on the Cross I swear I won't, I promise that from now on I'll take more care of the flock."

When Don Quixote saw what was happening, he fired up and said:

"Discourteous knight: it ill becomes you to assault one who cannot defend himself; mount your steed and take up your lance," (for the man also had a lance leaning up against the oak to which his mare was tethered) "and I shall force you to recognize that your actions are those of a coward."

The farmer, seeing such a figure bearing down on him, encased in armour and brandishing a lance under his nose, gave himself up for dead and meekly replied:

"This lad I'm punishing, sir knight, is one of my servants, and his job is to look after a flock of sheep for me, but he's so careless that every day one of them goes missing; and although what I'm punishing is his carelessness, or his wickedness, he says I'm doing it because I'm a skinflint, so as not to pay him his wages—but I swear by God and by my eternal soul that he's lying."

"You dare to use that word in my presence, you villainous wretch?"[1] said Don Quixote. "I swear by the sun that shines down on us that I am minded to run you through with this lance. Pay him immediately, and do not answer back; otherwise, by God who rules us, I shall exterminate and annihilate you this very instant. Untie him."

The farmer bowed his head and, without uttering a word, untied his servant, whom Don Quixote asked how much his master owed him. The reply was nine months at seven reals a month. Don Quixote worked it out and found that it came to seventy-three reals, which he told the farmer to hand over there and then, if he didn't want to die. The fearful countryman swore by the tight corner he was in and by the oath he'd already sworn (he hadn't sworn any oath at all), that it wasn't as much as all that, because an allowance and deduction had to be made for three pairs of shoes he'd given the lad, and one real paid for two blood-lettings when he'd been ill.

"That is all very well," replied Don Quixote, "but the shoes and the blood-lettings will be set against the flogging you have given him without due cause: for if he has done some damage to the hide of the shoes that you bought him, you have damaged his own hide, and if the barber bled him when he was ill, you have done the same to him in good health; so that on this account be owes you nothing."

"The problem is, sir knight, I haven't got any money on me; if Andrés would like to come home with me, I'll pay him every single real I owe him."

"Me, go with him, ever again?" said the lad. "No fear! No sir, I wouldn't even dream of it—so that as soon as we're alone again he can flay me like St Bartholomew?"[2]

"He shall do no such thing," replied Don Quixote. "My command will be sufficient to ensure his obedience; and provided that he gives me his oath by the laws of the order of chivalry into which he has been admitted, I shall allow him to go free, and personally guarantee the payment."

"Think what you're saying, sir," said the lad. "My master here isn't a knight at all, and he's never been admitted into any order of chivalry—he's just Juan Haldudo, the rich farmer from Quintanar."

"That is of little consequence," replied Don Quixote, "there is no reason why someone with a plebeian name should not be a knight, for every man is the child of his own deeds."

"That's as may be," said Andrés, "but this master of mine, what deeds is he the child of, seeing as how he refuses to pay me any wages for my sweat and toil?"

"I'm not refusing you anything at all, my dear Andrés," replied the farmer. "Please do be so kind as to come with me—I swear by all the orders of chivalry in the world to pay you, as I said, every single real I owe you, and with brass knobs on too."

"You may dispense with the brass knobs," said Don Quixote. "Pay him in silver reals, and that will satisfy me; and take good care to do exactly as you have sworn to do, for otherwise, by that same oath, I swear that I will come back to punish you, and that I will find you, even if you hide yourself away like a lizard. And if you wish to know who is issuing these commands, so as to be the more obliged to obey them,

1. The word in question is "lying"; Don Quixote takes the farmer's words as a personal assault, since he has chosen to defend the young boy.
2. A martyr who was flayed alive.

know that I am the valiant Don Quixote de la Mancha, the righter of wrongs and injustices; and God be with you, and do not forget for one moment what you have promised and sworn, under pain of the penalties prescribed."

And as he said this he spurred Rocinante, and before very long he had got under way. The farmer followed him with his gaze, and as soon as he was certain that he'd ridden out of the wood and was out of sight, he turned to his servant Andrés and said:

"Come here, my son, I want to pay you what I owe you, just as that righter of wrongs has ordered."

"I swear you will, too," said Andrés, "and you'll do well to obey that good knight's commands, God bless him, because he's such a brave man and such a good judge, by all that's holy, that if you don't pay me he'll come back and do what he said he'd do."

"And I swear I will, too," said the farmer, "but, since I'm so very fond of you, I think I'll increase the debt first, just so as to increase the repayment."

And seizing him by the arm, he tied him back to the evergreen oak and flogged him half dead.

"And now, Señor Andrés," said the farmer, "you can call upon your righter of wrongs. As you'll see, he isn't going to right this particular wrong in a hurry. But I don't think I've done with the wronging quite yet, because I'm feeling the urge to skin you alive, just as you feared I would."

But at length he untied him and told him he could go off in search of his judge so that this gentleman could carry out the sentence he'd pronounced. Andrés crept sullenly away, swearing that he was going in search of the brave Don Quixote de la Mancha to tell him exactly what had happened, and that the farmer would pay for it sevenfold. But, for all that, Andrés departed in tears and his master was left laughing.

This was how the valiant Don Quixote redressed that wrong; and delighted with what had happened, and considering that he had made a most happy and glorious beginning to his knight-errantry, he rode towards his village full of satisfaction, and murmuring:

"Well may you call yourself fortunate above all women who dwell on this earth, O Dulcinea del Toboso, fairest of the fair, for it has befallen your lot to hold subjected and enslaved to your every wish and desire a knight as valiant and far-famed as is and shall be Don Quixote de la Mancha, who (as all the world knows) was but yesterday admitted to the order of chivalry and today has righted the greatest injury and wrong ever devised by unreason and perpetrated by cruelty: today he has wrested the scourge from the hand of that pitiless enemy who was so unjustly flogging that delicate child."

As he was saying this he came to a crossroads, and this brought to his mind those other crossroads where knights errant would pause to consider which way to go; and, to imitate them, he remained motionless for a while; but after careful thought he let go of the reins, surrendering his will to that of his nag, which followed its original inclination—to head for its stable. After a couple of miles, Don Quixote spotted a throng of people who, as it afterwards transpired, were merchants from Toledo on their way to Murcia to buy silk.[3] There were six of them, each beneath his sunshade, accompanied by four servants on horseback and three footmen. As soon as Don Quixote saw them, he imagined that here was the opportunity for a new adventure; and, wishing to imitate in every way he believed he could the passages of arms he'd

3. Murcia is on the southwest coast of Spain.

read about in his books, he decided that one he had in mind was perfect for this situation. And so, with a gallant bearing and a resolute air, he steadied himself in his stirrups, clutched his lance, lifted his leather shield to his chest and, taking up his position in the middle of the highway, awaited the arrival of these knights errant, for this was what he judged them to be; and when they came within sight and earshot, Don Quixote raised his voice and, striking a haughty posture, declared:

"You will none of you advance one step further unless all of you confess that in all the world there is no maiden more beauteous than the Empress of La Mancha, the peerless Dulcinea del Toboso."

The merchants halted when they heard these words and saw the strange figure uttering them, and from the figure and the words they realized that the man was mad; but they had a mind to stay and see what would be the outcome of the required confession and one of them, waggish and sharp-witted, said:

"Sir knight, we don't know who this worthy lady is; do let us see her, because if she's as beautiful as you claim she is, we'll most freely and willingly confess that what you say is true."

"If I were to let you see her," retorted Don Quixote, "what merit would there be in confessing so manifest a truth? The whole point is that, without seeing her, you must believe, confess, affirm, swear and uphold it; if not, monstrous and arrogant wretches, you shall face me in battle forthwith. For whether you present yourselves one by one, as the order of chivalry requires, or all together, as is the custom and wicked practice of those of your ilk, here I stand and wait for you, confident in the justice of my cause."

"Sir knight," replied the merchant, "I beg you, in the name of all us princes gathered here, that—so as not to burden our consciences by confessing something never seen or heard by any of us, particularly since it is so detrimental to the Empresses and Queens of La Alcarria and Extremadura[4]—you be pleased to show us a portrait of that lady, even if no bigger than a grain of wheat; because the skein can be judged by the thread, as they say, and this will leave us satisfied and reassured, and leave you pleased and contented; indeed I believe we are already so far inclined in her favour that, even if her portrait shows that one of her eyes has gone skew-whiff and that sulphur and cinnabar ooze out of the other one, we will, just to please you, say in her favour whatever you want us to say."

"It does not ooze, you infamous knaves," replied Don Quixote, burning with anger. "It does not ooze, I repeat, with what you say, but with ambergris and civet kept in finest cotton; and she is not skew-whiff or hunch-backed, but straighter than a Guadarrama spindle.[5] And you shall pay for the great blasphemy you have uttered against such beauty as that of my lady!"

And so saying he charged with lowered lance at the blasphemer in such fury that, if good fortune hadn't made Rocinante trip and fall on the way, things would have gone badly for the reckless merchant. But Rocinante did fall, and his master rolled over the ground for some distance, and he tried to get up, but he couldn't, so encumbered was he by his lance, his leather shield, his spurs and his helmet, together with the burden of all the rest of his ancient armour. And as he struggled in vain to rise he cried:

4. La Alcarria, known for its production of honey, and Extremadura, on the border of Portugal, are relatively underdeveloped regions in Spain; the designation is thus vaguely insulting.

5. Guadarrama is a mountainous area outside of Madrid well-known for its cloth production.

"Flee not, you paltry cowards; you wretches, bide your time. 'Tis my horse's fault and not my own that I am lying here."

One of the footmen—not, it seems, a very well-intentioned one—on hearing all this bluster from the poor fallen fellow, couldn't resist giving him an answer on his ribs. And coming up to him he grabbed his lance and, breaking it into pieces, took one of them and began to give our Don Quixote such a pounding that, in spite of all his armour, he ended up as well threshed as the finest chaff. The muleteer's masters were shouting to him not to hit so hard, and to stop, but the lad was by now so caught up in his game that he wouldn't leave it until he'd played all the cards of his fury, and, picking up the other pieces of the lance, he shattered them, too, on the poor fallen man who, in the face of the storm of blows raining down, never stopped shouting as he threatened heaven and earth and those brigands, as he imagined them to be.

The lad grew tired, and the merchants continued their journey, supplied with enough to talk about throughout it on the subject of the poor pounded knight. Once he found himself alone, he again tried to get up; but if he hadn't been able to do so when fit and well, how was he going to manage it now that he was pummelled to pieces? Even so he considered himself lucky, in the belief that this was a fitting misfortune for knights errant, and he blamed his horse for it all; and it was impossible to get up, so very bruised and battered was his body.

Chapter 5

In which the story of our knight's misfortune is continued

Finding, then, that he couldn't move, it occurred to him to resort to his usual remedy, which was to think about some passage from his books; and his madness brought to his memory the episode from the story of Baldwin and the Marquis of Mantua in which Carloto leaves Baldwin wounded in the forest, a tale known to every little boy, not unfamiliar to youths, celebrated and even believed by old men, yet with no more truth in it than the miracles of Muhammad.[1] It was perfect for the predicament in which he found himself; and so, with many manifestations of extreme suffering, he began to writhe about on the ground and to say in the faintest of voices what the wounded knight of the forest is said to have said:

Where are you, mistress of my heart?
Are you not pained by my distress?
Maybe you know not of my plight,
Maybe you're false and pitiless.

And on he went reciting the ballad right up to the lines that go:

O noble Marquis, gentle sire,
My uncle and my lord by blood . . .

Fortune decreed that at this point a farmer from his own village, one of his neighbours, happened to be returning home after taking a hundredweight of wheat to the mill. Seeing a man lying there the farmer came up and asked him who he was and what was the matter with him, moaning away like that. No doubt Don Quixote

1. Don Quixote is thinking of a ballad about the son of Charlemagne (Carloto), who wounds the nephew of the Marquis of Mantua; the Marquis in turn will seek perpetual revenge. The anti-Islamic sentiment is not unusual in the period.

thought that this was the Marquis of Mantua, his uncle, and so his only response was to continue reciting his ballad, informing the man of his misfortune and of the love that the Emperor's son felt for his wife, exactly as the ballad relates.

The farmer was astonished to hear all this nonsense; and, removing the man's visor, which had been battered to pieces, he wiped his face, which was covered in dust. And once he'd done wiping he recognized him and said:

"Señor Quixana," (for this must have been his name when he was sane and hadn't yet turned from a placid hidalgo into a knight errant) "who's done this to you?"

But he continued to reply with his ballad to everything he was asked. Sizing up the situation, the farmer took his back and breast plates off as best he could, to see if he was wounded, but couldn't see any blood or signs of any hurt. He managed to lift him up, and with great difficulty hoisted him on to the donkey, since this seemed the more tranquil animal. He picked up the armour and arms, including the fragments of the lance, and tied them on to Rocinante, which he took by the reins, and taking his donkey by the halter he set off in the direction of his village, deep in thought as he heard the nonsense being spoken by Don Quixote, who was no less pensive and so badly bruised that he couldn't keep his seat on the donkey, and every so often breathed sighs loud enough to reach heaven; so that the farmer again felt he should ask what was wrong, and it must have been the devil himself who made Don Quixote recall tales to fit the events, because at that moment, forgetting all about Baldwin, he remembered Abindarráez the Moor being captured and taken as a prisoner to his castle by the Governor of Antequera, Rodrigo de Narváez. So that when the farmer asked him again how he felt and what was the matter with him, he replied with the very same words and arguments used by the captive Moor to reply to Rodrigo de Narváez, as he'd read the story in Jorge de Montemayor's *Diana,*[2] making such appropriate use of it that the farmer wished himself to the devil for having to listen to such a pack of absurdities. He realized his neighbour was mad, and hurried on to the village so as not to have to put up with Don Quixote's interminable harangue more than necessary. It concluded like this:

"You must know, Señor Don Rodrigo de Narváez, that this fair Jarifa I have mentioned is now the beauteous Dulcinea del Toboso, for whom I have performed, do perform and shall perform the most famous deeds of chivalry that have been witnessed, are witnessed and shall be witnessed in this world."

The farmer replied:

"Look here sir, as I'm a sinner I'm not Don Rodrigo de Narváez, nor the Marquis of Mantua, but Pedro Alonso, your neighbour; and you aren't Baldwin, nor Abindarráez, but the honourable hidalgo Señor Quixana."

"I know who I am," retorted Don Quixote, "and I know that I can be not only all those whom I have mentioned, but every one of the Twelve Peers of France, and every one of the Nine Worthies as well, because all the deeds performed by them both singly and together will be exceeded by mine."[3]

2. A popular pastoral romance; begun by Gil Polo, its second part was written by Jorge de Montemayor in the mid-16th century. The episode about Abindarráez, the captive Moor, is from the novel.

3. The 12 peers were the warriors of Charlemagne's court in late 8th-century France. The nine worthies consisted of three groups of Christians, Jews, and Gentiles; Charlemagne, David, and Alexander are among them. Along with the Knights of the Round Table, a band of worthies assembled by the legendary King Arthur of England, these three groups of warriors provide constant (even interchangeable) points of comparison for the deluded Quixote.

With these exchanges and other similar ones they approached the village at nightfall, but the farmer waited until it was darker so that nobody could see the battered hidalgo so wretchedly mounted. When he thought the time had come he entered the village and went straight to Don Quixote's house, which was in an uproar: the priest and the barber, great friends of Don Quixote's, were there, and his housekeeper was shouting:

"And what's your opinion, Father Pero Pérez sir," (for this was the priest's name) "about my master's misfortune? Three days it's been now without a trace of him, his nag, his leather shield, his lance or his armour. A fine pickle I'm in! It's my belief, as sure as I was born to die, that his brain's been turned by those damned chivalry books of his he reads all the time—I remember often hearing him say to himself that he wanted to be a knight errant and go off in search of adventures. The devil take all those books, and Barabbas[4] take them too, for scrambling the finest mind in all La Mancha!"

The niece said much the same and even more:

"And let me tell you this, Master Nicolás," (for this was the barber's name). "My uncle would often be reading those evil books of misadventure for two whole days and nights on end, and then he'd throw his book down, grab his sword and slash the walls of his room, and once he was exhausted he'd say that he'd killed four giants as big as four towers, and that the sweat pouring from him was blood from the wounds received in battle, and then he'd drink a pitcher of cold water and feel calm and well again, claiming that the water was a most precious draught brought by the famous sage Squiffy, a great enchanter and friend of his.[5] But I'm the one to blame for it all, not telling you gentlemen about my uncle's madness so you could have done something about it and burned those unchristian books of his before it came to all this; he's got lots and lots of them, and they do deserve to be put to the flames, like heretics."

"I agree with that," said the priest, "and I swear that before another day has passed they'll be put on public trial and condemned to the flames so that they can't make anyone reading them do what my friend must have done."

All this was overheard by Don Quixote and the farmer, who could no longer have any doubts about his neighbour's illness, and so he began to shout:

"Open up to Sir Baldwin and the Marquis of Mantua, who's sore wounded here, and to the Moor Abindarráez, brought captive by the valiant Rodrigo de Narváez, the Governor of Antequera."

These shouts brought all four running into the porch, and as the men recognized their friend, and the women their master and uncle, who hadn't dismounted from the donkey because he couldn't, they ran to embrace him. He said:

"Stop, all of you, for I am sore wounded through the fault of my steed. Carry me to my bed and, if you are able, summon the wise Urganda[6] to heed and tend my wounds."

"Just look at him, in the name of the devil!" cried the housekeeper. "Didn't I know in the marrow of my bones what was wrong with the master? Up you go, sir, up you go to bed, we'll cure you well enough without any need for that there Ugandan woman. Damn those chivalry books, damn the lot of them, getting you into such a state!"

4. The thief whom Pilate released to the Jews when they requested that he be freed rather than Jesus.

5. An enchanter (Alquife) from *Amadis of Gaul.*

6. Alquife's wife.

They took him to his bed and, examining him for wounds, couldn't find any; he told them that it had been a general, overall battering sustained when he and his steed Rocinante suffered a terrible fall as he was doing battle with ten giants, the most lawless and reckless giants to be found almost anywhere on the face of the earth.

"I see, I see!" said the priest. "So there are giants in the game as well, are there? I swear by this Holy Cross that I'll burn them tomorrow, before the day is over."

They asked Don Quixote a thousand questions, and his only reply was to request food and to be allowed to sleep, for this was his greatest need. And then the priest asked the farmer to tell him exactly how he'd found Don Quixote. The farmer told him the whole story, including the nonsense that on being discovered and transported the knight had uttered, which made the priest even more anxious to do what the very next day he did do: call on his friend the barber Master Nicolás, with whom he walked to Don Quixote's house.

from *Chapter 6*

About the amusing and exhaustive scrutiny that the priest and the barber made in the library of our ingenious hidalgo

Who was still asleep. The priest asked the niece for the keys of the room where the books, the authors of the mischief, were kept, and she was happy to hand them over. They went in, the housekeeper too, and found more than a hundred large volumes, finely bound, and some small ones; and as soon as the housekeeper saw them, she ran out of the room and back again clutching a bowl of holy water and some hyssop, and said:

"Here you are, reverend father, you take this and sprinkle the room with it, just in case there's one of those hordes of enchanters from those books in here, and he puts a spell on us as a punishment for the torments they'll undergo once we've wiped them off the face of the earth."

The priest laughed at the housekeeper's simple-mindedness, and told the barber to hand him the books one by one so that he could see what was in them, since he might find some that didn't deserve to be committed to the flames.[1]

"No," said the niece, "there's no reason to let any of them off, they're all to blame. Better throw the whole lot of them out of the windows into the courtyard, and make a pile of them, and set fire to them, or take them to the backyard and make the bonfire there, where the smoke won't be such a nuisance."

The housekeeper said much the same, so anxious were both women to see those innocents massacred, but the priest wouldn't agree without at least reading the titles. The first one that Master Nicolás put into his hands was *The Four Books of Amadis of Gaul,* and the priest said:

"This is a strange coincidence: I've heard that this was the very first chivalry romance to be printed in Spain, and that all the others have their origin and beginning in it; so it seems to me that, as the prophet of such a pernicious sect, it should be condemned to the flames without delay."

1. The auto-de-fé which the priest is orchestrating—a public exhibition of those convicted of heresy—would have been a familiar sight in the days of the Inquisition; at times such an exhibition culminated in the death by fire of the heretic. There were calls to burn chivalric books as well in the mid-16th century when the fashion of chivalric romances was at its height.

"No, no," said the barber. "I've also heard that it's the very best of all the books of this kind that have ever been written; and so, being unique in its artistry, it ought to be pardoned."

"You're right," said the priest, "so its life is spared for the time being. Let's see that one next to it."

"This," said the barber, "is *The Exploits of Esplandian,* Amadis of Gaul's legitimate son."[2]

"Well, to be sure," said the priest, "the excellence of the father isn't going to be of any avail to the son. Here you are, ma'am, open that window and throw it into the yard, the first faggot on the bonfire we're going to make."

The housekeeper was delighted to do so, and the good Esplandian flew out into the courtyard, where he patiently awaited the flames with which he was threatened.

"Let's see the next one," said the priest.

"This," said the barber, "is *Amadis of Greece,* and all the books on this side, I think, are members of that same family."[3]

"Then out into the yard with the lot of them," said the priest. "Just to be able to burn Queen Pintiquiniestra, and the shepherd Darinel, and his eclogues, and his author's devilish, contorted language, I'll burn the father that begot me, too, if I catch him going about as a knight errant."

"I agree," said the barber.

"So do I," added the niece.

"That being so," said the housekeeper, "let's have them here, and out into the courtyard they all go."

They gave them to her, and since there were so many of them she spared herself the stairs again and flung them out of the window. . . .

And not wanting to weary himself any more reading chivalry romances, the priest ordered the housekeeper to take all the big books and throw them out into the yard. His command didn't fall on deaf ears, because she'd rather have been burning those books than weaving the finest and largest piece of fabric in the world, and, seizing about eight of them, she heaved them out of the window. But because she took up so many of them together, one fell at the barber's feet and, curious to know what it was, he saw: *History of the Famous Knight Tirante the White.*[4]

"Good heavens!" cried the priest. "Fancy Tirante the White being here! Give it to me, my friend: I reckon I've found in this book a treasure of delight and a mine of entertainment. In it you'll discover Don Quirieleisón de Montalbán, a most courageous knight, and his brother Tomás de Montalbán, and the knight Fonseca, together with the fight that the brave Tirante had with the mastiff, and the witticisms of the maiden Placerdemivida, and the amours and the trickery of the widow Reposada, and the lady empress in love with her squire Hipólito. Let me tell you this, my friend; as far as its style is concerned this is the best book in the world. In it knights eat and sleep and die in their beds and make wills before they die, and other such things that are usually omitted from books of this sort. But in spite of all this I do have to say that the man who wrote it deserved to be sent to the galleys for life, for not knowing what he was doing when he was writing such nonsense. Take it home and read it, and you'll see that what I say is true."

"That I'll do," replied the barber, "but what about these other little books here?"

2. Written by the author of *Amadis of Gaul* and published two years later.

3. The Amadis story provoked a number of imitations.

4. A late 15th-century Catalan chivalric romance.

"They can't be books of chivalry," said the priest, "but books of poetry."

And, opening one of them he saw that it was Jorge de Montemayor's *Diana* and, convinced that they were all of the same sort, he said:

"These don't deserve to be burned with the others, because they aren't and never will be as damaging as those books of chivalry have been—these are books for the intellect, and do nobody any harm."

"Oh sir," cried the niece, "please have them burned like the rest, because it could well happen that once my uncle gets over his chivalry illness he starts reading all these other books and takes it into his head to become a shepherd and wander about the forests and meadows singing and playing music and, what would be even worse than that, turn into a poet, which they say is a catching and incurable disease."

"The girl's right," said the priest, "and it'll be a good idea to remove this dangerous stumbling-block from our friend's way."

* * *

Chapter 7

About our worthy knight Don Quixote de la Mancha's second sally

And now Don Quixote began to bellow:

"Come, come, you valiant knights; 'tis now you must display the worth of your mighty arms, for the courtiers are getting the better of the tourney."

They ran to see what the commotion was all about, and this put a stop to the scrutiny of the remaining books; as a result it's believed that *Carolea* and *The Lion of Spain,* together with *The Exploits of the Emperor* by Luis de Avila,[1] went to the flames without any trial at all, because they must have been among the remainder; and perhaps if the priest had examined them they wouldn't have received such a severe sentence.

By the time they reached Don Quixote's room he was out of bed, shouting and raving, laying about him with his sword in all directions with slashes and backstrokes, as wide awake as if he'd never slept. They wrestled him back to bed, and once he'd calmed down a little, he turned to the priest and said:

"Indeed, my Lord Archbishop Turpin, it is a disgrace for us, who call ourselves the Twelve Peers, so meekly to allow those knights courtiers to carry off the victory in this tournament, after we knights adventurers had won all the honours on the previous three days."[2]

"Hush, my friend," said the priest, "God will grant a change of fortune so that what is lost today is won tomorrow, and for the moment you should look to your health—you seem to be overtired, if not sore wounded."

"Wounded I am not," said Don Quixote, "but weak and exhausted I am indeed, for the bastard Roland has been pounding me with the trunk of an evergreen oak, and all out of envy, because he can see that I am the only man who opposes his bravado. But my name would not be Reynald of Montalbán if, as soon as I rise from this bed, I did not make him pay for it, in spite of all his magic spells.[3] For the present, however,

1. *La Carolea* and *The Lion of Spain* were heroic poems about Charles V (1500–1558), who was both Holy Roman Emperor and king of Spain; *The Exploits of the Emperor* chronicled Charles V's deeds in prose.

2. Turpin was archbishop at Charlemagne's court and the fabled author of the *Song of Roland.*

3. Reynald (Rinaldo) was Roland's cousin; Roland (Orlando) is conceived as virtually invulnerable to injury in the Italian romance tradition.

bring me victuals, for they, I know, will be more to my purpose, and leave it to me to seek my revenge."

And that's what they did: they gave him some food, and he fell asleep again, and they fell to marvelling at his madness.

That night the housekeeper burned to ashes all the books in the courtyard and the house, and some must have perished that deserved to be treasured in perpetual archives; but fate, and the scrutineer's laziness, wouldn't permit it, and in them was fulfilled the proverb which says that the just sometimes pay for sinners.

One of the remedies that the priest and the barber had prescribed at that time for their friend's malady was to have his library walled up and sealed off, so that he couldn't find his books when he got up—maybe if the cause was removed the effect might cease—and to tell him that an enchanter had carried them off, with the library and all; and this was done without delay. Two days later Don Quixote did get up, and his first action was to go and look at his books; and, since he couldn't find the room in which he'd left them, he wandered all over the house searching for it. He kept going up to the place where the door used to be, and feeling for it with his hands, and running his eyes backwards and forwards over the walls without uttering a word; and after some time doing this he asked his housekeeper where his library was. Well trained in her answer, she said:

"And what library do you think you're looking for? There's no library and no books left in this house, because the devil himself took them away."

"No it wasn't the devil," replied the niece, "it was an enchanter who came one night on a cloud, after you'd gone away, and he climbed off a serpent he was riding and he went into the library and I don't know what he got up to in there, because a bit later he flew away over the roof and left the house full of smoke; and when we made up our minds to go and see what he'd done, we couldn't find any books or any library. All we remember is that as that wicked old man flew away he shouted that because of a secret grudge he bore the owner of the books and the library, he'd done the house the damage that we were about to discover. He also said that he was called the sage Munaton."

"Frestón is what he must have said," said Don Quixote.

"I don't know," said the housekeeper, "whether he was called Frestón or Piston or whatever, all I know is his name ended in ton."[4]

"That is indeed his name," said Don Quixote, "and he is a wise enchanter, a great enemy of mine, who bears me much malice, because he knows by his arts and his learning that the time will come when I shall engage in single combat a knight who is a favourite of his, and defeat him, without his being able to do anything to prevent it, and for this reason he tries to make as much mischief for me as he can; but I can promise him that he is powerless to gainsay or avert what heaven has decreed."

"Who can doubt that?" said the niece. "But uncle, why do you have to go and get involved in these arguments? Wouldn't it be better to stay quietly at home instead of looking for better bread than what's made from wheat, and forgetting that many a man's gone out shearing and come back shorn?"

"My dear niece!" replied Don Quixote. "How wrong you are! Before anyone shears me I will pluck the beards off the chins of all those who even contemplate touching a single hair of mine!"

4. Probably Frestón, an enchanter in the chivalric romance *Don Belianís de Grecia.*

Neither woman answered him back, because they could see that he was growing heated.

And yet he did stay quietly at home for a whole fortnight without showing any signs of wanting to re-enact his former follies, and during this time he talked all kinds of amusing bunkum with his friends the priest and the barber, as he declared that what the world most needed was knights errant and a rebirth of knight-errantry. Sometimes the priest contradicted him and sometimes he gave in to him, because if he didn't make use of this tactic it would be impossible to restore his sanity.

During this fortnight Don Quixote set to work on a farmer who was a neighbour of his, an honourable man (if a poor man can be called honourable) but a little short of salt in the brain-pan. To be brief, Don Quixote told him, reasoned with him and promised him so much that the poor villager decided to go away with him and serve him as squire. Don Quixote told the man, among other things, that he ought to be delighted to go, because at some time or other he could well have an adventure in which he won an island in the twinkling of an eye and installed his squire as governor. These and other similar promises persuaded Sancho Panza, for this was the farmer's name, to leave his wife and children and go into service as his neighbour's squire.

Don Quixote immediately set about raising money, and by selling one possession, pawning another, and always making a bad bargain, he scraped together a reasonable sum. He also found himself a little round infantryman's shield, borrowed from a friend, and, patching up his shattered helmet as best he could, he told his squire Sancho the day and time he intended to set out, so that he too could obtain whatever he considered most necessary. Don Quixote was particularly insistent on saddle-bags, and Sancho said that indeed he would bring some, and he'd bring a very fine donkey of his too, because he wasn't all that much given to going very far on foot. At this Don Quixote hesitated, racking his brains to try and remember if any knight errant had ever been escorted by a donkey-mounted squire, but none came to mind; yet for all that he decided that Sancho should ride his donkey, proposing to provide him with a more honourable mount at the earliest opportunity, by unhorsing the first discourteous knight he came across. Don Quixote stocked up with shirts and everything else he could, following the advice that the innkeeper had given him; and once all these preparations had been made, without Panza saying goodbye to his wife and children, or Don Quixote to his housekeeper and niece, they left the village unseen one night, and by daybreak they'd ridden so far they felt certain no one would be able to find them however hard he looked.

Sancho Panza rode his ass like a patriarch, complete with saddle-bags and leather bottle, longing to be the governor of the island his master had promised him. Don Quixote happened to take the same road he'd followed on his first sally, across the plain of Montiel, with less discomfort than before, because it was early morning and the sun, being low, didn't bother them. Sancho Panza said to his master:

"You'll be sure, won't you, sir knight, not to forget what you promised me about the island. I'll be up to governing it all right, however big it is."

To which Don Quixote replied:

"I would have you know, my good friend Sancho Panza, that it was a custom much in use among the knights errant of old to make their squires the governors of the islands or kingdoms that they conquered, and I have determined that such an ancient usage shall not lapse through my fault. Quite on the contrary, I intend to improve upon it: for those knights would sometimes—more often than not, perhaps—wait until their squires were old men and, once they were tired of serving and of suffering bad days and worse nights, give them some title, such as count or at the most marquis of some valley or paltry province; but if your life and mine are spared, it could well be that within six days I shall conquer a kingdom with others annexed, any one of which would be perfect for you to be crowned king of it. And you must not think that there would be anything extraordinary about that: incidents and accidents befall us knights in such unprecedented and unimagined ways that I might easily be able to give you even more than I have promised."

"And so," said Sancho Panza, "if by one of those miracles you've just said I became king, then Juana Gutiérrez, my old woman, would be queen no less, and the kids would be princes and princesses."

"Who can doubt it?" replied Don Quixote.

"I can," retorted Sancho Panza. "To my mind, even if God rained kingdoms down on this earth none of them would sit well on my Mari Gutiérrez's head. Look here, sir, she wouldn't be worth two brass farthings as a queen—countess would suit her better, and even that'd be hard going for her."

"Commend the matter to God, Sancho," replied Don Quixote, "and he will give her what is best for her; but you must not be so daunted that you agree to content yourself with anything less than being a provincial governor."

"I shan't do that, sir," replied Sancho, "not with such a fine master as you, who'll be able to give me everything that's good for me and I can cope with."

Chapter 8

About the brave Don Quixote's success in the dreadful and unimaginable adventure of the windmills, together with other events worthy of happy memory

As he was saying this, they caught sight of thirty or forty windmills standing on the plain, and as soon as Don Quixote saw them he said to his squire:

"Fortune is directing our affairs even better than we could have wished: for you can see over there, good friend Sancho Panza, a place where stand thirty or more monstrous giants with whom I intend to fight a battle and whose lives I intend to take; and with the booty we shall begin to prosper. For this is a just war, and it is a great service to God to wipe such a wicked breed from the face of the earth."

"What giants?" said Sancho Panza.

"Those giants that you can see over there," replied his master, "with long arms: there are giants with arms almost six miles long."

"Look you here," Sancho retorted, "those over there aren't giants, they're windmills, and what look to you like arms are sails—when the wind turns them they make the millstones go round."

"It is perfectly clear," replied Don Quixote, "that you are but a raw novice in this matter of adventures. They are giants; and if you are frightened, you can take yourself away and say your prayers while I engage them in fierce and arduous combat."

And so saying he set spurs to his steed Rocinante, not paying any attention to his squire Sancho Panza, who was shouting that what he was charging were definitely windmills not giants. But Don Quixote was so convinced that they were giants that he neither heard his squire Sancho's shouts nor saw what stood in front of him, even though he was by now upon them; instead he cried:

"Flee not, O vile and cowardly creatures, for it is but one solitary knight who attacks you."

A gust of wind arose, the great sails began to move, and Don Quixote yelled:

"Though you flourish more arms than the giant Briareus,[1] I will make you pay for it."

So saying, and commending himself with all his heart to his lady Dulcinea, begging her to succour him in his plight, well protected by his little round infantryman's shield, and with his lance couched, he advanced at Rocinante's top speed and charged at the windmill nearest him. As he thrust his lance into its sail the wind turned it with such violence that it smashed the lance into pieces and dragged the horse and his rider with it, and Don Quixote went rolling over the plain in a very sore predicament. Sancho Panza rushed to help his master at his donkey's fastest trot and found that he couldn't stir, such was the toss that Rocinante had given him.

"For God's sake!" said Sancho. "Didn't I tell you to be careful what you were doing, didn't I tell you they were only windmills? And only someone with windmills on the brain could have failed to see that!"

"Not at all, friend Sancho," replied Don Quixote. "Affairs of war, even more than others, are subject to continual change. All the more so as I believe, indeed I am certain, that the same sage Frestón who stole my library and my books has just turned these giants into windmills, to deprive me of the glory of my victory, such is the enmity he feels for me; but in the end his evil arts will avail him little against the might of my sword."

"God's will be done," replied Sancho Panza.

He helped his master to his feet, and his master remounted Rocinante, whose shoulder was half dislocated. And talking about this adventure they followed the road towards the Pass of Lápice, because Don Quixote said they couldn't fail to encounter plentiful and varied adventures there, as it was a much frequented spot. But he was dejected by the destruction of his lance, and he told his squire so, and added:

"I remember reading that a Spanish knight called Diego Pérez de Vargas, having broken his sword in battle, tore a weighty bough or trunk from an evergreen oak, and did such deeds with it that day, and thrashed so many Moors, that he was nicknamed Machuca, that is to say, the thrasher; and from that day onwards his surname and that of his descendants was changed to Vargas y Machuca.[2] I have told you this because from the first oak tree that comes before me I intend to tear off another such trunk, as good as the one I have in mind, and with it I intend to do such deeds as to make you consider yourself most fortunate to be deemed worthy to behold them, and to witness that which can hardly be believed."

"God's will be done," said Sancho. "I believe every word you say. But do sit up straighter, you're riding all lopsided, it must be that hammering you got when you fell off your horse."

"That is indeed the case," replied Don Quixote, "and if I do not utter any complaint about the pain it is because knights errant are not permitted to complain about wounds, even if their entrails are spilling out of them."

"If that's so there's nothing more for me to say," replied Sancho, "but God knows I'd like you to complain if anything hurts. As for me, I can tell you I'm going to moan like anything about the slightest little pain, unless that stuff about not complaining goes for knight errants' squires as well."

1. One of the mythological Titans, Briareus had 100 arms.

2. "Machuca" was the subject of ballads; he was instrumental at the 13th-century battle of Jerez.

Don Quixote couldn't help laughing at his squire's simple-mindedness, and declared that he could moan as and when he pleased, whether he felt any pain or not, for he had not yet read anything to the contrary in the order of chivalry. Sancho pointed out that it was time to eat. His master replied that he didn't need any food yet, but that Sancho could eat whenever he liked. So Sancho settled himself down as best he could on his donkey and, taking out of his saddle-bags what he'd put into them, he jogged along and munched away behind his master, and every so often he'd take a swig from his leather bottle with such relish that the most self-indulgent innkeeper in Malaga[3] would have envied him. And as Sancho trotted on, drinking his fill, he didn't remember any of the promises his master had made him, and reckoned that going in search of adventures, however dangerous they might be, was more like good fun than hard work.

To cut a long story short, they spent that night under some trees, and from one of them Don Quixote tore a dead branch that might almost serve as a lance, and fastened on to it the iron head that he'd taken off the broken one. He didn't sleep in all the night, thinking about his lady Dulcinea, to conform with what he'd read in his books, where knights errant spent many sleepless nights in glades and deserts, engrossed in the recollection of their ladies. Not so Sancho Panza who, with his stomach full, and not of chicory water either, slept right through until morning; and, if his master hadn't called him, neither the rays of the sun, falling full on his face, nor the songs of the birds that, in great throngs and with expansive joy, greeted the coming of the new day, would have been capable of awaking him. He got up, had his breakfast swig and found his leather bottle rather slimmer than the evening before; and his heart sank, because it didn't look as if this lack was going to be remedied as soon as he'd have liked. Don Quixote refused breakfast because, as we know, he had decided to subsist on savoury recollections. They continued along the road to the Pass of Lápice, and at about three o'clock in the afternoon they sighted it.

"Over there, brother Sancho Panza," said Don Quixote when he saw it, "we can dip our arms right up to our elbows in what people call adventures. But take note that, even if you see me in the greatest peril imaginable, you must not seize your sword to defend me, unless you should see that those who attack me are rabble and common people, in which case you can most certainly come to my aid; but should they be knights and gentlemen, it is on no account licit or permitted by the laws of chivalry for you to assist me, until you yourself be knighted."

"You can be sure, sir," replied Sancho, "of being fully obeyed there, specially since I'm a peaceful man by nature and don't like getting involved in rows and brawls. Though I do have to say that when it comes to defending myself I'm not going to take much notice of those there laws of yours, because divine and human justice both let anyone defend himself against attack."

"I do not disagree in the slightest," replied Don Quixote, "but as regards assisting me against knights, you must keep your natural impetuosity under control."

"I'll do that all right," replied Sancho. "I'll keep that particular promise as strictly as the Sabbath."

As they talked away like this, two friars of the order of St Benedict appeared on the road, each seated upon a dromedary: their mules were no less tall than that. They came complete with their riding masks and their sunshades. Behind them was a coach

3. A port-town on the southern coast of Spain.

with four or five horsemen escorting it, and two footmen walking. In the coach, as was later discovered, there was a Basque lady on her way to Seville to join her husband, who was going to America to take up an important post. The friars weren't travelling with her, they just happened to be on the same road; but as soon as Don Quixote caught sight of them he said to his squire:

"Either I am much mistaken or this will be the most famous adventure ever witnessed; for those black figures over there must be and no doubt are enchanters abducting a princess in that coach, and I must redress this wrong to the utmost of my power."

"This'll be worse than the windmills," said Sancho. "Look here, sir, those there are Benedictine friars, and the coach must just be taking some travellers on their way. Look, look, do take care what you're doing, this could be one of the devil's own tricks."

"I have already told you, Sancho," replied Don Quixote, "that you know next to nothing on the subject of adventures. What I say is true, as you will soon see."

So saying, he rode forward and planted himself in the middle of the road down which the friars were plodding and, when he thought they were near enough to hear him, he cried:

"Diabolical and monstrous wretches, release this very moment the noble princesses whom you are abducting in that coach, or prepare to be killed this instant as a just punishment for your wicked works."

The friars reined in their mules and sat there in astonishment at the figure cut by Don Quixote and at the words he'd spoken, to which they replied:

"Sir knight, we aren't diabolical or monstrous at all, we're just two Benedictine friars going about our business, and we haven't the faintest idea whether there are any abducted princesses in this coach."

"Soft words will not work with me, for I know you only too well, perfidious knaves!" said Don Quixote.

And without awaiting any more replies he spurred Rocinante and charged with levelled lance at the friar in front with such determination and fury that, if the friar hadn't thrown himself from his mule, the knight would have brought him to the ground sore vexed and indeed sore wounded, if not stone dead. The other friar, seeing how his companion was being treated, dug his heels into his castle of a mule and made off across the plain faster than the wind.

Sancho Panza, seeing the friar sprawling on the ground, slipped off his donkey, ran over to him and began to strip him of his habits. And now two of the friars' servants came up and asked what he thought he was doing stripping their master like that. Sancho replied that the clothes were rightly his, the spoils of the battle his master Don Quixote had won. The servant-lads, who lacked a sense of humour and knew nothing about spoils and battles, seeing that Don Quixote had gone off to talk to the ladies in the coach, fell upon Sancho, knocked him to the ground, gave his beard a thorough plucking and his body a merciless kicking, and left him lying there breathless and senseless. Without pausing for an instant the friar remounted, terrified and trembling and drained of all colour, and spurred his mule in the direction of his companion, who was waiting a good distance away to see what would be the outcome of this nightmare; and not wanting to stop for the conclusion of the incident they continued on their way, making more signs of the cross than if they had the very devil at their backs.

Don Quixote, as has been said, was talking to the lady in the coach, and saying:

"You may now, in your ineffable loveliness, my lady, dispose of your person as best pleases you, for the pride of your ravishers lies on the ground, o'erthrown by this mighty arm of mine; and that you may not pine to know the name of your deliverer, be informed that I am Don Quixote de la Mancha, knight adventurer and errant, and captive to the peerless and beauteous Doña Dulcinea del Toboso; and in requital of the benefit you have received from me, all I desire is that you turn back to El Toboso and on my behalf present yourself before that lady and inform her of what I have accomplished for your deliverance."

Everything that Don Quixote said was overheard by one of the squires escorting the coach, a Basque; who, seeing that the man didn't want to let the coach continue on its way, but was saying that it must turn back at once to El Toboso, rode up to Don Quixote and, seizing him by the lance, said in bad Castilian and worse Basque:[4]

"Go on way, knight, and go with devil. By God made me, if not leaving coach, you as killed by Basque as stand there."

Don Quixote understood him perfectly, and with great composure he replied:

"If you were a knight and a gentleman, which you are not, I should already have punished your folly and audacity, you wretched creature."

To which the Basque replied:

"Me not gentleman? I swear God you lie as me Christian. If leaving lance and taking sword, soon see you monkey making! Basque on land, gentleman on sea, gentleman for devil, and see lie if other saying."

"'Now you shall see,' quoth Agrages,"[5] quoted Don Quixote.

And throwing his lance to the ground, he drew his sword, took up his little round shield and set upon the Basque, intending to kill him. The Basque, seeing the knight advance, would have preferred to dismount from his mule, which was a hired one and therefore a bad one and not to be trusted, but all he had time to do was to draw his sword; and it was lucky for him that he happened to be next to the coach, from which he was able to snatch a cushion to serve as a shield; and then the two men went for each other as if they were mortal enemies. The rest of the party would have made peace between them but they couldn't, because the Basque was saying in his topsy-turvy tongue that if they didn't let him finish his battle he'd kill his mistress and anyone else who got in his way. The lady in the coach, astonished and terrified at this sight, made the coachman drive a safe distance off, and then settled down to watch the desperate struggle, in the course of which the Basque dealt Don Quixote such a mighty blow on the shoulder, over the top of his shield, that if he hadn't been wearing armour he'd have been split down the middle. When Don Quixote felt the impact of the terrible stroke he cried:

"O lady of my soul, Dulcinea, flower of all beauty, succour this your knight who, through his desire to satisfy your great goodness, finds himself in this dire peril!"

Uttering these words, gripping his sword, raising his shield and launching himself at the Basque was the work of a moment, as Don Quixote resolved to venture everything on the fortune of a single blow. The Basque, seeing Don Quixote advance, could see from his spirited bearing what a brave man he was, and decided to follow his example; so he stood his ground, well protected by his cushion but unable to turn the mule one way or the other because by now, exhausted and unaccustomed to such pranks, it couldn't budge a single step.

4. The Basque region is in northern Spain. Basques were renowned for their fighting abilities, and their traditional limberness also made them good dancers. Their language is unrelated to Spanish. Castilian is another word for what has become the Spanish language.

5. A warrior from the *Amadis de Gaul* who typically says this phrase at the start of a fight.

So Don Quixote was advancing, as described, on the well-shielded Basque, with his sword aloft, determined to split him in half, and the Basque was awaiting him with his sword also aloft, and upholstered in his protective cushion, and all the bystanders were terrified and wondering what was going to be the outcome of the prodigious blows with which the two men were threatening each other; and the lady in the coach and her maids were making a thousand vows and offerings to all the images and holy places in Spain for God to deliver their squire and themselves from this great peril. But the trouble is that at this very point the author of this history leaves the battle unfinished, excusing himself on the ground that he hasn't found anything more written about these exploits of Don Quixote than what he has narrated. It is true, though, that the second author of this work refused to believe that such a fascinating history had been abandoned to the laws of oblivion, or that the chroniclers of La Mancha had been so lacking in curiosity that they hadn't kept papers relating to this famous knight in their archives or their desks; and so, with this in mind, he didn't despair of finding the end of this delectable history, which indeed, with heaven's help, he did find in the way that will be narrated in the second part.

Second Part of the Ingenious Hidalgo DON QUIXOTE de la Mancha

Chapter 9

In which the stupendous battle between the gallant Basque and the valiant man from La Mancha is brought to a conclusion

In the first part of this history we left the valiant Basque and the famous Don Quixote with naked swords aloft, about to deliver two such devastating downstrokes that if their aim was true they would at the very least split each other from top to bottom and cut each other open like pomegranates; and at this critical point the delightful history stopped short and was left truncated, without any indication from its author about where the missing section might be found.

This worried me, because the pleasure afforded by the little I had read turned to displeasure as I considered what an uphill task awaited me if I wanted to find the great bulk of material that, as I imagined, was missing from this delectable tale. It seemed impossible and contrary to all good practice that such an excellent knight shouldn't have had some sage who'd have made it his job to record his unprecedented deeds, something never lacked by any of those knights errant

> Who go, as people say,
> Adventuring their way,[1]

because every one of them had one or two sages, made to measure for him, who not only recorded his exploits but also depicted his least thoughts and most trivial actions, however hidden from the public gaze they were; and such an excellent knight couldn't have been so unfortunate as to be totally lacking in what Platir and the like had more than enough of.[2] So I couldn't bring myself to believe that such a superb history had been left maimed and mutilated, and I laid the blame on malicious time,

1. Likely to be a refrain from a contemporary ballad, one repeated several times in the novel.

2. A knight whose deeds were supposedly recorded.

the devourer and demolisher of all things, which had either hidden or destroyed what was missing.

It also struck me that, since modern books like *The Undeceptions of Jealousy* and *The Nymphs and Shepherds of Henares* had been found in his library, his history must also be a recent one, and that, even if it hadn't been put into writing, it must live on in the memory of the people of his village and others near by. All these thoughts left me feeling puzzled and eager for exact and authentic knowledge of the complete life and works of our famous Spaniard Don Quixote de la Mancha, the light and mirror of the chivalry of that land, and the first man in our times, in these calamitous times of ours, to devote himself to the toils and exercise of knight-errantry, and to the redressing of wrongs, the succouring of widows and the protecting of maidens, those maidens who used to ride about, up hill and down dale, with their whips and their palfreys, carrying their maidenhead with them; for unless raped by some blackguard, or by some peasant with his hatchet and his iron skullcap, or by some monstrous giant, there were maidens in those times gone by who, at the age of eighty and not having slept a single night under a roof, went to their graves with their maidenheads as intact as the mothers who'd borne them. I say, then, that for these and many other reasons our gallant Don Quixote is worthy of continuous and memorable praise—which shouldn't be denied me, either, for all the hard work and diligence I devoted to searching out the conclusion to this agreeable history; although I'm well aware that if heaven, chance and fortune hadn't helped me, the world would have been left without the pleasurable entertainment that an attentive reader of this work can enjoy for nearly two hours. And this is how I found the missing part:

One day when I was in the main shopping street in Toledo, a lad appeared, on his way to sell some old notebooks and loose sheets of paper to a silk merchant; and since I'll read anything, even scraps of paper lying in the gutter, this leaning of mine led me to pick up one of the notebooks that the lad had for sale, and I saw it was written in characters that I recognized as Arabic. Although I knew that much, I couldn't read them, and so I looked around to see if there was some Spanish-speaking Moor in the street, and it wasn't very hard to find one, because even if I'd been looking for a translator from another better and older language,[3] I should have found him, too. In short, chance provided me with a man who, when I told him what I wanted and put the book in his hands, opened it in the middle and after reading a little began to laugh. I asked him why, and he replied that he was laughing at something written in the margin of the book by way of annotation. I told him to tell me what it was and, still laughing, he replied:

"As I said, this is written here in the margin: 'This woman Dulcinea del Toboso, so often mentioned in this book, is said to have been a dabber hand at salting pork than any other woman in La Mancha.'"

When I heard "Dulcinea del Toboso" I was dumbfounded, because it immediately suggested that the notebooks contained the history of Don Quixote. So I told him to read me the title-page that very instant and he did so, making an extempore translation from the Arabic, and it said: *History of Don Quixote de la Mancha, written by Cide Hamete Benengeli, an Arab historian.*[4] I had to draw on all the discretion

3. Hebrew. Despite the supposed banishing of both Moors and Jews from Spain in the late 15th and early 16th centuries, quite a few remained; many had become converts or *conversos*.

4. "Cide" (as in El Cid) means "Lord" in Arabic, and "Hamete" means "He who praises." "Benengeli," on the other hand, derives from the Spanish word for eggplant.

I possess not to reveal how happy I felt when I heard the title of the book; and, getting in ahead of the silk merchant, I bought all the papers and notebooks from the lad for half a real; and if the lad himself had had any discretion and had noticed how much I wanted them, he could well have expected and indeed exacted more than six reals. Then I went off with the Moor to the cathedral cloister and asked him to translate the notebooks, or at least all those that had to do with Don Quixote, into Castilian, without adding or omitting a single word, and I offered to pay him whatever he asked. He was satisfied with fifty pounds of raisins and two bushels of wheat, and promised to make a good, faithful translation, and to be quick about it, too. But to ensure the smooth working of our agreement, and not to let such a find out of my sight, I brought the Moor home with me, and in little more than a month and a half he translated the whole text just as it is set down here.

In the first notebook there was a realistic picture of Don Quixote's battle with the Basque, with both of them in the positions described in the history, their swords aloft, one protected by his little round infantry man's shield and the other by his cushion, and the Basque's mule so lifelike that you could tell from a mile off that it was a hired one. At the Basque's feet were written the words *Don Sancho de Azpetia,* which must have been his name; and at Rocinante's feet were these other words: *Don Quixote.* Rocinante was depicted in such wonderful detail—as long as a wet week and as lean as a lath, with a jutting spine and far gone in consumption—that it was easy to see how appropriately he had been named Rocinante. Next to him stood Sancho Panza, holding his ass by the halter, and at his feet were the words *Sancho Zancas;* and he must, to judge from the picture, have had a short body, a plump paunch and long shanks, these last two features being expressed in the words Panza and Zancas[5] respectively, because he's given both these surnames at different points in this history. Other details could be observed, but none of them is important, or relevant to the truthful narration of this history—and no history is bad so long as it is truthful.

If there is any objection to be made about the truthfulness of this history, it can only be that its author was an Arab, and it's a well-known feature of Arabs that they're all liars; but since they're such enemies of ours, it's to be supposed that he fell short of the truth rather than exaggerating it. And this is, indeed, what I suspect he did, because where he could and should have launched into the praises of such an excellent knight, he seems to have been careful to pass them over in silence, which is something he shouldn't have done or even thought of doing, because historians should and must be precise, truthful and unprejudiced, without allowing self-interest or fear, hostility or affection, to turn them away from the path of truth, whose mother is history: the imitator of time, the storehouse of actions and the witness to the past, an example and a lesson to the present and a warning to the future. In this history I know that everything anyone could want to find in the most delectable history is to be found; and if anything worthwhile is missing from it, it's my belief that it's the dog of an author who wrote it that's to blame, rather than any defect in the subject. At all events the second part began like this, according to the translation:

The keen-edged swords of the two valiant and enraged combatants, thus raised aloft, seemed to be threatening the very heavens, earth and watery abysses, such was the determination displayed by both men. The first to deliver his blow was the wrathful Basque, and he did so with such force and fury that, if his sword had not twisted in

5. "Panza" means belly or paunch; "zancas" means legs.

the course of its descent, that stroke alone would have been enough to put an end to the fearful fight and to all our knight's adventures; but fortune, which had better things in store for him, turned his opponent's blade aside so that, although it struck his left shoulder, all the damage it did was to disarm him on that side, carrying with it a large part of his helmet together with half his ear, all of which tumbled to the ground in hideous ruin, leaving him in a sorry state indeed.

By God, who could describe the rage that took possession of the heart of the man of La Mancha on seeing himself treated in this way? All that can be said is that it was so great that he rose at last in his stirrups and, gripping his sword with both hands, brought it down with such fury full on the Basque's cushion and head that his admirable protection was of no avail and, as if a mountain had fallen on top of him, blood began to trickle from his nose, and from his mouth, and from his ears, and he started to slide off his mule, from which he would no doubt have fallen had he not clung to its neck; but even so he lost his stirrups and dropped his reins, and the animal, terrified by the awful blow, began to gallop this way and that, and soon bucked its rider off.

Don Quixote was calmly watching this scene, and when he saw the Basque fall he jumped from his horse, ran up to him and, putting the tip of his sword between his eyes, told him to surrender or he would cut off his head. The Basque was so stunned that he could not reply, and his fate would have been sealed, so blind with rage was Don Quixote, if the ladies in the coach, who had been watching the fight in consternation, had not hastened to where he stood and pleaded with him to do them the great kindness and favour of sparing their squire's life. To which Don Quixote, haughty and grave, replied:

"To be sure, fair ladies, I am well content to do as you request; but I insist on one condition to which you must agree, which is that this knight promise me to repair to the village of El Toboso and present himself on my behalf before the peerless Doña Dulcinea, that she may dispose of him according to her pleasure."

The fearful, disconsolate ladies, without stopping to think about what Don Quixote was demanding or even asking who Dulcinea was, promised that the squire would do whatever was required of him.

"Since you have given me your word, I shall do him no further harm, even though he richly merits it."

Chapter 10

About what happened next between Don Quixote and the Basque, and the peril with which he was threatened by a mob of men from Yanguas

By this time Sancho Panza had struggled to his feet, somewhat mauled by the friars' servants, and had stood watching Don Quixote's battle, as in his heart he prayed to God to be so kind as to give his master the victory and let him win some island of which he could make his squire the governor, as promised. So once Sancho saw that the fight was over and that his master was about to remount Rocinante, he went over to hold his stirrup and, before he started climbing, knelt down before him and, grasping his hand, kissed it and said:

"Don Quixote sir, please make me the governor of the island you've just won in this dreadful battle. However big it is, I'm sure I'll be strong enough to govern it as well as anyone who ever governed islands anywhere in the world."

To which Don Quixote replied:

"I would have you know, brother Sancho, that this adventure and others like it are not island adventures but roadside adventures, in which there is nothing to be won but a broken head and a missing ear. Be patient, for there will be adventures that will enable me to make you not only a governor but something greater still."

Sancho thanked him profusely and, again kissing his hand, and the skirts of his armour too, helped him on to Rocinante, and himself mounted his donkey and set out after his master, who, without a word of farewell to the ladies in the coach, rode off at a brisk pace into a nearby wood. Sancho followed as fast as his donkey could trot, but Rocinante's speed was such that Sancho fell further and further behind and had to call out to his master to wait for him. Don Quixote did so, reining Rocinante in until his weary squire caught up with him, and said:

"What I'm thinking, sir, is that it'd be a good idea to go and take refuge in some church somewhere, because that man you fought is in a really bad way, and it wouldn't surprise me if we were reported to the Holy Brotherhood and they came to arrest us.[1] And by God, if they do that, we'll sweat blood before we get out of prison."

"Not at all, Sancho," said Don Quixote. "Where have you ever seen or read of a knight errant standing trial, whatever outrages he is accused of?"

"I don't know anything about getting out of rages, I've never been in one in my life—all I do know is that people who go fighting in the fields are dealt with by the Holy Brotherhood, and I'm not going to poke my nose into that other thing you said."

"Do not worry, my friend," replied Don Quixote, "for I shall rescue you from the Chaldeans themselves if need be,[2] let alone the Holy Brotherhood. But tell me, pray: have you ever seen a knight more valiant than I on all the face of the earth? Have you ever read in histories of any knight who is or has been more spirited in the attack, more persevering in the pursuit, more dexterous in the wounding or more skilful in the unhorsing?"

"To tell you the honest truth," replied Sancho, "I haven't ever read a history, because I can't read or write, but what I will dare bet is that in all the days of my born life I've never served a braver master than you—and I pray God these braveries of yours aren't paid for where I just said. And what I pray you to do is to see to that ear of yours, you're losing a lot of blood from it. Here in my saddle-bags I've got some lint and white ointment."

"All this would have been quite unnecessary," replied Don Quixote, "if I had remembered to make a flask of the Balsam of Fierabras: for but one drop of it would have saved us both time and medicine."[3]

"What flask and what balsam is that?" said Sancho Panza.

"It is," said Don Quixote, "a balsam the recipe for which I carry in my memory, and if provided with it one need not fear death or contemplate dying from any kind of wound. And so, once I make some and give it to you, all you have to do when you see that in some battle I have been cut in two (as often happens) is to take the part of my body that has fallen to the ground and, before the blood congeals, neatly and carefully place it on top of the part remaining in the saddle, being quite sure to make it fit exactly. Then you will have me drink just two mouthfuls of the balsam, and I shall be as sound as a bell."

1. Created during Ferdinand's and Isabella's reign, the Holy Brotherhood dealt largely with rural criminals and highway robbers.

2. The Chaldeans were a group of tribes who became dominant in Babylonia and were regarded as enemies of the Israelites.

3. The balsam in which Christ's body was embalmed, supposedly possessed of miraculous powers of healing. Fierabras is a giant who steals the balsam from the Christians in the legends surrounding the history of Charlemagne; Charlemagne himself eventually retrieves it.

"If that's so," said Sancho, "I here and now renounce being governor of the island you've promised me, and all I want in payment for my many good services is for you to let me have the recipe for that wonderful potion—to my mind it'll fetch more than two reals an ounce anywhere, so it's all I need to live an honourable and easy life. But first I'd better know if it costs a lot to make."

"For less than three reals you can make twelve pints of it," replied Don Quixote.

"Strike me blind!" replied Sancho. "What are you waiting for, why not make some here and now and show me how?"

"Enough of that, my friend," replied Don Quixote. "I intend in due course to show you even greater secrets and do you even greater favours. But now let us see to this ear of mine, for it is hurting more than I should like."

Sancho took lint and ointment out of his saddle-bags. But when Don Quixote saw his broken helmet he was on the point of going berserk, and, placing his hand on his sword and raising his eyes to heaven, he said:

"I swear by the Creator of all things, and by the four evangelists and all their holy writings, that I will lead the life led by the great Marquis of Mantua when he swore to avenge his nephew Baldwin's death, and until then 'ne'er at table to eat bread nor with his wife to lie,' and other such things that, although I cannot remember them now, can be taken as spoken, until I have exacted full vengeance on the perpetrator of this outrage."

When Sancho heard this he said:

"I'd just like to point out, Don Quixote sir, that if that knight has done as he was told and has gone to present himself before my lady Dulcinea del Toboso, then he's done his duty and doesn't deserve another punishment unless he commits another crime."

"You have spoken well and to the purpose," replied Don Quixote, "and so I hereby annul my oath as regards exacting fresh vengeance on him; but I swear anew and confirm that I will lead the life I have just described until I wrest from some knight another helmet at least as fine as this. And do not imagine, Sancho, that I am doing this without a solid basis, for I have a clear model to follow: exactly the same thing happened, down to the very last detail, with Mambrino's helmet, which cost Sacripante so dear."[4]

"You just send all those oaths of yours to the devil, sir," retorted Sancho, "they're bad for your health and worse for your conscience. Or else tell me this—supposing days and days go by and we don't come across anyone in a helmet, what then? Have we got to honour the oath, regardless of all the inconvenience and discomfort, always sleeping in our clothes, never under a roof, and those hundreds of other penances in the mad old Marquis of Mantua's vow, that you're so set on reviving? Just think about it, sir—it isn't men in armour you'll find on these here roads but carters and muleteers, who not only don't wear helmets but have probably never even heard of them."

"You are mistaken about that," said Don Quixote, "because before we have been riding along these highways and byways for two hours we shall see more men in arms than fell upon Albracca to carry off the fair Angelica."[5]

4. Rinaldo, elsewhere cited as Reynaldo of Montelban, steals the enchanted helmet of the Moorish king Sacripante in Book 1 of Boiardo's *Orlando Innamorato.*

5. Daughter of a Moorish king who dwells in the castle of Albracca; in Boiardo's poem, the castle is beseiged by Agricane and his men.

"All right, then, so be it," said Sancho, "and please God we come well out of all this and the time soon arrives to conquer this island that's going to cost me so dear—and then I can die happy."

"I have already told you, Sancho, not to worry about all that; for if finding an island presents any problems, there is always the kingdom of Denmark or the kingdom of Soliadisa,[6] which would fit you like a glove, and still more so being as it is on terra firma, which should make you even happier. But let us leave these matters until it is time to deal with them; and now see if you have anything to eat in your saddle-bags, so that we can go without delay in search of some castle where we can stay for the night and make the balsam about which I have told you; for I swear to God that my ear is very painful."

"There's an onion here, and a bit of cheese, and a few scraps of bread," said Sancho, "but that isn't food for a valiant knight like you."

"How mistaken you are!" replied Don Quixote. "I would have you know, Sancho, that it is an honour for knights errant not to eat for a whole month, and if they do eat, it must be what they find readiest to hand, and you would know this well enough if you had read as many histories as I have; for in all those very very many that I have read, I have not found any mention of knights errant eating, except when it happened that some sumptuous banquet was held for them, but otherwise they used to live on next to nothing. And although it is evident that they could not have gone without eating and satisfying all the other needs of nature, because, after all, they were men like us, it is also evident that since they spent most of their time wandering in woods and wildernesses, without cooks, their everyday food must have been country fare, like that which you are offering me now. And so, friend Sancho, do not be afflicted by what pleases me; do not seek to build the world anew, or to turn knight-errantry on its head."

"I'm sorry I'm sure," said Sancho. "Not knowing how to read or write, as I said before, I haven't been able to find out about all these rules of knighthood. From now on I'll put all sorts of nuts and raisins into the saddle-bags for you, being as you are a knight, and for me, not being one, I'll put in feathered provisions of greater substance."

"I am not saying, Sancho," replied Don Quixote, "that it is obligatory for knights errant not to eat anything other than those nuts to which you refer; but that they must have been their usual sustenance, together with certain herbs, known to them and to me, which they found in the fields."

"It's a good idea," said Sancho, "to know about those there herbs. I fancy we're going to need that knowledge one fine day."

Then he took out what he'd said he'd brought, and the two men ate together in peace and good fellowship. But anxious to find somewhere to stay that night they didn't linger over their dry and frugal meal. They remounted and hurried on, to try and reach a village before nightfall, but both the day and their hopes of doing so came to an end as they were passing some goatherds' huts, and they decided to spend the night there. Sancho's sorrow at not reaching a village was matched by his master's delight at sleeping in the open air, because he considered that each time he did so he performed an act of possession that provided fresh proof of his chivalry.

6. Perhaps Cervantes (or Quixote) is confusing names here; Soliadisa is a princess, not a kingdom, in a 16th-century romance.

from *Chapter 11*

About what happened to Don Quixote with some goatherds

He received a hearty welcome from the goatherds. Once Sancho had accommodated Rocinante and the donkey as best he could, he set off on the trail of the smell being given out by some chunks of goat meat that were boiling in a pot over the fire; and, although he'd have liked to find out there and then if they were ready to be transferred from the pot to the stomach, this wasn't possible, because the goatherds took them off the fire and, spreading some sheepskins on the ground, made haste to lay their rustic table and, showing great goodwill, invited them to share their meal. There were six goatherds using that fold and they all sat down around the skins, after begging Don Quixote, with rough ceremony, to sit on an upside-down bowl that they placed there for him. Don Quixote did so, and Sancho stayed standing to serve him the drinking horn. When Don Quixote saw his squire on his feet, he said:

"So that you may see, Sancho, what great good there is in knight-errantry, and how close those exercising any of its ministries always are to being honoured and esteemed by the world, it is my wish that you should come and sit by my side in the company of these excellent people, and be one with me, your natural lord and master—that you should eat from my very own plate and drink from my very own cup: for of knight-errantry may be said what is said of love, that it makes all things equal."

"What a great honour!" said Sancho. "But just let me tell you one thing, sir—if I had plenty to eat, I'd eat it as well or even better standing up and by myself as sitting down next to an emperor. The truth is that what I eat in my own little corner without any fuss or bother, even if it is only bread and onions, tastes much better to me than all the fine turkeys on other tables where I'd have to chew slowly, drink hardly a drop, wipe my mouth all the time, never sneeze or cough if I felt like it, or do all those other things that being by yourself and free and easy lets you do. So, sir, as for these honours that you want to confer on me for being a follower and servant of knight-errantry, which is what I am as your squire, I'd rather you turned them into something more practical and useful, and I renounce all your honours from here to eternity—though I'm very grateful to you I'm sure."

"You shall sit down all the same; for he that humbleth himself shall be exalted."

And seizing Sancho by the arm he forced him to squat by his side.

The goatherds couldn't make head or tail of this gibberish about squires and knights errant, and they just sat there eating in silence and staring at their guests who, with great elegance and even greater appetite, were stowing away chunks of meat as big as their fists. Once the meat course was finished, a quantity of sweet acorns was spread on the sheepskins together with half a cheese, harder than if it had been made of mortar. Meanwhile the drinking horn was being kept busy, circulating so often (now full, now empty, like a bucket on a water wheel) that it soon exhausted one of the two wineskins hanging near by. * * *

Chapter 12

About what a goatherd told Don Quixote and the others

And now one of the lads who brought provisions from the village appeared and said:

"Hey, do you know what's happened down in the village?"

"How are we supposed to know that?" replied one of them.

"Well, it's like this," the lad continued. "That famous student-shepherd Grisóstomo died this morning, and it's rumoured he died of love for that fiendish Marcela, rich Guillermo's daughter, that girl who wanders about all those God-forsaken places dressed up as a shepherdess."

"Marcela you said?" asked one of them.

"Marcela I said," the lad replied. "And the best part is he's left in his will that he wants to be buried out in the wilds, like some Moor, at the foot of the rock by the cork-oak spring, because rumour has it that's where he first saw her, and they say he said so himself. And he's left other things to be done, too, but the village priests say they won't be done, and that it wouldn't be right to do them, because they're more like what pagans get up to. To all this, that great friend of his, Ambrosio—you know, that student who dressed up as a shepherd with him—replies that it'll all be done just as Grisóstomo ordered, and the village is in an uproar about it, but, to judge from what everyone's saying, they're going to end up doing what Ambrosio and all his shepherd friends want, and tomorrow they're coming to bury him with great pomp and ceremony where I said. And it's my belief it's going to be well worth seeing—at least I'm not going to miss it, not even if it means that I can't get back to the village tomorrow."

"That's what we'll all do," added the goatherds, "and we'll draw lots to see who'll stay behind to look after the goats."

"A good idea, Pedro," said one, "but there won't be any need for that, I'll stay behind with everybody's goats. And don't put it down to virtue or lack of curiosity on my part, but to me not being able to walk, because of that broken branch that went through my foot the other day."

"Thanks all the same," replied Pedro.

Don Quixote asked this Pedro to tell him about the dead man and the shepherdess, to which Pedro replied that all he knew was that the dead man was a rich hidalgo who lived in a village in the sierra and who'd been a student at Salamanca University for many years, after which he'd come back to the village with a reputation for being wise and well-read.[1]

"In particular, people said he knew all about the science of the stars, and what the sun and the moon do up there in the sky, because he used to tell us exactly when the clips were going to come."

"*Eclipse* is the word, my friend, not *clips,* for the obscuration of the two great luminaries," said Don Quixote.

But Pedro, not troubling himself with trifles, went on with his story:

"And he also used to predict whether a year was going to be fruitful or hysterical."

"You mean *sterile,* my friend," said Don Quixote.

"Sterile or hysterical," replied Pedro, "it all boils down to the same thing. As I was saying, with all this predicting his father and his friends grew very rich, because they believed him and did as he advised when he said: 'Sow barley this year, not wheat; this year you'd better sow chick-peas, not barley; next year there's going to be a bumper crop of olives, but the following three there won't be any at all.'"

1. A sierra is a mountain range. Don Quixote will shortly wander into the Sierra Morena, a name given to the southcentral stretch of Spain that encompasses parts of the provinces of Cordoba and Sevilla and separates La Mancha from Andalucia. Salamanca University was respected as the foremost university in Spain and received strong royal support.

"That science is called astrology," said Don Quixote.

"I haven't the faintest idea what it's called," retorted Pedro, "but what I do know is that he knew all this and more besides. In the end, not very many months after he came back from Salamanca, he took off his long scholar's gown one day and appeared dressed as a shepherd, with his crook and his sheepskin jacket—and this other man, his great friend Ambrosio, who'd studied with him, he dressed himself up as a shepherd too. I was forgetting to say that Grisóstomo, the dead man, was very good at writing poems—he even used to write the carols for Christmas Eve, and the mystery plays for Corpus Christi[2] that the village lads performed, and everyone said they were brilliant. When the people in the village saw the two scholars suddenly dressed as shepherds they were amazed, and couldn't work out what had led them to make such an odd change. By this time Grisóstomo's father had died and he'd inherited piles of property—royal estate, goods and cattles, cows and horses, sheep and goats, as well as masses of money, and the lad was left the absolute lord of it all, and the truth is he deserved it, because he was a fine companion and very charitable, a good friend to all good men, with a face like an angel. Later it was known that he'd only changed clothes to wander all about these wild places after that shepherdess Marcela the young lad mentioned before, because poor Grisóstomo, God rest his soul, had fallen in love with her. And now I'm going to tell you, because it's something you should know, who that lass is—it's possible, and more than possible, that you won't hear anything like it in all the days of your life, even if you live to be older than noses."

"*Moses* you should have said," interrupted Don Quixote, who couldn't abide the goatherd's word-mangling.

"Noses have been around for quite a while, too," retorted Pedro, "and if you're going to be picking on every other word I use, sir, we shan't be done in a twelvemonth."

"Forgive me, my friend," said Don Quixote. "I only mentioned it because there is such a difference between noses and Moses; but your reply was an excellent one, for noses are indeed older than Moses; and do continue your history, and I will not interrupt you ever again."

"I was about to say, my dear good sir," said the goatherd, "that there was one farmer in our village even richer than Grisóstomo's father, and he was called Guillermo, and God had given him not only vast riches but also a daughter whose mother, the most honourable woman in all these parts, had died giving birth to her. I can see her even now, that lovely face of hers with the sun in one cheek and the moon in the other. And what a fine housewife she was, and so good to the poor—I do believe that at this very moment her soul must be enjoying God in the other world. Guillermo was heartbroken at the death of such an excellent wife and he died, too, leaving his daughter Marcela young and rich and in the care of one of her uncles, a priest in our village. The girl grew up so beautiful that she put us in mind of her mother, such a great beauty herself, although everyone thought that her daughter was going to be even lovelier. And so she was, and by the time she was fourteen or fifteen all who set eyes on her praised God for making her so beautiful, and most fell hopelessly in love. Her uncle kept her shut up indoors, very bashful and demure, but the fame of her great beauty spread far and wide—and this, and her fortune, brought the men not only of our own village but of all the villages for many miles around, the very best of them too, flocking to ask, beg and pester her uncle for her hand in

2. The feast of Corpus Christi, celebrated in early June, was always an occasion for *autos sacramentales*—mystery plays on a religious theme.

marriage. But even though he'd have liked to marry her off straight away, since she was of the right age, being a true and good Christian he was unwilling to do so without her consent—and no, he didn't have an eye on the gains to be made from delaying the girl's marriage and keeping control of her property. This, I can promise you, was said in praise of the good priest in more than one circle of commentators in the village. For I should tell you, errant sir, that in these tiny places everything's discussed and everything's gossiped about; and you can be quite certain, just as I am, that a priest has to be a saint to make his flock speak well of him, especially in a village."

"That is quite true," said Don Quixote, "but do continue, for the story is a very good one, and you, my dear Pedro, are telling it with a certain stylish grace."

"It's the grace of Our Lord God that I'm in need of, which is more to the purpose. Anyway, what happened was that although the priest described to his niece, in detail, the qualities of each one of her many suitors, begging her to choose and marry whichever she preferred, all she ever replied was that she didn't want to marry yet because, being so young, she didn't feel strong enough to bear the burden of matrimony. Faced with excuses as good as these appeared to be, her uncle stopped pressing her, and decided to wait until she was older and able to choose a companion to her taste. For as he said, and said rightly, parents shouldn't provide for their children's future against their will. But lo and behold, like a bolt from the blue, meticulous modest Marcela appears one day converted into a shepherdess, and, despite all the efforts of her uncle and the other villagers to dissuade her, off she goes into the fields with the other shepherdesses in the village to mind her own flock. And once she came into the public gaze and her beauty was exposed to all eyes, I couldn't tell you how many rich youths, hidalgos and farmers dressed up just like Grisóstomo, and wandered about the fields wooing her—among them, as I've said, our deceased friend, who people said no longer loved her, but adored her.

"But you mustn't suppose, just because Marcela has given herself over to this free and easy life, with little privacy or rather none at all, that she's done anything to bring the least discredit upon her modesty or chastity; quite the opposite, she watches so closely over her own honour that of all her suitors and pursuers not one has boasted, or could boast without lying, of having been given the slightest hope of fulfilling his desire. Because although she doesn't avoid the company of shepherds, and treats them with courteous friendliness, as soon as any of them reveals his intentions, even if in a proper and holy proposal of marriage, she hurls him from her like a boulder from a catapult. And in this mood she's wreaking more havoc on these lands than if they'd been invaded by the plague; because her affability and beauty encourage those who know her to serve her and to love her, but her disdainful destruction of their hopes drives them to the brink of suicide; and so they don't know what to say, and only cry that she's cruel and an ingrate, and other similar words that describe her character all too accurately. And if you were to stay here awhile, sir, you'd hear these mountains and these valleys echoing with the laments of the broken-hearted wretches who pursue her.

"Not far from here is a place where there are almost two dozen lofty beeches, and there is not one on whose smooth bark is not engraved the name of Marcela, and above some a crown with which a lover affirms that Marcela wears and deserves to wear the crown of all human beauty.[3] Here a shepherd sighs, there another moans; here songs of love are to be heard, there dirges of despair. There's one who spends

3. Writing poems to one's beloved on the bark of a tree was common in pastoral romance.

every hour of the night seated at the foot of some oak or crag, and there, never allowing his tear-filled eyes a moment's rest, sunk and lost in his thoughts, he's found by the morning sun; there's another who, finding no relief or respite for his sighs, stretched out on the burning sand in the racking noonday heat of summer, sends his complaints up to merciful heaven. And over every single one of them the lovely Marcela triumphs, footloose and fancy-free, and all of us who know her are waiting to see where her arrogance will lead, and who will be the fortunate man to tame such ferocity and enjoy such perfect beauty. Since everything I've narrated is the proven truth, I can well believe that what this young lad here said they're saying about the cause of Grisóstomo's death is also true. And so I advise you, sir, not to miss his burial tomorrow—it'll be well worth seeing, because Grisóstomo has lots of friends, and it isn't a couple of miles from here to where he said he wanted to be buried."

"That is indeed what I intend to do," said Don Quixote, "and I thank you for the pleasure you have afforded me by telling me such a delightful story."

"Oh no!" replied the goatherd. "I don't know half the things that have happened to Marcela's suitors, but it could be that tomorrow we come across some shepherd who can tell us about them. And now it'll be a good idea for you to go and sleep under cover, because sleeping in the damp night air could be bad for your wound—though the remedy you've been given is so effective that there's no fear of an infection setting in."

Sancho Panza, who was wishing that the goatherd would take his endless talk with him to the devil, also asked his master to go and sleep in Pedro's hut. He did so, and there he spent most of the night remembering his lady Dulcinea, in imitation of Marcela's suitors. Sancho Panza settled down between Rocinante and his donkey, and there he slept the sleep not so much of a star-crossed lover as of a hoof-hammered squire.

from *Chapter 13*

Which concludes the story about the shepherdess Marcela, together with other events

But hardly had the day begun to show itself on the balconies of the east when five of the six goatherds got up and went to wake Don Quixote, to ask him if he still intended to go and see the famous burial of Grisóstomo, and to tell him that if he did they would keep him company. Don Quixote, who was longing to go, rose and told Sancho to saddle the horse and fit the pack-saddle on to the donkey immediately, which he did with great diligence; and with the same diligence they all set out on their way. And they'd ridden less than a mile when, as they crossed another path, they saw half a dozen shepherds coming towards them clothed in black sheepskin jackets and with wreaths of cypress and bitter oleander crowning their heads. Each had a stout holly stave in his hand. With them came two gentlemen on horseback, splendidly dressed for travelling, accompanied by three servants on foot. When the two parties met they exchanged courteous greetings, and when they asked each other where they were going they discovered that they were all on their way to the burial, so they travelled together.

One of the horsemen said to his companion:

"It seems to me, Señor Vivaldo, that we're going to count however much time we spend on this famous burial as having been time well spent: it is indeed going to be famous, considering the extraordinary things these shepherds have been telling us about the dead shepherd and the death-dealing shepherdess."

"I think so, too," replied Vivaldo, "and I'm not talking about taking just one day over it, either—I'd happily take four days off for the sake of witnessing it."

Don Quixote asked what it was that they had heard about Marcela and Grisóstomo. The horseman replied that they'd joined up with the shepherds earlier that morning and that, seeing them in such mournful attire, they'd asked why they were dressed like that; and that one of the shepherds had told them all about the secluded life and the beauty of a shepherdess called Marcela, and about the love she inspired in the many men who wooed her, and about the death of that Grisóstomo to whose burial they were going. In short, he told them everything that Pedro had told Don Quixote the day before.

So this conversation came to an end, and another one began when the man called Vivaldo asked Don Quixote what it was that prompted him to ride about such a peaceful part of the world armed in that fashion. And Don Quixote replied:

"The profession that I exercise does not allow me to ride in any other way. Easy living, luxury and repose were invented for effete courtiers; toil, disquiet and arms were created solely for those the world calls knights errant, of whom I, unworthy as I am, am the very least."

On hearing this they all concluded that he was mad; and to make quite certain, and to find out what sort of madness he suffered from, Vivaldo went on to ask him what knights errant were.

"Have you not read," replied Don Quixote, "the annals and histories of England, which treat of the famous exploits of King Arthur, commonly known in our Castilian tongue as Artús, who, according to an ancient tradition divulged throughout that kingdom of Great Britain, did not die but was, by sorcerer's art, turned into a raven, and who, in due course, will recover his sceptre and kingdom, and reign again; for which reason no Englishman has ever been known from that day to this to kill a raven? Well, in the days of that good king the famous order of chivalry of the Knights of the Round Table was founded, and the love between Sir Lancelot of the Lake and Queen Guinevere was consummated as is there recorded, the go-between and confidante being that honourable duenna Quintañona, all of which gave rise to the ballad that is so well known and so highly praised in Spain:

And never sure was any knight
So served by damsel or by dame
As Lancelot, that man of might,
When here from Brittany he came,

with its smooth and gentle unfolding of its deeds of love and war.[1] Well, from that time onwards, handed on down the generations, the order of chivalry gradually extended and spread throughout many different parts of the world, and its members were famous for their exploits: the valiant Amadis of Gaul with all his sons and grandsons to the fifth generation, and the valorous Felixmarte of Hyrcania, and the never sufficiently praised Tirante the White, and the brave and invincible knight Belianis of Greece, whom we have very nearly been able to see and speak with and hear

1. Quixote accurately summarizes the famed legends of Arthur, Lancelot, and Guinevere. Quintañona was added in the Spanish versions of Lancelot's and Guinevere's unchaste love.

in our own times.[2] This, then, gentlemen, is what it is to be a knight errant, and this is the order of chivalry, in which I, as I have said, although a sinner, have professed; and I do profess everything professed by the knights of whom I have told you. And so I roam these lonely and deserted places in search of adventures, with the firm intention to employ my arm and indeed my whole person in the most perilous adventures that fortune sends my way, in aid of the weak and needy."

These words showed the travellers that Don Quixote was indeed out of his wits, and they could now see what kind of madness had taken him over, which astonished them as much as it did everybody else who made this discovery. And, to while away the time during the short journey said to remain, Vivaldo, who was a clever man with a cheerful disposition, decided, when they reached the sierra where the burial was to take place, to provide him with the opportunity to expand on his nonsense. So he said: "It seems to me, sir knight errant, that you profess one of the very strictest professions in the world, and it's my belief that not even being a Carthusian monk is as strict."[3]

"It may be that it is as strict," replied our Don Quixote, "but whether it is as necessary to the world is something that I am within a hair's breadth of doubting. For, if truth is to be told, the soldier who carries out his captain's orders contributes no less than the captain who gives him those orders. What I mean to say is that monks, in peace and tranquillity, pray to heaven for the well-being of the world; but we soldiers and knights put into practice what they pray for, defending the world with the prowess of our arms and the blades of our swords, and not under cover but in the open air, the targets for unbearable sun-rays in the summer and for the piercing frosts of winter. So we are ministers of God on earth, the arms through which his justice is executed here. . . ."

As they continued on their way engrossed in this conversation they saw, coming down a gorge between two great hills, about twenty shepherds, all wearing black sheepskin jackets and crowned with wreaths some of which were later discovered to be of yew and the others of cypress. Six of the shepherds were carrying a bier covered with a great variety of flowers and branches. At this sight one of the goatherds said:

"Those men over there are bringing Grisóstomo's body, and at the foot of that mountain is the spot where he said he was to be buried."

So they hurried there, just in time, because the shepherds had placed the bier on the ground and four of them had begun digging a grave beside a hard rock with their sharp pickaxes.

The two parties exchanged courteous greetings, and then Don Quixote and those who had come with him went to examine the bier, and on it, covered in flowers, they saw the corpse, dressed as a shepherd, of a man who seemed to be about thirty; and even though he was dead, it was plain to see that in life he'd had handsome features and a gallant disposition. Scattered around him on the bier there were some books and many papers, some open and some folded up. The onlookers, the grave-diggers and all the others kept an extraordinary silence, until one of those who'd brought the body said to another:

"You'd better make quite certain, Ambrosio, that this is the place Grisóstomo said, since you're so concerned for everything in his will to be carried out exactly as he instructed."

2. Amadis and Tirante have already been mentioned; Felixmarte is also known as Florismarte of Hircania, the hero of a chivalric work bearing his name (1556). Belianis also appears as hero of a Spanish chivalric romance.

3. Carthusian monks were rigorous contemplatives bound by strict orders of fasting.

"Yes, this is the place," replied Ambrosio, "because it was here that my unhappy friend often told me the story of his misadventures. He told me it was here that he first saw that mortal enemy of the human race; here that he first declared his love, as honourable as it was ardent; and here, at their last meeting, that Marcela sealed her scornful rejection, which led him to put an end to the tragedy of his wretched existence. And here, in remembrance of so many misfortunes, he wished to be laid in the bowels of eternal oblivion."

And, turning to Don Quixote and the travellers, Ambrosio continued:

"This body, gentlemen, that you are contemplating with compassionate eyes, was the dwelling-place of a soul in which heaven placed an infinite portion of its riches. This is the body of Grisóstomo, who was unmatched in intelligence, peerless in courtesy, perfect in politeness, a phoenix in friendship, generous beyond measure, grave without presumptuousness, joyful without vulgarity, and, all in all, the first in virtue, and second to none in misfortune. He loved and was hated; he adored and was disdained; he entreated a dragon, pleaded with marble, chased the wind, cried out in the wilderness and served ingratitude, whose reward was to make him the prey of death in the midst of the course of his life, which was ended by a shepherdess whom he wished to make immortal in the memory of mankind, as those papers at which you are looking could demonstrate, if he had not instructed me to commit them to the flames as soon as I have committed his body to the earth."

"If you do that," said Vivaldo, "you'll be treating them with even harsher cruelty than their owner himself, because it's neither just nor proper to carry out the wishes of a man who orders something that no rational arguments can justify. Augustus Caesar would have been out of his mind if he'd agreed to what the divine Mantuan poet ordered in his will.[4] And so, Señor Ambrosio, even though you are committing your friend's body to the earth, don't commit his writings to oblivion; for if he was so aggrieved as to command it, you shouldn't be so foolish as to obey him. Rather let these papers live, and Marcela's cruelty with them, for ever, as an example to the living, in times to come, so that they can avoid such pitfalls; because I and these friends of mine know the history of this enamoured and desperate friend of yours, and we know about your friendship, and what caused his death, and the instructions he left when he died; from all of which lamentable history it is easy to judge how great was Marcela's cruelty, Grisóstomo's love and your faithful friendship, and also to see what happens to people who rush headlong down the path that delirious love places before their eyes. Last night we learned that Grisóstomo had died and was to be buried in this place, and so, moved by curiosity and compassion, we departed from our route and agreed to come and see for ourselves what we'd been so sad to hear about. And in recognition of this compassion, and of our desire to do something about it if we could, we beg you, O Ambrosio,—or at least I for my part beg you—not to burn these papers and to let me have some of them."

And without waiting for the shepherd to reply, Vivaldo stretched out his hand and took some of the papers closest to him. Seeing which Ambrosio said:

"Courtesy obliges me, sir, to let you keep the papers you've just taken, but it would be vain for you to think I shall not burn the rest."

Vivaldo, longing to see what was written on the papers, opened one of them and saw that its title was *Song of Despair.* On hearing this Ambrosio said:

4. Virgil asked from his deathbed that his unfinished *Aeneid* be destroyed.

"This is the last thing the unfortunate man wrote. And so that all can hear, sir, to what a pass his misfortune had brought him, please read it aloud: there'll be time enough to do so while the grave is being dug."

"That I shall do with pleasure," said Vivaldo.

And since all the others were equally curious, they gathered around him, and he read the following in a clear and ringing voice:

from *Chapter 14*

In which the dead shepherd's verses of despair are given, together with other unexpected events

Grisóstomo's Song

Since you would have me publish, cruel maid,
From tongue to tongue, in this and every nation,
The news of your implacable disdain,
I'll call on hell itself to come and aid
My grieving breast with howls of lamentation,
And bend and break my voice with grief and pain.
And as I strive and labour to explain
My sorrow and your cold and heartless deed,
Forth shall the terrifying clamour stream,
And in it fragments of my bowels shall teem
To make my torture exquisite indeed.
So give me your attention: listen now
Not to harmonious sounds, but to the row
That from my bosom's depths in desolation,
Stirred up by bitter frenzy without measure,
Flows for my pleasure and for your vexation. . . .

And now the hour has struck: from deepest hell
Come, thirsting Tantalus, to my ordeal;
Rolling your mighty stone along its way
Come, Sisyphus; come, Tityus, come as well,
And bring your vulture; Ixion, bring your wheel;[1]
Come too, you sisters toiling night and day;[2]
And now let all of you as one convey
Your mortal anguish to my breast, and sigh
(If it's allowed to victims of despair)
Your harrowing laments over my bare
Carcass, refused a shroud in which to lie.[3]
Come, three-faced guardian of the dreadful gate[4]
And all hell's brood of fiends, and celebrate
And sing the doleful descant of your grief;

1. The four names illustrate vivid punishments in the afterworld from Greek mythology. Tantalus must forever be suspended between a stream and a cluster of fruit; Sisphyus is doomed to roll a stone up a mountain only to watch it roll back down; Tityus has his liver eaten by a vulture each day only to have it grow back by night; Ixion is strapped to a wheel that never stops turning.

2. Probably the Danaids, condemned to Hades for killing their husbands on their wedding night; their punishment is to try to fill leaky jars for all eternity.

3. Suicides were not permitted burial in consecrated ground.

4. Cerberus, the three-headed dog who guards the entrance to the underworld.

No better tribute can, I think, be due
To lovers who have won death's cold relief.

O Song of Desperation, do not grieve
Now that in desolation I must leave;
But rather, since the cause that gave you birth
By my misfortune grows and grows in gladness,
Be free from sadness, even in the earth.

The members of the audience quite liked Grisóstomo's song, even though the reader said he didn't think it accorded with the account he'd heard of Marcela's modesty and virtue, because Grisóstomo complained about jealousy, suspicion and absence, all to the prejudice of Marcela's good name and reputation. To which Ambrosio replied, as one who knew his friend's most hidden thoughts:

"To satisfy that doubt, sir, I should tell you that when this unfortunate man wrote this song he was far from Marcela, having taken himself away to see if absence would have its customary effect; and, since there's nothing that doesn't worry an absent lover and no fear that doesn't assail him, Grisóstomo was worried by imagined jealousies and suspicions that he feared as if they were real. And so everything that fame affirms about Marcela's virtue is true: except for some cruelty, and a little arrogance, and more than a little disdain, there are no faults at all for envy itself to find in her."

"That's true enough," replied Vivaldo.

As he was about to read another of the papers he'd saved from the fire, he was halted by a miraculous vision (that was what it seemed to be) which came before their eyes: on top of the crag by which the grave was being dug the shepherdess Marcela appeared, so beautiful that her beauty was even greater than it was famed to be. Those who had never seen her before gazed at her in silent amazement, and those who were used to seeing her stood in no less awe. But as soon as Ambrosio saw her he said, with indignation in his looks:

"Have you come, perhaps, fierce basilisk of these mountains, to see if your presence will make the wounds of this poor man slain by your cruelty spout blood? Or have you come to gloat over the achievements of your barbarity; or to contemplate from those heights, like another pitiless Nero, the flames of burning Rome; or to ride roughshod in your arrogance over this luckless corpse, as the ungrateful daughter did over her father Tarquin?[5] Tell us now why you've come and what you want; because knowing that Grisóstomo's very thoughts never failed to obey you when he was alive, I shall ensure that, even though he's dead, you'll be obeyed by the thoughts of all those who called themselves his friends."

"I haven't come, Ambrosio, for any of the reasons you've mentioned," replied Marcela, "but to defend myself and to demonstrate how wrong are all those who blame me for Grisóstomo's death and for their grief; and so I beg all of you here to give me your attention, because it won't take me very long nor shall I need many words to bring the truth home to people of good sense.

"You all say that heaven made me beautiful, so much so that this beauty of mine, with a force you can't resist, makes you love me; and you say and even demand that, in return for the love you show me, I must love you. By the natural understanding

5. The emperor Nero was rumored to have fiddled while Rome burned. The wicked Tullia persuaded her husband to murder her father, and when he was dead, she drove her chariot over his body. Her husband, however, was named Tarquin, her father Servius Tullius.

which God has granted me I know that whatever is beautiful is lovable; but I can't conceive why, for this reason alone, a woman who's loved for her beauty should be obliged to love whoever loves her. What's more, it could happen that the lover of beauty is ugly, and since that which is ugly is loathsome, it isn't very fitting for him to say: 'I love you because you're beautiful; you must love me even though I'm ugly.' And even if they are well-matched as far as beauty goes, that doesn't mean that the attraction's going to be mutual, because not all beauty inspires love. Some beauties delight the eye but don't captivate the heart; just as well, because if all beauty did inspire love and conquer hearts, people's affections would be forever wandering this way and that without knowing where to come to rest—there's an infinite number of beautiful people, so the affections would be infinite, too. And, according to what I've heard, true love can't be divided, and must be voluntary, not forced on you. If this is so, as I believe it is, why do you think I should be obliged to give in to you, just because you say you love me dearly? Or else tell me this: if heaven had made me ugly instead of beautiful, would I have been right to complain about you for not loving me? What's more, you must remember that I didn't choose this beauty of mine—heaven gave it to me, exactly as you see it, quite freely, without my asking for it or picking it. And just as the viper doesn't deserve to be blamed for her poison, even though she kills with it, because nature gave it to her, so I don't deserve to be blamed for being beautiful; because beauty in a virtuous woman is like a distant fire or sharp sword, which don't burn or cut anyone who doesn't come too close. Honour and virtue are ornaments of the soul, and without them the body, even if it is beautiful, shouldn't seem beautiful. Well then, if chastity is one of the virtues that most embellish the soul and the body, why should the woman who's loved for her beauty lose her chastity by responding to the advances of the man who, merely for his own pleasure, employs all his strength and cunning to make her lose it?

"I was born free, and to live free I chose the solitude of the countryside. The trees on these mountains are my company, the clear waters of these streams are my mirrors; and to the trees and the waters I reveal my thoughts and my beauty. I am the distant fire and the far-off sword. Those who have loved me for my looks I have disabused with my words. And if desires are kept alive on hope, I have never given any hope to Grisóstomo or fulfilled any man's desires, so it can truly be said of all of them that they were killed by their own obstinacy rather than by my cruelty. And if it's objected that his intentions were honourable and that for this reason I should have been more responsive to him, I reply that when, in that very place where his grave is being dug now, he revealed those honourable intentions of his to me, I told him that mine were to live in perpetual solitude and to allow nothing but the earth to enjoy the fruits of my seclusion and the remains of my beauty. If, after I'd spoken as plainly as that, he still chose to persevere against all hope and sail against the wind, is it surprising that he sank in the middle of the gulf of his own folly? If I'd encouraged him, I should have been false; if I'd gratified him, I should have been acting against my own intentions, better than his. He persisted although disabused, he despaired although not hated: and now you tell me whether it's just for me to be blamed for his grief! Let the man I deceive complain, let the victim of broken promises despair, let the man I entice nurse hope, let the man I accept rejoice: but let me not be called cruel or murderous by any man whom I have never deceived, made promises to, enticed or accepted.

"Heaven hasn't yet made it my destiny to love, and it's vain to think I'd ever love out of choice. Let this general warning serve for the individual benefit of each of my pursuers; and let it also be understood from now on that if any man dies because of me, he isn't dying from jealousy or mistreatment, because a woman who doesn't love any man can't make any man jealous, and disabuse must not be confused with disdain. He who calls me fierce and a basilisk can leave me alone, as something evil and dangerous; he who calls me an ingrate can stop courting me; he who calls me distant can keep his distance; he who calls me cruel can stop following me: because this fierce basilisk, this ingrate, this cruel and distant woman is most certainly not going to seek, court, approach or follow any of them. If Grisóstomo was killed by his own impatience and uncontrolled passion, why should anyone blame my modest and circumspect behaviour for that? If I keep my purity in the company of the trees, why should anyone want me to lose it in the company of men? As you all know, I have wealth of my own and I don't covet anyone else's; I live in freedom and I don't like to be constrained; I neither love nor hate anybody. I neither deceive this man nor run after that; I neither toy with one, nor amuse myself with another. The innocent company of the village shepherdesses and the care of my goats keep me happy. These mountains mark the limits of my desires, and if they do extend any further it is only for the contemplation of the beauty of the heavens, the way along which the soul travels back to its first abode."

And as she said this she turned and disappeared into the thick of a nearby forest without waiting for an answer, leaving everyone astonished as much at her intelligence as at her beauty. And some of them, wounded by the powerful arrows of the rays flashing from her lovely eyes, made to follow her, heedless of the clear warning that they'd heard. Don Quixote, seeing this, and thinking it a good moment to make use of his chivalry by succouring a maiden in distress, cried in a ringing voice and with his hand on the hilt of his sword:

"Let no man, of whatever estate or condition, dare to follow the beautiful Marcela, under pain of incurring my furious indignation. She has shown with clear and sufficient reasons that she bears little or no blame for Grisóstomo's death, and that she is far from reciprocating the desires of any of her suitors; for which reason it is right that, instead of being pursued and persecuted, she should be honoured and held in esteem by all good men, for she has shown that she is the only woman in the world who lives such a chaste life."

Whether because of Don Quixote's threats or because Ambrosio told them to finish what they were doing for their dead friend, none of the shepherds left the spot until, with the grave dug and Grisóstomo's papers burned, they placed his body in it, not without shedding many tears. They sealed the grave with a thick slab of rock, to be replaced in due course by a tombstone which Ambrosio said he was going to have made, with the following epitaph engraved on it:

In here, earth's cold and paltry prize,
The body of a lover lies,
A shepherd who was cruelly slain
By one who paid love with disdain.
Ungrateful, haughty, cold and fair
Was she who drove him to despair:
More triumph for man's deadly foe
As tyrant Love's dominions grow.

They strewed flowers and branches over the grave, condoled with their friend Ambrosio and took their leave of him. Vivaldo and his companion did the same, and Don Quixote said goodbye to his hosts and to the travellers, who begged him to come with them to Seville, because it's just the place to find adventures—on every street and round every corner they're simply waiting for you, more of them than anywhere else in the world.[6] Don Quixote thanked them for the information and for their disposition to extend such courtesies to him, but said that for the time being he did not wish to go to Seville and indeed could not go there, until he had rid all those sierras of foul robbers, with which they were said to be infested. In view of his firm intentions the travellers decided not to pester him any more and, repeating their farewells, they left him and continued their journey, during which they weren't short of things to talk about, what with Marcela's history and Don Quixote's mad deeds. He resolved to go in search of the shepherdess Marcela and offer her all the services in his power. But events didn't turn out as he expected, according to what is related in the course of this true history, the second part of which ends here.

Third Part of the Ingenious Hidalgo DON QUIXOTE de la Mancha

Chapter 15

Which relates the unfortunate adventure that came Don Quixote's way when he came the way of some wicked men from Yanguas

The wise Cide Hamete Benengeli says that as soon as Don Quixote had taken his leave of his hosts and of everyone else at Grisóstomo's burial, he and his squire rode off into the forest where Marcela had disappeared; and, after they'd wandered about it searching for her in vain for over two hours, they reached a meadow of fresh grass, with a cool, tranquil stream running alongside, which invited and indeed compelled them to spend the hours of early afternoon there, because the heat was beginning to be excessive.

Don Quixote and Sancho dismounted and, leaving the donkey and Rocinante free to graze as they pleased on the lush grass, they ransacked the saddle-bags; and, without ceremony, in peace and good fellowship, master and servant ate what they found in them.

Sancho hadn't bothered to hobble Rocinante, safe in the knowledge that the nag was so meek and chaste that all the fillies in the pastures of Cordoba wouldn't lead him astray. But as fate—or the devil, who isn't always asleep—would have it, there was also in that valley a herd of Galician pony-mares belonging to some muleteers from Yanguas, whose custom it is to take their siesta with their animals wherever there is grass and water. And that place where Don Quixote happened to find himself suited these men from Yanguas very well.

It happened, then, that Rocinante felt the urge to enjoy some fun and games with their ladyships the pony-mares and, abandoning his natural habits and his normal gait the moment he scented them, without requesting his master's permission, he broke into a lively trot and went to inform them of his needs. But it seems that they must have been feeling more like grazing, because they gave him such a welcome with their hooves and their teeth that his girths soon snapped and he was left saddleless and naked. Yet what must have affected him most was that when the muleteers saw the

6. Seville's reputation as a city of adventure may have come from its size; it had over 90,000 inhabitants by 1600, making it the fourth largest city in Europe. Proclaimed the central port for all ships bound for the New World, it grew quickly from a provincial town to a commerical capital.

attack that was being made on their mares, they ran over with their walking-staffs and gave him such a good hiding that they left him sprawling on the grass. At this point Don Quixote and Sancho, having witnessed Rocinante's thrashing, arrived breathless on the scene, and Don Quixote said to Sancho:

"From what I can see, friend Sancho, these are not knights, but base and low-born men. I say this because it means that you can freely help me to take due vengeance for the affront to which Rocinante has been subjected before our very eyes."

"How the devil are we going to take vengeance," replied Sancho, "when there are more than twenty of them and just the two of us—or just the one and a half of us, more like?"

"I am the equal of a hundred men," retorted Don Quixote.

And without further thought he seized his sword and attacked the men from Yanguas, and so did Sancho Panza, encouraged by his master's example. Don Quixote dealt one of them a blow that slashed open both his leather smock and a large part of his shoulder.

The muleteers, seeing so many of themselves so rudely handled by only two men, resorted to their walking-staffs, surrounded the pair and began to lay into them for all they were worth. The truth is that with the second blow they knocked Sancho to the ground, and Don Quixote went the same way in spite of all his eager dexterity. As fate would have it, he fell at the prostrate Rocinante's feet, from which one can judge the furious pounding that walking-staffs can give when wielded by wrathful rustic hands. When the men from Yanguas realized what they'd done, they loaded their animals as fast as they could and hurried on their way, leaving the two adventurers looking a sorry sight and feeling in an even worse temper.

Sancho Panza, lying by his master's side, was the first to start groaning, and he said in a feeble, doleful voice:

"Don Quixote sir! Oh, Don Quixote sir!"

"What do you want, brother Sancho?" replied Don Quixote, in the same weak, languishing tones.

"If it's at all possible," replied Sancho Panza, "I'd like a couple of swigs of that Fairy Brass's drink, if you've got some handy. Maybe it's good for broken bones as well as for sore wounds."

"If I had some here, wretch that I am, what more could we want?" replied Don Quixote. "But I swear to you, Sancho Panza, on my word as a knight errant, that before two days have elapsed, if fortune does not ordain otherwise, I shall have some in my possession; given a modicum of luck I shall manage this in the turning of a hand."

"And how long do you think it'll be before we can move our feet?" replied Sancho Panza.

"For myself," said the battered knight Don Quixote, "I must say that I cannot tell how long. But I am to blame for it all, for I should not have drawn my sword against men who are not knights, as I am; and so I believe that, as a penalty for having broken the laws of chivalry, the god of battles has allowed me to be punished in this way. For this reason, Sancho Panza, you must always bear in mind what I am about to tell you, because it concerns the well-being of us both: whenever you see rabble of this kind offering us some affront, do not wait for me to draw my sword against them, for I shall most certainly not do so, but you draw your sword and punish them to your heart's content; and if any knights come to their aid and defence, I shall then defend you and attack them with all my power. You have already had a thousand signs and demonstrations of how far the powers of this mighty arm of mine extend."

This was how arrogant the poor gentleman had become after his victory over the brave Basque. But his warning didn't impress Sancho Panza enough to prevent him from responding, and he said:

"I'm a peaceful man, sir, meek and mild, and I can overlook any insult, because I've got a wife to support and children to bring up. So even though it isn't up to me to give any orders, you bear this in mind, too—in no way am I going to draw my sword against anyone, peasant or knight, and I hereby, before God my Maker, forgive all affronts that anybody ever has offered me or ever will offer me, whether the person who has offered them, offers them or will offer them is of high or low birth, rich or poor, a gentleman or a commoner, not excepting any estate or condition whatsoever."

On hearing this his master replied:

"If only I had breath enough in my body to speak a few words to you at my ease, and if only this pain in my ribs would abate a little, so that I could make you understand, Panza, how wrong you are. Look here, you rogue: should the winds of fortune, hitherto so adverse, turn in our favour, driving the sails of our desire so that with a constant breeze behind us, and in perfect safety, we reach harbour on one of the islands I have promised you, what would become of you if, after conquering it, I made you its lord? Well, you would render things impossible for yourself, through not being a knight or even wanting to be one, or having the courage or the desire to avenge affronts and defend your dominions. For I would have you know that in freshly conquered provinces and kingdoms, the hearts of the natives are never so subdued or so well disposed towards their new master as to leave no fear that they might play some trick, to reverse the state of affairs once more and, as people say, try their luck again; and so the new master must have understanding to be able to govern, and courage to attack and defend in any crisis."

"In this particular crisis we've just been in," replied Sancho, "I do wish I'd had that understanding and courage you're going on about, but I can swear, on my word as a poor man, that I'm in more of a state for plasters than for chit-chat. You try and see if you can get up, and we'll give Rocinante a hand, though he doesn't deserve it, because he was the main cause of all this battering. I never would have believed it of him, I always took him for a pure-minded character, and as peaceful as me. Still, as they say, you need time to get to know people, and there's nothing certain in this life. Who'd have said that after you'd cut that poor knight errant about like that, the follow-up was going to be this great storm of a thumping that's just rained down on our ribs?"

"Your ribs, Sancho," replied Don Quixote, "must at least be accustomed to such squalls; but it is clear that mine, nurtured as they were between cambric and holland-cloth,[1] feel the pain of this misfortune more keenly. And if it were not that I imagine . . .—no, I do not imagine: I know for a certain fact—that all these discomforts are inseparable from the exercise of arms, I should be ready to die of sheer rage, here and now."

To this his squire replied:

"Sir, seeing as how all these disasters are as you might say the harvest of chivalry, I'd be grateful if you'd tell me whether they happen very often, or just at certain set times, because to my mind after two harvests like this one we're going to be useless for the third, unless God in his infinite mercy helps us."

"Let me tell you, friend Sancho," replied Don Quixote, "that the life of a knight errant is subject to a thousand dangers and misfortunes, and it is equally true that

1. Two kinds of fine linen, made in the Netherlands.

knights errant are potential emperors and kings, as is shown by the experience of many different knights, about whose histories I am fully informed. And I could tell you now, if the pain would allow me, about some who by the might of their arms alone have risen to the high estate I have just mentioned; and yet these selfsame knights, both before and afterwards, were engulfed in various calamities and misfortunes. The valiant Amadis of Gaul once found himself in the power of his mortal enemy the enchanter Arcalaus, who, it is attested, had him tied to a column in his courtyard and gave him more than two hundred lashes with the reins of his horse. And there is an anonymous author of no small credit who says that after the Knight of the Sun had been caught in a trap by a door that opened under his feet in a certain castle, and found himself bound hand and foot in a deep pit underground, there he was given what is known as an enema, of snow-water and sand, which was nearly the end of him; and if he had not been succoured in that sore extremity by a sage who was a great friend of his, the poor knight would have fared very ill.[2] So I can well have patience, being as I am in such good company; for they suffered greater affronts than those which we have undergone. And I would have you know, Sancho, that wounds received from weapons that happen accidentally to be in the assailants' hands are not dishonourable, and this is explicitly stated in the law of challenges: if a shoemaker hits a man with the last he is holding, that man cannot be said to have been birched, even if the last is made of this particular wood. I am only telling you this to prevent you from thinking that, just because we have taken a battering in this dispute, we have been dishonoured, for the arms borne by those men, with which they belaboured us, were only their walking-staffs, and none of them, so far as I can remember, was carrying a rapier, a sword or a dagger."

"They didn't give me a chance to look into details like that," replied Sancho. "I'd hardly drawn my own trusty blade when they gave my shoulders such a thrashing with those pine trees of theirs that they knocked the sight out of my eyes and the strength out of my feet and left me where I'm lying now, and where wondering whether the beating was dishonourable or not doesn't bother me in the slightest—all that does bother me is the pain of those staff-blows, and they're going to be as deeply engraved in my memory as they are on my shoulders."

"For all that, brother Panza," replied Don Quixote, "allow me to remind you that there is no memory that time does not efface, no pain that death does not destroy."

"Well, what bigger disaster could there ever be," retorted Panza, "than the one that has to wait for time to efface it and for death to destroy it? If this mishap of ours was one of those that can be cured with a couple of plasters it wouldn't be so bad, but I'm beginning to think that all the bandages in a hospital aren't going to be enough to even begin to sort us two out."

"Stop that talk, Sancho, and attempt to make the best of a bad business," replied Don Quixote, "because that is what I shall do; and now let us see how Rocinante is, because it seems to me that not the least part of this misfortune has fallen to the poor fellow's share."

"There's nothing surprising about that," retorted Sancho, "seeing as how he's such a fine knight errant. But what does surprise me is that my donkey's still in the pink, while we're black and blue all over."

"Fortune always leaves a door open in adversity, to provide a remedy," said Don Quixote. "I say this because that creature of yours can now replace Rocinante, and bear me to some castle where I can be cured of my wounds. Furthermore, I shall not

2. Apparently an episode of Don Quixote's own invention.

count it dishonourable to ride on such a beast, for I remember reading that when good old Silenus, the tutor of the merry god of laughter, rode into the city of the hundred gates, he did so, much to his satisfaction, on a handsome ass."[3]

"I expect it's true he rode on an ass, as you say," replied Sancho, "but there's a big difference between riding an ass and being slung across an ass's back like a sack of rubbish."

To which Don Quixote replied:

"Wounds received in battle do not detract from honour, but bestow it; and so, friend Panza, stop answering me back and do as you are told, get up as best you can and put me on top of your donkey in the posture that most pleases you; and let us be gone from here before night falls and catches us in this wild place."

"Well, well," said Panza, "I have heard you say that it's right and proper for knight errants to sleep on open plains and deserts for most of the year, and that they count themselves lucky to do it."

"All that," said Don Quixote, "is when there is no alternative, or when they are in love; and this is so true that there have been knights who have remained on top of a crag, in sunlight and shadow and all the inclemencies of the heavens, for two whole years, unknown to their ladies. And one of these was Amadis, when he called himself Beltenebros and took up his quarters on the Peña Pobre, for eight years or eight months—I cannot quite remember which, but all that matters is that he was doing penance there for some vexation or other that the lady Oriana had caused him.[4] But let us leave these matters, Sancho, and do make haste, before some misfortune like Rocinante's befalls the donkey."

"Then there'd be the devil and all to do," said Sancho.

And letting out thirty groans and sixty sighs and one hundred and twenty curses on the head of the person who'd brought him there, he hauled himself to his feet, but he was so exhausted that he stopped half way up, bent over in the form of a Turkish bow and incapable of straightening himself any further; yet despite all these troubles he harnessed his donkey, which had also taken advantage of the day's excess of liberty to go a little astray. Then he righted Rocinante, who, if he'd had a tongue to complain with, certainly wouldn't have been matched by Sancho or his master.

from *Chapter 18*

Which relates the conversation that Sancho Panza had with his master Don Quixote, and other adventures worth relating

* * * As Don Quixote and his squire discussed these matters, Don Quixote saw that a huge, dense cloud of dust was approaching them along the road, and he turned to Sancho and said:

"This is the day, O Sancho, when will be seen the good that fortune has in store for me; this is the day, I say, when the might of my arm will be displayed as never before, and when I shall do deeds that will remain written in the book of fame for the ages to come. Do you see that cloud of dust rising up over there, Sancho? Well,

3. The merry god of laughter (and drunkeness) is Bacchus, god of the vine; the elderly satyr Silenus who rode into Thebes astride an ass was his tutor.

4. An episode from the *Amadis de Gaul,* it treats of the penance that Amadis believes he must do for his beloved Oriana. Because of the imprudence of his dwarf, Ardian, Amadis has been banished from Oriana's sight, and he retreats to the Peña Pobre; she later repents and sends a messenger asking that Amadis come to her at once. Dulcinea is mentioned later in *Don Quixote* as coming from a lesser family than Oriana.

it is being raised by a vast army from countless different nations, marching towards us."

"In that case there must be two armies," said Sancho, "because opposite it, back there behind us, there's another dust cloud just like it."

Don Quixote turned round and saw that Sancho was right; and then he was beside himself with joy, because he knew that these were two armies marching to clash in the middle of that broad plain. Every minute of every hour his imagination was filled with those battles, enchantments, adventures, extravagances, loves and challenges that books of chivalry recount, and everything he said, thought or did was channelled into such affairs. And the dust clouds were being raised by two great droves of sheep approaching from opposite directions along the same road, but the dust prevented the sheep from being seen until they came close. And Don Quixote was so insistent they were armies that Sancho believed him, and said:

"So what are we going to do now, sir?"

"What are we going to do?" said Don Quixote. "Favour and assist the needy and helpless. And you should know, Sancho, that this army approaching from in front of us is led and directed by the great Emperor Alifanfarón, lord of the great island of Taprobana;[1] the other army coming up behind me belongs to his enemy, the King of the Garamantes, known as Pentapolín of the Uprolled Sleeve, because he always goes into battle with his right arm bare."[2]

"But why do these two lords hate each other so much?" asked Sancho.

"They hate each other," replied Don Quixote, "because this Alifanfarón is a wild pagan, and he is in love with Pentapolín's daughter, who is a very beauteous and, moreover, charming lady, and a Christian, and her father will not give her in marriage to the pagan king unless this man first abjures the religion of his false prophet Muhammad and is converted to Christianity."

"My eye!" said Sancho. "Pentapolín's doing just the right thing, and I'm going to help him in every way I can."

"Then you will be doing your duty, Sancho," said Don Quixote, "because to take part in battles of this kind it is not necessary to be knighted."

"I'm very well aware of that," replied Sancho, "but where are we going to put this ass of mine so that we can be sure of finding it again once the fighting's over? Because I don't expect going into battle on something like this is what people usually do."

"That is true," said Don Quixote. "What you can do with the ass is to leave it free to have its own adventures, whether it goes missing or not, because we shall possess so many horses when we emerge victorious that even Rocinante will be in danger of being replaced by another. But now pay attention to me and keep your eyes open, for I am going to inform you about the most important knights in these two armies. And so that you can see and observe them better, let us withdraw to that hill over there, from where both armies must be visible."

This they did, and from the hill they would indeed have had a clear view of the two flocks that were armies for Don Quixote, if the clouds of dust they were raising hadn't interfered with the view. Yet seeing in his imagination what he didn't see and didn't exist, he began to proclaim:

1. Taprobana is Sri Lanka, the emperor a fantasy of Don Quixote's.

2. The Garamantes were a fierce people from Africa; Pentapolín is another invention of Don Quixote.

"That knight you can see over there in yellow armour, with a crowned lion lying submissive at a damsel's feet on his shield, is the valiant Laurcalco, Lord of the Silver Bridge; the other one, with golden flowers on his armour, and on his shield three silver crowns on a blue field, is the much-feared Micocolembo, the Grand Duke of Quirocia; that other one on his right, with gigantic limbs, is the fearless Brandabarbarán de Boliche, Lord of the Three Arabias, wearing that serpent's skin for armour and, instead of a shield, bearing a door which is reputed to be one of the doors of the temple pulled down by Samson when in dying he avenged himself on his enemies.[3] But look in the other direction and you will see at the front of the other army the ever victorious, never vanquished Timonel de Carcajona, the Prince of Nueva Vizcaya, with his armour quartered blue, green, white and yellow, and on his shield he has a golden cat on a tawny field with the word *Miau,* which is the beginning of his lady's name, for it is said that she is the peerless Miulina, the daughter of Duke Alfeñiquén of the Algarve; that other knight who burdens the back of that powerful steed, with armour as white as snow and white arms—that is to say a shield without any device on it—is a novice knight from France, called Pierres Papin, Lord of the Baronies of Utrique; that other one, striking his iron spurs into the flanks of that dazzling, fleet zebra, and with armour of blue vair,[4] is the powerful Duke of Nerbia, Espartafilardo of the Wood, who bears on his shield the device of an asparagus plant, with a motto in Castilian that says: 'Divine my fortune.'"

And he went on naming imaginary knights from one army and the other and, swept along by the fancies of his unique madness, he improvised armour, colours, devices and mottoes for all of them; and without a pause he continued:

"This other army, facing us, is formed of people of many races: here are those who have drunk the sweet waters of famous Xanthus; mountaineers who tread the Massilian fields; those who sift fine gold dust in Arabia Felix; those who enjoy the famous, cool banks of clear Thermodon; those who bleed golden Pactolus along many different channels; and the Numidians, breakers of promises; the Persians, bowmen of great renown; the Parthians and the Medes, who fight as they flee; the Arabs, who move their dwellings; the Scythians, as cruel as they are pale; the Ethiopians, with pierced lips, and other infinite peoples, whose faces I see and recognize, even though I do not remember their names. In this other squadron come those who drink the crystalline waters of olive-bearing Betis; those who wash their faces in the liquor of the ever rich and golden Tagus; those who enjoy the beneficent waters of the divine Genil; those who tread the lush pastures of the Tartesian fields; those who take delight in the Elysian meadows of Jerez; men of La Mancha, rich and crowned with yellow ears of corn; men clad in iron, ancient relics of Gothic blood; those who bathe in the Pisuerga, renowned for the gentleness of its current; those who graze their flocks and herds on the broad meadows of winding Guadiana, famous for its secret course; those who shiver in the cold of the bosky Pyrenees and among the white snowflakes of the lofty Apennines: in short, all those whom Europe contains and encloses within its boundaries."[5]

3. Once again, for most of this paragraph Don Quixote is indulging in his own fictions. Samson was the Hebrew warrior who was blinded by Delilah and pulled down a temple on top of himself and his enemies, the Philistines.

4. Weasel fur.

5. In this paragraph, Don Quixote mentions real places and warlike peoples. In the "first squadron" are found the Trojans, who lived near the river Xanthus, and numerous other races from countries in Africa and Asia, including Turkey (site of the Thermodon River) and Lydia (site of the Pactolus). The "other squadron" includes peoples from Spain and Italy; all the rivers he lists here run through the Iberian peninsula, including the "winding Guadiana," which flows through La Mancha and frequently makes its "secret course" underground. The Pyrenees are the mountains on the border between Spain and France; the Apennines are mountains running down the center of Italy.

Great God, how many provinces he mentioned, how many races he named, giving to each one of them, with wonderful readiness, its own attributes, steeped as he was in everything he'd read in his lying books! Sancho Panza was hanging on his every word, and didn't utter a single one himself, and every so often he'd turn his head to try to spot the knights and giants his master was naming; and since he couldn't see any of them, he said:

"Look sir, the devil can take any of those men or giants or knights you say there are hereabouts—at least I can't see them, perhaps it's all a magic spell, like those ghosts last night."

"How can you say that?" retorted Don Quixote. "Do you not hear the neighing of the horses, the sounding of the bugles, the beating of the drums?"

"All I can hear," replied Sancho, "is lots of sheep bleating."

And he was right, because the two flocks were coming close.

"It is your fear, Sancho," said Don Quixote, "that is preventing you from seeing or hearing properly; because one of the effects of fear is to muddle the senses and make things seem to be what they are not; and if you are so frightened, stand aside and leave me alone, for I am sufficient by myself to give the victory to whichever army I decide to support."

As he said this he put spurs to Rocinante and, with his lance at the ready, he sped down the hill like a thunderbolt. Sancho shouted after him:

"Come back, come back, Don Quixote sir, I swear to God they're sheep you're charging! Come back! By the bones of my poor old father! What madness is this? Look, there aren't any giants or knights, or cats, or armour, or shields quartered or left in one piece, or blue vairs, or the devil. What are you doing? Lord have mercy on us sinners!"

But nothing would make Don Quixote turn back. Instead he galloped on, crying:

"Come, you knights, fighting beneath the banners of the valiant Emperor Pentapolín of the Uprolled Sleeve, follow me, and you shall see with what ease I give him his revenge over his enemy Alifanfarón of Taprobana!"

With this he rode into the army of sheep and began to spear them with as much fury and determination as if he really were attacking mortal enemies. The shepherds and farmers accompanying the flock were screaming at him to stop, but, seeing that this didn't have any effect, they drew their slings from their belts and started to salute him about the ears with stones the size of fists. Don Quixote didn't take any notice of the stones; instead he galloped this way and that, crying:

"Where are you, proud Alifanfarón? Come here: a lone knight am I, who wishes, in single combat, to try your strength and take your life, as punishment for the distress you have caused the valiant Pentapolín the Garamante."

As he said this a large smooth pebble came and struck him in the side and buried two of his ribs in his body. This left him in such a state that he felt certain he was either dead or sore wounded and, remembering his remedy, he took out the oil-bottle, put it to his mouth and began to pour the liquor into his stomach;[6] but before he could swallow what he considered to be a sufficient amount, another of those sugared almonds came and hit his hand and his bottle with such force that it smashed the bottle, taking out three or four teeth as well, and crushing two fingers.

6. This is the holy balsam of Fierebras that cures all ills, which Don Quixote managed to concoct in Chapter 17 after he and Sancho Panza were badly beaten at an inn Don Quixote took for a castle. Sancho drinks the potion as a cure, and undergoes such "seizures and spasms" that not only he but everyone else in the inn "thought that his end had come."

Such was the first blow, and such was the second, that the poor knight couldn't stop himself from sliding off his horse. The shepherds came up to look at him, and thought they'd killed him, so they made haste to round up their flock, pick up the dead sheep, of which there were more than a few, and make themselves scarce, without looking any further into the matter.

All this time Sancho had been on the hill, watching his master's follies, tearing his beard and cursing the moment when fortune had brought them together. When he saw that Don Quixote was lying on the ground and that the shepherds had gone away, he ventured down the hill and approached him, and found him in a terrible state, although still conscious. And Sancho said:

"Didn't I tell you, Don Quixote sir, to turn back, because what you were attacking wasn't armies, it was flocks of sheep?"

"This just shows how my enemy, that scoundrel of an enchanter, can transform things and make them disappear. I would have you know, Sancho, that it is very easy for such people to make us look like whatever they want, and this villain who is persecuting me, envious of the glory he saw I was about to conquer in this battle, turned the armies of enemy forces into flocks of sheep. If you do not believe me, Sancho, I beg you to do something that will correct your mistake and make you see that I am telling you the truth: mount your ass and stalk them, and you will soon see how, once they have gone a little way, they turn back into what they were at first and, ceasing to be sheep, become real men again, just as I described them to you. But do not go yet, because I have need of your assistance: come here and see how many of my teeth are missing, for it seems to me that there is not one left in my mouth."

Sancho came so close that his eyes were nearly inside his master's mouth; and by now the balsam had done its work in Don Quixote's stomach, and, just as Sancho was peering in, he discharged all its contents with the violence of a shotgun and they exploded in the face of the compassionate squire.

"Holy Mother of God!" cried Sancho. "What's up now? The man's dying, he must be—he's spewing blood!"

But when he examined the evidence more closely he could tell from the colour, taste and smell that it wasn't blood but the balsam he'd seen him drinking from the oil-bottle, and this disgusting discovery so turned his stomach that he vomited his guts all over his master, and both of them were left in the same fine mess. Sancho staggered over to his ass to look in the saddle-bags for something with which to clean himself and see to his master's wounds, and when he couldn't find them he almost went insane. He cursed himself again, and decided in his heart to leave his master and go back home, even if that did mean forfeiting what he was owed for services rendered and his hopes of governing the promised island.

Don Quixote now struggled to his feet, with his left hand clapped to his mouth to stop his remaining teeth from falling out, took hold with the other hand of the reins of the faithful Rocinante, who was so loyal and good-natured that he hadn't budged from his master's side, and went over to his squire, who was leaning over his ass with his hand on his cheek, in the posture of a man overwhelmed by thought. And when Don Quixote saw all these signs of deep distress, he said:

"Allow me to remind you, Sancho, that no man is worth more than any other, unless he achieves more than the other. All these storms falling upon us are signs that the weather will soon clear and that things will go well for us; for neither good nor bad can last for ever, and from this we can deduce that since this bad spell has lasted for a long time, a good one cannot be far away. So you must not be distressed about the misfortunes that I undergo, for you have no part in them."

"No part in them?" retorted Sancho. "The bloke who got blanket-tossed yesterday—was he by any chance any other than my own father's son? And the saddle-bags I've lost today, with all my valuables in them—do they belong to any other than the same?"[7]

"You have lost your saddle-bags, Sancho?" said Don Quixote.

"Yes I have," replied Sancho.

"So we have nothing to eat today," replied Don Quixote.

"We wouldn't have," replied Sancho, "if it wasn't for those herbs you say you know all about growing in the fields, the ones that unfortunate knight errants like you go and pick to make up for lack of food in fixes like this."

"For all that," replied Don Quixote, "I would sooner have a two-pound loaf of white bread or indeed an eight-pound loaf of bran bread and a couple of dozen salted pilchards, than all the herbs described by Dioscorides, even in Dr. Laguna's magnificent edition.[8] But anyway, climb on to your donkey, good Sancho, and follow me, because God, who is the provider of all things, will not fail us, especially since we are engaged in his service; because he does not fail the gnats in the air, or the worms in the earth, or the tadpoles in the water. And he is so merciful that he makes his sun rise on the evil and on the good, and sends his rain on the just and on the unjust."

"You'd have done better as a preacher," said Sancho, "than as a knight errant."

"Knights errant have always known and still must know about everything, Sancho," said Don Quixote, "for there were knights errant in centuries past who would stop to preach a sermon or deliver a speech in the middle of a fair just as if they were graduates of the University of Paris; from which we can infer that the sword has never blunted the pen, nor the pen the sword."[9]

"All right, I'll take your word for it," replied Sancho, "and now let's get going and find somewhere to stay the night, and God grant it's a place where there aren't any blankets, or blanket-tossers, or ghosts, or enchanted Moors—because if there are any of those, I'll send this adventuring lark to the devil, lock, stock and barrel."

"You must pray to God for that, my son," said Don Quixote. "And now guide us where you will, for on this occasion I wish to leave the choice of a lodging to you. But first lend me your hand and feel with your finger how many teeth are missing on this upper right side, because that is where I feel the pain."

Sancho put his fingers in and, as he felt around, he asked:

"How many back teeth did you use to have on this side?"

"Four," replied Don Quixote, "apart from the wisdom tooth, all of them whole and sound."

"Are you quite sure of what you're saying, sir?" said Sancho.

"Yes, four, if not five," replied Don Quixote, "because I have never had any teeth extracted, nor have any fallen out or been destroyed by decay or infection."

"Well, down here below," said Sancho, "you've only got two and a half now, and up above not even half a tooth, it's as smooth as the palm of my hand."

7. When Don Quixote leaves the inn without paying, others staying at the inn pull Sancho from his ass, throw him into a blanket, and toss the poor squire up and down in the middle of the yard. Unbeknownst to Sancho, the innkeeper seizes his saddle-bags in exchange for the missing payment.

8. Dioscorides was a Greek physician during Nero's reign; his botanical treatise was a crucial source for the science of pharmacy, and was translated from the Greek by the doctor Andrés Laguna in 1555.

9. There were ongoing debates in the Renaissance as to the respective merits of the pen (the privilege of the scholars and clerics) and the sword (that of knights).

"Oh, unhappy me!" said Don Quixote as he heard the sad news his squire was giving him. "I would rather have lost an arm, so long as it was not my sword arm. For I would have you know, Sancho, that a mouth without teeth is like a mill without a millstone, and that a tooth is much more worthy of esteem than a diamond. But those of us who profess the order of chivalry in all its severity are subject to this. Mount your donkey, my friend, and lead the way, and I shall follow at whatever pace you prefer."

Sancho did so, heading towards where he thought they might find a place to stay without leaving the highway, which was uninterrupted in that part.

As they plodded along, because the pain in Don Quixote's jaws didn't give him any respite or any inclination to ride faster, Sancho tried to amuse him and cheer him up by chatting to him, and said, among other things, what is recorded in the next chapter.

* * *

Chapter 20

ABOUT THE UNPRECEDENTED AND UNIQUE ADVENTURE UNDERTAKEN BY THE VALIANT DON QUIXOTE DE LA MANCHA, THE ONE THAT WITH THE LEAST DANGER WAS EVER BROUGHT TO A HAPPY CONCLUSION BY ANY FAMOUS KNIGHT IN THE WORLD

"All this grass, sir, must be a sign that there's a spring or a stream near here watering it, so it'll be a good plan to carry on a little further, and we'll find somewhere we can quench this terrible thirst of ours—I'm sure thirst hurts even more than hunger does."

Don Quixote thought this was good advice, and he took Rocinante by the reins, and Sancho loaded his ass with all the left-overs and took it by the halter, and they began to feel their way up the meadow, because the darkness of the night prevented them from seeing anything; but they hadn't gone a couple of hundred paces when a sound of thundering water reached their ears, as if it were crashing down from some great cliff. They were overjoyed at this but, when they stopped to work out where the sound was coming from, they suddenly heard another noise that diluted the pleasure of the water, especially for Sancho, with his timid, fearful nature. What they heard was a steady pounding and some sort of a clanking of iron and chains that, added to the water's furious roaring, would have struck fear into any other heart than that of Don Quixote.

In this dark night they'd wandered in among some tall trees whose leaves, blown by the breeze, rustled eerily; and the combination of the solitude, the surroundings, the darkness, the noise of the water and the rustling of the leaves filled them with fear and dread, all the more so when they found that the pounding didn't cease, the breeze didn't die down and the morning didn't come; and, on top of all this, they had no idea where they were. But Don Quixote, steeled by his intrepid heart, leapt upon Rocinante, grasped his little round shield, clasped his pike and said:

"Friend Sancho, I would have you know that I was born, by the will of heaven, in this iron age of ours, to revive in it the age of gold, or golden age, as it is often called. I am the man for whom dangers, great exploits, valiant deeds are reserved. I am, I repeat, the man who will revive the Knights of the Round Table, the Twelve Peers of France and the Nine Worthies, and who will consign to oblivion the Platirs, the Tablantes, the Olivantes and Tirantes, the Phoebuses and Belianises, together with the whole crowd of illustrious knights errant of olden times, by performing in this age in which I live such prodigies, such wonders, such feats of arms as to eclipse the most brilliant deeds that they ever accomplished. You are aware, faithful and trusty squire, of the darkness of this night, its unearthly silence, the confused and muffled hubbub of the trees, the fearsome roar of the water that we have come to seek and that seems to crash down from the heights of the Mountains of the Moon,[1] and the incessant pounding that assails and wounds our ears; all of which together, and indeed each by itself, would be enough to infuse fear and terror and dismay into the breast of Mars himself, let alone one unaccustomed to such occurrences and adventures. Now all of this that I depict for you is an incentive and a stimulant for my spirit, making this heart of mine burst in my breast with a desire to launch out on this adventure, however difficult it seems to be. So tighten Rocinante's girths a little, and God be with you, and await me here for just three days, after which, if I should not return, you may go back to our village, and from thence, as a favour and a service to me, you shall go to El Toboso, where you shall inform my incomparable lady Dulcinea that her hapless knight died attempting exploits which would make him worthy to call himself hers."

When Sancho heard his master's words he began to weep tears of infinite tenderness and said:

"Sir, I don't know why you want to take on this fearful adventure—it's night now, nobody can see us here, we can easily ride the other way and avoid the danger, even if we have to go for three days without a drink, and since there's no one to see us, there's no one to think we're cowards, either. What's more, I've heard our village priest, who you know well, saying in a sermon that danger loved is death won, so it isn't a good idea to go tempting God by taking on such a tremendous feat that you can only get out of alive by some miracle—you ought to be content with the ones that heaven worked on you when it stopped you from being tossed in a blanket, as I was, and when it brought you out safe, sound and victorious from among all those enemies that were riding with that corpse. And if all this doesn't move or soften that hard heart of yours, let's see if this does—just think that as soon as you've gone away I'll be ready to give up the ghost to whoever wants to take it, out of pure fear. I left my village and my children and my wife to come and serve you, in the belief that I'd be better for it rather than the opposite, but greed breaks the sack and it's broken all my hopes, because just when they were brightest and I thought I was going to get my hands on that damned island you've promised me so often, I find that instead you want to leave me in a place like this, far from all human company. In the name of the one true God, sir, let not this wrong be done unto me, and if you just can't hold yourself back from doing this daring deed, at least put it off till morning—according to the lore I learned as a shepherd, dawn can't be three hours away, because the Little Bear's mouth is on top of its head, and at midnight it's in line with its left arm."[2]

"But Sancho," asked Don Quixote, "how can you tell where that line goes, or where that mouth or small bear is, when the night is so dark that there is not a star to be seen in the sky?"

"That's true enough," said Sancho, "but fear has many eyes, and it can see things under the ground so it's got even more reason to see them up in the sky, but anyway you only need to use your head to realize that it isn't long till daybreak."

"However long it is," replied Don Quixote, "it shall not be said of me, now or ever, that tears and pleas deflected me from acting as I should, in a true knightly fashion; so I beg you, Sancho, to hold your tongue; for God, who has placed in my heart the desire to undertake this unique and dreadful adventure, will be sure to watch over my well-being and console your grief. What you must do is to make

1. The Nile was believed to have its source in the "Mountains of the Moon," in Ethiopia.

2. Sancho is imagining that he sees the constellation Ursa Minor, or "Little Bear."

Rocinante's girths as tight as may be, and wait here, for I shall soon return, alive or dead."

Sancho realized that this was his master's final decision, and that tears, advice and pleas weren't having any effect, so he decided to make use of his cunning to force him to wait until daybreak, if he could: as he was tightening the horse's girths he took his ass's halter and, ever so carefully and quietly so as not to be noticed, he tied Rocinante's hind legs together, so that when Don Quixote tried to set off he couldn't, because the only way in which the horse could move was in fits and starts. When Sancho saw that his trick had worked, he said:

"There you are, sir—the heavens, moved by my tears and my prayers, have ordained that Rocinante can't move, and if you keep on spurring him again and again like that you'll only annoy fortune and, as they say, kick against the pricks."

Don Quixote was close to despair, and the more he gave his horse the spur the less it budged; and, not suspecting the ligature, he resigned himself to calming down and waiting either for dawn to come or for Rocinante to move, ascribing the problem to everything except Sancho's cunning. And so he said:

"Since the fact is, Sancho, that Rocinante cannot move, I am content to wait until dawn smiles on us, even though I weep at her delay."

"No, you mustn't weep," replied Sancho. "I'll keep you amused by telling you stories till daybreak, unless you'd rather get off your horse and lie down for a little nap on the green grass, as knight errants often do, so as to feel nice and fresh when day comes and it's time to go off on that enormous adventure that's in store for you."

"What do you mean, get off my horse and lie down for a little nap?" said Don Quixote. "Am I, perchance, one of those knights who repose in the midst of danger? You can sleep, for you were born to sleep—indeed you can do as you wish—but I shall behave as I consider befits my aspirations."

"Don't be angry, sir," replied Sancho, "I didn't mean it like that."

And coming up to him he held on to the front of his saddle with one hand and on to the back of it with the other, so that he was left embracing his master's left thigh, not daring to stir one inch from it, so scared was he of the pounding, which continued unabated. Don Quixote asked him to tell a story to while the time away, as he had promised, to which Sancho replied that he would, if his fear of what he was hearing let him.

"But in spite of that I will try my hardest to tell you a true story that, if I manage to tell it properly and don't get interrupted, is the best true story there ever was, and now you must pay attention because I'm about to begin. 'Once upon a time and may good befall us all and evil come to him that evil seeks . . .' And you can see, sir, that in those ancient times they didn't start their stories any old way, but with a saying by Cato the Senseless of Rome,[3] who says 'And evil come to him that evil seeks,' which just about fits the bill here, to persuade you to stay put and not wander off seeking evil, and let's go the other way instead, sir, because nobody's forcing us to carry on in this direction, with all these terrors putting the fear of God into us."

"Continue with your story, Sancho," said Don Quixote, "and leave me to worry about the direction in which we are travelling."

"I was saying, then," continued Sancho, "that in a village in Extremadura there once lived a goat-shepherd, in other words a man who looked after goats, and this shepherd or goat-shepherd my story's all about was called Lope Ruiz, and this

3. Sancho means Cato the Censor, known for his moral austerity during the days of Rome's republic as well as his many pithy sayings.

Lope Ruiz was in love with a shepherdess called Torralba, and this shepherdess called Torralba was the daughter of a rich stock farmer, and this rich stock farmer . . ."

"If that is the way in which you tell your story, Sancho," said Don Quixote, "repeating everything you say, in two days' time you still will not have finished; either tell it straightforwardly, like a man of good sense, or do not tell it at all."

"The way I'm telling it," retorted Sancho, "is the way tales are always told where I come from, and I don't know any other way to tell it, and it isn't fair to expect me to learn new habits."

"Tell it however you like, then," replied Don Quixote, "and since fate decrees that I cannot avoid listening, you had better continue."

"And so, my dear good sir," continued Sancho, "as I was saying, this herdsman was in love with Torralba the shepherdess, who was a plump lass, unruly and a bit mannish, because she had the beginnings of a moustache—I can almost see her even now."

"So you knew her, did you?" said Don Quixote.

"I didn't know her as such," replied Sancho, "but the person who told me the story said it was so very true that when I told it to anyone else I could swear blind I'd seen it all for myself. So the days came and the days went and the devil, who doesn't sleep and meddles and muddles in everything, made the love that the herdsman felt for the shepherdess turn into deadly hatred, and the cause, so the gossips said, was a dose of jealousy-pangs she gave him, that went well beyond the pale; and the herdsman hated her so much from then on that, so as never to see her again, he decided to leave that land and go where he wouldn't ever clap eyes on her. As soon as Torralba saw that Lope scorned her, she fell in love with him, even though she'd never been at all fond of him before that."

"That is the way with woman," said Don Quixote: "to disdain the man who loves her, and to love the man who disdains her. Continue, Sancho."

"What happened," said Sancho, "was that the herdsman put his plan into action, and he drove his goats in front of him through the fields of Extremadura to cross over into the Kingdom of Portugal. The Torralba woman found out and went after him, and followed him at a distance on her bare feet, with her staff in her hand and her two satchels hanging from her neck and containing, so it's said, a piece of a mirror and a piece of a comb and some sort of jar of face lotion, but whatever it was she was carrying, and I'm not going to start trying to find that out now, all I will say is that it's said that the herdsman and his goats reached the River Guadiana,[4] and it was swollen almost to overflowing, and there wasn't any ferry or any other boat to take him and his animals across, which put him in a tizzy because he could see that the Torralba woman was getting close and she was going to make a nuisance of herself with all her pleading and moaning, but he kept looking so hard that he saw a fisherman with a boat by his side, so small that there was only room in it for one person and one goat, and in spite of this he spoke to him and bargained with him and they agreed that the fisherman would ferry him and his three hundred goats across to the other bank. The fisherman climbed into his boat and took one goat across, and he came back and took another goat across, and he came back again and took another goat across. You've got to keep count of the goats that the fisherman takes across, because if you let just one of them slip from

4. A river that runs through La Mancha and into southern Portugal.

your memory the story will come to an end and I won't be able to tell you another word of it. To continue, then, I ought to say that the landing-stage on the other side was very muddy and slippery, and the fisherman was taking a long time going to and fro. All the same, he came for another goat, and another goat, and another goat . . ."

"Just assume that he has ferried them all across," said Don Quixote. "Don't keep coming and going like that—you won't get them to the other side in a year."

"How many goats has he taken across so far?" asked Sancho.

"How the devil do you expect me to know that?" replied Don Quixote.

"That's just what I told you—to keep good count. Well, by God, the story's over, I'm not going on."

"How can that be?" replied Don Quixote. "Is it so essential to the story to know exactly how many goats have gone across that if we are so much as one out you cannot continue telling it?"

"No, sir, not at all," replied Sancho. "It's just that when I asked you to tell me how many goats had gone and you replied that you didn't know, at that very instant I clean forgot what I had left to say, and it was full of good things, I can tell you that much."

"So your story is finished?" said Don Quixote.

"As sure as my mother is," said Sancho.

"I can honestly say," replied Don Quixote, "that you have just told one of the most original tales, true or false, that anybody could ever have dreamed of, and that your way of telling it and concluding it is something never heard before nor to be heard again, although I did expect no less from your fine mind. But this does not surprise me, because that incessant pounding must have turned your brain."

"That's as may be," replied Sancho, "all I know is, that's the end of my story—it finishes where you start to make mistakes in counting the goats."

"It is welcome to finish wherever it wishes," said Don Quixote. "Now let us see if Rocinante can move."

He set spurs to his horse again, and again the horse jumped and froze, for Sancho's knots were good knots.

It appears that at this moment, either because of the cold of the morning, which was fast approaching, or because Sancho had eaten something loosening for his supper, or because of natural processes (which seems most likely), he felt the urgent need to do the job of work that nobody could do for him; but so great was the fear which had entered his heart that he didn't dare to move as much as a hair's-breadth from his master's side. Yet not doing what he had to do wasn't a possibility, either; and so what he did, for the sake of peace and concord, was to draw his right hand away from the back of Don Quixote's saddle and use it with great stealth to loosen the running knot that was all that held his breeches up, at which they slid down and encircled his ankles like fetters. Then he lifted up his shirt as best he could, and thrust two ample buttocks into the night air. Once he'd done this, which he'd thought was all he needed to do to escape from his harrowing predicament, he found himself in another even worse plight: he thought that he wasn't going to be able to relieve himself in silence, and he began to grit his teeth and hunch his shoulders and hold his breath for as long as he could, but in spite of all these precautions he was unfortunate enough, in the end, to make a small noise, quite different from the noise causing him such great fear. Don Quixote heard it and said:

"What murmuring is that, Sancho?"

"I don't know, sir," he replied. "It must be some new business, because adventures and misadventures never come singly."

He tried his luck again, and such was his success that, with no greater noise than the previous time, he relieved himself of the burden that had been weighing so heavily upon him. But since Don Quixote's sense of smell was as acute as his sense of hearing, and since Sancho was clinging so very close to him, it was inevitable that some of the fumes, rising almost in a straight line, would reach his nostrils, whereupon he went to their rescue by squeezing them between finger and thumb, and said in somewhat nasal tones:

"It seems to me, Sancho, that you are very frightened."

"That I am," replied Sancho, "but what makes you notice it now more than at other times?"

"The fact that now, more than at other times, you smell, and not of ambergris," replied Don Quixote.

"You could well be right," said Sancho, "but I'm not the one to blame—you are, for dragging me into such wild places at these unearthly hours."

"Move three or maybe four places backwards, my friend," said Don Quixote, without taking his hand from his nose, "and from now on be more careful with your person and with what is due to mine; for it is my familiarity with you that has given rise to this contempt."

"I bet you're thinking," said Sancho, "that I've done something with my person that I didn't ought to have done."

"The more you stir it the worse it gets, friend Sancho," replied Don Quixote.

In this and other similar conversations master and servant spent the night; but when Sancho saw that morning was fast approaching, he very quietly untied Rocinante and tied his breeches. Once Rocinante found himself free it seems that, although he wasn't a high-spirited animal, the after-effects of his confinement made him begin pawing, because prancing (begging his pardon) was beyond him. And when Don Quixote noticed that Rocinante could move again, he considered it to be a favourable sign indicating, he believed, that it was time for him to undertake that terrible adventure.

And now dawn broke at last, and objects began to be clearly visible, and Don Quixote saw that he was beneath some tall trees, chestnuts, which cast a deep, dark shade. He also noticed that the pounding didn't cease, but he couldn't see what was causing it; and so, without further delay, he let Rocinante feel the spur and, saying goodbye again to Sancho, told him to wait there for three days, at the most, just as he had told him before, and, if by the end of them he hadn't returned, to take it as certain that it had been God's will that he should end his life in that perilous adventure. He repeated his instructions about the message to be taken on his behalf to his lady Dulcinea, and told Sancho not to worry about the matter of the payment for his services, because he had made his will before leaving home and in it he had made full provision for wages covering the time served, *pro rata;*[5] and he added that, if God brought him out of that peril safe and sound and ransomless, Sancho could count with total certainty on receiving the promised island.

Sancho wept again as he heard his good master's doleful words once more, and he resolved not to leave him until the absolute final end of that particular incident. From these tears of Sancho Panza's and from this honourable decision of his the author of this history concludes that he must have been of good family and, at the very

5. At the going rate.

least, of pure old Christian stock. And his master was moved by his feelings, but not so much as to make him waver in the slightest; on the contrary he hid his emotion as best he could and began to ride in the direction from which he thought the noise of the water and the pounding were coming. Sancho followed on foot, leading his donkey—his perpetual companion in prosperous and adverse fortune—by the halter, as he so often did; and after they'd advanced some way under those gloomy chestnut trees, they came to a little meadow at the foot of a high cliff from which a great waterfall came tumbling down. Beneath the cliff there were some roughly constructed buildings that looked more like ruins than anything else, and the two men realized that the ceaseless pounding din was coming from over there. Rocinante started at the racket of the water and the pounding, and Don Quixote soothed him and then inched his way towards the buildings, commending himself with all his heart to his lady and imploring her to favour him in this dreadful enterprise, and while he was about it he also commended himself to God and asked not to be forgotten by him. Sancho never strayed from his side, and he poked his neck out as far as he could and he peered as hard as he could between Rocinante's legs, to try to make out what it was that was filling him with such dread.

They must have advanced another hundred paces when, as they came round the side of a hillock, they saw, starkly exposed to their gaze, without any room for doubt, the cause of that hideous and, for them, horrendous din that had kept them so bewildered and scared throughout the night. And it was (please don't take this amiss, dear reader) six fulling-hammers making all the noise with their alternating blows.[6]

When Don Quixote saw what it was he fell silent and stiffened from top to toe. Sancho looked up at Don Quixote and saw that his head was sunk on his breast in manifest mortification. Don Quixote looked down at Sancho and saw that his cheeks were puffed up and his mouth was filled with mirth, about to explode with it; and the knight's dejection was not so great that it could prevent him from laughing at the sight of Sancho, and when Sancho saw that his master had begun to laugh, he released his own captive so suddenly that he had to press his fists to his sides so as not to explode. Four times he calmed down, and four times he started laughing again, every bit as hard as the first time, and Don Quixote was becoming more and more enraged, particularly when he heard Sancho say by way of mockery:

"'I would have you know, friend Sancho, that I was born, by the will of heaven, in this iron age of ours, to revive in it the age of gold, or golden age. I am the man for whom dangers, great exploits, valiant deeds are reserved . . .'"

And he went on to repeat most of what Don Quixote had said when they'd first heard the dreadful pounding. Seeing Sancho making fun of him, Don Quixote was so furious that he raised his pike and struck him two such blows that if they'd connected with his head instead of his shoulders there wouldn't have been any need to pay any wages, except to his heirs. Now that his jolly jest had turned into ugly earnest, and fearful that his master might give him some more of the same, Sancho grovelled:

"Calm down, do, sir, please—I swear to God I was only joking."

"You may be joking, sir, but I am not," retorted Don Quixote. "Look here, my merry fellow: do you fancy that, if these were not fulling-hammers but some perilous

6. "Fulling" is the process by which cloth is thickened and cleaned; in a fulling-mill, cloth is first beaten with heavy wooden mallets or hammers, and then cleansed with soap.

new adventure, I should have failed to display the courage needed to undertake and conclude it? Am I, perchance, sir, obliged—being, as I am, a knight and a gentleman—to identify and distinguish between sounds, and tell whether they come from fulling-mills or not? And furthermore it could be the case, as indeed it is, that I have never seen such things in my life, just as you must have seen them often, being a miserable peasant, born and brought up among them. Or else, sir, you just turn these six hammers into six giants, and set them on me one by one or all together, and if I do not topple each and every one of them, then you can laugh at me as much as you please."

"Enough said, sir," said Sancho, "I will admit I was a bit free with my giggles. But tell me, now we're at peace again, and may God get you out of all your adventures to come as safe and sound as out of this one—wasn't it a great joke, and won't it make a fine story, this enormous fear of ours? My fear I mean, because I'm aware you don't even know what fear is, sir, or what it feels like to be afraid."

"I do not deny," replied Don Quixote, "that what has happened to us is worth laughing at; but it is not worth telling, because not all people are intelligent enough to see things in the right perspective."

"At least you got your pike in the right perspective," replied Sancho, "aiming at my head and hitting my shoulders, thanks to God and the care I took to duck. But there we are, it all comes out in the wash, and I've often heard people say 'you've got to be cruel to be kind,' and what's more, when important gentlemen give their servants a good talking-to, they normally give them a pair of breeches afterwards, though I don't know what they give them after beatings, but maybe what knight errants give after beatings are islands, or kingdoms on dry land."

"The dice could well fall in such a way," said Don Quixote, "that what you say comes true; and forgive me for what has just happened, because you are intelligent and so you understand that man's first impulses are beyond his control; and pay heed from now on to what I am about to say, so that you refrain from talking to me excessively: in all the books of chivalry I have read, an infinity of them, I have never come across any squire who talked to his master as much as you do to yours. And in truth I consider it a great fault in both you and me; in you, because you show me scant respect; in me, because I do not make you respect me more. Yes, indeed: Gandalin, Amadis of Gaul's squire, was the Count of the Firm Isle, yet we read that he always addressed his master cap in hand, with his head bowed and his body bent double, in the Turkish fashion. And what shall we say of Gasabal, Sir Galaor's squire, who was so quiet that to convey the excellence of his miraculous silence his name is only mentioned once in the whole of that great and true history?[7] From all that I have said you should infer, Sancho, that a distance must be kept between master and man, between lord and lackey, between knight and squire. So from now on we must behave with more respect, and not indulge in our little jokes, for in whatever way I become annoyed with you, sir, take note that it is always the pitcher that is broken. The boons and favours that I have promised you will arrive in good time, and if they do not arrive you will not, at least, forfeit your wages, as I have already informed you."

"All you say is very well said," replied Sancho, "but what I'd like to know, just in case the time of the favours never does come round and I have to fall back on wages, is how much knights' squires used to earn in those olden days, and whether they were hired by the month or on a daily basis like builders' labourers."

7. In *Amadis of Gaul,* Don Galaor is Amadis's brother, although ignorant of his legacy; Gasabal is his squire.

"I do not believe," replied Don Quixote, "that such squires were ever paid wages: they depended upon favour. And if I have provided for you to be paid wages, in the sealed will I left in my house, that was only because of what might happen; for I do not yet know how chivalry will fare in these calamitous times of ours, and I should not want my soul to suffer in the other world for the sake of a mere trifle. For I would have you know, Sancho, that there is no profession in this world more hazardous than that of knight adventurer."

"That's true enough," said Sancho, "because it only needed the sound of some hammers in a fulling-mill to strike fear and terror into the heart of a really brave errant adventurer like yourself. But you can take it from me that from this moment on I won't open my mouth to make fun of your doings, but only to honour you as my master and natural lord."

"In that case," replied Don Quixote, "your days will be long on the face of the earth, because next to our parents, our masters should be respected as if they were our parents."

* * *

Chapter 22

About how Don Quixote freed many wretches who, much against their will, were being taken where they would have preferred not to go

Cide Hamete Benengeli, the Arab author from La Mancha, relates in this most grave, grandiloquent, meticulous, delightful and imaginative history that after the conversation between the famous Don Quixote de la Mancha and his squire Sancho Panza recorded at the end of the twenty-first chapter, Don Quixote raised his eyes and saw that some twelve men on foot, strung by the neck, like beads, on a great iron chain, and with shackles on their hands, were plodding towards them along the road. Two men on horseback and two others on foot were escorting them. The mounted men were carrying firelocks and the others swords and spears, and as soon as Sancho Panza saw them he said:

"Here comes a chain-gang of convicts, on their forced march to the King's galleys."

"What do you mean, forced march?" demanded Don Quixote. "Is it possible that the King uses force on anyone?"

"I don't mean that," replied Sancho, "just that they've been sentenced to serve the King in his galleys for their crimes, and they've got a long walk to get there."

"In short," replied Don Quixote, "whatever the details may be, these people, wherever they are going, are being forced to march there, and are not doing it of their own free will."

"That's right," said Sancho.

"In that case," said his master, "this situation is calling out for the exercise of my profession: the redressing of outrages and the succour and relief of the wretched."

"Look, sir," said Sancho. "Justice, and that means the King himself, isn't doing these people any outrages, only punishing them for their crimes."

At this point the chain-gang came up, and Don Quixote, in courteous language, asked the guards to be so kind as to inform him of the reason or reasons why they were bearing those people off in that way. One of the guards on horseback replied that they were all convicts, detained at His Majesty's pleasure and on their way to the galleys, and that there was nothing else to be said and nothing else that he had any business to know.

"All the same," said Don Quixote, "I should like to hear from each one of them individually the cause of his misfortune."

He added other such polite expressions to persuade them to tell him what he wanted to know that the other guard on horseback said:

"We do have here the documents and certificates with the sentences that each of these wretches has been given, but this is no time to stop to take them out and read them; so you'd better come and ask the men yourself, and they'll tell you if they want to—and they will want to, because these are fellows who really enjoy getting up to their evil tricks and bragging about them afterwards."

With this permission, which Don Quixote would have taken for himself if it hadn't been given him, he approached the chain-gang and asked the first convict what sins had put him in that plight. The convict replied that he was there for being in love.

"For no more than that?" replied Don Quixote. "If they send men to the galleys for being in love, I could have been rowing in them for a long time by now."

"It isn't love of the sort you think," said the convict. "Mine was for a washing-basket that was chock-a-block with linen, and I loved it so much, and I hugged it so tight, that if the law hadn't taken it off me by force I still wouldn't have let go of it of my own freewill to this day. I was caught red-handed, there wasn't any need for torture, the trial's over and done with, they gave me a hundred of the best plus three in the tubs and that's that."

"What are tubs?" asked Don Quixote.

"Tubs is galleys," replied the convict.

He was a young man of maybe twenty-four, and he said he was a native of Piedrahita. Don Quixote put the same question to the second convict, who was so overcome by melancholy that he didn't offer a word in reply, but the first one answered for him and said:

"This one, sir, is here for being a canary-bird, that is to say for being a singer and musician."

"What?" said Don Quixote. "Do men go to the galleys for being singers and musicians, too?"

"Yes, sir," replied the convict, "because there's nothing worse than singing in your throes."

"On the contrary," said Don Quixote, "I have often heard it said that one can sing away sorrows and cast away care."

"Here it's the opposite," said the convict. "Sing just that once and you'll weep for the rest of your life."

"I fail to understand," said Don Quixote.

But one of the guards explained:

"Sir knight, among these ungodly people singing in your throes means confessing under torture. This sinner was tortured and he confessed to his crime—he's a prigger of prancers, in other words a horse-thief—and because he confessed he was sentenced to six years in the galleys and two hundred strokes of the lash, and these he's already been given; and he's always sad and lost in his thoughts, because the other criminals back there in prison and here in the chain-gang despise and mock and maltreat him and make his life impossible for confessing and not having the guts to keep saying no. They say, you see, that "nay" has no more letters in it than "aye," and that a delinquent's a lucky man if his life or death depends on his own tongue and not on witnesses or evidence, and it's my belief they aren't far wrong."

"That is my understanding, too," replied Don Quixote.

He moved on to the third convict and put the same question to him; the reply was ready and assured:

"I'm off to our old friends the tubs for five years, for the lack of ten ducats."

"I will most gladly give you twenty," said Don Quixote, "to relieve you of such distress."

"That looks to me," replied the convict, "like having money in the middle of the ocean when you're starving and there isn't anywhere to buy what you need. I'm saying this because if I'd had those twenty ducats you're offering me when I needed them, I'd have used them to grease the clerk's pen and liven up my lawyer's wits, and now I'd be in the middle of Zocodover Square in Toledo instead of in the middle of this road, like a greyhound on a leash. But God is good, and you've just got to be patient."

Don Quixote went on to the fourth convict, a man with a venerable face and a white beard reaching below his chest who, when asked why he was there, began to weep and didn't reply; but the fifth convict acted as interpreter and said:

"This honourable man is going to the galleys for four years, having been paraded in state through the customary streets, all dressed up and on a fine horse."

"That means, I think," said Sancho, "that he was exposed to public shame."[1]

"That's right," said the convict, "and the crime he was given this punishment for was stockbroking, or to be more exact bodybroking. What I mean to say is that this gentleman's here for being a pimp, and also for having a touch of the sorcerer about him."

"If it were not for the touch of the sorcerer," said Don Quixote, "for being a pimp alone he does not deserve to go to row in the galleys, but rather to be the admiral in charge of them. Because the pimp's trade is no ordinary trade; it must be carried out by intelligent people and it is absolutely essential to any well-ordered society, and only the well-born should exercise it; and there should be an official inspector of pimps, as there is of other trades, and a maximum permitted number of them established and published, as is the case with stockbrokers, and this would be the way to forestall many evils that arise from the fact that this trade is in the hands of untrained and unqualified people such as little strumpets, page-boys and other scoundrels of no age or experience who, when at a critical moment some decisive action is called for, make a mess of the whole thing because they cannot tell their right hands from their left. I should like to go on to give the reasons why it would be advisable to make a careful selection of those who do such a necessary job in society, but this is not the place: one day I shall present my ideas to the proper authorities. All I shall say now is that the distress caused me by the sight of these white hairs and this venerable face in such a plight through his being a pimp is dissipated by the addition of his being a sorcerer. I know, of course, that there are no spells in the world that can control a person's will, as some simple people believe; for our free will is sovereign, and there is no herb or enchantment that can control it. What some silly little strumpets and deceitful rogues do is to make certain poisonous mixtures that they use to turn men mad, claiming that they have the power to make them fall in love, whereas it is, as I have just said, impossible to coerce the will."

"Right you are," said the old man, "and honestly, sir, I wasn't guilty of being a sorcerer, though I couldn't deny the charge of being a pimp. But I never thought I was doing any harm, all I wanted was for everyone to be happy and live in peace and

1. A common form of punishment in early modern Europe; he would have been flogged and then paraded through the city's main streets with a placard denouncing his crimes.

quiet, without any quarrels or sadness—but these good intentions weren't any use to prevent me from being sent where I don't expect to come back from, what with my advanced age and my bladder trouble, that doesn't give me a moment's peace."

And here he started weeping again, and Sancho felt so sorry for him that he took a real from inside his shirt and handed it over. Don Quixote moved on to the next man and asked what was his crime, and he replied with no less brio than the last, indeed with rather more of it:

"I'm here because I fooled around too much with two girl-cousins of mine, and with two girl-cousins of somebody else's; and, in short, I fooled around so much with the lot of them that as a result the family tree's become so complicated that I don't know who the devil would be able to work it out. It was all proved against me, there weren't any strings for me to pull, I hadn't got any money, I was within an inch of having my neck stretched, I was sentenced to the galleys for six years and I accepted my fate: it's the punishment for my crime, I'm still young, long live life, while there's life there's hope. If, sir knight, you've got anything on you that you could spare for us poor wretches, God will repay you for it in heaven, and here on earth we'll take care to pray to God that your life and your health may be as long and as good as you obviously deserve."

He was wearing a student's gown, and one of the guards said that he was a great talker and a first-rate latiner.

Behind all of these was a man of thirty, very good-looking except that he squinted a little. He was shackled in a different way from the others: he had a chain on his ankle so long that he'd wound it all round his body, and two neck-irons, one linking him to the other convicts and the other, one of the sort called a keep-friend or friend's foot, from which descended two bars to his waist, where his wrists were manacled to them with great padlocks, so that he could neither raise his hands to his mouth nor lower his head to his hands. Don Quixote asked why this man was wearing so many more fetters than the others. The guard replied that it was because he'd committed more crimes than all the others put together, and that he was so reckless and such a villain that, even though he was shackled up like that, they didn't feel at all safe with him, and feared he was going to escape.

"What crimes can he have committed, though," asked Don Quixote, "if he was not given a worse punishment than the galleys?"

"He's going for ten years," replied the guard, "which is civil death, more or less. All you need to know is that this man is the famous Ginés de Pasamonte, also known as Ginesillo de Parapilla."[2]

"Look you here, sergeant," said the convict, "just watch your step, and don't be in such a hurry to fix names and nicknames on to people. I'm called Ginés, not Ginesillo, and my family name is Pasamonte, not the Parapilla you said, and I'd advise you lot to stop poking your noses into other people's business."

"Less impudence, you double-dyed villain," replied the sergeant, "unless you want me to shut your mouth for you."

"It isn't hard to spot," replied the convict, "that at the moment I'm reduced to what God has seen fit to send me; but one day somebody's going to find out whether I'm called Ginesillo de Parapilla or not."

2. Ginesillo is the diminutive for Ginés, and implies a lack of respect.

"Isn't that what people call you, then, you liar?" said the guard.

"Yes, that's what they call me," replied Ginés, "but I'll stop them calling me that, or else I'll pull out every single hair from my I know what. If you've got something to give us, sir knight, let's have it, and then you can clear off, because you're beginning to get on my nerves with all your prying into other people's lives—and if you want to know about mine, let me tell you I'm Ginés de Pasamonte, and my life has been written by these very fingers here."

"Now he's telling the truth," said the sergeant. "He's written his own life-history himself and a good one it is, too, and he pawned the book in prison for two hundred reals."

"And I mean to redeem it," said Ginés. "And I would, even if I'd pawned it for two hundred ducats."

"Is it as good as all that?" said Don Quixote.

"It's so good," replied Ginés, "that I wouldn't give a fig for *Lazarillo de Tormes* and all the others of that kind that have been or ever will be written.[3] What I can tell you is that it deals with facts, and that they're such fine and funny facts no lies could ever match them."

"And what is the title of your book?" asked Don Quixote.

"*The Life of Ginés de Pasamonte,*" replied the man of that name.

"And have you finished it?" asked Don Quixote.

"How can I have finished it," he replied, "if my life hasn't finished yet? What's written so far is from my birth to when I was sentenced to the galleys this last time."

"Have you been to the galleys before, then?" asked Don Quixote.

"I have, serving God and the King for four years, so I know what biscuits taste like and I know what the lash tastes like," replied Ginés. "And I'm not too worried about going back, because it'll give me a chance to finish my book—there are lots of things left for me to say, and in Spanish galleys there's more than enough peace and quiet, not that I need much of that for what I've got left to write, because I know it all by heart."

"You seem to be an able fellow," said Don Quixote.

"And an unfortunate one, too," replied Ginés, "because misfortunes always pursue men of genius."

"They pursue villains," said the sergeant.

"I've already told you, sergeant," replied Pasamonte, "to watch your step—you weren't given that staff to ill-treat us poor wretches, but to guide and take us to where His Majesty commands. Otherwise—by the blood of . . .!—all sorts of things might come out in the wash one day, like those stains that were made at the inn, for example. So everyone keep his mouth shut, and live a good life, and speak even better words, and let's get moving, because this little joke has been going on for far too long."

The sergeant raised his staff to hit Pasamonte in reply to his threats, but Don Quixote thrust himself between them and begged the sergeant not to maltreat the fellow, for it was only to be expected that one whose hands were so tightly bound would loosen his tongue a little. And turning to the chain-gang he said:

"From everything that you have told me, dearly beloved brethren, I have gathered that, although it is for your crimes you have been sentenced, the punishments

3. *The Life of Lazarillo of Tormes* was a popular novel in mid–16th-century Spain about a young boy forced to make his way in the world. The anonymous novel, written as an autobiography, launched the genre of the "picaresque," or works about down-and-out rogues (*picaro* means rascal). Ginés is obviously capitalizing on the public's thirst for such works.

you are to suffer give you little pleasure, and that you are on your way to receive them with reluctance and against your will; and it could be that one man's lack of courage under torture, another's lack of money, another's lack of strings to pull and, to be brief, the judge's perverse decisions, were the causes of your downfall and of his failure to recognize the right that was on your side. All of which is now so powerfully present in my mind that it is persuading, telling and even obliging me to demonstrate on you the purpose for which heaven sent me into this world and made me profess in it the order of chivalry that I do profess, and the vow that I made to favour the needy and those oppressed by the powerful. But because I know that one essential part of prudence is never to do by force what can be achieved by consent, I hereby request these guards and this sergeant to be so kind as to release you and allow you to go in peace, for there will be no lack of other men to serve the King in happier circumstances, and it does seem excessively harsh to make slaves of those whom God and nature made free. What is more, guards," added Don Quixote, "these poor men have done nothing to you. Let each answer for his sins in the other world; there is a God in heaven who does not neglect to punish the wicked and reward the virtuous, and it is not right for honourable men to be the executioners of others, if they have no personal concern in the matter. I am making my request in this mild and measured manner so that, if you accede to it, I shall have reason for thanking you; but if you do not accede voluntarily, this lance and this sword and the might of my arm will force you to comply."

"That's a good one that is!" said the sergeant. "That's a fine joke he's come out with at long last! He wants us to hand the King's prisoners over to him, as if we had the authority to let them go or he had the authority to tell us to! You'd better clear off and make tracks, sir, and straighten that chamber-pot you've got on your head, and don't go around trying to put the cat among the pigeons."

"You are the cat, and the rat, and the villain, too!" retorted Don Quixote. He matched his deeds to his words and his attack was such a sudden one that he tumbled the man to the ground with a pike-wound before he had a chance to defend himself; and it was fortunate for Don Quixote that this was the guard with the firelock. The other guards were amazed and disconcerted by this unexpected development, but they rallied, and those on horseback seized their swords, and those on foot their spears, and they all fell upon Don Quixote, who was calmly awaiting them; yet he'd have fared badly if the convicts, seeing their chance to be free, hadn't succeeded by breaking the chain on which they were threaded. The hurly-burly was such that the guards, trying both to control the convicts, who were unshackling themselves, and to attack Don Quixote, who was attacking them, chased around in circles and achieved nothing.

Sancho, for his part, helped with the freeing of Ginés de Pasamonte, who was the first to spring into action as he launched himself at the fallen sergeant, snatched up his sword and his firelock and, pointing this at one man and then at another, without firing it, made all the guards disappear as they fled both from the gun and from the stones being hurled at them by the escaped convicts.

This incident saddened Sancho, because he supposed that the fleeing men would go and inform the Holy Brotherhood, who would sound the alarm and come out in pursuit of the wrongdoers; and Sancho said so to his master, and begged him to agree to a quick getaway to hide in the forests in the nearby sierra.

"That is a good idea," said Don Quixote, "but there is something I must do first."

And he called out to the convicts, who were creating a furor as they stripped the sergeant naked; they gathered around to see what he wanted, and he said:

"It is a mark of well-born people to be grateful for benefits received, and one of the sins most offensive to God is ingratitude. I am saying this because you have seen, gentlemen, manifest before your eyes, the benefit that you have received from me; in payment of which it is my wish and desire that you should set out without delay, bearing that chain that I have taken from your necks, for the city of El Toboso, and present yourselves before the lady Dulcinea del Toboso, and tell her that her knight, the Knight of the Sorry Face,[4] presents his compliments, and relate to her, stage by stage, every detail of this famous adventure up to and including my restoration of the liberty that you so desired; and once you have done this you can go wherever you like, and may good fortune attend you."

Ginés de Pasamonte replied on behalf of them all, and said:

"This that you order us to do, dear lord and liberator, is utterly and totally out of the question, because we can't travel together—we've got to split up and go alone, each along his own road, and try to find a way into the very bowels of the earth so as not to be caught by the Holy Brotherhood, who'll be coming out after us, for certain. What you can do and what it'd be right for you to do is to replace that toll or tax payable to the lady Dulcinea del Toboso by a certain number of Ave Marias and Credos, which we'll say for your kindness, and this is something that can be done by night and by day, running away and resting, in peace and in war; but to think that we're going back to the flesh-pots of Egypt,[5] in other words picking up our chain again and setting off for El Toboso, is like thinking it's night-time already when it isn't yet ten in the morning—it's like trying to get figs from thistles."

"By my faith," cried Don Quixote, by now in a fury, "you little bastard, Don Ginesillo de Paropillo or whatever you're called—now you shall go there alone, with your tail between your legs and the whole chain on your back!"

Pasamonte wasn't a long-suffering sort, and from Don Quixote's absurd desire to set them free he'd realized that the man wasn't very sane, so when he found himself thus addressed, he tipped his companions the wink and they edged away and began to rain so many stones on Don Quixote that, however he ducked and dodged behind his little round shield, he couldn't fend them off; and poor Rocinante paid no more attention to the spurs than if he'd been made of bronze. Sancho sheltered behind his ass from the hailstorm falling on them both. Don Quixote couldn't prevent countless stones from hitting his body with enough force to knock him to the ground, and as soon as he did fall the student leapt on him, snatched the basin from his head and smashed it three or four times on his back and as many more times on the earth, pounding it almost to pieces. Then they stripped him of a surcoat he was wearing over his armour and would have stripped him of his stockings, too, if his leg armour hadn't made this impossible. They took Sancho's topcoat and left him in his shirtsleeves, and they shared the rest of the spoils of battle, and each went his own way, more concerned to escape from the dreaded Holy Brotherhood than to burden himself with the chain and go to present himself before the lady Dulcinea del Toboso.

The ass and Rocinante, Sancho and Don Quixote were left alone: the ass hanging its head, lost in its thoughts, flapping its ears every so often in the belief that the storm of stones wasn't yet over, because it was still raging inside its skull; Rocinante

4. In Chapter 19, Sancho hits upon a fitting epithet for Don Quixote: *Caballero de la Triste Figura,* or Knight of the Sad or Sorry Face. Don Quixote immediately takes a liking to the name, declaring that "the sage whose task it is to write the history of my exploits must have thought it right for me to take some appellation, as all previous knights have done": he therefore magically must have placed the epithet in Sancho's mind.

5. Back to the lap of luxury; the phrase is from Exodus 16.

stretched out by his master's side, because he'd also been brought down by a stone; Sancho in his shirtsleeves and fearful of the Holy Brotherhood; and Don Quixote sulking at being left in such a sorry state by men for whom he had done so much.

* * *

from *Chapter 25*

Concerning the strange things that happened to the brave knight of La Mancha in the Sierra Morena, and his imitation of the penance of Beltenebros[1]

* * * "What I say, Sancho," replied Don Quixote, "is that you must do as you please, for your idea does not seem a bad one; and I also say that you shall depart three days from now, because I want you to spend this time witnessing what I do and say for her sake, so that you can tell her about it."

"And what else have I got to see," asked Sancho, "apart from what I've seen already?"

"You are well informed about these matters, I must say!" Don Quixote retorted. "Now I must tear my garments, scatter my armour and dash my head against these rocks, and perform other similar actions that will amaze you."

"For God's sake," said Sancho Panza, "do be careful how you go around dashing your head, because you could pick on such a rock and hit it in such a place that you put paid to the whole penance business with the very first knock you gave it. And if you really think head-dashing's essential and this job can't be done without it, to my mind you ought to be content, since it's all make-believe, a fake and a sham, to dash your head against the water, or something soft like cotton, and leave the rest to me—I'll tell my lady you were knocking it against a jutting crag, harder than diamonds."

"I am grateful to you for meaning well, friend Sancho," replied Don Quixote, "but I would have you know that I am doing all these things not in jest but very much in earnest; for to behave otherwise would be to contravene the commands of chivalry, which instruct one never to tell a lie, on pain of being punished as a recidivist;[2] and to do one thing instead of another is the same as lying. So my blows on the head must be real, firm and effective, with no element of the sophistical or the fantastic about them. And you will have to leave me some lint to cure my wounds, for fate has left us without our balsam."

"Losing the ass was worse," replied Sancho, "because the lint and all was lost with it. And I'd ask you very kindly not to bring that damned potion up again—just hearing it mentioned turns not only my stomach but my very soul inside-out. And I'd also ask you, as regards those three days you allocated for watching the crazy things you're going to do, to make believe they're over and done with, because I'll be happy to take them for granted as if seen and approved, and I'll tell my lady wonders. So you write your letter and then send me packing, because I'm longing to come back and get you out of this purgatory where I'm leaving you."

"Purgatory you call it, Sancho?" said Don Quixote. "You would do better to call it hell, or worse, if there is anything worse."

1. Don Quixote and Sancho have reached the desolate region of the Sierra Morena, where Don Quixote prepares to perform penance in imitation of Amadis de Gaul, who took the name "Beltenebros," or "beautiful shadows." Sancho is preparing to depart to report to Dulcinea what he has seen of his master's penitence.

2. A backslider or repeat offender.

"In hell," replied Sancho, "*nulla est retentio,* so I've heard say."[3]

"I do not understand what you mean by *retentio,*" said Don Quixote.

"*Retentio* means," replied Sancho, "that people in hell never get out, and can't get out. It'll be the reverse with you, though, so long as I get my heels working, if I'm wearing spurs to make Rocinante move, that is—and you just wait till I reach El Toboso, and come before my lady Dulcinea, and then I'll tell her such stories about the acts of madness and stupidity, which comes to the same thing, that you've done and are doing as will make her as sweet as a nut, even if she's as hard as a cork-oak when I start work on her. And I'll come back through the air like a sorcerer with her honeyed answer, and I'll rescue you from this purgatory that seems like hell but isn't, because there's a hope of getting out of it, which people in hell haven't got, as I've just said, and I don't suppose you'll want to disagree with that."

"True," said the Knight of the Sorry Face, "but how are we going to manage to write that letter?"

"And that donkey-warrant," added Sancho.

"It will all be included," said Don Quixote, "and, since we have no paper, it would be appropriate to write it, as the ancients did, on leaves from the trees, or on tablets of wax; yet it would be as difficult to find these now as paper itself. But I have just thought of a good place, indeed an excellent one, to write it: the notebook that used to belong to Cardenio,[4] and you must take care to have it copied in a clear hand on to a sheet of paper in the first village with a schoolmaster, or else any sexton will copy it for you; but do not ask a clerk to copy it, because they use a corrupt and degenerate hand that Satan himself would not be able to read."

"And what's to be done about your signature?" asked Sancho.

"The letters of Amadis are never signed," replied Don Quixote.

"That's as may be," replied Sancho, "but the warrant must be signed, and if it's copied out they'll say the signature's a fake and I'll be left without my donkeys."

"The warrant will be signed in the notebook, and when my niece sees it she will not raise any objections about complying with it. And as regards the love-letter, you will have it signed: 'Yours until death, The Knight of the Sorry Face.' It will matter little that it is signed in another hand, because as far as I remember Dulcinea cannot read or write, and she has never seen a letter written by me, because the love between us has always been platonic, never going beyond a modest glance. And even this has been so occasional that I can truly swear that, in the twelve years I have loved her more than the light of these eyes that the earth will one day devour, I have not seen her as many as four times; and it is possible that on those four occasions she has not even once noticed that I was looking at her, such is the reserve and seclusion in which her father Lorenzo Corchuelo and her mother Aldonza Nogales have brought her up."

"Oho!" said Sancho. "So Lorenzo Corchuelo's daughter is the lady Dulcinea del Toboso, also known as Aldonza Lorenzo, is she?"

"She is," said Don Quixote, "and she it is who deserves to be the mistress of the entire universe."

"I know her well," said Sancho, "and let me tell you she pitches a bar as far as the strongest lad in all the village. Good God, she's a lusty lass all right, hale and hearty, strong as an ox, and any knight errant who has her as his lady now or in the future can

3. While Sancho's explanation is a canny one, his Latin is mangled; he should have said "in hell, *nulla est redemptio*" (nothing is redeemed) rather than "nothing is retained." The line is from the service for the dead.

4. Sancho and Don Quixote were first alerted to Cardenio's whereabouts when they discovered a satchel with his notebooks in Chapter 23.

count on her to pull him out of the mire! The little baggage, what muscles she's got on her, and what a voice! Let me tell you she climbed up one day to the top of the church belfry to call to some lads of hers who were in a fallow field of her father's, and even though they were a good couple of miles off they could hear her just as if they'd been standing at the foot of the tower. And the best thing about her is she isn't at all priggish, she's a real courtly lass, enjoys a joke with everyone and turns everything into a good laugh. And now I can say, Sir Knight of the Sorry Face, that not only is it very right and proper for you to get up to your mad tricks for her sake—you've got every reason to give way to despair and hang yourself, too, and nobody who knows about it will say you weren't justified, even if it does send you to the devil. And I wish I was on my way already, just to take a look at her, because I haven't seen her for days, and she must be changed by now, because women's faces get spoiled by always being out in the fields, in the sun and the wind. And I must be honest with you, Don Quixote sir—until now I've been completely mistaken, because I really and truly believed that the lady Dulcinea must be some princess you were in love with, or at least someone who deserved all those fine gifts you've sent her, that Basque and those convicts, and lots of others that there must have been, too, considering how many victories you must have won before I became your squire. But all things considered, what will the lady Aldonza Lorenzo I mean the lady Dulcinea del Toboso care whether the knights you defeat and send to her get down on their bended knees before her? Because when they turn up she might be combing flax or threshing wheat in the yard, and then they'd be all embarrassed and she'd burst out laughing and turn up her nose at the gift."

"I have often told you before now, Sancho," said Don Quixote, "that you are a chatterbox and that, although you are a dim-witted fellow, you often try to be too clever by half; but, so that you can see how stupid you are and how intelligent I am, I want you to listen to a little story. There was once a widow who was beautiful, young, unattached, rich and, above all, carefree, and who fell in love with a certain lay brother, a well-fleshed, corpulent young man; his superior found out, and said to the good widow one day, by way of friarly reprehension:

"'I am surprised, madam, and not without good reason, that a woman of your quality, as beautiful and as wealthy as you are, should have fallen in love with such a low, vulgar and ignorant fellow, when in this house there are so many bachelors, masters and doctors of divinity among whom you could have chosen as among pears at a fruit-stall, saying: "I'll have this one; no, not that."'

"But she replied to him with wit and dash:

"'You are much mistaken, sir, and very old-fashioned in your ideas, if you think I have made a bad choice, however stupid he may seem to you; because for what I want of him he knows as much philosophy as Aristotle, and more.'"

"And so, Sancho, for what I want of Dulcinea del Toboso, she is as good as the most exalted princess in the world. Yes indeed, for not all poets who praise ladies under a name that they choose for them really have any such mistresses at all. Do you really believe that the Amaryllises, Phyllises, Sylvias, Dianas, Galateas, Alidas and others that fill books, ballads, barbers' shops and theatre stages were real ladies of flesh and blood, and the mistresses of those that praise and have praised them?[5] No, of course not, the poets themselves invent most of them, to have something to write

5. All names of female characters from the many pastoral romances written in the second half of the 16th century. Cervantes' own pastoral romance was called *La Galatea*.

their poetry about, and to make people think that they are in love and that they have it in them to be lovers. And so it is enough for me to be convinced that the good Aldonza Lorenzo is beautiful and virtuous, and the question of lineage is not very important, because nobody is going to be enquiring into it to see whether she is entitled to robes of nobility, and for me she is the greatest princess in the world. For I would have you know, Sancho, if you do not know it already, that there are just two qualities that inspire love more than any others, and these are great beauty and good repute, and these two qualities are to be found in abundance in Dulcinea, because no woman can equal her in beauty, and few can approach her in good repute. And to put it in a nutshell, I imagine that everything I say is precisely as I say it is, and I depict her in my imagination as I wish her to be, both in beauty and in rank, and Helen cannot rival her, nor can Lucretia or any other of the famous women of past ages, whether Greek, Barbarian or Roman, equal her.[6] And people can say what they like, because if I am reproached by the ignorant for this, I shall not be punished by even the most severe judges."

"And I say you're right as right can be," replied Sancho, "and I'm an ass—but I don't know why I'm talking about asses, because you don't mention ropes in the house of the man that hanged himself. Let's have the letter, though, and then I'll be off."

Don Quixote took out the notebook and, drawing a little aside, he began with great deliberation to write the letter; and as he finished he called Sancho and said that he was going to read it aloud, so that Sancho could learn it by heart, in case he lost it on the way, because with his bad luck anything could happen. To which Sancho replied:

"You just write it down two or three times in the book and then let me have it, and I'll take good care of it—it's madness to think I'm going to learn it by heart, because my memory's so bad I often forget my own name. But read it to me all the same, I'll enjoy listening to it, because it must be a beauty."

"Listen, then; it goes like this," said Don Quixote.

Letter from Don Quixote to Dulcinea del Toboso

Sovereign and noble lady,

One sore-wounded by the dart of absence and lacerated to the very fabric of his heart, O sweetest Dulcinea del Toboso, wishes you the good health that he does not enjoy. If your beauteousness scorns me, if your worth does not favour me, if your disdain is my humiliation, I shall ill be able, albeit I am well furnished with longanimity,[7] to suffer a grief that is not merely intense but protracted. My good squire Sancho will render you a full account, O lovely ingrate, O beloved enemy of mine, of the state to which I am reduced for your sake. If it be your wish to succour me, I am yours, and if not, do what you will, for by ending my life I shall satisfy your cruelty and my desire.

Yours until death,

THE KNIGHT OF THE SORRY FACE

"By my dear father's bones!" cried Sancho. "That's the very finest thing I ever did hear! Damn it all, how well you say everything you want to say, and how well it

6. Lucretia was the chaste wife of the Roman Collatinus; when raped by Sextus Tarquinius, son of the despot Tarquinius Superbus, she killed herself, after calling on her family to bring down Rome's king. They did so, founding the Roman republic.

7. Long-suffering or forbearance.

all suits the signature 'The Knight of the Sorry Face'! To be sure you're the very devil, there isn't anything you don't know!"

"Everything is needed," replied Don Quixote, "in the profession that I follow."

"Come on, then," said Sancho, "turn over the page and write the warrant for the three donkeys, and sign it clear as clear, so they know your signature as soon as they see it."

"Very well," said Don Quixote.

And once he'd written it he read it out:

On receipt of this my first donkey-warrant, please order that three of the five that I left at home in your charge be given to my squire Sancho Panza. Which three donkeys I hereby order to be delivered to him and duly paid for, in return for the like number received from him here; and this bill, together with his receipt, will be sufficient for this transaction. Given in the heart of the Sierra Morena on the twenty-second of August of the current year.

"That's good," said Sancho. "Now sign it."

"There is no need for me to sign it," said Don Quixote. "All I have to do is to append my flourish, which counts as a signature, and that is sufficient for three asses, and even for three hundred."

"I'll believe you," replied Sancho. "Now let me go and saddle Rocinante, and you get ready to give me your blessing, because I'm leaving straight away, without waiting to see any of these antics you're going to get up to, though I'll tell her I saw you do so many of them that she'll be more than satisfied."

"At least, Sancho, I want you, because it is essential—what I mean to say is that I want you to see me naked, performing a dozen or two dozen mad deeds, which will only take me half an hour, so that having seen them with your own eyes you can safely swear to any others that you may care to add; and I can assure you that you will not tell her of as many as I intend to perform."

"For the love of God, sir, don't make me see you naked, I'll feel so sorry for you I shan't be able to help crying. And my head's in such a state after crying so much last night for my dun that I'm in no condition for any more tears, so if you want me to see some of your antics, do them with your clothes on—quick antics, just the most relevant ones. What's more, there isn't any need for all this as far as I'm concerned, and, as I said, it would mean I'd come back all the sooner with the news that you want and deserve to hear. If not, the lady Dulcinea had better look out, because if she doesn't reply as she ought to, I take my solemn oath that I'll kick and punch the right answer out of her guts. Because who can put up with a famous knight errant like you going mad, without any reason at all, for a . . .? And the lady had better not make me say it, or else by God I'll upset the apple cart, and hang the consequences! And I can! She doesn't know what I'm like! If she did, she'd stand in fear of me, she would!"

"And so, Sancho," said Don Quixote, "it seems that you are no saner than I am."

"No, I'm not as mad as you," said Sancho, "but I am angrier. Leaving all that aside, though, what are you going to eat while I'm away? Are you going to waylay goatherds and steal your food, like Cardenio?"

"You must not worry about that," replied Don Quixote, "for even if I had any food, all I should eat would be whatever herbs and other fruit of the land this meadow and these trees provide; for the beauty of my plan lies precisely in not eating and in other equivalent mortifications. And so goodbye."

"But do you know what I'm scared of? Not finding the way back here where I'm leaving you, because it's so secluded."

"You take good note of the landmarks, and I shall try not to move far off," said Don Quixote, "and I shall even take the precaution of climbing the highest of these crags here to see if I can spot you when you return. In addition, your surest way of not getting lost and missing me will be to cut some of this broom growing so abundantly hereabouts, and to drop a branch every so often until you reach the plain, and they will serve as guide-marks on your return, like the thread in Perseus's labyrinth."[8]

"That's what I'll do," replied Sancho Panza.

He cut some broom, asked his master for his blessing and, not without many tears on both sides, said goodbye. And climbing on to Rocinante, whom Don Quixote warmly entrusted to Sancho's safe-keeping, with the instruction to take as good care of him as of his own person, he headed off towards the plain, scattering broom-branches every so often, as his master had advised. And so he rode away, even though Don Quixote was still insisting that he should watch a couple of his wild deeds, at least. But Sancho hadn't gone a hundred steps when he turned and came back and said:

"I think you were right, sir, and to be able to swear with a clear conscience that I've seen you doing mad deeds, I'd better see one of them at least, although I must say I've seen a big enough one already—you staying here."

"Did I not tell you so?" said Don Quixote. "Just wait a minute, Sancho, I shall perform them in the saying of a creed."

And pulling down his breeches as fast as ever he could, he stood there in his shirt and then did two leaps in the air followed by two somersaults, revealing things that made Sancho turn Rocinante so as not to have to see them again; and he felt fully satisfied that he could swear his master was mad. And we shall allow him to go his way until his return, which was speedy.

* * *

from *Chapter 52*

About Don Quixote's fight with the goatherd, and the singular adventure of the penitents, which he brought to a happy conclusion by the sweat of his brow[1]

* * * The goatherd[2] looked at Don Quixote, and finding him such a sorry sight he asked the barber—who was sitting next to him—in some bewilderment:

"Who is this man, sir, that cuts such a figure and speaks in such a way?"

"Who should he be," answered the barber, "but the famous Don Quixote de la Mancha, the redresser of injuries, the righter of wrongs, the protector of damsels, the terror of giants and the victor in battles?"

8. A reference to the labyrinth in which the Minotaur was housed, and which Theseus (not Perseus) successfully navigated by means of a thread.

1. In the intervening chapters, Don Quixote leaves the Sierra Morena, hears a variety of tales from Cardenio and others, and suffers the effects of an enchantment orchestrated by the barber and the priest, who are trying to bring him back to La Mancha. Don Quixote is bound hand and foot while sleeping in an inn and placed as a captive in an ox-cart, with which the disguised barber and priest will take him home. A canon from Toledo, along with his servants and several "peace-officers" or members of the Holy Brotherhood, have joined the company as well.

2. The goatherd is a young man named Eugenio, who has just finished telling a story about his love for a woman who eloped with a trickster and has been put by her father in a convent. The current discussion is taking place in an inn, after Don Quixote is let temporarily out of his cage and promises not to run away: "I do indeed give my word," he says, "and in any case, a person who is enchanted, as I am, is not at liberty to dispose of his person as he wishes, because the man who enchanted him can prevent him from moving for three centuries on end, and if he flees he will bring him back in the twinkling of an eye."

"That sounds to me," replied the goatherd, "like what you read in books about knights errant, who used to do all those things you said this man does, but it's my opinion that either you're joking or some of the rooms in this character's upper storey are empty."

"You are a villainous wretch," Don Quixote burst out, "and you are the one who is empty and a fool, and I am fuller than the whore of a bitch who bore you ever was."

And with these words he snatched up a loaf and hurled it at the goatherd's face with such furious force that he flattened his nose; and the goatherd, who couldn't take a jest and found himself being assaulted in earnest, disregarded the carpet and the tablecloths and all the people who were eating, and leapt upon Don Quixote, seized him by the throat with both hands and wouldn't have hesitated to throttle him if Sancho Panza hadn't rushed over, grabbed the goatherd by the shoulders and flung him down on the table, breaking plates, smashing cups and overturning and scattering everything else. As soon as Don Quixote found himself free he jumped on top of the goatherd, who, bloody-faced and pounded by Sancho's feet, was crawling over the tablecloths in search of a knife with which to take some gory revenge, but the canon and the priest were making sure this couldn't happen; and then the barber intervened to enable the goatherd to climb on top of Don Quixote, at whom he flailed away until as much blood was pouring from the poor knight's face as from his own. The canon and the priest were laughing fit to burst, the peace-officers were jumping with joy, everyone was cheering the two men on as dogs are cheered on when they're fighting; only Sancho Panza was in despair, because he couldn't wriggle free of the grasp of one of the canon's servants who was preventing him from going to help his master.

In short, just when everyone was enjoying this festival of fun, except the two battered, scratching warriors, they heard a trumpet call, so mournful that it made them all turn towards where it seemed to be coming from; but the man who was most affected by the sound was Don Quixote who, although he was under the goatherd, much against his will and most severely mauled, said to him:

"Brother devil, for that is what you must be, since you have found the resolve and the strength to overpower me: I request that we agree on a truce for just one hour, because the sorrowful sound of that trumpet which we can hear appears to be summoning me to a new adventure."

The goatherd, who by now was tired of thumping and being thumped, climbed off without more ado, and Don Quixote stood up and looked with the others in the direction of the sounds, and as he did so a horde of men dressed as penitents in white suddenly came into sight as they descended one of the sides of the valley. What had happened was that the clouds had withheld their moisture from the earth that year, and processions, public prayers and acts of penitence were being organized in all the villages in the area to entreat God to open the hands of his mercy and send down some rain; and to this end the people from a nearby village were coming in a procession to a holy chapel on one side of the valley.[3] Don Quixote, seeing the processionists' strange dress, and not pausing to remember that he must have seen such penitents many times before, imagined that this was the subject for an adventure, and that it was his task alone, as a knight errant, to undertake it; and he was further confirmed in this belief when he saw a holy image swathed in mourning that they were carrying, and

3. Such processions to pray for changes in weather were fairly common, particularly in rural areas. The participants would generally pray and sing while flogging themselves in penitence for sins of the community, and would often carry with them large statues or images of Mary and the saints.

thought it was some eminent lady whom those arrant and insolent knaves were bearing off against her will; and no sooner had this idea found its way into his head than he charged over to where Rocinante was grazing, unhooked both the horse's bit and his own shield from the pommel, put the bit in its place in the twinkling of an eye, told Sancho to give him his sword, mounted Rocinante, took up his shield and cried to all present:

"And now, O doughty company, you shall perceive how important it is that knights who profess the order of knight-errantry should exist in the world; now, I say, you shall perceive, in the freeing of that good lady who is being carried away captive, whether or not knights errant are worthy of esteem."

And as he said this he put thighs to Rocinante, because he wasn't wearing any spurs, and at a canter, because we don't read anywhere in this true history that Rocinante ever ventured on a full gallop, he advanced on the penitents, despite all the efforts of the priest and the canon and the barber to stop him; but it was impossible, and Sancho couldn't do anything to dissuade him, either, by yelling:

"What are you going to do now, Don Quixote sir? What demons have you got inside your breast egging you on against our holy Catholic faith? I'll be damned—look, look, that's a penitents' procession, and that lady they're carrying on the platform is the blessed image of the immaculate Virgin. Be careful, sir, what you're doing—this time I'm really sure it isn't what you think it is."

But Sancho laboured in vain, because his master was so set on confronting the men in white and freeing the lady in black that he didn't hear a word; and even if he had heard one he wouldn't have turned back, not if it had been the King himself ordering him. So on he cantered towards the procession and then he halted Rocinante, who was by now ready to take a rest, and he cried in a hoarse and agitated voice:

"O you who hide your faces, perchance because you are evil: pay attention and listen to what I have to say to you."

The first to stop were the men carrying the image, and one of the four priests chanting the litanies took one look at Don Quixote's strange figure, Rocinante's thinness and other ludicrous aspects of the knight's appearance, and replied with the words:

"If you want to say something to us, my good man, say it quickly, because our brethren here are tearing their flesh to shreds, and we cannot and must not stop to listen to anything unless it's brief enough to be said in a couple of words."

"I shall say it all in one word," replied Don Quixote, "and it is this: you must at this very instant set free that beautiful lady, whose tears and sorrowful face are clear proof that you are bearing her off against her will and that you have done her some very great mischief; and I, who came into this world to redress such injuries, will not permit you to take one step forward unless you give her the liberty that she desires and deserves."

These words made all those who heard them realize that Don Quixote must be some madman, and they burst into hearty laughter, which was like pouring gunpowder on to the fire of Don Quixote's wrath: without another word he drew his sword and charged at the platform. One of the men carrying it left his companions holding it up, came out to meet Don Quixote brandishing the forked prop on which he helped to support it whenever they paused for a rest, used this prop to ward off a mighty sword-stroke that the knight aimed at him and that cut it in two and then, with the part left in his hand, delivered such a blow to the shoulder of his enemy's sword arm, which the shield couldn't protect against brute strength, that poor Don Quixote tumbled to the ground in dire straits. Sancho Panza, who came puffing after his master, saw him fall and cried out to his demolisher not to hit him again, he was only a poor enchanted knight who'd never done anyone any harm in all the days of his born life. But what stopped the peasant wasn't Sancho's shouts but seeing that Don Quixote wasn't stirring, not so much as a hand or a foot; and so, in the belief that he'd killed him, he hoisted his tunic up to his waist and ran away across the fields like a deer.

And now Don Quixote's companions arrived on the scene, as did the other processionists, who saw their opponents come running up with the peace-officers clutching their crossbows, feared the worst and swarmed around the holy image with their hoods raised from their faces, brandishing their scourges while the priests wielded their great processional candle-sticks, awaiting the assault in the determination to defend themselves and even attack their assailants if they could; but fortune treated them better than they'd thought it would, because all Sancho did was to throw himself upon his master's body and pour over him the most piteous and laughable lament ever heard, in the belief that he was dead. Our priest was recognized by one of the priests in the procession, and this calmed the fears that had developed in both squadrons. The first priest gave the second one a brief account of Don Quixote, and then he went with the throng of penitents to see whether the poor knight was dead, and they all heard Sancho Panza saying, with tears in his eyes:

"O flower of chivalry, whose well-spent life just one thump with a cudgel has done for! O pride of your family, honour and glory of all La Mancha and all the world—now that you've gone from it, it'll fill up with evil-doers who won't be frightened of being punished for their wicked ways! O you who were more open-handed than all the Alexanders, because for only eight months' service you said you'd give me the best island that ever had the sea all round it! O you who were humble to the haughty and haughty to the humble, tackler of dangers, taker of insults, in love without a cause, imitator of the good, scourge of the wicked, enemy of villains—in a word, knight errant, and that says it all!"

Sancho's cries and groans revived Don Quixote, and what he first said was:

"He who lives absent from you, sweetest Dulcinea, is subject to even greater calamities than this. Help me, dear Sancho, to climb on to the enchanted cart: I am no longer in any fit state to burden Rocinante's saddle, for this shoulder of mine has been smashed to smithereens."

"I'll do that with a will, sir," replied Sancho, "and let's go back to our village with these gentlemen, who only want what's best for you, and there we'll work out a way to make another sally that'll bring us more profit and renown."

"You are speaking sound sense," replied Don Quixote, "and it will be wise indeed to wait for the presently prevailing malign influence of the stars to dissipate."

The canon and the priest and the barber told him that he would be quite right to do as he'd said; and so, having been most wonderfully entertained by Sancho Panza's absurdities, they put Don Quixote back on the cart. The religious procession formed up again, and went on its way. The goatherd said goodbye to everyone. The peace-officers refused to go any further, and the priest paid them what he owed them. The canon asked the priest to let him know what happened to Don Quixote, whether he recovered from his madness or continued in the same state, and then begged their leave to continue his journey.

And so the party split up and each followed his own road, leaving the priest and the barber, Don Quixote and Panza and the good Rocinante, as patient as his master in the face of everything he'd undergone. The carter yoked his oxen, put Don Quixote on top of a truss of hay, followed with his usual sedateness the route indicated by the priest; and six days later they reached their village, which they entered at noon, and as it happened to be a Sunday everybody was in the square, through the middle of which the cart trundled on its way. Everyone went over to see what was in the cart, and when they recognized their neighbour they were astonished, and a lad ran to tell the housekeeper and the niece that their master and uncle had come back, thin and pale, and lying on top of a pile of hay in an ox-cart. It was pitiful to hear the cries these two good ladies let loose, the slaps they gave themselves, the curses they again directed at those damned books of chivalry; all of which they renewed when they saw Don Quixote coming in through the door.

At the news of Don Quixote's arrival Sancho Panza's wife hurried to his house, because she had discovered that her husband had gone away with him as his squire, and when she saw Sancho the first thing she asked was whether the ass was well. Sancho replied that the ass was better than its master was.[4]

"Thanks be to God for his great goodness to me," she replied. "And now tell me, husband, what have you got out of all this squiring of yours? How many fine skirts have you brought back for me? How many pairs of shoes for your children?"

"I haven't brought any of all that, wife," said Sancho. "But I've got other stuff that's much more special and important."

"I'm very pleased to hear it, too," his wife replied. "Now show me this stuff that's so much more important and special, husband—I'd love to see it to cheer up this heart of mine that's been so sad and out of sorts all these ages that you've been away."

"I'll let you see it when we get home," said Panza, "and meantime you can count yourself lucky, because if it's God's will for us to go off again in search of adventures you'll soon see me made an earl or the governor of an island, and not any old island either but the very best island there is."

"May heaven grant it, husband, we need it badly enough. But tell me, what's all this about islands? I don't understand you."

"Honey wasn't made for the mouths of asses," Sancho retorted. "You'll see in due course, wife, and you'll get a surprise, I can tell you, when you hear all your vassals calling you your ladyship."

"What's this you're saying, Sancho, about ladyships, islands and vassals?" replied Juana Panza, for this was the name of Sancho's wife, not that they were blood relations but because it's the custom in La Mancha for women to take their husbands' surnames.

"Don't you be in such a hurry, Juana, to know about all these things; I'm telling you the truth, and that's enough for you, so shut up. All I will say, since I'm on the subject, is that there's nothing better in life than being an honest man who's the squire of a knight errant who goes in search of adventures. It is true that most of the adventures you find don't turn out as well as what you'd like them to, because out of a hundred you come across ninety-nine usually go skew-whiff. I know that from experience, because I've ended up blanket-tossed in some and beaten black and blue in others. But in spite of all that, it's great to be waiting to see what's going to happen next as you ride across mountains, explore forests, climb crags, visit castles and put up at inns as and when you like, and not the devil a farthing to pay."

While Sancho Panza and his wife Juana Panza chatted away like this, Don Quixote's housekeeper and niece welcomed their master, undressed him and laid him

4. The ass mysteriously returns to Sancho after its theft by Ginés de Pasamonte, an oversight that Cervantes will make fun of in Part 2.

on his ancient bed. He was peering at them through unfocused eyes, and couldn't fathom where on earth he was. The priest told the niece to make sure to pamper her uncle and have him watched so that he didn't escape again, and described what they'd had to do to bring him back home. And then the two women again raised the roof with their outcry; again they renewed their cursing of the books of chivalry; again they implored heaven to cast the authors of all those lies and absurdities into the depths of the bottomless pit. All this left them bewildered and fearful that as soon as their master and uncle felt a little better they'd lose him again; and that was indeed what happened.

But although the author of this history has searched with the most meticulous care for an account of the deeds performed by Don Quixote during his third sally, he hasn't been able to find any information about them, not at least in writings by reputable authors; tradition alone has preserved, in the memory of La Mancha, the belief that the third time Don Quixote left home he went to Saragossa, where he took part in some famous jousts and underwent experiences worthy of his courage and intelligence. But the author could not discover any information about how Don Quixote met his end, nor would he ever have even known about it if good fortune had not sent him an aged doctor who had in his possession a lead casket which, he said, had been found among the foundations of an old, ruined chapel that was being rebuilt. In this casket there were some parchments with texts written in Roman letters but in Castilian verse, describing many of his exploits and giving accounts of Dulcinea del Toboso's beauty, Rocinante's looks, Sancho Panza's loyalty and Don Quixote's grave, in various epitaphs and eulogies about his life and works. And those that could be read and understood have been set down here by the trustworthy author of this original and matchless history, who only asks from his readers, in recompense for the immense trouble that he has taken to scrutinize and explore all the archives in La Mancha so as to be able to bring it to the light of day, that they give it the same credit that people of good sense give to books of chivalry, so highly prized by all; and this will make him feel well rewarded and satisfied, and encourage him to search out other histories, perhaps less authentic than this one but no less ingenious or entertaining.

[*Several verses by local wits praising Don Quixote and Sancho follow, ending with the following poems.*]

HOBGOBLIN, A MEMBER OF THE ARGAMASILLA ACADEMY,[5] ON THE GRAVE OF DON QUIXOTE

EPITAPH

Here lies a knight, a man of pluck,
Rich in thumpings, poor in luck,
Who, perched on Rocinante's back,
Rode up this path and down that track.
And Sancho Panza is the dolt
Who lies beside him in this vault;
The loyallest man in our empire
Who ever earned the name of squire.

5. Argamasilla is a village in La Mancha; this may be the "forgotten" town from which Don Quixote hails. Academies were men's clubs that convened on civic and festive occasions, and churned out mediocre verses to honor important events; the academy mentioned here is completely imaginary, as the silly names of its members attest.

Ding-dong, a member of the Argamasilla Academy,
on the grave of Dulcinea del Toboso

Epitaph

Fair Dulcinea here is laid
And though she was a meaty maid
Death turned her into dust and clay
In his horrendous, dreadful way.
Of a true breed she surely came,
She was the great Don Quixote's flame,
She wore with style a lady's gown:
The glory of Toboso town.

These were the verses that were legible; since the others were worm-eaten, they were handed to an academician for him to decipher. It is reported that he has done so, after long vigils and much toil, and that he intends to publish them, as we await Don Quixote's third sally.

Forse altri canterà con miglior plectio.[6]

Part 2[1]

Chapter 3

About the ridiculous discussion between Don Quixote, Sancho Panza and Sansón Carrasco, BA

Don Quixote remained deep in thought as he awaited the young graduate Carrasco, from whom he was expecting to hear news about himself published in a book, as Sancho had said; and he couldn't persuade himself that such a history existed—the blood of the enemies that he had killed was not yet dry on the blade of his sword, and people were already claiming that his noble deeds of chivalry had appeared in print! Despite this, though, it did occur to him that some sage, friendly or hostile, must have published his deeds by way of enchantment: if friendly, to exalt them and place them above the most renowned exploits ever performed by any knight errant; if hostile, to dismiss them and present them as being meaner than the wretchedest deeds that the basest squire had ever been described as doing, but then again (he said to himself), squires' exploits had never been recorded; and if it was true that this history did exist, the fact that it concerned a knight errant was a guarantee that it would be grandiloquent, lofty, illustrious, magnificent and true.

This thought offered him some consolation, but then he lost heart again when he remembered that the name Cide suggested that the author was a Moor, and not a word of truth was to be expected from any of those, since the whole lot of them are deceivers, liars and story-tellers. He was afraid that the author might have handled his

6. "Perhaps others will sing with better lyre than I." From *Orlando furioso* (canto 30, stanza 16).

1. Part 2 of *Don Quixote* was published in 1615, ten years after Part 1. After an introductory chapter, Chapter 2 has Don Quixote eager to discover what others are saying about him, and he urges Sancho to sally forth to find one Sansón Carrasco. Carrasco has just returned from his studies at Salamanca University and has told Sancho that his story has been put into a book called *The Ingenious Hidalgo Don Quixote de la Mancha.* As Sancho reports to Don Quixote, "he says I'm named in it with my very own name of Sancho Panza, and the lady Dulcinea del Toboso too, and things are even mentioned when you and I were alone when we did them"—prompting Don Quixote to declare "that the author of our history must be some wise enchanter."

love affair in an indelicate manner that would cause detraction and damage to the chastity of his lady Dulcinea del Toboso; he hoped that he had portrayed his faithfulness and the unswerving correctness of his behaviour towards her, snubbing queens, empresses and damsels of all ranks, and holding in leash the powerful urges of his natural passions; and in this state, engrossed in these and many other thoughts careering about his brain, he was found by Sancho and Carrasco, whom Don Quixote greeted with gracious courtesy.

Despite his name[2] the new graduate wasn't a big man, although he was a great leg-puller; his complexion was dull but his wits were sharp; he'd have been about twenty-four, with a moon face, a snub nose and a large mouth, all signs that he had a waggish disposition and loved joking and jesting, as he showed when he saw Don Quixote by throwing himself on to his knees before him and saying:

"Pray give me your hands, Don Quixote de la Mancha; I swear by this habit of St Peter that I'm wearing, even though I've only taken minor orders,[3] that you are one of the most famous knights errant that have ever existed or indeed ever will exist in the whole wide world. A blessing on Cide Hamete Benengeli for having written the history of your great deeds, and a double blessing on the diligent man who took care to have it translated from Arabic into our Castilian vernacular, for the amusement and entertainment of all."

Don Quixote brought him to his feet and said:

"It is true, then, is it, that a history of me exists, and that it was a Moor and a sage who wrote it?"

"It's so true, sir," said Sansón, "that I'm to understand that more than twelve thousand copies of the history are in print at this moment; and if you don't believe me, just ask Portugal, Barcelona and Valencia, where they were printed; and there's a report that it's being printed now in Antwerp, and all the signs are that there's no language in the world into which it won't be translated."[4]

"One of the things," Don Quixote put in, "that must give the greatest happiness to a virtuous and eminent man is to find himself with a good name on everybody's lips, and in print, while he is still alive. I said "with a good name" because, if the opposite were the case, no death could equal it."

"As far as good names and good reputations are concerned," the young graduate said, "you have gained the palm from all other knights errant, because the Moor in his language, and the Christian in his, took good care to depict most vividly for us your gallantry, your courage in confronting perils, your patience in adversity, your long-suffering in misfortune and when wounded, and your chastity and continence in that most platonic love-affair between you and my lady Doña Dulcinea del Toboso."

"I've never heard anyone," Sancho butted in, "calling my lady Dulcinea Doña, but just the lady Dulcinea del Toboso—so the history's wrong about that, for starters."

"That isn't an important objection," Carrasco replied.

"Certainly not," said Don Quixote, "but tell me, sir, which of my deeds are most highly praised in the history?"

"About that," the young graduate replied, "opinions differ, as tastes do: some prefer the adventure of the windmills, which you thought were Briareuses and giants;

2. Sansón is Spanish for Samson, the Hebrew warrior who possessed great strength as long as he didn't cut his hair.
3. Carrasco would have been wearing a habit of someone who was a minor cleric.
4. By 1615, *Don Quixote* had already been translated into English as well as French; numerous editions in Spanish had been published in Valencia, Barcelona, Lisbon, and Madrid as well as Brussels and Milan.

others, the adventure of the fulling-mill; others, the description of the two armies that turned out to be two flocks of sheep; one man praises the adventure of the corpse being taken to Segovia to be buried; another says that the best one of them all is the freeing of the convicts; yet another that none of them equals the adventure of the two Benedictine giants and the fight with the brave Basque."

"Could you please tell me, sir," Sancho put in, "whether they've included the adventure of the men from Yanguas, when good old Rocinante had the bright idea of reaching for the stars?"

"The sage didn't leave anything out," replied Sansón. "He includes and describes it all, even the capers cut by Sancho in the blanket."

"I didn't cut any capers in the blanket," Sancho retorted. "I cut them in the air, and more of them than I'd have chosen to."

"I suppose," added Don Quixote, "that every history that has ever been written has its ups and its downs, especially those that deal with chivalric exploits, for they cannot recount successful adventures alone."

"For all that," the young graduate replied, "some of those who've read the history say that they'd have been happier if its authors had overlooked some of the countless beatings that Don Quixote received in various confrontations."

"That's where the truth of the history comes in," said Sancho.

"But they could, in all fairness, have kept quiet about them," said Don Quixote, "because there is no need to narrate actions that do not alter or undermine the truth of the history, if they are going to result in the discrediting of the hero. I am sure that Aeneas was not as pious as Virgil depicts him, nor was Ulysses as prudent as Homer says."

"That's true," Sansón replied, "but it's one thing to write as a poet and quite another to write as a historian: the poet can narrate or sing events not as they were but as they should have been, and the historian must record them not as they should have been but as they were, without adding anything to the truth or taking anything away from it."

"Well if this Moorish bloke's after telling the truth," said Sancho, "I bet the thumpings they handed out to me will be in there among the ones my master got, because they never took the measure of his shoulders without taking it of my whole body. But that's no surprise, because as my master says, all the limbs have got to share the headache."

"You are a sly dog, Sancho," replied Don Quixote. "I must say your memory works well enough when you want it to."

"Even if I did want to forget the thrashings I've been given," said Sancho, "the bruises wouldn't let me, still fresh here on my ribs."

"Keep quiet, Sancho," said Don Quixote, "and stop interrupting our friend from the university, whom I entreat to continue telling me what is said about me in this history."

"And about me, too," said Sancho. "They say I'm one of the main caricatures in it, too."

"*Characters,* not *caricatures,* friend Sancho," said Sansón.

"Oh no, not another blunders-expert!" said Sancho. "If you two start up on that again, we'll all be here till the ends of our lives."

"May God give me a bad life, Sancho," replied the young graduate, "if you aren't the second most important character in the history, and there are those who'd rather hear you talk than the finest of the others, even though there are also people who say you were too gullible in believing you could ever become governor of that island offered you by Don Quixote here."

"All is not yet lost," said Don Quixote, "and as Sancho matures he will, with the experience that only the passing years can bring, become more suited and better qualified for the post of governor than he is at present."

"For God's sake, sir," said Sancho, "the island I can't govern at my age. I shan't be able to govern when I'm as old as Moses. The problem is that this island of yours is biding its time God only knows where, not that I haven't got the gumption to govern it."

"Entrust the matter to God's good care, Sancho," said Don Quixote, "for everything will turn out well, better perhaps than you think: not a leaf stirs on a tree unless God wishes it to."

"That's true enough," said Sansón, "and, if it is God's will, there shall be a thousand islands for Sancho to govern, let alone one."

"I've seen governors about the place," said Sancho, "that to my mind can't hold a candle to me, yet, for all that, they get called my lord and they eat off plates of silver."

"Those aren't governors of islands," replied Sansón, "but of other less demanding things; because those who govern islands must at the very least have some knowledge of syntax."

"I could cope with the sin," said Sancho, "but I'll pass on the tax—it's something I haven't ever come to grips with. But to leave me being governor in God's hands, and may he send me where I can be of most service to him—what I say, Sansón Carrasco sir, is that I'm very very glad that the author of this here history has talked about me in such a way that what he says doesn't give offence, because I swear to you as a loyal squire that if he'd said anything that wasn't fit to be said about a pure-bred Christian, which is what I am, the deafest of the deaf would have heard what I'd have had to say to him."

"That would have been a miracle," Sansón replied.

"Miracle or no miracle," said Sancho, "everyone should watch out how he talks or writes about the next man and not just shove down the first thing that comes into his brain-box."

"One of the faults that have been found in this history," said the young graduate, "is that the author included a tale called *Inappropriate Curiosity;* not that it's a bad one or badly told, but it's out of place and has nothing to do with the history of the great Don Quixote."[5]

"I bet," replied Sancho, "that the bastard's gone and made a right old hotchpotch."

"I do now have to say," said Don Quixote, "that the author of my history is no sage but some ignorant prattler, who started writing it in a haphazard and unplanned way and let it turn out however it would, like Orbaneja, the famous artist of Úbeda,[6] who, when asked what he was painting, replied: 'Whatever emerges.' On one occasion he was painting a cockerel so badly and so unlike a real cockerel that he had to write in capital letters by its side: 'This is a cockerel.' My history must be like that, needing a commentary to make it intelligible."

"No, no," replied Sansón, "it's so very intelligible that it doesn't pose any difficulties at all: children leaf through it, adolescents read it, grown men understand it and old men praise it, and, in short, it's so well-thumbed and well-perused and well-known by all kinds of people that as soon as they see a skinny nag pass by they say: 'Look, there goes Rocinante.' And the people who have most taken to it are the page-boys. There's not a lord's antechamber without its *Quixote:* if one person puts it

5. In Chapters 33–35, the priest read aloud to the company a tale that the innkeeper found among some other papers; it concerns the exploits of two Florentine gentlemen who are best friends.

6. An unknown Spanish painter.

aside, another picks it up; some ask to be lent it, others run up and snatch it away. All in all, this history provides the most delightful and least harmful entertainment ever, because nowhere in it can one find the slightest suspicion of language that isn't wholesome or thoughts that aren't Catholic."

"To write in any other way," said Don Quixote, "would be to write not truths but falsehoods, and historians who have recourse to falsehoods should be burnt, like counterfeiters; and I do not know what could have made the author turn to stories about other people when there was so much to write about me: I suppose he was relying on the saying, 'It's all fish that comes to the net.' Yet the truth of the matter is that just by recording my thoughts, my sighs, my tears, my worthy designs and my missions he could have written a volume bigger than all the works of El Tostado[7] put together, or at any rate as big. Be that as it may, my understanding of the matter, my dear sir, is that to write histories and other books one needs a fine mind and a mature understanding. To tell jokes and write wittily is the work of geniuses; the most intelligent character in a play is the fool, because the actor playing the part of a simpleton must not be one. History is, as it were, sacred, because it must be truthful, and where there is truth there is God, because he is truth; and yet, in spite of all this, there are those who toss off books as if they were pancakes."

"There's no book so bad," said the young graduate, "that there isn't something good in it."

"About that there is no doubt," Don Quixote replied, "but it often happens that men who have deservedly achieved and won fame by their writings lose it completely or find it diminished in part as soon as they publish them."

"The reason for that," said Sansón, "is that printed works are read at leisure and their defects are easily spotted, and the more famous the author the more closely they're scrutinized. Men renowned for their genius—great poets, illustrious historians—are usually envied by those whose pleasure and pastime is to pass judgement on what others have written, without ever having published anything themselves."

"That is not surprising," said Don Quixote, "because there are many theologians who cannot preach, yet are experts at identifying the faults and the excesses of those who can."

"It is exactly as you say, Don Quixote," said Carrasco, "but I do wish that such critics were more forgiving and less censorious, and did not pay such attention to the spots on the brilliant sun of the work they grumble at; for if *aliquando bonus dormitat Homerus,*[8] they should also remember how very long Homer stayed awake to give us the light of his work with the least possible shadow; and it could even be that what they think are faults are in reality beauty spots, which often increase the loveliness of a face; so, you see, anyone publishing a book exposes himself to enormous risk, because it's absolutely impossible to write one in such a way that it satisfies and pleases all those who read it."

"The book that has been written about me," said Don Quixote, "will not have pleased many people."

"Quite the contrary: since *stultorum infinitus est numerus,*[9] innumerable are those who have relished this history. Some have found fault with the author's memory and accused him of deception because he forgets to tell us who was the thief that stole

7. Alonso de Madrigal, bishop of Avila in the 15th century who wrote a large number of religious works.

8. "Even the good Homer sometimes nods"; from Horace's *Art of Poetry.*

9. "The number of fools is infinite."

Sancho's dun[1]—the incident isn't narrated and we just have to infer that somebody has stolen it, and a little later we find Sancho riding the very same donkey without having recovered it. They also say that the author forgot to state what Sancho did with the hundred escudos he found in the travelling bag in the Sierra Morena, which are never mentioned again; and there are many people who would like to know what happened to them, or what he spent them on, which is one of the essential points omitted from the book."

Sancho replied:

"Right now, Señor Carrasco, I'm in no state to go into any accounts or explanations, because I've just gone all a-flutter in my tummy, and if I don't get a couple of swigs of the old stuff inside me to put it right I'll soon be nothing but skin and bone. I'll have to go home for it, and the wife's waiting for me—as soon as I've done eating I'll come back and answer all the questions you and anyone else want to put to me, both about the loss of the ass and about the spending of the hundred escudos."

And without awaiting a reply or saying another word he went home. Don Quixote insisted that the graduate must share his humble board. The graduate accepted the invitation and stayed for the meal, a couple of squabs were added to the pot, the conversation at table was about deeds of chivalry, Carrasco played along with his host, the banquet came to an end, they had their afternoon nap, Sancho returned and the previous conversation was resumed.

Chapter 4

In which Sancho Panza provides the answers to the young graduate Sansón Carrasco's doubts and questions; together with other events worth knowing and telling

Sancho Panza returned to Don Quixote's house and to the previous conversation, and he said:

"To what Señor Sansón said about people wanting to know who stole my donkey, and how and when, it is my reply that on the very same night when we went to hide from the Holy Brotherhood in the Sierra Morena, after the adventure or misadventure of the convicts, and the other one of the dead body being taken to Segovia, me and my master rode into a clump of trees where my master leaned on his lance and I sat on my dun, both of us dead beat after the fights we'd had, and we dozed off just as if we were lying on half-a-dozen feather mattresses, and in particular I fell so very fast asleep that whoever it was managed to come and prop up the pack-saddle, with me sitting there and all, on top of four poles one in each corner, and get the dun out from underneath without me noticing a thing."

That is easy enough to do, and no new occurrence: it is what happened to Sacripante when he was at the siege of Albracca and that famous thief Brunello removed his horse from between his legs using the same trick.[1]

"Dawn broke," Sancho resumed, "and as soon as I gave myself a good shake the poles caved in and I came down with an almighty thump, and I looked around for my donkey and I couldn't find it, and the tears filled my eyes and I made such a lament that if the author of our history hasn't put it in he can take it from me he hasn't put anything worthwhile in. A few days later, I can't rightly remember how many, I was

1. Cervantes actually corrected this oversight in Book 1, reporting on Ginés's theft.

1. In *Orlando furioso,* Brunello is notorious for his thievery; he steals Sacripante's horse in Canto 27.

walking along with Princess Micomicona when I spotted my donkey, and on top of it wearing gipsy clothes was that character Ginés de Pasamonte, that crook, that great villain me and my master set free from the chain."[2]

"That isn't the mistake," Sansón replied. "The mistake is that before the ass has reappeared the author says Sancho's riding it!"

"I don't know what to say to that," said Sancho, "but maybe the historian got it wrong, or it might have been a slip of the printer's."

"I'm sure you're right," said Sansón, "but what happened to the hundred escudos? Did they disappear into thin air?"

Sancho replied:

"I laid them out on the well-being of my person and of my wife and children, and those escudos are the only reason why my wife's putting up with me going off along all those highways and byways serving my master Don Quixote, because if after all that time I'd come back home penniless and donkeyless I'd have been in for it—and if there's anything else you want to know about me here I am, and I'll answer to the King himself in person, and there's no cause for anybody to be poking their noses into whether I brought money back with me or not and whether I spent it or not. Because if the thumpings I was given on my travels had to be paid for in hard cash, even if they were only priced at four maravedís apiece another hundred escudos wouldn't be enough to pay for the half of them, and people can put their hands on their hearts and say what they'd have done, and stop making out that what's white's black and what's black's white—each of us is how God made him and many are much worse."

"I'll take care," said Carrasco, "to warn the author of the history that if he prints it again he mustn't forget what the worthy Sancho has just said—for this will carry it to even greater heights."

"Are there any other features of this book that need correcting, my dear young graduate?" Don Quixote asked.

"Yes, there must be," he replied, "but none of them can be as important as those that I have mentioned."

"And does the author," Don Quixote asked, "by any chance promise a second part?"

"Yes, he does," Sansón replied, "but he says he hasn't found it and doesn't know who's got it, so we can't tell whether it'll come out or not—and both because of this and because some people are saying, 'Second parts are never any good,' and others are saying, 'What's already been written about Don Quixote is quite enough,' there are doubts about the appearance of this second part; although other people who are jovial rather than saturnine say, 'Let's have more quixotry—let Don Quixote charge and Sancho Panza talk, and that'll keep us happy, whatever he writes.'"

"And what is the author's position?"

"He says," Sansón replied, "that as soon as he does find the history, for which he's searching with the utmost diligence, he's going to have it printed immediately, more for the profit he can make out of it than to win anybody's praise."

At which Sancho remarked:

"So the author's hoping to make some money out of it, is he? That'd be a miracle, because it'll be hurry, hurry, hurry, like a tailor on the day before a fiesta, and rushed jobs are never as well done as they ought to be. That Moorish bloke, or whatever he is,

2. In Chapter 44 of Book 1. Princess Micomicona is really the young Dorotea, an accomplice in the priest's and barber's elaborate plans to lure Don Quixote out of the Sierra Morena. She pretends to be a princess who needs her kingdom restored to her by none other than Don Quixote himself.

had better take care to be on his mettle—me and my master are going to hand him such a supply of raw materials in the shape of adventures and all kinds of other doings that he'll be able to write not just one second part but a hundred of them. I suppose that character thinks we're resting on our laurels here—well, if he holds up our feet to be shod he'll soon see if there's anything wrong with our hooves. All I can say is that if my master took my advice we'd be out in the fields by now, redressing grievances and righting wrongs as all the best knight errants do."

Sancho had hardly finished speaking when they heard Rocinante neighing, which Don Quixote took as a most happy omen, so he decided to make another sally in three or four days' time. He informed the young graduate of his decision, and asked his advice about where to start the campaign; and the reply was that they should travel to the kingdom of Aragon and the city of Saragossa, where solemn jousts were soon to be held to celebrate St George's day[3]—and these would give Don Quixote the chance to outshine all the knights in Aragon, which would be the same as outshining all the knights in the world. Sansón commended Don Quixote's decision as a most honourable and courageous one, and warned him to be more cautious when he confronted dangers, because his life was not his own: it belonged to all those who needed his aid and protection in their misfortunes. * * *

Chapter 10

Which describes Sancho's cunning enchantment of the lady Dulcinea, and other events as ridiculous as they are true

As the author of this great history reaches the events that he narrates in this chapter, he says that he'd have preferred to pass over them in silence, fearing he wouldn't be believed, because here Don Quixote's mad deeds approached the limits of the imaginable, and indeed went a couple of bowshots beyond them. But in the end, and in spite of these fears and misgivings, he described those deeds exactly as they happened, without adding or subtracting one atom of truth or concerning himself with any accusations that might be made that he was lying; and he was right to do so, because the truth might be stretched thin but it never breaks, and it always surfaces above lies, as oil floats on water.

And so, continuing his history, he says that as soon as Don Quixote had hidden in the glade, wood or oak-grove close to El Toboso, he ordered Sancho to return to the city and not to appear in his presence again without having spoken on his behalf to his lady and besought her to be so gracious as to grant her hapless knight an audience and deign to bestow her blessing on him, so that he could hope for the greatest success in all his undertakings and difficult enterprises, thanks to her. Sancho agreed to do exactly as he was told, and to bring back as good a reply as he had brought back the first time.[1]

"On your way, then, my friend," replied Don Quixote, "and do not be plunged into confusion when you find yourself in the presence of the light of the sun of beauty that you are now going to seek. Happy are you above all the squires in the world! Stay alert, and make sure that you do not fail to observe the way in which she receives you: whether her colour changes as you deliver my message; whether

3. April 23, feast day of the proverbial slayer of dragons.

1. This was in Part 1 when Don Quixote was in the Sierra Morena; Sancho returns to Don Quixote in Chapter 27 with instructions by the priest and barber to tell him that Dulcinea had replied by word of mouth, commanding Don Quixote to come and see her at once.

she seems disturbed or disquieted on hearing my name; whether her cushion seems not to be able to hold her, if perchance you find her seated upon the rich dais proper to her dignity—and if she is standing, watch her to see whether she shifts her weight from one foot to the other; whether she repeats her answer maybe two or three times; whether she changes it from a kind one to a harsh one, or from a cruel one to a loving one; whether she raises her hand to her hair to pat it into place, even though it is not untidy; and in short, my son, watch her every action, her every movement, because if you tell me about them I shall deduce how she feels in the most secret places of her heart about my love for her; for I would have you know, Sancho, if you do not know it already, that the external actions and movements made by lovers while the conversation concerns their love are messengers between them giving totally reliable accounts of what is happening in their souls. So off you go, my friend, and may better fortune than mine guide you and send you a happier outcome than that which I, here in this my bleak solitude, fear and expect."

"Yes, I'm going, and I'll soon be back," said Sancho. "And do try and stop that poor little heart of yours from shrinking so, it must be about the size of a hazel nut by now, and remember what they say, a good heart conquers ill fortune, and where there isn't any bacon there aren't any hooks to hang it from and, as they also say, the hare leaps up where you least expect it to. I'm only mentioning all this because if we didn't find my lady's palace or castle last night, now it's daytime I do intend to find it, when I'm least expecting to, and once I've found it, you just leave her to me."

"This I will say, Sancho," said Don Quixote. "I do hope that God gives me even better fortune in my aspirations than you have in choosing proverbs appropriate to our discussions."

After this, Sancho turned away and gave his dun the stick, and Don Quixote was left sitting on his nag, resting in his stirrups and leaning on his lance, overwhelmed by sorrowful and confused musings, where we shall leave him and go off with Sancho Panza, who was no less pensive and bewildered than his master; so much so, that he was hardly out of the wood when, looking back and seeing that Don Quixote was no longer in sight, he climbed off his donkey, sat down at the foot of a tree, and began to talk to himself and to say:

"Pray be so good as to tell us, brother Sancho, where it is that you're going. To look for some donkey that you've lost? No, most certainly not. So what are you looking for? Oh, I'm just going to look for some princess, that's all, the sun of beauty and the whole of heaven in one person. And where do you expect to find all that, Sancho? Where? In the great city of El Toboso. Very well, and on whose behalf are you going to look for her? On behalf of the famous knight Don Quixote de la Mancha, who rights wrongs and gives food to the thirsty and drink to the hungry. That is all most commendable. And do you know where she lives, Sancho? My master says she must live in a royal palace or a splendid castle. And have you ever seen her by any chance? Neither me nor my master have ever clapped eyes on the woman. And do you think it would be right and proper for the men of El Toboso, if they found out that you're here intending to spirit away their princesses and raise a rumpus among their ladies, to come and give you such a going-over that they didn't leave a bone unbroken in your body? Yes, they'd be in the right, unless they bore in mind that I'm just an errand-boy, and

> You're but a messenger, my friend,
> You don't deserve the blame.[2]

2. From a ballad about the hero Bernardo del Carpio, the Castilian who defeats Roland.

No, you can't rely on that, Sancho, because the people of La Mancha are as hot-tempered as they're honourable, and they won't let anyone play around with them. God Almighty, if they suspect what you're up to, I can promise you a bad time of it! No, you can get lost, Old Nick, you're not catching me in a hurry! Oh yes, I'm going to go stirring up a hornet's nest for the sake of somebody else's pleasure, I am! What's more, looking for Dulcinea in El Toboso would be like looking for a student in Salamanca or a girl called María in Madrid. Yes, yes, it was the devil, the devil and 'nobody else that got me into this mess!'"

The result of Sancho's soliloquy was that he talked to himself again, and said:

"On the other hand, there's a remedy for all things but death, under whose yoke we must all pass, like it or not, at the end of our lives. I've seen a thousand signs that this master of mine is a raving lunatic, and I'm not much better myself, because I'm even stupider than he is, following him and serving him as I do, if there's any truth in the proverb that says a man is known by the company he keeps, and that other one about birds of a feather flocking together. So him being as he is mad, and with a madness that usually makes him take one thing for another and think that white is black and black is white, as anyone could see when he said that those windmills were giants, and those friars' mules were dromedaries, and those flocks of sheep were enemy armies, and all sorts of other stuff like that, it won't be all that difficult to make him believe that some peasant girl, the very first one I come across, is lady Dulcinea—and if he doesn't believe it I'll swear she is, and if he swears she isn't I'll swear she is again, and if he insists I'll insist even more, and so I'll make sure I always have the last word, come what may. Maybe by insisting like this I'll make him stop sending me off on all these errands, seeing what a mess I make of them—or on the other hand maybe he'll think, as I expect he will, that one of those evil enchanters that he says hate him so much has changed her looks to spite him and do him harm."

These thoughts calmed Sancho's breast, and he counted the business as good as settled; and he waited where he was until the afternoon, to leave enough time for Don Quixote to believe that he'd gone to El Toboso and come back; and events fell out so well for him that when he got up to climb on his dun he saw three peasant girls coming towards him from El Toboso on three jackasses, or she-asses, because the author isn't explicit on this point, though it's more likely that they were she-asses, this being what peasant girls usually ride on; but since it doesn't matter much one way or the other, there's no need to stop to elucidate the matter. So, to cut a long story short, as soon as Sancho saw the peasant girls he rode back to his master Don Quixote as fast as he could go, and found him sighing and breathing a thousand amorous laments. When Don Quixote saw Sancho he said:

"What news, Sancho my friend? Can I mark this day with a white stone or with a black stone?"[3]

"It'll be best," Sancho replied, "for you to mark it in bright red paint, like new professors' names on college walls, so that everyone who sees it sees it clearly."

"That means," said Don Quixote, "that you bring good news."

"Such good news," Sancho replied, "that all you've got to do to find the lady Dulcinea del Toboso is to clap spurs to Rocinante and ride out of the wood—she's on her way with two of her maids to see you."

3. From the Roman practice of using white stones to mark lucky days, black stones unlucky ones.

"Good God! What are you saying, friend Sancho?" said Don Quixote. "You had better not be deceiving me, or attempting to beguile my real grief with false joy."

"What would I gain from deceiving you?" Sancho replied, "specially now I'm so close to showing you the truth of what I'm saying. Just get your spurs into action, sir, and come with me, and you'll see the princess, our mistress, on her way here, dressed and bedecked just like what she is. She and her maids are all one blaze of flaming gold, all spindlefuls of pearls, they're all diamonds, all rubies, all brocade more than ten levels deep, with their hair flowing over their shoulders like sunbeams playing with the wind, and what's more each of them's riding her piebald poultry, a sight for sore eyes."

"I think you mean *palfrey,* Sancho."

"There isn't that much of a difference," Sancho replied, "between poultry and palfrey, but whatever they're riding they're looking as spruce and ladylike as you could ever wish, specially my lady Princess Dulcinea—she fair takes your breath away, she does."

"Let us go, Sancho my son," Don Quixote said, "and as a reward for this news, as splendid as it is unexpected, I hereby promise you the best spoils I win in the first adventure that I undertake, and if this does not satisfy you I promise you all the foals born this year to my three mares: as you know, they are awaiting the happy event on the village green."

"I'll take the foals," replied Sancho, "because it isn't too clear that the spoils of the first adventure are going to be that brilliant."

As he said this, they emerged from the wood and saw the three peasant girls not far away. Don Quixote surveyed the road to El Toboso, and since all he could see was these three peasants he became alarmed and asked Sancho if the ladies had been outside the city when he'd left them.

"What do you mean, outside the city?" Sancho replied. "Do you keep your eyes in the back of your head or something, to stop you from seeing that they're these ladies here, shining like the very sun at noon?"

"All I can see, Sancho," said Don Quixote, "is three peasant girls on three donkeys."

"God save my soul from damnation!" Sancho replied. "Is it possible for three palfreys or whatever they're called, as white as the driven snow, to seem to you like donkeys? Good Lord, I'd pull out every single hair on my chin if that was true!"

"Well, I am telling you, friend Sancho," said Don Quixote, "that it is as true that they are asses, or maybe she-asses, as it is that I am Don Quixote and you are Sancho Panza; or at least this is how it seems to me."

"Hush, sir," said Sancho, "you mustn't talk like that—open those eyes of yours and come and do homage to the lady of your life, now she's so close at hand."

And as he said this he rode forward to greet the three peasant girls, and, dismounting from his dun, he seized one of their asses by the halter, fell to his knees and said: "O queen and princess and duchess of beauty, may your highness and your mightiness be pleased to receive into your grace and goodwill this your hapless knight, standing over there like a marble statue, all flustered and flummoxed at finding himself in your magnificent presence. I am his squire Sancho Panza, and he is the harassed knight Don Quixote de la Mancha, also known as the Knight of the Sorry Face."

Don Quixote had by now knelt at Sancho's side and was staring with clouded vision and bulging eyes at the woman whom Sancho called queen and lady; and since all he could see there was a peasant girl, and not a very pretty one at that, because she was moon-faced and flat-nosed, he was dumbstruck and didn't dare open his mouth. The peasant girls were equally astonished, at the sight of such an ill-assorted pair kneeling in front of one of them and impeding her progress. But she broke the silence and spoke with neither goodwill nor grace:

"Get out of the bloody way and let us through, we're in a hurry!"

To which Sancho replied:

"O princess and universal lady of El Toboso! How is it that your magnanimous heart is not melted by the sight of the column and foundation of knight-errantry kneeling here in your sublimated presence?"

When one of the other girls heard this, she said:

"Come to cast pearls before swine, have we? Look at these fine gents trying to make fun of us village girls, as if we didn't know how to take the piss as well! You two go on your way, and let us go on ours, if you want to stay in one piece."

"Arise, Sancho," Don Quixote put in. "I can see that fortune, not content with my sufferings, has blocked all the roads along which some happiness might have come to this wretched soul contained within my flesh. And you, O perfection of all the excellence that the heart can desire, acme of human courtesy, the sole remedy of this afflicted heart that adores you: even though the malicious enchanter is hounding me, and has placed clouds and cataracts over my eyes, and for them alone and not for other eyes has altered and transformed your face of peerless beauty into that of some poor peasant wench, I beg you—so long as he has not also changed my face into that of some monster, to make me abominable in your sight—not to refuse to look on me with gentleness and love, seeing in my position of submission and prostration before your disguised beauty the self-humiliation of my soul's adoration."

"Hark at old grandad!" the village girl replied. "Don't I just love oily eyewash like that! Come on, shift over and let us through, thank you very much."

Sancho shifted over and let her through, delighted to have extricated himself from that particular muddle. As soon as the peasant girl who'd played the part of Dulcinea found herself free she prodded her poultry with a nail on a stick that she was carrying and it broke into a canter across the field. And feeling the nail, which annoyed it more than usual, it started to prance and buck, and dumped Lady Dulcinea among the daisies; Don Quixote rushed to pick her up and Sancho hurried to put the pack-saddle, which had slipped round under the ass's belly, back into place. Once Sancho had done this, Don Quixote went to lift his enchanted lady in his arms and place her on the ass; but the lady saved him the trouble by jumping to her feet, taking a couple of strides backwards, bounding up to the ass, bringing both hands down on to its rump and vaulting, as swift as a falcon, on to the pack-saddle, where she sat astride as if she were a man; and then Sancho said:

"By holy St Roch,[4] our lady and mistress is nimbler than a hobby-hawk, and she could teach the best rider from Cordova or Mexico how to jump on to a horse Arab-style! Over the crupper she went in one leap, and without any spurs she's making her palfrey gallop like a zebra. And her maids aren't being outdone, they're going like the wind, too."

4. Saint Roch (or Roque), 14th-century figure from Montpellier who healed plague victims and who is invoked against disease.

And Sancho was right, because once Dulcinea was mounted the other two girls spurred after her, not turning their heads back for more than a mile. Don Quixote pursued them with his gaze, and when they were out of sight he turned to Sancho and said:

"Sancho, what is your opinion about this grudge that the enchanters bear me? You can see how far their malice and hatred extend, for they have deprived me of the joy that I could have experienced on beholding my lady in her true being. I was indeed born to be a mirror of misfortune, the eternal target for the arrows of adversity. And you should also note, Sancho, that those traitors were not content just to transform my Dulcinea, but had to transform her into a figure as wretched and ugly as that peasant wench, and at the same time they took away from her what is so characteristic of fine ladies; the sweet smell that they derive from living among ambergris and flowers. Because I would have you know, Sancho, that when I went to replace Dulcinea on her palfrey (as you call it, although I thought it was a donkey), I was half suffocated by a blast of raw garlic that poisoned my very soul."

"Oh you miserable wretches!" Sancho burst out. "Oh you fateful and spiteful enchanters, I'd like to see you all hanging by your gills like pilchards on a string! Aren't you clever, aren't you powerful and aren't you bloody well active! You ought to have been happy, you villains, with turning those eyes of pearl of my lady's into oak-apples, and her tresses of purest gold into hairs from the tail of a sorrel ox, and, all in all, every one of her features from good to bad, without messing about with her smell, too—from her smell we'd at least have been able to work out what was hidden under that ugly outside although, to tell you the truth, I never did see her ugliness but only her beauty, which was boosted no end by a mole she had on the right side of her lip, a bit like a moustache, with seven or eight blond hairs like threads of gold growing out of it, more than a handsbreadth long."

"According to the rules of correspondence between facial moles and bodily moles," said Don Quixote, "Dulcinea must have another mole on the thick of the thigh on the same side as the one on her face; but hairs of the length that you have indicated are very long indeed for moles."

"Well, I can tell you," Sancho replied, "they were there all right, just as if she'd been born with them."

"I believe you, my friend," replied Don Quixote, "because nature has given Dulcinea nothing that is not complete and perfect; and so, if she had a hundred moles like the one you have described, on her they would not be moles but moons—resplendent moons and shining stars. But tell me, Sancho, the object that seemed to me like a pack-saddle, which you straightened for her—was it an ordinary saddle or a lady's saddle with arms?"

"It was nothing less than a great tall Arab-style saddle," Sancho replied, "with a saddle-cloth so precious it's worth half a kingdom."

"And to think that I could not see any of that, Sancho!" said Don Quixote. "I say it again, and I shall say it a thousand times: I am the most unfortunate of men."

The sly rogue Sancho had his work cut out to hide his laughter as he listened to the nonsense being blurted by his master, whom he had deceived with such finesse. In the end, after the two had talked for a good while longer, they remounted and followed the road that led towards Saragossa, where they planned to arrive in time for the solemn festivities held each year in that famous city. But before they arrived certain things happened to them, so many, so important and so strange, that they deserve to be written and read about, as will be seen in what follows.

* * *

from *Chapter 25*

WHICH BEGINS THE AMUSING ADVENTURE OF THE PUPPETEER, TOGETHER WITH THE MEMORABLE DIVINATIONS OF THE FORTUNE-TELLING APE

* * * "And that's quite enough of this matter for now; so let us go and see Master Pedro's puppet show, for I imagine that it might offer a certain novelty," said Don Quixote.[1]

"What do you mean, a certain novelty?" Master Pedro replied. "This puppet show of mine offers sixty thousand novelties—I'm telling you, Don Quixote sir, it's one of the sights most worth seeing in the whole wide world, but *operibus credite, et non verbis,*[2] so let's set to work, because it's getting late and we have a lot to do, and say, and show."

Don Quixote and Sancho did as they were told, and walked over to where the puppet theatre had been erected and uncovered, glowing all over with wax tapers that made it a glittering, resplendent sight. Master Pedro disappeared inside it, because he was the one who worked the puppets, and in front of it stood a boy, Master Pedro's servant, to act as announcer and interpreter of the mysteries of the show: he held a pointer to indicate the puppets as they emerged. With everyone at the inn in front of the puppet theatre, some of them standing, and with Don Quixote, Sancho, the page and the cousin in the best seats, the announcer began to say what anyone who reads the next chapter or has it read to him will see or hear.

Chapter 26

WHICH CONTINUES THE AMUSING ADVENTURE OF THE PUPPETEER, TOGETHER WITH OTHER REALLY VERY GOOD THINGS

The Tyrians and the Trojans all were silent,[1]

what I mean to say is that everyone in the audience was hanging, as it were, on the lips of the announcer of the marvels of the puppet show, when the sounds of war-drums and trumpets and artillery fire rang out from inside the theatre and suddenly died down again, and the boy proclaimed:

"This true history that is about to be performed before your very eyes has been taken word for word from the French chronicles and from the Spanish ballads that people sing, and boys too, in the street. It's about how Don Gaiferos freed his wife Melisendra, who was a prisoner of the Moors in Spain, in the city of Sansueña, which is what Saragossa was called then; and here you can see Don Gaiferos playing backgammon, as that song goes:

And Don Gaiferos, playing at the tables,
Has not a thought for Melisendra now.[2]

1. Earlier in this chapter, Don Quixote and Sancho encounter in an inn a famous puppeteer named Master Pedro, accompanied by an ape who can predict the future. Remarkably, he instantly recognizes Don Quixote as the "illustrious reviver of the forgotten order of knight-errantry."
2. "Believe works, not words"; an echo from John 10:38 in which Jesus says that actions are heeded more than words.
1. From the beginning of *Aeneid* 2, as the Trojans and Tyrians (Dido's people) fall silent to hear Aeneas's tale of the fall of Troy and his subsequent travels.
2. Melisendra, daughter of Charlemagne, was captured by the Moors because of the negligence of her husband, Don Gaiferos, who then rescued her in a daring mission and took her to France. Subject of a popular ballad in Spain, the story had originally derived from the medieval stories around Charlemagne's court.

And that character coming into view over there with a crown on his head and a sceptre in his hands—he's the Emperor Charlemagne, Melisendra's foster father, who's angry at his son-in-law's laziness and negligence and is coming to scold him; and see with what warmth and feeling he does it, it looks as if he's going to bang him on the head half a dozen times with his sceptre, and some authorities reckon that's exactly what he did, good and hard; and after telling him all sorts of things about the danger his honour is in from not trying to free his wife, it's said that he said:

> I've said enough; see to it now.

You can also see how the Emperor turns away and leaves Don Gaiferos fuming, and now you see him in his rage hurling the backgammon board far from him and calling for his arms and armour, and he asks his cousin Roland to lend him his sword Durandal, and Roland refuses, offering him instead his company in the difficult task ahead; but our angry hero will not accept this, and says he's quite capable of rescuing his wife alone even if she's imprisoned deep in the centre of the earth; and then he goes away to don his armour and set off. Now look at that tower you can see over there, which we must imagine is one of the towers of Saragossa Castle, today called the Aljafería; and that lady in Moorish clothes on that balcony is the matchless Melisendra, who often used to come out on to it to gaze at the road to France, and to console herself in her imprisonment by daydreaming about Paris and her husband. And now watch out for a new incident that's about to happen, maybe never seen before. Can't you see that Moor sneaking up behind Melisendra with his forefinger over his lips? Well, now look how he gives her a kiss slap on the mouth, and how soon she spits and wipes her lips with the white sleeve of her blouse, and how she wails and tears her lovely hair in grief, as if her hair were to blame for that evil deed. And see that grave Moor on that balcony, King Marsilio of Sansueña: he spotted the Moor's insolent action and, even though the fellow was a relative and a great favourite of his, ordered him to be arrested and given two hundred lashes, after being paraded through the city along the customary streets,

> With squawkers before him
> And truncheons behind,

and now you can see they're coming to carry out the sentence, and the crime's hardly even been committed yet, because the Moors don't go in for notification of the charge or detention on remand, as we do."

"Come, boy," exclaimed Don Quixote, "proceed with your story in a straight line, and don't go wandering round bends or up side-roads; for to reach the truth about something like that, proof upon proof is needed."

And Master Pedro said from inside the theatre:

"Look here, my lad, I don't want any flourishes, just do as the gentleman says, that'll be the wisest course—stick to plain chant without any counterpoint,[3] and don't you go and spin the thread so fine you break it."

"All right," the lad replied, and he continued: "this figure appearing here on horseback, muffled in a Gascon cape, is Don Gaiferos himself; and here his wife, avenged for the amorous Moor's effrontery, with a happier and calmer look on her

3. Plain chant was sung in unison by monks; counterpoint was the practice of adding one or more melodies to a plainsong. The accompanying notes (or "points") were set "against" those of the original song.

face, has come out on to the tower balcony and is talking to her husband in the belief that he's some passer-by, and they had that conversation in that ballad that goes:

Sir knight, if it's to France you go,
Pray ask for Don Gaiferos.

"But I shan't repeat the conversation now, because long-windedness breeds boredom; it's enough to see how Don Gaiferos reveals who he is, and from Melisendra's gestures of joy we're given to understand that she's recognized him, and even more so now that we see her letting herself down from the balcony to sit on the crupper of her good husband's horse. But oh how unlucky, look, the hem of her skirt's got caught on one of the balcony railings, and she's been left hanging in the air and can't reach the ground. But now you can see that merciful heaven sends aid at times of greatest need, because up comes Don Gaiferos and without worrying about tearing her fine skirt he seizes her and tugs her down whether she likes it or not, and with a leap he puts her on to the crupper of his horse, astride, just like a man, and tells her to hold on tight and put her arms over his shoulders and across his chest so as not to fall off, because madam Melisendra wasn't used to galloping around like that. Observe, too, how the neighing of the horse shows how happy it is with the burden of bravery and beauty it bears in the shape of its master and mistress. Observe how they turn and leave the city, and full of joy and happiness they take the road to Paris. Go in peace, O peerless pair of true lovers! May you arrive safely in your longed-for homeland, and may fortune raise no barrier to hinder your happy journey! May your friends and relations see you enjoying the remainder of your life in peace and tranquillity, and may your days be as many as Nestor's!"[4]

Here Master Pedro shouted out again:

"Keep it simple, boy, none of those flights of yours! Affectation's always bad!"

The announcer didn't reply, but continued:

"Idle eyes see everything, and there they were to see Melisendra getting down and then getting up, and off they went to tell King Marsilio, who ordered the alarm to be sounded, and look how fast—the whole city's shaking with the bells being rung from all the mosque towers!"

"No, no," Don Quixote intervened. "Those bells are a grave blunder by Master Pedro, because Moors do not use bells but kettle drums, and a kind of pipe rather like our shawm;[5] and to have bells ringing in Sansueña is most definitely a gross absurdity."

When Master Pedro heard this he stopped ringing his bells and said:

"Don't worry about trivialities, Don Quixote sir—you can't make anything without making mistakes. Aren't thousands of plays performed all the time full of thousands of blunders and absurdities, and despite that they have a good run and are greeted not only with applause but with admiration too? You carry on, my lad, and let them say what they like—so long as I fill my money bags it doesn't matter if I make more blunders than there are atoms in the sun."

"That is true enough," Don Quixote replied.

And the boy said:

4. Elderly Greek statesman and counselor in Homer.

5. Medieval musical instrument with a double reed, like an oboe.

"See all the resplendent cavalry riding out of the city in pursuit of the two Christian lovers; how many trumpets blaring, how many pipes rather like shawms playing, how many kettle drums and other sorts of drums beating. I'm afraid they're going to catch up with them and return with them tied to the tail of their own horse, which would be a horrendous sight."

Seeing such hordes of Moors and hearing such a racket, Don Quixote thought it would be a good idea to help the fugitives, and he sprang to his feet and cried:

"Never while there is still breath in my body will I consent to such an insult being offered in my presence to such a famous knight and bold innamorato[6] as Don Gaiferos. Desist, you low-born rabble; do not follow him, do not pursue him, or you shall do battle with me!"

And acting even as he spoke he drew his sword and with one leap positioned himself in front of the stage, and with speedy and unprecedented fury began to hack at the hordes of puppet Moors, knocking some over, beheading others, wrecking this one, destroying that; and one down-stroke among many others would have lopped Master Pedro's head off as easily as if it had been made of marzipan, if he hadn't ducked and crouched and made himself into a ball. Master Pedro was crying:

"Stop, stop, Don Quixote sir, look, these you're knocking down and smashing and killing aren't real Moors but papier mâché figures. I'll be damned, you're destroying everything I own in the world!"

But this didn't stop Don Quixote from raining down his cuts and thrusts and two-handers and fore-strokes and back-strokes. And in the time it takes to say a couple of creeds he left the whole show in a heap on the floor, with the puppets and the fittings cut into little pieces, King Marsilio critically injured, and the Emperor Charlemagne with his head and his crown split in two. The senate of spectators was in an uproar, the monkey escaped through the window on to the roof, the cousin was frightened, the page was panic-stricken and even Sancho Panza was petrified because, as he swore once the storm was over, he'd never seen his master in such a temper. Once the demolition of the puppet show was complete, Don Quixote grew somewhat calmer and said:

"I should like to have here before me all those who do not and will not believe how beneficial knights errant are to society: for look—if I had not been present, what would have become of the worthy Don Gaiferos and the lovely Melisendra? By now those dogs would most certainly have caught up with them and done them some mischief. Long live knight-errantry, then, above all else on earth!"

"Yes, long live knight-errantry," Master Pedro commented, in feeble tones, "and quick death to me, so wretched that I can well say with King Rodrigo:

> But yesterday the lord of Spain . . .
> Today not one embattlement
> That I can call my own![7]

Not half an hour ago, indeed not half a minute ago, I was the master of kings and emperors, and my stables, my coffers and my bags were full of countless horses and innumerable pieces of finery; and now I'm abject and desolate, poverty-stricken and a beggar and, what's worst of all, monkeyless, for I'll have to sweat blood to get that animal back,

6. Lover (Italian).
7. From a famous ballad about King Rodrigo, the last Visigoth king of Spain; in 713, thanks to his losses in battle, Spain was completely absorbed within the dominion of the Muslims.

all because of the wrongheaded fury of this knight here, who's said to succour orphans, and right wrongs, and do other charitable works, yet only with me have his good intentions misfired—blessed and praised be heaven above in the highest of the high. I suppose it had to be the Knight of the Sorry Face who came to deface the faces of my puppets."

Sancho was moved by Master Pedro's words, and said:

"Don't cry like that, Master Pedro, don't wail so, you're breaking my heart—and I can tell you my master Don Quixote's such a scrupulous and Catholic Christian that if he realizes he's done you any harm he'll say so and pay you double."

"If Don Quixote paid me for just half the figures of mine he's disfigured I'd be happy enough, and that would clear his conscience—because there's no salvation for the man who's holding on to something against its owner's will and doesn't give it back to him."

"That is true enough," said Don Quixote, "but I am not aware that I am retaining anything of yours, Master Pedro."

"What do you mean?" replied Master Pedro. "And all these relics scattered about this hard and sterile soil—what was it that smashed and scattered them if not the invincible power of that mighty arm of yours? And who did they belong to if not to me? And how did I support myself except with them?"

"Now I am utterly convinced," Don Quixote inserted, "of what I have many times thought might be true: the ploy of these enchanters who pursue me is to place before my eyes things as they are, and then change them into what they want them to be. I can assure you really and truly, all you who hear me, that I did believe that everything happening here happened exactly as it seemed to happen: that Melisendra was Melisendra, Don Gaiferos was Don Gaiferos, Marsilio was Marsilio and Charlemagne was Charlemagne. That is why I lost my temper and, to do what I had to do as a knight errant, I decided to aid and assist the people who were fleeing, and with that worthy aim in mind I did what you have seen me do; if it has all turned out the opposite of how I intended, that is not my fault, but the fault of the wicked ones who pursue me; and despite all this, although my mistake did not proceed from malice aforethought, I hereby award costs against myself: so Master Pedro must assess what he wants for his broken puppets, and I will pay for them in good current Castilian coin."[8]

Master Pedro bowed and said:

"I expected no less from the unprecedented Christian virtue of the brave Don Quixote de la Mancha, true help and support of all needy and distressed vagrants; and the good innkeeper and the worthy Sancho will be assessors and arbiters between you and me of what the broken puppets are worth, or rather were worth."

The innkeeper and Sancho agreed to this, and Master Pedro picked up King Marsilio of Saragossa, minus his head, and said:

"You can see how impossible it is to restore this king to his original state; and so it seems to me, and subject to your better judgement, that for his sad demise and sorry end I should be given four and a half reals."

"Continue!" said Don Quixote.

"And for this crack from top to bottom," Master Pedro continued, picking up the broken Emperor Charlemagne, "I wouldn't be asking very much if I asked for five and a quarter reals."

"That's no small sum," said Sancho.

8. When he leaves La Mancha again in Part 2, Don Quixote furnishes himself with money, and his dealings with others are thus different than when he was the penurious knight of Part 1.

"Not a large one either," replied the innkeeper. "Split the difference and give him five reals."

"Give him the full five and a quarter," said Don Quixote, "because this notable misfortune is not to be measured in quarters of a real; and I wish Master Pedro would hurry up, it is time for supper and I am beginning to feel the pangs of hunger."

"For this figure," said Master Pedro, "minus its nose and an eye, the figure of the lovely Melisendra, I want two reals and twelve maravedís, and that's only fair."

"There will be the devil and all to do," said Don Quixote, "if Melisendra and her husband are not on the French border by now, at least, because I thought the horse they were riding was flying rather than galloping; so don't you come trying to sell me a pig in a poke, and presenting me with a noseless Melisendra when she must, if given half a chance, be frolicking in France with her husband to her heart's content. God help each of us to what is rightly his, Master Pedro, and let us all march on with a firm foot and honest intentions. Pray continue."

Master Pedro could see that Don Quixote was beginning to rave again and to return to his earlier fixation, and didn't want to let him off the hook, and so he said:

"This one can't be Melisendra, then, but one of her maidservants, so if I'm given sixty maravedís for her I'll be happy enough."

And in this way he put prices to many other wrecked puppets, which the arbitrators moderated to the satisfaction of the two parties, and it came to a total of forty and three-quarter reals; and on top of this sum, which Sancho paid out immediately, Master Pedro asked for two reals for the trouble of going for his ape.

"Give them to him, Sancho," said Don Quixote, "although what he'll go for with them has more to do with grapes than with apes; and I would give two hundred reals this very moment as a reward to anyone who could tell me for certain that Doña Melisendra and Don Gaiferos are in France among their own people."

"Nobody will be able to tell us that better than my monkey," said Master Pedro, "but the devil himself wouldn't be able to catch him now; though I imagine that his affection for me, and his hunger, will force him to come back to look for me tonight—and God will send us his light, and then we'll see."

So the storm over the puppet show died down and all had supper together in peace and good fellowship, at the expense of Don Quixote, who was an extremely generous man.

The man transporting the lances and halberds left before dawn, and once it was light the cousin and the page came to take their leave of Don Quixote, one to go back home and the other to continue on his way, as a help with which Don Quixote gave him a dozen reals. Master Pedro didn't want any more argy-bargy with Don Quixote, whom he knew all too well,[9] and so he rose before the sun, took his monkey and the remains of his puppet theatre, and went off in search of his own adventures. The innkeeper, who didn't know Don Quixote, was as amazed at his capers as at his generosity. And Sancho paid him well, on his master's orders, and at a little before eight o'clock in the morning they left the inn and took to the road, where we shall leave them to go on their way, as we must in order to provide an opportunity to record other matters that are relevant to the narration of this famous history.

* * *

9. As Cervantes reveals in Chapter 27, Master Pedro is Ginés de Pasamonte, the notorious criminal and writer of autobiography with whom Quixote has had earlier dealings.

Chapter 59

About the strangest and most singular experience undergone by Don Quixote in the whole course of this great history

* * * So suppertime came round, Don Quixote retired to his room and the landlord brought the stew, just as it was, and Don Quixote sat down to eat it with a will.[1] It seems that in a room next to Don Quixote's, divided from it only by a flimsy partition, he heard someone saying:

"I beg you, Don Jerónimo—while dinner's being fetched do let's read another chapter of the second part of *Don Quixote de la Mancha.*"[2]

The instant Don Quixote heard his name he started to his feet and pricked up his ears to listen to what these people were saying, and he heard Don Jerónimo's reply:

"Why do you want to us read all that nonsense, Don Juan? Nobody who has read the first part of the history of Don Quixote de la Mancha can possibly derive any pleasure from reading this second part."

"All the same," said Don Juan, "it'll be as well to read it, because there's no book so bad that there isn't something good in it. What I most dislike about this one is that it describes Don Quixote as no longer in love with Dulcinea del Toboso."

When Don Quixote heard this he flared up and cried:

"If anyone claims that Don Quixote de la Mancha has forgotten or can forget Dulcinea del Toboso, I shall, with equal arms, force him to acknowledge that he is very far from the truth, because neither can the peerless Dulcinea del Toboso be forgotten, nor is Don Quixote capable of forgetting. His motto is constancy, and his profession is to observe this principle with ease and without constraint."

"Who is that answering us?" came the reply from the other room.

"Who do you think it is," Sancho replied, "if not the very same Don Quixote de la Mancha? And he'll make good everything he's just said and everything he hasn't said yet, too, because a good payer's a good pledger."

Hardly had Sancho finished speaking when two gentlemen, as they gave every sign of being, walked in through the door, and one of them put his arms round Don Quixote's neck and said:

"Neither can your presence belie your name, nor can your name fail to accredit your presence: there can be no doubt that you, sir, are the real Don Quixote de la Mancha, guide and lodestar of knight-errantry, in spite and in defiance of the one who has attempted to usurp your name and obliterate your deeds, as has the author of this book I have here."

And taking a book from his companion he handed it to Don Quixote, who began to thumb through it in silence, and after a short while he returned it with the words:

"In the little I have seen I have found three aspects of this author's work that are worthy of rebuke. First, certain statements in the prologue;[3] secondly, the fact that the

1. Following numerous adventures—such as Sancho's being rewarded with governorship of a (fake) island by a Duke and Duchess who have enjoyed teasing Don Quixote and his squire—the pair find themselves, finally alone, at an inn en route to Saragossa, where Don Quixote plans to participate in the jousts for St. George's Day.

2. A spurious Book 2 of Don Quixote's story (*Segundo tomo del ingenioso hidalgo don Quixote de la Mancha*) was published in 1614, by one Alonso Fernández de Avellaneda, a pseudonym for an unidentified author. Beginning with this episode, Cervantes has a great deal of fun with the book that spurred him into publishing his own sequel a year later.

3. Most likely attacks made on Cervantes, which Cervantes himself mentions in the prologue to Part 2. Thus he writes, "Avellaneda attacks me for being old and one-handed, as if it had been in my power to halt time and prevent it from ravaging me, or as if I had been maimed in some tavern brawl rather than at the greatest battle that past or present ages have ever seen or that future ages can ever hope to see" (the battle at Lepanto, against the Moors).

language is Aragonese, because he often omits the article;[4] and thirdly, and this is what most confirms his ignorance, he blunders and strays from the truth in the most central feature of the whole history, because he says here that my squire Sancho Panza's wife is called Mari Gutiérrez, when she is called nothing of the sort, but Teresa Panza; and if someone can make a mistake about such an important matter we can well fear that he is mistaken in everything else that he says in his history."[5]

To which Sancho added:

"That's a fine thing in a historian! He must be really clued up on our doings if he calls my wife Teresa Panza Mari Gutiérrez! Take another look at the book, sir, and see if I'm in it, and if he's changed my name too."

"From what I have heard, my friend," said Don Jerónimo, "you must be Sancho Panza, Don Quixote's squire."

"That's me," Sancho replied, "and proud of it."

"Well the fact is," the gentleman said, "that this novice author doesn't treat you with the scrupulosity that you display in your person: he represents you as a glutton, and simple-minded, and not at all funny, very different from the Sancho described in the first part of the history of your master."

"God forgive him," said Sancho. "He should have left me in my corner and forgotten all about me, because you've got to know your strings before you pluck them, and St Peter's all right in Rome."

The two gentlemen asked Don Quixote into their room to share their dinner, as they were well aware that there was no food to be had at that inn fit for him to consume. Don Quixote, courteous as always, acceded to their request and dined with them; Sancho was left with the stew, absolute lord and master of it all, and sat himself at the head of the table, and by his side sat the innkeeper, no less fond than Sancho of his heels and of his feet.

During dinner Don Juan asked Don Quixote what news he had of his lady Dulcinea del Toboso: whether she had married, whether she had given birth or was pregnant, or whether on the contrary she was still intact and still remembered (always preserving her decorum and propriety) Don Quixote's amorous intentions. To which he replied:

"Dulcinea is indeed intact, and my intentions are firmer than ever; our communications are as unsatisfactory as they ever were; her beauty has been transformed into that of a coarse peasant girl."

And he went on to give a detailed account of Dulcinea's enchantment, and what had happened in the Cave of Montesinos, together with the arrangements made by the sage Merlin for her to be disenchanted, in other words Sancho's self-flagellation.[6] It gave the two gentlemen great pleasure to hear Don Quixote narrating the strange events of his own history, and they were as astonished by his mad antics as by the elegant manner in which he described them. One minute they thought him an intelligent

4. The Aragonese dialect is used in the region (at one time the kingdom) of Aragon, in northeast Spain.

5. Cervantes himself had made this "mistake" in Part 1.

6. Shortly before meeting up with Master Pedro, Don Quixote descends into the great cave of Montesinos (Chapters 22 and 23), where he has a vision of the great warrior Montesinos himself, who confirms for him the fact of Dulcinea's enchantment. Upon telling this to Sancho Panza, Sancho breaks out in laughter, "he himself having been the enchanter and the concocter of evidence." In Chapter 35 of Part 2, the sage Merlin, riding in a triumphal cart designed by the Duke and Duchess who have continued to orchestrate the majority of events in the second half of Part 2, appears before Sancho Panza and Don Quixote. Merlin instructs Sancho that in order for Dulcinea to be transformed from the coarse peasant girl encountered in Chapter 10 to the beautiful lady of El Toboso, he must flog himself "on both his buttocks, big and bold and bare," 3,300 times. Naturally, Sancho wants nothing to do with this act of penitence, but he finally agrees, assuming some conditions are met such as "I'm not to have to make myself bleed, and if some of the lashes turn out to be more like swatting flies they're still valid."

man, the next minute he skidded off into absurdity, and they couldn't decide where to place him between sound sense and madness.

Sancho finished his supper and, leaving the innkeeper pie-eyed and tangle-footed, he went through to the room where his master was, and as he walked in he said:

"I'll be blowed, gents, if the author of that book you've got there doesn't want to get on bad terms with me—and if he calls me a greedy-guts, as you say he does, I only hope he doesn't call me a boozer into the bargain."

"Oh yes he does," said Don Jerónimo, "but I don't remember his exact words, although I do know that they're offensive ones and, what's more, quite untrue, as I can plainly see from the physiognomy of the worthy Sancho who stands before me."

"You mark my words," said Sancho, "the Sancho and the Don Quixote in that there history can't be the same as the ones in the history by Cide Hamete Benengeli, which is us—my master, brave and wise and in love, and me, a down-to-earth funny man, and not a greedy-guts or a boozer either."

"That's what I think, too," said Don Juan, "and if it were possible a law ought to be passed that nobody should presume to write about the doings of the great Don Quixote, except the first author Cide Hamete, just as Alexander ordered that nobody should presume to represent him on canvas except Apelles."[7]

"Anyone who so wishes can represent me," said Don Quixote, "but not misrepresent me; for patience often fails when it is overloaded with insults."

"No insult can be offered to Don Quixote," said Don Juan, "that he cannot avenge, unless he wards it off with the shield of his patience, which, in my belief, is large and strong."

They spent a great part of that night in conversation of this sort, and, although Don Juan would have liked Don Quixote to read some more of the book, to see what other comments he made, they couldn't persuade him to, and he said that he took it as read and assumed that it was absurd through and through; for if by any chance the author discovered that he had held it in his hands, he was unwilling to give that man the pleasure of knowing that he had read it; because our thoughts, and still more our eyes, must be kept aloof from everything lewd and obscene.

They asked Don Quixote where he was intending to go next. He replied that he was on his way to Saragossa, to take part in the jousts for the suit of armour that is held in that city each year. Don Juan told him that the new history related how Don Quixote, or whoever it was, had participated there in the riding at the ring, an episode depicted without imagination, with poor mottoes, even poorer costumes, and rich only in absurdities.

"Well, for that very reason," Don Quixote replied, "I shall not set foot in Saragossa, and thus I shall announce that novice historian's lie to the whole world, and people will be made aware that I am not the Don Quixote about whom he writes."

"That will be an excellent move," said Don Jerónimo, "and they hold other jousts in Barcelona, where Don Quixote will be able to display his prowess."

"And that is what I intend to do," said Don Quixote, "and now, with your permission, it is time for me to retire to bed, and please count me in the number of your firmest friends and most devoted servants."

"Me too," said Sancho, "who knows, I might come in handy sometime."

7. Alexander the Great's favorite painter.

And so they said goodnight, and Don Quixote and Sancho returned to their room, leaving Don Juan and Don Jerónimo lost in amazement at the mixture that the knight had contrived of sound sense and sheer madness; and they felt quite certain that these, and not the pair described by the Aragonese author, were the real Don Quixote and Sancho.

Don Quixote rose early next morning and, knocking on the partition, said goodbye to the men in the other room. Sancho showered wealth upon the innkeeper and advised him that in future he should either be less boastful about the provision at his inn, or keep it better provided.

* * *

Chapter 72

Concerning the arrival of Don Quixote and Sancho at their village[1]

Don Quixote and Sancho spent all that day at the village inn, waiting for nightfall: one of them to bring his exercise in flagellation to a conclusion in the open air, and the other to witness its completion and with it the accomplishment of his desires. Meanwhile a traveller arrived on horseback with three or four servants, one of whom said to the man who seemed to be their master:

"You can rest here, Don Álvaro Tarfe sir, while the sun is high—the inn seems clean and cool."

When Don Quixote heard this he said to Sancho:

"Look, Sancho, when I thumbed through that book containing the second part of my history, I think I came across the name Don Álvaro Tarfe."

"You could be right," Sancho replied. "Let's wait for him to dismount and then we'll ask him."

The gentleman dismounted, and the innkeeper's wife gave him a ground-floor room opposite Don Quixote's, decorated with painted cloths of the same sort. The recent arrival went to change into more comfortable clothes and, strolling out into the cool, spacious porch, where Don Quixote was pacing up and down, he asked:

"And where might you be bound for, my dear sir?"

And Don Quixote replied:

"To a village near here, where I live. And where are you going?"

"I am on my way to Granada, sir," the gentleman replied, "my home town."

"And a very fine town it is, too!" Don Quixote replied. "But please be so kind as to tell me your name; because I think it is going to be of more interest to me to know it than I can well explain."

"My name is Don Álvaro Tarfe," the guest said.

To which Don Quixote replied:

"I do believe you must be the very same Don Álvaro Tarfe who appears in the second part of the *History of Don Quixote de la Mancha,* recently printed and published by a novice author."

"Indeed I am," the gentleman replied, "and that man Don Quixote, the protagonist of the history, was a very close friend of mine, and I was the one who took him

1. In Barcelona, Don Quixote experiences humiliating defeat at the hands of the Knight of the White Moon, who is really the graduate Sansón Carrasco in disguise. Carrasco exacts from him the promise that for one year hence, he will remain in his village. The dejected Quixote starts toward La Mancha, and in Chapter 71 Sancho approaches the end of his "penance," adminstering in the dark such a severe flogging to a nearby tree that Don Quixote, unaware of the trick, fears for his squire's life.

away from home, or at least I persuaded him to travel to Saragossa to take part in jousts held there, where I was going; and the truth of the matter is that I did him many favours and prevented the executioner from tickling his ribs for his recklessness."

"And please tell me, Señor Don Álvaro, am I at all like that Don Quixote to whom you refer?"

"No, certainly not," the guest replied, "not in the slightest."

"And did that Don Quixote," said our one, "have with him a squire called Sancho Panza?"

"Yes, he did," Don Álvaro replied, "and although he had the reputation of being a comical fellow, not one of his attempts to be funny that I heard ever succeeded."

"I can believe that all right," Sancho butted in, "because not everybody's good at being funny, and that Sancho you're talking about, my good sir, must be some great scoundrel, as much a crook as he's unfunny; I'm the real Sancho Panza, and I'm so funny it's as if fun had rained down on me from heaven, and if you don't believe me just give me a try, and follow me around for a year or so, and you'll see how the fun gushes out of me at every turn, so much of it and such high quality that even though most of the time I don't know what I'm saying I make everyone listening to me laugh. And the real Don Quixote de la Mancha, the famous one, the brave and wise one, the lover, the righter of wrongs, the guardian of minors and orphans, the protector of widows and the slaughterer of maidens, the one whose only lady is the peerless Dulcinea del Toboso, is this gentleman here present, who's my master. All other Don Quixotes and all other Sancho Panzas besides us two are so much jiggery-pokery, figures from dreamland."

"And I believe you too, by God!" Don Álvaro Tarfe replied. "Because you've said more funny things, my friend, in the half-a-dozen words you've just spoken than the other Sancho Panza managed in all the words I heard from him. He was better at gorging himself than at talking, and was more foolish than funny, and I consider it a certain fact that the enchanters who pursue Don Quixote the Good have been chasing after me with Don Quixote the Bad. But I don't know what to say—I'd go as far as to swear that I left him in the Toledo madhouse awaiting treatment, and now another Don Quixote pops up here, quite different from mine."

"I do not know," said Don Quixote, "whether I am good, but I do know that I am not the bad Quixote, as proof of which I should like you to know, Don Álvaro Tarfe sir, that I have never in my life set foot in Saragossa; on the contrary, having been told that the fantasy Don Quixote had taken part in the jousts in that city, I refused to go there, to prove to all the world that he is a fraud; and so I went straight on to Barcelona, the storehouse of courtesy, the refuge of strangers, the hospital of the poor, the homeland of the brave, the avenger of the affronted and the appreciative returner of firm friendship, unique in its setting and its beauty. And although what happened to me there was not very pleasant, indeed was most disagreeable, I can bear it all without heaviness of heart, just for the sake of having seen Barcelona. In short, Don Álvaro Tarfe sir, I am the Don Quixote de la Mancha of whom fame speaks—not that wretch who sought to usurp my name and exalt himself with my thoughts. I entreat you, sir, as you are a gentleman, to be so kind as to make a formal declaration before the mayor of this village to the effect that you have never in all the days of your life seen me until now, and that I am not the Don Quixote who appears in the second part, nor is this squire of mine Sancho Panza the man whom you knew."

"I shall be delighted to do so," Don Álvaro replied, "even though it amazes me to see two Don Quixotes and two Sancho Panzas at the same time, as identical in name as they are antithetical in action; and I repeat and confirm that I have not seen what I have seen and that what has happened to me has not happened."

"I'm sure," said Sancho, "that you must be under a spell too, like my lady Dulcinea, and would to God I could get rid of it for you by giving myself another three thousand odd lashes like the ones I'm giving myself for her—and I'd do it without expecting anything for it, either."

"I don't understand this talk of lashes," said Don Álvaro.

And Sancho replied that it was a long story, but he'd tell it if they happened to be going the same way. By now it was time for lunch; Don Quixote and Don Álvaro ate together. The village mayor happened to walk into the inn with a notary, and to the said mayor Don Quixote presented a petition to the effect that it was his wish and right that Don Álvaro Tarfe, the gentleman who was there present, should depose before His Worship that the said deponent did not know Don Quixote de la Mancha, who was also there present, and that the said Don Quixote was not the man who appeared in print in a history entitled *The Second Part of Don Quixote de la Mancha* written by one Avellaneda, from Tordesillas. And the mayor took all the appropriate steps: the deposition was drawn up with all the legal requisites, as is proper in such cases, which delighted Don Quixote and Sancho, as if such a deposition were vital to their welfare, and as if their deeds and their words didn't clearly show the difference between the two Don Quixotes and between the two Sanchos. Many courtesies and offers were exchanged between Don Álvaro and Don Quixote, in the course of which the great man of La Mancha displayed such good sense that he disabused Don Álvaro of his error; and Don Álvaro reached the conclusion that he must indeed have been enchanted, since he'd seen with his own eyes two such contrasting Don Quixotes.

Evening came, they left the village and after a couple of miles the road forked, one way leading to Don Quixote's village and the other to where Don Álvaro was going. In this short interval Don Quixote told him about his calamitous defeat, and about Dulcinea's enchantment and disenchantment, all of which filled Don Álvaro with fresh amazement; and then he embraced Don Quixote and Sancho and went on his way, as did Don Quixote, who spent that night among some more trees, to give Sancho the opportunity to complete his penance, which he did as he had on the previous night, at the expense of the bark of the beeches rather than the skin of his back, of which he took such good care that the lashes wouldn't have brushed a fly off it if there had been one there. The deluded Don Quixote didn't fail to count a single stroke, and found that together with the previous night's score the total was three thousand and twenty-nine. It seems that the sun rose early to witness the sacrifice, and by its light the pair continued on their way, discussing Don Álvaro's delusion and what a good idea it had been to have him make his deposition before the proper authorities in such a correct and formal manner. That day and that night they pressed on, and nothing worth mentioning happened to them, except that during the night Sancho completed his task, to Don Quixote's unutterable joy, and he waited eagerly for daylight, to see if he could find his lady Dulcinea along the way, disenchanted; and as he rode there was not a woman whom he did not approach to examine her and discover whether she was Dulcinea del Toboso, because he was absolutely certain that Merlin's promises could not be false. Full of these thoughts and expectations they climbed a hill, from the top of which they could see their village, and Sancho fell to his knees, exclaiming:

"Open your eyes, my longed-for village, and see your son Sancho Panza returning, not very rich but very well lashed. Open your arms, too, to welcome your son Don Quixote, who has been conquered by another's arm but comes here as the conqueror of himself; and that, he's told me, is the best conquering you can wish for. I've got some money with me, because if I've been given a good lashing I've had a ride on a good horse, as the thief said to the executioner."

"Stop all that nonsense," said Don Quixote, "and let's put our best feet forward as we make our entry into the village, where we'll give free play to our imaginations and settle our plans for the pastoral life that we're going to lead."

And with this they went down the hill towards their village.

Chapter 73

About the omens that Don Quixote encountered as he entered his village, together with other events that adorn and authenticate this great history

As they approached it, according to Cide Hamete Benengeli, Don Quixote saw two boys squabbling on the threshing floor, and one said to the other:

"Don't keep on, Periquillo—that's something that's never ever going to happen."

Don Quixote overheard him, and said to Sancho:

"Didn't you hear, friend Sancho, what that boy said—'that's something that's never ever going to happen'?"

"And who cares," said Sancho, "what the boy said?"

"Who cares?" replied Don Quixote. "Can't you see that if you apply these words to my hopes, they mean that I'll never see Dulcinea again?"

Sancho was about to reply when he was stopped by the sight of a hare dashing across the fields, chased by many greyhounds and huntsmen, and in its terror it sought shelter and squatted between the dun's feet. Sancho picked it up and presented it to Don Quixote, who was saying:

"*Malum signum! Malum signum!*[1] Hare flees, greyhounds chase: Dulcinea appears not!"

"You're a strange one," said Sancho. "Let's suppose that this here hare is Dulcinea del Toboso and those there greyhounds chasing it are the knavish enchanters that turned her into a peasant girl—she runs away, I grab her and put her into your charge, and now she's in your arms and you're caring for her, so how can that be a bad sign, and what bad omen can you see in that?"

The two squabbling boys came to look at the hare, and Sancho asked one of them why they'd been quarrelling. The answer came from the one who'd said "that's something that's never ever going to happen"—he had taken a cricket cage from the other boy and was never ever going to give it back to him. Sancho took four quarter-reals out of his waist-pouch and gave them to the boy for the cage, which he placed in Don Quixote's hands, saying:

"Here you are, sir—your omens foiled and come to nought, and I might be a fool but to my mind they haven't got any more to do with our affairs than last year's clouds. And if I'm not much mistaken, I've heard the village priest saying that sensible Christian persons shouldn't pay any attention to such nonsense, and you yourself told me the same thing a few days back, and showed me that all Christians who heeded omens were idiots. But there's no need for me to keep on about it—let's go into the village."

The huntsmen came up and asked for their hare, and Don Quixote gave it back to them; the pair continued, and in a meadow on the outskirts of the village they found

1. "A bad sign, a bad sign!", often uttered by doctors. Hares were bad omens.

the priest and the graduate Carrasco at their devotions. It should be mentioned that Sancho Panza had draped over his dun and the bundle of armour, as a kind of sumpter-cloth, the buckram robe with flames painted all over it that he'd been made to wear in the Duke's castle on the night Altisidora came back to life.[2] And he'd also put the inquisitional cardboard cone on the donkey's head, the most original transformation and adornment ever effected on any ass in the world.[3] The pair were immediately recognized by the priest and the graduate, who ran over to them with open arms. Don Quixote dismounted and embraced them warmly, while the village boys—boys' lynx eyes see everything—spotted the donkey's headgear and came to stare at it, calling to each other:

"Come over here, lads, if you want to see an ass looking as spruce as a sparrow and an old hack as skinny as a skeleton—and then you can have a good giggle at the dun and Rocinante, too."

Finally, surrounded by boys and accompanied by the priest and the graduate, they entered the village and went to Don Quixote's house, and at the door they found the housekeeper and the niece, who'd already been told of his arrival. So too had Teresa Panza, Sancho's wife, who, dishevelled and half naked, clutching her daughter Sanchica by the hand, hurried out to meet her husband; and when she saw that he wasn't as smart as she thought a governor ought to be, she said:

"Why are you looking like that, husband? I'd say you've come here on foot and it hasn't done your feet much good either—you look more unruly, than a ruler."

"Shut up, Teresa," Sancho replied. "Often where there are hooks there isn't any bacon to hang on them, so let's go home, and then you'll hear marvels. I've brought some money back with me, and that's what counts, and I've earned it with my own wiles, without doing any harm to anybody."

"So long as you've brought some money back, good husband," Teresa said, "you can have earned it this way or that for all I care—however you've earned it you won't have started up any new customs in the world."

Sanchica hugged her father and asked him if he'd brought anything for her, she'd been longing to see him like rain in a drought; and with her hanging on to one side of his belt and pulling his dun along behind her, and his wife holding his hand, they made for their house, leaving Don Quixote in his, in the care of his niece and his housekeeper, and in the company of the priest and the graduate.

Without a moment's delay, Don Quixote took the graduate and the priest aside and gave them a brief account of his defeat and of the promise that he'd made not to leave the village for a year,[4] which he intended to keep to the letter, without breaking it in the slightest detail, as became a true knight errant, bound by all the discipline and order of knight-errantry—and he added that his intention was to become a shepherd for the year, and amuse himself in the solitude of the fields, where he could give free rein to his thoughts of love as he practised that virtuous pastoral way of life, and that he entreated them, if they didn't have too much to do and weren't prevented by more important matters, to consent to be his companions; he'd buy sheep enough to qualify

2. Reference to a recent episode (Chapter 69) in which, as part of yet another plan engineered by the Duke and Duchess, Altisidora had feigned to be in love with Don Quixote. In fact, the episode prompts Cide Hamete himself to say in Chapter 70 that he "considers that the perpetrators of the hoax were as mad as the victims, and that the Duke and Duchess, going to such lengths to make fun of two fools, were within a hairsbreadth of looking like fools themselves."

3. Those denounced by the Inquisition and forced to repent publicly had to wear tall white cones on their heads, along with a sign stating their sin.

4. The promise exacted of Don Quixote by the supposed Knight of the White Moon, Carrasco himself.

them as shepherds, and he could tell them that the most essential part of the business was already settled, because he'd provided them with names that would fit like gloves. The priest told him to say what they were. Don Quixote replied that he himself was going to be called the shepherd Quixotiz, the graduate the shepherd Carrascón, the priest the shepherd Curambro and Sancho Panza the shepherd Panzino.[5]

They were both astonished at Don Quixote's latest delusion; but to prevent him from wandering away from the village again on his chivalric exploits, and in the hope that during the year he might be cured, they consented to his new project, acclaimed his folly as sound sense and agreed to join him in his new way of life.

"And what's more," said Sansón Carrasco, "as everybody knows, I'm a famous poet and at every turn I'll write pastoral verse or courtly verse or whatever verse best suits my purpose, to keep us amused in the Godforsaken places where we're going a-wandering; and what's most essential, gentlemen, is for each of us to choose the name of the shepherdess he's going to honour in his verses, and for us not to leave a single tree, however hard the wood, where her name isn't carved, as is the habit and custom among shepherds in love."

"That is most fitting," Don Quixote replied, "even though I have no need to search for the name of a fictitious shepherdess, because I already have the peerless Dulcinea del Toboso, the glory of these riverbanks, the ornament of these meadows, the mainstay of beauty, the cream of all the graces, and, in short, one worthy to receive all praise, however hyperbolical it might appear to be."

"Quite right too," said the priest, "but the rest of us will look for nice obliging shepherdesses who'll be just what the doctor ordered."

To which Sansón Carrasco added:

"And if they haven't got appropriate names, we'll give them the names of the shepherdesses that come printed in all those books—the world's full of them: Phyllises, Amaryllises, Dianas, Fléridas, Galateas, Belisardas; and since they're sold in the market squares, we've got every right to buy them and keep them for ourselves. If my lady or, more accurately, my shepherdess happens to be called Ana, I'll sing her praises under the name of Anarda; if she's Francisca, I'll call her Francenia; if she's Lucía, Lucinda; and so on and so forth. And if Sancho Panza is going to join the club, he can sing his wife's praises with the name Teresaina."

Don Quixote laughed at the invention of the name, and the priest lauded his virtuous and honourable decision, and again offered to accompany them for as long as he could spare from his unavoidable duties. With this they took their leave and advised and begged him to take care of his health, and to indulge in everything that was good for him. As fate would have it, his niece and housekeeper overheard the conversation between the three men, and as soon as Don Quixote was alone they walked in, and the niece said:

"What's all this, uncle? Just when we were thinking you'd come back home to stay, and to live a quiet and honourable life here, you want to go off into yet more labyrinths, turning yourself into a

> Little Shepherd, coming, coming,
> Little Shepherd, going, going?[6]

Well, the plain fact is the straw's a bit old for making whistles."

5. All diminutives, reflective of shepherds' lowly status. 6. From a Christmas carol.

To which the housekeeper added:

"And are you going to be able to put up with the heat of the summer afternoons, the damp of the winter nights, the howling of the wolves, out there in the country? Of course not—that's a job for strong men, brought up and hardened to it pretty well since they were babes in arms. And of the two evils it's better to be a knight errant than a shepherd. Look, sir, take my advice, which I'm not giving you on a belly full of bread and wine but on an empty stomach and fifty years of experience—stay at home, look after your property, go often to confession, give alms to the poor, and on my conscience be it if I'm wrong."

"Hush, my daughters," Don Quixote replied, "I know what's good for me. Take me to my bed now, because I don't feel very well, and rest assured that, whether an actual knight errant or a would-be shepherd, I shall never fail to provide for your needs, as you will see for yourselves."

And his good daughters (as the housekeeper and the niece surely were) took him to his bed, where they gave him some food and lavished all possible attentions on him.

Chapter 74

Concerning how Don Quixote fell ill, the will that he made, and his death

Since what is human is not eternal, but is in continuous decline from its beginnings to its conclusion, this being particularly true of men's lives, and since Don Quixote's life had not been granted any special privilege by heaven to halt the course of its decline, it reached its end when he was least expecting it to; because, either out of the depression brought on by his defeat or by divine ordination, he was seized by a fever that kept him in bed for six days, during which time he was often visited by his friends the priest, the graduate and the barber, while his good squire Sancho Panza never left his bedside. In the belief that dejection at his defeat and the disappointment of his hopes for Dulcinea's deliverance and disenchantment had brought him to this state, they tried in every way they knew to raise his spirits; and the graduate told him to cheer up and get out of bed to make a start on the pastoral life, for which he'd already written an eclogue that would be bad news for all the eclogues Sannazaro had ever produced[1]—and with his own money he'd bought two splendid dogs to keep watch over the flock, one of them called Barcino and the other Butrón, which a herdsman from Quintanar had sold him. But none of this roused Don Quixote from his melancholy.

His friends called in the doctor, who felt his pulse and wasn't happy with what he found, and said that to be on the safe side he should look to the well-being of his soul, because the well-being of his body was in some danger. Don Quixote listened with great composure, but not so his housekeeper, his niece and his squire, who started to weep tender tears as if he were already lying dead before them. The doctor's opinion was that depression and despondency were killing him. Don Quixote asked to be left alone, because he needed a little sleep. They did as he asked, and he slept for more than six hours at a stretch, as the saying goes: indeed he slept for so long that the housekeeper and the niece thought that he was going to die in his sleep. But he did eventually awake, and he bellowed:

1. The Neapolitan Jacopo Sannazaro wrote *Arcadia,* the first pastoral romance; published in 1504, it juxtaposes verse eclogues with a prose sequence that tells the story of a desperate lover's attempts to escape his sorrow and live among the shepherds. It inspired more than a century's worth of pastoral literature.

"Blessed be Almighty God, who has done me such good! Indeed his mercy knows no bounds, and the sins of men do not lessen or obstruct it."

The niece paid careful attention to her uncle's words, and they seemed more rational than usual, during his recent illness at least, and she asked him:

"What are you saying, sir? Has something happened? What's this mercy you're on about, and these sins of men?"

"The mercy, niece," Don Quixote replied, "is that which God has this instant shown me, unobstructed, as I said, by my sins. My mind has been restored to me, and it is now clear and free, without those gloomy shadows of ignorance cast over me by my wretched, obsessive reading of those detestable books of chivalry. Now I can recognize their absurdity and their deceitfulness, and my only regret is that this discovery has come so late that it leaves me no time to make amends by reading other books that might be a light for my soul. It is my belief, niece, that I am at death's door; I should like to make myself ready to die in such a way as to indicate that my life has not been so very wicked as to leave me with a reputation as a madman; for even though this is exactly what I have been, I'd rather not confirm this truth in the way in which I die. Call my good friends, my dear: the priest, the graduate Sansón Carrasco, and Master Nicolás the barber, because I want to confess my sins and make my will."

But she was saved her trouble by the entrance of all three. As soon as Don Quixote saw them he said:

"You must congratulate me, my good sirs, because I am no longer Don Quixote de la Mancha but Alonso Quixano, for whom my way of life earned me the nickname of 'the Good.' I am now the enemy of Amadis of Gaul and the whole infinite horde of his descendants; now all those profane histories of knight-errantry are odious to me; now I acknowledge my folly and the peril in which I was placed by reading them; now, by God's mercy, having at long last learned my lesson, I abominate them all."

When the three heard all this they were certain that he was in the grips of some new madness. And Sansón said:

"Now that we've had news, Don Quixote sir, that the lady Dulcinea has been disenchanted, you come out with all that? Now that we're on the point of becoming shepherds, to spend all our time singing and living like lords, you want to turn yourself into a hermit? Stop it for goodness sake, and come to your senses, and forget all that idle nonsense."

"The nonsense in which I have been involved so far," Don Quixote replied, "has been real enough as regards the harm it has done me, but my death will, with heaven's help, turn it to my benefit. Gentlemen: I can feel that I am dying, and dying quickly; please leave jests aside and bring me a confessor to confess me and a notary to write down my will, because at times like this a man must not trifle with his soul. And so I implore you to send someone for the notary while the priest confesses me."

They looked at each other, amazed at Don Quixote's words, and although they didn't know what to think they ended up by believing him; and one of the signs that led them to conclude that he really was dying was the ease with which he had turned from a madman into a sane man; for to what he had already said he added some more that was so well expressed, so Christian and so coherent that it removed all doubt from their minds and convinced them that he was indeed sane.

The priest ordered everybody out of the room and was left alone with him, and confessed him.

The graduate went to fetch the notary and returned a little later with him and with Sancho Panza, who had been told by the graduate about the state his master was in and who, finding the housekeeper and the niece in tears, began to pucker his lips and shed some of his own. The confession ended and the priest emerged, saying:

"Alonso Quixano the Good really is dying, and he really is sane; we'd better go back in so that he can make his will."

This news was a terrible stimulus for the housekeeper's, the niece's and the good squire Sancho Panza's swollen eyes, so much so that it made the tears burst from them, and a thousand deep sighs burst from their breasts; because the truth is, as has been said before, that while Don Quixote was plain Alonso Quixano the Good—and while he was Don Quixote, too—he was always of gentle disposition and affable behaviour, and well loved not only by his own household but by everybody who knew him. The notary went in with the others and once he had drawn up the heading and Don Quixote had disposed of his soul with all the necessary Christian formalities, they reached the part concerning the disposal of property, and he said:

"Likewise it is my will that with respect to certain monies in the possession of Sancho Panza, whom in my madness I made my squire, inasmuch as between the two of us there has been a certain amount of haggling, of give and take, he should not be held accountable for them, nor should any claim be made against him but that, if anything remains after he has paid himself what I owe him, it should all be his, although there will be little enough of it, and much good may it do him; and if, just as when I was mad I helped to procure for him the governorship of an island, I could now that I am sane make him the ruler of a kingdom, I would do it, because the straightforwardness of his character and the fidelity of his conduct deserve it."

And turning his face towards Sancho, he said:

"Forgive me, my friend, for making you seem mad, like me, and for making you fall into my own error of believing that knights errant ever have existed or do exist."

"Oh no, don't die, master!" Sancho replied, crying. "Take my advice and live for a long long time, because the maddest thing a man can do in this life is to let himself die, just like that, without anybody killing him or any other hands except the hands of depression doing away with him. Come on, don't be lazy, get out of that bed of yours, and let's go off into the countryside dressed up as shepherds as we said we would—and perhaps behind some bush or other we'll find the lady Dulcinea, disenchanted and looking as pretty as a picture. If you're dying from sadness because you were defeated, you just blame me and say you were knocked down because I didn't girth Rocinante properly—and what's more you must have read in your books of chivalry that it's an everyday event for knights to knock each other down, and for the one who's defeated today to be the victor tomorrow."

"Very true," said Sansón, "and the worthy Sancho Panza has hit the nail right on the head."

"Not so fast, gentlemen," said Don Quixote: "you won't find this year's birds in last year's nests. I was mad, and now I am sane: I was Don Quixote de la Mancha and now, as I said, I am Alonso Quixano the Good. May my repentance and my sincerity restore me in your eyes to the esteem in which I used to be held, and let the notary continue taking down my will:

"Likewise I bequeath all my estate in its entirety to my niece Antonia Quixana, here present, once what is needed for my other bequests has been deducted from the most readily disposable part of it; and it is my will that the first of these shall be the payment of the wages that I owe my housekeeper for all the time that she has been serving me, and in addition twenty ducats for a dress. I appoint the priest and the graduate Sansón Carrasco, here present, to be my executors.

"Likewise it is my will that if my niece Antonia Quixana should wish to marry, it must be to a man about whom it has first been formally established that he does not so much as know what books of chivalry are; and if it is discovered that he does, and, despite that, my niece still insists on marrying him, and she does so, she is to forfeit everything that I have left her, and my executors can distribute it in pious works as they see fit.

"Likewise I request the aforementioned gentlemen, my executors, if they are fortunate enough to meet the author who is said to have written a history that is circulating under the title of *The Second Part of the Exploits of Don Quixote de la Mancha,* to beg him on my behalf, as earnestly as they can, to forgive me for unintentionally having provided him with the opportunity to write all the gross absurdities contained in that book; because I am leaving this life with scruples of conscience for having given him an excuse for writing them."

Here he ended his testament, and was overcome by a fainting fit that prostrated him on his bed. The company was thrown into alarm and hurried to help him, and during the three days that he lived after making his will he fainted frequently. The whole house was in turmoil; but still the niece ate, the housekeeper toasted and Sancho Panza enjoyed himself; because inheriting always does something to dispel or temper in the heir the thoughts of the grief that the dead man will, of course, leave behind him.

Eventually Don Quixote's last day on earth arrived, after he had received all the sacraments and had expressed, in many powerful words, his loathing of books of chivalry. The notary was present, and he said that he'd never read in any book of chivalry of any knight errant dying in his bed in such a calm and Christian manner as Don Quixote, who, amidst the tears and lamentations of everybody present, gave up the ghost; by which I mean to say he died.

At which the priest asked the notary to write out a certificate to the effect that Alonso Quixano the Good, commonly known as Don Quixote de la Mancha, had passed on from this life, and died from natural causes. And he said that he was requesting this certificate to deprive any author other than Cide Hamete Benengeli of the opportunity to bring him falsely back to life and write endless histories of his exploits.

This was the end of the Ingenious Hidalgo of La Mancha, the name of whose village Cide Hamete couldn't quite recall, so that all the towns and villages of La Mancha could fight among themselves for the right to adopt him and make him their own son, just as the seven cities of Greece contended for Homer.[2] The lamentations of Sancho, the niece and the housekeeper are omitted from this account, as are the fresh epitaphs that were placed upon his tomb, although Sansón Carrasco did have this one put there:

> This is a doughty knight's repose;
> So high his matchless courage rose
> That, as it's plain enough to see,
> He granted death no victory,
> Not even when in death's last throes.
> This world he didn't ever prize:
> He was a scarecrow in its eyes,
> And yet he was its bugbear, too.
> He had the luck, with much ado,
> To live a madman, yet die wise.

2. The birthplace of the poet called Homer is unknown.

And the sage Cide Hamete said to his pen:

"Here you shall rest, hanging from this rack on this length of brass wire, O quill of mine—whether well trimmed or not I do not know—and here you shall live on for many centuries, unless presumptuous and knavish historians take you down to profane you. But before they touch you, you can warn them and tell them as best you can:

> 'Hands off, hands off, you paltry knaves;
> My noble king, let none
> Attempt this enterprise: you know
> It's kept for me alone.'[3]

For me alone was Don Quixote born, and I for him; it was for him to act, for me to write; we two are as one, in spite of that false writer from Tordesillas who has had and may even again have the effrontery to write with a coarse and clumsy ostrich quill about my valiant knight's deeds, because this is not a burden for his shoulders or a subject for his torpid wit. And you can warn him, if you do happen to meet him, to leave Don Quixote's weary mouldering bones at rest in his tomb, and not to try to take him, in the face of all the prerogatives of death, to Old Castile,[4] making him rise from the grave where he really and truly does lie stretched out at full length, quite incapable of any third sally or fresh campaign; because to make fun of all those campaigns waged by so very many knights errant his two are quite sufficient, such has been the approval and delight of all those who have known of them, both in Spain and in foreign realms. And so you will have carried out your Christian mission, giving good advice to one who wishes you ill, and I shall feel proud and satisfied to have been the first author to enjoy the full fruit of his writings, as I desired, because my only desire has been to make men hate those false, absurd histories in books of chivalry, which thanks to the exploits of my real Don Quixote are even now tottering, and without any doubt will soon tumble to the ground. Farewell."

William Shakespeare

1564–1616

Like his contemporary Montaigne, whose remarkable essay "Of Cannibals" informs *The Tempest,* William Shakespeare was an armchair traveler. And like Montaigne, he seldom took anything at face value. For his plays, he devoured novellas by Italians, chapbooks by Englishmen, snatches of songs by Spaniards, and tourist propaganda by the New Virginians, who in 1610 were boasting that "after some planting and husbanding the Americas could supply not only England's needs but those of other nations as well." Virginia, that is to say, could be Carthage to England's Rome: the breadbasket for a Europe that still perenially suffered from plague and bad harvests. First performed in 1611, *The Tempest* is a recasting and rigorous questioning of pamphlets such as these, as it explores the anxieties that accompanied England's belated foray

3. Lines from a popular ballad about the siege of Granada, the last part of the Moorish kingdom to fall into Christian hands (in 1492).

4. A northern region of central Spain, formerly part of the Kingdom of Castile. This may be an ironic gesture on Cervantes' part; almost all of *Don Quixote* takes place in what was once Castile, and almost all of the characters except for the meddling Duke and Duchess are from Castile.

into a New World already occupied by Spanish plantations to the south and French missionaries to the north, not to mention by the native peoples themselves. Shipwreck and drowning, drunken brawls, seditious murder, tense confrontations between natives and Europeans, tender romance, and all within three hours: *The Tempest* is one of only two of Shakespeare's plays that respect the unities of time and place. And all of it is orchestrated by an exiled duke named Prospero, whose exceptional skills at magic and theatrical arts have resulted in many an audience seeing him as a self-portrait of his notoriously elusive creator.

Traditionally read as the culmination of Shakespeare's career, *The Tempest* is a retrospective of earlier plays, and thus of a long and successful theatrical career. It was a career marked by shrewd business practice and shrewd relationships with figures in authority, and one for which the young Will Shakespeare (or Shaxpeare, or Shakyspere, or Shakspere, or Shackspeare—there are over two dozen different spellings of his name) seemed well-prepared. The oldest of five siblings, Shakespeare enjoyed a relatively comfortable bourgeois childhood in Stratford-on-Avon. His mother, Mary Arden, was the daughter of an affluent farmer; his father was a wool-dealer and glover who went into local politics. Stratford-on-Avon was a booming country town on a river that brought in a great deal of traffic, and the town's general prosperity enabled it to hire first-class teachers for the grammar school, where its most famous citizen became well-read in classics, history, and rhetoric.

Little is known of the period between Shakespeare's departure from Stratford Grammar School in 1578 and his marriage in 1582 to Anne Hathaway—he may have apprenticed as a glover for his father—and there are again no records of him until 1587, when he shows up in London, acting and possibly already writing plays. His extraordinarily rapid rise to the top of the competitive theater industry is attested by his success in purchasing a coat-of-arms in 1596 and, a year later, the biggest house in Stratford. In 1599, he was one of five actors in the Lord Chamberlain's Men to hold half the lease for the new Globe Theatre, built by the acting company after their lease at James Burbage's Theatre had expired. By then not only was he listed as "principal comedian" for the company, but he had already written and produced his great history plays and his comedies, one of them—*The Merry Wives of Windsor,* with the burly Falstaff as its protagonist and a town not unlike his native Stratford as its setting—at the specific request of his Queen, Elizabeth I. It may have been Elizabeth's formidable presence that inspired Shakespeare to create for his other comedies some of the classiest heroines in dramatic literature, albeit ones played by boys: notably, the self-possessed Rosalynde, who commandeers the events that transpire in Arden in *As You Like It,* and Viola, in *Twelfth Night,* who wins for herself a duke.

The season of Shakespeare's great tragedies followed, and with it, a change of monarchs and a corresponding change in Shakespeare's status. King James I, formerly James VI of Scotland, ruled England after Elizabeth's death in 1603, and promptly elevated Shakespeare's troupe to the King's Men, authorizing the actors to wear livery and inviting them to play some thirteen times a year at court. *Julius Caesar* and *Hamlet* predate James's succession, while *Othello, Macbeth,* and *King Lear* were written shortly after James became king. They were followed by works that do not fit nicely into distinct categories. *Antony and Cleopatra,* with its flirtatious Egyptian queen, lacks the momentum and drive of the earlier tragedies, and *Measure for Measure* ends too uneasily to be confused with the earlier comedies. Shakespeare's increasing interest in experimenting with dramatic structure is evident in the final plays of his career: *Winter's Tale, Cymbeline, Pericles,* and *The Tempest.* With their exotic settings and fantastic plots, their mixture of deaths and comic rebirths, they represent yet again a sharp departure from what had come before, while returning to themes that had always sparked Shakespeare's interest—jealousy, the trials of kingship, the possibilities afforded by escape to a pastoral world. Shakespeare officially retired from the stage in 1613, the year the capacious Globe Theatre burned down while *Henry VIII,* which Shakespeare wrote in collaboration with John Fletcher, was being performed. In April of 1616 he died in Stratford, having bequeathed to the

English-speaking world several long narrative poems, over a hundred and fifty sonnets, and thirty-seven plays (see page 1497 for a selection of the sonnets).

The Tempest opened the voluminous collection overseen and published by Shakespeare's fellow actors in 1623. The First Folio, as it has been traditionally called, groups Shakespeare's works by genre. The fact that *The Tempest* is followed by *Two Gentlemen of Verona* and *Merry Wives of Windsor* suggests that the actors perceived it as a comedy. And so, in many respects, it is. It celebrates the magician's powers and those of the theater in which Shakespeare spent his adult life. It effects reconciliations undreamed of and lures us and its characters into brave new worlds; written on the edge of the baroque, it remarks throughout on theater's capacity to use illusion for peaceful resolutions—the most resounding of which is the love affair between Prospero's daughter Miranda and the dashing Ferdinand. An island spirit named Ariel is Prospero's Puckish servant, who does his master's bidding by transforming himself into (mostly female) roles and controlling characters as though they were puppets, first befuddling them, then bringing them together on the stage for revelations of life and death. Yet Shakespeare is also conscious of art's limitations, especially when confronted by the messiness of politics and family affairs. *The Tempest* is relentlessly realistic with respect to the extent to which "human nature" resists even the most artful Machiavellian tactics. Indeed, Prospero, the play's reigning Machiavellian, while provoking sympathy for his plight at his brother Antonio's hands, was a bad ruler who ignored office of state to pursue his magical arts; and it is only on the island that Prospero finds a means of bringing statecraft and witchcraft together for manipulative, at times, sadistic effect. The doubleness of Prospero's achievement is highlighted at the play's end, when Prospero must address the gaping Europeans' wonder not over a beautiful Miranda but over his "deformed" slave: "the thing of darkness" that he acknowledges, in a perplexing moment, as his own. Indeed, Caliban, whose name may be an anagram for "cannibal," represents a terrain which Machiavelli, in his cynical portrait of the ideal Renaissance ruler of a century earlier, had barely imagined: colonial encounters abroad with defiant indigenous peoples. The tumultuous relationship between Prospero and Caliban would inspire the later meditations of Caribbean and Latin American writers, especially Aimé Césaire, whose own twentieth-century *Tempest* is excerpted in the Resonance that follows.

Yet Caliban is no "cannibal," and some of his lines—as when he reminds Prospero that once he "lov'd thee, / And show'd thee all the qualities o'th'isle, / The fresh springs, brine-pits, barren place and fertile"—are some of the most poetic in the play. At the same time, he is versatile enough to speak in bantering prose with the "jester" Trinculo and with Stephano, a "drunken butler," who contemplate taking the island over as theirs. Shakespeare's own ability to move back and forth between stunning poetry and prosaic wit distinguishes almost his entire dramatic canon, as he draws for his characters on extremely diverse segments of society and convincingly creates a world through their language; Elizabethans said they would go to *hear,* not *see,* a play, and this emphasis on the ear suggests for us the power that the dramatic word could have. But Shakespeare also derives his fast-paced dialogues and moving verse from a wealth of literary and dramatic traditions, both ancient and contemporary. The vibrant practices of the Italian professional theater or the *commedia dell'arte*—literally, the actor's guild, although the expression has come to designate the improvised scenarios of masked actors such as the hunchbacked merchant, the bumbling doctor, the wily servant—have long been considered an influence particularly on *The Tempest,* with its slapstick scenes of low life. On the other hand, Rome's most accomplished poet, Virgil, furnished not only the source of the wondering lines spoken by Ferdinand when he imagines Miranda to be a goddess, but the chaotic storm with which both the *Aeneid* and *The Tempest* open. And Ovid's *Metamorphoses* gave Shakespeare the powerful verses recited by Prospero when he abjures his "rough magic" and promises to drown his book: they are the words of Medea, the vengeful sorceress of Greek and Roman myth. If Shakespeare on the one hand lends to his characters' language the cadences of everyday life, on the other he infuses it with the resonant poetry of earlier literary geniuses, and thereby participates in the broader cultural project of the English Renaissance, making the legacy of Roman empire and the European Renaissance alike England's own.

And yet not entirely its own. The haunting poetry of the waif Ariel—"Full fathom five thy father lies, / Of his bones are coral made"—would have been sung to an uncomprehending Ferdinand and audience alike, as though Shakespeare was making us and Ferdinand experience the unsettling feeling of what it is like to be in a place where we have lost our normal bearings. But this may in fact be what all of Shakespeare's theater tries to accomplish. The geography of London was such that the public theaters were on the other side—the wrong side—of the Thames River from the city's official neighborhoods, and the entertainment district was in some sense discontinuous with the real London. Similarly, *The Tempest* takes place like so many of Shakespeare's plays not at "home" but somewhere else: in this case, on an unnamed island in the Mediterranean that vanishes off the surface of the map as soon as the play is done. In remarking again and again on the insubstantialities of a play that has given us a narrative about marriage between old world and new, between the seasoned colonist Ferdinand and the innocent Miranda, Shakespeare points to the strange insubstantialities of stories about love and conquest alike. At the same time, in calling attention to the extent to which the problematic figure of Prospero is behind those stories, Shakespeare takes care to insinuate that he, like his audience, bears responsibility for what can happen to narratives once they are set in motion.

PRONUNCIATIONS:

Prospero: PROS-pe-ro
Trinculo: TRIN-coo-lo

The Tempest

The Names of the Actors

ALONSO, *King of Naples*
SEBASTIAN, *his brother*
PROSPERO, *the right Duke of Milan*
ANTONIO, *his brother, the usurping Duke of Milan*
FERDINAND, *son to the King of Naples*
GONZALO, *an honest old councillor*
ADRIAN *and* FRANCISCO, *lords*
CALIBAN, *a savage and deformed slave*
TRINCULO, *a jester*
STEPHANO, *a drunken butler*
MASTER *of a ship*
BOATSWAIN
MARINERS
MIRANDA, *daughter to Prospero*
ARIEL, *an airy spirit*
IRIS, CERES, JUNO, NYMPHS, REAPERS *(presented by) spirits*
[*Other Spirits attending on Prospero*]

Scene: An uninhabited island

ACT 1

Scene 1

[*A tempestuous noise of thunder and lightning heard. Enter a Shipmaster and a Boatswain.*][1]

MASTER: Boatswain!
BOATSWAIN: Here, Master. What cheer?

1. Location: On board ship.

MASTER: Good, speak to the mariners. Fall to 't yarely,[2] or we run ourselves aground. Bestir, bestir!

[*Exit.*]

[*Enter Mariners.*]

BOATSWAIN: Heigh, my hearts! Cheerly, cheerly, my hearts! Yare, yare! Take in the topsail. Tend[3] to the Master's whistle.—Blow[4] till thou burst thy wind, if room enough![5]

[*Enter Alonso, Sebastian, Antonio, Ferdinand, Gonzalo, and others.*]

ALONSO: Good Boatswain, have care. Where's the Master? Play[6] the men.

BOATSWAIN: I pray now, keep below.

ANTONIO: Where is the Master, Boatswain?

BOATSWAIN: Do you not hear him? You mar our labor. Keep your cabins! You do assist the storm.

GONZALO: Nay, good, be patient.

BOATSWAIN: When the sea is. Hence! What cares these roarers[7] for the name of king? To cabin! Silence! Trouble us not.

GONZALO: Good, yet remember whom thou hast aboard.

BOATSWAIN: None that I more love than myself. You are a councillor; if you can command these elements to silence and work the peace of the present, we will not hand[8] a rope more. Use your authority. If you cannot, give thanks you have lived so long and make yourself ready in your cabin for the mischance of the hour, if it so hap.—Cheerly, good hearts!—Out of our way, I say.

[*Exit.*]

GONZALO: I have great comfort from this fellow. Methinks he hath no drowning mark upon him; his complexion is perfect gallows.[9] Stand fast, good Fate, to his hanging! Make the rope of his destiny our cable, for our own doth little advantage.[1] If he be not born to be hanged, our case is miserable.

[*Exeunt (courtiers).*]

[*Enter Boatswain.*]

BOATSWAIN: Down with the topmast! Yare! Lower, lower! Bring her to try wi' the main course.[2] [*A cry within.*] A plague upon this howling! They are louder than the weather or our office.[3]

[*Enter Sebastian, Antonio, and Gonzalo.*]

Yet again? What do you here? Shall we give o'er and drown? Have you a mind to sink?

SEBASTIAN: A pox o'your throat, you bawling, blasphemous, incharitable dog!

BOATSWAIN: Work you, then.

2. Quickly.
3. Attend.
4. Addressed to the wind.
5. As long as we have sea room enough.
6. Ply? Urge the men to exert themselves.
7. Waves or wind.
8. Handle.
9. Alludes to the proverb "He that's born to be hanged need fear no drowning."
1. Doesn't do much good.
2. Sail her close to the wind.
3. The noise we make at our work.

ANTONIO: Hang, cur! Hang, you whoreson, insolent noisemaker! We are less afraid to be drowned than thou art.

GONZALO: I'll warrant him for drowning,[4] though the ship were no stronger than a nutshell and as leaky as an unstanched[5] wench.

BOATSWAIN: Lay her ahold,[6] ahold! Set her two courses.[7]
Off to sea again! Lay her off!

[*Enter Mariners, wet.*]

MARINERS: All lost! To prayers, to prayers! All lost!

[*The Mariners run about in confusion, exiting at random.*]

BOATSWAIN: What, must our mouths be cold?[8]
GONZALO: The King and Prince at prayers! Let's assist them,
For our case is as theirs.
SEBASTIAN: I am out of patience.
ANTONIO: We are merely° cheated of our lives by drunkards. *utterly*
This wide-chapped° rascal! Would thou mightst lie drowning *wide-jawed*
The washing of ten tides![9]
GONZALO: He'll be hanged yet,
Though every drop of water swear against it
And gape at wid'st to glut° him. *gobble*
[*A confused noise within.*] "Mercy on us!"—
"We split, we split!"—"Farewell my wife and children!"—
"Farewell, brother!"—"We split, we split, we split!"

[*Exit Boatswain.*]

ANTONIO: Let's all sink wi' the King.
SEBASTIAN: Let's take leave of him.

[*Exit* (*with Antonio*).]

GONZALO: Now would I give a thousand furlongs of sea for an acre of barren ground: long heath, brown furze; anything. The wills above be done! But I would fain die a dry death.

[*Exit.*]

Scene 2[1]

[*Enter Prospero* (*in his magic cloak*) *and Miranda.*]

MIRANDA: If by your art, my dearest father, you have
Put the wild waters in this roar, allay them.
The sky, it seems, would pour down stinking pitch,
But that the sea, mounting to th' welkin's cheek,° *the sky's face*
Dashes the fire out. O, I have suffered

4. Guarantee against.
5. Loose (suggesting also "menstrual").
6. Close to the wind.
7. Sets of sails.
8. Must we drown in the cold sea; or, let us heat up our mouths with liquor.
9. Pirates were hanged on the shore and left until three tides had come in.
1. Location: The island, near Prospero's cell.

With those that I saw suffer! A brave° vessel, *splendid*
Who had, no doubt, some noble creature in her,
Dashed all to pieces. O, the cry did knock
Against my very heart! Poor souls, they perished.
Had I been any god of power, I would
Have sunk the sea within the earth or ere° *before*
It should the good ship so have swallowed and
The freighting° souls within her. *forming the cargo*

PROSPERO: Be collected.° *composed*
No more amazement.° Tell your piteous° heart *consternation / pitying*
There's no harm done.

MIRANDA: O, woe the day!

PROSPERO: No harm.
I have done nothing but in care of thee,
Of thee, my dear one, thee, my daughter, who
Art ignorant of what thou art, naught knowing
Of whence I am, nor that I am more better
Than Prospero, master of a full° poor cell, *very*
And thy no greater father.

MIRANDA: More to know
Did never meddle° with my thoughts. *mingle*

PROSPERO: 'Tis time
I should inform thee farther. Lend thy hand
And pluck my magic garment from me. So,

[*laying down his magic cloak and staff*]

Lie there, my art.—Wipe thou thine eyes. Have comfort.
The direful spectacle of the wreck,° which touched *shipwreck*
The very virtue° of compassion in thee, *essence*
I have with such provision° in mine art *foresight*
So safely ordered that there is no soul—
No, not so much perdition° as an hair *loss*
Betid° to any creature in the vessel *happened*
Which thou heard'st cry, which thou saw'st sink. Sit down.
For thou must now know farther.

MIRANDA [*sitting*]: You have often
Begun to tell me what I am, but stopped
And left me to a bootless inquisition,° *fruitless inquiry*
Concluding, "Stay, not yet."

PROSPERO: The hour's now come;
The very minute bids thee ope thine ear.
Obey, and be attentive. Canst thou remember
A time before we came unto this cell?
I do not think thou canst, for then thou wast not
Out° three years old. *fully*

MIRANDA: Certainly, sir, I can.

PROSPERO: By what? By any other house or person?
Of anything the image, tell me, that
Hath kept with thy remembrance.

MIRANDA: 'Tis far off,
And rather like a dream than an assurance
That my remembrance warrants.[2] Had I not
Four or five women once that tended me?
PROSPERO: Thou hadst, and more, Miranda. But how is it
That this lives in thy mind? What seest thou else
In the dark backward and abysm of time?[3]
If thou rememberest aught ere thou carn'st here,
How thou cam'st here thou mayst.
MIRANDA: But that I do not.
PROSPERO: Twelve year since, Miranda, twelve year since,
Thy father was the Duke of Milan and
A prince of power.
MIRANDA: Sir, are not you my father?
PROSPERO: Thy mother was a piece° of virtue, and *masterpiece*
She said thou wast my daughter; and thy father
Was Duke of Milan, and his only heir
And princess no worse issued.° *no less nobly born*
MIRANDA: O the heavens!
What foul play had we, that we came from thence?
Or blessèd was 't we did?
PROSPERO: Both, both, my girl.
By foul play, as thou sayst, were we heaved thence,
But blessedly holp° hither. *helped*
MIRANDA: O, my heart bleeds
To think o' the teen° that I have turned you to,[4] *trouble*
Which is from° my remembrance! Please you, farther. *out of*
PROSPERO: My brother and thy uncle, called Antonio—
I pray thee mark me—that a brother should
Be so perfidious!—he whom next° thyself *next to*
Of all the world I loved, and to him put
The manage° of my state, as at that time *management*
Through all the seigniories[5] it was the first,
And Prospero the prime duke, being so reputed
In dignity, and for the liberal arts
Without a parallel; those being all my study,
The government I cast upon my brother
And to my state grew stranger,[6] being transported° *carried away*
And rapt in secret studies. Thy false uncle—
Dost thou attend me?
MIRANDA: Sir, most heedfully.
PROSPERO: Being once perfected° how to grant suits, *grown skillful*
How to deny them, who t' advance and who
To trash for overtopping,[7] new created
The creatures that were mine, I say, or° changed 'em, *either*

2. A certainty that my memory guarantees.
3. Abyss of the past.
4. I've caused you to remember.
5. City-states of northern Italy.
6. Withdrew from my responsibilities as a duke.
7. To check for going too fast, like hounds.

Or else new formed 'em; having both the key[8]
Of officer and office, set all hearts i' the state
To what tune pleased his ear, that° now he was *so that*
The ivy which had hid my princely trunk
And sucked my verdure out on 't. Thou attend'st not.

MIRANDA: O, good sir, I do.

PROSPERO: I pray thee, mark me.
I, thus neglecting worldly ends, all dedicated
To closeness° and the bettering of my mind *seclusion*
With that which, but by being so retired,
O'erprized° all popular rate,° in my false brother *outvalued / estimation*
Awaked an evil nature; and my trust,
Like a good parent,[9] did beget of° him *in*
A falsehood in its contrary as great
As my trust was, which had indeed no limit,
A confidence sans° bound. He being thus lorded° *without / made a lord*
Not only with what my revenue yielded
But what my power might else exact, like one
Who, having into° truth by telling of it, *unto*
Made such a sinner of his memory
To° credit his own lie,[1] he did believe *as to*
He was indeed the Duke, out° o' the substitution *as a result*
And executing th' outward face of royalty
With all prerogative. Hence his ambition growing—
Dost thou hear?

MIRANDA: Your tale, sir, would cure deafness.

PROSPERO: To have no screen between this part he played
And him he played it for, he needs will be° *insisted on becoming*
Absolute Milan.[2] Me, poor man, my library
Was dukedom large enough. Of temporal royalties
He thinks me now incapable; confederates°— *allies himself*
So dry° he was for sway—wi' the King of Naples *thirsty*
To give him annual tribute, do him homage,
Subject his coronet to his crown, and bend
The dukedom yet° unbowed—alas, poor Milan!— *previously*
To most ignoble stooping.

MIRANDA: O the heavens!

PROSPERO: Mark his condition° and th' event,° then tell me *pact / outcome*
If this might be a brother.

MIRANDA: I should sin
To think but nobly of my grandmother.
Good wombs have borne bad sons.

PROSPERO: Now the condition.
This King of Naples, being an enemy
To me inveterate, hearkens° my brother's suit, *listens to*

8. Key for unlocking; tool for tuning stringed instruments.
9. Alludes to the proverb that good parents often bear bad children; see line 120.
1. Who starts to believe his own lie.
2. Duke of Milan in fact.

Which was that he, in lieu o' the premises[3]
Of homage and I know not how much tribute,
Should presently° extirpate° me and mine *immediately / remove*
Out of the dukedom and confer fair Milan,
With all the honors, on my brother. Whereon,
A treacherous army levied, one midnight
Fated° to th' purpose did Antonio open *devoted*
The gates of Milan, and, i' the dead of darkness,
The ministers° for the purpose hurried thence *agents*
Me and thy crying self.

MIRANDA: Alack, for pity!
I, not remembering how I cried out then,
Will cry it o'er again. It is a hint° *occasion*
That wrings[4] mine eyes to 't.

PROSPERO: Hear a little further,
And then I'll bring thee to the present business
Which now's upon 's, without the which this story
Were most impertinent.° *irrelevant*

MIRANDA: Wherefore° did they not *why*
That hour destroy us?

PROSPERO: Well demanded,° wench. *asked*
My tale provokes that question. Dear, they durst not,
So dear the love my people bore me, nor set
A mark so bloody on the business, but
With colors fairer painted their foul ends.
In few,° they hurried us aboard a bark,° *few words / ship*
Bore us some leagues to sea, where they prepared
A rotten carcass of a butt,° not rigged, *tub*
Nor tackle, sail, nor mast; the very rats
Instinctively have quit it. There they hoist us,
To cry to th' sea that roared to us, to sigh
To th' winds whose pity, sighing back again,
Did us but loving wrong.

MIRANDA: Alack, what trouble
Was I then to you!

PROSPERO: O, a cherubin
Thou wast that did preserve me. Thou didst smile,
Infusèd with a fortitude from heaven,
When I have decked° the sea with drops full salt, *adorned*
Under my burden groaned, which raised in me
An undergoing stomach,° to bear up *courage to endure*
Against what should ensue.

MIRANDA: How came we ashore?

PROSPERO: By Providence divine.
Some food we had, and some fresh water, that
A noble Neapolitan, Gonzalo,

3. In exchange for the guarantee.

4. Constrains; wrings tears from.

Out of his charity, who being then appointed
Master of this design, did give us, with
Rich garments, linens, stuffs,° and necessaries, — *supplies*
Which since have steaded much.° So, of his gentleness, — *been of much use*
Knowing I loved my books, he furnished me
From mine own library with volumes that
I prize above my dukedom.

MIRANDA: Would I might
But ever see that man!

PROSPERO: Now I arise. [*He puts on his magic cloak.*]
Sit still, and hear the last of our sea sorrow.
Here in this island we arrived; and here
Have I, thy schoolmaster, made thee more profit° — *profit more*
Than other princes'° can, that have more time — *princesses*
For vainer hours and tutors not so careful.

MIRANDA: Heavens thank you for 't! And now, I pray you, sir—
For still 'tis beating in my mind—your reason
For raising this sea storm?

PROSPERO: Know thus far forth:
By accident most strange, bountiful Fortune,
Now my dear lady, hath mine enemies
Brought to this shore; and by my prescience
I find my zenith° doth depend upon — *apex of fortune*
A most auspicious star, whose influence
If now I court not, but omit,° my fortunes — *neglect*
Will ever after droop. Here cease more questions.
Thou art inclined to sleep. 'Tis a good dullness,° — *drowsiness*
And give it way. I know thou canst not choose.

[*Miranda sleeps.*]

Come away,° servant, come! I am ready now. — *come here*
Approach, my Ariel, come.

[*Enter Ariel.*]

ARIEL: All hail, great master, grave sir, hail! I come
To answer thy best pleasure; be 't to fly,
To swim, to dive into the fire, to ride
On the curled clouds, to thy strong bidding task° — *make demands upon*
Ariel and all his quality.° — *cohorts or abilities*

PROSPERO: Hast thou, spirit,
Performed to point° the tempest that I bade thee? — *in detail*

ARIEL: To every article.
I boarded the King's ship. Now on the beak,° — *prow*
Now in the waist,° the deck,° in every cabin, — *midships / poop*
I flamed amazement.[5] Sometimes I'd divide
And burn in many places; on the topmast,

5. Struck terror by appearing as St. Elmo's fire, an electric discharge seen at the prominent parts of ships in stormy weather.

The yards, and bowsprit would I flame distinctly,° *in different places*
Then meet and join. Jove's lightning, the precursors
O' the dreadful thunderclaps, more momentary
And sight-outrunning° were not. The fire and cracks *swifter than sight*
Of sulfurous roaring the most mighty Neptune
Seem to besiege and make his bold waves tremble,
Yea, his dread trident shake.

PROSPERO: My brave spirit!
Who was so firm, so constant, that this coil° *uproar*
Would not infect his reason?

ARIEL: Not a soul
But felt a fever of the mad and played
Some tricks of desperation. All but mariners
Plunged in the foaming brine and quit the vessel,
Then all afire with me. The King's son, Ferdinand,
With hair up-staring°—then like reeds, not hair— *standing on end*
Was the first man that leapt; cried, "Hell is empty,
And all the devils are here!"

PROSPERO: Why, that's my spirit!
But was not this nigh shore?

ARIEL: Close by, my master.

PROSPERO: But are they, Ariel, safe?

ARIEL: Not a hair perished.
On their sustaining garments[6] not a blemish,
But fresher than before; and, as thou bad'st me,
In troops I have dispersed them 'bout the isle.
The King's son have I landed by himself,
Whom I left cooling of the air with sighs
In an odd angle° of the isle, and sitting, *corner*
His arms in this sad knot. [*He folds his arms.*]

PROSPERO: Of the King's ship,
The mariners, say how thou hast disposed,
And all the rest o' the fleet.

ARIEL: Safely in harbor
Is the King's ship; in the deep nook,° where once *bay*
Thou called'st me up at midnight to fetch dew[7]
From the still-vexed° Bermudas,[8] there she's hid; *ever stormy*
The mariners all under hatches stowed,
Who, with a charm joined to their suffered° labor, *undergone*
I have left asleep. And for the rest o' the fleet,
Which I dispersed, they all have met again
And are upon the Mediterranean float° *sea*
Bound sadly home for Naples,
Supposing that they saw the King's ship wrecked

6. Garments that buoyed them up in the sea.
7. For magical purposes; see line 322.
8. Perhaps refers to the then-recent Bermuda shipwreck of 1609, when one of nine ships sailing from England to Virginia was driven onto the Bermuda coast in a severe storm. As in *The Tempest,* all on board survived, although the news took a while to reach those in England, who had presumed the crew lost.

And his great person perish.
PROSPERO: Ariel, thy charge
Exactly is performed. But there's more work.
What is the time o' the day?
ARIEL: Past the mid season.° *noon*
PROSPERO: At least two glasses.° The time twixt six and now *hourglasses*
Must by us both be spent most preciously.
ARIEL: Is there more toil? Since thou dost give me pains,° *labors*
Let me remember° thee what thou hast promised, *remind*
Which is not yet performed me.
PROSPERO: How now? Moody?
What is't thou canst demand?
ARIEL: My liberty.
PROSPERO: Before the time be out? No more!
ARIEL: I prithee,
Remember I have done thee worthy service,
Told thee no lies, made thee no mistakings, served
Without or grudge or grumblings. Thou did promise
To bate° me a full year. *remit*
PROSPERO: Dost thou forget
From what a torment I did free thee?
ARIEL: No.
PROSPERO: Thou dost, and think'st it much to tread the ooze
Of the salt deep,
To run upon the sharp wind of the north,
To do me° business in the veins[9] o' the earth *do for me*
When it is baked° with frost. *hardened*
ARIEL: I do not, sir.
PROSPERO: Thou liest, malignant thing! Hast thou forgot
The foul witch Sycorax, who with age and envy° *malice*
Was grown into a hoop?[1] Hast thou forgot her?
ARIEL: No, sir.
PROSPERO: Thou hast. Where was she born? Speak. Tell me.
ARIEL: Sir, in Argier.° *Algiers*
PROSPERO: O, was she so? I must
Once in a month recount what thou hast been,
Which thou forget'st. This damned witch Sycorax,
For mischiefs manifold and sorceries terrible
To enter human hearing, from Argier,
Thou know'st, was banished. For one thing she did° *becoming pregnant*
They would not take her life. Is not this true?
ARIEL: Ay, sir.
PROSPERO: This blue-eyed[2] hag was hither brought with child° *pregnant*
And here was left by the sailors. Thou, my slave,
As thou report'st thyself, was then her servant;
And, for° thou wast a spirit too delicate *because*

9. Of minerals, or underground streams.
1. So bent with age as to resemble a hoop.
2. With dark circles under her eyes, implying pregnancy.

To act her earthy and abhorred commands,
Refusing her grand hests,° she did confine thee, *orders*
By help of her more potent ministers
And in her most unmitigable rage,
Into a cloven pine, within which rift
Imprisoned thou didst painfully remain
A dozen years; within which space she died
And left thee there, where thou didst vent thy groans
As fast as mill wheels strike.[3] Then was this island—
Save° for the son that she did litter° here, *except / give birth to*
A freckled whelp,° hag-born—not honored with *animal offspring*
A human shape.

ARIEL: Yes, Caliban her son.

PROSPERO: Dull thing, I say so:[4] he, that Caliban
Whom now I keep in service. Thou best know'st
What torment I did find thee in. Thy groans
Did make wolves howl, and penetrate the breasts
Of ever-angry bears. It was a torment
To lay upon the damned, which Sycorax
Could not again undo. It was mine art,
When I arrived and heard thee, that made gape° *open wide*
The pine and let thee out.

ARIEL: I thank thee, master.

PROSPERO: If thou more murmur'st, I will rend an oak
And peg thee in his° knotty entrails till *its*
Thou hast howled away twelve winters.

ARIEL: Pardon, master.
I will be correspondent° to command *obedient*
And do my spriting[5] gently.° *graciously*

PROSPERO: Do so, and after two days
I will discharge thee.

ARIEL: That's my noble master!
What shall I do? Say what? What shall I do?

PROSPERO: Go make thyself like a nymph o' the sea. Be subject
To no sight but thine and mine, invisible
To every eyeball else. Go take this shape
And hither come in 't. Go, hence with diligence!

[*Exit* (*Ariel*).]

Awake, dear heart, awake! Thou hast slept well.
Awake!

MIRANDA: The strangeness of your story put
Heaviness° in me. *drowsiness*

PROSPERO: Shake it off. Come on,
We'll visit Caliban, my slave, who never
Yields us kind answer.

3. As the blades of a mill wheel strike water.
4. Exactly, that's what I said, you dimwit.
5. Duties as a spirit.

MIRANDA: 'Tis a villain, sir,
I do not love to look on.
PROSPERO: But, as 'tis,
We cannot miss° him. He does make our fire, *do without*
Fetch in our wood, and serves in offices° *functions*
That profit us.—What ho! Slave! Caliban!
Thou earth, thou! Speak.
CALIBAN [*within*]: There's wood enough within.
PROSPERO: Come forth, I say! There's other business for thee.
Come, thou tortoise! When?[6]

[*Enter Ariel like a water nymph.*]

Fine apparition! My quaint° Ariel, *ingenious*
Hark in thine ear. [*He whispers.*]
ARIEL: My lord, it shall be done.

[*Exit.*]

PROSPERO: Thou poisonous slave, got° by the devil himself *begotten*
Upon thy wicked dam,° come forth! *mother*

[*Enter Caliban.*]

CALIBAN: As wicked dew as e'er my mother brushed
With raven's feather from unwholesome fen° *marsh*
Drop on you both! A southwest° blow on ye *diseased wind*
And blister you all o'er!
PROSPERO: For this, be sure, tonight thou shalt have cramps,
Side-stitches that shall pen thy breath up. Urchins[7]
Shall forth at vast° of night that they may work[8] *desolate time*
All exercise on thee. Thou shalt be pinched
As thick as honeycomb, each pinch more stinging
Than bees that made 'em.
CALIBAN: I must eat my dinner.
This island's mine, by Sycorax my mother,
Which thou tak'st from me. When thou cam'st first,
Thou strok'st me and made much of me, wouldst give me
Water with berries in 't, and teach me how
To name the bigger light, and how the less,
That burn by day and night. And then I loved thee
And showed thee all the qualities° o' th' isle, *resources*
The fresh springs, brine pits, barren place and fertile.
Cursed be I that did so! All the charms° *spells*
Of Sycorax, toads, beetles, bats, light on you!
For I am all the subjects that you have,
Which first was mine own king; and here you, sty° me *put me in a sty*
In this hard rock, whiles you do keep from me
The rest o' th' island.

6. Expression of impatience.
7. Hedgehogs (here, goblins in the shape of hedgehogs).
8. Malignant spirits were thought to prowl at night.

PROSPERO: Thou most lying slave,
Whom stripes° may move, not kindness! I have used thee, *lashes*
Filth as thou art, with humane care, and lodged thee
In mine own cell, till thou didst seek to violate
The honor of my child.

CALIBAN: O ho, O ho! Would't had been done!
Thou didst prevent me; I had peopled else° *otherwise populated*
This isle with Calibans.

MIRANDA:[9] Abhorrèd slave,
Which any print° of goodness wilt not take, *imprint*
Being capable of all ill! I pitied thee,
Took pains to make thee speak, taught thee each hour
One thing or other. When thou didst not, savage,
Know thine own meaning, but wouldst gabble like
A thing most brutish, I endowed thy purposes° *meanings*
With words that made them known. But thy vile race,° *nature*
Though thou didst learn, had that in 't which good natures
Could not abide to be with; therefore wast thou
Deservedly confined into this rock,
Who hadst deserved more than a prison.

CALIBAN: You taught me language, and my profit on 't
Is I know how to curse. The red° plague rid° you *bubonic / destroy*
For learning me your language!

PROSPERO: Hagseed, hence!
Fetch us in fuel, and be quick, thou'rt best,[1]
To answer other business:[2] Shrugg'st thou, malice?
If thou neglect'st or dost unwillingly
What I command, I'll rack thee with old[3] cramps,
Fill all thy bones with aches,[4] make thee roar
That beasts shall tremble at thy din.

CALIBAN: No, pray thee.
[*Aside.*] I must obey. His art is of such power
It would control my dam's god, Setebos,[5]
And make a vassal of him.

PROSPERO: So, slave, hence!

[*Exit Caliban.*]

[*Enter Ferdinand; and Ariel, invisible,*[6] *playing and singing.* (*Ferdinand does not see Prospero and Miranda.*)]

[*Ariel's Song.*]

ARIEL: *Come unto these yellow sands,*
And then take hands;
Curtsied when you have, and kissed

9. This speech is sometimes assigned by editors to Prospero.
1. You'd be well advised.
2. Perform other tasks.
3. Such as old people have.
4. Pronounced "aitches."
5. A god of the Patagonians, at the tip of South America, named in Richard Eden's *History of Travel,* 1577.
6. To the other characters.

The wild waves whist;[7]
Foot it featly° *here and there,* (dance nimbly)
And, sweet sprites, bear
The burden. Hark, hark!
[Burden,° dispersedly (within): *Bow-wow.*] (Refrain)
The watchdogs bark.
[Burden, dispersedly within: *Bow-wow.*]
Hark, hark! I hear
The strain of strutting chanticleer
Cry Cock-a-diddle-dow.

FERDINAND: Where should this music be? I' th' air or th' earth?
It sounds no more; and sure it waits upon
Some god o' th' island. Sitting on a bank,
Weeping again the King my father's wreck,
This music crept by me upon the waters,
Allaying both their fury and my passion° (lamentation)
With its sweet air. Thence I have followed it,
Or it hath drawn me rather. But 'tis gone.
No, it begins again.

[*Ariel's Song.*]

ARIEL: *Full fathom five thy father lies.*
Of his bones are coral made.
Those are pearls that were his eyes.
Nothing of him that doth fade
But doth suffer a sea change
Into something rich and strange.
Sea nymphs hourly ring his knell.
[Burden (within): *Ding dong.*]
Hark, now I hear them, ding dong bell.

FERDINAND: The ditty does remember° my drowned father. (allude to)
This is no mortal business, nor no sound
That the earth owes.° I hear it now above me. (owns)

PROSPERO [*to Miranda*]: The fringèd curtains of thine eye advance° (raise)
And say what thou seest yond.

MIRANDA: What is 't? A spirit?
Lord, how it looks about! Believe me, sir,
It carries a brave° form. But 'tis a spirit. (excellent)

PROSPERO: No, wench, it eats and sleeps and hath such senses
As we have, such. This gallant which thou seest
Was in the wreck; and, but he's something stained° (disfigured)
With grief, that's beauty's canker,° thou mightst call him (cankerworm)
A goodly person. He hath lost his fellows
And strays about to find 'em.

MIRANDA: I might call him
A thing divine, for nothing natural

7. Kissed the waves into silence.

I ever saw so noble.
PROSPERO [*aside*]: It goes on, I see,
As my soul prompts° it.—Spirit, fine spirit, I'll free thee *would like*
Within two days for this.
FERDINAND [*seeing Miranda*]: Most sure,° the goddess *this is certainly*
On whom these airs° attend!—Vouchsafe° my prayer *songs / grant*
May know if you remain° upon this island, *dwell*
And that you will some good instruction give
How I may bear me° here. My prime request, *conduct myself*
Which I do last pronounce, is—O you wonder![8]—
If you be maid[9] or no?
MIRANDA: No wonder, sir,
But certainly a maid.
FERDINAND: My language? Heavens!
I am the best° of them that speak this speech, *in birth*
Were I but where 'tis spoken.
PROSPERO [*coming forward*]: How? The best?
What wert thou if the King of Naples heard thee?
FERDINAND: A single[1] thing, as I am now, that wonders
To hear thee speak of Naples.° He does hear me, *King of Naples*
And that he does I weep. Myself am Naples,
Who with mine eyes, never since at ebb,° beheld *dry*
The King my father wrecked.
MIRANDA: Alack, for mercy!
FERDINAND: Yes, faith, and all his lords, the Duke of Milan
And his brave son[2] being twain.
PROSPERO [*aside*]: The Duke of Milan
And his more braver° daughter could control° thee, *splendid / refute*
If now 'twere fit to do 't. At the first sight
They have changed eyes.°—Delicate Ariel, *exchanged love looks*
I'll set thee free for this. [*To Ferdinand.*] A word, good sir.
I fear you have done yourself some wrong.° A word! *told a lie*
MIRANDA [*aside*]: Why speaks my father so ungently? This
Is the third man that e'er I saw, the first
That e'er I sighed for. Pity move my father
To be inclined my way!
FERDINAND: O, if a virgin,
And your affection not gone forth, I'll make you
The Queen of Naples.
PROSPERO: Soft, sir! One word more.
[*Aside.*] They are both in either's power's; but this swift business
I must uneasy° make, lest too light winning *difficult*
Make the prize light. [*To Ferdinand.*] One word more: I charge thee
That thou attend° me. Thou dost here usurp *listen to*
The name thou ow'st° not, and hast put thyself *ownest*

8. Miranda's name means "to be wondered at."
9. As opposed to either a goddess or a married woman.
1. Solitary, being at once King of Naples and myself; feeble.
2. Antonio's son is not mentioned elsewhere.

Upon this island as a spy, to win it
From me, the lord on 't.
FERDINAND: No, as I am a man.
MIRANDA: There's nothing ill can dwell in such a temple.
If the ill spirit have so fair a house,
Good things will strive to dwell with 't.
PROSPERO: Follow me.—
Speak not you for him; he's a traitor.—Come,
I'll manacle thy neck and feet together.
Seawater shalt thou drink; thy food shall be
The fresh-brook mussels, withered roots, and husks
Wherein the acorn cradled. Follow.
FERDINAND: No!
I will resist such entertainment° till — *treatment*
Mine enemy has more power. [*He draws, and is charmed from moving.*]
MIRANDA: O dear father,
Make not too rash° a trial° of him, for — *harsh / judgment*
He's gentle,° and not fearful.[3] — *noble*
PROSPERO: What, I say,
My foot° my tutor?—Put thy sword up, traitor, — *subordinate*
Who mak'st a show but dar'st not strike, thy conscience
Is so possessed with guilt. Come, from thy ward,° — *defensive posture*
For I can here disarm thee with this stick
And make thy weapon drop. [*He brandishes his staff.*]
MIRANDA [*trying to hinder him*]: Beseech you, father!
PROSPERO: Hence! Hang not on my garments.
MIRANDA: Sir, have pity!
I'll be his surety.° — *guarantee*
PROSPERO: Silence! One word more
Shall make me chide thee, if not hate thee. What,
An advocate for an impostor? Hush!
Thou think'st there is no more such shapes as he,
Having seen but him and Caliban. Foolish wench,
To° the most of men this is a Caliban, — *compared to*
And they to him are angels.
MIRANDA: My affections
Are then most humble; I have no ambition
To see a goodlier man.
PROSPERO [*to Ferdinand*]: Come on, obey.
Thy nerves° are in their infancy again — *sinews*
And have no vigor in them.
FERDINAND: So they are.
My spirits,° as in a dream, are all bound up. — *vital powers*
My father's loss, the weakness which I feel,
The wreck of all my friends, nor this man's threats
To whom I am subdued, are but light° to me, — *unimportant*

3. Frightening; cowardly.

Might I but through my prison once a day
Behold this maid. All corners else° o' th' earth *other regions*
Let liberty make use of; space enough
Have I in such a prison.

PROSPERO [*aside*]: It works. [*To Ferdinand.*] Come on.—
Thou hast done well, fine Ariel! [*To Ferdinand.*] Follow me.
[*To Ariel.*] Hark what thou else shalt do me.° *for me*

MIRANDA [*to Ferdinand*]: Be of comfort.
My father's of a better nature, sir,
Than he appears by speech. This is unwonted° *unusual*
Which now came from him.

PROSPERO [*to Ariel*]: Thou shalt be as free
As mountain winds; but then° exactly do *until then*
All points of my command.

ARIEL: To th' syllable.

PROSPERO [*to Ferdinand*]: Come, follow. [*To Miranda.*] Speak not for him.

[*Exeunt.*]

ACT 2

Scene 1[1]

[*Enter Alonso, Sebastian, Antonio, Gonzalo, Adrian, Francisco, and others.*]

GONZALO [*to Alonso*]: Beseech you, sir, be merry. You have cause,
So have we all, of joy, for our escape
Is much beyond our loss. Our hint° of woe *occasion*
Is common; every day some sailor's wife,
The masters of some merchant, and the merchant,[2]
Have just our theme of woe. But for the miracle,
I mean our preservation, few in millions
Can speak like us. Then wisely, good sir, weigh
Our sorrow with our comfort.

ALONSO: Prithee, peace.

SEBASTIAN [*aside to Antonio*]: He receives comfort like cold porridge.[3]

ANTONIO [*aside to Sebastian*]: The visitor[4] will not give him o'er[5] so.

SEBASTIAN: Look, he's winding up the watch of his wit; by and by it will strike.

GONZALO [*to Alonso*]: Sir—

SEBASTIAN [*aside to Antonio*]: One. Tell.° *keep count*

GONZALO: When every grief is entertained
That's offered, comes to th' entertainer—

SEBASTIAN: A dollar.[6]

GONZALO: Dolor comes to him, indeed. You have spoken truer than you purposed.

SEBASTIAN: You have taken it wiselier than I meant you should.

GONZALO [*to Alonso*]: Therefore, my lord—

1. Location: Another part of the island.
2. Officers of some merchant vessel and the owner himself.
3. Broth, with a pun on *peace* (peas), often used in porridge.
4. One taking comfort to the sick, as Gonzalo is doing.
5. Let him alone.
6. Widely circulated coin. (Sebastian puns on *entertainer* in the sense of inn-keeper; to Gonzalo, *dollar* suggests "dolor," or grief.)

ANTONIO: Fie, what a spendthrift is he of his tongue!
ALONSO [*to Gonzalo*]: I prithee, spare.° *forbear*
GONZALO: Well, I have done. But yet—
SEBASTIAN [*aside to Antonio*]: He will be talking.
ANTONIO [*aside to Sebastian*]: Which, of he or Adrian, for a good wager, first begins to crow?[7]
SEBASTIAN: The old cock.° *Gonzalo*
ANTONIO: The cockerel.° *Adrian*
SEBASTIAN: Done. The wager?
ANTONIO: A laughter.[8]
SEBASTIAN: A match!° *agreed*
ADRIAN: Though this island seem to be desert°— *uninhabited*
ANTONIO: Ha, ha, ha!
SEBASTIAN: So, you're paid.
ADRIAN: Uninhabitable and almost inaccessible—
SEBASTIAN: Yet—
ADRIAN: Yet—
ANTONIO: He could not miss 't.
ADRIAN: It must needs be of subtle, tender, and delicate temperance.° *climate*
ANTONIO: Temperance° was a delicate wench.[9] *girl's name*
SEBASTIAN: Ay, and a subtle,° as he most learnedly delivered.[1] *sexually tricky*
ADRIAN: The air breathes upon us here most sweetly.
SEBASTIAN: As if it had lungs, and rotten ones.
ANTONIO: Or as 'twere perfumed by a fen.
GONZALO: Here is everything advantageous to life.
ANTONIO: True, save° means to live. *except*
SEBASTIAN: Of that there's none, or little.
GONZALO: How lush and lusty° the grass looks! How green! *healthy*
ANTONIO: The ground indeed is tawny.° *dull brown*
SEBASTIAN: With an eye° of green in 't. *spot*
ANTONIO: He misses not much.
SEBASTIAN: No. He doth but° mistake the truth totally. *merely*
GONZALO: But the rarity of it is—which is indeed almost beyond credit—
SEBASTIAN: As many vouched rarities[2] are.
GONZALO: That our garments, being, as they were, drenched in the sea, hold notwithstanding their freshness and glosses, being rather new-dyed than stained with salt water.
ANTONIO: If but one of his pockets[3] could speak, would it not say he lies?
SEBASTIAN: Ay, or very falsely pocket up[4] his report.
GONZALO: Methinks our garments are now as fresh as when we put them on first in Afric, at the marriage of the King's fair daughter Claribel to the King of Tunis.
SEBASTIAN: 'Twas a sweet marriage, and we prosper well in our return.

7. Speak.
8. Whoever laughs, wins.
9. Antonio is mocking Adrian's Puritan phrase, *tender, and delicate temperance,* by applying it to a young woman.
1. Puritan cant for "well-phrased." (Sebastian joins Antonio in baiting the Puritans.)
2. Wonders guaranteed to be true.
3. I.e., because they are muddy.
4. Suppress.

ADRIAN: Tunis was never graced before with such a paragon to[5] their queen.
GONZALO: Not since widow Dido's[6] time.
ANTONIO [*aside to Sebastian*]: Widow? A pox o' that! How came that "widow" in? Widow Dido!
SEBASTIAN: What if he had said "widower Aeneas" too? Good Lord, how you take it!
ADRIAN [*to Gonzalo*]: "Widow Dido" said you? You make me study of that. She was of Carthage, not of Tunis.
GONZALO: This Tunis, sir, was Carthage.
ADRIAN: Carthage?
GONZALO: I assure you, Carthage.
ANTONIO: His word is more than the miraculous harp.[7]
SEBASTIAN: He hath raised the wall, and houses too.
ANTONIO: What impossible matter will he make easy next?
SEBASTIAN: I think he will carry this island home in his pocket and give it his son for an apple.
ANTONIO: And, sowing the kernels of it in the sea, bring forth more islands.
GONZALO: Ay.[8]
ANTONIO: Why, in good time.
GONZALO [*to Alonso*]: Sir, we were talking that our garments seem now as fresh as when we were at Tunis at the marriage of your daughter, who is now queen.
ANTONIO: And the rarest that e'er came there.
SEBASTIAN: Bate,° I beseech you, widow Dido. *except*
ANTONIO: O, widow Dido? Ay, widow Dido.
GONZALO: Is not, sir, my doublet as fresh as the first day I wore it? I mean, in a sort.[9]
ANTONIO: That "sort"[1] was well fished for.
GONZALO: When I wore it at your daughter's marriage.
ALONSO: You cram these words into mine ears against
The stomach of my sense.[2] Would I had never
Married° my daughter there! For, coming thence, *married off*
My son is lost and, in my rate,° she too, *estimation*
Who is so far from Italy removed
I ne'er again shall see her. O thou mine heir
Of Naples and of Milan, what strange fish
Hath made his meal on thee?
FRANCISCO: Sir, he may live.
I saw him beat the surges° under him *waves*
And ride upon their backs. He trod the water,
Whose enmity he flung aside, and breasted
The surge most swoll'n that met him. His bold head
'Bove the contentious waves he kept, and oared
Himself with his good arms in lusty stroke

5. For.
6. Queen of Carthage, deserted by Aeneas. (She was, in fact, a widow when Aeneas, a widower, met her, but Antonio may be amused at Gonzalo's prudish use of "widow" for a woman deserted by her lover.)
7. The harp of Amphion, which raised the walls of Thebes; Gonzalo has exceeded that deed by recreating ancient Carthage mistakenly on the site of modern-day Tunis.
8. This and Antonio's rejoinder have not been satisfactorily explained.
9. Comparatively.
1. Play on the idea of drawing lots, or else fishing for something to say.
2. My appetite to hear them.

To th' shore, that o'er his° wave-worn basis° bowed, *its / base*
As° stooping to relieve him. I not doubt *as if*
He came alive to land.
ALONSO: No, no, he's gone.
SEBASTIAN [*to Alonso*]: Sir, you may thank yourself for this great loss,
That° would not bless our Europe with your daughter, *you who*
But rather loose° her to an African, *release; lose*
Where she at least is banished from your eye,
Who hath cause to wet the grief on 't.
ALONSO: Prithee, peace.
SEBASTIAN: You were kneeled to and importuned otherwise
By all of us, and the fair soul herself
Weighed between loathness and obedience at
Which end o' the beam should bow.[3] We have lost your son,
I fear, forever. Milan and Naples have
More widows in them of this business' making
Than we bring men to comfort them.
The fault's your own.
ALONSO: So is the dear'st° o' the loss. *heaviest*
GONZALO: My lord Sebastian,
The truth you speak doth lack some gentleness
And time to speak it in. You rub the sore
When you should bring the plaster.° *bandage*
SEBASTIAN: Very well.
ANTONIO: And most chirurgeonly.° *like a surgeon*
GONZALO [*to Alonso*]: It is foul weather in us all, good sir,
When you are cloudy.
SEBASTIAN [*to Antonio*]: Fowl weather?
ANTONIO [*to Sebastian*]: Very foul.
GONZALO: Had I plantation[4] of this isle, my lord—
ANTONIO [*to Sebastian*]: He'd sow 't with nettle seed.
SEBASTIAN: Or docks, or mallows.[5]
GONZALO: And were the king on 't, what would I do?
SEBASTIAN: Scape° being drunk for want° of wine. *escape / only for lack*
GONZALO: I' the commonwealth I would by contraries[6]
Execute all things; for no kind of traffic° *trade*
Would I admit; no name of magistrate;
Letters° should not be known; riches, poverty, *learning*
And use of service,° none; contract, succession,° *servants / inheritance*
Bourn,° bound of land, tilth,° vineyard, none; *borders / tilled soil*
No use of metal, corn,° or wine, or oil; *grain*
No occupation; all men idle, all,
And women too, but innocent and pure;
No sovereignty—
SEBASTIAN: Yet he would be king on 't.
ANTONIO: The latter end of his commonwealth forgets the beginning.

3. Which side of the moral scale was heavier.
4. Colonization; planting.
5. Antidotes to nettle stings.
6. In contrast to custom.

GONZALO: All things in common nature should produce
Without sweat or endeavor. Treason, felony,
Sword, pike,° knife, gun, or need of any engine° *lance / weapon*
Would I not have; but nature should bring forth,
Of its own kind, all foison,° all abundance, *plenty*
To feed my innocent people.

SEBASTIAN: No marrying 'mong his subjects?

ANTONIO: None, man, all idle—whores and knaves.

GONZALO: I would with such perfection govern, sir,
T' excel the Golden Age.[7]

SEBASTIAN: 'Save° His Majesty! *God save*

ANTONIO: Long live Gonzalo!

GONZALO: And—do you mark me, sir?

ALONSO: Prithee, no more. Thou dost talk nothing to me.

GONZALO: I do well believe Your Highness, and did it to minister occasion[8] to these gentlemen, who are of such sensible[9] and nimble lungs that they always use to laugh at nothing.

ANTONIO: 'Twas you we laughed at.

GONZALO: Who in this kind of merry fooling am nothing to you; so you may continue, and laugh at nothing still.

ANTONIO: What a blow was there given!

SEBASTIAN: An[1] it had not fallen flat-long.[2]

GONZALO: You are gentlemen of brave mettle; you would lift the moon out of her sphere if she would continue in it five weeks without changing.

[*Enter Ariel* (*invisible*) *playing solemn music.*]

SEBASTIAN: We would so, and then go a-batfowling.[3]

ANTONIO: Nay, good my lord, be not angry.

GONZALO: No, I warrant you, I will not adventure my discretion[4] so weakly. Will you laugh me asleep? For I am very heavy.[5]

ANTONIO: Go sleep, and hear us.

[*All sleep except Alonso, Sebastian, and Antonio.*]

ALONSO: What, all so soon asleep? I wish mine eyes
Would, with themselves, shut up my thoughts. I find
They are inclined to do so.

SEBASTIAN: Please you, sir,
Do not omit° the heavy offer of it. *neglect*
It seldom visits sorrow; when it doth,
It is a comforter.

ANTONIO: We two, my lord,
Will guard your person while you take your rest,
And watch your safety.

7. In Hesiod, an age of innocence and abundance.
8. Provide opportunity.
9. Sensitive.
1. If.
2. Fallen flat.
3. Hunting birds at night with sticks (bats); duping a fool (Gonzalo).
4. Risk my reputation for discretion.
5. Sleepy.

ALONSO: Thank you. Wondrous heavy.

[*Alonso sleeps. Exit Ariel.*]

SEBASTIAN: What a strange drowsiness possesses them!
ANTONIO: It is the quality o' the climate.
SEBASTIAN: Why
Doth it not then our eyelids sink? I find not
Myself disposed to sleep.
ANTONIO: Nor I. My spirits are nimble.
They fell together all, as by consent;° *agreement*
They dropped, as by a thunderstroke. What might,
Worthy Sebastian, O, what might—? No more.
And yet methinks I see it in thy face,
What thou shouldst be. Th' occasion speaks° thee, and *summons*
My strong imagination sees a crown
Dropping upon thy head.
SEBASTIAN: What, art thou waking?
ANTONIO: Do you not hear me speak?
SEBASTIAN: I do, and surely
It is a sleepy language, and thou speak'st
Out of thy sleep. What is it thou didst say?
This is a strange repose, to be asleep
With eyes wide open—standing, speaking, moving—
And yet so fast asleep.
ANTONIO: Noble Sebastian,
Thou lett'st thy fortune sleep—die, rather; wink'st° *shut your eyes*
Whiles thou art waking.
SEBASTIAN: Thou dost snore distinctly;° *articulately*
There's meaning in thy snores.
ANTONIO: I am more serious than my custom. You
Must be so too if heed° me, which to do *you heed*
Trebles thee o'er.[6]
SEBASTIAN: Well, I am standing water.
ANTONIO: I'll teach you how to flow.
SEBASTIAN: Do so. To ebb
Hereditary sloth[7] instructs me.
ANTONIO: O,
If you but knew how you the purpose cherish° *enrich*
Whiles thus you mock it! How, in stripping it,
You more invest° it! Ebbing men, indeed, *clothe*
Most often do so near the bottom run
By their own fear or sloth.
SEBASTIAN: Prithee, say on:
The setting° of thine eye and cheek proclaim *expression*
A matter from thee, and a birth indeed
Which throes° thee much to yield. *pains*

6. Will make you three times as powerful.

7. Natural laziness; the position of younger son.

ANTONIO: Thus, sir:
Although this lord of weak remembrance,° this — *memory*
Who shall be of as little memory° — *as little remembered*
When he is earthed,° hath here almost persuaded— — *buried*
For he's a spirit of persuasion, only
Professes° to persuade—the King his son's alive, — *functions*
'Tis as impossible that he's undrowned
As he that sleeps here swims.
SEBASTIAN: I have no hope
That he's undrowned.
ANTONIO: O, out of that "no hope"
What great hope have you! No hope that way is
Another way so high a hope that even
Ambition cannot pierce a wink° beyond, — *glimpse*
But doubt discovery there. Will you grant with me
That Ferdinand is drowned?
SEBASTIAN: He's gone.
ANTONIO: Then tell me,
Who's the next heir of Naples?
SEBASTIAN: Claribel.
ANTONIO: She that is Queen of Tunis; she that dwells
Ten leagues beyond man's life; she that from Naples
Can have no note,° unless the sun were post°— — *news / messenger*
The Man i' the Moon's too slow—till newborn chins
Be rough and razorable; she that from° whom — *leaving*
We all were sea-swallowed, though some cast[8] again,
And by that destiny to perform an act
Whereof what's past is prologue, what to come
In yours and my discharge.° — *business*
SEBASTIAN: What stuff is this? How say you?
'Tis true my brother's daughter's Queen of Tunis,
So is she heir of Naples, twixt which regions
There is some space.
ANTONIO: A space whose every cubit° — *unit of length*
Seems to cry out, "How shall that Claribel
Measure us° back to Naples? Keep in Tunis, — *the cubits*
And let Sebastian wake." Say this were death
That now hath seized them, why, they were no worse
Than now they are. There be that can rule Naples
As well as he that sleeps, lords that can prate° — *prattle*
As amply and unnecessarily
As this Gonzalo. I myself could make
A chough° of as deep chat. O, that you bore — *jackdaw*
The mind that I do! What a sleep were this
For your advancement! Do you understand me?
SEBASTIAN: Methinks I do.

8. Thrown up; cast, as in a play.

ANTONIO: And how does your content° *desire*
Tender° your own good fortune? *regard*
SEBASTIAN: I remember
You did supplant your brother Prospero.
ANTONIO: True.
And look how well my garments sit upon me,
Much feater° than before. My brother's servants *more suitably*
Were then my fellows.° Now they are my men.° *equals / servants*
SEBASTIAN: But, for your conscience?
ANTONIO: Ay, sir, where lies that? If 'twere a kibe,° *sore on the heel*
'Twould put me to° my slipper; but I feel not *make me wear*
This deity in my bosom. Twenty consciences
That stand twixt me and Milan, candied° be they *sugared*
And melt ere they molest!° Here lies your brother, *interfere*
No better than the earth he lies upon,
If he were that which now he's like—that's dead,
Whom I, with this obedient steel, three inches of it,
Can lay to bed forever; whiles you, doing thus,
To the perpetual wink° for aye° might put *sleep / ever*
This ancient morsel, this Sir Prudence, who
Should not° upbraid our course. For all the rest, *would not be able to*
They'll take° suggestion as a cat laps milk; *respond to*
They'll tell the clock° to any business that *chime in*
We say befits the hour.
SEBASTIAN: Thy case, dear friend,
Shall be my precedent. As thou gott'st Milan,
I'll come by Naples. Draw thy sword. One stroke
Shall free thee from the tribute which thou payest,
And I the king shall love thee.
ANTONIO: Draw together;
And when I rear my hand, do you the like
To fall it° on Gonzalo. [*They draw.*] *let it fall*
SEBASTIAN: O, but one word. [*They talk apart.*]

[*Enter Ariel (invisible), with music and song.*]

ARIEL [*to Gonzalo*]: My master through his art foresees the danger
That you, his friend, are in, and sends me forth—
For else his project dies—to keep them living.

[*Sings in Gonzalo's ear.*]

While you here do snoring lie,
Open-eyed conspiracy
His time° doth take. *opportunity*
If of life you keep a care,
Shake off slumber, and beware.
Awake, awake!

ANTONIO: Then let us both be sudden.° *quick*
GONZALO [*waking*]: Now, good angels preserve the King!

[*The others wake.*]

ALONSO: Why, how now, ho, awake? Why are you drawn?
Wherefore this ghastly looking?

GONZALO: What's the matter?

SEBASTIAN: Whiles we stood here securing° your repose, *guarding*
Even now, we heard a hollow burst of bellowing
Like bulls, or rather lions. Did 't not wake you?
It struck mine ear most terribly.

ALONSO: I heard nothing.

ANTONIO: O, 'twas a din to fright a monster's ear,
To make an earthquake! Sure it was the roar
Of a whole herd of lions.

ALONSO: Heard you this, Gonzalo?

GONZALO: Upon mine honor, sir, I heard a humming,
And that a strange one too, which did awake me.
I shaked you, sir, and cried. As mine eyes opened,
I saw their weapons drawn. There was a noise,
That's verily.° 'Tis best we stand upon our guard, *true*
Or that we quit this place. Let's draw our weapons.

ALONSO: Lead off this ground, and let's make further search
For my poor son.

GONZALO: Heavens keep him from these beasts!
For he is, sure, i' th' island.

ALONSO: Lead away.

ARIEL [*aside*]: Prospero my lord shall know what I have done.
So, King, go safely on to seek thy son.

[*Exeunt (separately).*]

SCENE 2[9]

[*Enter Caliban with a burden of wood. A noise of thunder heard.*]

CALIBAN: All the infections that the sun sucks up
From bogs, fens, flats,° on Prosper fall, and make him *swamps*
By inchmeal° a disease! His spirits hear me, *inch by inch*
And yet I needs must° curse. But they'll nor° pinch, *have to / neither*
Fright me with urchin shows,° pitch me i' the mire, *hedgehog goblins*
Nor lead me, like a firebrand,[1] in the dark
Out of my way, unless he bid 'em. But
For every trifle are they set upon me,
Sometimes like apes, that mow° and chatter at me *make faces*
And after bite me; then like hedgehogs, which
Lie tumbling in my barefoot way and mount
Their pricks at my footfall. Sometimes am I
All wound with adders, who with cloven tongues

9. Location: another part of the island.
1. In the form of a will-'o-th'-wisp, a light that appears at night over marshy ground, often a metaphor for false hope.

Do hiss me into madness.

[*Enter Trinculo.*]

Lo, now, lo!
Here comes a spirit of his, and to torment me
For bringing wood in slowly. I'll fall flat.
Perchance he will not mind° me. [*He lies down.*] *notice*

TRINCULO: Here's neither bush nor shrub to bear off[2] any weather at all. And another storm brewing; I hear it sing i' the wind. Yond same black cloud, yond huge one, looks like a foul bombard[3] that would shed his[4] liquor. If it should thunder as it did before, I know not where to hide my head. Yond same cloud cannot choose but fall by pailfuls. [*Seeing Caliban.*] What have we here, a man or a fish? Dead or alive? A fish, he smells like a fish; a very ancient and fishlike smell; a kind of not-of-the-newest poor-John.[5] A strange fish! Were I in England now, as once I was, and had but this fish painted,[6] not a holiday fool there but would give a piece of silver. There would this monster make a man.[7] Any strange beast there makes a man. When they will not give a doit[8] to relieve a lame beggar, they will lay out ten to see a dead Indian. Legged like a man, and his fins like arms! Warm, o' my troth! I do now let loose my opinion, hold it no longer: this is no fish, but an islander, that hath lately suffered[9] by a thunderbolt. [*Thunder.*] Alas, the storm is come again! My best way is to creep under his gaberdine.[1] There is no other shelter hereabout. Misery acquaints a man with strange bedfellows. I will here shroud[2] till the dregs of the storm be past. [*He creeps under Caliban's garment.*]

[*Enter Stephano, singing, (a bottle in his hand).*]

STEPHANO: "I shall no more to sea, to sea,
Here shall I die ashore—"
This is a very scurvy tune to sing at a man's funeral.
Well, here's my comfort. [*Drinks.*]

[*Sings.*]

"The master, the swabber, the boatswain, and I,
The gunner and his mate,
Loved Mall, Meg, and Marian, and Margery,
But none of us cared for Kate.
For she had a tongue with a tang,
Would cry to a sailor, 'Go hang!'
She loved not the savor of tar nor of pitch,
Yet a tailor might scratch her where'er she did itch.
Then to sea, boys, and let her go hang!"

This is a scurvy tune too. But here's my comfort. [*Drinks.*]

2. Ward off.
3. Leather bottle.
4. Its.
5. Salted fish.
6. Painted on a sign outside a booth at a fair.
7. Make a man's fortune; be indistinguishible from an Englishman.
8. Small coin.
9. Died.
1. Cloak.
2. Take shelter.

CALIBAN: Do not torment me! O!

STEPHANO: What's the matter?[3] Have we devils here? Do you put tricks upon 's with savages and men of Ind,[4] ha? I have not scaped drowning to be afeard now of your four legs. For it hath been said, "As proper[5] a man as ever went on four[6] legs cannot make him give ground"; and it shall be said so again while Stephano breathes at' nostrils.

CALIBAN: This spirit torments me! O!

STEPHANO: This is some monster of the isle with four legs, who hath got, as I take it, an ague. Where the devil should he learn[7] our language? I will give him some relief, if it be but for that.[8] If I can recover[9] him and keep him tame and get to Naples with him, he's a present for any emperor that ever trod on neat's leather.[1]

CALIBAN: Do not torment me, prithee. I'll bring my wood home faster.

STEPHANO: He's in his fit now and does not talk after the wisest. He shall taste of my bottle. If he have never drunk wine afore, it will go near to remove his fit. If I can recover him and keep him tame, I will not take too much[2] for him. He shall pay for him that hath him, and that soundly.

CALIBAN: Thou dost me yet but little hurt; thou wilt anon,[3] I know it by thy trembling. Now Prosper works upon thee.

STEPHANO: Come on your ways. Open your mouth. Here is that which will give language to you, cat.[4] Open your mouth. This will shake your shaking, I can tell you, and that soundly. [*Giving Caliban a drink.*] You cannot tell who's your friend. Open your chaps[5] again.

TRINCULO: I should know that voice. It should be—but he is drowned, and these are devils. O, defend me!

STEPHANO: Four legs and two voices—a most delicate[6] monster! His forward voice now is to speak well of his friend; his backward voice is to utter foul speeches and to detract. If all the wine in my bottle will recover him, I will help[7] his ague. Come. [*Giving a drink.*] Amen! I will pour some in thy other mouth.

TRINCULO: Stephano!

STEPHANO: Doth thy other mouth call me?[8] Mercy, mercy! This is a devil, and no monster. I will leave him. I have no long spoon.[9]

TRINCULO: Stephano! If thou beest Stephano, touch me and speak to me, for I am Trinculo—be not afeard—thy good friend Trinculo.

STEPHANO: If thou beest Trinculo, come forth. I'll pull thee by the lesser legs. If any be Trinculo's legs, these are they. [*Pulling him out.*] Thou art very Trinculo indeed! How cam'st thou to be the siege[1] of this mooncalf?[2] Can he vent[3] Trinculos?

TRINCULO: I took him to be killed with a thunderstroke. But art thou not drowned, Stephano? I hope now thou art not drowned. Is the storm overblown?[4]

3. What's going on here?
4. India.
5. Handsome.
6. The expression supplies *two* legs, but Stephano thinks he sees a creature with four.
7. Could he have learned.
8. His speaking our language.
9. Restore.
1. Cowhide.
2. No price will be too much.
3. Presently.
4. Allusion to the proverb "Liquor will make a cat talk."
5. Jaws.
6. Ingenious.
7. Cure.
8. Call my name (know who I am).
9. Allusion to the proverb "He who sups with the devil must have a long spoon."
1. Excrement.
2. Monster.
3. Excrete.
4. Blown over.

I hid me under the dead mooncalf's gaberdine for fear of the storm. And art thou living, Stephano? O Stephano, two Neapolitans scaped! [*He capers with Stephano.*]

STEPHANO: Prithee, do not turn me about. My stomach is not constant.[5]

CALIBAN: These be fine things, an if[6] they be not spirits.
That's a brave[7] god, and bears celestial liquor.
I will kneel to him.

STEPHANO: How didst thou scape? How cam'st thou hither? Swear by this bottle how thou cam'st hither. I escaped upon a butt of sack[8] which the sailors heaved o'erboard—by this bottle, which I made of the bark of a tree with mine own hands since I was cast ashore.

CALIBAN [*kneeling*]: I'll swear upon that bottle to be thy true subject, for the liquor is not earthly.

STEPHANO: Here. Swear then how thou escapedst.

TRINCULO: Swum ashore, man, like a duck. I can swim like a duck, I'll be sworn.

STEPHANO: Here, kiss the book.[9] Though thou canst swim like a duck, thou art made like a goose.[1] [*Giving him a drink.*]

TRINCULO: O Stephano, hast any more of this?

STEPHANO: The whole butt, man. My cellar is in a rock by the seaside, where my wine is hid.—How now, mooncalf? How does thine ague?

CALIBAN: Hast thou not dropped from heaven?

STEPHANO: Out o' the moon, I do assure thee. I was the Man i' the Moon when time was.[2]

CALIBAN: I have seen thee in her, and I do adore thee.
My mistress showed me thee, and thy dog, and thy bush.[3]

STEPHANO: Come, swear to that. Kiss the book. I will furnish it anon with new contents. Swear. [*Giving him a drink.*]

TRINCULO: By this good light, this is a very shallow monster! I afeard of him? A very weak monster! The Man i' the Moon? A most poor credulous monster! Well drawn,[4] monster, in good sooth!

CALIBAN [*to Stephano*]: I'll show thee every fertile inch o' th' island,
And I will kiss thy foot. I prithee, be my god.

TRINCULO: By this light, a most perfidious and drunken monster! When 's god's asleep, he'll rob his bottle.

CALIBAN: I'll kiss thy foot. I'll swear myself thy subject.

STEPHANO: Come on then. Down, and swear.

[*Caliban kneels.*]

TRINCULO: I shall laugh myself to death at this puppy-headed monster. A most scurvy monster! I could find in my heart to beat him—

STEPHANO: Come, kiss.

TRINCULO: But that the poor monster's in drink.[5] An abominable monster!

CALIBAN: I'll show thee the best springs. I'll pluck thee berries.

5. Unsteady.
6. If.
7. Magnificent.
8. Barrel of Canary wine.
9. I.e., the bottle (ironic allusion to swearing on the Bible).
1. With a long neck.
2. Once upon a time.
3. The Man in the Moon was popularly imagined to have with him a dog and a thorn-bush.
4. Drawn from the bottle.
5. Drunk.

I'll fish for thee and get thee wood enough.
A plague upon the tyrant that I serve!
I'll bear him no more sticks, but follow thee,
Thou wondrous man.

TRINCULO: A most ridiculous monster, to make a wonder of a poor drunkard!

CALIBAN: I prithee, let me bring thee where crabs° grow, *crab apples*
And I with my long nails will dig thee pignuts,° *peanuts*
Show thee a jay's nest, and instruct thee how
To snare the nimble marmoset.° I'll bring thee *small monkey*
To clustering filberts, and sometimes I'll get thee
Young scamels[6] from the rock. Wilt thou go with me?

STEPHANO: I prithee now, lead the way without any more talking.—Trinculo, the King and all our company else being drowned, we will inherit[7] here.—Here, bear my bottle.—Fellow Trinculo, we'll fill him by and by[8] again.

CALIBAN [*sings drunkenly*]: Farewell, master, farewell, farewell!

TRINCULO: A howling monster; a drunken monster!

CALIBAN:
No more dams I'll make for fish,
Nor fetch in firing° *firewood*
At requiring,
Nor scrape trenchering,° nor wash dish. *wooden plates*
'Ban, 'Ban, Ca-Caliban
Has a new master. Get a new man!° *servant*

Freedom, high-day![9] High-day, freedom! Freedom, high-day, freedom!

STEPHANO: O brave monster! Lead the way. [*Exeunt.*]

ACT 3

Scene 1[1]

[*Enter Ferdinand, bearing a log.*]

FERDINAND: There be some sports are painful,° and their labor *strenuous*
Delight in them sets off.° Some kinds of baseness *compensates*
Are nobly undergone, and most poor matters° *poorest affairs*
Point to rich ends. This my mean° task *lowly*
Would be as heavy to me as odious, but° *but that*
The mistress which I serve quickens° what's dead *brings to life*
And makes my labors pleasures. O, she is
Ten times more gentle than her father's crabbed,
And he's composed of harshness. I must remove
Some thousands of these logs and pile them up,
Upon a sore injunction.° My sweet mistress *severe command*
Weeps when she sees me work and says such baseness
Had never like executor. I forget;
But these sweet thoughts do even refresh my labors,
Most busy lest[2] when I do it.

6. Unexplained, but either a shellfish or a rock-nesting bird.
7. Take possession.
8. Soon.
9. Holiday.
1. Location: Before Prospero's cell.
2. Busy, but with my mind on other things.

[*Enter Miranda; and Prospero (at a distance, unseen).*]

MIRANDA: Alas now, pray you,
Work not so hard. I would the lightning had
Burnt up those logs that you are enjoined° to pile! — *commanded*
Pray, set it down and rest you. When this burns,
'Twill weep° for having wearied you. My father — *exude resin*
Is hard at study. Pray now, rest yourself.
He's safe for these three hours.

FERDINAND: O most dear mistress,
The sun will set before I shall discharge
What I must strive to do.

MIRANDA: If you'll sit down,
I'll bear your logs the while. Pray, give me that.
I'll carry it to the pile.

FERDINAND: No, precious creature,
I had rather crack my sinews, break my back,
Than you should such dishonor undergo
While I sit lazy by.

MIRANDA: It would become me
As well as it does you; and I should do it
With much more ease, for my good will is to it,
And yours it is against.

PROSPERO [*aside*]: Poor worm, thou art infected!
This visitation[3] shows it.

MIRANDA: You look wearily.

FERDINAND: No, noble mistress, 'tis fresh morning with me
When you are by° at night. I do beseech you— — *nearby*
Chiefly that I might set it in my prayers—
What is your name?

MIRANDA: Miranda.—O my father,
I have broke your hest° to say so. — *command*

FERDINAND: Admired Miranda![4]
Indeed the top of admiration, worth
What's dearest to the world! Full many a lady
I have eyed with best regard, and many a time
The harmony of their tongues hath into bondage
Brought my too diligent° ear. For several° virtues — *attentive / different*
Have I liked several women, never any
With so full soul° but some defect in her — *so wholeheartedly*
Did quarrel with the noblest grace she owed° — *owned*
And put it to the foil.[5] But you, O you,
So perfect and so peerless, are created
Of every creature's best!

MIRANDA: I do not know
One of my sex; no woman's face remember,

3. Visit; attack of plague (in the metaphor of *infected*).
4. Her name means "to be admired or wondered at."
5. Overthrow; contrast.

Save, from my glass, mine own. Nor have I seen
More that I may call men than you, good friend,
And my dear father. How features are abroad° *elsewhere*
I am skilless° of; but, by my modesty,° *ignorant / virginity*
The jewel in my dower, I would not wish
Any companion in the world but you;
Nor can imagination form a shape,
Besides yourself, to like of.° But I prattle *care for*
Something° too wildly, and my father's precepts *somewhat*
I therein do forget.

FERDINAND: I am in my condition° *rank*
A prince, Miranda; I do think, a king—
I would,° not so!—and would no more endure *wish*
This wooden slavery than to suffer
The flesh-fly[6] blow° my mouth. Hear my soul speak: *lay eggs*
The very instant that I saw you did
My heart fly to your service, there resides
To make me slave to it, and for your sake
Am I this patient log-man.

MIRANDA: Do you love me?

FERDINAND: O heaven, O earth, bear witness to this sound,
And crown what I profess with kind event° *favorable outcome*
If I speak true! If hollowly,° invert° *falsely / turn*
What best is boded° me to mischief!° I *in store for / harm*
Beyond all limit of what else i' the world
Do love, prize, honor you.

MIRANDA [*weeping*]: I am a fool
To weep at what I am glad of.

PROSPERO [*aside*]: Fair encounter
Of two most rare affections! Heavens rain grace
On that which breeds between 'em!

FERDINAND: Wherefore weep you?

MIRANDA: At mine unworthiness, that dare not offer
What I desire to give, and much less take
What I shall die[7] to want.° But this is trifling, *lack*
And all the more it seeks to hide itself
The bigger bulk it shows. Hence, bashful cunning,° *coyness*
And prompt me, plain and holy innocence!
I am your wife, if you will marry me;
If not, I'll die your maid.[8] To be your fellow° *equal*
You may deny me, but I'll be your servant
Whether you will° or no. *desire it*

FERDINAND: My mistress, dearest,
And I thus humble ever.

MIRANDA: My husband, then?

FERDINAND: Ay, with a heart as willing

6. Insect that lays eggs in dead flesh.
7. Probably with unconscious sexual meaning.
8. Servant; virgin.

As bondage e'er of freedom.° Here's my hand. *to win freedom*

MIRANDA [*clasping his hand*]:
And mine, with my heart in 't. And now farewell
Till half an hour hence.

FERDINAND: A thousand thousand!° *farewells*

[*Exeunt (Ferdinand and Miranda, separately).*]

PROSPERO: So glad of this as they I cannot be,
Who are surprised with all; but my rejoicing
At nothing can be more. I'll to my book,
For yet ere suppertime must I perform
Much business appertaining.° *relevant*

[*Exit.*]

SCENE 2[9]

[*Enter Caliban, Stephano, and Trinculo.*]

STEPHANO: Tell not me. When the butt is out,[1] we will drink water, not a drop before. Therefore bear up and board 'em.[2] Servant monster, drink to me.

TRINCULO: Servant monster? The folly of this island! They say there's but five upon this isle. We are three of them; if th' other two be brained[3] like us, the state totters.

STEPHANO: Drink, servant monster, when I bid thee. Thy eyes are almost set[4] in thy head. [*Giving a drink.*]

TRINCULO: Where should they be set[5] else? He were a brave[6] monster indeed if they were set in his tail.

STEPHANO: My man-monster hath drowned his tongue in sack. For my part, the sea cannot drown me. I swam, ere I could recover[7] the shore, five and thirty leagues off and on. By this light, thou shalt be my lieutenant, monster, or my standard.[8]

TRINCULO: Your lieutenant, if you list;[9] he's no standard.[1]

STEPHANO: We'll not run,[2] Monsieur Monster.

TRINCULO: Nor go[3] neither, but you'll lie[4] like dogs and yet say nothing neither.

STEPHANO: Mooncalf, speak once in thy life, if thou beest a good mooncalf.

CALIBAN: How does thy honor? Let me lick thy shoe.
I'll not serve him. He is not valiant.

TRINCULO: Thou liest, most ignorant monster, I am in case[5] to jostle a constable. Why, thou debauched fish, thou, was there ever man a coward that hath drunk so much sack[6] as I today? Wilt thou tell a monstrous lie, being but half a fish and half a monster?

CALIBAN: Lo, how he mocks me! Wilt thou let him, my lord?

9. Location: Another part of the island.
1. Empty.
2. Drink up (using the language of a nautical assault).
3. Have brains.
4. Sunk, like the sun.
5. Placed.
6. Fine.
7. Reach.
8. Standard-bearer.
9. Prefer.
1. Not able to stand up.
2. Retreat; urinate.
3. Walk.
4. Tell lies; lie down; excrete.
5. Fit condition.
6. Spanish white wine.

TRINCULO: "Lord," quoth he? That a monster should be such a natural![7]

CALIBAN: Lo, lo, again! Bite him to death, I prithee.

STEPHANO: Trinculo, keep a good tongue in your head. If you prove a mutineer—the next tree![8] The poor monster's my subject, and he shall not suffer indignity.

CALIBAN: I thank my noble lord. Wilt thou be pleased
To hearken once again to the suit I made to thee?

STEPHANO: Marry, will I. Kneel and repeat it. I will stand, and so shall Trinculo.

[*Caliban kneels.*]

[*Enter Ariel, invisible.*]

CALIBAN: As I told thee before, I am subject to a tyrant,
A sorcerer, that by his cunning hath
Cheated me of the island.

ARIEL [*mimicking Trinculo*]: Thou liest.

CALIBAN: Thou liest, thou jesting monkey, thou!
I would my valiant master would destroy thee.
I do not lie.

STEPHANO: Trinculo, if you trouble him any more in 's tale, by this hand, I will supplant[9] some of your teeth.

TRINCULO: Why, I said nothing.

STEPHANO: Mum, then, and no more.—Proceed.

CALIBAN: I say by sorcery he got this isle;
From me he got it. If thy greatness will
Revenge it on him—for I know thou dar'st,
But this thing° dare not— *Trinculo*

STEPHANO: That's most certain.

CALIBAN: Thou shalt be lord of it, and I'll serve thee.

STEPHANO: How now shall this be compassed? Canst thou bring me to the party?[1]

CALIBAN: Yea, yea, my lord. I'll yield him thee asleep,
Where thou mayst knock a nail into his head.

ARIEL: Thou liest; thou canst not.

CALIBAN: What a pied ninny's° this! Thou scurvy patch!°— *motley fool / clown*
I do beseech thy greatness, give him blows
And take his bottle from him. When that's gone
He shall drink naught but brine, for I'll not show him
Where the quick freshes° are. *freshwater springs*

STEPHANO: Trinculo, run into no further danger. Interrupt the monster one word further and, by this hand, I'll turn my mercy out o' doors and make a stockfish[2] of thee.

TRINCULO: Why, what did I? I did nothing. I'll go farther off.

STEPHANO: Didst thou not say he lied?

ARIEL: Thou liest.

STEPHANO: Do I so? Take thou that. [*He beats Trinculo.*] As you like this, give me the lie[3] another time.

7. Fool; as opposed to "unnatural."
8. I.e., you'll hang.
9. Remove.
1. Person.
2. Dried cod, prepared by beating.
3. Call me a liar.

TRINCULO: I did not give the lie. Out o' your wits and hearing too? A pox o' your bottle! This can sack and drinking do. A murrain[4] on your monster, and the devil take your fingers!

CALIBAN: Ha, ha, ha!

STEPHANO: Now, forward with your tale. [*To Trinculo.*] Prithee, stand further off.

CALIBAN: Beat him enough. After a little time
I'll beat him too.

STEPHANO: Stand farther.—Come, proceed.

CALIBAN: Why, as I told thee, 'tis a custom with him
I' th' afternoon to sleep. There thou mayst brain him,
Having first seized his books; or with a log
Batter his skull, or paunch° him with a stake, *stab in the belly*
Or cut his weasand° with thy knife. Remember *windpipe*
First to possess his books, for without them
He's but a sot,° as I am, nor hath not *fool*
One spirit to command. They all do hate him
As rootedly as I. Burn but his books.
He has brave utensils°—for so he calls them— *furnishings*
Which, when he has a house, he'll deck withal.° *furnish with them*
And that most deeply to consider is
The beauty of his daughter. He himself
Calls her a nonpareil. I never saw a woman
But only Sycorax my dam and she;
But she as far surpasseth Sycorax
As great'st does least.

STEPHANO: Is it so brave° a lass? *splendid*

CALIBAN: Ay, lord. She will become° thy bed, I warrant, *suit (sexually)*
And bring thee forth brave brood.

STEPHANO: Monster, I will kill this man. His daughter and I will be king and queen—save Our Graces!—and Trinculo and thyself shall be viceroys. Dost thou like the plot, Trinculo?

TRINCULO: Excellent.

STEPHANO: Give me thy hand. I am sorry I beat thee; but, while thou liv'st, keep a good tongue in thy head.

CALIBAN: Within this half hour will he be asleep.
Wilt thou destroy him then?

STEPHANO: Ay, on mine honor.

ARIEL [*aside*]: This will I tell my master.

CALIBAN: Thou mak'st me merry; I am full of pleasure.
Let us be jocund. Will you troll the catch° *sing the song*
You taught me but whilere?° *just now*

STEPHANO: At thy request, monster, I will do reason, any reason.[5]—
Come on, Trinculo, let us sing. [*Sings.*]

"Flout° 'em and scout° 'em *scoff at / deride*
And scout 'em and flout 'em!
Thought is free."

4. Cattle disease.

5. Anything reasonable.

CALIBAN: That's not the tune.

[*Ariel plays the tune on a tabor° and pipe.*] *small drum*

STEPHANO: What is this same?

TRINCULO: This is the tune of our catch, played by the picture of Nobody.[6]

STEPHANO: If thou beest a man, show thyself in thy likeness. If thou beest a devil, take 't as thou list.[7]

TRINCULO: O, forgive me my sins!

STEPHANO: He that dies pays all debts. I defy thee. Mercy upon us!

CALIBAN: Art thou afeard?

STEPHANO: No, monster, not I.

CALIBAN: Be not afeard. The isle is full of noises,
Sounds, and sweet airs, that give delight and hurt not.
Sometimes a thousand twangling instruments
Will hum about mine ears, and sometimes voices
That, if I then had waked after long sleep,
Will make me sleep again; and then, in dreaming,
The clouds methought would open and show riches
Ready to drop upon me, that when I waked
I cried to dream again.

STEPHANO: This will prove a brave kingdom to me, where I shall have my music for nothing.

CALIBAN: When Prospero is destroyed.

STEPHANO: That shall be by and by.° I remember the story. *right away*

TRINCULO: The sound is going away. Let's follow it, and after do our work.

STEPHANO: Lead, monster; we'll follow. I would I could see this taborer! He lays it on.[8]

TRINCULO: Wilt come? I'll follow, Stephano.

[*Exeunt* (*following Ariel's music*).]

SCENE 3[9]

[*Enter Alonso, Sebastian, Antonio, Gonzalo, Adrian, Francisco, etc.*]

GONZALO: By'r lakin,[1] I can go no further, sir.
My old bones aches. Here's a maze trod indeed
Through forthrights° and meanders! By your patience, *straight paths*
I needs must rest me.

ALONSO: Old lord, I cannot blame thee,
Who am myself attached° with weariness, *seized*
To th' dulling of my spirits. Sit down and rest.
Even here I will put off my hope, and keep it
No longer for° my flatterer. He is drowned *as*
Whom thus we stray to find, and the sea mocks
Our frustrate° search on land. Well, let him go. *frustrated*

[*Alonso and Gonzalo sit.*]

6. Familiar image with head, arms, legs, but no trunk.
7. Suit yourself.
8. I.e., plays the drum vigorously.
9. Location: Another part of the island.
1. By our Ladykin (Virgin Mary).

ANTONIO [*aside to Sebastian*]: I am right glad that he's so out of hope.
Do not, for° one repulse, forgo the purpose *because of*
That you resolved t' effect.
SEBASTIAN [*to Antonio*]: The next advantage
Will we take throughly.° *thoroughly*
ANTONIO [*to Sebastian*]: Let it be tonight,
For, now they are oppressed with travel, they
Will not, nor cannot, use such vigilance
As when they are fresh.
SEBASTIAN [*to Antonio*]: I say tonight. No more.

[*Solemn and strange music; and Prospero on the top,*[2] *invisible.*]

ALONSO: What harmony is this? My good friends, hark!
GONZALO: Marvelous sweet music!

[*Enter several strange shapes, bringing in a banquet, and dance about it with gentle actions of salutations; and, inviting the King, etc., to eat, they depart.*]

ALONSO: Give us kind keepers,° heavens! What were these? *guardian angels*
SEBASTIAN: A living drollery.[3] Now I will believe
That there are unicorns; that in Arabia
There is one tree, the phoenix' throne, one phoenix
At this hour reigning there.
ANTONIO: I'll believe both;
And what does else want credit,° come to me *lack credibility*
And I'll be sworn 'tis true. Travelers ne'er did lie,
Though fools at home condemn 'em.
GONZALO: If in Naples
I should report this now, would they believe me
If I should say I saw such islanders?
For, certes,° these are people of the island, *certainly*
Who, though they are of monstrous shape, yet note,
Their manners are more gentle, kind, than of
Our human generation you shall find
Many, nay, almost any.
PROSPERO [*aside*]: Honest lord,
Thou hast said well, for some of you there present
Are worse than devils.
ALONSO: I cannot too much muse
Such shapes, such gesture, and such sound, expressing—
Although they want° the use of tongue—a kind *lack*
Of excellent dumb discourse.
PROSPERO [*aside*]: Praise in departing.[4]
FRANCISCO: They vanished strangely.
SEBASTIAN: No matter, since
They have left their viands° behind, for we have stomachs.° *food / appetites*
Will't please you taste of what is here?

2. An upper level of the theater.
3. Puppet show with live actors.
4. Save your praise for the end of the performance (proverbial).

ALONSO: Not I.
GONZALO: Faith, sir, you need not fear. When we were boys,
Who would believe that there were mountaineers
Dewlapped[5] like bulls, whose throats had hanging at 'em
Wallets° of flesh? Or that there were such men *wattles*
Whose heads stood in their breasts?[6] Which now we find
Each putter-out of five for one[7] will bring us
Good warrant of.
ALONSO: I will stand to° and feed, *take the risk*
Although my last[8]—no matter, since I feel
The best is past. Brother, my lord the Duke,
Stand to, and do as we. [*They approach the table.*]

[*Thunder and lightning. Enter Ariel, like a harpy,*[9] *claps his wings upon the table, and with a quaint*[1] *device the banquet*[2] *vanishes.*]

ARIEL: You are three men of sin, whom Destiny—
That hath to° instrument this lower world *as its*
And what is in 't—the never-surfeited sea
Hath caused to belch up you, and on this island
Where man doth not inhabit, you 'mongst men
Being most unfit to live. I have made you mad;
And even with suchlike valor men hang and drown
Their proper° selves. *own*

[*Alonso, Sebastian, and Antonio draw their swords.*]

You fools! I and my fellows
Are ministers of Fate. The elements
Of whom° your swords are tempered° may as well *which / composed*
Wound the loud winds, or with bemocked-at° stabs *scorned*
Kill the still-closing° waters, as diminish *ever-closing*
One dowl° that's in my plume. My fellow ministers *feather*
Are like° invulnerable. If you could hurt, *likewise*
Your swords are now too massy° for your strengths *massive*
And will not be uplifted. But remember—
For that's my business to you—that you three
From Milan did supplant good Prospero;
Exposed unto the sea, which hath requit° it, *avenged*
Him and his innocent child; for which foul deed
The powers, delaying, not forgetting, have
Incensed the seas and shores, yea, all the creatures,
Against your peace. Thee of thy son, Alonso,
They have bereft; and do pronounce by me
Ling'ring perdition,° worse than any death *ruin*
Can be at once, shall step by step attend

5. With folds of flesh at the neck.
6. Like the Anthropophagi described in *Othello* 1.3.146.
7. Traveler whose insurance policy guarantees five to one repayment on his return.
8. Even if this were my last meal.
9. Monster with a woman's face and breasts and a vulture's body, supposed to bring divine vengeance.
1. Ingenious.
2. The food only.

You and your ways; whose wraths to guard you from—
Which here, in this most desolate isle, else° falls — *or else*
Upon your heads—is nothing° but heart's sorrow — *there is no way*
And a clear° life ensuing. — *innocent*

[*He vanishes in thunder; then, to soft music, enter the shapes again, and dance, with mocks and mows,*[3] *and carrying out the table.*]

PROSPERO: Bravely the figure of this harpy hast thou
Performed, my Ariel; a grace it had devouring.[4]
Of my instruction hast thou nothing bated° — *omitted*
In what thou hadst to say. So,° with good life° — *similarly / acting*
And observation strange,° my meaner ministers — *close attention*
Their several kinds° have done. My high charms work, — *separate parts*
And these mine enemies are all knit up
In their distractions.° They now are in my power; — *trances*
And in these fits I leave them, while I visit
Young Ferdinand, whom they suppose is drowned,
And his and mine loved darling.

[*Exit above.*]

GONZALO: I' the name of something holy, sir, why stand you
In this strange stare?

ALONSO: O, it is monstrous, monstrous!
Methought the billows° spoke and told me of it;° — *waves / my sin*
The winds did sing it to me, and the thunder,
That deep and dreadful organ pipe, pronounced
The name of Prosper; it did bass° my trespass. — *boom*
Therefore my son i' th' ooze is bedded; and
I'll seek him deeper than e'er plummet sounded,° — *probed*
And with him there lie mudded.

[*Exit.*]

SEBASTIAN: But one fiend at a time,
I'll fight their legions o'er.° — *one by one*

ANTONIO: I'll be thy second.

[*Exeunt (Sebastian and Antonio).*]

GONZALO: All three of them are desperate. Their great guilt,
Like poison given to work a great time after,
Now 'gins to bite the spirits. I do beseech you,
That are of suppler joints, follow them swiftly
And hinder them from what this ecstasy° — *madness*
May now provoke them to.

ADRIAN: Follow, I pray you.

[*Exeunt omnes.*]

3. Grimaces and gestures.
4. Causing the banquet to disappear, with puns on "grace" as the blessing at meals and "devouring" as in "ravishing grace."

ACT 4

Scene 1[1]

[*Enter Prospero, Ferdinand, and Miranda.*]

PROSPERO: If I have too austerely punished you,
Your compensation makes amends, for I
Have given you here a third[2] of mine own life,
Or that for which I live; who once again
I tender° to thy hand. All thy vexations *offer*
Were but my trials of thy love, and thou
Hast strangely° stood the test. Here, afore heaven, *extraordinarily*
I ratify this my rich gift. O Ferdinand,
Do not smile at me that I boast her off;° *boast of her*
For thou shalt find she will outstrip all praise
And make it halt° behind her. *limp*

FERDINAND: I do believe it
Against an oracle.[3]

PROSPERO: Then, as my gift and thine own acquisition
Worthily purchased, take my daughter. But
If thou dost break her virgin-knot before
All sanctimonious° ceremonies may *sacred*
With full and holy rite be ministered,
No sweet aspersion° shall the heavens let fall *blessing*
To make this contract grow; but barren hate,
Sour-eyed disdain, and discord shall bestrew
The union of your bed with weeds[4] so loathly
That you shall hate it both. Therefore take heed,
As Hymen's lamps shall light you.[5]

FERDINAND: As I hope
For quiet days, fair issue,° and long life, *offspring*
With such love as 'tis now, the murkiest den,
The most opportune place, the strong'st suggestion° *temptation*
Our worser genius can,° shall never melt *bad angel can make*
Mine honor into lust, to take away
The edge of that day's celebration
When I shall think or Phoebus' steeds are foundered[6]
Or Night kept chained below.

PROSPERO: Fairly spoke.
Sit then and talk with her. She is thine own.

[*Ferdinand and Miranda sit and talk together.*]

What, Ariel! My industrious servant, Ariel!

[*Enter Ariel.*]

1. Location: Before Prospero's cell.
2. The other two thirds being his knowledge and his power?
3. Even if an oracle should deny it.
4. As opposed to flowers.
5. Hymen was the Greek and Roman god of marriage, whose torches burned brightly for a happy marriage and smokily for a troubled one.
6. Either the sun-god's horses are lame.

ARIEL: What would my potent master? Here I am.
PROSPERO: Thou and thy meaner fellows° your last service — *subordinates*
Did worthily perform, and I must use you
In such another trick. Go bring the rabble,
O'er whom I give thee power, here to this place.
Incite them to quick motion, for I must
Bestow upon the eyes of this young couple
Some vanity° of mine art. It is my promise, — *show*
And they expect it from me.
ARIEL: Presently?° — *now*
PROSPERO: Ay, with a twink.° — *now*
ARIEL: Before you can say "Come" and "Go,"
And breathe twice, and cry "So, so,"
Each one, tripping on his toe,
Will be here with mop and mow.° — *antics and gestures*
Do you love me, master? No?
PROSPERO: Dearly, my delicate Ariel. Do not approach
Till thou dost hear me call.
ARIEL: Well; I conceive.° — *understand*

[*Exit.*]

PROSPERO: Look thou be true;° do not give dalliance — *true to your word*
Too much the rein. The strongest oaths are straw
To the fire i' the blood. Be more abstemious,
Or else good night your vow!
FERDINAND: I warrant you, sir,
The white cold virgin snow upon my heart
Abates the ardor of my liver.[7]
PROSPERO: Well.
Now come, my Ariel! Bring a corollary,° — *surplus*
Rather than want° a spirit. Appear, and pertly!°— — *lack / briskly*
No tongue! All eyes! Be silent. [*Soft music.*]

[*Enter Iris.*[8]]

IRIS: Ceres,[9] most bounteous lady, thy rich leas° — *meadows*
Of wheat, rye, barley, vetches,° oats, and peas; — *fodder*
Thy turfy mountains, where live nibbling sheep,
And flat meads° thatched with stover,° them to keep; — *meadows / fodder*
Thy banks with pionèd and twillèd brims,[1]
Which spongy° April at thy hest° betrims — *wet / command*
To make cold nymphs chaste crowns; and thy broom groves,° — *clumps of gorse*
Whose shadow the dismissèd° bachelor loves, — *rejected*
Being lass-lorn; thy poll-clipped° vineyard; — *pruned*
And thy sea marge,° sterile and rocky hard, — *shore*
Where thou thyself dost air: the queen o' the sky,° — *Juno*

7. Supposed seat of the passions.
8. Goddess of the rainbow and Juno's messenger.
9. Goddess of fertility.
1. Dug under by the current and protected by woven layers of branches.

Whose watery arch° and messenger am I, *rainbow*
Bids thee leave these, and with her sovereign grace,

[*Juno descends* (*slowly in her car*).]

Here on this grass plot, in this very place,
To come and sport. Her peacocks[2] fly amain.° *at full speed*
Approach, rich Ceres, her to entertain.° *receive*

[*Enter Ceres.*]

CERES: Hail, many-colored messenger, that ne'er
Dost disobey the wife of Jupiter,
Who with thy saffron° wings upon my flowers *yellow*
Diffusest honeydrops, refreshing showers,
And with each end of thy blue bow° dost crown *rainbow*
My bosky° acres and my unshrubbed down, *wooded*
Rich scarf to my proud earth. Why hath thy queen
Summoned me hither to this short-grassed green?

IRIS: A contract of true love to celebrate,
And some donation freely to estate° *bestow*
On the blest lovers.

CERES: Tell me, heavenly bow,
If Venus or her son,[3] as thou dost know,
Do now attend the Queen? Since they did plot
The means that dusky Dis my daughter got,[4]
Her and her blind boy's scandaled° company *disgraceful*
I have forsworn.

IRIS: Of her society
Be not afraid. I met her deity° *her Divine Majesty*
Cutting the clouds towards Paphos,[5] and her son
Dove-drawn with her. Here thought they to have done° *placed*
Some wanton charm upon this man and maid,
Whose vows are that no bed-right shall be paid
Till Hymen's torch be lighted; but in vain.
Mars's hot minion° is returned again; *Venus*
Her waspish-headed° son has broke his arrows, *spiteful*
Swears he will shoot no more, but play with sparrows[6]
And be a boy right out.° *outright*

[*Juno alights.*]

CERES: Highest Queen of state,
Great Juno, comes; I know her by her gait.

JUNO: How does my bounteous sister?° Go with me *fellow goddess*
To bless this twain, that they may prosperous be,
And honored in their issue.° *offspring*

[*They sing.*]

2. Birds sacred to Juno, that drew her chariot.
3. Cupid, often portrayed as blind-folded.
4. Pluto (Dis), god of the underworld, kidnapped Ceres's daughter Prosperpina.
5. In Cyprus, center of Venus's cult.
6. Thought to be lustful, sparrows were sacred to Venus.

JUNO: *Honor, riches, marriage blessing,*
Long continuance, and increasing,
Hourly joys be still° upon you! — *constantly*
Juno sings her blessings on you.

CERES: *Earth's increase, foison° plenty,* — *abundance*
Barns and garners° never empty, — *granaries*
Vines with clustering bunches growing,
Plants with goodly burden bowing;
Spring come to you at the farthest
In the very end of harvest![7]
Scarcity and want shall shun you;
Ceres' blessing so is on you.

FERDINAND: This is a most majestic vision, and
Harmonious charmingly. May I be bold
To think these spirits?

PROSPERO: Spirits, which by mine art
I have from their confines called to enact
My present fancies.

FERDINAND: Let me live here ever!
So rare a wondered° father and a wife — *wonderful*
Makes this place Paradise.

[*Juno and Ceres whisper, and send Iris on employment.*]

PROSPERO: Sweet now, silence!
Juno and Ceres whisper seriously;
There's something else to do. Hush and be mute,
Or else our spell is marred.

IRIS [*calling offstage*]:
You nymphs, called naiads, of the windring° brooks, — *winding*
With your sedged° crowns and ever-harmless looks, — *made of reeds*
Leave your crisp° channels, and on this green land — *rippling*
Answer your summons; Juno does command.
Come, temperate° nymphs, and help to celebrate — *chaste*
A contract of true love. Be not too late.

[*Enter certain nymphs.*]

You sunburned sicklemen, of August° weary, — *the harvest*
Come hither from the furrow and be merry.
Make holiday; your rye-straw hats put on,
And these fresh nymphs encounter every one
In country footing.° — *dancing*

[*Enter certain reapers, properly habited. They join with the nymphs in a graceful dance, towards the end whereof Prospero starts suddenly, and speaks; after which, to a strange, hollow, and confused noise, they heavily vanish.*]

PROSPERO [*aside*]: I had forgot that foul conspiracy

7. I.e., with no winter in between.

Of the beast Caliban and his confederates
Against my life. The minute of their plot
Is almost come. [*To the Spirits.*] Well done! Avoid;° no more! *be off*
FERDINAND [*to Miranda*]: This is strange. Your father's in some passion
That works° him strongly. *affects*
MIRANDA: Never till this day
Saw I him touched with anger so distempered.
PROSPERO: You do look, my son, in a moved sort,° *troubled state*
As if you were dismayed. Be cheerful, sir.
Our revels now are ended. These our actors,
As I foretold you, were all spirits and
Are melted into air, into thin air;
And, like the baseless° fabric of this vision, *insubstantial*
The cloud-capped towers, the gorgeous palaces,
The solemn temples, the great globe itself,° *(glances at theater)*
Yea, all which it inherit,° shall dissolve, *occupy it*
And, like this insubstantial pageant faded,
Leave not a rack° behind. We are such stuff *cloud*
As dreams are made on,° and our little life *of*
Is rounded° with a sleep. Sir, I am vexed. *surrounded*
Bear with my weakness. My old brain is troubled.
Be not disturbed with my infirmity.
If you be pleased, retire into my cell
And there repose. A turn or two I'll walk
To still my beating° mind. *agitated*
FERDINAND, MIRANDA: We wish your peace.

[*Exeunt (Ferdinand and Miranda).*]

PROSPERO: Come with a thought!° I thank thee, Ariel. Come. *right now*

[*Enter Ariel.*]

ARIEL: Thy thoughts I cleave to. What's thy pleasure?
PROSPERO: Spirit,
We must prepare to meet with Caliban.
ARIEL: Ay, my commander. When I presented° Ceres, *played; introduced*
I thought to have told thee of it, but I feared
Lest I might anger thee.
PROSPERO: Say again, where didst thou leave these varlets?
ARIEL: I told you, sir, they were red-hot with drinking;
So full of valor that they smote the air
For breathing in their faces, beat the ground
For kissing of their feet; yet always bending
Towards their project. Then I beat my tabor,
At which, like unbacked° colts, they pricked their ears, *unbroken*
Advanced° their eyelids, lifted up their noses *raised*
As they smelt music. So I charmed their ears
That calflike they my lowing followed through
Toothed briers, sharp furzes, pricking gorse, and thorns,
Which entered their frail shins. At last I left them

I' the filthy-mantled° pool beyond your cell, *scummed*
There dancing up to the chins, that the foul lake
O'erstunk their feet.

PROSPERO: This was well done, my bird.
Thy shape invisible retain thou still.
The trumpery° in my house, go bring it hither, *cheap goods*
For stale° to catch these thieves. *decoy*

ARIEL: I go, I go.

[*Exit.*]

PROSPERO: A devil, a born devil, on whose nature
Nurture can never stick; on whom my pains,
Humanely taken, all, all lost, quite lost!
And as with age his body uglier grows,
So his mind cankers.° I will plague them all, *festers*
Even to roaring.

[*Enter Ariel, loaden with glistering apparel, etc.*]

Come, hang them on this line.° *lime tree*

[*(Ariel hangs up the showy finery; Prospero and Ariel remain, invisible.) Enter Caliban, Stephano, and Trinculo, all wet.*]

CALIBAN: Pray you, tread softly, that the blind mole may
Not hear a foot fall. We now are near his cell.

STEPHANO: Monster, your fairy, which you say is a harmless fairy, has done little better than played the jack[8] with us.

TRINCULO: Monster, I do smell all horse piss, at which my nose is in great indignation.

STEPHANO: So is mine. Do you hear, monster? If I should take a displeasure against you, look you—

TRINCULO: Thou wert but a lost monster.

CALIBAN: Good my lord, give me thy favor still.
Be patient, for the prize I'll bring thee to
Shall hoodwink° this mischance. Therefore speak softly. *cover over*
All's hushed as midnight yet.

TRINCULO: Ay, but to lose our bottles in the pool—

STEPHANO: There is not only disgrace and dishonor in that, monster, but an infinite loss.

TRINCULO: That's more to me than my wetting. Yet this is your harmless fairy, monster!

STEPHANO: I will fetch off my bottle, though I be o'er ears[9] for my labor.

CALIBAN: Prithee, my king, be quiet. Seest thou here,
This is the mouth o' the cell. No noise, and enter.
Do that good mischief which may make this island
Thine own forever, and I thy Caliban
For aye thy footlicker.

8. Knave; jack o' lantern, will o' th' wisp.

9. Submerged or drowned.

STEPHANO: Give me thy hand. I do begin to have bloody thoughts.

TRINCULO [*seeing the finery*]: O King Stephano! O peer![1]
O worthy Stephano! Look what a wardrobe here is for thee!

CALIBAN: Let it alone, thou fool, it is but trash.

TRINCULO: O ho, monster! We know what belongs to a frippery.[2] O King Stephano! [*He puts on a gown.*]

STEPHANO: Put off that gown, Trinculo. By this hand, I'll have that gown.

TRINCULO: Thy Grace shall have it.

CALIBAN: The dropsy[3] drown this fool! What do you mean
To dote thus on such luggage? Let 't alone
And do the murder first. If he awake,
From toe to crown he'll fill our skins with pinches,
Make us strange stuff.

STEPHANO: Be you quiet, monster.—Mistress line, is not this my jerkin?[4] [*He takes it down.*] Now is the jerkin under the line.[5] Now, jerkin, you are like to lose your hair and prove a bald jerkin.

TRINCULO: Do, do! We steal by line and level,[6] an 't like[7] your Grace.

STEPHANO: I thank thee for that jest. Here's a garment for 't. [*He gives a garment.*] Wit shall not go unrewarded while I am king of this country. "Steal by line and level" is an excellent pass of pate.[8] There's another garment for 't.

TRINCULO: Monster, come, put some lime[9] upon your fingers, and away with the rest.

CALIBAN: I will have none on 't. We shall lose our time,
And all be turned to barnacles,[1] or to apes
With foreheads villainous low.

STEPHANO: Monster, lay to[2] your fingers. Help to bear this away where my hogshead of wine is, or I'll turn you out of my kingdom. Go to, carry this.

TRINCULO: And this.

STEPHANO: Ay, and this.

[*They load Caliban with more and more garments.*]

[*A noise of hunters heard. Enter divers spirits, in shape of dogs and hounds, hunting them about, Prospero and Ariel setting them on.*]

PROSPERO: Hey, Mountain, hey!

ARIEL: Silver! There it goes, Silver!

PROSPERO: Fury, Fury! There, Tyrant, there! Hark! Hark! [*Caliban, Stephano, and Trinculo are driven out.*]
Go, charge my goblins that they grind their joints
With dry[3] convulsions, shorten up their sinews
With agèd cramps, and more pinch-spotted make them
Than pard or cat o'mountain.[4]

1. Alludes to the ballad beginning "King Stephen was a worthy peer . . ."
2. Old-clothes shop.
3. Disease in which joints fill with fluid.
4. Leather jacket.
5. Lime tree; pun on the equator, south of which sailors supposedly caught scurvy and lost their hair.
6. Methodically (pun on *line*).
7. If it please.
8. Witticism.
9. Bird-lime (sticky and good for stealing).
1. Geese.
2. Start using.
3. Aged.
4. Leopard or wildcat.

ARIEL: Hark, they roar!
PROSPERO: Let them be hunted soundly. At this hour
Lies at my mercy all mine enemies.
Shortly shall all my labors end, and thou
Shalt have the air at freedom. For a little
Follow, and do me service.

[*Exeunt.*]

ACT 5

Scene 1[1]

[*Enter Prospero in his magic robes,* (*with his staff,*) *and Ariel.*]

PROSPERO: Now does my project gather to a head.
My charms crack° not, my spirits obey, and Time — *fail*
Goes upright with his carriage.[2] How's the day?
ARIEL: On the sixth hour, at which time, my lord,
You said our work should cease.
PROSPERO: I did say so,
When first I raised the tempest. Say, my spirit,
How fares the King and 's followers?
ARIEL: Confined together
In the same fashion as you gave in charge,
Just as you left them; all prisoners, sir,
In the line grove which weather-fends° your cell. — *protects from weather*
They cannot budge till your release.° The King, — *you release them*
His brother, and yours abide all three distracted,° — *mad*
And the remainder mourning over them,
Brim full of sorrow and dismay; but chiefly
Him that you termed, sir, the good old lord, Gonzalo.
His tears runs down his beard like winter's drops
From eaves of reeds.° Your charm so strongly works 'em — *thatched roof*
That if you now beheld them your affections° — *feelings*
Would become tender.
PROSPERO: Dost thou think so, spirit?
ARIEL: Mine would, sir, were I human.
PROSPERO: And mine shall.
Hast thou, which art but air, a touch,° a feeling — *a sense*
Of their afflictions, and shall not myself,
One of their kind, that relish° all° as sharply — *feel / quite*
Passion as they, be kindlier moved than thou art?
Though with their high wrongs I am struck to the quick,
Yet with my nobler reason 'gainst my fury
Do I take part. The rarer° action is — *nobler*
In virtue than in vengeance. They being penitent,
The sole drift of my purpose doth extend
Not a frown further. Go release them, Ariel.

1. Location: Before Prospero's cell.
2. Time's burden is light.

My charms I'll break, their senses I'll restore,
And they shall be themselves.

ARIEL: I'll fetch them, sir.

[*Exit.*]

[*Prospero traces a charmed circle with his staff.*]

PROSPERO:[3] Ye elves of hills, brooks, standing lakes, and groves,
And ye that on the sands with printless foot
Do chase the ebbing Neptune, and do fly him
When he comes back; you demi-puppets° that *fairies*
By moonshine do the green sour ringlets° make, *circles in grass*
Whereof the ewe not bites; and you whose pastime
Is to make midnight mushrooms, that rejoice
To hear the solemn curfew;° by whose aid, *evening bell*
Weak masters° though ye be, I have bedimmed *forces*
The noontide sun, called forth the mutinous winds,
And twixt the green sea and the azured vault° *the sky*
Set roaring war; to the dread rattling thunder
Have I given fire, and rifted° Jove's stout oak[4] *split*
With his own bolt; the strong-based promontory
Have I made shake, and by the spurs° plucked up *roots*
The pine and cedar; graves at my command
Have waked their sleepers, oped, and let 'em forth
By my so potent art. But this rough magic
I here abjure, and when I have required° *requested*
Some heavenly music—which even now I do—
To work mine end upon their senses that[5]
This airy charm° is for, I'll break my staff, *music*
Bury it certain fathoms in the earth,
And deeper than did ever plummet sound
I'll drown my book. [*Solemn music.*]

[*Here enters Ariel before; then Alonso, with a frantic gesture, attended by Gonzalo; Sebastian and Antonio in like manner, attended by Adrian and Francisco. They all enter the circle which Prospero had made, and there stand charmed; which Prospero observing, speaks:*]

[*To Alonso.*] A solemn air,° and° the best comforter *song / which is*
To an unsettled fancy, cure thy brains,
Now useless, boiled within thy skull! [*To Sebastian and Antonio.*] There stand,
For you are spell-stopped.—
Holy Gonzalo, honorable man,
Mine eyes, e'en sociable° to the show° of thine, *sympathetic / sight*
Fall° fellowly drops. [*Aside.*] The charm dissolves apace, *let fall*
And as the morning steals upon the night,

3. This famous passage, lines 33–50, is an embellished paraphrase of Golding's translation of Ovid's *Metamorphoses* 7.197–219.

4. Tree sacred to Jove.

5. The senses of those whom.

Melting the darkness, so their rising senses
Begin to chase the ignorant fumes that mantle° *envelop*
Their clearer reason.—O good Gonzalo,
My true preserver, and a loyal sir
To him thou follow'st! I will pay thy graces° *favors*
Home° both in word and deed.—Most cruelly *fully*
Didst thou, Alonso, use me and my daughter.
Thy brother was a furtherer° in the act.— *accomplice*
Thou art pinched for 't now, Sebastian. [*To Antonio.*] Flesh and blood,
You, brother mine, that entertained ambition,
Expelled remorse° and nature,° whom, with Sebastian, *pity / natural feeling*
Whose inward pinches therefore are most strong,
Would here have killed your king, I do forgive thee,
Unnatural though thou art.—Their understanding
Begins to swell, and the approaching tide
Will shortly fill the reasonable shore° *shore of the mind*
That now lies foul and muddy. Not one of them
That yet looks on me, or would know me.—Ariel,
Fetch me the hat and rapier in my cell.

[*Ariel goes to the cell and returns immediately.*]

I will discase° me and myself present *disrobe*
As I was sometime Milan.[6] Quickly, spirit!
Thou shalt ere long be free.

[*Ariel sings and helps to attire him.*]

ARIEL: *Where the bee sucks, there suck I.*
In a cowslip's bell I lie;
There I couch° when owls do cry. *lie*
On the bat's back I do fly
After° summer merrily. *pursuing*
Merrily, merrily shall I live now
Under the blossom that hangs on the bough.

PROSPERO: Why, that's my dainty Ariel! I shall miss thee,
But yet thou shalt have freedom. So, so, so.
To the King's ship, invisible as thou art!
There shalt thou find the mariners asleep
Under the hatches. The Master and the Boatswain
Being awake, enforce them to this place,
And presently,° I prithee. *right away*

ARIEL: I drink the air° before me and return *consume space*
Or ere° your pulse twice beat. *before*

[*Exit.*]

GONZALO: All torment, trouble, wonder, and amazement
Inhabits here. Some heavenly power guide us

6. As I looked when I was Duke of Milan.

Out of this fearful° country! *frightening*
PROSPERO: Behold, sir King,
The wrongèd Duke of Milan, Prospero.
For more assurance that a living prince
Does now speak to thee, I embrace thy body;
And to thee and thy company I bid
A hearty welcome. [*Embracing him.*]
ALONSO: Whe'er thou be'st he or no,
Or some enchanted trifle° to abuse° me, *trick / deceive*
As late° I have been, I not know. Thy pulse *lately*
Beats as of flesh and blood; and, since I saw thee,
Th' affliction of my mind amends, with which
I fear a madness held me. This must crave°— *require*
An if this be° at all—a most strange story. *is happening*
Thy dukedom I resign, and do entreat
Thou pardon me my wrongs. But how should Prospero
Be living, and be here?
PROSPERO [*to Gonzalo*]: First, noble friend,
Let me embrace thine age,° whose honor cannot *yourself*
Be measured or confined. [*Embracing him.*]
GONZALO: Whether this be
Or be not, I'll not swear.
PROSPERO: You do yet taste
Some subtleties° o' th' isle, that will not let you *illusions*
Believe things certain. Welcome, my friends all!

[*Aside to Sebastian and Antonio.*]

But you, my brace° of lords, were I so minded, *pair*
I here could pluck° his Highness' frown upon you *pull down*
And justify° you traitors. At this time *prove*
I will tell no tales.
SEBASTIAN: The devil speaks in him.
PROSPERO: No.
[*To Antonio.*] For you, most wicked sir, whom to call brother
Would even infect my mouth, I do forgive
Thy rankest fault—all of them; and require
My dukedom of thee, which perforce° I know *necessarily*
Thou must restore.
ALONSO: If thou be'st Prospero,
Give us particulars of thy preservation,
How thou hast met us here, whom three hours since
Were wrecked upon this shore; where I have lost—
How sharp the point of this remembrance is!—
My dear son Ferdinand.
PROSPERO: I am woe° for 't, sir. *sorry*
ALONSO: Irreparable is the loss, and patience
Says it is past her cure.
PROSPERO: I rather think
You have not sought her help, of whose soft grace

For the like loss I have her sovereign° aid *effective*
And rest myself content.
ALONSO: You the like loss?
PROSPERO: As great to me as late,° and supportable *recent*
To make the dear° loss, have I means much weaker *grievous*
Than you may call to comfort you; for I
Have lost my daughter.
ALONSO: A daughter?
O heavens, that they were living both in Naples,
The king and queen there! That° they were, I wish *so that*
Myself were mudded° in that oozy bed *buried in mud*
Where my son lies. When did you lose your daughter?
PROSPERO: In this last tempest. I perceive these lords
At this encounter do so much admire° *wonder*
That they devour their reason° and scarce think *are open-mouthed*
Their eyes do offices° of truth, their words *perform services*
Are natural breath. But, howsoever you have
Been jostled from your senses, know for certain
That I am Prospero and that very duke
Which was thrust forth of Milan, who most strangely
Upon this shore, where you were wrecked, was landed
To be the lord on 't. No more yet of this,
For 'tis a chronicle of day by day,° *many days' telling*
Not a relation for a breakfast nor
Befitting this first meeting. Welcome, sir.
This cell's my court. Here have I few attendants,
And subjects none abroad.° Pray you, look in. *elsewhere*
My dukedom since you have given me again,
I will requite° you with as good a thing, *repay*
At least bring forth a wonder to content ye
As much as me my dukedom.

[*Here Prospero discovers° Ferdinand and Miranda, playing at chess.*] *discloses*

MIRANDA: Sweet lord, you play me false.
FERDINAND: No, my dearest love,
I would not for the world.
MIRANDA: Yes, for a score of kingdoms you should wrangle,
And I would call it fair play.[7]
ALONSO: If this prove
A vision° of the island, one dear son *illusion*
Shall I twice lose.
SEBASTIAN: A most high miracle!
FERDINAND [*approaching his father*]: Though the seas threaten, they are merciful;
I have cursed them without cause. [*He kneels.*]
ALONSO: Now all the blessings
Of a glad father compass° thee about! *encompass*
Arise, and say how thou cam'st here.

7. Miranda would still love Ferdinand, even if he did not play fair.

[*Ferdinand rises.*]

MIRANDA: O, wonder!
How many goodly creatures are there here!
How beauteous mankind is! O brave° new world *splendid*
That has such people in 't!

PROSPERO: 'Tis new to thee.

ALONSO: What is this maid with whom thou wast at play?
Your eld'st° acquaintance cannot be three hours. *longest*
Is she the goddess that hath severed us,
And brought us thus together?

FERDINAND: Sir, she is mortal;
But by immortal Providence she's mine.
I chose her when I could not ask my father
For his advice, nor thought I had one. She
Is daughter to this famous Duke of Milan,
Of whom so often I have heard renown,
But never saw before; of whom I have
Received a second life; and second father
This lady makes him to me.

ALONSO: I am hers.
But O, how oddly will it sound that I
Must ask my child forgiveness!

PROSPERO: There, sir, stop.
Let us not burden our remembrances with
A heaviness° that's gone. *sadness*

GONZALO: I have inly° wept, *inwardly*
Or should have spoke ere this. Look down, you gods,
And on this couple drop a blessèd crown!
For it is you that have chalked forth the way
Which brought us hither.

ALONSO: I say amen, Gonzalo!

GONZALO: Was Milan° thrust from Milan, that his issue *the Duke of Milan*
Should become kings of Naples? O, rejoice
Beyond a common joy, and set it down
With gold on lasting pillars: In one voyage
Did Claribel her husband find at Tunis,
And Ferdinand, her brother, found a wife
Where he himself was lost; Prospero his dukedom
In a poor isle; and all of us ourselves° *our senses*
When no man was his own.° *sane*

ALONSO [*to Ferdinand and Miranda*]: Give me your hands.
Let grief and sorrow still° embrace his heart *always*
That doth not wish you joy!

GONZALO: Be it so! Amen!

[*Enter Ariel, with the Master and Boatswain amazedly following.*]

O, look, sir, look, sir! Here is more of us.
I prophesied, if a gallows were on land,
This fellow could not drown.—Now, blasphemy,° *blasphemer*

That swear'st grace o'erboard, not an oath on shore?
Hast thou no mouth by land? What is the news?
BOATSWAIN: The best news is that we have safely found
Our King and company; the next, our ship—
Which, but three glasses° since, we gave out° split— *hours / reported*
Is tight and yare° and bravely rigged as when *shipshape*
We first put out to sea.
ARIEL [*aside to Prospero*]: Sir, all this service
Have I done since I went.
PROSPERO [*aside to Ariel*]: My tricksy° spirit! *ingenious*
ALONSO: These are not natural events; they strengthen
From strange to stranger. Say, how came you hither?
BOATSWAIN: If I did think, sir, I were well awake,
I'd strive to tell you. We were dead of sleep,
And—how we know not—all clapped under hatches,
Where but even now, with strange and several° noises *various*
Of roaring, shrieking, howling, jingling chains,
And more diversity of sounds, all horrible,
We were awaked; straightway at liberty;
Where we, in all her trim,° freshly beheld *sail*
Our royal, good, and gallant ship, our Master
Cap'ring° to eye° her. On a trice, so please you, *dancing / see*
Even in a dream, were we divided from them
And were brought moping° hither. *in a daze*
ARIEL [*aside to Prospero*]: Was't well done?
PROSPERO [*aside to Ariel*]: Bravely, my diligence. Thou shalt be free.
ALONSO: This is as strange a maze as e'er men trod,
And there is in this business more than nature
Was ever conduct° of. Some oracle *conductor*
Must rectify our knowledge.
PROSPERO: Sir, my liege,
Do not infest° your mind with beating on *bother*
The strangeness of this business. At picked° leisure, *chosen*
Which shall be shortly, single° I'll resolve° you, *privately / explain*
Which to you shall seem probable, of every° *every one of*
These happened accidents;° till when, be cheerfull *incidents*
And think of each thing well. [*Aside to Ariel.*] Come hither, spirit.
Set Caliban and his companions free.
Untie the spell. [*Exit Ariel.*] How fares my gracious sir?
There are yet missing of your company
Some few odd lads that you remember not.

[*Enter Ariel, driving in Caliban, Stephano, and Trinculo, in their stolen apparel.*]

STEPHANO: Every man shift[8] for all the rest,[9] and let no man take care for himself; for all is but fortune. Coragio,[1] bully monster,[2] coragio!

8. Provide.
9. Stephano drunkenly gets wrong the saying "Every man for himself."
1. Courage.
2. Gallant monster (ironical).

TRINCULO: If these be true spies[3] which I wear in my head, here's a goodly sight.
CALIBAN: O Setebos, these be brave° spirits indeed! *handsome*
How fine° my master is! I am afraid *well-dressed*
He will chastise me.
SEBASTIAN: Ha, ha!
What things are these, my lord Antonio?
Will money buy 'em?
ANTONIO: Very like. One of them
Is a plain fish, and no doubt marketable.
PROSPERO: Mark but the badges of these men,° my lords, *servants*
Then say if they be true.° This misshapen knave, *honest*
His mother was a witch, and one so strong
That could control the moon, make flows and ebbs,
And deal in her° command without° her power. *the moon's / beyond*
These three have robbed me, and this demidevil—
For he's a bastard° one—had plotted with them *counterfeit*
To take my life. Two of these fellows you
Must know and own.° This thing of darkness I *acknowledge*
Acknowledge mine.
CALIBAN: I shall be pinched to death.
ALONSO: Is not this Stephano, my drunken butler?
SEBASTIAN: He is drunk now. Where had he wine?
ALONSO: And Trinculo is reeling ripe.° Where should they *stumbling drunk*
Find this grand liquor that hath gilded[4] 'em?
[*To Trinculo.*] How cam'st thou in this pickle?[5]
TRINCULO: I have been in such a pickle since I saw you last that, I fear me, will never out of my bones. I shall not fear flyblowing.[6]
SEBASTIAN: Why, how now, Stephano?
STEPHANO: O, touch me not! I am not Stephano, but a cramp.
PROSPERO: You'd be king o' the isle, sirrah?[7]
STEPHANO: I should have been a sore[8] one, then.
ALONSO [*pointing to Caliban*]: This is a strange thing as e'er I looked on.
PROSPERO: He is as disproportioned in his manners
As in his shape.—Go, sirrah, to my cell.
Take with you your companions. As you look
To have my pardon, trim° it handsomely. *decorate*
CALIBAN: Ay, that I will; and I'll be wise hereafter
And seek for grace.° What a thrice-double ass *favor*
Was I to take this drunkard for a god
And worship this dull fool!
PROSPERO: Go to. Away!
ALONSO: Hence, and bestow your luggage where you found it.
SEBASTIAN: Or stole it, rather.

[*Exeunt Caliban, Stephano, and Trinculo.*]

3. Sharp eyes.
4. Intoxicated; covered with gold (suggesting horse urine).
5. Predicament; pickling brine (here, horse urine).
6. Being soiled by fly eggs (he is protected by being pickled).
7. Address to an inferior (here, a reprimand).
8. Tyrannical; sorry; aching.

PROSPERO: Sir, I invite Your Highness and your train
To my poor cell, where you shall take your rest
For this one night; which, part of it, I'll waste° *spend*
With such discourse as, I not doubt, shall make it
Go quick away: the story of my life,
And the particular accidents° gone by *events*
Since I came to this isle. And in the morn
I'll bring you to your ship, and so to Naples,
Where I have hope to see the nuptial
Of these our dear-belovèd solemnized;
And thence retire me to my Milan, where
Every third thought shall be my grave.
ALONSO: I long
To hear the story of your life, which must
Take° the ear strangely. *captivate*
PROSPERO: I'll deliver° all; *tell*
And promise you calm seas, auspicious gales,
And sail so expeditious that shall catch
Your royal fleet far off. [*Aside to Ariel.*] My Ariel, chick,
That is thy charge. Then to the elements
Be free, and fare thou well!—Please you, draw near.
[*Exeunt omnes* (*except Prospero*).]

EPILOGUE

[*Spoken by Prospero.*]

Now my charms are all o'erthrown,
And what strength I have's mine own,
Which is most faint. Now, 'tis true,
I must be here confined by you
Or sent to Naples. Let me not,
Since I have my dukedom got
And pardoned the deceiver, dwell
In this bare island by your spell,° *silence*
But release me from my bands° *bonds*
With the help of your good hands.° *applause*
Gentle breath of yours my sails
Must fill, or else my project fails,
Which was to please. Now I want° *lack*
Spirits to enforce,° art to enchant, *control*
And my ending is despair,
Unless I be relieved by prayer,° *this very speech*
Which pierces so that it assaults° *gains the attention of*
Mercy itself, and frees° all faults. *earns pardon for*
As you from crimes° would pardoned be, *sins*
Let your indulgence° set me free. *humoring; pardon*
[*Exit.*]

RESONANCE

Aimé Césaire: from *A Tempest*[1]

Characters as in Shakespeare

Two alterations: Ariel, a mulatto slave
Caliban, a black slave[2]

ACT I, SCENE 2

Prospero with Ariel and Caliban[3]

[*Enter Caliban.*]

CALIBAN: Uhuru![4]

PROSPERO: What did you say?

CALIBAN: I said, Uhuru!

PROSPERO: Back to your native language again. I've already told you, I don't like it. You could be polite, at least; a simple "hello" wouldn't kill you.

CALIBAN: Oh, I forgot. . . . But as froggy, waspish, pustular and dung-filled a "hello" as possible. May today hasten by a decade the day when all the birds of the sky and beasts of the earth will feast upon your corpse!

PROSPERO: Gracious as always, you ugly ape! How can anyone *be* so ugly?

CALIBAN: You think I'm ugly . . . well, I don't think you're handsome either. With that big hooked nose, you look just like some old vulture. [*Laughing.*] An old vulture with a scrawny neck!

PROSPERO: Since you're so fond of invective, you could at least thank me for having taught you to speak at all. You savage . . . a dumb animal, a beast I educated, trained, dragged up from the bestiality that still sticks out all over you!

CALIBAN: In the first place, that's not true. You didn't teach me a thing! Except to jabber in your own language so that I could understand your orders—chop the wood, wash the dishes, fish for food, plant vegetables, all because you're too lazy to do it yourself.[5] And as for your learning, did you ever impart any of *that* to me? No, you

1. Translated by Emile Snyder and Sanford Upson. The full title is *A Tempest Based on Shakespeare's "The Tempest": Adaptation for a Black Theatre.* Aimé Césaire was born to an impoverished black family in Martinique in 1913. Along with the Senegalese poet Léopold Senghor, he established the influential movement of "négritude," which encouraged a return to African roots and a reaction against European values. While Césaire writes in French, he often infuses his language with words of African origin and distorts original meanings and syntax. *A Tempest,* written in 1969, takes Shakespeare's late romance as a model to be subverted, although Césaire was also arguably influenced by an 1878 play entitled *Caliban* by the French intellectual Ernest Renan.

2. Césaire maintains the list of characters in Shakespeare's play, but specifies that Ariel is a mulatto (of mixed ancestry) and Caliban is black or African. The setting is unspecified; in his notes to the "Characters," Césaire suggests that the atmosphere is one of a "psychodrama" in which the actors enter "one after the other and each chooses a mask of his liking."

3. The play opens with a flashback to Prospero's exile from Milan, and a discussion of the storm produced by Prospero, with Ariel's assistance, in which the Neapolitans—portrayed by Césaire as ruthless conquerors—are tempest-tossed and in danger of death. At the beginning of Act I, Scene 2, Ariel asks Prospero to be released from having to do such work in the future, and after Prospero sternly rebukes his slave ("Ingrate!. . . . As for your freedom, you'll have it when I'm good and ready") he summons Caliban to the cave: "I've been keeping my eye on him and he's getting a little too emancipated."

4. Swahili word for freedom.

5. Césaire bases the exchange on *The Tempest,* 1.2.322–75 in which Caliban argues with both Prospero and Miranda.

took care not to. All your science and know-how you keep for yourself alone, shut up in big books like those.

PROSPERO: What would you be without me?

CALIBAN: Without you? I'd be the king, that's what I'd be, the King of the Island. The king of the island I inherited from my mother, Sycorax.

PROSPERO: There are some family trees it's better not to climb! She's a ghoul! A witch from whom—and may God be praised—death has delivered us.

CALIBAN: Dead or alive, she was my mother, and I won't deny her! Anyhow, you only think she's dead because you think the earth itself is dead. . . . It's so much simpler that way! Dead, you can walk on it, pollute it, you can tread upon it with the steps of a conqueror. I respect the earth, because I know that it is alive, and I know that Sycorax is alive. Sycorax. Mother.

> Serpent, rain, lightning.
> And I see thee everywhere!
> In the eye of the stagnant pool into which I gaze
> unflinching,
> through the rushes,
> in the gesture made by twisted root and its awaiting thrust.
> In the night, the all-seeing blinded night,
> the nostril-less all-smelling night!

. . . Often, in my dreams, she speaks to me and warns me. . . . Yesterday, even, when I was lying by the stream on my belly lapping at the muddy water, when the Beast was about to spring upon me with that huge stone in his hand. . . .

PROSPERO: If you keep on like that even your sorcery won't save you from punishment!

CALIBAN: That's right, that's right! In the beginning, he was all sweet talk: dear Caliban here, my little Caliban there! And what do you think you'd have done without me in this strange land? Ingrate! I taught you the trees, fruits, birds, the seasons, and now you don't give a damn. . . . Caliban the animal, Caliban the slave! I know that story! Once you've squeezed the juice from the orange, you toss the rind away!

PROSPERO: Oh!

CALIBAN: Do I lie? Isn't it true that you threw me out of your house and made me live in a filthy cave, a hovel, a slum, a ghetto?

PROSPERO: It's easy to say "ghetto"! It wouldn't be such a ghetto if you took the trouble to keep it clean! And there's something you forgot, which is that what forced me to get rid of you was your lust. Good God, you tried to rape my daughter!

CALIBAN: Rape! Rape! Listen, you old goat, you're the one that puts those sexy thoughts in my head. Let me tell you something: I couldn't care less about your daughter, or about your cave, for that matter. If I complain, it's on principle, because I didn't like living with you at all, as a matter of fact. Your feet stink!

PROSPERO: I did not summon you here to argue. Away with you! Back to work! Wood, water, and lots of both! I'm expecting company today.

CALIBAN: I've had just about enough. There's already a pile of wood that high. . . .

PROSPERO: Enough! Take care, Caliban! If you keep grumbling you will be thrashed. And if you don't step lively, if you try to go on strike or to sabotage things, I'll beat you. Beating is the only language you really understand. So much the worse for you: I'll speak it, loud and clear. Off with you, and hurry!

CALIBAN: All right, I'm going . . . but this is the last time. It's the last time, do you hear me? Oh . . . I forgot: I've got something important to tell you.

PROSPERO: Important? Well, out with it.

CALIBAN: It's this: I've decided I don't want to be called Caliban any longer.

PROSPERO: What kind of rot is that? I don't understand.

CALIBAN: Put it this way: I'm *telling* you that from now on I won't answer to the name Caliban.

PROSPERO: What put that notion into your head?

CALIBAN: Well, because Caliban isn't my name. It's as simple as that.

PROSPERO: It's mine, I suppose!

CALIBAN: It's the name given me by hatred, and every time it's spoken it's an insult.

PROSPERO: My, how sensitive we're getting to be! All right, suggest something else. . . . I've got to call you something. What will it be? Cannibal would suit you, but I'm sure you wouldn't like that, would you? Let's see . . . what about Hannibal?[6] That fits. And why not . . . they all seem to like historical names.

CALIBAN: Call me X.[7] That would be best. Like a man without a name. Or, to be more precise, a man whose name has been *stolen.* You talk about history . . . well, that's history, and everyone knows it! Every time you call me it reminds me of a basic fact, the fact that you've stolen everything from me, even my identity! Uhuru! [*He exits.*]

[*Enter Ariel as a sea-nymph.*]

PROSPERO: My dear Ariel, did you see how he looked at me, that glint in his eye? That's something new. Well, let me tell you, Caliban is the enemy. As for those people on the boat, I've changed my mind about them. Give them a scare, but for God's sake don't touch a hair of their heads! You'll answer to me if you do!

ARIEL: I've suffered too much myself from having had to be the agent of their sufferings not to be pleased at your mercy. You can count on me, Master.

PROSPERO: Yes, however great their crimes, if they repent you can assure them of my forgiveness. They are men of my race, and of high rank. As for me, at my age one must rise above disputes and quarrels and think about the future. I have a daughter. Alonso has a son. If they were to love each other, I would give my consent. Let Ferdinand marry Miranda, and may their marriage bring us harmony and peace. That is my plan. I wish to see it carried out. As for Caliban, does it matter what that villain plots against me? All the nobility of Italy, Naples and Milan henceforth combined, will protect my person. Go!

ARIEL: Yes, Master. Your orders will be fully carried out.

[*Ariel sings.*][8]

Sandy seashore, deep blue sky,
Surf is rising, sea birds fly
Here the lover finds delight,
Sun at noontime, moon at night.
Join hands lovers, join the dance,
Find contentment, find romance.

Sandy seashore, deep blue sky,
Cares will vanish . . . so can I . . .

6. Famous general from Carthage in North Africa and a bitter enemy of Rome in the Punic Wars.

7. A possible allusion to Malcolm X, who rejected his name Malcom Little as a relic of slavery; he converted to the Nation of Islam while in prison and was assassinated in 1965.

8. Ariel's song and Ferdinand's subsequent appearance are also from Act 1, Scene 2, of *The Tempest.*

FERDINAND: What is this music? It has led me here and now it stops. . . . No, there it is again. . . .

ARIEL [*singing*]:

Waters move, the ocean flows,
Nothing comes and nothing goes . . .
Strange days are upon us . . .

Oysters stare through pearly eyes
Heart-shaped corals gently beat
In the crystal undersea
Here the journey ends—oh see:
Waters move and ocean flows,
Nothing comes and nothing goes . . .
Strange days are upon us . . .

FERDINAND: What do I see before me? A goddess? A mortal?

MIRANDA: I know what *I'm* seeing: a flatterer. Young man, your ability to pay compliments in the situation in which you find yourself at least proves your courage. Who are you?

FERDINAND: As you see, a poor shipwrecked soul.

MIRANDA: But one of high degree!

FERDINAND: In other surroundings I might be called "Prince," "son of the King". . . . But, no, I was forgetting . . . not "Prince" but "King," alas. . . . "King" because my father has just perished in the disaster.

MIRANDA: Poor young man! Here, you'll be received with hospitality and we'll support you in your misfortune.

FERDINAND: Alas, my father. . . . Can it be that I am an unnatural son? Your pity would make the greatest of sorrows seem sweet.

MIRANDA: I hope you'll like it here with us. The island is pretty. I'll show you the beaches and the forests, I'll tell you the names of fruits and flowers, I'll introduce you to a whole world of insects, of lizards of every hue, of birds. . . . Oh, you cannot imagine! The birds! . . .

PROSPERO: That's enough, daughter! I find your chatter irritating . . . and let me assure you, it's not at all fitting. You are doing too much honor to an imposter. Young man, you are a traitor, a spy, and a woman-chaser to boot! No sooner has he escaped the perils of the sea than he's sweet-talking the first girl he meets! You won't get round me that way. Your arrival is convenient, because I need more manpower: you shall be my house servant.

FERDINAND: Seeing the young lady, more beautiful than any wood-nymph, I thought I was Ulysses on Nausicaa's isle.[9] But hearing you, Sir, I now understand my fate a little better—I see I have come ashore on the Barbary Coast and am in the hands of a cruel pirate.[1] [*Drawing his sword.*] However, a gentleman prefers death to dishonor! I shall defend my life with my freedom!

PROSPERO: Poor fool: your arm is growing weak, your knees are trembling! Traitor! I could kill you now . . . but I need help. Follow me.

9. In the *Odyssey,* Ulysses was shipwrecked on the island of the Phaiakians; naked and hungry, he appeals to Nausicaa, daughter of the king, for help.

1. The Barbary Coast is in North Africa.

ARIEL: It's no use trying to resist, young man. My master is a sorcerer: neither your passion nor your youth can prevail against him. Your best course would be to follow and obey him.

FERDINAND: Oh God! What sorcery is this? Vanquished, a captive—yet far from rebelling against my fate, I am finding my servitude sweet. Oh, I would be imprisoned for life if only heaven will grant me a glimpse of my sun each day, the face of my own sun. Farewell, Nausicaa.

[*They exit.*]

from ACT 2, SCENE 1

Caliban's cave. Caliban is singing as he works when Ariel enters. He listens to him for a moment.

CALIBAN [*singing*]:

May he who eats his corn heedless of Shango[2]
Be accursed! May Shango creep beneath
His nails and into his every pore!
Shango, Shango ho!

Forget to give him room if you dare!
He will make himself at home on your nose!

Refuse to have him under your roof at your own risk!
He'll tear off your roof and wear it as a hat!
Whoever tries to mislead Shango
Will suffer for it!
Shango, Shango ho!

* * *

from ACT 3, SCENE 5[3]

* * *

PROSPERO: Enough! Today is a day to be benevolent, and it will do no good to try to talk sense to you in the state you're in. . . . Leave us. Go sleep it off, drunkards. We raise sail tomorrow.

TRINCULO: Raise sail! But that's what we do all the time, Sire, raise things, Stephano and I . . . at least, we raise our glasses, from dawn till dusk till dawn. . . . The hard part is putting them down, decking, as you might say.

PROSPERO: Scoundrels, would that in your voyage through life you might one day put in at the harbor of Temperance and Sobriety!

ALONSO [*indicating Caliban*]: That is the strangest creature I've ever seen!

PROSPERO: And the most devilish too!

GONZALO: What's that? Devilish! You've reprimanded him, preached at him, you've given orders and made him obey, and you say he is still indomitable!

PROSPERO: Honest Gonzalo, it is as I have said.

2. Shango is a Yoruba god of thunder and war, worshipped in the Antilles, Africa, and Brazil.

3. The final scene brings to a culmination the various threads of the play, much as in *The Tempest*. As the scene opens, Ferdinand and Miranda are playing chess, and Prospero tells the entire group, assembled in his grotto, that they will all set sail for Italy on the following day; with that, he sets Ariel free.

GONZALO: Well—and forgive me, Counsellor, if I give counsel—on the basis of my long experience the only thing left is exorcism. "Begone, unclean spirit, in the name of the Father, of the Son and of the Holy Ghost." That's all there is to it!

[*Caliban bursts out laughing.*]

GONZALO: You were absolutely right! And more so than you thought. . . . He's not just a rebel, he's a hardened criminal! [*To Caliban.*] So much the worse for you, my friend. I have tried to save you. I give up. I leave you to the secular arm![4]

PROSPERO: Draw near, Caliban. What say you in your own defense? Take advantage of my good humor. Today, I feel in a forgiving mood.

CALIBAN: I'm not interested in defending myself. My only regret is that I've failed.

PROSPERO: What were you hoping for?

CALIBAN: To get back my island and regain my freedom.

PROSPERO: And what would you do all alone here on this island, haunted by the devil, tempest tossed?

CALIBAN: First of all, I'd get rid of you! I'd spew you out, all your works and pomps! Your "white" magic!

PROSPERO: That is a fairly negative program. . . .

CALIBAN: You don't understand it. . . . I say I'm going to spew you out, and that's very positive. . . .

PROSPERO: Well, the world is really upside down. . . . We've seen everything now: Caliban as a dialectician! However, in spite of everything I'm fond of you, Caliban. Come, let's make peace. We've lived together for ten years and worked side by side! Ten years count for something, after all! We've ended up by becoming compatriots!

CALIBAN: You know very well that I'm not interested in peace. I'm interested in being free! Free, you hear?

PROSPERO: It's odd . . . no matter what you do, you won't succeed in making me believe that I'm a tyrant!

CALIBAN: Understand what I say, Prospero:

For years I bowed my head
for years I took it, all of it—
your insults, your ingratitude . . .
and worst of all, more degrading than all the rest,
your condescension,
But now, it's over!
Over, do you hear?
Of course, at the moment
You're still stronger than I am.
But I don't give a damn for your power
or for your dogs or your police or your inventions!
And do you know why?
It's because I know I'll get you!
I'll impale you! And on a stake that you've
sharpened yourself!

4. Having played at being the exorcist, Gonzalo "releases" Caliban to the "state."

You'll have impaled yourself!
Prospero, you're a great magician:
you're an old hand at deception.
And you lied to me so much,
about the world, about yourself,
that you ended up by imposing on me
an image of myself:
underdeveloped, in your words, incompetent,
that's how you made me see myself!
And I loathe that image . . . and it's false!
But now I know you, you old cancer,
And I also know myself!

And I know that one day my bare fist, just that, will be enough to crush your world. The old world is falling apart!

Isn't it true? Just look. It even bores *you* to death.
And by the way . . . you have a chance to get
it over with: you can fuck off.
You can go back to Europe. But in a pig's eye you will!
I'm sure you won't leave. You make me laugh
with your "mission"!
Your "vocation"!
Your vocation is to give me shit.
And that's why you'll stay . . . just like those
guys who founded the colonies
and who now can't live anywhere else.
You're just an old colonial addict, that's what you are!

PROSPERO: Poor Caliban! You know that you're headed toward your own ruin. You're sliding toward suicide! You know I will be the stronger, and stronger all the time. I pity you!

CALIBAN: And I hate you!

PROSPERO: Beware! My generosity has its limits.

CALIBAN [*shouting*]:

Shango marches with strength
along his path, the sky!
Shango is a fire-bearer,
his arms shake the heavens
and the earth
Oh, Shango! Shango!

PROSPERO: I have uprooted the oak and raised the sea,
I have caused the mountain to tremble and have bared my chest to adversity.
With Jove I have traded thunderbolt for thunderbolt.
Better yet—from a brutish monster I have made man!
But ah! To have failed to find the path to man's heart . . .
if that be where man is.
[*To Caliban.*] Well, I hate you as well!
For it is you who have made me doubt myself for the first time.

[*To the Nobles.*] My friends, draw near. I take my leave of you . . . I shall not be going. My fate is here: I shall not run from it.

ANTONIO: What, Sire?

PROSPERO: Hear me well. I am not in any ordinary sense a master,
as this savage thinks,
but rather the conductor of a boundless score—
this isle,
summoning voices—I alone—
and mingling them at my pleasure,
arranging out of confusion
one intelligible line.
Without me, who would be able to draw music from all that?
This isle is mute without me.
My duty, thus, is here, and here I shall stay.

GONZALO: Oh day full rich in miracles!

PROSPERO: Do not be distressed. Antonio, be you the lieutenant of my goods and make use of them as procurator until that time when Ferdinand and Miranda may take effective possession of them, joining them with the Kingdom of Naples. Nothing of that which has been set for them must be postponed: let their marriage be celebrated at Naples with all royal splendor. Honest Gonzalo, I place my trust in your word. You shall stand as father to our Princess at this ceremony.

GONZALO: Count on me, Sire.

PROSPERO: Gentlemen, farewell.

[*They exit.*]

And now Caliban, it's you and me!
What I have to tell you will be brief:
Ten times, a hundred times, I've tried to save you,
above all from yourself.
But you have always answered me with wrath and venom,
like the opossum that pulls itself up by its own tail
the better to bite the hand that tears it from the darkness.
Well, my boy, I shall set aside my indulgent nature
and henceforth I will answer your violence
with violence!

[*Time passes, symbolized by the curtain's being lowered halfway and reraised. In semi-darkness Prospero appears, aged and weary. His gestures are jerky and automatic, his speech weak, toneless.*]

PROSPERO: Odd, but for some time now we seem to be overrun with opossums. Peccarys,[5] wild boar, all of the unpleasant animals! But mainly opossums. With those eyes! And the vile grin they have! It's as though the jungle was laying siege to the cave. . . . But I shall stand firm . . . I shall not let my work perish! [*Shouting.*] I shall protect civilization! [*He fires in all directions.*] They're done for! Now, this

5. A piglike, hoofed mammal with long dark bristles, found in the Americas; from the Carib word *pekira.*

way I'll be able to have some peace and calm for a while. But it's cold. Odd how the climate's changed. Cold on this island. . . . Have to think about making a fire. . . . Well, Caliban, old fellow, it's just us two now, here on the island . . . only you and me. You and me. You-me . . . me-you! What in the hell is he up to? [*Shouting.*] Caliban!

[*In the distance, above the sound of the surf and the chirping of birds, we hear snatches of Caliban's song.*]

FREEDOM HI-DAY, FREEDOM HI-DAY!!

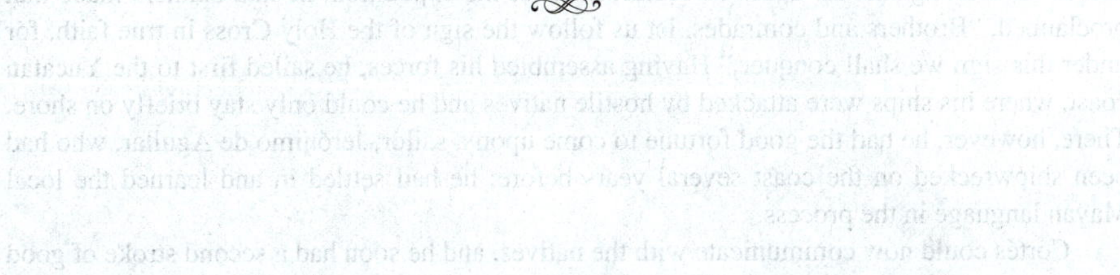

PERSPECTIVES
The Conquest and Its Aftermath

When Hernán Cortés sailed from Cuba in 1519 to invade Mexico with his little army, he went in defiance of his superior Diego Velázquez, the governor of the recently established Spanish colony at Cuba. Velázquez was well aware of the precariousness of his foothold in the area and was not yet ready to attempt a major invasion on the mainland; at most, Cortés was authorized simply to establish an outlying base colony. Any sensible person, in fact, would never have thought of doing more with so small a force, but Cortés was convinced that God would enable him to succeed against all odds. To recruit men for his expedition, he had banners made that proclaimed, "Brothers and comrades, let us follow the sign of the Holy Cross in true faith, for under this sign we shall conquer." Having assembled his forces, he sailed first to the Yucatan coast, where his ships were attacked by hostile natives and he could only stay briefly on shore. There, however, he had the good fortune to come upon a sailor, Jerónimo de Aguilar, who had been shipwrecked on the coast several years before; he had settled in and learned the local Mayan language in the process.

Cortés could now communicate with the natives, and he soon had a second stroke of good fortune: he took on board a young Mexican noblewoman who was fluent in Mayan as well as in her native Nahuatl. Now Cortés could communicate with the Aztecs, through a double process of translation: Jerónimo de Aguilar could translate from Spanish into Mayan, and she could translate from Mayan into Nahuatl. Having her baptized as Doña Maria, Cortés made her his common-law wife, interpreter, and confidante; she became known to the Indians as "La Malinche."

Cortés next made a successful landing on the gulf coast of Mexico, at a swampy site he grandly dubbed La Villa Rica de la Vera Cruz, "The Rich Town of the True Cross." Though by all rights his mission should have ended there, he burned his boats so as to keep his troops from leaving. In letters to Charles V, Cortés claimed that his men had threatened to desert the new colony, but probably he was really preventing anyone from returning to Cuba to help his great rival, Diego Velázquez, establish authority on the mainland. The ships destroyed, Cortés and some four hundred men began the march into the interior. As they made their way toward the Aztec capital of Tenochtitlán, Cortés began to hear of the natives' widespread anger against their Aztec overlords. He also soon received ambassadors from the Aztec king, Moctezuma II, who was concerned to learn whether Cortés might possibly be the returning god Quetzalcoatl, as rumored, or whether he was an impostor.

Later accounts both by Spanish historians and by native chroniclers probed the enigma of Moctezuma's shifting responses to the news of Cortés's approach, which he alternately welcomed and rebuffed. Once Cortés reached the capital, he succeeded in placing Moctezuma under house arrest, a development that fatally damaged Moctezuma's prestige among his allies. Some sources describe the Aztec king as gullibly convinced that Cortés was indeed the returning Quetzalcoatl, yet a different picture emerges from close reading of accounts such as those given here by Bernal Díaz del Castillo. Even as he appears to welcome Cortés with open arms, Moctezuma tries a variety of strategies to put him off from approaching the capital. As the historian Davíd Carrasco has argued in a book called *Quetzalcoatl and the Irony of Empire,* the Aztec ruling house had shorn up its political power by claiming to be ruling on behalf of the absent divine Toltec king. Moctezuma could hardly refuse to welcome him outright, particularly after Cortés got wind of the old legend and began to intimate that he was indeed the returned monarch, or at least his ambassador (with the Spanish king Charles V in place of Quetzalcoatl). Further, even though it soon became clear that Cortés and his rough-and-ready troops were no divinities, it appears likely that Moctezuma hoped to use the newcomers to reinforce his fragile position at home among his restive allies. He was unaware that Cortés—who protested

Cortés accepting the Aztecs' surrender, from a native chronicle called the *Lienzo de Tlaxcala,* (1550). Wearing an improbable feathered headdress, Cortés is shown with La Malinche standing behind him as translator, as he accepts the surrender of the Aztec leader Cuauhtemoc. The Tlaxcalans, who had sided with the Spanish, are shown with a Spanish soldier in the lower right. The Nahuatl caption says *Yc poliuhque mexica,* "Here perished the Mexica."

friendship and admiration for him—was actively negotiating with his neighbors to destroy his empire.

After several months of a sort of standoff in Tenochtitlán, Cortés was forced to return to the coast to defeat a Spanish force sent from Cuba to bring him to heel. He left behind his hotheaded captain Pedro de Alvarado to keep watch over Moctezuma; while Cortés was away, however, Alvarado rightly or wrongly concluded that the natives were about to rise against him, and he engineered a massacre of many of the nobility in the midst of a religious festival. The enraged Aztecs retaliated in full force. During a bloody night known as the *noche triste* ("night of sorrows"), they succeeded in driving the Spaniards from the city. As they regrouped onshore, the would-be conquistadors could see captured comrades, high on the summit of Huitzilopochtli's temple, made to dance in the war god's honor before having their hearts cut out.

Undeterred by this disaster, Cortés soon returned to the Valley of Mexico with more men, and began campaigning among the Aztecs' neighbors to make a decisive strike against the capital. Aided by a combined force of 200,000 native warriors, Cortés mounted a long siege of Tenochtitlán, whose position out in Lake Texcoco, ordinarily very secure, became a trap once the inhabitants lost control of the causeways linking the city to the mainland. Starvation began to set in, and the situation became still more grave when plague broke out in the crowded city. By August of 1521, after weeks of street-to-street fighting, Cortés had destroyed the Aztecs' capital and was master of their empire. As an anonymous account from Tlatelolco recalled in 1528,

> Broken spears lie in the roads;
> we have torn our hair in our grief.
> The houses are roofless now,
> and their walls are red with blood.
>
> . . . . . .
>
> We have pounded our hands in despair
> against the adobe walls,
> for our inheritance, our city, is lost and dead.
> The shields of our warriors were its defense,
> but they could not save it.

In his *True History of the Conquest of New Spain,* Cortés's soldier Bernal Díaz del Castillo describes with real regret the destruction of the capital and the neighboring cities, cities so magnificent that when they first saw them, he and his comrades thought they must be dreaming. "Today," he wrote in 1564, "everything is torn down, lost, so there is nothing left." He was right that much had been destroyed: palaces and temples were pulled down, their stones used to build churches; "idolatrous" native books were burned en masse; over the course of the century as much as ninety percent of the native population perished from warfare, brutal mistreatment, and imported diseases like smallpox and plague. Yet more of the culture survived than either Bernal Díaz or the Tlatelolcan chronicler believed: religious and medical practices carried on out of Spanish view or recast into Spanish forms; historical traditions preserved in native languages with the convenient technology of the Roman alphabet; poems old and new, sung in memory of past greatness and in response to present struggles. Even amid the destruction of Tenochtitlán, one post-Conquest poem says, poetry sustained the Aztec nobles as the Spaniards tortured them in search of gold:

> Yet peacefully were Motelchiuh and Tlacotzin taken away.
> They fortified themselves with song in Acachinanco
> when they went to be delivered to the fire in Coyohuacan.

PRONUNCIATIONS:

Hernán Cortés: air-NAHN core-TEZ
Malinche: mah-LEAN-chay
Moctezuma: mock-tay-ZOO-mah
Tenochtitlán: tay-nokh-tea-TLAN
Tlatelolco: tlah-tell-OLE-co

Bernal Díaz del Castillo

1492–1584

Born in the very year in which Christopher Columbus made his momentous first voyage across the Atlantic, Bernal Díaz grew up to become a soldier, adventurer, and the most vivid chronicler of the conquest of Mexico. Son of a magistrate in a provincial city in Spain, he received enough education to develop a fluent prose style and an enduring love of adventure stories and knightly romances, including the tales of Amadis of Gaul whose fictional exploits would later inspire Cervantes's hero Don Quixote. In his early twenties he sailed for the newly discovered New World, taking part in an unsuccessful quest for gold in Panama in 1514 and then attempting to establish himself in Cuba. There he signed on as a soldier serving Hernán Cortés, becoming part of the force with which Cortés invaded Mexico in 1519. After the two and a half years of struggle and hardship that culminated in the fall of Tenochtitlán, Bernal Díaz sought to achieve fame and fortune in Spain's new empire, but with only moderate success. The major political offices and land grants went to others with closer links to Cortés or with higher social standing and better connections at the royal court in Madrid.

Eventually, Bernal Díaz had to content himself with a modest position in Guatemala, where he served as a magistrate, carrying on his father's profession in a very different world. In the 1560s—irritated by an early history of the Conquest that gave credit largely to Cortés alone—Bernal Díaz decided to record his own reminiscences and set the record straight. His account didn't arouse the interest he had hoped; it remained unpublished until 1632, long after his death in Guatemala in 1584 at the age of ninety-two. As he wrote in a preface to his manuscript, "as luck would have it, I have gained nothing of value to leave to my children and descendants but this my true story, and they will presently find out what a wonderful story it is."

Writing with lively directness and with remarkably clear recall of events forty years before, Bernal Díaz didn't hesitate to reconstruct or even invent speeches, but comparison with other sources shows that he rarely seems to have misremembered events. He gives unforgettable portraits of Cortés and of Moctezuma ("Montezuma," as he calls him). He details Cortés's bold moves and shrewd negotiations while also criticizing his high-handedness and greed, and he gives us the fullest contemporary account of Doña Marina, also known as "La Malinche," the Aztec noblewoman who became Cortés's interpreter and wife. He records as well both Moctezuma's ambivalent, shifting responses and the heroic valor of the Aztec warriors in the face of the Spanish invasion. Altogether, *The True History of the Conquest of New Spain* is an unparalleled, soldier's-eye view of the Conquest, and a prime testimony to the wonder and mystery of the first European encounters with the great civilizations of Mesoamerica.

PRONUNCIATIONS:

Coyoacan: coy-oh-AH-cahn
Huexotzingo: way-shot-ZINC-go
Huichilobos: we-chill-LOW-bose
Iztapalapa: eats-tah-pah-LAH-pah
Malinche: mah-LEAN-chay
Montezuma: mon-tay-ZOU-mah
Narvaez: nar-VAH-yez
Texcoco: tesh-COH-coh
Tezcatepuca: tez-cat-eh-POU-cah
Tlaxcala: tlash-CAH-la

from The True History of the Conquest of New Spain[1]

[PREFACE]

I have observed that the most celebrated chroniclers, before they begin to write their histories, first set forth a Prologue and Preface with the argument expressed in lofty rhetoric in order to give lustre and repute to their statements, so that the studious readers who peruse them may partake of their melody and flavour. But I, being no Latin scholar, dare not venture on such a preamble or prologue, for in order properly to extol the adventures which we met with and the heroic deeds we accomplished during the Conquest of New Spain and its provinces in the company of that valiant and

1. Translated by Alfred Percival Maudslay.

doughty Captain, Don Hernando Cortés (who later on, on account of his heroic deeds, was made Marqués del Valle) there would be needed an eloquence and rhetoric far beyond my powers. That which I have myself seen and the fighting I have gone through, with the help of God, I will describe quite simply, as a fair eye witness without twisting events one way or another. I am now an old man, over eighty-four years of age, and I have lost my sight and hearing, and, as luck would have it, I have gained nothing of value to leave to my children and descendants but this my true story, and they will presently find out what a wonderful story it is.

[CORTÉS PREPARES HIS EXPEDITION]

As soon as Hernando Cortés had been appointed General he began to search for all sorts of arms, guns, powder and crossbows, and every kind of warlike stores which he could get together, and all sorts of articles to be used for barter, and other things necessary for the expedition.

Moreover he began to adorn himself and be more careful of his appearance than before, and he wore a plume of feathers with a medal, and a gold chain, and a velvet cloak trimmed with knots of gold, in fact he looked like a gallant and courageous Captain. However, he had no money to defray the expenses I have spoken about, for at that time he was very poor and much in debt, although he had a good *encomienda*[2] of Indians who were getting him a return from his gold mines, but he spent all of it on his person and on finery for his wife, whom he had recently married, and on entertaining some guests who had come to visit him. For he was affable in his manner and a good talker, and he had twice been chosen mayor of the town of Santiago Baracoa where he had settled, and in that country it is esteemed a great honour to be chosen as mayor.

When some merchant friends of his saw that he had obtained this command as Captain General, they lent him four thousand gold dollars in coin and gave him merchandise worth another four thousand dollars secured on his Indians and estates. Then he ordered two standards and banners to be made, worked in gold with the royal arms and a cross on each side with a legend which said, "Comrades, let us follow the sign of the holy Cross with true faith, and through it we shall conquer." And he ordered a proclamation to be made with the sound of drums and trumpets in the name of His Majesty and by Diego Velásquez in the King's name, and in his own as Captain General, to the effect that whatsoever person might wish to go in his company to the newly discovered lands to conquer them and to settle there, should receive his share of the gold, silver and riches which might be gained, and an *encomienda* of Indians after the country had been pacified, and that to do these things Diego Velásquez held authority from His Majesty. * * *

We continued to enlist soldiers and to buy horses, which at that time were both scarce and costly, and as Alonzo Hernándes Puertocarrero neither possessed a horse nor the wherewithal to buy one, Hernando Cortés bought him a gray mare, and paid for it with some of the golden knots off the velvet cloak which as I have said he had made at Santiago de Cuba.

[*Cortés's expedition sails along the Yucatan coast. They are driven off from some places, but find Jerónimo de Aguilar and take him on board as interpreter. They land further along the coast and fight a major battle, killing eight hundred natives. Their chiefs ("Caciques") then come to make peace.*]

2. A royal grant of peasants and land.

Early the next morning many Caciques and chiefs of Tabasco and the neighbouring towns arrived and paid great respect to us all, and they brought a present of gold, consisting of four diadems and some gold lizards, and two ornaments like little dogs, and earrings and five ducks, and two masks with Indian faces and two gold soles for sandals, and some other things of little value. I do not remember how much the things were worth; and they brought cloth, such as they make and wear, which was quilted stuff.

This present, however, was worth nothing in comparison with the twenty women that were given us, among them one very excellent woman called Doña Marina, for so she was named when she became a Christian. Cortés received this present with pleasure. * * * Cortés allotted one of the women to each of his captains and Doña Marina, as she was good looking and intelligent and without embarrassment, he gave to Alonzo Hernández Puertocarrero. When Puertocarrero went to Spain, Doña Marina lived with Cortés, and bore him a son named Don Martin Cortés. * * *

Before telling about the great Montezuma and his famous City of Mexico and the Mexicans, I wish to give some account of Doña Marina, who from her childhood had been the mistress and Cacica of towns and vassals. It happened in this way:

Her father and mother were chiefs and Caciques of a town called Paynala, which had other towns subject to it, and stood about eight leagues from the town of Coatzacoalcos.[3] Her father died while she was still a little child, and her mother married another Cacique, a young man, and bore him a son. It seems that the father and mother had a great affection for this son and it was agreed between them that he should succeed to their honours when their days were done. So that there should be no impediment to this, they gave the little girl, Doña Marina, to some Indians from Xicalango, and this they did by night so as to escape observation, and they then spread the report that she had died, and as it happened at this time that a child of one of their Indian slaves died they gave out that it was their daughter and the heiress who was dead.

The Indians of Xicalango gave the child to the people of Tabasco and the Tabasco people gave her to Cortés. I myself knew her mother, and the old woman's son and her halfbrother, when he was already grown up and ruled the town jointly with his mother, for the second husband of the old lady was dead. When they became Christians, the old lady was called Marta and the son Lázaro. I knew all this very well because in the year 1523 after the conquest of Mexico and the other provinces, when Cristóbal de Olid revolted in Honduras, and Cortés was on his way there, he passed through Coatzacoalcos and I and the greater number of the settlers of that town accompanied him on that expedition as I shall relate in the proper time and place. As Doña Marina proved herself such an excellent woman and good interpreter throughout the wars in New Spain, Tlaxcala, and Mexico (as I shall show later on) Cortés always took her with him, and during that expedition she was married to a gentleman named Juan Jaramillo at the town of Orizaba.

Doña Marina was a person of the greatest importance and was obeyed without question by the Indians throughout New Spain. * * * Doña Marina knew the language of Coatzacoalcos, which is that common to Mexico, and she knew the language of Tabasco, as did also Jerónimo de Aguilar, who spoke the language of Yucatan and Tabasco, which is one and the same. So that these two could understand one another clearly, and Aguilar translated into Castilian for Cortés.

3. A Nahuatl-speaking coastal city near the beginning of the Mayan-speaking Yucatan Peninsula.

This was the great beginning of our conquests and thus, thanks be to God, things prospered with us. I have made a point of explaining this matter, because without the help of Doña Marina we could not have understood the language of New Spain and Mexico.

* * *

During the morning, we arrived at a broad Causeway and continued our march towards Iztapalapa,[4] and when we saw so many cities and villages built in the water and other great towns on dry land and that straight and level Causeway going towards Mexico, we were amazed and said that it was like the enchantments they tell of in the legend of Amadis, on account of the great towers and cues and buildings rising from the water, and all built of masonry. And some of our soldiers even asked whether the things that we saw were not a dream. It is not to be wondered at that I here write it down in this manner, for there is so much to think over that I do not know how to describe it, seeing things as we did that had never been heard of or seen before, not even dreamed about.

Thus, we arrived near Iztapalapa, to behold the splendour of the other Caciques who came out to meet us, who were the Lord of the town named Cuitlahuac, and the Lord of Culuacan, both of them near relations of Montezuma. And then when we entered the city of Iztapalapa, the appearance of the palaces in which they lodged us! How spacious and well built they were, of beautiful stone work and cedar wood, and the wood of other sweet-scented trees, with great rooms and courts, wonderful to behold, covered with awnings of cotton cloth.

When we had looked well at all of this, we went to the orchard and garden, which was such a wonderful thing to see and walk in, that I was never tired of looking at the diversity of the trees, and noting the scent which each one had, and the paths full of roses and flowers, and the many fruit trees and native roses, and the pond of fresh water. There was another thing to observe, that great canoes were able to pass into the garden from the lake through an opening that had been made so that there was no need for their occupants to land. And all was cemented and very splendid with many kinds of stone monuments with pictures on them, which gave much to think about. Then the birds of many kinds and breeds which came into the pond. I say again that I stood looking at it and thought that never in the world would there be discovered other lands such as these, for at that time there was no Peru, nor any thought of it. Of all these wonders that I then beheld to-day all is overthrown and lost, nothing left standing.

Let us go on, and I will relate that the Caciques of that town and of Coyoacan brought us a present of gold, worth more than two thousand pesos.

Early next day we left Iztapalapa with a large escort of those great Caciques whom I have already mentioned. We proceeded along the Causeway which is here eight paces in width and runs so straight to the City of Mexico that it does not seem to me to turn either much or little, but, broad as it is, it was so crowded with people that there was hardly room for them all, some of them going to and others returning from Mexico, besides those who had come out to see us, so that we were hardly able to pass by the crowds of them that came; and the towers and cues[5] were full of people as well as the

4. City on the southern shore of Lake Texcoco; endpoint of one of the three main causeways linking Tenochtitlán to the mainland.

5. Pyramids.

canoes from all parts of the lake. It was not to be wondered at, for they had never before seen horses or men such as we are.

Gazing on such wonderful sights, we did not know what to say, or whether what appeared before us was real, for on one side, on the land, there were great cities, and in the lake ever so many more, and the lake itself was crowded with canoes, and in the Causeway were many bridges at intervals, and in front of us stood the great City of Mexico, and we—we did not even number four hundred soldiers! and we well remembered the words and warnings given us by the people of Huexotzingo and Tlaxcala, and the many other warnings that had been given that we should beware of entering Mexico, where they would kill us, as soon as they had us inside.

Let the curious readers consider whether there is not much to ponder over in this that I am writing. What men have there been in the world who have shown such daring? But let us get on, and march along the Causeway. When we arrived where another small causeway branches off (leading to Coyoacan, which is another city) where there were some buildings like towers, which are their oratories, many more chieftains and Caciques approached clad in very rich mantles, the brilliant liveries of one chieftain differing from those of another, and the causeways were crowded with them. The Great Montezuma had sent these great Caciques in advance to receive us, and when they came before Cortés they bade us welcome in their language, and as a sign of peace, they touched their hands against the ground, and kissed the ground with the hand.

There we halted for a good while, and Cacamatzin, the Lord of Texcoco, and the Lord of Iztapalapa and the Lord of Tacuba and the Lord of Coyoacan went on in advance to meet the Great Montezuma, who was approaching in a rich litter accompanied by other great Lords and Caciques, who owned vassals. When we arrived near to Mexico, where there were some other small towers, the Great Montezuma got down from his litter, and those great Caciques supported him with their arms beneath a marvellously rich canopy of green coloured feathers with much gold and silver embroidery and with pearls and chalchihuites suspended from a sort of bordering, which was wonderful to look at. The Great Montezuma was richly attired according to his usage, and he was shod with sandals, the soles were of gold and the upper part adorned with precious stones. The four Chieftains who supported his arms were also richly clothed according to their usage, in garments which were apparently held ready for them on the road to enable them to accompany their prince, for they did not appear in such attire when they came to receive us. Besides these four Chieftains, there were four other great Caciques who supported the canopy over their heads, and many other Lords who walked before the Great Montezuma, sweeping the ground where he would tread and spreading cloths on it, so that he should not tread on the earth. Not one of these Chieftains dared even to think of looking him in the face, but kept their eyes lowered with great reverence, except those four relations, his nephews, who supported him with their arms.

When Cortés was told that the Great Montezuma was approaching, and he saw him coming, he dismounted from his horse, and when he was near Montezuma, they simultaneously paid great reverence to one another. Montezuma bade him welcome and our Cortés replied through Doña Marina wishing him very good health. And it seems to me that Cortés, through Doña Marina, offered him his right hand, and Montezuma did not wish to take it, but he did give his hand to Cortés and then Cortés brought out a necklace which he had ready at hand, made of glass stones, which I have already said are called Margaritas, which have within them many patterns of diverse colours, these were strung on a cord of gold and with musk so that it should have a sweet scent, and he placed it round the neck of the Great Montezuma and when he had so placed it he was going to embrace him, and those great Princes who accompanied Montezuma held back Cortés by the arm so that he should not embrace him, for they considered it an indignity.

Then Cortés through the mouth of Doña Marina told him that now his heart rejoiced at having seen such a great Prince, and that he took it as a great honour that he had come in person to meet him and had frequently shown him such favour.

Then Montezuma spoke other words of politeness to him, and told two of his nephews who supported his arms, the Lord of Texcoco and the Lord of Coyoacan, to go with us and show us to our quarters, and Montezuma with his other two relations, the Lord of Cuitlahuac and the Lord of Tacuba who accompanied him, returned to the city, and all those grand companies of Caciques and chieftains who had come with him returned in his train. As they turned back after their Prince we stood watching them and observed how they all marched with their eyes fixed on the ground without looking at him, keeping close to the wall, following him with great reverence. Thus space was made for us to enter the streets of Mexico, without being so much crowded. But who could now count the multitude of men and women and boys who were in the streets and on the azoteas,[6] and in canoes on the canals, who had come out to see us. It was indeed wonderful, and, now that I am writing about it, it all comes before my eyes as though it had happened but yesterday. Coming to think it over it seems to be a great mercy that our Lord Jesus Christ was pleased to give us grace and courage to dare to enter into such a city; and for the many times He has saved me from danger of death, as will be seen later on, I give Him sincere thanks, and in that He has preserved me to write about it, although I cannot do it as fully as is fitting or the subject needs. Let us make no words about it, for deeds are the best witnesses to what I say here and elsewhere.

* * *

[*Hearing of a skirmish between native warriors and the men he had left behind at Vera Curz, Cortés decides to use the excuse to take Montezuma prisoner.*]

When Cortés entered, after having made his usual salutations, he said to him through our interpreters: "Señor Montezuma, I am very much astonished that you, who are such a valiant Prince, after having declared that you are our friend, should order your Captains, whom you have stationed on the coast near to Tuxpan, to take arms against my Spaniards, and that they should dare to rob the towns which are in the keeping and under the protection of our King and master and to demand of them Indian men and women for sacrifice, and should kill a Spaniard, one of my brothers, and a horse." (He did not wish to speak of the Captain nor of the six soldiers who died as soon as they arrived at Villa Rica, for Montezuma did not know about it, nor did the Indian Captains who had attacked them.) Cortés went on to say: "Being such a friend of yours I ordered my Captains to do all that was possible to help and serve you, and you have done exactly the contrary to us. Also in the affair at Cholula your Captains and a large force of warriors had received your own commands to kill us. I forgave it at the time out of my great regard for you, but now again your vassals and Captains have become insolent, and hold secret consultations stating that you wish us to be killed. I do not wish to begin a war on this account nor to destroy this city, I am

6. Roof terraces.

willing to forgive it all, if silently and without raising any disturbance you will come with us to our quarters, where you will be as well served and attended to as though you were in your own house, but if you cry out or make any disturbance you will immediately be killed by these my Captains, whom I brought solely for this purpose."

When Montezuma heard this he was terrified and dumbfounded, and replied that he had never ordered his people to take arms against us, and that he would at once send to summon his Captains so that the truth should be known, and he would chastise them, and at that very moment he took from his arm and wrist the sign and seal of Huichilobos, which was only done when he gave an important and weighty command which was to be carried out at once. With regard to being taken prisoner and leaving his Palace against his will, he said that he was not the person to whom such an order could be given, and that he would not go. Cortés replied to him with very good arguments and Montezuma answered him with even better, showing that he ought not to leave his house. In this way more than half an hour was spent over talk, and when Juan Velásquez de Leon and the other Captains saw that they were wasting time over it and could not longer await the moment when they should remove him from his house and hold him a prisoner, they spoke to Cortés somewhat angrily and said: "What is the good of your making so many words, let us either take him prisoner, or stab him, tell him once more that if he cries out or makes an uproar we will kill him, for it is better at once to save our lives or to lose them," and as Juan Velásquez said this with a loud and rather terrifying voice, for such was his way of speaking, Montezuma, who saw that our Captains were angered, asked Doña Marina what they were saying in such loud tones.

As Doña Marina was very clever, she said: "Señor Montezuma, what I counsel you is to go at once to their quarters without any disturbance at all, for I know that they will pay you much honour as a great Prince such as you are, otherwise you will remain here a dead man, but in their quarters you will learn the truth." Then Montezuma said to Cortés: "Señor Malinche, if this is what you desire, I have a son and two legitimate daughters, take them as hostages, and do not put this affront on me, what will my chieftains say if they see me taken off as a prisoner?" Cortés replied to him that he must come with them himself and there was no alternative. At the end of much more discussion that took place, Montezuma said that he would go willingly, and then Cortés and our Captains bestowed many caresses on him and told him that they begged him not to be annoyed, and to tell his captains and the men of his guard that he was going of his own free will, because he had spoken to his Idol Huichilobos and the priests who attended him, and that it was beneficial for his health and the safety of his life that he should be with us. His rich litter, in which he was used to go out with all the Captains who accompanied him, was promptly brought, and he went to our quarters where we placed guards and watchmen over him.

All the attentions and amusements which it was possible for him to have, both Cortés and all of us did our best to afford him, and he was not put under any personal restraint, and soon all the principal Mexican Chieftains and his nephews came to talk with him, and to learn the reason of his seizure, and whether he wished them to attack us. Montezuma answered them that he was delighted to be here some days with us of his own free will and not by force, and that when he wished for anything he would tell them so, and that they must not excite themselves nor the City, nor were they to take it to heart, for what had happened about his being there was agreeable to his Huichilobos, and certain priests who knew had told him so, for they had spoken to the Idol about it. In this way which I have now related the capture of the Great Montezuma was effected.

There, where he remained, he had his service and his women and his baths in which he bathed himself, and twenty great chiefs always stayed in his company holding their ancient offices, as well as his councillors and captains, and he stayed there a prisoner without showing any anger at it, and Ambassadors from distant lands came there with their suites, and brought him his tribute, and he carried on his important business.

I will not say anything more at present about this imprisonment, and will relate how the messengers whom Montezuma sent with his sign and seal to summon the Captains who had killed our soldiers, brought them before him as prisoners and what he said to them I do not know, but he sent them on to Cortés, so that he might do justice to them, and their confession was taken when Montezuma was not present and they confessed that what I have already stated was true, that their Prince had ordered them to wage war and to extract tribute, and that if any Teules should appear in defence of the towns, they too should be attacked or killed. When Cortés heard this confession he sent to inform Montezuma how it implicated him in the affair, and Montezuma made all the excuses he could, and our captain sent him word that he believed the confession himself, but that although Montezuma deserved punishment in conformity with the ordinances of our King, to the effect that any person causing others, whether guilty or innocent, to be killed, shall die for it, yet he was so fond of him and wished him so well, that even if that crime lay at his door, he, Cortés, would pay the penalty with his own life sooner than allow Montezuma's to pass away. With all this that Cortés sent to tell him, Montezuma felt anxious, and without any further discussion Cortés sentenced those captains to death and to be burned in front of Montezuma's palace. This sentence was promptly carried out, and, so that there could be no obstruction while they were being burned, Cortés ordered shackles to be put on Montezuma himself, and when this was done Montezuma roared with rage, and if before this he was scared, he was then much more so.

After the burning was over our Cortés with five of our captains went to Montezuma's apartment and Cortés himself took off the fetters, and he spoke such loving words to him that his anger soon passed off, for our Cortés told him that he not only regarded him as a brother, but much more, and that, as he was already Lord and King of so many towns and provinces, if it were possible he would make him Lord of many more countries as time went on, such as he had not been able to subdue, and which did not now obey him, and he told him that if he now wished to go to his Palace, that he would give him leave to go. Cortés told him this through our interpreters and while Cortés was saying it the tears apparently sprang to Montezuma's eyes. He answered with great courtesy, that he thanked him for it (but he well knew that Cortés' speech was mere words), and that now at present it was better for him to stay there a prisoner, for there was danger, as his chieftains were numerous, and his nephews and relations came every day to him to say that it would be a good thing to attack us and free him from prison, that as soon as they saw him outside they might drive him to it. He did not wish to see revolutions in his city, but if he did not comply with their wishes possibly they would want to set up another Prince in his place. And so he was putting those thoughts out of their heads by saying that Huichilobos had sent him word that he should remain a prisoner.

[*As Cortés solidified his position in Mexico, he sent letters and gold directly to the king in Spain, ignoring his superior, Diego Velázquez, governor of Cuba. Angered, Velázquez sent a force of four hundred men, commanded by his lieutenant Pánfilo de Narvaez, to Vera Cruz to supplant Cortés. Cortés hurried to the coast with most of his men, leaving Pedro de Alvarado and a small force to keep Montezuma under house arrest. Cortés defeated Narvaez, and enlisted most of Narvaez's men in his own service.*]

Let us return now to Narvaez and a black man whom he brought covered with smallpox, and a very black affair it was for New Spain, for it was owing to him that the whole country was stricken and filled with it, from which there was great mortality, for according to what the Indians said they had never had such a disease, and, as they did not understand it, they bathed very often, and on that account a great number of them died; so that dark as was the lot of Narvaez, still blacker was the death of so many persons who were not Christians.

Let me say how ill luck suddenly turns the wheel, and after great good fortune and pleasure follows sadness; it so happened that at this moment came the news that Mexico was in revolt, and that Pedro de Alvarado was besieged in his fortress and quarters, and that they had set fire to this same fortress in two places, and had killed seven of his soldiers and wounded many others, and he sent to demand assistance with great urgency and haste. This news was brought by two Tlaxcalans without any letter, but a letter soon arrived by two other Tlaxcalans sent by Pedro de Alvarado in which he told the same story. When we heard this bad news, God knows how greatly it depressed us.

By forced marches we began our journey to Mexico, Narvaez and Salvatierra remaining as prisoners in Villa Rica.

Just at this moment, as we were ready to start, there arrived four great chieftains sent to Cortés by the great Montezuma to complain to him of Pedro de Alvarado, and what they said, with tears streaming from their eyes, was that Pedro de Alvarado sallied out from his quarters with all the soldiers that Cortés had left with him, and, for no reason at all, fell on their chieftains and Caciques who were dancing and celebrating a feast in honour of their Idols Huichilobos and Tezcatepuca, Pedro de Alvarado having given them leave to do so. He killed and wounded many of them and in defending themselves they had killed six of his soldiers. Thus they made many complaints against Pedro de Alvarado, and Cortés, somewhat disgusted, replied to the messengers that he would go to Mexico and put it all to rights. So they went off with that reply to their great Montezuma, who it is said, resented it as a very bad one and was enraged at it.

[The Battle for the City]

Diego de Ordás set out in the way that he was ordered with his four hundred soldiers, but he had hardly reached the middle of the street along which he was to march, when so many squadrons of Mexican warriors fell on him and so many more were on the roofs of the houses, and they made such fierce attacks that on the first assault they killed eight soldiers and wounded all the rest, and Diego de Ordás himself was wounded in three places, and in this manner he could not advance one step further but had to return little by little to his quarters. During the retreat they killed another good soldier named Lyscano who, with a broadsword, had done the work of a very valiant man.

At that moment, while many squadrons came out against Ordás, many more approached our quarters and shot off so many javelins and stones from slings, and arrows, that they wounded on that occasion alone over forty-six of our men, and twelve of them died of their wounds; and such a number of warriors fell upon us that Diego de Ordás, who was coming in retreat, could not reach our quarters on account of the fierce assaults they made on him, some from the rear and others in front and others from the roofs.

Little availed our cannon, or our muskets, crossbows and lances, or the thrusts we gave them, or our good fighting, for although we killed and wounded many of them, yet they managed to reach us by pushing forward over the points of our swords and lances, and closing up their squadrons never desisted from their brave attack, nor could we push them away from us. * * *

We passed the night in dressing wounds and in mending the breaches in the walls that the enemy had made, and in getting ready for the next day. Then, as soon as it was dawn, our Captain decided that all of us and Narvaez' men should sally out to fight with them and that we should take the cannon and muskets and crossbows and endeavour to defeat them, or at least to make them feel our strength and valour better than the day before. I may state that when we came to this decision, the Mexicans were arranging the very same thing. We fought very well, but they were so strong, and had so many squadrons which relieved each other from time to time, that even if ten thousand Trojan Hectors and as many more Roldans[7] had been there, they would not have been able to break through them.

* * *

We made attacks on the Mexicans every day and succeeded in capturing many idol towers, houses, canals, and other openings and bridges which they had constructed from house to house, and we filled them all up with adobes and the timbers from the houses that we pulled down and destroyed and we kept guard over them, but notwithstanding all this trouble that we took, the enemy came back and deepened them and widened the openings and erected more barricades. * * *

I well understand that interested readers will be surfeited with seeing so many fights every day but one cannot do less, for during the ninety and three days that we besieged this strong and great City we had war and combats every day and every night as well. However, when it seemed to us that we were victorious, great disasters were really coming upon us, and we were in the greatest danger of perishing in all three camps, as will be seen later on. * * *

When we had retreated near to our quarters and had already crossed a great opening where there was much water the arrows, javelins and stones could no longer reach us. Sandoval, Francisco de Lugo and Andrés de Tápia were standing with Pedro de Alvarado each one relating what had happened to him and what Cortés had ordered, when again there was sounded the dismal drum of Huichilobos and many other shells and horns and things like trumpets and the sound of them all was terrifying, and we all looked towards the lofty Cue where they were being sounded, and saw that our comrades whom they had captured when they defeated Cortés were being carried by force up the steps, and they were taking them to be sacrificed. When they got them up to a small square in front of the oratory, where their accursed idols are kept, we saw them place plumes on the heads of many of them and with things like fans in their hands they forced them to dance before Huichilobos, and after they had danced they immediately placed them on their backs on some rather narrow stones which had been prepared as places for sacrifice, and with stone knives they sawed open their chests and drew out their palpitating hearts and offered them to the idols that were there, and they kicked the bodies down the steps, and Indian butchers who were waiting below cut off the arms and feet and flayed the skin off the faces, and prepared it afterwards like glove leather with the beards on, and kept those for the festivals when they celebrated drunken orgies, and the flesh they ate in *chilmole*.[8] In the same way they sacrificed all the others

7. Rolandor, a great hero of medieval romance.

8. Chili sauce.

and ate the legs and arms and offered the hearts and blood to their idols, as I have said, and the bodies, that is their entrails and feet, they threw to the tigers and lions which they kept in the house of the carnivores which I have spoken about in an earlier chapter.

When we saw those cruelties all of us in our camp said the one to the other: "Thank God that they are not carrying me off to-day to be sacrificed."

It should also be noted that we were not far away from them, yet we could render them no help, and could only pray God to guard us from such a death.

* * *

From all three camps we were now advancing into the City, Cortés on his side, Sandoval on his and Pedro de Alvarado on our side, and we reached the spot where the spring was, that I have already spoken about, where the Mexicans drank the brackish water, and we broke it up and destroyed it so that they might not make use of it. Some Mexicans were guarding it and we had a good skirmish with them. We could already move freely through all parts of the streets we had captured, for they were already levelled and free from water and openings and the horses could move very easily.

Thus the ten Companies of Pedro de Alvarado advanced fighting and reached Tlatelolco, and there were so many Mexicans guarding their Idols and lofty cues, and they had raised so many barricades that we were fully two hours before we were able to capture them and get inside. Now that the horses had space to gallop, although most of them were wounded, they helped us very much, and the horsemen speared many Mexicans.

[*Day after day, the Spanish penetrate further into the city, systematically levelling blocks of houses as they proceed. As they take the last districts of the city, the new ruler Cuauhtemoc ("Guatemoc") tries to flee by canoe. He is caught and brought to Cortés.*]

While they were bringing him, Cortés ordered a guest chamber to be prepared as well as could be done at the time, with mats and cloths and seats, and a good supply of the food which Cortés had reserved for himself. Sandoval and Holguin soon arrived with Guatemoc, and the two captains between them led him up to Cortés, and when he came in front of him he paid him great respect, and Cortés embraced Guatemoc with delight, and was very affectionate to him and his captains. Then Guatemoc said to Cortés: "Señor Malinche, I have surely done my duty in defence of my City, and I can do no more and I come by force and a prisoner into your presence and into your power. Take that dagger that you have in your belt and kill me at once with it," and when he said this he wept tears and sobbed and other great Lords whom he had brought with him also wept. Cortés answered him through Doña Marina and Aguilar very affectionately, that he esteemed him all the more for having been so brave as to defend the City, and he was deserving of no blame, on the contrary it was more in his favour than otherwise.

What he wished was that Guatemoc had made peace of his own free will before the city had been so far destroyed, and so many of his Mexicans had died, but now that both had happened there was no help for it and it could not be mended, let his spirit and the spirit of his Captains take rest, and he should rule in Mexico and over his provinces as he did before. Then Guatemoc and his Captains said that they accepted his favour, and Cortés asked after his wife and other great ladies, the wives of other Captains who, he had been told, had come with Guatemoc. Guatemoc himself answered and said that he had begged Gonzalo de Sandoval and García Holguin that they might remain in the canoes while he came to see what orders Malinche gave them. Cortés at once sent for them and ordered them all to be given of the best that at that time there was in the camp to eat, and as it was late and was beginning to rain, Cortés arranged for them to go to Coyoacan, and took Guatemoc and all his family and household and many chieftains with him, and he ordered Pedro de Alvarado, Gonzalo de Sandoval and the other captains each to go to his own quarters and camp, and we went to Tacuba, Sandoval to Tepeaquilla and Cortés to Coyoacan. Guatemoc and his captains were captured on the thirteenth day of August at the time of vespers on the day of Señor San Hipólito in the year one thousand five hundred and twenty-one, thanks to our Lord Jesus Christ and our Lady the Virgin Santa Maria, His Blessed Mother. Amen.

The Aztec-Spanish Dialogues of 1524

Following the military conquest of Mexico, it soon became clear that the spiritual conquest of the population was going to involve a much longer struggle. In 1524 the Pope authorized the Spanish emperor Charles V to send a select band of "twelve Apostles" to Mexico to oversee this process. Not long after their arrival, the twelve staged a public disputation with a group of Aztec priests and nobles; this extraordinary text is the result of those debates. Over several days, the Spanish friars and the Aztec spokesmen took turns in making the case for and against conversion. Hoping for a decisive and exemplary success, the friars arranged for extensive notes to be taken in Nahuatl, to provide a written record that could be used to persuade groups elsewhere. Forty years later, the tireless Bernardino de Sahagún organized the transcript and enlisted the aid of several of his native seminarians and four native elders "to transcribe it into suitably polished Nahuatl," as he wrote in a preface to the compilation. This revised manuscript was never published, perhaps because it proved to give such eloquent expression to the Aztec priests' reasons for remaining loyal to their gods even after their spectacular defeat by the Europeans. Preserved in secret archives at the Vatican and long forgotten, it was rediscovered and published only in 1924.

According to a Spanish summary that Sahagún wrote at the beginning of the manuscript, the dialogues did conclude with the conversion of the native speakers, but the second half of the manuscript has been lost. In the fourteen surviving chapters, the friars argue that the native gods are really devils who have rightly been overthrown by God, while the native elders defend their loyalty to the gods who have sustained their culture over many centuries. Jorge Klor de Alva's sensitive translation divides the elevated rhetoric of the speeches into units of sense, approximating the effect that oral delivery might have had, as the Aztec nobles attempt to negotiate a space for traditional beliefs and values in a radically changed world.

from The Aztec-Spanish Dialogues of 1524[1]

[THE FRIARS' OPENING SPEECH]

Listen well, our beloved,
you who caused yourselves to bear witness here,
you who came out together here,
you Mexicas, you Tenochcas, you lords, you speakers,
please approach hither and consider well.
If only it be able to settle where your heart makes a home,

1. Translated by Jorge Klor de Alva.

(when we set it forth, when we say it)
the word of the message.

Let us not disconcert you as to something,
take care lest you see us as something superior,
indeed, we are only your peers, we are only common people,
we are men such as you are, we are surely not gods.
We are also inhabitants on the earth, we also drink, we also eat,
we also die of cold, we are also overwhelmed by heat,
we are also mortal, we are also destructible.
Indeed, we are only messengers, we were only sent here,
to the place of your homeland, to your water, to your mountain.
We came bearing it, his honorable breath, his honorable word,
of this one who everywhere in the world, on the earth,
is the great speaker of divine things,
his name is Holy Father Pope.

* * *

And it is not something else for which we came,
for which we were sent hither;
only on account of spiritual compassion for you,
for your salvation.
Then, nothing earthly does he desire,
the great speaker of divine things,
hence, neither jade, nor gold,
nor quetzal plumes, nor anything precious.
Now, only your completely total salvation he desires.

* * *

But, perhaps, you ask, now, perhaps, you say,
this one, the divine word you mention with reverence,
where did it come from? Where did it appear?
Who gave it to you? Who showed it to you?
Where did the great speaker of divine things acquire it?
Be so kind as to raise your ears, so you will be able to hear,
from where came the divine word we come to give you,
we come to make you comprehend.
Understand and pursue earnestly the truth of it,
that your heart may be properly filled.
Indeed, already it has been a long time,
since He, the True God, Speaker,[2]
Possessor of the Near, Possessor of the Surrounding,[3]
He by Whom All Live, showed it to His most beloved,
to His servants, these whose heart was very good, upright,
His great knowledge, His choices,
their name is patriarchs, prophets.
And, indeed, here on the earth a man He came to make Himself,
He was able, as a man, to appeal to them,

2. *Tlatoani* in Nahuatl, the traditional term for "ruler."

3. Epithets of the god Tezcatlipoca, now transferred to the Christian God.

the apostles, the evangelists.
And they are those to whom He gave
His venerable breath, His venerable word, the divine word.
And He commanded them so they will paint it,
so that it will be preserved on the earth,
so that the men on the earth will be instructed by the divine word.
And the Holy Father guards all the divine words they left,
these formerly mentioned, His beloved of Our Lord, God.
All is in the divine book, it lies blackened, it lies colored.
All is there, everything is conserved,
these which now are the very marvelous divine words.
And likewise, he made us bear it hither now, he, the Holy Father,
so that we will give it to you, we will notify you of it.
Indeed, this one, the divine word,
does not resemble the speech of the common people on the earth.
Indeed, very marvelous, true is His venerable breath, His venerable word,
the Creator of Men's and this one of the Savior of Men,
the One Sole God, the Speaker,
Possessor of the Near, Possessor of the Surrounding,
On account of that it is properly named divine word;
very truly the one followed.
Absolutely no one will be able to contradict it,
even though he is a great knower of things on earth.

* * *

There it is told, indeed, how on the earth,
there, is His precious dominion as a man, Our Lord Jesus Christ.
He, the Only True God, Speaker,
Creator of Men, and Savior of Men, Jesus Christ,
here on the earth He founded His precious dominion,
His honorable mat, His honorable seat, He set down,
and it is this whose name is dominion of heaven,
moreover, its name is Holy Catholic Church.[4]
Because of that, it is called the dominion of heaven,
indeed, absolutely no one will enter heaven
if he will not belong to it, the Holy Church.

* * *

There where He resides, He by Whom All Live, Jesus Christ,
it is very necessary for you that you detest them,
you despise them, you hate them, and you spit on them,
these whom you have always regarded as gods.
These gods which you esteemed, indeed, are truly not gods,
indeed, they only make a mockery of anyone.
Furthermore, moreover, it is very necessary that you avoid them,
that you abandon them, all these various transgressions,
these injuries to the heart of the Possessor of the Near,
Possessor of the Surrounding,
He by Whom All Live, which you have continually caused.

4. *Sancta yglesia catholica* in the Nahuatl text.

[The Aztecs' Reply]

After it ended, it terminated,
this the venerable speech of the twelve Fathers,
at once one of those lords, speakers,
stood up, he greeted the divine guardians,
and a little bit, one lip, two lips,
by this he returned their venerable breath, their venerable words.
He said: Our lords, you have endured much,
indeed, when you came to approach us on this land,
indeed, when you came to govern it
from your honorable water, your honorable mountain.
From where? What kind of place is it, the place of our lords,
there, from where you came?
Indeed, from among the clouds, from among the mist, you have come out.
Indeed, before you, about you we carefully observe, admire,
the possessors of the water, the possessors of the mountain.
Here we acquire it, we seize it, the new word,
as if it were something celestial, that which you say.
And here it is shown to us, it is opened for us,
His precious coffer, His precious hamper,
that of the Man, Our Lord, Possessor of Heaven, Possessor of Earth.
And, thus, he sends you hither, the man, the great speaker,
from where his breath is made known,
from the place of our lords, the Holy Father, and the Emperor.
Indeed, here before us you place the turquoise, the bracelet,
here we marvel at it as if it were a round jade
able to shine without its shade, without its defect,
and as if it were a large precious quetzal plume, extremely green.
Indeed, they left, He destroyed them,
He burnt them, the Man, Our Lord,
the speakers, these who came to be,
these who came to live on the earth,
and who came to guard it, who came to govern it,
your honorable mat, your honorable seat,
for a brief day, for a moment,
here in Mexico, in Tenochtitlan,
and here in Aculhuacan, Tetzcoco, here in Tlacopan:
Motecuhzomatzin,[5]
Ahuitzotzin, Axayacatzin, Tizocicatzin, and Itzcoatzin,
the elder Motecuhzoma and Nezahualcoyotzin,
Nezahualpilli, Totoquihuaztli, and the elder Tezozomoctli.
If it had occurred during their time,
indeed, they would have returned
your precious breath, your precious word.
Likewise, they would have entreated you
by reason of your precious love for people,
which we admire here.

5. A list follows of ten earlier kings.

But, we, what now, immediately, will we say?
Supposing that we, we are those who shelter the people,
we are mothers to the people, we are fathers to the people,
perchance, then, are we, here before you, to destroy it, the ancient law;
the one which was greatly esteemed by our grandparents, our women;
the one which they would go speaking of favorably,
the one which they would go admiring, the lords, the speakers?

And these, oh our lords,
indeed, they are there, they still guide us,
these who carry us, these who govern us,
in relation to these being served,
indeed, these who are our gods, these who have their merit,
that of the tail, of the wing,
the ones who offer things, the ones who offer incense,
and those named the feathered serpents.
These are knowers of the word,
and their charge with which they trouble themselves,
by night, by day, is the act of burning *copal,*
the act of offering incense, thorns, *acxoyatl,*[6] the act of blood letting.
These see, these trouble themselves,
with the journey, the orderly course of the heavens,
according to how the night is divided.
And these continually look at it, these continually relate it,
these continually cause the book to cackle.
The black, the color, is in the paintings they continually carry.
Indeed, they are the ones who continually carry us,
they guide us, they cause the path to speak to us.
They are the ones who put it in order,
such as how a year falls,
such as how the count of the destinies-feasts follows its path,
and each one of the complete counts.
They trouble themselves with it,
they have their charge, their commission,
their duty which is the divine word.
And we are those, indeed, who but have as our sole task
(what is called) divine water, fire. And only we speak on it,
we trouble ourselves with the tribute, of the tail, the wing;
so that it seizes its headdress of heron feathers, its jacket of cords,
and its digging stick, its tumpline;[7]
that which is placed in front of the hearth;
in this way people are made "slaves."
Let us, for now, assemble them,
the ones who offer things, the feathered serpents.
Let us give them His precious breath, His precious word,
this one of the Man, Our Lord.
So that they, perhaps, will restore it, will return it,

6. Needles used for ritual bloodletting.

7. A band running across the forehead and back behind the shoulders to support a pack.

this which we have seized, this which we have grasped,
from your honorable breasts, your honorable heads,
we will elevate it, our lords.
If only you would calm your precious hearts, your precious flesh;
remain on your honorable mat, your honorable seat.

[The Aztecs' Second Speech][8]

And now, what, in what manner, what sort of thing will we say,
which we will raise to your honorable ears?

* * *

Have we, perhaps, been negligent in doing things?
Oh, where, by chance, are we truly to go?
Indeed, we are common people, we are destructible, we are mortal.
Oh, indeed, let us die, oh, indeed, let us perish,
since, indeed, the gods have been defeated!
If only it would settle itself,
your honorable heart, your honorable flesh (Oh, our lords).
Indeed, on account of this, we divide something very little,
now, on account of this, we open it very little,
his coffer, his hamper, this one of the man, our lord.

You tell them, indeed, that we do not know Him,
the Possessor of the Near, Possessor of the Surrounding,
the Possessor of Heaven, Possessor of Earth.
You tell them, indeed, that our gods are not real gods.
It is a new word, this one you tell them,
and because of it we are distressed,
because of it we are extremely frightened.
Indeed, these our makers,
these who came to be, these who came to live on the earth,
did not speak in this way.
Verily, they gave us their law.
They followed them as true, they served them,
they honored them, the gods.
They taught us all their forms of serving, their modes of honoring.
Thus, before them we eat earth, thus, we bleed ourselves,
thus, we discharge the debt ourselves, thus, we burn *copal,*
and, thus, we cause something to be killed.
They used to say that, verily, they, the gods, by whose grace one lives,
they merited us.
When? Where? While it was still night.
And they used to say, indeed, they give us our supper, our breakfast,
and all that is drinkable, edible,
this our meat, the corn, the bean,
the wild amaranth, the lime-leaved sage.
They are those from whom we request the water, the rain,
by which the things of the earth are made.

8. After hearing renewed Spanish arguments that their gods are really devils, the Aztecs take time to consult and then return to speak further.

Furthermore, they are rich themselves, they are happy themselves,
they are possessors of goods, they are owners of goods,
by which always, forever, it germinates there, it grows green in their house.
Where? What kind of place is it, the place of Tlaloc?[9]
Hunger never occurs there, nothing is diseased, nothing is poor.
And also, they give to the people prowess, courage, the chase, and the lip-grass,
the instrument by which something is bound, the loincloth, the mantle,
the flowers, the tobacco,
the jade, the quetzal plumes, the gold.

And when, where were these thus summoned,
when implored, when held as gods, when honored?
It is already a very long time.
When? At another time it was in Tula.
When? At another time it was in Huapalcalco.
When? At another time it was in Xochitlalpan.
When? At another time it was in Tamoanchan.
At another time it was in Yoallichan.
When? At another time it was in Teotihuacan.
Indeed, they, everywhere in the world,
they caused the people to construct with stones their mat, their seat.
They gave to the people the lordship, the dominion, the fame, the glory.

And, perchance, now, are we those who will destroy it, the ancient law?
The law of the Chichimecs? The law of the Toltecs?
The law of the Colhuaque? The law of the Tepanecs?
Already our heart is this way:
through him one is made to live,
through him one is given birth,
on account of him one is made to grow,
on account of him one is made to mature,
by means of this one, who is summoned,
by means of this one, who is implored.
Hear, our lords, beware of doing something to them,
this your precious tail, your precious wing,
so much the more so that it will be abandoned,
so much the more so that it will be destroyed.
In this way also the old man,
in this way also the old woman had her growth, had her increase in age.
Oh, that the gods be not angry with us.
Oh, that their anger, their wrath, not come.
And let us beware that on account of that
it not rise before us, on us, the tail, the wing.
Let us beware that on account of that we not stir it up,
let us beware that on account of that we not provoke it,
by saying to it: no longer will it summon them,
no longer will it implore them.

9. The heavenly realm of Tlaloc, god of rain.

In the meantime, calmly, peacefully,
consider it, our lords, whatever is necessary.
Indeed, our heart is not able to be full.
And, indeed, absolutely we do not yet agree to it ourselves,
we do not yet make it true for ourselves.
We ourselves will cause you injury to the heart.
Indeed, here they lie, the possessors of water, the possessors of mountains,
the lords, the speakers, these who carry it, these who bear it, the world.
It is enough that we have already left it alone,
we have lost it, we have had it taken away,
we have had it prohibited, the mat, the seat.
Indeed, if we will only remain there,
we will only cause them to be restricted.
Do it to us, whatever it is you will desire.
Indeed, we return it all by this, by this we respond to it,
your precious breath, your precious word, our lords.

[THE FRIARS REPLY]

Indeed, we will tell you everything,
we will cause you to hear it, if you desire it.
And we will be able to cause you to have a full heart,
because we guard it, the divine book, the divine word,
there where it lies visible, it lies painted,
it lies arranged, all that which is His precious word,
this one of the Possessor of the Near, Possessor of the Surrounding.

* * *

You did not guard it, the divine book, the divine word.
It never came to reach you,
His precious breath, His precious word,
this one of the Possessor of Heaven, the Possessor of Earth.
And, then, you are blind, you are deaf,
as if in darkness, in gloom, you live.
On account of this your faults are, furthermore, not very great.
But now, if you do not desire to hear it,
the precious breath, the precious word of God
(this one He gives to you), you will be in much danger.
And God, Who has commenced your destruction,
will conclude it, you will be completely lost.

Our beloved, so that you may hear it rightly, that which you desire,
likewise, so that your heart will be able to be full,
it is necessary that first we will cause you to hear,
we will manifest to you, of what precious sort is Our Lord God,
He by Whom All Live, This One we came to show you.
And, indeed, already it is late, now, already, the time to eat is distant.
Tomorrow at dawn, when the sun comes out,
everybody will come hither,
here one will be assembled, something will be heard.
For now all may depart, please go, eat something.
For now rest, let your heart be settled.

Songs of the Aztec Nobility
15th–16th century

The court poets of the Aztecs and their allies created the most extensive and exquisite body of poetry ever known to have existed in Mesoamerica. Many of these lyrics are marked by a gentle melancholy and a delicate aestheticism, with poems often taking poetry itself as their subject. Poetry was commonly described metaphorically in Nahuatl as *in xochitl in cuicatl,* "flowers and birdsong," emblems of beauty in a transient world. The poets delighted in creating beautiful images and in elegant plays on words, and often intertwined friendship and poetry together as the greatest human values. As one poem puts it in the collection known as *Cantares Mexicanos:*

> We lift our songs, our flowers,
> these songs of the Only Spirit.
> Then friends embrace,
> the companions in each others' arms.
> So it has been said by Tochihuitzin,
> so it has been said by Coyolchiuqui:
> We come here only to sleep,
> we come here only to dream.

The same images and methods came to be used for very different purposes as the Aztec empire grew over the course of the century before the Spanish conquest. Court poets began to celebrate the beauties of conquest, and death in battle became an act of almost poetic virtue: "Jaguar flowers are opening," one poem declares; "knife-death flowers are becoming delicious upon the field." As another poem puts it, "We'll dare to go where fame, where glory, is gotten, where nobility is gotten, where flower death is won."

Aztec poetry underwent a further revolution with the coming of Cortés and the fall of the Aztec empire. Now the surviving poets had to consider the brevity of human life in a new way, involving not only individual mortality but the swift defeat of the greatest empire the region had ever known. Both the traditional themes and the unsettling colonial context are apparent in the poems as they have come down to us, chiefly in two manuscripts compiled between 1550 and 1585: the *Cantares Mexicanos* ("Songs of the Mexicans") and the *Romances de los Señores de la Nueva España* ("Ballads of the Lords of New Spain"). Written in the Roman alphabet but in the Aztecs' language, Nahuatl, these collections of close to two hundred poems record songs that likely come from a range of times. Some appear to be purely pre-Conquest poems, showing no trace of later events; others seem to be traditional poems revised in light of the Conquest; others (like the "Fish Song" and the "Water-Pouring Song" below) were clearly composed as direct responses to the Conquest itself.

The poems interweave the natural imagery of brightly colored tropical birds and flowers with a social landscape of great nobles, such as the Aztec king Moctezuma and the pre-Conquest ruler Nezahualcoyotl (1402–1472), king of the allied city of Texcoco. Often the poet sings in the name of these rulers or other nobles, and traditionally many poems were ascribed to Nezahualcoyotl himself, much as the Hebrew psalms were ascribed to King David. In post-Conquest times, the poems at times refer to still living figures, at other times recall great heroes of the past, invoking their aid in the ongoing struggle for life and liberty. Even the most pressing historical events are seen through the prism of metaphor, as in the "Fish Song," whose speaker presents the Aztecs as fish, hoping the new bishop will stop eating them now that Lent is over and Easter has come. The long, haunting "Water-Pouring Song" shows the nobles pressed into service hauling water, and the poet turns their water jugs into images of Aztec culture and finally of the poem itself.

The "Water-Pouring Song" extends its range abroad, recounting a trip across the ocean by the Mexican leader Martin Ecatl in 1525 to meet Spain's emperor Charles V, and it includes a surreal encounter with Pope Clement VII, sitting on his mat with his turquoise blowgun. The post-Conquest poems often speak directly to the new God whom the Spaniards have brought, Dios (or Tios, or Tiox, as they call him) and his companions Jesus, Mary, and the Holy Spirit (*spilitu xanto* in the manuscript). Often God is addressed as Ipalnemoani, "Giver of Life," or as Tloque Nahuaque, "The Ever Present, Ever Near," traditional names for the great god Tezcatlipoca. Never named outright or seen directly, the old gods often seem still to be in the wings in these poems.

As it is set down in the manuscripts, Aztec poetry is written not in verse form but in paragraphs of varying lengths, sometimes prefaced with syllables that indicate rhythms to be used (*titico titico titico, toco toco toti*). A modern translator has a choice: to break these paragraphs into shorter lines corresponding to verses, usually guided by repetitions and variations in phrasing; or to retain the paragraphing of the manuscripts, presenting the poems as chants rather than as lyric utterances. The first selection here is set in verse form, which is how the poems have usually been published by Mexican scholars; the rest of the selections are given in paragraph form, in the eloquent contemporary translations of John Bierhorst.

The largest compilation of Aztec poetry, the *Cantares* manuscript, was apparently assembled by native informants under the direction of the Spanish friar Bernardino de Sahagún, compiler of the great historical and cultural survey called the *General History of the Affairs of New Spain*. Sahagún was evidently seeking to collect the poems to serve as a sort of sourcebook he could use in composing hymns and psalms in Nahuatl for his parishioners to use. Fascinated by the native cultures and deeply learned in Nahuatl, Sahagún had no interest in preserving the poems for their own sake; on the contrary, in his preface to his book of psalms he wrote that his parishioners' "persistence in singing their old songs arouses a good deal of suspicion as to the sincerity of their Christian Faith." It is a fitting poetic irony that these poems have been preserved for us today thanks to Sahagún's effort to study and then replace them so that "the praises of idols and idolatry be buried as they deserve."

PRONUNCIATIONS:

Dozens of names of people and places appear in the following poems; only a few of the most common are listed here. Generally Nahuatl names are pronounced as they are spelled, following Spanish usage at the time; *x* is pronounced *sh; h* is silent (*hua* has the sound *wa*); and *que* has the sound *kay*. Names are usually accented on the next to last syllable.

cuicatl: KWEE-cah'l
Cantares Mexicanos: cahn-TAR-race may-he-CAH-nohs
Huexotzinco: way-show-TZEEN-coh
Moctezuma: mock-tay-ZOOM-ah
Nahuatl: NAH-waht'l
Nezahualcoyotl: nets-ah-wahl-COY-yaht'l
Tezozomoc: tet-zoh-TZOH-mock
xochitl: SHOW-cheet'l
Sahagún: sah-ah-GOUN

SONGS OF THE AZTEC NOBILITY

Make your beginning, you who sing[1]

Xi huel om pehua
ti cuicanitl.
Ma oc xocon tzotzona
moxochihuehueuh.
Ma ic xi quimahuiltia
in tepilhuan
in cuauhtin in ocelo.
Cuel achic tiquitotlanehuia.

Make your beginning,
you who sing.
May you beat again
your flowered drum,
may you give joy
to my lords,
the eagles, the jaguars.[2]
Briefly are we here together.

In zan iyollo ya quinequi
in ipal nemohuani
in cozcatli in quetzalli
in quipuztequiz oncan.
in quimmonequiz
quimontepehuatiuh
in cuauhtin in ocelo.
Cuel achic tiquitotlanehuia.

The one heart's desire
of the Giver of Life
is jewels, is quetzal plumes—
to tear them apart.
This is his desire:
to scatter apart
the eagles, the jaguars.
Briefly are we here together.

Quexquich cozcatli
quexquich quetzalli
tlatilo. Oo
ac a chalchiuhitli
ac a teocuitlatl.
In ma ye ica on xon ahuiyacan
ma ye ica on popolihui
a in totlaocol antepilhuan.
Auh in tocuic
auh in toxochiuh
ya in tonequimilol
xon ahuiyacan
ic malinticac
cuauhyotl ocelyotl
ica tiyazque
in canon ye yuhcan.

How many jewels,
how many quetzal plumes,
have been destroyed? Ah,
though it was jade,
though it was gold.
So may you now be happy:
for surely too will perish
our sorrow, my lords.
And these our songs,
these our flowers,
they are our shrouds.
So be happy:
woven into them
is the eagle, the jaguar;
we will go with them
there where it is all the same.

Zaniyo ye nican
titocnihua in tlalticpac.
Zan cuel achica tontiximati
zan titotlanehuico ye nican.
Ohua zan cuel achic
in inahuac in ipal nemoani
zan tocontlanehuico
ichimalxochiuh
a ixtlahuacateca.

It is only here
we have friends, on earth.
Only briefly do we know one another,
only here are we together
Ah, only briefly here
do we share with the Giver of Life;
we are only given a loan
of his flowered shield—
soon it must be returned.

1. Translated by David Damrosch.

2. Orders of warriors.

In ma oc ompa papaqui in toyollo
yeehuaya in tlalticpac
zan cuel achica tontiximati
zan titotlanehuico ye nican.
Maca xi tlaocoyacan antepilhuan
ayac ayac
mocauhtiaz in tlalticpac.

So let us rejoice within our hearts,
all who are on earth;
only briefly do we know one another,
only here are we together.
So do not be saddened, my lords:
no one, no one
is left behind on earth.

from Water-Pouring Song[1]

1

There were plume willows at the turquoise-green waters in Chapolco. We Mexicans had reached jade water's flowing-out place. Ah! And the waters are His, and He drinks them, it's true. Drinks them, it's true. And ah, this Mexico arrives in that Chapolco yonder. Aya!

It resembles that time of our utmost eagerness when we Mexicans set out from Acocolco[2] to reach this place that is here. And ah, the waters are His, and He drinks them, it's true.

When the Captain arrived in Mexico and Moctezuma went out to meet him, then he got down from his horse; and he adorned him with a gold necklace, spoke to him, and embraced him. And the waters are His, and He drinks them, it's true.

And right away he says to him, "You've wearied yourself in reaching your city, this Mexico. You've come to govern your mat and your seat. For but a moment and a day I've tended things for you. Poor is your vassal." He speaks to him, embraces him. And the waters are His, and He drinks them, it's true.

Now woe! He gives off smoke! This is how he enters, this conquistador, this Captain. Now all the lords are yet alive: Commander Atlixcatzin and the troop chief Tepehuatzin. And as these princes come forth pouring water, Mexico is handed over. Oh! the waters are His, and He drinks them, it's true.

"We who've come to Water's Midst to marvel are Tlaxcalans: Mexican princes are pouring out their waters!" Lord Moctezuma's hauling vats of water. And the city passes on, ensconced in water-whorl flowers. Thus Mexico is handed over. Oh! the waters are His, and He drinks them, it's true.

Iye! The lady María[3] comes shouting. María comes saying, "O Mexicans, your water jars go here! Let all the lords come carrying." And Acolhuacan's Quetzalacxoyatl arrives. And Cuauhpopoca. Oh! the waters are His, and He drinks them, it's true.

O Life Giver, these urgently required ones have been broken, these, our water jars, and we are Mexicans. A cry goes up. They're picking them off at Eagle Gate, where recognition is achieved. Oh! the waters are His, and He drinks them, it's true.

They've been ruined with water hauling, and they're smoking—Nezahualquentzin and the troop chief Tepehuatzin. It's because we Mexicans are hauling water. And the waters are His, and He drinks them, it's true.

And so they're flowing. Indeed the ruler Moctezuma himself comes forth to pour one out. As roseate-swan flowers, as flower shoots, as trogons, as pine flowers, would

1. Translated by John Bierhorst.
2. As the Aztecs' ancestors migrated south into the Valley of Mexico, they lived for a time at Acocolco.
3. Cortés's interpreter and common-law wife Doña María or Malinche.

he go off whirling his garlands: thus he glorifies Tenochcans. Oh! the waters are His, and He drinks them, it's true.

Oh never would our water pitchers be destroyed. These broad ones, these turquoise gems, are strewn as gold. Ensconced in roseate-swan hand-flowers, he's moved on to You. Shattered, he's moved on to Water's Midst, where waters and the navel lie: and so he glorifies Tenochcans. Oh! the waters are His, and He drinks them, it's true.

3

O nephews, hail! And hear a work assignment: we've come to do our water pouring. Now who will go and fetch the jadestone jars that we must carry? And yonder we're assembled, at Shore of the Bells, at the Place of Green Waters.

Oh none with us shall work for tribute. We're to pass away. Our guardian Don Diego Tehuetzquiti is to lead us. And yonder we're assembled, at Shore of the Bells, at the Place of Green Waters.

Our cups are born. It seems they're twirling—and as maize flowers—at the water's edge. These jade-water drums! At Chapultepec's side! Let all our brothers pour. Clean waters, then, will flow in beauty.

But I wonder, am I blessed? And so I grieve. O friends, where am I to go that I might pour these? For my heart desires them. Let Yonder be the church![4]

I weep, I sorrow, and I sing: I've broken these, my turquoise gems, my pearls, these water jars.

And merely in this manner let it be that I return them. Chirping for these flowers, let me head for home. At Flower Waters let me weep, composing them: I've broken these, my turquoise gems, my pearls, these water jars.

Indeed I seek those lords who drew the water. Nezahualtecolotl and Lord Coaihuitl. In serenity I come to pour these waters at the emperor's. And may you all take heart. Hey Don Pedrotli![5]

Nobility will flow in beauty here. Could our carried waters perish then? Take heart. Hey Don Pedrotli!

4

God and Only Spirit, you and you alone lay down the mirror and the flame that stands here in the world,[6]

Where there used to be the black and color of your creatures who were carried-water masters, who were lords.

I pass, I pass away, I pass beyond, that I might reach the plume-shore turquoise lode. There I'll fetch my limpid green one. Ah!

"O Ixtlilxochitl! O Mexicans!" So it is that they who were swallowed are painted as shields—these hidden ones.

O charges of the flood-and-blaze! And so it is that they shall pour them. And it's in this manner that Tenochcans are to labor. Oh it seems that they themselves are done for, they, Cuauhtemoc, Coanacoch, ah! and Tetlepanquetzatzin: they've heard the multitude.

4. *Iquelexia* in the manuscript, from the Spanish *iglesia*, "church."

5. Don Pedro Temilotzin, a leader of resistance after the Conquest.

6. God ("Tiox") has taken over the power of Tezcatlipoca, "Smoking Mirror."

So it is that they who were swallowed are painted as spears. Indeed, the lord Captain[7] has said it: "Paint them as turquoise pictures: the Mexicans' labor's in pictures!" And oh it would seem that this labor's been taken from everywhere into the city.

Now they who've wept in sadness are the lords and rulers. It's our destiny and circumstance: they've painted them as turquoise pictures!

We must go to hear them. Ho, Cuauhtemoc! Oquiztzin! Huanitl! He's handed down His judgment: our carried waters will never be destroyed. Take heart. And where in time are we to go? To the emperor![8]

Take heart, nephews. Cuauhtemoc! Let's go have these captured ones, our pitchers, be a raining mist of trogons. Off they go to fall as dew. Let our garlands flow profusely and as gold. Let us make our entry side by side with these, our carried waters. Off to the emperor!

Indeed I seek those lords who drew the water: Nezahualtecolotl and Lord Coaihuitl. In serenity I come to pour these waters at the emperor's. May you all take heart.

Thus nobility will flow in beauty. Could our babes then perish? May you all take heart.

5

I, Lord Xicotencatl, am the one who's saying, "Pass away, and not in vain! Fetch your shields, flowers, water jars. They're your pitchers—that is, your well-wrought blade-jar urns!" With these we'll carry water: we'll go get water there in Mexico—Chapolco! Yes, in Water's Midst.

"Pass away, and not in vain, O nephew." Brothers! Nephews! Princes of the flood!

I'm pouring water, Lord Cuauhtencoz. Let's all go and carry water. Yes, we'll get the water. Hey!

Now brother Motelchiuh must shout. O friends, it's said that we're to fetch him in the dawn, him, our carried water, this very limpid one, this limpid green one, gleaming like an emerald. And yonder we arrive. O cup!

Pass away, and not in vain! Must Nanahuatl have a craving? O brother, O Commander Cuitlachihuitl! Truly he's well wrought, like gold, this painted one, our water jar—and he's gone painting Lord Axayacatl. Scattered, we're to pass beyond. And yonder we arrive. O cup!

Jade water sprinkles. My adornments fall in a raining mist. My Tlaxcalan uncles have come to give me Huanitl, my flower-water charge. O Chichimecs, pass away, and not in vain.

Blaze flowers, shield flowers, are blossoming in quantity: these flower shoots are bursting: they're scattered plentifully, because it seems they've come to take them, these, these golden ones, as captives. And yes, in bearing off these precious water jars of mine, I fetch those painted green ones. O my great ones!

O Acolhuacan's Don Antonio! Let me take you away! Hail, nephew! O Tehuetzquiti! And they pass away reviving as reed flowers, as colored banners, pass away as captives. This is how I carry off these painted green ones, these precious water jars of mine. See me, O great ones!

And I who recall these painted ones, these precious water jars—am Fray Pedro! Before he went away, the bishop Don Fray Juan purified this city with a golden balm and sprinkled it with water.

7. Cortés, who had illustrated reports prepared to send home to Spain.

8. In 1525 Cortés brought a group of Aztec nobles to Spain; some went on to Rome, where they met Pope Clement VII.

Yes, it seems that our beloved father, the bishop, has gone away. And before he went, he purified this city with a golden balm and sprinkled it with water.

Let's be off to Plume-Shore Chapultepec! And these handflowers? They pass away as turquoise swans reviving, for they've been captured, they, our pitcher jades. Hail, brothers! But be cautious. Beware of being broken, for Our Lord would scold us.

So let them follow onward. Go carefully! And yonder we're assembled. To Mexico, where tunas[9] lie, they're off to be revived as turquoise swans.

Friends, willow men, behold the pope, who's representing God, who speaks for him.

The pope is on God's mat and seat and speaks for him.

Who is this reclining on a golden chair? Look! It's the pope. He has his turquoise blowgun and he's shooting in the world.

It seems it's true: it seems he has his cross and golden staff, and these are shining in the world.

I grieve in Rome and see his flesh, and he's San Pedro, San Pablo![1]

It seems that from the four directions they've been captured: you've made them enter the golden refuge, and it's shining.

It seems the pope's home lies painted in golden butterflies. It's beaming.

6

Wind arises, roaring, hissing. The ocean seethes, and the boat goes creaking along.

We see great waves flowing over us, wonderful things of God. It's raining flowers, and the boat goes creaking along.

Friends, rejoice in these waters. You're splitting it open, O Don Martín! It's broken to pieces here on the ocean.

O Life Giver, you're alive in this place of fear. The waves are rolling over us. Let's go perish at the navel, at the roundel.

"No one in this boat is precious, friends. Can we return?" Let's go be counted at the navel, at the roundel!

Alas, I grieve. The emerald dew is on us. And where are we to go?

Life Giver causes grief. If only He were my friend, if only He were a kinsman. No one cares anymore about anyone here in the boat.

Inside this boat, this place of fear, jade waters are flowing over us, seething. Ah, these garlands roar, these fish are flying. See them!

Ah, and yonder stands the tree of sustenance, stands our palace. And these garlands roar, these fish are flying. See them!

9

We've been required right here, and this would seem to be the emperor's home. Would that His waters might make an appearance. They're being recited! Would God agree?

Let's call to the Only Spirit. It may be that in this manner we, the vassals, are allowed to spend a day near him and in his presence.

We, mere Mexicans, are off to marvel on the sea, the emperor commanding us: he's told us, "Go and see the holy father."

He's said: What do I need? Gold! Everybody bow down! Call out to God in excelsis![2]

9. Prickly pears, grown for their fruit.

1. The Pope was regarded as the successor of the apostles Peter and Paul.

2. In the highest (Latin).

And it's just for this that he sends us to Rome. He's told us, "Go and see the holy father."

Our hearts will be content, for he sends us on to Rome. He's told us, "Go and see the holy father."

It would seem that at the pope's, where the cavern house of colors stands, are golden words that give us life.

On account of trumpets there's a stirring. Aya! And they're honored where it stands: God's words, these trogons! They're ensconced in war capes. Ah, they give us life.

Bring them in, you princes. They're our comrades. Where? With God in Rome! Aya, there the pope is paying honor.

There in Rome she dwells, she the mother called Santa Cecelia! Aya, there the pope is paying honor.

Your flowers, it would seem, are budding, greening, in Willow Place, O Axayacatl. Indeed, you went away deserving. It's where the tunas lie!

White feather flowers are sifting down at Water Face. And it would seem that they're your flowers, Lord Axayacatl. Indeed, you went away deserving. It's where the tunas lie!

In the Place Unknown, where all are shorn, in heaven and as jades, perhaps, or turquoises, they're marshaled, they, the princes. They're with God.

Lord Oquiztzin flies along, perhaps, as a roscate swan. Perhaps Tlacotzin is an eagle plume. Yes, all are alive, and they're with God.

Take a look at the Only Spirit's flower field. There's a freshening in that place of heart pleasers: there's a plume dew raining all around.

Yonder dwells the turquoise swan-bird Don Martín. An egret bird is pleasured, and it's Coaihuitl. There's Don Juan!

Red feather trees are blossoming in God's home, and princes are inhaling them. Lord Anahuacatl and perhaps Commander Cuitlachihuitl are rejoicing in heaven.

They've been broken as plume jades or perhaps as turquoise gems: they're princes, and they're Mexicans, these Huexotzincans. Lord Anahuacatl and perhaps Commander Cuitlachihuitl are rejoicing in heaven.

Moctezuma, you creature of heaven, you sing in Mexico[1]

Moctezuma, you creature of heaven, you sing in Mexico, in Tenochtitlan.

Here where eagle multitudes were ruined, your bracelet house stands shining—there in the home of God our father.

There and in that place they come alive, ah! on the field! For a moment they come whirling, they the eagles, ah! the nobles Ixtlilcuechahuac and Matlaccuiatzin.

And in that place these nobles gain renown and honor: bells are scattered, dust and lords grow golden.

Onward, friends! We'll dare to go where fame, where glory's, gotten, where nobility is gotten, where flower death is won.

Your name and honor live, O princes. Prince Tlacahuepan! Ixtlilcuechahuac! You've gone and won war death.

Sky dawn is rising up. The multitude, the birds, are shrilling. Precious swans are being created. Turquoise troupials are being created.

Lucky you, arrayed in chalk and plumes. O flower-drunk Moctezuma! Precious swans are being created. Turquoise troupials are being created.

1. Translated by John Bierhorst.

Sor Juana Inés de la Cruz

c. 1651–1695

Cortés's venture in Mexico was primarily military, but not exclusively so. Accompanying Cortés on his entrance into Mexico City in 1520 were several Franciscan friars, whose presence marked a secondary reason for Spanish intervention in the New World: the spreading of Catholicism. For those Indians who survived death by disease or guns, there was another kind of subjection: to the missions, comprised of colleges and "seminaries" where the native peoples were instructed through catechism, preaching, and perhaps surprisingly, theater, often presented on feast days such as Corpus Christi.

In the hands of Sor Juana, the Mexican nun who would write over 150 years after Cortés, such theater drew on not one but two vibrant traditions: that of seventeenth-century Spain, particularly the *auto sacramental* or religious drama, and the rituals of the indigenous Aztecs, marked by considerable pageantry and dance. Written in 1688, *The Divine Narcissus,* if it was performed at all, was shown only in Madrid, not Mexico. Part of the *loa* or prefatory act (excerpted below) explicitly debates its propriety for the Spanish stage, since it was written in the "backward" colonies. But the *loa* is also strikingly anticolonial. Like so many Mexican works, it commemorates the conquest of New World by Old (represented by the figures of Zeal and Religion). Yet the new-world characters of Occident and America are dignified in their resistance to these European figures revealed, by turns, as unnecessarily violent and hypocritical. Perhaps most intriguing is Sor Juana's grasp of Aztec customs and her occasional use of Nahuatl words in the play, as well as the final triumph of the *dios de las Semillas* whom America praises at the beginning of the *loa* as the Aztec fertility god. As much as he can be seen as a hybrid of Christ and an Aztec deity, his name—"the god of seeds"—persists at the end of the *loa,* despite the fact that the Europeans have obviously emerged victorious.

from The Loa for the Auto Sacramental of the Divine Narcissus[1]

An Allegory[2]

Speaking Characters

Occident	Religion
America	Musician
Zeal	Soldiers

SCENE 1

[*Enter Occident, a gallant-looking Aztec, wearing a crown. By his side is America, an Aztec woman of poised self-possession. They are dressed in the* mantas *and* huipiles *worn for singing a* tocotín.[3] *They seat themselves on two chairs. On each side, Aztec men and women dance with feathers and rattles in their hands, as is customary for those doing this dance. While they dance, Music sings.*]

1. Translated by Patricia A. Peters and Renée Domeier, O.S.B. The *loa* was the often lengthy preamble to a play, in this case an *auto sacramental* or one-act sacramental or Eucharist play performed for a religious feast day.

2. *Por alegorías* suggests that the play should be read allegorically—that is, using the characters to represent something else.

3. *Manta* is the Spanish word for a blanket or poncho, while *huipile* is a blouse. A *tocotín* was a traditional Nahuatl ballad, of which Sor Juana wrote at least two.

MUSIC: O, Noble Mexicans,
whose ancient ancestry
comes forth from the clear light
and brilliance of the Sun,[4]
since this, of all the year,
is your most happy feast
in which you venerate
your greatest deity,
come and adorn yourselves
with vestments of your rank;
let your holy fervor be
made one with jubilation;
and celebrate in festive pomp
the great God of the Seeds![5]

Since the abundance of
our native fields and farms
is owed to him alone
who gives fertility,
then offer him your thanks,
for it is right and just
to give from what has grown,
the first of the new fruits.
From your own veins, draw out
and give, without reserve,
the best blood, mixed with seed,
so that his cult be served,
and celebrate in festive pomp,
the great God of the Seeds!

[*Occident and America sit, and Music ceases.*]

OCCIDENT: Of all the deities to whom
our rites demand I bend my knee—
among two thousand gods or more
who dwell within this royal city
and who require the sacrifice
of human victims still entreating
for life until their blood is drawn
and gushes forth from hearts still beating
and bowels still pulsing—I declare,
among all these, (it bears repeating),
whose ceremonies we observe,

4. The Mexicans believed that the Sun was their original "father": "The Sun cast down an arrow and made a hole, from which a man emerged . . . and following, a woman," a story Sor Juana could have read about in the writings of Franciscans such as Father Juan de Torquemada, published in Spain in the early 17th century.

5. There were several Aztec fertility gods, among them, Centéotl, god of corn; Xiuhteuctli, god of the grass; and Tláloc, god of water and the fecundity of the earth. However, in the context of the *loa,* it seems that Sor Juana is referring to Huitzilopochtli, who was the god of war and the most powerful deity of Tenochtitlán, the Aztecs' capital and what is now Mexico City. Identified with the sun, he was the one who demanded the blood sacrifices that will be referred to by Music.

the greatest is, surpassing all
this pantheon's immensity
the great God of the Seeds.

AMERICA: And you are right, since he alone
daily sustains our monarchy
because our lives depend on his
providing crops abundantly;
and since he gives us graciously
the gift from which all gifts proceed,
our fields rich with golden maize,
the source of life through daily bread,
we render him our highest praise.
Then how will it improve our lives
if rich America abounds
in gold from mines whose smoke deprives
the fields of their fertility
and with their clouds of filthy soot
will not allow the crops to grow
which blossom now so fruitfully
from seeded earth?[6] Moreover, his
protection of our people far
exceeds our daily food and drink,
the body's sustenance. Indeed,
he feeds us with his very flesh
(first purified of every stain).
We eat his body, drink his blood,
and by this sacred meal are freed
and cleansed from all that is profane,
and thus, he purifies our soul.[7]
And now, attentive to his rites,
together let us all proclaim:

THEY [*OCCIDENT, AMERICA, DANCERS*] AND MUSIC: We celebrate in festive pomp,
the great God of the Seeds!

SCENE 2

[*They exit dancing. Enter Christian Religion as a Spanish lady, Zeal as a Captain General in armor, and Spanish soldiers.*][8]

RELIGION: How, being Zeal, can you suppress
the flames of righteous Christian wrath
when here before your very eyes
idolatry, so blind with pride,
adores, with superstitious rites
an idol, leaving your own bride,

6. An allusion to the extensive mining being practiced by the Spaniards throughout Mexico.

7. Sor Juana may be referring to the Aztec ritual of sacrifice in which those who had imbibed the "god" were slaughtered on the altar.

8. "Religion" represents the missionaries and the spiritual conquest of the Mexicans; "Zeal" the military wing of the conquest.

the holy faith of Christ disgraced?
ZEAL: Religion, trouble not your mind
or grieve my failure to attack,
complaining that my love is slack,
for now the sword I wear is bared,
its hilt in hand, clasped ready and
my arm raised high to take revenge.
Please stand aside and deign to wait
till I requite your grievances.

[*Enter Occident and America dancing, and accompanied by Music, who enters from the other side.*]

MUSIC: And celebrate in festive pomp,
the great God of the Seeds!
ZEAL: Here they come! I will confront them.
RELIGION: And I, in peace, will also go
(before your fury lays them low)
for justice must with mercy kiss;
I shall invite them to arise
from superstitious depths to faith.
ZEAL: Let us approach while they are still
absorbed in their lewd rituals.
MUSIC: And celebrate in festive pomp,
the great God of the Seeds!

[*Zeal and Religion cross the stage.*]

RELIGION: Great Occident, most powerful;
America, so beautiful
and rich; you live in poverty
amid the treasures of your land.
Abandon this irreverent cult
with which the demon has waylaid you.
Open your eyes! Follow the path
that leads straightforwardly to truth,
to which my love yearns to persuade you.
OCCIDENT: Who are these unknown people, so
intrusive in my sight, who dare
to stop us in our ecstasy?
Heaven forbid such infamy!
AMERICA: Who are these nations, never seen,
that wish, by force, to pit themselves
against my ancient power supreme?
OCCIDENT: Oh, you alien beauty fair;
oh, pilgrim woman from afar,
who comes to interrupt my prayer,
please speak and tell me who you are.
RELIGION: Christian Religion is my name,
and I intend that all this realm
will make obeisance unto me.

OCCIDENT: An impossible concession!
AMERICA: Yours is but a mad obsession!
OCCIDENT: You will meet with swift repression.
AMERICA: Pay no attention; she is mad!
Let us go on with our procession.
MUSIC AND ALL [*Aztecs on stage*]: And celebrate in festive pomp,
the great God of the Seeds!
ZEAL: How is this, barbarous Occident?
Can it be, sightless Idolatry,
that you insult Religion,
the spouse I cherish tenderly?
Abomination fills your cup
and overruns the brim, but see
that God will not permit you to
continue drinking down delight,
and I am sent to deal your doom.
OCCIDENT: And who are you who frightens all
who only look upon your face?
ZEAL: I am Zeal. Does that surprise you?
Take heed! for when your excesses
bring disgrace to fair Religion,
then will Zeal arise to vengeance;
for insolence I will chastise you.
I am the minister of God,
Who growing weary with the sight
of overreaching tyrannies
so sinful that they reach the height
of error, practiced many years,
has sent me forth to penalize you.
And thus, these military hosts
with flashing thunderbolts of steel,
the ministers of His great wrath
are sent, His anger to reveal.
OCCIDENT: What god? What sin? What tyranny?
What punishment do you foresee?
Your reasons make no sense to me,
nor can I make the slightest guess
who you might be with your insistence
on tolerating no resistance,
impeding us with rash persistence
from lawful worship as we sing.
MUSIC: And celebrate with festive pomp,
the great God of the Seeds!
AMERICA: Madman, blind, and barbarous,
with mystifying messages
you try to mar our calm and peace,
destroying the tranquility
that we enjoy. Your plots must cease,

unless, of course, you wish to be
reduced to ashes, whose existence
even the winds will never sense.

[*to Occident*]

And you, my spouse, and your cohort,
close off your hearing and your sight
to all their words; refuse to heed
their fantasies of zealous might;
proceed to carry out your rite.
Do not concede to insolence
from foreigners intent to dull
our ritual's magnificence.

MUSIC: And celebrate with festive pomp,
the great God of the Seeds!

ZEAL: Since our initial offering
of peaceful terms, you held so cheap,
the dire alternative of war,
I guarantee you'll count more dear.
Take up your arms! To war! To war!

[*Drums and trumpets sound.*]

OCCIDENT: What miscarriages of justice
has heaven sent against me?
What are these weapons, blazing fire,
before my unbelieving eyes?
Get ready, guards! Aim well, my troops,
Your arrows at this enemy!

AMERICA: What lightening bolts does heaven send
to lay me low? What molten balls
of burning lead so fiercely rain?
What centaurs crush with monstrous force
and cause my people such great pain?

[*within*]

To arms! To arms! War! War!

[(*Drums and trumpets*) *sound.*]

Long life to Spain! Long live her king!

[*The battle begins. Indians enter through one door and flee through another with the Spanish pursuing at their heels. From back stage, Occident backs away from Religion and America retreats before Zeal's onslaught.*]

* * *

SCENE 4[9]

AMERICA: There is much more I want to see,
and my desire to know is now
by holy inspiration led.
OCCIDENT: And I desire more keenly still
to know about the life and death
of the God you say is in the bread.
RELIGION: Then come along with me, and I
shall make for you a metaphor,
a concept clothed in rhetoric
so colorful that what I show
to you, your eyes will clearly see;
for now I know that you require
objects of sight instead of words,
by which faith whispers in your ears
too deaf to hear; I understand,
for you necessity demands
that through the eyes, faith find her way
to her reception in your hearts.[1]
OCCIDENT: Exactly so. I do prefer
to see the things you would impart.

SCENE 5

RELIGION: Then come.
ZEAL: Religion, answer me:
what metaphor will you employ
to represent these mysteries?
RELIGION: An *auto*[2] will make visible
through allegory images
of what America must learn
and Occident implores to know
about the questions that now burn
within him so.
ZEAL: What will you call
this play in allegory cast?
RELIGION: *Divine Narcissus,* let it be,
because if that unhappy maid
adored an idol which disguised
in such strange symbols the attempt
the demon made to counterfeit

9. In the ensuing scene, America and the Occident are defeated. Zeal is ready to annihilate them, but Religion protests that they be kept alive, insisting that they can be converted. Claiming that she will speak like St. Paul, Religion suggests to Occident and America that the many miracles they recount of fertility and growth are the work not of their "mendacious deities" but of "the One True God" who gave his life for theirs. Particularly striking are the numerous similarities Religion elucidates between the Aztecs' religion and Christianity.

1. Illustrations were often used by the missionaries to teach the indigenous Mexicans, as made clear in a work such as *Rhetorica Christiana* by the missionary Diego Valadés. Theater too, particularly the *autos sacramentales* of which Sor Juana's work is an example, was thought to be a highly effective teaching tool.

2. An *auto sacramental* or "Mystery Play."

the great and lofty mystery
of the most Blessed Eucharist,[3]
then there were also, I surmise,
among more ancient pagans hints
of such high marvels symbolized.

ZEAL: Where will your drama be performed?

RELIGION: In the crown city of Madrid,
which is the center of the Faith,
the seat of Catholic majesty,
to whom the Indies owe their best
beneficence, the blessed gift
of Holy Writ, the Gospel light
illuminating all the West.[4]

ZEAL: That you should write in Mexico
for royal patrons don't you see
to be an impropriety?[5]

RELIGION: Is it beyond imagination
that something made in one location
can in another be of use?
Furthermore, my writing it
comes, not of whimsical caprice,
but from my vowed obedience
to do what seems beyond my reach.[6]
Well, then, this work, however rough
and little polished it might be,
results from my obedience,
and not from any arrogance.

ZEAL: Then answer me, Religion, how
(before you leave the matter now),
will you respond when you are chid
for loading the whole Indies on
a stage to transport to Madrid?

RELIGION: The purpose of my play can be
none other than to glorify
the Eucharistic Mystery;
and since the cast of characters
are no more than abstractions which
depict the theme with clarity,

3. Possibly an allusion to the one-act play that will follow the *loa*, for which Sor Juana drew on the myth of Narcissus. In her rendition, Narcissus is Christ, in love with the semblance of himself that is humanity, while the figure of Echo is the demonic fallen Angel who tries to tempt him from his love for *naturaleza Humana* or humankind. The work ends with Narcissus's death and resurrection and a hymn celebrating the Eucharist.

4. The performance history of *The Divine Narcissus* is unclear, although it was published in a separate edition in 1690. Madrid is called "center of the faith" because it was the religious and publishing center for the evangelization of the Indies.

5. Probably because the Mexicans were deemed inferior to the Spaniards.

6. Sor Juana was asked to write the *loa* by her close friend María Luisa Manrique de Lara y Gonzaga, the Condesa of Pardes. Sor Juana addresses her as "Phyllis" in several poems, and the countess in turn would take Sor Juana's poems to Spain and arrange for their first publication in 1689.

then surely no one should object
if they are taken to Madrid;
distance can never hinder thought
with persons of intelligence,
nor seas impede exchange of sense.
ZEAL: Then, prostrate at his royal feet,
beneath whose strength two worlds are joined
we beg for pardon of the King;
RELIGION: and from her eminence, the Queen;[7]
AMERICA: whose sovereign and anointed feet
the humble Indies bow to kiss;
ZEAL: and from the Royal High Council;
RELIGION: and from the ladies, who bring light
into their hemisphere;
AMERICA: and from
their poets, I most humbly beg
forgiveness for my crude attempt,
desiring with these awkward lines
to represent the Mystery.[8]
OCCIDENT: Let's go, for anxiously I long to see
exactly how this God of yours
will give Himself as food to me.

[*America, Occident, and Zeal sing:*]

The Indies know
and do concede
who is the true
God of the Seeds.
In loving tears
which joy prolongs
we gladly sing
our happy songs.
ALL: Blest be the day
when I could see
and worship the
great God of Seeds.

[*They all exit, dancing and singing.*]

END OF PERSPECTIVES: THE CONQUEST AND ITS AFTERMATH

7. Many *loas* close with such a request for pardon directed to the king, queen, the Royal Council, and the women and poets of the court.

8. Note America's use of the first person in speaking of the "crude attempt" of the *loa;* perhaps a personal allusion to Sor Juana, who is herself, of course, "American."

John Milton

1608–1674

> What will betide the few
> His faithful, left among the unfaithful herd,
> The enemies of truth . . .? (*Paradise Lost* 12.480–482)

John Milton wrote against the backdrop of the most violent period in English history: a civil war that dominated the decade of the 1640s. King was turned against Parliament, Anglican against Puritan, and too often—as in Milton's own family—brother against brother. The war ended in 1649 with the triumph of the anti-Royalists and the public execution of both King Charles I and his Archbishop, William Laud. Milton himself, whose reputation rested at this point on a series of fiery prose tracts advocating reformation, liberty of conscience, and divorce, was called in to write a treatise defending regicide. He willingly complied with *Eikonoklastes,* in which he likens Charles to the wicked Pharaoh: beseiged by the plagues sent by God, Pharaoh "soon found that evil which before slept, came suddenly upon him, by the preposterous way he took to shun it. Passing by examples between, and not shutting willfully our eyes, we may see the like story brought to pass in our own land."

A Protectorate was established—a Puritan Republic under Oliver Cromwell, whom Milton would serve as Secretary from an office in Scotland Yard—but it was short-lived. Within ten years, a new Pharaoh, Charles's son, returned from France (where he had become acquainted with Parisian culture, including its many actresses), and Milton, calling still for a republic, was imprisoned. In light of what must have seemed to him the permanent victory of the Royalists, he has Adam plaintively ask the archangel Michael, sent below to admonish and console the sinners with a vision of the future, what will happen to the chosen "few" once Christ reascends to heaven. In the difficult years after Charles' restoration, Milton may well have imagined himself to be one of those few: opposed to monarchy, an intolerant state religion too close to the Catholicism England had forsworn long ago, and any regulation that would prevent him from following his conscience in the pursuit of "truth"—always "strong," Milton had written, "next to the Almighty." Burdened moreover by blindness, he no doubt felt that his many efforts to allow for truth's pursuit had borne little fruit. Like the Florentine Machiavelli, in many ways his antithesis, Milton turned from active political engagement after 1659 to writing poetry, cast into figurative if not physical exile.

Yet this image of Milton is not wholly accurate. *Paradise Lost,* probably completed in 1664 and published in 1667, had been in Milton's thoughts for decades, as had his desire to excel as a poet. While still studying at Christ's College, Cambridge, Milton published a poem for Shakespeare's Fourth Folio; his first major literary "event" was the performance of *Comus, A Masque,* in 1634, for the aging patroness of Edmund Spenser. Four years later he published his moving pastoral poem "Lycidas," in honor of a drowned fellow-student. Refusing upon graduation to enter the corrupt Anglican clergy, Milton took a seminal voyage to Italy, where he met, among others, Galileo. But plans to continue to Sicily and Greece were abandoned when he heard of the death of his close friend Charles Diodati as well as of growing turmoil in England. In 1645 he published his collected poems, among them "Lycidas" and a number of sonnets. But if Milton had not perservered in his plans to write on the theme of "Adam Unparadiz'd," first conceived as a tragedy in the early 1640s, his reputation would be primarily that of the polemical prose-writer who criticized his king and the Anglican church and tirelessly defended the Puritan cause throughout twenty years of turmoil. It was only toward the end of those two decades that Milton returned to more youthful plans to compose a poem that would, as he forthrightly declared in the opening lines, "justify the ways of God to man."

Such a line suggests much about *Paradise Lost* and Milton's intentions for it. For one thing, it cannot simply be read as a commentary on recent events, as much as those events may have stirred Milton to write about the bitterness of loss and hope for redemption. (It is hard not to imaging an aging, dour Milton, married by 1663 to his third wife, reciting to his amanuensis the despairing lines in Book 7 as though they were pure autobiography: "On evil days though fallen, and evil tongues.") The poem's subject matter far exceeds any narrowly conceived nationalistic lore such as "the fables of knights" with which Milton had once flirted, or the defeat of the Puritan republic. Instead, it reaches back to the epic par excellence of the European Renaissance: the Bible, Old Testament as well as New, retold in Milton's translation, as bold as that of Wycliff or Tyndale before him. Moreover, in taking the Bible as his primary model, Milton forces a reconsideration of both the classical epics and the medieval romances that had inspired his contemporaries.

Milton, in fact, is at pains to underscore how anti-epic his poem truly is. There is indeed a battle (the war in heaven), a great journey (Satan's flight out of hell), rousing speeches (Satan's plea to the devils in Book 1) and acts of heroism (Raphael's challenge to Satan). But the poem's main action takes place in a garden, and its primary characters are a naked man and woman whose goal is relatively dull: to "stand fast." Milton opposes this Christian inheritance to the bloodthirsty wrath of an Achilles or the deceptiveness of an Odysseus. (A suffering Aeneas was more to Milton's liking—and Virgil's Latinity is everywhere evident in Milton's sonorous English—but even Aeneas ultimately yields to bloodthirsty revenge, and the empire his acts presage is altogether too worldly.) It is Satan to whom Milton entrusts the overreaching of epic and tragic characters—hence Satan's reassuring familiarity and his charm that has infected many listeners beside Eve. Yet his slinking away from Eden after Eve's fall is symptomatic of the banality of evil and the limitations, for Milton, of classical epic. Something more must, and does, come following Satan's triumph over man, and that is a different kind of heroics. When Adam learns from Michael that Christ will ultimately defeat Satan, he demands breathlessly, "Say where and when the fight," and Michael can only instruct him—and us—"Dream not of their fight / As of a duel." Christ's birth in a stable and ensuing sacrifice forecast a very different kind of epic poetry, the kind that Dante had crafted in his *Divine Comedy* and to which Milton himself would turn in *Paradise Regained,* a poem, as critics have frequently commented, in which "nothing happens," as Satan unsuccessfully tries to tempt Jesus to sin.

Paradise Lost would also, ideally, have been a poem in which "nothing happens," had it not been for Eve's yielding to her desire to be equal to God and Adam's yielding to "female charms." All of the poem is, in some sense, preparatory to the "tragic notes" that mark Book 9, the book of the fall; and therein the reader is forced to wrestle with questions that were fundamental to the era itself—among them, at what point man first sinned, and whether Adam should have divorced Eve after she ate the apple. But few questions are more central than the one Milton had asked twenty years earlier in his classic defense of freedom from censorship, *Areopagitica:* "what were vertue but a name" unless it is put through trial? (*Areopagitica,* it should be added, didn't defend freedom for everyone; Milton excludes protection for Catholicism, "which, as it extirpates all religious and civil supremacies, so itself should be extirpate.") This question about "vertue" is one Eve herself asks, as she fearlessly abandons Adam in the protective shade of the bower to labor on her own, despite the imminent threat of an escapee from hell: "And what is faith, love, virtue unassayed / Alone, without exterior help sustained"? (9:335–36). How, in short, is one to know if one is virtuous unless faced by the "assays" or "trials" to which Eve—and, of course, Milton and his contemporaries—are put? Moved by Eve's and Adam's plight, Christ provides one answer: it would have been far, far better if man had known "good by itself / evil not at all" (11.85). Yet Milton and his readers, unlike Adam and Eve, have no choice. Thus if the poem on one level indicts its once-innocent protagonists, on another it vindicates the active component of a faith tried and made resilient in the rough and tumble of public life.

At the same time, *Paradise Lost* looks toward the necessary inwardness of faith set apart from any physical or worldly manifestation, as well as from bondage to creeds and external restrictions of any kind. Milton claims in his 1668 Preface that in abandoning rhyme, his poem "is to be esteemed an example set, the first in English, of ancient liberty recovered to heroic poem from the troublesome and modern bondage of rhyming." "God attributes to place no sanctity," Michael informs Adam; and while his lines attack the idolatry that pervaded Catholicism and Anglicanism alike, they also free Adam and Eve to live where they wish, to carry within them even in exile their own paradise in the same way that Satan, lamenting his distance from the beauties of earth, must always bring with him his murky home: "myself am Hell" (4:75). This separation from the world was even more manifest in Milton's last two poems: Christ in *Paradise Regained* is ethereal next to the increasingly frustrated Satan, and in Milton's tragedy, *Samson Agonistes,* Samson's blindness becomes metaphorical for his indifference to place. The political freedoms that Milton had not succeeded in bringing about for the English people, the religious freedoms he could not experience for himself under a monarchy, are finally inconsequential compared to the radical freedom of the individual will. As Raphael tells Adam minutes before the "tragic notes" begin, "To stand or fall / Free in thine own arbitrement it lies" (8.640).

All of Milton's writings, in some sense, are an attempt to cultivate the sharpened awareness one must have in order to be responsive to Raphael's dictum: the belief that one can—and must—choose "to stand." The necessary exercising of the will is hardly novel in a period that includes a multitude of Machiavellis. Yet rarely had it been framed within such a tense and accessible human drama. Such accessibility derives from both the stance of the narrator—confiding, as no epic narrator before him, his weaknesses, his limitations, his despair—and the characters of Adam and Eve: immediate in their coyness, their blandishments, their quarrels, their misery and tearful repentance, too late. This particular couple, of course, is a trifle unusual insofar as they dwell for a time in the world's most beautiful garden, and have angels as dinner guests; nor will the modern reader find Eve's apparent inferiority to Adam the poem's most attractive feature. Yet the compelling poetry of *Paradise Lost* is not only that of Satan awakening his fellow fallen, or of Michael as he patiently explains to Adam the future of Christ's sacrifice while God grants Eve the same vision through a dream. Equally it is in the ordinary exchanges between husband and wife as they trim bushes, discuss breakfast, and revel in the beauties of the bower and each other—as well as in their wrestling together as they try to comprehend the wonder and mystery of the universe they have lost.

from PARADISE LOST[1]

Book 9

The Argument

Satan *having compast the Earth, with meditated guile returns as a mist by Night into Paradise, enters into the Serpent sleeping.* Adam *and* Eve *in the Morning go forth to thir labors, which* Eve *proposes to divide in several places, each laboring apart:* Adam *consents not, alleging the danger, lest that Enemy, of whom they were forewarn'd, should attempt her found alone:* Eve *loath to be thought not circumspect or firm enough, urges her going apart, the rather desirous to make trial of her strength;* Adam *at last yields: The Serpent finds her alone; his subtle approach, first gazing, then speaking, with much flattery extolling* Eve *above all other Creatures.* Eve *wond'ring to hear the Serpent speak, asks how he attain'd to human speech and such understanding not till now; the Serpent answers, that by tasting of a certain Tree in the Garden he attain'd both to Speech and Reason, till then void of both:* Eve *requires*

1. Our text is taken, and the notes are adapted, from John Carey and Alastair Fowler, eds., *The Poems of John Milton.*

him to bring her to that Tree, and finds it to be the Tree of Knowledge forbidden: The Serpent now grown bolder, with many wiles and arguments induces her at length to eat; she pleas'd with the taste deliberates awhile whether to impart thereof to Adam *or not, at last brings him of the Fruit, relates what persuaded her to eat thereof:* Adam *at first amaz'd, but perceiving her lost, resolves through vehemence*[2] *of love to perish with her; and extenuating*[3] *the trespass, eats also of the Fruit: The effects thereof in them both; they seek to cover thir nakedness; then fall to variance and accusation of one another.*

No more of talk where God or Angel Guest
With Man, as with his Friend, familiar us'd
To sit indulgent, and with him partake
Rural repast, permitting him the while
Venial° discourse unblam'd: I now must change *permissible*
Those Notes to Tragic; foul distrust, and breach
Disloyal on the part of Man, revolt,
And disobedience: On the part of Heav'n
Now alienated, distance and distaste,
Anger and just rebuke, and judgment giv'n,
That brought into this World a world of woe,
Sin and her shadow Death, and Misery
Death's Harbinger: Sad task, yet argument
Not less but more Heroic than the wrath
Of stern *Achilles* on his Foe pursu'd
Thrice Fugitive about *Troy* Wall; or rage
Of *Turnus* for *Lavinia* disespous'd,
Or *Neptune's* ire or *Juno's,* that so long
Perplex'd the *Greek* and *Cytherea's* Son;[4]
If answerable° style I can obtain *equal, accountable*
Of my Celestial Patroness,[5] who deigns
Her nightly visitation unimplor'd,
And dictates to me slumb'ring, or inspires
Easy my unpremeditated Verse:
Since first this Subject for Heroic Song
Pleas'd me long choosing, and beginning late;
Not sedulous by Nature to indite
Wars, hitherto the only Argument
Heroic deem'd, chief maistry to dissect
With long and tedious havoc fabl'd Knights
In Battles feign'd; the better fortitude
Of Patience and Heroic Martyrdom

2. The root meaning of Latin "vehementia" is mindlessness.

3. Carrying further, drawing out.

4. Achilles is "stern" in his "wrath" because he refused any covenant with Hector, and Turnus dies fighting Aeneas for the hand of Lavinia, whereas Messiah, more heroically, is not implacable in his anger. He issued his sole commandment "sternly" (8.333); but when it is disobeyed, he works for reconciliation. Similarly, God's anger is distinguished from "Neptune's ire" and "Juno's" (which merely "perplexed" Odysseus and Aeneas) in that it is expressed in justice rather than in victimization.

5. The heavenly Muse, Urania. Both ancient and modern epics had always had war, or at least fighting, as a principal ingredient. (So has *Paradise Lost,* in the first half of the poem; but in the second half this subject is transcended.) Milton now glances unfavorably at the typical matter of the romantic epic.

Unsung; or to describe Races and Games,
Or tilting Furniture, emblazon'd Shields,
Impreses[6] quaint, Caparisons[7] and Steeds;
Bases and tinsel Trappings, gorgeous Knights
At Joust and Tournament; then marshall'd Feast
Serv'd up in Hall with Sewers,° and Seneschals;° *waiters / stewards*
The skill of Artifice or Office mean,
Not that which justly gives Heroic name
To Person or to Poem.[8] Mee of these
Nor skill'd nor studious, higher Argument
Remains, sufficient of itself to raise
That name,[9] unless an age too late, or cold
Climate, or Years damp my intended wing
Deprest; and much they may, if all be mine,
    Not Hers who brings it nightly to my Ear.
The Sun was sunk, and after him the Star
Of *Hesperus,*° whose Office is to bring *the planet Venus*
Twilight upon the Earth, short Arbiter
Twixt Day and Night, and now from end to end
Night's Hemisphere had veil'd the Horizon round:
When *Satan* who late fled before the threats
Of *Gabriel* out of *Eden,*[1] now improv'd° *intensified*
In meditated fraud and malice, bent
On Man's destruction, maugre what might hap
Of heavier on himself,[2] fearless return'd.
By Night he fled, and at Midnight return'd
From compassing the Earth, cautious of day,
Since *Uriel* Regent of the Sun descri'd
His entrance, and forewarn'd the Cherubim
That kept thir watch; thence full of anguish driv'n,
The space of seven continu'd Nights he rode
With darkness, thrice the Equinoctial Line
He circl'd, four times cross'd the Car of Night
From Pole to Pole, traversing each Colure;[3]
On th'eighth return'd, and on the Coast averse
From entrance or Cherubic Watch, by stealth
Found unsuspected way. There was a place,
Now not, though Sin, not Time, first wrought the change,
Where *Tigris* at the foot of Paradise
Into a Gulf shot under ground, till part
Rose up a Fountain by the Tree of Life;

6. Heraldic devices, often with accompanying mottos.

7. Ornamented coverings spread over the saddle of a horse.

8. Artifice implies mechanic or applied art. It is beneath the dignity of epic to teach etiquette and social ceremony and heraldry.

9. The name of epic.

1. At the end of Book 4, a week earlier.

2. Despite the danger of heavier punishment.

3. By keeping to earth's shadow, Satan contrives to experience a whole week of darkness. The two colures were great circles, intersecting at right angels at the poles and dividing the equinoctial circle (the equator) into four equal parts.

In with the River sunk, and with it rose
Satan involv'd in rising Mist, then sought
Where to lie hid; Sea he had searcht and Land
From *Eden* over *Pontus,* and the Pool
Maeotis, up beyond the River *Ob;*[4]
Downward as far Antarctic; and in length
West from *Orontes* to the Ocean barr'd
At *Darien,* thence to the Land where flows
Ganges and *Indus:*[5] thus the Orb he roam'd
With narrow search; and with inspection deep
Consider'd every Creature, which of all
Most opportune might serve his Wiles, and found
The Serpent subtlest Beast of all the Field.[6]
Him after long debate, irresolute° *undecided*
Of thoughts revolv'd, his final sentence° chose *judgment*
Fit Vessel, fittest Imp° of fraud, in whom *offshoot*
To enter, and his dark suggestions hide
From sharpest sight: for in the wily Snake,
Whatever sleights none would suspicious mark,
As from his wit and native subtlety
Proceeding, which in other Beasts observ'd
Doubt° might beget of Diabolic pow'r *suspicion*
Active within beyond the sense of brute.
Thus he resolv'd, but first from inward grief
His bursting passion into plaints thus pour'd:
O Earth, how like to Heav'n, if not preferr'd
More justly, Seat worthier of Gods, as built
With second thoughts, reforming what was old!
For what God after better worse would build?
Terrestrial Heav'n, danc't round by other Heav'ns
That shine, yet bear thir bright officious Lamps,
Light above Light, for thee alone, as seems,
In thee concentring all thir precious beams
Of sacred influence:[7] As God in Heav'n
Is Centre, yet extends to all, so thou
Centring receiv'st from all those Orbs; in thee,
Not in themselves, all thir known virtue appears
Productive in Herb, Plant, and nobler birth
Of Creatures animate with gradual life
Of Growth, Sense, Reason, all summ'd up in Man.[8]
With what delight could I have walkt thee round,

4. In his north-south circles, Satan passed Pontus (the Black Sea), the "pool / Maeotis" (the Sea of Azov), and the Siberian River Ob, which flows north into the Gulf of Ob and from there into the Arctic Ocean.

5. In his westward circling of the equinoctial line, he crossed the Syrian River Orontes, then the Pacific ("peaceful") "Ocean barred" by the Isthmus of Darien (Panama) and India.

6. See Genesis 3:1.

7. The case for an earth-centered universe, put at 8.86–114 by Raphael, is now put by Satan.

8. "Growth, sense, reason" are the activities of the vegetable, animal, and rational souls, respectively, in humans.

If I could joy in aught, sweet interchange
Of Hill and Valley, Rivers, Woods and Plains,
Now Land, now Sea, and Shores with Forest crown'd,
Rocks, Dens, and Caves; but I in none of these
Find place or refuge; and the more I see
Pleasures about me, so much more I feel
Torment within me, as from the hateful siege° *conflict*
Of contraries; all good to me becomes
Bane,° and in Heav'n much worse would be my state. *poison*
But neither here seek I, no nor in Heav'n
To dwell, unless by maistring Heav'n's Supreme;
Nor hope to be myself less miserable
By what I seek, but others to make such
As I, though thereby worse to me redound:
For only in destroying I find ease
To my relentless thoughts; and him destroy'd,
Or won to what may work his utter loss,
For whom all this was made, all this will soon
Follow, as to him linkt in weal or woe,
In woe then: that destruction wide may range:[9]
To mee shall be the glory sole among
Th'infernal Powers, in one day to have marr'd
What he *Almight* styl'd, six Nights and Days
Continu'd making, and who knows how long
Before had been contriving, though perhaps
Not longer than since I in one Night freed
From servitude inglorious well nigh half
Th' Angelic Name, and thinner left the throng
Of his adorers: hee to be aveng'd,
And to repair his numbers thus impair'd,
Whether such virtue° spent of old now fail'd *power*
More Angels to Create, if they at least
Are his Created, or to spite us more,
Determin'd to advance into our room
A Creature form'd of Earth, and him endow,
Exalted from so base original,
With Heav'nly spoils, our spoils; What he decreed
He effected; Man he made, and for him built
Magnificent this World, and Earth his seat,
Him Lord pronounc'd, and, O indignity!
Subjected to his service Angel wings,
And flaming Ministers to watch and tend
Thir earthy Charge: Of these the vigilance
I dread, and to elude, thus wrapt in mist
Of midnight vapor glide obscure, and pry
In every Bush and Brake, where hap may find

9. The created cosmos will follow humans to destruction.

The Serpent sleeping, in whose mazy folds
To hide me, and the dark intent I bring.
O foul descent! that I who erst contended
With Gods to sit the highest, am now constrain'd
Into a Beast, and mixt with bestial slime,
This essence to incarnate and imbrute,
That to the highth of Deity aspir'd;
But what will not Ambition and Revenge
Descend to? who aspires must down as low
As high he soar'd, obnoxious° first or last *exposed*
To basest things. Revenge, at first though sweet,
Bitter ere long back on itself recoils;
Let it, I reck not, so it light well aim'd,
Since higher I fall short, on him who next
Provokes my envy, this new Favorite
Of Heav'n, this Man of Clay, Son of despite,
Whom us the more to spite his Maker rais'd
From dust: spite then with spite is best repaid.
So saying, through each Thicket Dank or Dry,
Like a black mist low creeping, he held on
His midnight search, where soonest he might find
The Serpent: him fast sleeping soon he found
In Labyrinth of many a round self-roll'd,
His head the midst, well stor'd with subtle wiles:
Not yet in horrid Shade or dismal Den,
Nor nocent° yet, but on the grassy Herb *harmful, guilty*
Fearless unfear'd he slept: in at his Mouth
The Devil enter'd, and his brutal sense,
In heart or head, possessing soon inspir'd
With act intelligential; but his sleep
Disturb'd not, waiting close° th' approach of Morn. *concealed*
Now whenas sacred Light began to dawn
In *Eden* on the humid Flow'rs, that breath'd
Thir morning incense, when all things that breathe,
From th' Earth's great Altar send up silent praise
To the Creator, and his Nostrils fill
With grateful Smell, forth came the human pair
And join'd thir vocal Worship to the Choir
Of Creatures wanting voice; that done, partake
The season, prime for sweetest Scents and Airs:
Then cómmune how that day they best may ply
Thir growing work: for much thir work outgrew
The hands' dispatch of two Gard'ning so wide.
And *Eve* first to her Husband thus began.
Adam, well may we labor still to dress
This Garden, still to tend Plant, Herb and Flow'r,
Our pleasant task enjoin'd, but till more hands
Aid us, the work under our labor grows,
Luxurious by restraint; what we by day

Lop overgrown, or prune, or prop, or bind,
One night or two with wanton growth derides
Tending to wild. Thou therefore now advise
Or hear what to my mind first thoughts present,
Let us divide our labors, thou where choice
Leads thee, or where most needs, whether to wind
The Woodbine round this Arbor, or direct
The clasping Ivy where to climb, while I
In yonder Spring of Roses intermixt
With Myrtle, find what to redress till Noon:
For while so near each other thus all day
Our task we choose, what wonder if so near
Looks intervene and smiles, or object new
Casual discourse draw on, which intermits
Our day's work brought to little, though begun
Early, and th' hour of Supper comes unearn'd.
  To whom mild answer *Adam* thus return'd.
Sole *Eve,* Associate sole, to me beyond
Compare above all living Creatures dear,
Well hast thou motion'd,° well thy thoughts imploy'd *proposed*
How we might best fulfil the work which here
God hath assign'd us, nor of me shalt pass
Unprais'd: for nothing lovelier can be found
In Woman, than to study household good,
And good works in her Husband to promote.
Yet not so strictly hath our Lord impos'd
Labor, as to debar us when we need
Refreshment, whether food, or talk between,
Food of the mind, or this sweet intercourse
Of looks and smiles, for smiles from Reason flow,
To brute deni'd, and are of Love the food,
Love not the lowest end of human life.
For not to irksome toil, but to delight
He made us, and delight to Reason join'd.
These paths and Bowers doubt not but our joint hands
Will keep from Wilderness with ease, as wide
As we need walk, till younger hands ere long
Assist us: But if much converse perhaps
Thee satiate, to short absence I could yield.
For solitude sometimes is best society,
And short retirement urges sweet return.
But other doubt possesses me, lest harm
Befall thee sever'd from me; for thou know'st
What hath been warn'd us, what malicious Foe
Envying our happiness, and of his own
Despairing, seeks to work us woe and shame
By sly assault; and somewhere nigh at hand
Watches, no doubt, with greedy hope to find
His wish and best advantage, us asunder,

Hopeless to circumvent us join'd, where each
To other speedy aid might lend at need;
Whether his first design be to withdraw
Our fealty from God, or to disturb
Conjugal Love, than which perhaps no bliss
Enjoy'd by us excites his envy more;
Or this, or worse,[1] leave not the faithful side
That gave thee being, still shades thee and protects.
The Wife, where danger or dishonor lurks,
Safest and seemliest by her Husband stays,
Who guards her, or with her the worst endures.
    To whom the Virgin° Majesty of *Eve,* *chaste, innocent*
As one who loves, and some unkindness meets,
With sweet austere composure thus repli'd.
    Offspring of Heav'n and Earth, and all Earth's Lord,
That such an Enemy we have, who seeks
Our ruin, both by thee inform'd I learn,
And from the parting Angel over-heard
As in a shady nook I stood behind,
Just then return'd at shut of Ev'ning Flow'rs.
But that thou shouldst my firmness therefore doubt
To God or thee, because we have a foe
May tempt it, I expected not to hear.
His violence thou fear'st not, being such,
As wee, not capable of death or pain,
Can either not receive, or can repel.
His fraud is then thy fear, which plain infers
Thy equal fear that my firm Faith and Love
Can by his fraud be shak'n or seduc't;
Thoughts, which how found they harbor in thy breast,
Adam, misthought of her to thee so dear?
    To whom with healing words *Adam* repli'd.
Daughter of God and Man, immortal *Eve,*
For such thou art, from sin and blame entire:° *free*
Not diffident° of thee do I dissuade *mistrustful*
Thy absence from my sight, but to avoid
Th' attempt itself, intended by our Foe.
For hee who tempts, though in vain, at least asperses° *falsely charges*
The tempted with dishonor foul, suppos'd
Not incorruptible of Faith, not proof
Against temptation: thou thyself with scorn
And anger wouldst resent the offer'd wrong,
Though ineffectual found: misdeem not then,
If such affront I labor to avert
From thee alone, which on us both at once
The Enemy, though bold, will hardly dare,

1. Whether this or worse (be his first design).

Or daring, first on mee th' assault shall light.
Nor thou his malice and false guile contemn;
Subtle he needs must be, who could seduce
Angels, nor think superfluous others' aid.
I from the influence of thy looks receive
Access° in every Virtue, in thy sight *increase*
More wise, more watchful, stronger, if need were
Of outward strength; while shame, thou looking on,
Shame to be overcome or over-reacht
Would utmost vigor raise, and rais'd unite.
Why shouldst not thou like sense within thee feel
When I am present, and thy trial choose
With me, best witness of thy Virtue tri'd.
 So spake domestic *Adam* in his care
And Matrimonial Love; but *Eve,* who thought
Less° attribúted to her Faith sincere, *too little*
Thus her reply with accent sweet renew'd.
 If this be our condition, thus to dwell
In narrow circuit strait'n'd by a Foe,
Subtle or violent, we not endu'd
Single with like defense, wherever met,
How are we happy, still in fear of harm?
But harm precedes not sin: only our Foe
Tempting affronts us with his foul esteem
Of our integrity: his foul esteem
Sticks no dishonor on our Front,° but turns *face*
Foul on himself; then wherefore shunn'd or fear'd
By us? who rather double honor gain
From his surmise prov'd false, find peace within,
Favor from Heav'n, our witness from th' event.
And what is Faith, Love, Virtue unassay'd
Alone, without exterior help sustain'd?
Let us not then suspect our happy State
Left so imperfet by the Maker wise,
As not secure to single or combin'd.
Frail is our happiness, if this be so,
And *Eden* were no Eden[2] thus expos'd.
 To whom thus Adam fervently repli'd.
O Woman, best are all things as the will
Of God ordain'd them, his creating hand
Nothing imperfet or deficient left
Of all that he Created, much less Man,
Or aught that might his happy State secure,
Secure from outward force; within himself
The danger lies, yet lies within his power:
Against his will he can receive no harm.

2. No pleasure, the literal Hebrew meaning of "Eden."

But God left free the Will, for what obeys
Reason, is free, and Reason he made right,
But bid her well beware, and still erect,[3]
Lest by some fair appearing good surpris'd
She dictate false, and misinform the Will
To do what God expressly hath forbid.
Not then mistrust, but tender love enjoins,
That I should mind thee oft, and mind thou me.
Firm we subsist, yet possible to swerve,
Since Reason not impossibly may meet
Some specious object by the Foe suborn'd,
And fall into deception unaware,
Not keeping strictest watch, as she was warn'd.
Seek not temptation then, which to avoid
Were better, and most likely if from mee
Thou sever not: Trial will come unsought.
Wouldst thou approve° thy constancy, approve *demonstrate*
First thy obedience; th' other who can know,
Not seeing thee attempted, who attest?
But if thou think, trial unsought may find
Us both securer° than thus warn'd thou seem'st, *more careless*
Go; for thy stay, not free, absents thee more;
Go in thy native innocence, rely
On what thou hast of virtue, summon all,
For God towards thee hath done his part, do thine.
  So spake the Patriarch of Mankind, but *Eve*
Persisted, yet submiss, though last, repli'd.
  With thy permission then, and thus forewarn'd
Chiefly by what thy own last reasoning words
Touch'd only, that our trial, when least sought,
May find us both perhaps far less prepar'd,
The willinger I go, nor much expect
A Foe so proud will first the weaker seek;
So bent, the more shall shame him his repulse.
Thus saying, from her Husband's hand her hand
Soft she withdrew, and like a Wood-Nymph light,
Oread or *Dryad,* or of *Delia's* Train,[4]
Betook her to the Groves, but *Delia's* self
In gait surpass'd and Goddess-like deport,
Though not as shee with Bow and Quiver arm'd,
But with such Gard'ning Tools as Art yet rude,
Guiltless° of fire had form'd, or Angels brought.[5] *innocent, ignorant*
To Pales, or Pomona, thus adorn'd,
Likest she seem'd, Pomona when she fled
Vertumnus, or to *Ceres* in her Prime,

3. Always attentive, but also with a glance at upright.
4. Oreads, were mountain nymphs, such as attended on Diana; dryads were wood nymphs. Neither class of nymphs were immortal.
5. Only as a result of the Fall did it become necessary for humans to have some means of warming themselves. There may also be an allusion to the fire stolen from heaven by Prometheus.

Yet Virgin of *Proserpina* from *Jove.*[6]
Her long and ardent look his Eye pursu'd
Delighted, but desiring more her stay.
Oft he to her his charge of quick return
Repeated, shee to him as oft engag'd
To be return'd by Noon amid the Bow'r,
And all things in best order to invite
Noontide repast, or Afternoon's repose.
O much deceiv'd, much failing, hapless *Eve,*
Of thy presum'd return! event perverse!
Thou never from that hour in Paradise
Found'st either sweet repast, or sound repose;
Such ambush hid among sweet Flow'rs and Shades
Waited with hellish rancor imminent
To intercept thy way, or send thee back
Despoil'd of Innocence, of Faith, of Bliss.
For now, and since first break of dawn the Fiend,
Mere° Serpent in appearance, forth was come, *plain*
And on his Quest, where likeliest he might find
The only two of Mankind, but in them
The whole included Race, his purpos'd prey.
In Bow'r and Field he sought, where any tuft
Of Grove or Garden-Plot more pleasant lay,
Thir tendance° or Plantation for delight, *object of care*
By Fountain or by shady Rivulet,
He sought them both, but wish'd his hap° might find *chance*
Eve separate, he wish'd, but not with hope
Of what so seldom chanc'd, when to his wish,
Beyond his hope, *Eve* separate he spies,
Veil'd in a Cloud of Fragrance, where she stood,
Half spi'd, so thick the Roses bushing round
About her glow'd, oft stooping to support
Each Flow'r of slender stalk, whose head though gay
Carnation, Purple, Azure, or speckt with Gold,
Hung drooping unsustain'd, them she upstays
Gently with Myrtle band, mindless the while,
Herself, though fairest unsupported Flow'r,
From her best prop so far, and storm so nigh.
Nearer he drew, and many a walk travers'd
Of stateliest Covert, Cedar, Pine, or Palm,
Then voluble and bold, now hid, now seen
Among thick-wov'n Arborets and Flow'rs
Imborder'd on each Bank, the hand° of *Eve:* *handiwork*
Spot more delicious than those Gardens feign'd

6. Pales was the Roman goddess of pastures; Pomona was the nymph or goddess of fruit trees, seduced by the disguised Vertumnus; Ceres was the goddess of corn and agriculture who bore Proserpina to Jove.

Or of reviv'd *Adonis,* or renown'd
Alcinoüs, host of old *Laertes'* Son,
Or that, not Mystic, where the Sapient King
Held dalliance with his fair *Egyptian* Spouse.[7]
Much hee the Place admir'd, the Person more.
As one who long in populous City pent,
Where Houses thick and Sewers annoy the Air,
Forth issuing on a Summer's Morn to breathe
Among the pleasant Villages and Farms
Adjoin'd, from each thing met conceives delight,
The smell of Grain, or tedded° Grass, or Kine,° *mown / cows*
Or Dairy, each rural sight, each rural sound;
If chance with Nymphlike step fair Virgin pass,
What pleasing seem'd, for her now pleases more,
She most, and in her look sums all Delight.
Such Pleasure took the Serpent to behold
This Flow'ry Plat,° the sweet recess of *Eve* *piece of ground*
Thus early, thus alone; her Heav'nly form
Angelic, but more soft, and Feminine,
Her graceful Innocence, her every Air
Of gesture or least action overaw'd
His Malice, and with rapine sweet bereav'd
His fierceness of the fierce intent it brought:
That space the Evil one abstracted stood
From his own evil, and for the time remain'd
Stupidly good, of enmity disarm'd,
Of guile, of hate, of envy, of revenge;
But the hot Hell that always in him burns,
Though in mid Heav'n, soon ended his delight,
And tortures him now more, the more he sees
Of pleasure not for him ordain'd: then soon
Fierce hate he recollects, and all his thoughts
Of mischief, gratulating,° thus excites. *rejoicing*
    Thoughts, whither have ye led me, with what sweet
Compulsion thus transported to forget
What hither brought us, hate, not love, nor hope
Of Paradise for Hell, hope here to taste
Of pleasure, but all pleasure to destroy,
Save what is in destroying, other joy
To me is lost. Then let me not let pass
Occasion which now smiles, behold alone
The Woman, opportune° to all attempts, *exposed*
Her Husband, for I view far round, not nigh,
Whose higher intellectual more I shun,
And strength, of courage haughty, and of limb

7. "The sapient king" was Solomon (Song of Songs 6:2). Milton alludes to Spenser's addition to the myth of Adonis, that Venus keeps Adonis hidden in a secret garden (*The Faerie Queene* 3.6). "Laertes' son" was Odysseus; much-traveled as he was, he marveled when he saw the Garden of Alcinoüs (Homer, *Odyssey* 7).

Heroic built, though of terrestrial mould,° *formed of earth*
Foe not informidable, exempt from wound,
I not; so much hath Hell debas'd, and pain
Infeebl'd me, to what I was in Heav'n.
Shee fair, divinely fair, fit Love for Gods,
Not terrible, though terror be in Love
And beauty, not approacht by stronger hate,
Hate stronger, under show of Love well feign'd,
The way which to her ruin now I tend.
So spake the Enemy of Mankind, enclos'd
In Serpent, Inmate bad, and toward *Eve*
Address'd his way, not with indented wave,
Prone on the ground, as since, but on his rear,
Circular base of rising folds, that tow'r'd
Fold above fold a surging Maze, his Head
Crested aloft, and Carbuncle his Eyes;[8]
With burnisht Neck of verdant Gold, erect
Amidst his circling Spires,° that on the grass *coils*
Floated redundant:° pleasing was his shape, *abundant to excess*
And lovely, never since of Serpent kind
Lovelier, not those that in *Illyria* chang'd
Hermione and *Cadmus,* or the God
In *Epidaurus;*[9] nor to which transform'd
Ammonian Jove, or *Capitoline* was seen,
Hee with *Olympias,* this with her who bore
Scipio the highth of Rome.[1] With tract oblique
At first, as one who sought access, but fear'd
To interrupt, side-long he works his way.
As when a Ship by skilful Steersman wrought
Nigh River's mouth or Foreland, where the Wind
Veers oft, as oft so steers, and shifts her Sail;
So varied hee, and of his tortuous Train
Curl'd many a wanton wreath in sight of *Eve,*
To lure her Eye; shee busied heard the sound
Of rustling Leaves, but minded not, as us'd
To such disport before her through the Field,
From every Beast, more duteous at her call,
Than at *Circean* call the Herd disguis'd.[2]
Hee bolder now, uncall'd before her stood;
But as in gaze admiring: Oft he bow'd
His turret Crest, and sleek enamell'd Neck,
Fawning, and lick'd the ground whereon she trod.

8. "Carbuncle" or reddish eyes denoted rage.

9. Cadmus was turned into a serpent first; only after he had embraced his wife Hermione (Harmonia) in his new form did she too change (Ovid, *Metamorphoses* 4.572–603). Aesculapius, the god of healing, once changed into a serpent to help the Romans in that form (Ovid, *Metamorphoses* 15.626–744).

1. Jupiter Ammon, the "Lybian Jove," as a serpent mated with Olympias to father Alexander the Great, just as the Roman Jupiter, Capitolinus, took the form of a snake to father the great general Scipio.

2. Homer's Circe changed men into beasts who surprised Odysseus's company by fawning on them like dogs (*Odyssey* 10.212–19).

His gentle dumb expression turn'd at length
The Eye of *Eve* to mark his play; he glad
Of her attention gain'd, with Serpent Tongue
Organic, or impulse of vocal Air,
His fraudulent temptation thus began.
 Wonder not, sovran Mistress, if perhaps
Thou canst, who are sole Wonder, much less arm
Thy looks, the Heav'n of mildness, with disdain,
Displeas'd that I approach thee thus, and gaze
Insatiate, I thus single, nor have fear'd
Thy awful brow, more awful thus retir'd.
Fairest resemblance of thy Maker fair,
Thee all things living gaze on, all things thine
By gift, and thy Celestial Beauty adore
With ravishment beheld, there best beheld
Where universally admir'd: but here
In this enclosure wild, these Beasts among,
Beholders rude, and shallow to discern
Half what in thee is fair, one man except,
Who sees thee? (and what is one?) who shouldst be seen
A Goddess among Gods, ador'd and serv'd
By Angels numberless, thy daily Train.
 So gloz'd° the Tempter, and his Proem° tun'd; *flattered / prelude*
Into the Heart of *Eve* his words made way,
Though at the voice much marvelling; at length
Not unamaz'd she thus in answer spake.
 What may this mean? Language of Man pronounc't
By Tongue of Brute, and human sense exprest?[3]
The first at least of these I thought deni'd
To Beasts, whom God on thir Creation-Day
Created mute to all articulate sound;
The latter I demur,° for in thir looks *hesitate about*
Much reason, and in thir actions oft appears.
Thee, Serpent, subtlest beast of all the field
I knew, but not with human voice endu'd;
Redouble then this miracle, and say,
How cam'st thou speakable of mute,[4] and how
To me so friendly grown above the rest
Of brutal kind, that daily are in sight?
Say, for such wonder claims attention due.
 To whom the guileful Tempter thus repli'd.
Empress of this fair World, resplendent *Eve,*
Easy to mee it is to tell thee all
What thou command'st and right thou should'st be obey'd:
I was at first as other Beasts that graze

3. Milton is unusually favorable to Eve in making her ask the serpent how it came by its voice. The Eve of Scriptural exegesis, by contrast, is carried away by the words and makes no inquiry into their source.

4. How did you become capable of speech from being dumb?

The trodden Herb, of abject° thoughts and low, *mean-spirited*
As was my food, nor aught but food discern'd
Or Sex, and apprehended nothing high:
Till on a day roving the field, I chanc'd
A goodly Tree far distant to behold
Loaden with fruit of fairest colors mixt,
Ruddy and Gold: I nearer drew to gaze;
When from the boughs a savory odor blown,
Grateful to appetite, more pleas'd my sense
Than smell of sweetest Fennel, or the Teats
Of Ewe or Goat dropping with Milk at Ev'n,
Unsuckt of Lamb or Kid, that tend thir play.
To satisfy the sharp desire I had
Of tasting those fair Apples, I resolv'd
Not to defer; hunger and thirst at once,
Powerful persuaders, quick'n'd at the scent
Of that alluring fruit, urg'd me so keen.
About the mossy Trunk I wound me soon,
For high from ground the branches would require
Thy utmost reach or *Adam's:* Round the Tree
All other Beasts that saw, with like desire
Longing and envying stood, but could not reach.
Amid the Tree now got, where plenty hung
Tempting so nigh, to pluck and eat my fill
I spar'd not, for such pleasure till that hour
At Feed or Fountain never had I found.
Sated at length, ere long I might perceive
Strange alteration in me, to degree
Of Reason in my inward Powers, and Speech
Wanted not long, though to this shape retain'd.
Thenceforth to Speculations high or deep
I turn'd my thoughts, and with capacious mind
Consider'd all things visible in Heav'n,
Or Earth, or Middle, all things fair and good;
But all that fair and good in thy Divine
Semblance, and in thy Beauty's heav'nly Ray
United I beheld; no Fair° to thine *beauty*
Equivalent or second, which compell'd
Mee thus, though importune perhaps, to come
And gaze, and worship thee of right declar'd
Sovran of Creatures, universal Dame.
So talk'd the spirited[5] sly Snake; and *Eve,*
Yet more amaz'd unwary thus repli'd.
Serpent, thy overpraising leaves in doubt
The virtue° of that Fruit, in thee first prov'd: *power*
But say, where grows the Tree, from hence how far?

5. Endowed with an animating spirit, stirred up; also energetic, enterprising, possessed by a spirit.

For many are the Trees of God that grow
In Paradise, and various, yet unknown
To us, in such abundance lies our choice,
As leaves a greater store of Fruit untoucht,
Still hanging incorruptible, till men
Grow up to thir provision, and more hands
Help to disburden Nature of her Birth.
To whom the wily Adder, blithe and glad.
Empress, the way is ready, and not long,
Beyond a row of Myrtles, on a Flat,
Fast by a Fountain, one small Thicket past
Of blowing° Myrrh and Balm; if thou accept *blooming*
My conduct,° I can bring thee thither soon. *guidance*
Lead then, said Eve. Hee leading swiftly roll'd
In tangles, and made intricate seem straight,
To mischief swift. Hope elevates, and joy
Bright'ns his Crest, as when a wand'ring Fire,
Compact° of unctuous vapor, which the Night *made up*
Condenses, and the cold invirons round,
Kindl'd through agitation to a Flame,
Which oft, they say, some evil Spirit attends,
Hovering and blazing with delusive Light,
Misleads th' amaz'd Night-wanderer from his way
To Bogs and Mires, and oft through Pond or Pool,
There swallow'd up and lost, from succor far.
So glister'd the dire Snake, and into fraud
Led *Eve* our credulous Mother, to the Tree
Of prohibition, root of all our woe;
Which when she saw, thus to her guide she spake.
Serpent, we might have spar'd our coming hither,
Fruitless to mee, though Fruit be here to excess,
The credit of whose virtue rest with thee,
Wondrous indeed, if cause of such effects.
But of this Tree we may not taste nor touch;
God so commanded, and left that Command
Sole Daughter of his voice;[6] the rest, we live
Law to ourselves, our Reason is our Law.
To whom the Tempter guilefully repli'd.
Indeed? hath God then said that of the Fruit
Of all these Garden Trees ye shall not eat,
Yet Lords declar'd of all in Earth or Air?[7]
To whom thus *Eve* yet sinless. Of the Fruit
Of each Tree in the Garden we may eat,
But of the Fruit of this fair Tree amidst
The Garden, God hath said, Ye shall not eat
Thereof, nor shall ye touch it, lest ye die.

6. A Hebraism for "voice sent from heaven."

7. Lines 655–58 closely follow Genesis 3:1.

She scarce had said, though brief, when now more bold
The Tempter, but with show of Zeal and Love
To Man, and indignation at his wrong,
New part puts on, and as to passion mov'd,
Fluctuates disturb'd, yet comely, and in act
Rais'd, as of some great matter to begin.
As when of old some Orator renown'd
In *Athens* or free *Rome,* where Eloquence
Flourish'd, since mute, to some great cause addrest,
Stood in himself collected, while each part,
Motion, each act won audience ere the tongue,
Sometimes in highth began, as no delay
Of Preface brooking through his Zeal of Right.[8]
So standing, moving, or to highth upgrown
The Tempter all impassion'd thus began.
O Sacred, Wise, and Wisdom-giving Plant,
Mother of Science,° now I feel thy Power *knowledge*
Within me clear, not only to discern
Things in thir Causes, but to trace the ways
Of highest Agents, deem'd however wise.
Queen of this Universe, do not believe
Those rigid threats of Death; ye shall not Die:
How should ye? by the Fruit? it gives you Life
To° Knowledge: By the Threat'ner? look on mee, *in addition to*
Mee who have touch'd and tasted, yet both live,
And life more perfet have attain'd than Fate
Meant mee, by vent'ring higher than my Lot.
Shall that be shut to Man, which to the Beast
Is open? or will God incense his ire
For such a petty Trespass, and not praise
Rather your dauntless virtue, whom the pain
Of Death denounc't, whatever thing Death be,
Deterr'd not from achieving what might lead
To happier life, knowledge of Good and Evil;
Of good, how just? of evil, if what is evil
Be real, why not known, since easier shunn'd?[9]
God therefore cannot hurt ye, and be just;
Not just, not God; not fear'd then, nor obey'd:
Your fear itself of Death removes the fear.
Why then was this forbid? Why but to awe,
Why but to keep ye low and ignorant,
His worshippers; he knows that in the day
Ye Eat thereof, your Eyes that seem so clear,

8. This simile blends oratorical, theatrical, and theological meanings. Thus "part" means "part of the body," "dramatic role," and "moral act"; "motion" means "gesture," "mime" (or "puppet-show"), and "instigation, persuasive force, inclination"; "act" means "action," "performance of a play," and "the accomplished deed itself."

9. If the knowledge is good, how is it just to prohibit it? Here occurs the most egregious logical fallacy in speech. (For evil to be "shunned," it is not at all necessary that it should be "known" in the sense of being experienced.)

Yet are but dim, shall perfetly be then
Op'n'd and clear'd, and ye shall be as Gods,
Knowing both Good and Evil as they know.[1]
That ye should be as Gods, since I as Man,
Internal Man,[2] is but proportion meet,
I of brute human, thee of human Gods.
So ye shall die perhaps, by putting off
Human, to put on Gods, death to be wisht,
Though threat'n'd, which no worse than this can bring.[3]
And what are Gods that Man may not become
As they, participating° God-like food? *sharing*
The Gods are first, and that advantage use
On our belief, that all from them proceeds;
I question it, for this fair Earth I see,
Warm'd by the Sun, producing every kind,
Them nothing: If they° all things, who enclos'd *if they produce*
Knowledge of Good and Evil in this Tree,
That who so eats thereof, forthwith attains
Wisdom without their leave? and wherein lies
Th' offense, that Man should thus attain to know?
What can your knowledge hurt him, or this Tree
Impart against his will if all be his?
Or is it envy, and can envy dwell
In heav'nly breasts?[4] these, these and many more
Causes import° your need of this fair Fruit. *suggest*
Goddess humane, reach then, and freely taste.
He ended, and his words replete with guile
Into her heart too easy entrance won:
Fixt on the Fruit she gaz'd, which to behold
Might tempt alone, and in her ears the sound
Yet rung of his persuasive words, impregn'd° *impregnated*
With Reason, to her seeming, and with Truth;
Meanwhile the hour of Noon drew on, and wak'd
An eager appetite, rais'd by the smell
So savory of that Fruit, which with desire,
Inclinable now grown to touch or taste,
Solicited her longing eye;[5] yet first
Pausing a while, thus to herself she mus'd.
Great are thy Virtues, doubtless, best of Fruits,
Though kept from Man, and worthy to be admir'd,
Whose taste, too long forborne, at first assay
Gave elocution to the mute, and taught

1. See Genesis 3:5.
2. The serpent's pretence is that his "inward powers" are human.
3. Satan offers a travesty of Christian mortification and death to sin; see Colossians 3:1–15: "ye have put off the old man with his deeds; And have put on the new man, which is renewed in knowledge after the image of him that created him."
4. See Virgil, *Aeneid* 1.11; Satan is inviting Eve to participate in a pagan epic, complete with machinery of jealous gods.
5. For lines 735–43, see Genesis 3:6.

The Tongue not made for Speech to speak thy praise:[6]
Thy praise hee also who forbids thy use,
Conceals not from us, naming thee the Tree
Of Knowledge, knowledge both of good and evil;
Forbids us then to taste, but his forbidding
Commends thee more, while it infers the good
By thee communicated, and our want:
For good unknown, sure is not had, or had
And yet unknown, is as not had at all.
In plain° then, what forbids he but to know, *plainly*
Forbids us good, forbids us to be wise?
Such prohibitions bind not. But if Death
Bind us with after-bands, what profits then
Our inward freedom? In the day we eat
Of this fair Fruit, our doom is, we shall die.
How dies the Serpent? hee hath eat'n and lives,
And knows, and speaks, and reasons, and discerns,
Irrational till then. For us alone
Was death invented? or to us deni'd
This intellectual food, for beasts reserv'd?
For Beasts it seems: yet that one Beast which first
Hath tasted, envies not, but brings with joy
The good befall'n him, Author unsuspect,[7]
Friendly to man, far from deceit or guile.
What fear I then, rather what know to fear[8]
Under this ignorance of Good and Evil,
Of God or Death, of Law or Penalty?
Here grows the Cure of all, this Fruit Divine,
Fair to the Eye, inviting to the Taste,
Of virtue° to make wise: what hinders then *power*
To reach, and feed at once both Body and Mind?
So saying, her rash hand in evil hour
Forth reaching to the Fruit, she pluck'd, she eat:° *ate*
Earth felt the wound, and Nature from her seat
Sighing through all her Works gave signs of woe,
That all was lost. Back to the Thicket slunk
The guilty Serpent, and well might, for *Eve,*
Intent now wholly on her taste, naught else
Regarded, such delight till then, as seem'd,
In Fruit she never tasted, whether true
Or fancied so, through expectation high
Of knowledge, nor was God-head from her thought.[9]
Greedily she ingorg'd without restraint,

6. Eve has trusted Satan's account of the fruit and consequently argues from false premises, such as its magical power.
7. Eve means "informant not subject to suspicion."
8. What fear I, then—or rather (since I'm not allowed to know anything) what do I know that is to be feared?
9. She expected to achieve godhead.

And knew not eating Death:[1] Satiate at length,
And hight'n'd as with Wine, jocund and boon,° *jolly*
Thus to herself she pleasingly began.
O Sovran, virtuous, precious of all Trees
In Paradise, of operation blest
To Sapience,[2] hitherto obscur'd, infam'd,° *defamed*
And thy fair Fruit let hang, as to no end
Created; but henceforth my early care,
Not without Song, each Morning, and due praise
Shall tend thee, and the fertile burden ease
Of thy full branches offer'd free to all;
Till dieted by thee I grow mature
In knowledge, as the Gods who all things know;
Though others[3] envy what they cannot give;
For had the gift been theirs, it had not here
Thus grown. Experience, next to thee I owe,
Best guide; not following thee, I had remain'd
In ignorance, thou op'n'st Wisdom's way,
And giv'st access, though secret she retire.
And I perhaps am secret; Heav'n is high,
High and remote to see from thence distinct
Each thing on Earth; and other care perhaps
May have diverted from continual watch
Our great Forbidder, safe with all his Spies
About him. But to *Adam* in what sort
Shall I appear? shall I to him make known
As yet my change, and give him to partake
Full happiness with mee, or rather not.
But keep the odds of Knowledge in my power
Without Copartner? so to add what wants
In Female Sex, the more to draw his Love,
And render me more equal, and perhaps,
A thing not undesirable, sometime
Superior: for inferior who is free?
This may be well: but what if God have seen,
And Death ensue? then I shall be no more,
And *Adam* wedded to another *Eve,*
Shall live with her enjoying, I extinct;
A death to think. Confirm'd then I resolve,
Adam shall share with me in bliss or woe:
So dear I love him, that with him all deaths
I could endure, without him live no life.
So saying, from the Tree her step she turn'd,
But first low Reverence done, as to the power

1. She knew not that she was eating death; "she was unaware, while she ate death" or even "she 'knew'; not eating (immediate) death."
2. "Sapience" is derived from Latin *sapientia* (discernment, taste) and ultimately from *sapere* (to taste).
3. I.e., God. Eve's language is now full of lapses in logic and evasions in theology.

That dwelt within, whose presence had infus'd
Into the plant sciential[4] sap, deriv'd
From Nectar, drink of Gods. *Adam* the while
Waiting desirous her return, had wove
Of choicest Flow'rs a Garland to adorn
Her Tresses, and her rural labors crown,
As Reapers oft are wont thir Harvest Queen.
Great joy he promis'd to his thoughts, and new
Solace in her return, so long delay'd;
Yet oft his heart, divine° of something ill, *prophet*
Misgave him; hee the falt'ring measure[5] felt;
And forth to meet her went, the way she took
That Morn when first they parted; by the Tree
Of Knowledge he must pass; there he her met,
Scarce from the Tree returning; in her hand
A bough of fairest fruit that downy smil'd,
New gather'd, and ambrosial smell diffus'd.
To him she hasted, in her face excuse
Came Prologue, and Apology to prompt,[6]
Which with bland words at will she thus addrest.
    Hast thou not wonder'd, *Adam,* at my stay?
Thee I have misst, and thought it long, depriv'd
Thy presence, agony of love till now
Not felt, nor shall be twice, for never more
Mean I to try, what rash untri'd I sought,
The pain of absence from thy sight. But strange
Hath been the cause, and wonderful to hear:
This Tree is not as we are told, a Tree
Of danger tasted,° nor to evil unknown *if tasted*
Op'ning the way, but of Divine effect
To open Eyes, and make them Gods who taste;
And hath been tasted such: the Serpent wise,
Or not restrain'd as wee, or not obeying,
Hath eat'n of the fruit, and is become,
Not dead, as we are threat'n'd, but thenceforth
Endu'd with human voice and human sense,
Reasoning to admiration, and with mee
Persuasively hath so prevail'd, that I
Have also tasted, and have also found
Th' effects to correspond, opener mine Eyes,
Dim erst, dilated Spirits, ampler Heart,
And growing up to Godhead; which for thee
Chiefly I sought, without thee can despise.
For bliss, as thou hast part, to me is bliss,

4. Endowed with knowledge.
5. The rhythm of his own heart.
6. The expression on Eve's face is visible in advance as she approaches and so is like the prologue-speaker of a play. But it also remains on her face as she speaks, to help out her words, and so is like the prompter of the play. The actor prompted is Apology, i.e., justification or defense personified.

Tedious, unshar'd with thee, and odious soon.
Thou therefore also taste, that equal Lot
May join us, equal Joy, as equal Love;
Lest thou not tasting, different degree[7]
Disjoin us, and I then too late renounce
Deity for thee, when Fate will not permit.
  Thus *Eve* with Count'nance blithe her story told;
But in her Cheek distemper[8] flushing glow'd.
On th' other side, *Adam,* soon as he heard
The fatal Trespass done by *Eve,* amaz'd,
Astonied° stood and Blank, while horror chill *stunned*
Ran through his veins, and all his joints relax'd;
From his slack hand the Garland wreath'd for *Eve,*
Down dropp'd, and all the faded Roses shed:
Speechless he stood and pale, till thus at length
First to himself he inward silence broke.
  O fairest of Creation, last and best
Of all God's Works, Creature in whom excell'd
Whatever can to sight or thought be form'd,
Holy, divine, good, amiable, or sweet!
How art thou lost, how on a sudden lost,
Defac't, deflow'r'd, and now to death devote?° *given over*
Rather how hast thou yielded to transgress
The strict forbiddance, how to violate
The sacred Fruit forbidd'n! some cursed fraud
Of Enemy hath beguil'd thee, yet unknown,
And mee with thee hath ruin'd, for with thee
Certain my resolution is to Die;
How can I live without thee, how forgo
Thy sweet Converse and Love so dearly join'd,
To live again in these wild Woods forlorn?
Should God create another *Eve,* and I
Another Rib afford, yet loss of thee
Would never from my heart; no no, I feel
The Link of Nature draw me: Flesh of Flesh,
Bone of my Bone thou art, and from thy State
Mine never shall be parted, bliss or woe.
  So having said, as one from sad dismay
Recomforted, and after thoughts disturb'd
Submitting to what seem'd remediless,
Thus in calm mood his Words to *Eve* he turn'd.
  Bold deed thou hast presum'd, advent'rous *Eve,*
And peril great provok't, who thus hath dar'd
Had it been only coveting to Eye
That sacred Fruit, sacred° to abstinence, *devoted*

7. Differing position in the scale of creatures.

8. A disordered condition due to disturbance of the temperament of the bodily humors.

Much more to taste it under ban to touch.
But past who can recall, or done undo?
Not God Omnipotent, nor Fate; yet so
Perhaps thou shalt not Die, perhaps the Fact° *crime, deed*
Is not so heinous now, foretasted Fruit,
Profan'd first by the Serpent, by him first
Made common and unhallow'd ere our taste;
Nor yet on him found deadly, he yet lives,
Lives, as thou said'st, and gains to live as Man
Higher degree of Life, inducement strong
To us, as likely tasting to attain
Proportional ascent, which cannot be
But to be Gods, or Angels Demi-gods.
Nor can I think that God, Creator wise,
Though threat'ning, will in earnest so destroy
Us his prime Creatures, dignifi'd so high,
Set over all his Works, which in our Fall,
For us created, needs with us must fail,
Dependent made; so God shall uncreate,
Be frustrate, do, undo, and labor lose,
Not well conceiv'd of God, who though his Power
Creation could repeat, yet would be loath
Us to abolish, lest the Adversary
Triumph and say; Fickle their State whom God
Most Favors, who can please him long? Mee first
He ruin'd, now Mankind; whom will he next?
Matter of scorn, not to be given the Foe.
However I with thee have fixt my Lot,
Certain to undergo like doom;[9] if Death
Consort with thee, Death is to mee as Life;
So forcible within my heart I feel
The Bond of Nature draw me to my own,
My own in thee, for what thou art is mine;
Our State cannot be sever'd, we are one,
One Flesh; to lose thee were to lose myself.
   So *Adam,* and thus *Eve* to him repli'd.
O glorious trial of exceeding Love,
Illustrious evidence, example high!
Ingaging me to emulate, but short
   Of thy perfection, how shall I attain,
Adam, from whose dear side I boast me sprung,
And gladly of our Union hear thee speak,
One Heart, one Soul in both; whereof good proof
This day affords, declaring thee resolv'd,
Rather than Death or aught than Death more dread
Shall separate us, linkt in Love so dear,
To undergo with mee one Guilt, one Crime,

9. Three separate meanings are possible: judgment, irrevocable destiny, and death.

If any be, of tasting this fair Fruit,
Whose virtue, for of good still good proceeds,
Direct, or by occasion[1] hath presented
This happy trial of thy Love, which else
So eminently never had been known.
Were it I thought Death menac't would ensue
This my attempt, I would sustain alone
The worst, and not persuade thee, rather die
Deserted, than oblige° thee with a fact *make liable*
Pernicious to thy Peace, chiefly assur'd
Remarkably so late of thy so true,
So faithful Love unequall'd; but I feel
Far otherwise th' event,° nor Death, but Life *result*
Augmented, op'n'd Eyes, new Hopes, new Joys,
Taste so Divine, that what of sweet before
Hath toucht my sense, flat seems to this, and harsh.
On my experience, *Adam,* freely taste,
And fear of Death deliver to the Winds.
So saying, she embrac'd him, and for joy
Tenderly wept, much won that he his Love
Had so ennobl'd, as of choice to incur
Divine displeasure for her sake, or Death.
In recompense (for such compliance bad
Such recompense best merits) from the bough
She gave him of that fair enticing Fruit
With liberal hand: he scrupl'd not to eat
Against his better knowledge, not deceiv'd,
But fondly overcome with Female charm.[2]
Earth trembl'd from her entrails, as again
In pangs, and Nature gave a second groan,
Sky low'r'd, and muttering Thunder, some sad drops
Wept at completing of the mortal Sin
Original;[3] while *Adam* took no thought,
Eating his fill, nor *Eve* to iterate
Her former trespass fear'd, the more to soothe
Him with her lov'd society, that now
As with new Wine intoxicated both
They swim in mirth, and fancy that they feel
Divinity within them breeding wings
Wherewith to scorn the Earth: but that false Fruit
Far other operation first display'd,
Carnal desire inflaming, hee on *Eve*
Began to cast lascivious Eyes, she him
As wantonly repaid; in Lust they burn:
Till *Adam* thus 'gan *Eve* to dalliance move.

1. I.e., directly or indirectly.
2. See 1 Timothy 2:14: "And Adam was not deceived, but the woman being deceived was in the transgression."
3. The only occurrence in *Paradise Lost* of the term "Original Sin." In his *De doctrina* (1.11), Milton defines Original Sin as "the sin which is common to all men, that which our first parents, and in them all their posterity committed, when, casting off their obedience to God, they tasted the fruit of the forbidden tree."

Eve, now I see thou are exact of taste,
And elegant, of Sapience[4] no small part,
Since to each meaning savor[5] we apply,
And Palate call judicious; I the praise
Yield thee, so well this day thou hast purvey'd.° *provided*
Much pleasure we have lost, while we abstain'd
From this delightful Fruit, nor known till now
True relish, tasting; if such pleasure be
In things to us forbidden, it might be wish'd,
For this one Tree had been forbidden ten.
But come, so well refresh't, now let us play,
As meet is, after such delicious Fare;
For never did thy Beauty since the day
I saw thee first and wedded thee, adorn'd
With all perfections, so inflame my sense
With ardor to enjoy thee, fairer now
Than ever, bounty of this virtuous Tree.[6]
So said he, and forbore not glance or toy° *caress*
Of amorous intent, well understood
Of° *Eve,* whose Eye darted contagious Fire. *by*
Her hand he seiz'd, and to a shady bank,
Thick overhead with verdant roof imbowr'd
He led her nothing loath; Flow'rs were the Couch,
Pansies, and Violets, and Asphodel,
And Hyacinth, Earth's freshest softest lap.
There they thir fill of Love and Love's disport
Took largely, of thir mutual guilt the Seal,
The solace of thir sin, till dewy sleep
Oppress'd them, wearied with thir amorous play.
Soon as the force of that fallacious Fruit,
That with exhilarating vapor bland° *pleasing*
About thir spirits had play'd, and inmost powers
Made err, was now exhal'd, and grosser sleep
Bred of unkindly fumes,[7] with conscious dreams
Encumber'd, now had left them, up they rose
As from unrest, and each the other viewing,
Soon found thir Eyes how op'n'd, and thir minds
How dark'n'd;[8] innocence, that as a veil
Had shadow'd them from knowing ill, was gone,
Just confidence, and native righteousness,
And honor from about them, naked left
To guilty shame: hee cover'd, but his Robe
Uncover'd more. So rose the *Danite* strong

4. Wisdom, from Latin *sapere,* to taste.
5. Tastiness, understanding.
6. See Homer, *Iliad* 14, where Hera, bent on deceiving Zeus, comes to him wearing Aphrodite's belt and seems more charming to him than ever before.
7. Unnatural vapors or exhalations rising from the stomach to the brain.
8. See Genesis 3:7: "The eyes of them both were opened, and they knew that they were naked."

Herculean Samson from the Harlot-lap
Of *Philistean Dalilah,* and wak'd
Shorn of his strength, They destitute and bare
Of all thir virtue:[9] silent, and in face
Confounded long they sat, as struck'n mute,
Till *Adam,* though not less than *Eve* abasht,
At length gave utterance to these words constrain'd.
O *Eve,* in evil hour thou didst give ear
To that false Worm, of whomsoever taught
To counterfeit Man's voice, true in our Fall,
False in our promis'd Rising; since our Eyes
Op'n'd we find indeed, and find we know
Both Good and Evil, Good lost, and Evil got,
Bad Fruit of Knowledge, if this be to know,
Which leaves us naked thus, of Honor void,
Of Innocence, of Faith, of Purity,
Our wonted Ornaments now soil'd and stain'd,
And in our Faces evident the signs
Of foul concupiscence; whence evil store;
Even shame, the last of evils; of the first
Be sure then. How shall I behold the face
Henceforth of God or Angel, erst with joy
And rapture so oft beheld? those heav'nly shapes
Will dazzle now this earthly, with thir blaze
Insufferably bright. O might I here
In solitude live savage, in some glade
Obscur'd, where highest Woods impenetrable
To Star or Sun-light, spread thir umbrage broad,
And brown as Evening: Cover me ye Pines,
Ye Cedars, with innumerable boughs
Hide me, where I may never see them more.
But let us now, as in bad plight, devise
What best may for the present serve to hide
The Parts of each from other, that seem most
To shame obnoxious,° and unseemliest seen, *exposed*
Some Tree whose broad smooth Leaves together sew'd,
And girded on our loins, may cover round
Those middle parts, that this new comer, Shame,
There sit not, and reproach us as unclean.[1]
So counsell'd hee, and both together went
Into the thickest Wood, there soon they chose
The Figtree,[2] not that kind for Fruit renown'd,
But such as at this day to *Indians* known
In *Malabar* or *Decan* spreads her Arms

9. See Judges 16 for the story of Samson's betrayal by Delilah.
1. See Genesis 3:7.
2. Milton's description of the banyan or Indian fig comes from Gerard's *Herball* (1597).

Branching so broad and long, that in the ground
The bended Twigs take root, and Daughters grow
About the Mother Tree, a Pillar'd shade
High overarch't, and echoing Walks between;
There oft the *Indian* Herdsman shunning heat
Shelters in cool, and tends his pasturing Herds
At Loopholes cut through thickest shade: Those Leaves
They gather'd, broad as Amazonian Targe,° *shield*
And with what skill they had, together sew'd,
To gird thir waist, vain Covering if to hide
Thir guilt and dreaded shame; O how unlike
To that first naked Glory. Such of late
Columbus found th' *American* so girt
With feather'd Cincture,° naked else and wild *belt*
Among the Trees on Isles and woody Shores.
Thus fenc't, and as they thought, thir shame in part
Cover'd, but not at rest or ease of Mind,
They sat them down to weep, nor only Tears
Rain'd at thir Eyes, but high Winds worse within
Began to rise, high Passions, Anger, Hate,
Mistrust, Suspicion, Discord, and shook sore
Thir inward State of Mind, calm Region once
And full of Peace, now toss't and turbulent:
For Understanding rul'd not, and the Will
Heard not her lore, both in subjection now
To sensual Appetite, who from beneath
Usurping over sovran Reason claim'd
Superior sway: From thus distemper'd breast,
Adam, estrang'd in look and alter'd style,
Speech intermitted thus to *Eve* renew'd.
  Would thou hadst heark'n'd to my words, and stay'd
With me, as I besought thee, when that strange
Desire of wand'ring this unhappy Morn,
I know not whence possess'd thee; we had then
Remain'd still happy, not as now, despoil'd
Of all our good, sham'd, naked, miserable.
Let none henceforth seek needless cause to approve° *give proof of*
The Faith they owe;[3] when earnestly they seek
Such proof, conclude, they then begin to fail.
  To whom soon mov'd with touch of blame thus *Eve.*
What words have past thy Lips,[4] *Adam* severe,
Imput'st thou that to my default, or will
Of wand'ring, as thou call'st it, which who knows
But might as ill have happ'n'd thou being by,
Or to thyself perhaps: hadst thou been there,

3. Be under obligation to render or possess.

4. Echoes Odysseus's disapproval of a speech of Agamemnon (*Iliad* 14.83).

Or here th' attempt, thou couldst not have discern'd
Fraud in the Serpent, speaking as he spake;
No ground of enmity between us known,
Why hee should mean me ill, or seek to harm.
Was I to have never parted from thy side?
As good have grown there still a lifeless Rib.
Being as I am, why didst not thou the Head[5]
Command me absolutely not to go,
Going into such danger as thou said'st?
Too facile° then thou didst not much gainsay, *permissive*
Nay, didst permit, approve, and fair dismiss.
Hadst thou been firm and fixt in thy dissent,
Neither had I transgress'd, nor thou with mee.
To whom then first incenst Adam repli'd.
Is this the Love, is this the recompense
Of mine to thee, ingrateful *Eve,* express't
Immutable° when thou wert lost, not I, *unchangeable*
Who might have liv'd and joy'd immortal bliss,
Yet willingly chose rather Death with thee:
And am I now upbraided, as the cause
Of thy transgressing? not enough severe,
It seems, in thy restraint: what could I more?
I warn'd thee, I admonish'd thee, foretold
The danger, and the lurking Enemy
That lay in wait; beyond this had been force,
And force upon free Will hath here no place.
But confidence then bore thee on, secure
Either to meet no danger, or to find
Matter of glorious trial; and perhaps
I also err'd in overmuch admiring
What seem'd in thee so perfet, that I thought
No evil durst attempt thee, but I rue
That error now, which is become my crime,
And thou th' accuser. Thus it shall befall
Him who to worth in Woman overtrusting
Lets her Will rule; restraint she will not brook,
And left to herself, if evil thence ensue,
Shee first his weak indulgence will accuse.
Thus they in mutual accusation spent
The fruitless hours, but neither self-condemning,
And of thir vain contést appear'd no end.[6]

5. Alludes to 1 Corinthians 11:3: "The head of every man is Christ; and the head of the woman is the man; and the head of Christ is God."

6. God visits his judgment on Adam and Eve, as well as on Satan and his followers, who are turned into serpents. Adam and Eve languish in despair, turning to God in "sorrow unfeign'd," and at Christ's request, God sends Michael to show Adam what will happen before the flood (Book 11) and then to tell him of Christ and man's redemption in Book 12.

Anonymous drawing of Louis XIV as the "Sun King." The verses below the image are a masterpiece of propaganda, describing the French king's conservative Counter-Reformation policy, reversing earlier religious tolerance in the new terms of the Enlightenment: the power of Louis' "sun" will enlighten heretics, evaporating the mists of John Calvin's Protestant teachings—not because of any religious zeal, but to conceal his subtle political strategy.

The Age of the Enlightenment

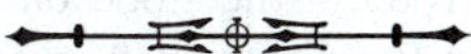

The middle decades of the 1600s marked a time of transition in many parts of the world. The Manchu dynasty came to power in China in 1644 and continued to rule the world's most populous country until 1912. In Japan, the Tokugawa clan of warlords, or shoguns, had begun to establish themselves in 1600; they cemented their control over the country in the next few decades. By midcentury they had succeeded in their ambition of closing Japan to outside influence, and after 1641 the sole foreign presence in Japan was a small Dutch trade mission confined to an island in Nagasaki Harbor—a situation that wouldn't change for over two hundred years. Both local and colonial rule began to assume new forms in Africa and the Americas: the great Bambara kingdom was established in midcentury along the upper reaches of the Niger River, and in 1652 Dutch settlers founded a colony at Capetown in what would become the English colony of South Africa. While the Dutch gained in Africa, they lost in the Western hemisphere: in 1654 Portugal took back Brazil from them, and a decade later the English expelled them from their colony of New Amsterdam, renaming it New York.

Europe too saw sweeping changes during these years. A long period of conflict in and around Germany, the Thirty Years War, finally ended in 1648, while in France the "Sun King" Louis XIV ascended the throne at age five in 1643 and began to rule in his own right in 1661; he remained the dominant political figure of his era until his death in 1715, after a record-breaking reign of seventy-two years. Gathering the French nobility into the gilded cage of his lavish palace complex at Versailles, Louis proclaimed absolute authority granted by divine right, asserting "L'état, c'est moi"—"I am the state." The Mughal Empire reached its height under a similarly absolutist monarch, Aurangzeb (r. 1685–1707), who extended his realm to include most of India and what is now Pakistan. Yet neither monarch bequeathed a stable situation to his successors: Louis's unrestrained spending on frequent wars and on lavish palaces left France's treasuries depleted on his death, while his insistence on Catholicism as the sole permitted religion led to the departure of tens of thousands of French Protestants, many of them enterprising small manufacturers and artisans, seriously weakening the French economy. Growing popular discontent in France would lead to revolution by the end of the century. In India, Aurangzeb tried to unify his widened realm by making Islam the state religion and repressing the practice of Hinduism; his restless Hindu subjects repeatedly revolted and his sons fought each other, and the empire declined after his death.

The splendor of courts like Versailles in France, Saint Petersburg in Russia, and Delhi in India was underwritten by the growing economic contributions of traders and manufacturers, who provided new sources of wealth beyond the traditional base of peasant agriculture. A new "middle class" was growing up between the aristocracy and the peasantry, often congregating in towns and known on the Continent as Bürger or bourgeois (from the German and French terms for "town"). The new bourgeoisie often favored self-government and flexibility over aristocratic authority, and increasingly proposed that laws, not monarchs, should have the final say. As the philosopher John Locke wrote in 1690, "Wherever Law ends, Tyranny begins." Or as an antiroyal rebel, Richard Rumbold, declared in 1685, as he stood on the scaffold waiting to be executed: "I never could believe that Providence had sent a few men into the world, ready booted and spurred to ride, and millions ready saddled and bridled to be ridden."

Commerce and Industry

Some small countries, such as Holland and Switzerland, asserted their freedom by abolishing monarchy altogether and becoming republics. In England, the unpopular monarch Charles I was beheaded by Puritan rebels in 1649; though the monarchy was restored in 1660, Charles II and his successors were increasingly subject to parliamentary control. Elsewhere, monarchs such as Russia's Peter the Great prospered by working closely with the bourgeoisie to modernize agriculture and establish the rudiments of modern industry. In Persia, the ruler Karim Khan developed his capital of Shiraz as a commercial center accessible to the Persian Gulf and trade with India. A driving force in the changing expectations of middle-class subjects, in fact, was the opening up of the world through rapidly expanding travel and trade. Though the Dutch East India Company maintained only a tenuous foothold in Japan, it assumed greater and greater influence in Indonesia, while French and British trading companies jostled for influence in India. In 1661 the British East India Company took control of Bombay, and in 1690 the company founded the major city of Calcutta. Gradually the East India Company became the *de facto* ruler of much of the Indian subcontinent. Trade steadily increased as well between Europe and the Americas, which now provided not only gold and silver but also a growing bulk of goods like sugar, cotton, hides, and timber. England and other nations developed a further trade, in human bodies, to support these enterprises: the "triangular trade" of slaves from Africa to the Americas and of slave-produced sugar and cotton from the Americas to Europe, which in turn manufactured finished goods to sell back to Africa and the Americas.

This was a new sort of empire: developed and maintained less by governments and guns than by companies and invoices. As the Scottish economic theorist Adam Smith said in his 1776 book *The Wealth of Nations:* "To found a great empire for the sole purpose of raising up a people of customers, may at first sight appear a project fit for a nation of shopkeepers; but extremely fit for a nation whose Government is influenced by shopkeepers." Elsewhere in the world, too, there was a growing sense of social life as a changing and changeable reality, subject to personal initiative more than to inherited status or direct divine intervention. The writers of this era responded to these new circumstances in realistic accounts of the new social mobility and in fictional or literal travel narratives as well. Voltaire's comic hero Candide ventures from a Europe torn by war to South America, searching for happiness and security in what his teacher Pangloss asserts is "the best of all possible worlds." The great Japanese poet and traveler Matsuo Bashō sees travel as the condition of life itself, shared even by the passing seasons: "The months and days are the travelers of eternity. The years that come and go are also voyagers. . . . I too for years past have been stirred by the sight of a solitary cloud drifting with the wind to ceaseless thoughts of roaming."

Science and Technology

The growth of commerce and industry was fed by rapid developments in science and technology, and commerce fed the advance of science in turn. The scientific revolution inaugurated during the early modern period took on new force in the late seventeenth century. In a period of three years in the 1660s, for example, England's Isaac Newton made three major discoveries: he discovered the theory of gravitation; determined that white light is composed of colored rays; and invented calculus. Far from resting on his laurels, Newton continued to press for new understanding. As he famously remarked,

> I do not know what I may appear in the world; but to myself I seem to have been only like a boy playing on the seashore, and diverting myself in now and then finding a smoother pebble or a prettier shell than ordinary, whilst the great ocean of truth lay all undiscovered before me.

Major practical advances in technology followed from the new research. The spinning and weaving of cloth, formerly laborious handwork, became mechanized with the invention of the flying shuttle in 1733 and the spinning jenny in 1764. The first modern factories were built, and their output grew enormously with the invention of the steam engine, perfected by James Watt in 1769. Steam power vastly multiplied the work that an individual could accomplish, and humanity seemed poised to rise above its traditional limits—literally so, when the Montgolfier brothers launched the first hot air balloon in France in 1783.

The rapidly increasing grasp of the laws of nature prompted major shifts in religious understanding. Many scientists—Newton included—saw their discoveries as illuminating God's sublime handiwork; as one early scientist, Sir Thomas Pope Blount, asserted in 1693, "Every flower of the field, every fiber of a plant, every particle of an insect, carries with it the impress of its Maker, and can—if duly considered—read us lectures of ethics or divinity." Others took a more skeptical view, and increasingly began to view religious beliefs as projections of human needs and understanding: as the French philosopher Montesquieu put it in 1721, "If triangles had a god, he would have three sides."

Increasingly the ideals of science and rational planning came to be applied to the social world as well as to the world of nature. In Europe, this broad movement became known as "the Enlightenment." By the late eighteenth century, Enlightenment ideas of political, economic, and intellectual liberty stimulated and shaped the revolutionary movements that led to America's declaration of independence from England and the French Revolution of 1789. The outlines of our modern world were beginning to emerge, along with the increasingly visible figure of the modern artist as a skeptical observer, independent of royal patronage or received ideas, even of received literary forms. Alexander Pope used the mock-epic to satirize English court culture, while Lady Mary Wortley Montagu used sharply pointed couplets to mock Jonathan Swift's own mockery of women. Everywhere the period's writers vanquished their enemies in print if not in fact: as Voltaire wrote to a friend late in life: "I have never made but one prayer to God, a very short one: 'O Lord, make my enemies ridiculous.' And God granted it.'"

The Enlightenment

France and England were the two primary poles generating the massive charge of intellectual and political energy that spread so much "light" in Europe and beyond. Many other countries contributed to the Enlightenment and experienced its profound influence, but in general all were responding to the social, scientific, industrial, and intellectual revolutions that accompanied the political ones in France and England, the two most centralized and powerful nations in Europe at the time. What eighteenth-century philosophers themselves baptized as "the Enlightenment" was the continued trend in Europe, after the early modern wars of religion, to question received authority—religious, political, moral, and intellectual. Absolute, received authority was to be tempered or even replaced by the guidance of reason, understood as a faculty common to all humankind. Such questioning brought with it an increasing recognition that reason must also master the passions that drove the wars of religion by fostering religious tolerance alongside free intellectual experimentation and argument.

Many Enlightenment thinkers, from Locke and Leibniz in the late seventeenth century through Voltaire to Jean-Jacques Rousseau and the leaders of the American Revolution toward the end of the eighteenth century, adopted a stance of Christian theism as a solution to the fundamental tension between religious dogma and freethinking. Theism, as Leibniz put it, meant that, "We believe the Scriptures … but reason controls our interpretation of them." More radical thinkers, such as David Hume, Denis Diderot, and William Godwin, rejected the authority of received religious doctrine altogether. As in the early modern period, religious reformation was tied to political revolution. Rousseau described the "social contract" as a bond willingly built up from below by individuals in need of mutual support, rather than imposed upon them from above. His concept crystallized the long-standing critique of monarchical rule by divine right that went back at least as far as Locke, and prepared the philosophical justification for the French Revolution a century after Locke. Rousseau's rather pessimistic outlook held that humankind had been happiest in a lost state of nature. The German philosopher Immanuel Kant's more optimistic view was more representative of the widespread Enlightenment belief in progress and the infinite perfectibility of mankind. It was the idea of fundamental human equality, most forcefully formulated by Rousseau and Kant, that gave rise to the concept of inalienable political rights upon which both the French and American Revolutions were based, and which still drives the civil rights movement in the United States and human rights activism around the world.

The opening up of the whole world, as it seemed to many Europeans, to the power of reason fostered an encyclopedic approach to knowledge. Diderot and D'Alembert's *Encylclopédie* (1751–1765) was only the most ambitious and influential of a long series of attempts to catalogue systematically the entirety of human knowledge and experience. In Britain, Samuel Johnson added his famous *Dictionary* (1755) to Chambers' *Cyclopaedia* (London, 1728), followed by the *Encyclopedia Britannica* (Edinburgh, 1768–1771). Modern readers may wonder how such sober reference books could once have been so revolutionary as to provoke attacks by the clergy and government censorship. The revolutionary aim of the *Encyclopédie* was the unification of knowledge centered around humankind rather than God. Its anatomical illustrations offended morality. Its description of non-Western cultures called European norms into question. Its explanations of recent scientific discoveries challenged traditional and religious beliefs. Even its detailed descriptions of industrial processes unveiled trade secrets closely guarded by guilds for centuries. But the most revolutionary aspect of encyclopedias and dictionaries was their widespread distribution in print.

If the Enlightenment was an age of revolution, it was so because all this burgeoning progress was not free simply to happen. When control was suddenly released or overcome, decadence, bloodshed, and new abuses of power often ensued. Literature played a crucial role in these revolutionary power struggles, often deployed directly as a weapon through a revival of the classical genre of satire. It is hard for readers of the twenty-first century to appreciate the power of satire in the eighteenth. Writing was dangerous, and therefore important. Royal spies filled court circles, salons, and coffeehouses, and opened private letters, trying to control the circulation of unpublished writings. The theater was such a good medium for Molière's social satire because during his time any material could be staged at least once—before the theater was shut down. A few satirists, such as Lady Mary Wortley Montagu, were aristocrats, but most were not: Molière and Voltaire in France, and in Britain Jonathan Swift and Alexander Pope, "the Wasp of Twickenham." They judged their targets by the measures of virtue and reason, showing shocking disrespect for social hierarchies. The upper classes weren't their only objects of derision; the satirists attacked vice and folly wherever they found it. And they found it so universally that Dr. Johnson wrote of Swift and Pope: "whoever should form his opinion of the age from their representation, would suppose them to have lived amidst ignorance and barbarity, unable to find among their contemporaries either virtue or intelligence, and persecuted by those that could not understand them."

It was during the Enlightenment that women in large numbers began reading and writing secular and imaginative literature in all genres—drama, poetry, letters. Above all, and increasingly as the period wore on, women employed the new experimental and popular genre of plausible prose fiction that came to be called the novel. Paradoxically, the very age that saw unprecedented access by women to literacy and publishing was also one that transformed the conventional European image of femininity from one of barely controlled sexual power and cunning into one of relatively desexualized passivity combined with a new moral rectitude. The long literary career of Eliza Haywood illustrates how rapidly and thoroughly the shift took hold: she began by publishing best-selling novels about dangerously desirous heroines such as "Fantomina" (1724), but then the success of Samuel Richardson's sentimental novels of the 1740s forced her to take a sudden turn to similarly domestic and sentimental fiction about passively virtuous heroines, in order to stay in business as a novelist.

Just as the characteristic concerns of the Enlightenment didn't emerge suddenly with the English Revolution in 1642, neither did they vanish with the French one in 1789. By the end of the Enlightenment period, political liberation was only just beginning in earnest, with the French and American Revolutions—for European men of property at least. It had scarcely begun for women of any class, and for slaves it was only a faint and distant glimmer of hope. Even for European men of the laboring classes, the famous battle cry of "liberty, equality, fraternity" referred to ideals that remained largely abstract. The struggles of all of these groups to realize the best promise of the Enlightenment would continue to gather force over the course of the nineteenth century, with the movements for the abolition of slavery, for women's education and suffrage, and for the liberation of workers from the new capitalist oppression—as analyzed by Karl Marx—that was fast replacing the feudal kind. For better and worse, most

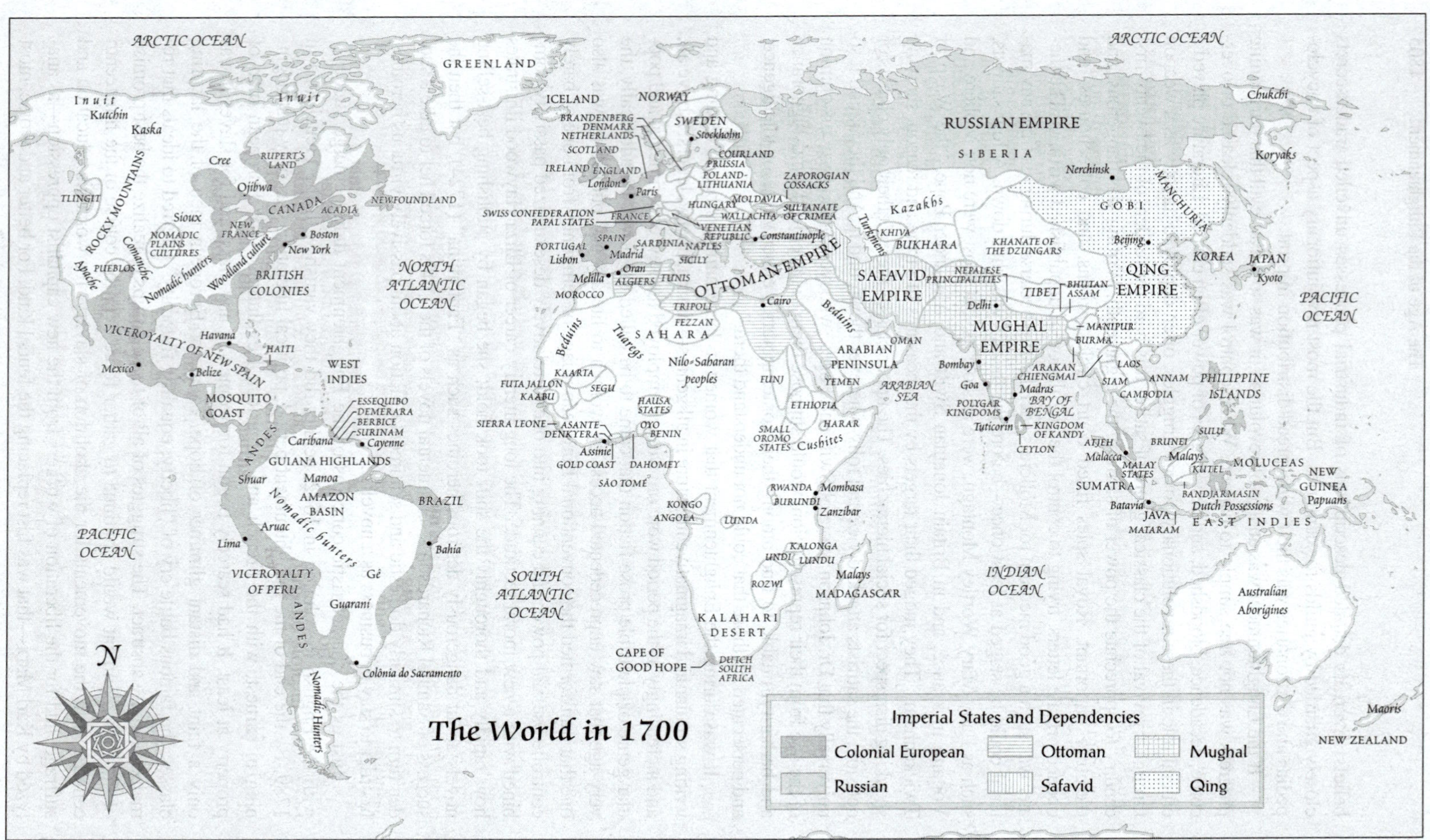

The World in 1700
Imperial States and Dependencies
Colonial European
Russian
Ottoman
Safavid
Mughal
Qing
ARCTIC OCEAN
GREENLAND
Inuit
Kutchin
Kaska
TLINGIT
ROCKY MOUNTAINS
Cree
RUPERT'S LAND
Ojibwa
CANADA
ACADIA
NEWFOUNDLAND
Sioux
NEW FRANCE
NOMADIC PLAINS CULTURES
Comanche
Apache
PUEBLOS
Nomadic hunters
Woodland culture
Boston
New York
BRITISH COLONIES
NORTH ATLANTIC OCEAN
VICEROYALTY OF NEW SPAIN
Havana
HAITI
Mexico
Belize
WEST INDIES
MOSQUITO COAST
ESSEQUIBO
DEMERARA
BERBICE
SURINAM
Cayenne
Caribana
ANDES
GUIANA HIGHLANDS
Shuar
Manoa
AMAZON BASIN
BRAZIL
Aruac
Lima
Bahia
PACIFIC OCEAN
VICEROYALTY OF PERU
Gê
Guaraní
Colônia do Sacramento
Nomadic Hunters
SOUTH ATLANTIC OCEAN
ICELAND
NORWAY
SWEDEN
Stockholm
BRANDENBERG
DENMARK
NETHERLANDS
SCOTLAND
IRELAND
ENGLAND
London
Paris
COURLAND
PRUSSIA
POLAND-LITHUANIA
ZAPOROGIAN COSSACKS
HUNGARY
MOLDAVIA
SULTANATE OF CRIMEA
WALLACHIA
SWISS CONFEDERATION
PAPAL STATES
FRANCE
VENETIAN REPUBLIC
Constantinople
PORTUGAL
Lisbon
SPAIN
Madrid
SARDINIA
NAPLES
SICILY
Melilla
Oran
ALGIERS
TUNIS
MOROCCO
OTTOMAN EMPIRE
TRIPOLI
FEZZAN
Cairo
SAHARA
Beduins
Tuaregs
Nilo-Saharan peoples
KAARTA
FUTA JALLON
KAABU
SEGU
HAUSA STATES
SIERRA LEONE
ASANTE
DENKYERA
OYO
BENIN
Assinie
GOLD COAST
DAHOMEY
SÃO TOMÉ
FUNJ
ETHIOPIA
HARAR
SMALL OROMO STATES
Cushites
YEMEN
ARABIAN PENINSULA
OMAN
ARABIAN SEA
RWANDA
BURUNDI
Mombasa
Zanzibar
KONGO
ANGOLA
LUNDA
KALONGA
UNDI
LUNDU
Malays
MADAGASCAR
ROZWI
KALAHARI DESERT
CAPE OF GOOD HOPE
DUTCH SOUTH AFRICA
RUSSIAN EMPIRE
SIBERIA
Nerchinsk
Kazakhs
Turkmens
KHIVA
BUKHARA
SAFAVID EMPIRE
KHANATE OF THE DZUNGARS
GOBI
MANCHURIA
Beijing
KOREA
JAPAN
Kyoto
QING EMPIRE
NEPALESE PRINCIPALITIES
TIBET
BHUTAN
ASSAM
Delhi
MUGHAL EMPIRE
MANIPUR
BURMA
Bombay
Goa
Madras
ARAKAN
CHIENGMAI
BAY OF BENGAL
POLYGAR KINGDOMS
Tuticorin
KINGDOM OF KANDY
CEYLON
LAOS
SIAM
ANNAM
CAMBODIA
PHILIPPINE ISLANDS
SULU
BRUNEI
AJJEH
Malacca
MALAY STATES
Malays
KUTEL
MOLUCEAS
SUMATRA
BANDJARMASIN
Dutch Possessions
Batavia
JAVA
MATARAM
EAST INDIES
NEW GUINEA
Papuans
INDIAN OCEAN
Chukchi
Koryaks
PACIFIC OCEAN
Australian Aborigines
Maoris
NEW ZEALAND
N

of the world is still deeply affected by Enlightenment ideas today. Wherever popular democracy and individual civil liberties are valued, or the scientific method and the technological advances produced by it; wherever debate rages over the effects of colonialism, the economic principles of free trade and enlightened self-interest; wherever novels are enjoyed; and even wherever the pervasive fear is expressed that young people cannot help but be corrupted by the bad examples they encounter in fictional representations, from pornography to violent television shows—in all these instances and more, the Enlightenment endures.

The Seventeenth and Eighteenth Centuries

Year	The World	Literature
1600	**1603** Death of Elizabeth I of England, accession of James I **1605** Death of Akbar; Jahangir ascends Mughal throne **1607** British settlement of Virginia **1608–1648** Marquise de Rambouillet's "Blue Room," first important Parisian salon **1609** Tokugawa Shogunate founded in Japan	**1605, 1615** Cervantes, *Don Quixote*
1610	**1618** Bohemian revolt against Habsburgs initiates Thirty Years' War **1619** First African slaves taken to Virginia	**1616** Death of Shakespeare
1620	**1620** English Pilgrims begin migration to New England	**1624** Babur, *Memoirs of Babur*
1630	**1633** Tokugawa shoguns close Japan to foreigners **1634** First official meeting of the Académie Française	**1637** Maria de Zayas, *Amorous and Exemplary Novellas*
1640	**1642** English Civil War begins; Tasman discovers New Zealand and Tasmania **1643** Shah Jahan rules much of India; Taj Mahal completed **1644** Manchu dynasty begins in China (to 1912) **1648** The Fronde, civil war in France; Treaty of Westphalia ends Thirty Years' War **1649** Execution of Charles I of England, which becomes a republic under Oliver Cromwell and Parliament	**1641** René Descartes, *Meditations on First Philosophy;* Banarasidas, *Half a Life*
1650	**1652** Dutch establish colony in South Africa **1653** Louis XIV returns to Paris from exile with his powerful minister Cardinal Mazarin, ending the Fronde rebellion **1658** Oliver Cromwell dies	**1651** Thomas Hobbes, *Leviathan* **1654–1660** Madeleine de Scudéry, *Clélie*

Year	The World	Literature
1660	**1660** Restoration of Charles II to the English throne; Royal Society founded; rise of Bambara kingdom on upper Niger River	**1660** Pierre Corneille, collected plays and discourses on the art of the theater
	1661 Louis XIV, aged 23, assumes the full government of France after the death of his protector Cardinal Mazarin and the arrest of his finance minister, Fouquet	
	1662 English Royal Society receives its charter from Charles II	**1662–1663** Molière, *The School for Wives*
	1663 Brazil becomes Portuguese Viceroyalty	
	1664 England seizes New Amsterdam from Dutch, changes name to New York	
	1665 Last "Great Plague" in England	**1665** Katherine Philips, *Poems;* George Warren, *An Impartial Description of Surinam*
	1666 Great Fire of London destroys the city, which is rebuilt on a neoclassical plan; Isaac Newton formulates the law of gravity	**1667** John Milton, *Paradise Lost*
		1668 Jean de la Fontaine, *Fables*
1670	**1670** Hudson's Bay Company incorporated in London to conduct trade in North America	
		1678 Comtesse de Lafayette, *The Princess of Clèves*
1680		**1680** Unauthorized posthumous edition of the Earl of Rochester's poems
	1683 Ottoman siege of Vienna fails after intervention of the Poles	
	1685 Death of Charles II of England, accession of James II; Louis XIV revokes the Edict of Nantes, ending tolerance for Protestants in France	
	1686 The English establish Calcutta as a factory and port settlement in Bengal	**1686** Ihara Saikaku, *Life of a Sensuous Woman*
	1688 "Glorious Revolution" in England: Mary, daughter of James II of England, and her spouse the Dutch Prince William of Orange oust her father in a bloodless coup	**1687** Isaac Newton, *Principia Mathematica*
		1688 Aphra Behn, *Oroonoko;* Ihara Saikaku, *Japan's Eternal Storehouse*
	1689 Treaty of Nerchinsk between Russian and Qing Empires	
1690		**1690** John Locke, *Essay Concerning Human Understanding*
		1694 *Dictionary* of the French Academy
	1698 Omani Arabs capture Mombasa and Zanzibar in Africa	**1697** Charles Perrault, *Tales of Past Times, with Morals* (*Mother Goose Tales*); Pierre Bayle, *Historical and Critical Dictionary*
1700	**1700** Charles II of Spain dies, leaving the kingdom to the French duke of Anjou	**1701** Mary Chudleigh, *The Ladies Defence*
	1702 War of Spanish Succession; Holy Roman Emperor Charles XII invades Poland; death of William III of England and accession of Queen Anne	
	1703 St. Petersburg founded by Czar Peter the Great, who has just visited Western Europe and vowed to modernize Russia	
	1704 English capture Gibraltar (in War of the Spanish Succession)	**1704–1717** Galland's French translation of *The Thousand and One Nights,* its first translation into a European language

YEAR	THE WORLD	LITERATURE
	1707 United Kingdom links formerly separate kingdoms of England and Scotland; death of Aurangzeb in India, leading to the decline of the Mughal Empire; first pipe organ built by Gottfried Silbermann in Germany	
	1708 Robert Walpole, first to use title of Prime Minister, takes charge of the Whig government in London	
	1709 Technique for making Chinese porcelain first replicated in Europe, Meissen factory established the following year; modern piano invented in Padua by Bartolomeo Cristofori	
1710		**1710** Gottfried Wilhelm von Leibniz, *Theodicy*
	1712 German composer Georg Friedrich Händel moves permanently to London	**1712, 1717** Alexander Pope, *The Rape of the Lock*
	1713 Treaty of Utrecht ends the War of the Spanish Succession for Britain and the Netherlands: France cedes most Canadian holdings to Britain; Pope Clement XI condemns the powerful Jansenist sect as heretical	**1713** Anne Finch, Countess of Winchilsea, *Miscellaneous Poems on Several Occasions, Written by a Lady*
	1714 Death of Queen Anne and accession of George I of Great Britain; Tripoli becomes independent from the Ottoman Empire; France makes peace with Austria, Bavaria, and the Holy Roman Empire; Fahrenheit invents the mercury thermometer	
	1715 Death of Louis XIV; partisans of the exiled Stuart heir (Jacobites) rebel and are suppressed in Britain	
	1716 Ottoman Turks defeated by forces of the Holy Roman Empire at the Battle of Peterwardein	
	1717 France, Britain, and Holland form the Triple Alliance; Walpole resigns as prime minister of Great Britain	**1717–1724** Lady Mary Wortley Montagu, *The Turkish Embassy Letters*
	1718 Ottoman and Holy Roman Empires sign Treaty of Passarowitz; Triple Alliance becomes Quadruple Alliance when Holy Roman Emperor Charles VI joins it	**1718, 1724** Comtesse de Lafayette, *The Countess of Tende* (published posthumously)
1720		
	1720 "South Sea Bubble" bursts in Britain, ruining many; Manchus seize control of Xinjiang	**1721** Chikamatsu Mon'zaemon, *Love Suicides at Amijima;* Baron de Montesquieu, *Persian Letters*
	1722 Dutch East India Company founded by Holy Roman Emperor Charles VI	
	1723 French Regency ends with majority of Louis XV; Ottoman Empire attacks Persia	
	1724 Treaty of Constantinople: Russian and Ottoman Empires partition Persia	**1724** Eliza Haywood, *Fantomina*
		1725, 1754 Marquise de Sévigné, *Correspondence* (written 1648–1696)
		1726 Jonathan Swift, *Gulliver's Travels; Dictionary* of the Spanish Academy
	1727 Oxygen isolated by Stephen Hales in England	
	1728 Bering Strait first explored by Europeans	
		1729 First secular Turkish literature published in Constantinople

YEAR	THE WORLD	LITERATURE
1730		
	1730 Ottoman Emperor Achmet III deposed in favor of Mahmud I	
	1731 John Hadley invents the sextant, improving navigation	**1732** Swift, "The Lady's Dressing Room"
	1733 War of the Polish Succession	**1733–1734** Alexander Pope, *An Essay on Man*
		1734 Lady Mary Wortley Montagu, "The Reasons that Induced Doctor S. to Write a Poem called The Lady's Dressing Room"
		1735 Alexander Pope, *Epistle II: To a Lady* (*Of the Characters of Women*)
	1736 War between Ottoman, Holy Roman, and Russian Empires	
	1738 War of the Polish Succession ends	
	1739 Nadir Shah of Persia sacks Delhi; slave rebellion in South Carolina	
1740		
	1740 Holy Roman Emperor Charles VI dies; Frederick II the Great crowned king of Prussia; invading Silesia, he begins the War of the Austrian Succession	**1740** Samuel Richardson, *Pamela*
	1742 Händel's *Messiah* first performed in Dublin	
	1746 Uprising in western Szechuan province, China; French conquer Madras, India	
	1747 Achmed Khan Abdali establishes kingdom of Afghanistan and invades India	**1747** Françoise de Graffigny, *Letters from a Peruvian Woman*
	1748 War of the Austrian Succession ends, confirming the taking of Silesia from Austria by Prussia, while Britain surrenders Asiento (Italy) to Spain	**1748** Baron de Montesquieu, *The Spirit of the Laws* 1748
1750		
	1750s Emergence of Wahhabi movement in Arabia	**1750–1760** Cao Xueqin, *The Story of the Stone*
	1751 Chinese invade Tibet; Portugal and Spain divide their South American colonies by treaty	**1751** First volume of Diderot's *Encyclopedia* published
	1752 Benjamin Franklin proves that lightning is electricity; start of Konbuang Dynasty in Burma	
	1753 British Museum founded; Swedish Academy of Letters founded	
		1754 Etienne Bonnot de Condillac, *Treaty on the senses*
	1755 Lisbon earthquake kills 30,000–40,000 people	**1755** Samuel Johnson, *Dictionary of the English Language*
	1756 Seven Years' War begins when Frederick the Great of Prussia invades Saxony; English lose settlement at Calcutta to the nawab of Bengal, suffering great loss of life in the "Black Hole of Calcutta"	
	1757 British regain Calcutta; start of British imperial rule in India	
	1758 Invention of the threshing machine	
		1759 Voltaire, *Candide*
		1759–1767 Laurence Sterne, *Tristram Shandy*

Year	The World	Literature
1760		
	1760s Start of Industrial Revolution, inventions of Hargreaves's "spinning jenny" in 1765 and Watt's improved steam engine in 1769 help to mechanize the textile industry	
	1760 George III succeeds George II as King of Great Britain	
	1762 Catherine II the Great crowned Empress of Russia	**1762** Jean-Jacques Rousseau, *The Social Contract*
	1763 Seven Years' War ends; France is awarded Guadeloupe, Martinique, and parts of Africa and India; Britain takes over Canada and Florida; Spain takes Cuba and the Philippines	**1763** Lady Mary Wortley Montagu, *Turkish Embassy Letters* (written 1716–1718)
	1764 Jesuits expelled from France	**1764** Voltaire, *Philosophical Dictionary*; Horace Walpole, *The Castle of Otranto*
	1765 British East India Company wins control of Bengal and Bihar	
	1766 Britain occupies the Falkland Islands; hydrogen discovered by Henry Cavendish	
	1766–1769 Louis Antoine de Bougainville circumnavigates the world	
	1767 Jesuits expelled from Spain, Parma, and Sicily	
	1768–1771 Captain James Cook explores Australia and New Zealand	
1770		
	1770 The Boston Massacre; Spain seizes Falklands from Britain; famine in Bengal kills one-third of the population	**1771** Louis Antoine de Bougainville, *Voyage around the World*
	1772 War between Russian and Ottoman Empires ends with First Partition of Poland; nitrogen discovered by Daniel Rutherford; Captain James Cook begins a three-year voyage of the South Seas	**1772** Gotthold Lessing, *Emilia Galotti*
	1773 Boston Tea Party; Jesuit order abolished by Pope Clement XIV	
	1774 Louis XVI succeeds Louis XV in France; Joseph Priestley isolates oxygen; Karl Scheele identifies chlorine; Nguyen Anh becomes emperor of Vietnam	**1774** Johann Wolfgang Goethe, *The Sufferings of Young Werther*
	1775 Start of American Revolution	**1775** Pierre de Beaumarchais, *The Barber of Seville*
	1776 Declaration of Independence adopted by the Continental Congress in Philadelphia; first submarine, David Bushnell's *Turtle;* the following year he invents the torpedo	
	1778 War of the Bavarian Succession begins; hypnotism first used by Friedrich Mesmer in Paris	**1778** Frances Burney, *Evelina*
	1779 Captain James Cook killed in Hawaii; First Kaffir War between Dutch Boer settlers and the Xhosa of South Africa	
1780		
	1780 Anti-Catholic "Gordon Riots" in England; waltz invented in Germany and Austria	
	1781 Continental Army defeats British at Yorktown, Virginia; Uranus, first planet discovered since antiquity, identified by William Herschel	**1781** First Polish encyclopedia; Sauda, *Satires*

YEAR	THE WORLD	LITERATURE
	1782 Irish gain legislative independence	**1782** Pierre Choderlos de Laclos, *Les Liaisons dangereuses*; first volume of Jean-Jacques Rousseau's *Confessions*
	1783 Treaty of Versailles ends war between Britain, France, and Spain, recognizes American independence and extends borders of the United States as far as the Mississippi River and the Great Lakes; first demonstrations of the hot air balloon and the steamboat	
	1784 Ottoman Empire cedes Crimea to Russians	**1784** Immanuel Kant, "An Answer to the Question: What Is Enlightenment?"
		1785 Charles Wilkins translates the *Bhagavad-Gita* into English (first translation of an important Sanskrit text into a European language); Ann Yearsley, *Poems, on Several Occasions*
	1786 Death of Frederick the Great of Prussia	**1786** Robert Burns, *Poems Chiefly in the Scottish Dialect*; Ann Yearsley, *Poems, on Various Subjects*
	1787 Constitution of the United States of America; British begin to settle freed slaves in Sierra Leone	**1787** Lorenzo Da Ponte and Wolfgang Amadeus Mozart, *Don Giovanni*
	1788 First British settlement in Australia	
	1789 Declaration of the Rights of Man and Citizen adopted by the French National Assembly; storming of the Bastille political prison in Paris; Antoine Lavoisier creates first table of elements; start of French Revolution	**1789** Olaudah Equiano, *Interesting Narrative of the Life of Olaudah Equiano* **1789–1792** Benedikte Naubert, *New German Folk Tales*
1790		
	1791 French National Assembly abolishes royal censorship; start of Haitian Revolution	
	1792 France declared a republic; Revolutionary Assembly legalizes divorce; Manchus invade Nepal	**1792** Mary Wollstonecraft, *A Vindication of the Rights of Woman*
	1793 Execution of Louis XVI of France; the Louvre palace becomes a public art gallery; France at war against Britain, Holland, Spain, Portugal, Tuscany, and the Holy Roman Empire; Second Kaffir War between Boer settlers and Xhosa of South Africa	
	1794 Fall of Robespierre ends French "Reign of Terror"; Qajar Dynasty founded in Persia (to 1925); Eli Whitney invents the cotton gin in the United States	**1794** Ann Radcliffe, *The Mysteries of Udolpho*
	1795 White Lotus Uprising in China; Mungo Park explores West Africa and River Niger	**1795** Anna Letitia Barbauld, "The Rights of Woman"; Marquis de Sade, *Philosophy in the Boudoir*
	1796 Death of Russian Empress Catherine the Great; Dr. Edward Jenner introduces smallpox vaccine; first exhibition of paintings by J.M.W. Turner	**1796** Denis Diderot, *Supplement to the Voyage of Bougainville* (written 1772)
	1798–1799 Napoleon's expedition to Egypt results in discovery of Rosetta Stone and naval defeat by British	**1798** William Wordsworth and Samuel Taylor Coleridge, *Lyrical Ballads*
	1799 War of the Second Coalition (Great Britain, Portugal, and Naples, with the Holy Roman, Russian, and Ottoman Empires) against France, where the Directory Government is overthrown and Napoleon Bonaparte is named First Consul	

PRONUNCIATIONS:

Académie Française: ah-kah-day-MEE frahn-SEZ
l'Age des Lumières: LAHZH day leu-mee-AYR
d'Alembert: da-lahm-BAYR
Candide: kahn-DEED
Pierre Corneille: pee-AYR kohr-NEH
Denis Diderot: duh-NEE DEE-duh-ROH
Don Juan: don HWAHN
Fronde: FROND
François, duc de La Rochefoucauld: frahnh-SWAH deuk duh lah rohsh-foo-KOH
Gottfried Wilhelm von Leibniz: got-freed vil-helm fon LAIB-nits
Mazarin: MA-za-RANH
Molière: moh-LYEHR
philosophe: fee-loh-ZOF
privilège du roi: pree-vee-LEZH deu RWAH
querelle des femmes: kay-rel day FUM
Marquise de Rambouillet: mahr-KEEZ duh RAHM-boo-YAY
Jean-Jacques Rousseau: zhahnh-ZHAHK ROO-SOH
Versailles: vehr-SAI

Jean-Baptiste Poquelin [Molière]

1622–1673

Molière's great ambition in life was to distinguish himself in the preeminent genre of the golden age of French literature: tragedy. He failed miserably—but just as his stage career seemed to be over for good, he made the king laugh. From that moment, he became one of the greatest French authors of all time by creating a new kind of comedy, which he elevated to the status of high literary art.

Jean-Baptiste Poquelin was born and raised to cover with silk damask the ornate gilded chairs on which the king sat with his court. His father and both grandfathers had amassed such a fortune in upholstery that by 1631 M. Poquelin senior was able to purchase the office of upholsterer-in-ordinary to the King. This meant access to court society and a hereditary monopoly for his eldest son, Jean-Baptiste, who was accordingly groomed to hobnob with the aristocracy through an elite education, including law school. His classical training at a Jesuit college known for freethinking nurtured his independence along with his interest in drama (he is said to have memorized all the Latin comedies of Terence—which owed much to ancient mime show situations that survived in the *commedia dell'arte* so popular in Molière's Paris). Upon graduation at twenty-one he replaced his father in the service of Louis XIII for one year. That was enough. Adopting the stage name "Molière" in 1643, he abandoned the family business to run off to the theater, becoming a founding member of the "Illustre Théâtre." Funded by the Béjart theatrical family and managed by the young actress Madeleine Béjart, this upstart company staged the great neoclassical tragedies in a converted tennis court. The venture failed disastrously. Molière's stutter was no obstacle in *commedia dell'arte* mime, but was a serious one to his ambition as a tragic actor. Within two years, bankrupt, he was thrown into debtor's prison. Released when his father paid off his debts, he fled Paris with other members of the original troupe to tour the southern provinces for the next thirteen years as its star, alongside Madeleine as business manager and female lead. By 1650 he was directing the company, and began writing original plays for it.

Molière's company was at last invited back to Paris in 1658 to perform for the young king Louis XIV at the Louvre. Their production of Corneille's tragedy *Nicomède* did not impress, and Molière was judged a mediocre actor. He snatched victory from the jaws of defeat by persuading the king, in a witty closing speech, to allow his company to close by presenting his original farce *The Doctor in Love,* in which he played the lead. The king couldn't stop laughing, so his courtiers all tittered along with him. The result was that the company was allowed to share a royal theater with an Italian company of *commedia dell'arte* mimes led by the renowned "Scaramouche" (Tiberio Fiorelli), who had been Molière's drama teacher, and who left the space entirely to his former student the following year. That year Molière came through with his first major success, *Les Précieuses ridicules* (1659), in which he satirized ladies who imitated the linguistic and literary pretensions, rarefied manners, and ideals of platonic love cultivated in the salons of such important literary women as the Marquise de Rambouillet, Madeleine de Scudéry, Marie-Madeleine de Lafayette, and the Marquise de Sévigné—known as *précieuses.* No mere farce like his earlier comedies, this play addressed contemporary ideas. So incendiary was it considered that it was temporarily withdrawn, probably under pressure from influential *précieuses* or offended members of their circles. This play was perhaps the first modern comedy of manners, in which Molière's innovation was to employ more recognizably realistic characters, speaking a more straightforward language than was customary in tragedy. His satire of the mannered language of the *précieuses* was also indirectly a satire on the stilted verse of neoclassical tragedy.

A writer who achieves fame by exposing recognizable people to public ridicule is bound to make enemies, and Molière made many powerful ones. The year after his inaugural Parisian success (and its suppression), intriguers against him managed to have his theater demolished. His company moved the following year to the Palais-Royal theater, and followed up with another hit which brought Molière to the peak of his career: *The School for Wives* (1662), about the absurd and futile jealousies of a forty-two-year-old man (rather ancient in those days) who wants to marry a young girl. Molière himself was forty and had just wed nineteen-year-old Armande Béjart, who had replaced Madeleine—probably her mother—as Molière's costar, and the newlyweds played the husband and wife roles in the new piece. His marriage actually was troubled by jealousy and differences in age and temperament. Even during their repeated separations, however, the couple continued to act together on stage. Molière often drew on his personal troubles and vulnerabilities for comic material—making fun not only of jealous husbands but of middle-class men who, like himself, mixed with the aristocracy; playing the hypochondriac in *The Imaginary Invalid* when he was really at death's door; and even making two plays out of the extended controversy that arose in response to *The School for Wives,* which included charges of bad art and bad morals. In March 1663 he published the text of *The School for Wives,* dedicating it to "Madame" (Elizabeth Charlotte, Duchess of Orléans), the king's sister-in-law, which resulted in a generous royal pension, citing Molière as an "excellent comic poet." His company was soon renamed "The King's Company." That December the controversy reached its nadir when a rival actor wrote to the king accusing Molière of having "married the daughter and slept with the mother." This was effectively rebuffed when Louis XIV himself served as godfather in February 1664 to the son Armande had just borne Molière (the baby died soon after).

Tartuffe premiered later in 1664, a satire on religious hypocrisy. Another brilliant success, it added to Molière's roster of powerful enemies the clergy, who now denounced him as a blasphemous libertine. *Dom Juan* (1665), yet another success, was also attacked as impious, so much so that it was withdrawn and never again presented in Molière's lifetime. A daughter, Esprit-Madeleine (his only child to survive), was born the same year. By the next year he was continually ill and estranged from his wife. Yet the several years following saw more than one version of *Tartuffe,* first banned under pressure from the clergy but then revived to acclaim, and another of his greatest plays, *The Bourgeois Gentleman* (1670). In 1672 Madeleine Béjart died, Molière was reconciled with Armande, and a second son was born, who also died in infancy. He wrote *The Imaginary Invalid* so that he could perform the lead role even with his horrible cough. A theatrical rival, Lully, succeeded in having the play rejected for court performance; nevertheless it was a success at the Palais-Royal. Molière was overcome by coughing in the middle of the fourth performance on February seventeenth, and died soon after. Burial in consecrated ground was at first refused by the Archbishop of Paris, as it would be later to Voltaire, but on the King's petition it was permitted, albeit at night and without ceremony. Lully took over the Palais-Royal theater after Molière's death, but in 1680 his former company, having merged with its rivals, formed the *Comédie Française,* which remains to this day France's leading company for classical theater.

THE SCHOOL FOR WIVES In *The School for Wives* Molière first perfected his original contribution to drama, combining poetic yet plain language with the broad, physical routines of farce and the stock situations of the ancient *commedia dell'arte* theater to create plausible plots about recognizably current character types. Contemporaries indeed found the plot and characters of this play all too plausible and recognizable: the situation of the man who is so afraid of wives' infidelity that he wants to marry a young girl he has raised in complete ignorance of the world struck many as scandalously close to Molière's own private life. This premise was nevertheless taken from a contemporary French novella, Scarron's *Useless Precaution,* where such a man raises the infant daughter of his unfaithful lover for the same purpose, and with the same result. Molière's French enemies accused him of plagiarizing Scarron, not observing that Scarron's tale was itself adapted from "Forewarned but Not Forearmed" by Maria de Zayas (see page 1860), who in turn borrowed some of her motifs from a medieval Italian source. Molière combined the Zayas/Scarron story with a stock *commedia dell'arte* situation in which a young lover confides the progress of his efforts at seduction to an older man without realizing it is the same man he is attempting to cuckold. The strong influence of the *commedia* tradition on the play can also be seen in the fact that the ending, which may seem rather abrupt to modern readers, would have been extended by a concluding dance, as was customary in the *commedia.*

Within this plot framework, Molière fleshes out a plausible character type of the bourgeois merchant whose fear of the public humiliation of cuckoldry blinds him to the fact that he himself is destroying his own happiness by attempting to destroy the adult independence of his bride. Thus *The School for Wives* presented the first of the major satirical character types that came to characterize Molière's mature work, which later included the spendthrift, the miser, the snob, the vulgar social climber, the learned lady, the hypocrite, and the hypochondriac. The aesthetic norms of the period held that literature should instruct as well as delight, rendering comedy morally suspect as more frivolous and less instructive than tragedy; but Molière sought to teach through the cautionary character types he created. His major protagonists are governed by their fears of loss of control. As Molière so often drew on his own personal griefs to supply comic material, so his characters' personal tragedies furnish the comedy of his plays.

Molière's innovative, modern approach to theater in *The School for Wives* was fabulously successful. It was also his first play of many to send shock waves of scandal and bitter aesthetic and moral controversy through Parisian society. For his plays use stock characters and comic plot devices to afford commentary on the contemporary social scene. While *Les Précieuses ridicules* had ruffled feathers as early as 1659, *The School for Wives* was the first of Molière's plays to engender a sustained critical controversy, dubbed by one participant "The Comic War," exploding theatrical as well as literary rivalries while fueling the antagonisms of literary women and religious prudes. These disputes had everything to do with the immense popular appeal of Molière's plays. The critic Boileau's response to the controversy, addressed to Molière a mere week after the first performance of *The School for Wives,* reassured him, "If you pleased a bit less, you would not displease so much." For several years thereafter, the play was attacked in a whole series of critical dialogues and satirical one-act plays published by numerous rival writers and actors. His critics accused him of plagiarism from literary sources and memoirs of acquaintances; of being, like his protagonist, a jealous, cuckolded, or even incestuous husband; of violating literary decorum; and of being an untalented actor with a speech impediment.

Molière replied with his own brief plays, first, *The Critique of the School for Wives,* in which he represents his critics as extravagant *précieuses,* empty-headed noblemen, prudes mired in prejudice, or pedantic men of letters, and proposes that comedy is no less difficult or demanding an art than tragedy. In *Versailles Impromptu,* he rebuts rivals in the established theater by satirizing the mannered and emphatic tragic delivery then in vogue, using his own more natural acting style. The force and duration of this controversy shows how new and how threatening to the social and literary establishment were Molière's innovations in creating serious literary drama with broad popular appeal, as he altered the conventional styles of language and acting then dominating the established theater, and boldly attacked powerful social groups. A new theater, and a new society, were being born.

PRONUNCIATIONS:

Agnès: ah-NYES
Alain: a-LANH
Arnolphe: ar-NOLF
Billet-doux: bee-yay DOO
Chrysalde: kree-SALD
Enrique: ahnh-REEK
Horace: oh-RAHS
Oronte: oh-RONT
Jean-Baptiste Poquelin: zhahnh-bap-TEEST poh-kuh-LANH

The School for Wives[1]

Characters[2]

CHRYSALDE
ARNOLPHE
ALAIN
GEORGETTE
AGNÈS
HORACE
NOTARY
ORONTE
ENRIQUE

The scene throughout is a square in a provincial town.

ACT 1

Scene 1

CHRYSALDE, ARNOLPHE

CHRYSALDE: You're coming back to marry her, you said.
ARNOLPHE: Tomorrow it'll all be . . . put to bed.
CHRYSALDE: Arnolphe, perhaps I ought to have a word
Since we're alone and can't be overheard.
Speaking friend to friend and man to man
It makes me frightened for you does this plan.
Looked at from whatever point of view
Marriage is a dangerous step for you.

1. Translated by Ranjit Bolt. First performed at the theater of the Palais-Royal on 26 December 1662.

2. Arnolphe was played by Molière himself. The name refers to the medieval saint Arnulphus, the traditional patron saint of deceived husbands. Horace: the name of the lover was traditionally Horatio in Italian romantic comedies.

ARNOLPHE: You think so, friend. Perhaps, at home, you see
Some goings on that make you fear for *me*.
Have *you* perhaps been given *horns*[3] to wear
And want to think all husbands have a pair?
CHRYSALDE: Horns? A misfortune; there's no guarantee
Against: concern about them seems to me
Futile. In *your* case, what I worry about
Is the fierce mockery you've meted out
To hundreds of poor husbands. Every sort
Of cuckold, fat and thin and tall and short,
Has had to undergo your railery.
Your chief delight, wherever you may be,
Is to make countless secret intrigues known.
ARNOLPHE: Quite so. But then, show me another town
With such long-suffering husbands as our own?
Fat, thin, and short and tall, yes all are found
Being given an atrocious run-around.
These days we churn out cuckolds by the score.
One man in two is married to a whore.
Yes, horns, that badge of shame, are so widespread
A herd of goats has fewer, head for head.
One man has money? *His* wife doles it out
To sundry men who've caused his horns to sprout!
Another may be somewhat luckier—
His wife is having money spent on her—
But as she tells him it's rewards for virtue
The danger's something he is not alert to.
One's loud in his complaints—pointlessly so.
Another meekly leaves things status quo—
Some handsome man drops by—he knows what for—
To get what he's not getting any more—
He dons his coat and leaves by the back door.
A really cunning wife informs her spouse
That a young man's been coming to the house
But says he isn't getting anywhere.
And so the spouse rests easy, unaware
That two small bumps are peeping through his hair.
It's the saddest thing you ever saw,
One wife is such a cunning little whore
She'll tell her spouse she's got a youth in tow.
She also says he's getting nowhere, though.
The spouse rests easy, pitying the Hell
Of the poor youth . . . who's doing *pretty* well.
Or—just as clever—to explain away
Suspicious new accoutrements, she'll say:
"I simply *cannot lose* at cards these days."

3. The traditional symbol of cuckolds (husbands of unfaithful wives).

So, little knowing just what game she plays,
Her idiot spouse gives thanks to Providence
Because his wife has saved him some expense!
Subjects for satire seem to multiply
Each day. I watch. I laugh. Why shouldn't I?

CHRYSALDE: But when you laugh at cuckolds, please beware:
They'll laugh at *you* soon, if you don't take care.
Of course I hear the gossip. Everyone
Loves to discuss these sorts of goings-on,
But *I*, no matter what I might hear said,
Have never let it swell my hornless head,
Or bragged about my own good fortune. When
I might have censured certain tolerant men
For suffering in docile silence what
I'd *never* suffer, silently or not,
I've held my peace instead because the boot
Might very well be on the other foot
Eventually—that's how it goes, and who
Can tell what *his* wife might or mightn't do
Some day? But should *I* share the common fate,
And horns, the husband's lot, adorn *my* pate,° *scalp*
Since I've been tactful, I've a shrewd idea
People will think it's quite enough to sneer
Behind their hands, and surreptitiously,
And one or two may even pity me.
Your case will be quite different, I'm afraid.
You're in tremendous danger, as I've said:
Since you have quite outrageously abused
Each and every husband who's accused
Of tolerance—hounded them like some mad fiend
You'll have to tread *so* softly. Yes, my friend,
Steer a straight course or how the world will mock!
Give it the least grounds and a laughing stock
Is what you'll be. A byword. Furthermore . . .

ARNOLPHE: Oh, Heavens, have no worries on that score.
Nobody's ever going to catch me out.
There's not one trick that I don't know about.
No, not a single super-subtle ruse
That wives who want to horn their husbands use.
My grasp of conjugal cunning is complete.
I'm an expert on uxorial deceit.
I've taken steps, moreover, to prevent
My cuckolding. She's wholly innocent
Is *my* bride. Yes, a clot.° *idiot*

CHRYSALDE: I can't quite see . . .

ARNOLPHE: I'm marrying a fool. No flies on me.
I'm sure your wife's as virtuous as can be.
But one with *brains* is *not* a good idea

And certain husbands I could name pay dear
For taking on the intellectual type.
Spare me the clever-clogses who spout tripe° *nonsense*
About their coteries;[4] write nice poetry
And prose; play host to wits and counts. And me?
Just Madame's husband. Just a sort of saint
Who won't be canonised for his restraint.
Wives on a higher plane? Save *me* from such.
Women who write things always know too much.
I'd like a wife whose thoughts are *not* sublime;
One who wouldn't even know a rhyme
From a rhinoceros, and when we play
The rhyming *game,* and someone says—oo, say,
Something suggestive, such as: "What I mean is . . ."
She definitely won't reply with "Penis."
The sort of wife I want is one, in short,
Who couldn't think a single knowing thought.
As for her pastimes, I'll allow her three:
Sewing; church-going; loving me.

CHRYSALDE: You want a total imbecile. I see.

ARNOLPHE: I'd rather someone stupid and quite plain
Than absolutely gorgeous with a brain.

CHRYSALDE: Beauty, intelligence . . .?

ARNOLPHE: Chastity's enough.

CHRYSALDE: How will you ever be quite certain, though,
That such a dunderhead is going to know
The meaning of the *word* "chaste"? Let's ignore
The fact that life would be an utter bore
With your rank cretin°—are you sure you're *right*? *idiot*
Your anti-horn scheme—*is* it water-tight?
A clever wife may well deceive you—true;
But if she does she will at least mean to,
Whereas a dunce could always cuckold one
Without even knowing what she'd done.

ARNOLPHE: A trenchant diatribe, to which I say:
Preach at me from now until Domesday
On why my wife ought not to be a twit—
You'll find the sermon, when you've finished it,
Has *not* persuaded me. Amazing, eh?!
Each to his method.

CHRYSALDE: I've no more to say.

ARNOLPHE: I'll wed, as I do everything, *my* way.
I have sufficient means, one might suppose,
To pick myself a better half who owes
All that she has to me, and will have made me
Her lord and master, and cannot upbraid me
With stuff about the wealth and pedigree

4. Exclusive groups, cliques, usually featuring women writers.

That she has graciously bestowed on me.
Among the many children that I saw
Agnès stood out (this was when she was four)
Because she seemed submissive and demure.
Her mother's finances were not secure
And it occurred to me: suppose I bought her?
The good soul read my mind and sold her daughter
Without a qualm. I then designed my wife:
She would be raised in ignorance of life,
In a small convent, where I gave the nuns
Guidelines for turning out a total dunce.
My hopes have been attended by success,
I thank the Lord for it. I find Agnès
Has grown into the absolute nitwit
That was my dearest wish; for granting it
I'm on my knees to Heaven—yes, indeed—
For sending me the very wife I need.
The convent? I've now taken her away,
And since my house is bustling, night and day,
With Tom and Dick and Harry, she's been put
Here in this other one, where no one, but
No one, comes calling on me. Can one be
Too careful? Lest the girl's simplicity—
Her Nature—which is open through and through—
Be spoiled, the menials here are morons too.
You ask: "What does this long narration mean?"
I wanted you to know how wise I've been.
To round things off, as an old friend and true,
This very evening I'm inviting you
To dine with her, so you can scrutinise
My choice, and judge if it was so unwise.

CHRYSALDE: Thank you!

ARNOLPHE: This meeting will enable you
To gauge her innocence, and her person too.

CHRYSALDE: To judge from your report one must suppose . . .

ARNOLPHE: Agnès is poetry. My report was prose.
She's so . . . so *simple.* Time and time again
I'm moved to wonder at her. Now and then
The child comes out with things that, I must say,
Just make me piss myself. The other day
(Can you believe it?!) she was all distrait° *upset*
And came and asked me with a quite exquisite
Naïveté: "Where do babies come from? Is it
Something that happens through the ear or what?"[5]

CHRYSALDE: Well, well, it *is* a wondrous bride you've got,
Arnolphe. I'm happy for you.

5. Some religious belief held that Christ entered Mary's body through her ear during the Annunciation, along with the angel's message to her that she was bearing the child of God. Since Agnès has been brought up in a convent, it may be imagined she learned this theory there.

ARNOLPHE: All the same
Must you keep calling me by my old name?
CHRYSALDE: I try to stop myself but out it slips.
De la Souche[6] is *not* a name that trips
Off *my* tongue. Really! What got into you—
Re-christening yourself at forty-two?
Borrowing from a tree-stump on your land
A name that should belong to someone grand?
ARNOLPHE: La Souche, though, is the name of my estate.
What's more I *like* La Souche—Arnolphe I hate.
CHRYSALDE: To drop the name we got from our forebears
And take another, just to put on airs—
It's *wrong!* Though, granted, in this day and age
Trumping a title up is all the rage:
Gros-pierre, the peasant, lately did the same.
He's barely got an acre to *his* name.
He's dug a moat, though, and the imbecile
Insists that he be called "Monsieur de l'Isle"![7]
I hope the parallel doesn't anger you.
ARNOLPHE: Don't drag up people to compare me to.
Monsieur de la Souche is now my name.
It's one to which I have a damned good claim.
I like it, and I'm most displeased with you
For still "Arnolphe"ing me the way you do.
CHRYSALDE: As yet the new name's not in general use.
ARNOLPHE: But you've been told and so have no excuse.
CHRYSALDE: I've noticed people often still address
Letters to you as . . .
ARNOLPHE: *Can* we drop this?
CHRYSALDE: Yes.
We'll say no more about it. I shall train
My tongue to call you nothing, ever again,
But Monsieur . . . Monsieur de la Souche.
ARNOLPHE: Bravo. I'm going to knock here now, to say "Hello"
And let her know I'm back.
CHRYSALDE [*going*]: Good gracious me!
Just how affected can a fellow be?!
He's mad!
ARNOLPHE: That man has some peculiar views.
Really, the curious stances people choose
And stick to—with a passion! Weird! [*Calls.*] Hello!

6. "Tree stump"; the name Monsieur de la Souche indicates ridiculous attempt to imply ancient lineage. There is also a sexual innuendo.

7. A reference to the two playwrights Pierre Corneille (1625–1709) and his brother Thomas (1606–1684). Thomas took the name de l'Isle—it was common practice for a younger son in a freshly ennobled family to take a new name in this manner. Pierre Corneille had difficulty being ennobled, especially after the King's 1661 proclamation that persons unlawfully assuming noble titles would be punished.

Scene 2

ALAIN, GEORGETTE, ARNOLPHE

ALAIN: Who's there?!
ARNOLPHE [*to audience*]: I've been away a week or so.
She should be pleased to . . . [*Aloud.*] Open up! What ho!
ALAIN: Who's there?
ARNOLPHE: ME!
ALAIN: Georgette!
GEORGETTE: Yeah?
ALAIN: A man below.
Let him in.
GEORGETTE: You go.
ALAIN: *You* go!
GEORGETTE: Can't.
ALAIN: Nor me.
ARNOLPHE: What a palaver! Come on, somebody!
GEORGETTE: Who's there?
ARNOLPHE: Your master.
GEORGETTE: Alain!
ALAIN: What?
GEORGETTE: He's back!
ALAIN/GEORGETTE: Open up!
GEORGETTE: I've got dishes here to stack.
ALAIN: What if the cat gets my canary?
ARNOLPHE: Hey!
Whoever doesn't open right away
Won't get a bite to eat till Saturday!
HA!
GEORGETTE: Don't move Alain! I'm on my way!
ALAIN: Correction. *I'm* on *my* way. But nice try!
GEORGETTE: Gedardervit!° *get out of the way*
ALAIN: *You* gedardervit!
GEORGETTE: Look *you: I*
Am damn well opening that frigging door!
ALAIN: *I'm* sodding opening it!
GEORGETTE: You're not!
ALAIN: Well nor
Are you!
GEORGETTE: Nor you!
ARNOLPHE: *What* am I waiting for?!
ALAIN: Here, sir!
GEORGETTE: It's me, sir! At your service, sir!
ALAIN: But for Monsieur, I'd . . .
[*He aims a clout at her and gets Arnolphe.*]
ARNOLPHE: Pest!
ALAIN: Eh?

ARNOLPHE: Clot!
ALAIN: Blame *her!*
ARNOLPHE: *Will* you just pipe down, the pair of you!
I have questions I want answers to
So stop this nonsense. Now, how have things been?
Alain?

[*Each time Alain attempts to speak Arnolphe removes his hat and he puts it back on.*]

ALAIN: Well, sir . . . Well, sir . . . Well . . .
ARNOLPHE: What d'you mean
By keeping that on when you speak to *me?*!
ALAIN: Well said, sir! What got into me? Sorry!
ARNOLPHE: Go upstairs and send Agnès out here. [*Alain goes.*]
[*To Georgette.*] After we parted, how did she appear?
Sad?
GEORGETTE: Sad! No!
ARNOLPHE: No?!
GEORGETTE: Yes!
ARNOLPHE: Yes? Then why . . . ?
GEORGETTE: I'll say!
Waited for your return each day, *all* day.
Yes, every donkey, horse or mule that's been
She thought was you—you riding it, I mean.

[*Agnès emerges with Alain from the house.*]

Scene 3

ARNOLPHE [*aside*]: She's brought her work down. I approve. [*Aloud.*] Agnès
My pet, I trust you're pleased to see me?
AGNÈS: Yes.
Of course. Thanks be to God.
ARNOLPHE: It's sheer delight
To see you too. How have you been? All right?
AGNÈS: The bed-bugs have been bothering me all night.
ARNOLPHE: I'll soon be there to chase the bugs away.
AGNÈS: That'll be nice.
ARNOLPHE: That'll be nice? I'll say!
What's that work?
AGNÈS: A bonnet. Your nightcaps
And night-shirts are all done.
ARNOLPHE: Good girl! Perhaps
You'd better go upstairs, though. Don't despair,
In next to no time I'll rejoin you there.
We've things to talk about. Important things.

[*The others go.*]

[*Alone.*] Oh, you viragos!° Oh, you blue-stockings,° *domineering women* / *intellectual women*
Peddling emotions and fine sentiments,
Love-letters; poems; novels—all nonsense
Compared with honest, ignorant chastity.

She's poor. So bloody what?

Scene 4

[*Enter Horace.*]

It seems to me,
As long as honour . . . But what's this I see?
No! Is it? Yes! It is! No. It can't be.
It *is*! Hora . . .

HORACE: Monsieur Arnol . . .

ARNOLPHE: What joy!
Horace!

HORACE: Monsieur Arnolphe!

ARNOLPHE: My dear, *dear* boy!
So when did *you* get here?

HORACE: A week ago.
I called. You weren't in.

ARNOLPHE: Been away.

HORACE: I know.

ARNOLPHE: Oronte—your splendid father—how is *he?*
My god, an age we go back, him and me.
We haven't seen each other in four years.

HORACE: Or even corresponded, it appears.
He's happier than we are now. For you.
A letter from him. I've received one too.
A note informing me of his return.
The reason for it, though, I've yet to learn.
But tell me, have you heard of somebody—
A citizen of *this* town, recently
Returned from the New World, where he has made
A quite enormous fortune?

ARNOLPHE: I'm afraid
It rings no bells. His name?

HORACE: Enrique.

ARNOLPHE: Hmmm . . . No.

HORACE: My father does refer to him as though
He's somebody I really ought to know.
They're travelling together, so he says—
"On business." What, though, one can only guess.

ARNOLPHE: Oronte! Can't wait to see him.
[*Peruses the letter.*]
Compliments?
Between old friends? Well, really. What nonsense.
He didn't need to write. My purse is yours.

HORACE: Lend me a hundred Louis,° then. *gold pieces*

ARNOLPHE: Of course.
Thank God I've got them on me.
[*Gives purse.*] Keep the lot.

HORACE: I can't express my . . .

ARNOLPHE: No more formal rot.[8]
Now then: tell me how you like it here.
HORACE: Plenty of fun about—that much is clear.
ARNOLPHE: Pleasure depends on what one has in mind.
But if you're what they call a "beau,"° you'll find *playboy*
A plentiful supply of young coquettes.° *flirtatious women*
Really juicy ones—blondes *and* brunettes.
And oh, such docile husbands! Splendid sport
We offer; watching everyone cavort
Affords me mountains of amusement. Yeees . . .
You've got a girl already. That's *my* guess.
You've had some sort of amorous success.
A boy with looks and a physique like yours
Doesn't need money to begin amours.
You're a born cuckolder, and no mistake.
HORACE: It's a confession I'm prepared to make.
I've had an amorous adventure, yes,
I'll share it with you too, in friendliness.
ARNOLPHE: Aha! Horns sprouting on *another* crown!
My tables! Meet it is I set it down!
HORACE: I trust it's going to be our secret . . .
ARNOLPHE: Oh!
HORACE: A confidence betrayed can, as you know,
Prove fatal in these matters. Very well:
A beauty in this quarter's cast a spell
On me. I've had a measure of success
Right at the outset, having gained access
To the girl's house. With all due modesty
And respect to her, it seems to me
Extremely promising.
ARNOLPHE: And who is she?
HORACE: She lives there. Such a sweet girl. Simple too.
And this simplicity, it appears, is due
To a mistake made by some idiot man
Who hides her from the world. This fellow's plan
Is to preserve her ignorance, but that trait
Serves as a foil to charms that captivate
And thrill—to such a soft, engaging air—
The sort that wins hearts. Have you seen her there?
Her name's Agnès.
ARNOLPHE: Oh, God!
HORACE: And this fellow
Is de la Soup or Soot or some such . . . no,
Still haven't got it. Rich he is, but *not*
The most intelligent of men. A clot—
At least, that's how he's been described to me.
Know him?
ARNOLPHE: Sweet Jesus! This is agony!

8. It was customary to give a receipt for loans—Arnolphe here dismisses Horace's attempt to write one out for the large loan.

HORACE: Well?
ARNOLPHE: Yes! I know the fellow.
HORACE: And it's true?
He *is* quite potty? Totally cuckoo?
ARNOLPHE: Aaarggghh!
HORACE: Am I to take that as a Yes?
Ridiculous in his possessiveness?
So: my sources were correct, I see.
Well, the fair Agnès has conquered me.
She is a veritable jewel, Monsieur.
It would be heinous to abandon her
To the designs of this—this crazy-man
And I'll be doing everything I can
To thwart the jealous fool, make *her* my own.
That's why I've bluntly asked you for a loan—
To fund this scheme. You know as well as I:
That daring enterprises go awry
Without hard cash. The metal men adore
Makes conquests possible in love and war.
What's the matter though? You've gone quite wan.
Are you disapproving of my plan?
ARNOLPHE: No. I was thinking . . .
HORACE: If I'm boring you
I'll drop round later. Right, that's what I'll do—
To thank you. [*Going.*]
ARNOLPHE: Christ almi . . .
HORACE [*coming back*]: Remember, though:
This is a secret—*nobody* must know. [*Going.*]
ARNOLPHE: I feel . . .
HORACE [*coming back*]: My father *mustn't* hear of it.
If he does find out he'll throw a fit. [*Goes.*]
ARNOLPHE: Oh! Oh! That conversation was sheer HELL!
What induced the brainless brat to tell
Me? *Me*? My new name threw him off the scent,
But still, how stupid. On and on he went.
After all the pain I'd just been through
I should have forced myself to let him spew
The rest up. Wasn't that the way to learn
Whether there's grounds for really grave concern
And ascertain how intimate they are?
Better catch up with him. He won't be far.
I'll worm the whole thing out of him. But, ah,
I hate to think what horrors are in store
And dread to find the thing I'm looking for!

ACT 2

Scene 1

ARNOLPHE: I've lost him, and perhaps it's for the best.
This sort of torment cannot be suppressed

And if he saw me he'd be sure to guess
That I'm in—well, in pretty dire distress.
He of all people simply *must* not know.
Meanwhile, I don't intend to lie doggo
And let my young opponent play about:
I want to thwart him right now. I'll find out
Just how far their . . . intercourse has gone.
Guarding my honour is my number one
Priority. In my view she's my wife
In all but name, and I'm disgraced for life
If she . . . if she . . . Oh, *why* did I leave town?

Scene 2

[*Enter Alain and Georgette.*]

ALAIN: Monsieur! This time we really will . . .
ARNOLPHE: Calm down.
Come here, you two. Come on! Do as you're told!
GEORGETTE: You're frightening me. You make my blood run cold.
ARNOLPHE: I give my orders—here's how you obey me:
I'm away a week and you betray me!
GEORGETTE: Monsieur, I beg of you, don't bawl at me.
ALAIN [*aside*]: Bite from a rabid dog this is. Must be.
ARNOLPHE: Oof! I'm so furious I can hardly speak.
I'm almost suffocating from sheer pique.
I've got to get these clothes off! To allow
That man in *my* house! SCUM! Come back here—NOW!
Tell me at once . . . Stay where you are! Tell me . . .
Ahh! . . . I demand that you immediately . . .
Move and I'll kill you! . . . I demand to know
How that marauder gained admittance, so
SPEAK—clearly and concisely . . . out with it!
AT ONCE!!
ALAIN/GEORGETTE: MY GOD!!
GEORGETTE: My heart, it's thumping!
ALAIN: Shit!
He's mad!
ARNOLPHE: I'm drowning! . . . I need air! . . . Cool down!
Have to cool down! . . . A walk . . . Could I have known
When that . . . that little darling came my way
She'd grow into a . . . what she is today?
I'm palpitating! I must just extract
A full confession from her—but with *tact*—
And try to moderate my bitterness—
Softly softly catchee monkey—yes . . .
[*To them.*] Go back in now, and send out Agnès.
HOLD IT! Then her surprise won't be as great.
You'll only warn her that I'm in a state.
I'll get her. [*Goes in.*]

Scene 3

GEORGETTE: Jesus! He's well off his tree!
He scared the living daylights out of me!
He's a monster! And that ugly mug of his!

ALAIN: Monsieur Horace—that must be what it is
That's riled him. Told you.

GEORGETTE: Yes, but what's he at,
Making us keep her locked away like that?
What's he hide her from the whole world for?
And not let anybody near our door?

ALAIN: He's jealous.

GEORGETTE: Why?

ALAIN: Because . . . because he is.

GEORGETTE: But how do you explain this rage of his?

ALAIN: Well now . . . jealousy . . . you see, Georgette,
It's something that . . . that makes a fellow fret.
It's why male visitors are often banned.
A comparison might help you understand:
Suppose you're having soup and somebody
Comes up and says: "I'm hungry! Give it me!"
And grabs it? You'd be angry, wouldn't you?
You'd want to hit him . . .

GEORGETTE: Got it . . .

ALAIN: Get this too:
Likewise, a man's wife is his soup, you see?[1]
And he'll be well pissed off if somebody
Starts dunking his baguette in it.

GEORGETTE: That's true.
Though husbands can be easy-going too.
Some of them even seem delighted when
Their wives are visited by handsome men.

ALAIN: Yes. Easy-going types are sometimes found.
Just as some people pass their soup around.

GEORGETTE: He's coming back. He still looks pretty grim.

ALAIN: Must be anger that's upsetting him.

Scene 4

[*Enter Arnolphe.*]

ARNOLPHE: Augustus Caesar got from a Greek sage
A sovereign remedy for fits of rage:
If something riles us we should just repeat
Our ABC, he said, until the heat
Of wrath has died down, and before we do
Anything stupid. Well, I've said mine through,
Over this business with Agnès, and now
I've sent for her—for a walk; anyhow,

1. It was a peasant custom that the suitor would sit next to his beloved and share the food from her bowl.

A walk's the pretext, but I mean to charm
Her into spilling all the beans; to calm
My poor, tormented mind I'll sound her out,
But *gently*—then at least there's no more doubt.
[*To Agnès, who is emerging from the house.*]
Agnès, come here, child.
[*To Alain and Georgette.*]
Go back in you two.
[*They go.*]

Scene 5

ARNOLPHE: Nice day.
AGNÈS: It is.
ARNOLPHE: For walking.
AGNÈS: Yes.
ARNOLPHE: What's new?
AGNÈS: My kitten died.
ARNOLPHE: Oh dear. But there again,
All flesh is grass, and so forth. Get much rain
During my absence?
AGNÈS: No.
ARNOLPHE: Not bored, eh?
AGNÈS: No.
I never *am* bored.
ARNOLPHE: Ten whole, long days, though—
What *did* you do?
AGNÈS: I sewed an awful lot.
ARNOLPHE: People can be malicious, can they not?
Eager to gossip and to interfere?
Somebody told me a young man was here
While I was gone—that he paid court to you
And you allowed this—but it can't be true.
AGNÈS: Oh, but it is too.
ARNOLPHE: What?! You mean to say
A man . . .?
AGNÈS: Was here? Yes. Came here every day.
ARNOLPHE [*aside*]: Hmm. This confession's certainly sincere:
She *is* an ingenue—that much is clear.
[*Aloud.*] I did forbid this, though, as I recall:
I said no visitors, didn't I? None at all?
AGNÈS: You did. You don't know why I saw him, though.
You would have done the same as me, I know.
ARNOLPHE: Perhaps. Let's hear.
AGNÈS: All this'll sound a bit
Far-fetched at first—you mightn't credit it . . .
Well, I was sitting on my balcony
Doing some needlework, when suddenly
I saw a handsome youth go strolling by

Under the trees, and when he caught my eye
He bowed low. I politely *curtsied* low.
He bowed again. I curtsied. A third bow
From him. From me another curtsey. Now
He's walking up and down and every time
He passes me he's bowing low and I'm
Responding with a curtsey. I, for one,
Would certainly have curtseyed on and on
Rather than have him think me less polite
Than him. I'd not have given in. But night
Did fall at last, and stop us.

ARNOLPHE: Tell me more.

AGNÈS: Well, the next day I'm outside our front door
When this old crone comes up to me and says:
"God bless you child, and keep you *all* your days
As lovely as you are now. Don't forget,
Your beauty is a gift from Him, my pet;
The gifts He gives are not for wasting, though.
And that is why I thought you ought to know
You've wounded someone's heart and brought him woe."

ARNOLPHE [*aside*]: Ah! The old fiend! The hell-hound! Damn her eyes!

AGNÈS: "Wounded by *me!*" says I, in great surprise.
"That's right," she says, "as wounded as can be—
The youth you spotted from your balcony
Yesterday afternoon." "But how?" I said.
"What did I do? Drop something on his head?"
"Oh, no, my pet," the good old soul replies,
"Oh, no; the culprit was your sparkling eyes."
"Well, you astonish me. It can't be true.
Are my eyes evil? What harm could they do!"
Says I. Says she: "Those eyes of yours give out
A lethal poison you don't know about.
In short, the wretched boy is languishing.
And if you're cruel and don't do anything
To help, within these two days he will die."
"La! That would make me miserable!" says I.
"What sort of help does he require?" "Just this:
To meet and talk," she answers, "just that bliss.
Only your eyes can keep him from the grave.
If they've a poison then they also have
An antidote." "Why, willingly!" says I.
"If this is so, let the poor boy drop by
When he so pleases."

ARNOLPHE: Ah! A poisoner
Of innocent minds, this *hag*! My curse on her
For all her foul wiles: may she rot in Hell!

AGNÈS: That's why he came to see me—to get well.
And surely you agree I did right now?
I mean, in conscience, how could I allow

The boy to die, when I had just the thing
To save him? I who pity suffering
Of any kind, and have been known to cry
On seeing something like a chicken die?

ARNOLPHE [*aside*]: She's acted in all innocence. It's my fault
For swanning off like that—I'm such a dolt:
She's artless and must stay under my thumb
Or else she's always liable to succumb
To some hawk-eyed seducer. I'm afraid
It mightn't be an innocent game they've played.
The lecherous swine may well have gone a mite
Further than that.

AGNÈS: I say, are you all right?
You're muttering. Have I really done wrong?

ARNOLPHE: Nooooo . . .
Let's hear what happened next. How did this beau . . .
This *boy* behave when he was here? Hm?

AGNÈS: Oh,
If only you had seen his sheer delight;
How, when we met, at once he felt all right;
The pretty jewellery-box he's given me;
And his amazing generosity.
[*To Alain and Georgette.*]
We all adore him,
And if you met you'd share our feelings for him,
I'm certain of it.

ARNOLPHE: Yes, but what's he done?
When he was with you? When you were alone?

AGNÈS: Well, he told me that he loved me more
Than any boy'd loved any girl before
And said such things! So *tender!* Each sweet word—
How shall I put this?—tickled me and stirred
Something inside me—yes, I'm bound to say
I *was* moved, in a most peculiar way.

ARNOLPHE [*aside*]: Bizarre, this: *I'm* interrogating *her,*
Or meant to be, but *she's* the torturer!
[*Aloud.*] Besides this talk; besides this tenderness;
Did he . . . did he . . . look, did he kiss you?

AGNÈS: Yes!
He took my hands and arms and kissed and kissed.
Not one opportunity was missed.

ARNOLPHE: Your hands and arms are all he's taken though?
Oof!

AGNÈS: Weeeell, he . . .

ARNOLPHE: Yes?

AGNÈS: He took my . . .

ARNOLPHE: Tell me!

AGNÈS: No.
You'll just be angry with me.

ARNOLPHE: I will not!
AGNÈS: You will.
ARNOLPHE: I won't!
AGNÈS: You promise?
ARNOLPHE: Yes!
AGNÈS: He got . . .
You *really* won't be angry?
ARNOLPHE: NO! NO!! NO!!!
Good God above, girl, must you tease me so?
What did he get from you?
AGNÈS: He . . .
ARNOLPHE [*aside*]: Now I know
What's meant by Hell on earth!
AGNÈS: All right, here goes:
The ribbons you once gave me?—one of those.
But there was no way of refusing it . . .
ARNOLPHE [*taking deep breaths*]: The ribbon doesn't bother me a bit.
You say he kissed you—the odd arm or hand—
What else?
AGNÈS: What else? I don't quite understand.
Are there other things that young men do?
ARNOLPHE: NO! But this remedy he had from you—
What . . . Christ! . . . What else did it involve?
AGNÈS: Nothing.
Although, to ease the poor boy's suffering,
I'd've done anything.
ARNOLPHE [*aside*]: I've come out of it,
Smelling, if not of roses, not of shit.
But if I make the same mistake again
May I be pilloried by my fellow men.
[*Aloud.*] Agnès, I can explain how this occurred:
You're innocent. It was innocence, in a word.
Let's call the subject closed. What's happened has.
But all that lecherous toad was after was
To trick you, have his wicked way with you,
And then to laugh about it.
AGNÈS: That's not true!
So many times he swore he wanted . . .
ARNOLPHE: Ah!
But *you* don't know what tricksters these chaps are.
Beware! Accepting presents; listening
To pretty speeches, and that sort of thing—
Letting yourself be wooed and even kissed
Because you can't be bothered to resist—
It's mortal sin.
AGNÈS: A sin? Why should it be?
ARNOLPHE: Because it's been determined by decree:
Heaven abhors it.
AGNÈS: Why would Heaven abhor

Something so pleasurable? Whatever for?
I never knew about such things before
And I'm amazed to find how much delight
They give.
ARNOLPHE: Oh, yes, they're pleasurable all right.
Very much so—all these tendernesses
And soft seductive talk and sweet caresses
But still they must be lawfully enjoyed.
One must be married first, and thus avoid
The taint of sin.
AGNÈS: That takes the sin away?
ARNOLPHE: Yes.
AGNÈS: Let us marry then, without delay.
ARNOLPHE: Well, if that's what you want, I want it too.
AGNÈS: You really mean it?
ARNOLPHE: But of course I do.
AGNÈS: You'll make me happy. Oh, *so* happy.
ARNOLPHE: Yes
I'm offering you *unequalled* happiness.
AGNÈS: You really want us . . .?
ARNOLPHE: Must I say again:
Yes!
AGNÈS: Married! My, but how I'll kiss you then!
ARNOLPHE: And how I'll kiss you back!
AGNÈS: I can't make out
When somebody's just messing me about.
You really, really, *really* mean . . .?
ARNOLPHE: That's right.
Isn't it obvious?
AGNÈS: Married! When?
ARNOLPHE: Tonight.
AGNÈS: Tonight!
ARNOLPHE: Tonight. That makes you laugh, eh?
AGNÈS: Yes.
ARNOLPHE: That's all I ever want: your happiness.
AGNÈS: Well, I'll be deeply in your debt for this.
Me and him together! Oh, what bliss!
ARNOLPHE: You and who?
AGNÈS: Hora . . . Horoo . . . Hoorah!
ARNOLPHE: No, that's not the chappy, and you're far
Too hasty choosing husbands. Now I've *got*
A man in mind for you, but it is *not*
Hoorah. Regarding him (and may he die
Of this . . . this so-called "wound" you've been duped by)
Oblige me and don't see him any more.
If he should call again, just slam the door
Right in his face; and if he whines, you'll throw
A big stone down at him through your window
Thereby ensuring that he won't come here

Ever again—I've made myself quite clear
I hope. I'll watch your each and every move
Hiding in some dark corner.

AGNÈS: Made for love
He was. Oh, God!

ARNOLPHE: What kind of talk is this?

AGNÈS: I wouldn't have the . . .

ARNOLPHE: Go upstairs please, miss,
And no more moaning.

AGNÈS: But . . .?

ARNOLPHE: Enough, I say!
I've spoken. I'm your master. Go! Obey!

ACT 3

Scene 1

ARNOLPHE, AGNÈS, GEORGETTE, ALAIN

ARNOLPHE [*to Agnès*]: I gave my orders and I'm gratified,
No, *thrilled,* to see how promptly you've complied.
You showed that smooth seducer what was what.
Wise guardians have their uses, do we not?
Your innocence was ambushed. Yes, Agnès,
You were on the primrose path and didn't guess
Where you were going. I know fops: they've got
Ribbons and ruffs and plumes and God knows what—
Fine teeth; enormous wigs; great charm, of course—
But these are like the pads on a cat's paws
And underneath those pads there are sharp claws.
They're ravening fiends whose thirst is not for blood
But female chastity. But I have stood
Between you and the Devil's work once more.
Your honour's still intact, and what I saw—
The vicious way you hurled that great big stone—
Well, it was one less reason to postpone
Our marriage a day longer. First things first
However, and some precepts I've rehearsed
To toughen up your virtue. So—a chair—
[*This to Alain, who brings one.*]
I'll sit out here a while and take the air.
[*To Georgette and Alain.*]
And as for you . . .

GEORGETTE: We've learned our lesson well.
We're out from under that young wizard's spell.

ALAIN: If he gets in again I'll give up booze.
'sides, he's a berk:° he slipped me two écus *fool*
Last time—and bloody bogus coin they were.[1]

1. The coins were underweight: people used to shave bits off gold coins and pass them off as full-weight.

ARNOLPHE: About the marriage—I want you or her
To fetch the notary. Get the supper too—
The various dishes I described to you.
[*Georgette and Alain go.*]

Scene 2

ARNOLPHE: Now, put your work down and attend to me.
Head up; look at me; listen carefully;
Absolutely rapt attention please.
I'm marrying you. You should be on your knees
A hundred times a day to Providence.
Think of the humble circumstances whence
I generously raised you—after all
You were in the mire, if you recall—
A village girl, and would be now. Instead
You're a good burgher and you'll share the bed
And the embraces of a man who turned—
What—twenty offers down? a man who spurned
Attractive girls and honoured *you*. Recall
I say, that you were something, oh, *so* small,
And strive to earn what I've bestowed on you.
To know thyself and see that I don't rue
The step I'm taking now. Marriage, Agnès,
Is an extremely serious matter. Yes,
You're going to have stern duties as a wife—
Your new, exalted station—and the life
Of pleasure doesn't feature in the plan:
The woman is subordinate to the man.
One sex is born to rule; one to obey;
One to assert; the other to give way;
The private truckles to the officer;
Insignificant friars will defer
To reverend fathers; servants have to do
Exactly what their masters tell them to . . .
But none of this obedience can compare
With the complete docility, the rare
Humility, submission and respect
Wives owe their husbands, who are, in effect,
The only lords and masters they can know.
She sees him frown on her? That means: eyes low.
If, and *only* if, she's favoured by
Kind looks is she allowed to meet his eye.
There's too much flirting going on today.
Coquettes abound. Beware. It's a bad way.
The devil's work. My honour's in your hands.
A fragile charge is Honour—it demands
Such careful keeping. Wives must guard it well
Or else be punished in the fires of Hell
For living wicked lives. Get what I've said

Properly into that pretty head:
A bright, white lily—that must be your soul:
Play false and it becomes as black as coal.
You'll be anathema to everyone
And rot in Hell when your sad race is run.
Now curtsey.
In a convent a young novice
Takes infinite pains to con by rote her office;
A wife has her equivalent of it—
I've got a copy on me—holy writ [2]
This is, for wives—I want it to become
Your constant study. Take it. Read out some.

AGNÈS: *Marital Maxims*
Or: The Duties Of A Wife

ARNOLPHE: I shall expound them to you later on.
For now just read them out, please, one by one.

AGNÈS: What's a wife allowed to do?
What her husband tells her to.
She's as much a good or chattel
As his house and land and cattle.
She must never leave the house
Unless accompanied by her spouse:
Girls who venture out of doors
Meet young men and end up whores.
Balls, walks, parties, picnics and
Games of any kind are banned.
Many a wife who lost at loo° *a card game*
Forfeited her honour too.

ARNOLPHE: Now finish on your own and I'll explain
Their meaning to you when we meet again.
I've got some business to attend to—just
A trivial thing—I shan't be long I trust.
You guard that with your life.
[*Indicates book.*] And if I'm late
Just tell the notary, when he comes, to wait.

[*Agnès goes in.*]

Scene 3

ARNOLPHE: The model of a wife? Well this is it.
I'm going to mould her mind as I see fit.
Putty in my hands—that's what she is
And I can give to her that shape or this
As whim dictates. I almost lost her, true,
But then at least the little slip was due
To innocence. It isn't hard to find

2. Molière may be parodying St. Gregory of Nazianzus' *Marriage Precepts,* translated into French in 1640 by Desmarets de Saint-Sorlin. In the original version Molière made up a treatise of ten maxims satirizing the Ten Commandments, which led some contemporaries to accuse him of sacrilege.

A remedy for lapses of that kind.
A simple girl is easily put back
By two words on the straight and narrow track.
But clever ones are different kettles of fishes
Our fate will be attendant on *their* wishes,
If a party's what they want they'll damn well give it
And wise instruction only leaves them livid.
They'll make a virtue out of any crime,
And nonsense of our maxims every time,
By clever argument. Try how we may
To stop them sinning, they will find a way.
And once their whim has whispered the decree:
"Let Honour die" then what will be will be.
This fop will *not* be crowing over *me*
However, since he gave the game away—
He couldn't keep his boastfulness at bay.
Conceited sod! It *must* be Satan's work
When women want this sort of brainless berk
And . . . here he is. Deception—that's the thing—
Let's just find out how much he's suffering.

Scene 4

[*Enter Horace.*]

HORACE: I came to call on you, and yet again
You weren't at home: Fate's foiling me, that's plain.
But I'll be coming twenty times a day—
Until at last, on *one* occasion . . .

ARNOLPHE: Hey!
No more of this absurd politeness, *please!*
If there's one thing I hate it's *forms* like these
And if I had my way they'd all be banned.
It's a quite execrable custom, and
People waste *too* much time with such hot air.
I want to hear about your love affair—
Where . . . where are you *up* to? May I learn?
Our last encounter? Some sort of turn.
I'm better now, I've pondered, and indeed
Am simply flabbergasted by the speed
Of your initial progress. How you fare—
Well, I almost feel it's *my* affair.

HORACE: All right, I'll tell you, since you're in the know.
I've just had something of a setback.

ARNOLPHE: Oh?
Such as?

HORACE: Her guardian has returned. Moreover
It seems he's ascertained that I'm her lover.

ARNOLPHE: So soon! But how?

HORACE: I don't know. I do know

He has, though. At my usual hour or so
I thought I'd drop in on my little darling
Only to find the maid and valet snarling,
Barring my way. "Don't want you here no more!"
They said, and then they rudely slammed the door
Right in my face!

ARNOLPHE: They did?!!

HORACE: Yes.

ARNOLPHE: What a bore!

HORACE: And when I tried to parley with them through it.
No matter what I said, their answer to it
Was: "You're not coming in. Monsieur said so."

ARNOLPHE: Neither of them opened up then?

HORACE: No.
And then Agnès appeared at her window
And, in a haughty tone, told me to go,
Which proved to me that *he* was back—her tone
Plus the fact that then she threw a stone.

ARNOLPHE: A *STONE??!!*

HORACE: A stone, yes. Quite a good-sized one,
Some welcome, eh?

ARNOLPHE: Gosh!! Nasty!! And I'm sad
On your account.

HORACE: The outlook's pretty bad
Now that he's back.

ARNOLPHE: It's awful. Really dire.

HORACE: He's wrecked things.

ARNOLPHE: But you'll get out of the mire
It's nothing, this.

HORACE: The man's so vigilant,
So jealous—an insider's what I want—
Then I can thwart him.

ARNOLPHE: Easier than pie.
She loves you, doesn't she?

HORACE: That I can't deny.

ARNOLPHE: Well then, you're bound to get there.

HORACE: I hope to.

ARNOLPHE: The stone has—*what's* it done?—deflected you.
You mustn't be disheartened.

HORACE: This is true.
And then I knew at once *our friend* was there
Master-minding the entire affair,
Unseen. What really did surprise me, though—
And will surprise you too, sir, when you know—
Was a great stroke of daring and finesse
Which, from a girl as innocent as Agnès,
I call incredible. Believe you me,
Love's a great teacher, and will let us be
Some person that we've never been before.

You wouldn't recognise us any more
And yet the change was almost instant? Why?
Because it's love we've been instructed by.
Love breaks the mould of character—like that!
Will make a brave man of a scaredy-cat;
Or the worst miser give his gold away;
Or ingenues cunning—as it has today:
"GO!" she said. "Don't call again! GoodBYE!
I know just what you'll say. Here's my reply."
Then came the stone that so astonished you—
But *with* it—what d'you think? A billet-doux!° *love letter*
They landed at my feet together. Now:
That was what I found amazing—how
The sort of word-play worked—how she'd referred
To stone and letter with a single word—
"Reply"! Now go on, tell me, aren't you stunned?
Under love's tutelage *Agnès* had *punned!*
As for the part that nincompoop had played . . .
Hilarious! No?

ARNOLPHE: A hoot.

HORACE: Don't be afraid
To laugh.

[*Forced laughter from Arnolphe.*]

I mean, the man behaved as though
I was a bloody army, not a beau;
Why, he was ready for an ambuscade;° *ambush*
Petrified, and mustering his maid
And manservant, and mounting a charade
With stones . . . and hoisted with his own petard![3]
Yes, his return *is* going to make this hard,
But all the same, a scream! I laugh out loud
Each time I think of it. And *you're* allowed.
Go on then, laugh! You haven't really yet.

ARNOLPHE [*more forced laughter*]:
I'm trying to.

HORACE: But as a friend, I'll bet
You'll want to see the letter. Agnès' heart
Was in her pen. She's managed to impart
The pangs of first love.

ARNOLPHE [*aside*]: Filthy little whore!
What did I keep the bitch illiterate for
If not to . . .

HORACE [*reads*]:

"I want to write to you but I've no idea how to go about it. I need to tell you how I feel but I can't find the words. I realise now how ignorant he's made me and I'm

3. Explosive device formerly used in warfare. Hoisted (blown up) by his own petard: destroyed by the very device or plot he designed for another.

afraid of saying the wrong thing, or saying more than I ought. You've had such a weird and wonderful effect on me! But I've been forced to turn you away. It makes me mad! I can't live without you. I'm yours. But ought I to say that? Well, I can't help myself. How I wish he wasn't against it! He says all young men are the same. 'Beaus' he calls them. It seems they're all seducers and I shouldn't listen to you. But I know you're not that type. Everything you say is full of love. How could you be lying? Please tell me what it all means. I couldn't wish you any ill. It would be wrong to lead me on. In fact it would kill me."

ARNOLPHE: Phwarggh!
HORACE: What's up?
ARNOLPHE: I've got a cough.
HORACE: Ever heard anything so tender, though.
Ruled by an evil tyrant, even so
Her sweetness has emerged. And what a crime
For anyone to stifle so sublime
A soul as this is, and to set about
Snuffing the bright flame of her spirit out
With ignorance and stupidity. Love's begun
To rip the veil up. Some star, some kind one,
May shine its influence on me—then I can,
I know, defeat this NASTY, GHASTLY man.
ARNOLPHE: Good day to you.
HORACE: But where are you off to?!
ARNOLPHE: Just thought of something that I have to do.
And it's extremely urgent.
HORACE: Hey! Hang on!
He keeps her so confined—is there no one
Of your acquaintance who might possibly
Have access there? It may be crass of me
To ask, but after all, we're friends, aren't we?
All I've got there now are enemies.
I mean the maid and valet are *his* spies.
I *was* assisted by an ancient crone—
A supernaturally ingenious one
Who served me well at first. Four days ago
The poor thing passed away. You'll help me?
ARNOLPHE: No.
Sorry. You don't need *me*. You'll muddle through.
HORACE: Goodbye, then. Mum's the word. I'm trusting you . . .
You're not to let a word of this get out. [*Goes.*]

Scene 5

ARNOLPHE: How I do suffer when that boy's about!
It's hard to hide that I'm being torn to bits.
But can my ingenue have such quick wits?
Either she *acts* the innocent with me
Or else that stroke of ingenuity
Was inspiration from the Devil. Well,

Thanks to that wretched letter I'm in Hell.
He's got possession of her soul—that's plain.
I'm out. He's in. Which spells despair and pain
For *me.* Her heart's been stolen. My distress
Is two-fold: love is suffering no less
Than honour: being ousted makes me mad;
So does discovering that I've been had
Despite my prudence. Now, it's clear to me
That to punish her for her lechery
All I need do is leave the adultress' fate
To do its work: I only have to wait
To be revenged on her *by* her . . . although
To lose the thing we love is dreadful. Oh,
Sweet Heaven! When I chose my partner so . . .
So *systematically,* to find myself
Besotted with her charms! Friends, parents, wealth—
Agnès has none of them; she cuckolds me
Although I've cared for her so lovingly,
Yet I adore her—after this vile trick—
Yes, I'm obsessed! Christ, I'm a lunatic!
Have I no shame? I'll burst! I'll throw a fit!
Bash my own face in! Go in for a bit—
That's best. Yes. Just to see what sort of face
She'll show me after this. But keep disgrace
Away from my poor forehead, Heaven! Or,
If such a doom is what I'm destined for,
Bestow on me the strength to bear a stroke
Like this—a strength I've seen in other folk.

ACT 4

Scene 1

ARNOLPHE: I've got the jitters now, I must admit.
My mind! The worry churning round in it!
You see, I'm wildly searching for a way
Of beating back that bastard. No dismay—
No, not a trace of it did Agnès betray
At what she's done. She looked me in the eye—
She's all but killed me, and to see her, why,
You'd think she was as pure as driven snow!
By Christ, I seethed with rage to see her so . . .
So *calm!* This over-boiling passion, though,
Only appeared to make my ardour grow
Even as it seared my heart. I felt such bile,
Despair and rage at her, yet all the while
It seemed she'd never looked so lovely! No,
Her eyes had never met my eyes with so
Piercing a gaze, or managed to inspire
In me so overwhelming a desire.

I'll die—I'm bound to—if my sorry case
Does bring with it the customary disgrace.
But am I to have seen her educated
With so much loving care? Had her instated
Here in my house, as a child? Palpitated
Over her charms as they were burgeoning?
Cherished such tender hopes of the sweet thing?
Thought I was moulding her for *me,* for—what?
Thirteen whole years, so some . . . some cloth-eared clot
Whom she's besotted with can come and whisk her
Away beneath my nose, and just a whisker
Away from being my wife she was. You'll not,
Repeat *not* get her you, you little twot,
No matter how you scheme and plan and plot,
By thunder, NO! I'll blight your hopes, you'll see.
I won't allow you the last laugh on *me!*

Scene 2

NOTARY [*entering*]:
Ah! There he is. Good day. I'm here to draw
That contract up that you were asking for.

ARNOLPHE [*not seeing him*]:
How to proceed?

NOTARY: The standard formulae
Should do the trick.

ARNOLPHE [*same business*]: I'm going to have to see
Exactly what precautions I must take.

NOTARY: Sir, not one move do I intend to make
That hurts your interests.

ARNOLPHE [*same*]: I must guarantee
That I can*not* be caught out.

NOTARY: Just trust *me*
With all your side of it. If you're afraid
Of being cheated, till the dowry's paid
You're not to sign the contract, sir.

ARNOLPHE [*same*]: Let out
Some detail and the thing gets talked about
All over town.

NOTARY: Oh, no—it needn't be:
The contract can be drawn up secretly.

ARNOLPHE [*same.*] How can we reach some sort of compromise?

NOTARY: The settlement's determined by the size
Of Madame's dowry.[1]

1. Upon marriage the wife's property normally became her husband's (hence the need to pay for gambling debts with alternate means). The husband made arrangements to provide for his wife should he die first. This is what the notary proceeds to explain to Arnolphe.

ARNOLPHE [*same*]: I'm in love with her—
There lies the problem.
NOTARY: Well, in that case, sir,
We'll give the bride the best terms.
ARNOLPHE [*same*]: How on earth
Am I to deal with her?
NOTARY: The wife's share's worth
One third part of the dowry; so it goes
Generally speaking, but the husband shows
More generosity if he's fond . . .
ARNOLPHE [*same*]: If she . . .
NOTARY [*as Arnolphe notices him*]:
Concerning either party's property:
No real distinction's made in law, i.e.
He can endow the bride as he sees fit.
ARNOLPHE: Eh?
NOTARY: He can fix things for her benefit
If he wants *her* to have the best of it
(Being in love) by jointure which may lapse
Upon his wife's demise or may perhaps
Revert to the aforesaid's heirs or may
Be reapportioned in some other way
By settlement or else in common law
As per what either party holds out for
Or else by deed of gift contiguous
To the said instrument and drawn up thus
a) Subject to agreement or if not
b) Outright . . .
[*Arnolphe shrugs.*] What's wrong? Am I talking rot?
So I suppose I'm not equipped to draw
A contract up? Lessons in contract law—
That's what I need is it? I don't *think* so.
Regarding all such settlements, I know,
I think, that party A and party B
Hold chattels, fixed and unfixed property
In common, or at any rate *unless*
Such terms are nullified by an express
Agreement. That of everything the bride
May own, a third is taken to reside
Within the joint estate . . .
ARNOLPHE: You know. You know.
Who said a sodding word about it, though?
NOTARY: *You* did! You're mocking me, or why grimace
And shrug?
ARNOLPHE [*aside*]: To Hell with him and his dog's face!
[*To Notary.*] Goodbye, if that's the way to shut you up.
NOTARY: You sent for me to draft a contract?
ARNOLPHE: Yup.
There's been a hitch though. [*Aside.*] *What* a bag of wind!

NOTARY: This man is not, repeat *not* of sound mind.
ARNOLPHE: I'll fetch you when the time comes.
NOTARY: Cracked. Must be.

Scene 3

[*Enter Alain and Georgette.*]

NOTARY: He sent you to collect me didn't he?
ALAIN: Yes.
NOTARY: Tell him he's an imbecile from me.
GEORGETTE: Will do.
[*Exit Notary.*]

Scene 4

ARNOLPHE: Come here, please. Faithful friends and true
You are, and recent news confirms it too.
ALAIN: The notary said to say . . .
ARNOLPHE: Another time.
Somebody's planning to commit a crime
Against my honour. What an insult, eh?
To *you,* I mean, if someone took away
Your master's good name? How could you appear
In public? Wouldn't everybody peer
And point at you? Then since it's your concern
As much as mine, you must, at every turn
Be vigilant, or else this gallant may . . .
It's more than possible that in some way . . .
GEORGETTE: You've told us what to do ten times today!
ARNOLPHE: What if his weasel words should win you round?
ALAIN: Don't worry: *we* know how to stand our ground.
ARNOLPHE: But if he wheedled—said to you: [*to Alain.*] Alain!
My poor, *poor* heart—*please* help me—*ease* my pain!"
ALAIN: I'd say: "You twerp!"
ARNOLPHE: That's good. Or there again:
"My *dear* Georgette, you seemed so sweet—so *kind* . . . !"
GEORGETTE: You idiot!
ARNOLPHE: Good girl! Or again: [*to Alain.*] "I'm *not*
A man to think that something can be got
For nothing . . . Help me, and I won't forget.
Meanwhile, by way of an advance, Georgette . . .
That's for a dress—Alain, that's for a beer . . ."
[*He holds out some coins which they grab.*]

ALAIN [*pushing Arnolphe violently*]:
Thanks. Now hop it!
ARNOLPHE: Hmm. That's the idea . . .
I . . .
GEORGETTE: [*same business*]: Scram!
ARNOLPHE: [*same*]: Shove off! At once!

ALAIN: How did we do?
ARNOLPHE: Excellent . . . I'm very pleased with you . . .
You weren't supposed to take the money, though.
GEORGETTE: Ah. Sorry.
ALAIN: Shall we try again, then?
ARNOLPHE: NO!
But you can keep the cash. Now, off you go.
Inside.
GEORGETTE: But if . . .?
ARNOLPHE: I *WANT* you both indoors.
Be *very* watchful, and defend my cause.
[*They go.*]

Scene 5

ARNOLPHE: I'll keep her in the house, and keep *away*
Such people as coiffeurs, and perruquiers,° *wigmakers*
Vendors of ribbons, handkerchiefs and gloves—
Creatures of Satan, furtherers of love's
Infernal mysteries. Yes indeed. You see
The world—its wicked ways—are known to me—
Our little friend is going to need great skill—
If he's to get a letter in he will.

Scene 6

[*Enter Horace.*]

HORACE: I'm glad I've found you. I've been in a scrape.
I've never had a narrower escape.
After I'd left you, I just chanced to see
Agnès; she was out on her balcony,
Immediately she made a sign to me
And then, contriving to insinuate
Herself downstairs, unlocked the garden gate
And let me in. We're in her room . . . no time
When she hears her jealous monster climb
The stairs. In such a dire emergency
What could she do but quickly bundle me
Into a wardrobe. Now, in a twinkling,
He's in the room. I can't see anything
But I can hear the fellow thundering
Around the place—stride after giant stride—
But saying nothing, though he sometimes sighed—
Such sad sighs!—thumps a table-top perhaps—
Or aims a kick at a small dog that yaps
In terror—then starts chucking things around—
Anything of Agnès's that he found—
And even smashes, in his frenzied state,
Some vases, lovely ones, that decorate

(Or did) her mantle-piece. And there's no doubt
About it, the old billy-goat's found out—
He knows what she's been up to. So he vents
His wrath on things that offer no defence,
Pacing around the place for, ooh, maybe
A hundred circuits, and then finally,
Having remained as silent as the tomb
About what's bothering him, he leaves the room,
Enabling *me* to leave my hiding-place.
The prospect of him's more than we can face.
It's far too dangerous for me to remain
One minute with her. I'll be back again
Tonight, though—late—when I intend to clamber
Stealthily, mind you, up to her bed-chamber:
I'll cough three times—a sign to let her know
That I've arrived—she'll open her window,
And, aided by a ladder and Agnès,
Love *will* gain access to her. Happiness
Increases when disclosed—I must disclose it—
You *are* a friend—if nobody else knows it
One might have tasted bliss that's Heaven-sent—
Completely perfect, and not be content.
My joy is surely something that you share.
Goodbye. I'm off to think now, and prepare.

[*He goes.*]

Scene 7

ARNOLPHE: Fate seems intent on one thing: my despair.
It's unrelenting: every step I take
Is rendered futile by the plans *they* make!
At my age must I be the tool, the toy
Of a young ingenue and an idiot boy?
For twenty years and more the grisly fate
Of husbands was a thing I'd contemplate
So sagely; and I came to recognise
The pitfalls waiting even for the wise.
I learned from other men's disgrace. My aim?
To find some method whereby, when *I* came
To marry, I could somehow guarantee
That those dread horns would never sprout on *me.*
But, as if Fate had issued a decree
That there is *no* escaping cuckoldry,
I find that I am in the very place
I'd been avoiding—face the same disgrace
As other husbands. Well, I now defy
That cursed Fate! I've still got her, haven't I?
And if that bloody boy has pinched her heart
He isn't pinching any other part!

This amorous adventure won't end *quite*
As pleasurably as he'd hoped it might.

Scene 8

CHRYSALDE [*entering*]: Supper and then a stroll? What do you say?
ARNOLPHE: I don't want any supper. Not today.
CHRYSALDE: I see. Feeling a touch off colour, eh?
ARNOLPHE: I've other things on *my* plate, haven't I.
CHRYSALDE: Indeed? Your marriage plans have gone awry?
ARNOLPHE: None of your bleeding business. Please don't pry.
CHRYSALDE: Oh! Tetchy! Hmmm. To look at you, I'd say
It *is* the marriage plan that's gung aglay.° *gone wrong*
ARNOLPHE: Well I won't take it like the others. No,
I'm hitting back at *my* wife's Romeo.
CHRYSALDE: It's odd to see a man as wise as you
Getting as over-heated as you do
About all this. Happiness; honour, too,
Just means avoiding horns. Yes, that's your view:
Whatever sort of life a man has led,
As long as he retains a hornless head
He's honourable—a random circumstance
Determines our good name—that's right, mere chance—
Likewise a decent man receives a blow
He couldn't have prevented, even so
He has to blame himself. I don't see why.
We choose a wife we're later cheated by?
How is blame, *or* praise, implied here, pray?
Is cuckoldom so awful *anyway*?
It is entirely random, as I say,
And then there's nothing good or bad, you know—
Not even horns—but thinking makes it so.
Of course one doesn't want to rush about
Reading long lists of one's wife's lovers out,
And saying what amazing men they are,
And going on picnics with them—going too *far*
In one direction. But it's just as grave
A crime against good sense to rant and rave
And weep and wail about one's marital woes
Et cetera, until the whole world knows.
Between these two poles lies the middle way
On which the prudent husband tries to stay.
Follow it and your wife can do her worst—
You needn't feel ashamed, or somehow cursed.
Just make the best of it. Steady as you go.
That's the wise way.
ARNOLPHE: Splendid speech! Bravo!
Recruiting officer for cuckoldom.
That's what you ought to be, Chrysalde.

CHRYSALDE: Come come.
All I mean is that one ought to view
The business like a game of dice—you threw
Unluckily? Well play with extra skill
And caution—draw your horns in, if you will.
ARNOLPHE: Oh, *excellent* advice! Eat well, sleep well,
Try to persuade yourself you're not in Hell.
CHRYSALDE: Sarcasm, eh? Well, let's just get this clear:
There are far worse predicaments to fear
Than horns. For instance, you may well suppose
That, if I had to choose between two woes,
I'd rather have a slut than one of those
Dragons of virtue, devils of rectitude,
Who, because of one sin they've eschewed,
One wrong they haven't done them, claim the right
To treat their spouse like . . . well, like so much shite.
ARNOLPHE: Then cuckoldom's your bag, or seems to be.
It certainly does *not* appeal to *me.*
Rather than have a pair of horns to wear . . .
CHRYSALDE: Don't say it, or you'll promptly get a pair!
ARNOLPHE: Me!
CHRYSALDE: Yes. They sprout on men whose pedigree
Wealth, stature, far exceed yours.
ARNOLPHE: Oh, I see!
So you've decided to start riling me!
Let's drop this please.
CHRYSALDE: Ah, well, you're in a pet.
I'll find out why. But meanwhile, don't forget
A man who vows he'll keep the plague at bay
May well go down with it the following day.
ARNOLPHE: Well, *I* shall find a remedy, right away.

[*He knocks at his door. Exit Chrysalde.*]

[*Enter Georgette and Alain.*]

Scene 9

ARNOLPHE: I need your help, you two, quite desperately.
Your devotion really touches me
And you must show it in the present case.
Justify the confidence I place
In you, and you will be rewarded. Now . . .
(Secrecy's vital too) . . . this youth—you know—
I'm told he has a ladder and intends
To climb up to Agnès tonight. My friends,
We have to set a trap. I want you each
To take a good sized stick, and let him reach
The top rung (I'll have opened the window)
Then thrash the little shit—blow after blow,

Leaving a lasting imprint with each thwack.
Teach him a lesson so he won't come back.
Well? Can you do it?

ALAIN: Can a rose-bush grow?
I haven't got a withered arm, you know.

GEORGETTE: Monsieur, my arm might not look quite as strong,
But Christ, I'll wallop him—wallop him hard and long.

ARNOLPHE: Go in then. There's to be no blabbing, mind.
[*They go.*]
This is a useful lesson for mankind:
If every little bastard beau was shown
The stick by every husband in this town
The cuckolds' numbers would come crashing down.

ACT 5

Scene 1

ARNOLPHE, GEORGETTE, ALAIN

ARNOLPHE: What did you have to go and kill him for?!

ALAIN: We only did as we were told. No more,
No less.

ARNOLPHE: I said to leave him bruised, not dead!
To break his back perhaps but not his head!
What a disaster! Go in. Not a word
About the cock-up that has just occurred.
It'll be day soon. Then I'll have to see
Just how to deal with this catastrophe.
Oh Jesus Christ, what*ever's* to be done?
How do I tell Oronte I've killed his son?

Scene 2

HORACE [*entering*]: Who's this, then . . .?

ARNOLPHE: How could I . . .? Who might *this* be?

HORACE: Monsieur Arnolphe, is that you?

ARNOLPHE: Yes, it's me.
Who's that?

HORACE: Horace. And I was on my way
To ask a favour . . . *You're* up early!

ARNOLPHE: EH?!
[*Low voice.*] Is he a ghost? Has someone cast a spell?

HORACE: Monsieur, I *have* gone through a spot of Hell
But everything seems to have turned out well.
Better than I dared hope and what is more
Just when it seemed that I was, well, done for.
I can't think how, but that mad bastard knew
That we'd arranged a midnight rendez-vous—
I'd reached the window, or was almost there
When somebody appeared out of thin air—
Two bodies—and they raised their hands, as though

Preparing to repulse me with a blow—
With sticks or some such. Now, this made me lose
My footing and fall—I got a nasty bruise
Or two, but I escaped a thrashing. Well,
They thought they must have hit me since I fell
(*Our friend* was there, as far as I could tell)
And I remained completely motionless,
Being in agony—leading them to guess
They must have murdered me. As well they might
They started panicking—in the silent night
I heard them arguing—without a light—
Accusing one another of killing me—
Still squabbling loudly—they crept out to see
If I was really dead—I *acted* dead—
Easy enough as it was dark—they fled
In terror—back inside they went—to flee
Did also seem the wisest course to *me*—
I would have done, but then Agnès came out,
All of a flutter, having learned, no doubt,
Of my "demise" from their ferocious row.
She flew to me, found me alive, and now
Her jubilation—words cannot convey
The half of it—of course there was no way
She could return—that's what love taught her—so
She placed herself in *my* hands. Goes to show,
This innocent decision, what he's done
With his outrageous schemes: she might have run
A huge risk, had I been a different sort—
I mean ensnaring her instead of caught—
But a chaste flame is burning in my heart—
We are a pair that only death can part—
I'd *rather* die than . . . no, her hold on me
Is not at all of that kind. I foresee
A problem, as my father's bound to frown
On such a choice—his anger will die down—
We shall appease him—she's the only wife
For me—one tries to be content in life—
She's poor? So what? Here's what I want from *you*—
And once again it's just between us two:
I'd like to leave her with you. Could she stay
In *your* house, as a safe retreat, for say
Two days, perhaps more?—hidden well away
From prying eyes? She'll surely be pursued—
Then there's the world's suspicious attitude
To a young girl, with a young man, alone . . .
You're truly wise, and you're the only one
I've told—you've been a friend to me all through—
Who else could I entrust my treasure to?

ARNOLPHE: I'm at your service. You can count on me.
HORACE: You *angel!* Then you'll do it?!
ARNOLPHE: Willingly.
Delighted I can help, I mean, help *you*—
Can't think of anything I'd rather do—
Thank Heaven for a chance to.
HORACE: I shall owe
Such a tremendous debt to you. You know
I really thought you mightn't have played ball—
But *you're* not hard on young love—after all
You're very wise and worldly. She's close by—
I told a man of mine to keep an eye
On her.
ARNOLPHE: But what to do? I've no idea.
You can't exactly hand her to me here—
It's almost day and somebody may see—
On the other hand, bring her round to me,
The servants start to talk. We have to play
Completely safe—somewhere out of the way
We want—my garden!—I shall wait for her.
In *my* back garden.
HORACE: Wise precaution, sir.
I'll leave her with you there and then go home.
ARNOLPHE [*alone*]: HA! At last a stroke of luck has come.
This makes up for everything—and some!
[*He lifts cloak up to the bridge of his nose.*]

Scene 3

[*Enter Agnès and Horace.*]

HORACE: You're safe. You needn't worry any more.
I've picked a good place. Come on—through this door.
We couldn't live together yet, Agnès—
We'd ruin everything. Go where he says.
[*Arnolphe takes her hand. She doesn't recognise him.*]

AGNÈS: You're leaving me.
HORACE: This is the only way.
AGNÈS: You *will* be back soon, won't you?
HORACE: Come what may.
I love you.
AGNÈS: When you're gone, I'm sad.
HORACE: Me too.
AGNÈS: You wouldn't go away if that was true.
HORACE: You doubt my love?
AGNÈS: I know mine's greater.
[*Arnolphe pulls her.*]

Ow!

HORACE: It's curtains if we're seen together now.
This man's our friend. He wants our happiness.
He's wise. That's why he's pulling you, Agnès.
AGNÈS: Who is he?
HORACE: Don't be frightened. You've no cause.
You're in safe hands.
AGNÈS: I'd rather be in yours.
HORACE: And I . . .
AGNÈS [*to Arnolphe, who is still pulling her*]:
Wait!
HORACE: Day-break. I must disappear.
AGNÈS: When shall I see you?
HORACE: Very soon, I swear.
AGNÈS: And till you *are* back *I'll* be in despair.
[*Horace goes.*]

Scene 4

ARNOLPHE: Not that way—this is where you're going to stay.
You'll be quite safe, dear. Recognise me?
AGNÈS [*calls*]: Hey!
ARNOLPHE: You little slut! Not frightening you am I?
Not pleased to see me? Found a nasty fly
In our nice ointment, have we?
[*Agnès is looking for Horace.*]
No use, dear.
Looking for your young Romeo. I fear
He cannot help you now. He's on his way.
But ah! Ah! What a beastly trick to play,
And so young too! You managed to appear
So *innocent*. Asked if it was through the ear
That we make babies. Yet you meet young men
At midnight don't you, all the while, and then
Creep off with them! Your words caress him so!
Where did you learn all that? A good school, no?
This sudden change—who has your teacher been?
Not scared of ghosts now? Why not? Does this mean
Your boy's emboldened you? Perfidious . . . WHORE!
I'm so benevolent with you, and *you're*
So false to *me!* A viper at my breast
Biting the hand by which it was caressed![1]
That's what you've been to me your whole life long!
AGNÈS: Why do you scream?
ARNOLPHE: Why do you do me wrong?

1. Allusion to an ancient fable told by Aesop and later by Molière's friend La Fontaine. A kindly peasant, while traveling in the dead of winter, finds a snake nearly frozen to death and tries to warm the snake inside his shirt. Once revived, the snake's evil nature returns and it bites the peasant, who in his anger cuts the snake to pieces with a knife.

AGNÈS: Just name a single wicked thing I've done!
ARNOLPHE: Isn't eloping with your lover one?
AGNÈS: He wants to marry me. Didn't you say
You *have* to marry? Take the sin away?
I'm doing what you told me.
ARNOLPHE: I said so.
It's me that you were meant to marry, though!
I rather thought I'd dinned that into you.
AGNÈS: Perhaps, but frankly—just between us two—
You're not my type and *he* is. What's your view
Of marriage? Something nasty, something grim.
That's *not* the picture that I get from *him.*
He makes it seem desirable, and fun.
ARNOLPHE: So he's the one for you.
AGNÈS: The *only* one.
ARNOLPHE: You say that to my face you huzzy, you!
AGNÈS: I say it to your face because it's true.
ARNOLPHE: Why can't you love me?
AGNÈS: You should ask *him* that.
I loved before I knew what I was at.
ARNOLPHE: You should have tried to drive away desire.
AGNÈS: How can you do that when your heart's on fire?
ARNOLPHE: Didn't you realise it would anger me?
AGNÈS: What grievance you could have, I fail to see.
ARNOLPHE: Grievance? Of course not! I'm in ecstasy!
I take it you don't love me.
AGNÈS: You.
ARNOLPHE: Yes.
AGNÈS: No.
ARNOLPHE: What do you mean, no?
AGNÈS: I'm supposed to lie?
ARNOLPHE: How dare you! But why *can't* you love me? WHY?
AGNÈS: I don't see what you're carping at *me* for
If he's the sort of man that girls adore.
Why not be *like* him? *I'm* not stopping you.
ARNOLPHE: Being adorable? I *have tried* to.
I've tried my level best, and all in vain.
AGNÈS: He's got what *you* don't have—that much is plain:
He didn't *have* to try.
ARNOLPHE [*to himself*]: Well here's a thing!
The slut can wrangle like a blue-stocking!
She's *not* a nitwit. Otherwise, is love
One subject that a fool can know more of
Than any sage? [*Aloud.*] Argument's your forte?
All right, miss reasoner: would you care to say
Why I have spent a fortune raising you?
AGNÈS: He'll compensate you down to the last sou.° *cent*
ARNOLPHE: Can he discharge, although he's stinking rich,
Your countless obligations to me, bitch?

AGNÈS: I've countless obligations, then, have I?
ARNOLPHE: Haven't I raised you, since you were so high?
AGNÈS: And what an *education* I've received!
You don't suppose I've ever once believed
That I was anything other than a clot?
ARNOLPHE: You're going to learn from *him,* though—God knows what!
AGNÈS: Yes.
ARNOLPHE: I should strike the girl. This pert address—
Why, it enrages me—this *frostiness:*
What she could do with is a damned good clout—
Or two—or three—to let my anger out.
AGNÈS: You want to wallop me? Wallop me then!
ARNOLPHE: That voice, that look—they calm my rage again,
Filling my heart with the old tenderness
And making an enormous wrong seem less.
Ah, what a mystifying thing love is!
So *weak* men are with faithless fiends like this!
Better make up. [*To her.*] All right then, I surrender.
Such love I'll give you. I'll be oh, *so* tender
From now on. I'm besotted with you. See?
I'm being an angel, *please* be one to me.
AGNÈS: Oh, but I want to please you desperately.
What would it take to do it?
ARNOLPHE: Sweetypie!
You can do it. [*Sighs.*] Listen to that sigh!
So amorous! Isn't it a giveaway,
This doleful look? Reject the poppinjay
And spurn his love. Bewitched is what you are
And I can make you happier by far.
It's all you ever want is happiness.
You'll have it constantly. I'll stroke, caress
And smother you in kisses night and day.
In everything I'll let you have your way.
There then. I've said my piece. [*Aside.*] I just don't know
How far obsession mightn't make me go!
[*To her.*] Where will you find the equal of my love?
Heartless girl! How would you have me prove
My passion? Must I weep? Or beat my breast?
Tear out my hair? Or kill myself? What test
Am I to pass? Just name it? I'm your man.
I'll show my love in any way I can.
AGNÈS: Nothing you say will touch my heart at all.
It's touched by every word that he lets fall.
ARNOLPHE: Why must you flout me and outrage me so?
An untamed animal that *will* not know
The curb is what you are: this very day
I'll carry out my plan: send you away—
You spurn me; cross me; so: a convent cell—
That's my revenge on you—a long, long spell.

Scene 5

[*Enter Alain.*]

ALAIN: Monsieur, the girl!—she's gone! And if I'm right,
She's hopped it with the bloke we killed last night!

ARNOLPHE: Here she is. Lock her in my room. Nowhere
The boy's unlikelier to look than there.
Only a half an hour this should be for.
Then I intend to take her somewhere more . . .
Secure. I'll find a carriage. To remove
The girl from here might cure her of her *love*.

[*Alain goes, taking Agnès out.*]

Scene 6

[*Enter Horace.*]

HORACE: Ah, there you are! Now I'm in *dire* distress.
Heaven just doesn't want my happiness.
Disaster's struck. It's really most unjust.
My darling girl and I are to be thrust
Apart for good. My father's coming here
On foot (his carriage left him somewhere near)
And why's he come? He's found a *wife* for me!
What's more it's here the wedding is to be!
Could this have been worse timed? I hope you share
My utter misery. This sad affair
Is all the doing of Enrique—you know—
Mentioned him yesterday. Yes, he's in tow.
Together they'll destroy me, for you see
His only daughter is the bride to be.
I bloody nearly fainted when I heard,
I couldn't listen to another word.
They were to call on you, my father said.
In great alarm I hurried on ahead.
Keep mum—about Agnès. He'd throw a fit.
And also, try dissuading him from it—
I mean this marriage—since he sets great store
By your opinion.

ARNOLPHE: Will do.

HORACE: Try to pour
Cold water on the project. A delay—
That's what I need.

ARNOLPHE: I'll do it.

HORACE: Need I say
I'm counting on you.

ARNOLPHE: Good.

HORACE: You know, somehow
I feel I'm more *your* son than . . . [*Voices off.*] That's him now.
Here are some arguments I've got for you.

[*They go into a corner.*]

Scene 7

[*Enter Oronte, Enrique, Chrysalde.*]

ENRIQUE [*to Chrysalde*]:
As soon as I caught sight of you I knew
Without being told exactly who you were—
Your sister—how you do resemble her—
My loving wife. How happy I should be
Had cruel Fate let me bring her back with me
To share the joy of seeing her family
Once more, after the hardships we endured.
But Destiny's all-powerful hand ensured
That I should lose this jewel. I must, therefore,
Be happy with the fruit our union bore—
Our one child. This concerns you, and I need
Your blessing for the marriage to proceed—
I've made an excellent choice in Oronte's son,
But I want *you* to feel it's the right one.

CHRYSALDE: Enrique, I hope you don't consider me
A fool—for that is what I'd have to be
To question such a wise choice!

ARNOLPHE [*to Horace*]: I'm your man.

HORACE: And as we said, you won't . . .

ARNOLPHE: Your little plan?
Our secret.

[*Arnolphe taps his nose, then comes forward. He and Oronte embrace.*]

ORONTE: That's a warm embrace all right!

ARNOLPHE: But seeing you again is sheer delight.

ORONTE: I've come . . .

ARNOLPHE: I know.

ORONTE: My son has told you?

ARNOLPHE: Yes.

ORONTE: I'm glad.

ARNOLPHE: He couldn't want this marriage less.
He sees it as a . . . as a "sad affair,"
And his affections are engaged elsewhere.
He's asked me to ask *you* for a delay—
Here's my advice: proceed—and right away—
Oughtn't a father to govern a son?
One must be firm with youngsters, mustn't one?
Indulging them is bad for them.

HORACE: Youuuuuuu . . . SHIT!!!

CHRYSALDE [*to Oronte*]: Maybe, if the boy objects to it
We shouldn't force him into it . . . should we?
My brother-in-law ought surely to agree . . . ?

ARNOLPHE: What? Will he let his son rule over him
And gratify his every foolish whim?
Will he, at the age he's reached today,
And when he ought to stand his ground, give way?

He's a close friend. My reputation is—
Well, it's more or less bound up with his:
He's made a promise—he must honour it,
He must be firm—twist the boy's arm a bit—
Even in love.

ORONTE: Arnolphe, you're talking sense.
I want and I *expect* obedience.
He marries.

CHRYSALDE [*to Arnolphe*]:
I'm amazed that *you're* so keen
To see this marriage. Can't think what you mean
By this int . . . ?

ARNOLPHE: Oh, I know what I'm about.
I've said what needed to be said.

CHRYSALDE: No doubt.

ORONTE: Monsieur Arnolphe . . .

CHRYSALDE: He doesn't like that name.
Call him De la Souche.

ARNOLPHE: It's all the same
To me.

HORACE: De la . . . De la . . . but . . . oh, my god!

ARNOLPHE: [*to Horace*]: Now my behaviour doesn't seem so odd.
The mystery's solved.

HORACE: HELL!

Scene 8

[*Enter Georgette.*]

GEORGETTE: Please come quickly, sir.
We've had the Devil's own job controlling her.
She keeps on trying to leg it and she *may*
Jump out the window!

ARNOLPHE: She'll be sent away
At once. Fetch her.
[*Georgette goes back in.*]
[*To Horace.*] Don't fret. We *need* bad days
Or we get cocky. And the proverb says
That every *dog* has *his*.

HORACE: It's the abyss!
What calamity could equal this?

ARNOLPHE: Well now, when's the wedding going to be.
It couldn't be a second too soon for me.
Trust I'm invited?

Scene 9

[*Enter Alain with Agnès.*]

ARNOLPHE [*to Agnès*]: Playing up are we,
My darling? Come along. Console your beau

With a brief curtsey. [*To the others.*] Well, we have to go:
And so a burgeoning romance bites the dust.
As burgeoning romance sometimes must.

AGNÈS: [*to Horace*]: Will you abandon me?

HORACE: I barely know
Where in the world I am, I'm suffering so.

ARNOLPHE: [*to Agnès*]:
Come. No more talk. We're off.

AGNÈS: I'm staying here!

ORONTE: Could someone get the fog I'm in to clear?

ARNOLPHE: I can explain the whole affair to you
At greater leisure. [*Going.*]

ORONTE: Where are you off to?

ARNOLPHE: Just get him married.

ORONTE: But that can't be done . . .
Without . . . you said he'd told you . . . *she's* the one—
The bride. Her father's this man here—Enrique,
Whose wife was *this* man's sister,
[*Points to Chrysalde.*]
Angelique.
They'd married secretly. Now please explain
Your strange behaviour.

CHRYSALDE: Quite right!

ARNOLPHE: Come again?

CHRYSALDE: My sister married secretly, you see,
And had a daughter which her family,
Needless to say, was never told about.

ORONTE: To hide the birth the baby was put out
With an old peasant-woman to be reared.

CHRYSALDE: A little later Enrique disappeared.
Sundry disasters drove him to New Spain.

ORONTE: And there he built his fortunes up again.

CHRYSALDE: On finally returning from the West . . .

ORONTE: He found that peasant woman.

CHRYSALDE: Who confessed
To having sold his child to *you*, aged four.

ORONTE: (In fairness, she was desperately poor.)

CHRYSALDE [*to Arnolphe*]:
Oh, I can well imagine you're in Hell.
Looked at another way, things have turned out well:
Avoiding cuckoldom is all, you say—
Not getting married seems the surest way.

ARNOLPHE: Ahhhhhhhhhhhh! [*Goes.*]

ORONTE: He disappeared without a word! But why?

HORACE: These are matters I can clarify.
The chief point is that I'm already tied
By bonds of love to *this* girl—to the bride
You've wisely chosen for me. And I'm glad:

God knows what sort of row we would have had!
[*To Enrique.*] I trust that *you* have no objection, sir . . .
ENRIQUE: Of course not. I was certain it was her.
I didn't dare believe it. Dear Agnès!
Come here and let me hold you. Happiness
Could scarcely reach a greater pitch than this.
Past sorrows only heighten present bliss!
[*Enrique embraces Agnès.*]

CHRYSALDE: Here's not the place, though, for displays like these.
We'll clear up all remaining mysteries
Indoors and, when *his* wrongs have been redressed,
Praise Heaven, which settles all things for the best.
[*Curtain*]

RESONANCE

Maria de Zayas y Sotomayor: from *The Enchantments of Love: Amorous and Exemplary Novels*[1]

PRONUNCIATIONS:

Don Fadrique: don fa-DREE-kay
Scarron: skahr-ROHNH
Don Vicente: dohn vee-SEN-tay
Doña Violante: doh-nya vee-oh-LAHN-tay
Maria de Zayas y Sotomayor: mah-REE-ah day ZAI-yahss ee soh-toh-mai-YOHRH

from *Enchantments of Love: Amorous and Exemplary Novels*[1]

[*A young and dashing nobleman of Granada, Don Fadrique, is disappointed in love after witnessing his fiancée, Serafina, give birth to another man's child, the baby girl Doña Garcia. Since then, Don Fadrique has spent sixteen years traveling through Spain and Italy, encountering so many examples of female infidelity that he concludes: "I intend to avoid that kind of thing if I can, either by not marrying or by finding a woman so simple and innocent that she'll know nothing of love and scorn, a woman who doesn't know the meaning of cleverness or deception."*]

From Madrid don Fadrique set out for Granada, where he was received like a favorite son of the city. He went to his aunt's house and she welcomed him with a

1. Like Aphra Behn in seventeenth-century England, Maria de Zayas published acclaimed poetry, plays, and novellas in a great literary era when it was extraordinary for a woman to publish at all. Like Behn, too, her life is much more a matter of speculation than documentation. All that is really known is that she lived and wrote in Madrid during the first half of the seventeenth century—the "Golden Age" of Spanish literature—and became the first secular woman in Spain to achieve literary fame. Her famous contemporary, Lope de Vega, praised "her rare and unique genius." Her two novella collections were best-sellers rivaled only by those of Cervantes. "Forewarned but not Forearmed" is told by a male character in Zayas's first collection, *Enchantments of Love: Amorous and Exemplary Novels* (1637). A man who fears a clever woman might cuckold him marries an ignoramus, but the joke is on him. This and other Zayas novellas were translated into French without attribution (a common practice of the time), and Molière adapted Scarron's translation of it for *The School for Wives* (see page 1817).

1. Translated by H. Patsy Boyer.

thousand kind words. He learned everything that had happened during his absence: Serafina had become a nun, was leading a penitent life, and everyone considered her a saint; don Vicente, feeling guilty for having abandoned her after she'd entrusted her honor to him, had died of remorse at seeing her a nun. Don Vicente had tried to take her out of the convent to marry her, but Serafina was determined never to marry. Five days after his fruitless attempt to marry Serafina had failed and helped along by a sudden fever, he paid for his ingratitude with his life. Don Fadrique learned that doña Gracia, the little baby he'd left in his aunt's custody and who was now sixteen, had lived in the convent since she was four.

The very next day he accompanied his aunt to visit doña Gracia. In her beauty, in her innocence and simplicity, he saw the image of an angel. She looked like a lovely statue, but a statue without a soul, which was surprising, given that she'd been brought up by nuns and they're not stupid. As don Fadrique talked with her, he found in her conversation and ignorance precisely the woman he was looking for. He felt very attracted to the beautiful Gracia and his love was increased by the fact that she looked just like her mother, Serafina.

Don Fadrique told his aunt the whole story. When she learned that Gracia wasn't his daughter as she'd thought all along, she approved of his choice for a wife. Gracia accepted this good fortune placidly, like one who knows neither pleasure or displeasure, good or evil. She was naturally stupid, the only flaw in her beauty, although it was precisely the flaw her husband required.

Don Fadrique arranged the wedding, bought finery and jewels for his bride, and set up the house he'd inherited from his parents to be their home. He wanted his wife to live in her own house and not with his aunt, for he didn't want her primitive intelligence to develop. Given his obsessive belief that intelligence leads women to fall into a thousand errors, he hired all her maids with great care, selecting the least cunning and the most ignorant. I may have stated otherwise at the beginning of this story, but now I realize that he wasn't a wise man. I can't understand how a discreet man can desire his opposite. But perhaps his fears about his honor explain his error; perhaps, in order to protect his honor, he felt compelled to deny his pleasure.

The day of the wedding arrived and Gracia left the convent. Her beauty amazed all eyes, her innocence all sense. The wedding was celebrated with a banquet and party attended by all the principal citizens of Granada, as befitted the groom's nobility. The day passed by more quickly than the bride would've liked because she didn't ever want to take off all her finery and jewels. At last don Fadrique bade farewell to the guests, and the members of his family left him alone with Gracia. Determined to test his wife's ignorance, he took her into the bedroom and sat down on the bed. She had on her small clothes, as the saying goes, wearing only her bodice and pettiskirt and divested of her jewels. Fadrique asked Gracia to listen carefully to what he had to say, which was this or something equally foolish:

"My lady, you are now my wife, for which I give thanks to heaven! So long as we live, you must do what I'm about to tell you, and you must always perform this duty faithfully to keep from displeasing me and offending against God."

Gracia humbly replied that she would gladly do as he said.

"Do you know," don Fadrique asked, "what married life is?"

"No, my lord, I have no idea," Gracia said. "But you explain it to me and I'll learn it like the Hail Mary."

Don Fadrique was delighted with her simplicity. He showed her some golden armor and then put it on over her bodice: the breastplate and the backpiece, the gorget and the armplates, without omitting the gauntlets. He gave her a lance and told her that married life meant that, while he slept, she was to keep watch over him, pacing back and forth around the room.

Dressed in her golden armor, Gracia was a sight to see, so fetching and lovely was she! Whatever she didn't possess in the way of intelligence she made up for in her striking appearance; with the helmet pressed down over her curly locks and the sword in its sheath, she was the very image of Pallas Athena.[2]

After the lovely lady was fully armed as I've described, don Fadrique commanded her to keep watch while he slept. Happily he went to bed and slept peacefully until five o'clock. He got up and, after he dressed, he took Gracia gently in his arms and very tenderly undressed her and put her to bed, telling her to rest and sleep. He ordered the servants not to wake her until eleven. He went off to hear mass and tend his business affairs, which were many, since he'd bought himself a position on the city council. More than a week went by with this routine, and don Fadrique never led Gracia to think married life might be any different. She was so innocent that she believed this was what all married women did.

Then it happened that some problems arose with city affairs and the council ordered don Fadrique to depart by the next stage to go speak with the king. Because of the urgency of the case and because they knew he had many friends at court, having spent so much time in Madrid, they didn't observe the usual courtesy toward newlyweds in this instance. The suddenness of this development left him time only to rush home, pack for the journey, and tell his new wife to be sure to keep up her married duties while he was gone just as she'd done before, for it was a great sin to breach them in any way. Gracia promised to do her duty regularly and devoutly, so don Fadrique departed quite happily. But, of course, one intends to go to court for a short time and ends up staying for a long time. That's what happened with don Fadrique. His stay lasted not days but months; his case dragged on for over six months. Gracia faithfully performed her marital duty.

One day a gentleman from Cordoba came to Granada to file a lawsuit before the chancellery. He was in no way stupid or unattractive. When he was idle, he would stroll through the streets of the city. One day, he saw doña Gracia out on her balcony where she spent her afternoons embroidering. The sight of her captivated him. He was stricken by the vision of her beauty and, suffice it to say, he began to frequent her street. The lady, being ignorant of all these things and knowing nothing about the laws of love and courtship, neither accepted nor rejected his attentions. Her lack of response saddened the gentleman from Cordoba.

One of doña Gracia's neighbors was observing this course of events, and she realized that the gentleman had fallen in love with the young bride. One day she called out to him and, discovering the truth of her supposition, promised to intercede with doña Gracia for him. There's always some abyss for virtue to fall into. The neighbor went to see doña Gracia. Extravagantly she praised the young bride's beauty, which marked the first step leading to doña Gracia's downfall. Then the neighbor told her how the gentleman who spent so much time in her street loved her greatly and desired to serve her.

"I truly appreciate that," the lady replied. "But I already have a lot of servants and, until one of them leaves, I shan't be able to satisfy his wish although, if he likes, I can write my husband to see if he might hire him just to please me."

2. The Greek goddess of wisdom. A famous statue by Phidias, erected in the Parthenon in Athens in the 5th century B.C.E., represented her clad in golden armor.

"Oh, no, my lady," the crafty matchmaker exclaimed, beginning to realize how ignorant the young bride was. "This gentleman is very rich and noble; he has great estates. He doesn't want you to hire him as a servant, he wants to serve you with all his wealth, to send you some gift or jewel, if you'd like."

"Oh, my friend," doña Gracia replied. "I already have so much jewelry I don't even know where to put it all."

"Well, if that's the way it is," the matchmaker said, "and you don't want him to send you anything, then at least give him permission to visit you, which he greatly desires."

"Of course! Let him come!" the foolish lady said. "What prevents him from coming to visit me?"

"My lady," the neighbor answered, "don't you understand that the servants, if they see him come openly during the daytime, might think ill of it?"

"Well, then, here," doña Gracia said, "this key opens the back door entering from the garden and, indeed, I think it opens every door in the house because it's a master key. Give it to him and tell him to come tonight and climb the circular staircase that comes right up to the room where I sleep."

The woman could hardly believe such ignorance, but she didn't want to probe further. She took the key and went to get the reward for her work, which was a heavy gold chain. That night don Alvaro—this was his name—came through the garden as he'd been instructed, climbed the stairs, and was about to enter the room, when he saw doña Gracia in her elaborate armor holding aloft her lance. She looked like an Amazon. The light was dim and, since don Alvaro couldn't begin to imagine, let alone believe, the truth of what he was seeing, he thought he'd been betrayed. As quickly as he could, he turned tail and fled and the next minute he was in the street.

The following morning he described this scene to the matchmaker and immediately she went to see doña Gracia. The moment she entered, doña Gracia inquired about the gentleman. He must have been terribly ill since he hadn't come as he'd been instructed.

"Oh, my lady," she said, "of course he came. But he said he found a man in armor, carrying a lance and marching around the room."

"Good heavens!" doña Gracia answered, laughing merrily, "doesn't he know I was just doing my married duty? That gentleman must not be married if he thought I was a man! Tell him it's me and not to be afraid."

The matchmaker took this explanation to don Alvaro. That night he went again to visit his lady and, when he found her in her armor, he asked her to explain. Laughing, she said:

"Well, how else should I lead a married life if not like this?"

"What do you mean, married life, my lady?" don Alvaro asked. "You've been deceived; this isn't what married life is."

"Well, my lord," said doña Gracia, "this is how my husband taught me, and he says it's a terrible sin to violate it. But if you know an easier way, in truth I'd love to know what it is and learn how to do it, for this life I lead is very tiresome."

When the cavalier youth heard this naive request, he himself undressed her and took her to bed and enjoyed everything that her foolish husband had postponed in his desire to test his wife's ignorance. All the time don Fadrique was at court, don Alvaro and doña Gracia lived a true married life. At last don Fadrique finished his business and wrote that he was coming home. Don Alvaro finished up his business and returned to Cordoba.

Don Fadrique arrived home and was greeted by his wife with much pleasure for, just as she had no intelligence, she had no sense either. They dined together and, because don Fadrique was tired from his journey, he went right to bed. He assumed that doña Gracia would put on her armor as he'd commanded. When he saw her come out naked and get into bed with him, he was astounded at this novelty, and asked:

"Well, my lady, how is it that you don't perform your married duty as I taught you?"

"My, my, sir," she said, "what do you mean married duty and all that nonsense! I learned a much better way with my other husband who took me to bed with him and caressed me more than you do."

"You mean," don Fadrique asked, "you've had another husband?"

"Yes, my lord," doña Gracia answered. "After you left, another handsome, charming husband came along and told me he'd show me a different married life, better than yours."

She told him everything that had happened with the gentleman from Cordoba. But she couldn't understand what had become of him. After she'd received don Fadrique's letter with news of his return, she hadn't seen him again. In despair, the foolish don Fadrique asked her what the man's name was and where he was from. But doña Gracia answered that she didn't know, she never called him anything but husband.

Don Fadrique understood that in trying to prevent his dishonor, he had purposely married a fool who had not only offended against his honor but who even told him all about it. He realized the error in his thinking and recalled the duchess's words: discreet women know how to keep the laws of honor and, if ever they break them, they know how to keep their error secret.

For the rest of his life, don Fadrique praised discreet women who are virtuous, saying that they are priceless beyond all thought and, if they're not virtuous, at least they know how to behave prudently and modestly.

Realizing that nothing could be done about what had happened because it was his fault, don Fadrique covered up his misfortune. If discreet women sometimes fail in the test, what could he expect of a foolish woman? Trying not to let his wife out of his sight so she wouldn't offend against him again, he lived for several more years. When he died, since they had no children, he left all his wealth to doña Gracia, with the provision that she become a nun in the same convent as Serafina. He wrote a letter to Serafina explaining that this was her long-lost daughter. He also wrote his cousin don Juan in Madrid telling this story just as it is set down here.

In the end, no matter how don Fadrique tried to prevent the catastrophe he'd been forewarned about, in spite of all the lands he'd visited and all the adventures he'd had, he fell into the very situation he feared, and it was a foolish woman who ruined his honor.

Doña Gracia became a nun in the same convent with her mother, and the two were happy to know each other. Because doña Gracia was foolish, she readily found happiness and spent the huge fortune at her disposal in building a grand convent where she spent her days pleasantly.

I now take pleasure in ending this enchantment by warning all the ignorant people who condemn discretion in women: there can be no virtue where intelligence is lacking. Furthermore, if a woman is going to be bad, it doesn't matter whether she's foolish or not, but a good woman, if she's discreet, will know how to take care of herself. Be warned, you who would put a woman to the test, of the risk you take.

Chikamatsu Mon'zaemon

1653–1725

Japanese puppet theater emerged in the early seventeenth century and flourished thereafter as popular entertainment. In contrast to noh—a medieval dramatic genre that continued to be staged but whose audience was largely samurai or merchant elite—puppet theater was aimed at a wide audience. Puppet theater consists of three elements that are closely coordinated: the puppets, the music (played by a banjo-like *shamisen*), and the chanting (*jōruri*) performed by a chanter who sits to the side of the stage and who speaks or sings all the roles of the puppets, including the third-person narration. Puppet theater began with one-man puppets, but by the eighteenth century it had evolved into a complex art with three-man puppets whose handlers are visible to the audience: the head puppeteer controls the head and right hand, the second manipulates the left hand, and the third is in charge of the feet. Of the three elements—puppets, music, and chanting—the chanting is the most important, so much so that the chanter is usually the star performer and the chanting is sometimes performed alone, without the puppets.

Chikamatsu Mon'zaemon was the greatest of the puppet theater playwrights. He came from a relatively well-off samurai (warrior) family and served in the households of royalty and aristocrats in Kyoto in his youth, before going into the theater and moving to Osaka, the city of merchants and urban commoners. One consequence is that Chikamatsu describes the life of townspeople but is deeply interested in samurai values and society. Chikamatsu's earliest play on contemporary social life was the one-act *Love Suicides at Sonezaki* (1703), which depicts an actual incident of the time and which became a model for subsequent contemporary life plays.

Love Suicides at Amijima, first performed at the Takemoto Theater in Osaka in 1721, is widely considered to be Chikamatsu Mon'zaemon's best puppet play concerning contemporary life. The source for the play is unclear, but the incident inspired a number of later plays. In the play, Kamiya (literally, "paper merchant") Jihei, an Osaka paper merchant with a wife and children, falls in love with Koharu, a prostitute under contract to the Kinokuniya House in Sonezaki (a licensed quarter in Osaka). Forced into tragic circumstances, the two of them commit suicide at a temple in Amijima, in Osaka.

About half of Chikamatsu's twenty-four contemporary-life plays focus on an incident concerning an Osaka urban commoner. Almost all the male protagonists are young and of low social station, either an adopted son or a shop clerk, and most of them become involved with a low-level prostitute. In that the lovers have already decided to commit double suicide at the beginning, *The Love Suicides at Amijima* differs from such double-suicide plays as *The Love Suicides at Sonezaki,* which show the tragic chain of events that lead to death. Instead, the focus in *Amijima* is on the desperate efforts of those who attempt to prevent the suicide of the two lovers. Chikamatsu places the tragedy in a tight web of urban commoner social relationships and obligations, particularly the hierarchical relations between master and apprentice, parent and child, and husband and wife, as well as in the context of the new monetary economy and commercial life of Osaka. Jihei and Koharu bear a great social burden, particularly as Jihei is a pillar of the family business, and the tragic result pulls down not only the two lovers but others in the family. Here Chikamatsu develops one of the central themes of his contemporary-life plays: the conflict between those who try to preserve the family *and* the individual, driven by his or her own desires, who works against that social order.

Chikamatsu focuses on *giri*, or sense of social obligation, including that between women, between Koharu and Jihei's wife Osan, whose conflicted relationship develops into a tense mutual understanding. Not only does Chikamatsu create complex conflicts between individual desire and obligation, he focuses on conflicts between competing obligations that result in extreme pathos. Desire and obligation are also reflected in the settings: the first act occurs in the pleasure quarters, a world of desire, passion, and the individual; and the second act takes place in the paper shop, a world of responsibility, reason, and the family, with Jihei caught between the two. The third act focuses on a journey in which the lovers leave behind both places and travel toward death.

In the poetic journey in the third act there is a double movement: a downward movement, the Buddhist cycle of *samsara*, of birth and death, of suffering, which leads to hell; and an upward movement, leading from hell to possible salvation. The fundamental assumption behind the two movements, which is symbolically mapped out, is that awakening is the result of some profound crisis or suffering. Accordingly, the lovers initially pass such places as Tenma Bridge and the River of the Three Fords—which represent places in hell—before they cross over Kyō (Sutra) Bridge and Onari (Becoming a Buddha) Bridge. The final scene has the added function of praying for the spirits of the dead—that is, the play implicitly recalls to this world the spirits or ghosts of the two lovers, who have recently died a gruesome death, and now sends them off again to the world of the dead.

PRONUNCIATIONS:

Chikamatsu Mon'zaemon: chi-ka-mah-tsu mon-ZAH-e-mon
Gozaemon: go-zah-e-mon
Jihei: ji-hay
Koharu: ko-hah-reu
Osan: o-sahn
Tahei: tah-hay

The Love Suicides at Amijima[1]

Characters

JIHEI, *aged twenty-eight, a paper merchant*
MAGOEMON, *his brother, a flour merchant*
GOZAEMON, *Jihei's father-in-law*
TAHEI, *a rival for Koharu*
DENBEI, *proprietor of the Yamato House*
SANGORŌ, *Jihei's servant*
KANTARŌ, *aged six, Jihei's son*
KOHARU, *aged nineteen, a courtesan belonging to the Kinokuni House in Sonezaki, a new licensed quarter in the north part of Ōsaka*
OSAN, *Jihei's wife*
OSAN'S MOTHER (*who is also Jihei's aunt*), *aged fifty-six*
OSUE, *aged four, Jihei's daughter*

ACT 1

[*In an opening scene, which is rarely performed and is omitted here, Koharu makes her way to the Kawashō Teahouse in Sonezaki licensed quarter to meet Tahei, a samurai customer. We learn that Koharu is in love with Jihei and that Tahei, a man*

1. Translated by Donald Keene.

that she dislikes immensely, is trying to buy out her contract. Koharu sees Tahei in the street and flees.]

The Kawashō, a Teahouse in Sonezaki.

CHANTER: Koharu slips away, under cover of the crowd, and hurries into the Kawashō Teahouse.

[PROPRIETRESS]: Well, well, I hadn't expected you so soon—It's been ages since I've even heard your name mentioned. What a rare visitor you are, Koharu! And what a long time it's been!

CHANTER: The proprietress greets Koharu cheerfully.

[KOHARU]: Oh—you can be heard as far as the gate. Please don't call me Koharu in such a loud voice. That horrible Ri Tōten[2] is out there. I beg you, keep your voice down.

CHANTER: Were her words overheard? In bursts a party of three men.

[TAHEI]: I must thank you first of all, dear Koharu, for bestowing a new name on me, Ri Tōten. I never was called *that* before. Well, friends, this is the Koharu I've confided to you about—the good-hearted, good-natured, good-in-bed Koharu. Step up and meet the whore who's started all the rivalry! Will I soon be the lucky man and get Koharu for my wife? Or will Kamiya Jihei ransom her?

CHANTER: He swaggers up.

[KOHARU]: I don't want to hear another word. If you think it's such an achievement to start unfounded rumors about someone you don't even know, go ahead; say what you please. But I don't want to hear.

CHANTER: She steps away suddenly, but he sidles up again.

[TAHEI]: You may not want to hear me, but the clink of my gold coins will make you listen! What a lucky girl you are! Just think—of all the many men in Tenma and the rest of Ōsaka, you chose Jihei the paper dealer, the father of two children, with his cousin for his wife and his uncle for his father-in-law! A man whose business is so tight he's at his wits' end every sixty days merely to pay the wholesalers' bills! Do you think he'll be able to fork over nearly ten *kanme* to ransom you? That reminds me of the mantis who picked a fight with an oncoming vehicle![3] But look at me—I don't have a wife, a father-in-law, a father, or even an uncle, for that matter. Tahei the Lone Wolf—that's the name I'm known by. I admit that I'm no match for Jihei when it comes to bragging about myself in the Quarter, but when it comes to money, I'm an easy winner. If I pushed with all the strength of my money, who knows what I might conquer?—How about it, men?—Your customer tonight, I'm sure, is none other than Jihei, but I'm taking over. The Lone Wolf's taking over. Hostess! Bring on the saké! On with the saké!

[PROPRIETRESS]: What are you saying? Her customer tonight is a samurai, and he'll be here any moment. Please amuse yourself elsewhere.

CHANTER: But Tahei's look is playful.

[TAHEI]: A customer's a customer, whether he's a samurai or a townsman. The only difference is that one wears swords and the other doesn't. But even if this samurai wears his swords, he won't have five or six—there'll only be two, the broadsword and dirk. I'll take care of the samurai and borrow Koharu afterward.

2. The villain of the play *Battles of Coxinga.*

3. A simile, derived from ancient Chinese texts, for someone who doesn't know his own limitations.

[*To Koharu.*] You may try to avoid me all you please, but some special connection from a former life must have brought us together. I owe everything to that ballad-singing priest—what a wonderful thing the power of prayer is! I think I'll recite a prayer of my own. Here, this ashtray will be my bell, and my pipe the hammer. This is fun.

Chan Chan Cha Chan Chan.
Ei Ei Ei Ei Ei.
Jihei the paper dealer—
Too much love for Koharu
Has made him a foolscap,
He wastepapers sheets of gold
Till his fortune's shredded to confetti
And Jihei himself is like scrap paper
You can't even blow your nose on!
Hail, Hail Amida Buddha!
Namaida Namaida Namaida.

CHANTER: As he prances wildly, roaring his song, a man appears at the gate, so anxious not to be recognized that he wears, even at night, a wicker hat.[4]

[TAHEI]: Well, Toilet Paper's showed up! That's quite a disguise! Why don't you come in, Toilet Paper? If my prayer's frightened you, say a Hail Amida![5] Here, I'll take off your hat!

CHANTER: He drags the man in and examines him: it is the genuine article, a two-sworded samurai, somber in dress and expression, who glares at Tahei through his woven hat, his eyeballs round as gongs. Tahei, unable to utter either a Hail or an Amida, gasps "Haaa!" in dismay, but his face is unflinching.

[TAHEI]: Koharu, I'm a townsman. I've never worn a sword, but I've lots of New Silver[6] at my place, and I think that the glint could twist a mere couple of swords out of joint. Imagine that wretch from the toilet paper shop, with a capital as thin as tissue, trying to compete with the Lone Wolf! That's the height of impertinence! I'll wander down now from Sakura Bridge to Middle Street, and if I meet that Wastepaper along the way, I'll trample him under foot. Come on, men.

CHANTER: Their gestures, at least, have a cavalier assurance as they swagger off, taking up the whole street. The samurai customer patiently endures the fool, indifferent to his remarks because of the surroundings, but every word of gossip about Jihei, whether for good or ill, affects Koharu. She is so depressed that she stands there blankly, unable even to greet her guest. Sugi, the maid from the Kinokuni House, runs up from home, looking annoyed.

[SUGI]: When I left you here a while ago, Miss Koharu, your guest hadn't appeared yet, and they gave me a terrible scolding when I got back for not having checked on him. I'm very sorry, sir, but please excuse me a minute.

3. A simile, derived from ancient Chinese texts, for someone who doesn't know his own limitations.

4. Customers visiting the licensed quarter by day wear these deep wicker hats (which virtually conceal the face) in order to preserve the secrecy of their visits. But this customer wears a hat even at night.

5. A play on words centering on the syllables *ami*, part of the name Amida Buddha, and on *amigasa*, meaning "woven hat."

6. Good-quality coinage of about 1720.

CHANTER: She lifts the woven hat and examines the face.

[SUGI]: Oh—it's not him! There's nothing to worry about, Koharu. Ask your guest to keep you for the whole night, and show him how sweet you can be. Give him a barrelful of nectar![7] Good-bye, madam, I'll see you later, honey.

CHANTER: She takes her leave with a cloying stream of puns. The extremely hard baked[8] samurai is furious.

[SAMURAI]: What's the meaning of this? You'd think from the way she appraised my face that I was a tea canister or a porcelain cup! I didn't come here to be trifled with. It's difficult enough for me to leave the residence even by day, and in order to spend the night away I had to ask the senior officer's permission and sign the register. You can see how complicated the regulations make things. But I'm in love, miss, just from hearing about you, and I wanted very badly to spend a night with you. I came here a while ago without an escort and made the arrangements with the teahouse. I had been looking forward to your kind reception, a memory to last me a lifetime, but you haven't so much as smiled at me or said a word of greeting. You keep your head down as if you were counting money in your lap. Aren't you afraid of getting a stiff neck? Madam—I've never heard the like. Here I come to a teahouse, and I must play the part of night nurse in a maternity room!

[PROPRIETRESS]: You're quite right, sir. Your surprise is entirely justified, considering that you don't know the reasons. This girl is deeply in love with a customer named Kamiji. It's been Kamiji today and Kamiji tomorrow, with nobody else allowed a chance at her. Her other customers have scattered in every direction, like leaves in a storm. When two people get so carried away with each other, it often leads to trouble, for both the customer and the girl. In the first place, it interferes with business, and the owner, whoever he may be, must prevent it. That's why all her guests are examined. Koharu is naturally depressed—it's only to be expected. You are annoyed, which is equally to be expected. But speaking as the proprietress here, it seems to me that the essential thing is for you to meet each other halfway and cheer up. Come, have a drink.—Act a little more lively, Koharu.

CHANTER: Koharu, without answering, lifts her tear-stained face.

[KOHARU]: Tell me, samurai, they say that if you're going to kill yourself anyway, people who die during the Ten Nights[9] are sure to become Buddhas. Is that really true?

[SAMURAI]: How should I know? Ask the priest at your family temple.

[KOHARU]: Yes, that's right. But there's something I'd like to ask a samurai. If you're committing suicide, it'd be a lot more painful, wouldn't it, to cut your throat rather than hang yourself?

[SAMURAI]: I've never tried cutting my throat to see whether or not it hurt. Please ask more sensible questions.—What an unpleasant girl!

CHANTER: Samurai though he is, he looks nonplussed.

[PROPRIETRESS]: Koharu, that's a shocking way to treat a guest the first time you meet him. I'll go and get my husband. We'll have some saké together. That ought to liven things up a bit.

7. The imagery used by the maid has been altered from puns on saltiness (soy sauce, green vegetables, and so forth) to puns on sweetness.

8. A technical term of pottery making, meaning "hard-fired."

9. A period in the Tenth Month when special Buddhist services were conducted in temples of the Pure Land (Jōdo) sect. It was believed that persons who died during this period immediately became Buddhas.

CHANTER: The gate she leaves is lighted by the evening moon low in the sky; the clouds and the passers in the street have thinned.

For long years there has lived in Tenma, the seat of the mighty god,[1] though not a god himself, Kamiji,[2] a name often bruited by the gongs of worldly gossip, so deeply, hopelessly, is he tied to Koharu by the ropes[3] of an ill-starred love. Now is the tenth moon, the month when no gods will unite them;[4] they are thwarted in their love, unable to meet. They swore in the last letters they exchanged that if only they could meet, that day would be their last. Night after night Jihei, ready for death, trudges to the Quarter, distracted, as though his soul had left a body consumed by the fires of love.

At a roadside eating stand he hears people gossiping about Koharu. "She's at Kawashō with a samurai customer," someone says, and immediately Jihei decides, "It will be tonight!"

He peers through the latticework window and sees a guest in the inside room, his face obscured by a hood. Only the moving chin is visible, and Jihei cannot hear what is said.

[JIHEI]: Poor Koharu! How thin her face is! She keeps it turned away from the lamp. In her heart she's thinking only of me. I'll signal her that I'm here, and we'll run off together. Then which will it be—Umeda or Kitano?[5] Oh—I want to tell her I'm here. I want to call her.

CHANTER: He beckons with his heart, his spirit flies to her; but his body, like a cicada's cast-off shell, clings to the latticework. He weeps with impatience. The guest in the inside room gives a great yawn.

[SAMURAI]: What a bore, playing nursemaid to a prostitute with worries on her mind!—The street seems quiet now. Let's go to the end room. We can at least distract ourselves by looking at the lanterns. Come with me.

CHANTER: They go together to the outer room. Jihei, alarmed, squeezes into the patch of shadow under the lattice window. Inside they do not realize that anyone is eavesdropping.

[SAMURAI]: I've been noticing your behavior and the little things you've said this evening. It's plain to me that you intend a love suicide with Kamiji, or whatever his name is—the man the hostess mentioned. I'm sure I'm right. I realize that no amount of advice or reasoning is likely to penetrate the ears of somebody bewitched by the god of death, but I must say that you're exceedingly foolish. The boy's family won't blame him for his recklessness, but they will blame and hate you. You'll be shamed by the public exposure of your body. Your parents may be dead, for all I know, but if they're alive, you'll be punished in hell as a wicked daughter. Do you think you'll become a buddha? You and your lover won't even be able to fall smoothly into hell together! What a pity—and what a tragedy! This is only our first meeting, but as a samurai, I can't let you die without trying to save you. No doubt money's the problem. I'd like to help, if five or ten *ryō* would be of service. I swear by the god Hachiman and by my good

1. Tenma, one of the principal districts of Ōsaka, was the site of the Tenjin Shrine, for the worship of the deified Sugawara no Michizane (845–903).

2. The word *kami,* for "paper," sounds like *kami,* "god." We have thus "Kami who is not a *kami*"—the paper dealer who isn't a god.

3. The sacred ropes at a Shintō shrine.

4. The Tenth Month was a time when the gods were believed to gather at Izumo; they thus were absent from the rest of Japan.

5. Both places had well-known cemeteries.

fortune as a samurai that I will never reveal to anyone what you tell me. Open your heart without fear.

CHANTER: He whispers these words. She joins her hands and bows.

[KOHARU]: I'm extremely grateful. Thank you for your kind words and for swearing an oath to me, someone you've never had for a lover or even a friend. I'm so grateful that I'm crying.—Yes, it's as they say, when you've something on your mind it shows on your face. You were right. I have promised Kamiji to die with him. But we've been completely prevented from meeting by my master, and Jihei, for various reasons, can't ransom me at once. My contracts with my former master[6] and my present one still have five years to run. If somebody else claimed me during that time, it would be a blow to me, of course, but a worse disgrace to Jihei's honor. He suggested that it would be better if we killed ourselves, and I agreed. I was caught by obligations from which I could not withdraw, and I promised him before I knew what I was doing. I said, "We'll watch for a chance, and I'll slip out when you give the signal." "Yes," he said, "slip out somehow." Ever since then I've been leading a life of uncertainty, never knowing from one day to the next when my last hour will come.

I have a mother living in a back alley south of here. She has no one but me to depend on, and she does piecework to eke out a living. I keep thinking that after I'm dead she'll become a beggar or an outcast, and maybe she'll die of starvation. That's the only sad part about dying. I have just this one life. I'm ashamed that you may think me a coldhearted woman, but I must endure the shame. The most important thing is that I don't want to die. I beg you, please help me stay alive.

CHANTER: As she speaks, the samurai nods thoughtfully. Jihei, crouching outside, hears her words with astonishment; they are so unexpected to his manly heart that he feels like a monkey who has tumbled from a tree. He is frantic with agitation.

[JIHEI, *to himself*]: Then was everything a lie? Ahhh—I'm furious! For two whole years I've been bewitched by that rotten she-fox! Shall I break in and kill her with one blow of my sword? Or shall I satisfy my anger by shaming her to her face?

CHANTER: He gnashes his teeth and weeps in chagrin. Inside the house Koharu speaks through her tears.

[KOHARU]: It's a curious thing to ask, but would you please show the kindness of a samurai and become my customer for the rest of this year and into next spring? Whenever Jihei comes, intent on death, please step in and force him to postpone his plan. In this way our relations can be broken quite naturally. He won't have to kill himself, and my life will also be saved.—What evil connection from a former existence made us promise to die? How I regret it now!

CHANTER: She weeps, leaning on the samurai's knee.

[SAMURAI]: Very well, I'll do as you ask. I think I can help you.—But I feel a breeze. Somebody may be watching.

CHANTER: He slams shut the latticework *shōji*. Jihei, listening outside, is in a frenzy.

[JIHEI]: Exactly what you'd expect from a whore, a cheap whore! I misjudged her foul nature. She robbed the soul from my body, the thieving harlot! Shall I slash her or run her through? What am I to do?

CHANTER: The shadows of two profiles fall on the *shōji*.

6. The master at the bathhouse where Koharu formerly worked.

[JIHEI]: I'd like to give her a taste of my fist and trample her.—What are they chattering about? See how they nod to each other! Now she's bowing to him, whispering and sniveling. I've tried to control myself—I've pressed my chest, I've stroked it—but I can't stand any more. This is too much to endure!

CHANTER: His heart pounds wildly as he unsheathes his dirk, a Magoroku of Seki. "Koharu's side must be here," he judges, and stabs through an opening in the latticework. But Koharu is too far away for his thrust, and although she cries out in terror, she remains unharmed. Her guest instantly leaps at Jihei, grabs his hands, and jerks them through the latticework. With his sword knot he quickly and securely fastens Jihei's hands to the window upright.

[SAMURAI]: Don't scream, Koharu. Don't look at him.

CHANTER: At this moment the proprietor and his wife return. They exclaim in alarm.

[SAMURAI]: This needn't concern you. Some ruffian ran his sword through the *shōji,* and I've tied his arms to the latticework. I have my own way of dealing with him. Don't untie the cord. If you attract a crowd, the place is sure to be thrown in an uproar. Let's all go inside. Come with me, Koharu. We'll go to bed.

CHANTER: Koharu answers yes, but she recognizes the handle of the dirk, and the memory—if not the blade—transfixes her breast.

[KOHARU]: There're always people doing crazy things in the Quarter when they've had too much to drink. Why don't you let him go without making any trouble? I think that's best, don't you?

[SAMURAI]: Out of the question. Do as I say—inside, all of you. Koharu, come along.

CHANTER: Jihei can still see their shadows even after they enter the inner room, but he is bound to the spot, his hands held in fetters that grip him more tightly as he struggles, his body beset by suffering as he tastes a living shame worse than a dog's.[7] More determined than ever to die, he sheds tears of blood, a pitiful sight.

Tahei the Lone Wolf returns from his carousing.

[TAHEI]: That's Jihei standing by Kawashō's window. I'll give him a thrashing.

CHANTER: He catches Jihei by the collar and starts to lift him over his back.

[JIHEI]: Owww!

[TAHEI]: Owww? What kind of weakling are you? Oh, I see—you're tied here. You must've been pulling off a robbery. You dirty pickpocket! You rotten pickpocket!

CHANTER: He beats Jihei mercilessly.

[TAHEI]: You burglar! You convict!

CHANTER: He kicks him wildly.

[TAHEI]: Kamiya Jihei's been caught burgling, and they've tied him up!

CHANTER: Passersby and people of the neighborhood, attracted by his shouts, quickly gather. The samurai rushes from the house.

[SAMURAI]: Who's calling him a burglar? You? Tell me what Jihei's stolen! Out with it!

CHANTER: He seizes Tahei and forces him into the dirt. Tahei rises to his feet only for the samurai to kick him down again and again. He grabs Tahei.

[SAMURAI]: Jihei! Kick him to your heart's content!

CHANTER: He pushes Tahei under Jihei's feet. Bound though he is, Jihei stamps furiously on Tahei's face. Tahei, thoroughly kicked and covered with muck, gets to his feet and glares around him.

7. A proverb of Buddhist origin: "Suffering follows one like a dog."

[TAHEI, *to bystander*]: How could you fools just stand there and let him step on me? I know every one of your faces, and I intend to pay you back. Remember that!

CHANTER: He makes his escape, still determined to have the last word. The spectators burst out laughing.

[VOICES]: Listen to him brag, even after he's been beaten up! Let's throw him from the bridge and give him a drink of water! Don't let him get away!

CHANTER: They chase after him. When the crowd has dispersed, the samurai goes to Jihei and unfastens the knots. He shows his face with his hood removed.

[JIHEI]: Magoemon! My brother! How shameful!

CHANTER: He sinks to the ground and weeps, prostrating himself in the dirt.

[KOHARU]: Are you his brother, sir?

CHANTER: Koharu runs to them. Jihei, catching her by the front of the kimono, forces her to the ground.

[JIHEI]: Beast! She-fox! I'd sooner kick you than Tahei!

CHANTER: He raises his foot, but Magoemon calls out.

[MAGOEMON]: That's the kind of foolishness that's gotten you into all this trouble. A prostitute's business is to deceive men. Are you just realizing that? I could see to the bottom of her heart the very first time I met her, but you're so scatter-brained that in more than two years of sleeping with this woman you never figured out what she was thinking. Instead of kicking Koharu, why don't you use your feet on your own misguided disposition?—It's deplorable. You may be my younger brother, but you're almost thirty, and you've got a six-year-old boy and a four-year-old girl, Kantarō and Osue. You run a shop with a thirty-six-foot frontage,[8] but you don't seem to realize that your whole fortune's collapsing. You shouldn't have to be lectured to by your brother. Your father-in-law is your aunt's husband, and your mother-in-law is your aunt. They've always been like real parents to you. Your wife Osan is my cousin, too. The ties of marriage are multiplied by those of blood. But when the family has a reunion, the only subject of discussion is our mortification over your incessant visits to Sonezaki. I feel sorry for our poor aunt. You know what a stiff-necked gentleman of the old school her husband Gozaemon is. He's forever flying into a rage and saying, "We've been tricked by your nephew. He's deserted our daughter. I'll take Osan back and ruin Jihei's reputation throughout Tenma." Our aunt, with all the heartache to bear herself, sometimes sides with him and sometimes with you. She's worried herself sick. What an ingrate not to appreciate how she's defended you in your shame! This one offense is enough to make you the target for Heaven's future punishment!

I realized that your marriage couldn't last much longer at this rate. So I decided, in the hopes of relieving our aunt's worries, that I'd see with my own eyes what kind of woman Koharu was and work out some sort of solution afterward. I consulted the proprietor here, then came myself to investigate the cause of your sickness. I see now how easy it was for you to desert your wife and children. What a faithful prostitute you discovered! I congratulate you!

And here I am, Magoemon the Miller,[9] known far and wide for my paragon of a brother, dressed up like a masquerader at a festival or maybe a lunatic! I put on

8. A large shop.

9. Magoemon is a dealer in flour (for noodles). His shop name Konaya—"the flour merchant"—is used almost as a surname.

swords for the first time in my life and announced myself, like a bit player in a costume piece, as an officer at a residence. I feel like an absolute idiot with these swords, but there's nowhere I can dispose of them now.—It's so infuriating—and ridiculous—that it's given me a pain in the chest.

CHANTER: He gnashes his teeth and grimaces, attempting to hide his tears. Koharu, choking all the while with emotion, can only say:

[KOHARU]: Yes, you're entirely right.

CHANTER: The rest is lost in tears. Jihei pounds the ground with his fist.

[JIHEI]: I was wrong. Forgive me, Magoemon. For three years I've been possessed by that witch. I've neglected my parents, relatives—even my wife and children—and wrecked my fortune, all because I was deceived by Koharu, that sneak thief! I'm utterly mortified. But I'm through with her now, and I'll never set foot here again. Weasel! Vixen! Sneak thief! Here's proof that I've broken with her!

CHANTER: He pulls out the amulet bag that has rested next to his skin.

[JIHEI]: Here are the written oaths we've exchanged, one at the beginning of each month, twenty-nine in all. I am returning them. This means our love and affection are over. Take them.

CHANTER: He flings the notes at her.

[JIHEI]: Magoemon, get my pledges from her. Please make sure you get them all. Then burn them with your own hands. [*To Koharu.*] Give them to my brother.

[KOHARU]: As you wish.

CHANTER: In tears, she surrenders the amulet bag. Magoemon opens it.

[MAGOEMON]: One, two, three, four . . . ten . . . twenty-nine. They're all here. There's also a letter from a woman. What's this?

CHANTER: He starts to unfold it.

[KOHARU]: That's an important letter. I can't let you see it.

CHANTER: She clings to Magoemon's arm, but he pushes her away. He holds the letter to the lamplight and examines the address, "To Miss Koharu from Kamiya Osan." As soon as he reads the words, he casually thrusts the letter into his kimono.

[MAGOEMON]: Koharu. A while ago I swore by my good fortune as a samurai, but now Magoemon the Miller swears by his good fortune as a businessman that he will show this letter to no one, not even his wife. I alone will read it, then burn it with the oaths. You can trust me. I will not break this oath.

[KOHARU]: Thank you. You save my honor.

CHANTER: She bursts into tears again.

[JIHEI *laughs contemptuously*]: Save your honor! You talk like a human being! [*To Magoemon.*] I don't want to see her cursed face another minute. Let's go. No—I can't hold so much resentment and bitterness! I'll kick her one in the face, a memory to treasure for the rest of my life. Excuse me, please.

CHANTER: He strides up to Koharu and stamps on the ground.

[JIHEI]: For three years I've loved you, delighted in you, longed for you, adored you; but today my foot will say my only farewells.

CHANTER: He kicks her sharply on the forehead and bursts into tears. The brothers leave, forlorn figures. Koharu, unhappy woman, raises her voice in lament as she watches them go. Is she faithful or unfaithful? Her true feelings are hidden in the words penned by Jihei's wife, a letter that no one has seen. Jihei goes his separate way without learning the truth.

ACT 2

Scene 1

Scene: The house and shop of Kamiya Jihei. Time: Ten days later.

CHANTER: The busy street that runs straight to Tenjin Bridge,[1] named for the god of Tenma, bringer of good fortune, is known as the Street Before the Kami,[2] and here a paper shop does business under the name Kamiya Jihei. The paper is honestly sold, and the shop is well situated; it is a long-established firm, and customers come thick as raindrops.

Outside, crowds pass in the street, on their way to the Ten Nights service, while inside, the husband dozes in the kotatsu,[3] shielded from drafts by a screen at his pillow. His wife Osan keeps solitary, anxious watch over shop and house.

[OSAN]: The days are so short—it's dinnertime already, but Tama still hasn't returned from her errand to Ichinokawa.[4] I wonder what can be keeping her. That scamp Sangorō isn't back either. The wind is freezing. I'm sure both the children will be cold. He doesn't even realize that it's time for Osue to be nursed. Heaven preserve me from ever becoming such a fool! What an infuriating creature!

CHANTER: She speaks to herself.

[KANTARŌ]: Mama, I've come back all by myself.

CHANTER: Her son, the older child, runs up to the house.

[OSAN]: Kantarō—is that you? What's happened to Osue and Sangorō?

[KANTARŌ]: They're playing by the shrine. Osue wanted her milk, and she was bawling her head off.

[OSAN]: I was sure she would. Oh—your hands and feet are frozen stiff as nails! Go and warm yourself at the kotatsu. Your father's sleeping there.—What am I to do with that idiot?

CHANTER: She runs out impatiently to the shop just as Sangorō shuffles back, alone.

[OSAN]: Come here, you fool! Where have you left Osue?

[SANGORŌ]: You know, I must've lost her somewhere. Maybe somebody's picked her up. Should I go back for her?

[OSAN]: How could you! If any harm has come to my precious child, I'll beat you to death!

CHANTER: But while she is screaming at him, the maid Tama returns with Osue on her back.

[TAMA]: The poor child—I found her in tears at the corner. Sangorō, when you're supposed to look after the child, do it properly.

[OSAN]: You poor dear. You must want your milk.

CHANTER: She joins the others by the kotatsu and nurses the child.

[OSAN]: Tama—give that fool a taste of something that he'll remember![5]

CHANTER: Sangorō shakes his head.

[SANGORŌ]: No, thanks. I gave each of the children two tangerines just a while ago at the shrine, and I tasted five myself.

1. The reference is to Tenma Tenjin, a deified form of Sugawara no Michizane.

2. Again, a play on the words *kami* (god) and *kami* (paper).

3. A source of heat in which a charcoal burner is placed under a low, quilt-covered table.

4. The site of a large vegetable market near the north end of Tenjin Bridge.

5. A pun on the two meanings of *kurawasu:* "to cause to eat" and "to beat."

CHANTER: Fool though he is, bad puns come from him nimbly enough, and the others can only smile despite themselves.

[TAMA]: Oh—I've become so involved with this half-wit that I almost forgot to tell you, ma'am, that Mr. Magoemon and his aunt[6] are on their way here from the west.

[OSAN]: Oh dear! In that case, I'll have to wake Jihei. [*To Jihei*] Please get up. Mother and Magoemon are coming. They'll be upset again if you let them see you, a businessman, sleeping in the afternoon, with the day as short as it is.

[JIHEI]: All right.

CHANTER: He struggles to a sitting position and, with his abacus in one hand, pulls his account book to him with the other.

[JIHEI]: Two into ten goes five, three into nine goes three, three into six goes two, seven times eight is fifty-six.

CHANTER: His fifty-six-year-old aunt enters with Magoemon.

[JIHEI]: Magoemon, aunt. How good of you. Please come in. I was in the midst of some urgent calculations. Four nines makes thirty-six *monme.* Three sixes make eighteen *fun*. That's two *monme* less two *fun*.[7] Kantarō! Osue! Granny and Uncle have come! Bring the tobacco tray! One times three makes three. Osan, serve the tea.[8]

CHANTER: He jabbers away.

[AUNT]: We haven't come for tea or tobacco. Osan, you're young, I know, but you're the mother of two children, and your excessive forbearance does you no credit. A man's dissipation can always be traced to his wife's carelessness. Remember, it's not only the man who's disgraced when he goes bankrupt and his marriage breaks up. You'd do well to take notice of what's going on and assert yourself a bit more.

[MAGOEMON]: It's foolish to hope for any results, aunt. The scoundrel deceives even me, his elder brother. Why should he take to heart criticism from his wife? Jihei—you played me for a fool. After showing me how you returned Koharu's pledges, here you are, not ten days later, redeeming her! What does this mean? I suppose your urgent calculations are of Koharu's debts! I've had enough!

CHANTER: He snatches away the abacus and flings it clattering into the hallway.

[JIHEI]: You're making an enormous fuss without any cause. I haven't left the house since the last time I saw you, except to go twice to the wholesalers in Imabashi and once to the Tenjin Shrine. I haven't even thought of Koharu, much less redeemed her.

[AUNT]: None of your evasions! Last evening at the Ten Nights service I heard the people in the congregation gossiping. Everybody was talking about the great patron from Tenma who'd fallen in love with a prostitute named Koharu from the Kinokuni House in Sonezaki. They said he'd driven away her other guests and was going to ransom her in the next couple of days. There was all kinds of gossip about the abundance of money and fools even in these days of high prices.

My husband Gozaemon has been hearing about Koharu constantly, and he's sure that her great patron from Tenma must be you, Jihei. He told me, "He's your nephew, but to me he's a stranger, and my daughter's happiness is my chief con-

6. Magoemon's (and Jihei's) aunt but Osan's mother.

7. Meaningless calculations. Twenty *fun* made two *monme*.

8. The name Osan echoes the word *san* (three).

cern. Once he ransoms the prostitute he'll no doubt sell his wife to a brothel. I intend to take her back before he starts selling her clothes."

He was halfway out of the house before I could stop him. "Don't get so excited. We can settle this calmly. First we must make sure whether or not the rumors are true."

That's why Magoemon and I are here now. He was telling me a while ago that the Jihei of today was not the Jihei of yesterday—that you'd broken all connections with Sonezaki and completely reformed. But now I hear that you've had a relapse. What disease can this be?

Your father was my brother. When the poor man was on his deathbed, he lifted his head from the pillow and begged me to look after you, as my son-in-law and nephew. I've never forgotten those last words, but your perversity has made a mockery of his request!

CHANTER: She collapses in tears of resentment. Jihei claps his hands in sudden recognition.

[JIHEI]: I have it! The Koharu everybody's gossiping about is the same Koharu, but the great patron who's to redeem her is a different man. The other day, as my brother can tell you, Tahei—they call him the Lone Wolf because he hasn't any family or relations—started a fight and was beaten up. He gets all the money he needs from his home town, and he's been trying for a long time to redeem Koharu. I've always prevented him, but I'm sure he's decided that now is his chance. I have nothing to do with it.

CHANTER: Osan brightens at his words.

[OSAN]: No matter how forbearing I might be—even if I were an angel—you don't suppose I'd encourage my husband to redeem a prostitute! In this instance at any rate there's not a word of untruth in what my husband has said. I'll be a witness to that, Mother.

CHANTER: Husband's and wife's words tally perfectly.

[AUNT]: Then it's true?

CHANTER: The aunt and nephew clap their hands with relief.

[MAGOEMON]: Well, I'm happy it's over, anyway. To make us feel doubly reassured, will you write an affidavit that will dispel any doubts your stubborn uncle may have?

[JIHEI]: Certainly. I'll write a thousand if you like.

[MAGOEMON]: Splendid! I happen to have bought this on the way here.

CHANTER: Magoemon takes from the fold of his kimono a sheet of oath-paper from Kumano, the sacred characters formed by flocks of crows.[9] Instead of vows of eternal love, Jihei now signs under penalty of Heaven's wrath an oath that he will sever all ties and affections with Koharu. "If I should lie, may Bonten and Taishaku above, and the Four Great Kings below, afflict me!"[1] So the text runs and to it is appended the names of many Buddhas and gods. He signs his name, Kamiya Jihei, in bold characters, seals the oath with blood, and hands it over.

[OSAN]: It's a great relief to me too. Mother, I have you and Magoemon to thank. Jihei and I have had two children, but this is his firmest pledge of affection. I hope you share my joy.

9. The charms issued by the Shintō shrine at Kumano were printed with six Chinese characters, whose strokes were in the shape of crows. The reverse side of these charms was used for writing oaths.

1. A formal oath. Bonten (Brahma) and Taishaku (Indra), though Hindu gods, were considered to be protective deities of the Buddhist law. The four Deva kings served under Indra and were also protectors of Buddhism.

[AUNT]: Indeed we do. I'm sure that Jihei will settle down and his business will improve, now that he's in this frame of mind. It's been entirely for his sake and for love of the grandchildren that we've intervened. Come, Magoemon, let's be on our way. I'm anxious to set my husband's mind at ease.—It's become chilly here. See that the children don't catch cold.—This, too, we owe to the Buddha of the Ten Nights. I'll say a prayer of thanks before I go. Hail, Amida Buddha!

CHANTER: She leaves, her heart innocent as Buddha's. Jihei is perfunctory even about seeing them to the door. Hardly have they crossed the threshold than he slumps down again at the kotatsu. He pulls the checked quilting over his head.

[OSAN]: You still haven't forgotten Sonezaki, have you?

CHANTER: She goes up to him in disgust and tears away the quilting. He is weeping; a waterfall of tears streams along the pillow, deep enough to bear him afloat. She tugs him upright and props his body against the kotatsu frame. She stares into his face.

[OSAN]: You're acting outrageously, Jihei. You shouldn't have signed that oath if you felt so reluctant to leave her. The year before last, on the middle day of the boar of the Tenth Month,[2] we lit the first fire in the kotatsu and celebrated by sleeping here together, pillow to pillow. Ever since then—did some demon or snake creep into my bosom that night?—for two whole years I've been condemned to keep watch over an empty nest. I thought that tonight at least, thanks to Mother and Magoemon, we'd share sweet words in bed as husbands and wives do, but my pleasure didn't last long. How cruel of you, how utterly heartless! Go ahead, cry your eyes out, if you're so attached to her. Your tears will flow into Shijimi River, and Koharu, no doubt, will ladle them out and drink them! You're ignoble, inhuman.

CHANTER: She embraces his knees and throws herself over him, moaning in supplication. Jihei wipes his eyes.

[JIHEI]: If tears of grief flowed from the eyes and tears of anger from the ears, I could show my heart without saying a word. But my tears all pour in the same way from my eyes, and there's no difference in their color. It's not surprising that you can't tell what's in my heart. I have not a shred of attachment left for that vampire in human skin, but I bear a grudge against Tahei. He has all the money he wants and no wife or children. He's schemed again and again to redeem her, but Koharu refused to give in, at least until I broke with her. She told me time and again, "You have nothing to worry about. I'll never let myself be redeemed by Tahei, not even if my ties with you are ended and I can no longer stay by your side. If my master is induced by Tahei's money to deliver me to him, I'll kill myself in a way that'll do you credit!" But think—not ten days have passed since I broke with her, and she's to be redeemed by Tahei! That rotten whore! That animal! No, I haven't a trace of affection left for her, but I can just hear how Tahei will be boasting. He'll spread the word around Ōsaka that my business has come to a standstill and I'm hard pressed for money. I'll meet with contemptuous stares from the wholesalers. I'll be dishonored. My heart is broken, and my body burns with shame. What a disgrace! How maddening! I've passed the stage of shedding hot tears, tears of blood, sticky tears—my tears now are of molten iron!

CHANTER: He collapses, weeping. Osan turns pale with alarm.

[OSAN]: If that's the situation, poor Koharu will surely kill herself.

2. It was customary to light the first fire of the winter on this day.

[JIHEI]: You're too well bred, despite your intelligence, to understand someone like her! What makes you suppose that faithless creature would kill herself? Far from it—she's probably taking moxa treatments and medicine to prolong her life!

[OSAN]: No, that's not true. I was determined never to tell you so long as I lived, but I'm afraid of the crime I'd be committing if I concealed the facts and let her die with my knowledge. I will reveal my great secret. There is not a grain of deceit in Koharu. It was I who schemed to end the relations between you. I could see signs that you were drifting toward suicide. I felt so unhappy that I wrote a letter, begging her as one woman to another to break with you, even though I knew how painful it would be. I asked her to save your life. The letter must have moved her. She answered that she would give you up, even though you were more precious than life itself, because she could not shirk her duty to me. I've kept her letter with me ever since—it's been like a protective charm. Would such a noble-hearted woman break her promise and brazenly marry Tahei? When a woman—I no less than another—has given herself completely to a man, she does not change. I'm sure she'll kill herself. I'm sure of it. Ahhh—what a dreadful thing to have happened! Save her, please.

CHANTER: Her voice rises in agitation. Her husband is thrown into a turmoil.

[JIHEI]: There was a letter in an unknown woman's hand among the written oaths she surrendered to my brother. It must have been from you. If that's the case, Koharu will surely commit suicide.

[OSAN]: Alas! I'd be failing in the obligations I owe her as another woman if I allowed her to die. Please go to her at once. Don't let her kill herself.

CHANTER: Clinging to her husband, she melts in tears.

[JIHEI]: But what can I possibly do? It'd take half the amount of her ransom in earnest money merely to keep her out of Tahei's clutches. I can't save Koharu's life without administering a dose of 750 *monme* in New Silver.[3] How could I raise that much money in my present financial straits? Even if I crush my body to powder, where will the money come from?

[OSAN]: Don't exaggerate the difficulties. If that's all you need, it's simple enough.

CHANTER: She goes to the wardrobe, and opening a small drawer takes out a bag fastened with cords of twisted silk. She unhesitatingly tears it open and throws down a packet which Jihei retrieves.

[JIHEI]: What's this? Money? Four hundred *monme* in New Silver? How in the world—

CHANTER: He stares astonished at this money he never put there.

[OSAN]: I'll tell you later where this money came from. I've scraped it together to pay the bill for Iwakuni paper that falls due the day after tomorrow. We'll have to ask Magoemon to help us keep the business from going bankrupt. But Koharu comes first. The packet contains 400 *monme*. That leaves 350 *monme* to raise.

CHANTER: She unlocks a large drawer. From the wardrobe lightly fly kite-colored Hachijō silks; a Kyōto crepe kimono lined in pale brown, insubstantial as her husband's life, which flickers today and may vanish tomorrow; a padded kimono of Osue's, a flaming scarlet inside and out—Osan flushes with pain to part with it; Kantarō's sleeveless, unlined jacket—if she pawns this, he'll be cold this winter.

3. Koharu's plight is described as a sickness. If 750 *me* is half the sum needed to redeem Koharu, the total of 1,500 *me* (or 6,000 *me* in Old Silver) is considerably less than the 10 *kanme,* or 10,000 *me* in Old Silver, mentioned by Tahei.

Next comes a garment of striped Gunnai silk lined in pale blue and never worn, and then her best formal costume—heavy black silk dyed with her family crest, an ivy leaf in a ring. They say that those joined by marriage ties can even go naked at home, although outside the house clothes make the man: she snatches up even her husband's finery, a silken cloak, making fifteen articles in all.

[OSAN]: The very least the pawnshop can offer is 350 *monme* in New Silver.

CHANTER: Her face glows as though she already held the money she needs; she hides in the one bundle her husband's shame and her own obligation and puts her love in besides.

[OSAN]: It doesn't matter if the children and I have nothing to wear. My husband's reputation concerns me more. Ransom Koharu. Save her. Assert your honor before Tahei.

CHANTER: But Jihei's eyes remain downcast all the while, and he is silently weeping.

[JIHEI]: Yes, I can pay the earnest money and keep her out of Tahei's hands. But once I've redeemed her, I'll either have to maintain her in a separate establishment or bring her here. Then what will become of you?

CHANTER: Osan is at a loss to answer.

[OSAN]: Yes, what shall I do? Shall I become your children's nurse or the cook? Or perhaps the retired mistress of the house?

CHANTER: She falls to the floor with a cry of woe.

[JIHEI]: That would be too selfish. I'd be afraid to accept such generosity. Even if the punishment for my crimes against my parents, against Heaven, against the gods and the Buddhas fails to strike me, the punishment for my crimes against my wife alone will be sufficient to destroy all hope for the future life. Forgive me, I beg you.

CHANTER: He joins his hands in tearful entreaty.

[OSAN]: Why should you bow before me? I don't deserve it. I'd be glad to rip the nails from my fingers and toes, to do anything that might serve my husband. I've been pawning my clothes for some time in order to scrape together the money for the paper wholesalers' bills. My wardrobe is empty, but I don't regret it in the least. But it's too late now to talk of such things. Hurry, change your cloak and go to her with a smile.

CHANTER: He puts on an underkimono of Gunnai silk, a robe of heavy black silk, and a striped cloak. His sash of figured damask holds a dirk of middle length worked in gold: Buddha surely knows that tonight it will be stained with Koharu's blood.

[JIHEI]: Sangorō! Come here!

CHANTER: Jihei loads the bundle on the servant's back, intending to take him along. Then he firmly thrusts the wallet next to his skin and starts toward the gate.

[VOICE]: Is Jihei at home?

CHANTER: A man enters, removing his fur cap. They see—good heavens!—that it is Gozaemon.

[OSAN and JIHEI]: Ahhh—how fortunate that you should come at this moment!

CHANTER: Husband and wife are upset and confused. Gozaemon snatches away Sangorō's bundle and sits heavily. His voice is sharp.

[GOZAEMON]: Stay where you are, harlot!—My esteemed son-in-law, what a rare pleasure to see you dressed in your finest attire, with a dirk and a silken cloak! Ahhh—that's how a gentleman of means spends his money! No one would take you for a paper dealer. Are you perchance on your way to the New Quarter? What commendable perseverance! You have no need for your wife, I take it.—Give her a divorce. I've come to take her home with me.

CHANTER: He speaks needles and his voice is bitter. Jihei has not a word to reply.

[OSAN]: How kind of you, Father, to walk here on such a cold day. Do have a cup of tea.

CHANTER: Offering the teacup serves as an excuse for edging closer.

[OSAN]: Mother and Magoemon came here a while ago, and they told my husband how much they disapproved of his visits to the New Quarter. Jihei was in tears and he wrote out an oath swearing he had reformed. He gave it to Mother. Haven't you seen it yet?

[GOZAEMON]: His written oath? Do you mean this?

CHANTER: He takes the paper from his kimono.

[GOZAEMON]: Libertines scatter vows and oaths wherever they go, as if they were monthly statements of accounts. I thought there was something peculiar about this oath, and now that I am here I can see I was right. Do you still swear to Bonten and Taishaku? Instead of such nonsense, write out a bill of divorcement!

CHANTER: He rips the oath to shreds and throws down the pieces. Husband and wife exchange looks of alarm, stunned into silence. Jihei touches his hands to the floor and bows his head.

[JIHEI]: Your anger is justified. If I were still my former self, I would try to offer explanations, but today I appeal entirely to your generosity. Please let me stay with Osan. I promise that even if I become a beggar or an outcast and must sustain life with the scraps that fall from other people's chopsticks, I will hold Osan in high honor and protect her from every harsh and bitter experience. I feel so deeply indebted to Osan that I cannot divorce her. You will understand that this is true as time passes and I show you how I apply myself to my work and restore my fortune. Until then please shut your eyes and allow us to remain together.

CHANTER: Tears of blood stream from his eyes and his face is pressed to the matting in contrition.

[GOZAEMON]: The wife of an outcast! That's all the worse. Write the bill of divorcement at once! I will verify and seal the furniture and clothes Osan brought in her dowry.

CHANTER: He goes to the wardrobe. Osan is alarmed.

[OSAN]: All my clothes are here. There's no need to examine them.

CHANTER: She runs up to stop him, but Gozaemon pushes her aside and jerks open a drawer.

[GOZAEMON]: What does this mean?

CHANTER: He opens another drawer: it too is empty. He pulls out every last drawer, but not so much as a foot of patchwork cloth is to be seen. He tears open the wicker hampers, long boxes, and clothes chests.

[GOZAEMON]: Stripped bare, are they?

CHANTER: His eyes set in fury. Jihei and Osan huddle under the striped kotatsu quilts, ready to sink into the fire with humiliation.

[GOZAEMON]: This bundle looks suspicious.

CHANTER: He unties the knots and dumps out the contents.

[GOZAEMON]: As I thought! You were sending these to the pawnshop, I take it. Jihei—you'd strip the skin from your wife's and your children's bodies to squander the money on your whore! Dirty thief! You're my wife's nephew, but an utter stranger to me, and I'm under no obligation to suffer for your sake. I'll explain to Magoemon what has happened and ask him to make good on whatever you've already stolen from Osan's belongings. But first, the bill of divorcement!

CHANTER: Even if Jihei could escape through seven padlocked doors, eight layers of chains, and a hundred retention walls, he could not escape so stringent a demand.

[JIHEI]: I won't use a brush to write the bill of divorcement. Here's what I'll do instead! Good-bye, Osan.

CHANTER: He lays his hand on his dirk, but Osan clings to him.

[OSAN]: Father—Jihei admits that he's done wrong and he's apologized in every way. You press your advantage too hard. Jihei may be a stranger, but his children are your grandchildren. Have you no affection for them? I will not accept a bill of divorcement.

CHANTER: She embraces her husband and raises her voice in tears.

[GOZAEMON]: Very well. I won't insist on it. Come with me, woman.

CHANTER: He pulls her to her feet.

[OSAN]: No, I won't go. What bitterness makes you expose to such shame a man and wife who still love each other? I will not suffer it.

CHANTER: She pleads with him, weeping, but he pays her no heed.

[GOZAEMON]: Is there some greater shame? I'll shout it through the town!

CHANTER: He pulls her up, but she shakes free. Caught by the wrist she totters forward when—alas!—her toes brush against her sleeping children. They open their eyes.

[CHILDREN]: Mother dear, why is Grandfather, the bad man, taking you away? Whom will we sleep beside now?

CHANTER: They call out after her.

[OSAN]: My poor dears! You've never spent a night away from Mother's side since you were born. Sleep tonight beside your father. [*To Jihei.*] Please don't forget to give the children their tonic before breakfast.—Oh, my heart is broken!

CHANTER: These are her parting words. She leaves her children behind, abandoned as in the woods; the twin-trunked bamboo of conjugal love is sundered forever.

ACT 3

Scene 1

In Sonezaki, in front of the Yamato Teahouse.

CHANTER: This is Shijimi River, the haunt of love and affection. Its flowing water and the feet of passersby are stilled now at two in the morning, and the full moon shines clear in the sky. Here in the street a dim doorway lantern is marked "Yamatoya Denbei" in a single scrawl. The night watchman's clappers take on a sleepy cadence as he totters by on uncertain legs. The very thickness of his voice crying, "Beware of fire! Beware of fire!" tells how far advanced the night is. A serving woman from the upper town comes along, followed by a palanquin. "It's terribly late," she remarks to the bearers as she clatters open the side door of the Yamato Teahouse and steps inside.

[SERVANT]: I've come to take back Koharu of the Kinokuni House.

CHANTER: Her voice is faintly heard outside. A few moments later, after hardly time enough to exchange three or four words of greeting, she emerges.

[SERVANT]: Koharu is spending the night. Bearers, you may leave now and get some rest. [*To proprietress, inside the doorway.*] Oh, I forgot to tell you, madam. Please keep an eye on Koharu. Now that the ransom to Tahei has been arranged and the money's been accepted, we're merely her custodians. Please don't let her drink too much saké.

CHANTER: She leaves, having scattered at the doorway the seeds that before morning will turn Jihei and Koharu to dust.

At night between two and four even the teahouse kettle rests; the flame flickering in the low candle stand narrows; and the frost spreads in the cold river-wind of the deepening night. The master's voice breaks the stillness.

[DENBEI, *to Jihei*]: It's still the middle of the night. I'll send somebody with you. [*To the servants.*] Mr. Jihei is leaving. Wake Koharu. Call her here.

CHANTER: Jihei slides open the side door.

[JIHEI]: No, Denbei, not a word to Koharu. I'll be trapped here until dawn if she hears I'm leaving. That's why I'm letting her sleep and slipping off this way. Wake her up after sunrise and send her back then. I'm returning home now and will leave for Kyōto immediately on business. I have so many engagements that I may not be able to return in time for the interim payment.[4] Please use the money I gave you earlier this evening to clear my account. I'd like you also to send 150 *me* of Old Silver to Kawashō for the moon-viewing party last month. Please get a receipt. Give Saietsubō[5] from Fukushima one piece of silver as a contribution to the Buddhist altar he's bought, and tell him to use it for a memorial service. Wasn't there something else? Oh yes—give Isoichi a tip of four silver coins. That's the lot. Now you can close up and get to bed. Good-bye. I'll see you when I return from Kyōto.

CHANTER: Hardly has he taken two or three steps than he turns back.

[JIHEI]: I forgot my dirk. Fetch it for me, won't you?—Yes, Denbei, this is one respect in which it's easier being a townsman. If I were a samurai and forgot my sword, I'd probably commit suicide on the spot!

[DENBEI]: I completely forgot that I was keeping it for you. Yes, here's the knife with it.

CHANTER: He gives the dirk to Jihei, who fastens it firmly into his sash.

[JIHEI]: I feel secure as long as I have this. Good night!

CHANTER: He goes off.

[DENBEI]: Please come back to Ōsaka soon! Thank you for your patronage!

CHANTER: With this hasty farewell Dembei rattles the door bolt shut; then not another sound is heard as the silence deepens. Jihei pretends to leave, only to creep back again with stealthy steps. He clings to the door of the Yamato Teahouse. As he peeps inside he is startled by shadows moving toward him. He takes cover at the house across the way until the figures pass.

Magoemon the Miller, his heart pulverized with anxiety over his younger brother, comes first, followed by the apprentice Sangorō with Jihei's son Kantarō on his back. They hurry along until they see the lantern of the Yamato Teahouse. Magoemon pounds on the door.

[MAGOEMON]: Excuse me. Kamiya Jihei's here, isn't he? I'd like to see him a moment.

CHANTER: Jihei thinks, "It's my brother!" but dares not stir from his place of concealment. From inside a man's sleep-laden voice is heard.

[DENBEI]: Jihei left a while ago saying he was going up to Kyōto. He's not here.

CHANTER: Not another sound is heard. Magoemon's tears fall unchecked.

[MAGOEMON, *to himself.*]: I ought to have met him on the way if he'd been going home. I can't understand what would take him to Kyōto. Ahhh—I'm shivering all over with worry. I wonder whether he took Koharu with him.

CHANTER: The thought pierces his heart; unable to bear the pain, he pounds again on the door.

4. On the last day of the Tenth Month, one of the times during the year for making payments.

5. The name of a male entertainer in the quarter. Fukushima was west of Sonezaki.

[DENBEI]: Who is it, so late at night? We've gone to bed.

[MAGOEMON]: I'm sorry to disturb you, but I'd like to ask one more thing. Has Koharu of the Kinokuni House left? I was wondering whether she might have gone with Jihei.

[DENBEI]: What's that? Koharu's upstairs, sound asleep.

[MAGOEMON]: That's a relief, anyway. There's no fear of a lovers' suicide. But where is he hiding himself, causing me all this anxiety? He can't imagine the agony of suspense that the whole family is going through on his account. I'm afraid that bitterness toward his father-in-law may make him forget himself and do something rash. I brought Kantarō along, hoping he would help to dissuade Jihei, but the gesture was in vain. I wonder why I never saw him?

CHANTER: He murmurs to himself, his eyes wet with tears. Jihei's hiding place is close enough for him to hear every word. He chokes with emotion but can only swallow his tears.

[MAGOEMON]: Sangorō! Where does the fool go night after night? Don't you know anywhere else?

CHANTER: Sangorō imagines that he himself is the fool referred to.

[SANGORŌ]: I know a couple of places, but I'm too embarrassed to mention them.

[MAGOEMON]: You know them? Where are they? Tell me.

[SANGORŌ]: Please don't scold me when you've heard. Every night I wander down below the warehouses by the market.

[MAGOEMON]: Imbecile! Who's asking about that? Come on, let's search the back streets. Don't let Kantarō catch a chill. The poor kid's having a hard time of it, thanks to that useless father of his. Still, if the worst the boy experiences is the cold, I won't complain. I'm afraid that Jihei may cause him much greater pain. The scoundrel!

CHANTER: But beneath the rancor in his heart of hearts is profound pity.

[MAGOEMON]: Let's look at the back street!

CHANTER: They pass on. As soon as their figures have gone off a distance, Jihei runs from his hiding place. Standing on tiptoes he gazes with yearning after them and cries out in his heart.

[JIHEI]: He cannot leave me to my death, even though I am the worst of sinners! I remain to the last a burden to him! I'm unworthy of such kindness!

CHANTER: He joins his hands and kneels in prayer.

[JIHEI]: If I may make one further request of your mercy, look after my children!

CHANTER: These are his only words; for a while he chokes with tears.

[JIHEI]: At any rate, our decision's been made. Koharu must be waiting.

CHANTER: He peers through a crack in the side door of the Yamato Teahouse and glimpses a figure.

[JIHEI]: That's Koharu, isn't it? I'll let her know I'm here.

CHANTER: He clears his throat, their signal. "Ahem, ahem"—the sound blends with the clack of wooden clappers as the watchman comes from the upper street, coughing in the night wind. He hurries on his round of fire warning, "Take care! Beware!" Even this cry has a dismal sound to one in hiding. Jihei, concealing himself like the god of Katsuragi,[6] lets the watchman pass. He sees his chance and rushes to the side door, which softly opens from within.

[JIHEI]: Koharu?

[KOHARU]: Were you waiting? Jihei—I want to leave quickly.

6. The god was so ashamed of his ugliness that he ventured forth only at night.

CHANTER: She is all impatience, but the more quickly they open the door, the more likely people will be to hear the casters turning. They lift the door; it makes a moaning sound that thunders in their ears and in their hearts. Jihei lends a hand from the outside, but his fingertips tremble with the trembling of his heart. The door opens a quarter of an inch, a half, an inch—an inch ahead are the tortures of hell, but more than hell itself they fear the guardian-demon's eyes. At last the door opens, and with the joy of New Year's morning[7] Koharu slips out. They catch each other's hands. Shall they go north or south, west or east? Their pounding hearts urge them on, though they know not to what destination: turning their backs on the moon reflected in Shijimi River, they hurry eastward as fast as their legs will carry them.

Scene 2

The farewell journey of many bridges.

CHANTER: *The running hand in texts of nō is always Konoe style;*
An actor in a woman's part is sure to wear a purple hat.
Does some teaching of the Buddha as rigidly decree
That men who spend their days in evil haunts must end like this?

Poor creatures, although they would discover today their destiny in the Sutra of Cause and Effect,[8] tomorrow the gossip of the world will scatter like blossoms the scandal of Kamiya Jihei's love suicide, and carved in cherry wood,[9] his story to the last detail will be printed in illustrated sheets.

Jihei, led on by the spirit of death—if such there be among the gods—is resigned to this punishment for neglect of his trade. But at times—who could blame him?—his heart is drawn to those he has left behind, and it is hard to keep walking on. Even in the full moon's light, this fifteenth night of the Tenth Month,[1] he cannot see his way ahead—a sign perhaps of the darkness in his heart? The frost now falling will melt by dawn, but even more quickly than this symbol of human frailty, the lovers themselves will melt away. What will become of the fragrance that lingered when he held her tenderly at night in their bedchamber?

This bridge, Tenjin Bridge, he has crossed every day, morning and night, gazing at Shijimi River to the west. Long ago, when Tenjin, then called Michizane,[2] was exiled to Tsukushi, his plum tree, following its master, flew in one bound to Dazaifu, and here is Plum-Field Bridge.[3] Green Bridge recalls the aged pine that

7. Mention of New Year is connected with Koharu's name, in which *haru* means "spring."

8. A sacred text of Buddhism, which states: "If you wish to know the past cause, look at the present effect; if you wish to know the future effect, look at the present cause."

9. The blocks from which illustrated books were printed were frequently made of cherry wood. The illustrated sheets mentioned here featured current scandals, such as lovers' suicides.

1. November 14, 1720. In the lunar calendar the full moon occurs on the fifteenth of the month.

2. Sugawara no Michizane, unfairly abused at court, was exiled to Dazaifu in Kyūshū. When he was about to depart, he composed a poem of farewell to his favorite plum tree. The tree, moved by this honor, flew after him to Kyūshū. The cherry tree in his garden withered away in grief. Only the pine seemed indifferent, as Michizane complained in another poem. The pine thereupon also flew to Kyūshū.

3. Umeda Bridge. "Green Bridge" is Midori-bashi.

followed later, and Cherry Bridge the tree that withered away in grief over parting. Such are the tales still told, demonstrating the power of a single poem.[4]

[JIHEI]: Though born the parishioner of so holy and mighty a god, I shall kill you and then myself. If you ask the cause, it was that I lacked even the wisdom that might fill a tiny Shell Bridge.[5] Our stay in this world has been short as an autumn day. This evening will be the last of your nineteen, of my twenty-eight years. The time has come to cast away our lives. We promised we'd remain together faithfully until you were an old woman and I an old man, but before we knew each other three full years, we have met this disaster. Look, there is Ōe Bridge. We will follow the river from Little Naniwa Bridge to Funairi Bridge. The farther we journey, the closer we approach the road to death.

CHANTER: He laments. She clings to him.

[KOHARU]: Is this already the road to death?

CHANTER: Falling tears obscure from each the other's face and threaten to immerse even the Horikawa bridges.

[JIHEI]: A few steps north and I could glimpse my house, but I will not turn back. I will bury in my breast all thoughts of my children's future, all pity for my wife. We cross southward over the river. Why did they call a place with as many buildings as a bridge has piers "Eight Houses"? Hurry, we want to arrive before the downriver boat from Fushimi comes—with what happy couples sleeping aboard!

Next is Tenma Bridge, a frightening name[6] for us about to depart this world. Here the two streams Yodo and Yamato join in one great river, as fish with water, and as Koharu and I, dying on one blade, will cross together the River of Three Fords.[7] I would like this water for our tomb offering!

[KOHARU]: What have we to grieve about? Although in this world we could not stay together, in the next and through each successive world to come until the end of time we shall be husband and wife. Every summer for my devotions[8] I have copied the All Compassionate and All Merciful Chapter of the Lotus Sutra, in the hope that we may be reborn on one lotus.

CHANTER: They cross over Sutra Bridge and reach the opposite shore.[9]

[KOHARU]: If I can save living creatures at will when once I mount a lotus calyx in Paradise and become a Buddha, I want to protect women of my profession, so that never again will there be love suicides.

CHANTER: This unattainable prayer stems from worldly attachment, but it touchingly reveals her heart. They cross Onari Bridge.[1] The waters of Noda Creek are shrouded with morning haze; the mountain tips show faintly white.

4. The poem by Michizane bewailing the inconstancy of his pine tree.

5. The lovers' journey takes them along the north bank of Shijimi River ("Shell River") to Shijimi Bridge, where they cross to Dōjima. At Little Naniwa Bridge they cross back again to Sonezaki. Continuing eastward, they cross Horikawa, then cross the Tenma Bridge over the Ōkawa. At "Eight Houses" (Hakkenya) they journey eastward along the south bank of the river as far as Kyō Bridge. They cross this bridge to the tip of land at Katamachi and then take the Onari Bridge to Amijima.

6. The characters used for "Tenma" literally mean "demon."

7. A river in the Buddhist underworld that had to be crossed to reach the world of the dead. This is arithmetic association: one blade plus two people equals three fords.

8. It was customary for Buddhist monks to observe a three-month summer retreat during which they practiced various austerities.

9. Kyōbashi is literally "Sutra Bridge." "Opposite Shore" implies the Buddhist term for nirvana.

1. The name Onari means "to become a Buddha."

[JIHEI]: Listen—the voices of the temple bells begin to boom. How much farther can we go on this way? We are not fated to live any longer—let us end it quickly. Come this way.

CHANTER: Tears are strung with the 108 beads of the rosaries in their hands. They have come now to Amijima, to the Daichō Temple. The overflowing sluice gate of a little stream beside a bamboo thicket will be their place of death.

Scene 3

Amijima.

[JIHEI]: No matter how far we walk, there'll never be a spot marked "For Suicides." Let us kill ourselves here.

CHANTER: He takes her hand and sits on the ground.

[KOHARU]: Yes, that's true. One place is as good as another to die. But I've been thinking on the way that if they find our dead bodies together, people will say that Koharu and Jihei committed a lovers' suicide. Osan will think then that I treated as mere scrap paper the letter I sent promising her, when she asked me not to kill you, that I would not and vowing to break off all relations with you. She will be sure that I lured her precious husband into a lovers' suicide. She will despise me as a one-night prostitute, a false woman with no sense of decency. I fear her contempt more than the slander of a thousand or ten thousand strangers. I can imagine how she will resent and envy me. That is the greatest obstacle to my salvation. Kill me here, then choose another spot, far away, for yourself.

CHANTER: She leans against him. Jihei joins in her tears of pleading.

[JIHEI]: What foolish worries! Osan has been taken back by my father-in-law. I've divorced her. She and I are strangers now. Why should you feel obliged to a divorced woman? You were saying on the way that you and I will be husband and wife through each successive world until the end of time. Who can criticize us, who can be jealous if we die side by side?

[KOHARU]: But who is responsible for your divorce? You're even less reasonable than I. Do you suppose that our bodies will accompany us to the afterworld? We may die in different places, our bodies may be pecked by kites and crows, but what does it matter as long as our souls are twined together? Take me with you to heaven or to hell!

CHANTER: She sinks again in tears.

[JIHEI]: You're right. Our bodies are made of earth, water, fire, and wind, and when we die they revert to emptiness. But our souls will not decay, no matter how often they're reborn. And here's a guarantee that our souls will be married and never part!

CHANTER: He whips out his dirk and slashes off his black locks at the base of the topknot.

[JIHEI]: Look, Koharu. As long as I had this hair, I was Kamiya Jihei, Osan's husband, but cutting it has made me a monk. I have fled the burning house of the three worlds of delusion; I am a priest, unencumbered by wife, children, or worldly possessions. Now that I no longer have a wife named Osan, you owe her no obligations either.

CHANTER: In tears he flings away the hair.

[KOHARU]: I am happy.

CHANTER: Koharu takes up the dirk and ruthlessly, unhesitatingly, slices through her flowing Shimada coiffure. She casts aside the tresses she has so often washed and combed and stroked. How heartbreaking to see their locks tangled with the weeds and midnight frost of this desolate field!

[JIHEI]: We have escaped the inconstant world, a nun and a priest. Our duties as husband and wife belong to our profane past. It would be best to choose quite separate places for our deaths, a mountain for one, the river for the other. We will pretend that the ground above this sluice gate is a mountain. You will die there. I shall hang myself by this stream. The time of our deaths will be the same, but the method and place will differ. In this way we can honor to the end our duty to Osan. Give me your undersash.

CHANTER: Its fresh violet color and fragrance will be lost in the winds of impermanence; the crinkled silk long enough to wind twice round her body will bind two worlds, this and the next. He firmly fastens one end to the crosspiece of the sluice, then twists the other into a noose for his neck. He will hang for love of his wife like the "pheasant in the hunting grounds."[2] Koharu watches Jihei prepare for his death. Her eyes swim with tears, her mind is distraught.

[KOHARU]: Is that how you're going to kill yourself?—If we are to die apart, I have only a little while longer by your side. Come near me.

CHANTER: They take each other's hands.

[KOHARU]: It's over in a moment with a sword, but I'm sure you'll suffer. My poor darling!

CHANTER: She cannot stop the silent tears.

[JIHEI]: Can suicide ever be pleasant, whether by hanging or cutting the throat? You mustn't let worries over trifles disturb the prayers of your last moments. Keep your eyes on the westward-moving moon, and worship it as Amida himself.[3] Concentrate your thoughts on the Western Paradise. If you have any regrets about leaving the world, tell me now, then die.

[KOHARU]: I have none at all, none at all. But I'm sure you must be worried about your children.

[JIHEI]: You make me cry all over again by mentioning them. I can almost see their faces, sleeping peacefully, unaware, poor dears, that their father is about to kill himself. They're the one thing I can't forget.

CHANTER: He droops to the ground with weeping. The voices of the crows leaving their nests at dawn rival his sobs. Are the crows mourning his fate? The thought brings more tears.

[JIHEI]: Listen to them. The crows have come to guide us to the world of the dead. There's an old saying that every time somebody writes an oath on the back of a Kumano charm, three crows of Kumano die on the holy mountain. The first words we've written each New Year have been vows of love, and how often we've made oaths at the beginning of the month! If each oath has killed three crows, what a multitude must have perished! Their cries have always sounded like "beloved, beloved," but hatred for our crime of taking life makes their voices ring tonight "revenge, revenge!"[4] Whose fault is it they demand revenge? Because of me you will die a painful death. Forgive me!

2. A reference to a poem by Ōtomo no Yakamochi (718–785): "The pheasant foraging in the fields of spring reveals his whereabouts to man as he cries for his mate."

3. Amida's paradise lies in the west. The moon is often used as a symbol of Buddhist enlightenment.

4. The cries have always sounded like *kawai, kawai* (beloved), but now they sound like *mukui, mukui* (revenge).

CHANTER: He takes her in his arms.

[KOHARU]: No, it's my fault!

CHANTER: They cling to each other, face pressed to face; their sidelocks, drenched with tears, freeze in the winds blowing over the fields. Behind them echoes the voice of the Daichō Temple.

[JIHEI]: Even the long winter night seems as short as our lives.

CHANTER: Dawn is already breaking, and matins can be heard. He draws her to him.

[JIHEI]: The moment has come for our glorious end. Let there be no tears on your face when they find you later.

[KOHARU]: There won't be any.

CHANTER: She smiles. His hands, numbed by the frost, tremble before the pale vision of her face, and his eyes are first to cloud. He is weeping so profusely that he cannot control the blade.

[KOHARU]: Compose yourself—but be quick!

CHANTER: Her encouragement lends him strength; the invocations to Amida carried by the wind urge a final prayer. *Namu Amida Butsu.* He thrusts in the savaging sword.[5] Stabbed, she falls backward, despite his staying hand, and struggles in terrible pain. The point of the blade has missed her windpipe, and these are the final tortures before she can die. He writhes with her in agony, then painfully summons his strength again. He draws her to him and plunges his dirk to the hilt. He twists the blade in the wound, and her life fades away like an unfinished dream at dawning.

He arranges her body with her head to the north, face to the west, lying on her right side,[6] and throws his cloak over her. He turns away at last, unable to exhaust with tears his grief over parting. He pulls the sash to him and fastens the noose around his neck. The service in the temple has reached the closing section, the prayers for the dead. "Believers and unbelievers will equally share in the divine grace," the voices proclaim, and at the final words Jihei jumps from the sluice gate.

[JIHEI]: May we be reborn on one lotus! Hail Amida Buddha!

CHANTER: For a few moments he writhes like a gourd swinging in the wind, but gradually the passage of his breath is blocked as the stream is dammed by the sluice gate, where his ties with this life are snapped. Fishermen out for the morning catch find the body in their net.[7]

[FISHERMEN]: A dead man! Look, a dead man! Come here, everybody!

CHANTER: The tale is spread from mouth to mouth. People say that they who were caught in the net of Buddha's vow immediately gained salvation and deliverance, and all who hear the tale of the Love Suicides at Amijima are moved to tears.

5. The invocation of Amida's name freed one from spiritual obstacles, just as a sword freed one from physical obstacles. Here the two images are blended.

6. The dead were arranged in this manner because Shakyamuni Buddha chose this position when he died.

7. "Net" (*ami*) is echoed a few lines later in the name Amijima. The vow of the Buddha to save all living creatures is likened to a net that catches people in its meshes.

Matsuo Bashō
1644–1694

Matsuo Bashō was born in the castle town of Ueno, southeast of Kyōto. Bashō's grandfather and great-grandfather belonged to the samurai class, but by Bashō's generation, the family had fallen so low that they had become farmers with only tenuous ties to the samurai class. Bashō at first served as a domestic employee of the Tōdō house, presumably as a companion to the son of the Tōdō lord. During this time, Bashō began to write linked verse (*haikai*). The linked verse sequence, usually consisting of 36 or 100 linked verses, began with the seventeen-syllable poetic form now known as haiku.

In the spring of 1672, at the age of twenty-nine, Bashō moved to Edo to establish himself as a linked-verse and haiku master who could charge fees for his services. By the mid-1670s Bashō had attracted the nucleus of his disciples and patrons who played a major role in the formation of what came to be known as the Bashō circle. In the winter of 1680, at the age of thirty-seven, Bashō left Edo and retreated to Fukagawa, on the banks of the Sumida River, on the outskirts of Edo. During the next four years he wrote in the so-called Chinese style, creating the persona of the recluse poet who was opposed to the materialism and social ambitions of the new urban culture. One of Bashō's literary achievements was fusing the earlier recluse poet tradition with the new commoner genre of haiku. He took his poetic name from the *bashō* plant, or Japanese plantain, whose large leaves sometimes tear in the wind, thus representing the fragility of the hermit-traveler's life.

In the fall of 1684, Bashō began the first of a series of journeys that occupied much of the remaining ten years of his life. On his first journey, commemorated in his travel diary *Skeleton in the Fields*, Bashō traveled to several western provinces, recruiting followers before returning to Edo in the summer of 1685. In the spring of 1689, Bashō departed once again, this time with his disciple Sora, for Michinoku ("Deep North") in the northeast, in an expedition later commemorated in *Narrow Road to the Deep North*. For the next two years, Bashō remained in the Kyōto-Ōsaka area. Together with two disciples in Kyōto, Bashō then edited *Monkey's Straw Coat*, the magnum opus of the Bashō school, which was published in the summer of 1691. Bashō died in 1694 on a journey to Ōsaka.

Bashō and the Art of Haiku

The seventeen-syllable haiku, which is usually translated into English in three lines, requires a cutting word and a seasonal word. The cutting word, often indicated in English translation by a dash, divides the haiku into two parts, which constitute two parts of the same scene while at the same time resonating with each other (often in a contrastive or parallel structure). The seasonal word is a word that, as a result of a long tradition of poetic use, not only indicates a specific season but usually possesses a cluster of associations that the poet draws on to widen the scope and complexity of the poem. For example, the seasonal word "evening in autumn" (*aki no kure*), which can also be translated as "end of autumn," is associated in the Japanese poetic tradition with loneliness. In the following haiku by Bashō, the cutting word, marked by a dash, creates a resonance between the implicit loneliness of the crow(s) on a withered branch and the implicit loneliness of an autumn evening or the end of autumn (also implying the end of life).

kareeda ni	Crows resting
karasu no tomarikeri	on a withered branch—
aki no kure	evening in autumn

In Bashō's time, the spirit of haiku meant taking pleasure in seeing things freshly: both dislocating habitual, conventionalized perceptions *and* also recasting established poetic topics

A *haiga* (haikai sketch), on the Chinese painting theme of cold crows on a withered branch. The painting is by Morikawa Kyoriku, 1656–1715, Bashō's disciple and his painting instructor, and the calligraphy and poem are by Bashō: "On a withered branch, a crow comes to rest—evening in autumn" (*Kareeda ni / karasu no tomarikeri / aki no kure*). Probably done around 1692/1693 while Kyoriku, a samurai from Hikone, was in Edo. Signed "Bashō Tōsei." (42.1 in. × 12.2 in.)

into contemporary language and culture. In the previous haiku, the topic of "evening in autumn," which classical poets from the Heian and medieval periods had composed on, is given new life by juxtaposing it with the surprising image of "crows on a withered branch," which had hitherto appeared only in Chinese ink painting.

Of particular interest here is the complex relationship between haiku and tradition. Bashō looked to classical and medieval poets for poetic and spiritual inspiration. He especially admired Saigyō (1118–1190) and Sōgi (1421–1502)—who were travelers and poet-priests—and he was strongly influenced by Chinese poetry and poetics. At the same time, Bashō was a poet of haiku (called haikai at the time), which, by its very nature, was parodic, oppositional, and immersed in popular culture. One result was the emergence in the seventeenth century of a culture of *mitate* (literally, seeing by comparison), which moved back and forth between the two starkly different worlds, that of the Japanese classics and that of the new popular literature and drama, each providing a lens or filter with which to view the other. Artists such as Hishikawa Moronobu (1618–1694), a pioneer of *ukiyo-e* prints, used the technique of *mitate* in the visual arts, both alluding to and radically transforming the topics and imagery of the classical tradition into a contemporary form.

Bashō's haiku differed from the *mitate* found in Moronobu's *ukiyo-e* woodblock prints in that the popular culture in his poetry and prose was not that of the stylish men and women of the great urban centers but, rather, that of the mundane, everyday lives of farmers and fishermen in the provinces. Bashō himself was a socially marginal figure, and his poetry and prose are pervaded by marginal figures such as the beggar, the old man, the outcast, and the traveler, no doubt reflecting his own provincial origins. Likewise, his allusions were not to famous lovers like the shining Genji but, rather, to medieval traveler poets such as Saigyō and Sōgi.

In the seventeenth century, the popular vernacular genres such as Saikaku's tales frequently parodied their classical predecessors by borrowing the elegant, aristocratic forms of traditional literature and giving them a popular, vulgar, or erotic content. In a reverse movement, Bashō gave a popular, vernacular genre (haiku) a spiritual or refined content, or more accurately, he sought out the spiritual and poetic in commoner culture, giving to contemporary language and provincial subject matter the kind of nuances and sentiments hitherto found only in classical or Chinese poetry. In this way, Bashō was able to raise haiku—which until then had been considered a form of light entertainment—into a serious literary genre and a vehicle for cultural transmission.

[Selected Haiku][1]

kareeda ni
karasu no tomarikeri
aki no kure

On a withered branch
a crow comes to rest—
evening in autumn[2]

Going out on the beach while the light is still faint:

akebono ya—
shirauo shiroki
koto issun

early dawn—
whitefish, an inch
of whiteness[3]

1. Translated by Haruo Shirane.
2. Bashō first composed this haiku in the spring of 1681, during his late Chinese-style period. *Aki no kure* can be read as either "end of autumn" or "autumn nightfall." In a 1698 collection of Bashō's haiku, this haiku is preceded by the title "On Evening in Autumn" (*aki no kure to wa*), indicating that the poem was written on a seasonal topic closely associated with Fujiwara Shunzei (d. 1204) and his medieval aesthetics of quiet, meditative loneliness. Crows perched on a withered branch, on the other hand, was a popular subject in Chinese ink painting. In this context, Bashō's haiku juxtaposes a medieval poetic topic with a Chinese painting motif, causing the two to resonate in montage fashion.
3. Bashō composed this haiku in the Eleventh Month of 1684 while visiting the Ise area during the *Skeleton in the Fields* journey. Drawing on the phonic connotations of *shirauo* (literally, white fish), Bashō establishes a connotative correspondence between the semi-translucent "whiteness" (*shiroki koto*) of the tiny fish and the pale, faint light of early dawn (*akebono*). The poem has a melodic rhythm, resulting from the repeated "o" vowel mixed with the consonantal "s."

Having stayed once more at the residence of Master Tōyō, I was about to leave for the Eastern Provinces.

botan shibe fukaku *wakeizuru hachi no—* *nagori kana*	From deep within the peony pistils, withdrawing regretfully, the bee[4]

Spending a whole day on the beach:

umi kurete *kamo no koe* *honoka ni shiroshi*	The sea darkening— the voice of a wild duck faintly white[5]
furuike ya *kawazu tobikomu* *mizu no oto*	An old pond— a frog leaps in, the sound of water[6]

On the road:

kutabirete *yado karu koro ya* *fuji no hana*	Exhausted, time to find a lodging— hanging wisteria[7]

Lodging for the night at Akashi:

takotsubo ya *hakanaki yume o* *natsu no tsuki*	Octopus traps— fleeting dreams under the summer moon[8]

4. This is a good example of a semi-allegorical poetic greeting. Bashō composed the haiku, which appears in *Skeleton in the Fields*, when he left the house of his friend Tōyō in the Fourth Month of 1685. The bee, representing Bashō, is resting peacefully in the peony, an elegant summer flower that symbolizes Tōyō's residence, joyfully imbibing the rich pollen of the pistils, but now, with much reluctance, it must leave. The haiku is an expression of gratitude and a farewell not only to Tōyō but to all the Nagoya-area poets who have hosted him on this journey.

5. The opening verse of a linked-verse sequence composed in Atsuta, in Nagoya, in 1685. The poet looks out toward the voice of the wild duck (*kamo*), which has disappeared with the approaching darkness, and sees only a faint whiteness (*shiroshi* implies a kind of translucency), which may be the waves or the reflection of the sea in the dusk. *Kamo* is a seasonal word for winter.

6. Written in 1686 and collected in *Spring Days.* Since the ancient period, the frog had been admired for its singing and its beautiful voice. In the Heian period it became associated with spring, the *yamabuki*—the bright yellow globeflower—and limpid mountain streams. According to one source, Kikaku, one of Bashō's disciples, suggested that Bashō use *yamabuki* in the opening phrase. Instead, Bashō works against the classical associations of the frog. In place of the plaintive voice of the frog singing in the rapids or calling out for its lover, Bashō evokes the sound of the frog jumping into the water. And instead of the elegant image of a frog in a fresh mountain stream beneath the *yamabuki,* the haiku presents a stagnant pond. At the same time, the haiku offers a fresh twist to the seasonal association of the frog with spring: the sudden movement of the frog, which suggests rebirth and the awakening of life in spring, is contrasted with the implicit winter stillness of the old pond.

7. This haiku, which Bashō composed in 1688, appears in *Backpack Notes.* The wisteria (*fuji no hana*), with its long drooping flowers, is blooming outside the lodge even as it functions as a metaphor for the traveler's heart.

8. Bashō composed this poem, which appears in *Backpack Notes,* in the Fourth Month of 1688. The octopus traps were lowered in the afternoon and raised the next morning, after the octopus had crawled inside. The octopus in the jars implicitly suggest the troops of the Heike clan that were massacred on these shores at the end of the 12th century and whose ghosts subsequently appear before the traveler in *Backpack Notes.* Now these octopi are having "fleeting dreams," not knowing they are about to be harvested. Bashō juxtaposes the "summer moon" (*natsu no tsuki*), which the classical tradition deemed to be as brief as the summer night and thus associated with ephemerality, and the "octopus traps" (*takotsubo*), a vernacular word, giving new life to the theme of impermanence. The poem is intended to be humorous and sad at the same time.

hototogisu	The cuckoo—
kieyuku kata ya	where it disappears
shima hitotsu	a single island[9]

While sleeping in a lodge in the capital and hearing each night the sorrowful chanting of the Kūya pilgrims:

karazake mo	Dried salmon
Kūya no yase mo	the gauntness of a Kūya pilgrim
kan no uchi	in the cold season[1]
kogarashi ya	Withering winds—
hohobare itamu	the face of a man
hito no kao	pained by swollen cheeks[2]
mugimeshi ni	A cat's wife—
yatsururu koi ka	grown thin from
neko no tsuma—	love and barley?[3]
hototogisu	A cuckoo—
koe yokotau ya	the voice lies stretched
mizu no ue	over the water[4]
hiyahiya to	Taking a midday nap
kabe o fumaete	feet planted
hirune kana	on a cool wall[5]

9. Diverging from the classical poetic association of the cuckoo (*hototogisu*), which was its singing, Bashō focuses here on its arrow-like flight. In this poem, which Bashō wrote in 1688 during his *Backpack Notes* journey, the speaker implicitly hears the cuckoo, but by the time he looks up, it has disappeared, replaced by a single island, presumably Awajishima, the small island across the bay from Suma and Akashi, where the speaker stands. The haiku is also parodic, twisting a well-known classical poem in the *Senzaishū* (1188): "When I gaze in the direction of the crying cuckoo, only the moon lingers in the dawn." Another possible pretext is the following poem in the classic collection: "Faintly, in the morning mist on Akashi Bay, it disappears behind an island, the boat I long for." In Bashō's haiku, the flight of the disappearing cuckoo, which the poet implicitly longs to see, becomes the path of the ship, which "disappears behind" (*shimagakureyuku*) Awajishima, the "one island."

1. Bashō composed this haiku while visiting Kyōto in the Twelfth Month of 1690 and later included it in *Monkey's Straw Coat*. Kūya were lay monks or pilgrims who commemorated the anniversary of the death of Priest Kūya by begging and chanting Buddhist songs in the streets of Kyōto for 48 days beginning in the middle of the Eleventh Month. *Kan* (cold season), a roughly 30-day period from the Twelfth Month through the beginning of the First Month (February), was the coldest part of the year. The three parts—dried salmon (*karazake*), the gauntness of the Kūya pilgrim (*Kūya no yase*), and the cold season (*kan no uchi*), each of which is accentuated by a hard beginning "k" consonant and by the repeated *mo* (also)—suggest three different dimensions (material, human, and seasonal) of the loneliness of a traveler on a distant journey.

2. Composed in the winter of 1691. The two parts of the haiku—separated by the cutting word *ya*—can be read together as one continuous scene or separately as two parts reverberating against each other. In the first part, a person suffering from mumps (*hohobare,* literally, swollen cheeks) stands outside, his or her face contorted by the *kogarashi,* the strong winds that blow the leaves off the trees in the winter. In the second part, the person's face inflamed by and suffering from mumps echoes the cold, stinging wind. The expectations generated by withering winds, a classical seasonal topic associated with cold winter landscapes, are humorously undercut by the haiku phrase *hohobare itamu* (pained by swollen cheeks), which then leads to a double reversal: after the initial collision, the reader discovers a fusion between the withering winds and the painfully swollen cheeks.

3. "Cat's love for its mate" (*neko no tsumagoi*), later simply called cat's love (*neko no koi*), was a haiku seasonal topic that became popular in the Edo period. Bashō composed this haiku in 1691 and included it in *Monkey's Straw Coat*. Bashō humorously depicts a female cat that has grown emaciated not only from being fed only barley—a situation that suggests a poor farmhouse—but from intense lovemaking. (*Yatsururu* modifies both *mugimeshi* and *koi,* implying "emaciating barley and love.")

4. Bashō apparently wrote this haiku in the Fourth Month of 1693 after being urged by his disciples to compose on the topic of "cuckoos on the water's edge." As the cuckoo flies overhead, it makes a sharp penetrating cry, which "lies sideways" (*yokotau*), hanging over the quiet surface of the water, probably at dusk or night when it traditionally sings. The cuckoo quickly disappears, but the sound lingers, like an overtone.

5. This haiku appears in *Backpack Diary;* Bashō composed it in 1694 at the residence of Mokusetsu in Ōtsu (near Lake Biwa). This poem uses *hiyahiya* (cool) as a seasonal word for autumn. The speaker, cooling the bottoms of his bare feet on the wall, has fallen asleep on a hot afternoon. The implied topic is lingering summer heat (*zansho*), which is captured from a humorous, haiku angle, in the feet, through which the speaker feels the arrival of autumn.

kiku no ka ya *Nara ni wa furuki* *hotoketachi*	Chrysanthemum scent— in Nara ancient statues of the Buddha[6]
aki fukaki *tonari wa nani o* *suru hito zo*	Autumn deepening— my neighbor how does he live, I wonder?[7]
kono michi ya *yuku hito nashi ni* *aki no kure*	This road— no one goes down it autumn's end[8]

Composed while ill:

tabi ni yande *yume wa kareno o* *kakemeguru*	Sick on a journey dreams roam about on a withered moor[9]

Narrow Road to the Deep North

In the spring of 1689, Bashō and his companion Sora departed for Michinoku, or Oku (Interior), the relatively unsettled area of Japan's northeastern Honshū. Bashō traveled north to present-day Sendai, crossed west over the mountains to the Japan Sea side, then moved south, down the coast, through Kanazawa, and arrived at Ōgaki in Mino Province (Gifu), after a five-month journey (see map on page 1898). Although *Narrow Road to the Deep North* is often read as a faithful travel account, it is best regarded as a kind of fiction loosely based on the actual journey. Bashō depicts an ideal world in which the traveler devotes himself to poetic life in a manner that Bashō himself probably aspired to but found impossible in the busy world of a linked-verse and haiku master.

The text consists of fifty or so discrete sections strung together like a linked-verse sequence. They describe a series of interrelated journeys: a search for noted poetic places, especially the traces of ancient poets such as Saigyō, the medieval poet-priest to whom this account pays special homage; a journey into the past to such historical places as the old battlefield at Hiraizumi; an ascetic journey and a pilgrimage to sacred places; and interesting encounters with individuals and poetic partners, with whom he exchanges poetic greetings.

The interest of travel literature, at least in the Anglo-European tradition, generally lies in the unknown, new worlds, new knowledge, new perspectives, and new experiences. But for Japanese medieval poets, the object of travel was to confirm what already existed, to reinforce

6. Bashō composed this haiku in 1694, on Chrysanthemum Festival Day (Chōyō), which fell on the ninth day of the Ninth Month, while stopping at Nara on the way to Ōsaka on his last journey. Nara, the capital of Japan in the 8th century, is known for its many temples and buddha statues. The chrysanthemum, considered the aristocrat of flowers in classical poetry and a seasonal word for late autumn, possess a strong but refined fragrance. The many buddhas in the ancient capital of Nara evoke a similar sense of dignity, solemnity, and refinement as well as nostalgia for a bygone era.

7. Bashō composed this haiku, which appears in *Backpack Diary,* in the autumn of 1694, shortly before he died in Ōsaka. Bashō had been invited to a poem party at the home of one of his close followers, but he didn't feel well enough to go and instead sent a poem which subtly expresses his deep regret at not being able to meet this friends. In highly colloquial language, the poem suggests the loneliness of a traveler implicitly seeking companionship, or the loneliness of those who live together and yet apart in urban society, or the loneliness of life itself, particularly in the face of death—all of which resonate with late autumn (*aki fukaki*), associated in classical poetry with loneliness and sorrow.

8. Bashō composed this in the late autumn of 1694, at the end of his life, at a large haiku gathering. The poem can be read as an expression of disappointment that, at the end of his life, in the autumn of his career—*aki no kure* can mean either "autumn's end" or "autumn evening"—he is alone, and/or as an expression of disappointment at the lack of sympathetic poetic partners, as an expression of desire for those who can engage in the poetic dialogue necessary to continue on this difficult journey.

9. Bashō's last poem, written four days before his death on the twelfth day of the Tenth Month of 1694, during a journey in Ōsaka.

the roots of cultural memory. By visiting noted poetic locales, the poet-traveler hoped to relive the experience of his or her literary predecessors, to be moved to compose poetry on the same landscape, thereby joining his or her cultural forebears. The travel diary itself became a link in a chain of poetic and literary transmission.

In contrast to medieval Japanese poets, however, who attempted to preserve the classical associations of the poetic topics, Bashō sought out new poetic associations in classic sites and discovered new poetic places. In the passage on Muro-no-yashima, toward the beginning, Bashō suggests that *Narrow Road* will take a new approach, exploring both the local place and its historical and poetic roots in an effort to re-envision the landscape. A contrast can be seen between the places visited in the first half of *Narrow Road*, which tend to be major poetic sites and which bear the weight of the classical tradition, and those found along the Japan Sea side in the second half, such as Kisagata, which tend to be lesser poetic locales or even unknown in the classical tradition. In writing *Narrow Road*, Bashō sought a Chinese poetic ideal of "landscape in human emotion, and human emotion in landscape," in which the landscape becomes infused with cultural memory and a wide variety of human emotions and associations, from the sensual to the spiritual.

A number of the early sections imply that the journey also is a form of ascetic practice. The title of *Narrow Road to the Deep North* (*Oku no hosomichi*) implies not only the narrow and difficult roads (*hosomichi*) of Michinoku but the difficulty of the spiritual journey "within" (*oku*). Pilgrimages to sacred places, to temples and shrines, were popular from as early as the medieval Heian period and formed an integral part of travel literature, particularly those written by hermit-priests, a persona that Bashō adopts here. *Narrow Road,* in fact, has far more sections on this topic than usually found in medieval travel diaries. A typical passage begins with a description of the place and a history of the shrine or temple, usually giving some detail about the founder or the name. The climactic haiku, which may be a poetic greeting to the divine spirit or head of the temple/shrine, usually conveys a sense of the sacred quality or efficacy of the place.

Bashō wrote *Narrow Road* a considerable time after the actual journey, probably in 1694 at the end of his life, when he was developing his new ideal of *haibun*, or haiku-prose, in which haiku was embedded in poetic prose. *Narrow Road to the Deep North* is marked by a great variety of prose styles, and it may best be understood as an attempt to reveal the different possibilities of *haibun* in the form of travel literature. The resulting fusion of vernacular Japanese, classical Japanese, and classical Chinese, with its parallel and contrastive couplet-like phrases, had a profound impact on the development of Japanese prose. Of particular interest is the close fusion between the prose and the poetry, in which the prose creates a dramatic context for many of the best haiku that Bashō wrote.

PRONUNCIATIONS:

Hiraizumi: hee-rye-zou-mee
Ise: ee-say
Matsuo Bashō: mah-tsu-oh bah-show
Saigyō: sigh-gyoh

from Narrow Road to the Deep North[1]

The months and days, the travelers of a hundred ages;
the years that come and go, voyagers too.
floating away their lives on boats,
growing old as they lead horses by the bit,
for them, each day a journey, travel their home.
Many, too, are the ancients who perished on the road.

1. Translated by Haruo Shirane.

Some years ago, seized by wanderlust, I wandered along the shores of the sea. Then, last autumn, I swept away the old cobwebs in my dilapidated dwelling on the river's edge.

As the year gradually came to an end and spring arrived, filling the sky with mist, I longed to cross the Shirakawa Barrier, the most revered of poetic places. Somehow or other, I became possessed by a spirit, which crazed my soul. Unable to sit still, I accepted the summons of the Deity of the Road. No sooner had I repaired the holes in my trousers, attached a new cord to my rain hat, and cauterized my legs with moxa than my thoughts were on the famous moon at Matsushima. I turned my dwelling over to others and moved to Sanpū's villa.

kusa no to mo	Time even for the grass hut
sumikawaru yo zo	to change owners—
hina no ie	house of dolls[2]

I left a sheet of eight linked verses on the pillar of the hermitage.

I started out on the twenty-seventh day of the Third Month.

The dawn sky was misting over; the moon lingered, giving off a pale light; the peak of Mount Fuji appeared faintly in the distance. I felt uncertain, wondering whether I would see again the cherry blossoms on the boughs at Ueno and Yanaka. My friends had gathered the night before to see me off and joined me on the boat. When I disembarked at a place called Senju, my breast was overwhelmed by thoughts of the "three thousand leagues ahead," and standing at the crossroads of the illusory world, I wept at the parting.

yuku haru ya	Spring going—
tori naki uo no	birds crying and tears
me wa namida	in the eyes of the fish[3]

Making this my first journal entry, we set off but made little progress. People lined the sides of the street, seeing us off, it seemed, as long as they could see our backs.

Was it the second year of Genroku? On a mere whim, I had resolved that I would make a long journey to the Deep North. Although I knew I would probably suffer, my hair growing white under the distant skies of Wu, I wanted to view those places that I had heard of but never seen and placed my faith in an uncertain future, not knowing if I would return alive. We barely managed to reach the Sōka post station that night. The luggage that I carried over my bony shoulders began to cause me pain. I had departed on the journey thinking that I need bring only myself, but I ended up carrying a coat to keep me warm at night, a night robe, rain gear, inkstone, brush, and the like, as well as the farewell presents that I could not refuse. All these became a burden on the road.

We paid our respects to the shrine at Muro-no-yashima, Eight Islands of the Sealed Room. Sora, my travel companion, noted: "This deity is called the Goddess of the Blooming Cherry Tree and is the same as that worshiped at Mount Fuji. Since the goddess entered a sealed hut and burned herself giving birth to Hohodemi, the God of Emitting Fire, and proving her vow, they call the place Eight Islands of the Sealed Room.

2. *Hina* (dolls), a new seasonal word for late spring, meant Hinamatsuri, the girls' festival on the third of the Third Month, when families with daughters displayed dolls in their houses. The time has come for even the recluse hut—symbolized by the "grass door"—to become a domestic, secular dwelling, with family and daughter(s).

3. The birds and fish mourn the passing of spring and, by implication, the departure of the travelers. Some commentators see the fish as the disciples left behind and the birds as the departing travelers (Bashō and Sora); others interpret the departing spring as the traveler. *Yuku,* a key word in *Narrow Road,* means both "to go" and "to pass time," thereby fusing passings in time and in space.

In spring 1687, Bashō and his disciple Sora departed Edo, the capital of Tokagawa Japan, for Michinoku (Deep North). Their five month journey concluded at Ōgaki.

The custom of including smoke in poems on this place also derives from this story. It is forbidden to consume a fish called *konoshiro,* or shad, which is thought to smell like flesh when burned. The essence of this shrine history is already known to the world."[4]

On the thirtieth, stopped at the foot of Nikkō Mountain. The owner said, "My name is Buddha Gozaemon. People have given me this name because I make honesty my first concern in all matters. As a consequence, you can relax for one night on the road. Please stay here." I wondered what kind of buddha had manifested itself in this

4. A typical classical poem on Muro-no-yashima, by Fujiwara Sanekata, reads: "How could I let you know of my longing were it not for the smoke of Muro-no-yashima?" Classical poets believed that the steam from a stream in Muro-no-yashima looked like smoke. However, Sora, who came from a family of Shintō priests, presents here a different explanation, taking a revisionary approach to *utamakura,* or poetic places.

soiled world to help someone like me, traveling like a beggar priest on a pilgrimage. I observed the actions of the innkeeper carefully and saw that he was neither clever nor calculating. He was nothing but honesty—the type of person that Confucius referred to when he said, "Those who are strong in will and without pretension are close to humanity." I had nothing but respect for the purity of his character.

On the first of the Fourth Month, we paid our respects to the holy mountain. In the distant past, the name of this sacred mountain was written with the characters Nikkōzan, Two Rough Mountain, but when Priest Kūkai established a temple here, he changed the name to Nikkō, Light of the Sun. Perhaps he was able to see a thousand years into the future. Now this venerable light shines throughout the land, and its benevolence flows to the eight corners of the earth, and the four classes—warrior, samurai, artisan, and merchant—all live in peace. Out of a sense of reverence and awe, I put my brush down here.

aratōto	Awe inspiring!
aoba wakaba no	on the green leaves, budding leaves
hi no hikari	light of the sun

Black Hair Mountain, enshrouded in mist, the snow still white.

sorisutete	Shaving my head
Kurokamiyama ni	at Black Hair Mountain—
koromogae	time for summer clothes[5]
	[Sora]

Sora's family name is Kawai; his personal name is Sōgoro. He lived near me, helping me gather wood and heat water, and was delighted at the thought of sharing with me the sights of Matsushima and Kisagata. At the same time, he wanted to help me overcome the hardships of travel. On the morning of the departure, he shaved his hair, changed to dark black robes, and took on the Buddhist name of Sōgo. That is why he wrote the Black Hair Mountain poem. I thought that the words "time for summer clothes" were particularly effective.

Climbing more than a mile up a mountain, we came to a waterfall. From the top of the cavern, the water flew down a hundred feet, falling into a blue pool of a thousand rocks. I squeezed into a hole in the rocks and entered the cavern: they say that this is called Back-View Falls because you can see the waterfall from the back, from inside the cavern.

shibaraku wa	Secluded for a while
taki ni komoru ya	in a waterfall—
ge no hajime	beginning of summer austerities[6]

There is a mountain-priest temple called Kōmyōji. We were invited there and prayed at the Hall of Gyōja.

natsuyama ni	Summer mountains—
ashida o ogamu	praying to the tall clogs
kadode kana	at journey's start[7]

5. Embarking on a journey becomes synonymous with entering the Buddhist path: both imply a firm resolve and a new life, symbolized here by the seasonal word *koromogae* (change of clothes at the beginning of summer).

6. This line refers both to the beginning of summer and to the Buddhist austerities of summer, in which Buddhist practitioners remained indoors for three months fasting, reciting sutras, and carrying out such ascetic and purification practices as standing under a waterfall. The traveler stands behind the waterfall, which gives him the cool, pure feeling of being cleansed of the dirt of the world.

7. At the beginning of the journey, the traveler bows before the high clogs, a prayer for the foot strength of En no Gyōja, the founder of a mountain priest sect and an "austerity man" (gyōja) believed to have acquired superhuman power from rigorous mountain training.

The willow that was the subject of Saigyō's poem, "Where a Crystal Stream Flows,"[8] still stood in the village of Ashino, on a footpath in a rice field. The lord of the manor of this village had repeatedly said, "I would like to show you this willow," and I had wondered where it was. Today I was able to stand in its very shade.

ta ichimai *uete tachisaru* *yanagi kana*	Whole field of rice seedlings planted—I part from the willow[9]

The days of uncertainty piled one on the other, and when we came upon the Shirakawa Barrier, I finally felt as if I had settled into the journey. I can understand why that poet had written, "Had I a messenger, I would send a missive to the capital!" One of three noted barriers, the Shirakawa Barrier captured the hearts of poets. With the sound of the autumn wind in my ears and the image of the autumn leaves in my mind, I was moved all the more by the tops of the green-leafed trees.[1] The flowering of the wild rose amid the white deutzia clusters made me feel as if I were crossing over snow.

At the Sukagawa post station, we visited a man named Tōkyū. He insisted that we stay for four or five days and asked me how I had found the Shirakawa Barrier. I replied, "My body and spirit were tired from the pain of the long journey; my heart overwhelmed by the landscape. The thoughts of the distant past tore through me, and I couldn't think straight." But feeling it would be a pity to cross the barrier without producing a single verse, I wrote:

fūryū no *hajime ya oku no* *taue uta*	Beginnings of poetry— rice-planting songs of the Deep North[2]

This opening verse was followed by a second verse and then a third; before we knew it, three sequences.

The next day we went to Shinobu Village and visited Shinobu Mottling Rock. The rock was in a small village, half buried, deep in the shade of the mountain. A child from the village came and told us, "In the distant past, the rock was on top of

8. Poem by Saigyō in the *Shinkokinshū* collection (1205): "I thought to pause on the roadside where a crystal stream flows beneath a willow and stood rooted to the spot."

9. The entire passage alludes to *The Wandering Priest and the Willow,* a nō play based on Saigyō's poem just referred to, in which an itinerant priest, retracing the steps of Saigyō through the Deep North, meets an old man who shows him the withered willow about which Saigyō wrote his famous poem. The old man later turns out to be the spirit of that willow. At the end of the play the priest offers prayers to the spirit of the willow, thereby enabling it to achieve salvation. When the district officer offers to introduce Saigyō's willow to the traveler, the passage takes on the atmosphere of a nō dream play in which the traveler encounters the spirit of Saigyō, embodied in the willow. In contrast to Saigyō's classical poem, in which time passes as the traveler rests near a beautiful stream, in Bashō's haiku, time passes as the traveler journeys to meet Saigyō's spirit.

1. The Shirakawa Barrier here exists almost entirely in the traveler's imagination as a circle of poetic associations. Taira Kanemori (d. 990), referred to as "that poet," was the first in a long line of classical poets to compose on the barrier: "Had I a messenger I would send a missive to the capital!" A poem by Priest Nōin, who first traveled to the Deep North in 1025, created the association of the Shirakawa Barrier with autumn wind. At a poetry contest in 1170, Minamoto Yorimasa composed a variation on Nōin's poem that also linked the Shirakawa Barrier with bright autumn leaves: "In the capital the leaves were still green when I saw them, but bright autumn leaves now scatter at the Shirakawa Barrier." Now Bashō follows the traces of Saigyō, Yorimasa, and others who had earlier sought the traces of Nōin, who in turn had followed the traces of Kanemori.

2. This haiku, which Bashō composed in the summer of 1689 and later placed in *Narrow Road*, is a greeting to his friend and host Tōkyō (1638–1715), a station master at Sukagawa, at the entrance to the Deep North (*oku*), the northeast region. Hearing the rice-planting songs in the fields (probably owned by Tōkyō), Bashō composes a poem that compliments the host on the elegance of his home and region. The poem also expresses Bashō's joy and gratitude at being able to compose linked verse for the first time in the Interior.

this mountain, but the villagers, angered by the visitors who had been tearing up the barley grass to test the rock, pushed it down into the valley, where it lies face down." Perhaps that was the way it had to be.

sanae toru	Planting rice seedlings
temoto ya mukashi	the hands—in the distant past pressing
shinobuzuri	the grass of longing[3]

* * *

The Courtyard Inscribed-Stone was in Taga Castle in the Village of Ichikawa. More than six feet tall and about three feet wide; the moss had eaten away the rock, and the letters were faint. On the memorial, which listed the number of miles to the four borders of the province: "This castle was built in 724 by Lord Ōno Azumabito, the Provincial Governor and General of the Barbarian-Subduing Headquarters. In 762, on the first of the Twelfth Month, it was rebuilt by the Councillor and Military Commander of the Eastern Seaboard, Lord Emi Asakari." The memorial belonged to the era of the sovereign Shōmu.[4] Famous places in poetry have been collected and preserved; but mountains crumble, rivers shift, roads change, rock are buried in dirt; trees age, saplings replace them; times change, generations come and go. But here, without a doubt, was a memorial of a thousand years: I was peering into the heart of the ancients. The virtues of travel, the joys of life, forgetting the weariness of travel, I shed only tears. * * *

It was already close to noon when we borrowed a boat and crossed over to Matsushima. The distance was more than two leagues, and we landed on the shore of Ojima. It has been said many times, but Matsushima is the most beautiful place in all of Japan. First of all, it can hold its head up to Dongting Lake or West Lake. Letting in the sea from the southeast, it fills the bay, three leagues wide, with the tide of Zhejiang. Matsushima has gathered countless islands: the high ones point their fingers to heaven; those lying down crawl over the waves. Some are piled two deep; some, three deep. To the left, the islands are separated from one another; to the right, they are linked. Some seem to be carrying islands on their backs; others, to be embracing them like a person caressing a child. The green of the pine is dark and dense, the branches and leaves bent by the salty sea breeze—as if they were deliberately twisted. A soft, tranquil landscape, like a beautiful lady powdering her face. Did the god of the mountain create this long ago, in the age of the gods? Is this the work of the Creator? What words to describe this?

The rocky shore of Ojima extended out from the coast and became an island protruding in the sea. Here were the remains of Priest Ungo's dwelling and the rock on which he meditated. Again, one could see, scattered widely in the shadow of the pines, people who had turned their backs on the world. They lived quietly in grass huts, the smoke from burning rice ears and pinecones rising from the huts. I didn't know what kind of people they were, but I was drawn to them, and when I approached, the moon was reflected on the sea, and the scenery changed

3. Shinobu was the most famous *utamakura,* or poetic place, in the Deep North. Women there would rub ferns onto woven cloth so as to create a wild pattern or design, which became associated with uncontrolled longing. The traveler in *Narrow Road* is disappointed to discover that an *utamakura* that had given birth to countless poems has been neglected and abused, but the powerful memory of that poetic place enables the poet to find new poetry in the mundane, as Bashō sees the women's hands planting seedlings instead of rubbing the famous ferns.

4. Emperor Shōmu, r. 724–748. In actuality, Shōmu wasn't alive at the time of this memorial.

again, different from the afternoon landscape. When we returned to the shore and took lodgings, I opened the window. It was a two-story building, and I felt like a traveler sleeping amid the wind and the clouds: to a strange degree it was a good feeling.

Matsushima ya	Matsushima—
tsuru ni mi kare	borrow the body of a crane
hototogisu	cuckoo!!

[Sora]

I closed my mouth and tried to sleep but couldn't. When I left my old hermitage, Sodō had given me a Chinese poem on Matsushima, and Hara Anteki had sent me a waka on Matsugaurashima. Opening my knapsack, I made those poems my friends for the night. There also were hokku by Sanpū and Jokushi.

On the eleventh, made a pilgrimage to Zuiganji temple. Thirty-two generations ago, Makabe Heishirō took holy vows, went to China, returned, and founded this temple. Owing to his good works, the seven halls of the temple have been splendidly rebuilt, the gold-foiled walls and the grand decorations casting a light on everything. The temple, a realization of the land of the buddha in this world. Wondered where that temple of the famous Kenbutsu sage was.

On the twelfth we headed for Hiraizumi. We had heard of such places as the Pine at Anewa and the Thread-Broken Bridge, but there were few human traces, and finding it difficult to recognize the path normally used by the rabbit hunters and woodcutters, we ended up losing our way and came out at a harbor called Ishi no maki. Across the water we could see Kinkazan, the Golden Flower Mountain, where the "Blooming of the Golden Flower" poem had been composed as an offering to the emperor. Several hundred ferry boats gathered in the inlet; human dwellings fought for space on the shore; and the smoke from the ovens rose high. Never occurred to me I would come across such a prosperous place. Attempted to find a lodging, but no one gave us a place for the night. Finally, spent the night in an impoverished hovel and, at dawn, wandered off again onto an unknown road. Looking afar at Sode no watari, Obuchi no maki, Mano no kayahara, and other famous places, made our way over a dike that extended into the distance. Followed the edge of a lonely and narrow marsh, lodged for the night at a place called Toima and then arrived at Hiraizumi: a distance, I think, of more than twenty leagues.

The glory of three generations of Fujiwara vanished in the space of a dream; the remains of the Great Gate stood two miles in the distance. Hidehira's headquarters had turned into rice paddies and wild fields. Only Kinkeizan, Golden Fowl Hill, remained as it was. First, we climbed Takadachi, Castle-on-the Heights, from where we could see the Kitakami, a broad river that flowed from the south. The Koromo River rounded Izumi Castle, and at a point beneath Castle-on-the-Heights, it dropped into the broad river. The ancient ruins of Yasuhira and others, lying behind Koromo Barrier, appear to close off the southern entrance and guard against the Ainu barbarians. Selecting his loyal retainers, Yoshitsune fortified himself in the castle, but his glory quickly turned to grass. "The state is destroyed; rivers and hills remain. The city walls turn to spring; grasses and trees are green." With these lines from Du Fu in my head, I lay down my bamboo hat, letting the time and tears flow.

natsugusa ya	Summer grasses—
tsuwamonodomo ga	the traces of dreams
yume no ato	of ancient warriors[5]

unohana ni	In the deutzia
Kanefusa miyuru	Kanefusa appears
shiraga kana	white haired[6]

[Sora]

The two halls about which we had heard such wonderful things were open. The Sutra Hall held the statues of the three chieftains, and the Hall of Light contained the coffins of three generations, preserving three sacred images. The seven precious substances were scattered and lost; the doors of jewels, torn by the wind; the pillars of gold, rotted in the snow. The hall should have turned into a mound of empty, abandoned grass, but the four sides were enclosed, covering the roof with shingles, surviving the snow and rain. For a while, it became a memorial to a thousand years.

samidare no	Have the summer rains
furinokoshite	come and gone, sparing
hikaridō	the Hall of Light?

Gazing afar at the road that extended to the south, we stopped at the village of Iwade. We passed Ogurazaki and Mizu no ojima, and from Narugo Hot Springs we proceeded to Passing-Water Barrier and attempted to cross into Dewa Province. Since there were few travelers on this road, we were regarded with suspicion by the barrier guards, and it was only after considerable effort that we were able to cross the barrier. We climbed a large mountain, and since it had already grown dark, we caught sight of a house of a border guard and asked for lodging. For three days, the wind and rain were severe, forcing us to stay in the middle of a boring mountain.

nomi shirami	Fleas, lice—
uma no shito suru	a horse passes water
makuramoto	by my pillow

I visited a person named Seifū at Obanazawa. Though wealthy, he had the spirit of a recluse. Having traveled repeatedly to the capital, he understood the tribulations of travel and gave me shelter for a number of days. He eased the pain of the long journey.

5. The four successive heavy "o" syllables in *tsuwamonodomo* ("warriors") suggest the ponderous march of soldiers or the thunder of battle. This haiku depends on multiple meanings: *ato* can mean "site," "aftermath," "trace," or "track"; and *yume* can mean "dream," "ambition," or "glory." The traveler here takes on the aura of the traveling priest in a nō warrior play who visits the site of a former battlefield and then, as if in a dream, watches the ghost of the slain warrior reenact his most tragic moments on the battlefield. Through the reference to Tang Dynasty poet Du Fu's noted Chinese poem on the impermanence of civilization—"The state is destroyed, rivers and hills remain / The city walls turn to spring, grasses and trees are green"—Bashō transforms these classical associations of eroticism and fertility into those of battle and the larger theme of the ephemerality of human ambitions.

6. The white flowers of the deutzia, a kind of brier, appear in the midst of a field of summer grass, from which the figure of Kanefusa rises like a ghost. According to the *Record of Yoshitsune,* Kanefusa, Yoshitsune's loyal retainer, helped Yoshitsune's wife and children commit suicide; saw his master to his end; set fire to the fort at Takadachi; slew an enemy captain; and then leaped into the flames—a sense of frenzy captured in the image of the white hair.

suzushisa o	Taking coolness
waga yado ni shite	for my lodging
nemaru nari	I relax[7]

In Yamagata there was a mountain temple, the Ryūshakuji, founded by the high priest Jikaku, an especially pure and tranquil place. People had urged us to see this place at least once, so we backtracked from Obanazawa, a distance of about seven leagues. It was still light when we arrived. We borrowed a room at a temple at the mountain foot and climbed to the Buddha hall at the top. Boulders were piled on boulders; the pines and cypress had grown old; the soil and rocks were aged, covered with smooth moss. The doors to the temple buildings at the top were closed, not a sound to be heard. I followed the edge of the cliff, crawling over the boulders, and then prayed at the Buddhist hall. It was a stunning scene wrapped in quiet—I felt my spirit being purified.

shizukasa ya	Stillness—
iwa ni shimiiru	sinking deep into the rocks
semi no koe	cries of the cicada[8]

The Mogami River originates in the Deep North; its upper reaches are in Yamagata. As we descended, we encountered frightening rapids with names like Scattered Go Stones and Flying Eagle. The river skirts the north side of Mount Itajiki and then finally pours into the sea at Sakata. As I descended, passing through the dense foliage, I felt as if the mountains were covering the river on both sides. When filled with rice, these boats are apparently called "rice boats." Through the green leaves, I could see the falling waters of White-Thread Cascade. Sennindō, Hall of the Wizard, stood on the banks, directly facing the water. The river was swollen with rain, making the boat journey perilous.

samidare wo	Gathering the rains
atsumete hayashi	of the wet season—swift
Mogamigawa	the Mogami River[9]

Haguroyama, Gassan, and Yudono are called the Three Mountains of Dewa. At Haguroyama, Feather Black Mountain—which belongs to the Tōeizan Temple in Edo, in Musashi Province—the moon of Tendai concentration and contemplation shines, and the lamp of the Buddhist Law of instant enlightenment glows. The temple quarters stand side by side, and the ascetics devote themselves to their calling. The efficacy of the divine mountain, whose prosperity will last forever, fills people with awe and fear.

On the eighth, we climbed Gassan, Moon Mountain. With purification cords around our necks and white cloth wrapped around our heads, we were led up the mountain by a person called a "strongman." Surrounded by clouds and mist, we walked over ice and snow and climbed for twenty miles. Wondering if we had passed Cloud Barrier, beyond which the sun and moon move back and forth, I ran out of breath, my body

7. Bashō, exhausted from a difficult journey, finds Seifū's residence and hospitality to be "coolness" itself and "relaxes" (*nemaru*)—a word in the local dialect—as if he were at home. In an age without air conditioners, the word "cool" (*suzushisa*), a seasonal word for summer, was the ultimate compliment that could be paid to the host of a summer's lodging.

8. In classical poetry, the cicada was associated with its raucous, unpleasant cries. In a paradoxical twist, the sharp, high-pitched cries of the cicada deepen the stillness by penetrating the rocks on top of the mountain.

9. Here Bashō gives a new "poetic essence," based on personal experience, to the Mogami River, an *utamakura* (poetic place) long associated with rice-grain boats, which were thought to ply the river.

frozen. By the time we reached the top, the sun had set and the moon had come out. We spread bamboo grass on the ground and lay down, waiting for the dawn. When the sun emerged and the clouds cleared away, we descended to Yudono, Bathhouse Mountain.

On the side of the valley were the so-called Blacksmith Huts. Here blacksmiths collect divine water, purify their bodies and minds, forge swords admired by the world, and engrave them with "Moon Mountain." I hear that in China they harden swords in the sacred water at Dragon Spring, and I was reminded of the ancient story of Gan Jiang and Mo Ye, the two Chinese who crafted famous swords. The devotion of these masters to the art was extraordinary. Sitting down on a large rock for a short rest, I saw a cherry tree about three feet high, its buds half open. The tough spirit of the late-blooming cherry tree, buried beneath the accumulated snow, remembering the spring, moved me. It was as if I could smell the "plum blossom in the summer heat," and I remembered the pathos of the poem by Priest Gyōson.[1] Forbidden to speak of the details of this sacred mountain, I put down my brush.

When we returned to the temple quarters, at priest Egaku's behest, we wrote down verses about our pilgrimage to the Three Mountains.

suzushisa ya *hono mikazuki no* *Haguroyama*	Coolness— faintly a crescent moon over Feather Black Mountain[2]
kumo no mine *ikutsu kuzurete* *tsuki no yama*	Cloud peaks crumbling one after another— Moon Mountain[3]
katararenu *yudono ni nurasu* *tamoto kana*	Forbidden to speak— wetting my sleeves at Bathhouse Mountain![4]

Left Haguro and at the castle town of Tsurugaoka were welcomed by the samurai Nagayama Shigeyuki. Composed a round of haikai. Sakichi accompanied us this far. Boarded a boat and went down to the port of Sakata. Stayed at the house of a doctor named En'an Fugyoku.

1. "Plum blossoms in summer heat" is a Zen phrase for the unusual ability to achieve enlightenment. The plum tree blooms in early spring and generally never lasts until the summer. The poem by the priest Gyōson (1055–1135) is "think of us as feeling sympathy for each other! Mountain cherry blossoms! I know of no one beside you here."
2. Greetings to the spirit of the land often employed complex wordplay and associative words, which interweave the place-name into the physical description. Here the prefix *hono* (faintly or barely) and *mikazuki* (third-day moon) create a visual contrast between the thin light of the crescent moon and the blackness of the night, implied in the name Feather Black Mountain. The silver hook of the moon, which casts a thin ray of light through the darkness, brings a sense of "coolness" amid the summer heat, suggesting both the hospitality and the spiritual purity of the sacred mountain.
3. *Kumo no mine* (literally, cloud peak) is a high, cumulus cloud that results from intense moisture and heat. The mountain-shaped clouds, which have gathered during midday at the peak of Gassan, or Moon Mountain, crumble or collapse one after another until they are finally gone, leaving the moon shining over the mountain (*tsuki no yama*), a Japanese reading for "Gassan." Movement occurs from midday, when the clouds block the view, to night, when the mountain stands unobscured, and from mental obscurity to enlightenment.
4. In contrast to the first two mountains, which never appeared in classical poetry, Yudono (literally, Bathhouse) was often referred to in classical poetry as Koi-no-yama, Mountain of Love. The body of the Yudono deity was a huge red rock that spouted hot water and was said to resemble sexual organs. "Forbidden to speak" refers to the rule that all visitors to Yudono are forbidden to speak about the appearance of the mountain to others. The wetting of the sleeves echoes the erotic association with love and bathing and also suggests the speaker's tears of awe at the holiness of the mountain.

Atsumiyama ya	From Hot Springs Mountain
Fukuura kakete	to the Bay of Breezes,
yusuzumi	the evening cool

atsuki hi o	Pouring the hot day
umi ni iretari	into the sea—
Mogamigawa	Mogami River[5]

Having seen all the beautiful landscapes—rivers, mountains, seas, and coasts—I now prepared my heart for Kisagata. From the port at Sakata moving northeast, we crossed over a mountain, followed the rocky shore, and walked across the sand—all for a distance of ten miles. The sun was on the verge of setting when we arrived. The sea wind blew sand into the air; the rain turned everything to mist, hiding Chōkai Mountain. I groped in the darkness. Having heard that the landscape was exceptional in the rain, I decided that it must also be worth seeing after the rain, too, and squeezed into a fisherman's thatched hut to wait for the rain to pass.

By the next morning the skies had cleared, and with the morning sun shining brightly, we took a boat to Kisagata. Our first stop was Nōin Island, where we visited the place where Nōin had secluded himself for three years. We docked our boat on the far shore and visited the old cherry tree on which Saigyō had written the poem about "a fisherman's boat rowing over the flowers."[6] On the shore of the river was an imperial mausoleum, the gravestone of Empress Jingū. The temple was called Kanmanju Temple. I wondered why I had yet to hear of an imperial procession to this place.

We sat down in the front room of the temple and raised the blinds, taking in the entire landscape at one glance. To the south, Chōkai Mountain held up the heavens, its shadow reflected on the bay of Kisagata; to the west, the road came to an end at Muyamuya Barrier; and to the east, there was a dike. The road to Akita stretched into the distance. To the north was the sea, the waves pounding into the bay at Shiogoshi, Tide-Crossing. The face of the bay, about two and a half miles in width and length, resembled Matsushima but with a different mood. If Matsushima was like someone laughing, Kisagata resembled a resentful person filled with sorrow and loneliness. The land was as if in a state of anguish.

Kisagata ya	Kisagata—
ame ni Seishi ga	Xi Shi asleep in the rain
nebu no hana	flowers of the silk tree[7]

5. The first version was composed by Bashō at the residence of Terajima Hikosuke, a wealthy merchant at Sakata: "Coolness— / pouring into the sea, / Mogami River." The haiku praises the view from Hikosuke's house, which overlooks the great Mogami River where it flows into the Japan Sea. In the revised version, the Mogami River is pouring the *atsuki hi,* "hot sun" or "hot day," suggesting both a setting sun washed by the waves at sea and a hot summer's day coming to a dramatic close in the sea. Bashō drops the word "coolness" and the constraints of the greeting to his host to create a more dramatic image, one that suggests coolness without using the word.

6. The poem attributed to Saigyō is "The cherry trees at Kisakata are buried in waves—a fisherman's boat rowing over the flowers."

7. Kisagata was an *utamakura* (poetic place) associated, particularly as a result of the famous poem by Nōin (d. 1050), with wandering, the thatched huts of fisherfolk, lodgings, and a rocky shore. The traveler relives these classical associations, but in the end, he draws on Chinese poet Su Dongpo's "West Lake," which compares the noted lake to Xi Shi, a legendary Chinese beauty who was forced to debauch an enemy emperor and cause his defeat. She was thought to have a constant frown, her eyes half closed, as a result of her tragic fate. Dampened and shriveled by the rain, the silk tree flower echoes the resentful Chinese consort: both in turn became a metaphor for the rain-enshrouded, emotionally dark bay.

shiogoshi ya	In the shallows—
tsuru hagi nurete	cranes wetting their legs
umi suzushi	coolness of the sea[8]

Reluctant to leave Sakata, the days piled up; now I turn my gaze to the far-off clouds of the northern provinces. Thoughts of the distant road ahead fill me with anxiety; I hear it is more than 325 miles to the castle town in Kaga. After we crossed Nezu-no-seki, Mouse Barrier, we hurried toward Echigo and came to Ichiburi, in Etchū Province. During these nine days, I suffered from the extreme heat, fell ill, and did not record anything.

fumizuki ya	The Seventh Month—
muika mo tsune no	the sixth day, too, is different
yo ni wa nizu	from the usual night[9]
araumi ya	A wild sea—
Sado ni yokotau	stretching to Sado Isle
Amanogawa	the River of Heaven[1]

Today, exhausted from crossing the most dangerous places in the north country—places with names like Children Forget Parents, Parents Forget Children, Dogs Turn Back, Horses Sent Back—I drew up my pillow and lay down to sleep, only to hear in the adjoining room the voices of two young women. An elderly man joined in the conversation, and I gathered that they were women of pleasure from a place called Niigata in Echigo Province. They were on a pilgrimage to Ise Shrine, and the man was seeing them off as far as the barrier here at Ichiburi. They seemed to be writing letters and giving him other trivial messages to take back to Niigata tomorrow. Like "the daughters of the fishermen, passing their lives on the shore where the white waves roll in,"[2] they had fallen low in this world, exchanging vows with every passerby. What terrible lives they must have had in their previous existence for this to occur. I fell asleep as I listened to them talk. The next morning, they came up to us as we departed. "The difficulties of road, not knowing our destination, the uncertainty and sorrow—it makes us want to follow your tracks. We'll be inconspicuous. Please bless us with your robes of compassion, link us to the Buddha," they said tearfully.

"We sympathize with you, but we have many stops on the way. Just follow the others. The gods will make sure that no harm occurs to you." Shaking them off with these remarks, we left, but the pathos of their situation lingered with us.

hitotsu ya ni	Under the same roof
yūjo mo netari	women of pleasure also sleep—
hagi to tsuki	bush clover and moon[3]

I dictated this to Sora, who wrote it down.

8. Bashō here describes Kisagata after the rains, closing out a series of contrasts: between lightness and darkness, laughter and resentment, the dark brooding atmosphere of Kisagata during the rains and the cool, light atmosphere that follows.

9. The seventh night of the Seventh Month was when the legendary constellations, the Herd Boy and Weaver Girl, two separated lovers, cross over the Milky Way for their annual meeting. Even the night before is unusual.

1. Sado, an island across the water from Izumozaki (Izumo Point), was known for its long history of political exiles. Here the island, standing under the vast River of Heaven or Milky Way, comes to embody the feeling of loneliness, both of the exiles and of the traveler himself.

2. From the anonymous *Shinkokinshū* poem "Since I am the daughter of a fisherman, passing my life on the shore where the white waves roll in, I have no home."

3. The haiku suggests Bashō's surprise that two very different parties—the young prostitutes and the male priest-travelers—have something in common, implicitly the uncertainty of life and of travel. The bush clover (*hagi*), the object of love in classical poetry, suggests the prostitutes, while the moon, associated with enlightenment and clarity, may imply Bashō and his priest friend.

We visited Tada Shrine where Sanemori's helmet and a piece of his brocade robe were stored. They say that long ago when Sanemori belonged to the Genji clan, Lord Yoshitomo offered him the helmet. Indeed, it was not the armor of a common soldier. A chrysanthemum and vine carved design inlaid with gold extended from the visor to the ear flaps, and a two-horn frontpiece was attached to the dragon head. After Sanemori died in battle, Kiso Yoshinaka attached a prayer sheet to the helmet and offered it to the shrine. Higuchi Jirō had acted as Kiso's messenger. It was as if the past were appearing before my very eyes.

muzan ya na	"How pitiful!"
kabuto no shita no	beneath the warrior helmet
kirigirisu	cries of a cricket[4]

The sixteenth. The skies had cleared, and we decided to gather little red shells at Iro-no-hama, Color Beach, seven leagues across the water. A man named Ten'ya made elaborate preparations—lunch boxes, wine flasks, and the like—and ordered a number of servants to go with us on the boat. Enjoying a tailwind, we arrived quickly. The beach was dotted with a few fisherman's huts and a dilapidated Lotus Flower temple. We drank tea, warmed up saké, and were overwhelmed by the loneliness of the evening.

sabishisa ya	Loneliness—
Suma ni kachitaru	an autumn beach judged
hama no aki	superior to Suma's[5]
nami no ma ya	Between the waves—
kogai ni majiru	mixed with small shells
hagi no chiri	petals of bush clover

I had Tōsai write down the main events of that day and left it at the temple.

Rotsū came as far as the Tsuruga harbor to greet me, and together we went to Mino Province. With the aid of horses, we traveled to Ōgaki. Sora joined us from Ise. Etsujin galloped in on horseback, and we gathered at the house of Jokō. Zensenshi, Keiko, Keiko's sons, and other intimate acquaintances visited day and night. For them, it was like meeting someone who had returned from the dead. They were both overjoyed and sympathetic. Although I had not yet recovered from the weariness of the journey, we set off again on the sixth of the Ninth Month. Thinking to pay our respects to the great shrine at Ise, we boarded a boat.

hamaguri no	Autumn going—
futami ni wakare	parting for Futami
yuku aki zo	a clam pried from its shell[6]

4. In *The Tales of Heike*, Saitō Sanemori, not wanting other soldiers to realize his advanced age, dyed his white hair black and fought valiantly before being slain by the retainers of Kiso Yoshinaka (1154–1184). According to legend, Yoshinaka, who had been saved by Sanemori as a child, wept at seeing the washed head of the slain warrior and subsequently made an offering of the helmet and brocade to Tada Shrine. The cricket, a seasonal word for autumn, was associated in classical poetry with pathos and the loneliness that comes from inevitable decline.

5. Suma was closely associated with the poetry of Ariwara no Yukihira (d. 893), who was exiled to Suma, and the hero of *The Tale of Genji,* who was also exiled there, and so it was considered to be the embodiment of loneliness in the classical tradition.

6. Bashō's closing haiku turns on a series of puns: *wakaru* means both "to depart for" and "to tear from," and Futami refers to a noted place on the coast of Ise Province (the traveler's next destination and a place known for clams) as well as the shell (*futa*) and body (*mi*) of the clam (*hamaguri*). The phrase "autumn going" (*yuku aki*) directly echoes the phrase "spring going" (*yuku haru*) in the poem at the beginning of the narrative.

François-Marie Arouet [Voltaire]

1694–1778

Voltaire's life and writings embody the philosophy of the Enlightenment—yet his contemporaries in the Age of Reason forced him into a life of exile. Like his fellow *philosophes* Diderot and Rousseau, François-Marie Arouet was born into a middle-class family. Finding an entrée into aristocratic Parisian society—where wit sparkled, ideas were circulated, and connections were made—was therefore a challenge. The Arouets were engaged in farming and trade, but François's father had become a lawyer and minor government official in Paris, and his son was meant to follow in his footsteps. He received a Jesuit education—the best to be had—but soon thereafter abandoned the study of law, pursuing literary satire as a better way to get the attention of Parisian high society. When he was only twenty-two he began unleashing his satirical wit in anti-aristocratic verses and was exiled from Paris on suspicion of having written a satire against Philippe d'Orléans, Regent of France since the death the previous year of Louis XIV. The next year he did it again, and on this second offense the regent, ready to display some wit of his own, wagered that he could show the unruly author something he had never seen before. When young Arouet asked, "What is that?" he received the reply, "The inside of the Bastille." He spent nearly a year studying the interior of this famous dungeon for political prisoners. He was allowed to bring his books with him, however, to dine frequently with the prison governor, and to write his tragedy *Oedipe* there.

Upon his release in 1718, exiled again to the suburbs outside Paris, Arouet adopted the pen name Voltaire, staged the play he had written in prison, and upon its brilliant success received a gold medal and an annuity from the very Regent who had imprisoned him. In 1723 he cemented his literary reputation with the publication of a poem received as both a masterpiece and the first French national epic, *La Henriade,* a work on the theme of religious tolerance centered around Henri IV, the great Protestant king of the previous century. The same year Voltaire almost died of smallpox, a disease that ravaged Europe and the Americas; he claimed to have saved himself by drinking two hundred pints of lemonade. Over the next several years he added wealth to his new fame and social status by shrewd investments in the period's colonial exploitations. Yet in 1726, just at the moment when his speculations in the stock of the Compagnie des Indes were making him a rich man, Voltaire was forced to renew his acquaintance with the inside of the Bastille. The Chevalier de Rohan, insulted by Voltaire in return for having cast aspersions on the celebrated author's humble origins, retorted by ordering his footmen to beat up the young upstart as he watched from his carriage, and then had him thrown once more into prison. This time Voltaire was released only on condition of exile, not just from Paris but from France.

Far from teaching him to keep to his proper station, his time in prison made Voltaire realize that he would forever remain an outsider to French society, grounded as it was in inherited privilege and unquestioned authority. Having begun as something of a social climber, he became a leader in the great Enlightenment battle against *préjugé,* or "prejudice," in the original sense of that word: literally pre-judgment, the blind acceptance of received ideas without having subjected them to the judgment of reason. Like many other thinkers of the period, Voltaire devoted his career to the critique of traditional, received authority, whether intellectual, religious, or political, which culminated in the American and French revolutions toward the end of the century. He adopted the motto *Ecrasez l'infame!* (Crush infamy!) by which he meant the infamous injustices perpetrated in the name of organized religion—whether Roman Catholicism or Calvinist Protestantism—and of absolute power.

Voltaire spent his exile in London, where he found himself welcomed at all levels of society. The English had beheaded their king nearly a century earlier, and although the monarchy had been restored it clung to legitimacy through anxious attempts to square its authority with the principles of individual freedom from tyranny. By the eighteenth century England had an international reputation for religious and political liberty, and especially for freedom of speech. By contrast with France and many other European countries, this reputation was deserved. Voltaire saw literary men like Joseph Addison entrusted with political responsibilities, and Sir Isaac Newton honored for his scientific achievements in Westminster Abbey. He met John Locke, his predecessor among the foremost philosophers of political liberty and human reason, as well as Pope and Swift, who preceded him as the most important satirists of the age. King George I, who had given Voltaire a gold medal and a watch on the success of *Oedipe,* also welcomed him to England.

Allowed to return to France after several years, Voltaire published his *Letters Concerning the English Nation* begun in exile. This book appeared first in England (1733) and the following year in a French version. This time his French publisher was thrown into the Bastille, the books condemned by the Parliament of Paris and burnt. Voltaire himself retreated to the château of the philosopher Madame du Châtelet at Cirey in Champagne, where he spent much of his time over the next fifteen years living in a ménage à trois with her and her husband. In the 1740s he gained the protection of the king's mistress, Madame de Pompadour, and was again received at court—even appointed Historiographer to the King (1745) and elected to the Académie Française (1746), as he had been to the Royal Society in London in 1743. Shortly after Madame du Châtelet's death in childbirth, Voltaire left France again in 1750 to accept an invitation to the court of Prussia's King Frederick the Great. Within a few years he had angered this king too, fleeing Prussia in 1753, but detained for a time in Germany by Frederick's soldiers on his way back to France. After his experiences at royal courts Voltaire bought two houses near the republic of Geneva during the later 1750s, Les Délices (1755) and later Ferney, just over the Swiss border in France (1759). There he held court himself, continuing to disseminate his revolutionary ideas. It was the custom for young men of the upper crust to crown their educations with the Grand Tour of Europe, and many visited Voltaire at Ferney to learn the new ideas of the Enlightenment firsthand from one of its most famous exponents.

Voltaire returned to Paris one last time in 1778 for the production of his final tragedy, *Irène*. He arrived to find himself celebrated by the entire capital; saw the opening of his play, met Benjamin Franklin, and addressed the Académie Française. All this overwhelmed the aged exile, who died shortly thereafter. Back at Ferney he had already made plans for his tomb to be placed half in and half out of the chapel he had built there and engraved with the dedication, "Deo erexit Voltaire" ("Voltaire erected [it] to God")—"a fine word between two great names," as he quipped. He was never to rest there, however, as neither transportation nor embalming were quite what they are now. The Archbishop of Paris refused him Christian burial, as it had been refused to Molière; Voltaire's body was disguised and smuggled under cover of darkness to be buried at an abbey outside the city limits. The itinerary of Voltaire's corpse reflects that of his life: at first seemingly exiled forever, in the end he was brought back to Paris in triumph—where his remains are still enshrined in the Pantheon, a neoclassical secular temple dedicated on its frieze AUX GRANDS HOMMES. Voltaire's status as the original "Great Man" is literally written in stone.

Candide, or Optimism: Translated from the German of Dr. Ralph Together with the Addenda which were found in the Doctor's packet when he died at Minden in the year of grace 1759 This is the full title readers found when they opened the first edition of *Candide* in 1759. Even though he at first denied authorship of the work, no one who read it had much trouble guessing that it was written by Voltaire, who was already well known for using pseudonyms. This was a strategy to protect himself while publishing his merciless satires exposing established religious and secular power structures—and even the thought of some of his fellow Enlightenment philosophers—as irrational and absurd. Like his other works, *Candide* champions the cause of reason and freedom against superstition, intolerance, and privilege. When he published *Candide* at the age of sixty-five, Voltaire was perhaps the most famous living author in Europe. He had already distinguished himself in all the most respected literary genres—tragedy, history, and epic—and was renowned also for his satires and philosophical works. In an encyclopedic age he had written a dictionary and contributed to Diderot's *Encyclopédie*. He had even previously invented the philosophical tale with *Zadig* (1748) and *Micromégas* (1750), perfecting this new genre in *Candide*. It was an immediate bestseller, reprinted about forty times during its first year and soon translated into several European languages.

The eighteenth century was fond of tales of simpleton protagonists whose misadventures expose the folly and vice of all they encounter and the absurdities of the philosophical systems they take to heart. Such, for example, are Sarah Fielding's *The Adventures of David Simple* and Henry Mackenzie's *The Man of Feeling*. The type goes back much further, however, the most famous example being Cervantes' *Don Quixote* (1605); even earlier, several of the tales in Boccaccio's *Decameron* relate the adventures of fools in order to poke fun at the corrupt clergy who take advantage of them. Voltaire also mocks the church, but like other eighteenth-century writers, he used the device of the foolish protagonist to expose the dangers of contemporary philosophical systems. *Candide* attacks the widespread idealist system of philosophical optimism, which could be seen as justifying human suffering as a necessary part of a cosmic order beyond human ken, implicitly condoning a passive resistance to the effort required to prevent or alleviate suffering. The Resonances following *Candide* give famous expressions of such ideas by the philosopher G. W. von Leibniz, who argued that God has created "the best of all possible worlds," and the poet Alexander Pope, who roundly declared that "Whatever Is, is Right."

The age was also fond of romance, a genre of prose fiction going back to late antiquity, featuring amazing adventures, disguises, enslavements, escapes, and world-wanderings, and often winding up with miraculous reunions under the most unlikely circumstances. Probability is not necessary in a world ordered by Providence. In *Candide* Voltaire exposes the irrationality of this form of narrative, which was beginning to be challenged by the novel, an emerging form of fiction governed by standards of verisimilitude, or plausibility. By putting his tale in romance form, however, he is also taking advantage of its lingering popularity.

The parody of romance in *Candide* also helps Voltaire make a point shared by Cervantes and by the authors of many novels in their attack on romance: an emphasis on firsthand experience, rather than idealism, reading or instruction, as the ultimate means to truth. Romance was the product of an aesthetic that held that art should represent the world as it should be, rather than as it is. Everything Candide's teacher Dr. Pangloss tells him about the "best of all possible worlds" is belied by Candide's own experiences of the world he actually inhabits. This stress on individual experience and judgment as the only true path to knowledge characterizes the Enlightenment's more general challenge to received wisdom and authority, as well as its reliance on the senses, rather than the soul, as the way to truth: a vast shift that gave us, among other things, the scientific method. It also gave us one of the Western world's most enduringly delightful and instructive fictions.

PRONUNCIATIONS:

Abare: ah-BAHRH
François-Marie Arouet: frahnh-SWAH mah-REE ah-ROO-AY
Cacambo: kah-KAHM-boh
Candide: cahn-DEED
Madame du Châtelet: mah-DAHM deu SHAH-te-LAY
Cunégonde: keu-nay-GOND
Giroflée: zhee-roh-FLAY
Issachar: ee-sah-KAHR
Pangloss: PAN-gloss
Paquette: pah-KET
Pococurante: poh-koh-keu-RAHN-tay
Thunder-Ten-Tronckh: TUHN-dayr-ten-TROHNK

Candide, or Optimism[1]

Translated from the German of Dr. Ralph
Together with the addenda which were found in the Doctor's pocket when he died at Minden in the year of grace 1759

CHAPTER 1

How Candide was brought up in a beautiful castle, and how he was kicked out of the same

Once upon a time in Westphalia,[2] in the castle of Baron Thunder-ten-tronckh, there lived a young boy whom nature had endowed with the gentlest of dispositions. His soul was written upon his countenance. He was quite sound in his judgement, and he had the most straightforward of minds. It is for this reason, I believe, that he was called Candide. The older servants of the household suspected that he was the son of the Baron's sister by a kind and upright gentleman of the neighbourhood, a man whom this lady had consistently refused to marry because he had only ever been able to establish seventy-one heraldic quarterings,[3] the rest of his family tree having been destroyed by the ravages of time.

The Baron was one of the most powerful noblemen in Westphalia, for his castle had a door and windows. His great hall was even adorned with a tapestry. All the dogs in his farmyards would combine, when the need arose, to make up a pack of hounds: his grooms were his whippers-in, and the local vicar his great almoner.[4] They all called him "Your Lordship," and laughed at his jokes.

The Baroness, who weighed approximately 350 pounds, therefore enjoyed a large measure of public esteem; and she performed the honours of the house with a degree of dignified aplomb that rendered her all the more respectable. Her daughter Cunégonde,[5] being seventeen and of a high complexion, looked fresh, chubby, and toothsome. The Baron's son seemed in every way worthy of his father. Pangloss,[6] the tutor, was the oracle of the household, and little Candide would listen to his lessons with all the good faith of his age and character.

1. Translated by Roger Pearson.
2. Region of western Germany.
3. Each quartering or division of a coat of arms represented a separate line of noble ancestry.
4. Grooms care for horses, but here have to double as the beaters who scare small game animals and birds out of the underbrush during a hunt. A truly powerful nobleman would also maintain a separate servant to distribute his alms to the poor.
5. This name puns on the French and Latin words for female genitalia.
6. All tongues (Greek).

Pangloss taught metaphysico-theologico-cosmo-codology. He could prove wonderfully that there is no effect without cause and that, in this best of all possible worlds, His Lordship the Baron's castle was the most beautiful of castles and Madam the best of all possible baronesses.

"It is demonstrably true," he would say, "that things cannot be other than as they are. For, everything having been made for a purpose, everything is necessarily for the best purpose. Observe how noses were made to bear spectacles, and so we have spectacles. Legs are evidently devised to be clad in breeches, and breeches we have. Stones were formed in such a way that they can be hewn and made into castles, and so His Lordship has a very beautiful castle. The greatest baron in the province must be the best lodged. And since pigs were made to be eaten, we eat pork all the year round. Consequently, those who have argued that all is well have been talking nonsense. They should have said that all is for the best."

Candide would listen attentively, and innocently he would believe: for he found Miss Cunégonde extremely beautiful, though he had never made bold to tell her so. His conclusion was that, next to the happiness of being born Baron Thunder-ten-tronckh, the second degree of happiness was being Miss Cunégonde, the third was seeing her every day, and the fourth was listening to Maître Pangloss, the greatest philosopher in the province and therefore in the whole world.

One day, as Cunégonde was taking a stroll near the castle in the little wood they referred to as their "parkland," she caught a glimpse through the bushes of Dr. Pangloss giving a lesson in applied physiology to her mother's maid, a very pretty and very receptive little brunette. As Miss Cunégonde had quite a gift for science, she noted in breathless silence the repeated experiments to which she was witness. She saw clearly the doctor's sufficient reason, the effects and the causes, and returned home all agitated, her thoughts provoked, and filled with desire to be a scientist, musing that she might well be able to be young Candide's sufficient reason, just as he could well be hers.

She met Candide on her return to the castle and blushed. Candide blushed too. She greeted him in a choked voice, and Candide spoke to her without knowing what he was saying. The next day after dinner, as they were leaving the table, Cunégonde and Candide found themselves behind a screen. Cunégonde dropped her handkerchief, Candide picked it up. Innocently she took his hand, innocently the young man kissed the young lady's hand, and with quite singular vivacity, sensibility, and grace. Their mouths met, their eyes shone, their knees trembled, their hands strayed. Baron Thunder-ten-tronckh passed by the screen and, seeing this cause and this effect, chased Candide out of the castle with a number of hefty kicks up the backside. Cunégonde fainted. As soon as she recovered her senses, the Baroness slapped her. And all was consternation in the most beautiful and most agreeable of all possible castles.

Chapter 2

What became of Candide among the Bulgars

Candide, thus expelled from paradise on earth, walked on for a long time, not knowing where he was going, weeping, raising his eyes to heaven, and turning them often in the direction of the most beautiful of castles, which contained the most beautiful of barons' daughters. He went to sleep in the middle of the fields, supperless, in a furrow. The snow fell in large flakes. Next day, soaked to the skin, Candide dragged himself as far as the neighbouring town, which was called

Wald-berghoff-trarbk-dikdorff. He had no money, and he was dying of hunger and exhaustion. He stopped wistfully at the door of a small hostelry. Two men dressed in blue spotted him.

"Comrade," said one, "there's a fine figure of a young man, and he's the right height."

They went up to Candide and very civilly invited him to dine with them.

"Gentlemen," said Candide with charming modesty, "you do me great honour, but I have not the means to pay my corner."

"Oh, sir," replied one of the men in blue, "people of your looks and quality[7] never pay. Are you not five feet five inches tall?"

"Yes, gentlemen, that is my height," he said with a bow.

"Oh sir, come, do sit yourself down at the table. Not only will we pay for you, but we will not see a man such as yourself go short either. Man was made that he might help his fellow-man."

"You are right," said Candide. "That's what Mr. Pangloss always told me, and I can see that everything is for the best."

They pressed him to accept a few crowns. He took them and wanted to make out a receipt. It was not required. They all sat down at the table.

"Don't you love . . .?"

"Oh, yes," he replied. "I love Miss Cunégonde."

"No," said one of the gentlemen, "what we want to know is whether you love the King of the Bulgars[8] or not."

"Not in the least," he said, "for I have never met him."

"What! He is the most charming of kings and we must drink to his health."

"Oh, very willingly, gentlemen," and he drank.

"That will do nicely," he was told. "That makes you a supporter, a defender, a champion, nay a hero of the Bulgars. Your fortune is made and your glory assured."

His feet were promptly clapped in irons and he was taken off to the regiment. They made him do right turns, left turns, draw ramrods, replace ramrods, take aim, fire, quick march, and then they gave him thirty strokes of the birch. Next day he performed the drill a little less badly, and he received only twenty. The next day they gave him only ten, and his comrades thought him a prodigy.

Candide, totally bewildered, could not yet quite make out how he was a hero. One fine day in spring he took it into his head to go for a stroll, simply walking straight ahead, in the belief that it was the privilege of the human, as of the animal species to use its legs how it wanted. He had not gone two leagues when up came four other heroes, each six feet tall, who tied him up and carted him off to a dungeon. They asked him which, juridically speaking, he preferred: whether to run the gauntlet of the entire regiment thirty-six times, or to have twelve lead bullets shot through his brains at one go. It did no good his talking about the freedom of the individual and saying that, personally, he wished for neither: a choice had to be made. He resolved, by virtue of that gift of God called "freedom," to run the gauntlet thirty-six times. He managed two. The regiment numbered two thousand men. For him that meant four thousand birch strokes, which laid bare every muscle and sinew in his body from the nape of his neck right down to his butt. As they were preparing for his third run, Candide, quite done for, implored them to be so kind as to do him the favour of bashing his head in.

7. Social class.

8. An allusion to Frederick the Great, 1712–1786, King of Prussia.

This favour was granted. His eyes were bandaged, he was made to kneel. At that moment the King of the Bulgars passed by and inquired what crime the condemned man had committed. As this King was a great genius, he understood from everything that Candide told him that here was a young metaphysician much in ignorance of the ways of the world: and he pardoned him with a clemency that will be praised in every newspaper and in every century. A splendid surgeon cured Candide in three weeks with the emollients prescribed by Dioscorides.[9] He already had a little skin and could walk when the King of the Bulgars joined battle with the King of the Abars.[1]

CHAPTER 3

How Candide escaped from the Bulgars and what became of him

Never was there anything so fine, so dashing, so glittering, or so well-regulated as those two armies. The trumpets, the fifes, the oboes, the drums, and the cannon produced a harmony such as was never heard in hell. First the cannon felled about six thousand men on each side. Then the musketry removed from the best of all worlds nine or ten thousand ruffians who were polluting its surface. The bayonet, too, was the sufficient reason for the death of a few thousand. The sum total may well have come to about thirty thousand souls. Candide, who was trembling like a philosopher, hid himself as best he could during this heroic butchery.

At length, while the two Kings were having *Te Deums*[2] sung in their respective camps, he made up his mind to go and think about cause and effect elsewhere. He climbed over the heaps of dead and dying, and came first to a neighbouring village. It was in ashes. This was an Abar village which the Bulgars had burnt to the ground in accordance with international law. In one part, old men riddled with shot looked on as their wives lay dying, their throats slit, and clutching their children to blood-spattered breasts. In another, young girls lay disembowelled, having satisfied the natural urges of a hero or two, breathing their last; others, half burnt to death, cried out for someone to finish them off. Brains lay scattered on the ground beside severed arms and legs.

Candide fled as fast as he could to another village. It belonged to Bulgars, and Abar heroes had given it the same treatment. Candide, continually stepping over quivering limbs or through the midst of ruins, eventually left the battlefield behind, taking with him some few provisions in his bag and with Miss Cunégonde never far from his thoughts. His provisions had run out by the time he reached Holland but, having heard that the people there were all rich and all Christians, he had no doubt that he would be treated as well as he had been in the Baron's castle before he had been turned out on account of Miss Cunégonde's pretty eyes.

He begged alms of several solemn personages, who all replied that if he continued in this occupation, he would be locked up in a house of correction and taught how to earn a living.

He then spoke to a man who, all on his own, had just been addressing a large gathering for a whole hour on the subject of charity. This orator scowled at him and said.

"What are you doing here? Do you support the good cause?"

"There is no effect without a cause," replied Candide humbly. "Everything is connected in a chain of necessity, and has all been arranged for the best. It was

9. Famous ancient Greek doctor.

1. Likely a reference to the Seven Years' War, with the "Bulgars" and the "Abars" representing the Prussians and the French.

2. Hymns of thanks to God.

necessary that I should be separated from Miss Cunégonde and that I should run the gauntlet, and it is necessary that I should beg for my bread until such time as I can earn it. All this could not have been otherwise."

"My friend," said the orator, "do you believe that the Pope is the Antichrist?"

"I've never heard that before," replied Candide. "But whether he is or he isn't, I need bread."

"You don't deserve to eat it," said the other. "Be off with you, you rogue! Away with you, you miserable wretch! And don't you come near me ever again."

The orator's wife, having stuck her head out of the window and set eyes on a man who could doubt that the Pope was the Antichrist, poured a pot full of . . . over his head. Heavens! To what lengths the ladies do carry their religious zeal!

A man who had never been baptized, a worthy Anabaptist named Jacques,[3] saw the cruel and ignominious treatment being meted out in this way to one of his brothers, a living being with two feet, no feathers, and possessed of a soul.[4] He took him home with him, cleaned him up, gave him some bread and beer, presented him with two florins, and even wanted to train him for work in his factories, which produced that "Persian" material[5] that is made in Holland. Candide, almost prostrate before him, exclaimed:

"Maître Pangloss was quite right when he told me that everything in this world is for the best. For I am infinitely more touched by your extreme generosity than by the harshness of that gentleman with the black hat and his lady wife."

The next day, while out walking, he met a beggar all covered in sores. His eyes were glazed, the end of his nose was eaten away, his mouth was askew, his teeth black, and he spoke from the back of his throat. He was racked by a violent cough and spat out a tooth with every spasm.

Chapter 4

How Candide chanced upon his old philosophy tutor, Dr. Pangloss, and what came of it

Candide, again more moved by compassion than by disgust, gave this appalling beggar the two florins which he had received from his worthy Anabaptist, Jacques. The phantom stared at him, wept, and fell upon his neck. Candide, startled, recoiled.

"Alas!" said the one unfortunate to the other, "do you no longer recognize your dear Pangloss?"

"What do I hear? You? My dear tutor?! You in this dreadful state?! But what misfortune has befallen you? Why are you no longer in the most beautiful of castles? What has become of Miss Cunégonde, that pearl of a daughter, that masterpiece of nature?"

"I'm famished," said Pangloss.

Whereupon Candide took him to the Anabaptist's stable, where he gave him a little bread to eat and, when Pangloss had recovered, said:

"Well? What about Cunégonde?"

"She is dead," replied the other.

Candide fainted on hearing this. His friend brought him round with some old vinegar that was lying about in the stable. Candide opened his eyes.

3. Anabaptists, known for their peacefulness and charitability, rejected infant baptism.

4. Jacques follows Aristotle's definition of common humanity.

5. Silk.

"Cunégonde is dead! Ah, best of all worlds, where are you now? But what did she die of? It wouldn't have been at seeing me kicked out of her father's beautiful castle, would it?"

"No," said Pangloss. "She was eviscerated by Bulgar soldiers after they'd raped her as many times as anyone can be. They smashed the Baron's head in as he tried to protect her, the Baroness was hacked to pieces, my poor pupil received precisely the same treatment as his sister, and as for the castle, not one stone remains standing on another. Not a single barn, or sheep, or duck, or tree is left. But we had our revenge, for the Abars did exactly the same to the neighbouring barony of a Bulgar lord."

At this account Candide fainted again. But having recovered his senses and said everything one should say in such circumstances, he enquired as to the cause and the effect and the sufficient reason which had reduced Pangloss to such a woeful state.

"Alas," said the other, "the answer is love: love, the solace and comfort of the human race, the preserver of the universe, the soul of all sentient beings, tender love."

"Alas," said Candide, "I too have known it, this love of yours, this sovereign ruler of the heart, this soul of our soul. All the good it ever did me was one kiss and a score of kicks up the backside. How can this fine cause have had such an abominable effect on you?"

Pangloss replied in these terms:

"O my dear Candide! You knew Paquette, that pretty lady's maid to our noble Baroness. In her arms I tasted the delights of paradise, and in turn they have led me to these torments of hell by which you see me now devoured. She had the disease,[6] and may have died of it by now. Paquette was made a present of it by a very knowledgeable Franciscan who had traced it back to its source. For he had got it from an old countess, who had contracted it from a captain in the cavalry, who owed it to a marchioness, who had it from a page, who had caught it from a Jesuit, who, during his noviciate, had inherited it in a direct line from one of Christopher Columbus's shipmates. For my part I shall give it to no one, because I'm dying."

"O Pangloss!" cried Candide. "What a strange genealogy! Was it not the devil who began it?"

"Not at all," replied the great man. "It was an indispensable part of the best of all worlds, a necessary ingredient. For if Columbus, on an island in the Americas, had not caught this disease which poisons the spring of procreation, which often even prevents procreation, and which is evidently the opposite of what nature intended, we would have neither chocolate nor cochineal.[7] Moreover one must remember that up till now this disease has been unique to the inhabitants of our continent, like controversy. The Turks, the Indians, the Persians, the Chinese, the Siamese, the Japanese, they have all yet to know it. But there is sufficient reason for them to know it in their turn a few centuries hence. In the mean time it is making spectacular progress among our population, and especially among those great armies of fine, upstanding, well-bred mercenaries who decide the destiny of nations. One can be sure that when thirty thousand soldiers are fighting against a similar number in pitched battle, there are about twenty thousand cases of the pox on either side."

6. Syphilis.

7. A scarlet dye, imported, like chocolate, from the Americas.

"Well, isn't that extraordinary," said Candide. "But you must go and get treated."

"And how am I supposed to do that?" said Pangloss. "I haven't a penny, my friend, and in the whole wide world you can't so much as be bled or have an enema without paying for it, or without someone else paying for you."

These last remarks decided Candide. He went and threw himself at the feet of his charitable Anabaptist, Jacques, and painted such a poignant picture of the state to which his friend was reduced that the good fellow did not hesitate to take Dr. Pangloss under his roof: and he had him cured at his own expense. In the process Pangloss lost but one eye and one ear. He could write well and had a perfect grasp of arithmetic. Jacques the Anabaptist made him his bookkeeper. Two months later, having to go to Lisbon on business, he took his two philosophers with him on the ship. Pangloss explained to him how things could not be better. Jacques was not of this opinion.

"Men must surely have corrupted nature a little," he would say, "for they were not born wolves, and yet wolves they have become. God gave them neither twenty-four pounders nor bayonets, and they have made bayonets and twenty-four pounders in order to destroy each other. I could also mention bankruptcies, and the courts who seize the assets of bankrupts and cheat their creditors of them."

"That was all indispensable," was the one-eyed doctor's reply. "Individual misfortunes contribute to the general good with the result that the more individual misfortunes there are, the more all is well."

While he was presenting his argument, the air grew thick, the winds blew from the four corners of the earth, and the ship was assailed by the most terrible storm, within sight of the port of Lisbon.

Chapter 5

Storm, shipwreck, earthquake, and what became of Dr. Pangloss, Candide, and Jacques the Anabaptist

Half the passengers on board, weakened and near dead from those unimaginable spasms that the rolling of a ship can induce in every nerve and humour of the body by tossing them in opposite directions, did not even have the strength to worry about the danger. The other half shrieked and prayed. The sails were rent, the masts were smashed, the ship broke up. Work as they might, no one could make himself understood, and there was no one in charge. The Anabaptist was helping out with the rigging down on the decks. Furious, a sailor came up, gave him a good clout, and laid him flat on the boards. But the force of the blow jerked him so violently that he himself fell head first overboard and ended up suspended in mid-air, hanging from a piece of broken mast. Kind Jacques ran to his rescue, helped him back on board, and in the process was precipitated into the sea in full view of the sailor—who left him to perish without so much as a backward glance. Along came Candide, saw his benefactor momentarily reappear on the surface and then sink without trace, and wanted to jump in after him. Pangloss the philosopher prevented him, arguing that Lisbon harbour had been created expressly so that the Anabaptist would be drowned in it. While he was proving this a priori,[8] the ship foundered and everyone perished, except for Pangloss, Candide, and the brute of a sailor who had drowned the virtuous Anabaptist. The

8. By logic as opposed to experience.

blackguard swam safely to the very shore where Pangloss and Candide were also carried on a plank.

When they had recovered a little, they proceeded on foot towards Lisbon. They had some money left and hoped with this to escape hunger, just as they had survived the storm.

Scarcely had they set foot in the city, still weeping over the death of their benefactor, than they felt the earth quake beneath their feet. In the port a boiling sea rose up and smashed the ships lying at anchor. Whirlwinds of flame and ash covered the streets and public squares: houses disintegrated, roofs were upended upon foundations, and foundations crumbled.

Thirty thousand inhabitants of both sexes and all ages were crushed beneath the ruins. The sailor said with a whistle and an oath:

"There'll be some rich pickings here."

"What can be the sufficient reason for this phenomenon?" wondered Pangloss.

"The end of the world is come!" Candide shouted.

The sailor forthwith dashed into the midst of the rubble, braving death in search of money; he duly found some, grabbed it, got drunk and, having slept it off, bought the favours of the first willing girl he met among the remains of the ruined houses, among the dying and the dead.

Pangloss, however, took him aside:

"My friend," he said, "this is not right. You are in breach of universal reason, and this is hardly the moment."

"Hell's teeth!" replied the other. "I'm a sailor and I come from Batavia. Four times I've trampled on the crucifix, on four separate voyages to Japan.[9] You've picked the wrong man, you and your universal reason!"

One or two fragments of stone had injured Candide. He was lying in the street covered in rubble. He kept calling out to Pangloss:

"Help! Get me some wine and oil. I'm dying."

"This earthquake is nothing new," replied Pangloss. "The city of Lima felt the same tremors in America last year. Same causes, same effects. There must be a vein of sulphur running underground from Lima to Lisbon."[1]

"Nothing is more probable," said Candide, "but for God's sake get me some oil and wine."

"What do you mean, probable?" the philosopher retorted. "I maintain that the thing is proven."

Candide lost consciousness, and Pangloss brought him some water from a nearby fountain.

The next day, having located some food by crawling about among the rubble, they recovered their strength a little. Then they worked like everyone else at giving assistance to the inhabitants who had survived. One group of citizens they had helped gave them as good a dinner as was possible in such a disaster. It is true that the meal was a sad one, and the company wept over their bread; but Pangloss consoled them by assuring them that things could not be otherwise:

"For all this is the best there is. If the volcanic activity is in Lisbon, it means it could not have been anywhere else. For it is impossible for things not to be where they are. For all is well."

9. In the 18th century Dutch traders could enter Japan only after renouncing Christianity in this way.

1. Lima was destroyed by an earthquake in 1746, and Lisbon suffered a catastrophic earthquake in 1755.

A little man in black, an agent of the Inquisition,[2] was sitting next to him. He intervened politely and said:

"Apparently sir does not believe in original sin. For if everything is as well as can be, there has been neither Fall nor punishment."

"I most humbly beg Your Excellency's pardon," replied Pangloss even more politely, "but the Fall of man and the curse entered necessarily into the scheme of the best of all possible worlds."

"So sir does not believe in freedom?" said the agent.

"Your Excellency will forgive me," said Pangloss. "Freedom can exist alongside absolute necessity, for it was necessary for us to be free. For ultimately, the will once determined . . ."

Pangloss was in the middle of his sentence when the agent nodded to his henchman, who was pouring him some port, or rather Oporto, wine.

Chapter 6

How they had a splendid auto-da-fé[3] *to prevent earthquakes, and how Candide was flogged*

After the earthquake which had destroyed three quarters of Lisbon, the wise men of the country had not been able to come up with any more effective means of preventing total ruin than to give the people a splendid *auto-da-fé*. It was decided by the University of Coimbra that the spectacle of a few people being ceremonially burnt over a low flame is the infallible secret of preventing earthquakes.

Consequently they had arrested a man from Biscay who had been found guilty of marrying his fellow godparent, and two Portuguese who had removed the bacon when eating a chicken.[4] After dinner men came and tied up Dr. Pangloss and his disciple Candide, one for what he had said, and the other for having listened with an air of approval. Both were led away to separate apartments, which were extremely cool and where the sun was never troublesome. A week later they were both dressed in a *san-benito*,[5] and paper mitres were placed upon their heads. Candide's mitre and *san-benito* were painted with flames that were upside down and with devils which had neither claws nor tails, but Pangloss's devils had claws and tails, and his flames were the right way up. So dressed, they walked in procession and listened to a very moving sermon, followed by a beautiful recital of plainchant. Candide was flogged in time to the singing; the man from Biscay and the two men who had not wanted to eat bacon were burned; and Pangloss was hanged, despite the fact that this was not the custom. The very same day the earth quaked once more: the din was fearful.

Terrified, confounded, thoroughly distraught, all bleeding and trembling, Candide reflected to himself:

"If this is the best of all possible worlds, then what must the others be like? I wouldn't mind if I'd only been flogged. That happened with the Bulgars. But, o my dear Pangloss! You, the greatest of philosophers! Did I have to see you hanged without my knowing why?! O my dear Anabaptist! You, the best of men! Did you have to

2. The tribunal that violently persecuted persons accused of religious heresy.

3. "Act of faith," the public judgment (and often burning) of an accused authorized by the Inquisition.

4. Implying that they were Jewish; chickens were frequently covered with bacon strips to keep the meat moist while roasting.

5. A shirt worn by condemned heretics, usually with painted flames to indicate whether the heretic had confessed (upside down) or remained unrepentant (upright).

drown in the port?! O Miss Cunégonde! You pearl among daughters! Did you have to get your stomach slit open?!"

He was just leaving the scene afterwards, scarcely able to stand up, and having been preached at, flogged, absolved, and blessed, when an old woman came up to him and said:

"Take courage, my son, follow me."

Chapter 7

How an old woman took care of Candide, and how he was reunited with the one he loved

Candide did not take courage, but he did follow the old woman into a hovel. She gave him a pot of ointment to rub on himself, set things out for him to eat and drink, and indicated a small, moderately clean bed, beside which lay a full set of clothes.

"Eat, drink, and sleep," she said, "and may Our Lady of Atocha, His Eminence Saint Anthony of Padua, and His Eminence Saint James of Compostella[6] watch over you. I'll be back tomorrow."

Candide, still astonished at all he had seen and suffered, and even more astonished at the charity of the old woman, wanted to kiss her hand.

"It's not my hand you should be kissing. I'll be back tomorrow. Rub yourself with ointment, eat, and sleep."

Candide, despite so many misfortunes, ate and slept. The next day the old woman brought him breakfast, inspected his back, and rubbed a different ointment on it herself. Then she brought him dinner, and in the evening she returned with supper. The day after that she went through the same ritual again.

"Who are you?" Candide kept asking her. "What has made you so kind? How can I repay you?"

The good woman did not answer. She returned that evening bringing nothing for supper.

"Come with me," she said, "and not a word."

She took him by the arm and walked with him for about a quarter of a mile into the country. They arrived at a house standing on its own, surrounded by gardens and waterways. The old woman knocked at a little door. Someone opened it. She led Candide up a secret staircase into a small gilded room, left him sitting on a brocaded couch, shut the door after her, and departed. Candide thought he was dreaming; his whole life seemed to him like a bad dream, and the present moment a sweet one.

The old woman soon reappeared. She was supporting with some difficulty the trembling figure of a majestic-looking woman, all sparkling with jewels and hidden by a veil.

"Remove this veil," the old woman told Candide.

The young man drew near. With a timid hand he lifted the veil. What a moment! What a surprise! He thought he was looking at Miss Cunégonde. He was indeed looking at her, for it was she. His strength failed him, words failed him, and he fell at her feet. Cunégonde fell on the couch. The old woman showered them with various waters. They came to their senses. They spoke to each other. At first it was all half-finished

6. Patron saints of Portugal and Spain.

sentences, and questions and answers getting crossed, and sighs, and tears, and exclamations. The old woman suggested they make less noise and left them to it.

"What! It is you!" said Candide. "You're alive! To think that I should find you in Portugal! So you weren't raped? So you didn't have your stomach slit open as Pangloss the philosopher assured me you did?"

"I certainly was, and did," said the fair Cunégonde. "But those two particular misfortunes are not always fatal."

"But were your father and mother killed?"

"That is only too true," said Cunégonde tearfully.

"And your brother?"

"My brother was killed, too."

"And why are you in Portugal? And how did you know that I was here? And how on earth did you arrange to have me brought to this house?"

"I will tell you all these things," the young lady replied. "But first you must tell me all that has happened to you since that innocent kiss you gave me and those kicks you got."

With deep respect Candide obeyed her, and although he was at a loss for words, and his voice was weak and quavering, and his spine still hurt a little, he gave her the most artless account of all that had happened to him since the moment of their separation. Cunégonde raised her eyes to heaven, and she shed tears at the deaths of the good Anabaptist and Pangloss; after which she spoke in these terms to Candide, who missed not a word and devoured her with his eyes.

Chapter 8

Cunégonde's story

"I was in bed fast asleep when it pleased heaven to send the Bulgars into our beautiful castle of Thunder-ten-tronckh. They slit the throats of my father and brother, and hacked my mother to pieces. A great big Bulgar, six feet tall, seeing that I had passed out at the sight of all this, began to rape me. That brought me round. I came to, screamed, struggled, bit him, scratched him. I wanted to tear that big Bulgar's eyes out, little realizing that what was taking place in my father's castle was standard practice. The brute knifed me in the left side, and I still have the scar."

"Dear, oh dear! I hope I may see it," said the guileless Candide.

"You shall," said Cunégonde, "but let me continue."

"Go on," said Candide.

She took up the thread of her story thus:

"A Bulgar captain came into the room and saw me all covered in blood. The soldier didn't take any notice. The captain became angry at this lack of respect being shown him by the brute and killed him where he lay on top of me. Then he had me bandaged up and took me to his quarters as a prisoner of war. I used to wash what few shirts he had, and I cooked for him. He found me very pretty, I must admit, and I won't deny he was a good-looking man himself, with skin that was white and soft. Apart from that, not much brain, not much of a thinker. You could tell he hadn't been educated by Dr. Pangloss. Three months later, having lost all his money and grown tired of me, he sold me to a Jew called Don Issacar, who was a dealer in Holland and Portugal, and who was passionately fond of women. This Jew became much attached to my person, but he was unable to get the better of it. I resisted his advances more successfully than I had the Bulgar soldier's. A woman of honour may be raped once, but her virtue is all the stronger for it. In an attempt to win me over, the Jew brought me here to this country house. I had previously thought that there was nothing in the world as beautiful as the castle of Thunder-ten-tronckh. I have been disabused.

"The Grand Inquisitor noticed me one day during Mass. He kept eyeing me, and then sent word that he had to speak to me on a confidential matter. I was taken to his palace. I told him who I was. He pointed out how far beneath my station it was to belong to an Israelite. It was suggested on his behalf to Don Issacar that he should cede me to His Eminence. Don Issacar, who is the Court's banker and a man of some influence, would have none of it. The Inquisitor threatened him with an *auto-da-fé*. In the end, under intimidation, my Jew agreed to a deal whereby the house and I would belong to both of them jointly. The Jew would have Mondays, Wednesdays, and the sabbath, and the Inquisitor would have the other days of the week. This convention has been operating for six months now. It has not been without its quarrels, for it has often been a moot point which sabbath the period from Saturday night to Sunday morning belongs to, the Old Testament one or the New. For my own part I have resisted both men up till now, and I'm sure that's why they still love me.

"Anyway, in order to ward off the scourge of the earthquakes and to intimidate Don Issacar, it pleased my lord and master the Inquisitor to celebrate an *auto-da-fé*. He did me the honour of inviting me. I had a very good seat, and the ladies were served refreshments between the Mass and the execution. I was horrified, it must be said, to see those two Jews being burnt, as well as that nice man from Biscay who had married his fellow godparent. But how surprised, how shocked, how upset I was to see someone that looked like Pangloss in a *san-benito* and wearing a mitre! I rubbed my eyes, stared, saw him hanged, and fainted. I had hardly come to when I saw you standing there stark naked. That was my moment of greatest horror and consternation, the moment of greatest pain and despair. I can tell you truthfully, your skin is even fairer and more perfectly pink than my Bulgar captain's. The sight of it lent added force to all the feelings which were surging through me and devouring me. I screamed, I wanted to shout out: 'Stop, you animals!,' but nothing came out, and anyway my screaming and shouting would have done no good. 'How is it,' I said to myself, when you had been well and truly flogged, 'that nice Candide and wise Pangloss come to be in Lisbon, and that one of them gets a hundred lashes, and the other is hanged by order of His Eminence the Inquisitor, who in turn is in love with me? So Pangloss deceived me cruelly when he told me that all was well with the world.'

"Distressed, agitated, beside myself with anger one minute and ready to faint clean away the next, all I could think about was the massacre of my father and mother and brother, the insolence of my ugly Bulgar soldier, and the knife wound he gave me, my bondage, my menial work as a cook, my Bulgar captain, my ugly Don Issacar, my abominable Inquisitor, the hanging of Dr. Pangloss, that great *Miserere* they sang in plainchant while you were being flogged, and above all that kiss I gave you behind a screen the day I last saw you. I praised God for bringing you back to me after so many trials and tribulations. I instructed my old servant to tend to you and to bring you here as soon as she could. She has carried out my commission most capably. I have had the indescribable pleasure of seeing you again, of hearing you and speaking to you. You must have a terrible hunger, and I have a large appetite. Let's begin with supper."

With which they both sat down to eat. After supper they resumed their positions on the aforementioned beautiful couch. There they were when Señor Don Issacar, one of the masters of the house, arrived. It was the sabbath. He had come to enjoy his rights and press his suit.

Chapter 9

What became of Cunégonde, Candide, the Grand Inquisitor, and a Jew

This Issacar was the most irascible Hebrew in the tribe of Israel since the time of the Captivity in Babylon.[7]

"What!" he said, "you whore of Galilee! So Mr. Inquisitor isn't enough for you then? I've got to share you with this infidel too?"

With these words he drew a long dagger which he always carried with him and, not thinking his adversary would be armed, attacked Candide. But the old woman had given our good Westphalian a fine sword with his suit of clothes. Gentle though his disposition was, he drew his sword, and that was it: one Israelite stone dead on the floor at the feet of the fair Cunégonde.

"Holy Virgin!" cried she. "What is to become of us? A man killed in my house! If the police come, we're lost!"

"If Pangloss had not been hanged," said Candide, "he would have given us some good advice in this predicament, for he was a great philosopher. Since he's not here, let's ask the old woman."

She was a most prudent sort, and was just beginning to give her opinion when another little door opened. It was one hour after midnight: Sunday was beginning. This day belonged to His Eminence the Inquisitor. In he came to find Candide, who had been flogged, now standing sword in hand, with a corpse stretched out on the ground, Cunégonde in a fluster, and the old woman giving advice.

Here is what went through Candide's mind at that moment, and how he reasoned: "If this holy man calls for help, he will certainly have me burned. He may well do the same to Cunégonde. He has already had me mercilessly whipped. He is my rival. I've already started killing. There's nothing else for it."

This reasoning was clear and quick, and without giving the Inquisitor the time to recover from his surprise, he ran him through and hurled him down beside the Jew.

"Well, here's a fine mess," said Cunégonde. "There's no going back now. That's us excommunicated. Our last hour has come. How is it that someone as soft-hearted as you can have ended up killing a Jew and a prelate in a matter of minutes?"

"My dear girl," replied Candide, "when a man's in love, jealous, and flogged by the Inquisition, there's no knowing what he may do."

The old woman then broke in and said:

"There are three Andalusian horses in the stable, as well as saddles and bridles. Let brave Candide get them ready. Madam has moidores[8] and diamonds. Let us mount quickly—though my seat is but one buttock—and ride to Cadiz.[9] The weather is of the best, and it is always a great pleasure to travel in the cool of the night."

At once Candide saddled up the three horses. Cunégonde, the old woman, and he covered thirty miles without stopping. While they were making their escape, the Holy Hermandad[1] reached the house. They buried His Eminence in a beautiful church, and threw Issacar on to the rubbish-heap.

Candide, Cunégonde, and the old woman had by this time reached the small town of Avacena, in the middle of the Sierra Morena mountains, where they had the following conversation in an inn.

7. The period of Hebrew captivity in the 6th century B.C.E.

8. Portuguese coins.

9. Coastal town in southwestern Spain.

1. The "Holy Brotherhood," agents of the Inquisition.

Chapter 10

In what distress Candide, Cunégonde, and the old woman arrived in Cadiz, and of their embarkation

"But who can possibly have stolen my pistoles[2] and diamonds?" sobbed Cunégonde. "What will we live on? How shall we manage? Where will I find the Inquisitors and the Jews to replace them?"

"Alas!" said the old woman, "I have a strong suspicion it was that Franciscan monk who spent yesterday night in the same inn as us in Badajoz. God preserve me from jumping to conclusions, but he did come into our room twice and he did leave long before us."

"Oh dear!" said Candide. "Good Pangloss often used to argue that the fruits of the earth are common to all and that everyone has an equal right to them. According to his principles, that Franciscan ought to have left us enough money behind to finish our journey. Have you really not got anything left, my fair Cunégonde?"

"Not a maravedi,"[3] said she.

"What shall we do?" said Candide.

"Let's sell one of our horses," said the old woman. "I can ride behind Miss Cunégonde, even though I have only one buttock to sit on, and we'll make it to Cadiz."

There was a Benedictine prior staying in the same hostelry. He bought the horse cheaply. Candide, Cunégonde, and the old woman passed through Lucena, Chillas, and Lebrija, and came at last to Cadiz. There a fleet was being fitted out and troops were being mustered to go and knock some sense into the Jesuit reverend fathers in Paraguay, who were accused of having incited one of their local native hordes to revolt against the Kings of Spain and Portugal near the town of San Sacramento.[4] Candide, having served with the Bulgars, performed the Bulgar drill for the general of this little army with so much grace, speed, skill, agility, and panache that he was given command of a company of foot. So there he was a captain. He boarded ship with Miss Cunégonde, the old woman, two valets, and the two Andalusian horses which had belonged to the Grand Inquisitor of Portugal.

During the crossing they discussed poor Pangloss's philosophy a great deal.

"We're going to another world," Candide would say. "I expect it must be there that all is well. For you have to admit, one could grumble rather at what goes on in our one, both physically and morally."

"I love you with all my heart," Cunégonde would say, "but my soul is still in something of a state, what with all I've seen and been through."

"All will be well," was Candide's reply. "Already the sea in this new world is better than those we have in Europe. It's calmer, and the winds are more constant. It is assuredly the new world which is the best of all possible worlds."

"God willing!" said Cunégonde. "But I have been so horribly unfortunate in my own that my heart is almost closed to hope."

"*You're* complaining!" said the old woman. "Alas! You haven't had the misfortunes I have."

2. Spanish gold coins.
3. Spanish copper coin.
4. Jesuit missionaries who controlled Paraguay resisted Spain's attempt to transfer this territory to Portugal. Spain sent troops from Cadiz to crush the rebellion; Voltaire invested in this expedition as part owner of one of the ships.

Cunégonde almost burst out laughing and found it extremely droll of this little old woman to claim to be more unfortunate than she.

"I'm afraid, my good woman," she said to her, "that unless you have been raped by two Bulgars, stabbed twice in the stomach, had two of your castles demolished, seen two mothers' and two fathers' throats slit before your very eyes, and watched two of your lovers being flogged at an *auto-da-fé,* then I don't see you bettering me. Added to which, I was born a Baroness with seventy-two heraldic quarterings and yet I have been a cook."

"My young lady," replied the old woman, "you do not know who I am by birth, and if I were to show you my bottom, you would not speak as you do, and you would reserve judgement."

This declaration aroused the deepest curiosity in the minds of Cunégonde and Candide. The old woman had this to say to them.

CHAPTER 11

The old woman's story

"My eyes haven't always been bloodshot and red-rimmed, my nose hasn't always come down to my chin, and I haven't always been a servant. I am the daughter of Pope Urban X[5] and the Princess of Palestrina. Until the age of fourteen I was brought up in a palace, next to which not one of your German barons' castles would even have done as a stable. And any single one of my dresses was worth more than all the treasures of Westphalia put together. As I grew older, so I grew in beauty, grace, and fine accomplishments. I took pleasure in life; I commanded respect; I had prospects. I was already able to inspire love, and my breasts were forming. And what breasts they were! White and firm, just like those of the Medici Venus.[6] And what eyes! What eyelids! What black eyebrows! What fire burned in my pupils and outshone the sparkling of the stars, as the poets in that part of the world used to tell me. The women who dressed and undressed me would go into ecstasies when they saw me, back and front, and all the men would love to have changed places with them.

"I was engaged to be married to a sovereign prince of Massa-Carrara. What a prince! As handsome as I was beautiful, gentle and charming to a fault, brilliant in mind and ardent in love. I loved him as one does love for the first time, I worshipped him with passionate abandon. Arrangements were made for the wedding. The pomp and magnificence of it! No one had seen their like before. It was one continual round of entertainments, tournaments, opera buffa. And all Italy composed sonnets for me, though not one of them was any good. My moment of bliss was at hand when an old marchioness, who had been my prince's mistress, invited him to take chocolate with her. He died less than two hours later after appalling convulsions. But that was a trifle. My mother, being in despair and yet much less grief-stricken than I, wanted to absent herself for a time from so dreadful a scene. She had a very fine property near Gaeta.[7] We took ship on a local galley, which was all covered in gilt like the altar of Saint Peter's in Rome. What happens but a corsair from Salé[8] makes straight for us and boards us. Our soldiers defended themselves as if they were the Pope's own: they all knelt down, cast their weapons aside, and asked the corsair for absolution *in articulo mortis.*[9]

5. A fictional pope (the joke is that popes were of course expected to remain celibate).
6. A famous white marble sculpture.
7. A port in southern Italy.
8. A port in Morocco which was a center of piracy in the 18th century.
9. "At the point of death."

"At once they were stripped as naked as monkeys, as were my mother, and our ladies-in-waiting, and I also. It is a remarkable thing, the eagerness of these gentlemen to undress everybody. But what surprised me more was that they put a finger up all of us in a place where we women ordinarily allow only enema nozzles to enter. This ritual struck me as being most odd. But that's how one judges everything when one's never been abroad. I soon gathered that it was to see if we'd hadn't hidden any diamonds up there. It has been established practice among civilized seafaring nations since time immemorial. I discovered that those religious gentlemen, the Knights of Malta,[1] never fail to do it when they capture any Turks, men or women. It is one article of the law of nations which has never been infringed.

"I needn't tell you how hard it is for a young princess to be taken to Morocco as a slave with her mother. You can well imagine all we had to suffer on the pirate ship. My mother was still very beautiful. Our ladies-in-waiting, even our maids, had more charms than are to be found in the whole of Africa. As for me, I was ravishing. I was beauty, grace itself, and I was a virgin. I wasn't one for long. The flower which had been kept for the handsome prince of Massa-Carrara was ravished by the pirate captain. He was a loathsome Negro, who even thought he was doing me a great honour. Yes indeed, the Princess of Palestrina and I had to be extremely tough to survive everything we went through up until our arrival in Morocco. But enough of this. Such things are so commonplace they're not worth talking about.

"Morocco was bathed in blood when we arrived. The fifty sons of the Emperor Muley-Ismael each had his own followers, which in effect meant fifty civil wars—blacks against blacks, blacks against browns, browns against browns, mulattos against mulattos. It was one long bloodbath from one end of the empire to the other.

"We had scarcely disembarked when some blacks belonging to a faction opposed to that of my pirate appeared on the scene wanting to relieve him of his booty. After the diamonds and the gold, we were the most precious things he had. I was witness to a fight the like of which you in your European climates just never see. The Northern races are simply not hot-blooded enough. They don't have that thirst for women that they have in Africa. It's as if you Europeans had milk in your veins, whereas it is vitriol, fire, that flows in the veins of the inhabitants of Mount Atlas and that part of the world. They fought with the fury of the lions and tigers and serpents of their own country to decide which of them should have us. A Moor grabbed my mother by the right arm, my pirate's lieutenant held on to her left, a Moorish soldier took her by one leg, and one of our other pirates held her by the other. In an instant almost all our ladies-in-waiting found themselves being torn like this between four soldiers. My captain kept me hidden behind him. Scimitar in hand, he was killing anything that stood in the way of his own particular thirst. In the end I saw all our Italian women and my mother torn apart, cut to pieces, massacred by the monsters who were fighting over them. My fellow captives and their captors, soldiers, sailors, blacks, browns, whites, mulattos, and finally my captain, all were killed, and I lay dying on top of a pile of corpses. Similar scenes were taking place, as you know, over an area more than three hundred leagues across: and never once did they fail to say the five daily prayers ordered by Mahomet.

"I extricated myself with great difficulty from the piled heap of all these blood-soaked corpses, and dragged myself over to a tall orange-tree next to a nearby stream.

1. An old religious order active in the Crusades.

There I collapsed in shock, exhaustion, horror, hunger, and despair. Soon afterwards my shattered senses gave themselves up to a sleep that was more like unconsciousness than rest. I was in this enfeebled and insensible state, halfway between life and death, when I felt myself being pressed down on by something squirming on my body. I opened my eyes and saw a white man with a friendly face sighing and muttering between his teeth: '*O che sciagura d'essere senza coglioni!*'[2]

Chapter 12

The continuing story of the old woman's misfortunes

"Astonished and delighted to hear my native tongue, and no less surprised at the words the man was uttering, I replied that there were greater misfortunes than that of which he complained. I informed him in a few words of the horrors to which I had been subjected, and passed out. He carried me to a house nearby, had me put to bed and given something to eat, waited on me, comforted me, flattered me, told me that he had never seen anything so beautiful, and that never had he so much regretted the loss of that which no one could restore to him.

"'I was born in Naples,' he told me. 'They castrate two or three thousand children every year there. Some die, some develop a voice more beautiful than any woman's, and some go off and govern the Papal States.[3] They carried out this operation most successfully on me, and I sang in the chapel of the Princess of Palestrina.'

"'My mother!' cried I.

"'Your mother!' cried he, with tears in his eyes. 'What! Then you would be that young princess I taught till she was six, and who promised even then to be as beautiful as you are?'

"'I am she. My mother lies not four hundred yards from here, in four pieces, beneath a pile of corpses . . .'

"I told him everything that had happened to me. He told me his adventures too, and about how one of the Christian powers had sent him as an envoy to sign a treaty with the King of Morocco, whereby this monarch would be supplied with powder, cannon, and ships to assist him in putting an end to the trading of the other Christian powers.

"'My mission is complete,' the worthy eunuch told me. 'I am on my way to board ship at Ceuta, and I will take you back to Italy. *Ma che sciagura d'essere senza coglioni!*'

"I thanked him with tears of tender gratitude: instead of taking me to Italy, he took me to Algiers and sold me to the local dey.[4] Hardly had I been sold than the plague which was going round Africa, Asia, and Europe broke out with a vengeance in Algiers. You have seen earthquakes; but you, my young lady, have you ever had the plague?"

"Never," the Baron's daughter replied.

"If you had," the old woman went on, "you would agree that it comes well above an earthquake. It is extremely rife in Africa, and I caught it. Can you imagine? What a situation for the fifteen-year-old daughter of a pope to be in, and for one who in the

2. "O what calamity it is to lack testicles" (editions after 1759 usually abbreviated the last word); many Italian boys were castrated to give them a future as male sopranos.

3. In the 18th century Farinelli, a castrato, became a top adviser to the king of Spain. At this time, much of northern Italy was governed by the Pope and known as the Papal States.

4. A ruling official of the Ottoman Empire.

space of three months had suffered poverty and enslavement, been raped almost daily, seen her mother torn limb from limb, survived starvation and war, and was now dying of the plague in Algiers. Die, however, I did not. But my eunuch and the dey and almost the entire seraglio at Algiers perished.

"When the first wave of this appalling plague had passed, they sold the dey's slaves. A merchant bought me and took me to Tunis. He sold me to another merchant who in turn sold me in Tripoli. After Tripoli I was resold in Alexandria, after Alexandria I was resold in Smyrna, and after Smyrna in Constantinople. In the end I became the property of an aga in the janissaries,[5] who shortly afterwards received orders to go and defend Azov against the Russians, who were laying siege to it.[6]

"This aga, who was quite a ladies" man, took his whole seraglio with him, and housed us in a little fort on the Palus-Meotides under the guard of two black eunuchs and twenty soldiers. An enormous number of Russians were killed, but they gave as good as they got. Azov was put to fire and sword, and no quarter was given either as to sex or to age. All that was left was our little fort. The enemy determined to starve us out. The twenty janissaries had sworn not to surrender. The extremes of hunger to which they were reduced forced them to eat our two eunuchs, for fear of breaking their oath. After a few days they decided to eat the women.

"We had a very pious and very understanding imam,[7] who preached a fine sermon to them persuading them not to kill us outright.

"'Cut off one buttock from each of these ladies,' he said, 'and you will eat well. If you have to come back for more in a few days' time, you'll still be able to have the same again. Heaven will be grateful to you for such a charitable deed, and you will be saved.'

"He was very eloquent: he convinced them. They performed this dreadful operation on us. The imam rubbed on us the ointment they use on children who have just been circumcised. We were all at death's door.

"Hardly had the janissaries finished the meal with which we'd provided them than the Russians turn up in flat-bottomed boats. Not one janissary got away. The Russians paid not a blind bit of notice to the state we were in. There are French surgeons all over the world, and a very skilful one took charge of us and made us better. And I shall never forget how, once my wounds were well and truly healed, he then propositioned me. That apart, he told us all to cheer up and assured us that this sort of thing happened in lots of sieges, and that it was one of the laws of warfare.

"As soon as my companions could walk, they were sent to Moscow. I was part of a boyar's share of the spoils, and he put me to work in his garden and gave me twenty lashes a day. But after this nobleman was broken on the wheel two years later, along with thirty other boyars, because of some trouble or other at court, I took my chance and made my escape. I crossed the whole of Russia. For a long time I served in inns, first in Riga, then in Rostock, Wismar, Leipzig, Kassel, Utrecht, Leiden, The Hague, and Rotterdam. I grew old in poverty and dishonour, having but half a bottom, yet always mindful that I was the daughter of a pope. A hundred times I wanted to kill myself, but still I loved life. This ridiculous weakness for living is perhaps one of our most fatal tendencies. For can anything be sillier than to insist on carrying a burden one would continually much rather throw to the ground? Sillier than to feel disgust at

5. Turkish soldiers; an aga is a commanding officer.
6. In the 17th century the Russians invaded the sea of Azov, the northern arm of the Black Sea, which contained the islands of Palus-Meotides.
7. Leader of a mosque.

one's own existence and yet cling to it? Sillier, in short, than to clasp to our bosom the serpent that devours us until it has gnawed away our heart? In the countries through which it has been my fate to travel and in the inns where I have served, I have seen a huge number of people who felt abhorrence for their own lives. But I've seen only a dozen voluntarily put an end to their wretchedness: three Negroes, four Englishmen, four Genevans, and a German professor called Robeck.[8]

"In the end I finished up as one of the servants in the household of Don Issacar the Jew. He gave me to you, my fair young lady, as your maid. I have become involved in your destiny and been more concerned with your adventures than with my own. Indeed I would never have mentioned my misfortunes if you hadn't provoked me to it a little, and if it were not the custom on board ship to tell stories to pass the time. So there you are, Miss. I have lived, and I know the world. Just for fun, why not get each passenger to tell you the story of his life, and if there is one single one of them who hasn't often cursed the day he was born and hasn't often said to himself that he was the most unfortunate man alive, then you can throw me into the sea head first."

Chapter 13

How Candide was obliged to part from fair Cunégonde and the old woman

Fair Cunégonde, having heard the old woman's story, treated her with all the civilities due to a person of her rank and quality. She accepted her suggestion and got all the passengers one after another to tell her their adventures. Candide and she conceded that the old woman was right.

"It's a great pity," said Candide, "that wise Pangloss was hanged, contrary to the usual custom, during an *auto-da-fé*. He would have some remarkable things to tell us about the physical and moral evil that prevails over land and sea—and I would feel able to venture a few respectful objections."

While each person told his story, the ship continued on its way. They docked at Buenos Aires. Cunégonde, Captain Candide, and the old woman went to call on the Governor, Don Fernando d'Ibaraa y Figueora y Mascarenes y Lampourdos y Souza. This grandee had a pride to match his many names. He spoke to people with the most noble disdain, sticking his nose so far in the air, speaking in such a mercilessly loud voice, adopting so high and mighty a tone, and affecting so haughty a gait, that all who greeted him were also tempted to hit him. He loved women to distraction. Cunégonde seemed to him more beautiful than any he had ever seen. The first thing he did was to ask if she were not by any chance the Captain's wife. The air with which he put this question alarmed Candide. He did not dare say she was his wife, because in fact she was not. He did not dare say she was his sister, because she was not that either. And although this white lie had once been very fashionable among the Ancients,[9] and could still come in very useful to the Moderns, his soul was too pure to be unfaithful to the truth.

"Miss Cunégonde," he said, "is to do me the honour of marrying me, and we humbly beseech Your Excellency to condescend to officiate at our wedding."

With a twirl of his moustache Don Fernando d'Ibaraa y Figueora y Mascarenes y Lampourdos y Souza smiled a bitter smile, and ordered Captain Candide to go and review his company. Candide obeyed. The Governor remained with Miss Cunégonde.

8. Author of a book promoting suicide who drowned himself in 1739.

9. The patriarchs Abraham and Isaac passed off their wives as their sisters when in hostile territory (Genesis 12 and 26).

He declared his love for her and made protestations that on the morrow he would marry her, in the eyes of the Church or anyone else's, just as it might please her lovely self. Cunégonde asked him for a quarter of an hour in which to collect herself, consult with the old woman, and come to a decision.

The old woman said to Cunégonde:

"Miss, you have seventy-two quarterings, and not a penny to your name. You can be the wife of the greatest nobleman in South America, who also has a very fine moustache. Are you in any position to make a point of unswerving fidelity? You have been raped by the Bulgars. A Jew and an Inquisitor have enjoyed your favours. Misfortune does give people some rights. Frankly, if I were in your position, I would have no scruples about marrying the Governor and making Captain Candide's fortune for him."

While the old woman was speaking with all the prudence of age and experience, a small ship was seen entering the port. On board were an alcalde and some alguazils:[1] what had happened was this.

The old woman had quite rightly guessed that it had been the Cordelier[2] with the loose sleeves who had stolen the money and jewels from Cunégonde in the town of Badajoz, when she was making her rapid escape with Candide. This monk tried to sell some of the stones to a jeweller. The merchant recognized them as belonging to the Grand Inquisitor. The Franciscan, before being hanged, confessed that he had stolen them. He gave a description of the people concerned and the route they were taking. Cunégonde and Candide were already known to have escaped. They were followed to Cadiz. No time was lost in sending a ship after them, and this ship was already in the port of Buenos Aires. Rumour spread that an alcalde was about to come ashore, and that they were after the Grand Inquisitor's murderers. The prudent old woman saw at once what was to be done.

"You cannot run away," she told Cunégonde, "and you have nothing to fear. It wasn't you who killed His Eminence and, anyway, the Governor loves you and won't allow any harm to come to you. Stay here."

Whereupon she rushed off to Candide: "Quick, off you go," she said, "or in an hour you'll be burnt."

There was not a moment to lose. But how could he leave Cunégonde, and where was he to hide?

Chapter 14

How Candide and Cacambo were received by the Jesuits of Paraguay

Candide had brought a manservant with him from Cadiz of the kind frequently found along the coasts of Spain and in the colonies. He was a quarter Spanish, the son of a half-breed in the Tucuman.[3] He had been a choir-boy, sexton, sailor, monk, commercial agent, soldier, and lackey. His name was Cacambo, and he loved his master very much, because his master was a very good man. He saddled up the two Andalusian horses as quickly as he could.

"Come on, master, let's do as the old woman says and be off. Let's ride away, and no looking back."

Candide burst out crying.

1. A Spanish mayor and some officers.
2. A Franciscan friar who typically wore a loose habit as a sign of poverty.
3. Region in Argentina.

"O my darling Cunégonde! Must I abandon you just when the Governor was going to marry us! Cunégonde, what will become of you so far from home?"

"She'll become what she can," said Cacambo. "Women are never stuck. God sees to that. Let's go."

"Where are you taking me? Where are we going? What will we do without Cunégonde?" said Candide.

"By Saint James of Compostella," said Cacambo, "you were going to fight against the Jesuits. Let's go and fight for them instead. I know the roads well enough. I'll take you to their kingdom. They'll be delighted to have a captain who can do drill the Bulgar way. You'll be all the rage. If one doesn't get what one wants in one world, one can always get it in another. It's always a great pleasure to see new places and do different things."

"So you've already been to Paraguay then?" said Candide.

"I've been there all right!" said Cacambo. "I used to be a servant at the College of the Assumption, and I know los Padres' way of running things like I know the streets of Cadiz. It's a wonderful way of governing they have. Their kingdom is already more than three hundred leagues wide, and it's been divided into thirty provinces. Los Padres own everything in it, and the people nothing—a masterpiece of reason and justice. If you ask me, nothing could be more divine than los Padres making war on the Kings of Spain and Portugal over here and being confessors to the very same Kings back in Europe, or than killing Spaniards here and speeding them on their way to heaven back in Madrid. It appeals to me, that does. Come on, let's go. You're about to become the happiest man alive. How pleased los Padres are going to be when they discover there's a captain coming who knows the Bulgar drill!"

The moment they arrived at the first border post, Cacambo told the advance guard that a captain was asking to speak to His Eminence, the commanding officer. The main guard was notified. A Paraguayan officer made haste to go and kneel at the feet of the commanding officer and inform him of the news. Candide and Cacambo were first disarmed, and then their two Andalusian horses were taken from them. Both strangers were ushered between two lines of soldiers. The commanding officer was standing at the far end, with the three-cornered hat on his head, his cassock hitched up, a sword at his side, and a halberd in his hand. He made a sign. Instantly twenty-four soldiers surrounded the two newcomers. A sergeant told them they must wait, that the commanding officer could not speak to them, that the Reverend Father Provincial did not permit Spaniards to open their mouths unless he was present, or to remain in the country for more than three hours.

"And where is the Reverend Father Provincial?" asked Cacambo.

"He has said Mass, and now he's taking parade," replied the sergeant. "And you won't be able to kiss his spurs for another three hours yet."

"But," said Cacambo, "the Captain—who incidentally is dying of hunger, as indeed I am—isn't Spanish. He's German. Couldn't we have lunch while we wait for His Reverence?"

With this the sergeant went off to tell the commanding officer what had been said.

"May God be praised!" said this reverend gentleman. "Since he's German, I can speak to him. Show him to my arbour."

At once Candide was led into a closet of greenery, embellished with a very pretty colonnade of green and gold marble, and trellis-work containing parrots, colibris, humming-birds, guinea-fowl, and all manner of rare birds. An excellent lunch had been laid out in vessels of gold, and while the Paraguayans ate maize from wooden bowls out in the open in the full glare of the sun, the reverend father-in-command entered the arbour.

He was a very handsome young man, rather pale-skinned, with a round, ruddy face, arched eyebrows, a keen gaze, red ears, vermilion lips, and a proud demeanour—though proud in a way quite unlike a Spaniard or a Jesuit. Candide and Cacambo were given back the weapons which had been taken from them, as well as their two Andalusian horses. Cacambo gave the latter their oats near the arbour and kept a watchful eye on them in case of surprise.

First Candide kissed the hem of the commanding officer's cassock, and then they all sat down to table.

"So you're German, you say?" said the Jesuit in that language.

"Yes, reverend father," said Candide.

As they uttered these words, they looked at each other in absolute astonishment and with a degree of emotion which it was beyond them to control.

"And from which part of Germany do you come?" said the Jesuit.

"From the filthy province of Westphalia," said Candide. "I was born in the castle of Thunder-ten-tronckh."

"Good heavens! It's not possible?" exclaimed the commanding officer.

"It's a miracle!" exclaimed Candide.

"Can it really be you?" said the commanding officer.

"It's impossible," said Candide.

They both fell back in amazement, and kissed each other, and wept buckets of tears.

"What! Can it really be you, reverend father? You, the brother of the fair Cunégonde! You who were killed by the Bulgars! You the son of the Baron! You a Jesuit in Paraguay! The world really is a very strange place, I must say. O Pangloss! Pangloss! how pleased you would be now if you hadn't been hanged!"

The commanding officer dismissed the Negro slaves and the Paraguayans who were serving drinks in goblets of rock-crystal. He thanked God and Saint Ignatius[4] a thousand times, and he hugged Candide. Their faces were bathed in tears.

"You will be even more astonished, even more moved, even more beside yourself," said Candide, "when I tell you that Miss Cunégonde, your sister whom you thought disembowelled, is in the best of health."

"Where?"

"Not far from here, with the Governor of Buenos Aires. And I was coming over here to fight against you."

Each word they uttered in this long conversation piled wonder upon wonder. The soul of each took wing upon his tongue, paid careful heed with either ear, and sparkled in his eyes. Being Germans, they sat on at table for a long time; and while they waited for the Reverend Father Provincial, the commanding officer spoke thus to his dear Candide.

Chapter 15

How Candide killed the brother of his dear Cunégonde

"For as long as I live I shall always remember that dreadful day when I saw my father and mother killed and my sister raped. When the Bulgars had gone, my adorable sister was nowhere to be found, and my mother and father and I, together with two

4. Ignatius of Loyola (1491–1556), founder of the Jesuit order.

servant girls and three little boys who'd had their throats slit, were placed on a cart to be taken for burial at a Jesuit chapel two leagues from our ancestral home. A Jesuit threw some holy water over us. It was horribly salty. A few drops of it went in my eyes. The reverend father saw my eyelids quiver. He put his hand on my heart and felt it beating. I was saved, and three weeks later you wouldn't have known there'd been anything the matter. You know how good-looking I was, my dear Candide. I became even more so, with the result that the reverend father Croust,[5] who was Father Superior, developed the most tender affection for me. He initiated me as a novice. Some time later I was sent to Rome. The Father General had need of a batch of young German Jesuit recruits. The rulers of Paraguay admit as few Spanish Jesuits as they can. They prefer foreign ones in the belief that they can control them better. The Father General thought I was just the right sort of person to go and toil in this particular vineyard. So off we went, a Pole, a Tyrolean,[6] and myself. On arrival I had the honour of being made sub-deacon and lieutenant. Today I am colonel and priest. We shall give the King of Spain's troops a warm reception. They will be excommunicated and beaten, I can promise you. Providence has sent you here to help us. But is it really true that my dear sister Cunégonde is not far away, at the Governor's in Buenos Aires?"

Candide swore to him that nothing could be more true. Their tears began once more to flow.

The Baron could not desist from embracing Candide. He called him his brother, his saviour.

"Ah, my dear Candide," he said, "perhaps we can enter the city as victors, the two of us together, and rescue my dear sister Cunégonde."

"There's nothing I'd like better," said Candide, "for I was intending to marry her, and I still hope to."

"You insolent man!" retorted the Baron. "You would have the audacity to marry my sister who has seventy-two quarterings! I consider it great effrontery on your part to dare speak to me of so rash an intention!"

Candide's blood turned to stone at such a statement. He answered him: "Reverend father, all the quarterings in the world have nothing to do with it. I have rescued your sister from the arms of a Jew and an Inquisitor. She owes me a number of debts, and she intends to marry me. Maître Pangloss always told me that men are equal, and marry her I most assuredly will."

"We'll see about that, you scoundrel!" said the Jesuit Baron of Thunder-ten-tronckh and, so saying, struck him a heavy blow across the face with the flat of his sword.

Candide, quick as a flash, drew his own and plunged it up to the hilt into the Jesuit Baron's gut. But as he withdrew it, all steaming, he began to cry.

"Dear God," he said, "I've killed my former master, my friend, my brother-in-law. I am the best fellow in the world, and already that makes three men I've killed, and two of them priests!"

Cacambo, who had been standing guard at the door of the arbour, came running.

"There's nothing for it but to sell our lives dearly," his master said to him. "They're bound to come into the arbour, so we'll have to die fighting."

5. Name of a Jesuit who had helped drive Voltaire from Colmar in 1754.

6. Tyrol: Alpine region in present-day Austria and Italy.

Cacambo, who had seen a thing or two, kept his head. He removed the Baron's Jesuit cassock, put it on Candide, handed him the dead man's biretta,[7] and made him mount his horse. This was all done in a trice.

"Quickly, master, at the gallop. Everyone will take you for a Jesuit dashing off to give orders, and we'll have passed the frontier before they can give chase."

He was already riding like the wind when he said this, shouting out in Spanish: "Make way, make way for the reverend father colonel."

Chapter 16

What became of the two travellers with two girls, two monkeys, and the savages called the Lobeiros

Candide and his manservant were past the frontier, and still no one in the camp knew the German Jesuit was dead. The vigilant Cacambo had taken care to fill his bag with bread, chocolate, ham, fruit, and a quantity of wine. They rode their Andalusian horses deep into unknown country where they found no sign of a track. Eventually a beautiful stretch of grassland, criss-crossed with streams, opened up before them. Our two travellers halted to allow their mounts to graze. Cacambo suggested to his master that they eat something and duly set him an example.

"How do you expect me to eat ham," said Candide, "when I have killed the Baron's son and see myself doomed never to see fair Cunégonde again in my life? What's the use of prolonging my miserable existence if I must drag it out, far away from her, in remorse and despair? And what will the *Journal de Trévoux* say?"[8]

So saying, he did not abstain from eating. The sun was setting. The two lost travellers heard one or two faint cries which sounded as though they came from women. They could not tell if they were cries of joy or pain, but they quickly sprang to their feet, full of that apprehension and alarm which anything in a strange land can arouse. The clamour was emanating from two completely naked girls who were scampering along the edge of the meadow pursued by two monkeys who were nibbling at their bottoms. Candide was moved to pity. He had learnt to shoot with the Bulgars, and he could have downed a hazelnut in a thicket without so much as touching a single leaf. He raised his Spanish double-barrelled gun, fired, and killed the two monkeys.

"God be praised, my dear Cacambo! I have delivered those two poor creatures from great peril. If it was a sin to kill an Inquisitor and a Jesuit, I've certainly atoned for it by saving the lives of these two girls. Perhaps the two young ladies are well-to-do and this chance episode will prove to be of great advantage to us hereabouts."

He was about to continue, but he was struck dumb when he saw the two girls throw loving arms around the two monkeys, dissolve into tears over their dead bodies, and rend the air with wails of utmost grief.

"I didn't expect the kindness of their hearts to go that far," Candide said at last to Cacambo, who replied:

"A fine thing you've done there, master. You've just killed those two young ladies' lovers."

"Their lovers! Impossible! You're joking, Cacambo. How can they possibly be?"

7. Priest's square hat.

8. This was a Jesuit publication that had been critical of Voltaire.

"My dear master," continued Cacambo, "you're always surprised by everything. Why do you find it so strange that in some countries monkeys should enjoy the favours of the ladies? They're a quarter human, just as I am a quarter Spanish."

"Oh, dear!" replied Candide, "I remember now Maître Pangloss saying that such accidents did use to happen once upon a time, and that these couplings produced centaurs, fauns, and satyrs, and that several of the great names of antiquity had seen them. But I used to think that it only happened in fables."

"Well, you ought to be convinced now that it's true," said Cacambo. "You see how people behave when they haven't had a bit of education. All I hope is that these ladies don't cause us any trouble."

These solid reflections persuaded Candide to leave the meadow and plunge into a wood. There he supped with Cacambo and, having cursed the Inquisitor of Portugal, the Governor of Buenos Aires, and the Baron, they both fell asleep on some moss. When they awoke, they felt unable to move. The reason was that during the night the Lobeiros,[9] who inhabit that country, and to whom the two ladies had denounced them, had pinioned them with rope made of bark. They were surrounded by some fifty naked Lobeiros armed with arrows, cudgels, and hatchets made of flint. Some of them were warming a large cauldron, others were preparing skewers, and they were all chanting:

"It's a Jesuit! It's a Jesuit! We will be avenged, our stomachs will be full. Let's eat Jesuit! Let's eat Jesuit!"

"I told you so, my dear master," cried Cacambo sadly. "I told you those two girls would play us false."

Candide, seeing the cauldron and the skewers, exclaimed:

"We're going to be roasted or boiled, that's for certain. Ah! what would Maître Pangloss say if he could see how human nature is in its pure state? All is well. So it may be. But I must say it's pretty rotten to have lost Miss Cunégonde and be spit-roasted by Lobeiros."

Cacambo was not one to lose his head.

"Don't despair," he said to the disconsolate Candide. "I know these people's lingo a bit. I'll have a word with them."

"Make sure you point out to them," said Candide, "how frightfully inhuman it is to cook people, and how unchristian it is too."

"So, gentlemen," said Cacambo, "you think you're going to have Jesuit today. That's fine by me. Nothing could be fairer than to treat your enemies this way. The laws of nature do indeed tell us to kill our neighbour, and that is the way people behave throughout the world. If we ourselves do not exercise our right to eat our neighbour, that's because we've got better things to eat. But you haven't the same resources as we have. Certainly it is better to eat one's enemies than to leave the fruits of one's victory for the rooks and the crows. But, gentlemen, you would not want to eat your friends. You think you're about to skewer a Jesuit, while in fact it's your defender, the enemy of your enemies, that you'll be roasting. Me, I was born in these parts. This gentleman here is my master and, far from being a Jesuit, he has just killed a Jesuit and is wearing the spoils of combat. That's how you came to be mistaken. If you want to check the truth of what I say, take his cassock to the nearest frontier post of the kingdom of los Padres. Ask them if my master didn't kill a Jesuit officer. It

9. Tribe in Paraguay.

won't take you long, and you'll always be able to eat us anyway if you discover I've lied to you. But if I've told you the truth, you are too well acquainted with the principles, articles, and procedures of international law not to pardon us."

The Lobeiros found this speech very reasonable. They deputed two eminent persons to proceed post-haste to find out the truth. The two deputies carried out their commission like intelligent men and soon returned bearing good tidings. The Lobeiros untied their two prisoners, did them all kinds of honour, offered them girls, gave them refreshments, and escorted them back to the boundary of their lands merrily chanting: "He isn't a Jesuit, he isn't a Jesuit!"

Candide could not get over the manner of his deliverance.

"What a people!" he was saying. "What men! What manners! If I hadn't had the good fortune to run Miss Cunégonde's brother through with a hefty thrust of my sword, I would have been eaten, and without remission of sentence. But human nature in its pure state is good after all, since these people, instead of eating me, were all sweetness and light the minute they knew I wasn't a Jesuit."

CHAPTER 17

The arrival of Candide and his manservant in Eldorado,[1] *and what they saw there*

When they reached the Lobeiro frontier, Cacambo said to Candide:

"You see, this half of the world is no better than the other. Take my advice, let's head back to Europe by the shortest route possible."

"But how?" said Candide, "and where to? If I go back to my own country, I'll find the Bulgars and Abars busy cutting everyone's throats. If I return to Portugal, I'll be burnt at the stake. And if we stay here, we may end up on a spit at any moment. But how can I bring myself to leave the part of the world that contains Miss Cunégonde?"

"Let's make for Cayenne,"[2] said Cacambo. "We'll find the French there. They travel all over the place. They'll be able to help us. Perhaps God will have pity on us."

Getting to Cayenne was no simple matter. They knew roughly which direction to take, but what with mountains, rivers, precipices, brigands, and savages, terrible obstacles presented themselves at every turn. Their horses died of exhaustion, they ran out of provisions, and for a whole month they survived on wild fruits, before they eventually found themselves by a small river lined with coconut palms, which kept both them and their hopes alive.

Cacambo, whose advice was always as good as the old woman's had been, said to Candide:

"We've had it, we've walked as far as we can. I see an empty canoe on the bank. Let's fill it with coconuts, get in and let the current take us. A river always leads to some kind of habitation. If we don't find anything nice, at least we'll find something new,"

"All right," said Candide. "Let's trust in Providence."

They drifted downstream for a few leagues between riverbanks now covered in flowers, now bare of vegetation, now flat, now steep. The river grew wider and wider. At length it ran under a vault of fearsome-looking rocks that reached high into the

1. A rumored city of gold deep in the interior, sought by Sir Walter Raleigh and others. Voltaire's description draws heavily from Garcilaso de la Vega's *History of the Inca.*

2. The capital of French Guiana.

sky. The two travellers had the pluck to let the water carry them under this vault. The river, which narrowed at this point, swept them along with horrifying speed and made a terrifying din. Twenty-four hours later they saw the light of day once more, but their boat was dashed to pieces in the rapids. They had to drag themselves from rock to rock for a whole league. Eventually they came to a vast open space surrounded by impassable peaks. The land had been cultivated as much to give pleasure as to serve a need. Everywhere whatever was useful was also agreeable. The roads were covered, or rather adorned, with conveyances of the most lustrous form and substance, bearing men and women of singular beauty, and drawn at great speed by large red sheep who could outpace the finest horses in Andalusia, Tetuan, or Mequinez.[3]

"This, on the other hand," said Candide, "is something of an improvement on Westphalia."

He and Cacambo stepped ashore at the first village they came to. A few village children, covered in tattered gold brocade, were playing quoits[4] at the entrance to the settlement. Our two men from the other world stopped to watch them. Their quoits were fairly large round objects, some of them yellow, some red, some green, and they gleamed in an odd way. The travellers were prompted to pick some of them up. They were pieces of gold, emerald, and ruby, and the smallest of them would have been the greatest ornament on the Mogul's throne.

"No doubt," said Candide, "these children playing quoits are the sons of the King of this country."

The village schoolmaster appeared at that moment to call them back to the classroom.

"That," said Candide, "must be the royal family's private tutor."

The little urchins stopped their game at once, leaving their quoits and everything else they had been playing with lying on the ground. Candide picked them up, ran to the tutor, and humbly presented him with them, explaining in sign language that their Royal Highnesses had forgotten their gold and their precious stones. The village schoolmaster threw them on the ground with a smile, stared at Candide for a moment in great surprise, and walked off.

The travellers did not fail to gather up the gold, rubies, and emeralds.

"Where can we be?" exclaimed Candide. "The royal children here must be very well brought up if they're taught to turn their noses up at gold and precious stones."

Cacambo was just as surprised as Candide. At length they drew near to the first house in the village. It was built like a European palace. There was a crowd of people at the door, and an even bigger one inside. Some very pleasant music could be heard, and there was a mouth-watering smell of cooking. Cacambo went up to the door and heard Peruvian being spoken. This was his native tongue; for, as everyone knows, Cacambo was born in the Tucuman in a village where this was the only language they knew.

"I'll interpret for you," he told Candide. "Let's go inside. This is an inn."

At once two waiters and two waitresses, dressed in cloth of gold and wearing ribbons in their hair, showed them to a table and offered them the table d'hôte. The meal consisted of four different soups, each garnished with a couple of parrots, then a boiled condor weighing two hundred pounds, two excellent roast monkeys, one platter of three hundred colibris, and another of six hundred humming-birds, some exquisite casseroles, and delicious pastries. Everything was served on dishes made of a

3. These last two are towns in Morocco.

4. A game similar to ring toss.

kind of rock-crystal. The waiters and waitresses poured out a variety of liqueurs made from sugar-cane.

The guests were tradesmen and waggoners for the most part, all of them extremely polite. They asked Cacambo one or two questions with the most scrupulous discretion, and returned full answers to those he put to them.

When the meal was over, Cacambo thought, as Candide did, that he could more than cover the cost of their meal by tossing two of the large pieces of gold he had picked up on to the table. The landlord and his wife burst out laughing and held their sides for a long time. Finally they recovered themselves:

"Gentlemen," said the host, "we can see you're strangers. We're not used to them here. Forgive us if we started laughing when you offered to pay with the stones off our roads. Presumably you don't have any of the local currency, but you don't need any to dine here. All inns set up for the convenience of those engaged in commerce are paid for by the government. The meal wasn't very good here because this is a poor village, but anywhere else you'll get the kind of reception you deserve."

Cacambo interpreted for Candide all that the landlord had said, and Candide was as amazed and bewildered to hear it as Cacambo was to tell it.

"What is this place," said one to the other, "which is unknown to the rest of the world and where the whole nature of things is so different from ours? It's probably the place where all goes well, for there absolutely must be such a place. And whatever Maître Pangloss might have said, I often observed that everything went rather badly in Westphalia."

Chapter 18

What they saw in the land of Eldorado

Cacambo gave the landlord to understand how curious he was to know more. The landlord said:

"I know very little about things, and that suits me well enough. But we have an old man living in the village who used to be at court and who is the most knowledgeable man in the kingdom, as well as the most communicative."

Thereupon he took Cacambo to see the old man. Candide was playing second fiddle now, and it was he who accompanied his servant. They entered a house of a very modest sort, for its front door was only of silver and the panelling of its room merely gold, though the workmanship was in such good taste that more opulent panelling could not have outshone it. It has to be said that the antechamber was studded only with rubies and emeralds, but the pattern in which they had all been arranged more than made up for this extreme simplicity.

The old man received the two strangers on a sofa stuffed with colibri feathers and gave orders for them to be served various liquors in diamond goblets. After which he satisfied their curiosity in the following fashion:

"I am one hundred and seventy-two years old, and I learnt from my late father, who was a crown equerry,[5] of the extraordinary upheavals which he witnessed in Peru. This kingdom we are in now is the former homeland of the Incas, who most imprudently left it to go and conquer another part of the world and ended up being wiped out by the Spanish.

5. Master of the royal horses.

"The princes of their race who remained behind in their native country were wiser. They ordained, with the consent of the nation, that no inhabitant was ever to leave our little kingdom. And that's how we've managed to remain innocent and happy. The Spanish knew vaguely about the place and called it Eldorado, and an English knight called Raleigh even came fairly near it about a hundred years ago. But since we are surrounded by unclimbable rocks and cliffs, we have always hitherto been safe from the rapacity of European nations with their unaccountable fondness for the pebbles and dirt off our land, and who would kill us to the very last man just to lay their hands on the stuff."

Their conversation was a long one and touched on the form of government there, on local customs, on women, public entertainment, and the arts. Eventually Candide, ever one for metaphysics, asked through Cacambo if there was a religion in this country.

The old man flushed a little.

"But how could you suppose there might not be?" he said. "What do you take us for? Ungrateful wretches?"

Cacambo humbly asked what the religion of Eldorado was. The old man flushed again.

"Can there be more than one religion?" he asked. "As far as I know, we have the same religion as everyone else. We worship God from dusk till dawn."

"Do you worship only one God?" asked Cacambo, who was still acting as interpreter to the doubting Candide.

"Obviously," said the old man. "There aren't two Gods, or three, or four. I must say people from your part of the world do ask some very strange questions."

Candide persisted in having further questions put to this genial old man. He wanted to know how they prayed to God in Eldorado.

"We don't pray to God," said the good and worthy sage. "We have nothing to ask him for. He has given us all we need, and we never cease to thank him."

Candide was curious to see the priests. He had Cacambo ask where they were. The kindly old man smiled.

"My friends," he said, "we are all priests. The King and the head of each family sing hymns of thanksgiving solemnly every morning, to the accompaniment of five or six thousand musicians."

"What! You mean you don't have any monks to teach and dispute and govern and intrigue and burn people to death who don't agree with them?"

"We'd be mad to," said the old man. "We're all of like mind here, and we can't see the point of your monks."

Each of these remarks left Candide in raptures, and he kept thinking to himself: "This is all rather different from Westphalia and His Lordship's castle. If our friend Pangloss had seen Eldorado, he would no longer have said that the castle of Thunder-ten-tronckh was the best place on earth. It just goes to show: travel's the thing."

After this long conversation the kind old man had six sheep harnessed to a carriage and lent the two travellers twelve of his servants to take them to the court.

"Forgive me," he said to them, "if my advancing years deprive me of the honour of accompanying you. You will not be dissatisfied with the way the King receives you, and I am sure you will be tolerant of our customs if any are not to your liking."

Candide and Cacambo stepped into the carriage. The six sheep went like the wind, and in less than four hours they had arrived at the palace of the King, situated at one end of the capital. The main entrance was two hundred and twenty feet high and one hundred wide. There are no words to describe what it was made of, which in itself gives some idea of just how prodigiously superior it was to the sand and pebbles we call "gold" and "precious stones."

Twenty beautiful guardswomen received Candide and Cacambo upon arrival, escorted them to the baths, and dressed them in robes of humming-bird down, after which the Grand Officers and the Grand Dames of the Crown led them to His Majesty's apartments between two lines of musicians each a thousand strong, in accordance with normal protocol. As they approached the throne-room, Cacambo asked one of the Grand Officers what to do when being presented to His Majesty. Should one fall on one's knees or flat on the ground; should one put one's hands on one's head or over one's backside; should one lick the dust off the floor? In a word, what was the done thing?

"It is customary," said the Grand Officer, "to embrace the King and kiss him on both cheeks."

Candide and Cacambo fell upon His Majesty's neck. He welcomed them with all imaginable graciousness and politely asked them to supper.

Before then they were shown round the city, with its public buildings raised (and praised) to the skies, its market-places decorated with a thousand columns, its fountains of spring-water and rose-water and sugar-cane liquors, all playing ceaselessly in the middle of large squares paved with special stones which gave off an aroma similar to that of clove and cinnamon. Candide asked to see the law courts. He was told there weren't any, and that there were never any cases to hear. He asked if there were any prisons, and he was told there weren't. What surprised him most and gave him the greatest pleasure was the Palace of Science, in which he saw a gallery two thousand feet long all full of instruments for the study of mathematics and physics.

Having seen about a thousandth part of the city in the course of the entire afternoon, they were then brought back to the King. Candide sat down to table next to His Majesty, his servant Cacambo, and several ladies. Never did anyone dine better, and never was anyone wittier at supper than His Majesty. Cacambo interpreted the King's 'bons mots'[6] for Candide, and even in translation they still seemed "bons." Of all the things that surprised Candide, this was not what surprised him the least.

They spent a month in this hospice. Candide never stopped saying to Cacambo: "It's true, my friend, and I'll say it again. The castle where I was born is nothing compared to this place. But still, Miss Cunégonde isn't here, and doubtless you have some sweetheart back in Europe. If we stay on here, we'll simply be the same as everyone else, whereas if we return to Europe with even a mere dozen sheep loaded up with Eldorado pebbles, then we'll be richer than all the kings put together, we'll have no more inquisitors to worry about, and we'll easily be able to get Miss Cunégonde back."

Cacambo liked what he heard. Such is the desire to be always on the move, to be somebody, and to show off about what you've seen on your travels, that the two happy men resolved to be happy no longer and to ask leave of His Majesty to depart.

"You're making a great mistake," the King told them. "I know my country isn't up to much, but when one is reasonably content in a place, one ought to stay there. But I certainly have no right to stop strangers from leaving. That is a piece of tyranny which has no part in our customs or our laws. All men are free. Leave when you wish, though getting out is difficult. It is impossible to return up the rapids which, by a

6. Witty remarks.

miracle, you managed to come down: the river runs under vault after vault of rock. The mountains which surround my kingdom are ten thousand feet high and as sheer as a city wall. Each one is about ten leagues thick, and the only way down the other side is one long cliff-face. However, since you are absolutely determined to leave, I shall give orders for the machine intendants to make one which will transport you in comfort. When they've got you to the other side of the mountains, no one will be able to accompany you any further, for my subjects have vowed never to set foot outside these boundaries, and they are too sensible to break their vow. Apart from that you can ask me for whatever you want."

"All we ask of Your Majesty," said Cacambo, "is a few sheep laden with provisions and pebbles and some of the local dirt."

The King laughed.

"I really don't understand this passion you Europeans have for our yellow dirt," said the King, "but take all you want, and much good may it do you."

He immediately ordered his engineers to make a machine to windlass these two extraordinary men out of his kingdom. Three thousand of the best scientists worked on it. It was ready in a fortnight and cost no more than the equivalent of twenty thousand pounds sterling in local currency. Candide and Cacambo were installed on the machine, together with two large red sheep saddled up for them to ride when they had crossed the mountains, twenty pack-sheep laden with provisions, thirty carrying a selection of the best local curios and gifts the country could offer, and fifty loaded up with gold, diamonds, and other precious stones. The King embraced the two wanderers and bid them a fond farewell.

They presented quite a sight as they departed, as did the ingenious way in which they were hoisted, men and sheep together, to the top of the mountains. The scientists took their leave of them once they were safely across, and Candide was left with no other desire or object but to go and present Miss Cunégonde with his sheep.

"We have the wherewithal to pay the Governor of Buenos Aires now," he said, "if a price can be put on Miss Cunégonde, that is. Let's head for Cayenne and take ship there, and then we'll see what kingdom we're going to buy."

Chapter 19

What happened to them in Surinam and how Candide met Martin

For our two travellers the first day's journey passed pleasantly enough. They were spurred on by the prospect of themselves as owners of more treasures than Asia, Europe, and Africa can muster between them. Candide, quite carried away, carved the name of Cunégonde on trees as he passed. On the second day, two of their sheep became bogged down in a swamp and were swallowed up with their entire load. A few days afterwards two more sheep died of exhaustion. Seven or eight then starved to death in a desert. Others fell down some mountain-sides a day or two later. In the end, after a hundred days of journeying, they had only two sheep left.

Said Candide to Cacambo:

"My friend, you see how perishable are the riches of this world. The only sure thing is virtue and the happiness of seeing Miss Cunégonde again."

"I'm sure," said Cacambo. "But we do still have two sheep left and more treasure than the King of Spain will ever have, and in the distance I can see a town which, I suspect, is Surinam, where the Dutch are. Our troubles are over and the good times are just beginning."

As they drew near to the town, they came on a Negro lying on the ground half-naked, which in his case meant in half a pair of short denim breeches. The poor man was missing his left leg and his right hand.

"My God!" said Candide in Dutch, "what are you doing lying here, my friend, in this dreadful state?"

"I'm waiting for my master, Mr. Van der Hartbargin,[7] the well-known trader," replied the Negro.

"And is it Mr. Van der Hartbargin," said Candide, "who has treated you like this?"

"Yes, sir," said the Negro, "it is the custom. We are given one pair of short denim breeches twice a year, and that's all we have to wear. When we're working at the sugar-mill and catch our finger in the grinding-wheel, they cut off our hand. When we try to run away, they cut off a leg. I have been in both these situations. This is the price you pay for the sugar you eat in Europe. However, when my mother sold me for ten Patagonian crowns on the coast of Guinea, she said to me: 'My dear child, bless our fetishes,[8] worship them always, they will bring you a happy life. You have the honour of being a slave to our lords and masters the Whites and, by so being, you are making your father's and mother's fortune.' Alas! I don't know if I made their fortune, but they didn't make mine. Dogs, monkeys, parrots, they're all a thousand times less wretched than we are. The Dutch fetishes who converted me tell me every Sunday that we are all the sons of Adam, Whites and Blacks alike. I'm no genealogist, but if these preachers are right, we are all cousins born of first-cousins. Well, you will grant me that you can't treat a relative much worse than this."

"O Pangloss!" cried Candide, "this is one abomination you never thought of. That does it. I shall finally have to renounce your Optimism."

"What's Optimism?" asked Cacambo.

"I'm afraid to say," said Candide, "that it's a mania for insisting that all is well when things are going badly."

And he began to weep as he gazed at his Negro, and he entered Surinam in tears.

The first thing they enquired about was whether there were a ship in the port which could be sent to Buenos Aires. The person they approached happened to be a Spanish skipper, who offered to name them a fair price himself. He arranged to meet them in an inn. Candide and the faithful Cacambo went to wait for him there along with their two sheep.

Candide, whose heart was always on his lips, told the Spaniard all about his adventures and confessed that he wished to carry off Miss Cunégonde.

"I'm not taking you to Buenos Aires, that's for sure," said the skipper. "I'd be hanged, and so would you. The fair Cunégonde is His Excellency's favourite mistress."

This came as a bolt from the blue to Candide. He wept for a long time. Eventually he took Cacambo to one side:

"Look, my dear friend," he said to him, "this is what you must do. We've each got about five or six million in diamonds in our pockets. You're cleverer than I am. Go and fetch Miss Cunégonde from Buenos Aires. If the Governor makes difficulties about it, give him a million. If he won't budge, give him two. You haven't killed any

7. In the original French Voltaire has "Vanderdendur," thought to be a dig at a Dutch bookseller, Van Duren, who had driven a hard bargain with Voltaire over a manuscript.

8. Objects thought to possess magical protective power.

inquisitors, they won't be suspicious of you. I'll have another ship made ready. I'll go and wait for you in Venice. Theirs is a free country where one has nothing to fear from Bulgars or Abars or Jews or Inquisitors."

Cacambo applauded this wise decision. He was in despair at the thought of parting from so good a master, who had become his close friend. But the pleasure of being of use to him outweighed the pain of leaving him. They tearfully embraced each other. Candide told him to make sure and not forget the kind old woman. Cacambo left the same day. He was a very fine fellow, Cacambo.

Candide stayed some while longer in Surinam, waiting to find another skipper who would be prepared to take him and his two remaining sheep to Italy. He engaged servants and bought everything he needed for a long voyage. At last Mr. Van der Hartbargin, the master of a large ship, came and introduced himself.

"How much will you charge," he asked this man, "to take myself, my servants, my baggage, and these two sheep directly to Venice?"

The master asked ten thousand piastres. Candide did not hesitate.

"Hallo," the careful Van der Hartbargin said to himself, "this stranger parts with ten thousand piastres just like that! He must be pretty rich."

He came back at him a moment later and indicated that he could not sail for less than twenty thousand.

"Very well, then, you shall have them," said Candide.

"Blow me!" said the merchant under his breath. "This man parts with twenty thousand piastres as easily as ten."

He came back at him once more and said that he could not take him to Venice for less than thirty thousand piastres.

"Then thirty thousand it is," replied Candide.

"Hallo, indeed!" the Dutch merchant said to himself again. "Thirty thousand piastres are nothing to this man. Those two sheep must be carrying immense treasures. Better not press things any further. Let's get paid the thirty thousand piastres first, and then we'll see."

Candide sold two little diamonds, the smaller of which was worth more than all the money the shipmaster was asking. He paid him in advance. The two sheep were loaded on board. Candide was following behind in a small boat to join the ship moored out in the roads,[9] when the master calmly set his sails and weighed anchor. The wind favoured him. Candide, helpless and quite flabbergasted, soon lost sight of him.

"Alas!" he lamented, "that's just the kind of dirty trick you'd expect from the old world."

He returned to the shore deep in misery, for, after all, he had lost what would have been enough to make the fortune of twenty monarchs.

He took himself off to the Dutch Resident Magistrate and, as he was a little upset, knocked rather peremptorily on the door. In he went, explained what had happened to him, and shouted rather more loudly than was proper. The magistrate began by fining him ten thousand piastres for the noise he had made. Then he listened to him patiently, promised to look into his case as soon as the merchant returned, and charged a further ten thousand piastres for the cost of the hearing.

This treatment was the last straw for Candide in his despair. To be sure, he had suffered misfortunes a thousand times more grievous, but the sang-froid of the magistrate, and of that shipmaster who had robbed him, stirred his bile and plunged

9. Sheltered water near shore.

him into a black melancholy. The wickedness of men struck him in all its ugliness, and his mind fed on images of gloom. Finally, there being a French vessel all ready to sail for Bordeaux, and as he had no more sheep laden with diamonds to place aboard, he paid for a cabin on the ship at the standard price, and made it known in the town that he would pay passage and board for, and give two thousand piastres to, any respectable person who would make the journey with him, on condition that this person was the most disgusted with his lot and the unhappiest man in the province.

A crowd of applicants came forward such as an entire fleet could not have carried. Wanting to choose among the most likely candidates, Candide selected twenty who seemed to him fairly companionable and who all claimed to deserve preference. He got them together in his inn and gave them supper on condition that each would swear to give a faithful version of his story. He undertook to choose the one who would seem to him most to be pitied and to have the greatest reason for being the most dissatisfied with his lot. To the others he promised a small consideration.

The session lasted until four o'clock in the morning. Candide, as he listened to all their adventures, recalled what the old woman had said to him on their way to Buenos Aires and how she had wagered that not a single person on board would not have suffered very great misfortunes. He thought of Pangloss with every story he was told.

"Pangloss," he said, "would be hard put to it to prove his system. I wish he were here. One thing's certain: if all is going well, it's happening in Eldorado and not in the rest of the world."

In the end he decided in favour of a poor scholar who had spent ten years working for the publishing houses of Amsterdam. He took the view that there was no form of employment in the world with which one could possibly be more disgusted.[1]

This man of learning, who was a perfectly decent fellow moreover, had been robbed by his wife, assaulted by his son, and abandoned by his daughter, who had eloped with a Portuguese. He had just been removed from a small post which had provided him with a living, and the preachers of Surinam were persecuting him because they took him for a Socinian.[2] It must be admitted that the other applicants were at least as unhappy as him, but Candide hoped that the scholar would keep him amused on the voyage. All his rivals considered that Candide was doing them a great injustice, but he pacified them by giving them a hundred piastres each.

Chapter 20

What happened to Candide and Martin at sea

So the old scholar, who was called Martin, took ship for Bordeaux with Candide. Both had seen much and suffered much, and even if the ship had had to sail all the way from Surinam to Japan via the Cape of Good Hope, they would still have had matter enough to sustain their discussion of physical and moral evil throughout the entire voyage.

However, Candide had one great advantage over Martin, which was that he was still hoping to see Miss Cunégonde again, while Martin had nothing to hope for. Moreover, he had gold and diamonds, and although he had lost a hundred large sheep laden with the greatest treasure on earth, and although the Dutch master's villainy still

1. Voltaire had had difficult dealings with Dutch publishers.

2. A sect resembling present-day Unitarians who denied the Trinity and Christ's divinity.

rankled, nevertheless when he thought about what he had left in his pockets, and when he talked about Cunégonde, especially at the end of a meal, then he would be inclined to favour the philosophical system of Pangloss.

"But you, Mr. Martin," he said to the scholar, "what are your thoughts on all this? How do you see physical and moral evil?"

"Sir," replied Martin, "my priests accused me of being a Socinian, but the fact of the matter is that I am a Manichean."[3]

"You're pulling my leg," said Candide. "There aren't any Manicheans left any more."

"There's me," said Martin. "I can't help it. I just can't see things any other way."

"It's the devil in you," said Candide.

"He's mixed up in the affairs of this world to such an extent," said Martin, "that he may well be in me, just as he's in everything else. But to be frank, when I look about me on this globe, or rather this globule, I begin to think God has abandoned it to some malign being—apart from Eldorado, that is. I've scarcely seen one town that did not wish the ruination of its neighbour, or one family that did not want to see the end of another. Everywhere you look, the weak execrate the strong while they grovel at their feet, and the strong treat them like so many sheep, providing wool and meat to be sold. One million regimented assassins, rushing from one end of Europe to the other, commit murder and brigandage by the rule book in order to earn their daily bread, because there is no more respectable profession; and in the cities, where people appear to live in peace and the arts flourish, men are devoured by more envy, worry, and dissatisfaction than all the scourges of a city under siege. Secret sorrows are more cruel even than public tribulations. In short, I have seen so many of them, and suffered so many, that I am a Manichean."

"Yet there is good," Candide would answer.

"That's as may be," Martin would say, "but I've never met it."

In the middle of this debate, they heard the sound of cannon fire. The noise increased by the moment. Each of them grabbed his telescope. Two ships were to be seen engaging at a distance of about three miles. The wind brought both of these ships so close to the French vessel that they had the pleasure of seeing the engagement in perfect comfort. Eventually one ship let fly a broadside at the other that was so low and so accurate that it sank it. Candide and Martin could distinctly see a hundred men on the deck of the ship which was going down. They were all raising their hands heavenwards and letting out the most appalling screams. In an instant everything disappeared beneath the waves.

"Well, there you are," said Martin. "That's how men treat each other."

"It is true," said Candide. "The devil has had a hand in this business."

So saying, he noticed something bright red swimming near their ship. The ship's launch was lowered to go and see what it could be. It was one of his sheep. There was more joy in Candide at finding this one sheep than there had been sorrow at losing an hundredfold all laden with large Eldorado diamonds.

The French captain soon observed that the captain of the sinker was Spanish, while the captain of the sunk was a Dutch pirate. It was the very man who had robbed Candide. The immense riches with which this villain had absconded had gone down with him, and all that had been saved was one sheep.

3. Ancient religious philosophy that posits two equal forces of good and evil governing the world; one of the earliest Christian heresies.

"You see," Candide said to Martin, "crime is sometimes punished. That scoundrel of a Dutch skipper got the fate he deserved."

"Yes," said Martin, "but did the passengers on his ship have to perish also? God punished the rogue: the devil drowned the rest."

Meanwhile the French and Spanish ships resumed their voyages, and Candide and Martin their conversations. They argued for a solid fortnight, and at the end of the fortnight they were as far forward as the day they began. But, well, they talked, and exchanged ideas, and consoled each other. Candide would stroke his sheep and say: "I have found you, so I may well be able to find Cunégonde."

CHAPTER 21

Candide and Martin approach the French coast and reason together

At last they came in sight of the French coast.

"Have you ever been to France, Mr. Martin?" said Candide.

"Yes," said Martin, "I've travelled through several of its provinces. There are some where half the inhabitants are mad, one or two where they're too clever by half, some where they're generally quite gentle and rather stupid, and others where they try to be witty. And in all of them the principal occupation is love. Next comes slander and gossip, and third comes talking nonsense."

"But, Mr. Martin, have you been to Paris?"

"Yes, I've been to Paris. There they have all of these types. It's chaos there, a throng in which everyone is searching for pleasure and where practically no one finds it, at least not as far as I could see. I haven't spent much time there. When I arrived, I was robbed of everything I had by pickpockets at the Saint-Germain fair. I myself was taken for a thief and spent a week in prison, after which I did some proof-reading to earn enough to be able to return to Holland on foot. I got to know the pen-pushing brigade, and the political intriguers, and the religious convulsions crowd.[4] They say there are some very well-mannered people in that city. I dare say there are."

"Personally I have no desire to see France," said Candide. "As I'm sure you can imagine, when one's spent a month in Eldorado, there's nothing in the world one much wants to see other than Miss Cunégonde. I'm on my way to wait for her in Venice. We will be going through France to get to Italy. Why don't you come with me?"

"Delighted to," said Martin. "They say Venice is only fit to live in if you're a Venetian nobleman, but that foreigners are well looked after none the less, providing they have a lot of money. I haven't, you have; I'll follow you anywhere."

"Incidentally," said Candide, "do you believe the Earth was originally a sea, as they say it was in that big book the captain has?"[5]

"I don't believe anything of the sort," said Martin, "no more than I believe any of the other rubbish they've been coming out with recently."

"But for what purpose was this world created then?" said Candide.

"To drive us mad," replied Martin.

"Don't you find it absolutely amazing," Candide went on, "the way the two girls I told you about, the ones who lived in the land of the Lobeiros, loved those two monkeys?"

4. Jansenist extremists, who were known for convulsions and trances, through which they supposedly performed miracles.

5. Probably the Bible, in which God creates the sea before dry land (Genesis 1).

"Not at all," said Martin. "I don't see what's odd about that particular passion. I've seen so many extraordinary things that nothing's extraordinary any more."

"Do you think," said Candide, "that men have always massacred each other the way they do now? that they've always been liars, cheats, traitors, ingrates, brigands? that they've always been feeble, fickle, envious, gluttonous, drunken, avaricious, ambitious, bloodthirsty, slanderous, debauched, fanatical, hypocritical, and stupid?"

"Do you think," said Martin, "that hawks have always eaten pigeons when they find them?"

"Yes, no doubt," said Candide.

"Well, then," said Martin, "if hawks have always had the same character, why do you expect men to have changed theirs?"

"Oh!" said Candide, "there's a big difference, because free will . . ." Arguing thus the while, they arrived in Bordeaux.

Chapter 22

What happened to Candide and Martin in France

Candide broke his journey in Bordeaux just long enough to sell a few Eldorado pebbles and to procure a good post-chaise with two seats, for he could no longer be without Martin, his philosopher. He was only very sorry to be parted from his sheep, which he left with the Academy of Science at Bordeaux. They set as the subject of that year's prize the question why the wool of this sheep was red, and the prize was awarded to a scientist from the North[6] who proved by A plus B minus C divided by Z that the sheep had necessarily to be red, and to die of sheep-pox.

Meanwhile all the travellers Candide met in the inns along the way told him: "We're off to Paris." In the end this universal eagerness made him want to see that capital city. It would not take him much out of his way on his journey to Venice.

He entered by the Faubourg Saint-Marceau and thought he was in the ugliest village in Westphalia.

Scarce had Candide put up at his inn than he was laid low by a minor indisposition brought on by his exertions. As he had an enormous diamond on his finger, and as an extremely heavy strong box had been noticed among his luggage, he soon had by him two doctors whom he had not sent for, a number of bosom companions who never left his side, and two ladies of good works who were heating up his broth.

Martin said:

"I remember being ill on my first trip to Paris too. I was very poor, so I had no friends or do-gooders or doctors, and I got better."

Meanwhile, by dint of many potions and bloodlettings, Candide's illness became serious. A local priest came and kindly asked him for a confessional note payable to bearer in the other world.[7] Candide would have none of it. The ladies of good works assured him that it was the new fashion. Candide replied that he was not a one for fashion. Martin was for throwing the priest out of the window. The cleric swore that Candide would not be granted burial. Martin swore that he would bury the cleric if he continued to bother them. The quarrel grew more heated. Martin took him by the

6. A reference to Maupertuis, the president of Frederick the Great's Berlin Academy of Sciences, who was often ridiculed by Voltaire.

7. In order to receive the last sacraments, Parisians were required to present a note from their confessor indicating they had subscribed to the Papal Bull *Unigenitus*, which condemned the Jansenist heresy.

shoulders and unceremoniously ejected him. This caused a great scandal, which was the subject of an official enquiry.

Candide recovered, and during his convalescence he had some very fine company to supper with him. There was gambling for high stakes. Candide was most surprised never to get a single ace, and Martin was not surprised.

Among those who did him the honours of the city was a little abbé[8] from Périgord, one of those busy little, pushy, fawning, frightfully accommodating types, always on the make, always ready to please, who lie in wait for strangers passing through and give them all the local gossip and scandal and offer them entertainments at all sorts of prices. This one took Candide and Martin to the theatre first. A new tragedy was on. Candide found himself sitting next to some of the intellectual smart set. This did not prevent him from crying at scenes that were played to perfection.

One of these arbiters of taste sitting near him said to him during an interval:

"You are quite wrong to cry. That actress is very bad. The actor playing opposite her is still worse. The play is even worse than the actors. The author doesn't know a word of Arabic, and yet the play is set in Arabia.[9] And what's more, the man doesn't believe in innate ideas. Tomorrow I can bring you twenty pamphlets criticizing him."

"Sir, how many plays do you have in France?" Candide asked the abbé, who replied:

"Five or six thousand."

"That's a lot," said Candide. "How many of them are any good?"

"Fifteen or sixteen," was the answer.

"That's a lot," said Martin.

Candide was much taken with an actress who was playing Queen Elizabeth in a rather dull tragedy which is sometimes put on.

"I do like that actress," he said to Martin. "She looks a bit like Miss Cunégonde. I should be rather pleased to call on her."

The abbé from Périgord offered to effect an introduction. Candide, brought up in Germany, asked what the form was and how queens of England were treated in France.

"We must distinguish," said the abbé. "In the provinces you take them to an inn. In Paris you respect them when they're beautiful, and you throw them on to the rubbish-heap when they're dead."[1]

"Queens on the rubbish-heap!" said Candide.

"Yes, really," said Martin. "The abbé is right. I was in Paris when Mlle Monime passed, as they say, from this life to the next. She was refused what people here call 'the honours of the grave,' that is to say of rotting in a filthy cemetery with all the beggars of the neighbourhood. Unlike the rest of her troupe she was buried alone at the corner of the rue de Bourgogne, which must have pained her exceedingly, for she thought very nobly."

"That's not a very nice way to treat people," said Candide.

"What can you expect?" said Martin. "That's the way they are round here. Take any contradiction or inconsistency you can think of, and you will find it in the government, the courts, the churches, or the theatres of this strange nation."

"Is it true that people in Paris are always laughing?" enquired Candide.

8. French clergyman.

9. Voltaire himself had written a play, *Mahomet*, set in Arabia.

1. Actors and actresses were denied Christian burial in France at this time; Voltaire had assisted in the secret burial of an actress in 1730.

"Yes," said the abbé, "but through gritted teeth. For they complain about everything with great gales of laughter, and they laugh even when doing the most detestable things."

"Who," asked Candide, "was the fat pig who was telling me so many bad things about that play I cried such a lot at, and about those actors I liked so much?"

"He is evil incarnate," replied the abbé. "He earns his living by decrying all new plays and books. He hates the up-and-coming writer, just as eunuchs hate the up-and-coming lover. He's one of those vipers of literature that feeds off filth and venom. He's a hack."

"What do you mean by 'hack'?" said Candide.

"I mean," said the abbé, "someone who churns out articles by the dozen, a Fréron."[2]

Such was the discussion between Candide, Martin, and the man from Périgord as they stood on the staircase, watching people pass by on their way out after the play.

"Although I can't wait to see Miss Cunégonde again," said Candide, "nevertheless I would like to have supper with Mlle Clairon,[3] for she did seem quite admirable to me."

The abbé was not the right man for an approach to Mlle Clairon, who moved only in the best circles.

"She has a prior engagement this evening," he said, "but if you will allow me the honour of taking you to a lady of quality, there you will get to meet Paris society as if you'd already been living here for years."

Candide, who was curious by nature, allowed himself to be taken to the lady, at the bottom end of the Faubourg Saint-Honoré.[4] There they were busy playing faro.[5] Twelve sad punters each held a small hand of cards, the dog-eared register of their misfortunes. A profound silence reigned; pallor was upon the punters' brows, anxiety upon that of the banker; and the lady of the house, seated beside this implacable banker, noted with the eyes of a lynx all the doubling up and any illegal antes whenever each player turned down the corner of his card. She would make them turn the corners back with firm but polite insistence, and never lost her temper for fear of losing her clients. This lady called herself the Marchioness of Dubelauchwitz. Her daughter, aged fifteen, was one of the punters and would indicate with a wink any cheating on the part of these poor people endeavouring to repair the cruel blows of fate. The abbé from Périgord, Candide, and Martin walked in. No one got up, or greeted them, or looked at them; they were all deeply engrossed in their cards.

"The Baroness of Thunder-ten-tronckh was more civil," said Candide.

Meanwhile the abbé had a word in the ear of the Marchioness, who half rose and honoured Candide with a gracious smile and Martin with a thoroughly grand tilt of the head. She had Candide given a seat and dealt a hand: he lost fifty thousand francs in two rounds. Afterwards they supped merrily, and everyone was surprised that Candide was not more upset about his losses. The lackeys said to each other in their own lackey language:

"He must be one of your English lords."

The supper was like most suppers in Paris. First, silence; then a cacaphonous welter of words which no one can make out; and then jokes, which mostly fall flat,

2. Name of one of Voltaire's harshest critics, who had panned his play *Tancrède.*

3. An actress who often performed in Voltaire's plays.

4. A wealthy section of Paris.

5. Popular card game in which "punters" bet against the bank.

false rumours, false arguments, a smattering of politics, and a quantity of slander. They even talked about the latest books.

"Have you read," said the abbé from Périgord, "that nonsense by Master Gauchat,[6] doctor of theology?"

"Yes," replied one of the party, "but I couldn't finish it. There's enough irrelevant rubbish in print as it is, but the whole lot put together doesn't come anywhere near the irrelevance of Master Gauchat, doctor of theology. I'm so sick of this great flood of detestable books that I've taken to punting at faro."

"And the *Miscellany* of Archdeacon T . . .?[7] What do you think of that?" said the abbé.

"Oh," said the Marchioness of Dubelauchwitz, "that crashing bore! The way he tells you with great interest what everybody knows already! The ponderous discussion of points that aren't even worth a passing reference! The witless way he borrows other people's wit! How he ruins what he filches! How he disgusts me! But he won't disgust me any further. One or two pages of the archdeacon are quite enough."

At table there was a man of taste and learning, who agreed with what the Marchioness was saying. Conversation then moved on to tragedies. The lady asked why it was that some tragedies were staged from time to time but were totally unreadable. The man of taste explained very well how a play could be of some interest but of almost no merit. He showed in a few words how it was not enough to contrive one or two of the stock situations which can be found in any novel, and which always captivate the audience, but that one had to be original without being far-fetched; often sublime and always natural; to know the human heart and to make it speak; to be a great poet without any of the characters in the play appearing to be poets themselves; to have perfect command of one's own language, and to use it with fluent euphony, without forcing it, and without ever sacrificing the sense to the rhyme.

"Whoever fails to follow every one of these rules," he added, "may produce one or two tragedies that are applauded in the theatre, but he will never be counted a good writer. There are very few good tragedies. Some are simply idylls in a dialogue that happens to be well-written and well-rhymed; some have political messages, and send you to sleep, while others are so overdone they fail to move; and some are the fantasies of fanatics, written in a barbarous style with broken-off sentences and long speeches to the gods—because they don't know how to communicate with human beings—and full of false maxims and pompous platitudes."

Candide listened attentively to these remarks and formed a high opinion of the speaker. As the Marchioness had taken good care to place Candide next to her, he took the liberty of asking, by means of a whisper in her ear, who this man was who spoke so well.

"He's a man of learning," said the lady, "who doesn't gamble and whom the abbé brings to supper sometimes. He knows all about tragedies and books, and he has himself written a tragedy, which was whistled off the stage, and a book, of which but one copy has ever been seen outside a bookshop, and that was the one he presented to me with a dedication."

"A great man!" said Candide. "He's another Pangloss."

Then, turning to him, he said:

6. Author of a series of refutations of Voltaire's *Encyclopédie*.

7. Trublet, another critic of Voltaire.

"Sir, doubtless you think that everything is for the best in the physical and moral worlds, and that things could not be other than as they are?"

"I, sir?" replied the man of learning. "I don't think anything of the sort. I find that everything in our world is amiss, that nobody knows his place or his responsibility, or what he's doing or what he should do, and that, except for supper parties, which are quite jolly and where people seem to get on reasonably well, the rest of the time is spent in pointless quarrelling: Jansenists with Molinists,[8] parliamentarians with churchmen, men of letters with men of letters, courtiers with courtiers, financiers with the general public, wives with husbands, relatives with relatives. It's one battle after another."

Candide answered him:

"I've seen worse ones. But a wise man, who has since had the misfortune to be hanged, told me that that's all fine. Those are just the shadows in a beautiful painting."

"Your hanged man was having people on," said Martin. "What you call shadows are horrible stains."

"It's human beings who make the stains," said Candide. "They can't help it."

"So it's not their fault," said Martin.

The majority of the punters, who did not understand a word of all this, were drinking. Martin had a discussion with the man of learning; and Candide recounted some of his adventures to the lady of the house.

After supper the Marchioness took Candide to her room and bid him be seated on a couch.

"Well, then," she said to him, "so you're still madly in love with Miss Cunégonde de Thunder-ten-tronckh?"

"Yes, madame."

The Marchioness returned a tender smile:

"You answer like the young man from Westphalia you are. A Frenchman would have said to me: 'It is true that I did once love Miss Cunégonde, but on seeing you, madame, I fear that I love her no longer.'"

"Oh, dear," said Candide. "Madame, I shall answer as you please."

"Your passion for her began," said the Marchioness, "when you picked up her handkerchief. I want you to pick up my garter."

"With all my heart," said Candide, and he picked it up.

"But I want you to put it back for me," said the lady, and Candide put it back for her.

"You see," she said, "you are a foreigner. Sometimes I make my Parisian lovers wait a whole fortnight, but here I am giving myself to you on the very first night, because one must do the honours of one's country to a young man from Westphalia."

The fair lady, having noticed two enormous diamonds on the hands of her young foreigner, enthused about them with such sincerity that from Candide's fingers they passed on to the fingers of the Marchioness.

Candide, as he returned home with his abbé from Périgord, felt some remorse at having been unfaithful to Miss Cunégonde. The abbé commiserated with him; he was only slightly responsible for the fifty thousand francs Candide had lost at cards and the value of the two brilliants which had been half given and half extorted. His object was to profit as much as he possibly could from the advantages that knowing Candide

8. Followers of Luis Molina (1535–1600), a Spanish Jesuit who promoted the doctrine of free will. Jansenists, on the other hand, believed in predestination.

might bring him. He asked him all about Cunégonde, and Candide told him that he would certainly beg that fair lady's pardon for his infidelity when he saw her in Venice.

The man from Périgord became even more courteous and attentive and took a touching interest in everything that Candide said, or did, or wanted to do.

"So you have arranged to meet in Venice then, sir?" he said.

"Yes, Monsieur l'abbé," said Candide. "I really must go and find Miss Cunégonde."

Then, drawn on by the pleasure of talking about the one he loved, he recounted, as was his wont, a part of his adventures with this illustrious Westphalian lady.

"I expect Miss Cunégonde is witty and clever," said the abbé, "and that she writes charming letters?"

"I've never had any from her," said Candide. "The thing is, you see, having been kicked out of the castle for loving her, I couldn't write to her, and then I learnt soon afterwards that she was dead, and then I found her again, and then I lost her, and then I sent an express messenger two thousand five hundred leagues to her, and I am still awaiting a reply."

The abbé listened attentively and seemed somewhat lost in thought. Soon he took his leave of the two strangers, after embracing them warmly. The next day, upon waking, Candide received the following letter:

> My very dear and beloved sir, I have been lying ill in this city for the past week. I discover that you are here too. I would fly to your arms if I could move. I heard in Bordeaux that you had passed through. I left the faithful Cacambo there and the old woman, and they are soon to follow on after me. The Governor of Buenos Aires took everything, but I still have your heart. Come to me. Your presence will restore me to life, or make me die of pleasure.

This charming, this unexpected letter sent Candide into transports of inexpressible joy, while the illness of his dear Cunégonde weighed him down with grief. Torn between these two emotions, he grabbed his gold and diamonds and had someone take him and Martin to the hotel where Miss Cunégonde was staying. He entered the room trembling with emotion, his heart aflutter, his voice choked. He made to open the curtains round the bed and was about to send for a lamp.

"Do no such thing," said the maid, "the light will kill her." And at once she shut the curtains:

"My dear Cunégonde," wept Candide, "How are you? If you cannot look at me, at least speak to me."

"She cannot speak," said the maid. The lady then drew from the bedclothes a chubby little hand, which Candide bathed with his tears for a long time and subsequently filled with diamonds, leaving a pouch full of gold on the chair.

In the midst of his transports an officer of the watch arrived, followed by the abbé from Périgord and a squad of men.

"Are these the two suspicious foreigners then?" he said.

He had them arrested on the spot and ordered his lads to haul them off to prison.

"This is not how they treat travellers in Eldorado," said Candide.

"I feel more Manichean than ever," said Martin.

"But, sir, where are you taking us?" said Candide.

"To the deepest of dark dungeons," said the officer.

Martin, having recovered his sang-froid, judged that the lady claiming to be Cunégonde was a fraud, the abbé from Périgord a scoundrel who had taken advantage of Candide's innocence at the earliest opportunity, and the officer another scoundrel, whom it would be easy to be rid of.

Rather than be exposed to the process of law, Candide, enlightened by Martin's counsel and, more especially, ever impatient to see the real Miss Cunégonde again, offered the officer three little diamonds worth about three thousand pistoles each.

"Ah, sir," the man with the ivory baton said to him, "had you committed every crime in the book, you'd still be the most honest man alive. Three diamonds! And each worth three thousand pistoles! Sir, I'd sooner die for you than take you to a dungeon. There are orders to arrest all foreigners, but leave it to me. I have a brother in Normandy, in Dieppe, I'll take you there. And if you have a diamond or two to give him, he'll take care of you as if it were myself he was looking after."

"And why are they arresting all foreigners?" says Candide.

The abbé from Périgord intervened:

"It's because a wretch from Atrabatia listened to some silly talk, which was all it took to make him commit parricide—not like the one in May 1610 but like the one in December 1594, and like several others committed in other months and other years by other wretches who had listened to similar silly talk."[9]

The officer then explained what this was all about.

"Ah, the monsters!" exclaimed Candide. "What! Such horrors, and from a people that loves singing and dancing! Can't I leave this very minute? Let me out of this country where monkeys provoke tigers. I have seen bears in my own country; I have seen men only in Eldorado. In the name of God, officer, take me to Venice, where I am to wait for Miss Cunégonde."

"Lower Normandy is the best I can do," said the right arm of the law.

Thereupon he had his irons removed, said he must have made a mistake, dismissed his men, and took Candide and Martin to Dieppe and left them in the hands of his brother. There was a small Dutch ship out in the roads. The Norman, who with the help of three more diamonds had now become the most obliging of men, put Candide and his servants aboard the ship, which was about to set sail for Portsmouth in England. It was not the way to Venice, but Candide felt as though he was being delivered from hell, and he fully intended to rejoin the route to Venice at the first opportunity.

Chapter 23

Candide and Martin proceed to the shores of England; what they see there

"Ah, Pangloss! Pangloss! Ah, Martin! Martin! Ah, my dear Cunégonde! What sort of a world is this?" Candide was asking on board the Dutch ship.

"A rather mad and rather awful one," answered Martin.

"You know England. Are they as mad there as they are in France?"

"It's a different kind of madness," said Martin. "As you know, the two countries are at war over a few acres of snow across in Canada, and they're spending more on this war than the whole of Canada is worth.[1] To tell you exactly if there are more people who should be locked up in one country than in the other is something my feeble

9. Atrabatia is the Latin name for the French province Artois, the birthplace of Damiens, who attempted to assassinate Louis XV in 1757. Châtel attempted to assassinate Henry IV in December 1594, and in May 1610 Ravaillac assassinated Henry IV.

1. This colonial struggle between Britain and France culminated in the French and Indian War. It was resolved in 1763 by the Treaty of Paris, which transferred Canada from French to British control.

lights do not permit. All I know is that, by and large, the people we are going to see are extremely glum."[2]

Thus conversing, they landed at Portsmouth. A multitude of people covered the shore, all gazing intently at a rather stout man who was kneeling blindfold on the deck of one of the naval ships. Four soldiers, posted opposite this man, each fired three shots into his skull, as calmly as you please, and the assembled multitude then dispersed, thoroughly satisfied.

"What is all this?" said Candide. "And what demon is it that holds such universal sway?"

He asked who this stout man was who had just been ceremonially killed.

"He's an admiral," came the answer.[3]

"And why kill this admiral?"

"Because he didn't kill enough people," Candide was told. "He gave battle to a French admiral, and it has been found that he wasn't close enough."

"But," said Candide, "the French admiral was just as far away from the English admiral as he was from him!"

"Unquestionably," came the reply. "But in this country it is considered a good thing to kill an admiral from time to time so as to encourage the others."

Candide was so dumbfounded and so shocked by what he was seeing and hearing that he refused even to set foot ashore, and he negotiated with the Dutch master of the ship (it was just too bad if he fleeced him like the one in Surinam) to take him to Venice as soon as possible.

The master was ready in two days. They sailed down the French coast. They passed within sight of Lisbon, and Candide shuddered. They entered the straits and the Mediterranean. At last they put in at Venice.

"God be praised!" said Candide, embracing Martin. "This is where I shall see fair Cunégonde again. I trust Cacambo as I would myself. All is well, all is going well, all is going as well as it possibly can."

CHAPTER 24

Of Paquette and Brother Giroflée

As soon as he reached Venice, he instigated a search for Cacambo in every inn and coffee house, and in all the brothels. He was nowhere to be found. Each day he had enquiries made of every new ship or boat that came in. No sign of Cacambo.

"I don't know," he was saying to Martin. "I have had time to cross from Surinam to Bordeaux, to go from Bordeaux to Paris, from Paris to Dieppe, from Dieppe to Portsmouth, to sail the length of Portugal and Spain, to cross the entire Mediterranean, to spend several months in Venice, and fair Cunégonde has still not got here! All I've encountered instead is some hussy and an abbé from Périgord. Cunégonde is probably dead, so I may as well die too. Ah! it would have been better to remain in the paradise of Eldorado than come back to this accursed Europe. How right you are, my dear Martin! All is but illusion and calamity."

2. The British were thought to be characteristically melancholic.

3. Admiral Byng, who had been in charge of British naval forces during their defeat by the French in a battle off Minorca, was court-martialed and tried for cowardice. He was executed by firing squad on his own quarterdeck in 1757; Voltaire had unsuccessfully attempted to intercede on Byng's behalf.

He sank into a dark melancholy and took no part in the opera *alla moda* or in any of the other carnival entertainments. Not a single lady caused him a moment's temptation.

Martin said to him:

"You really are rather simple to imagine that a half-caste[4] manservant with five or six millions in his pocket will go and look for your lady-love on the other side of the world and bring her to you in Venice. He'll take her for himself if he finds her. If he doesn't find her, he'll take somebody else. My advice to you is to forget your manservant Cacambo and your beloved Cunégonde."

Martin was not consoling. Candide's melancholy deepened, and Martin kept on proving to him that there was little virtue and little happiness in this world—except perhaps in Eldorado, where no one could ever go.

While they disputed this important subject and waited for Cunégonde, Candide noticed a young Theatine[5] monk in Saint Mark's Square, who was walking with a girl on his arm. The Theatine had a fresh, chubby, robust appearance. His eyes shone, and there was an air of assurance about him. His expression was haughty, his gait proud. The girl, who was very pretty, was singing. She gazed lovingly at her Theatine, and tweaked his pudgy cheeks from time to time.

"You'll grant me at least," Candide said to Martin, "that those two are happy. So far, throughout the inhabited world, I have encountered only unfortunates—except in Eldorado, that is. But as for that girl and her Theatine, I bet they are very happy creatures."

"I bet they're not," said Martin.

"All we have to do is to invite them to dinner," said Candide, "and you'll see if I'm wrong."

Thereupon he went up to them, presented his compliments, and invited them back to his hostelry for some macaroni, Lombardy partridge, and caviar, washed down with Montepulciano, lachryma Christi,[6] and some of the wines of Cyprus and Samos. The young lady blushed, the Theatine accepted the invitation, and the girl followed him, glancing at Candide with eyes wide in surprise and embarrassment and clouded with tears.

Scarcely had she entered Candide's room than she said to him:

"Well? Doesn't Master Candide recognize Paquette any more?"

At these words Candide, who had not looked at her closely until then (because he had thoughts only for Cunégonde), said to her:

"Oh dear, my poor girl, so you are the one who got Dr. Pangloss into the fine state I saw him in?"

"Alas, sir, I am indeed," said Paquette. "I see you know all about it. I heard about the dreadful misfortunes that befell Her Ladyship's household and the fair Miss Cunégonde. I swear to you, my own fate has hardly been less wretched. I was utterly innocent when last you saw me. A Franciscan monk who was my confessor had no difficulty in seducing me. The consequences were terrible. I was obliged to leave the castle not long after His Lordship kicked you up the backside and sent you packing. If a famous doctor had not taken pity on me, I'd have had it. For a time I became the doctor's mistress, as a way of showing my gratitude. His wife, who was madly jealous, beat me every day

4. Mixed-race.
5. An order founded in 1524.
6. Fine Italian wines.

without mercy. She was a fury. This doctor was the ugliest of men, and I the unhappiest of creatures to be continually beaten for a man I did not love. As you know, sir, it's very dangerous for a shrewish woman to have a doctor for a husband. One day, sick and tired of the way his wife was behaving, he treated her for a slight cold by giving her some medicine, which proved so effective that within two hours she was dead, having had some horrible convulsions. The mistress's family brought an action against the master. He upped and fled, and I was put in prison. My innocence would not have saved me had I not been reasonably pretty. The judge let me go on condition that he would succeed the doctor. I was soon supplanted by a rival, dismissed without a penny, and obliged to continue in this unspeakable profession which seems so harmless to you men, and which for us is nothing but a vale of tears. I chose Venice to practise my profession in. Oh, sir, if you could imagine what it's like having to caress just anybody, an old merchant, a lawyer, a monk, a gondolier, an abbé; to be exposed to all manner of insult and degradation; to be reduced often to having to borrow a skirt, only then to go and have it lifted up by some disgusting man or other; to be robbed by one of what one's earned with another; to be held to ransom by officers of the law, and to have nothing to look forward to but a gruesome old age, the workhouse, and the rubbish-heap; then you would agree that I am one of the unhappiest and most unfortunate creatures alive."

This was how, in a private room in the hostelry, Paquette opened her heart to good Candide in the presence of Martin, who said to Candide:

"You see, I've already won half my bet."

Brother Giroflée had remained in the dining-room, and was having a drink as he waited for dinner.

"But," Candide said to Paquette, "you were looking so gay, so happy, when I ran into you. You were singing, you were fondling the Theatine quite naturally and willingly. You seemed to me every bit as happy as you say you are unhappy."

"Ah, sir," replied Paquette, "that's another of the awful things about our profession. Yesterday I was robbed and beaten by an officer, and today I have to appear to be in a good mood just to please a monk."

That was enough for Candide; he admitted that Martin was right. They sat down to dinner with Paquette and the Theatine. The meal was quite good-humoured, and at the end they were all talking to each other with some degree of freedom.

"Father," Candide said to the monk, "you seem to me to be enjoying the kind of life everyone must envy. You are the picture of health, you have a happy face, you have a very pretty girl to keep you amused, and you seem perfectly content with your monastic condition."

"By my faith, sir," said Brother Giroflée, "I wish all Theatines were at the bottom of the sea. I've been tempted a hundred times to set fire to the monastery and to go and turn Turk.[7] My parents forced me to don this detestable habit at the age of fifteen so that I would leave a bigger fortune for my damned elder brother, may God confound him! The monastery is rife with jealousy, and backbiting, and bad feeling. It's true that I have preached a few miserable sermons that have brought me in some money, half of which the Prior steals—the rest I use for keeping girls. But when I get back to the monastery in the evening, I'm ready to beat my head in on the dormitory walls. And all the brothers feel the same way."

7. A common expression signifying the ultimate infidelity or treachery.

Martin turned to Candide with his usual sang-froid:

"Well?" he said. "Have I not won the whole bet?"

Candide gave Paquette two thousand piastres, and Brother Giroflée a thousand. "I guarantee you," he said, "that with this money they'll be happy."

"I shouldn't think so for a minute," said Martin. "With these piastres you may make them even more unhappy still."

"Whatever shall be, shall be," said Candide. "But one thing consoles me. I see that people one never thought to see again often do turn up. It may well turn out that, having run into my red sheep and Paquette, I will also run into Cunégonde."

"I wish," said Martin, "that she may one day make you happy. But I very much doubt she will."

"You are a bit hard," said Candide.

"That's because I've lived," said Martin.

"But look at those gondoliers," said Candide. "They're always singing, aren't they?"

"You don't see them at home with their wives and screaming children," said Martin. "The doge[8] has his problems, the gondoliers have theirs. It is true that, all things considered, the life of a gondolier is preferable to that of a doge, but I think there's so little in it that it's not worth arguing about."

"I've heard people talk," said Candide, "about a Senator Pococurante[9] who lives in that beautiful palace on the Brenta, and who's very hospitable to visiting foreigners. They say he's a man who's never had any troubles."

"I'd like to meet such a rare breed," said Martin.

Candide at once sent someone to ask the noble Signor Pococurante's permission to call on him the following day.

Chapter 25

The visit to Signor Pococurante, a Venetian nobleman

Candide and Martin proceeded down the Brenta by gondola and came to the palace of the noble Pococurante. The gardens were well laid out and embellished with beautiful marble statues, while the palace itself was a fine piece of architecture. The master of the house, a man of sixty, and very rich, received the two curious visitors most politely but with very little fuss, which disconcerted Candide and did not displease Martin.

First, two pretty and neatly dressed girls poured out some chocolate, managing to give it a good frothy top. Candide could not help but compliment them on their beauty, their kindness, and their skill.

"They're not bad creatures," said Senator Pococurante. "I have them sleep with me sometimes, because I'm rather tired of the society ladies here with all their flirting, and their jealousy, and their quarrelling, and their moods, and their petty-mindedness, and their arrogance, and their silliness, not to mention the sonnets you have to compose, or have composed, for them. But, well, in the end I'm beginning to find these two girls exceedingly boring too."

Candide, walking in a long gallery after lunch, was surprised at the beauty of the paintings. He asked which master had painted the first two.

"They're by Raphael,"[1] said the Senator. "I bought them out of vanity some years ago for a considerable amount of money. They are said to be the finest in Italy, but I

8. Chief magistrate of Venice.
9. "Caring little."

1. Famous Renaissance painter whose works were known for their clarity of form and subtle gravity.

don't like them at all. The colouring is very dark, the faces aren't sufficiently rounded and don't stand out enough, and the draperies don't bear the slightest resemblance to any real cloth. Basically, whatever anyone may say, I don't consider they're a true imitation of nature. You'll only get me to like a picture when I think I'm looking at nature itself—and there aren't any like that. I have lots of paintings, but I don't look at them any more."

As they waited for dinner, Pococurante gave orders for a concerto to be played. Candide found the music delightful.

"This sort of noise helps pass the odd half-hour," said Pococurante, "but if it goes on any longer, everybody finds it tedious, though no one dares say so. Nowadays music is simply nothing more than the art of playing difficult pieces, and that which is merely difficult gives no pleasure in the end.

"Perhaps I'd prefer opera, if they hadn't found a way of turning it into a monstrous hybrid which I find quite repugnant. Let anyone who wishes go and see bad tragedies set to music, with all those scenes that have been put together simply as pretexts—and pretty poor ones at that—for two or three ridiculous songs which allow an actress to show off her vocal cords. Let anyone that wants to—and that can—go and swoon away with ecstasy at the sight of a *castrato* humming the roles of Caesar and Cato[2] and strutting about the stage in that ungainly fashion. For my part I have long since given up going to these paltry affairs, even though nowadays they are the glory of Italy and put its ruling princes to so much expense."

Candide demurred somewhat, though with tact. Martin was entirely of the Senator's opinion.

They sat down to eat, and after an excellent dinner, they went into the library. Candide, on seeing a magnificently bound edition of Homer, complimented his most illustrious host on his good taste.

"This book," he said, "used to delight the great Pangloss, the finest philosopher in Germany."

"It doesn't delight me," said Pococurante coolly. "They did once have me believe that I took pleasure in reading it. But that endless repetition of combats which all seem the same, those gods who are always doing things but never getting anywhere, that Helen who causes the war and then plays scarcely any part in the thing, that Troy they besiege and never take, I found all that deadly boring. I've sometimes asked men of learning if they found reading it as boring as I did. The honest ones admitted that the book used to drop from their hands, but said that you had to have it in your library, like an ancient monument, or like those rusty medals that have no commercial value."

"Your Excellency doesn't think the same about Virgil?" said Candide.

"I agree that the second, fourth, and sixth books of the *Aeneid* are excellent," said Pococurante. "But as for his pious Aeneas, and valiant Cloanthus, and faithful Achates, and little Ascanius, not to mention half-witted King Latinus, and parochial Amata, and insipid Lavinia, I can think of nothing more disagreeable or more likely to leave one absolutely cold. I prefer Tasso and those improbable tales of Ariosto."[3]

"Dare I ask, sir," said Candide, "whether Horace does not afford you considerable pleasure?"

2. Caesar and Cato are the two principal roles in Vivaldi's 1735 opera *Catone in Utica;* such serious heroic roles were commonly sung by castrati. The joke is that Roman statesmen are represented by eunuchs.

3. Voltaire faithfully traces the history of the epic here. Homer's *Iliad* (which recounts the Trojan War) and *Odyssey* were imitated by Virgil's *Aeneid.* Ariosto's *Orlando Furioso* and Tasso's *Gerusalemme Liberata* in turn were partly modeled on the *Aeneid.*

"There are one or two maxims," said Pococurante, "which a man of the world may profit by, and which fix themselves more readily in the memory for being compressed in powerful verse. But I care very little for his journey to Brindisi, or the description of that poor dinner he had, or that foulmouthed quarrel between someone or other called Pupilus, whose language, he says, 'was full of pus,' and someone else whose language 'was like vinegar.' It was only with extreme distaste that I read his crude verses against old women and witches, and I cannot see what merit there can be in telling his friend Maecenas that if he were to place him among the ranks of the lyric poets, he would bang his sublime forehead on the stars in the heavens.[4] Fools admire everything in a respected author. I read only for myself. I like only what may be of use to me."

Candide, who had been brought up never to judge things for himself, was much astonished by what he heard; and Martin found Pococurante's way of thinking rather sensible.

"Oh, look! Here's a copy of Cicero," said Candide. "I'm sure when it comes to this great man, you never tire of reading him?"

"I never read him," replied the Venetian. "What does it matter to me whether he defended Rabirius or Cluentius?[5] What with the cases I try myself, I have quite enough of all that as it is. I might have got on better with his philosophical works, but when I saw that he doubted everything, I decided that I knew as much as he did, and that I didn't need anyone else's help if I was going to be ignorant."

"Ah, look, eighty volumes of the proceedings of an Academy of Science," exclaimed Martin. "There may be something worthwhile there."

"There would be," said Pococurante, "if but one of the authors of all that rubbish had so much as invented the art of making pins. But in every one of those books there's nothing but pointless theorizing, and not a single thing that's useful."

"What a lot of plays there are!" said Candide; "in Italian, in Spanish, in French!"

"Yes," said the Senator, "there are three thousand of them, and not three dozen good ones. As for the collected sermons, which between them aren't worth one page of Seneca, and all those fat tomes on theology, well, you can be sure I never open them, not I, not anyone."

Martin noticed some shelves full of English books.

"I imagine," he said, "that a republican[6] must find most of these enjoyable to read, given how free the authors were to write them?"

"Yes," answered Pococurante, "it is a fine thing to write what one thinks. It is man's privilege. Throughout this Italy of ours, people write only what they do not think. Those who live in the land of the Caesars and the Antonines dare not have an idea without obtaining permission from a Dominican friar. I would be content with the freedom which inspires these English men of genius if their passion for the party interest didn't spoil all the estimable things that would otherwise flow from this precious freedom."

Candide, catching sight of a copy of Milton, asked him if he did not regard this author as a great man.

"Who?" said Pococurante, "that barbarian with his long commentary on the first book of *Genesis* in ten books of difficult verse?[7] That crude imitator of the Greeks

4. These refer to passages in Horace's *Satires* 1.5, 2.8, 1.7 (Voltaire changes Rupilius to Pupilus), *Epodes* 5, 8, 12, and *Odes* 1.1.

5. Referring to orations by Ciceros.

6. A citizen of a free republic like Venice.

7. *Paradise Lost,* the first edition of which was in ten books, and later in twelve books. As Pococurante implies, Milton's poem at points imitates the epics of Tasso and Ariosto (as well as those of Homer and Virgil). Voltaire criticized Milton along similar lines in his *Essay on Epic Poetry* and *Age of Louis XIV.*

who gives such a distorted view of the Creation and, where Moses shows the Eternal Being producing the world with the spoken word, has the Messiah take a great big compass out of a tool-chest in heaven and start drawing a plan? Me, admire the man who ruined Tasso's vision of hell and the devil; who has Lucifer appear disguised variously as a toad or a pygmy; who makes him say the same things over and over again; who makes him discuss theological points; who takes Ariosto's bit of comic invention about the fire-arms seriously and has the devils firing the cannon into heaven? Neither I nor anyone else in Italy has ever been able to enjoy all these extravagant absurdities. The marriage of Sin and Death, and the adders to which Sin gives birth, are enough to make anyone with a delicate stomach vomit. And his long description of a hospital is fit only for a grave-digger. That obscure, bizarre, disgusting poem was spurned at birth. Now I treat it the way it was treated in its own time by the readers in its own country. Anyway, I say what I think, and I couldn't care less whether anyone thinks the way I do or not."

Candide was distressed to hear all this. He admired Homer, and he had a sneaking fondness for Milton.

"Oh, dear!" he said to Martin under his breath, "I'm very much afraid that this man may have a sovereign disregard for our German poets."

"There would be no great harm in that," said Martin.

"Oh, what a great man!" Candide continued to mutter to himself. "What a great genius this Pococurante is! There is no pleasing him."

Having thus inspected all the books, they went down into the garden. Candide praised all its finer features.

"I know of nothing that could be in worse possible taste," said the master of the house. "All you see here are just pretty bits and pieces. But, as from tomorrow, I'm going to have a new one planted along much nobler lines."

When the two curious visitors had taken their leave of His Excellency, Candide turned to Martin:

"Well, there you are," he said. "You will agree that there is the happiest of men, for he is above all that he owns."

"Don't you see", said Martin, "that he's sated on everything he owns? Plato said a long time ago that the best stomachs are not those which reject all foods."

"But," said Candide, "isn't there pleasure in criticizing everything, in finding fault where other men think they find beauty?"

"Which is to say," rejoined Martin, "that there's pleasure in not having pleasure?"

"Oh, all right. Have it your way then," said Candide. "So the only one who's happy is me, when I see Miss Cunégonde again."

"One does well to hope," said Martin.

Meanwhile the days, the weeks went by. Still Cacambo did not return, and Candide was so sunk in misery that it did not even occur to him that Paquette and Brother Giroflée had not so much as come to thank him.

Chapter 26

Of a supper that Candide and Martin ate in the company of six strangers, and who they were

One evening as Candide, accompanied by Martin, was about to sit down to table with the other passing strangers staying in the same hostelry, a man with a face the colour of soot came up behind him and, taking him by the arm, said:

"Be ready to leave when we do, and do not fail."

He turned round: it was Cacambo. Only the sight of Cunégonde could have surprised and pleased him more. He went nearly mad with joy. He embraced his dear friend.

"Cunégonde must be here, then. Where is she? Take me to her. Let me die of joy with her."

"Cunégonde is not here," said Cacambo. "She's in Constantinople."

"Ah, heavens! In Constantinople! But were she in China, I should fly to her! Let's go!"

"We will leave after supper," replied Cacambo. "I can't say any more. I'm a slave and my master's waiting for me. I've got to go and wait on him at table. Don't breathe a word. Have supper, and then be ready and waiting."

Candide, torn between joy and pain, absolutely delighted to have seen his faithful agent again, surprised to see him now a slave, full of the idea of being reunited with his beloved, his heart in tumult and his mind in a spin, sat down to eat in the company of Martin, who was watching all these goings-on with equanimity, and of the six strangers who had come to spend carnival in Venice.

Cacambo, who was filling the glass of one of these strangers, drew near to his master's ear at the end of the meal and said to him:

"Sire, Your Majesty may depart when he wishes. The ship is ready."

Having said this, he left the room. Astonished, the supper guests were exchanging silent glances, when another servant came up to his master and said:

"Sire, Your Majesty's carriage is at Padua, and the boat is ready."

His master made a sign, and the servant left. All the guests stared at each other again, and the general amazement increased. A third servant, coming up to a third stranger, said to him:

"Believe me, Sire, Your Majesty must not stay here a moment longer. I shall go and get everything ready."

And he disappeared at once.

Candide and Martin now had no doubt that this was some masquerade to do with the carnival. A fourth servant said to a fourth master:

"Your Majesty may depart at his convenience," and left the room like the others.

The fifth servant said the same to the fifth master. But the sixth servant spoke differently to the sixth stranger, who was sitting next to Candide.

He said to him:

"Lor me, Sire, they're refusing to let Your Majesty have any more credit, nor me neither, and the pair of us'll as like be carted off to the clink this very night. I'm off to look after number one, thank you very much. Good-bye."

The servants having all vanished, the six strangers, Candide and Martin remained deep in silence. Finally Candide broke it:

"Gentlemen," he said, "this is some strange joke. How is it that you are all Kings? For my part I must tell you that neither I nor Martin are anything of the sort."

Cacambo's master then intervened gravely and said in Italian:

"I am no joke, my name is Achmed III.[8] I was Grand Sultan for several years; I dethroned my brother; my nephew has dethroned me; my viziers have had their heads cut off; I am spending the rest of my days in the old seraglio; my nephew the

8. Sultan of the Ottoman Empire from 1703 until 1730, when he was deposed by a military coup.

Grand Sultan Mahmood occasionally allows me to travel for my health, and I have come to spend carnival in Venice."

A young man who was next to Achmed spoke after him and said:

"My name is Ivan, I was Emperor of all the Russias.[9] I was dethroned in my cradle; my father and mother were locked up; I was brought up in prison; I occasionally get permission to travel, accompanied by my guards, and I have come to spend carnival in Venice."

The third said:

"I am Charles Edward, King of England.[1] My father renounced his claim to the throne in my favour; I have fought many battles to make good my claim; eight hundred of my supporters had their hearts ripped out and their cheeks slapped with them; I was put in prison; I am on my way to Rome to visit my father the King, dethroned like me and my grandfather, and I have come to spend carnival in Venice."

The fourth then spoke up and said:

"I am the King of Poland.[2] The fortunes of war have dispossessed me of my ancestral domains; my father suffered the same reverses; I am resigned to Providence like Sultan Achmed, Emperor Ivan, and King Charles Edward, whom God preserve, and I have come to spend carnival in Venice."

The fifth said: "I too am the King of Poland.[3] I have lost my kingdom twice; but Providence has given me another domain, in which I have done more good than all the Kings of Sarmatia put together have ever been able to manage on the banks of the Vistula. I too am resigned to Providence, and I have come to spend carnival in Venice."

It remained for the sixth monarch to speak.

"Gentlemen," he said, "I am not so great a lord as any of you but, well, I have been a King just like everyone else. I am Theodore;[4] I was elected King in Corsica; they called me "Your Majesty," and now they hardly call me "Sir"; once I minted money, and now I haven't a penny; once I had two secretaries of state, and now I have scarcely a valet; I once sat on a throne, and I have spent a long time in prison in London, with straw for a bed. I am much afraid I shall be treated in the same way here, although I came like Your Majesties to spend carnival in Venice."

The other five Kings listened to this speech with a noble compassion. Each of them gave King Theodore twenty sequins[5] to buy coats and shirts, and Candide made him a present of a diamond worth two thousand sequins.

"Who can this be then," said the five Kings, "a mere private individual who is in a position to give a hundred times as much as each of us, and who gives it?"

Just as they were leaving the table, there arrived in the same hostelry four Serene Highnesses who had also lost their domains through the fortunes of war, and who were coming to spend what was left of the carnival in Venice. But Candide did not even notice these new arrivals. All he could think about was going to find his dear Cunégonde in Constantinople.

9. Ivan VI, whom Catherine the Great imprisoned and ultimately put to death in 1764.

1. The "Young Pretender" (1720–1788), son of James Stuart (the "Old Pretender") and grandson of King James II of England; called "Bonnie Prince Charlie" by the Scots supporters of the uprising he led against the English crown, disastrously defeated at the Battle of Culloden in 1746.

2. Augustus III, Elector of Saxony and King of Poland, was driven from Saxony by Frederick the Great in 1756. His father Augustus II had similarly been dispossessed by Charles XII of Sweden.

3. Stanislas Lesczinski, King of Poland from 1704 to 1709, when he was driven out by the Russians. He unsuccessfully attempted to regain the Polish throne in 1733 and was made Duke of Lorraine in 1735.

4. The representative of Holy Roman Emperor Charles VI, who led a revolt in Corsica against the Genoese in the 1730s.

5. Venetian coins.

Chapter 27

Candide's journey to Constantinople

Faithful Cacambo had already obtained permission from the Turkish captain who was to take Sultan Achmed back to Constantinople for Candide and Martin to join them on board. Together they made their way to the ship, having prostrated themselves before His unhappy Highness.

On the way Candide was saying to Martin:

"There you are, you see. That was six dethroned Kings we had supper with. And that's not all. Among those six Kings there was one I could give alms to. Perhaps there are lots more princes who are even more unfortunate. Whereas me, all I've lost is a hundred sheep, and I'm flying to the arms of Cunégonde. My dear Martin, once more, Pangloss was right: all is well."

"I certainly hope so," said Martin.

"But," said Candide, "that was a pretty unlikely adventure we had in Venice. Who ever saw or heard tell of six dethroned kings having supper together in a tavern."

"It's no more extraordinary," said Martin, "than most of the things that have happened to us. It's very common for kings to be dethroned, and as for the honour of having supper with them, there's nothing special about that."

Scarce was Candide aboard than he fell upon the neck of his former manservant, his friend Cacambo.

"Well, then," said Candide, "what's Cunégonde doing? Is she still a paragon of beauty? Does she still love me? How is she? Presumably you bought her a palace in Constantinople?"

"My dear master," replied Cacambo, "Cunégonde is washing dishes on the shores of the Sea of Marmara for a prince who has very few dishes. She's a slave in the household of an ex-ruler called Ragotsky,[6] to whom in his exile the Grand Turk gives three crowns a day. But, worse than that, she has lost her beauty and become horribly ugly."

"Ah, beautiful or ugly," said Candide, "I'm a man of honour, and my duty is to love her always. But how can she possibly have fallen so low with the five or six millions you took her?"

"Look here," said Cacambo. "Didn't I have to give two million to Señor don Fernando d'Ibaraa y Figueora y Mascarenes y Lampourdos y Souza, Governor of Buenos Aires, for permission to take Miss Cunégonde back? And didn't a pirate very kindly relieve us of the rest? And didn't the same pirate take us to Cape Matapan, Milo, Nicaria, Samos, Petra, the Dardanelles, Marmara, and Scutari? Cunégonde and the old woman are now working as servants to the prince I told you about, and I am a slave of the dethroned sultan."

"What a chain of appalling calamities one after another," said Candide. "But after all, I do still have some diamonds left. I will easily secure Cunégonde's release. It really is a pity that she has become so ugly."

Then, turning to Martin:

"Who do you think one should feel most sorry for," he said, "Emperor Achmed, Emperor Ivan, King Charles Edward, or me?"

"I've no idea," said Martin. "I'd have to see inside all your hearts to know the answer to that."

6. Rákóczy (1676–1735), prince of Transylvania, led an unsuccessful uprising against Joseph I in Hungary in the early 1700s and subsequently fled to the Sea of Marmara.

"Ah!" said Candide, "if Pangloss were here, he would know, he would tell us the answer."

"I don't know what sort of scales your Pangloss could have used to weigh the misfortunes of men and calculate their sufferings," said Martin. "All I presume is that there are millions of people on this earth one might feel a hundred times sorrier for than King Charles Edward, Emperor Ivan, and Sultan Achmed."

"That may well be so," said Candide.

In a few days they reached the channel leading to the Black Sea. The first thing Candide did was to buy Cacambo back at a very high price, and then without delay he and his companions quickly boarded a galley and made for the shores of the Sea of Marmara in search of Cunégonde, ugly though she might be.

Amongst the galley-slaves were two prisoners who rowed extremely badly, and to whose naked shoulders the Levantine captain would periodically apply a few lashes of his bull's pizzle. Candide's natural reaction was to pay more attention to them than to the other galley-slaves, and he drew near them with compassion. One or two features on their disfigured faces seemed to him to bear some resemblance to those of Pangloss and that unfortunate Jesuit, Miss Cunégonde's brother, the Baron. The thought touched and saddened him. He watched them even more closely.

"Quite honestly," he said to Cacambo, "if I hadn't seen Maître Pangloss hanged and if I hadn't had the misfortune to kill the Baron, I could swear it was them rowing on this galley."

On hearing the names of the Baron and Pangloss, the two galley-slaves gave a great shout, stopped still on their bench, and dropped their oars. The Levantine captain rushed up to them, and the lashes from his bull's pizzle rained down anew.

"Stop, stop, good sir," screamed Candide. "I will give you all the money you want."

"Why, it's Candide!" said one of the two galley-slaves.

"Why, it's Candide!" said the other.

"Am I dreaming all this?" said Candide. "Am I awake? Am I really here on this galley? Is that the Baron I killed? Is that the Maître Pangloss I saw hanged?"

"It is we, it is we," they replied.

"What, so that's the great philosopher?" said Martin.

"Look here, Mr. Levantine captain," said Candide, "how much ransom do you want for Mr. von Thunder-ten-tronckh, one of the foremost barons of the Empire, and for Mr. Pangloss, the profoundest metaphysician in Germany?"

"You Christian cur," replied the Levantine slave-driver. "Since these two Christian slave dogs are barons and metaphysicians, which is no doubt a great honour where they come from, you can give me fifty thousand sequins."

"You shall have them, sir. Get me to Constantinople as fast as you possibly can, and you will be paid on the spot. On second thoughts, take me to Miss Cunégonde."

The Levantine captain, at Candide's first offer, had already altered course for the city, and he bid the crew row faster than a bird may cleave the air.

Candide embraced the Baron and Pangloss a hundred times.

"And how did I not kill you, my dear Baron? And you, my dear Pangloss, how is it that you are alive after being hanged? And what are you both doing on a galley in Turkey?"

"Is it really true that my dear sister is here in this country?" said the Baron.

"Yes," replied Cacambo.

"So here is my dear Candide again," exclaimed Pangloss.

Candide introduced them to Martin and Cacambo. They all embraced; everybody talked at once. The galley was flying along; they were already in port. A Jew was summoned, to whom Candide sold a diamond worth a hundred thousand sequins for fifty thousand, and who swore by Abraham that he could offer not a sequin more. Thereupon Candide paid the ransom for the Baron and Pangloss. The latter threw himself at the feet of his liberator and bathed them in tears; the other thanked him with a nod of his head and promised to reimburse him at the earliest opportunity.

"But can it really be that my sister is in Turkey?" he said.

"It really can," retorted Cacambo, "seeing as how she's washing dishes for a Prince of Transylvania."

At once two Jews were sent for. Candide sold some more diamonds, and they all left by another galley to go and deliver Cunégonde from bondage.

Chapter 28

What happened to Candide, Cunégonde, Pangloss, Martin, and co.

"Once more, forgive me," Candide said to the Baron. "Forgive me, reverend father, for running you through with my sword like that."

"We'll say no more about it," said the Baron. "I did speak rather sharply, I admit. But since you want to know how you came to find me on a galley, I will tell you that after being cured of my wounds by the college's apothecary monk, I was set upon and abducted by a group of Spaniards. I was put in prison in Buenos Aires just after my sister left there. I asked to be allowed to return to Rome to be with the Father General: I was appointed almoner to His Excellency the ambassador of France in Constantinople. I hadn't been in post more than a week when one evening I ran into a young icoglan,[7] who was very good-looking. It was extremely hot: the young man wanted to go for a swim; I took the opportunity to go swimming too. I did not know that it was a capital offence for a Christian to be found stark naked with a young Muslim. A cadi[8] had me birched a hundred times on the soles of the feet and sent me to the galleys. I don't believe there's ever been a more ghastly miscarriage of justice. But what I'd like to know is why my sister is working in the kitchens of a Transylvanian ruler in exile among the Turks."

"But you, my dear Pangloss," said Candide, "how is it that we meet again?"

"It is true that you did see me hanged," said Pangloss. "I was, of course, to have been burned but, as you will remember, it poured with rain just as they were about to roast me. The storm was so violent that they gave up trying to light the fire, and I was hanged for want of a better alternative. A surgeon bought my body, took me home with him, and dissected me. First he made a cruciform incision in me from my navel to my collar-bone. One can't have a worse hanging than I'd had. The executive arm of the high works of the Holy Inquisition, namely a sub-deacon, certainly did a splendid job when it came to burning people, but he wasn't used to hanging. The rope was wet and wouldn't slip through properly, and it got caught. So I was still breathing. The crucial incision made me give such an enormous shriek that my surgeon fell over backwards and, thinking it was the devil himself he was dissecting, rushed away, nearly dying of fright, and then, to cap it all, fell down the stairs in his flight. His wife came running from the next room at the noise, saw me stretched out on the table with my crucial incision, took even greater fright than her husband, fled, and fell over him.

7. A page of the Sultan, often employed in the seraglio.

8. A ranking Muslim official.

"When they had collected their wits a little, I heard the surgeon's wife say to her husband: "My dear, what on earth were you thinking of, dissecting a heretic like that? Don't you know those sort of people always have the devil in them? I'm going to fetch a priest this minute to exorcize him." I shuddered to hear this, and I mustered what little strength I had left and cried out: "Have mercy on me!" In the end the Portuguese barber plucked up courage.[9] He sewed me up again, and his wife even nursed me. I was up and about again in a fortnight. The barber found me a position and made me lackey to a Knight of Malta who was going to Venice. But since my master had not the means to pay me, I entered service with a merchant of Venice and followed him to Constantinople.

"One day I happened to enter a mosque. There was no one in there apart from an old imam and a very pretty young worshipper, who was saying her paternosters. Her bosom was uncovered for all to see, and in her cleavage was a lovely posy of tulips, roses, anemones, buttercups, hyacinths, and auriculas. She dropped her posy; I picked it up and replaced it for her with respectful zeal. I took so long about replacing it that the imam became angry and, seeing I was a Christian, called for help. I was taken to the cadi, who sentenced me to a hundred strokes of the lath on the soles of my feet and sent me to the galleys. I was chained up in precisely the same galley and on precisely the same bench as His Lordship the Baron. On the galley were four young men from Marseilles, five Neapolitan priests, and two monks from Corfu, who all told us that this sort of thing happened every day. His Lordship claimed he'd been more unjustly treated than I had. I maintained for my part that it was much more permissible putting a posy back on a woman's bosom than being stark naked with an icoglan. We used to argue the whole time, and were getting twenty lashes a day with the bull's pizzle when, by a turn in the chain of events that governs this universe, you were led to our galley and bought us back."

"Now then, my dear Pangloss!" Candide said to him. "When you were being hanged, and dissected, and beaten, and made to row in a galley, did you continue to think that things were turning out for the best?"

"I still feel now as I did at the outset," replied Pangloss. "I am a philosopher after all. It wouldn't do for me to go back on what I said before, what with Leibniz not being able to be wrong, and pre-established harmony being the finest thing in the world, not to mention the *plenum* and *materia subtilis."*[1]

CHAPTER 29

How Candide was reunited with Cunégonde and the old woman

While Candide, the Baron, Pangloss, Martin, and Cacambo were recounting their adventures, and philosophizing about which events in the universe are contingent and which not contingent, and arguing about effects and causes, moral and physical evil, freedom and necessity, and about what consolations are to be had on board a Turkish galley, they landed on the shores of the Sea of Marmara at the house of the Prince of Transylvania. The first thing they saw was Cunégonde and the old woman hanging towels out on a line to dry.

The Baron went pale at the sight. Candide, the tender-hearted lover, on seeing his fair Cunégonde all brown, with her eyes bloodshot, her bosom shrivelled, her cheeks

9. Barbers often did minor surgery.

1. Leibniz posited the idea of a pre-established harmony to describe the correspondence between the physical and spiritual realms. Leibniz and Descartes argued that the universe was a *plenum* ("fullness"), meaning there is no empty space in the universe, and that the space between planets was filled by an ethereal *materia subtilis* ("fine matter"). This philosophy was discredited by Newton.

wrinkled, and her arms red and peeling, recoiled three paces in horror, and then went forward out of sheer good manners. She embraced Candide and her brother. They embraced the old woman. Candide bought them both free.

There was a small farm in the vicinity. The old woman suggested to Candide that it would do them nicely while they waited for the whole company to fall on better times. Cunégonde did not know that she had become ugly; no one had told her. She reminded Candide of his promises in such a firm tone that good Candide did not dare refuse her. He intimated to the Baron, therefore, that he was going to marry his sister.

"I will not tolerate such a demeaning act on her part," he said, "nor such insolence from you. Never shall it be said that I allowed such infamy: my wife's children would never be able to mix in Germany's noble chapters.[2] No, my sister will marry no one but a baron of the Empire."

Cunégonde threw herself at his feet and bathed them with her tears; he was inflexible.

"You great numskull," said Candide, "I've saved you from the galleys, I've paid your ransom, and I've paid your sister's. She was washing dishes here, she's ugly, I have the goodness to make her my wife, and you still think you're going to stand in our way! I'd kill you all over again if I let my anger have its way."

"You can kill me all over again if you want," said the Baron, "but you won't marry my sister so long as I live."

Chapter 30

Conclusion

Candide, in his heart of hearts, had no desire to marry Cunégonde. But the extreme impertinence of the Baron made him decide to go through with the marriage, and Cunégonde was pressing him so keenly that he could not go back on his word. He consulted Pangloss, Martin, and the faithful Cacambo. Pangloss wrote a fine dissertation in which he proved that the Baron had no rights over his sister, and that it was open to her, under all the laws of the Empire, to marry Candide with the left hand.[3] Martin was for throwing the Baron into the sea. Cacambo decided they should return him to the Levantine captain and have him put back in the galleys, after which he was to be packed off to the Father General in Rome on the first available ship. This view of the matter was thought to be very sound. The old woman approved, nothing was said to his sister, the thing was done with the help of a little money, and they had the pleasure of bettering a Jesuit and punishing the arrogance of a German baron.

It was quite natural to imagine that, after so many disasters, Candide, now married to his sweetheart and living with the philosophical Pangloss, the philosophical Martin, the prudent Cacambo and the old woman and, moreover, having brought back so many diamonds from the land of the ancient Incas, would be leading the most agreeable of all possible lives. But he was swindled so many times by the Jews that all he had left in the end was his little farm; his wife, who grew uglier with every day that passed, became shrewish and impossible to live with; the old woman was infirm and even more bad-tempered than Cunégonde; Cacambo, who worked in the garden and travelled to Constantinople to sell vegetables, was worn out with work and cursed his fate; Pangloss was in despair at not being a luminary in some German

2. Assemblies of the nobility.

3. A marriage between persons of different rank in which the inferior's status is not raised.

university. As for Martin, he was firmly persuaded that one is just as badly off wherever one is; he put up with things as they were. Candide, Martin, and Pangloss would argue sometimes about metaphysics and ethics. They would often see boats passing beneath the windows of the farm-house laden with effendis, pashas, and cadis,[4] who were being exiled to Lemnos or Mytilene or Erzerum. They would see more cadis, more pashas, and more effendis coming to take the place of those who had been expelled, and being themselves in their turn expelled. They would see heads duly stuffed with straw being taken for display before the Sublime Porte.[5] Such sights would give rise to yet further disquisitions, and when they were not arguing, the boredom was so excessive that the old woman made bold to say to them one day:

"I would like to know which is worse: being raped a hundred times by negro pirates, having a buttock chopped off, running the gauntlet of the Bulgars, being flogged and hanged in an *auto-da-fé,* being dissected, rowing in a galley, in short, suffering all the misfortunes we've all suffered, or simply being stuck here doing nothing?"

"That is a good question," said Candide.

This speech gave rise to renewed speculation, and Martin in particular came to the conclusion that man was born to spend his life alternately a prey to the throes of anxiety and the lethargy of boredom. Candide did not agree, but asserted nothing. Pangloss admitted that he had always suffered horribly; but having once maintained that everything was going marvellously, he still maintained it, and believed nothing of the sort.

One thing finally confirmed Martin in his detestable principles, gave Candide more than ever pause, and embarrassed Pangloss. This was the sight one day of Paquette and Brother Giroflée arriving at their farm in a state of extreme wretchedness. They had very quickly gone through their three thousand piastres, left each other, patched things up, quarrelled again, been put in prison, escaped; and in the end Brother Giroflée had turned Turk. Paquette still pursued her profession, and no longer earned any money at it.

"I told you so," Martin said to Candide. "I knew what you gave them would soon be gone and would only make them even more wretched. You had more piastres than you knew what to do with, you and Cacambo, and you are no happier than Brother Giroflée and Paquette."

"Aha!" said Pangloss to Paquette, "so heaven brings you back here among us, my poor child! Do you know, you've cost me the tip of my nose, an eye and an ear? And you, just look at the state you're in! What a world we live in!"

This new turn of events led them to philosophize more than ever.

There lived in the neighbourhood a very famous dervish,[6] who passed for the greatest philosopher in Turkey. They went to consult him. Pangloss acted as their spokesman and said to him:

"Master, we have come to ask you to tell us why such a strange animal as man was created."

"What's that to you?" said the dervish. "Is it any of your business?"

"But, reverend father," said Candide, "there's an awful lot of evil in the world."

4. Men of high rank.
5. The gate of the Turkish court.
6. Muslim holy man.

"What does it matter whether there's evil or there's good," said the dervish. "When His Highness sends a ship to Egypt, does he worry whether the mice on board are comfortable or not?"

"So what must we do then?" said Pangloss.

"Be silent," said the dervish.

"I had flattered myself," said Pangloss, "that we might have a talk about effects and causes, the best of all possible worlds, the origin of evil, the nature of the soul, and pre-established harmony."

The dervish, at these words, slammed the door in their faces.

During this conversation news had spread that two viziers of the bench and the mufti[7] had been strangled in Constantinople, and several of their friends impaled. This catastrophe made a great stir everywhere for some hours. On their way back to the farm Pangloss, Candide, and Martin met a kindly old man who was taking the air at his door beneath an arbour of orange-trees. Pangloss, who was as curious as he was prone to philosophizing, asked him the name of the mufti who had just been strangled.

"I have no idea," replied the fellow, "and I never have known what any mufti or vizier was called. What you have just told me means absolutely nothing to me. I have no doubt that in general those who get involved in public affairs do sometimes come to a sad end and that they deserve it. But I never enquire what's going on in Constantinople. I am content to send my fruit for sale there from the garden I cultivate."

Having said this, he invited the strangers into his house. His two daughters and two sons offered them several kinds of sorbet which they made themselves, some *kaïmak*[8] sharpened with the zest of candied citron, some oranges, lemons, limes, pineapple, and pistachio nuts, and some Mocha coffee which had not been blended with that awful coffee from Batavia and the islands. After which the two daughters of this good Muslim perfumed the beards of Candide, Pangloss, and Martin.

"You must have a vast and magnificent property," said Candide to the Turk.

"I have but twenty acres," replied the Turk. "I cultivate them with my children. Work keeps us from three great evils: boredom, vice, and need."

Candide, on his way back to his farm, thought long and hard about what the Turk had said, and commented to Pangloss and Martin:

"That kind old man seems to me to have made a life for himself which is much preferable to that of those six Kings with whom we had the honour of having supper."

"High rank can be very dangerous," said Pangloss; "all the philosophers say so. For the fact is, Eglon, King of the Moabites, was slain by Ehud; Absalom was hanged by the hair on his head and had three darts thrust through his heart; King Nadab, son of Jeroboam, was smitten by Baasha; King Elah by Zimri; Joram by Jehu; Athaliah by Jehoiada; and Kings Jehoiakim, Jehoiachin, and Zedekiah entered into captivity.[9] You know what sort of deaths befell Croesus, Astyages, Darius, Dionysius of Syracuse, Pyrrhus, Perseus, Hannibal, Jugurtha, Ariovistus, Caesar, Pompey, Nero, Otho, Vitellius, Domitian, Richard II of England, Edward II, Henry VI, Richard III, Mary Stuart, Charles I, France's three Henris, and the Emperor Henri IV? You know . . ."

"I also know," said Candide, "that we must cultivate our garden."

7. Judge.
8. Sweet cream.
9. Having given a string of biblical examples, Pangloss next turns to classical and then modern cases.

"You're right," said Pangloss; "for when man was placed in the garden of Eden, he was placed there *ut operaretur eum*—that he might work[1]—which proves that man was not born to rest."

"Let's get down to work and stop all this philosophizing," said Martin. "It's the only way to make life bearable."

The little society all fell in with this laudable plan. Each began to exercise his talents. Their small amount of land produced a great deal. Cunégonde was in truth very ugly, but she became an excellent pastry-cook. Paquette embroidered. The old woman took care of the linen. Everyone made himself useful, including Brother Giroflée; he was a very fine carpenter, and even became quite the gentleman. And sometimes Pangloss would say to Candide:

"All events form a chain in the best of all possible worlds. For in the end, if you had not been given a good kick up the backside and chased out of a beautiful castle for loving Miss Cunégonde, and if you hadn't been subjected to the Inquisition, and if you hadn't wandered about America on foot, and if you hadn't dealt the Baron a good blow with your sword, and if you hadn't lost all your sheep from that fine country of Eldorado, you wouldn't be here now eating candied citron and pistachio nuts."

"That is well put," replied Candide, "but we must cultivate our garden."

Alexander Pope

1688–1744

Alexander Pope was perhaps the most celebrated poet of the eighteenth century. He was also a tiny hunchback and a Catholic during a rabidly anti-Catholic time in England. The sufferings he endured because of his deformity and religion jaundiced his view of humanity. Satire became his preferred mode. Yet this "hunch-backed toad," as one critic called him (toads were believed to spit poison) was also known for his "general benevolence and particular fondness," in the words of another. Like the philosopher Kant, he cultivated close friendships in the absence of sexual relationships. Aside from his satiric genius, he was acknowledged a master of all the neoclassical genres that predominated in the poetic practice of his age. Through them all he developed what remains his signature style: the rhyming "heroic couplets" in which he delivers nuggets of wisdom.

For Pope, Fate took the form of a wayward cow. He was trampled by one at age twelve, severely wounded, and thereafter developed a spinal infection that within a few years transformed a pretty child into a "little, tender, and crazy Carcass," as one of his early mentors, the playwright William Wycherley, lamented. Thus began what Pope later described as "this long disease, my life." His weakness and deformity made him unable to dress or undress himself; a maid had to help him in and out of the fur undergarment he wore because of his extreme sensitivity to cold, lace up the corset without which he could not stand upright, and cover it all with a warm shirt and flannel waistcoat, shortened on one side. At table he had to have his seat raised, like a child's. Worse than all this, he was in constant pain. He suffered especially from headaches, which he tried to treat by inhaling coffee vapors (like his character the Baron in his great mock-epic satire, *The Rape of the Lock*).

1. Genesis 2:15.

It was no mere accident that the young Alexander was out roaming the countryside, dangerously exposed to rural misadventures. His parents, a London linen merchant and his second wife, had just been forced to leave the city for the country village of Binfield, near Windsor. They were complying with recent laws designed to bar Catholics like themselves from any significant resources or advantages, and especially from government—so that they were no longer allowed to live within ten miles of the royal seat in London. The Protestant rulers William and Mary, who ousted Mary's Catholic father King James II in their "Glorious Revolution" the year of Pope's birth, intended to end forever the long and bloody history of struggle between Catholic and Protestant factions for control of the English throne, which stretched back to the heirs of Henry VIII in the sixteenth century. They succeeded—partly by encouraging the enactment of particularly harsh anti-Catholic legislation. In addition to being exiled from London and forbidden to celebrate mass in public, Catholics were excluded from attending public schools or universities, from holding public office or voting in elections, and from owning real estate or inheriting it. The severity of these restrictions varied even during Pope's lifetime, but Catholics would not regain equal rights with other British subjects until 1829: one year after Protestant dissenters, four years before slaves, and eighty-nine years before women of any persuasion or social standing. Meanwhile widespread prejudice saw all Catholics in Britain as potential traitors. Pope suffered as much under this social disability as he did under his physical one.

Luckily young Alexander encountered some human neighbors in the countryside who influenced the course of his life in positive ways. There he met William Wycherley and through him his fellow-dramatist William Congreve, the poet William Walsh, and the statesman Sir William Trumbull. With a little help from these and other friends Pope continued his study of classical languages and literature on his own, and traveled to London to study French and Italian. By these efforts he became as able a classicist as any trained at Oxford or Cambridge. When Pope was still only seventeen, through the good offices of Walsh and Congreve his poetry came to the attention of prominent publisher Jacob Tonson, who brought out Pope's first publication several years later. Several early publications, including a first version of *The Rape of the Lock,* gave him an entree to London literary circles, and he tried to maintain good relations with the Whig associates of the essayists Addison and Steele even as he became closely associated with Jonathan Swift and the other Tory members of the Scriblerus Club, a short-lived but influential group of satirists.

It is a tried–and–true strategy of writers who would become great men to edit or translate the great men of yore, thus elevating themselves by association. This strategy worked brilliantly for Pope. By 1713, having made enough of a name for himself with his first publications to attract subscribers to his next, he agreed to translate Homer's *Iliad* and *Odyssey.* "What terrible moments does one feel, after one has engaged for large work!" he later wrote. "In the beginning of my translating the *Iliad,* I wished anybody would hang me, a hundred times." The hard work paid off, however, for it was this translation that made Pope truly famous, and moreover made him rich. It made him the first commercially successful English poet: the first, that is, to earn enough from the sale of his published works to dispense with the previously indispensable noble patrons, royal pension, or politically appointed sinecure. "Thanks to Homer," as he acknowledged in his *Imitations of Horace* (*Epistle* 2.2), he could henceforth "live and thrive,/ Indebted to no Prince or Peer alive."

So established was Pope's reputation by the first volumes of his *Iliad* that he soon ventured to publish his collected *Works of Alexander Pope* (1717), though he was still in his twenties. That same year Pope's father died, and during the next he moved into a rented villa called Twickenham, at the regulation distance from London. It became famous for the gardens he created there. Its five acres of land were unfortunately separated from the house by the highway to London, and Pope, declaring that "what we cannot *overcome,* we must *undergo,*" caused the two areas to be joined by a tunnel, which he grandiosely christened his "Grotto of Friendship and Liberty." This burrow actually became the most elaborate and most celebrated part of his whole landscape garden. He decorated its surfaces with semiprecious and other exotic stones, marble, glass, and shells. Comparing it favorably to his poetic creations, he called it his "best imitation of nature," and invited only his best friends to share this favorite retreat from the outside world.

While finishing his translation of the *Odyssey* Pope tried to repeat the marketing strategy that had worked so well for him, by editing the works of Shakespeare (1725). He thought even less of this type of literary labor than he had of translating, lamenting that he had sunk, "by due gradation of dulness, from a poet a translator, and from a translator, a mere editor." Indeed his bowdlerized versions of the plays were soon discredited by contemporary Shakespeare scholars. Pope lashed out in revenge against anyone who had ever made him feel small in *The Dunciad* (1728), in which he attacked his former friend Lady Mary Wortley Montagu, the popular novelist Eliza Haywood, and nearly every other writer alive. This satirical mock-epic purported to trace "the Progress of Dulness" in the characters of the hack writers, or "dunces" of the day—authors who, like Pope himself, were attempting to make writing a commercially successful enterprise. Pope continued another fifteen years engaged in his brilliantly successful manipulation of the medium of print to disparage other writers and enhance his own image. He published *An Essay on Man* anonymously in 1733–1734, for fear of attacks by the hordes of literary enemies he'd made with his earlier satires, and even got his friends to rally his enemies to support its unknown author as a new "rival" to Pope's literary supremacy. He then published his own letters while he was still alive (1737), after strategically editing them. Not many years later he died, surrounded by friends in spite of his printed vituperations. Some of these friends feared that he had hastened his demise by his habit of using a silver saucepan to heat his favorite dish of potted lampreys. When asked on his deathbed by a Catholic friend whether a priest should be called so that he could "die like his father and mother," Pope replied, "I do not think it essential, but it will be very right; and I thank you for putting me in mind of it." He left the fortune he had amassed to his dear friend Martha Blount, with whom he had been in love all his life.

The Rape of the Lock (1712–1717) *The Rape of the Lock* is Pope's mocking response to a real-life incident in which two Catholic families of high standing feuded after the scion of one, Robert, Lord Petre, snipped a love-lock from the unwilling daughter of the other, Miss Arabella Fermor. Their mutual friend John Caryll asked Pope to try and "laugh them together again" by writing a poem that would make a joke of the whole affair.

Pope's method was to highlight the absurdity of this tempest in a teapot by comparing small things to great: writing an epic on the model of Homer and Virgil with this minor social squabble as its subject and the trivial, domestic world of English high society as its setting. In this plan he had in mind recent models of comic mock-epics, notably Boileau's *Le Lutrin,* (1674, 1683), which similarly satirized a dispute among priests over an object of little more than symbolic significance (a lectern). Pope published his first version in 1712, which seemed only to aggravate the original quarrel by the public attention it attracted. In 1714 and 1717, as he progressed in his work of translating Homer, he offered the public revised and expanded versions, each time adding more specific—and thus more ludicrous—parallels to the classical epics. The Homeric rape of Helen—the abduction that led to the Trojan War—becomes the violation of a modern society belle's elaborate coiffure. Her lament, "Oh hadst thou, cruel! been content to seize / Hairs less in sight, or any hairs but these!" exposes with ribald humor the misplaced value with which, Pope implies, his contemporaries invested outward signs of honor and status to the neglect of real virtue. In keeping with its original conciliatory intent, however, this poem is far lighter in tone, less bitter and brittle than more ruthless satires like *The Dunciad.* As Pope himself described it to friend, "'Tis a sort of writing very like tickling."

The Rape of the Lock

An Heroi-Comical Poem in Five Cantos

Nolueram, Belinda, *tuos violare capillos*
Sed juvat hoc precibus me tribuisse tuis.

Martial[1]

TO MRS. ARABELLA FERMOR

MADAM,

It will be in vain to deny that I have some regard for this piece, since I dedicate it to you. Yet you may bear me witness, it was intended only to divert a few young ladies, who have good sense and good humour enough to laugh not only at their sex's little unguarded follies, but at their own.[2] But as it was communicated with the air of a secret, it soon found its way into the world. An imperfect copy having been offered to a bookseller, you had the good-nature, for my sake, to consent to the publication of one more correct. This I was forced to, before I had executed half my design, for the machinery was entirely wanting to complete it.

The machinery, Madam, is a term invented by the critics, to signify that part which the deities, angels, or demons, are made to act in a poem. For the ancient poets are in one respect like many modern ladies, let an action be never so trivial in itself, they always make it appear of the utmost importance. These machines I determined to raise on a very new and odd foundation, the Rosicrucian[3] doctrine of spirits.

I know how disagreeable it is to make use of hard words before a lady; but it is so much the concern of a poet to have his works understood, and particularly by your sex, that you must give me leave to explain two or three difficult terms.

The Rosicrucians are a people I must bring you acquainted with. The best account I know of them is in a French book, called Le Comte de Gabalis,[4] which both in its title and size is so like a novel, that many of the fair sex have read it for one by mistake. According to these gentlemen the four elements are inhabited by spirits, which they call sylphs, gnomes, nymphs, and salamanders.[5] The gnomes or demons of earth delight in mischief; but the sylphs, whose habitation is in the air, are the best conditioned[6] creatures imaginable. For they say, any mortals may enjoy the most intimate familiarities with these gentle spirits, upon a condition very easy to all true adepts, an inviolate preservation of chastity.

As to the following cantos, all the passages of them are as fabulous,[7] as the vision at the beginning, or the transformation at the end, except the loss of your hair, which I always mention with reverence. The human persons are as fictitious as the airy ones; and the character of Belinda, as it is now managed, resembles you in nothing but in beauty.

If this poem had as many graces as there are in your person, or in your mind, yet I could never hope it should pass through the world half so uncensured as you have

1. "I did not wish, [Belinda,] to violate your locks, but I rejoice to have yielded this to your wishes" (Martial, *Epigrams* 12.84). Pope has substituted "Belinda" for Martial's "Polytimus."
2. I.e., at their own individual follies as well.
3. A secret society of the 17th and 18th centuries, devoted to the study of ancient religious, philosophical, and mystical doctrines.
4. Written in 1670 by the Abbé de Monfaucon de Villars, its approach to Rosicrucian philosophy was lighthearted.
5. Elemental spirits living in fire.
6. Best natured.
7. Fictional.

done. But let its fortune be what it will, mine is happy enough, to have given me this occasion of assuring you that I am, with the truest esteem,

Madam,
Your most obedient, humble servant,
A. Pope

Canto 1

What dire offence from am'rous causes springs,
What mighty contests rise from trivial things,
I sing[8]—This verse to Caryll,[9] Muse! is due:
This, ev'n Belinda may vouchsafe to view:
Slight is the subject, but not so the praise,
If she inspire, and he approve my lays.° *verses*
Say what strange motive, goddess!° could compel *his Muse*
A well-bred lord t' assault a gentle belle?
O say what stranger cause, yet unexplored,
Could make a gentle belle reject a lord?
In tasks so bold, can little men engage,
And in soft bosoms, dwells such mighty rage?
Sol through white curtains shot a tim'rous ray,
And ope'd those eyes that must eclipse the day:
Now lap-dogs[1] give themselves the rousing shake,
And sleepless lovers, just at twelve, awake:
Thrice rung the bell, the slipper knocked the ground,[2]
And the pressed watch returned a silver sound.[3]
Belinda still her downy pillow pressed,
Her guardian sylph prolonged the balmy rest:
'Twas he had summoned to her silent bed
The morning dream that hovered o'er her head,
A youth more glitt'ring than a birth-night beau,[4]
(That ev'n in slumber caused her cheek to glow)
Seemed to her ear his winning lips to lay,
And thus in whispers said, or seemed to say.[5]
"Fairest of mortals, thou distinguished care
Of thousand bright inhabitants of air!
If e'er one vision touched thy infant thought,
Of all the nurse and all the priest have taught;[6]
Of airy elves by moonlight shadows seen,

8. Pope begins with the ancient epic formula of "proposition" of the work as a whole, and "invocation" of the gods' assistance, continuing with the traditional epic questions.
9. John Caryll, a mutual friend of Pope and the Fermor family. See page 1973.
1. Small dogs imported from Asia were highly fashionable ladies' pets at this time.
2. Belinda rings the bell and then finally bangs her slipper on the floor to call her maid.
3. The popular "pressed watch" chimed the hour and quarter hours when its stem was pressed, saving its owner from striking a match to see the time.
4. On a royal birthday, courtiers' clothes were particularly extravagant.
5. His whispering recalls the serpent's temptation of Eve in Milton's *Paradise Lost.*
6. The nurse and priest were seen as two standard sources of superstition.

The silver token, and the circled green,[7]
Or virgins visited by angel-pow'rs[8]
With golden crowns and wreaths of heav'nly flow'rs;
Hear and believe! thy own importance know,
Nor bound thy narrow views to things below.
Some secret truths, from learned pride concealed,
To maids alone and children are revealed.
What though no credit doubting wits may give?[9]
The fair and innocent shall still believe.
Know then, unnumbered spirits round thee fly,
The light militia of the lower sky:
These, though unseen, are ever on the wing,
Hang o'er the box, and hover round the ring.[1]
Think what an equipage[2] thou hast in air,
And view with scorn two pages and a chair.[3]
As now your own, our beings were of old,
And once inclosed in woman's beauteous mould;
Thence, by a soft transition, we repair
From earthly vehicles[4] to these of air.
Think not, when woman's transient breath is fled,
That all her vanities at once are dead;
Succeeding vanities she still regards,
And though she plays no more, o'erlooks the cards.
Her joy in gilded chariots, when alive,
And love of ombre,[5] after death survive.
For when the fair in all their pride expire,
To their first elements,[6] their souls retire:
The sprites of fiery termagants° in flame *scolding women*
Mount up, and take a salamander's name.
Soft yielding minds to water glide away,
And sip, with nymphs, their elemental tea.
The graver prude sinks downward to a gnome,
In search of mischief still on earth to roam.
The light coquettes in sylphs aloft repair,
And sport and flutter in the fields of air.
"Know further yet; whoever fair and chaste
Rejects mankind, is by some sylph embraced:
For spirits, freed from mortal laws, with ease
Assume what sexes and what shapes they please.[7]

7. Withered circles in the grass and silver coins were supposed to be signs of fairies' presence.
8. Belinda is reminded of the many virgin saints, and particularly the Annunciation to the Virgin Mary.
9. Religious skepticism was on the increase.
1. The theater box and the equally fashionable drive round Hyde Park.
2. Carriage, horses, and attendants.
3. A sedan chair, carried by two chairmen.
4. Both the carriage, and the physical body.
5. Ombre (pronounced "Omber") was an elaborate card game. Pope may also be punning on the origin of the word "Ombre," from the Spanish *hombre,* meaning "man."
6. The four elements of fire, water, earth, and air were thought to make up all things; so an individual's character was determined by whichever element dominated his or her soul.
7. Cf. *Paradise Lost,* "For spirits when they please / Can either sex assume, or both" (1.423–24).

What guards the purity of melting maids,
In courtly balls, and midnight masquerades,
Safe from the treach'rous friend, the daring spark,° *bold young man*
The glance by day, the whisper in the dark,
When kind occasion prompts their warm desires,
When music softens, and when dancing fires?
"'Tis but their sylph, the wise celestials know,
Though honour is the word with men below.
"Some nymphs there are, too conscious of their face,
For life predestined to the gnomes' embrace.
These swell their prospects and exalt their pride,
When offers are disdained, and love denied:
Then gay ideas crowd the vacant brain,
While peers° and dukes, and all their sweeping train, *aristocrats*
And garters, stars, and coronets[8] appear,
And in soft sounds 'Your Grace'[9] salutes their ear.
'Tis these that early taint the female soul,
Instruct the eyes of young coquettes to roll,
Teach infant-cheeks a bidden° blush to know, *deliberate*
And little hearts to flutter at a beau.
"Oft, when the world imagine women stray,
The sylphs through mystic mazes guide their way,
Through all the giddy circle they pursue,
And old impertinence° expel by new. *frivolity*
What tender maid but must a victim fall
To one man's treat, but for another's ball?
When Florio speaks, what virgin could withstand,
If gentle Damon did not squeeze her hand?
With varying vanities, from ev'ry part,
They shift the moving toyshop[1] of their heart;
Where wigs with wigs, with sword-knots sword-knots strive,[2]
Beaux banish beaux, and coaches coaches drive.[3]
This erring mortals levity may call;
Oh blind to truth! the sylphs contrive it all.
"Of these am I, who thy protection claim,
A watchful sprite, and Ariel is my name.
Late, as I ranged the crystal wilds of air,
In the clear mirror of thy ruling star
I saw, alas! some dread event impend,
Ere to the main° this morning sun descend. *sea*
But heaven reveals not what, or how, or where:
Warned by the sylph, oh pious maid, beware!
This to disclose is all thy guardian can:
Beware of all, but most beware of man!"

8. Emblems of noble rank.
9. Form of address for a duke or a duchess.
1. Where toys and trinkets are sold; "moving" here means easily changed, unstable.
2. Most men wore wigs in public; formally dressed men tied ribbons to the hilt of their swords.
3. These two lines mimic both Homer's and Ovid's description of heroic combat.

He said; when Shock,° who thought she slept too long, *her poodle*
Leaped up, and waked his mistress with his tongue;
'Twas then, Belinda, if report say true,
Thy eyes first opened on a billet-doux;° *love letter*
Wounds, charms, and ardours, were no sooner read,
But all the vision vanished from thy head.
And now, unveiled, the toilet° stands displayed, *dressing table*
Each silver vase in mystic order laid.
First, robed in white, the nymph intent adores,
With head uncovered, the cosmetic pow'rs.
A heav'nly image[4] in the glass appears,
To that she bends, to that her eyes she rears° *raises*
Th' inferior priestess,[5] at her altar's side,
Trembling begins the sacred rites of pride.
Unnumbered treasures ope at once, and here
The various off'rings of the world appear;
From each she nicely culls with curious° toil, *careful*
And decks the goddess with the glitt'ring spoil.
This casket India's glowing gems unlocks,
And all Arabia° breathes from yonder box. *eastern perfume*
The tortoise here and elephant unite,
Transformed to combs, the speckled, and the white.[6]
Here files of pins extend their shining rows,
Puffs, powders, patches, bibles,[7] billets-doux.
Now awful° beauty puts on all its arms; *awe-inspiring*
The fair each moment rises in her charms,
Repairs her smiles, awakens ev'ry grace,
And calls forth all the wonders of her face;
Sees by degrees a purer blush° arise, *rouge*
And keener lightnings[8] quicken in her eyes.
The busy sylphs surround their darling care,
These set the head, and those divide the hair,
Some fold the sleeve, whilst others plait° the gown; *pleat*
And Betty's praised for labours not her own.

Canto 2

Not with more glories, in th' ethereal plain,° *sky*
The sun first rises o'er the purpled main,
Than, issuing forth, the rival of his beams
Launched on the bosom of the silver Thames.[1]
Fair nymphs, and well-dressed youths around her shone,
But ev'ry eye was fixed on her alone.

4. I.e., Belinda herself.
5. Belinda's maid, Betty.
6. Tortoise-shell and ivory.
7. Patches were small beauty spots of black silk, pasted onto the face to make the skin appear whiter. It was fashionable to own Bibles in very small format.
8. Caused by drops of belladonna (deadly nightshade), which dilates the pupils.
1. Belinda takes a boat from London to Hampton Court, avoiding the dirt and squalor of the streets; her voyage compares with Aeneas's up the Tiber (*Aeneid* 7), or Cleopatra's up the Nile (*Antony and Cleopatra* 2.2).

On her white breast a sparkling cross she wore,
Which Jews might kiss, and infidels adore.
Her lively looks a sprightly mind disclose,
Quick as her eyes, and as unfixed as those;
Favours to none, to all she smiles extends;
Oft she rejects, but never once offends.
Bright as the sun, her eyes the gazers strike,
And, like the sun, they shine on all alike.
Yet graceful ease, and sweetness void of pride,
Might hide her faults, if belles had faults to hide;
If to her share some female errors fall,
Look on her face, and you'll forget 'em all.
    This nymph, to the destruction of mankind,
Nourished two locks, which graceful hung behind
In equal curls, and well conspired to deck,
With shining ringlets, the smooth iv'ry neck.
Love in these labyrinths his slaves detains,
And mighty hearts are held in slender chains.
With hairy springes° we the birds betray, *noose traps*
Slight lines° of hair surprise the finny prey, *fishing lines*
Fair tresses man's imperial race insnare,
And beauty draws us with a single hair.
    Th' advent'rous baron[2] the bright locks admired;
He saw, he wished, and to the prize aspired.
Resolved to win, he meditates the way,
By force to ravish, or by fraud betray;
For when success a lover's toil attends,
Few ask, if fraud or force attained his ends.
    For this, ere Phoebus[3] rose, he had implored
Propitious heav'n, and ev'ry pow'r adored,° *worshipped*
But chiefly Love—to Love an altar built,
Of twelve vast French romances, neatly gilt.
There lay three garters, half a pair of gloves,
And all the trophies of his former loves;
With tender billets-doux he lights the pyre,
And breathes three am'rous sighs to raise the fire.
Then prostrate falls, and begs with ardent eyes
Soon to obtain, and long possess the prize:
The pow'rs gave ear, and granted half his pray'r,
The rest, the winds dispersed in empty air.[4]
    But now secure the painted vessel glides,
The sun-beams trembling on the floating tides:
While melting music steals upon the sky,
And softened sounds along the waters die;
Smooth flow the waves, the zephyrs° gently play, *breezes*

2. Robert, Lord Petre (1690–1713), responsible for the original incident.
3. Phoebus Apollo, Greek sun god.
4. Cf. *The Aeneid* 2.794–95, which Dryden translated: "Apollo heard, and granting half his pray'r, / Shuffled in winds the rest, and toss'd in empty air."

Belinda smiled, and all the world was gay.
All but the sylph—with careful° thoughts oppressed, *worried*
Th' impending woe sat heavy on his breast.
He summons straight his denizens° of air; *residents*
The lucid squadrons round the sails repair:
Soft o'er the shrouds° aërial whispers breathe, *ropes*
That seemed but zephyrs to the train beneath.
Some to the sun their insect-wings unfold,
Waft on the breeze, or sink in clouds of gold;
Transparent forms, too fine for mortal sight,
Their fluid bodies half dissolved in light.
Loose to the wind their airy garments flew,
Thin glitt'ring textures of the filmy dew,
Dipped in the richest tincture of the skies,
Where light disports in ever-mingling dyes;
While ev'ry beam new transient colours flings,
Colours that change whene'er they wave their wings.
Amid the circle, on the gilded mast,
Superior by the head, was Ariel placed;[5]
His purple pinions opening to the sun,
He raised his azure wand, and thus begun.
"Ye sylphs and sylphids,° to your chief give ear! *female sylphs*
Fays, fairies, genii, elves, and demons, hear!
Ye know the spheres, and various tasks assigned
By laws eternal to th' aërial kind.
Some in the fields of purest ether[6] play,
And bask and whiten in the blaze of day.
Some guide the course of wand'ring orbs° on high, *comets*
Or roll the planets through the boundless sky.
Some less refined, beneath the moon's pale light
Pursue the stars that shoot athwart the night,
Or suck the mists in grosser° air below, *heavier*
Or dip their pinions in the painted bow,° *rainbow*
Or brew fierce tempests on the wintry main,
Or o'er the glebe° distil the kindly rain. *farmland*
Others on earth o'er human race preside,
Watch all their ways, and all their actions guide:
Of these the chief the care of nations own,
And guard with arms divine the British throne.
"Our humbler province is to tend the fair,
Not a less pleasing, though less glorious care;
To save the powder from too rude° a gale, *rough*
Nor let th' imprisoned essences° exhale; *perfumes*
To draw fresh colours from the vernal flow'rs;
To steal from rainbows ere they drop in show'rs
A brighter wash;[7] to curl their waving hairs,

5. Heroes of epics were typically taller than their men.
6. Air beyond the moon.
7. A cosmetic rinse.

Assist their blushes, and inspire their airs;
Nay oft, in dreams, invention we bestow,
To change a flounce, or add a furbelow.° *ruffle*
"This day, black omens threat the brightest fair
That e'er deserved a watchful spirit's care;
Some dire disaster, or° by force, or slight;° *either / trick*
But what, or where, the fates have wrapped in night.
Whether the nymph shall break Diana's law,° *virginity*
Or some frail china jar receive a flaw;
Or stain her honour, or her new brocade;
Forget her pray'rs, or miss a masquerade;
Or lose her heart, or necklace at a ball;
Or whether heav'n has doomed that Shock must fall.
Haste then, ye spirits! to your charge° repair: *duty*
The flutt'ring fan be Zephyretta's care;
The drops° to thee, Brillante, we consign; *earrings*
And, Momentilla, let the watch be thine;
Do thou, Crispissa,[8] tend her fav'rite lock;
Ariel himself shall be the guard of Shock.
"To fifty chosen Sylphs, of special note,
We trust th' important charge, the petticoat:
Oft have we known that seven-fold fence[9] to fail,
Though stiff with hoops and armed with ribs of whale;
Form a strong line about the silver bound,
And guard the wide circumference around.
"Whatever spirit, careless of his charge,
His post neglects, or leaves the fair at large,
Shall feel sharp vengeance soon o'ertake his sins,
Be stopped in vials, or transfixed with pins;
Or plunged in lakes of bitter washes lie,
Or wedged, whole ages, in a bodkin's[1] eye:
Gums and pomatums° shall his flight restrain, *ointments*
While clogged he beats his silken wings in vain;
Or alum styptics[2] with contracting pow'r
Shrink his thin essence like a rivelled° flow'r: *shriveled*
Or, as Ixion fixed, the wretch shall feel
The giddy motion of the whirling mill,[3]
In fumes of burning chocolate shall glow,
And tremble at the sea that froths below!"
He spoke; the spirits from the sails descend:
Some, orb in orb, around the nymph extend;
Some thrid° the mazy ringlets of her hair; *slid through*

8. The Latin *crispere* means "to curl."

9. Serving Belinda like the epic warrior's shield, her petticoat has seven layers bound together with a silver band (cf. *Iliad* 18 or *Aeneid* 8).

1. Blunt, thick needle; the Sylph, like the camel in Matthew 19:24, has difficulty getting through. Pope later plays on the various meanings of "bodkin," which also include a hair ornament and a dagger.

2. Astringents that stopped bleeding.

3. For grinding cocoa beans for chocolate, a new and highly fashionable drink. Ixion was punished by being tied to a revolving wheel of fire, after trying to seduce the goddess Hera.

Some hang upon the pendants of her ear;
With beating hearts the dire event they wait,
Anxious, and trembling for the birth of fate.

CANTO 3

CLOSE by those meads, for ever crowned with flow'rs,
Where Thames with pride surveys his rising tow'rs,
There stands a structure of majestic frame,
Which from the neighb'ring Hampton takes its name.[1]
Here Britain's statesmen oft the fall foredoom
Of foreign tyrants, and of nymphs at home;
Here thou, great ANNA! whom three realms obey,[2]
Dost sometimes counsel take—and sometimes tea.
Hither the heroes and the nymphs resort,
To taste awhile the pleasures of a court;
In various talk th' instructive hours they passed,
Who gave the ball, or paid the visit last;
One speaks the glory of the British Queen,
And one describes a charming Indian screen;
A third interprets motions, looks, and eyes;
At ev'ry word a reputation dies.
Snuff, or the fan, supply each pause of chat,
With singing, laughing, ogling, and all that.
Meanwhile, declining from the noon of day,
The sun obliquely shoots his burning ray;
The hungry judges soon the sentence sign,
And wretches hang that jury-men may dine;
The merchant from th' Exchange° returns in peace, *market*
And the long labours of the toilet cease.
Belinda now, whom thirst of fame invites,
Burns to encounter two advent'rous knights,
At ombre[3] singly to decide their doom;
And swells her breast with conquests yet to come.
Straight the three bands prepare in arms to join,
Each band the number of the sacred nine.[4]
Soon as she spreads her hand, th' aërial guard
Descend, and sit on each important card:
First Ariel perched upon a Matadore,[5]
Then each according to the rank they bore;
For sylphs, yet mindful of their ancient race,
Are, as when women, wondrous fond of place.° *rank*

1. Hampton Court, about 15 miles upriver from London, was built in the 16th century by Cardinal Wolsey, and by Queen Anne's day was associated with wits as well as with statesmen.
2. England, Scotland, and Ireland.
3. A card game played with 40 cards, similar to modern bridge: three players hold nine cards each and bid for tricks, with the highest bidder becoming the "ombre" (man) and choosing trumps.
4. Pope links the nine Muses to the nine cards each player holds.
5. The Matadores are the three cards of highest value; Belinda holds all three: when trumps are black, they are the Spadillio (ace of spades), Manillio (deuce of spades), and Basto (ace of clubs).

Behold, four kings, in majesty revered,
With hoary whiskers[6] and a forky beard;
And four fair queens whose hands sustain° a flow'r, *hold*
Th' expressive emblem of their softer pow'r;
Four knaves in garbs succinct,° a trusty band; *girded up*
Caps on their heads, and halberts in their hand;
And parti-coloured troops, a shining train,
Draw forth to combat on the velvet plain.[7]
The skilful nymph reviews her force with care:
Let spades be trumps! she said, and trumps they were.[8]
Now move to war her sable Matadores,
In show like leaders of the swarthy Moors.
Spadillio first, unconquerable lord!
Led off two captive trumps, and swept the board.
As many more Manillio forced to yield,
And marched a victor from the verdant field.
Him Basto followed, but his fate more hard
Gained but one trump and one plebeian card.
With his broad sabre next, a chief in years,
The hoary majesty of spades appears,
Puts forth one manly leg, to sight revealed,
The rest, his many-coloured robe concealed.
The rebel knave, who dares his prince engage,
Proves the just victim of his royal rage.
Ev'n mighty Pam,[9] that kings and queens o'erthrew,
And mowed down armies in the fights of loo,
Sad chance of war! now destitute of aid,
Falls undistinguished by the victor spade!
Thus far both armies to Belinda yield;
Now to the baron fate inclines the field.
His warlike Amazon her host invades,
Th' imperial consort of the crown of spades.
The club's black tyrant first her victim died,
Spite of his haughty mien, and barb'rous pride:
What boots the regal circle on his head,
His giant limbs, in state unwieldy spread;
That long behind he trails his pompous robe,
And of all monarchs only grasps the globe?
The baron now his diamonds pours apace!
Th' embroidered king who shows but half his face,
And his refulgent queen, with pow'rs combined,
Of broken troops, an easy conquest find.
Clubs, diamonds, hearts, in wild disorder seen,

6. Gray mustache. The royal figures on the cards now conduct a mock-epic review of their forces, and the whole game is described as an epic battle, with the characters appearing as on the cards.
7. The green velvet card table.
8. "Then God said, 'Let there be light'; and there was light" (Genesis 1:3).
9. The knave or jack of clubs, which took precedence over all trumps in the game of Lu, or Loo.

With throngs promiscuous strew the level green.
Thus when dispersed a routed army runs,
Of Asia's troops, and Afric's sable sons,
With like confusion different nations fly,
Of various habit, and of various dye;
The pierced battalions disunited fall,
In heaps on heaps; one fate o'erwhelms them all.
    The knave of diamonds tries his wily arts,
And wins (oh shameful chance!) the queen of hearts.
At this, the blood the virgin's cheek forsook,
A livid paleness spreads o'er all her look;
She sees, and trembles at th' approaching ill,
Just in the jaws of ruin, and codille.[1]
And now (as oft in some distempered state)
On one nice trick[2] depends the gen'ral fate:
An ace of hearts steps forth: the king[3] unseen
Lurked in her hand, and mourned his captive queen:
He springs to vengeance with an eager pace,
And falls like thunder on the prostrate ace.
The nymph exulting fills with shouts the sky;
The walls, the woods, and long canals reply.
    Oh thoughtless mortals! ever blind to fate,
Too soon dejected, and too soon elate.
Sudden these honours shall be snatched away,
And cursed for ever this victorious day.
    For lo! the board with cups and spoons is crowned;
The berries crackle, and the mill turns round;[4]
On shining altars of japan[5] they raise
The silver lamp; the fiery spirits blaze:
From silver spouts the grateful° liquors glide, *pleasing*
While China's earth receives the smoking tide:
At once they gratify their scent and taste,
And frequent cups prolong the rich repast.
Straight° hover round the fair her airy band; *immediately*
Some, as she sipped, the fuming liquor fanned,
Some o'er her lap their careful plumes displayed,
Trembling, and conscious of the rich brocade.
Coffee (which makes the politician wise,
And see through all things with his half-shut eyes)
Sent up in vapours[6] to the baron's brain
New stratagems, the radiant lock to gain.
Ah cease, rash youth! desist ere 'tis too late,
Fear the just gods, and think of Scylla's fate![7]

1. Literally "elbow": the defeat suffered by the ombre if another player wins more tricks.
2. Trick applies in both its technical and general senses as Belinda makes this careful maneuver.
3. The King of Hearts.
4. Grinding coffee beans.
5. Lacquered tables.
6. Both steam and vain imaginations.
7. Scylla plucked purple hair from the head of her father, King Nisus, to offer to her lover, Minos, so destroying her father's power. Minos rejected her impiety, and Scylla was transformed into a bird.

Changed to a bird, and sent to flit in air,
She dearly pays for Nisus' injured hair!
But when to mischief mortals bend their will,
How soon they find fit instruments of ill!
Just then, Clarissa drew with tempting grace
A two-edged weapon from her shining case:
So ladies in romance assist their knight,
Present the spear, and arm him for the fight.
He takes the gift with rev'rence, and extends
The little engine° on his fingers' ends; *instrument*
This just behind Belinda's neck he spread,
As o'er the fragrant steams she bends her head.
Swift to the lock a thousand sprites repair,
A thousand wings, by turns, blow back the hair;
And thrice they twitched the diamond in her ear;
Thrice she looked back, and thrice the foe drew near.
Just in that instant, anxious Ariel sought
The close recesses of the virgin's thought:
As on the nosegay in her breast reclined,
He watched th' ideas rising in her mind,
Sudden he viewed in spite of all her art,
An earthly lover° lurking at her heart. *Lord Petre*
Amazed, confused, he found his pow'r expired,
Resigned to fate, and with a sigh retired.
The peer now spreads the glitt'ring forfex° wide, *scissors*
T' inclose the lock; now joins it, to divide.
Ev'n then, before the fatal engine closed,
A wretched sylph too fondly interposed;
Fate urged the shears, and cut the sylph in twain,
(But airy substance soon unites again,)[8]
The meeting points the sacred hair dissever
From the fair head, for ever, and for ever!
Then flashed the living lightning from her eyes,
And screams of horror rend th' affrighted skies,
Not louder shrieks to pitying heav'n are cast,
When husbands, or when lap-dogs breathe their last;
Or when rich china vessels fall'n from high,
In glitt'ring dust, and painted fragments lie!
"Let wreaths of triumph now my temples twine,"
(The victor cried,) "the glorious prize is mine!
While fish in streams, or birds delight in air,
Or in a coach and six[9] the British fair,
As long as Atalantis shall be read,[1]

8. *Milton* lib. 6 [Pope's note], citing *Paradise Lost* 6.329–31, "The girding sword with discontinuous wound / Passed through him, but the ethereal substance closed / Not long divisible. . . ."

9. A carriage drawn by six horses; a symbol of wealth and prestige.

1. The scandalous *Atalantis: Secret Memoirs and Manners of Several Persons of Quality* (1709), by Mary Delarivière Manley.

Or the small pillow grace a lady's bed,[2]
While visits shall be paid on solemn days,
When num'rous wax-lights[3] in bright order blaze,
While nymphs take treats, or assignations give,
So long my honour, name, and praise shall live!"
  What time would spare, from steel receives its date,° *end*
And monuments, like men, submit to fate!
Steel could the labour of the gods destroy,
And strike to dust th' imperial tow'rs of Troy,[4]
Steel could the works of mortal pride confound,
And hew triumphal arches to the ground,
What wonder then, fair nymph! thy hairs should feel
The conqu'ring force of unresisted steel?

CANTO 4

BUT anxious cares the pensive nymph oppressed,
And secret passions laboured in her breast.
Not youthful kings in battle seized alive,
Not scornful virgins who their charms survive,
Not ardent lovers robbed of all their bliss,
Not ancient ladies when refused a kiss,
Not tyrants fierce that unrepenting die,
Not Cynthia when her manteau's° pinned awry, *gown's*
E'er felt such rage, resentment, and despair,
As thou, sad virgin! for thy ravished hair.
  For, that sad moment, when the sylphs withdrew,
And Ariel weeping from Belinda flew,
Umbriel, a dusky, melancholy sprite,
As ever sullied the fair face of light,
Down to the central earth, his proper scene,
Repaired to search the gloomy cave of Spleen.[1]
  Swift on his sooty pinions flits the gnome,
And in a vapour[2] reached the dismal dome.
No cheerful breeze this sullen region knows,
The dreaded east[3] is all the wind that blows.
Here in a grotto, sheltered close from air,
And screened in shades° from day's detested glare, *shadows*
She sighs for ever on her pensive bed,
Pain at her side, and Megrim° at her head. *migraine*
  Two handmaids wait' the throne: alike in place,
But diff'ring far in figure and in face.
Here stood Ill-nature like an ancient maid,

2. Said to be a place where ladies hid romance novels and other contraband.

3. Candles made of wax, rather than the cheaper tallow. Evening social visits were an essential part of the fashionable woman's routine.

4. Even Troy, fabled to have been built by Apollo and Poseidon, was destroyed by arms.

1. Named after the bodily organ, "spleen" was the current name for the fashionable affliction of melancholy or ill-humor. Umbriel's descent into the womb-like Cave of Spleen suggests the epic commonplace of the journey to the underworld.

2. "The spleen" was also called "the vapors."

3. The east wind was supposed to induce fits of spleen.

Her wrinkled form in black and white arrayed;
With store of pray'rs, for mornings, nights, and noons,
Her hand is filled; her bosom with lampoons.
There Affectation with a sickly mien,
Shows in her cheek the roses of eighteen,
Practised to lisp, and hang the head aside,
Faints into airs, and languishes with pride,
On the rich quilt sinks with becoming woe,
Wrapped in a gown, for sickness, and for show.
The fair ones feel such maladies as these,
When each new night-dress gives a new disease.
A constant vapour o'er the palace flies;
Strange phantoms rising as the mists arise;
Dreadful, as hermits' dreams in haunted shades,
Or bright, as visions of expiring maids.[4]
Now glaring fiends, and snakes on rolling spires,° *coils*
Pale spectres, gaping tombs, and purple fires:
Now lakes of liquid gold, Elysian scenes,[5]
And crystal domes, and angels in machines.
Unnumbered throngs, on ev'ry side are seen,
Of bodies changed to various forms by Spleen.[6]
Here living tea-pots stand, one arm held out,
One bent; the handle this, and that the spout:
A pipkin[7] there, like Homer's tripod walks;
Here sighs a jar, and there a goose-pye talks;[8]
Men prove with child, as pow'rful fancy works,
And maids turned bottles, call aloud for corks.
Safe past the gnome through this fantastic band,
A branch of healing spleenwort in his hand.[9]
Then thus addressed the pow'r—"Hail, wayward queen!
Who rule the sex to fifty from fifteen:
Parent of vapours and of female wit,
Who give th' hysteric, or poetic fit,
On various tempers act by various ways,
Make some take physic,° others scribble plays;[1] *medicine*
Who cause the proud their visits to delay,
And send the godly in a pet° to pray; *ill-humor*
A nymph there is, that all thy pow'r disdains,
And thousands more in equal mirth maintains.
But oh! if e'er thy gnome could spoil a grace,
Or raise a pimple on a beauteous face,
Like citron-waters° matrons' cheeks inflame, *flavored brandy*

4. Religious visions of hell and heaven.
5. Elysium was the classical paradise, but this also recalls contemporary theater, which made much of scenic spectacle and the use of machinery.
6. Hallucinations similar to those described in the following lines were common to those afflicted with spleen.
7. Small pot or pan. Hephaistos's "walking" tripods are described in the *Iliad* 18.439ff.
8. Alludes to a real fact, a Lady of distinction imagin'd herself in this condition [Pope's note].
9. Pope changes the golden bough that protected Aeneas on his trip through the underworld into an herb that was supposed to be good for the spleen.
1. Melancholy was associated with artistic creativity.

Or change complexions at a losing game;
If e'er with airy horns I planted heads,[2]
Or rumpled petticoats, or tumbled beds,
Or caused suspicion when no soul was rude,
Or discomposed the head-dress of a prude,
Or e'er to costive° lap-dog gave disease, *constipated*
Which not the tears of brightest eyes could ease:
Hear me, and touch Belinda with chagrin,
That single act gives half the world the spleen."
    The goddess with a discontented air
Seems to reject him, though she grants his pray'r.
A wondrous bag with both her hands she binds,
Like that where once Ulysses held the winds;[3]
There she collects the force of female lungs,
Sighs, sobs, and passions, and the war of tongues.
A phial next she fills with fainting fears,
Soft sorrows, melting griefs, and flowing tears.
The gnome rejoicing bears her gifts away,
Spreads his black wings, and slowly mounts to day.
    Sunk in Thalestris'[4] arms the nymph he found,
Her eyes dejected, and her hair unbound.
Full o'er their heads the swelling bag he rent,
And all the furies issued at the vent.
Belinda burns with more than mortal ire,
And fierce Thalestris fans the rising fire.
"O wretched maid!" she spread her hands, and cried,
(While Hampton's echoes, "Wretched maid!" replied)
"Was it for this you took such constant care
The bodkin, comb, and essence to prepare?
For this your locks in paper durance° bound? *curling papers*
For this with tort'ring irons wreathed around?
For this with fillets[5] strained your tender head,
And bravely bore the double loads of lead?° *curl fasteners*
Gods! shall the ravisher display your hair,
While the fops envy, and the ladies stare!
Honour forbid! at whose unrivalled shrine
Ease, pleasure, virtue, all our sex resign.
Methinks already I your tears survey,
Already hear the horrid things they say,
Already see you a degraded toast,[6]
And all your honour in a whisper lost!
How shall I, then, your helpless fame defend?
'Twill then be infamy to seem your friend!
And shall this prize, th' inestimable prize,

2. A sign that a husband had been cuckolded.
3. Given to him by the wind god Aeolus (*Odyssey* 10.19ff.).
4. A queen of the Amazons; here Mrs. Morley, Arabella's second cousin.
5. Headbands, with reference to priestesses in the *Aeneid*.
6. A woman whose toast is often drunk, and who by implication is all too well known to her (male) toasters.

Exposed through crystal to the gazing eyes,
And heightened by the diamond's circling rays,
On that rapacious hand for ever blaze?[7]
Sooner shall grass in Hyde-Park Circus grow,[8]
And wits take lodgings in the sound of Bow;[9]
Sooner let earth, air, sea, to chaos fall,
Men, monkeys, lap-dogs, parrots, perish all!"
She said; then raging to Sir Plume[1] repairs,
And bids her beau demand the precious hairs:
(Sir Plume, of amber snuff-box justly vain,
And the nice conduct of a clouded cane)[2]
With earnest eyes, and round unthinking face,
He first the snuff-box opened, then the case,
And thus broke out—"My Lord, why, what the devil!
Zounds![3] damn the lock! 'fore Gad, you must be civil.
Plague on't! 'tis past a jest—nay prithee, pox!
Give her the hair"—he spoke, and rapped his box.
"It grieves me much," replied the peer again,
"Who speaks so well should ever speak in vain,
But by this lock, this sacred lock I swear,
(Which never more shall join its parted hair;
Which never more its honours shall renew,
Clipped from the lovely head where late it grew)
That while my nostrils draw the vital air,
This hand, which won it, shall for ever wear."
He spoke, and speaking, in proud triumph spread
The long-contended honours of her head.[4]
But Umbriel, hateful gnome! forbears not so;
He breaks the phial whence the sorrows flow.
Then see! the nymph in beauteous grief appears,
Her eyes half languishing, half drowned in tears;
On her heaved bosom hung her drooping head,
Which, with a sigh, she raised; and thus she said.
"For ever cursed be this detested day,[5]
Which snatched my best, my fav'rite curl away!
Happy! ah ten times happy had I been,
If Hampton-Court these eyes had never seen!
Yet am not I the first mistaken maid,
By love of courts to num'rous ills betrayed.
Oh had I rather unadmired remained
In some lone isle, or distant northern land;
Where the gilt chariot never marks the way,
Where none learn ombre, none e'er taste bohea!° *the finest tea*

7. I.e., mounted in a ring.
8. The fashion for driving coaches around Hyde Park prevented grass from growing there.
9. A commercial area around St. Mary-le-Bow, and not at all fashionable.
1. Sir George Browne, cousin of Arabella's mother.
2. Skilled use of a cane with a head of dark polished stone.
3. A Corruption of "God's wounds," a mild oath.
4. Her beautiful hair.
5. Echoing Achilles' lament for his slain friend Patroclus (*Iliad* 18.107ff.).

There kept my charms concealed from mortal eye,
Like roses, that in deserts bloom and die.
What moved my mind with youthful lords to roam?
O had I stayed, and said my pray'rs at home!
'Twas this the morning omens seemed to tell,
Thrice from my trembling hand the patch-box fell;
The tott'ring china shook without a wind,
Nay, Poll° sat mute, and Shock was most unkind! *her parrot*
A sylph too warned me of the threats of fate,
In mystic visions, now believed too late!
See the poor remnants of these slighted hairs!
My hands shall rend what ev'n thy rapine spares:
These in two sable ringlets taught to break,° *divide*
Once gave new beauties to the snowy neck;
The sister-lock now sits uncouth, alone,
And in its fellow's fate foresees its own;
Uncurled it hangs, the fatal shears demands,
And tempts, once more, thy sacrilegious hands.
Oh hadst thou, cruel! been content to seize
Hairs less in sight, or any hairs but these!"

CANTO 5

SHE said: the pitying audience melt in tears,
But Fate and Jove had stopped the baron's ears.
In vain Thalestris with reproach assails,
For who can move when fair Belinda fails?
Not half so fixed the Trojan could remain,[1]
While Anna begged and Dido raged in vain.
Then grave Clarissa[2] graceful waved her fan;
Silence ensued, and thus the nymph began.
"Say, why are beauties praised and honoured most,
The wise man's passion, and the vain man's toast?
Why decked with all that land and sea afford,
Why angels called, and angel-like adored?
Why round our coaches crowd the white-gloved beaux,
Why bows the side-box from its inmost rows?[3]
How vain are all these glories, ill our pains,
Unless good sense preserve what beauty gains:
That men may say, when we the front box grace,
Behold the first in virtue as in face!
Oh! if to dance all night, and dress all day,
Charmed the small-pox,[4] or chased old age away;

1. Aeneas, fixed on his decision to leave Carthage and abandon Dido despite her pleas and those of her sister Anna (*Aeneid* 4.269–449).

2. A new character introduced . . . to open more clearly the moral of the poem, in a parody of the speech of Sarpedon to Glaucus in Homer [Pope's note in the 1717 edition]. Sarpedon's speech (*Iliad* 12) is a famous reflection on glory.

3. At the theater, gentlemen sat in the side boxes, ladies in the front boxes facing the stage.

4. A common disease, which often left permanent facial scars.

Who would not scorn what housewifes' cares produce,
Or who would learn one earthly thing of use?
To patch, nay ogle, might become a saint,
Nor could it sure be such a sin to paint.
But since, alas! frail beauty must decay,
Curled or uncurled, since locks will turn to grey;
Since painted, or not painted, all shall fade,
And she who scorns a man, must die a maid;
What then remains but well our pow'r to use,
And keep good humour still, whate'er we lose?
And trust me, dear! good humour can prevail,
When airs, and flights, and screams, and scolding fail.
Beauties in vain their pretty eyes may roll;
Charms strike the sight, but merit wins the soul."
So spoke the dame, but no applause ensued;
Belinda frowned, Thalestris called her prude.
To arms, to arms! the fierce virago[5] cries,
And swift as lightning to the combat flies.
All side in parties, and begin th' attack;
Fans clap, silks rustle, and tough whalebones crack;
Heroes' and heroines' shouts confus'dly rise,
And base and treble voices strike the skies.
No common weapons in their hands are found,
Like gods they fight, nor dread a mortal wound.
So when bold Homer makes the gods engage,
And heav'nly breasts with human passions rage;
'Gainst Pallas,° Mars; Latona,[6] Hermes arms; *Athena*
And all Olympus rings with loud alarms:
Jove's thunder roars, heav'n trembles all around,
Blue Neptune storms, the bellowing deeps resound:
Earth shakes her nodding tow'rs, the ground gives way,
And the pale ghosts start at the flash of day!
Triumphant Umbriel on a sconce's[7] height
Clapped his glad wings, and sate to view the fight.
Propped on their bodkin spears, the sprites survey
The growing combat, or assist the fray.
While through the press enraged Thalestris flies,
And scatters death around from both her eyes,
A beau and witling° perished in the throng, *little wit*
One died in metaphor, and one in song.
"O cruel nymph! a living death I bear,"
Cried Dapperwit, and sunk beside his chair.
A mournful glance Sir Fopling upwards cast,
"Those eyes are made so killing"[8]—was his last.

5. Woman who behaves like a man.
6. Mother of Diana and Apollo.
7. Candlestick attached to the wall.
8. A line from Giovanni Bononcini's opera, *Camilla* (1696), popular in London.

Thus on Maeander's flow'ry margin lies
Th' expiring swan, and as he sings he dies.[9]
When bold Sir Plume had drawn Clarissa down,
Chloe stepped in, and killed him with a frown;
She smiled to see the doughty hero slain,
But, at her smile, the beau revived again.
Now Jove suspends his golden scales in air,[1]
Weighs the men's wits against the lady's hair;
The doubtful beam long nods from side to side;
At length the wits mount up, the hairs subside.
See fierce Belinda on the baron flies,
With more than usual lightning in her eyes:
Nor feared the chief th' unequal fight to try,
Who sought no more than on his foe to die.[2]
But this bold lord with manly strength endued,
She with one finger and a thumb subdued;
Just where the breath of life his nostrils drew,
A charge of snuff the wily virgin threw;
The gnomes direct, to ev'ry atom just,
The pungent grains of titillating dust.
Sudden, with starting tears each eye o'erflows,
And the high dome re-echoes to his nose.[3]
"Now meet thy fate," incensed Belinda cried,
And drew a deadly bodkin[4] from her side.
(The same, his ancient personage to deck,
Her great great grandsire wore about his neck,
In three seal-rings; which after, melted down,
Formed a vast buckle for his widow's gown:
Her infant grandame's° whistle next it grew, *grandmother's*
The bell she jingled, and the whistle blew;
Then in a bodkin graced her mother's hairs,
Which long she wore, and now Belinda wears.)
"Boast not my fall," he cried, "insulting foe!
Thou by some other shalt be laid as low:
Nor think, to die dejects my lofty mind;
All that I dread is leaving you behind!
Rather than so, ah let me still survive,
And burn in Cupid's flames—but burn alive."
"Restore the Lock!" she cries; and all around
"Restore the Lock!" the vaulted roofs rebound.
Not fierce Othello in so loud a strain
Roared for the handkerchief that caused his pain.
But see how oft ambitious aims are crossed,
And chiefs contend till all the prize is lost!

9. Meander: a river in Asia Minor. Swans were believed to sing only on their death. This simile refers to Ovid's *Heroides* 7, a lament from Dido to Aeneas.

1. To determine victory in battle; a convention found in both Homer and Virgil.

2. A standard metaphor for sexual climax.

3. See his boast, 4.133–38.

4. A decorative pin, shaped like a dagger.

The lock, obtained with guilt, and kept with pain,
In ev'ry place is sought, but sought in vain:
With such a prize no mortal must be blessed,
So heav'n decrees! with heav'n who can contest?
Some thought it mounted to the Lunar sphere,[5]
Since all things lost on earth are treasured there.
There heroes' wits are kept in pond'rous vases,
And beaus' in snuff-boxes and tweezer-cases.
There broken vows, and death-bed alms are found,
And lovers' hearts with ends of ribbon bound,
The courtier's promises, and sick man's pray'rs,
The smiles of harlots, and the tears of heirs,
Cages for gnats, and chains to yoke a flea,
Dried butterflies, and tomes of casuistry.[6]
  But trust the muse—she saw it upward rise,
Though marked by none but quick, poetic eyes:
(So Rome's great founder to the heav'ns withdrew,
To Proculus alone confessed in view)[7]
A sudden star, it shot through liquid air,
And drew behind a radiant trail of hair.
Not Berenice's locks first rose so bright,[8]
The heav'ns bespangling with dishevelled light.
The sylphs behold it kindling as it flies,
And pleased pursue its progress through the skies.
  This the beau monde shall from the Mall[9] survey,
And hail with music its propitious ray;
This the bless'd lover shall for Venus° take, *the planet*
And send up vows from Rosamonda's lake;[1]
This Partridge[2] soon shall view in cloudless skies,
When next he looks through Galileo's eyes;° *a telescope*
And hence th' egregious wizard shall foredoom
The fate of Louis, and the fall of Rome.
  Then cease, bright nymph! to mourn thy ravished hair,
Which adds new glory to the shining sphere!
Not all the tresses that fair head can boast,
Shall draw such envy as the lock you lost.
For after all the murders of your eye,
When, after millions slain, yourself shall die;
When those fair suns° shall set, as set they must, *her eyes*
And all those tresses shall be laid in dust,
This lock the muse shall consecrate to fame,
And 'midst the stars inscribe Belinda's name.

5. In Ariosto's *Orlando Furioso* (1516–1532), Orlando's lost wits are sought on the moon.

6. Subtle reasoning (often used of arguments justifying immoral conduct).

7. When Romulus was killed mysteriously, Proculus soothed popular grief by asserting that he had been taken up to heaven.

8. The Egyptian queen Berenice made an offering of her hair after her husband returned victorious from the wars; when it disappeared from the temple, the court astronomer claimed it had been made into a new constellation.

9. A fashionable walk in St. James's Park.

1. Where lovers met in St. James's Park.

2. John Partridge was a ridiculous star-gazer, who in his almanacs every year never failed to predict the downfall of the Pope and the King of France, then at war with the English [Pope's note].

Jonathan Swift

1667–1745

Jonathan Swift was born in Ireland, where his English father had moved the family in an unsuccessful quest for better business. The father died before Jonathan's birth; his mother moved back to England when the boy was six, leaving him in a school near Dublin. At twenty-two, Swift was still at his studies in Dublin, granted a bachelor's degree from Trinity College even though he didn't pass his exams. Beginning a career of disappointment and frustrated ambition, Swift moved to England as personal secretary to a family friend, the retired Whig statesman William Temple, who died the following year. Swift moved back to Dublin to be ordained in the Church of Ireland, although he returned to London to be with "Stella,"—Esther Johnson, the young daughter of a servant of Temple whom he had begun tutoring on his arrival there, when she was eight and he twenty-two. It was a lifelong love affair, although it remains uncertain whether it ever involved legal marriage or physical love. In 1701, Swift invited her and a chaperone to join him in Dublin. They accepted and lived in close contact with him there, although in a separate house, for the rest of their lives.

In 1704, Swift published two of his most famous works, the elaborately structured prose satires, *A Tale of Tub*—an assault upon religious dissenters and fanatics which also savaged the established church—and *The Battle of the Books*—which compared "modern" writers who did not follow classical models to spiders spinning poison from their own guts. Published more than twenty years later, Swift's political satire, *Gulliver's Travels* (1726) describes the adventures of the narrator Gulliver in four bizarre countries as a way of dramatizing one of the fundamental oppositions informing Enlightenment thought: reason versus passion.

"The Lady's Dressing Room" is the earliest of the scatological poems for which Swift is distinguished, although it recalls previous descriptions of female bodies in his novel *Gulliver's Travels*. In it he takes up the same popular theme that Pope explores in *The Rape of the Lock* (page 1973)—the mysterious operation of dressing, by which, with the aid of "puffs, powders, and patches," imperfect bodies of flesh and blood were transformed into dazzling objects of desire. But Swift takes us from Pope's airy realm, where the battle of the sexes is fought by sylphs and gnomes, back to the physical world where the divinest pleasures of love remain always disturbingly close to less romanticized bodily functions. Swift's obscenity shocked many contemporaries and later readers, but it is not so different from such verses of the libertine poet Rochester's as, "Fair nasty nymph, be clean and kind / And all my joys restore / By using paper still behind / And sponges for before." The discoveries of Swift's Strephon in Celia's chamber pot come as a shock only to one who buys into representations of upper-class women not as mortal human subjects, but as fantastic creatures somewhere between goddesses and dolls.

The Lady's Dressing Room

Five hours (and who can do it less in?)
By haughty Celia spent in dressing;
The goddess from her chamber issues,
Arrayed in lace, brocade, and tissues:
Strephon,[1] who found the room was void,
And Betty[2] otherwise employed,

1. Strephon and Celia are names usually associated with pastoral poetry, and are therefore used mockingly here.

2. A typical maidservant's name.

Stole in, and took a strict survey,
Of all the litter as it lay:
Whereof, to make the matter clear,
An *inventory* follows here.

And first, a dirty smock appeared,
Beneath the arm-pits well besmeared;
Strephon, the rogue, displayed it wide,
And turned it round on every side.
In such a case few words are best,
And Strephon bids us guess the rest;
But swears how damnably the men lie,
In calling Celia sweet and cleanly.

Now listen while he next produces
The various combs for various uses,
Filled up with dirt so closely fixed,
No brush could force a way betwixt;
A paste of composition rare,
Sweat, dandruff, powder, lead,[3] and hair,
A forehead cloth with oil upon't
To smooth the wrinkles on her front;
Here alum flour[4] to stop the steams,
Exhaled from sour, unsavory streams;
There night-gloves made of Tripsy's[5] hide,
Bequeathed by Tripsy when she died;
With puppy water,[6] beauty's help,
Distilled from Tripsy's darling whelp.
Here gallipots° and vials placed, *ointment jars*
Some filled with washes, some with paste;
Some with pomatum,° paints, and slops, *hair ointment*
And ointments good for scabby chops.° *lips or cheeks*
Hard° by a filthy basin stands, *close*
Fouled with the scouring of her hands;
The basin takes whatever comes,
The scrapings of her teeth and gums,
A nasty compound of all hues,
For here she spits, and here she spews.

But oh! it turned poor Strephon's bowels,
When he beheld and smelt the towels;
Begummed, bemattered, and beslimed;
With dirt, and sweat, and ear-wax grimed.
No object Strephon's eye escapes,

3. White lead face paint, used to whiten the skin.
4. Powdered alum used like modern antiperspirant.
5. Celia's lapdog; no fashionable lady was without such a pet.
6. A recipe for this cosmetic, made from the innards of a pig or a fat puppy, was given in the "Fop's Dictionary" in *Mundus Muliebris* [Womanly Make-up]: *Or, the Ladies' Dressing Room Unlocked* (1690), which Swift also used for other terms.

Here, petticoats in frowzy° heaps; *unkempt*
Nor be the handkerchiefs forgot,
All varnished o'er with snuff[7] and snot.
The stockings why should I expose,
Stained with the moisture of her toes;
Or greasy coifs and pinners° reeking, *night caps*
Which Celia slept at least a week in?
A pair of tweezers next he found
To pluck her brows in arches round,
Or hairs that sink the forehead low,
Or on her chin like bristles grow.

The virtues we must not let pass
Of Celia's magnifying glass;
When frighted Strephon cast his eye on't,
It showed the visage of a giant:[8]
A glass that can to sight disclose
The smallest worm in Celia's nose,
And faithfully direct her nail
To squeeze it out from head to tail;
For catch it nicely by the head,
It must come out alive or dead.

Why, Strephon, will you tell the rest?
And must you needs describe the chest?
That careless wench! no creature warn her
To move it out from yonder corner,
But leave it standing full in sight,
For you to exercise your spite!
In vain the workman showed his wit
With rings and hinges counterfeit
To make it seem in this disguise
A cabinet to vulgar eyes;
Which Strephon ventured to look in,
Resolved to go through *thick and thin;*
He lifts the lid: there need no more,
He smelt it all the time before.

As, from within Pandora's box,
When Epimethus oped the locks,
A sudden universal crew
Of human evils upward flew;[9]
He still was comforted to find
That hope at last remained behind.

7. Powdered tobacco, sniffed by fashionable men and women alike.

8. Cf. *Gulliver's Travels,* Part 2, "A Voyage to Brobdingnag," ch. 1: "This made me reflect upon the fair skins of our *English* ladies, who appear so beautiful to us, only because they are of our own size, and their defects not to be seen but through magnifying glass, where we find by experiment that the smoothest and whitest skins look rough and coarse, and ill colored."

9. In Greek mythology, Epimetheus, acting against advice, opened the box Jove had given his wife Pandora, and all the evils and vices of the world flew out, leaving only hope in the box.

So, Strephon, lifting up the lid
To view what in the chest was hid,
The vapors flew from out the vent,
But Strephon cautious never meant
The bottom of the pan to grope,
And foul his hands in search of hope.

O! ne'er may such a vile machine° *construction*
Be once in Celia's chamber seen!
O! may she better learn to keep
"Those secrets of the hoary deep."[1]

As mutton cutlets, prime of meat,
Which though with art you salt and beat
As laws of cookery require,
And roast them at the clearest fire;
If from adown the hopeful chops
The fat upon a cinder drops,
To stinking smoke it turns the flame
Poisoning the flesh from whence it came;
And up exhales a greasy stench
For which you curse the careless wench:
So things which must not be expressed,
When plumped° into the reeking chest, *dropped*
Send up an excremental smell
To taint the parts from which they fell:
The petticoats and gown perfume,
And waft a stink round every room.

Thus finishing his grand survey,
The swain disgusted slunk away,
Repeating in his amorous fits,
"Oh! Celia, Celia, Celia shits!"

But Vengeance, goddess never sleeping,
Soon punished Strephon for his peeping.
His foul imagination links
Each dame he sees with all her stinks:
And if unsavory odors fly,
Conceives a lady standing by:
All women his description fits,
And both ideas jump° like wits *join together*
By vicious fancy coupled fast,
And still appearing in contrast.

I pity wretched Strephon, blind
To all the charms of womankind;
Should I the queen of love refuse,
Because she rose from stinking ooze?[2]

1. Quoting Milton's *Paradise Lost* 2.891, in which Sin is unleashing the chaotic forces of her infernal realm.

2. Venus, Roman goddess of sexual love and physical beauty, rose from the sea.

To him that looks behind the scene,
Statira's but some pocky quean.[3]

When Celia in her glory shows,
If Strephon would but stop his nose,
Who now so impiously blasphemes
Her ointments, daubs, and paints and creams;
Her washes, slops, and every clout,[4]
With which she makes so foul a rout;[5]
He soon would learn to think like me,
And bless his ravished eyes to see
Such order from confusion sprung,
Such gaudy *tulips* raised from *dung*.

RESONANCE

Lady Mary Wortley Montagu: The Reasons that Induced Dr. S. to write a Poem called The Lady's Dressing Room[1]

The Doctor in a clean starched band,
His golden snuff box in his hand,
With care his diamond ring displays
And artful shows its various rays,
While grave he stalks down——street
His dearest Betty——to meet.[2]
Long had he waited for this hour,
Nor gained admittance to the bower,
Had joked and punned, and swore and writ,
Tried all his gallantry and wit,[3]
Had told her oft what part he bore
In Oxford's schemes in days of yore,[4]
But bawdy,° politics, nor satire *obscenity*
Could move this dull hard hearted creature.
Jenny her maid could taste° a rhyme *enjoy*
And, grieved to see him lose his time,
Had kindly whispered in his ear,

3. One of the heroines of Nathaniel Lee's highly popular tragedy *The Rival Queens* (1677); Swift's common slattern (quean) has had either smallpox or venereal disease.
4. Washes were either treated water used for the complexion or stale urine used as a detergent; clouts were rags.
5. Both of her skin and, presumably, of the men.

1. Lady Mary Wortley Montagu (1689–1762) educated herself to become a classical scholar, translator, and poet, but her lasting literary fame rests at least as much on her personal letters, especially the Turkish Embassy Letters (1717), written while her husband, Edward Wortley Montagu, was ambassador to Constantinople (modern Istanbul). His status as great friend of Alexander Pope did not prevent the poet from lampooning her for wearing "diamonds with her dirty smock" in his "Epistle II: To a Lady." Montagu's riposte to Swift's "The Lady's Dressing Room" mimics her model's iambic tetrameter and other mannerisms, nor does she hesitate to identity, with great comic effect, Dean Swift's well-known lack of ease with women as the source of his unflattering verses.
2. In Swift's poem, Betty is the maid's name, Celia, the mistress's.
3. Montagu echoes Swift's poem *Cadenus and Vanessa,* where the clumsy lover "Had sighed and languished, vowed, and writ, / For pastime, or to show his wit" (lines 542–543).
4. Swift had collaborated closely in the political schemes of Robert Harley, first Earl of Oxford (1661–1724).

"For twice two pound you enter here;
My lady vows without that sum
It is in vain you write or come."
The destined offering now he brought,
And in a paradise of thought,
With a low bow approached the dame,
Who smiling heard him preach his flame.
His gold she takes (such proofs as these
Convince most unbelieving shes)
And in her trunk rose up to lock it
(Too wise to trust it in her pocket)
And then, returned with blushing grace,
Expects the doctor's warm embrace.
But now this is the proper place
Where morals stare me in the face,
And for the sake of fine expression
I'm forced to make a small digression.
Alas for wretched humankind,
With learning mad, with wisdom blind!
The ox thinks he's for saddle fit
(As long ago friend Horace writ[5])
And men their talents still mistaking,
The stutterer fancies his is speaking.
With admiration oft we see
Hard features heightened by toupée,
The beau affects° the politician, *pretends to be*
Wit is the citizen's ambition,
Poor Pope philosophy displays on
With so much rhyme and little reason,
And though he argues ne'er so long
That all is right, his head is wrong.[6]
None strive to know their proper merit
But strain for wisdom, beauty, spirit,
And lose the praise that is their due
While they've th' impossible in view.
So have I seen the injudicious heir
To add one window the whole house impair.
Instinct the hound does better teach,
Who never undertook to preach;
The frighted hare from dogs does run
But not attempts to bear a gun.
Here many noble thoughts occur
But I prolixity abhor,
And will pursue th' instructive tale
To show the wise in some things fail.
The reverend lover with surprise

5. "The ox desires the saddle" (Horace, *Epistles* 1.14.43).

6. Montagu ridicules Pope's famous conclusion to *An Essay on Man:* "Whatever IS, is RIGHT."

Peeps in her bubbies, and her eyes,
And kisses both, and tries—and tries.
The evening in this hellish play,
Beside his guineas thrown away,
Provoked the priest to that degree
He swore, "The fault is not in me.
Your damned close stool° so near my nose, *chamber pot*
Your dirty smock, and stinking toes
Would make a Hercules as tame
As any beau that you can name."
The nymph grown furious roared, "By God
The blame lies all in sixty odd,"[7]
And scornful pointing to the door
Cried, "Fumbler, see my face no more."
"With all my heart I'll go away,
But nothing done, I'll nothing pay.
Give back the money." "How," cried she,
"Would you palm such a cheat on me!
For poor four pound to roar and bellow—
Why sure you want some new Prunella?"[8]
"I'll be revenged, you saucy quean"° *whore*
(Replies the disappointed Dean)
"I'll so describe your dressing room
The very Irish shall not come."
She answered short, "I'm glad you'll write.
You'll furnish paper when I shite."[9]

Eliza Haywood

c. 1693–1756

Eliza Haywood was possibly the most prolific of all the verbose writers of the eighteenth century, and also one of the most famous and widely read. She was so good at constructing fictional personae, however, and masking her private identity—much like her character, "Fantomina"—that virtually nothing is known for certain about her life. That she was born, married, and divorced or separated in England in the early part of the century are uncontested, but where and to whom, and whether she had children, are matters of debate. Like many women novelists of her century, she began her public career as an actress, first in Dublin at the Smock Alley Theatre and then in London. She soon tried her hand at fiction, and her first novel, *Love in Excess* (1719), was one of three major bestsellers published in English within the next few years, alongside Defoe's *Robinson Crusoe* (1719) and Swift's *Gulliver's Travels* (1726). Over the next forty years she published more than sixty titles in many genres: novels, short fiction, plays, poetry, translations, political tracts, and entire periodical series that she wrote and edited herself.

7. I.e., Swift's impotence derives not from her odors but from his age (65 at the time the poem was written).

8. "Prunella" is both a fabric used in clergy vestments (Swift was a clergyman), and the name of the promiscuous, low-born heroine in Richard Estcourt's comic interlude *Prunella* (1708).

9. Compare line 118 of Swift's poem, page 1997.

Haywood became so successful during the 1720s as a writer of "scandalous" narratives that she was mocked by fellow novelist Henry Fielding as "Mrs. Novel," and viciously lampooned by Pope in his *Dunciad* (1728). These attacks had their effect on Haywood, and she temporarily stopped publishing novels. Moreover, the general tone of British fiction changed markedly in the direction of moralizing prudishness after the success of Samuel Richardson's sentimental novels of the 1740s, which Haywood first satirized (as did Fielding), and then imitated. "Fantomina" (1724) characterizes Haywood's best early fiction, with its open expression of female sexual desire—which, nevertheless, must always be masked, and finally punished.

PRONUNCIATIONS:

Beauplaisir: BOH-play-ZEER
Fantomina: fan-to-MAI-nah

Fantomina: Or, Love in a Maze

Being a Secret History of an Amour Between Two Persons of Condition[1]

In love the victors from the vanquished fly.
They fly that wound, and they pursue that die.

—Waller[2]

A young lady of distinguished birth, beauty, wit, and spirit, happened to be in a box one night at the playhouse; where, though there were a great number of celebrated toasts,[3] she perceived several gentlemen extremely pleased themselves with entertaining a woman who sat in a corner of the pit,[4] and, by her air and manner of receiving them, might easily be known to be one of those who come there for no other purpose than to create acquaintance with as many as seem desirous of it. She could not help testifying her contempt of men who, regardless either of the play or circle, threw away their time in such a manner, to some ladies that sat by her: but they, either less surprised by being more accustomed to such sights than she who had been bred for the most part in the country, or not of a disposition to consider anything very deeply, took but little notice of it. She still thought of it, however; and the longer she reflected on it, the greater was her wonder that men, some of whom she knew were accounted to have wit,[5] should have tastes so very depraved.—This excited a curiosity in her to know in what manner these creatures were addressed:[6]—she was young, a stranger to the world, and consequently to the dangers of it; and having nobody in town at that time to whom she was obliged to be accountable for her actions, did in everything as her inclinations or humors rendered most agreeable to her: therefore thought it not in the least a fault to put in practice a little whim which came immediately into her head, to dress herself as near as she could in the fashion of those women who make sale of their favors, and set herself in the way of being accosted as such a one, having at that time no other aim, than the gratification of an innocent curiosity.—She no sooner designed this frolic than she put it in execution; and muffling her hoods

1. Upper-class rank.
2. The final lines of Edmund Waller's "To a Friend, on the different success of their loves" (1645), in which a man describes how his infatuation with a proud woman named Celia met with her rejection, while his subsequent loss of interest turned the tables and made her solicitous of him. "To die" here also means "to experience orgasm."
3. Belles, fine young ladies (whose health was commonly drunk by gentlemen in toasts).
4. The area below the stage generally occupied by gentlemen, law students, professional or literary types, and (in this case) prostitutes. Aristocracy generally sat in the boxes above.
5. Intelligence, good taste, judgment.
6. Creatures: common term of disrespect for women of low birth or reputation. Addressed: approached, solicited.

over her face, went the next night into the gallery-box, and practicing as much as she had observed at that distance the behavior of that woman, was not long before she found her disguise had answered the ends she wore it for.—A crowd of purchasers of all degrees and capacities were in a moment gathered about her, each endeavoring to outbid the other in offering her a price for her embraces.—She listened to 'em all, and was not a little diverted in her mind at the disappointment she should give to so many, each of which thought himself secure of gaining her.—She was told by 'em all that she was the most lovely woman in the world; and some cried, *Gad, she is mighty like my fine Lady Such-a-one*—naming her own name. She was naturally vain, and received no small pleasure in hearing herself praised, though in the person of another, and a supposed prostitute; but she dispatched as soon as she could all that had hitherto attacked her, when she saw the accomplished *Beauplaisir*[7] was making his way through the crowd as fast as he was able, to reach the bench she sat on. She had often seen him in the drawing-room, had talked with him; but then her quality[8] and reputed virtue kept him from using her with that freedom she now expected he would do, and had discovered something in him which had made her often think she should not be displeased, if he would abate some part of his reserve.—Now was the time to have her wishes answered:—he looked in her face, and fancied, as many others had done, that she very much resembled that lady whom she really was; but the vast disparity there appeared between their characters prevented him from entertaining even the most distant thought that they could be the same.—He addressed her at first with the usual salutations of her pretended profession, as, *Are you engaged, Madam?—Will you permit me to wait on you home after the play?—By Heaven, you are a fine girl!—How long have you used this house?*—and such like questions; but perceiving she had a turn of wit, and a genteel manner in her raillery, beyond what is frequently to be found among those wretches, who are for the most part gentlewomen but by necessity, few of 'em having had an education suitable to what they affect to appear, he changed the form of his conversation, and showed her it was not because he understood no better that he had made use of expressions so little polite.—In fine, they were infinitely charmed with each other: he was transported to find so much beauty and wit in a woman, who he doubted not but on very easy terms he might enjoy; and she found a vast deal of pleasure in conversing with him in this free and unrestrained manner. They passed their time all the play with an equal satisfaction; but when it was over, she found herself involved in a difficulty, which before never entered into her head, but which she knew not well how to get over.—The passion he professed for her, was not of that humble nature which can be content with distant adorations:—he resolved not to part from her without the gratifications of those desires she had inspired; and presuming on the liberties which her supposed function allowed of, told her she must either go with him to some convenient house of his procuring, or permit him to wait on her to her own lodgings.—Never had she been in such a *dilemma:* three or four times did she open her mouth to confess her real quality; but the influence of her ill stars prevented it, by putting an excuse into her head, which did the business as well, and at the same time did not take from her the power of seeing and entertaining him a second time with the same freedom she had done this.—She told him, she was under obligations to a man who maintained her, and whom she durst not disappoint, having promised to meet him that night at a house hard by.[9]—This story

7. Lovely pleasure (French).

8. High social station.

9. Nearby.

so like what those ladies sometimes tell was not at all suspected by *Beauplaisir;* and assuring her he would be far from doing her a prejudice,[1] desired that in return for the pain he should suffer in being deprived of her company that night, that she would order her affairs, so as not to render him unhappy the next. She gave a solemn promise to be in the same box on the morrow evening; and they took leave of each other; he to the tavern to drown the remembrance of his disappointment; she in a hackney-chair[2] hurried home to indulge contemplation on the frolic she had taken, designing nothing less on her first reflections than to keep the promise she had made him, and hugging herself with joy, that she had the good luck to come off undiscovered.

But these cogitations were but of a short continuance; they vanished with the hurry of her spirits, and were succeeded by others vastly different and ruinous:—all the charms of *Beauplaisir* came fresh into her mind; she languished, she almost died for another opportunity of conversing with him; and not all the admonitions of her discretion were effectual to oblige her to deny laying hold of that which offered itself the next night.—She depended on the strength of her virtue, to bear her fate through trials more dangerous than she apprehended this to be, and never having been addressed by him as Lady —— was resolved to receive his devoirs[3] as a town-mistress, imagining a world of satisfaction to herself in engaging him in the character of such a one, observing the surprise he would be in to find himself refused by a woman, who he supposed granted her favors without exception.—Strange and unaccountable were the whimsies she was possessed of—wild and incoherent her desires—unfixed and undetermined her resolutions, but in that of seeing *Beauplaisir* in the manner she had lately done. As for her proceedings with him, or how a second time to escape him, without discovering who she was, she could neither assure herself, nor whether or not in the last extremity she would do so.—Bent, however, on meeting him, whatever should be the consequence, she went out some hours before the time of going to the playhouse, and took lodgings in a house not very far from it, intending, that if he should insist on passing some part of the night with her, to carry him there, thinking she might with more security to her honor entertain him at a place where she was mistress, than at any of his own choosing.

The appointed hour being arrived, she had the satisfaction to find his love in his assiduity: he was there before her; and nothing could be more tender than the manner in which he accosted her: but from the first moment she came in, to that of the play being done, he continued to assure her no consideration should prevail with him to part from her again, as she had done the night before; and she rejoiced to think she had taken that precaution of providing herself with a lodging, to which she thought she might invite him, without running any risk, either of her virtue or reputation.—Having told him she would admit of his accompanying her home, he seemed perfectly satisfied; and leading her to the place, which was not above twenty houses distant, would have ordered a collation[4] to be brought after them. But she would not permit it, telling him she was not one of those who suffered themselves to be treated at their own lodgings; and as soon she was come in, sent a servant, belonging to the house, to provide a very handsome supper, and wine, and everything was served to table in a manner which showed the director neither wanted money, nor was ignorant how it should be laid out.

1. Injury.
2. Hired sedan chair carried by two men.
3. Respects.
4. Light meal.

This proceeding, though it did not take from him the opinion that she was what she appeared to be, yet it gave him thoughts of her, which he had not before.—He believed her a *mistress,* but believed her to be one of a superior rank, and began to imagine the possession of her would be much more expensive than at first he had expected: but not being of a humor to grudge anything for his pleasures, he gave himself no farther trouble than what were occasioned by fears of not having money enough to reach her price, about him.

Supper being over, which was intermixed with a vast deal of amorous conversation, he began to explain himself more than he had done; and both by his words and behavior let her know he would not be denied that happiness the freedoms she allowed had made him hope.—It was in vain; she would have retracted the encouragement she had given:—in vain she endeavored to delay, till the next meeting, the fulfilling of his wishes:—she had now gone too far to retreat:—*he* was bold;—he was resolute: *she* fearful—confused, altogether unprepared to resist in such encounters, and rendered more so, by the extreme liking she had to him.—Shocked, however, at the apprehension of really losing her honor, she struggled all she could, and was just going to reveal the whole secret of her name and quality, when the thoughts of the liberty he had taken with her, and those he still continued to prosecute, prevented her, with representing[5] the danger of being exposed, and the whole affair made a theme for public ridicule.—Thus much, indeed, she told him, that she was a virgin, and had assumed this manner of behavior only to engage him. But that he little regarded, or if he had, would have been far from obliging him to desist;—nay, in the present burning eagerness of desire, 'tis probable, that had he been acquainted both with who and what she really was, the knowledge of her birth would not have influenced him with respect sufficient to have curbed the wild exuberance of his luxurious wishes, or made him in that longing—that impatient moment, change the form of his addresses. In fine, she was undone; and he gained a victory, so highly rapturous, that had he known over whom, scarce could he have triumphed more. Her tears, however, and the distraction she appeared in, after the ruinous ecstasy was past, as it heightened his wonder, so it abated his satisfaction:—he could not imagine for what reason a woman, who, if she intended not to be a *mistress,* had counterfeited the part of one, and taken so much pains to engage him, should lament a consequence which she could not but expect, and till the last test, seemed inclinable to grant; and was both surprised and troubled at the mystery.—He omitted nothing that he thought might make her easy; and still retaining an opinion that the hope of interest had been the chief motive which had led her to act in the manner she had done, and believing that she might know so little of him, as to suppose, now she had nothing left to give, he might not make that recompense she expected for her favors: to put her out of that pain, he pulled out of his pocket a purse of gold, entreating her to accept of that as an earnest of what he intended to do for her; assuring her, with ten thousand protestations, that he would spare nothing, which his whole estate could purchase, to procure her content and happiness. This treatment made her quite forget the part she had assumed, and throwing it from her with an air of disdain, Is this a reward (*said she*) for condescensions,[6] such as I have yielded to?—Can all the wealth you are possessed of make a reparation for my loss of honor?—Oh! no, I am undone beyond the power of heaven itself to help me!—She uttered many more such exclamations; which the

5. By calling to mind.

6. Unworthiness, vice.

amazed *Beauplaisir* heard without being able to reply to, till by degrees sinking from that rage of temper, her eyes resumed their softening glances, and guessing at the consternation he was in, No, my dear *Beauplaisir,* (*added she*) your love alone can compensate for the shame you have involved me in; be you sincere and constant, and I hereafter shall, perhaps, be satisfied with my fate, and forgive myself the folly that betrayed me to you.

Beauplaisir thought he could not have a better opportunity than these words gave him of inquiring who she was, and wherefore she had feigned herself to be of a profession which he was now convinced she was not; and after he had made her a thousand vows of an affection, as inviolable and ardent as she could wish to find in him, entreated she would inform him by what means his happiness had been brought about, and also to whom he was indebted for the bliss he had enjoyed.—Some remains of yet unextinguished modesty, and sense of shame, made her blush exceedingly at this demand; but recollecting herself in a little time, she told him so much of the truth, as to what related to the frolic she had taken of satisfying her curiosity in what manner *mistresses,* of the sort she appeared to be were treated by those who addressed them; but forbore discovering her true name and quality, for the reasons she had done before, resolving, if he boasted of this affair, he should not have it in his power to touch her character: she therefore said she was the daughter of a country gentleman, who was come to town to buy clothes, and that she was called *Fantomina.* He had no reason to distrust the truth of this story, and was therefore satisfied with it; but did not doubt by the beginning of her conduct, but that in the end she would be in reality, the thing she so artfully had counterfeited; and had good nature enough to pity the misfortunes he imagined would be her lot: but to tell her so, or offer his advice in that point, was not his business, at least, as yet.

They parted not till towards morning; and she obliged him to a willing vow of visiting her the next day at three in the afternoon. It was too late for her to go home that night, therefore contented herself with lying there. In the morning she sent for the woman of the house to come up to her; and easily perceiving, by her manner, that she was a woman who might be influenced by gifts, made her a present of a couple of broad pieces,[7] and desired her, that if the gentleman, who had been there the night before, should ask any questions concerning her, that he should be told, she was lately come out of the country, had lodged there about a fortnight, and that her name was *Fantomina.* I shall (*also added she*) lie but seldom here; nor, indeed, ever come but in those times when I expect to meet him: I would, therefore, have you order it so, that he may think I am but just gone out, if he should happen by any accident to call when I am not here; for I would not, for the world, have him imagine I do not constantly lodge here. The landlady assured her she would do everything as she desired, and gave her to understand she wanted not the gift of secrecy.

Everything being ordered at this home for the security of her reputation, she repaired to the other, where she easily excused to an unsuspecting aunt, with whom she boarded, her having been abroad all night, saying, she went with a gentleman and his lady in a barge, to a little country seat of theirs up the river, all of them designing to return the same evening; but that one of the bargemen happening to be taken ill on the sudden, and no other waterman to be got that night, they were obliged to tarry till morning. Thus did this lady's wit and vivacity assist her in all, but where it was most needed.—She had discernment to foresee, and avoid all those ills which might attend

7. Gold coins.

the loss of her *reputation,* but was wholly blind to those of the ruin of her *virtue;* and having managed her affairs so as to secure the *one,* grew perfectly easy with the remembrance she had forfeited the *other.*—The more she reflected on the merits of *Beauplaisir,* the more she excused herself for what she had done; and the prospect of that continued bliss she expected to share with him took from her all remorse for having engaged in an affair which promised her so much satisfaction, and in which she found not the least danger of misfortune.—If he is really (*said she, to herself*) the faithful, the constant lover he has sworn to be, how charming will be our amor?—And if he should be false, grow satiated, like other men, I shall but, at the worst, have the private vexation of knowing I have lost him;—the intrigue being a secret, my disgrace will be so too:—I shall hear no whispers as I pass—She is forsaken:—the odious word *forsaken* will never wound my ears; nor will my wrongs excite either the mirth or pity of the talking world:—it would not be even in the power of my undoer himself to triumph over me; and while he laughs at, and perhaps despises the fond, the yielding *Fantomina,* he will revere and esteem the virtuous, the reserved lady.—In this manner did she applaud her own conduct, and exult with the imagination that she had more prudence than all her sex beside. And it must be confessed, indeed, that she preserved an economy in the management of this intrigue beyond what almost any woman but herself ever did: in the first place, by making no person in the world a confidant in it; and in the next, in concealing from *Beauplaisir* himself the knowledge who she was; for though she met him three or four days in a week, at that lodging she had taken for that purpose, yet as much as he employed her time and thoughts, she was never missed from any assembly she had been accustomed to frequent.—The business of her love has engrossed her till six in the evening, and before seven she has been dressed in a different habit, and in another place.—Slippers, and a night-gown loosely flowing, has been the garb in which he has left the languishing *Fantomina;*—laced and adorned with all the blaze of jewels has he, in less than an hour after, beheld at the royal chapel, the palace gardens, drawing-room, opera, or play, the haughty awe-inspiring lady—a thousand times has he stood amazed at the prodigious likeness between his little mistress and this court beauty; but was still as far from imagining they were the same as he was the first hour he had accosted her in the playhouse, though it is not impossible but that her resemblance to this celebrated lady might keep his inclination alive something longer than otherwise they would have been; and that it was to the thoughts of this (as he supposed) unenjoyed charmer she owed in great measure the vigor of his latter caresses.

But he varied not so much from his sex as to be able to prolong desire to any great length after possession: the rifled charms of *Fantomina* soon lost their potency, and grew tasteless and insipid; and when the season of the year inviting the company to the *Bath,*[8] she offered to accompany him, he made an excuse to go without her. She easily perceived his coldness, and the reason why he pretended her going would be inconvenient, and endured as much from the discovery as any of her sex could do: she dissembled it, however, before him, and took her leave of him with the show of no other concern than his absence occasioned: but this she did to take from him all suspicion of her following him, as she intended, and had already laid a scheme for.—From her first finding out that he designed to leave her behind, she plainly saw it was for no other reason, than that being tired of her conversation, he was willing to be at liberty to pursue new conquests; and wisely considering that complaints, tears, swoonings,

8. Town in southwestern England, popular as a resort because of its hot springs.

and all the extravagancies which women make use of in such cases, have little prevalence over a heart inclined to rove, and only serve to render those who practice them more contemptible, by robbing them of that beauty which alone can bring back the fugitive lover, she resolved to take another course; and remembering the height of transport she enjoyed when the agreeable *Beauplaisir* kneeled at her feet, imploring her first favors, she longed to prove the same again. Not but a woman of her beauty and accomplishments might have beheld a thousand in that condition *Beauplaisir* had been; but with her sex's modesty, she had not also thrown off another virtue equally valuable, though generally unfortunate, *constancy:* she loved *Beauplaisir;* it was only he whose solicitations could give her pleasure; and had she seen the whole species despairing, dying for her sake, it might, perhaps, have been a satisfaction to her pride, but none to her more tender inclination.—Her design was once more to engage him, to hear him sigh, to see him languish, to feel the strenuous pressures of his eager arms, to be compelled, to be sweetly forced to what she wished with equal ardor, was what she wanted, and what she had formed a stratagem to obtain, in which she promised herself success.

She no sooner heard he had left the town, than making a pretense to her aunt, that she was going to visit a relation in the country, went towards *Bath,* attended but by two servants, who she found reasons to quarrel with on the road and discharged: clothing herself in a habit she had brought with her, she forsook the coach, and went into a wagon, in which equipage she arrived at *Bath.* The dress she was in was a round-eared cap,[9] a short red petticoat, and a little jacket of gray stuff;[1] all the rest of her accoutrements were answerable to these, and joined with a broad country dialect, a rude unpolished air, which she, having been bred in these parts, knew very well how to imitate, with her hair and eye-brows blacked, made it impossible for her to be known, or taken for any other than what she seemed. Thus disguised did she offer herself to service in the house where *Beauplaisir* lodged, having made it her business to find out immediately where he was. Notwithstanding this metamorphosis she was still extremely pretty; and the mistress of the house happening at that time to want a maid was very glad of the opportunity of taking her. She was presently received into the family; and had a post in it (such as she would have chose, had she been left at her liberty), that of making the gentlemen's beds, getting them their breakfasts, and waiting on them in their chambers. Fortune in this exploit was extremely on her side; there were no others of the male-sex in the house than an old gentleman, who had lost the use of his limbs with the rheumatism, and had come thither for the benefit of the waters, and her beloved *Beauplaisir;* so that she was in no apprehensions of any amorous violence, but where she wished to find it. Nor were her designs disappointed: He was fired with the first sight of her; and though he did not presently take any farther notice of her, than giving her two or three hearty kisses, yet she, who now understood that language but too well, easily saw they were the prelude to more substantial joys.—Coming the next morning to bring his chocolate, as he had ordered, he catched her by the pretty leg, which the shortness of her petticoat did not in the least oppose; then pulling her gently to him, asked her, how long she had been at service?—How many sweethearts she had? If she had ever been in love? and many other such questions, befitting one of the degree she appeared to be: all which she answered with such seeming innocence, as more enflamed the amorous heart of him who talked

9. Style of cap associated with country women.

1. Coarse wool fabric.

to her. He compelled her to sit in his lap; and gazing on her blushing beauties, which, if possible, received addition from her plain and rural dress, he soon lost the power of containing himself.—His wild desires burst out in all his words and actions: he called her little angel, cherubim, swore he must enjoy her, though death were to be the consequence, devoured her lips, her breasts with greedy kisses, held to his burning bosom her half-yielding, half-reluctant body, nor suffered her to get loose, till he had ravaged all, and glutted each rapacious sense with the sweet beauties of the pretty *Celia,*[2] for that was the name she bore in this second expedition.—Generous as liberality itself to all who gave him joy this way, he gave her a handsome sum of gold, which she durst not now refuse, for fear of creating some mistrust, and losing the heart she so lately had regained; therefore taking it with an humble courtesy, and a well counterfeited show of surprise and joy, cried, O law, Sir! what must I do for all this? He laughed at her simplicity, and kissing her again, though less fervently than he had done before, bad her not be out of the way when he came home at night. She promised she would not, and very obediently kept her word.

His stay at *Bath* exceeded not a month; but in that time his supposed country lass had persecuted him so much with her fondness, that in spite of the eagerness with which he first enjoyed her, he was at last grown more weary of her, than he had been of *Fantomina;* which she perceiving, would not be troublesome, but quitting her service, remained privately in the town till she heard he was on his return; and in that time provided herself of another disguise to carry on a third plot, which her inventing brain had furnished her with, once more to renew his twice-decayed ardors. The dress she had ordered to be made, was such as widows wear in their first mourning, which, together with the most afflicted and penitential countenance that ever was seen, was no small alteration to her who used to seem all gaiety.—To add to this, her hair, which she was accustomed to wear very loose, both when *Fantomina* and *Celia,* was now tied back so straight, and her pinners[3] coming so very forward, that there was none of it to be seen. In fine, her habit and her air were so much changed, that she was not more difficult to be known in the rude country *girl,* than she was now in the sorrowful *widow.*

She knew that *Beauplaisir* came alone in his chariot to the *Bath,* and in the time of her being servant in the house where he lodged, heard nothing of any body that was to accompany him to *London,* and hoped he would return in the same manner he had gone: She therefore hired horses and a man to attend her to an inn about ten miles on this side of *Bath,* where having discharged them, she waited till the chariot should come by; which when it did, and she saw that he was alone in it, she called to him that drove it to stop a moment, and going to the door saluted the master with these words:

The distressed and wretched, Sir (*said she*), never fail to excite compassion in a generous mind; and I hope I am not deceived in my opinion that yours is such:—You have the appearance of a gentleman, and cannot, when you hear my story, refuse that assistance which is in your power to give to an unhappy woman, who without it, may be rendered the most miserable of all created beings.

It would not be very easy to represent the surprise, so odd an address created in the mind of him to whom it was made.—She had not the appearance of one who

2. In Renaissance literature the name Celia is frequently associated with vanity or pride, as in Lyly's *Love's Metamorphosis* as well as Waller's "To Phyllis" and "To a Friend" (quoted in the epigraph); similarly, in Swift's "The Lady's Dressing Room" (see page 1994) Celia is the woman who spends five hours in her dressing room each day in an effort to conceal her natural nastiness.

3. The side flaps of a close-fitting hat, usually worn by women of higher rank.

wanted charity; and what other favor she required he could not conceive: but telling her she might command any thing in his power gave her encouragement to declare herself in this manner: You may judge (*resumed she*), by the melancholy garb I am in, that I have lately lost all that ought to be valuable to womankind; but it is impossible for you to guess the greatness of my misfortune, unless you had known my husband, who was master of every perfection to endear him to a wife's affections.—But, notwithstanding, I look on myself as the most unhappy of my sex in out-living him, I must so far obey the dictates of my discretion, as to take care of the little fortune he left behind him, which being in the hands of a brother of his in *London,* will be all carried off to *Holland,*[4] where he is going to settle; if I reach not the town before he leaves it, I am undone for ever.—To which end I left *Bristol,* the place where we lived, hoping to get a place in the stage at *Bath,* but they were all taken up before I came; and being, by a hurt I got in a fall, rendered incapable of traveling any long journey on horseback, I have no way to go to *London,* and must be inevitably ruined in the loss of all I have on earth, without you have good nature enough to admit me to take part of your chariot.

Here the feigned widow ended her sorrowful tale, which had been several times interrupted by a parenthesis of sighs and groans; and *Beauplaisir,* with a complaisant and tender air, assured her of his readiness to serve her in things of much greater consequence than what she desired of him; and told her it would be an impossibility of denying a place in his chariot to a lady who he could not behold without yielding one in his heart. She answered the compliments he made her but with tears, which seemed to stream in such abundance from her eyes, that she could not keep her handkerchief from her face one moment. Being come into the chariot, *Beauplaisir* said a thousand handsome things to persuade her from giving way to so violent a grief; which, he told her, would not only be destructive to her beauty, but likewise her health. But all his endeavors for consolement appeared ineffectual, and he began to think he should have but a dull journey, in the company of one who seemed so obstinately devoted to the memory of her dead husband, that there was no getting a word from her on any other theme:—but bethinking himself of the celebrated story of the *Ephesian* matron,[5] it came into his head to make trial, she who seemed equally susceptible of *sorrow,* might not also be so too of *love:* and having began a discourse on almost every other topic, and finding her still incapable of answering, resolved to put it to the proof, if this would have no more effect to rouse her sleeping spirits:—with a gay air, therefore, though accompanied with the greatest modesty and respect, he turned the conversation, as though without design, on that joy-giving passion, and soon discovered that was indeed the subject she was best pleased to be entertained with; for on his giving her a hint to begin upon, never any tongue run more voluble than hers, on the prodigious power it had to influence the souls of those possessed of it, to actions even the most distant from their intentions, principles, or humors.—From that she passed to a description of the happiness of mutual affection;—the unspeakable ecstasy of those who meet with equal ardency; and represented it in colors so lively, and disclosed by the gestures with which her words were accompanied, and the accent of her voice so true a feeling of what she said, that *Beauplaisir,* without being as stupid, as he was really the contrary, could not avoid perceiving there were seeds of fire, not yet extinguished, in this fair widow's soul, which wanted but the kindling

4. Holland had been a frequent destination for English religious dissenters in exile.

5. In Petronius's *Satyricon,* the Ephesian matron is a faithful wife who stays by her dead husband's burial vault day and night until she is seduced by a soldier who guards the nearby bodies of crucified criminals. When one of the bodies is stolen, the matron gives her own husband's body to the soldier to save him from punishment.

breath of tender sighs to light into a blaze.—He now thought himself as fortunate, as some moments before he had the reverse; and doubted not, but, that before they parted, he should find a way to dry the tears of this lovely mourner, to the satisfaction of them both. He did not, however, offer, as he had done to *Fantomina* and *Celia,* to urge his passion directly to her, but by a thousand little softening artifices, which he well knew how to use, gave her leave to guess he was enamored. When they came to the inn where they were to lie, he declared himself somewhat more freely, and perceiving she did not resent it past forgiveness, grew more encroaching still:—he now took the liberty of kissing away her tears, and catching the sighs as they issued from her lips; telling her if grief was infectious, he was resolved to have his share; protesting he would gladly exchange passions with her, and be content to bear her load of *sorrow,* if she would as willingly ease the burden of his *love.*—She said little in answer to the strenuous pressures with which at last he ventured to enfold her, but not thinking it decent, for the character she had assumed, to yield so suddenly, and unable to deny both his and her own inclinations, she counterfeited a fainting, and fell motionless upon his breast.—He had no great notion that she was in a real fit, and the room they supped in happening to have a bed in it, he took her in his arms and laid her on it, believing, that whatever her distemper was, that was the most proper place to convey her to.—He laid himself down by her, and endeavored to bring her to herself; and she was too grateful to her kind physician at her returning sense, to remove from the posture he had put her in, without his leave.

It may, perhaps, seem strange that *Beauplaisir* should in such near intimacies continue still deceived: I know there are men who will swear it is an impossibility, and that no disguise could hinder them from knowing a woman they had once enjoyed. In answer to these scruples, I can only say, that besides the alteration which the change of dress made in her, she was so admirably skilled in the art of feigning, that she had the power of putting on almost what face she pleased, and knew so exactly how to form her behavior to the character she represented, that all the comedians at both playhouses[6] are infinitely short of her performances: she could vary her very glances, tune her voice to accents the most different imaginable from those in which she spoke when she appeared herself.—These aids from nature, joined to the wiles of art, and the distance between the places where the imagined *Fantomina* and *Celia* were, might very well prevent his having any thought that they were the same, or that the fair *widow* was either of them: it never so much as entered his head, and though he did fancy he observed in the face of the latter, features which were not altogether unknown to him, yet he could not recollect when or where he had known them;—and being told by her, that from her birth, she had never removed from *Bristol,* a place where he never was, he rejected the belief of having seen her, and supposed his mind had been deluded by an idea of some other, whom she might have a resemblance of.

They passed the time of their journey in as much happiness as the most luxurious gratification of wild desires could make them; and when they came to the end of it, parted not without a mutual promise of seeing each other often.—He told her to what place she should direct a letter to him; and she assured him she would send to let him know where to come to her, as soon as she was fixed in lodgings.

She kept her promise; and charmed with the continuance of his eager fondness, went not home, but into private lodgings, whence she wrote to him to visit her the first opportunity, and inquire for the Widow *Bloomer.*—She had no sooner dispatched this billet,[7] than she repaired to the house where she had lodged as *Fantomina,*

6. Comedians are actors. There were only two public playhouses in London, established by royal decree in 1660.

7. Note, brief letter.

charging the people if *Beauplaisir* should come there, not to let him know she had been out of town. From thence she wrote to him, in a different hand, a long letter of complaint, that he had been so cruel in not sending one letter to her all the time he had been absent, entreated to see him, and concluded with subscribing herself his unalterably affectionate *Fantomina.* She received in one day answers to both these. The first contained these lines:

To the Charming Mrs. Bloomer,

It would be impossible, my Angel! for me to express the thousandth part of that infinity of transport, the sight of your dear letter gave me.—Never was woman formed to charm like you: never did any look like you,—write like you,—bless like you;—nor did ever man adore as I do.—Since yesterday we parted, I have seemed a body without a soul; and had you not by this inspiring billet, gave me new life, I know not what by tomorrow I should have been.—I will be with you this evening about five:—O, 'tis an age till then!—But the cursed formalities of duty oblige me to dine with my lord —— who never rises from table till that hour;—therefore adieu till then sweet lovely mistress of the soul and all the faculties of

Your most faithful,
Beauplaisir.

The other was in this manner:

To the Lovely Fantomina,

If you were half so sensible as you ought of your own power of charming, you would be assured, that to be unfaithful or unkind to you, would be among the things that are in their very natures impossibilities.—It was my misfortune, not my fault, that you were not persecuted every post with a declaration of my unchanging passion; but I had unluckily forgot the name of the woman at whose house you are, and knew not how to form a direction that it might come safe to your hands.—And, indeed, the reflection how you might misconstrue my silence, brought me to town some weeks sooner than I intended—If you knew how I have languished to renew those blessings I am permitted to enjoy in your society, you would rather pity than condemn

Your ever faithful,
Beauplaisir.

P.S. *I fear I cannot see you till tomorrow; some business has unluckily fallen out that will engross my hours till then.—Once more, my dear,* Adieu.

Traitor! (*cried she*) as soon as she had read them, 'tis thus our silly, fond, believing sex are served when they put faith in man: so had I been deceived and cheated, had I like the rest believed, and sat down mourning in absence, and vainly waiting recovered tendernesses.—How do some women (*continued she*) make their life a hell, burning in fruitless expectations, and dreaming out their days in hopes and fears, then wake at last to all the horror of despair?—But I have outwitted even the most subtle of the deceiving kind, and while he thinks to fool me, is himself the only beguiled person.

She made herself, most certainly, extremely happy in the reflection on the success of her stratagems; and while the knowledge of his inconstancy and levity of nature kept her from having that real tenderness for him she would else have had, she found the means of gratifying the inclination she had for his agreeable person, in as full a manner as she could wish. She had all the sweets of love, but as yet had tasted none of the gall, and was in a state of contentment, which might be envied by the more delicate.

When the expected hour arrived, she found that her lover had lost no part of the fervency with which he had parted from her; but when the next day she received him as *Fantomina,* she perceived a prodigious difference; which led her again into reflections on the unaccountableness of men's fancies, who still prefer the last conquest, only because it is the last.—Here was an evident proof of it; for there could not be a difference in merit, because they were the same person; but the Widow *Bloomer* was a more new acquaintance than *Fantomina,* and therefore esteemed more valuable. This, indeed, must be said of *Beauplaisir,* that he had a greater share of good nature than most of his sex, who, for the most part, when they are weary of an intrigue, break it entirely off, without any regard to the despair of the abandoned nymph. Though he retained no more than a bare pity and complaisance for *Fantomina,* yet believing she loved him to an excess, would not entirely forsake her, though the continuance of his visits was now become rather a penance than a pleasure.

The Widow *Bloomer* triumphed some time longer over the heart of this inconstant, but at length her sway was at an end, and she sunk in this character, to the same degree of tastelessness, as she had done before in that of *Fantomina* and *Celia.*—She presently perceived it, but bore it as she had always done; it being but what she expected, she had prepared herself for it, and had another project in embryo, which she soon ripened into action. She did not, indeed, complete it altogether so suddenly as she had done the others, by reason there must be persons employed in it; and the aversion she had to any confidants in her affairs, and the caution with which she had hitherto acted, and which she was still determined to continue, made it very difficult for her to find a way without breaking through that resolution to compass what she wished.—She got over the difficulty at last, however, by proceeding in a manner, if possible, more extraordinary than all her former behavior:—muffling herself up in her hood one day, she went into the park about the hour when there are a great many necessitous gentlemen,[8] who think themselves above doing what they call little things for a maintenance, walking in the *Mall,*[9] to take a *Camelion* Treat,[1] and fill their stomachs with air instead of meat. Two of those, who by their physiognomy she thought most proper for her purpose, she beckoned to come to her; and taking them into a walk more remote from company, began to communicate the business she had with them in these words: I am sensible, gentlemen (*said she*), that, through the blindness of fortune, and partiality of the world, merit frequently goes unrewarded, and that those of the best pretentions meet with the least encouragement:—I ask your pardon (*continued she*), perceiving they seemed surprised, if I am mistaken in the notion, that you two may, perhaps, be of the number of those who have reason to complain of the injustice of fate; but if you are such as I take you for, I have a proposal to make you, which may be of some little advantage to you. Neither of them made any immediate answer, but appeared buried in consideration for some moments. At length, We should, doubtless, madam (*said one of them*), willingly come into any measures to oblige you, provided they are such as may bring us into no danger, either as to our persons or reputations. That which I require of you (*resumed she*), has nothing in it criminal: All that I desire is *secrecy* in what you are entrusted, and to disguise yourselves in such a manner as you cannot be known, if hereafter seen by the person on whom you are to impose.—In fine, the business is only an innocent frolic, but if blazed abroad, might be taken for too great a freedom in me:—Therefore, if you

8. Poor men.

9. A popular walk in St. James's Park.

1. Chameleons were thought to subsist on air.

resolve to assist me, here are five pieces to drink my health, and assure you, that I have not discoursed you[2] on an affair, I design not to proceed in; and when it is accomplished fifty more lie ready for your acceptance. These words, and, above all, the money, which was a sum which, 'tis probable, they had not seen of a long time, made them immediately assent to all she desired, and press for the beginning of their employment: but things were not yet ripe for execution; and she told them, that the next day they should be let into the secret, charging them to meet her in the same place at an hour she appointed. 'Tis hard to say, which of these parties went away best pleased; *they,* that fortune had sent them so unexpected a windfall; or *she,* that she had found persons, who appeared so well qualified to serve her.

Indefatigable in the pursuit of whatsoever her humor was bent upon, she had no sooner left her new-engaged emissaries, than she went in search of a house for the completing of her project.—She pitched on one very large, and magnificently furnished, which she hired by the week, giving them the money beforehand, to prevent any inquiries. The next day she repaired to the park, where she met the punctual 'squires of low degree; and ordering them to follow her to the house she had taken, told them they must condescend to appear like servants, and gave each of them a very rich livery. Then writing a letter to *Beauplaisir,* in a character vastly different from either of those she had made use of, as *Fantomina,* or the fair Widow *Bloomer,* ordered one of them to deliver it into his own hands, to bring back an answer, and to be careful that he sifted out nothing of the truth.—I do not fear (*said she*), that you should discover to him who I am, because that is a secret, of which you yourselves are ignorant; but I would have you be so careful in your replies, that he may not think the concealment springs from any other reasons than your great integrity to your trust.—Seem therefore to know my whole affairs; and let your refusing to make him partaker in the secret, appear to be only the effect of your zeal for my interest and reputation. Promises of entire fidelity on the one side, and reward on the other, being past, the messenger made what haste he could to the house of *Beauplaisir;* and being there told where he might find him, performed exactly the injunction that had been given him. But never astonishment exceeded that which *Beauplaisir* felt at the reading this billet, in which he found these lines:

To the All-conquering Beauplaisir.

I imagine not that 'tis a new thing to you, to be told, you are the greatest charm in nature to our sex: I shall therefore, not to fill up my letter with any impertinent praises on your wit or person, only tell you, that I am infinite in love with both, and if you have a heart not too deeply engaged, should think myself the happiest of my sex in being capable of inspiring it with some tenderness.—There is but one thing in my power to refuse you, which is the knowledge of my name, which believing the sight of my face will render no secret, you must not take it ill that I conceal from you.—The bearer of this is a person I can trust; send by him your answer; but endeavor not to dive into the meaning of this mystery, which will be impossible for you to unravel, and at the same time very much disoblige me:—But that you may be in no apprehensions of being imposed on by a woman unworthy of your regard, I will venture to assure you, the first and greatest men in the kingdom would think themselves blessed to have that influence over me you have, though unknown to yourself, acquired.—But I need not go about to raise your curiosity, by giving you any idea of what my person is; if you think fit to be satisfied, resolve to visit me tomorrow

2. Talked to you.

about three in the afternoon; and though my face is hid, you shall not want sufficient demonstration, that she who takes these unusual measures to commence a friendship with you, is neither old, nor deformed. Till then I am,

Yours,
Incognita.[3]

He had scarce come to the conclusion, before he asked the person who brought it, from what place he came;—the name of the lady he served;—if she were a wife, or widow, and several other questions directly opposite to the directions of the letter; but silence would have availed him as much as did all those testimonies of curiosity: no *Italian Bravo,*[4] employed in a business of the like nature, performed his office with more artifice; and the impatient inquirer was convinced, that nothing but doing as he was desired, could give him any light into the character of the woman who declared so violent a passion for him; and little fearing any consequence which could ensue from such an encounter, resolved to rest satisfied till he was informed of everything from herself, not imagining this *Incognita* varied so much from the generality of her sex, as to be able to refuse the knowledge of anything to the man she loved with that transcendency of passion she professed, and which his many successes with the ladies gave him encouragement enough to believe. He therefore took pen and paper, and answered her letter in terms tender enough for a man who had never seen the person to whom he wrote. The words were as follows:

To the Obliging and Witty Incognita.

Though to tell me I am happy enough to be liked by a woman, such, as by your manner of writing, I imagine you to be, is an honor which I can never sufficiently acknowledge, yet I know not how I am able to content myself with admiring the wonders of your wit alone: I am certain, a soul like yours must shine in your eyes with a vivacity, which must bless all they look on.—I shall, however, endeavor to restrain myself in those bounds you are pleased to set me, till by the knowledge of my inviolable fidelity, I may be thought worthy of gazing on that heaven I am now but to enjoy in contemplation.—You need not doubt my glad compliance with your obliging summons: there is a charm in your lines, which gives too sweet an idea of their lovely author to be resisted.—I am all impatient for the blissful moment, which is to throw me at your feet, and give me an opportunity of convincing you that I am,

Your everlasting slave,
Beauplaisir.

Nothing could be more pleased than she, to whom it was directed, at the receipt of this letter; but when she was told how inquisitive he had been concerning her character and circumstances, she could not forbear laughing heartily to think of the tricks she had played him, and applauding her own strength of genius, and force of resolution, which by such unthought-of ways could triumph over her lover's inconstancy, and render that very temper, which to other women is the greatest curse, a means to make herself more blessed.—Had he been faithful to me (*said she, to herself*), either as *Fantomina,* or *Celia,* or the Widow *Bloomer,* the most violent passion, if it does not change its object, in time will wither: possession naturally abates the vigor of desire, and I should have had, at best, but a cold, insipid, husband-like lover in my arms; but by these arts of passing on him as a new mistress whenever the ardor, which alone

3. Unknown woman (Latin); i.e., a woman in disguise.

4. Hired assassin.

makes love a blessing, begins to diminish, for the former one, I have him always raving, wild, impatient, longing, dying.—O that all neglected wives, and fond abandoned nymphs would take this method!—Men would be caught in their own snare, and have no cause to scorn our easy, weeping, wailing sex! Thus did she pride herself as if secure she never should have any reason to repent the present gaiety of her humor. The hour drawing near in which he was to come, she dressed herself in as magnificent a manner, as if she were to be that night at a ball at court, endeavoring to repair the want of those beauties which the vizard[5] should conceal, by setting forth the others with the greatest care and exactness. Her fine shape, and air, and neck appeared to great advantage; and by that which was to be seen of her, one might believe the rest to be perfectly agreeable. *Beauplaisir* was prodigiously charmed, as well with her appearance, as with the manner she entertained him: but though he was wild with impatience for the sight of a face which belonged to so exquisite a body, yet he would not immediately press for it, believing before he left her he should easily obtain that satisfaction.—A noble collation being over, he began to sue for the performance of her promise of granting everything he could ask, excepting the sight of her face, and knowledge of her name. It would have been a ridiculous piece of affectation in her to have seemed coy in complying with what she herself had been the first in desiring: she yielded without even a show of reluctance: and if there be any true felicity in an amour such as theirs, both here enjoyed it to the full. But not in the height of all their mutual raptures, could he prevail on her to satisfy his curiosity with the sight of her face: she told him that she hoped he knew so much of her, as might serve to convince him, she was not unworthy of his tenderest regard; and if he could not content himself with that which she was willing to reveal, and which was the conditions of their meeting, dear as he was to her, she would rather part with him for ever, than consent to gratify an inquisitiveness, which, in her opinion, had no business with his love. It was in vain that he endeavored to make her sensible of her mistake; and that this restraint was the greatest enemy imaginable to the happiness of them both: she was not to be persuaded, and he was obliged to desist his solicitations, though determined in his mind to compass what he so ardently desired, before he left the house. He then turned the discourse wholly on the violence of the passion he had for her; and expressed the greatest discontent in the world at the apprehensions of being separated;—swore he could dwell for ever in her arms, and with such an undeniable earnestness pressed to be permitted to tarry with her the whole night, that had she been less charmed with his renewed eagerness of desire, she scarce would have had the power of resisting him; but in granting this request, she was not without a thought that he had another reason for making it besides the extremity of his passion, and had it immediately in her head how to disappoint him.

The hours of repose being arrived, he begged she would retire to her chamber, to which she consented, but obliged him to go to bed first; which he did not much oppose, because he supposed she would not lie in her mask, and doubted not but the morning's dawn would bring the wished discovery.—The two imagined servants ushered him to his new lodging; where he lay some moments in all the perplexity imaginable at the oddness of this adventure. But she suffered not these cogitations to be of any long continuance: she came, but came in the dark; which being no more than he expected by the former part of her proceedings, he said nothing of; but as much satisfaction as he found in her embraces, nothing ever longed for the approach of day with

5. Mask or veil.

more impatience than he did. At last it came; but how great was his disappointment, when by the noises he heard in the street, the hurry of the coaches, and the cries of penny-merchants,[6] he was convinced it was night nowhere but with him? He was still in the same darkness as before; for she had taken care to blind the windows in such a manner, that not the least chink was left to let in day.—He complained of her behavior in terms that she would not have been able to resist yielding to, if she had not been certain it would have been the ruin of her passion:—she, therefore, answered him only as she had done before; and getting out of the bed from him, flew out of the room with too much swiftness for him to have overtaken her, if he had attempted it. The moment she left him, the two attendants entered the chamber, and plucking down the implements which had screened him from the knowledge of that which he so much desired to find out, restored his eyes once more to day:—they attended to assist him in dressing, brought him tea, and by their obsequiousness, let him see there was but one thing which the mistress of them would not gladly oblige him in.—He was so much out of humor, however, at the disappointment of his curiosity, that he resolved never to make a second visit.—Finding her in an outer room, he made no scruple of expressing the sense he had of the little trust she reposed in him, and at last plainly told her, he could not submit to receive obligations from a lady, who thought him uncapable of keeping a secret, which she made no difficulty of letting her servants into.—He resented—he once more entreated—he said all that man could do, to prevail on her to unfold the mystery; but all his adjurations were fruitless; and he went out of the house determined never to re-enter it, till she should pay the price of his company with the discovery of her face and circumstances.—She suffered him to go with this resolution, and doubted not but he would recede from it, when he reflected on the happy moments they had passed together; but if he did not, she comforted herself with the design of forming some other stratagem, with which to impose on him a fourth time.

She kept the house, and her gentlemen-equipage[7] for about a fortnight, in which time she continued to write to him as *Fantomina* and the Widow *Bloomer,* and received the visits he sometimes made to each; but his behavior to both was grown so cold, that she began to grow as weary of receiving his now insipid caresses as he was of offering them: she was beginning to think in what manner she should drop these two characters, when the sudden arrival of her mother, who had been some time in a foreign country, obliged her to put an immediate stop to the course of her whimsical adventures.—That lady, who was severely virtuous, did not approve of many things she had been told of the conduct of her daughter; and though it was not in the power of any person in the world to inform her of the truth of what she had been guilty of, yet she heard enough to make her keep her afterwards in a restraint, little agreeable to her humor, and the liberties to which she had been accustomed.

But this confinement was not the greatest part of the trouble of this now afflicted lady: she found the consequences of her amorous follies would be, without almost a miracle, impossible to be concealed:—she was with child; and though she would easily have found means to have screened even this from the knowledge of the world, had she been at liberty to have acted with the same unquestionable authority over herself, as she did before the coming of her mother, yet now all her invention was at a loss for a stratagem to impose on a woman of her penetration:—by eating little, lacing

6. Street vendors of cheap wares.

7. Retinue of footmen.

prodigious straight, and the advantage of a great hoop-petticoat, however, her bigness was not taken notice of, and, perhaps, she would not have been suspected till the time of her going into the country, where her mother designed to send her, and from whence she intended to make her escape to some place where she might be delivered with secrecy, if the time of it had not happened much sooner than she expected.—A ball being at court, the good old lady was willing she should partake of the diversion of it as a farewell to the town.—It was there she was seized with those pangs, which none in her condition are exempt from:—she could not conceal the sudden rack which all at once invaded her; or had her tongue been mute, her wildly rolling eyes, the distortion of her features, and the convulsions which shook her whole frame, in spite of her, would have revealed she labored under some terrible shock of nature.—Everybody was surprised, everybody was concerned, but few guessed at the occasion.—Her mother grieved beyond expression, doubted not but she was struck with the hand of death; and ordered her to be carried home in a chair, while herself followed in another.—A physician was immediately sent for: but he presently perceiving what was her distemper, called the old lady aside, and told her, it was not a doctor of his sex, but one of her own, her daughter stood in need of.—Never was astonishment and horror greater than that which seized the soul of this afflicted parent at these words: she could not for a time believe the truth of what she heard; but he insisting on it, and conjuring her to send for a midwife, she was at length convinced of it.—All the pity and tenderness she had been for some moment before possessed of now vanished, and were succeeded by an adequate[8] shame and indignation:—she flew to the bed where her daughter was lying, and telling her what she had been informed of, and which she was now far from doubting, commanded her to reveal the name of the person whose insinuations had drawn her to this dishonor.—It was a great while before she could be brought to confess anything, and much longer before she could be prevailed on to name the man whom she so fatally had loved; but the rack of nature growing more fierce, and the enraged old lady protesting no help should be afforded her while she persisted in her obstinacy, she, with great difficulty and hesitation in her speech, at last pronounced the name of *Beauplaisir.* She had no sooner satisfied her weeping mother, than that sorrowful lady sent messengers at the same time, for a midwife, and for that gentleman who had occasioned the other's being wanted.—He happened by accident to be at home, and immediately obeyed the summons, though prodigiously surprised what business a lady so much a stranger to him could have to impart.—But how much greater was his amazement, when taking him into her closet, she there acquainted him with her daughter's misfortune, of the discovery she had made, and how far he was concerned in it?—All the idea one can form of wild astonishment, was mean to what he felt:—he assured her, that the young lady her daughter was a person whom he had never, more than at a distance, admired:—that he had indeed, spoke to her in public company, but that he never had a thought which tended to her dishonor.—His denials, if possible, added to the indignation she was before enflamed with:—she had no longer patience; and carrying him into the chamber, where she was just delivered of a fine girl, cried out, I will not be imposed on: the truth by one of you shall be revealed.—*Beauplaisir* being brought to the bedside, was beginning to address himself to the lady in it, to beg she could clear the mistake her mother was involved in; when she, covering herself with the cloths, and ready to die a second time with the inward agitations of her soul, shrieked out, Oh, I am undone!—I cannot live,

8. Equal.

and bear this shame!—But the old lady believing that now or never was the time to dive into the bottom of this mystery, forcing her to rear her head, told her, she should not hope to escape the scrutiny of a parent she had dishonored in such a manner, and pointing to *Beauplaisir,* Is this the gentleman (*said she*), to whom you owe your ruin? or have you deceived me by a fictitious tale? Oh! no (*resumed the trembling creature*), he is, indeed, the innocent cause of my undoing:—Promise me your pardon (*continued she*), and I will relate the means. Here she ceased, expecting what she would reply, which, on hearing *Beauplaisir* cry out, What mean you, madam? I your undoing, who never harbored the least design on you in my life, she did in these words, Though the injury you have done your family (*said she*), is of a nature which cannot justly hope forgiveness, yet be assured, I shall much sooner excuse you when satisfied of the truth, than while I am kept in a suspense, if possible, as vexatious as the crime itself is to me. Encouraged by this she related the whole truth. And 'tis difficult to determine, if *Beauplaisir,* or the lady, were most surprised at what they heard; he, that he should have been blinded so often by her artifices; or she, that so young a creature should have the skill to make use of them. Both sat for some time in a profound reverie; till at length she broke it first in these words: Pardon, sir (*said she*),[9] the trouble I have given you: I must confess it was with a design to oblige you to repair the supposed injury you had done this unfortunate girl, by marrying her, but now I know not what to say:—The blame is wholly hers, and I have nothing to request further of you, than that you will not divulge the distracted folly she has been guilty of.—He answered her in terms perfectly polite; but made no offer of that which, perhaps, she expected, though could not, now informed of her daughter's proceedings, demand. He assured her, however, that if she would commit the newborn lady to his care, he would discharge it faithfully. But neither of them would consent to that; and he took his leave, full of cogitations,[1] more confused than ever he had known in his whole life. He continued to visit there, to inquire after her health every day; but the old lady perceiving there was nothing likely to ensue from these civilities, but, perhaps, a renewing of the crime, she entreated him to refrain; and as soon as her daughter was in a condition, sent her to a monastery in *France,* the abbess of which had been her particular friend. And thus ended an intrigue, which, considering the time it lasted, was as full of variety as any, perhaps, that many ages have produced.

9. I.e., the elder lady.

1. Anxious thoughts.

The Pilgrim's Vision. Frontispiece to Mark Twain, *The Innocents Abroad,* 1869.

The Nineteenth Century

Toward the end of the eighteenth century things heated up in and around Europe. Not the climate—cold weather and bad harvests in the 1780s and 1790s contributed to the anguish of the French Revolution—but socially and politically. After the many political and religious upheavals of the seventeenth century, the century that followed saw long, stable reigns in eighteenth-century England, France, the rapidly westernizing Russia, and the self-isolated Spain, punctuated by relatively local, short-lived conflicts and accompanied by fairly steady economic progress. Under the surface, however, discontent grew as early industrial development increased the gap between the rich and the working poor and as increasing literacy, especially among craftsmen and laborers, raised expectations and hopes. The ringing words that open Rousseau's *Social Contract* fired a flame that spread across the continents and through the century: "Man is born free, and everywhere he is in chains."

The term *revolution* itself originally means rotation. It first came to mean rebellion in 1688 when the "Glorious Revolution" drove the crypto-Catholic James II off the English throne. After that there were no comparable events until the Americans revolted in 1776. The century that followed was strongly marked by turmoil and warfare around Europe, lasting from the fall of the Bastille in 1789 through the definitive fall of Napoleon in 1815, the Greek War of Independence (1821–1828), the Revolution of 1830 in France that replaced the restored Bourbon monarchy with the "Citizen King" Louis-Philippe, the continent-wide revolutions of 1848 that mostly failed but left strong democratic and even communist movements in their wake while overthrowing the French monarchy for good, and the blitzkrieg Franco-Prussian War of 1870, an early salvo in nearly a century of German expansionism.

Meanwhile, the New World was struggling to shake off the yoke of the old, with Haiti rising up soon after the United States, followed by all the major mainland Spanish possessions and, late in the century, trailed peacefully by Canada and violently by Cuba. There had never before been a mass war such as Napoleon led, but then the American Civil War of 1861–1865 and the Paris Commune of 1871 broke out with unprecedented internecine violence. Clearly a whole new kind of energy was on the loose, accompanied and symbolized by the power of steam and the speed of railroads, and reflected, steered, and resisted by the influential and imaginative writers of the era.

Romanticism

"The three great tendencies of the age are the French Revolution, Fichte's *Doctrine of Knowledge*, and Wilhelm Meister." So wrote Friedrich Schlegel in 1798 (in a collection of so-called "Fragments" in his journal *Athenaeum*), one of the cluster of incandescent intellectuals who drove German culture to unprecedented heights around 1800. Schlegel is as responsible as any individual for the label that we attach to the culture and writing of the early decades of the century, and unpacking his utterances can give us a way to organize the multifariousness of the period. Willfully, Schlegel aligns the mass political outburst in France with the latest philosophical blockbuster and the title figure of a massive new novel by Goethe. In the middle of things it was hard to see what was really happening, and indeed modern scholars continue to differ radically about the thrust of the French Revolution, its chronological limits, and even its outcome. Schlegel's brilliance was to see the revolution not as a thing—whether a political event or a social manifestation—but as a "tendency," an ongoing process, escaping definition. And, as Schlegel suggests, books can work on us as powerfully as external actions, if not as dramatically. Johann Gottlieb Fichte was the first great successor to Immanuel Kant's "Copernican revolution" in philosophy; in abstract treatises and fiery moral and political lectures Fichte preached a doctrine of the absolute primacy of the self which must, however, strive for self-fulfillment through the most demanding individual and community discipline. "Tendency" is just the term to capture the perpetual unrest driving a philosopher whose emotions radiated through Thomas Carlyle and Ralph Waldo Emerson into the Victorian soul and through Ludwig Feuerbach and Karl Marx into the social thought of central and eastern Europe.

Schlegel's third "tendency" refers to Goethe's novel *Wilhelm Meister's Apprenticeship*. The title is ironic, since "Meister" means "master," while Wilhelm is in fact just an overprotected bourgeois adolescent. Goethe's novel reflects a focus on individual development; it begins with childhood infatuations as few novels before Rousseau had (but many later ones by Dickens, Flaubert, Joyce, and countless others would), and it proceeds to tell of Wilhelm's unfinished development toward becoming a functioning member of a far-flung society. Individual psychology is thus discovered to be as crucial as mass movements to the destinies of civilization. Like most educated German speakers in subsequent generations, Sigmund Freud was a passionate admirer of Goethe, and his studies in infantile sexuality and his writings on culture stand at the end of tendencies originating in the romantic period. Schlegel's aphorism implies a recognition that mass movements and individual ideals are inseparably connected.

Romantic striving took many forms, all of them intense but not all noisy. "Near is / And hard to grasp / The god," wrote the great German mythic poet Friedrich Hölderlin at the start of his ode "Patmos" (1803), using the simplest words in typically contorted grammar to express everyman's struggle toward comprehension. John Keats and Percy Bysshe Shelley wrote poems to nightingale and skylark, dreaming of flying in the age that invented balloons: "Hail to thee, blithe spirit, / Bird thou never wert," as Shelley wrote in "To a Sky-Lark," with exuberant disrespect for his addressee's identity. Wordsworth counseled humane alertness to the quietest signs of life—the hermit's smoke of "Tintern Abbey," or the quiet play of lights in the late sonnet, "Mark the Concent'red Hazels." William Blake, meanwhile, wrote massive epics of social and sexual struggle, confronting private and public demons such as those imaged in the fearful symmetry of his "tyger."

Parallels can be found in the other arts. Beethoven was composing some of the loudest music yet heard on the face of the earth, to be performed by huge orchestras and choruses in front of vast publics, and explicitly preaching heroism (*Eroica* Symphony), liberation from tyranny (the opera *Fidelio*) and brotherhood (the choral setting of Friedrich Schiller's "Ode to Joy" in the Ninth Symphony). At the same time, romantic exaltation finds quiet expression in Franz Schubert's many hundreds of art-songs (a new musical form), in William Constable's many paintings of the heaven-directed, pastorally sited spire of Salisbury Cathedral and in the natural cathedrals of Caspar David Friedrich's sublime landscapes (see page 2152). Some modern readers complain of too much self-assertion in one kind of Romanticism, others of too much complacency in alternative kinds. But the various moods are best considered to be a dialogue reflecting different attempts to confront the spirit of the age—its vital forces, its electricity (another newly discovered phenomenon). "Spirit of the age" is itself a Romantic idea, the notion that a hidden inner force rather than a rational ideal or external guide permeates and motivates individuals and groups. They share an innovative awareness even where they may disagree about responses.

In another pithy formula, Schlegel called Romanticism "a progressive universal poetry." What did he mean by this? Colonial expansion had been in progress for centuries by then, and not even Goethe's *Faust* could be more cosmic than Dante's *Divine Comedy,* Shakespeare's *King Lear*, or Milton's *Paradise Lost.* But universal doesn't mean overwhelming—an ambition that would be inconsistent with the open-ended striving of Romanticism. Goethe's Faust is a highly educated old man; unlike Renaissance versions of the legend, he wants to know and experience everything, not to have ultimate power, and he dies after a fit of blind philanthropy. Even in the demonic forms of the French Revolution at its worst, universality implies an ideal of brotherhood—a universal embrace rather than a world-order.

The word *Romanticism* itself has universal overtones in this sense. In its derivation from Rome it evokes the grand world-empire of the classical past, and more broadly the glories of thought and imagination of the classical world. But romances (as then conceived) were medieval tales of knighthood and adventure and ballads of the common people. Romance in this sense evokes national histories and traditions, preserved in unschooled writings and obsolete dialects, and in the rural folktales and folk songs that were collected starting gradually from the mid-eighteenth century. Romances suggest the aura of mystery and magic that is part of the transhuman universality of Romanticism, and they also suggest the nation mystically rooted not in political and military history but in the essence of a popular spirit. Then, at an individual level, romance means love. To the eighteenth century, physical love tended to seem irrational (in novels of uncontrolled passion) or ridiculous (as in Lemuel Gulliver's scornful horror at the different kinds of affection he encounters in his various voyages), if not straightforwardly animalistic, as in the many casual marriages of Daniel Defoe's *Moll Flanders.* To the nineteenth century, love was a magical and spiritual passion like that of Wagner's Tristan and Isolde, edifying or terrifying (or both at once, as in much of Baudelaire's poetry), but always a force implicated in moral good or evil, at times even transcending both. Finally, in German as in French, Italian, and Russian, "Roman" or its near equivalent is the term for what English and Spanish call a "novel." Hence the quintessentially "romantic" form of progressive universal poetry is the novel as the story of the new. The great Russian writer Pushkin subtitled *Eugene Onegin* a "Novel in Verse," while Gogol subtitled his comic novel *Dead Souls* a "Poem." Novels are detailed stories based in the everyday world, and romantic writers prepared the way for the great realistic novels that dominated literary production in the second half of the century. Often drawing their inspiration from the

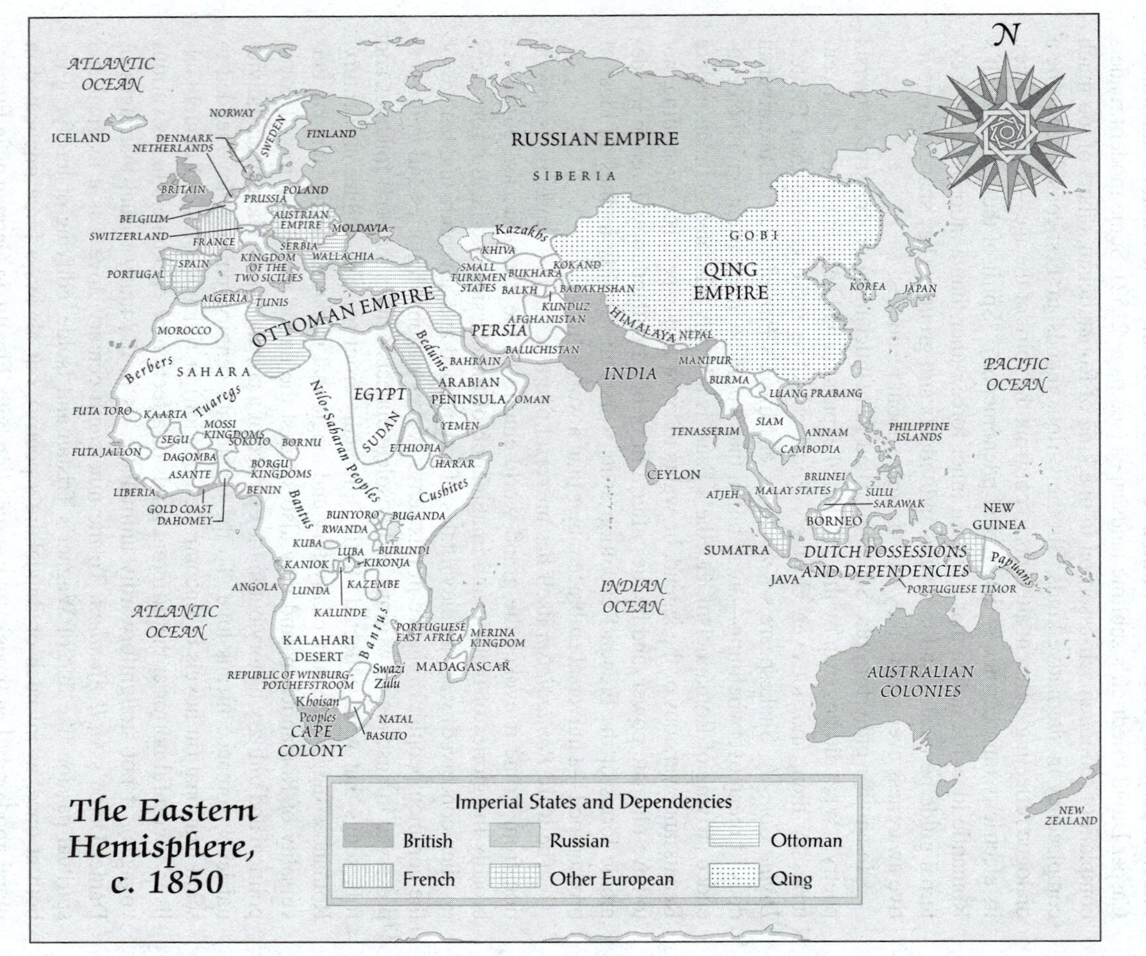
The Eastern Hemisphere, c. 1850
Imperial States and Dependencies
British
Russian
Ottoman
French
Other European
Qing
N
ATLANTIC OCEAN
ICELAND
NORWAY
SWEDEN
FINLAND
DENMARK
NETHERLANDS
BRITAIN
BELGIUM
SWITZERLAND
PRUSSIA
POLAND
AUSTRIAN EMPIRE
MOLDAVIA
FRANCE
SERBIA
WALLACHIA
KINGDOM OF THE TWO SICILIES
SPAIN
PORTUGAL
ALGERIA
TUNIS
MOROCCO
OTTOMAN EMPIRE
RUSSIAN EMPIRE
SIBERIA
Kazakhs
KHIVA
SMALL TURKMEN STATES
BUKHARA
KOKAND
BALKH
BADAKHSHAN
KUNDUZ
AFGHANISTAN
PERSIA
BALUCHISTAN
HIMALAYA
NEPAL
GOBI
QING EMPIRE
KOREA
JAPAN
Berbers
SAHARA
Tuaregs
FUTA TORO
KAARTA
MOSSI KINGDOMS
SEGU
SOKOTO
BORNU
FUTA JALLON
DAGOMBA
ASANTE
BORGU KINGDOMS
LIBERIA
BENIN
GOLD COAST
DAHOMEY
Nilo-Saharan Peoples
EGYPT
SUDAN
Beduins
BAHRAIN
ARABIAN PENINSULA
OMAN
YEMEN
ETHIOPIA
HARAR
Cushites
Bantus
BUNYORO
BUGANDA
RWANDA
KUBA
LUBA
BURUNDI
KANIOK
KIKONJA
ANGOLA
LUNDA
KAZEMBE
KALUNDE
ATLANTIC OCEAN
KALAHARI DESERT
Bantus
PORTUGUESE EAST AFRICA
MERINA KINGDOM
MADAGASCAR
REPUBLIC OF WINBURG-POTCHEFSTROOM
Swazi
Zulu
Khoisan Peoples
NATAL
CAPE COLONY
BASUTO
INDIA
MANIPUR
BURMA
LUANG PRABANG
TENASSERIM
SIAM
ANNAM
CAMBODIA
PHILIPPINE ISLANDS
CEYLON
BRUNEI
ATJEH
MALAY STATES
SULU
SARAWAK
BORNEO
SUMATRA
DUTCH POSSESSIONS AND DEPENDENCIES
JAVA
PORTUGUESE TIMOR
NEW GUINEA
Papuans
PACIFIC OCEAN
INDIAN OCEAN
AUSTRALIAN COLONIES
NEW ZEALAND

comprehensive social vision of Shakespeare, who was just then being rediscovered and translated on the Continent, Romantic writers wanted to bring all things to all people, linking the past with the present, the individual with the nation, Europe with the rest of humanity, the soul with the body, nature with culture.

A World Within the World

Another typical genius in this age of geniuses was Wilhelm von Humboldt—brother of the great explorer and naturalist Alexander von Humboldt. Wilhelm wrote on aesthetics, politics, anthropology, and classical civilization, composed and translated poetry, served as Prussian ambassador to Rome, and founded the University of Berlin that now bears his name and that established the model for university education to the present day. Of course, every age has its universal intellects. But Wilhelm von Humboldt's greatest passion was distinctive to his age, for he made himself into the founder of modern linguistic study. Linguists from the later eighteenth century had been discovering the seemingly universal relationships of human languages and hence of human cultures. Goethe (who read at least seven languages and explored the literatures of many others) coined the term *world literature*; Schlegel (poet, literary critic, philosopher, historian of culture, theologian) studied Sanskrit, the oldest relic of the Indo-European language family, and wrote an influential book on the language and wisdom of the Indians. But Humboldt's striving for universality outdid them all. He went into unrelated territory, learning well over a hundred languages including the most exotic that could be investigated—Basque, American Indian languages, and the Kavi language of what is now Indonesia.

When the globe was opened on this scale, it was no longer possible to comprehend the commonality of humankind, and that was not Humboldt's goal. Rather he (like his close friend Goethe) sought to understand the differences among cultures. Respect for difference was as much a part of romantic striving as global ambition. It extended even to new kinds of reverence for the animal and plant worlds, familial pets, and ecological treasures such as Wordsworth and Dickinson celebrated in verse, and Rousseau and Thoreau studied in their intensive botanizing.

For Humboldt, as for many others, however, social difference was crucial, and above all the difference among societies that arise from linguistic difference. Humboldt famously referred to language as a "world within the world": the language that you speak governs all of your perceptions. Kant had earlier argued that there are no "things in themselves" accessible to our awareness, but only subjective perceptions of things, and Humboldt asserted that there aren't even perceptions in themselves, but only the words we give to them, and these vary radically among languages, as do the grammatical structures that create meaning. Modern linguistics continues to split sharply between Humboldtians who believe in linguistic relativity and anti-Humboldtians (including artificial intelligence specialists) who believe in a common basis for language that allows for an ideal of perfect equivalence and translation among them. For a Humboldtian, progress then comes to mean either learning and understanding more and more different linguistic and cultural worlds, or else, as in some of the more notorious projects for colonial education, suppressing difference in favor of English (or Spanish or French) as a universal medium of communication and civilization.

Through Humboldt we can see how Romanticism develops into the kind of mystical nationalism that first emerged in the later stages of the French Revolution. A country isn't just where you happen to live, not just family and community, but a spiritual essence that grounds your whole being. In 1847, on the threshold of a new revolutionary movement that he avidly supported, Jules Michelet prefaced his great history of the French Revolution with the words: "The Revolution is inside us, in our souls; it has no external monument. Living spirit of France, where shall I seize thee, if not within myself?" Such a spirit can seem noble, or it can seem tyrannical. The first great English historian of the French Revolution, the "Victorian sage" Thomas Carlyle, imagines that, "as a thing *without* order, . . . it must work and welter, not as a Regularity but as a Chaos; destructive and self-destructive."

Thus the great writers of the nineteenth century are united only in confronting a problem. The electric tendencies of self, nature, language, and national culture no longer seemed masterable in a comprehensive formula such as many had imagined in the eighteenth-century Age of Enlightenment. Karl Marx's greatness as an economic theorist, for instance, was to understand economic relations as mysteriously spiritual forces—describing prices, for example, as "wooing glances cast at money by commodities." By tying national and individual destinies to national and idiosyncratic languages, Walter Scott's novels determined how nineteenth-century Europeans conceived of cooperation or dissension in constructing their polities. Americans explored similar issues via James Fenimore Cooper's fascination with Indian speech. The stirring choruses of Verdi's operas *Nabucco* and *Il Trovatore* caught the pulse of a people and stirred them to action toward Italian independence. Hopeful visionaries like Emerson or Nietzsche looked forward to a reconstructed humanity; pessimists like Leopardi and (sometimes) Melville looked down a tunnel into darkness. Meanwhile, rapid material progress in a century that opened with horse-drawn coaches and ended with telephones and automobiles put the question of what was real to its inhabitants with ever-increasing urgency.

Realism

It has been argued that realism came into being when Walter Scott wrote his novels of historical ambivalence about the downfall of feudalism in the Scottish Highlands and its replacement by the humdrum commercial civilization of the Lowlands and of England. Scott's loyalties were divided between the generously heroic, doomed figures of the old aristocratic order and the rational but mean-spirited representatives of modernity, which promised both greater democracy and a lower, narrowly self-interested view of human motives and aspirations. Realism did not result, as one might think, from a sudden and unprecedented desire to see the world clearly and accurately. Nor did it represent a major break with Romanticism. Rather, it emerged from a conviction (shared with the Romantics) that the social world itself had been set irrevocably in motion. Realists saw that historical change was powered by social contradictions such as those between feudalism and capitalism, and they understood that these contradictions did not just affect society's leaders, but worked themselves out in everyday feelings and relationships. Unlike previous stories of the rise and fall of kings, history now reached down deep into the lives of ordinary people. Thus the ethical meaning of ordinary lives—increasingly the subject literature took for itself—was now increasingly hard to agree upon.

Honoré de Balzac, who sought to understand the passage from an aristocratic to a bourgeois order in France after the fall of Napoleon, was one of many writers inspired by Scott's example. Examining the moral and emotional meaning of this immense transformation, Balzac gave his own loyalty to the reactionaries calling for a return to the old monarchy and its tried-and-true values. But as Friedrich Engels wrote in a famous letter, Balzac's distaste for the direction history was taking did not stop him from becoming a brilliant chronicler of its contradictions—far more useful, Engels went on, than the well-intentioned but tendentious socialism of his successor Émile Zola. Like many other observers, Engels disliked Zola's dark determinism. The coal miners of Zola's *Germinal* were innocent victims, but they were also passive victims, caught up and inevitably destroyed by huge, obscure forces that seemed beyond anyone's control. Naturalism, the more pessimistic variant of realism that was gaining force in the second half of the nineteenth century, was in part an accommodation to the rising authority of natural science, in part a delayed reaction to the general sense of helplessness that followed the failure of the 1848 revolutions.

Revolutions had indeed broken out in 1848 all across Europe and beyond, a "springtime of peoples" seeming to promise that the world could at last be remade in the name of the democratic ideals of 1789. But they also expressed the specific discontent of the new industrial working class, and that is why in early 1848 Alexis de Tocqueville told the Chamber of Deputies in Paris, "We are sleeping on a volcano." Both the sense of hope and the threat to private property that made so many property-holders draw back from this eruption are captured in Marx and Engels's *Communist Manifesto,* which came out the same year. This was a key moment for Gustave Flaubert, who narrates the Paris street fighting in his *Sentimental Education,* as well as for Elizabeth Gaskell, whose novel *Mary Barton* (1848) describes industrial conflict with serious and unprecedented sympathy for the workers. More indirectly, in Charles Dickens's *Bleak House* (1851–1852) a revolution that doesn't happen is displaced onto plague, murder, and "spontaneous combustion."

Science and Technology

The political upheavals of midcentury were matched by a revolutionary ferment in natural science. The period of Charles Darwin's treatise *On the Origin of Species by Means of Natural Selection* (1859) also saw the development of antiseptics by Lister and pasteurization by Pasteur as well as Clerk Maxwell's electromagnetic theory of light (1862), Mendeleyev's presentation of the periodic table of the elements in 1869, and many other breakthroughs of almost incalculable importance. It was perhaps inevitable that such advances would generate a certain overconfidence. The celebrated physicist Lord Kelvin announced, somewhat prematurely, that all the basic problems of physics had been solved. Though scientific advances and their technological applications were gradually responsible for improving the lives of ordinary people in numerous ways, especially in health, transportation, and communication, Antonio Machado de Assis's "The Psychiatrist" and Charlotte Gilman's "The Yellow Wallpaper" testify to a growing awareness of the danger that the authority attributed to science might easily be abused. Though Darwin himself was cautiously modest about the social implications of his discovery, others like Herbert Spencer (1820–1903) hastened to seize his authority on behalf of so-called "Social Darwinism," the belief that competition for survival was as natural in human society as it was among animal species and that, if not meddled with by governments, it would lead to the evolutionary progress of humankind. This political philosophy preexisted Darwin—it had inspired British authorities to let the victims of the Irish famine starve in the 1840s—but with new support from the theory of evolution it became a widespread tool of imperial expansion, generating convenient contempt for peoples held to be below or behind on the evolutionary ladder.

An Age of Empire

A period of relative European stability followed the crushing of the 1848 revolutions, felt by many artists and writers as the defeat of creativity by conformity and philistinism. This calm at home coincided with, and was perhaps made possible by, an enormous expansion of European control over the non-European world. More and more, the social disparities and conflicts that had led to 1848 could in effect be exported to the colonies. Algeria, the first Arabic-speaking country to be conquered, fell to France in 1847. The rest of Africa was swiftly divided up by the various powers, and soon Ethiopia was the only African country that remained unconquered. Colonialism extended across the Pacific as well, and after the Opium War of 1840–1842 (the result of China's refusal to buy English opium imported from India), China was forced to cede Hong Kong to England and to open itself to European traders. Britain took over official control of India after the so-called Mutiny of 1857–1859, better described perhaps as the first Indian war of independence. By the end of the century, Britain alone controlled one quarter of the earth's land area. Between 1804 and 1827, Russia defeated Iran in three wars, thus annexing Georgia and Azerbaijan, and Russian troops were still fighting for control over the mountain tribes of the Caucasus in the late 1830s when the novelist Lermontov's unit was posted there. Russia expanded eastward through Central Asia toward the Pacific, which was soon all that separated it from the westward-expanding United States. In the 1860s, slavery ended in the United States and serfdom ended in Russia, but neither society worried too much about the racially different natives it was subjugating or exterminating. Meanwhile, the settler colonies of Latin America, which had won their independence in the first half of the century, likewise continued their campaigns to seize land from their remaining indigenous populations and make it commercially profitable. From a global perspective, the most striking fact about the nineteenth century is not its proud technological achievements or real if uneven lurches toward domestic democracy, but the fact that it made most of the surface of the earth into colonies, protectorates, and spheres of influence for European states or European settlers. It was, and was seen to be, an age of empire.

The consolidation and clashing of nations and empires came at a high cost even for the Europeans themselves. In the Crimean War (1854–1856), Russia's territorial aspirations ran up against British interests in India and the Middle East, leading to its confrontation with an alliance of British, French, and Ottoman armies in the Crimea—to nineteenth-century Russians, a zone of the mysterious Orient. The war is best known to students of English literature for Alfred Lord Tennyson's poem "The

Charge of the Light Brigade," a poem about military courage in the face of mismanagement and, perhaps, the meaninglessness of one's own cause—"Theirs not to reason why, / Theirs but to do and die." On the Russian side, the combatants included Count Leo Tolstoy. In the midst of the war, the great poet and patriot Adam Mickiewicz traveled to Istanbul to organize Polish and Jewish troops to fight with the Ottomans on behalf of his fellow Poles, who remained subject to Russia. Mickiewicz died there of cholera in 1855. As soldiers in the Crimea died like flies, more from disease than from enemy fire, the nurse Florence Nightingale became famous for her struggles on behalf of rational sanitation, thus striking a blow on behalf of professional careers for middle-class women. This brief and inconclusive war resulted in approximately 600,000 casualties, about the same as the American Civil War and many more than the fierce battles for the unification of Germany and Italy that were happening during the same period.

A journey around the world in eighty days, as imagined by Jules Verne, would have been impossible in 1848. With so few railways in operation, it would have taken at least eleven months. By 1872, however, railways had connected huge tracts of territory, and a round-the-world journey in eleven weeks had become quite feasible. Yet the cultural consequences of this new global interconnectedness are complex and often difficult to ascertain with any certainty. Better informed about other regions than they had ever been, thanks to such inventions as the steamship, the telegraph, and the camera, European readers nevertheless had little difficulty embracing Rudyard Kipling's assertion of the absolute difference between civilizations: "East is East and West is West." Imperialist enjoyment of the exotic became an increasing part of everyday European consciousness via the mass market success of boys' adventure novels such as those of the Englishman H. Rider Haggard and the German Karl May, Oriental stereotypes such as Sax Rohmer's Dr. Fu Manchu, and Buffalo Bill's Wild West Show.

On the other hand, some British writers identified with aspirations to national independence even at the expense of Britain's allies. Tennyson's sonnet "Montenegro" (1877)—repeatedly translated into Serbian—glorified the struggles of the Montenegrins, friends of the Russians and enemies of the Ottomans. English became the official language of instruction of India in 1835, replacing Sanskrit, Arabic, and Persian. The intention was to form an English-educated native class through whom much of the administration could be handled. But the results would include an extraordinary cultural flowering, as for example in the bilingual and multicultural writing of Rabindranath Tagore.

Even as nation-states unified themselves, their literary cultures were becoming more and more varied, and writers took inspiration across regions and borders alike. Emerson and his fellow American Transcendentalists were inspired by the new interpretations of Hinduism coming out of British-occupied India; in Paris, Adam Mickiewicz lent his copy of Emerson's *Nature* to his fellow republican Edgar Quinet; Parisian modernism revealed itself to Rubén Darío when he was given Lautréamont's poetry to read on a visit to El Salvador. Industrialization in Britain and political revolutions in France were world-historical events. Unprecedented anywhere in the world, they were extraordinarily and inevitably influential almost everywhere in the world. And so were their cultural sequels.

But it would be a mistake to think of literary schools and fashions as simply emanating out from a center in Europe. Many South American countries became

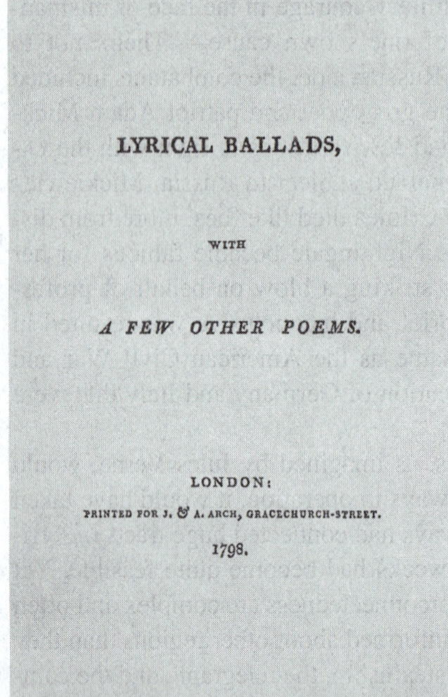

LYRICAL BALLADS,

WITH

A FEW OTHER POEMS.

LONDON:

PRINTED FOR J. & A. ARCH, GRACECHURCH-STREET.

1798.

SENSE AND SENSIBILITY.

A NOVEL,

BY

JANE AUSTEN.

Marianne, suddenly awakened by some accidental noise in the house, started hastily up, and with feverish wildness, cried out "Is mamma coming?"

LONDON:

RICHARD BENTLEY,

NEW BURLINGTON STREET.

CUMMING, DUBLIN.—BELL & BRADFUTE, EDINBURGH.

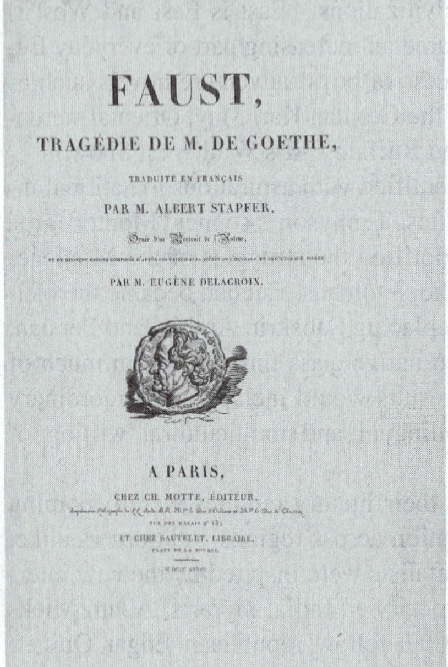

FAUST,

TRAGÉDIE DE M. DE GOETHE,

TRADUITE EN FRANÇAIS

PAR M. ALBERT STAPFER,

Orné d'un Portrait de l'Auteur,

PAR M. EUGÈNE DELACROIX.

A PARIS,

CHEZ CH. MOTTE, ÉDITEUR,

ET CHEZ SAUTELET, LIBRAIRE,

WALDEN;

OR,

LIFE IN THE WOODS.

By HENRY D. THOREAU,

AUTHOR OF "A WEEK ON THE CONCORD AND MERRIMACK RIVERS."

I do not propose to write an ode to dejection, but to brag as lustily as chanticleer in the morning, standing on his roost, if only to wake my neighbors up.—Page 92.

BOSTON:

TICKNOR AND FIELDS.

M DCCC LIV.

Like book jackets today, title pages promoted and advertised older books, which were sold unbound. Earlier title pages were typically illustrated and typographically lavish, often containing epigraphs and lengthy descriptions of their contents. Spare title pages like that reproduced on the upper left give only the title, author's name (and not even always that), genre, and publisher. They illustrate how books had become ordinary objects of commerce rather than valuable possessions and were intended for private reading of the contents more than for fashion or display. *Sense and Sensibility* and *Walden,* typical of a later day, illustrate a simple, rather bourgeois nostalgia for earlier modes of book production.

independent before some of the European states that carried out the project of imperialism, and their literatures are thus on a different timetable. There was also a Latin American turn to the folk—including a celebration of the same natives the colonizers were still in the process of subduing and assimilating—in order to define a positive national identity distinct from the European motherland. We find as well a Latin-American tendency (for example, in the Argentine writers Esteban Echevarría and Domingo Sarmiento) to be more enthusiastic about modernizing thought like the positivism of Auguste Comte (1798–1857). The same might be said about the energetic upsurge of thinking in the nineteenth-century Arab world, pondering both its Ottoman and its European masters in relation to its Muslim heritage, and in Asia, particularly in China, though there much of the new thought came through Japan. Warnings against the Romantic illusions of national continuity came from the Frenchman Renan and the German Nietzsche but also (later) the Martiniquan Frantz Fanon. When Mahatma Gandhi read the Victorian art critic John Ruskin, he assimilated him to Hindu thought, which went back centuries and was undergoing a recent renaissance. The self-educated Brazilian writer Machado de Assis quoted many and various European authors but dug deep into Brazilian popular culture for the prime resources of his fiction.

Cities, Women, Artists

Among the common threads that do run through the world literature of the nineteenth century, one of the foremost is the tension between the country and the city. On every continent, an abyss opened up between the modernizing tendencies of the capital and the traditional culture of the hinterland. The sparkling coastal cosmopolitanism of cities like Alexandria and Beirut did not always resonate with small farmers in the interior. The Petersburg of Gogol and Dostoevsky, the New York of Melville and Whitman, the Paris of Baudelaire would have seemed to many of their compatriots as foreign as European cities seemed to the Muslim travelers of the time.

In trying to make sense of urban life, nineteenth-century writers were also trying to make sense of their writerly vocation. The century's second half sees Romantic nature poetry succeeded in part by a new poetry of the city. To Baudelaire and his successors, Paris is as mysterious, inviting, dangerous, and sublime as Romantic nature. Yet its buildings and crowds, its novel rhythms of companionship and perception, also remind the poet of ways of shaping his or her art. The same insight made a home for itself in fiction. "Oh for a good spirit who would take the housetops off," Dickens appealed in *Dombey and Son*. The city should be made to reveal the hidden, often sordid interconnections that held society in place. The spiritlike narrators and complicated plots of Dickens's novels could be seen as an answer to this appeal, especially when they anticipate Conan Doyle's Sherlock Holmes and the urban genre of the detective story. As urbanization inches closer to being a social norm for the first time in history, the poet and the novelist become two of its heroic figures.

As does the new independent woman. One would never guess it from the novels of Emily and Charlotte Brontë, set as they are on the wild Yorkshire heath, but the distinct nineteenth-century rise in literary and political attention to the condition of women has much to do with the rise of cities. In cities children were less of an economic asset to their families than they had been on the farm, in part because of compulsory schooling, in part because of a new separation of the workplace from the place of residence. One result was lower birth rates and the emancipation of at least some women from the burdensome tasks of child rearing. Most women in Europe and elsewhere remained subject to the will of men and to labor both in the house and in the workplace, but for increasing numbers, there was new leisure and new access to education. Thus the emancipation of women could be imagined with new energy and, increasingly, acted upon in movements for women's suffrage. In literature, the questioning of assumptions about women's proper place, feelings, and aspirations is expressed in stories of adultery, one of nineteenth-century fiction's greatest themes, as in Flaubert's *Madame Bovary* and Tolstoy's *Anna Karenina,* as well as by such revolutionary texts as Emily Dickinson's poetry, Charlotte Perkins Gilman's "The Yellow Wallpaper," and Henrik Ibsen's *A Doll's House*.

It was also in the city that the artist's new and reluctant submission to market forces was most visible. Angry reactions to the increasing dominance of culture by mass production and the profit-motive included the Arts and Crafts movement, as represented for example by William Morris, and a turn against a perceived cheapening of art in the direction of "art for art's sake." For the first time in history, perhaps, artists began to boast of their *lack* of popular success. By the *fin de siècle,* many of Europe's artists, increasingly hostile to a mass public they saw as incapable of understanding them, were increasingly interested in the exotic civilizations of the East and the "primitive" art of Africa and Oceania, which reinforced their sense of distance from the status quo at home and its empty claims of progress. The global awareness that Goethe foresaw when he coined the term "world literature" in 1832 was becoming a marked feature of literature at the century's end.

THE NINETEENTH CENTURY

YEAR	THE WORLD	LITERATURE
1770		**1774, 1786** Goethe, *Werther*
1780	**1783** First balloon flight **1789** Fall of the Bastille (beginning of the French Revolution)	**1781, 1788, 1790** Immanuel Kant, *Critique of Pure Reason, Critique of Practical Reason, Critique of Judgment* **1782, 1789** J. J. Rousseau, *Confessions, Reveries* **1789, 1794** William Blake, *Songs of Innocence, Songs of Experience*
1790	**1792** Discovery of electromagnetism **1793** Execution of the king and queen of France	**1795–1796** Goethe, *Wilhelm Meister's Apprenticeship* **1796** Ludwig Tieck, "Fair Eckbert" **1798–1799** Friedrich Schiller, *Wallenstein* (translated by Coleridge in 1800) **1798** Wordsworth and Coleridge, *Lyrical Ballads*
1800	**1800** Volta's invention of the electric battery **1803** Louisiana Purchase **1804** Haitian declaration of independence **1806** Mungo Park expedition to the Niger River **1806** Dissolution of the Holy Roman Empire **1807** Fulton sails a steamboat on the Hudson River **1809–1825** Independence movements in South America	**1804** Ludwig von Beethoven, *Eroica* Symphony **1805** Wordsworth, first version of *Prelude* completed (published, much revised, in 1850) **1807** G. W. F. Hegel, *Phenomenology of Mind* **1808** Goethe, *Faust, Part 1*
1810	**1815** Final defeat of Napoleon; restoration of the Bourbon monarchy in France	**1810** Madame de Staël, *On Germany* **1812, 1815** J. and W. Grimm, *Fairy Tales* **1813–1822** E. T. A. Hoffmann's tales published in various collections **1814** Walter Scott, *Waverley* **1819–1824** Lord Byron, *Don Juan*
1820	**1825** Failed "Decembrist" Revolution in Russia **1825** First scheduled railroad	**1820** John Keats, *Lamia, Isabella, The Eve of St. Agnes, and Other Poems*
1830	**1830** Revolution of 1830 in France ; Louis-Philippe become the "Citizen King" **1830** France seizes Algiers: beginning of French colonization of North Africa	**1831** Stendhal (Henri Beyle), *The Red and the Black: A Chronicle of 1830* **1831** Honoré de Balzac, *The Wild Ass's Skin* (first work designed as part of the collective *Human Comedy*) **1832** Goethe, *Faust, Part 2*

Year	The World	Literature
	1832 Death of Goethe; death of Scott; English Reform Bill	
	1832 Greek Independence achieved after war of 1821–1828	
	1833 Abolition of slavery in Britain's colonies	**1833** Alexander Pushkin, *Eugene Onegin*
	1838 Slave mutiny aboard the *Amistad*	**1836** Ralph Waldo Emerson, *Nature*
	1839–1842 Opium War in China	
1840		
		1840 Mikhail Lermontov, *A Hero of Our Time*
		1842 Nikolai Gogol, "The Overcoat"
		1845 Edgar Allan Poe, "The Raven"
	1848 Revolutions throughout Europe, mostly suppressed, but leading to the end of the French monarchy	
	1848 War between United States and Mexico	
1850		
	1850–1864 Taiping Uprising in China, eventually put down with Western intervention	
	1851 Sojourner Truth delivers her "And Ain't I a Woman Speech" at the Woman's Rights Convention in Akron, Ohio	**1851** Herman Melville, *Moby Dick;* first issue of *New York Times*
		1852 Harriet Beecher Stowe, *Uncle Tom's Cabin*
	1853–1856 Crimean War	**1854** Alfred Tennyson, "The Charge of the Light Brigade"
		1854 Henry David Thoreau, *Walden*
		1855 Walt Whitman, *Leaves of Grass*
	1856–1857 British-Persian War	**1856** Elizabeth Barrett Browning, *Aurora Leigh*
	1857 Indian revolt known as "Mutiny"	
	1858 Chinese ports opened to Western trade	**1857** Gustave Flaubert, *Madame Bovary*
	1859–1861 Wars of national unification in Italy	**1859** Charles Darwin, *On the Origin of Species by Natural Selection*
1860		
	1860 Anglo-French troops occupy Beijing and burn Summer Palace	
	1861 Emancipation of serfs in Russia; outbreak of Civil War in United States	
	1862 Richard Gatling patents machine-gun	
	1863 French troops occupy Mexico City	**1864** Leo Tolstoy, *War and Peace*
	1868 Meiji restoration in Japan, abolition of Shogunate	**1866** Fyodor Dostoevsky, *Crime and Punishment*
		1867 Marx, *Das Kapital,* Volume 1
1870		
	1870–1871 Franco-Prussian War, Paris Commune	**1871–1872** George Eliot, *Middlemarch*
	1873 Ashanti tribes fight British in West Africa	**1872** Jules Verne, *Around the World in 80 Days*
	1874 Iceland becomes independent from Denmark	
	1875 Korea becomes independent from China	

Year	The World	Literature
	1876 Schliemann excavates Mycenae in Greece; massacre of Bulgarians by Turkish troops; General Custer defeated by Sioux at Little Big Horn	**1876** George Sand, *Marianne*
	1877 Samurai revolt suppressed in Japan	
	1879 Edison invents electric lightbulb; Britain invades Afghanistan; Chile defeats Bolivia and Peru in "Nitrate War"	
1880		
	1880 France annexes Tahiti	**1882** Henrik Ibsen, *An Enemy of the People*
		1883 Friedrich Nietzsche, *Thus Spake Zarathustra*
		1884 Mark Twain, *Huckleberry Finn*
		1885 Emile Zola, *Germinal*
	1886 First meeting of Indian National Congress	
1890		
	1890 New Zealand is the first nation to give women suffrage	**1890** Knut Hamsun, *Hunger*
	1894–1895 War between China and Japan; China loses Formosa and Port Arthur	
	1895 Cuban revolution against Spanish rule	**1895** Oscar Wilde, *The Importance of Being Earnest*
	1896 Italy is defeated in war with Abyssinia and withdraws	**1896** Anton Chekhov, *The Seagull*
	1897 First Zionist congress, Basel, Switzerland	
	1898 Spanish-American War	
		1899 Joseph Conrad, *Heart of Darkness*
1900		
		1900 Sigmund Freud, *The Interpretation of Dreams*

Johann Wolfgang Goethe

1749–1832

Johann Wolfgang Goethe was an amazing figure by anyone's standards. Not only did he write *Faust,* the epic drama of the scholar's pact with the devil that has come to embody the West and its fatal love affair with knowledge and technology, but he wrote seven other major plays and innumerable smaller ones. He wrote the most popular novel of the eighteenth century (*The Sorrows of Young Werther*), one of the most influential novels of the nineteenth century (*Wilhelm Meister's Apprenticeship*), and a profoundly modern novel of adultery (*Elective Affinities*) that has been widely influential in the twentieth century. He wrote more than a thousand pages of odes, ballads, songs, sonnets, bawdy love elegies, didactic poems, satires, short epics, and other verse. The standard edition of his works and letters runs to 144 volumes.

Goethe was born in 1749 but didn't settle down to literature as his real vocation until he was fifty years old, and he continued to pursue many other interests until his death in 1832. He drew, painted, sculpted, and collected art; he directed the Weimar court theater and personally trained the actors; he published contributions in geology, botany, comparative anatomy, chemistry, meteorology, and especially optics; he was a government official in the small duchy of Saxe-Weimar-Eisenach in central Germany, responsible at different times for mines, roads, finances, the university and all libraries and museums. And from age twenty-five until his death he was Germany's most famous personality and most visited cultural attraction. In his day the French Revolution brought an end to the old feudal order of Europe and ushered in the earliest version of the modern mass society in which we live today: as the greatest European writer of his age he is the cultural figure who embodies for us most clearly the beginning of the modern world.

Goethe was educated at home by his wealthy father, who intended his son to be a lawyer and eventually an influential member of the government in the free city of Frankfurt am Main, where Goethe's maternal grandfather had been the mayor. The son had other ideas. He did finally earn a law degree, but spent most of his time at the universities of Leipzig and Strasbourg studying drawing and medicine, as well as socializing and writing poetry. Under the influence of his friend Johann Gottfried Herder (1744–1803), who coined the term "folk song," Goethe scoured the countryside collecting songs—and pursuing his love life. From the combination of his superb schooling and the language of the people, he forged a poetry previously unheard in European culture, in which an individual voice spoke its most personal feelings without constraint in simple song or even in the apparent spontaneity of free verse. Already a quarter of a century before Wordsworth his poetry seemed to express human experience directly, and for the next two hundred years his example convinced scholars and general readers that true poetry was autobiographical.

In 1775 Goethe took advantage of his status as Germany's most famous writer (he was twenty-six!) to leave Frankfurt and settle in Weimar, long an artistic and cultural center, where the young Duke soon invited him to join the government. He threw himself into governing and practical activity and, gradually, science. In 1782 he was ennobled, adding "von" to his name. By 1786, tired of governing and of his platonic relationship with the difficult (and married) lady-in-waiting Charlotte von Stein, he fled to Italy, where for eighteen months he studied the art, the geology, and the people. He returned from Italy a changed man: he resigned his political responsibilities (but kept his salary), and he also entered into a common-law marriage with Christiane Vulpius, a young woman from the lower middle class. Goethe lived in Weimar for the remainder of his life. Milestones were the 1792 military campaign against France in which he accompanied the Duke and which he chronicled movingly; a profound friendship established in 1794 with the great dramatist Friedrich Schiller (1759–1804); the German defeat of 1806 by Napoleon at Jena, the neighboring city in the Duchy, followed immediately by formalizing his relationship with Christiane. He began a vast autobiography, *Poetry and Truth* (published in installments beginning in 1810), and devoted himself to his longest book, the thousand-page *Treatise on Optics* (1810). Christiane died in 1816. The major books published in his last years were the *West-Easterly Divan* (1819), a volume of verse written in the manner of the great fourteenth-century Persian poet Hafiz, and an experimental antinovel (*Wilhelm Meister's Journeyman Years,* 1832). The second part of *Faust,* last retouched only weeks before his death, was reserved for posthumous publication.

Assessments of Goethe as a person vary. To some he has seemed aloof, "Olympian," conservative in an era of change; to others he has appeared broadly tolerant, concerned for the welfare of citizens, supportive of countless rival and younger artists even if he did not share their tastes, a nation-builder who was at the same time a committed internationalist. The fifth act of *Faust II* displays his compassionate insight into the ravages of industrialization; earlier, anti-Napoleonic works were powerful pleas for peace in a time of war-mongering. He was an advocate for authentic cultural artifacts worldwide, inventing the term "world literature" and taking an active interest in poetic production from beyond Europe. Religious readers used to consider him immoral, while some recent biographers have suspected frigidity. He has been blamed for condescension toward Christiane and praised for insisting that she be accepted among his friends; he married her late and mourned her death less than that of his close friend Friedrich Schiller, but then few ministers of state married their lower-class mistresses at all. All seem to agree on his commitment to the famous last lines of *Faust,* "Eternal Womanhood / Draws us on high."

FAUST What remains beyond question is the power of Goethe's literary achievement, which is embodied above all in *Faust,* the epic drama to which he kept returning from age twenty-three until his death. Georg Faust was a wandering charlatan who lived from about 1480 to 1540. An anonymous chapbook—a cheap pamphlet for popular consumption—appeared in 1587 recounting his pact with the devil, adventures, and eventual death and damnation. In England the playwright Christopher Marlowe wrote his famous version, *The Tragical History of Dr. Faustus,* about 1590, though Goethe probably didn't read it until 1818, decades after he took up the theme. In Germany the Faust legend lived on in numerous versions of the chapbook and in street theater and puppet plays, the form in which Goethe first became acquainted with the story. Along with other contemporaries, he imagined it as the vehicle for a grand work, though unlike them he treated it as a European legend more than as a strictly Germanic one. He began work on it in 1773. Scenes amounting to about half of the eventual first part were published in 1790 as *Faust: A Fragment.* The entire first part appeared in print in 1808, though it was staged only in 1829. Around the turn of the century he began work on the second part, which he worked on at intervals for the rest of his life, putting the final touches to the manuscript just weeks before he died in 1832. It was published shortly after his death. The first and only complete theatrical performance, a two-day, twenty-two-hour spectacle, ran successively in three cities (Hannover, Berlin, and Vienna) between 1999 and 2001.

Faust is incredibly varied, yet consistent in its intense human sympathies. Goethe didn't hesitate to juxtapose the individual tragedy of Margareta, the heroine of Part I, with the ribald humor of the apes of Witch's Kitchen. He strove to integrate both normal and eccentric people into social and natural totalities. His devil is humane, his god tolerant. From Shakespeare he learned to portray the interactions of all different social classes on stage. Whereas Marlowe had presented Faust's story as high tragedy in his play *Dr. Faustus,* Goethe transforms the scholar's pact with the devil into a sporting bet, endorsed by the Lord in person. Marlowe's Faustus sells his soul for twenty-four years of service leading to wealth and power, but Goethe's Faust will receive from the devil access to all of human experience—its joys and woes—and only when he ceases to desire more experience will he die. And far from embodying a grim vision of degradation, the devil Mephistopheles is urbane and witty as well as immoral, and is often referred to by the almost friendly nickname "Mephisto." In this radically secular revision of the traditional myth, human experience is all.

Unique to Goethe's sense for the human is the way he always foregrounds ordinary people against larger contexts of nature, culture, and history. Nature is not only the object of veneration, as for Rousseau, or the eternal ground of human existence, as for Wordsworth, but the essential creative force that makes all things exist in time. It embraces the entry of all things into life, their departure from it, and all their developmental transformations in between. Thus does Faust's opening monologue express his greatest desire:

I ought rather to ask,
To grant me a vision of Nature's forces
That bind the world, all its seeds and sources
And innermost life.

Nature encompasses all being from the inanimate, the geological and elemental up the entire chain of being. All manifestations of nature are connected by a web of analogies that can be described with the same basic spiral of development: the forces that Goethe names polarity and enhancement govern phenomena as diverse as the polarization of light, the development of plants, and the weaving of damask linen. All around us, nature is nevertheless ineffable, not fully accessible to human understanding. In the human sphere its force is often represented by love. Animal spirits, sexual attraction, the desire for knowledge, the mystique of childhood, and above all the eternal feminine—these are all forms of the teeming life of nature. Nature's creative power, in turn, finds a conscious equivalent in culture; as a result art becomes an object worthy of the same attention as nature. Through art, as through nature, Goethe's characters, and by implication his readers, learn to know their essential humanity, their place in nature and in the cosmos. The philosopher Immanuel Kant (whose works Goethe studied carefully) argued that the world in which we live is the world constructed through our faculties of perception; just so, Faust discovers that he must learn about nature through representations of it, mostly plays-within-plays, that he himself constructs, and that are preceded by the elaborately stagy Prelude on the Stage and the Prologue in Heaven that follows.

Since nature is constantly changing, it can be comprehended only as a historical phenomenon. *Poetry and Truth* is the first autobiography to explain the development of the author's identity through generous analysis of the history—political, social, cultural—of his times. Nature itself has a history of change; Goethe's concern with the history of the earth and with what came to be called evolution was widely recognized, by Darwin among many others. History not only enters the details of plot but pervades Goethe's style at every point. His works are so varied precisely because they explore so many different historical modes. In *Faust* Goethe evokes and often parodies a vast range of styles: the Bible, Greek tragedy and comedy, medieval troubadour lyric, Dante, Shakespeare, sixteenth-century German comedy, folk song, Renaissance masque, Spanish Golden Age drama, French neoclassicism, the sentimentalism of eighteenth-century Germany and England all the way up to Lord Byron, for whose death in 1824 he set a eulogy at the end of the third act of Part II. That every age and society is a distinct culture with its own value was one of the great insights of the late eighteenth century. Goethe's friend Herder was one of the great early proponents of this "historicism" that refused to judge different societies by a uniform yardstick, while Goethe gave it its most memorable poetic incarnation.

Goethe's concerns thus extend from the depths of the human psyche to the limits of the universe, from the most profound kind of interiority to the most patient and attentive external observation. All objects of knowledge for Goethe are at once external and internal, objective and subjective. Like all the Romantics, Goethe grappled unceasingly with the division between self and world opened up by Kant's metaphysics, and he reflects the dominant philosophy constantly in the opposed pairs that people *Faust.* A work that stretches (as the Prelude says) "from heaven, through the world, right down to hell," that ranges from the mythic origins of classical antiquity to modern industrial society, that mixes popular and ritual forms with the latest in theatrical fashion and technical advances, is the prototype of what has come to be known, not surprisingly, as cosmic drama.

PRONUNCIATIONS:

Altmayer: ALT-mai-er
Baucis: BOW-tsis
Brander: BRAHN-der
Faust: fowst
Goethe: GER-te
Gretchen: GRAYT-shen
Lieschen: LEEZ-shen
Lynceus: LINK-oys
Mephistopheles: me-fis-TO-fe-leez
Mignon: MIN-yohn
Philemon: phi-LAY-mohn
Siebel: ZEE-bel
Wagner: VAG-ner

Faust[1]

PART I

Dedication[2]

Uncertain shapes, visitors from the past
At whom I darkly gazed so long ago,
My heart's mad fleeting visions—now at last
Shall I embrace you, must I let you go?
Again you haunt me: come then, hold me fast!
Out of the mist and murk you rise, who so
Besiege me, and with magic breath restore,
Stirring my soul, lost youth to me once more.

You bring back memories of happier days
And many a well-loved ghost again I greet;
As when some old half-faded legend plays
About our ears, lamenting strains repeat

1. Translated by David Luke.
2. Written in 1797, when Goethe was contemplating finishing Part 1 of *Faust,* about eight years after the most recently composed sections. Early portions had been written in the 1770s, with other scenes at intervals through the 1780s. He subsequently continued working on the first part, finally completing it in 1806.

My journey through life's labyrinthine maze,
Old griefs revive, old friends, old loves I meet,
Those dear companions, by their fate's unkind
Decree cut short, who left me here behind.

They cannot hear my present music, those
Few souls who listened to my early song:
They are far from me now who were so close,
And their first answering echo has so long
Been silent. Now my voice is heard, who knows
By whom? I shudder as the nameless throng
Applauds it. Are they living still, those friends
Whom once it moved, scattered to the world's ends?

And I am seized by long unwonted yearning
For that still, solemn spirit-realm which then
Was mine: these hovering lisping tones returning
Sigh as from some Aeolian harp,[3] as when
I sang them first: I tremble, and my burning
Tears flow, my stern heart melts to love again.
All that I now possess seems far away
And vanished worlds are real to me today.

Prelude on the Stage

[*The Director. The Poet. The Clown*[4]]

DIRECTOR: Well, here we are on German soil,
My friends. Tell me, you two have stood
By me in bad times and in good:
How shall we prosper now? My toil,
Indeed my pleasure, is to please the mob;
And they're a tolerant public, I'll admit.
The posts and boards are up, and it's our job
To give them all a merry time of it.
They're in their seats, relaxed, eyes opened wide,
Waiting already to be mystified.
I know how to content popular taste;
But I've a problem here, it must be said:
Their customary fare's not of the best—
And yet they are appallingly well-read.
How shall we give them something fresh and new,
That's entertaining and instructive too?
I like to see them all throng through the gate
Into our wooden paradise, to watch
Them push and shove and labor up that straight
And narrow way, like babes about to hatch!

3. A wind harp, frequently associated with poetic inspiration.

4. Actor. Frequently played by the same actor as Mephistopheles. Similarly, Faust and the Lord often play the Poet and the Director, respectively.

Our box-office, while it's still broad daylight,
Is under siege; before it's even four
They want their tickets. Tooth and nail they fight,
Like some half-famished crowd outside a baker's door.
Only the poet's magic so holds sway
Over them all: make it, my friend, today!

POET: Do not remind me of that motley throng,
Spare me the sight of them! Our spirits fail
And flounder in that stream, we are swept along,
Against the unruly flood what can prevail?
Give me the quietness where I belong,
The poet's place, the stillness never stale,
The love and friendship! Only there our art
Thrives on the blessed nurture of the heart.
Deep in the soul an impulse there can flow,
An early song still lisping and unclear;
Well-formed or ill, its momentary show
Too soon from Time's wild crest will disappear.
Often unseen and darkly it must grow,
Reaching its ripeness after many a year.
What glisters is the moment's, born to be
Soon lost; true gold lives for posterity.

CLOWN: Must we bring in posterity? Suppose
Posterity were all I thought about,
Who'd keep the present public's boredom out?
They must be entertained, it's what one owes
To them. And with a lad like me
Performing, they're enjoying what they see!
Communicate and please! You'll not retire
Then into semi-solitude,
Resentful of the public's fickle mood;
The wider circle's easier to inspire.
So do what's needed, be a model poet!
Let Fancy's choirs all sing, and interweave
Reason, sense, feeling, passion—but, by your leave,
Let a good vein of folly still run through it!

DIRECTOR: And let's have enough action, above all!
They come to look, they want a spectacle.
Let many things unfold before their eyes,
Let the crowd stare and be amazed, for then
You'll win their hearts, and that's to win the prize;
You'll join the ranks of famous men.
Mass alone charms the masses; each man finds
Something to suit him, something to take home.
Give much, and you'll have given to many minds;
They'll all leave here contented to have come.
And let your piece be all in pieces too!
You'll not go wrong if you compose a stew:
It's quick to make and easy to present.

Why offer them a whole? They'll just fragment
It anyway, the public always do.
POET: I note you don't despise such a *métier,*[5]
And have no sense of how it ill beseems
True art. If I were to do things your way,
I'd join the bungling amateurs, it seems.
DIRECTOR: Such a reproach offends me not a whit.
My aim is our success: I must adopt
The proper method of achieving it.
What tool's best, when there's soft wood to be chopped?
Consider who you're writing for! They come,
Some of them, from sheer boredom; some
Arrive here fully sated after feeding;
Others again have just been reading
The newspapers, God help us all.
They come with absent thoughts, as if to a masked ball;
Mere curiosity brings them. As for the display
Of ladies and their finery, why, they
Eke out the show, and ask me for no pay!
Why do you dream your lofty dreams of art?
Why do full houses flatter you as well?
Take a look at our patrons: you can tell
Half of them have no taste, and half no heart.
One will be looking forward to a game
Of cards after the play, another to a night
In some girl's arms. Poor foolish poet, why invite
Your Muse to toil for this? Make it your aim
Merely to give them more—give them excess!
It's such a hard job to amuse them
That your best plan is to confuse them:
Do that, and you'll be certain of success—
Now what's the matter? Pain, or ecstasy?
POET: Leave me, and find some other willing slave!
Must the poet forgo what Nature gave
Him as his birthright, forfeit wantonly
For you that noble gift? How else does he
Move all men's hearts, what power but his invents
The conquest of the elements?
Song bursts forth from him, a harmonious whole
Engulfs the world and draws it back into his soul.
Nature spins out her thread, endlessly long,
At random on her careless spindle wound;[6]
All individual lives in chaos throng
Together, mixed like harsh discordant sound.
Who divides up this dull monotonous drift
Into a living rhythm? Who can lift

5. Job, trade.

6. In contrast to the classical Fates, who measured out people's destiny on their spindles.

Particular things into a general sense
Of some great music's sacred congruence?
When passions rage, who makes the tempest sing,
The sunset glow when solemn thought prevails?
Who scatters all the blossoms of the spring
On his beloved's path? Who makes a crown
Of mere green leaves the symbol of renown
For high distinction? What is this that fills
Olympus, joins the gods in unity?—
The power of Man, revealed in Poetry!

CLOWN: Use them then, these delightful powers,
And do your poet's work, rather as when
One falls in love to pass the amorous hours.
One meets by chance, one lingers, one is smitten,
And one's involvement gradually increases;
Happiness grows, but soon enough it ceases;
Joy ends in tears. And somehow then
It all becomes a novel, ready written.
Let's give them that, let's make that kind of show!
Use real life and its rich variety!
They're living it, but unreflectingly;
They'll notice this or that they didn't know.
Colorful changing scenes and little sense,
Much error, mixed with just a grain of truth—
That's the best drink for such an audience;
They'll be refreshed and edified. That way
It will attract the flower of our youth:
They'll hear your words, and think them revelation,
And every tender soul suck from your play
A sustenance of melancholy sensation.
Each will find something in it to excite him
For what he'll see's already there inside him.
They're young yet, ready still to laugh or cry;
Fancy still pleases, rhetoric lifts them high.
The old and hardened are a thankless brood,
But growing minds can still show gratitude.

POET: Ah, give me back those years when I
Myself was still developing,
When songs poured forth unceasingly
And thick and fast as from a spring!
Then still my world was misty-veiled,
Then promised wonders were in bud;
I picked the myriad flowers that filled
Those valleys in such plenitude.
My poverty was rich profusion;
I longed for truth and loved illusion.
Give unchecked passion back to me,
Those deep delights I suffered then,
Love's power, and hatred's energy—

Give back my youth to me again!

CLOWN: My friend, youth's what one needs, of course, when one
Is in the thick of battle with the foe,
Or when sweet girls are hanging on
One's neck and simply won't let go,
Or when the finish of a race
Beckons far off to victory,
Or when one's danced at furious pace
Then spends the night in revelry:
But boldly, gracefully to play
Upon the lyre, choose one's own goal
And reach it by some charming way
On random motions of the soul—
Such is the older poet's task; and we
Respect you none the less. The proverb's wrong, you see:
Age is no second childhood—age makes plain,
Children we were, true children we remain.

DIRECTOR: Come, that's enough of words! What I
Want now is deeds. While you, my friends,
Exchange these well-turned compliments,
The time for useful work slips by.
Why all this talk of the right mood?
It won't just come by dithering.
Command your Muses, and they'll sing
To order, if you're any good!
You know what we expect of you:
We're thirsty for a potent brew.
Prepare it now! What's not begun
Today will still be left undone
Tomorrow. Never miss a day,
But boldly and with resolution
Seize Chance's forelock and waylay
The possible before it slips away;
A started task compels completion.

On German stages, as you know no doubt,
Producers like to try things out;
So make sure now we have machines
And plenty of spectacular scenes!
Use the sunshine and moonshine lights,
Use starlight—we have stars galore,
Water and fire and rocky heights,
And birds and animals by the score!
Thus on these narrow boards[7] you'll seem
To explore the entire creation's scheme—
And with swift steps, yet wise and slow
From heaven, through the world, right down to hell you'll go!

7. The stage.

Prologue in Heaven

[*The Lord. The Heavenly Hosts, then Mephistopheles. The three Archangels advance.*]

RAPHAEL: The sun proclaims its old devotion
In rival song with brother spheres,
And still completes in thunderous motion
The circuits of its destined years.
Angelic powers, uncomprehending.
Are strengthened as they gaze their fill;
Thy works, unfathomed and unending,
Retain the first day's splendor still.

GABRIEL: The glorious earth, with mind-appalling
Swiftness, upon itself rotates,
And with the deep night's dreadful falling
Its primal radiance alternates.
High cliffs stand deep in ocean weather,
Wide foaming waves flood out and in,
And cliffs and seas rush on together
Caught in the globe's unceasing spin.

MICHAEL: And turn by turn the tempests raging
From sea to land, from land to sea,
Build up, in passion unassuaging,[8]
Their chain of furious energy.
The thunder strikes, its flash is faster,
It spreads destruction on its way—
But we, thy messengers,[9] O master,
Revere thy gently circling day.

THE THREE IN CHORUS: And each of us, uncomprehending,
Is strengthened as we gaze our fill;
For all thy works, sublime, unending,
Retain their first day's splendor still.

MEPHISTOPHELES: Your Grace, since you have called on us again
To see how things are going, and since you
Have been quite pleased to meet me now and then,
I thought I'd come and join your retinue.
Forgive me, but grand words are not my trick;
I cut a sorry figure here, I know,
But you would laugh at my high rhetoric
If you'd not left off laughing long ago.
The solar system I must leave unsung,
And to mankind's woes lend my humbler tongue.
The little earth-god still persists in his old ways,
Ridiculous as ever, as in his first days.
He'd have improved if you'd not given

8. Uncalmable.

9. "Angel" comes from the Greek word for "messenger."

Him a mere glimmer of the light of heaven;
He calls it Reason, and it only has increased
His power to be beastlier than a beast.
He is—if I may say so, sir—
A little like the long-legged grasshopper,
Which hops and flies, and sings its silly songs
And flies, and drops straight back to grass where it belongs.
Indeed, if only he would stick to grass!
He pokes his nose in all the filth he finds, alas.

THE LORD: And that is all you have to say?
Must you complain each time you come my way?
Is nothing right on your terrestrial scene?

MEPHISTOPHELES: No, sir! The earth's as bad as it has always been.
I really feel quite sorry for mankind;
Tormenting them myself's no fun, I find.

THE LORD: Do you know Faust?

MEPHISTOPHELES: The doctor? Do you mean—

THE LORD: My servant.

MEPHISTOPHELES: Ah, he serves you well, indeed!
He scorns earth's fare and drinks celestial mead.
Poor fool, his ferment drives him far!
He half knows his own madness, I'll be bound.
He'd pillage heaven for its brightest star,
And earth for every last delight that's to be found;
Not all that's near nor all that's far
Can satisfy a heart so restless and profound.

THE LORD: He serves me, but still serves me in confusion;
I will soon lead him into clarity.
A gardener knows, one day this young green tree
Will blossom and bear fruit in rich profusion.

MEPHISTOPHELES: If I may be his guide, you'll lose him yet;
I'll subtly lead him my way, if you'll let
Me do so; shall we have a bet?

THE LORD: He lives on earth, and while he is alive
You have my leave for the attempt;
Man errs, till he has ceased to strive.

MEPHISTOPHELES: I thank your Grace; for dead men never tempt
Me greatly, I confess. In this connection
I like to see a full and fresh complexion;
A corpse is an unwelcome visitor.
The cat-and-mouse game is what I prefer.

THE LORD: Well, go and try what you can do!
Entice that spirit from its primal source,
And lead him, if he's not too hard for you
To grasp, on your own downward course—
And then, when you have failed, with shame confess:
A good man, in his dark, bewildered stress,
Well knows the path from which he should not stray.

MEPHISTOPHELES: No doubt; it's a short journey anyway.

I'll win my wager without much delay.
And when I do, then, if I may,
I'll come back here and boast of my success.
I'll make him greedy for the dust, the way
The serpent was, my famous ancestress![1]

THE LORD: Indeed, you may feel free to come and call.
You are a type I never learnt to hate;
Among the spirits who negate,
The ironic scold offends me least of all.
Man is too apt to sink into mere satisfaction,
A total standstill is his constant wish:
Therefore your company, busily devilish,
Serves well to stimulate him into action.
But you, the authentic sons of God, enfold
With praise the abundant beauty of the world;
Love, as you do, the eternal Process, which
Is ever living and forever rich;
Its vanishing phenomena will last,
By your angelic thoughts made firm and fast.

[*The heavens close, the Archangels disperse.*]

MEPHISTOPHELES: I like to see him sometimes, and take care
Not to fall out with him. It's civil
Of the old fellow, such a *grand seigneur,*° *noble lord*
To have these man-to-man talks with the Devil!

The First Part of the Tragedy

NIGHT

[*A high-vaulted, narrow Gothic room.*]

FAUST [*sitting restlessly at his desk*]:
Well, that's Philosophy I've read,
And Law and Medicine, and I fear
Theology too, from A to Z;
Hard studies all, that have cost me dear.
And so I sit, poor silly man,
No wiser now than when I began.
They call me Professor and Doctor, forsooth.
For misleading many an innocent youth
These last ten years now, I suppose,
Pulling them to and fro by the nose;
And I see all our search for knowledge is vain,
And this burns my heart with bitter pain.
I've more sense, to be sure, than the learned fools,

1. In Genesis 3:14 God punishes the serpent for tempting Eve by condemning him to crawl forever on his belly: "and dust you shall eat, all the days of your life."

The masters and pastors, the scribes from the schools;
No scruples to plague me, no irksome doubt,
No hell-fire or devil to worry about—
Yet I take no pleasure in anything now;
For I know I know nothing, I wonder how
I can still keep up the pretense of teaching
Or bettering mankind with my empty preaching.
Can I even boast any worldly success?
What fame or riches do I possess?
No dog would put up with such an existence!
And so I am seeking magic's assistance,
Calling on spirits and their might
To show me many a secret sight,
To relieve me of the wretched task
Of telling things I ought rather to ask,
To grant me a vision of Nature's forces
That bind the world, all its seeds and sources
And innermost life—all this I shall see,
And stop peddling in words that mean nothing to me.
Oh sad full moon, my friend, why must
You see me suffer? Look your last!
Here at this desk so many a night
I've watched and waited for your light
To visit me again and shine
Over this paper world of mine.
Oh, take me to the hilltops, there
To wander in the sweet moonlit air,
By mountain caves, through fields to roam,
Hovering with spirits in your gloam,
Cleansed of book-learning's fog and stew
And healed by bathing in your dew!

God, how these walls still cramp my soul,
This cursèd, stifling prison-hole
Where even heaven's dear light must pass
Dimly through panes of painted glass!
Hemmed in by books to left and right
Which worms have gnawed, which dust-layers choke,
And round them all, to ceiling-height,
This paper stained by candle-smoke,
These glasses, boxes, instruments,
All stuffed and cluttered anyhow,
Ancestral junk—look at it now,
Your world, this world your brain invents!

And can you still ask why your heart
Is pent and pining in your breast,
Why you obscurely ache and smart.
Robbed of all energy and zest?
For here you sit, surrounded not

By living Nature, not as when
God made us, but by reek and rot
And mouldering bones of beasts and men.

Come, flee into the open land!
And this great book of magic lore,
By Nostradamus'[2] very hand,
Shall be my guide, I'll need no more;
By it I'll see the stars in course,
And as great Nature rules my mind
Discover the inner psychic force,
The spirit speaking to its kind!
This arid speculation's vain,
The sacred diagrams are clear:
Spirits, you hover close—be plain
And answer me, if you can hear!

[*He throws open the book and sees the Sign of the Macrocosm.*[3]]

Ha! as I look, what sudden ecstasy
Floods all my senses, how I feel it flowing
Through every vein, through every nerve in me,
Life's sacred joy and youth's renewal glowing!
Did not some god write these mysterious
Signs, by whose might my soul is filled
With peace again, my poor heart healed,
And by whose secret impetus
The powers of Nature all about me are revealed?
Am I a god? Light fills my mind;
In these pure lines and forms appear
All Nature's workings, to my inner sense made clear.
That sage's words at last I understand:
"The spirit-world is open wide,
Only your heart has closed and died;
Come, earth-disciple, boldly lave
Your bosom in the dawn's red wave!"

[*He gazes at the sign.*]

How it all lives and moves and weaves
Into a whole! Each part gives and receives,
Angelic powers ascend and redescend
And each to each their golden vessels lend;
Fragrant with blessing, as on wings
From heaven through the earth and through all things
Their movement thrusts, and all in harmony it sings!
How great a spectacle! But that, I fear,
Is all it is. Oh, endless Nature, where
Shall I embrace you? Where, you breasts that flow

2. Author of a 16th-century collection of prophecies.

3. A mystical diagram in a book of alchemy, showing the solar system.

With life's whole life? All earth and heaven hangs
On you, who slake the thirsty pangs
Of every heart—and must I languish vainly so?

[*He turns impatiently to another page of the book and sees the Sign of the Earth Spirit.*[4]]

How differently this sign affects me! You,
Spirit of Earth, are closer to me,
Fresh strength already pulses through me,
I glow already from wine so new!
Now, to go out into the world and bear
The earth's whole pain and joy, all this I dare;
To fight with tempests anywhere,
And in the grinding shipwreck stand and not despair!
Clouds gather over me—
The full moon hides its face—
My lamp burns low!
Mist rises—red fire flashes round
My head, and from the vaulted roof
A chill breathes down and strikes
A shudder into me!
Spirit I long to summon, now I feel
You hovering round me, oh reveal
Yourself! Ha, this pain tears my heart!
A new sensation
Stirs all my senses into perturbation!
I am committed: you shall come, you must
Appear to me, though you may strike me into dust!

[*He seizes the book and secretly pronounces the spirit's sign. A red flame flashes, the spirit appears in the flame.*]

THE SPIRIT: Who is calling me?
FAUST [*turning away*]: Ah, you are too terrible!
THE SPIRIT: You have drawn me to you with mighty power,
Sucked at my sphere for many an hour,
And now—
FAUST: Alas, this sight's unbearable!
THE SPIRIT: You groan and sigh to have me appear,
To hear my voice, to behold my face:
Your soul's great plea compels me to this place
And I have come! What pitiable fear
Seizes you, Faust the superman! Where is the call
Of your creative heart, that carried all
The world and gave it birth, that shook with ecstasy,
Swelling, upsurging to the heights where we,
The spirits, live? Where are you, you whose song
I heard besieging me so loud and strong?

4. The Earth Spirit is Goethe's invention.

Can this be you? Now that my breath blows round you,
In the depths of terror I have found you,
Shrinking and writhing like a worm!

FAUST: Am I to quail before you, shape of flame?
It is I, Faust! you and I are the same!

THE SPIRIT: In life like a flood, in deeds like a storm
I surge to and fro,
Up and down I flow!
Birth and the grave
An eternal wave,
Turning, returning,
A life ever burning:
At Time's whirring loom I work and play
God's living garment I weave and display.

FAUST: Oh busy spirit! from end to end
Of the world you roam: how close you are to me!

THE SPIRIT: You match the spirit you can comprehend:
I am not he. [*It vanishes.*]

FAUST [*collapsing*]: Not you!
Who is he then?
I, made in God's image
And not even like you!

[*There is a knock at the door.*]

Oh, devil take him, it's that dry-as-dust
Toady, my famulus![5] Why must
He interrupt me and destroy
This supreme hour of visionary joy?

[*Enter Wagner in a nightgown and nightcap, carrying a lamp. Faust turns to him impatiently.*]

WAGNER: Excuse me, sir! I heard your declamation:
You were reading a Greek tragedy, no doubt?
That art is one of powerful persuasion
These days; I'd like to learn what it's about.
I've often heard it said an actor might
Give lessons to a parson.

FAUST: You are right,
If the parson himself's an actor too;
As sometimes is the case.

WAGNER: Oh dear, what can one do,
Sitting day after day among one's books!
The world's so distant, and one never looks
Even through a spyglass at it; so how can
One learn to bring about the betterment of man?

FAUST: Give up pursuing eloquence, unless
You can speak as you feel! One's very heart

5. Assistant.

Must pour it out, with primal power address
One's hearers and compel them with an art
Deeper than words. Clip and compile, and brew
From the leavings of others your ragoût
Of rhetoric, pump from your embers
A few poor sparks that nobody remembers!
Children will gape and fools admire,
If that's the audience to which you aspire.
But what can blend all hearts into a whole?
Only the language of the soul.

WAGNER: But one must know how to deliver a tirade.[6]
I fear my training still is uncompleted.

FAUST: Why don't you learn to ply an honest trade?
Why be a fool with tinkling bells?
Stick to right thinking and sound sense, it tells
Its own tale, little artifice is needed;
If you have something serious to say,
Drop the pursuit of words! This play
Of dazzling oratory, this paper decoration
You fiddle with and offer to the world—
Why, the dry leaves in autumn, whirled
About by foggy winds, carry more inspiration!

WAGNER: Alas, our life is short,
And art is long, they say!
My scholarly pursuits, how sore they weigh
Upon my heart and mind! One ought
To learn the means of mounting to the sources,
Yet even this task almost passes my resources;
For we poor devils, by the time we've got
Less than halfway, we die, as like as not.

FAUST: A manuscript—is that the sacred spring
That stills one's thirst for evermore?
Refreshment! It's your own soul that must pour
It through you, if it's to be anything.

WAGNER: Excuse me, but it's very pleasant
Studying epochs other than the present,
Entering their spirit, reading what they say,
And seeing how much wiser we have grown today.

FAUST: Oh yes indeed, a wisdom most sublime!—
My friend, the spirit of an earlier time,
To us it is a seven-sealed mystery;
And what you learned gentlemen would call
Its spirit, is its image, that is all,
Reflected in your own mind's history.
And what a sight it often is! Enough
To run a mile from at first glance. A vast
Old rubbish-dump, an attic of the past,

6. A speech in a play.

At best a royal tragedy—bombastic stuff
Full of old saws, most edifying for us,
The strutting speeches of a puppet-chorus!

WAGNER: But the great world! The heart and mind of man!
We all seek what enlightenment we can.

FAUST: Ah yes, we say "enlightenment," forsooth!
Which of us dares to call things by their names?
Those few who had some knowledge of the truth,
Whose full heart's rashness drove them to disclose
Their passion and their vision to the mob, all those
Died nailed to crosses or consigned to flames.
You must excuse me, friend, the night's half through.
We shall speak further on the next occasion.

WAGNER: I'd stay awake all night, and gladly too,
Enjoying such a learned conversation.
Tomorrow morning, being Easter Day,
I'll ask you some more questions, if I may.
I've studied now for years with zeal and zest;
Already I know much I must know all the rest. [*Exit.*]

FAUST: Why does he not despair? A mind so void
And blinkered, so benighted and earthbound!
Greedy for gold, he scratches in the ground,
And when he finds some worms he's overjoyed.

Why, when those spirit-voices filled the air
About me, must the speech of such a man
Intrude? And yet for once I can
Thank you, poor mortal wretch: for when despair
Was close to me and madness had assailed
My mind, when like a dwarf I seemed to shrink
Before that giant vision, and I quailed,
Dwindling to nothingness—you snatched me from the brink.

I, God's own image! Ah, how close it shone,
The mirror of eternal verity!
I fed upon its light and clarity
Within myself, all mortal limits gone,
And with presumption too extreme
Of free, superangelic strength, divine
Creative life, thought even now to stream
Through Nature's veins—what sudden shame was mine!
A voice of thunder dashed me from that dream.

Not close to you, not like you; this I dare
No longer claim to be. I had the power
To summon you, but could not hold you there.
I felt in that ecstatic hour
So small, and yet so great: and then
You hurled me back so cruelly
Into the changeful common state of men.
What must I do now? who shall counsel me?

What urge claims my obedience?
Alas, not only pain, even activity
Itself can stop our life's advance.

The spirit's noblest moments, rare and high,
Are choked by matter's alien obtrusion,
And rich with this world's goods, we cry
Scorn on those better things as mere illusion.
Life-giving intuitions of great worth
Are stifled in the muddle of the earth.
Imagination, once a flight sublime
That soared in hope beyond the swirl of time,
Now, as each joy is drowned beyond redress,
Sinks down inside us into pettiness:
Care makes its nest in the heart's deepest hole
And secretly torments the soul;
Its restless rocking motion mars our mind's content.
Its masks are ever-changing, it appears
As house and home, as wife and child, it will invent
Wounds, poisons, fires and floods—from all
These blows we flinch before they ever fall,
And for imagined losses shed continual tears.

I am not like a god! Too deeply now I feel
This truth. I am a worm stuck in the dust,
Burrowing and feeding, where at last I must
Be crushed and buried by some rambler's heel.

Is this not dust, filling a hundred shelves
On these high walls that hem me in?
These thousand useless toys that thrust themselves
At me in this moth-mumbled rubbish-bin?
How shall I find fulfillment in this jail,
Reading the thousand-times-reprinted tale
Of man's perpetual strife and stress
And rare occasional happiness?—
You hollow skull, what does your grinning say?
That brain, in the confusion of its youth,
Like mine, once sought the ethereal dawn of truth
But in the heavy dusk went piteously astray.
And you old instruments, how you too mock,
What scorn your wheels, cogs, pulleys pour on me!
I reached the gate, you were to be the key:
Your bit's a well-curled beard, but it won't fit the lock.
We snatch in vain at Nature's veil,
She is mysterious in broad daylight,
No screws or levers can compel her to reveal
The secrets she has hidden from our sight.
Useless mechanical contrivances, retained
Because my father used them, old smoke-stained

Parchments that have lain here, untouched by toil,
Since my dull lamp first burnt its midnight oil!
I should have squandered all my poor inheritance,
Not sat here sweating while it weighed me down.
What we are born with, we must make our own
Or it remains a mere appurtenance
And is not ours: a load of unused things,
Not the live moment's need, raised on the moment's wings.

But what is this? My eyes, magnetically drawn,
Are fixed on that one spot, where I can see
That little flask: why does sweet light break over me,
As when in a dark wood the gentle moonbeams dawn?
Unique alembic![7] Reverently I lift
You down and greet you. Now, most subtle gift
Compounded of the wit and art of man,
Distillment of all drowsy syrups, kind
Quintessence of all deadly and refined
Elixirs, come, and serve your master as you can!
I see you, and am healed as with a balm,
I seize you, and my striving soul grows calm;
And borne upon my spirit's ebbing tide,
Little by little drifting out to sea,
I tread on its bright mirror—far and wide
As new dawn breaks, new shores are beckoning me!

A fiery chariot[8] on light wings descends
And hovers by me! I will set forth here
On a new journey to the heaven's ends,
To pure activity in a new sphere!
O sublime life, o godlike joy! And how
Do I, the ertswhile worm, deserve it now?
I will be resolute, and turn away
For ever from the earth's sweet day.
Dread doors, though all men sneak and shuffle past
You, I'll confront you, tear you open wide!
Here it is time for me to prove at last
That by his noble deeds a man is deified;
Time not to shrink from the dark cavern where
Our fancy damns itself to its own tortured fate;
Time to approach the narrow gate
Ringed by the eternal flames of hell's despair;
Time to step gladly over this great brink,
And if it is the void, into the void to sink!

7. Distilling apparatus.
8. The sunrise is here described using an image that is both biblical and classical (Apollo, god of light and reason, drives the sun across the sky) and biblical (a fiery chariot takes the prophet Elijah up to heaven, 2 Kings 2:11).

Old goblet of pure crystal, come, now let
Me take you from your shelf and sheath. Long years
Have passed since last I thought of you; and yet
At bygone feasts you were the cup that cheers
The solemn guests, the gleaming beaker
Raised to the toast by many a speaker!
Your rich engraved pictorial decorations,
The drinker's task, his rhyming explanations
Before in one long draught he drained you down—
These I recall, from revels long ago;
I passed you round, I praised your art to show
My wit. Now I shall not do so.
I have a potion here whose work's soon done;
Its dizzying liquid fills you, dark and brown.
I made and mixed it well, as I know how.
And so, with all my heart, I raise it now:
With this last festive drink I greet the rising sun!

[*He sets the cup to his lips. There is a peal of bells and a sound of choral singing.*]

CHORUS OF ANGELS: Christ is ris'n from the dead!
Hail to all mortal men,
From sin's insidious bane,
From their inherited
Bondage set free again!

FAUST: What lilting tones are these, what notes profound
Cry to me: Do not drink! Have they such power?
And do these bells with their dull booming sound
Announce the Easter festival's first hour?
Is this already the angelic song
Of solace, heard above the grave that night so long
Ago, when the new covenant was sealed and bound?

CHORUS OF WOMEN: Spices we brought and myrrh,
We who befriended him,
Faithfully laid him here,
Lovingly tended him;
Clean linen, swaddling-bands,
We wound with our own hands.
Who can have come today
Taking our Lord away?

CHORUS OF ANGELS: Christ is raised, Christ is blest!
He bore mankind's ordeal,
Loving their joys to feel,
Suffering the stripes that heal:
He passed the test!

FAUST: You gentle, puissant choirs of heaven, why
Do you come seeking me? The dust is stronger!
Go, chant elsewhere to tenderer souls! For I

Can hear the message, but believe no longer.
Wonders are dear to faith, by it they live and die.
I cannot venture to those far-off spheres,
Their sweet evangel[9] is not for my ears.
And yet—these strains, so long familiar, still
They call me back to life. There was a time
Of quiet, solemn sabbaths when heaven's kiss would fill
Me with its love's descent, when a bell's chime
Was deep mysterious music, and to pray
Was fervent ecstasy. I could not understand
The sweet desire that drove me far away
Out through the woods, over the meadowland:
There I would weep a thousand tears and feel
A whole world come to birth, my own yet real.
Those hymns would herald youthful games we played
To celebrate the spring. As I recall
That childhood, I am moved, my hand is stayed,
I cannot take this last and gravest step of all.
Oh sing, dear heaven-voices, as before!
Now my tears flow, I love the earth once more!

CHORUS OF DISCIPLES: Now from his burial
Christ has gone up on high,
Living, no more to die,
Glorious, imperial;
He in creative zest
Into the heavens has grown.
On the earth-mother's breast
We still must weep alone;
Yet though we here endure
Exile and anguish,
Master, it is in your
Joy that we languish!

CHORUS OF ANGELS: Christ is raised from the tomb,
Snatched from corruption's womb!
Rise and be joyful, all
You whom earth's bonds enthrall!
Brothers, o blessed few,
Sharers of love's food, who
Praise him in deeds you do,
Pilgrims whose words renew
Man's hope of glory: you
Know that your Lord is near,
See, he is here!

9. Gospel, good news.

from OUTSIDE THE TOWN WALL[1]

AN OLD PEASANT: Why, Doctor, now that's very kind
To join us for your Easter walk,
Being such a learned gentleman,
And not look down on us poor folk!
Now, here's a jug of finest ale;
You are the man we've filled it for,
And in your honor this we wish,
That it may quench your thirst, and more:
There's many a drop in this cup I raise—
May their number be added to your days!

FAUST: I thank you all; this drink refreshes,
And I return your kind good wishes.

[*The people gather round.*]

THE OLD PEASANT: Yes, sir, indeed! we all are glad
To see you on this day of cheer,
For long ago, when times were bad,
You wished us well for many a year.
There's many of us might now be dead
Who've lived on to a healthy age
Because your father stopped the spread
Of plague, and cooled the fever's rage.
You were young then, you went about
Visiting every hospital:
So many corpses they brought out,
But you came out alive and well;
Though many a hard time you had too.
You helped us, and the Lord helped you.

ALL: Long life to our good doctor! May
He help us yet for many a day.

FAUST: Give thanks to Him who gave these skills
And helps mankind in all its ills.

[*He walks on with Wagner.*]

WAGNER: Ah, what a sense of your own greatness must
You have as all these people honor you!
Happy the man whose gifts bring him such true
Advantage, as is only just!
They all ask questions, fathers point you out
To sons, they all rush up to see
You pass, the fiddling stops, they stand about
To stare instead of dancing, and the sky
Is full of cheers and caps thrown high;
They very nearly drop on bended knee
As if the Sacred Host were being carried by!

1. Faust and Wagner walk out among the peasants celebrating the spring and Easter.

FAUST: A few steps further, to that rock up there;
Now let us rest here from our walk. This place is one
Where I would often sit and meditate alone,
Keeping strict fast, in anguished prayer.
Here, full of hope, firm in belief,
I sought to alter heaven's will;
I groaned, I wrung my hands in grief—
The pestilence continued still.
Now I feel mocked by this mob's adulation.
If only you could read my mind and know
How little we did, so long ago,
I and my father, to deserve such commendation!
My father was a man respected, yet obscure,
Who labored honestly with never a pause,
Though by his own eccentric methods to be sure,
Studying Nature's sacred cyclic laws.
With the initiated few
He practiced in the Black Laboratory,[2]
Mixing, by this or that strange recipe,
Elements in an ill-assorted brew.
Thus in tepid immersion he would wed
The Lily to the Lion bold and red;
Then with intenser heat he forced this bridal pair
From one glass chamber to the other—by and by
The Young Queen was engendered there,
The rainbow-hued precipitate: this, then,
Was our specific. Still the sick would die,
But no one asked why none got well again.
So in these valleys and these villages,
With those hell-syrups as our remedies,
We, worse than any plague, raged far and wide.
I myself poisoned thousands, I saw how
They all wasted away and perished—now
Men praise that cynical mass-homicide.
WAGNER: Sir, do not let that trouble you!
To practice a transmitted skill
With a good conscience and good will
Is all an honest man need do.
If one respects one's father in one's youth,
One will have learnt from him with pleasure;
If as a man one then adds to our store of truth,
One's own son will do this in even greater measure.
FAUST: Happy are they who still hope this is so,
While ignorance surrounds us like an ocean!
The very thing one needs one does not know,

2. Faust here describes chemical operations in the language of alchemy. In his laboratory Faust's father produced his failed "specific" (medication: the precipitate called the Young Queen) by marrying (combining) the Red Lion (mercuric oxide) with the Lily (hydrochloric acid).

And what one knows is needless information.
But let us put these gloomy thoughts away
And let the precious present hour confound them!
Look how they gleam in the last light of day,
Those little huts with green all round them!
Evening has come, our sun is westering now—
But it speeds on to bring new life elsewhere.
Oh if some wings would raise me, if somehow
I could follow its circuit through the air!
For then as I strove onwards I should see
A silent sunset world for ever under me,
The hills aglow, the valleys lost in dreams,
The silver brooks poured into golden streams;
No mountain-range would stop me, not with all
Its rugged chasms; at divine speed I fly,
The sea already greets my wondering eye
With its warm gulfs where now the sun's rays fall.
Now the god seems at last to sink and set,
But a new impulse drives me yet:
I hasten on to drink his endless light,
The day ahead, behind my back the night,
The sky above me and the waves below . . .
A pleasing dream; but the sun vanishes
And it is over. Wings, alas, may grow
Upon our soul, but still our body is
Earthbound. And yet, by inborn instinct given
To each of us, our hearts rise up and soar
For ever onwards, when we hear the lark outpour
Its warbling song, lost in the blue of heaven,
Or when we see the wing-spread eagle hover
Above wild cliffs which pine-trees cover,
Or across marsh and lakeland watch the crane
Fly homeward to its native haunts again.

WAGNER: I too have known fanciful states of mind,
But to such moods as yours I never was inclined.
One soon grows tired of forests and of fields;
I never envied any bird its wings.
But the pursuit of intellectual things
From book to book, from page to page—what joys that yields!
How fine and snug the winter nights become,
What sweet life courses through one's veins!
Is an old parchment not a whole compendium
Of paradise itself, rewarding all our pains?

FAUST: Only one of our needs is known to you;
You must not learn the other, oh beware!
In me there are two souls, alas, and their
Division tears my life in two.
One loves the world, it clutches her, it binds
Itself to her, clinging with furious lust:

The other longs to soar beyond the dust
Into the realm of high ancestral minds.
Are there no spirits moving in the air,
Ruling the region between earth and sky?
Come down then to me from your golden mists on high,
And to new, many-colored life, oh take me there!
Give me a magic cloak to carry me
Away to some far place, some land untold,
And I'd not part with it for silk or gold
Or a king's crown, so precious it would be!

WAGNER: Oh do not call the dreaded host that swarms
And streams abroad throughout the atmosphere![3]
They bring men danger in a thousand forms,
From the earth's ends they come to plague us here.
Out of the north the sharp-toothed demons fly,
Attacking us with arrow-pointed tongues:
On the east wind they ride to drain us dry
And slake their hunger on our lungs;
The southern desert sends them to beat down
Upon our heads with fiery beams;
The west will bring refreshment, as it seems,
Till in their flooding rains we and the fields must drown.
Their spiteful ears are open to obey
Our summons, for they love to harm and cheat;
They pose as heaven's angels, and though all they say
Is false, their lisping voice is sweet.
But come, the air grows chill, the world is gray
With dusk and mist already; come away!
When evening falls, indoors is best.—
Why do you stand and stare with such surprise?
What twilight thing has seized your interest?

FAUST: There—in the corn and stubble, do you see
That black dog?

WAGNER: Why, of course; of what account is he?

FAUST: What do you take him for? Come, use your eyes!

WAGNER: A poodle, acting as a dog will do
When it has lost its master, I suppose.

FAUST: He's getting closer; round and round he goes
In a narrowing spiral; no, there's no mistake!
And as he comes—look, can't you see it too?—
A streak of fire follows in his wake!

WAGNER: An ordinary black poodle is all I
Can see; no doubt some trick of light deceives your eye.

FAUST: It is some magic he is weaving, so
Subtly about our feet, some future knot!

WAGNER: He's nervous, jumping round us, since we're not
His master, but two men he doesn't know.

3. True to his pedantic nature, Wagner misunderstands Faust's mystical nature spirits as mere weather demons.

FAUST: The circle shrinks; now he is on our ground.
WAGNER: You see! he's not a phantom, just a hound.
He's doubtful still, he growls, he lies down flat,
He wags his tail. All dogs do that.
FAUST: Come to us! Come to heel! Come here!
WAGNER: He's just a foolish poodle-beast, I fear.
Stand still, and he will dance attendance on you;
Speak to him, and he'll put his forepaws on you;
Drop something, and he'll find it, that's his trick—
He'll jump into the water for your stick.
FAUST: No doubt you're right; no spirit after all,
But merely a conditioned animal.
WAGNER: A well-trained dog is one who can
Find favor even with a learned man.
Our students taught him to behave this way;
He far excels his teachers, I must say.

[*They pass through the gate into the town.*]

FAUST'S STUDY (1)

FAUST [*entering with the poodle*]:
Now I have left the fields and hills
Where now the night's dark veil is spread;
Night wakes our better part, and fills
Our prescient soul with holy dread.
The active turmoil leaves my mind,
All wilder passions sleep and cease;
Now I am moved to love mankind,
To love God too, and am at peace.
Stop running about, you poodle-clown!
Why are you snuffling there by the door?
Go behind the stove! Keep still, lie down!
You have my best cushion, I can't do more.
On that path down the hill you jumped and ran
For our delectation, and that was fun;
I will entertain you now if I can,
As a welcome guest, but a silent one.
Back in our little narrow cell
We sit, the lamp glows soft and bright,
And in our heart and mind as well
Self-knowledge sheds its kindly light.
Reason once more begins to speak,
And hope once more is blossoming;
We long to find life's source, to seek
Life's fountainhead, to taste life's spring.
Poodle, stop growling! It does not agree
With my high tone, and my soul's sacred joys
Are interrupted by your animal noise.
We know what scorn and mockery

Uncomprehending man will pour
On anything he has not heard before—
The good, the beautiful, the true;
Must dogs start muttering at it too?

But now, that deep contentment in my breast,
Alas, wells up no more, in spite of all my best
Endeavors. Oh, how soon the stream runs dry,
And in what parching thirst again we lie!
How often this has happened to me!
And yet, there is a remedy:
We learn to seek a higher inspiration,
A supernatural revelation—
And where does this shine in its fullest glory.
If not in that old Gospel story?
Here is the Greek text; I am moved to read
Its sacred words, I feel the need
Now to translate them true and clear
Into the German tongue I hold so dear.

[*He opens a volume and prepares to write.*]

"In the beginning was the Word":[4] why, now
I'm stuck already! I must change that; how?
Is then "the word" so great and high a thing?
There is some other rendering,
Which with the spirit's guidance I must find.
We read: "In the beginning was the Mind."
Before you write this first phrase, think again;
Good sense eludes the overhasty pen.
Does "mind" set worlds on their creative course?
It means: "In the beginning was the Force."
So it should be—but as I write this too,
Some instinct warns me that it will not do.
The spirit speaks! I see how it must read,
And boldly write: "In the beginning was the Deed!"

If we are to share this room in peace,
Poodle, this noise has got to cease,
This howling and barking has got to end!
My invitation did not extend
To so cacophonous a friend.
In my study I won't put up with it.
One of us two will have to quit.
I am sorry that we must part so;
The door stands open, you may go.
But what is this I see?
Can it be happening naturally?

4. The opening line of John's Gospel.

Is it real? Is it a dream or not?
How long and broad my poodle has got!
He heaves himself upright:
This is no dog, if I trust my sight!
What hobgoblin have I brought home somehow?
He looks like a hippopotamus now,
With fearsome jaws and fiery eyes.
Aha! you'll get a surprise!
With this hybrid half-brood of hell
King Solomon's Key[5] works very well.

SPIRITS [*outside in the passage*]:
He's caught! There's one caught in there!
Don't follow him, don't go in!
Like a fox in a gin
An old hell-lynx is trapped; beware!
But now wait and see!
Hover round, hover
Up and down, he'll recover,
He'll set himself free;
We'll lend a hand to him,
We'll not abandon him;
He's been polite to us,
Always done right by us!

FAUST: First, to defeat this beast,
I need the Spell of the Four,[6] at least.
Salamander, burn!
Water-nymph, twist and turn!
Sylph of the air, dissolve!
Goblin, dig and delve!
When the elements are known,
Each in its own
Qualities and powers,
The mastery is ours
Over all and each,
By this knowledge and speech.
Salamander, in flame
Vanish as you came!
Murmur and mingle,
Nymph of the sea-dingle![7]
Blaze like a meteor,
Sylph-creature!
Serve in the house for us,
Incubus, incubus!
Come out of him, show yourself thus or thus!
None of those four

5. A magic book popular from the 16th to the 18th century.
6. The four elements: fire (salamander), water (nymph), air (sylph), and earth (goblin or incubus).
7. Dell or hollow.

Rembrandt van Rijn, *The Scholar in His Study,* c. 1652, often known as *Faust in His Study,* was used as the frontispiece to *Faust: A Fragment* (1790), Goethe's first publication of scenes from Part 1.

Has passed through my door.
The beast just lies there grinning at me.
I've not yet hurt him, evidently.
Wait! I can sing
A more powerful spell!
Are you from hell,
You fugitive thing?
Then behold this Sign
Which they fear and know,
The black hosts below!
Now he swells up with bristling spine.
Vile reprobate!
Do you read this name?
He who is nameless,
Uncreated, timeless,
In all worlds the same,
Pierced in impious hate?
Behind the stove he shrinks from my spells;
Like an elephant he swells.

The whole room is filled by this devil-dog.
He wants to dissolve into a fog.
Do not rise to the ceiling, I forbid you!
Lie down at your master's feet, I bid you!
You will see that I utter no idle warning;
With sacred fire I shall set you burning!
Do not dare the might
Of the Thrice-Effulgent Light![8]
Do not dare the might
Of my strongest magic of all!

MEPHISTOPHELES [*stepping out from behind the stove as the mist disperses, dressed as a medieval wandering student*]:
Why all this fuss? How can I serve you, sir?

FAUST: So that was the quintessence of the cur!
A student-tramp! How very comical.

MEPHISTOPHELES: Sir, I salute your learning and your wit!
You made me sweat, I must admit.

FAUST: What is your name?

MEPHISTOPHELES: The question is absurd,
Surely, in one who seeks to know
The inmost essence, not the outward show,
And has such deep contempt for the mere word.

FAUST: Ah, with such gentlemen as you
The name often conveys the essence too,
Clearly enough; we say Lord of the Flies,[9]
Destroyer, Liar—each most fittingly applies.
Well then, who are you?

MEPHISTOPHELES: Part of that Power which would
Do evil constantly, and constantly does good.

FAUST: This riddle has, no doubt, some explanation.

MEPHISTOPHELES: I am the spirit of perpetual negation;
And rightly so, for all things that exist
Deserve to perish, and would not be missed—
Much better it would be if nothing were
Brought into being. Thus, what you men call
Destruction, sin, evil in short, is all
My sphere, the element I most prefer.

FAUST: You seem complete and whole, yet say you are a part?

MEPHISTOPHELES: I speak the modest truth, I use no art.
Let foolish little human souls
Delude themselves that they are wholes.
I am part of that part which once, when all began,
Was all there was; part of the Darkness before man
Whence light was born, proud light, which now makes futile war
To wrest from Night, its mother, what before
Was hers, her ancient place and space. For light depends

8. The sign of the Trinity.

9. Translates Beelzebub, a biblical name for the devil.

On the corporeal worlds—matter that sends
Visible light out, stops light in its stride
And by reflected light is beautified.
So, light will not last long, I fear;
Matter shall be destroyed, and light shall disappear.

FAUST: Well! now I know your high vocation:
Failing that grand annihilation
You try it on a smaller scale.

MEPHISTOPHELES: And frankly, I must own, here too I fail.
The Something, this coarse world, this mess,
Stands in the way of Nothingness,
And despite all I've undertaken,
This solid lump cannot be shaken—
Storms, earthquakes, fire and flood assail the land
And sea, yet firmly as before they stand!
And as for that damned stuff, the brood of beasts and men,
That too is indestructible, I've found;
I've buried millions—they're no sooner underground
Than new fresh blood will circulate again.
So it goes on; it drives me mad. The earth,
The air, the water, all give birth:
It germinates a thousandfold,
In dry or wet, in hot or cold!
Fire is still mine, that element alone—
Without it, I could call no place my own.

FAUST: And so the ever-stirring, wholesome energy
Of life is your arch-enemy;
So in cold rage you raise in vain
Your clenched satanic fist. Why, you
Strange son of chaos! think again,
And look for something else to do!

MEPHISTOPHELES: On such a point there's much to say;
We'll talk again another day.
This time I'll take my leave—if, by your leave, I may.

FAUST: Why not? We are acquainted now,
And you are welcome to come back
And visit me some time, somehow.
Here is the window, there's the door;
I even have a chimney-stack.

MEPHISTOPHELES: I must confess that on the floor,
Across your threshold, you have put
A certain obstacle—a witch's foot—

FAUST: You mean, that pentagram[1] I drew
Hinders a gentleman from hell?
Then how did you get in? Well, well!
How did I fool a sprite like you?

1. A five-pointed star.

MEPHISTOPHELES: It's not well drawn; look closely, sir!
One of the outside angles—there,
You see? the lines do not quite meet.
FAUST: How curious! how very neat!
And so you are my prisoner.
A lucky chance, I do declare!
MEPHISTOPHELES: The poodle skipped in without noticing,
But now it's quite another thing:
The Devil can't skip out again.
FAUST: Why don't you use the window, then?
MEPHISTOPHELES: Devils and spirits have a law, as you may know:
They must use the same route to come and go.
We enter as we please; leaving, we have no choice.
FAUST: So even hell has laws? Good; in that case
One might conclude a pact with you
Gentlemen, and a guaranteed one too?
MEPHISTOPHELES: Whatever is promised, you shall have your due,
There'll be no quibbling, no tergiversation.
But that all needs mature consideration;
We shall discuss it by and by.
Meanwhile I must most earnestly
Repeat my plea to be released.
FAUST: Come, stay a little while at least,
To edify me with your conversation.
MEPHISTOPHELES: Excuse me now: I soon will reappear
And tell you anything you wish to hear.
FAUST: I did not pursue you, you know;
You put your own head in the noose.
Don't catch the Devil and let go,
They say—it's harder when he's on the loose.
MEPHISTOPHELES: Very well, if you wish, I will remain
And help you while the time away;
But I insist you let me entertain
You with my arts in a befitting way.
FAUST: Certainly, you are welcome to do so;
But you must make it an amusing show.
MEPHISTOPHELES: My friend, you shall in this one night,
In this one hour, know greater sensuous delight
Than in a whole monotonous year!
Delicate spirits now will bring
You visions, and will charm your ear
With song; theirs is no empty conjuring.
Your palate also shall be sated,
Your nostrils sweetly stimulated,
Your sense of touch exhilarated.
We are all ready, all are in
Our places—come, at once, begin!
SPIRITS:
Vanish, you darkling

Vaults there above us!
Now let the sweeter
Blue of the ether
Gaze in and love us!
Are not the darkling
Clouds disappearing?
Starlight is sparkling,
Suns of a gentler
Brightness appearing.
Children of light dance
Past in their radiance,
Swaying, inclining,
Hovering, shining:
Passionate yearning
Follows them burning.
And their long vesture
Streams out and flutters,
Streams out and covers
Arbor and pasture,
Where lovers ponder
As they surrender
Each to each other.
Arbor and bower,
Full fruit and flower!
Vines shed their burden
Into the winepress
Rich with their ripeness;
Wines foam unending
In streams descending,
Through precious gleaming
Stones they are streaming,
Leaving behind them
Heights that confined them,
Pleasantly winding
Round the surrounding
Hills and their verdure,
To lakes expanding.
Birds drink their pleasure,
Soaring to sunlight,
Flying to far bright
Islands that shimmer,
Trembling, enticing,
Where the waves glimmer,
Where echo answers
Songs of rejoicing
Shouted in chorus,
Where we see dancers
Leaping before us
Out over green fields;

Over the green hills
Some of them climbing,
Some of them over
Lake-waters swimming,
Some of them hover;
All seeking life, each
Seeking a distant star
Where love and beauty are
Far beyond speech.

MEPHISTOPHELES: He sleeps! Well done, my airy cherubim!
How soon your lullaby enchanted him!
This concert puts me in your debt.
Faust, you are not the man to hold the Devil yet!
Go on deluding him with sweet dream-shapes,
Plunge him into a sea where he escapes
Reality. As for this threshold, I know how
To split the spell: I need a rat's tooth now.
No need to conjure in this place for long!
I hear them scuttling, soon they'll hear my song.

The master of all rats and mice,
All flies and frogs and bugs and lice,
Commands you to poke forth your snout
And gnaw this floor to let me out!
I'll smear it for you with some drops
Of oil. Aha! see, out he hops!
Now set to work. The point where I was stuck
Is at the front here. What a piece of luck!
One little bite more and it's done.[2]—
Now, Faust, until we meet again, dream on!

FAUST [*waking*]: Have I been twice deluded in one day?
The spirit-orgy vanishes: it seems
I merely saw the Devil in my dreams,
And had a dog that ran away!

from FAUST'S STUDY (2)

FAUST: A knock? Come in!—Who is this bothering me
Again?

MEPHISTOPHELES: I'm back!

FAUST: Come in!

MEPHISTOPHELES: You must say it three
Times over.

FAUST: Well, come in!

MEPHISTOPHELES [*entering*]: Well done!
I think we're going to get on
Together, you and I. To cheer

2. At Mephisto's command the rat gnaws a large enough hole in the pentagram for him to wiggle past.

You up, I've come dressed as a cavalier:
In scarlet, with gold trimmings, cloak
Of good stiff silk, and in my hat
The usual cock's feather; take
A fine long pointed rapier,
And one's complete. So, my dear sir,
Be ruled by me and do just that:
Wear clothes like mine, strike out, be free,
And learn what the good life can be.

FAUST: The earth's a prison—one can't get away
From it, whatever clothes one wears.
I'm still too young to lack desires,
Not young enough now for mere play.
What satisfaction can life hold?
Do without, do without! That old
Command pursues us down the years
Endlessly echoing in our ears—
The same old hoarse repeated song
Heard hour by hour our whole life long!
With each new dawn I wake aghast,
My eyes with bitter tears are filled
To think that when this day has passed
I'll not have had one single wish fulfilled,
That even my presentiments of joy
Will die of nagging scruples, and life's mess
Of trivial impediments destroy
My active soul's creativeness.
When the night falls, I seek my bed
With anxious fears, with many a sigh,
But find no peace: with sights of dread
Wild dreams torment me as I lie.
And though a god lives in my heart,
Though all my powers waken at his word,
Though he can move my every inmost part—
Yet nothing in the outer world is stirred.
Thus by existence tortured and oppressed
I crave for death, I long for rest.

MEPHISTOPHELES: And yet death never is a wholly welcome guest.

FAUST: Happy the man whom glorious death has crowned
With bloodstained victor's laurels, happy he
Whose sudden sweet surcease is found
In some girl's arms, after wild revelry!
And I, who saw that mighty Spirit's power,
Why did I not expire with joy in that same hour!

MEPHISTOPHELES: And yet, in that same night, someone who mixed a brown
Elixir did not drink it down.

FAUST: You seem to like eavesdropping.

MEPHISTOPHELES: I am not
Omniscient, but I know a lot.

FAUST: In that great turmoil and distress
Sweet well-known echoing notes deceived
My ear, old childhood joys relieved
My homesick heart—this I confess.
But now I curse all flattering spells
That tempt our souls with consolation,
All that beguilingly compels
Us to endure earth's tribulation!
A curse first on the high pretences
Of our own intellectual pride!
A curse on our deluded senses
That keep life's surface beautified!
A curse upon our dreams of fame,
Of honor and a lasting name!
A curse upon vain property,
On wife and child and husbandry!
A curse on Mammon,[3] when his gold
Lures us to rash heroic deeds,
Or when his easeful arms enfold
Us softly, pampering all our needs!
I curse the nectar of the grape,
I curse love's sweet transcendent call,
My curse on faith! My curse on hope!
My curse on patience above all!

CHORUS OF INVISIBLE SPIRITS: Alas, alas,
You have destroyed
The beautiful world!
At a blow of your clenched fist
It falls, struck down
By a demigod, it disappears.[4]
Into the void
We carry its fragments, with our tears
We mourn
The beauty that is lost.
Mightiest
Of the sons of earth,
Let it be built anew
More splendidly, let it come to birth
Again, within you:
Begin new
Ways of living,
With your mind clear,
New light receiving,
New music to hear.

3. The god of evil wealth.
4. Not a literal destruction (such as the baboon imagines at line 2406), but a metaphorical destruction of beauty through Faust's curse. The name Faust derives from the Latin for "blessed" (*faustus*); Goethe here puns on "Faust," the German word for fist.

MEPHISTOPHELES: My little sprites
Are performing their rites:
Full of wise exhortations
And invitations
To worlds unknown
Of living and doing.
Why sit here alone,
They say, stifling and stewing?
Stop playing with your misery,
That gnaws your vitals like some carrion-bird!
Even the worst human society
Where you feel human, is to be preferred!
I don't of course propose that we
Should merely mingle with the common herd;
I'm not exactly a grandee,
But if you'd fancy getting through
Your life in partnership with me,
I shall with pleasure, without more ado,
Wholly devote myself to you.
You shall have my company,
And if you are satisfied,
I shall be your servant, always at your side!
FAUST: And what is your reward for this to be?
MEPHISTOPHELES: Long years will pass till we need think of that.
FAUST: No, no! The Devil has his tit-for-tat;
He is an egoist, he'll not work for free,
Merely to benefit humanity.
State your conditions, make them plain and clear!
Servants like you can cost one dear.
MEPHISTOPHELES: In this world I will bind myself to cater
For all your whims, to serve and wait on you;
When we meet in the next world, some time later,
Wages in the same kind will then fall due.
FAUST: The next world? Well, that's no great matter;
Here is a world for you to shatter—
Smash this one first, then let the next be born!
Out of this earth all my contentment springs,
This sun shines on my sufferings;
First wean me from all earthly things—
What happens then's not my concern.
That's something I've no wish to hear:
Whether there's hatred still or love
In that remote supernal sphere,
And who's below and who's above.
MEPHISTOPHELES: Why, in that case, be bold and dare!
Bind yourself to me, begin life anew:
You soon will see what I can do.
No man has ever known a spectacle so rare.
FAUST: Poor devil! What can you offer to me?

A mind like yours, how can it comprehend
A human spirit's high activity?
But have you food that leaves one still unsatisfied,
Quicksilver-gold that breaks up in
One's very hands? Can you provide
A game that I can never win,
Procure a girl whose roving eye
Invites the next man even as I lie
In her embrace? A meteoric fame
That fades as quickly as it came?
Show me the fruit that rots before it's plucked
And trees that change their foliage every day!

MEPHISTOPHELES: I shall perform as you instruct;
All these delights I can purvey.
But there are times in life, my friend,
When one enjoys mere quiet satisfaction.

FAUST: If ever I lie down in sloth and base inaction,
Then let that moment be my end!
If by your false cajolery
You lull me into self-sufficiency,
If any pleasure you can give
Deludes me, let me cease to live!
I offer you this wager!

MEPHISTOPHELES: Done!

FAUST: And done again!
If ever to the moment I shall say:
Beautiful moment, do not pass away!
Then you may forge your chains to bind me,
Then I will put my life behind me,
Then let them hear my death-knell toll,
Then from your labors you'll be free,
The clock may stop, the clock-hands fall,
And time come to an end for me!

MEPHISTOPHELES: We shall remember this; think well what you are doing.

FAUST: That is your right. This bet, which I may lose,
Is no bravado. I must be pursuing
My purpose: once I stand still, I shall be
A slave—yours or no matter whose.

MEPHISTOPHELES: At the doctoral feast I shall display
My willing servitude to you this very day.
One small request—I am sure you'll understand;
It's just in case—I'd like a line or two in your own hand.

FAUST: Poor pedant! Must it be in writing too?
Is a man's plighted word a thing unknown to you?
My spoken word must rule my life's whole course
For ever: is this not enough?
The world streams on with headlong force,
And a promise arrests me. What strange stuff
Of dreams composes us! A pledge that binds

Is a thing rooted in our minds,
And we accept this. Happy is the man
Of pure and constant heart, who can
Regret no choice, no loss! But parchments signed and sealed
Are ghosts that haunt and daunt us; the word dies
Upon the very pen we wield,
And wax and leather tyrannize
Our lives. Well, devil, which is it to be:
Bronze, marble, parchment, paper? Answer me:
What pen, what tool, what chisel shall I use?
The medium is yours to choose!

MEPHISTOPHELES: Come, come, sir, this excited flood
Of rhetoric's quite out of place.
The merest scrap of paper meets the case.
And—for your signature, a drop of blood.

FAUST: If that is all you want, I'll willingly go through
With such a farce to humor you.

MEPHISTOPHELES: Blood is a juice with curious properties.

FAUST: But you need have no fear that I will break
This bond. To strive with all my energies—
Just that is what I undertake.
I have been too puffed up with pride:
I see now I belong beside
Merely the likes of you. With scorn
That mighty Spirit spurned me, Nature's door
Is closed, the thread of thought is torn,
Books sicken me, I'll learn no more.
Now let us slake hot passions in
The depths of sweet and sensual sin!
Make me your magics—I'll not care to know
What lies behind their outward show.
Let us plunge into the rush of things,
Of time and all its happenings!
And then let pleasure and distress,
Disappointment and success,
Succeed each other as they will;
Man cannot act if he is standing still.

MEPHISTOPHELES: Nothing shall limit you; if you wish, sir,
To sample every possible delight,
To snatch your pleasures in full flight,
Then let it be as you prefer.
Enjoy them boldly, grasp at what you want!

FAUST: I tell you, the mere pleasure's not the point!
To dizzying, painful joy I dedicate
Myself, to refreshing frustration, loving hate!
I've purged the lust for knowledge from my soul;
Now the full range of suffering it shall face,
And in my inner self I will embrace
The experience allotted to the whole

Race of mankind; my mind shall grasp the heights
And depths, my heart know all their sorrows and delights.
Thus I'll expand myself, and their self I shall be,
And perish in the end, like all humanity.

MEPHISTOPHELES: Oh, take my word for it, I who have chewed
For centuries on this stale food—
From birth to death a man may do his best,
But this old leavened lump he'll not digest!
We do assure you, such totality
Is only for a god; perpetual light
Is God's alone, me and my kind
He has banished to darkness, and you'll find
You men must live with day and night.

FAUST: Yet I swear I'll achieve it!

MEPHISTOPHELES: Bravely said!
But there's a problem, I'm afraid;
For time is short, and art is long.[5]
Might I suggest you take along
With you some well-known poet? He will teach
You many things: his thoughts will reach
Out far and wide, all sorts of virtues crown
Your noble head at his behest:
The courage of the lion,
The stag's velocity,
The Italian's fiery zest,
The north's tenacity!
He'll find out for you how to mingle guile
With magnanimity, and while
You're still a young warm-blooded man,
How to fall in love by a prearranged plan.
The result, I'm sure, would be well worth meeting;
"Mr. Microcosm!" shall be my respectful greeting.

FAUST: What am I then, if it's impossible
To win that crown of our humanity,
To be what all my senses ache to be?

MEPHISTOPHELES: You are just what you are. Do what you will;
Wear wigs, full-bottomed, each with a million locks,
Stand up yards high on stilts or actor's socks—
You're what you are, you'll be the same man still.

FAUST: How uselessly I've laboured to collect
The treasures of the human intellect,
And now I sit and wonder what I've done.
I feel no new strength surging in my soul
I'm not a hairsbreadth taller, I'm not one
Step nearer to the infinite goal.

5. The Christian devil Mephistopheles here quotes a classical adage.

MEPHISTOPHELES: My dear good sir, I fear your view
Of things is all too common in our day.
Revise it; and let's see what we can do
Before life's pleasures fleet away.
Confound it, man, one's hands and feet of course
Belong to one, so do one's head and arse!
But all the things that give me pleasure,
Are they not mine too, for good measure?
Suppose I keep six stallions, don't you see
The strength of each of them's a part of me?
What a fine fellow I have grown,
Trotting with twenty-four feet of my own!
So come, drop all this cogitation, stir
Yourself, explore the world with me. I say
A philosophic ponderer
Is like a poor beast led astray
By some malignant sprite, to graze on desert ground
When fine green grass is growing all around!

FAUST: How do we start?

MEPHISTOPHELES: First we get out of here!
What sort of prison-hole is this? What mere
Shadow of life you live, when all you do
Just bores your pupils and bores you!
Let your fat colleagues take the strain!
Stop threshing empty straw! Why, even when
There's really something you could teach the poor lads, then
It's something you're forbidden to explain.
Ah, I hear one of them outside your door!

FAUST: I can't see any students now.

MEPHISTOPHELES: He's waited a long time, poor chap,
We'll have to comfort him somehow.
Come, let me have your gown and cap.
What a disguise! I'll look my best in it.

[*He dresses up as Faust.*]

Now leave all this to me and to my native wit.
I'll only need a quarter of an hour.
Meanwhile, make ready for our great Grand Tour!

[*Exit Faust.*]

MEPHISTOPHELES [*in Faust's long gown*]:
Scorn reason, despise learning, man's supreme
Powers and faculties; let your vain dream
Of magic arts be fortified with sweet
Flatteries by the Spirit of Deceit,
And you're mine, signature or none!—
Fate has endowed him with the blind
Impatience of an ever-striving mind;
In headlong haste it drives him on,

He skips the earth and leaves its joys behind.
I'll drag him through life's wastes, through every kind
Of meaningless banality;
He'll struggle like a bird stuck fast, I'll bind
Him hand and foot; in his voracity
He'll cry in vain for food and drink, he'll find
Them dangling out of reach—ah, yes!
Even without this devil's bond that he has signed
He's doomed to perish nonetheless![6]

* * *

A Witch's Kitchen

[*A low hearth with a large cauldron hanging over the fire. In the steam that rises from it various apparitions are seen. A female baboon is sitting by the cauldron skimming it, taking care not to let it run over. The male baboon with their young sits nearby warming himself. The walls and ceiling are decorated with strange witch-paraphernalia. Faust and Mephistopheles enter.*]

FAUST: I'm sick of all this crazy magic stuff!
Is this your vaunted therapy,
This mess of raving mad absurdity?
Advice from an old witch! Am I to slough
Off thirty years, become as good as new,
By swallowing her stinking brew?
God help me now, if that's the best
Hope you can offer! Has man's mind
Devised no other method, can we find
No nobler balm in Nature's treasure-chest?

MEPHISTOPHELES: You're talking sense again now, my dear sir!
There is another means to your rejuvenation,
But it's a very different operation;
I doubt if it's what you'd prefer.

FAUST: I wish to know it.

MEPHISTOPHELES: Very well;
You'll need no fee, no doctor and no spell.
Go out onto the land at once, begin
To dig and delve, be primitive
In body and mind, be bound within
Some altogether narrower sphere;
Eat food that's plain and simple, live
Like cattle with the cattle, humbly reap
The fields you have manured with your own dung;
Believe me, that will make you young
And keep you young until your eightieth year!

6. In the omitted scenes Mephistopheles, impersonating Faust, makes fun of a newly arrived student, then sets out with Faust on their adventures. They begin with the raucous low life of a Leipzig tavern, where Mephisto scares the drunken patrons with fire, then deludes them with visions of happiness while he escapes with Faust, bringing him to visit a witch.

FAUST: I'm not used to all that; it's no good now
Trying to learn the simple life. A spade
Is something I could never use.

MEPHISTOPHELES: Then I'm afraid
The witch will have to show us how.

FAUST: Why do we need this hag? Can't you
Prepare the necessary brew?

MEPHISTOPHELES: The Devil's busy, sir! Why, I could build
A thousand bridges by the time that stuff's distilled!
I have the secret art, indeed,
But not the patience I should need.
Quiet laborious years must run their course;
Time alone can ferment that subtle force.
And there's a deal of ceremony
To go with it—too weird for me.
The Devil taught the witch her tricks,
But she makes potions he can't mix.

[*Seeing the animals.*]

Why, look! what charming kith and kin!
This is her manservant, that's her maid.

[*To the animals.*]

It seems your mistress is not in?

THE ANIMALS: Dining out!
Up the chimney-spout!
She's been delayed!

MEPHISTOPHELES: How long do her trips last, if I may be told?

THE ANIMALS: Till we leave the fire, till our paws get cold.

MEPHISTOPHELES [*to Faust*]: Delightful creatures, don't you agree?

FAUST: I think they're dreary disgusting brutes.

MEPHISTOPHELES: Not at all; their conversation suits
Me very well, as you can see.

[*To the animals.*]

So, what are you stirring there in that pot,
You damnable apes? What mess have you got?

THE ANIMALS: It's charity soup, very light to digest.

MEPHISTOPHELES: I'm sure your public will be impressed.

THE MALE BABOON [*bounding up to Mephistopheles and coaxing him*]:
O please, throw the dice!
To be rich is so nice,
It's so nice to be winning!
Being poor isn't funny,
And if I had money
My head would stop spinning!

MEPHISTOPHELES: This monkey thinks a lucky thing to do
Would be to play the lottery too!

[*Meanwhile the young baboons have been playing with a large globe, which they roll forward.*]

THE MALE BABOON: The world is this ball:
See it rise and fall
And roll round and round!
It's glass, it will break,
It's an empty fake—
Hear the hollow sound!
See it glow here and shine,
See it glitter so fine!
"I'm alive!" it sings.
O my son, beware of it,
Keep clear of it:
You must die, like all things!
It's made of clay;
Clay gets broken, they say.

MEPHISTOPHELES: What's the use of that sieve?

THE MALE BABOON [*lifting it down*]: If you were a thief
I could tell straight away![7]

[*He scampers across to the female and makes her look through it.*]

Look through the sieve!
You can name the thief,
And you mustn't say.

MEPHISTOPHELES [*approaching the fire*]: And what's this pot?

THE BABOONS: Poor ignorant sot!

Doesn't know why the pot,
Why the cauldron's there!

MEPHISTOPHELES: You insolent beast!

THE MALE BABOON: Take this whisk, at least,
And sit down in the chair!

[*He makes Mephistopheles sit down.*]

FAUST [*who in the meantime has been standing in front of a mirror, alternately moving towards it and backing away from it*]:
Oh, heavenly image! What is this I see
Appearing to me in this magic glass?
Love, carry me to where she dwells, alas,
Oh, lend the swiftest of your wings to me!
If I so much as move from this one spot,
If I dare to approach her, then she seems
To fade, I see her as in misty dreams!
The loveliest image of a woman! Is this not
Impossible, can woman be so fair?

7. A folk belief.

I see in that sweet body lying there
The quintessence of paradise! How can one
Believe such things exist beneath the sun?
MEPHISTOPHELES: Well, if a god has worked hard for six days
And on the seventh gives himself high praise,
You'd think it would be reasonably well done!—
Look your fill at her now. I'll find
A little darling for you of that kind;
Then you can try your luck. If you succeed
In winning her, you'll be a happy man indeed!

[*Faust keeps gazing into the mirror. Mephistopheles, lolling in the chair and playing with the whisk, goes on talking.*]

Well, here I sit, a king enthroned in state;
My sceptre's in my hand, my crown I still await.
THE ANIMALS [*who have been scampering about with each other in a bizarre fashion and now bring a crown for Mephistopheles, offering it to him with loud screeches*]:
Oh sir, be so good
As to mend this old crown
With sweat and with blood!

[*They handle the crown clumsily and break it into two pieces, which they then scamper about with.*]

Now it's done! It falls down!—
We can talk, see and hear,
We can rhyme loud and clear!
FAUST [*gazing at the mirror*]:
Oh God! have I gone mad? I'm quite distraught!
MEPHISTOPHELES [*indicating the animals*]:
I think I'm going a bit crazy too.
THE ANIMALS: And when our rhymes fit
We're in luck: that's the thought,
That's the meaning of it!
FAUST [*as above*]: My heart's on fire, what shall I do?
Quick, let's leave now, let's get away!
MEPHISTOPHELES [*remaining seated, as above*]:
Well, one must certainly admit
These apes are honest poets, in their way!

[*The cauldron, which the female baboon has been neglecting, begins to boil over, and a great tongue of flame blazes up into the chimney. The witch comes down through the flame, screaming hideously.*]

THE WITCH: Ow! ow! ow! ow!
You damned brute, you damned filthy sow!
Not minding the pot! You've burnt me now,
You filthy brute!

[*Seeing Faust and Mephistopheles.*]

What's this here? Who
The hell are you?
Who let you in?
What does this mean?
May hell's hot pains
Burn in your bones!

[*She plunges the skimming-ladle into the cauldron and splashes flames at Faust, Mephistopheles, and the animals. The animals whine.*]

MEPHISTOPHELES [*reversing the whisk in his hand and striking out with the handle at the glasses and pots*]:
Split! Split in two!
That's spilt your stew!
That's spoilt your cooking!
I'm only joking,
Hell-hag! You croon,
I beat the tune!

[*The witch recoils in rage and terror.*]

Do you know me now? Skinny, cadaverous bitch,
Do you know your lord and master? Why don't I
Smash you to pieces, tell me why,
You and your ape-familiars? Must I teach
You some respect for my red doublet? What
Is this cock's feather, eh? My face,
Have I been hiding it? You learn your place,
Old hag! Am I to name myself or not?

THE WITCH: Oh master, pardon my rude greeting!
But where's your cloven hoof, your horse's leg?
And your two ravens? Sir, I beg
To be excused!

MEPHISTOPHELES: Well, well, and so
You are for once; it's true, I know,
Some time has passed since our last meeting.
Besides, civilization, which now licks
Us all so smooth, has taught even the Devil tricks;
The northern fiend's becoming a lost cause—
Where are his horns these days, his tail, his claws?
As for my foot, which I can't do without,
People would think me odd to go about
With that; and so, like some young gentlemen,
I've worn false calves since God knows when.

THE WITCH [*capering about*]: I'm crazy with excitement now I see
Our young Lord Satan's back again!

MEPHISTOPHELES: Woman, don't use that name to me!

THE WITCH: Why, sir, what harm's it ever done?

MEPHISTOPHELES: The name has been a myth too long.
Not that man's any better off—the Evil One
They're rid of, evil is still going strong.

Please call me "Baron," that will do.
I'm just a gentleman, like others of my kind.
My blood's entirely noble, you will find;
My coat of arms may be inspected too.

[*He makes an indecent gesture.*]

THE WITCH [*shrieking with laughter*]: Ha! ha! You haven't changed a bit!
Still the same bad lad, by the looks of it!

MEPHISTOPHELES [*to Faust*]: Mark well, my dear sir! This is how
One deals with witches.

THE WITCH: Tell me now,
Gentlemen, what might be your pleasure?

MEPHISTOPHELES: A good glass of the you-know-what;
But please, the oldest vintage you have got—
Years give it strength in double measure.

THE WITCH: Certainly! I've a bottle on this shelf,
I sometimes take a swig from it myself;
By now it's even quite stopped stinking.
A glass for you can well be spared.
[*Aside.*] But as you know, it's not for casual drinking—
This man will die of it unless he's been prepared.

MEPHISTOPHELES: No, it will do him good—he's a good friend
Of ours, and I can safely recommend
Your kitchen to him. Draw your circle, say
Your spells, pour him a cup without delay!

[*The witch, with strange gestures, draws a circle and places magic objects in it; as she does so the glasses and pots begin to ring and hum and make music. Finally she fetches a massive tome and puts the baboons in the circle, where they are made to act as a reading-desk for her and hold the torch. She beckons Faust to approach her.*]

FAUST [*to Mephistopheles*]: Look, what use is all this to me?
These crazy antics, all that stupid stuff,
The woman's vulgar trickery—
I know and hate them well enough!

MEPHISTOPHELES: Rubbish, man! Can't you see a joke?
Don't be pedantic! You must understand,
As a doctor she's got to hoke and poke
If her medicine's to take effect as planned.

[*He makes Faust step into the circle.*]

THE WITCH [*beginning to declaim from the book with great emphasis*]:

Now hear and see!
From one make ten,
Take two, and then
At once take three,
And you are rich!
Four doesn't score.
But, says the witch,

From five and six
Make seven and eight;
That puts it straight.
And nine is one,
And ten is none.
The witch's twice-times-table's done.

FAUST: She's obviously raving mad.

MEPHISTOPHELES: Oh, she has still much more to say!
I know it well, the whole book reads that way.
It's cost me more time than I had.
A complete paradox, you see,
Fills fools and wise men with a sense of mystery.
My friend, the art's both new and old:
Let error, not the truth be told—
Make one of three and three of one;
That's how it always has been done.
Thus to their heart's content they dogmatize,
Plague take the silly chattering crew!
Men hear mere words, yet commonly surmise
Words must have intellectual content too.

THE WITCH [*continuing*]:
The lofty might
Of wisdom's light,
Hid from the vulgar throng:
It costs no thought,
It's freely taught,
We know it all along!

FAUST: What rubbish is the crone repeating?
My head's half split by this entire
Performance; it's like some massed choir
Of fifty thousand idiots bleating.

MEPHISTOPHELES: Enough, enough, excellent sibyl! Bring
Your cocktail, pour it, fill the cup
Right to the brim, quick, fill it up!
This drink won't harm my friend, he knows a thing
Or two already; many a strong potation
He's swallowed during his initiation!

[*The witch, with great ceremony, pours the potion into a cup; as Faust raises it to his lips it flames up a little.*]

Come, down with it! Don't dither so!
Soon it will warm the cockles of your heart.
You're practically the Devil's bedfellow,
And fire still makes you flinch and start!

[*The witch opens the circle. Faust steps out of it.*]

Let's go! You must keep moving now.

THE WITCH: I hope my potion whets your appetite!

MEPHISTOPHELES [*to the Witch*]: And if I can do you a good turn somehow,

Just tell me on Walpurgis Night.[8]
THE WITCH: Here is a song, sir, you might like to sing;
You'll find it has a special virtue in it.
MEPHISTOPHELES [*to Faust*]: Do as I say, come, let's be off this minute;
You must let yourself sweat, this thing
Must soak right through your guts. Then you shall learn
How to appreciate your noble leisure,
And soon, to your consummate pleasure,
Cupid[9] will stir in you, you'll feel him dance and burn.
FAUST: Let me look once more in the glass before we go—
That woman's lovely shape entrances me.
MEPHISTOPHELES: No, no!
Before you in the flesh you soon will see
The very paragon of femininity.

[*Aside.*] With that elixir coursing through him,
Soon any woman will be Helen[1] to him.

* * *[2]

Evening

[*A small well-kept room.*]

MARGARETA [*plaiting and binding up her hair*]:
I'd like to find out, I must say,
Who that gentleman was today.
A handsome man, I do admit,
And a nobleman by the looks of it.
I could tell by something in his eyes.
And he wouldn't have had the cheek otherwise.

[*Exit. Mephistopheles and Faust enter.*]

MEPHISTOPHELES: Come in, keep quiet! Come, don't delay!
FAUST [*after a pause*]: Leave me alone, please go away.
MEPHISTOPHELES [*taking a look round the room*]:
Very neat and tidy, I must say. [*Exit.*]
FAUST [*gazing up and about him*]:
Welcome, sweet twilight, shining dim all through
This sanctuary! Now let love's sweet pain
That lives on hope's refreshing dew
Seize and consume my heart again!
How this whole place breathes deep content
And order and tranquillity!
What riches in this poverty,
What happiness in this imprisonment!

[*He sinks into the leather armchair by the bed.*]

8. The night of April 30, when witches were supposed to engage in Satanic rituals on the Brocken, the highest peak of the Harz Mountains.
9. God of love.
1. Helen of Troy, famous for her fatal beauty.
2. Faust, transformed into a dashing youth, meets Margareta, a lower-class girl, and demands that Mephisto seduce her for him. (Later she is also called by her nickname Gretchen.)

Oh let me rest here: long ago, among
Their joys and sorrows, others sat on you,
Embraced and welcomed! Ah, how often too
Round this, their grandsire's throne, the children clung!
My love herself, at Christmas time, a young
Rosy-cheeked child, glad at some gift, knelt here
Perhaps, and kissed his wrinkled hand so dear!
What order, what completeness I am made
To sense in these surroundings! It is yours,
Dear girl, your native spirit that ensures
Maternal daily care, the table neatly laid,
The crisp white sand strewn on the floors!
Oh godlike hand, by whose dear skill and love
This little hut matches the heavens above!
And here!

[*He draws aside a curtain from the bed.*]

What fierce joy seizes me! I could
Stand gazing here for ever. Nature, you
Worked this sweet wonder, here the inborn angel grew
Through gentle dreams to womanhood.
Here the child lay, her tender heart
Full of warm life, here the pure love
Of God's creative forces wove
His likeness by their sacred art!

And I! What purpose brings me? What
Profound emotion stirs me! What did I
Come here to do? Why do I sigh?
Poor wretch! Am I now Faust or not?

Is there some magic hovering round me here?
I was resolved, my lust brooked no delay—
And now in dreams of love I wilt and melt away!
Are we mere playthings of the atmosphere?

If she came in this instant, ah, my sweet,
How she would punish me! How small
The great Don Juan would feel, how he would fall
In tears of languor at her feet!

MEPHISTOPHELES [*entering*]: Quick, she's down there, she'll be here any minute.
FAUST: Take me away! I'll never come again!
MEPHISTOPHELES: Here's quite a heavy box with nice things in it;
I got it—somewhere else. Now then,
Into her cupboard with it, quick, before we're seen.
I tell you, when she finds that stuff
She'll go out of her mind; I've put enough
Jewelry in there to seduce a queen.
A child's a child, of course, and play's just play.
FAUST: I don't know if I should—

MEPHISTOPHELES: Now what's the fuss about?
You'd like to keep it for yourself, no doubt?
Let me advise you then, Sir Lecher-Lust,
Stop wasting the fine time of day,
And spare me further tasks! I trust
You're not a miser too? I scratch my pate
And bite my nails and calculate—

[*He puts the jewel-case in the cupboard and locks it up again.*]

Quick, we must go!—
How I'm to please your sweetheart for you
And make her want you and adore you;
And now you hesitate
As if this were your lecture-room
Where in gray professorial gloom
Physics and metaphysics wait!
We must go! [*They leave.*]

MARGARETA [*coming in with a lamp*]:
It's so hot and sultry in here somehow,

[*She opens the window.*]

And yet it's quite cool outside just now.
I've got a feeling something's wrong—
I hope my mother won't be long.
It's a sort of scare coming over me—
What a silly baby I must be!

[*She begins singing as she undresses.*]

There once was a king of Thule.[3]
Of the far north land of old:
His dying lady he loved so truly
She gave him a cup of gold.

There was no thing so dear to the king,
And every time he wept
As he drained that cup at each banqueting,
So truly his faith he kept.

And at last, they say, on his dying day
His kingdom was willed and told,
And his son and heir got all his share—
But the king kept the cup of gold.

They feasted long with wine and song,
And there with his knights sat he,
In the ancestral hall, in his castle tall
On the cliffs high over the sea.

3. Ultima Thule was the ancient name for the far north.

The old man still drank as his life's flame sank,
Then above the waves he stood,
And the sacred cup he raised it up,
Threw it down to the raging flood.

He watched it fall to the distant shore
And sink in the waters deep;
And never a drop that king drank more,
For he'd closed his eyes to sleep.

[*She opens the cupboard to put her clothes in, and sees the jewel case.*]

However did this pretty box get here?
I left the cupboard locked; how very queer!
Whatever can be in it? Perhaps my mother lent
Some money on it, and it's meant
As a security. Oh dear!
It's got a ribbon with a little key—
I think I'll open it, just to see!
What's this? Oh God in heaven, just look!
I've never seen such things before!
These jewels would be what a princess wore
At the highest feast in the feast-day book!
I wonder how that necklace would suit me?
Whose can these wonderful things be?

[*She puts on some of the jewelry and looks at herself in the glass.*]

If even the earrings were only mine!
My, what a difference it makes!
We young girls have to learn, it takes
More than just beauty; that's all very fine,
But everyone just says "she's pretty,"
And they seem to say it out of pity.
Gold's all they care
About, gold's wanted everywhere;
For us poor folk there's none to spare.

A Promenade

[*Faust walking up and down deep in thought. Enter Mephistopheles.*]

MEPHISTOPHELES: By the pangs of despised love! By the fires of hell!
I wish I knew something worse, to curse it as well!
FAUST: Whatever's the matter? You do look odd
What a sour face for a fine day!
MEPHISTOPHELES: May the devil take me, I would say,
If I weren't the Devil myself, by God.
FAUST: Are you right in the head? Excuse me if I smile;
These rages aren't your usual style.
MEPHISTOPHELES: Just think: those jewels for Gretchen that I got,
A priest has been and swiped the lot!—

Her mother took one look, and hey!
She had the horrors straight away.
That woman's got a good nose all right,
Snuffling her prayer-book day and night,
With any commodity she can tell
Profane from sacred by the smell:
And as for those jewels, she knew soon enough
There was something unholy about that stuff.
"My child," she exclaimed, ill-gotten wealth
Poisons one's spiritual health.
To God's blessed Mother it must be given,
And she will reward us with manna from heaven!
How Meg's face fell, poor little minx!
It's a gift-horse after all, she thinks,
And whoever so kindly brought it—how can
There be anything godless about such a man?
Ma sends for the priest, and he, by glory!
Has no sooner heard their little story
And studied the spoils with great delight,
Than he says: "Dear ladies, you are quite right!
Who resists the tempter shall gain a crown.
The Church can digest all manner of meat,
It's never been known to over-eat
Although it has gulped whole empires down;
Holy Church's stomach alone can take
Ill-gotten goods without stomach-ache!"

FAUST: It's common; many a king and Jew
Has a well-filled belly of that kind too.

MEPHISTOPHELES: So he sweeps every ring and chain and brooch,
As if they were peanuts, into his pouch:
Takes it no less for granted, indeed,
Than if it were all just chickenfeed—
Promises them celestial reward
And leaves them thanking the blessed Lord.

FAUST: And Gretchen?

MEPHISTOPHELES: Sitting there all of a dither,
Doesn't know what to do or why or whether.
Can't get the jewels out of her mind—
Or the gentleman who had been so kind.

FAUST: I can't bear my darling to be sad.
Get another lot for her! The ones she had
Weren't all that remarkable anyway.

MEPHISTOPHELES: Oh indeed, for my lord it's mere child's play!

FAUST: Do as I tell you!—And one thing more:
Get to know that friend of hers next door!
Do something, devil, stir your feet!
And get some more jewels for my sweet!

MEPHISTOPHELES: With pleasure, sir, whatever you say.

[*Exit Faust.*]

He's just like all the lovesick fools I know;
To please their darlings they would blow
The sun and moon and stars out at one go. [*Exit.*]

THE NEIGHBOR'S HOUSE

MARTHA [*alone*]: My husband, may God pardon him!
He didn't treat me right. For shame!
Just went off into the world one day.
Left me a grass widow, as they say.
Yet I've never done him any wrong;
I loved him truly all along. [*She weeps.*]
He may even be dead. Oh, my poor heart bleeds!
—A death certificate's what one needs.

[*Enter Margareta*]

MARGARETA: Martha!
MARTHA: Gretchen dear! What a face!
MARGARETA: Martha, I feel quite faint! There's been
This second box—I found it in
My cupboard there—an ebony case
Of the grandest jewels you ever saw;
Much richer than the one before!
MARTHA: Now this time you mustn't tell your mother,
Or the priest'll get it, just like the other.
MARGARETA: Oh, look at this! Just look at this!
MARTHA [*trying out some of the jewels on her*]:
Aren't you a lucky little miss!
MARGARETA: But I can't wear them in the street, or go
To church and be seen in them, you know.[4]
MARTHA: Just come whenever you can to me,
And put on your jewels secretly—
Walk about in front of the looking-glass here,
And we'll enjoy them together, my dear.
Then when there's a feast-day or some occasion,
Let people see one little thing, then another,
A necklace at first, a pearl earring; your mother
May not notice, or we'll make up some explanation.
MARGARETA: But all this jewelry—who can have brought it?
I think there's something funny about it.

[*There is a knock at the door.*]

Oh God, perhaps that's my mother!
MARTHA [*looking through the peep-hole*]: No!

4. Clothing and ornamentation were regulated by law, according to the social rank of the wearer.

It's some gentleman I don't know—
Come in!

[*Enter Mephistopheles*]

MEPHISTOPHELES: If I may make so bold!
Forgive me, ladies; I'm looking for
Frau Martha Schwertlein,[5] who lives here, I'm told.

[*He steps back respectfully on seeing Margareta*]

MARTHA: That's me; how can I oblige you, sir?
MEPHISTOPHELES [*aside to her*]: Now that I know you, that will do;
You have a fine lady visiting you.
Excuse my taking the liberty;
I'll call again later when you're free.
MARTHA [*aloud*]: Do you hear that, child! What a rigmarole!
He takes you for a lady, bless your soul!
MARGARETA: Oh sir, you're much too kind to me;
I'm a poor young woman—this jewelry
I'm trying on, it isn't mine.
MEPHISTOPHELES: Why, it's not just the jewels that are fine;
You have a manner, a look in your eyes.
Then I may stay? What a pleasant surprise.
MARTHA: Now, I'm sure your business is interesting—
MEPHISTOPHELES: I hope you'll pardon the news I bring;
I'm sorry to grieve you at our first meeting.
Your husband is dead, and sends his greeting.
MARTHA: What, dead? My true love! Alas the day!
My husband's dead! I shall pass away!
MARGARETA: Oh, don't despair, Frau Martha dear!
MEPHISTOPHELES: Well, it's a sad tale you shall hear.
MARGARETA: I hope I shall never love; I know
It would kill me with grief to lose someone so.
MEPHISTOPHELES: Joy and grief need each other, they can't be parted.
MARTHA: Good sir, pray tell me how he died.
MEPHISTOPHELES: In Padua, by St. Anthony's[6] side,
There they interred your late departed,
In a spot well suited, by God's grace,
To be his last cool resting-place.
MARTHA: And have you brought nothing else for me?
MEPHISTOPHELES: Ah, yes: he requests you solemnly
To have three hundred masses sung for his repose.
For the rest, my hands are empty, I fear.
MARTHA: What! No old medal, not a souvenir
Or trinket any poor apprentice will lay by,
Stuffed in his satchel, and would rather die
In penury than sell or lose?

5. "Schwertlein" means "little sword," an off-color joke.

6. St. Anthony of Padua, the patron saint of brides and wives.

MEPHISTOPHELES: I much regret it, ma'am; but truthfully,
Your husband wasn't one to waste his property.
And he rued his faults, but his luck he cursed—
The second more bitterly than the first.
MARGARETA: Oh, why have people such ill luck! I'm sad for them.
I promise to pray for him with many a requiem.
MEPHISTOPHELES: What a charming child you are! I'd say
You deserve to be married straight away.
MARGARETA: Oh, I'm still too young, that wouldn't be right.
MEPHISTOPHELES: If a husband won't do, then a lover might.
Why not? It's life's greatest blessing and pleasure
To lie in the arms of so sweet a treasure.
MARGARETA: That's not the custom in this country, sir.
MEPHISTOPHELES: Custom or not, it does occur.
MARTHA: Tell me the rest!
MEPHISTOPHELES: I stood by his deathbed;
It was pretty filthy, it must be said.
But he died as a Christian, on half-rotten straw.
His sins were absolved, though he felt he had many more.
"I hate myself," he cried, "for what I've done;
Away from my trade, away from my wife to run.
I'm tormented by that memory.
If only she could forgive me in this life!—"
MARTHA [*weeping*]: Oh, he's long been forgiven by his loving wife!
MEPHISTOPHELES: "—But God knows, she was more to blame than me."
MARTHA: Why, that's a lie! What, lie at the point of death!
MEPHISTOPHELES: He was delirious at his last breath,
If I am any judge of such events.
"I had my time cut out," he said,
"Providing her with children, then with bread—
Which meant bread in the very widest sense.
And then I got no peace to eat my share."
MARTHA: Had he forgotten all my faithful loving care,
Slaving for him all day and night?
MEPHISTOPHELES: Why no, he had remembered that all right.
He told me: "When we sailed away from Malta,
For my wife and brats I said a fervent prayer,
And by heaven's will, our luck began to alter:
We took a Turkish ship and boarded her—
The mighty Sultan's treasure-ship! We fought
Them bravely and deserved our prize.
And as for me, this bold adventure brought
Me in a dividend of some size."
MARTHA: What's that? Where is it? Has he buried it?
MEPHISTOPHELES: Who knows now where the four winds carried it!
He fell in with a lovely lady-friend
In Naples, visiting the place for fun;
And fun he got—the kindnesses she'd done,

They left their mark on him till his life's end.[7]
MARTHA: The scoundrel! Stealing his own children's bread!
Not even want and poverty
Could stop his vices and debauchery!
MEPHISTOPHELES: Well, there you are, you see; so now he's dead.
If I were in your place, you know,
I'd mourn him for a decent twelvemonth, then,
Having looked round a little, choose another beau.
MARTHA: Oh dear, after my first, it will be hard
To find a second man like him again!
He was a jolly fellow—everyone enjoyed him;
He just was far too fond of wandering abroad,
And foreign women, foreign wine,
And it was that damned gambling that destroyed him.
MEPHISTOPHELES: Well, I daresay it was a fine
Arrangement, if for his part he
Allowed you equal liberty.
On such terms, I would hardly hesitate
Myself to be your second mate.
MARTHA: Oh, sir, you like to have your little joke with me!
MEPHISTOPHELES [*aside*]: While there's still time I'd best get out of here;
She'd hold the Devil to his word, that's clear.

[*To Gretchen.*]

And you, my child, are you still fancy-free?
MARGARETA: I don't quite understand.
MEPHISTOPHELES [*aside*]: Now there's sweet innocence!
[*Aloud.*] Ladies, good day to you!
MARGARETA: Good day!
MARTHA: Sir, one more thing:
I'd like to have some proper evidence—
The details of my husband's death and burying.
I've always liked things orderly and neat;
I want to read it in the weekly notice-sheet.
MEPHISTOPHELES: Indeed, ma'am; when two witnesses agree,
The truth's revealed infallibly.
I have a companion; he and I
Can go before the judge to testify.
I'll bring him here.
MARTHA: Oh by all means do!
MEPHISTOPHELES: And this young miss will be here too?—
He's a fine lad; seen the world all right;
Very nice to ladies, very polite.
MARGARETA: I shall blush with shame to meet him, I fear.
MEPHISTOPHELES: You need blush before no king, my dear.

7. Syphilis was known as "the Naples disease."

MARTHA: I've a garden at the back; so, gentlemen.
Please come this evening, we'll expect you then.

A STREET

FAUST: Well, what news now? Is it going ahead?
MEPHISTOPHELES: Ah, bravo! So you're well alight!
Gretchen will soon be in your bed.
We're to meet her at her neighbour's house tonight.
That Martha's a proper witch, good Lord,
I couldn't have picked you a better bawd.
FAUST: Good.
MEPHISTOPHELES: But she asks a service of us too.
FAUST: That's fair enough; what do we have to do?
MEPHISTOPHELES: We swear a deposition, warranting
That her late husband's bones now are
Buried in hallowed ground in Padua.
FAUST: Brilliant; so first we have to travel there.
MEPHISTOPHELES: *Sancta simplicitas!*[8] Why should we care?
Just testify; no need to make the visit.
FAUST: If that's your scheme, then I'll do no such thing.
MEPHISTOPHELES: Oh, holy Willie! That's your scruple, is it?
So this is the first time in your career
That you'll have borne false witness? Have you not
Laid down authoritative definitions
Of God and of the world, of all that's there and here,
Man's mind and heart, his motives and conditions,
With brazen confidence, with all the pride you've got?
But pause to think—confess, as you draw breath:
Of all those matters you knew not a jot
More than of Martha Schwertlein's husband's death!
FAUST: You are, and always were, a sophist[9] and a liar.
MEPHISTOPHELES: And your standards of truth, I know, are so much higher.
In all good faith, tomorrow, we shall find
You turning little Gretchen's mind
With vows of love, and nonsense of that kind.
FAUST: It will come from my heart.
MEPHISTOPHELES: A splendid vow!
Eternal love, faithfulness to the end,
Unique all-powerful passion—yes, my friend,
That will come from the heart too, will it now?
FAUST: Yes! Let me be! It shall!—This deep commotion
And turmoil in me, I would speak
Its name, find words for this emotion—
Through the whole world my soul and senses seek

8. Holy simplicity!

9. False reasoner.

The loftiest words for it: this flame
That burns me, it must have a name!
And so I say: eternal, endless, endless—why,
You devil, do you call all that a lie?

MEPHISTOPHELES: I am right nonetheless.

FAUST: Listen to me—
And understand, before I burst a lung:
Insist on being right, and merely have a tongue,
And right you'll be.
But now let's go, I'm sick of all this chatter.
And you are right; I've no choice in the matter.

A Garden

[*Margareta walking up and down with Faust, Martha with Mephistopheles.*]

MARGARETA: I'm quite ashamed, I feel you're being so kind
And condescending, just to spare
My feelings, sir! A traveler
Must be polite, and take what he can find.
I know quite well that my poor conversation
Can't entertain a man of education.

FAUST: One look, one word from you—that entertains
Me more than any this wise world contains.

[*He kisses her hand.*]

MARGARETA: Sir, you put yourself out! How can you kiss my hand?
It's so nasty and rough; I have to do
Such a lot of housework with it. If you knew
How fussy Mother is, you'd understand!

[*They pass on.*]

MARTHA: So, sir, you're always traveling, I believe?

MEPHISTOPHELES: Alas, constraints of duty and vocation!
Sometimes a place is very hard to leave—
But it's just not one's destination.

MARTHA: I dare say, when one's young and strong,
It's good to roam the world and to be free;
But there are bad times coming before long,
And creeping to one's grave alone—oh, you'd be wrong
To be a bachelor then, sir, believe me!

MEPHISTOPHELES: I view with horror that approaching fate.

MARTHA: Then think again, while it's not yet too late!

[*They pass on.*]

MARGARETA: Yes, out of sight out of mind it will be!
And though you talk politely—after all,
You've many friends, and I'm sure they are all
More intellectual than me.

FAUST: My sweet, believe me, what's called intellect
Is often shallowness and vanity.
MARGARETA: How so?
FAUST: Oh, why can simple innocence not know
Itself, or humble lowliness respect
Its own great value, feel the awe that's due
To generous Nature's dearest, greatest boon—
MARGARETA: You'll sometimes think of me, and then forget me soon;
But I'll have time enough to think of you.
FAUST: So you're alone a lot?
MARGARETA: Oh yes, you see, our household's not
Big, but one has to see to it;
And we've no maid. I cook and sweep and knit
And sew, all day I'm on my feet.
And my mother insists everything's got
To be so neat!
Not that she's really poor in any way,
In fact, we're better off than most folk, I should say.
We got some money when my father died,
A little house and garden just outside
The town. But mine's a quiet life now, that's true.
My brother's a soldier, he's not here.
My little sister, she died too.
I had such trouble with her, the poor little dear,
And yet I'd gladly have it all again to do,
I loved her so.
FAUST: A darling, just like you.
MARGARETA: I brought her up: she got so fond of me.
She was born after Father's death, you see,
And Mother was so desperately ill then
We thought she never would be well again,
And she got better slowly, very gradually.
She couldn't possibly, you know,
Give the baby her breast; and so
I had to feed her, all alone,
With milk and water; she became my own,
And in my arms and on my breast
She smiled and wriggled and grew and grew.
FAUST: That must have been great happiness for you.
MARGARETA: But very hard as well, although I did my best.
At night she had her little cradle by
My bed; she'd hardly need to move, and I
Was wide awake.
Then I would have to feed her, or else take
Her into bed with me, or if she went
On crying, I'd get up and jog her to and fro.
And then, the washing started at cock-crow;
Then I would shop and cook. That's how I spent
The whole of every blessed day.

So you see, sir, it's not all play!
But you eat well, and you sleep well that way.

[*They pass on.*]

MARTHA: We women do have an unlucky fate!
A confirmed bachelor's hard to educate.
MEPHISTOPHELES: I'm sure it takes a lady of your kind,
Madam, to make one change one's mind.
MARTHA: But tell me truly now, sir: have you never
Lost your hard heart to any woman ever?
MEPHISTOPHELES: One's own fireside, we are so often told,
And a good wife, are worth silver and gold.[1]
MARTHA: I'm asking: have you never felt the inclination—?
MEPHISTOPHELES: I've always been treated with great consideration.
MARTHA: I meant: have things not been serious at any time?
MEPHISTOPHELES: Trifling with ladies is a very serious crime.
MARTHA: Oh, you don't understand!
MEPHISTOPHELES: That grieves me, I confess!
But I do understand—your great obligingness.

[*They pass on.*]

FAUST: You knew me again, sweetheart, immediately,
Here in the garden? Is it really true?
MARGARETA: You saw me cast my eyes down, didn't you.
FAUST: And you've forgiven the liberty
I took outside the church, the insulting way
I spoke to you the other day?
MARGARETA: It was a shock—you see, it never had
Happened before. No one ever says bad
Things of me, and I thought: did I somehow
Seem lacking in modesty to him just now?
He suddenly just thinks, quite without shame:
"I'll pick this girl up;" maybe I'm to blame?
I must confess that something in my heart,
I don't know what, began quite soon to take your part;
In fact I got quite cross with myself, too,
For not being quite cross enough with you.
FAUST: Oh my sweet!
MARGARETA: Wait!

[*She picks a daisy and begins pulling off the petals one by one.*]

FAUST: What's this for? A bouquet?
MARGARETA: No!
FAUST: What?
MARGARETA: You'll laugh at me; it's just a game we play.

[*She murmurs as she picks off the petals.*]

1. Mephisto's proverbial wisdom partly derives from the Bible: "Who can find a virtuous woman? For her price is far above rubies" (Proverbs 31:10).

FAUST: What's this you're murmuring?
MARGARETA [*half aloud*]: He loves me—loves me not
FAUST: You dear beloved little thing!
MARGARETA [*continuing*]: Loves me—not—loves me—not—

[*Pulling off the last petal and exclaiming with joy.*]

He loves me!
FAUST: Yes, my love! The flower speaks,
And let it be your oracle! He loves you:
Do you know what that means? He loves you!

[*He clasps both her hands in his.*]

MARGARETA: I'm trembling all over!
FAUST: Don't be afraid! Oh, let my eyes,
My hands on your hands tell you what
No words can say:
To give oneself entirely and to feel
Ecstasy that must last for ever!
For ever!—For its end would be despair.
No, never-ending! Never-ending!

[*Margareta presses his hands, frees herself and runs away. He stands lost in thought for a moment, then follows her. Martha enters with Mephistopheles*]

MARTHA: It's getting dark.
MEPHISTOPHELES: Yes, and we must be gone.
MARTHA: I would gladly invite you to stay on,
But this place has sharp eyes, and sharp tongues too.
It's as if they all had nothing else to do,
Day in, day out,
But try to sniff their neighbors' business out.
It's wicked! But one can't escape their talk.
And our young pair?
MEPHISTOPHELES: Gone fluttering up that garden walk;
Wild wayward butterflies!
MARTHA: He seems to have found
His true love.
MEPHISTOPHELES: So has she. That's how the world goes round!

A Summerhouse

[*Margareta runs in, hides behind the door, puts a fingertip to her lips and peeps through a crack.*]

MARGARETA: He's coming!
FAUST [*entering*]: Little rogue! I've caught you now,
You tease! [*He kisses her.*]
MARGARETA [*throwing her arms round him and returning his kiss*]:
Darling, I love you so. I can't say how!

[*Mephistopheles knocks at the door.*]

FAUST [*stamping his foot*]: Who's there?

MEPHISTOPHELES: A friend!
FAUST: A beast!
MEPHISTOPHELES: It's time to leave, I fear.
MARTHA [*entering*]: Yes, sir, it's getting late.
FAUST: May I not escort you, then?
MARGARETA: My mother would—Goodbye!
FAUST: Then I must go, my dear?
Goodbye!
MARTHA: Adieu!
MARGARETA: Till we soon meet again!

[*Faust and Mephistopheles leave.*]

Oh goodness gracious, what a lot
Of clever thoughts in his head he's got!
I'm so ashamed, I just agree
With all he says, poor silly me.
I'm just a child and don't know a thing,
How can he find me so interesting?

from A FOREST CAVERN

FAUST [*alone*]: Oh sublime Spirit![2] You have given me,
Given me all I asked for. From the fire
You turned your face to me, and not in vain.
You gave me Nature's splendor for my kingdom,
And strength to grasp it with my heart. No mere
Cold curious inspection was the privilege
You granted me, but to gaze deep, as into
The heart of a dear friend. Before my eyes,
Opened by you, all living creatures move
In sequence: in the quiet woods, the air,
The water, now I recognize my brothers.
And when the storm-struck forest roars and jars,
When giant pines crash down, whose crushing fall
Tears neighboring branches, neighboring tree-trunks with them,
And drones like hollow thunder through the hills:
Then in this cavern's refuge, where you lead me,
You show me to myself, and my own heart's
Profound mysterious wonders are disclosed.
And when the pure moon lifts its soothing light
As I look skywards, then from rocky cliffs
And dewy thickets the ensilvered shapes
Of a lost world, hovering there before me,
Assuage the austere joy of my contemplation.

Oh now I feel this truth, that for mankind
No boon is perfect. To such happiness,

2. The Earth Spirit (lines 460–513).

Which brings me ever nearer to the gods,
You added a companion, who already
Is indispensable to me, although
With one cold mocking breath he can degrade me
In my own eyes, and turn your gifts to nothing.
He stirs my heart into a burning fire
Of passion for that lovely woman's image.
Thus from my lust I stumble to fulfilment,
And in fulfilment for more lust I languish.

* * *[3]

Gretchen's Room

[*Gretchen at her spinning-wheel, alone.*]

GRETCHEN: My heart's so heavy,
My heart's so sore,
How can ever my heart
Be at peace any more?

How dead the whole world is,
How dark the day,
How bitter my life is
Now he's away!

My poor head's troubled,
Oh what shall I do?
My poor mind's broken
And torn in two.

My heart's so heavy,
My heart's so sore,
How can ever my heart
Be at peace any more?

When I look from my window
It's him I must see;
I walk out wondering
Where can he be?

Oh his step so proud
And his head so high
And the smile on his lips
And the spell of his eye,

And his voice, like a stream
Of magic it is,
And his hand pressing mine
And his kiss, his kiss!

My heart's so heavy,
My heart's so sore,

3. In the omitted lines Faust complains to Mephisto that he is torn by pity for Gretchen.

How can ever my heart
Be at peace any more?

My body's on fire
With wanting him so;
Oh when shall I hold him
And never let go

And kiss him at last
As I long to do,
And swoon on his kisses
And die there too!

MARTHA'S GARDEN

[*Margareta. Faust.*]

MARGARETA Promise me, Heinrich.
FAUST: Whatever I can!
MARGARETA: Then tell me what you think about religion.
I know you are a dear good man,
But it means little to you, I imagine.
FAUST: My darling, let's not talk of that. You know
I'd give my life for you, I love you so:
I wouldn't want to take anyone's faith away.
MARGARETA: One must believe! That's not right what you say!
FAUST: Ah, must one?
MARGARETA: Oh, if only I could show you!
You don't respect the holy Sacraments, do you?
FAUST: I do.
MARGARETA: But you don't want them! You don't go
To Mass or to confession, that I know.
Do you believe in God?
FAUST: My dear, how can
Anyone dare to say: I believe in Him?
Ask a priest how, ask a learned man,
And all their answers merely seem
To mock the questioner.
MARGARETA: Then you don't believe?
FAUST: My sweet beloved child, don't misconceive
My meaning! Who dare say God's name?
Who dares to claim
That he believes in God?
And whose heart is so dead
That he has ever boldly said:
No, I do not believe?
Embracing all things,
Holding all things in being,
Does He not hold and keep
You, me, even Himself?
Is not the heavens' great vault up there on high,

And here below, does not the earth stand fast?
Do everlasting stars, gleaming with love,
Not rise above us through the sky?
Are we not here and gazing eye to eye?
Does all this not besiege
Your mind and heart,
And weave in unseen visibility
All round you its eternal mystery?
Oh, fill your heart right up with all of this,
And when you're brimming over with the bliss
Of such a feeling, call it what you like!
Call it joy, or your heart, or love, or God!
I have no name for it. The feeling's all there is:
The name's mere noise and smoke—what does it do
But cloud the heavenly radiance?

MARGARETA: Well, I suppose all that makes sense;
I think the priest says something like that too—
Just in the wording there's a difference.

FAUST: It is what all men say,
All human hearts under the blessed day
Speak the same message, each
In its own speech:
May I not speak in mine?

MARGARETA: It sounds all very well, all very fine
But there's still something wrong about it,
For you're not a Christian, I truly doubt it!

FAUST: Sweetheart!

MARGARETA: It's always worried me
To see you keep such company.

FAUST: What do you mean?

MARGARETA: That man you have with you—
I hate him, upon my soul I do!
It pierces me to the heart like a knife.
I've seen nothing so dreadful in all my life
As that man's face and its ugly sneer.

FAUST: My poor child, why, there's nothing to fear!

MARGARETA: It's just that his presence offends me so!
I don't usually dislike people, you know!
And I'd gaze at you just as long as I can,
But it makes my blood freeze to see that man—
And I think he's a scoundrel, anyway.
If I wrong him, God pardon what I say!

FAUST: Well, you know, some people just are rather odd.

MARGARETA: I wouldn't live with a man like that!
As soon as he steps through the door, you can tell
You're being looked so mockingly at
And half fiercely as well;
And he cares for nothing, not man nor God.
It's as if he'd a mark on his brow that said

That he never has loved, that his heart is dead.
Each time you put your arms round me
I'm yours so completely, so warm, so free!
But I close up inside at the sight of him.

FAUST: Dear fancy, sweet foreboding whim!

MARGARETA: It upsets me so much, each time I see
Him coming, that I even doubt
If I still love you, when he's about.
Besides, when he's there, I never could pray,
And that's what's eating my heart away.
Dear Heinrich, tell me you feel the same way!

FAUST: You've just taken against him, and that's all.

MARGARETA: I must go home now.

FAUST: Oh, tell me whether
We can have some peaceful hour together,
Lie breast to breast and mingle soul with soul!

MARGARETA: Oh, if only I slept alone it would be all right,
I'd leave you my door unbolted tonight.
But my mother sleeps lightly, and if she
Were to wake up and catch us, oh goodness me,
I'd drop down dead on the very spot!

FAUST: My darling, there need be no such surprise.
Look, take this little flask I've got:
You must put just three drops in her drink
And into a sweet, sound sleep she'll sink.

MARGARETA: What would I not do for your sake!
But she'll be all right again, she'll wake?

FAUST: Would I suggest it otherwise?

MARGARETA: I look at you, dear Heinrich, and somehow
My will is yours, it's not my own will now.
Already I've done so many things for you,
There's—almost nothing left to do.

[*Exit. Enter Mephistopheles*]

MEPHISTOPHELES: Pert monkey! Has she gone?

FAUST: Still eavesdropping and spying?

MEPHISTOPHELES: I listened to it all most carefully.
The learned Doctor was catechized![4]
I hope he will find it edifying.
Girls always check up, if they're well-advised,
On one's simple old-world piety;
Their theory is, if he swallows all
That stuff, he'll be at our beck and call.

FAUST: To your vile mind, of course, it's merely quaint
That that dear loving soul, filled with her faith,
The only road to heaven that she knows,

4. Quizzed concerning his faith.

Should so torment herself, poor saint,
Thinking her lover's damned to everlasting death!
MEPHISTOPHELES: You supersensual sensual wooer,
A pretty maid has led you by the nose.
FAUST: You misborn monster, spawn of fire and shit!
MEPHISTOPHELES: And physiognomy,[5] how well she's mastered it!
When I'm around she feels—just what, she's not quite sure;
My face, forsooth! conceals some runic spell;
She guesses I'm a genius certainly,
Perhaps indeed the Devil as well.
So, it's to be tonight—?
FAUST: What's that to you?
MEPHISTOPHELES: I take a certain pleasure in it too!

At the Well

[*Gretchen and Lieschen with water jugs.*]

LIESCHEN: You've heard about Barbara, haven't you?
GRETCHEN: No; I hardly see anyone.
LIESCHEN: Well, it's true!
She's done it at last; Sybil told me today.
Made a fool of herself. That's always the way
With those airs and graces.
GRETCHEN: But what?
LIESCHEN: It stinks!
There's two to feed now when she eats and drinks!
GRETCHEN: Oh! . . .
LIESCHEN: And serve her right at last, I say.
Throwing herself at the lad for so long!
Always on his arm, always walking along,
Off to the villages, off to the dance;
Oh, she had an eye to the main chance!
Such a beauty, of course, she must lead the way!
He courts her with pastries and wine every day;
She's even so shameless, the little minx,
That she can accept presents from him, she thinks!
Cuddling and petting hour by hour—
Well, now she's lost her little flower!
GRETCHEN: Poor thing!
LIESCHEN: Don't tell me you're sorry for her!
Why, all the rest of us, there we were,
Spinning, our mothers not letting us out
In the evenings, while she's sitting about
In dark doorways with her fancy man,
Lingering in alleys as long as they can!
Well, now she'll have her church penance to do,

5. The "science" of discerning character from the face.

And sit in her smock on the sinner's pew!
GRETCHEN: But surely he'll marry her now!
LIESCHEN: Not he!
A smart boy like that, there are fish in the sea
In plenty for him; he's not such a fool!
Anyway, he's left.
GRETCHEN: That's wrong of him!
LIESCHEN: Well,
If she gets him, she'll get the rest of it too.
The boys'll snatch the flowers from her head,
And we'll throw her none, just chopped straw instead![6] [*Exit.*]

GRETCHEN [*as she walks home*]: What angry things I used to say
When some poor girl had gone astray!
I used to rack my brains to find
Words to condemn sins of that kind;
Blacker than black they seemed to be,
And were still not black enough for me,
And I crossed myself and made such a to-do—
Now that sin of others is my sin too!
Oh God! but all that made me do it
Was good, such dear love drove me to it!

By a Shrine Inside the Town Wall

[*An icon of the Mater Dolorosa stands in the above with vases of flowers in front of it. Gretchen puts fresh flowers into the vases, then prays.*]

GRETCHEN:
O Virgin Mother, thou
Who art full of sorrows, bow
Thy face in mercy to my anguish now!

O Lady standing by
Thy Son to watch Him die,
Thy heart is pierced to hear His bitter cry.

Seeking the Father there
Thy sighs rise through the air
From his death-agony, from thy despair.

Who else can know
The pain that so
Burns in my bones like fire from hell?
How my wretched heart is bleeding,
What it's dreading, what it's needing,
Lady, only you can tell!

6. Traditional behavior when an unwed mother married.

Wherever I go, wherever,
It never stops, just never;
Oh how it hurts and aches!
When I'm alone, I'm crying,
I cry as if I'm dying,
I cry as my heart breaks.

The flower-pots by my window
I watered with tears like dew
When in the early morning
I picked these flowers for you.

The early sun was gleaming,
I sat up in my bed
My eyes already streaming
As the new dawn turned red.
Help! Save me from shame and death!—O thou
Who art full of sorrows, thou
Most holy Virgin, bow
Thy face in mercy to my anguish now!

NIGHT. THE STREET OUTSIDE GRETCHEN'S DOOR

VALENTINE [*a soldier, Gretchen's brother*]:
I used to drink with the other chaps;
That's when one likes to boast. Perhaps
They'd start to sing their girl-friends' praises—
All lovely girls, like a ring of roses;
And round and round the full toasts went.
I'd sit there calm and confident,
With my elbows on the table-top;
Sit there and stroke my beard meanwhile,
Wait for their blethering to stop,
Then fill my glass and with a smile
I'd say: All honor where honor's due!
But in this whole land is there one girl who
Can compare with Meg, my sister so sweet,
One worthy to fasten the shoes to her feet?
Then clink! The toasts went round again,
And some of the fellows exclaimed: he's right!
She's the pride of her sex, she's the heart's delight!
And the boasters and praisers sat silent then.
And now—what now?—Shall I tear my hair,
Shall I run up the walls?—I could despair.
Every one of those blackguards now is free
To sneer and wrinkle his nose at me;
I must sweat, like a debtor who can't pay,
At each chance remark that drops my way!
Oh, yes! I could knock out their brains! But why?
I still couldn't tell them they're telling a lie!

Who's there? Who's sneaking to her door?
There are two of them, if I know the score.
If it's him, I'll take him while I can—
He'll not leave here a living man!

[*Enter Faust and Mephistopheles.*]

FAUST: Look, through the window of the sacristy
The sanctuary lamp gleams up and glows,
Yet to each side, how dim, how weak it shows,
As darkness clusters round it! So in me
Night falls and thickens in my heart.

MEPHISTOPHELES: Well, I could act a tom-cat's part,
Slinking the streets to find a way
Up to the rooftops where I'll play!
I feel a healthy appetite
For some thieving, some lechery tonight.
Walpurgis, Night of the Wild Witching,[7]
Is coming soon; already I'm twitching
With expectation. Just you wait!
One doesn't sleep through that fine date.

FAUST: Is that your buried gold that's rising now,[8]
Back there? It blooms, it shines at us somehow!

MEPHISTOPHELES: Quite so; you soon will have the pleasure
Of lifting out the pot of treasure.
I took a squint into it too;
Fine silver coins I've raised for you.

FAUST: Was there no jewelry you could find?
My mistress loves those golden toys.

MEPHISTOPHELES: I did see something of the kind;
A necklace. Pearls that are her eyes.[9]

FAUST: That's good; it makes me sad to go
Without a gift to her, you know.

MEPHISTOPHELES: Come now, you should get used to ladies;
Sometimes one enjoys their favors gratis.
But look! The stars are in the sky,
And being a gifted artist, I
Will now sing her a moral song,
To confuse her sense of right and wrong.

[*He sings, accompanying himself on a zither.*]

Who stands before
Her sweetheart's door
Once more, once more,

7. See note to line 2590.
8. In lines 2675–77 (omitted from our selection) Mephisto has implied that he will locate buried treasure to seduce Gretchen. There was a folk belief that buried treasure would shine at night.
9. This allusion to a famous song in Shakespeare's *Tempest* does not originate with Goethe but was added by the translator, in the spirit of the many other Shakespeare allusions in *Faust.*

With early morning starting?
Poor Kate, beware!
You'll enter there
A maid so fair—
No maid you'll be departing!

Men must have fun,
But when it's done
They'll up and run—
They're thieves, why should they linger?
Poor darlings all,
Beware your fall:
Do nothing at all
Till you've got the ring on your finger!

VALENTINE: Who are you serenading here?
Damned ratcatcher![1] The devil take
Your zither first; God's blood! I'll make
Him take the singer next, d'you hear?
MEPHISTOPHELES: The instrument's a write-off, I'm afraid.
VALENTINE: Now draw, and there'll be corpses made!
MEPHISTOPHELES: Doctor, don't back away! Now, quick!
Keep close to me, move as I do.
Come on, out with your tickle-stick!
Now lunge! I'll parry him for you.
VALENTINE: Well, parry this one!
MEPHISTOPHELES: Certainly!
VALENTINE: And that!
MEPHISTOPHELES: Why not?
VALENTINE: The devil it must be!
What fencing's this? I think my hand's gone lame.
MEPHISTOPHELES [*to Faust*]: Strike now!
VALENTINE [*falling*]: Oh God!
MEPHISTOPHELES: Now the poor lout is tame!
But now let's go! We must get out of here;
They'll start a hue and cry, and all that chatter.
The police I can deal with, but I fear
The High Assize is quite another matter.[2]

[*Exit with Faust.*]

MARTHA [*at her window*]: Come out! Come out!
GRETCHEN [*at her window*]: Please, fetch a light!
MARTHA: They're cursing and shouting! There's a fight!
THE CROWD [*gathering*]: There's someone dead, there's one!
MARTHA [*coming out of her house*]: Where did the murderers run?

1. A triple allusion: (1) to Mephisto's self-description as a "tomcat" a few lines earlier, though Valentine cannot actually hear the conversation between Mephisto and Faust; (2) to the Pied Piper of Hamelin, subject of a ballad by Goethe; (3) to a line in Shakespeare's *Midsummer Night's Dream* (3.1.75) leading up to a deadly duel: "Tybalt, you ratcatcher, will you walk?"
2. The high court pronounced sentence in God's name, causing problems for Mephisto.

GRETCHEN [*coming out of her house*]: Who's lying here?
THE CROWD: Your mother's son.
GRETCHEN: Oh God in heaven! What have they done!
VALENTINE: I'm dying; it's a thing soon said,
And even sooner the thing's real.
You women-folk, why weep and wail?
Just hear me speak before I'm dead.

[*They all gather round him.*]

Meg, listen: you're still a poor young chit,
You've not yet got the hang of it,
You're bungling things, d'you see?
Just let me tell you in confidence:
Since you're a whore now, have some sense
And do it properly!
GRETCHEN: My brother! God! What do you mean?
VALENTINE: Leave God out of this little scene!
What's done is done, I'm sorry to say,
And things must go their usual way.
You started in secret with one man;
Soon others will come where he began,
And when a dozen have joined the queue
The whole town will be having you!

Let me tell you about disgrace:
It enters the world as a secret shame,
Born in the dark without a name,
With the hood of night about its face.
It's something that you'll long to kill.
But as it grows, it makes its way
Even into the light of day;
It's bigger, but it's ugly still!
The filthier its face has grown,
The more it must be seen and shown.

There'll come a time, and this I know,
All decent folk will abhor you so,
You slut! That like a plague-infected
Corpse you'll be shunned, you'll be rejected,
They'll look at you and your heart will quail,
Their eyes will all tell the same tale!
You'll have no gold chains or jewelry then,
Never stand in church by the altar again,
Never have any pretty lace to wear
At the dance, for you'll not be dancing there!
Into some dark corner may you creep
Among beggars and cripples to hide and weep;
And let God forgive you as he may—
But on earth be cursed till your dying day!

MARTHA: Commend your soul to God's mercy too!
Will you die with blasphemy on you?
VALENTINE: Vile hag, vile bawd! If I could take
You by the skinny throat and shake
The life out of you, that alone,
For all my sins it would atone.
GRETCHEN: Oh, brother—how can I bear it—how—
VALENTINE: I tell you, tears won't mend things now.
When you and your honor came to part,
That's when you stabbed me to the heart.
I'll meet my Maker presently—
As the soldier I'm still proud to be.

[*He dies.*]

A Cathedral

[*A Mass for the Dead. Organ and choral singing. Gretchen in a large congregation. An Evil Spirit behind Gretchen.*]

THE EVIL SPIRIT: How different things were for you, Gretchen,
When you were still all innocence,
Approaching that altar,
Lisping prayers from your little
Worn prayer-book;
Your heart had nothing in it
But God and child's play!
Gretchen!
What are you thinking?
What misdeed burdens
Your heart now? Are you praying
For your mother's soul, who by your doing
Overslept into long, long purgatorial pains?
Whose blood stains your doorstep?
—And under your heart is there not
Something stirring, welling up already,
A foreboding presence,
Feared by you and by itself?
GRETCHEN: Oh God! Oh God!
If I could get rid of these thoughts
That move across me and through me,
Against my will!
THE CHOIR: *Dies irae, dies illa*
Solvet saeclum in favilla.[3]

[*Organ.*]

THE EVIL SPIRIT: God's wrath seizes you!
The Last Trumpet scatters its sound!

3. A Latin hymn, part of the Requiem Mass for the dead: "Day of wrath, that day / Shall dissolve the world into cinders."

The graves shudder open!
And your heart
That was at rest in its ashes
Is resurrected in fear,
Fanned again to the flames
Of its torment!

GRETCHEN: Let me get away from here!
It's as if the organ
Were choking me
And the singing melting
The heart deep down in me!

THE CHOIR: *Judex ergo cum sedebit,*
Quidquid latet adparebit,
Nil inultum remanebit.[4]

GRETCHEN: I can't breathe!
The great pillars
Are stifling me,
The vaulted roof
Crushes me!—Give me air!

THE EVIL SPIRIT: Hide yourself! Sin and shame
Cannot be hidden,
Air? Light?
Woe on you!

THE CHOIR: *Quid sum miser tunc dicturus?*
Quem patronum rogaturus,
Cum vix justus sit securus?[5]

THE EVIL SPIRIT: Souls in bliss
Have turned their faces from you.
They shrink from touching you,
For they are pure!
Woe!

THE CHOIR:
Quid sum miser tunc dicturus?

GRETCHEN: Neighbor! Your smelling-salts!

[*She faints.*]

* * *[6]

A Gloomy Day. Open Country.

[*Faust and Mephistopheles.*]

FAUST: In misery! In despair! Pitiably wandering about the country for so long, and now a prisoner! Locked up in prison as a criminal and suffering such torment, the sweet hapless creature! So this is what it has come to! This!—Vile treacherous

4. "Thus when the judge sits, / everything hidden will be manifest / and nothing will remain unavenged."

5. "What am I, miserable, then to say? / What patron shall I call on? / When scarcely the just man is secure?"

6. Mephisto next leads Faust to the orgy at the Walpurgis Night (see note to line 2590). Faust is caught up in the wild dancing until distracted by a vision of Gretchen.

demon, and you told me nothing!—Yes, stand there, stand there and roll your devilish eyes in fury! Stand and affront me by your unendurable presence! A prisoner! In utter ruin, delivered over to evil spirits and the judgment of cold heartless mankind! And meanwhile you lull me with vulgar diversions, hide her growing plight from me and leave her helpless to her fate!

MEPHISTOPHELES: She is not the first.

FAUST: You dog! You repulsive monster! Oh infinite Spirit, change him back, change this reptile back into the form of a dog, the shape he used so often when it amused him to trot along ahead of me at night, suddenly rolling at the feet of innocent wayfarers and leaping on their backs as they fell! Change him back into his favorite shape, let him crawl before me in the sand on his belly, let me trample this reprobate under my feet!—Not the first!—Oh grief, grief that no human soul can grasp, to think that more than one creature has sunk to such depths of wretchedness, that the sins of all the others were not expiated even by the first, as it writhed in its death-agony before the eyes of the eternally merciful God! I am stricken to my life's very marrow by the misery of this one girl—and you calmly sneer at the fate of thousands!

MEPHISTOPHELES: Well, here we are again at the end of our wit's tether, the point where your poor human brains always snap! Why do you make common cause with us, if you can't stand the pace? Why try to fly if you've no head for heights? Did we force ourselves on you, or you on us?

FAUST: Stop baring your greedy fangs at me, it makes me sick!—Oh you great splendid Spirit, who deigned to appear to me, who know my heart and my soul, why did you chain me to this vile companion, who gorges his appetite on ruin and drinks refreshment from destruction?

MEPHISTOPHELES: Have you done talking?

FAUST: Save her! Or woe betide you! May the most hideous curse lie upon you for thousands of years!

MEPHISTOPHELES: I cannot loose the Avenger's bonds or open his bolts!—Save her!—Who was it who ruined her? I, or you?

[*Faust glares about him in speechless rage.*]

Are you snatching for the thunder? A good thing it was not given to you wretched mortals, to blast your adversary when he makes an innocent reply! That's the way of tyrants, venting their spleen when they're in an embarrassing pass.

FAUST: Take me to her! I'll have her set free!

MEPHISTOPHELES: And what of the risk you'll run? I tell you, on that town there lies blood-guilt by your hand. Over the grave of the man you killed there hover avenging spirits, waiting for the murderer to return.

FAUST: Must I hear that from you too? May the murder and death of a world come upon you, you monster! Take me to her, I tell you, and free her!

MEPHISTOPHELES: I will take you, and I will tell you what I can do. Have I all the power in heaven and earth? I will bemuse the jailer's senses, you can take his keys and bring her out with your own human hand! I'll keep watch, the magic horses will be ready, and I'll carry you both to safety. That I can do.

FAUST: Let's go at once!

Night. In Open Country.

[*Faust and Mephistopheles storming past on black horses.*]

FAUST: What's that moving around on the gallows-mound?
MEPHISTOPHELES: I don't know what they're doing and stewing.
FAUST: Up and down they hover, they stoop, they swoop.
MEPHISTOPHELES: A guild of witches!
FAUST: They're scattering something, it's a ritual deed.
MEPHISTOPHELES: Ride on! Ride on!

A Prison

FAUST [*with a bundle of keys and a lamp, by a small iron door*]:
That shudder comes again—how long a time
Since last I felt this grief for all man's woe!
She lies behind this cold, damp wall, I know;
And her loving heart's illusion was her crime.
Do I pause as I enter this place?
Am I afraid to see her face?
Quick! She must die if I keep hesitating so.

[*He grasps the lock. Margareta's voice sings from inside.*]

MARGARETA: Who killed me dead?
My mother, the whore!
Who ate my flesh?
My father, for sure!
Little sister gathered
The bones he scattered;
In a cool, cool place they lie.
And then I became a birdie so fine,
And away I fly—away I fly.
FAUST [*unlocking the door*]:
She doesn't know her lover's listening at the door,
Hearing the clank of chains, straw rustling on the floor.

[*He enters the cell.*]

MARGARETA [*hiding her face on her straw mattress*]:
Oh! Oh! They're coming! Bitter death!
FAUST [*softly*]: Quiet! Quiet! I've come to set you free.
MARGARETA [*crawling towards his feet*]: If you are human, then have pity on me!
FAUST: You'll waken the jailers, speak under your breath!

[*He takes up her chains to unlock them.*]

MARGARETA [*on her knees*]: Oh, hangman, who gave you this power
Over me? Who said
You could fetch me at this midnight hour?
Have pity! Tomorrow morning I'll be dead,
Isn't that soon enough for you?

[*She stands up.*]

I'm still so young, still so young too!
And already I must die!
I was pretty too, and that's the reason why.
My lover was with me, now he's far away.
They tore my garland off, and threw the flowers away.
Why are you clutching at me like this?
Oh spare me! What have I done amiss?
Let me live! Must I beg you, must I implore
You in vain? I've never even seen you before!

FAUST: How can I bear this any more!

MARGARETA: I'm in your power now, I'm ready to go.
Just let me feed my baby first.
I was cuddling it all last night, you know.
They took it from me; that was just
To hurt me. I killed it, is what they say.
Now things will never be the same.
They're wicked people: they sing songs against me!
There's an old tale that ends that way—
Who told them it meant me?

FAUST [*throwing himself at her feet*]:
It's your lover, I'm here at your feet, I came
To free you from this dreadful place!

MARGARETA [*kneeling down beside him*]:
Oh, let's kneel, and call on the saints for grace!
Look, under that stair,
Under the door,
Hell's boiling there!
You can hear the voice
Of his angry roar!

FAUST [*aloud*]: Gretchen! Gretchen!

MARGARETA [*hearing her name*]: That was my lover's voice!

[*She jumps to her feet. Her chains fall off.*]

Where is he? I heard him call to me.
No one shall stop me, I am free!
To his arms I'll fly,
On his breast I'll lie!
He stood and called "Gretchen"! I recognized him!
Through the wailing and gnashing of Hell so grim,
Through the Devil's rage, through his scorn and sneer,
I knew it was his voice, so loving and dear!

FAUST: I am here!

MARGARETA: It is you! Oh, tell me once again!
[*Embracing him.*] It's him! It's him! Where's all my suffering, then?
Where are my chains, my prison and my fear?
It's you! You've come to rescue me from here
And I am saved!—

I think it's here again, that street
Where I first saw you; and by and by
We're waiting again, Martha and I,
In that lovely garden where we used to meet.

FAUST [*trying to leave with her*]: Come! Come with me!

MARGARETA: Oh stay!
I love being anywhere when you're not away!

[*Caressing him.*]

FAUST: No, don't delay!
Or we shall have to pay
Most bitterly for this!

MARGARETA: What, you've forgotten so soon how to kiss?
We're together again, my sweetest friend,
And our kissing's come to an end?
In your arms, why do I tremble so?
A whole heaven used to close in on me,
You spoke and you looked so lovingly;
I was stifled with kisses, you'd never let go.
Oh kiss me now!
Or I'll show you how!

[*She embraces him.*]

Oh! Your lips are dumb,
They've nothing to say!
Why has your love gone cold?
Who can have come
Between us to take it away?

[*She turns away from him.*]

FAUST: Come! Follow me! Darling, you must be bold!
I'll hug you later on ten-thousandfold,
Just follow me now! It's all I ask of you!

MARGARETA [*turning to him*]: But is it you, can it be really true?

FAUST: It's me! Come!

MARGARETA: You undid my chains, they fell apart,
And you will take me back to your heart.
How is it you don't find me a vile thing?
Do you really know, my dear, who you are rescuing?

FAUST: Come! Come! The deep night's giving way to dawn!

MARGARETA: My mother's dead; I poisoned her, you see.
I drowned my child when it was born.
Hadn't it been God's gift to you and me?
To you as well—It is you! Can I trust
This not to be a dream?
Your hand! Your dear hand!—Ugh, but it's wet! You must
Wipe off the blood! To me there seem
To be bloodstains on it. Oh my God,
What did you do!

Put away your sword,
I beg of you!
FAUST: Forget what happened, let it be!
You are killing me.
MARGARETA: Oh no, you must survive!
I'll tell you about the graves now, I'll describe
Them to you. You must arrange all this,
Tomorrow as ever is.
You must choose the places. Mother must have the best,
And my brother right next to her with his,
And me a little further off—
But not too far! Just far enough.
And my little baby at my right breast.
There'll be no one else to lie with me!—
When I clung to your side so tenderly,
Oh, that was so blessed, a joy so sweet!
But I can't seem to do it now as I could;
When I come, I seem to be dragging my feet,
And you seem to be pushing me back somehow.
Yet it's still you, you're still gentle and good!
FAUST: If you feel that it's me, come with me now!
MARGARETA: Out there?
FAUST: Into freedom!
MARGARETA: If my grave's out there,
If death is waiting, come with me! No,
From here to my everlasting tomb
And not one step further I'll go!—
You're leaving? Oh Heinrich, if only I could come!
FAUST: You can! Just want to! I've opened the door!
MARGARETA: I can't leave; for me there's no hope any more.
What's the use of escaping? They'll be watching for me.
It's so wretched to have to beg one's way
Through life, and with a bad conscience too,
And to wander abroad; and if I do,
In the end they'll catch me anyway!
FAUST: I'll stay with you always!
MARGARETA: Quick, oh, quick!
Save your poor baby!
Just follow the path
Up the stream, uphill,
Over the bridge,
The wood's just beyond;
In there, on the left, by the fence—
He's in the pond!
Oh, catch hold of him!
He's struggling still,
He's trying to swim!
Save him! Save him!
FAUST: Oh, stop, stop! Think what it is you say!

Just one step, and we're on our way.
MARGARETA: Oh, quick, let's get to the other side
Of the hill! My mother sits on a stone
Up there—oh it's cold, I'm so terrified!—
My mother's sitting up there on a stone,
She's wagging her head, she's all alone,
Not beckoning, not nodding her poor heavy head;
She slept so long that she'll never wake.
She slept so that we could be happy in bed!
Oh, those were good times, and no mistake.
FAUST: If persuasion's no use, if that's how it must be,
I'll have to carry you off with me.
MARGARETA: Don't touch me! Put me down! No, no!
I'll not be compelled! Don't clutch me so!
I was always willing, as well you know.
FAUST: The day's dawning! Oh sweetheart! Sweetheart!
MARGARETA: The day! Yes, it's day! The last day dawning!
I thought it would be my wedding morning.
Now you've been with Gretchen, don't tell anyone.
Oh, my garland's spoilt!
What's done is done!
We'll meet later on;
But I shan't be dancing.
I can't hear them, but the crowd's advancing.
There are so many there,
The streets and the square
Are all full; the bell tolls; they break the white rod.[7]
Oh how they bind me and seize me, oh God!
Now I'm on the execution-chair,
And at every neck in this whole great throng
The blade strikes when that sword is swung.
The world lies silent as the grave.
FAUST: Oh why was I born, at such a cost!
MEPHISTOPHELES [*appearing outside the door*]:
Come! One more moment and you're lost!
What's all this dallying, parleying and dithering!
My night-steeds are quivering,
The sun's nearly risen.
MARGARETA: What's that? It came out of the floor of my prison!
It's him! It's him! Send him away!
He can't come! This place is sacred today!
He wants me!
FAUST: You're to live!
MARGARETA: Oh my God, I await
Your righteous judgment!
MEPHISTOPHELES [*to Faust*]:
Come! Come! Or I'll leave

7. Sign of final condemnation.

You both to your fate!
MARGARETA: Oh Father, save me, do not reject me,
I am yours! Oh holy angels, receive
Me under your wings, surround me, protect me!—
Heinrich! You frighten me.
MEPHISTOPHELES: She is condemned!
A VOICE [*from above*]: She is redeemed!
MEPHISTOPHELES [*to Faust*]: Come to me!

[*He vanishes with Faust.*]

[*Margareta's*] VOICE [*from the cell, dying away*]: Heinrich! Heinrich!

Faust

PART II

ACT 1

A BEAUTIFUL LANDSCAPE

[*Faust, lying among grass and flowers, exhausted and restless, trying to sleep. Dusk. Spirits, graceful little shapes, hovering and circling round.*]

ARIEL[1] [*his song accompanied by Aeolian harps*]:

When the blossoms hovering
Rain on meadows green and new,
All earth's children feel the spring,
Bright with universal dew.
Come then, little elfin spirits,
All alike to help and bless;
Ours to heed no sins or merits
But to pity man's distress.
You, round this mortal's head circling in air,
Heal now his heart, in noble elfin fashion:
Soothe its fierce conflict and the bitter passion
Of self-reproach's burning darts, make clean
His soul of all the horrors it has seen.
Four are night's vigils:[2] now with fair
Contentment fill each one immediately.
First lay his head where it is soft and cool,
Then bathe him in the dew of Lethe:[3] see,
His clenched limbs will relax, he will be free,
As he gains strength and feels the day before him.
Obey the highest elfin rule,
And to the sacred light restore him!

1. The spirit of the air in Shakespeare's *Tempest.* The wind harps that accompany him are associated with poetic inspiration.

2. The three-hour segments into which the night watch was divided.

3. The classical river of forgetfulness between the land of the living and the land of the dead.

CHORUS [*singly and in two or more voices, by turns and together*]:

When a fragrance has descended
All about the green-girt plain,
Richer air with mist-clouds blended,
Evening dusk comes down again;
Lulls to infant-sweet reposing,
Rocks the heart with whispering sighs,
And this wanderer feels it closing
On his daylight-weary eyes.

Now to night the world surrenders,
Sacred love joins star to star;
Little sparkles, greater splendors,
Glitter near and gleam from far,
Glitter in the lake reflecting,
Gleam against the clear night sky;
Deepest seals of rest protecting
Glows the full moon strong and high.

Soon the hours have slipped away,
Pain and happiness are past;
Trust the light of the new day,
Feel your sickness will not last!
Green the valleys, hillsides swelling,
Bushing thick to restful shade,
And the fields, their wealth foretelling,
Rippling ripe and silver-swayed!

Have you wishes without number?
Watch the promise of the dawn!
Lightly you are wrapped in slumber:
Shed this husk and be reborn!
Venture boldly; hesitation
Is for lesser men—when deeds
Are a noble mind's creation,
All his enterprise succeeds.

[*A tremendous roaring sound heralds the approach of the sun.*]

ARIEL: Hear the tempest of the Hours![4]

For to spirit-ears like ours
Day makes music at its birth.
Hear it! Gates of rock are sundering
And the sun-god's wheels are thundering:
See, with noise light shakes the earth!
Hear it blare, its trumpets calling,
Dazzling eyes and ears appalling,
Speechless sound unheard for dread!

4. Greek goddesses of the seasons, often associated with the sun-god.

Quickly, into flowers deep,
Into rocks and foliage creep,
Hide where elves in silence sleep:
Ear it strikes is stricken dead.

FAUST: How strong and pure the pulse of life is beating!
Dear earth, this night has left you still unshaken,
And at my feet you breathe refreshed; my greeting
To you, ethereal dawn! New joys awaken
All round me at your bidding: beckoning distance,
New-stirring strength, new resolution taken
To strive on still towards supreme existence.—
A gloaming-shine reveals the reborn world,
The forest sings with myriad-voiced insistence,
Through vale and dale the morning mists have curled,
But heaven's radiance pierces them, descending,
And branch and bough appear, revived, unfurled
From the vaporous chasm, their slumber ending,
Now deep-down colors grow distinct, as flower
And leaf gleam moistly, tremulous pearls suspending.
Oh paradise again, oh encircling power!

Let me look up!—Each giant summit-height
Proclaims already this most solemn hour:
They are the first to taste the eternal light,
As we shall, when its downward course is ended.
Now the green-slanting meadow-slopes are bright
Again, each detail new and clear and splendid,
And day spreads stepwise with the dark's downsinking:
See, the sun rises!—But my eyes offended
Turn away dazzled, from this great sight shrinking.

And thus, when with our heart's whole hope for guide
Towards our goal we have struggled on unthinking,
And find fulfilment's portals open wide—
From those unfathomed depths a sudden mass
Of fire bursts forth, we stand amazed: we tried
To set the torch of life alight—alas,
A sea of flame engulfs us, ah what flame
Of love or hate, burning, consuming us
With pain and joy, which strangely seem the same!
We look back earthwards, hiding from this blaze
Behind a youthful veil of awestruck shame.

So be it! I will turn from the sun's rays.
At that rock-riving torrent, with increasing
Ecstasy at that waterfall I gaze:
From cliff to cliff it pours down never-ceasing,
It foams and streams a thousand thousandfold,
Spray upon spray high in the air releasing.
But from this tumult, marvelous to behold,
The rainbow blooms, changing yet ever still;

Now vanishing and now drawn clear and bold.
How cool the moisture of its scattering spill!
I watch a mirror here of man's whole story,
And plain it speaks, ponder it as you will:
Our life's a spectrum-sheen of borrowed glory.

* * *[5]

A Dark Gallery

[*Faust. Mephistopheles.*]

MEPHISTOPHELES: These gloomy passages! Why do you drag me here?
Was all that high society
Not fun enough? There's plenty of good cheer
Still to enjoy, and much fine trickery!

FAUST: No need to speak of it; in the old days
You played that game a hundred tedious ways.
Now stop your slithering to and fro
And tell me what I need to know.
They're pestering me now for action:
The Steward, the Chamberlain want satisfaction.
The Emperor demands to see
Helen and Paris, here, immediately;
The ideal man and woman, to appear
Before his eyes, in figures plain and clear.
So get to work! I mustn't break my word.

MEPHISTOPHELES: You promised that? How frivolous, how absurd!

FAUST: Let me inform you that your pranks
Have consequences, my good friend.
We made him rich and earned his thanks,
And now he must be entertained.

MEPHISTOPHELES: You think this task's a simple one;
But it's a steeper stair to climb,
A stranger region than you've ever known,
Which by your new commitments you now dare
To tread, conjuring Helen out of time
Like phantom paper-money from the air.
Easy, you think?—Witches I can supply,
Ghost-goblins, changelings, curious succubi;
But Satan-sweethearts, though quite charming in their way,
Can't pass for Homer's heroines even today.

FAUST: So, here we go again, your old lament!
With you there's never any guarantee;
Nothing gets done without an extra fee,
Everything is a problem you invent.

5. In omitted scenes Mephisto, posing as jester at a decadent Renaissance court, leads Faust in an elaborate masque. Fire breaks out and Faust saves the Emperor by extinguishing it. Mephisto has printed paper money to "magically" revive the failing economy. During the festivities, the Emperor has commanded Mephisto and Faust to show him the Greek beauty Helen, over whom the Trojan War was fought after the Trojan prince Paris abducted her. Since Helen is a classical figure beyond the reach of the Christian devil, Mephisto enlists Faust's aid.

She'll come at once, as I know very well!
Two mumbled words from you will summon her.
MEPHISTOPHELES: Pagans are not my period, sir;
They're lodged in their own special hell.
But there's a way.
FAUST: Divulge it instantly!
MEPHISTOPHELES: I do not like to; this is high mystery.
Enthroned in solitude are goddesses—
No place, no space around them, time still less;
I mention them with some uneasiness.
They are *the Mothers.*[6]
FAUST [*startled*]: Mothers!
MEPHISTOPHELES: You dread the name?
FAUST: The Mothers! But how strange "the mothers" sounds!
MEPHISTOPHELES: Indeed; we hesitate ourselves to speak
Of these great goddesses, and your mortal minds
Have never known them. Go to the depths to seek
Their dwelling! If we need them, you're to blame.
FAUST: Which is the way?
MEPHISTOPHELES: No way! A path untrodden
Which none may tread; a way to the forbidden,
The unmoved, the inexorable. Make preparation!
There'll be no locks to unlock, no bolts to slide:
On solitudes you will drift far and wide.
Do you know solitude and desolation?
FAUST: If these are your wise saws, you might as well
Not speak. They've a witch-kitchen smell;
This is all stuff from long ago.
The world was with me, was it not? And there
I learnt and taught nothing but empty air.
If ever I talked sense, told what I know,
They'd shout me down still louder; finally,
Embracing desert solitude to flee
From the vile tricks society played on me,
Rather than have no company at all
I invoked the Devil, as you will recall.
MEPHISTOPHELES: Yet even if you'd swum the ocean through
And known its boundlessness, even then
You would see waves roll by and roll again;
Even at the dreadful drowning-point, there too
You would see something. In the still sea-green
There would be darting dolphins to be seen;
There'd be the clouds, sun, moon and starry sky—
But in the eternal void you'll say goodbye
To sight, not hear the step that steps so far,
Not rest a foot on where you are.

6. Goethe apparently drew the name "the Mothers" from vague Classical sources, but there is no precedent for Mephisto's fantastic and comic use of the name.

FAUST: You talk like any ancient mystagogue[7]
Addressing neophytes with words to fog
Their simple minds; but here *per contra.*[8] I
Am sent into your void to magnify
My art and strength there; I am to cat's-paw
Your chestnuts from the fire. Come then! let's claw
The meaning out of this. I hope to see
Your Nothing turn to Everything for me.

MEPHISTOPHELES: My compliments, sir, as you take your leave;
You know the Devil well, I do believe.
Now take this key.

FAUST: That little thing!

MEPHISTOPHELES: First seize
It firmly, and respect it, if you please.

FAUST: It grows in my hand! It shines, it's all a-glitter!

MEPHISTOPHELES: Perhaps you now appreciate it better.
Follow it downwards, for this key can read
The hidden map: to the Mothers it will lead.

FAUST [*shuddering*]: The Mothers! Every time it strikes such fear
Into my heart, this word I dare not hear.

MEPHISTOPHELES: Are you so limited, that a new word
Disturbs you, merely one you've not yet heard?
Let nothing trouble you in sound or sense:
By now you should be used to strange events.

FAUST: Yet must I turn to stone? Not so I'll thrive!
Our sense of awe's what keeps us most alive.
The world chokes human feeling more and more,
But deep dread still can move us to the core.

MEPHISTOPHELES: Descend then! I could say ascend; there's no
Distinction. Flee from all that has been born
To the unbound realm of empty shapes; return
To savor what has vanished long ago.
Like drifting coils of cloud they will approach you:
Brandish the key, for then they cannot touch you.

FAUST [*with enthusiasm*]: I seize it, and at once my spirits rise,
I feel new strength for this great enterprise.

MEPHISTOPHELES: A glowing tripod will alert your fall
That it has reached the deepest depth of all.
And by that tripod's light you'll see the Mothers;
Some sitting, as the case may be, and others
Who stand or walk. Formation, transformation,
The eternal Mind's eternal delectation.
You'll pass unseen: the whole world of creatures swarms
As images round them; they see empty forms
And nothing else. But you will be in great

7. Leader of a mystic cult.

8. On the contrary.

Peril still, and you must be bold: go straight
To the tripod, touch it with the key.

[*Faust strikes a decisive commanding attitude with the key.*]

MEPHISTOPHELES [*watching him*]: Just so!
Then, slave-like, it will follow where you go;
Good fortune's wings will raise you, never fear!
Before they miss it, you'll be back up here.
And once you've got that brazier, then you may
Summon the famous pair into the day.
No one has ever dared before to do
This deed, and it will be achieved by you.
The incense-cloud, with magic to compel it,
Will assume any godlike shape you tell it.
FAUST: Well then, what now?
MEPHISTOPHELES: Strive downwards; stamp, and you
Will sink; you'll rise again by stamping too.

[*Faust stamps and disappears into the earth.*]

I hope he's well protected by that key.
Will he get back, I wonder? We shall see.

* * *[9]

ACT 2

A LABORATORY

[*In medieval style, with elaborate clumsy apparatus for fantastic purposes.*]

WAGNER [*at his furnace*]: That dreadful bell's reverberation
Comes shuddering through the sooty walls.
Too long my doubtful expectation
Has waited for what now befalls.
From blackness to illumination
The deep alembic[1] now has passed,
And like a living coal at last
A fine carbuncular[2] fire is glowing,
Into the dark its brilliance throwing:
An incandescent white shines through!
Let me succeed, just this once more!—
Oh God, who's rattling at my door?
MEPHISTOPHELES [*entering*]: A well-meant greeting, sir, to you!
WAGNER [*anxiously*]: Greetings, by this hour's ruling star!
[*sotto voce*[3]]: But hold your words and breath: I am not far
From a great work's goal, now to be displayed.
MEPHISTOPHELES [*sotto voce*]: What great work's that?
WAGNER [*in a whisper*]: A man is being made.

9. Faust projects an image of Helen on a screen. He falls in love with her, as do the men at court. Chaos and an explosion ensue. Mephisto brings Faust back to his old laboratory, where Wagner is now making an artificial man.

1. Distilling apparatus.
2. Fiery red.
3. Under his breath.

MEPHISTOPHELES: A man? So you have locked an amorous pair
Up in your chimney-stack somehow?
WAGNER: Why, God forbid! That method's out of fashion now:
Procreation's sheer nonsense, we declare!
That tender point where life used to begin,
That gentle power springing from within,
Taking and giving, programmed to portray
Itself, to assimilate what came its way
From near or far—all that's now null and void;
By animals, no doubt, it's still enjoyed,
But man henceforth, being so highly gifted,
Must have an origin much more uplifted.

[*Turning to the furnace.*]

See how it gleams!—Now we may hope to see
Results. The ingredients—our manifold
Materia anthropica,[4] they are called—
We mix in a retort most patiently,
With all due care, and so by perlutation[5]
And proper double-distillation,
They quietly reach their consummation.

[*Turning to the furnace again.*]

It works! The moving mass is clarified,
And our conviction fortified:
These mysteries we thought only great Nature knew,
Our expertise now dares attempt them too!
Her way with living matter was to organize it,
And we have learnt to crystallize it.
MEPHISTOPHELES: When we live long, we learn a thing
Or two; nothing surprises any more.
I have, in my long years of wandering,
Seen crystallized humanity before.
WAGNER [*who has been staring intently at the retort*]:
It flashes, swells and rises! One
More moment and it will be done.
Great plans seem mad at first, but one day we
Shall laugh at what is bred haphazardly;
And one day, too, some great brain will create
A brain designed to think and cerebrate!

[*Gazing at the retort in delight.*]

The glass is struck into harmonious sound.
Ah, now it cannot fail! It clouds and clears:
And moving daintily around
A well-formed tiny little man appears.

4. Human matter.

5. Cementing together.

What more do I, what more does the world need?
The secret is at last made known.
Now hear this music: it has grown
To a voice, and into speech, indeed!
THE HOMUNCULUS[6] [*in the retort, to Wagner*]:
Well, dad! It worked, you see! And how are you?
Come now, embrace me tenderly—but do
Be careful, please, my glass must not be cracked.
That is the way things are, in fact:
For natural growth the world's too small a place,
But art must be enclosed in its own space.

[*To Mephistopheles.*]

So you are here as well, my mocking cousin?
I am much obliged; the moment was well chosen.
Our good luck brings this timely call by you.
Since I exist, I must find things to do:
I'd like to set to work this very day,
And you know how to set me on my way.
WAGNER: Just one word, please! It's so embarrassing,
The way I'm questioned on this sort of thing.
For instance: no one yet can understand
How soul and body seem to have been planned
To fit so perfectly and cling so tight,
Yet each torments the other day and night.
Furthermore—
MEPHISTOPHELES: Stop, stop! One should ask him rather
Why man and woman can't endure each other.
My friend, you'll never get such matters straight.
There's work to do here: our small guest can't wait.
THE HOMUNCULUS: What's to be done?
MEPHISTOPHELES [*pointing to a side-door*]: A case for you to cure.
WAGNER [*still gazing into the retort*]:
You are a little darling, to be sure!

[*The side-door opens, Faust is seen lying on the couch.*]

THE HOMUNCULUS [*astonished*]: Remarkable!—

[*The retort slips out of Wagner's hands, hovers over Faust and illuminates him.*]

Delightful place![7]—Clear streams
In a dense grove, and women making ready
To bathe; enchanting! Better still already!
But one shines brighter than them all, she seems
Descended from great heroes, gods perhaps.
She sets her foot in the translucent pool;
Life's noble flame in her sweet body dips

6. Little man.
7. Homunculus now describes Faust's dream of Leda, Queen of Sparta, who gave birth to Helen of Troy after Zeus, in the shape of a swan, made love to her.

Into the yielding crystal and grows cool.—
But now, what flurry of quick wings, what whirring
Is this, in the smooth surface splashing, stirring?
The girls flee in alarm: the queen, calm-eyed,
Remains alone, but her heart fills with pride
And womanly contentment as she sees
The prince of swans come nestling to her knees,
Docile yet bold. He seems to like it there.—
And round them all at once has risen a veil
Of mist, thick-woven to conceal
The loves of this most charming pair.

MEPHISTOPHELES: What a strange tale! Your fantasies at least
Are out of all proportion to your size.
I can see nothing—

THE HOMUNCULUS: Why should you! Your eyes
Are northern, steeped in medieval mist;
In that mad world of monks and armor-plated
Knights, naturally your vision's obfuscated.
Dark ages are your proper habitat.

[*Looking round.*]

Black mouldering stones, arches in Gothic style
And absurd curlicues—how drab, how vile!
If he wakes up here, like as not
He'll drop dead on the very spot.
Nude women, swans and woodland streams
I saw in his prophetic dreams.
In this dank hole he'd have no future;
Neither would I, despite my unfastidious nature.
Away with him!

MEPHISTOPHELES: I welcome this solution.

THE HOMUNCULUS: Order a warrior to fight,
Or a young girl to dance all night,
And things soon reach their right conclusion.
And let me see—tonight is Classical
Walpurgis Night,[8] as I recall.
A lucky chance, I do declare!
He'll be in his own element there.

MEPHISTOPHELES: I know of no such date.

THE HOMUNCULUS: Indeed!
You'll not have heard of it, you and your breed.
Romantic ghosts are all they know in hell;
A proper ghost is classical as well.

MEPHISTOPHELES: But where do we go, where do we start exploring?
My ancient history colleagues are so boring.

8. A scene of Goethe's invention (omitted from our selections) as an analogue to the Walpurgis Night of Part 1 (see note to line 3833). It takes place on the Thessalian Fields, on the bank of the Peneus River, a noted resort of witches and also the location where Caesar defeated Pompey in the battle of Pharsalus in 48 B.C.E.

THE HOMUNCULUS: Satan, the north-west is your stamping-ground!
But for this trip, south-eastward we are bound,
To the great plain where the Peneus flows;
Tree-lined, bush-lined its moist meandering goes.
Out to the mountain glens the lowlands rise,
And up there, old and new, Pharsalus lies.
MEPHISTOPHELES: Ugh! why do you remind me of those gory
Wars between slaves and tyrants? That old story,
How stale it is! Their battle is begun
All over again as soon as it is done;
They never guess they merely are the dupes
Of Asmodeus,[9] who really rules the troops.
They call it fighting for their liberty;
Slaves against slaves in fact, it seems to me.
THE HOMUNCULUS: Just let them squabble; men will never mend.
Each one asserts himself as best he can
From boyhood on, and so becomes a man.
The question here is how to cure our friend.
If you've a remedy, then try it now;
If not, leave it to me to find out how.
MEPHISTOPHELES: My Blocksberg[1] magic might be what he'd need
But pagan rules forbid me to proceed.
The Greeks were never much good anyway!
But you are charmed by their free sensuous play,[2]
They lure mankind to many a sinful blessing;
The sins we sell are gloomy and depressing.
And so, what now?
THE HOMUNCULUS: But you do like some sport,
I think; Thessalian witches are the sort
Of thing that might appeal to you.
MEPHISTOPHELES [*lustfully*]: Thessalian witches! If I've heard aright,
They're persons well worth meeting, that is true;
Not for concubinage night after night,
I hardly think that that would do.
But for a visit, for a try—
THE HOMUNCULUS: We need
Your cloak! And wrap it round our gentleman!
This cloth will bear you, as you know it can,
And carry both of you with speed;
I'll light the way ahead.
WAGNER [*anxiously*]: And I?
THE HOMUNCULUS: Why, you
Must stay at home: you have great things to do.
Study old manuscripts, learn from their lore

9. A Jewish spirit of marital discord.

1. A reference to the Walpurgis Night in Part 1; see the notes to lines 2590 and 4222.

2. Mephisto here makes fun of Goethe's ideal of the Greek spirit, which combined erotic sensuousness with the perfected freedom ("play") of the body as perceived by the senses.

How to collect life's elements together
And carefully compose them each to other;
Consider *what,* consider *how* still more.
I meanwhile, traveling the world about,
Shall light on some essential point, no doubt.
Then our great work will have achieved its end;
Such striving merits such reward, my friend!
Gold, honor, fame, health and longevity;
Service to science, virtue too—maybe!
Farewell!

WAGNER [*sadly*]:
Farewell! This parting's pain
And grief; I fear we'll never meet again.

MEPHISTOPHELES: So, off to Greece then!—Judging by your arts,
Cousin, you are a mannikin of parts.
[*Ad spectatores.*°] *to the spectators*
Just fancy that! One does depend
On one's own creatures, in the end.

* * *[3]

from Act 5

Open Country

A WANDERER: There they are, so dark and strong,
Those old lindens, as before;
I have wandered for so long,
Now I find them here once more!
And the hut that sheltered me,
Tempest-tossed as I was then,
On the sand-dunes here I see:
This is the same place again!
And my hosts? That fine old couple
Rescued me with ready will:
They were pious gentle people—
Can I hope to find them still?
They were old at our first meeting.
Shall I knock or call?—My greeting
To you, if the gods still bless
You with your life of kindliness!

3. The lengthy and raucous Classical Walpurgis Night, occupying most of Act 2, culminates in three forms of love: Mephisto finds his obscene Classical counterparts; Homunculus is "born" by breaking out of his glass vessel, crashes into the sea, and dies; and Faust witnesses an ecstatic celebration of the four elements celebrating the birth of Galatea, the successor to Venus as goddess of beauty. Act 3 opens in the style of a Greek tragedy, with Helen and a chorus suffering in time of war. Later, Faust acts on the side of the northern tribes that overthrew the Roman Empire and rescues the ancient Greek beauty into the modern world. In the conclusion to Act 3, Faust and Helen have a son, Euphorion (modeled on Lord Byron), who dies attempting to fly and is followed into the underworld by Helen. Act 4 returns to Germany for battles between rival emperors. Faust, helped by Mephisto's magic, aids one of the emperors to win and is awarded a fiefdom in the Netherlands, where he glories in helping mankind by building dikes to create new farmland.

BAUCIS [*a very old little woman*]:[4]
Stranger dear, speak softly please,
Softly! My old husband, he's
Resting still. He needs the length
Of his nights, for short days' strength.

THE WANDERER: Dear old woman, is it true,
Can I still be thanking you
For my young life you and he
Long ago saved from the sea?
Baucis! You, who when death coldly
Kissed me, warmed my freezing blood?

[*The husband enters.*]

You, Philemon, who so boldly
Snatched my treasure from the flood?
Yours the hospitable fire,
Yours the bell with silver tone,
You, my rescuers from dire
Peril, you my help alone!
Now, to ease my heart's emotion,
I must look upon this shore;
I must kneel and pray once more,
Gazing on the boundless ocean.

[*He steps forward across the sand-dune.*]

PHILEMON [*to Baucis*]: Quickly now, let's lay the table
Here among the flowers and trees.
Let him go; he'll stare, unable
To believe the change he sees.

[*Standing by The Wanderer.*]

Look! Your enemies of old,
The fierce foaming waves, have been
Turned into a park; behold
Now this paradisal scene!
I was not young enough to lend
My helping hands to this endeavor;
Soon my strength was at an end;
The sea was further off than ever.
Those wise lords, they sent bold slaves:
Dams and dikes built in a day
Stole the birthright of the waves
And usurped the ocean's sway.
Now green fields and gardens lie,

4. The aged couple Baucis and Philemon are the subjects of a tale in Ovid's Latin mythological epic *Metamorphoses.* They offered hospitality to Zeus and Hermes, who were refused shelter by all others while traveling in disguise. The gods flooded the lands, except for the hut belonging to the old couple, which became a temple; Philemon was transformed into an oak and Baucis into a linden.

Woods and villages have grown
Up all round. But come, the sun
Will be setting by and by,
Let us eat. Those distant white
Sails seek haven for the night;
Now like nesting birds they know
Here's a port where they can go.
Thus it is; you must look far
Now to find the sea's blue shore,
For dense between, on wide new land,
New human habitations stand.

[*The three sit at table in the little garden.*]

BAUCIS: You are silent? And no food
Has refreshed you, stranger dear?
PHILEMON: Tell him about the wonders; you'd
Like to talk, he'd like to hear.
BAUCIS: Yes, the wonders. I'm still worried
By strange doings we have seen.
Things unnaturally hurried;
Things not as they should have been.
PHILEMON: Can the Emperor sin? He named him° *Faust*
Feudal lord of all the coast;
Even a herald, marching past
With his trumpet-call, proclaimed him.
It began here near the dune,
That first foothold on the flood;
There were tents and huts. But soon
In green fields a palace stood.
BAUCIS: Slaves toiled vainly: blow by blow,
Pick and shovel made no way.
Then we saw the night-flames glow—
And a dam stood there next day.
They used human sacrifice:
Fire ran down, like rivers burning.
All night long we heard the cries—
A canal was built by morning.
He is godless, for he sorely
Wants our hut, our clump of trees.
As a neighbor he's too lordly;
We must serve him, if you please!
PHILEMON: Yet a fine new house he's found
For us on the polder-ground.
BAUCIS: I'd not trust that soil for long.
Stay up here where you belong!
PHILEMON: Come, let's watch the sun's last ray,
When our chapel bell we've tolled.
Let us kneel there, let us pray,
Trusting our God, as of old.

A Palace

[*A large ornamental park, with a long straight canal. Faust in extreme old age, walking about pensively. Lynceus the watchman speaks through a megaphone.*]

LYNCEUS: The sun sinks, the last ships appear,
Gaily they pass the harbor bar,
Soon a tall vessel will be here
In the canal; how merry are
Those fluttering pennants! Each one plays
From a proud standing mast; the crew
Are sharing the good fortune too
That greets you in your latter days.

[*The chapel bell sounds from the sand dune.*]

FAUST [*starting up angrily*]:
Damned bell! A treacherous wound that flies
As from a sniper's shot behind me!
Out there my endless kingdom lies,
But this vexation at my back,
These teasing envious sounds remind me
My great estate's not pure! That line
Of linden-trees, that little shack,
That crumbling chapel, are not mine.
On that green place I may not tread
Another's shadow falls like dread;
It irks my feet, my eyes, my ear—
How can I get away from here!

LYNCEUS THE WATCHMAN [*as above*]:
Now, in the evening breeze, all hail
To this fine ship with swelling sail!
How swift it glides, its load how high—
Sacks, boxes, piled against the sky!

[*A splendid boat appears, richly loaded with a variety of products from distant lands. Enter Mephistopheles and The Three Mighty Men.*[5]]

CHORUS: Welcome ashore!
We're back again!
Long live the master,
Say his men!

[*They land; the cargo is brought ashore.*]

MEPHISTOPHELES: We have done well and had good sport;
We hope my lord will be content.
We'd only two ships when we went,
With twenty now we're back in port.
Our cargo richly testifies

5. Mephisto's assistants.

To our great deeds that won this prize.
The ocean sets one's notions free:
Who's plagued by scruple out at sea?
To catch a fish, to catch a ship,
The only way is grab and grip;
And once three ships have come one's way,
A fourth is easy grappling-prey.
Then guess what chance a fifth will stand!
For might is right, by sea or land.
Not *how* but *how much*—that's what's counted!
What seaman does not take for granted
The undivided trinity
Of war and trade and piracy?

THE THREE MIGHTY MEN: No thanks to meet us,
No word to greet us!
Our master thinks
Our cargo stinks.
His face expresses
Great displeasure;
He does not like
This princely treasure.

MEPHISTOPHELES: There's no more for you
On the house.
You took your cut,
So what's the grouse?

THE THREE: That's mere penny
For our pains:
We ask fair shares
Of all the gains!

MEPHISTOPHELES: Go up there first
And set out all
The valuables
Hall by hall.
He'll see the richest
Show on earth;
Then he'll work out
Just what it's worth,
Decide he can
Afford a treat,
And order a feast-day
For the fleet.
Tomorrow the pretty birds° we'll see; *prostitutes*
They're my responsibility.

[*The cargo is removed.*]

MEPHISTOPHELES [*to Faust*]: Why these dark looks, this frowning brow?
Sublime good fortune greets you now:
By your high wisdom, the sea-shore
And sea are reconciled once more;

Now from the land in easy motion
The ships glide swiftly to the ocean;
And thus, here in this royal place,
The whole world lies in your embrace!
Your kingdom started on this spot;
The first shed stood here, did it not?
Here the first shallow trench was tried
Where now the plashing oars are plied.
Your lofty plan, our industry,
Have made you lord of land and sea.
From here—

FAUST: *Here!* That damned word again,
The theme and burden of my pain!
You are no fool: I must tell you
It cuts my very heart in two,
I'll not bear it another day!
Yet as I say it, even I
Feel shame. The old couple must give way!
I chose that linden clump as my
Retreat: those few trees not my own
Spoil the whole world that is my throne.
From branch to branch I planned to build
Great platforms, to look far afield,
From panoramic points to gaze
At all I've done; as one surveys
From an all-mastering elevation
A masterpiece of man's creation.
I'd see it all as I have planned:
Man's gain of habitable land.

This is the sharpest torment: what
A rich man feels he has not got!
That linden-scent, that chapel-chime
Haunt me like some grim funeral-time.
My will, my sovereign command
Is broken on that mound of sand!
How shall I cure my mental hell
That rages at that little bell!

MEPHISTOPHELES: Indeed, such matter for distress
Must turn your life to bitterness.
These cursèd tinkling sounds we hear
Must stink in every noble ear.
Ding-donging, tintinnabulating,
Clear evening skies obnubilating:° *clouding over*
Every event of life it blights.
From that first bath to our last rites—
As if life were some dream-like thing
That fades away from dong to ding!

FAUST: Their stubbornness, their opposition
Ruins my finest acquisition;

And in fierce agony I must
Grow weary now of being just.

MEPHISTOPHELES: Why scruple then at this late hour?
Are you not—a colonial power?

FAUST: Well, do it! Clear them from my path!—
A fine new cottage, as you know,
I've built, where the old folk can go.

MEPHISTOPHELES: We'll lift them up and whisk them to it;
A moment's work, they'll scarcely know it.
They'll suffer it with a good grace
And settle down in their new place.

[*At his shrill whistle, The Three Mighty Men appear.*]

Come, we have orders from my lord;
Tomorrow there'll be a feast on board.

THE THREE: We've had a poor reception here;
A feast's an excellent idea. [*Exeunt.*]

MEPHISTOPHELES [*ad spectatores*]:° *aside*
The same old story! No doubt you
Have heard of Naboth's vineyard too. (*I Kgs.* 21)[6]

Deep Night

LYNCEUS THE WATCHMAN [*on the castle tower, singing*]:
A watchman by calling,
Far-sighted by birth,
From this tower, my dwelling,
I gaze at the earth:

At the earth near and far,
At the world far and near,
At the moon and the stars,
At the woods and the deer.

A beauty eternal
In all things I see,
And the world and myself
Are both pleasing to me.

Oh blest are these eyes,
All they've seen and can tell:
Let it be as it may—
They have loved it so well!

[*A pause.*]

But I keep my watch so high,
Alas, not only for delight!

6. King Ahab, helped by Queen Jezebel in a murderous seizure of Naboth's vineyard, was denounced by the prophet Elijah. The biblical reference appears in Goethe's text: the devil here does not merely quote scripture, but even annotates his citation.

What dread terror of the night
Spreads its threat across the sky?[7]
Fiery sparks are scattering, spraying
Through the twin-dark linden-trees:
Higher still the flames are playing,
Fanned to heat by their own breeze!
Now the hut's ablaze all through,
That was moist and mossy green;
Too late now for rescue—who
Can bring help to such a scene?
Smoke will choke the good old couple,
At their hearth so carefully
Kept and tended, poor old people,
What a dreadful tragedy!
Flames lick up, black mossy beams
Now are turned to burning red:
How grim this wild inferno seems!
Can they escape it? Have they fled?
Tongues of fearful lightning rise
Through those leaves and branches tall;
Dried-up boughs burn flickerwise;
Charred and breaking, soon they fall.
Cursèd eyes, why must I see?
Take your gift away from me!—
By their downward-crashing weight
Now the little chapel's crushed;
Snaking pointed flames have rushed
Up to crown the tree-tops' fate.
Hollow trunks in fiery showing
To their very roots are glowing.

[*A long pause; singing.*]

Something lovely to behold
Has vanished like an old tale told.

FAUST [*on the balcony, looking towards the sand-dunes*]:
From overhead, what song of woe?
Its words and music came too slow.
My watchman wails: and inwardly
The impatient deed now vexes me.
What if the linden-trees are gone,
Their trunks half-charred, a direful sight—
I'll quickly build a watch-tower on
That place, and scan the infinite!
I see the new house over there,
That soon will shelter that old pair;
They'll praise my generous patronage

7. The watchman's speech, reporting disaster, is a common device in Classical tragedy.

And pass a peaceable old age.
MEPHISTOPHELES and THE THREE [*from below*]:
We're back, sir, with due promptitude;
Regrettably, they misconstrued
Our meaning, and some force was needed.
We knocked and banged, but were not heeded.
We rattled on, and banged some more,
Till there it lay, the rotten door.
We threatened them and made a din:
They would not budge, or ask us in,
And as is common in such cases
They just sat on with stolid faces.
On your behalf, our zeal not lacking,
We grabbed them then and sent them packing.
They didn't linger long—the pair
Dropped dead of terror then and there.
A stranger, lurking with them, drew
His sword and was soon dealt with too.
The fight was brief and violent;
Some coals were scattered, and up went
Some straw; the merry blazing fire
Is now a triple funeral pyre.
FAUST: And this you claim to have done for me?
I said exchange, not robbery!
Deaf savages! I curse this deed;
Now share my curse, your folly's meed!
THE OTHERS, IN CHORUS: The moral's plain, hear it who can:
Never resist the powerful man.
Don't put up a bold fight, or you
Risk house and home, and your life too. [*Exeunt.*]
FAUST [*on the balcony*]: The stars have hid their gleam and glow,
The fire sinks and glimmers low;
A breeze still fans its embers free
And blows the reek across to me.
A rash command, too soon obeyed!—
What comes now, like a hovering shade?

MIDNIGHT

[*Enter Four Gray Women.*]

THE FIRST: My name is Want.
THE SECOND: My name is Debt.
THE THIRD: My name is Care.
THE FOURTH: My name is Need.
THREE OF THEM: The door will not open, we'll never get in.
This is a rich man's house, there's no way in.
WANT: I am a shadow there.
DEBT: I am as nothing there.

NEED: They pay no heed to me, for they need nothing there.
CARE: You are locked out, sisters, you cannot stay.
But through his keyhole Care finds a way.

[*Care vanishes.*]

WANT: Come then, my gray sisters, for you must be gone.
DEBT: I'll follow you closely, sister, lead on!
NEED: Need follows you, sister, as close as a breath.
ALL THREE: The dark clouds are drifting, the stars disappearing:
From far off, from far off, another is nearing!
Our brother is coming; he comes—brother Death.

[*Exeunt.*]

FAUST [*in the palace*]: I saw four come, I only saw three go.
What their speech meant I do not know.
They talked of *debt,* and then another word
That almost rhymed—could it be *death* I heard?
A dark and hollow sound, a ghostly sigh.
I have not broken through to freedom yet.
I must clear magic from my path, forget
All magic conjurations—for then I
Would be confronting Nature all alone:
Man's life worth while, man standing on his own!

So it was once, before I probed the gloom
And dared to curse myself, with words of doom
That cursed the world. The air is swarming now
With ghosts we would avoid if we knew how.
How logical and clear the daylight seems
Till the night weaves us in its web of dreams!
As we return from dewy fields, dusk falls
And birds of mischief croak their ominous calls.
All round us lurks this superstition's snare;
Some haunting, half-seen thing cries out Beware!
We shrink back in alarm, and are alone.
Doors creak, and no one enters.

[*In sudden alarm.*]

Is someone
There at the door?
CARE: You ask, need I reply?
FAUST: And who are you?
CARE: I am here, here am I.
FAUST: Go away!
CARE: I am here where I should be.
FAUST [*at first angry, then calmer, to himself*]:
I must take care to use no sorcery.
CARE: Though no human ear can hear me,

Yet the echoing heart must fear me;
In an ever-changed disguise
All men's lives I tyrannize.
On the roads and on the sea
Anxiously they ride with me;
Never looked for, always there,
Cursed and flattered. I am Care:
Have I never crossed your path?

FAUST: I merely raced across the earth,
Seized by the hair each passing joy,
Discarded all that did not satisfy;
What slipped my grasp, I let it go again.
I have merely desired, achieved, and then
Desired some other thing. Thus I have stormed
Through life; at first with pride and violence,
But now less rashly, with more sober sense.
I've seen enough of this terrestrial sphere.
There is no view to the Beyond from here:
A fool will seek it, peer with mortal eyes
And dream of human life above the skies!
Let him stand fast in this world, and look round
With courage: here so much is to be found!
Why must he wander into timelessness?
What his mind grasps, he may possess.
Thus let him travel all his earthly day:
Though spirits haunt him, let him walk his way,
Let both his pain and joy be in his forward stride—
Each moment leave him still unsatisfied!

CARE: When a man is in my keeping,
All his world is dead or sleeping;
Everlasting dusk descending,
Sun not moving, dark not ending.
Though each outward sense be whole,
Night has nested in his soul;
Riches stand around him staling,
Unpossessed and unavailing;
Gladness, sadness are mere whim,
Plenty cannot nourish him,
He delays both joy and pain
Till the day has passed again,
And on time-to-come intent
Comes to no accomplishment.

FAUST: Stop! You'll not put that blight on me!
I will not listen to such stuff.
Leave me! Your wretched litany
Can drive wise men to madness soon enough.

CARE: Shall he come or shall he go?
He can't choose, he does not know.
In the middle of the road,

See, he staggers, tremble-toed!
Wanders deeper in the maze,
Sees the whole world crookedways,
Burdening himself and others;
Still he breathes, yet chokes and smothers—
Not quite choked, yet life-bereft,
Stubborn, though with hope still left.
Such a ceaseless downward course,
Bitter may not, must by force,
Now released, now re-pursued,
Restless sleep and tasteless food,
Binds him in a static state,
Makes him hell's initiate.

FAUST: Horrible phantoms! Thus you still conspire
Again against mankind and yet again;
Even indifferent days you turn into a dire
Chaotic nexus of entangling pain.
Demons, I know, are hard to exorcize,
The spirit-bond is loath to separate:
But though the creeping power of Care be great,
This power I will never recognize!

CARE: Suffer it then; for as I go
I leave a curse where I have passed.
Men live their lives in blindness: so
Shall even Faust be blinded at the last!

[*She breathes on him. Exit.*]

FAUST [*blinded*]: Night seems to close upon me deeper still,
But in my inmost soul a bright light shines.
I hasten to complete my great designs:
My words alone can work my mastering will.
Rise from your sleep, my servants, every man!
Give visible success to my bold plan!
Set to work now with shovel and with spade:
I have marked it all out, let it be made!
With a well-ordered project and with hard
Toil we shall win supreme reward;
Until the edifice of this achievement stands,
One mind shall move a thousand hands.

The Great Forecourt of the Palace

[*Torches. Mephistopheles as overseer leading a gang of Lemures.*[8]]

MEPHISTOPHELES: Come now, my lemur-goblins, patched-Up semi-skeletons,
With mouldering sinews still attached
To move your rattling bones!

8. Not the monkeys called lemurs, but Classical spirits of the evil dead.

LEMURS [*in chorus*]: We came at once, sir, when you called;
Is there—we did half hear of it—
A plot of land here to be sold,
And shall we get our share of it?
Here are the chains, here are the posts
To measure out the site.
Why did you summon us poor ghosts?
We can't remember quite.

MEPHISTOPHELES: There's no need for these mysteries;
Just use yourselves as measuring-rods!
The tallest of you can lie down lengthwise,
The rest stand round and cut away the sods.
A rectangle of earth dug deep,
A good old-fashioned place to sleep!
From palace to this narrow house descending—
That always was the stupid story's ending.

LEMURS [*digging with mocking gestures*]:

In youth when I did love, did love
Methought 'twas very sweet,
And night and day to music gay
I danced with nimble feet.
But Age with his crutch and cunning clutch
Has come to trip me now.
By a grave I stumbled, and in I tumbled;
They'd left it open somehow.

FAUST [*comes out of the palace, groping at the doorpost*]:
The clash of spades: how it delights my heart!
These are my many workmen; here they toil,
The alienated earth to reconcile,
To keep the ocean and the land apart,
To rule the unruly waves once more.

MEPHISTOPHELES [*aside*]: And yet it's us you're working for
With all your foolish dams and dikes;
Neptune,° the water-devil, likes *sea god*
To think of the great feast there'll be
When they collapse. Do what you will, my friend,
You all are doomed! They are in league with me,
The elements, and shall destroy you in the end.

FAUST: Overseer!

MEPHISTOPHELES: Sir!

FAUST: I need more workers; bring
Them to me by the hundred! Use persuasion,
Cajole or bully them, try everything,
Inducements, money, force! This excavation
Must go ahead; the ditch I've now begun—
I must know daily how much has been done.

MEPHISTOPHELES [*sotto voce*]:° *under his breath*
The digging has gone well today;

No ditch or dike, but dust to dust,[9] they say.
FAUST: A swamp surrounds the mountains' base;
It poisons all I have achieved till now.
I'll drain it too; that rotten place
Shall be my last great project. I see how
To give those millions a new living-space:
They'll not be safe, but active, free at least.
I see green fields, so fertile: man and beast
At once shall settle that new pleasant earth,
Bastioned by great embankments that will rise
About them, by bold labor brought to birth.
Here there shall be an inland paradise:
Outside, the sea, as high as it can reach,
May rage and gnaw; and yet a common will,
Should it intrude, will act to close the breach.
Yes! to this vision I am wedded still,
And this as wisdom's final word I teach:
Only that man earns freedom, merits life,
Who must reconquer both in constant daily strife.
In such a place, by danger still surrounded,
Youth, manhood, age, their brave new world have founded.
I long to see that multitude, and stand
With a free people on free land!
Then to the moment I might say:
Beautiful moment, do not pass away!
Till many ages shall have passed
This record of my earthly life shall last.
And in anticipation of such bliss
What moment could give me greater joy than this?

[*Faust sinks back, the Lemures seize him and lay him on the ground.*]

MEPHISTOPHELES: Poor fool! Unpleasured and unsatisfied,
Still whoring after changeful fantasies,
This last, poor, empty moment he would seize,
Content with nothing else beside.
How he resisted me! But in the end
Time wins; so here you lie, my senile friend.
The clock has stopped—
CHORUS: Has stopped! Like midnight it is stilled.
The clock-hands fall.
MEPHISTOPHELES: They fall. All is fulfilled.[1]
CHORUS: All's over now.
MEPHISTOPHELES: Over! A stupid word! Why "over"? What can be
"Over" is just not there; it's all the same to me!
Why bother to go on creating?
Making, then endlessly annihilating!

9. Once again the devil quotes Christian material, this time the prayer for the dead.

1. Mephisto echoes the last words of Jesus on the Cross (John 19:30).

"Over and past!" What's that supposed to mean?
It's no more than if it had never been,
Yet it goes bumbling round as if it were.
The Eternal Void is what I'd much prefer.

Burial Rites

A LEMUR [*solo*]: Why is the house so poorly made,
And hempen the shrouding-sheet?
LEMURS [*in chorus*]: 'Twas built with pickaxe and with spade,
And for such a guest 'tis meet.
A LEMUR [*solo*]: Who furnished it so ill, who took
The table and chairs away?
LEMURS [*in chorus*]: Not yours to own, 'twas all on loan,
The creditors came today.
MEPHISTOPHELES: The body's down, the spirit I'll soon fix,
I'll show him his own blood-scribed document—
Yet souls come hard these days, their friends invent
Loopholes, and try to play the Devil tricks.
Our older methods gave offense,
Our new ones don't commend us greatly;
I used to do it all myself, but lately
I've had to send for adjutants.
Things are no longer what they were!
Traditional custom, the old rules inspire
No confidence now; there's nothing one can trust.
In former times a man would breathe his last,
Out popped the soul as quick as any mouse,
And snap! my waiting claws would close on it.
But nowadays it hesitates to quit
The gloomy corpse, its dark disgusting house;
Till in the end the elements at strife
Drive out the wretched scrap of life.
I rack my brains about it night and day:
When, how, and *where*'s the question—who can say?
Old Death has lost his old decisive style;
Even the *whether*'s doubtful a long while.[2]
Often I've watched stiff limbs with lustful eyes—
Sham-dead again! They twitch and squirm and rise.

[*He makes fantastic summoning gestures, like a flank-man drilling troops.*]

Come on then, at the double now, my friends,
Straight-horns and crooked-horns! Good solid fiends
Of the old school. And bring the jaws of hell,[3]

2. Premature burial was a topic for lively discussion in late 18th-century Germany.

3. A common setting in medieval drama, anticipated at the end of Prelude on the Stage, line 242.

Please, gentlemen, along with you as well!
Hell has a multiplicity of jaws, it's true,
And swallows up by rank and by degree;
Although in future those rules too
Will be relaxed, presumably.

[*The frightful jaws of hell open up on the left.*]

The fangs gape; through the arching orifice
Hell's maw spews up a fiery ocean,
And in the seething murk of the abyss
I see the Infernal City's ceaseless conflagration.
The red surf surges to the teeth: "At last,"
Think damned souls, swimming up, "here's rescue!" But the vast
Hyena-crunch reclaims them; with dismay
They must pursue their incandescent way.
Amusing those odd corners look as well;
What horrors a small area can contain!
It's supposed to scare sinners; they remain,
However, total skeptics about hell.

[*To the fat devils with short straight horns.*]

Now, you pot-bellied red-faced rascals, you!
How fat you are! Hot brimstone in your guts,
No doubt; you stiff-necked lumps, you no-necked clots!
Watch here for a sudden phosphorescent glow:
It's called the soul, "Psyche"[4]—pull off its wings!
Without them, souls are nasty worm-like things.
I'll stamp it with my seal; off with it then
Into the fire-storm!
                                        You, the gentlemen
Resembling bladders, guard his lower parts!
Don't let our prey squeeze out there—we don't know
Exactly, but it might live where he farts;
Perhaps its whimsy takes it to do so—
Or in the navel maybe; that's a place
It likes. Watch that, or you'll be in disgrace!

[*To the thin devils with long crooked horns.*]

You, flanking giants, you tall gangling fools,
Snatch at the air—keep practicing, and keep
Your arms straight! Spread your claws, they're good sharp tools;
Don't let our fluttering bird give you the slip!
It must be tired of its old lodging now;
And genius, too—that must soar up somehow.

[*A flash of glory from above right.*]

4. "Psyche" is the Greek for both soul and butterfly.

THE HEAVENLY HOST: Follow, bright envoys,
Companions of heaven,
Unhurriedly soaring:
Let sin be forgiven,
Earth-creatures restoring,
All natures partaking;
Let each feel the trace
As you pause at the place
Of your hovering grace!

MEPHISTOPHELES: Now what cacophony is this, what jangling
Noise from above, unwelcome as that light?
A boyish-girlish callow twing-a-twangling,
Fit for some pious nun or acolyte!
In vain we hatched that supersubtle plot
To lay the human population waste;
Our most outrageous trick, just fancy what?
Exactly suits their dim religious taste.
The hypocrites, the riff-raff! Here they are!
That's how they've cheated us of many a prize;
They fight with our own weapons in this war—
They're devils too, but in disguise.
You there! Hold firm, on your eternal shame!
Stand round the grave, and guard it like hell's flame!

CHORUS OF ANGELS [*scattering roses*]:
Roses resplendent,
Roses balm-redolent,
Floating and hovering,
Stem-wing and petal-wing,
Rosebuds reopening,
Blossom recovering,
Secretly succouring:
Hasten to him and bring
Crimson and green of spring,
Make him a paradise
Here where he lies!

MEPHISTOPHELES [*to the demons*]:
What's all this flinching, twitching? Did they teach
You that in hell? Stand fast, and let them throw
Bouquets about! To battle-stations, each
Ugly man-jack of you! They think they'll snow
Hot fiends up under flower-power! Blow,
And they'll all wither, they'll all fade and bleach!
Snuff them out, snuffle-snouts!—Enough, enough!
The whole flight's blighted with your stinking puff!
Just take it easy! Shut your mouths and noses!
Damn you, you're blowing far too hard!
Can't you learn moderation? Look, those roses,
They're not just withering, they're all black and charred—
They're burning! Here they come, the poisoned flames.

Stand and resist, in the three devils' names!—
They're losing heart, they might as well retire.
My devils smell a new, insinuating fire!

ANGELS [*in chorus*]: Flowers of blessedness,
Flames with your dancing light,
Spreaders of happiness,
Powers of love that bless,
Givers of heart's delight:
True words that shine and last,
Brightness in ether lost,
For the eternal host
World without night!

MEPHISTOPHELES: Damn you, my satan-wimps! Now, by my wrath,
They're standing on their heads; oh, shame on you!
The louts are turning cartwheels—the whole crew
Goes plunging arsewise back into perdition.
May you enjoy your well-deserved hot bath!
But I'll not budge from my position.

[*Striking out at the roses as they float down.*]

Begone, will-o'-the-wisps! You're bright lights, yes,
But once I catch you, you're a sticky mess.
Ugh! Get away from me, you fluttering pack!—
They cling like pitch and sulphur to my back.

ANGELS [*in chorus*]: What has no part in you
You have no need of it,
What frets the heart in you
Do not take heed of it.
If the defenses fail
Our strength must then prevail.
Love: for by love alone
Heaven is won.

MEPHISTOPHELES: My head's on fire, my heart and guts as well:
This is worse than the flames of hell!
Some superdiabolic element
Is piercing me. Is this the pain that's meant,
Why unrequited lovers wail Alas!
And crane their necks to see their mistress pass?

Even I! What twists my head towards them somehow?
I was their mortal enemy till now:
Even the sight of them was more than I could bear.
Am I possessed, then, by some alien force?
I like the look of these nice boys—of course
I do! What's this? Why can't I curse and swear?
I'd like to know who's going to be
The fool in future, if they make a fool of me!
Young ruffians, how I hate them all! Yet I confess
They're damned attractive none the less!—
My dears, would I be wrong to guess you are

By any chance cousins of Lucifer?
You're pretty! I must give you all a kiss!
I think you'll suit me at a time like this.
I feel so comfy and so natural,
As if I'd seen you many times before;
So curiously cat-randy, and the more
I contemplate you, the more beautiful
You get. Come closer, please! Just one sweet glance!

THE ANGELS: We are coming; why do you shrink as we advance?
As we draw near, stand your ground if you can!

[*The Angels circle round, filling the entire stage.*]

MEPHISTOPHELES [*pushed forward to the proscenium*]:
You give us a bad name as sprites of hell,
And yet the witchcraft's yours: your goblin-spell
Seduces woman and seduces man!
Damn this for an adventure! Can this be
The element of love, can it be real?
I burn all over, I can scarcely feel
My burnt hump where those flowers got at me.
You dither about so, my dears: come down!
Those lovely limbs should move more worldly-wise.
It's true it suits you well, that serious frown;
But to see you smile would be a sweet surprise!
Just once, please! It would give me such delight!
Just smile the little smile that lovers use—
A modulation of the mouth, that's right!
You tall boy there, now you I'd not refuse;
But why this unbecoming priestly air?
Give me a lustful look instead, ah yes!
And please, be all a little nakeder!
Those flowing robes are decent to excess.
They turn—the rear view is too tantalizing!
Delicious monkeys! ah, how appetizing!

CHORUS OF ANGELS: Turn, burning flames of love,
Turn into clarity!
So to the self-condemned
Truth shall bring liberty;
Freed from the evil spell
They shall win through as well
Into the blessed throng
Where all belong.

MEPHISTOPHELES [*pulling himself together*]:
What's wrong with me? I'm out in boils all over,
Like Job![5] A self-repugnant spectacle;
And yet a triumph, when one sees the whole

5. The man tormented by Satan to test his faith with God. His story is told in the biblical Book of Job.

Depths of oneself, and trusts them to recover.
My noble devil-parts are saved alive!
Those love-charms, as mere eczema they thrive;
The whole damned bonfire's now a burnt-out case,
And once again I curse the whole angelic race!

CHORUS OF ANGELS: Blaze, holy fire! These
Whom you surround here
Sweet life have found here
For all to share.
With single voice now
Cry and rejoice now!
The spirit breathes
In a purified air.

[*They soar upwards, carrying Faust's immortal part.*]

MEPHISTOPHELES [*looking round*]:
But what is this? They've gone! Where can they be?
You halflings, I've been caught off duty!
You've hovered off to heaven with my booty!
That's why they snuffled round this grave; I see!
I've lost my greatest, my most precious prize.
That lofty soul who pledged himself to me—
Filched cunningly before my very eyes!
Now who shall I complain to? Who
Will give me justice, give me back what's mine?
Poor fool, at your age you've been tricked. A fine
Mess you are in, and well deserve it too!
I've misbehaved, there's no one else to blame,
I'm in disgrace. The whole investment lost;
All that good work for nothing! Common lust,
Absurd infatuation puts to shame
The hard-boiled Devil. And if even my
Wisdom's no match for such tomfoolery—
Then to this strange love-madness I extend
My compliments, since it could catch me in the end!

* * *

from MOUNTAIN GORGES[6]

DOCTOR MARIANUS [*prostrated in adoration*]:
Gaze aloft—the saving eyes
See you all, such tender
Penitents; look up and render
Thanks, to blest renewal rise!
May each nobler spirit never
Fail to serve thee; Virgin, Mother,

6. In the final scene Faust's redemption is celebrated by the soul of Gretchen, the Holy Virgin, and Catholic holy figures. Included here is the famous hymn to the feminine that closes the play.

Queen, oh keep us in thy favor,
Goddess, kind for ever!

CHORUS MYSTICUS:

All that must disappear
Is but a parable;
What lay beyond us, here
All is made visible;
Here deeds have understood
Words they were darkened by;
Eternal Womanhood
Draws us on high.

PERSPECTIVES
Romantic Nature

"Love of Nature Leading to Love of Mankind." The title of Book 8 of Wordsworth's epic poem *The Prelude* could serve as a label for much of the enterprise of Romanticism. Birds and flowers, rivers and mountains form the subjects of many of the most famous poems of the era, of key stretches of the novels, vast amounts of travel writing, the most characteristic painting in England and Germany, and important philosophical and scientific works. Of course, poets and artists have always admired nature and depicted the scenery in their writings and paintings. But nature was newly central to the Romantic sensibility, and in ways that continue to form our ecological sensibility today.

Chaucer's medieval *Canterbury Tales* opens with a beautiful spring scene. The point, however, is to set the pilgrims on their journey; nature bears a moral and religious impress: "So pricketh hem nature in hir courages. / Than longen folk to goon on pilgrimages." Dante similarly notes the landscape as he starts underway, in the second canto of the *Inferno.* But here the pilgrim is set apart from nature: "The day was now departing; the dark air released the living beings of the earth from work and weariness; and I myself alone . . ." There is nature, and there is the heart of man, and nature (or the goddess Natura) sends man on his way, or holds him back from his heavenly destination. Nature is setting or mediator, but never end in itself. Only late in the sixteenth century, and then very gradually, did painters even began to depict landscape scenes without humans or divinities in them.

The history of gardening is instructive and important. In the seventeenth century the French set the fashion, with architecturally inspired gardens of neat squares and fountains and rigidly pruned trees. In the eighteenth century the so-called English garden came into style, with informal vistas, lawns, and brooks. Still, and in a succession of different modes, gardens remained tamed and carefully manicured. In his "Epistle to Burlington" (1731) Alexander Pope, a famous gardener in his own right, blamed one kind—"Grove nods at grove, each alley has a brother, / And half the platform just reflects the other"—and praised a more informal and more productive scene, "Whose ample lawns are not ashamed to feed / The milky heifer and deserving steed." But it would never have occurred to Pope to write poems celebrating a field mouse, as did Robert Burns, or a cuckoo or weed as did Wordsworth. Pope may have preferred a more natural garden, but it was still a garden. In contrast, the park in Coleridge's "Kubla Khan" is watered by brooks as meandering as the raw countryside of England.

Perhaps the most famous lines in all of eighteenth-century poetry are found in Thomas Gray's "Elegy Written in a Country Churchyard" (1751):

> Full many a gem of purest ray serene,
> The dark unfathomed caves of ocean bear:
> Full many a flower is born to blush unseen,
> And waste its sweetness on the desert air.

Poems of sensibility like this one drew attention to the hidden, unnoticed beauties of nature. Still, even Gray and his contemporaries wanted to extract the gems for human use, to bring flowers where they wouldn't be wasted. The natural scene remains an allegory: the flower and gem represent the country dwellers who lack the proper education and opportunities to develop their gifts. Things have changed by the time Wordsworth praises a mysterious girl he called Lucy in 1798, in his song "She dwelt among th' untrodden ways." Now the comparisons go the other way; it's not that the isolated beauties of nature are like people but that she is like them:

> A Violet by a mossy stone,
> Half hidden from the Eye!

—Fair, as a star when only one
Is shining in the sky!

Most surprising to us about older attitudes toward nature is perhaps the fear of mountains. In his *Sacred Theory of the Earth* (first published in Latin in 1681) Bishop Thomas Burnet notoriously called them "wild, vast and indigested Heaps of Stone and Earth," and the "Ruins of a broken World." There are obvious reasons. Nights were dark, roads were bad, there were no snowplows, carriages were unheated, there was always the risk in unpoliced border regions of encountering savage animals or even more savage people. Many residues of this old terror survive—for instance, in the haunted Sleepy Hollow portrayed by Washington Irving, or in the mysterious forest of Ludwig Tieck's "Blond Eckbert," and in Kubla Khan's ice caves. But the Romantics were learning not just to delight in nature's unadorned beauties but equally to revere the grandest and even the most forbidding regions. Rousseau, Swiss by birth, retreated into natural isolation in times of stress. Wordsworth crossed the Alps and climbed Mount Snowdon (the highest peak in the British Isles), and he and Coleridge loved to hike the most isolated and remote reaches of the Lake District, in the far northwest of England. For Emerson, nature displays the power of divinity, and Thoreau caps the turn to nature in all her majestic savagery with the spring vision that climaxes *Walden* and with his famous cry, "We need the tonic of wildness."

Three characteristics of nature might be identified as elements of the Romantic vision. First, Romantic nature is particular. While it may still retain the aura that earlier surrounded nature as either a Paradise or a fallen realm, it is watched and understood first in its own right. Rousseau was never happier than when cataloguing the plants of his retreat on the Island of Saint-Pierre, Goethe amassed an enormous and meticulously inventoried rock collection, Droste-Hülshoff and Thoreau were scrupulous and knowledgeable observers of the characteristics and habits of the plants and animals around them. This was the age of natural history, when scientists and laypeople refined the catalogue of species originally drawn up by Linnaeus (Carl von Linné, 1707–1778), when paleontologists studied fossils and geologists first began speculating about the ages of the earth, and when some daring writers on astronomy, beginning with the young Immanuel Kant, even started imagining histories of the universe. The Romantics localized nature in both place and time.

Second, Romantic nature isn't just composed of living beings but is itself a living thing. In "Tintern Abbey" Wordsworth says, "We see into the life of things," while Goethe has Faust describe the ecstasy of the waterfall at the end of "A Beautiful Landscape," the first scene of *Faust, Part 2,* and Thoreau writes, "I love to see that Nature is so rife with life that myriads can be afforded to be sacrificed and suffered to prey on one another." In each of these cases, the writer celebrates a life force larger than any individual. Notice how old the scene often looks to Romantic writers. Keats's nightingale has sung for millennia, and his autumn seems to live beyond its limits when the "soft-dying day" becomes the home for "gathering swallows"; Droste-Hülshoff's "In the Grass" is a moment that "hastens" and yet "lingers," as she drowses while nature lives on. *Vitalism* is the formal name for the belief in a life that is larger than life and an age that is older yet more continuous than any recorded time. The Romantics were vitalists to their very core, with an instinctive belief that nature is holier and more valuable than any mere sign or evidence of divinity.

Third, Romantic nature is grand. Even its tiniest elements are of infinite value, and its most imposing monuments are less threatening than inspiring. The period's name for this grandeur is sublimity. In its oldest English usage, the term "sublime" meant uplifting, and that sense remained the underpinning for all later meanings. Earlier writers and painters certainly also admired nature's grandeurs but typically found them intimidating; the Romantics found them elevating. Nature was no longer a realm of occult powers to be mastered by magicians like Shakespeare's Prospero or the legendary Renaissance wonder-worker Dr. Faustus, but rather a domain of wondrous, living order to be penetrated by the human intellect and experienced by

Caspar David Friedrich, *Wanderer Above Sea of Fog,* 1818.

the human body. Each of the three main divisions of Dante's *Divine Comedy* ends with the word "stars" in witness of the pilgrim's humility before God. When Kant contemplates the stars, he allies them with his own exaltation of spirit. Emerson's nature-ecstasy is the culmination of the Romantic cult of the particular, living grandeur of nature that has become so much a part of our modern sense of the nature's incomparable value in all its forms, in itself and for our cultural and spiritual lives. "Standing on the bare ground—my head bathed by the blithe air and uplifted into infinite space—all mean egotism vanishes. I become a transparent eyeball; I am nothing; I see all; the currents of the Universal being circulate through me; I am part or parcel of God."

William Blake
1757–1827

"When the Sun rises do you not see a round Disk of fire somewhat like a Guinea? O no no, I see an Innumerable company of the Heavenly host crying 'Holy Holy Holy is the Lord God Almighty.' I question not my Corporeal or Vegetative Eye any more than I would Question a Window concerning a Sight. I look through it & not with it." So William Blake, the visionary engraver and poet, commented on his painting of the Last Judgment. A favorite phrase in his mystical epic poems is "He became what he beheld." Sights mesmerized and transported Blake. A uniquely skilled craftsman and a radical thinker never content with religious, political, or sexual orthodoxies, he found the natural world inspiring (as in "The Ecchoing Green," from his "Songs of Innocence") and terrifying (as in "The Tyger," from the "Songs of Experience"). The Tyger's "fearful symmetry" evokes the art of the engraver who arduously incises a steel plate to make a reverse image of the eventual picture; it evokes the exhilarating but frightening correspondence of a powerless man with the vital flux of the universe; and it evokes the almost Kantian sublimity of a supposed constellation that might guide him through the dark night of his labors—or might threaten him under a social regime that he considered unfeeling and repressive. Blake shared with his tamer contemporaries a devotion to the natural world, but he rejected naturalism in favor of his eccentric kind of religious exaltation.

The Ecchoing Green

The Sun does arise,
And make happy the skies.
The merry bells ring
To welcome the Spring.
The sky-lark and thrush,
The birds of the bush,
Sing louder around,
To the bells chearful sound
While our sports shall be seen
On the Ecchoing Green.

Old John with white hair
Does laugh away care,
Sitting under the oak,
Among the old folk,
They laugh at our play,
And soon they all say,
Such such were the joys
When we all girls & boys,
In our youth-time were seen,
On the Ecchoing Green.

Till the little ones weary
No more can be merry
The sun does descend,
And our sports have an end:

Round the laps of their mothers
Many sisters and brothers,
Like birds in their nest,
Are ready for rest;
And sport no more seen,
On the darkening Green.

The Tyger

Tyger Tyger, burning bright,
In the forests of the night;
What immortal hand or eye,
Could frame thy fearful symmetry?

In what distant deeps or skies,
Burnt the fire of thine eyes?
On what wings dare he aspire?[1]
What the hand, dare sieze the fire?

And what shoulder, & what art,
Could twist the sinews of thy heart?
And when thy heart began to beat,
What dread hand? & what dread feet?

What the hammer? what the chain,
In what furnace was thy brain?
What the anvil? what dread grasp,
Dare its deadly terrors clasp!

When the stars threw down their spears
And water'd heaven with their tears:[2]
Did he smile his work to see?
Did he who made the Lamb make thee?[3]

Tyger Tyger burning bright,
In the forests of the night:
What immortal hand or eye,
Dare frame thy fearful symmetry?

William Wordsworth
1770–1850

Wordsworth spent his twenties restlessly, wandering about England and France, suspected of radical political activities possibly extending even to spying for the French, and writing his

1. An allusion to Icarus, who, with his father Dedalus, fashioned wings of feathers and wax to escape from prison. Icarus became enchanted with flight and, ignoring his father's cautions, soared too close to the sun; the wax melted and he fell to his death in the sea.
2. In the war in Heaven, in Book 6 of Milton's *Paradise Lost*, Satan, rebelling against God's authority, is defeated by the Son and driven down to Hell. Blake's verb leaves it undecidable whether the stars "threw down their spears" in deseperate surrender or in defiance.
3. An allusion to Jesus, "The Lamb of God" (John 1:29 and 1:36).

earliest poetry. A bequest allowed him to settle modestly in the countryside with his talented sister Dorothy. In 1797 he met the younger, more precocious Coleridge, and in 1798 they published *Lyrical Ballads,* a joint collection of poems that enjoyed moderate and growing success, becoming the foundation of Wordsworth's reputation as the greatest English poet of the nineteenth century.

His poetical output was steady and various: songs and ballads, long narrative poems, formal odes and elevated philosophical meditations, and over 500 sonnets, often on political and religious topics including the injustices of slavery and of the death penalty. He slowly advanced from his early poverty to considerable wealth and retreated from revolutionary politics into staunch conservatism; in 1802 he married a childhood friend; in 1813 the growing family moved to a grand house in the Lakes; in 1843 he was finally named Poet Laureate.

Before Wordsworth in England and Goethe in Germany it had never occurred to anyone to make a cult of simplicity. Poetry was supposed to be learned, "to instruct and to delight," as the Latin poet Horace had written. Wordsworth doesn't so much reject such traditional values as completely transform them. "Tintern Abbey," one of Wordsworth's greatest achievements, looks to a sublime natural scene, records the loss and recovery of childhood feelings with great complexity and in multiple stages, and pits the impoverished inhabitants of its Welsh setting against the dehumanizing "din" of cities. In the Westminster Bridge sonnet, a majestic calm hides intimations of death ("And all that mighty heart is lying still") in a poem associated with Wordsworth's farewell journey to Annette Vallon. Poems like this one can be as indispensable to understanding the crosscurrents of natural piety as are Goethe's critique of modernization at the end of *Faust* or Thoreau's cultivation of wildness.

No other writer so richly expresses the struggles of a newly industrialized and highly stratified urban culture to retain its anchor in unforced relations among humans and in contact with natural and local settings. Perhaps the poet's mixture of simplicity and arrogance was necessary to capture these contending impulses to their fullest. At the end of one of his grandest short poems, "Ode: Intimations of Immortality from Recollections of Early Childhood," Wordsworth puts lines that memorably combine his capacious philanthropy, his indulgent sympathy for the humble creatures of the human and natural worlds, and his intricate psychological insight into sadness and joy, taking his own feelings as the model for the universe:

Thanks to the human heart by which we live,
Thanks to its tenderness, its joys, and fears,
To me the meanest flower that blows can give
Thoughts that do often lie too deep for tears.

Lines Composed a Few Miles above Tintern Abbey

On Revisiting the Banks of the Wye During a Tour, July 13, 1798

Five years have past; five summers, with the length
Of five long winters! and again I hear
These waters, rolling from their mountain-springs
With a soft inland murmur.—Once again
Do I behold these steep and lofty cliffs,
That on a wild secluded scene impress
Thoughts of more deep seclusion; and connect
The landscape with the quiet of the sky.
The day is come when I again repose
Here, under this dark sycamore, and view
These plots of cottage-ground, these orchard-tufts,
Which at this season, with their unripe fruits,

Are clad in one green hue, and lose themselves
'Mid groves and copses. Once again I see
These hedge-rows, hardly hedge-rows, little lines
Of sportive wood run wild: these pastoral farms,
Green to the very door; and wreaths of smoke
Sent up, in silence, from among the trees!
With some uncertain notice, as might seem
Of vagrant dwellers in the houseless woods,
Or of some Hermit's cave, where by his fire
The Hermit sits alone.

These beauteous forms,
Through a long absence, have not been to me
As is a landscape to a blind man's eye:
But oft, in lonely rooms, and 'mid the din
Of towns and cities, I have owed to them
In hours of weariness, sensations sweet,
Felt in the blood, and felt along the heart;
And passing even into my purer mind,
With tranquil restoration:—feelings too
Of unremembered pleasure: such, perhaps,
As have no slight or trivial influence
On that best portion of a good man's life,
His little, nameless, unremembered, acts
Of kindness and of love. Nor less, I trust,
To them I may have owed another gift,
Of aspect more sublime; that blessed mood
In which the burthen of the mystery,
In which the heavy and the weary weight
Of all this unintelligible world,
Is lightened:—that serene and blessed mood,
In which the affections gently lead us on,—
Until, the breath of this corporeal frame
And even the motion of our human blood
Almost suspended, we are laid asleep
In body, and become a living soul:
While with an eye made quiet by the power
Of harmony, and the deep power of joy,
We see into the life of things.

If this
Be but a vain belief, yet, oh! how oft—
In darkness and amid the many shapes
Of joyless daylight; when the fretful stir
Unprofitable, and the fever of the world,
Have hung upon the beatings of my heart—
How oft, in spirit, have I turned to thee,
O sylvan Wye! thou wanderer thro' the woods,
How often has my spirit turned to thee!

And now, with gleams of half-extinguished thought,
With many recognitions dim and faint,
And somewhat of a sad perplexity,
The picture of the mind revives again:
While here I stand, not only with the sense
Of present pleasure, but with pleasing thoughts
That in this moment there is life and food
For future years. And so I dare to hope,
Though changed, no doubt, from what I was when first
I came among these hills; when like a roe
I bounded o'er the mountains, by the sides
Of the deep rivers, and the lonely streams,
Wherever nature led: more like a man
Flying from something that he dreads than one
Who sought the thing he loved. For nature then
(The coarser pleasures of my boyish days,
And their glad animal movements all gone by)
To me was all in all.—I cannot paint
What then I was. The sounding cataract
Haunted me like a passion: the tall rock,
The mountain, and the deep and gloomy wood,
Their colours and their forms, were then to me
An appetite; a feeling and a love,
That had no need of a remoter charm,
By thought supplied, nor any interest
Unborrowed from the eye.—That time is past,
And all its aching joys are now no more,
And all its dizzy raptures. Not for this
Faint° I, nor mourn nor murmur; other gifts *lose heart*
Have followed; for such loss, I would believe,
Abundant recompense. For I have learned
To look on nature, not as in the hour
Of thoughtless youth; but hearing oftentimes
The still, sad music of humanity,
Nor harsh nor grating, though of ample power
To chasten and subdue. And I have felt
A presence that disturbs me with the joy
Of elevated thoughts; a sense sublime
Of something far more deeply interfused,
Whose dwelling is the light of setting suns,
And the round ocean and the living air,
And the blue sky, and in the mind of man:
A motion and a spirit, that impels
All thinking things, all objects of all thought,
And rolls through all things. Therefore am I still
A lover of the meadows and the woods,
And mountains; and of all that we behold
From thus green earth; of all the mighty world

Of eye, and ear,—both what they half create,[1]
And what perceive; well pleased to recognise
In nature and the language of the sense
The anchor of my purest thoughts, the nurse,
The guide, the guardian of my heart, and soul
Of all my moral being.

Nor perchance,
If I were not thus taught, should I the more
Suffer my genial° spirits to decay: *creative*
For thou art with me here upon the banks
Of this fair river; thou my dearest Friend,
My dear, dear Friend; and in thy voice I catch
The language of my former heart, and read
My former pleasures in the shooting lights
Of thy wild eyes. Oh! yet a little while
May I behold in thee what I was once,
My dear, dear Sister! and this prayer I make,
Knowing that Nature never did betray
The heart that loved her; 'tis her privilege,
Through all the years of this our life, to lead
From joy to joy: for she can so inform
The mind that is within us, so impress
With quietness and beauty, and so feed
With lofty thoughts, that neither evil tongues,
Rash judgments, nor the sneers of selfish men,
Nor greetings where no kindness is, nor all
The dreary intercourse of daily life,
Shall e'er prevail against us, or disturb
Our cheerful faith, that all which we behold
Is full of blessings. Therefore let the moon
Shine on thee in thy solitary walk;
And let the misty mountain-winds be free
To blow against thee: and, in after years,
When these wild ecstasies shall be matured
Into a sober pleasure; when thy mind
Shall be a mansion for all lovely forms,
Thy memory be as a dwelling-place
For all sweet sounds and harmonies; oh! then,
If solitude, or fear, or pain, or grief,
Should be thy portion,° with what healing thoughts *dowry*
Of tender joy wilt thou remember me,
And these my exhortations! Nor, perchance—
If I should be where I no more can hear
Thy voice, nor catch from thy wild eyes these gleams
Of past existence—wilt thou then forget
That on the banks of this delightful stream

1. In a note Wordsworth signals that this phrase is borrowed from the popular long meditative poem *Night Thoughts* (1742–1746) by Edward Young: The senses "half create the wondrous world they see" (6.427).

We stood together; and that I, so long
A worshipper of Nature, hither came
Unwearied in that service: rather say
With warmer love—oh! with far deeper zeal
Of holier love. Nor wilt thou then forget,
That after many wanderings, many years
Of absence, these steep woods and lofty cliffs,
And this green pastoral landscape, were to me
More dear, both for themselves and for thy sake!

Composed upon Westminster Bridge, Sept. 3, 1802[1]

Earth has not anything to show more fair:
Dull would he be of soul who could pass by
A sight so touching in its majesty:
This City now doth, like a garment, wear
The beauty of the morning; silent, bare,
Ships, towers, domes, theatres, and temples lie
Open unto the fields, and to the sky;
All bright and glittering in the smokeless air.
Never did sun more beautifully steep
In his first splendour, valley, rock, or hill;
Ne'er saw I, never felt, a calm so deep!
The river glideth at his own sweet will:
Dear God! the very houses seem asleep;
And all that mighty heart is lying still!

John Keats
1795–1821

The short and chubby son of a successful stable-keeper who died before his son was ten, John Keats spent his life aspiring for recognition from the same classes that the well-born Percy Shelley (a close friend) and Lord Byron rebelled against. Hence Keats goes in for self-display while shunning self-assertion. "A poet . . . has no identity," he writes in one of his eloquent letters, and another praises "*Negative Capability,* that is when man is capable of being in uncertainties, Mysteries, doubts, without an irritable reaching after fact & reason." Via ardent self-suppression he sought the eternal validation of artistic perfection, opening his dream epic *Endymion* with the famous line, "A thing of beauty is a joy forever." His poetry expresses radical humanitarianism that bemoans "where men grow pale and spectre-thin and die," without sacrificing formal rigor and stylistic polish. In his odes he mimics ancient ritual formulas: he addresses the nightingale and autumn as divinities to be approached with the greatest hesitation; he tells their histories, imagines their advent as if a god has descended to earth, prays to them, and absorbs their lessons. While the speaker remains static—contemplating the urn, caught in half-slumber while listening to the nightingale—his negative capability embroiders the encounters with richly imagined scenes, hints of romantic adventure, mythical situations,

1. Composed on the roof of a coach, on my way to France [Wordsworth's note, 1843].

biblical legend, Virgilian pastoral, Miltonic paradise. No other poet so densely sums up both the pagan and the Christian cultural heritage in such intricately ornamented small poems. Jointly obsessed with mortality and with eternity, Keats seems destined to have endured the tragic death he suffered from tuberculosis at the age of twenty-five.

Ode to a Nightingale[1]

1

My heart aches, and a drowsy numbness pains
My sense, as though of hemlock I had drunk,
Or emptied some dull opiate to the drains
One minute past, and Lethe-wards had sunk:[2]
'Tis not through envy of thy happy lot,
But being too happy in thine happiness,—
That thou, light-wingèd Dryad° of the trees, *wood-nymph*
In some melodious plot
Of beechen green, and shadows numberless,
Singest of summer in full-throated ease.

2

O, for a draught of vintage!° that hath been *wine*
Cool'd a long age in the deep-delvèd° earth, *dug*
Tasting of Flora° and the country green, *goddess of flowers*
Dance, and Provençal[3] song, and sunburnt mirth!
O for a beaker full of the warm South,
Full of the true, the blushful Hippocrene,[4]
With beaded bubbles winking at the brim,
And purple-stainèd mouth;
That I might drink, and leave the world unseen,[5]
And with thee fade away into the forest dim:

3

Fade far away, dissolve, and quite forget
What thou among the leaves hast never known,
The weariness, the fever, and the fret
Here, where men sit and hear each other groan;
Where palsy shakes a few, sad, last gray hairs,
Where youth grows pale, and spectre-thin, and dies;
Where but to think is to be full of sorrow
And leaden-eyed despairs,
Where Beauty cannot keep her lustrous eyes,
Or new Love pine at them beyond to-morrow.

1. In Greek legend Philomela had been raped by her brother-in-law Tereus, who cut out her tongue to ensure her silence. After she revealed the crime by weaving the story into a robe, the gods changed her into a nightingale.

2. Hemlock (extracted from a flowering plant unrelated to the North American tree) is a sedative; in large doses, such as Socrates', it is fatal; an opiate is any sense-duller, particularly opium, widely used as a painkiller; Lethe is the mythic river of the underworld whose waters produce forgetfulness of previous life.

3. Provence is a region in southern France famed for troubadours (see p. 1179).

4. The fountain of the muses on Mount Helicon.

5. "Unseen" can modify both "I" and "world."

4

Away! away! for I will fly to thee,
 Not charioted by Bacchus and his pards,[6]
But on the viewless wings of Poesy,
 Though the dull brain perplexes and retards:
Already with thee! tender is the night,
 And haply° the Queen-Moon is on her throne, *happily, perhaps*
  Cluster'd around by all her starry Fays;° *fairies*
   But here there is no light,
 Save what from heaven is with the breezes blown
  Through verdurous glooms and winding mossy ways.

5

I cannot see what flowers are at my feet,
 Nor what soft incense hangs upon the boughs,
But, in embalmed darkness, guess each sweet
 Wherewith the seasonable month endows
The grass, the thicket, and the fruit-tree wild;
 White hawthorn, and the pastoral eglantine;
  Fast fading violets cover'd up in leaves;
   And mid-May's eldest child,
 The coming musk-rose, full of dewy wine,
  The murmurous haunt of flies on summer eves.

6

Darkling° I listen; and, for many a time *in the dark*
 I have been half in love with easeful Death,
Call'd him soft names in many a mused rhyme,
 To take into the air my quiet breath;
Now more than ever seems it rich to die,
 To cease upon the midnight with no pain,
  While thou art pouring forth thy soul abroad
   In such an ecstasy!
 Still wouldst thou sing, and I have ears in vain—
  To thy high requiem° become a sod. *funeral mass*

7

Thou wast not born for death, immortal Bird!
 No hungry generations tread thee down;
The voice I hear this passing night was heard
 In ancient days by emperor and clown:° *rustic, peasant*
Perhaps the self-same song that found a path
 Through the sad heart of Ruth, when, sick for home,
  She stood in tears amid the alien corn;[7]
   The same that oft-times hath
 Charm'd magic casements, opening on the foam
  Of perilous seas, in faery lands forlorn.

6. Bacchus, god of wine and revelry, whose chariot is drawn by leopards.

7. See Ruth 1–2: compelled by famine to leave her home, Ruth eked out a living as a gleaner in faraway fields.

8

Forlorn! the very word is like a bell
  To toll me back from thee to my sole self!
Adieu! the fancy cannot cheat so well
  As she is fam'd to do, deceiving elf.
Adieu! adieu! thy plaintive anthem fades
  Past the near meadows, over the still stream,
    Up the hill-side; and now 'tis buried deep
      In the next valley-glades:
  Was it a vision, or a waking dream?
    Fled is that music:—Do I wake or sleep?

To Autumn[1]

1

Season of mists and mellow fruitfulness,
  Close bosom-friend of the maturing sun;
Conspiring with him how to load and bless
  With fruit the vines that round the thatch-eaves[2] run;
To bend with apples the moss'd cottage-trees,
  And fill all fruit with ripeness to the core;
    To swell the gourd, and plump the hazel shells
  With a sweet kernel; to set budding more,
  And still more, later flowers for the bees,
  Until they think warm days will never cease,
    For Summer has o'er-brimm'd their clammy cells.

2

Who hath not seen thee oft amid thy store?
  Sometimes whoever seeks abroad may find
Thee sitting careless on a granary floor,
  Thy hair soft-lifted by the winnowing wind;
Or on a half-reap'd furrow sound asleep,
  Drows'd with the fume of poppies while thy hook° *scythe*
    Spares the next swath and all its twined flowers:
And sometimes like a gleaner thou dost keep
  Steady thy laden head across a brook;
  Or by a cyder-press, with patient look,
    Thou watchest the last oozings hours by hours.

3

Where are the songs of Spring? Ay, where are they?
  Think not of them, thou hast thy music too,—
While barred clouds bloom the soft-dying day,
  And touch the stubble-plains with rosy hue;
Then in a wailful choir the small gnats mourn

1. Composed 19–21 September 1819 in Winchester, a tranquil town in southern England, from which Keats wrote to a friend: "How beautiful the season is now—How fine the air. A temperate sharpness about it. . . . I never lik'd stubble fields so much as now—Aye better than the chilly green of the spring. Somehow a stubble plain looks warm—in the same way that some pictures look warm—this struck me so much in my Sunday's walk that I composed upon it."

2. The eaves of thatched cottage roofs.

Among the river sallows,[3] borne aloft
Or sinking as the light wind lives or dies;
And full-grown lambs loud bleat from hilly bourn;° *boundary, region*
Hedge-crickets sing; and now with treble soft° *faint high pitch*
The red-breast whistles from a garden-croft;° *enclosure*
And gathering swallows twitter in the skies.

Annette von Droste-Hülshoff
1797–1848

German artists tended to feel marginal in the first half of the nineteenth century, and none more so than Annette von Droste-Hülshoff. The unmarried daughter of declining nobility, she cared for her widowed mother and other ailing family members, though she herself was often in ill health. Her mother selected appropriate contacts for her lively daughter and only grudgingly allowed her first collection of poems to appear in 1838. As a female Catholic kept cloistered by her aristocratic relatives, Droste suffered more than the usual ambivalence in relationships with intellectuals of her generation, mostly Protestant bourgeois. Nevertheless, her poems commanded immediate respect and lasting fame. A larger collected edition appeared in 1844; Robert Schumann asked her for an opera libretto in the following year. She has remained the most honored woman poet of the century from Continental Europe. Unusually well educated in both music and natural history, Droste combines precise realistic detail with a compelling need to overcome the boundaries of individuality. Her speakers suffer from the limitation of their senses and point of view; they long to move from the margins to the centers of being that had become so inaccessible for late Romantics.

PRONUNCIATION:
Annette von Droste-Hülshoff: ahn-NET-tuh fon DRO-stuh HILZ-hoff

The Heath-Man[1]

"Go children, shun the quarry's depths,
The sun is setting, weaker hums
The bee's flight now, befogged in sleep,
An ashen cloth floats on the deep,
The heath-man comes."

Along the bank the boys play on,
They pluck at grass stems, skip a stone,
They paddle at the water's edge,
Catch dragon flies above the bog
And watch with joy the water spinner
Long-legged flee into the sedge.

"You children, don't lie in the grass!—
Look, where just now the bee flew past,
How steaming mist engulfs the bells.

3. Willows (an emblem of death).

1. Translated by Jane K. Brown.

The hare peers shyly from the bush,
The heath-man swells!"

The reed scarce lifts its heavy head
Above the fog, the beetle sneaks
Into its hole, and on the stalk
The torpid moth yet higher creeps,
To flee before the humid smoke
That rises underneath its wings.

"You children, stay here close to home!
Don't go beyond the quarry's edge;
See how grey the thornbush grows,
The song thrush groans upon its nest,
The heath-man brews!"—

You see the herdsman's pipe now glowing,
Ahead of him his herd is flowing,
As Proteus[2] homeward drives his flock
Of seals across the greying waves.
The swallows twitter round the eaves,
And melancholy crows the cock.

"You children, stay close by the house!
See how the damp flat band of mist
About the garden gate-latch twines;
A false light floats now in the depths,
The heath-man climbs!"—

Now just the pine trees' highest tips
Protrude green summits from the mist,
Like junipers above the snow;
A gentle bubbling swells the moor,
A feeble whine, a sighing hiss
From out the hollow surges forth.

"You children, come, come quickly in!
The Jack-o'-lantern lights his lamp,
The toad puffs up, snake in the fen;
It's eerie now to be abroad,
The heath-man walks!"—

The topmost needle sinks, the spruce
Dissolves in smoke, the fog-sprites come,
Upwelling slowly from the moor,
Then glide away on giant limbs;
A mad light flickers in the sedge,
The toads strike up at water's edge.

2. A subject or son of Poseidon, god of the sea.

And now a feeble glowing seems
To penetrate the giant's limbs;
It boils up, it tints the waves,
The north, the north bursts into flame—
Arrows burning, fire-spears fly,
Horizon all a lava stream!
"God save us! how it flares and booms,
And sulphur burns atop the dunes!
You children, fold your hands and pray,
That brings us plague and troubled times—
The heath-man's ablaze!"

In the Grass

Sweet repose, sweet reeling in grass,
Enveloped in fragrance of green,
Deep stream, deep deep drunken stream,
When the cloud dissolves in the blue,
When on my tired, swimming head
Sweetly laughter flutters down,
Dear voice murmurs, and trickles
Down like linden blooms onto a grave.

When in the breast the dead ones then,
Every corpse stretches and stirs,
Quietly, quietly draws its breath,
Moves its tight-drawn lashes,
Dead love, dead joy, dead time,
All the treasures, immured in the dust
Touch one another, timidly sounding,
As tiny bells wave in the breeze.

Hours, more fleeting are you than the kiss
Of a beam on the sorrowing lake,
Than the song of the passing bird,
That drops like dew from the heights,
Than the glittering beetle's flash,
As it hastes through the sun's path,
Than the ardent clasp of a hand
As it lingers a final time.

Yet, o heaven, this alone
Ever for me: for the song
Of each bird free in the sky
Please, a soul, to fly with him,
But for each scanty beam
This my iridescent hem,
For each warm hand my clasp,
And for every joy my dream.

Alexander Sergeyevich Pushkin
1799–1837

Russia wanted a national poet, and Pushkin filled the bill to perfection. In the previous century Catherine the Great, who ruled from 1762–1796, had worked to westernize and modernize the country, importing leading French and German intellectuals. The upper classes were culturally French. But the failed Napoleonic invasion of 1812 led the once liberal tsar Alexander I to retreat into reaction, leaving the country at Nicholas's accession with much ferment and little direction. There were plenty of writers in Western European modes, but none to capture the popular imagination until Pushkin came along. He wrote with equal success lyric poems, Byronic narratives with native themes, plays, and prose narratives, the longest of which, "The Captain's Daughter," is a historical fiction in Scott's panoramic manner concerning a Cossack rebel against Catherine the Great. He became the founding figure of Russian national literature, as well as the inspiration for the Russian musical school; operas based on his works were composed by Glinka (*Russlan and Ludmilla,* 1842), Mussorgsky (*Boris Godunov,* 1870, rev. 1872), Tchaikovsky (*Eugene Onegin,* 1877; *Queen of Spades,* 1890), Rimsky-Korsakov (*Mozart and Salieri,* 1897), Stravinsky (*Mavra,* 1922), and others.

With his French education and his facility in English and Italian, his deep Russian pedigree, and his "Oriental" ancestry, Pushkin was the perfect figure to represent imperial aspirations. He was fiercely liberal at times, yet ultimately compliant. He wrote in polished Western forms such as the couplets of "The Bronze Horseman." His lyrics show a responsiveness to a nature sensibility resembling Wordsworth's; his story "The Queen of Spades" plays into the fashion for the fantastic tale. At the same time, his Russian themes elevate his native country to all the beauty, sublimity, and dignity of the long-established realms of Europe. All these elements can be found in perfection in his last and most eloquent verse tale, "The Bronze Horseman."

PRONUNCIATIONS:
Pushkin: PUSH-kin
Onegin: ahn-YAY-gin
Nevá: nye-VAH

The Bronze Horseman[1]
A Petersburg Tale
INTRODUCTION[2]

Upon the brink of the wild stream
He[3] stood, and dreamt a mighty dream.
He gazed far off. Near him the spreading
river poured by; with flood abeam,
alone, a flimsy skiff was treading.
Scattered along those shores of bog

1. Translated by Charles Johnston.
2. "The Bronze Horseman" tells a story founded on a real flood in November 1824. The grand modern city of Saint Petersburg was built on swampland on the Baltic Sea, looking out toward Finland and the then powerful kingdom of Sweden.
3. Peter the Great, who founded Saint Petersburg in 1703.

and moss were huts of blackened log,
the wretched fisher's squalid dwelling;
forests, impervious in the fog
to hidden suns, all round were telling
their whispered tale.
And so thought He:
"From here, proud Sweden will get warning;
just here is where a city'll be
founded to stop our foes from scorning;
here Nature destines us to throw
out over Europe a window;
to stand steadfast beside the waters;
across waves unknown to the West,
all flags will come, to be our guest—
and we shall feast in spacious quarters."

A century went by—a young
city, of Northern lands the glory
and pride, from marsh and overhung
forest arose, story on story:
where, earlier, Finland's fisher sank—
of Nature's brood the most downhearted—
alone on the low-lying bank,
his ropy net in the uncharted
current, today, on brinks that hum
with life and movement, there have come
enormous mansions that are justling
with graceful towers; and vessels here
from earth's extremities will steer
until the rich quayside is bustling.
Nevá[4] now sports a granite face;
bridges are strung across her waters;
in darkly verdant garden-quarters
her isles have vanished without trace;
old Moscow's paled before this other
metropolis; it's just the same
as when a widowed Empress-Mother
bows to a young Tsaritsa's° claim. *Princess's*

I love you, Peter's own creation;
I love your stern, your stately air,
Nevá's majestical pulsation,
the granite that her quaysides wear,
your railings with their iron shimmer,
your pensive nights in the half-gloom,

4. The river along which the city is built.

translucent twilight, moonless glimmer,
when, sitting lampless in my room,
I write and read; when, faintly shining,
the streets in their immense outlining
are empty, given up to dreams;
when Admiralty's needle gleams;
when not admitting shades infernal
into the golden sky, one glow
succeeds another, and nocturnal
tenure has one half-hour to go;
I love your brutal winter, freezing
the air to so much windless space;
by broad Nevá the sledges breezing;
brighter than roses each girl's face;
the ball, its brilliance, din, and malice;
bachelor banquets and the due
hiss of the overflowing chalice,
and punch's radiance burning blue.
I love it when some warlike duty
livens the Field of Mars, and horse
and foot impose on that concourse
their monolithic brand of beauty;
above the smooth-swaying vanguard
victorious, tattered flags are streaming,
on brazen helmets light is gleaming,
helmets that war has pierced and scarred.
I love the martial detonation,
the citadel in smoke and roar,
when the North's Empress to the nation
has given a son for empire, or
when there's some new triumph in war
victorious Russia's celebrating;
or when Nevá breaks the blue ice,
sweeps it to seaward, slice on slice,
and smells that days of spring are waiting.

Metropolis of Peter, stand,
steadfast as Russia, stand in splendor!
Even the elements by your hand
have been subdued and made surrender;
let Finland's waves forget the band
of hate and bondage down the ages,
nor trouble with their fruitless rages
Peter the Great's eternal sleep!

A fearful time there was: I keep
its memory fresh in retrospection . . .
My friends, let me turn up for you
the dossiers of recollection.
Grievous the tale will be, it's true . . .

PART ONE

On Petrograd,° the darkened city, *Saint Petersburg*
November, chill and without pity,
blasted; against its noble brink
Nevá was splashing noisy billows;
its restless mood would make one think
of sufferers tossing on their pillows.
The hour was late and dark; the rain
angrily lashed the window-pane,
the wind blew, pitifully shrieking.
From house of friends, about this time,
young Evgeny came home . . .
My rhyme
selects this name to use in speaking
of our young hero. It's a sound
I like; my pen has long been bound
in some way with it; further naming
is not required, though lustre flaming
in years gone by might have lit on
his forebears, and perhaps their story
under Karamzin's[5] pen had shone,
resounding to the nation's glory;
but now by all, both high and low,
it's quite forgotten. Our hero
lives in Kolomna,[6] has employment
in some bureau, tastes no enjoyment
of wealth or fashion's world, and no
regret for tales of long ago.

So Evgeny came home and, shaking
his greatcoat, got undressed for bed—
but lay long hours awake, his head
with various thoughts disturbed and aching.
What did he think about? The fact
that he was penniless; that packed
mountains of work must be surmounted
to earn him freedom, fame, and ease;
that wit and money might be counted
to him from God; and that one sees
fellows on permanent vacation,
dull-witted, idle, in whose station
life runs as smooth as in a dream;
that he'd served two years altogether . . .
And he thought also that the weather
had got no gentler; that the stream

5. Nikolai Mikhailovich Karamzin (1766–1826), prose writer.

6. A part of Saint Petersburg.

was rising, ever higher lifting;
that soon the bridges might be shifting;
that maybe from Parasha° he *his beloved*
would be cut off, two days or three.

These were his dreams. And a great sadness
came over him that night; he wished
the raindrops with less raging madness
would lash the glass, that the wind swished
less drearily . . .
At last his failing
eyes closed in sleep. But look, the gloom
of that foul-weather night is paling,
and a weak daylight fills the room . . .
A dreadful day it was!
All night
Nevá against the gales to seaward
had battled, but been blown to leeward
by their ungovernable might . . .
That morning, on the quayside, fountains
of spray held an admiring crowd,
that pressed to watch the watery mountains,
the foaming waves that roared so loud.
But now, blocked by the headwinds blowing
in from the Gulf, Nevá turned back,
in sullen, thunderous fury flowing,
and flooded all the islands; black,
still blacker grew the day; still swelling,
Nevá exploded, raging, yelling,
in kettle-like outbursts of steam—
until, mad as a beast, the stream
pounced on the city. From its path
everyone fled, and all around
was sudden desert . . . At a bound
cellars were under inundation,
canals leapt rails, forgot their station—
and Triton-Petropol[7] surfaced
with waters lapping round his waist.

Siege and assault! The waves, malicious,
like thieves, burst in through windows; vicious
rowboats, careering, smash the panes;
stalls are engulfed; piteous remains,
débris of cabins, roofing, boarding,
wares that a thrifty trade's been hoarding,
poor household goods, dashed all astray,

7. Triton is a Greek sea god who rides the waves on sea horses. Petropol is a Greek form of the name Petersburg.

bridges the storm has snatched away,
and scooped-up coffins, helter-skelter
swim down the streets!
All sense alike
God's wrath, and wait for doom to strike.
Everything's ruined: bread and shelter!
and where to find them?
That deathlike,
that frightful year, Tsar Alexander[8]
still ruled in glory. He came out
on the balcony, in grief, in doubt,
and said: "A Tsar is no commander
against God's elements." Deep in thought
he gazed with sorrow and confusion,
gazed at the wreck the floods had wrought.
The city squares gave the illusion
of lakes kept brimming to profusion
by torrent-streets. The palace stood
sad as an island in the ocean.
And then the Tsar spoke out, for good
or evil set in farflung motion
his generals on their dangerous way
along those streets of boisterous waters
to save the people in their quarters,
drowning, unhinged by terror's sway.

And then in Peter's square, where lately
a corner-mansion rose, and stately
from its high porch, on either side,
caught as in life, with paws suspended,
two lions,[9] sentry-like, attended—
perched up on one, as if to ride,
arms folded, motionless, astride,
hatless, and pale with apprehension,
Evgeny sat. His fear's intention
not for himself, he never knew
just how the greedy waters grew,
how at his boots the waves were sucking,
how in his face the raindrops flew;
or how the stormwind, howling, bucking,
had snatched his hat away. His view
was fixed in darkest desperation,
immobile, on a single spot.
Mountainous, from the perturbation
down in the depths, the waves had got
on their high horses, raging, pouncing;

8. Alexander I (1777–1825).

9. Statues at the entrance to the War Ministry.

the gale blew up, and, with it, bouncing
wreckage . . . Oh, God, oh God! for there—
close to the seashore—almost where
the Gulf ran in, right on the billow—
a fence, untouched by paint, a willow,
a flimsy cottage; *there* were they,
a widow and his dream, her daughter,
Parasha . . . or perhaps he may
have dreamt it all? Fickle as water,
our life is as dreamlike as smoke—
at our expense, fate's private joke.
As if by sorcery enchanted,
high on the marble fixed and planted,
he can't dismount! And all about
is only water. Looking out,
with back turned to him, on the retching
waves of Nevá in their wild course
from his fast summit, arm outstretching,
the Giant rides on his bronze horse.[1]

PART TWO

But by now, tired of helter-skelter
ruin and sheer rampaging, back
Nevá was flowing, in its track
admiring its own hideous welter;
its booty, as it made for shelter,
it slung away. With his grim crew
so any robber chief will do;
bursting his way into a village,
he'll hack and thrust and snatch and pillage;
rape, havoc, terror, howl and wail!
Then, loaded down with loot, and weary—
fear of pursuers makes them leery—
the robbers take the homeward trail
and as they flee they scatter plunder.

So, while the water fell asunder,
the road came up. And fainting, pale,
in hope and yearning, fear and wonder,
Evgeny hurries at full steam
down to the scarcely falling stream.
And yet, still proud, and still exulting,
the waves, still furious and insulting,
boiled as if over flames alight;
they still were lathered, foaming, seething
and deeply the Nevá was breathing

1. Monument to Peter the Great.

just like a horse flown from a fight.
Evgeny looks: a skiff is waiting—
Godsent—he rushes, invocating
the ferryman, who without a care
for just a few copecks quite gladly
agrees to take him, though still madly
the floods are boiling everywhere.
The boatman fought the agonizing
billows like an experienced hand;
the cockboat with its enterprising
crew was quite ready for capsizing
at any moment—but dry land
at last it gained.
Evgeny, tearful,
rushes along the well-known ways
towards the well-known scene. His gaze
finds nothing it can grasp: too fearful
the sight! before him all is drowned,
or swept away, or tossed around;
cottages are askew, some crumbled
to sheer destruction, others tumbled
off by the waves; and all about,
as on a field of martial rout,
bodies lie weltered. Blankly staring,
Evgeny, uncomprehending, flies,
faint from a torment past all bearing,
runs to where fate will meet his eyes,
fate whose unknown adjudication
still waits as under seal of wax.
And now he's near his destination
and here's the Gulf, here . . . in his tracks
Evgeny halts . . . the house . . . where ever?
he goes back, he returns. He'd never. . .
he looks . . . he walks . . . he looks again:
here's where their cottage stood; and then
here was the willow. Gates were standing
just here—swept off, for sure. But where's
the cottage gone? Not understanding,
he walked round, full of boding cares,
he talked to himself loud and gruffly,
and then he struck his forehead roughly
and laughed and laughed.
In deepest night
the city trembled at its plight;
long time that day's events were keeping
the citizenry all unsleeping
as they rehearsed them.
Daylight's ray
fell out of tired, pale clouds to play

over a scene of calm—at dawning
yesterday's hell had left no trace.
The purple radiance of the morning
had covered up the dire event.
All in its previous order went.
Upon highways no longer flowing,
people as everyday were going
in cold indifference, and the clerk
left where he'd sheltered in the dark
and went to work. The daring bosses
of commerce, unperturbed, explore
Nevá's inroads upon their store,
and plan to take their heavy losses
out on their neighbor. From backyards
boats are removed.
That bard of bards,
Count Khvostov,[2] great poetic master,
begins to sing Nevá's disaster
in unforgettable ballades.

But spare, I pray you, spare some pity
for my poor, poor Evgeny, who
by the sad happenings in the city
had wits unhinged. Still the halloo
of tempest and Nevá was shrieking
into his ear; pierced through and through
by frightful thoughts, he roamed unspeaking;
some nightmare held him in its thrall.
A week went by, a month—and all
the time he never once was seeking
his home. That small deserted nook,
its lease expired, his landlord took
for a poor poet. His possessions
Evgeny never went to claim.
Soon to the world and its professions
a stranger, all day long he came
and went on foot, slept by the water;
scraps thrown from windows of the quarter
his only food; always the same,
his clothes wore out to shreds. Malicious
children would stone him; he received
from time to time the coachman's vicious
whiplash, for he no more perceived
which way was which, or what direction
led where; he never seemed to know
where he was going, he was so
plunged in tumult of introspection.

2. Count D. I. Khvostov (1757–1835), a minor poet.

And so his life's unhappy span
he eked out—neither beast nor man—
not this, nor that—not really living
nor yet a ghost . . .
He slept one night
by the Nevá. Summer was giving
its place to autumn. Full of spite,
a bad wind blew. In mournful fight
against the embankment, waves were splashing,
their crests on the smooth steps were smashing
for all the world like suppliant poor
at some hard-hearted judge's door.
Evgeny woke. Raindrops were falling
in midnight gloom; the wind was calling
piteously—on it, far off, hark,
the cry of sentries in the dark . . .
Evgeny rose, and recollection
brought up past horrors for inspection;
he stood in haste, walked off from there,
then halted, and began to stare
in silence, with an insensately
wild look of terror on his face.
He was beside the pillared, stately
front of a mansion. In their place,
caught as in life, with paws suspended,
two lions, sentry-like, attended,
and there, above the river's course,
atop his rock, fenced-off, defended
on his dark summit, arm extended,
the Idol rode on his bronze horse.

Evgeny shuddered. Thoughts were hatching
in frightful clarity. He knew
that spot, where floods ran raging through—
where waves had massed, voracious, snatching,
a riot-mob, vindictive, grim—
the lions, and the square, and him
who, motionless and without pity,
lifted his bronze head in the gloom,
whose will, implacable as doom,
had chosen seashore for his city.
Fearful he looked in that half-light!
Upon his forehead, what a might
of thought, what strength of concentration!
what fire, what passion, and what force
are all compact in that proud horse!
He gallops—to what destination?
On the cliff-edge, O lord of fate,
was it not you, O giant idol,

who, pulling on your iron bridle,
checked Russia, made her rear up straight?

Around the hero's plinth of granite
wretched Evgeny, in a daze,
wandered, and turned a savage gaze
on the autocrat of half the planet.
A steely pressure gripped his chest.
His brow on the cold railing pressed,
over his eyes a mist was lowering,
and through his heart there ran a flame;
his blood was seething; so he came
to stand before the overpowering
image, with teeth and fists again
clenched as if some dark force possessed him.
"Take care," he whisperingly addressed him,
"you marvel-working builder, when . . ."
He shivered with bitter fury, then
took headlong flight. He had the impression
that the grim Tsar, in sudden race
of blazing anger, turned his face
quietly and without expression . . .
and through the empty square he runs,
but hears behind him, loud as guns
or thunderclap's reverberation,
ponderous hooves in detonation
along the shuddering roadway—
as, lighted by the pale moon-ray,
one arm stretched up, on headlong course,
after him gallops the Bronze Rider,
after him clatters the Bronze Horse.
So all night long, demented strider,
wherever he might turn his head—
everywhere gallops the Bronze Rider
pursuing him with thunderous tread.

And from then on, if he was chancing
at any time to cross that square,
a look of wild distress came glancing
across his features; he would there
press hand to heart, in tearing hurry,
as if to chase away a worry;
take his worn cap off; never raise
up from the ground his distraught gaze,
but sidle off.

A small isle rises
close to the foreshore. Now and then,
a fisher moors alongside, when
late from his catch, with nets and prizes,

and cooks his poor meal on the sand;
or some official comes to land,
out for a Sunday's pleasure-boating,
on the wild islet. Not a blade
of grass is seen. There, gaily floating,
the floods had washed up as they played
a flimsy cottage. Above water
it showed up like a bush, quite black—
last spring they moved it. The small quarter,
empty, was shipped away, all rack
and ruin. Near it, my dim-witted
my mad Evgeny there they found . . .
His cold corpse in that self-same ground
to God's good mercy they committed.

Henry David Thoreau
1817–1862

"The fact will one day flower out into a truth." Much is packed into this aphorism from Thoreau's voluminous and meticulous journals. A Harvard graduate of good family and modest means, partly supported by his close friend Ralph Waldo Emerson, he went to live for two years in a cabin on Walden Pond, just outside Concord, Massachusetts, collecting facts, looking for nature and, through nature, toward Truth. Thoreau doesn't represent a back-to-nature movement, any more than Wordsworth does, and perhaps less than Rousseau, his most obvious model. One chapter of his great book *Walden* is called "Reading," another is "Higher Laws," and even as the book increasingly concentrates on animals and plants, it is in the service of exalted hopes for humanity. "We need the tonic of wildness," he says near the end of "Spring," in the curiously matter-of-fact tone that makes him the soberest and most reflective of visionaries; that is, we need a cure but also a bracing wake-up. Thoreau's most famous books (mostly, apart from *Walden,* published posthumously) concern his wanderings, as does his famous essay "Walking," which speaks for American destiny: "We go eastward to realize history and study the workings of art and literature, retracing the steps of the race; we go westward as into the future, with a spirit of enterprise and adventure." The spirit of enterprise led him to a ringing defense of individual conscience in "Civil Disobedience," as well as to the millennial hopes that he shares—though in a distinctive voice—with Wordsworth on Mount Snowdon, as with many other hopeful spirits: "There is more day to dawn. The sun is but a morning star."

from *Walden*
from Spring

Our village life would stagnate if it were not for the unexplored forests and meadows which surround it. We need the tonic of wildness,—to wade sometimes in marshes where the bittern and the meadow-hen lurk, and hear the booming of the snipe; to smell the whispering sedge where only some wilder and more solitary fowl builds her nest, and the mink crawls with its belly close to the ground. At the same time that we are earnest to explore and learn all things, we require that all things be mysterious and unexplorable, that land and sea be infinitely wild, unsurveyed and unfathomed by us because unfathomable. We can never have enough of Nature. We must be refreshed by the sight of inexhaustible vigor, vast and Titanic features, the sea-coast with its wrecks, the wilderness with its living and its decaying trees, the thunder cloud, and the rain which lasts three weeks and produces freshets.[1] We need to witness our own limits transgressed, and some life pasturing freely where we never wander. We are cheered when we observe the vulture feeding on the carrion which disgusts and disheartens us and deriving health and strength from the repast. There was a dead horse in the hollow by the path to my house, which compelled me sometimes to go out of my way, especially in the night when the air was heavy, but the assurance it gave me of the strong appetite and inviolable health of Nature was my compensation for this. I love to see that Nature is so rife with life that myriads can be afforded to be sacrificed and suffered to prey on one another; that tender organizations can be so serenely squashed out of existence like pulp,—tadpoles which herons gobble up, and tortoises and toads run over in the road; and that sometimes it has rained flesh and blood! With the liability to accident, we must see how little account is to be made of it. The impression made on a wise man is that of universal innocence. Poison is not poisonous after all, nor are any wounds fatal. Compassion is a very untenable ground. It must be expeditious. Its pleadings will not bear to be stereotyped.

Early in May, the oaks, hickories, maples, and other trees, just putting out amidst the pine woods around the pond, imparted a brightness like sunshine to the landscape, especially in cloudy days, as if the sun were breaking through mists and shining faintly on the hill-sides here and there. On the third or fourth of May I saw a loon in the pond, and during the first week of the month I heard the whippoorwill, the brown-thrasher, the veery, the wood-pewee, the che-wink, and other birds. I had heard the wood-thrush long before. The phoebe had already come once more and looked in at my door and window, to see if my house was cavern-like enough for her, sustaining herself on humming wings with clinched talons, as if she were held by the air, while she surveyed the premises. The sulphur-like pollen of the pitch-pine soon covered the pond and the stones and rotten wood along the shore, so that you could have collected a barrel-ful. This is the "sulphur showers" we hear of. Even in Calidas'[2] drama of Sacontala, we read of "rills dyed yellow with the golden dust of the lotus." And so the seasons went rolling on into summer, as one rambles in high and higher grass.

Thus was my first year's life in the woods completed; and the second year was similar to it. I finally left Walden September 6th, 1847.

from Conclusion

To the sick the doctors wisely recommend a change of air and scenery. Thank Heaven, here is not all the world. The buck-eye does not grow in New England, and the mocking-bird is rarely heard here. The wild goose is more of a cosmopolite than we; he breaks his fast in Canada, takes a luncheon in the Ohio, and plumes himself for the night in a southern bayou. Even the bison, to some extent, keeps pace with the seasons, cropping the pastures of the Colorado only till a greener and sweeter grass awaits him by the Yellowstone. Yet we think that if rail fences are pulled down, and stone-walls piled up on our farms, bounds are henceforth set to our lives and our fates decided. If you are chosen

1. Rushing streams.

2. Thoreau knew the ancient Indian drama Sakuntala in a version published by Sir William Jones in 1789.

town-clerk, forsooth, you cannot go to Tierra del Fuego[1] this summer: but you may go to the land of infernal fire nevertheless. The universe is wider than our views of it.

Yet we should oftener look over the tafferel[2] of our craft, like curious passengers, and not make the voyage like stupid sailors picking oakum. The other side of the globe is but the home of our correspondent. Our voyaging is only great-circle sailing, and the doctors prescribe for diseases of the skin merely. One hastens to Southern Africa to chase the giraffe; but surely that is not the game he would be after. How long, pray, would a man hunt giraffes if he could? Snipes and woodcocks also may afford rare sport; but I trust it would be nobler game to shoot one's self.—

> Direct your eye right inward, and you'll find
> A thousand regions in your mind
> Yet undiscovered. Travel them, and be
> Expert in home-cosmography.[3]

What does Africa,—what does the West stand for? Is not our own interior white[4] on the chart? black though it may prove, like the coast, when discovered. Is it the source of the Nile, or the Niger, or the Mississippi, or a North-West Passage around this continent, that we would find? Are these the problems which most concern mankind? Is Franklin the only man who is lost, that his wife should be so earnest to find him? Does Mr. Grinnell know where he himself is?[5] Be rather the Mungo Park, the Lewis and Clarke and Frobisher,[6] of your own streams and oceans; explore your own higher latitudes,—with shiploads of preserved meats to support you, if they be necessary; and pile the empty cans sky-high for a sign. Were preserved meats invented to preserve meat merely? Nay, be a Columbus to whole new continents and worlds within you, opening new channels, not of trade, but of thought. Every man is the lord of a realm beside which the earthly empire of the Czar is but a petty state, a hummock left by the ice. Yet some can be patriotic who have no *self*-respect, and sacrifice the greater to the less. They love the soil which makes their graves, but have no sympathy with the spirit which may still animate their clay. Patriotism is a maggot in their heads. What was the meaning of that South-Sea Exploring Expedition,[7] with all its parade and expense, but an indirect recognition of the fact, that there are continents and seas in the moral world, to which every man is an isthmus or an inlet, yet unexplored by him, but that it is easier to sail many thousand miles through cold and storm and cannibals, in a government ship, with five hundred men and boys to assist one, than it is to explore the private sea, the Atlantic and Pacific Ocean of one's being alone.

> "Erret, et extremos alter scrutetur Iberos.
> Plus habet hic vitae, plus habet ille viae."
>
> Let them wander and scrutinize the outlandish Australians.
> I have more of God, they more of the road.[8]

1. "The land of fire," the southern tip of South America.
2. Taffrail, the rail at the stern of a ship.
3. From "To My Honoured Friend Sir Ed. P. Knight," by William Habington (1605–1664), a minor Catholic poet.
4. An unexplored blank space on a map.
5. Sir John Franklin (1786–1847), a British explorer lost trying to find the Northwest Passage (open water through the Arctic) and sought by Henry Grinnell (1799–1874), among others.
6. Mungo Park (1771–1806), a Scotsman who explored the Niger basin in Africa. William Clark (1770–1838) and Meriwether Lewis (1774–1809) explored the Columbia River. Sir Martin Frobisher (1535–1594), an Englishman, sought the Northwest Passage.
7. A U.S. Navy expedition conducted between 1829 and 1842.
8. An epigram by the 4th century Latin poet Claudian. Note that in place of the Roman reference to the passage past Spain ("Iberos," the Iberians) into the open ocean Thoreau puts Australia, which an American of his day might have considered similarly exotic.

It is not worth the while to go round the world to count the cats in Zanzibar. Yet do this even till you can do better, and you may perhaps find some "Symmes' Hole"[9] by which to get at the inside at last. England and France, Spain and Portugal, Gold Coast and Slave Coast, all front on this private sea; but no bark from them has ventured out of sight of land, though it is without doubt the direct way to India. If you would learn to speak all tongues and conform to the customs of all nations, if you would travel farther than all travelers, be naturalized in all climes, and cause the Sphinx to dash her head against a stone, even obey the precept of the old philosopher, and Explore thyself.[1] Herein are demanded the eye and the nerve. Only the defeated and deserters go to the wars, cowards that run away and enlist. Start now on that farthest western way, which does not pause at the Mississippi or the Pacific, nor conduct toward a worn-out China or Japan, but leads on direct, a tangent to this sphere, summer and winter, day and night, sun down, moon down, and at last earth down too.

It is said that Mirabeau[2] took to highway robbery "to ascertain what degree of resolution was necessary in order to place one's self in formal opposition to the most sacred laws of society." He declared that "a soldier who fights in the ranks does not require half so much courage as a foot-pad"—"that honor and religion have never stood in the way of a well-considered and firm resolve." This was manly, as the world goes; and yet it was idle, if not desperate. A saner man would have found himself often enough "in formal opposition" to what are deemed "the most sacred laws of society," through obedience to yet more sacred laws, and so have tested his resolution without going out of his way. It is not for a man to put himself in such an attitude to society, but to maintain himself in whatever attitude he find himself through obedience to the laws of his being, which will never be one of opposition to a just government, if he should chance to meet with such.

I left the woods for as good a reason as I went there. Perhaps it seemed to me that I had several more lives to live, and could not spare any more time for that one. It is remarkable how easily and insensibly we fall into a particular route, and make a beaten track for ourselves. I had not lived there a week before my feet wore a path from my door to the pond-side; and though it is five or six years since I trod it, it is still quite distinct. It is true, I fear that others may have fallen into it, and so helped to keep it open. The surface of the earth is soft and impressible by the feet of men; and so with the paths which the mind travels. How worn and dusty, then, must be the highways of the world, how deep the ruts of tradition and conformity! I did not wish to take a cabin passage, but rather to go before the mast and on the deck of the world, for there I could best see the moonlight amid the mountains. I do not wish to go below now.

I learned this, at least, by my experiment; that if one advances confidently in the direction of his dreams, and endeavors to live the life which he has imagined, he will meet with a success unexpected in common hours. He will put some things behind, will pass an invisible boundary; new, universal, and more liberal laws will begin to establish themselves around and within him; or the old laws be expanded, and interpreted in his favor in a more liberal sense, and he will live with the license of a higher order of beings. In proportion as he simplifies his life, the laws of the universe will

9. Captain John Symmes declared in 1818 that the earth was hollow and open at both poles.

1. When Oedipus answered the riddle of the Sphinx, she killed herself by dashing her head against a rock. Thoreau then varies the proverbial maxim "Know thyself," chiseled into the Temple of Apollo and echoed by many Greek philosophers.

2. Honoré Gabriel Riqueti, Comte de Mirabeau (1749–1791), a moderate leader in the French Revolution.

appear less complex, and solitude will not be solitude, nor poverty poverty, nor weakness weakness. If you have built castles in the air, your work need not be lost; that is where they should be. Now put the foundations under them.

It is a ridiculous demand which England and America make, that you shall speak so that they can understand you. Neither men nor toadstools grow so. As if that were important, and there were not enough to understand you without them. As if Nature could support but one order of understandings, could not sustain birds as well as quadrupeds, flying as well as creeping things, and *hush* and *who,* which Bright[3] can understand, were the best English. As if there were safety in stupidity alone. I fear chiefly lest my expression may not be *extra-vagant* enough, may not wander far enough beyond the narrow limits of my daily experience, so as to be adequate to the truth of which I have been convinced. *Extra vagance!* it depends on how you are yarded. The migrating buffalo, which seeks new pastures in another latitude, is not extravagant like the cow which kicks over the pail, leaps the cow-yard fence, and runs after her calf, in milking time. I desire to speak somewhere *without* bounds; like a man in a waking moment, to men in their waking moments; for I am convinced that I cannot exaggerate enough even to lay the foundation of a true expression. Who that has heard a strain of music feared then lest he should speak extravagantly any more forever? In view of the future or possible, we should live quite laxly and undefined in front, our outlines dim and misty on that side; as our shadows reveal an insensible perspiration toward the sun. The volatile truth of our words should continually betray the inadequacy of the residual statement. Their truth is instantly *translated;* its literal monument alone remains. The words which express our faith and piety are not definite; yet they are significant and fragrant like frankincense to superior natures.

Why level downward to our dullest perception always, and praise that as common sense? The commonest sense is the sense of men asleep, which they express by snoring. Sometimes we are inclined to class those who are one-and-a-half witted with the half-witted, because we appreciate only a third part of their wit. Some would find fault with the morning-red, if they ever got up early enough. "They pretend," as I hear, "that the verses of Kabir[4] have four different senses; illusion, spirit, intellect, and the exoteric doctrine of the Vedas;" but in this part of the world it is considered a ground for complaint if a man's writings admit of more than one interpretation. While England endeavors to cure the potato-rot, will not any endeavor to cure the brain-rot, which prevails so much more widely and fatally?

I do not suppose that I have attained to obscurity, but I should be proud if no more fatal fault were found with my pages on this score than was found with the Walden ice. Southern customers objected to its blue color, which is the evidence of its purity, as if it were muddy, and preferred the Cambridge ice, which is white, but tastes of weeds. The purity men love is like the mists which envelop the earth, and not like the azure ether beyond.

Some are dinning in our ears that we Americans, and moderns generally, are intellectual dwarfs compared with the ancients, or even the Elizabethan men. But what is that to the purpose? A living dog is better than a dead lion.[5] Shall a man go and hang himself because he belongs to the race of pygmies, and not be the biggest

3. Conventional name for an ox. "Hush" and "who" are cattlemen's lingo for go and stop.

4. A 15th-century mystic, known to Thoreau from a French history of Hindu literature. The Vedas are the oldest Hindu scriptures.

5. Ecclesiastes 9:4.

pygmy that he can? Let every one mind his own business, and endeavor to be what he was made.

Why should we be in such desperate haste to succeed, and in such desperate enterprises? If a man does not keep pace with his companions, perhaps it is because he hears a different drummer. Let him step to the music which he hears, however measured or far away. It is not important that he should mature as soon as an apple-tree or an oak. Shall he turn spring into summer? If the condition of things which we were made for is not yet, what were any reality which we can substitute? We will not be shipwrecked on a vain reality. Shall we with pains erect a heaven of blue glass over ourselves, though when it is done we shall be sure to gaze still at the true ethereal heaven far above, as if the former were not?

* * *

There is an incessant influx of novelty into the world, and yet we tolerate incredible dulness. I need only suggest what kind of sermons are still listened to in the most enlightened countries. There are such words and joy and sorrow, but they are only the burden of a psalm, sung with a nasal twang, while we believe in the ordinary and mean. We think that we can change our clothes only. It is said that the British Empire is very large and respectable, and that the United States are a first-rate power. We do not believe that a tide rises and falls behind every man which can float the British Empire like a chip, if he should ever harbor it in his mind. Who knows what sort of seventeen-year locust will next come out of the ground? The government of the world I live in was not framed, like that of Britain, in after-dinner conversations over the wine.

The life in us is like the water in the river. It may rise this year higher than man has ever known it, and flood the parched uplands; even this may be the eventful year, which will drown out all our muskrats. It was not always dry land where we dwell. I see far inland the banks which the stream anciently washed, before science began to record its freshets.[6] Every one has heard the story which has gone the rounds of New England, of a strong and beautiful bug which came out of the dry leaf of an old table of apple-tree wood, which had stood in a farmer's kitchen for sixty years, first in Connecticut, and afterwards in Massachusetts,—from an egg deposited in the living tree many years earlier still, as appeared by counting the annual layers beyond it; which was heard gnawing out for several weeks, hatched perchance by the heat of an urn. Who does not feel his faith in a resurrection and immortality strengthened by hearing of this? Who knows what beautiful and winged life, whose egg has been buried for ages under many concentric layers of woodenness in the dead dry life of society, deposited at first in the alburnum[7] of the green and living tree, which has been gradually converted into the semblance of its well-seasoned tomb,—heard perchance gnawing out now for years by the astonished family of man, as they sat round the festive board,—may unexpectedly come forth from amidst society's most trivial and handselled[8] furniture, to enjoy its perfect summer life at last!

I do not say that John or Jonathan[9] will realize all this; but such is the character of that morrow which mere lapse of time can never make to dawn. The light which puts out our eyes is darkness to us. Only that day dawns to which we are awake. There is more day to dawn. The sun is but a morning star.

END OF PERSPECTIVES: ROMANTIC NATURE

6. Rushing streams.
7. Soft wood, close to the bark.
8. Shoddy.
9. John (Bull), a stock name for an Englishman; Jonathan, an American.

Ghalib

1797–1869

One of the greatest poets of modern times in two different languages, Persian and Urdu, Ghalib was a religious skeptic whose verses are filled with echoes of the Qur'an. A court poet with little reverence for power, Ghalib was a writer of passionate love poetry and an ironic observer of his own passion. He was born in Agra, in Muslim northern India, as Mirza Asadullah Beg Khan, a descendant of Turkish aristocrats who had come to India seeking to improve their fortunes. His father was killed in battle when he was four years old; his mother and her children then moved in with a wealthy brother, who soon died as well. The children received the education of aristocrats, but they had little wealth of their own. At age thirteen, Ghalib was married into a noble family in Delhi, then the capital of the Mughal Empire. He wrote much of his most famous Urdu poetry over the next several years, shifting to Persian at around age twenty. Though the young poet took the lofty pen name of Ghalib ("Victorious"), he was financially dependent on inconsistent patrons, and his own love of wine and gambling left him often in debt. In a capital of lavish homes, Ghalib never owned a home himself, and even possessed few books, often borrowing from friends and storing his own poems in their libraries.

Ghalib's patrons didn't really know what to make of him, in part because of his unorthodox personal habits and his skeptical, tolerant religious beliefs, and in part for the mysterious beauty of his poems. By the age of eleven he had begun composing poetry in both Persian and Urdu (the common speech of much of north India, derived from Hindi and written in the Arabic alphabet). By his late teens he was already writing many of his most striking and original poems, particularly in the verse form of the *ghazal* or "conversation with the beloved." Such poems could be addressed either to an earthly beloved or to God; in Ghalib's verse, it is often difficult to say which is the case, or whether the poem is addressed to both at once. (In the translations below, the translators use the term "the Great One" to keep these possibilities open.) The *ghazal* is a highly structured poetic form, with strict rules of rhyme and repetition of a key phrase in each of its couplets. In lesser hands, the rhymes can drive the meaning, and the imagery may remain simple or even hackneyed, but Ghalib fashioned his couplets into individual gems, linked together in ways that can be hard to sort out but that cumulatively create powerful images of desire and loss. Ghalib was well aware that his poems weren't generally easy to grasp on a first hearing, and he wrote a *ghazal*—pointedly brief and direct—about this very problem:

I agree, O heart, that my ghazals are not easy to take in.
When they hear my work, experienced poets

Tell me I should write something easier to understand.
I have to write what's difficult, otherwise it is difficult to write.

Like Byron, his contemporary, Ghalib was an aristocratic rebel, a self-styled outsider who sought and enjoyed the admiration of the more conventional readers who read him despite their discomfort with his free-living and free-thinking ways. Like Byron as well, Ghalib made himself a leading figure within his own poems. *Ghazals* had traditionally ended with a coda mentioning the poet's name, often in relatively impersonal fashion, but Ghalib's poems build up a powerful persona of a witty, sophisticated, melancholy commentator on his own life and on life in general. Ghalib is typically indirect in his social and political references, but his verses reflect his ambivalent skepticism toward secular power and religious orthodoxy. Seen in the context of his times, his poems become a personal mirror (a recurrent image in his lyrics) of the declining decades of the Mughal Empire, at a time when British involvement in India was rapidly increasing.

Ghalib was deeply critical of the harshness of British rule, yet he also admired the city planning and prosperity they had introduced in Calcutta. He didn't support the 1857 revolt (or as the British called it, the "Mutiny") against colonial rule, and was shocked at the extent of British reprisals, in which many of his friends were hanged or exiled. An added personal loss was the destruction of the homes and libraries of two friends where many of his poems were housed. Hundreds survived, though, scattered about on paper and in people's memories; one poem was said to have been preserved when a beggar, seeking alms, came to his door and recited it.

Though he wrote for the Mughal emperor and other aristocrats, Ghalib was never a model court poet, and he didn't conceal his lack of admiration for the emperor's own poetry. For the middle decades of his life he enjoyed less royal favor than the emperor's less talented poetry teacher, Zauq; finally, upon Zauq's death in 1847, the emperor rather reluctantly appointed Ghalib his court poet. Ghalib wrote Persian poems in praise of the king, while once again turning to writing *ghazals* in Urdu, until his death in 1869 at the age of seventy-two. Since then, Ghalib has been regarded as the greatest writer of Urdu *ghazals* of any era.

In a classic *ghazal,* both lines of the poem's opening couplet must end with the same word or phrase, which then serves as a refrain at the end of each succeeding couplet. A rhyming word or phrase must appear just before this refrain, and the same rhyme must be carried through the entire poem. The *ghazal* has no set length and no fixed meter, but all the lines in a given *ghazal* have to be of the same length. The translations below strive to convey the condensed, revelatory beauty of Ghalib's verse rather than the formal patterning of rhymes, but this patterning can be experienced directly in the Resonance section that follow Ghalib's verses.

These poems were written in English by the contemporary Kashmiri-American poet Agha Shahid Ali, and they brilliantly transmute Ghalib's favored form, often responding to Ghalib's work either explicitly or indirectly. "Of Snow," for example, published posthumously after Ali's early death in 2001, brings Ghalib's classic themes of wine, poetry, lost love, and religious doubt into the world of jet travel and modernist poetry. Like Ghalib's poems, Ali's *ghazals* are deeply personal, even contemplative, and full of charm and sly wit, seen especially in the turns of phrase producing each new version of the poem's rhyme, and in the personal couplet that concludes the poem and gives a final twist to its themes. Unlike Ghalib, Ali often gives his verse an openly social and political force, describing his own personal dislocation across continents and cultures. In his 1997 collection *The Country Without a Post Office,* he wrote about the ongoing strife in his homeland of Kashmir—still bitterly disputed between India and Pakistan. In other poems he meditates on the struggles of displaced peoples elsewhere, evoking a wide range of exiles, from Jews and Palestinians, to medieval mystics, to Oscar Wilde. Like Ghalib, Shahid Ali was finally at home only in his own verses.

I'm neither the loosening of song[1]

I'm neither the loosening of song nor the close-drawn tent of music;
I'm the sound, simply, of my own breaking.[2]

You were meant to sit in the shade of your rippling hair;
I was made to look further, into a blacker tangle.

1. Translated by Adrienne Rich.

2. The term used, *shikast,* means defeat or breaking; it is also used for a note out of tune.

All my self-possession is self-delusion;
what violent effort, to maintain this nonchalance!

Now that you've come, let me touch you in greeting
as the forehead of the beggar touches the ground.

No wonder you came looking for me, you
who care for the grieving, and I the sound of grief.

Come now: I want you: my only peace[1]

Come now: I want you: my only peace.
I've passed the age of fencing and teasing.

This life: a night of drinking and poetry.
Paradise: a long hangover.

Tears sting my eyes; I'm leaving
lest the other guests see my weakness.

I is another, the rose no rose this year;
without a meaning to perceive, what is perception?

Ghalib: no hangover will cure a man like you
knowing as you do the aftertaste of all sweetness.

When I look out, I see no hope for change[1]

When I look out, I see no hope for change.
I don't see how anything in my life can end well.

Their funeral date is already decided, but still
People complain that they can't sleep.

When young, my love-disasters made me burst out laughing.
Now even funny things seem sober to me.

I know the answer—that's what keeps me quiet.
Beyond that it's clear I know how to speak.

Why shouldn't I scream? I can stop. Perhaps
The Great One notices Ghalib only when he stops screaming.

This is the spiritual state I am in:
About myself, there isn't any news.

I do die; the longing for death is so strong it's killing me.
Such a death comes, but the other death doesn't come.

What face will you wear when you visit the Kaaba?[2]
Ghalib, you are shameless even to think of that.

1. Translated by Adrienne Rich.

1. Translated by Robert Bly and Sunil Dutta, as are the rest of the Ghalib poems.

2. Sacred shrine in Mecca, which every Muslim hopes to visit at least once.

If King Jamshid's diamond cup breaks that's it

If King Jamshid's diamond cup breaks, that's it.[1]
But my clay cup I can easily replace, so it's better.

The delight of giving is deeper when the gift hasn't been demanded.
I like the God-seeker who doesn't make a profession of begging.

When I see God, color comes into my cheeks.
God thinks—this is a bad mistake—that I'm in good shape.

When a drop falls in the river, it becomes the river.
When a deed is done well, it becomes the future.

I know that Heaven doesn't exist, but the idea
Is one of Ghalib's favorite fantasies.

One can sigh, but a lifetime is needed to finish it

One can sigh, but a lifetime is needed to finish it.
We'll die before we see the tangles in your hair loosened.

There are dangers in waves, in all those crocodiles with their jaws open.
The drop of water goes through many difficulties before it becomes a pearl.

Love requires waiting, but desire doesn't want to wait.
The heart has no patience; it would rather bleed to death.

I know you will respond when you understand the state of my soul,
But I'll probably become earth before all that is clear to you.

When the sun arrives the dew on the petal passes through existence.
I am also me until your kind eye catches sight of me.

How long is our life? How long does an eyelash flutter?
The warmth of a poetry gathering is like a single spark.[1]

Oh Ghalib, the sorrows of existence, what can cure them but death?
There are so many colors in the candle flame, and then the day comes.

When the Great One gestures to me

When the Great One gestures to me, the message does not become clear.
When love words are spoken, I get six or seven meanings.

I must tell you, God, this woman doesn't grasp my meaning.
Give her a second heart, please, if you don't give me a second tongue.

Her eyebrows do make a bow, but the rest is unclear.
What are her eyes? An arrow or something else?

You come into town, and I still grieve. Of course I can go
To the market and buy another heart and another life.

1. The legendary Persian king Jamshid could see the future inside his jeweled cup.

1. Poets and their friends would gather for long evenings of poetry and feasting.

I'm good at smashing rocks with my head, but it looks as if
Someone on this street has been strewing boulders.

My soul is full and it would be good to drain the blood.
The problem is limits; I have only two eyes.

Even though my head flies off, I love to hear her voice
As she remarks to the executioner: "You're doing well."

People get a real sense of what the sun is like
When I let the light reflect off one of my scars.

I could have had some peace, had I not fallen in love with you.
If I hadn't died, I could have done a lot more crying and sighing.

A river keeps rising when its bed is not available.
When my nature becomes dammed, it just keeps moving.

We know there is more than one good poet in the world,
But the experts say that Ghalib's little jests are great.

For tomorrow's sake, don't skimp with me on wine today

For tomorrow's sake, don't skimp with me on wine today.
A stingy portion implies a suspicion of heaven's abundance.

The horse of life is galloping; we'll never know the stopping place.
Our hands are not touching the reins, nor our feet the stirrups.

I keep a certain distance from the reality of things.
It's the same distance between me and utter confusion.

The scene, the one looking, and the ability to see are all the same.
If that is so, why am I confused about what is in front of me?

The greatness of a river depends on its magnificent face.
If we break it into bubbles and drops and waves, we are lost.

She is not free from her ways to increase her beauty.
The mirror she sees is on the inside of her veil.

What we think is obvious is so far beyond our comprehension.
We are still dreaming even when we dream we are awake.

From the smell of my friend's friend I get the smell of my friend.
Listen, Ghalib, you are busy worshiping God's friend.

I am confused: should I cry over my heart, or slap my chest?

I am confused: should I cry over my heart, or slap my chest?
If I could afford it, I'd have a man paid to cry.

My jealousy is so strong that I refuse to name the street where you live.
In view of that, "How do I get there?" doesn't make much sense.

I was forced to walk to his house a thousand times.
I wish I'd never known about that path you like so much.

It's clear to her that my fate is nothing and nobody.
If I had known that, I would not have thrown away my house.

Fools typically mistake simple desire for a form of worship.
Do I desire a hard woman or do I worship a stone?[1]

I walk for a short distance with each fast-moving stream.
But that's because I don't know who the guide is.

I was so carefree I forgot the roads to my friend's house.
Now how can I discover who I am?

I judge the whole world on the basis of my imagination.
I think that every person loves a true work of art.

She has a habit of torture, but doesn't mean to end the love

She has a habit of torture, but doesn't mean to end the love.
Such oppression is only teasing; we don't imagine it as a test.

Which of my mouths shall I use to thank her for this delight?
I know she inquires about me even though no word is exchanged.

The one who tortures likes us, and we like the torturers.
So if she's not kind, we have to say she's not unkind.

If you don't give me a kiss, at least curse at me.
That means you have a tongue if you don't have a mouth.

If your heart is still in one piece, cut your chest with a dagger.
If eyelashes are not soaked with blood, put a knife in your heart.

The heart is an embarrassment to the chest if it's not on fire.
Releasing a breath brings shame if it's not a fountain of flame.

Well, it's not a loss for me if my madness has destroyed our house.
Giving up a large house for a wilderness is a good bargain.

You ask me what is written on my forehead? It shows marks
From being rubbed on the stone floor before some god.

Gabriel[1] sends praise to me for my poems;
That happens even though Gabriel speaks a different language.

For the price of one kiss she sets my whole life—
Because she knows Ghalib is only about half alive.

For my weak heart this living in the sorrow house

For my weak heart this living in the sorrow house is more than enough.
The shortage of rose-colored wine is also more than enough.

1. Perhaps alluding to the Black Stone enshrined at Mecca, which Muslim pilgrims kiss to obtain forgiveness of sin; it is said to have been given to Adam on his expulsion from Paradise.

1. Archangel who brought divine revelations to Muhammad, "guidance and glad tidings for those who believe" (*Qur'an* 2:97).

I'm embarrassed, otherwise I'd tell the wine-server
That even the leftovers in the cup are, for me, enough.

No arrow comes flying in; I am safe from hunters.
The comfort level I experience in this cage is more than enough.

I don't see why the so-called elite people are so proud
When the ropes of custom that tie them down are clear enough.

It's hard for me to distinguish sacrifice from hypocrisy,
When the greed for reward in pious actions is obvious enough.

Leave me alone at the Zam Zam Well; I won't circle the Kaaba.[1]
The wine stains on my robe are already numerous enough.

If we can't resolve this, it will be a great injustice.
She is not unwilling and my desire is more than strong enough.

The blood of my heart has not completely exited through my eyes.
O death, let me stay a while, the work we have to do is abundant enough.

It's difficult to find a person who has no opinion about Ghalib.
He is a good poet, but the dark rumors about him are more than enough.

Religious people are always praising the Garden of Paradise

Religious people are always praising the Garden of Paradise.
To us ecstatics it's a bouquet left on the bedstand of forgetfulness.

Her eyelashes are so sharp it's hard to describe the pain.
Each drop of eye blood is like a necklace made of coral.

If this world gave me free time, I could show you fireworks.
My heart has many scars; each scar signifies a tree all on fire.

You know what the reflected sunlight does to dewdrops.
Your beauty has the same effect on the house of mirrors.

In my beginning there was already the essence of my end.
Lightning doesn't care about the crop, it wants the farmer.

In my silence there are thousands of blood-soaked desires.
I am like a candle that has gone out on the grave of a poor man.

I think you must be making love today with that man I hate.
Otherwise why would you smile so mischievously in my dream?

Ghalib, I think we have caught sight of the road to death now.
Death is a string that binds together the scattered beads of the universe.

Only a few faces show up as roses

Only a few faces show up as roses; where are the rest?
This dust must be concealing so many poets and saints.

1. The poet will remain at an oasis short of the pilgrim's destination of the Kaaba, the sacred shrine at Mecca.

The Seven Pleiades hid behind a veil all day.[1]
At night they changed their minds, and became naked.

During the night of separation red tears flow from my eyes.
I will imagine my eyes as two burning candles.

We'll seek revenge in heaven from these hard-hearted beauties.
Of course that presupposes that their destination is heaven.

That man on whose arm your hair is spread out
Owns three things: sleep, a quiet mind, and night.

When I visited the Garden, it was as if I started a school.
Even the birds gave poetry readings after hearing me cry.

O God, why do these glances of hers keep invading my heart?
What luck do I have? When I look, I see her lids.

All the good words I could remember I gave to the doorman.
How can I change her painful jibes now into blessings?

Whenever a man's hand closes around a cup of wine,
That energy-enhancer, he believes the lines in his palm are life's rivers.

I believe in one God only, and my religion is breaking rules:
When all sects go to pieces, they'll become part of the true religion.

When a human being becomes used to sorrow, then sorrow disappears;
Obstacle after obstacle fell on me, and the road was easy.

If Ghalib keeps pouring out the salt of his tears,
Dear people, I say the whole world will become a ruin.

I agree that I'm in a cage, and I'm crying

I agree that I'm in a cage, and I'm crying.
But my crying doesn't affect the happy birds in the garden.

The wound I have in my chest did not bring one tear from you.
But that wound made even the eye of the needle weep.

When people began to talk about chains for my ankles,
The gold under the ground began to twist, pushing the iron away.

The essence of faith is loyalty and devotion.
It's all right to bury in the Kaaba the Brahman who died worshiping in the
temple.[1]

My destiny was always to have my head cut off.
Whenever I see a sword, my neck bends by habit.

I can sleep well at night because I was robbed during the day.
I have to thank the robber for providing such a relaxed sleep.

1. The translators use the Pleiades as an equivalent to a cluster of three stars called "Daughters of the Bier" in Urdu.

1. A Brahman is a member of the Hindu priestly caste, who would never ordinarily be admitted to the precincts of the Muslim shrine at Mecca.

Why should we bother about diamonds if we can write poems?
We have our own chests to dig in; why bother traveling to the mines?

Each time I open my mouth, the Great One says

Each time I open my mouth, the Great One says: "You—you, who are you?"
Help me, how would you describe the style of such a conversation?

A spark is lacking in awe. Lightning lacks playfulness.
Neither has the Great One's adroit fierceness.

My jealousy arises because my rival gets to speak to you;
Otherwise it's okay if he ruins my reputation.

Blood makes my whole shirt stick to my body.
The good thing is I don't have to repair my collar.

With the whole body cindered, the heart was clearly burnt.
Digging into the ashes, what's the point of that?

Blood flowing along through the veins doesn't impress us.
If blood doesn't drop from the eyes, it's not real blood.

My main attraction to Heaven has always been its wine—
That musky, fuschia-colored wine we've been promised.

If it's drinking time, I need large containers.
Let's put away these mingy cups and flagons.

My gift of speech is gone but even if I still had it
What reason would I have to put desire into words?

Since he's a friend of the Emperor, he oozes arrogance.[1]
How else can Ghalib gain any respect?

My heart is becoming restless again

My heart is becoming restless again;
And my fingernails start looking for my chest.

My fingernails are clawing down toward my heart again.
It must be the right time for planting red tulips.

The eyes that are filled with desire have a goal—
The curtained hoodah[1] where the elegant rider sits.

The eye's habit is to buy and sell disreputable goods.
The heart is an enthusiastic purchaser of humiliation.

1. Said to be an allusion to the favored court poet Zauq.

1. A canopied seat for nobility riding on an elephant.

I'm still giving out the same hundred colorful complaints.
Tears are falling now, but a hundred times more.

Because my heart wants so much to look at my lover's beautiful feet,
It has become a scene of great unrest like the paintings of the Last Day.

Beauty is passing by once more and showing her style
So we know that someone will shortly die in the public square.

We die over and over for the same unfaithful person.
Our life has fallen back into the old familiar ways.

The whole world is sinking into darkness and corruption
Because she has just thrown back her beautiful hair.

Once more the mashed pieces of the heart send in their petitions
Asking why the pain in this world is so repetitive.

The amount of ecstasy has to make some sense, Ghalib.
There must be something hiding behind the curtain.

RESONANCE

Agha Shahid Ali[1]
Ghazal

Pale hands I loved beside the Shalimar
—Laurence Hope[2]

Where are you now? Who lies beneath your spell tonight
before you agonize him in farewell tonight?

Pale hands that once loved me beside the Shalimar:
Whom else from rapture's road will you expel tonight?

Those "Fabrics of Cashmere—" "to make Me beautiful—"
"Trinket"—to gem—"Me to adorn—How—tell"—tonight?

I beg for haven: Prisons, let open your gates—
A refugee from Belief seeks a cell tonight.

Executioners near the woman at the window.
Damn you, Elijah, I'll bless Jezebel tonight.[3]

1. Born in New Delhi in 1949, Agha Shahid Ali was raised a Muslim in the northern Indian region of Kashmir, site of prolonged, ongoing conflicts between Hindu nationalists and Muslim separatists. After completing college in India, he emigrated to the United States, where he earned a Ph.D. and an M.F.A. in the 1980s. Before his death in 2001 he directed several creative writing programs and published seven volumes of poetry. Ali wrote many *ghazals* in English, using the classical form to reflect on contemporary romantic, social, and political conflicts.

2. Pen name of Adela Nicolson (1865–1904), whose *Indian Love Lyrics* freely adapted Indian poets, in melodramatic style: "To have—to hold—and—in time—let go!" Her poem "Kashmiri Song" begins, "Pale hands I loved beside the Shalimar, / Where are you now? Who lies beneath your spell?"

3. In 1 Kings 21, the prophet Elijah announces God's condemnation of Queen Jezebel, who serves the god Ba'al and has slain God's prophets.

Lord, cried out the idols, *Don't let us be broken;*
Only we can convert the infidel tonight.[4]

Has God's vintage loneliness turned to vinegar?
He's poured rust into the Sacred Well tonight.

In the heart's veined temple all statues have been smashed.
No priest in saffron's left to toll its knell tonight.[5]

He's freed some fire from ice, in pity for Heaven;
he's left open—for God—the doors of Hell tonight.

And I, Shahid, only am escaped to tell thee—
God sobs in my arms. Call me Ishmael tonight.[6]

Of Snow

Husband of Water, where is your Concubine of Snow?
Has she laced your flooded desert with a wine of snow?

What a desert we met in—the foliage was lush!—
a cactus was dipped into every moonshine of snow.

One song is so solitaire in our ring of mountains,
its echo climbs to cut itself at each line of snow.

The sky beyond its means is always beside itself
till (by the plane) each peak rises, a shrine of snow.

Snowmen, inexplicably, have gathered in the Sahara
to melt and melt and melt for a Palestine of snow.

Kali[1] turned to ice one winter, her veins transparent—
on her lips blood froze. A ruby wine of snow!

If Lorca were alive he would again come to New York,[2]
bringing back to my life that one Valentine of snow.

Do you need to make angels, really, who then vanish
or are angels all you can undermine of snow?

I who believe in prayer but could never in God
place roses at your grave with nothing to divine of snow.

When he drinks in winter, Shahid kisses his enemies.
For Peace, then, let bars open at the first sign of snow.

4. Muhammad purified the shrine of Mecca by destroying the idols that had been set there in pre-Islamic times.
5. Hindu priests wear saffron-colored robes.
6. "Call me Ishmael" is the opening sentence of Melville's *Moby-Dick,* whose narrator alone survived the wrecking of his ship. In the Bible and the Qur'an, Ishmael is the traditional forefather of the Arabs.
1. Hindu goddess of destruction.
2. Federico García Lorca, Spanish surrealist poet .

Charles Baudelaire

1821–1867

Charles Baudelaire was the consummate modern city-dweller, a bohemian slummer who devoted himself to sex, drugs, alcohol, art, and poetry. His background was typical for an upper-middle-class child in nineteenth-century France: the young second wife adored by her son, the father an ancient civil servant (and poet and painter) dead before his son was ten, the detested and disciplinarian stepfather who sent the boy away to various schools from which he was quickly expelled for bad behavior, the inheritance squandered on a dandy's finery and on every debauchery the city could offer, the enforced South Seas voyage to straighten him out, and the return to Paris more determined than ever to live to the fullest the life of the penniless artist. Baudelaire fell tumultuously in love with the mulatta actress Jeanne Duval, among others; he drank to excess while experimenting with hashish and other intoxicants; he accumulated enormous debts, and contracted syphilis in the bargain while exploring the low life of Paris. He also wrote, constantly.

In the mid-1840s, Baudelaire began publishing reviews of the annual *Salons* (art exhibitions), and composing the poems that he would eventually collect in *Les Fleurs du Mal* (*The Flowers of Evil*). He was involved briefly in radical politics, manning the barricades during the Revolution of 1848, where his primary contribution was to exhort the Republicans to shoot down his stepfather, the General Aupick. He achieved his first literary celebrity with a series of translations of the American writer Edgar Allan Poe. When the first edition of *Les Fleurs du Mal* was finally published in 1857, it was immediately prosecuted for obscenity, the author was fined, and six of the poems were ordered to be excised from further editions. Over the last ten years of his life, as his health deteriorated, Baudelaire revised *Les Fleurs du Mal,* continued publishing criticism, including influential manifesto of modernism, *The Painter of Modern Life,* and began work on a series of prose poems, *Paris Spleen,* which were published posthumously. By the last years of his life, syphilis had rendered him mute and partially paralyzed; he died an invalid at age forty-six, his mother by his side.

The subject matter of Baudelaire's poetry has retained much of its capacity to shock: the necrophilia of "A Martyr," the rotting corpse of "Carrion," the sheer cruelty of "Ragpicker's Wine." But the key to its power is the decorous language and melodic rhythms with which the poems describe the depravity of modern life. In "Carrion," for example, the poet begins with the familiar theme of a lover remembering a walk in a park alongside his beloved, before bringing his reader face-to-face with a different sort of nature:

> Remember, my soul, the thing we saw
> that lovely summer day?
> On a pile of stones where the path turned off,
> that hideous carrion.

Baudelaire favored regular and often intricate rhyme schemes, short and highly structured verse forms such as the sonnet, and the classically French twelve-syllable line called the alexandrine. In the quatrain quoted above, the narrative alexandrines (1 and 3) alternate with the singsong counterpoint of the brief eight-syllable lines (2 and 4):

> Rappelez-vous l'objet que nous vîmes, mon âme,
> Ce beau matin d'été si doux:
> Au détour d'un sentier une charogne infame
> Sur un lit semé de cailloux.

Just as modern life hid unpleasant surprises behind pleasing exteriors, just as the industrial city brought stark contrasts of experience into close proximity, so the *Fleurs du Mal* wrapped cruel and cynical insights inside perfect poetic artifacts of great beauty.

Although the desire to shock the middle class was a fundamental tenet of Baudelaire's bohemianism, his poetry extended that rebellious impulse into a profound expression of despair. Baudelaire is one of the great love poets of the French language, and yet his poetry is more about the impossibility of love in Paris than about its wonders and delights. The poet appears rooted to Paris, but can conceive of love only outside of its bounds, in an exotic place he will never actually see but where he can hope to escape in his imagination: "All is order there, and elegance, / pleasure, peace, and opulence" ("Invitation to the Voyage"). By contrast, love in reality takes place in the fallen world of Paris, sullied by money and spoiled by boredom, a world where "Man is tired of writing, Woman of love" ("Twilight: Daybreak"). The only joy offered by love in the city lies in a momentary glance or a dream of what might have been, as in the sonnet, "In Passing." Once tasted, passion turns to boredom, and novelty gives way to spleen, the bile of someone who yearns for genuine experience but is convinced he will never find it.

Among the citydwellers who inhabit the world of these poems there is scarcely a glimpse of the figures of elegance, wealth, and beauty for which mid-nineteenth-century Paris was renowned; instead, the poet turns his caustic eye to society's exiles, throwing into the face of his bourgeois readers what they would have seen around them every day but never actually registered: the ragpicking beggars, the prostitutes, the drunkards, and the rundown slums. Whatever his society defined as evil or excluded as diseased, Baudelaire placed in his poetry as a figure of warped beauty. Not for the bohemian the easy pleasures of the summer day and the innocent sweetheart of the traditional lyric; the only response to the cruelty of modern life was a crueler beauty and a fiercely ironic gaze on the world.

Baudelaire brought lyric poetry into the modern world; he invented the persona of the *poète maudit*, the cursed artist who transforms despair into a tool for stripping away the hypocrisies of existence, and who trades in the niceties of society for the grit of the slums. And he perfected another hallmark of modern culture—irony—for he never forgot the fundamentally ridiculous fact that his audience, the "hypocrite reader" of the opening poem of the *Fleurs du Mal,* was not the downtrodden marginals and perverse bohemians of whom he wrote, but the respectable bourgeoisie whom he wanted so desperately to shock. The mythic persona and ironic gaze of Baudelaire's writing resonates through modern poetry from Symbolist admirers such as Rimbaud and Mallarmé to modernist poets such as Pound and Eliot through the American Beat poets of the 1950s all the way to such martyrs to rock music as Jim Morrison, Janis Joplin, and Kurt Cobain.

from The Flowers of Evil[1]

To the Reader

Stupidity, delusion, selfishness and lust
torment our bodies and possess our minds,
and we sustain our affable remorse
the way a beggar nourishes his lice.

Our sins are stubborn, our contrition lame;
we want our scruples to be worth our while—
how cheerfully we crawl back to the mire:
a few cheap tears will wash our stains away!

1. Translated by Richard Howard.

Satan Trismegistus[2] subtly rocks
our ravished spirits on his wicked bed
until the precious metal of our will
is leached out° by this cunning alchemist:[3] *filtered out*
the Devil's hand directs our every move—
the things we loathed become the things we love;
day by day we drop through stinking shades
quite undeterred on our descent to Hell.

Like a poor profligate who sucks and bites
the withered breast of some well-seasoned trull,° *prostitute*
we snatch in passing at clandestine joys
and squeeze the oldest orange harder yet.

Wriggling in our brains like a million worms,
a demon demos° holds its revels there, *populace*
and when we breathe, the Lethe[4] in our lungs
trickles sighing on its secret course.

If rape and arson, poison and the knife
have not yet stitched their ludicrous designs
onto the banal buckram° of our fates, *coarse linen*
it is because our souls lack enterprise!

But here among the scorpions and the hounds,
the jackals, apes and vultures, snakes and wolves,
monsters that howl and growl and squeal and crawl
in all the squalid zoo of vices, one

is even uglier and fouler than the rest,
although the least flamboyant of the lot;
this beast would gladly undermine the earth
and swallow all creation in a yawn;

I speak of Boredom[5] which with ready tears
dreams of hangings as it puffs its pipe.
Reader, you know this squeamish monster well,
—hypocrite reader,—my alias,—my twin!

The Albatross[1]

Often, to pass the time on board, the crew
will catch an albatross, one of those big birds
which nonchalantly chaperone a ship
across the bitter fathoms of the sea.

2. Meaning "triply great," Trismegistus was usually applied to Hermes Trismegistus, legendary author of the Hermetic writings of Egypt and inventor of alchemy.
3. Alchemy manipulates base metals with corrosive acids and water preparations to yield precious metals such as gold and silver.
4. The river of forgetting in the classical underworld.
5. Here as elsewhere in *The Flowers of Evil,* Baudelaire personifies states of mind and other abstractions as active forces or characters.
1. Large seabirds with a wingspan reaching over ten feet, albatrosses spend nearly their entire lives at sea. In sailors' lore, to cause the death of an albatross was considered extremely bad luck.

Tied to the deck, this sovereign of space,
as if embarrassed by its clumsiness,
pitiably lets its great white wings
drag at its sides like a pair of unshipped oars.

How weak and awkward, even comical
this traveller but lately so adroit—
one deckhand sticks a pipestem in its beak,
another mocks the cripple that once flew!

The Poet is like this monarch of the clouds
riding the storm above the marksman's range;
exiled on the ground, hooted and jeered,
he cannot walk because of his great wings.

Correspondences

The pillars of Nature's temple are alive
and sometimes yield perplexing messages;
forests of symbols between us and the shrine
remark our passage with accustomed eyes.

Like long-held echoes, blending somewhere else
into one deep and shadowy unison
as limitless as darkness and as day,
the sounds, the scents, the colors correspond.[1]

There are odors succulent as young flesh,
sweet as flutes, and green as any grass,
while others—rich, corrupt and masterful—

possess the power of such infinite things
as incense, amber, benjamin[2] and musk,
to praise the senses' raptures and the mind's.

The Head of Hair

Ecstatic fleece that ripples to your nape
and reeks of negligence in every curl!
To people my dim cubicle tonight
with memories shrouded in that head of hair,
I'd have it flutter like a handkerchief!

For torpid Asia, torrid Africa
—the wilderness I thought a world away—
survive at the heart of this dark continent . . .

1. The theory of a universal analogy between sounds, scents, and colors was frequently voiced in mid-19th-century literary circles; among its proponents were the German writer of fantastic stories, E. T. A. Hoffmann, the French novelist Honoré de Balzac, the eccentric poet Alphonse Esquiros, and Alphonse-Louis Constant, who published occult works under the pseudonym Eliphas Levi.

2. Gum benjamin, the resin of the benzoin tree of Southeast Asia, is used as an aromatic in perfumes.

As other souls set sail to music, mine,
O my love! embarks on your redolent hair.

Take me, tousled current, to where men
as mighty as the trees they live among
submit like them to the sun's long tyranny;
ebony sea, you bear a brilliant dream
of sails and pennants, mariners and masts,

a harbor where my soul can slake its thirst
for color, sound and smell—where ships that glide
among the seas of golden silk throw wide
their yardarms to embrace a glorious sky
palpitating in eternal heat.

Drunk, and in love with drunkenness, I'll dive
into this ocean where the other lurks,
and solaced by these waves, my restlessness
will find a fruitful lethargy at last,
rocking forever at aromatic ease.

Blue hair, vault of shadows, be for me
the canopy of overarching sky;
here at the downy roots of every strand
I stupefy myself on the mingled scent
of musk and tar and coconut oil for hours . . .

For hours? Forever! Into that splendid mane
let me braid rubies, ropes of pearls to bind
you indissolubly to my desire—
you the oasis where I dream, the gourd
from which I gulp the wine of memory.

Carrion

Remember, my soul, the thing we saw
  that lovely summer day?
On a pile of stones where the path turned off,
  the hideous carrion—

legs in the air, like a whore—displayed,
  indifferent to the last,
a belly slick with lethal sweat
  and swollen with foul gas.

The sun lit up that rottenness
  as though to roast it through,
restoring to Nature a hundredfold
  what she had here made one.

And heaven watched the splendid corpse
  like a flower open wide—

you nearly fainted dead away
at the perfume it gave off.

Flies kept humming over the guts
from which a gleaming clot
of maggots poured to finish off
what scraps of flesh remained.

The tide of trembling vermin sank,
then bubbled up afresh
as if the carcass, drawing breath,
by *their* lives lived again

and made a curious music there—
like running water, or wind,
or the rattle of chaff the winnower
loosens in his fan.[1]

Shapeless—nothing was left but a dream
the artist had sketched in,
forgotten, and only later on
finished from memory.

Behind the rocks an anxious bitch
eyed us reproachfully,
waiting for the chance to resume
her interrupted feast.

—Yet you will come to this offence,
this horrible decay,
you, the light of my life, the sun
and moon and stars of my love!

Yes, you will come to this, my queen,
after the sacraments,° *funeral rites*
when you rot underground among
the bones already there.

But as their kisses eat you up,
my Beauty, tell the worms
I've kept the sacred essence, saved
the form of my rotted loves!

Invitation to the Voyage

Imagine the magic
of living together
there, with all the time in the world
for loving each other,

1. A winnower uses a special fan to toss corn or wheat into the air to separate the lighter husks, the chaff, from the edible grain.

for loving and dying
where even the landscape resembles you:
the suns dissolved
in overcast skies
have the same mysterious charm for me
as your wayward eyes
through crystal tears,
my sister, my child!

All is order there, and elegance,
pleasure, peace, and opulence.

Furniture gleaming
with the patina
of time itself in the room we would share;
the rarest flowers
mingling aromas
with amber's uncertain redolence;
encrusted ceilings
echoed in mirrors
and Eastern splendor on the walls—
here all would whisper
to the soul in secret
her sweet mother tongue.

All is order there, and elegance,
pleasure, peace, and opulence.

On these still canals
the freighters doze
fitfully: their mood is for roving,
and only to flatter
a lover's fancy
have they put in from the ends of the earth.
By late afternoon
the canals catch fire
as sunset glorifies the town;
the world turns to gold
as it falls asleep
in a fervent light.

All is order there, and elegance,
pleasure, peace, and opulence.

Spleen (II)[1]

Souvenirs?
More than if I had lived a thousand years!

1. In medieval medicine, the spleen was associated with the black bile said to cause melancholy. Baudelaire adapted the English word to express the feeling of bitterness and boredom ("ennui") he considered to be characteristic of modern life.

No chest of drawers crammed with documents,
love-letters, wedding-invitations, wills,
a lock of someone's hair rolled up in a deed,
hides so many secrets as my brain.
This branching catacombs, this pyramid
contains more corpses than the potter's field:[2]
I am a graveyard that the moon abhors,
where long worms like regrets come out to feed
most ravenously on my dearest dead.
I am an old boudoir where a rack of gowns,
perfumed by withered roses, rots to dust;
where only faint pastels and pale Bouchers[3]
inhale the scent of long-unstoppered flasks.

Nothing is slower than the limping days
when under the heavy weather of the years
Boredom, the fruit of glum indifference,
gains the dimension of eternity . . .
Hereafter, mortal clay, you are no more
than a rock encircled by a nameless dread,
an ancient sphinx omitted from the map,
forgotten by the world, and whose fierce moods
sing only to the rays of setting suns.

The Swan

to Victor Hugo[1]

1

Andromache, I think of you! That stream,
the sometime witness to your widowhood's
enormous majesty of mourning—that
mimic Simoïs salted by your tears[2]

suddenly inundates my memory
as I cross the new Place du Carrousel.[3]
Old Paris is gone (no human heart
changes half so fast as a city's face)[4]

2. In French *fosse commune,* a burial ground for the poor and for strangers.
3. The French painter François Boucher (1703–1770) was famous for his delicate colors, easy style, and frivolous subjects, and especially for his female nudes.
1. Celebrated French Romantic poet, novelist and dramatist (1802–1885). Baudelaire sent a manuscript copy of the poem to Hugo, who was in political exile at the time on the Channel Islands.
2. The wife of Hector of Troy, Andromache was claimed as prize of war by Achilles' son Pyrrhus. Abandoned by him, she eventually came to settle in Epirus, where Aeneas visits her in Book 3 of Virgil's *Aeneid.* She and her new husband, Hector's brother Helenus, have built a miniature Troy, complete with a replica of its river, Simois, at the shores of which she weeps over the empty grave of her dead husband.
3. The bohemian artists' quarter where Baudelaire and others of his circle had lived had been demolished in 1849 in order to connect the Louvre with the Tuileries Palace. The Place du Carrousel was established in its place.
4. The loss of *vieux Paris*, the narrow winding streets and old buildings dating back to the medieval city, to the demolitions of 19th-century speculation and improvements, was a refrain through most of the century, especially the second half.

and only in my mind's eye can I see
The junk laid out to glitter in the booths
among the weeds and splintered capitals,° *columns*
blocks of marble blackened by the mud;

there used to be a poultry-market here,
and one cold morning—with the sky swept clean,
the ground, too, swept by garbage-men who raised
clouds of soot in the icy air—I saw

a swan that had broken out of its cage,
webbed feet clumsy on the cobblestones,
white feathers dragging in the uneven ruts,
and obstinately pecking at the drains,

drenching its enormous wings in the filth
as if in its own lovely lake, crying
'Where is the thunder, when will it rain?'
I see it still, inevitable myth,

like Daedalus dead-set against the sky[5]—
the sky quite blue and blank and unconcerned—
that straining neck and that voracious beak,
as if the swan were castigating God!

2

Paris changes . . . But in sadness like mine
nothing stirs—new buildings, old
neighborhoods turn to allegory,
and memories weigh more than stone.

One image, near the Louvre, will not dissolve:
I think of that great swan in its torment,
silly, like all exiles, and sublime,
endlessly longing . . . And again I think

of you, Andromache, dragged off
to be the booty of Achilles' son,
Hector's widow now the wife of Helenus,
crouching blindly over an empty grave!

I think of some black woman, starving
and consumptive in the muddy streets,
peering through a wall of fog for those
missing palms of splendid Africa;

I think of orphans withering like flowers;
of those who lose what never can be found
again—never! swallowing their tears
and nursing at the she-wolf Sorrow's dugs;

5. According to legend, the Greek inventor Daedalus had escaped with his son Icarus from imprisonment in Crete with the help of artificial wings stuck with wax.

and in the forest of my mind's exile
a merciless memory winds its horn:
I hear it and I think of prisoners,
of the shipwrecked, the beaten—and so many more!

In Passing

The traffic roared around me, deafening!
Tall, slender, in mourning—noble grief—
a woman passed, and with a jewelled hand
gathered up her black embroidered hem;

stately yet lithe, as if a statue walked . . .
And trembling like a fool, I drank from eyes
as ashen as the clouds before a gale
the grace that beckons and the joy that kills.

Lightning . . . then darkness! Lovely fugitive
whose glance has brought me back to life! But where
is life—not this side of eternity?

Elsewhere! Too far, too late, or never at all!
Of me you know nothing, I nothing of you—you
whom I might have loved and who knew that too!

Twilight: Evening

It comes as an accomplice, stealthily,
the lovely hour that is the felon's friend;
the sky, like curtains round a bed, draws close,
and man prepares to become a beast of prey.

Longed for by those whose aching arms confess:
we earned our daily bread, at last it comes,
evening and the anodyne° it brings *relief*
to workmen free to sleep and dream of sleep,
to stubborn scholars puzzling over texts,
to minds consumed by one tormenting pain . . .
Meantime, foul demons in the atmosphere
dutifully waken—they have work to do—
rattling shutters as they take the sky.
Under the gaslamps shaken by that wind
whoredom invades and everywhere at once
debouches° on invisible thoroughfares, *pours out*
as if the enemy had launched a raid;
it fidgets like a worm in the city's filth,
filching its portion of Man's daily bread.

Listen! Now you can hear the kitchens hiss,
the stages yelp, the music drown it all!
The dens that specialize in gambling fill
with trollops and their vague confederates,

and thieves untroubled by a second thought
will soon be hard at work (they also serve)
softly forcing doors and secret drawers
to dress their sluts and live a few days more.

This is the hour to compose yourself, my soul;
ignore the noise they make; avert your eyes.
Now comes the time when invalids grow worse
and darkness takes them by the throat; they end
their fate in the usual way, and all their sighs
turn hospitals into a cave of the winds.
More than one will not come back for broth
warmed at the fireside by devoted hands.

Most of them, in fact, have never known
a hearth to come to, and have never lived.

Twilight: Daybreak

The morning wind rattles the windowpanes
and over the barracks reveille rings out.

Dreams come now, bad dreams, and teen-age boys
burrow into their pillows. Now the lamp
that glowed at midnight seems, like a bloodshot eye,
to throb and throw a red stain on the room;
balked by the stubborn body's weight, the soul
mimics the lamplight's struggles with the dawn.
Like a face in tears—the tears effaced by wind—
the air is tremulous with escaping things,
and Man is tired of writing, Woman of love.

Here and there, chimneys begin to smoke.
Whores, mouths gaping, eyelids gray as ash,
sleep on their feet, leaning against the walls,
and beggar-women, hunched over sagging breasts,
blow on burning sticks, then on their hands.
Now, the hungry feel the cold the worst,
and women in labor suffer the sharpest pains;
now, like a sob cut short by a clot of blood,
a rooster crows somewhere; a sea of mist
swirls around the buildings; in the Hôtel-Dieu[1]
the dying breathe their last, while the debauched,
spent by their exertions, sleep alone.

Shivering dawn, in a wisp of pink and green,
totters slowly across the empty Seine,

1. A municipal hospital; the one in Paris dates back to the very early Middle Ages, and was demolished in the late 19th century. It stood on the south side of the Ile de la Cité, catercornered to the Notre Dame Cathedral.

and dingy Paris—old drudge rubbing its eyes—
picks up its tools to begin another day.

Ragpickers' Wine[1]

Look—there! in the streetlamp's dingy glow
—wind rattling the glass, lashing the flame—
out of the muddy labyrinth of streets
teeming with unruly, sordid types,

a ragpicker stumbles past, wagging his head
and bumping into walls with a poet's grace,
pouring out his heartfelt schemes to one
and all, including spies of the police.[2]

He swears to wonders, lays down noble laws,
reforms the wicked, raises up their prey,
and under the lowering canopy of heaven
intoxicates himself on his own boasts.

More such creatures—who knows where they live?—
wracked by drudgery, ruined by the years,
staggering under enormous sacks of junk
—the vomit of surfeited Paris—now appear,

whole armies of them, reeking of sour wine,
comrades in arms, whitened by their wars,
whiskers dropping like surrendered flags . . .
Before them wave the banners and the palms—

as if by magic, arches of triumph rise
and in the chaos of exploding flares,
bugle-calls and battle-cries and drums,
they march in glory past a cheering mob!

So it is, through frivolous mankind,
that wine like a bright Pactolus pours its gold;[3]
with human tongues it glorifies its deeds
and rules by what it gives, as true kings do.

To drown the spleen and pacify the sloth
of these old wrecks who die without a word,
God, taking pity, created Sleep; to which
Man added Wine, the sun's anointed son!

1. Ragpickers, or *chiffonniers,* lived off what they scavenged at night from the rags and the garbage of the city. The *chiffonnier* was an important figure for many writers of the many marginal occupations of the nocturnal city, both positive and negative, including poetry.

2. *Mouchards,* or police and government spies, were omnipresent under the July Monarchy of Louis-Philippe (1830–1848) and the Second Empire of Napoleon III (1852–1870). *Chiffonniers* were frequently identified with radical politics.

3. According to Greek myth, King Midas was released from the enchantment that caused whatever he touched to become gold by bathing in the river Pactolus, filling it with gold.

A Martyr

Drawing by an Unknown Master[1]

Among decanters, ivories and gems,
sumptuous divans[2]
with gold-brocaded silks and fragrant gowns
trailing languid folds,

where lilies sorrowing in crystal urns
exhale their final sigh
and where, as if the room were under glass,
the air is pestilent,

a headless corpse emits a stream of blood
the sopping pillows shed
onto thirsty sheets which drink it up
as greedily as sand.

Pale as the visions which our captive eyes
discover in the dark,
the head, enveloped in its sombre mane,
emeralds still in its ears,

watches from a stool, a thing apart,
and from the eyes rolled back
to whiteness blank as daybreak emanates
an alabaster stare.[3]

The carcass sprawling naked on the bed
displays without a qualm
the splendid cynosure[4] which prodigal
Nature bestowed—betrayed;

pink with gold clocks, one stocking clings—
a souvenir, it seems;
the garter, gleaming like a secret eye,
darts a jewelled glance.

Doubled by a full-length portrait drawn
in the same provocative pose,
the strange demeanor of this solitude
reveals love's darker side—

profligate practices and guilty joys,
embraces bound to please

1. Rather than referring to a particular work of art, the subtitle emphasizes the visual focus of the poem. The style is of the exotic Romanticism of artists such as Eugène Delacroix, about whose works Baudelaire wrote regularly as an art critic.

2. A decanter is a glass bottle with a stopper in its top; wine is stored in it after it has been decanted, or poured off slowly to eliminate sediment. A divan is a low couch or bed without back or ends; the word comes from the Persian, and the divan was associated with the Orient.

3. Alabaster is a translucent form of gypsum, usually white, used for carving. The adjective is used as a poetic term to describe something white and smooth, such as skin, or, here, in a more symbolic way, the gaze of a dead eye.

4. A brilliant or beautiful focus of attraction or of admiration.

the swarm of naughty angels frolicking
in the curtains overhead;

yet judging from the narrow elegance
of her shoulders sloping down
past the serpentine curve of her waist
to the almost bony hips,

she still is young!—What torment in her soul,
what tedium that stung
her senses gave this body to the throng
of wandering, lost desires?[5]
In spite of so much love, did the vengeful man
she could not, living, sate
assuage on her inert and docile flesh
the measure of his lust?

And did he, gripping her blood-stiffened hair
lift up that dripping head
and press on her cold teeth one final kiss?
The sullied corpse is still.
—Far from a scornful world of jeering crowds
and peering magistrates,
sleep in peace, lovely enigma, sleep
in your mysterious tomb:

your bridegroom roves, and your immortal form
keeps vigil when he sleeps;
like you, no doubt, he will be constant too,
and faithful unto death.

Gustave Flaubert

1821–1880

Gustave Flaubert was almost twenty-eight when he left France for what was then called "the Orient," a journey that was to last from November 1849 to June 1851. Journeys to the Middle East were in fashion. This was partly because Napoleon's expedition to Egypt (1798–1801) and France's strong continuing influence had opened the region to tourism, which increased after France conquered Algeria in 1847. In part, too, people had become full of disgust with the sordid money- and title-grubbing and the social inertia that had followed the epoch of Napoleonic glory. Many of the alienated escaped into exoticism. But in the profundity of his personal alienation, Flaubert had few if any competitors.

Born in 1821 in Rouen, the son of a doctor, Flaubert abandoned the study of law after a brief and not very successful experience. Supported by a private income, he devoted himself with an almost theological intensity to writing. He never married or had an ordinary job,

5. Opinion at the time had it that the real-life model was a singer, Rosine Stoltz, of whom Baudelaire was enamored, and whose profile evidently matched this description.

and it was largely writing (including voluminous letters to lovers who were also talented writers) that gave shape to the rest of his life. A perfectionist who worked to discipline his romantic flamboyance, he tried to achieve perfect sentences and perfect detachment. His most famous novel, *Madame Bovary* (1857), scandalized and confused its readers, who couldn't tell whether its author condemned the hungrily misguided aspirations of its adulterous heroine, or secretly identified with them. Prosecuted for "offense to public and religious morality," Flaubert was acquitted but given a severe reprimand and forced to pay the costs of the trial. Subsequent novels added to the sense of public incomprehension, for Flaubert remained absent from his work, refusing to give directions as to how readers were supposed to feel. About *Salammbô* (1862), which fled from the banality of contemporary France into the archaeologically precise strangeness of ancient Carthage, Flaubert famously remarked that few would ever guess how sad he had to be in order to resuscitate this lost kingdom.

Sentimental Education (1869) is set in Paris in the 1840s (the period of Flaubert's own beginnings as a writer) and roughly follows his early passion for an older married woman. But it, too, is distinguished by an apparent disaffection from nearly everything the characters say and do. Franz Kafka, who sets the twentieth-century standard for disaffection, once said that each time he opened Flaubert's book, he felt perfectly at home. *Three Tales* (1877), which includes "A Simple Heart," was a success with the public, but it is simpler only in appearance. Readers have never decided whether Flaubert is or isn't ironic about the servant protagonist of "A Simple Heart," whose life seems empty and who worships a stuffed parrot. Convinced that it was style rather than content that should be decisive, Flaubert once expressed the desire to write a text about "nothing." His extreme horror of cliché and sense of the nothingness lurking behind everyday life are exemplified in two further works, *Bouvard and Pécuchet* and the *Dictionary of Received Ideas,* which were published after his death in 1880.

In 1876, at the funeral of George Sand, a pioneer feminist writer and one of the most famous figures of her generation, Flaubert wept for the loss of his dear friend and long-time correspondent—and for the bad timing that took her away just as he was writing something "exclusively" for her. Sand, who couldn't understand Flaubert's unwillingness to take a moral stand in his fiction, had urged him to write "something down to earth that everybody can enjoy." "A Simple Heart" was his attempt to fulfill her wish. Flaubert insisted that the story was not ironic but intended "to move tender hearts to pity and tears"—just as Sand would have desired. Flaubert would no doubt have appreciated the further irony that we don't know whether or not to trust his own opinion of his story.

PRONUNCIATIONS:
Aubain: oh-BAHNG
Félicité: fay-lee-cee-TAY
Gustave Flaubert: gous-TAHV flow-BARE

A Simple Heart[1]

1

Madame Aubain's servant Félicité was the envy of the ladies of Pont-l'Évêque for half a century.

1. Translated by Arthur McDowall.

She received four pounds a year. For that she was cook and general servant, and did the sewing, washing, and ironing; she could bridle a horse, fatten poultry, and churn butter—and she remained faithful to her mistress, unamiable as the latter was.

Mme. Aubain had married a gay bachelor without money who died at the beginning of 1809, leaving her with two small children and a quantity of debts. She then sold all her property except the farms of Toucques and Geffosses, which brought in two hundred pounds a year at most, and left her house in Saint-Melaine for a less expensive one that had belonged to her family and was situated behind the market.

This house had a slate roof and stood between an alley and a lane that went down to the river. There was an unevenness in the levels of the rooms which made you stumble. A narrow hall divided the kitchen from the "parlour" where Mme. Aubain spent her day, sitting in a wicker easy chair by the window. Against the panels, which were painted white, was a row of eight mahogany chairs. On an old piano under the barometer a heap of wooden and cardboard boxes rose like a pyramid. A stuffed armchair stood on either side of the Louis-Quinze chimney-piece, which was in yellow marble with a clock in the middle of it modelled like a temple of Vesta.[2] The whole room was a little musty, as the floor was lower than the garden.

The first floor began with "Madame's" room: very large, with a pale-flowered wallpaper and a portrait of "Monsieur" as a dandy of the period. It led to a smaller room, where there were two children's cots without mattresses. Next came the drawing-room, which was always shut up and full of furniture covered with sheets. Then there was a corridor leading to a study. The shelves of a large bookcase were respectably lined with books and papers, and its three wings surrounded a broad writing-table in darkwood. The two panels at the end of the room were covered with pen-drawings, water-colour landscapes, and engravings by Audran, all relics of better days and vanished splendour. Félicité's room on the top floor got its light from a dormer-window, which looked over the meadows.

She rose at daybreak to be in time for Mass, and worked till evening without stopping. Then, when dinner was over, the plates and dishes in order, and the door shut fast, she thrust the log under the ashes and went to sleep in front of the hearth with her rosary in her hand. Félicité was the stubbornest of all bargainers; and as for cleanness, the polish on her saucepans was the despair of other servants. Thrifty in all things, she ate slowly, gathering off the table in her fingers the crumbs of her loaf—a twelve-pound loaf expressly baked for her, which lasted for three weeks.

At all times of year she wore a print hand-kerchief fastened with a pin behind, a bonnet that covered her hair, grey stockings, a red skirt, and a bibbed apron—such as hospital nurses wear—over her jacket.

Her face was thin and her voice sharp. At twenty-five she looked like forty. From fifty onwards she seemed of no particular age; and with her silence, straight figure, and precise movements she was like a woman made of wood, and going by clockwork.

2

She had had her love-story like another.

Her father, a mason, had been killed by falling off some scaffolding. Then her mother died, her sisters scattered, and a farmer took her in and employed her, while

2. Roman goddess of hearth and home.

she was still quite little, to herd the cows at pasture. She shivered in rags and would lie flat on the ground to drink water from the ponds; she was beaten for nothing, and finally turned out for the theft of a shilling which she did not steal. She went to another farm, where she became dairy-maid; and as she was liked by her employers her companions were jealous of her.

One evening in August (she was then eighteen) they took her to the assembly at Colleville. She was dazed and stupefied in an instant by the noise of the fiddlers, the lights in the trees, the gay medley of dresses, the lace, the gold crosses, and the throng of people jigging all together. While she kept shyly apart a young man with a well-to-do air, who was leaning on the shaft of a cart and smoking his pipe, came up to ask her to dance. He treated her to cider, coffee, and cake, and bought her a silk handkerchief; and then, imagining she had guessed his meaning, offered to see her home. At the edge of a field of oats he pushed her roughly down. She was frightened and began to cry out; and he went off.

One evening later she was on the Beaumont road. A big hay-wagon was moving slowly along; she wanted to get in front of it, and as she brushed past the wheels she recognized Theodore. He greeted her quite calmly, saying she must excuse it all because it was "the fault of the drink." She could not think of any answer and wanted to run away.

He began at once to talk about the harvest and the worthies of the commune, for his father had left Colleville for the farm at Les Écots, so that now he and she were neighbours. "Ah!" she said. He added that they thought of settling him in life. Well, he was in no hurry; he was waiting for a wife to his fancy. She dropped her head; and then he asked her if she thought of marrying. She answered with a smile that it was mean to make fun of her.

"But I am not, I swear!"—and he passed his left hand round her waist. She walked in the support of his embrace; their steps grew slower. The wind was soft, the stars glittered, the huge wagon-load of hay swayed in front of them, and dust rose from the dragging steps of the four horses. Then, without a word of command, they turned to the right. He clasped her once more in his arms, and she disappeared into the shadow.

The week after Theodore secured some assignations with her.

They met at the end of farmyards, behind a wall, or under a solitary tree. She was not innocent as young ladies are—she had learned knowledge from the animals—but her reason and the instinct of her honour would not let her fall. Her resistance exasperated Theodore's passion; so much so that to satisfy it—or perhaps quite artlessly—he made her an offer of marriage. She was in doubt whether to trust him, but he swore great oaths of fidelity.

Soon he confessed to something troublesome; the year before his parents had bought him a substitute for the army, but any day he might be taken again, and the idea of serving was a terror to him. Félicité took this cowardice of his as a sign of affection, and it redoubled hers. She stole away at night to see him, and when she reached their meeting-place Theodore racked her with his anxieties and urgings.

At last he declared that he would go himself to the prefecture for information, and would tell her the result on the following Sunday, between eleven and midnight.

When the moment came she sped towards her lover. Instead of him she found one of his friends.

He told her that she would not see Theodore any more. To ensure himself against conscription he had married an old woman, Madame Lehoussais, of Toucques, who was very rich.

There was an uncontrollable burst of grief. She threw herself on the ground, screamed, called to the God of mercy, and moaned by herself in the fields till daylight came. Then she came back to the farm and announced that she was going to leave; and at the end of the month she received her wages, tied all her small belongings with a handkerchief, and went to Pont-l'Évêque.

In front of the inn there she made inquiries of a woman in a widow's cap, who, as it happened, was just looking for a cook. The girl did not know much, but her willingness seemed so great and her demands so small that Mme. Aubain ended by saying:

"Very well, then, I will take you."

A quarter of an hour afterwards Félicité was installed in her house.

She lived there at first in a tremble, as it were, at "the style of the house" and the memory of "Monsieur" floating over it all. Paul and Virginie, the first aged seven and the other hardly four, seemed to her beings of a precious substance; she carried them on her back like a horse; it was a sorrow to her that Mme. Aubain would not let her kiss them every minute. And yet she was happy there. Her grief had melted in the pleasantness of things all round.

Every Thursday regular visitors came in for a game of boston,[3] and Félicité got the cards and foot-warmers ready beforehand. They arrived punctually at eight and left before the stroke of eleven.

On Monday mornings the dealer who lodged in the covered passage spread out all his old iron on the ground. Then a hum of voices began to fill the town, mingled with the neighing of horses, bleating of lambs, grunting of pigs, and the sharp rattle of carts along the street. About noon, when the market was at its height, you might see a tall, hook-nosed old countryman with his cap pushed back making his appearance at the door. It was Robelin, the farmer of Geffosses. A little later came Liébard, the farmer from Toucques—short, red, and corpulent—in a grey jacket and gaiters shod with spurs.

Both had poultry or cheese to offer their landlord. Félicité was invariably a match for their cunning, and they went away filled with respect for her.

At vague intervals Mme. Aubain had a visit from the Marquis de Gremanville, one of her uncles, who had ruined himself by debauchery and now lived at Falaise on his last remaining morsel of land. He invariably came at the luncheon hour, with a dreadful poodle whose paws left all the furniture in a mess. In spite of efforts to show his breeding, which he carried to the point of raising his hat every time he mentioned "my late father," habit was too strong for him; he poured himself out glass after glass and fired off improper remarks. Félicité edged him politely out of the house—"You have had enough, Monsieur de Gremanville! Another time!"—and she shut the door on him.

She opened it with pleasure to M. Bourais, who had been a lawyer. His baldness, his white stock, frilled shirt, and roomy brown coat, his way of rounding the arm as he took snuff—his whole person, in fact, created that disturbance of mind which overtakes us at the sight of extraordinary men.

As he looked after the property of "Madame" he remained shut up with her for hours in "Monsieur's" study, though all the time he was afraid of compromising himself. He respected the magistracy immensely, and had some pretensions to Latin.

To combine instruction and amusement he gave the children a geography book made up of a series of prints. They represented scenes in different parts of the world:

3. A fashionable card game.

cannibals with feathers on their heads, a monkey carrying off a young lady, Bedouins in the desert, the harpooning of a whale, and so on. Paul explained these engravings to Félicité; and that, in fact, was the whole of her literary education. The children's education was undertaken by Guyot, a poor creature employed at the town hall, who was famous for his beautiful hand and sharpened his penknife on his boots.

When the weather was bright the household set off early for a day at Geffosses Farm.

Its courtyard is on a slope, with the farmhouse in the middle, and the sea looks like a grey streak in the distance.

Félicité brought slices of cold meat out of her basket, and they breakfasted in a room adjoining the dairy. It was the only surviving fragment of a country house which was now no more. The wall-paper hung in tatters, and quivered in the draughts. Mme. Aubain sat with bowed head, overcome by her memories; the children became afraid to speak. "Why don't you play, then?" she would say, and off they went.

Paul climbed into the barn, caught birds, played at ducks and drakes over the pond, or hammered with his stick on the big casks which boomed like drums. Virginie fed the rabbits or dashed off to pick cornflowers, her quick legs showing their embroidered little drawers.

One autumn evening they went home by the fields. The moon was in its first quarter, lighting part of the sky; and mist floated like a scarf over the windings of the Toucques. Cattle, lying out in the middle of the grass, looked quietly at the four people as they passed. In the third meadow some of them got up and made a half-circle in front of the walkers. "There's nothing to be afraid of," said Félicité, as she stroked the nearest on the back with a kind of crooning song; he wheeled round and the others did the same. But when they crossed the next pasture there was a formidable bellow. It was a bull, hidden by the mist. Mme. Aubain was about to run. "No! no! don't go so fast!" They mended their pace, however, and heard a loud breathing behind them which came nearer. His hoofs thudded on the meadow grass like hammers; why, he was galloping now! Félicité turned round, and tore up clods of earth with both hands and threw them in his eyes. He lowered his muzzle, waved his horns, and quivered with fury, bellowing terribly. Mme. Aubain, now at the end of the pasture with her two little ones, was looking wildly for a place to get over the high bank. Félicité was retreating, still with her face to the bull, keeping up a shower of clods which blinded him, and crying all the time, "Be quick! be quick!"

Mme. Aubain went down into the ditch, pushed Virginie first and then Paul, fell several times as she tried to climb the bank, and managed it at last by dint of courage.

The bull had driven Félicité to bay against a rail-fence; his slaver was streaming into her face; another second, and he would have gored her. She had just time to slip between two of the rails, and the big animal stopped short in amazement.

This adventure was talked of at Pont-l'Évêque for many a year. Félicité did not pride herself on it in the least, not having the barest suspicion that she had done anything heroic.

Virginie was the sole object of her thoughts, for the child developed a nervous complaint as a result of her fright, and M. Poupart, the doctor, advised sea-bathing at Trouville. It was not a frequented place then. Mme. Aubain collected information, consulted Bourais, and made preparations as though for a long journey.

Her luggage started a day in advance, in Liébard's cart. The next day he brought round two horses, one of which had a lady's saddle with a velvet back to it, while a cloak was rolled up to make a kind of seat on the crupper of the other. Mme. Aubain rode on that, behind the farmer. Félicité took charge of Virginie, and Paul mounted M. Lechaptois' donkey, lent on condition that great care was taken of it.

The road was so bad that its five miles took two hours. The horses sank in the mud up to their pasterns, and their haunches jerked abruptly in the effort to get out; or else they stumbled in the ruts, and at other moments had to jump. In some places Liébard's mare came suddenly to a halt. He waited patiently until she went on again, talking about the people who had properties along the road, and adding moral reflections to their history. So it was that as they were in the middle of Toucques, and passed under some windows bowered with nasturtiums, he shrugged his shoulders and said: "There's a Mme. Lehoussais lives there; instead of taking a young man she . . ." Félicité did not hear the rest; the horses were trotting and the donkey galloping. They all turned down a bypath; a gate swung open and two boys appeared; and the party dismounted in front of a manure-heap at the very threshold of the farmhouse door.

When Mme. Liébard saw her mistress she gave lavish signs of joy. She served her a luncheon with a sirloin of beef, tripe, black-pudding, a fricassee of chicken, sparkling cider, a fruit tart, and brandied plums; seasoning it all with compliments to Madame, who seemed in better health; Mademoiselle, who was "splendid" now; and Monsieur Paul, who had "filled out" wonderfully. Nor did she forget their deceased grandparents, whom the Liébards had known, as they had been in the service of the family for several generations. The farm, like them, had the stamp of antiquity. The beams on the ceiling were worm-eaten, the walls blackened with smoke, and the window-panes grey with dust. There was an oak dresser laden with every sort of useful article—jugs, plates, pewter bowls, wolf-traps, and sheep-shears; and a huge syringe made the children laugh. There was not a tree in the three courtyards without mushrooms growing at the bottom of it or a tuft of mistletoe on its boughs. Several of them had been thrown down by the wind. They had taken root again at the middle; and all were bending under their wealth of apples. The thatched roofs, like brown velvet and of varying thickness, withstood the heaviest squalls. The cart-shed, however, was falling into ruin. Mme. Aubain said she would see about it, and ordered the animals to be saddled again.

It was another half-hour before they reached Trouville. The little caravan dismounted to pass Écores—it was an overhanging cliff with boats below it—and three minutes later they were at the end of the quay and entered the courtyard of the Golden Lamb, kept by good Mme. David.

From the first days of their stay Virginie began to feel less weak, thanks to the change of air and the effect of the sea-baths. These, for want of a bathing-dress, she took in her chemise; and her nurse dressed her afterwards in a coastguard's cabin which was used by the bathers.

In the afternoons they took the donkey and went off beyond the Black Rocks, in the direction of Hennequeville. The path climbed at first through ground with dells in it like the green sward of a park, and then reached a plateau where grass fields and arable lay side by side. Hollies rose stiffly out of the briary tangle at the edge of the road; and here and there a great withered tree made zigzags in the blue air with its branches.

They nearly always rested in a meadow, with Deauville on their left, Havre on their right, and the open sea in front. It glittered in the sunshine, smooth as a mirror and so quiet that its murmur was scarcely to be heard; sparrows chirped in hiding and the immense sky arched over it all. Mme. Aubain sat doing her needlework; Virginie plaited rushes by her side; Félicité pulled up lavender, and Paul was bored and anxious to start home.

Other days they crossed the Toucques in a boat and looked for shells. When the tide went out sea-urchins, starfish, and jelly-fish were left exposed; and the children ran in pursuit of the foam-flakes which scudded in the wind. The sleepy waves broke on the sand and unrolled all along the beach; it stretched away out of sight, bounded on the land-side by the dunes which parted it from the Marsh, a wide meadow shaped like an arena. As they came home that way, Trouville, on the hill-slope in the background, grew bigger at every step, and its miscellaneous throng of houses seemed to break into a gay disorder.

On days when it was too hot they did not leave their room. From the dazzling brilliance outside light fell in streaks between the laths of the blinds. There were no sounds in the village; and on the pavement below not a soul. This silence round them deepened the quietness of things. In the distance, where men were caulking, there was a tap of hammers as they plugged the hulls, and a sluggish breeze wafted up the smell of tar.

The chief amusement was the return of the fishing-boats. They began to tack as soon as they had passed the buoys. The sails came down on two of the three masts; and they drew on with the foresail swelling like a balloon, glided through the splash of the waves, and when they had reached the middle of the harbour suddenly dropped anchor. Then the boats drew up against the quay. The sailors threw quivering fish over the side; a row of carts was waiting, and women in cotton bonnets darted out to take the baskets and give their men a kiss.

One of them came up to Félicité one day, and she entered the lodgings a little later in a state of delight. She had found a sister again—and then Nastasie Barette, "wife of Leroux," appeared, holding an infant at her breast and another child with her right hand, while on her left was a little cabin boy with his hands on his hips and a cap over his ear.

After a quarter of an hour Mme. Aubain sent them off; but they were always to be found hanging about the kitchen, or encountered in the course of a walk. The husband never appeared.

Félicité was seized with affection for them. She bought them a blanket, some shirts, and a stove; it was clear that they were making a good thing out of her. Mme. Aubain was annoyed by this weakness of hers, and she did not like the liberties taken by the nephew, who said "thee" and "thou" to Paul. So as Virginie was coughing and the fine weather gone, she returned to Pont-l'Évêque.

There M. Bourais enlightened her on the choice of a boys' school. The one at Caen was reputed to be the best, and Paul was sent to it. He said his good-byes bravely, content enough at going to live in a house where he would have companions.

Mme. Aubain resigned herself to her son's absence as a thing that had to be. Virginie thought about it less and less. Félicité missed the noise he made. But she found an occupation to distract her; from Christmas onward she took the little girl to catechism every day.

3

After making a genuflexion at the door she walked up between the double row of chairs under the lofty nave, opened Mme. Aubain's pew, sat down, and began to look about her. The choir stalls were filled with the boys on the right and the girls on the left, and the curé stood by the lectern. On a painted window in the apse the Holy Ghost looked down upon the Virgin. Another window showed her on her knees before the child Jesus, and a group carved in wood behind the altarshrine represented St. Michael overthrowing the dragon.

The priest began with a sketch of sacred history. The Garden, the Flood, the Tower of Babel, cities in flames, dying nations, and overturned idols passed like a dream before her eyes; and the dizzying vision left her with reverence for the Most High and fear of his wrath. Then she wept at the story of the Passion. Why had they crucified Him, when He loved the children, fed the multitudes, healed the blind, and had willed, in His meekness, to be born among the poor, on the dungheap of a stable? The sowings, harvests, wine-presses, all the familiar things the Gospel speaks of, were a part of her life. They had been made holy by God's passing; and she loved the lambs more tenderly for her love of the Lamb, and the doves because of the Holy Ghost.

She found it hard to imagine Him in person, for He was not merely a bird, but a flame as well, and a breath at other times. It may be His light, she thought, which flits at night about the edge of the marshes, His breathing which drives on the clouds, His voice which gives harmony to the bells; and she would sit rapt in adoration, enjoying the cool walls and the quiet of the church.

Of doctrines she understood nothing—did not even try to understand. The curé discoursed, the children repeated their lesson, and finally she went to sleep, waking up with a start when their wooden shoes clattered on the flagstones as they went away.

It was thus that Félicité, whose religious education had been neglected in her youth, learned the catechism by dint of hearing it; and from that time she copied all Virginie's observances, fasting as she did and confessing with her. On Corpus Christi Day they made a festal altar together.

The first communion loomed distractingly ahead. She fussed over the shoes, the rosary, the book and gloves; and how she trembled as she helped Virginie's mother to dress her!

All through the mass she was racked with anxiety. She could not see one side of the choir because of M. Bourais; but straight in front of her was the flock of maidens, with white crowns above their hanging veils, making the impression of a field of snow; and she knew her dear child at a distance by her dainty neck and thoughtful air. The bell tinkled. The heads bowed, and there was silence. As the organ pealed, singers and congregation took up the "Agnus Dei"; then the procession of the boys began, and after them the girls rose. Step by step, with their hands joined in prayer, they went towards the lighted altar, knelt on the first step, received the sacrament in turn, and came back in the same order to their places. When Virginie's turn came Félicité leaned forward to see her; and with the imaginativeness of deep and tender feeling it seemed to her that she actually was the child; Virginie's face became hers, she was dressed in her clothes, it was her heart beating in her breast. As the moment came to open her mouth she closed her eyes and nearly fainted.

She appeared early in the sacristy next morning for Monsieur the curé to give her the communion. She took it with devotion, but it did not give her the same exquisite delight.

Mme. Aubain wanted to make her daughter into an accomplished person; and as Guyot could not teach her music or English she decided to place her in the Ursuline Convent at Honfleur as a boarder. The child made no objection. Félicité sighed and thought that Madame lacked feeling. Then she reflected that her mistress might be right; matters of this kind were beyond her.

So one day an old spring-van drew up at the door, and out of it stepped a nun to fetch the young lady. Félicité hoisted the luggage on to the top, admonished the driver, and put six pots of preserves, a dozen pears, and a bunch of violets under the seat.

At the last moment Virginie broke into a fit of sobbing; she threw her arms round her mother, who kissed her on the forehead, saying over and over "Come, be brave! be brave!" The step was raised, and the carriage drove off.

Then Mme. Aubain's strength gave way; and in the evening all her friends—the Lormeau family, Mme. Lechaptois, the Rochefeuille ladies, M. de Houppeville, and Bourais—came in to console her.

To be without her daughter was very painful for her at first. But she heard from Virginie three times a week, wrote to her on the other days, walked in the garden, and so filled up the empty hours.

From sheer habit Félicité went into Virginie's room in the mornings and gazed at the walls. It was boredom to her not to have to comb the child's hair now, lace up her boots, tuck her into bed—and not to see her charming face perpetually and hold her hand when they went out together. In this idle condition she tried making lace. But her fingers were too heavy and broke the threads; she could not attend to anything, she had lost her sleep, and was, in her own words, "destroyed."

To "divert herself" she asked leave to have visits from her nephew Victor.

He arrived on Sundays after mass, rosy-cheeked, bare-chested, with the scent of the country he had walked through still about him. She laid her table promptly and they had lunch, sitting opposite each other. She ate as little as possible herself to save expense, but stuffed him with food so generously that at last he went to sleep. At the first stroke of vespers she woke him up, brushed his trousers, fastened his tie, and went to church, leaning on his arm with maternal pride.

Victor was always instructed by his parents to get something out of her—a packet of moist sugar, it might be, a cake of soap, spirits, or even money at times. He brought his things for her to mend and she took over the task, only too glad to have a reason for making him come back.

In August his father took him off on a coasting voyage. It was holiday time, and she was consoled by the arrival of the children. Paul, however, was getting selfish, and Virginie was too old to be called "thou" any longer; this put a constraint and barrier between them.

Victor went to Morlaix, Dunkirk, and Brighton in succession and made Félicité a present on his return from each voyage. It was a box made of shells the first time, a coffee cup the next, and on the third occasion a large gingerbread man. Victor was growing handsome. He was well made, had a hint of a moustache, good honest eyes, and a small leather hat pushed backwards like a pilot's. He entertained her by telling stories embroidered with nautical terms.

On a Monday, July 14, 1819 (she never forgot the date), he told her that he had signed on for the big voyage and next night but one he would take the Honfleur boat and join his schooner, which was to weigh anchor from Havre before long. Perhaps he would be gone two years.

The prospect of this long absence threw Félicité into deep distress; one more good-bye she must have, and on the Wednesday evening, when Madame's dinner was finished, she put on her clogs and made short work of the twelve miles between Pont-l'Évêque and Honfleur.

When she arrived in front of the Calvary she took the turn to the right instead of the left, got lost in the timber-yards, and retraced her steps; some people to whom she spoke advised her to be quick. She went all round the harbour basin, full of ships, and knocked against hawsers; then the ground fell away, lights flashed across each other, and she thought her wits had left her, for she saw horses up in the sky.

Others were neighing by the quay-side, frightened at the sea. They were lifted by a tackle and deposited in a boat, where passengers jostled each other among cider casks, cheese baskets, and sacks of grain; fowls could be heard clucking, the captain swore; and a cabin-boy stood leaning over the bows, indifferent to it all. Félicité, who had not recognized him, called "Victor!" and he raised his head; all at once, as she was darting forwards, the gangway was drawn back.

The Honfleur packet, women singing as they hauled it, passed out of harbour. Its framework creaked and the heavy waves whipped its bows. The canvas had swung round, no one could be seen on board now; and on the moonsilvered sea the boat made a black speck which paled gradually, dipped, and vanished.

As Félicité passed by the Calvary she had a wish to commend to God what she cherished most, and she stood there praying a long time with her face bathed in tears and her eyes towards the clouds. The town was asleep, coastguards were walking to and fro; and water poured without cessation through the holes in the sluice, with the noise of a torrent. The clocks struck two.

The convent parlour would not be open before day. If Félicité were late Madame would most certainly be annoyed; and in spite of her desire to kiss the other child she turned home. The maids at the inn were waking up as she came in to Pont-l'Évêque.

So the poor slip of a boy was going to toss for months and months at sea! She had not been frightened by his previous voyages. From England or Brittany you came back safe enough; but America, the colonies, the islands—these were lost in a dim region at the other end of the world.

Félicité's thoughts from that moment ran entirely on her nephew. On sunny days she was harassed by the idea of thirst; when there was a storm she was afraid of the lightning on his account. As she listened to the wind growling in the chimney or carrying off the slates she pictured him lashed by that same tempest, at the top of a shattered mast, with his body thrown backwards under a sheet of foam; or else (with a reminiscence of the illustrated geography) he was being eaten by savages, captured in a wood by monkeys, or dying on a desert shore. And never did she mention her anxieties.

Mme. Aubain had anxieties of her own, about her daughter. The good sisters found her an affectionate but delicate child. The slightest emotion unnerved her. She had to give up the piano.

Her mother stipulated for regular letters from the convent. She lost patience one morning when the postman did not come, and walked to and fro in the parlour from her armchair to the window. It was really amazing; not a word for four days!

To console Mme. Aubain by her own example Félicité remarked:

"As for me, Madame, it's six months since I heard . . ."

"From whom, pray?"

"Why . . . from my nephew," the servant answered gently.

"Oh! your nephew!" And Mme. Aubain resumed her walk with a shrug of the shoulders, as much as to say: "I was not thinking of him! And what is more, it's absurd! A scamp of a cabin-boy—what does he matter? . . . whereas my daughter . . . why, just think!"

Félicité, though she had been brought up on harshness, felt indignant with Madame—and then forgot. It seemed the simplest thing in the world to her to lose one's head over the little girl. For her the two children were equally important; a bond in her heart made them one, and their destinies must be the same.

She heard from the chemist that Victor's ship had arrived at Havana. He had read this piece of news in a gazette.

Cigars—they made her imagine Havana as a place where no one does anything but smoke, and there was Victor moving among the negroes in a cloud of tobacco. Could you, she wondered, "in case you needed,' return by land? What was the distance from Pont-l'Évêque? She questioned M. Bourais to find out.

He reached for his atlas and began explaining the longitudes; Félicité's consternation provoked a fine pedantic smile. Finally he marked with his pencil a black, imperceptible point in the indentations of an oval spot, and said as he did so, "Here it is." She bent over the map; the maze of coloured lines wearied her eyes without conveying anything; and on an invitation from Bourais to tell him her difficulty she begged him to show her the house where Victor was living. Bourais threw up his arms, sneezed, and laughed immensely: a simplicity like hers was a positive joy. And Félicité did not understand the reason; how could she when she expected, very likely, to see the actual image of her nephew—so stunted was her mind!

A fortnight afterwards Liébard came into the kitchen at market-time as usual and handed her a letter from her brother-in-law. As neither of them could read she took it to her mistress.

Mme. Aubain, who was counting the stitches in her knitting, put the work down by her side, broke the seal of the letter, started, and said in a low voice, with a look of meaning:

"It is bad news . . . that they have to tell you. Your nephew . . ."

He was dead. The letter said no more.

Félicité fell on to a chair, leaning her head against the wainscot; and she closed her eyelids, which suddenly flushed pink. Then with bent forehead, hands hanging, and fixed eyes, she said at intervals:

"Poor little lad! poor little lad!"

Liébard watched her and heaved sighs. Mme. Aubain trembled a little.

She suggested that Félicité should go to see her sister at Trouville. Félicité answered by a gesture that she had no need.

There was a silence. The worthy Liébard thought it was time for them to withdraw. Then Félicité said:

"They don't care, not they!"

Her head dropped again; and she took up mechanically, from time to time, the long needles on her work-table.

Women passed in the yard with a barrow of dripping linen.

As she saw them through the window-panes she remembered her washing; she had put it to soak the day before, to-day she must wring it out; and she left the room.

Her plank and tub were at the edge of the Toucques. She threw a pile of linen on the bank, rolled up her sleeves, and taking her wooden beater dealt lusty blows whose sound carried to the neighbouring gardens. The meadows were empty, the river stirred in the wind; and down below long grasses wavered, like the hair of corpses floating in the water. She kept her grief down and was very brave until the evening; but once in her room she surrendered to it utterly, lying stretched on the mattress with her face in the pillow and her hands clenched against her temples.

Much later she heard, from the captain himself, the circumstances of Victor's end. They had bled him too much at the hospital for yellow fever. Four doctors held him at once. He had died instantly, and the chief had said:

"Bah! there goes another!"

His parents had always been brutal to him. She preferred not to see them again; and they made no advances, either because they forgot her or from the callousness of the wretchedly poor.

Virginie began to grow weaker.

Tightness in her chest, coughing, continual fever, and veinings on her cheek-bones betrayed some deep-seated complaint. M. Poupart had advised a stay in Provence. Mme. Aubain determined on it, and would have brought her daughter home at once but for the climate of Pont-l'Évêque.

She made an arrangement with a job-master, and he drove her to the convent every Tuesday. There is a terrace in the garden, with a view over the Seine. Virginie took walks there over the fallen vine-leaves, on her mother's arm. A shaft of sunlight through the clouds made her blink sometimes, as she gazed at the sails in the distance and the whole horizon from the castle of Tancarville to the lighthouses at Havre. Afterwards they rested in the arbour. Her mother had secured a little cask of excellent Malaga; and Virginie, laughing at the idea of getting tipsy, drank a thimble-full of it, no more.

Her strength came back visibly. The autumn glided gently away. Félicité reassured Mme. Aubain. But one evening, when she had been out on a commission in the neighbourhood, she found M. Poupart's gig at the door. He was in the hall, and Mme. Aubain was tying her bonnet.

"Give me my foot-warmer, purse, gloves! Quicker, come!"

Virginie had inflammation of the lungs; perhaps it was hopeless.

"Not yet!" said the doctor, and they both got into the carriage under whirling flakes of snow. Night was coming on and it was very cold.

Félicité rushed into the church to light a taper. Then she ran after the gig, came up with it in an hour, and jumped lightly in behind. As she hung on by the fringes a thought came into her mind: "The courtyard has not been shut up; supposing burglars got in!" And she jumped down.

At dawn next day she presented herself at the doctor's. He had come in and started for the country again. Then she waited in the inn, thinking that a letter would come by some hand or other. Finally, when it was twilight, she took the Lisieux coach.

The convent was at the end of a steep lane. When she was about half-way up it she heard strange sounds—a death-bell tolling. "It is for someone else," thought Félicité, and she pulled the knocker violently.

After some minutes there was a sound of trailing slippers, the door opened ajar, and a nun appeared.

The good sister, with an air of compunction, said that "she had just passed away." On the instant the bell of St. Leonard's tolled twice as fast.

Félicité went up to the second floor.

From the doorway she saw Virginie stretched on her back, with her hands joined, her mouth open, and head thrown back under a black crucifix that leaned towards her, between curtains that hung stiffly, less pale than was her face. Mme. Aubain, at the foot of the bed which she clasped with her arms, was choking with sobs of agony. The mother superior stood on the right. Three candlesticks on the chest of drawers made spots of red, and the mist came whitely through the windows. Nuns came and took Mme. Aubain away.

For two nights Félicité never left the dead child. She repeated the same prayers, sprinkled holy water over the sheets, came and sat down again, and watched her. At the end of the first vigil she noticed that the face had grown yellow, the lips turned blue, the nose was sharper, and the eyes sunk in. She kissed them several times, and would not have been immensely surprised if Virginie had opened them again; to minds like hers the supernatural is quite simple. She made the girl's toilette, wrapped her in her shroud, lifted her down into her bier, put a garland on her head, and spread out her hair. It was fair, and extraordinarily long for her age. Félicité cut off a big lock and slipped half of it into her bosom, determined that she should never part with it.

The body was brought back to Pont-l'Évêque, as Mme. Aubain intended; she followed the hearse in a closed carriage.

It took another three-quarters of an hour after the mass to reach the cemetery. Paul walked in front, sobbing. M. Bourais was behind, and then came the chief residents, the women shrouded in black mantles, and Félicité. She thought of her nephew; and because she had not been able to pay these honours to him her grief was doubled, as though the one were being buried with the other.

Mme. Aubain's despair was boundless. It was against God that she first rebelled, thinking it unjust of Him to have taken her daughter from her—she had never done evil and her conscience was so clear! Ah, no!—she ought to have taken Virginie off to the south. Other doctors would have saved her. She accused herself now, wanted to join her child, and broke into cries of distress in the middle of her dreams. One dream haunted her above all. Her husband, dressed as a sailor, was returning from a long voyage, and shedding tears he told her that he had been ordered to take Virginie away. Then they consulted how to hide her somewhere.

She came in once from the garden quite upset. A moment ago—and she pointed out the place—the father and daughter had appeared to her, standing side by side, and they did nothing, but they looked at her.

For several months after this she stayed inertly in her room. Félicité lectured her gently; she must live for her son's sake, and for the other, in remembrance of "her."

"Her?" answered Mme. Aubain, as though she were just waking up. "Ah, yes! . . . yes! . . . You do not forget her!" This was an allusion to the cemetery, where she was strictly forbidden to go.

Félicité went there every day.

Precisely at four she skirted the houses, climbed the hill, opened the gate, and came to Virginie's grave. It was a little column of pink marble with a stone underneath and a garden plot enclosed by chains. The beds were hidden under a coverlet of flowers. She watered their leaves, freshened the gravel, and knelt down to break up the earth better. When Mme. Aubain was able to come there she felt a relief and a sort of consolation.

Then years slipped away, one like another, and their only episodes were the great festivals as they recurred—Easter, the Assumption, All Saints' Day. Household occurrences marked dates that were referred to after-wards. In 1825, for instance, two glaziers whitewashed the hall; in 1827 a piece of the roof fell into the courtyard and nearly killed a man. In the summer of 1828 it was Madame's turn to offer the consecrated bread; Bourais, about this time, mysteriously absented himself; and one by one the old acquaintances passed away: Guyot, Liébard, Mme. Lechaptois, Robelin, and Uncle Gremanville, who had been paralysed for a long time.

One night the driver of the mail-coach announced the Revolution of July in Pont-l'Évêque.[4] A new sub-prefect was appointed a few days later—Baron de Larsonnière,

4. The July Revolution overthrew King Charles X, marking the ascendancy of the middle class, who installed a king (Louis-Philippe) more to their liking.

who had been consul in America, and brought with him, besides his wife, a sister-in-law and three young ladies, already growing up. They were to be seen about on their lawn, in loose blouses, and they had a negro and a parrot. They paid a call on Mme. Aubain which she did not fail to return. The moment they were seen in the distance Félicité ran to let her mistress know. But only one thing could really move her feelings—the letters from her son.

He was swallowed up in a tavern life and could follow no career. She paid his debts, he made new ones; and the sighs that Mme. Aubain uttered as she sat knitting by the window reached Félicité at her spinning-wheel in the kitchen.

They took walks together along the espaliered wall, always talking of Virginie and wondering if such and such a thing would have pleased her and what, on some occasion, she would have been likely to say.

All her small belongings filled a cupboard in the two-bedded room. Mme. Aubain inspected them as seldom as she could. One summer day she made up her mind to it—and some moths flew out of the wardrobe.

Virginie's dresses were in a row underneath a shelf, on which there were three dolls, some hoops, a set of toy pots and pans, and the basin that she used. They took out her petticoats as well, and the stockings and handkerchiefs, and laid them out on the two beds before folding them up again. The sunshine lit up these poor things, bringing out their stains and the creases made by the body's movements. The air was warm and blue, a blackbird warbled, life seemed bathed in a deep sweetness. They found a little plush hat with thick, chestnut-coloured pile; but it was eaten all over by moth. Félicité begged it for her own. Their eyes met fixedly and filled with tears; at last the mistress opened her arms, the servant threw herself into them, and they embraced each other, satisfying their grief in a kiss that made them equal.

It was the first time in their lives, Mme. Aubain's nature not being expansive. Félicité was as grateful as though she had received a favour, and cherished her mistress from that moment with the devotion of an animal and a religious worship.

The kindness of her heart unfolded.

When she heard the drums of a marching regiment in the street she posted herself at the door with a pitcher of cider and asked the soldiers to drink. She nursed cholera patients and protected the Polish refugees; one of these even declared that he wished to marry her. They quarrelled, however; for when she came back from the Angelus one morning she found that he had got into her kitchen and made himself a vinegar salad which he was quietly eating.

After the Poles came father Colmiche, an old man who was supposed to have committed atrocities in '93.[5] He lived by the side of the river in the ruins of a pigsty. The little boys watched him through the cracks in the wall, and threw pebbles at him which fell on the pallet where he lay constantly shaken by a catarrh;[6] his hair was very long, his eyes inflamed, and there was a tumour on his arm bigger than his head. She got him some linen and tried to clean up his miserable hole; her dream was to establish him in the bakehouse, without letting him annoy Madame. When the tumour burst she dressed it every day; sometimes she brought him cake, and would put him in the sunshine on a truss of straw. The poor old man, slobbering and trembling, thanked her in his worn-out voice, was terrified that he might lose her, and stretched out his

5. During the Reign of Terror at the height of the French Revolution.

6. Racking cough.

hands when he saw her go away. He died; and she had a mass said for the repose of his soul.

That very day a great happiness befell her; just at dinner-time appeared Mme. de Larsonnière's negro, carrying the parrot in its cage, with perch, chain, and padlock. A note from the baroness informed Mme. Aubain that her husband had been raised to a prefecture and they were starting that evening; she begged her to accept the bird as a memento and mark of her regard.

For a long time he had absorbed Félicité's imagination, because he came from America; and that name reminded her of Victor, so much so that she made inquiries of the negro. She had once gone so far as to say "How Madame would enjoy having him!"

The negro repeated the remark to his mistress; and as she could not take the bird away with her she chose this way of getting rid of him.

4

His name was Loulou. His body was green and the tips of his wings rose-pink; his fore-head was blue and his throat golden.

But he had the tiresome habits of biting his perch, tearing out his feathers, sprinkling his dirt about, and spattering the water of his tub. He annoyed Mme. Aubain, and she gave him to Félicité for good.

She endeavoured to train him; soon he could repeat "Nice boy! Your servant, sir! Good morning, Marie!" He was placed by the side of the door, and astonished several people by not answering to the name Jacquot, for all parrots are called Jacquot. People compared him to a turkey and a log of wood, and stabbed Félicité to the heart each time. Strange obstinacy on Loulou's part!—directly you looked at him he refused to speak.

None the less he was eager for society; for on Sundays, while the Rochefeuille ladies, M. de Houppeville, and new familiars—Onfroy the apothecary, Monsieur Varin, and Captain Mathieu—were playing their game of cards, he beat the windows with his wings and threw himself about so frantically that they could not hear each other speak.

Bourais' face, undoubtedly, struck him as extremely droll. Directly he saw it he began to laugh—and laugh with all his might. His peals rang through the courtyard and were repeated by the echo; the neighbours came to their windows and laughed too; while M. Bourais, gliding along under the wall to escape the parrot's eye, and hiding his profile with his hat, got to the river and then entered by the garden gate. There was a lack of tenderness in the looks which he darted at the bird.

Loulou had been slapped by the butcher-boy for making so free as to plunge his head into his basket; and since then he was always trying to nip him through his shirt. Fabu threatened to wring his neck, although he was not cruel, for all his tattooed arms and large whiskers. Far from it; he really rather liked the parrot, and in a jovial humour even wanted to teach him to swear. Félicité, who was alarmed by such proceedings, put the bird in the kitchen. His little chain was taken off and he roamed about the house.

His way of going downstairs was to lean on each step with the curve of his beak, raise the right foot, and then the left; and Félicité was afraid that these gymnastics brought on fits of giddiness. He fell ill and could not talk or eat any longer. There was a growth under his tongue, such as fowls have sometimes. She cured him by tearing the pellicle off with her finger-nails. Mr. Paul was thoughtless enough one day to blow some cigar smoke into his nostrils, and another time when Mme. Lormeau was teasing him with the end of her umbrella he snapped at the ferrule. Finally he got lost.

Félicité had put him on the grass to refresh him, and gone away for a minute, and when she came back—no sign of the parrot! She began by looking for him in the shrubs, by the waterside, and over the roofs, without listening to her mistress's cries of "Take care, do! You are out of your wits!" Then she investigated all the gardens in Pont-l'Évêque, and stopped the passers-by. "You don't ever happen to have seen my parrot, by any chance, do you?" And she gave a description of the parrot to those who did not know him. Suddenly, behind the mills at the foot of the hill she thought she could make out something green that fluttered. But on the top of the hill there was nothing. A hawker assured her that he had come across the parrot just before, at Saint-Melaine, in Mère Simon's shop. She rushed there; they had no idea of what she meant. At last she came home exhausted, with her slippers in shreds and despair in her soul; and as she was sitting in the middle of the garden-seat at Madame's side, telling the whole story of her efforts, a light weight dropped on to her shoulder—it was Loulou! What on earth had he been doing? Taking a walk in the neighbourhood, perhaps!

She had some trouble in recovering from this, or rather never did recover. As the result of a chill she had an attack of quinsy,[7] and soon afterwards an earache. Three years later she was deaf; and she spoke very loud, even in church. Though Félicité's sins might have been published in every corner of the diocese without dishonour to her or scandal to anybody, his Reverence the priest thought it right now to hear her confession in the sacristy only.

Imaginary noises in the head completed her upset. Her mistress often said to her, "Heavens! how stupid you are!" "Yes, Madame," she replied, and looked about for something.

Her little circle of ideas grew still narrower; the peal of church-bells and the lowing of cattle ceased to exist for her. All living beings moved as silently as ghosts. One sound only reached her ears now—the parrot's voice.

Loulou, as though to amuse her, reproduced the click-clack of the turn-spit, the shrill call of a man selling fish, and the noise of the saw in the joiner's house opposite; when the bell rang he imitated Mme. Aubain's "Félicité! the door! the door!"

They carried on conversations, he endlessly reciting the three phrases in his repertory, to which she replied with words that were just as disconnected but uttered what was in her heart. Loulou was almost a son and a lover to her in her isolated state. He climbed up her fingers, nibbled at her lips, and clung to her kerchief; and when she bent her forehead and shook her head gently to and fro, as nurses do, the great wings of her bonnet and the bird's wings quivered together.

When the clouds massed and the thunder rumbled Loulou broke into cries, perhaps remembering the downpours in his native forests. The streaming rain made him absolutely mad; he fluttered wildly about, dashed up to the ceiling, upset everything, and went out through the window to dabble in the garden; but he was back quickly to perch on one of the fire-dogs and hopped about to dry himself, exhibiting his tail and his beak in turn.

One morning in the terrible winter of 1837 she had put him in front of the fireplace because of the cold. She found him dead, in the middle of his cage: head

7. Tonsillitis.

downwards, with his claws in the wires. He had died from congestion, no doubt. But Félicité thought he had been poisoned with parsley, and though there was no proof of any kind her suspicions inclined to Fabu.

She wept so piteously that her mistress said to her, "Well, then, have him stuffed!"

She asked advice from the chemist, who had always been kind to the parrot. He wrote to Havre, and a person called Fellacher undertook the business. But as parcels sometimes got lost in the coach she decided to take the parrot as far as Honfleur herself.

Along the sides of the road were leafless apple-trees, one after the other. Ice covered the ditches. Dogs barked about the farms; and Félicité, with her hands under her cloak, her little black sabots and her basket, walked briskly in the middle of the road.

She crossed the forest, passed High Oak, and reached St. Gatien.

A cloud of dust rose behind her, and in it a mail-coach, carried away by the steep hill, rushed down at full gallop like a hurricane. Seeing this woman who would not get out of the way, the driver stood up in front and the positilion shouted too. He could not hold in his four horses, which increased their pace, and the two leaders were grazing her when he threw them to one side with a jerk of the reins. But he was wild with rage, and lifting his arm as he passed at full speed, gave her such a lash from waist to neck with his big whip that she fell on her back.

Her first act, when she recovered consciousness, was to open her basket. Loulou was happily none the worse. She felt a burn in her right cheek, and when she put her hands against it they were red; the blood was flowing.

She sat down on a heap of stones and bound up her face with her handkerchief. Then she ate a crust of bread which she had put in the basket as a precaution, and found a consolation for her wound in gazing at the bird.

When she reached the crest of Ecquemauville she saw the Honfleur lights sparkling in the night sky like a company of stars; beyond, the sea stretched dimly. Then a faintness overtook her and she stopped; her wretched childhood, the disillusion of her first love, her nephew's going away, and Virginie's death all came back to her at once like the waves of an oncoming tide, rose to her throat, and choked her.

Afterwards, at the boat, she made a point of speaking to the captain, begging him to take care of the parcel, though she did not tell him what was in it.

Fellacher kept the parrot a long time. He was always promising it for the following week. After six months he announced that a packing-case had started, and then nothing more was heard of it. It really seemed as though Loulou was never coming back. "Ah, they have stolen him!" she thought.

He arrived at last, and looked superb. There he was, erect upon a branch which screwed into a mahogany socket, with a foot in the air and his head on one side, biting a nut which the bird-stuffer—with a taste for impressiveness—had gilded.

Félicité shut him up in her room. It was a place to which few people were admitted, and held so many religious objects and miscellaneous things that it looked like a chapel and bazaar in one.

A big cupboard impeded you as you opened the door. Opposite the window commanding the garden a little round one looked into the court; there was a table by the folding-bed with a water-jug, two combs, and a cube of blue soap in a chipped plate. On the walls hung rosaries, medals, several benign Virgins, and a holy water vessel made out of cocoa-nut; on the chest of drawers, which was covered with a cloth like an altar, was the shell box that Victor had given her, and after that a watering-can, a toy-balloon, exercise-books, the illustrated geography, and a pair of young lady's boots; and, fastened by its ribbons to the nail of the looking-glass, hung the little plush hat! Félicité carried observances of this kind so far as to keep one of Monsieur's frock-coats. All the old rubbish which Mme. Aubain did not want any longer she laid hands on for her room. That was why there were artificial flowers along the edge of the chest of drawers and a portrait of the Comte d'Artois[8] in the little window recess.

With the aid of a bracket Loulou was established over the chimney, which jutted into the room. Every morning when she woke up she saw him there in the dawning light, and recalled old days and the smallest details of insignificant acts in a deep quietness which knew no pain.

Holding, as she did, no communication with anyone, Félicité lived as insensibly as if she were walking in her sleep. The Corpus Christi processions roused her to life again. Then she went round begging mats and candlesticks from the neighbours to decorate the altar they put up in the street.

In church she was always gazing at the Holy Ghost in the window, and observed that there was something of the parrot in him. The likeness was still clearer, she thought, on a crude colour-print representing the baptism of Our Lord. With his purple wings and emerald body he was the very image of Loulou.

She bought him, and hung him up instead of the Comte d'Artois, so that she could see them both together in one glance. They were linked in her thoughts; and the parrot was consecrated by his association with the Holy Ghost, which became more vivid to her eye and more intelligible. The Father could not have chosen to express Himself through a dove, for such creatures cannot speak; it must have been one of Loulou's ancestors, surely. And though Félicité looked at the picture while she said her prayers she swerved a little from time to time towards the parrot.

She wanted to join the Ladies of the Virgin, but Mme. Aubain dissuaded her.

And then a great event loomed up before them—Paul's marriage.

He had been a solicitor's clerk to begin with, and then tried business, the Customs, the Inland Revenue, and made efforts, even, to get into the Rivers and Forests. By an inspiration from heaven he had suddenly, at thirty-six, discovered his real line—the Registrar's Office. And there he showed such marked capacity that an inspector had offered him his daughter's hand and promised him his influence.

So Paul, grown serious, brought the lady to see his mother.

She sniffed at the ways of Pont-l'Évêque, gave herself great airs, and wounded Félicité's feelings. Mme. Aubain was relieved at her departure.

The week after came news of M. Bourais' death in an inn in Lower Brittany. The rumour of suicide was confirmed, and doubts arose as to his honesty. Mme. Aubain studied his accounts, and soon found out the whole tale of his misdoings—embezzled arrears, secret sales of wood, forged receipts, etc. Besides that he had an illegitimate child, and "relations with a person at Dozulé."

These shameful facts distressed her greatly. In March 1853 she was seized with a pain in the chest; her tongue seemed to be covered with film, and leeches did not ease the difficult breathing. On the ninth evening of her illness she died, just at seventy-two.

8. The deposed king Charles X.

She passed as being younger, owing to the bands of brown hair which framed her pale, pock-marked face. There were few friends to regret her, for she had a stiffness of manner which kept people at a distance.

But Félicité mourned for her as one seldom mourns for a master. It upset her ideas and seemed contrary to the order of things, impossible and monstrous, that Madame should die before her.

Ten days afterwards, which was the time it took to hurry there from Besançon, the heirs arrived. The daughter-in-law ransacked the drawers, chose some furniture, and sold the rest; and then they went back to their registering.

Madame's armchair, her small round table, her foot-warmer, and the eight chairs were gone! Yellow patches in the middle of the panels showed where the engravings had hung. They had carried off the two little beds and the mattresses, and all Virginie's belongings had disappeared from the cupboard. Félicité went from floor to floor dazed with sorrow.

The next day there was a notice on the door, and the apothecary shouted in her ear that the house was for sale.

She tottered, and was obliged to sit down. What distressed her most of all was to give up her room, so suitable as it was for poor Loulou. She enveloped him with a look of anguish when she was imploring the Holy Ghost, and formed the idolatrous habit of kneeling in front of the parrot to say her prayers. Sometimes the sun shone in at the attic window and caught his glass eye, and a great luminous ray shot out of it and put her in an ecstasy.

She had a pension of fifteen pounds a year which her mistress had left her. The garden gave her a supply of vegetables. As for clothes, she had enough to last her to the end of her days, and she economized in candles by going to bed at dusk.

She hardly ever went out, as she did not like passing the dealer's shop, where some of the old furniture was exposed for sale. Since her fit of giddiness she dragged one leg; and as her strength was failing Mère Simon, whose grocery business had collapsed, came every morning to split the wood and pump water for her.

Her eyes grew feeble. The shutters ceased to be thrown open. Years and years passed, and the house was neither let nor sold.

Félicité never asked for repairs because she was afraid of being sent away. The boards on the roof rotted; her bolster was wet for a whole winter. After Easter she spat blood.

Then Mère Simon called in a doctor. Félicité wanted to know what was the matter with her. But she was too deaf to hear, and the only word which reached her was "pneumonia." It was a word she knew, and she answered softly "Ah! like Madame," thinking it natural that she should follow her mistress.

The time for the festal shrines was coming near. The first one was always at the bottom of the hill, the second in front of the post-office, and the third towards the middle of the street. There was some rivalry in the matter of this one, and the women of the parish ended by choosing Mme. Aubain's courtyard.

The hard breathing and fever increased. Félicité was vexed at doing nothing for the altar. If only she could at least have put something there! Then she thought of the parrot. The neighbours objected that it would not be decent. But the priest gave her permission, which so intensely delighted her that she begged him to accept Loulou, her sole possession, when she died.

From Tuesday to Saturday, the eve of the festival, she coughed more often. By the evening her face had shrivelled, her lips stuck to her gums, and she had vomitings; and at twilight next morning, feeling herself very low, she sent for a priest.

Three kindly women were round her during the extreme unction. Then she announced that she must speak to Fabu. He arrived in his Sunday clothes, by no means at his ease in the funereal atmosphere.

"Forgive me," she said, with an effort to stretch out her arm; "I thought it was you who had killed him."

What did she mean by such stories? She suspected him of murder—a man like him! He waxed indignant, and was on the point of making a row.

"There," said the women, "she is no longer in her senses, you can see it well enough!"

Félicité spoke to shadows of her own from time to time. The women went away, and Mère Simon had breakfast. A little later she took Loulou and brought him close to Félicité with the words:

"Come, now, say good-bye to him!"

Loulou was not a corpse, but the worms devoured him; one of his wings was broken, and the tow was coming out of his stomach. But she was blind now; she kissed him on the forehead and kept him close against her cheek. Mère Simon took him back from her to put him on the altar.

5

Summer scents came up from the meadows; flies buzzed; the sun made the river glitter and heated the slates. Mère Simon came back into the room and fell softly asleep.

She woke at the noise of bells; the people were coming out from vespers. Félicité's delirium subsided. She thought of the procession and saw it as if she had been there.

All the school children, the church-singers, and the firemen walked on the pavement, while in the middle of the road the verger armed with his hallebard and the beadle with a large cross advanced in front. Then came the schoolmaster, with an eye on the boys, and the sister, anxious about her little girls; three of the daintiest, with angelic curls, scattered rosepetals in the air; the deacon controlled the band with outstretched arms; and two censerbearers turned back at every step towards the Holy Sacrament, which was borne by Monsieur the curé, wearing his beautiful chasuble, under a canopy of dark-red velvet held up by four churchwardens. A crowd of people pressed behind, between the white cloths covering the house walls, and they reached the bottom of the hill.

A cold sweat moistened Félicité's temples. Mère Simon sponged her with a piece of linen, saying to herself that one day she would have to go that way.

The hum of the crowd increased, was very loud for an instant, and then went further away.

A fusillade shook the window-panes. It was the postilions saluting the monstrance.[9] Félicité rolled her eyes and said as audibly as she could: "Does he look well?" The parrot was weighing on her mind.

Her agony began. A death-rattle that grew more and more convulsed made her sides heave. Bubbles of froth came at the corners of her mouth and her whole body trembled.

Soon the booming of the ophicleides,[1] the high voices of the children, and the deep voices of the men were distinguishable. At intervals all was silent, and the tread of feet, deadened by the flowers they walked on, sounded like a flock pattering on grass.

9. Golden container displaying the consecrated communion bread.

1. Brass wind instruments.

The clergy appeared in the courtyard. Mère Simon clambered on to a chair to reach the attic window, and so looked down straight upon the shrine. Green garlands hung over the altar, which was decked with a flounce of English lace. In the middle was a small frame with relics in it; there were two orange-trees at the corners, and all along stood silver candlesticks and china vases, with sunflowers, lilies, peonies, foxgloves, and tufts of hortensia. This heap of blazing colour slanted from the level of the altar to the carpet which went on over the pavement; and some rare objects caught the eye. There was a silver-gilt sugar-basin with a crown of violets; pendants of Alençon stone glittered on the moss, and two Chinese screens displayed their landscapes. Loulou was hidden under roses, and showed nothing but his blue forehead, like a plaque of lapis lazuli.

The churchwardens, singers, and children took their places round the three sides of the court. The priest went slowly up the steps, and placed his great, radiant golden sun upon the lace. Everyone knelt down. There was a deep silence; and the censers glided to and fro on the full swing of their chains.

An azure vapour rose up into Félicité's room. Her nostrils met it; she inhaled it sensuously, mystically; and then closed her eyes. Her lips smiled. The beats of her heart lessened one by one, vaguer each time and softer, as a fountain sinks, an echo disappears; and when she sighed her last breath she thought she saw an opening in the heavens, and a gigantic parrot hovering above her head.

Fyodor Dostoevsky

1821–1881

"I am a sick man. . . . I am a spiteful man. I am an unpleasant man." The first words of Fyodor Dostoevsky's *Notes from Underground* (1864) announced a new voice and defined a new epoch. Who had ever dared introduce his story by trying to alienate his readers, listing reasons why we shouldn't listen to him? So as not to be identified with his character, Dostoevsky added a footnote reminding us that this speaker is a fiction. But the note also says that characters like him "not only may, but must exist in our society." In this unnamed hero, or rather antihero (as he calls himself), Dostoevsky was trying to sum up the meaning of the nineteenth century.

His own life looks much like an unpleasant preparation for this enterprise. Born in Moscow in 1821, the son of an army doctor, Dostoevsky was destined by his family for the Army Engineering Corps. However, he soon revolted against the study of engineering and threw himself instead into literature and politics. Both interests led him to European writers like Goethe, Hugo, and Balzac, who seemed to embody the spirit of modernity that had produced the French Revolution and continued to shake many of society's deeply rooted ethical values and political structures. Convinced that Russia needed this spiritual agitation, Dostoevsky spent much time and energy translating Balzac's novel *Eugénie Grandet*. And in his own fiction, too, he turned to the new urban realities, writing about the underpaid, rootless, resentful inhabitants of cities like Petersburg who had been forgotten by Russia's "literature of landowners." His great predecessor Nikolai Gogol had already discovered the poor government clerk as a comic figure for Russia's backwardness. "We have all emerged," Dostoevsky wrote, "from under Gogol's *Overcoat*." But Dostoevsky took this figure more seriously. Wandering the streets of Petersburg at night, especially in the less prosperous sections, he was seeking to integrate clerks and prostitutes, the insulted and the injured, into literature's conversation about the fate

Leonid Petrovich Grossman, *Caricature of Dostoevsky.*

of the nation, a conversation that had been restricted to the fashionable salons. Though he used his income from his family to pursue a bohemian life of alternating prodigality and indebtedness, studiously avoiding the middle-class model of hardworking frugality, Dostoevsky was astonishingly productive. In the five years after giving up his army career in 1844, he published ten novels and short stories. He was a celebrity from the age of twenty-four, when his first novel, *Poor Folk* (1845), was hailed by the most important critics of the age.

The next stage in his life is also the most famous. Having joined a left-wing student group centered around a rich young man named Petrashevsky, Dostoevsky was arrested along with the rest of the group in 1849, imprisoned for eight months, and sentenced to death. The eight men were led out in front of a firing squad, then told at the last minute that their lives would be spared. The sentence was commuted to prison in Siberia, where he served four years. There has naturally been much speculation about the impact this near-death experience must have had. Dostoevsky had been troubled by childhood bouts of epilepsy; in Siberia his epilepsy worsened. Politically, he gave up his hopes of progressive reform. Released from prison in 1854, he married in 1857 and finally returned to Petersburg in 1859, where despite continuing government suspicion and interference, he resumed a successful career as novelist and journalist.

He was forty years old, and had been a famous writer for a decade and a half, when the emancipation of the serfs in 1861 marked the beginning of the end of the old landowners' order (two years before Lincoln's Emancipation Proclamation abolished slavery in the United States). Dostoevsky—whose father had been murdered by serfs—wasn't enthusiastic about this democratic transformation. Like other members of the Westernized elite, he watched uneasily the social processes in the materialist West that brought, along with political democracy, a disintegration of age-old moral certainties and a huge, desperate mass of urban poor. Should Russia follow this example? Many thought not, turning against their own Westernized education and even against the self-consciousness it had stimulated in them. Dostoevsky's political ideas became reactionary even by the standards of the day. He wrote odes to members of the Czar's family and expressed a somewhat paranoid fear that socialists and Roman Catholics were conspiring together to destroy the Russian Orthodox Church. For him, Orthodoxy was a desperately needed cultural heritage that set the Russian nation apart from the increasingly godless West, but he saw nothing un-christian in calling on patriotic Russians to invade Turkey and win back Constantinople from the Muslim Turks.

His most directly political novel, *The Possessed* (1867), made use of his early radical experiences in order to satirize progressives, especially wealthy ones like Petrashevsky, with merciless brilliance. Journeys abroad, in part to flee his creditors, provided compelling evidence against the arrogance and spiritual emptiness of the West. These travels also encouraged his compulsive penchant for gambling, which gave self-destructive expression to his belief in free will and contingency, his revolt against the European creed of scientific determinism. But if anti-Western and Slavophile ideas are present in the masterpieces Dostoevsky wrote in the following years, like *The Idiot, Crime and Punishment,* and *The Brothers Karamazov,* they are by no means the single key to the meaning of those novels. Many readers have felt that though he vigorously opposed the subversive modernity of the West, fearing its effect on established values, he knew deep down that established values were weak and indefensible and that humanity would eventually have to face the enormous challenge of what Nietzsche called the revaluation of all values. As he wrote in *The Brothers Karamazov,* Dostoevsky was afraid people would conclude that if there is no God, everything is permitted. Yet to someone like the philosopher Jean-Paul Sartre, it is precisely that existential truth that Dostoevsky forces us to recognize.

The enduring power of *Notes from Underground* comes in part from its ability to hold this question open. The text seems to have been intended as a critique of progressive Westernized intellectuals like Nicolai Chernyshevsky, whose extremely influential novel of ideas *What Is to Be Done?* had argued that society can be improved by following the principle of rational self-interest. Unsurprisingly, it was the aristocratic landowners who preached self-sacrifice rather than self-interest, and Underground Man's contempt for self-interest and "model flats" makes him sound at times like a spokesman for their party. To Dostoevsky's protagonist, it is better to be irrational and free than rational and thus ruled by a calculating materialism. But by putting his ideas in the mouth of such an unreliable narrator, Dostoevsky doesn't permit us simply to agree. He gives us no firm footing anywhere. Like Nietzsche, he asks unpleasantly searching questions about values that seem self-evident. Modern humanity prides itself on its self-consciousness. But what after all is the value of self-consciousness? Does it really lead, as it claims, to change for the better? Wouldn't it be better *not* to be Hamlet, to be able simply to act, even in revenge, rather than asking endless philosophical questions about everything? Is the nineteenth century making a tragic mistake when it seizes on Hamlet as an exemplary figure, celebrating consciousness over action?

Clerks, like the former employee of the Civil Service in the story, are Dostoevsky's characteristic types because they are spiteful: hemmed in by the rules and regulations of an archaic, irrational bureaucracy in which they don't believe, always in danger from the eyes and ears of those around them, unable to act independently, yet also unable to imagine any alternative. As a writer, Dostoevsky had a bizarre intimacy with the bureaucracy. His reactionary ideas didn't stop the journal he ran with his brother from being suppressed by the government. Seemingly random parts of *Notes from Underground* were cut by the official censor. The knowledge that he would be read and judged by unfriendly and uncomprehending bureaucrats no doubt adds a certain spice to Underground Man's self-consciousness. "I want to tell you, gentlemen, whether you care to hear it or not, why I could not even become an insect." This extraordinary voice

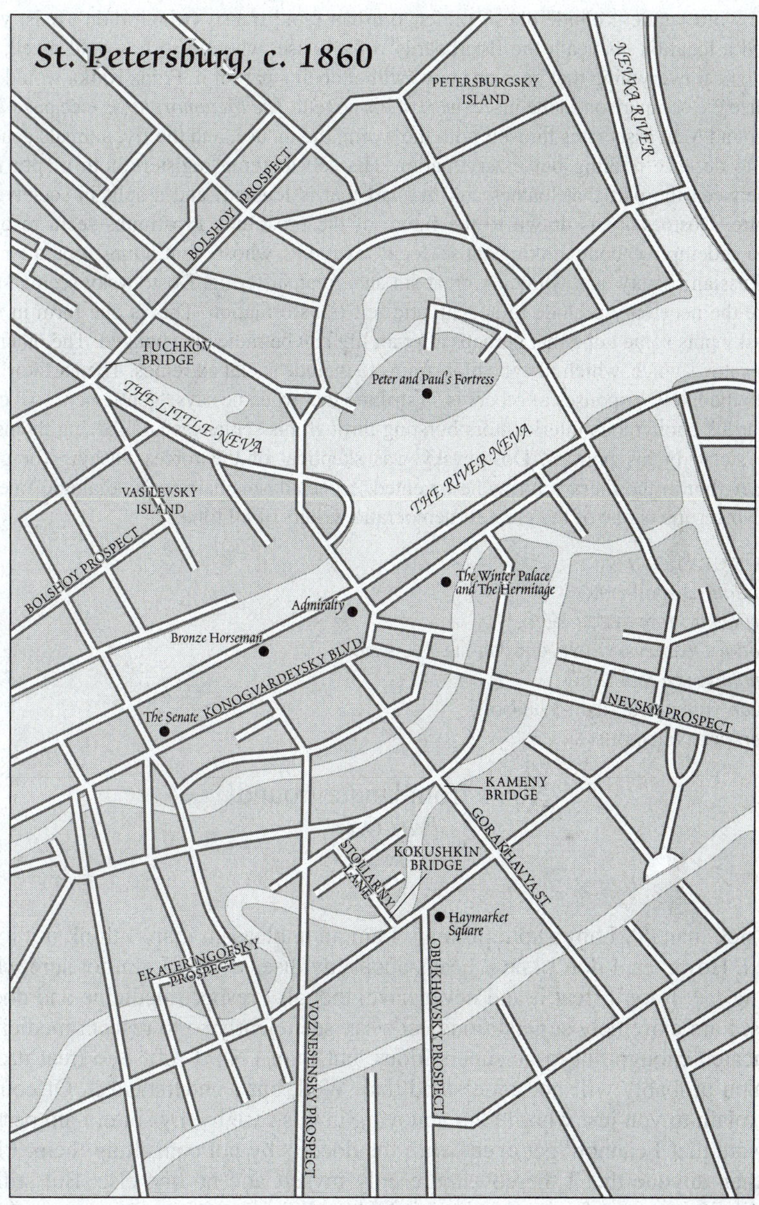

foresees the indifference of those whom it nevertheless seems obstinately obliged to address. The Underground Man has internalized, made a part of himself, both the hostility of the government and the contrary hostility of the intellectuals who had launched Dostoevsky's own career. In a time of great social and ideological unrest, Russia's intellectuals wielded a degree of influence unparalleled either before or since. It is not for nothing that the word "intelligentsia" comes to English from the Russian. Yet Dostoevsky saw them as fatefully cut off from the lives of clerks and other ordinary people.

The word "underground" doesn't refer to urban rapid transit (which didn't exist yet); it suggested a location "beneath the floorboards" of a house, where insects would dwell, close enough to hear everything that goes on above without being part of it. Franz Kafka would go on to literalize the comparison in the insect hero of his novella *The Metamorphosis* (see page 2598). Underground Man associates himself with the worm, the mouse, and the fly, animals generally thought to deserve nothing but extermination. His self-loathing registers both a split in the mind (between the part that loathes and the part that is loathed) and a split in society. Like Baudelaire, Dostoevsky is drawn to the figure of the prostitute. Prostitutes seem to offer a bridge, a redemptive bond linking those social extremes whose continuing separation condemns Russian society as a whole. A great sin and great suffering, Dostoevsky seemed to believe, are the necessary prelude to apocalyptic self-transformation. This is one form in which Dostoevsky puts some hope that perhaps after all life *can* be radically changed. The other form is the narrator's voice, which like the plot strains to include social extremes. The narrator's sensitivity to the likely responses of others is so striking that when he says "gentlemen," we can almost hear his anonymous interlocutors bursting through his sentences and forcing themselves into the story. In his politics, Dostoevsky was skeptical of the forces pushing for greater democracy, but in the literary forms he invented, especially his narrator's "dialogic"openness to other voices, he is one of the greatest democratic writers of all time.

PRONUNCIATIONS:

Apollon: ah-poll-OHN
Ferfichkin: fare-FEECH-keen
Fyodor Dostoevsky: FYO-dur dah-sta-YEF-skee
Simonov: see-MOHN-off
Trudolyubov: true-dahl-YOU-boff
Zverkov: ZVAIR-KOHF

Notes from Underground[1]

Part One

UNDERGROUND

I

I am a sick man . . . I am a spiteful man. I am an unpleasant man. I think my liver is diseased. However, I don't know beans about my disease, and I am not sure what is bothering me. I don't treat it and never have, though I respect medicine and doctors. Besides, I am extremely superstitious, let's say sufficiently so to respect medicine. (I am educated enough not to be superstitious, but I am.) No, I refuse to treat it out of spite. You probably will not understand that. Well, but *I* understand it. Of course, I can't explain to you just whom I am annoying in this case by my spite. I am perfectly well aware that I cannot "get even" with the doctors by not consulting them. I know better than anyone that I thereby injure only myself and no one else. But still, if I don't treat it, it is out of spite. My liver is bad, well then—let it get even worse!

I have been living like that for a long time now—twenty years. I am forty now. I used to be in the civil service, but no longer am. I was a spiteful official. I was rude and took pleasure in being so. After all, I did not accept bribes, so I was bound to find a compensation in that, at least. (A bad joke but I will not cross it out, I wrote it thinking it would sound very witty; but now that I see myself that I only wanted to show off in a despicable way, I will purposely not cross it out!) When petitioners would come to my desk for information I would gnash my teeth at them, and feel intense

1. Translated by Ralph E. Matlaw.

enjoyment when I succeeded in distressing some one. I was almost always successful. For the most part they were all timid people—of course, they were petitioners. But among the fops there was one officer in particular I could not endure. He simply would not be humble, and clanked his sword in a disgusting way. I carried on a war with him for eighteen months over that sword. At last I got the better of him. He left off clanking it. However, that happened when I was still young. But do you know, gentlemen, what the real point of my spite was? Why, the whole trick, the real vileness of it lay in the fact that continually, even in moments of the worst spleen, I was inwardly conscious with shame that I was not only not spiteful but not even an embittered man, that I was simply frightening sparrows at random and amusing myself by it. I might foam at the mouth, but bring me some kind of toy, give me a cup of tea with sugar, and I would be appeased. My heart might even be touched, though probably I would gnash my teeth at myself after ward and lie awake at night with shame for months after. That is the way I am.

I was lying when I said just now that I was a spiteful official. I was lying out of spite. I was simply indulging myself with the petitioners and with the officer, but I could never really become spiteful. Every moment I was conscious in myself of many, very many elements completely opposite to that. I felt them positively teeming in me, these opposite elements. I knew that they had been teeming in me all my life, begging to be let out, but I would not let them, would not let them, purposely would not let them out. They tormented me till I was ashamed; they drove me to convulsions, and finally, they bored me, how they bored me! Well, are you not imagining, gentlemen, that I am repenting for something now, that I am asking your forgiveness for something? I am sure you are imagining that. However, I assure you it does not matter to me if you are.

Not only could I not become spiteful, I could not even become anything: neither spiteful nor kind, neither a rascal nor an honest man, neither a hero nor an insect. Now, I am living out my life in my corner, taunting myself with the spiteful and useless consolation that an intelligent man cannot seriously become anything and that only a fool can become something. Yes, an intelligent man in the nineteenth century must and morally ought to be pre-eminently a characterless creature; a man of character, an active man, is pre-eminently a limited creature. That is the conviction of my forty years. I am forty years old now, and forty years, after all, is a whole lifetime; after all, that is extreme old age. To live longer than forty years is bad manners; it is vulgar, immoral. Who does live beyond forty? Answer that, sincerely and honestly. I will tell you who do: fools and worthless people do. I tell all old men that to their face, all those respectable old men, all those silver-haired and reverend old men! I tell the whole world that to its face. I have a right to say so, for I'll go on living to sixty myself. I'll live till seventy! Till eighty! Wait, let me catch my breath.

No doubt you think, gentlemen, that I want to amuse you. You are mistaken in that, too. I am not at all such a merry person as you imagine, or as you may imagine; however, if irritated by all this babble (and I can feel that you are irritated) you decide to ask me just who I am—then my answer is, I am a certain low-ranked civil servant. I was in the service in order to have something to eat (but only for that reason), and when last year a distant relation left me six thousand roubles in his will I immediately retired from the service and settled down in my corner. I used to live in this corner before, but now I have settled down in it. My room is a wretched, horrid one on the outskirts of town. My servant is an old country-woman, spiteful out of stupidity, and, moreover, she always smells bad. I am told that the Petersburg climate is bad for me, and that with my paltry means it is very expensive to live in Petersburg. I know all that better than all these sage and experienced counsellors and monitors. But I am going to stay in Petersburg. I will not leave Petersburg! I will not leave because . . . Bah, after all it does not matter in the least whether I leave or stay.

But incidentally, what can a decent man speak about with the greatest pleasure?

Answer: About himself.

Well, then, I will talk about myself.

II

Now I want to tell you, gentlemen, whether you care to hear it or not, why I could not even become an insect. I tell you solemnly that I wanted to become an insect many times. But I was not even worthy of that. I swear to you, gentlemen, that to be hyperconscious is a disease, a real positive disease. Ordinary human consciousness would be too much for man's everyday needs, that is, half or a quarter of the amount which falls to the lot of a cultivated man of our unfortunate nineteenth century, especially one who has the particular misfortune to inhabit Petersburg, the most abstract and intentional city in the whole world.[2] (There are intentional and unintentional cities.) It would have been quite enough, for instance, to have the consciousness by which all so-called straightforward persons and men of action live. I'll bet you think I am writing all this to show off, to be witty at the expense of men of action; and what is more, that out of ill-bred showing-off, I am clanking a sword, like my officer. But, gentlemen, whoever can pride himself on his diseases and even show off with them?

However, what am I talking about? Everyone does that. They do pride themselves on their diseases, and I, perhaps, more than any one. There is no doubt about it: my objection was absurd. Yet just the same, I am firmly convinced not only that a great deal of consciousness, but that any consciousness is a disease. I insist on it. Let us drop that, too, for a minute. Tell me this: why did it happen that at the very, yes, at the very moment when I was most capable of recognizing every refinement of "all the sublime and beautiful," as we used to say at one time, I would, as though purposely, not only feel but do such hideous things, such that—well, in short, such as everyone probably does but which, as though purposely, occurred to me at the very time when I was most conscious that they ought not to be done. The more conscious I was of goodness, and of all that "sublime and beautiful," the more deeply I sank into my mire and the more capable I became of sinking into it completely. But the main thing was that all this did not seem to occur in me accidentally, but as though it had to be so. As though it were my most normal condition, and not in the least disease or depravity, so that finally I even lost the desire to struggle against this depravity. It ended by my almost believing (perhaps actually believing) that probably this was really my normal condition. But at first, in the beginning, that is, what agonies I suffered in that struggle! I did not believe that others went through the same things, and therefore I hid this fact about myself as a secret all my life. I was ashamed (perhaps I am even ashamed now). I reached the point of feeling a sort of secret abnormal, despicable enjoyment in returning home to my corner on some disgusting Petersburg night, and being acutely conscious that that day I had again done something loathsome, that what was done could never be undone, and secretly, inwardly gnaw, gnaw at myself for it, nagging

2. One of the youngest European cities, Petersburg was established at the beginning of the 18th century by the decree of Tsar Peter the Great, who wanted a "window on the west." Peter's ambition was to turn a marshy wasteland into a harmonious and perfectly ordered Enlightenment capital.

and consuming myself till at last the bitterness turned into a sort of shameful accursed sweetness, and finally into real positive enjoyment! Yes, into enjoyment, into enjoyment! I insist upon that. And that is why I have started to speak, because I keep wanting to know for a fact whether other people feel such an enjoyment. Let me explain: the enjoyment here consisted precisely in the hyperconsciousness of one's own degradation; it was from feeling oneself that one had reached the last barrier, that it was nasty, but that it could not be otherwise; that you no longer had an escape; that you could never become a different person; that even if there remained enough time and faith for you to change into something else you probably would not want to change; or if you did want to, even then you would do nothing; because perhaps in reality there was nothing for you to change into. And the worst of it, and the root of it all, was that it all proceeded according to the normal and fundamental laws of hyperconsciousness, and with the inertia that was the direct result of those laws, and that consequently one could not only not change but one could do absolutely nothing. Thus it would follow, as the result of hyperconsciousness, that one is not to blame for being a scoundrel, as though that were any consolation to the scoundrel once he himself has come to realize that he actually is a scoundrel. But enough. Bah, I have talked a lot of nonsense, but what have I explained? Can this enjoyment be explained? But I will explain it! I will get to the bottom of it! That is why I have taken up my pen.

To take an instance, I am terribly vain. I am as suspicious and touchy as a hunchback or a dwarf. But to tell the truth, there have been moments when if someone had happened to slap my face I would, perhaps, have even been glad of that. I say, very seriously, that I would probably have been able to discover a peculiar sort of enjoyment even in that—the enjoyment, of course, of despair; but in despair occur the most intense enjoyments, especially when one is very acutely conscious of one's hopeless position. As for the slap in the face—why then the consciousness of being beaten to a pulp would positively overwhelm one. The worst of it is, no matter how I tried, it still turned out that I was always the most to blame in everything, and what is most humiliating of all, to blame for no fault of my own but, so to say, through the laws of nature. In the first place, to blame because I am cleverer than any of the people surrounding me. (I have always considered myself cleverer than any of the people surrounding me, and sometimes, would you believe it, I have even been ashamed of that. At any rate, all my life, I have, as it were, looked away and I could never look people straight in the eye.) To blame, finally, because even if I were magnanimous, I would only have suffered more from the consciousness of all its uselessness. After all, I would probably never have been able to do anything with my magnanimity—neither to forgive, for my assailant may have slapped me because of the laws of nature, and one cannot forgive the laws of nature; nor to forget, for even if it were the laws of nature, it is insulting all the same. Finally, even if I had wanted to be anything but magnanimous, had desired on the contrary to revenge myself on the man who insulted me, I could not have revenged myself on anyone nor anything because I would certainly never have made up my mind to do anything, even if I had been able to. Why would I not have made up my mind? I want to say a few words about that in particular.

III

After all, people who know how to revenge themselves and to take care of themselves in general, how do they do it? After all, when they are possessed, let us suppose, by the feeling of revenge, then for the time there is nothing else but that feeling left in their whole being. Such a man simply rushes straight toward his object like an infuriated bull with its horns down, and nothing but a wall will stop him. (By the way: facing the wall, such people—that is, the straightforward persons and men of action—are genuinely nonplussed. For them a wall is not an evasion, as for example for us people who think and consequently do nothing; it is not an excuse for turning aside, an excuse for which our kind is always very glad, though we scarcely believe in it ourselves, usually. No, they are nonplussed in all sincerity. The wall has for them something tranquilizing, morally soothing, final—maybe even something mysterious . . . but of the wall later.) Well, such a direct person I regard as the real normal man, as his tender mother nature wished to see him when she graciously brought him into being on the earth. I envy such a man till I am green in the face. He is stupid. I am not disputing that, but perhaps the normal man should be stupid, how do you know? Perhaps it is very beautiful, in fact. And I am all the more convinced of that suspicion, if one can call it so, by the fact that if, for instance, you take the antithesis of the normal man, that is, the hyperconscious man, who has come, of course, not out of the lap of nature but out of a retort (this is almost mysticism, gentlemen, but I suspect this, too), this retort-made man is sometimes so nonplussed in the presence of his antithesis that with his hyperconsciousness he genuinely thinks of himself a mouse and not a man. It may be a hyperconscious mouse, yet it is a mouse, while the other is a man, are therefore, etc. And the worst is, he himself, his very ownself, looks upon himself as a mouse. No one asks him to do so. And that is an important point. Now let us look at this mouse in action. Let us suppose, for instance, that it feels insulted, too (and it almost always does feel insulted), and wants to revenge itself too. There may even be a greater accumulation of spite in it than in *l'homme de la nature et de la vérité.*[3] The base, nasty desire to repay with spite whoever has offended it, rankles perhaps even more nastily in it than in *l'homme de la nature et de la vérité,* because *l'homme de la nature et de la vérité,* through his innate stupidity looks upon his revenge as justice pure and simple; while in consequence of his hyperconsciousness the mouse does not believe in the justice of it. To come at last to the deed itself, to the very act of revenge. Apart from the one fundamental nastiness the unfortunate mouse succeeds in creating around it so many other nastinesses in the form of doubts and questions, adds to the one question so many unsettled questions, that there inevitably works up around it a sort of fatal brew, a stinking mess, made up of its doubts, agitations and lastly of the contempt spat upon it by the straightforward men of action who stand solemnly about it as judges and arbitrators, laughing at it till their healthy sides ache. Of course the only thing left for it is to dismiss all that with a wave of its paw, and, with a smile of assumed contempt in which it does not even believe itself, creep ignominiously into its mouse-hole. There, in its nasty, stinking, underground home our insulted, crushed and ridiculed mouse promptly becomes absorbed in cold, malignant and, above all, everlasting spite. For forty years together it will remember its injury down to the smallest, most shameful detail, and every time will add, of itself, details still more shameful, spitefully teasing and irritating itself with its own imagination. It will be ashamed of its own fancies, but yet it will recall everything, it will go over it again and again, it will invent lies against itself pretending that worse things might have happened, and will forgive anything. Maybe it will begin to revenge itself, too, but, as it were, piecemeal, in trivial ways, from behind the stove, incognito, without believing either in its own right to vengeance, or in the success of its revenge, knowing

3. A man of nature and of truth (French), ideal of Enlightenment philosophers like Jean-Jacques Rousseau.

beforehand that from all its efforts at revenge it will suffer a hundred times more than he on whom it revenges itself, while he, probably will not even feel it. On its deathbed it will recall it all over again, with interest accumulated over all the years. But it is just in that cold, abominable half-despair, half-belief, in that conscious burying oneself alive for grief in the underworld for forty years, in that hyperconsciousness and yet to some extent doubtful hopelessness of one's position, in that hell of unsatisfied desires turned inward, in that lever of oscillations, of resolutions taken for ever and regretted again a minute later—that the savor of that strange enjoyment of which I have spoken lies. It is so subtle, sometimes so difficult to analyze consciously, that somewhat limited people, or simply people with strong nerves, will not understand anything at all in it. "Possibly," you will add on your own account with a grin, "people who have never received a slap in the face will not understand it either," and in that way you will politely hint to me that I, too, perhaps, have been slapped in the face in my life, and so I speak as an expert. I'll bet that you are thinking that. But set your minds at rest, gentlemen, I have not received a slap in the face, though it doesn't matter to me at all what you may think about it. Possibly, I even myself regret that I have given so few slaps in the face during my life. But enough, not another word on the subject of such extreme interest to you.

I will continue calmly about people with strong nerves who do not understand a certain refinement of enjoyment. Though in certain circumstances these gentlemen bellow their loudest like bulls, though this, let us suppose, does them the greatest honor, yet, as I have already said, confronted with the impossible they at once resign themselves. Does the impossible mean the stone wall? What stone wall? Why, of course, the laws of nature, the conclusions of natural science, of mathematics. As soon as they prove to you, for instance, that you are descended from a monkey, then it is no use scowling, accept it as a fact. When they prove to you that in reality one drop of your own fat must be dearer to you than a hundred thousand of your fellow creatures, and that this conclusion is the final solution of all so-called virtues and duties and all such ravings and prejudices, then you might as well accept it, you can't do anything about it, because two times two is a law of mathematics. Just try refuting it.

"But really," they will shout at you, "there is no use protesting; it is a case of two times two makes four. Nature does not ask your permission, your wishes, and whether you like or dislike her laws does not concern her. You are bound to accept her as she is, and consequently also all her conclusions. A wall, you see, is a wall—etc., etc." Good God! but what do I care about the laws of nature and arithmetic, when, for some reason, I dislike those laws and the fact that two times two makes four? Of course I cannot break through a wall by battering my head against it if I really do not have the strength to break through it, but I am not going to resign myself to it simply because it is a stone wall and I am not strong enough.

As though such a stone wall really were a consolation, and really did contain some word of conciliation, if only because it is as true as two times two makes four. Oh, absurdity of absurdities! How much better it is to understand it all, to be conscious of it all, all the impossibilities and the stone walls, not to resign yourself to a single one of those impossibilities and stone walls if it disgusts you to resign yourself; to reach, through the most inevitable, logical combinations, the most revolting conclusions on the everlasting theme that you are yourself somehow to blame even for the stone wall, though again it is as clear as day you are not to blame in the least, and therefore grinding your teeth in silent impotence sensuously to sink into inertia, brooding on the fact that it turns out that there is even no one for you to feel vindictive against, that you have not, and perhaps never will have, an object for your spite, that it is a sleight-of-hand, a bit of juggling, a card-sharper's trick, that it is simply a mess, no knowing what and no knowing who, but in spite of all these uncertainties, and jugglings, still there is an ache in you, and the more you do not know, the worse the ache.

IV

"Ha, ha, ha! Next you will find enjoyment in a toothache," you cry with a laugh.

"Well? So what? There is enjoyment even in a toothache," I answer. I had a toothache for a whole month and I know there is. In that case, of course, people are not spiteful in silence, they moan; but these are not sincere moans, they are malicious moans, and the maliciousness is the whole point. The sufferer's enjoyment finds expression in those moans; if he did not feel enjoyment in them he would not moan. It is a good example, gentlemen, and I will develop it. The moans express in the first place all the aimlessness of your pain, which is so humiliating to your consciousness; the whole legal system of Nature on which you spit disdainfully, of course, but from which you suffer all the same while she does not. They express the consciousness that you have no enemy, but that you do have a pain; the consciousness that in spite of all the dentists in the world you are in complete slavery to your teeth; that if someone wishes it, your teeth will leave off aching, and if he does not, they will go on aching another three months; and that finally if you still disagree and still protest, all that is left you for your own gratification is to thrash yourself or beat your wall with your fist as hard as you can, and absolutely nothing more. Well then, these mortal insults, these jeers on the part of someone unknown, end at last in an enjoyment which sometimes reaches the highest degree of sensuality. I beg you, gentlemen, to listen sometimes to the moans of an educated man of the nineteenth century who is suffering from a toothache, particularly on the second or third day of the attack, when he has already begun to moan not as he moaned on the first day, that is, not simply because he has a toothache, not just as any coarse peasant might moan, but as a man affected by progress and European civilization, a man who is "divorced from the soil and the nation of principles," as they call it these days. His moans become nasty, disgustingly spiteful, and go on for whole days and nights. And, after all, he himself knows that he does not benefit at all from his moans; he knows better than any one that he is only lacerating and irritating himself and others in vain; he knows that even the audience for whom he is exerting himself and his whole family now listen to him with loathing, do not believe him for the second, and that deep down they understand that he could moan differently, more simply, without trills and flourishes, and that he is only indulging himself like that out of spite, out of malice. Well, sensuality exists precisely in all these consciousnesses and infamies. "It seems I am troubling you, I am lacerating your hearts, I am keeping everyone in the house awake. Well, stay awake then, you, too, feel every minute that I have a toothache, I am no longer the hero to you now that I tried to appear before, but simply a nasty person, a scoundrel. Well, let it be that way, then! I am very glad that you see through me. Is it nasty for you to hear my foul moans? Well, let it be nasty. Here I will let you have an even nastier flourish in a minute. . . ." You still do not understand, gentlemen? No, it seems our development and our consciousness must go further to understand all the intricacies of this sensuality. You laugh? I am delighted. My jokes, gentlemen, are of course in bad taste, uneven, involved, lacking self-confidence. But of course that is because I do not respect myself. Can a man with consciousness respect himself at all?

V

Come, can a man who even attempts to find enjoyment in the very feeling of self-degradation really have any respect for himself at all? I am not saying this now from any insipid kind of remorse. And, indeed, I could never endure to say, "Forgive me, Daddy, I won't do it again," not because I was incapable of saying it, but, on the contrary, perhaps just because I was too capable of it, and in what a way, too! As though on purpose I used to get into trouble on occasions when I was not to blame in the faintest way. That was the nastiest part of it. At the same time I was genuinely touched and repentant, I used to shed tears and, of course, tricked even myself, though it was not acting in the least and there was a sick feeling in my heart at the time. For that one could not even blame the laws of nature, though the laws of nature have offended me continually all my life more than anything. It is loathsome to remember it all, but it was loathsome even then. Of course, in a minute or so I would realize with spite that it was all a lie, a lie, an affected, revolting lie, that is, all this repentance, all these emotions, these vows to reform. And if you ask why I worried and tortured myself that way, the answer is because it was very dull to twiddle one's thumbs, and so one began cutting capers. That is really it. Observe yourselves more carefully, gentlemen, then you will understand that that's right! I invented adventures for myself and made up a life, so as to live at least in some way. How many times it has happened to me—well, for instance, to take offence at nothing, simply on purpose; and one knows oneself, of course, that one is offended at nothing, that one is pretending, but yet one brings oneself, at last, to the point of really being offended. All my life I have had an impulse to play such pranks, so that in the end, I could not control it in myself. Another time, twice, in fact, I tried to force myself to fall in love. I even suffered, gentlemen, I assure you. In the depth of my heart I did not believe in my suffering, there was a stir of mockery, but yet I did suffer, and in the real, regular way I was jealous, I was beside myself, and it was all out of boredom, gentlemen, all out of boredom; inertia overcame me. After all, the direct, legitimate, immediate fruit of consciousness is inertia, that is, conscious thumb twiddling. I have referred to it already, I repeat, I repeat it emphatically: all straightforward persons and men of action are active just because they are stupid and limited. How can that be explained? This way: as a result of their limitation they take immediate and secondary causes for primary ones, and in that way persuade themselves more quickly and easily than other people do that they have found an infallible basis for their activity, and their minds are at ease and that, you know, is the most important thing. To begin to act, you know, you must first have your mind completely at ease and without a trace of doubt left in it. Well, how am I, for example, to set my mind at rest? Where are the primary causes on which I am to build? Where are my bases? Where am I to get them from? I exercise myself in the process of thinking, and consequently with me every primary cause at once draws after itself another still more primary, and so on to infinity. That is precisely the essence of every sort of consciousness and thinking. It must be a case of the laws of nature again. In what does it finally result? Why, just the same. Remember I spoke just now of vengeance. (I am sure you did not grasp that.) I said that a man revenges himself because he finds justice in it. Therefore he has found a primary cause, found a basis, to wit, justice. And so he is completely set at rest, and consequently he carries out his revenge calmly and successfully, as he is convinced that he is doing a just and honest thing. But, after all, I see no justice in it, I find no sort of virtue in it either, and consequently if I attempt to revenge myself, it would only be out of spite. Spite, of course, might overcome everything, all my doubts, and could consequently serve quite successfully in a place of a primary cause, precisely because it is not a cause. But what can be done if I do not even have spite (after all, I began with that just now)? Again, in consequence of those accursed laws of consciousness, my spite is subject to chemical disintegration. You look into it, the object flies off into air, your reasons evaporate, the criminal is not to be found, the insult becomes fate rather than an insult, something like the toothache, for which no one is to blame, and consequently there is only the same outlet left again—that is, to beat the wall as hard as you can. So you give it up as hopeless because you have not found a fundamental cause. And try letting yourself be carried away by your feelings, blindly, without reflection, without a primary cause, repelling consciousness at least for a time; hate or love, if only not to sit and twiddle your thumbs. The day after tomorrow, at the latest, you will begin despising yourself for having knowingly deceived yourself. The result—a soap-bubble and inertia. Oh, gentlemen, after all, perhaps I consider myself an intelligent man only because all my life I have been able neither to begin nor to finish anything. Granted, granted I am a babbler, a harmless annoying babbler, like all of us. But what is to be done if the direct and sole vocation of every intelligent man is babble, that is, the intentional pouring of water through a sieve?

VI

Oh, if I had done nothing simply out of laziness! Heavens, how I would have respected myself then. I would have respected myself because I would at least have been capable of being lazy; there would at least have been in me one positive quality, as it were, in which I could have believed myself. Question: Who is he? Answer: A loafer. After all, it would have been pleasant to hear that about oneself! It would mean that I was positively defined, it would mean that there was something to be said about me. "Loafer"—why, after all, it is a calling and an appointment, it is a career, gentlemen. Do not joke, it is so. I would then, by rights, be a member of the best club, and would occupy myself only in continually respecting myself. I knew a gentleman who prided himself all his life on being a connoisseur of Lafitte.[4] He considered this as his positive virtue, and never doubted himself. He died, not simply with a tranquil but with a triumphant conscience, and he was completely right. I should have chosen a career for myself then too: I would have been a loafer and a glutton, not a simple one, but, for instance, one in sympathy with everything good and beautiful. How do you like that? I have long had visions of it. That "sublime and beautiful" weighs heavily on my mind at forty. But that is when I am forty, while then—oh, then it would have been different! I would have found myself an appropriate occupation, namely, to drink to the health of everything sublime and beautiful. I would have seized every opportunity to drop a tear into my glass and then to drain it to all that is sublime and beautiful. I would then have turned everything into the sublime and the beautiful; I would have sought out the sublime and the beautiful in the nastiest, most unquestionable trash. I would have become as tearful as a wet sponge. An artist, for instance, paints Ge's picture. At once I drink to the health of the artist who painted Ge's picture, because I love all that is "sublime and beautiful." An author writes "Whatever You Like"; at once I drink to the health of "Whatever You Like" because I love all that is "sublime and beautiful." I would demand respect for doing so, I

4. A fine wine.

would persecute anyone who would not show me respect. I would live at ease, I would die triumphantly—why, after all, it is charming, perfectly charming! And what a belly I would have grown, what a triple chin I would have established, what a red nose I would have produced for myself, so that every passer-by would have said, looking at me: "Here is an asset! Here is something really positive!" And, after all, say what you like, it is very pleasant to hear such remarks about oneself in this negative age, gentlemen.

VII

But these are all golden dreams. Oh, tell me, who first declared, who first proclaimed, that man only does nasty things because he does not know his own real interests; and that if he were enlightened, if his eyes were opened to his real normal interests, man would at once cease to do nasty things, would at once become good and noble because, being enlightened and understanding his real advantage, he would see his own advantage in the good and nothing else, and we all know that not a single man can knowingly act to his own disadvantage. Consequently, so to say, he would begin doing good through necessity. Oh, the babe! Oh, the pure, innocent child! Why, in the first place, when in all these thousands of years has there ever been a time when man has acted only for his own advantage? What is to be done with the millions of facts that bear witness that men, *knowingly*, that is, fully understanding their real advantages, have left them in the background and have rushed headlong on another path, to risk, to chance, compelled to this course by nobody and by nothing, but, as it were, precisely because they did not want the beaten track, and stubbornly, wilfully, went off on another difficult, absurd way seeking it almost in the darkness. After all, it means that this stubbornness and willfulness were more pleasant to them than any advantage. Advantage! What is advantage? And will you take it upon yourself to define with perfect accuracy in exactly what the advantage of man consists of? And what if it so happens that a man's advantage *sometimes* not only may, but even must, consist exactly in his desiring under certain conditions what is harmful to himself and not what is advantageous. And if so, if there can be such a condition then the whole principle becomes worthless. What do you think—are there such cases? You laugh; laugh away, gentlemen, so long as you answer me: have man's advantages been calculated with perfect certainty? Are there not some which not only have been included but cannot possibly be included under any classification? After all, you, gentlemen, so far as I know, have taken your whole register of human advantages from the average of statistical figures and scientific-economic formulas. After all, your advantages are prosperity, wealth, freedom, peace—and so on, and so on. So that a man who, for instance, would openly and knowingly oppose that whole list would, to your thinking, and indeed to mine too, of course, be an obscurantist or an absolute madman, would he not? But, after all, here is something amazing: why does it happen that all these statisticians, sages and lovers of humanity, when they calculate human advantages invariably leave one out? They don't even take it into their calculation in the form in which it should be taken, and the whole reckoning depends upon that. There would be no great harm to take it, this advantage, and to add it to the list. But the trouble is, that this strange advantage does not fall under any classification and does not figure in any list. For instance, I have a friend. Bah, gentlemen! But after all he is your friend, too; and indeed there is no one, no one to whom he is not a friend! When he prepares for any undertaking this gentleman immediately explains to you, pompously and clearly, exactly how he must act in accordance with the laws of reason and truth. What is more, he will talk to you with excitement and passion of the real normal interests of man; with irony he will reproach the short-sighted fools who do not understand their own advantage, for the true significance of virtue; and, within a quarter of an hour, without any sudden outside provocation, but precisely through that something internal which is stronger than all his advantages, he will go off on quite a different tack—that is, act directly opposite to what he has just been saying himself, in opposition to the laws of reason, in opposition to his own advantage—in fact, in opposition to everything. I warn you that my friend is a compound personality, and therefore it is somehow difficult to blame him as an individual. The fact is, gentlemen, it seems that something that is dearer to almost every man than his greatest advantages must really exist, or (not to be illogical) there is one most advantageous advantage (the very one omitted of which we spoke just now) which is more important and more advantageous than all other advantages, for which, if necessary, a man is ready to act in opposition to all laws, that is, in opposition to reason, honor, peace, prosperity—in short, in opposition to all those wonderful and useful things if only he can attain that fundamental, most advantageous advantage which is dearer to him than all.

"Well, but it is still advantage just the same," you will retort. But excuse me, I'll make the point clear, and it is not a case of a play on words, but what really matters is that this advantage is remarkable from the very fact that it breaks down all our classifications, and continually shatters all the systems evolved by lovers of mankind for the happiness of mankind. In short, it interferes with everything. But before I mention this advantage to you, I want to compromise myself personally, and therefore I boldly declare that all these fine systems—all these theories for explaining to mankind its real normal interests, so that inevitably striving to obtain these interests, it may at once become good and noble—are, in my opinion, so far, mere logical exercises! Yes, logical exercises. After all, to maintain even this theory of the regeneration of mankind by means of its own advantage, is, after all, to my mind almost the same thing as—as to claim, for instance, with Buckle, that through civilization mankind becomes softer, and consequently less blood-thirsty, and less fitted for warfare.[5] Logically it does not seem to follow from his arguments. But man is so fond of systems and abstract deductions that he is ready to distort the truth intentionally, he is ready to deny what he can see and hear just to justify his logic. I take this example because it is the most glaring instance of it. Only look about you: blood is being spilled in streams, and in the merriest way, as though it were champagne. Take the whole of the nineteenth century in which Buckle lived. Take Napoleon—both the Great and the present one.[6] Take North America—the eternal union. Take farcical Schleswig-Holstein.[7] And what is it that civilization softens in us? Civilization only produces a greater variety of sensations in man—and absolutely nothing more. And through the development of this variety, man may even come to find enjoyment in bloodshed. After all, it has already happened to him. Have you noticed that the subtlest slaughterers have almost always been the most civilized gentlemen, to whom the various Attilas and Stenka Razins[8] could never hold a candle, and if they are not so conspicuous as

5. Thomas Buckle (1821–1862) argued in his *History of Civilization in England* that modern society was becoming more and more rational and less dependent on violence to solve disputes.

6. The reference is to Napoleon Bonaparte and his nephew, Louis-Napoleon or Napoleon III, who ruled France as president and then emperor from 1850 to 1870.

7. An area disputed between Denmark and Prussia in the 19th century and eventually seized by Prussia; after World War II it was divided between Denmark and Germany.

8. Leader of a major Cossack and peasant rebellion, 1670–1671.

the Attilas and Stenka Razins it is precisely because they are so often met with, are so ordinary and have become so familiar to us. In any case if civilization has not made man more bloodthirsty, it has at least made him more abominably, more loathsomely bloodthirsty than before. Formerly he saw justice in bloodshed and with his conscience at peace exterminated whomever he thought he should. And now while we consider bloodshed an abomination, we nevertheless engage in this abomination and even more than ever before. Which is worse? Decide that for yourselves. It is said that Cleopatra (pardon the example from Roman history) was found of sticking gold pins into her slave-girls' breasts and derived enjoyment from their screams and writhing. You will say that that occurred in comparatively barbarous times; that these are barbarous times too, because (also comparatively speaking) pins are stuck in even now; that even though man has now learned to see more clearly occasionally than in barbarous times, he is still far from having *accustomed* himself to act as reason and science would dictate. But all the same you are fully convinced that he will inevitably accustom himself to it when he gets completely rid of certain old bad habits, and when common sense and science have completely re-educated human nature and turned it in a normal direction. You are confident that man will then refrain from erring *intentionally,* and will, so to say, willy-nilly, not want to set his will against his normal interests. More than that: then, you say, science itself will teach man (though to my mind that is a luxury) that he does not really have either caprice or will of his own and that he has never had it, and that he himself is something like a piano key or an organ stop, and that, moreover, laws of nature exist in this world, so that everything he does is not done by his will at all, but is done by itself, according to the laws of nature. Consequently we have only to discover these laws of nature, and man will no longer be responsible for his actions and life will become exceedingly easy for him. All human actions will then, of course, be tabulated according to these laws, mathematically, like tables of logarithms up to 108,000, and entered in a table; or, better still, there would be published certain edifying works like the present encyclopedic lexicons, in which everything will be so clearly calculated and designated that there will be no more incidents or adventures in the world.

Then—it is still you speaking—new economic relations will be established, all ready-made and computed with mathematical exactitude, so that every possible question will vanish in a twinkling, simply because every possible answer to it will be provided. Then the crystal palace will be built. Then—well, in short, those will be halcyon days. Of course there is no guaranteeing (this is my comment now) that it will not be, for instance, terribly boring then (for what will one have to do when everything is calculated according to the table?) but on the other hand everything will be extraordinarily rational. Of course boredom may lead you to anything. After all, boredom even sets one to sticking gold pins into people, but all that would not matter. What is bad (this is my comment again) is that for all I know people will be thankful for the gold pins then. After all, man is stupid, phenomenally stupid. Or rather he is not stupid at all, but he is so ungrateful that you could not find another like him in all creation. After all, it would not surprise me in the least, if, for instance, suddenly for no reason at all, general rationalism in the midst of the future, a gentleman with an ignoble, or rather with a reactionary and ironical, countenance were to arise and, putting his arms akimbo, say to us all: "What do you think, gentlemen, hadn't we better kick over all that rationalism at one blow, scatter it to the winds, just to send these logarithms to the devil, and to let us live once more according to our own foolish will!" That again would not matter; but what is annoying is that after all he would be sure to find followers—such is the nature of man. And all that for the most foolish reason, which, one would think, was hardly worth mentioning: that is, that man everywhere and always, whoever he may be, has preferred to act as he wished and not in the least as his reason and advantage dictated. Why, one may choose what is contrary to one's own interests, and sometimes one *positively ought* (that is my idea). One's own free unfettered choice, one's own fancy, however wild it may be, one's own fancy worked up at times to frenzy—why that is that very "most advantageous advantage" which we have overlooked, which comes under no classification and through which all systems and theories are continually being sent to the devil. And how do these sages know that man must necessarily need a rationally advantageous choice? What man needs is simply *independent* choice, whatever that independence may cost and wherever it may lead. Well, choice, after all, the devil only knows . . .

VIII

"Ha! ha! ha! But after all, if you like, in reality, there is no such thing as choice," you will interrupt with a laugh. "Science has even now succeeded in analyzing man to such an extent that we know already that choice and what is called freedom of will are nothing other than—"

Wait, gentlemen, I meant to begin with that myself. I admit that I was even frightened. I was just going to shout that after all the devil only knows what choice depends on, and that perhaps that was a very good thing, but I remembered the teaching of science—and pulled myself up. And here you have begun to speak. After all, really, well, if some day they truly discover a formula for all our desires and caprices—that is, an explanation of what they depend upon, by what laws they arise, just how they develop, what they are aiming at in one case or another and so on, and so on, that is, a real mathematical formula—then, after all, man would most likely at once stop to feel desire, indeed, he will be certain to. For who would want to choose by rule? Besides, he will at once be transformed from a human being into an organ stop or something of the sort; for what is a man without desire, without free will and without choice, if not a stop in an organ? What do you think? Let us consider the probability—can such a thing happen or not?

"H'm!" you decide. "Our choice is usually mistaken through a mistaken notion of our advantage. We sometimes choose absolute nonsense because in our stupidity we see in that nonsense the easiest means for attaining an advantage assumed beforehand. But when all that is explained and worked out on paper (which is perfectly possible, for it is contemptible and senseless to assume in advance that man will never understand some laws of nature), then, of course, so-called desires will not exist. After all, if desire should at any time come to terms completely with reason, we shall then, of course, reason and not desire, simply because, after all, it will be impossible to retain reason and *desire* something senseless, and in that way knowingly act against reason and desire to injure ourselves. And as all choice and reasoning can really be calculated, because some day they will discover the laws of our so-called free will—so joking aside, there may one day probably be something like a table of desires so that we really shall choose in accordance with it. After all, if, for instance, some day they calculate and prove to me that I stuck my tongue out at someone because I could not help sticking my tongue out at him and that I had to do it in that particular way, what sort of *freedom* is left me, especially if I am a learned man and have taken my degree somewhere? After all, then I would be able to calculate my whole life for thirty years in advance. In short, if that comes about, then, after all, we could do nothing about it. We would have to accept it just the same. And, in fact, we ought to repeat to ourselves incessantly that at such and such a time and under such and such circumstances. Nature does not ask our leave; that we must accept her as she is and not as we imagine her to be, and if we really aspire to tables and indices and well, even—well, let us say to the chemical retort, then it cannot be helped. We must accept the retort, too, or else it will be accepted without our consent."

Yes, but here I come to a stop! Gentlemen, you must excuse me for philosophizing; it's the result of forty years underground! Allow me to indulge my fancy for a minute. You see, gentlemen, reason, gentlemen, is an excellent thing, there is no disputing that, but reason is only reason and can only satisfy man's rational faculty, while will is a manifestation of all life, that is, of all human life including reason as well as all impulses. And although our life, in this manifestation of it, is often worthless, yet it is life nevertheless and not simply extracting square roots. After all, here I, for instance, quite naturally want to live, in order to satisfy all my faculties for life, and not simply my rational faculty, that is, not simply one-twentieth of all my faculties for life. What does reason know? Reason only knows what it has succeeded in learning (some things it will perhaps never learn; while this is nevertheless no comfort, why not say so frankly?) and human nature acts as a whole, with everything that is in it, consciously or unconsciously, and, even if it goes wrong, it lives. I suspect, gentlemen, that you are looking at me with compassion; you repeat to me that an enlightened and developed man, such, in short, as the future man will be, cannot knowingly desire anything disadvantageous to himself, that this can be proved mathematically. I thoroughly agree, it really can—by mathematics. But I repeat for the hundredth time, there is one case, one only, when man may purposely consciously, desire what is injurious to himself, which is stupid, very stupid—simply in order *to have the right* to desire for himself even what is very stupid and not to be bound by an obligation to desire only what is rational. After all, this very stupid thing, after all, this caprice of ours, may really be more advantageous for us, gentlemen than anything else on earth, especially in some cases. And in particular it may be more advantageous than any advantages even when it does us obvious harm, and contradicts the soundest conclusions of our reason about our advantage—because in any case it preserves for us what is most precious and most important—that is, our personality, our individuality. Some, you see, maintain that this really is the most precious thing for man; desire can, of course, if it desires, be in agreement with reason; particularly if it does not abuse this practice but does so in moderation, it is both useful and sometimes even praiseworthy. But very often, and even most often, desire completely and stubbornly opposes reason, and . . . and . . . and do you know that that, too, is useful and sometimes even praiseworthy? Gentlemen, let us suppose that man is not stupid. (Indeed, after all, one cannot say that about him anyway, if only for the one consideration that, if man is stupid, then, after all, who is wise?) But if he is not stupid, he is just the same monstrously ungrateful! Phenomenally ungrateful. I even believe that the best definition of man is—a creature that walks on two legs and is ungrateful. But that is not all, that is not his worst defect; his worst defect is his perpetual immorality, perpetual—from the days of the Flood to the Schleswig-Holstein period of human destiny. Immorality, and consequently lack of good sense; for it has long been accepted that lack of good sense is due to no other cause than immorality. Try it, and cast a look upon the history of mankind. Well, what will you see? Is it a grand spectacle?

All right, grand, if you like. The Colossus of Rhodes,[9] for instance, that is worth something. Mr. Anaevsky may well testify that some say it is the work of human hands, while others maintain that it was created by Nature herself. Is it variegated? Very well, it may be variegated too. If one only took the dress uniforms, military and civilian, of all peoples in all ages—that alone is worth something, and if you take the undress uniforms you will never get to the end of it; no historian could keep up with it. Is it monotonous? Very well. It may be monotonous, too; they fight and fight; they are fighting now, they fought first and they fought last—you will admit that it is almost too monotonous. In short, one may say anything about the history of the world—anything that might enter the most disordered imagination. The only thing one cannot say is that it is rational. The very word sticks in one's throat. And, indeed, this is even the kind of thing that continually happens. After all, there are continually turning up in life moral and rational people, sages, and lovers of humanity, who make it their goal for life to live as morally and rationally as possible, to be, so to speak, a light to their neighbors, simply in order to show them that it is really possible to live morally and rationally in this world. And so what? We all know that those very people sooner or later toward the end of their lives have been false to themselves, playing some trick, often a most indecent one. Now I ask you: What can one expect from man since he is a creature endowed with such strange qualities? Shower upon him every earthly blessing, drown him in bliss so that nothing but bubbles would dance on the surface of his bliss, as on a sea; give him such economic prosperity that he would have nothing else to do but sleep, eat cakes and busy himself with ensuring the continuation of world history and even then man, out of sheer ingratitude, sheer libel, would play you some loathsome trick. He would even risk his cakes and would deliberately desire the most fatal rubbish, the most uneconomical absurdity, simply to introduce into all this positive rationality his fatal fantastic element. It is just his fantastic dreams, his vulgar folly, that he will desire to retain, simply in order to prove to himself (as though that were so necessary) that men still are men and not piano keys, which even if played by the laws of nature themselves threaten to be controlled so completely that soon one will be able to desire nothing but by the calendar. And, after all, that is not all: even if man really were nothing but a piano key, even if this were proved to him by natural science and mathematics, even then he would not become reasonable, but would purposely do something perverse out of sheer ingratitude, simply to have his own way. And if he does not find any means he will devise destruction and chaos, will devise sufferings of all sorts, and will thereby have his own way. He will launch a curse upon the world, and, as only man can curse (it is his privilege, the primary distinction between him and other animals) then, after all, perhaps only by his curse will he attain his object, that is, really convince himself that he is a man and not a piano key! If you say that all this, too, can be calculated and tabulated, chaos and darkness and curses, so that the mere possibility of calculating it all beforehand would stop it all, and reason would reassert itself—then man would purposely go mad in order to be rid of reason and have his own way! I believe in that, I vouch for it, because, after all, the whole work of man seems really to consist in nothing but proving to himself continually that he is a man and not an organ stop. It may be at the cost of his skin! But he has proved it; he may become a caveman, but he will have proved it. And after that can one help sinning, rejoicing that it has not yet come, and that desire still depends on the devil knows what!

You will shout at me (that is, if you will still favor me with your shout) that, after all, no one is depriving me of my will, that all they are concerned with is that my will

9. One of the wonders of the ancient world.

should somehow of itself, of its own free will, coincide with my own normal interests, with the laws of nature and arithmetic.

Bah, gentlemen, what sort of free will is left when we come to tables and arithmetic, when it will all be a case of two times two makes four? Two times two makes four even without my will. As if free will meant that!

IX

Gentlemen, I am joking, of course, and I know myself that I'm joking badly, but after all you know, one can't take everything as a joke. I am, perhaps, joking with a heavy heart. Gentlemen, I am tormented by questions; answer them for me. Now you, for instance, want to cure men or their old habits and reform their will in accordance with science and common sense. But how do you know, not only that it is possible, but also that it is *desirable,* to reform man in that way? And what leads you to the conclusion that it is so *necessary* to reform man's desires? In short, how do you know that such a reformation will really be advantageous to man? And to go to the heart of the matter, why are you *so sure* of your conviction that not to act against his real normal advantages guaranteed by the conclusions of reason and arithmetic is always advantageous for man and must be a law for all mankind? After all, up to now it is only your supposition. Let us assume it to be a law of logic, but perhaps not a law of humanity at all. You gentlemen perhaps think that I am mad? Allow me to defend myself. I agree that man is pre-eminently a creative animal, predestined to strive consciously toward a goal, and to engage in engineering; that is, eternally and incessantly, to build new roads, *wherever they may lead.* But the reason why he sometimes wants to swerve aside may be precisely that he is *forced* to make that road, and perhaps, too, because however stupid the straightforward practical man may be in general, the thought nevertheless will sometimes occur to him that the road, it would seem, almost always does lead *somewhere,* and that the destination it leads to is less important than the process of making it, and that the chief thing is to save the well-behaved child from despising engineering, and so giving way to the fatal idleness, which, as we all know, is the mother of all vices. Man likes to create and build roads, that is beyond dispute. But why does he also have such a passionate love for destruction and chaos? Now tell me that! But on that point I want to say a few special words myself. May it not be that he loves chaos and destruction (after all, he sometimes unquestionably likes it very much, that is surely so) because he is instinctively afraid of attaining his goal and completing the edifice he is constructing? How do you know, perhaps he only likes that edifice from a distance, and not at all at close range, perhaps he only likes to build it and does not want to live in it, but will leave it, when completed, *aux animaux domestiques*[1]—such as the ants, the sheep, and so on, and so on. Now the ants have quite a different taste. They have an amazing edifice of that type, that endures forever—the anthill.

With the anthill, the respectable race of ants began and with the anthill they will probably end, which does the greatest credit to their perseverence and staidness. But man is a frivolous and incongruous creature, and perhaps, like a chessplayer, loves only the process of the game, not the end of it. And who knows (one cannot swear to it), perhaps the only goal on earth to which mankind is striving lies in this incessant process of attaining, or in other words, in life itself, and not particularly in the goal which of course must always be two times two makes four, that is a formula, and after all, two times two makes four is no longer life, gentlemen, but is the beginning of death. Anyway, man has always been somehow afraid of this two times two makes

1. Domestic animals (French).

four, and I am afraid of it even now. Granted that man does nothing but seek that two times two makes four, that he sails the oceans, sacrifices his life in the quest, but to succeed, really to find it—he is somehow afraid, I assure you. He feels that as soon as he has found it there will be nothing for him to look for. When workmen have finished their work they at least receive their pay, they go to the tavern, then they wind up at the police station—and there is an occupation for a week. But where can man go? Anyway, one can observe a certain awkwardness about him every time he attains such goals. He likes the process of attaining, but does not quite like to have attained, and that, of course, is terribly funny. In short, man is a comical creature; there seems to be a kind of pun in it all. But two times two makes four is, after all, something insufferable. Two times two makes four seems to me simply a piece of insolence. Two times two makes four is a fop standing with arms akimbo barring your path and spitting. I admit that two times two makes four is an excellent thing, but if we are going to praise everything, two times two makes five is sometimes also a very charming little thing.

And why are you so firmly, so triumphantly convinced that only the normal and the positive—in short, only prosperity—is to the advantage of man? Is not reason mistaken about advantage? After all, perhaps man likes something besides prosperity? Perhaps he likes suffering just as much? Perhaps suffering is just as great an advantage to him as prosperity? Man is sometimes fearfully, passionately in love with suffering and that is a fact. There is no need to appeal to universal history to prove that; only ask yourself, if only you are a man and have lived at all. As far as my own personal opinion is concerned, to care only for prosperity seems to me somehow even ill-bred. Whether it's good or bad, it is sometimes very pleasant to smash things, too. After all, I do not really insist on suffering or on prosperity either. I insist on my caprice, and its being guaranteed to me when necessary. Suffering would be out of place in vaudevilles, for instance; I know that. In the crystal palace it is even unthinkable; suffering means doubt, means negation, and what would be the good of a crystal palace if there could be any doubt about it? And yet I am sure man will never renounce real suffering, that is, destruction and chaos. Why, after all, suffering is the sole origin of consciousness. Though I stated at the beginning that consciousness, in my opinion, is the greatest misfortune for man, yet I know man loves it and would not give it up for any satisfaction. Consciousness, for instance, is infinitely superior to two times two makes four. Once you have two times two makes four, there is nothing left to do or to understand. There will be nothing left but to bottle up your five senses and plunge into contemplation. While if you stick to consciousness, even though you attain the same result, you can at least flog yourself at times, and that will, at any rate, liven you up. It may be reactionary, but corporal punishment is still better than nothing.

X

You believe in a crystal edifice that can never be destroyed; that is, an edifice at which one would neither be able to stick out one's tongue nor thumb one's nose on the sly. And perhaps I am afraid of this edifice just because it is of crystal and can never be destroyed and that one could not even put one's tongue out at it even on the sly.

You see, if it were not a palace but a chicken coop and rain started, I might creep into the chicken coop to avoid getting wet, and yet I would not call the chicken coop a palace out of gratitude to it for sheltering me from the rain. You laugh, you even say that in such circumstances a chicken coop is as good as a mansion. Yes, I answer, if one had to live simply to avoid getting wet.

But what is to be done if I have taken it into my head that this is not the only object in life, and that if one must live one may as well live in a mansion. That is my choice, my desire. You will only eradicate it when you have changed my desire. Well, do change it, tempt me with something else, give me another ideal. But in the meantime, I will not take a chicken coop for a palace. Let the crystal edifice even be an idle dream, say it is inconsistent with the laws of nature and that I have invented it only through my own stupidity, through some old-fashioned irrational habits of my generation. But what do I care if it is inconsistent? Does it matter at all, since it exists in my desires, or rather exists as long as my desires exist? Perhaps you are laughing again? Laugh away; I will put up with all your laughter rather than pretend that I am satisfied when I am hungry. I know, anyway, that I will not be appeased with a compromise, with an endlessly recurring zero, simply because it is consistent with the laws of nature and *really* exists. I will not accept as the crown of my desires a block of buildings with apartments for the poor on a lease of a thousand years and, to take care of any contingency, a dentist's shingle hanging out. Destroy my desires, eradicate my ideals, show me something better, and I will follow you. You may say, perhaps, that it is not worth your getting involved in it; but in that case, after all, I can give you the same answer. We are discussing things seriously; but if you won't deign to give me your attention, then, after all, I won't speak to you, I do have my underground.

But while I am still alive and have desires I would rather my hand were withered than to let it bring one brick to such a building! Don't remind me that I have just rejected the crystal edifice for the sole reason that one cannot put out one's tongue at it. I did not say it at all because I am so fond of putting my tongue out. Perhaps the only thing I resented was that of all your edifices up to now, there has not been a single one at which one could not put out one's tongue. On the contrary, I would let my tongue be cut off out of sheer gratitude if things could be so arranged that I myself would lose all desire to put it out. What do I care that things cannot be so arranged, and that one must be satisfied with model apartments? Why then am I made with such desires? Can I have been made simply in order to come to the conclusion that the whole way I am made is a swindle? Can this be my whole purpose? I do not believe it.

But do you know what? I am convinced that we underground folk ought to be kept in tow. Though we may be able to sit underground forty years without speaking, when we do come out into the light of day and break out we talk and talk and talk.

XI

The long and the short of it is, gentlemen, that it is better to do nothing! Better conscious inertia!! And so hurrah for underground!

Though I have said that I envy the normal man to the point of exasperation, yet I would not care to be in his place as he is now (though I will not stop envying him. No, no; anyway the underground life is more advantageous!) There, at any rate, one can—Bah! But after all, even now I am lying! I am lying because I know myself as surely as two times two makes four, that it is not at all underground that is better, but something different, quite different, for which I long but which I cannot find! Damn underground!

I will tell you another thing that would be better, and that is, if I myself believed even an iota of what I have just written. I swear to you, gentlemen, that I do not really believe one thing, not even one word, of what I have just written. That is, I believe it, perhaps, but at the same time, I feel and suspect that I am lying myself blue in the face.

"Then why have you written all this?" you will say to me.

"I ought to put you underground for forty years without anything to do and then come to you to find out what stage you have reached! How can a man be left alone with nothing to do for forty years?"

"Isn't that shameful, isn't that humiliating?" you will say, perhaps, shaking your heads contemptuously. "You long for life and try to settle the problems of life by a logical tangle. And how tiresome, how insolent your outbursts are, and at the same time, how scared you are. You talk nonsense and are pleased with it; you say impudent things and are constantly afraid of them and apologizing for them. You declare that you are afraid of nothing and at the same time try to ingratiate yourself with us. You declare that you are gnashing your teeth and at the same time you try to be witty so as to amuse us. You know that your witticisms are not witty, but you are evidently well satisfied with their literary value. You may perhaps really have suffered, but you have no respect whatsoever for your own suffering. You may be truthful in what you have said but you have no modesty; out of the pettiest vanity you bring your truth to public exposure, to the market place, to ignominy. You doubtlessly mean to say something, but hide your real meaning for fear, because you lack the resolution to say it, and only have a cowardly impudence. You boast of consciousness, but you are unsure of your ground, for though your mind works, yet your heart is corrupted by depravity, and you cannot have a full, genuine consciousness without a pure heart. And how tiresome you are, how you thrust yourself on people and grimace! Lies, lies, lies!"

Of course I myself have made up just now all the things you say. That, too, is from underground. For forty years I have been listening to your words there through a crack under the floor. I have invented them myself. After all there was nothing else I could invent. It is no wonder that I have learned them by heart and that it has taken a literary form.

But can you really be so credulous as to think that I will print all this and give it to you to read too? And another problem; why do I really call you "gentlemen," Why do I address you as though you really were my readers? Such declarations as I intend to make are never printed nor given to other people to read. Anyway, I am not strong-minded enough for that, and I don't see why I should be. But you see a fancy has occurred to me and I want to fulfill it at all costs. Let me explain.

Every man has some reminiscences which he would not tell to everyone, but only to his friends. He has others which he would not reveal even to his friends, but only to himself, and that in secret. But finally there are still others which a man is even afraid to tell himself, and every decent man has a considerable number of such things stored away. That is, one can even say that the more decent he is, the greater the number of such things in his mind. Anyway, I have only lately decided to remember some of my early adventures. Till now I have always avoided them, even with a certain uneasiness. Now, however, when I am not only recalling them, but have actually decided to write them down, I want to try the experiment whether one can be perfectly frank, even with oneself, and not take fright at the whole truth. I will observe, parenthetically, that Heine maintains that a true autobiography is almost an impossibility, and that man is bound to lie about himself. He considers that Rousseau certainly told lies about himself in his confessions, and even intentionally lied, out of vanity. I am convinced that Heine is right; I understand very well that sometimes one may, just out of sheer vanity, attribute regular crimes to oneself, and indeed I can very well conceive that kind of vanity. But Heine judged people who made their confessions to the public. I, however, am writing for myself, and wish to declare once and for all that if I write as though I were addressing readers, that is simply because it is easier for me to write in that way. It is merely a question of form, only an empty form—I shall never have readers. I have made this plain already.

I don't wish to be hampered by any restrictions in compiling my notes. I shall not attempt any system or method. I will jot things down as I remember them.

But here, perhaps, someone will take me at my word and ask me: if you really don't count on readers, why do you make such compacts with yourself—and on paper too—that is, that you won't attempt any system or method, that you will jot things down as you remember them, etc., etc.? Why do you keep explaining? Why do you keep apologizing?

Well, there it is, I answer.

Incidentally, there is a whole psychological system in this. Or, perhaps, I am simply a coward. And perhaps also, that I purposely imagine an audience before me in order to conduct myself in a more dignified manner while I am jotting things down. There are perhaps thousands of reasons.

And here is still something else. What precisely is my object in writing? If it is not for the public, then after all, why should I not simply recall these incidents in my own mind without putting them down on paper?

Quite so; but yet it is somehow more dignified on paper. There is something more impressive in it; I will be able to criticize myself better and improve my style. Besides, perhaps I will really get relief from writing. Today, for instance, I am particularly oppressed by a certain memory from the distant past. It came back to my mind vividly a few days ago, and since then, has remained with me like an annoying tune that one cannot get rid of. And yet I must get rid of it. I have hundreds of such memories, but at times some single one stands out from the hundreds and oppresses me. For some reason I believe that if I write it down I will get rid of it. Why not try?

Besides, I am bored, and I never do anything. Writing will really be a sort of work. They say work makes man kindhearted and honest. Well, here is a chance for me, anyway.

It is snowing today. A wet, yellow, dingy snow. It fell yesterday too and a few days ago. I rather think that I remembered that incident which I cannot shake off now, apropos of the wet snow. And so let it be a story apropos of the wet snow.

Part Two

Apropos of the Wet Snow

When from the gloom of corruption
I delivered your fallen soul
With the ardent speech of conviction;
And, full of profound torment,
Wringing your hands, you cursed
The vice that ensnared you;
When, with memories punishing
Forgetful conscience
You told me the tale
Of all that happened before me,
And suddenly, covering your face,
Full of shame and horror,
You tearfully resolved,
Outraged, shocked. . . .
Etc., etc., etc.

From the poetry of N. A. Nekrasov[2]

2. A poet and journalist (1827–1878) known for his compassionate attention to the sufferings of the peasantry.

I

At that time I was only twenty-four. My life was even then gloomy, disorganized, and solitary to the point of savagery. I made friends with no one and even avoided talking, and hid myself in my corner more and more. At work in the office I even tried never to look at anyone, and I was very well aware that my colleagues looked upon me, not only as a crank, but looked upon me—so I always thought—seemed to look upon me with a sort of loathing. I sometimes wondered why no one except me thought that he was looked upon with loathing. One of our clerks had a repulsive, pock-marked face, which even looked villainous. I believe I would not have dared to look at anyone with such an unsightly face. Another had a uniform so worn that there was an unpleasant smell near him. Yet not one of these gentlemen was disconcerted either by his clothes or his face or in some moral sense. Neither of them imagined that he was looked at with loathing, and even if he had imagined it, it would not have mattered to him, so long as his superiors did not look at him in that way. It is perfectly clear to me now that, owing to my unbounded vanity and, probably, to the high standard I set for myself, I very often looked at myself with furious discontent, which verged on loathing, and so I inwardly attributed the same view to everyone. For instance, I hated my face; I thought it disgusting, and even suspected that there was something base in its expression and therefore every time I turned up at the office I painfully tried to behave as independently as possible so that I might not be suspected of being base, and to give my face as noble an expression as possible. "Let my face even be ugly," I thought, "but let it be noble, expressive, and, above all, *extremely* intelligent." But I was absolutely and painfully certain that my face could never express those perfections; but what was worst of all, I thought it positively stupid-looking. And I would have been quite satisfied if I could have looked intelligent. In fact, I would even have put up with looking base if, at the same time, my face could have been thought terribly intelligent.

Of course, I hated all my fellow-clerks, one and all, and I despised them all, yet at the same time I was, as it were, afraid of them. It happened at times that I even thought more highly of them than of myself. It somehow happened quite suddenly then that I alternated between despising them and thinking them superior to myself. A cultivated and decent man cannot be vain without setting an inordinately high standard for himself, and without despising himself at certain moments to the point of hatred. But whether I despised them or thought them superior I dropped my eyes almost every time I met anyone. I even made experiments whether I could face So-and-So's looking at me, and I was always the first to drop my eyes. This tormented me to the point of frenzy. I was also morbidly afraid of being ridiculous, and so I slavishly worshipped the conventional in everything external. I loved to fall into the common rut, and had a whole-hearted terror of any kind of eccentricity in myself. But how could I live up to it? I was morbidly cultivated as a cultivated man of our age should be. They were all dull, and as like one another as so many sheep. Perhaps I was the only one in the office who constantly thought that I was a coward and a slave, and I thought it precisely because I was cultivated. But I did not only think it, in actuality it was really so. I was a coward and a slave. I say this without the slightest embarrassment. Every decent man in our age must be a coward and a slave. That is his normal condition. I am profoundly convinced of that. He is made that way and is constructed for that very purpose. And not only at the present time owing to some casual circumstances, but always, at all times, a decent man must be a coward and a slave. That is the law of nature for all decent people on the earth. If any one of them happens to be brave about something, he need not be comforted or carried away by that; he will funk out just the same before something else. That is how it invariably and inevitably ends. Only asses and mules are brave, and even they are so only until they come up against the wall. It is not even worth while to pay attention to them. Because they don't mean anything at all.

Still another circumstance tormented me in those days: that no one resembled me and that I resembled no one else. "I am alone and they are *every one,*" I thought—and pondered.

From that it can be seen that I was still an absolute child.

The very opposite sometimes happened. After all, how vile it sometimes seemed to have to go to the office; things reached such a point that I often came home ill. But all at once, for no rhyme or reason, there would come a phase of skepticism and indifference (everything happened to me in phases), and I would myself laugh at my intolerance and fastidiousness. I would reproach myself with being *romantic.* Sometimes I was unwilling to speak to anyone, while at other times I would not only talk, but even think of forming a friendship with them. All my fastidiousness would suddenly vanish for no rhyme or reason. Who knows, perhaps I never had really had it, and it had simply been affected, and gotten out of books. I have still not decided that question even now. Once I quite made friends with them, visited their homes, played preference, drank vodka, talked of promotions . . . But here let me make a digression.

We Russians, speaking generally, have never had those foolish transcendental German, and still more, French, romantics on whom nothing produces any effect; if there were an earthquake, if all France perished at the barricades, they would still be the same, they would not even change for decency's sake, but would still go on singing their transcendental songs, so to speak, to the hour of their death, because they are fools. We, in Russia, have no fools; that is well known. That is what distinguishes us from foreign lands. Consequently those transcendental natures do not exist among us in their pure form. We only think they do because our "positivistic" journalists and critics of that time, always on the hunt for Kostanzhoglos and Uncle Peter Ivaniches and foolishly accepting them as our ideal,[3] slandered our romantics taking them for the same transcendental sort that exists in Germany or France. On the contrary, the characteristics of our romantics are absolutely and directly opposed to the transcendental European type, and not a single European standard can be applied to them. (Allow me to make use of this word "romantic"—an old fashioned and much-respected word which has done good service and is familiar to all.) The characteristics of our romantics are to understand everything, *to see everything and often to see it incomparably more clearly than our most positivistic minds see it;* to refuse to accept anyone or anything, but at the same time not to despise anything; to give way, to yield, from policy; never to lose sight of a useful practical goal (such as rent-free government quarters, pensions, decorations), to keep their eye on that object through all the enthusiasms and volumes of lyrical poems, and at the same time to preserve "the sublime and the beautiful" inviolate within them to the hour of their death, and also, incidentally, to preserve themselves wrapped in cotton, like some precious jewel if only for the benefit of "the sublime and the beautiful." Our romantic is a man of great breadth and the greatest rogue of all our rogues, I assure you. I can even assure you from experience. Of course all that occurs if he is intelligent. But what am I saying!

3. Good-hearted, efficient administrators in novels by Dostoevsky's older contemporaries Nikolai Gogol and Ivan Goncharov.

The romantic is always intelligent, and I only meant to observe that although we have had foolish romantics they don't count, and they were only so because in the flower of their youth they degenerated completely into Germans, and to preserve their precious jewel more comfortably, settled somewhere out there—by preference in Weimar or the Black Forest. I, for instance, genuinely despised my official work and did not openly abuse it simply through necessity because I was in it myself and got a salary for it. And, as a result, take note, I did not openly abuse it. Our romantic would rather go out of his mind (which incidentally happened very rarely) than abuse it, unless he had some other career in view; and he is never kicked out, unless, of course, he is taken to the lunatic asylum as "the King of Spain" and then only if he went very mad. But after all, it is only the thin, fair people who go out of their minds in Russia. Innumerable romantics later in life rise to considerable rank in the service. Their versatility is remarkable! And what a faculty they have for the most contradictory sensations! I was comforted by those thoughts even in those days, and I am so still. That is why there are so many "broad natures" among us who never lose their ideal even in the depths of degradation; and though they never lift a finger for their ideal, though they are arrant thieves and robbers, yet they tearfully cherish their first ideal and are extraordinarily honest at heart. Yes, only among us can the most arrant rogue be absolutely and even loftily honest at heart without in the least ceasing to be a rogue. I repeat, our romantics, after all, frequently become such accomplished rascals (I use the term "rascals" affectionately), suddenly display such a sense of reality and practical knowledge, that their bewildered superiors and the public can only gape in amazement at them.

Their many-sidedness is really astounding, and goodness knows what it may turn itself into under future circumstances, and what lies in store for us later on. They are good stuff! I do not say this out of any foolish or boastful patriotism. But I feel sure that you are again imagining that I am joking. Or perhaps it's just the contrary, and you are convinced that I really think so. Anyway, gentlemen, I shall welcome both views as an honor and a special favor. And do forgive my digression.

I did not, of course, maintain a friendship with my comrades and soon was at loggerheads with them, and in my youthful inexperience I even gave up bowing to them, as though I had cut off all relations. That, however, only happened to me once. As a rule, I was always alone.

In the first place, at home, I spent most of my time reading. I tried to stifle all that was continually seething within me by means of external sensations. And the only source of external sensation possible for me was reading. Reading was a great help, of course, it excited, delighted and tormented me. But at times it bored me terribly. One longed for movement just the same, and I plunged all at once into dark, subterranean, loathsome—not vice but petty vice. My petty passions were acute, smarting, from my continual sickly irritability. I had hysterical fits, with tears and convulsions. I had no resource except reading—that is, there was then nothing in my surroundings which I could respect and which attracted me. I was overwhelmed with depression, too; I had an hysterical craving for contradictions and for contrast, and so I took to vice. I have not said all this to justify myself, after all—but no, I am lying. I did want to justify myself. I make that little observation for my own benefit, gentlemen. I don't want to lie. I vowed to myself I would not.

I indulged my vice in solitude at night, furtively, timidly, filthily, with a feeling of shame which never deserted me, even at the most loathsome moments, and which at such moments drove me to curses. Even then I already had the underground in my soul. I was terribly afraid of being seen, of being met, of being recognized. I visited various completely obscure places.

One night as I was passing a tavern, I saw through a lighted window some gentlemen fighting with billiard cues, and saw one of them thrown out of the window. At another time I would have felt very much disgusted, but then I was suddenly in such a mood that I actually envied the gentleman thrown out of the window, and I envied him so much that I even went into the tavern and into the billiard-room. "Perhaps," I thought, "I'll have a fight, too, and they'll throw me out of the window."

I was not drunk, but what is one to do—after all, depression will drive a man to such a pitch of hysteria. But nothing happened. It seemed that I was not even equal to being thrown out of the window and I went away without having fought.

An officer put me in my place from the very first moment.

I was standing by the billiard-table and in my ignorance blocking up the way, and he wanted to pass; he took me by the shoulders and without a word—without a warning or an explanation—moved me from where I was standing to another spot and passed by as though he had not noticed me. I could even have forgiven blows, but I absolutely could not forgive his having moved me and so completely failing to notice me.

Devil knows what I would then have given for a real regular quarrel—a more decent, a more *literary* one, so to speak. I had been treated like a fly. This officer was over six feet, while I am short and thin. But the quarrel was in my hands. I had only to protest and I certainly would have been thrown out of the window. But I changed my mind and preferred to beat a resentful retreat.

I went out of the tavern straight home, confused and troubled, and the next night I continued with my petty vices, still more furtively, abjectly and miserably than before, as it were, with tears in my eyes—but still I did continue them. Don't imagine, though, that I funked out on the officer through cowardice. I have never been a coward at heart, though I have always been a coward in action. Don't be in a hurry to laugh. There is an explanation for it. I have an explanation for everything, you may be sure.

Oh, if only that officer had been one of the sort who would consent to fight a duel! But no, he was one of those gentlemen (alas, long extinct!) who preferred fighting with cues, or, like Gogol's Lieutenant Pirogov,[4] appealing to the police. They did not fight duels and would have thought a duel with a civilian like me an utterly unseemly procedure in any case—and they looked upon the duel altogether as something impossible, something free-thinking and French, but they were quite ready to insult people, especially when they were over six feet.

I did not funk out through cowardice here but through unbounded vanity. I was not afraid of his six feet, not of getting a sound thrashing and being thrown out of the window; I would probably have had sufficient physical courage; but I lacked sufficient moral courage. What I was afraid of was that everyone present, from the insolent marker down to the lowest little stinking pimply clerk hanging around in a greasy collar, would jeer at me and fail to understand when I began to protest and to address them in literary language. For even now we cannot, after all, speak of the point of honor—not of honor, but of the point of honor (*point d'honneur*)—except in literary language. You cannot allude to the "point of honor" in ordinary language. I was fully

4. A cowardly officer in Gogol's story "Nevsky Prospect," who doesn't stand up for his own honor.

convinced (the sense of reality, in spite of all romanticism!) that they would all simply split their sides with laughter and that the officer would not simply, that is, not uninsultingly, beat me, but would certainly prod me in the back with his knee, kick me round the billiard-table that way and only then perhaps have pity and throw me out of the window. Of course, this trivial incident could not have ended like that with me. I often met that officer afterward in the street and observed him very carefully. I am not quite sure whether he recognized me. I imagine not; I judge from certain signs. But I—I stared at him with spite and hatred and so it went on—for several years! My resentment even grew deeper with the years. At first I began making stealthy inquiries about this officer. It was difficult for me to do so, for I knew no one. But one day I heard someone call him by his name in the street when I was following him at a distance, just as though I were tied to him—and so I learned his surname. Another time I followed him to his flat, and for a few pennies learned from the porter where he lived, on which floor, whether he lived alone or with others, and so on—in fact, everything one could learn from a porter. One morning, though I had never tried to write anything before, it suddenly occurred to me to describe this officer in the form of an exposé, in a satire, in a tale. I wrote the tale with relish. I did expose him. I slandered him; at first I so altered his name that it could easily be recognized but on second thought I changed it, and sent the story to the *Annals of the Fatherland.* But at that time such exposés were not yet the fashion and my story was not printed. That was a great vexation to me. Sometimes I was positively choked with resentment. At last I decided to challenge my enemy to a duel. I composed a splendid, charming letter to him, imploring him to apologize to me, and hinting rather plainly at a duel in case of refusal. The letter was so composed that if the officer had had the least understanding of the "sublime and the beautiful" he would certainly have rushed to me to fling himself on my neck and to offer me his friendship. And how fine that would have been! How we would have gotten along! How we would have gotten along! "He could have shielded me with his higher rank, while I could have improved his mind with my culture, and, well—my ideas, and all sorts of things might have happened." Just think, this was two years after his insult to me, and my challenge was the most ridiculous anachronism, in spite of all the ingenuity of my letter in disguising and explaining away the anachronism. But, thank God (to this day I thank the Almighty with tears in my eyes), I did not send the letter to him. Cold shivers run down my back when I think of what might have happened if I had sent it. And all at once I revenged myself in the simplest way, by a stroke of genius! A brilliant thought suddenly dawned upon me. Sometimes on holidays I used to stroll along the sunny side of the Nevsky between three and four in the afternoon. That is, I did not stroll so much as experience innumerable torments, humiliations and resentments; but no doubt that was just what I wanted. I used to wriggle like an eel among the passers-by in the most unbecoming fashion, continually moving aside to make way for generals, for officers of the Guards and the Hussars, or for ladies. In those minutes I used to feel a convulsive twinge at my heart, and hot all the way down my back at the mere thought of the wretchedness of my dress, of the wretchedness and vulgarity of my little wriggling figure. This was a regular martyrdom, a continual, intolerable humiliation at the thought, which passed into an incessant and direct sensation, that I was a fly in the eyes of this whole world, a nasty, disgusting fly—more intelligent, more cultured, more noble than any of them, of course, but a fly that was continually making way for everyone, insulted and humiliated by everyone. Why I inflicted this torment upon myself, why I went to the Nevsky, I don't know. I felt simply *drawn* there at every possible opportunity.

Already then I began to experience a rush of the enjoyment of which I spoke in the first chapter. After my affair with the officer I felt even more drawn there than before: it was on the Nevsky that I met him most frequently, it was *there* that I could admire him. He, too, went there chiefly on holidays. He, too, made way for generals and persons of high rank, and he, too, shifted among them like an eel; but people like me, or even neater than I, he simply walked over; he made straight for them as though there was nothing but empty space before him, and never, under any circumstances, moved aside. I gloated over my resentment watching him and—resentfully made way for him every time. It tormented me that even in the street I could not be on an even footing with him. "Why must you invariably be the first to move aside?" I kept asking myself in hysterical rage, waking up sometimes at three o'clock in the morning. "Why precisely you and not he? After all, there's no regulation about it; after all, there's no written law about it. Let the making way be equal as it usually is when refined people meet; he moves halfway and you move halfway; you pass with mutual respect." But that never happened, and I always made way, while he did not even notice I moved aside for him. And lo and behold the most astounding idea dawned upon me! "What," I thought, "if I meet him and—don't move aside? What if I don't move aside on purpose, even if I were to bump into him? How would that be?" This audacious idea little by little took such a hold on me that it gave me no peace. I dreamt of it continually, terribly, and I purposely went to the Nevsky more frequently in order to picture more vividly how I would do it when I did do it. I was delighted. This plan seemed to me more and more practical and possible. "Of course I will not really bump him," I thought, already more good-natured in my joy. "I will simply not turn aside, will bump against him, not very violently, but just shouldering each other—just as much as decency permits. I will bump him just as much as he bumps me." At last I made up my mind completely. But my preparations took a great deal of time. To begin with, when I carried out my plan I would have to look rather more decent, and I had to think of my clothes. "In any case, if, for instance, there were any sort of public scandal (and the public there is of the most *superflu*:[5] the Countess walks there; Prince D. walks there; the whole literary world is there), I would have to be well dressed; that inspires respect and of itself puts us in some way on equal footing in the eyes of high society." With that in mind I asked for my salary in advance, and bought at Churkin's a pair of black gloves and a decent hat. Black gloves seemed to me both more dignified and *bon ton* than the lemon-colored ones which I had contemplated at first. "The color is too gaudy, it looks as though one were trying to be conspicuous," and I did not take the lemon-colored ones. I had gotten ready a good shirt, with the bone studs, long beforehand; but my overcoat very much delayed me. The coat in itself was a very good one, it kept me warm; but it was wadded and it had a raccoon collar which was the height of vulgarity. I had to change the collar at any sacrifice, and to have a beaver one like an officer's. For this purpose I began visiting the Gostiny Dvor and after several attempts I lit on a piece of cheap German beaver. Though these German beavers very soon wear out and look shabby, at first, when new, they look exceedingly well, and after all, I only needed it for one occasion. I asked the price; even so, it was too expensive. After thinking it over thoroughly I decided to sell my raccoon collar. The rest of the money—a considerable sum for me, I decided to borrow from Anton Antonich Syetochkin, my superior, an unassuming person, but grave and dependable. He never lent money to anyone, but I had, on

5. Useless, redundant (French).

entering the service, been specially recommended to him by an important personage who had got me my job. I was terribly worried. To borrow from Anton Antonich seemed to me monstrous and shameful. I did not sleep for two or three nights, and indeed I did not sleep well in general at that time, I was in a fever; I had a vague sinking at my heart or suddenly it would start to throb, throb, throb! Anton Antonich was at first surprised, then he frowned, then he reflected, and did after all lend me the money, receiving from me a written authorization to take from my salary a fortnight later the sum that he had lent me. In this way everything was at last ready. The handsome beaver was established in place of the mean-looking raccoon, and I began by degrees to get to work. It would never have done to act offhand, at random; the plan had to be carried out skillfully, by degrees. But I must confess that after many efforts I almost even began to despair; we could not run into each other and that is all there was to it. I made every preparation, I was quite determined—it seemed as though we would run into one another directly—and before I knew what I was doing I had stepped aside for him again and he had passed without noticing me. I even prayed as I approached him that God would grant me determination. One time I had made up my mind thoroughly, but it ended in my stumbling and falling at his feet because at the very last instant when I was only some six inches from him my courage failed me. He very calmly stepped over me, while I flew to one side like a ball. That night I was ill again, feverish and delirious. And suddenly it ended most happily. The night before I had made up my mind not to carry out my fatal plan and to abandon it all, and with that goal in mind I went to the Nevsky for the last time, just to see how I would abandon it all. Suddenly, three paces from my enemy, I unexpectedly made up my mind—I closed my eyes, and we ran full tilt, shoulder to shoulder, into each other! I did not budge an inch and passed him on a perfectly equal footing! He did not even look round and pretended not to notice it; but he was only pretending, I am convinced of that. I am convinced of that to this day! Of course, I got the worst of it—he was stronger, but that was not the point. The point was that I had attained my goal, I had kept up my dignity. I had not yielded a step, and had put myself publicly on an equal social footing with him. I returned home feeling that I was perfectly avenged for everything. I was delighted. I was triumphant and sang Italian arias. Of course, I will not describe to you what happened to me three days later; if you have read my first chapter "Underground," you can guess for yourself. The officer was afterward transferred; I have not seen him now for fourteen years. What is the dear fellow doing now? Whom is he walking over?

II

But the period of my dissipation would end and I always felt terribly sick afterward. It was followed by remorse—I tried to drive it away; I felt too sick. By degrees, however, I grew used to that, too. I grew used to everything, that is, I did not really grow used to it, but rather I voluntarily resigned myself to enduring it. But I had a means of escape that reconciled everything—that was to find refuge in "the sublime and the beautiful," in dreams. Of course I was a terrible dreamer. I would dream for three months on end, tucked away in my corner, and you may believe me that at those moments I had no resemblance to the gentleman who, in his chicken-hearted anxiety, put a German beaver collar on his greatcoat. I suddenly became a hero. I would not have received my six-foot lieutenant even if he had called on me. I could not even picture him before me then. What were my dreams and how I could satisfy myself with them, it is hard to say now, but at the time I did satisfy myself with them, to some extent. Dreams were particularly sweet and vivid after a little vice; they came with remorse and with tears, with curses and transports. There were moments of such positive intoxication, of such happiness, that there was not the faintest trace of irony within me, on my honor. I had faith, hope, love. That is just it. I believed blindly at such times that by some miracle, through some external circumstance, all this would suddenly open out, expand; that suddenly a vista of suitable activity—beneficial, good, and above all, *ready-made* (what sort of activity I had no idea, but the great thing was that it should be all ready for me)—would rise up before me, and I should come out into the light of day, almost riding a white horse and crowned with laurel. I could not conceive of a secondary role for myself, and for that reason I quite contentedly played the lowest one in reality. Either to be a hero or to grovel in the mud—there was nothing between. That was my ruin, for when I was in the mud I comforted myself with the thought that at other times I was a hero, and I took refuge in this hero for the mud: for an ordinary man, say, it is shameful to defile himself, but a hero is too noble to be utterly defiled, and so he might defile himself. It is worth noting that these attacks of "the sublime and the beautiful" visited me even during the period of vice and just at the times when I had sunk to the very bottom. They came in separate spurts, as though reminding me of themselves, but did not banish the vice by their appearance. On the contrary, they seemed to add a zest to it by contrast, and were only sufficiently present to serve as an appetizing sauce. That sauce was made up of contradictions and sufferings, of agonizing inward analysis, and all these torments and pin-pricks lent my vice a certain piquancy, even a significance—in short, completely fulfilled the function of a good sauce. There was even a certain depth of meaning in it. And I could hardly have restrained myself to the simple, vulgar, direct clerk-like vice and have endured all the filthiness of it. What could have attracted me about it then and have driven me at night into the street? No, I had a noble loophole for everything.

And what love, oh Lord, what love I felt at times in those dreams of mine! In those "flights into the sublime and the beautiful"; though it was fantastic love, though it was never applied to anything human in reality, yet there was so much of this love that afterward one did not even feel the impulse to apply it in reality; that would have been a superfluous luxury. Everything, however, always passed satisfactorily by a lazy and fascinating transition into the sphere of art; that is, into the beautiful forms of life, ready made, violently stolen from the poets and novelists and adapted to all sorts of needs and uses. I, for instance, was triumphant over everyone; everyone, of course, lay in the dust and was forced to recognize my superiority spontaneously, and I forgave them all. I, a famous poet, and a courtier, fell in love; I inherited countless millions and immediately devoted them to humanity, and at the same time I confessed before all the people my shameful deeds, which, of course, were not merely shameful, but contained an enormous amount of "the sublime and the beautiful," something in the Manfred[6] style. Everyone would weep and kiss me (what idiots they would be if they did not), while I would go barefoot and hungry preaching new ideas and fighting a victorious Austerlitz against the reactionaries. Then a march would sound, an amnesty would be declared, the Pope would agree to retire from Rome to Brazil; then there would be a ball for the whole of Italy at the Villa Borghese on the shores of Lake Como, Lake Como being for that purpose transferred to the neighborhood of Rome; then would come a scene in the bushes, etc., etc.—as though you did not know

6. Brooding, romantic title character in a verse tragedy by Byron.

all about it! You will say that it is vulgar and base to drag all this into public after all the tears and raptures I have myself admitted. But why is it base? Can you imagine that I am ashamed of it all, and that is was stupider than anything in your life, gentlemen? And I can assure you that some of these fancies were by no means badly composed. Not everything took place on the shores of Lake Como. And yet you are right—it really is vulgar and base. And what is most base of all is that I have now started to justify myself to you. And even more base than that is my making this remark now. But that's enough, or, after all, there will be no end to it; each step will be more base than the last.

I could never stand more than three months of dreaming at a time without feeling an irresistible desire to plunge into society. To plunge into society meant to visit my superior, Anton Antonich Syetochkin. He was the only permanent acquaintance I have had in my life, and I even wonder at the fact myself now. But I even went to see him only when that phase came over me, and when my dreams had reached such a point of bliss that it became essential to embrace my fellows and all mankind immediately. And for that purpose I needed at least one human being at hand who actually existed. I had to call on Anton Antonich, however, on Tuesday—his at-home day; so I always had to adjust my passionate desire to embrace humanity so that it might fall on a Tuesday. This Anton Antonich lived on the fourth floor in a house in Five Corners, in four low-pitched rooms of a particularly frugal and sallow appearance, one smaller than the next. He had two daughters and their aunt, who used to pour out the tea. Of the daughters one was thirteen and another fourteen, they both had snub noses, and I was terribly embarrassed by them because they were always whispering and giggling together. The master of the house usually sat in his study on a leather couch in front of the table, with some gray-headed gentleman, usually a colleague from our office or even some other department. I never saw more than two or three visitors there, and those always the same. They talked about the excise duty, about business in the senate, about salaries, about promotions, about His Excellency, and the best means of pleasing him, and so on, and so on. I had the patience to sit like a fool beside these people for four hours at a stretch, listening to them without knowing what to say to them or venturing to say a word. I became stupefied; several times I felt myself perspiring. I was overcome by a sort of paralysis; but that was pleasant and useful for me. On returning home I deferred for a time my desire to embrace all mankind.

I had, however, one other acquaintence of a sort, Simonov, who was an old schoolfellow. Indeed I had a number of schoolfellows in Petersburg, but I did not associate with them and had even given up nodding to them in the street. Perhaps I even transferred into the department I was in simply to avoid their company and to cut off at one stroke all connection with my hateful childhood. Curses on that school and all those terrible years of penal servitude! In short, I parted from my schoolfellows as soon as I got out into the world. There were two or three left to whom I nodded in the street. One of them was Simonov, who had been in no way distinguished at school, was of a quiet and even disposition; but I discovered in him a certain independence of character and even honesty. I don't even suppose that he was particularly limited. I had at one time spent some rather soulful moments with him, but these had not lasted long and had somehow been suddenly clouded over. He was evidently uncomfortable at these reminiscences, and was, it seemed, always afraid that I might take up the same tone again. I suspected that he had an aversion for me, but I still went on going to see him, not being completely certain of it.

And so on one occasion, on a Thursday, unable to endure my solitude and knowing that it was Thursday Anton Antonich's door would be closed, I thought of Simonov. Climbing up four floors to his place, I was thinking that I made the man uncomfortable and that it was a mistake to go to see him. But as it always happened that such reflections impelled me even more strongly, as though purposely, to put myself into a false position, I went in. It was almost a year since I had last seen Simonov.

III

I found two more of my old schoolfellows with him. They seemed to be discussing an important matter. All of them scarcely took any notice of my entrance, which was strange, for I had not seen them for years. Evidently they looked upon me as something on the level of a common fly. I had not been treated like that even at school, although everybody hated me there. I knew, of course, that they must despise me now for my lack of success in the service, and for having let myself sink so low, going about badly dressed and so on which seemed to them a sign of my inaptitude and insignificance. But nevertheless I had not expected such contempt. Simonov even seemed surprised at my turning up. Even in the old days he had always seemed surprised at my coming. All this disconcerted me; I sat down, feeling rather miserable, and began listening to what they were saying.

They were engaged in an earnest and even heated discussion about a farewell dinner these gentlemen wanted to arrange together the very next day for their friend Zverkov, an officer in the army, who was going away to a distant province. Monsieur Zverkov had been all the time at school with me too. I had begun to hate him particularly in the upper classes. In the lower classes he had simply been a pretty, playful boy whom everybody liked. I had hated him, however, even in the lower classes, just because he was a pretty and playful boy. He was always consistently poor in his work, and got worse and worse as he went on; nevertheless he was successfully graduated as influence was exerted on his behalf. During his last year at school he inherited an estate of two hundred serfs, and as almost all of us were poor he even started to boast before us. He was vulgar to the worst degree, but nevertheless he was a good-natured fellow, even when he boasted. In spite of superficial, fantastic and rhetorical notions of honor and dignity, all but a very few of us positively grovelled before Zverkov, and the more so the more he boasted. And they did not grovel for any advantage, but simply because he had been favored by the gifts of nature. Moreover, we came somehow to accept the idea that Zverkov was a specialist in regard to tact and good manners. That particularly infuriated me. I hated the sharp, self-confident tone of his voice, his admiration for his own witticisms, which were terribly stupid, though he was bold in his expressions; I hated his handsome but stupid face (for which I would, however, have gladly exchanged my *intelligent* one), and the free-and-easy military manners in fashion in the 'forties. I hated the way in which he used to talk of his future conquests of women (he did not venture to begin with women until he had officer's epaulettes and was looking forward to them with impatience), and boasted of the duels he would constantly be fighting. I remember how I, invariably so taciturn, suddenly attacked Zverkov, when one day he talked at a leisure moment with his schoolfellows of the affairs he would have in the future and growing as sportive as a puppy in the sun, he all at once declared that he would not leave a single village girl on his estate unnoticed, that that was his *droit de seigneur,*[7] and that if the peasants dared to protest he

7. A feudal lord's right to have sex with women on his estate on their wedding night.

would have them all flogged and double their taxes, the bearded rascals. Our servile rabble applauded, but I attacked him, not at all out of compassion for the girls and their fathers, but simply because they were applauding such a beetle. I got the better of him on that occasion, but though Zverkov was stupid he was lively and impudent, and so laughed it off, and even in such a way that my victory was not really complete: the laugh was on his side. He got the better of me on several occasions afterward, but without malice, somehow just in jest, casually, in fun. I remained maliciously and contemptuously silent. When we left school he made advances to me; I did not rebuff them much, for I was flattered, but we soon parted naturally. Afterward I heard of his barrack-room success as a lieutenant, and of the *fast life* he was leading. Then there came other rumors—of his *successes* in the service. By then he no longer greeted me in the street, and I suspected that he was afraid of compromising himself by greeting a person as insignificant as I. I also saw him once in the theatre, in the third tier of boxes. By then he was a staff officer. He was twisting and twirling about, ingratiating himself with the daughters of an ancient general. In three years his looks had gotten considerably worse, though he was still rather handsome and smart. He had somehow swelled, started to put on weight. One could see that by the time he was thirty he would be completely fat. So it was, finally, to this Zverkov that my schoolfellows were going to give a dinner on his departure. They had kept up with him for those three years, though privately they did not consider themselves on an equal footing with him, I am convinced of that.

Of Simonov's two visitors, one was Ferfichkin, a Russianized German—a little fellow with the face of a monkey, a blockhead who was always deriding everyone, a very bitter enemy of mine from our days in the lower classes—a vulgar, impudent, boastful fellow, who affected a most sensitive feeling of personal honor, though, of course, he was a wretched little coward at heart. He was one of those admirers of Zverkov who made up to the latter out of calculation, and often borrowed money from him. Simonov's other visitor, Trudolyubov, was a person in no way remarkable—a military lad, tall with a cold face, quite honest. But he worshipped success of every sort, and was only capable of thinking of promotion. He was some distant relation of Zverkov and this, foolish as it seems, gave him a certain importance among us. He never thought me of any consequence whatever; while his behavior to me was not quite courteous, it was tolerable.

"Well then, with seven roubles each," said Trudolyubov, "twenty-one *roups* from the three of us, we can dine well. Zverkov, of course, won't pay."

"Of course not, since we are inviting him," Simonov decided.

"Can you imagine," Ferfichkin interrupted hotly and conceitedly, like some insolent flunky boasting of his master the general's decorations, "can you imagine that Zverkov will let us pay alone? He will accept from delicacy, but he will order *a half case* on his own."

"Why do we need half a case for the four of us?" observed Trudolyubov, taking notice only of the half case.

"So the three of us, with Zverkov for the fourth, twenty-one roubles, at the Hôtel de Paris at five o'clock tomorrow," Simonov, who had been asked to make the arrangements, concluded finally.

"How about twenty-one roubles?" I asked in some agitation, even offended, apparently; "if you count me it will be twenty-eight, not twenty-one roubles."

It seemed to me that to invite myself so suddenly and unexpectedly would be positively graceful, and that they would all be conquered at once and would look at me with respect.

"Do you want to join, too?" Simonov observed, with displeasure, and seemed to avoid looking at me. He knew me inside out.

It infuriated me that he knew me inside out.

"Why not? After all, I am an old schoolfellow of his too, I believe, and I must admit I feel offended that you have left me out," I said, boiling over again.

"And where were we to find you?" Ferfichkin put in roughly.

"You were never on good terms with Zverkov," Trudolyubov added, frowning. But I had already clutched at the idea and would not let go.

"I do not think that anyone has a right to judge that," I retorted in a shaking voice, as though God only knows what had happened. "Perhaps that is just my reason for wishing it now, that I have not always been on good terms with him."

"Oh, there's no making you out—with these refinements," Trudolyubov jeered.

"We'll put your name down," Simonov decided, addressing me. "Tomorrow at five o'clock at the Hotel de Paris."

"What about the money?" Ferfichkin began in an undertone, indicating me to Simonov, but he broke off, for even Simonov was embarrassed.

"That will do," said Trudolyubov, getting up. "If he wants to come so much, let him."

"But after all it's a private thing, between us friends," Ferfichkin said crossly, as he too picked up his hat. "It's not an official meeting. Perhaps we do not want you at all—"

They went away. Ferfichkin did not salute me in any way as he went out. Trudolyubov barely nodded. Simonov, with whom I remained alone, was in some state of vexed perplexity, and looked at me strangely. He did not sit down and did not ask me to.

"H'm—yes—tomorrow, then. Will you pay your share now? I just ask so as to know," he muttered in embarrassment.

I blazed up in anger but as I did so I remembered that I had owed Simonov fifteen roubles for ages—which I had, indeed, never forgotten, though I had not paid it.

"You will understand, Simonov, that I could have had no idea when I came here—I am very much vexed that I have forgotten—"

"All right, all right, it doesn't matter. You can pay tomorrow after the dinner. After all, I simply wanted to know—Please don't—"

He broke off and began pacing the room still more vexed. As he walked he began to thump with his heels and stomped even louder.

"Am I keeping you?" I asked, after two minutes of silence.

"Oh, no!" he said, starting, "that is—to be truthful—yes. I have to go and see someone—not far from here," he added in a sort of apologetic voice, somewhat ashamed.

"My goodness, but why didn't you say so?" I cried, seizing my cap with, incidentally, an astonishingly free-and-easy air, which was the last thing I would have expected of myself.

"After all, it's close by—not two paces away," Simonov repeated, accompanying me to the front door with a fussy air which did not suit him at all. "So five o'clock, punctually, tomorrow," he called down the stairs after me. He was very glad to get rid of me. I was in a fury.

"What possessed me, what possessed me to force myself upon them?" I gnashed my teeth, as I strode along the street. "For a scoundrel, a pig like that Zverkov! Of course, I had better not go; of course, I can just snap my fingers at them. I am not bound in any way. I'll send Simonov a note by tomorrow's post—"

But what made me furious was that I knew for certain that I would go, that I would purposely go; and the more tactless, the more ill-mannered my going would be, the more certainly I would go.

And there was even a positive obstacle to my going: I had no money. All I had altogether, was nine roubles. But I had to give seven of that to my servant, Apollon, for his monthly wages. That was all I paid him—he had to keep himself.

Not to pay him was impossible, considering his character. But I will talk about that fellow, about that plague of mine, another time.

However, I knew I would go after all and would not pay him his wages.

That night I had the most hideous dreams. No wonder; the whole evening I had been oppressed by memories of my days of penal servitude at school, and I could not shake them off. I was sent to the school by distant relations, upon whom I was dependent and of whom I have heard nothing since—they sent me there, a lonely, silent boy, already crushed by their reproaches, already troubled by doubt, and looking savagely at everything around him. My schoolfellows met me with spiteful and merciless jibes because I was not like any of them. But I could not endure their taunts; I could not give in to them as cheaply as they gave in to one another. I hated them from the first, and shut myself away from everyone in timid, wounded and disproportionate pride. Their coarseness revolted me. They laughed, cynically at my face, at my clumsy figure; and yet what stupid faces they themselves had. In our school the boys' faces somehow degenerated and grew stupider particularly. How many fine-looking boys came to us? In a few years they became repulsive looking. Even at sixteen I wondered at them morosely; even then I was struck by the pettiness of their thoughts, the stupidity of their pursuits, their games, their conversations. They had no understanding of such essential things, they took no interest in such striking, impressive subjects, that I could not help considering them inferior to myself. It was not wounded vanity that drove me to it, and for God's sake do not thrust upon me your hackneyed remarks, repeated to nausea, that "I was only a dreamer, while they even then understood real life." They understood nothing, they had no idea of real life, and I swear that that was what made me most indignant with them. On the contrary, the most obvious, striking reality they accepted with fantastic stupidity and even then had already begun to respect only success. Everything that was just, but oppressed and looked down upon, they laughed at cruelly and shamefully. They took rank for intelligence; even at sixteen they were already talking about a snug berth. Of course a great deal of it was due to their stupidity, to the bad examples that constantly surrounded them in their childhood and boyhood. They were monstrously depraved. Of course much of that, too, was superficial and much was only affected cynicism; of course there were glimpses of youth and freshness in them even beneath their depravity; but even that freshness was not attractive in them, and showed itself in a certain rakishness. I hated them terribly, though perhaps I was worse than any of them. They repaid me in kind, and did not conceal their aversion for me. But by then I did not want them to like me; on the contrary, I continually longed for them to humiliate me. To escape from their derision I purposely began to make all the progress I could with my studies and forced my way to the very top. This impressed them. Moreover, they all began to grasp slowly that I was already reading books none of them could read, and understood things (not forming part of our school curriculum) of which they had not even heard. They took a savage and sarcastic view of it, but were morally impressed, especially as the teachers began to notice me on those grounds. The mockery ceased but the hostility remained, and cold and strained relations were formed between us. In the end I could not stand it myself; with years a craving for society, for friends, developed in me. I attempted to get on friendly terms with some of my schoolfellows; but somehow or other my intimacy with them was always strained and soon ended of itself.

Once, indeed, I did have a friend. But I was already a tyrant at heart; I wanted to exercise unlimited power over him; I tried to instil into him a contempt for his surroundings; I required of him a disdainful and complete break with those surroundings. I frightened him with my passionate affection; I reduced him to tears, to convulsions. He was a simple and devoted soul; but when he submitted to me completely I began to hate him immediately and rejected him—as though all I needed him for was to win a victory over him, to subjugate him and nothing else. But I could not subjugate all of them; my friend was not at all like them either, he was, in fact, a rare exception. The first thing I did on leaving school was to give up the special job for which I had been destined so as to break all ties, to curse my past and scatter it to the winds—And goodness knows why, after all that, I should drag myself to that Simonov!

Early next morning I roused myself and jumped out of bed with excitement, as though it were all about to happen at once. But I believed that some radical change in my life was coming, and would inevitably come that day. Owing to its rarity, perhaps, any external event, however trivial, always made me feel as though some radical change in my life would occur immediately. I went to the office as usual, however, but slipped away home two hours early to get ready. The important thing, I thought, is not to be the first to arrive, or they will think I was overjoyed at coming. But there were thousands of such important points to consider, and they all agitated me to the point of impotence. I polished my boots a second time with my own hands; nothing in the world would have induced Apollon to clean them twice a day, as he considered that it was more than his duties required of him. I stole the brushes to clean them from the passage, so that he would not detect it and then start to despise me. Then I minutely examined my clothes, and found that everything looked old, worn and threadbare. I had let myself get too slovenly. My uniform, perhaps, was in good shape, but I could hardly go out to dinner in my uniform. And the worst thing was that on the knee of my trousers was a big yellow stain. I had a foreboding that that stain would in itself deprive me of nine-tenths of my personal dignity. I knew, too, that it was stopping very low to think so. "But this is no time for thinking: now the real thing is beginning," I thought, and my heart sank. I knew, too, perfectly well even then, that I was monstrously exaggerating the facts. But how could I help it? I could not control myself and I was already shaking with fever. With despair I pictured to myself how coldly and disdainfully that "scoundrel" Zverkov would greet me; with what dull-witted, absolutely profound contempt the blockhead Trudolyubov would look at me; with what nasty insolence the beetle Ferfichkin would snigger at me in order to curry favor with Zverkov; how completely Simonov would take it all in, and how he would despise me for the abjectness of my vanity and faint-heartedness, and worst of all how paltry, *unliterary,* commonplace it would all be. Of course the best thing would be not to go at all. But that was the most impossible of all: once I feel impelled to do anything, I am completely drawn into it, head first. I would have jeered at myself ever afterward: "So you funked it, you funked the *real thing,* you funked it!" On the contrary, I passionately longed to show all that "rabble" that I was not at all such a coward as I pictured myself. What is more, even in the acutest paroxysm of this cowardly fever, I dreamed of getting the upper hand, of overcoming them, carrying them away, making them like me—if only for my "elevation of thought and unmistakable wit." They would abandon Zverkov, he would sit on one side, silent and ashamed, while I would crush Zverkov. Then, perhaps, I would be reconciled to him and toast our camaraderie; but what was most spiteful and insulting for me was that I knew even then, knew completely and for certain, that I needed nothing of all this really, that I did not really want to crush, to subdue, to attract them, and that I would be the first not to care a straw, really, for the result, even if I did achieve it. Oh, how I prayed to God for the day to pass quickly! In inexpressible anguish I went to the window, opened a pane and looked out into the turbid darkness of the thickly falling wet snow.

At last my wretched little wall clock hissed out five. I seized my hat trying not to look at Apollon, who had been all day expecting his month's wages, but in his pride was unwilling to be the first to speak about it. I slipped past him and out the door, and jumping into a high-class sledge, on which I spent my last half-rouble, I drove up in grand style to the Hôtel de Paris.

IV

I had already known the day before that I would be the first to arrive. But it was no longer a question of precedence.

Not only were they not there, but I even had difficulty finding our room. The table had still not been completely set. What did it mean? After a good many questions I finally ascertained from the waiters that the dinner had been ordered not for five, but for six o'clock. This was confirmed at the buffet too. I even felt ashamed to go on questioning them. It was still only twenty-five minutes past five. If they changed the dinner hour they ought in any case to have let me know—that is what the post is for, and not to have subjected me to "shame" both in my own eyes and—well, before the waiters. I sat down: the servant began to set the table; I felt even more insulted when he was present. Toward six o'clock they brought in candles, though there were lamps burning in the room. It had not occurred to the waiter, however, to bring them in at once when I arrived. In the next room, two gloomy, angry-looking persons were eating their dinners in silence at two different tables. There was a great deal of noise, even shouting, in a room farther away; one could hear the laughter of a crowd of people, and nasty little shrieks in French; there were ladies at the dinner. In short, it was sickening. I rarely passed a more unpleasant time, so much so that when they did arrive all together punctually at six I was for the first moment overjoyed to see them, as though they were my deliverers, and almost forgot it was incumbent upon me to look insulted.

Zverkov walked in at the head of them; evidently he was the leading spirit. He and all of them were laughing; but, seeing me, Zverkov drew himself up, walked up to me unhurriedly with a slight, rather jaunty bend from the waist, and shook hands with me in a friendly but not over-friendly fashion, with a sort of circumspect courtesy almost like a general's as though in giving me his hand he were warding off something. I had imagined, on the contrary, that as soon as he came in he would immediately break into his former thin, shrieking laugh and fall to making his insipid jokes and witticisms. I had been preparing for them ever since the previous day, but I had never expected such condescension, such high-official courtesy. So, then, he felt himself immeasurably superior to me in every respect! If he had only meant to insult me by that high-official tone, it would still not have mattered, I thought—I could pay him back for it one way or another. But what if, in reality, without the least desire to be offensive, that sheep's-head had seriously acquired the notion that he was immeasurably superior to me and could only look at me in a patronizing way? The very supposition made me gasp.

"I was surprised to hear of your desire to join us," he began, lisping and drawling, which was something new. "You and I seem to have seen nothing of one another. You fight shy of us. You shouldn't. We are not such terrible people as you think. Well, anyway, I am glad to renew our acquaintance."

And he turned carelessly to put down his hat on the window sill.

"Have you been waiting long?" Trudolyubov inquired.

"I arrived punctually at five o'clock as I was informed yesterday," I answered aloud, with an irritability that promised an imminent explosion.

"Didn't you let him know that we had changed the hour?" said Trudolyubov to Simonov.

"No, I didn't. I forgot," the latter replied, with no sign of regret, and without even apologizing to me he went off to order the *hors d'oeuvres.*

"So you've been here a whole hour? Oh, you poor fellow!" Zverkov cried ironically, for according to his notions this was bound to be extremely funny. That scoundrel Ferfichkin followed with his nasty little snigger like a puppy yapping. My position struck him, too, as extremely ludicrous and embarrassing.

"It isn't funny at all!" I cried to Ferfichkin, more and more irritated. "It wasn't my fault, but other people's. They neglected to let me know. It was—it was—it was simply absurd."

"It's not only absurd, but something else as well," muttered Trudolyubov, naïvely taking my part. "You are too complacent about it. It was simply rudeness—unintentional, of course. And how could Simonov—h'm!"

"If a trick like that had been played on me," observed Ferfichkin, "I would—"

"But you should have ordered yourself something," Zverkov interrupted, "or simply asked for dinner without waiting for us."

"You will allow that I might have done that without your permission," I rapped out. "If I waited, it was—"

"Let us sit down, gentlemen," cried Simonov, coming in. "Everything is ready; I can answer for the champagne; it is capitally chilled.—After all, I did not know your address. Where was I to look for you?" He suddenly turned to me, but again he seemed to avoid looking at me. Evidently he had something against me. He must have made up his mind after what happened yesterday.

Everybody sat down: I did the same. It was a round table. Trudolyubov was on my left, Simonov on my right. Zverkov was sitting opposite, Ferfichkin next to him, between him and Trudolyubov.

"Te-e-ell me, are you—in a government agency?" Zverkov went on, attending to me. Seeing that I was embarrassed, he seriously thought that he ought to be friendly to me, and, so to speak, cheer me up. "Does he want me to throw a bottle at his head or something?" I thought, in a fury. In my unaccustomed surroundings I was unnaturally quick to be irritated.

"In the N—office," I answered jerkily, with my eyes on my plate.

"And—ha-ave you a go-od berth? Te-e-ll me, what ma-a-de you leave your former job?"

"What ma-a-de me was that I wanted to leave my original job," I drawled twice as much as he, hardly able to control myself. Ferfichkin snorted. Simonov looked at me ironically. Trudolyubov stopped eating and began looking at me with curiosity.

Zverkov was jarred but he pretended not to notice it.

"A-a-and the remuneration?"

"What remuneration?"

"I mean, your sa-a-lary?"

"Why are you cross-examining me?"

However, I told him at once what my salary was. I blushed terribly.

"It is not very handsome," Zverkov observed majestically.

"Yes, you can't afford to dine in restaurants on that," Ferfichkin added insolently.

"I think it's very low," Trudolyubov observed gravely.

"And how thin you have grown! How you have changed!" added Zverkov, with a shade of venom in his voice, scanning me and my attire with a sort of insolent compassion.

"Oh, spare his blushes," cried Ferfichkin, sniggering.

"My dear sir, permit me to tell you I am not blushing," I broke out at last; "do you hear? I am dining here, at this restaurant, at my own expense, at mine, not at other people's—note that, Monsieur Ferfichkin."

"Wha-at do you mean? Isn't everyone here dining at his own expense? You seem to be—" Ferfichkin let fly at me, turning as red as a lobster, and looking me in the face with fury.

"Tha-at's what I mean," I answered, feeling I had gone too far, "and I imagine it would be better to talk of something more intelligent."

"You intend to show off your intelligence, I suppose?"

"Don't disturb yourself, that would be quite out of place here."

"What are you clacking away like that for, my good sir, eh? Have you gone out of your wits in your *dumb*partment?"

"Enough, gentlemen, enough!" Zverkov cried, authoritatively.

"How stupid it is," muttered Simonov.

"It really is stupid. We have met here, a company of friends, for a farewell dinner to a good comrade and you are settling old scores," said Trudolyubov, rudely addressing himself to me alone. "Yesterday you invited yourself to join us, so don't disturb the general harmony."

"Enough, enough!" cried Zverkov. "Stop it, gentlemen, it's out of place. Better let me tell you how I nearly got married the day before yesterday . . ."

And then followed a burlesque narrative of how this gentleman had almost been married two days before. There was not a word about marriage, however, but the story was adorned with generals, colonels and high courtiers while Zverkov practically took the lead among them. It was greeted with approving laughter; Ferfichkin even squealed.

No one paid any attention to me, and I sat crushed and humiliated.

"Good heavens, these are not the people for me!" I thought. "And what a fool I have made of myself before them! I let Ferfichkin go too far, though. The brutes imagine that it is an honor for me to sit down with them. They don't understand that I do them an honor. I to them and not they to me! I've grown thinner! My clothes! Oh, damn my trousers! Zverkov long ago noticed the yellow stain on the knee . . . But what's the use! I must get up at once, this very minute, take my hat and simply go without a word—out of contempt! And tomorrow I can send a challenge. The scoundrels! After all, I don't care about the seven roubles. They may think . . . Damn it! I don't care about the seven roubles. I'll go this minute!"

Of course I remained.

I drank sherry and Lafitte by the glassful in my distress. Being unaccustomed to it, I quickly became intoxicated and my annoyance increased with the intoxication. I longed all at once to insult them all in a most flagrant manner and then go away. To seize the moment and show what I could do, so that they would say, "Though he is absurd, he's clever," and—and—in short, damn them all!

I scanned them all insolently with my dulled eyes. But they seemed to have forgotten me altogether. *They* were noisy, vociferous, cheerful. Zverkov kept talking. I began to listen. Zverkov was talking about some sumptuous lady whom he had at last led on to declaring her love (of course, he was lying like a horse), and how he had been helped in this affair by an intimate friend of his, a Prince Kolya, an officer in the Hussars, who had three thousand serfs.

"And yet, this Kolya, who has three thousand serfs, has not put in an appearance here tonight at all to see you off," I cut in suddenly. For a minute everyone was silent.

"You are drunk already." Trudolyubov deigned to notice me at last, glancing contemptuously in my direction. Zverkov, without a word, examined me as though I were a little beetle. I dropped my eyes. Simonov made haste to fill up the glasses with champagne.

Trudolyubov raised his glass, as did everyone else but me.

"Your health and good luck on the journey!" he cried to Zverkov. "To old times, gentlemen, to our future, hurrah!"

They all tossed off their glasses, and crowded round Zverkov to kiss him. I did not move; my full glass stood untouched before me.

"Why, aren't you going to drink it?" roared Trudolyubov, losing patience and turning menacingly to me.

"I want to make a toast separately, on my own account . . . and then I'll drink it, Mr. Trudolyubov."

"Disgusting crank!" muttered Simonov.

I drew myself up in my chair and feverishly seized my glass, prepared for something extraordinary, though I did not know myself precisely what I was going to say.

"*Silence!*" cried Ferfichkin, in French. "Now for a display of wit!"

Zverkov waited very gravely, knowing what was coming.

"Lieutenant Zverkov," I began, "let me tell you that I hate phrases, phrasemongers and corseted waists—that's the first point, and there is a second one to follow it."

There was a general stir.

"The second point is: I hate dirty stories and people who tell dirty stories. Especially people who tell dirty stories!

"The third point: I love truth, sincerity and honesty," I went on almost mechanically, for I was beginning to shiver with horror and had no idea how I came to be talking like this. "I love thought, Monsieur Zverkov; I love true comradeship, on an equal footing and not—h'm—I love—but, however, why not? I will drink to your health, too, Monsieur Zverkov. Seduce the Circassian girls, shoot the enemies of the fatherland and—and—to your health, Monsieur Zverkov!"

Zverkov got up from his seat, bowed to me and said:

"I am very much obliged to you."

He was frightfully offended and even turned pale.

"Damn the fellow!" roared Trudolyubov, bringing his fist down on the table.

"Well, he ought to be punched in the nose for that," squealed Ferfichkin.

"We ought to turn him out," muttered Simonov.

"Not a word, gentlemen, not a movement!" cried Zverkov solemnly, checking the general indignation. "I thank you all, but I can show him for myself how much value I attach to his words."

"Mr. Ferfichkin, you will give me satisfaction tomorrow at the latest for your words just now!" I said aloud, turning with dignity to Ferfichkin.

"A duel, you mean? Certainly," he answered. But probably I was so ridiculous as I challenged him and it was so out of keeping with my appearance that everyone, including Ferfichkin, roared with laughter.

"Yes, let him alone, of course! After all, he is completely drunk," Trudolyubov said with disgust.

"I will never forgive myself for letting him join us," Simonov muttered again.

"Now is the time to throw a bottle at their heads," I thought to myself. I picked up the bottle . . . and poured myself a full glass.

"No, I had better sit on to the end," I went on thinking; "you would be pleased, my friends, if I left. Nothing will induce me to go. I'll go on sitting here, and drinking to the end, on purpose, as a sign that I don't attach the slightest importance to you. I will go on sitting and drinking, because this is a public-house and I paid my entrance money. I'll sit here and drink, for I look upon you as so many pawns, as inanimate pawns. I'll sit here and drink—and sing if I want to, yes, sing, for I have the right to—to sing—h'm!"

But I did not sing. I simply tried not to look at any of them. I assumed most unconcerned attitudes and waited with impatience for them to speak *first,* of their own accord. But alas, they did not speak! And oh, how I wished, how I wished at that moment to be reconciled to them! It struck eight, at last nine. They moved from the table to the sofa. Zverkov stretched himself on a couch and put one foot on a round table. The wine was brought there. He did, as a matter of fact, order three bottles on his own account. He didn't, of course, invite me to join them. They all sat round him on the sofa. They listened to him, almost with reverence. It was evident that they were fond of him. "For what? For what?" I wondered. From time to time they were moved to drunken enthusiasm and kissed each other. They talked of the Caucasus, of the nature of true passion, of advantageous jobs in the service, of the income of a Hussar called Podkharzhevsky, whom none of them knew personally and rejoiced that he had a large income; of the extraordinary grace and beauty of a Princess D., whom none of them had ever seen; then it came to Shakespeare's being immortal.

I smiled contemptuously and walked up and down the other side of the room, opposite the sofa, along the wall, from the table to the stove and back again. I tried my very utmost to show them that I could do without them, and yet I purposely stomped with my boots, thumping with my heels. But it was all in vain. They paid no attention at all. I had the patience to walk up and down in front of them that way from eight o'clock till eleven, in one and the same place, from the table to the stove and from the stove back again to the table. "I walk up and down to please myself and no one can prevent me." The waiter who came into the room several times stopped to look at me. I was somewhat giddy from turning round so often; at moments it seemed to me that I was in delirium. During those three hours I was three times soaked with sweat, and then dry again. At times, with an intense, acute pang, I was stabbed to the heart by the thought that ten years, twenty years, forty years would pass, and that even in forty years I would remember with loathing and humiliation those filthiest, most ludicrous, and most terrible moments of my life. No one could have gone out of his way to degrade himself more shamelessly and voluntarily, and I fully realized it, fully, and yet I went on pacing up and down from the table to the stove. "Oh, if you only knew what thoughts and feelings I am capable of, how cultured I am!" I thought at moments, mentally addressing the sofa on which my enemies were sitting. But my enemies behaved as though I did not exist in the room. Once—only once—they turned toward me, just when Zverkov was talking about Shakespeare, and I suddenly gave a contemptuous laugh. I snorted in such an effected and nasty way that they all at once broke off their conversation, and silently and gravely for two minutes watched me walking up and down from the table to the stove, *paying no attention whatsoever to them.* But nothing came of it; they said nothing, and two minutes later they ceased to notice me again. It struck eleven.

"Gentlemen," cried Zverkov, getting up from the sofa, "let us all go there *now!*"

"Of course, of course," the others said.

I turned sharply to Zverkov. I was so exhausted, so broken, that I would have cut my throat to put an end to it. I was in a fever; my hair, soaked with perspiration, stuck to my forehead and temples.

"Zverkov, I beg your pardon," I said abruptly and resolutely. "Ferfichkin, yours too, and everyone's, everyone's; I have insulted you all!"

"Aha! A duel is not in your line, old man," Ferfichkin hissed venomously.

It sent a deep pang to my heart.

"No, it's not the duel I am afraid of, Ferfichkin! I am ready to fight you tomorrow, after we are reconciled. I insist upon it, in fact, and you cannot refuse. I want to show you that I am not afraid of a duel. You will fire first and I will fire into the air."

"He is comforting himself," remarked Simonov.

"He's simply raving," declared Trudolyubov.

"But let us pass. Why are you barring our way? Well, what do you want?" Zverkov answered disdainfully. They were all flushed; their eyes were bright; they had been drinking heavily.

"I asked for your friendship, Zverkov; I insulted you, but—"

"Insulted? You-u insulted me-e-e! Permit me to tell you, sir, that you never, under any circumstances, could possibly insult *me.*"

"And that's enough of you. Out of the way!" concluded Trudolyubov. "Let's go."

"Olympia is mine, gentlemen, that's agreed!" cried Zverkov.

"We won't dispute your right, we won't dispute your right," the others answered, laughing.

I stood as though spat upon. The party went noisily out of the room. Trudolyubov struck up some stupid song. Simonov remained behind for a moment to tip the waiters. I suddenly went up to him.

"Simonov! give me six roubles!" I said, decisively and desperately.

He looked at me in extreme amazement, with dulled eyes. He, too, was drunk.

"You don't mean you are even coming with us *there?*"

"Yes."

"I've no money," he snapped out, and with a scornful laugh he went out of the room.

I clutched at his overcoat. It was a nightmare.

"Simonov! I saw you had money, why do you refuse me? Am I a scoundrel? Beware of refusing me; if you knew, if you knew why I am asking! Everything depends upon it! My whole future, my whole plans!"

Simonov pulled out the money and almost flung it at me.

"Take it, if you have no sense of shame!" he pronounced pitilessly, and ran to overtake them.

I was left alone for a moment. Disorder, the remains of dinner, a broken wine-glass on the floor, spilt wine, cigarette butts, intoxication and delirium in my brain, an agonizing misery in my heart and finally the waiter, who had seen and heard all and was looking inquisitively into my face.

"I am going *there!*" I shouted. "Either they will all fall down on their knees to beg for my friendship—or I will give Zverkov a slap in the face!"

V

"So this is it, so this is it at last, a clash with reality," I muttered as I ran headlong downstairs. "This, it seems, is very different from the Pope's leaving Rome and going to Brazil; this, it seems, is very different from the ball on the shores of Lake Como!"

"You are a scoundrel," flashed through my mind, "if you laugh at this now."

"No matter!" I cried, answering myself. "Now everything is lost!"

There was no trace of them left, but that made no difference—I knew where they had gone.

At the steps was standing a solitary night sledge-driver in a rough peasant coat, powdered over with the wet, and, as it were, warm snow that was still falling thickly. It was sultry and warm. The little shaggy piebald horse was also powdered with snow and was coughing, I remember that very well. I made a rush for the roughly made sledge; but as soon as I raised my foot to get into it, the recollection of how Simonov had just given me six roubles seemed to double me up and I tumbled into the sledge like a sack.

"No, I must do a great deal to make up for all that," I cried. "But I will make up for it or perish on the spot this very night. Start!"

We set off. There was an absolute whirl in my head.

"They won't go down on their knees to beg for my friendship. That is a mirage, a cheap mirage, revolting, romantic and fantastical—that is another ball at Lake Como. And so I have to slap Zverkov's face! It is my duty to. And so it is settled; I am flying to give him a slap in the face. Hurry up!"

The cabby tugged at the reins.

"As soon as I go in I'll give it to him. Ought I to say a few words by way of preface before giving him the slap? No, I'll simply go in and give it to him. They will all be sitting in the drawing-room, and he with Olympia on the sofa. That damned Olympia! She laughed at my looks on one occasion and refused me. I'll pull Olympia's hair, pull Zverkov's ears! No, better one ear, and pull him by it round the room. Maybe they will all begin beating me and will kick me out. That is even very likely. No matter! Anyway, I will slap him first; the initiative will be mine; and according to the code of honor that is everything: he will be branded and no blows can wipe off the slap, nothing but a duel can. He will be forced to fight. And let them beat me then. Let them, the ungrateful wretches! Trudolyubov will beat me hardest, he is so strong; Ferfichkin is sure to catch hold from the side and tug at my hair. But no matter, no matter! That's what I am going for. The blockheads will be forced at last to see the tragedy of it all! When they drag me to the door I shall call out to them that in reality they are not worth my little finger." "Get on, driver, get on!" I cried to the driver. He started and flicked his whip, I shouted so savagely.

"We shall fight at daybreak, that's a settled thing. I am through with the Department. Ferfichkin called the Department 'Dumbpartment' before. But where can I get pistols? Nonsense! I'll call my salary in advance and buy them. And powder, and bullets? That's the second's business. And how can it all be done by daybreak? And where am I to get a second? I have no friends. Nonsense!" I cried, lashing myself more and more into a fury. "Nonsense! the first person I meet in the street is bound to be my second, just as he would be bound to pull a drowning man out of water. The strangest things may happen. Even if I were to ask the Director himself to be my second tomorrow, even he would be bound to consent, if only from a feeling of chivalry, and to keep the secret! Anton Antonich—"

The fact is that at that very minute the disgusting absurdity of my plans and the other side of the question were clearer and more vivid to my imagination than they could be to anyone on earth, but—

"Get on, driver, get on, you rascal, get on!"

"Ugh, sir!" said the son of toil.

Cold shivers suddenly ran down me.

"Wouldn't it be better . . . wouldn't it be better . . . to go straight home now? Oh, my God! Why, why did I invite myself to this dinner yesterday? But no, it's impossible. And my three hours' walk from the table to the stove? No, they, they and no one else must pay for my walking up and down! They must wipe out this dishonor! Drive on!"

"And what if they hand me over to the police? They won't dare! They'll be afraid of the scandal. And what if Zverkov is so contemptuous that he refuses to fight a duel? That is even sure to happen, but in that case I'll show them—I will turn up at the posting station when he is setting off tomorrow—I'll catch him by the leg, I'll pull off his coat when he gets into the carriage. I'll get my teeth into his hand, I'll bite him. See to what lengths you can drive a desperate man! He may hit me on the head and they may pummel me from behind. I will shout to the whole crowd of spectators: 'Look at this young puppy who is driving off to captivate the Circassian girls after letting me spit in his face!'

"Of course, after that everything will be over! The Department will have vanished off the face of the earth. I will be arrested. I will be tried, I will be dismissed from the service, thrown in prison, sent to Siberia, deported. Never mind! In fifteen years when they let me out of prison I will trudge off to him, a begger in rags, I shall find him in some provincial city. He will be married and happy. He will have a grown-up daughter . . . I will say to him: 'Look, monster, at my hollow cheeks and my rags! I've lost everything—my career, my happiness, art, science, *the woman I loved,* and all through you. Here are pistols. I have come to discharge my pistol and—and I . . . forgive you.' Then I will fire into the air and he will hear nothing more of me."

I was actually on the point of tears, though I knew perfectly well at that very moment that all this was out of Pushkin's Silvio and Lermontov's *Masquerade.*[8] And all at once I felt terribly ashamed, so ashamed that I stopped the sledge, stepped out of it and stood still in the snow in the middle of the street. The driver sighed and gazed at me in astonishment.

What was I to do? I could not go on there—that was clearly absurd, and I could not leave things as they were, because that would seem as though—"Heavens, how could I leave things! And after such insults!" "No!" I cried, throwing myself into the sledge again. "It is ordained! It is fate! Drive on, drive on to that place!"

And in my impatience I punched the sledge-driver on the back of the neck.

"What are you up to? What are you hitting me for?" the poor man shouted, but he whipped up his nag so that it began to kick out.

The wet snow was falling in big flakes; I unbuttoned myself. I did not care about it. I forgot everything else, for I had finally decided on the slap, and felt with horror that after all it was going to happen *now, at once,* that it would happen immediately and that *no force could stop it.* The deserted street lamps gleamed sullenly in the snowy darkness like torches at a funeral. The snow drifted under my greatcoat, under my coat, under my necktie, and melted there. I did not cover myself up—after all, all was already lost, anyway. At last we arrived. I jumped out, almost fainting, ran up the steps and began knocking and kicking at the door. My legs, particularly at the knee, felt terribly weak. The door was opened quickly as though they knew I was coming. As a matter of fact, Simonov had warned them that perhaps another would arrive, and

8. An 1835 play by Mikhail Lermontov about love, duty, and honor. Silvio is the vengeful hero of a story by Alexander Pushkin, "The Shot" (1830).

this was a place in which one had to give notice and to observe certain precautions. It was one of the "millinery establishments" which were abolished by the police a long time ago. By day it really was a shop; but at night, if one had an introduction, one might visit it for other purposes.

I walked rapidly through the dark shop into the familiar drawing-room, where there was only one candle burning, and stopped in amazement; there was no one there.

"Where are they?" I asked somebody.

But by now, of course, they had separated.

Before me stood a person with a stupid smile, the "madam" herself, who had seen me before. A minute later a door opened and another person came in.

Paying no attention to anything, I strode about the room, and, I believe, I talked to myself. I felt as though I had been saved from death and was conscious of it, joyfully, all over: after all, I would have given that slap. I would certainly, certainly have given it! But now they were not here and—everything had vanished and changed! I looked round. I could not realize my condition yet. I looked mechanically at the girl who had come in and had a glimpse of a fresh, young, rather pale face, with straight, dark eyebrows, and with a grave, as it were, amazed glance, eyes that attracted me at once. I would have hated her if she had been smiling. I began looking at her more intently and, as it were, with effort. I had not fully collected my thoughts. There was something simple and good-natured in her face, but something strangely serious. I am sure that this stood in her way here, and that not one of those fools had noticed her. She could not, however, have been called a beauty, though she was tall, strong-looking, and well built. She was very simply dressed. Something loathsome stirred within me. I went straight up to her—

I happened to look at myself in the mirror. My harassed face struck me as extremely revolting, pale, spiteful, nasty, with disheveled hair. "No matter, I am glad of it," I thought; "I am glad that I shall seem revolting to her; I like that."

VI

. . . Somewhere behind a screen a clock began wheezing, as though under some great pressure, as though someone were strangling it. After an unnaturally prolonged wheezing there followed a shrill, nasty and, as it were, unexpectedly rapid chime—as though someone were suddenly jumping forward. It struck two. I woke up, though I had not really been asleep but only lay semi-conscious.

It was almost completely dark in the narrow, cramped, low-pitched room, cluttered up with an enormous wardrobe and piles of cardboard boxes and all sorts of frippery and litter. The candle stump that had been burning on the table was going out and it gave a faint flicker from time to time. In a few minutes it would be completely dark.

I was not long in coming to myself; everything came back to my mind at once, without an effort, as though it had been in ambush to pounce upon me again. And, indeed, even while I was unconscious, a point continually seemed to remain in my memory that could not ever be forgotten, and around it my dreams moved drearily. But strange to say, everything that had happened to me during that day seemed to me now, on waking, to be in the far, far-away distant past, as though I had long, long ago lived all that down.

My head was heavy. Something seemed to be hovering over me, provoking me, rousing me and making me restless. Misery and gall seemed to surge up in me again and to seek an outlet. Suddenly I saw beside me two wide-open eyes scrutinizing me curiously and persistently. The look in those eyes was coldly detached, sullen, utterly detached, as it were; it weighed heavily on me.

A grim idea came into my brain and passed all over my body, like some nasty sensation, such as one feels when one goes into a damp and mouldy cellar. It was somehow unnatural that those two eyes only now thought of beginning to examine me. I recalled, too, that during those two hours I had not said a single word to this creature, and had, in fact, considered it entirely unnecessary; it had even for some reason gratified me before. Now I suddenly realized vividly how absurd, revolting as a spider, was the idea of vice which, without love, grossly and shamelessly begins directly with that in which true love finds its consummation. For a long time we gazed at each other like that, but she did not drop her eyes before mine and did not change her expression, so that at last, somehow, I felt uncomfortable.

"What is your name?" I asked abruptly, to put an end to it quickly.

"Liza," she answered almost in a whisper, but somehow without any friendliness; she turned her eyes away.

I was silent.

"What weather today—the snow—it's abominable!" I said, almost to myself, putting my arm under my head despondently, and gazing at the ceiling.

She made no answer. This was all outrageous.

"Are you a local girl?" I asked a minute later, almost angrily, turning my head slightly toward her.

"No."

"Where do you come from?"

"From Riga," she answered reluctantly.

"Are you a German?"

"No, Russian."

"Have you been here long?"

"Where?"

"In this house?"

"A fortnight."

She spoke more and more jerkily. The candle went out: I could no longer distinguish her face.

"Have you a father and mother?"

"Yes—no—I have."

"Where are they?"

"There—in Riga."

"What are they?"

"Oh, nothing."

"Nothing? Why, what do they do?"

"Tradespeople."

"Have you always lived with them?"

"Yes."

"How old are you?"

"Twenty."

"Why did you leave them?"

"Oh, for no reason."

That answer meant "Let me alone; I feel wretched." We were silent.

God knows why I did not go away. I felt myself more and more wretched and dreary. The images of the previous day started to flit through my mind in confusion independently of my will. I suddenly recalled something I had seen that morning when, full of anxious thoughts, I was hurrying to the office.

"I saw them carrying a coffin out yesterday and they nearly dropped it," I suddenly said aloud with no desire at all to start a conversation, but just so, almost by accident.

"A coffin?"

"Yes, in the Haymarket; they were bringing it up out of a cellar."

"From a cellar?"

"Not from a cellar, but from a basement. Oh, you know—down below—from a house of ill-fame. It was filthy all round—eggshells, litter—a stench. It was loathsome."

Silence.

"A nasty day to be buried," I began, simply to avoid being silent.

"Nasty, in what way?"

"The snow, the wet." (I yawned.)

"It doesn't matter," she said suddenly, after a brief silence.

"No, it's abominable." (I yawned again.) "The gravediggers must have sworn at getting drenched by the snow. And there must have been water in the grave."

"Why would there be water in the grave?" she asked, with a sort of curiosity, but speaking even more harshly and abruptly than before. I suddenly began to feel provoked.

"Why, there must have been water at the bottom a foot deep. You can't dig a dry grave in Volkovo Cemetery."

"Why?"

"Why? Why, the place is waterlogged. It's a regular marsh. So they bury them in water. I've seen it myself—many times."

(I had never seen it at all, and I had never even been in Volkovo, but had only heard stories of it.)

"Do you mean to say it doesn't matter to you whether you die?"

"But why should I die?" she answered, as though defending herself.

"Why, some day you will die, and you will die just the same as that dead woman. She was—a girl like you. She died of consumption."

"The wench would have died in a hospital, too . . . (She knows all about it already; she said "wench," not "girl.")

"She was in debt to her madam," I retorted, more and more provoked by the discussion; "and went on earning money for her almost up to the very end, though she was in consumption. Some coachmen standing by were talking about her to some soldiers and telling them so. No doubt her former acquaintances. They were laughing. They were going to meet in a pot-house to drink to her memory." (I lied a great deal here.)

Silence followed, profound silence. She did not even stir.

"And is it better to die in a hospital?"

"Isn't it just the same? Besides, why should I die?" she added irritably.

"If not now, a little later."

"Why a little later?"

"Why, indeed? Now you are young, pretty, fresh, you fetch a high price. But after another year of this life you will be very different—you will fade."

"In a year?"

"Anyway, in a year you will be worth less," I continued malignantly. "You will go from here to something lower, another house; a year later—to a third, lower and lower, and in seven years you will come to a basement in the Haymarket. And that's if you are lucky. But it would be much worse if you got some disease, consumption, say—and caught a chill, or something or other. It's not easy to get over an illness in your way of life. If you catch anything you may not get rid of it. And so you would die."

"Oh, well, then I will die," she answered, quite vindictively, and she made a quick movement.

"But after all, it's a pity."

"For whom?"

"Pity for life."

Silence.

"Were you engaged? Eh?"

"What's that to you?"

"Oh, I am not cross-examining you. It's nothing to me. Why are you so cross? Of course you may have had your own troubles. What is it to me? I simply felt sorry."

"For whom?"

"Sorry for you."

"No need," she whispered hardly audibly, and again made a faint movement.

That incensed me at once. What! I was so gentle with her, and she—

"Why, what do you think? Are you on the right path, ah?"

"I don't think anything."

"That's what's wrong, that you don't think. Wake up while there is still time. And there is still time. You are still young, good-looking; you might love, be married, be happy—"

"Not all married women are happy," she snapped out in the rude, fast way she had spoken before.

"Not all, of course, but anyway it is much better than the life here. Infinitely better. Besides, with love one can live even without happiness. Even in sorrow life is sweet; life is sweet, however one lives. But here you have nothing except foulness. Phew!"

I turned away with disgust; I was no longer reasoning coldly. I began to feel myself what I was saying and warmed to the subject. I was already longing to expound the cherished *little ideas* I had brooded over in my corner. Something suddenly flared up in me. An object had "appeared" before me.

"Never mind my being here. I am not an example for you. I am, perhaps, even worse than you are. I was drunk when I came here, though," I hastened, however, to say in self-defense. "Besides, a man is no example for a woman. It's a different thing. I may degrade and defile myself, but I am not anyone's slave. I come and go, and there's an end to it. I shake it off, and I am a different man. But you are a slave from the start. Yes, a slave! You give up everything, your whole freedom. If you want to break your chains afterward, you won't be able to; you will be caught more and more in the snares. It is an accursed bondage. I know it. I won't mention anything else, maybe you won't understand it, but tell me: after all, surely you are in debt to your madam already? There, you see," I added, though she made no answer, but only listened in silence, entirely absorbed, "that's bondage for you! You will never buy your freedom. They will see to that. It's like selling your soul to the devil—

"And besides—perhaps I, too, am just as unfortunate, how do you know—and wallow in the mud on purpose, also out of misery? After all, men take to drink out of grief; well, maybe I am here out of grief. Come, tell me, what good is there here? Here you and I—were intimate—just now and did not say one word to one another all the time, and it was only afterward you began staring at me like a wild creature, and I at you. Is that loving? Is that how human beings are intimate? It's hideous, that's what it is!"

"Yes!" she assented sharply and hurriedly.

I was even amazed by the eagerness of this "yes." So the same thought may have been straying through her mind when she was staring at me just before. So she, too, was capable of certain thoughts? "Damn it all, this was curious, this was *kinship?*" I thought, almost rubbing my hands. And indeed how can one fail to manage a young soul like that?

The sport in it attracted me most.

She turned her head nearer to me, and it seemed to me in the darkness that she propped herself on her arm. Perhaps she was scrutinizing me. How I regretted that I could not see her eyes. I heard her deep breathing.

"Why did you come here?" I asked her, with a note of authority already in my voice.

"Oh, I don't know."

"But after all how nice it would be to be living in your own father's house! It's warm and free; you have a nest of your own."

"But what if it's worse than this?"

"I must take the right tone," flashed through my mind. "I may not get far with sentimentality."

But it was only a momentary thought. I swear she really did interest me. Besides, I was exhausted and moody. And after all, cunning so easily goes hand in hand with feeling.

"Who denies it?" I hastened to answer. "Anything may happen. I am, after all, convinced that someone has wronged you and is guiltier toward you than you toward them. After all, I know nothing of your story, but it's not likely a girl like you has come here of her own inclination—"

"What kind of girl am I?" she whispered, hardly audible, but I heard it.

Damn it all, I was flattering her. That was abominable. But perhaps it was a good thing—She was silent.

"See, Liza, I will tell you about myself. If I had had a home from childhood, I shouldn't be what I am now. I often think about that. After all, no matter how bad it may be at home, at least they are your father and mother, and not enemies, strangers. Once a year, at least, they'll show their love for you. Anyway, you know you are at home. I grew up without a home; and perhaps that's why I've turned so—unfeeling."

I waited again.

"Perhaps she doesn't understand," I thought, "and, indeed, it is absurd, this moralizing."

"If I were a father and had a daughter, I believe I should love my daughter more than my sons, really," I began indirectly, as though talking of something else, in order to distract her attention. I confess I blushed.

"Why so?" she asked.

Ah! so she was listening!

"I don't know, Liza. I knew a father who was a stern, strict man, but he used to go down on his knees to his daughter, used to kiss her hands and feet, he couldn't make enough of her, really. When she danced at parties he used to stand for five hours at a stretch without taking his eyes off her. He was mad about her; I understand that! She would fall asleep tired at night, and he would get up to kiss her in her sleep and make the sign of the cross over her. He would go about in a dirty old coat, he was stingy to everyone else, but would spend his last penny for her, giving her expensive presents, and it was a delight to him when she was pleased with what he gave her. Fathers always love their daughters more than mothers do. Some girls live happily at home! And I believe I would never let my daughter marry."

"What next?" she said with a faint smile.

"I would be jealous, I really would. To think that she should kiss anyone else! That she should love a stranger more than her father! It's painful to imagine it. Of course, that's all nonsense, of course every father would be reasonable at last. But I believe before I would let her marry, I would worry myself to death; I would find fault with all her suitors. But I would end by letting her marry whom she herself loved. After all, the one whom the daughter loves always seems the worst to the father. That is always so. So many families get into trouble with that."

"Some are glad to sell their daughters, rather than to marry them honorably."

Ah! So that was it!

"Such a thing, Liza, happens in those accursed families in which there is neither love nor God," I retorted warmly, "and where there is no love, there is no sense either. There are such families, it's true, but I am not speaking of them. You must have seen wickedness in your own family, if you talk like that. You must have been genuinely unlucky. H'm!—that sort of thing mostly comes about through poverty."

"And is it any better among the rich? Even among the poor, honest people live happily."

"H'm—yes. Perhaps. Another thing, Liza, man only likes to count his troubles, but he does not count his joys. If he counted them up as he ought, he would see that every lot has enough happiness provided for it. And what if all goes well with the family, if the blessing of God is upon it, if the husband is a good one, loves you, cherishes you, never leaves you! There is happiness in such a family! Sometimes there is happiness even in the midst of sorrow; and indeed sorrow is everywhere. If you marry *you will find out for yourself.* But think of the first years of married life with one you love: what happiness, what happiness there sometimes is in it! And indeed it's the ordinary thing. In those early days even quarrels with one's husband end happily. Some women get up more quarrels with their husbands the more they love them. Indeed, I knew a woman like that: she seemed to say that because she loved him deeply, she would torment him out of love so that he'd feel it. Did you know that you may torment a man on purpose out of love? Women are particularly given to that, thinking to themselves, 'I will love him so much afterward, I will make so much of him, that it's no sin to torment him a little now.' And everyone in the house rejoices in the sight of you, and you are happy and gay and peaceful and honorable. Then there are some women who are jealous. If the husband goes off someplace—I knew one such woman, she couldn't restrain herself, but would jump up at night and would run off on the sly to find out where he was, whether he was with some other woman. That's already bad. And the woman knows herself it's wrong, and her heart fails her and she suffers, but, after all, she loves—it's all through love. And how sweet it is to make up after quarrels, to admit she was wrong, or to forgive him! And they are both so happy, all at once they become so happy, as though they had met anew, been married over again; as though their love had begun anew. And no one, no one should know what passes between husband and wife if they love one another. And no matter how their quarrels ended they ought not to call in even their own mothers to judge between them and tell tales of one another. They are their own judges. Love is a holy mystery and ought to be hidden from all other eyes, no matter what happens. That makes it holier and better. They respect one another more, and much is built on respect. And if once there has been love, if they have been married for love, why should love pass away?

Surely one can keep it! It is rare that one cannot keep it. And if the husband is kind and straightforward, why should not love last? The first phase of married love will pass, it is true, but then there will come a love that is better still. Then there will be the union of souls, they will have everything in common, there will be no secrets between them. And once they have children, the most difficult times will seem to them happy, so long as there is love and courage. Even toil will be a joy, you may deny yourself bread for your children and even that will be a joy. After all, they will love you for it afterward; so you are laying by for your future. As the children grow up you feel that you are an example, a support for them; that even after you die your children will always cherish your thoughts and feelings, because they have received them from you, they will take on your semblance and likeness. So you see it is a great duty. How can it fail to draw the father and mother closer? People say it's a trial to have children. Who says that? It is heavenly joy! Are you fond of little children, Liza? I am awfully fond of them. You know—a little rosy baby boy at your bosom, and what husband's heart is not touched, seeing his wife nursing his child! A plump little rosy baby, sprawling and snuggling, chubby little hands and feet, clean tiny little nails, so tiny that it makes one laugh to look at them; eyes that look as if they understand everything. And while it sucks it clutches at your bosom with its little hand, plays. When its father comes up, the child tears itself away from the bosom, flings itself back, looks at its father, laughs, as though it were God knows how funny, and falls to sucking again. Or it will bite its mother's breast when it is cutting its little teeth while it looks sideways at her with its little eyes as though to say, 'Look, I am biting!' Is not all that a joy when they are all three together, husband, wife and child? One can forgive a great deal for the sake of such moments. Yes, Liza, one must first learn to live oneself before one blames others!"

"It's by pictures, pictures like that one must get at you," I thought to myself, though I did not speak with real feeling, and all at once I flushed crimson. "What if she were suddenly to burst out laughing, what would I do then?" That idea drove me to fury. Toward the end of my speech I really was excited, and now my vanity was somehow wounded. The silence continued. I almost wanted to nudge her.

"Why are you . . ." she began, and stopped. But I understood: there was a quiver of something different in her voice, not abrupt, harsh and unyielding as before, but something soft and shamefaced, so shamefaced that I suddenly felt ashamed and guilty.

"What?" I asked with tender curiosity.

"Why, you . . ."

"What?"

"Why you—speak exactly like a book," she said, and something sarcastic was heard in her voice.

That remark sent a pang to my heart. It was not what I was expecting.

I did not understand that she was hiding her feelings by sarcasm and that this is usually the last refuge of modest and chaste-souled people when the privacy of their soul is coarsely and intrusively invaded, and that their pride makes them refuse to surrender till the last moment and shrink from expressing their feelings to you. I ought to have guessed the truth for the timidity with which she had a number of times attempted her sarcasm, only bringing herself to utter it at last with an effort. But I did not guess, and a spiteful feeling took possession of me.

"Wait a bit!" I thought.

VII

"Oh, hush, Liza! How can you talk about my speaking like a book when it makes even me, an outsider, feel sick? Though I don't look at it as an outsider, for, indeed, all that has touched me to the heart. Is it possible, is it possible that you do not feel sick at being here yourself? Evidently habit does wonders! God knows what habit can do with anyone. Can you really and seriously think that you will never grow old, that you will always be good-looking, and that they will keep you here forever and ever? I say nothing of the filth here. Though let me tell you this about it; about your present life, I mean; even though you are young now, attractive, nice, with soul and feeling, yet you know, as soon as I came to myself just now, I felt at once sick at being here with you! After all, one can only come here when one is drunk. But if you were anywhere else, living as decent people live, I would perhaps be more than attracted by you, I would fall in love with you, would be glad of a look from you, let alone a word. I would hang about your door, would go down on my knees to you, we would become engaged and I would even consider it an honor to do so. I would not dare to have an impure thought about you. But here, after all, I know that I have only to whistle and you have to come with me whether you like it or not. I don't consult your wishes, but you mine. The lowest laborer hires himself as a workman but he doesn't make a slave of himself altogether; besides, he knows that he will be free again. But when will you be free? Only think what you are giving up here! What is it you are making a slave of? It is your soul, together with your body; you are selling your soul which you have no right to dispose of! You give your love to be outraged by every drunkard! Love! But after all, that's everything, but after all, it's a jewel, it's a maiden's treasure, love—why, after all a man would be ready to give his soul, to face death to gain that love. But how much is your love worth now? You can be bought, all of you, body and soul, and there is no need to strive for love when you can have everything without love. And after all, there is no greater insult for a girl than that, do you understand? To be sure, I have heard that they comfort you, poor fools, they let you have lovers of your own here. But after all, that's simply a farce, that's simply a sham, it's just laughing at you, and you are taken in by it! Why, do you suppose he really loves you, that lover of yours? I don't believe it. How can he love you when he knows that you may be called away from him any minute? He would be a vile fellow if he did! Would he have a grain of respect for you? What have you in common with him? He laughs at you and robs you—that is all his love amounts to! You are lucky if he does not beat you. Very likely he does beat you, too. Ask him, if you have one, whether he will marry you. He will laugh in your face, if he doesn't spit in it or give you a blow—yet he may not be worth a plugged nickel himself. And for what have you ruined your life, if you come to think of it? For the coffee they give you to drink and the plentiful meals? But after all, why do they feed you? An honest girl couldn't swallow the food, she would know why she was being fed. You are in debt here, and, of course, you will always be in debt, and you will go on in debt to the end, till the visitors here begin to scorn you. And that will soon happen, don't rely upon your youth—all that flies by, like an express train here, after all. You will be kicked out. And not simply kicked out; long before that they will begin to nag you, scold you, abuse you, as though you had not sacrificed your health for her, had not ruined your youth and your soul for her benefit, but as though you had ruined her, ravaged her, robbed her. And don't expect anyone to take your part; the others, your companions, will attack you, too, to win her favor, for all are in slavery here, and have lost all conscience and pity long ago. They have become utterly vile, and nothing on earth is viler, more loathsome and more insulting than their abuse. And you are laying down everything here, everything unconditionally, youth and health and beauty and hope, and at twenty-two you will look like a woman of thirty-five, and you will be lucky if you are not diseased, pray to God for that! No doubt you are thinking now after all that you have a lark and no work to do! Yet there is no harder or more dreadful work in the world or ever has been. One would think that the heart alone would be worn out with tears. And you won't dare to say a word, not half a word, when they drive you away from here: you will go away as though you were to blame. You will change to another house, then to a third, then somewhere else, till you come down at last to the Haymarket. There you will be beaten at every turn; that is a courtesy there, the visitors there don't know how to be friendly without beating you. You don't believe that it is so hateful there? Go and look for yourself some time, you can see with your own eyes. Once, one New Year's Day, I saw a woman at a door. Her own kind had turned her out as a joke, to give her a taste of the frost because she had been howling too much, and they shut the door behind her. At nine o'clock in the morning she was already completely drunk, dishevelled, half-naked, covered with bruises, her face was powdered, but she had a black eye, blood was trickling from her nose and her teeth; some cabman had just beaten her. She was sitting on the stone steps, a salt fish of some sort was in her hand; she was howling, wailing something about her 'fate' and beating with the fish on the steps, and cabmen and drunken soldiers were crowding in the doorway taunting her. You don't believe that you will ever be like that? I would not like to believe it, either, but how do you know, maybe ten years, eight years ago that very woman with that salt fish came here fresh as a little cherub, innocent, pure, knowing no evil, blushing at every word. Perhaps she was like you, proud, ready to take offence, not like the others; perhaps she looked like a queen, and knew what happiness was in store for the man who would love her and whom she would love. Do you see how it ended? And what if at that very minute when she was beating on the filthy steps with that fish, drunken and dishevelled—what if at that very minute she recalled the pure early days in her father's house, when she used to go to school and the neighbor's son watched for her on the way, declaring that he would love her as long as he lived, that he would devote his life to her, and when they vowed to love one another for ever and be married as soon as they were grown up! No, Liza, it would be a joy for you, a joy if you were to die soon of consumption in some corner, in some cellar like that woman just now. In the hospital, do you say? You will be lucky if they take you, but what if you are still of use to the madam here? Consumption is a queer disease, it is not like fever. The patient goes on hoping till the last minute and says he is all right. He deludes himself. And that's just advantageous for your madam. Don't doubt it, that's how it is; you have sold your soul, and what is more you owe money, so you don't even dare to say a word. But when you are dying, everyone will abandon you, everyone will turn away from you, for then there will be nothing to get from you. What's more, they will reproach you for taking up space, for taking so long to die. You won't even be able to beg for a drink of water without getting abuse. 'Aren't you going to die, you foul wench; you won't let us sleep with your moaning, you make the gentlemen sick.' That's true. I have heard such things said myself. When you are really dying they will push you into the filthiest corner in the cellar; in the damp and darkness; what will your thoughts be, lying there alone? When you die, strange hands will lay you out, with grumbling and impatience; no one will bless you, no one will sigh for you, they will only want to get rid of you as soon as possible; they will buy a coffin, take you to the grave as they did that poor woman today, and celebrate your memory at the tavern. There is slush, filth, wet snow in the grave—no need to put themselves out for you: 'Let her down, Vanyukha; it's just like her "fate" after all, here she goes in, head first, the wench. Shorten the cord, you rascal.' 'It's all right as it is.' 'All right, is it? Why, she's on her side! Wasn't she a human being, too? Well, never mind, cover her up.' And they won't care to waste much time quarreling over you. They will scatter the wet blue clay as quickly as they can and go off to the tavern—and there your memory on earth will end; other women have children who visit their graves, fathers, husbands. While for you there will be neither tear, nor sigh, nor remembrance; no one, no one in the whole wide world will ever come to you; your name will vanish from the face of the earth as though you had never existed, had never been born at all! Nothing but filth and mud, no matter how much you knock on your coffin lid at night, when the dead arise, however you cry: 'Let me out, kind people, to live in the light of day! My life was no life at all; my life has been thrown away like a dirty rag; it was drunk away in the tavern at the Haymarket; let me out, kind people, to live in the world again!'"

And I worked myself up to such a pitch that I began to have a lump in my throat myself and—and suddenly I stopped, sat up in dismay, and bending over apprehensively, began to listen with a beating heart. I had reason to be worried.

I felt for some time that I was turning her soul upside down and breaking her heart, and the more I was convinced of it, the more I wanted to gain my end as quickly and as effectively as possible. The sport, the sport attracted me; yet it was not merely the sport.

I knew I was speaking stiffly, artificially, even bookishly, in short I did not know how to speak except "just like a book." But that did not bother me: after all I knew, I felt, that I would be understood and that this very bookishness would perhaps even be a help. But now, having achieved my effect, I was suddenly panic-stricken. No, I had never, never before witnessed such despair! She was lying face down, pressing her face deep into the pillow and clutching it in both hands. Her heart was being torn. Her youthful body was shuddering all over as though in convulsions. Suppressed sobs rent her bosom and suddenly burst out in weeping and wailing, then she pressed even deeper into the pillow: she did not want anyone here, not a single living soul, to know of her anguish and her tears. She bit the pillow, bit her hand till it bled (I saw that afterward), or, thrusting her fingers into her dishevelled hair, seemed rigid with the effort to restrain herself, holding her breath and clenching her teeth. I began to say something to her, to beg her to calm herself, but felt that I did not dare; and suddenly, all in a sort of chill, almost in terror, began fumbling in the dark, trying hurriedly to get dressed to go. It was dark: try as I would, I could not finish dressing quickly. Suddenly I felt a box of matches and a candlestick with a whole new candle in it. As soon as the room was lighted up, Liza sprang up, sat up in bed, and with a contorted face, with a half-insane smile, looked at me almost senselessly. I sat down beside her and took her hands; she came to herself, made a movement toward me, would have clasped me, but did not dare, and slowly bowed her head before me.

"Liza, my dear, I was wrong to—Forgive me," I began but she squeezed my hand in her fingers so tightly that I felt I was saying the wrong thing and stopped.

"This is my address, Liza, come to me."

"I will come," she whispered resolutely, her head still bowed.

"But now I am going, good-by—till we meet again."

I got up; she, too, stood up and suddenly flushed all over, shuddered, snatched up a shawl that was lying on a chair and muffled herself in it to her chin. As she did this she gave another sickly smile, blushed and looked at me strangely. I felt wretched; I was in haste to get away—to disappear.

"Wait a minute," she said suddenly, in the passage just at the doorway, stopping me with her hand on my overcoat. She put down the candle hastily and ran off; evidently she had thought of something or wanted to show me something. As she ran away she flushed, her eyes shone, and a smile appeared on her lips—what was the meaning of it? Against my will I waited; she came back a minute later with an expression that seemed to ask forgiveness for something. In fact, it was not the same face, nor the same look it had been before: sullen, mistrustful and obstinate. Her look was now imploring, soft, and at the same time trustful, caressing, timid. Children look that way at people they are very fond of, of whom they are asking a favor. Her eyes were a light hazel, they were lovely eyes, full of life, capable of expressing love as well as sullen hatred.

Making no explanation, as though I, as a sort of higher being, must understand everything without explanations, she held out a piece of paper to me. Her whole face was positively beaming at that instant with naïve, almost childish, triumph. I unfolded it. It was a letter to her from a medical student or someone of that sort—a very high-flown and flowery, but extremely respectful, declaration of love. I don't recall the words now, but I remember well enough that through the high-flown phrases there was apparent a genuine feeling, which cannot be feigned. When I had finished reading it I met her glowing, questioning, and childishly impatient eyes fixed upon me. She fastened her eyes upon my face and waited impatiently for what I would say. In a few words, hurriedly, but with a sort of joy and pride, she explained to me that she had been to a dance somewhere, in a private house, at some "very, very nice people's house, a *family* who *still know nothing,* absolutely nothing," for she had only come here so lately and it had all happened—and she hadn't made up her mind to stay and was certainly going away as soon as she had paid her debt—"and at that party there had been that student who had danced with her the whole evening, had talked to her, and it turned out that he had known her in the old days at Riga when he was a child, they had played together, but a very long time ago—and he knew her parents, but *about this* he knew nothing, nothing, nothing whatever, and had no suspicion! And the day after the dance (three days ago) he had sent her that letter through the friend with whom she had gone to the party—and—well, that was all."

She dropped her shining eyes with a sort of bashfulness as she finished.

The poor girl was keeping that student's letter as a treasure and had run to fetch it, her only treasure, because she did not want me to go away without knowing that she, too, was honestly and genuinely loved; that she, too, was addressed respectfully. No doubt that letter was destined to lie in her box and lead to nothing. But it doesn't matter, I am certain that she would guard it as a treasure all her life, as her pride and justification, and now at such a minute she had thought of that letter and brought it with naïve pride to raise herself in my eyes that I might see, that I, too, might think well of her. I said nothing, pressed her hand and went out. I so longed to get away. I walked home all the way in spite of the fact that the wet snow was still falling in large flakes. I was exhausted, shattered, in bewilderment. But behind the bewilderment the truth was already gleaming. The loathsome truth!

VIII

It was some time, however, before I consented to recognize that truth. Waking up in the morning after some hours of heavy, leaden sleep, and immediately realizing all that had happened on the previous day, I was positively amazed at my last night's *sentimentality* with Liza, at all those "horrors and pity of yesterday." After all, to have such an attack of womanish hysteria, pah! I concluded. "And why did I force my address upon her? What if she comes? Let her come, though; it is all right—" But *obviously* that was not now the chief and the most important matter: I had to make haste and at all costs save my reputation in the eyes of Zverkov and Simonov as quickly as possible; that was the chief business. And I was so taken up that morning that I actually forgot all about Liza.

First of all I had to repay at once what I had borrowed the day before from Simonov. I resolved on a desperate course: to borrow fifteen roubles from Anton Antonich. As luck would have it he was in the best of humors that morning, and gave it to me at once, as soon as I asked. I was so delighted at this that, as I signed the I O U with a swaggering air, I told him *casually* that the night before "I had been making merry with some friends at the Hôtel de Paris; we were giving a farewell party to a comrade, in fact, I might say a friend of my childhood, and you know—a desperate rake, spoilt—of course, he belongs to a good family, and has considerable means, a brilliant career; he is witty, charming, carries on affairs with certain ladies, you understand; we drank an extra 'half-a-case' and—" And after all it went off all right; all this was said very lightly, unconstrainedly and complacently.

On reaching home I promptly wrote to Simonov.

To this hour I am lost in admiration when I recall the truly gentlemanly, good-humored, candid tone of my letter. With tact and good taste, and, above all, entirely without superfluous words, I blamed myself for all that had happened. I defended myself, "if only I may still be allowed to defend myself," by alleging that being utterly unaccustomed to wine, I had been intoxicated by the first glass which (I claimed) I had drunk before they arrived, while I was waiting for them at the Hotel de Paris between five and six o'clock. I particularly begged Simonov's pardon; I asked him also to convey my explanations to all the others, especially to Zverkov whom "I remember as though in a dream" I seem to have insulted. I added that I would have called upon all of them myself, but that my head ached, and that besides, I was rather ashamed. I was especially pleased with that "certain lightness," almost carelessness (strictly within the bounds of politeness, however), which was suddenly reflected in my style, and better than any possible arguments, gave them at once to understand that I took rather an independent view of "all that unpleasantness last night"; that I was by no means so utterly crushed as you, gentlemen, probably imagine; but on the contrary that I looked at it as a gentleman serenely respecting himself should. "On a young hero's past no censure is cast!"

"There is, after all, even an aristocratic playfulness about it!" I thought admiringly, as I read over the letter. "And it's all because I am a cultured and educated man! Others in my place would not have known how to extricate themselves, but here I have gotten out of it and am as gay as ever again, and all because I am a cultured and educated man of our day." And, indeed, perhaps, everything really was due to the wine yesterday. H'm!—well, no, it was not the wine. I drank nothing at all between five and six while I was waiting for them. I had lied to Simonov; lied shamelessly; and even now I wasn't ashamed—

Hang it all, though! The important thing was that I was rid of it.

I put six roubles in the letter, sealed it up, and asked Apollon to take it to Simonov. When he learned that there was money in the letter, Apollon became more respectful and agreed to take it. Toward evening I went out for a walk. My head was still aching and giddy, after yesterday. But as evening came on and the twilight grew thicker, my impressions changed and grew more and more confused and, after them, my thoughts. Something was not dead within me, in the depths of my heart and conscience it would not die, and it expressed itself as a burning anguish. For the most part I jostled my way through the most crowded business streets, along Meshchansky Street, along Sadovy Street and in the Yusupov Garden. I always particularly liked to stroll along these streets at dusk just when they become more crowded with people of all sorts, merchants and artisans going home from their day's work, with faces looking malicious out of anxiety. What I liked was just that cheap bustle, that bare, humdrum prosaic quality. On this occasion all that bustling in the streets irritated me more than ever. I could not make out what was wrong with me, I could not find the clue. Something was rising up, rising up continually in my soul, painfully, and refusing to be appeased. I returned home completely upset; it was just as though some crime were lying on my conscience.

The thought that Liza was coming worried me continually. It seemed queer to me that of all yesterday's memories, the memory of her tormented me as it were, particularly, quite separately, as it were. I had succeeded in forgetting everything else by evening time. I dismissed it all and was still perfectly satisfied with my letter to Simonov. But on this point I was not satisfied at all. It was as though I were worried only by Liza. "What if she comes," I thought incessantly. "Well, so what, it's all right, let her come! H'm! it's horrid that she should see how I live for instance. Yesterday I seemed such a—hero to her, while now, H'm! It's horrid, though, that I have let myself sink so low, the room looks like a beggar's. And I brought myself to go out to dinner in such a suit! And my oilcloth sofa with the stuffing sticking out. And my robe, which will not cover me! What tatters. And she will see all this and she will see Apollon. That beast is certain to insult her. He will fasten upon her in order to be rude to me. And I, of course, will be panic-stricken as usual. I will begin to bow and scrape before her and to pull my robe around me, I will begin to smile, to lie. Oh, how foul! And it isn't the foulness of it that matters most! There is something more important, more loathsome, viler! Yes, viler! And to put on that dishonest lying mask again!"

When I reached that thought I flared up all at once.

"Why dishonest? How dishonest? I was speaking sincerely last night. I remember there was real feeling in me, too. What I wanted was to awake noble feelings in her. Her crying was a good thing, it will have a good effect."

Yet I could not feel at ease.

All that evening, even when I had come back home, even after nine o'clock, when I calculated that Liza could not possibly come, she still haunted me, and what was worse, she always came back to my mind in the same position. One moment out of all that had happened last night presented itself before me vividly: the moment when I struck a match and saw her pale, distorted face, with its tortured look. And what a pitiful, what an unnatural, what a distorted smile she had at that moment! But I did not know then that even fifteen years later I would still always picture Liza to myself with that pitiful, distorted, inappropriate smile which was on her face at that minute.

Next day I was ready again to look upon it all as nonsense, due to over-excited nerves, and, above all, as *exaggerated.* I always recognized that as a weak point of mine, and was sometimes very much afraid of it. "I exaggerate everything, that is where I go wrong," I repeated to myself every hour. But, nevertheless, Liza will very likely come still, nevertheless, was the refrain with which all my reflections ended then. I was so uneasy that I sometimes flew into a fury. "She'll come, she is certain to come!" I cried, running about the room, "if not today, she will come tomorrow; she'll seek me out! The damnable romanticism of these *pure hearts!* Oh, the vileness—oh, the silliness—oh, the stupidity of these 'wretched sentimental souls'! Why, how could one fail to understand? How could one possibly fail to understand?"

But at this point I stopped short, and even in great confusion.

"And how few, how few words," I thought, in passing, "were needed; how little of the idyllic (and affectedly, bookishly, artificially idyllic too) had sufficed to turn a whole human life at once according to my will. That's innocence for you! That's virgin soil for you!"

At times the thought occurred to me to go to her, "to tell her all" and beg her not to come to me. But this thought stirred such wrath in me that I believed I would have crushed that "damned" Liza if she had happened to be near me at the time. I would have insulted her, have spat at her, have turned her out, have struck her!

One day passed, however, a second and a third; she did not come and I began to grow calmer, I felt particularly bold and cheerful after nine o'clock, I even began sometimes to dream, and rather sweetly: I, for instance, became the salvation of Liza, simply through her coming to me and my talking to her. I develop her, educate her. Finally, I notice that she loves me, loves me passionately. I pretend not to understand (I don't know, however, why I pretend, just for effect, perhaps). At last all confusion, beautiful, trembling and sobbing, she flings herself at my feet and tells me that I am her savior, and that she loves me better than anything in the world. I am amazed, but—"Liza," I say, "can you really believe that I have noticed your love? I saw it all, I divined it, but I did not dare to approach you first, because I had an influence over you and was afraid that you would force yourself, out of gratitude, to respond to my love, would try to rouse in your heart a feeling which was perhaps absent, and I did not wish that because it would be—tyranny. It would be indelicate (in short, I launch off at that point into European, inexplicably lofty subtleties, *à la* George Sand),[9] but now, now you are mine, you are my creation, you are pure, you are beautiful, you are my beautiful wife.

> And into my house come bold and free,
> Its rightful mistress there to be.[1]

Then we begin to live together happily, go abroad, etc., etc. In short, in the end it seemed vulgar to me myself, and I began to put out my tongue at myself.

Besides, they won't let her out, "the hussy!" I thought. After all, they don't let them go out very readily, especially in the evening (for some reason I fancied she would have to come in the evening, and precisely at seven o'clock). Though she did say she was not altogether a slave there yet, and had certain rights; so, h'm! Damn it all, she will come, she is sure to come!

It was a good thing, in fact, that Apollon distracted my attention at that time by his rudeness. He drove me beyond all patience! He was the bane of my life, the curse laid upon me by Providence. We had been squabbling continually for years, and I hated him. My God, how I hated him! I believe I had never hated anyone in my life as I hated him, especially at some moments. He was an elderly, dignified man, who worked part of his time as a tailor. But for some unknown reason, he despised me beyond all measure, and looked down upon me insufferably. Though indeed, he looked down upon everyone. Simply to glance at that flaxen, smoothly brushed head, at the tuft of hair he combed up on his forehead and oiled with sunflower oil, at that dignified mouth, always pursed, made one feel one was confronting a man who never doubted himself. He was an insufferable pedant, the greatest pedant I had met on earth, and with that had a vanity only befitting Alexander the Great. He was in love

9. George Sand (1804–1876), French woman writer concerned with the liberation of women.

1. These are the concluding lines of the poem by Nekrasov that opens this section (page 2251).

with every button on his coat, every nail on his fingers—absolutely in love with them, and he looked it! In his behavior to me he was an absolute tyrant, spoke very little to me, and if he chanced to glance at me he gave me a firm, majestically self-confident and invariably ironical look that sometimes drove me to fury. He did his work with the air of doing me the greatest favor. Though he did scarcely anything for me, and did not, indeed, consider himself obliged to do anything, there could be no doubt that he looked upon me as the greatest fool on earth, and that the reason he did not "get rid of me" was simply that he could get wages from me every month. He consented "to do nothing" for me for seven roubles a month. Many sins should be forgiven me for what I suffered from him. My hatred reached such a point that sometimes his very walk almost threw me into convulsions. What I loathed particularly was his lisp. His tongue must have been a little too long or something of that sort, for he continually lisped, and seemed to be very proud of it, imagining that it greatly added to his dignity. He spoke in a slow, measured tone, with his hands behind his back and his eyes fixed on the ground. He maddened me particularly when he read the Psalms aloud to himself behind his partition. I waged many a battle over that reading! But he was awfully fond of reading aloud in the evenings, in a slow, even, chanting voice, as though over the dead. It is interesting that he has ended up that way. He hires himself out to read the Psalms over the dead, and at the same time he kills rats and makes shoe polish. But at that time I could not get rid of him, it was as though he were chemically combined with my existence. Besides, nothing would have induced him to consent to leave me. I could not live in a furnished room: my apartment was my privacy, my shell, my cave, in which I concealed myself from all mankind, and Apollon seemed to me, God only knows why, an integral part of that apartment, and for seven whole years I could not get rid of him.

For example, to be two or three days late with his wages was impossible. He would have made such a fuss, I would not have known where to hide my head. But I was so exasperated with everyone during that period, that I made up my mind for some reason and with some object to *punish* Apollon and not to pay him for a fortnight the wages I owed him. I had intended to do this for a long time, for the last two years, simply in order to teach him not to give himself airs with me, and to show him that if I liked I could withhold his wages. I decided to say nothing to him about it, and even to be silent purposely in order to conquer his pride and force him to be the first to speak of his wages. Then I would take the seven roubles out of a drawer, show him I have the money and have put it aside purposely, but that I don't want, I don't want, I simply don't want to pay him his wages, I don't want to just because that is *what I want,* because "I am master and it is for me to decide," because he has been disrespectful, because he is a ruffian; but if he were to ask respectfully I might be softened and give it to him, otherwise he might wait another fortnight, another three weeks, a whole month . . .

But no matter how angry I was, he always got the better of me. I could not even hold out for four days. He began as he always did begin such cases, for there had been such cases already, there had been attempts (and it may be observed I knew all this beforehand, I knew his nasty tactics by heart), to wit: he would begin by fixing upon me an exceedingly severe stare, keeping it up for several minutes at a time, particularly on meeting me or seeing me out of the house. If I held out and pretended not to notice these stares, he would, still in silence, proceed to further tortures. All at once, for no reason at all, he would softly and smoothly walk into my room when I was pacing up and down, or reading, stand at the door, one hand behind his back and one foot forward, and fix upon me a stare more than severe, utterly contemptuous. If I suddenly asked him what he wanted, he would not answer, but continue to stare at me persistently for some seconds longer, then, with a peculiar compression of his lips and a very significant air, deliberately turn round and deliberately go back to his room. Two hours later he would come out again and again present himself before me in the same way. It has happened that in my fury I did not even ask him what he wanted, but simply raised my head sharply and imperiously and began staring back at him. So we stared at one another for two minutes; at last he turned with deliberation and dignity and went back again for two hours.

If I were still not brought to reason by all this, but persisted in my revolt, he would suddenly begin sighing while he looked at me, long, deep sighs as though measuring by them the depths of my moral degradation, and, of course, it ended at last by his triumphing completely: I raged and shouted, but was still forced to do what he wanted.

This time the usual maneuvers of "severe staring" had scarcely begun when I lost my temper and flew at him in a fury. I was irritated beyond endurance even without him.

"Wait," I shouted in a frenzy, as he was slowly and silently turning with one hand behind his back, to go to his room. "Wait! Come back, come back, I tell you!" and I must have bawled so unnaturally, that he turned round and even looked at me with a certain amazement. However, he persisted in saying nothing, and that infuriated me.

"How dare you come and look at me like that without being sent for? Answer!"

After looking at me calmly for half a minute, he began turning round again.

"Wait!" I roared, running up to him. "Don't stir! There. Answer, now: what did you come in to look at?"

"If you have any order to give me at the moment, it is my duty to carry it out," he answered, after another silent pause, with a slow, measured lisp, raising his eyebrows and calmly twisting his head from one side to another, all this with exasperating composure.

"That's not it, that is not what I am asking you about, you torturer!" I shouted, shaking with anger. "I'll tell you myself, you torturer, why you came here: you see, I don't give you your wages, you are so proud you don't want to bow down and ask for it, and so you have come to punish me with your stupid stares, to torture me, and you have no suspicion, you torturer, how stupid it is—stupid, stupid, stupid, stupid!"

He would have turned round again without a word, but I seized him.

"Listen," I shouted to him. "Here's the money, do you see, here it is" (I took it out of the table drawer) "here's the whole seven roubles but you are not going to have it, you . . . are . . . not . . . going . . . to . . . have it until you come respectfully with bowed head to beg my pardon. Do you hear?"

"That cannot be," he answered, with the most unnatural self-confidence.

"It will be so," I said. "I give you my word of honor, it will be!"

"And there's nothing for me to beg your pardon for," he went on, as though he had not noticed my exclamations at all. "Why, besides, you called me a 'torturer,' for which I can summon you at the police station at any time for insulting behavior."

"Go, summon me," I roared, "go at once, this very minute, this very second! You are a torturer all the same! A torturer! A torturer!" But he merely looked at me, then turned, and regardless of my loud calls to him, he walked to his room with an even step and without looking round.

"If it had not been for Liza nothing of this would have happened," I decided inwardly. Then, after waiting a minute, I myself went behind the screen with a dignified and solemn air, though my heart was beating slowly and violently.

"Apollon," I said quietly and emphatically, though I was breathless, "go at once without a minute's delay and fetch the police officer."

He had meanwhile settled himself at his table, put on his spectacles and taken up something to tailor. But, hearing my order, he burst into a guffaw.

"At once, go this minute! Go on, or else you can't imagine what will happen."

"You are certainly not in your right mind," he observed, without even raising his head, lisping as deliberately as ever and threading his needle. "Whoever heard of a man sending for the police against himself? And as for being frightened—you are upsetting yourself about nothing, for nothing will come of it."

"Go!" I shrieked, grabbing him by the shoulder. I felt that in another minute I would hit him.

But I did not notice that suddenly the door from the passage softly and slowly opened at that instant and a figure came in, stopped short, and began staring at us in amazement. I glanced, nearly died with shame, and rushed back to my room. There, clutching at my hair with both hands, I leaned my head against the wall and stood motionless in that position.

Two minutes later I heard Apollon's deliberate footsteps.

"There is *some woman* asking for you," he said, looking at me with peculiar severity. Then he stood aside and let in—Liza. He would not go away, but stared at us sarcastically.

"Go away, go away," I commanded in desperation. At that moment my clock began whirring and wheezing and struck seven.

IX

And into my house come bold and free,
Its rightful mistress there to be.

From the same poetic work

I stood before her crushed, crestfallen, revoltingly embarrassed, and I believe I smiled as I did my utmost to wrap myself in the skirts of my ragged wadded robe—just exactly as I had imagined the scene not long before in a fit of depression. After standing over us for a couple of minutes Apollon went away, but that did not make me more comfortable. What made it worse was that suddenly, she, too, became embarrassed, more so, in fact, than I would have expected. At the sight of me, of course.

"Sit down," I said mechanically, moving a chair up to the table, and I sat down on the sofa. She obediently sat down at once and gazed at me open-eyed, evidently expecting something from me at once. This naïveté of expectation drove me to fury, but I restrained myself.

She ought to have tried not to notice, as though everything had been as usual, while instead she . . . and I dimly felt that I would make her pay dearly for *all this.*

"You have found me in a strange position, Liza," I began, stammering and knowing that this was the wrong way to begin.

"No, no, don't imagine anything," I cried, seeing that she had suddenly flushed. "I am not ashamed of my poverty. On the contrary, I look on my poverty with pride. I am poor but honorable. One can be poor and honorable," I muttered. "However—would you like tea?"

"No—" she was beginning.

"Wait a minute."

I leapt up and ran to Apollon. I had to get out of the room somehow.

"Apollon," I whispered in feverish haste, flinging down before him the seven roubles which had remained all the time in my clenched fist, "here are your wages. You see I give them to you; but for that you must come to my rescue: bring me tea and a dozen rusks from the restaurant. If you won't go, you'll make a man miserable! You don't know what this woman is. This is—everything! You may be imagining something, but you don't know what a woman she is!"

Apollon, who had already sat down to his work and put on his spectacles again, at first glanced askance at the money without speaking or putting down his needle; then, without paying the slightest attention to me, or making any answer, he went on busying himself with his needle, which he had not yet threaded. I waited before him for several minutes with my arms crossed *à la Napoleon.* My temples were moist with sweat. I was pale, I felt it. But, thank God, he must have been moved to pity, looking at me. Having threaded his needle, he deliberately got up from his seat, deliberately moved back his chair, deliberately took off his spectacles, deliberately counted the money, and finally asking me over his shoulder: "Shall I get a whole pot?" deliberately walked out of the room. As I was going back to Liza, the thought occurred to me on the way: shouldn't I run away just as I was in my robe, no matter where, and let come what may?

I sat down again. She looked at me uneasily. For some minutes we were silent.

"I will kill him," I shouted suddenly, striking the table with my fist so that the ink spurted out of the inkstand.

"What are you saying!" she cried, starting.

"I will kill him! kill him!" I shrieked, suddenly striking the table in absolute frenzy, and at the same time fully understanding how stupid it was to be in such a frenzy.

"You don't know, Liza, what that torturer is to me. He is my torturer. He has gone now to fetch some rusks; he—"

And suddenly I burst into tears. It was an hysterical attack. How ashamed I felt in the midst of my sobs; but still I could not restrain them.

She was frightened. "What is the matter? What is wrong?" she shrieked, fussing around me.

"Water, give me water, over there!" I muttered in a faint voice, though I was inwardly conscious that I could easily have done without water and without muttering in a faint voice. But I was what is called *putting it on,* to save appearances, though the attack was a genuine one.

She gave me water, looking at me in bewilderment. At that moment Apollon brought in the tea. It suddenly seemed to me that this commonplace and prosaic tea was terribly undignified and paltry after all that had happened, and I blushed. Liza even looked at Apollon with alarm. He went out without a glance at us.

"Liza, do you despise me?" I asked, looking at her fixedly, trembling with impatience to know what she was thinking.

She was embarrassed and did not know what to answer.

"Drink your tea," I said to her angrily. I was angry with myself, but, of course, it was she who would have to pay for it. A horrible spite against her suddenly surged up in my heart; I believe I could have killed her. To revenge myself on her I swore inwardly not to say a word to her all the time. "She is the cause of it all," I thought.

Our silence lasted for five minutes. The tea stood on the table; we did not touch it. I had got to the point of purposely refraining from beginning to drink in order to embarrass her further; it was awkward for her to begin alone. Several times she glanced at me with mournful perplexity. I was obstinately silent. I was, of course, myself the chief sufferer, because I was fully conscious of the disgusting meanness of my spiteful stupidity, and yet at the same time I absolutely could not restrain myself.

"I want to—get away—from there altogether," she began, to break the silence in some way, but, poor girl, that was just what she ought not to have spoken about at such a moment, stupid enough even without that to a man so stupid as I was. My heart positively ached with pity for her tactless and unnecessary straightforwardness. But something hideous at once stifled all compassion in me; it even provoked me to greater venom. Let the whole world go to pot. Another five minutes passed.

"Perhaps I am in your way?" she began timidly, hardly audibly, and was getting up.

But as soon as I saw this first impulse of wounded dignity I positively trembled with spite, and at once burst out.

"Why did you come to me, tell me that, please?" I began, gasping for breath and regardless of all logical connection in my words. I longed to have it all out at once, at one burst: I did not even trouble how to begin.

"Why did you come? Answer, answer," I cried, hardly knowing what I was doing. "I'll tell you, my good girl, why you came. You came because I talked *fine sentiments* to you then. So now you are soft as butter and longing for fine sentiments again. So you may as well know, know that I was laughing at you then. And I am laughing at you now. Why are you shuddering? Yes, I was laughing at you! I had been insulted just before, at dinner, by the fellows who came that evening before me. I came to you, meaning to thrash one of them, an officer; but I didn't succeed. I didn't find him; I had to avenge the insult on someone to get my own back again; you turned up, I vented my spleen on you and laughed at you. I had been humiliated, so I wanted to humiliate; I had been treated like a rag, so I wanted to show my power. That's what it was, and you imagined I had come there on purpose to save you, didn't you? Did you imagine that? Did you imagine that?"

I knew that she would perhaps get muddled and not grasp all the details, but I knew, too, that she would grasp the gist of it very well. And so, indeed, she did. She turned white as a handkerchief, tried to say something, and distorted her mouth painfully but she sank on a chair as though she had been felled by an ax. And all the time afterward she listened to me with her lips parted and her eyes wide open, shuddering with awful terror. The cynicism, the cynicism of my words overwhelmed her—

"Save you!" I went on, jumping up from my chair and running up and down the room before her. "Save you from what? But perhaps I am worse than you myself. Why didn't you throw it in my teeth when I was giving you that sermon: 'But you, what did you come here for yourself? Was it to read us a sermon?' Power, power was what I wanted then, sport was what I wanted, I wanted to wring out your tears, your humiliation, your hysteria—that was what I wanted then! After all, I couldn't keep it up then, because I am a wretch, I was frightened, and the devil knows why, gave you my address in my folly. Afterward, before I got home, I was cursing and swearing at you because of that address. I hated you already because of the lies I had told you. Because I only like to play with words, to dream in my mind, but, do you know, what I really want is that you would all go to hell, that is what I want. I want peace; yes, I'd sell the whole world for a farthing right now, so long as I was left in peace. Is the world to go to pot, or am I to go without my tea? I say let the world go to pot as long as I get my tea every time. Did you know that, or not? Well, anyway, I know that I am a blackguard, a scoundrel, an egotist, a sluggard. Here I have been shuddering for the last three days at the thought of your coming. And do you know what has worried me particularly for these three days? That I posed as such a hero to you then, and now you would see me in a wretched torn robe, a beggar, an abomination. I told you just now that I was not ashamed of my poverty; you may as well know that I am ashamed of it; I am more ashamed of it than of anything, more afraid of it than of being found out if I were a thief, because I am as vain as though I had been skinned and the very air blowing on me hurt. Surely by now even you must have realized that I will never forgive you for having found me in this wretched robe, just as I was flying at Apollon like a spiteful sheep-dog at his lackey, and the lackey was jeering at him! And I shall never forgive you for the tears I could not help shedding before you just now, like some silly woman put to shame! And for what I am confessing to you now, I shall never forgive *you,* either! Yes—you must answer for it all because you turned up like this, because I am a blackguard, because I am the nastiest, stupidest, pettiest, absurdest and most envious of all worms on earth, none of whom is a bit better than I am, but who, the devil only knows why, are never embarrassed; while I will always be insulted by every louse, that is my doom! And what is it to me that you don't understand a word of this! And what do I care, what do I care about you, and whether you go to ruin there or not? Do you understand how I will hate you now after saying this, for having been here and listening? After all, a man speaks out like this once in a lifetime and then it is in hysterics! What more do you want? Why, after all, do you still stand there in front of me? Why do you torment me? Why don't you go?"

But at this point a strange thing happened.

I was so accustomed to think and imagine everything from books, and to picture everything in the world to myself just as I had made it up in my dreams beforehand, that I could not even take in this strange circumstance all at once. What happened was this: Liza, wounded and crushed by me, understood a great deal more than I imagined. She understood from all this what a woman understands first of all, if she feels genuine love, that is, that I was myself unhappy.

The frightened and wounded expression on her face was followed first by a look of sorrowful perplexity. When I began to call myself a scoundrel and a blackguard and my tears flowed (that tirade was accompanied throughout by tears) her whole face worked convulsively. She was on the point of getting up and stopping me; when I finished she took no notice of my shouting: "Why are you here, why don't you go away?" but realized only that it must have been very bitter to me to say all this. Besides, she was so crushed, poor girl; she considered herself infinitely beneath me; how could she feel anger or resentment? Suddenly she leapt up from her chair with an irresistible impulse and held out her hands, yearning toward me, though still timid and not daring to stir. At this point there was an upheaval in my heart too. Then she suddenly rushed to me, threw her arms round me and burst into tears. I, too, could not restrain myself, and sobbed as I never had before.

"They won't let me—I can't be—good!" I managed to say, then I went to the sofa, fell on it, face downward, and sobbed on it for a quarter of an hour in genuine hysterics. She knelt near me, put her arms round me and stayed motionless in that position.

But the trouble was that the hysterics could not go on for ever. And (after all, I am writing the loathsome truth) lying face downward on the sofa with my face thrust into my nasty leather pillow, I began by degrees to be aware of a far-away, involuntary but irresistible feeling that after all it would be awkward for me to raise my head now and look Liza straight in the face. Why was I ashamed? I don't know, but I was ashamed. In my overwrought brain the thought also occurred that our parts were after all completely reversed now, that she was now the heroine, while I was just a crushed and humiliated creature as she had been before me that night—four days before . . . And all this came into my mind during the minutes I was lying face down on the sofa!

My God! surely I was not envious of her then?

I don't know, to this day I cannot decide, and at the time, of course, I was still less able to understand what I was feeling than now. I cannot get on without domineering and tyrannizing over someone, after all, but—but, after all, there is no explaining anything by reasoning and consequently it is useless to reason.

I conquered myself, however, and raised my head—I had to do so sooner or later—and I am convinced to this day that it was just because I was ashamed to look at her that another feeling was suddenly kindled and flamed up in my heart—a feeling of mastery and possession. My eyes gleamed with passion, and I gripped her hands tightly. How I hated her and how I was drawn to her at that minute! The one feeling intensified the other. It was almost like an act of vengeance! At first there was a look of amazement, even of terror, on her face, but only for one instant. She warmly and rapturously embraced me.

X

A quarter of an hour later I was rushing up and down the room in frenzied impatience, from minute to minute I went up to the screen and peeped through the crack at Liza. She was sitting on the floor with her head leaning against the bed, and must have been crying. But she did not go away, and that irritated me. This time she understood it all. I had insulted her once and for all, but—there's no need to describe it. She realized that my outburst of passion had been simply revenge, a new humiliation for her and that to my earlier, almost generalized hatred was added now a *personal, envious* hatred—though I do not maintain positively that she understood all this distinctly; but she certainly did fully understand that I was a despicable man, and what was worse, incapable of loving her.

I know I shall be told that this is incredible; that it is incredible to be as spiteful and stupid as I was; it may be added it was strange that I would not love her, or at any rate, appreciate her love. Why is it strange? In the first place, by then I was incapable of love, for, I repeat, with me loving meant tyrannizing and showing my moral superiority. I have never in my life ever been able to imagine any other sort of love, and have nowadays come to the point of sometimes thinking that love really consists in the right—freely given by the beloved object—to be tyrannized over. Even in my underground dreams I did not imagine love in any form except as a struggle. I always began it with hatred and ended it with moral subjugation, and afterward I could never imagine what to do with the subjugated object. And what is there incredible in that, since I had so succeeded in corrupting myself morally, since I was so out of touch with "real life," that I had just thought of reproaching her and putting her to shame for having come to me to hear "fine sentiments," and I did not even guess that she had come not at all to hear fine sentiments, but to love me, because to a woman true resurrection, true salvation from any sort of ruin, and true moral regeneration is contained in love and can only show itself in that form. I no longer hated her so much, however, when I was running about the room and peeping through the crack in the screen. I was only insufferably oppressed by her being here. I wanted her to disappear. I wanted "peace," I wanted to be left alone in my underground world. "Real life" oppressed me with its novelty so much that I could hardly breathe.

But several minutes passed and she still remained without stirring, as though she were unconscious. I had the shamelessness to tap softly at the screen as though to remind her. She started, sprang up, and flew to seek her shawl, her hat, her coat, just as though she were making her escape from me. Two minutes later she came from behind the screen and looked with heavy eyes at me. I gave a spiteful grin, which was forced, however, to *keep up appearances,* and I turned away from her look.

"Good-by," she said, going toward the door.

I ran up to her, seized her hand, opened it, thrust something in it—and closed it again. Then I turned immediately and hurriedly rushed to the other corner of the room, to avoid seeing, anyway—

I meant to lie a moment ago—to write that I did this accidentally, not knowing what I was doing, through foolishness, through losing my head. But I don't want to lie, and so I will say straight out that I opened her hand and put the money in it—from spite. It came into my head to do so while I was running up and down the room and she was sitting behind the screen. But I can say this for certain: though I did that cruel thing purposely, it was not an impulse from the heart, but came from my evil brain. This cruelty was so affected, so purposely made up, so completely a product of the brain, of *books,* that I could not even keep it up for a minute—first I rushed to the corner to avoid seeing her, and then in shame and despair rushed after Liza. I opened the door in the passage and began listening.

"Liza! Liza!" I cried on the stairs, but in a low voice, not boldly.

There was no answer, but it seemed to me I heard her footsteps, lower down on the stairs.

"Liza!" I cried, more loudly.

No answer. But at that minute I heard the stiff outer glass door open heavily with a creak and slam violently. The roar echoed up the stairs.

She had gone. I went back to my room in hesitation. I felt horribly oppressed.

I stood still at the table beside the chair on which she had sat and looked aimlessly before me. A minute passed. Suddenly I started; straight before me on the table I saw—in short, I saw a crumpled blue five-rouble note, the one I had thrust into her hand a minute before. It was the same note; it could be no other, there was no other in the apartment. So she had managed to fling it from her hand on the table at the moment when I had rushed into the farther corner.

So what? I might have expected that she would do that. Might I have expected it? No, I was such an egotist, I was so lacking in respect for people in actuality, that I could not even imagine she would do so. I could not endure it. A moment later I flew like a madman to get dressed, flinging on what I could at random and ran headlong after her. She could not have got two hundred paces away when I ran out into the street.

It was a still night and the snow was coming down in masses and falling almost perpendicularly, blanketing the pavement and the empty street. There was no one in the street, no sound was to be heard. The street lamps gave a disconsolate and useless glimmer. I ran two hundred paces to the intersection and stopped short. Where had she gone? And why was I running after her?

Why? To fall down before her, to sob with remorse, to kiss her feet, to beg her forgiveness! I longed for that. My whole heart was being rent to pieces, and never, never will I recall that minute with indifference. But—what for? I thought. Would I not begin to hate her, perhaps, even tomorrow, just because I had kissed her feet today? Would I give her happiness? Had I not again recognized that day, for the hundredth time, what I was worth? Would I not torment her?

I stood in the snow, gazing into the troubled darkness and pondered this.

"And will it not be better? *Will it not be better?*" I fantasied afterward at home, stifling the living pang of my heart with fantastic dreams. "Will it not be better that she carry the outrage with her forever? Outrage—why, after all, that is purification: it is the most stinging and painful consciousness! Tomorrow I would have defiled her soul and have exhausted her heart, while now the feeling of humiliation will never die in her, and however loathsome the filth awaiting her, that outrage will elevate and purify her—by hatred—h'm!—perhaps by forgiveness also. But will all that make things easier for her, though? . . ."

And, indeed, I will at this point ask an idle question on my own account: which is better—cheap happiness or exalted sufferings? Well, which is better?

So I dreamed as I sat at home that evening, almost dead with the pain in my soul. Never yet had I endured such suffering and remorse, but could there possibly have been the faintest doubt when I ran out from my lodging that I would turn back halfway? I never met Liza again and I have heard nothing about her. I will add, too, that for a long time afterward I remained pleased with the *phrase* about the utility of outrage and hatred, in spite of the fact that I almost fell ill from misery.

Even now, many years later, I somehow remember all this as very bad. I have many bad memories now, but—hadn't I better end my "Notes" here? I believe I made a mistake in beginning to write this *story;* so it's hardly literature so much as corrective punishment. After all, to tell long stories, for example, showing how I have ruined my life by morally rotting in my corner, through lack of fitting environment, through divorce from reality, and vainglorious spite in my underground world, would certainly not be interesting; a novel needs a hero, and all the traits of an anti-hero are *expressly* gathered together here, and what matters most, it all produces an unpleasant impression, for we are all divorced from life, we are all cripples, every one of us, more or less. We are so far divorced from it that we immediately feel a sort of loathing for actual "real life," and so cannot even stand to be reminded of it. After all, we have reached the point of almost looking at actual "real life" as an effort, almost as hard work, and we are all privately agreed that it is better in books. And why do we sometimes fret, why are we perverse and ask for something else? We don't know why ourselves. It would be worse for us if our capricious requests were granted. Come, try, come give anyone of us, for instance, a little more independence, untie our hands, widen the spheres of our activity, relax the controls and we—yes, I assure you—we would immediately beg to be under control again. I know that you will very likely be angry with me for that, and will begin to shout and stamp your feet. "Speak for yourself," you will say, "and for your miseries in your underground holes, but don't dare to say 'all of us.'" Excuse me, gentlemen, after all I do not mean to justify myself with that "all of us." As for what concerns me in particular I have only, after all, in my life carried to an extreme what you have not dared to carry halfway, and what's more, you have taken your cowardice for good sense, and have found comfort in deceiving yourselves. So that perhaps, after all, there is more "life" in me than in you. Look into it more carefully! After all, we don't even know where living exists now, what it is, and what it is called! Leave us alone without books and we will be lost and in a confusion at once—we will not know what to join, what to cling to, what to love and what to hate, what to respect and what to despise. We are even oppressed by being men—men with real *individual* body and blood. We are ashamed of it, we think it a disgrace and try to contrive to be some sort of impossible generalized man. We are still-born, and for many years we have not been begotten by living fathers, and that suits us better and better. We are developing a taste for it. Soon we shall somehow contrive to be born from an idea. But enough; I don't want to write more from "underground" . . .

The "notes" of this paradoxalist do not end here, however. He could not resist and continued them. But it also seems to me that we may stop here.

RESONANCES

Friedrich Nietzsche: from *Daybreak*[1]

In this book you will discover a "subterranean man" at work, one who tunnels and mines and undermines. You will see him—presupposing you have eyes capable of seeing this work in the depths—going forward slowly, cautiously, gently inexorable, without betraying very much of the distress which any protracted deprivation of light and air must entail; you might even call him contented, working there in the dark. Does it not seem as though some faith were leading him on, some consolation offering him compensation? As though he perhaps desires this prolonged obscurity, desires to be incomprehensible, concealed, enigmatic, because he knows what he will thereby also acquire: his own morning, his own redemption, his own *daybreak?* . . . He will return, that is certain: do not ask him what he is looking for down there, he will tell you himself of his own accord; this seeming Trophonius[2] and subterranean, as soon as he has 'become a man' again. Being silent is something one completely unlearns if, like him, one has been for so long a solitary mole———

And indeed, my patient friends, I shall now tell you what I was after down there—here in this late preface which could easily have become a funeral oration: for I have returned and, believe it or not, returned safe and sound. Do not think for a moment that I intend to invite you to the same hazardous enterprise! Or even only to the same solitude! For he who proceeds on his own path in this fashion encounters no one: that is inherent in "proceeding on one's own path." No one comes along to help him: all the perils, accidents, malice and bad weather which assail him he has to tackle by himself. For his path is *his alone*—as is, of course, the bitterness and occasional ill-humour he feels at this "his alone": among which is included, for instance, the knowledge that

1. Translated by R. J. Hollingdale. Whereas Dostoevsky wrote highly philosophical novels, the radically skeptical German philosopher Friedrich Nietzsche (1844–1900) wrote philosophy with a novelist's eye and a poet's ear. He shared Dostoevsky's sense of estrangement from the optimistic rationalism of the bourgeois society around him, though unlike Dostoevsky he was deeply opposed to the "slave morality" of Christianity, as he described it. After a brief early career as a professor of philology, he lived in seclusion in Switzerland, Italy, and the south of France, writing searching analyses of morality, rationality, and language, including *Beyond Good and Evil* and *The Genealogy of Morals.* He pays direct tribute to Dostoevsky in the preface to his 1881 collection *Daybreak,* a shifting blend of aphorisms and philosophical mediations by a philosopher turned underground man.

2. In Greek myth, an oracle consulted by descending into a chasm.

even his friends are unable to divine where he is or whither he is going, that they will sometimes ask themselves: "what? is he going at all? does he still have—a path?"— At that time I undertook something not everyone may undertake: I descended into the depths, I tunnelled into the foundations, I commenced an investigation and digging out of an ancient *faith,* one upon which we philosophers have for a couple of millennia been accustomed to build as if upon the firmest of all foundations—and have continued to do so even though every building hitherto erected on them has fallen down: I commenced to undermine our *faith in morality.* But you do not understand me?

* * *

Do not forget!—The higher we soar, the smaller we seem to those who cannot fly.

We aeronauts of the spirit!—All those brave birds which fly out into the distance, into the farthest distance—it is certain! somewhere or other they will be unable to go on and will perch on a mast or a bare cliff-face—and they will even be thankful for this miserable accommodation! But who could venture to infer from that, that there was *not* an immense open space before them, that they had flown as far as one *could* fly! All our great teachers and predecessors have at last come to a stop and it is not with the noblest or most graceful of gestures that weariness comes to a stop: it will be the same with you and me! But what does that matter to you and me! *Other birds will fly farther!* This insight and faith of ours vies with them in flying up and away; it rises above our heads and above our impotence into the heights and from there surveys the distance and sees before it the flocks of birds which, far stronger than we, still strive whither we have striven, and where everything is still sea, sea, sea![3]—And whither then would we go? Would we *cross* the sea? Whither does this mighty longing draw us, this longing that is worth more to us than any pleasure? Why just in this direction, thither where all the suns of humanity have hitherto *gone down?* Will it perhaps be said of us one day that we too, *steering westward, hoped to reach an India*—but that it was our fate to be wrecked against infinity? Or, my brothers. Or?—

Ishikawa Takuboku: from *The Romaji Diary*[1]

7th April 1909

This morning a violent west wind was roaring through the sky. The windows on the third floor were all rattling, and a dustlike sand from the street below came blowing in the cracks. But in spite of the wind the scattered clouds were motionless.

A springlike sunshine was warming the windowpanes. It was the sort of day when you might be sweating if it weren't for the wind. The old man from the lending

3. "Still sea," *noch Meer* in German, plays on the striving to have *noch mehr*—still more.

1. Translated by Donald Keene. Born in 1885 on the island of Hokkaido, in the far north of Japan, Ishikawa Takuboku had set his sights on becoming a poet and novelist. Married and with a young daughter, he left them at home when he came to Tokyo hoping to establish himself. He rented a room and found a low-paying job as a newspaper proofreader, unable to afford to bring his family to join him. In the spring of 1909, consumed with self-doubt, he kept a secret diary from April to June, writing it in Japanese but using "romaji"—the Roman alphabet—so that his family wouldn't be able to read it. The diary records his sharp, ironic observations of life in late Meiji Tokyo, his ambitions, and his despair for the future. A real-life "underground man," Ishikawa was in fact reading widely in Russian literature at the time he wrote this diary. In 1910 he published a volume of experimental poetry, *A Handful of Sand,* and brought his family to Tokyo. All three contracted tuberculosis; Takuboku died of it in 1912.

library came in, wiping his nose with the palm of his hand. "Terrible wind," said he. "Still, the cherry blossoms all over Tokyo will be opening today. Wind or no wind, it's fine weather."

"Spring has come at last," I said, but of course he couldn't understand my feelings. "Eh! Eh!" answered the old man, "Spring, you know, is a loss as far as we're concerned. Lending books is finished for the season. All my customers would rather go out for a walk than read a book, and I can't say I blame them. The few people who do read books naturally take their time over it."

There is a five-yen bill in my wallet, the remains of what I borrowed yesterday of next month's pay from the company. All morning long I couldn't think about anything else. It must be the way people who normally have money feel when they are suddenly deprived of it. Both situations are funny, but though they're funny in quite the same way, there's a big difference in the happiness or grief involved!

Having nothing else to do, I tried to make a table of Romaji. From time to time the memory of my mother and my wife in Hokkaido leapt out of the middle of the table and took possession of me. "Spring has come. It's April! Spring! Spring! The blossoms are opening! It's already a year since I came to Tokyo . . . ! And still I haven't been able to make any arrangements to send for my family." That's the problem that keeps tormenting me, I don't know how many times a day.

Why did I decide to keep this diary in Romaji? Why? I love my wife, and it's precisely because I love her that I don't want her to read this diary. No, that's a lie! It's true that I love her, and it's true that I don't want her to read this, but the two facts are not necessarily related.

Am I a weakling then? No, my trouble comes entirely from the mistaken institution of marriage. Marriage! What an idiotic institution! What's to be done about it?

Today the members of the tennis team from Kyoto University, who are staying in the next room, are having their last day of play. They went off in high spirits.

After eating lunch I went by streetcar as usual to the office, where I corrected proofs with the old men in a corner of the editorial room. About five o'clock in the evening the proofs for the first edition were finished and I went back home: this is my daily stint to earn a living.

On the way back I walked along a street in Hongō, intending to do a little shopping. The cherry trees of the university campus had half-opened their blossoms in just one day.

The world is now completely given over to the spring.

The sound of the footsteps of the people going back and forth crowding the streets somehow exhilarated me. I couldn't help wondering where they had so suddenly appeared from, those beautiful people in beautiful clothes who were streaming by. It's spring, I thought. Then I thought of my wife and little Kyōko.

I had promised myself that I would send for them by April and I haven't—no, I can't.

Oh, my writing is my enemy, and my philosophy nothing but empty logic that I myself ridicule. I seem to desire so many things, but don't they boil down to one small one? Money!

When I got back after ten tonight there was a tremendous racket in the next room. One of the tennis players, having returned drunk from a dinner given in their honor, had smashed the light and was breaking up the frames of the sliding doors.

I met one of the students at the entrance to his room. He was a classmate of mine in high school and is now studying engineering in Kyoto. We carried on a childish conversation until about one in the morning. In the meantime the uproar in the next room had subsided. The spring night deepened, the night of a day which had opened the blossoms all over the city.

In the midst of a city quiet in sleep, I lay awake alone, and, counting the breaths of the calm spring night, I felt how dull and meaningless my life in this little room has been. What must I look like sleeping here all alone in this tiny room, overcome by an indescribable fatigue? The final discovery of human beings must be that the human being itself is not of the slightest importance.

I have lived a long time—over two hundred days—in this little room, filled with heavy uneasiness, and with the shallow hope that I may find something to interest me. How long will it last . . .? No!

I read in bed the *Collected Stories of Turgenev*.[2]

* * *

9th, Friday

The cherry blossoms are almost in full bloom: it is a warm, calm, perfectly springlike day; the sky in the distance is veiled in mist.

On the tram going back this evening I saw a child who looked just as Kyōko did when I parted from her last spring. She was making a squeak with a toy flute, and as she did so she looked at me bashfully, hiding her laughing face. She was so adorable I felt like taking her in my arms.

The face of the child's mother looked the way I imagine my mother's did when she was young. The nose, the cheeks, the eyes—the whole face was like hers. It wasn't a very refined face!

It is a spring evening sweet as milk. In the distance a frog is croaking. The first frog of the year!

10th, Saturday

Last night I read until past three, and I got up today after ten. A wind from the south is blowing in the clear sky.

The fact that recent short stories have come to be no more than a kind of new form of sketches from life—no—the fact that we have stopped wanting to read them—in other words, the fact that we are dissatisfied with them—shows that the authority of Naturalistic philosophy as a view of life is gradually dying out.

How times change! It cannot be denied that Naturalism[3] was the philosophy we sought out with the greatest eagerness. But before we knew it we had discovered the logical contradictions in it. Then when we had surmounted these contradictions and moved forward, the sword we held in our hands was no longer the sword of Naturalism. I for one am no longer able to content myself with an attitude of detachment. The attitude of the writer toward humanity cannot be one of detachment. He must be a critic. Or a planner for mankind.

The positive Naturalism I have reached is a new idealism. For a long time we despised the word "ideal." As a matter of fact, the kind of ideals we were then holding were, as we discovered, no more than pitiful illusions—no more than a *life illusion*. But we are alive and we must live. The ideal of destroying everything and then building

2. Ivan Turgenev (1818–1883), Russian writer of tragic, realistic tales, often focusing on the quandaries of Russian intellectuals in a stagnant society.
3. Aesthetic movement championed by Emile Zola and other 19th-century French novelists, who sought to depict social life with scientific detachment, often showing how individual choices and happiness are constrained by social forces.

anew with our own hands is no longer just a pitiful illusion. Even if the ideal itself is just a *life illusion,* we cannot live without it. If this deep internal need must also be discarded, there is nothing left for me to do but to die.

What I wrote this morning is a lie. At least in so far as I am concerned it is not a first principle. I do not consider that any human achievement, regardless of the field, is of consequence. I used to think that literature was more admirable and valuable than other things, but that was before I knew what "admirable" meant. Is it possible that anything done by a human being can be admirable? The human being itself is neither admirable nor valuable.

What I desire is peace of mind. I realized it this evening for the first time. Yes, it is exactly that, beyond any doubt.

I wonder what real assurance—the feeling that there is nothing to worry about—must be like. It has been such a long time since I experienced it—not since I became conscious of what was going on in the world—that I have forgotten.

Of late the most tranquil moments in my life have been the ones spent going back and forth to work on the streetcar. When I am at home doing nothing, I feel as if I should be doing something. But what? That's the problem. Read? Write? But there seems to be nothing to read or write. No, reading and writing are only a part of that "something." Is there anything else I can do besides read and write? That I don't know. But I feel, anyway, as though I should do something. Even when I am thinking of quite carefree things, I feel as if I am always being pursued by that "something." And as a result I can't seem to put my hand to anything.

At the office I wish the time would pass more quickly. It's not that there's anything I especially dislike about the work, or that the surroundings are disagreeable: when I return home early I am pursued by that feeling that I must do "something." I don't know what it is I should be doing, but I'm haunted by that compulsion.

* * *

Of late I have been tempted from time to time by the desire to go where there is no one else. A place with no one else—or at least where no voices are heard, where nothing can be heard which has the remotest connection with me, a place where there is no fear of anyone coming and looking at me—oh, I would like to go there all by myself for a week, ten days, no, even for a day, even for half a day.

I should like to rest my body as I please in a place where no matter what expression I have on my face, no matter what appearance I make, there is no fear of being noticed.

Sometimes, trying to forget this thought, I go to places where there are many people, like the motion pictures. And sometimes, on the other hand, I go when I feel a yearning for people—for young women. But I can't find any satisfaction there either. While I am watching the film, especially if it is the most stupid, childish kind, I do manage to return to the heart of a child, and I can forget everything; but as soon as the film is over and the lights flash on, and I see the countless swarming people, the desire to seek some gayer, more amusing place rises all the stronger within my breast. Sometimes I can smell right in front of my nose the fragrance of hair, or I can feel a warm hand in mine. But at such times my mind is calculating the contents of my pocketbook—or, rather, thinking of how to borrow some money! When I hold a warm hand or breathe the strong perfume of hair, I have the feeling not merely of holding a hand, but of taking in my arms a soft, warm, white body. And how lonely I feel when I return home without having done so! It is not just the loneliness that comes from having been unable to obtain sexual satisfaction: it is the deep terrible despair at not being able to get everything I want.

When I have had a little money I have without hesitation gone, filled with the voice of lust, to those narrow dirty streets.

Since last autumn I have gone thirteen or fourteen times, and I have bought about ten prostitutes. Mitsu, Masa, Kiyo, Mine, Tsuyu, Hana, Aki. . . . I have forgotten the names of some of them. What I sought was a warm, soft, white body: a pleasure in which my body and mind would melt. But those women, the old ones and the ones of fifteen who were still children, had all slept with hundreds or thousands of men.

There is no luster to their faces, their skin is cold and rough, they are so used to men that they feel no excitement. All it amounts to is that for a little while they hire out their private parts to men, and receive a pittance in exchange. Without even bothering to undo their sashes, they say "All right," and lie down just as they are, without the slightest embarrassment.

It doesn't make the least difference to them whether or not there is anyone on the other side of the partition who hears them. All it amounts to is that an excretory process has been effected with thousands of men. They have no desire to heal themselves with a pleasure in which the body and mind melt.

The nervous desire to seek strong excitement did not leave me even when I was receiving the excitement. I have spent the night three or four times.

It is no longer possible for me to go off somewhere all by myself, and yet I can obtain no satisfaction from people. I can't stand the agony of human life itself, but I can't do anything about it. Everything is in shackles, and there is heavy responsibility. What should I do? Hamlet said, *To be or not to be?* But in the present world the question of death has become more complicated than in Hamlet's time. Oh, Ilya![4] Ilya's plan was the greatest plan that any human being could conceive. He tried to escape from life, no, he did escape, and then with all his strength he rushed from life—from this life of ours—into a limitless path of darkness. He dashed out his brains against a stone wall.

Ilya was a bachelor. I always think: how lucky Ilya was to have been a bachelor! There's the difference between the unhappy Ilya and myself.

I am worn out now. And I am seeking peace of mind. What sort of thing is "peace of mind?" Where is it? I can't return to the blank mind I had long ago before I knew pain, not if a hundred years were to elapse. Where is peace of mind?

I want to be sick. For a long time this desire has been lurking in my head. Sick! This word that other people hate sounds as sweet to me as the name of the mountain where I was born. A free life, released from all responsibilities!

Sickness is the only way we have to obtain peace of mind.

* * *

11th, Sunday

Today I had to go to a poetry gathering at Yosano's house.[5] Naturally, there was no likelihood of anything amusing taking place. Hiraide was telling what a big success last night's "Devotees of Pan"[6] had been. Yoshii, who came in late, was saying, "Last

4. Suicidal hero of "The Three of Them," a story by the radical, working-class Russian writer Maxim Gorky (1868–1936).

5. Yosano Tekkan (1873–1935), a young experimental poet, as was his wife Akiko, mentioned below.

6. A literary club whose members sought to blend European and Japanese traditions.

night when I got drunk and pissed from Eitai Bridge, a policeman bawled me out." Everybody seems to have been drunk and had a wild time.

As usual we wrote poems on given themes. It must have been about nine o'clock when the selection of poems was completed. Recently I haven't felt like writing serious *uta,*[7] and as usual turned out some mock verses. Here are a couple:

When I wear shoes
That make a squeak
I feel unpleasant, as if
I tread upon a frog.

Your eyes must have
The mechanism of
A fountain pen—
You are always shedding tears.

The man
Whose hands tremble and voice breaks
At sight of a woman
No longer exists.

Akiko suggested that we sit up all night composing poetry. I made some silly excuse and left.

Another precious day wasted. Suddenly a feeling of regret surged up within me. If I was going to look at the cherry blossoms, why didn't I go by myself and look at them as I wanted? A poetry gathering! Of all the stupid things!

* * *

13th, Tuesday

Early this morning I opened my eyes, momentarily wakened by the noise of the maid opening the shutters. Hearing nothing else, I dozed off again, the unconscious sleep of spring. It is a cloudy calm day. All over the city the blossoms are gradually beginning to fall.

A sad letter came from my mother.

Dear Mr. Ishikawa,

I was so happy with the letter you sent to Mr. Miyazaki. I have been waiting every day since, hoping word would come from you, and now it is April already. I am taking care of Kyōko and feeding her, which I have never done before. She is getting bigger every day, and is almost too much for me. Can't you send for her? I beg the favor of a reply. On the sixth and seventh there was a terrible rainstorm. The rain leaked in and we had nowhere to stay. Kyōko was so upset she couldn't sleep. She caught a cold on the second of April and is still not better. Setsuko[8] leaves for work every morning at eight o'clock and doesn't return until five or six. It's so hard for me when she is not here. There's no more household money left. Even one yen will be appreciated. I beg you kindly to send something soon. When do you think we will be able to go to Tokyo? Please let me know. If we don't get an answer from you, it's all over with us. We are all coming, so please make preparations.

Katsu

7. Formal poems.

8. Takuboku's wife.

My mother's letter, in shaky characters, full of spelling mistakes! I don't suppose very many people besides myself could read it. They say Mother was the best student at school when she was a girl. But in forty years of married life with my father, she probably never once wrote a letter. The first one I received from her was two summers ago. I had left Mother alone in Shibutami. She couldn't stand that dreadful town any longer, and she had written out of loneliness, searching in her memory for the completely forgotten characters. Today was the fifth letter I have received since coming to Tokyo. There are fewer mistakes, and the characters are better formed. How sad—my mother's letter!

14th, Wednesday

I decided to take off today and tomorrow, and started a story. I'm calling it "The Wooden Horse."

Inspiration in writing seems to be something like sexual desire. The man from the lending library came today and offered me some "unusual" books. Somehow I wanted to read them, and I borrowed two. One is called *The Misty Night in the Blossoms,* the other *The Secrets of Love.* I wasted three hours copying out in Romaji *The Misty Night.*

At night Nakajima came here, together with a minor poet named Uchiyama. Uchiyama's nose has the most extraordinary shape! It looks as if a deformed sweet potato had been stuck in the middle of his face, with a few parings and flattenings here and there. An endless flow of chatter comes from him: he's like one of those unshaven beggars one sees clowning in the streets. On top of everything else, he is practically a midget. I have never seen anyone quite so pathetic-looking. A truly pitiful, farcical innocent—excessively so, perhaps: I felt a strange impulse to smash him in the face. Every serious utterance he makes sounds funny, and when he says something humorous with a sniff of his grotesque nose, he looks as if he is crying.

It started to rain a little before ten. Nakajima professes to be a Socialist, but his is a very aristocratic socialism—he left in a rickshaw. Uchiyama—the poet is a real Socialist—went home under a borrowed umbrella. He really looked a poet.

I wrote three pages of "The Wooden Horse." I longed for Setsuko—not because of the lonely patter of the rain, but because I had been reading *The Misty Night in the Blossoms.*

15th, Thursday

No! Does my need for Setsuko arise simply out of sexual desire? No! No!

My love for her has cooled. That is a fact, a not surprising fact—regrettable but inescapable.

Love is only a part, not the entirety of human life, a diversion, something like a song. Everyone wants at times to sing, and it is a pleasant thing to do. But man cannot spend his whole life in song, and to sing the same tune all the time, however joyous it may be, is sating.

My love has cooled; I am tired of singing that song—it's not that I dislike it. Setsuko is really a good woman. Is there in all the world another such good, gentle, sensible woman? I cannot imagine a better wife than Setsuko. Sometimes, even while I was actually sleeping with Setsuko, I have hungered for other women. But what has that to do with Setsuko? I was not dissatisfied with her. It is simply that men have complex desires.

I have not changed in my love for Setsuko. She was not the only woman I loved, but the one I loved most. Even now, especially during the last few days, I often think of her.

The present marriage system—the whole social system—is riddled with errors. Why must I be tied down because of parents, a wife, or a child? Why must they be victimized because of me? But that, naturally, is quite apart from the fact that I love my parents, Setsuko, and Kyōko.

16th, Friday

What an idiotic thing! Last night I stayed up until three copying in my notebook that pornographic old novel *The Misty Night in the Blossoms*. Ah, me!

I could not control my craving for that intense pleasure!

When I woke about ten this morning I felt a strange mental fatigue. I read the letter from Miyazaki.

Will they all please die, or must I? It's one or the other! I really thought that as I sat down to write an answer. I assured Miyazaki that I am now able to make a living, and said that all I need is the money to move from these lodgings, to rent a house, and to pay the traveling expenses for my family! When I finished writing, I wished I were dead.

I finally got off the one yen to my mother. Out of dislike for writing, out of fear, I have neglected to send it until today. I enclosed it in the letter to Miyazaki.

Tonight Kindaichi[9] came to my room. He talked about all kinds of things, hoping to stir up some literary inspiration in me. I didn't answer—instead, I indulged in a variety of absurd pranks which eventually drove Kindaichi away. I took up my pen immediately. Half an hour went by. I was obliged to give serious consideration again to my inability to write a novel and to the fact that my future is devoid of hope. I went to Kindaichi's room and performed my whole repertory of silly tricks. I painted a huge face on my chest and made all kinds of grimaces, whistled like a thrush, and, in conclusion, took out my knife and acted out the part of the murderer in a play. Kindaichi fled from the room! I certainly must have been thinking something horrible!

I had switched off the light in his room, and stood in the doorway brandishing my knife.

Later, back in my room, we looked at each other in dismay at what had happened. I thought that suicide could not frighten me.

Then, at night, what did I do? *Misty Night in the Blossoms!*

It is about two o'clock. Somewhere off beyond Koishigawa there is a fire, a single dull red line of smoke climbing perpendicularly into the black sky.

A fire!

17th, Saturday

I did not go to work today because I was sure I would be able to write—no, it was because I wanted to take the day off that I decided to write. I attempted to describe

9. A linguist and scholar of Japan's Ainu minority population, who was living in the room next to Takuboku's.

last night's thoughts about suicide. I wrote three pages and couldn't think of another line.

I tried to correct some poems, but just spreading out the paper was enough to make me sick.

I thought of writing a story about a man who is arrested by a policeman for sleeping in a vacant house, but couldn't find the energy to lift my pen.

I said to myself, "I positively will give up my literary career."

"If I give up literature, what shall I do?"

Death! That's the only answer.

Either I must have money or else be released from all responsibilities.

Probably this problem will haunt me until I die—I'll think about it in bed!

* * *

21st, Wednesday

The cherry trees are in full leaf. When I opened the window this morning, a smoky color of young leaves met my eyes. Yesterday I saw two people in summer hats. It's summer!

At nine o'clock I went to the public bath in Daimachi. I often used to go there when I first came to Tokyo last year. Nothing has changed, except that the seventeen-year-old girl-attendant, the one who seemed fond of me, is no longer there. I could see through the window the shadows of young leaves in the fresh morning sunlight. I returned to all my feelings of a year ago. Then the memory of the dreadful Tokyo summer came back with painful vividness, that summer I spent in lodgings. I was in terrible financial straits, but happy to be escaping even briefly the responsibility of providing for my family. Yes, I was enjoying the sensation of being a "semi-bachelor." I soon abandoned the woman with whom I was having an affair at the time. She's now a geisha in Asakusa. A great deal has changed. I have made a number of new friends and discarded them.

As I scrubbed my body, healthier than it was then, I lost myself in recollections—a year of terrible struggle! *The dreadful summer is coming again on me—the penniless novelist! The dreadful summer! alas! with great pains and deep sorrows of physical struggle, and, other young with the bottomless rapture of hand, Nihilist!*

As I come out of the gate of the bathhouse, the expressful faced woman who sold me the soap yesterday said to me "Good morning" with something calm and favourable gesture.

The bath and the memories bring me some hot and young lightness. I am young, and, at last, the life is not so dark and so painful. The sun shines, and moon is calm. If I do not send the money, or call up them to Tokyo, they—my mother and wife will take other manner to eat. I am young, and young, and young: and I have the pen, the brain, the eyes, the heart and the mind. That is all. All of all. If the inn-master take me out of this room, I will go everywhere—where are many inns and hotels in this capital. Today, I have only one piece of change: but what then? Nonsence! There are many, many writers in Tokyo. What is that to me? There is nothing. They are writing with their finger-bones and the brush: but I must write with the ink and the G pen! That is all. Ah, the burning summer and the green-coloured struggle!

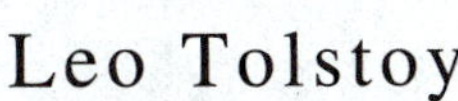

Leo Tolstoy

1828–1910

Count Leo Tolstoy was born and raised at Yasnaya Polyana, his family's estate located near Moscow. After an early and unsuccessful attempt to reform the estate, he volunteered for the army. He served first with Russian forces seeking to conquer what were called "mountain tribesmen" in the Caucasus, and then in the Crimean War (1853–1856), in which Russian expansion southward into Orthodox areas of the Ottoman Empire was defeated at great cost by combined Turkish and British armies. Already a published author before beginning his military career, Tolstoy achieved solid success by making use of his military experience to tell realistic, unglamorous tales of the war. He left the army in 1856, traveled around Europe, and before reaching the age of thirty had retired to his estate; its revenues made it possible for him to spend the rest of his life writing. It was there that he wrote his masterpieces, the novels *War and Peace* (1863–1869) and *Anna Karenina* (1875–1877). After a personal crisis (described in *Confession* [1879]), he formulated a philosophy involving nonviolence, the renunciation of wealth, and the value of physical labor. The philosophy was an inspiration to such world figures as Mahatma Gandhi. In *What Is Art?* (1897) Tolstoy renounced much of his earlier fiction on moral grounds. But some of his last works are among his greatest, including "The Death of Ivan Ilych" (1886) and "The Kreutzer Sonata" (1890). In "Hadji Murad" (1896–1904), he returned to the subject of Russia's war of conquest in the Caucasus, but chose a Caucasian protagonist. By the end of Tolstoy's long life, Yasnaya Polyana had become a place of pilgrimage. After a violent quarrel with his wife, Sofia, he left the estate in October 1910, fell ill, and died at a nearby town.

Tolstoy's great counterpart, Dostoevsky, once described Russian literature as "a literature of landowners." He was announcing his desire to write fiction about Russia's urban poor. But the remark also helps explain why, like classical Greece, nineteenth-century Russia sometimes seems to set an unmatchable standard for literary greatness. Russian landowners turned to literature with such passionate seriousness because they could see that their way of life was doomed. The most prophetic, like Tolstoy, could even see that they deserved no better. Their power, based on their ownership of serfs and supporting in turn the increasingly antiquated bureaucratic empire headed by the Czar, appeared to almost everyone as a sign of Russia's backwardness by comparison with Europe. Unless there was some fundamental change, Russia seemed condemned to ongoing feebleness and disrespect, and more humiliations like the Crimean War. Yet what kind of change should there be? Slavophiles, supporters of native Russian traditions, fell back with nationalist fervor on the certainties of the Russian Orthodox tradition or romanticized views of the Russian peasant. But even devout Westernizers joined with them in being critical of the West's version of industrial modernity. There were more questions than answers. Russian writers could see, as their more complacent European contemporaries often did not, that their society had ceased to function, that revolution of some sort was on the horizon, that everything was up in the air. Blocked at the level of political action by the Czarist autocracy, the energy of criticizing the status quo and imagining alternatives went into literature, which took as its ambitious task the largest and most tantalizing mysteries of human existence.

Tolstoy's celebration of peasantlike simplicity and hard work—evident in the character of Gerasim in "The Death of Ivan Ilych"—shares something with Slavophile primitivism, but this story shows that Tolstoy's disaffection was both deeper and more complex, as his dying hero belatedly reflects on the world he is about to leave.

The Death of Ivan Ilych[1]

I

During an interval in the Melvinski trial in the large building of the Law Courts the members and public prosecutor met in Ivan Egorovich Shebek's private room, where the conversation turned on the celebrated Krasovski case. Fedor Vasilievich warmly maintained that it was not subject to their jurisdiction, Ivan Egorovich maintained the contrary, while Peter Ivanovich, not having entered into the discussion at the start, took no part in it but looked through the *Gazette* which had just been handed in.

"Gentlemen," he said, "Ivan Ilych has died!"

"You don't say so!"

"Here, read it yourself," replied Peter Ivanovich, handing Fedor Vasilievich the paper still damp from the press. Surrounded by a black border were the words: "Praskovya Fedorovna Golovina, with profound sorrow, informs relatives and friends of the demise of her beloved husband Ivan Ilych Golovin, Member of the Court of Justice, which occurred on February the 4th of this year 1882. The funeral will take place on Friday at one o'clock in the afternoon."

Ivan Ilych had been a colleague of the gentlemen present and was liked by them all. He had been ill for some weeks with an illness said to be incurable. His post had been kept open for him, but there had been conjectures that in case of his death Alexeev might receive his appointment, and that either Vinnikov or Shtabel would succeed Alexeev. So on receiving the news of Ivan Ilych's death the first thought of each of the gentlemen in that private room was of the changes and promotions it might occasion among themselves or their acquaintances.

"I shall be sure to get Shtabel's place or Vinnikov's," thought Fedor Vasilievich. "I was promised that long ago, and the promotion means an extra eight hundred rubles a year for me besides the allowance."

"Now I must apply for my brother-in-law's transfer from Kaluga[2]," thought Peter Ivanovich. "My wife will be very glad, and then she won't be able to say that I never do anything for her relations."

"I thought he would never leave his bed again," said Peter Ivanovich aloud. "It's very sad."

"But what really was the matter with him?"

"The doctors couldn't say—at least they could, but each of them said something different. When last I saw him I thought he was getting better."

"And I haven't been to see him since the holidays. I always meant to go."

"Had he any property?"

"I think his wife had a little—but something quiet trifling."

"We shall have to go to see her, but they live so terribly far away."

"Far away from you, you mean. Everything's far away from your place."

1. Translated by Louise Maude and Aylmer Maude.

2 A city in central Russia, about 90 miles southwest of Moscow.

"You see, he never can forgive my living on the other side of the river," said Peter Ivanovich, smiling at Shebek. Then, still talking of the distances between different parts of the city, they returned to the Court.

Besides considerations as to the possible transfers and promotions likely to result from Ivan Ilych's death, the mere fact of the death of a near acquaintance aroused, as usual, in all who heard of it the complacent feeling that, "It is he who is dead and not I." Each one thought or felt, "Well, he's dead but I'm alive!" But the more intimate of Ivan Ilych's acquaintances, his so-called friends, could not help thinking also that they would now have to fulfil the very tiresome demands of propriety by attending the funeral service and paying a visit of condolence to the widow.

Fedor Vasilievich and Peter Ivanovich had been his nearest acquaintances. Peter Ivanovich had studied law with Ivan Ilych and had considered himself to be under obligations to him.

Having told his wife at dinner-time of Ivan Ilych's death, and of his conjecture that it might be possible to get her brother transferred to their circuit, Peter Ivanovich sacrificed his usual nap, put on his evening clothes and drove to Ivan Ilych's house.

At the entrance stood a carriage and two cabs. Leaning against the wall in the hall downstairs near the cloakstand was a coffin-lid covered with cloth of gold, ornamented with gold cord and tassels, that had been polished up with metal powder. Two ladies in black were taking off their fur cloaks. Peter Ivanovich recognized one of them as Ivan Ilych's sister, but the other was a stranger to him. His colleague Schwartz was just coming downstairs, but on seeing Peter Ivanovich enter he stopped and winked at him, as if to say: "Ivan Ilych has made a mess of things — not like you and me."

Schwartz's face with his Piccadilly whiskers, and his slim figure in evening dress, had as usual an air of elegant solemnity which contrasted with the playfulness of his character and had a special piquancy here, or so it seemed to Peter Ivanovich.

Peter Ivanovich allowed the ladies to precede him and slowly followed them upstairs. Schwartz did not come down but remained where he was, and Peter Ivanovich understood that he wanted to arrange where they should play bridge that evening. The ladies went upstairs to the widow's room, and Schwartz with seriously compressed lips but a playful look in his eyes, indicated by a twist of his eyebrows the room to the right where the body lay.

Peter Ivanovich, like everyone else on such occasions, entered feeling uncertain what he would have to do. All he knew was that at such times it is always safe to cross oneself. But he was not quite sure whether one should make obeisances while doing so. He therefore adopted a middle course. On entering the room he began crossing himself and made a slight movement resembling a bow. At the same time, as far as the motion of his head and arm allowed, he surveyed the room. Two young men—apparently nephews, one of whom was a high-school pupil—were leaving the room, crossing themselves as they did so. An old woman was standing motionless, and a lady with strangely arched eyebrows was saying something to her in a whisper. A vigorous, resolute Church Reader, in a frock-coat, was reading something in a loud voice with an expression that precluded any contradiction. The butler's assistant, Gerasim, stepping lightly in front of Peter Ivanovich, was strewing something on the floor.

Noticing this, Peter Ivanovich was immediately aware of a faint odour of a decomposing body.

The last time he had called on Ivan Ilych, Peter Ivanovich had seen Gerasim in the study. Ivan Ilych had been particularly fond of him and he was performing the duty of a sick nurse.

Peter Ivanovich continued to make the sign of the cross slightly inclining his head in an intermediate direction between the coffin, the Reader, and the icons on the table in a corner of the room. Afterwards, when it seemed to him that this movement of his arm in crossing himself had gone on too long, he stopped and began to look at the corpse.

The dead man lay, as dead men always lie, in a specially heavy way, his rigid limbs sunk in the soft cushions of the coffin, with the head forever bowed on the pillow. His yellow waxen brow with bald patches over his sunken temples was thrust up in the way peculiar to the dead, the protruding nose seeming to press on the upper lip. He was much changed and grown even thinner since Peter Ivanovich had last seen him, but, as is always the case with the dead, his face was handsomer and above all more dignified than when he was alive. The expression on the face said that what was necessary had been accomplished, and accomplished rightly. Besides this there was in that expression a reproach and a warning to the living. This warning seemed to Peter Ivanovich out of place, or at least not applicable to him. He felt a certain discomfort and so he hurriedly crossed himself once more and turned and went out of the door—too hurriedly and too regardless of propriety, as he himself was aware.

Schwartz was waiting for him in the adjoining room with legs spread wide apart and both hands toying with his top-hat behind his back. The mere sight of that playful, well-groomed, and elegant figure refreshed Peter Ivanovich. He felt that Schwartz was above all these happenings and would not surrender to any depressing influences. His very look said that this incident of a church service for Ivan Ilych could not be a sufficient reason for infringing the order of the session—in other words, that it would certainly not prevent his unwrapping a new pack of cards and shuffling them that evening while a footman placed fresh candles on the table: in fact, that there was no reason for supposing that this incident would hinder their spending the evening agreeably. Indeed he said this in a whisper as Peter Ivanovich passed him, proposing that they should meet for a game at Fedor Vasilievich's. But apparently Peter Ivanovich was not destined to play bridge that evening. Praskovya Fedorovna (a short, fat woman who despite all efforts to the contrary had continued to broaden steadily from her shoulders downwards and who had the same extraordinarily arched eyebrows as the lady who had been standing by the coffin), dressed all in black, her head covered with lace, came out of her own room with some other ladies, conducted them to the room where the dead body lay, and said: "The service will begin immediately. Please go in."

Schwartz, making an indefinite bow, stood still, evidently neither accepting nor declining this invitation. Praskovya Fedorovna recognizing Peter Ivanovich, sighed, went close up to him, took his hand, and said: "I know you were a true friend to Ivan Ilych . . ." and looked at him awaiting some suitable response. And Peter Ivanovich knew that, just as it had been the right thing to cross himself in that room, so what he had to do here was to press her hand, sigh, and say, "Believe me . . ." So he did all this and as he did it felt that the desired result had been achieved: that both he and she were touched.

"Come with me. I want to speak to you before it begins," said the widow. "Give me your arm."

Peter Ivanovich gave her his arm and they went to the inner rooms, passing Schwartz who winked at Peter Ivanovich compassionately.

"That does for our bridge! Don't object if we find another player. Perhaps you can cut in when you do escape," said his playful look.

Peter Ivanovich sighed still more deeply and despondently, and Praskovya Fedorovna pressed his arm gratefully. When they reached the drawing-room, upholstered in pink cretonne and lighted by a dim lamp, they sat down at the table—she on a sofa and Peter Ivanovich on a low pouffe, the springs of which yielded spasmodically under his weight. Praskovya Fedorovna had been on the point of warning him to take another seat, but felt that such a warning was out of keeping with her present condition and so changed her mind. As he sat down on the pouffe Peter Ivanovich recalled how Ivan Ilych had arranged this room and had consulted him regarding this pink cretonne with green leaves. The whole room was full of furniture and knick-knacks, and on her way to the sofa the lace of the widow's black shawl caught on the edge of the table. Peter Ivanovich rose to detach it, and the springs of the pouffe, relieved of his weight, rose also and gave him a push. The widow began detaching her shawl herself, and Peter Ivanovich again sat down, suppressing the rebellious springs of the pouffe under him. But the widow had not quite freed herself and Peter Ivanovich got up again, and again the pouffe rebelled and even creaked. When this was all over she took out a clean cambric handkerchief and began to weep. The episode with the shawl and the struggle with the pouffe had cooled Peter Ivanovich's emotions and he sat there with a sullen look on his face. This awkward situation was interrupted by Sokolov, Ivan Ilych's butler, who came to report that the plot in the cemetery that Praskovya Fedorovna had chosen would cost two hundred rubles. She stopped weeping and, looking at Peter Ivanovich with the air of a victim, remarked in French that it was very hard for her. Peter Ivanovich made a silent gesture signifying his full conviction that it must indeed be so.

"Please smoke," she said in a magnanimous yet crushed voice, and turned to discuss with Sokolov the price of the plot for the grave.

Peter Ivanovich while lighting his cigarette heard her inquiring very circumstantially into the prices of different plots in the cemetery and finally decide which she would take. When that was done she gave instructions about engaging the choir. Sokolov then left the room.

"I look after everything myself," she told Peter Ivanovich, shifting the albums that lay on the table; and noticing that the table was endangered by his cigarette-ash, she immediately passed him an ash-tray, saying as she did so: "I consider it an affectation to say that my grief prevents my attending to practical affairs. On the contrary, if anything can—I won't say console me, but—distract me, it is seeing to everything concerning him." She again took out her handkerchief as if preparing to cry, but suddenly, as if mastering her feeling, she shook herself and began to speak calmly. "But there is something I want to talk to you about."

Peter Ivanovich bowed, keeping control of the springs of the pouffe, which immediately began quivering under him.

"He suffered terribly the last few days."

"Did he?" said Peter Ivanovich.

"Oh, terribly! He screamed unceasingly, not for minutes but for hours. For the last three days he screamed incessantly. It was unendurable. I cannot understand how I bore it; you could hear him three rooms off. Oh, what I have suffered!"

"Is it possible that he was conscious all that time?" asked Peter Ivanovich.

"Yes," she whispered. "To the last moment. He took leave of us a quarter of an hour before he died, and asked us to take Volodya away."

The thought of the suffering of this man he had known so intimately, first as a merry little boy, then as a schoolmate, and later as a grown-up colleague, suddenly struck Peter Ivanovich with horror, despite an unpleasant consciousness of his own and this woman's dissimulation. He again saw that brow, and that nose pressing down on the lip, and felt afraid for himself.

"Three days of frightful suffering and the death! Why, that might suddenly, at any time, happen to me," he thought, and for a moment felt terrified. But—he did not himself know how—the customary reflection at once occurred to him that this had happened to Ivan Ilych and not to him, and that it should not and could not happen to him, and that to think that it could would be yielding to depression which he ought not to do, as Schwartz's expression plainly showed. After which reflection Peter Ivanovich felt reassured, and began to ask with interest about the details of Ivan Ilych's death, as though death was an accident natural to Ivan Ilych but certainly not to himself.

After many details of the really dreadful physical sufferings Ivan Ilych had endured (which details he learnt only from the effect those sufferings had produced on Praskovya Fedorovna's nerves) the widow apparently found it necessary to get to business.

"Oh, Peter Ivanovich, how hard it is! How terribly, terribly hard!" and she again began to weep.

Peter Ivanovich sighed and waited for her to finish blowing her nose. When she had done so he said, "Believe me . . ." and she again began talking and brought out what was evidently her chief concern with him—namely, to question him as to how she could obtain a grant of money from the government on the occasion of her husband's death. She made it appear that she was asking Peter Ivanovich's advice about her pension, but he soon saw that she already knew about that to the minutest detail, more even than he did himself. She knew how much could be got out of the government in consequence of her husband's death, but wanted to find out whether she could not possibly extract something more. Peter Ivanovich tried to think of some means of doing so, but after reflecting for a while and, out of propriety, condemning the government for its niggardliness, he said he thought that nothing more could be got. Then she sighed and evidently began to devise means of getting rid of her visitor. Noticing this, he put out his cigarette, rose, pressed her hand, and went out into the anteroom.

In the dining-room where the clock stood that Ivan Ilych had liked so much and had bought at an antique shop, Peter Ivanovich met a priest and a few acquaintances who had come to attend the service, and he recognized Ivan Ilych's daughter, a handsome young woman. She was in black and her slim figure appeared slimmer than ever. She had a gloomy, determined, almost angry expression, and bowed to Peter Ivanovich as though he were in some way to blame. Behind her, with the same offended look, stood a wealthy young man, and examining magistrate, whom Peter Ivanovich also knew and who was her fiance, as he had heard. He bowed mournfully to them and was about to pass into the death-chamber, when from under the stairs appeared the figure of Ivan Ilych's schoolboy son, who was extremely like his father. He seemed a little Ivan Ilych, such as Peter Ivanovich remembered when they studied law together. His tear-stained eyes had in them the look that is seen in the eyes of boys of thirteen or fourteen who are not pure-minded. When he saw Peter Ivanovich he scowled morosely and shamefacedly. Peter Ivanovich nodded to him and entered the death-chamber. The service began: candles, groans, incense, tears, and sobs. Peter Ivanovich stood looking gloomily down at his feet. He did not look once at the dead man, did not yield to any depressing influence, and was one of the first to leave the room. There was no one in the anteroom, but Gerasim darted out of the dead man's room, rummaged with his strong hands among the fur coats to find Peter Ivanovich's and helped him on with it.

"Well, friend Gerasim," said Peter Ivanovich, so as to say something. "It's a sad affair, isn't it?"

"It's God will. We shall all come to it some day," said Gerasim, displaying his teeth—the even white teeth of a healthy peasant—and, like a man in the thick of urgent work, he briskly opened the front door, called the coachman, helped Peter Ivanovich into the sledge, and sprang back to the porch as if in readiness for what he had to do next. Peter Ivanovich found the fresh air particularly pleasant after the smell of incense, the dead body, and carbolic acid.

"Where to sir?" asked the coachman.

"It's not too late even now. . . . I'll call round on Fedor Vasilievich."

He accordingly drove there and found them just finishing the first rubber, so that it was quite convenient for him to cut in.

II

Ivan Ilych's life had been most simple and most ordinary and therefore most terrible. He had been a member of the Court of Justice, and died at the age of forty-five. His father had been an official who after serving in various ministries and departments in Petersburg had made the sort of career which brings men to positions from which by reason of their long service they cannot be dismissed, though they are obviously unfit to hold any responsible position, and for whom therefore posts are specially created, which though fictitious carry salaries of from six to ten thousand rubles that are not fictitious, and in receipt of which they live on to a great age.

Such was the Privy Councillor and superfluous member of various superfluous institutions, Ilya Epimovich Golovin.

He had three sons, of whom Ivan Ilych was the second. The eldest son was following in his father's footsteps only in another department, and was already approaching that stage in the service at which a similar sinecure would be reached. The third son was a failure. He had ruined his prospects in a number of positions and was not serving in the railway department. His father and brothers, and still more their wives, not merely disliked meeting him, but avoided remembering his existence unless compelled to do so. His sister had married Baron Greff, a Petersburg official of her father's type. Ivan Ilych was *le phenix de la famille*[3] as people

3. The pride of the family (French).

said. He was neither as cold and formal as his elder brother nor as wild as the younger, but was a happy mean between them—an intelligent polished, lively and agreeable man. He had studied with his younger brother at the School of Law, but the latter had failed to complete the course and was expelled when he was in the fifth class. Ivan Ilych finished the course well. Even when he was at the School of Law he was just what he remained for the rest of his life: a capable, cheerful, good-natured, and sociable man, though strict in the fulfillment of what he considered to be his duty: and he considered his duty to be what was so considered by those in authority. Neither as a boy nor as a man was he a toady, but from early youth was by nature attracted to people of high station as a fly is drawn to the light, assimilating their ways and views of life and establishing friendly relations with them. All the enthusiasms of childhood and youth passed without leaving much trace on him; he succumbed to sensuality, to vanity, and latterly among the highest classes to liberalism, but always within limits which his instinct unfailingly indicated to him as correct.

At school he had done things which had formerly seemed to him very horrid and made him feel disgusted with himself when he did them; but when later on he saw that such actions were done by people of good position and that they did not regard them as wrong, he was able not exactly to regard them as right, but to forget about them entirely or not be at all troubled at remembering them.

Having graduated from the School of Law and qualified for the tenth rank of the civil service, and having received money from his father for his equipment, Ivan Ilych ordered himself clothes at Scharmer's, the fashionable tailor, hung a medallion inscribed *respice finem*[4] on his watch-chain, took leave of his professor and the prince who was patron of the school, had a farewell dinner with his comrades at Donon's first-class restaurant, and with his new and fashionable portmanteau, linen, clothes, shaving and other toilet appliances, and a travelling rug, all purchased at the best shops, he set off for one of the provinces where through his father's influence, he had been attached to the governor as an official for special service.

In the province Ivan Ilych soon arranged as easy and agreeable a position for himself as he had had at the School of Law. He performed his official task, made his career, and at the same time amused himself pleasantly and decorously. Occasionally he paid official visits to country districts where he behaved with dignity both to his superiors and inferiors, and performed the duties entrusted to him, which related chiefly to the sectarians[5], with an exactness and incorruptible honesty of which he could not but feel proud.

In official matters, despite his youth and taste for frivolous gaiety, he was exceedingly reserved, punctilious, and even severe; but in society he was often amusing and witty, and always good-natured, correct in his manner, and *bon enfant*[6], as the governor and his wife—with whom he was like one of the family—used to say of him. In the province he had an affair with a lady who made advances to the elegant young lawyer, and there was also a milliner; and there were carousals with aides-de-camp who visited the district, and after-supper visits to a certain outlying street of

4. Look to the end (Latin).
5. Christians who had repudiated the Orthodox church.
6. Easygoing, a good citizen; literally, a "good child" (French).

doubtful reputation; and there was too some obsequiousness to his chief and even to his chief's wife, but all this was done with such a tone of good breeding that no hard names could be applied to it. It all came under the heading of the French saying: "*Il faut que jeunesse se passe.*"[7] It was all done with clean hands, in clean linen, with French phrases, and above all among people of the best society and consequently with the approval of people of rank.

So Ivan Ilych served for five years and then came a change in his official life. The new and reformed judicial institutions were introduced, and new men were needed. Ivan Ilych became such a new man. He was offered the post of examining magistrate, and he accepted it though the post was in another province and obliged him to give up the connexions he had formed and to make new ones. His friends met to give him a send-off; they had a group photograph taken and presented him with a silver cigarette-case, and he set off to his new post.

As examining magistrate Ivan Ilych was just as *comme il faut* and decorous a man, inspiring general respect and capable of separating his official duties from his private life, as he had been when acting as an official on special service. His duties now as examining magistrate were far more interesting and attractive than before. In his former position it had been pleasant to wear an undress uniform made by Scharmer, and to pass through the crowd of petitioners and officials who were timorously awaiting an audience with the governor, and who envied him as with free and easy gait he went straight into his chief's private room to have a cup of tea and a cigarette with him. But not many people had then been directly dependent on him—only police officials and the sectarians when he went on special missions—and he liked to treat them politely, almost as comrades, as if he were letting them feel that he who had the power to crush them was treating them in this simple, friendly way. There were then but few such people. But now, as an examining magistrate, Ivan Ilych felt that everyone without exception, even the most important and self-satisfied, was in his power, and that he need only write a few words on a sheet of paper with a certain heading, and this or that important, self-satisfied person would be brought before him in the role of an accused person or a witness, and if he did not choose to allow him to sit down, would have to stand before him and answer his questions. Ivan Ilych never abused his power; he tried on the contrary to soften its expression, but the consciousness of it and the possibility of softening its effect, supplied the chief interest and attraction of his office. In his work itself, especially in his examinations, he very soon acquired a method of eliminating all considerations irrelevant to the legal aspect of the case, and reducing even the most complicated case to a form in which it would be presented on paper only in its externals, completely excluding his personal opinion of the matter, while above all observing every prescribed formality. The work was new and Ivan Ilych was one of the first men to apply the new Code of 1864.[8]

On taking up the post of examining magistrate in a new town, he made new acquaintances and connexions, placed himself on a new footing and assumed a somewhat different tone. He took up an attitude of rather dignified aloofness towards the provincial authorities, but picked out the best circle of legal gentlemen and wealthy gentry living in the town and assumed a tone of slight dissatisfaction with the government,

7. "Youth must have its day" (French).

8. A legal reform.

of moderate liberalism, and of enlightened citizenship. At the same time, without at all altering the elegance of his toilet, he ceased shaving his chin and allowed his beard to grow as it pleased.

Ivan Ilych settled down very pleasantly in this new town. The society there, which inclined towards opposition to the governor was friendly, his salary was larger, and he began to play vint,[9] which he found added not a little to the pleasure of life, for he had a capacity for cards, played good-humouredly, and calculated rapidly and astutely, so that he usually won.

After living there for two years he met his future wife, Praskovya Fedorovna Mikhel, who was the most attractive, clever, and brilliant girl of the set in which he moved, and among other amusements and relaxations from his labours as examining magistrate, Ivan Ilych established light and playful relations with her.

While he had been an official on special service he had been accustomed to dance, but now as an examining magistrate it was exceptional for him to do so. If he danced now, he did it as if to show that though he served under the reformed order of things, and had reached the fifth official rank, yet when it came to dancing he could do it better than most people. So at the end of an evening he sometimes danced with Praskovya Fedorovna, and it was chiefly during these dances that he captivated her. She fell in love with him. Ivan Ilych had at first no definite intention of marrying, but when the girl fell in love with him he said to himself: "Really, why shouldn't I marry?"

Praskovya Fedorovna came of a good family, was not bad looking, and had some little property. Ivan Ilych might have aspired to a more brilliant match, but even this was good. He had his salary, and she, he hoped, would have an equal income. She was well connected, and was a sweet, pretty, and thoroughly correct young woman. To say that Ivan Ilych married because he fell in love with Praskovya Fedorovna and found that she sympathized with his views of life would be as incorrect as to say that he married because his social circle approved of the match. He was swayed by both these considerations: the marriage gave him personal satisfaction, and at the same time it was considered the right thing by the most highly placed of his associates.

So Ivan Ilych got married.

The preparations for marriage and the beginning of married life, with its conjugal caresses, the new furniture, new crockery, and new linen, were very pleasant until his wife became pregnant—so that Ivan Ilych had begun to think that marriage would not impair the easy, agreeable, gay and always decorous character of his life, approved of by society and regarded by himself as natural, but would even improve it. But from the first months of his wife's pregnancy, something new, unpleasant, depressing, and unseemly, and from which there was no way of escape, unexpectedly showed itself.

His wife, without any reason—*de gaiete de coeur*[1] as Ivan Ilych expressed it to himself—began to disturb the pleasure and propriety of their life. She began to be jealous without any cause, expected him to devote his whole attention to her, found fault with everything, and made coarse and ill-mannered scenes.

At first Ivan Ilych hoped to escape from the unpleasantness of this state of affairs by the same easy and decorous relation to life that had served him heretofore: he tried to ignore his wife's disagreeable moods, continued to live in his usual easy and pleasant way, invited friends to his house for a game of cards, and also tried going out to

9. A form of bridge.

1. Out of sheer exuberance (French).

his club or spending his evenings with friends. But one day his wife began upbraiding him so vigorously, using such coarse words, and continued to abuse him every time he did not fulfil her demands, so resolutely and with such evident determination not to give way till he submitted—that is, till he stayed at home and was bored just as she was—that he became alarmed. He now realized that matrimony—at any rate with Praskovya Fedorovna—was not always conducive to the pleasures and amenities of life, but on the contrary often infringed both comfort and propriety, and that he must therefore entrench himself against such infringement. And Ivan Ilych began to seek for means of doing so. His official duties were the one thing that imposed upon Praskovya Fedorovna, and by means of his official work and the duties attached to it he began struggling with his wife to secure his own independence.

With the birth of their child, the attempts to feed it and the various failures in doing so, and with the real and imaginary illnesses of mother and child, in which Ivan Ilych's sympathy was demanded but about which he understood nothing, the need of securing for himself an existence outside his family life became still more imperative. As his wife grew more irritable and exacting and Ivan Ilych transferred the center of gravity of his life more and more to his official work, so did he grow to like his work better and became more ambitious than before.

Very soon, within a year of his wedding, Ivan Ilych had realized that marriage, though it may add some comforts to life, is in fact a very intricate and difficult affair towards which in order to perform one's duty, that is, to lead a decorous life approved of by society, one must adopt a definite attitude just as towards one's official duties.

And Ivan Ilych evolved such an attitude towards married life. He only required of it those conveniences—dinner at home, housewife, and bed—which it could give him, and above all that propriety of external forms required by public opinion. For the rest he looked for lighthearted pleasure and propriety, and was very thankful when he found them, but if he met with antagonism and querulousness he at once retired into his separate fenced-off world of official duties, where he found satisfaction.

Ivan Ilych was esteemed a good official, and after three years was made Assistant Public Prosecutor. His new duties, their importance, the possibility of indicting and imprisoning anyone he chose, the publicity his speeches received, and the success he had in all these things, made his work still more attractive.

More children came. His wife became more and more querulous and ill-tempered, but the attitude Ivan Ilych had adopted towards his home life rendered him almost impervious to her grumbling.

After seven years' service in that town he was transferred to another province as Public Prosecutor. They moved, but were short of money and his wife did not like the place they moved to. Though the salary was higher the cost of living was greater, besides which two of their children died and family life became still more unpleasant for him. Praskovya Fedorovna blamed her husband for every inconvenience they encountered in their new home. Most of the conversations between husband and wife, especially as to the children's education, led to topics which recalled former disputes, and these disputes were apt to flare up again at any moment. There remained only those rare periods of amorousness which still came to them at times but did not last long. These were islets at which they anchored for a while and then again set out upon that ocean of veiled hostility which showed itself in their aloofness from one another. This aloofness might have grieved Ivan Ilych had he considered that it ought not to exist, but he now regarded the position as normal, and even made it the goal at which he aimed in family life. His aim was to free himself more and more from those unpleasantnesses and to give them a semblance of harmlessness and propriety. He attained this by spending less and less time with his family, and when obliged to be at home he tried to safeguard his position by the presence of outsiders. The chief thing however was that he had his official duties. The whole interest of his life now centered in the official world and that interest absorbed him. The consciousness of his power, being able to ruin anybody he wished to ruin, the importance, even the external dignity of his entry into court, or meetings with his subordinates, his success with superiors and inferiors, and above all his masterly handling of cases, of which he was conscious—all this gave him pleasure and filled his life, together with chats with his colleagues, dinners, and bridge. So that on the whole Ivan Ilych's life continued to flow as he considered it should do — pleasantly and properly.

So things continued for another seven years. His eldest daughter was already sixteen, another child had died, and only one son was left, a schoolboy and a subject of dissension. Ivan Ilych wanted to put him in the School of Law, but to spite him Praskovya Fedorovna entered him at the High School. The daughter had been educated at home and had turned out well: the boy did not learn badly either.

III

So Ivan Ilych lived for seventeen years after his marriage. He was already a Public Prosecutor of long standing, and had declined several proposed transfers while awaiting a more desirable post, when an unanticipated and unpleasant occurrence quite upset the peaceful course of his life. He was expecting to be offered the post of presiding judge in a University town, but Happe somehow came to the front and obtained the appointment instead. Ivan Ilych became irritable, reproached Happe, and quarrelled both with him and with his immediate superiors—who became colder to him and again passed him over when other appointments were made.

This was in 1880, the hardest year of Ivan Ilych's life. It was then that it became evident on the one hand that his salary was insufficient for them to live on, and on the other that he had been forgotten, and not only this, but that what was for him the greatest and most cruel injustice appeared to others a quite ordinary occurrence. Even his father did not consider it his duty to help him. Ivan Ilych felt himself abandoned by everyone, and that they regarded his position with a salary of 3,500 rubles as quite normal and even fortunate. He alone knew that with the consciousness of the injustices done him, with his wife's incessant nagging, and with the debts he had contracted by living beyond his means, his position was far from normal.

In order to save money that summer he obtained leave of absence and went with his wife to live in the country at her brother's place.

In the country, without his work, he experienced *ennui* for the first time in his life, and not only *ennui* but intolerable depression, and he decided that it was impossible to go on living like that, and that it was necessary to take energetic measures.

Having passed a sleepless night pacing up and down the veranda, he decided to go to Petersburg and bestir himself, in order to punish those who had failed to appreciate him and to get transferred to another ministry.

Next day, despite many protests from his wife and her brother, he started for Petersburg with the sole object of obtaining a post with a salary of five thousand rubles a year. He was no longer bent on any particular department, or tendency, or kind of activity. All he now wanted was an appointment to another post with a salary of five thousand rubles, either in the administration, in the banks, with the railways in one of the Empress Marya's Institutions[2], or even in the customs—but it had to carry with it a salary of five thousand rubles and be in a ministry other than that in which they had failed to appreciate him.

And this quest of Ivan Ilych's was crowned with remarkable and unexpected success. At Kursk[3] an acquaintance of his, F. I. Ilyin, got into the first-class carriage, sat down beside Ivan Ilych, and told him of a telegram just received by the governor of Kursk announcing that a change was about to take place in the ministry: Peter Ivanovich was to be superseded by Ivan Semonovich.

The proposed change, apart from its significance for Russia, had a special significance for Ivan Ilych, because by bringing forward a new man, Peter Petrovich, and consequently his friend Zachar Ivanovich, it was highly favourable for Ivan Ilych, since Sachar Ivanovich was a friend and colleague of his.

In Moscow this news was confirmed, and on reaching Petersburg Ivan Ilych found Zachar Ivanovich and received a definite promise of an appointment in his former Department of Justice.

A week later he telegraphed to his wife: "Zachar in Miller's place. I shall receive appointment on presentation of report."

Thanks to this change of personnel, Ivan Ilych had unexpectedly obtained an appointment in his former ministry which placed him two states above his former colleagues besides giving him five thousand rubles salary and three thousand five hundred rubles for expenses connected with his removal. All his ill humour towards his former enemies and the whole department vanished, and Ivan Ilych was completely happy.

He returned to the country more cheerful and contented than he had been for a long time. Praskovya Fedorovna also cheered up and a truce was arranged between them. Ivan Ilych told of how he had been feted by everybody in Petersburg, how all those who had been his enemies were put to shame and now fawned on him, how envious they were of his appointment, and how much everybody in Petersburg had liked him.

Praskovya Fedorovna listened to all this and appeared to believe it. She did not contradict anything, but only made plans for their life in the town to which they were going. Ivan Ilych saw with delight that these plans were his plans, that he and his wife agreed, and that, after a stumble, his life was regaining its due and natural character of pleasant lightheartedness and decorum.

Ivan Ilych had come back for a short time only, for he had to take up his new duties on the 10th of September. Moreover, he needed time to settle into the new place, to move all his belongings from the province, and to buy and order many additional things: in a word, to make such arrangements as he had resolved on, which were almost exactly what Praskovya Fedorovna too had decided on.

Now that everything had happened so fortunately, and that he and his wife were at one in their aims and moreover saw so little of one another, they got on together better than they had done since the first years of marriage. Ivan Ilych had thought of taking his family away with him at once, but the insistence of his wife's brother and her sister-in-law, who had suddenly become particularly amiable and friendly to him and his family, induced him to depart alone.

So he departed, and the cheerful state of mind induced by his success and by the harmony between his wife and himself, the one intensifying the other, did not leave

2. Marya Fyodorovna (1759–1828), second wife of Tsar Paul I, founded a number of orphanages.

3. An administrative center and railway hub in central Russia.

him. He found a delightful house, just the thing both he and his wife had dreamt of. Spacious, lofty reception rooms in the old style, a convenient and dignified study, rooms for his wife and daughter, a study for his son—it might have been specially built for them. Ivan Ilych himself superintended the arrangements, chose the wallpapers, supplemented the furniture (preferably with antiques which he considered particularly *comme il faut*), and supervised the upholstering. Everything progressed and progressed and approached the ideal he had set himself: even when things were only half completed they exceeded his expectations. He saw what a refined and elegant character, free from vulgarity, it would all have when it was ready. On falling asleep he pictured to himself how the reception room would look. Looking at the yet unfinished drawing room he could see the fireplace, the screen, the what-not, the little chairs dotted here and there, the dishes and plates on the walls, and the bronzes, as they would be when everything was in place. He was pleased by the thought of how his wife and daughter, who shared his taste in this matter, would be impressed by it. They were certainly not expecting as much. He had been particularly successful in finding, and buying cheaply, antiques which gave a particularly aristocratic character to the whole place. But in his letters he intentionally understated everything in order to be able to surprise them. All this so absorbed him that his new duties—though he liked his official work—interested him less than he had expected. Sometimes he even had moments of absent-mindedness during the court sessions and would consider whether he should have straight or curved cornices for his curtains. He was so interested in it all that he often did things himself, rearranging the furniture, or rehanging the curtains. Once when mounting a step-ladder to show the upholsterer, who did not understand, how he wanted the hangings draped, he made a false step and slipped, but being a strong and agile man he clung on and only knocked his side against the knob of the window frame. The bruised place was painful but the pain soon passed, and he felt particularly bright and well just then. He wrote: "I feel fifteen years younger." He thought he would have everything ready by September, but it dragged on till mid-October. But the result was charming not only in his eyes but to everyone who saw it.

In reality it was just what is usually seen in the houses of people of moderate means who want to appear rich, and therefore succeed only in resembling others like themselves: there are damasks, dark wood, plants, rugs, and dull and polished bronzes—all the things people of a certain class have in order to resemble other people of that class. His house was so like the others that it would never have been noticed, but to him it all seemed to be quite exceptional. He was very happy when he met his family at the station and brought them to the newly furnished house all lit up, where a footman in a white tie opened the door into the hall decorated with plants, and when they went on into the drawing-room and the study uttering exclamations of delight. He conducted them everywhere, drank in their praises eagerly, and beamed with pleasure. At tea that evening, when Praskovya Fedorovna among others things asked him about his fall, he laughed, and showed them how he had gone flying and had frightened the upholsterer.

"It's a good thing I'm a bit of an athlete. Another man might have been killed, but I merely knocked myself, just here; it hurts when it's touched, but it's passing off already—it's only a bruise."

So they began living in their new home—in which, as always happens, when they got thoroughly settled in they found they were just one room short—and with the increased income, which as always was just a little (some five hundred rubles) too little, but it was all very nice.

Things went particularly well at first, before everything was finally arranged and while something had still to be done: this thing bought, that thing ordered, another thing moved, and something else adjusted. Though there were some disputes between husband and wife, they were both so well satisfied and had so much to do that it all passed off without any serious quarrels. When nothing was left to arrange it became rather dull and something seemed to be lacking, but they were then making acquaintances, forming habits, and life was growing fuller.

Ivan Ilych spent his mornings at the law court and came home to dinner, and at first he was generally in a good humour, though he occasionally became irritable just on account of his house. (Every spot on the tablecloth or the upholstery, and every broken window-blind string, irritated him. He had devoted so much trouble to arranging it all that every disturbance of it distressed him.) But on the whole his life ran its course as he believed life should do: easily, pleasantly, and decorously.

He got up at nine, drank his coffee, read the paper, and then put on his undress uniform and went to the law courts. There the harness in which he worked had already been stretched to fit him and he donned it without a hitch: petitioners, inquiries at the chancery, the chancery itself, and the sittings public and administrative. In all this the thing was to exclude everything fresh and vital, which always disturbs the regular course of official business, and to admit only official relations with people, and then only on official grounds. A man would come, for instance, wanting some information. Ivan Ilych, as one in whose sphere the matter did not lie, would have nothing to do with him: but if the man had some business with him in his official capacity, something that could be expressed on officially stamped paper, he would do everything, positively everything he could within the limits of such relations, and in doing so would maintain the semblance of friendly human relations, that is, would observe the courtesies of life. As soon as the official relations ended, so did everything else. Ivan Ilych possessed this capacity to separate his real life from the official side of affairs and not mix the two, in the highest degree, and by long practice and natural aptitude had brought it to such a pitch that sometimes, in the manner of a virtuoso, he would even allow himself to let the human and official relations mingle. He let himself do this just because he felt that he could at any time he chose resume the strictly official attitude again and drop the human relation. And he did it all easily, pleasantly, correctly, and even artistically. In the intervals between the sessions he smoked, drank tea, chatted a little about politics, a little about general topics, a little about cards, but most of all about official appointments. Tired, but with the feelings of a virtuoso—one of the first violins who has played his part in an orchestra with precision—he would return home to find that his wife and daughter had been out paying calls, or had a visitor, and that his son had been to school, had done his homework with his tutor, and was surely learning what is taught at High Schools.

Everything was as it should be. After dinner, if they had no visitors, Ivan Ilych sometimes read a book that was being much discussed at the time, and in the evening settled down to work, that is, read official papers, compared the depositions of witnesses, and noted paragraphs of the Code applying to them. This was neither dull nor amusing. It was dull when he might have been playing bridge, but if no bridge was available it was at any rate better than doing nothing or sitting with his wife. Ivan Ilych's chief pleasure was giving little dinners to which he invited men and women of good social position, and just as his drawing-room resembled all other drawing-rooms so did his enjoyable little parties resemble all other such parties.

Once they even gave a dance. Ivan Ilych enjoyed it and everything went off well, except that it led to a violent quarrel with his wife about the cakes and sweets. Praskovya Fedorovna had made her own plans, but Ivan Ilych insisted on getting everything from an expensive confectioner and ordered too many cakes, and the quarrel occurred because some of those cakes were left over and the confectioner's bill came to forty-five rubles. It was a great and disagreeable quarrel. Praskovya Fedorovna called him "a fool and an imbecile," and he clutched at his head and made angry allusions to divorce.

But the dance itself had been enjoyable. The best people were there, and Ivan Ilych had danced with Princess Trufonova, a sister of the distinguished founder of the Society "Bear My Burden."

The pleasures connected with his work were pleasures of ambition; his social pleasures were those of vanity; but Ivan Ilych's greatest pleasure was playing bridge. He acknowledged that whatever disagreeable incident happened in his life, the pleasure that beamed like a ray of light above everything else was to sit down to bridge with good players, not noisy partners, and of course to four-handed bridge (with five players it was annoying to have to stand out, though one pretended not to mind), to play a clever and serious game (when the cards allowed it) and then to have supper and drink a glass of wine. After a game of bridge, especially if he had won a little (to win a large sum was unpleasant), Ivan Ilych went to bed in a specially good humour.

So they lived. They formed a circle of acquaintances among the best people and were visited by people of importance and by young folk. In their views as to their acquaintances, husband, wife and daughter were entirely agreed, and tacitly and unanimously kept at arm's length and shook off the various shabby friends and relations who, with much show of affection, gushed into the drawing-room with its Japanese plates on the walls. Soon these shabby friends ceased to obtrude themselves and only the best people remained in the Golovins' set.

Young men made up to Lisa, and Petrishchev, an examining magistrate and Dmitri Ivanovich Petrishchev's son and sole heir, began to be so attentive to her that Ivan Ilych had already spoken to Praskovya Fedorovna about it, and considered whether they should not arrange a party for them, or get up some private theatricals.

So they lived, and all went well, without change, and life flowed pleasantly.

IV

They were all in good health. It could not be called ill health if Ivan Ilych sometimes said that he had a queer taste in his mouth and felt some discomfort in his left side.

But this discomfort increased and, though not exactly painful, grew into a sense of pressure in his side accompanied by ill humour. And his irritability became worse and worse and began to mar the agreeable, easy, and correct life that had established itself in the Golovin family. Quarrels between husband and wife became more and more frequent, and soon the ease and amenity disappeared and even the decorum was barely maintained. Scenes again became frequent, and very few of those islets remained on which husband and wife could meet without an explosion. Praskovya Fedorovna now had good reason to say that her husband's temper was trying. With characteristic exaggeration she said he had always had a dreadful temper, and that it had needed all her good nature to put up with it for twenty years. It was true that now the quarrels were started by him. His bursts of temper always came just before dinner, often just as he began to eat his soup. Sometimes he noticed that a plate or dish was chipped, or the food was not right, or his son put his elbow on the table, or his daughter's hair was not done as he liked it, and for all this he blamed Praskovya Fedorovna. At first she retorted and said disagreeable things to him, but once or twice he fell into such a rage at the beginning of dinner that she realized it was due to some physical derangement brought on by taking food, and so she restrained herself and did not answer, but only hurried to get the dinner over. She regarded this self-restraint as highly praiseworthy. Having come to the conclusion that her husband had a dreadful temper and made her life miserable, she began to feel sorry for herself, and the more she pitied herself the more she hated her husband. She began to wish he would die; yet she did not want him to die because then his salary would cease. And this irritated her against him still more. She considered herself dreadfully unhappy just because not even his death could save her, and though she concealed her exasperation, that hidden exasperation of hers increased his irritation also.

After one scene in which Ivan Ilych had been particularly unfair and after which he had said in explanation that he certainly was irritable but that it was due to his not being well, she said that if he was ill it should be attended to, and insisted on his going to see a celebrated doctor.

He went. Everything took place as he had expected and as it always does. There was the usual waiting and the important air assumed by the doctor, with which he was so familiar (resembling that which he himself assumed in court), and the sounding and listening, and the questions which called for answers that were foregone conclusions and were evidently unnecessary, and the look of importance which implied that "if only you put yourself in our hands we will arrange everything—we know indubitably how it has to be done, always in the same way for everybody alike." It was all just as it was in the law courts. The doctor put on just the same air towards him as he himself put on towards an accused person.

The doctor said that so-and-so indicated that there was so-and-so inside the patient, but if the investigation of so-and-so did not confirm this, then he must assume that and that. If he assumed that and that, then . . . and so on. To Ivan Ilych only one question was important: was his case serious or not? But the doctor ignored that inappropriate question. From his point of view it was not the one under consideration, the real question was to decide between a floating kidney, chronic catarrh, or appendicitis. It was a question the doctor solved brilliantly, as it seemed to Ivan Ilych, in favour of the appendix, with the reservation that should an examination of the urine give fresh indications the matter would be reconsidered. All this was just what Ivan Ilych had himself brilliantly accomplished a thousand times in dealing with men on trial. The doctor summed up just as brilliantly, looking over his spectacles triumphantly and even gaily at the accused. From the doctor's summing up Ivan Ilych concluded that things were bad, but that for the doctor, and perhaps for everybody else, it was a matter of indifference, though for him it was bad. And this conclusion struck him painfully, arousing in him a great feeling of pity for himself and of bitterness towards the doctor's indifference to a matter of such importance.

He said nothing of this, but rose, placed the doctor's fee on the table, and remarked with a sigh: "We sick people probably often put inappropriate questions. But tell me, in general, is this complaint dangerous, or not? . . ."

The doctor looked at him sternly over his spectacles with one eye, as if to say: "Prisoner, if you will not keep to the questions put to you, I shall be obliged to have you removed from the court."

"I have already told you what I consider necessary and proper. The analysis may show something more." And the doctor bowed.

Ivan Ilych went out slowly, seated himself disconsolately in his sledge, and drove home. All the way home he was going over what the doctor had said, trying to translate those complicated, obscure, scientific phrases into plain language and find in them an answer to the question: "Is my condition bad? Is it very bad? Or is there as yet nothing much wrong?" And it seemed to him that the meaning of what the doctor had said was that it was very bad. Everything in the streets seemed depressing. The cabmen, the houses, the passers-by, and the shops, were dismal. His ache, this dull gnawing ache that never ceased for a moment, seemed to have acquired a new and more serious significance from the doctor's dubious remarks. Ivan Ilych now watched it with a new and oppressive feeling.

He reached home and began to tell his wife about it. She listened, but in the middle of his account his daughter came in with her hat on, ready to go out with her mother. She sat down reluctantly to listen to this tedious story, but could not stand it long, and her mother too did not hear him to the end.

"Well, I am very glad," she said. "Mind now to take your medicine regularly. Give me the prescription and I'll send Gerasim to the chemist's." And she went to get ready to go out.

While she was in the room Ivan Ilych had hardly taken time to breathe, but he sighed deeply when she left it.

"Well," he thought, "perhaps it isn't so bad after all."

He began taking his medicine and following the doctor's directions, which had been altered after the examination of the urine. But then it happened that there was a contradiction between the indications drawn from the examination of the urine and the symptoms that showed themselves. It turned out that what was happening differed from what the doctor had told him, and that he had either forgotten or blundered, or hidden something from him. He could not, however, be blamed for that, and Ivan Ilych still obeyed his orders implicitly and at first derived some comfort from doing so.

From the time of his visit to the doctor, Ivan Ilych's chief occupation was the exact fulfillment of the doctor's instructions regarding hygiene and the taking of medicine, and the observation of his pain and his excretions. His chief interest came to be people's ailments and people's health. When sickness, deaths, or recoveries were mentioned in his presence, especially when the illness resembled his own, he listened with agitation which he tried to hide, asked questions, and applied what he heard to his own case.

The pain did not grow less, but Ivan Ilych made efforts to force himself to think that he was better. And he could do this so long as nothing agitated him. But as soon as he had any unpleasantness with his wife, any lack of success in his official work, or held bad cards at bridge, he was at once acutely sensible of his disease. He had formerly borne such mischances, hoping soon to adjust what was wrong, to master it and attain success, or make a grand slam. But now every mischance upset him and plunged him into despair. He would say to himself: "there now, just as I was beginning to get better and the medicine had begun to take effect, comes this accursed misfortune, or unpleasantness . . .". And he was furious with the mishap, or with the people who were causing the unpleasantness and killing him, for he felt that this fury was killing him but he could not restrain it. One would have thought that it should have been clear to him that this exasperation with circumstances and people aggravated his illness, and that he ought therefore to ignore unpleasant occurrences. But he drew the very opposite conclusion: he said that he needed peace, and he watched for everything that might disturb it and became irritable at the slightest infringement of it. His condition was rendered worse by the fact that he read medical books and consulted doctors. The progress of his disease was so gradual that he could deceive himself when comparing one day with another — the difference was so slight. But when he consulted the doctors it seemed to him that he was getting worse, and even very rapidly. Yet despite this he was continually consulting them.

That month he went to see another celebrity, who told him almost the same as the first had done but put his questions rather differently, and the interview with this celebrity only increased Ivan Ilych's doubts and fears. A friend of a friend of his, a very good doctor, diagnosed his illness again quite differently from the others, and though he predicted recovery, his questions and suppositions bewildered Ivan Ilych still more and increased his doubts. A homeopathist diagnosed the disease in yet another way, and prescribed medicine which Ivan Ilych took secretly for a week. But after a week, not feeling any improvement and having lost confidence both in the former doctor's treatment and in this one's, he became still more despondent. One day a lady acquaintance mentioned a cure effected by a wonder-working icon. Ivan Ilych caught himself listening attentively and beginning to believe that it had occurred. This incident alarmed him. "Has my mind really weakened to such an extent?" he asked himself. "Nonsense! It's all rubbish. I mustn't give way to nervous fears but having chosen a doctor must keep strictly to his treatment. That is what I will do. Now it's all settled. I won't think about it, but will follow the treatment seriously till summer, and then we shall see. From now there must be no more of this wavering!" This was easy to say but impossible to carry out. The pain in his side oppressed him and seemed to grow worse and more incessant, while the taste in his mouth grew stranger and stranger. It seemed to him that his breath had a disgusting smell, and he was conscious of a loss of appetite and strength. There was no deceiving himself: something terrible, new, and more important than anything before in his life, was taking place within him of which he alone was aware. Those about him did not understand or would not understand it, but thought everything in the world was going on as usual. That tormented Ivan Ilych more than anything. He saw that his household, especially his wife and daughter who were in a perfect whirl of visiting, did not understand anything of it and were annoyed that he was so depressed and so exacting, as if he were to blame for it. Though they tried to disguise it he saw that he was an obstacle in their path, and that his wife had adopted a definite line in regard to his illness and kept to it regardless of anything he said or did. Her attitude was this: "You know," she would say to her friends, "Ivan Ilych can't do as other people do, and keep to the treatment prescribed for him. One day he'll take his drops and keep strictly to his diet and go to bed in good time, but the next day unless I watch him he'll suddenly forget his medicine, eat sturgeon — which is forbidden — and sit up playing cards till one o'clock in the morning."

"Oh, come, when was that?" Ivan Ilych would ask in vexation. "Only once at Peter Ivanovich's."

"And yesterday with Shebek."

"Well, even if I hadn't stayed up, this pain would have kept me awake."

"Be that as it may you'll never get well like that, but will always make us wretched."

Praskovya Fedorovna's attitude to Ivan Ilych's illness, as she expressed it both to others and to him, was that it was his own fault and was another of the annoyances he caused her. Ivan Ilych felt that this opinion escaped her involuntarily — but that did not make it easier for him.

At the law courts too, Ivan Ilych noticed, or thought he noticed, a strange attitude towards himself. It sometimes seemed to him that people were watching him inquisitively as a man whose place might soon be vacant. Then again, his friends would suddenly begin to chaff him in a friendly way about his low spirits, as if the awful, horrible, and unheard-of thing that was going on within him, incessantly gnawing at him and irresistibly drawing him away, was a very agreeable subject for jests. Schwartz in particular irritated him by his jocularity, vivacity, and *savoir-faire*, which reminded him of what he himself had been ten years ago.

Friends came to make up a set and they sat down to cards. They dealt, bending the new cards to soften them, and he sorted the diamonds in his hand and found he had seven. His partner said "No trumps" and supported him with two diamonds. What more could be wished for? It ought to be jolly and lively. They would make a grand slam. But suddenly Ivan Ilych was conscious of that gnawing pain, that taste in his mouth, and it seemed ridiculous that in such circumstances he should be pleased to make a grand slam.

He looked at his partner Mikhail Mikhaylovich, who rapped the table with his strong hand and instead of snatching up the tricks pushed the cards courteously and indulgently towards Ivan Ilych that he might have the pleasure of gathering them up without the trouble of stretching out his hand for them. "Does he think I am too weak to stretch out my arm?" thought Ivan Ilych, and forgetting what he was doing he over-trumped his partner, missing the grand slam by three tricks. And what was most awful of all was that he saw how upset Mikhail Mikhaylovich was about it but did not himself care. And it was dreadful to realize why he did not care.

They all saw that he was suffering, and said: "We can stop if you are tired. Take a rest." Lie down? No, he was not at all tired, and he finished the rubber. All were gloomy and silent. Ivan Ilych felt that he had diffused this gloom over them and could not dispel it. They had supper and went away, and Ivan Ilych was left alone with the consciousness that his life was poisoned and was poisoning the lives of others, and that this poison did not weaken but penetrated more and more deeply into his whole being.

With this consciousness, and with physical pain besides the terror, he must go to bed, often to lie awake the greater part of the night. Next morning he had to get up again, dress, go to the law courts, speak, and write; or if he did not go out, spend at home those twenty-four hours a day each of which was a torture. And he had to live thus all alone on the brink of an abyss, with no one who understood or pitied him.

V

So one month passed and then another. Just before the New Year his brother-in-law came to town and stayed at their house. Ivan Ilych was at the law courts and Praskovya Fedorovna had gone shopping. When Ivan Ilych came home and entered his study he found his brother-in-law there—a healthy, florid man—unpacking his portmanteau himself. He raised his head on hearing Ivan Ilych's footsteps and looked up at him for a moment without a word. That stare told Ivan Ilych everything. His brother-in-law opened his mouth to utter an exclamation of surprise but checked himself, and that action confirmed it all.

"I have changed, eh?"

"Yes, there is a change."

And after that, try as he would to get his brother-in-law to return to the subject of his looks, the latter would say nothing about it. Praskovya Fedorovna came home and her brother went out to her. Ivan Ilych locked the door and began to examine himself in the glass, first full face, then in profile. He took up a portrait of himself taken with his wife, and compared it with what he saw in the glass. The change in him was immense. Then he bared his arms to the elbow, looked at them, drew the sleeves down again, sat down on an ottoman, and grew blacker than night.

"No, no, this won't do!" he said to himself, and jumped up, went to the table, took up some law papers and began to read them, but could not continue. He unlocked the door and went into the reception-room. The door leading to the drawing-room was shut. He approached it on tiptoe and listened.

"No, you are exaggerating!" Praskovya Fedorovna was saying.

"Exaggerating! Don't you see it? Why, he's a dead man! Look at his eyes—there's no life in them. But what is it that is wrong with him?"

"No one knows. Nikolaevich said something, but I don't know what. And Seshchetitsky said quite the contrary . . ."

Ivan Ilych walked away, went to his own room, lay down, and began musing; "The kidney, a floating kidney." He recalled all the doctors had told him of how it detached itself and swayed about. And by an effort of imagination he tried to catch that kidney and arrest it and support it. So little was needed for this, it seemed to him. "No, I'll go to see Peter Ivanovich again." He rang, ordered the carriage, and got ready to go.

"Where are you going, Jean?" asked his wife with a specially sad and exceptionally kind look.

This exceptionally kind look irritated him. He looked morosely at her.

"I must go to see Peter Ivanovich."

He went to see Peter Ivanovich, and together they went to see his friend, the doctor. He was in, and Ivan Ilych had a long talk with him.

Reviewing the anatomical and physiological details of what in the doctor's opinion was going on inside him, he understood it all.

There was something, a small thing, in the vermiform appendix. It might all come right. Only stimulate the energy of one organ and check the activity of another, then absorption would take place and everything would come right. He got home rather late for dinner, ate his dinner, and conversed cheerfully, but could not for a long time bring himself to go back to work in his room. At last, however, he went to his study and did what was necessary, but the consciousness that he had put something aside — an important, intimate matter which he would revert to when his work was done — never left him. When he had finished his work he remembered that this intimate matter was the thought of his vermiform appendix. But he did not give himself up to it, and went to the drawing-room for tea. There were callers there, including the examining magistrate who was a desirable match for his daughter, and they were conversing, playing the piano, and singing. Ivan Ilych, as Praskovya Fedorovna remarked, spent that evening more cheerfully than usual, but he never for a moment forgot that he had postponed the important matter of the appendix. At eleven o'clock he said goodnight and went to his bedroom. Since his illness he had slept alone in a small room next to his study. He undressed and took up a novel by Zola,[4] but instead of reading it he fell into thought, and in his imagination that desired improvement in the vermiform appendix occurred. There was the absorption and evacuation and the re-establishment of normal activity. "Yes, that's it!" he said to himself. "One need only assist nature, that's all." He remembered his medicine, rose, took it, and lay down on his back watching for the beneficent action of the medicine and for it to lessen the pain. "I need only take it regularly and avoid all injurious influences. I am already feeling better, much better." He began touching his side: it was not painful to the touch. "There, I really don't feel it. It's much better already." He put out the light and turned on his side . . . "The appendix is getting better, absorption is occurring." Suddenly he felt the old, familiar, dull, gnawing pain, stubborn and serious. There was the same familiar loathsome taste in his mouth. His heart sank and he felt dazed. "My God! My God!" he muttered. "Again, again! And it will never cease." And suddenly the matter presented itself in a quite different aspect. "Vermiform appendix! Kidney!" he said to himself. "It's not a question of appendix or kidney, but of life and . . . death. Yes, life was there and now it is going, going and I cannot stop it. Yes. Why deceive myself? Isn't it obvious to everyone but me that I'm dying, and that it's only a question of weeks, days . . . it may happen this moment. There was light and now there is darkness. I was here and now I'm going there! Where?" A chill came over him, his breathing ceased, and he felt only the throbbing of his heart.

"When I am not, what will there be? There will be nothing. Then where shall I be when I am no more? Can this be dying? No, I don't want to!" He jumped up and tried to light the candle, felt for it with trembling hands, dropped candle and candlestick on the floor, and fell back on his pillow.

"What's the use? It makes no difference," he said to himself, staring with wide-open eyes into the darkness. "Death. Yes, death. And none of them knows or wishes to know it, and they have no pity for me. Now they are playing." (He heard through the door the distant sound of a song and its accompaniment.) "It's all the same to them, but they will die too! Fools! I first, and they later, but it will be the same for them. And now they are merry . . . the beasts!"

Anger choked him and he was agonizingly, unbearably miserable. "It is impossible that all men have been doomed to suffer this awful horror!" He raised himself.

"Something must be wrong. I must calm myself—must think it all over from the beginning." And he again began thinking. "Yes, the beginning of my illness: I knocked my side, but I was still quite well that day and the next. It hurt a little, then rather more. I saw the doctors, then followed despondency and anguish, more doctors, and I drew nearer to the abyss. My strength grew less and I kept coming nearer and nearer, and now I have wasted away and there is no light in my eyes. I think of the appendix—but this is death! I think of mending the appendix, and all the while here is death! Can it really be death?" Again terror seized him and he gasped for breath. He leant down and began feeling for the matches, pressing with his elbow on the stand beside the bed. It was in his way and hurt him, he grew furious with it, pressed on it still harder, and upset it. Breathless and in despair he fell on his back, expecting death to come immediately.

Meanwhile the visitors were leaving. Praskovya Fedorovna was seeing them off. She heard something fall and came in.

"What has happened?"

"Nothing. I knocked it over accidentally."

4. The French novelist Emile Zola (1840–1902) was a proponent of the school of naturalism and a virtuoso portraitist of gruesome death from disease.

She went out and returned with a candle. He lay there panting heavily, like a man who has run a thousand yards, and stared upwards at her with a fixed look.

"What is it, Jean?"

"No . . . o . . . thing. I upset it." ("Why speak of it? She won't understand," he thought.)

And in truth she did not understand. She picked up the stand, lit his candle, and hurried away to see another visitor off. When she came back he still lay on his back, looking upwards.

"What is it? Do you feel worse?"

"Yes."

She shook her head and sat down.

"Do you know, Jean, I think we must ask Leshchetitsky to come and see you here."

This meant calling in the famous specialist, regardless of expense. He smiled malignantly and said "No." She remained a little longer and then went up to him and kissed his forehead.

While she was kissing him he hated her from the bottom of his soul and with difficulty refrained from pushing her away.

"Good night. Please God you'll sleep."

"Yes."

VI

Ivan Ilych saw that he was dying, and he was in continual despair.

In the depth of his heart he knew he was dying, but not only was he not accustomed to the thought, he simply did not and could not grasp it.

The syllogism he had learnt from Kiesewetter's Logic: "Caius is a man, men are mortal, therefore Caius is mortal," had always seemed to him correct as applied to Caius, but certainly not as applied to himself. That Caius—man in the abstract—was mortal, was perfectly correct, but he was not Caius, not an abstract man, but a creature quite, quite separate from all others. He had been little Vanya, with a mamma and a papa, with Mitya and Volodya, with the toys, a coachman and a nurse, afterwards with Katenka and with all the joys, griefs, and delights of childhood, boyhood, and youth. What did Caius know of the smell of that striped leather ball Vanya had been so fond of? Had Caius kissed his mother's hand like that, and did the silk of her dress rustle so for Caius? Had he rioted like that at school when the pastry was bad? Had Caius been in love like that? Could Caius preside at a session as he did? "Caius really was mortal, and it was right for him to die; but for me, little Vanya, Ivan Ilych, with all my thoughts and emotions, it's altogether a different matter. It cannot be that I ought to die. That would be too terrible." Such was his feeling.

"If I had to die like Caius I would have known it was so. An inner voice would have told me so, but there was nothing of the sort in me and I and all my friends felt that our case was quite different from that of Caius. And now here it is!" he said to himself. "It can't be. It's impossible! But here it is. How is this? How is one to understand it?" He could not understand it, and tried to drive this false, incorrect, morbid thought away and to replace it by other proper and healthy thoughts. But that thought, and not the thought only but the reality itself, seemed to come and confront him.

And to replace that thought he called up a succession of others, hoping to find in them some support. He tried to get back into the former current of thoughts that had once screened the thought of death from him. But strange to say, all that had formerly shut off, hidden, and destroyed his consciousness of death, no longer had that effect. Ivan Ilych now spent most of his time in attempting to re-establish that old current. He would say to himself: "I will take up my duties again—after all I used to live by them." And banishing all doubts he would go to the law courts, enter into conversation with his colleagues, and sit carelessly as was his wont, scanning the crowd with a thoughtful look and leaning both his emaciated arms on the arms of his oak chair; bending over as usual to a colleague and drawing his papers nearer he would interchange whispers with him, and then suddenly raising his eyes and sitting erect would pronounce certain words and open the proceedings. But suddenly in the midst of those proceedings the pain in his side, regardless of the stage the proceedings had reached, would begin its own gnawing work. Ivan Ilych would turn his attention to it and try to drive the thought of it away, but without success. *It* would come and stand before him and look at him, and he would be petrified and the light would die out of his eyes, and he would again begin asking himself whether *It* alone was true. And his colleagues and subordinates would see with surprise and distress that he, the brilliant and subtle judge, was becoming confused and making mistakes. He would shake himself, try to pull himself together, manage somehow to bring the sitting to a close, and return home with the sorrowful consciousness that his judicial labours could not as formerly hide from him what he wanted them to hide, and could not deliver him from *It*. And what was worst of all was that *It* drew his attention to itself not in order to make him take some action but only that he should look at *It*, look it straight in the face: look at it and without doing anything, suffer inexpressibly.

And to save himself from this condition Ivan Ilych looked for consolations—new screens—and new screens were found and for a while seemed to save him, but then they immediately fell to pieces or rather became transparent, as if *It* penetrated them and nothing could veil *It*.

In these latter days he would go into the drawing-room he had arranged—that drawing-room where he had fallen and for the sake of which (how bitterly ridiculous it seemed) he had sacrificed his life—for he knew that his illness originated with that knock. He would enter and see that something had scratched the polished table. He would look for the cause of this and find that it was the bronze ornamentation of an album, that had got bent. He would take up the expensive album which he had lovingly arranged, and feel vexed with his daughter and her friends for their untidiness—for the album was torn here and there and some of the photographs turned upside down. He would put it carefully in order and bend the ornamentation back into position. Then it would occur to him to place all those things in another corner of the room, near the plants. He would call the footman, but his daughter or wife would come to help him. They would not agree, and his wife would contradict him, and he would dispute and grow angry. But that was all right, for then he did not think about *It*. *It* was invisible.

But then, when he was moving something himself, his wife would say: "Let the servants do it. You will hurt yourself again." And suddenly *It* would flash through the screen and he would see it. It was just a flash, and he hoped it would disappear, but he would involuntarily pay attention to his side. "It sits there as before, gnawing just the same!" And he could no longer forget *It*, but could distinctly see it looking at him from behind the flowers. "What is it all for?"

"It really is so! I lost my life over that curtain as I might have done when storming a fort. Is that possible? How terrible and how stupid. It can't be true! It can't, but it is." He would go to his study, lie down, and again be alone with *It*: face to face with *It*. And nothing could be done with *It* except to look at it and shudder.

VII

How it happened it is impossible to say because it came about step by step, unnoticed, but in the third month of Ivan Ilych's illness, his wife, his daughter, his son, his acquaintances, the doctors, the servants, and above all he himself, were aware that the whole interest he had for other people was whether he would soon vacate his place, and at last release the living from the discomfort caused by his presence and be himself released from his sufferings.

He slept less and less. He was given opium and hypodermic injections of morphine, but this did not relieve him. The dull depression he experienced in a somnolent condition at first gave him a little relief, but only as something new, afterwards it became as distressing as the pain itself or even more so.

Special foods were prepared for him by the doctors' orders, but all those foods became increasingly distasteful and disgusting to him.

For his excretions also special arrangements had to be made, and this was a torment to him every time—a torment from the uncleanliness, the unseemliness, and the smell, and from knowing that another person had to take part in it.

But just through his most unpleasant matter, Ivan Ilych obtained comfort. Gerasim, the butler's young assistant, always came in to carry the things out. Gerasim was a clean, fresh peasant lad, grown stout on town food and always cheerful and bright. At first the sight of him, in his clean Russian peasant costume, engaged on that disgusting task embarrassed Ivan Ilych.

Once when he got up from the commode too weak to draw up his trousers, he dropped into a soft armchair and looked with horror at his bare, enfeebled thighs with the muscles so sharply marked on them.

Gerasim with a firm light tread, his heavy boots emitting a pleasant smell of tar and fresh winter air, came in wearing a clean Hessian apron, the sleeves of his print shirt tucked up over his strong bare young arms; and refraining from looking at his sick master out of consideration for his feelings, and restraining the joy of life that beamed from his face, he went up to the commode.

"Gerasim!" said Ivan Ilych in a weak voice.

Gerasim started, evidently afraid he might have committed some blunder, and with a rapid movement turned his fresh, kind, simple young face which just showed the first downy signs of a beard.

"Yes, sir?"

"That must be very unpleasant for you. You must forgive me. I am helpless."

"Oh, why, sir," and Gerasim's eyes beamed and he showed his glistening white teeth, "what's a little trouble? It's a case of illness with you, sir."

And his deft strong hands did their accustomed task, and he went out of the room stepping lightly. Five minutes later he as lightly returned.

Ivan Ilych was still sitting in the same position in the armchair.

"Gerasim," he said when the latter had replaced the freshly-washed utensil. "Please come here and help me." Gerasim went up to him. "Lift me up. It is hard for me to get up, and I have sent Dmitri away."

Gerasim went up to him, grasped his master with his strong arms deftly but gently, in the same way that he stepped—lifted him, supported him with one hand, and with the other drew up his trousers and would have set him down again, but Ivan Ilych asked to be led to the sofa. Gerasim, without an effort and without apparent pressure, led him, almost lifting him, to the sofa and placed him on it.

"Thank you. How easily and well you do it all!"

Gerasim smiled again and turned to leave the room. But Ivan Ilych felt his presence such a comfort that he did not want to let him go.

"One thing more, please move up that chair. No, the other one—under my feet. It is easier for me when my feet are raised."

Gerasim brought the chair, set it down gently in place, and raised Ivan Ilych's legs on it. It seemed to Ivan Ilych that he felt better while Gerasim was holding up his legs.

"It's better when my legs are higher," he said. "Place that cushion under them."

Gerasim did so. He again lifted the legs and placed them, and again Ivan Ilych felt better while Gerasim held his legs. When he set them down Ivan Ilych fancied he felt worse.

"Gerasim," he said. "Are you busy now?"

"Not at all, sir," said Gerasim, who had learnt from the townsfolk how to speak to gentlefolk.

"What have you still to do?"

"What have I to do? I've done everything except chopping the logs for tomorrow."

"Then hold my legs up a bit higher, can you?"

"Of course I can. Why not?" and Gerasim raised his master's legs higher and Ivan Ilych thought that in that position he did not feel any pain at all.

"And how about the logs?"

"Don't trouble about that, sir. There's plenty of time."

Ivan Ilych told Gerasim to sit down and hold his legs, and began to talk to him. And strange to say it seemed to him that he felt better while Gerasim held his legs up.

After that Ivan Ilych would sometimes call Gerasim and get him to hold his legs on his shoulders, and he liked talking to him. Gerasim did it all easily, willingly, simply, and with a good nature that touched Ivan Ilych. Health, strength, and vitality in other people were offensive to him, but Gerasim's strength and vitality did not mortify but soothed him.

What tormented Ivan Ilych most was the deception, the lie, which for some reason they all accepted, that he was not dying but was simply ill, and that he only need keep quiet and undergo a treatment and then something very good would result. He however knew that do what they would nothing would come of it, only still more agonizing suffering and death. This deception tortured him—their not wishing to admit what they all knew and what he knew, but wanting to lie to him concerning his terrible condition, and wishing and forcing him to participate in that lie. Those lies—lies enacted over him on the eve of his death and destined to degrade this awful, solemn act to the level of their visitings, their curtains, their sturgeon for dinner—were a terrible agony for Ivan Ilych. And strangely enough, many times when they were going through their antics over him he had been within a hairbreadth of calling out to them: "Stop lying! You know and I know that I am dying. Then at least stop lying about it!" But he had never had the spirit to do it. The awful, terrible act of his dying was, he could see, reduced by those about him to the level of a casual, unpleasant, and almost indecorous incident (as if someone entered a drawing room defusing an unpleasant odour) and this was done by that very decorum which he had served all his life long. He saw that no one felt for him, because no one even wished to grasp his position. Only Gerasim recognized it and pitied him. And so Ivan Ilych felt at ease only with him. He felt comforted when Gerasim supported his legs (sometimes all night long) and refused to go to bed, saying: "Don't you worry, Ivan Ilych. I'll get sleep enough later on," or when he suddenly became familiar and exclaimed: "If you weren't sick it would be another matter, but as it is, why should I grudge a little trouble?" Gerasim alone did not lie; everything showed that he alone understood the facts of the case and did not consider it necessary to disguise them, but simply felt sorry for his emaciated and enfeebled master. Once when Ivan Ilych was sending him away he even said straight out: "We shall all of us die, so why should I grudge a little trouble?"—expressing the fact that he did not think his work burdensome, because he was doing it for a dying man and hoped someone would do the same for him when his time came.

Apart from this lying, or because of it, what most tormented Ivan Ilych was that no one pitied him as he wished to be pitied. At certain moments after prolonged suffering he wished most of all (though he would have been ashamed to confess it) for someone to pity him as a sick child is pitied. He longed to be petted and comforted. He knew he was an important functionary, that he had a beard turning grey, and that therefore what he longed for was impossible, but still he longed for it. And in Gerasim's attitude towards him there was something akin to what he wished for, and so that attitude comforted him. Ivan Ilych wanted to weep, wanted to be petted and cried over, and then his colleague Shebek would come, and instead of weeping and being petted, Ivan Ilych would assume a serious, severe, and profound air, and by force of habit would express his opinion on a decision of the Court of Cassation and would stubbornly insist on that view. This falsity around him and within him did more than anything else to poison his last days.

VIII

It was morning. He knew it was morning because Gerasim had gone, and Peter the footman had come and put out the candles, drawn back one of the curtains, and begun quietly to tidy up. Whether it was morning or evening, Friday or Sunday, made no difference, it was all just the same: the gnawing, unmitigated, agonizing pain, never ceasing for an instant, the consciousness of life inexorably waning but not yet extinguished, the approach of that ever dreaded and hateful Death which was the only reality, and always the same falsity. What were days, weeks, hours, in such a case?

"Will you have some tea, sir?"

"He wants things to be regular, and wishes the gentlefolk to drink tea in the morning," thought Ivan Ilych, and only said "No."

"Wouldn't you like to move onto the sofa, sir?"

"He wants to tidy up the room, and I'm in the way. I am uncleanliness and disorder," he thought, and said only:

"No, leave me alone."

The man went on bustling about. Ivan Ilych stretched out his hand. Peter came up, ready to help.

"What is it, sir?"

"My watch."

Peter took the watch which was close at hand and gave it to his master.

"Half-past eight. Are they up?"

"No sir, except Vladimir Ivanovich" (the son) "who has gone to school. Praskovya Fedorovna ordered me to wake her if you asked for her. Shall I do so?"

"No, there's no need to." "Perhaps I'd better have some tea," he thought, and added aloud: "Yes, bring me some tea."

Peter went to the door, but Ivan Ilych dreaded being left alone. "How can I keep him here? Oh yes, my medicine." "Peter, give me my medicine." "Why not? Perhaps it may still do some good." He took a spoonful and swallowed it. "No, it won't help. It's all tomfoolery, all deception," he decided as soon as he became aware of the familiar, sickly, hopeless taste. "No, I can't believe in it any longer. But the pain, why this pain? If it would only cease just for a moment!" And he moaned. Peter turned towards him. "It's all right. Go and fetch me some tea."

Peter went out. Left alone Ivan Ilych groaned not so much with pain, terrible though that was, as from mental anguish. Always and forever the same, always these endless days and nights. If only it would come quicker! If only *what* would come quicker? Death, darkness? . . . No, no! anything rather than death!

When Peter returned with the tea on a tray, Ivan Ilych stared at him for a time in perplexity, not realizing who and what he was. Peter was disconcerted by that look and his embarrassment brought Ivan Ilych to himself.

"Oh, tea! All right, put it down. Only help me to wash and put on a clean shirt."

And Ivan Ilych began to wash. With pauses for rest, he washed his hands and then his face, cleaned his teeth, brushed his hair, looked in the glass. He was terrified by what he saw, especially by the limp way in which his hair clung to his pallid forehead.

While his shirt was being changed he knew that he would be still more frightened at the sight of his body, so he avoided looking at it. Finally he was ready. He drew on a dressing-gown, wrapped himself in a plaid, and sat down in the armchair to take his tea. For a moment he felt refreshed, but as soon as he began to drink the tea he was again aware of the same taste, and the pain also returned. He finished it with an effort, and then lay down stretching out his legs, and dismissed Peter.

Always the same. Now a spark of hope flashes up, then a sea of despair rages, and always pain; always pain, always despair, and always the same. When alone he had a dreadful and distressing desire to call someone, but he knew beforehand that with others present it would be still worse. "Another dose of morphine—to lose consciousness. I will tell him, the doctor, that he must think of something else. It's impossible, impossible, to go on like this."

An hour and another pass like that. But now there is a ring at the door bell. Perhaps it's the doctor? It is. He comes in fresh, hearty, plump, and cheerful, with that look on his face that seems to say: "There now, you're in a panic about something, but we'll arrange it all for you directly!" The doctor knows this expression is out of place here, but he has put it on once for all and can't take it off—like a man who has put on a frock-coat in the morning to pay a round of calls.

The doctor rubs his hands vigorously and reassuringly.

"Brr! How cold it is! There's such a sharp frost; just let me warm myself!" he says, as if it were only a matter of waiting till he was warm, and then he would put everything right.

"Well now, how are you?"

Ivan Ilych feels that the doctor would like to say: "Well, how are our affairs?" but that even he feels that this would not do, and says instead: "What sort of a night have you had?"

Ivan Ilych looks at him as much as to say: "Are you really never ashamed of lying?" But the doctor does not wish to understand this question, and Ivan Ilych says: "Just as terrible as ever. The pain never leaves me and never subsides. If only something . . ."

"Yes, you sick people are always like that. . . . There, now I think I am warm enough. Even Praskovya Fedorovna, who is so particular, could find no fault with my temperature. Well, now I can say good-morning," and the doctor presses his patient's hand.

Then dropping his former playfulness, he begins with a most serious face to examine the patient, feeling his pulse and taking his temperature, and then begins the sounding and auscultation.

Ivan Ilych knows quite well and definitely that all this is nonsense and pure deception, but when the doctor, getting down on his knee, leans over him, putting his ear first higher then lower, and performs various gymnastic movements over him with a significant expression on his face, Ivan Ilych submits to it all as he used to submit to the speeches of the lawyers, though he knew very well that they were all lying and why they were lying.

The doctor, kneeling on the sofa, is still sounding him when Praskovya Fedorovna's silk dress rustles at the door and she is heard scolding Peter for not having let her know of the doctor's arrival.

She comes in, kisses her husband, and at once proceeds to prove that she has been up a long time already, and only owing to a misunderstanding failed to be there when the doctor arrived.

Ivan Ilych looks at her, scans her all over, sets against her the whiteness and plumpness and cleanness of her hands and neck, the gloss of her hair, and the sparkle of her vivacious eyes. He hates her with his whole soul. And the thrill of hatred he feels for her makes him suffer from her touch.

Her attitude towards him and his diseases is still the same. Just as the doctor had adopted a certain relation to his patient which he could not abandon, so had she formed one towards him—that he was not doing something he ought to do and was himself to blame, and that she reproached him lovingly for this—and she could not now change that attitude.

"You see he doesn't listen to me and doesn't take his medicine at the proper time. And above all he lies in a position that is no doubt bad for him—with his legs up."

She described how he made Gerasim hold his legs up.

The doctor smiled with a contemptuous affability that said: "What's to be done? These sick people do have foolish fancies of that kind, but we must forgive them."

When the examination was over the doctor looked at his watch, and then Praskovya Fedorovna announced to Ivan Ilych that it was of course as he pleased, but she had sent today for a celebrated specialist who would examine him and have a consultation with Michael Danilovich (their regular doctor).

"Please don't raise any objections. I am doing this for my own sake," she said ironically, letting it be felt that she was doing it all for his sake and only said this to leave him no right to refuse. He remained silent, knitting his brows. He felt that he was surrounded and involved in a mesh of falsity that it was hard to unravel anything. Everything she did for him was entirely for her own sake, and she told him she was doing for herself what she actually was doing for herself, as if that was so incredible that he must understand the opposite.

At half-past eleven the celebrated specialist arrived. Again the sounding began and the significant conversations in his presence and in another room, about the kidneys and the appendix, and the questions and answers, with such an air of importance that again, instead of the real question of life and death which now alone confronted him, the question arose of the kidney and appendix which were not behaving as they ought to and would now be attacked by Michael Danilovich and the specialist and forced to amend their ways.

The celebrated specialist took leave of him with a serious though not hopeless look, and in reply to the timid question Ivan Ilych, with eyes glistening with fear and hope, put to him as to whether there was a chance of recovery, said that he could not vouch for it but there was a possibility. The look of hope with which Ivan Ilych watched the doctor out was so pathetic that Praskovya Fedorovna, seeing it, even wept as she left the room to hand the doctor his fee.

The gleam of hope kindled by the doctor's encouragement did not last long. The same room, the same pictures, curtains, wallpaper, medicine bottles, were all there, and the same aching suffering body, and Ivan Ilych began to moan. They gave him a subcutaneous injection and he sank into oblivion.

It was twilight when he came to. They brought him his dinner and he swallowed some beef tea with difficulty, and then everything was the same again and night was coming on.

After dinner, at seven o'clock, Praskovya Fedorovna came into the room in evening dress, her full bosom pushed up by her corset, and with traces of powder on her face. She had reminded him in the morning that they were going to the theatre. Sarah Bernhardt[5] was visiting the town and they had a box, which he had insisted on their taking. Now he had forgotten about it and her toilet offended him, but he concealed his vexation when he remembered that he had himself insisted on their securing a box and going because it would be an instructive and aesthetic pleasure for the children.

Praskovya Fedorovna came in, self-satisfied but yet with a rather guilty air. She sat down and asked how he was, but, as he saw, only for the sake of asking and not in order to learn about it, knowing that there was nothing to learn—and then went on to what she really wanted to say: that she would not on any account have gone but that the box had been taken and Helen and their daughter were going, as well as Petrishchev (the examining magistrate, their daughter's fiance) and that it was out of the question to let them go alone; but that she would have much preferred to sit with him for a while; and he must be sure to follow the doctor's orders while she was away.

"Oh, and Fedor Petrovich" (the fiance) "would like to come in. May he? And Lisa?"

"All right."

5. "The Divine Sarah" was the most celebrated actress of her century.

Their daughter came in in full evening dress, her fresh young flesh exposed (making a show of that very flesh which in his own case caused so much suffering), strong, healthy, evidently in love, and impatient with illness, suffering, and death, because they interfered with her happiness.

Fedor Petrovich came in too, in evening dress, his hair curled *a la Capoul*,[6] a tight stiff collar round his long sinewy neck, an enormous white shirt-front and narrow black trousers tightly stretched over his strong thighs. He had one white glove tightly drawn on, and was holding his opera hat in his hand.

Following him the schoolboy crept in unnoticed, in a new uniform, poor little fellow, and wearing gloves. Terribly dark shadows showed under his eyes, the meaning of which Ivan Ilych knew well.

His son had always seemed pathetic to him, and now it was dreadful to see the boy's frightened look of pity. It seemed to Ivan Ilych that Vasya was the only one besides Gerasim who understood and pitied him.

They all sat down and again asked how he was. A silence followed. Lisa asked her mother about the opera glasses, and there was an altercation between mother and daughter as to who had taken them and where they had been put. This occasioned some unpleasantness.

Fedor Petrovich inquired of Ivan Ilych whether he had ever seen Sarah Bernhardt. Ivan Ilych did not at first catch the question, but then replied: "No, have you seen her before?"

"Yes, in *Adrienne Lecouvreur*.[7]"

Praskovya Fedorovna mentioned some roles in which Sarah Bernhardt was particularly good. Her daughter disagreed. Conversation sprang up as to the elegance and realism of her acting—the sort of conversation that is always repeated and is always the same.

In the midst of the conversation Fedor Petrovich glanced at Ivan Ilych and became silent. The others also looked at him and grew silent. Ivan Ilych was staring with glittering eyes straight before him, evidently indignant with them. This had to be rectified, but it was impossible to do so. The silence had to be broken, but for a time no one dared to break it and they all became afraid that the conventional deception would suddenly become obvious and the truth become plain to all. Lisa was the first to pluck up courage and break that silence, but by trying to hide what everybody was feeling, she betrayed it.

"Well, if we are going it's time to start," she said, looking at her watch, a present from her father, and with a faint and significant smile at Fedor Petrovich relating to something known only to them. She got up with a rustle of her dress.

They all rose, said good-night, and went away.

When they had gone it seemed to Ivan Ilych that he felt better; the falsity had gone with them. But the pain remained—that same pain and that same fear that made everything monotonously alike, nothing harder and nothing easier. Everything was worse.

Again minute followed minute and hour followed hour. Everything remained the same and there was no cessation. And the inevitable end of it all became more and more terrible.

"Yes, send Gerasim here," he replied to a question Peter asked.

6. An elaborate style named after a French singer.

7. An tragic drama based on the life and early death of an eighteenth-century actress.

IX

His wife returned late at night. She came in on tiptoe, but he heard her, opened his eyes, and made haste to close them again. She wished to send Gerasim away and to sit with him herself, but he opened his eyes and said: "No, go away."

"Are you in great pain?"

"Always the same."

"Take some opium."

He agreed and took some. She went away.

Till about three in the morning he was in a state of stupefied misery. It seemed to him that he and his pain were being thrust into a narrow, deep black sack, but though they were pushed further and further in they could not be pushed to the bottom. And this, terrible enough in itself, was accompanied by suffering. He was frightened yet wanted to fall through the sack, he struggled but yet cooperated. And suddenly he broke through, fell, and regained consciousness. Gerasim was sitting at the foot of the bed dozing quietly and patiently, while he himself lay with his emaciated stockinged legs resting on Gerasim's shoulders; the same shaded candle was there and the same unceasing pain.

"Go away, Gerasim," he whispered.

"It's all right, sir. I'll stay a while."

"No. Go away."

He removed his legs from Gerasim's shoulders, turned sideways onto his arm, and felt sorry for himself. He only waited till Gerasim had gone into the next room and then restrained himself no longer but wept like a child. He wept on account of his helplessness, his terrible loneliness, the cruelty of man, the cruelty of God, and the absence of God.

"Why hast Thou done all this? Why hast Thou brought me here? Why, why dost Thou torment me so terribly?"

He did not expect an answer and yet wept because there was no answer and could be none. The pain again grew more acute, but he did not stir and did not call. He said to himself: "Go on! Strike me! But what is it for? What have I done to Thee? What is it for?"

Then he grew quiet and not only ceased weeping but even held his breath and became all attention. It was as though he were listening not to an audible voice but to the voice of his soul, to the current of thoughts arising within him.

"What is it you want?" was the first clear conception capable of expression in words, that he heard.

"What do you want? What do you want?" he repeated to himself.

"What do I want? To live and not to suffer," he answered.

And again he listened with such concentrated attention that even his pain did not distract him.

"To live? How?" asked his inner voice.

"Why, to live as I used to—well and pleasantly."

"As you lived before, well and pleasantly?" the voice repeated.

And in imagination he began to recall the best moments of his pleasant life. But strange to say none of those best moments of his pleasant life now seemed at all what they had then seemed—none of them except the first recollections of childhood. There, in childhood, there had been something really pleasant with which it would be possible to live if it could return. But the child who had experienced that happiness existed no longer, it was like a reminiscence of somebody else.

As soon as the period began which had produced the present Ivan Ilych, all that had then seemed joys now melted before his sight and turned into something trivial and often nasty.

And the further he departed from childhood and the nearer he came to the present the more worthless and doubtful were the joys. This began with the School of Law. A little that was really good was still found there—there was lightheartedness, friendship, and hope. But in the upper classes there had already been fewer of such good moments. Then during the first years of his official career, when he was in the service of the governor, some pleasant moments again occurred: they were the memories of love for a woman. Then all became confused and there was still less of what was good; later on again there was still less that was good, and the further he went the less there was. His marriage, a mere accident, then the disenchantment that followed it, his wife's bad breath and the sensuality and hypocrisy: then that deadly official life and those preoccupations about money, a year of it, and two, and ten, and twenty, and always the same thing. And the longer it lasted the more deadly it became. "It is as if I had been going downhill while I imagined I was going up. And that is really what it was. I was going up in public opinion, but to the same extent life was ebbing away from me. And now it is all done and there is only death.

"Then what does it mean? Why? It can't be that life is so senseless and horrible. But if it really has been so horrible and senseless, why must I die and die in agony? There is something wrong!

"Maybe I did not live as I ought to have done," it suddenly occurred to him. "But how could that be, when I did everything properly?" he replied, and immediately dismissed from his mind this, the sole solution of all the riddles of life and death, as something quite impossible.

"Then what do you want now? To live? Live how? Live as you lived in the law courts when the usher proclaimed 'The judge is coming!' The judge is coming, the judge!" he repeated to himself. "Here he is, the judge. But I am not guilty!" he exclaimed angrily. "What is it for?" And he ceased crying, but turning his face to the wall continued to ponder on the same question: Why, and for what purpose, is there all this horror? But however much he pondered he found no answer. And whenever the thought occurred to him, as it often did, that it all resulted from his not having lived as he ought to have done, he at once recalled the correctness of his whole life and dismissed so strange an idea.

X

Another fortnight passed. Ivan Ilych now no longer left his sofa. He would not lie in bed but lay on the sofa, facing the wall nearly all the time. He suffered ever the same unceasing agonies and in his loneliness pondered always on the same insoluble question: "What is this? Can it be that it is Death?" And the inner voice answered: "Yes, it is Death."

"Why these sufferings?" And the voice answered, "For no reason—they just are so." Beyond and besides this there was nothing.

From the very beginning of his illness, ever since he had first been to see the doctor, Ivan Ilych's life had been divided between two contrary and alternating moods: now it was despair and the expectation of this uncomprehended and terrible death, and now hope and an intently interested observation of the functioning of his organs. Now before his eyes there was only a kidney or an intestine that temporarily evaded its duty, and now only that incomprehensible and dreadful death from which it was impossible to escape.

These two states of mind had alternated from the very beginning of his illness, but the further it progressed the more doubtful and fantastic became the conception of the kidney, and the more real the sense of impending death.

He had but to call to mind what he had been three months before and what he was now, to call to mind with what regularity he had been going downhill, for every possibility of hope to be shattered.

Latterly during the loneliness in which he found himself as he lay facing the back of the sofa, a loneliness in the midst of a populous town and surrounded by numerous acquaintances and relations but that yet could not have been more complete anywhere—either at the bottom of the sea or under the earth—during that terrible loneliness Ivan Ilych had lived only in memories of the past. Pictures of his past rose before him one after another. They always began with what was nearest in time and then went back to what was most remote—to his childhood—and rested there. If he thought of the stewed prunes that had been offered him that day, his mind went back to the raw shrivelled French plums of his childhood, their peculiar flavour and the flow of saliva when he sucked their stones, and along with the memory of that taste came a whole series of memories of those days: his nurse, his brother, and their toys. "No, I mustn't think of that. . . . It is too painful," Ivan Ilych said to himself, and brought himself back to the present—to the button on the back of the sofa and the creases in its morocco. "Morocco is expensive, but it does not wear well: there had been a quarrel about it. It was a different kind of quarrel and a different kind of morocco that time when we tore father's portfolio and were punished, and mamma brought us some tarts. . . ." And again his thoughts dwelt on his childhood, and again it was painful and he tried to banish them and fix his mind on something else.

Then again together with that chain of memories another series passed through his mind—of how his illness had progressed and grown worse. There also the further back he looked the more life there had been. There had been more of what was good in life and more of life itself. The two merged together. "Just as the pain went on getting worse and worse, so my life grew worse and worse," he thought. "There is one bright spot there at the back, at the beginning of life, and afterwards all becomes blacker and blacker and proceeds more and more rapidly—in inverse ratio to the square of the distance from death," thought Ivan Ilych. And the example of a stone falling downwards with increasing velocity entered his mind. Life, a series of increasing sufferings, flies further and further towards its end—the most terrible suffering. "I am flying. . . ." He shuddered, shifted himself, and tried to resist, but was already aware that resistance was impossible, and again with eyes weary of gazing but unable to cease seeing what was before them, he stared at the back of the sofa and waited—awaiting that dreadful fall and shock and destruction.

"Resistance is impossible!" he said to himself. "If I could only understand what it is all for! But that too is impossible. An explanation would be possible if it could be said that I have not lived as I ought to. But it is impossible to say that," and he remembered all the legality, correctitude, and propriety of his life. "That at any rate can certainly not be admitted," he thought, and his lips smiled ironically as if someone could see that smile and be taken in by it. "There is no explanation! Agony, death. . . . What for?"

XI

Another two weeks went by in this way and during that fortnight an event occurred that Ivan Ilych and his wife had desired. Petrishchev formally proposed. It happened in the evening. The next day Praskovya Fedorovna came into her husband's room considering how best to inform him of it, but that very night there had been a fresh change for the worse in his condition. She found him still lying on the sofa but in a different position. He lay on his back, groaning and staring fixedly straight in front of him.

She began to remind him of his medicines, but he turned his eyes towards her with such a look that she did not finish what she was saying; so great an animosity, to her in particular, did that look express.

"For Christ's sake let me die in peace!" he said.

She would have gone away, but just then their daughter came in and went up to say good morning. He looked at her as he had done at his wife, and in reply to her inquiry about his health said dryly that he would soon free them all of himself. They were both silent and after sitting with him for a while went away.

"Is it our fault?" Lisa said to her mother. "It's as if we were to blame! I am sorry for papa, but why should we be tortured?"

The doctor came at his usual time. Ivan Ilych answered "Yes" and "No," never taking his angry eyes from him, and at last said: "You know you can do nothing for me, so leave me alone."

"We can ease your sufferings."

"You can't even do that. Let me be."

The doctor went into the drawing room and told Praskovya Fedorovna that the case was very serious and that the only resource left was opium to allay her husband's sufferings, which must be terrible.

It was true, as the doctor said, that Ivan Ilych's physical sufferings were terrible, but worse than the physical sufferings were his mental sufferings which were his chief torture.

His mental sufferings were due to the fact that that night, as he looked at Gerasim's sleepy, good-natured face with its prominent cheek-bones, the question suddenly occurred to him: "What if my whole life has been wrong?"

It occurred to him that what had appeared perfectly impossible before, namely that he had not spent his life as he should have done, might after all be true. It occurred to him that his scarcely perceptible attempts to struggle against what was considered good by the most highly placed people, those scarcely noticeable impulses which he had immediately suppressed, might have been the real thing, and all the rest false. And his professional duties and the whole arrangement of his life and of his family, and all his social and official interests, might all have been false. He tried to defend all those things to himself and suddenly felt the weakness of what he was defending. There was nothing to defend.

"But if that is so," he said to himself, "and I am leaving this life with the consciousness that I have lost all that was given me and it is impossible to rectify it—what then?"

He lay on his back and began to pass his life in review in quite a new way. In the morning when he saw first his footman, then his wife, then his daughter, and then the doctor, their every word and movement confirmed to him the awful truth that had been revealed to him during the night. In them he saw himself—all that for which he had lived—and saw clearly that it was not real at all, but a terrible and huge deception which had hidden both life and death. This consciousness intensified his physical suffering tenfold. He groaned and tossed about, and pulled at his clothing which choked and stifled him. And he hated them on that account.

He was given a large dose of opium and became unconscious, but at noon his sufferings began again. He drove everybody away and tossed from side to side. His wife came to him and said:

"Jean, my dear, do this for me. It can't do any harm and often helps. Healthy people often do it."

He opened his eyes wide.

"What? Take communion? Why? It's unnecessary! However . . . ".

She began to cry.

"Yes, do, my dear. I'll send for our priest. He is such a nice man."

"All right. Very well," he muttered.

When the priest came and heard his confession, Ivan Ilych was softened and seemed to feel a relief from his doubts and consequently from his sufferings, and for a moment there came a ray of hope. He again began to think of the vermiform appendix and the possibility of correcting it. He received the sacrament with tears in his eyes.

When they laid him down again afterwards he felt a moment's ease, and the hope that he might live awoke in him again. He began to think of the operation that had been suggested to him. "To live! I want to live!" he said to himself.

His wife came in to congratulate him after his communion, and when uttering the usual conventional words she added:

"You feel better, don't you?"

Without looking at her he said "Yes."

Her dress, her figure, the expression of her face, the tone of her voice, all revealed the same thing. "This is wrong, it is not as it should be. All you have lived for and still live for is falsehood and deception, hiding life and death from you." And as soon as he admitted that thought, his hatred and his agonizing physical suffering again sprang up, and with that suffering a consciousness of the unavoidable, approaching end. And to this was added a new sensation of grinding shooting pain and a feeling of suffocation.

The expression of his face when he uttered that "Yes" was dreadful. Having uttered it, he looked her straight in the eyes, turned on his face with a rapidity extraordinary in his weak state and shouted:

"Go away! Go away and leave me alone!"

XII

From that moment the screaming began that continued for three days, and was so terrible that one could not hear it through two closed doors without horror. At the moment he answered his wife realized that he was lost, that there was no return, that the end had come, the very end, and his doubts were still unsolved and remained doubts.

"Oh! Oh! Oh!" he cried in various intonations. He had begun by screaming "I won't!" and continued screaming on the letter "O."

For three whole days, during which time did not exist for him, he struggled in that black sack into which he was being thrust by an invisible, resistless force. He struggled as a man condemned to death struggles in the hands of the executioner, knowing that he cannot save himself. And every moment he felt that despite all his efforts he was drawing nearer and nearer to what terrified him. He felt that his agony was due to his being thrust into that black hole and still more to his not being able to get right into it. He was hindered from getting into it by his conviction that his life had been a good one. That very justification of his life held him fast and prevented his moving forward, and it caused him most torment of all.

Suddenly some force struck him in the chest and side, making it still harder to breathe, and he fell through the hole and there at the bottom was a light. What had happened to him was like the sensation one sometimes experiences in a railway carriage when one thinks one is going backwards while one is really going forwards and suddenly becomes aware of the real direction.

"Yes, it was not the right thing," he said to himself, "but that's no matter. It can be done. But what *is* the right thing?" He asked himself, and suddenly grew quiet.

This occurred at the end of the third day, two hours before his death. Just then his schoolboy son had crept softly in and gone up to the bedside. The dying man was still screaming desperately and waving his arms. His hand fell on the boy's head, and the boy caught it, pressed it to his lips, and began to cry.

At that very moment Ivan Ilych fell through and caught sight of the light, and it was revealed to him that though his life had not been what it should have been, this could still be rectified. He asked himself, "What *is* the right thing?" and grew still, listening. Then he felt that someone was kissing his hand. He opened his eyes, looked at his son, and felt sorry for him. His wife came up to him and he glanced at her. She was gazing at him open-mouthed, with undried tears on her nose and cheek and a despairing look on her face. He felt sorry for her too.

"Yes, I am making them wretched," he thought. "They are sorry, but it will be better for them when I die." He wished to say this but had not the strength to utter it. "Besides, why speak? I must act," he thought. With a look at his wife he indicated his son and said: "Take him away . . . sorry for him . . . sorry for you too. . . ." He tried to add, "Forgive me," but said "Forego" and waved his hand, knowing that He whose understanding mattered would understand.

And suddenly it grew clear to him that what had been oppressing him and would not leave him was all dropping away at once from two sides, from ten sides, and from all sides. He was sorry for them, he must act so as not to hurt them: release them and free himself from these sufferings. "How good and how simple!" he thought. "And the pain?" he asked himself. "What has become of it? Where are you, pain?"

He turned his attention to it.

"Yes, here it is. Well, what of it? Let the pain be."

"And death . . . where is it?"

He sought his former accustomed fear of death and did not find it. "Where is it? What death?" There was no fear because there was no death.

In place of death there was light.

"So that's what it is!" he suddenly exclaimed aloud. "What joy!"

To him all this happened in a single instant, and the meaning of that instant did not change. For those present his agony continued for another two hours. Something rattled in his throat, his emaciated body twitched, then the gasping and rattle became less and less frequent.

"It is finished!" said someone near him.

He heard these words and repeated them in his soul.

"Death is finished," he said to himself. "It is no more!"

He drew in a breath, stopped in the midst of a sigh, stretched out, and died.

Charlotte Perkins Gilman

1860–1935

One of the leading intellectuals of the early American women's movement, Charlotte Perkins Gilman was forgotten for several decades in the mid-twentieth century, then rediscovered in the 1970s by feminists who found virtues in her fiction that had been less obvious to earlier readers. Thus *Herland* (1915), one of Gilman's three utopian novels, has become a landmark in the imagining of alternative sexual relationships. "The Yellow Wallpaper" (1892), with its extraordinary analysis of "normal" marriage and the pathologizing of feminine emotion as "hysterical," has acquired the status of an unquestioned literary classic.

Born in 1860 in Connecticut, Gilman was raised by her mother at the edge of poverty after her father abandoned the family. As soon as she was old enough, she began contributing to the family finances. She studied art and in 1884 married a fellow artist. The birth of a daughter one year later left her in a state of severe depression. Gilman consulted the prominent Dr. S. Weir Mitchell, mentioned by name in "The Yellow Wallpaper," and underwent his so-called "rest cure," which involved total bed rest, confinement, and isolation. Echoing much of the (male) medical opinion of the day, Mitchell advised Gilman after the cure to devote herself entirely to her child and domestic duties—in his view, the proper role for a woman—and avoid all intellectual and artistic work. Unable to follow this advice, Gilman chose instead a trial separation from her husband and a trip to California. Her health was restored, and she and her husband were amicably divorced. A second marriage in 1900 endured until her husband died in 1934, a year before her own death.

During this period, Gilman worked happily and productively as a writer and lecturer on behalf of both women's rights and the political reforms advocated by Edward Bellamy, whose influential utopian novel *Looking Backward* had appeared in 1888. In 1898 Gilman won international fame with *Women and Economics;* inspired in part by the newly developing social sciences, this pioneering work of what is now called interdisciplinary research explored the historical reasons for women's subordination. Her emphasis on the economic dimension of sexual inequality, or how women's status is determined by the fact that their labor inside the family is unpaid, led her to propose a radical solution: cooking, cleaning, and child care should henceforth be managed by paid professionals, thus leaving women free to choose if they desired to work outside the home. Gilman's sympathy for professionalism sheds an interesting light on the critique of professional medicine that many readers have found in "The Yellow Wallpaper." She elaborated and championed this analysis in a series of further books and in seven years of work on a periodical called *The Forerunner,* which she founded and for which she did virtually all the work of writing and editing.

While suggesting that even loving marriage is too often a punishing form of solitary confinement for women, that every husband in a sense plays the role of doctor, "The Yellow Wallpaper" is also an allegory of the situation of the woman writer. The protagonist is forbidden to exercise her craft on the grounds that it is harmful for her, and she finds allegories of her own situation in what she has access to, the furnishings of the room. But Gilman's premise of the narrator-as-mad(wo)man, shared with such rough contemporaries as Tolstoy and Lu Xun, lends itself to a multiplicity of interpretations.

The Yellow Wallpaper

It is very seldom that mere ordinary people like John and myself secure ancestral halls for the summer.

A colonial mansion, a hereditary estate, I would say a haunted house, and reach the height of romantic felicity—but that would be asking too much of fate!

Still I will proudly declare that there is something queer about it.

Else, why should it be let so cheaply? And why have stood so long untenanted?

John laughs at me, of course, but one expects that in marriage.

John is practical in the extreme. He has no patience with faith, an intense horror of superstition, and he scoffs openly at any talk of things not to be felt and seen and put down in figures.

John is a physician, and *perhaps*—(I would not say it to a living soul, of course, but this is dead paper and a great relief to my mind)—*perhaps* that is one reason I do not get well faster.

You see he does not believe I am sick!

And what can one do?

If a physician of high standing, and one's own husband, assures friends and relatives that there is really nothing the matter with one but temporary nervous depression—a slight hysterical tendency—what is one to do?

My brother is also a physician, and also of high standing, and he says the same thing.

So I take phosphates or phosphites—whichever it is, and tonics, and journeys, and air, and exercise, and am absolutely forbidden to "work" until I am well again.

Personally, I disagree with their ideas.

Personally, I believe that congenial work, with excitement and change, would do me good.

But what is one to do?

I did write for a while in spite of them; but it *does* exhaust me a good deal—having to be so sly about it, or else meet with heavy opposition.

I sometimes fancy that in my condition if I had less opposition and more society and stimulus—but John says the very worst thing I can do is to think about my condition, and I confess it always makes me feel bad.

So I will let it alone and talk about the house.

The most beautiful place! It is quite alone, standing well back from the road, quite three miles from the village. It makes me think of English places that you read about, for there are hedges and walls and gates that lock, and lots of separate little houses for the gardeners and people.

There is a *delicious* garden! I never saw such a garden—large and shady, full of box-bordered paths, and lined with long grape-covered arbors with seats under them.

There were greenhouses, too, but they are all broken now.

There was some legal trouble, I believe, something about the heirs and coheirs; anyhow, the place has been empty for years.

That spoils my ghostliness, I am afraid, but I don't care—there is something strange about the house—I can feel it.

I even said so to John one moonlight evening, but he said what I felt was a *draught,* and shut the window.

I get unreasonably angry with John sometimes. I'm sure I never used to be so sensitive. I think it is due to this nervous condition.

But John says if I feel so, I shall neglect proper self-control; so I take pains to control myself—before him, at least, and that makes me very tired.

I don't like our room a bit. I wanted one downstairs that opened on the piazza and had roses all over the window, and such pretty old-fashioned chintz hangings! but John would not hear of it.

He said there was only one window and not room for two beds, and no near room for him if he took another.

He is very careful and loving, and hardly lets me stir without special direction.

I have a schedule prescription for each hour in the day; he takes all care from me, and so I feel basely ungrateful not to value it more.

He said we came here solely on my account, that I was to have perfect rest and all the air I could get. "Your exercise depends on your strength, my dear," said he, "and your food somewhat on your appetite; but air you can absorb all the time." So we took the nursery at the top of the house.

It is a big, airy room, the whole floor nearly, with windows that look all ways, and air and sunshine galore. It was nursery first and then playroom and gymnasium, I should judge; for the windows are barred for little children, and there are rings and things in the walls.

The paint and paper look as if a boys' school had used it. It is stripped off—the paper—in great patches all around the head of my bed, about as far as I can reach, and in a great place on the other side of the room low down. I never saw a worse paper in my life.

One of those sprawling flamboyant patterns committing every artistic sin.

It is dull enough to confuse the eye in following, pronounced enough to constantly irritate and provoke study, and when you follow the lame uncertain curves for a little distance they suddenly commit suicide—plunge off at outrageous angles, destroy themselves in unheard of contradictions.

The color is repellent, almost revolting; a smouldering unclean yellow, strangely faded by the slow-turning sunlight.

It is a dull yet lurid orange in some places, a sickly sulphur tint in others.

No wonder the children hated it! I should hate it myself if I had to live in this room long.

There comes John, and I must put this away,—he hates to have me write a word.

We have been here two weeks, and I haven't felt like writing before, since that first day.

I am sitting by the window now, up in this atrocious nursery, and there is nothing to hinder my writing as much as I please, save lack of strength.

John is away all day, and even some nights when his cases are serious.

I am glad my case is not serious!

But these nervous troubles are dreadfully depressing.

John does not know how much I really suffer. He knows there is no *reason* to suffer, and that satisfies him.

Of course it is only nervousness. It does weigh on me so not to do my duty in any way!

I meant to be such a help to John, such a real rest and comfort, and here I am a comparative burden already!

Nobody would believe what an effort it is to do what little I am able,—to dress and entertain, and order things.

It is fortunate Mary is so good with the baby. Such a dear baby!

And yet I *cannot* be with him, it makes me so nervous.

I suppose John never was nervous in his life. He laughs at me so about this wallpaper!

At first he meant to repaper the room, but afterwards he said that I was letting it get the better of me, and that nothing was worse for a nervous patient than to give way to such fancies.

He said that after the wallpaper was changed it would be the heavy bedstead, and then the barred windows, and then that gate at the head of the stairs, and so on.

"You know the place is doing you good," he said, "and really, dear, I don't care to renovate the house just for a three months' rental."

"Then do let us go downstairs," I said, "there are such pretty rooms there."

Then he took me in his arms and called me a blessed little goose, and said he would go down to the cellar, if I wished, and have it whitewashed into the bargain.

But he is right enough about the beds and windows and things.

It is an airy and comfortable room as any one need wish, and, of course, I would not be so silly as to make him uncomfortable just for a whim.

I'm really getting quite fond of the big room, all but that horrid paper.

Out of one window I can see the garden, those mysterious deepshaded arbors, the riotous old-fashioned flowers, and bushes and gnarly trees.

Out of another I get a lovely view of the bay and a little private wharf belonging to the estate. There is a beautiful shaded lane that runs down there from the house. I always fancy I see people walking in these numerous paths and arbors, but John has cautioned me not to give way to fancy in the least. He says that with my imaginative power and habit of story-making, a nervous weakness like mine is sure to lead to all manner of excited fancies, and that I ought to use my will and good sense to check the tendency. So I try.

I think sometimes that if I were only well enough to write a little it would relieve the press of ideas and rest me.

But I find I get pretty tired when I try.

It is so discouraging not to have any advice and companionship about my work. When I get really well, John says we will ask Cousin Henry and Julia down for a long visit; but he says he would as soon put fireworks in my pillow-case as to let me have those stimulating people about now.

I wish I could get well faster.

But I must not think about that. This paper looks to me as if it *knew* what a vicious influence it had!

There is a recurrent spot where the pattern lolls like a broken neck and two bulbous eyes stare at you upside down.

I get positively angry with the impertinence of it and the everlastingness. Up and down and sideways they crawl, and those absurd, unblinking eyes are everywhere. There is one place where two breaths didn't match, and the eyes go all up and down the line, one a little higher than the other.

I never saw so much expression in an inanimate thing before, and we all know how much expression they have! I used to lie awake as a child and get more entertainment and terror out of blank walls and plain furniture than most children could find in a toy-store.

I remember what a kindly wink the knobs of our big, old bureau used to have, and there was one chair that always seemed like a strong friend.

I used to feel that if any of the other things looked too fierce I could always hop into that chair and be safe.

The furniture in this room is no worse than inharmonious, however, for we had to bring it all from downstairs. I suppose when this was used as a playroom they had to take the nursery things out, and no wonder! I never saw such ravages as the children have made here.

The wallpaper, as I said before, is torn off in spots, and it sticketh closer than a brother—they must have had perseverance as well as hatred.

Then the floor is scratched and gouged and splintered, the plaster itself is dug out here and there, and this great heavy bed which is all we found in the room, looks as if it had been through the wars.

But I don't mind it a bit—only the paper.

There comes John's sister. Such a dear girl as she is, and so careful of me! I must not let her find me writing.

She is a perfect and enthusiastic housekeeper, and hopes for no better profession. I verily believe she thinks it is the writing which made me sick!

But I can write when she is out, and see her a long way off from these windows.

There is one that commands the road, a lovely shaded winding road, and one that just looks off over the country. A lovely country, too, full of great elms and velvet meadows.

This wallpaper has a kind of sub-pattern in a different shade, a particularly irritating one, for you can only see it in certain lights, and not clearly then.

But in the places where it isn't faded and where the sun is just so—I can see a strange, provoking, formless sort of figure, that seems to skulk about behind that silly and conspicuous front design.

There's sister on the stairs!

Well, the Fourth of July is over! The people are all gone and I am tired out. John thought it might do me good to see a little company, so we just had Mother and Nellie and the children down for a week.

Of course I didn't do a thing. Jennie sees to everything now.

But it tired me all the same.

John says if I don't pick up faster he shall send me to Weir Mitchell in the fall.

But I don't want to go there at all. I had a friend who was in his hands once, and she says he is just like John and my brother, only more so!

Besides, it is such an undertaking to go so far.

I don't feel as if it was worthwhile to turn my hand over for anything, and I'm getting dreadfully fretful and querulous.

I cry at nothing, and cry most of the time.

Of course I don't when John is here, or anybody else, but when I am alone.

And I am alone a good deal just now. John is kept in town very often by serious cases, and Jennie is good and lets me alone when I want her to.

So I walk a little in the garden or down that lovely lane, sit on the porch under the roses, and lie down up here a good deal.

I'm getting really fond of the room in spite of the wallpaper. Perhaps *because* of the wallpaper.

It dwells in my mind so!

I lie here on this great immovable bed—it is nailed down, I believe—and follow that pattern about by the hour. It is as good as gymnastics, I assure you. I start, we'll say, at the bottom, down in the corner over there where it has not been touched, and I determine for the thousandth time that I *will* follow that pointless pattern to some sort of a conclusion.

I know a little of the principle of design, and I know this thing was not arranged on any laws of radiation, or alternation, or repetition, or symmetry, or anything else that I ever heard of.

It is repeated, of course, by the breadths, but not otherwise.

Looked at in one way each breadth stands alone, the bloated curves and flourishes—a kind of "debased Romanesque" with *delirium tremens*—go waddling up and down in isolated columns of fatuity.

But, on the other hand, they connect diagonally, and the sprawling outlines run off in great slanting waves of optic horror, like a lot of wallowing seaweeds in full chase.

The whole thing goes horizontally, too, at least it seems so, and I exhaust myself in trying to distinguish the order of its going in that direction.

They have used a horizontal breadth for a frieze, and that adds wonderfully to the confusion.

There is one end of the room where it is almost intact, and there, when the crosslights fade and the low sun shines directly upon it, I can almost fancy radiation after all,—the interminable grotesques seem to form around a common centre and rush off in headlong plunges of equal distraction.

It makes me tired to follow it. I will take a nap I guess.

I don't know why I should write this.

I don't want to.

I don't feel able.

And I know John would think it absurd. But I *must* say what I feel and think in some way—it is such a relief!

But the effort is getting to be greater than the relief.

Half the time now I am awfully lazy, and lie down ever so much.

John says I mustn't lose my strength, and has me take cod liver oil and lots of tonics and things, to say nothing of ale and wine and rare meat.

Dear John! He loves me very dearly, and hates to have me sick. I tried to have a real earnest reasonable talk with him the other day, and tell him how I wish he would let me go and make a visit to Cousin Henry and Julia.

But he said I wasn't able to go, nor able to stand it after I got there; and I did not make out a very good case for myself, for I was crying before I had finished.

It is getting to be a great effort for me to think straight. Just this nervous weakness I suppose.

And dear John gathered me up in his arms, and just carried me upstairs and laid me on the bed, and sat by me and read to me till it tired my head.

He said I was his darling and his comfort and all he had, and that I must take care of myself for his sake, and keep well.

He says no one but myself can help me out of it, that I must use my will and self-control and not let any silly fancies run away with me.

There's one comfort, the baby is well and happy, and does not have to occupy this nursery with the horrid wallpaper.

If we had not used it, that blessed child would have! What a fortunate escape! Why, I wouldn't have a child of mine, an impressionable little thing, live in such a room for worlds.

I never thought of it before, but it is lucky that John kept me here after all, I can stand it so much easier than a baby, you see.

Of course I never mention it to them any more—I am too wise,—but I keep watch of it all the same.

There are things in that paper that nobody knows but me, or ever will.

Behind that outside pattern the dim shapes get clearer every day.

It is always the same shape, only very numerous.

And it is like a woman stooping down and creeping about behind that pattern. I don't like it a bit. I wonder—I begin to think—I wish John would take me away from here!

It is so hard to talk with John about my case, because he is so wise, and because he loves me so.

But I tried it last night.

It was moonlight. The moon shines in all around just as the sun does.

I hate to see it sometimes, it creeps so slowly, and always comes in by one window or another.

John was asleep and I hated to waken him, so I kept still and watched the moonlight on that undulating wallpaper till I felt creepy.

The faint figure behind seemed to shake the pattern, just as if she wanted to get out.

I got up softly and went to feel and see if the paper *did* move, and when I came back John was awake.

"What is it, little girl?" he said. "Don't go walking about like that—you'll get cold."

I thought it was a good time to talk, so I told him that I really was not gaining here, and that I wished he would take me away.

"Why darling!" said he, "our lease will be up in three weeks, and I can't see how to leave before.

"The repairs are not done at home, and I cannot possibly leave town just now. Of course if you were in any danger, I could and would, but you really are better, dear, whether you can see it or not. I am a doctor, dear, and I know. You are gaining flesh and color, your appetite is better, I feel really much easier about you."

"I don't weigh a bit more," said I, "nor as much; and my appetite may be better in the evening when you are here, but it is worse in the morning when you are away!"

"Bless her little heart!" said he with a big hug, "she shall be as sick as she pleases! But now let's improve the shining hours by going to sleep, and talk about it in the morning!"

"And you won't go away?" I asked gloomily.

"Why, how can I, dear? It is only three weeks more and then we will take a nice little trip of a few days while Jennie is getting the house ready. Really dear you are better!"

"Better in body perhaps—" I began, and stopped short, for he sat up straight and looked at me with such a stern, reproachful look that I could not say another word.

"My darling," said he, "I beg of you, for my sake and for our child's sake, as well as for your own, that you will never for one instant let that idea enter your mind! There is nothing so dangerous, so fascinating, to a temperament like yours. It is a false and foolish fancy. Can you not trust me as a physician when I tell you so?"

So of course I said no more on that score, and we went to sleep before long. He thought I was asleep first, but I wasn't, and lay there for hours trying to decide whether that front pattern and the back pattern really did move together or separately.

On a pattern like this, by daylight, there is a lack of sequence, a defiance of law, that is a constant irritant to a normal mind.

The color is hideous enough, and unreliable enough, and infuriating enough, but the pattern is torturing.

You think you have mastered it, but just as you get well underway in following, it turns a back-somersault and there you are. It slaps you in the face, knocks you down, and tramples upon you. It is like a bad dream.

The outside pattern is a florid arabesque, reminding one of a fungus. If you can imagine a toadstool in joints, an interminable string of toadstools, budding and sprouting in endless convolutions—why, that is something like it.

That is, sometimes!

There is one marked peculiarity about this paper, a thing nobody seems to notice but myself, and that is that it changes as the light changes.

When the sun shoots in through the east window—I always watch for that first long, straight ray—it changes so quickly that I never can quite believe it.

That is why I watch it always.

By moonlight—the moon shines in all night when there is a moon—I wouldn't know it was the same paper.

At night in any kind of light, in twilight, candle light, lamplight, and worst of all by moonlight, it becomes bars! The outside pattern I mean, and the woman behind it is as plain as can be.

I didn't realize for a long time what the thing was that showed behind, that dim sub-pattern, but now I am quite sure it is a woman.

By daylight she is subdued, quiet. I fancy it is the pattern that keeps her so still. It is so puzzling. It keeps me quiet by the hour.

I lie down ever so much now. John says it is good for me, and to sleep all I can.

Indeed he started the habit by making me lie down for an hour after each meal.

It is a very bad habit I am convinced, for you see I don't sleep.

And that cultivates deceit, for I don't tell them I'm awake—O no!

The fact is I am getting a little afraid of John.

He seems very queer sometimes, and even Jennie has an inexplicable look.

It strikes me occasionally, just as a scientific hypothesis,—that perhaps it is the paper!

I have watched John when he did not know I was looking, and come into the room suddenly on the most innocent excuses, and I've caught him several times *looking at the paper!* And Jennie too. I caught Jennie with her hand on it once.

She didn't know I was in the room, and when I asked her in a quiet, a very quiet voice, with the most restrained manner possible, what she was doing with the paper—she turned around as if she had been caught stealing, and looked quite angry—asked me why I should frighten her so!

Then she said that the paper stained everything it touched, that she had found yellow smooches on all my clothes and John's, and she wished we would be more careful!

Did not that sound innocent? But I know she was studying that pattern, and I am determined that nobody shall find it out but myself!

Life is very much more exciting now than it used to be. You see I have something more to expect, to look forward to, to watch. I really do eat better, and am more quiet than I was.

John is so pleased to see me improve! He laughed a little the other day, and said I seemed to be flourishing in spite of my wallpaper.

I turned it off with a laugh. I had no intention of telling him it was *because* of the wallpaper—he would make fun of me. He might even want to take me away.

I don't want to leave now until I have found it out. There is a week more, and I think that will be enough.

I'm feeling ever so much better! I don't sleep much at night, for it is so interesting to watch developments; but I sleep a good deal in the daytime.

In the daytime it is tiresome and perplexing.

There are always new shoots on the fungus, and new shades of yellow all over it. I cannot keep count of them, though I have tried conscientiously.

It is the strangest yellow, that wallpaper! It makes me think of all the yellow things I ever saw—not beautiful ones like buttercups, but old foul, bad yellow things.

But there is something else about that paper—the smell! I noticed it the moment we came into the room, but with so much air and sun it was not bad. Now we have had a week of fog and rain, and whether the windows are open or not, the smell is here.

It creeps all over the house.

I find it hovering in the dining-room, skulking in the parlor, hiding in the hall, lying in wait for me on the stairs.

It gets into my hair.

Even when I go to ride, if I turn my head suddenly and surprise it—there is that smell!

Such a peculiar odor, too! I have spent hours in trying to analyze it, to find what it smelled like.

It is not bad—at first, and very gentle, but quite the subtlest, most enduring odor I ever met.

In this damp weather it is awful, I wake up in the night and find it hanging over me.

It used to disturb me at first. I thought seriously of burning the house—to reach the smell.

But now I am used to it. The only thing I can think of that it is like is the *color* of the paper! A yellow smell.

There is a very funny mark on this wall, low down, near the mopboard. A streak that runs round the room. It goes behind every piece of furniture, except the bed, a long, straight, even *smooch,* as if it had been rubbed over and over.

I wonder how it was done and who did it, and what they did it for. Round and round and round—round and round and round—it makes me dizzy!

I really have discovered something at last.

Through watching so much at night, when it changes so, I have finally found out.

The front pattern *does* move—and no wonder! The woman behind shakes it!

Sometimes I think there are a great many women behind, and sometimes only one, and she crawls around fast, and her crawling shakes it all over.

Then in the very bright spots she keeps still, and in the very shady spots she just takes hold of the bars and shakes them hard.

And she is all the time trying to climb through. But nobody could climb through that pattern—it strangles so; I think that is why it has so many heads.

They get through, and then the pattern strangles them off and turns them upside down, and makes their eyes white!

If those heads were covered or taken off it would not be half so bad.

I think that woman gets out in the daytime!

And I'll tell you why—privately—I've seen her!

I can see her out of every one of my windows!

It is the same woman, I know, for she is always creeping, and most women do not creep by daylight.

I see her on that long road under the trees, creeping along, and when a carriage comes she hides under the blackberry vines.

I don't blame her a bit. It must be very humiliating to be caught creeping by daylight!

I always lock the door when I creep by daylight. I can't do it at night, for I know John would suspect something at once.

And John is so queer now, that I don't want to irritate him. I wish he would take another room! Besides, I don't want anybody to get that woman out at night but myself.

I often wonder if I could see her out of all the windows at once.

But, turn as fast as I can, I can only see out of one at one time.

And though I always see her, she *may* be able to creep faster than I can turn!

I have watched her sometimes away off in the open country, creeping as fast as a cloud shadow in a high wind.

If only that top pattern could be gotten off from the under one! I mean to try it, little by little.

I have found out another funny thing, but I shan't tell it this time! It does not do to trust people too much.

There are only two more days to get this paper off, and I believe John is beginning to notice. I don't like the look in his eyes.

And I heard him ask Jennie a lot of professional questions about me. She had a very good report to give.

She said I slept a good deal in the daytime.

John knows I don't sleep very well at night, for all I'm so quiet!

He asked me all sorts of questions, too, and pretended to be very loving and kind.

As if I couldn't see through him!

Still, I don't wonder he acts so, sleeping under this paper for three months.

It only interests me, but I feel sure John and Jennie are secretly affected by it.

Hurrah! This is the last day, but it is enough. John is to stay in town over night, and won't be out until this evening.

Jennie wanted to sleep with me—the sly thing! but I told her I should undoubtedly rest better for a night all alone.

That was clever, for really I wasn't alone a bit! As soon as it was moonlight and that poor thing began to crawl and shake the pattern, I got up and ran to help her.

I pulled and she shook, I shook and she pulled, and before morning we had peeled off yards of that paper.

A strip about as high as my head and half around the room.

And then when the sun came and that awful pattern began to laugh at me, I declared I would finish it to-day!

We go away to-morrow, and they are moving all my furniture down again to leave things as they were before.

Jennie looked at the wall in amazement, but I told her merrily that I did it out of pure spite at the vicious thing.

She laughed and said she wouldn't mind doing it herself, but I must not get tired.

How she betrayed herself that time!

But I am here, and no person touches this paper but me,—not *alive!*

She tried to get me out of the room—it was too patent! But I said it was so quiet and empty and clean now that I believed I would lie down again and sleep all I could; and not to wake me even for dinner—I would call when I woke.

So now she is gone, and the servants are gone, and the things are gone, and there is nothing left but that great bedstead nailed down, with the canvas mattress we found on it.

We shall sleep downstairs to-night, and take the boat home to-morrow.

I quite enjoy the room, now it is bare again.

How those children did tear about here!

This bedstead is fairly gnawed!

But I must get to work.

I have locked the door and thrown the key down into the front path.

I don't want to go out, and I don't want to have anybody come in, till John comes.

I want to astonish him.

I've got a rope up here that even Jennie did not find. If that woman does get out, and tries to get away, I can tie her!

But I forgot I could not reach far without anything to stand on!

This bed will *not* move!

I tried to lift and push it until I was lame, and then I got so angry I bit off a little piece at one corner—but it hurt my teeth.

Then I peeled off all the paper I could reach standing on the floor. It sticks horribly and the pattern just enjoys it! All those strangled heads and bulbous eyes and waddling fungus growths just shriek with derision!

I am getting angry enough to do something desperate. To jump out of the window would be admirable exercise, but the bars are too strong even to try.

Besides I wouldn't do it. Of course not. I know well enough that a step like that is improper and might be misconstrued.

I don't like to *look* out of the windows even—there are so many of those creeping women, and they creep so fast.

I wonder if they all come out of that wallpaper as I did?

But I am securely fastened now by my well-hidden rope—you don't get *me* out in the road there!

I suppose I shall have to get back behind the pattern when it comes night, and that is hard!

It is so pleasant to be out in this great room and creep around as I please!

I don't want to go outside. I won't, even if Jennie asks me to.

For outside you have to creep on the ground, and everything is green instead of yellow.

But here I can creep smoothly on the floor, and my shoulder just fits in that long smooch around the wall, so I cannot lose my way.

Why there's John at the door!

It is no use, young man, you can't open it!

How he does call and pound!

Now he's crying for an axe.

It would be a shame to break down that beautiful door!

"John dear!" said I in the gentlest voice, "the key is down by the front steps, under a plantain leaf!"

That silenced him for a few moments.

Then he said—very quietly indeed, "Open the door, my darling!"

"I can't," said I. "The key is down by the front door under a plantain leaf!"

And then I said it again, several times, very gently and slowly, and said it so often that he had to go and see, and he got it of course, and came in. He stopped short by the door.

"What is the matter?" he cried. "For God's sake, what are you doing!"

I kept on creeping just the same, but I looked at him over my shoulder.

"I've got out at last," said I, "in spite of you and Jane. And I've pulled off most of the paper, so you can't put me back!"

Now why should that man have fainted? But he did, and right across my path by the wall, so that I had to creep over him every time!

Henrik Ibsen

1828–1906

In 1850, when Henrik Ibsen began writing, theater was largely a form of entertainment, a sort of doll's house where stock figures and neatly contrived plots were expected to provide an evening's innocent amusement. By 1899, when his last play was published, it had become an adult art form comparable to poetry and the novel, shocking and disorienting, giving more strenuous and instructive kinds of pleasure. With the twenty-five plays he wrote in that half century, Ibsen did more than any other single dramatist to bring about this upheaval. The transformation we see in Nora in *A Doll's House* bears a family resemblance to the transformation Ibsen brought to the theater itself.

Born in a small Norwegian town in 1828, Ibsen grew up (like many other nineteenth-century writers, including Dickens and Melville) facing a failure of paternal authority. His father, who had been a prosperous merchant, went bankrupt when Ibsen was a small child, leaving his eldest son to fend for himself in a state of poverty made more bitter by the memory of better days. Ibsen's sense of injustice expressed itself in poems to the European revolutionaries of 1848. Apprenticed to a pharmacist in a small town fifty miles from home, he became involved with a local servant ten years older than himself, got her pregnant, and spent fourteen years paying child support. He had dreams of becoming a doctor, but while studying at night to enter the university in Christiania (now Oslo), he gave them up to join a small theater in Bergen. There he contributed to a radical journal that was suppressed, learned the dramatist's craft, and collected local ballads and legends. Romantic nationalism was in fashion, and for good reason. Norway, which had won its independence from Denmark in 1814, was now united with the more powerful Sweden (it would not become fully independent until 1905), and it still had no national theater. Nor did it have national agreement on its language; it was during these same years that the philologist Ivar Aasen, traveling around the rural west of the country to collect dialects, fashioned a *landsmål* or "national language" to compete with the Dano-Norwegian, or *bokmål,* spoken by eastern urbanites. Of the 145 plays produced in Bergen during Ibsen's years of apprenticeship there, over half were translated from French. What was demanded was a generic, blandly international "well-made play," with a complicated plot involving confidential documents, babies identified by birthmarks, poisoned goblets quaffed by the wrong party, and other devices that had little to do with everyday Norwegian life.

Ibsen married Susannah Thoresen, the daughter of a pastor, in 1858. The couple traveled to Rome on a scholarship in 1864, and it was there that Ibsen wrote *Brand* (1866) and *Peer Gynt* (1867), a play inhabited by trolls and other materials of Nordic legend. These plays established his reputation as his country's first national dramatist. Apart from two short visits to Norway, however, Ibsen spent the next quarter century living in Italy and Germany. Like his admirer James Joyce (who learned Norwegian in order to read his hero in the original), Ibsen was that strange sort of exile, a national poet who felt obliged to examine his homeland from a distance. He became friends with the Danish critic Georg Brandes, author of *Main Currents of Nineteenth-Century Literature* (1872) and translator of John Stuart Mill's *On the Subjection of Women* (in 1869, the same year it came out in English), and Brandes helped turn Ibsen away from verse and toward the realistic wrestling with modern topics for which he was soon to become famous. It's been said that all the poetry Ibsen wrote after 1875 could be put on a single sheet of paper.

Ibsen's treatment of the emancipation of women in *A Doll's House* (1879) marks his full mastery of this new realistic mode. First performed in Copenhagen, Denmark, *A Doll's House* created an immediate sensation. Many found it almost unthinkable that Ibsen should endorse a woman who pays so little heed to her sacred duty as a wife and mother and so much to her own development as an individual. Ten years later, when the play was first presented in London, mainstream reviewers found it morally loathsome; one compared it to a view of an open sewer.

Plays like *A Doll's House*, *Ghosts* (1881), and *An Enemy of the People* (1882) are sometimes described as "naturalist" rather than realist, perhaps because they set their characters in the midst of the large historical processes that define the modern moment and fatally determine the outcome. It was this topical or "problem-play" side of Ibsen that George Bernard Shaw defended in *The Quintessence of Ibsenism* (1891). But *Hedda Gabler* (1890), *The Master Builder* (1892), and *When We Dead Awaken* (1899) returned to a less realistic mode, refashioning the theatrical parable so as to explore high individual aspiration, outside the conventions of society, as Ibsen had already done in *Peer Gynt.* These plays were taken by many to herald the new literary tendency of Symbolism. Older than the other major playwrights of the 1880s and 1890s, the Swedish August Strindberg and the Russian Anton Chekhov, Ibsen nonetheless continued to keep pace with them, and at times to set the pace for them. His last plays were written in Norway, to which he had returned in 1891, and he died there in 1906.

Shocking as *A Doll's House* was to its first audiences, it had an ambiguous relation to the feminism of the time. From the perspective of the two women who had the most direct influence on *A Doll's House,* what is striking is Ibsen's complex and contradictory relations to their cause. Camilla Collett, a pioneering Norwegian novelist and campaigner for women's rights, visited the Ibsens in Germany in the 1870s and, though Ibsen later acknowledged his debt to her, was unimpressed with the playwright's views on the woman question. Laura Kieler wrote a fictional sequel to Ibsen's *Brand* called *Brand's Daughters* (1869) when she was only twenty. It was Kieler's own life story that Ibsen retold in *A Doll's House,* though with changes. When Kieler was attacked as a result of Ibsen's stage portrait of her, she begged him to declare in public that she had acted honorably. He refused. One of his greatest virtues as a dramatist was his ability to separate himself off from unattractive aspects of his personality and put them into his characters.

A Doll's House is after all a well-made play. Like the romantic melodramas Ibsen helped put on in Bergen, it has stock characters (the flighty woman, the heavy insensitive husband, the faithful friend), guilty secrets, sealed lips, and fateful documents. But all these familiar stereotypes are reversed and revalued. After learning to see Nora as a stereotype of silly, childish, thoughtless femininity, we are suddenly asked to reinterpret this stereotype as a piece of theater that for various reasons Nora herself has been staging. In the person of Dr. Rank, we are offered tantalizing hints of the convention by which a rich old gentleman leaves money to the needy heroine and magically resolves all difficulties. Yet instead of the magical denouement that audiences had come to expect, Ibsen offers us, of all things, a serious discussion. We are asked to find the same emotional intensity in ideas about marriage and freedom that we had learned to expect from the discovery of long-lost brothers and sudden inheritances.

Freedom was, of course, more than an issue of sexual justice to Ibsen. Given his mixed feelings about the women's movement, it seems probable that he could make such a strong theatrical statement on Nora's behalf only because in his eyes she was not just a woman, but a figure for his own aspirations as an individual and an artist. Nora's story stood for the artist's defiance of conventional morality and the wishes of those around them, the sacrifice of children in exchange for individual self-realization. It was a defiance and a sacrifice about which he remained ambivalent. In his original notes for the play, Ibsen described it as "a tragedy of modern times." The notes suggest that he knew Nora would have to pay a large price for her liberation, that the story did not end (though this is perhaps the most famous ending in the history of the modern theater) with the slamming of the door.

A Doll's House[1]

ACT 1

Characters

TORVALD HELMER
NORA, *his wife*
DOCTOR RANK
MRS. LINDEN
NILS KROGSTAD
THE HELMERS' THREE CHILDREN
ANNA, *their nurse*
A MAID-SERVANT (Ellen)
A PORTER

The action passes in Helmer's house (an apartment) in Christiania.

A room, comfortably and tastefully, but not expensively, furnished. In the back, on the right, a door leads to the hall; on the left another door leads to Helmer's study. Between the two doors a pianoforte. In the middle of the left wall a door, and nearer the front a window. Near the window a round table with arm-chairs and a small sofa. In the right wall, somewhat to the back, a door, and against the same wall, further forward, a procelain stove; in front of it a couple of arm-chairs and a rocking-chair. Between the stove and the side-door a small table. Engravings on the walls. A what-not with china and bric-à-brac. A small bookcase filled with handsomely bound books. Carpet. A fire in the stove. It is a winter day.

A bell rings in the hall outside. Presently the outer door of the flat is heard to open. Then Nora enters, humming gaily. She is in outdoor dress, and carries several parcels, which she lays on the right-hand table. She leaves the door into the hall open, and a Porter is seen outside, carrying a Christmas-tree and a basket, which he gives to the Maid-servant who has opened the door.

NORA: Hide the Christmas-tree carefully, Ellen; the children must on no account see it before this evening, when it's lighted up. [*To the Porter, taking out her purse.*] How much?

PORTER: Fifty öre.[2]

NORA: There is a crown. No, keep the change.

[*The Porter thanks her and goes. Nora shuts the door. She continues smiling in quiet glee as she takes off her outdoor things. Taking from her pocket a bag of macaroons, she eats one or two. Then she goes on tip-toe to her husband's door and listens.*]

1. Translated by William Archer.

2. A hundred öre equal one crown (*krone*), equivalent to a few dollars today.

NORA: Yes; he is at home.

[*She begins humming again, crossing to the table on the right.*]

HELMER [*in his room*]: Is that my lark twittering there?

NORA [*busy opening some of her parcels*]: Yes, it is.

HELMER: Is it the squirrel frisking around?

NORA: Yes!

HELMER: When did the squirrel get home?

NORA: Just this minute. [*Hides the bag of macaroons in her pocket and wipes her mouth.*] Come here, Torvald, and see what I've been buying.

HELMER: Don't interrupt me. [*A little later he opens the door and looks in, pen in hand.*] Buying, did you say? What! All that? Has my little spend-thrift been making the money fly again?

NORA: Why, Torvald, surely we can afford to launch out a little now. It's the first Christmas we haven't had to pinch.

HELMER: Come come; we can't afford to squander money.

NORA: Oh yes, Torvald, do let us squander a little, now—just the least little bit! You know you'll soon be earning heaps of money.

HELMER: Yes, from New Year's Day. But there's a whole quarter before my first salary is due.

NORA: Never mind; we can borrow in the meantime.

HELMER: Nora! [*He goes up to her and takes her playfully by the ear.*] Still my little featherbrain! Supposing I borrowed a thousand crowns to-day, and you made ducks and drakes of them during Christmas week, and then on New Year's Eve a tile blew off the roof and knocked my brains out—

NORA [*laying her hand on his mouth*]: Hush! How can you talk so horridly?

HELMER: But supposing it were to happen—what then?

NORA: If anything so dreadful happened, it would be all the same to me whether I was in debt or not.

HELMER: But what about the creditors?

NORA: They! Who cares for them? They're only strangers.

HELMER: Nora, Nora! What a woman you are! But seriously, Nora, you know my principles on these points. No debts! No borrowing! Home life ceases to be free and beautiful as soon as it is founded on borrowing and debt. We two have held out bravely till now, and we are not going to give in at the last.

NORA [*going to the fireplace*]: Very well—as you please, Torvald.

HELMER [*following her*]: Come come; my little lark mustn't droop her wings like that. What? Is my squirrel in the sulks? [*Takes out his purse.*] Nora, what do you think I have here?

NORA [*turning round quickly*]: Money!

HELMER: There! [*Gives her some notes.*] Of course, I know all sorts of things are wanted at Christmas.

NORA [*counting*]: Ten, twenty, thirty, forty. Oh, thank you, thank you, Torvald! This will go a long way.

HELMER: I should hope so.

NORA: Yes, indeed; a long way! But come here, and let me show you all I've been buying. And so cheap! Look, here's a new suit for Ivar, and a little sword. Here are a horse and a trumpet for Bob. And here are a doll and a cradle for Emmy. They're only common; but they're good enough for her to pull to pieces. And dress-stuffs and kerchiefs for the servants. I ought to have got something better for old Anna.

HELMER: And what's in that other parcel?

NORA [*crying out*]: No, Torvald, you're not to see that until this evening!

HELMER: Oh! Ah! But now tell me, you little spendthrift, have you thought of anything for yourself?

NORA: For myself! Oh, I don't want anything.

HELMER: Nonsense! Just tell me something sensible you would like to have.

NORA: No, really I don't know of anything—Well, listen, Torvald—

HELMER: Well?

NORA [*playing with his coat-buttons, without looking him in the face*]: If you really want to give me something, you might, you know—you might—

HELMER: Well? Out with it!

NORA [*quickly*]: You might give me money, Torvald. Only just what you think you can spare; then I can buy something with it later on.

HELMER: But, Nora—

NORA: Oh, please do, dear Torvald, please do! I should hang the money in lovely gilt paper on the Christmas-tree. Wouldn't that be fun?

HELMER: What do they call the birds that are always making the money fly?

NORA: Yes, I know—spendthrifts, of course. But please do as I ask you, Torvald. Then I shall have time to think what I want most. Isn't that very sensible, now?

HELMER [*smiling*]: Certainly; that is to say, if you really kept the money I gave you, and really spent it on something for yourself. But it all goes in housekeeping, and for all manner of useless things, and then I have to pay up again.

NORA: But, Torvald—

HELMER: Can you deny it, Nora dear? [*He puts his arm round her.*] It's a sweet little lark, but it gets through a lot of money. No one would believe how much it costs a man to keep such a little bird as you.

NORA: For shame! How can you say so? Why, I save as much as ever I can.

HELMER [*laughing*]: Very true—as much as you can—but that's precisely nothing.

NORA [*hums and smiles with covert glee*]: H'm! It you only knew, Torvald, what expenses we larks and squirrels have.

HELMER: You're a strange little being! Just like your father—always on the look-out for all the money you can lay your hands on; but the moment you have it, it seems to slip through your fingers; you never know what becomes of it. Well, one must take you as you are. It's in the blood. Yes, Nora, that sort of thing is hereditary.

NORA: I wish I had inherited many of papa's qualities.

HELMER: And I don't wish you anything but just what you are—my own, sweet little song-bird. But I say—it strikes me you look so—so—what shall I call it?—so suspicious to-day—

NORA: Do I?

HELMER: You do, indeed. Look me full in the face.

NORA [*looking at him*]: Well?

HELMER [*threatening with his finger*]: Hasn't the little sweet-tooth been playing pranks to-day?

NORA: No; how can you think such a thing!

HELMER: Didn't she just look in at the confectioner's?

NORA: No, Torvald; really—

HELMER: Not to sip a little jelly?

NORA: No; certainly not.

HELMER: Hasn't she even nibbled a macaroon or two?

NORA: No, Torvald, indeed, indeed!

HELMER: Well, well, well; of course I'm only joking.

NORA [*goes to the table on the right*]: I shouldn't think of doing what you disapprove of.

HELMER: No, I'm sure of that; and, besides, you've given me your word—[*Going towards her.*] Well, keep your little Christmas secrets to yourself, Nora darling. The Christmas-tree will bring them all to light, I daresay.

NORA: Have you remembered to invite Doctor Rank?

HELMER: No. But it's not necessary; he'll come as a matter of course. Besides, I shall ask him when he looks in to-day. I've ordered some capital wine. Nora, you can't think how I look forward to this evening.

NORA: And I too. How the children will enjoy themselves, Torvald!

HELMER: Ah, it's glorious to feel that one has an assured position and ample means. Isn't it delightful to think of?

NORA: Oh, it's wonderful!

HELMER: Do you remember last Christmas? For three whole weeks beforehand you shut yourself up every evening till long past midnight to make flowers for the Christmas-tree, and all sorts of other marvels that were to have astonished us. I was never so bored in my life.

NORA: I didn't bore myself at all.

HELMER [*smiling*]: But it came to little enough in the end, Nora.

NORA: Oh, are you going to tease me about that again? How could I help the cat getting in and pulling it all to pieces?

HELMER: To be sure you couldn't, my poor little Nora. You did your best to give us all pleasure, and that's the main point. But, all the same, it's a good thing the hard times are over.

NORA: Oh, isn't it wonderful?

HELMER: Now I needn't sit here boring myself all alone; and you needn't tire your blessed eyes and your delicate little fingers—

NORA [*clapping her hands*]: No, I needn't, need I, Torvald? Oh, how wonderful it is to think of? [*takes his arm*] And now I'll tell you how I think we ought to manage, Torvald. As soon as Christmas is over—[*The hall-door bell rings.*] Oh, there's a ring! [*Arranging the room.*] That's somebody come to call. How tiresome!

HELMER: I'm "not at home" to callers; remember that.

ELLEN [*in the doorway*]: A lady to see you, ma'am.

NORA: Show her in.

ELLEN [*to Helmer*]: And the doctor has just come, sir.

HELMER: Has he gone into my study?

ELLEN: Yes, sir.

[*Helmer goes into his study. Ellen ushers in Mrs. Linden, in travelling costume, and goes out, closing the door.*]

MRS. LINDEN [*embarrassed and hesitating*]: How do you do, Nora?

NORA [*doubtfully*]: How do you do?

MRS. LINDEN: I see you don't recognise me.

NORA: No, I don't think—oh yes!—I believe—[*Suddenly brightening.*] What, Christina! Is it really you?

MRS. LINDEN: Yes; really I!

NORA: Christina! And to think I didn't know you! But how could I—[*More softly.*] How changed you are, Christina!

MRS. LINDEN: Yes, no doubt. In nine or ten years—

NORA: Is it really so long since we met? Yes, so it is. Oh, the last eight years have been a happy time, I can tell you. And now you have come to town? All that long journey in mid-winter! How brave of you!

MRS. LINDEN: I arrived by this morning's steamer.

NORA: To have a merry Christmas, of course. Oh, how delightful! Yes, we will have a merry Christmas. Do take your things off. Aren't you frozen? [*Helping her.*] There; now we'll sit cosily by the fire. No, you take the arm-chair; I shall sit in this rocking-chair. [*Seizes her hands.*] Yes, now I can see the dear old face again. It was only at the first glance—But you're a little paler, Christina—and perhaps a little thinner.

MRS. LINDEN: And much, much older, Nora.

NORA: Yes, perhaps a little older—not much—ever so little. [*She suddenly checks herself; seriously.*] Oh, what a thoughtless wretch I am! Here I sit chattering on, and—Dear, dear Christina, can you forgive me!

MRS. LINDEN: What do you mean, Nora?

NORA [*softly*]: Poor Christina! I forgot; you are a widow.

MRS. LINDEN: Yes; my husband died three years ago.

NORA: I know, I know; I saw it in the papers. Oh, believe me, Christina, I did mean to write to you; but I kept putting it off, and something always came in the way.

MRS. LINDEN: I can quite understand that, Nora, dear.

NORA: No, Christina; it was horrid of me. Oh, you poor darling! how much you must have gone through!—And he left you nothing?

MRS. LINDEN: Nothing.

NORA: And no children?

MRS. LINDEN: None.

NORA: Nothing, nothing at all?

MRS. LINDEN: Not even a sorrow or a longing to dwell upon.

NORA [*looking at her incredulously*]: My dear Christina, how is that possible?

MRS. LINDEN [*smiling sadly and stroking her hair*]: Oh, it happens so sometimes, Nora.

NORA: So utterly alone! How dreadful that must be! I have three of the loveliest children. I can't show them to you just now; they're out with their nurse. But now you must tell me everything.

MRS. LINDEN: No, no; I want you to tell me—

NORA: No, you must begin; I won't be egotistical to-day. To-day I'll think only of you. Oh! but I must tell you one thing—perhaps you've heard of our great stroke of fortune?

MRS. LINDEN: No. What is it?

NORA: Only think! my husband has been made manager of the Joint Stock Bank.

MRS. LINDEN: Your husband! Oh, how fortunate!

NORA: Yes; isn't it? A lawyer's position is so uncertain, you see, especially when he won't touch any business that's the least bit—shady, as of course Torvald never would; and there I quite agree with him. Oh! you can imagine how glad we are. He is to enter on his new position at the New Year, and then he'll have a large salary, and percentages. In future we shall be able to live quite differently—just as we please, in fact. Oh, Christina, I feel so lighthearted and happy! It's delightful to have lots of money, and no need to worry about things, isn't it?

MRS. LINDEN: Yes; at any rate it must be delightful to have what you need.

NORA: No, not only what you need, but heaps of money—heaps!

MRS. LINDEN [*smiling*]: Nora, Nora, haven't you learnt reason yet? In our schooldays you were a shocking little spendthrift.

NORA [*quietly smiling*]: Yes; that's what Torvald says I am still. [*Holding up her forefinger.*] But "Nora, Nora" is not so silly as you all think. Oh! I haven't had the chance to be much of a spendthrift. We have both had to work.

MRS. LINDEN: You, too?

NORA: Yes, light fancy work: crochet, and embroidery, and things of that sort; [*Carelessly*] and other work too. You know, of course, that Torvald left the Government service when we were married. He had little chance of promotion, and of course he required to make more money. But in the first year after our marriage he overworked himself terribly. He had to undertake all sorts of extra work, you know, and to slave early and late. He couldn't stand it, and fell dangerously ill. Then the doctors declared he must go to the South.

MRS. LINDEN: You spent a whole year in Italy, didn't you?

NORA: Yes, we did. It wasn't easy to manage, I can tell you. It was just after Ivar's birth. But of course we had to go. Oh, it was a wonderful, delicious journey! And it saved Torvald's life. But it cost a frightful lot of money, Christina.

MRS. LINDEN: So I should think.

NORA: Twelve hundred dollars! Four thousand eight hundred crowns! Isn't that a lot of money?

MRS. LINDEN: How lucky you had the money to spend.

NORA: We got it from father, you must know.

MRS. LINDEN: Ah, I see. He died just about that time, didn't he?

NORA: Yes, Christina, just then. And only think! I couldn't go and nurse him! I was expecting little Ivar's birth daily; and then I had my poor sick Torvald to attend to. Dear, kind old father! I never saw him again, Christina. Oh! that's the hardest thing I have had to bear since my marriage.

MRS. LINDEN: I know how fond you were of him. But then you went to Italy?

NORA: Yes; you see, we had the money, and the doctors said we must lose no time. We started a month later.

MRS. LINDEN: And your husband came back completely cured.

NORA: Sound as a bell.

MRS. LINDEN: But—the doctor?

NORA: What do you mean?

MRS. LINDEN: I thought as I came in your servant announced the doctor—

NORA: Oh, yes; Doctor Rank. But he doesn't come professionally. He is our best friend, and never lets a day pass without looking in. No, Torvald hasn't had an hour's illness since that time. And the children are so healthy and well, and so am I. [*Jumps up and claps her hands.*] Oh, Christina, Christina, what a wonderful thing it is to live and to be happy!—Oh, but it's really too horrid of me! Here am I talking about nothing but my own concerns. [*Seats herself upon a footstool close to Christina, and lays her arms on her friend's lap.*] Oh, don't be angry with me! Now tell me, is it really true that you didn't love your husband? What made you marry him, then?

MRS. LINDEN: My mother was still alive, you see, bedridden and helpless; and then I had my two younger brothers to think of. I didn't think it would be right for me to refuse him.

NORA: Perhaps it wouldn't have been. I suppose he was rich then?

MRS. LINDEN: Very well off, I believe. But his business was uncertain. It fell to pieces at his death, and there was nothing left.

NORA: And then—?

MRS. LINDEN: Then I had to fight my way by keeping a shop, a little school, anything I could turn my hand to. The last three years have been one long struggle for me. But now it is over, Nora. My poor mother no longer needs me; she is at rest. And the boys are in business, and can look after themselves.

NORA: How free your life must feel!

MRS. LINDEN: No, Nora; only inexpressibly empty. No one to live for! [*Stands up restlessly.*] That's why I could not bear to stay any longer in that out-of-the-way corner. Here it must be easier to find something to take one up—to occupy one's thoughts. If I could only get some settled employment—some office work.

NORA: But, Christina, that's such drudgery, and you look worn out already. It would be ever so much better for you to go to some watering-place and rest.

MRS. LINDEN [*going to the window*]: I have no father to give me the money, Nora.

NORA [*rising*]: Oh, don't be vexed with me.

MRS. LINDEN [*going to her*]: My dear Nora, don't you be vexed with me. The worst of a position like mine is that it makes one so bitter. You have no one to work for, yet you have to be always on the strain. You must live; and so you become selfish. When I heard of the happy change in your fortunes—can you believe it?—I was glad for my own sake more than for yours.

NORA: How do you mean? Ah, I see! You think Torvald can perhaps do something for you.

MRS. LINDEN: Yes; I thought so.

NORA: And so he shall, Christina. Just you leave it all to me. I shall lead up to it beautifully!—I shall think of some delightful plan to put him in a good humour! Oh, I should so love to help you.

MRS. LINDEN: How good of you, Nora, to stand by me so warmly! Doubly good in you, who know so little of the troubles and burdens of life.

NORA: I? I know so little of—?

MRS. LINDEN [*smiling*]: Oh, well—a little fancy-work, and so forth.—You're a child, Nora.

NORA [*tosses her head and paces the room*]: Oh, come, you mustn't be so patronising!

MRS. LINDEN: No?

NORA: You're like the rest. You all think I'm fit for nothing really serious—

MRS. LINDEN: Well, well—

NORA: You think I've had no troubles in this weary world.

MRS. LINDEN: My dear Nora, you've just told me all your troubles.

NORA: Pooh—those trifles! [*Softly.*] I haven't told you the great thing.

MRS. LINDEN: The great thing? What do you mean?

NORA: I know you look down upon me, Christina; but you have no right to. You are proud of having worked so hard and so long for your mother.

MRS. LINDEN: I am sure I don't look down upon any one; but it's true I am both proud and glad when I remember that I was able to keep my mother's last days free from care.

NORA: And you're proud to think of what you have done for your brothers, too.

MRS. LINDEN: Have I not the right to be?

NORA: Yes, indeed. But now let me tell you, Christina—I, too, have something to be proud and glad of.

MRS. LINDEN: I don't doubt it. But what do you mean?

NORA: Hush! Not so loud. Only think, if Torvald were to hear! He mustn't—not for worlds! No one must know about it, Christina—no one but you.

MRS. LINDEN: Why, what can it be?

NORA: Come over here. [*Draws her down beside her on the sofa.*] Yes, Christina—I, too, have something to be proud and glad of. I saved Torvald's life.

MRS. LINDEN: Saved his life? How?

NORA: I told you about our going to Italy. Torvald would have died but for that.

MRS. LINDEN: Well—and your father gave you the money.

NORA [*smiling*]: Yes, so Torvald and every one believes; but—

MRS. LINDEN: But—?

NORA: Papa didn't give us one penny. It was *I* that found the money.

MRS. LINDEN: You? All that money?

NORA: Twelve hundred dollars. Four thousand eight hundred crowns. What do you say to that?

MRS. LINDEN: My dear Nora, how did you manage it? Did you win it in the lottery?

NORA [*contemptuously*]: In the lottery? Pooh! Any one could have done that!

MRS. LINDEN: Then wherever did you get it from?

NORA [*hums and smiles mysteriously*]: H'm; tra-la-la-la.

MRS. LINDEN: Of course you couldn't borrow it.

NORA: No? Why not?

MRS. LINDEN: Why, a wife can't borrow without her husband's consent.

NORA [*tossing her head*]: Oh! when the wife has some idea of business, and knows how to set about things—

MRS. LINDEN: But, Nora, I don't understand—

NORA: Well, you needn't. I never said I borrowed the money. There are many ways I may have got it. [*Throws herself back on the sofa.*] I may have got it from some admirer. When one is so—attractive as I am—

MRS. LINDEN: You're too silly, Nora.

NORA: Now I'm sure you're dying of curiosity, Christina—

MRS. LINDEN: Listen to me, Nora dear: haven't you been a little rash?

NORA [*sitting upright again*]: Is it rash to save one's husband's life?

MRS. LINDEN: I think it was rash of you, without his knowledge—

NORA: But it would have been fatal for him to know! Can't you understand that? He wasn't even to suspect how ill he was. The doctors came to me privately and told me his life was in danger—that nothing could save him but a winter in the South. Do you think I didn't try diplomacy first? I told him how I longed to have a trip abroad, like other young wives; I wept and prayed; I said he ought to think of my condition, and not to thwart me; and then I hinted that he could borrow the money. But then, Christina, he got almost angry. He said I was frivolous, and that it was his duty as a husband not to yield to my whims and fancies—so he called them. Very well, thought I, but saved you must be; and then I found the way to do it.

MRS. LINDEN: And did your husband never learn from your father that the money was not from him?

NORA: No; never. Papa died at that very time. I meant to have told him all about it, and begged him to say nothing. But he was so ill—unhappily, it wasn't necessary.

MRS. LINDEN: And you have never confessed to your husband?

NORA: Good heavens! What can you be thinking of? Tell him, when he has such a loathing of debt! And besides—how painful and humiliating it would be for Torvald, with his manly self-respect, to know that he owed anything to me! It would utterly upset the relation between us; our beautiful, happy home would never again be what it is.

MRS. LINDEN: Will you never tell him?

NORA [*thoughtfully, half-smiling*]: Yes, some time, perhaps—many, many years hence, when I'm—not so pretty. You mustn't laugh at me! Of course I mean when Torvald is not so much in love with me as he is now; when it doesn't amuse him any longer to see me dancing about, and dressing up and acting. Then it might be well to have something in reserve. [*Breaking off.*] Nonsense! nonsense! That time will never come. Now, what do you say to my grand secret, Christina? Am I fit for nothing now? You may believe it has cost me a lot of anxiety. It has been no joke to meet my engagements punctually. You must know, Christina, that in business there are things called instalments, and quarterly interest, that are terribly hard to provide for. So I've had to pinch a little here and there, wherever I could. I couldn't save much out of the housekeeping, for, of course. Torvald had to live well. And I couldn't let the children go about badly dressed; all I got for them, I spent on them, the blessed darlings!

MRS. LINDEN: Poor Nora! So it had to come out of your own pocket-money.

NORA: Yes, of course. After all, the whole thing was my doing. When Torvald gave me money for clothes, and so on, I never spent more than half of it; I always bought the simplest and cheapest things. It's a mercy that everything suits me so well—Torvald never had any suspicions. But it was often very hard, Christina dear. For it's nice to be beautifully dressed—now, isn't it?

MRS. LINDEN: Indeed it is.

NORA: Well, and besides that, I made money in other ways. Last winter I was so lucky—I got a heap of copying to do. I shut myself up every evening and wrote far into the night. Oh, sometimes I was so tired, so tired. And yet it was splendid to work in that way and earn money. I almost felt as if I was a man.

MRS. LINDEN: Then how much have you been able to pay off?

NORA: Well, I can't precisely say. It's difficult to keep that sort of business clear. I only know that I've paid everything I could scrape together. Sometimes I really didn't know where to turn. [*Smiles.*] Then I used to sit here and pretend that a rich old gentleman was in love with me—

MRS. LINDEN: What! What gentleman?

NORA: Oh, nobody!—that he was dead now, and that when his will was opened, there stood in large letters: "Pay over at once everything of which I die possessed to that charming person, Mrs. Nora Helmer."

MRS. LINDEN: But, my dear Nora—what gentleman do you mean?

NORA: Oh, dear, can't you understand? There wasn't any old gentleman: it was only what I used to dream and dream when I was at my wits' end for money. But it doesn't matter now—the tiresome old creature may stay where he is for me. I care nothing for him or his will; for now my troubles are over. [*Springing up.*] Oh, Christina, how glorious it is to think of! Free from all anxiety! Free, quite free. To be able to play and romp about with the children; to have things tasteful and pretty in the house, exactly as Torvald likes it! And then the spring will soon be here, with the great blue sky. Perhaps then we shall have a little holiday. Perhaps I shall see the sea again. Oh, what a wonderful thing it is to live and to be happy!

[*The hall-door bell rings.*]

MRS. LINDEN [*rising*]: There's a ring. Perhaps I had better go.

NORA: No; do stay. No one will come here. It's sure to be some one for Torvald.

ELLEN [*in the doorway*]: If you please, ma'am, there's a gentleman to speak to Mr. Helmer.

NORA: Who is the gentleman?

KROGSTAD [*in the doorway*]: It is I, Mrs. Helmer.

[*Mrs. Linden starts and turns away to the window.*]

NORA [*goes a step towards him, anxiously, speaking low*]: You? What is it? What do you want with my husband?

KROGSTAD: Bank business—in a way. I hold a small post in the Joint Stock Bank, and your husband is to be our new chief, I hear.

NORA: Then it is—?

KROGSTAD: Only tiresome business, Mrs. Helmer; nothing more.

NORA: Then will you please go to his study.

[*Krogstad goes. She bows indifferently while she closes the door into the hall. Then she goes to the stove and looks to the fire.*]

MRS. LINDEN: Nora—who was that man?

NORA: A Mr. Krogstad—a lawyer.

MRS. LINDEN: Then it was really he?

NORA: Do you know him?

MRS. LINDEN: I used to know him—many years ago. He was in a lawyer's office in our town.

NORA: Yes, so he was.

MRS. LINDEN: How he has changed!

NORA: I believe his marriage was unhappy.

MRS. LINDEN: And he is a widower now?

NORA: With a lot of children. There! Now it will burn up.

[*She closes the stove, and pushes the rocking-chair a little aside.*]

MRS. LINDEN: His business is not of the most creditable, they say?

NORA: Isn't it? I daresay not. I don't know. But don't let us think of business—it's so tiresome.

[*Dr. Rank comes out of Helmer*'s *room.*]

RANK [*still in the doorway*]: No, no; I'm in your way. I shall go and have a chat with your wife. [*Shuts the door and sees Mrs. Linden.*] Oh, I beg your pardon. I'm in the way here too.

NORA: No, not in the least. [*Introduces them.*] Doctor Rank—Mrs. Linden.

RANK: Oh, indeed; I've often heard Mrs. Linden's name; I think I passed you on the stairs as I came up.

MRS. LINDEN: Yes; I go so very slowly. Stairs try me so much.

RANK: Ah—you are not very strong?

MRS. LINDEN: Only overworked.

RANK: Nothing more? Then no doubt you've come to town to find rest in a round of dissipation?

MRS. LINDEN: I have come to look for employment.

RANK: Is that an approved remedy for overwork?

MRS. LINDEN: One must live, Doctor Rank.

RANK: Yes, that seems to be the general opinion.

NORA: Come, Doctor Rank—you want to live yourself.

RANK: To be sure I do. However wretched I may be, I want to drag on as long as possible. All my patients, too, have the same mania. And it's the same with people whose complaint is moral. At this very moment Helmer is talking to just such a moral incurable—

MRS. LINDEN [*softly*]: Ah!

NORA: Whom do you mean?

RANK: Oh, a fellow named Krogstad, a man you know nothing about—corrupt to the very core of his character. But even he began by announcing, as a matter of vast importance, that he must live.

NORA: Indeed? And what did he want with Torvald?

RANK: I haven't an idea; I only gathered that it was some bank business.

NORA: I didn't know that Krog—that this Mr. Krogstad had anything to do with the Bank?

RANK: Yes. He has got some sort of place there. [*To Mrs. Linden.*] I don't know whether, in your part of the country, you have people who go grubbing and sniffing around in search of moral rottenness—and then, when they have found a "case," don't rest till they have got their man into some good position, where they can keep a watch upon him. Men with a clean bill of health they leave out in the cold.

MRS. LINDEN: Well, I suppose the—delicate characters require most care.

RANK [*shrugs his shoulders*]: There we have it! It's that notion that makes society a hospital.

[*Nora. deep in her own thoughts, breaks into half-stifled laughter and claps her hands.*]

RANK: Why do you laugh at that? Have you any idea what "society" is?

NORA: What do I care for your tiresome society? I was laughing at something else—something excessively amusing. Tell me, Doctor Rank, are all the employees at the Bank dependent on Torvald now?

RANK: Is that what strikes you as excessively amusing?

NORA [*smiles and hums*]: Never mind, never mind! [*Walks about the room.*] Yes, it is funny to think that we—that Torvald has such power over so many people. [*Takes the bag from her pocket.*] Doctor Rank, will you have a macaroon?

RANK: What!—macaroons! I thought they were contraband here.

NORA: Yes; but Christina brought me these.

MRS. LINDEN: What! I—?

NORA: Oh, well! Don't be frightened. You couldn't possibly know that Torvald had forbidden them. The fact is, he's afraid of me spoiling my teeth. But, oh bother, just for once!—That's for you, Doctor Rank! [*Puts a macaroon into his mouth.*] And you too, Christina. And I'll have one while we're about it—only a tiny one, or at most two. [*Walks about again.*] Oh dear, I am happy! There's only one thing in the world I really want.

RANK: Well; what's that?

NORA: There's something I should so like to say—in Torvald's hearing.

RANK: Then why don't you say it?

NORA: Because I daren't, it's so ugly.

MRS. LINDEN: Ugly?

RANK: In that case you'd better not. But to us you might—What is it you would so like to say in Helmer's hearing?

NORA: I should so love to say "Damn it all!"

RANK: Are you out of your mind?

MRS. LINDEN: Good gracious, Nora—!

RANK: Say it—there he is!

NORA [*hides the macaroons*]: Hush—sh—sh

[*Helmer comes out of his room, hat in hand, with his overcoat on his arm.*]

NORA [*going to him*]: Well, Torvald dear, have you got rid of him?

HELMER: Yes; he has just gone.

NORA: Let me introduce you—this is Christina, who has come to town—

HELMER: Christina? Pardon me, I don't know—

NORA: Mrs. Linden, Torvald dear—Christina Linden.

HELMER [*to Mrs. Linden*]: Indeed! A school-friend of my wife's, no doubt?

MRS. LINDEN: Yes; we knew each other as girls.

NORA: And only think! she has taken this long journey on purpose to speak to you.

HELMER: To speak to me!

MRS. LINDEN: Well, not quite—

NORA: You see, Christina is tremendously clever at office work, and she's so anxious to work under a first-rate man of business in order to learn still more—

HELMER [*to Mrs. Linden*]: Very sensible indeed.

NORA: And when she heard you were appointed manager—it was telegraphed, you know—she started off at once, and—Torvald, dear, for my sake, you must do something for Christina. Now, can't you?

HELMER: It's not impossible. I presume Mrs. Linden is a widow?

MRS. LINDEN: Yes.

HELMER: And you have already had some experience of business?

MRS. LINDEN: A good deal.

HELMER: Well, then, it's very likely I may be able to find a place for you.

NORA [*clapping her hands*]: There now! There now!

HELMER: You have come at a fortunate moment, Mrs. Linden.

MRS. LINDEN: Oh, how can I thank you—?

HELMER [*smiling*]: There is no occasion. [*Puts on his overcoat.*] But for the present you must excuse me—

RANK: Wait; I am going with you.

[*Fetches his fur coat from the hall and warms it at the fire.*]

NORA: Don't be long, Torvald dear.

HELMER: Only an hour; not more.

NORA: Are you going too, Christina?

MRS. LINDEN [*putting on her walking things*]: Yes; I must set about looking for lodgings.

HELMER: Then perhaps we can go together?

NORA [*helping her*]: What a pity we haven't a spare room for you; but it's impossible—

MRS. LINDEN: I shouldn't think of troubling you. Goodbye, dear Nora, and thank you for all your kindness.

NORA: Good-bye for the present. Of course, you'll come back this evening. And you, too, Doctor Rank. What! If you're well enough? Of course you'll be well enough. Only wrap up warmly. [*They go out, talking, into the hall. Outside on the stairs are heard children's voices.*] There they are! There they are! [*She runs to the outer door and opens it. The nurse, Anna, enters the hall with the children.*] Come in! Come in! [*Stoops down and kisses the children.*] Oh, my sweet darlings! Do you see them, Christina? Aren't they lovely?

RANK: Don't let us stand here chattering in the draught.

HELMER: Come, Mrs. Linden; only mothers can stand such a temperature.

[*Dr. Rank, Helmer, and Mrs. Linden go down the stairs; Anna enters the room with the children; Nora also, shutting the door.*]

NORA: How fresh and bright you look! And what red cheeks you've got! Like apples and roses. [*The children chatter to her during what follows.*] Have you had great fun? That's splendid! Oh, really! You've been giving Emmy and Bob a ride on your sledge!—both at once, only think! Why, you're quite a man, Ivar. Oh, give her to me a little, Anna. My sweet little dolly! [*Takes the smallest from the nurse and dances with her.*] Yes, yes; mother will dance with Bob too. What! Did you have a game of snowballs? Oh, I wish I'd been there. No; leave them, Anna; I'll take their things off. Oh, yes, let me do it; it's such fun. Go to the nursery; you look frozen. You'll find some hot coffee on the stove.

[*The Nurse goes into the room on the left. Nora takes off the children's things and throws them down anywhere, while the children talk all together.*]

Really! A big dog ran after you? But he didn't bite you? No; dogs don't bite dear little dolly children. Don't peep into those parcels, Ivar. What is it? Wouldn't you like to know? Take care—it'll bite! What? Shall we have a game? What shall we play at? Hide-and-seek? Yes, let's play hide-and-seek. Bob shall hide first. Am I to? Yes, let me hide first.

[*She and the children play, with laughter and shouting, in the room and the adjacent one to the right. At last Nora hides under the table; the children come rushing in, look for her, but cannot find her, hear her half-choked laughter, rush to the table, lift up the cover and see her. Loud shouts. She creeps out, as though to frighten them. Fresh shouts. Meanwhile there has been a knock at the door leading into the hall. No one has heard it. Now the door is half opened and Krogstad appears. He waits a little; the game is renewed.*]

KROGSTAD: I beg your pardon, Mrs. Helmer—

NORA [*with a suppressed cry, turns round and half jumps up*]: Ah! What do you want?

KROGSTAD: Excuse me; the outer door was ajar—somebody must have forgotten to shut it—

NORA [*standing up*]: My husband is not at home, Mr. Krogstad.

KROGSTAD: I know it.

NORA: Then what do you want here?

KROGSTAD: To say a few words to you.

NORA: To me? [*To the children, softly.*] Go in to Anna. What? No, the strange man won't hurt mamma. When he's gone we'll go on playing. [*She leads the children into the left-hand room, and shuts the door behind them. Uneasy, in suspense.*] It is to me you wish to speak?

KROGSTAD: Yes, to you.

NORA: To-day? But it's not the first yet—

KROGSTAD: No, to-day is Christmas Eve. It will depend upon yourself whether you have a merry Christmas.

NORA: What do you want? I'm not ready to-day—

KROGSTAD: Never mind that just now. I have come about another matter. You have a minute to spare?

NORA: Oh, yes, I suppose so; although—

KROGSTAD: Good. I was sitting in the restaurant opposite, and I saw your husband go down the street—

NORA: Well?

KROGSTAD: —with a lady.

NORA: What then?

KROGSTAD: May I ask if the lady was a Mrs. Linden?

NORA: Yes.

KROGSTAD: Who has just come to town?

NORA: Yes. To-day.

KROGSTAD: I believe she is an intimate friend of yours.

NORA: Certainly. But I don't understand—

KROGSTAD: I used to know her too.

NORA: I know you did.

KROGSTAD: Ah! You know all about it. I thought as much. Now, frankly, is Mrs. Linden to have a place in the Bank?

NORA: How dare you catechise me in this way, Mr. Krogstad—you, a subordinate of my husband's? But since you ask, you shall know. Yes, Mrs. Linden is to be employed. And it is I who recommended her, Mr. Krogstad. Now you know.

KROGSTAD: Then my guess was right.

NORA [*walking up and down*]: You see one has a wee bit of influence, after all. It doesn't follow because one's only a woman—When people are in a subordinate position, Mr. Krogstad, they ought really to be careful how they offend anybody who—h'm—

KROGSTAD: —who has influence?

NORA: Exactly.

KROGSTAD [*taking another tone*]: Mrs. Helmer, will you have the kindness to employ your influence on my behalf?

NORA: What? How do you mean?

KROGSTAD: Will you be so good as to see that I retain my subordinate position in the Bank?

NORA: What do you mean? Who wants to take it from you?

KROGSTAD: Oh, you needn't pretend ignorance. I can very well understand that it cannot be pleasant for your friend to meet me; and I can also understand now for whose sake I am to be hounded out.

NORA: But I assure you—

KROGSTAD: Come, come, now, once for all: there is time yet, and I advise you to use your influence to prevent it.

NORA: But, Mr. Krogstad, I have no influence—absolutely none.

KROGSTAD: None? I thought you said a moment ago—

NORA: Of course, not in that sense. I! How can you imagine that I should have any such influence over my husband?

KROGSTAD: Oh, I know your husband from our college days. I don't think he is any more inflexible than other husbands.

NORA: If you talk disrespectfully of my husband, I must request you to leave the house.

KROGSTAD: You are bold, madam.

NORA: I am afraid of you no longer. When New Year's Day is over, I shall soon be out of the whole business.

KROGSTAD [*controlling himself*]: Listen to me, Mrs. Helmer. If need be, I shall fight as though for my life to keep my little place in the Bank.

NORA: Yes, so it seems.

KROGSTAD: It's not only for the salary: that is what I care least about. It's something else—Well, I had better make a clean breast of it. Of course, you know, like every one else, that some years ago I—got into trouble.

NORA: I think I've heard something of the sort.

KROGSTAD: The matter never came into court; but from that moment all paths were barred to me. Then I took up the business you know about. I had to turn my hand to something; and I don't think I've been one of the worst. But now I must get clear of it all. My sons are growing up; for their sake I must try to recover my character as well as I can. This place in the Bank was the first step; and now your husband wants to kick me off the ladder, back into the mire.

NORA: But I assure you, Mr. Krogstad, I haven't the least power to help you.

KROGSTAD: That is because you have not the will; but I can compel you.

NORA: You won't tell my husband that I owe you money?

KROGSTAD: H'm; suppose I were to?

NORA: It would be shameful of you. [*With tears in her voice.*] The secret that is my joy and my pride—that he should learn it in such an ugly, coarse way—and from you. It would involve me in all sorts of unpleasantness—

KROGSTAD: Only unpleasantness?

NORA [*hotly*]: But just do it. It's you that will come off worst, for then my husband will see what a bad man you are, and then you certainly won't keep your place.

KROGSTAD: I asked whether it was only domestic unpleasantness you feared?

NORA: If my husband gets to know about it, he will, of course pay you off at once, and then we shall have nothing more to do with you.

KROGSTAD [*coming a pace nearer*]: Listen, Mrs. Helmer: either your memory is defective, or you don't know much about business. I must make the position a little clearer to you.

NORA: How so?

KROGSTAD: When your husband was ill, you came to me to borrow twelve hundred dollars.

NORA: I knew of nobody else.

KROGSTAD: I promised to find you the money—

NORA: And you did find it.

KROGSTAD: I promised to find you the money, on certain conditions. You were so much taken up at the time about your husband's illness, and so eager to have the wherewithal for your journey, that you probably did not give much thought to the details. Allow me to remind you of them. I promised to find you the amount in exchange for a note of hand, which I drew up.

NORA: Yes, and I signed it.

KROGSTAD: Quite right. But then I added a few lines, making your father security for the debt. Your father was to sign this.

NORA: Was to—? He did sign it!

KROGSTAD: I had left the date blank. That is to say, your father was himself to date his signature. Do you recollect that?

NORA: Yes, I believe—

KROGSTAD: Then I gave you the paper to send to your father, by post. Is not that so?

NORA: Yes.

KROGSTAD: And of course you did so at once; for within five or six days you brought me back the document with your father's signature; and I handed you the money.

NORA: Well? Have I not made my payments punctually?

KROGSTAD: Fairly—yes. But to return to the point: You were in great trouble at the time, Mrs. Helmer.

NORA: I was indeed!

KROGSTAD: Your father was very ill, I believe?

NORA: He was on his death-bed.

KROGSTAD: And died soon after?

NORA: Yes.

KROGSTAD: Tell me, Mrs. Helmer: do you happen to recollect the day of his death? The day of the month, I mean?

NORA: Father died on the 29th of September.

KROGSTAD: Quite correct. I have made inquiries. And here comes in the remarkable point—[*produces a paper*] which I cannot explain.

NORA: What remarkable point? I don't know—

KROGSTAD: The remarkable point, madam, that your father signed this paper three days after his death!

NORA: What! I don't understand—

KROGSTAD: Your father died on the 29th of September. But look here: he has dated his signature October 2nd! Is not that remarkable, Mrs. Helmer? [*Nora is silent.*] Can you explain it? [*Nora continues silent.*] It is noteworthy, too, that the words "October 2nd" and the year are not in your father's handwriting, but in one which I believe I know. Well, this may be explained; your father may have forgotten to date his signature, and somebody may have added the date at random, before the fact of your father's death was known. There is nothing wrong in that. Everything depends on the signature. Of course it is genuine, Mrs. Helmer? It was really your father himself who wrote his name here?

NORA [*after a short silence, throws her head back and looks defiantly at him*]: No, it was not. *I* wrote father's name.

KROGSTAD: Ah!—Are you aware, madam, that that is a dangerous admission?

NORA: How so? You will soon get your money.

KROGSTAD: May I ask you one more question? Why did you not send the paper to your father?

NORA: It was impossible. Father was ill. If I had asked him for his signature, I should have had to tell him why I wanted the money; but he was so ill I really could not tell him that my husband's life was in danger. It was impossible.

KROGSTAD: Then it would have been better to have given up your tour.

NORA: No, I couldn't do that; my husband's life depended on that journey. I couldn't give it up.

KROGSTAD: And did it never occur to you that you were playing me false?

NORA: That was nothing to me. I didn't care in the least about you. I couldn't endure you for all the cruel difficulties you made, although you knew how ill my husband was.

KROGSTAD: Mrs. Helmer, you evidently do not realise what you have been guilty of. But I can assure you it was nothing more and nothing worse that made me an outcast from society.

NORA: You! You want me to believe that you did a brave thing to save your wife's life?

KROGSTAD: The law takes no account of motives.

NORA: Then it must be a very bad law.

KROGSTAD: Bad or not, if I produce this document in court, you will be condemned according to law.

NORA: I don't believe that. Do you mean to tell me that a daughter has no right to spare her dying father trouble and anxiety?—that a wife has no right to save her husband's life? I don't know much about the law, but I'm sure you'll find, somewhere or another, that that is allowed. And you don't know that—you, a lawyer! You must be a bad one, Mr. Krogstad.

KROGSTAD: Possibly. But business—such business as ours—I do understand. You believe that? Very well; now, do as you please. But this I may tell you, that if I am flung into the gutter a second time, you shall keep me company.

[*Bows and goes out through hall.*]

NORA [*stands a while thinking, then tosses her head*]: Oh nonsense! He wants to frighten me. I'm not so foolish as that. [*Begins folding the children's clothes. Pauses.*] But—? No, it's impossible! Why, I did it for love!

CHILDREN [*at the door, left*]: Mamma, the strange man has gone now.

NORA: Yes, yes, I know. But don't tell anyone about the strange man. Do you hear? Not even papa!

CHILDREN: No, mamma; and now will you play with us again?

NORA: No, no; not now.

CHILDREN: Oh, do, mamma; you know you promised.

NORA: Yes, but I can't just now. Run to the nursery; I have so much to do. Run along, run along, and be good, my darlings! [*She pushes them gently into the inner room, and closes the door behind them. Sits on the sofa, embroiders a few stitches, but soon pauses.*] No! [*Throws down the work, rises, goes to the hall door and calls out.*] Ellen, bring in the Christmas-tree! [*Goes to table, left, and opens the drawer; again pauses.*] No, it's quite impossible!

ELLEN [*with Christmas-tree*]: Where shall I stand it, ma'am?

NORA: There, in the middle of the room.

ELLEN: Shall I bring in anything else?

NORA: No, thank you, I have all I want.

[*Ellen, having put down the tree, goes out.*]

NORA [*busy dressing the tree*]: There must be a candle here—and flowers there.—That horrible man! Nonsense, nonsense! there's nothing to be afraid of. The Christmas-tree shall be beautiful. I'll do everything to please you, Torvald; I'll sing and dance, and—

[*Enter Helmer by the hall door, with a bundle of documents.*]

NORA: Oh! You're back already?

HELMER: Yes. Has anybody been here.

NORA: Here? No.

HELMER: That's odd. I saw Krogstad come out of the house.

NORA: Did you? Oh, yes, by-the-bye, he was here for a minute.

HELMER: Nora, I can see by your manner that he has been begging you to put in a good word for him.

NORA: Yes.

HELMER: And you were to do it as if of your own accord? You were to say nothing to me of his having been here. Didn't he suggest that, too?

NORA: Yes, Torvald; but—

HELMER: Nora, Nora! And you could condescend to that! To speak to such a man, to make him a promise! And then to tell me an untruth about it!

NORA: An untruth!

HELMER: Didn't you say that nobody had been here? [*Threatens with his finger.*] My little bird must never do that again! A song-bird must sing clear and true; no false notes. [*Puts his arm round her.*] That's so, isn't it? Yes, I was sure of it. [*Lets her go.*] And now we'll say no more about it. [*Sits down before the fire.*] Oh, how cosy and quiet it is here!

[*Glances into his documents.*]

NORA [*busy with the tree, after a short silence*]: Torvald!

HELMER: Yes.

NORA: I'm looking forward so much to the Stenborgs' fancy ball the day after tomorrow.

HELMER: And I'm on tenterhooks to see what surprise you have in store for me.

NORA: Oh, it's too tiresome!

HELMER: What is?

NORA: I can't think of anything good. Everything seems so foolish and meaningless.

HELMER: Has little Nora made that discovery?

NORA [*behind his chair, with her arms on the back*]: Are you very busy, Torvald?

HELMER: Well—

NORA: What papers are those?

HELMER: Bank business.

NORA: Already!

HELMER: I have got the retiring manager to let me make some necessary changes in the staff and the organization. I can do this during Christmas week. I want to have everything straight by the New Year.

NORA: Then that's why that poor Krogstad—

HELMER: H'm.

NORA [*still leaning over the chair-back and slowly stroking his hair*]: If you hadn't been so very busy, I should have asked you a great, great favour, Torvald.

HELMER: What can it be? Out with it.

NORA: Nobody has such perfect taste as you; and I should so love to look well at the fancy ball. Torvald, dear, couldn't you take me in hand, and settle what I'm to be, and arrange my costume for me?

HELMER: Aha! So my willful little woman is at a loss, and making signals of distress.

NORA: Yes, please, Torvald. I can't get on without your help.

HELMER: Well, well, I'll think it over, and we'll soon hit upon something.

NORA: Oh, how good that is of you! [*Goes to the tree again; pause.*] How well the red flowers show.—Tell me, was it anything so very dreadful this Krogstad got into trouble about?

HELMER: Forgery, that's all. Don't you know what that means?

NORA: Mayn't he have been driven to it by need?

HELMER: Yes; or, like so many others, he may have done it in pure heedlessness. I am not so hard-hearted as to condemn a man absolutely for a single fault.

NORA: No, surely not, Torvald!

HELMER: Many a man can retrieve his character, if he owns his crime and takes the punishment.

NORA: Punishment—?

HELMER: But Krogstad didn't do that. He evaded the law by means of tricks and subterfuges; and that is what has morally ruined him.

NORA: Do you think that—?

HELMER: Just think how a man with a thing of that sort on his conscience must be always lying and canting and shamming. Think of the mask he must wear even towards those who stand nearest him—towards his own wife and children. The effect on the children—that's the most terrible part of it, Nora.

NORA: Why?

HELMER: Because in such an atmosphere of lies home life is poisoned and contaminated in every fibre. Every breath the children draw contains some germ of evil.

NORA [*closer behind him*]: Are you sure of that?

HELMER: As a lawyer, my dear, I have seen it often enough. Nearly all cases of early corruption may be traced to lying mothers.

NORA: Why—mothers?

HELMER: It generally comes from the mother's side; but of course the father's influence may act in the same way. Every lawyer knows it too well. And here has this Krogstad been poisoning his own children for years past by a life of lies and hypocrisy—that is why I call him morally ruined. [*Holds out both hands to her.*] So my sweet little Nora must promise not to plead his cause. Shake hands upon it. Come, come, what's this? Give me your hand. That's right. Then it's a bargain. I assure you it would have been impossible for me to work with him. It gives me a positive sense of physical discomfort to come in contact with such people.

[*Nora draws her hand away, and moves to the other side of the Christmas-tree.*]

NORA: How warm it is here. And I have so much to do.

HELMER [*rises and gathers up his papers*]: Yes, and I must try to get some of these papers looked through before dinner. And I shall think over your costume too. Perhaps I may even find something to hang in gilt paper on the Christmas-tree. [*Lays his hand on her head.*] My precious little song-bird!

[*He goes into his room and shuts the door.*]

NORA [*softly, after a pause*]: It can't be. It's impossible. It must be impossible!

ANNA [*at the door, left*]: The little ones are begging so prettily to come to mamma.

NORA: No, no, no; don't let them come to me! Keep them with you, Anna.

ANNA: Very well, ma'am.

[*Shuts the door.*]

NORA [*pale with terror*]: Corrupt my children!—Poison my home! [*Short pause. She throws back her head.*] It's not true! It can never, never be true!

ACT 2

The same room. In the corner, beside the piano, stands the Christmas-tree, stripped, and with the candles burnt out. Nora's outdoor things lie on the sofa.

Nora, alone, is walking about restlessly. At last she stops by the sofa, and takes up her cloak.

NORA [*dropping the cloak*]: There's somebody coming! [*Goes to the hall door and listens.*] Nobody; of course nobody will come to-day, Christmas-day; nor tomorrow either. But perhaps——[*Opens the door and looks out.*]—No, nothing in the letter box; quite empty. [*Comes forward.*] Stuff and nonsense! Of course he won't really do anything. Such a thing couldn't happen. It's impossible! Why, I have three little children.

[*Anna enters from the left, with a large cardboard box.*]

ANNA: I've found the box with the fancy dress at last.

NORA: Thanks; put it down on the table.

ANNA [*does so*]: But I'm afraid it's very much out of order.

NORA: Oh, I wish I could tear it into a hundred thousand pieces!

ANNA: Oh, no. It can easily be put to rights—just a little patience.

NORA: I shall go and get Mrs. Linden to help me.

ANNA: Going out again? In such weather as this! You'll catch cold, ma'am, and be ill.

NORA: Worse things might happen.—What are the children doing?

ANNA: They're playing with their Christmas presents, poor little dears; but—

NORA: Do they often ask for me?

ANNA: You see they've been so used to having their mamma with them.

NORA: Yes; but, Anna, I can't have them so much with me in future.

ANNA: Well, little children get used to anything.

NORA: Do you think they do? Do you believe they would forget their mother if she went quite away?

ANNA: Gracious me! Quite away?

NORA: Tell me, Anna—I've so often wondered about it—how could you bring yourself to give your child up to strangers?

ANNA: I had to when I came to nurse my little Miss Nora.

NORA: But how could you make up your mind to it?

ANNA: When I had the chance of such a good place? A poor girl who's been in trouble must take what comes. That wicked man did nothing for me.

NORA: But your daughter must have forgotten you.

ANNA: Oh, no, ma'am, that she hasn't. She wrote to me both when she was confirmed and when she was married.

NORA [*embracing her*]: Dear old Anna—you were a good mother to me when I was little.

ANNA: My poor little Nora had no mother but me.

NORA: And if my little ones had nobody else, I'm sure you would—Nonsense, nonsense! [*Opens the box.*] Go in to the children. Now I must—You'll see how lovely I shall be to-morrow.

ANNA: I'm sure there will be no one at the ball so lovely as my Miss Nora.

[*She goes into the room on the left.*]

NORA [*takes the costume out of the box, but soon throws it down again*]: Oh, if I dared go out. If only nobody would come. If only nothing would happen here in the meantime. Rubbish; nobody is coming. Only not to think. What a delicious muff! Beautiful gloves, beautiful gloves! To forget—to forget! One, two, three, four, five, six—[*With a scream.*] Ah, there they come.

[*Goes towards the door, then stands irresolute.*]

[*Mrs. Linden enters from the hall, where she has taken off her things.*]

NORA: Oh, it's you, Christina. There's nobody else there? I'm so glad you have come.

MRS. LINDEN: I hear you called at my lodgings.

NORA: Yes, I was just passing. There's something you must help me with. Let us sit here on the sofa—so. To-morrow evening there's to be a fancy ball at Consul Stenborg's overhead, and Torvald wants me to appear as a Neapolitan fisher-girl, and dance the tarantella; I learned it at Capri.

MRS. LINDEN: I see—quite a performance.

NORA: Yes, Torvald wishes it. Look, this is the costume; Torvald had it made for me in Italy. But now it's all so torn, I don't know—

MRS. LINDEN: Oh, we shall soon set that to rights. It's only the trimming that has come loose here and there. Have you a needle and thread? Ah, here's the very thing.

NORA: Oh, how kind of you.

MRS. LINDEN [*sewing*]: So you're to be in costume to-morrow, Nora? I'll tell you what—I shall come in for a moment to see you in all your glory. But I've quite forgotten to thank you for the pleasant evening yesterday.

NORA [*rises and walks across the room*]: Oh, yesterday, it didn't seem so pleasant as usual.—You should have come to town a little sooner, Christina.—Torvald has certainly the art of making home bright and beautiful.

MRS. LINDEN: You, too, I should think, or you wouldn't be your father's daughter. But tell me—is Doctor Rank always so depressed as he was last evening?

NORA: No, yesterday it was particularly noticeable. You see, he suffers from a dreadful illness. He has spinal consumption, poor fellow. They say his father was a horrible man, who kept mistresses and all sorts of things—so the son has been sickly from his childhood, you understand.

MRS. LINDEN [*lets her sewing fall into her lap*]: Why, my darling Nora, how do you come to know such things?

NORA [*moving about the room*]: Oh, when one has three children, one sometimes has visits from women who are half—half doctors—and they talk of one thing and another.

MRS. LINDEN [*goes on sewing; a short pause*]: Does Doctor Rank come here every day?

NORA: Every day of his life. He has been Torvald's most intimate friend from boyhood, and he's a good friend of mine, too. Doctor Rank is quite one of the family.

MRS. LINDEN: But tell me—is he quite sincere? I mean, isn't he rather given to flattering people?

NORA: No, quite the contrary. Why should you think so?

MRS. LINDEN: When you introduced us yesterday he said he had often heard my name; but I noticed afterwards that your husband had no notion who I was. How could Doctor Rank—?

NORA: He was quite right, Christina. You see, Torvald loves me so indescribably, he wants to have me all to himself, as he says. When we were first married, he was almost jealous if I even mentioned any of my old friends at home; so naturally I gave up doing it. But I often talk of the old times to Doctor Rank, for he likes to hear about them.

MRS. LINDEN: Listen to me, Nora! You are still a child in many ways. I am older than you, and have had more experience. I'll tell you something? You ought to get clear of all this with Doctor Rank.

NORA: Get clear of what?

MRS. LINDEN: The whole affair, I should say. You were talking yesterday of a rich admirer who was to find you money—

NORA: Yes, one who never existed, worse luck. What then?

MRS. LINDEN: Has Doctor Rank money?

NORA: Yes, he has.

MRS. LINDEN: And nobody to provide for?

NORA: Nobody. But—?

MRS. LINDEN: And he comes here every day?

NORA: Yes, I told you so.

MRS. LINDEN: I should have thought he would have had better taste.

NORA: I don't understand you a bit.

MRS. LINDEN: Don't pretend, Nora. Do you suppose I can't guess who lent you the twelve hundred dollars?

NORA: Are you out of your senses? How can you think such a thing? A friend who comes here every day! Why, the position would be unbearable!

MRS. LINDEN: Then it really is not he?

NORA: No, I assure you. It never for a moment occurred to me—Besides, at that time he had nothing to lend; he came into his property afterwards.

MRS. LINDEN: Well, I believe that was lucky for you, Nora, dear.

NORA: No, really, it would never have struck me to ask Doctor Rank—And yet, I'm certain that if I did—

MRS. LINDEN: But of course you never would.

NORA: Of course not. It's inconceivable that it should ever be necessary. But I'm quite sure that if I spoke to Doctor Rank—

MRS. LINDEN: Behind your husband's back?

NORA: I must get clear of the other thing; that's behind his back too. I must get clear of that.

MRS. LINDEN: Yes, yes, I told you so yesterday; but—

NORA [*walking up and down*]: A man can manage these things much better than a woman.

MRS. LINDEN: One's own husband, yes.

NORA: Nonsense. [*Stands still.*] When everything is paid, one gets back the paper.

MRS. LINDEN: Of course.

NORA: And can tear it into a hundred thousand pieces, and burn it up, the nasty, filthy thing!

MRS. LINDEN [*looks at her fixedly, lays down her work, and rises slowly*]: Nora, you are hiding something from me.

NORA: Can you see it in my face?

MRS. LINDEN: Something has happened since yesterday morning. Nora, what is it?

NORA [*going towards her*]: Christina—! [*Listens.*] Hush! There's Torvald coming home. Do you mind going into the nursery for the present? Torvald can't bear to see dressmaking going on. Get Anna to help you.

MRS. LINDEN [*gathers some of the things together*]: Very well; but I shan't go away until you have told me all about it.

[*She goes out to the left, as Helmer enters from the hall.*]

NORA [*runs to meet him*]: Oh, how I've been longing for you to come, Torvald, dear!

HELMER: Was that the dressmaker—?

NORA: No, Christina. She's helping me with my costume. You'll see how nice I shall look.

HELMER: Yes, wasn't that a happy thought of mine?

NORA: Splendid! But isn't it good of me, too, to have given in to you about the tarantella?

HELMER [*takes her under the chin*]: Good of you! To give in to your own husband? Well, well, you little madcap, I know you don't mean it. But I won't disturb you. I daresay you want to be "trying on."

NORA: And you are going to work, I suppose?

HELMER: Yes. [*Shows her a bundle of papers.*] Look here. I've just come from the Bank—

[*Goes towards his room.*]

NORA: Torvald.

HELMER [*stopping*]: Yes?

NORA: If your little squirrel were to beg you for something so prettily—

HELMER: Well?

NORA: Would you do it?

HELMER: I must know first what it is.

NORA: The squirrel would skip about and play all sorts of tricks if you would only be nice and kind.

HELMER: Come, then, out with it.

NORA: Your lark would twitter from morning till night—

HELMER: Oh, that she does in any case.

NORA: I'll be an elf and dance in the moonlight for you, Torvald.

HELMER: Nora—you can't mean what you were hinting at this morning?

NORA [*coming nearer*]: Yes, Torvald, I beg and implore you!

HELMER: Have you really the courage to begin that again?

NORA: Yes, yes; for my sake, you must let Krogstad keep his place in the Bank.

HELMER: My dear Nora, it's his place I intend for Mrs. Linden.

NORA: Yes, that's so good of you. But instead of Krogstad, you could dismiss some other clerk.

HELMER: Why, this is incredible obstinacy! Because you have thoughtlessly promised to put in a word for him, I am to—!

NORA: It's not that, Torvald. It's for your own sake. This man writes for the most scurrilous newspapers; you said so yourself. He can do you no end of harm. I'm so terribly afraid of him—

HELMER: Ah, I understand; it's old recollections that are frightening you.

NORA: What do you mean?

HELMER: Of course you're thinking of your father.

NORA: Yes—yes, of course. Only think of the shameful slanders wicked people used to write about father. I believe they would have got him dismissed if you hadn't been sent to look into the thing, and been kind to him, and helped him.

HELMER: My little Nora, between your father and me there is all the difference in the world. Your father was not altogether unimpeachable. I am; and I hope to remain so.

NORA: Oh, no one knows what wicked men may hit upon. We could live so quietly and happily now, in our cosy, peaceful home, you and I and the children, Torvald! That's why I beg and implore you—

HELMER: And it is just by pleading his cause that you make it impossible for me to keep him. It's already known at the Bank that I intend to dismiss Krogstad. If it were now reported that the new manager let himself be turned round his wife's little finger—

NORA: What then?

HELMER: Oh, nothing, so long as a wilful woman can have her way—! I am to make myself a laughing-stock to the whole staff, and set people saying that I am open to all sorts of outside influence? Take my word for it, I should soon feel the consequences. And besides—there is one thing that makes Krogstad impossible for me to work with—

NORA: What thing?

HELMER: I could perhaps have overlooked his moral failings at a pinch—

NORA: Yes, couldn't you, Torvald?

HELMER: And I hear he is good at his work. But the fact is, he was a college chum of mine—there was one of those rash friendships between us that one so often repents of later. I may as well confess it at once—he calls me by my Christian name; and he is tactless enough to do it even when others are present. He delights in putting on airs of familiarity—Torvald here, Torvald there! I assure you it's most painful to me. He would make my position at the Bank perfectly unendurable.

NORA: Torvald, surely you're not serious?

HELMER: No? Why not?

NORA: That's such a petty reason.

HELMER: What! Petty! Do you consider me petty!

NORA: No, on the contrary, Torvald, dear; and that's just why—

HELMER: Never mind; you call my motives petty; then I must be petty too. Petty! Very well!—Now we'll put an end to this, once for all. [*Goes to the door into the hall and calls.*] Ellen!

NORA: What do you want?

HELMER [*searching among his papers*]: To settle the thing. [*Ellen enters.*] Here; take this letter; give it to a messenger. See that he takes it at once. The address is on it. Here's the money.

ELLEN: Very well, sir. [*Goes with the letter.*]

HELMER [*putting his papers together*]: There, Madam Obstinacy.

NORA [*breathless*]: Torvald—what was in the letter?

HELMER: Krogstad's dismissal.

NORA: Call it back again, Torvald! There's still time. Oh, Torvald, call it back again! For my sake, for your own, for the children's sake! Do you hear, Torvald? Do it! You don't know what that letter may bring upon us all.

HELMER: Too late.

NORA: Yes, too late.

HELMER: My dear Nora, I forgive your anxiety, though it's anything but flattering to me. Why should you suppose that *I* would be afraid of a wretched scribbler's spite? But I forgive you all the same, for it's a proof of your great love for me. [*Takes her in his arms.*] That's as it should be, my own dear Nora. Let what will happen—when it comes to the pinch, I shall have strength and courage enough. You shall see: my shoulders are broad enough to bear the whole burden.

NORA [*terror-struck*]: What do you mean by that?

HELMER: The whole burden, I say—

NORA [*with decision*]: That you shall never, never do!

HELMER: Very well; then we'll share it, Nora, as man and wife. That is how it should be. [*Petting her.*] Are you satisfied now? Come, come, come, don't look like a scared dove. It's all nothing—foolish fancies.—Now you ought to play the tarantella through and practise with the tambourine. I shall sit in my inner room and shut both doors, so that I shall hear nothing. You can make as much noise as you please. [*Turns round in doorway.*] And when Rank comes, just tell him where I'm to be found.

[*He nods to her, and goes with his papers into his room, closing the door.*]

NORA [*bewildered with terror, stands as though rooted to the ground, and whispers*]: He would do it. Yes, he would do it. He would do it, in spite of all the world.—No, never that, never, never! Anything rather than that! Oh, for some way of escape! What shall I do—! [*Hall bell rings.*] Doctor Rank—! —Anything, anything, rather than—!

[*Nora draws her hands over her face, pulls herself together, goes to the door and opens it. Rank stands outside hanging up his fur coat. During what follows it begins to grow dark.*]

NORA: Good-afternoon, Doctor Rank. I knew you by your ring. But you mustn't go to Torvald now. I believe he's busy.

RANK: And you? [*Enters and closes the door.*]

NORA: Oh, you know very well, I have always time for you.

RANK: Thank you. I shall avail myself of your kindness as long as I can.

NORA: What do you mean? As long as you can?

RANK: Yes. Does that frighten you?

NORA: I think it's an odd expression. Do you expect anything to happen?

RANK: Something I have long been prepared for; but I didn't think it would come so soon.

NORA [*catching at his arm*]: What have you discovered? Doctor Rank, you must tell me!

RANK [*sitting down by the stove*]: I am running down hill. There's no help for it.

NORA [*drank a long breath of relief*]: It's you—?

RANK: Who else should it be?—Why lie to one's self? I am the most wretched of all my patients, Mrs. Helmer. In these last days I have been auditing my life-account—bankrupt! Perhaps before a month is over, I shall lie rotting in the churchyard.

NORA: Oh! What an ugly way to talk.

RANK: The thing itself is so confoundedly ugly, you see. But the worst of it is, so many other ugly things have to be gone through first. There is only one last investigation to be made, and when that is over I shall know pretty certainly when the break-up will begin. There's one thing I want to say to you: Helmer's delicate nature shrinks so from all that is horrible: I will not have him in my sick-room—

NORA: But, Doctor Rank—

RANK: I won't have him, I say—not on any account. I shall lock my door against him.—As soon as I am quite certain of the worst, I shall send you my visiting-card with a black cross on it; and then you will know that the final horror has begun.

NORA: Why, you're perfectly unreasonable to-day; and I did so want you to be in a really good humour.

RANK: With death staring me in the face?—And to suffer thus for another's sin! Where's the justice of it? And in one way or another you can trace in every family some such inexorable retribution—

NORA [*stopping her ears*]: Nonsense, nonsense! Now, cheer up!

RANK: Well, after all, the whole thing's only worth laughing at. My poor innocent spine must do penance for my father's wild oats.

NORA [*at table, left*]: I suppose he was too fond of asparagus and Strasbourg pâté, wasn't he?

RANK: Yes; and truffles.

NORA: Yes, truffles, to be sure. And oysters, I believe?

RANK: Yes, oysters; oysters, of course.

NORA: And then all the port and champagne! It's sad that all these good things should attack the spine.

RANK: Especially when the luckless spine attacked never had any good of them.

NORA: Ah, yes, that's the worst of it.

RANK [*looks at her searchingly*]: H'm—

NORA [*a moment later*]: Why did you smile?

RANK: No; it was you that laughed.

NORA: No; it was you that smiled, Doctor Rank.

RANK [*standing up*]: I see you're deeper than I thought.

NORA: I'm in such a crazy mood to-day.

RANK: So it seems.

NORA [*with her hands on his shoulders*]: Dear, dear Doctor Rank, death shall not take you away from Torvald and me.

RANK: Oh, you'll easily get over the loss. The absent are soon forgotten.

NORA [*looks at him anxiously*]: Do you think so?

RANK: People make fresh ties, and then—

NORA: Who make fresh ties?

RANK: You and Helmer will, when I am gone. You yourself are taking time by the forelock, it seems to me. What was that Mrs. Linden doing here yesterday?

NORA: Oh!—you're surely not jealous of poor Christina?

RANK: Yes, I am. She will be my successor in this house. When I am out of the way, this woman will, perhaps—

NORA: Hush! Not so loud! She's in there.

RANK: Today as well? You see!

NORA: Only to put my costume in order—dear me, how unreasonable you are! [*Sits on sofa.*] Now, do be good, Doctor Rank! Tomorrow you shall see how beautifully I shall dance; and then you may fancy that I'm doing it all to please you—and of course Torvald as well. [*Takes various things out of box.*] Doctor Rank, sit down here, and I'll show you something.

RANK [*sitting*]: What is it?

NORA: Look here. Look!

RANK: Silk stockings.

NORA: Flesh-coloured. Aren't they lovely? It's so dark here now; but to-morrow— No, no, no; you must only look at the feet. Oh, well, I suppose you may look at the rest too.

RANK: H'm—

NORA: What are you looking so critical about? Do you think they won't fit me?

RANK: I can't possibly give any competent opinion on that point.

NORA [*looking at him a moment*]: For shame! [*Hits him lightly on the ear with the stockings.*] Take that. [*Rolls them up again.*]

RANK: And what other wonders am I to see?

NORA: You shan't see anything more; for you don't behave nicely.

[*She hums a little and searches among the things.*]

RANK [*after a short silence*]: When I sit here gossiping with you, I can't imagine—I simply cannot conceive—what would have become of me if I had never entered this house.

NORA [*smiling*]: Yes, I think you do feel at home with us.

RANK [*more softly—looking straight before him*]: And now to have to leave it all—

NORA: Nonsense. You sha'n't leave us.

RANK [*in the same tone*]: And not to be able to leave behind the slightest token of gratitude; scarcely even a passing regret—nothing but an empty place, that can be filled by the first comer.

NORA: And if I were to ask you for—? No—

RANK: For what?

NORA: For a great proof of your friendship.

RANK: Yes—yes?

NORA: I mean—for a very, very great service—

RANK: Would you really, for once, make me so happy?

NORA: Oh, you don't know what it is.

RANK: Then tell me.

NORA: No, I really can't, Doctor Rank. It's far, far too much—not only a service, but help and advice, besides—

RANK: So much the better. I can't think what you can mean. But go on. Don't you trust me?

NORA: As I trust no one else. I know you are my best and truest friend. So I will tell you. Well, then, Doctor Rank, there is something you must help me to prevent. You know how deeply, how wonderfully Torvald loves me; he wouldn't hesitate a moment to give his very life for my sake.

RANK [*bending towards her*]: Nora—do you think he is the only one who—?

NORA [*with a slight start*]: Who—?

RANK: Who would gladly give his life for you?

NORA [*sadly*]: Oh!

RANK: I have sworn that you shall know it before I—go. I shall never find a better opportunity.—Yes, Nora, now I have told you; and now you know that you can trust me as you can no one else.

NORA [*standing up; simply and calmly*]: Let me pass, please.

RANK [*makes way for her, but remains sitting*]: Nora—

NORA [*in the doorway*]: Ellen, bring the lamp. [*crosses to the stove*] Oh dear, Doctor Rank, that was too bad of you.

RANK [*rising*]: That I have loved you as deeply as—anyone else? Was that too bad of me?

NORA: No, but that you should have told me so. It was so unnecessary—

RANK: What do you mean? Did you know—?

[*Ellen enters with the lamp; sets it on the table and goes out again.*]

RANK: Nora—Mrs. Helmer—I ask you, did you know?

NORA: Oh, how can I tell what I knew or didn't know? I really can't say—How could you be so clumsy, Doctor Rank? It was all so nice!

RANK: Well, at any rate, you know now that I am at your service, body and soul. And now, go on.

NORA [*looking at him*]: Go on—now?

RANK: I beg you to tell me what you want.

NORA: I can tell you nothing now.

RANK: Yes, yes! You mustn't punish me in that way. Let me do for you whatever a man can.

NORA: You can do nothing for me now.—Besides, I really want no help. You shall see it was only my fancy. Yes, it must be so. Of course! [*Sits in the rocking-chair, looks at him and smiles.*] You are a nice person, Doctor Rank! Aren't you ashamed of yourself, now that the lamp is on the table?

RANK: No; not exactly. But perhaps I ought to go—for ever.

NORA: No, indeed you mustn't. Of course you must come and go as you've always done. You know very well that Torvald can't do without you.

RANK: Yes, but you?

NORA: Oh, you know I always like to have you here.

RANK: That is just what led me astray. You are a riddle to me. It has often seemed to me as if you liked being with me almost as much as being with Helmer.

NORA: Yes; don't you see? There are people one loves, and others one likes to talk to.

RANK: Yes—there's something in that.

NORA: When I was a girl, of course I loved papa best. But it always delighted me to steal into the servants' room. In the first place they never lectured me, and in the second it was such fun to hear them talk.

RANK: Ah, I see; then it's their place I have taken?

NORA [*jumps up and hurries towards him*]: Oh, my dear Doctor Rank, I don't mean that. But you understand, with Torvald it's the same as with papa—

[*Ellen enters from the hall.*]

ELLEN: Please, ma'am—[*Whispers to Nora, and gives her a card.*]

NORA [*glancing at card*]: Ah! [*Puts it in her pocket.*]

RANK: Anything wrong?

NORA: No, no, not in the least. It's only—it's my new costume—

RANK: Your costume! Why, it's there.

NORA: Oh, that one, yes. But this is another that—I have ordered it—Torvald mustn't know—

RANK: Aha! So that's the great secret.

NORA: Yes, of course. Please go to him; he's in the inner room. Do keep him while I—

RANK: Don't be alarmed; he sha'n't escape.

[*Goes into Helmer's room.*]

NORA [*to Ellen*]: Is he waiting in the kitchen?

ELLEN: Yes, he came up the back stair—

NORA: Didn't you tell him I was engaged?

ELLEN: Yes, but it was no use.

NORA: He won't go away?

ELLEN: No, ma'am, not until he has spoken to you.

NORA: Then let him come in; but quietly. And, Ellen—say nothing about it; it's a surprise for my husband.

ELLEN: Oh, yes, ma'am, I understand. [*She goes out.*]

NORA: It is coming! The dreadful thing is coming, after all. No, no, no, it can never be; it shall not!

[*She goes to Helmer's door and slips the bolt. Ellen opens the hall door for Krogstad, and shuts it after him. He wears a travelling-coat, high boots, and a fur cap.*]

NORA [*goes towards him*]: Speak softly; my husband is at home.

KROGSTAD: All right. That's nothing to me.

NORA: What do you want?

KROGSTAD: A little information.

NORA: Be quick, then. What is it?

KROGSTAD: You know I have got my dismissal.

NORA: I couldn't prevent it, Mr. Krogstad. I fought for you to the last, but it was of no use.

KROGSTAD: Does your husband care for you so little? He knows what I can bring upon you, and yet he dares—

NORA: How could you think I should tell him?

KROGSTAD: Well, as a matter of fact, I didn't think it. It wasn't like my friend Torvald Helmer to show so much courage—

NORA: Mr. Krogstad, be good enough to speak respectfully of my husband.

KROGSTAD: Certainly, with all due respect. But since you are so anxious to keep the matter secret, I suppose you are a little clearer than yesterday as to what you have done.

NORA: Clearer than you could ever make me.

KROGSTAD: Yes, such a bad lawyer as I—

NORA: What is it you want?

KROGSTAD: Only to see how you are getting on, Mrs. Helmer. I've been thinking about you all day. Even a mere money-lender, a gutter-journalist, a—in short, a creature like me—has a little bit of what people call feeling.

NORA: Then show it; think of my little children.

KROGSTAD: Did you and your husband think of mine? But enough of that. I only wanted to tell you that you needn't take this matter too seriously. I shall not lodge any information, for the present.

NORA: No, surely not. I knew you wouldn't.

KROGSTAD: The whole thing can be settled quite amicably. Nobody need know. It can remain among us three.

NORA: My husband must never know.

KROGSTAD: How can you prevent it? Can you pay off the balance?

NORA: No, not at once.

KROGSTAD: Or have you any means of raising the money in the next few days?

NORA: None—that I will make use of.

KROGSTAD: And if you had, it would not help you now. If you offered me ever so much money down, you should not get back your I.O.U.

NORA: Tell me what you want to do with it.

KROGSTAD: I only want to keep it—to have it in my possession. No outsider shall hear anything of it. So, if you have any desperate scheme in your head—

NORA: What if I have?

KROGSTAD: If you should think of leaving your husband and children—

NORA: What if I do?

KROGSTAD: Or if you should think of—something worse—

NORA: How do you know that?

KROGSTAD: Put all that out of your head.

NORA: How did you know what I had in my mind?

KROGSTAD: Most of us think of that at first. I thought of it, too; but I hadn't the courage—

NORA [*tonelessly*]: Nor I.

KROGSTAD [*relieved*]: No, one hasn't. You haven't the courage either, have you?

NORA: I haven't, I haven't.

KROGSTAD: Besides, it would be very foolish.—Just one domestic storm, and it's all over. I have a letter in my pocket for your husband—

NORA: Telling him everything?

KROGSTAD: Sparing you as much as possible.

NORA [*quickly*]: He must never read that letter. Tear it up. I will manage to get the money somehow—

KROGSTAD: Pardon me, Mrs. Helmer, but I believe I told you—

NORA: Oh, I'm not talking about the money I owe you. Tell me how much you demand from my husband—I will get it.

KROGSTAD: I demand no money from your husband.

NORA: What do you demand then?

KROGSTAD: I will tell you. I want to regain my footing in the world. I want to rise; and your husband shall help me to do it. For the last eighteen months my record has been spotless; I have been in bitter need all the time; but I was content to fight my way up, step by step. Now, I've been thrust down again, and I will not be satisfied with merely being reinstated as a matter of grace. I want to rise, I tell you. I must get into the Bank again, in a higher position than before. Your husband shall create a place on purpose for me—

NORA: He will never do that!

KROGSTAD: He will do it; I know him—he won't dare to show fight! And when he and I are together there, you shall soon see! Before a year is out I shall be the manager's right hand. It won't be Torvald Helmer, but Nils Krogstad, that manages the Joint Stock Bank.

NORA: That shall never be.

KROGSTAD: Perhaps you will—?

NORA: Now I have the courage for it.

KROGSTAD: Oh, you don't frighten me! A sensitive, petted creature like you—

NORA: You shall see, you shall see!

KROGSTAD: Under the ice, perhaps? Down into the cold, black water? And next spring to come up again, ugly, hairless, unrecognisable—

NORA: You can't terrify me.

KROGSTAD: Nor you me. People don't do that sort of thing, Mrs. Helmer. And, after all, what would be the use of it? I have your husband in my pocket, all the same.

NORA: Afterwards? When I am no longer—?

KROGSTAD: You forget, your reputation remains in my hands! [*Nora stands speechless and looks at him.*] Well, now you are prepared. Do nothing foolish. As soon as Helmer has received my letter, I shall expect to hear from him. And remember that it is your husband himself who has forced me back again into such paths. That I will never forgive him. Good-bye, Mrs. Helmer.

[*Goes out through the hall. Nora hurries to the door, opens it a little, and listens.*]

NORA: He's going. He's not putting the letter into the box. No, no, it would be impossible! [*Opens the door further and further.*] What's that. He's standing still; not going down stairs. Has he changed his mind? Is he—? [*A letter falls into the box. Krogstad's footsteps are heard gradually receding down the stair. Nora utters a suppressed shriek, and rushes forward towards the sofa-table; pause.*] In the letter-box! [*Slips shrinkingly up to the hall door.*] There it lies.—Torvald, Torvald—now we are lost!

[*Mrs. Linden enters from the left with the costume.*]

MRS. LINDEN: There, I think it's all right now. Shall we just try it on?

NORA [*hoarsely and softly*]: Christina, come here.

MRS. LINDEN [*throws down the dress on the sofa*]: What's the matter? You look quite distracted.

NORA: Come here. Do you see that letter? There, see—through the glass of the letter-box.

MRS. LINDEN: Yes, yes, I see it.

NORA: That latter is from Krogstad—

MRS. LINDEN: Nora—it was Krogstad who lent you the money?

NORA: Yes; and now Torvald will know everything.

MRS. LINDEN: Believe me, Nora, it's the best thing for both of you.

NORA: You don't know all yet. I have forged a name—

MRS. LINDEN: Good heavens!

NORA: Now, listen to me, Christina; you shall bear me witness—

MRS. LINDEN: How "witness"? What am I to—?

NORA: If I should go out of my mind—it might easily happen—

MRS. LINDEN: Nora!

NORA: Or if anything else should happen to me—so that I couldn't be here—!

MRS. LINDEN: Nora, Nora, you're quite beside yourself!

NORA: In case any one wanted to take it all upon himself—the whole blame—you understand—

MRS. LINDEN: Yes, yes; but how can you think—?

NORA: You shall bear witness that it's not true, Christina. I'm not out of my mind at all; I know quite well what I'm saying; and I tell you nobody else knew anything about it; I did the whole thing, I myself. Remember that.

MRS. LINDEN: I shall remember. But I don't understand what you mean—

NORA: Oh, how should you? It's the miracle coming to pass.

MRS. LINDEN: The miracle?

NORA: Yes, the miracle. But it's so terrible, Christina; it mustn't happen for all the world.

MRS. LINDEN: I shall go straight to Krogstad and talk to him.

NORA: Don't; he'll do you some harm.

MRS. LINDEN: Once he would have done anything for me.

NORA: He?

MRS. LINDEN: Where does he live?

NORA: Oh, how can I tell—? Yes—[*Feels in her pocket.*] Here's his card. But the letter, the letter—!

HELMER [*knocking outside*]: Nora!

NORA [*shrieks in terror*]: Oh, what is it? What do you want?

HELMER: Well, well, don't be frightened. We're not coming in; you've bolted the door. Are you trying on your dress?

NORA: Yes, yes, I'm trying it on. It suits me so well, Torvald.

MRS. LINDEN [*who has read the card*]: Why, he lives close by here.

NORA: Yes, but it's no use now. We are lost. The letter is there in the box.

MRS. LINDEN: And your husband has the key?

NORA: Always.

MRS. LINDEN: Krogstad must demand his letter back, unread. He must find some pretext—

NORA: But this is the very time when Torvald generally—

MRS. LINDEN: Prevent him. Keep him occupied. I shall come back as quickly as I can.

[*She goes out hastily by the hall door.*]

NORA [*opens Helmer's door and peeps in*]: Torvald!

HELMER: Well, may one come into one's own room again at last? Come, Rank, we'll have a look—[*in the doorway*] But how's this?

NORA: What, Torvald dear?

HELMER: Rank led me to expect a grand transformation.

RANK [*in the doorway*]: So I understood. I suppose I was mistaken.

NORA: No, no one shall see me in my glory till tomorrow evening.

HELMER: Why, Nora dear, you look so tired. Have you been practising too hard?

NORA: No, I haven't practised at all yet.

HELMER: But you'll have to—

NORA: Oh, yes, I must, I must! But, Torvald, I can't get on at all without your help. I've forgotten everything.

HELMER: Oh, we shall soon freshen it up again.

NORA: Yes, do help me, Torvald. You must promise me—Oh, I'm so nervous about it. Before so many people—This evening you must give yourself up entirely to me. You mustn't do a stroke of work; you musn't even touch a pen. Do promise, Torvald dear!

HELMER: I promise. All this evening I shall be your slave. Little helpless thing—! But, by-the-bye, I must just—[*Going to hall door.*]

NORA: What do you want there?

HELMER: Only to see if there are any letters.

NORA: No, no, don't do that, Torvald.

HELMER: Why not?

NORA: Torvald, I beg you not to. There are none there.

HELMER: Let me just see.[*Is going.*]

[*Nora, at the piano, plays the first bars of the tarantella.*]

HELMER [*at the door, stops*]: Aha!

NORA: I can't dance to-morrow if I don't rehearse with you first.

HELMER [*going to her*]: Are you really so nervous, dear Nora?

NORA: Yes, dreadfully! Let me rehearse at once. We have time before dinner. Oh, do sit down and play for me, Torvald dear; direct me and put me right, as you used to do.

HELMER: With all the pleasure in life, since you wish it.

[*Sits at piano. Nora snatches the tambourine out of the box, and hurriedly drapes herself in a long parti-coloured shawl; then, with a bound, stands in the middle of the floor.*]

NORA: Now play for me! Now I'll dance!

[*Helmer plays and Nora dances. Rank stands at the piano behind Helmer and looks on.*]

HELMER [*playing*]: Slower! Slower!

NORA: Can't do it slower!

HELMER: Not so violently, Nora.

NORA: I must! I must!

HELMER [*stops*]: No, no, Nora—that will never do.

NORA [*laughs and swings her tambourine*]: Didn't I tell you so!

RANK: Let me play for her.

HELMER [*rising*]: Yes, do—then I can direct her better.

[*Rank sits down to the piano and plays; Nora dances more and more wildly. Helmer stands by the stove and addresses frequent corrections to her; she seems not to hear. Her hair breaks loose, and falls over her shoulders. She does not notice it, but goes on dancing. Mrs. Linden enters and stands spellbound in the doorway.*]

MRS. LINDEN: Ah—!

NORA [*dancing*]: We're having such fun here, Christina!

HELMER: Why, Nora, dear, you're dancing as if it were a matter of life and death.

NORA: So it is.

HELMER: Rank, stop! This is the merest madness, Stop, I say!

[*Rank stops playing, and Nora comes to a sudden standstill.*]

HELMER [*going towards her*]: I couldn't have believed it. You've positively forgotten all I taught you.

NORA [*throws the tambourine away*]: You see for yourself.

HELMER: You really do want teaching.

NORA: Yes, you see how much I need it. You must practise with me up to the last moment. Will you promise me, Torvald?

HELMER: Certainly, certainly.

NORA: Neither today nor tomorrow must you think of anything but me. You mustn't open a single letter—mustn't look at the letter-box.

HELMER: Ah, you're still afraid of that man—

NORA: Oh, yes, yes, I am.

HELMER: Nora, I can see it in your face—there's a letter from him in the box.

NORA: I don't know, I believe so. But you're not to read anything now; nothing ugly must come between us until all is over.

RANK [*softly, to Helmer*]: You mustn't contradict her.

HELMER [*putting his arm around her*]: The child shall have her own way. But tomorrow night, when the dance is over—

NORA: Then you shall be free.

[*Ellen appears in the doorway, right.*]

ELLEN: Dinner is on the table, ma'am.

NORA: We'll have some champagne, Ellen.

ELLEN: Yes, ma'am.

[*Goes out.*]

HELMER: Dear me! Quite a banquet.

NORA: Yes, and we'll keep it up till morning [*Calling out.*] And macaroons, Ellen—plenty—just this once.

HELMER [*seizing her hand.*]: Come, come, don't let us have this wild excitement! Be my own little lark again.

NORA: Oh yes, I will. But now go into the dining-room; and you, too, Doctor Rank. Christina, you must help me to do up my hair.

RANK [*softly, as they go*]: There's nothing in the wind? Nothing—I mean—?

HELMER: Oh no, nothing of the kind. It's merely this babyish anxiety I was telling you about.

[*They go out to the right.*]

NORA: Well?

MRS. LINDEN: He's gone out of town.

NORA: I saw it in your face.

MRS. LINDEN: He comes back tomorrow evening. I left a note for him.

NORA: You shouldn't have done that. Things must take their course. After all, there's something glorious in waiting for the miracle.

MRS. LINDEN: What is it you're waiting for?

NORA: Oh, you can't understand. Go to them in the dining-room; I shall come in a moment.

[*Mrs. Linden goes into the dining-room. Nora stands for a moment as though collecting her thoughts; then looks at her watch.*]

NORA: Five. Seven hours till midnight. Then twenty-four hours till the next midnight. Then the tarantella will be over. Twenty-four and seven? Thirty-one hours to live.

[*Helmer appears at the door, right.*]

HELMER: What has become of my little lark?

NORA [*runs to him with open arms*]: Here she is!

ACT 3

The same room. The table, with the chairs around it, in the middle. A lighted lamp on the table. The door to the hall stands open. Dance music is heard from the floor above.

Mrs. Linden sits by the table and absently turns the pages of a book. She tries to read, but seems unable to fix her attention; she frequently listens and looks anxiously towards the hall door.

MRS. LINDEN [*looks at her watch*]: Not here yet; and the time is nearly up. If only he hasn't—[*listens again*] Ah, there he is. [*She goes into the hall and cautiously opens the outer door; soft footsteps are heard on the stairs; she whispers.*] Come in; there is no one here.

KROGSTAD [*in the doorway*]: I found a note from you at my house. What does it mean?

MRS. LINDEN: I must speak to you.

KROGSTAD: Indeed? And in this house?

MRS. LINDEN: I could not see you at my rooms. They have no separate entrance. Come in; we are quite alone. The servants are asleep, and the Helmers are at the ball upstairs.

KROGSTAD [*coming into the room*]: Ah! So the Helmers are dancing this evening? Really?

MRS. LINDEN: Yes. Why not?

KROGSTAD: Quite right. Why not?

MRS. LINDEN: And now let us talk a little.

KROGSTAD: Have we two anything to say to each other?

MRS. LINDEN: A great deal.

KROGSTAD: I should not have thought so.

MRS. LINDEN: Because you have never really understood me.

KROGSTAD: What was there to understand? The most natural thing in the world—a heartless woman throws a man over when a better match offers.

MRS. LINDEN: Do you really think me so heartless? Do you think I broke with you lightly?

KROGSTAD: Did you not?

MRS. LINDEN: Do you really think so?

KROGSTAD: If not, why did you write me that letter?

MRS. LINDEN: Was it not best? Since I had to break with you, was it not right that I should try to put an end to all that you felt for me?

KROGSTAD [*clenching his hands together*]: So that was it? And all this—for the sake of money!

MRS. LINDEN: You ought not to forget that I had a helpless mother and two little brothers. We could not wait for you, Nils, as your prospects then stood.

KROGSTAD: Perhaps not; but you had no right to cast me off for the sake of others, whoever the others might be.

MRS. LINDEN: I don't know. I have often asked myself whether I had the right.

KROGSTAD [*more softly*]: When I had lost you, I seemed to have no firm ground left under my feet. Look at me now. I am a shipwrecked man clinging to a spar.

MRS. LINDEN: Rescue may be at hand.

KROGSTAD: It was at hand; but then you came and stood in the way.

MRS. LINDEN: Without my knowledge, Nils. I did not know till today that it was you I was to replace in the Bank.

KROGSTAD: Well, I take your word for it. But now that you do know, do you mean to give way?

MRS. LINDEN: No, for that would not help you in the least.

KROGSTAD: Oh, help, help—! I should do it whether or no.

MRS. LINDEN: I have learnt prudence. Life and bitter necessity have schooled me.

KROGSTAD: And life has taught me not to trust fine speeches.

MRS. LINDEN: Then life has taught you a very sensible thing. But deeds you will trust?

KROGSTAD: What do you mean?

MRS. LINDEN: You said you were a shipwrecked man, clinging to a spar.

KROGSTAD: I have good reason to say so.

MRS. LINDEN: I too am shipwrecked, and clinging to a spar. I have no one to mourn for, no one to care for.

KROGSTAD: You made your own choice.

MRS. LINDEN: No choice was left me.

KROGSTAD: Well, what then?

MRS. LINDEN: Nils, how if we two shipwrecked people could join hands?

KROGSTAD: What!

MRS. LINDEN: Two on a raft have a better chance than if each clings to a separate spar.

KROGSTAD: Christina!

MRS. LINDEN: What do you think brought me to town?

KROGSTAD: Had you any thought of me?

MRS. LINDEN: I must have work or I can't bear to live. All my life, as long as I can remember, I have worked; work has been my one great joy. Now I stand quite alone in the world, aimless and forlorn. There is no happiness in working for one self. Nils, give me somebody and something to work for.

KROGSTAD: I cannot believe in all this. It is simply a woman's romantic craving for self-sacrifice.

MRS. LINDEN: Have you ever found me romantic?

KROGSTAD: Would you really—? Tell me: do you know all my past?

MRS. LINDEN: Yes.

KROGSTAD: And do you know what people say of me?

MRS. LINDEN: Did you not say just now that with me you could have been another man?

KROGSTAD: I am sure of it.

MRS. LINDEN: Is it too late?

KROGSTAD: Christina, do you know what you are doing? Yes, you do; I see it in your face. Have you the courage then—?

MRS. LINDEN: I need some one to be a mother to, and your children need a mother. You need me, and I—I need you. Nils, I believe in your better self. With you I fear nothing.

KROGSTAD [*seizing her hands*]: Thank you—thank you, Christina. Now I shall make others see me as you do.—Ah, I forgot—

MRS. LINDEN [*listening*]: Hush! The tarantella! Go! go!

KROGSTAD: Why? What is it?

MRS. LINDEN: Don't you hear the dancing overhead? As soon as that is over they will be here.

KROGSTAD: Oh yes, I shall go. Nothing will come of this, after all. Of course, you don't know the step I have taken against the Helmers.

MRS. LINDEN: Yes, Nils, I do know.

KROGSTAD: And yet you have the courage to—?

MRS. LINDEN: I know to what lengths despair can drive a man.

KROGSTAD: Oh, if I could only undo it!

MRS. LINDEN: You could. Your letter is still in the box.

KROGSTAD: Are you sure?

MRS. LINDEN: Yes; but—

KROGSTAD [*looking to her searchingly*]: Is that what it all means? You want to save your friend at any price. Say it out—is that your idea?

MRS. LINDEN: Nils, a woman who has once sold herself for the sake of others, does not do so again.

KROGSTAD: I shall demand my letter back again.

MRS. LINDEN: No, no.

KROGSTAD: Yes, of course. I shall wait till Helmer comes; I shall tell him to give it back to me—that it's only about my dismissal—that I don't want it read—

MRS. LINDEN: No, Nils, you must not recall the letter.

KROGSTAD: But tell me, wasn't that just why you got me to come here?

MRS. LINDEN: Yes, in my first alarm. But a day has passed since then, and in that day I have seen incredible things in this house. Helmer must know everything; there must be an end to this unhappy secret. These two must come to a full understanding. They must have done with all these shifts and subterfuges.

KROGSTAD: Very well, if you like to risk it. But one thing I can do, and at once—

MRS. LINDEN [*listening*]: Make haste! Go, go! The dance is over; we're not safe another moment.

KROGSTAD: I shall wait for you in the street.

MRS. LINDEN: Yes, do; you must see me home.

KROGSTAD: I never was so happy in all my life!

[*Krogstad goes out by the outer door. The door between the room and the hall remains open.*]

MRS. LINDEN [*arranging the room and getting her outdoor things together*]: What a change! What a change! To have some one to work for, to live for; a home to make happy! Well, it shall not be my fault if I fail.—I wish they would come.—[*Listens.*] Ah, here they are! I must get my things on.

[*Takes bonnet and cloak. Helmer's and Nora's voices are heard outside, a key is turned in the lock, and Helmer drags Nora almost by force into the hall. She wears the Italian costume with a large black shawl over it. He is in evening dress and wears a black domino,*[3] *open.*]

NORA [*struggling with him in the doorway*]: No, no, no! I won't go in! I want to go upstairs again; I don't want to leave so early!

HELMER: But, my dearest girl—!

NORA: Oh, please, please, Torvald, I beseech you—only one hour more!

HELMER: Not one minute more, Nora dear; you know what we agreed. Come, come in; you're catching cold here.

[*He leads her gently into the room in spite of her resistance.*]

MRS. LINDEN: Good evening.

NORA: Christina!

HELMER: What, Mrs. Linden! You here so late?

MRS. LINDEN: Yes, I ought to apologise. I did so want to see Nora in her costume.

NORA: Have you been sitting here waiting for me?

MRS. LINDEN: Yes; unfortunately, I came too late. You had gone upstairs already, and I felt I couldn't go away without seeing you.

3. A hooded robe with a mask for the eyes.

HELMER [*taking Nora's shawl off*]: Well, then, just look at her! I assure you she's worth it. Isn't she lovely, Mrs. Linden?

MRS LINDEN: Yes, I must say—

HELMER: Isn't she exquisite? Every one said so. But she's dreadfully obstinate, dear little creature. What's to be done with her? Just think, I had almost to force her away.

NORA: Oh, Torvald, you'll be sorry some day that you didn't let me stay, if only for one half-hour more.

HELMER: There! You hear her, Mrs. Linden? She dances her tarantella with wild applause, and well she deserved it, I must say—though there was, perhaps, a little too much nature in her rendering of the idea—more than was, strictly speaking, artistic. But never mind—the point is, she made a great success, a tremendous success. Was I to let her remain after that—to weaken the impression? Not if I know it. I took my sweet little Capri girl—my capricious little Capri girl, I might say—under my arm; a rapid turn round the room, a curtsey to all sides, and—as they say in novels—the lovely apparition vanished! An exit should always be effective, Mrs. Linden; but I can't get Nora to see it. By Jove! it's warm here. [*Throws his domino on a chair and opens the door to his room.*] What! No light there? Oh, of course. Excuse me—

[*Goes in and lights candles.*]

NORA [*whispers breathlessly*]: Well?

MRS. LINDEN [*softly*]: I've spoken to him.

NORA: And—?

MRS. LINDEN: Nora—you must tell your husband everything—

NORA [*tonelessly*]: I knew it!

MRS. LINDEN: You have nothing to fear from Krogstad; but you must speak out.

NORA: I shall not speak!

MRS. LINDEN: Then the letter will.

NORA: Thank you, Christina. Now I know what I have to do. Hush—!

HELMER [*coming back*]: Well, Mrs. Linden, have you admired her?

MRS. LINDEN: Yes; and now I must say good-night.

HELMER: What, already? Does this knitting belong to you?

MRS. LINDEN [*takes it*]: Yes, thanks; I was nearly forgetting it.

HELMER: Then you do knit?

MRS. LINDEN: Yes.

HELMER: Do you know, you ought to embroider instead?

MRS. LINDEN: Indeed! Why?

HELMER: Because it's so much prettier. Look now! You hold the embroidery in the left hand, so, and then work the needle with the right hand, in a long, graceful curve—don't you?

MRS. LINDEN: Yes, I suppose so.

HELMER: But knitting is always ugly. Just look—your arms close to your sides, and the needles going up and down—there's something Chinese about it.—They really gave us splendid champagne tonight.

MRS. LINDEN: Well, good-night, Nora, and don't be obstinate any more.

HELMER: Well said, Mrs. Linden!

MRS. LINDEN: Good-night, Mr. Helmer.

HELMER [*accompanying her to the door*]: Good-night, good-night; I hope you'll get safely home. I should be glad to—but you have such a short way to go. Good-night, good-night. [*She goes; Helmer shuts the door after her and comes forward again.*] At last we've got rid of her; she's a terrible bore.

NORA: Aren't you very tired, Torvald?

HELMER: No, not in the least.

NORA: Nor sleepy?

HELMER: Not a bit. I feel particularly lively. But you? You do look tired and sleepy.

NORA: Yes, very tired. I shall soon sleep now.

HELMER: There, you see. I was right, after all, not to let you stay longer.

NORA: Oh, everything you do is right.

HELMER [*kissing her forehead*]: Now my lark is speaking like a reasonable being. Did you notice how jolly Rank was this evening?

NORA: Indeed? Was he? I had no chance of speaking to him.

HELMER: Nor I, much; but I haven't seen him in such good spirits for a long time. [*Looks at Nora a little, then comes nearer her.*] It's splendid to be back in our own home, to be quite alone together!—Oh, you enchanting creature!

NORA: Don't look at me in that way, Torvald.

HELMER: I am not to look at my dearest treasure?—at all the loveliness that is mine, mine only, wholly and entirely mine?

NORA [*goes to the other side of the table*]: You mustn't say these things to me this evening.

HELMER [*following*]: I see you have the tarantella still in your blood—and that makes you all the more enticing. Listen! the other people are going now. [*More softly.*] Nora—soon the whole house will be still.

NORA: Yes, I hope so.

HELMER: Yes, don't you, Nora darling? When we are among strangers, do you know why I speak so little to you, and keep so far away, and only steal a glance at you now and then—do you know why I do it? Because I am fancying that we love each other in secret, that I am secretly betrothed to you, and that no one dreams that there is anything between us.

NORA: Yes, yes, yes. I know all your thoughts are with me.

HELMER: And then, when the time comes to go, and I put the shawl about your smooth, soft shoulders, and this glorious neck of yours, I imagine you are my bride, that our marriage is just over, that I am bringing you for the first time to my home—that I am alone with you for the first time—quite alone with you, in your trembling loveliness! All this evening I have been longing for you, and you only. When I watched you swaying and whirling in the tarantella—my blood boiled—I could endure it no longer; and that's why I made you come home with me so early—

NORA: Go now, Torvald! Go away from me. I won't have all this.

HELMER: What do you mean? Ah, I see you're teasing me, little Nora! Won't—won't! Am I not your husband—?

[*A knock at the outer door.*]

NORA [*starts*]: Did you hear—?

HELMER [*going towards the hall*]: Who's there?

RANK [*outside*]: It is I; may I come in for a moment?

HELMER [*in a low tone, annoyed*]: Oh! what can he want just now? [*Aloud.*] Wait a moment. [*Opens door.*] Come, it's nice of you to look in.

RANK: I thought I heard your voice, and that put it into my head. [*Looks round.*] Ah, this dear old place! How cosy you two are here!

HELMER: You seemed to find it pleasant enough upstairs, too.

RANK: Exceedingly. Why not? Why shouldn't one take one's share of everything in this world? All one can, at least, and as long as one can. The wine was splendid—

HELMER: Especially the champagne.

RANK: Did you notice it? It's incredible the quantity I contrived to get down.

NORA: Torvald drank plenty of champagne, too.

RANK: Did he?

NORA: Yes, and it always puts him in such spirits.

RANK: Well, why shouldn't one have a jolly evening after a well-spent day?

HELMER: Well-spent! Well, I haven't much to boast of in that respect.

RANK [*slapping him on the shoulder*]: But I have, don't you see?

NORA: I suppose you have been engaged in a scientific investigation, Doctor Rank?

RANK: Quite right.

HELMER: Bless me! Little Nora talking about scientific investigations!

NORA: Am I to congratulate you on the result?

RANK: By all means.

NORA: It was good then?

RANK: The best possible, both for doctor and patient—certainty.

NORA [*quickly and searchingly*]: Certainty?

RANK: Absolute certainty. Wasn't I right to enjoy myself after that?

NORA: Yes, quite right, Doctor Rank.

HELMER: And so say I, provided you don't have to pay for it tomorrow.

RANK: Well, in this life nothing is to be had for nothing.

NORA: Doctor Rank—I'm sure you are very fond of masquerades?

RANK: Yes, when there are plenty of amusing disguises—

NORA: Tell me, what shall we two be at our next masquerade?

HELMER: Little featherbrain! Thinking of your next already!

RANK: We two? I'll tell you. You must go as a good fairy.

HELMER: Ah, but what costume would indicate that?

RANK: She has simply to wear her everyday dress.

HELMER: Capital! But don't you know what you will be yourself?

RANK: Yes, my dear friend, I am perfectly clear upon that point.

HELMER: Well?

RANK: At the next masquerade I shall be invisible.

HELMER: What a comical idea!

RANK: There's a big black hat—haven't you heard of the invisible hat? It comes down all over you, and then no one can see you.

HELMER [*with a suppressed smile*]: No, you're right there.

RANK: But I'm quite forgetting what I came for, Helmer, give me a cigar—one of the dark Havanas.

HELMER: With the greatest pleasure. [*Hands cigar-case.*]

RANK [*takes one and cuts the end off*]: Thank you.

NORA [*striking a wax match*]: Let me give you a light.

RANK: A thousand thanks.

[*She holds the match. He lights his cigar at it.*]

RANK: And now, good-bye!

HELMER: Good-bye, good-bye, my dear fellow.

NORA: Sleep well, Doctor Rank.

RANK: Thanks for the wish.

NORA: Wish me the same.

RANK: You? Very well, since you ask me—Sleep well. And thanks for the light.

[*He nods to them both and goes out.*]

HELMER [*in an undertone*]: He's been drinking a good deal.

NORA [*absently*]: I daresay. [*Helmer takes his bunch of keys from his pocket and goes into the hall.*] Torvald, what are you doing there?

HELMER: I must empty the letter-box; it's quite full; there will be no room for the newspapers tomorrow morning.

NORA: Are you going to work tonight?

HELMER: You know very well I am not.—Why, how is this? Some one has been at the lock.

NORA: The lock—?

HELMER: I'm sure of it. What does it mean? I can't think that the servants—? Here's a broken hair-pin. Nora, it's one of yours.

NORA [*quickly*]: It must have been the children—

HELMER: Then you must break them of such tricks.—There! At last I've got it open. [*Takes contents out and calls into the kitchen.*] Ellen!—Ellen, just put the hall door lamp out.

[*He returns with letters in his hand, and shuts the inner door.*]

HELMER: Just see how they've accumulated. [*Turning them over.*] Why, what's this?

NORA [*at the window*]: The letter! Oh no, no, Torvald!

HELMER: Two visiting-cards—from Rank.

NORA: From Doctor Rank?

HELMER [*looking at them*]: Doctor Rank. They were on the top. He must just have put them in.

NORA: Is there anything on them?

HELMER: There's a black cross over the name. Look at it. What an unpleasant idea! It looks just as if he were announcing his own death.

NORA: So he is.

HELMER: What! Do you know anything? Has he told you anything?

NORA: Yes. These cards mean that he has taken his last leave of us. He is going to shut himself up and die.

HELMER: Poor fellow! Of course. I knew we couldn't hope to keep him long. But so soon—! And to go and creep into his lair like a wounded animal—

NORA: When we must go, it is best to go silently. Don't you think so, Torvald?

HELMER [*walking up and down*]: He had so grown into our lives, I can't realise that he is gone. He and his sufferings and his loneliness formed a sort of cloudy background to the sunshine of our happiness.—Well, perhaps it's best as it is—at any rate for him. [*Stands still.*] And perhaps for us, too, Nora. Now we two are thrown entirely upon each other. [*Takes her in his arms.*] My darling wife! I feel as if I could never hold you close enough. Do you know, Nora, I often wish some danger might threaten you, that I might risk body and soul, and everything, everything, for your dear sake.

NORA [*tears herself from him and says firmly*]: Now you shall read your letters, Torvald.

HELMER: No, no; not tonight. I want to be with you, my sweet wife.

NORA: With the thought of your dying friend—?

HELMER: You are right. This has shaken us both. Unloveliness has come between us—thoughts of death and decay. We must seek to cast them off. Till then—we will remain apart.

NORA [*her arms round his neck*]: Torvald! Good-night! good-night!

HELMER [*kissing her forehead*]: Good-night, my little song-bird. Sleep well, Nora. Now I shall go and read my letters.

[*He goes with the letters in his hand into his room and shuts the door.*]

NORA [*with wild eyes, gropes about her, seizes Helmer's domino, throws it round her, and whispers quickly, hoarsely, and brokenly*]: Never to see him again. Never, never, never. [*Throws her shawl over her head.*] Never to see the children again. Never, never.—Oh that black, icy water! Oh that bottomless—! If it were only over! Now he has it; he's reading it. Oh, no, no, no, not yet. Torvald, good-bye—! Good-bye, my little ones—!

[*She is rushing out by the hall; at the same moment Helmer flings his door open, and stands there with an open letter in his hand*]

HELMER: Nora!

NORA [*shrieks*]: Ah—!

HELMER: What is this? Do you know what is in this letter?

NORA: Yes, I know. Let me go! Let me pass!

HELMER [*holds her back*]: Where do you want to go?

NORA [*tries to break away from him*]: You shall not save me, Torvald.

HELMER [*falling back*]: True! Is what he writes true? No, no, it is impossible that this can be true.

NORA: It is true. I have loved you beyond all else in the world.

HELMER: Pshaw—no silly evasions!

NORA [*a step nearer him*]: Torvald—!

HELMER: Wretched woman—what have you done?

NORA: Let me go—you shall not save me! You shall not take my guilt upon yourself!

HELMER: I don't want any melodramatic airs. [*Locks the outer door.*] Here you shall stay and give an account of yourself. Do you understand what you have done? Answer! Do you understand it?

NORA [*looks at him fixedly, and says with a stiffening expression*]: Yes; now I begin fully to understand it.

HELMER [*walking up and down*]: Oh! what an awful awakening! During all these eight years—she who was my pride and my joy—a hypocrite, a liar—worse, worse—a criminal. Oh, the unfathomable hideousness of it all! Ugh! Ugh!

[*Nora says nothing, and continues to look fixedly at him.*]

HELMER: I ought to have known how it would be. I ought to have foreseen it. All your father's want of principle—be silent!—all your father's want of principle you have inherited—no religion, no morality, no sense of duty. How I am punished for screening him! I did it for your sake; and you reward me like this.

NORA: Yes—like this.

HELMER: You have destroyed my whole happiness. You have ruined my future. Oh, it's frightful to think of! I am in the power of a scoundrel; he can do whatever he pleases with me, demand whatever he chooses; he can domineer over me as much as he likes, and I must submit. And all this disaster and ruin is brought upon me by an unprincipled woman!

NORA: When I am out of the world, you will be free.

HELMER: Oh, no fine phrases. Your father, too, was always ready with them. What good would it do me, if you were "out of the world," as you say? No good whatever! He can publish the story all the same; I might even be suspected of collusion. People will think I was at the bottom of it all and egged you on. And for all this I have you to thank—you whom I have done nothing but pet and spoil during our whole married life. Do you understand now what you have done to me?

NORA [*with cold calmness*]: Yes.

HELMER: The thing is so incredible, I can't grasp it. But we must come to an understanding. Take that shawl off. Take it off, I say! I must try to pacify him in one way or another—the matter must be hushed up, cost what it may.—As for you and me, we must make no outward change in our way of life—no outward change, you understand. Of course, you will continue to live here. But the children cannot be left in your care. I dare not trust them to you.—Oh, to have to say this to one I have loved so tenderly—whom I still—! But that must be a thing of the past. Henceforward there can be no question of happiness, but merely of saving the ruins, the shreds, the show—[*A ring; Helmer starts.*] What's that? So late! Can it be the worst? Can he—? Hide yourself, Nora; say you are ill.

[*Nora stands motionless. Helmer goes to the door and opens it.*]

ELLEN [*half dressed, in the hall*]: Here is a letter for you, ma'am.

HELMER: Give it to me. [*Seizes the letter and shuts the door.*] Yes, from him. You shall not have it. I shall read it.

NORA: Read it!

HELMER [*by the lamp*]: I have hardly the courage to. We may both be lost, both you and I. Ah! I must know. [*Hastily tears the letter open; reads a few lines, looks at an enclosure; with a cry of joy.*] Nora!

[*Nora looks inquiringly at him.*]

HELMER: Nora!—Oh! I must read it again.—Yes, yes, it is so. I am saved! Nora, I am saved!

NORA: And I?

HELMER: You too, of course; we are both saved, both of us. Look here—he sends you back your promissory note. He writes that he regrets and apologises that a happy turn in his life—Oh, what matter what he writes. We are saved, Nora! No one can harm you. Oh, Nora, Nora—; but first to get rid of this hateful thing. I'll just see—[*Glances at the I.O.U.*] No, I will not look at it; the whole thing shall be nothing but a dream to me. [*Tears the I.O.U. and both letters in pieces. Throws them into the fire and watches them burn.*] There! it's gone!—He said that ever since Christmas Eve—Oh, Nora, they must have been three terrible days for you!

NORA: I have fought a hard fight for the last three days.

HELMER: And in your agony you saw no other outlet but—No; we won't think of that horror. We will only rejoice and repeat—it's over, all over! Don't you hear, Nora? You don't seem able to grasp it. Yes, it's over. What is this set look on your face? Oh, my poor Nora, I understand you cannot believe that I have forgiven you. But I have, Nora; I swear it. I have forgiven everything. I know that what you did was all for love of me.

NORA: That is true.

HELMER: You loved me as a wife should love her husband. It was only the means that, in your inexperience, you misjudged. But do you think I love you the less because you cannot do without guidance? No, no. Only lean on me; I will counsel you, and guide you. I should be no true man if this very womanly helplessness did not make you doubly dear in my eyes. You mustn't dwell upon the hard things I said in my first moment of terror, when the world seemed to be tumbling about my ears. I have forgiven you, Nora—I swear I have forgiven you.

NORA: I thank you for your forgiveness.

[*Goes out, to the right.*]

HELMER: No, stay—! [*Looking through the doorway.*] What are you going to do?

NORA [*inside*]: To take off my masquerade dress.

HELMER [*in the doorway*]: Yes, do, dear. Try to calm down, and recover your balance, my scared little song-bird. You may rest secure. I have broad wings to shield you. [*Walking up and down near the door.*] Oh, how lovely—how cosy our home is, Nora! Here you are safe; here I can shelter you like a hunted dove whom I have saved from the claws of the hawk. I shall soon bring your poor beating heart to rest; believe me, Nora, very soon. Tomorrow all this will seem quite different—everything will be as before. I shall not need to tell you again that I forgive you; you will feel for yourself that it is true. How could you think I could find it in my heart to drive you away, or even so much as to reproach you? Oh, you don't know a true man's heart, Nora. There is something indescribably sweet and soothing to a man in having forgiven his wife—honestly forgiven her, from the bottom of his heart. She becomes his property in a double sense. She is as though born again; she has become, so to speak, at once his wife and his child. That is what you shall henceforth be to me, my bewildered, helpless darling. Don't be troubled about anything, Nora; only open your heart to me, and I will be both will and conscience to you. [*Nora enters in everyday dress.*] Why, what's this? Not gone to bed? You have changed your dress?

NORA: Yes, Torvald; now I have changed my dress.

HELMER: But why now, so late—?

NORA: I shall not sleep to-night.

HELMER: But, Nora dear—

NORA [*looking at her watch*]: It's not so late yet. Sit down, Torvald; you and I have much to say to each other.[*She sits at one side of the table.*]

HELMER: Nora—what does this mean? Your cold, set face—

NORA: Sit down. It will take some time. I have much to talk over with you.

[*Helmer sits at the other side of the table.*]

HELMER: You alarm me, Nora. I don't understand you.

NORA: No, that is just it. You don't understand me; and I have never understood you—till tonight. No, don't interrupt. Only listen to what I say.—We must come to a final settlement, Torvald.

HELMER: How do you mean?

NORA [*after a short silence*]: Does not one thing strike you as we sit here?

HELMER: What should strike me?

NORA: We have been married eight years. Does it not strike you that this is the first time we two, you and I, man and wife, have talked together seriously?

HELMER: Seriously! What do you call seriously?

NORA: During eight whole years, and more—ever since the day we first met—we have never exchanged one serious word about serious things.

HELMER: Was I always to trouble you with the cares you could not help me to bear?

NORA: I am not talking of cares. I say that we have never yet set ourselves seriously to get to the bottom of anything.

HELMER: Why, my dearest Nora, what have you to do with serious things?

NORA: There we have it! You have never understood me.—I have had great injustice done me, Torvald; first by father, and then by you.

HELMER: What! By your father and me?—By us, who have loved you more than all the world?

NORA [*shaking her head*]: You have never loved me. You only thought it amusing to be in love with me.

HELMER: Why, Nora, what a thing to say!

NORA: Yes, it is so, Torvald. While I was at home with father, he used to tell me all his opinions, and I held the same opinions. If I had others, I said nothing about them, because he wouldn't have liked it. He used to call me his doll-child, and played with me as I played with my dolls. Then I came to live in your house—

HELMER: What an expression to use about our marriage!

NORA [*undisturbed*]: I mean I passed from father's hands into yours. You arranged everything according to your taste; and I got the same tastes as you; or I pretended to—I don't know which—both ways, perhaps; sometimes one and sometimes the other. When I look back on it now, I seem to have been living here like a beggar, from hand to mouth. I lived by performing tricks for you, Torvald. But you would have it so. You and father have done me a great wrong. It is your fault that my life has come to nothing.

HELMER: Why, Nora, how unreasonable and ungrateful you are! Have you not been happy here?

NORA: No, never. I thought I was; but I never was.

HELMER: Not—not happy!

NORA: No; only merry. And you have always been so kind to me. But our house has been nothing but a play-room. Here I have been your doll-wife, just as at home I used to be papa's doll-child. And the children, in their turn, have been my dolls. I thought it fun when you played with me, just as the children did when I played with them. That has been our marriage, Torvald.

HELMER: There is some truth in what you say, exaggerated and overstrained though it be. But henceforth it shall be different. Play-time is over; now comes the time for education.

NORA: Whose education? Mine, or the children's?

HELMER: Both, my dear Nora.

NORA: Oh, Torvald, you are not the man to teach me to be a fit wife for you.

HELMER: And you can say that?

NORA: And I—how have I prepared myself to educate the children?

HELMER: Nora!

NORA: Did you not say yourself, a few minutes ago, you dared not trust them to me?

HELMER: In the excitement of the moment! Why should you dwell upon that?

NORA: No—you were perfectly right. That problem is beyond me. There is another to be solved first—I must try to educate myself. You are not the man to help me in that. I must set about it alone. And that is why I am leaving you.

HELMER [*jumping up*]: What—do you mean to say—?

NORA: I must stand quite alone if I am ever to know myself and my surroundings; so I cannot stay with you.

HELMER: Nora! Nora!

NORA: I am going at once. I daresay Christina will take me in for tonight—

HELMER: You are mad! I shall not allow it! I forbid it!

NORA: It is of no use your forbidding me anything now. I shall take with me what belongs to me. From you I will accept nothing, either now or afterwards.

HELMER: What madness this is!

NORA: Tomorrow I shall go home—I mean to what was my home. It will be easier for me to find some opening there.

HELMER: Oh, in your blind inexperience—

NORA: I must try to gain experience, Torvald.

HELMER: To forsake your home, your husband, and your children! And you don't consider what the world will say.

NORA: I can pay no heed to that. I only know that I must do it.

HELMER: This is monstrous! Can you forsake your holiest duties in this way?

NORA: What do you consider my holiest duties?

HELMER: Do I need to tell you that? Your duties to your husband and your children.

NORA: I have other duties equally sacred.

HELMER: Impossible! What duties do you mean?

NORA: My duties towards myself.

HELMER: Before all else you are a wife and a mother.

NORA: That I no longer believe. I believe that before all else I am a human being, just as much as you are—or at least that I should try to become one. I know that most people agree with you, Torvald, and that they say so in books. But henceforth I can't be satisfied with what most people say, and what is in books. I must think things out for myself, and try to get clear about them.

HELMER: Are you not clear about your place in your own home? Have you not an infallible guide in questions like these? Have you not religion?

NORA: Oh, Torvald, I don't really know what religion is.

HELMER: What do you mean?

NORA: I know nothing but what Pastor Hansen told me when I was confirmed. He explained that religion was this and that. When I get away from all this and stand alone, I will look into that matter too. I will see whether what he taught me is right, or, at any rate, whether it is right for me.

HELMER: Oh, this is unheard of! And from so young a woman! But if religion cannot keep you right, let me appeal to your conscience—for I suppose you have some moral feeling? Or, answer me: perhaps you have none?

NORA: Well, Torvald, it's not easy to say. I really don't know—I am all at sea about these things. I only know that I think quite differently from you about them. I hear, too, that the laws are different from what I thought; but I can't believe that they can be right. It appears that a woman has no right to spare her dying father, or to save her husband's life! I don't believe that.

HELMER: You talk like a child. You don't understand the society in which you live.

NORA: No, I do not. But now I shall try to learn. I must make up my mind which is right—society or I.

HELMER: Nora, you are ill; you are feverish; I almost think you are out of your senses.

NORA: I have never felt so much clearness and certainty as tonight.

HELMER: You are clear and certain enough to forsake husband and children?

NORA: Yes, I am.

HELMER: Then there is only one explanation possible.

NORA: What is that?

HELMER: You no longer love me.

NORA: No; that is just it.

HELMER: Nora!—Can you say so!

NORA: Oh, I'm so sorry, Torvald; for you've always been so kind to me. But I can't help it. I do not love you any longer.

HELMER [*mastering himself with difficulty*]: Are you clear and certain on this point too?

NORA: Yes, quite. That is why I will not stay here any longer.

HELMER: And can you also make clear to me how I have forfeited your love?

NORA: Yes, I can. It was this evening, when the miracle did not happen; for then I saw you were not the man I had imagined.

HELMER: Explain yourself more clearly; I don't understand.

NORA: I have waited so patiently all these eight years; for of course, I saw clearly enough that miracles don't happen every day. When this crushing blow threatened me, I said to myself so confidently, "Now comes the miracle!" When Krogstad's letter lay in the box, it never for a moment occurred to me that you would think of submitting to that man's conditions. I was convinced that you would say to him, "Make it known to all the world"; and that then—

HELMER: Well? When I had given my own wife's name up to disgrace and shame—?

NORA: Then I firmly believed that you would come forward, take everything upon yourself, and say, "I am the guilty one."

HELMER: Nora—!

NORA: You mean I would never have accepted such a sacrifice? No, certainly not. But what would my assertions have been worth in opposition to yours?—That was the miracle that I hoped for and dreaded. And it was to hinder that that I wanted to die.

HELMER: I would gladly work for you day and night, Nora—bear sorrow and want for your sake. But no man sacrifices his honour, even for one he loves.

NORA: Millions of women have done so.

HELMER: Oh, you think and talk like a silly child.

NORA: Very likely. But you neither think nor talk like the man I can share my life with. When your terror was over—not for what threatened me, but for yourself—when there was nothing more to fear—then it seemed to you as though nothing had happened. I was your lark again, your doll, just as before—whom you would take twice as much care of in future, because she was so weak and fragile. [*Stands up.*] Torvald—in that moment it burst upon me that I had been living here these eight years with a strange man, and had borne him three children.—Oh, I can't bear to think of it! I could tear myself to pieces!

HELMER [*sadly*]: I see it, I see it; an abyss has opened between us.—But, Nora, can it never be filled up?

NORA: As I now am, I am no wife for you.

HELMER: I have strength to become another man.

NORA: Perhaps—when your doll is taken away from you.

HELMER: To part—to part from you! No, Nora, no; I can't grasp the thought.

NORA [*going out, right*]: All the more reason why is has to be. [*She reenters with her coat and a traveling-bag, which she puts on a chair by the table.*]

HELMER: Nora, Nora, not now! Wait until tomorrow.

NORA: I can't spend the night in a strange man's room.

HELMER: But couldn't we live here like brother and sister—

NORA: You know very well how long that would last. [*Throws her shawl over her shoulders.*] Good-bye, Torvald. I won't look in on the children. I know they're in better hands than mine. The way I am now, I'm no use to them.

HELMER: But someday, Nora—someday—?

NORA: How can I tell? I haven't the least idea what'll become of me.

HELMER: But you're my wife, now and wherever you go.

NORA: Listen, Torvald—when a wife deserts her husband's house, as I am doing, I have heard that in the eyes of the law he is free from all duties toward her. At any rate, I release you from all duties. You must not feel yourself bound, any more than I shall. There must be perfect freedom on both sides. There, I give you back your ring. Give me mine.

HELMER: That too?

NORA: That too.

HELMER: Here it is.

NORA: Very well. Now it is all over. I lay the keys here. The servants know about everything in the house—better than I do. Tomorrow, when I have started, Christina will come to pack up the things I brought with me from home. I will have them sent after me.

HELMER: All over! All over! Nora, will you never think of me again?

NORA: Oh, I shall often think of you, and the children, and this house.

HELMER: May I write to you, Nora?

NORA: No—never. You must not.

HELMER: But I must send you—

NORA: Nothing, nothing.

HELMER: I must help you if you need it.

NORA: No, I say. I take nothing from strangers.

HELMER: Nora—can I never be more than a stranger to you?

NORA [*taking her traveling-bag*]: Oh, Torvald, then the miracle of miracles would have to happen—

HELMER: What is the miracle of miracles?

NORA: Both of us would have to change so that—Oh, Torvald, I no longer believe in miracles.

HELMER: But I will believe. Tell me! We must so change that—?

NORA: That communion between us shall be a marriage. Good-bye. [*She goes out by the hall door.*]

HELMER [*sinks into a chair by the door with his face in his hands*]: Nora! Nora! [*He looks around and rises.*] Empty. She is gone. [*A hope springs up in him.*] Ah! The miracle of miracles—?!

[*From below is heard the reverberation of a heavy door closing.*]

THE END

Anton Chekhov

1860–1904

"All I wanted was to say honestly to people: 'Have a look at yourselves and see how bad and dreary your lives are!' The important thing is that people should realize that, for when they do, they will most certainly create another and better life for themselves. I will not live to see it, but I know that it will be quite different, quite unlike our present life. And so long as this different life does not exist, I shall go on saying to people again and again: 'Please, understand that your life is bad and dreary!'"

A doctor whose own life was weighed down and then cut short at the age of forty-four by tuberculosis, Chekhov was by all accounts anything but dreary himself. Born in southern Russia, son of a merchant and grandson of a freed serf, Chekhov came to Moscow in 1879 to study medicine, receiving his degree in 1884. A lover of games, banter, comic nicknames, vaudeville, and French farce, he began to write jokes and comic sketches for journals to help support himself and his family while he was in school. In time, he wrote a number of hilarious one-act plays for the Moscow stage and hundreds of comic stories. The longer plays that made him famous, masterpieces of the world theater like *The Seagull* (1897), *Uncle Vanya* (1899), *The Three Sisters* (1901), and *The Cherry Orchard* (1904), are often described as tragedies, but Chekhov quarreled with the tragic style in which they were staged by the great director Constantin Stanislavsky, insisting that they were really comedies. The plots alone can't decide this question; as Virginia Woolf once remarked, Chekhov's endings seem "as if a tune had stopped short without the expected chords to close it." Everything depends on the perspective.

The perspective that has come to be called "Chekhovian" is usually characterized by understatement and concealed meaning, scenes of autumn and twilight when things are winding down rather than starting up, prematurely aging heroes who hope for very little and don't know what they want, or perhaps don't even really want what they think they want. Overpowering desire is not Chekhov's trademark effect. What matters is less the actions taken and their consequences than how we look at those actions, whether taken or not. In its outlines, "The Lady with the Dog" might be described as a story about the abrupt and awesome power of passionate love. In its sentence-by-sentence texture, however, it seems easily distracted by other, more mundane matters. Something like the threat of ultimate dreariness seems to hang over even the happiest moments. Can love save us from the hopelessness of everyday banality? Or is love too a farce, nothing but more of that banality? It's as if Chekhov wants us to ask but refuses any conclusive answer.

The Lady with the Dog[1]

1

It was said that a new person had appeared on the sea-front: a lady with a little dog. Dmitri Dmitritch Gurov, who had by then been a fortnight at Yalta, and so was fairly at home there, had begun to take an interest in new arrivals. Sitting in Verney's pavilion, he saw, walking on the sea-front, a fair-haired young lady of medium height, wearing a *béret;* a white Pomeranian dog was running behind her.

1. Translated by Constance Garnett.

And afterwards he met her in the public gardens and in the square several times a day. She was walking alone, always wearing the same *béret,* and always with the same white dog; no one knew who she was, and every one called her simply "the lady with the dog."

"If she is here alone without a husband or friends, it wouldn't be amiss to make her acquaintance," Gurov reflected.

He was under forty, but he had a daughter already twelve years old, and two sons at school. He had been married young, when he was a student in his second year, and by now his wife seemed half as old again as he. She was a tall, erect woman with dark eyebrows, staid and dignified, and, as she said of herself, intellectual. She read a great deal, used phonetic spelling,[2] called her husband, not Dmitri, but Dimitri, and he secretly considered her unintelligent, narrow, inelegant, was afraid of her, and did not like to be at home. He had begun being unfaithful to her long ago—had been unfaithful to her often, and, probably on that account, almost always spoke ill of women, and when they were talked about in his presence, used to call them "the lower race."

It seemed to him that he had been so schooled by bitter experience that he might call them what he liked, and yet he could not get on for two days together without "the lower race." In the society of men he was bored and not himself, with them he was cold and uncommunicative; but when he was in the company of women he felt free, and knew what to say to them and how to behave; and he was at ease with them even when he was silent. In his appearance, in his character, in his whole nature, there was something attractive and elusive which allured women and disposed them in his favour; he knew that, and some force seemed to draw him, too, to them.

Experience often repeated, truly bitter experience, had taught him long ago that with decent people, especially Moscow people—always slow to move and irresolute—every intimacy, which at first so agreeably diversifies life and appears a light and charming adventure, inevitably grows into a regular problem of extreme intricacy, and in the long run the situation becomes unbearable. But at every fresh meeting with an interesting woman this experience seemed to slip out of his memory, and he was eager for life, and everything seemed simple and amusing.

One evening he was dining in the gardens, and the lady in the *béret* came up slowly to take the next table. Her expression, her gait, her dress, and the way she did her hair told him that she was a lady, that she was married, that she was in Yalta for the first time and alone, and that she was dull there. . . . The stories told of the immorality in such places as Yalta are to a great extent untrue; he despised them, and knew that such stories were for the most part made up by persons who would themselves have been glad to sin if they had been able; but when the lady sat down at the next table three paces from him, he remembered these tales of easy conquests, of trips to the mountains, and the tempting thought of a swift, fleeting love affair, a romance with an unknown woman, whose name he did not know, suddenly took possession of him.

He beckoned coaxingly to the Pomeranian, and when the dog came up to him he shook his finger at it. The Pomeranian growled: Gurov shook his finger at it again.

The lady looked at him and at once dropped her eyes.

2. Literally, "omitted the 'hard sign,'" a characteristic of a progressive intellectual (this anticipated the reform of the Russian alphabet).

"He doesn't bite," she said, and blushed.

"May I give him a bone?" he asked; and when she nodded he asked courteously, "Have you been long in Yalta?"

"Five days."

"And I have already dragged out a fortnight here."

There was a brief silence.

"Time goes fast, and yet it is so dull here!" she said, not looking at him.

"That's only the fashion to say it is dull here. A provincial will live in Belyov or Zhidra and not be dull, and when he comes here it's 'Oh, the dulness! Oh, the dust!' One would think he came from Grenada."

She laughed. Then both continued eating in silence, like strangers, but after dinner they walked side by side; and there sprang up between them the light jesting conversation of people who are free and satisfied, to whom it does not matter where they go or what they talk about. They walked and talked of the strange light on the sea: the water was of a soft warm lilac hue, and there was a golden streak from the moon upon it. They talked of how sultry it was after a hot day. Gurov told her that he came from Moscow, that he had taken his degree in Arts, but had a post in a bank; that he had trained as an opera-singer, but had given it up, that he owned two houses in Moscow. . . . And from her he learnt that she had grown up in Petersburg, but had lived in S—— since her marriage two years before, that she was staying another month in Yalta, and that her husband, who needed a holiday too, might perhaps come and fetch her. She was not sure whether her husband had a post in a Crown Department or under the Provincial Council—and was amused by her own ignorance. And Gurov learnt, too, that she was called Anna Sergeyevna.

Afterwards he thought about her in his room at the hotel—thought she would certainly meet him next day; it would be sure to happen. As he got into bed he thought how lately she had been a girl at school, doing lessons like his own daughter; he recalled the diffidence, the angularity, that was still manifest in her laugh and her manner of talking with a stranger. This must have been the first time in her life she had been alone in surroundings in which she was followed, looked at, and spoken to merely from a secret motive which she could hardly fail to guess. He recalled her slender, delicate neck, her lovely grey eyes.

"There's something pathetic about her, anyway," he thought, and fell asleep.

2

A week had passed since they had made acquaintance. It was a holiday. It was sultry indoors, while in the street the wind whirled the dust round and round, and blew people's hats off. It was a thirsty day, and Gurov often went into the pavilion, and pressed Anna Sergeyevna to have syrup and water or an ice. One did not know what to do with oneself.

In the evening when the wind had dropped a little, they went out on the groyne[3] to see the steamer come in. There were a great many people walking about the harbour; they had gathered to welcome some one, bringing bouquets. And two peculiarities of a well-dressed Yalta crowd were very conspicuous: the elderly ladies were dressed like young ones, and there were great numbers of generals.

Owing to the roughness of the sea, the steamer arrived late, after the sun had set, and it was a long time turning about before it reached the groyne. Anna Sergeyevna

3. Pier.

looked through her lorgnette at the steamer and the passengers as though looking for acquaintances, and when she turned to Gurov her eyes were shining. She talked a great deal and asked disconnected questions, forgetting next moment what she had asked; then she dropped her lorgnette in the crush.

The festive crowd began to disperse; it was too dark to see people's faces. The wind had completely dropped, but Gurov and Anna Sergeyevna still stood as though waiting to see some one else come from the steamer. Anna Sergeyevna was silent now, and sniffed the flowers without looking at Gurov.

"The weather is better this evening," he said. "Where shall we go now? Shall we drive somewhere?"

She made no answer.

Then he looked at her intently, and all at once put his arm round her and kissed her on the lips, and breathed in the moisture and the fragrance of the flowers; and he immediately looked round him, anxiously wondering whether any one had seen them.

"Let us go to your hotel," he said softly. And both walked quickly.

The room was close and smelt of the scent she had bought at the Japanese shop. Gurov looked at her and thought: "What different people one meets in the world!" From the past he preserved memories of careless, good-natured women, who loved cheerfully and were grateful to him for the happiness he gave them, however brief it might be; and of women like his wife who loved without any genuine feeling, with superfluous phrases, affectedly, hysterically, with an expression that suggested that it as not love nor passion, but something more significant; and of two or three others, very beautiful, cold women, on whose faces he had caught a glimpse of a rapacious expression—an obstinate desire to snatch from life more than it could give, and these were capricious, unreflecting, domineering, unintelligent women not in their first youth, and when Gurov grew cold to them their beauty excited his hatred, and the lace on their linen seemed to him like scales.

But in this case there was still the diffidence, the angularity of inexperienced youth, an awkward feeling; and there was a sense of consternation as though some one had suddenly knocked at the door. The attitude of Anna Sergeyevna—"the lady with the dog" —to what had happened was somehow peculiar, very grave, as though it were her fall—so it seemed, and it was strange and inappropriate. Her face dropped and faded, and on both sides of it her long hair hung down mournfully; she mused in a dejected attitude like "the woman who was a sinner" in an old-fashioned picture.

"It's wrong," she said. "You will be the first to despise me now."

There was a water-melon on the table. Gurov cut himself a slice and began eating it without haste. There followed at least half an hour of silence.

Anna Sergeyevna was touching; there was about her the purity of a good, simple woman who had seen little of life. The solitary candle burning on the table threw a faint light on her face, yet it was clear that she was very unhappy.

"How could I despise you?" asked Gurov. "You don't know what you are saying."

"God forgive me," she said, and her eyes filled with tears. "It's awful."

"You seem to feel you need to be forgiven."

"Forgiven? No. I am a bad, low woman; I despise myself and don't attempt to justify myself. It's not my husband but myself I have deceived. And not only just now; I have been deceiving myself for a long time. My husband may be a good, honest man, but he is a flunkey! I don't know what he does there, what his work is, but I know he is a flunkey! I was twenty when I was married to him. I have been tormented by curiosity; I wanted something better. 'There must be a different sort of life,' I said to myself. I wanted to live! To live, to live! . . . I was fired by curiosity . . . you don't understand it, but, I swear to God, I could not control myself; something happened to me: I could not be restrained. I told my husband I was ill, and came here. . . . And here I have been walking about as though I were dazed, like a mad creature; . . . and now I have become a vulgar, contemptible woman whom any one may despise."

Gurov felt bored already, listening to her. He was irritated by the naive tone, by this remorse, so unexpected and inopportune; but for the tears in her eyes, he might have thought she was jesting or playing a part.

"I don't understand," he said softly. "What is it you want?"

She hid her face on his breast and pressed close to him.

"Believe me, believe me, I beseech you . . ." she said. "I love a pure, honest life, and sin is loathsome to me. I don't know what I am doing. Simple people say: 'The Evil One has beguiled me.' And I may say of myself now that the Evil One has beguiled me."

"Hush, hush! . . ." he muttered.

He looked at her fixed, scared eyes, kissed her, talked softly and affectionately, and by degrees she was comforted, and her gaiety returned; they both began laughing.

Afterwards when they went out there was not a soul on the sea-front. The town with its cypresses had quite a deathlike air, but the sea still broke noisily on the shore; a single barge was rocking on the waves, and a lantern was blinking sleepily on it.

They found a cab and drove to Oreanda.

"I found out your surname in the hall just now: it was written on the board—Von Diderits," said Gurov. "Is your husband a German?"

"No; I believe his grandfather was a German, but he is an Orthodox Russian himself."

At Oreanda they sat on a seat not far from the church, looked down at the sea, and were silent. Yalta was hardly visible through the morning mist; white clouds stood motionless on the mountain-tops. The leaves did not stir on the trees, grasshoppers chirruped, and the monotonous hollow sound of the sea rising up from below, spoke of the peace, of the eternal sleep awaiting us. So it must have sounded when there was no Yalta, no Oreanda here; so it sounds now, and it will sound as indifferently and monotonously when we are all no more. And in this constancy, in this complete indifference to the life and death of each of us, there lies hid, perhaps, a pledge of our eternal salvation, of the unceasing movement of life upon earth, of unceasing progress towards perfection. Sitting Beside a young woman who in the dawn seemed so lovely, soothed and spellbound in these magical surroundings—the sea, mountains, clouds, the open sky—Gurov thought how in reality everything is beautiful in this world when one reflects: everything except what we think or do ourselves when we forget our human dignity and the higher aims of our existence.

A man walked up to them—probably a keeper—looked at them and walked away. And this detail seemed mysterious and beautiful, too. They saw a steamer come from Theodosia, with its lights out in the glow of dawn.

"There is dew on the grass," said Anna Sergeyevna, after a silence.

"Yes. It's time to go home."

They went back to the town.

Then they met every day at twelve o'clock on the sea-front, lunched and dined together, went for walks, admired the sea. She complained that she slept badly, that her heart throbbed violently; asked the same questions, troubled now by jealousy and now by the fear that he did not respect her sufficiently. And often in the square or gardens, when there was no one near them, he suddenly drew her to him and kissed her passionately. Complete idleness, these kisses in broad daylight while he looked round in dread of some one's seeing them, the heat, the smell of the sea, and the continual passing to and fro before him of idle, well-dressed, well-fed people, made a new man of him; he told Anna Sergeyevna how beautiful she was, how fascinating. He was impatiently passionate, he would not move a step away from her, while she was often pensive and continually urged him to confess that he did not respect her, did not love her in the least, and thought of her as nothing but a common woman. Rather late almost every evening they drove somewhere out of town, to Oreanda or to the waterfall; and the expedition was always a success, the scenery invariably impressed them as grand and beautiful.

They were expecting her husband to come, but a letter came from him, saying that there was something wrong with his eyes, and he entreated his wife to come home as quickly as possible. Anna Sergeyevna made haste to go.

"It's a good thing I am going away," she said to Gurov. "It's the finger of destiny!"

She went by coach and he went with her. They were driving the whole day. When she had got into a compartment of the express, and when the second bell had rung, she said:

"Let me look at you once more . . . look at you once again. That's right."

She did not shed tears, but was so sad that she seemed ill, and her face was quivering.

"I shall remember you . . . think of you," she said. "God be with you; be happy. Don't remember evil against me. We are parting forever—it must be so, for we ought never to have met. Well, God be with you."

The train moved off rapidly, its lights soon vanished from sight, and a minute later there was no sound of it, as though everything had conspired together to end as quickly as possible that sweet delirium, that madness. Left alone on the platform, and gazing into the dark distance, Gurov listened to the chirrup of the grasshoppers and the hum of the telegraph wires, feeling as though he had only just waked up. And he thought, musing, that there had been another episode or adventure in his life, and it, too, was at an end, and nothing was left of it but a memory. . . . He was moved, sad, and conscious of a slight remorse. This young woman whom he would never meet again had not been happy with him; he was genuinely warm and affectionate with her, but yet in his manner, his tone, and his caresses there had been a shade of light irony, the coarse condescension of a happy man who was, besides, almost twice her age. All the time she had called him kind, exceptional, lofty; obviously he had seemed to her different from what he really was, so he had unintentionally deceived her. . . .

Here at the station was already a scent of autumn; it was a cold evening.

"It's time for me to go north," thought Gurov as he left the platform. "High time!"

3

At home in Moscow everything was in its winter routine; the stoves were heated, and in the morning it was still dark when the children were having breakfast and getting ready for school, and the nurse would light the lamp for a short time. The frosts had begun already. When the first snow has fallen, on the first day of sledge-driving it is pleasant to see the white earth, the white roofs, to draw soft, delicious breath, and the season brings back the days of one's youth. The old limes and birches, white with hoar-frost, have a good-natured expression; they are nearer to one's heart than cypresses and palms, and near them one doesn't want to be thinking of the sea and the mountains.

Gurov was Moscow born; he arrived in Moscow on a fine frosty day, and when he put on his fur coat and warm gloves, and walked along Petrovka, and when on Saturday evening he heard the ringing of the bells, his recent trip and the places he had seen lost all charm for him. Little by little he became absorbed in Moscow life, greedily read three newspapers a day, and declared he did not read the Moscow papers on principle! He already felt a longing to go to restaurants, clubs, dinner-parties, anniversary celebrations, and he felt flattered at entertaining distinguished lawyers and artists, and at playing cards with a professor at the doctors' club. He could already eat a whole plateful of salt fish and cabbage. . . .

In another month, he fancied, the image of Anna Sergeyevna would be shrouded in a mist in his memory, and only from time to time would visit him in his dreams with a touching smile as others did. But more than a month passed, real winter had come, and everything was still clear in his memory as though he had parted with Anna Sergeyevna only the day before. And his memories glowed more and more vividly. When in the evening stillness he heard from his study the voices of his children, preparing their lessons, or when he listened to a song or the organ at the restaurant, or the storm howled in the chimney, suddenly everything would rise up in his memory: what had happened on the groyne, and the early morning with the mist on the mountains, and the steamer coming from Theodosia, and the kisses. He would pace a long time about his room, remembering it all and smiling; then his memories passed into dreams, and in his fancy the past was mingled with what was to come. Anna Sergeyevna did not visit him in dreams, but followed him about everywhere like a shadow and haunted him. When he shut his eyes he saw her as though she were living before him, and she seemed to him lovelier, younger, tenderer than she was; and he imagined himself finer than he had been in Yalta. In the evenings she peeped out at him from the bookcase, from the fireplace, from the corner—he heard her breathing, the caressing rustle of her dress. In the street he watched the women, looking for some one like her.

He was tormented by an intense desire to confide his memories to some one. But in his home it was impossible to talk of his love, and he had no one outside; he could not talk to his tenants nor to any one at the bank. And what had he to talk of? Had he been in love, then? Had there been anything beautiful, poetical, or edifying or simply interesting in his relations with Anna Sergeyevna? And there was nothing for him but to talk vaguely of love, of woman, and no one guessed what it meant; only his wife twitched her black eyebrows, and said: "The part of a lady-killer does not suit you all, Dimitri."

One evening, coming out of the doctors' club with an official with whom he had been playing cards, he could not resist saying:

"If only you knew what a fascinating woman I made the acquaintance of in Yalta!"

The official got into his sledge and was driving away, but turned suddenly and shouted:

"Dmitri Dmitritch!"

"What?"

"You were right this evening: the sturgeon was a bit too strong!"

These words, so ordinary, for some reason moved Gurov to indignation, and struck him as degrading and unclean. What savage manners, what people! What senseless nights, what uninteresting, uneventful days! The rage for card-playing, the gluttony, the drunkenness, the continual talk always about the same thing. Useless pursuits and conversations always about the same things absorb the better part of one's time, the better part of one's strength, and in the end there is left a life grovelling and curtailed, worthless and trivial, and there is no escaping or getting away from it—just as though one were in a madhouse or a prison.

Gurov did not sleep all night, and was filled with indignation. And he had a headache all next day. And the next night he slept badly; he sat up in bed, thinking, or paced up and down his room. He was sick of his children, sick of the bank; he had no desire to go anywhere or to talk of anything.

In the holidays in December he prepared for a journey, and told his wife he was going to Petersburg to do something in the interests of a young friend—and he set off for S——. What for? He did not very well know himself. He wanted to see Anna Sergeyevna and to talk with her—to arrange a meeting, if possible.

He reached S—— in the morning, and took the best room at the hotel, in which the floor was covered with grey army cloth, and on the table was an inkstand, grey with dust and adorned with a figure on horseback, with its hat in its hand and its head broken off. The hotel porter gave him the necessary information; Von Diderits lived in a house of his own in Old Gontcharny Street—it was not far from the hotel: he was rich and lived in good style, and had his own horses; every one in the town knew him. The porter pronounced the name "Dridirits."

Gurov went without haste to Old Gontcharny Street and found the house. Just opposite the house stretched a long grey fence adorned with nails.

"One would run away from a fence like that," thought Gurov, looking from the fence to the windows of the house and back again.

He considered: to-day was a holiday, and the husband would probably be at home. And in any case it would be tactless to go into the house and upset her. If he were to send her a note it might fall into her husband's hands, and then it might ruin everything. The best thing was to trust to chance. And he kept walking up and down the street by the fence, waiting for the chance. He saw a beggar go in at the gate and dogs fly at him; then an hour later he heard a piano, and the sounds were faint and indistinct. Probably it was Anna Sergeyevna playing. The front door suddenly opened, and an old woman came out, followed by the familiar white Pomeranian. Gurov was on the point of calling to the dog, but his heart began beating violently, and in his excitement he could not remember the dog's name.

He walked up and down, and loathed the grey fence more and more, and by now he thought irritably that Anna Sergeyevna had forgotten him, and was perhaps already amusing herself with some one else, and that that was very natural in a young woman who had nothing to look at from morning till night but that confounded fence. He went back to his hotel room and sat for a long while on the sofa, not knowing what to do, then he had dinner and a long nap.

"How stupid and worrying it is!" he thought when he woke and looked at the dark windows: it was already evening. "Here I've had a good sleep for some reason. What shall I do in the night?"

He sat on the bed, which was covered by a cheap grey blanket, such as one sees in hospitals, and he taunted himself in his vexation:

"So much for the lady with the dog . . . so much for the adventure. . . . You're in a nice fix. . . ."

That morning at the station a poster in large letters had caught his eye. "The Geisha"[4] was to be performed for the first time. He thought of this and went to the theatre.

4. An 1896 operetta by the Englishman Sidney Jones.

"It's quite possible she may go to the first performance," he thought.

The theatre was full. As in all provincial theatres, there was a fog above the chandelier, the gallery was noisy and restless; in the front row the local dandies were standing up before the beginning of the performance, with their hands behind them; in the Governor's box the Governor's daughter, wearing a boa, was sitting in the front seat, while the Governor himself lurked modestly behind the curtain with only his hands visible; the orchestra was a long time tuning up; the stage curtain swayed. All the time the audience were coming in and taking their seats Gurov looked at them eagerly.

Anna Sergeyevna, too, came in. She sat down in the third row, and when Gurov looked at her his heart contracted, and he understood clearly that for him there was in the whole world no creature so near, so precious, and so important to him; she, this little woman, in no way remarkable, lost in a provincial crowd, with a vulgar lorgnette[5] in her hand, filled his whole life now, was his sorrow and his joy, the one happiness that he now desired for himself, and to the sounds of the inferior orchestra, of the wretched provincial violins, he thought how lovely she was. He thought and dreamed.

A young man with small side-whiskers, tall and stooping, came in with Anna Sergeyevna and sat down beside her; he bent his head at every step and seemed to be continually bowing. Most likely this was the husband whom at Yalta, in a rush of bitter feeling, she had called a flunkey. And there really was in his long figure, his side-whiskers, and the small bald patch on his head, something of the flunkey's obsequiousness; his smile was sugary, and in his buttonhole there was some badge of distinction like the number on a waiter.

During the first interval the husband went away to smoke; she remained alone in her stall. Gurov, who was sitting in the stalls, too, went up to her and said in a trembling voice, with a forced smile:

"Good-evening."

She glanced at him and turned pale, then glanced again with horror, unable to believe her eyes, and tightly gripped the fan and the lorgnette in her hands, evidently struggling with herself not to faint. Both were silent. She was sitting, he was standing, frightened by her confusion and not venturing to sit down beside her. The violins and the flute began tuning up. He felt suddenly frightened; it seemed as though all the people in the boxes were looking at them. She got up and went quickly to the door; he followed her, and both walked senselessly along passages, and up and down stairs, and figures in legal, scholastic, and civil service uniforms, all wearing badges, flitted before their eyes. They caught glimpses of ladies, of fur coats hanging on pegs; the draughts blew on them, bringing a smell of stale tobacco. And Gurov, whose heart was beating violently, thought:

"Oh, heavens! Why are these people here and this orchestra! . . ."

And at that instant he recalled how when he had seen Anna Sergeyevna off at the station he had thought that everything was over and they would never meet again. But how far they were still from the end!

On the narrow, gloomy staircase over which was written, "To the Amphitheatre," she stopped.

"How you have frightened me!" she said, breathing hard, still pale and overwhelmed. "Oh, how you have frightened me! I am half dead. Why have you come? Why?"

5. A pair of eyeglasses with a short handle.

"But do understand, Anna, do understand . . ." he said hastily in a low voice. "I entreat you to understand . . ."

She looked at him with dread, with entreaty, with love; she looked at him intently, to keep his features more distinctly in her memory.

"I m so unhappy," she went on, not heeding him. "I have thought of nothing but you all the time; I live only in the thought of you. And I wanted to forget, to forget you; but why, oh why, have you come?"

On the landing above them two schoolboys were smoking and looking down, but that was nothing to Gurov; he drew Anna Sergeyevna to him, and began kissing her face, her cheeks, and her hands.

"What are you doing, what are you doing!" she cried in horror, pushing him away. "We are mad. Go away to-day; go away at once . . . I beseech you by all that is sacred, I implore you. . . . There are people coming this way!"

Some one was coming up the stairs.

"You must go away," Ann Sergeyevna went on in a whisper. "Do you hear, Dmitri Dmitritch? I will come and see you in Moscow. I have never been happy; I am miserable now, and I never, never shall be happy, never! Don't make me suffer still more! I swear I'll come to Moscow. But now let us part. My precious, good, dear one, we must part!"

She pressed his hand and began rapidly going downstairs, looking round at him, and from her eyes he could see that she really was unhappy. Gurov stood for a little while, listened, then, when all sound had died away, he found his coat and left the theatre.

4

And Anna Sergeyevna began coming to see him in Moscow. Once in two or three months she left S——, telling her husband that she was going to consult a doctor about an internal complaint—and her husband believed her, and did not believe her. In Moscow she stayed at the Slaviansky Bazaar hotel, and at once sent a man in a red cap to Gurov. Gurov went to see her, and no one in Moscow knew of it.

Once he was going to see her in this way on a winter morning (the messenger had come the evening before when he was out). With him walked his daughter, whom he wanted to take to school: it was on the way. Snow was falling in big wet flakes.

"It's three degrees above freezing-point, and yet it is snowing," said Gurov to his daughter. "The thaw is only on the surface of the earth; there is quite a different temperature at a greater height in the atmosphere."

"And why are there no thunderstorms in the winter, father?"

He explained that, too. He talked, thinking all the while that he was going to see *her,* and no living soul knew of it, and probably never would know. He had two lives: one, open, seen and known by all who cared to know, full of relative truth and of relative falsehood, exactly like the lives of his friends and acquaintances; and another life running its course in secret. And through some strange, perhaps accidental, conjunction of circumstances, everything that was essential, of interest and of value to him, everything in which he was sincere and did not deceive himself, everything that made the kernel of his life, was hidden from other people; and all that was false in him, the sheath in which he hid himself to conceal the truth—such, for instance, as his work in the bank, his discussions at the club, his "lower race," his presence with his wife at anniversary festivities—all that was open. And he judged of others by himself, not believing in what he saw, and always believing that every man had his real, most interesting life under the cover of secrecy and under the cover of night. All personal life rested on secrecy, and possibly it was partly on that account that civilized man was so nervously anxious that personal privacy should be respected.

After leaving his daughter at school, Gurov went on to the Slaviansky Bazaar. He took off his fur coat below, went upstairs, and softly knocked at the door. Anna Sergeyenva, wearing his favourite grey dress, exhausted by the journey and the suspense, had been expecting him since the evening before. She was pale; she looked at him, and did not smile, and he had hardly come in when she fell on his breast. Their kiss was slow and prolonged, as though they had not met for two years.

"Well, how are you getting on there?" he asked. "What news?"

"Wait; I'll tell you directly . . . I can't talk."

She could not speak; she was crying. She turned away from him, and pressed her handkerchief to her eyes.

"Let her have her cry out. I'll sit down and wait," he thought, and he sat down in an arm-chair.

Then he rang and asked for tea to be brought him, and while he drank his tea she remained standing at the window with her back to him. She was crying from emotion, from the miserable consciousness that their life was so hard for them; they could only meet in secret, hiding themselves from people, like thieves! Was not their life shattered?

"Come, do stop!" he said.

It was evident to him that this love of their would not soon be over, that he could not see the end of it. Anna Sergeyevna grew more and more attached to him. She adored him, and it was unthinkable to say to her that it was bound to have an end some day; besides, she would not have believed it!

He went up to her and took her by the shoulders to say something affectionate and cheering, and at that moment he saw himself in the looking-glass.

His hair was already beginning to turn grey. And it seemed strange to him that he had grown so much older, so much plainer during the last few years. The shoulders on which his hands rested were warm and quivering. He felt compassion for this life, still so warm and lovely, but probably already not far from beginning to fade and wither like his own. Why did she love him so much? He always seemed to women different form what he was, and they loved in him not himself, but the man created by their imagination, whom they had been eagerly seeking all their lives; and afterwards, when they noticed their mistake, they loved him all the same. And not one of them had been happy with him. Time passed, he had made their acquaintance, got on with them, parted, but he had never once loved; it was anything you like, but not love.

And only now when his head was grey he had fallen properly, really in love—for the first time in his life.

Anna Sergeyevna and he loved each other like people very close and akin, like husband and wife, like tender friends; it seemed to them that fate itself had meant them for one another, and they could not understand why he had a wife and she a husband; and it was as though they were a pair of birds of passage, caught and forced to live in different cages. They forgave each other for what they were ashamed of in their past, they forgave everything in the present, and felt that this love of theirs had changed them both.

In moments of depression in the past he had comforted himself with any arguments that came into his mind, but now he no longer cared for arguments; he felt profound compassion, he wanted to be sincere and tender. . . .

"Don't cry, my darling," he said "You've had your cry; that's enough . . . Let us talk now, let us think of some plan."

Then they spent a long while taking counsel together, talked of how to avoid the necessity for secrecy, for deception, for living in different towns and not seeing each other for long at a time. How could they be free from this intolerable bondage?

"How? How?" he asked, clutching his head. "How?"

And it seemed as though in a little while the solution would be found, and then a new and splendid life would begin; and it was clear to both of them that they had still a long, long road before them, and that the most complicated and difficult part of it was only just beginning.

Rabindranath Tagore

1861–1941

In the course of a long and immensely distinguished life, the Bengali writer Rabindranath Tagore was a leading figure in the Indian nationalist movement, an antagonist and intimate of Gandhi, the composer of India's national anthem along with many other popular songs, an educational reformer, and winner of the Nobel Prize for Literature. Born in Calcutta three years after Britain took over the government of India, he died six years before national independence in 1947. It is difficult to describe his life and achievements without linking them at every point with the emergence of modern India.

Tagore's father, the son of one of India's richest men, was a noted religious thinker, and Tagore was encouraged to begin publishing at the age of nineteen in a journal run by his family. The foremost Bengali writer of the day, Bankim Chandra Chatterji (1838–1894), acclaimed his youthful poems. He benefited as well from the example of the Bengali reformer Ram Mohan Roy (1772–1833), who offered an early synthesis of European enlightenment with brilliantly reinterpreted Hindu tradition. Roy helped inspire Tagore's lifelong struggle to eliminate prejudice against women, foreigners, and non-Hindus. The Bengali poems of *Gitanjali* (translated into English in 1912) captured the imagination of W. B. Yeats, Ezra Pound, André Gide, and then the Nobel Prize committee, which gave Tagore its prize for literature in 1913. He was knighted in 1915. Tagore's lectures against the dangers of militaristic nationalism, delivered in the midst of World War I, gave grave offense to many British readers, as did his decision to return his knighthood in protest against the Amritsar massacre by the British army in 1919. Still, his international celebrity continued to grow.

An early leader in the movement for India's national liberation, Tagore was the first to call Gandhi "Mahatma," or "Great Soul." No less generous to one who frequently disagreed with him, Gandhi spoke of Tagore as the "Great Sentinel." Repelled by the violence and coercion spawned by Gandhi's Swaraj or self-rule campaign, Tagore withdrew from it in 1921. This withdrawal is the background to his best-known novel, *The Home and the World,* in which a cosmopolitan landowner and his nationalist rival struggle for the affections of the landowner's wife. To some, Tagore's stubborn faith in the unity of mankind has seemed idealistic. To others his life remains a practical inspiration.

PRONUNCIATION:

Rabindranath Tagore: rah-BIN-dra-nath tah-GORE

The Conclusion[1]

1

Apurba Krishna had just passed his BA examination in Calcutta and was returning to his village. On the way his boat had to cross a small river. Later in the year, after the close of the rainy season, it would have been almost dry. Now at the end of Shraban, the monsoon month, it had reached the edge of the village and was lapping at the ruins of the bamboo grove. But after days and days of heavy rain, the sun shone in a cloudless sky.

Apurba's thoughts as he sat in the boat were brimming too. Had we access to the pictures in his young mind we would have seen them dancing like the sun's rays on the wind-ruffled water.

The boat drew up at the usual ghat.[2] From the riverbank Apurba could see the tiled roof of his house through a gap in the trees. No one there knew of his arrival, and so no one had come to meet him. The boatman offered a hand with the luggage, but Apurba refused it and stepped gaily ashore. His feet touched the mud of the ghat, and he fell over, luggage and all. At that instant a melodious peal of high-pitched laughter came from somewhere and startled the birds in a nearby peepul tree.

Extremely embarrassed, Apurba quickly recovered his balance and looked about him. On top of a pile of bricks in course of being unloaded for the local money-lender, a girl sat doubled up with giggles. Apurba recognized her as Mrinmayi, daughter of their recently arrived neighbours. He knew they had previously lived by a big river some distance away, but when the river had swallowed their land they had settled in the village two or three years ago.

Apurba knew much about this girl's reputation. The men of the village referred to her affectionately as Pagli—"Madcap"—but their wives were in a constant state of alarm at her wayward behaviour. All her playmates were boys, and she had vast scorn for girls her own age. In the ranks of biddable children she was regarded as a scourge.

Being her father's favourite made her all the more unruly. Her mother never stopped grumbling about it to her friends. Yet because the father loved Mrinmayi, her tears would have hurt him deeply if he had been at home. That fact, and natural deference to her absent husband, kept the mother from imposing too strict a discipline.

Mrinmayi was dark complexioned with wavy hair that straggled over her shoulders. Her expression was boyish. Her enormous black eyes held no shame or fear, and not the slightest coyness. She was tall, well built, healthy, strong—but of an age people found hard to estimate; otherwise they would have criticized her parents because she was still unmarried. If the boat of some distant zamindar[3] arrived at the ghat, the villagers became impressively alert. As if at a signal, the women pulled their veils down to the tips of their noses, thus concealing their faces like curtains on a stage. But Mrinmayi would arrive holding a naked child to her chest, her unbound hair hanging free. She would stand like a young doe gazing inquisitively in a land where there was neither hunter nor danger. Eventually she would return to her boy playmates and give them elaborate descriptions of the new arrival's manners and mores.

Our Apurba had set eyes on this untamed creature several times during holidays at home, and had occasionally thought of her in a casual way, and sometimes in a not-so-casual way. In the course of life one sees a great many faces, but only a few

1. Translated by Krishna Dutta and Andrew Robinson.
2. Broad riverside stairway.
3. Tax collector.

become fixed in the mind, not for their external appeal but for some other quality—a transparency perhaps. Most faces do not give away much of the personality; but the transparent face—the face in a thousand—clearly reveals the mystery behind it and immediately impresses itself on the mind. Mrinmayi's face was one of these. Her eyes held all the wilful femininity of a nimble, unfettered fawn. It was a face that, once seen, was not easy to forget.

Of course its melodious laughter, however charming it might have been to others, sounded rather painful to the unlucky Apurba. Hastily handing the suitcase to the boatman, he set off red-faced towards home.

And so the scene was beautifully set, with the riverbank, the shady trees, the bird-song, the morning sun, the joy of being twenty—no need to mention a pile of bricks: but as for the person sitting on top of them, she bestowed grace even on that dull and solid heap. How cruel of fate to have turned poetry into farce at the first entrance of the first act.

2

The peal of laughter from that pile was still echoing in Apurba's ears when he picked up his mud-smeared case and chadar,[4] took the path beneath the trees, and arrived at his house. His widowed mother was ecstatic at his unexpected arrival. She sent out at once for rice pudding, curds and *rui* fish and caused a bit of a flurry in the neighbourhood. Once the meal was over she introduced the subject of marriage. Apurba had expected it. He had already received many proposals, and in keeping with the slogan of the day had obstinately insisted "BA pass before bride." But now he was a BA, and his mother had been expectant for so long that he knew further excuses would be useless. He said, "Very well, first let me see the girl. Then I'll decide."

His mother said, "I've seen her. You needn't give it a thought."

Apurba was quite prepared to give it a thought himself and said, "Bride must be seen before marriage." His mother thought she had never heard anything so outrageous, but she consented.

That night, after Apurba had put out the lamp and lain down to sleep in his solitary bed, he caught a sound from beyond the patter of midnight rain and the stillness of the village, the sound of sweet high-pitched laughter. His morning downfall bothered him very much, and he pondered how to rectify the impression he had created. The girl doesn't know that I, Apurba Krishna, am an erudite fellow, he thought, who has spent long periods in Calcutta—not a village bumpkin to be dismissed with a laugh because of a trifling slip in some mud.

The next day Apurba had to inspect the potential bride. She was not far away; the family lived in a neighbouring village. He dressed with some care. Discarding his usual dhoti and chadar, he wore a long silk *chapkan,* a puggree[5] on his head, and his best varnished shoes, and set out at dawn with a silk umbrella in his hand.

The instant he entered the prospective father-in-law's house, he was received with pomp and circumstance. In due time a trembling creature, painted and polished, tinsel round the bun in her hair, and wrapped in a fine colourful sari, was produced before him. She was led silently to a corner, where she remained with her head bent almost to her knees and an elderly maidservant at her back to give

4. Long shawl.

5. Turban.

her courage. Her small brother Rakhal now concentrated his total attention upon this latest intruder into the family and scrutinized its puggree, gold watch-chain and newly sprouted beard. After stroking this last a few times, Apurba finally asked with a solemn air, "What have you read?" The dumb-founded ornamented bundle made no response. After a few more questions and some encouraging prods in the ribs from the maid, the girl blurted out in a faint voice, "*Charupath*-Volume-Two-Grammar-Volume-One-Descriptive-Geography-Arithmetic-History-of-India." Simultaneously there came a sudden series of repeated thuds outside the room, and a moment later Mrinmayi raced breathlessly into the room with her hair flying. Without so much as a glance at Apurba Krishna, she grabbed the brother of the bride-to-be by the hand and began to pull him out of the room. But Rakhal refused to co-operate, so absorbing was the situation indoors. The maid did her best to retrieve this by berating Mrinmayi as sharply as propriety permitted. Apurba Krishna meanwhile preserved his own dignity as best he could by sitting bolt upright in his lofty turban and fiddling with the watch-chain across his stomach. When Mrinmayi finally grasped that she could not distract Rakhal, she slapped him loudly on the back, whipped the veil off the girl's head, and dashed out like a whirlwind. The maid growled in fury, and Rakhal tittered at the sudden sight of his sister minus her precious veil. The slap on the back he did not object to at all, for such exchanges often took place between them. Mrinmayi's hair, for instance, once hung halfway down her back, rather than to her shoulders. One day Rakhal had sneaked up behind her and snipped off a handful with a pair of scissors. She had grabbed the scissors from him in anger and finished the job with a few slashes. Waves of hair had fallen to the ground and lain there like clusters of black grapes. This was the system of discipline between them.

The inspection session fell silent and did not endure much longer. Somehow the girl uncurled herself, regained a perpendicular position and returned to the inner rooms escorted by the old maid. Apurba, still stroking his sparse moustache, rose as solemnly as possible and prepared to depart. But when he reached the door he saw that his new pair of varnished shoes had vanished, and no one could find them. Everyone in the house was frightfully put out and hurled endless reproaches in the direction of the culprit. Eventually a desperate Apurba borrowed an old, torn and flapping pair of slippers belonging to the master of the house. With this additional touch to his fancy *chapkan* and puggree, he very gingerly set out along the village path.

By the edge of a pond, at a deserted point on the path, the high-pitched laughter caught him again. It was as if some fun-loving nymph in the forest had seen the slippers and could not suppress her giggles. While Apurba stood hesitating, she emerged brazenly, placed his new pair of shoes on the path, and was about to take to her heels when Apurba managed to grab both her hands and capture her.

Twisting and turning, Mrinmayi tried to free herself but could not. A stray sunbeam slanted through the trees on to her full, mischievous face. Like a curious traveller stooping to see the sunlit bed of a moving stream through clear water, Apurba gravely gazed on Mrinmayi's upturned face with its sparkling eyes, very gradually loosened his grip on his prisoner, and released her. If he had struck her in anger Mrinmayi would not have been at all surprised, but this gentle sentence of punishment in this empty glade quite baffled her.

The whole sky seemed to ring with laughter like the sound of celestial ankle bells. Lost in thought Apurba Krishna plodded home.

3

All day Apurba made up excuses for not joining his mother in the inner rooms. He had an invitation elsewhere; he ate there. The fact is—though it may be hard to swallow—that even someone as erudite, serious minded and original as Apurba was remarkably eager to regain his lost dignity in the eyes of this simple village girl. What did it matter if she had momentarily reduced him to a laughing-stock, then ignored him in favour of some ignoramus named Rakhal? Must he prove to her that he reviewed books for a magazine called *Visvadip* and carried in his suitcase cologne, shoes, Rubini's camphor, coloured letter paper, and a book on how to play the harmonium, not to mention a notebook awaiting future publication like the dawn in the womb of night? Nevertheless, whatever common sense might say, Mr Apurba Krishna Ray was definitely unprepared to admit defeat at the hands of this flighty rustic girl.

When he appeared in the inner rooms that evening, his mother asked, "Well Apu, you saw the girl. Do you approve?"

Somewhat awkwardly Apurba replied, "I saw the girl, Mother, and there was one I liked."

Astounded, his mother said, "You saw *girls?*"

Then, after much shilly-shallying, he revealed that he had selected Mrinmayi, daughter of their neighbour. What a choice after so much education and study!

At first Apurba was considerably abashed, but he was no longer so when his mother began to object vehemently. He sat there insisting doggedly that he would marry no one but Mrinmayi. The more he thought of the dolled-up kind of girl, the more repulsive became the idea of marrying one.

Battle was joined between them, in the form of tiffs, sulks, fasts and sleepless nights, and after two or three days Apurba was victorious. His mother managed to convince herself that Mrinmayi was still immature, that her own mother had been unable to bring her up properly, but that if taken in hand after marriage Mrinmayi's nature would change. Gradually, she came to believe that the girl had a pretty face. It was when she thought of the girl's cropped hair that her heart filled with despair. Yet even that, she hoped, if tied up firmly and thoroughly soaked in oil, might in time respond to treatment.

To the village people Apurba's choice of bride quickly became labelled *apurba*—original. Many of them rather liked "Pagli Mrinmayi," but not, it had to be said, as a possible daughter-in-law.

Her father, Ishan Majumdar, was informed. He was a clerk in a steamship company, responsible for the correct loading and unloading of goods and the sale of tickets from a decrepit tin-roofed hut at a distant riverside station. When he heard the news, he shed tears of sorrow and joy, mingled in proportions unknown. He petitioned his boss, a head-office sahib, for leave of absence to attend his daughter's wedding. The sahib considered this insufficient grounds and turned down the request. Then, expecting a week's holiday at Puja time, Ishan wrote home to postpone the wedding. But Apurba's mother said, "The auspicious days fall in the present month, the wedding cannot be put off." Twice rejected, the distressed father protested no more and went back to weighing goods and selling tickets.

Whereupon Mrinmayi's mother and all the older women of the village assembled and began to instruct Mrinmayi day and night in her future duties. Their stern prohibitions against playfulness and frolicking around, loud laughter, gossip with boys, and eating when hungry succeeded in making marriage sound like a nightmare. An alarmed Mrinmayi thought she had been sentenced to life imprisonment with hanging at the end of it. Like an unbroken pony she stiffened her neck, reared back, and said, "I'm not going to get married."

4

Nevertheless, she did.

Then her lessons began. Overnight, Mrinmayi's world contracted to the confines of her mother-in-law's inner rooms. Her mother-in-law began the task of correcting her. Assuming a minatory expression, she said, "Look, dear, you are not a little girl any longer. We don't tolerate disgraceful manners in our house." Mrinmayi did not grasp what she meant. If my manners are not tolerated here, I'd better go elsewhere, she thought. That afternoon she went missing. A thorough search was launched. Finally the traitor Rakhal led them to her secret hideout, the abandoned old chariot of the village deity Radha Kanta under a banyan tree. It is easy to imagine how the mother-in-law and willing well-wishers set upon the girl.

That night the clouds gathered and rain began with a pattering sound. Apurba Krishna edged a little closer to Mrinmayi as she lay in bed and whispered in her ear, "Mrinmayi, don't you love me?"

"No!" she said violently, "I will never ever love you!" And then she unleashed all her rage and humiliation on Apurba's head like a thunderbolt.

In a wounded voice he said, "Why, what have I done?"

"Why did you marry me?"

A satisfactory counter to this accusation was tricky. But then and there Apurba decided he must win her over.

The next day the mother-in-law saw all the signs of rebellion and locked Mrinmayi in. At first and for some time she fluttered about the room like a newly captured bird. When she could not escape she shredded the bedsheets with her teeth in futile anger and then, lying prone on the floor, pined for her father and wept.

In time someone slowly came and sat beside her. Affectionately he tried to lift her hair off the floor and away from her face. Mrinmayi shook her head vigorously and threw off the hand. Then Apurba bent down to her and said softly, "I've opened the door. Come, let's get away to the back garden." But Mrinmayi's head shook vehemently and said, "No." Apurba tried to lift her chin and said, "Just look who's here." Rakhal, bewildered at seeing Mrinmayi prostrate on the floor, stood at the door. Without looking up she pushed away Apurba's hand. "Rakhal's come to play with you. Won't you go with him?" In a voice loud with irritation she repeated "No!" Rakhal realized he had chosen the wrong moment and fled with a sigh of relief. Apurba sat on in silence. Mrinmayi wept and wept, until she exhausted herself and fell asleep. Apurba tiptoed out and fastened the door behind him.

The next day she received a letter from her father. He grieved over his inability to attend his darling's marriage, and he sent the newly-weds his heartfelt blessings. Mrinmayi went to her mother-in-law and said, "I want to go to my father." The astonished woman exploded at this outlandish request. "Who knows where her father lives, and she wants to go to him! A fantastic notion!" Mrinmayi went away without replying. She went to her room, bolted the door, and in utter hopelessness began to pray to her father as if to God: "Father, come and take me away. I have no one here. I'll die if I stay here."

In the dead of night, while her husband slept, Mrinmayi very carefully opened the door and left the house. Clouds passed over now and then, but the paths were plain in the moonlight. How to choose one leading to her father was beyond her. She assumed that if she followed the route of the mail runner it would take her to any address in the world. She set off on this familiar path. After walking quite a way she grew weary, and night was nearly over. As a few birds uncertain of the time began to give tentative chirps, she found herself on a riverbank in a place like a large market. She paused to think, and then recognized the "jham jham' sound of the mail runner's ankle bells. Then he himself appeared, out of breath, with the mail bag on his shoulder. Mrinmayi rushed up to him and begged, "I want to go to my father at Kushiganj. Will you take me?"

"I don't know where Kushiganj is." With barely a pause for breath he roused the boatman on the mail boat tied up at the ghat, and the boat cast off. He was not allowed to take time to answer questions.

By and by the market awoke. Mrinmayi went down to the ghat and called to another boatman, "Will you take me to Kushiganj?" Before he could reply, someone in the next boat called out, "So it's you, Minu Ma? What are you doing here?" Bursting with impatience she called back, "Banamali, I'm going to my father at Kushiganj. Can you take me in your boat?" Banamali was a boatman from their village and knew this wilful girl very well. "You're going to your father? That's good. Come on, I'll take you." Mrinmayi jumped in.

The boatman cast off. The clouds descended and a torrential downpour began. The boat tossed in a current swollen with the rains of the month of Bhadra. Mrinmayi was overwhelmed with fatigue. She spread the loose end of her sari, lay down, and went tamely to sleep, rocked by the river like a baby in mother nature's arms.

She awoke in her bed in her married home. Seeing her eyes open the maid began to scold. This brought the mother-in-law and a stream of harsh words. Mrinmayi, wide-eyed, stared at her. But when she made a dig at Mrinmayi's father's bad training, Mrinmayi got up, went to the next room, and bolted the door.

Apurba forsook his usual timidity, went to his mother and said, "What harm is there in sending her to her father for a few days?"

His mother turned on him: "She's bewitched!" and then she took up an old theme: with so many girls to choose from, why had he brought home this bone-burning good-for-nothing?

5

All day the downpour continued, and the atmosphere indoors was equally foul. That night, in the early hours, Apurba woke Mrinmayi and said, "Do you want to go to your father?" Suddenly alert, she clutched his hand and said simply, "Yes!" Apurba whispered, "Come then. We'll escape very quietly. I've arranged a boat."

Mrinmayi looked at her husband with profound gratitude. She got up quickly, dressed, and prepared to leave. Apurba left a note to allay his mother's anxiety, and the two of them stepped out. In the dark, without a soul or a sound nearby, she first put her hand in her husband's of her own free will; the tingle of her excitement thrilled his every nerve.

The boat moved out into the night. In spite of her ecstasy Mrinmayi fell asleep almost at once. The next day, what freedom what delight! On both banks were so many villages, markets, fields of grain, forests, other boats passing back and forth. Soon she was plying her husband with a thousand questions about the tiniest and most trivial of sights. What is in that boat? Where have those people come from? What is the name of this place? Questions whose answers could not be found in any of Apurba's college books or extracted from his Calcutta experience. His friends there would have been embarrassed to know that he answered every one of them and that most of his replies did not tally with the truth. He asserted, for instance, that a boat carrying sesame carried linseed, and he called a magistrate's court a zamindar's warehouse and confused the town of Panchberia with that of Rainagar. His wrong replies did not impede in the slightest the satisfaction in the heart of his trustful questioner.

The following evening they reached Kushiganj. In a tin-roofed hut half lit by an oily old lantern Ishan Chandra sat bare-chested on a stool, bent over a huge leather-bound account book resting on a small desk. The newly-weds entered and Mrinmayi said, "Father!" in a tone of voice quite alien to that room. Ishan wept. He could not think what to say or what to do. His daughter and son-in-law were standing in his hut like the princess and prince of an empire, and all he could offer them for thrones were some bales of jute. He was absolutely disoriented. And what about food? As a poor clerk he cooked his own dal[6] and rice—but this was a joyous occasion. Mrinmayi said, "Father, today we'll all cook." Apurba agreed with alacrity.

The room was without space, servants and food, but joy sprang in abundance from the constricted circumstances of poverty, as a fountain gushes with increased force from a tiny aperture.

Three days went by. Twice the river steamer appeared on schedule with many passengers and much hubbub; but by evening the riverbank had emptied, and then the three of them were at liberty once more. They cooked together, making mistakes, and ended up with meals not quite what they had intended, which Mrinmayi, now the devoted wife, served to son-in-law and father-in-law, while they teased her about a thousand shortcomings in her household arrangements and she jingled her bangles in pretended pique. At last Apurba said they really had to leave. Though Mrinmayi pleaded with him for a few more days, her father said, "Better not."

On the last day he hugged his daughter, stroked her head, and said in a choked voice, "Darling, you must be a Lakshmi[7] to brighten your husband's home. Let no one find fault with my Minu." A sobbing Mrinmayi bade farewell and departed with her husband. Ishan turned and went back to his hut, now twice as cramped and cheerless, and resumed weighing goods, day after day, month after month.

6

When this guilty couple returned home, Apurba's mother wore a long face and said nothing. She blamed no one, and they did not try to exonerate themselves. Unspoken reproof and reproach sat sternly upon the house like a stone. At last the atmosphere became unbearable, and Apurba said, "Mother, college has opened, and I had better return to start my law degree."

His mother said indifferently, "What will you do with your wife?"

"She'll stay here."

"No son, it won't work. You must take her with you." She did not employ the usual affectionate form of address.

Apurba in a mortified tone said, "All right." He began to prepare. On the night before his departure he came to bed and found Mrinmayi in tears. Sorrowfully he asked, "I suppose you don't want to go with me to Calcutta?"

"No."

6. Lentils. 7. Celestial maiden.

"Don't you love me?" There was no answer. Sometimes an answer comes easily, but other times the psychology of it is so complex that a shy girl can only keep silent. Apurba asked, "Will you mind leaving Rakhal?"

"Yes," said Mrinmayi without hesitation.

A pang of jealousy as piercing as the point of a needle passed through this Bachelor of Arts at the thought of the boy Rakhal. He said, "I won't be able to return for a long time."

No reply.

"I think it could even be two years or more."

"When you return, bring a Rogers three-bladed knife for Rakhal," Mrinmayi ordered.

Apurba, who had been reclining against a bolster, rose a little at this and said, "So you really do want to stay here."

"Yes, I'll go and stay with my mother."

Apurba sighed and said, "All right, that's that. I won't come back until you write me a letter. Does that make you very happy?"

Mrinmayi felt that this question did not require a reply and dropped off to sleep. But Apurba did not sleep. He propped himself up with a pillow and remained alert.

Late at night the moon rose, and moonlight fell across the bed. Apurba looked at Mrinmayi and thought he saw a fairy princess put to sleep by the touch of a silver wand. If he could only find a wand of gold he could awaken her and exchange a garland of love. But he knew that such a wand would only bring him heartache instead of happiness, while the silver wand had turned her into a blissfully sleeping beauty.

At dawn he woke her and said, "Mrinmayi, it's time for me to go. Let me take you to your mother's house." She got out of bed and stood there, and Apurba took her hands. "I want you to grant me a wish. I have helped you many times. Now that I am going will you give me a reward?"

Mrinmayi was puzzled. "What?"

"Give me one loving kiss."

Apurba's ridiculous request and earnest voice made Mrinmayi burst into laughter. Then she pulled a long face and prepared to kiss him. She came close and could not, giggled and began to laugh again. Twice she tried, and at last gave up, muffling her hilarity with her sari. Apurba pulled her ears as a punishment but made a stern vow: he must not lower his dignity by snatching his reward by force. It must come spontaneously, as a sacred offering—or not at all.

Mrinmayi laughed no more. They set out together for her mother's house in the hush of early morning. When he returned he said to his own mother, "I thought it over and decided to take her to her mother. Having a wife with me in Calcutta would restrict my studies. She'd have no company there. You don't seem to want her here, so I left her with her own mother." In deep resentment, mother and son parted.

7

In her mother's house Mrinmayi found that she could not settle to anything. The entire house seemed to have altered. Time dragged. What to do, where to go, whom to see, she could not decide. It was as if the house and the village had been obliterated by a total eclipse of the sun at midday. And another thing: the desire to go to Calcutta that overwhelmed her now—where had that been last night? Only a day ago, she had had no conception that the life she loved could completely lose its savour. Today, like a mature leaf ready to detach itself from a tree, she effortlessly rejected her former existence.

There is a tale told of a swordsmith so skilled he could make a weapon keen enough to slice a man in two without his feeling a thing; only when he moved would the two parts divide. Mrinmayi was unaware when the Creator's sword severed her childhood from her youth. She looked around her, astonished and bruised, and saw herself anew. Her bedroom in her old home was no longer familiar. The girl who had lived there had disappeared. Now all her memorable moments gathered around another house, another room, another bed.

No one saw Mrinmayi out of doors any more. No one heard her peals of laughter. Rakhal was afraid even to look at her. Games together were out of the question. She said to her mother, "Take me back to my mother-in-law's house."

There Apurba's mother had been grieving, remembering her son's face at farewell. She agonized over his going away angry and leaving his wife with her own mother. Then the mournful Mrinmayi, veiled with due respect, came to touch her mother-in-law's feet. No wonder the old woman wept, embraced the younger, and in a moment was reconciled. Then the mother-in-law looked into the newly married girl's face and was amazed. The Mrinmayi she had known was no more. Could ordinary beings be so transformed? Such an enormous change would require enormous strength. The mother-in-law had intended to correct Mrinmayi's faults one by one, but an invisible Rectifier had taken charge of her and in one fell swoop had moulded her anew. Now Mrinmayi could understand her mother-in-law, and her mother-in-law Mrinmayi. They intertwined as one household like the branches and twigs of a tree.

A profound sense of womanhood filled every fibre of Mrinmayi and made her feel as tender as heartache. Tears of contrition welled up in her like the inky-black rain-clouds that herald the monsoon. They cast deep shadows beneath her eyelashes. She kept thinking to herself: I didn't know my own mind. You could see that. So why didn't you make it up for me? Why didn't you punish me? I didn't want to go to Calcutta with you and behaved like a witch. Why didn't you make me go? You shouldn't have taken any notice of me and my obstinacy.

She thought of that morning when Apurba had captured her on the lonely road by the pond, had said nothing, only looked at her. She saw the path, the spot beneath the trees, the morning sunbeams, the expression in his eyes and all of a sudden she sensed their full meaning. The half-kiss she had given him before he went away now tormented her like a thirsty bird in the desert darting forward and hesitating before a mirage. Over and over again she thought: I wish I'd done that then, I wish I'd said that, if only it had been like that!

Apurba was similarly despairing. He was telling himself: Mrinmayi has never seen my best self. While Mrinmayi was asking herself: what must he think of me? What must he take me for? A difficult, thoughtless, silly girl, not a mature woman capable of returning his love from an unquenchable heart. She felt sick with shame and remorse and began to repay all her debts to Apurba with kisses and caresses on his pillow.

When he had gone away he had said, "If you don't write, I won't come home." When she remembered that, she shut the door and began a letter on the gold-bordered coloured paper that he had given her. Very carefully she drew some lines and then, after smudging her fingers, without bothering to address her husband with a formal salutation she wrote: "Why don't you write to me? How are you?" and "You come home." What more could she say? Everything worth saying had surely been said, but not perhaps with quite the flair for expression to which humans are accustomed. Mrinmayi understood that and racked her brain for ways to put some new words together. “Now write me a letter, and write how you are and come home, mother is well, Bishu and Puti are well, yesterday our black cow had a calf.” With this she ended the letter. She put it in an envelope and in drops of love inscribed each letter: Shrijukta Babu Apurba Krishna Ray. But even so much love could not make the lines straight, the letters neatly formed, the spelling faultless. And on an envelope, besides the name, something else is required. This Mrinmayi did not know. To keep the letter private she gave it to a trusted maid for posting. Needless to say, nothing came of it. Apurba did not come home.

8

His mother knew he had a holiday, yet Apurba had not returned. She and Mrinmayi assumed that he was still angry, and when Mrinmayi thought of her letter she was overcome with shame. It had conveyed nothing she really wanted to say, and Apurba would think her even more immature and even less worthy of his efforts. She was transfixed with anxiety. Again and again she asked the maid, “That letter, did you post it?” A thousand times the maid reassured her, “Yes, I dropped it into the box myself. The master should have got it days ago.”

A day eventually came when Apurba’s mother called Mrinmayi and told her, “Daughter, Apu has been gone a long time, so I am thinking of going to Calcutta to see him. Will you come?” Mrinmayi nodded in agreement, went to her room, shut the door, fell on the bed, embraced the pillow and shook with silent laughter. Then all her pent-up emotion spilled out and she became serious, gloomy and apprehensive. Finally she started to cry.

With no prior warning these two repentant women set out for Calcutta to plead with Apurba for absolution. There they stayed at the home of his married sister.

That evening Apurba, who had given up hope of a letter from Mrinmayi, broke his vow and sat down to write to her. No words came. He groped for one to convey mingled love and hurt. Not finding it, he became contemptuous of his mother tongue. Just then a note arrived from his brother-in-law: “Mother is here. Come at once and have your meal with us. All is well.” In spite of this assurance, Apurba went along in a mood of gloomy apprehension. As he entered his sister’s house he promptly asked, “Mother, is everything all right?”

“Everything is perfectly all right. You didn’t come home for the holiday, so I have come to fetch you.”

“You needn’t have troubled,” Apurba said. “You know I have to prepare for the law exams . . .” And so on.

When it was time to eat his sister asked, “*Dada,* why isn’t your wife with you?”

“My studies, you know . . .” her brother said solemnly.

His brother-in-law laughed. “All these feeble excuses! You were afraid of us.”

The sister said, “You look ferocious enough to frighten any young person.”

The banter continued, but Apurba remained downcast. Nothing made him feel happier. All he could think was that since his mother had come, Mrinmayi could easily have come too if she had wished. Perhaps his mother had tried but been turned down. It was hardly something he felt he could question her about: one must simply accept that all human intercourse, in fact all creation, was a maze of deception and error.

After the meal a blustery wind arose and heavy rain came down. Apurba's sister proposed, "*Dada,* do stay with us tonight."

"No, I must get back. I have to work."

"What can you achieve at this hour?" asked his brother-in-law. "Stay. You're not obliged to anyone. Why worry?"

After more urging Apurba acquiesced. His sister said, "*Dada,* you look tired. Don't stay up. Go to bed." That was Apurba's wish as well. He wanted to be alone in bed in the dark and away from all this chatter. At the bedroom door he saw that the room was dark. His sister said, "That wind has blown out your lamp. Shall I bring another?"

"No need. I sleep without a lamp." His sister left.

Apurba began to feel his way towards the bed. He was about to climb into it when with a sudden sound of bangles, a soft arm took him in its embrace, and a pair of lips like a flowering bud smothered him with a flood of passionate kisses that left no space to express surprise. He was startled only for a moment. Then he knew that the half-kiss interrupted by fits of laughter was at long last being concluded among uninhibited tears.

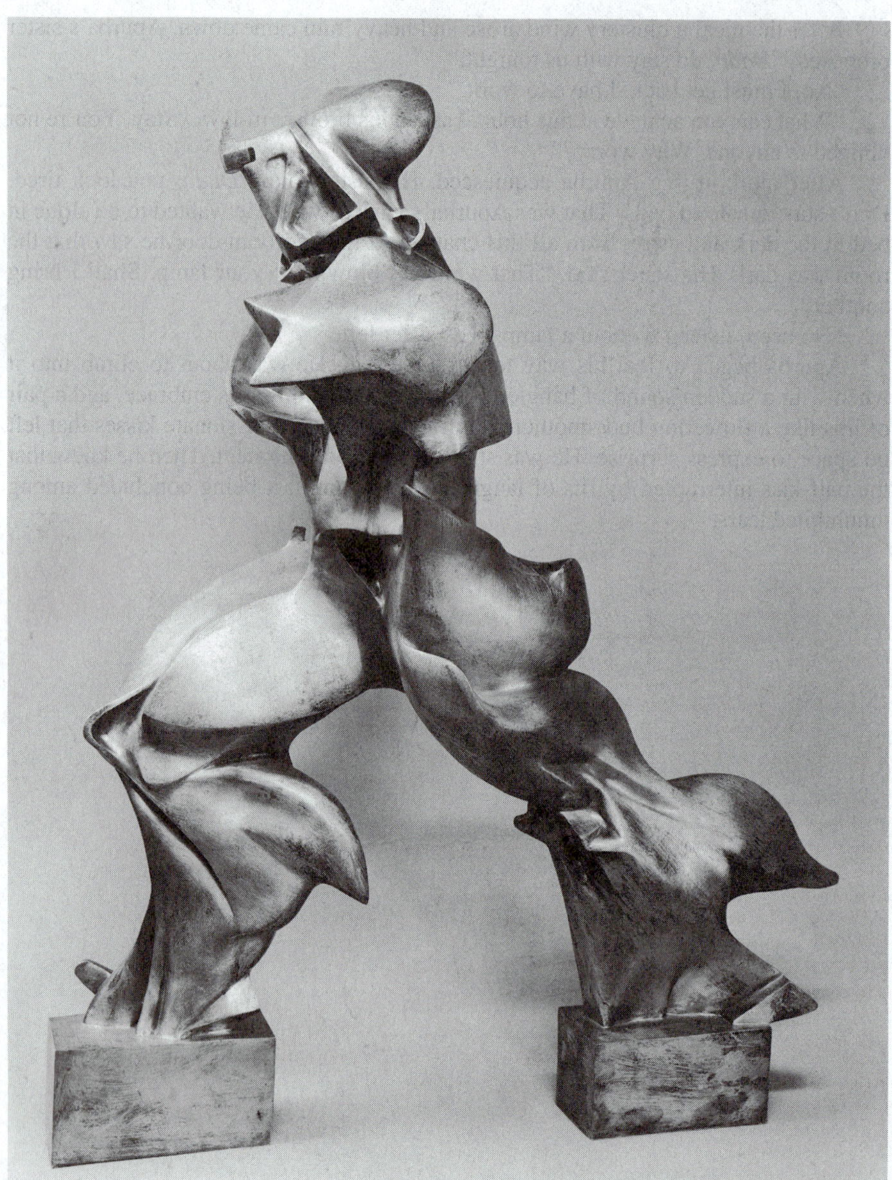

Umberto Boccioni's *Unique Forms of Continuity in Space,* 1913, is the Futurist Manifesto in Bronze. More than the suggested human form that is contained in the aerodynamic wrappings, Boccioni is praising technology and speed. His sculpture evokes the declaration of the Manifesto that "the roaring automobile is more beautiful than the Winged Victory" (the *Nike of Samothrace*). By the middle of the twentieth century, automobile design would indeed take on the winged fenders of Boccioni's sculpture. One year after the 1909 Futurist Manifesto of Marinetti, Boccioni was one of the signers of a Futurist painting manifesto, and author of "Manifesto of Futurist Sculpture" (1912).

The Twentieth Century

Human history is principally a record of strife. Few centuries in the history of humanity, though, can rival the magnitude, efficiency, and lethal intensity of the twentieth century's conflicts. No single decade, and few individual years in the course of the century, were free of war, revolutions, uprisings, or military and civil confrontation. The most advanced century in terms of its technological and scientific know-how was also marked by deadly results: two world wars, with a combined human death toll of over ninety million; numerous revolutions, at least a handful of which changed the course of history beyond their particular contexts—the Mexican Revolution of 1910, the Russian Revolution of 1917, the Chinese Revolutions between 1924 and 1949, the Cuban Revolution of 1959; wars of emancipation from colonial regimes that culminated in as many as seventeen new nation-states in a single year (1960) in Africa alone; the use of the deadliest weapon ever devised and deployed by humankind—the atomic bombs dropped on Hiroshima and Nagasaki in August 1945 by the United States; and then a so-called "Cold War" under the constant threat of worldwide nuclear conflagration for more than half of the twentieth century, during which 149 localized proxy wars on behalf of the rival ideologies of the superpowers killed more than twenty-three million people. By the end of the century, no part of the earth and no culture in it remained untouched by some external political and military force, cultural influence, or economic intrusion.

The Art of Strife

Like any art form, literature is neither immune to historical conflict nor is it simply symptomatic or reflective of strife that surrounds it. Art itself serves as instrument and as occasion for engagement, contestation, and struggle. And these struggles intensified in the early twentieth century with the eclipse of nineteenth-century ideals of historical progress and rational explanations of motives and wants. The twentieth century upended that orderliness and rationality in its pursuit of the underside of things and the far side of reason. Surface reality no longer sufficed. Twentieth-century art and science were bent on divulging reality's hidden faces, its surrealist para-realities. And while the nineteenth century may have privileged the role of the individual writer and originality of genius in the creation of science, art, and literature, in the twentieth century the cult of novelty and individuality placed a premium on disruption. Thus, the order of continuity was first subjected to the disorder of rupture, breakage, destruction, and eradication before a new generation of artists or writers, or a new school or mode of art, could feel that they had attained cultural legitimacy. The literature that ushered in and succeeded the conflagration of the Great War of 1914–1918 (it would be dubbed the First World War only in retrospect) would always be marked by an obsessive concern for the underside of reason and the darker side of human ingenuity. All subsequent literature to the end of the century would carry the signs of

David Alfaro Siqueiros, *Echo of a Scream,* 1937.

this ambivalence and equivocation, to the point where such ambiguity came to be prized as the mark of accomplished literature.

The language of war becomes also the language of artistic and aesthetic advancement and self-affirmation. The eruption of twentieth-century modernity becomes synonymous with the self-designation of "avant-garde," a military term for the front-line deployment of shock troops. And the self-announcement of a literary movement's arrival invariably is through the shrill proclamation of a "manifesto," or some other form of self-assertive declaration whose shock value spells more an interruption of one's antecedents than an affirmation of one's own program. "Revolution" loses its dictionary sense of returning, or turning over again, in favor of overturning and overthrow of what must be succeeded by the self-contradictory novelty of repetition, often couched in a descriptive language that revels in self-contradiction. Hence, paradoxical assertions like the "the tradition of the new" would be proclaimed by more than one poet and by even a greater number of historians and critics of art and literature. If rational evolution was the progressive cause of eighteenth-century enlightenment and of the science of the nineteenth century, then interruptive revolution was the explanatory method of twentieth-century scientific and artistic processes, especially so in the art of literature.

Modernity, Modernism, Modernization

Modulation and conformity, then, are not attributes one could associate with the twentieth century. Rather, the century elevated modernism, modernization, and modernity to a privileged status as the ultimate mode to which all human activity was destined to advance. Failure to achieve this mode of modes in art, literature, technology, science, or governance pegged a culture as underdeveloped, the opposite of progressive, or, at best, euphemistically designated as in the process of developing. Often judged by criteria of outwardly measurable material achievement, modernity came to be synonymous with the value of what made such material progress possible—namely, modernization.

Modernization moved with and beyond modernism in the arts to designate advancements in technology and industry, especially the scientific harnessing, ordering, and exploitation of natural resources and native populations, with "natural" being rooted in the same etymology as "native." The legacy of late nineteenth-century colonization in Africa and Asia, along with re-colonization in Latin America, neatly divided the world between the civilizing modern colonialist and the premodern native, who depended on the colonist for entry into the course of modern human history. Modernism in the arts was most often in tune with this newly global world order, thus consolidating the division between the modern and the modernizing, the developed and the developing, the arrived and the aspiring but not-yet-accomplished.

Decolonization/Recolonization

The emancipatory movements of decolonization starting at the mid-twentieth century aggravated the contest between the principal ideologies of the century—namely, the Marxist East and the capitalist West. The newly independent nations became the testing ground—and often the battleground—of the two systems competing to bring about the salvation of those new nations in the annals of history. Both systems put forth internationalist conceptions of culture. In the Marxist system, the world was viewed as a transnational culture without frontiers, a world order in which humanity would transcend local divisions and produce a world literature infinitely more meaningful than the bourgeois and parochial. The triumphant capitalist system, for its part, deemed its own cultural paradigm as the point of reference and standard for all world culture, with free capital moving unimpeded in a world without economic borders. In both ideologies, literature was valued in proportion to its universal appeal and its capacity to project the local and the particular onto the world stage and the higher order of humanity's shared cultural heritage.

In the nineteenth century, literature had been closely identified with the project of nation-building. During the twentieth century, as part of the process of decolonization, national literature as such became a subject of debate, as did the language in which literatures would be written and read, since geography, language, culture, and nation did not necessarily coincide as they were arrayed by colonial powers. And when nation, religion, race, ethnicity, and geography would be forcefully constructed as overlapping—secular and scientific history notwithstanding—colonialism and occupation would overflow from the twentieth into the twenty-first century in territorial and cultural struggles from southern Mexico to East Timor in Indonesia to Palestine and Israel.

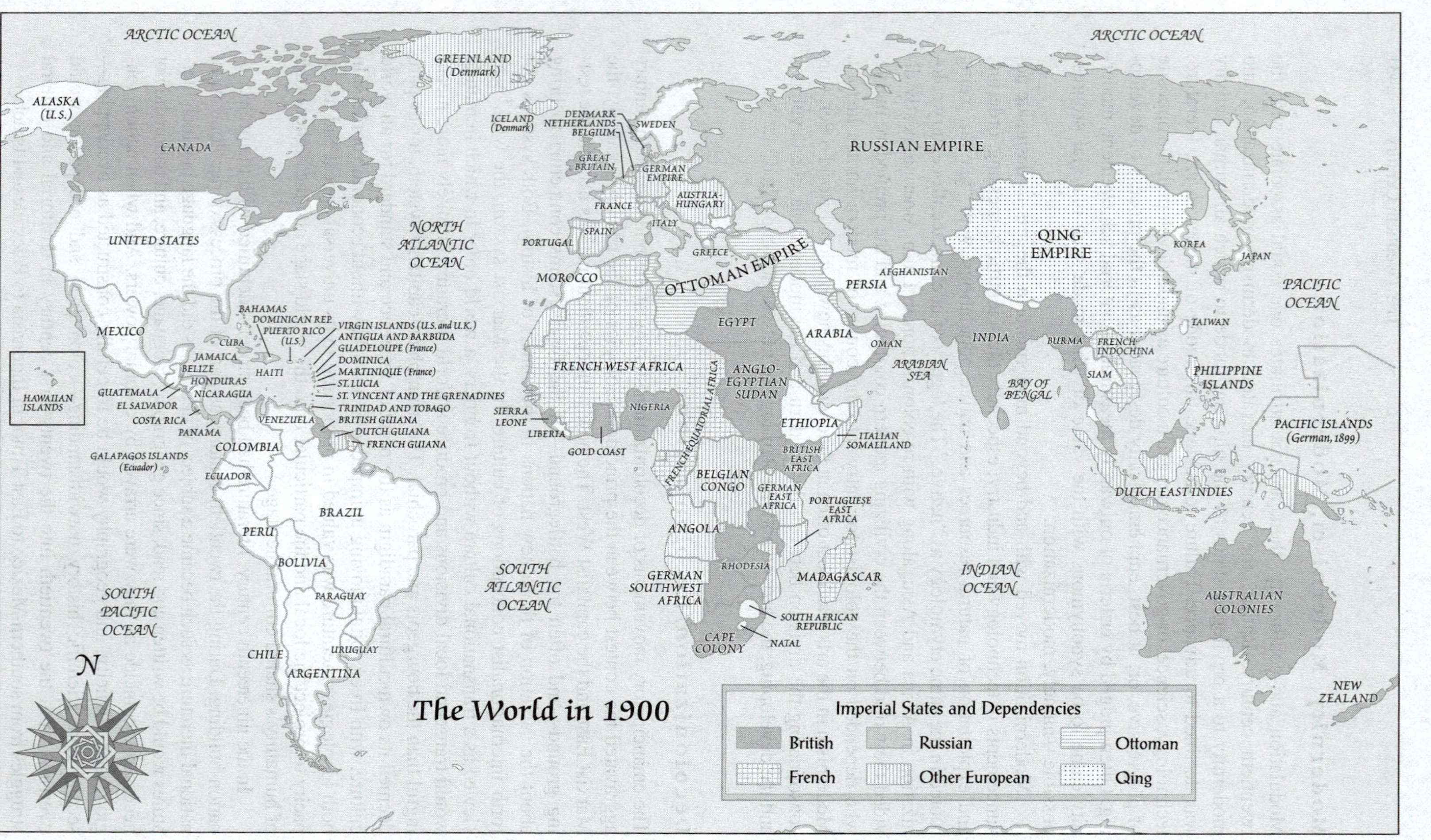

ARCTIC OCEAN
ARCTIC OCEAN
ALASKA (U.S.)
CANADA
GREENLAND (Denmark)
ICELAND (Denmark)
DENMARK
NETHERLANDS
BELGIUM
SWEDEN
GREAT BRITAIN
GERMAN EMPIRE
RUSSIAN EMPIRE
FRANCE
AUSTRIA-HUNGARY
ITALY
SPAIN
PORTUGAL
GREECE
UNITED STATES
NORTH ATLANTIC OCEAN
MOROCCO
OTTOMAN EMPIRE
QING EMPIRE
KOREA
JAPAN
AFGHANISTAN
PERSIA
PACIFIC OCEAN
BAHAMAS
DOMINICAN REP.
PUERTO RICO (U.S.)
VIRGIN ISLANDS (U.S. and U.K.)
ANTIGUA AND BARBUDA
GUADELOUPE (France)
DOMINICA
MARTINIQUE (France)
ST. LUCIA
ST. VINCENT AND THE GRENADINES
TRINIDAD AND TOBAGO
BRITISH GUIANA
DUTCH GUIANA
FRENCH GUIANA
MEXICO
CUBA
JAMAICA
BELIZE
HONDURAS
NICARAGUA
HAITI
GUATEMALA
EL SALVADOR
COSTA RICA
PANAMA
HAWAIIAN ISLANDS
EGYPT
ARABIA
OMAN
TAIWAN
INDIA
BURMA
FRENCH INDOCHINA
SIAM
FRENCH WEST AFRICA
ANGLO-EGYPTIAN SUDAN
ARABIAN SEA
PHILIPPINE ISLANDS
BAY OF BENGAL
SIERRA LEONE
LIBERIA
NIGERIA
FRENCH EQUATORIAL AFRICA
ETHIOPIA
ITALIAN SOMALILAND
PACIFIC ISLANDS (German, 1899)
VENEZUELA
COLOMBIA
GOLD COAST
BRITISH EAST AFRICA
GALAPAGOS ISLANDS (Ecuador)
ECUADOR
BELGIAN CONGO
GERMAN EAST AFRICA
PORTUGUESE EAST AFRICA
DUTCH EAST INDIES
BRAZIL
PERU
ANGOLA
BOLIVIA
SOUTH ATLANTIC OCEAN
RHODESIA
MADAGASCAR
INDIAN OCEAN
GERMAN SOUTHWEST AFRICA
SOUTH PACIFIC OCEAN
PARAGUAY
AUSTRALIAN COLONIES
SOUTH AFRICAN REPUBLIC
CHILE
URUGUAY
CAPE COLONY
NATAL
N
ARGENTINA
NEW ZEALAND
The World in 1900
Imperial States and Dependencies
British
Russian
Ottoman
French
Other European
Qing

History, Memory, and Trauma

Memory was of intense interest to the twentieth century, especially the ways in which remembering and forgetting can serve specific social, cultural, and political interests. Philosophy and psychoanalysis speculated on individual experiences of time and memory, even as technology, labor management, and political ideology strove to universalize and standardize such experiences in the early twentieth century. A unified time measuring system was introduced for the entire globe; the invention of the assembly line and new models of efficiency reshaped factory work; and wireless communication tied continents together without significant time delay.

In the economic sphere, pressures toward efficiency and standardization imposed increasing temporal homogeneity and speed. Countries that consisted of many different local time zones saw themselves forced to adopt a national standard to ensure reliable railway traffic, and international communication and commerce led to the creation of global time zones and the Greenwich Mean Time (GMT) standard. The efficiency expert Frederick Taylor discovered that industrial work could be sped up and made more efficient by breaking down complex processes into simpler ones, and distributing them over different workers who would perform one and the same task over and over again. This mode of work was complemented by Henry Ford's introduction, in 1913, of the assembly line in his car factory.

But this tendency toward ever-greater speed and standardization in industry and commerce was counterbalanced in the cultural sphere by in-depth inquiries into the complexity of individual time experience. Sigmund Freud's psychoanalytical theories introduced complexity into the simple notion of remembering. Philosophers William James and Henri Bergson explored the ways in which time is experienced in individual consciousness, as opposed to the regular progression of clock time and the institutional regularities of public time. While one set of social developments tended to streamline, homogenize, objectify and speed up time, another emphasized the irreducible idiosyncrasies of memory and expectation as they are actually experienced by individuals.

Einstein's relativity theory, which deals precisely with abstract and objective time, questioned time as an absolute measure as it was known from Newtonian mechanics. Einstein's theory was often misinterpreted as a parallel to attempts in the humanities and arts to represent the "relativity" of subjective time, even though Einstein was revising the laws of physics, not of psychology. Conversely, some artists and writers drew their inspiration not from psychological insights, but precisely from the hard mechanics of new technologies. The Italian Futurists, for example, exulted in speed and simultaneity, which became their inspiration for inventing innovative types of poetry and performance. Similarly, Dadaist and Surrealist artists were fascinated with the technological possibilities of photography and film, which for them became new ways of exploring the workings of memory and vision. The modernist period, then, opened up a variety of ways of thinking about time and memory, which different thinkers and artists appropriated in diverse ways.

If it was common for avant-gardists of all stripes to call for a complete break with the past, cataclysmic political events made violent rupture a reality in the historical arena. To many contemporaries, World War I appeared as the end of an era: the slaughter of millions, carried out by means of innovative technologies that superseded face-to-face confrontation, seemed to signal the end of a nineteenth-century vision of "civilized" human society. Many of the violent political upheavals of the time echoed the rhetorical proclamations of a historical ground zero: the Mexican Revolution, the Russian Revolution, and the rising fascist movements of Italy, Germany, and Japan, in their own ways, all aimed to wipe clean the slate of historical time and start the future anew. That such complete historical breaks were impossible in practice soon became obvious to those who lived under the new regimes, though the political structures often persisted long after the utopian impulse had vanished.

After World War II, as the rhetoric of historical rupture shifted to those nations that aimed to break away from colonial rule, literature became an important means of working through the history of colonialism and recuperating indigenous myths and memories. In the industrialized world, in the meantime, enormous technological innovations generated new waves of accelerated socioeconomic cycles that spread commercial models into art, information technologies, and scientific knowledge. Since commercialism in combination with new media such as television and the computer seemed to direct people's thinking mostly toward the present, some observers worried that historical thinking might become impossible in the nanosecond culture of the late twentieth century.

History, however, never ceased to be a central cultural concern, as communities and nations around the globe sought to come to terms with legacies of violence, oppression, and discrimination, and they attempted to develop forms of historical discourse that would incorporate a plurality of voices. In Western Europe and the United States, the Holocaust became the main paradigm in debates over how to write and rewrite history, especially as eyewitness testimony progressively succumbed to time's passage. In Spain and Latin America, memories of brutal dictatorial regimes, censorship, death squads, torture, and "disappeared" prisoners came into focus. In Eastern Europe and across the former Soviet Union, the collapse of communist and socialist governments raised a myraid of questions on how to deal with a historical legacy whose relevance to the present was suddenly uncertain. Questions of collaboration and resistance, of historical continuity and rupture emerged in this context in very different guises than in the West.

In countries such as Australia founded as settler colonies, violent controversies erupted over the history of white dominance and discrimination against aboriginals. Histories of racial oppression also occupied center stage in the United States. The South African Truth and Reconciliation Commission, a forum for working through the atrocities committed under white apartheid rule, was one of the most visible manifestations of similar concerns in much of what was formerly called the "Third World." In all of these struggles over what and how to remember historically, literary texts played a crucial role in articulating the perspective of those whose viewpoint had long been ignored, and for preserving the memories of communities that no longer exist.

In such contexts, the psychological notion of "trauma" has helped communities cope with the memory of painful and violent events. Literary texts, with their dual ability to make remote events come close to the reader and yet to preserve a sense of distance through their fictionalization, proved to be one way in which such traumatic histories could be worked through. But recent literature that focuses on the recuperation of history by no means always aims at its darker sides. Quite often, its purpose is simply to draw the readers' attention to individuals and communities

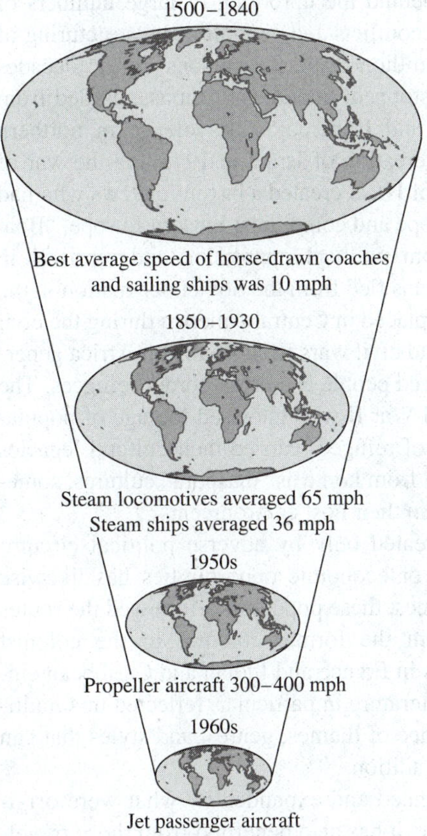

Global shrinkage: the effect of changing transport technologies on "real" distance.

that never occupied center stage in world history, but that nevertheless deserve to be remembered as part of a much more abundantly varied cultural legacy than textbook versions of history can convey. In the midst of what some call the "information glut" of the late twentieth and early twenty-first centuries, literature has remained a vital medium for embodying the memories, both individual and collective, that make for a rich and long-range sense of history, even in an era sometimes called posthistorical.

Cultures in Motion: Migration, Travel, and Displacement

In 1990, the anthropologist James Clifford called on ethnographers to shift their focus of study from traditional villages, conceived of as self-contained spatial and cultural entities, to the ways in which cultures traverse space. It was an apt moment for such a call, at the end of a century of unprecedented population movements around the planet. From millions of people displaced by war or political oppression and migrant workers in search of a livelihood to the millions of leisure travelers who seasonally moved between countries and continents, the 1900s were a century on the move.

Political upheaval was a major force behind the uprooting of large numbers of people throughout the century. The military conflicts and geopolitical restructuring of Europe in World War II created nearly a million displaced persons. In the decades since then, the flood of refugees has never stopped: hundreds of thousands fled from communist oppression in Eastern Europe and from colonial violence in northern Africa. Palestinians were dislocated by the creation of Israel in 1948 and the war of 1967, even as the establishment of the state of Israel created a haven for Jews who had been persecuted both in fascist Western Europe and communist Eastern Europe. "Boat people" took to the oceans to escape from political oppression and reprisals in Vietnam, Cuba, and Haiti. Millions of Afghans fled from the Soviet occupation in the 1980s, and over two million people were displaced in Central America during the civil wars of the same decade. Ethnic conflicts and civil wars in sub-Saharan Africa generated an unending stream of internally displaced people and cross-border refugees. The 1990s brought eerie reminiscences of World War II with televised footage of populations on the run in Kosovo. These millions of refugees carried their cultural legacies with them and often recreated them far away from home as "diaspora" cultures, sometimes triggering significant cultural changes in their host environments.

But such diaspora cultures weren't created only by adverse political circumstances. The search for better educational or economic opportunities has likewise taken populations around the globe. Sometimes, these populations followed the routes established by colonialism, migrating from the former colonies to the colonist metropolis, as in the case of Arab minorities in France and Indian and Caribbean emigrants to Britain. The arts in general, and literature in particular, reflected this multiplication of cultural identities in an abundance of themes, genres, and styles that can no longer be attributed to a single national tradition.

But if literature has been greatly enhanced and expanded by what were originally circumstances of dire human necessity, it has also benefited from those travelers who opted to seek different cultural settings. Throughout the twentieth century, artists and writers traveled in unprecedented numbers—sometimes temporarily, sometimes permanently—to places that they thought would better suit their imaginations. American poets and novelists traveled to London and Paris in the 1910s and 1920s, drawn by burgeoning avant-garde movements. In the 1950s and 1960s, they journeyed to India and Japan in search of innovative and perhaps more authentic forms of spiritual inspiration and literary expression. Latin American writers from the 1930s to the 1960s were drawn to Paris, by choice or by political necessity, bridging European literary aesthetics with those of their home countries. Such migrations increased as international communication and transportation became more easily accessible in the second half of the century, and cultural identities became likewise more dispersed. At the same time, a burgeoning global literary market has made international literature more available even to readers and writers who are not willing or able to engage in long-distance travel. James Joyce's *Ulysses*—judged obscene in Ireland and England—was first published in Paris, and the Latin American "boom" novels of the 1960s and 1970s were mostly published in Spain and avidly read by both European and Latin American audiences. Today, Hindi film romances are wildly successful across the Arab world, Brazilian soap operas are viewed by millions in Europe, and the novels of a writer like Salman Rushdie are read around the world.

The heady excitement of global culture traffic, though, should not obscure the fact that many writers' work remains hampered by the difficulties of translation into book markets that are mostly economically driven. When Chinese novelist and playwright Gao Xinjiang was awarded the Nobel Prize in literature in 2000, booksellers in Europe and the United States went scrambling in search of translations to offer their readers, since his work had not been given much attention by the international book market. By the same token, the celebration of cosmopolitan writers who live in one place, publish their work in another, and are read in several dozen countries should not let us forget that for many writers throughout the twentieth century international migration was a sad necessity rather than a choice. Writers in exile have left their mark on the course of literary history, and exile remained no less a reality for twentieth-century writers.

Science, Technology, and Progress

Few forces have transformed societies around the globe as much as science and technology in the twentieth century. For many, the increasing dependence on science and technology is intimately associated with the notion of progress in material, social, and intellectual terms, just as it was at the beginnings of the Industrial Revolution and throughout much of the nineteenth century. But while the twentieth century gave rise to an unprecedented number of scientific insights and technological innovations, science and technology also came to be questioned with a new intensity, both in terms of their intrinsic nature and in terms of their effects on human societies. This uneasy dependence on science and technology has significant consequences for many dimensions of cultural life, and particularly for literature. In the new millennium, literary creativity is redefining itself both in relation to new media that don't rely on printed text, and in relation to techno-scientific kinds of knowledge and imagination that were conventionally considered the antithesis of literary invention.

Science and technology themselves were transformed by numerous changes in theory and practice over the course of the twentieth century. For the cultural imagination, three changes have held particular significance: the shift in public scientific interest from physics in the early twentieth century to biology, the emergence of new media of communication, and the fusion of information and communication technology that took place during the "digital revolution" in the last quarter of the century. Developments in physical theory between the turn of the century and World War II profoundly changed not only the discipline itself, but exerted an almost magical attraction for the educated public as well as for artists and writers. The public imagination was engaged by concepts such as "relativity theory," "quantum mechanics," or the "uncertainty principle," even though their exact meaning and mathematical bases were often poorly understood. Such concepts led people to wonder what it might mean to live in a world ruled not by certain "laws of nature" but by statistical probabilities, where time and space were no longer the self-evident and self-identical foundations of experience that they had appeared to be.

Physics continued to hold public interest in the aftermath of World War II, as the invention of the atomic bomb and the civilian production of nuclear energy demonstrated its enormous power. But its unprecedented destructiveness in the attacks on Hiroshima and Nagasaki, as well as the long-term dangers associated with nuclear power plants, also aroused skepticism as to the desirability of such "progress," and led to public opposition that reached its peak in the student unrest of the 1960s. In the meantime, however, biology began to attract public attention with the widely publicized discovery of DNA in the 1950s, which promised a completely new understanding of life and reproduction. By the 1990s, public concerns had begun to focus on genetically modified foods and the implications of genetic cloning in some species, including humans. If radioactivity had long become associated with gothic images of deformed or oversized bodies, such images now shifted to the realm of biotechnology. The possibility of artificially created humans in particular called up echoes of literary and cultural motifs with deep roots in history, from Ovid's Pygmalion and the Jewish legend of the Golem to Mary Shelley's *Frankenstein* and the androids, replicants, and cyborgs of much twentieth-century science fiction. As so often in the history of technology, important innovations were accompanied by utopian hopes as well as fears of disaster that represent the latest technologies through age-old cultural templates.

Along with fundamental changes in scientific theory, a whole array of technological inventions transformed twentieth-century societies, from the mass production of automobiles to the invention of plastics, the vacuum tube, and the contraceptive pill. But it was the emergence of new media that proved particularly momentous for the cultural imagination in general and literary production in particular. The invention of the telephone, radio, film, television, the long-playing record, and finally the computer and the World Wide Web all contributed to change the ways in which we imagine space and time. Along with new transportation technologies, the media contributed to shortening distances across the globe and to speeding up the pace at which goods and services could be exchanged. Each new medium also subtly altered the ways in which already existing media functioned. If families in the 1930s would gather around the radio, they would assemble in front of the TV in the 1970s and may now disperse to use an ever-increasing variety of electronic devices conveying stories, images, and games of many sorts. But older media are for the most part not extinguished by the arrival of new ones. In fact, more literary texts are produced and distributed at the turn of the third millennium than ever before. Nevertheless, the social role of literature has changed, since in many literate societies it no longer stands alone as the crucial conveyor of cultural and human values.

New media also open up new possibilities for literary creation broadly understood, as the digital revolution in particular has demonstrated. The invention of computers—especially of the personal computer—and the rise of the Internet have become the latest icons of techno-scientific progress. These have given rise to utopian hopes for a better connected, better informed, more democratic, and more tolerant world society, not unlike the hopes expressed when the radio was invented. While concerns about privacy, surveillance, and commercialism have somewhat dampened the excitement that accompanied the burgeoning of computer culture in the late 1980s and early 1990s, the computer continues to attract those who think of technological innovation as a means for improved human futures. More subtly, the personal computer and the Internet seem to put in question the very meaning of the word "technology" as it was understood in the modern age, when it was mostly associated in the popular imagination with machines and heavy industry. Computers, which increase in power and connectivity even as they shrink in size and communicate by more and more invisible means, seem to defy conventional notions of the "machine," and appear better described by the metaphor of a new "environment." This new medium with its ability to merge text, image, sound, and touch is already beginning to reshape possibilities for story-telling, lyrical expression, and theatrical performance.

At the same time, starting in the 1960s, skepticism toward technology acquired even deeper resonance with the increasingly wide-spread perception that science and technology were contributing to the rapid despoliation of the natural environment. The environmental movement pointed out that technology-based lifestyles were increasingly leading to the destruction of habitats; the extinction of species, the pollution of air, water, and soil; and the rapid consumption of nonrenewable resources. In the former Communist bloc, such perceptions were compounded by the realization that even regimes that explicitly claimed to be acting on behalf of the common people wreaked havoc on nature. In the so-called Third World, environmentalist concerns form an explosive mix with resistance to the economic domination of Western chemical, pharmaceutical, and energy corporations. In all of these contexts, the notion that science and technology are associated with progress in any but the most superficial and material sense has come under intense scrutiny. While such views hardly constitute a majority view in any society, they have given rise to a generalized cultural unease and an ambivalence toward unchecked techno-scientific progress.

In the Romantic period, literature played an important part in formulating concerns over the Enlightenment emphasis on the rational faculties of humans, and over the ways in which science and technology were affecting human minds, bodies, and communities. To this day, literature has often been defined as the medium that best embodies the intuitive and affective faculties that science and technology seem to leave out of consideration. Yet the encounter between literature, science, and technology is a good deal more complicated today than it was at the turn of the nineteenth century. Much of "world literature" did not evolve out of the Western Romantic tradition and defines its relation to techno-scientific modernization quite differently. Even within the Western tradition, resistance to technological dehumanization competes with literary enthusiasm for technology. Literature is in the process redefining itself in an altered media landscape that sometimes limits the reach of literary expression and sometimes opens up new venues for it. Science, technology, media, and our ambivalence toward them make up part of the force field that shapes literary creation in the third millennium.

The Twentieth Century

Year	The World	Literature
1890		**1899, 1902** Joseph Conrad, *Heart of Darkness*
1900	**1900** Boxer Rebellion: nationalist forces rebel in China; suppressed by an international force	
	1901 Queen Victoria dies. Edward VII becomes king (to 1910)	**1901** Tomas Mann, *Buddenbrooks*
	1904 Belgian commission investigates atrocities in Congo	**1904** Alfred Jarry, *Ubu the King*
	1904–1905 Russo-Japanese War over rivalry in Korea and Manchuria, won by Japan	
	1906 Persian Shah Nasir ud-Din grants constitution	**1907** August Strindberg, *Ghost Sonata*
		1907 Premchand publishes first volume of stories, banned by the British as subversive
	1908–1913 Kamal Ataturk leads revolution establishing modernizing government in Turkey	**1909** F. I. Marinetti, *Futurist Manifesto*
1910	**1911–1912** Manchu dynasty overthrown in China; Sun Yat-sen elected president of Republic of China	**1911–1923** Rainer Maria Rilke, *Duino Elegies*
	1913 War in Balkans over Serbian claims to Macedonia	**1913** Rabindranath Tagore awarded Nobel Prize in Literature
		1913–1927 Marcel Proust, *A la recherche du temps perdu*
	1914–1918 World War I	**1914** James Joyce, *Dubliners*
		1915 Rupert Brooke, *1914 and Other Poems*
		1915 Virginia Woolf, *The Voyage Out*
		1916 Franz Kafka, *The Metamorphosis*
	1917–1922 Russian Revolution leads to establishment of Soviet Union	**1916** W. B. Yeats, *Easter 1916* and other poems on the Irish Rebellion
		1918 Lu Xun, "A Madman's Diary"
		1918 Tristan Tzara, *Dada Manifesto*
	1919 League of Nations formed	**1919–1931** Vicente Huidobro, *Altazor*
	1919 Mahatma Gandhi begins campaign of nonviolent resistance against British rule in India	
	1919–1922 Irish rebellion leads to formation of independent Republic of Ireland, with Northern Ireland remaining British	
1920	**1922** Fascist leader Benito Mussolini becomes Italian prime minister	**1922** César Vallejo, *Trilce*
		1922 James Joyce, *Ulysses*
	1922 Egypt achieves independence from Britain	**1922** T. S. Eliot, *The Waste Land*
		1922 Osip Mandelstam, *Tristia*
	1924 Vladimir Lenin dies; Joseph Stalin becomes Soviet leader	**1924** André Breton, *First Surrealist Manifesto*
		1925 Virginia Woolf, *Mrs Dalloway*
	1927 Charles Lindbergh completes first solo flight across the Atlantic	**1928** Mário de Andrade, *Macunaíma: The Hero Without Any Character*
	1929–mid-1930s Wall Street stock market crashes; worldwide depression follows	**1929** William Faulkner, *The Sound and the Fury*
	1929 First airplane flight over South Pole	

YEAR	THE WORLD	LITERATURE
1930		
	1933 Adolf Hitler becomes chancellor of Germany; Nazi party wins elections	
	1935–1949 Mao Zedong's Communist Party gains ascendancy in China	
	1936–1939 Spanish Civil War, won by fascist General Francisco Franco against the constitutional government	**1938** Jean-Paul Sartre, *Nausea*
		1939–1941 Bertolt Brecht, *Mother Courage and Her Children*
	1936 Italy takes over Ethiopia	**1939, 1954** Aimé Césaire, *Notebook of a Return to the Native Land*
	1939–1945 World War II	
1940		
	1940 Germany, Japan, and Italy form Axis alliance	**1940** Richard Wright, *Native Son*
		1940 Federico García Lorca, *Poet in New York*
		1942 Albert Camus, *The Stranger*
		1943 T. S. Eliot, *Four Quartets*
	1945 United States drops atomic bombs on Hiroshima and Nagasaki	**1944** Jorge Luis Borges, *Fictions*
	1945 United Nations established	
	1947 India achieves independence from England; Pakistan splits off as separate country	**1947** Thomas Mann, *Doktor Faustus*
	1947–1948 Partition of Palestine, creating State of Israel	**1948** Léopold Sédar Senghor, *Anthologie de la nouvelle poésie nègre et malgache*
	1948–1949 Soviets blockade West Berlin. U.S. and Western European nations form NATO to oppose Soviet expansion	**1948** T. S. Eliot awarded Nobel Prize in literature
	1949 Apartheid established as South African government policy	**1949** George Orwell, *1984*
		1949 Bertolt Brecht founds Berliner Ensemble in East Berlin
1950		
	1950–1953 Korean War, resulting in standoff between North and South Korea	
	1951 Chemist Carl Djerassi invents the birth control pill	**1952, 1957** Samuel Beckett, *Waiting for Godot* and *Endgame*
	1953 Stalin dies	
	1953 Watson and Crick discover DNA	
	1954–1962 Algerian War of Independence from France	**1955** Vladimir Nabokov, *Lolita*
		1955 Juan Rulfo, *Pedro Páramo*
	1956 Suez Crisis; Egypt defeats French and English efforts to maintain control of Suez Canal	**1956–1957** Naguib Mahfouz, *Cairo Trilogy*
	1956 Hungary's attempt to withdraw from the Warsaw Pact is ended through Soviet military intervention	
	1957 European Economic Community founded, creates the beginnings of a common market in Western Europe	**1957** Boris Pasternak, *Doctor Zhivago*
		1958 Primo Levi, *Survival in Auschwitz*
		1958 Chinua Achebe, *Things Fall Apart*
	1959 Fidel Castro overthrows Fulgencio Batista and ascends to power in Cuba	**1959** Günter Grass, *The Tin Drum*
1960		
	1960 Seventeen African colonies achieve independence from Europe	**1960** Clarice Lispector, *Family Ties*
	1960 Senghor becomes president of Senegal (through 1980)	
	1961 Russian Yuri Gagarin becomes first astronaut in space	**1961** Joseph Heller, *Catch-22*
		1961 V. S. Naipaul, *A House for Mr. Biswas*
	1961 Berlin Wall built, dividing East and West Berlin	

YEAR	THE WORLD	LITERATURE
	1962 Cuban missile crisis leads to the brink of nuclear confrontation between the United States and USSR	**1962** Derek Walcott, *In a Green Night*
	1962 Publication of Rachel Carson's *Silent Spring;* beginnings of the environmentalist movement	
	1963 U.S. President John F. Kennedy is assassinated	**1963** Anna Akhmatova, *Requiem*
		1963 Alain Robbe-Grillet, *Towards a New Novel*
	1965–1975 Vietnam War, won by Soviet-supported North against U.S.-supported South	**1963** Julio Cortázar, *Hopscotch*
	1967 Six-day War between Israel and Arab neighbors	**1967** Gabriel García Márquez, *A Hundred Years of Solitude*
	1968 Martin Luther King Jr. and Robert Kennedy are assassinated	
	1968 Soviet Union crushes the "Prague Spring" reformist movement	
	1968 Leftist student revolts in Paris, Berlin, and Mexico City; Tet offensive in Vietnam	
	1969 Civil unrest in Ireland leads to the intervention of British troops	**1969** Samuel Beckett awarded Nobel Prize in literature
	1969 American astronauts land on the moon	
1970		
		1972 Italo Calvino, *Invisible Cities*
	1973 Socialist government of Chilean president Salvador Allende overthrown through military coup backed by U.S.	**1973** Thomas Pynchon, *Gravity's Rainbow*
	1974 Personal computers begin to be marketed	**1974** Emile Habiby, *The Secret Life of Saeed the Pessoptimist*
	1974–1990 Military dictatorship of Augusto Pinochet in Chile	
	1975 General Franco dies; constitutional monarchy established in Spain	**1975** Wole Soyinka, *Death and the King's Horseman*
	1976 Mao Zedong dies in China	
	1978 The first "test-tube baby," Louise Brown, born in Britain	
	1979 Nicaraguan dictator Anastasio Somoza Debayle overthrown by Sandinistas	**1979** Nadine Gordimer, *Burger's Daughter*
		1979 Mariama Bâ, *So Long a Letter*
	1979 Shah of Iran deposed	
1980		
		1980 Mahasweta Devi, *Breast-Giver*
		1981 Salman Rushdie, *Midnight's Children*
		1981 Leslie Marmon Silko, *The Storyteller*
	1984 Bishop Desmond Tutu of South Africa awarded Nobel Peace Prize	**1982** Isabel Allende, *The House of the Spirits*
	1986 Philippine dictator Ferdinand Marcos overthrown	**1986** Ngugi wa Thiong'o, *Decolonizing the Mind*
	1989 Iran's Ayatollah Khomenei issues a decree of death against Salman Rushdie for *Satanic Verses*	**1988** Toni Morrison, *Beloved*
	1989 Eastern European nations begin to break free from Soviet bloc	
	1989 Fall of Berlin Wall; pro-democracy demonstration in Tiananmen Square, Beijing, ends in students' deaths	

YEAR	THE WORLD	LITERATURE
1990		
	1990 East Germany and West Germany reunified	**1990** Derek Walcott, *Omeros*
	1990 Iraq invades Kuwait, is repelled by U.S.-led coalition	
	1991 Breakup of Soviet Union	**1991** Nadine Gordimer awarded Nobel Prize in literature
	1992 Earth Summit convened in Rio de Janeiro to discuss global environment	**1992** Derek Walcott awarded Nobel Prize in literature
	1992 Signing of Maastricht Treaty creates European Union	
	1993 World Wide Web becomes accessible to broad public	
	1994 Civil War in Rwanda between Hutu and Tutsi; a half-million casualties	**1994** Salman Rushdie, *East, West*
	1994 Nelson Mandela elected first black president of South Africa	**1995** José Saramago, *Blindness*
	1996 Cloning of the sheep Dolly	
	1997 British rule ends in Hong Kong, which becomes part of China	
	1999 Adoption of the Euro as common currency by the European Union	**1999** Carlos Fuentes, *The Years with Laura Díaz*
2000		
		2000 Nobel Prize in literature awarded to Gao Xingjian, first Chinese recipient

Joseph Conrad

1857–1924

One of the greatest English-language novelists, Joseph Conrad didn't seriously begin to learn English until the age of twenty-one. He was already embarked on decades of world travel that would shape his fiction once he finally decided, in 1894, to become a full-time writer. By then, he had long lived in exile from his native Poland—a country no longer even present on the map at that time, carved up between Russia and the Austro-Hungarian empire. Born Josef Teodor Konrad Korzeniowski, he was the son of a noble-born Polish poet and patriot, Apollo, whose ardent nationalism led to his arrest by the Russian government in 1861. The four-year-old Josef and his mother Eva followed Apollo into exile in a bleak village in northern Russia. Ill with tuberculosis, Eva died there in 1865; Apollo also became ill, and was allowed to return to Cracow, wherehe died in 1869 when Josef was twelve. Josef was raised thereafter by his cultured, cosmopolitan uncle Tadeusz Bobrowski, but he was bored and restless in school in Cracow, and so his uncle eventually sent him to Switzerland with a private tutor. Before long, the tutor had resigned, and instead of returning to Cracow, the sixteen-year-old Josef slipped away to Marseilles and joined the French merchant navy.

He spent the following twenty years as a sailor and eventually as a merchant ship captain, working first for the French merchant marine and then for British companies. His ships took him around the world, to the eastern Mediterranean, Indonesia, China, Thailand, the Philippines, South America, the West Indies, and Africa, giving him the opportunity to see first-hand the unsettling effects of the rising tide of European imperial expansion. At one point he supplemented his observations with active involvement in political conflict: In 1878 he and several friends bought a ship to smuggle guns into Spain on behalf of a claimant to the throne. This effort collapsed, and Conrad was wounded not long after, either in a duel (as he claimed) or else (as his uncle believed) in a suicide attempt. Heavily in debt, he left France and switched into the British merchant marine, where he served for the next sixteen years.

Based in London in 1889 for several months between ships, he began to write *Almayer's Folly,* a novel closely based on some of his South Seas experiences, but in 1890 he interrupted this project to fulfill a childhood dream of sailing up the Congo River. Using an aunt's influence, he went to Brussels and gained an appointment to pilot an aging steamboat upriver—the basis for his most famous novella, *Heart of Darkness* (serialized in 1899, published in book form in 1902). The Congo at the time was controlled by a private corporation set up by King Leopold II of Belgium for personal profit. The king's company was being promoted as a perfect marriage of the noble work of civilization and the profits of free enterprise, a perspective advanced by the explorer-journalist Henry Morton Stanley in the Resonance below (page 2502). There, Stanley appeals to the businessmen of Manchester to support Leopold's unfettered control over the Congo, stressing both the higher goals of civilization and also the direct profits to be made by selling wedding dresses and burial clothes to the native inhabitants.

A diary Conrad kept during his journey (excerpted in the Resonance below, page 2500) shows his experience of a much grimmer reality. His work included transporting a sick agent of the Belgian Company downriver; his charge, Georges Klein, died en route. Conrad's encounter with Klein ("Little," in German) provided the germ of the plot of his novella, whose protagonist Marlow journeys upriver to encounter the mysterious, threatening, eloquent company agent Mister Kurtz. Conrad returned to England after four months in the Congo, beset with fever and with a deepening tragic sense of the imperial enterprise and of life overall.

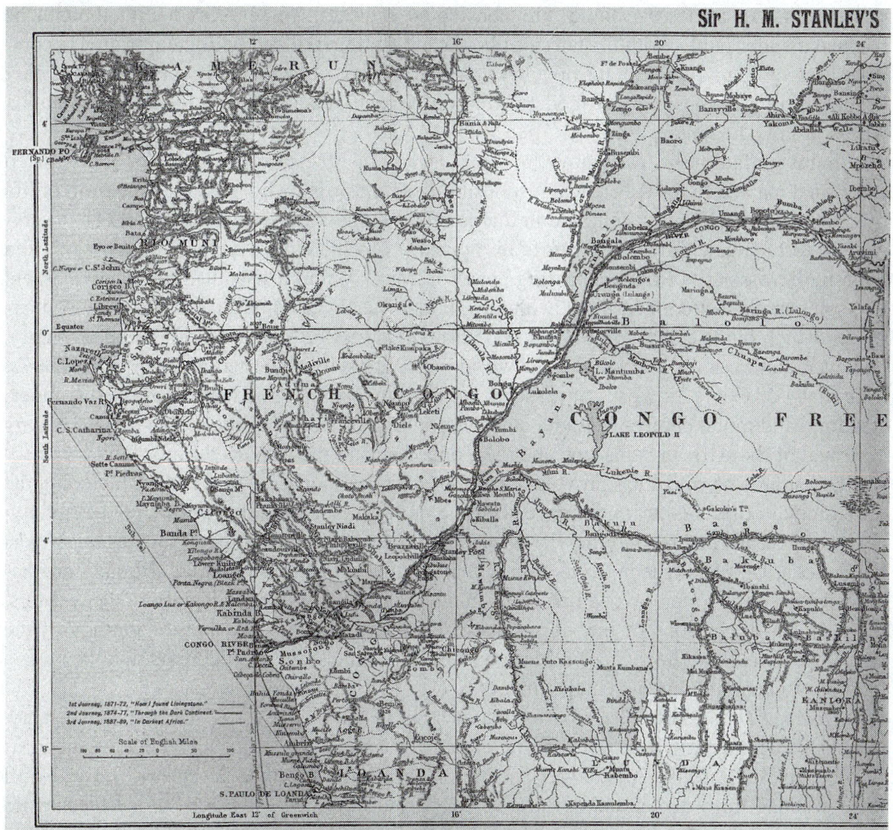

Sir H. M. Stanley's Three African Journeys, c. 1895; detail. When Conrad's Marlow dreamed of voyaging "into the yellow" of the empty spaces on African maps (page 2450), he would have been looking at a map like this one. The Congo Free State is shown in yellow on the map, with red, green and blue lines tracing Stanley's travels in the 1870s and 1880s across east and central Africa and up and down the Congo River, as he explored the borders of King Leopold's African domain.

"Before the Congo," he later wrote, "I was a mere animal." He became active in the efforts led by the Irish diplomat Roger Casement to expose the cruelty of imperial practices in the Congo, and in his fiction he explored the fatal slippage of idealism into corruption, in language and practice alike.

In 1894 Conrad's life changed in decisive ways. His uncle Bobrowski died, and Conrad decided to settle permanently in England; he Anglicized his name as "Joseph Conrad," and later married an Englishwoman, Jessie George. He also took a temporary break, which proved to be permanent, from sailing, and completed *Almayer's Folly,* which soon found a publisher. Determined to make a living as a writer, he began a second novel while the first was still in press, and was soon able to establish friendships with some of England's leading writers, including such figures as Bernard Shaw and H. G. Wells. His English friends regarded him with some bemusement as a master of English prose and yet an exotic foreigner; Wells described Conrad driving a carriage rapidly along a country lane, urging his horses on with imperious commands in Polish. General readers were slow to recognize the excellence of his fiction, and such major early works as *Lord Jim, Nostromo,* and *The Secret Agent* sold poorly. As late as 1910 Conrad still considered returning to sea. Gradually, though, he reached a wider public with his tales of the sea and of imperial and political intrigue, becoming a best-selling writer with his novels *Chance* (1910) and *Victory* (1915). World War I only deepened his pessimism about modern life, but he continued to pursue his artistic vocation with undiminished intensity.

In his preface to his early novella *The Nigger of the "Narcissus"* (1897), Conrad issued a personal manifesto for the critical responsibility of the artist, who must seek the truth of life by descending "within himself, and in that lonely region of stress and strife, if he be deserving and fortunate, he finds the terms of his appeal . . . to snatch in a moment of courage, from the remorseless rush of time, a passing phase of life." Conrad insists that this lonely descent into self is not a matter of aesthetic withdrawal but instead should be the basis for "the solidarity . . . which binds men to each other and all mankind to the visible world." That solidarity, however, and even the visibility of the world itself, are severely tested in *Heart of Darkness.* Like many of Conrad's works, it presents a world of shifting uncertainties of vision, understanding, and moral choice. From its multiple framing of stories inside stories to its uncanny portrayal of the African landscape and the Congolese and the displaced Europeans who people it, Conrad's narrative has provoked widely varying responses. Many critics, including the postcolonial critic Edward Said, have seen the novella as a pivotal exposure of the hollowness of imperial rhetoric and the viciousness of imperial practice; others, such as the Nigerian novelist Chinua Achebe, have argued that Conrad's heartfelt imperial critique nonetheless coexists with a stereotyped presentation of African racial primitivism. For other readers, the political dimensions of the story take a secondary place to the interior journey of the story's principal narrator, Charlie Marlow, for whom the African landscape may become a kind of projection of his own hallucinatory loss of psychic moorings.

Heart of Darkness has been one of the most influential narratives of the twentieth century. Chinua Achebe's own great novel *Things Fall Apart* (page 2694) is in part a response to Conrad, as Achebe gives a directly African perspective on the European imperial presence. The Nobel Prize–winning travel writer and novelist V. S. Naipaul has often expressed his indebtedness to Conrad's writing. A notable reuse of Conrad's novella can be found in Francis Ford Coppola's 1979 film *Apocalypse Now,* which cast Marlon Brando in the role of Kurtz and set the story in the midst of the Vietnam War. The novella's haunting blend of stark realities and multiplying uncertainties continues to unsettle and captivate readers today. As Marlow tells his tale to a group of friends aboard a pleasure yacht in the Thames River, his Congo—or King Leopold's Congo—oscillates between an image of all that is uncivilized, or the secret essence of civilization itself.

Heart of Darkness

1

The *Nellie,* a cruising yawl,[1] swung to her anchor without a flutter of the sails, and was at rest. The flood had made, the wind was nearly calm, and being bound down the river, the only thing for it was to come to and wait for the turn of the tide.

The sea-reach of the Thames stretched before us like the beginning of an interminable waterway. In the offing the sea and the sky were welded together without a joint, and in the luminous space the tanned sails of the barges drifting up with the tide seemed to stand still in red clusters of canvas sharply peaked, with gleams of varnished sprits. A haze rested on the low shores that ran out to sea in vanishing flatness. The air was dark above Gravesend, and farther back still seemed condensed into a mournful gloom, brooding motionless over the biggest, and the greatest, town on earth.[2]

1. A two-masted ship.

2. London. Gravesend is the last major town on the Thames estuary, from which the river joins the North Sea.

The Director of Companies was our captain and our host. We four affectionately watched his back as he stood in the bows looking to seaward. On the whole river there was nothing that looked half so nautical. He resembled a pilot, which to a seaman is trustworthiness personified. It was difficult to realise his work was not out there in the luminous estuary, but behind him, within the brooding gloom.

Between us there was, as I have already said somewhere, the bond of the sea. Besides holding our hearts together through long periods of separation, it had the effect of making us tolerant of each other's yarns—and even convictions. The Lawyer—the best of old fellows—had, because of his many years and many virtues, the only cushion on deck, and was lying on the only rug. The Accountant had brought out already a box of dominoes, and was toying architecturally with the bones. Marlow sat cross-legged right aft, leaning against the mizzen-mast.[3] He had sunken cheeks, a yellow complexion, a straight back, an ascetic aspect, and, with his arms dropped, the palms of hands outwards, resembled an idol. The Director, satisfied the anchor had good hold, made his way aft and sat down amongst us. We exchanged a few words lazily. Afterwards there was silence on board the yacht. For some reason or other we did not begin that game of dominoes. We felt meditative, and fit for nothing but placid staring. The day was ending in a serenity of still and exquisite brilliance. The water shone pacifically; the sky, without a speck, was a benign immensity of unstained light; the very mist on the Essex marshes was like a gauzy and radiant fabric, hung from the wooded rises inland, and draping the low shores in diaphanous folds. Only the gloom to the west, brooding over the upper reaches, became more sombre every minute, as if angered by the approach of the sun.

And at last, in its curved and imperceptible fall, the sun sank low, and from glowing white changed to a dull red without rays and without heat, as if about to go out suddenly, stricken to death by the touch of that gloom brooding over a crowd of men.

Forthwith a change came over the waters, and the serenity became less brilliant but more profound. The old river in its broad reach rested unruffled at the decline of day, after ages of good service done to the race that peopled its banks, spread out in the tranquil dignity of a waterway leading to the uttermost ends of the earth. We looked at the venerable stream not in the vivid flush of a short day that comes and departs for ever, but in the august light of abiding memories. And indeed nothing is easier for a man who has, as the phrase goes, "followed the sea" with reverence and affection, than to evoke the great spirit of the past upon the lower reaches of the Thames. The tidal current runs to and fro in its unceasing service, crowded with memories of men and ships it has borne to the rest of home or to the battles of the sea. It had known and served all the men of whom the nation is proud, from Sir Francis Drake to Sir John Franklin, knights all, titled and untitled—the great knights-errant of the sea.[4] It had borne all the ships whose names are like jewels flashing in the night of time, from the *Golden Hind* returning with her round flanks full of treasure, to be visited by the Queen's Highness and thus pass out of the gigantic tale, to the *Erebus* and *Terror,* bound on other conquests—and that never returned. It had known the ships and the men. They had sailed from Deptford, from Greenwich, from Erith—the adventurers and the settlers; kings' ships and the ships of men on 'Change; captains,

3. A secondary mast at the stern of the ship.

4. Sir Francis Drake (1540–1596) was captain of the *Golden Hind* in the service of Queen Elizabeth I; his reputation came from the successful raids he mounted against Spanish ships returning laden with gold from the New World (South America). In 1845 Sir John Franklin led an expedition in the *Erebus* and *Terror* in search of the Northwest Passage (to the Pacific); all perished.

admirals, the dark "interlopers" of the Eastern trade, and the commissioned "generals" of East India fleets.[5] Hunters for gold or pursuers of fame, they all had gone out on that stream, bearing the sword, and often the torch, messengers of the might within the land, bearers of a spark from the sacred fire. What greatness had not floated on the ebb of that river into the mystery of an unknown earth! . . . The dreams of men, the seed of commonwealths, the germs of empires.

The sun set; the dusk fell on the stream, and lights began to appear along the shore. The Chapman lighthouse, a three-legged thing erect on a mudflat, shone strongly. Lights of ships moved in the fairway—a great stir of lights going up and going down. And farther west on the upper reaches the place of the monstrous town was still marked ominously on the sky, a brooding gloom in sunshine, a lurid glare under the stars.

"And this also," said Marlow suddenly, "has been one of the dark places of the earth."

He was the only man of us who still "followed the sea." The worst that could be said of him was that he did not represent his class. He was a seaman, but he was a wanderer too, while most seamen lead, if one may so express it, a sedentary life. Their minds are of the stay-at-home order, and their home is always with them—the ship; and so is their country—the sea. One ship is very much like another, and the sea is always the same. In the immutability of their surroundings the foreign shores, the foreign faces, the changing immensity of life, glide past, veiled not by a sense of mystery but by a slightly disdainful ignorance; for there is nothing mysterious to a seaman unless it be the sea itself, which is the mistress of his existence and as inscrutable as Destiny. For the rest, after his hours of work, a casual stroll or a casual spree on shore suffices to unfold for him the secret of a whole continent, and generally he finds the secret not worth knowing. The yarns of seamen have a direct simplicity, the whole meaning of which lies within the shell of a cracked nut. But Marlow was not typical (if his propensity to spin yarns be excepted), and to him the meaning of an episode was not inside like a kernel but outside, enveloping the tale which brought it out only as a glow brings out a haze, in the likeness of one of these misty halos that sometimes are made visible by the spectral illumination of moonshine.

His remark did not seem at all surprising. It was just like Marlow. It was accepted in silence. No one took the trouble to grunt even; and presently he said, very slow,—

"I was thinking of very old times, when the Romans first came here, nineteen hundred years ago[6]—the other day. . . . Light came out of this river since—you say Knights? Yes; but it is like a running blaze on a plain, like a flash of lightning in the clouds. We live in the flicker—may it last as long as the old earth keeps rolling! But darkness was here yesterday. Imagine the feelings of a commander of a fine—what d'ye call 'em?—trireme in the Mediterranean, ordered suddenly to the north; run overland across the Gauls in a hurry;[7] put in charge of one of these craft the legionaries,—a wonderful lot of handy men they must have been too—used to build, apparently by the hundred, in a month or two, if we may believe what we read. Imagine him here—the very end of the world, a sea the colour of lead, a sky the colour of smoke, a kind of

5. Deptford, Greenwich, and Erith lie on the Thames between London and Gravesend; "men on 'Change" are brokers on the Stock Exchange; the East India Company, a commercial and trading concern, became *de facto* ruler of large tracts of India in the 18th and 19th centuries.

6. A Roman force under Julius Caesar landed in Britain in 55 B.C.E., but it was not until 43 C.E. that the Emperor Claudius decided to conquer the island.

7. A trireme is an ancient warship, propelled by oarsmen; the Gauls were the pre-Roman tribes who occupied present-day France; they were subdued by Julius Caesar between 58–50 B.C.E.

ship about as rigid as a concertina—and going up this river with stores, or orders, or what you like. Sandbanks, marshes, forests, savages,—precious little to eat fit for a civilised man, nothing but Thames water to drink. No Falernian wine here, no going ashore. Here and there a military camp lost in a wilderness, like a needle in a bundle of hay—cold, fog, tempests, disease, exile, and death,—death skulking in the air, in the water, in the bush. They must have been dying like flies here. Oh yes—he did it. Did it very well, too, no doubt, and without thinking much about it either, except afterwards to brag of what he had gone through in his time, perhaps. They were men enough to face the darkness. And perhaps he was cheered by keeping his eye on a chance of promotion to the fleet at Ravenna by-and-by, if he had good friends in Rome and survived the awful climate. Or think of a decent young citizen in a toga—perhaps too much dice, you know—coming out here in the train of some prefect, or tax-gatherer, or trader even, to mend his fortunes. Land in a swamp, march through the woods, and in some inland post feel the savagery, the utter savagery, had closed round him,—all that mysterious life of the wilderness that stirs in the forest, in the jungles, in the hearts of wild men. There's no initiation either into such mysteries. He has to live in the midst of the incomprehensible, which is also detestable. And it has a fascination, too, that goes to work upon him. The fascination of the abomination—you know. Imagine the growing regrets, the longing to escape, the powerless disgust, the surrender, the hate."

He paused.

"Mind," he began again, lifting one arm from the elbow, the palm of the hand outwards, so that, with his legs folded before him, he had the pose of a Buddha preaching in European clothes and without a lotus-flower—"Mind, none of us would feel exactly like this. What saves us is efficiency—the devotion to efficiency. But these chaps were not much account, really. They were no colonists; their administration was merely a squeeze, and nothing more, I suspect. They were conquerors, and for that you want only brute force—nothing to boast of, when you have it, since your strength is just an accident arising from the weakness of others. They grabbed what they could get for the sake of what was to be got. It was just robbery with violence, aggravated murder on a great scale, and men going at it blind—as is very proper for those who tackle a darkness. The conquest of the earth, which mostly means the taking it away from those who have a different complexion or slightly flatter noses than ourselves, is not a pretty thing when you look into it too much. What redeems it is the idea only. An idea at the back of it; not a sentimental pretence but an idea; and an unselfish belief in the idea—something you can set up, and bow down before, and offer a sacrifice to. . . ."

He broke off. Flames glided in the river, small green flames, red flames, white flames, pursuing, overtaking, joining, crossing each other—then separating slowly or hastily. The traffic of the great city went on in the deepening night upon the sleepless river. We looked on, waiting patiently—there was nothing else to do till the end of the flood; but it was only after a long silence, when he said, in a hesitating voice, "I suppose you fellows remember I did once turn fresh-water sailor for a bit," that we knew we were fated, before the ebb began to run, to hear about one of Marlow's inconclusive experiences.

"I don't want to bother you much with what happened to me personally," he began, showing in this remark the weakness of many tellers of tales who seem so often unaware of what their audience would best like to hear; "yet to understand the effect of it on me you ought to know how I got out there, what I saw, how I went up that river to the place where I first met the poor chap. It was the farthest point of navigation and the culminating point of my experience. It seemed somehow to throw a kind of light on everything about me—and into my thoughts. It was sombre enough too—and pitiful—not extraordinary in any way—not very clear either. No, not very clear. And yet it seemed to throw a kind of light.

"I had then, as you remember, just returned to London after a lot of Indian Ocean, Pacific, China Seas—a regular dose of the East—six years or so, and I was loafing about, hindering you fellows in your work and invading your homes, just as though I had got a heavenly mission to civilise you. It was very fine for a time, but after a bit I did get tired of resting. Then I began to look for a ship—I should think the hardest work on earth. But the ships wouldn't even look at me. And I got tired of that game too.

"Now when I was a little chap I had a passion for maps. I would look for hours at South America, or Africa, or Australia, and lose myself in all the glories of exploration. At that time there were many blank spaces on the earth, and when I saw one that looked particularly inviting on a map (but they all look that) I would put my finger on it and say, When I grow up I will go there. The North Pole was one of these places, I remember. Well, I haven't been there yet, and shall not try now. The glamour's off. Other places were scattered about the Equator, and in every sort of latitude all over the two hemispheres. I have been in some of them, and . . . well, we won't talk about that. But there was one yet—the biggest, the most blank, so to speak—that I had a hankering after.

"True, by this time it was not a blank space any more. It had got filled since my boyhood with rivers and lakes and names. It had ceased to be a blank space of delightful mystery—a white patch for a boy to dream gloriously over. It had become a place of darkness. But there was in it one river especially, a mighty big river, that you could see on the map, resembling an immense snake uncoiled, with its head in the sea, its body at rest curving afar over a vast country, and its tail lost in the depths of the land. And as I looked at the map of it in a shop-window, it fascinated me as a snake would a bird—a silly little bird. Then I remembered there was a big concern, a Company for trade on that river. Dash it all! I thought to myself, they can't trade without using some kind of craft on that lot of fresh water—steamboats! Why shouldn't I try to get charge of one. I went on along Fleet Street, but could not shake off the idea. The snake had charmed me.

"You understand it was a Continental concern, that Trading Society; but I have a lot of relations living on the Continent, because it's cheap and not so nasty as it looks, they say.

"I am sorry to own I began to worry them. This was already a fresh departure for me. I was not used to get things that way, you know. I always went my own road and on my own legs where I had a mind to go. I wouldn't have believed it of myself; but, then—you see—I felt somehow I must get there by hook or by crook. So I worried them. The men said 'My dear fellow,' and did nothing. Then—would you believe it?—I tried the women. I, Charlie Marlow, set the women to work—to get a job. Heavens! Well, you see, the notion drove me. I had an aunt, a dear enthusiastic soul. She wrote: 'It will be delightful. I am ready to do anything, anything for you. It is a glorious idea. I know the wife of a very high personage in the Administration, and also a man who has lots of influence with,' &c., &c. She was determined to make no end of fuss to get me appointed skipper of a river steamboat, if such was my fancy.

"I got my appointment—of course; and I got it very quick. It appears the Company had received news that one of their captains had been killed in a scuffle with the natives. This was my chance, and it made me the more anxious to go. It was only months and months afterwards, when I made the attempt to recover what was left of the body, that I heard the original quarrel arose from a misunderstanding about some hens. Yes, two black hens. Fresleven—that was the fellow's name, a Dane—thought himself wronged somehow in the bargain, so he went ashore and started to hammer the chief of the village with a stick. Oh, it didn't surprise me in the least to hear this, and at the same time to be told that Fresleven was the gentlest, quietest creature that ever walked on two legs. No doubt he was; but he had been a couple of years already out there engaged in the noble cause, you know, and he probably felt the need at last of asserting his self-respect in some way. Therefore he whacked the old nigger mercilessly, while a big crowd of his people watched him, thunderstruck, till some man,—I was told the chief's son,—in desperation at hearing the old chap yell, made a tentative jab with a spear at the white man—and of course it went quite easy between the shoulder-blades. Then the whole population cleared into the forest, expecting all kinds of calamities to happen, while, on the other hand, the steamer Fresleven commanded left also in a bad panic, in charge of the engineer, I believe. Afterwards nobody seemed to trouble much about Fresleven's remains, till I got out and stepped into his shoes. I couldn't let it rest, though; but when an opportunity offered at last to meet my predecessor, the grass growing through his ribs was tall enough to hide his bones. They were all there. The supernatural being had not been touched after he fell. And the village was deserted, the huts gaped black, rotting, all askew within the fallen enclosures. A calamity had come to it, sure enough. The people had vanished. Mad terror had scattered them, men, women, and children, through the bush, and they had never returned. What became of the hens I don't know either. I should think the cause of progress got them, anyhow. However, through this glorious affair I got my appointment, before I had fairly begun to hope for it.

"I flew around like mad to get ready, and before forty-eight hours I was crossing the Channel to show myself to my employers, and sign the contract. In a very few hours I arrived in a city that always makes me think of a whited sepulchre.[8] Prejudice no doubt. I had no difficulty in finding the Company's offices. It was the biggest thing in the town, and everybody I met was full of it. They were going to run an over-sea empire, and make no end of coin by trade.

"A narrow and deserted street in deep shadow, high houses, innumerable windows with venetian blinds, a dead silence, grass sprouting between the stones, imposing carriage archways right and left, immense double doors standing ponderously ajar. I slipped through one of these cracks, went up a swept and ungarnished staircase, as arid as a desert, and opened the first door I came to. Two women, one fat and the other slim, sat on straw-bottomed chairs, knitting black wool. The slim one got up and walked straight at me—still knitting with downcast eyes—and only just as I began to think of getting out of her way, as you would for a somnambulist, stood still, and looked up. Her dress was as plain as an umbrella-cover, and she turned round without a word and preceded me into a waiting-room. I gave my name, and looked about. Deal table in the middle, plain chairs all round the walls, on one end a large shining map, marked with all the colours of a rainbow. There was a vast amount of red—good

8. Brussels was the headquarters of the Société Anonyme Belge pour le Commerce du Haut-Congo (Belgian Corporation for Trade in the Upper Congo), with which Conrad obtained his post through the influence of his aunt, Marguerite Poradowska.

to see at any time, because one knows that some real work is done in there, a deuce of a lot of blue, a little green, smears of orange, and, on the East Coast, a purple patch, to show where the jolly pioneers of progress drink the jolly lager-beer.[9] However, I wasn't going into any of these. I was going into the yellow. Dead in the centre. And the river was there—fascinating—deadly—like a snake. Ough! A door opened, a white-haired secretarial head, but wearing a compassionate expression, appeared, and a skinny forefinger beckoned me into the sanctuary. Its light was dim, and a heavy writing-desk squatted in the middle. From behind that structure came out an impression of pale plumpness in a frock-coat. The great man himself. He was five feet six, I should judge, and had his grip on the handle-end of ever so many millions. He shook hands, I fancy, murmured vaguely, was satisfied with my French. *Bon voyage.*

"In about forty-five seconds I found myself again in the waiting-room with the compassionate secretary, who, full of desolation and sympathy, made me sign some document. I believe I undertook amongst other things not to disclose any trade secrets. Well, I am not going to.

"I began to feel slightly uneasy. You know I am not used to such ceremonies, and there was something ominous in the atmosphere. It was just as though I had been let into some conspiracy—I don't know—something not quite right; and I was glad to get out. In the outer room the two women knitted black wool feverishly. People were arriving, and the younger one was walking back and forth introducing them. The old one sat on her chair. Her flat cloth slippers were propped up on a foot-warmer, and a cat reposed on her lap. She wore a starched white affair on her head, had a wart on one cheek, and silver-rimmed spectacles hung on the tip of her nose. She glanced at me above the glasses. The swift and indifferent placidity of that look troubled me. Two youths with foolish and cheery countenances were being piloted over, and she threw at them the same quick glance of unconcerned wisdom. She seemed to know all about them and about me too. An eerie feeling came over me. She seemed uncanny and fateful. Often far away there I thought of these two, guarding the door of Darkness, knitting black wool as for a warm pall, one introducing, introducing continuously to the unknown, the other scrutinising the cheery and foolish faces with unconcerned old eyes. *Ave!* Old knitter of black wool. *Morituri te salutant.*[1] Not many of those she looked at ever saw her again—not half, by a long way.

"There was yet a visit to the doctor. 'A simple formality,' assured me the secretary, with an air of taking an immense part in all my sorrows. Accordingly a young chap wearing his hat over the left eyebrow, some clerk I suppose,—there must have been clerks in the business, though the house was as still as a house in a city of the dead,—came from somewhere upstairs, and led me forth. He was shabby and careless, with ink-stains on the sleeves of his jacket, and his cravat was large and billowy, under a chin shaped like the toe of an old boot. It was a little too early for the doctor, so I proposed a drink, and thereupon he developed a vein of joviality. As we sat over our vermouths he glorified the Company's business, and by-and-by I expressed casually my surprise at him not going out there. He became very cool and collected all at once. 'I am not such a fool as I look, quoth Plato to his disciples,' he said sententiously, emptied his glass with great resolution, and we rose.

9. British territories were traditionally marked in red on colonial maps; lager was originally a continental beer, not much drunk in England.

1. Hail! . . . Those who are about to die salute you!—traditional cry of Roman gladiators.

"The old doctor felt my pulse, evidently thinking of something else the while. 'Good, good for there,' he mumbled, and then with a certain eagerness asked me whether I would let him measure my head. Rather surprised, I said Yes, when he produced a thing like calipers and got the dimensions back and front and every way, taking notes carefully. He was an unshaven little man in a threadbare coat like a gaberdine, with his feet in slippers, and I thought him a harmless fool. 'I always ask leave, in the interests of science, to measure the crania of those going out there,' he said. 'And when they come back too?' I asked. 'Oh, I never see them,' he remarked; 'and moreover, the changes take place inside, you know.' He smiled, as if at some quiet joke. 'So you are going out there. Famous. Interesting too.' He gave me a searching glance, and made another note. 'Ever any madness in your family?' he asked, in a matter-of-fact tone. I felt very annoyed. 'Is that question in the interests of science too?' 'It would be,' he said, without taking notice of my irritation, 'interesting for science to watch the mental changes of individuals, on the spot, but . . .' 'Are you an alienist?'[2] I interrupted. 'Every doctor should be—a little,' answered that original, imperturbably. 'I have a little theory which you Messieurs who go out there must help me to prove. This is my share in the advantages my country shall reap from the possession of such a magnificent dependency. The mere wealth I leave to others. Pardon my questions, but you are the first Englishman coming under my observation . . .' I hastened to assure him I was not in the least typical. 'If I were,' said I, 'I wouldn't be talking like this with you.' 'What you say is rather profound, and probably erroneous,' he said, with a laugh. 'Avoid irritation more than exposure to the sun. Adieu. How do you English say, eh? Good-bye. Ah! Good-bye. Adieu. In the tropics one must before everything keep calm.' . . . He lifted a warning forefinger. . . . '*Du calme, du calme. Adieu.*'

"One thing more remained to do—say good-bye to my excellent aunt. I found her triumphant. I had a cup of tea—the last decent cup of tea for many days—and in a room that most soothingly looked just as you would expect a lady's drawing-room to look, we had a long quiet chat by the fireside. In the course of these confidences it became quite plain to me I had been represented to the wife of the high dignitary, and goodness knows to how many more people besides, as an exceptional and gifted creature—a piece of good fortune for the Company—a man you don't get hold of every day. Good heavens! and I was going to take charge of a twopenny-half-penny river-steamboat with a penny whistle attached! It appeared, however, I was also one of the Workers, with a capital—you know. Something like an emissary of light, something like a lower sort of apostle. There had been a lot of such rot let loose in print and talk just about that time, and the excellent woman, living right in the rush of all that humbug, got carried off her feet. She talked about 'weaning those ignorant millions from their horrid ways,' till, upon my word, she made me quite uncomfortable. I ventured to hint that the Company was run for profit.

"'You forget, dear Charlie, that the labourer is worthy of his hire,'[3] she said, brightly. It's queer how out of touch with truth women are. They live in a world of their own, and there had never been anything like it, and never can be. It is too beautiful altogether, and if they were to set it up it would go to pieces before the first sunset. Some confounded fact we men have been living contentedly with ever since the day of creation would start up and knock the whole thing over.

2. A psychologist.

3. 1 Timothy 5:18.

"After this I got embraced, told to wear flannel, be sure to write often, and so on—and I left. In the street—I don't know why—a queer feeling came to me that I was an impostor. Odd thing that I, who used to clear out for any part of the world at twenty-four hours' notice, with less thought than most men give to the crossing of a street, had a moment—I won't say of hesitation, but of startled pause, before this commonplace affair. The best way I can explain it to you is by saying that, for a second or two, I felt as though, instead of going to the centre of a continent, I were about to set off for the centre of the earth.

"I left in a French steamer, and she called in every blamed port they have out there, for, as far as I could see, the sole purpose of landing soldiers and custom-house officers. I watched the coast. Watching a coast as it slips by the ship is like thinking about an enigma. There it is before you—smiling, frowning, inviting, grand, mean, insipid, or savage, and always mute with an air of whispering, Come and find out. This one was almost featureless, as if still in the making, with an aspect of monotonous grimness. The edge of a colossal jungle, so dark-green as to be almost black, fringed with white surf, ran straight, like a ruled line, far, far away along a blue sea whose glitter was blurred by a creeping mist. The sun was fierce, the land seemed to glisten and drip with steam. Here and there greyish-whitish specks showed up, clustered inside the white surf, with a flag flying above them perhaps—settlements some centuries old, and still no bigger than pin-heads on the untouched expanse of their background. We pounded along, stopped, landed soldiers; went on, landed custom-house clerks to levy toll in what looked like a Godforsaken wilderness, with a tin shed and a flag-pole lost in it; landed more soldiers—to take care of the custom-house clerks, presumably. Some, I heard, got drowned in the surf; but whether they did or not, nobody seemed particularly to care. They were just flung out there, and on we went. Every day the coast looked the same, as though we had not moved; but we passed various places—trading places—with names like Gran' Bassam, Little Popo,[4] names that seemed to belong to some sordid farce acted in front of a sinister back-cloth. The idleness of a passenger, my isolation amongst all these men with whom I had no point of contact, the oily and languid sea, the uniform sombreness of the coast, seemed to keep me away from the truth of things, within the toil of a mournful and senseless delusion. The voice of the surf heard now and then was a positive pleasure, like the speech of a brother. It was something natural, that had its reason, that had a meaning. Now and then a boat from the shore gave one a momentary contact with reality. It was paddled by black fellows. You could see from afar the white of their eye-balls glistening. They shouted, sang; their bodies streamed with perspiration; they had faces like grotesque masks—these chaps; but they had bone, muscle, a wild vitality, an intense energy of movement, that was as natural and true as the surf along their coast. They wanted no excuse for being there. They were a great comfort to look at. For a time I would feel I belonged still to a world of straightforward facts; but the feeling would not last long. Something would turn up to scare it away. Once, I remember, we came upon a man-of-war anchored off the coast. There wasn't even a shed there, and she was shelling the bush. It appears the French had one of their wars going on thereabouts. Her ensign dropped limp like a rag; the muzzles of the long eight-inch guns stuck out all over the low hull; the greasy, slimy swell swung her up lazily and let her down, swaying her thin masts. In the empty immensity of earth, sky, and water, there she was, incomprehensible, firing into a continent. Pop, would go

4. Grand Bassam and Grand Popo are the names of ports where Conrad's ship called on its way to the Congo.

one of the eight-inch guns; a small flame would dart and vanish, a little white smoke would disappear, a tiny projectile would give a feeble screech—and nothing happened. Nothing could happen. There was a touch of insanity in the proceeding, a sense of lugubrious drollery in the sight; and it was not dissipated by somebody on board assuring me earnestly there was a camp of natives—he called them enemies!—hidden out of sight somewhere.

"We gave her letters (I heard the men in that lonely ship were dying of fever at the rate of three a day) and went on. We called at some more places with farcical names, where the merry dance of death and trade goes on in a still and earthy atmosphere as of an overheated catacomb;[5] all along the formless coast bordered by dangerous surf, as if Nature herself had tried to ward off intruders; in and out of rivers, streams of death in life, whose banks were rotting into mud, whose waters, thickened into slime, invaded the contorted mangroves, that seemed to writhe at us in the extremity of an impotent despair. Nowhere did we stop long enough to get a particularised impression, but the general sense of vague and oppressive wonder grew upon me. It was like a weary pilgrimage amongst hints for nightmares.

"It was upward of thirty days before I saw the mouth of the big river. We anchored off the seat of the government. But my work would not begin till some two hundred miles farther on. So as soon as I could I made a start for a place thirty miles higher up.

"I had my passage on a little sea-going steamer. Her captain was a Swede, and knowing me for a seaman, invited me on the bridge. He was a young man, lean, fair, and morose, with lanky hair and a shuffling gait. As we left the miserable little wharf, he tossed his head contemptuously at the shore. 'Been living there?' he asked. I said, 'Yes.' 'Fine lot these government chaps—are they not?' he went on, speaking English with great precision and considerable bitterness. 'It is funny what some people will do for a few francs a month. I wonder what becomes of that kind when it goes up country?' I said to him I expected to see that soon. 'So-o-o!' he exclaimed. He shuffled athwart, keeping one eye ahead vigilantly. 'Don't be too sure,' he continued. 'The other day I took up a man who hanged himself on the road. He was a Swede, too.' 'Hanged himself! Why, in God's name?' I cried. He kept on looking out watchfully. 'Who knows? The sun too much for him, or the country perhaps.'

"At last we opened a reach. A rocky cliff appeared, mounds of turned-up earth by the shore, houses on a hill, others, with iron roofs, amongst a waste of excavations, or hanging to the declivity. A continuous noise of the rapids above hovered over this scene of inhabited devastation. A lot of people, mostly black and naked, moved about like ants. A jetty projected into the river. A blinding sunlight drowned all this at times in a sudden recrudescence of glare. 'There's your Company's station,' said the Swede, pointing to three wooden barrack-like structures on the rocky slope. 'I will send your things up. Four boxes did you say? So. Farewell.'

"I came upon a boiler wallowing in the grass, then found a path leading up the hill. It turned aside for the boulders, and also for an undersized railway-truck lying there on its back with its wheels in the air. One was off. The thing looked as dead as the carcass of some animal. I came upon more pieces of decaying machinery, a stack

5. In a letter in May 1890 Conrad wrote: "What makes me rather uneasy is the information that 60 per cent. of our Company's employés return to Europe before they have completed even six months' service. Fever and dysentery! There are others who are sent home in a hurry at the end of a year, so that they shouldn't die in the Congo." According to a 1907 report, 150 out of every 2,000 native Congolese laborers died each month while in company employ; "All along the [railroad] track one would see corpses."

of rusty rails. To the left a clump of trees made a shady spot, where dark things seemed to stir feebly. I blinked, the path was steep. A horn tooted to the right, and I saw the black people run. A heavy and dull detonation shook the ground, a puff of smoke came out of the cliff, and that was all. No change appeared on the face of the rock. They were building a railway. The cliff was not in the way or anything; but this objectless blasting was all the work going on.

"A slight clinking behind me made me turn my head. Six black men advanced in a file, toiling up the path. They walked erect and slow, balancing small baskets full of earth on their heads, and the clink kept time with their footsteps. Black rags were wound round their loins, and the short ends behind wagged to and fro like tails. I could see every rib, the joints of their limbs were like knots in a rope; each had an iron collar on his neck, and all were connected together with a chain whose bights swung between them, rhythmically clinking. Another report from the cliff made me think suddenly of that ship of war I had seen firing into a continent. It was the same kind of ominous voice; but these men could by no stretch of imagination be called enemies. They were called criminals, and the outraged law, like the bursting shells, had come to them, an insoluble mystery from over the sea. All their meagre breasts panted together, the violently dilated nostrils quivered, the eyes stared stonily up-hill. They passed me within six inches, without a glance, with that complete, deathlike indifference of unhappy savages. Behind this raw matter one of the reclaimed, the product of the new forces at work, strolled despondently, carrying a rifle by its middle. He had a uniform jacket with one button off, and seeing a white man on the path, hoisted his weapon to his shoulder with alacrity. This was simple prudence, white men being so much alike at a distance that he could not tell who I might be. He was speedily reassured, and with a large, white, rascally grin, and a glance at his charge, seemed to take me into partnership in his exalted trust. After all, I also was a part of the great cause of these high and just proceedings.

"Instead of going up, I turned and descended to the left. My idea was to let that chain-gang get out of sight before I climbed the hill. You know I am not particularly tender; I've had to strike and to fend off. I've had to resist and to attack sometimes—that's only one way of resisting—without counting the exact cost, according to the demands of such sort of life as I had blundered into. I've seen the devil of violence, and the devil of greed, and the devil of hot desire; but, by all the stars! these were strong, lusty, red-eyed devils, that swayed and drove men—men, I tell you. But as I stood on this hillside, I foresaw that in the blinding sunshine of that land I would become acquainted with a flabby, pretending, weak-eyed devil of a rapacious and pitiless folly. How insidious he could be, too, I was only to find out several months later and a thousand miles farther. For a moment I stood appalled, as though by a warning. Finally I descended the hill, obliquely, towards the trees I had seen.

"I avoided a vast artificial hole somebody had been digging on the slope, the purpose of which I found it impossible to divine. It wasn't a quarry or a sandpit, anyhow. It was just a hole. It might have been connected with the philanthropic desire of giving the criminals something to do. I don't know. Then I nearly fell into a very narrow ravine, almost no more than a scar in the hillside. I discovered that a lot of imported drainage-pipes for the settlement had been tumbled in there. There wasn't one that was not broken. It was a wanton smash-up. At last I got under the trees. My purpose was to stroll into the shade for a moment; but no sooner within than it seemed to me I had stepped into the gloomy circle of some Inferno. The rapids were near, and an uninterrupted, uniform, headlong, rushing noise filled the mournful stillness of the grove, where not a breath stirred, not a leaf moved, with a mysterious sound—as though the tearing pace of the launched earth had suddenly become audible.

"Black shapes crouched, lay, sat between the trees, leaning against the trunks, clinging to the earth, half coming out, half effaced within the dim light, in all the attitudes of pain, abandonment, and despair. Another mine on the cliff went off, followed by a slight shudder of the soil under my feet. The work was going on. The work! And this was the place where some of the helpers had withdrawn to die.

"They were dying slowly—it was very clear. They were not enemies, they were not criminals, they were nothing earthly now,—nothing but black shadows of disease and starvation, lying confusedly in the greenish gloom. Brought from all the recesses of the coast in all the legality of time contracts, lost in uncongenial surroundings, fed on unfamiliar food, they sickened, became inefficient, and were then allowed to crawl away and rest. These moribund shapes were free as air—and nearly as thin. I began to distinguish the gleam of eyes under the trees. Then, glancing down, I saw a face near my hand. The black bones reclined at full length with one shoulder against the tree, and slowly the eyelids rose and the sunken eyes looked up at me, enormous and vacant, a kind of blind, white flicker in the depths of the orbs, which died out slowly. The man seemed young—almost a boy—but you know with them it's hard to tell. I found nothing else to do but to offer him one of my good Swede's ship's biscuits I had in my pocket. The fingers closed slowly on it and held—there was no other movement and no other glance. He had tied a bit of white worsted round his neck—Why? Where did he get it? Was it a badge—an ornament—a charm—a propitiatory act? Was there any idea at all connected with it? It looked startling round his black neck, this bit of white thread from beyond the seas.

"Near the same tree two more bundles of acute angles sat with their legs drawn up. One, with his chin propped on his knees, stared at nothing, in an intolerable and appalling manner: his brother phantom rested its forehead, as if overcome with a great weariness; and all about others were scattered in every pose of contorted collapse, as in some picture of a massacre or a pestilence. While I stood horror-struck, one of these creatures rose to his hands and knees, and went off on all-fours towards the river to drink. He lapped out of his hand, then sat up in the sunlight, crossing his shins in front of him, and after a time let his woolly head fall on his breastbone.

"I didn't want any more loitering in the shade, and I made haste towards the station. When near the buildings I met a white man, in such an unexpected elegance of get-up that in the first moment I took him for a sort of vision. I saw a high starched collar, white cuffs, a light alpaca jacket, snowy trousers, a clear silk necktie, and varnished boots. No hat. Hair parted, brushed, oiled, under a green-lined parasol held in a big white hand. He was amazing, and had a penholder behind his ear.

"I shook hands with this miracle, and I learned he was the Company's chief accountant, and that all the book-keeping was done at this station. He had come out for a moment, he said, 'to get a breath of fresh air.' The expression sounded wonderfully odd, with its suggestion of sedentary desk-life. I wouldn't have mentioned the fellow to you at all, only it was from his lips that I first heard the name of the man who is so indissolubly connected with the memories of that time. Moreover, I respected the fellow. Yes; I respected his collars, his vast cuffs, his brushed hair. His appearance was certainly that of a hairdresser's dummy; but in the great demoralisation of the land he kept up his appearance. That's backbone. His starched collars and got-up shirt-fronts were achievements of character. He had been out nearly three years; and, later on, I could not help asking him how he managed to sport such linen. He had just the faintest blush, and said modestly, 'I've been teaching one of the native women about the station. It was difficult. She had a distaste for the work.' Thus this man had verily accomplished something. And he was devoted to his books, which were in apple-pie order.

"Everything else in the station was in a muddle,—heads, things, buildings. Strings of dusty niggers with splay feet arrived and departed; a stream of manufactured goods, rubbishy cottons, beads, and brass-wire set into the depths of darkness, and in return came a precious trickle of ivory.

"I had to wait in the station for ten days—an eternity. I lived in a hut in the yard, but to be out of the chaos I would sometimes get into the accountant's office. It was built of horizontal planks, and so badly put together that, as he bent over his high desk, he was barred from neck to heels with narrow strips of sunlight. There was no need to open the big shutter to see. It was hot there too; big flies buzzed fiendishly, and did not sting, but stabbed. I sat generally on the floor, while, of faultless appearance (and even slightly scented), perching on a high stool, he wrote, he wrote. Sometimes he stood up for exercise. When a truckle-bed with a sick man (some invalided agent from up-country) was put in there, he exhibited a gentle annoyance. 'The groans of this sick person,' he said, 'distract my attention. And without that it is extremely difficult to guard against clerical errors in this climate.'

"One day he remarked, without lifting his head, 'In the interior you will no doubt meet Mr Kurtz.' On my asking who Mr Kurtz was, he said he was a first-class agent; and seeing my disappointment at this information, he added slowly, laying down his pen, 'He is a very remarkable person.' Further questions elicited from him that Mr Kurtz was at present in charge of a trading-post, a very important one, in the true ivory-country, at 'the very bottom of there. Sends in as much ivory as all the others put together . . .' He began to write again. The sick man was too ill to groan. The flies buzzed in a great peace.

"Suddenly there was a growing murmur of voices and a great tramping of feet. A caravan had come in. A violent babble of uncouth sounds burst out on the other side of the planks. All the carriers were speaking together, and in the midst of the uproar the lamentable voice of the chief agent was heard 'giving it up' tearfully for the twentieth time that day. . . . He rose slowly. 'What a frightful row,' he said. He crossed the room gently to look at the sick man, and returning, said to me, 'He does not hear.' 'What! Dead?' I asked, startled. 'No, not yet,' he answered, with great composure. Then, alluding with a toss of the head to the tumult in the station-yard, 'When one has got to make correct entries, one comes to hate those savages—hate them to the death.' He remained thoughtful for a moment. 'When you see Mr Kurtz,' he went on, 'tell him from me that everything here'—he glanced at the desk—'is very satisfactory. I don't like to write to him—with those messengers of ours you never know who may get hold of your letter—at that Central Station.' He stared at me for a moment with his mild, bulging eyes. 'Oh, he will go far, very far,' he began again. 'He will be a somebody in the Administration before long. They, above—the Council in Europe, you know—mean him to be.'

"He turned to his work. The noise outside had ceased, and presently in going out I stopped at the door. In the steady buzz of flies the homeward-bound agent was lying flushed and insensible; the other, bent over his books, was making correct entries of perfectly correct transactions; and fifty feet below the doorstep I could see the still tree-tops of the grove of death.

"Next day I left that station at last, with a caravan of sixty men, for a two-hundred-mile tramp.

"No use telling you much about that. Paths, paths, everywhere; a stamped-in network of paths spreading over the empty land, through long grass, through burnt grass, through thickets, down and up chilly ravines, up and down stony hills ablaze with heat; and a solitude, a solitude, nobody, not a hut. The population had cleared out a long time ago. Well, if a lot of mysterious niggers armed with all kinds of fearful weapons suddenly took to travelling on the road between Deal[6] and Gravesend, catching the yokels right and left to carry heavy loads for them, I fancy every farm and cottage thereabouts would get empty very soon. Only here the dwellings were gone too. Still, I passed through several abandoned villages. There's something pathetically childish in the ruins of grass walls. Day after day, with the stamp and shuffle of sixty pair of bare feet behind me, each pair under a 60-lb. load. Camp, cook, sleep, strike camp, march. Now and then a carrier dead in harness, at rest in the long grass near the path, with an empty water-gourd and his long staff lying by his side. A great silence around and above. Perhaps on some quiet night the tremor of far-off drums, sinking, swelling, a tremor vast, faint; a sound weird, appealing, suggestive, and wild—and perhaps with as profound a meaning as the sound of bells in a Christian country. Once a white man in an unbuttoned uniform, camping on the path with an armed escort of lank Zanzibaris,[7] very hospitable and festive—not to say drunk. Was looking after the upkeep of the road, he declared. Can't say I saw any road or any upkeep, unless the body of a middle-aged negro, with a bullet-hole in the forehead, upon which I absolutely stumbled three miles farther on, may be considered as a permanent improvement. I had a white companion too, not a bad chap, but rather too fleshy and with the exasperating habit of fainting on the hot hillsides, miles away from the least bit of shade and water. Annoying, you know, to hold your own coat like a parasol over a man's head while he is coming-to. I couldn't help asking him once what he meant by coming there at all. 'To make money, of course. What do you think?' he said, scornfully. Then he got fever, and had to be carried in a hammock slung under a pole. As he weighed sixteen stone I had no end of rows with the carriers. They jibbed, ran away, sneaked off with their loads in the night—quite a mutiny. So, one evening, I made a speech in English with gestures, not one of which was lost to the sixty pairs of eyes before me, and the next morning I started the hammock off in front all right. An hour afterwards I came upon the whole concern wrecked in a bush—man, hammock, groans, blankets, horrors. The heavy pole had skinned his poor nose. He was very anxious for me to kill somebody, but there wasn't the shadow of a carrier near. I remembered the old doctor,—'It would be interesting for science to watch the mental changes of individuals, on the spot.' I felt I was becoming scientifically interesting. However, all that is to no purpose. On the fifteenth day I came in sight of the big river again, and hobbled into the Central Station. It was on a back water surrounded by scrub and forest, with a pretty border of smelly mud on one side, and on the three others enclosed by a crazy fence of rushes. A neglected gap was all the gate it had, and the first glance at the place was enough to let you see the flabby devil was running that show. White men with long staves in their hands appeared languidly from amongst the buildings, strolling up to take a look at me, and then retired out of sight somewhere. One of them, a stout, excitable chap with black moustaches, informed me with great volubility and many digressions, as soon as I told him who I was, that my steamer was at the bottom of the river. I was thunderstruck. What, how, why? Oh, it

6. An English port.

7. Africans from Zanzibar, in East Africa; they were widely used as mercenaries.

was 'all right.' The 'manager himself' was there. All quite correct. 'Everybody had behaved splendidly! splendidly!'—'You must,' he said in agitation, 'go and see the general manager at once. He is waiting!'

"I did not see the real significance of that wreck at once. I fancy I see it now, but I am not sure—not at all. Certainly the affair was too stupid—when I think of it—to be altogether natural. Still. . . . But at the moment it presented itself simply as a confounded nuisance. The steamer was sunk. They had started two days before in a sudden hurry up the river with the manager on board, in charge of some volunteer skipper, and before they had been out three hours they tore the bottom out of her on stones, and she sank near the south bank. I asked myself what I was to do there, now my boat was lost. As a matter of fact, I had plenty to do in fishing my command out of the river. I had to set about it the very next day. That, and the repairs when I brought the pieces to the station, took some months.

"My first interview with the manager was curious. He did not ask me to sit down after my twenty-mile walk that morning. He was commonplace in complexion, in feature, in manners, and in voice. He was of middle size and of ordinary build. His eyes, of the usual blue, were perhaps remarkably cold, and he certainly could make his glance fall on one as trenchant and heavy as an axe. But even at these times the rest of his person seemed to disclaim the intention. Otherwise there was only an indefinable, faint expression of his lips, something stealthy—a smile—not a smile—I remember it, but I can't explain. It was unconscious, this smile was, though just after he had said something it got intensified for an instant. It came at the end of his speeches like a seal applied on the words to make the meaning of the commonest phrase appear absolutely inscrutable. He was a common trader, from his youth up employed in these parts—nothing more. He was obeyed, yet he inspired neither love nor fear, nor even respect. He inspired uneasiness. That was it! Uneasiness. Not a definite mistrust—just uneasiness—nothing more. You have no idea how effective such a . . . a . . . faculty can be. He had no genius for organising, for initiative, or for order even. That was evident in such things as the deplorable state of the station. He had no learning, and no intelligence. His position had come to him—why? Perhaps because he was never ill . . . He had served three terms of three years out there . . . Because triumphant health in the general rout of constitutions is a kind of power in itself. When he went home on leave he rioted on a large scale—pompously. Jack ashore—with a difference—in externals only. This one could gather from his casual talk. He originated nothing, he could keep the routine going—that's all. But he was great. He was great by this little thing that it was impossible to tell what could control such a man. He never gave that secret away. Perhaps there was nothing within him. Such a suspicion made one pause—for out there there were no external checks. Once when various tropical diseases had laid low almost every 'agent' in the station, he was heard to say, 'Men who come out here should have no entrails.' He sealed the utterance with that smile of his, as though it had been a door opening into a darkness he had in his keeping. You fancied you had seen things—but the seal was on. When annoyed at meal-times by the constant quarrels of the white men about precedence, he ordered an immense round table to be made, for which a special house had to be built. This was the station's mess-room. Where he sat was the first place—the rest were nowhere. One felt this to be his unalterable conviction. He was neither civil nor uncivil. He was quiet. He allowed his 'boy'—an overfed young negro from the coast—to treat the white men, under his very eyes, with provoking insolence.

"He began to speak as soon as he saw me. I had been very long on the road. He could not wait. Had to start without me. The up-river stations had to be relieved. There had been so many delays already that he did not know who was dead and who was alive, and how they got on—and so on, and so on. He paid no attention to my explanations, and, playing with a stick of sealing-wax, repeated several times that the situation was 'very grave, very grave.' There were rumours that a very important station was in jeopardy, and its chief, Mr Kurtz, was ill. Hoped it was not true. Mr Kurtz was . . . I felt weary and irritable. Hang Kurtz, I thought. I interrupted him by saying I had heard of Mr Kurtz on the coast. 'Ah! So they talk of him down there,' he murmured to himself. Then he began again, assuring me Mr Kurtz was the best agent he had, an exceptional man, of the greatest importance to the Company; therefore I could understand his anxiety. He was, he said, 'very, very uneasy.' Certainly he fidgeted on his chair a good deal, exclaimed, 'Ah, Mr Kurtz!' broke the stick of sealing-wax and seemed dumbfounded by the accident. Next thing he wanted to know 'how long it would take to' . . . I interrupted him again. Being hungry, you know, and kept on my feet too, I was getting savage. 'How can I tell?' I said. 'I haven't even seen the wreck yet—some months, no doubt.' All this talk seemed to me so futile. 'Some months,' he said. 'Well, let us say three months before we can make a start. Yes. That ought to do the affair.' I flung out of his hut (he lived all alone in a clay hut with a sort of verandah) muttering to myself my opinion of him. He was a chattering idiot. Afterwards I took it back when it was borne in upon me startlingly with what extreme nicety he had estimated the time requisite for the 'affair.'

"I went to work the next day, turning, so to speak, my back on that station. In that way only it seemed to me I could keep my hold on the redeeming facts of life. Still, one must look about sometimes; and then I saw this station, these men strolling aimlessly about in the sunshine of the yard. I asked myself sometimes what it all meant. They wandered here and there with their absurd long staves in their hands, like a lot of faithless pilgrims bewitched inside a rotten fence. The word 'ivory' rang in the air, was whispered, was sighed. You would think they were praying to it. A taint of imbecile rapacity blew through it all, like a whiff from some corpse. By Jove! I've never seen anything so unreal in my life. And outside, the silent wilderness surrounding this cleared speck on the earth struck me as something great and invincible, like evil or truth, waiting patiently for the passing away of this fantastic invasion.

"Oh, those months! Well, never mind. Various things happened. One evening a grass shed full of calico, cotton prints, beads, and I don't know what else, burst into a blaze so suddenly that you would have thought the earth had opened to let an avenging fire consume all that trash. I was smoking my pipe quietly by my dismantled steamer, and saw them all cutting capers in the light, with their arms lifted high, when the stout man with moustaches came tearing down to the river, a tin pail in his hand, assured me that everybody was 'behaving splendidly, splendidly,' dipped about a quart of water and tore back again. I noticed there was a hole in the bottom of his pail.

"I strolled up. There was no hurry. You see the thing had gone off like a box of matches. It had been hopeless from the very first. The flame had leaped high, driven everybody back, lighted up everything—and collapsed. The shed was already a heap of embers glowing fiercely. A nigger was being beaten near by. They said he had caused the fire in some way; be that as it may, he was screeching most horribly. I saw him, later on, for several days, sitting in a bit of shade looking very sick and trying to recover himself: afterwards he arose and went out—and the wilderness without a sound took him into its bosom again. As I approached the glow from the dark I found myself at the back of two men, talking. I heard the name of Kurtz pronounced, then the words, 'take advantage of this unfortunate accident.' One of the men was the manager. I wished him a good evening. 'Did you ever see anything like it—eh? it is incredible,' he said, and walked off. The other man remained. He was a first-class agent, young, gentlemanly, a bit reserved, with a forked little beard and a hooked nose. He was stand-offish with the other agents, and they on their side said he was the manager's spy upon them. As to me, I had hardly ever spoken to him before. We got into talk, and by-and-by we strolled away from the hissing ruins. Then he asked me to his room, which was in the main building of the station. He struck a match, and I perceived that this young aristocrat had not only a silver-mounted dressing-case but also a whole candle all to himself. Just at that time the manager was the only man supposed to have any right to candles. Native mats covered the clay walls; a collection of spears, assegais,[8] shields, knives was hung up in trophies. The business intrusted to this fellow was the making of bricks—so I had been informed; but there wasn't a fragment of a brick anywhere in the station, and he had been there more than a year—waiting. It seems he could not make bricks without something, I don't know what—straw maybe. Anyway, it could not be found there, and as it was not likely to be sent from Europe, it did not appear clear to me what he was waiting for. An act of special creation perhaps. However, they were all waiting—all the sixteen or twenty pilgrims of them—for something; and upon my word it did not seem an uncongenial occupation, from the way they took it, though the only thing that ever came to them was disease—as far as I could see. They beguiled the time by backbiting and intriguing against each other in a foolish kind of way. There was an air of plotting about that station, but nothing came of it, of course. It was as unreal as everything else—as the philanthropic pretence of the whole concern, as their talk, as their government, as their show of work. The only real feeling was a desire to get appointed to a trading-post where ivory was to be had, so that they could earn percentages. They intrigued and slandered and hated each other only on that account,—but as to effectually lifting a little finger—oh, no. By heavens! there is something after all in the world allowing one man to steal a horse while another must not look at a halter. Steal a horse straight out. Very well. He has done it. Perhaps he can ride. But there is a way of looking at a halter that would provoke the most charitable of saints into a kick.

"I had no idea why he wanted to be sociable, but as we chatted in there it suddenly occurred to me the fellow was trying to get at something—in fact, pumping me. He alluded constantly to Europe, to the people I was supposed to know there—putting leading questions as to my acquaintances in the sepulchral city, and so on. His little eyes glittered like mica discs—with curiosity,—though he tried to keep up a bit of superciliousness. At first I was astonished, but very soon I became awfully curious to see what he would find out from me. I couldn't possibly imagine what I had in me to make it worth his while. It was very pretty to see how he baffled himself, for in truth my body was full of chills, and my head had nothing in it but that wretched steamboat business. It was evident he took me for a perfectly shameless prevaricator. At last he got angry, and, to conceal a movement of furious annoyance, he yawned. I rose. Then I noticed a small sketch in oils, on a panel, representing a woman, draped and blind-folded, carrying a lighted torch. The background was sombre—almost black. The movement of the woman was stately, and the effect of the torchlight on the face was sinister.

8. Spears.

"It arrested me, and he stood by civilly, holding a half-pint champagne bottle (medical comforts) with the candle stuck in it. To my question he said Mr Kurtz had painted this—in this very station more than a year ago—while waiting for means to go to his trading-post. 'Tell me, pray,' said I, 'who is this Mr Kurtz?'

"'The chief of the Inner Station,' he answered in a short tone, looking away. 'Much obliged,' I said, laughing. 'And you are the brickmaker of the Central Station. Every one knows that.' He was silent for a while. 'He is a prodigy,' he said at last. 'He is an emissary of pity, and science, and progress, and devil knows what else. We want,' he began to declaim suddenly, 'for the guidance of the cause intrusted to us by Europe, so to speak, higher intelligence, wide sympathies, a singleness of purpose.' 'Who says that?' I asked. 'Lots of them,' he replied. 'Some even write that; and so *he* comes here, a special being, as you ought to know.' 'Why ought I to know?' I interrupted, really surprised. He paid no attention. 'Yes. To-day he is chief of the best station, next year he will be assistant-manager, two years more and . . . but I daresay you know what he will be in two years' time. You are of the new gang—the gang of virtue. The same people who sent him specially also recommended you. Oh, don't say no. I've my own eyes to trust.' Light dawned upon me. My dear aunt's influential acquaintances were producing an unexpected effect upon that young man. I nearly burst into a laugh. 'Do you read the Company's confidential correspondence?' I asked. He hadn't a word to say. It was great fun. 'When Mr Kurtz,' I continued severely, 'is General Manager, you won't have the opportunity.'

"He blew the candle out suddenly, and we went outside. The moon had risen. Black figures strolled about listlessly, pouring water on the glow, whence proceeded a sound of hissing; steam ascended in the moonlight; the beaten nigger groaned somewhere. 'What a row the brute makes!' said the indefatigable man with the moustaches, appearing near us. 'Serve him right. Transgression—punishment—bang! Pitiless, pitiless. That's the only way. This will prevent all conflagrations for the future. I was just telling the manager . . .' He noticed my companion, and became crestfallen all at once. 'Not in bed yet,' he said, with a kind of servile heartiness; 'it's so natural. Ha! Danger—agitation.' He vanished. I went on to the river-side, and the other followed me. I heard a scathing murmur at my ear, 'Heap of muffs—go to.' The pilgrims could be seen in knots gesticulating, discussing. Several had still their staves in their hands. I verily believe they took these sticks to bed with them. Beyond the fence the forest stood up spectrally in the moonlight, and through the dim stir, through the faint sounds of that lamentable courtyard, the silence of the land went home to one's very heart,—its mystery, its greatness, the amazing reality of its concealed life. The hurt nigger moaned feebly somewhere near by, and then fetched a deep sigh that made me mend my pace away from there. I felt a hand introducing itself under my arm. 'My dear sir,' said the fellow, 'I don't want to be misunderstood, and especially by you, who will see Mr Kurtz long before I can have that pleasure. I wouldn't like him to get a false idea of my disposition. . . .'

"I let him run on, this papier-mâché Mephistopheles, and it seemed to me that if I tried I could poke my forefinger through him, and would find nothing inside but a little loose dirt, maybe. He, don't you see, had been planning to be assistant-manager by-and-by under the present man, and I could see that the coming of that Kurtz had upset them both not a little. He talked precipitately, and I did not try to stop him. I had my shoulders against the wreck of my steamer, hauled up on the slope like a carcass of some big river animal. The smell of mud, of primeval mud, by Jove! was in my nostrils, the high stillness of primeval forest was before my eyes; there were shiny patches on the black creek. The moon had spread over everything a thin layer of silver—over the rank grass, over the mud, upon the wall of matted vegetation standing higher than the wall of a temple, over the great river I could see through a sombre gap glittering, glittering, as it flowed broadly by without a murmur. All this was great, expectant, mute, while the man jabbered about himself. I wondered whether the stillness on the face of the immensity looking at us two were meant as an appeal or as a menace. What were we who had strayed in here? Could we handle that dumb thing, or would it handle us? I felt how big, how confoundedly big, was that thing that couldn't talk, and perhaps was deaf as well. What was in there? I could see a little ivory coming out from there, and I had heard Mr Kurtz was in there. I had heard enough about it too—God knows! Yet somehow it didn't bring any image with it—no more than if I had been told an angel or a fiend was in there. I believed it in the same way one of you might believe there are inhabitants in the planet Mars. I knew once a Scotch sailmaker who was certain, dead sure, there were people in Mars. If you asked him for some idea how they looked and behaved, he would get shy and mutter something about 'walking on all-fours.' If you as much as smiled, he would—though a man of sixty—offer to fight you. I would not have gone so far as to fight for Kurtz, but I went for him near enough to a lie. You know I hate, detest, and can't bear a lie, not because I am straighter than the rest of us, but simply because it appals me. There is a taint of death, a flavour of mortality in lies,—which is exactly what I hate and detest in the world—what I want to forget. It makes me miserable and sick, like biting something rotten would do. Temperament, I suppose. Well, I went near enough to it by letting the young fool there believe anything he liked to imagine as to my influence in Europe. I became in an instant as much of a pretence as the rest of the bewitched pilgrims. This simply because I had a notion it somehow would be of help to that Kurtz whom at the time I did not see—you understand. He was just a word for me. I did not see the man in the name any more than you do. Do you see him? Do you see the story? Do you see anything? It seems to me I am trying to tell you a dream—making a vain attempt, because no relation of a dream can convey the dream-sensation, that commingling of absurdity, surprise, and bewilderment in a tremor of struggling revolt, that notion of being captured by the incredible which is of the very essence of dreams. . . ."

He was silent for a while.

". . . No, it is impossible; it is impossible to convey the life-sensation of any given epoch of one's existence,—that which makes its truth, its meaning—its subtle and penetrating essence. It is impossible. We live, as we dream—alone. . . ."

He paused again as if reflecting, then added—

"Of course in this you fellows see more than I could then. You see me, whom you know. . . ."

It had become so pitch dark that we listeners could hardly see one another. For a long time already he, sitting apart, had been no more to us than a voice. There was not a word from anybody. The others might have been asleep, but I was awake. I listened, I listened on the watch for the sentence, for the word, that would give me the clue to the faint uneasiness inspired by this narrative that seemed to shape itself without human lips in the heavy night-air of the river.

". . . Yes—I let him run on," Marlow began again, "and think what he pleased about the powers that were behind me. I did! And there was nothing behind me! There was nothing but that wretched, old, mangled steamboat I was leaning against, while he talked fluently about 'the necessity for every man to get on.' 'And when one comes out here, you conceive, it is not to gaze at the moon.' Mr Kurtz was a 'universal genius,' but even a genius would find it easier to work with 'adequate tools—intelligent men.' He did not make bricks—why, there was a physical impossibility in the way—as I was well aware; and if he did secretarial work for the manager, it was because 'no sensible man rejects wantonly the confidence of his superiors.' Did I see it? I saw it. What more did I want? What I really wanted was rivets, by heaven! Rivets. To get on with the work—to stop the hole. Rivets I wanted. There were cases of them down at the coast—cases—piled up—burst—split! You kicked a loose rivet at every second step in that station yard on the hillside. Rivets had rolled into the grove of death. You could fill your pockets with rivets for the trouble of stooping down—and there wasn't one rivet to be found where it was wanted. We had plates that would do, but nothing to fasten them with. And every week the messenger, a lone negro, letter-bag on shoulder and staff in hand, left our station for the coast. And several times a week a coast caravan came in with trade goods,—ghastly glazed calico that made you shudder only to look at it, glass beads value about a penny a quart, confounded spotted cotton handkerchiefs. And no rivets. Three carriers could have brought all that was wanted to set that steamboat afloat.

"He was becoming confidential now, but I fancy my unresponsive attitude must have exasperated him at last, for he judged it necessary to inform me he feared neither God nor devil, let alone any mere man. I said I could see that very well, but what I wanted was a certain quantity of rivets—and rivets were what really Mr Kurtz wanted, if he had only known it. Now letters went to the coast every week. . . . 'My dear sir,' he cried, 'I write from dictation.' I demanded rivets. There was a way—for an intelligent man. He changed his manner; became very cold, and suddenly began to talk about a hippopotamus; wondered whether sleeping on board the steamer (I stuck to my salvage night and day) I wasn't disturbed. There was an old hippo that had the bad habit of getting out on the bank and roaming at night over the station grounds. The pilgrims used to turn out in a body and empty every rifle they could lay hands on at him. Some even had sat up o' nights for him. All this energy was wasted, though. 'That animal has a charmed life,' he said; 'but you can say this only of brutes in this country. No man—you apprehend me?—no man here bears a charmed life.' He stood there for a moment in the moonlight with his delicate hooked nose set a little askew, and his mica eyes glittering without a wink, then, with a curt Good night, he strode off. I could see he was disturbed and considerably puzzled, which made me feel more hopeful than I had been for days. It was a great comfort to turn from that chap to my influential friend, the battered, twisted, ruined, tin-pot steamboat. I clambered on board. She rang under my feet like an empty Huntley & Palmer[9] biscuit-tin kicked along a gutter; she was nothing so solid in make, and rather less pretty in shape, but I had expended enough hard work on her to make me love her. No influential friend would have served me better. She had given me a chance to come out a bit—to find out what I could do. No, I don't like work. I had rather laze about and think of all the fine things that can be done. I don't like work—no man does—but I like what is in the work,—the chance to find yourself. Your own reality—for yourself, not for others—what no other man can ever know. They can only see the mere show, and never can tell what it really means.

"I was not surprised to see somebody sitting aft, on the deck, with his legs dangling over the mud. You see I rather chummed with the few mechanics there were in

9. A brand of English cookies.

that station, whom the other pilgrims naturally despised—on account of their imperfect manners, I suppose. This was the foreman—a boiler-maker by trade—a good worker. He was a lank, bony, yellow-faced man, with big intense eyes. His aspect was worried, and his head was as bald as the palm of my hand; but his hair in falling seemed to have stuck to his chin, and had prospered in the new locality, for his beard hung down to his waist. He was a widower with six young children (he had left them in charge of a sister of his to come out there), and the passion of his life was pigeon-flying. He was an enthusiast and a connoisseur. He would rave about pigeons. After work hours he used sometimes to come over from his hut for a talk about his children and his pigeons; at work, when he had to crawl in the mud under the bottom of the steamboat, he would tie up that beard of his in a kind of white serviette[1] he brought for the purpose. It had loops to go over his ears. In the evening he could be seen squatted on the bank rinsing that wrapper in the creek with great care, then spreading it solemnly on a bush to dry.

"I slapped him on the back and shouted 'We shall have rivets!' He scrambled to his feet exclaiming 'No! Rivets!' as though he couldn't believe his ears. Then in a low voice, 'You . . . eh?' I don't know why we behaved like lunatics. I put my finger to the side of my nose and nodded mysteriously. 'Good for you!' he cried, snapped his fingers above his head, lifting one foot. I tried a jig. We capered on the iron deck. A frightful clatter came out of that hulk, and the virgin forest on the other bank of the creek sent it back in a thundering roll upon the sleeping station. It must have made some of the pilgrims sit up in their hovels. A dark figure obscured the lighted doorway of the manager's hut, vanished, then, a second or so after, the doorway itself vanished too. We stopped, and the silence driven away by the stamping of our feet flowed back again from the recesses of the land. The great wall of vegetation, an exuberant and entangled mass of trunks, branches, leaves, boughs, festoons, motionless in the moonlight, was like a rioting invasion of soundless life, a rolling wave of plants, piled up, crested, ready to topple over the creek, to sweep every little man of us out of his little existence. And it moved not. A deadened burst of mighty splashes and snorts reached us from afar, as though an ichthyosaurus had been taking a bath of glitter in the great river. 'After all,' said the boiler-maker in a reasonable tone, 'why shouldn't we get the rivets?' Why not, indeed! I did not know of any reason why we shouldn't. 'They'll come in three weeks,' I said, confidently.

"But they didn't. Instead of rivets there came an invasion, an infliction, a visitation. It came in sections during the next three weeks, each section headed by a donkey carrying a white man in new clothes and tan shoes, bowing from that elevation right and left to the impressed pilgrims. A quarrelsome band of footsore sulky niggers trod on the heels of the donkey; a lot of tents, camp-stools, tin boxes, white cases, brown bales would be shot down in the courtyard, and the air of mystery would deepen a little over the muddle of the station. Five such instalments came, with their absurd air of disorderly flight with the loot of innumerable outfit shops and provision stores, that, one would think, they were lugging, after a raid, into the wilderness for equitable division. It was an inextricable mess of things decent in themselves but that human folly made look like the spoils of thieving.

"This devoted band called itself the Eldorado Exploring Expedition,[2] and I believe they were sworn to secrecy. Their talk, however, was the talk of sordid bucca-

1. Napkin.

2. Eldorado, legendary land of gold in South America and the object of many fruitless 16th-century Spanish expeditions.

neers: it was reckless without hardihood, greedy without audacity, and cruel without courage; there was not an atom of foresight or of serious intention in the whole batch of them, and they did not seem aware these things are wanted for the work of the world. To tear treasure out of the bowels of the land was their desire, with no more moral purpose at the back of it than there is in burglars breaking into a safe. Who paid the expenses of the noble enterprise I don't know; but the uncle of our manager was leader of that lot.

"In exterior he resembled a butcher in a poor neighbourhood, and his eyes had a look of sleepy cunning. He carried his fat paunch with ostentation on his short legs, and during the time his gang infested the station spoke to no one but his nephew. You could see these two roaming about all day long with their heads close together in an everlasting confab.

"I had given up worrying myself about the rivets. One's capacity for that kind of folly is more limited than you would suppose. I said Hang!—and let things slide. I had plenty of time for meditation, and now and then I would give some thought to Kurtz. I wasn't very interested in him. No. Still, I was curious to see whether this man, who had come out equipped with moral ideas of some sort, would climb to the top after all, and how he would set about his work when there."

2

"One evening as I was lying flat on the deck of my steamboat, I heard voices approaching—and there were the nephew and the uncle strolling along the bank. I laid my head on my arm again, and had nearly lost myself in a doze, when somebody said in my ear, as it were: 'I am as harmless as a little child, but I don't like to be dictated to. Am I the manager—or am I not? I was ordered to send him there. It's incredible.' . . . I became aware that the two were standing on the shore alongside the forepart of the steamboat, just below my head. I did not move; it did not occur to me to move: I was sleepy. 'It *is* unpleasant,' grunted the uncle. 'He has asked the Administration to be sent there,' said the other, 'with the idea of showing what he could do; and I was instructed accordingly. Look at the influence that man must have. Is it not frightful?' They both agreed it was frightful, then made several bizarre remarks: 'Make rain and fine weather—one man—the Council—by the nose'—bits of absurd sentences that got the better of my drowsiness, so that I had pretty near the whole of my wits about me when the uncle said, 'The climate may do away with this difficulty for you. Is he alone there?' 'Yes,' answered the manager; 'he sent his assistant down the river with a note to me in these terms: "Clear this poor devil out of the country, and don't bother sending more of that sort. I had rather be alone than have the kind of men you can dispose of with me." It was more than a year ago. Can you imagine such impudence?' 'Anything since then?' asked the other, hoarsely. 'Ivory,' jerked the nephew; 'lots of it—prime sort—lots—most annoying, from him.' 'And with that?' questioned the heavy rumble. 'Invoice,' was the reply fired out, so to speak. Then silence. They had been talking about Kurtz.

"I was broad awake by this time, but, lying perfectly at ease, remained still, having no inducement to change my position. 'How did that ivory come all this way?' growled the elder man, who seemed very vexed. The other explained that it had come with a fleet of canoes in charge of an English half-caste clerk Kurtz had with him; that Kurtz had apparently intended to return himself, the station being by that time bare of goods and stores, but after coming three hundred miles, had suddenly decided to go back, which he started to do alone in a small dug-out with four paddlers, leaving the half-caste to continue down the river with the ivory. The two fellows there seemed astounded at anybody attempting such a thing. They were at a loss for an adequate motive. As to me, I seemed to see Kurtz for the first time. It was a distinct glimpse: the dug-out, four paddling savages, and the lone white man turning his back suddenly on the headquarters, on relief, on thoughts of home—perhaps; setting his face towards the depths of the wilderness, towards his empty and desolate station. I did not know the motive. Perhaps he was just simply a fine fellow who stuck to his work for its own sake. His name, you understand, had not been pronounced once. He was 'that man.' The half-caste, who, as far as I could see, had conducted a difficult trip with great prudence and pluck, was invariably alluded to as 'that scoundrel.' The 'scoundrel' had reported that the 'man' had been very ill—had recovered imperfectly. . . . The two below me moved away then a few paces, and strolled back and forth at some little distance. I heard: 'Military post—doctor—two hundred miles—quite alone now—unavoidable delays—nine months—no news—strange rumours.' They approached again, just as the manager was saying, 'No one, as far as I know, unless a species of wandering trader—a pestilential fellow, snapping ivory from the natives.' Who was it they were talking about now? I gathered in snatches that this was some man supposed to be in Kurtz's district, and of whom the manager did not approve. 'We will not be free from unfair competition till one of these fellows is hanged for an example,' he said. 'Certainly,' grunted the other; 'get him hanged! Why not? Anything—anything can be done in this country. That's what I say; nobody here, you understand, *here,* can endanger your position. And why? You stand the climate—you outlast them all. The danger is in Europe; but there before I left I took care to—' They moved off and whispered, then their voices rose again. 'The extraordinary series of delays is not my fault. I did my possible.' The fat man sighed, 'Very sad.' 'And the pestiferous absurdity of his talk,' continued the other; 'he bothered me enough when he was here. "Each station should be like a beacon on the road towards better things, a centre for trade of course, but also for humanising, improving, instructing." Conceive you—that ass! And he wants to be manager! No, it's—' Here he got choked by excessive indignation, and I lifted my head the least bit. I was surprised to see how near they were—right under me. I could have spat upon their hats. They were looking on the ground, absorbed in thought. The manager was switching his leg with a slender twig: his sagacious relative lifted his head. 'You have been well since you came out this time?' he asked. The other gave a start. 'Who? I? Oh! Like a charm—like a charm. But the rest—oh, my goodness! All sick. They die so quick, too, that I haven't the time to send them out of the country—it's incredible!' 'H'm. Just so,' grunted the uncle. 'Ah! my boy, trust to this—I say, trust to this.' I saw him extend his short flipper of an arm for a gesture that took in the forest, the creek, the mud, the river,—seemed to beckon with a dishonouring flourish before the sunlit face of the land a treacherous appeal to the lurking death, to the hidden evil, to the profound darkness of its heart. It was so startling that I leaped to my feet and looked back at the edge of the forest, as though I had expected an answer of some sort to that black display of confidence. You know the foolish notions that come to one sometimes. The high stillness confronted these two figures with its ominous patience, waiting for the passing away of a fantastic invasion.

"They swore aloud together—out of sheer fright, I believe—then, pretending not to know anything of my existence, turned back to the station. The sun was low; and leaning forward side by side, they seemed to be tugging painfully uphill their two ridiculous shadows of unequal length, that trailed behind them slowly over the tall grass without bending a single blade.

"In a few days the Eldorado Expedition went into the patient wilderness, that closed upon it as the sea closes over a diver. Long afterwards the news came that all the donkeys were dead. I know nothing as to the fate of the less valuable animals. They, no doubt, like the rest of us, found what they deserved. I did not inquire. I was then rather excited at the prospect of meeting Kurtz very soon. When I say very soon I mean it comparatively. It was just two months from the day we left the creek when we came to the bank below Kurtz's station.

"Going up that river was like travelling back to the earliest beginnings of the world, when vegetation rioted on the earth and the big trees were kings. An empty stream, a great silence, an impenetrable forest. The air was warm, thick, heavy, sluggish. There was no joy in the brilliance of sunshine. The long stretches of the waterway ran on, deserted, into the gloom of overshadowed distances. On silvery sandbanks hippos and alligators sunned themselves side by side. The broadening waters flowed through a mob of wooded islands; you lost your way on that river as you would in a desert, and butted all day long against shoals, trying to find the channel, till you thought yourself bewitched and cut off for ever from everything you had known once—somewhere—far away—in another existence perhaps. There were moments when one's past came back to one, as it will sometimes when you have not a moment to spare to yourself; but it came in the shape of an unrestful and noisy dream, remembered with wonder amongst the overwhelming realities of this strange world of plants, and water, and silence. And this stillness of life did not in the least resemble a peace. It was the stillness of an implacable force brooding over an inscrutable intention. It looked at you with a vengeful aspect. I got used to it afterwards; I did not see it any more; I had no time. I had to keep guessing at the channel; I had to discern, mostly by inspiration, the signs of hidden banks; I watched for sunken stones; I was learning to clap my teeth smartly before my heart flew out, when I shaved by a fluke some infernal sly old snag that would have ripped the life out of the tin-pot steamboat and drowned all the pilgrims; I had to keep a look-out for the signs of dead wood we could cut up in the night for next day's steaming. When you have to attend to things of that sort, to the mere incidents of the surface, the reality—the reality, I tell you—fades. The inner truth is hidden—luckily, luckily. But I felt it all the same; I felt often its mysterious stillness watching me at my monkey tricks, just as it watches you fellows performing on your respective tight-ropes for—what is it? half-a-crown a tumble—"

"Try to be civil, Marlow," growled a voice, and I knew there was at least one listener awake besides myself.

"I beg your pardon. I forgot the heartache which makes up the rest of the price. And indeed what does the price matter, if the trick be well done? You do your tricks very well. And I didn't do badly either, since I managed not to sink that steamboat on my first trip. It's a wonder to me yet. Imagine a blindfolded man set to drive a van over a bad road. I sweated and shivered over that business considerably, I can tell you. After all, for a seaman, to scrape the bottom of the thing that's supposed to float all the time under his care is the unpardonable sin. No one may know of it, but you never forget the thump—eh? A blow on the very heart. You remember it, you dream of it, you wake up at night and think of it—years after—and go hot and cold all over. I don't pretend to say that steamboat floated all the time. More than once she had to wade for a bit, with twenty cannibals splashing around and pushing. We had enlisted some of these chaps on the way for a crew. Fine fellows—cannibals—in their place. They were men one could work with, and I am grateful to them. And, after all, they did not eat each other before my face: they had brought along a provision of hippo-meat which went rotten, and made the mystery of the wilderness stink in my nostrils. Phoo! I can sniff it now. I had the manager on board and three or four pilgrims with their staves—all complete. Sometimes we came upon a station close by the bank, clinging to the skirts of the unknown, and the white men rushing out of a tumble-down hovel, with great gestures of joy and surprise and welcome, seemed very strange,—had the appearance of being held there captive by a spell. The word 'ivory' would ring in the air for a while—and on we went again into the silence, along empty reaches, round the still bends, between the high walls of our winding way, reverberating in hollow claps the ponderous beat of the stern-wheel. Trees, trees, millions of trees, massive, immense, running up high; and at their foot, hugging the bank against the stream, crept the little begrimed steamboat, like a sluggish beetle crawling on the floor of a lofty portico. It made you feel very small, very lost, and yet it was not altogether depressing that feeling. After all, if you were small, the grimy beetle crawled on—which was just what you wanted it to do. Where the pilgrims imagined it crawled to I don't know. To some place where they expected to get something, I bet! For me it crawled towards Kurtz—exclusively; but when the steam-pipes started leaking we crawled very slow. The reaches opened before us and closed behind, as if the forest had stepped leisurely across the water to bar the way for our return. We penetrated deeper and deeper into the heart of darkness. It was very quiet there. At night sometimes the roll of drums behind the curtain of trees would run up the river and remain sustained faintly, as if hovering in the air high over our heads, till the first break of day. Whether it meant war, peace, or prayer we could not tell. The dawns were heralded by the descent of a chill stillness; the woodcutters slept, their fires burned low; the snapping of a twig would make you start. We were wanderers on a prehistoric earth, on an earth that wore the aspect of an unknown planet. We could have fancied ourselves the first of men taking possession of an accursed inheritance, to be subdued at the cost of profound anguish and of excessive toil. But suddenly, as we struggled round a bend, there would be a glimpse of rush walls, of peaked grass-roofs, a burst of yells, a whirl of black limbs, a mass of hands clapping, of feet stamping, of bodies swaying, of eyes rolling, under the droop of heavy and motionless foliage. The steamer toiled along slowly on the edge of a black and incomprehensible frenzy. The prehistoric man was cursing us, praying to us, welcoming us—who could tell? We were cut off from the comprehension of our surroundings; we glided past like phantoms, wondering and secretly appalled, as sane men would be before an enthusiastic outbreak in a madhouse. We could not understand, because we were too far and could not remember, because we were travelling in the night of first ages, of those ages that are gone, leaving hardly a sign—and no memories.

"The earth seemed unearthly. We are accustomed to look upon the shackled form of a conquered monster, but there—there you could look at a thing monstrous and free. It was unearthly, and the men were—No, they were not inhuman. Well, you know, that was the worst of it—this suspicion of their not being inhuman. It would come slowly to one. They howled, and leaped, and spun, and made horrid faces; but what thrilled you was just the thought of their humanity—like yours—the thought of your remote kinship with this wild and passionate uproar. Ugly. Yes, it was ugly enough; but if you were man enough you would admit to yourself that there was in you just the faintest trace of a response to the terrible frankness of that noise, a dim suspicion of there being a meaning in it which you—you so remote from the night of first ages—could comprehend. And why not? The mind of man is capable of anything—because everything is in it, all the past as well as all the future. What was there after all? Joy, fear, sorrow, devotion, valour, rage—who can tell?—but truth—truth stripped of its cloak of time. Let the fool gape and shudder—the man knows, and can look on without a wink. But he must at least be as much of a man as these on the shore. He must meet that truth with his own true stuff—with his own inborn strength. Principles? Principles won't do. Acquisitions, clothes, pretty rags—rags that would fly off at the first good shake. No; you want a deliberate belief. An appeal to me in this fiendish row—is there? Very well; I hear; I admit, but I have a voice too, and for good or evil mine is the speech that cannot be silenced. Of course, a fool, what with sheer fright and fine sentiments, is always safe. Who's that grunting? You wonder I didn't go ashore for a howl and a dance? Well, no—I didn't. Fine sentiments, you say? Fine sentiments be hanged! I had no time. I had to mess about with white-lead and strips of woollen blanket helping to put bandages on those leaky steam-pipes—I tell you. I had to watch the steering, and circumvent those snags, and get the tin-pot along by hook or by crook. There was surface-truth enough in these things to save a wiser man. And between whiles I had to look after the savage who was fireman. He was an improved specimen; he could fire up a vertical boiler. He was there below me, and, upon my word, to look at him was as edifying as seeing a dog in a parody of breeches and a feather hat, walking on his hind-legs. A few months of training had done for that really fine chap. He squinted at the steam-gauge and at the water-gauge with an evident effort of intrepidity—and he had filed teeth too, the poor devil, and the wool of his pate shaved into queer patterns, and three ornamental scars on each of his cheeks. He ought to have been clapping his hands and stamping his feet on the bank, instead of which he was hard at work, a thrall to strange witchcraft, full of improving knowledge. He was useful because he had been instructed; and what he knew was this—that should the water in that transparent thing disappear, the evil spirit inside the boiler would get angry through the greatness of his thirst, and take a terrible vengeance. So he sweated and fired up and watched the glass fearfully (with an impromptu charm, made of rags, tied to his arm, and a piece of polished bone, as big as a watch, stuck flatways through his lower lip), while the wooded banks slipped past us slowly, the short noise was left behind, the interminable miles of silence—and we crept on, towards Kurtz. But the snags were thick, the water was treacherous and shallow, the boiler seemed indeed to have a sulky devil in it, and thus neither that fireman nor I had any time to peer into our creepy thoughts.

"Some fifty miles below the Inner Station we came upon a hut of reeds, an inclined and melancholy pole, with the unrecognisable tatters of what had been a flag of some sort flying from it, and a neatly stacked wood-pile. This was unexpected. We came to the bank, and on the stack of firewood found a flat piece of board with some faded pencil-writing on it. When deciphered it said: 'Wood for you. Hurry up. Approach cautiously.' There was a signature, but it was illegible—not Kurtz—a much longer word. Hurry up. Where? Up the river? 'Approach cautiously.' We had not done so. But the warning could not have been meant for the place where it could be only found after approach. Something was wrong above. But what—and how much? That was the question. We commented adversely upon the imbecility of that telegraphic style. The bush around said nothing, and would not let us look very far, either. A torn curtain of red twill hung in the doorway of the hut, and flapped sadly in our faces. The dwelling was dismantled; but we could see a white man had lived there not very long ago. There remained a rude table—a plank on two posts; a heap of rubbish reposed in a dark corner, and by the door I picked up a book. It had lost its covers, and the pages had been thumbed into a state of extremely dirty softness; but the back had been lovingly stitched afresh with white cotton thread, which looked clean yet. It was an extraordinary find. Its title was, 'An Inquiry into some Points of Seamanship,' by a man Tower, Towson—some such name—Master in his Majesty's Navy. The matter looked dreary reading enough, with illustrative diagrams and repulsive tables of figures, and the copy was sixty years old. I handled this amazing antiquity with the greatest possible tenderness, lest it should dissolve in my hands. Within, Towson or Towser was inquiring earnestly into the breaking strain of ships' chains and tackle, and other such matters. Not a very enthralling book; but at the first glance you could see there a singleness of intention, an honest concern for the right way of going to work, which made these humble pages, thought out so many years ago, luminous with another than a professional light. The simple old sailor, with his talk of chains and purchases, made me forget the jungle and the pilgrims in a delicious sensation of having come upon something unmistakably real. Such a book being there was wonderful enough; but still more astounding were the notes pencilled in the margin, and plainly referring to the text. I couldn't believe my eyes! They were in cipher! Yes, it looked like cipher. Fancy a man lugging with him a book of that description into this nowhere and studying it—and making notes—in cipher at that! It was an extravagant mystery.

"I had been dimly aware for some time of a worrying noise, and when I lifted my eyes I saw the wood-pile was gone, and the manager, aided by all the pilgrims, was shouting at me from the river-side. I slipped the book into my pocket. I assure you to leave off reading was like tearing myself away from the shelter of an old and solid friendship.

"I started the lame engine ahead. 'It must be this miserable trader—this intruder,' exclaimed the manager, looking back malevolently at the place we had left. 'He must be English,' I said. 'It will not save him from getting into trouble if he is not careful,' muttered the manager darkly. I observed with assumed innocence that no man was safe from trouble in this world.

"The current was more rapid now, the steamer seemed at her last gasp, the sternwheel flopped languidly, and I caught myself listening on tiptoe for the next beat of the float, for in sober truth I expected the wretched thing to give up every moment. It was like watching the last flickers of a life. But still we crawled. Sometimes I would pick out a tree a little way ahead to measure our progress towards Kurtz by, but I lost it invariably before we got abreast. To keep the eyes so long on one thing was too much for human patience. The manager displayed a beautiful resignation. I fretted and fumed and took to arguing with myself whether or no I would talk openly with Kurtz; but before I could come to any conclusion it occurred to me that my speech or my silence, indeed any action of mine, would be a mere futility. What did it matter what any one knew or ignored? What did it matter who was manager? One gets sometimes such a flash of insight. The essentials of this affair lay deep under the surface, beyond my reach, and beyond my power of meddling.

"Towards the evening of the second day we judged ourselves about eight miles from Kurtz's station. I wanted to push on; but the manager looked grave, and told me the navigation up there was so dangerous that it would be advisable, the sun being very low already, to wait where we were till next morning. Moreover, he pointed out that if the warning to approach cautiously were to be followed, we must approach in daylight—not at dusk, or in the dark. This was sensible enough. Eight miles meant nearly three hours' steaming for us, and I could also see suspicious ripples at the upper end of the reach. Nevertheless, I was annoyed beyond expression at the delay, and most unreasonably too, since one night more could not matter much after so many months. As we had plenty of wood, and caution was the word, I brought up in the middle of the stream. The reach was narrow, straight, with high sides like a railway cutting. The dusk came gliding into it long before the sun had set. The current ran smooth and swift, but a dumb immobility sat on the banks. The living trees, lashed together by the creepers and every living bush of the undergrowth, might have been changed into stone, even to the slenderest twig, to the lightest leaf. It was not sleep—it seemed unnatural, like a state of trance. Not the faintest sound of any kind could be heard. You looked on amazed, and began to suspect yourself of being deaf—then the night came suddenly, and struck you blind as well. About three in the morning some large fish leaped, and the loud splash made me jump as though a gun had been fired. When the sun rose there was a white fog, very warm and clammy, and more blinding than the night. It did not shift or drive; it was just there, standing all round you like something solid. At eight or nine, perhaps, it lifted as a shutter lifts. We had a glimpse of the towering multitude of trees, of the immense matted jungle, with the blazing little ball of the sun hanging over it—all perfectly still—and then the white shutter came down again, smoothly, as if sliding in greased grooves. I ordered the chain, which we had begun to heave in, to be paid out again. Before it stopped running with a muffled rattle, a cry, a very loud cry, as of infinite desolation, soared slowly in the opaque air. It ceased. A complaining clamour, modulated in savage discords, filled our ears. The sheer unexpectedness of it made my hair stir under my cap. I don't know how it struck the others: to me it seemed as though the mist itself had screamed, so suddenly, and apparently from all sides at once, did this tumultuous and mournful uproar arise. It culminated in a hurried outbreak of almost intolerably excessive shrieking, which stopped short, leaving us stiffened in a variety of silly attitudes, and obstinately listening to the nearly as appalling and excessive silence. 'Good God! What is the meaning—?' stammered at my elbow one of the pilgrims,—a little fat man, with sandy hair and red whiskers, who wore side-spring boots, and pink pyjamas tucked into his socks. Two others remained open-mouthed a whole minute, then dashed into the little cabin, to rush out incontinently and stand darting scared glances, with Winchesters at 'ready' in their hands. What we could see was just the steamer we were on, her outlines blurred as though she had been on the point of dissolving, and a misty strip of water, perhaps two feet broad, around her—and that was all. The rest of the world was nowhere, as far as our eyes and ears were concerned. Just nowhere. Gone, disappeared; swept off without leaving a whisper or a shadow behind.

"I went forward, and ordered the chain to be hauled in short, so as to be ready to trip the anchor and move the steamboat at once if necessary. 'Will they attack?' whispered an awed voice. 'We will all be butchered in this fog,' murmured another. The faces twitched with the strain, the hands trembled slightly, the eyes forgot to wink. It was very curious to see the contrast of expressions of the white men and of the black fellows of our crew, who were as much strangers to that part of the river as we, though their homes were only eight hundred miles away. The whites, of course greatly discomposed, had besides a curious look of being painfully shocked by such an outrageous row. The others had an alert, naturally interested expression; but their faces were essentially quiet, even those of the one or two who grinned as they hauled at the chain. Several exchanged short, grunting phrases, which seemed to settle the matter to their satisfaction. Their headman, a young, broad-chested black, severely draped in dark-blue fringed cloths, with fierce nostrils and his hair all done up artfully in oily ringlets, stood near me. 'Aha!' I said, just for good fellowship's sake. 'Catch 'im,' he snapped, with a bloodshot widening of his eyes and a flash of sharp teeth—'catch 'im. Give 'im to us.' 'To you, eh?' I asked; 'what would you do with them?' 'Eat 'im!' he said, curtly, and, leaning his elbow on the rail, looked out into the fog in a dignified and profoundly pensive attitude. I would no doubt have been properly horrified, had it not occurred to me that he and his chaps must be very hungry: that they must have been growing increasingly hungry for at least this month past. They had been engaged for six months (I don't think a single one of them had any clear idea of time, as we at the end of countless ages have. They still belonged to the beginnings of time—had no inherited experience to teach them, as it were), and of course, as long as there was a piece of paper written over in accordance with some farcical law or other made down the river, it didn't enter anybody's head to trouble how they would live. Certainly they had brought with them some rotten hippo-meat, which couldn't have lasted very long, anyway, even if the pilgrims hadn't, in the midst of a shocking hullabaloo, thrown a considerable quantity of it overboard. It looked like a high-handed proceeding; but it was really a case of legitimate self-defence. You can't breathe dead hippo waking, sleeping, and eating, and at the same time keep your precarious grip on existence. Besides that, they had given them every week three pieces of brass wire, each about nine inches long; and the theory was they were to buy their provisions with that currency in river-side villages. You can see how *that* worked. There were either no villages, or the people were hostile, or the director, who like the rest of us fed out of tins, with an occasional old he-goat thrown in, didn't want to stop the steamer for some more or less recondite reason. So, unless they swallowed the wire itself, or made loops of it to snare the fishes with, I don't see what good their extravagant salary could be to them. I must say it was paid with a regularity worthy of a large and honourable trading company. For the rest, the only thing to eat—though it didn't look eatable in the least—I saw in their possession was a few lumps of some stuff like half-cooked dough, of a dirty lavender colour, they kept wrapped in leaves, and now and then swallowed a piece of, but so small that it seemed done more for the looks of the thing than for any serious purpose of sustenance. Why in the name of all the gnawing devils of hunger they didn't go for us—they were thirty to five—and have a good tuck-in for once, amazes me now when I think of it. They were big powerful men, with not much capacity to weigh the consequences, with courage, with strength, even yet, though their skins were no longer glossy and their muscles no longer hard. And I saw that something restraining, one of those human secrets that baffle probability, had come into play there. I looked at them with a swift quickening of interest—not because it occurred to me I might be eaten by them before very long, though I own to you that just then I perceived—in a new light, as it were—how unwholesome the pilgrims looked, and I hoped, yes, I positively hoped, that my aspect was not so—what shall I say?—so—unappetising: a touch of fantastic vanity which fitted well with the dream-sensation that pervaded all my days at that time. Perhaps I had a little fever too. One can't live with one's finger everlastingly on one's pulse. I had often 'a little fever,' or a little touch of other things—the playful paw-strokes of the wilderness, the preliminary trifling before the more serious onslaught which came in due course. Yes; I looked at them as you would on any human being, with a curiosity of their impulses, motives, capacities, weaknesses, when brought to the test of an inexorable physical necessity. Restraint! What possible restraint? Was it superstition, disgust, patience, fear—or some kind of primitive honour? No fear can stand up to hunger, no patience can wear it out, disgust simply does not exist where hunger is; and as to superstition, beliefs, and what you may call principles, they are less than chaff in a breeze. Don't you know the devilry of lingering starvation, its exasperating torment, its black thoughts, its sombre and brooding ferocity? Well, I do. It takes a man all his inborn strength to fight hunger properly. It's really easier to face bereavement, dishonour, and the perdition of one's soul—than this kind of prolonged hunger. Sad, but true. And these chaps too had no earthly reason for any kind of scruple. Restraint! I would just as soon have expected restraint from a hyena prowling amongst the corpses of a battlefield. But there was the fact facing me—the fact dazzling, to be seen, like the foam on the depths of the sea, like a ripple on an unfathomable enigma, a mystery greater—when I thought of it—than the curious, inexplicable note of desperate grief in this savage clamour that had swept by us on the river-bank, behind the blind whiteness of the fog.

"Two pilgrims were quarrelling in hurried whispers as to which bank. 'Left.' 'No, no; how can you? Right, right, of course.' 'It is very serious,' said the manager's voice behind me; 'I would be desolated if anything should happen to Mr Kurtz before we came up.' I looked at him, and had not the slightest doubt he was sincere. He was just the kind of man who would wish to preserve appearances. That was his restraint. But when he muttered something about going on at once, I did not even take the trouble to answer him. I knew, and he knew, that it was impossible. Were we to let go our hold of the bottom, we would be absolutely in the air—in space. We wouldn't be able to tell where we were going to—whether up or down stream, or across—till we fetched against one bank or the other,—and then we wouldn't know at first which it was. Of course I made no move. I had no mind for a smash-up. You couldn't imagine a more deadly place for a shipwreck. Whether drowned at once or not, we were sure to perish speedily in one way or another. 'I authorise you to take all the risks,' he said, after a short silence. 'I refuse to take any,' I said shortly; which was just the answer he expected, though its tone might have surprised him. 'Well, I must defer to your judgment. You are captain,' he said, with marked civility. I turned my shoulder to him in sign of my appreciation, and looked into the fog. How long would it last? It was the most hopeless look-out. The approach to this Kurtz grubbing for ivory in the wretched bush was beset by as many dangers as though he had been an enchanted princess sleeping in a fabulous castle. 'Will they attack, do you think?' asked the manager, in a confidential tone.

"I did not think they would attack, for several obvious reasons. The thick fog was one. If they left the bank in their canoes they would get lost in it, as we would be if we attempted to move. Still, I had also judged the jungle of both banks quite impenetrable—and yet eyes were in it, eyes that had seen us. The river-side bushes were certainly very thick; but the undergrowth behind was evidently penetrable. However, during the short lift I had seen no canoes anywhere in the reach—certainly not abreast of the steamer. But what made the idea of attack inconceivable to me was the nature of the noise—of the cries we had heard. They had not the fierce character boding of immediate hostile intention. Unexpected, wild, and violent as they had been, they had given me an irresistible impression of sorrow. The glimpse of the steamboat had for some reason filled those savages with unrestrained grief. The danger, if any, I expounded, was from our proximity to a great human passion let loose. Even extreme grief may ultimately vent itself in violence—but more generally takes the form of apathy. . . .

"You should have seen the pilgrims stare! They had no heart to grin, or even to revile me; but I believe they thought me gone mad—with fright, maybe. I delivered a regular lecture. My dear boys, it was no good bothering. Keep a look-out? Well, you may guess I watched the fog for the signs of lifting as a cat watches a mouse; but for anything else our eyes were of no more use to us than if we had been buried miles deep in a heap of cotton-wool. It felt like it too—choking, warm, stifling. Besides, all I said, though it sounded extravagant, was absolutely true to fact. What we afterwards alluded to as an attack was really an attempt at repulse. The action was very far from being aggressive—it was not even defensive, in the usual sense: it was undertaken under the stress of desperation, and in its essence was purely protective.

"It developed itself, I should say, two hours after the fog lifted, and its commencement was at a spot, roughly speaking, about a mile and a half below Kurtz's station. We had just floundered and flopped round a bend, when I saw an islet, a mere grassy hummock of bright green, in the middle of the stream. It was the only thing of the kind; but as we opened the reach more, I perceived it was the head of a long sand-bank, or rather of a chain of shallow patches stretching down the middle of the river. They were discoloured, just awash, and the whole lot was seen just under the water, exactly as a man's backbone is seen running down the middle of his back under the skin. Now, as far as I did see, I could go to the right or to the left of this. I didn't know either channel, of course. The banks looked pretty well alike, the depth appeared the same; but as I had been informed the station was on the west side, I naturally headed for the western passage.

"No sooner had we fairly entered it than I became aware it was much narrower than I had supposed. To the left of us there was the long uninterrupted shoal, and to the right a high, steep bank heavily overgrown with bushes. Above the bush the trees stood in serried ranks. The twigs overhung the current thickly, and from distance to distance a large limb of some tree projected rigidly over the stream. It was then well on in the afternoon, the face of the forest was gloomy, and a broad strip of shadow had already fallen on the water. In this shadow we steamed up—very slowly, as you may imagine. I sheered her well inshore—the water being deepest near the bank, as the sounding-pole informed me.

"One of my hungry and forbearing friends was sounding in the bows just below me. This steamboat was exactly like a decked scow.[3] On the deck there were two little teak-wood houses, with doors and windows. The boiler was in the fore-end, and the machinery right astern. Over the whole there was a light roof, supported on stanchions. The funnel projected through that roof, and in front of the funnel a small cabin built of light planks served for a pilot-house. It contained a couch, two camp-stools, a loaded Martini-Henry[4] leaning in one corner, a tiny table, and the steering-wheel. It had a wide door in front and a broad shutter at each side. All these were always thrown open, of course. I spent my days perched up there on the extreme fore-end of that roof, before the door. At night I slept, or tried to, on the couch. An athletic black belonging to some coast tribe, and educated by my poor predecessor, was the helmsman. He sported a pair of brass earrings, wore a blue cloth wrapper from the waist to the ankles, and thought all the world of himself. He was the most unstable kind of fool I had ever seen. He steered with no end of a swagger while you were by; but if he lost sight of you, he became instantly the prey of an abject funk, and would let that cripple of a steamboat get the upper hand of him in a minute.

"I was looking down at the sounding-pole, and feeling much annoyed to see at each try a little more of it stick out of that river, when I saw my poleman give up the business suddenly, and stretch himself flat on the deck, without even taking the trouble to haul his pole in. He kept hold on it though, and it trailed in the water. At the

3. A flat-bottomed boat.

4. A rifle.

same time the fireman, whom I could also see below me, sat down abruptly before his furnace and ducked his head. I was amazed. Then I had to look at the river mighty quick, because there was a snag in the fairway. Sticks, little sticks, were flying about—thick: they were whizzing before my nose, dropping below me, striking behind me against my pilot-house. All this time the river, the shore, the woods, were very quiet—perfectly quiet. I could only hear the heavy splashing thump of the stern-wheel and the patter of these things. We cleared the snag clumsily. Arrows, by Jove! We were being shot at! I stepped in quickly to close the shutter on the landside. That fool-helmsman, his hands on the spokes, was lifting his knees high, stamping his feet, champing his mouth, like a reined-in horse. Confound him! And we were staggering within ten feet of the bank. I had to lean right out to swing the heavy shutter, and I saw a face amongst the leaves on the level with my own, looking at me very fierce and steady; and then suddenly, as though a veil had been removed from my eyes, I made out, deep in the tangled gloom, naked breasts, arms, legs, glaring eyes,—the bush was swarming with human limbs in movement, glistening, of bronze colour. The twigs shook, swayed, and rustled, the arrows flew out of them, and then the shutter came to. 'Steer her straight,' I said to the helmsman. He held his head rigid, face forward; but his eyes rolled, he kept on lifting and setting down his feet gently, his mouth foamed a little. 'Keep quiet!' I said in a fury. I might just as well have ordered a tree not to sway in the wind. I darted out. Below me there was a great scuffle of feet on the iron deck; confused exclamations; a voice screamed, 'Can you turn back?' I caught sight of a V-shaped ripple on the water ahead. What? Another snag! A fusillade burst out under my feet. The pilgrims had opened with their Winchesters, and were simply squirting lead into that bush. A deuce of a lot of smoke came up and drove slowly forward. I swore at it. Now I couldn't see the ripple or the snag either. I stood in the doorway, peering, and the arrows came in swarms. They might have been poisoned, but they looked as though they wouldn't kill a cat. The bush began to howl. Our wood-cutters raised a warlike whoop; the report of a rifle just at my back deafened me. I glanced over my shoulder, and the pilot-house was yet full of noise and smoke when I made a dash at the wheel. The fool-nigger had dropped everything, to throw the shutter open and let off that Martini-Henry. He stood before the wide opening, glaring, and I yelled at him to come back, while I straightened the sudden twist out of that steamboat. There was no room to turn even if I had wanted to, the snag was somewhere very near ahead in that confounded smoke, there was no time to lose, so I just crowded her into the bank—right into the bank, where I knew the water was deep.

"We tore slowly along the overhanging bushes in a whirl of broken twigs and flying leaves. The fusillade below stopped short, as I had foreseen it would when the squirts got empty. I threw my head back to a glinting whizz that traversed the pilot-house, in at one shutter-hole and out at the other. Looking past that mad helmsman, who was shaking the empty rifle and yelling at the shore, I saw vague forms of men running bent double, leaping, gliding, distinct, incomplete, evanescent. Something big appeared in the air before the shutter, the rifle went overboard, and the man stepped back swiftly, looked at me over his shoulder in an extraordinary, profound, familiar manner, and fell upon my feet. The side of his head hit the wheel twice, and the end of what appeared a long cane clattered round and knocked over a little camp-stool. It looked as though after wrenching that thing from somebody ashore he had lost his balance in the effort. The thin smoke had blown away, we were clear of the snag, and looking ahead I could see that in another hundred yards or so I would be free to sheer off, away from the bank; but my feet felt so very warm and wet that I had to look down. The man had rolled on his back and stared straight up at me; both his hands clutched that cane. It was the shaft of a spear that, either thrown or lunged through the opening, had caught him in the side just below the ribs; the blade had gone in out of sight, after making a frightful gash; my shoes were full; a pool of blood lay very still, gleaming dark-red under the wheel; his eyes shone with an amazing lustre. The fusillade burst out again. He looked at me anxiously, gripping the spear like something precious, with an air of being afraid I would try to take it away from him. I had to make an effort to free my eyes from his gaze and attend to the steering. With one hand I felt above my head for the line of the steam-whistle, and jerked out screech after screech hurriedly. The tumult of angry and warlike yells was checked instantly, and then from the depths of the woods went out such a tremulous and prolonged wail of mournful fear and utter despair as may be imagined to follow the flight of the last hope from the earth. There was a great commotion in the bush; the shower of arrows stopped, a few dropping shots rang out sharply—then silence, in which the languid beat of the stern-wheel came plainly to my ears. I put the helm hard astarboard at the moment when the pilgrim in pink pyjamas, very hot and agitated, appeared in the doorway. 'The manager sends me—' he began in an official tone, and stopped short. 'Good God!' he said, glaring at the wounded man.

"We two whites stood over him, and his lustrous and inquiring glance enveloped us both. I declare it looked as though he would presently put to us some question in an understandable language; but he died without uttering a sound, without moving a limb, without twitching a muscle. Only in the very last moment, as though in response to some sign we could not see, to some whisper we could not hear, he frowned heavily, and that frown gave to his black death-mask an inconceivably sombre, brooding, and menacing expression. The lustre of inquiring glance faded swiftly into vacant glassiness. 'Can you steer?' I asked the agent eagerly. He looked very dubious; but I made a grab at his arm, and he understood at once I meant him to steer whether or no. To tell you the truth, I was morbidly anxious to change my shoes and socks. 'He is dead,' murmured the fellow, immensely impressed. 'No doubt about it,' said I, tugging like mad at the shoelaces. 'And, by the way, I suppose Mr Kurtz is dead as well by this time.'

"For the moment that was the dominant thought. There was a sense of extreme disappointment, as though I had found out I had been striving after something altogether without a substance. I couldn't have been more disgusted if I had travelled all this way for the sole purpose of talking with Mr Kurtz. Talking with . . . I flung one shoe overboard, and became aware that that was exactly what I had been looking forward to—a talk with Kurtz. I made the strange discovery that I had never imagined him as doing, you know, but as discoursing. I didn't say to myself, 'Now I will never see him,' or 'Now I will never shake him by the hand,' but, 'Now I will never hear him.' The man presented himself as a voice. Not of course that I did not connect him with some sort of action. Hadn't I been told in all the tones of jealousy and admiration that he had collected, bartered, swindled, or stolen more ivory than all the other agents together. That was not the point. The point was in his being a gifted creature, and that of all his gifts the one that stood out pre-eminently, that carried with it a sense of real presence, was his ability to talk, his words—the gift of expression, the bewildering, the illuminating, the most exalted and the most contemptible, the pulsating stream of light, or the deceitful flow from the heart of an impenetrable darkness.

"The other shoe went flying unto the devil-god of that river. I thought, By Jove! it's all over. We are too late; he has vanished—the gift has vanished, by means of some spear, arrow, or club. I will never hear that chap speak after all,—and my sorrow had a startling extravagance of emotion, even such as I had noticed in the howling sorrow of these savages in the bush. I couldn't have felt more of lonely desolation somehow, had I been robbed of a belief or had missed my destiny in life. . . . Why do you sigh in this beastly way, somebody? Absurd? Well, absurd. Good Lord! mustn't a man ever—Here, give me some tobacco." . . .

There was a pause of profound stillness, then a match flared, and Marlow's lean face appeared, worn, hollow, with downward folds and dropped eyelids, with an aspect of concentrated attention; and as he took vigorous draws at his pipe, it seemed to retreat and advance out of the night in the regular flicker of the tiny flame. The match went out.

"Absurd!" he cried. "This is the worst of trying to tell . . . Here you all are, each moored with two good addresses, like a hulk with two anchors, a butcher round one corner, a policeman round another, excellent appetites, and temperature normal—you hear—normal from year's end to year's end. And you say, Absurd! Absurd be—exploded! Absurd! My dear boys, what can you expect from a man who out of sheer nervousness had just flung overboard a pair of new shoes? Now I think of it, it is amazing I did not shed tears. I am, upon the whole, proud of my fortitude. I was cut to the quick at the idea of having lost the inestimable privilege of listening to the gifted Kurtz. Of course I was wrong. The privilege was waiting for me. Oh yes, I heard more than enough. And I was right, too. A voice. He was very little more than a voice. And I heard—him—it—this voice—other voices—all of them were so little more than voices—and the memory of that time itself lingers around me, impalpable, like a dying vibration of one immense jabber, silly, atrocious, sordid, savage, or simply mean, without any kind of sense. Voices, voices—even the girl herself—now—"

He was silent for a long time.

"I laid the ghost of his gifts at last with a lie," he began suddenly. "Girl! What? Did I mention a girl? Oh, she is out of it—completely. They—the women I mean—are out of it—should be out of it. We must help them to stay in that beautiful world of their own, lest ours gets worse. Oh, she had to be out of it. You should have heard the disinterred body of Mr Kurtz saying, 'My Intended.' You would have perceived directly then how completely she was out of it. And the lofty frontal bone of Mr Kurtz! They say the hair goes on growing sometimes, but this—ah—specimen was impressively bald. The wilderness had patted him on the head, and, behold, it was like a ball—an ivory ball; it had caressed him, and—lo!—he had withered; it had taken him, loved him, embraced him, got into his veins, consumed his flesh, and sealed his soul to its own by the inconceivable ceremonies of some devilish initiation. He was its spoiled and pampered favourite. Ivory? I should think so. Heaps of it, stacks of it. The old mud shanty was bursting with it. You would think there was not a single tusk left either above or below the ground in the whole country. 'Mostly fossil,' the manager had remarked disparagingly. It was no more fossil than I am; but they call it fossil when it is dug up. It appears these niggers do bury the tusks sometimes—but evidently they couldn't bury this parcel deep enough to save the gifted Mr Kurtz from his fate. We filled the steamboat with it, and had to pile a lot on the deck. Thus he could see and enjoy as long as he could see, because the appreciation of this favour had remained with him to the last. You should have heard him say, 'My ivory.' Oh yes, I heard him. 'My Intended, my ivory, my station, my river, my—' everything belonged to him. It made me hold my breath in expectation of hearing the wilderness burst into a prodigious peal of laughter that would shake the fixed stars in their places. Everything belonged to him—but that was a trifle. The thing was to know what he belonged to, how many powers of darkness claimed him for their own. That was the reflection that made you creepy all over. It was impossible—it was not good for one either—trying to imagine. He had taken a high seat amongst the devils of the land—I mean literally. You can't understand. How could you?—with solid pavement under your feet, surrounded by kind neighbours ready to cheer you or to fall on you, stepping delicately between the butcher and the policeman, in the holy terror of scandal and gallows and lunatic asylums—how can you imagine what particular region of the first ages a man's untrammelled feet may take him into by the way of solitude—utter solitude without a policeman—by the way of silence—utter silence, where no warning voice of a kind neighbour can be heard whispering of public opinion? These little things make all the great difference. When they are gone you must fall back upon your own innate strength, upon your own capacity for faithfulness. Of course you may be too much of a fool to go wrong—too dull even to know you are being assaulted by the powers of darkness. I take it, no fool ever made a bargain for his soul with the devil: the fool is too much of a fool, or the devil too much of a devil—I don't know which. Or you may be such a thunderingly exalted creature as to be altogether deaf and blind to anything but heavenly sights and sounds. Then the earth for you is only a standing place—and whether to be like this is your loss or your gain I won't pretend to say. But most of us are neither one nor the other. The earth for us is a place to live in, where we must put up with sights, with sounds, with smells too, by Jove!—breathe dead hippo, so to speak, and not be contaminated. And there, don't you see? your strength comes in, the faith in your ability for the digging of unostentatious holes to bury the stuff in—your power of devotion, not to yourself, but to an obscure, back-breaking business. And that's difficult enough. Mind, I am not trying to excuse or even explain—I am trying to account to myself for—for—Mr Kurtz—for the shade of Mr Kurtz. This initiated wraith from the back of Nowhere honoured me with its amazing confidence before it vanished altogether. This was because it could speak English to me. The original Kurtz had been educated partly in England, and—as he was good enough to say himself—his sympathies were in the right place. His mother was half-English, his father was half-French. All Europe contributed to the making of Kurtz; and by-and-by I learned that, most appropriately, the International Society for the Suppression of Savage Customs had intrusted him with the making of a report, for its future guidance. And he had written it too. I've seen it. I've read it. It was eloquent, vibrating with eloquence, but too high-strung, I think. Seventeen pages of close writing he had found time for! But this must have been before his—let us say—nerves went wrong, and caused him to preside at certain midnight dances ending with unspeakable rites, which—as far as I reluctantly gathered from what I heard at various times—were offered up to him—do you understand?—to Mr Kurtz himself. But it was a beautiful piece of writing. The opening paragraph, however, in the light of later information, strikes me now as ominous. He began with the argument that we whites, from the point of development we had arrived at, 'must necessarily appear to them [savages] in the nature of supernatural beings—we approach them with the might as of a deity,' and so on, and so on. 'By the simple exercise of our will we can exert a power for good practically unbounded,' &c., &c. From that point he soared and took me with him. The peroration was magnificent, though difficult to remember, you know. It gave me the notion of an exotic Immensity ruled by an august Benevolence. It made me tingle with enthusiasm. This was the unbounded power of eloquence—of words—of burning noble words. There were no practical hints to interrupt the magic current of phrases, unless a kind of note at the foot of the last page, scrawled evidently much later, in an unsteady hand, may be regarded as the exposition of a method. It was very simple, and at the end of that moving appeal to every altruistic sentiment it blazed at you, luminous and terrifying, like a flash of lightning in a serene sky: 'Exterminate all the brutes!' The curious part was that he had apparently forgotten all about that valuable postscriptum, because, later on, when he in a sense came to himself, he repeatedly entreated me to take good care of 'my pamphlet' (he called it), as it was sure to have in the future a good influence upon his career. I had full information about all these things, and, besides, as it turned out, I was to have the care of his memory. I've done enough for it to give me the indisputable right to lay it, if I choose, for an everlasting rest in the dust-bin of progress, amongst all the sweepings and, figuratively speaking, all the dead cats of civilisation. But then, you see, I can't choose. He won't be forgotten. Whatever he was, he was not common. He had the power to charm or frighten rudimentary souls into an aggravated witch-dance in his honour; he could also fill the small souls of the pilgrims with bitter misgivings: he had one devoted friend at least, and he had conquered one soul in the world that was neither rudimentary nor tainted with self-seeking. No; I can't forget him, though I am not prepared to affirm the fellow was exactly worth the life we lost in getting to him. I missed my late helmsman awfully,—I missed him even while his body was still lying in the pilot-house. Perhaps you will think it passing strange this regret for a savage who was no more account than a grain of sand in a black Sahara. Well, don't you see, he had done something, he had steered; for months I had him at my back—a help—an instrument. It was a kind of partnership. He steered for me—I had to look after him, I worried about his deficiencies, and thus a subtle bond had been created, of which I only became aware when it was suddenly broken. And the intimate profundity of that look he gave me when he received his hurt remains to this day in my memory—like a claim of distant kinship affirmed in a supreme moment.

"Poor fool! If he had only left that shutter alone. He had no restraint, no restraint—just like Kurtz—a tree swayed by the wind. As soon as I had put on a dry pair of slippers, I dragged him out, after first jerking the spear out of his side, which operation I confess I performed with my eyes shut tight. His heels leaped together over the little doorstep; his shoulders were pressed to my breast; I hugged him from behind desperately. Oh! he was heavy, heavy; heavier than any man on earth, I should imagine. Then without more ado I tipped him overboard. The current snatched him as though he had been a wisp of grass, and I saw the body roll over twice before I lost sight of it for ever. All the pilgrims and the manager were then congregated on the awning-deck about the pilot-house, chattering at each other like a flock of excited magpies, and there was a scandalised murmur at my heartless promptitude. What they wanted to keep that body hanging about for I can't guess. Embalm it, maybe. But I had also heard another, and a very ominous, murmur on the deck below. My friends the woodcutters were likewise scandalised, and with a better show of reason—though I admit that the reason itself was quite inadmissible. Oh, quite! I had made up my mind that if my late helmsman was to be eaten, the fishes alone should have him. He had been a very second-rate helmsman while alive, but now he was dead he might have become a first-class temptation, and possibly cause some startling trouble. Besides, I was anxious to take the wheel, the man in pink pyjamas showing himself a hopeless duffer at the business.

"This I did directly the simple funeral was over. We were going half-speed, keeping right in the middle of the stream, and I listened to the talk about me. They had given up Kurtz, they had given up the station; Kurtz was dead, and the station had been burnt—and so on—and so on. The red-haired pilgrim was beside himself with the thought that at least this poor Kurtz had been properly revenged. 'Say! We must have made a glorious slaughter of them in the bush. Eh? What do you think? Say?' He positively danced, the bloodthirsty little gingery beggar. And he had nearly fainted when he saw the wounded man! I could not help saying, 'You made a glorious lot of smoke, anyhow.' I had seen, from the way the tops of the bushes rustled and flew, that almost all the shots had gone too high. You can't hit anything unless you take aim and fire from the shoulder; but these chaps fired from the hip with their eyes shut. The retreat, I maintained—and I was right—was caused by the screeching of the steam-whistle. Upon this they forgot Kurtz, and began to howl at me with indignant protests.

"The manager stood by the wheel murmuring confidentially about the necessity of getting well away down the river before dark at all events, when I saw in the distance a clearing on the river-side and the outlines of some sort of building. 'What's this?' I asked. He clapped his hands in wonder. 'The station!' he cried. I edged in at once, still going half-speed.

"Through my glasses I saw the slope of a hill interspersed with rare trees and perfectly free from undergrowth. A long decaying building on the summit was half buried in the high grass; the large holes in the peaked roof gaped black from afar; the jungle and the woods made a background. There was no enclosure or fence of any kind; but there had been one apparently, for near the house half-a-dozen slim posts remained in a row, roughly trimmed, and with their upper ends ornamented with round carved balls. The rails, or whatever there had been between, had disappeared. Of course the forest surrounded all that. The river-bank was clear, and on the waterside I saw a white man under a hat like a cart-wheel beckoning persistently with his whole arm. Examining the edge of the forest above and below, I was almost certain I could see movements—human forms gliding here and there. I steamed past prudently, then stopped the engines and let her drift down. The man on the shore began to shout, urging us to land. 'We have been attacked,' screamed the manager. 'I know—I know. It's all right,' yelled back the other, as cheerful as you please. 'Come along. It's all right. I am glad.'

"His aspect reminded me of something I had seen—something funny I had seen somewhere. As I manoeuvred to get alongside, I was asking myself, 'What does this fellow look like?' Suddenly I got it. He looked like a harlequin. His clothes had been made of some stuff that was brown holland[5] probably, but it was covered with patches all over, with bright patches, blue, red, and yellow,—patches on the back, patches on front, patches on elbows, on knees; coloured binding round his jacket, scarlet edging at the bottom of his trousers; and the sunshine made him look extremely gay and wonderfully neat withal, because you could see how beautifully all this patching had been done. A beardless, boyish face, very fair, no features to speak of, nose peeling, little blue eyes, smiles and frowns chasing each other over that open countenance like sunshine and shadow on a wind-swept plain. 'Look out, captain!' he cried; 'there's a snag lodged in here last night.' What! Another snag? I confess I swore shamefully. I had nearly holed my cripple, to finish off that charming trip. The harlequin on the bank turned his little pug nose up to me. 'You English?' he asked, all smiles. 'Are you?' I shouted from the wheel. The smiles vanished, and he shook his head as if sorry for my disappointment. Then he brightened up. 'Never mind!' he cried encouragingly. 'Are we in time?' I asked. 'He is up there,' he replied, with a toss of the head up the hill, and becoming gloomy all of a sudden. His face was like the autumn sky, overcast one moment and bright the next.

5. A smooth linen fabric.

"When the manager, escorted by the pilgrims, all of them armed to the teeth, had gone to the house, this chap came on board. 'I say, I don't like this. These natives are in the bush,' I said. He assured me earnestly it was all right. 'They are simple people,' he added; 'well, I am glad you came. It took me all my time to keep them off.' 'But you said it was all right,' I cried. 'Oh, they meant no harm,' he said; and as I stared he corrected himself, 'Not exactly.' Then vivaciously, 'My faith, your pilot-house wants a clean-up!' In the next breath he advised me to keep enough steam on the boiler to blow the whistle in case of any trouble. 'One good screech will do more for you than all your rifles. They are simple people,' he repeated. He rattled away at such a rate he quite overwhelmed me. He seemed to be trying to make up for lots of silence, and actually hinted, laughing, that such was the case. 'Don't you talk with Mr Kurtz?' I said. 'You don't talk with that man—you listen to him,' he exclaimed with severe exaltation. 'But now—' He waved his arm, and in the twinkling of an eye was in the uttermost depths of despondency. In a moment he came up again with a jump, possessed himself of both my hands, shook them continuously, while he gabbled: 'Brother sailor . . . honour . . . pleasure . . . delight . . . introduce myself . . . Russian . . . son of an arch-priest . . . Government of Tambov[6] . . . What? Tobacco! English tobacco; the excellent English tobacco! Now, that's brotherly. Smoke? Where's a sailor that does not smoke?'

"The pipe soothed him, and gradually I made out he had run away from school, had gone to sea in a Russian ship; ran away again; served some time in English ships; was now reconciled with the arch-priest. He made a point of that. 'But when one is young one must see things, gather experience, ideas; enlarge the mind.' 'Here!' I interrupted. 'You can never tell! Here I have met Mr Kurtz,' he said, youthfully solemn and reproachful. I held my tongue after that. It appears he had persuaded a Dutch trading-house on the coast to fit him out with stores and goods, and had started for the interior with a light heart, and no more idea of what would happen to him than a baby. He had been wandering about that river for nearly two years alone, cut off from everybody and everything. 'I am not so young as I look. I am twenty-five,' he said. 'At first old Van Shuyten would tell me to go to the devil,' he narrated with keen enjoyment; 'but I stuck to him, and talked and talked, till at last he got afraid I would talk the hind-leg off his favorite dog, so he gave me some cheap things and a few guns, and told me he hoped he would never see my face again. Good old Dutchman, Van Shuyten. I sent him one small lot of ivory a year ago, so that he can't call me a little thief when I get back. I hope he got it. And for the rest, I don't care. I had some wood stacked for you. That was my old house. Did you see?'

"I gave him Towson's book. He made as though he would kiss me, but restrained himself. 'The only book I had left, and I thought I had lost it,' he said, looking at it ecstatically. 'So many accidents happen to a man going about alone, you know. Canoes get upset sometimes—and sometimes you've got to clear out so quick when the people get angry.' He thumbed the pages. 'You made notes in Russian?' I asked. He nodded. 'I thought they were written in cipher,' I said. He laughed, then became serious. 'I had lots of trouble to keep these people off,' he said. 'Did they want to kill you?' I asked. 'Oh no!' he cried, and checked himself. 'Why did they attack us?' I pursued. He hesitated, then said shamefacedly, 'They don't want him to go.' 'Don't they?' I said, curiously. He nodded a nod full of mystery and wisdom. 'I tell you,' he cried, 'this man has enlarged my mind.' He opened his arms wide, staring at me with his little blue eyes that were perfectly round."

6. A province of Western Russia.

3

"I looked at him, lost in astonishment. There he was before me, in motley, as though he had absconded from a troupe of mimes, enthusiastic, fabulous. His very existence was improbable, inexplicable, and altogether bewildering. He was an insoluble problem. It was inconceivable how he had existed, how he had succeeded in getting so far, how he had managed to remain—why he did not instantly disappear. 'I went a little farther,' he said, 'then still a little farther—till I had gone so far that I don't know how I'll ever get back. Never mind. Plenty time. I can manage. You take Kurtz away quick—quick—I tell you.' The glamour of youth enveloped his particoloured rags, his destitution, his loneliness, the essential desolation of his futile wanderings. For months—for years—his life hadn't been worth a day's purchase; and there he was gallantly, thoughtlessly alive, to all appearance indestructible solely by the virtue of his few years and of his unreflecting audacity. I was seduced into something like admiration—like envy. Glamour urged him on, glamour kept him unscathed. He surely wanted nothing from the wilderness but space to breathe in and to push on through. His need was to exist, and to move onwards at the greatest possible risk, and with a maximum of privation. If the absolutely pure, uncalculating, unpractical spirit of adventure had ever ruled a human being, it ruled this be-patched youth. I almost envied him the possession of this modest and clear flame. It seemed to have consumed all thought of self so completely, that, even while he was talking to you, you forgot that it was he—the man before your eyes—who had gone through these things. I did not envy him his devotion to Kurtz, though. He had not meditated over it. It came to him, and he accepted it with a sort of eager fatalism. I must say that to me it appeared about the most dangerous thing in every way he had come upon so far.

"They had come together unavoidably, like two ships becalmed near each other, and lay rubbing sides at last. I suppose Kurtz wanted an audience, because on a certain occasion, when encamped in the forest, they had talked all night, or more probably Kurtz had talked. 'We talked of everything,' he said, quite transported at the recollection. 'I forgot there was such a thing as sleep. The night did not seem to last an hour. Everything! Everything! . . . Of love too.' 'Ah, he talked to you of love!' I said, much amused. 'It isn't what you think,' he cried, almost passionately. 'It was in general. He made me see things—things.'

"He threw his arms up. We were on deck at the time, and the headman of my wood-cutters, lounging near by, turned upon him his heavy and glittering eyes. I looked around, and I don't know why, but I assure you that never, never before, did this land, this river, this jungle, the very arch of this blazing sky, appear to me so hopeless and so dark, so impenetrable to human thought, so pitiless to human weakness. 'And, ever since, you have been with him, of course?' I said.

"On the contrary. It appears their intercourse had been very much broken by various causes. He had, as he informed me proudly, managed to nurse Kurtz through two illnesses (he alluded to it as you would to some risky feat), but as a rule Kurtz wandered alone, far in the depths of the forest. 'Very often coming to this station, I had to wait days and days before he would turn up,' he said. 'Ah, it was worth waiting for!—sometimes.' 'What was he doing? exploring or what?' I asked. 'Oh yes, of course'; he had discovered lots of villages, a lake too—he did not know exactly in what direction; it was dangerous to inquire too much—but mostly his expeditions had been for ivory. 'But he had no goods to trade with by that time,' I objected. 'There's a good lot of cartridges left even yet,' he answered, looking away. 'To speak plainly, he raided the country,' I said. He nodded. 'Not alone, surely!' He muttered something about the villages round that lake. 'Kurtz got the tribe to follow him, did he?' I suggested. He fidgeted a little. 'They adored him,' he said. The tone of these words was so extraordinary that I looked at him searchingly. It was curious to see his mingled eagerness and reluctance to speak of Kurtz. The man filled his life, occupied his thoughts, swayed his emotions. 'What can you expect?' he burst out; 'he came to them with thunder and lightning, you know—and they had never seen anything like it—and very terrible. He could be very terrible. You can't judge Mr Kurtz as you would an ordinary man. No, no, no! Now—just to give you an idea—I don't mind telling you, he wanted to shoot me too one day—but I don't judge him.' 'Shoot you!' I cried. 'What for?' 'Well, I had a small lot of ivory the chief of that village near my house gave me. You see I used to shoot game for them. Well, he wanted it, and wouldn't hear reason. He declared he would shoot me unless I gave him the ivory and then cleared out of the country, because he could do so, and had a fancy for it, and there was nothing on earth to prevent him killing whom he jolly well pleased. And it was true too. I gave him the ivory. What did I care! But I didn't clear out. No, no. I couldn't leave him. I had to be careful, of course, till we got friendly again for a time. He had his second illness then. Afterwards I had to keep out of the way; but I didn't mind. He was living for the most part in those villages on the lake. When he came down to the river, sometimes he would take to me, and sometimes it was better for me to be careful. This man suffered too much. He hated all this, and somehow he couldn't get away. When I had a chance I begged him to try and leave while there was time; I offered to go back with him. And he would say yes, and then he would remain; go off on another ivory hunt; disappear for weeks; forget himself amongst these people—forget himself—you know.' 'Why! he's mad,' I said. He protested indignantly. Mr Kurtz couldn't be mad. If I had heard him talk, only two days ago, I wouldn't dare hint at such a thing. . . . I had taken up my binoculars while we talked, and was looking at the shore, sweeping the limit of the forest at each side and at the back of the house. The consciousness of there being people in that bush, so silent, so quiet—as silent and quiet as the ruined house on the hill—made me uneasy. There was no sign on the face of nature of this amazing tale that was not so much told as suggested to me in desolate exclamations, completed by shrugs, in interrupted phrases, in hints ending in deep sighs. The woods were unmoved, like a mask—heavy, like the closed door of a prison—they looked with their air of hidden knowledge, of patient expectation, of unapproachable silence. The Russian was explaining to me that it was only lately that Mr Kurtz had come down to the river, bringing along with him all the fighting men of that lake tribe. He had been absent for several months—getting himself adored, I suppose—and had come down unexpectedly, with the intention to all appearance of making a raid either across the river or down stream. Evidently the appetite for more ivory had got the better of the—what shall I say?—less material aspirations. However, he had got much worse suddenly. 'I heard he was lying helpless, and so I came up—took my chance,' said the Russian. 'Oh, he is bad, very bad.' I directed my glass to the house. There were no signs of life, but there was the ruined roof, the long mud wall peeping above the grass, with three little square window-holes, no two of the same size; all this brought within reach of my hand, as it were. And then I made a brusque movement, and one of the remaining posts of that vanished fence leaped up in the field of my glass. You remember I told you I had been struck at the distance by certain attempts at ornamentation, rather remarkable in the ruinous aspect of the place. Now I had suddenly a nearer view, and its first result was to make me throw my head back as if before a blow. Then I went carefully from post to post with my glass, and I saw my mistake. These round knobs were not ornamental but symbolic; they were expressive and puzzling, striking and disturbing—food for thought and also for the vultures if there had been any looking down from the sky; but at all events for such ants as were industrious enough to ascend the pole. They would have been even more impressive, those heads on the stakes, if their faces had not been turned to the house. Only one, the first I had made out, was facing my way. I was not so shocked as you may think. The start back I had given was really nothing but a movement of surprise. I had expected to see a knob of wood there, you know. I returned deliberately to the first I had seen—and there it was, black, dried, sunken, with closed eyelids,—a head that seemed to sleep at the top of that pole, and, with the shrunken dry lips showing a narrow white line of the teeth, was smiling too, smiling continuously at some endless and jocose dream of that eternal slumber.

"I am not disclosing any trade secrets. In fact the manager said afterwards that Mr Kurtz's methods had ruined the district. I have no opinion on that point, but I want you clearly to understand that there was nothing exactly profitable in these heads being there. They only showed that Mr Kurtz lacked restraint in the gratification of his various lusts, that there was something wanting in him—some small matter which, when the pressing need arose, could not be found under his magnificent eloquence. Whether he knew of this deficiency himself I can't say. I think the knowledge came to him at last—only at the very last. But the wilderness had found him out early, and had taken on him a terrible vengeance for the fantastic invasion. I think it had whispered to him things about himself which he did not know, things of which he had no conception till he took counsel with this great solitude—and the whisper had proved irresistibly fascinating. It echoed loudly within him because he was hollow at the core. . . . I put down the glass, and the head that had appeared near enough to be spoken to seemed at once to have leaped away from me into inaccessible distance.

"The admirer of Mr Kurtz was a bit crestfallen. In a hurried, indistinct voice he began to assure me he had not dared to take these—say, symbols—down. He was not afraid of the natives; they would not stir till Mr Kurtz gave the word. His ascendancy was extraordinary. The camps of these people surrounded the place, and the chiefs came every day to see him. They would crawl . . . 'I don't want to know anything of the ceremonies used when approaching Mr Kurtz,' I shouted. Curious, this feeling that came over me that such details would be more intolerable than those heads drying on the stakes under Mr Kurtz's windows. After all, that was only a savage sight, while I seemed at one bound to have been transported into some lightless region of subtle horrors, where pure, uncomplicated savagery was a positive relief, being something that had a right to exist—obviously—in the sunshine. The young man looked at me with surprise. I suppose it did not occur to him Mr Kurtz was no idol of mine. He forgot I hadn't heard any of these splendid monologues on, what was it? on love, justice, conduct of life—or what not. If it had come to crawling before Mr Kurtz, he crawled as much as the veriest savage of them all. I had no idea of the conditions, he said: these heads were the heads of rebels. I shocked him excessively by laughing. Rebels! What would be the next definition I was to hear? There had been enemies, criminals, workers—and these were rebels. Those rebellious heads looked very subdued to me on their sticks. 'You don't know how such a life tries a man like Kurtz,' cried Kurtz's last disciple. 'Well, and you?' I said. 'I! I! I am a simple man. I have no great thoughts. I want nothing from anybody. How can you compare me to . . .?' His feelings were too much for speech, and suddenly he broke down. 'I don't understand,' he groaned. 'I've been doing my best to keep him alive, and that's enough. I had no hand in all this. I have no abilities. There hasn't been a drop of medicine or a mouthful of invalid food for months here. He was shamefully abandoned. A man like this, with such ideas. Shamefully! Shamefully! I—I—haven't slept for the last ten nights. . . .'

"His voice lost itself in the calm of the evening. The long shadows of the forest had slipped down-hill while we talked, had gone far beyond the ruined hovel, beyond the symbolic row of stakes. All this was in the gloom, while we down there were yet in the sunshine, and the stretch of the river abreast of the clearing glittered in a still and dazzling splendour, with a murky and overshadowed bend above and below. Not a living soul was seen on the shore. The bushes did not rustle.

"Suddenly round the corner of the house a group of men appeared, as though they had come up from the ground. They waded waist-deep in the grass, in a compact body, bearing an improvised stretcher in their midst. Instantly, in the emptiness of the landscape, a cry arose whose shrillness pierced the still air like a sharp arrow flying straight to the very heart of the land; and, as if by enchantment, streams of human beings—of naked human beings—with spears in their hands, with bows, with shields, with wild glances and savage movements, were poured into the clearing by the dark-faced and pensive forest. The bushes shook, the grass swayed for a time, and then everything stood still in attentive immobility.

"'Now, if he does not say the right thing to them we are all done for,' said the Russian at my elbow. The knot of men with the stretcher had stopped too, half-way to the steamer, as if petrified. I saw the man on the stretcher sit up, lank and with an uplifted arm, above the shoulders of the bearers. 'Let us hope that the man who can talk so well of love in general will find some particular reason to spare us this time,' I said. I resented bitterly the absurd danger of our situation, as if to be at the mercy of that atrocious phantom had been a dishonouring necessity. I could not hear a sound, but through my glasses I saw the thin arm extended commandingly, the lower jaw moving, the eyes of that apparition shining darkly far in its bony head that nodded with grotesque jerks. Kurtz—Kurtz—that means 'short' in German—don't it? Well, the name was as true as everything else in his life—and death. He looked at least seven feet long. His covering had fallen off, and his body emerged from it pitiful and appalling as from a winding-sheet. I could see the cage of his ribs all astir, the bones of his arm waving. It was as though an animated image of death carved out of old ivory had been shaking its hand with menaces at a motionless crowd of men made of dark and glittering bronze. I saw him open his mouth wide—it gave him a weirdly voracious aspect, as though he had wanted to swallow all the air, all the earth, all the men before him. A deep voice reached me faintly. He must have been shouting. He fell back suddenly. The stretcher shook as the bearers staggered forward again, and almost at the same time I noticed that the crowd of savages was vanishing without any perceptible movement of retreat, as if the forest that had ejected these beings so suddenly had drawn them in again as the breath is drawn in a long aspiration.

"Some of the pilgrims behind the stretcher carried his arms—two shot-guns, a heavy rifle, and a light revolver-carbine—the thunderbolts of that pitiful Jupiter. The manager bent over him murmuring as he walked beside his head. They laid him down in one of the little cabins—just a room for a bed-place and a camp-stool or two, you know. We had brought his belated correspondence, and a lot of torn envelopes and open letters littered his bed. His hand roamed feebly amongst these papers. I was struck by the fire of his eyes and the composed languor of his expression. It was not so much the exhaustion of disease. He did not seem in pain. This shadow looked satiated and calm, as though for the moment it had had its fill of all the emotions.

"He rustled one of the letters, and looking straight in my face said, 'I am glad.' Somebody had been writing to him about me. These special recommendations were turning up again. The volume of tone he emitted without effort, almost without the trouble of moving his lips, amazed me. A voice! a voice! It was grave, profound, vibrating, while the man did not seem capable of a whisper. However, he had enough strength in him—factitious no doubt—to very nearly make an end of us, as you shall hear directly.

"The manager appeared silently in the doorway; I stepped out at once and he drew the curtain after me. The Russian, eyed curiously by the pilgrims, was staring at the shore. I followed the direction of his glance.

"Dark human shapes could be made out in the distance, flitting indistinctly against the gloomy border of the forest, and near the river two bronze figures, leaning on tall spears, stood in the sunlight under fantastic head-dresses of spotted skins, warlike and still in statuesque repose. And from right to left along the lighted shore moved a wild and gorgeous apparition of a woman.

"She walked with measured steps, draped in striped and fringed cloths, treading the earth proudly, with a slight jingle and flash of barbarous ornaments. She carried her head high; her hair was done in the shape of a helmet; she had brass leggings to the knee, brass wire gauntlets to the elbow, a crimson spot on her tawny cheek, innumerable necklaces of glass beads on her neck; bizarre things, charms, gifts of witchmen, that hung about her, glittered and trembled at every step. She must have had the value of several elephant tusks upon her. She was savage and superb, wild-eyed and magnificent; there was something ominous and stately in her deliberate progress. And in the hush that had fallen suddenly upon the whole sorrowful land, the immense wilderness, the colossal body of the fecund and mysterious life seemed to look at her, pensive, as though it had been looking at the image of its own tenebrous and passionate soul.

"She came abreast of the steamer, stood still, and faced us. Her long shadow fell to the water's edge. Her face had a tragic and fierce aspect of wild sorrow and of dumb pain mingled with the fear of some struggling, half-shaped resolve. She stood looking at us without a stir, and like the wilderness itself, with an air of brooding over an inscrutable purpose. A whole minute passed, and then she made a step forward. There was a low jingle, a glint of yellow metal, a sway of fringed draperies, and she stopped as if her heart had failed her. The young fellow by my side growled. The pilgrims murmured at my back. She looked at us all as if her life had depended upon the unswerving steadiness of her glance. Suddenly she opened her bared arms and threw them up rigid above her head, as though in an uncontrollable desire to touch the sky, and at the same time the swift shadows darted out on the earth, swept around on the river, gathering the steamer in a shadowy embrace. A formidable silence hung over the scene.

"She turned away slowly, walked on, following the bank, and passed into the bushes to the left. Once only her eyes gleamed back at us in the dusk of the thickets before she disappeared.

"'If she had offered to come aboard I really think I would have tried to shoot her,' said the man of patches, nervously. 'I had been risking my life every day for the last fortnight to keep her out of the house. She got in one day and kicked up a row about those miserable rags I picked up in the storeroom to mend my clothes with. I wasn't decent. At least it must have been that, for she talked like a fury to Kurtz for an hour, pointing at me now and then. I don't understand the dialect of this tribe. Luckily for me, I fancy Kurtz felt too ill that day to care, or there would have been mischief. I don't understand. . . . No—it's too much for me. Ah, well, it's all over now.'

"At this moment I heard Kurtz's deep voice behind the curtain, 'Save me!—save the ivory, you mean. Don't tell me. Save *me!* Why, I've had to save you. You are interrupting my plans now. Sick! Sick! Not so sick as you would like to believe. Never mind. I'll carry my ideas out yet—I will return. I'll show you what can be done. You with your little peddling notions—you are interfering with me. I will return. I . . .'

"The manager came out. He did me the honour to take me under the arm and lead me aside. 'He is very low, very low,' he said. He considered it necessary to sigh, but neglected to be consistently sorrowful. 'We have done all we could for him—haven't we? But there is no disguising the fact, Mr Kurtz has done more harm than good to the Company. He did not see the time was not ripe for vigorous action. Cautiously, cautiously—that's my principle. We must be cautious yet. The district is closed to us for a time. Deplorable! Upon the whole, the trade will suffer. I don't deny there is a remarkable quantity of ivory—mostly fossil. We must save it, at all events—but look how precarious the position is—and why? Because the method is unsound.' 'Do you,' said I, looking at the shore, 'call it "unsound method"?' 'Without doubt,' he exclaimed, hotly. 'Don't you?' . . . 'No method at all,' I murmured after a while. 'Exactly,' he exulted. 'I anticipated this. Shows a complete want of judgment. It is my duty to point it out in the proper quarter.' 'Oh,' said I, 'that fellow—what's his name?—the brickmaker, will make a readable report for you.' He appeared confounded for a moment. It seemed to me I had never breathed an atmosphere so vile, and I turned mentally to Kurtz for relief—positively for relief. 'Nevertheless, I think Mr Kurtz is a remarkable man,' I said with emphasis. He started, dropped on me a cold heavy glance, said very quietly, 'He was,' and turned his back on me. My hour of favour was over; I found myself lumped along with Kurtz as a partisan of methods for which the time was not ripe: I was unsound! Ah! but it was something to have at least a choice of nightmares.

"I had turned to the wilderness really, not to Mr Kurtz, who, I was ready to admit, was as good as buried. And for a moment it seemed to me as if I also were buried in a vast grave full of unspeakable secrets. I felt an intolerable weight oppressing my breast, the smell of the damp earth, the unseen presence of victorious corruption, the darkness of an impenetrable night. . . . The Russian tapped me on the shoulder. I heard him mumbling and stammering something about 'brother seaman—couldn't conceal—knowledge of matters that would affect Mr Kurtz's reputation.' I waited. For him evidently Mr Kurtz was not in his grave; I suspect that for him Mr Kurtz was one of the immortals. 'Well!' said I at last, 'speak out. As it happens, I am Mr Kurtz's friend—in a way.'

"He stated with a good deal of formality that had we not been 'of the same profession,' he would have kept the matter to himself without regard to consequences. He suspected 'there was an active ill-will towards him on the part of these white men that—' 'You are right,' I said, remembering a certain conversation I had overheard. 'The manager thinks you ought to be hanged.' He showed a concern at this intelligence which amused me at first. 'I had better get out of the way quietly,' he said, earnestly. 'I can do no more for Kurtz now, and they would soon find some excuse. What's to stop them? There's a military post three hundred miles from here.' 'Well, upon my word,' said I, 'perhaps you had better go if you have any friends amongst the savages near by.' 'Plenty,' he said. 'They are simple people—and I want nothing, you know.' He stood biting his lip, then: 'I don't want any harm to happen to these whites here, but of course I was thinking of Mr Kurtz's reputation—but you are a brother seaman and—' 'All right,' said I, after a time. 'Mr Kurtz's reputation is safe with me.' I did not know how truly I spoke.

"He informed me, lowering his voice, that it was Kurtz who had ordered the attack to be made on the steamer. 'He hated sometimes the idea of being taken away—and then again . . . But I don't understand these matters. I am a simple man. He thought it would scare you away—that you would give it up, thinking him dead. I could not stop him. Oh, I had an awful time of it this last month.' 'Very well,' I said. 'He is all right now.' 'Ye-e-es,' he muttered, not very convinced apparently. 'Thanks,' said I; 'I shall keep my eyes open.' 'But quiet—eh?' he urged, anxiously. 'It would be awful for his reputation if anybody here—' I promised a complete discretion with great gravity. 'I have a canoe and three black fellows waiting not very far. I am off. Could you give me a few Martini-Henry cartridges?' I could, and did, with proper secrecy. He helped himself, with a wink at me, to a handful of my tobacco. 'Between sailors—you know—good English tobacco.' At the door of the pilot-house he turned round—'I say, haven't you a pair of shoes you could spare?' He raised one leg. 'Look.' The soles were tied with knotted strings sandal-wise under his bare feet. I rooted out an old pair, at which he looked with admiration before tucking it under his left arm. One of his pockets (bright red) was bulging with cartridges, from the other (dark blue) peeped 'Towson's Inquiry,' &c., &c. He seemed to think himself excellently well equipped for a renewed encounter with the wilderness. 'Ah! I'll never, never meet such a man again. You ought to have heard him recite poetry—his own too it was, he told me. Poetry!' He rolled his eyes at the recollection of these delights. 'Oh, he enlarged my mind!' 'Good-bye,' said I. He shook hands and vanished in the night. Sometimes I ask myself whether I had ever really seen him—whether it was possible to meet such a phenomenon! . . .

"When I woke up shortly after midnight his warning came to my mind with its hint of danger that seemed, in the starred darkness, real enough to make me get up for the purpose of having a look round. On the hill a big fire burned, illuminating fitfully a crooked corner of the station-house. One of the agents with a picket of a few of our blacks, armed for the purpose, was keeping guard over the ivory; but deep within the forest, red gleams that wavered, that seemed to sink and rise from the ground amongst confused columnar shapes of intense blackness, showed the exact position of the camp where Mr Kurtz's adorers were keeping their uneasy vigil. The monotonous beating of a big drum filled the air with muffled shocks and a lingering vibration. A steady droning sound of many men chanting each to himself some weird incantation came out from the black, flat wall of the woods as the humming of bees comes out of a hive, and had a strange narcotic effect upon my half-awake senses. I believe I dozed off leaning over the rail, till an abrupt burst of yells, an overwhelming outbreak of a pent-up and mysterious frenzy, woke me up in a bewildered wonder. It was cut short all at once, and the low droning went on with an effect of audible and soothing silence. I glanced casually into the little cabin. A light was burning within, but Mr Kurtz was not there.

"I think I would have raised an outcry if I had believed my eyes. But I didn't believe them at first—the thing seemed so impossible. The fact is, I was completely unnerved by a sheer blank fright, pure abstract terror, unconnected with any distinct shape of physical danger. What made this emotion so overpowering was—how shall I define it?—the moral shock I received, as if something altogether monstrous, intolerable to thought and odious to the soul, had been thrust upon me unexpectedly. This lasted of course the merest fraction of a second, and then the usual sense of commonplace, deadly danger, the possibility of a sudden onslaught and massacre, or something of the kind, which I saw impending, was positively welcome and composing. It pacified me, in fact, so much, that I did not raise an alarm.

"There was an agent buttoned up inside an ulster[7] and sleeping on a chair on deck within three feet of me. The yells had not awakened him; he snored very slightly; I left him to his slumbers and leaped ashore. I did not betray Mr Kurtz—it was ordered I should never betray him—it was written I should be loyal to the nightmare of my choice. I was anxious to deal with this shadow by myself alone,—and to this day I don't know why I was so jealous of sharing with any one the peculiar blackness of that experience.

"As soon as I got on the bank I saw a trail—a broad trail through the grass. I remember the exultation with which I said to myself, 'He can't walk—he is crawling on all-fours—I've got him.' The grass was wet with dew. I strode rapidly with clenched fists. I fancy I had some vague notion of falling upon him and giving him a drubbing. I don't know. I had some imbecile thoughts. The knitting old woman with the cat obtruded herself upon my memory as a most improper person to be sitting at the other end of such an affair. I saw a row of pilgrims squirting lead in the air out of Winchesters held to the hip. I thought I would never get back to the steamer, and imagined myself living alone and unarmed in the woods to an advanced age. Such silly things—you know. And I remember I confounded the beat of the drum with the beating of my heart, and was pleased at its calm regularity.

"I kept to the track though—then stopped to listen. The night was very clear: a dark blue space, sparkling with dew and starlight, in which black things stood very still. I thought I could see a kind of motion ahead of me. I was strangely cocksure of everything that night. I actually left the track and ran in a wide semicircle (I verily believe chuckling to myself) so as to get in front of that stir, of that motion I had seen—if indeed I had seen anything. I was circumventing Kurtz as though it had been a boyish game.

"I came upon him, and, if he had not heard me coming, I would have fallen over him too, but he got up in time. He rose, unsteady, long, pale, indistinct, like a vapour exhaled by the earth, and swayed slightly, misty and silent before me; while at my back the fires loomed between the trees, and the murmur of many voices issued from the forest. I had cut him off cleverly; but when actually confronting him I seemed to come to my senses, I saw the danger in its right proportion. It was by no means over yet. Suppose he began to shout? Though he could hardly stand, there was still plenty of vigour in his voice. 'Go away—hide yourself,' he said, in that profound tone. It was very awful. I glanced back. We were within thirty yards from the nearest fire. A black figure stood up, strode on long black legs, waving long black arms, across the glow. It had horns—antelope horns, I think—on its head. Some sorcerer, some witch-man, no doubt: it looked fiend-like enough. 'Do you know what you are doing?' I whispered. 'Perfectly,' he answered, raising his voice for that single word: it sounded to me far off and yet loud, like a hail through a speaking-trumpet. If he makes a row we are lost, I thought to myself. This clearly was not a case for fisticuffs, even apart from the very natural aversion I had to beat that Shadow—this wandering and tormented thing. 'You will be lost,' I said—'utterly lost.' One gets sometimes such a flash of inspiration, you know. I did say the right thing, though indeed he could not have been more irretrievably lost than he was at this very moment, when the foundations of our intimacy were being laid—to endure—to endure—even to the end—even beyond.

"'I had immense plans,' he muttered irresolutely. 'Yes,' said I; 'but if you try to shout I'll smash your head with—' there was not a stick or a stone near. 'I will throttle you for good,' I corrected myself. 'I was on the threshold of great things,' he pleaded, in a voice of longing, with a wistfulness of tone that made my blood run cold. 'And

7. Long overcoat.

now for this stupid scoundrel—' 'Your success in Europe is assured in any case,' I affirmed, steadily. I did not want to have the throttling of him, you understand—and indeed it would have been very little use for any practical purpose. I tried to break the spell—the heavy, mute spell of the wilderness—that seemed to draw him to its pitiless breast by the awakening of forgotten and brutal instincts, by the memory of gratified and monstrous passions. This alone, I was convinced, had driven him out to the edge of the forest, to the bush, towards the gleam of fires, the throb of drums, the drone of weird incantations; this alone had beguiled his unlawful soul beyond the bounds of permitted aspirations. And, don't you see, the terror of the position was not in being knocked on the head—though I had a very lively sense of that danger too—but in this, that I had to deal with a being to whom I could not appeal in the name of anything high or low. I had, even like the niggers, to invoke him—himself—his own exalted and incredible degradation. There was nothing either above or below him, and I knew it. He had kicked himself loose of the earth. Confound the man! he had kicked the very earth to pieces. He was alone, and I before him did not know whether I stood on the ground or floated in the air. I've been telling you what we said—repeating the phrases we pronounced,—but what's the good? They were common everyday words,—the familiar, vague sounds exchanged on every waking day of life. But what of that? They had behind them, to my mind, the terrific suggestiveness of words heard in dreams, of phrases spoken in nightmares. Soul! If anybody had ever struggled with a soul, I am the man. And I wasn't arguing with a lunatic either. Believe me or not, his intelligence was perfectly clear—concentrated, it is true, upon himself with horrible intensity, yet clear; and therein was my only chance—barring, of course, the killing him there and then, which wasn't so good, on account of unavoidable noise. But his soul was mad. Being alone in the wilderness, it had looked within itself, and, by heavens! I tell you, it had gone mad. I had—for my sins, I suppose—to go through the ordeal of looking into it myself. No eloquence could have been so withering to one's belief in mankind as his final burst of sincerity. He struggled with himself, too. I saw it,—I heard it. I saw the inconceivable mystery of a soul that knew no restraint, no faith, and no fear, yet struggling blindly with itself. I kept my head pretty well; but when I had him at last stretched on the couch, I wiped my forehead, while my legs shook under me as though I had carried half a ton on my back down that hill. And yet I had only supported him, his bony arm clasped round my neck—and he was not much heavier than a child.

"When next day we left at noon, the crowd, of whose presence behind the curtain of trees I had been acutely conscious all the time, flowed out of the woods again, filled the clearing, covered the slope with a mass of naked, breathing, quivering, bronze bodies. I steamed up a bit, then swung down-stream, and two thousand eyes followed the evolutions of the splashing, thumping, fierce river-demon beating the water with its terrible tail and breathing black smoke into the air. In front of the first rank, along the river, three men, plastered with bright red earth from head to foot, strutted to and fro restlessly. When we came abreast again, they faced the river, stamped their feet, nodded their horned heads, swayed their scarlet bodies; they shook towards the fierce river-demon a bunch of black feathers, a mangy skin with a pendent tail—something that looked like a dried gourd; they shouted periodically together strings of amazing words that resembled no sounds of human language; and the deep murmurs of the crowd, interrupted suddenly, were like the responses of some satanic litany.

"We had carried Kurtz into the pilot-house: there was more air there. Lying on the couch, he stared through the open shutter. There was an eddy in the mass of human bodies, and the woman with helmeted head and tawny cheeks rushed out to the very brink of the stream. She put out her hands, shouted something, and all that wild mob took up the shout in a roaring chorus of articulated, rapid, breathless utterance.

"'Do you understand this?' I asked.

"He kept on looking out past me with fiery, longing eyes, with a mingled expression of wistfulness and hate. He made no answer, but I saw a smile, a smile of indefinable meaning, appear on his colourless lips that a moment after twitched convulsively. 'Do I not?' he said slowly, gasping, as if the words had been torn out of him by a supernatural power.

"I pulled the string of the whistle, and I did this because I saw the pilgrims on deck getting out their rifles with an air of anticipating a jolly lark. At the sudden screech there was a movement of abject terror through that wedged mass of bodies. 'Don't! don't! you frighten them away,' cried some one on deck disconsolately. I pulled the string time after time. They broke and ran, they leaped, they crouched, they swerved, they dodged the flying terror of the sound. The three red chaps had fallen flat, face down on the shore, as though they had been shot dead. Only the barbarous and superb woman did not so much as flinch, and stretched tragically her bare arms after us over the sombre and glittering river.

"And then that imbecile crowd down on the deck started their little fun, and I could see nothing more for smoke.

"The brown current ran swiftly out of the heart of darkness, bearing us down towards the sea with twice the speed of our upward progress; and Kurtz's life was running swiftly too, ebbing, ebbing out of his heart into the sea of inexorable time. The manager was very placid, he had no vital anxieties now, he took us both in with a comprehensive and satisfied glance: the 'affair' had come off as well as could be wished. I saw the time approaching when I would be left alone of the party of 'unsound method.' The pilgrims looked upon me with disfavour. I was, so to speak, numbered with the dead. It is strange how I accepted this unforeseen partnership, this choice of nightmares forced upon me in the tenebrous land invaded by these mean and greedy phantoms.

"Kurtz discoursed. A voice! a voice! It rang deep to the very last. It survived his strength to hide in the magnificent folds of eloquence the barren darkness of his heart. Oh, he struggled! he struggled! The wastes of his weary brain were haunted by shadowy images now—images of wealth and fame revolving obsequiously round his unextinguishable gift of noble and lofty expression. My Intended, my station, my career, my ideas—these were the subjects for the occasional utterances of elevated sentiments. The shade of the original Kurtz frequented the bedside of the hollow sham, whose fate it was to be buried presently in the mould of primeval earth. But both the diabolic love and the unearthly hate of the mysteries it had penetrated fought for the possession of that soul satiated with primitive emotions, avid of lying fame, of sham distinction, of all the appearances of success and power.

"Sometimes he was contemptibly childish. He desired to have kings meet him at railway-stations on his return from some ghastly Nowhere, where he intended to accomplish great things. 'You show them you have in you something that is really profitable, and then there will be no limits to the recognition of your ability,' he would say. 'Of course you must take care of the motives—right motives—always.' The long reaches that were like one and the same reach, monotonous bends that were exactly alike, slipped past the steamer with their multitude of secular[8] trees looking patiently after this grimy fragment of another world, the forerunner of

8. Ancient.

change, of conquest, of trade, of massacres, of blessings. I looked ahead—piloting. 'Close the shutter,' said Kurtz suddenly one day; 'I can't bear to look at this.' I did so. There was a silence. 'Oh, but I will wring your heart yet!' he cried at the invisible wilderness.

"We broke down—as I had expected—and had to lie up for repairs at the head of an island. This delay was the first thing that shook Kurtz's confidence. One morning he gave me a packet of papers and a photograph,—the lot tied together with a shoestring. 'Keep this for me,' he said. 'This noxious fool' (meaning the manager) 'is capable of prying into my boxes when I am not looking.' In the afternoon I saw him. He was lying on his back with closed eyes, and I withdrew quietly, but I heard him mutter, 'Live rightly, die, die . . .' I listened. There was nothing more. Was he rehearsing some speech in his sleep, or was it a fragment of a phrase from some newspaper article? He had been writing for the papers and meant to do so again, 'for the furthering of my ideas. It's a duty.'

"His was an impenetrable darkness. I looked at him as you peer down at a man who is lying at the bottom of a precipice where the sun never shines. But I had not much time to give him, because I was helping the engine-driver to take to pieces the leaky cylinders, to straighten a bent connecting-rod, and in other such matters. I lived in an infernal mess of rust, filings, nuts, bolts, spanners, hammers, ratchet-drills—things I abominate, because I don't get on with them. I tended the little forge we fortunately had aboard; I toiled wearily in a wretched scrap-heap—unless I had the shakes too bad to stand.

"One evening coming in with a candle I was startled to hear him say a little tremulously, 'I am lying here in the dark waiting for death.' The light was within a foot of his eyes. I forced myself to murmur, 'Oh, nonsense!' and stood over him as if transfixed.

"Anything approaching the change that came over his features I have never seen before, and hope never to see again. Oh, I wasn't touched. I was fascinated. It was as though a veil had been rent. I saw on that ivory face the expression of sombre pride, of ruthless power, of craven terror—of an intense and hopeless despair. Did he live his life again in every detail of desire, temptation, and surrender during that supreme moment of complete knowledge? He cried in a whisper at some image, at some vision,—he cried out twice, a cry that was no more than a breath—

"'The horror! The horror!'

"I blew the candle out and left the cabin. The pilgrims were dining in the mess-room, and I took my place opposite the manager, who lifted his eyes to give me a questioning glance, which I successfully ignored. He leaned back, serene, with that peculiar smile of his sealing the unexpressed depths of his meanness. A continuous shower of small flies streamed upon the lamp, upon the cloth, upon our hands and faces. Suddenly the manager's boy put his insolent black head in the doorway, and said in a tone of scathing contempt—

"'Mistah Kurtz—he dead.'

"All the pilgrims rushed out to see. I remained, and went on with my dinner. I believe I was considered brutally callous. However, I did not eat much. There was a lamp in there—light, don't you know—and outside it was so beastly, beastly dark. I went no more near the remarkable man who had pronounced a judgment upon the adventures of his soul on this earth. The voice was gone. What else had been there? But I am of course aware that next day the pilgrims buried something in a muddy hole.

"And then they very nearly buried me.

"However, as you see, I did not go to join Kurtz there and then. I did not. I remained to dream the nightmare out to the end, and to show my loyalty to Kurtz once more. Destiny. My destiny! Droll thing life is—that mysterious arrangement of merciless logic for a futile purpose. The most you can hope from it is some knowledge of yourself—that comes too late—a crop of unextinguishable regrets. I have wrestled with death. It is the most unexciting contest you can imagine. It takes place in an impalpable greyness, with nothing underfoot, with nothing around, without spectators, without clamour, without glory, without the great desire of victory, without the great fear of defeat, in a sickly atmosphere of tepid scepticism, without much belief in your own right, and still less in that of your adversary. If such is the form of ultimate wisdom, then life is a greater riddle than some of us think it to be. I was within a hair's-breadth of the last opportunity for pronouncement, and I found with humiliation that probably I would have nothing to say. This is the reason why I affirm that Kurtz was a remarkable man. He had something to say. He said it. Since I had peeped over the edge myself, I understand better the meaning of his stare, that could not see the flame of the candle, but was wide enough to embrace the whole universe, piercing enough to penetrate all the hearts that beat in the darkness. He had summed up—he had judged. 'The horror!' He was a remarkable man. After all, this was the expression of some sort of belief; it had candour, it had conviction, it had a vibrating note of revolt in its whisper, it had the appalling face of a glimpsed truth—the strange commingling of desire and hate. And it is not my own extremity I remember best—a vision of greyness without form filled with physical pain, and a careless contempt for the evanescence of all things—even of this pain itself. No! It is his extremity that I seem to have lived through. True, he had made that last stride, he had stepped over the edge, while I had been permitted to draw back my hesitating foot. And perhaps in this is the whole difference; perhaps all the wisdom, and all truth, and all sincerity, are just compressed into that inappreciable moment of time in which we step over the threshold of the invisible. Perhaps! I like to think my summing-up would not have been a word of careless contempt. Better his cry—much better. It was an affirmation, a moral victory paid for by innumerable defeats, by abominable terrors, by abominable satisfactions. But it was a victory! That is why I have remained loyal to Kurtz to the last, and even beyond, when a long time after I heard once more, not his own voice, but the echo of his magnificent eloquence thrown to me from a soul as translucently pure as a cliff of crystal.

"No, they did not bury me, though there is a period of time which I remember mistily, with a shuddering wonder, like a passage through some inconceivable world that had no hope in it and no desire. I found myself back in the sepulchral city resenting the sight of people hurrying through the streets to filch a little money from each other, to devour their infamous cookery, to gulp their unwholesome beer, to dream their insignificant and silly dreams. They trespassed upon my thoughts. They were intruders whose knowledge of life was to me an irritating pretence, because I felt so sure they could not possibly know the things I knew. Their bearing, which was simply the bearing of commonplace individuals going about their business in the assurance of perfect safety, was offensive to me like the outrageous flauntings of folly in the face of a danger it is unable to comprehend. I had no particular desire to enlighten them, but I had some difficulty in restraining myself from laughing in their faces, so full of stupid importance. I daresay I was not very well at that time. I tottered about the streets—there were various affairs to settle—grinning bitterly at perfectly respectable persons. I admit my behaviour was inexcusable, but then my temperature was seldom normal in these days. My dear aunt's endeavours to 'nurse up my strength' seemed altogether beside the mark. It was not my strength that wanted nursing, it was my imagination that wanted soothing. I kept the bundle of papers given me by Kurtz, not knowing exactly what to do with it. His mother had died lately, watched over, as I was told, by his Intended. A clean-shaved man, with an official manner and wearing gold-rimmed spectacles, called on me one day and made inquiries, at first circuitous, afterwards suavely pressing, about what he was pleased to denominate certain 'documents.' I was not surprised, because I had had two rows with the manager on the subject out there. I had refused to give up the smallest scrap out of that package, and I took the same attitude with the spectacled man. He became darkly menacing at last, and with much heat argued that the Company had the right to every bit of information about its 'territories.' And, said he, 'Mr Kurtz's knowledge of unexplored regions must have been necessarily extensive and peculiar—owing to his great abilities and to the deplorable circumstances in which he had been placed: therefore—' I assured him Mr Kurtz's knowledge, however extensive, did not bear upon the problems of commerce or administration. He invoked then the name of science. 'It would be an incalculable loss if,' &c., &c. I offered him the report on the 'Suppression of Savage Customs,' with the postscriptum torn off. He took it up eagerly, but ended by sniffing at it with an air of contempt. 'This is not what we had a right to expect,' he remarked. 'Expect nothing else,' I said. 'There are only private letters.' He withdrew upon some threat of legal proceedings, and I saw him no more; but another fellow, calling himself Kurtz's cousin, appeared two days later, and was anxious to hear all the details about his dear relative's last moments. Incidentally he gave me to understand that Kurtz had been essentially a great musician. 'There was the making of an immense success,' said the man, who was an organist, I believe, with lank grey hair flowing over a greasy coat-collar. I had no reason to doubt his statement; and to this day I am unable to say what was Kurtz's profession, whether he ever had any—which was the greatest of his talents. I had taken him for a painter who wrote for the papers, or else for a journalist who could paint—but even the cousin (who took snuff during the interview) could not tell me what he had been—exactly. He was a universal genius—on that point I agreed with the old chap, who thereupon blew his nose noisily into a large cotton handkerchief and withdrew in senile agitation, bearing off some family letters and memoranda without importance. Ultimately a journalist anxious to know something of the fate of his 'dear colleague' turned up. This visitor informed me Kurtz's proper sphere ought to have been politics 'on the popular side.' He had furry straight eyebrows, bristly hair cropped short, an eye-glass on a broad ribbon, and, becoming expansive, confessed his opinion that Kurtz really couldn't write a bit—'but heavens! how that man could talk! He electrified large meetings. He had faith—don't you see?—he had the faith. He could get himself to believe anything—anything. He would have been a splendid leader of an extreme party.' 'What party?' I asked. 'Any party,' answered the other. 'He was an—an—extremist.' Did I not think so? I assented. Did I know, he asked, with a sudden flash of curiosity, 'what it was that had induced him to go out there?' 'Yes,' said I, and forthwith handed him the famous Report for publication, if he thought fit. He glanced through it hurriedly, mumbling all the time, judged 'it would do,' and took himself off with this plunder.

"Thus I was left at last with a slim packet of letters and the girl's portrait. She struck me as beautiful—I mean she had a beautiful expression. I know that the sunlight can be made to lie too, yet one felt that no manipulation of light and pose could have conveyed the delicate shade of truthfulness upon those features. She seemed ready to listen without mental reservation, without suspicion, without a thought for herself. I concluded I would go and give her back her portrait and those letters myself. Curiosity? Yes; and also some other feeling perhaps. All that had been Kurtz's had passed out of my hands: his soul, his body, his station, his plans, his ivory, his career. There remained only his memory and his Intended—and I wanted to give that up too to the past, in a way,—to surrender personally all that remained of him with me to that oblivion which is the last word of our common fate. I don't defend myself. I had no clear perception of what it was I really wanted. Perhaps it was an impulse of unconscious loyalty, or the fulfilment of one of those ironic necessities that lurk in the facts of human existence. I don't know. I can't tell. But I went.

"I thought his memory was like the other memories of the dead that accumulate in every man's life,—a vague impress on the brain of shadows that had fallen on it in their swift and final passage; but before the high and ponderous door, between the tall houses of a street as still and decorous as a well-kept alley in a cemetery, I had a vision of him on the stretcher, opening his mouth voraciously, as if to devour all the earth with all its mankind. He lived then before me; he lived as much as he had ever lived—a shadow insatiable of splendid appearances, of frightful realities; a shadow darker than the shadow of the night, and draped nobly in the folds of a gorgeous eloquence. The vision seemed to enter the house with me—the stretcher, the phantom-bearers, the wild crowd of obedient worshippers, the gloom of the forests, the glitter of the reach between the murky bends, the beat of the drum, regular and muffled like the beating of a heart—the heart of a conquering darkness. It was a moment of triumph for the wilderness, an invading and vengeful rush which, it seemed to me, I would have to keep back alone for the salvation of another soul. And the memory of what I had heard him say afar there, with the horned shapes stirring at my back, in the glow of fires, within the patient woods, those broken phrases came back to me, were heard again in their ominous and terrifying simplicity. I remembered his abject pleading, his abject threats, the colossal scale of his vile desires, the meanness, the torment, the tempestuous anguish of his soul. And later on I seemed to see his collected languid manner, when he said one day, 'This lot of ivory now is really mine. The Company did not pay for it. I collected it myself at a very great personal risk. I am afraid they will try to claim it as theirs though. H'm. It is a difficult case. What do you think I ought to do—resist? Eh? I want no more than justice.' . . . He wanted no more than justice—no more than justice. I rang the bell before a mahogany door on the first floor, and while I waited he seemed to stare at me out of the glassy panel—stare with that wide and immense stare embracing, condemning, loathing all the universe. I seemed to hear the whispered cry, 'The horror! The horror!'

"The dusk was falling. I had to wait in a lofty drawing-room with three long windows from floor to ceiling that were like three luminous and bedraped columns. The bent gilt legs and backs of the furniture shone in indistinct curves. The tall marble fireplace had a cold and monumental whiteness. A grand piano stood massively in a corner, with dark gleams on the flat surfaces like a sombre and polished sarcophagus. A high door opened—closed. I rose.

"She came forward, all in black, with a pale head, floating towards me in the dusk. She was in mourning. It was more than a year since his death, more than a year since the news came; she seemed as though she would remember and mourn for ever. She took both my hands in hers and murmured, 'I had heard you were coming.' I noticed she was not very young—I mean not girlish. She had a mature capacity for fidelity, for belief, for suffering. The room seemed to have grown darker, as if all the sad light of the cloudy evening had taken refuge on her forehead. This fair hair, this pale visage, this pure brow, seemed surrounded by an ashy halo from which the dark eyes looked out at me. Their glance was guileless, profound, confident, and trustful. She carried her sorrowful head as though she were proud of that sorrow, as though she would say, I—I alone know how to mourn for him as he deserves. But while we were still shaking hands, such a look of awful desolation came upon her face that I perceived she was one of those creatures that are not the playthings of Time. For her he had died only yesterday. And, by Jove! the impression was so powerful that for me too he seemed to have died only yesterday—nay, this very minute. I saw her and him in the same instant of time—his death and her sorrow—I saw her sorrow in the very moment of his death. Do you understand? I saw them together—I heard them together. She had said, with a deep catch of the breath, 'I have survived'; while my strained ears seemed to hear distinctly, mingled with her tone of despairing regret, the summing-up whisper of his eternal condemnation. I asked myself what I was doing there, with a sensation of panic in my heart as though I had blundered into a place of cruel and absurd mysteries not fit for a human being to behold. She motioned me to a chair. We sat down. I laid the packet gently on the little table, and she put her hand over it. . . . 'You knew him well,' she murmured, after a moment of mourning silence.

"'Intimacy grows quickly out there,' I said. 'I knew him as well as it is possible for one man to know another.'

"'And you admired him,' she said. 'It was impossible to know him and not to admire him. Was it?'

"'He was a remarkable man,' I said, unsteadily. Then before the appealing fixity of her gaze, that seemed to watch for more words on my lips, I went on, 'It was impossible not to—'

"'Love him,' she finished eagerly, silencing me into an appalled dumbness. 'How true! how true! But when you think that no one knew him so well as I! I had all his noble confidence. I knew him best.'

"'You knew him best,' I repeated. And perhaps she did. But with every word spoken the room was growing darker, and only her forehead, smooth and white, remained illumined by the unextinguishable light of belief and love.

"'You were his friend,' she went on. 'His friend,' she repeated, a little louder. 'You must have been, if he had given you this, and sent you to me. I feel I can speak to you—and oh! I must speak. I want you—you who have heard his last words—to know I have been worthy of him. . . . It is not pride. . . . Yes! I am proud to know I understood him better than any one on earth—he told me so himself. And since his mother died I have had no one—no one—to—to—'

"I listened. The darkness deepened. I was not even sure whether he had given me the right bundle. I rather suspect he wanted me to take care of another batch of his papers which, after his death, I saw the manager examining under the lamp. And the girl talked, easing her pain in the certitude of my sympathy; she talked as thirsty men drink. I had heard that her engagement with Kurtz had been disapproved by her people. He wasn't rich enough or something. And indeed I don't know whether he had not been a pauper all his life. He had given me some reason to infer that it was his impatience of comparative poverty that drove him out there.

"'. . . Who was not his friend who had heard him speak once?' she was saying. 'He drew men towards him by what was best in them.' She looked at me with intensity. 'It is the gift of the great,' she went on, and the sound of her low voice seemed to have the accompaniment of all the other sounds, full of mystery, desolation, and sorrow, I had ever heard—the ripple of the river, the soughing of the trees swayed by the wind, the murmurs of wild crowds, the faint ring of incomprehensible words cried from afar, the whisper of a voice speaking from beyond the threshold of an eternal darkness. 'But you have heard him! You know!' she cried.

"'Yes, I know,' I said with something like despair in my heart, but bowing my head before the faith that was in her, before that great and saving illusion that shone with an unearthly glow in the darkness, in the triumphant darkness from which I could not have defended her—from which I could not even defend myself.

"'What a loss to me—to us!'—she corrected herself with beautiful generosity; then added in a murmur, 'To the world.' By the last gleams of twilight I could see the glitter of her eyes, full of tears—of tears that would not fall.

"'I have been very happy—very fortunate—very proud,' she went on. 'Too fortunate. Too happy for a little while. And now I am unhappy for—for life.'

"She stood up; her fair hair seemed to catch all the remaining light in a glimmer of gold. I rose too.

"'And of all this,' she went on, mournfully, 'of all his promise, and of all his greatness, of his generous mind, of his noble heart, nothing remains—nothing but a memory. You and I—'

"'We shall always remember him,' I said, hastily.

"'No!' she cried. 'It is impossible that all this should be lost—that such a life should be sacrificed to leave nothing—but sorrow. You know what vast plans he had. I knew of them too—I could not perhaps understand,—but others knew of them. Something must remain. His words, at least, have not died.'

"'His words will remain,' I said.

"'And his example,' she whispered to herself. 'Men looked up to him,—his goodness shone in every act. His example—'

"'True,' I said; 'his example too. Yes, his example. I forgot that.'

"'But I do not. I cannot—I cannot believe—not yet. I cannot believe that I shall never see him again, that nobody will see him again, never, never, never.'

"She put out her arms as if after a retreating figure, stretching them black and with clasped pale hands across the fading and narrow sheen of the window. Never see him! I saw him clearly enough then. I shall see this eloquent phantom as long as I live, and I shall see her too, a tragic and familiar Shade, resembling in this gesture another one, tragic also, and bedecked with powerless charms, stretching bare brown arms over the glitter of the infernal stream, the stream of darkness. She said suddenly very low, 'He died as he lived.'

"'His end,' said I, with dull anger stirring in me, 'was in every way worthy of his life.'

"'And I was not with him,' she murmured. My anger subsided before a feeling of infinite pity.

"'Everything that could be done—' I mumbled.

"'Ah, but I believed in him more than any one on earth—more than his own mother, more than—himself. He needed me! Me! I would have treasured every sigh, every word, every sign, every glance.'

"I felt like a chill grip on my chest. 'Don't,' I said, in a muffled voice.

"'Forgive me. I—I—have mourned so long in silence—in silence. . . . You were with him—to the last? I think of his loneliness. Nobody near to understand him as I would have understood. Perhaps no one to hear. . . .'

"'To the very end,' I said, shakily. 'I heard his very last words. . . .' I stopped in a fright.

"'Repeat them,' she said in a heart-broken tone. 'I want—I want—something—something—to—to live with.'

"I was on the point of crying at her, 'Don't you hear them?' The dusk was repeating them in a persistent whisper all around us, in a whisper that seemed to swell menacingly like the first whisper of a rising wind. 'The horror! the horror!'

"'His last word—to live with,' she murmured. 'Don't you understand I loved him—I loved him—I loved him!'

"I pulled myself together and spoke slowly.

"'The last word he pronounced was—your name.'

"I heard a light sigh, and then my heart stood still, stopped dead short by an exulting and terrible cry, by the cry of inconceivable triumph and of unspeakable pain. 'I knew it—I was sure!' . . . She knew. She was sure. I heard her weeping; she had hidden her face in her hands. It seemed to me that the house would collapse before I could escape, that the heavens would fall upon my head. But nothing happened. The heavens do not fall for such a trifle. Would they have fallen, I wonder, if I had rendered Kurtz that justice which was his due? Hadn't he said he wanted only justice? But I couldn't. I could not tell her. It would have been too dark—too dark altogether. . . ."

Marlow ceased, and sat apart, indistinct and silent, in the pose of a meditating Buddha. Nobody moved for a time. "We have lost the first of the ebb," said the Director, suddenly. I raised my head. The offing was barred by a black bank of clouds, and the tranquil waterway leading to the uttermost ends of the earth flowed sombre under an overcast sky—seemed to lead into the heart of an immense darkness.

RESONANCES

Joseph Conrad: from *Congo Diary*

Arrived at Matadi[1] on the 13th of June, 1890.

Mr Gosse, chief of the station (O.K.) retaining us for some reason of his own.

Made the acquaintance of Mr Roger Casement,[2] which I should consider as a great pleasure under any circumstances and now it becomes a positive piece of luck.

Thinks, speaks well, most intelligent and very sympathetic.

Feel considerably in doubt about the future. Think just now that my life amongst the people (white) around here cannot be very comfortable. Intend avoid acquaintances as much as possible. * * *

1. Colonial station near the mouth of the Congo River. Conrad arrived there on his way to take up his command of a steamship upriver at Kinshasa.

2. Casement (1864–1916) and Conrad were working for the same company. Casement later served as British consul in various parts of Africa, and was the author of a report on the Congo (1904) that did much to make public the terrible conditions there. He was knighted in 1912. In 1916 he was executed by the British for his part in the Easter Rebellion in Ireland.

24th. Gosse and R.C. gone with a large lot of ivory down to Boma. On G.['s] return to start to up the river. Have been myself busy packing ivory in casks. Idiotic employment. Health good up to now. * * *

Prominent characteristic of the social life here: people speaking ill of each other.

* * *

Friday, 4th July.

Left camp at 6h a.m. after a very unpleasant night. Marching across a chain of hills and then in a maze of hills. At 8:15 opened out into an undulating plain. Took bearings of a break in the chain of mountains on the other side. * * *

Saw another dead body lying by the path in an attitude of meditative repose.

In the evening three women of whom one albino passed our camp. Horrid chalky white with pink blotches. Red eyes. Red hair. Features very Negroid and ugly. Mosquitos. At night when the moon rose heard shouts and drumming in distant villages. Passed a bad night.

Saturday, 5th July. go.

Left at 6:15. Morning cool, even cold and very damp. Sky densely overcast. Gentle breeze from NE. Road through a narrow plain up to R. Kwilu. Swift-flowing and deep, 50 yds. wide. Passed in canoes. After[war]ds up and down very steep hills intersected by deep ravines. Main chain of heights running mostly NW-SE or W and E at times. Stopped at Manyamba. Camp[in]g place bad—in hollow—water very indifferent. Tent set at 10:15.

Section of today's road. NNE Distance 12 m. [a drawing]

Today fell into a muddy puddle. Beastly. The fault of the man that carried me. After camp[in]g went to a small stream, bathed and washed clothes. Getting jolly well sick of this fun.

Tomorrow expect a long march to get to Nsona, 2 days from Manyanga. No sunshine today.

* * *

Saturday, 26th.

Left very early. Road ascending all the time. Passed villages. Country seems thickly inhabited. At 11h arrived at large market place. Left at noon and camped at 1h p.m.

[section of the day's march with notes]

a camp—a white man died here—market—govt. post—mount—crocodile pond—Mafiesa. * * *

Sunday, 27th.

Left at 8h am. Sent luggage carriers straight on to Luasi and went ourselves round by the Mission of Sutili.

Hospitable reception by Mrs Comber. All the missio[naries] absent.

The looks of the whole establishment eminently civilized and very refreshing to see after the lots of tumble-down hovels in which the State and Company agents are content to live—fine buildings. Position on a hill. Rather breezy.

Left at 3h pm. At the first heavy ascent met Mr Davis, miss[ionary] returning from a preaching trip. Rev. Bentley away in the South with his wife. * * *

Tuesday, 29th.

Left camp at 7h after a good night's rest. Continuous ascent; rather easy at first. Crossed wooded ravines and the river Lunzadi by a very decent bridge.

At 9h met Mr Louette escorting a sick agent of the Comp[an]y back to Matadi. Looking very well. Bad news from up the river. All the steamers disabled. One wrecked. Country wooded. At 10:30 camped at Inkissi. * * *

Today did not set the tent but put up in Gov[ernmen]t shimbek.[3] Zanzibari in charge—very obliging. Met ripe pineapple for the first time. On the road today passed a skeleton tied up to a post. Also white man's grave—no name. Heap of stones in the form of a cross.

Health good now.

Wednesday, 30th.

Left at 6 a.m. intending to camp at Kinfumu. Two hours' sharp walk brought me to Nsona na Nsefe. Market. ½ hour after, Harou arrived very ill with billious [sic] attack and fever. Laid him down in Gov[ernmen]t shimbek. Dose of Ipeca.[4] Vomiting bile in enormous quantities. At 11h gave him 1 gramme of quinine and lots of hot tea. Hot fit ending in heavy perspiration. At 2 p.m. put him in hammock and started for Kinfumu. Row with carriers all the way. Harou suffering much through the jerks of the hammock. Camped at a small stream.

At 4h Harou better. Fever gone. * * *

Up till noon, sky clouded and strong NW wind very chilling. From 1h pm to 4h pm sky clear and very hot day. Expect lots of bother with carriers tomorrow. Had them all called and made a speech which they did not understand. They promise good behaviour. * * *

Friday, 1st of August 1890.

*** Row between the carriers and a man stating himself in Gov[ernmen]t employ, about a mat. Blows with sticks raining hard. Stopped it. Chief came with a youth about 13 suffering from gunshot wound in the head. Bullet entered about an inch above the right eyebrow and came out a little inside. The roots of the hair, fairly in the middle of the brow in a line with the bridge of the nose. Bone not damaged apparently. Gave him a little glycerine to put on the wound made by the bullet on coming out. Harou not very well. Mosquitos. Frogs. Beastly. Glad to see the end of this stupid tramp. Feel rather seedy. Sun rose red. Very hot day. Wind S[ou]th.

Sir Henry Morton Stanley:
from *Address to the Manchester Chamber of Commerce*[1]

There is not one manufacturer here present who could not tell me if he had the opportunity how much he personally suffered through the slackness of trade; and I dare say that you have all some vague idea that if things remain as they are the future of the

3. A group of huts.

4. A medicine.

1. The journalist-adventurer Henry Morton Stanley wrote *Through the Dark Continent* and other best-selling accounts of his exploits in Africa, including the finding of the lost missionary Doctor Livingstone. He delivered this address to the textile manufacturers of Manchester, England, in 1886, seeking their support for the commercial exploitation of the Congo. His speech gives a striking example of the outlook—and the rhetoric—of the people who created the conditions Conrad encountered when he went to the Congo a few years later.

cotton manufacture is not very brilliant. New inventions are continually cropping up, so that your power of producing, if stimulated, is almost incalculable; but new markets for the sale of your products are not of rapid growth, and as other nations, by prohibitive tariffs, are bent upon fostering native manufacturers to the exclusion of your own, such markets as are now open to you are likely to be taken away from you in course of time. Well, then, I come to you with at least one market where there are at present, perhaps, 6,250,000 yards of cheap cottons sold every year on the Congo banks and in the Congo markets.[2]

I was interested the other day in making a curious calculation, which was, supposing that all the inhabitants of the Congo basin were simply to have one Sunday dress each, how many yards of Manchester cloth would be required; and the amazing number was 320,000,000 yards, just for one Sunday dress! (Cheers.) Proceeding still further with these figures I found that two Sunday dresses and four everyday dresses would in one year amount to 3,840,000,000 yards, which at 2d. [two pence] per yard would be of the value of £16,000,000. The more I pondered upon these things I discovered that I could not limit these stores of cotton cloth to day dresses. I would have to provide for night dresses also—(laughter)—and these would consume 160,000,000 yards. (Cheers.) Then the grave cloths came into mind, and, as a poor lunatic, who burned Bolobo Station,[3] destroyed 30,000 yards of cloth in order that he should not be cheated out of a respectable burial, I really feared for a time that the millions would get beyond measurable calculation. However, putting such accidents aside, I estimate that, if my figures of population are approximately correct, 2,000,000 die every year, and to bury these decently, and according to the custom of those who possess cloth, 16,000,000 yards will be required, while the 40,000 chiefs will require an average of 100 yards each, or 4,000,000 yards. I regarded these figures with great satisfaction, and I was about to close my remarks upon the millions of yards of cloth that Manchester would perhaps be required to produce when I discovered that I had neglected to provide for the family wardrobe or currency chest, for you must know that in the Lower Congo there is scarcely a family that has not a cloth fund of about a dozen pieces of about 24 yards each. This is a very important institution, otherwise how are the family necessities to be provided for? How are the fathers and mothers of families to go to market to buy greens, bread, oil, ground nuts, chickens, fish, and goats, and how is the petty trade to be conducted? How is ivory to be purchased, the gums, rubber, dye powders, gunpowder, copper slugs, guns, trinkets, knives, and swords to be bought without a supply of cloth? Now, 8,000,000 families at 300 yards each will require 2,400,000,000. (Cheers.) You all know how perishable such currency must be; but if you sum up these several millions of yards, and value all of them at the average price of 2d. per yard, you will find that it will be possible for Manchester to create a trade—in the course of time—in cottons in the Congo basin amounting in value to about £26,000,000 annually. (Loud cheers.) I have said nothing about Rochdale savelist, or your own superior prints, your gorgeous handkerchiefs, with

2. The Congo Free State (later Zaire), a vast area of central Africa around the Congo River, was formally brought under the ownership of Leopold II of Belgium and other investors in the International Association of the Congo by the Berlin West Africa Conference of 1884–1885. Stanley's expeditions there (from 1876) had been financed by Leopold, and from 1879 Stanley had set up trading stations along the river to facilitate the exploitation of the area's natural resources.

3. The London *Times* carried frequent reports of disturbances in the Congo at this time; in March 1884, for example, Congolese attacks on foreign trading establishments at Nokki in the Lower Congo had caused the Europeans to "declare war against the natives."

their variegated patterns, your checks and striped cloths, your ticking and twills.[4] I must satisfy myself with suggesting them; your own imaginations will no doubt carry you to the limbo of immeasurable and incalculable millions. (Laughter and cheers.)

Now, if your sympathy for yourselves and the fate of Manchester has been excited sufficiently, your next natural question would be as follows: We acknowledge, sir, that you have contrived by an artful array of imposing millions to excite our attention, at least, to this field; but we beg to ask you what Manchester is to do in order that we may begin realising this sale of untold millions of yards of cotton cloth? I answer that the first thing to do is for you to ask the British Government to send a cruiser to the mouth of the Congo to keep watch and ward over that river until the European nations have agreed among themselves as to what shall be done with the river, lest one of these days you will hear that it is too late. (Hear, hear.) Secondly, to study whether, seeing that it will never do to permit Portugal to assume sovereignty over that river[5]—and England publicly disclaims any wish to possess that river for herself—it would not be as well to allow the International Association to act as guardians of international right to free trade and free entrance and exit into and out of the river. (Hear, hear.) The main point, remember, always is a guarantee that the lower river shall be free, that, however the Upper Congo may be developed, no Power, inspired by cupidity, shall seize upon the mouth of the river and build custom houses. (Hear, hear.) The Lower Congo in the future will only be valuable because down its waters will have to be floated the produce of the rich basin above to the ocean steamships. It will always have a fair trade of its own, but it bears no proportion to the almost limitless trade that the Upper Congo could furnish. If the Association could be assured that the road from Europe to Vivi[6] was for ever free, the first steps to realise the sale of those countless millions of yards of cotton cloth would be taken. Over six millions of yards are now used annually; but we have no means of absorbing more, owing to the difficulties of transport. Every man capable and willing to carry a load is employed. When human power was discovered to be not further available we tested animal power and discovered it to be feebler and more costly than the other; and we have come to the conclusion that steam power must now assist us or we remain *in statu quo* [as things now stand]. But before having recourse to this steam power, and building the iron road along which your bales of cotton fabrics may roll on to the absorbing markets of the Upper Congo unceasingly, the Association pauses to ask you, and the peoples of other English cities, such as London, Liverpool, Glasgow, Birmingham, Leeds, Preston, Sheffield, who profess to understand the importance of the work we have been doing, and the absorbing power of those markets we have reached, what help you will render us, for your own sakes, to make those markets accessible? (Hear, hear.) The Association will not build that railway to the Upper Congo, nor invest one piece of sterling gold in it, unless they are assured they will not be robbed of it, and the Lower Congo will be placed under some flag that shall be a guarantee to all the world that its waters and banks are absolutely free. (Cheers.)

4. Savelist is cheap fabric; ticking is a strong cotton or linen fabric; twill is a kind of textile weave.

5. The mouth of the Congo River had been discovered by the Portuguese in 1482.

6. A town on the Upper Congo River; from 1882 Stanley had been arguing that a railway should be built between the Lower and Upper Congo to facilitate the exploitation of the interior. It was completed in 1898.

You will agree with me, I am sure, that trade ought to expand and commerce grow, and if we can coax it into mature growth in this Congo basin that it would be a praiseworthy achievement, honoured by men and gods; for out of this trade, this intercourse caused by peaceful barter, proceed all those blessings which you and I enjoy. The more trade thrives, the more benefits to mankind are multipled, and nearer to gods do men become. (Hear, hear.) The builders of railroads through wildernesses generally require large concessions of lands; but the proposed builders of this railway to connect the Lower with the Upper Congo do not ask for any landed concessions; but they ask for a concession of authority over the Lower Congo in order that the beneficent policy which directs the civilising work on the Upper Congo may be extended to the Lower River, and that the mode of government and action may be uniform throughout. The beneficent policy referred to is explained in the treaty made and concluded with the United States Government.[7] That treaty says: "That with the object of enabling civilisation and commerce to penetrate into Equatorial Africa the Free States of the Congo have resolved to levy no customs duties whatever. The Free States also guarantee to all men who establish themselves in their territories the right of purchasing, selling, or leasing any land and buildings, of creating factories and of trade on the sole condition that they conform to the law. The International Association of the Congo is prepared to enter into engagements with other nations who desire to secure the free admission of their products on the same terms as those agreed upon with the United States."

Here you have in brief the whole policy. I might end here, satisfied with having reminded you of these facts, which probably you had forgotten. Obedience to the laws—that is, laws drawn for protection of all—is the common law of all civilised communities, without which men would soon become demoralised. Can anybody object to that condition? Probably many of you here recollect reading those interesting letters from the Congo which were written by an English clerk in charge of an English factory. They ended with the cry of "Let us alone." In few words he meant to say, "We are doing very well as we are, we do not wish to be protected, and least of all taxed—therefore, let us alone. Our customers, the natives, are satisfied with us. The native chiefs are friendly and in accord with us; the disturbances, if any occur, are local; they are not general, and they right themselves quickly enough, for the trader cannot exist here if he is not just and kind in his dealings. The obstreperous and violent white is left to himself and ruin. Therefore, let us alone." Most heartily do I echo this cry; but unfortunately the European nations will not heed this cry; they think that some mode of government is necessary to curb those inclined to be refractory, and if there is at present a necessity to exhibit judicial power and to restrict evil-minded and ill-conditioned whites, as the Congo basin becomes more and more populated this necessity will be still more apparent. At the same time, if power appears on the Congo with an arbitrary and unfeeling front—with a disposition to tax and levy burdensome tariffs just as trade begins to be established—the outlook for enterprise becomes dismal and dark indeed.[8] (Hear, hear.) * * *

No part of Africa, look where I might, appeared so promising to me as this neglected tenth part of the continent. I have often fancied myself—when I had nothing to do better than dream—gazing from some lofty height, and looking down upon this

7. The United States was the first country to recognize the right of the International Association to govern the Congo territories in April 1884.

8. The right of the International Association to govern the Congo was eventually ended in 1908, following widespread protests against the regime's brutality.

square compact patch of 800,000,000 acres, with its 80,000 native towns, its population of 40,000,000 souls, its 17,000 miles of river waters, and its 30,000 square miles of lakes, all lying torpid, lifeless, inert, soaked in brutishness and bestiality, and I have never yet descended from that airy perch in the empyrean and touched earth but I have felt a purpose glow in me to strive to do something to awaken it into life and movement, and I have sometimes half fancied that the face of aged Livingstone,[9] vague and indistinct as it were, shone through the warm, hazy atmosphere, with a benignant smile encouraging me in my purpose. ***

Yet, though examined from every point of view, a study of the Upper Congo and its capabilities produces these exciting arrays of figures and possibilities, I would not pay a two-shilling piece for it all so long as it remains as it is. It will absorb easily the revenue of the wealthiest nation in Europe without any return. I would personally one hundred times over prefer a snug little freehold in a suburb of Manchester to being the owner of the 1,300,000 English square miles of the Congo basin if it is to remain as inaccessible as it is to-day, or if it is to be blocked by that fearful tariff-loving nation, the Portuguese. (Hear, hear.) But if I were assured that the Lower Congo would remain free, and the flag of the Association guaranteed its freedom, I would if I were able build that railway myself—build it solid and strong—and connect the Lower Congo with the Upper Congo, perfectly satisfied that I should be followed by the traders and colonists of all nations. *** The Portuguese have had nearly 400 years given them to demonstrate to the world what they could do with the river whose mouth they discovered, and they have been proved to be incapable to do any good with it, and now civilisation is inclined to say to them, "Stand off from this broad highway into the regions beyond—(cheers); let others who are not paralytic strive to do what they can with it to bring it within the number of accessible markets. There are 40,000,000 of naked people beyond that gateway, and the cotton spinners of Manchester are waiting to clothe them. Rochdale and Preston women are waiting for the word to weave them warm blue and crimson savelist. Birmingham foundries are glowing with the red metal that shall presently be made into ironwork in every fashion and shape for them, and the trinkets that shall adorn those dusky bosoms; and the ministers of Christ are zealous to bring them, the poor benighted heathen, into the Christian fold." (Cheers.)

MR JACOB BRIGHT, M.P., who was received with loud cheers, said: I have listened with extreme interest to one of the ablest, one of the most eloquent addresses which have ever been delivered in this city—(cheers); and I have heard with uncommon pleasure the views of a man whose ability, whose splendid force of character, whose remarkable heroism, have given him a world-wide reputation. (Cheers.) ***

MR GRAFTON, M.P., moved:—

> That the best thanks of this meeting be and are hereby given to Mr H. M. Stanley for his address to the members of the Chamber, and for the interesting information conveyed by him respecting the Congo and prospects of international trade on the West Coast and interior of Africa.

9. David Livingstone (1813–1873), Scottish explorer and missionary. His expeditions into central Africa, in search of the source of the Nile River, were heavily publicized; when Livingstone "disappeared" in the course of what proved to be his last expedition, Stanley, then a correspondent for the *New York Herald,* was sent to find him. The two men met on the banks of Lake Tanganyika in East Africa in 1871; Stanley published an account of their meeting in *How I Found Livingstone* (1872).

He remarked that Mr Stanley's name was already enrolled in the pages of history, and would be handed down to posterity with the names of the greatest benefactors of our species, such as Columbus, who had opened out the pathways of the world. Long might Mr Stanley be spared to witness the benefit of his arduous and beneficent labours. (Cheers.)

Lu Xun

1881–1936

Widely considered the finest Chinese writer of his generation, Lu Xun (the pen name of Zhou Shuren) was born in 1881 to a family of scholar-officials on China's southeast coast. He received the classical education expected of someone with his pedigree, but a scandal during his youth sent his grandfather to prison and the family fortunes went into decline. Lu Xun studied in a school whose focus on science and technology was designed to "strengthen" a new generation of Chinese for the new century. He then received a government scholarship to continue his studies in Japan, where modern Western influences had already taken root. Blaming the death of his father some years before on the failed methods of traditional Chinese quacks, he entered medical school, choosing to study Western medicine. But he was shocked by photographs revealing the abject helplessness of even healthy Chinese before foreign armies fighting on their territory during the Russo-Japanese War of 1904–1905, and he decided that China's real diseases were of the spirit rather than the body. That realization, perhaps coupled with a rather undistinguished record in medical school, led him to embark on a literary career in hopes of effecting a spiritual transformation of the nation.

Lu Xun's publishing projects in Japan didn't elicit the hoped-for response, however, and in 1909 he returned disheartened to China, where he spent the next sixteen years teaching and working in the Ministry of Education. A friend introduced him to the New Culture Movement, which aimed to reform both literature and society by revolutionizing the language of writing itself, and urged Lu Xun to contribute something to the effort in 1917. His initial reaction, recorded in his preface to *A Call to Arms,* was one of apparent futility. But the following year his first short story, "A Madman's Diary," launched one of the movement's most trenchant critiques.

Over the next eight years Lu Xun wrote some two dozen stories, which were published in two volumes, *A Call to Arms* (1923) and *Wandering* (1926). In these works he wrestles with a number of recurring themes centering on the dilemmas and contradictions facing intellectuals committed to a thoroughgoing transformation of the culture. Recognizing the failings and abuses of traditional Chinese thought and practices, he was both unwilling to abandon them wholesale and skeptical of the ability of sweeping utopian reforms to effect real positive change. He was haunted as well by doubts about whether writing could in fact grasp and convey real knowledge, and about whether intellectuals in general could truly communicate with the common people, in whose interests they were presumably working. By 1926 these questions finally led him to abandon fiction writing altogether. Forced to flee Peking following a purge by the Nationalist government of Communists and Communist sympathizers, he turned to the more pointed essay form and to Marxist activism as a means of gaining a less ambiguous leverage over reality. His relations with leftist colleagues remained fraught, however, and he never joined the party, yet he continued writing and left behind a substantial body of work—from essays, poetry, short stories, translations, and works on premodern literature to collections of woodcuts.

PRONUNCIATIONS:

Li Shizhen: LEE SHEE-jen

Lu Xun: LOU SHOON

Zhao: ja'o

A Madman's Diary[1]

Two brothers, whose names I need not mention here, were both good friends of mine in high school; but after a separation of many years we gradually lost touch. Some time ago I happened to hear that one of them was seriously ill, and since I was going back to my old home I broke my journey to call on them. I saw only one, however, who told me that the invalid was his younger brother.

"I appreciate your coming such a long way to see us," he said, "but my brother recovered some time ago and has gone elsewhere to take up an official post." Then, laughing, he produced two volumes of his brother's diary, saying that from these the nature of his past illness could be seen and there was no harm in showing them to an old friend. I took the diary away, read it through, and found that he had suffered from a form of persecution complex. The writing was most confused and incoherent, and he had made many wild statements; moreover he had omitted to give any dates, so that only by the colour of the ink and the differences in the writing could one tell that it was not all written at one time. Certain sections, however, were not altogether disconnected, and I have copied out a part to serve as a subject for medical research. I have not altered a single illogicality in the diary and have changed only the names, even though the people referred to are all country folk, unknown to the world and of no consequence. As for the title, it was chosen by the diarist himself after his recovery, and I did not change it.

I

Tonight the moon is very bright.

I have not seen it for over thirty years, so today when I saw it I felt in unusually high spirits. I begin to realize that during the past thirty-odd years I have been in the dark; but now I must be extremely careful. Otherwise why should the Zhaos' dog have looked at me twice?

I have reason for my fear.

II

Tonight there is no moon at all, I know that this is a bad omen. This morning when I went out cautiously, Mr. Zhao had a strange look in his eyes, as if he were afraid of me, as if he wanted to murder me. There were seven or eight others who discussed me in a whisper. And they were afraid of my seeing them. So, indeed, were all the people I passed. The fiercest among them grinned at me; whereupon I shivered from head to foot, knowing that their preparations were complete.

I was not afraid, however, but continued on my way. A group of children in front were also discussing me, and the look in their eyes was just like that in Mr. Zhao's while their faces too were ghastly pale. I wondered what grudge these children could have against me to make them behave like this. I could not help calling out, "Tell me!" But then they ran away.

1. Translated by Yang Xianyi and Gladys Yang.

I wonder what grudge Mr. Zhao has against me, what grudge the people on the road have against me. I can think of nothing except that twenty years ago I trod on Mr. Gu Jiu's[2] old ledgers, and Mr. Gu was most displeased. Although Mr. Zhao does not know him, he must have heard talk of this and decided to avenge him, thus he is conspiring against me with the people on the road. But then what of the children? At that time they were not yet born, so why should they eye me so strangely today, as if they were afraid of me, as if they wanted to murder me? This really frightens me, it is so bewildering and upsetting.

I know. They must have learned this from their parents!

III

I can't sleep at night. Everything requires careful consideration if one is to understand it.

Those people, some of whom have been pilloried by the magistrate, slapped in the face by the local gentry, had their wives taken away by bailiffs or their parents driven to suicide by creditors, never looked as frightened and as fierce then as they did yesterday.

The most extraordinary thing was that woman on the street yesterday who was spanking her son. "Little devil!" she cried. "I'm so angry I could eat you!" Yet all the time it was me she was looking at. I gave a start, unable to hide my alarm. Then all those long-toothed people with livid faces began to hoot with laughter. Old Chen hurried forward and dragged me home.

He dragged me home. The folk at home all pretended not to know me; they had the same look in their eyes as all the others. When I went into the study, they locked me in as if cooping up a chicken or a duck. This incident left me even more bewildered.

A few days ago a tenant of ours from Wolf Cub Village came to report the failure of the crops and told my elder brother that a notorious character in their village had been beaten to death; then some people had taken out his heart and liver, fried them in oil, and eaten them as a means of increasing their courage. When I interrupted, the tenant and my brother both stared at me. Only today have I realized that they had exactly the same look in their eyes as those people outside.

Just to think of it sets me shivering from the crown of my head to the soles of my feet.

They eat human beings, so they may eat me.

I see that the woman's "eat you," the laughter of those long-toothed people with livid faces, and the tenant's story the other day are obviously secret signs. I realize all the poison in their speech, all the daggers in their laughter. Their teeth are white and glistening: they use these teeth to eat men.

Evidently, although I am not a bad man, ever since I trod on Mr. Gu's ledgers it has been touch-and-go with me. They seem to have secrets which I cannot guess, and once they are angry they will call anyone a bad character. I remember when my elder brother taught me to write compositions, no matter how good a man was, if I produced arguments to the contrary he would mark that passage to show his approval; while if I excused evildoers he would say, "Good for you, that shows originality." How can I possibly guess their secret thoughts—especially when they are ready to eat people?

Everything requires careful consideration if one is to understand it. In ancient times, as I recollect, people often ate human beings, but I am rather hazy about it. I tried to look this up, but my history has no chronology and scrawled all over each

2. Literally, Mr."Ancient Old."

page are the words: "Confucian Virtue and Morality." Since I could not sleep anyway, I read intently half the night until I began to see words between the lines. The whole book was filled with the two words—"Eat people."

All these words written in the book, all the words spoken by our tenant, eye me quizzically with an enigmatic smile.

I too am a man, and they want to eat me!

IV

In the morning I sat quietly for some time. Old Chen brought in lunch: one bowl of vegetables, one bowl of steamed fish. The eyes of the fish were white and hard, and its mouth was open just like those people who want to eat human beings. After a few mouthfuls I could not tell whether the slippery morsels were fish or human flesh, so I brought it all up.

I said, "Old Chen, tell my brother that I feel quite suffocated and want to have a stroll in the garden." Old Chen said nothing but went out, and presently he came back and opened the gate.

I did not move, but watched to see how they would treat me, feeling certain that they would not let me go. Sure enough! My elder brother came slowly out, leading an old man. There was a murderous gleam in his eyes, and fearing that I would see it he lowered his head, stealing side-glances at me from behind his glasses.

"You seem very well today," said my brother.

"Yes," said I.

"I have invited Mr. Ho here today to examine you."

"All right," I replied. Actually I knew quite well that this old man was the executioner in disguise! Feeling my pulse was simply a pretext for him to see how fat I was; for this would entitle him to a share of my flesh. Still I was not afraid. Although I do not eat men my courage is greater than theirs. I held out my two fists to see what he would do. The old man sat down, closed his eyes, fumbled for some time, remained motionless for a while; then opened his shifty eyes and said, "Don't let your imagination run away with you. Rest quietly for a few days, and you will be better."

Don't let your imagination run away with you! Rest quietly for a few days! By fattening me of course they'll have more to eat. But what good will it do me? How can it be "better"? The whole lot of them wanting to eat people yet stealthily trying to keep up appearances, not daring to do it outright, was really enough to make me die of laughter. I couldn't help it, I nearly split my sides, I was so amused. I knew that this laughter voiced courage and integrity. Both the old man and my brother turned pale, awed by my courage and integrity.

But my courage just makes them all the more eager to eat me, to acquire some of my courage for themselves. The old man went out of the gate, but before he had gone far he said to my brother in a low voice, "To be eaten at once!" My brother nodded. So you are in it too! This stupendous discovery, though it came as a shock, is no more than I might expect: the accomplice in eating me is my elder brother!

The eater of human flesh is my elder brother!

I am the younger brother of an eater of human flesh!

I, who will be eaten by others, am the younger brother of an eater of human flesh!

V

These few days I have been thinking again: suppose that old man were not an executioner in disguise, but a real doctor; he would be nonetheless an eater of human flesh. That book on herbs by his predecessor Li Shizhen[3] states explicitly that men's flesh can be boiled and eaten; how then can he still deny that he eats men?

As for my elder brother, I have also good reason to suspect him. When he was teaching me, he told me himself, "People exchange their sons to eat."[4] And once in discussing a bad man he said that not only did the fellow deserve to be killed, he should "have his flesh eaten and his hide slept on." I was still young at the time, and for quite a while my heart beat faster. That story our tenant from Wolf Cub Village told the other day about eating a man's heart and liver didn't surprise him at all—he kept nodding his head. He is evidently just as cruel as before. Since it is possible to "exchange sons to eat," then anything can be exchanged, anyone can be eaten. In the past I simply listened to his explanations and let it go at that; now I know that when he gave me these explanations, not only was there human fat at the corner of his lips, but his whole heart was set on eating men.

VI

Pitch dark. I don't know whether it is day or night. The Zhaos' dog has started barking again.

The fierceness of a lion, the timidity of a rabbit, the craftiness of a fox. . . .

VII

I know their way: they are not prepared to kill outright, nor would they dare, for fear of the consequences. Instead they have banded together and set traps everywhere, to force me to kill myself. The behaviour of the men and women in the street a few days ago and my elder brother's attitude these last few days make it quite obvious. What they like best is for a man to take off his belt and hang himself from a beam; for then they can enjoy their hearts' desire without being blamed for murder. Naturally that delights them and sets them roaring with laughter. On the other hand, if a man is frightened or worried to death, though that makes him rather thin, they still nod in approval.

They only eat dead flesh! I remember reading somewhere of a hideous beast with an ugly look in its eye called "hyena," which often eats dead flesh. Even the largest bones it crunches into fragments and swallows; the mere thought of this makes your hair stand on end. Hyenas are related to wolves, wolves belong to the canine species. The other day the Zhaos' dog eyed me several times: it is obviously in the plot too as their accomplice. The old man's eyes were cast down, but that did not deceive me.

The most deplorable is my elder brother. He's a man too, so why isn't he afraid, why is he plotting with others to eat me? Does force of habit blind a man to what's wrong? Or is he so heartless that he will knowingly commit a crime?

In cursing man-eaters, I shall start with my brother. In dissuading man-eaters, I shall start with him too.

3. Famous pharmacologist (1518–93). His *Compendium of Materia Medica* doesn't say that human flesh could be used as a medicine.

4. From a commentary on the canonical chronicle *Spring and Autumn Annals,* which describes the desperate conditions of a besieged population in 488 B.C.E.

VIII

Actually such arguments should have convinced them long ago. . . .

Suddenly someone came in. He was only about twenty years old and I did not see his features very clearly. His face was wreathed in smiles, but when he nodded to me his smile didn't seem genuine. I asked him, "Is it right to eat human beings?"

Still smiling, he replied, "When there is no famine how can one eat human beings?"

I realized at once he was one of them; but still I summoned up courage to repeat my question:

"Is it right?"

"What makes you ask such a thing? You really are . . . fond of a joke. . . . It is very fine today."

"It is fine, and the moon is very bright. But I want to ask you: Is it right?"

He looked disconcerted and muttered, "No. . . ."

"No? Then why do they still do it?"

"What are you talking about?"

"What am I talking about? They are eating men now in Wolf Cub Village, and you can see it written all over the books, in fresh red ink."

His expression changed. He grew ghastly pale. "It may be so," he said staring at me. "That's the way it's always been. . . ."

"Does that make it right?"

"I refuse to discuss it with you. Anyway, you shouldn't talk about it. It's wrong for anyone to talk about it."

I leaped up and opened my eyes wide, but the man had vanished. I was soaked with sweat. He was much younger than my elder brother, but even so he was in it. He must have been taught by his parents. And I am afraid he has already taught his son; that is why even the children look at me so fiercely.

IX

Wanting to eat men, at the same time afraid of being eaten themselves, they all eye each other with the deepest suspicion.

How comfortable life would be for them if they could rid themselves of such obsessions and go to work, walk, eat and sleep at ease. They have only this one step to take. Yet fathers and sons, husbands and wives, brothers, friends, teachers and students, sworn enemies and even strangers, have all joined in this conspiracy, discouraging and preventing each other from taking this step.

X

Early this morning I went to find my elder brother. He was standing outside the hall door looking at the sky when I walked up behind him, standing between him and the door, and addressed him with exceptional poise and politeness:

"Brother, I have something to say to you."

"Go ahead then." He turned quickly towards me, nodding.

"It's nothing much, but I find it hard to say. Brother, probably all primitive people ate a little human flesh to begin with. Later, because their views altered some of them stopped and tried so hard to do what was right that they changed into men, into real men. But some are still eating people—just like reptiles. Some have changed into fish, birds, monkeys, and finally men; but those who make no effort to do what's right are still reptiles. When those who eat men compare themselves with those who don't, how ashamed they must be. Probably much more ashamed than the reptiles are before monkeys.

"In ancient times Yi Ya boiled his son for Jie and Zhou to eat; that is the old story.[5] But actually since the creation of heaven and earth by Pan Gu[6] men have been eating each other, from the time of Yi Ya's son to the time of Xu Xilin,[7] and from the time of Xu Xilin down to the man caught in Wolf Cub Village. Last year they executed a criminal in the city, and a consumptive soaked a piece of bread in his blood and sucked it.

"They want to eat me, and of course you can do nothing about it single-handed; but why must you join them? As man-eaters they are capable of anything. If they eat me, they can eat you as well; members of the same group can still eat each other. But if you will just change your ways, change right away, then everyone will have peace. Although this has been going on since time immemorial, today we could make a special effort to do what is right, and say this can't be done! I'm sure you can say that, Brother. The other day when the tenant wanted the rent reduced, you said it couldn't be done."

At first he only smiled cynically, then a murderous gleam came into his eyes, and when I spoke of their secret he turned pale. Outside the gate quite a crowd had gathered, among them Mr. Zhao and his dog, all craning their necks to peer in. I could not see all their faces, some of them seemed to be masked; others were the old lot, long-toothed with livid faces, concealing their laughter. I knew they were one gang, all eaters of human flesh. But I also knew that they did not all think alike by any means. Some of them thought that since it had always been so, men should be eaten. Others knew they shouldn't eat men but still wanted to, and were afraid people might discover their secret; so although what I said made them angry they still smiled their cynical, tight-lipped smiles.

Suddenly my brother's face darkened.

"Clear off, the whole lot of you!" he roared. "What's the point of looking at a madman?"

Then I realized part of their cunning. They would never be willing to change their stand, and their plans were all laid: they had labelled me a madman. In future when I was eaten, not only would there be no trouble but people would probably be grateful to them. When our tenant spoke of the villagers eating a bad character, it was exactly the same device. This is their old trick.

Old Chen came in too in a towering temper. But they could not stop my mouth, I had to warn those people:

"You should change, change from the bottom of your hearts. You must realize that there will be no place for man-eaters in the world in future.

"If you don't change, you may all be eaten by each other. However many of you there are, you will be wiped out by the real men, just as wolves are killed by hunters—just like reptiles!"

Old Chen drove everybody away. My brother had disappeared. Old Chen advised me to go back to my room. It was pitch dark in there. The beams and rafters shook above my head. After shaking for a while they grew bigger and bigger. They piled on top of me.

5. Yi Ya, a favorite of Duke Huan of Qi in the seventh century B.C.E., was a good cook and sycophant. When the duke remarked that he had never tasted the flesh of children, Yi Ya cooked his own son for him to eat. Jie and Zhou were kings of earlier periods.

6. A mythological figure from whom, according to one legend, the entire universe derives.

7. A revolutionary executed in 1907 for assassinating a Qing official. His heart and liver were eaten.

The weight was so great, I couldn't move. They meant that I should die. However, knowing that the weight was false I struggled out, dripping with sweat. But I had to warn them:

"You must change at once, change from the bottom of your hearts! You must know that there'll be no place for man-eaters in future. . . ."

XI

The sun has stopped shining, the door is never opened. Just two meals day after day.

Picking up my chopsticks, I thought of my elder brother. I know now how my little sister died: it was all through him. My sister was only five at the time. I can still remember how sweet she looked, poor thing. Mother wept as if she would never stop, but he begged her not to cry, probably because he had eaten our sister himself and so this weeping made him rather ashamed. If he had any sense of shame. . . .

My sister was eaten by my brother, but I don't know whether Mother realized it or not.

I think Mother must have known, but when she wept she didn't say so outright, probably because she also thought it proper. I remember when I was four or five, sitting in the cool of the hall, my brother told me that if a man's parents were ill he should cut off a piece of his flesh and boil it for them, if he wanted to be considered a good son;[8] and Mother didn't contradict him. If one piece could be eaten, obviously so could the whole. And yet just to think of the weeping then still makes my heart bleed; that is the extraordinary thing about it!

XII

I can't bear to think of it.

It has only just dawned on me that all these years I have been living in a place where for four thousand years human flesh has been eaten. My brother had just taken over the charge of the house when our sister died, and he may well have used her flesh in our food, making us eat it unwittingly.

I may have eaten several pieces of my sister's flesh unwittingly, and now it is my turn. . . .

How can a man like myself, after four thousand years of man-eating history—even though I knew nothing about it at first—ever hope to face real men?

XIII

Perhaps there are still children who haven't eaten men?

Save the children. . . .

James Joyce

1882–1941

One of the greatest figures in European modernism, James Joyce emigrated from his native Ireland at the age of twenty-two, and spent his adult life in Italy, Switzerland, and France; yet this

8. Traditional doctrines instructed children to cut off their flesh to feed their parents, if necessary.

most cosmopolitan of writers continued to ground his fiction in the experiences of his early years in provincial Dublin. He had been born in a Dublin suburb, the eldest of "sixteen or seventeen children," as his father later hazily recalled, only ten of whom survived infancy. His father, John, worked for the Irish nationalist movement headed by Charles Stewart Parnell in the 1880s, until Parnell's influence collapsed after he was named as an adulterer in a divorce suit in 1889. The Irish Catholic hierarchy turned against him, as did many political supporters, and a broken Parnell died in 1891, an event that prompted the nine-year-old Joyce to compose his first published poem, "Et Tu, Healy?" John Joyce lost his political appointment as a tax collector (problems with alcohol and borrowings from his own tax receipts compounded his political difficulties), and the family moved frequently in the ensuing years, to a series of increasingly rundown lodgings.

Joyce spent his adolescence in the 1890s hoping to get away from what he saw as Dublin's spiritual, political, and intellectual paralysis. A prize-winning student at a Catholic boys' school—where for a time he considered entering the priesthood—Joyce won a scholarship to study at the Jesuit-run University College, Dublin, where he pursued his wide, eclectic reading in ancient and modern authors. By the age of eighteen, he had taught himself Dano-Norwegian in order to read the works of Henrik Ibsen in the original. That year, he published an article on Ibsen in the *Fortnightly Review,* an important London journal. A few months later, he learned that Ibsen had admired the article, and Joyce wrote his hero a glowing letter in Norwegian—never answered—congratulating the aging author on his work and indicating his intention to carry on Ibsen's struggle against social and artistic conventions.

Joyce always had an ambiguous relation to his Irish literary contemporaries. In 1901 he published "The Day of the Rabblement," an essay criticizing as provincial the Irish Literary Theatre recently started by W. B. Yeats and others to promote a revival of Irish culture. Yet in the following years, he sought out Yeats and the other leading literary figures of Dublin, hoping to establish himself as a writer and reviewer. Funds were a constant concern, and an attempt to study medicine in Paris was cut short both by lack of money and by the slow death by cancer of his mother in 1903. Joyce returned home for her final illness, and abandoned his projected medical career; after a desultory year of teaching and writing, he left permanently for the Continent, where he taught for several years in a Berlitz school in Trieste. He was accompanied by Nora Barnacle, whom he had met on 16 June 1904—a day he would immortalize as "Bloomsday," the day on which his great novel *Ulysses* is set. While in Trieste, he completed *Dubliners,* a series of short stories he had begun at the suggestion of a friend who had offered him £1 each for some simple stories for a newspaper called the *Irish Homestead.* He also began an autobiographical novel, first entitled *Stephen Hero* and then rewritten as *A Portrait of the Artist as a Young Man.*

Joyce had great difficulty getting both works published. He insisted on recording the actual language Dubliners used, including vulgarities and even occasional obscenities, and he included real people—often unflatteringly portrayed—along with his fictional characters. Dublin publishers hesitated to take his work, fearing both libel and obscenity charges, and though Joyce had impressed the Irish literary establishment with his talent (as well as his arrogance), he had no obvious group of supporters. At once anti-British and antinationalist, fiercely independent yet expecting others to support him, Joyce was hard to place. This difficulty only increased as time went on, as he continually reinvented himself throughout his career. As soon as one phase of his work finally found a publisher and a small group of fervent admirers, Joyce would abandon the kind of writing they had come to admire and would make new demands on his readers' creativity, intelligence, and sheer patience.

Dubliners was published in 1914, while *Portrait* was being serialized in a magazine of experimental writing run by Harriet Weaver, who became a longtime supporter of Joyce and his work. *Portrait* was published in book form in 1916—in the United States, no Irish or English publisher having been willing to take it. By that point, Joyce was deeply engaged in what was to become one of the most influential novels of the twentieth century—*Ulysses,* the story of several intertwined lives in Dublin on 16 June 1904, centering on the adventures of Leopold Bloom, advertising salesman, and his unfaithful wife Molly. *Ulysses* has direct links with Joyce's previous fiction, including the presence of its third lead character, Stephen Dedalus, the autobiographical hero of *Portrait.* Yet as he worked on his big new novel Joyce rapidly began to move beyond the symbolically charged realism that had characterized his earlier fiction. Like its predecessors, *Ulysses* is filled with realistic detail about Dublin life, but over the course of the book these details are increasingly caught up in an exploding universe of literary styles and cultural references—from an extended parallel with Homer's *Odyssey* to parodies of the entire history of English prose style, experiments in musical writing, and even a chapter in drama form. Arcane references to medieval scholastic philosophy intertwine with parodies of contemporary advertising language, and whole chains of reference to Dante, Shakespeare, and Mozart are developed amid visits to outhouses and brothels. Reading *Ulysses* after it was eventually published in 1922 in Paris—once again, no English or Irish publisher having been found willing to take it—a bemused Virginia Woolf was impressed by its virtuosity and ambition, but couldn't help feeling she was watching "an undergraduate scratching his pimples." T. S. Eliot, on the other hand, wrote an essay called "*Ulysses,* Order, and Myth," in which he praised the novel as one of the great achievements of modern literature, asserting that Joyce had succeeded in "giving a shape and a significance to the immense panorama of futility and anarchy which is contemporary history."

Joyce by this time was living in Paris, together with Nora—they would only formally marry late in life—and their two children. His great novel gradually came to find readers, including in the United States, where it was initially banned as obscene, until a landmark decision by a judge determined in 1928 that the book's obscenities served compelling artistic purposes. By then, Joyce was working on a yet more baffling work, *Finnegans Wake,* which would occupy him for seventeen years, until shortly before his death in 1941. An extraordinary kaleidoscope of styles and languages, the book is a riot of stories, rumors, and hearsay surrounding a series of comically embarrassing moments in the life of a hero of many names but constant initials, H.C.E.; his wife, Anna Livia Plurabelle; and their quarreling sons and daughter. At the same time, it is a compendium of Irish and world history, politics, and culture, a veritable "chaosmos of Alle," as it calls itself. Even this phantasmagoric book, though, remains set in Dublin, and it displays Joyce's abiding interest in intersections of sexual, textual, and political misfortunes, as H.C.E. loses a local election after seducing some girls, or being seduced by them, or exposing himself in Dublin's Phoenix Park, whereupon Anna Livia writes a long letter, her "mamafesta," in his defense.

When he received the commission to write some "simple stories" for the *Irish Homestead* in 1904, Joyce was already engaged in composing a series of short prose experiments that he called "epiphanies"—sketches of seemingly ordinary scenes in which the hidden truth about a person or situation is suddenly brought to the surface, often for the lead character to contemplate, sometimes only for the reader to perceive. Set on January 6, the Feast of the Epiphany, "The Dead" was written in 1907, two years after he had completed the rest of the book. This last and longest of the stories in *Dubliners* shows how its hero's world turns upside down over the course of a single evening, as Gabriel Conroy has a series of unsettling encounters with a servant, a nationalist friend, and his own wife. She reveals a past (based on actual experiences of Nora Barnacle) previously unknown to Gabriel, and dramatically different from the ordinary pleasures of food, drink, and hospitality that the story luminously evokes. As often happens in the stories and novels of Virginia Woolf, memory invades the present, breeding uncertainties that can be compared to those explored in Akutagawa Ryunosuke's modernist mystery stories as well. Like the tales that Premchand was beginning to write during the same period, the stories of *Dubliners* use close, understated observation of everyday objects and events to unfold abiding mysteries of loyalty and betrayal, rivalry and love.

from DUBLINERS

The Dead

Lily, the caretaker's daughter, was literally run off her feet. Hardly had she brought one gentleman into the little pantry behind the office on the ground floor and helped him off with his overcoat than the wheezy hall-door bell clanged again and she had to scamper along the bare hallway to let in another guest. It was well for her she had not to attend to the ladies also. But Miss Kate and Miss Julia had thought of that and had converted the bathroom upstairs into a ladies' dressing-room. Miss Kate and Miss Julia were there, gossiping and laughing and fussing, walking after each other to the head of the stairs, peering down over the banisters and calling down to Lily to ask her who had come.

It was always a great affair, the Misses Morkan's annual dance. Everybody who knew them came to it, members of the family, old friends of the family, the members of Julia's choir, any of Kate's pupils that were grown up enough and even some of Mary Jane's pupils too. Never once had it fallen flat. For years and years it had gone off in splendid style as long as anyone could remember; ever since Kate and Julia, after the death of their brother Pat, had left the house in Stoney Batter[1] and taken Mary Jane, their only niece, to live with them in the dark gaunt house on Usher's Island,[2] the upper part of which they had rented from Mr Fulham, the cornfactor on the ground floor. That was a good thirty years ago if it was a day. Mary Jane, who was then a little girl in short clothes, was now the main prop of the household for she had the organ in Haddington Road.[3] She had been through the Academy[4] and gave a pupils' concert every year in the upper room of the Antient Concert Rooms. Many of her pupils belonged to better-class families on the Kingstown and Dalkey line.[5] Old as they were, her aunts also did their share. Julia, though she was quite grey, was still the leading soprano in Adam and Eve's,[6] and Kate, being too feeble to go about much, gave music lessons to beginners on the old square piano in the back room. Lily, the caretaker's daughter, did housemaid's work for them. Though their life was modest they believed in eating well; the best of everything: diamond-bone sirloins, three-shilling tea and the best bottled stout.[7] But Lily seldom made a mistake in the orders so that she got on well with her three mistresses. They were fussy, that was all. But the only thing they would not stand was back answers.

Of course they had good reason to be fussy on such a night. And then it was long after ten o'clock and yet there was no sign of Gabriel and his wife. Besides they were dreadfully afraid that Freddy Malins might turn up screwed.[8] They would not wish for worlds that any of Mary Jane's pupils should see him under the influence; and when he was like that it was sometimes very hard to manage him. Freddy Malins always came late but they wondered what could be keeping Gabriel: and that was what brought them every two minutes to the banisters to ask Lily had Gabriel or Freddy come.

—O, Mr Conroy, said Lily to Gabriel when she opened the door for him, Miss Kate and Miss Julia thought you were never coming. Good-night, Mrs Conroy.

1. A district in northwest Dublin.
2. Two adjoining quays on the south side of the River Liffey.
3. Played the organ in a church on the Haddington Road.
4. Royal Academy of Music.
5. The train line connecting Dublin to the affluent suburbs south of the city.
6. A Dublin church.
7. An extra-strengh ale.
8. Drunk.

—I'll engage[9] they did, said Gabriel, but they forget that my wife here takes three mortal hours to dress herself.

He stood on the mat, scraping the snow from his goloshes, while Lily led his wife to the foot of the stairs and called out:

—Miss Kate, here's Mrs Conroy.

Kate and Julia came toddling down the dark stairs at once. Both of them kissed Gabriel's wife, said she must be perished alive and asked was Gabriel with her.

—Here I am as right as the mail, Aunt Kate! Go on up. I'll follow, called out Gabriel from the dark.

He continued scraping his feet vigorously while the three women went upstairs, laughing, to the ladies' dressing-room. A light fringe of snow lay like a cape on the shoulders of his overcoat and like toecaps on the toes of his goloshes; and, as the buttons of his overcoat slipped with a squeaking noise through the snow-stiffened frieze, a cold fragrant air from out-of-doors escaped from crevices and folds.

—Is it snowing again, Mr Conroy? asked Lily.

She had preceded him into the pantry to help him off with his overcoat. Gabriel smiled at the three syllables she had given his surname and glanced at her. She was a slim, growing girl, pale in complexion and with hay-coloured hair. The gas in the pantry made her look still paler. Gabriel had known her when she was a child and used to sit on the lowest step nursing a rag doll.

—Yes, Lily, he answered, and I think we're in for a night of it.

He looked up at the pantry ceiling, which was shaking with the stamping and shuffling of feet on the floor above, listened for a moment to the piano and then glanced at the girl, who was folding his overcoat carefully at the end of a shelf.

—Tell me, Lily, he said in a friendly tone, do you still go to school?

—O no, sir, she answered. I'm done schooling this year and more.

—O, then, said Gabriel gaily, I suppose we'll be going to your wedding one of these fine days with your young man, eh?

The girl glanced back at him over her shoulder and said with great bitterness:

—The men that is now is only all palaver[1] and what they can get out of you.

Gabriel coloured as if he felt he had made a mistake and, without looking at her, kicked off his goloshes and flicked actively with his muffler at his patent-leather shoes.

He was a stout tallish young man. The high colour of his cheeks pushed upwards even to his forehead where it scattered itself in a few formless patches of pale red; and on his hairless face there scintillated restlessly the polished lenses and the bright gilt rims of the glasses which screened his delicate and restless eyes. His glossy black hair was parted in the middle and brushed in a long curve behind his ears where it curled slightly beneath the groove left by his hat.

When he had flicked lustre into his shoes he stood up and pulled his waistcoat down more tightly on his plump body. Then he took a coin rapidly from his pocket.

—O Lily, he said, thrusting it into her hands, it's Christmas-time, isn't it? Just . . . here's a little. . . .

He walked rapidly towards the door.

—O no, sir! cried the girl, following him. Really, sir, I wouldn't take it.

—Christmas-time! Christmas-time! said Gabriel, almost trotting to the stairs and waving his hand to her in deprecation.

9. Wager.

1. Empty talk.

The girl, seeing that he had gained the stairs, called out after him:

—Well, thank you, sir.

He waited outside the drawing-room door until the waltz should finish, listening to the skirts that swept against it and to the shuffling of feet. He was still discomposed by the girl's bitter and sudden retort. It had cast a gloom over him which he tried to dispel by arranging his cuffs and the bows of his tie. Then he took from his waistcoat pocket a little paper and glanced at the headings he had made for his speech. He was undecided about the lines from Robert Browning for he feared they would be above the heads of his hearers. Some quotation that they could recognise from Shakespeare or from the Melodies[2] would be better. The indelicate clacking of the men's heels and the shuffling of their soles reminded him that their grade of culture differed from his. He would only make himself ridiculous by quoting poetry to them which they could not understand. They would think that he was airing his superior education. He would fail with them just as he had failed with the girl in the pantry. He had taken up a wrong tone. His whole speech was a mistake from first to last, an utter failure.

Just then his aunts and his wife came out of the ladies' dressing-room. His aunts were two small plainly dressed old women. Aunt Julia was an inch or so taller. Her hair, drawn low over the tops of her ears, was grey; and grey also, with darker shadows, was her large flaccid face. Though she was stout in build and stood erect her slow eyes and parted lips gave her the appearance of a woman who did not know where she was or where she was going. Aunt Kate was more vivacious. Her face, healthier than her sister's, was all puckers and creases, like a shrivelled red apple, and her hair, braided in the same old-fashioned way, had not lost its ripe nut colour.

They both kissed Gabriel frankly. He was their favourite nephew, the son of their dead elder sister, Ellen, who had married T.J. Conroy of the Port and Docks.

—Gretta tells me you're not going to take a cab back to Monkstown[3] to-night, Gabriel, said Aunt Kate.

—No, said Gabriel, turning to his wife, we had quite enough of that last year, hadn't we. Don't you remember, Aunt Kate, what a cold Gretta got out of it? Cab windows rattling all the way, and the east wind blowing in after we passed Merrion. Very jolly it was. Gretta caught a dreadful cold.

Aunt Kate frowned severely and nodded her head at every word.

—Quite right, Gabriel, quite right, she said. You can't be too careful.

—But as for Gretta there, said Gabriel, she'd walk home in the snow if she were let.

Mrs Conroy laughed.

—Don't mind him, Aunt Kate, she said. He's really an awful bother, what with green shades for Tom's eyes at night and making him do the dumb-bells, and forcing Eva to eat the stirabout.[4] The poor child! And she simply hates the sight of it! . . . O, but you'll never guess what he makes me wear now!

She broke out into a peal of laughter and glanced at her husband, whose admiring and happy eyes had been wandering from her dress to her face and hair. The two aunts laughed heartily too, for Gabriel's solicitude was a standing joke with them.

—Goloshes! said Mrs Conroy. That's the latest. Whenever it's wet underfoot I must put on my goloshes. Tonight even he wanted me to put them on, but I wouldn't. The next thing he'll buy me will be a diving suit.

2. Thomas Moore's *Irish Melodies,* a perennial favorite volume of poetry.

3. An elegant suburb south of Dublin.

4. Porridge.

Gabriel laughed nervously and patted his tie reassuringly while Aunt Kate nearly doubled herself, so heartily did she enjoy the joke. The smile soon faded from Aunt Julia's face and her mirthless eyes were directed towards her nephew's face. After a pause she asked:

—And what are goloshes, Gabriel?

—Goloshes, Julia! exclaimed her sister. Goodness me, don't you know what goloshes are? You wear them over your . . . over your boots, Gretta, isn't it?

—Yes, said Mrs Conroy. Guttapercha[5] things. We both have a pair now. Gabriel says everyone wears them on the continent.

—O, on the continent, murmured Aunt Julia, nodding her head slowly.

Gabriel knitted his brows and said, as if he were slightly angered:

—It's nothing very wonderful but Gretta thinks it very funny because she says the word reminds her of Christy Minstrels.[6]

—But tell me, Gabriel, said Aunt Kate, with brisk tact. Of course, you've seen about the room. Gretta was saying . . .

—O, the room is all right, replied Gabriel. I've taken one in the Gresham.[7]

—To be sure, said Aunt Kate, by far the best thing to do. And the children, Gretta, you're not anxious about them?

—O, for one night, said Mrs Conroy. Besides, Bessie will look after them.

—To be sure, said Aunt Kate again. What a comfort it is to have a girl like that, one you can depend on! There's that Lily, I'm sure I don't know what has come over her lately. She's not the girl she was at all.

Gabriel was about to ask his aunt some questions on this point but she broke off suddenly to gaze after her sister who had wandered down the stairs and was craning her neck over the banisters.

—Now, I ask you, she said, almost testily, where is Julia going? Julia! Julia! Where are you going?

Julia, who had gone halfway down one flight, came back and announced blandly:

—Here's Freddy.

At the same moment a clapping of hands and a final flourish of the pianist told that the waltz had ended. The drawing-room door was opened from within and some couples came out. Aunt Kate drew Gabriel aside hurriedly and whispered into his ear:

—Slip down, Gabriel, like a good fellow and see if he's all right, and don't let him up if he's screwed. I'm sure he's screwed. I'm sure he is.

Gabriel went to the stairs and listened over the banisters. He could hear two persons talking in the pantry. Then he recognised Freddy Malins' laugh. He went down the stairs noisily.

—It's such a relief, said Aunt Kate to Mrs Conroy, that Gabriel is here. I always feel easier in my mind when he's here. . . . Julia, there's Miss Daly and Miss Power will take some refreshment. Thanks for your beautiful waltz, Miss Daly. It made lovely time.

A tall wizen-faced man, with a stiff grizzled moustache and swarthy skin, who was passing out with his partner said:

—And may we have some refreshment, too, Miss Morkan?

—Julia, said Aunt Kate summarily, and here's Mr Browne and Miss Furlong. Take them in, Julia, with Miss Daly and Miss Power.

5. Rubberized fabric.
6. A 19th-century blackface minstrel show.
7. The most elegant hotel in Dublin.

—I'm the man for the ladies, said Mr Browne, pursing his lips until his moustache bristled and smiling in all his wrinkles. You know, Miss Morkan, the reason they are so fond of me is—

He did not finish his sentence, but, seeing that Aunt Kate was out of earshot, at once led the three young ladies into the back room. The middle of the room was occupied by two square tables placed end to end, and on these Aunt Julia and the caretaker were straightening and smoothing a large cloth. On the sideboard were arrayed dishes and plates, and glasses and bundles of knives and forks and spoons. The top of the closed square piano served also as a sideboard for viands[8] and sweets. At a smaller sideboard in one corner two young men were standing, drinking hop-bitters.[9]

Mr Browne led his charges thither and invited them all, in jest, to some ladies' punch, hot, strong and sweet. As they said they never took anything strong he opened three bottles of lemonade for them. Then he asked one of the young men to move aside, and, taking hold of the decanter, filled out for himself a goodly measure of whisky. The young men eyed him respectfully while he took a trial sip.

—God help me, he said, smiling, it's the doctor's orders.

His wizened face broke into a broader smile, and the three young ladies laughed in musical echo to his pleasantry, swaying their bodies to and fro, with nervous jerks of their shoulders. The boldest said:

—O, now, Mr Browne, I'm sure the doctor never ordered anything of the kind.

Mr Browne took another sip of his whisky and said, with sidling mimicry:

—Well, you see, I'm like the famous Mrs Cassidy, who is reported to have said: *Now, Mary Grimes, if I don't take it, make me take it, for I feel I want it.*

His hot face had leaned forward a little too confidentially and he had assumed a very low Dublin accent so that the young ladies, with one instinct, received his speech in silence. Miss Furlong, who was one of Mary Jane's pupils, asked Miss Daly what was the name of the pretty waltz she had played; and Mr Browne, seeing that he was ignored, turned promptly to the two young men who were more appreciative.

A red-faced young woman, dressed in pansy, came into the room, excitedly clapping her hands and crying:

—Quadrilles![1] Quadrilles!

Close on her heels came Aunt Kate, crying:

—Two gentlemen and three ladies, Mary Jane!

—O, here's Mr Bergin and Mr Kerrigan, said Mary Jane. Mr Kerrigan, will you take Miss Power? Miss Furlong, may I get you a partner, Mr Bergin. O, that'll just do now.

—Three ladies, Mary Jane, said Aunt Kate.

The two young gentlemen asked the ladies if they might have the pleasure, and Mary Jane turned to Miss Daly.

—O, Miss Daly, you're really awfully good, after playing for the last two dances, but really we're so short of ladies to-night.

—I don't mind in the least, Miss Morkan.

—But I've a nice partner for you, Mr Bartell D'Arcy, the tenor. I'll get him to sing later on. All Dublin is raving about him.

—Lovely voice, lovely voice! said Aunt Kate.

8. Meats.
9. Dry ale.
1. A French square dance.

As the piano had twice begun the prelude to the first figure Mary Jane led her recruits quickly from the room. They had hardly gone when Aunt Julia wandered slowly into the room, looking behind her at something.

—What is the matter, Julia? asked Aunt Kate anxiously. Who is it?

Julia, who was carrying in a column of table-napkins, turned to her sister and said, simply, as if the question had surprised her:

—It's only Freddy, Kate, and Gabriel with him.

In fact right behind her Gabriel could be seen piloting Freddy Malins across the landing. The latter, a young man of about forty, was of Gabriel's size and build, with very round shoulders. His face was fleshy and pallid, touched with colour only at the thick hanging lobes of his ears and at the wide wings of his nose. He had coarse features, a blunt nose, a convex and receding brow, tumid and protruded lips. His heavy-lidded eyes and the disorder of his scanty hair made him look sleepy. He was laughing heartily in a high key at a story which he had been telling Gabriel on the stairs and at the same time rubbing the knuckles of his left fist backwards and forwards into his left eye.

—Good-evening, Freddy, said Aunt Julia.

Freddy Malins bade the Misses Morkan good-evening in what seemed an off-hand fashion by reason of the habitual catch in his voice and then, seeing that Mr Browne was grinning at him from the sideboard, crossed the room on rather shaky legs and began to repeat in an undertone the story he had just told to Gabriel.

—He's not so bad, is he? said Aunt Kate to Gabriel.

Gabriel's brows were dark but he raised them quickly and answered:

—O no, hardly noticeable.

—Now, isn't he a terrible fellow! she said. And his poor mother made him take the pledge on New Year's Eve. But come on, Gabriel, into the drawing-room.

Before leaving the room with Gabriel she signalled to Mr Browne by frowning and shaking her forefinger in warning to and fro. Mr Browne nodded in answer and, when she had gone, said to Freddy Malins:

—Now, then, Teddy, I'm going to fill you out a good glass of lemonade just to buck you up.

Freddy Malins, who was nearing the climax of his story, waved the offer aside impatiently but Mr Browne, having first called Freddy Malins' attention to a disarray in his dress, filled out and handed him a full glass of lemonade. Freddy Malins' left hand accepted the glass mechanically, his right hand being engaged in the mechanical readjustment of his dress. Mr Browne, whose face was once more wrinkling with mirth, poured out for himself a glass of whisky while Freddy Malins exploded, before he had well reached the climax of his story, in a kink of high-pitched bronchitic laughter and, setting down his untasted and overflowing glass, began to rub the knuckles of his left fist backwards and forwards into his left eye, repeating words of his last phrase as well as his fit of laughter would allow him.

Gabriel could not listen while Mary Jane was playing her Academy piece, full of runs and difficult passages, to the hushed drawing-room. He liked music but the piece she was playing had no melody for him and he doubted whether it had any melody for the other listeners, though they had begged Mary Jane to play something. Four young men, who had come from the refreshment-room to stand in the doorway at the sound of the piano, had gone away quietly in couples after a few minutes. The only persons who seemed to follow the music were Mary Jane herself, her hands racing along the key-board or lifted from it at the pauses like those of a priestess in momentary imprecation, and Aunt Kate standing at her elbow to turn the page.

Gabriel's eyes, irritated by the floor, which glittered with beeswax under the heavy chandelier, wandered to the wall above the piano. A picture of the balcony scene in *Romeo and Juliet* hung there and beside it was a picture of the two murdered princes[2] in the Tower which Aunt Julia had worked in red, blue and brown wools when she was a girl. Probably in the school they had gone to as girls that kind of work had been taught, for one year his mother had worked for him as a birthday present a waistcoat of purple tabinet,[3] with little foxes' heads upon it, lined with brown satin and having round mulberry buttons. It was strange that his mother had had no musical talent though Aunt Kate used to call her the brains carrier of the Morkan family. Both she and Julia had always seemed a little proud of their serious and matronly sister. Her photograph stood before the pierglass.[4] She held an open book on her knees and was pointing out something in it to Constantine who, dressed in a man-o'-war suit, lay at her feet. It was she who had chosen the names for her sons for she was very sensible of the dignity of family life. Thanks to her, Constantine was now senior curate in Balbriggan[5] and, thanks to her, Gabriel himself had taken his degree in the Royal University.[6] A shadow passed over his face as he remembered her sullen opposition to his marriage. Some slighting phrases she had used still rankled in his memory; she had once spoken of Gretta as being country cute and that was not true of Gretta at all. It was Gretta who had nursed her during all her last long illness in their house at Monkstown.

He knew that Mary Jane must be near the end of her piece for she was playing again the opening melody with runs of scales after every bar and while he waited for the end the resentment died down in his heart. The piece ended with a trill of octaves in the treble and a final deep octave in the bass. Great applause greeted Mary Jane as, blushing and rolling up her music nervously, she escaped from the room. The most vigorous clapping came from the four young men in the doorway who had gone away to the refreshment-room at the beginning of the piece but had come back when the piano had stopped.

Lancers[7] were arranged. Gabriel found himself partnered with Miss Ivors. She was a frank-mannered talkative young lady, with a freckled face and prominent brown eyes. She did not wear a low-cut bodice and the large brooch which was fixed in the front of her collar bore on it an Irish device.

When they had taken their places she said abruptly:

—I have a crow to pluck with you.

—With me? said Gabriel.

She nodded her head gravely.

—What is it? asked Gabriel, smiling at her solemn manner.

—Who is G. C.? answered Miss Ivors, turning her eyes upon him.

Gabriel coloured and was about to knit his brows, as if he did not understand, when she said bluntly:

—O, innocent Amy! I have found out that you write for *The Daily Express*.[8] Now, aren't you ashamed of yourself?

2. The young sons of Edward IV, murdered in the Tower of London by order of their uncle, Edward III.
3. Silk and wool fabric.
4. A large high mirror.
5. A seaport southeast of Dublin.
6. The Royal University of Ireland, established in 1882.
7. A type of quadrille for 8 or 16 people.
8. A conservative paper opposed to the struggle for Irish independence.

—Why should I be ashamed of myself? asked Gabriel, blinking his eyes and trying to smile.

—Well, I'm ashamed of you, said Miss Ivors frankly. To say you'd write for a rag like that. I didn't think you were a West Briton.[9]

A look of perplexity appeared on Gabriel's face. It was true that he wrote a literary column every Wednesday in *The Daily Express,* for which he was paid fifteen shillings. But that did not make him a West Briton surely. The books he received for review were almost more welcome than the paltry cheque. He loved to feel the covers and turn over the pages of newly printed books. Nearly every day when his teaching in the college was ended he used to wander down the quays to the second-hand booksellers, to Hickey's on Bachelor's Walk, to Webb's or Massey's on Aston's Quay, or to O'Clohissey's in the by-street. He did not know how to meet her charge. He wanted to say that literature was above politics. But they were friends of many years' standing and their careers had been parallel, first at the University and then as teachers: he could not risk a grandiose phrase with her. He continued blinking his eyes and trying to smile and murmured lamely that he saw nothing political in writing reviews of books.

When their turn to cross had come he was still perplexed and inattentive. Miss Ivors promptly took his hand in a warm grasp and said in a soft friendly tone:

—Of course, I was only joking. Come, we cross now.

When they were together again she spoke of the University question[1] and Gabriel felt more at ease. A friend of hers had shown her his review of Browning's poems. That was how she had found out the secret: but she liked the review immensely. Then she said suddenly:

—O, Mr Conroy, will you come for an excursion to the Aran Isles[2] this summer? We're going to stay there a whole month. It will be splendid out in the Atlantic. You ought to come. Mr Clancy is coming, and Mr Kilkelly and Kathleen Kearney. It would be splendid for Gretta too if she'd come. She's from Connacht,[3] isn't she?

—Her people are, said Gabriel shortly.

—But you will come, won't you? said Miss Ivors, laying her warm hand eagerly on his arm.

—The fact is, said Gabriel, I have already arranged to go—

—Go where? asked Miss Ivors.

—Well, you know, every year I go for a cycling tour with some fellows and so—

—But where? asked Miss Ivors.

—Well, we usually go to France or Belgium or perhaps Germany, said Gabriel awkwardly.

—And why do you go to France and Belgium, said Miss Ivors, instead of visiting your own land?

—Well, said Gabriel, it's partly to keep in touch with the languages and partly for a change.

—And haven't you your own language to keep in touch with—Irish? asked Miss Ivors.

—Well, said Gabriel, if it comes to that, you know, Irish is not my language.

9. Disparaging term for people wishing to identify Ireland as British.

1. Ireland's oldest most and prestigious university, Trinity College, was open only to Protestants; the "University question" involved, in part, the provision of quality university education to Catholics.

2. Islands off the west coast of Ireland where the people still retained their traditional culture and spoke Irish.

3. A province on the west coast of Ireland.

Their neighbours had turned to listen to the cross-examination. Gabriel glanced right and left nervously and tried to keep his good humour under the ordeal which was making a blush invade his forehead.

—And haven't you your own land to visit, continued Miss Ivors, that you know nothing of, your own people, and your own country?

—O, to tell you the truth, retorted Gabriel suddenly, I'm sick of my own country, sick of it!

—Why? asked Miss Ivors.

Gabriel did not answer for his retort had heated him.

—Why? repeated Miss Ivors.

They had to go visiting together and, as he had not answered her, Miss Ivors said warmly:

—Of course, you've no answer.

Gabriel tried to cover his agitation by taking part in the dance with great energy. He avoided her eyes for he had seen a sour expression on her face. But when they met in the long chain he was surprised to feel his hand firmly pressed. She looked at him from under her brows for a moment quizzically until he smiled. Then, just as the chain was about to start again, she stood on tiptoe and whispered into his ear:

—West Briton!

When the lancers were over Gabriel went away to a remote corner of the room where Freddy Malins' mother was sitting. She was a stout feeble old woman with white hair. Her voice had a catch in it like her son's and she stuttered slightly. She had been told that Freddy had come and that he was nearly all right. Gabriel asked her whether she had had a good crossing. She lived with her married daughter in Glasgow and came to Dublin on a visit once a year. She answered placidly that she had had a beautiful crossing and that the captain had been most attentive to her. She spoke also of the beautiful house her daughter kept in Glasgow, and of all the nice friends they had there. While her tongue rambled on Gabriel tried to banish from his mind all memory of the unpleasant incident with Miss Ivors. Of course the girl or woman, or whatever she was, was an enthusiast but there was a time for all things. Perhaps he ought not to have answered her like that. But she had no right to call him a West Briton before people, even in joke. She had tried to make him ridiculous before people, heckling him and staring at him with her rabbit's eyes.

He saw his wife making her way towards him through the waltzing couples. When she reached him she said into his ear:

—Gabriel, Aunt Kate wants to know won't you carve the goose as usual. Miss Daly will carve the ham and I'll do the pudding.

—All right, said Gabriel.

—She's sending in the younger ones first as soon as this waltz is over so that we'll have the table to ourselves.

—Were you dancing? asked Gabriel.

—Of course I was. Didn't you see me? What words had you with Molly Ivors?

—No words. Why? Did she say so?

—Something like that. I'm trying to get that Mr D'Arcy to sing. He's full of conceit, I think.

—There were no words, said Gabriel moodily, only she wanted me to go for a trip to the west of Ireland and I said I wouldn't.

His wife clasped her hands excitedly and gave a little jump.

—O, do go, Gabriel, she cried. I'd love to see Galway again.

—You can go if you like, said Gabriel coldly.

She looked at him for a moment, then turned to Mrs Malins and said:

—There's a nice husband for you, Mrs Malins.

While she was threading her way back across the room Mrs Malins, without adverting to the interruption, went on to tell Gabriel what beautiful places there were in Scotland and beautiful scenery. Her son-in-law brought them every year to the lakes and they used to go fishing. Her son-in-law was a splendid fisher. One day he caught a fish, a beautiful big big fish, and the man in the hotel boiled it for their dinner.

Gabriel hardly heard what she said. Now that supper was coming near he began to think again about his speech and about the quotation. When he saw Freddy Malins coming across the room to visit his mother Gabriel left the chair free for him and retired into the embrasure of the window. The room had already cleared and from the back room came the clatter of plates and knives. Those who still remained in the drawing-room seemed tired of dancing and were conversing quietly in little groups. Gabriel's warm trembling fingers tapped the cold pane of the window. How cool it must be outside! How pleasant it would be to walk out alone, first along by the river and then through the park! The snow would be lying on the branches of the trees and forming a bright cap on the top of the Wellington Monument.[4] How much more pleasant it would be there than at the supper-table!

He ran over the headings of his speech: Irish hospitality, sad memories, the Three Graces, Paris, the quotation from Browning. He repeated to himself a phrase he had written in his review: *One feels that one is listening to a thought-tormented music.* Miss Ivors had praised the review. Was she sincere? Had she really any life of her own behind all her propagandism? There had never been any ill-feeling between them until that night. It unnerved him to think that she would be at the supper-table, looking up at him while he spoke with her critical quizzing eyes. Perhaps she would not be sorry to see him fail in his speech. An idea came into his mind and gave him courage. He would say, alluding to Aunt Kate and Aunt Julia: *Ladies and Gentlemen, the generation which is now on the wane among us may have had its faults but for my part I think it had certain qualities of hospitality, of humour, of humanity, which the new and very serious and hypereducated generation that is growing up around us seems to me to lack.* Very good: that was one for Miss Ivors. What did he care that his aunts were only two ignorant old women?

A murmur in the room attracted his attention. Mr Browne was advancing from the door, gallantly escorting Aunt Julia, who leaned upon his arm, smiling and hanging her head. An irregular musketry of applause escorted her also as far as the piano and then, as Mary Jane seated herself on the stool, and Aunt Julia, no longer smiling, half turned so as to pitch her voice fairly into the room, gradually ceased. Gabriel recognised the prelude. It was that of an old song of Aunt Julia's—*Arrayed for the Bridal.*[5] Her voice, strong and clear in tone, attacked with great spirit the runs which embellish the air and though she sang very rapidly she did not miss even the smallest of the grace notes. To follow the voice, without looking at the singer's face, was to feel and share the excitement of swift and secure flight. Gabriel applauded loudly with all the others at the close of the song and loud applause was borne in from the invisible supper-table. It sounded so genuine that a little colour struggled into Aunt Ju-

4. A monument to the Duke of Wellington, an Irish-born English military hero, located in Phoenix Park, Dublin's major public park.

5. A popular but challenging song set to music from Bellini's opera *I Puritani* (1835).

lia's face as she bent to replace in the music-stand the old leather-bound song-book that had her initials on the cover. Freddy Malins, who had listened with his head perched sideways to hear her better, was still applauding when everyone else had ceased and talking animatedly to his mother who nodded her head gravely and slowly in acquiescence. At last, when he could clap no more, he stood up suddenly and hurried across the room to Aunt Julia whose hand he seized and held in both his hands, shaking it when words failed him or the catch in his voice proved too much for him.

—I was just telling my mother, he said, I never heard you sing so well, never. No, I never heard your voice so good as it is to-night. Now! Would you believe that now? That's the truth. Upon my word and honour that's the truth. I never heard your voice sound so fresh and so . . . so clear and fresh, never.

Aunt Julia smiled broadly and murmured something about compliments as she released her hand from his grasp. Mr Browne extended his open hand towards her and said to those who were near him in the manner of a showman introducing a prodigy to an audience:

—Miss Julia Morkan, my latest discovery!

He was laughing very heartily at this himself when Freddy Malins turned to him and said:

—Well, Browne, if you're serious you might make a worse discovery. All I can say is I never heard her sing half so well as long as I am coming here. And that's the honest truth.

—Neither did I, said Mr. Browne. I think her voice has greatly improved.

Aunt Julia shrugged her shoulders and said with meek pride:

—Thirty years ago I hadn't a bad voice as voices go.

—I often told Julia, said Aunt Kate emphatically, that she was simply thrown away in that choir. But she never would be said by me.

She turned as if to appeal to the good sense of the others against a refractory child while Aunt Julia gazed in front of her, a vague smile of reminiscence playing on her face.

—No, continued Aunt Kate, she wouldn't be said or led by anyone, slaving there in that choir night and day, night and day. Six o'clock on Christmas morning! And all for what?

—Well, isn't it for the honour of God, Aunt Kate? asked Mary Jane, twisting round on the piano-stool and smiling.

Aunt Kate turned fiercely on her niece and said:

—I know all about the honour of God, Mary Jane, but I think it's not at all honourable for the pope to turn out the women out of the choirs that have slaved there all their lives and put little whipper-snappers of boys over their heads.[6] I suppose it is for the good of the Church if the pope does it. But it's not just, Mary Jane, and it's not right.

She had worked herself into a passion and would have continued in defence of her sister for it was a sore subject with her but Mary Jane, seeing that all the dancers had come back, intervened pacifically:

—Now, Aunt Kate, you're giving scandal to Mr Browne who is of the other persuasion.

Aunt Kate turned to Mr Browne, who was grinning at this allusion to his religion, and said hastily:

6. In 1903 the Pope had ordered all Catholic churches to start using all-male choirs.

—O, I don't question the pope's being right. I'm only a stupid old woman and I wouldn't presume to do such a thing. But there's such a thing as common everyday politeness and gratitude. And if I were in Julia's place I'd tell that Father Healy straight up to his face . . .

—And besides, Aunt Kate, said Mary Jane, we really are all hungry and when we are hungry we are all very quarrelsome.

—And when we are thirsty we are also quarrelsome, added Mr Browne.

—So that we had better go to supper, said Mary Jane, and finish the discussion afterwards.

On the landing outside the drawing-room Gabriel found his wife and Mary Jane trying to persuade Miss Ivors to stay for supper. But Miss Ivors, who had put on her hat and was buttoning her cloak, would not stay. She did not feel in the least hungry and she had already overstayed her time.

—But only for ten minutes, Molly, said Mrs Conroy. That won't delay you.

—To take a pick itself, said Mary Jane, after all your dancing.

—I really couldn't, said Miss Ivors.

—I am afraid you didn't enjoy yourself at all, said Mary Jane hopelessly.

—Ever so much, I assure you, said Miss Ivors, but you really must let me run off now.

—But how can you get home? asked Mrs Conroy.

—O, it's only two steps up the quay.

Gabriel hesitated a moment and said:

—If you will allow me, Miss Ivors, I'll see you home if you really are obliged to go.

But Miss Ivors broke away from them.

—I won't hear of it, she cried. For goodness sake go in to your suppers and don't mind me. I'm quite well able to take care of myself.

—Well, you're the comical girl, Molly, said Mrs Conroy frankly.

—*Beannacht libh,*[7] cried Miss Ivors, with a laugh, as she ran down the staircase.

Mary Jane gazed after her, a moody puzzled expression on her face, while Mrs Conroy leaned over the banisters to listen for the hall-door. Gabriel asked himself was he the cause of her abrupt departure. But she did not seem to be in ill humour: she had gone away laughing. He stared blankly down the staircase.

At that moment Aunt Kate came toddling out of the supper-room, almost wringing her hands in despair.

—Where is Gabriel? she cried. Where on earth is Gabriel? There's everyone waiting in there, stage to let, and nobody to carve the goose!

—Here I am, Aunt Kate! cried Gabriel, with sudden animation, ready to carve a flock of geese, if necessary.

A fat brown goose lay at one end of the table and at the other end, on a bed of creased paper strewn with sprigs of parsley, lay a great ham, stripped of its outer skin and peppered over with crust crumbs, a neat paper frill round its shin and beside this was a round of spiced beef. Between these rival ends ran parallel lines of side-dishes: two little minsters of jelly, red and yellow; a shallow dish full of blocks of blancmange and red jam, a large green leaf-shaped dish with a stalk-shaped handle, on which lay bunches of purple raisins and peeled almonds, a companion dish on which lay a solid rectangle of Smyrna figs, a dish of custard topped with grated nutmeg, a small bowl full of chocolates and sweets wrapped in gold and silver papers

7. Farewell (Irish).

and a glass vase in which stood some tall celery stalks. In the centre of the table there stood, as sentries to a fruit-stand which upheld a pyramid of oranges and American apples, two squat old-fashioned decanters of cut glass, one containing port and the other dark sherry. On the closed square piano a pudding in a huge yellow dish lay in waiting and behind it were three squads of bottles of stout and ale and minerals, drawn up according to the colours of their uniforms, the first two black, with brown and red labels, the third and smallest squad white, with transverse green sashes.

Gabriel took his seat boldly at the head of the table and, having looked to the edge of the carver, plunged his fork firmly into the goose. He felt quite at ease now for he was an expert carver and liked nothing better than to find himself at the head of a well-laden table.

—Miss Furlong, what shall I send you? he asked. A wing or a slice of the breast?

—Just a small slice of the breast.

—Miss Higgins, what for you?

—O, anything at all, Mr Conroy.

While Gabriel and Miss Daly exchanged plates of goose and plates of ham and spiced beef Lily went from guest to guest with a dish of hot floury potatoes wrapped in a white napkin. This was Mary Jane's idea and she had also suggested apple sauce for the goose but Aunt Kate had said that plain roast goose without apple sauce had always been good enough for her and she hoped she might never eat worse. Mary Jane waited on her pupils and saw that they got the best slices and Aunt Kate and Aunt Julia opened and carried across from the piano bottles of stout and ale for the gentlemen and bottles of minerals for the ladies. There was a great deal of confusion and laughter and noise, the noise of orders and counter-orders, of knives and forks, of corks and glass-stoppers. Gabriel began to carve second helpings as soon as he had finished the first round without serving himself. Everyone protested loudly so that he compromised by taking a long draught of stout for he had found the carving hot work. Mary Jane settled down quietly to her supper but Aunt Kate and Aunt Julia were still toddling round the table, walking on each other's heels, getting in each other's way and giving each other unheeded orders. Mr Browne begged of them to sit down and eat their suppers and so did Gabriel but they said there was time enough so that, at last, Freddy Malins stood up and, capturing Aunt Kate, plumped her down on her chair amid general laughter.

When everyone had been well served Gabriel said, smiling:

—Now, if anyone wants a little more of what vulgar people call stuffing let him or her speak.

A chorus of voices invited him to begin his own supper and Lily came forward with three potatoes which she had reserved for him.

—Very well, said Gabriel amiably, as he took another preparatory draught, kindly forget my existence, ladies and gentlemen, for a few minutes.

He set to his supper and took no part in the conversation with which the table covered Lily's removal of the plates. The subject of talk was the opera company which was then at the Theatre Royal. Mr Bartell D'Arcy, the tenor, a dark-complexioned young man with a smart moustache, praised very highly the leading contralto of the company but Miss Furlong thought she had a rather vulgar style of production. Freddy Malins said there was a negro chieftain singing in the second part of the Gaiety pantomime who had one of the finest tenor voices he had ever heard.

—Have you heard him? he asked Mr Bartell D'Arcy across the table.

—No, answered Mr Bartell D'Arcy carelessly.

—Because, Freddy Malins explained, now I'd be curious to hear your opinion of him. I think he has a grand voice.

—It takes Teddy to find out the really good things, said Mr Browne familiarly to the table.

—And why couldn't he have a voice too? asked Freddy Malins sharply. Is it because he's only a black?

Nobody answered this question and Mary Jane led the table back to the legitimate opera. One of her pupils had given her a pass for *Mignon.* Of course it was very fine, she said, but it made her think of poor Georgina Burns. Mr Browne could go back farther still, to the old Italian companies that used to come to Dublin—Tietjens, Ilma de Murzka, Campanini, the great Trebelli, Giuglini, Ravelli, Aramburo.[8] Those were the days, he said, when there was something like singing to be heard in Dublin. He told too of how the top gallery of the old Royal used to be packed night after night, of how one night an Italian tenor had sung five encores to *Let Me Like a Soldier Fall,* introducing a high C every time, and of how the gallery boys would sometimes in their enthusiasm unyoke the horses from the carriage of some great *prima donna* and pull her themselves through the streets to her hotel. Why did they never play the grand old operas now, he asked, *Dinorah, Lucrezia Borgia?* Because they could not get the voices to sing them: that was why.

—O, well, said Mr Bartell D'Arcy, I presume there are as good singers to-day as there were then.

—Where are they? asked Mr Browne defiantly.

—In London, Paris, Milan, said Mr Bartell D'Arcy warmly. I suppose Caruso,[9] for example, is quite as good, if not better than any of the men you have mentioned.

—Maybe so, said Mr Browne. But I may tell you I doubt it strongly.

—O, I'd give anything to hear Caruso sing, said Mary Jane.

—For me, said Aunt Kate, who had been picking a bone, there was only one tenor. To please me, I mean. But I suppose none of you ever heard of him.

—Who was he, Miss Morkan? asked Mr Bartell D'Arcy politely.

—His name, said Aunt Kate, was Parkinson. I heard him when he was in his prime and I think he had then the purest tenor voice that was ever put into a man's throat.

—Strange, said Mr Bartell D'Arcy. I never even heard of him.

—Yes, yes, Miss Morkan is right, said Mr Browne. I remember hearing of old Parkinson but he's too far back for me.

—A beautiful pure sweet mellow English tenor, said Aunt Kate with enthusiasm.

Gabriel having finished, the huge pudding was transferred to the table. The clatter of forks and spoons began again. Gabriel's wife served out spoonfuls of the pudding and passed the plates down the table. Midway down they were held up by Mary Jane, who replenished them with raspberry or orange jelly or with blancmange and jam. The pudding was of Aunt Julia's making and she received praises for it from all quarters. She herself said that it was not quite brown enough.

—Well, I hope, Miss Morkan, said Mr Browne, that I'm brown enough for you because, you know, I'm all brown.

All the gentlemen, except Gabriel, ate some of the pudding out of compliment to Aunt Julia. As Gabriel never ate sweets the celery had been left for him. Freddy Malins also took a stalk of celery and ate it with his pudding. He had been told that celery

8. Famous 19th-century opera singers.

9. Enrico Caruso (1874–1921), a famous tenor.

was a capital thing for the blood and he was just then under doctor's care. Mrs Malins, who had been silent all through the supper, said that her son was going down to Mount Melleray[1] in a week or so. The table then spoke to Mount Melleray, how bracing the air was down there, how hospitable the monks were and how they never asked for a penny-piece from their guests.

—And do you mean to say, asked Mr Browne incredulously, that a chap can go down there and put up there as if it were a hotel and live on the fat of the land and then come away without paying a farthing?

—O, most people give some donation to the monastery when they leave, said Mary Jane.

—I wish we had an institution like that in our Church, said Mr Browne candidly.

He was astonished to hear that the monks never spoke, got up at two in the morning and slept in their coffins. He asked what they did it for.

—That's the rule of the order, said Aunt Kate firmly.

—Yes, but why? asked Mr Browne.

Aunt Kate repeated that it was the rule, that was all. Mr Browne still seemed not to understand. Freddy Malins explained to him, as best he could, that the monks were trying to make up for the sins committed by all the sinners in the outside world. The explanation was not very clear for Mr Browne grinned and said:

—I like that idea very much but wouldn't a comfortable spring bed do them as well as a coffin?

—The coffin, said Mary Jane, is to remind them of their last end.

As the subject had grown lugubrious it was buried in a silence of the table during which Mrs Malins could be heard saying to her neighbour in an indistinct undertone:

—They are very good men, the monks, very pious men.

The raisins and almonds and figs and apples and oranges and chocolates and sweets were now passed about the table and Aunt Julia invited all the guests to have either port or sherry. At first Mr Bartell D'Arcy refused to take either but one of his neighbours nudged him and whispered something to him upon which he allowed his glass to be filled. Gradually as the last glasses were being filled the conversation ceased. A pause followed, broken only by the noise of the wine and by unsettlings of chairs. The Misses Morkan, all three, looked down at the tablecloth. Someone coughed once or twice and then a few gentlemen patted the table gently as a signal for silence. The silence came and Gabriel pushed back his chair and stood up.

The patting at once grew louder in encouragement and then ceased altogether. Gabriel leaned his ten trembling fingers on the tablecloth and smiled nervously at the company. Meeting a row of upturned faces he raised his eyes to the chandelier. The piano was playing a waltz tune and he could hear the skirts sweeping against the drawing-room door. People, perhaps, were standing in the snow on the quay outside, gazing up at the lighted windows and listening to the waltz music. The air was pure there. In the distance lay the park where the trees were weighted with snow. The Wellington Monument wore a gleaming cap of snow that flashed westward over the white field of Fifteen Acres.[2]

He began:

—Ladies and Gentlemen.

1. A monastery in southern Ireland, specializing in the treatment of alcoholics.

2. A section of Phoenix Park.

—It has fallen to my lot this evening, as in years past, to perform a very pleasing task but a task for which I am afraid my poor powers as a speaker are all too inadequate.

—No, no! said Mr Browne.

—But, however that may be, I can only ask you tonight to take the will for the deed and to lend me your attention for a few moments while I endeavour to express to you in words what my feelings are on this occasion.

—Ladies and Gentlemen. It is not the first time that we have gathered together under this hospitable roof, around this hospitable board. It is not the first time that we have been the recipients—or perhaps, I had better say, the victims—of the hospitality of certain good ladies.

He made a circle in the air with his arm and paused. Everyone laughed or smiled at Aunt Kate and Aunt Julia and Mary Jane who all turned crimson with pleasure. Gabriel went on more boldly:

—I feel more strongly with every recurring year that our country has no tradition which does it so much honour and which it should guard so jealously as that of its hospitality. It is a tradition that is unique as far as my experience goes (and I have visited not a few places abroad) among the modern nations. Some would say, perhaps, that with us it is rather a failing than anything to be boasted of. But granted even that, it is, to my mind, a princely failing, and one that I trust will long be cultivated among us. Of one thing, at least, I am sure. As long as this one roof shelters the good ladies aforesaid—and I wish from my heart it may do so for many and many a long year to come—the tradition of genuine warm-hearted courteous Irish hospitality, which our forefathers have handed down to us and which we in turn must hand down to our descendants, is still alive among us.

A hearty murmur of assent ran round the table. It shot through Gabriel's mind that Miss Ivors was not there and that she had gone away discourteously: and he said with confidence in himself:

—Ladies and Gentlemen.

—A new generation is growing up in our midst, a generation actuated by new ideas and new principles. It is serious and enthusiastic for these new ideas and its enthusiasm, even when it is misdirected, is, I believe, in the main sincere. But we are living in a sceptical and, if I may use the phrase, a thought-tormented age: and sometimes I fear that this new generation, educated or hypereducated as it is, will lack those qualities of humanity, of hospitality, of kindly humour which belonged to an older day. Listening to-night to the names of all those great singers of the past it seemed to me, I must confess, that we were living in a less spacious age. Those days might, without exaggeration, be called spacious days: and if they are gone beyond recall let us hope, at least, that in gatherings such as this we shall still speak of them with pride and affection, still cherish in our hearts the memory of those dead and gone great ones whose fame the world will not willingly let die.

—Hear, hear! said Mr Browne loudly.

—But yet, continued Gabriel, his voice falling into a softer inflection, there are always in gatherings such as this sadder thoughts that will recur to our minds: thoughts of the past, of youth, of changes, of absent faces that we miss here to-night. Our path through life is strewn with many such sad memories: and were we to brood upon them always we could not find the heart to go on bravely with our work among the living. We have all of us living duties and living affections which claim, and rightly claim, our strenuous endeavours.

—Therefore, I will not linger on the past. I will not let any gloomy moralising intrude upon us here to-night. Here we are gathered together for a brief moment from the bustle and rush of our everyday routine. We are met here as friends, in the spirit of good-fellowship, as colleagues, also to a certain extent, in the true spirit of *camaraderie,* and as the guests of—what shall I call them?—the Three Graces[3] of the Dublin musical world.

The table burst into applause and laughter at this sally. Aunt Julia vainly asked each of her neighbors in turn to tell her what Gabriel had said.

—He says we are the Three Graces, Aunt Julia, said Mary Jane.

Aunt Julia did not understand but she looked up, smiling, at Gabriel, who continued in the same vein:

—Ladies and Gentlemen.

—I will not attempt to play to-night the part that Paris[4] played on another occasion. I will not attempt to choose between them. The task would be an invidious one and one beyond my poor powers. For when I view them in turn, whether it be our chief hostess herself, whose good heart, whose too good heart, has become a byword with all who know her, or her sister, who seems to be gifted with perennial youth and whose singing must have been a surprise and a revelation to us all to-night, or, last but not least, when I consider our youngest hostess, talented, cheerful, hard-working and the best of nieces, I confess, Ladies and Gentlemen, that I do not know to which of them I should award the prize.

Gabriel glanced down at his aunts and, seeing the large smile on Aunt Julia's face and the tears which had risen to Aunt Kate's eyes, hastened to his close. He raised his glass of port gallantly, while every member of the company fingered a glass expectantly, and said loudly:

—Let us toast them all three together. Let us drink to their health, wealth, long life, happiness and prosperity and may they long continue to hold the proud and self-won position which they hold in their profession and the position of honour and affection which they hold in our hearts.

All the guests stood up, glass in hand, and, turning towards the three seated ladies, sang in unison, with Mr Browne as leader:

For they are jolly gay fellows,
For they are jolly gay fellows,
For they are jolly gay fellows,
Which nobody can deny.

Aunt Kate was making frank use of her handkerchief and even Aunt Julia seemed moved. Freddy Malins beat time with his pudding-fork and the singers turned towards one another, as if in melodious conference, while they sang, with emphasis:

Unless he tells a lie,
Unless he tells a lie.

Then, turning once more towards their hostesses, they sang:

For they are jolly gay fellows,
For they are jolly gay fellows,
For they are jolly gay fellows,

3. Companions to the Muses in Greek mythology.

4. Paris was the judge of a divine beauty contest in which Hera, Athena, and Aphrodite competed; his selection of Aphrodite was, indirectly, the cause of the Trojan War.

Which nobody can deny.

The acclamation which followed was taken up beyond the door of the supper-room by many of the other guests and renewed time after time, Freddy Malins acting as officer with his fork on high.

The piercing morning air came into the hall where they were standing so that Aunt Kate said:

—Close the door, somebody. Mrs Malins will get her death of cold.

—Browne is out there, Aunt Kate, said Mary Jane.

—Browne is everywhere, said Aunt Kate, lowering her voice.

Mary Jane laughed at her tone.

—Really, she said archly, he is very attentive.

—He has been laid on here like the gas, said Aunt Kate in the same tone, all during the Christmas.

She laughed herself this time good-humouredly and then added quickly:

—But tell him to come in, Mary Jane, and close the door. I hope to goodness he didn't hear me.

At that moment the hall-door was opened and Mr Browne came in from the doorstep, laughing as if his heart would break. He was dressed in a long green overcoat with mock astrakhan cuffs and collar and wore on his head an oval fur cap. He pointed down the snow-covered quay from where the sound of shrill prolonged whistling was borne in.

—Teddy will have all the cabs in Dublin out, he said.

Gabriel advanced from the little pantry behind the office, struggling into his overcoat and looking round the hall, said:

—Gretta not down yet?

—She's getting on her things, Gabriel, said Aunt Kate.

—Who's playing up there? asked Gabriel.

—Nobody. They're all gone.

—O no, Aunt Kate, said Mary Jane. Bartell D'Arcy and Miss O'Callaghan aren't gone yet.

—Someone is strumming at the piano, anyhow, said Gabriel.

Mary Jane glanced at Gabriel and Mr Browne and said with a shiver:

—It makes me feel cold to look at you two gentlemen muffled up like that. I wouldn't like to face your journey home at this hour.

—I'd like nothing better this minute, said Mr Browne stoutly, than a rattling fine walk in the country or a fast drive with a good spanking goer between the shafts.

—We used to have a very good horse and trap at home, said Aunt Julia sadly.

—The never-to-be-forgotten Johnny, said Mary Jane, laughing.

Aunt Kate and Gabriel laughed too.

—Why, what was wonderful about Johnny? asked Mr Browne.

—The late lamented Patrick Morkan, our grandfather, that is, explained Gabriel, commonly known in his later years as the old gentleman, was a glue-boiler.

—O, now, Gabriel, said Aunt Kate, laughing, he had a starch mill.

—Well, glue or starch, said Gabriel, the old gentleman had a horse by the name of Johnny. And Johnny used to work in the old gentleman's mill, walking round and round in order to drive the mill. That was all very well; but now comes the tragic part about Johnny. One fine day the old gentleman thought he'd like to drive out with the quality to a military review in the park.

—The Lord have mercy on his soul, said Aunt Kate compassionately.

—Amen, said Gabriel. So the old gentleman, as I said, harnessed Johnny and put on his very best tall hat and his very best stock collar and drove out in grand style from his ancestral mansion somewhere near Back Lane, I think.

Everyone laughed, even Mrs Malins, at Gabriel's manner and Aunt Kate said:

—O now, Gabriel, he didn't live in Back Lane, really. Only the mill was there.

—Out from the mansion of his forefathers, continued Gabriel, he drove with Johnny. And everything went on beautifully until Johnny came in sight of King Billy's statue:[5] and whether he fell in love with the horse King Billy sits on or whether he thought he was back again in the mill, anyhow he began to walk round the statue.

Gabriel paced in a circle round the hall in his goloshes amid the laughter of the others.

—Round and round he went, said Gabriel, and the old gentleman, who was a very pompous old gentleman, was highly indignant. *Go on, sir! What do you mean, sir? Johnny! Johnny! Most extraordinary conduct! Can't understand the horse!*

The peals of laughter which followed Gabriel's imitation of the incident were interrupted by a resounding knock at the hall-door. Mary Jane ran to open it and let in Freddy Malins. Freddy Malins, with his hat well back on his head and his shoulders humped with cold, was puffing and steaming after his exertions.

—I could only get one cab, he said.

—O, we'll find another along the quay, said Gabriel.

—Yes, said Aunt Kate. Better not keep Mrs Malins standing in the draught.

Mrs Malins was helped down the front steps by her son and Mr Browne and, after many manoeuvres, hoisted into the cab. Freddy Malins clambered in after her and spent a long time settling her on the seat, Mr Browne helping him with advice. At last she was settled comfortably and Freddy Malins invited Mr Browne into the cab. There was a good deal of confused talk, and then Mr Browne got into the cab. The cabman settled his rug over his knees, and bent down for the address. The confusion grew greater and the cabman was directed differently by Freddy Malins and Mr Browne, each of whom had his head out through a window of the cab. The difficulty was to know where to drop Mr Browne along the route and Aunt Kate, Aunt Julia and Mary Jane helped the discussion from the doorstep with cross-directions and contradictions and abundance of laughter. As for Freddy Malins he was speechless with laughter. He popped his head in and out of the window every moment, to the great danger of his hat, and told his mother how the discussion was progressing till at last Mr Browne shouted to the bewildered cabman above the din of everybody's laughter:

—Do you know Trinity College?

—Yes, sir, said the cabman.

—Well, drive bang up against Trinity College gates, said Mr Browne, and then we'll tell you where to go. You understand now?

—Yes, sir, said the cabman.

—Make like a bird for Trinity College.

—Right, sir, cried the cabman.

5. A statue of William of Orange, who defeated the Irish Catholic forces in the Battle of the Boyne in 1690, which stood in College Green in front of Trinity College in the heart of Dublin. It was seen as a symbol of British imperial oppression.

The horse was whipped up and the cab rattled off along the quay amid a chorus of laughter and adieus.

Gabriel had not gone to the door with the others. He was in a dark part of the hall gazing up the staircase. A woman was standing near the top of the first flight, in the shadow also. He could not see her face but he could see the terracotta and salmonpink panels of her skirt which the shadow made appear black and white. It was his wife. She was leaning on the banisters, listening to something. Gabriel was surprised at her stillness and strained his ear to listen also. But he could hear little save the noise of laughter and dispute on the front steps, a few chords struck on the piano and a few notes of a man's voice singing.

He stood still in the gloom of the hall, trying to catch the air that the voice was singing and gazing up at his wife. There was grace and mystery in her attitude as if she were a symbol of something. He asked himself what is a woman standing on the stairs in the shadow, listening to distant music, a symbol of. If he were a painter he would paint her in that attitude. Her blue felt hat would show off the bronze of her hair against the darkness and the dark panels of her skirt would show off the light ones. *Distant Music* he would call the picture if he were a painter.

The hall-door was closed; and Aunt Kate, Aunt Julia and Mary Jane came down the hall, still laughing.

—Well, isn't Freddy terrible? said Mary Jane. He's really terrible.

Gabriel said nothing but pointed up the stairs towards where his wife was standing. Now that the hall-door was closed the voice and the piano could be heard more clearly. Gabriel held up his hand for them to be silent. The song seemed to be in the old Irish tonality and the singer seemed uncertain both of his words and of his voice. The voice, made plaintive by distance and by the singer's hoarseness, faintly illuminated the cadence of the air with words expressing grief:

O, the rain falls on my heavy locks
And the dew wets my skin,
My babe lies cold . . .[6]

–O, exclaimed Mary Jane. It's Bartell D'Arcy singing and he wouldn't sing all the night. O, I'll get him to sing a song before he goes.

—O do, Mary Jane, said Aunt Kate.

Mary Jane brushed past the others and ran to the staircase but before she reached it the singing stopped and the piano was closed abruptly.

—O, what a pity! she cried. Is he coming down, Gretta?

Gabriel heard his wife answer yes and saw her come down towards them. A few steps behind her were Mr Bartell D'Arcy and Miss O'Callaghan.

—O, Mr D'Arcy, cried Mary Jane, it's downright mean of you to break off like that when we were all in raptures listening to you.

—I have been at him all the evening, said Miss O'Callaghan, and Mrs Conroy too and he told us he had a dreadful cold and couldn't sing.

—O, Mr D'Arcy, said Aunt Kate, now that was a great fib to tell.

—Can't you see that I'm as hoarse as a crow? said Mr D'Arcy roughly.

He went into the pantry hastily and put on his overcoat. The others, taken aback by his rude speech, could find nothing to say. Aunt Kate wrinkled her brows and

6. From a traditional ballad, *The Lass of Aughrim,* about a peasant girl seduced by a nobleman. She brings their baby to the castle door, only to be turned away; she and her child then die by drowning.

made signs to the others to drop the subject. Mr D'Arcy stood swathing his neck carefully and frowning.

—It's the weather, said Aunt Julia, after a pause.

—Yes, everybody has colds, said Aunt Kate readily, everybody.

—They say, said Mary Jane, we haven't had snow like it for thirty years; and I read this morning in the newspapers that the snow is general all over Ireland.

—I love the look of snow, said Aunt Julia sadly.

—So do I, said Miss O'Callaghan. I think Christmas is never really Christmas unless we have the snow on the ground.

—But poor Mr D'Arcy doesn't like the snow, said Aunt Kate, smiling.

Mr D'Arcy came from the pantry, full swathed and buttoned, and in a repentant tone told them the history of his cold. Everyone gave him advice and said it was a great pity and urged him to be very careful of his throat in the night air. Gabriel watched his wife who did not join in the conversation. She was standing right under the dusty fanlight and the flame of the gas lit up the rich bronze of her hair which he had seen her drying at the fire a few days before. She was in the same attitude and seemed unaware of the talk about her. At last she turned towards them and Gabriel saw that there was colour on her cheeks and that her eyes were shining. A sudden tide of joy went leaping out of his heart.

—Mr D'Arcy, she said, what is the name of that song you were singing?

—It's called *The Lass of Aughrim,* said Mr D'Arcy, but I couldn't remember it properly. Why? Do you know it?

—*The Lass of Aughrim,* she repeated. I couldn't think of the name.

—It's a very nice air, said Mary Jane. I'm sorry you were not in voice to-night.

—Now, Mary Jane, said Aunt Kate, don't annoy Mr D'Arcy. I won't have him annoyed.

Seeing that all were ready to start she shepherded them to the door where good-night was said:

—Well, good-night, Aunt Kate, and thanks for the pleasant evening.

—Good-night, Gabriel. Good-night, Gretta!

—Good-night, Aunt Kate, and thanks ever so much. Good-night, Aunt Julia.

—O, good-night, Gretta, I didn't see you.

—Good-night, Mr D'Arcy. Good-night, Miss O'Callaghan.

—Good-night, Miss Morkan.

—Good-night, again.

—Good-night, all. Safe home.

—Good-night. Good-night.

The morning was still dark. A dull yellow light brooded over the houses and the river; and the sky seemed to be descending. It was slushy underfoot; and only streaks and patches of snow lay on the roofs, on the parapets of the quay and on the area railings. The lamps were still burning redly in the murky air and, across the river, the palace of the Four Courts[7] stood out menacingly against the heavy sky.

She was walking on before him with Mr Bartell D'Arcy, her shoes in a brown parcel tucked under one arm and her hands holding her skirt up from the slush. She had no longer any grace of attitude but Gabriel's eyes were still bright with happiness. The blood went bounding along his veins; and the thoughts went rioting through his brain, proud, joyful, tender, valorous.

7. The Irish law courts.

She was walking on before him so lightly and so erect that he longed to run after her noiselessly, catch her by the shoulders and say something foolish and affectionate into her ear. She seemed to him so frail that he longed to defend her against something and then to be alone with her. Moments of their secret life together burst like stars upon his memory. A heliotrope envelope was lying beside his breakfast-cup and he was caressing it with his hand. Birds were twittering in the ivy and the sunny web of the curtain was shimmering along the floor: he could not eat for happiness. They were standing on the crowded platform and he was placing a ticket inside the warm palm of her glove. He was standing with her in the cold, looking in through a grated window at a man making bottles in a roaring furnace. It was very cold. Her face, fragrant in the cold air, was quite close to his; and suddenly she called out to the man at the furnace:

—Is the fire hot, sir?

But the man could not hear her with the noise of the furnace. It was just as well. He might have answered rudely.

A wave of yet more tender joy escaped from his heart and went coursing in warm flood along his arteries. Like the tender fires of stars moments of their life together, that no one knew of or would ever know of, broke upon and illumined his memory. He longed to recall to her those moments, to make her forget the years of their dull existence together and remember only their moments of ecstasy. For the years, he felt, had not quenched his soul or hers. Their children, his writing, her household cares had not quenched all their souls' tender fire. In one letter that he had written to her then he had said: *Why is it that words like these seem to me so dull and cold? Is it because there is no word tender enough to be your name?*

Like distant music these words that he had written years before were borne towards him from the past. He longed to be alone with her. When the others had gone away, when he and she were in their room in the hotel, then they would be alone together. He would call her softly:

—Gretta!

Perhaps she would not hear at once: she would be undressing. Then something in his voice would strike her. She would turn and look at him. . . .

At the corner of Winetavern Street they met a cab. He was glad of its rattling noise as it saved him from conversation. She was looking out of the window and seemed tired. The others spoke only a few words, pointing out some building or street. The horse galloped along wearily under the murky morning sky, dragging his old rattling box after his heels, and Gabriel was again in a cab with her, galloping to catch the boat, galloping to their honeymoon.

As the cab drove across O'Connell Bridge Miss O'Callaghan said:

—They say you never cross O'Connell Bridge without seeing a white horse.

—I see a white man this time, said Gabriel.

—Where? asked Mr Bartell D'Arcy.

Gabriel pointed to the statue, on which lay patches of snow.[8] Then he nodded familiarly to it and waved his hand.

—Good-night, Dan, he said gaily.

When the cab drew up before the hotel Gabriel jumped out and, in spite of Mr Bartell D'Arcy's protest, paid the driver. He gave the man a shilling over his fare. The man saluted and said:

8. A statue of Daniel O'Connell, 19th-century nationalist leader.

—A prosperous New Year to you, sir.

—The same to you, said Gabriel cordially.

She leaned for a moment on his arm in getting out of the cab and while standing at the curbstone, bidding the others good-night. She leaned lightly on his arm, as lightly as when she had danced with him a few hours before. He had felt proud and happy then, happy that she was his, proud of her grace and wifely carriage. But now, after the kindling again of so many memories, the first touch of her body, musical and strange and perfumed, sent through him a keen pang of lust. Under cover of her silence he pressed her arm closely to his side; and, as they stood at the hotel door, he felt that they had escaped from their lives and duties, escaped from home and friends and run away together with wild and radiant hearts to a new adventure.

An old man was dozing in a great hooded chair in the hall. He lit a candle in the office and went before them to the stairs. They followed him in silence, their feet falling in soft thuds on the thickly carpeted stairs. She mounted the stairs behind the porter, her head bowed in the ascent, her frail shoulders curved as with a burden, her skirt girt tightly about her. He could have flung his arms about her hips and held her still for his arms were trembling with desire to seize her and only the stress of his nails against the palms of his hands held the wild impulse of his body in check. The porter halted on the stairs to settle his guttering candle. They halted too on the steps below him. In the silence Gabriel could hear the falling of the molten wax into the tray and the thumping of his own heart against his ribs.

The porter led them along a corridor and opened a door. Then he set his unstable candle down on a toilet-table and asked at what hour they were to be called in the morning.

—Eight, said Gabriel.

The porter pointed to the tap of the electric-light and began a muttered apology but Gabriel cut him short.

—We don't want any light. We have light enough from the street. And I say, he added, pointing to the candle, you might remove that handsome article, like a good man.

The porter took up his candle again, but slowly for he was surprised by such a novel idea. Then he mumbled good-night and went out. Gabriel shot the lock to.

A ghostly light from the street lamp lay in a long shaft from one window to the door. Gabriel threw his overcoat and hat on a couch and crossed the room towards the window. He looked down into the street in order that his emotion might calm a little. Then he turned and leaned against a chest of drawers with his back to the light. She had taken off her hat and cloak and was standing before a large swinging mirror, unhooking her waist. Gabriel paused for a few moments, watching her, and then said:

—Gretta!

She turned away from the mirror slowly and walked along the shaft of light towards him. Her face looked so serious and weary that the words would not pass Gabriel's lips. No, it was not the moment yet.

—You looked tired, he said.

—I am a little, she answered.

—You don't feel ill or weak?

—No, tired: that's all.

She went on to the window and stood there, looking out. Gabriel waited again and then, fearing that diffidence was about to conquer him, he said abruptly:

—By the way, Gretta!

—What is it?

—You know that poor fellow Malins? he said quickly.

—Yes. What about him?

—Well, poor fellow, he's a decent sort of chap after all, continued Gabriel in a false voice. He gave me back that sovereign I lent him and I didn't expect it really. It's a pity he wouldn't keep away from that Browne, because he's not a bad fellow at heart.

He was trembling now with annoyance. Why did she seem so abstracted? He did not know how he could begin. Was she annoyed, too, about something? If she would only turn to him or come to him of her own accord! To take her as she was would be brutal. No, he must see some ardour in her eyes first. He longed to be master of her strange mood.

—When did you lend him the pound? she asked, after a pause.

Gabriel strove to restrain himself from breaking out into brutal language about the sottish Malins and his pound. He longed to cry to her from his soul, to crush her body against his, to overmaster her. But he said:

—O, at Christmas, when he opened that little Christmas-card shop in Henry Street.

He was in such a fever of rage and desire that he did not hear her come from the window. She stood before him for an instant, looking at him strangely. Then, suddenly raising herself on tiptoe and resting her hands lightly on his shoulders, she kissed him.

—You are a very generous person, Gabriel, she said.

Gabriel, trembling with delight at her sudden kiss and at the quaintness of her phrase, put his hands on her hair and began smoothing it back, scarcely touching it with his fingers. The washing had made it fine and brilliant. His heart was brimming over with happiness. Just when he was wishing for it she had come to him of her own accord. Perhaps her thoughts had been running with his. Perhaps she had felt the impetuous desire that was in him and then the yielding mood had come upon her. Now that she had fallen to him so easily he wondered why he had been so diffident.

He stood, holding her head between his hands. Then, slipping one arm swiftly about her body and drawing her towards him, he said softly:

—Gretta dear, what are you thinking about?

She did not answer nor yield wholly to his arm. He said again, softly:

—Tell me what it is, Gretta. I think I know what is the matter. Do I know?

She did not answer at once. Then she said in an outburst of tears:

—O, I am thinking about that song, *The Lass of Aughrim.*

She broke loose from him and ran to the bed and, throwing her arms across the bed-rail, hid her face. Gabriel stood stock-still for a moment in astonishment and then followed her. As he passed in the way of the cheval-glass he caught sight of himself in full length, his broad, well-filled shirt-front, the face whose expression always puzzled him when he saw it in a mirror and his glimmering gilt-rimmed eyeglasses. He halted a few paces from her and said:

—What about the song? Why does that make you cry?

She raised her head from her arms and dried her eyes with the back of her hand like a child. A kinder note than he had intended went into his voice.

—Why, Gretta? he asked.

—I am thinking about a person long ago who used to sing that song.

—And who was the person long ago? asked Gabriel, smiling.

—It was a person I used to know in Galway when I was living with my grandmother, she said.

The smile passed away from Gabriel's face. A dull anger began to gather again at the back of his mind and the dull fires of his lust began to glow angrily in his veins.

—Someone you were in love with? he asked ironically.

—It was a young boy I used to know, she answered, named Michael Furey. He used to sing that song, *The Lass of Aughrim.* He was very delicate.

Gabriel was silent. He did not wish her to think that he was interested in this delicate boy.

—I can see him so plainly, she said after a moment. Such eyes as he had: big dark eyes! And such an expression in them—an expression!

—O then, you were in love with him? said Gabriel.

—I used to go out walking with him, she said, when I was in Galway.

A thought flew across Gabriel's mind.

—Perhaps that was why you wanted to go to Galway with that Ivors girl? he said coldly.

She looked at him and asked in surprise:

—What for?

Her eyes made Gabriel feel awkward. He shrugged his shoulders and said:

—How do I know? To see him perhaps.

She looked away from him along the shaft of light towards the window in silence.

—He is dead, she said at length. He died when he was only seventeen. Isn't it a terrible thing to die so young as that?

—What was he? asked Gabriel, still ironically.

—He was in the gasworks, she said.

Gabriel felt humiliated by the failure of his irony and by the evocation of this figure from the dead, a boy in the gasworks. While he had been full of memories of their secret life together, full of tenderness and joy and desire, she had been comparing him in her mind with another. A shameful consciousness of his own person assailed him. He saw himself as a ludicrous figure, acting as a pennyboy[9] for his aunts, a nervous well-meaning sentimentalist, orating to vulgarians and idealising his own clownish lusts, the pitiable fatuous fellow he had caught a glimpse of in the mirror. Instinctively he turned his back more to the light lest she might see the shame that burned upon his forehead.

He tried to keep up his tone of cold interrogation but his voice when he spoke was humble and indifferent.

—I suppose you were in love with this Michael Furey, Gretta, he said.

—I was great with him at that time, she said.

Her voice was veiled and sad. Gabriel, feeling now how vain it would be to try to lead her whither he had purposed, caressed one of her hands and said, also sadly:

—And what did he die of so young, Gretta? Consumption, was it?

—I think he died for me, she answered.[1]

A vague terror seized Gabriel at this answer as if, at that hour when he had hoped to triumph, some impalpable and vindictive being was coming against him, gathering forces against him in its vague world. But he shook himself free of it with an effort of reason and continued to caress her hand. He did not question her again for he felt that she would tell him of herself. Her hand was warm and moist: it did not respond to his

9. Errand boy.

1. Gretta here echoes the words of Yeats's Cathleen ní Houlihan: "Singing I am about a man I knew one time, yellow-haired Donough that was hanged in Galway. . . . He died for love of me: many a man has died for love of me." The play was first performed in Dublin on 2 April 1902.

touch but he continued to caress it just as he had caressed her first letter to him that spring morning.

—It was in the winter, she said, about the beginning of the winter when I was going to leave my grandmother's and come up here to the convent. And he was ill at the time in his lodgings in Galway and wouldn't be let out and his people in Oughterard[2] were written to. He was in decline, they said, or something like that. I never knew rightly.

She paused for a moment and sighed.

—Poor fellow, she said. He was very fond of me and he was such a gentle boy. We used to go out together, walking, you know, Gabriel, like the way they do in the country. He was going to study singing only for his health. He had a very good voice, poor Michael Furey.

—Well; and then? asked Gabriel.

—And then when it came to the time for me to leave Galway and come up to the convent he was much worse and I wouldn't be let see him so I wrote a letter saying I was going up to Dublin and would be back in the summer and hoping he would be better then.

She paused for a moment to get her voice under control and then went on:

—Then the night before I left I was in my grandmother's house in Nuns' Island, packing up, and I heard gravel thrown up against the window. The window was so wet I couldn't see so I ran downstairs as I was and slipped out the back into the garden and there was the poor fellow at the end of the garden, shivering.

—And did you not tell him to go back? asked Gabriel.

—I implored him to go home at once and told him he would get his death in the rain. But he said he did not want to live. I can see his eyes as well as well! He was standing at the end of the wall where there was a tree.

—And did he go home? asked Gabriel.

—Yes, he went home. And when I was only a week in the convent he died and he was buried in Oughterard where his people came from. O, the day I heard that, that he was dead!

She stopped, choking with sobs, and, overcome by emotion, flung herself face downward on the bed, sobbing in the quilt. Gabriel held her hand for a moment longer, irresolutely, and then, shy of intruding on her grief, let it fall gently and walked quietly to the window.

She was fast asleep.

Gabriel, leaning on his elbow, looked for a few moments unresentfully on her tangled hair and half-open mouth, listening to her deep-drawn breath. So she had had that romance in her life: a man had died for her sake. It hardly pained him now to think how poor a part he, her husband, had played in her life. He watched her while she slept as though he and she had never lived together as man and wife. His curious eyes rested long upon her face and on her hair: and, as he thought of what she must have been then, in that time of her first girlish beauty, a strange friendly pity for her entered his soul. He did not like to say even to himself that her face was no longer beautiful but he knew that it was no longer the face for which Michael Furey had braved death.

Perhaps she had not told him all the story. His eyes moved to the chair over which she had thrown some of her clothes. A petticoat string dangled to the floor. One boot stood upright, its limp upper fallen down: the fellow of it lay upon its side. He

2. A small village in western Ireland.

wondered at his riot of emotions of an hour before. From what had it proceeded? From his aunt's supper, from his own foolish speech, from the wine and dancing, the merry-making when saying good-night in the hall, the pleasure of the walk along the river in the snow. Poor Aunt Julia! She, too, would soon be a shade with the shade of Patrick Morkan and his horse. He had caught that haggard look upon her face for a moment when she was singing *Arrayed for the Bridal.* Soon, perhaps, he would be sitting in that same drawing-room, dressed in black, his silk hat on his knees. The blinds would be drawn down and Aunt Kate would be sitting beside him, crying and blowing her nose and telling him how Julia had died. He would cast about in his mind for some words that might console her, and would find only lame and useless ones. Yes, yes: that would happen very soon.

The air of the room chilled his shoulders. He stretched himself cautiously along under the sheets and lay down beside his wife. One by one they were all becoming shades. Better pass boldly into that other world, in the full glory of some passion, than fade and wither dismally with age. He thought of how she who lay beside him had locked in her heart for so many years that image of her lover's eyes when he had told her that he did not wish to live.

Generous tears filled Gabriel's eyes. He had never felt like that himself towards any woman but he knew that such a feeling must be love. The tears gathered more thickly in his eyes and in the partial darkness he imagined he saw the form of a young man standing under a dripping tree. Other forms were near. His soul had approached that region where dwell the vast hosts of the dead. He was conscious of, but could not apprehend, their wayward and flickering existence. His own identity was fading out into a grey impalpable world: the solid world itself which these dead had one time reared and lived in was dissolving and dwindling.

A few light taps upon the pane made him turn to the window. It had begun to snow again. He watched sleepily the flakes, silver and dark, falling obliquely against the lamplight. The time had come for him to set out on his journey westward. Yes, the newspapers were right: snow was general all over Ireland. It was falling on every part of the dark central plain, on the treeless hills, falling softly upon the Bog of Allen and, farther westward, softly falling into the dark mutinous Shannon waves.[3] It was falling, too, upon every part of the lonely churchyard on the hill where Michael Furey lay buried. It lay thickly drifted on the crooked crosses and headstones, on the spears of the little gate, on the barren thorns. His soul swooned slowly as he heard the snow falling faintly through the universe and faintly falling, like the descent of their last end, upon all the living and the dead.

Virginia Woolf

1882–1941

"On or about December, 1910," Virginia Woolf once wrote in an essay on fiction, "human character changed." That month saw the opening of a major exhibit of post-Impressionist art in London, and it is characteristic of Woolf to consider that art has the power to change human nature itself. A proper Victorian by upbringing and an avant-garde artist by vocation, Virginia Woolf was deeply interested in the ways human nature was changing in her times, both through

3. Where Ireland's longest river, the Shannon, empties into the sea.

artistic revolutions and through the social upheavals that culminated in World War I and its aftermath. By 1910 her own life had changed in many ways from the life she had experienced in her childhood as the young Adeline Virginia Stephen, daughter of the prosperous editor and aspiring philosopher Sir Leslie Stephen, editor of the massive *Dictionary of National Biography.* Her mother, Julia—artistic in temperament, and a famous beauty often sketched by Pre-Raphaelite artist friends—died in 1895, when Virginia was thirteen. A mental breakdown, the first of what became Woolf's recurrent bouts of mental instability, quickly followed. Two years later, her half-sister Stella died in childbirth, and within another two years her brother Thoby died of typhoid.

Having grown up an intensely literary child in a pervasively literary and artistic household, the young Virginia Stephen was nevertheless kept away from the public routes to education offered to her brothers, who attended prestigious private schools and went on to Oxford. Like most upper-class British women of her generation, Woolf and her sisters were educated at home, and never went to college. Woolf read voraciously, and her independence of mind and habits fostered her later freedom to experiment, yet she remained keenly aware of her exclusion from the wealth of resources offered by Oxford and Cambridge. Her path-breaking essay *A Room of One's Own* (1928), on the intellectual and material conditions needed for women to write fiction, opens with a scene in which an angelic beadle prohibits her from entering an Edenlike university library. All her life, Woolf was to be a full member of upper-class British society and yet also in important ways an outsider to it: as a pacifist as World War II approached; as an entirely committed writer when women were supposed to devote most of their attention to husband and children; as someone romantically drawn to women as well as to men, notably to her intimate friend Vita Sackville-West, to whom she dedicated her 1928 novel *Orlando,* whose hero changes sex and becomes a heroine part way into the book.

Following her father's death in 1904, Virginia began to publish her work. Together with her surviving brother Adrian and her artist sister Vanessa, she set up house in Bloomsbury Square in London, forming the center for a loose group of free-thinking artists, writers, and other intellectuals. In 1912 she married Leonard Woolf, himself an outsider as a socialist, an anti-imperialist, and a Jew in the often genially anti-Semitic culture of Edwardian England. The Woolfs founded the Hogarth Press, which published their own books and those of many others, including work by their friends T. S. Eliot, E. M. Forster, and Katherine Mansfield, together with the first English translations of the works of Sigmund Freud.

Once she began publishing, Woolf was extraordinarily productive, creating a wide variety of work. She explored the finest nuances of consciousness and perception in her major novels, starting with *The Voyage Out* (1915). Her work became increasingly experimental as time went on; along with James Joyce she became a pioneering practitioner of the technique of "interior monologue," following the twists and turns of an individual's consciousness from within, most notably in her great novels *Mrs Dalloway* (1925) and *To the Lighthouse* (1927)—a loving, ironic recreation of her parents in the form of the charming, self-centered philosopher Mr. Ramsay and his magnetic, manipulative wife Mrs. Ramsay, who humors her husband and shelters her brood of eight children until her sudden, untimely death. Later Woolf experimented with a shifting, polyphonic multiplicity of voices in *The Waves* (1931) and used a fragmented, drama-based style for her last novel, *Between the Acts* (1941). The pressures for war were building as she was completing this novel, and Woolf grew increasingly depressed. She and Leonard anticipated that the Nazis would soon invade England; they expected that certainly Leonard—and probably Woolf herself, as well as many of their friends—would be killed if the invasion were to succeed. Fearing the onset of a new mental breakdown, Woolf drowned herself in a river near her country home in March of 1941.

By then she had produced not only a major body of fiction but also several volumes of sparkling essays and reviews for "the common reader," whom she hoped to reach even in her most experimental work. She also wrote voluminous diaries and masses of letters (several volumes have been published both of the diaries and of the letters). Together, these works show a life in which conversation, reflection, and writing were constant means of self-understanding and of engagement with the wider world.

The blending of social framing and psychological insight is fully evident in the two stories given here, two of her most compelling short fictions. Like the "epiphanies" of James Joyce, these stories center on an ordinary yet suddenly revelatory moment. "The Lady in the Looking-Glass: A Reflection" (1929) takes vision itself as its theme. The lady of the title is absent for most of the story; an invisible narrator builds a world around her absence by examining what can be seen, or inferred, in the mirror above her mantelpiece. Literature has long been described as "holding a mirror up to nature," though by Woolf's time writers were often revising this image to express less direct sorts of mirroring. In the 1890s, Oscar Wilde had described his art as a *cracked* looking-glass, while in *Ulysses,* Joyce went Wilde one better by having Stephen Dedalus describe Irish art as the cracked mirror "of a servant." Woolf's mirror in turn conceals as well as reveals, and the final appearance of the lady in the looking-glass yields a very different epiphany than we have been led to expect.

For Woolf, as for contemporaries of hers from Joseph Conrad in England to Akutagawa Ryunosuke in Japan, truth can't be reflected directly but must be perceived in fragments, by indirection. Seen rightly, even the smallest image or incident can reveal multiple facets and possibilities, as in "Mrs Dalloway in Bond Street" (1923), in which a woman simply goes out to buy a pair of gloves. This story was the germ of what was to become the novel *Mrs Dalloway.* As she was expanding this story, Woolf clearly had it in mind when writing an essay in 1925 on "Modern Fiction." "Examine for a moment an ordinary mind on an ordinary day," she says:

> The mind receives a myriad impressions—trivial, fantastic, evanescent, or engraved with the sharpness of steel. From all sides they come, an incessant shower of innumerable atom; and, as they fall, as they shape themselves into the life of Monday or Tuesday, the accent falls differently from of old; the moment of importance came not here but there; so that, if a writer were a free man and not a slave, if he could write what he chose, not what he must, if he could base his work upon his own feeling and not upon convention, there would be no plot, no comedy, no tragedy, no love interest or catastrophe in the accepted style, and perhaps not a single button sewn on as the Bond Street tailors would have it.

Mrs Dalloway in Bond Street

Mrs Dalloway said she would buy the gloves herself. Big Ben was striking as she stepped out into the street. It was eleven o'clock and the unused hour was fresh as if issued to children on a beach. But there was something solemn in the deliberate swing of the repeated strokes; something stirring in the murmur of wheels and the shuffle of footsteps.

No doubt they were not all bound on errands of happiness. There is much more to be said about us than that we walk the streets of Westminster.[1] Big Ben too is nothing but steel rods consumed by rust were it not for the care of H.M's Office of Works. Only for Mrs Dalloway the moment was complete; for Mrs Dalloway June was fresh. A happy childhood—and it was not to his daughters only that Justin Parry had seemed a fine fellow (weak of course on the Bench); flowers at evening, smoke rising; the caw of rooks falling from ever so high, down down through the October air—there is

1. District of central London, including the Houses of Parliament (with their famous clock tower "Big Ben"); it is also a fashionable residential area.

nothing to take the place of childhood. A leaf of mint brings it back: or a cup with a blue ring.

Poor little wretches, she sighed, and pressed forward. Oh, right under the horses' noses, you little demon! and there she was left on the kerb stretching her hand out, while Jimmy Dawes grinned on the further side.

A charming woman, posed, eager, strangely white-haired for her pink cheeks, so Scope Purvis, C.B., saw her as he hurried to his office. She stiffened a little, waiting for Durtnall's van to pass. Big Ben struck the tenth; struck the eleventh stroke. The leaden circles dissolved in the air. Pride held her erect, inheriting, handing on, acquainted with discipline and with suffering. How people suffered, how they suffered, she thought, thinking of Mrs Foxcroft at the Embassy last night decked with jewels, eating her heart out, because that nice boy was dead, and now the old Manor House (Durtnall's van passed) must go to a cousin.

"Good morning to you," said Hugh Whitbread raising his hat rather extravagantly by the china shop, for they had known each other as children. "Where are you off to?"

"I love walking in London," said Mrs Dalloway. "Really it's better than walking in the country!"

"We've just come up," said Hugh Whitbread. "Unfortunately to see doctors."

"Milly?" said Mrs Dalloway, instantly compassionate.

"Out of sorts," said Hugh Whitbread. "That sort of thing. Dick all right?"

"First rate!" said Clarissa.

Of course, she thought, walking on, Milly is about my age—fifty—fifty-two. So it is probably *that*. Hugh's manner had said so, said it perfectly—dear old Hugh, thought Mrs Dalloway, remembering with amusement, with gratitude, with emotion, how shy, like a brother—one would rather die than speak to one's brother—Hugh had always been, when he was at Oxford, and came over, and perhaps one of them (drat the thing!) couldn't ride. How then could women sit in Parliament? How could they do things with men? For there is this extraordinarily deep instinct, something inside one; you can't get over it; it's no use trying; and men like Hugh respect it without our saying it, which is what one loves, thought Clarissa, in dear old Hugh.

She had passed through the Admiralty Arch and saw at the end of the empty road with its thin trees Victoria's white mound, Victoria's billowing motherliness, amplitude and homeliness, always ridiculous, yet how sublime thought Mrs Dalloway, remembering Kensington Gardens and the old lady in horn spectacles and being told by Nanny to stop dead still and bow to the Queen. The flag flew above the Palace. The King and Queen were back then. Dick had met her at lunch the other day—a thoroughly nice woman. It matters so much to the poor, thought Clarissa, and to the soldiers. A man in bronze stood heroically on a pedestal with a gun on her left hand side—the South African war. It matters, thought Mrs Dalloway walking towards Buckingham Palace. There it stood four-square, in the broad sunshine, uncompromising, plain. But it was character she thought; something inborn in the race; what Indians respected. The Queen went to hospitals, opened bazaars—the Queen of England, thought Clarissa, looking at the Palace. Already at this hour a motor car passed out at the gates; soldiers saluted; the gates were shut. And Clarissa, crossing the road, entered the Park, holding herself upright.

June had drawn out every leaf on the trees. The mothers of Westminster with mottled breasts gave suck to their young. Quite respectable girls lay stretched on the grass. An elderly man, stooping very stiffly, picked up a crumpled paper, spread it out flat and flung it away. How horrible! Last night at the Embassy Sir Dighton had said,

"If I want a fellow to hold my horse, I have only to put up my hand." But the religious question is far more serious than the economic, Sir Dighton had said, which she thought extraordinarily interesting, from a man like Sir Dighton. "Oh, the country will never know what it has lost," he had said, talking, of his own accord, about dear Jack Stewart.

She mounted the little hill lightly. The air stirred with energy. Messages were passing from the Fleet to the Admiralty. Piccadilly and Arlington Street and the Mall seemed to chafe the very air in the Park and lift its leaves hotly, brilliantly, upon waves of that divine vitality which Clarissa loved. To ride; to dance; she had adored all that. Or going on long walks in the country, talking, about books, what to do with one's life, for young people were amazingly priggish—oh, the things one had said! But one had conviction. Middle age is the devil. People like Jack'll never know that, she thought; for he never once thought of death, never, they said, knew he was dying. And now can never mourn—how did it go?—a head grown grey. . . . From the contagion of the world's slow stain. . . . Have drunk their cup a round or two before. . . . From the contagion of the world's slow stain![2] She held herself upright.

But how Jack would have shouted! Quoting Shelley, in Piccadilly! "You want a pin," he would have said. He hated frumps. "My God Clarissa! My God Clarissa!"—she could hear him now at the Devonshire House party, about poor Sylvia Hunt in her amber necklace and that dowdy old silk. Clarissa held herself upright for she had spoken aloud and now she was in Piccadilly, passing the house with the slender green columns, and the balconies; passing club windows full of newspapers; passing old Lady Burdett Coutt's house where the glazed white parrot used to hang; and Devonshire House, without its gilt leopards; and Claridge's, where she must remember Dick wanted her to leave a card on Mrs Jepson or she would be gone. Rich Americans can be very charming. There was St James's Palace; like a child's game with bricks; and now—she had passed Bond Street—she was by Hatchard's book shop. The stream was endless—endless—endless. Lords, Ascot, Hurlingham[3]—what was it? What a duck, she thought, looking at the frontispiece of some book of memoirs spread wide in the bow window, Sir Joshua perhaps or Romney; arch, bright, demure; the sort of girl—like her own Elizabeth—the only *real* sort of girl. And there was that absurd book, *Soapy Sponge,* which Jum used to quote by the yard; and Shakespeare's Sonnets. She knew them by heart. Phil and she had argued all day about the Dark Lady, and Dick had said straight out at dinner that night that he had never heard of her. Really, she had married him for that! He had never read Shakespeare! There must be some little cheap book she could buy for Milly—*Cranford*[4] of course! Was there ever anything so enchanting as the cow in petticoats? If only people had that sort of humour, that sort of self-respect now, thought Clarissa, for she remembered the broad pages; the sentences ending; the characters—how one talked about them as if they were real. For all the great things one must go to the past, she thought. From the contagion of the world's slow stain. . . . Fear no more the heat o' the sun. . . . And now can never mourn, can never mourn, she repeated, her eyes straying over the window; for it ran in her head; the test of great poetry; the moderns had never written anything one wanted to read about death, she thought; and turned.

2. From *Adonais* (stanza 40), Percy Shelley's elegy on the early death of Keats.
3. Locations of fashionable sporting events (cricket, horse racing, and polo).
4. Popular novel by Elizabeth Gaskell (1810–1865).

Omnibuses joined motor cars; motor cars vans; vans taxicabs; taxicabs motor cars—here was an open motor car with a girl, alone. Up till four, her feet tingling, I know, thought Clarissa, for the girl looked washed out, half asleep, in the corner of the car after the dance. And another car came; and another. No! No! No! Clarissa smiled good-naturedly. The fat lady had taken every sort of trouble, but diamonds! orchids! at this hour of the morning! No! No! No! The excellent policeman would, when the time came, hold up his hand. Another motor car passed. How utterly unattractive! Why should a girl of that age paint black round her eyes? And a young man with a girl, at this hour, when the country—The admirable policeman raised his hand and Clarissa acknowledging his sway, taking her time, crossed, walked towards Bond Street; saw the narrow crooked street, the yellow banners; the thick notched telegraph wires stretched across the sky.

A hundred years ago her great-great-grandfather, Seymour Parry, who ran away with Conway's daughter, had walked down Bond Street. Down Bond Street the Parrys had walked for a hundred years, and might have met the Dalloways (Leighs on the mother's side) going up. Her father got his clothes from Hill's. There was a roll of cloth in the window, and here just one jar on a black table, incredibly expensive; like the thick pink salmon on the ice block at the fishmonger's. The jewels were exquisite—pink and orange stars, paste, Spanish, she thought, and chains of old gold; starry buckles, little brooches which had been worn on sea-green satin by ladies with high head-dresses. But no looking! One must economise. She must go on past the picture dealer's where one of the odd French pictures hung, as if people had thrown confetti—pink and blue—for a joke. If you had lived with pictures (and it's the same with books and music) thought Clarissa, passing the Aeolian Hall, you can't be taken in by a joke.

The river of Bond Street was clogged. There, like a queen at a tournament, raised, regal, was Lady Bexborough. She sat in her carriage, upright, alone, looking through her glasses. The white glove was loose at her wrist. She was in black, quite shabby, yet, thought Clarissa, how extraordinarily it tells, breeding, self-respect, never saying a word too much or letting people gossip; an astonishing friend; no one can pick a hole in her after all these years, and now, there she is, thought Clarissa, passing the Countess who waited powdered, perfectly still, and Clarissa would have given anything to be like that, the mistress of Clarefield, talking politics, like a man. But she never goes anywhere, thought Clarissa, and it's quite useless to ask her, and the carriage went on and Lady Bexborough was borne past like a queen at a tournament, though she had nothing to live for and the old man is failing and they say she is sick of it all, thought Clarissa and the tears actually rose to her eyes as she entered the shop.

"Good morning," said Clarissa in her charming voice. "Gloves," she said with her exquisite friendliness and putting her bag on the counter began, very slowly, to undo the buttons. "White gloves," she said. "Above the elbow," and she looked straight into the shopwoman's face—but this was not the girl she remembered? She looked quite old. "These really don't fit," said Clarissa. The shop-girl looked at them. "Madame wears bracelets?" Clarissa spread out her fingers. "Perhaps it's my rings," And the girl took the grey gloves with her to the end of the counter.

Yes, thought Clarissa, it's the girl I remember, she's twenty years older. . . . There was only one other customer, sitting sideways at the counter, her elbow poised, her bare hand drooping vacant; like a figure on a Japanese fan, thought Clarissa, too vacant perhaps, yet some men would adore her. The lady shook her head sadly.

Again the gloves were too large. She turned round the glass. "Above the wrist," she reproached the grey-headed woman, who looked and agreed.

They waited; a clock ticked; Bond Street hummed, dulled, distant; the woman went away holding gloves. "Above the wrist," said the lady, mournfully, raising her voice. And she would have to order chairs, ices, flowers, and cloak-room tickets, thought Clarissa. The people she didn't want would come; the others wouldn't. She would stand by the door. They sold stockings—silk stockings. A lady is known by her gloves and her shoes, old Uncle William used to say. And through the hanging silk stockings, quivering silver she looked at the lady, sloping shouldered, her hand drooping, her bag slipping, her eyes vacantly on the floor. It would be intolerable if dowdy women came to her party! Would one have liked Keats if he had worn red socks? Oh, at last—she drew into the counter and it flashed into her mind:

"Do you remember before the war you had gloves with pearl buttons?"

"French gloves, Madame?"

"Yes, they were French," said Clarissa. The other lady rose very sadly and took her bag, and looked at the gloves on the counter. But they were all too large—always too large at the wrist.

"With pearl buttons," said the shop-girl, who looked ever so much older. She split the lengths of tissue paper apart on the counter. With pearl buttons, thought Clarissa, perfectly simple—how French!

"Madame's hands are so slender," said the shop-girl, drawing the glove firmly, smoothly, down over her rings. And Clarissa looked at her arm in the looking-glass. The glove hardly came to the elbow. Were there others half an inch longer? Still it seemed tiresome to bother her—perhaps the one day in the month, thought Clarissa, when it's an agony to stand. "Oh, don't bother," she said. But the gloves were brought.

"Don't you get fearfully tired," she said in her charming voice, "standing? When d'you get your holiday?"

"In September, Madame, when we're not so busy."

When we're in the country thought Clarissa. Or shooting. She has a fortnight at Brighton. In some stuffy lodging. The landlady takes the sugar. Nothing would be easier than to send her to Mrs Lumley's right in the country (and it was on the tip of her tongue). But then she remembered how on their honeymoon Dick had shown her the folly of giving impulsively. It was much more important, he said, to get trade with China. Of course he was right. And she could feel the girl wouldn't like to be given things. There she was in her place. So was Dick. Selling gloves was her job. She had her own sorrows quite separate, "and now can never mourn, can never mourn," the words ran in her head, "From the contagion of the world's slow stain," thought Clarissa holding her arm stiff, for there are moments when it seems utterly futile (the glove was drawn off leaving her arm flecked with powder)—simply one doesn't believe, thought Clarissa, any more in God.

The traffic suddenly roared; the silk stockings brightened. A customer came in.

"White gloves," she said, with some ring in her voice that Clarissa remembered.

It used, thought Clarissa, to be so simple. Down, down through the air came the caw of the rooks. When Sylvia died, hundreds of years ago, the yew hedges looked so lovely with the diamond webs in the mist before early church. But if Dick were to die to-morrow? As for believing in God—no, she would let the children choose, but for herself, like Lady Bexborough, who opened the bazaar, they say, with the telegram in her hand—Roden, her favourite, killed—she would go on. But why, if one doesn't believe? For the sake of others, she thought taking the glove in her hand. The girl would be much more unhappy if she didn't believe.

"Thirty shillings," said the shop-woman. "No, pardon me Madame, thirty-five. The French gloves are more."

For one doesn't live for oneself, thought Clarissa.

And then the other customer took a glove, tugged it, and it split.

"There!" she exclaimed.

"A fault of the skin," said the grey-headed woman hurriedly. "Sometimes a drop of acid in tanning. Try this pair, Madame."

"But it's an awful swindle to ask two pound ten!"

Clarissa looked at the lady; the lady looked at Clarissa.

"Gloves have never been quite so reliable since the war," said the shop-girl, apologising, to Clarissa.

But where had she seen the other lady?—elderly, with a frill under her chin; wearing a black ribbon for gold eyeglasses; sensual, clever, like a Sargent drawing. How one can tell from a voice when people are in the habit, thought Clarissa, of making other people—"It's a shade too tight," she said—obey. The shop-woman went off again. Clarissa was left waiting. Fear no more she repeated, playing her finger on the counter. Fear no more the heat o' the sun. Fear no more she repeated. There were little brown spots on her arm. And the girl crawled like a snail. Thou thy wordly task hast done. Thousands of young men had died that things might go on. At last! Half an inch above the elbow; pearl buttons; five and a quarter. My dear slowcoach, thought Clarissa, do you think I can sit here the whole morning? Now you'll take twenty-five minutes to bring me my change!

There was a violent explosion in the street outside. The shop-women cowered behind the counters. But Clarissa, sitting very upright, smiled at the other lady. "Miss Anstruther!" she exclaimed.

The Lady in the Looking-Glass: A Reflection

People should not leave looking-glasses hanging in their rooms any more than they should leave open cheque books or letters confessing some hideous crime. One could not help looking, that summer afternoon, in the long glass that hung outside in the hall. Chance had so arranged it. From the depths of the sofa in the drawing-room one could see reflected in the Italian glass not only the marble-topped table opposite, but a stretch of the garden beyond. One could see a long grass path leading between banks of tall flowers until, slicing off an angle, the gold rim cut it off.

The house was empty, and one felt, since one was the only person in the drawing-room, like one of those naturalists who, covered with grass and leaves, lie watching the shyest animals—badgers, otters, kingfishers—moving about freely, themselves unseen. The room that afternoon was full of such shy creatures, lights and shadows, curtains blowing, petals falling—things that never happen, so it seems, if someone is looking. The quiet old country room with its rugs and stone chimney pieces, its sunken book-cases and red and gold lacquer cabinets, was full of such nocturnal creatures. They came pirouetting across the floor, stepping delicately with high-lifted feet and spread tails and pecking allusive beaks as if they had been cranes or flocks of elegant flamingoes whose pink was faded, or peacocks whose trains were veined with silver. And there were obscure flushes and darkenings too, as if a cuttlefish had suddenly suffused the air with purple; and the room had its passions and rages and envies and sorrows coming over it and clouding it, like a human being. Nothing stayed the same for two seconds together.

But, outside, the looking-glass reflected the hall table, the sunflowers, the garden path so accurately and so fixedly that they seemed held there in their reality unescapably. It was a strange contrast—all changing here, all stillness there. One could not help looking from one to the other. Meanwhile, since all the doors and windows were open in the heat, there was a perpetual sighing and ceasing sound, the voice of the transient and the perishing, it seemed, coming and going like human breath, while in the looking-glass things had ceased to breathe and lay still in the trance of immortality.

Half an hour ago the mistress of the house, Isabella Tyson, had gone down the grass path in her thin summer dress, carrying a basket, and had vanished, sliced off by the gilt rim of the looking-glass. She had gone presumably into the lower garden to pick flowers; or as it seemed more natural to suppose, to pick something light and fantastic and leafy and trailing, traveller's joy, or one of those elegant sprays of convolvulus that twine round ugly walls and burst here and there into white and violet blossoms. She suggested the fantastic and the tremulous convolvulus rather than the upright aster, the starched zinnia, or her own burning roses alight like lamps on the straight posts of their rose trees. The comparison showed how very little, after all these years, one knew about her; for it is impossible that any woman of flesh and blood of fifty-five or sixty should be really a wreath or a tendril. Such comparisons are worse than idle and superficial—they are cruel even, for they come like the convolvulus itself trembling between one's eyes and the truth. There must be truth; there must be a wall. Yet it was strange that after knowing her all these years one could not say what the truth about Isabella was; one still made up phrases like this about convolvulus and traveller's joy. As for facts, it was a fact that she was a spinster; that she was rich; that she had bought this house and collected with her own hands—often in the most obscure corners of the world and at great risk from poisonous stings and Oriental diseases—the rugs, the chairs, the cabinets which now lived their nocturnal life before one's eyes. Sometimes it seemed as if they knew more about her than we, who sat on them, wrote at them, and trod on them so carefully, were allowed to know. In each of these cabinets were many little drawers, and each almost certainly held letters, tied with bows of ribbon, sprinkled with sticks of lavender or rose leaves. For it was another fact—if facts were what one wanted—that Isabella had known many people, had had many friends; and thus if one had the audacity to open a drawer and read her letters, one would find the traces of many agitations, of appointments to meet, of upbraidings for not having met, long letters of intimacy and affection, violent letters of jealousy and reproach, terrible final words of parting—for all those interviews and assignations had led to nothing—that is, she had never married, and yet, judging from the mask-like indifference of her face, she had gone through twenty times more of passion and experience than those whose loves are trumpeted forth for all the world to hear. Under the stress of thinking about Isabella, her room became more shadowy and symbolic; the corners seemed darker, the legs of chairs and tables more spindly and hieroglyphic.

Suddenly these reflections were ended violently and yet without a sound. A large black form loomed into the looking-glass; blotted out everything, strewed the table with a packet of marble tablets veined with pink and grey, and was gone. But the picture was entirely altered. For the moment it was unrecognisable and irrational and entirely out of focus. One could not relate these tablets to any human purpose. And then by degrees some logical process set to work on them and began ordering and arranging them and bringing them into the fold of common experience. One realised at last that they were merely letters. The man had brought the post.

There they lay on the marble-topped table, all dripping with light and colour at first and crude and unabsorbed. And then it was strange to see how they were drawn in and arranged and composed and made part of the picture and granted that stillness and immortality which the looking-glass conferred. They lay there invested with a new reality and significance and with a greater heaviness, too, as if it would have needed a chisel to dislodge them from the table. And, whether it was fancy or not, they seemed to have become not merely a handful of casual letters but to be tablets graven with eternal truth—if one could read them, one would know everything there was to be known about Isabella, yes, and about life, too. The pages inside those marble-looking envelopes must be cut deep and scored thick with meaning. Isabella would come in, and take them, one by one, very slowly, and open them, and read them carefully word by word, and then with a profound sigh of comprehension, as if she had seen to the bottom of everything, she would tear the envelopes to little bits and tie the letters together and lock the cabinet drawer in her determination to conceal what she did not wish to be known.

The thought served as a challenge. Isabella did not wish to be known—but she should no longer escape. It was absurd, it was monstrous. If she concealed so much and knew so much one must prize her open with the first tool that came to hand—the imagination. One must fix one's mind upon her at that very moment. One must fasten her down there. One must refuse to be put off any longer with sayings and doings such as the moment brought forth—with dinners and visits and polite conversations. One must put oneself in her shoes. If one took the phrase literally, it was easy to see the shoes in which she stood, down in the lower garden, at this moment. They were very narrow and long and fashionable—they were made of the softest and most flexible leather. Like everything she wore, they were exquisite. And she would be standing under the high hedge in the lower part of the garden, raising the scissors that were tied to her waist to cut some dead flower, some overgrown branch. The sun would beat down on her face, into her eyes; but no, at the critical moment a veil of cloud covered the sun, making the expression of her eyes doubtful—was it mocking or tender, brilliant or dull? One could only see the indeterminate outline of her rather faded, fine face looking at the sky. She was thinking, perhaps, that she must order a new net for the strawberries; that she must send flowers to Johnson's widow; that it was time she drove over to see the Hippesleys in their new house. Those were the things she talked about at dinner certainly. But one was tired of the things that she talked about at dinner. It was her profounder state of being that one wanted to catch and turn to words, the state that is to the mind what breathing is to the body, what one calls happiness or unhappiness. At the mention of those words it became obvious, surely, that she must be happy. She was rich; she was distinguished; she had many friends; she travelled—she bought rugs in Turkey and blue pots in Persia. Avenues of pleasure radiated this way and that from where she stood with her scissors raised to cut the trembling branches while the lacy clouds veiled her face.

Here with a quick movement of her scissors she snipped the spray of traveller's joy and it fell to the ground. As it fell, surely some light came in too, surely one could penetrate a little farther into her being. Her mind then was filled with tenderness and regret. . . . To cut an overgrown branch saddened her because it had once lived, and life was dear to her. Yes, and at the same time the fall of the branch would suggest to her how she must die herself and all the futility and evanescence of things. And then again quickly catching this thought up, with her instant good sense, she thought life had treated her well; even if fall she must, it was to lie on the earth and moulder sweetly into the roots of violets. So she stood thinking. Without making any thought precise—for she was one of those reticent people whose minds hold their thoughts enmeshed in clouds of silence—she was filled with thoughts. Her mind was like her room, in which lights advanced and retreated, came pirouetting and stepping delicately, spread their tails, pecked their way; and then her whole being was suffused, like the room again, with a cloud of some profound knowledge, some unspoken regret, and then she was full of locked drawers, stuffed with letters, like her cabinets. To talk of "prizing her open" as if she were an oyster, to use any but the finest and subtlest and most pliable tools upon her was impious and absurd. One must imagine—here was she in the looking-glass. It made one start.

She was so far off at first that one could not see her clearly. She came lingering and pausing, here straightening a rose, there lifting a pink to smell it, but she never stopped; and all the time she became larger and larger in the looking-glass, more and more completely the person into whose mind one had been trying to penetrate. One verified her by degrees—fitted the qualities one had discovered into this visible body. There were her grey-green dress, and her long shoes, her basket, and something sparkling at her throat. She came so gradually that she did not seem to derange the pattern in the glass, but only to bring in some new element which gently moved and altered the other objects as if asking them, courteously, to make room for her. And the letters and the table and the grass walk and the sunflowers which had been waiting in the looking-glass separated and opened out so that she might be received among them. At last there she was, in the hall. She stopped dead. She stood by the table. She stood perfectly still. At once the looking-glass began to pour over her a light that seemed to fix her; that seemed like some acid to bite off the unessential and superficial and to leave only the truth. It was an enthralling spectacle. Everything dropped from her—clouds, dress, basket, diamond—all that one had called the creeper and convolvulus. Here was the hard wall beneath. Here was the woman herself. She stood naked in that pitiless light. And, there was nothing. Isabella was perfectly empty. She had no thoughts. She had no friends. She cared for nobody. As for her letters, they were all bills. Look, as she stood there, old and angular, veined and lined, with her high nose and her wrinkled neck, she did not even trouble to open them.

People should not leave looking-glasses hanging in their rooms.

A Room of One's Own In the fall of 1928 Virginia Woolf delivered lectures at two women's colleges at Cambridge University, where women were still not being admitted to the older, far better funded men's colleges, despite strong agitation for reform. Revised for publication, Woolf's talks became *A Room of One's Own* (1929), one of the most influential works in modern feminist writing. Woolf makes a double argument in her essay, both material and psychological. On the material level, Woolf insists that women writers have the need for the same degree of privacy and material support that the major male writers traditionally had. On the psychological level, she asserts that the great goal of literary work isn't a "separate but equal" status for women's writing but instead an inspired, transcendent "androgyny," in which the literary work can fuse the perspectives of both sexes, bound to neither alone.

Woolf's work has inspired many later feminist thinkers, while provoking controversy as well. Not all of Woolf's young audience at Newnham and Girton Colleges agreed with her claim that they would need an independent income to fuel their creative flame; and later feminists have questioned whether her advocacy of androgyny works against her claim that women's sentences are different from men's. Woolf's essayistic method has sparked debate as well: some readers have wanted her to come to her points more directly and clarify her terms more fully; many others, however, have responded to the essay's subtle weaving of images and ironies into deeply resonant patterns. Far from shunning controversy, Woolf herself welcomed it. As the book was about to appear, she wrote in her diary that what she really feared was "that I shall get no criticism, except the evasive jocular kind . . . that the press will be kind & talk of its charm, and sprightliness & also I shall be attacked for a feminist & hinted at for a sapphist. . . . I am afraid it will not be taken seriously." Her book did indeed receive such responses when it first appeared ("Mrs. Woolf speaks for her sex with as much fancy as logic," the *New York Times* brightly observed, while the *Yale Review* praised "its quiet, demure laughter"), but in the decades since then, *A Room of One's Own* has come to be seen as a foundational text for modern feminist thought and a masterpiece of creative nonfiction by a great novelist in her prime.

from A Room of One's Own

Chapter 1

But, you may say, we asked you to speak about women and fiction—what has that got to do with a room of one's own?[1] I will try to explain. When you asked me to speak about women and fiction I sat down on the banks of a river and began to wonder what the words meant. They might mean simply a few remarks about Fanny Burney; a few more about Jane Austen; a tribute to the Brontës and a sketch of Haworth Parsonage under snow; some witticisms if possible about Miss Mitford; a respectful allusion to George Eliot; a reference to Mrs Gaskell and one would have done.[2] But at second sight the words seemed not so simple. The title women and fiction might mean, and you may have meant it to mean, women and what they are like; or it might mean women and the fiction that they write; or it might mean women and the fiction that is written about them; or it might mean that somehow all three are inextricably mixed together and you want me to consider them in that light. But when I began to consider the subject in this last way, which seemed the most interesting, I soon saw that it had one fatal drawback. I should never be able to come to a conclusion. I should never be able to fulfil what is, I understand, the first duty of a lecturer—to hand you after an hour's discourse a nugget of pure truth to wrap up between the pages of your notebooks and keep on the mantelpiece for ever. All I could do was to offer you an opinion upon one minor point—a woman must have money and a room of her own if she is to write fiction; and that, as you will see, leaves the great problem of the true nature of woman and the true nature of fiction unsolved. I have shirked the duty of coming to a conclusion upon these two questions—women and fiction remain, so far as I am concerned, unsolved problems. But in order to make some amends I am going to do what I can to show you how I arrived at this opinion about the room and the money. I am going to develop in your presence as fully and freely as I can the train of thought which led me to think this. Perhaps if I lay bare the ideas, the prejudices, that lie behind this statement you will find that they have some bearing upon women and some upon fiction. At any rate, when a subject is highly controversial—and any question about sex is that—one cannot hope to tell the truth. One can only show how one came to hold whatever opinion one does hold. One can only give one's audience the chance of drawing their own conclusions as they observe the

1. Woolf delivered her essay in a shorter version to meetings first at two women's colleges, Newnham and Girton, Cambridge University, in October 1928.
2. Important 19th-century novelists.

limitations, the prejudices, the idiosyncrasies of the speaker. Fiction here is likely to contain more truth than fact. Therefore I propose, making use of all the liberties and licences of a novelist, to tell you the story of the two days that preceded my coming here—how, bowed down by the weight of the subject which you have laid upon my shoulders, I pondered it, and made it work in and out of my daily life. I need not say that what I am about to describe has no existence; Oxbridge is an invention; so is Fernham;[3] "I" is only a convenient term for somebody who has no real being. Lies will flow from my lips, but there may perhaps be some truth mixed up with them; it is for you to seek out this truth and to decide whether any part of it is worth keeping. If not, you will of course throw the whole of it into the wastepaper basket and forget all about it.

Here then was I (call me Mary Beton, Mary Seton, Mary Carmichael[4] or by any name you please—it is not a matter of any importance) sitting on the banks of a river a week or two ago in fine October weather, lost in thought. That collar I have spoken of, women and fiction, the need of coming to some conclusion on a subject that raises all sorts of prejudices and passions, bowed my head to the ground. To the right and left bushes of some sort, golden and crimson, glowed with the colour, even it seemed burnt with the heat, of fire. On the further bank the willows wept in perpetual lamentation, their hair about their shoulders. The river reflected whatever it chose of sky and bridge and burning tree, and when the undergraduate had oared his boat through the reflections they closed again, completely, as if he had never been. There one might have sat the clock round lost in thought. Thought—to call it by a prouder name than it deserved—had let its line down into the stream. It swayed, minute after minute, hither and thither among the reflections and the weeds, letting the water lift it and sink it, until—you know the little tug—the sudden conglomeration of an idea at the end of one's line: and then the cautious hauling of it in, and the careful laying of it out? Alas, laid on the grass how small, how insignificant this thought of mine looked; the sort of fish that a good fisherman puts back into the water so that it may grow fatter and be one day worth cooking and eating. I will not trouble you with that thought now, though if you look carefully you may find it for yourselves in the course of what I am going to say.

But however small it was, it had, nevertheless, the mysterious property of its kind—put back into the mind, it became at once very exciting, and important; and as it darted and sank, and flashed hither and thither, set up such a wash and tumult of ideas that it was impossible to sit still. It was thus that I found myself walking with extreme rapidity across a grass plot. Instantly a man's figure rose to intercept me. Nor did I at first understand that the gesticulations of a curious-looking object, in a cutaway coat and evening shirt, were aimed at me. His face expressed horror and indignation. Instinct rather than reason came to my help; he was a Beadle; I was a woman. This was the turf; there was the path. Only the Fellows and Scholars are allowed here; the gravel is the place for me.[5] Such thoughts were the work of a moment. As I regained the path the arms of the Beadle sank, his face assumed its usual repose, and though turf is better walking than gravel, no very great harm was done. The only charge I could bring against the Fellows and Scholars of whatever the college might

3. "Oxbridge" was in fact the common slang term for Oxford and Cambridge universities. "Fernham" suggests Newnham College.

4. Three of the four Marys who by tradition were attendants to Mary Queen of Scots (executed in 1567), and who figure in many Scottish ballads; the fourth was Mary Hamilton.

5. A beadle is a disciplinary officer. The fellows of Oxbridge colleges typically tutor the undergraduates, who are divided into scholars and commoners. The commoners form the majority of the student body.

happen to be was that in protection of their turf, which has been rolled for 300 years in succession, they had sent my little fish into hiding.

What idea it had been that had sent me so audaciously trespassing I could not now remember. The spirit of peace descended like a cloud from heaven, for if the spirit of peace dwells anywhere, it is in the courts and quadrangles of Oxbridge on a fine October morning. Strolling through those colleges past those ancient halls the roughness of the present seemed smoothed away; the body seemed contained in a miraculous glass cabinet through which no sound could penetrate, and the mind, freed from any contact with facts (unless one trespassed on the turf again), was at liberty to settle down upon whatever meditation was in harmony with the moment. As chance would have it, some stray memory of some old essay about revisiting Oxbridge in the long vacation brought Charles Lamb to mind—Saint Charles, said Thackeray,[6] putting a letter of Lamb's to his forehead. Indeed, among all the dead (I give you my thoughts as they came to me), Lamb is one of the most congenial; one to whom one would have liked to say, Tell me then how you wrote your essays? For his essays are superior even to Max Beerbohm's, I thought, with all their perfection, because of that wild flash of imagination, that lightning crack of genius in the middle of them which leaves them flawed and imperfect, but starred with poetry. Lamb then came to Oxbridge perhaps a hundred years ago. Certainly he wrote an essay—the name escapes me—about the manuscript of one of Milton's poems which he saw here.[7] It was *Lycidas* perhaps, and Lamb wrote how it shocked him to think it possible that any word in *Lycidas* could have been different from what it is. To think of Milton changing the words in that poem seemed to him a sort of sacrilege. This led me to remember what I could of *Lycidas* and to amuse myself with guessing which word it could have been that Milton had altered, and why. It then occurred to me that the very manuscript itself which Lamb had looked at was only a few hundred yards away, so that one could follow Lamb's footsteps across the quadrangle to that famous library where the treasure is kept. Moreover, I recollected, as I put this plan into execution, it is in this famous library that the manuscript of Thackeray's *Esmond* is also preserved. The critics often say that *Esmond* is Thackeray's most perfect novel. But the affectation of the style, with its imitation of the eighteenth century, hampers one, so far as I remember; unless indeed the eighteenth-century style was natural to Thackeray—a fact that one might prove by looking at the manuscript and seeing whether the alterations were for the benefit of the style or of the sense. But then one would have to decide what is style and what is meaning, a question which—but here I was actually at the door which leads into the library itself. I must have opened it, for instantly there issued, like a guardian angel barring the way with a flutter of black gown instead of white wings, a deprecating, silvery, kindly gentleman, who regretted in a low voice as he waved me back that ladies are only admitted to the library if accompanied by a Fellow of the College or furnished with a letter of introduction.

That a famous library has been cursed by a woman is a matter of complete indifference to a famous library. Venerable and calm, with all its treasures safe locked within its breast, it sleeps complacently and will, so far as I am concerned, so sleep for ever. Never will I wake those echoes, never will I ask for that hospitality again, I vowed as I descended the steps in anger. Still an hour remained before luncheon, and what was one to do? Stroll on the meadows? sit by the river? Certainly it was a lovely

6. William Makepeace Thackeray (1811–1863), novelist and journalist, Woolf's father's first father-in-law.

7. Lamb's *Oxford in the Vacation*—describing the locales Lamb himself was too poor to attend in term time. The manuscript of Milton's elegy *Lycidas* (1638) is in the Wren Library of Trinity College, Cambridge, together with that of Thackeray's novel *The History of Henry Esmond* (1852).

autumn morning; the leaves were fluttering red to the ground; there was no great hardship in doing either. But the sound of music reached my ear. Some service or celebration was going forward. The organ complained magnificently as I passed the chapel door. Even the sorrow of Christianity sounded in that serene air more like the recollection of sorrow than sorrow itself; even the groanings of the ancient organ seemed lapped in peace. I had no wish to enter had I the right, and this time the verger might have stopped me, demanding perhaps my baptismal certificate, or a letter of introduction from the Dean. But the outside of these magnificent buildings is often as beautiful as the inside. Moreover, it was amusing enough to watch the congregation assembling, coming in and going out again, busying themselves at the door of the chapel like bees at the mouth of a hive. Many were in cap and gown; some had tufts of fur on their shoulders; others were wheeled in bath-chairs; others, though not past middle age, seemed creased and crushed into shapes so singular that one was reminded of those giant crabs and crayfish who heave with difficulty across the sand of an aquarium. As I leant against the wall the University indeed seemed a sanctuary in which are preserved rare types which would soon be obsolete if left to fight for existence on the pavement of the Strand.[8] Old stories of old deans and old dons came back to mind, but before I had summoned up courage to whistle—it used to be said that at the sound of a whistle old Professor —— instantly broke into a gallop—the venerable congregation had gone inside. The outside of the chapel remained. As you know, its high domes and pinnacles can be seen, like a sailing-ship always voyaging never arriving, lit up at night and visible for miles, far away across the hills. Once, presumably, this quadrangle with its smooth lawns, its massive buildings, and the chapel itself was marsh too, where the grasses waved and the swine rootled. Teams of horses and oxen, I thought, must have hauled the stone in wagons from far countries, and then with infinite labour the grey blocks in whose shade I was now standing were poised in order one on top of another, and then the painters brought their glass for the windows, and the masons were busy for centuries up on that roof with putty and cement, spade and trowel. Every Saturday somebody must have poured gold and silver out of a leathern purse into their ancient fists, for they had their beer and skittles presumably of an evening. An unending stream of gold and silver, I thought, must have flowed into this court perpetually to keep the stones coming and the masons working; to level, to ditch, to dig and to drain. But it was then the age of faith, and money was poured liberally to set these stones on a deep foundation, and when the stones were raised, still more money was poured in from the coffers of kings and queens and great nobles to ensure that hymns should be sung here and scholars taught. Lands were granted; tithes were paid. And when the age of faith was over and the age of reason had come, still the same flow of gold and silver went on; fellowships were founded; lectureships endowed; only the gold and silver flowed now, not from the coffers of the king, but from the chests of merchants and manufacturers, from the purses of men who had made, say, a fortune from industry, and returned, in their wills, a bounteous share of it to endow more chairs, more lectureships, more fellowships in the university where they had learnt their craft. Hence the libraries and laboratories; the observatories; the splendid equipment of costly and delicate instruments which now stands on glass shelves, where centuries ago the grasses waved and the swine rootled. Certainly, as I strolled round the court, the foundation of gold and silver seemed deep enough; the pavement laid solidly over the wild grasses. Men with trays on their heads went busily from staircase to staircase. Gaudy blossoms

8. A thoroughfare in central London.

flowered in window-boxes. The strains of the gramophone blared out from the rooms within. It was impossible not to reflect—the reflection whatever it may have been was cut short. The clock struck. It was time to find one's way to luncheon.

It is a curious fact that novelists have a way of making us believe that luncheon parties are invariably memorable for something very witty that was said, or for something very wise that was done. But they seldom spare a word for what was eaten. It is part of the novelist's convention not to mention soup and salmon and ducklings, as if soup and salmon and ducklings were of no importance whatsoever, as if nobody ever smoked a cigar or drank a glass of wine. Here, however, I shall take the liberty to defy that convention and to tell you that the lunch on this occasion began with soles, sunk in a deep dish, over which the college cook had spread a counterpane of the whitest cream, save that it was branded here and there with brown spots like the spots on the flanks of a doe. After that came the partridges, but if this suggests a couple of bald, brown birds on a plate you are mistaken. The partridges, many and various, came with all their retinue of sauces and salads, the sharp and the sweet, each in its order; their potatoes, thin as coins but not so hard; their sprouts, foliated as rosebuds but more succulent. And no sooner had the roast and its retinue been done with than the silent serving-man, the Beadle himself perhaps in a milder manifestation, set before us, wreathed in napkins, a confection which rose all sugar from the waves. To call it pudding and so relate it to rice and tapioca would be an insult. Meanwhile the wineglasses had flushed yellow and flushed crimson; had been emptied; had been filled. And thus by degrees was lit, halfway down the spine, which is the seat of the soul, not that hard little electric light which we call brilliance, as it pops in and out upon our lips, but the more profound, subtle and subterranean glow, which is the rich yellow flame of rational intercourse. No need to hurry. No need to sparkle. No need to be anybody but oneself. We are all going to heaven and Vandyck[9] is of the company—in other words, how good life seemed, how sweet its rewards, how trivial this grudge or that grievance, how admirable friendship and the society of one's kind, as, lighting a good cigarette, one sunk among the cushions in the window-seat.

If by good luck there had been an ash-tray handy, if one had not knocked the ash out of the window in default, if things had been a little different from what they were, one would not have seen, presumably, a cat without a tail. The sight of that abrupt and truncated animal padding softly across the quadrangle changed by some fluke of the subconscious intelligence the emotional light for me. It was as if some one had let fall a shade. Perhaps the excellent hock was relinquishing its hold. Certainly, as I watched the Manx cat pause in the middle of the lawn as if it too questioned the universe, something seemed lacking, something seemed different. But what was lacking, what was different, I asked myself, listening to the talk. And to answer that question I had to think myself out of the room, back into the past, before the war indeed,[1] and to set before my eyes the model of another luncheon party held in rooms not very far distant from these; but different. Everything was different. Meanwhile the talk went on among the guests, who were many and young, some of this sex, some of that; it went on swimmingly, it went on agreeably, freely, amusingly. And as it went on I set it against the background of that other talk, and as I matched the two together I had no doubt that one was the descendant, the legitimate heir of the other. Nothing was changed; nothing was different save only—here I listened with all my ears not entirely to what was being

9. Sir Anthony Van Dyck, prominent 17th-century society painter.

1. World War I.

said, but to the murmur or current behind it. Yes, that was it—the change was there. Before the war at a luncheon party like this people would have said precisely the same things but they would have sounded different, because in those days they were accompanied by a sort of humming noise, not articulate, but musical, exciting, which changed the value of the words themselves. Could one set that humming noise to words? Perhaps with the help of the poets one could. A book lay beside me and, opening it, I turned casually enough to Tennyson. And here I found Tennyson was singing:

There has fallen a splendid tear
From the passion-flower at the gate.
She is coming, my dove, my dear;
She is coming, my life, my fate;
The red rose cries, "She is near, she is near";
And the white rose weeps, "She is late";
The larkspur listens, "I hear, I hear";
And the lily whispers, "I wait."[2]

Was that what men hummed at luncheon parties before the war? And the women?

My heart is like a singing bird
Whose nest is in a water'd shoot;
My heart is like an apple tree
Whose boughs are bent with thick-set fruit;
My heart is like a rainbow shell
That paddles in a halcyon sea;
My heart is gladder than all these
Because my love is come to me.[3]

Was that what women hummed at luncheon parties before the war?

There was something so ludicrous in thinking of people humming such things even under their breath at luncheon parties before the war that I burst out laughing, and had to explain my laughter by pointing at the Manx cat, who did look a little absurd, poor beast, without a tail, in the middle of the lawn. Was he really born so, or had he lost his tail in an accident? The tailless cat, though some are said to exist in the Isle of Man, is rarer than one thinks. It is a queer animal, quaint rather than beautiful. It is strange what a difference a tail makes—you know the sort of things one says as a lunch party breaks up and people are finding their coats and hats.

This one, thanks to the hospitality of the host, had lasted far into the afternoon. The beautiful October day was fading and the leaves were falling from the trees in the avenue as I walked through it. Gate after gate seemed to close with gentle finality behind me. Innumerable beadles were fitting innumerable keys into well-oiled locks; the treasure-house was being made secure for another night. After the avenue one comes out upon a road—I forget its name—which leads you, if you take the right turning, along to Fernham.[4] But there was plenty of time. Dinner was not till half-past seven. One could almost do without dinner after such a luncheon. It is strange how a

2. From Lord Alfred Tennyson's *Maud* (1855), lines 908–915.

3. The first stanza of Christina Rossetti's poem *A Birthday* (1857).

4. Both Girton and Newnham colleges, established only in the late 19th century, are outside the old university area of Cambridge.

scrap of poetry works in the mind and makes the legs move in time to it along the road. Those words—

There has fallen a splendid tear
From the passion-flower at the gate.
She is coming, my dove, my dear—

sang in my blood as I stepped quickly along towards Headingley. And then, switching off into the other measure, I sang, where the waters are churned up by the weir:

My heart is like a singing bird
Whose nest is in a water'd shoot;
My heart is like an apple tree—

What poets, I cried aloud, as one does in the dusk, what poets they were!

In a sort of jealousy, I suppose, for our own age, silly and absurd though these comparisons are, I went on to wonder if honestly one could name two living poets now as great as Tennyson and Christina Rossetti were then. Obviously it is impossible, I thought, looking into those foaming waters, to compare them. The very reason why the poetry excites one to such abandonment, such rapture, is that it celebrates some feeling that one used to have (at luncheon parties before the war perhaps), so that one responds easily, familiarly, without troubling to check the feeling, or to compare it with any that one has now. But the living poets express a feeling that is actually being made and torn out of us at the moment. One does not recognize it in the first place; often for some reason one fears it; one watches it with keenness and compares it jealously and suspiciously with the old feeling that one knew. Hence the difficulty of modern poetry; and it is because of this difficulty that one cannot remember more than two consecutive lines of any good modern poet. For this reason—that my memory failed me—the argument flagged for want of material. But why, I continued, moving on towards Headingley, have we stopped humming under our breath at luncheon parties? Why has Alfred ceased to sing

She is coming, my dove, my dear?

Why has Christina ceased to respond

My heart is gladder than all these
Because my love is come to me?

Shall we lay the blame on the war? When the guns fired in August 1914, did the faces of men and women show so plain in each other's eyes that romance was killed? Certainly it was a shock (to women in particular with their illusions about education, and so on) to see the faces of our rulers in the light of the shell-fire. So ugly they looked—German, English, French—so stupid. But lay the blame where one will, on whom one will, the illusion which inspired Tennyson and Christina Rossetti to sing so passionately about the coming of their loves is far rarer now than then. One has only to read, to look, to listen, to remember. But why say "blame"? Why, if it was an illusion, not praise the catastrophe, whatever it was, that destroyed illusion and put truth in its place? For truth . . . those dots mark the spot where, in search of truth, I missed the turning up to Fernham. Yes indeed, which was truth and which was illusion, I asked myself. What was the truth about these houses, for example, dim and festive now with their red windows in the dusk, but raw and red and squalid, with their sweets and their boot-laces, at nine o'clock in the morning? And the willows and the river and the gardens that run down to the river, vague now with the mist stealing over them, but gold and red in the sunlight—which was the truth, which was the illusion about them? I spare you the twists and turns of my cogitations, for no conclusion was found on the road to Headingley, and I ask you to suppose that I soon found out my mistake about the turning and retraced my steps to Fernham.

As I have said already that it was an October day, I dare not forfeit your respect and imperil the fair name of fiction by changing the season and describing lilacs hanging over garden walls, crocuses, tulips and other flowers of spring. Fiction must stick to facts, and the truer the facts the better the fiction—so we are told. Therefore it was still autumn and the leaves were still yellow and falling, if anything, a little faster than before, because it was now evening (seven twenty-three to be precise) and a breeze (from the south-west to be exact) had risen. But for all that there was something odd at work:

My heart is like a singing bird
Whose nest is in a water'd shoot;
My heart is like an apple tree
Whose boughs are bent with thick-set fruit—

perhaps the words of Christina Rossetti were partly responsible for the folly of the fancy—it was nothing of course but a fancy—that the lilac was shaking its flowers over the garden walls, and the brimstone butterflies were scudding hither and thither, and the dust of the pollen was in the air. A wind blew, from what quarter I know not, but it lifted the half-grown leaves so that there was a flash of silver grey in the air. It was the time between the lights when colours undergo their intensification and purples and golds burn in window-panes like the beat of an excitable heart; when for some reason the beauty of the world revealed and yet soon to perish (here I pushed into the garden, for, unwisely, the door was left open and no beadles seemed about), the beauty of the world which is so soon to perish, has two edges, one of laughter, one of anguish, cutting the heart asunder. The gardens of Fernham lay before me in the spring twilight, wild and open, and in the long grass, sprinkled and carelessly flung, were daffodils and bluebells, not orderly perhaps at the best of times, and now windblown and waving as they tugged at their roots. The windows of the building, curved like ships' windows among generous waves of red brick, changed from lemon to silver under the flight of the quick spring clouds. Somebody was in a hammock, somebody, but in this light they were phantoms only, half guessed, half seen, raced across the grass—would no one stop her?—and then on the terrace, as if popping out to breathe the air, to glance at the garden, came a bent figure, formidable yet humble, with her great forehead and her shabby dress—could it be the famous scholar, could it be J——H—— herself?[5] All was dim, yet intense too, as if the scarf which the dusk had flung over the garden were torn asunder by star or sword—the flash of some terrible reality leaping, as its way is, out of the heart of the spring. For youth——

Here was my soup. Dinner was being served in the great dining-hall. Far from being spring it was in fact an evening in October. Everybody was assembled in the big dining-room. Dinner was ready. Here was the soup. It was a plain gravy soup. There was nothing to stir the fancy in that. One could have seen through the transparent liquid any pattern that there might have been on the plate itself. But there was no pattern. The plate was plain. Next came beef with its attendant greens and potatoes—a

5. Jane Harrison, a famous classical scholar.

homely trinity, suggesting the rumps of cattle in a muddy market, and sprouts curled and yellowed at the edge, and bargaining and cheapening, and women with string bags on Monday morning. There was no reason to complain of human nature's daily food, seeing that the supply was sufficient and coal-miners doubtless were sitting down to less. Prunes and custard followed. And if any one complains that prunes, even when mitigated by custard, are an uncharitable vegetable (fruit they are not), stringy as a miser's heart and exuding a fluid such as might run in misers' veins who have denied themselves wine and warmth for eighty years and yet not given to the poor, he should reflect that there are people whose charity embraces even the prune. Biscuits and cheese came next, and here the water-jug was liberally passed round, for it is the nature of biscuits to be dry, and these were biscuits to the core. That was all. The meal was over. Everybody scraped their chairs back; the swing-doors swung violently to and fro; soon the hall was emptied of every sign of food and made ready no doubt for breakfast next morning. Down corridors and up staircases the youth of England went banging and singing. And was it for a guest, a stranger (for I had no more right here in Fernham than in Trinity or Somerville or Girton or Newnham or Christchurch),[6] to say, "The dinner was not good," or to say (we were now, Mary Seton and I, in her sitting-room), "Could we not have dined up here alone?" for if I had said anything of the kind I should have been prying and searching into the secret economies of a house which to the stranger wears so fine a front of gaiety and courage. No, one could say nothing of the sort. Indeed, conversation for a moment flagged. The human frame being what it is, heart, body and brain all mixed together, and not contained in separate compartments as they will be no doubt in another million years, a good dinner is of great importance to good talk. One cannot think well, love well, sleep well, if one has not dined well. The lamp in the spine does not light on beef and prunes. We are all *probably* going to heaven, and Vandyck is, we *hope,* to meet us round the next corner—that is the dubious and qualifying state of mind that beef and prunes at the end of the day's work breed between them. Happily my friend, who taught science, had a cupboard where there was a squat bottle and little glasses—(but there should have been sole and partridge to begin with)—so that we were able to draw up to the fire and repair some of the damages of the day's living. In a minute or so we were slipping freely in and out among all those objects of curiosity and interest which form in the mind in the absence of a particular person, and are naturally to be discussed on coming together again—how somebody has married, another has not; one thinks this, another that; one has improved out of all knowledge, the other most amazingly gone to the bad—with all those speculations upon human nature and the character of the amazing world we live in which spring naturally from such beginnings. While these things were being said, however, I became shamefacedly aware of a current setting in of its own accord and carrying everything forward to an end of its own. One might be talking of Spain or Portugal, of book or racehorse, but the real interest of whatever was said was none of those things, but a scene of masons on a high roof some five centuries ago. Kings and nobles brought treasure in huge sacks and poured it under the earth. This scene was for ever coming alive in my mind and placing itself by another of lean cows and a muddy market and withered greens and the stringy hearts of old men—these two pictures, disjointed and disconnected and nonsensical as they were, were for ever coming together and combating each other and had me entirely at their mercy. The best course, unless the whole talk was to be

6. Trinity, Girton, and Newnham are colleges of Cambridge University; Somerville and Christchurch are at Oxford.

distorted, was to expose what was in my mind to the air, when with good luck it would fade and crumble like the head of the dead king when they opened the coffin at Windsor. Briefly, then, I told Miss Seton about the masons who had been all those years on the roof of the chapel, and about the kings and queens and nobles bearing sacks of gold and silver on their shoulders, which they shovelled into the earth; and then how the great financial magnates of our own time came and laid cheques and bonds, I suppose, where the others had laid ingots and rough lumps of gold. All that lies beneath the colleges down there, I said; but this college, where we are now sitting, what lies beneath its gallant red brick and the wild unkempt grasses of the garden? What force is behind the plain china off which we dined, and (here it popped out of my mouth before I could stop it) the beef, the custard and the prunes?

Well, said Mary Seton, about the year 1860—Oh, but you know the story, she said, bored, I suppose, by the recital. And she told me—rooms were hired. Committees met. Envelopes were addressed. Circulars were drawn up. Meetings were held; letters were read out; so-and-so has promised so much; on the contrary, Mr——won't give a penny. The *Saturday Review* has been very rude. How can we raise a fund to pay for offices? Shall we hold a bazaar? Can't we find a pretty girl to sit in the front row? Let us look up what John Stuart Mill said on the subject.[7] Can any one persuade the editor of the——to print a letter? Can we get Lady——to sign it? Lady——is out of town. That was the way it was done, presumably, sixty years ago, and it was a prodigious effort, and a great deal of time was spent on it. And it was only after a long struggle and with the utmost difficulty that they got thirty thousand pounds together.[8] So obviously we cannot have wine and partridges and servants carrying tin dishes on their heads, she said. We cannot have sofas and separate rooms. "The amenities," she said, quoting from some book or other, "will have to wait."[9]

At the thought of all those women working year after year and finding it hard to get two thousand pounds together, and as much as they could do to get thirty thousand pounds, we burst out in scorn at the reprehensible poverty of our sex. What had our mothers been doing then that they had no wealth to leave us? Powdering their noses? Looking in at shop windows? Flaunting in the sun at Monte Carlo? There were some photographs on the mantel-piece. Mary's mother—if that was her picture—may have been a wastrel in her spare time (she had thirteen children by a minister of the church), but if so her gay and dissipated life had left too few traces of its pleasures on her face. She was a homely body; an old lady in a plaid shawl which was fastened by a large cameo; and she sat in a basket-chair, encouraging a spaniel to look at the camera, with the amused, yet strained expression of one who is sure that the dog will move directly the bulb is pressed. Now if she had gone into business; had become a manufacturer of artificial silk or a magnate on the Stock Exchange; if she had left two or three hundred thousand pounds to Fernham, we could have been sitting at our ease tonight and the subject of our talk might have been archaeology, botany, anthropology, physics, the nature of the atom, mathematics, astronomy, relativity, geography. If only Mrs Seton and her mother and her mother before her had learnt the great art of making money and had left their money, like their fathers and their grandfathers before them, to found

7. In 1869 Mill published his essay *The Subjection of Women,* which argued forcefully for women's suffrage and their right to equality with men.
8. "We are told that we ought to ask for £30,000 at least. . . . It is not a large sum, considering that there is to be but one college of this sort for Great Britain, Ireland and the Colonies, and considering how easy it is to raise immense sums for boys' schools. But considering how few people really wish women to be educated, it is a good deal."–Lady Stephen, *Life of Miss Emily Davies* [Woolf's note].
9. Every penny which could be scraped together was set aside for building, and the amenities had to be postponed.–R. Strachey, *The Cause* [Woolf's note].

fellowships and lectureships and prizes and scholarships appropriated to the use of their own sex, we might have dined very tolerably up here alone off a bird and a bottle of wine; we might have looked forward without undue confidence to a pleasant and honourable lifetime spent in the shelter of one of the liberally endowed professions. We might have been exploring or writing; mooning about the venerable places of the earth; sitting contemplative on the steps of the Parthenon, or going at ten to an office and coming home comfortably at half-past four to write a little poetry. Only, if Mrs Seton and her like had gone into business at the age of fifteen, there would have been—that was the snag in the argument—no Mary. What, I asked, did Mary think of that? There between the curtains was the October night, calm and lovely, with a star or two caught in the yellowing trees. Was she ready to resign her share of it and her memories (for they had been a happy family, though a large one) of games and quarrels up in Scotland, which she is never tired of praising for the fineness of its air and the quality of its cakes, in order that Fernham might have been endowed with fifty thousand pounds or so by a stroke of the pen? For, to endow a college would necessitate the suppression of families altogether. Making a fortune and bearing thirteen children—no human being could stand it. Consider the facts, we said. First there are nine months before the baby is born. Then the baby is born. Then there are three or four months spent in feeding the baby. After the baby is fed there are certainly five years spent in playing with the baby. You cannot, it seems, let children run about the streets. People who have seen them running wild in Russia say that the sight is not a pleasant one. People say, too, that human nature takes its shape in the years between one and five. If Mrs Seton, I said, had been making money, what sort of memories would you have had of games and quarrels? What would you have known of Scotland, and its fine air and cakes and all the rest of it? But it is useless to ask these questions, because you would never have come into existence at all. Moreover, it is equally useless to ask what might have happened if Mrs Seton and her mother and her mother before her had amassed great wealth and laid it under the foundations of college and library, because, in the first place, to earn money was impossible for them, and in the second, had it been possible, the law denied them the right to possess what money they earned. It is only for the last forty-eight years that Mrs Seton has had a penny of her own. For all the centuries before that it would have been her husband's property—a thought which, perhaps, may have had its share in keeping Mrs Seton and her mothers off the Stock Exchange.[1] Every penny I earn, they may have said, will be taken from me and disposed of according to my husband's wisdom—perhaps to found a scholarship or to endow a fellowship in Balliol or Kings,[2] so that to earn money, even if I could earn money, is not a matter that interests me very greatly. I had better leave it to my husband.

At any rate, whether or not the blame rested on the old lady who was looking at the spaniel, there could be no doubt that for some reason or other our mothers had mismanaged their affairs very gravely. Not a penny could be spared for "amenities"; for partridges and wine, beadles and turf, books and cigars, libraries and leisure. To raise bare walls out of the bare earth was the utmost they could do.

So we talked standing at the window and looking, as so many thousands look every night, down on the domes and towers of the famous city beneath us. It was very

1. The late 19th century saw the passage of legislation designed to improve the legal status of women. In 1870 the Married Women's Property Act allowed women to retain £200 of their own earnings (which previously had automatically become the property of her husband); in 1884 a further act gave married women the same rights over property as unmarried women, and allowed them to carry on trades or businesses using their property.

2. Balliol is a college of Oxford University; King's is at Cambridge.

beautiful, very mysterious in the autumn moonlight. The old stone looked very white and venerable. One thought of all the books that were assembled down there; of the pictures of old prelates and worthies hanging in the panelled rooms; of the painted windows that would be throwing strange globes and crescents on the pavement; of the tablets and memorials and inscriptions; of the fountains and the grass; of the quiet rooms looking across the quiet quadrangles. And (pardon me the thought) I thought, too, of the admirable smoke and drink and the deep armchairs and the pleasant carpets: of the urbanity, the geniality, the dignity which are the offspring of luxury and privacy and space. Certainly our mothers had not provided us with anything comparable to all this—our mothers who found it difficult to scrape together thirty thousand pounds, our mothers who bore thirteen children to ministers of religion at St Andrews.

So I went back to my inn, and as I walked through the dark streets I pondered this and that, as one does at the end of the day's work. I pondered why it was that Mrs Seton had no money to leave us; and what effect poverty has on the mind; and what effect wealth has on the mind; and I thought of the queer old gentlemen I had seen that morning with tufts of fur upon their shoulders; and I remembered how if one whistled one of them ran; and I thought of the organ booming in the chapel and of the shut doors of the library; and I thought how unpleasant it is to be locked out; and I thought how it is worse perhaps to be locked in; and, thinking of the safety and prosperity of the one sex and of the poverty and insecurity of the other and of the effect of tradition and of the lack of tradition upon the mind of a writer, I thought at last that it was time to roll up the crumpled skin of the day, with its arguments and its impressions and its anger and its laughter, and cast it into the hedge. A thousand stars were flashing across the blue wastes of the sky. One seemed alone with an inscrutable society. All human beings were laid asleep—prone, horizontal, dumb. Nobody seemed stirring in the streets of Oxbridge. Even the door of the hotel sprang open at the touch of an invisible hand—not a boots was sitting up to light me to bed, it was so late.

from *Chapter 3*

It would have been impossible, completely and entirely, for any woman to have written the plays of Shakespeare in the age of Shakespeare. Let me imagine, since facts are so hard to come by, what would have happened had Shakespeare had a wonderfully gifted sister, called Judith, let us say. Shakespeare himself went, very probably—his mother was an heiress—to the grammar school, where he may have learnt Latin—Ovid, Virgil, and Horace—and the elements of grammar and logic. He was, it is well known, a wild boy who poached rabbits, perhaps shot a deer, and had, rather sooner than he should have done, to marry a woman in the neighbourhood, who bore him a child rather quicker than was right. That escapade sent him to seek his fortune in London. He had, it seemed, a taste for the theatre; he began by holding horses at the stage door. Very soon he got work in the theatre, became a successful actor, and lived at the hub of the universe, meeting everybody, knowing everybody, practising his art on the boards, exercising his wits in the streets, and even getting access to the palace of the queen. Meanwhile his extraordinarily gifted sister, let us suppose, remained at home. She was as adventurous, as imaginative, as agog to see the world as he was. But she was not sent to school. She had no chance of learning grammar and logic, let alone of reading Horace and Virgil. She picked up a book now and then, one of her brother's perhaps, and read a few pages. But then her parents came in and told her to mend the stockings or mind the stew and not moon about with books and papers.

They would have spoken sharply but kindly, for they were substantial people who knew the conditions of life for a woman and loved their daughter—indeed, more likely than not she was the apple of her father's eye. Perhaps she scribbled some pages up in an apple loft on the sly, but was careful to hide them or set fire to them. Soon, however, before she was out of her teens, she was to be betrothed to the son of a neighbouring wool-stapler. She cried out that marriage was hateful to her, and for that she was severely beaten by her father. Then he ceased to scold her. He begged her instead not to hurt him, not to shame him in this matter of her marriage. He would give her a chain of beads or a fine petticoat, he said; and there were tears in his eyes. How could she disobey him? How could she break his heart? The force of her own gift alone drove her to it. She made up a small parcel of her belongings, let herself down by a rope one summer's night and took the road to London. She was not seventeen. The birds that sang in the hedge were not more musical than she was. She had the quickest fancy, a gift like her brother's, for the tune of words. Like him, she had a taste for the theatre. She stood at the stage door; she wanted to act, she said. Men laughed in her face. The manager—a fat, loose-lipped man—guffawed. He bellowed something about poodles dancing and women acting—no woman, he said, could possibly be an actress. He hinted—you can imagine what. She could get no training in her craft. Could she even seek her dinner in a tavern or roam the streets at midnight? Yet her genius was for fiction and lusted to feed abundantly upon the lives of men and women and the study of their ways. At last—for she was very young, oddly like Shakespeare the poet in her face, with the same grey eyes and rounded brows—at last Nick Greene the actor-manager took pity on her; she found herself with child by that gentleman and so—who shall measure the heat and violence of the poet's heart when caught and tangled in a woman's body?—killed herself one winter's night and lies buried at some cross-roads where the omnibuses now stop outside the Elephant and Castle.[3]

That, more or less, is how the story would run, I think, if a woman in Shakespeare's day had had Shakespeare's genius. But for my part, I agree with the deceased bishop, if such he was—it is unthinkable that any woman in Shakespeare's day should have had Shakespeare's genius. For genius like Shakespeare's is not born among labouring, uneducated, servile people. It was not born in England among the Saxons and the Britons. It is not born today among the working classes. How, then, could it have been born among women whose work began, according to Professor Trevelyan,[4] almost before they were out of the nursery, who were forced to it by their parents and held to it by all the power of law and custom? Yet genius of a sort must have existed among women as it must have existed among the working classes. Now and again an Emily Brontë or a Robert Burns blazes out and proves its presence. But certainly it never got itself on to paper. When, however, one reads of a witch being ducked, of a woman possessed by devils, of a wise woman selling herbs, or even of a very remarkable man who had a mother, then I think we are on the track of a lost novelist, a suppressed poet, of some mute and inglorious Jane Austen, some Emily Brontë who dashed her brains out on the moor or mopped and mowed about the highways crazed with the torture that her gift had put her to. Indeed, I would venture to guess that Anon, who wrote so many poems without signing them, was often a woman. It was a woman Edward Fitzgerald,[5] I think,

3. A tavern on the outskirts of South London.
4. George Trevelyan (1876–1962), historian.
5. Poet and translator (1809–1883).

suggested who made the ballads and the folk-songs, crooning them to her children, beguiling her spinning with them, or the length of the winter's night.

This may be true or it may be false—who can say?—but what is true in it, so it seemed to me, reviewing the story of Shakespeare's sister as I had made it, is that any woman born with a great gift in the sixteenth century would certainly have gone crazed, shot herself, or ended her days in some lonely cottage outside the village, half witch, half wizard, feared and mocked at. For it needs little skill in psychology to be sure that a highly gifted girl who had tried to use her gift for poetry would have been so thwarted and hindered by other people, so tortured and pulled asunder by her own contrary instincts, that she must have lost her health and sanity to a certainty. No girl could have walked to London and stood at a stage door and forced her way into the presence of actor-managers without doing herself a violence and suffering an anguish which may have been irrational—for chastity may be a fetish invented by certain societies for unknown reasons—but were none the less inevitable. Chastity had then, it has even now, a religious importance in a woman's life, and has so wrapped itself round with nerves and instincts that to cut it free and bring it to the light of day demands courage of the rarest. To have lived a free life in London in the sixteenth century would have meant for a woman who was poet and playwright a nervous stress and dilemma which might well have killed her. Had she survived, whatever she had written would have been twisted and deformed, issuing from a strained and morbid imagination. And undoubtedly, I thought, looking at the shelf where there are no plays by women, her work would have gone unsigned. That refuge she would have sought certainly. It was the relic of the sense of chastity that dictated anonymity to women even so late as the nineteenth century. Currer Bell, George Eliot, George Sand,[6] all the victims of inner strife as their writings prove, sought ineffectively to veil themselves by using the name of a man. Thus they did homage to the convention, which if not implanted by the other sex was liberally encouraged by them (the chief glory of a woman is not to be talked of, said Pericles, himself a much-talked-of man), that publicity in women is detestable.[7] Anonymity runs in their blood. The desire to be veiled still possesses them. They are not even now as concerned about the health of their fame as men are, and, speaking generally, will pass a tombstone or a signpost without feeling an irresistible desire to cut their names on it, as Alf, Bert or Chas. must do in obedience to their instinct, which murmurs if it sees a fine woman go by, or even a dog, Ce chien est à moi [that dog is mine]. And, of course, it may not be a dog, I thought, remembering Parliament Square, the Sieges Allee[8] and other avenues; it may be a piece of land or a man with curly black hair. It is one of the great advantages of being a woman that one can pass even a very fine negress without wishing to make an Englishwoman of her.

That woman, then, who was born with a gift of poetry in the sixteenth century, was an unhappy woman, a woman at strife against herself. All the conditions of her life, all her own instincts, were hostile to the state of mind which is needed to set free whatever is in the brain. * * * There would always have been that assertion—you cannot do this, you are incapable of doing that—to protest against, to overcome. Probably for a novelist this germ is no longer of much effect; for there have been women novelists of merit. But for painters it must still have some sting in it; and for musicians,

6. Currer Bell, pen name of Charlotte Brontë; George Eliot, pen name of Mary Ann Evans; George Sand, pen name of Amandine Aurore Lucille Dupin (1804–1876).

7. The Athenian statesman Pericles was reported by the historian Thucydides to have said, "That woman is most praiseworthy whose name is least bandied about on men's lips, whether for praise or dispraise."

8. Victory Road, a thoroughfare in Berlin.

I imagine, is even now active and poisonous in the extreme. The woman composer stands where the actress stood in the time of Shakespeare. Nick Greene, I thought, remembering the story I had made about Shakespeare's sister, said that a woman acting put him in mind of a dog dancing. Johnson repeated the phrase two hundred years later of women preaching.[9] And here, I said, opening a book about music, we have the very words used again in this year of grace, 1928, of women who try to write music. "Of Mlle. Germaine Tailleferre one can only repeat Dr. Johnson's dictum concerning a woman preacher, transposed into terms of music. 'Sir, a woman's composing is like a dog's walking on his hind legs. It is not done well, but you are surprised to find it done at all.'"[1] So accurately does history repeat itself.

Thus, I concluded, shutting Mr Oscar Browning's life and pushing away the rest, it is fairly evident that even in the nineteenth century a woman was not encouraged to be an artist. On the contrary, she was snubbed, slapped, lectured and exhorted. Her mind must have been strained and her vitality lowered by the need of opposing this, of disproving that. For here again we come within range of that very interesting and obscure masculine complex which has had so much influence upon the woman's movement; that deep-seated desire, not so much that she shall be inferior as that he shall be superior, which plants him wherever one looks, not only in front of the arts, but barring the way to politics too, even when the risk to himself seems infinitesimal and the suppliant humble and devoted. Even Lady Bessborough, I remembered, with all her passion for politics, must humbly bow herself and write to Lord Granville Leveson-Gower:[2] ". . . notwithstanding all my violence in politics and talking so much on that subject, I perfectly agree with you that no woman has any business to meddle with that or any other serious business, farther than giving her opinion (if she is ask'd)." And so she goes on to spend her enthusiasm where it meets with no obstacle whatsoever upon that immensely important subject, Lord Granville's maiden speech in the House of Commons. The spectacle is certainly a strange one, I thought. The history of men's opposition to women's emancipation is more interesting perhaps than the story of that emancipation itself. An amusing book might be made of it if some young student at Girton or Newnham would collect examples and deduce a theory—but she would need thick gloves on her hands, and bars to protect her of solid gold.

But what is amusing now, I recollected, shutting Lady Bessborough, had to be taken in desperate earnest once. Opinions that one now pastes in a book labelled cock-a-doodle-dum and keeps for reading to select audiences on summer nights once drew tears, I can assure you. Among your grandmothers and great-grandmothers there were many that wept their eyes out. Florence Nightingale shrieked aloud in her agony.[3] Moreover, it is all very well for you, who have got yourselves to college and enjoy sitting-rooms—or is it only bed-sitting-rooms?—of your own to say that genius should disregard such opinions; that genius should be above caring what is said of it. Unfortunately, it is precisely the men or women of genius who mind most what is said of them. Remember Keats. Remember the words he had cut on his tombstone. Think of Tennyson; think—but I need hardly multiply instances of the undeniable, if very unfortunate, fact that it is the nature of the artist to mind excessively what is said

9. Samuel Johnson (1709–1784), poet and man of letters.

1. *A Survey of Contemporary Music,* Cecil Gray, page 246 [Woolf's note].

2. Lady Bessborough (1761–1821), correspondent of the British statesman Lord Granville.

3. See *Cassandra,* by Florence Nightingale, printed in *The Cause,* by R. Strachey [Woolf's note].

about him. Literature is strewn with the wreckage of men who have minded beyond reason the opinions of others.

And this susceptibility of theirs is doubly unfortunate, I thought, returning again to my original enquiry into what state of mind is most propitious for creative work, because the mind of an artist, in order to achieve the prodigious effort of freeing whole and entire the work that is in him, must be incandescent, like Shakespeare's mind, I conjectured, looking at the book which lay open at *Antony and Cleopatra.* There must be no obstacle in it, no foreign matter unconsumed.

For though we say that we know nothing about Shakespeare's state of mind, even as we say that, we are saying something about Shakespeare's state of mind. The reason perhaps why we know so little of Shakespeare—compared with Donne or Ben Jonson or Milton—is that his grudges and spites and antipathies are hidden from us. We are not held up by some "revelation" which reminds us of the writer. All desire to protest, to preach, to proclaim an injury, to pay off a score, to make the world the witness of some hardship or grievance was fired out of him and consumed. Therefore his poetry flows from him free and unimpeded. If ever a human being got his work expressed completely, it was Shakespeare. If ever a mind was incandescent, unimpeded, I thought, turning again to the bookcase, it was Shakespeare's mind.

from *Chapter 4*

The extreme activity of mind which showed itself in the later eighteenth century among women—the talking, and the meeting, the writing of essays on Shakespeare, the translating of the classics—was founded on the solid fact that women could make money by writing. Money dignifies what is frivolous if unpaid for. It might still be well to sneer at "blue stockings with an itch for scribbling," but it could not be denied that they could put money in their purses. Thus, towards the end of the eighteenth century a change came about which, if I were rewriting history, I should describe more fully and think of greater importance than the Crusades or the Wars of the Roses. The middle-class woman began to write. For if *Pride and Prejudice* matters, and *Middlemarch* and *Villette* and *Wuthering Heights* matter,[4] then it matters far more than I can prove in an hour's discourse that women generally, and not merely the lonely aristocrat shut up in her country house among her folios and her flatterers, took to writing. Without those forerunners, Jane Austen and the Brontës and George Eliot could no more have written than Shakespeare could have written without Marlowe, or Marlowe without Chaucer, or Chaucer without those forgotten poets who paved the ways and tamed the natural savagery of the tongue. For masterpieces are not single and solitary births; they are the outcome of many years of thinking in common, of thinking by the body of the people, so that the experience of the mass is behind the single voice. Jane Austen should have laid a wreath upon the grave of Fanny Burney, and George Eliot done homage to the robust shade of Eliza Carter—the valiant old woman who tied a bell to her bedstead in order that she might wake early and learn Greek. All women together ought to let flowers fall upon the tomb of Aphra Behn[5] which is, most scandalously but rather appropriately, in Westminster Abbey, for it

4. *Pride and Prejudice* (1813), a novel by Jane Austen; *Middlemarch* (1871–1872) by George Eliot; *Villette* (1853) by Charlotte Brontë; *Wuthering Heights* (1847) by Emily Brontë.

5. A dramatist and the first English woman to earn a living by writing (1640–1689). Westminster Abbey, in central London, is the burial place of many of the English kings and queens, as well as of famous poets and statesmen.

was she who earned them the right to speak their minds. It is she—shady and amorous as she was—who makes it not quite fantastic for me to say to you tonight: Earn five hundred a year by your wits.

Here, then, one had reached the early nineteenth century. And here, for the first time, I found several shelves given up entirely to the works of women. But why, I could not help asking, as I ran my eyes over them, were they, with very few exceptions, all novels? The original impulse was to poetry. The "supreme head of song" was a poetess. Both in France and in England the women poets precede the women novelists. Moreover, I thought, looking at the four famous names, what had George Eliot in common with Emily Brontë? Did not Charlotte Brontë fail entirely to understand Jane Austen? Save for the possibly relevant fact that not one of them had a child, four more incongruous characters could not have met together in a room—so much so that it is tempting to invent a meeting and a dialogue between them. Yet by some strange force they were all compelled, when they wrote, to write novels. Had it something to do with being born of the middle class, I asked; and with the fact, which Miss Emily Davies a little later was so strikingly to demonstrate,[6] that the middle-class family in the early nineteenth century was possessed only of a single sitting-room between them? If a woman wrote, she would have to write in the common sitting-room. And, as Miss Nightingale was so vehemently to complain,—"women never have an half hour . . . that they can call their own"—she was always interrupted. Still it would be easier to write prose and fiction there than to write poetry or a play. Less concentration is required. Jane Austen wrote like that to the end of her days. "How she was able to effect all this," her nephew writes in his Memoir, "is surprising, for she had no separate study to repair to, and most of the work must have been done in the general sitting-room, subject to all kinds of casual interruptions. She was careful that her occupation should not be suspected by servants or visitors or any persons beyond her own family party."[7] Jane Austen hid her manuscripts or covered them with a piece of blotting-paper. Then, again, all the literary training that a woman had in the early nineteenth century was training in the observation of character, in the analysis of emotion. Her sensibility had been educated for centuries by the influences of the common sitting-room. People's feelings were impressed on her; personal relations were always before her eyes. Therefore, when the middle-class woman took to writing, she naturally wrote novels, even though, as seems evident enough, two of the four famous women here named were not by nature novelists. Emily Brontë should have written poetic plays; the overflow of George Eliot's capacious mind should have spread itself when the creative impulse was spent upon history or biography. They wrote novels, however; one may even go further, I said, taking *Pride and Prejudice* from the shelf, and say that they wrote good novels. Without boasting or giving pain to the opposite sex, one may say that *Pride and Prejudice* is a good book. At any rate, one would not have been ashamed to have been caught in the act of writing *Pride and Prejudice.* Yet Jane Austen was glad that a hinge creaked, so that she might hide her manuscript before any one came in. To Jane Austen there was something discreditable in writing *Pride and Prejudice.* And, I wondered, would *Pride and Prejudice* have been a better novel if Jane Austen had not thought it necessary to hide her manuscript from visitors? I read a page or two to see; but I could not find any signs that her circumstances had harmed her work in the slightest. That, perhaps, was the chief

6. (Sarah) Emily Davies was prominent in the movement to secure university education for women in the 19th century and was chief founder of Girton College, Cambridge (1873).

7. *Memoir of Jane Austen,* by her nephew, James Edward Austen-Leigh [Woolf's note].

miracle about it. Here was a woman about the year 1800 writing without hate, without bitterness, without fear, without protest, without preaching. That was how Shakespeare wrote, I thought, looking at *Antony and Cleopatra;* and when people compare Shakespeare and Jane Austen, they may mean that the minds of both had consumed all impediments; and for that reason we do not know Jane Austen and we do not know Shakespeare, and for that reason Jane Austen pervades every word that she wrote, and so does Shakespeare. If Jane Austen suffered in any way from her circumstances it was in the narrowness of life that was imposed upon her. It was impossible for a woman to go about alone. She never travelled; she never drove through London in an omnibus or had luncheon in a shop by herself. But perhaps it was the nature of Jane Austen not to want what she had not. Her gift and her circumstances matched each other completely. But I doubt whether that was true of Charlotte Brontë, I said, opening *Jane Eyre* and laying it beside *Pride and Prejudice.*[8]

I opened it at chapter twelve and my eye was caught by the phrase, "Anybody may blame me who likes." What were they blaming Charlotte Brontë for, I wondered? And I read how Jane Eyre used to go up on to the roof when Mrs Fairfax was making jellies and looked over the fields at the distant view. And then she longed—and it was for this that they blamed her—that "then I longed for a power of vision which might overpass that limit; which might reach the busy world, towns, regions full of life I had heard of but never seen: that then I desired more of practical experience than I possessed; more of intercourse with my kind, of acquaintance with variety of character than was here within my reach. I valued what was good in Mrs Fairfax, and what was good in Adèle; but I believed in the existence of other and more vivid kinds of goodness, and what I believed in I wished to behold.

"Who blames me? Many, no doubt, and I shall be called discontented. I could not help it: the restlessness was in my nature; it agitated me to pain sometimes. . . .

"It is vain to say human beings ought to be satisfied with tranquillity: they must have action; and they will make it if they cannot find it. Millions are condemned to a stiller doom than mine, and millions are in silent revolt against their lot. Nobody knows how many rebellions ferment in the masses of life which people earth. Women are supposed to be very calm generally: but women feel just as men feel; they need exercise for their faculties and a field for their efforts as much as their brothers do; they suffer from too rigid a restraint, too absolute a stagnation, precisely as men would suffer; and it is narrow-minded in their more privileged fellow-creatures to say that they ought to confine themselves to making puddings and knitting stockings, to playing on the piano and embroidering bags. It is thoughtless to condemn them, or laugh at them, if they seek to do more or learn more than custom has pronounced necessary for their sex.

"When thus alone I not unfrequently heard Grace Poole's laugh . . ."

That is an awkward break, I thought. It is upsetting to come upon Grace Poole all of a sudden. The continuity is disturbed. One might say, I continued, laying the book down beside *Pride and Prejudice,* that the woman who wrote those pages had more genius in her than Jane Austen; but if one reads them over and marks that jerk in them, that indignation, one sees that she will never get her genius expressed whole

8. Woolf now goes on to describe parts of the plot of *Jane Eyre;* Jane Eyre, a penniless orphan, having suffered greatly during her schooling, takes up the post of governess to Adèle, the daughter of Mr. Rochester, a man of strange moods. Rochester falls in love with Jane, who agrees to marry him; however this is prevented by Rochester's mad wife—whom Rochester has locked in the attic, concealing her existence from Jane—who tears Jane's wedding veil on the eve of the marriage. Rochester at first tells Jane that Grace Poole, a servant, had been responsible for this and other strange events, including the uncanny laughter occasionally heard in the house.

and entire. Her books will be deformed and twisted. She will write in a rage where she should write calmly. She will write foolishly where she should write wisely. She will write of herself where she should write of her characters. She is at war with her lot. How could she help but die young, cramped and thwarted?

One could not but play for a moment with the thought of what might have happened if Charlotte Brontë had possessed say three hundred a year—but the foolish woman sold the copyright of her novels outright for fifteen hundred pounds; had somehow possessed more knowledge of the busy world, and towns and regions full of life; more practical experience, and intercourse with her kind and acquaintance with a variety of character. In those words she puts her finger exactly not only upon her own defects as a novelist but upon those of her sex at that time. She knew, no one better, how enormously her genius would have profited if it had not spent itself in solitary visions over distant fields; if experience and intercourse and travel had been granted her. But they were not granted; they were withheld; and we must accept the fact that all those good novels, *Villette, Emma, Wuthering Heights, Middlemarch,* were written by women without more experience of life than could enter the house of a respectable clergyman; written too in the common sitting-room of that respectable house and by women so poor that they could not afford to buy more than a few quires of paper at a time upon which to write *Wuthering Heights* or *Jane Eyre.* One of them, it is true, George Eliot, escaped after much tribulation, but only to a secluded villa in St John's Wood. And there she settled down in the shadow of the world's disapproval.[9] "I wish it to be understood," she wrote, "that I should never invite any one to come and see me who did not ask for the invitation"; for was she not living in sin with a married man and might not the sight of her damage the chastity of Mrs Smith or whoever it might be that chanced to call? One must submit to the social convention, and be "cut off from what is called the world." At the same time, on the other side of Europe, there was a young man living freely with this gipsy or with that great lady; going to the wars; picking up unhindered and uncensored all that varied experience of human life which served him so splendidly later when he came to write his books. Had Tolstoi lived at the Priory in seclusion with a married lady "cut off from what is called the world," however edifying the moral lesson, he could scarcely, I thought, have written *War and Peace.* ***

I do not want, and I am sure that you do not want me, to broach that very dismal subject, the future of fiction, so that I will only pause here one moment to draw your attention to the great part which must be played in that future so far as women are concerned by physical conditions. The book has somehow to be adapted to the body, and at a venture one would say that women's books should be shorter, more concentrated, than those of men, and framed so that they do not need long hours of steady and uninterrupted work. For interruptions there will always be. Again, the nerves that feed the brain would seem to differ in men and women, and if you are going to make them work their best and hardest, you must find out what treatment suits them—whether these hours of lectures, for instance, which the monks devised, presumably, hundreds of years ago, suit them—what alternations of work and rest they need, interpreting rest not as doing nothing but as doing something but something that is different; and what should that difference be? All this should be discussed and discovered; all this is part of the question of women and fiction. And yet, I continued, approaching the bookcase again, where shall I find that elaborate study of the psychology

9. Following a strictly religious childhood, the novelist George Eliot lost her faith and eloped with G. H. Lewes, a married man, with whom she lived for the rest of his life; her family never forgave her.

of women by a woman? If through their incapacity to play football women are not going to be allowed to practise medicine——

Happily my thoughts were now given another turn.

from *Chapter 6*

Next day the light of the October morning was falling in dusty shafts through the uncurtained windows, and the hum of traffic rose from the street. London then was winding itself up again; the factory was astir; the machines were beginning. It was tempting, after all this reading, to look out of the window and see what London was doing on the morning of the twenty-sixth of October 1928. And what was London doing? Nobody, it seemed, was reading *Antony and Cleopatra.* London was wholly indifferent, it appeared, to Shakespeare's plays. Nobody cared a straw—and I do not blame them—for the future of fiction, the death of poetry or the development by the average woman of a prose style completely expressive of her mind. If opinions upon any of these matters had been chalked on the pavement, nobody would have stooped to read them. The nonchalance of the hurrying feet would have rubbed them out in half an hour. Here came an errand-boy; here a woman with a dog on a lead. The fascination of the London street is that no two people are ever alike; each seems bound on some private affair of his own. There were the business-like, with their little bags; there were the drifters rattling sticks upon area railings; there were affable characters to whom the streets serve for clubroom, hailing men in carts and giving information without being asked for it. Also there were funerals to which men, thus suddenly reminded of the passing of their own bodies, lifted their hats. And then a very distinguished gentleman came slowly down a doorstep and paused to avoid collision with a bustling lady who had, by some means or other, acquired a splendid fur coat and a bunch of Parma violets. They all seemed separate, self-absorbed, on business of their own.

At this moment, as so often happens in London, there was a complete lull and suspension of traffic. Nothing came down the street; nobody passed. A single leaf detached itself from the plane tree at the end of the street, and in that pause and suspension fell. Somehow it was like a signal falling, a signal pointing to a force in things which one had overlooked. It seemed to point to a river, which flowed past, invisibly, round the corner, down the street, and took people and eddied them along, as the stream at Oxbridge had taken the undergraduate in his boat and the dead leaves. Now it was bringing from one side of the street to the other diagonally a girl in patent leather boots, and then a young man in a maroon overcoat; it was also bringing a taxi-cab; and it brought all three together at a point directly beneath my window; where the taxi stopped; and the girl and the young man stopped; and they got into the taxi; and then the cab glided off as if it were swept on by the current elsewhere.

The sight was ordinary enough; what was strange was the rhythmical order with which my imagination had invested it; and the fact that the ordinary sight of two people getting into a cab had the power to communicate something of their own seeming satisfaction. The sight of two people coming down the street and meeting at the corner seems to ease the mind of some strain, I thought, watching the taxi turn and make off. Perhaps to think, as I had been thinking these two days, of one sex as distinct from the other is an effort. It interferes with the unity of the mind. Now that effort had ceased and that unity had been restored by seeing two people come together and get into a taxi-cab. The mind is certainly a very mysterious organ, I reflected, drawing my head in from the window, about which nothing whatever is known, though we depend upon it so completely. Why do I feel that there are severances and oppositions in the mind, as there are strains from obvious causes on the body? What does one mean by "the unity of the mind," I pondered, for clearly the mind has so great a power of concentrating at any point at any moment that it seems to have no single state of being. It can separate itself from the people in the street, for example, and think of itself as apart from them, at an upper window looking down on them. Or it can think with other people spontaneously, as, for instance, in a crowd waiting to hear some piece of news read out. It can think back through its fathers or through its mothers, as I have said that a woman writing thinks back through her mothers. Again if one is a woman one is often surprised by a sudden splitting off of consciousness, say in walking down Whitehall,[1] when from being the natural inheritor of that civilisation, she becomes, on the contrary, outside of it, alien and critical. Clearly the mind is always altering its focus, and bringing the world into different perspectives. But some of these states of mind seem, even if adopted spontaneously, to be less comfortable than others. In order to keep oneself continuing in them one is unconsciously holding something back, and gradually the repression becomes an effort. But there may be some state of mind in which one could continue without effort because nothing is required to be held back. And this perhaps, I thought, coming in from the window, is one of them. For certainly when I saw the couple get into the taxi-cab the mind felt as if, after being divided, it had come together again in a natural fusion. The obvious reason would be that it is natural for the sexes to co-operate. One has a profound, if irrational, instinct in favour of the theory that the union of man and woman makes for the greatest satisfaction, the most complete happiness. But the sight of the two people getting into the taxi and the satisfaction it gave me made me also ask whether there are two sexes in the mind corresponding to the two sexes in the body, and whether they also require to be united in order to get complete satisfaction and happiness. And I went on amateurishly to sketch a plan of the soul so that in each of us two powers preside, one male, one female; and in the man's brain, the man predominates over the woman, and in the woman's brain, the woman predominates over the man. The normal and comfortable state of being is that when the two live in harmony together, spiritually co-operating. If one is a man, still the woman part of the brain must have effect; and a woman also must have intercourse with the man in her. Coleridge perhaps meant this when he said that a great mind is androgynous.[2] It is when this fusion takes place that the mind is fully fertilised and uses all its faculties. Perhaps a mind that is purely masculine cannot create, any more than a mind that is purely feminine, I thought. * * *

One must turn back to Shakespeare then, for Shakespeare was androgynous; and so was Keats and Sterne and Cowper and Lamb and Coleridge. Shelley perhaps was sexless. Milton and Ben Jonson had a dash too much of the male in them. So had Wordsworth and Tolstoi. In our time Proust was wholly androgynous, if not perhaps a little too much of a woman. But that failing is too rare for one to complain of it, since without some mixture of the kind the intellect seems to predominate and the other faculties of the mind harden and become barren. However, I consoled myself with the reflection that this is perhaps a passing phase; much of what I have said in obedience to my promise to give you the course of my thoughts will seem out of date; much of what flames in my eyes will seem dubious to you who have not yet come of age.

1. A main thoroughfare in central London and site of government offices.

2. The poet Samuel Taylor Coleridge made the remark in September 1832—"a great mind must be androgynous"—and it was duly recorded in his *Table Talk*.

Even so, the very first sentence that I would write here, I said, crossing over to the writing-table and taking up the page headed Women and Fiction, is that it is fatal for any one who writes to think of their sex. It is fatal to be a man or woman pure and simple; one must be woman-manly or man-womanly. It is fatal for a woman to lay the least stress on any grievance; to plead even with justice any cause; in any way to speak consciously as a woman. And fatal is no figure of speech; for anything written with that conscious bias is doomed to death. It ceases to be fertilised. Brilliant and effective, powerful and masterly, as it may appear for a day or two, it must wither at nightfall; it cannot grow in the minds of others. Some collaboration has to take place in the mind between the woman and the man before the act of creation can be accomplished. Some marriage of opposites has to be consummated. The whole of the mind must lie wide open if we are to get the sense that the writer is communicating his experience with perfect fullness. There must be freedom and there must be peace. Not a wheel must grate, not a light glimmer. The curtains must be close drawn. The writer, I thought, once his experience is over, must lie back and let his mind celebrate its nuptials in darkness. He must not look or question what is being done. Rather, he must pluck the petals from a rose or watch the swans float calmly down the river. And I saw again the current which took the boat and the undergraduate and the dead leaves; and the taxi took the man and the woman, I thought, seeing them come together across the street, and the current swept them away, I thought, hearing far off the roar of London's traffic, into that tremendous stream.

Here, then, Mary Beton ceases to speak. She has told you how she reached the conclusion—the prosaic conclusion—that it is necessary to have five hundred a year and a room with a lock on the door if you are to write fiction or poetry. She has tried to lay bare the thoughts and impressions that led her to think this. She has asked you to follow her flying into the arms of a Beadle, lunching here, dining there, drawing pictures in the British Museum, taking books from the shelf, looking out of the window. While she has been doing all these things, you no doubt have been observing her failings and foibles and deciding what effect they have had on her opinions. You have been contradicting her and making whatever additions and deductions seem good to you. That is all as it should be, for in a question like this truth is only to be had by laying together many varieties of error. And I will end now in my own person by anticipating two criticisms, so obvious that you can hardly fail to make them.

No opinion has been expressed, you may say, upon the comparative merits of the sexes even as writers. That was done purposely, because, even if the time had come for such a valuation—and it is far more important at the moment to know how much money women had and how many rooms than to theorise about their capacities—even if the time had come I do not believe that gifts, whether of mind or character, can be weighed like sugar and butter, not even in Cambridge, where they are so adept at putting people into classes and fixing caps on their heads and letters after their names. I do not believe that even the Table of Precedency which you will find in Whitaker's *Almanac*[3] represents a final order of values, or that there is any sound reason to suppose that a Commander of the Bath will ultimately walk in to dinner behind a Master in Lunacy. All this pitting of sex against sex, of quality against quality; all this claiming of superiority and imputing of inferiority, belong to the private-school stage of human existence where there are "sides," and it is necessary for one side to beat another side, and of the utmost importance to walk up to a platform and receive from the hands of the Headmaster himself a highly ornamental pot. As people mature they cease to believe in sides or in

3. A compendium of general information first published in 1868.

Headmasters or in highly ornamental pots. At any rate, where books are concerned, it is notoriously difficult to fix labels of merit in such a way that they do not come off. Are not reviews of current literature a perpetual illustration of the difficulty of judgment? "This great book," "this worthless book," the same book is called by both names. Praise and blame alike mean nothing. No, delightful as the pastime of measuring may be, it is the most futile of all occupations, and to submit to the decrees of the measurers the most servile of attitudes. So long as you write what you wish to write, that is all that matters; and whether it matters for ages or only for hours, nobody can say. But to sacrifice a hair of the head of your vision, a shade of its colour, in deference to some Headmaster with a silver pot in his hand or to some professor with a measuring-rod up his sleeve, is the most abject treachery, and the sacrifice of wealth and chastity which used to be said to be the greatest of human disasters, a mere flea-bite in comparison.

Next I think that you may object that in all this I have made too much of the importance of material things. *** Intellectual freedom depends upon material things. Poetry depends upon intellectual freedom. And women have always been poor, not for two hundred years merely, but from the beginning of time. Women have had less intellectual freedom than the sons of Athenian slaves. Women, then, have not had a dog's chance of writing poetry. That is why I have laid so much stress on money and a room of one's own. However, thanks to the toils of those obscure women in the past, of whom I wish we knew more, thanks, curiously enough, to two wars, the Crimean which let Florence Nightingale out of her drawing-room, and the European War which opened the doors to the average woman some sixty years later, these evils are in the way to be bettered. Otherwise you would not be here tonight, and your chance of earning five hundred pounds a year, precarious as I am afraid that it still is, would be minute in the extreme. ***

Here I would stop, but the pressure of convention decrees that every speech must end with a peroration. And a peroration addressed to women should have something, you will agree, particularly exalting and ennobling about it. I should implore you to remember your responsibilities, to be higher, more spiritual; I should remind you how much depends upon you, and what an influence you can exert upon the future. But those exhortations can safely, I think, be left to the other sex, who will put them, and indeed have put them, with far greater eloquence than I can compass. When I rummage in my own mind I find no noble sentiments about being companions and equals and influencing the world to higher ends. I find myself saying briefly and prosaically that it is much more important to be oneself than anything else. Do not dream of influencing other people, I would say, if I knew how to make it sound exalted. Think of things in themselves.

And again I am reminded by dipping into newspapers and novels and biographies that when a woman speaks to women she should have something very unpleasant up her sleeve. Women are hard on women. Women dislike women. Women . . . but are you not sick to death of the word? I can assure you that I am. Let us agree, then, that a paper read by a woman to women should end with something particularly disagreeable.

But how does it go? What can I think of? The truth is, I often like women. I like their unconventionality. I like their subtlety. I like their anonymity. I like—but I must not run on in this way. That cupboard there,—you say it holds clean table-napkins only; but what if Sir Archibald Bodkin were concealed among them?[4] Let me then adopt a sterner tone. Have I, in the preceding words, conveyed to you sufficiently the

4. Sir Archibald Bodkin was then Director of Public Prosecutions; his office had been responsible for the 1928 prosecution of Radclyffe Hall's novel *The Well of Loneliness* on a charge of obscenity. It was subsequently banned. Woolf had wanted to give evidence in the book's defense at the trial, but expert witnesses were not allowed by the presiding magistrate.

warnings and reprobation of mankind? I have told you the very low opinion in which you were held by Mr Oscar Browning. I have indicated what Napoleon once thought of you and what Mussolini thinks now. Then, in case any of you aspire to fiction, I have copied out for your benefit the advice of the critic about courageously acknowledging the limitations of your sex. I have referred to Professor X and given prominence to his statement that women are intellectually, morally and physically inferior to men. I have handed on all that has come my way without going in search of it, and here is a final warning—from Mr John Langdon Davies.[5] Mr John Langdon Davies warns women "that when children cease to be altogether desirable, women cease to be altogether necessary." I hope you will make a note of it.

How can I further encourage you to go about the business of life? Young women, I would say, and please attend, for the peroration is beginning, you are, in my opinion, disgracefully ignorant. You have never made a discovery of any sort of importance. You have never shaken an empire or led an army into battle. The plays of Shakespeare are not by you, and you have never introduced a barbarous race to the blessings of civilisation. What is your excuse? It is all very well for you to say, pointing to the streets and squares and forests of the globe swarming with black and white and coffee-coloured inhabitants, all busily engaged in traffic and enterprise and love-_making, we have had other work on our hands. Without our doing, those seas would be unsailed and those fertile lands a desert. We have borne and bred and washed and taught, perhaps to the age of six or seven years, the one thousand six hundred and twenty-three million human beings who are, according to statistics, at present in existence, and that, allowing that some had help, takes time.

There is truth in what you say—I will not deny it. But at the same time may I remind you that there have been at least two colleges for women in existence in England since the year 1866; that after the year 1880 a married woman was allowed by law to possess her own property; and that in 1919—which is a whole nine years ago—she was given a vote? May I also remind you that the most of the professions have been open to you for close on ten years now? When you reflect upon these immense privileges and the length of time time during which they have been enjoyed, and the fact that there must be at this moment some two thousand women capable of earning over five hundred a year in one way or another, you will agree that the excuse of lack of opportunity, training, encouragement, leisure and money no longer holds good. Moreover, the economists are telling us that Mrs Seton has had too many children. You must, of course, go on bearing children, but, so they say, in twos and threes, not in tens and twelves.

Thus, with some time on your hands and with some book learning in your brains—you have had enough of the other kind, and are sent to college partly, I suspect, to be uneducated—surely you should embark upon another stage of your very long, very laborious and highly obscure career. A thousand pens are ready to suggest what you should do and what effect you will have. My own suggestion is a little fantastic, I admit; I prefer, therefore, to put it in the form of fiction.

I told you in the course of this paper that Shakespeare had a sister; but do not look for her in Sir Sidney Lee's life of the poet. She died young—alas, she never wrote a word. She lies buried where the omnibuses now stop, opposite the Elephant and Castle. Now my belief is that this poet who never wrote a word and was buried at the crossroads still lives. She lives in you and in me, and in many other women who are not here tonight, for they are washing up the dishes and putting the children to bed. But she lives; for great poets do not die; they are continuing presences; they need only the

5. *A Short History of Women,* by John Langford Davies [Woolf's note].

opportunity to walk among us in the flesh. This opportunity, as I think, it is now coming within your power to give her. For my belief is that if we live another century or so—I am talking of the common life which is the real life and not of the little separate lives which we live as individuals—and have five hundred a year each of us and rooms of our own; if we have the habit of freedom and the courage to write exactly what we think; if we escape a little from the common sitting-room and see human beings not always in their relation to each other but in relation to reality; and the sky, too, and the trees or whatever it may be in themselves; if we look past Milton's bogey, for no human being should shut out the view; if we face the fact, for it is a fact, that there is no arm to cling to, but that we go alone and that our relation is to the world of reality and not only to the world of men and women, then the opportunity will come and the dead poet who was Shakespeare's sister will put on the body which she has so often laid down. Drawing her life from the lives of the unknown who were her forerunners, as her brother did before her, she will be born. As for her coming without that preparation, without that effort on our part, without that determination that when she is born again she shall find it possible to live and write her poetry, that we cannot expect, for that would be impossible. But I maintain that she would come if we worked for her, and that so to work, even in poverty and obscurity, is worth while.

T. S. Eliot

1888–1965

Thomas Stearns Eliot, an American-born poet and playwright who became a British citizen, is one of the towering presences in modern literature. After its publication in 1922, his poem *The Waste Land* achieved international fame as one of the most poignant expressions of the alienation and despair of the modern age. Also revolutionary in the fragmentation of its lyrical form, *The Waste Land* is stitched together from textual fragments that echo a wide range of literary traditions from Sanskrit to Dante and that connect to each other by means of underlying mythological themes. Along with Eliot's poetic and dramatic work, his criticism equally accounts for his extraordinary stature in modernist literature. In hundreds of essays and reviews, Eliot revisited and partly redefined the British literary canon, setting out principles of literary criticism that were to become foundational for the New Criticism that dominated British and American universities from the early 1930s to the late 1950s. Forty years of work as an editor with the publisher Faber and Faber equally contributed to shaping the literary scene. While he was considered a revolutionary poet in the 1910s and 1920s, the combined weight of Eliot's poetry and criticism turned him into a prime representative of the literary establishment by the 1940s, a figure against whose influence a younger generation of poets rose up to rebel: His winning the Nobel Prize in literature in 1948 sealed the conversion of one of the foremost innovators of modern poetry into the figurehead of a new literary standard.

But it wasn't only Eliot's steadily growing reputation as a poet and critic that changed his status as a writer. His own worldview underwent a radical change only five years after the publication of *The Waste Land:* In 1927, Eliot converted to the Anglican church and only a few months later was naturalized as a British citizen. His literary mode of expression changed in similarly fundamental ways, moving away from the fragmentation, meaninglessness, and isolation portrayed in his earlier works to a much more centered and religious outlook. His greatest achievement in this later mode is a set of four poems called *Four Quartets* (1943); there is considerable debate among critics as to whether this work or the earlier *Waste Land* qualifies as his best poetry, and which one expresses the essence of modernist lyric more successfully.

"The Love Song of J. Alfred Prufrock" belongs to Eliot's earliest work, and it is in fact the poem that first made him visible on London's literary scene. Written between 1910 and 1911 and first published in the magazines *Poetry* and *Catholic Anthology* in 1915 with the help of fellow poet Ezra Pound, "Prufrock" addresses a middle-aged man's anxiety over the passing of time and his own aging; but this specific unease is associated in the poem with more diffuse fears over what the meaning of human existence might be and how it could be found or expressed in a society that exhausts itself in empty social rituals and linguistic clichés. Far from offering an alternative to these oppressive social conventions, however, Prufrock's own voice sounds hollow and uncertain. In counterpoint to nineteenth-century poet Robert Browning's dramatic monologues, on whose model Eliot draws in the poem, Prufrock is as fragmented and empty as the society that surrounds him; his condition prefigures the broader panorama of stagnation and estrangement Eliot was to portray in *The Waste Land.*

The Love Song of J. Alfred Prufrock

S'io credessi che mia risposta fosse
a persona che mai tornasse al mondo,
questa fiamma staria senza più scosse.
Ma per ciò che giammai di questo fondo
non tornò vivo alcun, s'i'odo il vero,
senza tema d'infamia ti rispondo.[1]

Let us go then, you and I,
When the evening is spread out against the sky
Like a patient etherised upon a table;
Let us go, through certain half-deserted streets,
The muttering retreats
Of restless nights in one-night cheap hotels
And sawdust restaurants with oyster-shells:
Streets that follow like a tedious argument
Of insidious intent
To lead you to an overwhelming question . . .
Oh, do not ask, "What is it?"
Let us go and make our visit.

In the room the women come and go
Talking of Michelangelo.

The yellow fog that rubs its back upon the window-panes,
The yellow smoke that rubs its muzzle on the window-panes,
Licked its tongue into the corners of the evening,
Lingered upon the pools that stand in drains,
Let fall upon its back the soot that falls from chimneys,
Slipped by the terrace, made a sudden leap,
And seeing that it was a soft October night,
Curled once about the house, and fell asleep.

1. From Dante's *Inferno* (27.61–66). Dante asks one of the damned souls for its name, and it replies: "If I thought my answer were for one who could return to the world, I would not reply, but as none ever did return alive from this depth, without fear of infamy I answer thee."

And indeed there will be time
For the yellow smoke that slides along the street
Rubbing its back upon the window-panes;
There will be time, there will be time
To prepare a face to meet the faces that you meet;
There will be time to murder and create,
And time for all the works and days of hands
That lift and drop a question on your plate;
Time for you and time for me,
And time yet for a hundred indecisions,
And for a hundred visions and revisions,
Before the taking of a toast and tea.

In the room the women come and go
Talking of Michelangelo.

And indeed there will be time
To wonder, "Do I dare?" and, "Do I dare?"
Time to turn back and descend the stair,
With a bald spot in the middle of my hair—
(They will say: "How his hair is growing thin!")
My morning coat, my collar mounting firmly to the chin,
My necktie rich and modest, but asserted by a simple pin—
(They will say: "But how his arms and legs are thin!")
Do I dare
Disturb the universe?
In a minute there is time
For decisions and revisions which a minute will reverse.

For I have known them all already, known them all—
Have known the evenings, mornings, afternoons,
I have measured out my life with coffee spoons;
I know the voices dying with a dying fall
Beneath the music from a farther room.
    So how should I presume?

And I have known the eyes already, known them all—
The eyes that fix you in a formulated phrase,
And when I am formulated, sprawling on a pin,
When I am pinned and wriggling on the wall,
Then how should I begin
To spit out all the butt-ends of my days and ways?
    And how should I presume?

And I have known the arms already, known them all—
Arms that are braceleted and white and bare
(But in the lamplight, downed with light brown hair!)
Is it perfume from a dress
That makes me so digress?
Arms that lie along a table, or wrap about a shawl.
    And should I then presume?

And how should I begin?

. . .

Shall I say, I have gone at dusk through narrow streets
And watched the smoke that rises from the pipes
Of lonely men in shirt-sleeves, leaning out of windows? . . .

I should have been a pair of ragged claws
Scuttling across the floors of silent seas.

. . .

And the afternoon, the evening, sleeps so peacefully!
Smoothed by long fingers,
Asleep . . . tired . . . or it malingers,
Stretched on the floor, here beside you and me.
Should I, after tea and cakes and ices,
Have the strength to force the moment to its crisis?
But though I have wept and fasted, wept and prayed,
Though I have seen my head (grown slightly bald) brought in upon a platter,[2]
I am no prophet—and here's no great matter;
I have seen the moment of my greatness flicker,
And I have seen the eternal Footman hold my coat, and snicker,
And in short, I was afraid.

And would it have been worth it, after all,
After the cups, the marmalade, the tea,
Among the porcelain, among some talk of you and me,
Would it have been worth while,
To have bitten off the matter with a smile,
To have squeezed the universe into a ball
To roll it towards some overwhelming question,
To say: "I am Lazarus, come from the dead,
Come back to tell you all, I shall tell you all"[3]—
If one, settling a pillow by her head,
Should say: "That is not what I meant at all.
That is not it, at all."

And would it have been worth it, after all,
Would it have been worth while,
After the sunsets and the dooryards and the sprinkled streets,
After the novels, after the teacups, after the skirts that trail along the floor—
And this, and so much more?—
It is impossible to say just what I mean!
But as if a magic lantern[4] threw the nerves in patterns on a screen:
Would it have been worth while
If one, settling a pillow or throwing off a shawl,
And turning toward the window, should say:

2. Cf. Matthew 14. John the Baptist was beheaded by Herod and his head was brought to his wife, Herodias, on a platter.

3. Cf. John 11. Jesus raised Lazarus from the grave after he had been dead four days.

4. A device that employs a candle to project images, rather like a slide projector.

"That is not it at all,
That is not what I meant, at all."

. . .

No! I am not Prince Hamlet, nor was meant to be;
Am an attendant lord, one that will do
To swell a progress, start a scene or two,
Advise the prince; no doubt, an easy tool,
Deferential, glad to be of use,
Politic, cautious, and meticulous;
Full of high sentence, but a bit obtuse;
At times, indeed, almost ridiculous—

Almost, at times, the Fool.
I grow old . . . I grow old . . .
I shall wear the bottoms of my trousers rolled.
Shall I part my hair behind? Do I dare to eat a peach?
I shall wear white flannel trousers, and walk upon the beach.
I have heard the mermaids singing, each to each.

I do not think that they will sing to me.
I have seen them riding seaward on the waves
Combing the white hair of the waves blown back
When the wind blows the water white and black.

We have lingered in the chambers of the sea
By sea-girls wreathed with seaweed red and brown
Till human voices wake us, and we drown.

The Waste Land[1]

"Nam Sibyllam quidem Cumis ego ipse oculis meis vidi in ampulla pendere, et cum illi pueri dicerent: Σίβυλλα τί θέλεις; respondebat illa: ἀποθανεῖν θέλω."[2]

For Ezra Pound
il miglior fabbro.[3]

I. The Burial of the Dead

April is the cruellest month, breeding
Lilacs out of the dead land, mixing

1. Not only the title, but the plan and a good deal of the incidental symbolism of the poem were suggested by Miss Jessie L. Weston's book on the Grail legend: *From Ritual to Romance* (Cambridge). Indeed, so deeply am I indebted, Miss Weston's book will elucidate the difficulties of the poem much better than my notes can do; and I recommend it (apart from the great interest of the book itself) to any who think such elucidation of the poem worth the trouble. To another work of anthropology I am indebted in general, one which has influenced our generation profoundly; I mean *The Golden Bough;* I have used especially the two volumes *Adonis, Attis, Osiris.* Anyone who is acquainted with these works will immediately recognize in the poem certain references to vegetation ceremonies [Eliot's note]. Sir James Frazer (1854–1941) brought out the 12 volumes of *The Golden Bough,* a vast work of anthropology, comparative mythology and religion, between 1890 and 1915, with a supplement published in 1936.

2. From the *Satyricon* of Petronius (1st century C.E.). "For once I myself saw with my own eyes the Sybil at Cumae hanging in a cage, and when the boys said to her, 'Sybil, what do you want?' she replied, 'I want to die.'" The Sybil was granted anything she wished by Apollo, if only she would be his; she made the mistake of asking for everlasting life, without asking for eternal youth.

3. "The better craftsman." Pound played a crucial role in editing *The Waste Land* before its publication.

Memory and desire, stirring
Dull roots with spring rain.
Winter kept us warm, covering
Earth in forgetful snow, feeding
A little life with dried tubers.
Summer surprised us, coming over the Starnbergersee[4]
With a shower of rain; we stopped in the colonnade,
And went on in sunlight, into the Hofgarten,[5]
And drank coffee, and talked for an hour.
Bin gar keine Russin, stamm' aus Litauen, echt deutsch.[6]
And when we were children, staying at the arch-duke's,
My cousin's, he took me out on a sled,
And I was frightened. He said, Marie,
Marie, hold on tight. And down we went.
In the mountains, there you feel free.
I read, much of the night, and go south in the winter.

What are the roots that clutch, what branches grow
Out of this stony rubbish? Son of man,[7]
You cannot say, or guess, for you know only
A heap of broken images, where the sun beats,
And the dead tree gives no shelter, the cricket no relief,[8]
And the dry stone no sound of water. Only
There is shadow under this red rock,
(Come in under the shadow of this red rock),
And I will show you something different from either
Your shadow at morning striding behind you
Or your shadow at evening rising to meet you;
I will show you fear in a handful of dust.

Frisch weht der Wind
Der Heimat zu
Mein Irisch Kind,
Wo weilest du?[9]

"You gave me hyacinths first a year ago;
They called me the hyacinth girl."
—Yet when we came back, late, from the hyacinth garden,
Your arms full, and your hair wet, I could not
Speak, and my eyes failed, I was neither
Living nor dead, and I knew nothing,

4. A lake near Munich.

5. A public park in Munich, with a zoo and cafés.

6. "I'm not a Russian at all; I come from Lithuania, a true German."

7. Cf. Ezekiel 2.7 [Eliot's note]. Ezekiel 2.8 reads: "But thou, son of man, hear what I say unto thee; Be not thou rebellious like that rebellious house: open thy mouth, and eat that I give thee."

8. Cf. Ecclesiastes 12.5 [Eliot's note]. "They shall be afraid of that which is high, and fears shall be in the way, and the almond tree shall flourish, and the grasshopper shall be a burden, and desire shall fail."

9. *V. Tristan and Isolde,* i, verses 5–8 [Eliot's note]. In Wagner's opera, Tristan sings this about Isolde, the woman he is leaving behind as he sails for home: "Fresh blows the wind to the homeland; my Irish child, where are you staying?"

Looking into the heart of light, the silence.
Oed' und leer das Meer.[1]

Madame Sosostris, famous clairvoyante,
Had a bad cold, nevertheless
Is known to be the wisest woman in Europe,
With a wicked pack of cards.[2] Here, said she,
Is your card, the drowned Phoenician Sailor,
(Those are pearls that were his eyes.[3] Look!)
Here is Belladonna, the Lady of the Rocks,
The lady of situations.
Here is the man with three staves, and here the Wheel,
And here is the one-eyed merchant, and this card,
Which is blank, is something he carries on his back,
Which I am forbidden to see. I do not find
The Hanged Man.[4] Fear death by water.
I see crowds of people, walking round in a ring.
Thank you. If you see dear Mrs. Equitone,
Tell her I bring the horoscope myself:
One must be so careful these days.

Unreal City,[5]
Under the brown fog of a winter dawn,
A crowd flowed over London Bridge, so many,
I had not thought death had undone so many.[6]
Sighs, short and infrequent, were exhaled,[7]
And each man fixed his eyes before his feet.
Flowed up the hill and down King William Street,
To where Saint Mary Woolnoth kept the hours
With a dead sound on the final stroke of nine.[8]
There I saw one I knew, and stopped him, crying: "Stetson!
You who were with me in the ships at Mylae![9]

1. Id. iii, verse 24 [Eliot's note]. Tristan is dying and waiting for Isolde to come to him, but a shepherd, whom Tristan has hired to keep watch for her ship, reports only "Desolate and empty the sea."

2. I am not familiar with the exact constitution of the Tarot pack of cards, from which I have obviously departed to suit my own convenience. The Hanged Man, a member of the traditional pack, fits my purpose in two ways: because he is associated in my mind with the Hanged God of Frazer, and because I associated him with the hooded figure in the passage of the disciples to Emmaus in Part V. The Phoenician Sailor and the Merchant appear later; also the "crowds of people," and Death by Water is executed in Part IV. The Man with Three Staves (an authentic member of the Tarot pack) I associate, quite arbitrarily, with the Fisher King Himself [Eliot's note].

3. From Ariel's song, in Shakespeare's *The Tempest:* "Full fathom five thy father lies; / Of his bones are coral made; / Those are pearls that were his eyes: / Nothing of him that doth fade, / But doth suffer a sea-change" (1.2.399–403).

4. The tarot card that depicts a man hanging by one foot from a cross.

5. Cf. Baudelaire: "Fourmillante cité, cité pleine de rêves, / Où le spectre en plein jour raccroche le passant" [Eliot's note]. From *The Flowers of Evil.* "Swarming city, city full of dreams, / where in plain daylight the spectre accosts the passer-by."

6. Cf. *Inferno,* iii.55–7: "si lunga tratta / di gente, ch'io non avrei mai creduto / che morte tanta n'avesse disfatta" [Eliot's note]. "Such an endless train, / Of people, it never would have entered in my head / There were so many men whom death had slain."

7. Cf. *Inferno,* iv. 25–7: "Ouivi, secondo che per ascoltare, / non avea pianto, ma' che di sospiri, / che l'aura eterna facevan tremare" [Eliot's note]. "We heard no loud complaint, no crying there, / No sound of grief except the sound of sighing / Quivering forever through the eternal air."

8. A phenomenon which I have often noticed [Eliot's note].

9. The Battle of Mylae (260 B.C.E.) in the First Punic War.

That corpse you planted last year in your garden,
Has it begun to sprout? Will it bloom this year?
Or has the sudden frost disturbed its bed?
O keep the Dog far hence, that's friend to men,[1]
Or with his nails he'll dig it up again!
You! hypocrite lecteur!—mon semblable,—mon frère!"[2]

II. A Game of Chess[3]

The Chair she sat in, like a burnished throne,[4]
Glowed on the marble, where the glass
Held up by standards wrought with fruited vines
From which a golden Cupidon peeped out
(Another hid his eyes behind his wing)
Doubled the flames of sevenbranched candelabra
Reflecting light upon the table as
The glitter of her jewels rose to meet it,
From satin cases poured in rich profusion.
In vials of ivory and coloured glass
Unstoppered, lurked her strange synthetic perfumes,
Unguent, powdered, or liquid—troubled, confused
And drowned the sense in odours; stirred by the air
That freshened from the window, these ascended
In fattening the prolonged candle-flames,
Flung their smoke into the laquearia,[5]
Stirring the pattern on the coffered ceiling.
Huge sea-wood fed with copper
Burned green and orange, framed by the coloured stone,
In which sad light a carvèd dolphin swam.
Above the antique mantel was displayed
As though a window gave upon the sylvan scene[6]
The change of Philomel, by the barbarous king[7]
So rudely forced; yet there the nightingale[8]
Filled all the desert with inviolable voice
And still she cried, and still the world pursues,
"Jug Jug" to dirty ears.
And other withered stumps of time

1. Cf. the Dirge in Webster's *White Devil* [Eliot's note].
2. *V.* Baudelaire, Preface to *Fleurs du Mal* [Eliot's note]. "Hypocrite reader—my double—my brother!"
3. Cf. Thomas Middleton's drama *A Game at Chess* (1625), a political satire.
4. Cf. *Antony and Cleopatra,* II. ii. 190 [Eliot's note].
5. "Laquearia. *V. Aeneid,* I.726: "dependent lychni laquearibus aureis / incensi, et noctem flammis funalia vincunt." [Eliot's note]. "Burning lamps hang from the gold-panelled ceiling / And torches dispel the night with their flames"; a *laquearia* is a panelled ceiling. The passage from Virgil's *Aeneid* describes the banquet given by Dido for her lover Aeneas.
6. "Sylvan scene. *V.* Milton, *Paradise Lost,* iv. 140 [Eliot's note]. "And over head up grew / Insuperable height of loftiest shade, / Cedar, and Pine, and Fir, and branching Palm, / A Silvan Scene, and as the ranks ascend / Shade above shade, a woody Theatre / Of stateliest view." The passage describes the Garden of Eden, as seen through Satan's eyes. A sylvan scene is one taking place in a forest.
7. *V.* Ovid, *Metamorphoses,* vi, Philomela [Eliot's note]. Philomela was raped by King Tereus, her sister's husband, and was then changed into a nightingale.
8. Cf. Part III, 1. 204 [Eliot's note].

Were told upon the walls; staring forms
Leaned out, leaning, hushing the room enclosed.
Footsteps shuffled on the stair.
Under the firelight, under the brush, her hair
Spread out in fiery points
Glowed into words, then would be savagely still.

"My nerves are bad to-night. Yes, bad. Stay with me.
Speak to me. Why do you never speak. Speak.
What are you thinking of? What thinking? What?
I never know what you are thinking. Think."

I think we are in rats' alley[9]
Where the dead men lost their bones.

"What is that noise?"
The wind under the door.[1]
"What is that noise now? What is the wind doing?"
Nothing again nothing.
"Do
"You know nothing? Do you see nothing? Do you remember
Nothing?"
I remember
Those are pearls that were his eyes.
"Are you alive, or not? Is there nothing in your head?"[2]
But
O O O O that Shakespeherian Rag[3]—
It's so elegant
So intelligent
"What shall I do now? What shall I do?"
"I shall rush out as I am, and walk the street
With my hair down, so. What shall we do tomorrow?
What shall we ever do?"
The hot water at ten.
And if it rains, a closed car at four.
And we shall play a game of chess,
Pressing lidless eyes and waiting for a knock upon the door.[4]

When Lil's husband got demobbed,° I said— *demobilized*
I didn't mince my words, I said to her myself,
HURRY UP PLEASE ITS TIME[5]
Now Albert's coming back, make yourself a bit smart.
He'll want to know what you done with that money he gave you
To get yourself some teeth. He did, I was there.

9. Cf. Part III, l. 195 [Eliot's note].
1. Cf. Webster: "Is the wind in that door still?" [Eliot's note]. From John Webster's *The Devil's Law Case,* 3.2.162. The doctor asks this question when he discovers that a "murder victim" is still breathing.
2. Cf. Part I, l. 37, 48 [Eliot's note].
3. Quoting an American ragtime song featured in Ziegfield's Follies of 1912.
4. Cf. the game of chess in Middleton's *Women beware Women* [Eliot's note].
5. A British pub-keeper's call for a last round before closing.

You have them all out, Lil, and get a nice set,
He said, I swear, I can't bear to look at you.
And no more can't I, I said, and think of poor Albert,
He's been in the army four years, he wants a good time,
And if you don't give it him, there's others will, I said.
Oh is there, she said. Something o' that, I said.
Then I'll know who to thank, she said, and give me a straight look.
HURRY UP PLEASE ITS TIME
If you don't like it you can get on with it, I said.
Others can pick and choose if you can't.
But if Albert makes off, it won't be for lack of telling.
You ought to be ashamed, I said, to look so antique.
(And her only thirty-one.)
I can't help it, she said, pulling a long face,
It's them pills I took, to bring it off, she said.
(She's had five already, and nearly died of young George.)
The chemist[6] said it would be all right, but I've never been the same.
You *are* a proper fool, I said.
Well, if Albert won't leave you alone, there it is, I said,
What you get married for if you don't want children?
HURRY UP PLEASE ITS TIME
Well, that Sunday Albert was home, they had a hot gammon,° *ham*
And they asked me in to dinner, to get the beauty of it hot—
HURRY UP PLEASE ITS TIME
HURRY UP PLEASE ITS TIME
Goonight Bill. Goonight Lou. Goonight May. Goonight.
Ta ta. Goonight. Goonight.
Good night, ladies, good night, sweet ladies, good night, good night.[7]

III. THE FIRE SERMON

The river's tent is broken; the last fingers of leaf
Clutch and sink into the wet bank. The wind
Crosses the brown land, unheard. The nymphs are departed.
Sweet Thames, run softly, till I end my song.[8]
The river bears no empty bottles, sandwich papers,
Silk handkerchiefs, cardboard boxes, cigarette ends
Or other testimony of summer nights. The nymphs are departed.
And their friends, the loitering heirs of City directors;
Departed, have left no addresses.
By the waters of Leman[9] I sat down and wept . . .
Sweet Thames, run softly till I end my song,

6. Pharmacist.
7. Ophelia speaks these words in Shakespeare's *Hamlet,* and they are understood by the King as certain evidence of her insanity: "Good night ladies, good night. Sweet ladies, good night, good night" (4.5.72–73).
8. V. Spenser, *Prothalamion* [Eliot's note]; Spenser's poem (1596) celebrates the double marriage of Lady Elizabeth and Lady Katherine Somerset.
9. Lake Geneva. The line echoes Psalm 137, in which, exiled in Babylon, the Hebrew poets are too full of grief to sing.

Sweet Thames, run softly, for I speak not loud or long.
But at my back in a cold blast I hear
The rattle of the bones, and chuckle spread from ear to ear.

A rat crept softly through the vegetation
Dragging its slimy belly on the bank
While I was fishing in the dull canal
On a winter evening round behind the gashouse
Musing upon the king my brother's wreck
And on the king my father's death before him.[1]
White bodies naked on the low damp ground
And bones cast in a little low dry garret,
Rattled by the rat's foot only, year to year.
But at my back from time to time I hear[2]
The sound of horns and motors, which shall bring[3]
Sweeney to Mrs. Porter in the spring.
O the moon shone bright on Mrs. Porter[4]
And on her daughter
They wash their feet in soda water
Et O ces voix d'enfants, chantant dans la coupole![5]

Twit twit twit
Jug jug jug jug jug jug
So rudely forc'd.
Tereu

Unreal City
Under the brown fog of a winter noon
Mr. Eugenides, the Smyrna[6] merchant
Unshaven, with a pocket full of currants
C.i.f.[7] London: documents at sight,
Asked me in demotic° French *vulgar*
To luncheon at the Cannon Street Hotel[8]
Followed by a weekend at the Metropole.[9]

At the violet hour, when the eyes and back
Turn upward from the desk, when the human engine waits
Like a taxi throbbing waiting,

1. Cf. *The Tempest,* I. ii [Eliot's note].
2. Cf. Marvell, *To His Coy Mistress* [Eliot's note]. "But at my back I always hear / Time's wingèd chariot hurrying near."
3. Cf. Day, *Parliament of Bees:* "When of the sudden, listening, you shall hear, / A noise of horns and hunting, which shall bring / Actaeon to Diana in the spring, / Where all shall see her naked skin . . ." [Eliot's note].
4. I do not know the origin of the ballad from which these are taken: it was reported to me from Sydney, Australia [Eliot's note]. Sung by Australian soldiers in World War I: "O the moon shone bright on Mrs. Porter / And on the daughter / Of Mrs. Porter / They wash their feet in soda water / And so they oughter / To keep them clean."
5. V. Verlaine, *Parsifal* [Eliot's note]. "And O those children's voices singing in the dome." Paul Verlaine's sonnet describes Parsifal, who keeps himself pure in hopes of seeing the holy grail, and has his feet washed before entering the castle.
6. Seaport in western Turkey.
7. The currants were quoted at a price "carriage and insurance free to London"; and the Bill of Lading, etc., were to be handed to the buyer upon payment of the sight draft [Eliot's note].
8. A Hotel in London near the train station used for travel to and from continental Europe.
9. An upscale seaside resort hotel in Brighton.

I Tiresias,[1] though blind, throbbing between two lives,
Old man with wrinkled female breasts, can see
At the violet hour, the evening hour that strives
Homeward, and brings the sailor home from sea,[2]
The typist home at teatime, clears her breakfast, lights
Her stove, and lays out food in tins.
Out of the window perilously spread
Her drying combinations touched by the sun's last rays,
On the divan are piled (at night her bed)
Stockings, slippers, camisoles, and stays.
I Tiresias, old man with wrinkled dugs
Perceived the scene, and foretold the rest—
I too awaited the expected guest.
He, the young man carbuncular,° arrives, *pimply*
A small house agent's clerk, with one bold stare,
One of the low on whom assurance sits
As a silk hat on a Bradford[3] millionaire.
The time is now propitious, as he guesses,
The meal is ended, she is bored and tired,
Endeavours to engage her in caresses
Which still are unreproved, if undesired.
Flushed and decided, he assaults at once;
Exploring hands encounter no defence;
His vanity requires no response,
And makes a welcome of indifference.
(And I Tiresias have foresuffered all
Enacted on this same divan or bed;
I who have sat by Thebes below the wall
And walked among the lowest of the dead.)

1. Tiresias, although a mere spectator and not indeed a "character," is yet the most important personage in the poem, uniting all the rest. Just as the one-eyed merchant, seller of currants, melts into the Phoenician Sailor, and the latter is not wholly distinct from Ferdinand Prince of Naples, so all the women are one woman, and the two sexes meet in Tiresias. What Tiresias *sees,* in fact, is the substance of the poem. The whole passage from Ovid is of great anthropological interest: ". . .Cum Iunone iocos et 'maior vestra profecto est / Quam, quae contingit maribus,' dixisse, 'voluptas.' / Illa negat; placuit quae sit sententia docti / Quaerere Tiresiae: venus huic erat utraque nota. / Nam duo magnorum viridi coeuntia silva / Corpora serpentum baculi violaverat ictu / Deque viro factus, mirabile, femina septem / Egerat autumnos; octavo rursus eosdem / Vidit et 'est vestrae si tanta potentia plagae,' / Dixit 'ut auctoris sortem in contraria mutet, / Nunc quoque vos feriam!' percussis anguibus isdem / Forma prior rediit genetivaque venit imago. / Arbiter hic igitur sumptus de lite iocosa / Dicta Iovis firmat; gravius Saturnia iusto / Nec pro materia fertur doluisse suique / Iudicis aeterna damnavit lumina nocte, / At pater omnipotens (neque enim licet inrita cuiquam / Facta dei fecisse deo) pro lumine adempto / Scire futura dedit poenamque levavit honore" [Eliot's note]. This passage from Ovid's *Metamorphoses* describes Tiresias's sex change: "[The story goes that once Jove, having drunk a great deal,] jested with Juno. He said, 'Your pleasure in love is really greater than that enjoyed by men.' She denied it; so they decided to seek the opinion of the wise Tiresias, for he knew both aspects of love. For once, with a blow of his staff, he had committed violence on two huge snakes as they copulated in the green forest; and—wonderful to tell—was turned from a man into a woman and thus spent seven years. In the eighth year he saw the same snakes again and said: 'If a blow struck at you is so powerful that it changes the sex of the giver, I will now strike at you again.' With these words he struck the snakes, and his former shape was restored to him and he became as he had been born. So he was appointed arbitrator in the playful quarrel, and supported Jove's statement. It is said that Saturnia [i.e., Juno] was quite disproportionately upset, and condemned the arbitrator to perpetual blindness. But the almighty father (for no god may undo what has been done by another god), in return for the sight that was taken away, gave him the power to know the future and so lightened the penalty paid by the honor."

2. This may not appear as exact as Sappho's lines but I had in mind the "longshore" or "dory" fisherman, who returns at nightfall [Eliot's note]. "Hesperus, thou bringst home all things bright morning scattered: thou bringest the sheep, the goat, the child to the mother."

3. An industrial town in Yorkshire; many of its residents became wealthy during World War I.

Bestows one final patronising kiss,
And gropes his way, finding the stairs unlit . . .

She turns and looks a moment in the glass,
Hardly aware of her departed lover;
Her brain allows one half-formed thought to pass:
"Well now that's done: and I'm glad it's over."
When lovely woman stoops to folly and[4]
Paces about her room again, alone,
She smoothes her hair with automatic hand,
And puts a record on the gramophone.

"This music crept by me upon the waters"[5]
And along the Strand, up Queen Victoria Street.
O City city, I can sometimes hear
Beside a public bar in Lower Thames Street,
The pleasant whining of a mandoline
And a clatter and a chatter from within
Where fishmen lounge at noon: where the walls
Of Magnus Martyr[6] hold
Inexplicable splendour of Ionian white and gold.

The river sweats[7]
Oil and tar
The barges drift
With the turning tide
Red sails
Wide
To leeward, swing on the heavy spar.
The barges wash
Drifting logs
Down Greenwich reach
Past the Isle of Dogs.[8]
Weialala leia
Wallala leialala

Elizabeth and Leicester[9]
Beating oars

4. V. Goldsmith, the song in *The Vicar of Wakefield* [Eliot's note]. Oliver Goldsmith's character Olivia, on returning to the place where she was seduced, sings, "When lovely woman stoops to folly / And finds too late that men betray / What charm can soothe her melancholy, / What art can wash her guilt away? / The only art her guilt to cover, / To hide her shame from every eye, / To give repentance to her lover / And wring his bosom—is to die."

5. *V. The Tempest,* as above [Eliot's note].

6. The interior of St. Magnus Martyr is to my mind one of the finest among Wren's interiors. See *The Proposed Demolition of Nineteen City Churches* (P.S. King & Son, Ltd.) [Eliot's note].

7. The Song of the (three) Thames-daughters begins here. From line 292 to 306 inclusive they speak in turn. *V. Götterdämmerung,* III.I: the Rhine-daughters [Eliot's note]. In Richard Wagner's opera *Twilight of the Gods,* the Rhine maidens, when their gold is stolen, lament that the beauty of the river is gone.

8. Greenwich is a borough on the south bank of the River Thames; the Isle of Dogs is a peninsula in East London formed by a sharp bend in the Thames called Greenwich Reach.

9. *V.* Froude, *Elizabeth,* vol. I, Ch. iv, letter of De Quadra to Philip of Spain: "In the afternoon we were in a barge, watching the games on the river. (The Queen) was alone with Lord Robert and myself on the poop, when they began to talk nonsense, and went so far that Lord Robert at last said, as I was on the spot there was no reason why they should not be married if the queen pleased" [Eliot's note].

The stern was formed
A gilded shell
Red and gold
The brisk swell
Rippled both shores
Southwest wind
Carried down stream
The peal of bells
White towers
        Weialala leia
        Wallala leialala

"Trams and dusty trees.
Highbury bore me. Richmond and Kew[1]
Undid me. By Richmond I raised my knees
Supine on the floor of a narrow canoe."

"My feet are at Moorgate,[2] and my heart
Under my feet. After the event
He wept. He promised 'a new start.'
I made no comment. What should I resent?"

"On Margate Sands.[3]
I can connect
Nothing with nothing.
The broken fingernails of dirty hands.
My people humble people who expect
Nothing."
        la la

To Carthage then I came[4]

Burning burning burning burning[5]
O Lord Thou pluckest me out[6]
O Lord Thou pluckest

burning

IV. Death by Water

Phlebas the Phoenician, a fortnight dead,
Forgot the cry of gulls, and the deep sea swell

1. "Cf. *Purgatorio,* V. 133: "Ricorditi di me, che son la Pia; / Siena mi fe', disfecemi Maremma." [Eliot's note]. "Remember me, that I am called Piety; / Sienna made me and Maremma undid me." Highbury, Richmond, and Kew are suburbs of London near the Thames.
2. A slum in East London.
3. A seaside resort in the Thames estuary.
4. *V.* St. Augustine's *Confessions:* "to Carthage then I came, where a cauldron of unholy loves sang all about mine ears" [Eliot's note].
5. The complete text of the Buddha's Fire Sermon (which corresponds in importance to the Sermon on the Mount) from which these words are taken, will be found translated in the late Henry Clarke Warren's *Buddhism in Translation* (Harvard Oriental Series). Mr. Warren was one of the great pioneers of Buddhist studies in the Occident [Eliot's note].
6. From St. Augustine's *Confessions* again. The collocation of these two representatives of eastern and western asceticism, as the culmination of this part of the poem, is not an accident [Eliot's note]. Augustine writes: "I entangle my steps with these outward beauties, but thou pluckest me out, O Lord, Thou pluckest me out."

And the profit and loss.
A current under sea
Picked his bones in whispers. As he rose and fell
He passed the stages of his age and youth
Entering the whirlpool.
Gentile or Jew
O you who turn the wheel and look to windward,
Consider Phlebas, who was once handsome and tall as you.

V. What the Thunder Said[7]

After the torchlight red on sweaty faces
After the frosty silence in the gardens
After the agony in stony places
The shouting and the crying
Prison and palace and reverberation
Of thunder of spring over distant mountains
He who was living is now dead
We who were living are now dying
With a little patience

Here is no water but only rock
Rock and no water and the sandy road
The road winding above among the mountains
Which are mountains of rock without water
If there were water we should stop and drink
Amongst the rock one cannot stop or think
Sweat is dry and feet are in the sand
If there were only water amongst the rock
Dead mountain mouth of carious° teeth that cannot spit *rotting*
Here one can neither stand nor lie nor sit
There is not even silence in the mountains
But dry sterile thunder without rain
There is not even solitude in the mountains
But red sullen faces sneer and snarl
From doors of mudcracked houses
If there were water
And no rock
If there were rock
And also water
And water
A spring
A pool among the rock
If there were the sound of water only
Not the cicada
And dry grass singing

7. In the first part of Part V three themes are employed: the journey to Emmaus, the approach to the Chapel Perilous (see Miss Weston's book), and the present decay of eastern Europe [Eliot's note].

But sound of water over a rock
Where the hermit-thrush sings in the pine trees
Drip drop drip drop drop drop drop[8]
But there is no water

Who is the third who walks always beside you?
When I count, there are only you and I together[9]
But when I look ahead up the white road
There is always another one walking beside you
Gliding wrapt in a brown mantle, hooded
I do not know whether a man or a woman
—But who is that on the other side of you?

What is that sound high in the air[1]
Murmur of maternal lamentation
Who are those hooded hordes swarming
Over endless plains, stumbling in cracked earth
Ringed by the flat horizon only
What is the city over the mountains
Cracks and reforms and bursts in the violet air
Falling towers
Jerusalem Athens Alexandria
Vienna London
Unreal

A woman drew her long black hair out tight
And fiddled whisper music on those strings
And bats with baby faces in the violet light
Whistled, and beat their wings
And crawled head downward down a blackened wall
And upside down in air were towers
Tolling reminiscent bells, that kept the hours
And voices singing out of empty cisterns and exhausted wells

In this decayed hole among the mountains
In the faint moonlight, the grass is singing
Over the tumbled graves, about the chapel
There is the empty chapel, only the wind's home.

8. This is *Turdus aonalaschkae pallasii,* the hermit-thrush which I have heard in Quebec County. Chapman says (*Handbook of Birds of Eastern North America*) "it is most at home in secluded woodland and thickety retreats. . . . Its notes are not remarkable for variety or volume, but in purity and sweetness of tone and exquisite modulation they are unequalled." Its "water-dripping song" is justly celebrated [Eliot's note].

9. The following lines were stimulated by the account of one of the Antarctic expeditions (I forget which, but I think one of Shackleton's): it was related that the party of explorers, at the extremity of their strength, had the constant delusion that there was one more member than could actually be counted [Eliot's note]. There seems also to be an echo of the account of Jesus meeting his disciples on the road to Emmaus: "Jesus himself drew near, and went with them. But their eyes were holden that they should not know him" (Luke 24.13–16).

1. Cf. Hermann Hesse, *Blick ins Chaos:* "Schon ist halb Europa, schon ist zumindest der halbe Osten Europas auf dem Wege zum Chaos, fährt betrunken im heiligen Wahn am Abgrund entlang und singt dazu, singt betrunken und hymnisch wie Dmitri Karamasoff sang. Ueber diese Lieder lacht der Bürger beleidigt, der Heilige und Seher hört sie mit Tränen" [Eliot's note]. "Already half of Europe, already at least half of Eastern Europe, on the way to chaos, drives drunk in sacred infatuation along the edge of the precipice, singing drunkenly, as though singing hymns, as Dmitri Karamazov sang. The offended bourgeois laughs at the songs; the saint and the seer hear them with tears."

It has no windows, and the door swings,
Dry bones can harm no one.
Only a cock stood on the rooftree
Co co rico co co rico
In a flash of lightning. Then a damp gust
Bringing rain

Ganga[2] was sunken, and the limp leaves
Waited for rain, while the black clouds
Gathered far distant, over Himavant.[3]
The jungle crouched, humped in silence.
Then spoke the thunder
Da
Datta: what have we given?[4]
My friend, blood shaking my heart
The awful daring of a moment's surrender
Which an age of prudence can never retract
By this, and this only, we have existed
Which is not to be found in our obituaries
Or in memories draped by the beneficent spider[5]
Or under seals broken by the lean solicitor
In our empty rooms
Da
Dayadhvam: I have heard the key[6]
Turn in the door once and turn once only
We think of the key, each in his prison
Thinking of the key, each confirms a prison
Only at nightfall, aethereal rumours
Revive for a moment a broken Coriolanus[7]
Da
Damyata: The boat responded
Gaily, to the hand expert with sail and oar
The sea was calm, your heart would have responded
Gaily, when invited, beating obedient
To controlling hands

2. The river Ganges.
3. The Himalayas.
4. "Datta, dayadhvam, damyata" (Give, sympathize, control). The fable of the meaning of the Thunder is found in the *Brihadaranyaka—Upanishad,* 5, I. A translation is found in Deussen's *Sechzig Upanishads des Veda,* p. 489 [Eliot's note]. "That very thing is repented even today by the heavenly voice, in the form of thunder, in the form of thunder as 'Da,' 'Da,' 'Da'. . . . Therefore one should practice these three things: self-control, alms-giving, and compassion."
5. Cf. Webster, *The White Devil,* v. vi: ". . . they'll remarry / Ere the worm pierce your winding-sheet, ere the spider / make a thin curtain for your epitaphs" [Eliot's note].
6. Cf. *Inferno,* xxxiii. 46: "ed io sentii chiavar l'uscio di sotto / all'orrible torre." Also F. H. *Bradley, Appearance and Reality,* p. 346: "My external sensations are no less private to myself than are my thoughts or my feelings. In either case my experience falls within my own circle, a circle closed on the outside; and, with all its elements alike, every sphere is opaque to the others which surround it. . . . In brief, regarded as an existence which appears in a soul, the whole world for each is peculiar and private to that soul." [Eliot's note]. In the passage from the *Inferno,* Ugolino tells Dante of his imprisonment and starvation until he became so desperate that he ate his children: "And I heard below me the door of the horrible tower being locked."
7. In Shakespeare's play of the same name, Coriolanus is a Roman general who is exiled and later leads the enemy in an attack against the Romans.

I sat upon the shore
Fishing, with the arid plain behind me[8]
Shall I at least set my lands in order?
London Bridge is falling down falling down falling down
Poi s'ascose nel foco che gli affina[9]
Quando fiam uti chelidon—O swallow swallow[1]
Le Prince d'Aquitaine à la tour abolie[2]
These fragments I have shored against my ruins
Why then Ile fit you. Hieronymo's mad againe.[3]
Datta. Dayadhvam. Damyata.
Shantih shantih shantih[4]

Franz Kafka

1883–1924

Compared to many other modern novelists, Franz Kafka wrote little, and three of his major novels remained incomplete at his death. Yet in spite of its small bulk, his fiction has become one of the most towering achievements of European modernism: Throughout the twentieth century, Kafka's stories deeply influenced writers across different continents and languages, from the Argentinean short-story writer Jorge Luis Borges to the Japanese novelist Abe Kobo and the American cartoon artist Art Spiegelman. Profoundly enigmatic, Kafka's novels and stories resist attempts at defining their meaning conclusively, but it is precisely their indeterminacy that allows readers from very different backgrounds to understand his works as reflecting a part of their own condition. Indeed, in several languages the adjective "kafkaesque" has become part of the common modern vocabulary as a description of situations that are difficult, intricate, alienating, or absurd.

This usage loosely reflects the kind of predicament Kafka's protagonists typically find themselves confronted with. An event occurs that can't really be explained in terms of ordinary experience and commonsense rationality; as they investigate what the meaning of this event might be, Kafka's characters move gradually away from normal life and become more and more deeply entangled with incomprehensible processes and authorities. In the encounter with immensely powerful but impenetrable structures of authority—whether they are familial, civic, legal, or religious—Kafka's characters come to question their own identities and beliefs about the world, but they are unable to formulate more adequate ones. Sometimes the protagonists die without ever having understood what it was that threw their lives off their normal course in the first place. As they find themselves in an environment that is unintelligible at best and hostile at worst,

8. *V.* Weston, *From Ritual to Romance;* chapter on the Fisher King [Eliot's note].

9. *V. Purgatorio,* xxvi.148: "Ara vos prec per aquella valor / que vos condus al som de l'escalina, / sovegna vos a temps de ma dolor." / Poi s'ascose nel foco che gli affina" [Eliot's note]. In this passage, the poet Arnaut Daniel speaks to Dante: "Now I pray you, by the goodness that guides you to the top of this staircase, be mindful in time of my suffering."

1. *V. Pervigilium Veneris.* Cf. Philomela in Parts II and III [Eliot's note]. Philomel asks, "When shall I be a swallow?"

2. *V.* Gerard de Nerval, Sonnet *El Desdichado* [Eliot's note]. "The Prince of Aquitaine in the ruined tower."

3. *V.* Kyd's *Spanish Tragedy* [Eliot's note]. The subtitle of Kyd's play is, "Hieronymo's Mad Againe." His son having been murdered, Hieronymo is asked to compose a court play, to which he responds "Why then Ile fit you"; his son's murder is avenged in the course of the play.

4. Shantih. Repeated as here, a formal ending to an Upanishad. "The Peace which passeth understanding" is a feeble translation of the content of this word [Eliot's note]. The Upanishads are poetic commentaries on the Hindu Scriptures.

Kafka's characters experience what is often considered one of the quintessentially modern conditions: *alienation,* the estrangement of the individual from normal social bonds and activities.

The reasons for this alienation in Kafka's fictional world have been hotly debated over the decades. Some readers (among them Max Brod, Kafka's friend and literary executor) have claimed that Kafka's characters exemplify the predicament of a humankind that needs and seeks out religious redemption but is forever cut off from divine mercy or access to salvation. Others emphasize that Kafka's descriptions of impersonal, inefficient, and incomprehensible institutions reflect some aspects of German sociologist Max Weber's famous characterization of modern bureaucracies. In this view, Kafka's characters would illustrate the condition of the typical modern citizen, whose life, in large part, is determined by abstract bureaucratic networks. Yet others have argued that Kafka's stories refer more specifically to the experience of a particular social group, the bourgeois middle class in an advanced capitalist society, and even more specifically to the double alienation implicit in Kafka's own status as a Jew of mixed German and Czech heritage living in Prague in the waning years of the Austro-Hungarian Empire. And finally, it has been suggested that the best way to approach Kafka's stories is through a psychoanalytical perspective that would foreground Kafka's own extremely troubled relation to his father as one of the basic sources of his characters' conflicted encounters with authority.

The reason that it is often difficult to decide which of these and other interpretations might be the most appropriate lies in the fact that many of Kafka's stories have the structure of a *parable,* a story that describes concrete and everyday events in order to illustrate an abstract concept or condition; unlike allegories, parables are usually not self-explanatory but require interpretive comment. Kafka's parables, however, stand on their own, and his brief reflection "On Parables" shows just how ambiguous the relation to the real can remain in this genre. An understanding of Kafka's texts is further complicated by the fact that even at the most literal level of the plot, they don't remain in the realm of ordinary experience in the way biblical parables do. Rather, many of them start out with what appears at first sight to be an everyday situation, which then mutates into nightmarish circumstances that clearly fall outside the realm of commonsense reality. In *The Trial,* Kafka's protagonist is informed by two officials on what seems like an ordinary morning that a lawsuit has been initiated against him, but he is not told what crime he is accused of, and still doesn't know months later when he is sentenced to death. In *The Metamorphosis,* Gregor Samsa wakes up in the morning with every intention of going to work, only to find himself transformed into a beetle lying on its back. Kafka's literary mastery is most obvious in his ability to make such fantastic occurrences appear perfectly real to the reader.

The apparent simplicity of Kafka's style subtly heightens the enigma of his works. Especially compared to other Prague authors writing in German at the same time, his style is strikingly concrete and literal, without any obvious display of metaphor, symbol, or ornate syntax. But precisely in stripping his fiction of the ordinary trappings of "literary" diction, Kafka often pushes language to an extreme where even very simple words become problematic: What, really, is a "trial" or a "judgment"? How are we to imagine the "singing" of the mouse performer in "Josephine the Singer," who hardly seems to make audible sounds at all? Since words like these don't seem to function in Kafka's texts in quite the way they do in ordinary language, readers have always been tempted to give a variety of symbolic meanings to them. But Kafka's own language stubbornly refuses to yield firm evidence of what these meanings might be. This has led some of his successors, such as the French novelist Alain Robbe-Grillet, to claim that, in fact, Kafka's fiction belongs to an entirely different kind of literature that does away with metaphor as the basis of narrative meaning.

Kafka's work consists not only of narrative fiction but also of extensive diaries and letters that he wrote during most of his life; indeed all of his life was accompanied by constant acts of writing. The diaries and letters reveal an intensely introspective mind that steadily scrutinizes itself and others: "Every person is lost in himself beyond hope of rescue, and one's sole consolation in this is to observe other people and the laws governing them and everything," he noted in a 1914 diary entry. Kafka felt and thought deeply about each of his family and friendship relations and often agonized over what he perceived as his own shortfalls in fulfilling others' expectations. But his letters and diaries are not only fascinating psychological documents; they are also quite often accomplished literary texts. The "Letter to His Father," beyond what it might reveal about Kafka's family experience, is a striking example of character construction, and some of the diary entries contain narrative fragments whose quality rivals that of Kafka's fiction. Though they were never meant for literary publication, they convey the sense of a man who lived almost every aspect of his life through writing. "My happiness, my abilities and every possibility of being useful in any way have always been in the literary field," he wrote in his diary in 1911.

The world that is reflected in Kafka's fiction as well as in his letters and diaries is that of Prague at the turn of the twentieth century, where Kafka was born in 1883 as the first child of Hermann Kafka, who came from a Czech-Jewish family, and his mother, Julie, who was German-Jewish. At the time, Prague formed part of the Empire of Austria-Hungary and was home to three different groups: the Czech majority and significant minorities of Jews and Germans. Jews occupied a somewhat ambiguous position between the Czech majority and the ruling German elite; Prague Jews had for a long time deeply identified with German culture, and it was not unusual for Jewish children to be sent to German-language schools. Kafka attended such a school in Prague from 1893 to 1901. In November 1901 he entered Prague's German University and studied law, graduating in June 1906. After the mandatory first year of unpaid practical experience in law, he started working for a private insurance company, Assicurazioni Generali, but he disliked the working atmosphere and long hours so much that less than a year later, he moved to the Workers' Accident Insurance Institute, for which he continued to work until shortly before his death in 1924.

Kafka's youth was overshadowed by personal, professional, and medical troubles. Some of the most important and intimate relationships in his life were also the most complex and conflicted. He had an intensely ambivalent relationship with his father, who first ran a small business selling women's clothing and later ran an asbestos factory in which his son sometimes helped out. Kafka's ambivalence emerges clearly in the "Letter to His Father," written in 1919 but never actually sent. According to this letter, the father's professional success, self-assurance, and willingness to ignore others' desires stood in stark contrast with the son's self-doubt and uncertainty regarding his success as a writer as well as in his relationships with women. This conflict led Kafka to a mixture of admiration and repulsion and to simultaneous desires to please his father and rebel against him, which precluded any effective communication or deep understanding. Kafka's relationship with his fiancée, Felice Bauer, was similarly troubled: in their five-year relationship between 1912 and 1917, the couple were twice engaged, but both times Kafka broke the engagement in intense self-doubt over his own inability to sustain a marriage and to reconcile it with his devotion to literature.

Kafka's professional life proved no less conflicted. He often agonized over the obligation to earn a living through legal work that he experienced as tedious and burdensome instead of devoting himself to the work that he considered to be his real vocation, writing. His attempt to carve out time to write outside of a long workday frequently led to sleepless nights and ill health during his time at Assicurazioni Generali, and he moved to the Workers' Accident Insurance Institute partly for the more moderate hours required there. Nevertheless, his life remained divided between tedious work that was financially necessary and the work he passionately cared about but was unable to live from. Illness was a constant presence in Kafka's life, starting in his childhood, but it gradually became a more and more serious threat to both his work and his life. From about 1912 on, he complained of insomnia and severe headaches, and symptoms of tuberculosis manifested themselves in 1917. In 1920 and 1921 he was forced to spend several months at a sanatorium. Only a few months before his death in March 1924, he wrote his haunting story "Josephine the Singer," which celebrates the profound significance of artistic creation, only to deny its social relevance. Perhaps not coincidentally, Kafka instructed his friend Max Brod shortly before his death to destroy all his literary works; Brod ignored this instruction and preserved Kafka's unpublished texts for posterity. Kafka died on 3 June 1924, from laryngeal tuberculosis, just a month short of his forty-first birthday.

The Metamorphosis[1]

1

When Gregor Samsa woke up one morning from unsettling dreams, he found himself changed in his bed into a monstrous vermin. He was lying on his back as hard as armor plate, and when he lifted his head a little, he saw his vaulted brown belly, sectioned by arch-shaped ribs, to whose dome the cover, about to slide off completely, could barely cling. His many legs, pitifully thin compared with the size of the rest of him, were waving helplessly before his eyes.

"What's happened to me?" he thought. It was no dream. His room, a regular human room, only a little on the small side, lay quiet between the four familiar walls. Over the table, on which an unpacked line of fabric samples was all spread out—Samsa was a traveling salesman—hung the picture which he had recently cut out of a glossy magazine and lodged in a pretty gilt frame. It showed a lady done up in a fur hat and a fur boa,[2] sitting upright and raising up against the viewer a heavy fur muff in which her whole forearm had disappeared.

Gregor's eyes then turned to the window, and the overcast weather—he could hear raindrops hitting against the metal window ledge—completely depressed him. "How about going back to sleep for a few minutes and forgetting all this nonsense," he thought, but that was completely impracticable, since he was used to sleeping on his right side and in his present state could not get into that position. No matter how hard he threw himself onto his right side, he always rocked onto his back again. He must have tried it a hundred times, closing his eyes so as not to have to see his squirming legs, and stopped only when he began to feel a slight, dull pain in his side, which he had never felt before.

"Oh God," he thought, "what a grueling job I've picked! Day in, day out—on the road. The upset of doing business is much worse than the actual business in the home office, and, besides, I've got the torture of traveling, worrying about changing trains, eating miserable food at all hours, constantly seeing new faces, no relationships that last or get more intimate. To the devil with it all!" He feld a slight itching up on top of his belly; shoved himself slowly on his back closer to the bedpost, so as to be able to lift his head better; found the itchy spot, studded with small white dots which he had no idea what to make of; and wanted to touch the spot with one of his legs but immediately pulled it back, for the contact sent a cold shiver through him.

He slid back again into his original position. "This getting up so early," he thought, "makes anyone a complete idiot. Human beings have to have their sleep. Other traveling salesmen live like harem women. For instance, when I go back to the hotel before lunch to write up the business I've done, these gentlemen are just having breakfast. That's all I'd have to try with my boss; I'd be fired on the spot. Anyway, who knows if that wouldn't be a very good thing for me. If I didn't hold back for my parents' sake, I would have quit long ago, I would have marched up to the boss and spoken my piece from the bottom of my heart. He would have fallen off the desk! It is funny, too, the way he sits on the desk and talks down from the heights to the employees, especially when they have to come right up close on account of the boss's being hard of hearing. Well, I haven't given up hope completely; once I've gotten the money together to pay off my parents' debt to him—that will probably take another

1. Translated by Stanley Corngold.

2. A long, thin scarf made of feathers or fur that women wear around their necks or shoulders.

five or six years—I'm going to do it without fail. Then I'm going to make the big break. But for the time being I'd better get up, since my train leaves at five."

And he looked over at the alarm clock, which was ticking on the chest of drawers. "God Almighty!" he thought. It was six-thirty, the hands were quietly moving forward, it was actually past the half-hour, it was already nearly a quarter to. Could it be that the alarm hadn't gone off? You could see from the bed that it was set correctly for four o'clock; it certainly had gone off, too. Yes, but was it possible to sleep quietly through a ringing that made the furniture shake? Well, he certainly hadn't slept quietly, but probably all the more soundly for that. But what should he do now? The next train left at seven o'clock; to make it he would have to hurry like a madman, and the line of samples wasn't packed yet, and he himself didn't feel especially fresh and ready to march around. And even if he did make the train, he could not avoid getting it from the boss, because the messenger boy had been waiting at the five-o'clock train and would have long ago reported his not showing up. He was a tool of the boss, without brains or backbone. What if he were to say he was sick? But that would be extremely embarrassing and suspicious because during his five years with the firm Gregor had not been sick even once. The boss would be sure to come with the health-insurance doctor, blame his parents for their lazy son, and cut off all excuses by quoting the health-insurance doctor, for whom the world consisted of people who were completely healthy but afraid to work. And, besides, in this case would he be so very wrong? In fact, Gregor felt fine, with the exception of his drowsiness, which was really unnecessary after sleeping so late, and he even had a ravenous appetite.

Just as he was thinking all this over at top speed, without being able to decide to get out of bed—the alarm clock had just struck a quarter to seven—he heard a cautious knocking at the door next to the head of his bed. "Gregor," someone called—it was his mother—"it's a quarter to seven. Didn't you want to catch the train?" What a soft voice! Gregor was shocked to hear his own voice answering, unmistakably his own voice, true, but in which, as if from below, an insistent distressed chirping intruded, which left the clarity of his words intact only for a moment really, before so badly garbling them as they carried that no one could be sure if he had heard right. Gregor had wanted to answer in detail and to explain everything, but given the circumstances, confined himself to saying, "Yes, yes, thanks, Mother, I'm just getting up." The wooden door must have prevented the change in Gregor's voice from being noticed outside, because his mother was satisfied with this explanation and shuffled off. But their little exchange had made the rest of the family aware that, contrary to expectations, Gregor was still in the house, and already his father was knocking on one of the side doors, feebly but with his fist. "Gregor, Gregor," he called, "what's going on?" And after a little while he called again in a deeper, warning voice, "Gregor! Gregor!" At the other side door, however, his sister moaned gently, "Gregor? Is something the matter with you? Do you want anything?" Toward both sides Gregor answered: "I'm all ready," and made an effort, by meticulous pronunciation and by inserting long pauses between individual words, to eliminate everything from his voice that might betray him. His father went back to his breakfast, but his sister whispered, "Gregor, open up, I'm pleading with you." But Gregor had absolutely no intention of opening the door and complimented himself instead on the precaution he had adopted from his business trips, of locking all the doors during the night even at home.

First of all he wanted to get up quietly, without any excitement; get dressed; and, the main thing, have breakfast, and only then think about what to do next, for he saw clearly that in bed he would never think things through to a rational conclusion. He remembered how even in the past he had often felt some kind of slight pain, possibly caused by lying in an uncomfortable position, which, when he got up, turned out to be purely imaginary, and he was eager to see how today's fantasy would gradually fade away. That the change in his voice was nothing more than the first sign of a bad cold, an occupational ailment of the traveling salesman, he had no doubt in the least.

It was very easy to throw off the cover; all he had to do was puff himself up a little, and it fell off by itself. But after this, things got difficult, especially since he was so unusually broad. He would have needed hands and arms to lift himself up, but instead of that he had only his numerous little legs, which were in every different kind of perpetual motion and which, besides, he could not control. If he wanted to bend one, the first thing that happened was that it stretched itself out; and if he finally succeeded in getting this leg to do what he wanted, all the others in the meantime, as if set free, began to work in the most intensely painful agitation. "Just don't stay in bed being useless," Gregor said to himself.

First he tried to get out of bed with the lower part of his body, but this lower part—which by the way he had not seen yet and which he could not form a clear picture of—proved too difficult to budge; it was taking so long; and when finally, almost out of his mind, he lunged forward with all his force, without caring, he had picked the wrong direction and slammed himself violently against the lower bedpost, and the searing pain he felt taught him that exactly the lower part of his body was, for the moment anyway, the most sensitive.

He therefore tried to get the upper part of his body out of bed first and warily turned his head toward the edge of the bed. This worked easily, and in spite of its width and weight, the mass of his body finally followed, slowly, the movement of his head. But when at last he stuck his head over the edge of the bed into the air, he got too scared to continue any further, since if he finally let himself fall in this position, it would be a miracle if he didn't injure his head. And just now he had better not for the life of him lose consciousness; he would rather stay in bed.

But when, once again, after the same exertion, he lay in his original position, sighing, and again watched his little legs struggling, if possible more fiercely, with each other and saw no way of bringing peace and order into this mindless motion, he again told himself that it was impossible for him to stay in bed and that the most rational thing was to make any sacrifice for even the smallest hope of freeing himself from the bed. But at the same time he did not forget to remind himself occasionally that thinking things over calmly—indeed, as calmly as possible—was much better than jumping to desperate decisions. At such moments he fixed his eyes as sharply as possible on the window, but unfortunately there was little confidence and cheer to be gotten from the view of the morning fog, which shrouded even the other side of the narrow street. "Seven o'clock already," he said to himself as the alarm clock struck again, "seven o'clock already and still such a fog." And for a little while he lay quietly, breathing shallowly, as if expecting, perhaps, from the complete silence the return of things to the way they really and naturally were.

But then he said to himself, "Before it strikes a quarter past seven, I must be completely out of bed without fail. Anyway, by that time someone from the firm will be here to find out where I am, since the office opens before seven." And now he started rocking the complete length of his body out of the bed with a smooth rhythm. If he let himself topple out of bed in this way, his head, which on falling he planned to lift up sharply, would presumably remain unharmed. His back seemed to be hard;

nothing was likely to happen to it when it fell onto the carpet. His biggest misgiving came from his concern about the loud crash that was bound to occur and would probably create, if not terror, at least anxiety behind all the doors. But that would have to be risked.

When Gregor's body already projected halfway out of bed—the new method was more of a game than a struggle, he only had to keep on rocking and jerking himself along—he thought how simple everything would be if he could get some help. Two strong persons—he thought of his father and the maid—would have been completely sufficient; they would only have had to shove their arms under his arched back, in this way scoop him off the bed, bend down with their burden, and then just be careful and patient while he managed to swing himself down onto the floor, where his little legs would hopefully acquire some purpose. Well, leaving out the fact that the doors were locked, should he really call for help? In spite of all his miseries, he could not repress a smile at this thought.

He was already so far along that when he rocked more strongly he could hardly keep his balance, and very soon he would have to commit himself, because in five minutes it would be a quarter past seven—when the doorbell rang. "It's someone from the firm," he said to himself and almost froze, while his little legs only danced more quickly. For a moment everything remained quiet. "They're not going to answer," Gregor said to himself, captivated by some senseless hope. But then, of course, the maid went to the door as usual with her firm stride and opened up. Gregor only had to hear the visitor's first word of greeting to know who it was—the office manager himself. Why was only Gregor condemned to work for a firm where at the slightest omission they immediately suspected the worst? Were all employees louts without exception, wasn't there a single loyal, dedicated worker among them who, when he had not fully utilized a few hours of the morning for the firm, was driven half-mad by pangs of conscience and was actually unable to get out of bed? Really, wouldn't it have been enough to send one of the apprentices to find out—if this prying were absolutely necessary—did the manager himself have to come, and did the whole innocent family have to be shown in this way that the investigation of this suspicious affair could be entrusted only to the intellect of the manager? And more as a result of the excitement produced in Gregor by these thoughts than as a result of any real decision, he swung himself out of bed with all his might. There was a loud thump, but it was not a real crash. The fall was broken a little by the carpet, and Gregor's back was more elastic than he had thought, which explained the not very noticeable muffled sound. Only he had not held his head carefully enough and hit it; he turned it and rubbed it on the carpet in anger and pain.

"Something fell in there," said the manager in the room on the left. Gregor tried to imagine whether something like what had happened to him today could one day happen even to the manager; you really had to grant the possibility. But as if in rude reply to this question, the manager took a few decisive steps in the next room and made his patent leather boots creak. From the room on the right his sister whispered, to inform Gregor, "Gregor, the manager is here." "I know," Gregor said to himself; but he did not dare raise his voice enough for his sister to hear.

"Gregor," his father now said from the room on the left, "the manager has come and wants to be informed why you didn't catch the early train. We don't know what we should say to him. Besides, he wants to speak to you personally. So please open the door. He will certainly be so kind as to excuse the disorder of the room." "Good morning, Mr. Samsa," the manager called in a friendly voice. "There's something the matter with him," his mother said to the manager while his father was still at the door, talking. "Believe me, sir, there's something the matter with him. Otherwise how would Gregor have missed a train? That boy has nothing on his mind but the business. It's almost begun to rile me that he never goes out nights. He's been back in the city for eight days now, but every night he's been home. He sits there with us at the table, quietly reading the paper or studying timetables. It's already a distraction for him when he's busy working with his fretsaw.[3] For instance, in the span of two or three evenings he carved a little frame. You'll be amazed how pretty it is; it's hanging inside his room. You'll see it right away when Gregor opens the door. You know, I'm glad that you've come, sir. We would never have gotten Gregor to open the door by ourselves; he's so stubborn. And there's certainly something wrong with him, even though he said this morning there wasn't." "I'm coming right away," said Gregor slowly and deliberately, not moving in order not to miss a word of the conversation. "I haven't any other explanation myself," said the manager. "I hope it's nothing serious. On the other hand, I must say that we businessmen—fortunately or unfortunately, whichever you prefer—very often simply have to overcome a slight indisposition for business reasons." "So can the manager come in now?" asked his father, impatient, and knocked on the door again. "No," said Gregor. In the room on the left there was an embarrassing silence; in the room on the right his sister began to sob.

Why didn't his sister go in to the others? She had probably just got out of bed and not even started to get dressed. Then what was she crying about? Because he didn't get up and didn't let the manager in, because he was in danger of losing his job, and because then the boss would start hounding his parents about the old debts? For the time being, certainly, her worries were unnecessary. Gregor was still here and hadn't the slightest intention of letting the family down. True, at the moment he was lying on the carpet, and no one knowing his condition could seriously have expected him to let the manager in. But just because of this slight discourtesy, for which an appropriate excuse would easily be found later on, Gregor could not simply be dismissed. And to Gregor it seemed much more sensible to leave him alone now than to bother him with crying and persuasion. But it was just the uncertainty that was tormenting the others and excused their behavior.

"Mr. Samsa," the manager now called, raising his voice, "what's the matter? You barricade yourself in your room, answer only 'yes' and 'no,' cause your parents serious, unnecessary worry, and you neglect—I mention this only in passing—your duties to the firm in a really shocking manner. I am speaking here in the name of your parents and of your employer and ask you in all seriousness for an immediate, clear explanation. I'm amazed, amazed. I thought I knew you to be a quiet, reasonable person, and now you suddenly seem to want to start strutting about, flaunting strange whims. The head of the firm did suggest to me this morning a possible explanation for your tardiness—it concerned the cash payments recently entrusted to you—but really, I practically gave my word of honor that this explanation could not be right. But now, seeing your incomprehensible obstinacy, I am about to lose even the slightest desire to stick up for you in any way at all. And your job is not the most secure. Originally I intended to tell you all this in private, but since you make me waste my time here for nothing, I don't see why your parents shouldn't hear too. Your performance of late has been very unsatisfactory; I know it is not the best season for doing business, we

3. A small fine-toothed saw that is used to cut creative, decorative patterns in wood.

all recognize that; but a season for not doing any business, there is no such thing, Mr. Samsa, such a thing cannot be tolerated."

"But, sir," cried Gregor, beside himself, in his excitement forgetting everything else, "I'm just opening up, in a minute. A slight indisposition, a dizzy spell, prevented me from getting up. I'm still in bed. But I already feel fine again. I'm just getting out of bed. Just be patient for a minute! I'm not as well as I thought yet. But really I'm fine. How something like this could just take a person by surprise! Only last night I was fine, my parents can tell you, or wait, last night I already had a slight premonition. They must have been able to tell by looking at me. Why didn't I report it to the office! But you always think that you'll get over a sickness without staying home. Sir! Spare my parents! There's no basis for any of the accusations that you're making against me now; no one has ever said a word to me about them. Perhaps you haven't seen the last orders I sent in. Anyway, I'm still going on the road with the eight o'clock train; these few hours of rest have done me good. Don't let me keep you, sir. I'll be at the office myself right away, and be so kind as to tell them this, and give my respects to the head of the firm."

And while Gregor hastily blurted all this out, hardly knowing what he was saying, he had easily approached the chest of drawers, probably as a result of the practice he had already gotten in bed, and now he tried to raise himself up against it. He actually intended to open the door, actually present himself and speak to the manager; he was eager to find out what the others, who were now so anxious to see him, would say at the sight of him. If they were shocked, then Gregor had no further responsibility and could be calm. But if they took everything calmly, then he, too, had no reason to get excited and could, if he hurried, actually be at the station by eight o'clock. At first he slid off the polished chest of drawers a few times, but at last, giving himself a final push, he stood upright; he no longer paid any attention to the pains in his abdomen, no matter how much they were burning. Now he let himself fall against the back of a nearby chair, clinging to its slats with his little legs. But by doing this he had gotten control of himself and fell silent, since he could now listen to what the manager was saying.

"Did you understand a word?" the manager was asking his parents. "He isn't trying to make fools of us, is he?" "My God," cried his mother, already in tears, "maybe he's seriously ill, and here we are, torturing him. Grete! Grete!" she then cried. "Mother?" called his sister from the other side. They communicated by way of Gregor's room. "Go to the doctor's immediately. Gregor is sick. Hurry, get the doctor. Did you just hear Gregor talking?" "That was the voice of an animal," said the manager, in a tone conspicuously soft compared with the mother's yelling. "Anna! Anna!" the father called through the foyer into the kitchen, clapping his hands, "get a locksmith right away!" And already the two girls were running with rustling skirts through the foyer—how could his sister have gotten dressed so quickly?—and tearing open the door to the apartment. The door could not be heard slamming; they had probably left it open, as is the custom in homes where a great misfortune has occurred.[4]

But Gregor had become much calmer. It was true that they no longer understood his words, though they had seemed clear enough to him, clearer than before, probably because his ear had grown accustomed to them. But still, the others now believed that there was something the matter with him and were ready to help him. The assurance

4. Kafka is referring to a common popular belief that opening a house's doors and windows after a stroke of ill fortune, especially a death, will help to clear bad influences and spirits from the residence.

and confidence with which the first measures had been taken did him good. He felt integrated into human society once again and hoped for marvelous, amazing feats from both the doctor and the locksmith, without really distinguishing sharply between them. In order to make his voice as clear as possible for the crucial discussions that were approaching, he cleared his throat a little—taking pains, of course, to do so in a very muffled manner, since this noise, too, might sound different from human coughing, a thing he no longer trusted himself to decide. In the next room, meanwhile, everything had become completely still. Perhaps his parents were sitting at the table with the manager, whispering; perhaps they were all leaning against the door and listening.

Gregor slowly lugged himself toward the door, pushing the chair in front of him, then let go of it, threw himself against the door, held himself upright against it—the pads on the bottom of his little legs exuded a little sticky substance—and for a moment rested there from the exertion. But then he got started turning the key in the lock with his mouth. Unfortunately it seemed that he had no real teeth—what was he supposed to grip the key with?—but in compensation his jaws, of course, were very strong; with their help he actually got the key moving and paid no attention to the fact that he was undoubtedly hurting himself in some way, for a brown liquid came out of his mouth, flowed over the key, and dripped onto the floor. "Listen," said the manager in the next room, "he's turning the key." This was great encouragement to Gregor; but everyone should have cheered him on, his father and mother too. "Go, Gregor," they should have called, "keep going, at that lock, harder, harder!" And in the delusion that they were all following his efforts with suspense, he clamped his jaws madly on the key with all the strength he could muster. Depending on the progress of the key, he danced around the lock; holding himself upright only by his mouth, he clung to the key, as the situation demanded, or pressed it down again with the whole weight of his body. The clearer click of the lock as it finally snapped back literally woke Gregor up. With a sigh of relief he said to himself, "So I didn't need the locksmith after all," and laid his head down on the handle in order to open wide one wing of the double doors.

Since he had to use this method of opening the door, it was really opened very wide while he himself was still invisible. He first had to edge slowly around the one wing of the door, and do so very carefully if he was not to fall flat on his back just before entering. He was still busy with this difficult maneuver and had no time to pay attention to anything else when he heard the manager burst out with a loud "Oh!"—it sounded like a rush of wind—and now he could see him, standing closest to the door, his hand pressed over his open mouth, slowly backing away, as if repulsed by an invisible, unrelenting force. His mother—in spite of the manager's presence she stood with her hair still unbraided from the night, sticking out in all directions—first looked at his father with her hands clasped, then took two steps toward Gregor, and sank down in the midst of her skirts spreading out around her, her face completely hidden on her breast. With a hostile expression his father clenched his fist, as if to drive Gregor back into his room, then looked uncertainly around the living room, shielded his eyes with his hands, and sobbed with heaves of his powerful chest.

Now Gregor did not enter the room after all but leaned against the inside of the firmly bolted wing of the door, so that only half his body was visible and his head above it, cocked to one side and peeping out at the others. In the meantime it had grown much lighter; across the street one could see clearly a section of the endless, grayish-black building opposite—it was a hospital—with its regular windows starkly piercing the façade; the rain was still coming down, but only in large, separately visible drops that were also pelting the ground literally one at a time. The breakfast dishes were laid out lavishly on the table, since for his father breakfast was the most important meal of the day, which he would prolong for hours while reading various newspapers. On the wall directly opposite hung a photograph of Gregor from his army days, in a lieutenant's uniform, his hand on his sword, a carefree smile on his lips, demanding respect for his bearing and his rank. The door to the foyer was open, and since the front door was open too, it was possible to see out onto the landing and the top of the stairs going down.

"Well," said Gregor—and he was thoroughly aware of being the only one who had kept calm—"I'll get dressed right away, pack up my samples, and go. Will you, will you please let me go? Now, sir, you see, I'm not stubborn and I'm willing to work; traveling is a hardship, but without it I couldn't live. Where are you going, sir? To the office? Yes? Will you give an honest report of everything? A man might find for a moment that he was unable to work, but that's exactly the right time to remember his past accomplishments and to consider that later on, when the obstacle has been removed, he's bound to work all the harder and more efficiently. I'm under so many obligations to the head of the firm, as you know very well. Besides, I also have my parents and my sister to worry about. I'm in a tight spot, but I'll also work my way out again. Don't make things harder for me than they already are. Stick up for me in the office, please. Traveling salesmen aren't well liked there, I know. People think they make a fortune leading the gay life. No one has any particular reason to rectify this prejudice. But you, sir, you have a better perspective on things than the rest of the office, an even better perspective, just between the two of us, than the head of the firm himself, who in his capacity as owner easily lets his judgment be swayed against an employee. And you also know very well that the traveling salesman, who is out of the office practically the whole year round, can so easily become the victim of gossip, coincidences, and unfounded accusations, against which he's completely unable to defend himself, since in most cases he knows nothing at all about them except when he returns exhausted from a trip, and back home gets to suffer on his own person the grim consequences, which can no longer be traced back to their causes. Sir, don't go away without a word to tell me you think I'm at least partly right!"

But at Gregor's first words the manager had already turned away and with curled lips looked back at Gregor only over his twitching shoulder. And during Gregor's speech he did not stand still for a minute but, without letting Gregor out of his sight, backed toward the door, yet very gradually, as if there were some secret prohibition against leaving the room. He was already in the foyer, and from the sudden movement with which he took his last step from the living room, one might have thought he had just burned the sole of his foot. In the foyer, however, he stretched his right hand far out toward the staircase, as if nothing less than an unearthly deliverance were awaiting him there.

Gregor realized that he must on no account let the manager go away in this mood if his position in the firm were not to be jeopardized in the extreme. His parents did not understand this too well; in the course of the years they had formed the conviction that Gregor was set for life in this firm; and furthermore, they were so preoccupied with their immediate troubles that they had lost all consideration for the future. But Gregor had this forethought. The manager must be detained, calmed down, convinced, and finally won over; Gregor's and the family's future depended on it! If only his sister had been there! She was perceptive; she had already begun to cry when Gregor was still lying calmly on his back. And certainly the manager, this ladies' man, would have listened to her; she would have shut the front door and in the foyer talked him out of his scare. But his sister was not there; Gregor had to handle the situation himself. And without stopping to realize that he had no idea what his new faculties of movement were, and without stopping to realize either that his speech had possibly—indeed, probably—not been understood again, he let go of the wing of the door; he shoved himself through the opening, intending to go to the manager, who was already on the landing, ridiculously holding onto the banisters with both hands; but groping for support, Gregor immediately fell down with a little cry onto his numerous little legs. This had hardly happened when for the first time that morning he had a feeling of physical well-being; his little legs were on firm ground; they obeyed him completely, as he noted to his joy; they even strained to carry him away wherever he wanted to go; and he already believed that final recovery from all his sufferings was imminent. But at that very moment, as he lay on the floor rocking with repressed motion, not far from his mother and just opposite her, she, who had seemed so completely self-absorbed, all at once jumped up, her arms stretched wide, her fingers spread, and cried, "Help, for God's sake, help!" held her head bent as if to see Gregor better, but inconsistently darted madly backward instead; had forgotten that the table laden with the breakfast dishes stood behind her; sat down on it hastily, as if her thoughts were elsewhere, when she reached it; and did not seem to notice at all that near her the big coffeepot had been knocked over and coffee was pouring in a steady stream onto the rug.

"Mother, Mother," said Gregor softly and looked up at her. For a minute the manager had completely slipped his mind; on the other hand at the sight of the spilling coffee he could not resist snapping his jaws several times in the air. At this his mother screamed once more, fled from the table, and fell into the arms of his father, who came rushing up to her. But Gregor had no time now for his parents; the manager was already on the stairs; with his chin on the banister, he was taking a last look back. Gregor was off to a running start, to be as sure as possible of catching up with him; the manager must have suspected something like this, for he leaped down several steps and disappeared; but still he shouted "Agh," and the sound carried through the whole staircase. Unfortunately the manager's flight now seemed to confuse his father completely, who had been relatively calm until now, for instead of running after the manager himself, or at least not hindering Gregor in his pursuit, he seized in his right hand the manager's cane, which had been left behind on a chair with his hat and overcoat, picked up in his left hand a heavy newspaper from the table, and stamping his feet, started brandishing the cane and the newspaper to drive Gregor back into his room. No plea of Gregor's helped, no plea was even understood; however humbly he might turn his head, his father merely stamped his feet more forcefully. Across the room his mother had thrown open a window in spite of the cool weather, and leaning out, she buried her face, far outside the window, in her hands. Between the alley and the staircase a strong draft was created, the window curtains blew in, the newspapers on the table rustled, single sheets fluttered across the floor. Pitilessly his father came on, hissing like a wild man. Now Gregor had not had any practice at all walking in reverse, it was really very slow going. If Gregor had only been allowed to turn around, he could have gotten into his room right away, but he was afraid to make his father impatient by this time-consuming gyration, and at any minute the cane in his father's hand threatened to come down on his back or his head with a deadly blow. Finally, however, Gregor had no choice, for he noticed with horror that in reverse he could not even keep going in one direction; and so, incessantly throwing uneasy side-glances at his father, he began to turn around as quickly as possible, in reality turning only very slowly. Perhaps his father realized his good intentions, for he did not interfere with him; instead, he even now and then directed the maneuver from afar with the tip of his cane. If only his father did not keep making this intolerable hissing sound! It made Gregor lose his head completely. He had almost finished the turn when—his mind continually on this hissing—he made a mistake and even started turning back around to his original position. But when he had at last successfully managed to get his head in front of the opened door, it turned out that his body was too broad to get through as it was. Of course in his father's present state of mind it did not even remotely occur to him to open the other wing of the door in order to give Gregor enough room to pass through. He had only the fixed idea that Gregor must return to his room as quickly as possible. He would never have allowed the complicated preliminaries Gregor needed to go through in order to stand up on one end and perhaps in this way fit through the door. Instead he drove Gregor on, as if there were no obstacle, with exceptional loudness; the voice behind Gregor did not sound like that of only a single father; now this was really no joke anymore, and Gregor forced himself—come what may—into the doorway. One side of his body rose up, he lay lop-sided in the opening, one of his flanks was scraped raw, ugly blotches marred the white door, soon he got stuck and could not have budged any more by himself, his little legs on one side dangled tremblingly in midair, those on the other were painfully crushed against the floor—when from behind his father gave him a hard shove, which was truly his salvation, and bleeding profusely, he flew far into his room. The door was slammed shut with the cane, then at last everything was quiet.

2

It was already dusk when Gregor awoke from his deep, comalike sleep. Even if he had not been disturbed, he would certainly not have woken up much later, for he felt that he had rested and slept long enough, but it seemed to him that a hurried step and a cautious shutting of the door leading to the foyer had awakened him. The light of the electric street-lamps lay in pallid streaks on the ceiling and on the upper parts of the furniture, but underneath, where Gregor was, it was dark. Groping clumsily with his antennae, which he was only now beginning to appreciate, he slowly dragged himself toward the door to see what had been happening there. His left side felt like one single long, unpleasantly tautening scar, and he actually had to limp on his two rows of legs. Besides, one little leg had been seriously injured in the course of the morning's events—it was almost a miracle that only one had been injured—and dragged along lifelessly.

Only after he got to the door did he notice what had really attracted him—the smell of something to eat. For there stood a bowl filled with fresh milk, in which small slices of white bread were floating. He could almost have laughed for joy, since he was even hungrier than he had been in the morning, and he immediately dipped his head into the milk, almost to over his eyes. But he soon drew it back again in disappointment; not only because he had difficulty eating on account of the soreness in his left side—and he could eat only if his whole panting body cooperated—but because he didn't like the milk at all, although it used to be his favorite drink, and that was certainly why his sister had put it in the room; in fact, he turned away from the bowl almost with repulsion and crawled back to the middle of the room.

In the living room, as Gregor saw through the crack in the door, the gas had been lit, but while at this hour of the day his father was in the habit of reading the afternoon newspaper in a loud voice to his mother and sometimes to his sister too, now there wasn't a sound. Well, perhaps this custom of reading aloud, which his sister was always telling him and writing him about, had recently been discontinued altogether. But in all the other rooms too it was just as still, although the apartment certainly was not empty. "What a quiet life the family has been leading," Gregor said to himself, and while he stared rigidly in front of him into the darkness, he felt very proud that he had been able to provide such a life in so nice an apartment for his parents and his sister. But what now if all the peace, the comfort, the contentment were to come to a horrible end? In order not to get involved in such thoughts, Gregor decided to keep moving, and he crawled up and down the room.

During the long evening, first one of the side doors and then the other was opened a small crack and quickly shut again; someone had probably had the urge to come in and then had had second thoughts. Gregor now settled into position right by the living-room door, determined somehow to get the hesitating visitor to come in, or at least to find out who it might be; but the door was not opened again, and Gregor waited in vain. In the morning, when the doors had been locked, everyone had wanted to come in; now that he had opened one of the doors and the others had evidently been opened during the day, no one came in, and now the keys were even inserted on the outside.

It was late at night when the light finally went out in the living room, and now it was easy for Gregor to tell that his parents and his sister had stayed up so long, since, as he could distinctly hear, all three were now retiring on tiptoe. Certainly no one would come in to Gregor until the morning; and so he had ample time to consider undisturbed how best to rearrange his life. But the empty high-ceilinged room in which he was forced to lie flat on the floor made him nervous, without his being able to tell why—since it was, after all, the room in which be had lived for the past five years—and turning half unconsciously and not without a slight feeling of shame, he scuttled under the couch where, although his back was a little crushed and he could not raise his head any more, he immediately felt very comfortable and was only sorry that his body was too wide to go completely under the couch.

There he stayed the whole night, which he spent partly in a sleepy trance, from which hunger pangs kept waking him with a start, partly in worries and vague hopes, all of which, however, led to the conclusion that for the time being he would have to lie low and, by being patient and showing his family every possible consideration, help them bear the inconvenience which he simply had to cause them in his present condition.

Early in the morning—it was still almost night—Gregor had the opportunity of testing the strength of the resolutions he had just made, for his sister, almost fully dressed, opened the door from the foyer and looked in eagerly. She did not see him right away, but when she caught sight of him under the couch—God, he had to be somewhere, he couldn't just fly away—she became so frightened that she lost control of herself and slammed the door shut again. But, as if she felt sorry for her behavior, she immediately opened the door again and came in on tiptoe, as if she were visiting someone seriously ill or perhaps even a stranger. Gregor had pushed his head forward just to the edge of the couch and was watching her. Would she notice that he had left the milk standing, and not because he hadn't been hungry, and would she bring in a dish of something he'd like better? If she were not going to do it of her own free will, he would rather starve than call it to her attention, although, really, he felt an enormous urge to shoot out from under the couch, throw himself at his sister's feet, and beg her for something good to eat. But his sister noticed at once, to her astonishment, that the bowl was still full, only a little milk was spilled around it; she picked it up immediately—not with her bare hands, of course, but with a rag—and carried it out. Gregor was extremely curious to know what she would bring him instead, and he racked his brains on the subject. But he would never have been able to guess what his sister, in the goodness of her heart, actually did. To find out his likes and dislikes, she brought him a wide assortment of things, all spread out on an old newspapers: old, half-rotten vegetables; bones left over from the evening meal, caked with congealed white sauce; some raisins and almonds; a piece of cheese, which two days before Gregor had declared inedible; a plain slice of bread, a slice of bread and butter, and one with butter and salt. In addition to all this she put down some water in the bowl apparently permanently earmarked for Gregor's use. And out of a sense of delicacy, since she knew that Gregor would not eat in front of her, she left hurriedly and even turned the key, just so that Gregor should know that he might make himself as comfortable as he wanted. Gregor's legs began whirring now that he was going to eat. Besides, his bruises must have completely healed, since he no longer felt any handicap, and marveling at this he thought how, over a month ago, he had cut his finger very slightly with a knife and how this wound was still hurting him only the day before yesterday. "Have I become less sensitive?" he thought, already sucking greedily at the cheese, which had immediately and forcibly attracted him ahead of all the other dishes. One right after the other, and with eyes streaming with tears of contentment, he devoured the cheese, the vegetables, and the sauce; the fresh foods, on the other hand, he did not care for; he couldn't even stand their smell and even dragged the things he wanted to eat a bit farther away. He had finished with everything long since and was just lying lazily at the same spot when his sister slowly turned the key as a sign for him to withdraw. That immediately startled him, although he was almost asleep, and he scuttled under the couch again. But it took great self-control for him to stay under the couch even for the short time his sister was in the room, since his body had become a little bloated from the heavy meal, and in his cramped position he could hardly breathe. In between slight attacks of suffocation he watched with bulging eyes as his unsuspecting sister took a broom and swept up, not only his leavings, but even the foods which Gregor had left completely untouched—as if they too were no longer usable—and dumping everything hastily into a pail, which she covered with a wooden lid, she carried everything out. She had hardly turned her back when Gregor came out from under the couch, stretching and puffing himself up.

This, then, was the way Gregor was fed each day, once in the morning, when his parents and the maid were still asleep, and a second time in the afternoon after everyone had had dinner, for then his parents took a short nap again, and the maid could be sent out by his sister on some errand. Certainly they did not want him to starve either, but perhaps they would not have been able to stand knowing any more about his meals than from hearsay, or perhaps his sister wanted to spare them even what was possibly only a minor torment, for really, they were suffering enough as it was.

Gregor could not find out what excuses had been made to get rid of the doctor and the locksmith on that first morning, for since the others could not understand what he said, it did not occur to any of them, not even to his sister, that he could understand what they said, and so he had to be satisfied, when his sister was in the room, with only occasionally hearing her sighs and appeals to the saints. It was only later, when she had begun to get used to everything—there could never, of course, be any question of a complete adjustment—that Gregor sometimes caught a remark which was meant to be friendly or could be interpreted as such. "Oh, he liked what he had today," she would say when Gregor had tucked away a good helping, and in the opposite case, which gradually occurred more and more frequently, she used to say, almost sadly, "He's left everything again."

But if Gregor could not get any news directly, he overheard a great deal from the neighboring rooms, and as soon as he heard voices, he would immediately run to the door concerned and press his whole body against it. Especially in the early days, there was no conversation that was not somehow about him, if only implicitly. For two whole days there were family consultations at every mealtime about how they should cope; this was also the topic of discussion between meals, for at least two members of the family were always at home, since no one probably wanted to stay home alone and it was impossible to leave the apartment completely empty. Besides, on the very first day the maid—it was not completely clear what and how much she knew of what had happened—had begged his mother on bended knees to dismiss her immediately; and when she said goodbye a quarter of an hour later, she thanked them in tears for the dismissal, as if for the greatest favor that had ever been done to her in this house, and made a solemn vow, without anyone asking her for it, not to give anything away to anyone.

Now his sister, working with her mother, had to do the cooking too; of course that did not cause her much trouble, since they hardly ate anything. Gregor was always hearing one of them pleading in vain with one of the others to eat and getting no answer except, "Thanks, I've had enough," or something similar. They did not seem to drink anything either. His sister often asked her father if he wanted any beer and gladly offered to go out for it herself; and when he did not answer, she said, in order to remove any hesitation on his part, that she could also send the janitor's wife to get it, but then his father finally answered with a definite "No," and that was the end of that.

In the course of the very first day his father explained the family's financial situation and prospects to both the mother and the sister. From time to time he got up from the table to get some kind of receipt or notebook out of the little strongbox he had rescued from the collapse of his business five years before. Gregor heard him open the complicated lock and secure it again after taking out what he had been looking for. These explanations by his father were to some extent the first pleasant news Gregor had heard since his imprisonment. He had always believed that his father had not been able to save a penny from the business, at least his father had never told him anything to the contrary, and Gregor, for his part, had never asked him any questions. In those days Gregor's sole concern had been to do everything in his power to make the family forget as quickly as possible the business disaster which had plunged everyone into a state of total despair. And so he had begun to work with special ardor and had risen almost overnight from stock clerk to traveling salesman, which of course had opened up very different moneymaking possibilities, and in no time his successes on the job were transformed, by means of commissions, into hard cash that could be plunked down on the table at home in front of his astonished and delighted family. Those had been wonderful times, and they had never returned, at least not with the same glory, although later on Gregor earned enough money to meet the expenses of the entire family and actually did so. They had just gotten used to it, the family as well as Gregor, the money was received with thanks and given with pleasure, but no special feeling of warmth went with it anymore. Only his sister had remained close to Gregor, and it was his secret plan that she, who, unlike him, loved music and could play the violin movingly, should be sent next year to the Conservatory, regardless of the great expense involved, which could surely be made up for in some other way. Often during Gregor's short stays in the city, the Conservatory would come up in his conversations with his sister, but always merely as a beautiful dream which was not supposed to come true, and his parents were not happy to hear even these innocent allusions; but Gregor had very concrete ideas on the subject and he intended solemnly to announce his plan on Christmas Eve.

Thoughts like these, completely useless in his present state, went through his head as he stood glued to the door, listening. Sometimes out of general exhaustion he could not listen anymore and let his head bump carelessly against the door, but immediately pulled it back again, for even the slight noise he made by doing this had been heard in the next room and made them all lapse into silence. "What's he carrying on about in there now?" said his father after a while, obviously turning toward the door, and only then would the interrupted conversation gradually be resumed.

Gregor now learned in a thorough way—for his father was in the habit of often repeating himself in his explanations, partly because he himself had not dealt with these matters for a long time, partly, too, because his mother did not understand everything the first time around—that in spite of all their misfortunes a bit of capital, a very little bit, certainly, was still intact from the old days, which in the meantime had increased a little through the untouched interest. But besides that, the money Gregor had brought home every month—he had kept only a few dollars for himself—had never been completely used up and had accumulated into a tidy principal. Behind his door Gregor nodded emphatically, delighted at this unexpected foresight and thrift. Of course he actually could have paid off more of his father's debt to the boss with this extra money, and the day on which he could have gotten rid of his job would have been much closer, but now things were undoubtedly better the way his father had arranged them.

Now this money was by no means enough to let the family live off the interest; the principal was perhaps enough to support the family for one year, or at the most two, but that was all there was. So it was just a sum that really should not be touched and that had to be put away for a rainy day; but the money to live on would have to be earned. Now his father was still healthy, certainly, but he was an old man who had not worked for the past five years and who in any case could not be expected to undertake too much; during these five years, which were the first vacation of his hard-working yet unsuccessful life, he had gained a lot of weight and as a result had become fairly sluggish. And was his old mother now supposed to go out and earn money, when she suffered from asthma, when a walk through the apartment was already an ordeal for her, and when she spent every other day lying on the sofa under the open window, gasping for breath? And was his sister supposed to work—who for all her seventeen years was still a child and whom it would be such a pity to deprive of the life she had led until now, which had consisted of wearing pretty clothes, sleeping late, helping in the house, enjoying a few modest amusements, and above all playing the violin? At first, whenever the conversation turned to the necessity of earning money, Gregor would let go of the door and throw himself down on the cool leather sofa which stood beside it, for he felt hot with shame and grief.

Often he lay there the whole long night through, not sleeping a wink and only scrabbling on the leather for hours on end. Or, not balking at the huge effort of pushing an armchair to the window, he would crawl up to the window sill and, propped up in the chair, lean against the window, evidently in some sort of remembrance of the feeling of freedom he used to have from looking out the window. For, in fact, from day to day he saw things even a short distance away less and less distinctly; the hospital opposite, which he used to curse because he saw so much of it, was now completely beyond his range of vision, and if he had not been positive that he was living in Charlotte Street—a quiet but still very much a city street—he might have believed that he was looking out of his window into a desert where the gray sky and the gray earth were indistinguishably fused. It took his observant sister only twice to notice that his armchair was standing by the window for her to push the chair back to the same place by the window each time she had finished cleaning the room, and from then on she even left the inside casement of the window open.

If Gregor had only been able to speak to his sister and thank her for everything she had to do for him, he could have accepted her services more easily; as it was, they caused him pain. Of course his sister tried to ease the embarrassment of the whole situation as much as possible, and as time went on, she naturally managed it better and better, but in time Gregor, too, saw things much more clearly. Even the way she came in was terrible for him. Hardly had she entered the room than she would run straight to the window without taking time to close the door—though she was usually so careful to spare everyone the sight of Gregor's room—then tear open the casements with eager hands, almost as if she were suffocating, and remain for a little while at the window even in the coldest weather, breathing deeply. With this racing and crashing she frightened Gregor twice a day; the whole time he cowered under the couch, and yet he knew very well that she would certainly have spared him this if only she had found it possible to stand being in a room with him with the window closed.

One time—it must have been a month since Gregor's metamorphosis, and there was certainly no particular reason any more for his sister to be astonished at Gregor's appearance—she came a little earlier than usual and caught Gregor still looking out the window, immobile and so in an excellent position to be terrifying. It would not have surprised Gregor if she had not come in, because his position prevented her from immediately opening the window, but not only did she not come in, she even sprang back and locked the door; a stranger might easily have thought that Gregor had been lying in wait for her, wanting to bite her. Of course Gregor immediately hid under the couch, but he had to wait until noon before his sister came again, and she seemed much more uneasy than usual. He realized from this that the sight of him was still repulsive to her and was bound to remain repulsive to her in the future, and that she probably had to overcome a lot of resistance not to run away at the sight of even the small part of his body that jutted out from under the couch. So, to spare her even this sight, one day he carried the sheet on his back to the couch—the job took four hours—and arranged it in such a way that he was now completely covered up and his sister could not see him even when she stooped. If she had considered this sheet unnecessary, then of course she could have removed it, for it was clear enough that it could not be for his own pleasure that Gregor shut himself off altogether, but she left the sheet the way it was, and Gregor thought that he had even caught a grateful look when one time he cautiously lifted the sheet a little with his head in order to see how his sister was taking the new arrangement.

During the first two weeks, his parents could not bring themselves to come in to him, and often he heard them say how much they appreciated his sister's work, whereas until now they had frequently been annoyed with her because she had struck them as being a little useless. But now both of them, his father and his mother, often waited outside Gregor's room while his sister straightened it up, and as soon as she came out she had to tell them in great detail how the room looked, what Gregor had eaten, how he had behaved this time, and whether he had perhaps shown a little improvement. His mother, incidentally, began relatively soon to want to visit Gregor, but his father and his sister at first held her back with reasonable arguments to which

Gregor listened very attentively and of which he whole-heartedly approved. But later she had to be restrained by force, and then when she cried out, "Let me go to Gregor, he is my unfortunate boy! Don't you understand that I have to go to him?" Gregor thought that it might be a good idea after all if his mother did come in, not every day of course, but perhaps once a week; she could still do everything much better than his sister, who, for all her courage, was still only a child and in the final analysis had perhaps taken on such a difficult assignment only out of childish flightiness.

Gregor's desire to see his mother was soon fulfilled. During the day Gregor did not want to show himself at the window, if only out of consideration for his parents, but he couldn't crawl very far on his few square yards of floor space, either; he could hardly put up with just lying still even at night; eating soon stopped giving him the slightest pleasure, so, as a distraction, he adopted the habit of crawling crisscross over the walls and the ceiling. He especially liked hanging from the ceiling; it was completely different from lying on the floor; one could breathe more freely; a faint swinging sensation went through the body; and in the almost happy absent-mindedness which Gregor felt up there, it could happen to his own surprise that he let go and plopped onto the floor. But now, of course, he had much better control of his body than before and did not hurt himself even from such a big drop. His sister immediately noticed the new entertainment Gregor had discovered for himself—after all, he left behind traces of his sticky substance wherever he crawled—and so she got it into her head to make it possible for Gregor to crawl on an altogether wider scale by taking out the furniture which stood in his way—mainly the chest of drawers and the desk. But she was not able to do this by herself; she did not dare ask her father for help; the maid would certainly not have helped her, for although this girl, who was about sixteen, was bravely sticking it out after the previous cook had left, she had asked for the favor of locking herself in the kitchen at all times and of only opening the door on special request. So there was nothing left for his sister to do except to get her mother one day when her father was out. And his mother did come, with exclamations of excited joy, but she grew silent at the door of Gregor's room. First his sister looked to see, of course, that everything in the room was in order; only then did she let her mother come in. Hurrying as fast as he could, Gregor had pulled the sheet down lower still and pleated it more tightly—it really looked just like a sheet accidentally thrown over the couch. This time Gregor also refrained from spying from under the sheet; he renounced seeing his mother for the time being and was simply happy that she had come after all. "Come on, you can't see him," his sister said, evidently leading her mother in by the hand. Now Gregor could hear the two frail women moving the old chest of drawers—heavy for anyone—from its place and his sister insisting on doing the harder part of the job herself, ignoring the warnings of her mother, who was afraid that she would overexert herself. It went on for a long time. After struggling for a good quarter of an hour, his mother said that they had better leave the chest where it was, because, in the first place, it was too heavy, they would not finish before his father came, and with the chest in the middle of the room, Gregor would be completely barricaded; and, in the second place, it was not at all certain that they were doing Gregor a favor by removing his furniture. To her the opposite seemed to be the case; the sight of the bare wall was heart-breaking; and why shouldn't Gregor also have the same feeling, since he had been used to his furniture for so long and would feel abandoned in the empty room. "And doesn't it look," his mother concluded very softly—in fact she had been almost whispering the whole time, as if she wanted to avoid letting Gregor, whose exact whereabouts she did not know, hear even the sound of her voice, for she was convinced that he did not understand the words—"and doesn't it look as if by removing his furniture we were showing him that we have given up all hope of his getting better and are leaving him to his own devices without any consideration? I think the best thing would be to try to keep the room exactly the way it was before, so that when Gregor comes back to us again, he'll find everything unchanged and can forget all the more easily what's happened in the meantime."

When he heard his mother's words, Gregor realized that the monotony of family life, combined with the fact that not a soul had addressed a word directly to him, must have addled his brain in the course of the past two months, for he could not explain to himself in any other way how in all seriousness he could have been anxious to have his room cleared out. Had he really wanted to have his warm room, comfortably fitted with furniture that had always been in the family, changed into a cave, in which, of course, he would be able to crawl around unhampered in all directions but at the cost of simultaneously, rapidly, and totally forgetting his human past? Even now he had been on the verge of forgetting, and only his mother's voice, which he had not heard for so long, had shaken him up. Nothing should be removed; everything had to stay; he could not do without the beneficial influence of the furniture on his state of mind; and if the furniture prevented him from carrying on this senseless crawling around, then that was no loss but rather a great advantage.

But his sister unfortunately had a different opinion; she had become accustomed, certainly not entirely without justification, to adopt with her parents the role of the particularly well-qualified expert whenever Gregor's affairs were being discussed; and so her mother's advice was now sufficient reason for her to insist, not only on the removal of the chest of drawers and the desk, which was all she had been planning at first, but also on the removal of all the furniture with the exception of the indispensable couch. Of course it was not only childish defiance and the self-confidence she had recently acquired so unexpectedly and at such a cost that led her to make this demand; she had in fact noticed that Gregor needed plenty of room to crawl around in; and on the other hand, as best she could tell, he never used the furniture at all. Perhaps, however, the romantic enthusiasm of girls her age, which seeks to indulge itself at every opportunity, played a part, by tempting her to make Gregor's situation even more terrifying in order that she might do even more for him. Into a room in which Gregor ruled the bare walls all alone, no human being beside Grete was ever likely to set foot.

And so she did not let herself be swerved from her decision by her mother, who, besides, from the sheer anxiety of being in Gregor's room, seemed unsure of herself, soon grew silent, and helped her daughter as best she could to get the chest of drawers out of the room. Well, in a pinch Gregor could do without the chest, but the desk had to stay. And hardly had the women left the room with the chest, squeezing against it and groaning, than Gregor stuck his head out from under the couch to see how he could feel his way into the situation as considerately as possible. But unfortunately it had to be his mother who came back first, while in the next room Grete was clasping the chest and rocking it back and forth by herself, without of course budging it from the spot. His mother, however, was not used to the sight of Gregor, he could have made her ill, and so Gregor, frightened, scuttled in reverse to the far end of the couch but could not stop the sheet from shifting a little at the front. That was enough to put his mother on the alert. She stopped, stood still for a moment, and then went back to Grete.

Although Gregor told himself over and over again that nothing special was happening, only a few pieces of furniture were being moved, he soon had to admit that this coming and going of the women, their little calls to each other, the scraping of the furniture along the floor had the effect on him of a great turmoil swelling on all sides, and as much as he tucked in his head and his legs and shrank until his belly touched the floor, he was forced to admit that he would not be able to stand it much longer. They were clearing out his room; depriving him of everything that he loved; they had already carried away the chest of drawers, in which he kept the fretsaw and other tools; were now budging the desk firmly embedded in the floor, the desk he had done his homework on when he was a student at business college, in high school, yes, even in public school—now he really had no more time to examine the good intentions of the two women, whose existence, besides, he had almost forgotten, for they were so exhausted that they were working in silence, and one could hear only the heavy shuffling of their feet.

And so he broke out—the women were just leaning against the desk in the next room to catch their breath for a minute—changed his course four times, he really didn't know what to salvage first, then he saw hanging conspicuously on the wall, which was otherwise bare already, the picture of the lady all dressed in furs, hurriedly crawled up on it and pressed himself against the glass, which gave a good surface to stick to and soothed his hot belly. At least no one would take away this picture, while Gregor completely covered it up. He turned his head toward the living-room door to watch the women when they returned.

They had not given themselves much of a rest and were already coming back; Grete had put her arm around her mother and was practically carrying her. "So what should we take now?" said Grete and looked around. At that her eyes met Gregor's as he clung to the wall. Probably only because of her mother's presence she kept her self-control, bent her head down to her mother to keep her from looking around, and said, though in a quavering and thoughtless voice: "Come, we'd better go back into the living room for a minute." Grete's intent was clear to Gregor, she wanted to bring his mother into safety and then chase him down from the wall. Well, just let her try! He squatted on his picture and would not give it up. He would rather fly in Grete's face.

But Grete's words had now made her mother really anxious; she stepped to one side, caught sight of the gigantic brown blotch on the flowered wallpaper, and before it really dawned on her that what she saw was Gregor, cried in a hoarse, bawling voice: "Oh, God, Oh, God!"; and as if giving up completely, she fell with outstretched arms across the couch and did not stir. "You, Gregor!" cried his sister with raised fist and piercing eyes. These were the first words she had addressed directly to him since his metamorphosis. She ran into the next room to get some kind of spirits to revive her mother; Gregor wanted to help too—there was time to rescue the picture—but he was stuck to the glass and had to tear himself loose by force; then he too ran into the next room, as if he could give his sister some sort of advice, as in the old days; but then had to stand behind her doing nothing while she rummaged among various little bottles; moreover, when she turned around she was startled, a bottle fell on the floor and broke, a splinter of glass wounded Gregor in the face, some kind of corrosive medicine flowed around him; now without waiting any longer, Grete grabbed as many little bottles as she could carry and ran with them inside to her mother; she slammed the door behind her with her foot. Now Gregor was cut off from his mother, who was perhaps near death through his fault; he could not dare open the door if he did not want to chase away his sister, who had to stay with his mother; now there was nothing for him to do except wait; and tormented by self-reproaches and worry, he began to crawl, crawled over everything, walls, furniture and ceiling, and finally in desperation, as the whole room was beginning to spin, fell down onto the middle of the big table.

A short time passed; Gregor lay there prostrate; all around, things were quiet, perhaps that was a good sign. Then the doorbell rang. The maid, of course, was locked up in her kitchen and so Grete had to answer the door. His father had come home. "What's happened?" were his first words; Grete's appearance must have told him everything. Grete answered in a muffled voice, her face was obviously pressed against her father's chest: "Mother fainted, but she's better now. Gregor's broken out." "I knew it," his father said. "I kept telling you, but you women don't want to listen." It was clear to Gregor that his father had put the worst interpretation on Grete's all-too-brief announcement and assumed that Gregor was guilty of some outrage. Therefore Gregor now had to try to calm his father down, since he had neither the time nor the ability to enlighten him. And so he fled to the door of his room and pressed himself against it for his father to see, as soon as he came into the foyer, that Gregor had the best intentions of returning to his room immediately and that it was not necessary to drive him back; if only the door were opened for him, he would disappear at once.

But his father was in no mood to notice such subtleties; "Ah!" he cried as he entered, in a tone that sounded as if he were at once furious and glad. Gregor turned his head away from the door and lifted it toward his father. He had not really imagined his father looking like this, as he stood in front of him now; admittedly Gregor had been too absorbed recently in his newfangled crawling to bother as much as before about events in the rest of the house and should really have been prepared to find some changes. And yet, and yet—was this still his father? Was this the same man who in the old days used to lie wearily buried in bed when Gregor left on a business trip; who greeted him on his return in the evening, sitting in his bathrobe in the armchair, who actually had difficulty getting to his feet but as a sign of joy only lifted up his arms; and who, on the rare occasions when the whole family went out for a walk, on a few Sundays in June and on the major holidays, used to shuffle along with great effort between Gregor and his mother, who were slow walkers themselves, always a little more slowly than they, wrapped in his old overcoat, always carefully planting down his crutch-handled cane, and, when he wanted to say something, nearly always stood still and assembled his escort around him? Now, however, he was holding himself very erect, dressed in a tight-fitting blue uniform with gold buttons, the kind worn by messengers at banking concerns; above the high stiff collar of the jacket his heavy chin protruded; under his bushy eyebrows his black eyes darted bright, piercing glances; his usually rumpled white hair was combed flat, with a scrupulously exact, gleaming part. He threw his cap—which was adorned with a gold monogram, probably that of a bank—in an arc across the entire room onto the couch, and with the tails of his long uniform jacket slapped back, his hands in his pants pockets, went for Gregor with a sullen look on his face. He probably did not know himself what he had in mind; still he lifted his feet unusually high off the floor, and Gregor staggered at the gigantic size of the soles of his boots. But he did not linger over this, he had known right from the first day of his new life that his father considered only the strictest treatment called for in dealing with him. And so he ran ahead of his father, stopped when his father stood still, and scooted ahead again when his father made even the slightest movement. In this way they made more than one tour of the room, without anything decisive happening; in fact the whole movement did not even have the appearance of a chase because of its slow tempo. So Gregor kept to the floor for the time being, especially since he was afraid that his father might interpret a flight onto the walls or the ceiling as a piece of particular nastiness. Of course Gregor had to admit that he would not be able to keep up even this running for long, for whenever his father took one step, Gregor had to execute countless movements. He was already beginning to feel winded, just as in the old days he had not had very reliable lungs. As he now staggered around, hardly keeping his eyes open in order to gather all his strength for the running; in his obtuseness not thinking of any escape other than by running; and having almost forgotten that the walls were at his disposal, though here of course they were blocked up with elaborately carved furniture full of notches and points—at that moment a lightly flung object hit the floor right near him and rolled in front of him. It was an apple; a second one came flying right after it; Gregor stopped dead with fear; further running was useless, for his father was determined to bombard him. He had filled his pockets from the fruit bowl on the buffet and was now pitching one apple after another, for the time being without taking good aim. These little red apples rolled around on the floor as if electrified, clicking into each another. One apple, thrown weakly, grazed Gregor's back and slid off harmlessly. But the very next one that came flying after it literally forced its way into Gregor's back; Gregor tried to drag himself away, as if the startling, unbelievable pain might disappear with a change of place; but he felt nailed to the spot and stretched out his body in a complete confusion of all his senses. With his last glance he saw the door of his room burst open as his mother rushed out ahead of his screaming sister, in her chemise, for his sister had partly undressed her while she was unconscious in order to let her breathe more freely; saw his mother run up to his father and on the way her unfastened petticoats slide to the floor one by one; and saw as, stumbling over the skirts, she forced herself onto his father, and embracing him, in complete union with him—but now Gregor's sight went dim—her hands clasping his father's neck, begged for Gregor's life.

3

Gregor's serious wound, from which he suffered for over a month—the apple remained imbedded in his flesh as a visible souvenir since no one dared to remove it—seemed to have reminded even his father that Gregor was a member of the family, in spite of his present pathetic and repulsive shape, who could not be treated as an enemy; that, on the contrary, it was the commandment of family duty to swallow their disgust and endure him, endure him and nothing more.

And now, although Gregor had lost some of his mobility probably for good because of his wound, and although for the time being he needed long, long minutes to get across his room, like an old war veteran—crawling above ground was out of the question—for this deterioration of his situation he was granted compensation which in his view was entirely satisfactory: every day around dusk the living-room door—which he was in the habit of watching closely for an hour or two beforehand—was opened, so that, lying in the darkness of his room, invisible from the living room, he could see the whole family sitting at the table under the lamp and could listen to their conversation, as it were with general permission; and so it was completely different from before.

Of course these were no longer the animated conversations of the old days, which Gregor used to remember with a certain nostalgia in small hotel rooms when he'd had to throw himself wearily into the damp bedding. Now things were mostly very quiet. Soon after supper his father would fall asleep in his armchair; his mother and sister would caution each other to be quiet; his mother, bent low under the light, sewed delicate lingerie for a clothing store; his sister, who had taken a job as a sales-girl, was learning shorthand and French in the evenings in order to attain a better position some time in the future. Sometimes his father woke up, and as if he had absolutely no idea that he had been asleep, said to his mother, "Look how long you're sewing again today!" and went right back to sleep, while mother and sister smiled wearily at each other.

With a kind of perverse obstinacy his father refused to take off his official uniform even in the house; and while his robe hung uselessly on the clothes hook, his father dozed, completely dressed, in his chair, as if he were always ready for duty and were waiting even here for the voice of his superior. As a result his uniform, which had not been new to start with, began to get dirty in spite of all the mother's and sister's care, and Gregor would often stare all evening long at this garment, covered with stains and gleaming with its constantly polished gold buttons, in which the old man slept most uncomfortably and yet peacefully.

As soon as the clock struck ten, his mother tried to awaken his father with soft encouraging words and then persuade him to go to bed, for this was no place to sleep properly, and his father badly needed his sleep, since he had to be at work at six o'clock. But with the obstinacy that had possessed him ever since he had become a messenger, he always insisted on staying at the table a little longer, although he invariably fell asleep and then could be persuaded only with the greatest effort to exchange his armchair for bed. However much mother and sister might pounce on him with little admonitions, he would slowly shake his head for a quarter of an hour at a time, keeping his eyes closed, and would not get up. Gregor's mother plucked him by the sleeves, whispered blandishments into his ear, his sister dropped her homework in order to help her mother, but all this was of no use. He only sank deeper into his armchair. Not until the women lifted him up under his arms did he open his eyes, look alternately at mother and sister, and usually say, "What a life. So this is the peace of my old age." And leaning on the two women, he would get up laboriously, as if he were the greatest weight on himself, and let the women lead him to the door, where, shrugging them off, he would proceed independently, while Gregor's mother threw down her sewing, and his sister her pen, as quickly as possible so as to run after his father and be of further assistance.

Who in this overworked and exhausted family had time to worry about Gregor any more than was absolutely necessary? The household was stinted more and more; now the maid was let go after all; a gigantic bony cleaning woman with white hair fluttering about her head came mornings and evenings to do the heaviest work; his mother took care of everything else, along with all her sewing. It even happened that various pieces of family jewelry, which in the old days his mother and sister had been overjoyed to wear at parties and celebrations, were sold, as Gregor found out one evening from the general discussion of the prices they had fetched. But the biggest complaint was always that they could not give up the apartment, which was much too big for their present needs, since no one could figure out how Gregor was supposed to be moved. But Gregor understood easily that it was not only consideration for him which prevented their moving, for he could easily have been transported in a suitable crate with a few air holes; what mainly prevented the family from moving was their complete hopelessness and the thought that they had been struck by a misfortune as none of their relatives and acquaintances had ever been hit. What the world demands of poor people they did to the utmost of their ability; his father brought breakfast for the minor officials at the bank, his mother sacrificed herself to the underwear of strangers, his sister ran back and forth behind the counter at the request of the customers; but for anything more than this they did not have the strength. And the wound in Gregor's back began to hurt anew when mother and sister, after getting his father to bed, now came back, dropped their work, pulled their chairs close to each other and sat cheek to cheek; when his mother, pointing to Gregor's room, said, "Close that door, Grete"; and when Gregor was back in darkness, while in the other room the women mingled their tears or stared dry-eyed at the table.

Gregor spent the days and nights almost entirely without sleep. Sometimes he thought that the next time the door opened he would take charge of the family's affairs again, just as he had done in the old days; after this long while there again appeared in his thoughts the boss and the manager, the salesmen and the trainees, the handyman who was so dense, two or three friends from other firms, a chambermaid in a provincial hotel—a happy fleeting memory—a cashier in a millinery store, whom he had courted earnestly but too slowly—they all appeared, intermingled with strangers or people he had already forgotten; but instead of helping him and his family, they were all inaccessible, and he was glad when they faded away. At other times he was in no mood to worry about his family, he was completely filled with rage at his miserable treatment, and although he could not imagine anything that would pique his appetite, he still made plans for getting into the pantry to take what was coming to him, even if he wasn't hungry. No longer considering what she could do to give Gregor a special treat, his sister, before running to business every morning and afternoon, hurriedly shoved any old food into Gregor's room with her foot; and in the evening, regardless of whether the food had only been toyed with or—the most usual case—had been left completely untouched, she swept it out with a swish of the broom. The cleaning up of Gregor's room, which she now always did in the evenings, could not be done more hastily. Streaks of dirt ran along the walls, fluffs of dust and filth lay here and there on the floor. At first, whenever his sister came in, Gregor would place himself in those corners which were particularly offending, meaning by his position in a sense to reproach her. But he could probably have stayed there for weeks without his sister's showing any improvement; she must have seen the dirt as clearly as he did, but she had just decided to leave it. At the same time she made sure—with an irritableness that was completely new to her and which had in fact infected the whole family—that the cleaning of Gregor's room remain her province. One time his mother had submitted Gregor's room to a major housecleaning, which she managed only after employing a couple of pails of water—all this dampness, of course, irritated Gregor too and he lay prostrate, sour and immobile, on the couch—but his mother's punishment was not long in coming. For hardly had his sister noticed the difference in Gregor's room that evening than, deeply insulted, she ran into the living room and, in spite of her mother's imploringly uplifted hands, burst out in a fit of crying, which his parents—his father had naturally been startled out of his armchair—at first watched in helpless amazement; until they too got going; turning to the right, his father blamed his mother for not letting his sister clean Gregor's room; but turning to the left, he screamed at his sister that she would never again be allowed to clean Gregor's room; while his mother tried to drag his father, who was out of his mind with excitement, into the bedroom; his sister, shaken with sobs, hammered the table with her small fists; and Gregor hissed loudly with rage because it did not occur to any of them to close the door and spare him such a scene and a row.

But even if his sister, exhausted from her work at the store, had gotten fed up with taking care of Gregor as she used to, it was not necessary at all for his mother to take her place and still Gregor did not have to be neglected. For now the cleaning woman was there. This old widow, who thanks to her strong bony frame had probably survived the worst in a long life, was not really repelled by Gregor. Without being in the least inquisitive, she had once accidentally opened the door of Gregor's room, and at the sight of Gregor—who, completely taken by surprise, began to race back and forth although no one was chasing him—she had remained standing, with her hands folded on her stomach, marveling. From that time on she never failed to open the door a crack every morning and every evening and peek in hurriedly at Gregor. In the beginning she also used to call him over to her with words she probably considered friendly, like, "Come over here for a minute, you old dung beetle!" or "Look at that old dung beetle!" To forms of address like these Gregor would not respond but remained immobile where he was, as if the door had not been opened. If only they had given this cleaning woman orders to clean up his room every day, instead of letting her disturb him uselessly whenever the mood took her. Once, early in the morning—heavy rain, perhaps already a sign of approaching spring, was beating on the window panes—Gregor was so exasperated when the cleaning woman started in again with her phrases that he turned on her, of course slowly and decrepitly, as if to attack. But the cleaning woman, instead of getting frightened, simply lifted up high a chair near the door, and as she stood there with her mouth wide open, her intention was clearly to shut her mouth only when the chair in her hand came crashing down on Gregor's back. "So, is that all there is?" she asked when Gregor turned around again, and she quietly put the chair back in the corner.

Gregor now hardly ate anything anymore. Only when he accidentally passed the food laid out for him would he take a bite into his mouth just for fun, hold it in for hours, and then mostly spit it out again. At first he thought that his grief at the state of his room kept him off food, but it was the very changes in his room to which he quickly became adjusted. His family had gotten into the habit of putting in this room things for which they could not find any other place, and now there were plenty of these, since one of the rooms in the apartment had been rented to three boarders. These serious gentlemen—all three had long beards, as Gregor was able to register once through a crack in the door—were obsessed with neatness, not only in their room, but since they had, after all, moved in here, throughout the entire household and especially in the kitchen. They could not stand useless, let alone dirty junk. Besides, they had brought along most of their own household goods. For this reason many things had become superfluous, and though they certainly weren't salable, on the other hand they could not just be thrown out. All these things migrated into Gregor's room. Likewise the ash can and the garbage can from the kitchen. Whatever was not being used at the moment was just flung into Gregor's room by the cleaning woman, who was always in a big hurry; fortunately Gregor generally saw only the object involved and the hand that held it. Maybe the cleaning woman intended to reclaim the things as soon as she had a chance or else to throw out everything together in one fell swoop, but in fact they would have remained lying wherever they had been thrown in the first place if Gregor had not squeezed through the junk and set it in motion, at first from necessity, because otherwise there would have been no room to crawl in, but later with growing pleasure, although after such excursions, tired to death and sad, he did not budge again for hours.

Since the roomers sometimes also had their supper at home in the common living room, the living-room door remained closed on certain evenings, but Gregor found it very easy to give up the open door, for on many evenings when it was opened he had not taken advantage of it, but instead, without the family's noticing, had lain in the darkest corner of his room. But once the cleaning woman had left the living-room door slightly open, and it also remained opened a little when the roomers came in in the evening and the lamp was lit. They sat down at the head of the table where in the old days his father, his mother, and Gregor had eaten, unfolded their napkins, and picked up their knives and forks. At once his mother appeared in the doorway with a platter of meat, and just behind her came his sister with a platter piled high with potatoes. A thick vapor steamed up from the food. The roomers bent over the platters set in front of them as if to examine them before eating, and in fact the one who sat in the middle, and who seemed to be regarded by the other two as an authority, cut into a piece of meat while it was still on the platter, evidently to find out whether it was tender enough or whether it should perhaps be sent back to the kitchen. He was satisfied, and mother and sister, who had been watching anxiously, sighed with relief and began to smile.

The family itself ate in the kitchen. Nevertheless, before going into the kitchen, his father came into this room and, bowing once, cap in hand, made a turn around the table. The roomers rose as one man and mumbled something into their beards. When they were alone again, they ate in almost complete silence. It seemed strange to Gregor that among all the different noises of eating he kept picking up the sound of their chewing teeth, as if this were a sign to Gregor that you needed teeth to eat with and that even with the best make of toothless jaws you couldn't do a thing. "I'm hungry enough," Gregor said to himself, full of grief, "but not for these things. Look how these roomers are gorging themselves, and I'm dying!"

On this same evening—Gregor could not remember having heard the violin during the whole time—the sound of violin playing came from the kitchen. The roomers had already finished their evening meal, the one in the middle had taken out a newspaper, given each of the two others a page, and now, leaning back, they read and smoked. When the violin began to play, they became attentive, got up, and went on tiptoe to the door leading to the foyer, where they stood in a huddle. They must have been heard in the kitchen, for his father called, "Perhaps the playing bothers you, gentlemen? It can be stopped right away." "On the contrary," said the middle roomer. "Wouldn't the young lady like to come in to us and play in here where it's much roomier and more comfortable?" "Oh, certainly," called Gregor's father, as if he were the violinist. The boarders went back into the room and waited. Soon Gregor's father came in with the music stand, his mother with the sheet music, and his sister with the violin. Calmly his sister got everything ready for playing; his parents—who had never rented out rooms before and therefore behaved toward the roomers with excessive politeness—did not even dare sit down on their own chairs; his father leaned against the door, his right hand inserted between two buttons of his uniform coat, which he kept closed; but his mother was offered a chair by one of the roomers, and since she left the chair where the roomer just happened to put it, she sat in a corner to one side.

His sister began to play. Father and mother, from either side, attentively followed the movements of her hands. Attracted by the playing, Gregor had dared to come out a little further and already had his head in the living room. It hardly surprised him that lately he was showing so little consideration for the others; once such consideration had been his greatest pride. And yet he would never have had better reason to keep hidden; for now, because of the dust which lay all over his room and blew around at the slightest movement, he too was completely covered with dust; he dragged around with him on his back and along his sides fluff and hairs and scraps of food; his indifference to everything was much too deep for him to have gotten on his back and scrubbed himself clean against the carpet, as once he had done several times a day. And in spite of his state, he was not ashamed to inch out a little farther on the immaculate living-room floor.

Admittedly no one paid any attention to him. The family was completely absorbed by the violin-playing; the roomers, on the other hand, who at first had stationed themselves, hands in pockets, much too close behind his sister's music stand, so that they could all have followed the score, which certainly must have upset his sister, soon withdrew to the window, talking to each other in an undertone, their heads lowered, where they remained, anxiously watched by his father. It now seemed only too obvious that they were disappointed in their expectation of hearing beautiful or entertaining violin-playing, had had enough of the whole performance, and continued to let their peace be disturbed only out of politeness. Especially the way they all blew the cigar smoke out of their nose and mouth toward the ceiling suggested great nervousness. And yet his sister was playing so beautifully. Her face was inclined to one side, sadly and probingly her eyes followed the lines of music. Gregor crawled forward a little farther, holding his head close to the floor, so that it might be possible to catch her eye. Was he an animal, that music could move him so? He felt as if the way to the unknown nourishment he longed for were coming to light. He was determined to force himself on until he reached his sister, to pluck at her skirt, and to let her know in this way that she should bring her violin into his room, for no one here appreciated her playing the way he would appreciate it. He would never again let her out of his room—at least not for as long as he lived; for once, his nightmarish looks would be of use to him; he would be at all the doors of his room at the same time and hiss and spit at the aggressors; his sister, however, should not be forced to stay with him, but would do so of her own free will; she should sit next to him on the couch, bending her ear down to him, and then he would confide to her that he had had the firm intention of sending her to the Conservatory, and that, if the catastrophe had not intervened, he would have announced this to everyone last Christmas—certainly Christmas had come and gone?—without taking notice of any objections. After this declaration his sister would burst into tears of emotion, and Gregor would raise himself up to her shoulder and kiss her on the neck which, ever since she started going out to work, she kept bare, without a ribbon or collar.

"Mr. Samsa!" the middle roomer called to Gregor's father and without wasting another word pointed his index finger at Gregor, who was slowly moving forward. The violin stopped, the middle roomer smiled first at his friends, shaking his head, and then looked at Gregor again. Rather than driving Gregor out, his father seemed to consider it more urgent to start by soothing the roomers although they were not at all upset, and Gregor seemed to be entertaining them more than the violin-playing. He rushed over to them and tried with outstretched arms to drive them into their room and at the same time with his body to block their view of Gregor. Now they actually did get a little angry—it was not clear whether because of his father's behavior or because of their dawning realization of having had without knowing it such a next door neighbor as Gregor. They demanded explanations from his father; in their turn they raised their arms, plucked excitedly at their beards, and, dragging their feet, backed off toward their room. In the meantime his sister had overcome the abstracted mood into which she had fallen after her playing had been so suddenly interrupted; and all at once, after holding violin and bow for a while in her slackly hanging hands and continuing to follow the score as if she were still playing, she pulled herself together, laid the instrument on the lap of her mother—who was still sitting in her chair, fighting for breath, her lungs violently heaving—and ran into the next room, which the roomers, under pressure from her father, were nearing more quickly than before. One could see the covers and bolsters on the beds, obeying his sister's practiced hands, fly up and arrange themselves. Before the boarders had reached the room, she had finished turning down the beds and had slipped out. Her father seemed once again to be gripped by his perverse obstinacy to such a degree that he completely forgot any respect still due his tenants. He drove them on and kept on driving until, already at the bedroom door, the middle boarder stamped his foot thunderingly and thus brought him to a standstill. "I herewith declare," he said, raising his hand and casting his eyes around for Gregor's mother and sister too, "that in view of the disgusting conditions prevailing in this apartment and family"—here he spat curtly and decisively on the floor—"I give notice as of now. Of course I won't pay a cent for the days I have been living here, either; on the contrary, I shall consider taking some sort of action against you with claims that—believe me—will be easy to substantiate." He stopped and looked straight in front of him, as if he were expecting something. And in fact his two friends at once chimed in with the words, "We too give notice as of now." Thereupon he grabbed the door knob and slammed the door with a bang.

Gregor's father, his hands groping, staggered to his armchair and collapsed into it; it looked as if he were stretching himself out for his usual evening nap, but the heavy drooping of his head, as if it had lost all support, showed that he was certainly not asleep. All this time Gregor had lain quietly at the spot where the roomers had surprised him. His disappointment at the failure of his plan—but perhaps also the weakness caused by so much fasting—made it impossible for him to move. He was afraid with some certainty that in the very next moment a general debacle would burst over him, and he waited. He was not even startled by the violin as it slipped from under his mother's trembling fingers and fell off her lap with a reverberating clang.

"My dear parents," said his sister and by way of an introduction pounded her hand on the table, "things can't go on like this. Maybe you don't realize it, but I do. I won't pronounce the name of my brother in front of this monster, and so all I say is: we have to try to get rid of it. We've done everything humanly possible to take care of it and to put up with it; I don't think anyone can blame us in the least."

"She's absolutely right," said his father to himself. His mother, who still could not catch her breath, began to cough dully behind her hand, a wild look in her eyes.

His sister rushed over to his mother and held her forehead. His father seemed to have been led by Grete's words to more definite thoughts, had sat up, was playing with the cap of his uniform among the plates which were still lying on the table from the roomers' supper, and from time to time looked at Gregor's motionless form.

"We must try to get rid of it," his sister now said exclusively to her father, since her mother was coughing too hard to hear anything. "It will be the death of you two, I can see it coming. People who already have to work as hard as we do can't put up with this constant torture at home, too. I can't stand it anymore either." And she broke out crying so bitterly that her tears poured down onto her mother's face, which she wiped off with mechanical movements of her hand.

"Child," said her father kindly and with unusual understanding, "but what can we do?"

Gregor's sister only shrugged her shoulders as a sign of the bewildered mood that had now gripped her as she cried, in contrast with her earlier confidence.

"If he could understand us," said her father, half questioning; in the midst of her crying Gregor's sister waved her hand violently as a sign that that was out of the question.

"If he could understand us," his father repeated and by closing his eyes, absorbed his daughter's conviction of the impossibility of the idea, "then maybe we could come to an agreement with him. But the way things are——"

"It has to go," cried his sister. "That's the only answer, Father. You just have to try to get rid of the idea that it's Gregor. Believing it for so long, that is our real misfortune.

But how can it be Gregor? If it were Gregor, he would have realized long ago that it isn't possible for human beings to live with such a creature, and he would have gone away of his own free will. Then we wouldn't have a brother, but we'd be able to go on living and honor his memory. But as things are, this animal persecutes us, drives the roomers away, obviously wants to occupy the whole apartment and for us to sleep in the gutter. Look, Father," she suddenly shrieked, "he's starting in again!" And in a fit of terror that was completely incomprehensible to Gregor, his sister abandoned even her mother, literally shoved herself off from her chair, as if she would rather sacrifice her mother than stay near Gregor, and rushed behind her father, who, upset only by her behavior, also stood up and half-lifted his arms in front of her as if to protect her.

But Gregor had absolutely no intention of frightening anyone, let alone his sister. He had only begun to turn around in order to trek back to his room; certainly his movements did look peculiar, since his ailing condition made him help the complicated turning maneuver along with his head, which he lifted up many times and knocked against the floor. He stopped and looked around. His good intention seemed to have been recognized; it had only been a momentary scare. Now they all watched him, silent and sad. His mother lay in her armchair, her legs stretched out and pressed together, her eyes almost closing from exhaustion; his father and his sister sat side by side, his sister had put her arm around her father's neck.

Now maybe they'll let me turn around, Gregor thought and began his labors again. He could not repress his panting from the exertion, and from time to time he had to rest. Otherwise no one harassed him; he was left completely on his own. When he had completed the turn, he immediately began to crawl back in a straight line. He was astonished at the great distance separating him from his room and could not understand at all how, given his weakness, he had covered the same distance a little while ago almost without realizing it. Constantly intent only on rapid crawling, he hardly noticed that not a word, not an exclamation from his family interrupted him. Only when he was already in the doorway did he turn his head—not completely, for he felt his neck stiffening; nevertheless he still saw that behind him nothing had changed except that his sister had gotten up. His last glance ranged over his mother, who was now fast asleep.

He was hardly inside his room when the door was hurriedly slammed shut, firmly bolted, and locked. Gregor was so frightened at the sudden noise behind him that his little legs gave way under him. It was his sister who had been in such a hurry. She had been standing up straight, ready and waiting, then she had leaped forward nimbly, Gregor had not even heard her coming, and she cried "Finally!" to her parents as she turned the key in the lock.

"And now?" Gregor asked himself, looking around in the darkness. He soon made the discovery that he could no longer move at all. It did not surprise him; rather, it seemed unnatural that until now he had actually been able to propel himself on these thin little legs. Otherwise he felt relatively comfortable. He had pains, of course, throughout his whole body, but it seemed to him that they were gradually getting fainter and fainter and would finally go away altogether. The rotten apple in his back and the inflamed area around it, which were completely covered with fluffy dust, already hardly bothered him. He thought back on his family with deep emotion and love. His conviction that he would have to disappear was, if possible, even firmer than his sister's. He remained in this state of empty and peaceful reflection until the tower clock struck three in the morning. He still saw that outside the window everything was beginning to grow light. Then, without his consent, his head sank down to the floor, and from his nostrils streamed his last weak breath.

When early in the morning the cleaning woman came—in sheer energy and impatience she would slam all the doors so hard although she had often been asked not to, that once she arrived, quiet sleep was no longer possible anywhere in the apartment—she did not at first find anything out of the ordinary on paying Gregor her usual short visit. She thought that he was deliberately lying motionless, pretending that his feelings were hurt; she credited him with unlimited intelligence. Because she happened to be holding the long broom, she tried from the doorway to tickle Gregor with it. When this too produced no results, she became annoyed and jabbed Gregor a little, and only when she had shoved him without any resistance to another spot did she begin to take notice. When she quickly became aware of the true state of things, she opened her eyes wide, whistled softly, but did not dawdle; instead, she tore open the door of the bedroom and shouted at the top of her voice into the darkness: "Come and have a look, it's croaked; it's lying there, dead as a doornail!"

The couple Mr. and Mrs. Samsa sat up in their marriage bed and had a struggle overcoming their shock at the cleaning woman before they could finally grasp her message. But then Mr. and Mrs. Samsa hastily scrambled out of bed, each on his side, Mr. Samsa threw the blanket around his shoulders, Mrs. Samsa came out in nothing but her nightgown; dressed this way, they entered Gregor's room. In the meantime the door of the living room had also opened, where Grete had been sleeping since the roomers had moved in; she was fully dressed, as if she had not been asleep at all; and her pale face seemed to confirm this. "Dead?" said Mrs. Samsa and look inquiringly at the cleaning woman, although she could scrutinize everything for herself and could recognize the truth even without scrunity. "I'll say," said the cleaning woman, and to prove it she pushed Gregor's corpse with her broom a good distance sideways. Mrs. Samsa made a movement as if to hold the broom back but did not do it. "Well," said Mr. Samsa, "now we can thank God!" He crossed himself, and the three women followed his example. Grete, who never took her eyes off the corpse, said, "Just look how thin he was. Of course he didn't eat anything for such a long time. The food came out again just the way it went in." As a matter of fact, Gregor's body was completely flat and dry; this was obvious now for the first time, really, since the body was no longer raised up by his little legs and nothing else distracted the eye.

"Come in with us for a little while, Grete," said Mrs. Samsa with a melancholy smile, and Grete, not without looking back at the corpse, followed her parents into their bedroom. The cleaning woman shut the door and opened the window wide. Although it was early in the morning, there was already some mildness mixed in with the fresh air. After all, it was already the end of March.

The three boarders came out of their room and looked around in astonishment for their breakfast; they had been forgotten. "Where's breakfast?" the middle roomer grumpily asked the cleaning woman. But she put her finger to her lips and then hastily and silently beckoned the boarders to follow her into Gregor's room. They came willingly and then stood, their hands in the pockets of their somewhat shabby jackets, in the now already very bright room, surrounding Gregor's corpse.

At that point the bedroom door opened, and Mr. Samsa appeared in his uniform, his wife on one arm, his daughter on the other. They all looked as if they had been crying; from time to time Grete pressed her face against her father's sleeve.

"Leave my house immediately," said Mr. Samsa and pointed to the door, without letting go of the women. "What do you mean by that?" said the middle roomer, somewhat nonplussed, and smiled with a sugary smile. The two others held their hands behind their back and incessantly rubbed them together, as if in joyful anticipation of a big argument, which could only turn out in their favor. "I mean just what I say," answered

Mr. Samsa and with his two companions marched in a straight line toward the roomer. At first the roomer stood still and looked at the floor, as if the thoughts inside his head were fitting themselves together in a new order. "So, we'll go, then," he said and looked up at Mr. Samsa as if, suddenly overcome by a fit of humility, he were asking for further permission even for this decision. Mr. Samsa merely nodded briefly several times, his eyes wide open. Thereupon the roomer actually went immediately into the foyer, taking long strides; his two friends had already been listening for a while, their hands completely still, and now they went hopping right after him, as if afraid that Mr. Samsa might get into the foyer ahead of them and interrupt the contact with their leader. In the foyer all three took their hats from the coatrack, pulled their canes from the umbrella stand, bowed silently, and left the apartment. In a suspicious mood which proved completely unfounded, Mr. Samsa led the two women out onto the landing; leaning over the banister, they watched the three roomers slowly but steadily going down the long flight of stairs, disappearing on each landing at a particular turn of the stairway and a few moments later emerging again; the farther down they got, the more the Samsa family's interest in them wore off, and when a butcher's boy with a carrier on his head came climbing up the stairs with a proud bearing, toward them and then up on past them, Mr. Samsa and the women quickly left the banister and all went back, as if relieved, into their apartment.

They decided to spend this day resting and going for a walk; they not only deserved a break in their work, they absolutely needed one. And so they sat down at the table and wrote three letters of excuse, Mr. Samsa to the management of the bank, Mrs. Samsa to her employer, and Grete to the store owner. While they were writing, the cleaning woman came in to say that she was going, since her morning's work was done. The three letter writers at first simply nodded without looking up, but as the cleaning woman still kept lingering, they looked up, annoyed. "Well?" asked Mr. Samsa. The cleaning woman stood smiling in the doorway, as if she had some great good news to announce to the family but would do so only if she were thoroughly questioned. The little ostrich feather which stood almost upright on her hat and which had irritated Mr. Samsa the whole time she had been with them swayed lightly in all directions. "What do you want?" asked Mrs. Samsa, who inspired the most respect in the cleaning woman. "Well," the cleaning woman answered, and for good-natured laughter could not immediately go on, "look, you don't have to worry about getting rid of the stuff next door. It's already been taken care of." Mrs. Samsa and Grete bent down over their letters, as if to continue writing; Mr. Samsa, who noticed that the cleaning woman was now about to start describing everything in detail, stopped her with a firmly outstretched hand. But since she was not going to be permitted to tell her story, she remembered that she was in a great hurry, cried, obviously insulted, "So long, everyone," whirled around wildly, and left the apartment with a terrible slamming of doors.

"We'll fire her tonight," said Mr. Samsa, but did not get an answer from either his wife or his daughter, for the cleaning woman seemed to have ruined their barely regained peace of mind. They got up, went to the window, and stayed there, holding each other tight. Mr. Samsa turned around in his chair toward them and watched them quietly for a while. Then he called, "Come on now, come over here. Stop brooding over the past. And have a little consideration for me, too." The women obeyed him at once, hurried over to him, fondled him, and quickly finished their letters.

Then all three of them left the apartment together, something they had not done in months, and took the trolley into the open country on the outskirts of the city. The car, in which they were the only passengers, was completely filled with warm sunshine. Leaning back comfortably in their seats, they discussed their prospects for the time to come, and it seemed on closer examination that these weren't bad at all, for all three positions—about which they had never really asked one another in any detail—were exceedingly advantageous and especially promising for the future. The greatest immediate improvement in their situation would come easily, of course, from a change in apartments; they would now take a smaller and cheaper apartment, but one better situated and in every way simpler to manage than the old one, which Gregor had picked for them. While they were talking in this vein, it occurred almost simultaneously to Mr. and Mrs. Samsa, as they watched their daughter getting livelier and livelier, that lately, in spite of all the troubles which had turned her cheeks pale, she had blossomed into a good-looking, shapely girl. Growing quieter and communicating almost unconsciously through glances, they thought that it would soon be time, too, to find her a good husband. And it was like a confirmation of their new dreams and good intentions when at the end of the ride their daughter got up first and stretched her young body.

Parables

The Trees[1]

For we are as treetrunks in the snow. They appear to lie flat on the surface, and with a little push one should be able to shift them. No, one cannot, for they are fixed firmly to the ground. But look, even that is mere appearance.

The Next Village[2]

My grandfather used to say: "Life is astoundingly short. To me, looking back over it, life seems so foreshortened that I scarcely understand, for instance, how a young man can decide to ride over to the next village without being afraid that—not to mention accidents—even the span of a normal happy life may fall far short of the time needed for such a journey."

The Cares of a Family Man[3]

Some say the word Odradek is of Slavonic origin, and try to account for it on that basis. Others again believe it to be of German origin, only influenced by Slavonic. The uncertainty of both interpretations allows one to assume with justice that neither is accurate, especially as neither of them provides an intelligent meaning of the word.

No one, of course, would occupy himself with such studies if there were not a creature called Odradek. At first glance it looks like a flat star-shaped spool for thread, and indeed it does seem to have thread wound upon it; to be sure, they are only old, broken-off bits of thread, knotted and tangled together, of the most varied sorts and colors. But it is not only a spool, for a small wooden crossbar sticks out of the middle of the star, and another small rod is joined to that at a right angle. By means of this latter rod on one side and one of the points of the star on the other, the whole thing can stand upright as if on two legs.

One is tempted to believe that the creature once had some sort of intelligible shape and is now only a broken-down remnant. Yet this does not seem to be the case; at least there is no sign of it; nowhere is there an unfinished or unbroken surface to suggest anything of the kind; the whole thing looks senseless enough, but in its own

1. Translated by J. A. Underwood.
2. Translated by Willa Muir and Edwin Muir.
3. Translated by Willa Muir and Edwin Muir.

way perfectly finished. In any case, closer scrutiny is impossible, since Odradek is extraordinarily nimble and can never be laid hold of.

He lurks by turns in the garret, the stairway, the lobbies, the entrance hall. Often for months on end he is not to be seen; then he has presumably moved into other houses; but he always comes faithfully back to our house again. Many a time when you go out of the door and he happens just to be leaning directly beneath you against the banisters you feel inclined to speak to him. Of course, you put no difficult questions to him, you treat him—he is so diminutive that you cannot help it—rather like a child. "Well, what's your name?" you ask him. "Odradek," he says. "And where do you live?" "No fixed abode," he says and laughs; but it is only the kind of laughter that has no lungs behind it. It sounds rather like the rustling of fallen leaves. And that is usually the end of the conversation. Even these answers are not always forthcoming; often he stays mute for a long time, as wooden as his appearance.

I ask myself, to no purpose, what is likely to happen to him? Can he possibly die? Anything that dies has had some kind of aim in life, some kind of activity, which has worn out; but that does not apply to Odradek. Am I to suppose, then, that he will always be rolling down the stairs, with ends of thread trailing after him, right before the feet of my children, and my children's children? He does no harm to anyone that one can see; but the idea that he is likely to survive me I find almost painful.

Give It Up![4]

It was very early in the morning, the streets clean and deserted, I was on my way to the station. As I compared the tower clock with my watch I realized it was much later than I had thought and that I had to hurry; the shock of this discovery made me feel uncertain of the way, I wasn't very well acquainted with the town as yet; fortunately, there was a policeman at hand, I ran to him and breathlessly asked him the way. He smiled and said: "You asking me the way?" "Yes," I said, "since I can't find it myself." "Give it up! Give it up!" said he, and turned with a sudden jerk, like someone who wants to be alone with his laughter.

On Parables[5]

Many complain that the words of the wise are always merely parables and of no use in daily life, which is the only life we have. When the sage says: "Go over," he does not mean that we should cross to some actual place, which we could do anyhow if the labor were worth it; he means some fabulous yonder, something unknown to us, something that he cannot designate more precisely either, and therefore cannot help us here in the very least. All these parables really set out to say merely that the incomprehensible is incomprehensible, and we know that already. But the cares we have to struggle with every day: that is a different matter.

Concerning this a man once said: Why such reluctance? If you only followed the parables you yourselves would become parables and with that rid of all your daily cares.

Another said: I bet that is also a parable.

The first said: You have won.

The second said: But unfortunately only in parable.

The first said: No, in reality: in parable you have lost.

4. Translated by Tania Stern and James Stern.

5. Translated by Willa Muir and Edwin Muir.

Jorge Luis Borges

1899–1986

One of the most cosmopolitan of modern writers, Jorge Luis Borges was born in Buenos Aires, Argentina, and spent his formative years in Geneva, Switzerland, after his family was trapped there during World War I while traveling in Europe. He learned German and French in addition to his native Spanish and English (his maternal ancestry was part English) and graduated from the Collège de Geneve. The family moved back to Buenos Aires following the war, after living for some time in Spain, where Borges came in contact with a number of avant-garde poets and where he published his first poem, "Hymn to the Sea," in the avant-garde journal *Grecia.* Borges's first published work was a translation into Spanish of Oscar Wilde's short story "The Happy Prince" when Borges was barely ten years old. Son of a psychology teacher with an extensive family library, Borges would spend most of his life in libraries, starting with his first job in 1939 as librarian in a municipal library in Buenos Aires. He held that position until the populist coup of the military strongman Juan Domingo Perón in 1946, at which time Borges was "promoted" to inspector of rabbits and poultry in the municipal market. Borges, whose rancor ran deep and proved implacable, never forgave Perón, and his politics, often anachronistic and deliberately provocative, were formed by this experience. Upon the fall of the Peronist regime in 1955, Borges was named Director of the National Library of Argentina, a post he held until his retirement in 1973, when Perón returned from exile to the presidency of Argentina. Genetically prone to blindness, Borges became the third director of his country's National Library to have this disability. As with most ironies, the irony of this was not lost on Borges, and several of his writings deal with this turn of fate.

While Borges began his career as a poet and wrote (or later dictated) poetry all his life, he is better known as a literary critic, essayist, and author of enigmatic short stories. His influence as a prose writer extends worldwide, with his works having been translated into many languages. As a critic, he introduced most of the Anglo-American and European modernists to the reading public of his country through his weekly column that appeared between 1936 and 1939 in a ladies' journal called *El Hogar* (The Home). During this period he was also writing some of his classic tales, which were gathered into a collection in 1941 under the title of *The Garden of the Forking Paths,* whose title story became one of his best known works.

Always fascinated by limit states of reason and rationality, Borges explores the thresholds between fantasy and reality, between the imagination and the materiality of the world. Deeply influenced by Idealist philosophers such as Arthur Schopenhauer and Bishop George Berkeley, whom he often cites, Borges speculates in his poetry and in his prose about the possibility that the world as we imagine it could well be a figment of someone else's imagination that imagines us imagining. In this sense, the authorship of the world is as compelling a problem for Borges as his and other writers' authorship of literary worlds. A self-proclaimed unbeliever, Borges doesn't view this as a religious problem but as a problem of the imagination. He is fascinated by creation, but he is not a creationist. The question of the creator, always with a lowercase "c," is of the same order as the question of a Creator with a capital "C." Very much in the metaphysical tradition of the Idealists and mathematicians, Borges sees creation as the product of an imaginative calculus. And he sees the world as a text—really, as a hypertext—whose myriad links could lead to an infinite number of other texts and other links. "The Garden of Forking Paths" and "The Library of Babel" printed here dramatize this open-ended nature of the world and its analog, writing, in Borges's characteristic fashion.

In this regard, Borges anticipated the possibilities of a "world wide web" much before this phenomenon became a commonplace part of our life. And in poems like "The Web" printed here, he had already speculated on what he refers to as "the fatal web of cause and effect / that no man can foresee, nor any god." There is much irony here, and ironic subterfuge, often self-directed, is everywhere in Borges. Even in his death, which he speculates about in this poem, he trumped fate ironically when he chose to go to Geneva upon realizing that he was dying.

Borges's essays on philosophy and literature are likewise speculative and hypertextual. He considers philosophy and metaphysics as branches of literature—that is, of imaginative creation. As a result, he always finds it more interesting to imagine the question rather than find the solution. And in this respect, he never ceases to be fascinated with the masters of the detective genre, Edgar Allan Poe, G. K. Chesterton, and the friend and mentor Borges inherited from his father in Buenos Aires, Macedonio Fernández, a writer who could never finish a novel because no single solution interested him as much as the problem the work explored. His only finished novel has fifty-nine different possible endings.

In addition to his own tales, Borges coauthored a number of stories with his lifetime friend and collaborator, Bioy Casares, publishing their joint productions in the detective genre under the pseudonym of "Bustos Domecq." Borges's translations include works by such authors as Virginia Woolf, Franz Kafka, and William Faulkner. A perennial candidate for the Nobel Prize, which eluded him, he shared the Prix Formentor with Samuel Beckett in 1961, a turning point in Borges's international recognition and world acclaim as one of the key literary figures of the twentieth century.

PRONUNCIATION:

Jorge Luis Borges: HOAR-hay lou-EES BOHR-hays

The Garden of Forking Paths[1]

For Victoria Ocampo

On page 242 of *The History of the World War,* Liddell Hart tells us that an Allied offensive against the Serre-Montauban line (to be mounted by thirteen British divisions backed by one thousand four hundred artillery pieces) had been planned for July 24, 1916, but had to be put off until the morning of the twenty-ninth. Torrential rains (notes Capt. Liddell Hart) were the cause of that delay—a delay that entailed no great consequences, as it turns out. The statement which follows—dictated, reread, and signed by Dr. Yu Tsun, former professor of English in the *Hochschule*[2] at Tsingtao—throws unexpected light on the case. The two first pages of the statement are missing.

. . . and I hung up the receiver. Immediately afterward, I recognised the voice that had answered in German. It was that of Capt. Richard Madden. Madden's presence in Viktor Runeberg's flat meant the end of our efforts and (though this seemed to me quite secondary, or *should have seemed*) our lives as well. It meant that Runeberg had been arrested, or murdered.[3] Before the sun set on that day, I would face the same fate. Madden was implacable—or rather, he was obliged to be implacable. An Irishman at the orders of the English, a man accused of a certain lack of zealousness, perhaps even treason, how could he fail to embrace and give thanks for this miraculous favour—the discovery, capture, perhaps death, of two agents of the German Empire?

1. Translated by Andrew Hurley.
2. "College" in German.
3. Here an "Editor's" footnote—by Borges— reads as follows: "A bizarre and despicable supposition. The Prussian spy Hans Rabener, alias Viktor Runeberg, had turned an automatic pistol on his arresting officer, Capt. Richard Madden. Madden, in self-defense, inflicted the wound on Rabener that caused his subsequent death."

I went upstairs to my room; absurdly, I locked the door, and then I threw myself, on my back, onto my narrow iron bed. Outside the window were the usual rooftops and the overcast six o'clock sun. I found it incredible that this day, lacking all omens and premonitions, should be the day of my implacable death. Despite my deceased father, despite my having been a child in a symmetrical garden in Hai Feng—was I, now, about to die? Then I reflected that all things happen to *oneself,* and happen precisely, precisely *now.* Century follows century, yet events occur only *in the present;* countless men in the air, on the land and sea, yet everything that truly happens, happens *to me. . . .* The almost unbearable memory of Madden's horsey face demolished those mental ramblings. In the midst of my hatred and my terror (now I don't mind talking about terror—now that I have foiled Richard Madden, now that my neck hungers for the rope), it occurred to me that that brawling and undoubtedly happy warrior did not suspect that I possessed the Secret—the name of the exact location of the new British artillery park on the Ancre.[4] A bird furrowed the grey sky, and I blindly translated it into an aeroplane, and that aeroplane into many (in the French sky), annihilating the artillery park with vertical bombs. If only my throat, before a bullet crushed it, could cry out that name so that it might be heard in Germany. . . . But my human voice was so terribly inadequate. How was I to make it reach the Leader's ear—the ear of that sick and hateful man who knew nothing of Runeberg and me save that we were in Staffordshire, and who was vainly awaiting word from us in his arid office in Berlin, poring infinitely through the newspapers? . . . *I must flee,* I said aloud. I sat up noiselessly, in needless but perfect silence, as though Madden were already just outside my door. Something—perhaps the mere show of proving that my resources were nonexistent—made me go through my pockets. I found what I knew I would find: the American watch, the nickel-plated chain and quadrangular coin, the key ring with the compromising and useless keys to Runeberg's flat, the notebook, a letter I resolved to destroy at once (and never did), the false passport, one crown, two shillings, and a few odd pence, the red-and-blue pencil, the handkerchief, the revolver with its single bullet. Absurdly, I picked it up and hefted it, to give myself courage. I vaguely reflected that a pistol shot can be heard at a considerable distance. In ten minutes, my plan was ripe. The telephone book gave me the name of the only person able to communicate the information: he lived in a suburb of Fenton, less than a half hour away by train.

I am a coward. I can say that, now that I have carried out a plan whose dangerousness and daring no man will deny. I know that it was a terrible thing to do. I did not do it for Germany. What do I care for a barbaric country that has forced me to the ignominy of spying? Furthermore, I know of a man of England—a modest man—who in my view is no less a genius than Goethe.[5] I spoke with him for no more than an hour, but for one hour he was Goethe. . . . No—I did it because I sensed that the Leader looked down on the people of my race—the countless ancestors whose blood flows through my veins. I wanted to prove to him that a yellow man could save his armies. And I had to escape from Madden. His hands, his voice, could beat upon my door at any moment. I silently dressed, said good-bye to myself in the mirror, made my way downstairs, looked up and down the quiet street, and set off. The train station was not far from my flat, but I thought it better to take a cab. I argued that I ran less chance of being recognised that way; the fact is, I felt I was visible and vulnerable—infinitely vulnerable—in the deserted street. I recall that I told the driver to stop a little

4. The River Ancre, France. Borges is also punning on "encre," "ink" in French.

5. Johann Wolfgang Goethe (1749–1832), German poet, novelist, dramatist, and essayist, often identified as Germany's greatest writer.

ways from the main entrance to the station. I got down from the cab with willed and almost painful slowness. I would be going to the village of Ashgrove, but I bought a ticket for a station farther down the line. The train was to leave at eight-fifty, scant minutes away. I had to hurry; the next train would not be until nine-thirty. There was almost no one on the platform. I walked through the cars; I recall a few workmen, a woman dressed in mourning weeds, a young man fervently reading Tacitus' *Annals,*[6] and a cheerful-looking wounded soldier. The train pulled out at last. A man I recognised ran, vainly, out to the end of the platform; it was Capt. Richard Madden. Shattered, trembling, I huddled on the other end of the seat, far from the feared window.

From that shattered state I passed into a state of almost abject cheerfulness. I told myself that my duel had begun, and that in dodging my adversary's thrust—even by forty minutes, even thanks to the slightest smile from fate—the first round had gone to me. I argued that this small win prefigured total victory. I argued that the win was not really even so small, since without the precious hour that the trains had given me, I'd be in gaol, or dead. I argued (no less sophistically) that my cowardly cheerfulness proved that I was a man capable of following this adventure through to its successful end. From that weakness I drew strength that was never to abandon me. I foresee that mankind will resign itself more and more fully every day to more and more horrendous undertakings; soon there will be nothing but warriors and brigands. I give them this piece of advice: *He who is to perform a horrendous act should imagine to himself that it is already done, should impose upon himself a future as irrevocable as the past.* That is what I did, while my eyes—the eyes of a man already dead—registered the flow of that day perhaps to be my last, and the spreading of the night. The train ran sweetly, gently, through woods of ash trees. It stopped virtually in the middle of the countryside. No one called out the name of the station. "Ashgrove?" I asked some boys on the platform. "Ashgrove," they said, nodding. I got off the train.

A lamp illuminated the platform, but the boys' faces remained within the area of shadow. "Are you going to Dr. Stephen Albert's house?" one queried. Without waiting for an answer, another of them said: "The house is a far way, but you'll not get lost if you follow that road there to the left, and turn left at every crossing." I tossed them a coin (my last), went down some stone steps, and started down the solitary road. It ran ever so slightly downhill and was of elemental dirt. Branches tangled overhead, and the low round moon seemed to walk along beside me.

For one instant, I feared that Richard Madden had somehow seen through my desperate plan, but I soon realized that that was impossible. The boy's advice to turn always to the left reminded me that that was the common way of discovering the central lawn of a certain type of maze. I am something of a *connoisseur* of mazes: not for nothing am I the great-grandson of that Ts'ui Pen who was governor of Yunan province and who renounced all temporal power in order to write a novel containing more characters than the *Hung Lu Meng*[7] and construct a labyrinth in which all men would lose their way. Ts'ui Pen devoted thirteen years to those disparate labours, but the hand of a foreigner murdered him and his novel made no sense and no one ever found the labyrinth. It was under English trees that I meditated on that lost labyrinth: I pictured it perfect and inviolate on the secret summit of a mountain; I pictured its

6. Cornelius Tacitus (c. 56–120 C.E.), historian of the Roman Empire. His *Annals* narrate the intrigue, corruption, and terror during the reigns of Tiberius, Claudius, and Nero.

7. Cao Xueqin's novel *Dream of the Red Chamber* (1791), China's elaborate family saga with more than 400 characters.

outlines blurred by rice paddies, or underwater; I pictured it as infinite—a labyrinth not of octagonal pavillions and paths that turn back upon themselves, but of rivers and provinces and kingdoms. . . . I imagined a labyrinth of labyrinths, a maze of mazes, a twisting, turning, ever-widening labyrinth that contained both past and future and somehow implied the stars. Absorbed in those illusory imaginings, I forgot that I was a pursued man; I felt myself, for an indefinite while, the abstract perceiver of the world. The vague, living countryside, the moon, the remains of the day did their work in me; so did the gently downward road, which forestalled all possibility of weariness. The evening was near, yet infinite.

The road dropped and forked as it cut through the now-formless meadows. A keen and vaguely syllabic song, blurred by leaves and distance, came and went on the gentle gusts of breeze. I was struck by the thought that a man may be the enemy of other men, the enemy of other men's other moments, yet not be the enemy of a country—of fireflies, words, gardens, watercourses, zephyrs. It was amidst such thoughts that I came to a high rusty gate. Through the iron bars I made out a drive lined with poplars, and a gazebo of some kind. Suddenly, I realised two things—the first trivial, the second almost incredible: the music I had heard was coming from that gazebo, or pavillion, and the music was Chinese. That was why unconsciously I had fully given myself over to it. I do not recall whether there was a bell or whether I had to clap my hands to make my arrival known.

The sputtering of the music continued, but from the rear of the intimate house, a lantern was making its way toward me—a lantern cross-hatched and sometimes blotted out altogether by the trees, a paper lantern the shape of a drum and the colour of the moon. It was carried by a tall man. I could not see his face because the light blinded me. He opened the gate and slowly spoke to me in my own language.

"I see that the compassionate Hsi P'eng has undertaken to remedy my solitude. You will no doubt wish to see the garden?"

I recognised the name of one of our consuls, but I could only disconcertedly repeat, "The garden?"

"The garden of forking paths."

Something stirred in my memory, and I spoke with incomprehensible assurance.

"The garden of my ancestor Ts'ui Pen."

"Your ancestor? Your illustrious ancestor? Please—come in."

The dew-drenched path meandered like the paths of my childhood. We came to a library of Western and Oriental books. I recognised, bound in yellow silk, several handwritten volumes of the Lost Encyclopedia compiled by the third emperor of the Luminous Dynasty but never printed.[8] The disk on the gramophone revolved near a bronze phoenix. I also recall a vase of *famille rose*[9] and another, earlier by several hundred years, of that blue colour our artificers copied from the potters of ancient Persia. . . .

Stephen Albert, with a smile, regarded me. He was, as I have said, quite tall, with sharp features, grey eyes, and a grey beard. There was something priestlike about him, somehow, but something sailorlike as well; later he told me he had been a missionary in Tientsin "before aspiring to be a Sinologist."

8. The third emperor of the Ming, or "Luminous," Dynasty was Yung-lo, and the Encyclopedia is one he commissioned between 1403 and 1408. Originally 11,000 volumes, only 370 volumes now survive.

9. Eighteenth-century pink enamel pottery.

We sat down, I on a long low divan, he with his back to the window and a tall circular clock. I figured that my pursuer, Richard Madden, could not possibly arrive for at least an hour. My irrevocable decision could wait.

"An amazing life, Ts'ui Pen's," Stephen Albert said. "Governor of the province in which he had been born, a man learned in astronomy, astrology, and the unwearying interpretation of canonical books, a chess player, a renowned poet and calligrapher—he abandoned it all in order to compose a book and a labyrinth. He renounced the pleasures of oppression, justice, the populous marriage bed, banquets, and even erudition in order to sequester himself for thirteen years in the Pavillion of Limpid Solitude. Upon his death, his heirs found nothing but chaotic manuscripts. The family, as you perhaps are aware, were about to deliver them to the fire, but his counsellor—a Taoist or Buddhist monk—insisted upon publishing them."

"To this day," I replied, "we who are descended from Ts'ui Pen execrate that monk. It was senseless to publish those manuscripts. The book is a contradictory jumble of irresolute drafts. I once examined it myself; in the third chapter the hero dies, yet in the fourth he is alive again. As for Ts'ui Pen's other labor, his Labyrinth . . ."

"Here is the Labyrinth," Albert said, gesturing towards a tall lacquered writing cabinet.

"An ivory labyrinth!" I exclaimed. "A very small sort of labyrinth . . ."

"A labyrinth of symbols," he corrected me. "An invisible labyrinth of time. I, an English barbarian, have somehow been chosen to unveil the diaphanous mystery. Now, more than a hundred years after the fact, the precise details are irrecoverable, but it is not difficult to surmise what happened, Ts'ui Pen must at one point have remarked, 'I shall retire to write a book,' and at another point, 'I shall retire to construct a labyrinth.' Everyone pictured two projects; it occurred to no one that book and labyrinth were one and the same. The Pavillion of Limpid Solitude was erected in the centre of a garden that was, perhaps, most intricately laid out; that fact might well have suggested a physical labyrinth. Ts'ui Pen died; no one in all the wide lands that had been his could find the labyrinth. The novel's confusion—confusedness, I mean, of course—suggested to me that it was that labyrinth. Two circumstances lent me the final solution of the problem—one, the curious legend that Ts'ui Pen had intended to construct a labyrinth which was truly infinite, and two, a fragment of a letter I discovered."

Albert stood. His back was turned to me for several moments; he opened a drawer in the black-and-gold writing cabinet. He turned back with a paper that had once been crimson but was now pink and delicate and rectangular. It was written in Ts'ui Pen's renowned calligraphy. Eagerly yet uncomprehendingly I read the words that a man of my own lineage had written with painstaking brushstrokes: *I leave to several futures (not to all) my garden of forking paths.* I wordlessly handed the paper back to Albert. He continued:

"Before unearthing this letter, I had wondered how a book could be infinite. The only way I could surmise was that it be a cyclical, or circular, volume, a volume whose last page would be identical to the first, so that one might go on indefinitely. I also recalled that night at the centre of the *1001 Nights,* when the queen Scheherazade (through some magical distractedness on the part of the copyist) begins to retell, verbatim, the story of the 1001 Nights, with the risk of returning once again to the night on which she is telling it—and so on, *ad infinitum.* I also pictured to myself a platonic, hereditary sort of work, passed down from father to son, in which each new individual would add a chapter or with reverent care correct his elders' pages. These imaginings amused and distracted me, but none of them seemed to correspond even remotely to Ts'ui Pen's contradictory chapters. As I was floundering about in the mire of these perplexities, I was sent from Oxford the document you have just examined. I paused, as you may well imagine, at the sentence 'I leave to several futures (not to all) my garden of forking paths.' Almost instantly, I saw it—the garden of forking paths was the chaotic novel; the phrase 'several futures (not all)' suggested to me the image of a forking in *time,* rather than in space. A full rereading of the book confirmed my theory. In all fictions, each time a man meets diverse alternatives, he chooses one and eliminates the others; in the work of the virtually impossible-to-disentangle Ts'ui Pen, the character chooses—simultaneously—all of them. *He creates,* thereby, 'several futures,' several *times,* which themselves proliferate and fork. That is the explanation for the novel's contradictions. Fang, let us say, has a secret; a stranger knocks at his door; Fang decides to kill him. Naturally, there are various possible outcomes—Fang can kill the intruder, the intruder can kill Fang, they can both live, they can both be killed, and so on. In Ts'ui Pen's novel, *all* the outcomes in fact occur; each is the starting point for further bifurcations. Once in a while, the paths of that labyrinth converge: for example, you come to this house, but in one of the possible pasts you are my enemy, in another my friend. If you can bear my incorrigible pronunciation, we shall read a few pages."

His face, in the vivid circle of the lamp, was undoubtedly that of an old man, though with something indomitable and even immortal about it. He read with slow precision two versions of a single epic chapter. In the first, an army marches off to battle through a mountain wilderness; the horror of the rocks and darkness inspires in them a disdain for life, and they go on to an easy victory. In the second, the same army passes through a palace in which a ball is being held; the brilliant battle seems to them a continuation of the *fête,* and they win it easily.

I listened with honourable veneration to those ancient fictions, which were themselves perhaps not as remarkable as the fact that a man of my blood had invented them and a man of a distant empire was restoring them to me on an island in the West in the course of a desperate mission. I recall the final words, repeated in each version like some secret commandment: "Thus the heroes fought, their admirable hearts calm, their swords violent, they themselves resigned to killing and to dying."

From that moment on, I felt all about me and within my obscure body an invisible, intangible pullulation—not that of the divergent, parallel, and finally coalescing armies, but an agitation more inaccessible, more inward than that, yet one those armies somehow prefigured. Albert went on:

"I do not believe that your venerable ancestor played at idle variations. I cannot think it probable that he would sacrifice thirteen years to the infinite performance of a rhetorical exercise. In your country, the novel is a subordinate genre; at that time it was a genre beneath contempt. Ts'ui Pen was a novelist of genius, but he was also a man of letters, and surely would not have considered himself a mere novelist. The testimony of his contemporaries proclaims his metaphysical, mystical leanings—and his life is their fullest confirmation. Philosophical debate consumes a good part of his novel. I know that of all problems, none disturbed him, none gnawed at him like the unfathomable problem of time. How strange, then, that that problem should be the *only* one that does not figure in the pages of his *Garden.* He never even uses the word. How do you explain that wilful omission?"

I proposed several solutions—all unsatisfactory. We discussed them; finally, Stephen Albert said:

"In a riddle whose answer is chess, what is the only word that must not be used?" I thought for a moment.

"The word 'chess,' " I replied.

"Exactly," Albert said. "*The Garden of Forking Paths* is a huge riddle, or parable, whose subject is time; that secret purpose forbids Ts'ui Pen the merest mention of its name. To *always* omit one word, to employ awkward metaphors and obvious circumlocutions, is perhaps the most emphatic way of calling attention to that word. It is, at any rate, the tortuous path chosen by the devious Ts'ui Pen at each and every one of the turnings of his inexhaustible novel. I have compared hundreds of manuscripts, I have corrected the errors introduced through the negligence of copyists, I have reached a hypothesis for the plan of that chaos, I have reestablished, or believe I've reestablished, its fundamental order—I have translated the entire work; and I know that not once does the word 'time' appear. The explanation is obvious: *The Garden of Forking Paths* is an incomplete, but not false, image of the universe as conceived by Ts'ui Pen. Unlike Newton and Schopenhauer,[1] your ancestor did not believe in a uniform and absolute time; he believed in an infinite series of times, a growing, dizzying web of divergent, convergent, and parallel times. That fabric of times that approach one another, fork, are snipped off, or are simply unknown for centuries, contains *all* possibilities. In most of those times, we do not exist; in some, you exist but I do not; in others, I do and you do not; in others still, we both do. In this one, which the favouring hand of chance has dealt me, you have come to my home; in another, when you come through my garden you find me dead; in another, I say these same words, but I am an error, a ghost."

"In all," I said, not without a tremble, "I am grateful for, and I venerate, your recreation of the garden of Ts'ui Pen."

"Not in all," he whispered with a smile. "Time forks, perpetually, into countless futures. In one of them, I am your enemy."

I felt again that pullulation I have mentioned. I sensed that the dew-drenched garden that surrounded the house was saturated, infinitely, with invisible persons. Those persons were Albert and myself—secret, busily at work, multiform—in other dimensions of time. I raised my eyes and the gossamer nightmare faded. In the yellow-and-black garden there was but a single man—but that man was as mighty as a statue, and that man was coming down the path, and he was Capt. Richard Madden.

"The future is with us," I replied, "but I am your friend. May I look at the letter again?"

Albert rose once again. He stood tall as he opened the drawer of the tall writing cabinet; he turned his back to me for a moment. I had cocked the revolver. With utmost care, I fired. Albert fell without a groan, without a sound, on the instant. I swear that he died instantly—one clap of thunder.

The rest is unreal, insignificant. Madden burst into the room and arrested me. I have been sentenced to hang. I have most abhorrently triumphed: I have communicated to Berlin the secret name of the city to be attacked. Yesterday it was bombed—I read about it in the same newspapers that posed to all of England the enigma of the murder of the eminent Sinologist Stephen Albert by a stranger, Yu Tsun. The Leader solved the riddle. He knew that my problem was how to report (over the deafening noise of the war) the name of the city named Albert, and that the only way I could

1. Isaac Newton (1642–1727), English physicist and mathematician who formulated laws of gravity and motion. Arthur Schopenhauer (1788–1860), German philosopher whose Idealist notions of the world as the individual's will and ideas are often cited by Borges.

find was murdering a person of that name. He does not know (no one can know) my endless contrition, and my weariness.

The Library of Babel[1]

By this art you may contemplate the variation of the 23 letters. . . .

Anatomy of Melancholy,[2] pt. 2, sec. 2, mem. 4

The universe (which others call the Library) is composed of an indefinite, perhaps infinite number of hexagonal galleries. In the center of each gallery is a ventilation shaft, bounded by a low railing. From any hexagon one can see the floors above and below—one after another, endlessly. The arrangement of the galleries is always the same: Twenty bookshelves, five to each side, line four of the hexagon's six sides; the height of the bookshelves, floor to ceiling, is hardly greater than the height of a normal librarian. One of the hexagon's free sides opens onto a narrow sort of vestibule, which in turn opens onto another gallery, identical to the first—identical in fact to all. To the left and right of the vestibule are two tiny compartments. One is for sleeping, upright; the other, for satisfying one's physical necessities. Through this space, too, there passes a spiral staircase, which winds upward and downward into the remotest distance. In the vestibule there is a mirror, which faithfully duplicates appearances. Men often infer from this mirror that the Library is not infinite—if it were, what need would there be for that illusory replication? I prefer to dream that burnished surfaces are a figuration and promise of the infinite. . . . Light is provided by certain spherical fruits that bear the name "bulbs." There are two of these bulbs in each hexagon, set crosswise. The light they give is insufficient, and unceasing.

Like all the men of the Library, in my younger days I traveled; I have journeyed in quest of a book, perhaps the catalog of catalogs. Now that my eyes can hardly make out what I myself have written, I am preparing to die, a few leagues from the hexagon where I was born. When I am dead, compassionate hands will throw me over the railing; my tomb will be the unfathomable air, my body will sink for ages, and will decay and dissolve in the wind engendered by my fall, which shall be infinite. I declare that the Library is endless. Idealists argue that the hexagonal rooms are the necessary shape of absolute space, or at least of our *perception* of space. They argue that a triangular or pentagonal chamber is inconceivable. (Mystics claim that their ecstasies reveal to them a circular chamber containing an enormous circular book with a continuous spine that goes completely around the walls. But their testimony is suspect, their words obscure. That cyclical book is God.) Let it suffice for the moment that I repeat the classic dictum: *The Library is a sphere whose exact center is any hexagon and whose circumference is unattainable.*

Each wall of each hexagon is furnished with five bookshelves; each bookshelf holds thirty-two books identical in format; each book contains four hundred ten pages; each page, forty lines; each line, approximately eighty black letters. There are also letters on the front cover of each book; those letters neither indicate nor prefigure what the pages inside will say. I am aware that that lack of correspondence once struck men as mysterious. Before summarizing the solution of the mystery (whose discovery, in spite of its tragic consequences, is perhaps the most important event in all history), I wish to recall a few axioms.

1. Translated by Andrew Hurley.
2. An ironic treatise published in 1621 by the bibliophile Robert Burton. Burton's private library contained more than 2,000 volumes. The epigraph refers to the alphabet, whose 23 letters and their possible combinations constitute any library.

First: *The Library has existed ab aeternitate.* That truth, whose immediate corollary is the future eternity of the world, no rational mind can doubt. Man, the imperfect librarian, may be the work of chance or of malevolent demiurges; the universe, with its elegant appointments—its bookshelves, its enigmatic books, its indefatigable staircases for the traveler, and its water closets for the seated librarian—can only be the handiwork of a god. In order to grasp the distance that separates the human and the divine, one has only to compare these crude trembling symbols which my fallible hand scrawls on the cover of a book with the organic letters inside—neat, delicate, deep black, and inimitably symmetrical.

Second: *There are twenty-five orthographic symbols.* That discovery enabled mankind, three hundred years ago, to formulate a general theory of the Library and thereby satisfactorily solve the riddle that no conjecture had been able to divine—the formless and chaotic nature of virtually all books. One book, which my father once saw in a hexagon in circuit 15–94, consisted of the letters M C V perversely repeated from the first line to the last. Another (much consulted in this zone) is a mere labyrinth of letters whose penultimate page contains the phrase *O Time thy pyramids.* This much is known: For every rational line or forthright statement there are leagues of senseless cacophony, verbal nonsense, and incoherency. (I know of one semi-barbarous zone whose librarians repudiate the "vain and superstitious habit" of trying to find sense in books, equating such a quest with attempting to find meaning in dreams or in the chaotic lines of the palm of one's hand. . . . They will acknowledge that the inventors of writing imitated the twenty-five natural symbols, but contend that that adoption was fortuitous, coincidental, and that books in themselves have no meaning. That argument, as we shall see, is not entirely fallacious.)

For many years it was believed that those impenetrable books were in ancient or far-distant languages. It is true that the most ancient peoples, the first librarians, employed a language quite different from the one we speak today; it is true that a few miles to the right, our language devolves into dialect and that ninety floors above, it becomes incomprehensible. All of that, I repeat, is true—but four hundred ten pages of unvarying M C V's cannot belong to any language, however dialectal or primitive it may be. Some have suggested that each letter influences the next, and that the value of M C V on page 71, line 3, is not the value of the same series on another line of another page, but that vague thesis has not met with any great acceptance. Others have mentioned the possibility of codes; that conjecture has been universally accepted, though not in the sense in which its originators formulated it.

Some five hundred years ago, the chief of one of the upper hexagons came across a book as jumbled as all the others, but containing almost two pages of homogeneous lines. He showed his find to a traveling decipherer, who told him that the lines were written in Portuguese; others said it was Yiddish. Within the century experts had determined what the language actually was: a Samoyed-Lithuanian dialect of Guaraní, with inflections from classical Arabic. The content was also determined: the rudiments of combinatory analysis, illustrated with examples of endlessly repeating variations. Those examples allowed a librarian of genius to discover the fundamental law of the Library. This philosopher observed that all books, however different from one another they might be, consist of identical elements: the space, the period, the comma, and the twenty-two letters of the alphabet. He also posited a fact which all travelers have since confirmed: *In all the Library, there are no two identical books.* From those incontrovertible premises, the librarian deduced that the Library is "total"—perfect, complete, and whole—and that its bookshelves contain all possible combinations of the twenty-two orthographic symbols (a number which, though unimaginably vast, is not infinite)—that is, all that is able to be expressed, in every language. *All*—the detailed history of the future, the autobiographies of the archangels, the faithful catalog of the Library, thousands and thousands of false catalogs, the proof of the falsity of those false catalogs, a proof of the falsity of the *true* catalog, the gnostic gospel of Basilides,[3] the commentary upon that gospel, the commentary on the commentary on that gospel, the true story of your death, the translation of every book into every language, the interpolations of every book into all books, the treatise Bede could have written (but did not) on the mythology of the Saxon people, the lost books of Tacitus.[4]

When it was announced that the Library contained all books, the first reaction was unbounded joy. All men felt themselves the possessors of an intact and secret treasure. There was no personal problem, no world problem, whose eloquent solution did not exist—somewhere in some hexagon. The universe was justified; the universe suddenly became congruent with the unlimited width and breadth of humankind's hope. At that period there was much talk of The Vindications—books of *apologiae* and prophecies that would vindicate for all time the actions of every person in the universe and that held wondrous arcana for men's futures. Thousands of greedy individuals abandoned their sweet native hexagons and rushed downstairs, upstairs, spurred by the vain desire to find their Vindication. These pilgrims squabbled in the narrow corridors, muttered dark imprecations, strangled one another on the divine staircases, threw deceiving volumes down ventilation shafts, were themselves hurled to their deaths by men of distant regions. Others went insane. . . . The Vindications do exist (I have seen two of them, which refer to persons in the future, persons perhaps not imaginary), but those who went in quest of them failed to recall that the chance of a man's finding his own Vindication, or some perfidious version of his own, can be calculated to be zero.

At that same period there was also hope that the fundamental mysteries of mankind—the origin of the Library and of time—might be revealed. In all likelihood those profound mysteries can indeed be explained in words; if the language of the philosophers is not sufficient, then the multiform Library must surely have produced the extraordinary language that is required, together with the words and grammar of that language. For four centuries, men have been scouring the hexagons. . . . There are official searchers, the "inquisitors." I have seen them about their tasks: they arrive exhausted at some hexagon, they talk about a staircase that nearly killed them—rungs were missing—they speak with the librarian about galleries and staircases, and, once in a while, they take up the nearest book and leaf through it, searching for disgraceful or dishonorable words. Clearly, no one expects to discover anything.

That unbridled hopefulness was succeeded, naturally enough, by a similarly disproportionate depression. The certainty that some bookshelf in some hexagon contained precious books, yet that those precious books were forever out of reach, was almost unbearable. One blasphemous sect proposed that the searches be discontinued and that all men shuffle letters and symbols until those canonical books, through some improbable stroke of chance, had been constructed. The authorities were forced to issue strict orders. The sect disappeared, but in my childhood I have seen old men

3. Scholar and teacher in 2nd-century C.E. Alexandria, Egypt. His *Exegetica,* a major commentary on the Bible, consisted of 24 books.

4. The Venerable Bede (c. 673–735) was an English historian and Benedictine monk. Cornelius Tacitus (c. 56–120 C.E.), historian of the Roman Empire.

who for long periods would hide in the latrines with metal disks and a forbidden dice cup, feebly mimicking the divine disorder.

Others, going about it in the opposite way, thought the first thing to do was eliminate all worthless books. They would invade the hexagons, show credentials that were not always false, leaf disgustedly through a volume, and condemn entire walls of books. It is to their hygienic, ascetic rage that we lay the senseless loss of millions of volumes. Their name is execrated today, but those who grieve over the "treasures" destroyed in that frenzy overlook two widely acknowledged facts: One, that the Library is so huge that any reduction by human hands must be infinitesimal. And two, that each book is unique and irreplaceable, but (since the Library is total) there are always several hundred thousand imperfect facsimiles—books that differ by no more than a single letter, or a comma. Despite general opinion, I daresay that the consequences of the depredations committed by the Purifiers have been exaggerated by the horror those same fanatics inspired. They were spurred on by the holy zeal to reach—someday, through unrelenting effort—the books of the Crimson Hexagon—books smaller than natural books, books omnipotent, illustrated, and magical.

We also have knowledge of another superstition from that period: belief in what was termed the Book-Man. On some shelf in some hexagon, it was argued, there must exist a book that is the cipher and perfect compendium *of all other books,* and some librarian must have examined that book; this librarian is analogous to a god. In the language of this zone there are still vestiges of the sect that worshiped that distant librarian. Many have gone in search of Him. For a hundred years, men beat every possible path—and every path in vain. How was one to locate the idolized secret hexagon that sheltered Him? Someone proposed searching by regression: To locate book A, first consult book B, which tells where book A can be found; to locate book B, first consult book C, and so on, to infinity. . . . It is in ventures such as these that I have squandered and spent my years. I cannot think it unlikely that there is such a total book on some shelf in the universe. I pray to the unknown gods that some man—even a single man, tens of centuries ago—has perused and read that book. If the honor and wisdom and joy of such a reading are not to be my own, then let them be for others. Let heaven exist, though my own place be in hell. Let me be tortured and battered and annihilated, but let there be one instant, one creature, wherein thy enormous Library may find its justification.

Infidels claim that the rule in the Library is not "sense," but "non-sense," and that "rationality" (even humble, pure coherence) is an almost miraculous exception. They speak, I know, of "the feverish Library, whose random volumes constantly threaten to transmogrify into others, so that they affirm all things, deny all things, and confound and confuse all things, like some mad and hallucinating deity." Those words, which not only proclaim disorder but exemplify it as well, prove, as all can see, the infidels' deplorable taste and desperate ignorance. For while the Library contains all verbal structures, all the variations allowed by the twenty-five orthographic symbols, it includes not a single absolute piece of nonsense. It would be pointless to observe that the finest volume of all the many hexagons that I myself administer is titled *Combed Thunder,* while another is titled *The Plaster Cramp,* and another, *Axaxaxas mlö.* Those phrases, at first apparently incoherent, are undoubtedly susceptible to cryptographic or allegorical "reading"; that reading, that justification of the words' order and existence, is itself verbal and, *ex hypothesi,* already contained somewhere in the Library. There is no combination of characters one can make—*dhcmrlchtdj,* for example—that the divine Library has not foreseen and that in one or more of its secret tongues does not hide a terrible significance. There is no syllable one can speak that is not filled with tenderness and terror, that is not, in one of those languages, the mighty name of a god. To speak is to commit tautologies. This pointless, verbose epistle already exists in one of the thirty volumes of the five bookshelves in one of the countless hexagons—as does its refutation. (A number *n* of the possible languages employ the same vocabulary; in some of them, the *symbol* "library" possesses the correct definition "everlasting, ubiquitous system of hexagonal galleries," while a library—the thing—is a loaf of bread or a pyramid or something else, and the six words that define it themselves have other definitions. You who read me—are you certain you understand my language?)

Methodical composition distracts me from the present condition of humanity. The certainty that everything has already been written annuls us, or renders us phantasmal. I know districts in which the young people prostrate themselves before books and like savages kiss their pages, though they cannot read a letter. Epidemics, heretical discords, pilgrimages that inevitably degenerate into brigandage have decimated the population. I believe I mentioned the suicides, which are more and more frequent every year. I am perhaps misled by old age and fear, but I suspect that the human species—the *only* species—teeters at the verge of extinction, yet that the Library—enlightened, solitary, infinite, perfectly unmoving, armed with precious volumes, pointless, incorruptible, and secret—will endure.

I have just written the word "infinite." I have not included that adjective out of mere rhetorical habit; I hereby state that it is not illogical to think that the world is infinite. Those who believe it to have limits hypothesize that in some remote place or places the corridors and staircases and hexagons may, inconceivably, end—which is absurd. And yet those who picture the world as unlimited forget that the number of possible books is *not.* I will be bold enough to suggest this solution to the ancient problem: *The Library is unlimited but periodic.* If an eternal traveler should journey in any direction, he would find after untold centuries that the same volumes are repeated in the same disorder—which, repeated, becomes order: the Order. My solitude is cheered by that elegant hope.

Borges and I[1]

It's Borges, the other one, that things happen to. I walk through Buenos Aires and I pause—mechanically now, perhaps—to gaze at the arch of an entryway and its inner door; news of Borges reaches me by mail, or I see his name on a list of academics or in some biographical dictionary. My taste runs to hourglasses, maps, seventeenth-century typefaces, etymologies, the taste of coffee, and the prose of Robert Louis Stevenson;[2] Borges shares those preferences, but in a vain sort of way that turns them into the accoutrements of an actor. It would be an exaggeration to say that our relationship is hostile—I live, I allow myself to live, so that Borges can spin out his literature, and that literature is my justification. I willingly admit that he has written a number of sound pages, but those pages will not save *me,* perhaps because the good in them no longer belongs to any individual, not even to that other man, but rather to language itself, or to tradition. Beyond that, I am doomed—utterly and inevitably—to oblivion, and fleeting moments will be all of me that survives in that other man. Little by little, I have been turning everything over to him, though I know the perverse way he has of distorting

1. Translated by Andrew Hurley.
2. Scottish author (1850–1894) of adventure tales and stories that explore embodiments of good and evil, often cited by Borges.

and magnifying everything. Spinoza[3] believed that all things wish to go on being what they are—stone wishes eternally to be stone, and tiger, to be tiger. I shall endure in Borges, not in myself (if, indeed, I am anybody at all), but I recognize myself less in his books than in many others', or in the tedious strumming of a guitar. Years ago I tried to free myself from him, and I moved on from the mythologies of the slums and outskirts of the city to games with time and infinity, but those games belong to Borges now, and I shall have to think up other things. So my life is a point-counterpoint, a kind of fugue, and a falling away—and everything winds up being lost to me, and everything falls into oblivion, or into the hands of the other man.

I am not sure which of us it is that's writing this page.

The Web[1]

Which of my cities will I die in?
Geneva, where revelation came to me
through Virgil and Tacitus, certainly not from Calvin?[2]
Montevideo, where Luis Melian Lafinur,[3]
blind and heavy with years, died among the archives
of that impartial history of Uruguay
he never wrote?
Nara, where in a Japanese inn
I slept on the floor and dreamed the terrible
image of Buddha I had touched sightlessly
but saw in my dream?
Buenos Aires, where I'm almost a foreigner,
given my many years, or else a habitual target
for autograph hunters?
Austin, Texas, where my mother and I
in the autumn of '61 discovered America?
Others will know it too and will forget it.
What language am I doomed to die in?
The Spanish my ancestors used
to call for the charge or bid at truco?° *a card game*
The English of that Bible
my grandmother read from at the desert's edge?
Others will know it too and will forget it.
What time will it be?
In the dove-colored twilight when color fades away
or in the twilight of the crow
when night abstracts and simplifies
all visible things, or at an odd moment—
two in the afternoon?
Others will know it too and will forget it.
These questions are digressions, not from fear
but from impatient hope,
part of the fatal web of cause and effect
that no man can foresee, nor any god.

3. Dutch philosopher Baruch Spinoza (1632–1677).
1. Translated by Alistair Reid.
2. Virgil and Tacitus, classical Rome's greatest poet and histrorian; John Calvin (1509–1564). French Protestant theologian whose sect emphasized strict morality in a sinful world.
3. One of Borges's ancestors.

Samuel Beckett
1906–1989

In Samuel Beckett's play *Endgame,* one of the characters asks anxiously, "We're not beginning to . . . to . . . mean something?" Whereupon another character responds, "Mean something! You and I, mean something! [Brief laugh.] Ah that's a good one!" This refusal of conventionally understood meaning—whether biographical, psychological, symbolic, or philosophical—characterizes Beckett's groundbreaking work in drama as well as his significant achievements in fiction. In both genres, Beckett persistently attempts to capture the human condition reduced to its barest essentials: through denuded landscapes or tightly enclosed spaces, sparse objects, handicapped or immobilized bodies, repeated gestures, and characters who have no way of escaping from their constrained existential situations. Sometimes they don't even have a voice of their own, functioning instead as an echo of other, perhaps imaginary voices. Yet their fatigue and boredom with their own suicidal despair are always counteracted by their irrepressible urge to keep on talking, adding yet another sentence to the dialogue, telling yet another story. Typically, such characters go back and forth between the assertion that all is over and that nothing will ever stop: "I can't go on, I'll go on," says the narrator in the very last line of Beckett's novel *The Unnamable* (1953), and the only character in his late play *Not I* (1973) is a disembodied mouth speaking incessantly.

The endeavor to get down to essentials and to subtract, reduce, and condense words is quite visible in the steadily diminishing bulk of Beckett's writing; while his works were never voluminous, in the 1940s he did write several full-length novels. By the 1960s and 1970s, he was publishing pieces whose very titles evoked brevity and inconsequence (such as *Ends and Odds* [1974–1976] or *Fizzles* [1976]), and they did indeed tend to become ever shorter: *Come and Go* (1967) and *Lessness* (1970) reduced their linguistic inventory to just a few dozen words or sentences, and some of his late plays such as *Quad* (1984) or *Acts Without Words I* and *Acts Without Words II* dispensed with language altogether, reducing theater to movement and gesture. Yet over a writing career that spanned four decades, Beckett never did stop writing. Instead, he invented ever-new ways to express the absence of meaning that lies at the core of his aesthetics: he once summarized his project as "the expression that there is nothing to express, nothing with which to express, nothing from which to express, no power to express, no desire to express, together with the obligation to express."

Yet this statement by no means implies that Beckett's works are tedious, bleak, and cheerless to read. On the contrary, many of them are uproariously funny, and some of his plays can be performed either as deadly serious drama or as vaudeville slapstick. A good example of this ambivalence is Beckett's most famous work, *Waiting for Godot,* which was an immediate success at its first performance in Paris in 1953 and established his reputation as a major playwright. Its four characters, Vladimir, Estragon, Lucky, and Pozzo, can be played either as existentialist heroes confronted with the absurdity of human life or as clowns who experience life's lack of meaning as a kind of cosmic comedy. The comedian Bert Lahr, in fact—best known as the Cowardly Lion in *The Wizard of Oz*—performed one of the roles in the play's Broadway debut. Beckett's fiction similarly oscillates between slapstick and bitter irony. A reader may be deeply disturbed at the spectacle of the character Molloy dragging himself through the mud with his crutches or laugh out loud at Molloy's insistence that even in this unlikely position, he never fails to doff his hat to passing ladies. While it isn't inappropriate to refer to Beckett as a pessimist, nihilist, or existentialist, he is also one of the twentieth century's great humorists, and his flair for comedy is what sets him apart from such writers as Franz Kafka, Jean-Paul Sartre, or Albert Camus, who also foreground the absurdity of an existence into which humans find themselves thrown without their consent.

Nor does Beckett's rejection of expression and meaning imply that his texts can't or shouldn't be interpreted. In fact, they challenge us to explore precisely the reasons and strategies through which they elude common procedures of sense making. Quite often, Beckett's texts take up problems of philosophy and language that have a long tradition in Western thought and pursue them to a logical impasse from which there is no conceptual escape. Many readers have noted the influence of French philosopher René Descartes on Beckett's work: Descartes's statement "I think, therefore I am" splits the thinking mind into the one who thinks and the one who observes the thinking, a self-referentiality that is often reflected in the relationship between similar or symbiotic characters in Beckett's fiction and plays. How the workings of human consciousness can be represented in literary language at all is a question that takes on a good deal of urgency in this context, one that was also explored by the Irish novelist James Joyce, whom Beckett met and worked with in Paris. In an early essay on the French novelist Marcel Proust, Beckett discussed the problematic connection between past and present self as they are established in the human mind by memory. His own works foreground this theme through characters who seem able to call up only fragments of their former lives. From Dante Alighieri, who is frequently alluded to, Beckett takes an interest in the various kinds of hell that people's lives can become and that they can create for each other—but without the sense of theological justice that informed Dante's *Inferno*. Frequently, then, what makes it difficult to attribute meaning to Beckett's texts is the fact that they question precisely the tools—rationality, logic, chronology, and transparent language—that we normally use to establish such meaning.

The multiple echoes of earlier writings in Beckett's texts point to a writer with a broad knowledge of varied languages and traditions. Born in a suburb of Dublin in 1906, he grew up in a middle-class, Anglo-Irish, Protestant family. From 1923 to 1927 he attended Trinity College in Dublin, where he studied French and Italian. In 1928 he went to Paris on a fellowship to teach English at the École Normale Supérieure and met his countryman James Joyce during his stay. Two years later, in 1930, he returned to Ireland to become a lecturer of French at Trinity College; he completed his master's degree in December 1931 and shortly afterward resigned from teaching, which he disliked intensely. In the following years, he lived and traveled in England, France, Italy, and Germany and finally settled in Paris in 1937. A year later he met Suzanne Deschevaux-Dumesnil, who became his life companion and, in 1961, his wife; she was an indispensable help in getting his first novel, *Murphy,* published in 1938 after it had been rejected by dozens of publishers.

Since Ireland was a neutral power in World War II, Beckett was able to remain in Paris during the Nazi occupation. But he joined an underground resistance group in 1941 and was forced to flee to Roussillon in the unoccupied south of France when some members of his group were arrested by the Germans in 1942. In Roussillon, he worked as a farm laborer until the end of the war and composed his novel *Watt*. In 1945 he worked for some time as an interpreter for the Irish Red Cross in Normandy. He returned to Paris in the winter of 1945, and was awarded the *Croix de guerre* and the *Médaille de la Résistance* for his participation in the French Resistance. Beckett lived and wrote in Paris for the rest of his life; while his main achievements continued to be in drama and narrative, he also ventured into radio plays, a television play, and a film script. He was awarded the Nobel Prize in literature in 1969, and at his eightieth birthday he was celebrated as one of the most important writers of the twentieth century. He died in Paris at the age of eighty-three.

The period following World War II was one of the most productive in Beckett's life: In the late 1940s, he switched from English to French as his principal literary medium and wrote his most important narrative work, a trilogy of novels entitled *Molloy*, *Malone Dies,* and *The Unnamable*, which were published between 1951 and 1953. He also completed *Waiting for Godot*, followed in 1957 by *Endgame,* which portrays a bunkerlike setting where human existences that have run far beyond meaning nevertheless stubbornly refuse to end. With its hints at a cultural landscape devastated perhaps by war, perhaps by holocaust, or maybe just by the sheer absurdity of life, *Endgame* is an even starker, more stripped-down play than *Godot.* Yet as in *Godot,* the moments of bleakest despair give rise to the most sweeping comedy.

Endgame[1]
A Play in One Act

Characters

NAGG
NELL
HAMM
CLOV

Bare interior.

Grey light.

Left and right back, high up, two small windows, curtains drawn. Front right, a door. Hanging near door, its face to wall, a picture. Front left, touching each other, covered with an old sheet, two ashbins. Center, in an armchair on castors, covered with an old sheet, Hamm. Motionless by the door, his eyes fixed on Hamm, Clov. Very red face. Brief tableau.

Clov goes and stands under window left. Stiff, staggering walk. He looks up at window left. He turns and looks at window right. He goes and stands under window right. He looks up at window right. He turns and looks at window left. He goes out, comes back immediately with a small step-ladder, carries it over and sets it down under window left, gets up on it, draws back curtain. He gets down, takes six steps (for example) towards window right, goes back for ladder, carries it over and sets it down under window right, gets up on it, draws back curtain. He gets down, takes three steps towards window left, goes back for ladder, carries it over and sets it down under window left, gets up on it, looks out of window. Brief laugh. He gets down, takes one step towards window right, goes back for ladder, carries it over and sets it down under window right, gets up on it, looks out of window. Brief laugh. He gets down, goes with ladder towards ashbins, halts, turns, carries back ladder and sets it down under window right, goes to ashbins, removes sheet covering them, folds it over his arm. He raises one lid, stoops and looks into bin. Brief laugh. He closes lid. Same with other bin. He goes to Hamm, removes sheet covering him, folds it over his arm. In a dressing-gown, a stiff toque[2] on his head, a large blood-stained handkerchief over his face, a whistle hanging from his neck, a rug over his knees, thick socks on his feet, Hamm seems to be asleep. Clov looks him over. Brief laugh. He goes to door, halts, turns towards auditorium.

CLOV [*fixed gaze, tonelessly*]: Finished, it's finished, nearly finished, it must be nearly finished. [*Pause.*] Grain upon grain, one by one, and one day, suddenly, there's a heap, a little heap, the impossible heap. [*Pause.*] I can't be punished any more. [*Pause.*] I'll go now to my kitchen, ten feet by ten feet by ten feet, and wait for him to whistle me. [*Pause.*] Nice dimensions, nice proportions, I'll lean on the table, and look at the wall, and wait for him to whistle me.

1. Written in French, then translated into English by Beckett himself. Beckett dedicated the play to its first director, Roger Blin.

2. A round brimless hat.

[*He remains a moment motionless, then goes out. He comes back immediately, goes to window right, takes up the ladder and carries it out. Pause. Hamm stirs. He yawns under the handkerchief. He removes the handkerchief from his face. Very red face. Black glasses.*]

HAMM: Me—[*he yawns*]—to play. [*He holds the handkerchief spread out before him.*]

Old stancher! [*He takes off his glasses, wipes his eyes, his face, the glasses, puts them on again, folds the handkerchief and puts it back neatly in the breast-pocket of his dressing-gown. He clears his throat, joins the tips of his fingers.*]

Can there be misery—[*he yawns*]—loftier than mine? No doubt. Formerly. But now? [*Pause.*] My father? [*Pause.*] My mother? [*Pause.*] My . . . dog? [*Pause.*] Oh I am willing to believe they suffer as much as such creatures can suffer. But does that mean their sufferings equal mine? No doubt. [*Pause.*] No, all is a—[*he yawns*]—bsolute, [*proudly*] the bigger a man is the fuller he is. [*Pause. Gloomily.*] And the emptier. [*He sniffs.*] Clov! [*Pause.*] No, alone. [*Pause.*] What dreams! Those forests! [*Pause.*] Enough, it's time it ended, in the shelter too. [*Pause.*] And yet I hesitate, I hesitate to . . . to end. Yes, there it is, it's time it ended and yet I hesitate to—[*he yawns*]—to end. [*Yawns.*] God, I'm tired, I'd be better off in bed.

[*He whistles. Enter Clov immediately. He halts beside the chair.*]

You pollute the air! [*Pause.*] Get me ready, I'm going to bed.

CLOV: I've just got you up.

HAMM: And what of it?

CLOV: I can't be getting you up and putting you to bed every five minutes, I have things to do. [*Pause.*]

HAMM: Did you ever see my eyes?

CLOV: No.

HAMM: Did you never have the curiosity, while I was sleeping, to take off my glasses and look at my eyes?

CLOV: Pulling back the lids? [*Pause.*] No.

HAMM: One of these days I'll show them to you. [*Pause.*] It seems they've gone all white. [*Pause.*] What time is it?

CLOV: The same as usual.

HAMM [*gesture towards window right*]: Have you looked?

CLOV: Yes.

HAMM: Well?

CLOV: Zero.

HAMM: It'd need to rain.

CLOV: It won't rain. [*Pause.*]

HAMM: Apart from that, how do you feel?

CLOV: I don't complain.

HAMM: You feel normal?

CLOV [*irritably*]: I tell you I don't complain.

HAMM: I feel a little queer. [*Pause.*] Clov!

CLOV: Yes.

HAMM: Have you not had enough?
CLOV: Yes! [*Pause.*] Of what?
HAMM: Of this . . . this . . . thing.
CLOV: I always had. [*Pause.*] Not you?
HAMM [*gloomily*]: Then there's no reason for it to change.
CLOV: It may end. [*Pause.*] All life long the same questions, the same answers.
HAMM: Get me ready.

[*Clov does not move.*]

Go and get the sheet.

[*Clov does not move.*]

Clov!
CLOV: Yes.
HAMM: I'll give you nothing more to eat.
CLOV: Then we'll die.
HAMM: I'll give you just enough to keep you from dying. You'll be hungry all the time.
CLOV: Then we won't die. [*Pause.*] I'll go and get the sheet.

[*He goes towards the door.*]

HAMM: No!

[*Clov halts.*]

I'll give you one biscuit per day. [*Pause.*] One and a half. [*Pause.*] Why do you stay with me?
CLOV: Why do you keep me?
HAMM: There's no one else.
CLOV: There's nowhere else. [*Pause.*]
HAMM: You're leaving me all the same.
CLOV: I'm trying.
HAMM: You don't love me.
CLOV: No.
HAMM: You loved me once.
CLOV: Once!
HAMM: I've made you suffer too much. [*Pause.*] Haven't I?
CLOV: It's not that.
HAMM [*shocked*]: I haven't made you suffer too much?
CLOV: Yes!
HAMM [*relieved*]: Ah you gave me a fright! [*Pause. Coldly.*] Forgive me. [*Pause. Louder.*] I said, Forgive me.
CLOV: I heard you. [*Pause.*] Have you bled?
HAMM: Less. [*Pause.*] Is it not time for my pain-killer?
CLOV: No. [*Pause.*]
HAMM: How are your eyes?
CLOV: Bad.
HAMM: How are your legs?
CLOV: Bad.

HAMM: But you can move.
CLOV: Yes.
HAMM [*violently*]: Then move!

[*Clov goes to back wall, leans against it with his forehead and hands.*]

Where are you?
CLOV: Here.
HAMM: Come back!

[*Clov returns to his place beside the chair.*]

Where are you?
CLOV: Here.
HAMM: Why don't you kill me?
CLOV: I don't know the combination of the cupboard. [*Pause.*]
HAMM: Go and get two bicycle-wheels.
CLOV: There are no more bicycle-wheels.
HAMM: What have you done with your bicycle?
CLOV: I never had a bicycle.
HAMM: The thing is impossible.
CLOV: When there were still bicycles I wept to have one. I crawled at your feet. You told me to go to hell. Now there are none.
HAMM: And your rounds? When you inspected my paupers. Always on foot?
CLOV: Sometimes on horse.

[*The lid of one of the bins lifts and the hands of Nagg appear, gripping the rim. Then his head emerges. Nightcap. Very white face. Nagg yawns, then listens.*]

I'll leave you, I have things to do.
HAMM: In your kitchen?
CLOV: Yes.
HAMM: Outside of here it's death. [*Pause.*] All right, be off.

[*Exit Clov. Pause.*]

We're getting on.
NAGG: Me pap!
HAMM: Accursed progenitor!
NAGG: Me pap!
HAMM: The old folks at home! No decency left! Guzzle, guzzle, that's all they think of.

[*He whistles. Enter Clov. He halts beside the chair.*]

Well! I thought you were leaving me.
CLOV: Oh not just yet, not just yet.
NAGG: Me pap!
HAMM: Give him his pap.
CLOV: There's no more pap.
HAMM [*to Nagg*]: Do you hear that? There's no more pap. You'll never get any more pap.
NAGG: I want me pap!

HAMM: Give him a biscuit.

[*Exit Clov.*]

Accursed fornicator! How are your stumps?
NAGG: Never mind me stumps.

[*Enter Clov with biscuit.*]

CLOV: I'm back again, with the biscuit.

[*He gives biscuit to Nagg who fingers it, sniffs it.*]

NAGG [*plaintively*]: What is it?
CLOV: Spratt's medium.
NAGG [*as before*]: It's hard! I can't!
HAMM: Bottle him!

[*Clov pushes Nagg back into the bin, closes the lid.*]

CLOV [*returning to his place beside the chair*]: If age but knew!
HAMM: Sit on him!
CLOV: I can't sit.
HAMM: True. And I can't stand.
CLOV: So it is.
HAMM: Every man his speciality. [*Pause.*] No phone calls? [*Pause.*] Don't we laugh?
CLOV [*after reflection*]: I don't feel like it.
HAMM [*after reflection*]: Nor I. [*Pause.*] Clov!
CLOV: Yes.
HAMM: Nature has forgotten us.
CLOV: There's no more nature.
HAMM: No more nature! You exaggerate.
CLOV: In the vicinity.
HAMM: But we breathe, we change! We lose our hair, our teeth! Our bloom! Our ideals!
CLOV: Then she hasn't forgotten us.
HAMM: But you say there is none.
CLOV [*sadly*]: No one that ever lived ever thought so crooked as we.
HAMM: We do what we can.
CLOV: We shouldn't. [*Pause.*]
HAMM: You're a bit of all right, aren't you?
CLOV: A smithereen. [*Pause.*]
HAMM: This is slow work. [*Pause.*] Is it not time for my pain-killer?
CLOV: No. [*Pause.*] I'll leave you, I have things to do.
HAMM: In your kitchen?
CLOV: Yes.
HAMM: What, I'd like to know.
CLOV: I look at the wall.
HAMM: The wall! And what do you see on your wall? Mene, mene?[3] Naked bodies?
CLOV: I see my light dying.

3. A phrase that appears written by a supernatural hand on a wall of the Babylonian king Belshazzar's palace in the book of Daniel. The inscription, "mene, mene, tekel, upharsin," is translated by the prophet Daniel as "God has numbered the days of your kingdom and brought it to an end" (Daniel 5:26); Belshazzar is killed the same night.

HAMM: Your light dying! Listen to that! Well, it can die just as well here, *your* light. Take a look at me and then come back and tell me what you think of *your* light. [*Pause.*]

CLOV: You shouldn't speak to me like that. [*Pause.*]

HAMM [*coldly*]: Forgive me. [*Pause. Louder.*] I said, Forgive me.

CLOV: I heard you.

[*The lid of Nagg's bin lifts. His hands appear, gripping the rim. Then his head emerges. In his mouth the biscuit. He listens.*]

HAMM: Did your seeds come up?

CLOV: No.

HAMM: Did you scratch round them to see if they had sprouted?

CLOV: They haven't sprouted.

HAMM: Perhaps it's still too early.

CLOV: If they were going to sprout they would have sprouted. [*Violently.*] They'll never sprout!

[*Pause. Nagg takes biscuit in his hand.*]

HAMM: This is not much fun. [*Pause.*] But that's always the way at the end of the day, isn't it, Clov?

CLOV: Always.

HAMM: It's the end of the day like any other day, isn't it, Clov?

CLOV: Looks like it. [*Pause.*]

HAMM [*anguished*]: What's happening, what's happening?

CLOV: Something is taking its course. [*Pause.*]

HAMM: All right, be off.

[*He leans back in his chair, remains motionless. Clov does not move, heaves a great groaning sigh. Hamm sits up.*]

I thought I told you to be off.

CLOV: I'm trying.

[*He goes to door, halts.*]

Ever since I was whelped.

[*Exit Clov.*]

HAMM: We're getting on.

[*He leans back in his chair, remains motionless. Nagg knocks on the lid of the other bin. Pause. He knocks harder. The lid lifts and the hands of Nell appear, gripping the rim. Then her head emerges. Lace cap. Very white face.*]

NELL: What is it, my pet? [*Pause.*] Time for love?

NAGG: Were you asleep?

NELL: Oh no!

NAGG: Kiss me.

NELL: We can't.

NAGG: Try.

[*Their heads strain towards each other, fail to meet, fall apart again.*]

NELL: Why this farce, day after day? [*Pause.*]
NAGG: I've lost me tooth.
NELL: When?
NAGG: I had it yesterday.
NELL [*elegiac*]: Ah yesterday!

[*They turn painfully towards each other.*]

NAGG: Can you see me?
NELL: Hardly. And you?
NAGG: What?
NELL: Can you see me?
NAGG: Hardly.
NELL: So much the better, so much the better.
NAGG: Don't say that. [*Pause.*] Our sight has failed.
NELL: Yes.

[*Pause. They turn away from each other.*]

NAGG: Can you hear me?
NELL: Yes. And you?
NAGG: Yes. [*Pause.*] Our hearing hasn't failed.
NELL: Our what?
NAGG: Our hearing.
NELL: No. [*Pause.*] Have you anything else to say to me?
NAGG: Do you remember—
NELL: No.
NAGG: When we crashed on our tandem and lost our shanks.

[*They laugh heartily.*]

NELL: It was in the Ardennes.

[*They laugh less heartily.*]

NAGG: On the road to Sedan.[4]

[*They laugh still less heartily.*]

Are you cold?
NELL: Yes, perished. And you?
NAGG: [*Pause.*] I'm freezing. [*Pause.*] Do you want to go in?
NELL: Yes.
NAGG: Then go in.

[*Nell does not move.*]

Why don't you go in?
NELL: I don't know. [*Pause.*]
NAGG: Has he changed your sawdust?
NELL: It isn't sawdust. [*Pause. Wearily.*] Can you not be a little accurate, Nagg?
NAGG: Your sand then. It's not important.
NELL: It is important. [*Pause.*]

4. A town in the Ardennes, a wooded region in northern France.

NAGG: It was sawdust once.

NELL: Once!

NAGG: And now it's sand. [*Pause.*] From the shore. [*Pause. Impatiently.*] Now it's sand he fetches from the shore.

NELL: Now it's sand.

NAGG: Has he changed yours?

NELL: No.

NAGG: Nor mine. [*Pause.*] I won't have it! [*Pause. Holding up the biscuit.*] Do you want a bit?

NELL: No. [*Pause.*] Of what?

NAGG: Biscuit. I've kept you half. [*He looks at the biscuit. Proudly.*] Three quarters. For you. Here. [*He proffers the biscuit.*] No? [*Pause.*] Do you not feel well?

HAMM [*wearily*]: Quiet, quiet, you're keeping me awake. [*Pause.*] Talk softer. [*Pause.*] If I could sleep I might make love. I'd go into the woods. My eyes would see . . . the sky, the earth. I'd run, run, they wouldn't catch me. [*Pause.*] Nature! [*Pause.*] There's something dripping in my head. [*Pause.*] A heart, a heart in my head. [*Pause.*]

NAGG [*soft*]: Do you hear him? A heart in his head! [*He chuckles cautiously.*]

NELL: One mustn't laugh at those things, Nagg. Why must you always laugh at them?

NAGG: Not so loud!

NELL [*without lowering her voice*]: Nothing is funnier than unhappiness, I grant you that. But—

NAGG [*shocked*]: Oh!

NELL: Yes, yes, it's the most comical thing in the world. And we laugh, we laugh, with a will, in the beginning. But it's always the same thing. Yes, it's like the funny story we have heard too often, we still find it funny, but we don't laugh any more. [*Pause.*] Have you anything else to say to me?

NAGG: No.

NELL: Are you quite sure? [*Pause.*] Then I'll leave you.

NAGG: Do you not want your biscuit? [*Pause.*] I'll keep it for you. [*Pause.*] I thought you were going to leave me.

NELL: I am going to leave you.

NAGG: Could you give me a scratch before you go?

NELL: No. [*Pause.*] Where?

NAGG: In the back.

NELL: No. [*Pause.*] Rub yourself against the rim.

NAGG: It's lower down. In the hollow.

NELL: What hollow?

NAGG: The hollow! [*Pause.*] Could you not? [*Pause.*] Yesterday you scratched me there.

NELL [*elegiac*]: Ah yesterday!

NAGG: Could you not? [*Pause.*] Would you like me to scratch you? [*Pause.*] Are you crying again?

NELL: I was trying. [*Pause.*]

HAMM: Perhaps it's a little vein. [*Pause.*]

NAGG: What was that he said?

NELL: Perhaps it's a little vein.

NAGG: What does that mean? [*Pause.*] That means nothing. [*Pause.*] Will I tell you the story of the tailor?

NELL: No. [*Pause.*] What for?
NAGG: To cheer you up.
NELL: It's not funny.
NAGG: It always made you laugh. [*Pause.*] The first time I thought you'd die.
NELL: It was on Lake Como.[5] [*Pause.*] One April afternoon. [*Pause.*] Can you believe it?
NAGG: What?
NELL: That we once went out rowing on Lake Como. [*Pause.*] One April afternoon.
NAGG: We had got engaged the day before.
NELL: Engaged!
NAGG: You were in such fits that we capsized. By rights we should have been drowned.
NELL: It was because I felt happy.
NAGG [*indignant*]: It was not, it was not, it was my story and nothing else. Happy! Don't you laugh at it still? Every time I tell it. Happy!
NELL: It was deep, deep. And you could see down to the bottom. So white. So clean.
NAGG: Let me tell it again. [*Raconteur's*[6] *voice.*] An Englishman, needing a pair of striped trousers in a hurry for the New Year festivities, goes to his tailor who takes his measurements.

[*Tailor's voice.*]

"That's the lot, come back in four days, I'll have it ready."
Good. Four days later.

[*Tailor's voice.*]

"So sorry, come back in a week, I've made a mess of the seat." Good, that's all right, a neat seat can be very ticklish. A week later.

[*Tailor's voice.*]

"Frightfully sorry, come back in ten days, I've made a hash of the crotch." Good, can't be helped, a snug crotch is always a teaser. Ten days later.

[*Tailor's voice.*]

"Dreadfully sorry, come back in a fortnight, I've made a balls of the fly." Good, at a pinch, a smart fly is a stiff proposition. [*Pause. Normal voice.*] I never told it worse. [*Pause. Gloomy.*] I tell this story worse and worse.

[*Pause. Raconteur's voice.*]

Well, to make it short, the bluebells are blowing and he ballockses the buttonholes.

[*Customer's voice.*]

"God damn you to hell, Sir, no, it's indecent, there are limits! In six days, do you hear me, six days, God made the world. Yes Sir, no less Sir, the WORLD! And you are not bloody well capable of making me a pair of trousers in three months!"

[*Tailor's voice, scandalized.*]

"But my dear Sir, my dear Sir, look—[*disdainful gesture, disgustedly*]—at the world—[*pause*] and look—[*loving gesture, proudly*]—at my TROUSERS!"

5. A scenic lake in northern Italy.

6. A talented storyteller.

[*Pause. He looks at Nell who has remained impassive, her eyes unseeing, breaks into a high forced laugh, cuts it short, pokes his head towards Nell, launches his laugh again.*]

HAMM: Silence!

[*Nagg starts, cuts short his laugh.*]

NELL: You could see down to the bottom.
HAMM [*exasperated*]: Have you not finished? Will you never finish? [*With sudden fury.*] Will this never finish?

[*Nagg disappears into his bin, closes the lid behind him. Nell does not move. Frenziedly.*]

My kingdom for a nightman![7]

[*He whistles. Enter Clov.*]

Clear away this muck! Chuck it in the sea!

[*Clov goes to bins, halts.*]

NELL: So white.
HAMM: What? What's she blathering about?

[*Clov stoops, takes Nell's hand, feels her pulse.*]

NELL [*to Clov*]: Desert!

[*Clov lets go her hand, pushes her back in the bin, closes the lid.*]

CLOV [*returning to his place beside the chair*]: She has no pulse.
HAMM: What was she drivelling about?
CLOV: She told me to go away, into the desert.
HAMM: Damn busybody! Is that all?
CLOV: No.
HAMM: What else?
CLOV: I didn't understand.
HAMM: Have you bottled her?
CLOV: Yes.
HAMM: Are they both bottled?
CLOV: Yes.
HAMM: Screw down the lids.

[*Clov goes towards door.*]

Time enough.

[*Clov halts.*]

My anger subsides, I'd like to pee.
CLOV [*with alacrity*]: I'll go and get the catheter.

[*He goes towards door.*]

7. Someone who empties outhouses. Hamm's phrasing alludes to Richard III's call, "My kingdom for a horse!" in Shakespeare's tragedy *Richard III* 5.4.

HAMM: Time enough.

[*Clov halts.*]

Give me my pain-killer.

CLOV: It's too soon. [*Pause.*] It's too soon on top of your tonic, it wouldn't act.

HAMM: In the morning they brace you up and in the evening they calm you down. Unless it's the other way round. [*Pause.*] That old doctor, he's dead naturally?

CLOV: He wasn't old.

HAMM: But he's dead?

CLOV: Naturally. [*Pause.*] *You* ask *me* that? [*Pause.*]

HAMM: Take me for a little turn.

[*Clov goes behind the chair and pushes it forward.*]

Not too fast!

[*Clov pushes chair.*]

Right round the world!

[*Clov pushes chair.*]

Hug the walls, then back to the center again.

[*Clov pushes chair.*]

I was right in the center, wasn't I?

CLOV [*pushing*]: Yes.

HAMM: We'd need a proper wheel-chair. With big wheels. Bicycle wheels! [*Pause.*] Are you hugging?

CLOV [*pushing*]: Yes.

HAMM [*groping for wall*]: It's a lie! Why do you lie to me?

CLOV [*bearing closer to wall*]: There! There!

HAMM: Stop!

[*Clov stops chair close to back wall. Hamm lays his hand against wall.*]

Old wall! [*Pause.*] Beyond is the . . . other hell. [*Pause. Violently.*] Closer! Closer! Up against!

CLOV: Take away your hand.

[*Hamm withdraws his hand. Clov rams chair against wall.*]

There!

[*Hamm leans towards wall, applies his ear to it.*]

HAMM: Do you hear?

[*He strikes the wall with his knuckles.*]

Do you hear? Hollow bricks!

[*He strikes again.*]

All that's hollow! [*Pause. He straightens up. Violently.*] That's enough. Back!

CLOV: We haven't done the round.

HAMM: Back to my place!

[*Clov pushes chair back to center.*]

Is that my place?
CLOV: Yes, that's your place.
HAMM: Am I right in the center?
CLOV: I'll measure it.
HAMM: More or less! More or less!
CLOV [*moving chair slightly*]: There!
HAMM: I'm more or less in the center?
CLOV: I'd say so.
HAMM: You'd say so! Put me right in the center!
CLOV: I'll go and get the tape.
HAMM: Roughly! Roughly!

[*Clov moves chair slightly.*]

Bang in the center!
CLOV: There! [*Pause.*]
HAMM: I feel a little too far to the left.

[*Clov moves chair slightly.*]

Now I feel a little too far to the right.

[*Clov moves chair slightly.*]

I feel a little too far forward.

[*Clov moves chair slightly.*]

Now I feel a little too far back.

[*Clov moves chair slightly.*]

Don't stay there [*i.e. behind the chair*], you give me the shivers.

[*Clov returns to his place beside the chair.*]

CLOV: If I could kill him I'd die happy. [*Pause.*]
HAMM: What's the weather like?
CLOV: As usual.
HAMM: Look at the earth.
CLOV: I've looked.
HAMM: With the glass?
CLOV: No need of the glass.
HAMM: Look at it with the glass.
CLOV: I'll go and get the glass

[*Exit Clov.*]

HAMM: No need for the glass!

[*Enter Clov with telescope.*]

CLOV: I'm back again, with the glass.

[*He goes to window right, looks up at it.*]

I need the steps.

HAMM: Why? Have you shrunk?

[*Exit Clov with telescope.*]

I don't like that, I don't like that.

[*Enter Clov with ladder, but without telescope.*]

CLOV: I'm back again, with the steps.

[*He sets down ladder under window right, gets up on it, realizes he has not the telescope, gets down.*]

I need the glass.

[*He goes towards door.*]

HAMM [*violently*]: But you have the glass!

CLOV [*halting, violently*]: No, I haven't the glass!

[*Exit Clov.*]

HAMM: This is deadly.

[*Enter Clov with telescope. He goes towards ladder.*]

CLOV: Things are livening up.

[*He gets up on the ladder, raises the telescope, lets it fall.*]

I did it on purpose.

[*He gets down, picks up the telescope, turns it on auditorium.*]

I see . . . a multitude . . . in transports . . . of joy. [*Pause.*] That's what I call a magnifier.

[*He lowers the telescope, turns towards Hamm.*]

Well? Don't we laugh?

HAMM [*after reflection*]: I don't.

CLOV [*after reflection*]: Nor I.

[*He gets up on ladder, turns the telescope on the without.*]

Let's see.

[*He looks, moving the telescope.*]

Zero . . . [*he looks*] . . . zero . . . [*he looks*] . . . and zero.

HAMM: Nothing stirs. All is—

CLOV: Zer—

HAMM [*violently*]: Wait till you're spoken to! [*Normal voice.*] All is . . . all is . . . all is what? [*Violently.*] All is what?

CLOV: What all is? In a word? Is that what you want to know? Just a moment.

[*He turns the telescope on the without, looks, lowers the telescope, turns towards Hamm.*]

Corpsed. [*Pause.*] Well? Content?
HAMM: Look at the sea.
CLOV: It's the same.
HAMM: Look at the ocean!

[*Clov gets down, takes a few steps towards window left, goes back for ladder, carries it over and sets it down under window left, gets up on it, turns the telescope on the without, looks at length. He starts, lowers the telescope, examines it, turns it again on the without.*]

CLOV: Never seen anything like that!
HAMM [*anxious*]: What? A sail? A fin? Smoke?
CLOV [*looking*]: The light is sunk.
HAMM [*relieved*]: Pah! We all knew that.
CLOV [*looking*]: There was a bit left.
HAMM: The base.
CLOV [*looking*]: Yes.
HAMM: And now?
CLOV [*looking*]: All gone.
HAMM: No gulls?
CLOV [*looking*]: Gulls!
HAMM: And the horizon? Nothing on the horizon?
CLOV [*lowering the telescope, turning towards Hamm, exasperated*]: What in God's name could there be on the horizon? [*Pause.*]
HAMM: The waves, how are the waves?
CLOV: The waves?

[*He turns the telescope on the waves.*]

Lead.
HAMM: And the sun?
CLOV [*looking*]: Zero.
HAMM: But it should be sinking. Look again.
CLOV [*looking*]: Damn the sun.
HAMM: Is it night already then?
CLOV [*looking*]: No.
HAMM: Then what is it?
CLOV [*looking*]: Gray.

[*Lowering the telescope, turning towards Hamm, louder.*]

Gray! [*Pause. Still louder.*] GRRAY! [*Pause. He gets down, approaches Hamm from behind, whispers in his ear.*]
HAMM [*starting*]: Gray! Did I hear you say gray?
CLOV: Light black. From pole to pole.
HAMM: You exaggerate. [*Pause.*] Don't stay there, you give me the shivers.

[*Clov returns to his place beside the chair.*]

CLOV: Why this farce, day after day?

HAMM: Routine. One never knows. [*Pause.*] Last night I saw inside my breast. There was a big sore.
CLOV: Pah! You saw your heart.
HAMM: No, it was living. [*Pause. Anguished.*] Clov!
CLOV: Yes.
HAMM: What's happening?
CLOV: Something is taking its course. [*Pause.*]
HAMM: Clov!
CLOV [*impatiently*]: What is it?
HAMM: We're not beginning to . . . to . . . mean something?
CLOV: Mean something! You and I, mean something! [*Brief laugh.*] Ah that's a good one!
HAMM: I wonder. [*Pause.*] Imagine if a rational being came back to earth, wouldn't he be liable to get ideas into his head if he observed us long enough. [*Voice of rational being.*] Ah, good, now I see what it is, yes, now I understand what they're at!

[*Clov starts, drops the telescope and begins to scratch his belly with both hands. Normal voice.*]

And without going so far as that, we ourselves . . . [*with emotion*] . . . we ourselves . . . at certain moments . . . [*Vehemently.*] To think perhaps it won't all have been for nothing!
CLOV [*anguished, scratching himself*]: I have a flea!
HAMM: A flea! Are there still fleas?
CLOV: On me there's one. [*Scratching.*] Unless it's a crablouse.
HAMM [*very perturbed*]: But humanity might start from there all over again! Catch him, for the love of God!
CLOV: I'll go and get the powder.

[*Exit Clov.*]

HAMM: A flea! This is awful! What a day!

[*Enter Clov with a sprinkling-tin.*]

CLOV: I'm back again, with the insecticide.
HAMM: Let him have it!

[*Clov loosens the top of his trousers, pulls it forward and shakes powder into the aperture. He stoops, looks, waits, starts, frenziedly shakes more powder, stoops, looks, waits.*]

CLOV: The bastard!
HAMM: Did you get him?
CLOV: Looks like it.

[*He drops the tin and adjusts his trousers.*]

Unless he's laying doggo.
HAMM: Laying! Lying you mean. Unless he's *lying* doggo.
CLOV: Ah? One says lying? One doesn't say laying?
HAMM: Use your head, can't you. If he was laying we'd be bitched.
CLOV: Ah. [*Pause.*] What about that pee?

HAMM: I'm having it.
CLOV: Ah that's the spirit, that's the spirit! [*Pause.*]
HAMM [*with ardour*]: Let's go from here, the two of us! South! You can make a raft and the currents will carry us away, far away, to other . . . mammals!
CLOV: God forbid!
HAMM: Alone, I'll embark alone! Get working on that raft immediately. Tomorrow I'll be gone for ever.
CLOV [*hastening towards door*]: I'll start straight away.
HAMM: Wait!

[*Clov halts.*]

Will there be sharks, do you think?
CLOV: Sharks? I don't know. If there are there will be.

[*He goes towards door.*]

HAMM: Wait!

[*Clov halts.*]

Is it not yet time for my pain-killer?
CLOV [*violently*]: No!

[*He goes towards door.*]

HAMM: Wait!

[*Clov halts.*]

How are your eyes?
CLOV: Bad.
HAMM: But you can see.
CLOV: All I want.
HAMM: How are your legs?
CLOV: Bad.
HAMM: But you can walk.
CLOV: I come . . . and go.
HAMM: In my house. [*Pause. With prophetic relish.*] One day you'll be blind, like me. You'll be sitting there, a speck in the void, in the dark, for ever, like me. [*Pause.*] One day you'll say to yourself, I'm tired, I'll sit down, and you'll go and sit down. Then you'll say, I'm hungry, I'll get up and get something to eat. But you won't get up. You'll say, I shouldn't have sat down, but since I have I'll sit on a little longer, then I'll get up and get something to eat. But you won't get up and you won't get anything to eat. [*Pause.*] You'll look at the wall a while, then you'll say, I'll close my eyes, perhaps have a little sleep, after that I'll feel better, and you'll close them. And when you open them again there'll be no wall any more. [*Pause.*] Infinite emptiness will be all around you, all the resurrected dead of all the ages wouldn't fill it, and there you'll be like a little bit of grit in the middle of the steppe. [*Pause.*] Yes, one day you'll know what it is, you'll be like me, except that you won't have anyone with you, because you won't have had pity on anyone and because there won't be anyone left to have pity on. [*Pause.*]
CLOV: It's not certain. [*Pause.*] And there's one thing you forget.

HAMM: Ah?

CLOV: I can't sit down.

HAMM [*impatiently*]: Well you'll lie down then, what the hell! Or you'll come to a standstill, simply stop and stand still, the way you are now. One day you'll say, I'm tired, I'll stop. What does the attitude matter? [*Pause.*]

CLOV: So you all want me to leave you.

HAMM: Naturally.

CLOV: Then I'll leave you.

HAMM: You can't leave us.

CLOV: Then I won't leave you. [*Pause.*]

HAMM: Why don't you finish us? [*Pause.*] I'll tell you the combination of the cupboard if you promise to finish me.

CLOV: I couldn't finish you.

HAMM: Then you won't finish me. [*Pause.*]

CLOV: I'll leave you, I have things to do.

HAMM: Do you remember when you came here?

CLOV: No. Too small, you told me.

HAMM: Do you remember your father.

CLOV [*wearily*]: Same answer. [*Pause.*] You've asked me these questions millions of times.

HAMM: I love the old questions. [*With fervour.*] Ah the old questions, the old answers, there's nothing like them! [*Pause.*] It was I was a father to you.

CLOV: Yes. [*He looks at Hamm fixedly.*] You were that to me.

HAMM: My house a home for you.

CLOV: Yes. [*He looks about him.*] This was that for me.

HAMM [*proudly*]: But for me, [*gesture towards himself*] no father. But for Hamm, [*gesture towards surroundings*] no home. [*Pause.*]

CLOV: I'll leave you.

HAMM: Did you ever think of one thing?

CLOV: Never.

HAMM: That here we're down in a hole. [*Pause.*] But beyond the hills? Eh? Perhaps it's still green. Eh? [*Pause.*] Flora! Pomona! [*Ecstatically.*] Ceres![8] [*Pause.*] Perhaps you won't need to go very far.

CLOV: I can't go very far. [*Pause.*] I'll leave you.

HAMM: Is my dog ready?

CLOV: He lacks a leg.

HAMM: Is he silky?

CLOV: He's a kind of Pomeranian.

HAMM: Go and get him.

CLOV: He lacks a leg.

HAMM: Go and get him!

[*Exit Clov.*]

We're getting on.

[*Enter Clov holding by one of its three legs a black toy dog.*]

CLOV: Your dogs are here.

8. Flora, Pomona, and Ceres: the Roman goddesses of flowering plants, fruits, and grains.

[*He hands the dog to Hamm who feels it, fondles it.*]

HAMM: He's white, isn't he?
CLOV: Nearly.
HAMM: What do you mean, nearly? Is he white or isn't he?
CLOV: He isn't. [*Pause.*]
HAMM: You've forgotten the sex.
CLOV [*vexed*]: But he isn't finished. The sex goes on at the end. [*Pause.*]
HAMM: You haven't put on his ribbon.
CLOV [*angrily*]: But he isn't finished, I tell you! First you finish your dog and then you put on his ribbon! [*Pause.*]
HAMM: Can he stand?
CLOV: I don't know.
HAMM: Try.

[*He hands the dog to Clov who places it on the ground.*]

Well?
CLOV: Wait!

[*He squats down and tries to get the dog to stand on its three legs, fails, lets it go. The dog falls on its side.*]

HAMM [*impatiently*]: Well?
CLOV: He's standing.
HAMM [*groping for the dog*]: Where? Where is he?

[*Clov holds up the dog in a standing position.*]

CLOV: There.

[*He takes Hamm's hand and guides it towards the dog's head.*]

HAMM [*his hand on the dog's head*]: Is he gazing at me?
CLOV: Yes.
HAMM [*proudly*]: As if he were asking me to take him for a walk?
CLOV: If you like.
HAMM [*as before*]: Or as if he were begging me for a bone.

[*He withdraws his hand.*]

Leave him like that, standing there imploring me.

[*Clov straightens up. The dog falls on its side.*]

CLOV: I'll leave you.
HAMM: Have you had your visions?
CLOV: Less.
HAMM: Is Mother Pegg's light on?
CLOV: Light! How could anyone's light be on?
HAMM: Extinguished!
CLOV: Naturally it's extinguished. If it's not on it's extinguished.
HAMM: No, I mean Mother Pegg.
CLOV: But naturally she's extinguished! [*Pause.*] What's the matter with you today?
HAMM: I'm taking my course. [*Pause.*] Is she buried?

CLOV: Buried! Who would have buried her?

HAMM: You.

CLOV: Me! Haven't I enough to do without burying people?

HAMM: But you'll bury me.

CLOV: No I won't bury you. [*Pause.*]

HAMM: She was bonny once, like a flower of the field. [*With reminiscent leer.*] And a great one for the men!

CLOV: We too were bonny—once. It's a rare thing not to have been bonny—once. [*Pause.*]

HAMM: Go and get the gaff.[9]

[*Clov goes to door, halts.*]

CLOV: Do this, do that, and I do it. I never refuse. Why?

HAMM: You're not able to.

CLOV: Soon I won't do it any more.

HAMM: You won't be able to any more.

[*Exit Clov.*]

Ah the creatures, the creatures, everything has to be explained to them.

[*Enter Clov with gaff.*]

CLOV: Here's your gaff. Stick it up.

[*He gives the gaff to Hamm who, wielding it like a puntpole, tries to move his chair.*]

HAMM: Did I move?

CLOV: No.

[*Hamm throws down the gaff.*]

HAMM: Go and get the oilcan.

CLOV: What for?

HAMM: To oil the castors.

CLOV: I oiled them yesterday.

HAMM: Yesterday! What does that mean? Yesterday!

CLOV [*violently*]: That means that bloody awful day, long ago, before this bloody awful day. I use the words you taught me. If they don't mean anything any more, teach me others. Or let me be silent. [*Pause.*]

HAMM: I once knew a madman who thought the end of the world had come. He was a painter—and engraver. I had a great fondness for him. I used to go and see him, in the asylum. I'd take him by the hand and drag him to the window. Look! There! All that rising corn! And there! Look! The sails of the herring fleet! All that loveliness! [*Pause.*] He'd snatch away his hand and go back into his corner. Appalled. All he had seen was ashes. [*Pause.*] He alone had been spared. [*Pause.*] Forgotten. [*Pause.*] It appears the case is . . . was not so . . . so unusual.

CLOV: A madman? When was that?

HAMM: Oh way back, way back, you weren't in the land of the living.

CLOV: God be with the days!

9. A fishing pole designed for catching large fish.

[*Pause. Hamm raises his toque.*]

HAMM: I had a great fondness for him.

[*Pause. He puts on his toque again.*]

He was a painter—and engraver.
CLOV: There are so many terrible things.
HAMM: No, no, there are not so many now. [*Pause.*] Clov!
CLOV: Yes.
HAMM: Do you not think this has gone on long enough?
CLOV: Yes! [*Pause.*] What?
HAMM: This . . . this . . . thing.
CLOV: I've always thought so. [*Pause.*] You not?
HAMM [*gloomily*]: Then it's a day like any other day.
CLOV: As long as it lasts. [*Pause.*] All life long the same inanities.
HAMM: I can't leave you.
CLOV: I know. And you can't follow me. [*Pause.*]
HAMM: If you leave me how shall I know?
CLOV [*briskly*]: Well you simply whistle me and if I don't come running it means I've left you. [*Pause.*]
HAMM: You won't come and kiss me goodbye?
CLOV: Oh I shouldn't think so. [*Pause.*]
HAMM: But you might be merely dead in your kitchen.
CLOV: The result would be the same.
HAMM: Yes, but how would I know, if you were merely dead in your kitchen?
CLOV: Well . . . sooner or later I'd start to stink.
HAMM: You stink already. The whole place stinks of corpses.
CLOV: The whole universe.
HAMM [*angrily*]: To hell with the universe. [*Pause.*] Think of something.
CLOV: What?
HAMM: An idea, have an idea. [*Angrily.*] A bright idea!
CLOV: Ah good.

[*He starts pacing to and fro, his eyes fixed on the ground, his hands behind his back. He halts.*]

The pains in my legs! It's unbelievable! Soon I won't be able to think any more.
HAMM: You won't be able to leave me.

[*Clov resumes his pacing.*]

What are you doing?
CLOV: Having an idea.

[*He paces.*]

Ah!

[*He halts.*]

HAMM: What a brain! [*Pause.*] Well?
CLOV: Wait! [*He meditates. Not very convinced.*] Yes . . . [*Pause. More convinced.*] Yes! [*He raises his head.*] I have it! I set the alarm. [*Pause.*]

HAMM: This is perhaps not one of my bright days, but frankly—

CLOV: You whistle me. I don't come. The alarm rings. I'm gone. It doesn't ring. I'm dead. [*Pause.*]

HAMM: Is it working? [*Pause. Impatiently.*] The alarm, is it working?

CLOV: Why wouldn't it be working?

HAMM: Because it's worked too much.

CLOV: But it's hardly worked at all.

HAMM [*angrily*]: Then because it's worked too little!

CLOV: I'll go and see.

[*Exit Clov. Brief ring of alarm off. Enter Clov with alarm-clock. He holds it against Hamm's ear and releases alarm. They listen to it ringing to the end. Pause.*]

Fit to wake the dead! Did you hear it?

HAMM: Vaguely.

CLOV: The end is terrific!

HAMM: I prefer the middle. [*Pause.*] Is it not time for my pain-killer?

CLOV: No! [*He goes to door, turns.*] I'll leave you.

HAMM: It's time for my story. Do you want to listen to my story?

CLOV: No.

HAMM: Ask my father if he wants to listen to my story.

[*Clov goes to bins, raises the lid of Nagg's, stoops, looks into it. Pause. He straightens up.*]

CLOV: He's asleep.

HAMM: Wake him.

[*Clov stoops, wakes Nagg with the alarm. Unintelligible words. Clov straightens up.*]

CLOV: He doesn't want to listen to your story.

HAMM: I'll give him a bon-bon.

[*Clov stoops. As before.*]

CLOV: He wants a sugar-plum.

HAMM: He'll get a sugar-plum.

[*Clov stoops. As before.*]

CLOV: It's a deal.

[*He goes towards door. Nagg's hands appear, gripping the rim. Then the head emerges. Clov reaches door, turns.*]

Do you believe in the life to come?

HAMM: Mine was always that.

[*Exit Clov.*]

Got him that time!

NAGG: I'm listening.

HAMM: Scoundrel! Why did you engender me?

NAGG: I didn't know.

HAMM: What? What didn't you know?

NAGG: That it'd be you. [*Pause.*] You'll give me a sugar-plum?
HAMM: After the audition.
NAGG: You swear?
HAMM: Yes.
NAGG: On what?
HAMM: My honor. [*Pause. They laugh heartily.*]
NAGG: Two.
HAMM: One.
NAGG: One for me and one for—
HAMM: One! Silence! [*Pause.*] Where was I? [*Pause. Gloomily.*] It's finished, we're finished. [*Pause.*] Nearly finished. [*Pause.*] There'll be no more speech. [*Pause.*] Something dripping in my head, ever since the fontanelles.[1] [*Stifled hilarity of Nagg.*] Splash, splash, always on the same spot. [*Pause.*] Perhaps it's a little vein. [*Pause.*] A little artery. [*Pause. More animated.*] Enough of that, it's story time, where was I? [*Pause. Narrative tone.*] The man came crawling towards me, on his belly. Pale, wonderfully pale and thin, he seemed on the point of—[*Pause. Normal tone.*] No, I've done that bit. [*Pause. Narrative tone.*] I calmly filled my pipe—the meerschaum, lit it with . . . let us say a vesta,[2] drew a few puffs. Aah! [*Pause.*] Well, what is it *you* want? [*Pause.*] It was an extra-ordinarily bitter day, I remember, zero by the thermometer. But considering it was Christmas Eve there was nothing . . . extra-ordinary about that. Seasonable weather, for once in a way. [*Pause.*] Well, what ill wind blows you my way? He raised his face to me, black with mingled dirt and tears. [*Pause. Normal tone.*] That should do it.

[*Narrative tone.*]

No no, don't look at me, don't look at me. He dropped his eyes and mumbled something, apologies I presume. [*Pause.*] I'm a busy man, you know, the final touches, before the festivities, you know what it is. [*Pause. Forcibly.*] Come on now, what is the object of this invasion? [*Pause.*] It was a glorious bright day, I remember, fifty by the heliometer, but already the sun was sinking down into the . . . down among the dead.

[*Normal tone.*]

Nicely put, that.

[*Narrative tone.*]

Come on now, come on, present your petition and let me resume my labors.

[*Pause. Normal tone.*]

There's English for you. Ah well . . .

[*Narrative tone.*]

It was then he took the plunge. It's my little one, he said. Tsstss, a little one, that's bad. My little boy, he said, as if the sex mattered. Where did he come from? He named the hole. A good half-day, on horse. What are you insinuating? That the place is still inhabited? No no, not a soul, except himself and the child—assuming

1. Soft gaps between an infant's skull bones.

2. A match.

he existed. Good. I enquired about the situation at Kov, beyond the gulf. Not a sinner. Good. And you expect me to believe you have left your little one back there, all alone, and alive into the bargain? Come now! [*Pause.*] It was a howling wild day, I remember, a hundred by the anenometer.[3] The wind was tearing up the dead pines and sweeping them . . . away.

[*Pause. Normal tone.*]

A bit feeble, that.

[*Narrative tone.*]

Come on, man, speak up, what is it you want from me, I have to put up my holly. [*Pause.*]

Well to make it short it finally transpired that what he wanted from me was . . . bread for his brat? Bread? But I have no bread, it doesn't agree with me. Good. Then perhaps a little corn?

[*Pause. Normal tone.*]

That should do it.

[*Narrative tone.*]

Corn, yes, I have corn, it's true, in my granaries. But use your head. I give you some corn, a pound, a pound and a half, you bring it back to your child and you make him—if he's still alive—a nice pot of porridge, [*Nagg reacts*] a nice pot and a half of porridge, full of nourishment. Good. The colors come back into his little cheeks—perhaps. And then? [*Pause.*] I lost patience. [*Violently.*] Use your head, can't you, use your head, you're on earth, there's no cure for that! [*Pause.*] It was an exceedingly dry day, I remember, zero by the hygrometer. Ideal weather, for my lumbago. [*Pause. Violently.*] But what in God's name do you imagine? That the earth will awake in spring? That the rivers and seas will run with fish again? That there's manna in heaven still for imbeciles like you? [*Pause.*] Gradually I cooled down, sufficiently at least to ask him how long he had taken on the way. Three whole days. Good. In what condition he had left the child. Deep in sleep. [*Forcibly.*] But deep in what sleep, deep in what sleep already? [*Pause.*] Well to make it short I finally offered to take him into my service. He had touched a chord. And then I imagined already that I wasn't much longer for this world. [*He laughs. Pause.*] Well? [*Pause.*] Well? Here if you were careful you might die a nice natural death, in peace and comfort. [*Pause.*] Well? [*Pause.*] In the end he asked me would I consent to take in the child as well—if he were still alive. [*Pause.*] It was the moment I was waiting for. [*Pause.*] Would I consent to take in the child . . . [*Pause.*] I can see him still, down on his knees, his hands flat on the ground, glaring at me with his mad eyes, in defiance of my wishes. [*Pause. Normal tone.*] I'll soon have finished with this story. [*Pause.*] Unless I bring in other characters. [*Pause.*] But where would I find them? [*Pause.*] Where would I look for them? [*Pause. He whistles. Enter Clov.*] Let us pray to God.

NAGG: Me sugar-plum!

CLOV: There's a rat in the kitchen!

3. An instrument used to measure wind speed.

HAMM: A rat! Are there still rats?
CLOV: In the kitchen there's one.
HAMM: And you haven't exterminated him?
CLOV: Half. You disturbed us.
HAMM: He can't get away?
CLOV: No.
HAMM: You'll finish him later. Let us pray to God.
CLOV: Again!
NAGG: Me sugar-plum!
HAMM: God first! [*Pause.*] Are you right?
CLOV [*resigned*]: Off we go.
HAMM [*to Nagg*]: And you?
NAGG [*clasping his hands, closing his eyes, in a gabble*]: Our Father which art—
HAMM: Silence! In silence! Where are your manners? [*Pause.*] Off we go. [*Attitudes of prayer. Silence. Abandoning his attitude, discouraged.*] Well?
CLOV [*abandoning his attitude*]: What a hope! And you?
HAMM: Sweet damn all! [*To Nagg.*] And you?
NAGG: Wait! [*Pause. Abandoning his attitude.*] Nothing doing!
HAMM: The bastard! He doesn't exist!
CLOV: Not yet.
NAGG: Me sugar-plum!
HAMM: There are no more sugar-plums! [*Pause.*]
NAGG: It's natural. After all I'm your father. It's true if it hadn't been me it would have been someone else. But that's no excuse. [*Pause.*] Turkish Delight, for example, which no longer exists, we all know that, there is nothing in the world I love more. And one day I'll ask you for some, in return for a kindness, and you'll promise it to me. One must live with the times. [*Pause.*] Whom did you call when you were a tiny boy, and were frightened, in the dark? Your mother? No. Me. We let you cry. Then we moved you out of earshot, so that we might sleep in peace. [*Pause.*] I was asleep, as happy as a king, and you woke me up to have me listen to you. It wasn't indispensable, you didn't really need to have me listen to you. Besides I didn't listen to you. [*Pause.*] I hope the day will come when you'll really need to have me listen to you, and need to hear my voice, any voice. [*Pause.*] Yes, I hope I'll live till then, to hear you calling me like when you were a tiny boy, and were frightened, in the dark, and I was your only hope. [*Pause. Nagg knocks on lid of Nell's bin. Pause.*] Nell! [*Pause. He knocks louder. Pause. Louder.*] Nell! [*Pause. Nagg sinks back into his bin, closes the lid behind him. Pause.*]
HAMM: Our revels now are ended.[4]

[*He gropes for the dog.*]

The dog's gone.
CLOV: He's not a real dog, he can't go.
HAMM [*groping*]: He's not there.
CLOV: He's lain down.
HAMM: Give him up to me.

4. Quoting the exiled magician Prospero in Shakespeare's *The Tempest* (4.1): "Our revels are now ended. These our actors / As I foretold you, were all spirits, and / Are melted into air, into thin air."

[*Clov picks up the dog and gives it to Hamm. Hamm holds it in his arms. Pause. Hamm throws away the dog.*]

Dirty brute!

[*Clov begins to pick up the objects lying on the ground.*]

What are you doing?

CLOV: Putting things in order. [*He straightens up. Fervently.*] I'm going to clear everything away! [*He starts picking up again.*]

HAMM: Order!

CLOV [*straightening up*]: I love order. It's my dream. A world where all would be silent and still and each thing in its last place, under the last dust. [*He starts picking up again.*]

HAMM [*exasperated*]: What in God's name do you think you are doing?

CLOV [*straightening up*]: I'm doing my best to create a little order.

HAMM: Drop it!

[*Clov drops the objects he has picked up.*]

CLOV: After all, there or elsewhere. [*He goes towards door.*]

HAMM [*irritably*]: What's wrong with your feet?

CLOV: My feet?

HAMM: Tramp! Tramp!

CLOV: I must have put on my boots.

HAMM: Your slippers were hurting you? [*Pause.*]

CLOV: I'll leave you.

HAMM: No!

CLOV: What is there to keep me here?

HAMM: The dialogue. [*Pause.*] I've got on with my story. [*Pause.*] I've got on with it well. [*Pause. Irritably.*] Ask me where I've got to.

CLOV: Oh, by the way, your story?

HAMM [*surprised*]: What story?

CLOV: The one you've been telling yourself all your days.

HAMM: Ah you mean my chronicle?

CLOV: That's the one. [*Pause.*]

HAMM [*angrily*]: Keep going, can't you, keep going!

CLOV: You've got on with it, I hope.

HAMM [*modestly*]: Oh not very far, not very far. [*He sighs.*] There are days like that, one isn't inspired. [*Pause.*] Nothing you can do about it, just wait for it to come. [*Pause.*] No forcing, no forcing, it's fatal. [*Pause.*] I've got on with it a little all the same. [*Pause.*] Technique, you know. [*Pause. Irritably.*] I say I've got on with it a little all the same.

CLOV [*admiringly*]: Well I never! In spite of everything you were able to get on with it!

HAMM [*modestly*]: Oh not very far, you know, not very far, but nevertheless, better than nothing.

CLOV: Better than nothing! Is it possible?

HAMM: I'll tell you how it goes. He comes crawling on his belly—

CLOV: Who?

HAMM: What?

CLOV: Who do you mean, he?

HAMM: Who do I mean! Yet another.
CLOV: Ah him! I wasn't sure.
HAMM: Crawling on his belly, whining for bread for his brat. He's offered a job as gardener. Before—

[*Clov bursts out laughing.*]

What is there so funny about that?
CLOV: A job as gardener!
HAMM: Is that what tickles you?
CLOV: It must be that.
HAMM: It wouldn't be the bread?
CLOV: Or the brat. [*Pause.*]
HAMM: The whole thing is comical, I grant you that. What about having a good guffaw the two of us together?
CLOV [*after reflection*]: I couldn't guffaw again today.
HAMM [*after reflection*]: Nor I. [*Pause.*] I continue then. Before accepting with gratitude he asks if he may have his little boy with him.
CLOV: What age?
HAMM: Oh tiny.
CLOV: He would have climbed the trees.
HAMM: All the little odd jobs.
CLOV: And then he would have grown up.
HAMM: Very likely. [*Pause.*]
CLOV: Keep going, can't you, keep going!
HAMM: That's all. I stopped there. [*Pause.*]
CLOV: Do you see how it goes on.
HAMM: More or less.
CLOV: Will it not soon be the end?
HAMM: I'm afraid it will.
CLOV: Pah! You'll make up another.
HAMM: I don't know. [*Pause.*] I feel rather drained. [*Pause.*] The prolonged creative effort. [*Pause.*] If I could drag myself down to the sea! I'd make a pillow of sand for my head and the tide would come.
CLOV: There's no more tide. [*Pause.*]
HAMM: Go and see is she dead.

[*Clov goes to bins, raises the lid of Nell's, stoops, looks into it. Pause.*]

CLOV: Looks like it.

[*He closes the lid, straightens up. Hamm raises his toque. Pause. He puts it on again.*]

HAMM [*with his hand to his toque*]: And Nagg?

[*Clov raises lid of Nagg's bin, stoops, looks into it. Pause.*]

CLOV: Doesn't look like it. [*He closes the lid, straightens up.*]
HAMM [*letting go his toque*]: What's he doing?

[*Clov raises lid of Nagg's bin, stoops, looks into it. Pause.*]

CLOV: He's crying. [*He closes lid, straightens up.*]

HAMM: Then he's living. [*Pause.*] Did you ever have an instant of happiness?
CLOV: Not to my knowledge. [*Pause.*]
HAMM: Bring me under the window.

[*Clov goes towards chair.*]

I want to feel the light on my face.

[*Clov pushes chair.*]

Do you remember, in the beginning, when you took me for a turn? You used to hold the chair too high. At every step you nearly tipped me out. [*With senile quaver.*] Ah great fun, we had, the two of us, great fun. [*Gloomily.*] And then we got into the way of it.

[*Clov stops the chair under window right.*]

There already? [*Pause. He tilts back his head.*] Is it light?
CLOV: It isn't dark.
HAMM [*angrily*]: I'm asking you is it light.
CLOV: Yes. [*Pause.*]
HAMM: The curtain isn't closed?
CLOV: No.
HAMM: What window is it?
CLOV: The earth.
HAMM: I knew it! [*Angrily.*] But there's no light there! The other!

[*Clov pushes chair towards window left.*]

The earth!

Clov stops the chair under window left. Hamm tilts back his head.]

That's what I call light! [*Pause.*] Feels like a ray of sunshine. [*Pause.*] No?
CLOV: No.
HAMM: It isn't a ray of sunshine I feel on my face?
CLOV: No. [*Pause.*]
HAMM: Am I very white? [*Pause. Angrily.*] I'm asking you am I very white!
CLOV: Not more so than usual. [*Pause.*]
HAMM: Open the window.
CLOV: What for?
HAMM: I want to hear the sea.
CLOV: You wouldn't hear it.
HAMM: Even if you opened the window?
CLOV: No.
HAMM: Then it's not worth while opening it?
CLOV: No.
HAMM [*violently*]: Then open it!

[*Clov gets up on the ladder, opens the window. Pause.*]

Have you opened it?
CLOV: Yes. [*Pause.*]
HAMM: You swear you've opened it?
CLOV: Yes. [*Pause.*]

HAMM: Well . . .! [*Pause.*] It must be very calm. [*Pause. Violently.*] I'm asking you is it very calm!

CLOV: Yes.

HAMM: It's because there are no more navigators. [*Pause.*] You haven't much conversation all of a sudden. Do you not feel well?

CLOV: I'm cold.

HAMM: What month are we? [*Pause.*] Close the window, we're going back.

[*Clov closes the window, gets down, pushes the chair back to its place, remains standing behind it, head bowed.*]

Don't stay there, you give me the shivers!

[*Clov returns to his place beside the chair.*]

Father! [*Pause. Louder.*] Father! [*Pause.*] Go and see did he hear me.

[*Clov goes to Nagg's bin, raises the lid, stoops. Unintelligible words. Clov straightens up.*]

CLOV: Yes.

HAMM: Both times?

[*Clov stoops. As before.*]

CLOV: Once only.

HAMM: The first time or the second?

[*Clov stoops. As before.*]

CLOV: He doesn't know.

HAMM: It must have been the second.

CLOV: We'll never know.

[*He closes lid.*]

HAMM: Is he still crying?

CLOV: No.

HAMM: The dead go fast. [*Pause.*] What's he doing?

CLOV: Sucking his biscuit.

HAMM: Life goes on.

[*Clov returns to his place beside the chair.*]

Give me a rug, I'm freezing.

CLOV: There are no more rugs. [*Pause.*]

HAMM: Kiss me. [*Pause.*] Will you not kiss me?

CLOV: No.

HAMM: On the forehead.

CLOV: I won't kiss you anywhere. [*Pause.*]

HAMM [*holding out his hand*]: Give me your hand at least. [*Pause.*] Will you not give me your hand?

CLOV: I won't touch you. [*Pause.*]

HAMM: Give me the dog.

[*Clov looks round for the dog.*]

No!

CLOV: Do you not want your dog?
HAMM: No.
CLOV: Then I'll leave you.
HAMM [*head bowed, absently*]: That's right.

[*Clov goes to door, turns.*]

CLOV: If I don't kill that rat he'll die.
HAMM [*as before*]: That's right.

[*Exit Clov. Pause.*]

Me to play.

[*He takes out his handkerchief, unfolds it, holds it spread out before him.*]

We're getting on. [*Pause.*] You weep, and weep, for nothing, so as not to laugh, and little by little . . . you begin to grieve.

[*He folds the handkerchief, puts it back in his pocket, raises his head.*]

All those I might have helped. [*Pause.*] Helped! [*Pause.*] Saved. [*Pause.*] Saved! [*Pause.*] The place was crawling with them! [*Pause. Violently.*] Use your head, can't you, use your head, you're on earth, there's no cure for that! [*Pause.*] Get out of here and love one another! Lick your neighbor as yourself! [*Pause. Calmer.*] When it wasn't bread they wanted it was crumpets. [*Pause. Violently.*] Out of my sight and back to your petting parties! [*Pause.*] All that, all that! [*Pause.*] Not even a real dog! [*Calmer.*] The end is in the beginning and yet you go on. [*Pause.*] Perhaps I could go on with my story, end it and begin another. [*Pause.*] Perhaps I could throw myself out on the floor.

[*He pushes himself painfully off his seat, falls back again.*]

Dig my nails into the cracks and drag myself forward with my fingers. [*Pause.*] It will be the end and there I'll be, wondering what can have brought it on and wondering what can have . . . [*he hesitates*] . . . why it was so long coming. [*Pause.*] There I'll be, in the old shelter, alone against the silence and . . . [*he hesitates*] . . . the stillness. If I can hold my peace, and sit quiet, it will be all over with sound, and motion, all over and done with. [*Pause.*] I'll have called my father and I'll have called my . . . [*he hesitates*] . . . my son. And even twice, or three times, in case they shouldn't have heard me, the first time, or the second. [*Pause.*] I'll say to myself, He'll come back. [*Pause.*] And then? [*Pause.*] And then? [*Pause.*] He couldn't, he has gone too far. [*Pause.*] And then? [*Pause. Very agitated.*] All kinds of fantasies! That I'm being watched! A rat! Steps! Breath held and then . . . [*He breathes out.*] Then babble, babble, words, like the solitary child who turns himself into children, two, three, so as to be together, and whisper together, in the dark. [*Pause.*] Moment upon moment, pattering down, like the millet grains of . . . [*he hesitates*] . . . that old Greek, and all life long you wait for that to mount up to a life.[5] [*Pause. He opens his mouth to continue, renounces.*] Ah let's get it over!

[*He whistles. Enter Clov with alarm-clock. He halts beside the chair.*]

What? Neither gone nor dead?
CLOV: In spirit only.
HAMM: Which?
CLOV: Both.
HAMM: Gone from me you'd be dead.
CLOV: And vice versa.
HAMM: Outside of here it's death! [*Pause.*] And the rat?
CLOV: He's got away.
HAMM: He can't go far. [*Pause. Anxious.*] Eh?
CLOV: He doesn't need to go far. [*Pause.*]
HAMM: Is it not time for my pain-killer?
CLOV: Yes.
HAMM: Ah! At last! Give it to me! Quick! [*Pause.*]
CLOV: There's no more pain-killer. [*Pause.*]
HAMM [*appalled*]: Good . . .! [*Pause.*] No more pain-killer!
CLOV: No more pain-killer. You'll never get any more pain-killer. [*Pause.*]
HAMM: But the little round box. It was full!
CLOV: Yes. But now it's empty.

[*Pause. Clov starts to move about the room. He is looking for a place to put down the alarm-clock.*]

HAMM [*soft*]: What'll I do? [*Pause. In a scream.*] What'll I do?

[*Clov sees the picture, takes it down, stands it on the floor with its face to the wall, hangs up the alarm-clock in its place.*]

What are you doing?
CLOV: Winding up.
HAMM: Look at the earth.
CLOV: Again!
HAMM: Since it's calling to you.
CLOV: Is your throat sore? [*Pause.*] Would you like a lozenge? [*Pause.*] No. [*Pause.*] Pity.

[*Clov goes, humming, towards window right, halts before it, looks up at it.*]

HAMM: Don't sing.
CLOV [*turning towards Hamm*]: One hasn't the right to sing any more?
HAMM: No.
CLOV: Then how can it end?
HAMM: You want it to end?
CLOV: I want to sing.
HAMM: I can't prevent you.

5. Hamm is referring to Zeno of Elea (5th century B.C.E.), who is known for his philosophical paradoxes. One of them is based on the sound a bushel of millet makes when it falls on the floor: since this sound is caused by the grains, each grain must make a sound when striking the ground. This sound, however, can't be heard, so the apparent sound is really an accumulation of silences.

[*Pause. Clov turns towards window right.*]

CLOV: What did I do with that steps? [*He looks around for ladder.*] You didn't see that steps? [*He sees it.*] Ah, about time. [*He goes towards window left.*] Sometimes I wonder if I'm in my right mind. Then it passes over and I'm as lucid as before. [*He gets up on ladder, looks out of window.*] Christ, she's under water! [*He looks.*] How can that be? [*He pokes forward his head, his hand above his eyes.*] It hasn't rained. [*He wipes the pane, looks. Pause.*] Ah what a fool I am! I'm on the wrong side! [*He gets down, takes a few steps towards window right.*] Under water! [*He goes back for ladder.*] What a fool I am! [*He carries ladder towards window right.*] Sometimes I wonder if I'm in my right senses. Then it passes off and I'm as intelligent as ever.

[*He sets down ladder under window right, gets up on it, looks out of window. He turns towards Hamm.*]

Any particular sector you fancy? Or merely the whole thing?

HAMM: Whole thing.

CLOV: The general effect? Just a moment. [*He looks out of window. Pause.*]

HAMM: Clov.

CLOV [*absorbed*]: Mmm.

HAMM: Do you know what it is?

CLOV [*as before*]: Mmm.

HAMM: I was never there. [*Pause.*] Clov!

CLOV [*turning towards Hamm, exasperated*]: What is it?

HAMM: I was never there.

CLOV: Lucky for you. [*He looks out of window.*]

HAMM: Absent, always. It all happened without me. I don't know what's happened. [*Pause.*] Do you know what's happened? [*Pause.*] Clov!

CLOV [*turning towards Hamm, exasperated*]: Do you want me to look at this muckheap, yes or no?

HAMM: Answer me first.

CLOV: What?

HAMM: Do you know what's happened?

CLOV: When? Where?

HAMM [*violently*]: When! What's happened? Use your head, can't you! What has happened?

CLOV: What for Christ's sake does it matter? [*He looks out of window.*]

HAMM: I don't know. [*Pause. Clov turns towards Hamm.*]

CLOV [*harshly*]: When old Mother Pegg asked you for oil for her lamp and you told her to get out to hell, you knew what was happening then, no? [*Pause.*] You know what she died of, Mother Pegg? Of darkness.

HAMM [*feebly*]: I hadn't any.

CLOV [*as before*]: Yes, you had. [*Pause.*]

HAMM: Have you the glass?

CLOV: No, it's clear enough as it is.

HAMM: Go and get it.

[*Pause. Clov casts up his eyes, brandishes his fists. He loses balance, clutches on to the ladder. He starts to get down, halts.*]

CLOV: There's one thing I'll never understand. [*He gets down.*] Why I always obey you. Can you explain that to me?

HAMM: No. . . . Perhaps it's compassion. [*Pause.*] A kind of great compassion. [*Pause.*] Oh you won't find it easy, you won't find it easy.

[*Pause. Clov begins to move about the room in search of the telescope.*]

CLOV: I'm tired of our goings on, very tired. [*He searches.*] You're not sitting on it?

[*He moves the chair, looks at the place where it stood, resumes his search.*]

HAMM [*anguished*]: Don't leave me there! [*Angrily Clov restores the chair to its place.*] Am I right in the center?

CLOV: You'd need a microscope to find this—[*He sees the telescope.*] Ah, about time.

[*He picks up the telescope, gets up on the ladder, turns the telescope on the without.*]

HAMM: Give me the dog.

CLOV [*looking*]: Quiet!

HAMM [*angrily*]: Give me the dog!

[*Clov drops the telescope, clasps his hands to his head. Pause. He gets down precipitately, looks for the dog, sees it, picks it up, hastens towards Hamm and strikes him violently on the head with the dog.*]

CLOV: There's your dog for you!

[*The dog falls to the ground. Pause.*]

HAMM: He hit me!

CLOV: You drive me mad, I'm mad!

HAMM: If you must hit me, hit me with the axe. [*Pause.*] Or with the gaff, hit me with the gaff. Not with the dog. With the gaff. Or with the axe.

[*Clov picks up the dog and gives it to Hamm who takes it in his arms.*]

CLOV [*imploringly*]: Let's stop playing!

HAMM: Never! [*Pause.*] Put me in my coffin.

CLOV: There are no more coffins.

HAMM: Then let it end!

[*Clov goes towards ladder.*]

With a bang!

[*Clov gets up on ladder, gets down again, looks for telescope, sees it, picks it up, gets up ladder, raises telescope.*]

Of darkness! And me? Did anyone ever have pity on me?

CLOV [*lowering the telescope, turning towards Hamm*]: What? [*Pause.*] Is it me you're referring to?

HAMM [*angrily*]: An aside, ape! Did you never hear an aside before? [*Pause.*] I'm warming up for my last soliloquy.

CLOV: I warn you. I'm going to look at this filth since it's an order. But it's the last time. [*He turns the telescope on the without.*] Let's see. [*He moves the telescope.*] Nothing . . . nothing . . . good . . . good . . . nothing . . . goo—[*He starts, lowers the telescope, examines it, turns it again on the without. Pause.*] Bad luck to it!

HAMM: More complications!

[*Clov gets down.*]

Not an underplot, I trust.

[*Clov moves ladder nearer window, gets up on it, turns telescope on the without.*]

CLOV [*dismayed*]: Looks like a small boy!
HAMM [*sarcastic*]: A small . . . boy!
CLOV: I'll go and see.

[*He gets down, drops the telescope, goes towards door, turns.*]

I'll take the gaff.

[*He looks for the gaff, sees it, picks it up, hastens towards door.*]

HAMM: No!

[*Clov halts.*]

CLOV: No? A potential procreator?
HAMM: If he exists he'll die there or he'll come here. And if he doesn't . . . [*Pause.*]
CLOV: You don't believe me? You think I'm inventing? [*Pause.*]
HAMM: It's the end, Clov, we've come to the end. I don't need you any more. [*Pause.*]
CLOV: Lucky for you. [*He goes towards door.*]
HAMM: Leave me the gaff.

[*Clov gives him the gaff, goes towards door, halts, looks at alarm-clock, takes it down, looks round for a better place to put it, goes to bins, puts it on lid of Nagg's bin. Pause.*]

CLOV: I'll leave you. [*He goes towards door.*]
HAMM: Before you go . . .

[*Clov halts near door.*]

. . . say something.
CLOV: There is nothing to say.
HAMM: A few words . . . to ponder . . . in my heart.
CLOV: Your heart!
HAMM: Yes. [*Pause. Forcibly.*] Yes! [*Pause.*] With the rest, in the end, the shadows, the murmurs, all the trouble, to end up with. [*Pause.*] Clov. . . . He never spoke to me. Then, in the end, before he went, without my having asked him, he spoke to me. He said . . .
CLOV [*despairingly*]: Ah . . .!
HAMM: Something . . . from your heart.
CLOV: My heart!
HAMM: A few words . . . from your heart. [*Pause.*]
CLOV [*fixed gaze, tonelessly, towards auditorium*]: They said to me, That's love, yes, yes, not a doubt, now you see how—
HAMM: Articulate!
CLOV [*as before*]: How easy it is. They said to me, That's friendship, yes, yes, no question, you've found it. They said to me, Here's the place, stop, raise your head and look at all that beauty. That order! They said to me, Come now, you're not a brute beast, think upon these things and you'll see how all becomes clear. And

simple! They said to me, What skilled attention they get, all these dying of their wounds.

HAMM: Enough!

CLOV [*as before*]: I say to myself—sometimes, Clov, you must learn to suffer better than that if you want them to weary of punishing you—one day. I say to myself—sometimes, Clov, you must be there better than that if you want them to let you go—one day. But I feel too old, and too far, to form new habits. Good, it'll never end, I'll never go. [*Pause.*] Then one day, suddenly, it ends, it changes, I don't understand, it dies, or it's me, I don't understand, that either. I ask the words that remain—sleeping, waking, morning, evening. They have nothing to say. [*Pause.*] I open the door of the cell and go. I am so bowed I only see my feet, if I open my eyes, and between my legs a little trail of black dust. I say to myself that the earth is extinguished, though I never saw it lit. [*Pause.*] It's easy going. [*Pause.*] When I fall I'll weep for happiness. [*Pause. He goes towards door.*]

HAMM: Clov!

[*Clov halts, without turning.*]

Nothing.

[*Clov moves on.*]

Clov!

[*Clov halts, without turning.*]

CLOV: This is what we call making an exit.

HAMM: I'm obliged to you, Clov. For your services.

CLOV [*turning, sharply*]: Ah pardon, it's I am obliged to you.

HAMM: It's we are obliged to each other.

[*Pause. Clov goes towards door.*]

One thing more.

[*Clov halts.*]

A last favor.

[*Exit Clov.*]

Cover me with the sheet. [*Long pause.*] No? Good. [*Pause.*] Me to play. [*Pause. Wearily.*] Old endgame lost of old, play and lose and have done with losing. [*Pause. More animated.*] Let me see. [*Pause.*] Ah yes!

[*He tries to move the chair, using the gaff as before. Enter Clov, dressed for the road. Panama hat, tweed coat, raincoat over his arm, umbrella, bag. He halts by the door and stands there, impassive and motionless, his eyes fixed on Hamm, till the end. Hamm gives up.*]

Good. [*Pause.*] Discard. [*He throws away the gaff, makes to throw away the dog, thinks better of it.*] Take it easy. [*Pause.*] And now? [*Pause.*] Raise hat. [*He raises his toque.*] Peace to our . . . arses. [*Pause.*] And put on again. [*He puts on his toque.*] Deuce. [*Pause. He takes off his glasses.*] Wipe. [*He takes out his *handkerchief and, without unfolding it, wipes his glasses.*] And put on again. [*He puts on his glasses, puts back the handkerchief in his pocket.*] We're coming. A few more squirms like that and I'll call. [*Pause.*] A little poetry. [*Pause.*] You prayed—[*Pause. He corrects himself.*] You CRIED for night; it comes—[*Pause. He corrects himself.*] It FALLS: now cry in darkness. [*He repeats, chanting.*] You cried for night; it falls: now cry in darkness. [*Pause.*] Nicely put, that. [*Pause.*] And now? [*Pause.*] Moments for nothing, now as always, time was never and time is over, reckoning closed and story ended. [*Pause. Narrative tone.*] If he could have his child with him. . . . [*Pause.*] It was the moment I was waiting for. [*Pause.*] You don't want to abandon him? You want him to bloom while you are withering? Be there to solace your last million last moments? [*Pause.*] He doesn't realize, all he knows is hunger, and cold, and death to crown it all. But you! You ought to know what the earth is like, nowadays. Oh I put him before his responsibilities! [*Pause. Normal tone.*] Well, there we are, there I am, that's enough. [*He raises the whistle to his lips, hesitates, drops it. Pause.*] Yes, truly! [*He whistles. Pause. Louder. Pause.*] Good. [*Pause.*] Father! [*Pause. Louder.*] Father! [*Pause.*] Good. [*Pause.*] We're coming. [*Pause.*] And to end up with? [*Pause.*] Discard. [*He throws away the dog. He tears the whistle from his neck.*] With my compliments.

[*He throws whistle towards auditorium. Pause. He sniffs. Soft.*]

Clov!

[*Long pause.*]

No? Good.

[*He takes out the handkerchief.*]

Since that's the way we're playing it . . .

[*He unfolds handkerchief*]

. . . let's play it that way . . .

[*He unfolds.*]

. . . and speak no more about it . . .

[*He finishes unfolding.*]

. . . speak no more.

[*He holds handkerchief spread out before him.*]

Old stancher!

[*Pause.*]

You . . . remain.

[*Pause. He covers his face with handkerchief, lowers his arms to armrests, remains motionless.*]

[*Brief tableau.*]

Curtain

Primo Levi

1919–1987

Primo Levi was born to a middle-class Jewish family in Turin, Italy. His family had long assimilated into Italian life, and Levy only discovered his Jewishness when he came up against the racial laws enacted in 1938 by Mussolini's Fascist regime. Levi graduated first in his class as a chemist from the University of Turin in 1941, the year in which Italy joined World War II as a German ally. Active in the resistance against the Fascist cause, Levi was captured in northern Italy in 1943 and imprisoned in an Italian transit camp, from which he was transferred to Auschwitz. He was one of fifteen men and nine women from the railroad convoy of 650 who survived. Levi's training as a chemist made him a valuable asset to the Germans, who spared him from the gas chamber and forced him to work in a laboratory. He was liberated by the Soviets in 1945 and returned to Turin, where he worked as a chemist, becoming general manager of a paint factory in 1961. In 1977 he retired to devote himself to writing full time. He committed suicide in 1987.

Primo Levi's life and writing are marked by his wartime experience and by the guilt of having survived when so many others perished in the German concentration camps. In matter-of-fact scientist's language, Levi recorded his prison recollections in a memoir in 1947 entitled *Se questo e un uomo (If This Is a Man*, translated into English as *Survival in Auschwitz).* There he details the dehumanizing conditions in the concentration camps. The book sold more than half a million copies in Italy and has been translated into many languages as a classic document of human cruelty and suffering at mid-twentieth century. In 1963, Levi published a sequel, *La tregua (The Truce / The Reawakening),* which documents his wanderings in Eastern Europe and the Soviet Union. The nightmares of Auschwitz never cease to haunt Levi in this picaresque itinerary. In *The Periodic Table* (1975), he organizes his haunting recollections into the Russian chemist Mendeleyev's periodic table, distilling his autobiography to correspond to each of the twenty-one chemical elements. In Levi's last completed work, *The Drowned and the Saved,* published the year before his death, he wonders how much of the concentration camp still forms part of modern life and how enduring it might be in human history. He explores the paradoxical similarities between those who perpetrate cruelty and those who must endure it, showing how violence and oppression dehumanize both victim and oppressor.

The Two Flags[1]

Bertrando was born and grew up in a country called Lantania that had a very beautiful flag: or at least that was how it seemed to Bertrando, to all of his friends and fellow students, and to the greater part of his compatriots. It was different from all the others: against a bright purple ground stood out an orange oval, and in this rose a volcano, green at the bottom and white with snow at its top, surmounted by a plume of smoke.

In Bertrando's country there were no volcanoes; but there was one in the bordering country, Gunduwia, with which Lantania had been for centuries at war, or at any rate in a hostile relationship. Indeed, the Lantanic national poem, in a passage of debatable interpretation, mentioned the volcano as the "Lantanic altar of fire."

1. Translated by Raymond Rosenthal.

In all of Lantania's schools it was taught that the annexation of the volcano by the Gunduwians had been an act of banditry, and that the first duty of every Lantanian was to train militarily, hate Gunduwia with all his might, and prepare for the inevitable and desirable war, which was going to bend Gunduwian arrogance and reconquer the volcano. That this volcano every three or four years devastated thousands of villages and every year caused disastrous earthquakes was of no importance: Lantanic it was and Lantanic it must be again.

In any case, how not hate a country like Gunduwia? That very name, so grim, so sepulchral, inspired aversion. The Lantanians were a contentious and litigious people, they brawled or knifed each other for the slightest divergence of opinion, but they all agreed on the fact that Gunduwia was a country of scoundrels and bullies.

As for their flag, it represented them perfectly: it could not have been uglier, it was flat and silly, clumsy both in colors and design. Nothing more than a brown disk in a yellow field: not an image, not a symbol. A coarse, vulgar, and excremental flag. The Gunduwians must really be imbeciles, must have been since time immemorial for having chosen it and drenched it with their blood when they died in battle, something that happened three or four times a century. Furthermore, they were notoriously avaricious and wasteful, lewd and prudish, reckless and cowardly.

Bertrando was a proper young man, respectful of laws and traditions, and the very sight of his country's flag caused a wave of pride and self-assurance to course through his veins. The combination of those three noble colors, green, orange, and purple, when he sometimes recognized them joined in a spring meadow, made him strong and happy, glad to be a Lantanian, glad to be in this world, but also ready to die for his flag, best if wrapped in it.

Conversely, since his earliest childhood, since his memory began, the Gunduwian yellow and brown had been odious to him: disagreeable if taken separately, hateful to the point of nausea when placed side by side. Bertrando was a sensitive and emotional youth, and the sight of the enemy flag reproduced for derision on wall posters or in satirical vignettes put him in a bad mood and gave him an itch at the nape of the neck and elbows, intense salivation, and a certain dizziness.

Once, during a concert, he had found himself next to a pretty girl who inadvertently, of course, was wearing a yellow blouse and a brown skirt; Bertrando had been compelled to get up and move away and, since there were no other seats, to listen to the concert standing up; if he hadn't been rather shy, he would have told that girl exactly what she deserved. Bertrando liked apricots and medlars, but he ate them with his eyes shut so as to avoid the disgusting sight of the brown pit that stood out against the yellowish pulp.

Also, the sound of the Gunduwian language, which was harsh, guttural, almost inarticulate, had similar effects on Bertrando. It seemed to him scandalous that in certain Lantanian schools the enemy tongue should be taught, and that there even should be academicians who studied its history and origins, its grammar and syntax, and translated its literature. What sort of literature could that be? What good could come from that yellow-brown land of perverts and degenerates?

And yet there had been a professor who claimed he could prove that Lantanian and Gunduwian descended from one and the same language, extinct now for three thousand years, documented by a number of inscriptions on tombstones. Absurd, or rather insufferable. There are things that *cannot* be true, that must be ignored, not mentioned, buried. If it had been up to Bertrando, all Gunduwophiles would be buried three meters deep under the ground, along with all those (unfortunately, almost all of them young!)

who, out of snobbism, surreptitiously listened to Gunduwian radio and repeated its obscene lies.

Not that the border between the two countries was hermetic. It was well patrolled on both sides by guards who shot readily, but there was a pass, and every so often trade delegations passed through it in both directions because the two economies were complementary. To everyone's surprise, there also passed through smugglers, with considerable loads that the border guards did not seem to notice.

Once Bertrando had watched a Gunduwian delegation pass through the main street of the capital. Those bastards were not really so different from the Lantanians: aside from their ridiculous way of dressing, they would have been difficult to pick out if not for their shifty eyes and their typically sly expressions. Bertrando had come closer, to sniff and find out whether it was true that they stank, but the police had prevented him. Of course, they had to stink. In the Lantanian subconscious there had been established for centuries an etymological nexus between Gunduwia and stench (*kumt* in Lantanian). Conversely, it was known to everyone that in Gunduwian *latnen* are boils, and to Lantanians this seemed a vicious buffoonery that must be washed in blood.

Now it so happened that, after long secret negotiations, the presidents of the two countries made it known that in the spring they would meet. After an embarrassed silence, the Lantanian daily newspaper began to leak unaccustomed material: photographs of the Gunduwian capital with its imposing cathedral and its beautiful parks; images of Gunduwian children, well groomed and with laughing eyes. A book was published in which it was shown how, in remote times, a Lantano-Gunduwian fleet had routed a ragtag fleet of pirate junks ten times stronger in number. And finally it became known that in the stadium of the Lantanian capital a soccer match would take place between each country's best teams.

Bertrando was one of the first to rush out and buy his ticket of admission, but it was already too late: he had to resign himself to spending five times as much buying from the scalpers. It was a splendid day, and the stadium was packed; there was not a breath of wind, and the two flags hung slack from the gigantic masts. At the appointed hour the umpire blew the starting whistle, and at the same instant there rose a sustained breeze. The two flags, side by side for the first time, fluttered gloriously: the Lantanian purple-orange-green next to the Gunduwian's yellow-brown.

Bertrando felt a gelid, searing shiver run down his spine, like a rapier threading his vertebrae. His eyes must be lying, they could not be transmitting to him that double message, that impossible, lacerating yes-no. He experienced revulsion and love to a degree that poisoned him. All around him he saw a crowd, as divided as he, explode. He felt all his muscles contract painfully, adductors and abductors, enemies to each other, the smooth and the striated, and the tireless muscles of the heart; all his glands secreted tumultuously, inundating him with warring hormones. His jaws locked as though from tetanus and he fell to the ground like a block of wood.

from Survival in Auschwitz[1]

The Journey

I was captured by the Fascist Militia on December 13, 1943. I was twenty-four, with little wisdom, no experience, and a decided tendency—encouraged by the life of

1. Translated by Stuart Woolf.

segregation forced on me for the previous four years by the racial laws—to live in an unrealistic world of my own, a world inhabited by civilized Cartesian phantoms,[2] by sincere male and bloodless female friendships. I cultivated a moderate and abstract sense of rebellion.

It had been by no means easy to flee into the mountains and to help set up what, both in my opinion and in that of friends little more experienced than myself, should have become a partisan band affiliated with the Resistance movement *Justice and Liberty*. Contacts, arms, money and the experience needed to acquire them were all missing. We lacked capable men, and instead we were swamped by a deluge of outcasts, in good or bad faith, who came from the plain in search of a non-existent military or political organization, of arms, or merely of protection, a hiding place, a fire, a pair of shoes.

At that time I had not yet been taught the doctrine I was later to learn so hurriedly in the Lager:[3] that man is bound to pursue his own ends by all possible means, while he who errs but once pays dearly. So that I can only consider the following sequence of events justified. Three Fascist Militia companies, which had set out in the night to surprise a much more powerful and dangerous band than ours, broke into our refuge one spectral snowy dawn and took me down to the valley as a suspect person.

During the interrogations that followed, I preferred to admit my status of "Italian citizen of Jewish race." I felt that otherwise I would be unable to justify my presence in places too secluded even for an evacuee; while I believed (wrongly as was subsequently seen) that the admission of my political activity would have meant torture and certain death. As a Jew, I was sent to Fossoli, near Modena,[4] where a vast detention camp, originally meant for English and American prisoners-of-war, collected all the numerous categories of people not approved of by the new-born Fascist Republic.[5]

At the moment of my arrival, that is, at the end of January, 1944, there were about one hundred and fifty Italian Jews in the camp, but within a few weeks their number rose to over six hundred. For the most part they consisted of entire families captured by the Fascists or Nazis through their imprudence or following secret accusations. A few had given themselves up spontaneously, reduced to desperation by the vagabond life, or because they lacked the means to survive, or to avoid separation from a captured relation, or even—absurdly—"to be in conformity with the law." There were also about a hundred Jugoslavian military internees and a few other foreigners who were politically suspect.

The arrival of a squad of German SS men[6] should have made even the optimists doubtful; but we still managed to interpret the novelty in various ways without drawing the most obvious conclusions. Thus, despite everything, the announcement of the deportation caught us all unawares.

On February 20, the Germans had inspected the camp with care and had publicly and loudly upbraided the Italian commissar for the defective organization of the kitchen service and for the scarce amount of wood distributed for heating; they even said that an infirmary would soon be opened. But on the morning of the 21st we learned that on the following day the Jews would be leaving. All the Jews, without

2. The French philosopher René Descartes (1596–1650) gave precedence to abstract reasoning as antidote to doubt.

3. Literally, "storage place." The "holding tank" for German prisoners destined for concentration camps.

4. Provincial capital in north-central Italy.

5. Fascist regime of Italy (1922–1943) under the dictatorship of Benito Mussolini.

6. The German SS, or "Storm Toopers," were the elite cadre of Hitler's military forces.

exception. Even the children, even the old, even the ill. Our destination? Nobody knew. We should be prepared for a fortnight of travel. For every person missing at the roll-call, ten would be shot.

Only a minority of ingenuous and deluded souls continued to hope; we others had often spoken with the Polish and Croat refugees and we knew what departure meant.

For people condemned to death, tradition prescribes an austere ceremony, calculated to emphasize that all passions and anger have died down, and that the act of justice represents only a sad duty towards society which moves even the executioner to pity for the victim. Thus the condemned man is shielded from all external cares, he is granted solitude and, should he want it, spiritual comfort; in short, care is taken that he should feel around him neither hatred nor arbitrariness, only necessity and justice, and by means of punishment, pardon.

But to us this was not granted, for we were many and time was short. And in any case, what had we to repent, for what crime did we need pardon? The Italian commissar accordingly decreed that all services should continue to function until the final notice: the kitchens remained open, the corvées[7] for cleaning worked as usual, and even the teachers of the little school gave lessons until the evening, as on other days. But that evening the children were given no homework.

And night came, and it was such a night that one knew that human eyes would not witness it and survive. Everyone felt this: not one of the guards, neither Italian nor German, had the courage to come and see what men do when they know they have to die.

All took leave from life in the manner which most suited them. Some praying, some deliberately drunk, others lustfully intoxicated for the last time. But the mothers stayed up to prepare the food for the journey with tender care, and washed their children and packed the luggage; and at dawn the barbed wire was full of children's washing hung out in the wind to dry. Nor did they forget the diapers, the toys, the cushions and the hundred other small things which mothers remember and which children always need. Would you not do the same? If you and your child were going to be killed tomorrow, would you not give him to eat today?

In hut 6A old Gattegno lived with his wife and numerous children and grandchildren and his sons and daughters-in-law. All the men were carpenters; they had come from Tripoli after many long journeys, and had always carried with them the tools of their trade, their kitchen utensils, and their accordions and violins to play and dance to after the day's work. They were happy and pious folk. Their women were the first to silently and rapidly finish the preparations for the journey in order to have time for mourning. When all was ready, the food cooked, the bundles tied together, they unloosened their hair, took off their shoes, placed the Yahrzeit[8] candles on the ground and lit them according to the customs of their fathers, and sat on the bare soil in a circle for the lamentations, praying and weeping all the night. We collected in a group in front of their door, and we experienced within ourselves a grief that was new for us, the ancient grief of the people that has no land, the grief without hope of the exodus which is renewed every century.

Dawn came on us like a betrayer; it seemed as though the new sun rose as an ally of our enemies to assist in our destruction. The different emotions that overcame us, of resignation, of futile rebellion, of religious abandon, of fear, of despair, now joined together after a sleepless night in a collective, uncontrolled panic. The time for

7. Unpaid workers.

8. In Judaism, the anniversary of the death of a relative, observed with mourning candles and religious recitations.

meditation, the time for decision was over, and all reason dissolved into a tumult, across which flashed the happy memories of our homes, still so near in time and space, as painful as the thrusts of a sword.

Many things were then said and done among us; but of these it is better that there remain no memory.

With the absurd precision to which we later had to accustom ourselves, the Germans held the roll-call. At the end the officer asked *"Wieviel Stück?"*[9] The corporal saluted smartly and replied that there were six hundred and fifty "pieces" and that all was in order. They then loaded us on to the buses and took us to the station of Carpi. Here the train was waiting for us, with our escort for the journey. Here we received the first blows: and it was so new and senseless that we felt no pain, neither in body nor in spirit. Only a profound amazement: how can one hit a man without anger?

There were twelve goods wagons for six hundred and fifty men; in mine we were only forty-five, but it was a small wagon. Here then, before our very eyes, under our very feet, was one of those notorious transport trains, those which never return, and of which, shuddering and always a little incredulous, we had so often heard speak. Exactly like this, detail for detail: goods wagons closed from the outside, with men, women and children pressed together without pity, like cheap merchandise, for a journey towards nothingness, a journey down there, towards the bottom. This time it is us who are inside.

Sooner or later in life everyone discovers that perfect happiness is unrealizable, but there are few who pause to consider the antithesis: that perfect unhappiness is equally unattainable. The obstacles preventing the realization of both these extreme states are of the same nature: they derive from our human condition which is opposed to everything infinite. Our ever-insufficient knowledge of the future opposes it: and this is called, in the one instance, hope, and in the other, uncertainty of the following day. The certainty of death opposes it: for it places a limit on every joy, but also on every grief. The inevitable material cares oppose it: for as they poison every lasting happiness, they equally assiduously distract us from our misfortunes, and make our consciousness of them intermittent and hence supportable.

It was the very discomfort, the blows, the cold, the thirst that kept us aloft in the void of bottomless despair, both during the journey and after. It was not the will to live, nor a conscious resignation; for few are the men capable of such resolution, and we were but a common sample of humanity.

The doors had been closed at once, but the train did not move until evening. We had learnt of our destination with relief. Auschwitz:[1] a name without significance for us at that time, but it at least implied some place on this earth.

The train travelled slowly, with long, unnerving halts. Through the slit we saw the tall pale cliffs of the Adige Valley and the names of the last Italian cities disappear behind us. We passed the Brenner[2] at midday of the second day and everyone stood up, but no one said a word. The thought of the return journey stuck in my heart, and I cruelly pictured to myself the inhuman joy of that other journey, with doors open, no one wanting to flee, and the first Italian names . . . and I looked around and wondered how many, among that poor human dust, would be struck by fate. Among the forty-five people in my wagon only four saw their homes again; and it was by far the most fortunate wagon.

We suffered from thirst and cold; at every stop we clamoured for water, or even a handful of snow, but we were rarely heard; the soldiers of the escort drove off

9. "How many pieces?"
1. City in southeast Poland, where the Nazis established concentration camps and forced labor camps.
2. Alpine pass between Austria and Italy.

anybody who tried to approach the convoy. Two young mothers, nursing their children, groaned night and day, begging for water. Our state of nervous tension made the hunger, exhaustion and lack of sleep seem less of a torment. But the hours of darkness were nightmares without end.

There are few men who know how to go to their deaths with dignity, and often they are not those whom one would expect. Few know how to remain silent and respect the silence of others. Our restless sleep was often interrupted by noisy and futile disputes, by curses, by kicks and blows blindly delivered to ward off some encroaching and inevitable contact. Then someone would light a candle, and its mournful flicker would reveal an obscure agitation, a human mass, extended across the floor, confused and continuous, sluggish and aching, rising here and there in sudden convulsions and immediately collapsing again in exhaustion.

Through the slit, known and unknown names of Austrian cities, Salzburg, Vienna, then Czech, finally Polish names. On the evening of the fourth day the cold became intense; the train ran through interminable black pine forests, climbing perceptibly. The snow was high. It must have been a branch line as the stations were small and almost deserted. During the halts, no one tried anymore to communicate with the outside world: we felt ourselves by now "on the other side." There was a long halt in open country. The train started up with extreme slowness, and the convoy stopped for the last time, in the dead of night, in the middle of a dark silent plain.

On both sides of the track rows of red and white lights appeared as far as the eye could see; but there was none of that confusion of sounds which betrays inhabited places even from a distance. By the wretched light of the last candle, with the rhythm of the wheels, with every human sound now silenced, we awaited what was to happen.

Next to me, crushed against me for the whole journey, there had been a woman. We had known each other for many years, and the misfortune had struck us together, but we knew little of each other. Now, in the hour of decision, we said to each other things that are never said among the living. We said farewell and it was short; everybody said farewell to life through his neighbour. We had no more fear.

The climax came suddenly. The door opened with a crash, and the dark echoed with outlandish orders in that curt, barbaric barking of Germans in command which seems to give vent to a millennial anger. A vast platform appeared before us, lit up by reflectors. A little beyond it, a row of lorries. Then everything was silent again. Someone translated: we had to climb down with our luggage and deposit it alongside the train. In a moment the platform was swarming with shadows. But we were afraid to break that silence: everyone busied himself with his luggage, searched for someone else, called to somebody, but timidly, in a whisper.

A dozen SS men stood around, legs akimbo, with an indifferent air. At a certain moment they moved among us, and in a subdued tone of voice, with faces of stone, began to interrogate us rapidly, one by one, in bad Italian. They did not interrogate everybody, only a few: "How old? Healthy or ill?" And on the basis of the reply they pointed in two different directions.

Everything was as silent as an aquarium, or as in certain dream sequences. We had expected something more apocalyptic: they seemed simple police agents. It was disconcerting and disarming. Someone dared to ask for his luggage: they replied, "luggage afterwards." Someone else did not want to leave his wife: they said, "together again afterwards." Many mothers did not want to be separated from their children: they said "good, good, stay with child." They behaved with the calm assurance of people doing their normal duty of every day. But Renzo stayed an instant too long to say goodbye to Francesca, his fiancée, and with a single blow they knocked him to the ground. It was their everyday duty.

In less than ten minutes all the fit men had been collected together in a group. What happened to the others, to the women, to the children, to the old men, we could establish neither then nor later: the night swallowed them up, purely and simply. To-day, however, we know that in that rapid and summary choice each one of us had been judged capable or not of working usefully for the Reich; we know that of our convoy no more than ninety-six men and twenty-nine women entered the respective camps of Monowitz-Buna and Birkenau, and that of all the others, more than five hundred in number, not one was living two days later. We also know that not even this tenuous principle of discrimination between fit and unfit was always followed, and that later the simpler method was often adopted of merely opening both doors of the wagon without warning or instructions to the new arrivals. Those who by chance climbed down on one side of the convoy entered the camp; the others went to the gas chamber.

This is the reason why three-year-old Emilia died: the historical necessity of killing the children of Jews was self-demonstrative to the Germans. Emilia, daughter of Aldo Levi of Milan, was a curious, ambitious, cheerful, intelligent child; her parents had succeeded in washing her during the journey in the packed car in a tub with tepid water which the degenerate German engineer had allowed them to draw from the engine that was dragging us all to death.

Thus, in an instant, our women, our parents, our children disappeared. We saw them for a short while as an obscure mass at the other end of the platform; then we saw nothing more.

Instead, two groups of strange individuals emerged into the light of the lamp. They walked in squads, in rows of three, with an odd, embarrassed step, head dangling in front, arms rigid. On their heads they wore comic berets and were all dressed in long striped overcoats, which even by night and from a distance looked filthy and in rags. They walked in a large circle around us, never drawing near, and in silence began to busy themselves with our luggage and to climb in and out of the empty wagons.

We looked at each other without a word. It was all incomprehensible and mad, but one thing we had understood. This was the metamorphosis that awaited us. To-morrow we would be like them.

Without knowing how I found myself loaded on to a lorry[3] with thirty others; the lorry sped into the night at full speed. It was covered and we could not see outside, but by the shaking we could tell that the road had many curves and bumps. Are we unguarded? Throw ourselves down? It is too late, too late, we are all "down." In any case we are soon aware that we are not without guard. He is a strange guard, a German soldier bristling with arms. We do not see him because of the thick darkness, but we feel the hard contact every time that a lurch of the lorry throws us all in a heap. At a certain point he switches on a pocket torch[4] and instead of shouting threats of damnation at us, he asks us courteously, one by one, in German and in pidgin language, if we have any money or watches to give him, seeing that they will not be useful to us anymore. This is no order, no regulation: it is obvious that it is a small private initiative of our Charon.[5] The matter stirs us to anger and laughter and brings relief. * * *

3. Truck.
4. Flashlight.
5. In Greek mythology, Charon is the ferryman who conveys the dead across the River Styx to the underworld.

The Canto of Ulysses

There were six of us, scraping and cleaning the inside of an underground petrol tank; the daylight only reached us through a small manhole. It was a luxury job because no one supervised us; but it was cold and damp. The powder of the rust burnt under our eyelids and coated our throats and mouths with a taste almost like blood.

The rope-ladder hanging from the manhole began to sway: someone was coming. Deutsch extinguished his cigarette, Goldner woke Sivadjan; we all began to vigorously scrape the resonant steelplate wall.

It was not the *Vorarbeiter,*[6] it was only Jean, the Pikolo of our Kommando. Jean was an Alsatian student; although he was already twenty-four, he was the youngest Häftling[7] of the Chemical Kommando. So that he was given the post of Pikolo, which meant the messenger-clerk, responsible for the cleaning of the hut, for the distribution of tools, for the washing of bowls, and for keeping record of the working hours of the Kommando.

Jean spoke French and German fluently: as soon as we recognized his shoes on the top step of the ladder we all stopped scraping.

"Also, Pikolo, was gibt es Neues?"[8]

"Qu'est ce qu'il-y-a comme soupe aujourd'hui?"[9]

. . . in what mood was the Kapo?[1] And the affair of the twenty-five lashes given to Stern? What was the weather like outside? Had he read the newspaper? What smell was coming from the civilian kitchen? What was the time?

Jean was liked a great deal by the Kommando. One must realize that the post of Pikolo represented a quite high rank in the hierarchy of the Prominents: the Pikolo (who is usually no more than seventeen years old) does no manual work, has an absolute right to the remainder of the daily ration to be found on the bottom of the vat, and can stay all day near the stove. He "therefore" has the right to a supplementary half-ration and has a good chance of becoming the friend and confidant of the Kapo, from whom he officially receives discarded clothes and shoes. Now Jean was an exceptional Pikolo. He was shrewd and physically robust, and at the same time gentle and friendly: although he continued his secret individual struggle against the camp and against death, he did not neglect his human relationships with less privileged comrades; at the same time he had been so able and persevering that he had managed to establish himself in the confidence of Alex, the Kapo.

Alex had kept all his promises. He had shown himself a violent and unreliable rogue, with an armour of solid and compact ignorance and stupidity, always excepting his intuition and consummate technique as convict-keeper. He never let slip an opportunity of proclaiming his pride in his pure blood and his green triangle, and displayed a lofty contempt for his ragged and starving chemists: *"Ihr Doktoren! Ihr Intelligenten!"*[2] he sneered every day, watching them crowd around with their bowls held out for the distribution of the ration. He was extremely compliant and servile before the civilian *Meister* and with the SS he kept up ties of cordial friendship.

He was clearly intimidated by the register of the Kommando and by the daily report of work, and this had been the path that Pikolo had chosen to make himself indispensable. It had been a long, cautious and subtle task which the entire Kommando had followed for a month with bated breath; but at the end the porcupine's defence was penetrated, and Pikolo confirmed in his office to the satisfaction of all concerned.

6. Foreman.
7. Underling.
8. "What's new?"
9. "What's today's soup?"
1. Chief.
2. "You doctors! You intellectuals!"

Although Jean had never abused his position, we had already been able to verify that a single word of his, said in the right tone of voice and at the right moment, had great power; many times already it had saved one of us from a whipping or from being denounced to the SS. We had been friends for a week: we discovered each other during the unusual occasion of an air-raid alarm, but then, swept by the fierce rhythm of the Lager, we had only been able to greet each other fleetingly, at the latrines, in the washroom.

Hanging with one hand on the swaying ladder, he pointed to me: *"Aujourd'hui c'est Primo qui viendra avec moi chercher la soupe."*[3]

Until yesterday it had been Stern, the squinting Transylvanian; now he had fallen into disgrace for some story of brooms stolen from the store, and Pikolo had managed to support my candidature as assistant to the *"Essenholen,"*[4] the daily corvée of the ration.

He climbed out and I followed him, blinking in the brightness of the day. It was warmish outside, the sun drew a faint smell of paint and tar from the greasy earth, which made me think of a holiday beach of my infancy. Pikolo gave me one of the two wooden poles, and we walked along under a clear June sky.

I began to thank him, but he stopped me: it was not necessary. One could see the Carpathians covered in snow. I breathed in the fresh air, I felt unusually light-hearted.

"Tu es fou de marcher si vite. On a le temps, tu sais,"[5] The ration was collected half a mile away; one had to return with the pot weighing over a hundred pounds supported on the two poles. It was quite a tiring task, but it meant a pleasant walk there without a load, and the ever-welcome chance of going near the kitchens.

We slowed down. Pikolo was expert. He had chosen the path cleverly so that we would have to make a long detour, walking at least for an hour, without arousing suspicion. We spoke of our houses, of Strasbourg and Turin, of the books we had read; of what we had studied, of our mothers: how all mothers resemble each other! His mother too had scolded him for never knowing how much money he had in his pocket; his mother too would have been amazed if she had known that he had found his feet, that day by day he was finding his feet.

An SS man passed on a bicycle. It is Rudi, the *Blockführer.*[6] Halt! Attention! Take off your beret! *"Sale brute, celui-là. Ein ganz gemeiner Hund."*[7] Can he speak French and German with equal facility? Yes, he thinks indifferently in both languages. He spent a month in Liguria,[8] he likes Italy, he would like to learn Italian: I would be pleased to teach him Italian: why not try? We can do it. Why not immediately, one thing is as good as another, the important thing is not to lose time, not to waste this hour.

Limentani from Rome walks by, dragging his feet, with a bowl hidden under his jacket. Pikolo listens carefully, picks up a few words of our conversation and repeats them smiling: *"Zup-pa, cam-po, acqua."*[9]

Frenkl the spy passes. Quicken our pace, one never knows, he does evil for evil's sake.

. . . The canto of Ulysses.[1] Who knows how or why it comes into my mind. But we have no time to change, this hour is already less than an hour. If Jean is intelligent he will understand. He *will* understand—today I feel capable of so much.

3. "Today Primo's the one who's getting the soup with me."

4. Mess hall.

5. "You're crazy to be walking so fast. There is time, you know."

6. Cell commander.

7. "A filthy brute, that one. Just a common mutt."

8. A region in northwest Italy that borders France.

9. "Soup, field, water."

1. The canto of Ulysses is the 26th Canto of Dante's *Inferno,* one of the three books of the *Divine Comedy* (see page 1351). The Homeric hero is condemned to one of the "malbolge" for having dared to go beyond the frontiers of the known world. In the pages that follow, Levi often cites from this canto.

. . . Who is Dante? What is the Comedy? That curious sensation of novelty which one feels if one tries to explain briefly what is the Divine Comedy. How the Inferno is divided up, what are its punishments. Virgil is Reason, Beatrice is Theology.

Jean pays great attention, and I begin slowly and accurately:

Then of that age-old fire the loftier horn
Began to mutter and move, as a wavering flame
Wrestles against the wind and is over-worn;
And, like a speaking tongue vibrant to frame
Language, the tip of it flickering to and fro
Threw out a voice and answered: "When I came . . ."

Here I stop and try to translate. Disastrous—poor Dante and poor French! All the same, the experience seems to promise well: Jean admires the bizarre simile of the tongue and suggests the appropriate word to translate "age-old."

And after "When I came?" Nothing. A hole in my memory. "Before Aeneas ever named it so." Another hole. A fragment floats into my mind, not relevant: ". . . nor piety To my old father, nor the wedded love That should have comforted Penelope . . . ," is it correct?

". . . So on the open sea I set forth."

Of this I am certain, I am sure, I can explain it to Pikolo, I can point out why "I set forth" is not *"je me mis,"* it is much stronger and more audacious, it is a chain which has been broken, it is throwing oneself on the other side of a barrier, we know the impulse well. The open sea: Pikolo has travelled by sea, and knows what it means: it is when the horizon closes in on itself, free, straight ahead and simple, and there is nothing but the smell of the sea; sweet things, ferociously far away.

We have arrived at Kraftwerk, where the cable-laying Kommando works. Engineer Levi must be here. Here he is, one can only see his head above the trench. He waves to me, he is a brave man, I have never seen his morale low, he never speaks of eating.

"Open sea, open sea." I know it rhymes with "left me": ". . . and that small band of comrades that had never left me," but I cannot remember if it comes before or after. And the journey as well, the foolhardy journey beyond the Pillars of Hercules, how sad, I have to tell it in prose—a sacrilege. I have only rescued two lines, but they are worth stopping for:

". . . that none should prove so hardy
To venture the uncharted distances . . ."

"to venture": I had to come to the Lager to realize that it is the same expression as before "I set forth." But I say nothing to Jean, I am not sure that it is an important observation. How many things there are to say, and the sun is already high, midday is near. I am in a hurry, a terrible hurry.

Here, listen Pikolo, open your ears and your mind, you have to understand, for my sake:

"Think of your breed; for brutish ignorance
Your mettle was not made; you were made men,
To follow after knowledge and excellence."

As if I also was hearing it for the first time: like the blast of a trumpet, like the voice of God. For a moment I forget who I am and where I am.

Pikolo begs me to repeat it. How good Pikolo is, he is aware that it is doing me good. Or perhaps it is something more: perhaps, despite the wan translation and the pedestrian, rushed commentary, he has received the message, he has felt that it has to do with him, that it has to do with all men who toil, and with us in particular; and that it has to do with us two, who dare to reason of these things with the poles for the soup on our shoulders.

"My little speech made every one so keen . . ."

. . . and I try, but in vain, to explain how many things this "keen" means. There is another lacuna here, this time irreparable. ". . . the light kindles and grows Beneath the moon" or something like it; but before it? . . . Not an idea, *"keine Ahnung"*[2] as they say here. Forgive me, Pikolo, I have forgotten at least four triplets.

"Ça ne fait rien, vas-y tout de même."[3]

". . . When at last hove up a mountain, grey
With distance, and so lofty and so steep,
I never had seen the like on any day."

Yes, yes, "so lofty and so steep," not "very steep," a consecutive proposition. And the mountains when one sees them in the distance . . . the mountains . . . oh, Pikolo, Pikolo, say something, speak, do not let me think of my mountains which used to show up against the dusk of evening as I returned by train from Milan to Turin!

Enough, one must go on, these are things that one thinks but does not say. Pikolo waits and looks at me.

I would give today's soup to know how to connect "the like on any day" to the last lines. I try to reconstruct it through the rhymes, I close my eyes, I bite my fingers—but it is no use, the rest is silence. Other verses dance in my head: ". . . The sodden ground belched wind . . . ," no, it is something else. It is late, it is late, we have reached the kitchen, I must finish;

"And three times round she went in roaring smother
With all the waters; at the fourth the poop
Rose, and the prow went down, as pleased Another."

I keep Pikolo back, it is vitally necessary and urgent that he listen, that he understand this "as pleased Another" before it is too late; tomorrow he or I might be dead, or we might never see each other again, I must tell him, I must explain to him about the Middle Ages, about the so human and so necessary and yet unexpected anachronism, but still more, something gigantic that I myself have only just seen, in a flash of intuition, perhaps the reason for our fate, for our being here today. . .

We are now in the soup queue, among the sordid, ragged crowd of soup-carriers from other Kommandos. Those just arrived press against our backs. *"Kraut und Rüben? Kraut und Rüben."* The official announcement is made that the soup today is of cabbages and turnips: *"Choux et navets. Kaposzta és répak."*

"And over our heads the hollow seas closed up."

2. No idea.

3. "No matter. Go on anyway."

Chinua Achebe

b. 1930

Chinua Achebe occupies a key position in the history of postcolonial African literature. Until the 1958 publication of his novel *Things Fall Apart,* readers outside Africa encountered Africa in fiction largely through European perspectives. Joseph Conrad's *Heart of Darkness* (page 2446) occupied a preeminent position in literature about Africa and its European colonization. Though incisive and critical of the European imperial enterprise in the continent, Conrad's remains a European perspective, and it was Achebe who presented an African reading of Africa to the wider world for the first time in the twentieth century. Some have felt that Achebe's narrative isn't actually African enough. Critics point out that the novel is written in one of the colonists' imperial languages, English, and, starting with the title of the novel (taken from W. B. Yeats), its literary antecedents and narrative strategies are as much European as the story is African. Achebe hasn't shied away from engaging in this discussion among critics and scholars of postcolonialism. As an African author and a Western academic and critic, he clearly is an interested party in more than one sense. As such, he can be seen as a writer who embodies simultaneously the cultures of the colonized and of the colonizer.

It is interesting, and also historically intriguing, that Achebe has viewed himself as an African insider, as attested to by his essay, included here, on the 1962 meeting of African intellectuals at Makarere University College in Uganda. That was an occasion for a "declaration of literary independence" by the African writers who gathered there, many of whom would in fact form the first cohort of postcolonial African authors. It would be some years before it came to light that Achebe along with the other African writers at that defining moment were indeed insiders, but they were also in the process of being turned inside out by the circumstances of the very occasion in which they were defining themselves. They would come to learn that their self-defining moment was in fact a move in a larger ideological and neocolonial chess game played by superpowers in the course of the Cold War. Unbeknownst to most of them, they were being gathered under the auspices of the U.S. Central Intelligence Agency through one of the proxy organizations it operated in Paris called the Society for Cultural Freedom.

Like his writing, Achebe himself is the product of an interesting mixture of educational institutions and religious traditions. Born in Ogidi, eastern Nigeria, an Igbo region, Achebe was the fifth of six children. His father was a teacher in an evangelical Protestant school of the Church Missionary Society. He was originally christened "Albert," after the son of England's Queen Victoria. Upon entering the university, he dropped his English name and kept his indigenous Igbo name, "Chinua." His secondary schooling was in Government College in Umuahia, which he entered in 1944. He received his university education at University College of Ibadan, from which he graduated in 1953 with a degree in English, history, and theology. Upon graduation he traveled throughout Africa and to America and then joined the Nigerian Broadcasting Company in 1954. Four years later he published his first novel, *Things Fall Apart,* in which he attempted to portray traditional life before the arrival of the colonizing Europeans. The work became a classic of African literature with translations into more than fifty languages. In 1960 he published his second novel, *No Longer at Ease,* followed by *Arrow of God* in 1964. These novels depict the clash of traditional Igbo life with colonial and missionary incursions by European powers.

Throughout the 1950s and 1960s Achebe worked in broadcasting, becoming director of External Services in charge of the Voice of Nigeria in 1961. He cofounded a publishing company in 1967 and was then appointed a research fellow at the University of Nigeria. Starting in

In 1885, British control was confined to Lagos and Niger Delta but would quickly advance upriver and into the interior under the direction of the Royal Niger Company. Missionaries such as Mr. Brown and Mr. Smith often preceded colonial administrators.

1971 he edited the journal *Okike,* which published and promoted new writing in Nigeria. Nigeria was torn by civil wars from 1966 to 1970, which were chiefly between his own Igbo people and the non-Igbo; these conflicts forced Achebe and his family to flee to Lagos, Nigeria's capital. His collection of poems based on his country's internecine strife won the Commonwealth Poetry Prize in 1972. In the same year Achebe published a collection of short stories, *Girls at War,* and traveled to the United States to teach at the University of Massachusetts in Amherst. He returned to Nigeria in 1976 to continue his engagement in the political life of his country, and in 1983 he published *The Trouble with Nigeria,* a scathing attack on the national corruption among Nigeria's leaders. Yet another military coup, the fifth, two years later became the basis for Achebe's fifth novel, *Anthills of the Savannah* (1987), an indictment of military power and dictatorship. The following year he was partially paralyzed as a result of a car accident but recovered enough to resume his writing career and to accept a teaching position at Bard College in New York, where he has taught since. *Things Fall Apart* has remained his best known and most influential work. Situated between a complex, traditional world and the European invasion and colonization that ensued, the narrative of *Things Fall Apart* has taken on much greater historical and cultural significance than usually accorded a work of fiction.

The pieces that follow Achebe's novel unfold the complexities of postcolonial cultural exchange, focusing especially on the issue of language. In his essay "The African Writer and the English Language," Achebe argues that African writers have a sovereign right to make use of colonial languages like English, which can unite audiences otherwise split among many local ethnic languages and cultures. Colonialism, Achebe says, gave Africans "a language with which to talk to one another. If it failed to give them a song, it at least gave them a tongue, for sighing." Now, a new generation will remake English for new purposes and new audiences.

In the first Resonance that follows Achebe's essay, Kenyan writer Ngugi wa Thiong'o offers a pointed rejoinder, recalling the same 1962 conference Achebe discusses, but describing it to very different effect as displaying a neocolonialist blindness to the central role of native African languages. Ngugi goes on to describe the mixed messages offered him by his own colonial education and his eventual decision to abandon the use of English for fiction, in favor of his native Gĩkũyũ.

The language debate has been carried out in fiction and poetry as much as in essays, as can be seen in the two Resonances following Ngugi's essay. First come excerpts from Congolese writer Mbwil Ngal's hilarious, satiric novel *Giambatista Viko: or, the Rape of African Discourse,* whose hero—a self–hating African writer and professor—is kidnapped by tribalists who demand that he renounce the French language and its culture. Finally, in the Perspectives section on Postcolonial conditions, white South African poet Jeremy Cronin (page 2794) gives a moving reflection on the challenge of representing a landscape marked by so many layers of language—Zulu and other native languages, Dutch-derived Afrikaans, and English. In his great novel, Conrad had carried out a searching exploration of the darkness at the heart of the European exploitation of Africa while hardly giving a single spoken line to an actual African character. In *Things Fall Apart,* and in the vigorous debates it has helped inspire, African writers have responded in many varied voices, in languages newly remade for a new world.

PRONUNCIATIONS:

Chinua Achebe: CHIN-ow-ah ah-CHAY-bay
Mbwil Ngal: m'BWEEL n'GAHL
Ngugi wa-Thiong'o: GOU-gie wah-tee-ON-go

Things Fall Apart

Principal Characters in the Novel[1]

Akueke (ah-KWAY-kay): Daughter of Obierika, whose marriage is negotiated
Anene (ah-NAY-nay): Ekwefi's first husband
Chielo (chee-AY-lah): The current priestess of the oracle
Chika (CHEE-kah): The former priestess of the oracle, during Unoka's time
Ekwefi (eh-KWAY-fee): Okonkwo's second wife; mother of Ezinma
Enoch: A Christian convert; a fanatic, who killed the sacred python and sought confrontation with Igbo traditionalists
Ezeani (ay-tsay-AH-nee): The priest of the earth goddess
Ezeudu (ay-TSEU-du): An important elder; the oldest man in Okonkwo's village
Ezeugo (ay-TSEU-gah): A powerful orator usually chosen as spokesman
Ezinma (ay-TSEEN-mah): Okonkwo's favorite daughter

1. Achebe prefaces his novel with this list of characters (pronunciations added) and definitions of the many Igbo terms that appear in the text.

Ikemefuna (ee-kay-may-FOO-nah): The boy from Mbaino given to Umuofia as compensation for murder
Maduka (MAH-dou-kah): Son of Obierika, a promising young wrestler
Mr. Brown: The first white missionary based in Umuofia
Mr. Kiaga: The Igbo missionary left in charge of the fledgling church in Mbanta
Mr. Smith: The zealous white missionary who replaced Mr. Brown
Ndulue (en-dou-LOO-ay): Husband who died at the same time as his wife
Nwakibie (nwah-key-BEE-ay): a big man in Umuofia, who helped Okonkwo get started in planting yams
Nwoye (NWO-yeh): Okonkwo's oldest son, who converts to Christianity and adopts the name Isaac
Obiageli (ah-bya-GAY-lee): Sister of Nwoye
Obierika (ah-byer-EE-kah): Okonkwo's good friend and confidant
Ogbuefi Udo (ag-BWAY-fee OU-dah): The man whose wife was murdered by the people of Mbaino
Ojiugo (ah-JYOU-go): One of Okonkwo's three wives, mother of Obiageli
Okagbue (ah-KAG-bway): The medicine man who finds and destroys Ezinma's *iyi-uwa*
Okonkwo (ah-CONK-wah): The main character, a strong, proud man
Okoye (ah-CO-yay): A friend of Okonkwo's father, who tries unsuccessfully to get back the money Unoka had borrowed
Ozoemena (ah-tso-ay-MAY-nah): Wife who dies at the same time as her husband
Uchendu (ou-CHEN-dou): Okonkwo's uncle, the senior man of Mbanta where Okonkwo's family lives in exile
Unoka (ou-NO-kah): Okonkwo's late father, an easygoing, rather lazy person

Glossary of Words and Phrases Used in the Text
(Igbo terms are in italics; *o* indicates "aw" sound as in *awful.*)

Afo: One of the four market days
agadi-nwayi: Old woman
agbala: Woman; also, an insulting term for a man who has taken no title
Agbala: The name of the oracle consulted by the people of Umuofia
Amadiora: The god of thunder and lightning
Ani: The earth goddess
bride-price: Or bridewealth; the gifts transferred from the groom's family to that of the bride, which cement the marriage and legitimize the children
chi: One's personal god, or guardian spirit
Chukwu: The supreme god
cowries: Shells imported from the Indian Ocean, widely used as currency in precolonial Africa
District Commissioner: The British official in charge of a particular African district
efulefu: An empty, worthless man
egwugwu: The masked spirits, representing the ancestral spirits of the village
Eke: One of the four market days
ekwe: A wooden drum
eneke-nti-oba: A kind of bird
eze-agai-nwayi: The teeth of an old woman
foo-foo: Or fufu; pounded yam eaten as part of most meals
harmattan: A cold, dry wind that blows from the North

iba: Fever
Ibo: The older spelling of "Igbo," less commonly used today
Idemili: One of the three most prestigious titles in Igboland
Ifejioku: The god of yams, the men's crop and principal food of the Igbo
Iguedo: Okonkwo's village, one of the nine villages that make up Umuofia
ikenga: A wooden carving that becomes imbued with a man's personal spirit
ilo: The village common, where meetings, ceremonies, and sports competitions take place
inyanga: Showing off; bragging
isa-ifi: A ceremony held to determine faithfulness if a woman had been separated from her fiancé or husband for some time and were then reunited with him
iyi-uwa: A special stone that forms the link between an *ogbanje* and the spirit world. The child would eventually die if the *iyi-uwa* were not discovered and destroyed.
jigida: A string of waist-beads
kite: A bird that appears during the dry season
kola nuts: Offered to guests on special occasions
kotma: "Court man," or court messenger; a corruption of the English term
kwenu: A shout of approval and greeting
maize: Corn
ndichie: The elders, who meet in council and make decisions binding the clan
nna ayi: Our father
nne: Mother
nno: An expression of welcome
nso-ani: Sacrilege
nza: A tiny bird
obi: The living quarters of the head of the family
obodo dike: The land of the brave
ochu: Murder or manslaughter
ogbanje: A changeling; a child who repeatedly dies and returns to its mother to be reborn
Ogbuefi: An honorific used before the name of a man who has taken the *ozo* title
ogene: A kind of gong
ogwu: Supernatural medicine
osu: An outcast; having been dedicated to a god, the *osu* was not allowed to mix with the freeborn, or to marry one of them
Oye: One of the four market days
ozo: One of the titles an important Igbo man could aspire to
palm kernels: The core of the fruit of the oil palm tree, which were cracked to release the oil
palm-oil: Used in cooking and for preparing food, also a major cash crop exported to Europe
palm-wine: A fermented drink prepared from the sap of certain palm trees
plantain: A starchy kind of banana, cooked as food
pottage: A stew
singlets: Men's undershirts
sisal: A kind of cactus plant with fibrous leaves
tufia: A curse or oath
udu: A type of drum made from pottery
uli: A dye used by women for drawing patterns on the skin

umuada: A family gathering of daughters, for which the female kinsfolk return to their village of origin
Umuofia: The clan Okonkwo belonged to, made up of nine villages
umunna: A wide group of kinsmen (the masculine form of *umuada*)
Uri: Part of the betrothal ceremony when the dowry or bridewealth is paid

Things Fall Apart

Turning and turning in the widening gyre
The falcon cannot hear the falconer;
Things fall apart; the centre cannot hold;
Mere anarchy is loosed upon the world.

W. B. Yeats, "The Second Coming"[1]

Part 1

Chapter 1

Okonkwo was well known throughout the nine villages and even beyond. His fame rested on solid personal achievements. As a young man of eighteen he had brought honour to his village by throwing Amalinze the Cat. Amalinze was the great wrestler who for seven years was unbeaten, from Umuofia to Mbaino. He was called the Cat because his back would never touch the earth. It was this man that Okonkwo threw in a fight which the old men agreed was one of the fiercest since the founder of their town engaged a spirit of the wild for seven days and seven nights.

The drums beat and the flutes sang and the spectators held their breath. Amalinze was a wily craftsman, but Okonkwo was as slippery as a fish in water. Every nerve and every muscle stood out on their arms, on their backs and their thighs, and one almost heard them stretching to breaking point. In the end Okonkwo threw the Cat.

That was many years ago, twenty years or more, and during this time Okonkwo's fame had grown like a bush-fire in the harmattan. He was tall and huge, and his bushy eyebrows and wide nose gave him a very severe look. He breathed heavily, and it was said that, when he slept, his wives and children in their out-houses could hear him breathe. When he walked, his heels hardly touched the ground and he seemed to walk on springs, as if he was going to pounce on somebody. And he did pounce on people quite often. He had a slight stammer and whenever he was angry and could not get his words out quickly enough, he would use his fists. He had no patience with unsuccessful men. He had had no patience with his father.

Unoka, for that was his father's name, had died ten years ago. In his day he was lazy and improvident and was quite incapable of thinking about tomorrow. If any money came his way, and it seldom did, he immediately bought gourds of palm-wine, called round his neighbours and made merry. He always said that whenever he saw a dead man's mouth he saw the folly of not eating what one had in one's lifetime. Unoka was, of course, a debtor, and he owed every neighbour some money, from a few cowries to quite substantial amounts.

1. The Irish poet, writing after World War I, refers to Judgment Day and the new age to commence with Christ's second coming as announced in Matthew 24:31–46, a cosmic recommencement that is preceded by apocalyptic calamity and cosmic catastrophe. With the title of his novel, Achebe alludes to the catastrophe in Yeats's poem and refers as well to the undoing of a traditional African order by the calamities of colonization, religious conversion, and imposed political transition from traditional society to a modernized order.

He was tall but very thin and had a slight stoop. He wore a haggard and mournful look except when he was drinking or playing on his flute. He was very good on his flute, and his happiest moments were the two or three moons after the harvest when the village musicians brought down their instruments, hung above the fireplace. Unoka would play with them, his face beaming with blessedness and peace. Sometimes another village would ask Unoka's band and their dancing *egwugwu* to come and stay with them and teach them their tunes. They would go to such hosts for as long as three or four markets, making music and feasting. Unoka loved the good fare and the good fellowship, and he loved this season of the year, when the rains had stopped and the sun rose every morning with dazzling beauty. And it was not too hot either, because the cold and dry harmattan wind was blowing down from the north. Some years the harmattan was very severe and a dense haze hung on the atmosphere. Old men and children would then sit round log fires, warming their bodies. Unoka loved it all, and he loved the first kites that returned with the dry season, and the children who sang songs of welcome to them. He would remember his own childhood, how he had often wandered around looking for a kite sailing leisurely against the blue sky. As soon as he found one he would sing with his whole being, welcoming it back from its long, long journey, and asking it if it had brought home any lengths of cloth.

That was years ago, when he was young. Unoka, the grown-up, was a failure. He was poor and his wife and children had barely enough to eat. People laughed at him because he was a loafer, and they swore never to lend him any more money because he never paid back. But Unoka was such a man that he always succeeded in borrowing more, and piling up his debts.

One day a neighbour called Okoye came in to see him. He was reclining on a mud bed in his hut playing on the flute. He immediately rose and shook hands with Okoye, who then unrolled the goatskin which he carried under his arm, and sat down. Unoka went into an inner room and soon returned with a small wooden disc containing a kola nut, some alligator pepper and a lump of white chalk.

"I have kola," he announced when he sat down, and passed the disc over to his guest.

"Thank you. He who brings kola brings life. But I think you ought to break it," replied Okoye passing back the disc.

"No, it is for you, I think," and they argued like this for a few moments before Unoka accepted the honour of breaking the kola. Okoye, meanwhile, took the lump of chalk, drew some lines on the floor, and then painted his big toe. As he broke the kola, Unoka prayed to their ancestors for life and health, and for protection against their enemies. When they had eaten they talked about many things: about the heavy rains which were drowning the yams, about the next ancestral feast and about the impending war with the village of Mbaino. Unoka was never happy when it came to wars. He was in fact a coward and could not bear the sight of blood. And so he changed the subject and talked about music, and his face beamed. He could hear in his mind's ear the blood-stirring and intricate rhythms of the *ekwe* and the *udu* and the *ogene,* and he could hear his own flute weaving in and out of them, decorating them with a colourful and plaintive tune. The total effect was gay and brisk, but if one picked out the flute as it went up and down and then broke up into short snatches, one saw that there was sorrow and grief there.

Okoye was also a musician. He played on the *ogene*. But he was not a failure like Unoka. He had a large barn full of yams and he had three wives. And now he was going to take the Idemili title, the third highest in the land. It was a very expensive ceremony and he was gathering all his resources together. That was in fact the reason why he had come to see Unoka. He cleared his throat and began:

"Thank you for the kola. You may have heard of the title I intend to take shortly."

Having spoken plainly so far, Okoye said the next half a dozen sentences in proverbs. Among the Ibo the art of conversation is regarded very highly, and proverbs are the palm-oil with which words are eaten. Okoye was a great talker and he spoke for a long time, skirting round the subject and then hitting it finally. In short, he was asking Unoka to return the two hundred cowries he had borrowed from him more than two years before. As soon as Unoka understood what his friend was driving at, he burst out laughing. He laughed loud and long and his voice rang out clear as the *ogene,* and tears stood in his eyes. His visitor was amazed, and sat speechless. At the end, Unoka was able to give an answer between fresh outbursts of mirth.

"Look at that wall," he said, pointing at the far wall of his hut, which was rubbed with red earth so that it shone. "Look at those lines of chalk;" and Okoye saw groups of short perpendicular lines drawn in chalk. There were five groups, and the smallest group had ten lines. Unoka had a sense of the dramatic and so he allowed a pause, in which he took a pinch of snuff and sneezed noisily, and then he continued: "Each group there represents a debt to someone, and each stroke is one hundred cowries. You see, I owe that man a thousand cowries. But he has not come to wake me up in the morning for it. I shall pay you, but not today. Our elders say that the sun will shine on those who stand before it shines on those who kneel under them. I shall pay my big debts first." And he took another pinch of snuff, as if that was paying the big debts first. Okoye rolled his goatskin and departed.

When Unoka died he had taken no title at all and he was heavily in debt. Any wonder then that his son Okonkwo was ashamed of him? Fortunately, among these people a man was judged according to his worth and not according to the worth of his father. Okonkwo was clearly cut out for great things. He was still young but he had won fame as the greatest wrestler in the nine villages. He was a wealthy farmer and had two barns full of yams, and had just married his third wife. To crown it all he had taken two titles and had shown incredible prowess in two inter-tribal wars. And so although Okonkwo was still young, he was already one of the greatest men of his time. Age was respected among his people, but achievement was revered. As the elders said, if a child washed his hands he could eat with kings. Okonkwo had clearly washed his hands and so he ate with kings and elders. And that was how he came to look after the doomed lad who was sacrificed to the village of Umuofia by their neighbours to avoid war and bloodshed. The ill-fated lad was called Ikemefuna.

Chapter 2

Okonkwo had just blown out the palm-oil lamp and stretched himself on his bamboo bed when he heard the *ogene* of the town-crier piercing the still night air. *Gome, gome, gome, gome,* boomed the hollow metal. Then the crier gave his message, and at the end of it beat his instrument again. And this was the message. Every man of Umuofia was asked to gather at the market-place tomorrow morning. Okonkwo wondered what was amiss, for he knew certainly, that something was amiss. He had discerned a clear overtone of tragedy in the crier's voice, and even now he could still hear it as it grew dimmer and dimmer in the distance.

The night was very quiet. It was always quiet except on moonlight nights. Darkness held a vague terror for these people, even the bravest among them. Children were warned not to whistle at night for fear of evil spirits. Dangerous animals became even more sinister and uncanny in the dark. A snake was never called by its name at night, because it would hear. It was called a string. And so on this particular night as the crier's voice was gradually swallowed up in the distance, silence returned to the world, a vibrant silence made more intense by the universal trill of a million million forest insects.

On a moonlight night it would be different. The happy voices of children playing in open fields would then be heard. And perhaps those not so young would be playing in pairs in less open places, and old men and women would remember their youth. As the Ibo say: "When the moon is shining the cripple becomes hungry for a walk."

But this particular night was dark and silent. And in all the nine villages of Umuofia a town-crier with his *ogene* asked every man to be present tomorrow morning. Okonkwo on his bamboo bed tried to figure out the nature of the emergency—war with a neighbouring clan? That seemed the most likely reason, and he was not afraid of war. He was a man of action, a man of war. Unlike his father he could stand the look of blood. In Umuofia's latest war he was the first to bring home a human head. That was his fifth head; and he was not an old man yet. On great occasions such as the funeral of a village celebrity he drank his palm-wine from his first human head.

In the morning the market-place was full. There must have been about ten thousand men there, all talking in low voices. At last Ogbuefi Ezeugo stood up in the midst of them and bellowed four times, "*Umuofia kwenu,*" and on each occasion he faced a different direction and seemed to push the air with a clenched fist. And ten thousand men answered "*Yaa!*" each time. Then there was perfect silence. Ogbuefi Ezeugo was a powerful orator and was always chosen to speak on such occasions. He moved his hand over his white head and stroked his white beard. He then adjusted his cloth, which was passed under his right arm-pit and tied above his left shoulder.

"*Umuofia kwenu,*" he bellowed a fifth time, and the crowd yelled in answer. And then suddenly like one possessed he shot out his left hand and pointed in the direction of Mbaino, and said through gleaming white teeth firmly clenched: "Those sons of wild animals have dared to murder a daughter of Umuofia." He threw his head down and gnashed his teeth, and allowed a murmur of suppressed anger to sweep the crowd. When he began again, the anger on his face was gone and in its place a sort of smile hovered, more terrible and more sinister than the anger. And in a clear unemotional voice he told Umuofia how their daughter had gone to market at Mbaino and had been killed. That woman, said Ezeugo, was the wife of Ogbuefi Udo, and he pointed to a man who sat near him with a bowed head. The crowd then shouted with anger and thirst for blood.

Many others spoke, and at the end it was decided to follow the normal course of action. An ultimatum was immediately dispatched to Mbaino asking them to choose between war on the one hand, and on the other the offer of a young man and a virgin as compensation.

Umuofia was feared by all its neighbours. It was powerful in war and in magic, and its priests and medicine-men were feared in all the surrounding country. Its most potent war-medicine was as old as the clan itself. Nobody knew how old. But on one point there was general agreement—the active principle in that medicine had been an old woman with one leg. In fact, the medicine itself was called *agadi-nwayi,* or old woman. It had its shrine in the centre of Umuofia, in a cleared spot. And if anybody was so foolhardy as to pass by the shrine after dusk he was sure to see the old woman hopping about.

And so the neighbouring clans who naturally knew of these things feared Umuofia, and would not go to war against it without first trying a peaceful settlement.

And in fairness to Umuofia it should be recorded that it never went to war unless its case was clear and just and was accepted as such by its Oracle—the Oracle of the Hills and the Caves. And there were indeed occasions when the Oracle had forbidden Umuofia to wage a war. If the clan had disobeyed the Oracle they would surely have been beaten, because their dreaded *agadi-nwayi* would never fight what the Ibo call *a fight of blame.*

But the war that now threatened was a just war. Even the enemy clan knew that. And so when Okonkwo of Umuofia arrived at Mbaino as the proud and imperious emissary of war, he was treated with great honour and respect, and two days later he returned home with a lad of fifteen and a young virgin. The lad's name was Ikemefuna, whose sad story is still told in Umuofia unto this day.

The elders, or *ndichie,* met to hear a report of Okonkwo's mission. At the end they decided, as everybody knew they would, that the girl should go to Ogbuefi Udo to replace his murdered wife. As for the boy, he belonged to the clan as a whole, and there was no hurry to decide his fate. Okonkwo was, therefore, asked on behalf of the clan to look after him in the interim. And so for three years Ikemefuna lived in Okonkwo's household.

Okonkwo ruled his household with a heavy hand. His wives, especially the youngest, lived in perpetual fear of his fiery temper, and so did his little children. Perhaps down in his heart Okonkwo was not a cruel man. But his whole life was dominated by fear, the fear of failure and of weakness. It was deeper and more intimate than the fear of evil and capricious gods and of magic, the fear of the forest, and the forces of nature, malevolent, red in tooth and claw. Okonkwo's fear was greater than these. It was not external but lay deep within himself. It was the fear of himself, lest he should be found to resemble his father. Even as a little boy he had resented his father's failure and weakness, and even now he still remembered how he had suffered when a playmate had told him that his father was *agbala.* That was how Okonkwo first came to know that *agbala* was not only another name for a woman, it could also mean a man who had taken no title. And so Okonkwo was ruled by one passion—to hate everything that his father Unoka had loved. One of those things was gentleness and another was idleness.

During the planting season Okonkwo worked daily on his farms from cock-crow until the chickens went to roost. He was a very strong man and rarely felt fatigue. But his wives and young children were not as strong, and so they suffered. But they dared not complain openly. Okonkwo's first son, Nwoye, was then twelve years old but was already causing his father great anxiety for his incipient laziness. At any rate, that was how it looked to his father, and he sought to correct him by constant nagging and beating. And so Nwoye was developing into a sad-faced youth.

Okonkwo's prosperity was visible in his household. He had a large compound enclosed by a thick wall of red earth. His own hut, or *obi,* stood immediately behind the only gate in the red walls. Each of his three wives had her own hut, which together formed a half moon behind the *obi.* The barn was built against one end of the red walls, and long stacks of yam stood out prosperously in it. At the opposite end of the compound was a shed for the goats, and each wife built a small attachment to her hut for the hens. Near the barn was a small house, the "medicine house" or shrine where Okonkwo kept the wooden symbols of his personal god and of his ancestral spirits. He worshipped them with sacrifices of kola nut, food and palm-wine, and offered prayers to them on behalf of himself, his three wives and eight children.

So when the daughter of Umuofia was killed in Mbaino, Ikemefuna came into Okonkwo's household. When Okonkwo brought him home that day he called his most senior wife and handed him over to her.

"He belongs to the clan," he told her. "So look after him."

"Is he staying long with us?" she asked.

"Do what you are told, woman," Okonkwo thundered, and stammered. "When did you become one of the *ndichie* of Umuofia?"

And so Nwoye's mother took Ikemefuna to her hut and asked no more questions.

As for the boy himself, he was terribly afraid. He could not understand what was happening to him or what he had done. How could he know that his father had taken a hand in killing a daughter of Umuofia? All he knew was that a few men had arrived at their house, conversing with his father in low tones, and at the end he had been taken out and handed over to a stranger. His mother had wept bitterly, but he had been too surprised to weep. And so the stranger had brought him, and a girl, a long, long way from home, through lonely forest paths. He did not know who the girl was, and he never saw her again.

Chapter 3

Okonkwo did not have the start in life which many young men usually had. He did not inherit a barn from his father. There was no barn to inherit. The story was told in Umuofia of how his father, Unoka, had gone to consult the Oracle of the Hills and the Caves to find out why he always had a miserable harvest.

The Oracle was called Agbala, and people came from far and near to consult it. They came when misfortune dogged their steps or when they had a dispute with their neighbours. They came to discover what the future held for them or to consult the spirits of their departed fathers.

The way into the shrine was a round hole at the side of a hill, just a little bigger than the round opening into a hen-house. Worshippers and those who came to seek knowledge from the god crawled on their belly through the hole and found themselves in a dark, endless space in the presence of Agbala. No one had ever beheld Agbala, except his priestess. But no one who had ever crawled into his awful shrine had come out without the fear of his power. His priestess stood by the sacred fire which she built in the heart of the cave and proclaimed the will of the god. The fire did not burn with a flame. The glowing logs only served to light up vaguely the dark figure of the priestess.

Sometimes a man came to consult the spirit of his dead father or relative. It was said that when such a spirit appeared, the man saw it vaguely in the darkness, but never heard its voice. Some people even said that they had heard the spirits flying and flapping their wings against the roof of the cave.

Many years ago when Okonkwo was still a boy his father, Unoka, had gone to consult Agbala. The priestess in those days was a woman called Chika. She was full of the power of her god, and she was greatly feared. Unoka stood before her and began his story.

"Every year," he said sadly, "before I put any crop in the earth, I sacrifice a cock to Ani, the owner of all land. It is the law of our fathers. I also kill a cock at the shrine of ioku, the god of yams. I clear the bush and set fire to it when it is dry. I sow the yams the first rain has fallen, and stake them when the young tendrils appear. I weed—"

old your peace!" screamed the priestess, her voice terrible as it echoed through void. "You have offended neither the gods nor your fathers. And when a man with his gods and his ancestors, his harvest will be good or bad according to the strength of his arm. You, Unoka, are known in all the clan for the weakness of your matchet and your hoe. When your neighbours go out with their axe to cut down virgin forests, you sow your yams on exhausted farms that take no labour to clear. They cross seven rivers to make their farms; you stay at home and offer sacrifices to a reluctant soil. Go home and work like a man."

Unoka was an ill-fated man. He had a bad *chi* or personal god, and evil fortune followed him to the grave, or rather to his death, for he had no grave. He died of the swelling which was an abomination to the earth goddess. When a man was afflicted with swelling in the stomach and the limbs he was not allowed to die in the house. He was carried to the Evil Forest and left there to die. There was a story of a very stubborn man who staggered back to his house and had to be carried again to the forest and tied to a tree. The sickness was an abomination to the earth, and so the victim could not be buried in her bowels. He died and rotted away above the earth, and was not given the first or the second burial. Such was Unoka's fate. When they carried him away, he took with him his flute.

With a father like Unoka, Okonkwo did not have the start in life which many young men had. He neither inherited a barn nor a title, nor even a young wife. But in spite of these disadvantages, he had begun even in his father's lifetime to lay the foundations of a prosperous future. It was slow and painful. But he threw himself into it like one possessed. And indeed he was possessed by the fear of his father's contemptible life and shameful death.

There was a wealthy man in Okonkwo's village who had three huge barns, nine wives and thirty children. His name was Nwakibie and he had taken the highest but one title which a man could take in the clan. It was for this man that Okonkwo worked to earn his first seed yams.

He took a pot of palm-wine and a cock of Nwakibie. Two elderly neighbours were sent for, and Nwakibie's two grown-up sons were also present in his *obi.* He presented a kola nut and an alligator pepper, which was passed round for all to see and then returned to him. He broke it, saying: "We shall all live. We pray for life, children, a good harvest and happiness. You will have what is good for you and I will have what is good for me. Let the kite perch and let the eagle perch too. If one says no to the other, let his wing break."

After the kola nut had been eaten Okonkwo brought his palm-wine from the corner of the hut where it had been placed and stood it in the centre of the group. He addressed Nwakibie, calling him "Our father."

"*Nna ayi,*" he said. "I have brought you this little kola. As our people say, a man who pays respect to the great paves the way for his own greatness. I have come to pay you my respects and also to ask a favour. But let us drink the wine first."

Everybody thanked Okonkwo and the neighbours brought out their drinking horns from the goatskin bags they carried. Nwakibie brought down his own horn, which was fastened to the rafters. The younger of his sons, who was also the youngest man in the group, moved to the centre, raised the pot on his left knee and began to pour out the wine. The first cup went to Okonkwo, who must taste his wine before anyone else. Then the group drank, beginning with the eldest man. When everyone had drunk two or three horns, Nwakibie sent for his wives. Some of them were not at home and only four came in.

"Is Anasi not in?" he asked them. They said she was coming. Anasi was the first wife and the others could not drink before her, and so they stood waiting.

Anasi was a middle-aged woman, tall and strongly built. There was authority in her bearing and she looked every inch the ruler of the womenfolk in a large and prosperous family. She wore the anklet of her husband's titles, which the first wife alone could wear.

She walked up to her husband and accepted the horn from him. She then went down on one knee, drank a little and handed back the horn. She rose, called him by his name and went back to her hut. The other wives drank in the same way, in their proper order, and went away.

The men then continued their drinking and talking. Ogbuefi Idigo was talking about the palm-wine tapper, Obiako, who suddenly gave up his trade.

"There must be something behind it," he said, wiping the foam of wine from his moustache with the back of his left hand. "There must be a reason for it. A toad does not run in the daytime for nothing."

"Some people say the Oracle warned him that he would fall off a palm tree and kill himself," said Akukalia.

"Obiako has always been a strange one," said Nwakibie. "I have heard that many years ago, when his father had not been dead very long, he had gone to consult the Oracle. The Oracle said to him, 'Your dead father wants you to sacrifice a goat to him.' Do you know what he told the Oracle? He said, 'Ask my dead father if he ever had a fowl when he was alive.'" Everybody laughed heartily except Okonkwo, who laughed uneasily because as the saying goes, an old woman is always uneasy when dry bones are mentioned in a proverb. Okonkwo remembered his own father.

At last the young man who was pouring out the wine held up half a horn of the thick, white dregs and said, "What we are eating is finished." "We have seen it," the others replied. "Who will drink the dregs?" he asked. "Whoever has a job in hand," said Idigo, looking at Nwakibie's elder son, Igwelo, with a mischievous twinkle in his eye.

Everybody agreed that Igwelo should drink the dregs. He accepted the half-full horn from his brother and drank it. As Idigo had said, Igwelo had a job in hand because he had married his first wife a month or two before. The thick dregs of palm-wine were supposed to be good for men who were going in to their wives.

After the wine had been drunk Okonkwo laid his difficulties before Nwakibie.

"I have come to you for help," he said. "Perhaps you can already guess what it is. I have cleared a farm but have no yams to sow. I know what it is to ask a man to trust another with his yams, especially these days when young men are afraid of hard work. I am not afraid of work. The lizard that jumped from the high iroko tree to the ground said he would praise himself if no one else did. I began to fend for myself at an age when most people still suck at their mothers' breasts. If you give me some yam seeds I shall not fail you."

Nwakibie cleared his throat. "It pleases me to see a young man like you these days when our youth have gone so soft. Many young men have come to me to ask for yams but I have refused because I knew they would just dump them in the earth and leave them to be choked by weeds. When I say no to them they think I am hard-hearted. But it is not so. Eneke the bird says that since men have learnt to shoot without missing, he has learnt to fly without perching. I have learnt to be stingy with my yams. But I can trust you. I know it as I look at you. As our fathers said, you can tell a ripe corn by its look. I shall give you twice four hundred yams. Go ahead and prepare your farm."

Okonkwo thanked him again and again and went home feeling happy. He knew that Nwakibie would not refuse him, but he had not expected he would be so generous.

He had not hoped to get more than four hundred seeds. He would now have to make a bigger farm. He hoped to get another four hundred yams from one of his father's friends at Isiuzo.

Share-cropping was a very slow way of building up a barn of one's own. After all the toil one only got a third of the harvest. But for a young man whose father had no yams, there was no other way. And what made it worse in Okonkwo's case was that he had to support his mother and two sisters from his meagre harvest. And supporting his mother also meant supporting his father. She could not be expected to cook and eat while her husband starved. And so at a very early age when he was striving desperately to build a barn through sharecropping Okonkwo was also fending for his father's house. It was like pouring grains of corn into a bag full of holes. His mother and sisters worked hard enough, but they grew women's crops, like coco-yams, beans and cassava. Yam, the king of crops, was a man's crop.

The year that Okonkwo took eight hundred seed-yams from Nwakibie was the worst year in living memory. Nothing happened at its proper time; it was either too early or too late. It seemed as if the world had gone mad. The first rains were late, and, when they came, lasted only a brief moment. The blazing sun returned, more fierce than it had ever been known, and scorched all the green that had appeared with the rains. The earth burned like hot coals and roasted all the yams that had been sown. Like all good farmers, Okonkwo had begun to sow with the first rains. He had sown four hundred seeds when the rains dried up and the heat returned. He watched the sky all day for signs of rain-clouds and lay awake all night. In the morning he went back to his farm and saw the withering tendrils. He had tried to protect them from the smouldering earth by making rings of thick sisal leaves around them. But by the end of the day the sisal rings were burnt dry and grey. He changed them every day, and prayed that the rain might fall in the night. But the drought continued for eight market weeks and the yams were killed.

Some farmers had not planted their yams yet. They were the lazy easy-going ones who always put off clearing their farms as long as they could. This year they were the wise ones. They sympathised with their neighbours with much shaking of the head, but inwardly they were happy for what they took to be their own foresight.

Okonkwo planted what was left of his seed-yams when the rains finally returned. He had one consolation. The yams he had sown before the drought were his own, the harvest of the previous year. He still had the eight hundred from Nwakibie and the four hundred from his father's friend. So he would make a fresh start.

But the year had gone mad. Rain fell as it had never fallen before. For days and nights together it poured down in violent torrents, and washed away the yam heaps. Trees were uprooted and deep gorges appeared everywhere. Then the rain became less violent. But it went on from day to day without a pause. The spell of sunshine which always came in the middle of the wet season did not appear. The yams put on luxuriant green leaves, but every farmer knew that without sunshine the tubers would not grow.

That year the harvest was sad, like a funeral, and many farmers wept as they dug up the miserable and rotting yams. One man tied his cloth to a tree branch and hanged himself.

Okonkwo remembered that tragic year with a cold shiver throughout the rest of his life. It always surprised him when he thought of it later that he did not sink under the load of despair. He knew he was a fierce fighter, but that year had been enough to break the heart of a lion.

"Since I survived that year," he always said, "I shall survive anything." He put it down to his inflexible will.

His father, Unoka, who was then an ailing man, had said to him during that terrible harvest month: "Do not despair. I know you will not despair. You have a manly and a proud heart. A proud heart can survive a general failure because such a failure does not prick its pride. It is more difficult and more bitter when a man fails *alone*."

Unoka was like that in his last days. His love of talk had grown with age and sickness. It tried Okonkwo's patience beyond words.

Chapter 4

"Looking at a king's mouth," said an old man, "one would think he never sucked at his mother's breast." He was talking about Okonkwo, who had risen so suddenly from great poverty and misfortune to be one of the lords of the clan. The old man bore no ill-will towards Okonkwo. Indeed he respected him for his industry and success. But he was struck, as most people were, by Okonkwo's brusqueness in dealing with less successful men. Only a week ago a man had contradicted him at a kindred meeting which they held to discuss the next ancestral feast. Without looking at the man Okonkwo had said: "This meeting is for men." The man who had contradicted him had no titles. That was why he had called him a woman. Okonkwo knew how to kill a man's spirit.

Everybody at the kindred meeting took sides with Osugo when Okonkwo called him a woman. The oldest man present said sternly that those whose palm-kernels were cracked for them by a benevolent spirit should not forget to be humble. Okonkwo said he was sorry for what he had said, and the meeting continued.

But it was really not true that Okonkwo's palm-kernels had been cracked for him by a benevolent spirit. He had cracked them himself. Anyone who knew his grim struggle against poverty and misfortune could not say he had been lucky. If ever a man deserved his success, that man was Okonkwo. At an early age he had achieved fame as the greatest wrestler in all the land. That was not luck. At the most one could say that his *chi* or personal god was good. But the Ibo people have a proverb that when a man says yes his *chi* says yes also. Okonkwo said yes very strongly; so his *chi* agreed. And not only his *chi* but his clan too, because it judged a man by the work of his hands. That was why Okonkwo had been chosen by the nine villages to carry a message of war to their enemies unless they agreed to give up a young man and a virgin to atone for the murder of Udo's wife. And such was the deep fear that their enemies had for Umuofia that they treated Okonkwo like a king and brought him a virgin who was given to Udo as wife, and the lad Ikemefuna.

The elders of the clan had decided that Ikemefuna should be in Okonkwo's care for a while. But no one thought it would be as long as three years. They seemed to forget all about him as soon as they had taken the decision.

At first Ikemefuna was very much afraid. Once or twice he tried to run away, but he did not know where to begin. He thought of his mother and his three-year-old sister and wept bitterly. Nwoye's mother was very kind to him and treated him as one of her own children. But all he said was: "When shall I go home?" When Okonkwo heard that he would not eat any food he came into the hut with a big stick in his hand and stood over him while he swallowed his yams, trembling. A few moments later he went behind the hut and began to vomit painfully. Nwoye's mother went to him and placed her hands on his chest and on his back. He was ill for three market weeks, and when he recovered he seemed to have overcome his great fear and sadness.

He was by nature a very lively boy and he gradually became popular in Okonkwo's household, especially with the children. Okonkwo's son, Nwoye, who was two years younger, became quite inseparable from him because he seemed to know everything. He could fashion out flutes from bamboo stems and even from the elephant grass. He knew the names of all the birds and could set clever traps for the little bush rodents. And he knew which trees made the strongest bows.

Even Okonkwo himself became very fond of the boy—inwardly of course. Okonkwo never showed any emotion openly, unless it be the emotion of anger. To show affection was a sign of weakness; the only thing worth demonstrating was strength. He therefore treated Ikemefuna as he treated everybody else—with a heavy hand. But there was no doubt that he liked the boy. Sometimes when he went to big village meetings or communal ancestral feasts he allowed Ikemefuna to accompany him, like a son, carrying his stool and his goatskin bag. And, indeed, Ikemefuna called him father.

Ikemefuna came to Umuofia at the end of the carefree season between harvest and planting. In fact he recovered from his illness only a few days before the Week of Peace began. And that was also the year Okonkwo broke the peace, and was punished, as was the custom, by Ezeani, the priest of the earth goddess.

Okonkwo was provoked to justifiable anger by his youngest wife, who went to plait her hair at her friend's house and did not return early enough to cook the afternoon meal. Okonkwo did not know at first that she was not at home. After waiting in vain for the dish he went to her hut to see what she was doing. There was nobody in the hut and the fireplace was cold.

"Where is Ojiugo?" he asked his second wife, who came out of her hut to draw water from the gigantic pot in the shade of a small tree in the middle of the compound.

"She has gone to plait her hair."

Okonkwo bit his lips as anger welled up within him.

"Where are her children? Did she take them?" he asked with unusual coolness and restraint.

"They are here," answered his first wife, Nwoye's mother. Okonkwo bent down and looked into her hut. Ojiugo's children were eating with the children of his first wife.

"Did she ask you to feed them before she went?"

"Yes," lied Nwoye's mother, trying to minimise Ojiugo's thoughtlessness.

Okonkwo knew she was not speaking the truth. He walked back to his *obi* to wait Ojiugo's return. And when she returned he beat her very heavily. In his anger he had forgotten that it was the Week of Peace. His first two wives ran out in great alarm pleading with him that it was the sacred week. But Okonkwo was not the man to stop beating somebody half-way through, not even for fear of a goddess.

Okonkwo's neighbours heard his wife crying and sent their voices over the compound walls to ask what was the matter. Some of them came over to see for themselves. It was unheard of to beat somebody during the sacred week.

Before it was dusk Ezeani, who was the priest of the earth goddess, Ani, called on Okonkwo in his *obi*. Okonkwo brought out kola nut and placed it before the priest.

"Take away your kola nut. I shall not eat in the house of a man who has no respect for our gods and ancestors."

Okonkwo tried to explain to him what his wife had done, but Ezeani seemed to pay no attention. He held a short staff in his hand which he brought down on the floor to emphasize his points.

"Listen to me," he said when Okonkwo had spoken. "You are not a stranger in Umuofia. You know as well as I do that our forefathers ordained that before we plant any crops in the earth we should observe a week in which a man does not say a harsh word to his neighbour. We live in peace with our fellows to honour our great goddess of the earth without whose blessing our crops will not grow. You have committed a great evil." He brought down his staff heavily on the floor. "You wife was at fault, but even if you came into your *obi* and found her lover on top of her, you would still have committed a great evil to beat her." His staff came down again. "The evil you have done can ruin the whole clan. The earth goddess whom you have insulted may refuse to give us her increase, and we shall all perish." His tone now changed from anger to command. "You will bring to the shrine of Ani tomorrow one she-goat, one hen, a length of cloth and a hundred cowries." He rose and left the hut.

Okonkwo did as the priest said. He also took with him a pot of palm-wine. Inwardly, he was repentant. But he was not the man to go about telling his neighbours that he was in error. And so people said he had no respect for the gods of the clan. His enemies said his good fortune had gone to his head. They called him the little bird *nza* who so far forgot himself after a heavy meal that he challenged his *chi.*

No work was done during the Week of Peace. People called on their neighbours and drank palm-wine. This year they talked of nothing else but the *nso-ani* which Okonkwo had committed. It was the first time for many years that a man had broken the sacred peace. Even the oldest men could only remember one or two other occasions somewhere in the dim past.

Ogbuefi Ezeudu, who was the oldest man in the village, was telling two other men who came to visit him that the punishment for breaking the Peace of Ani had become very mild in their clan.

"It has not always been so," he said. "My father told me that he had been told that in the past a man who broke the peace was dragged on the ground through the village until he died. But after a while this custom was stopped because it spoilt the peace which it was meant to preserve."

"Somebody told me yesterday," said one of the younger men, "that in some clans it is an abomination for a man to die during the Week of Peace."

"It is indeed true," said Ogbuefi Ezeudu. "They have that custom in Obodoani. If a man dies at this time he is not buried but cast into the Evil Forest. It is a bad custom which these people observe because they lack understanding. They throw away large numbers of men and women without burial. And what is the result? Their clan is full of the evil spirits of these unburied dead, hungry to do harm to the living."

After the Week of Peace every man and his family began to clear the bush to make new farms. The cut bush was left to dry and fire was then set to it. As the smoke rose into the sky kites appeared from different directions and hovered over the burning field in silent valediction. The rainy season was approaching when they would go away until the dry season returned.

Okonkwo spent the next few days preparing his seed-yams. He looked at each yam carefully to see whether it was good for sowing. Sometimes he decided that a yam was too big to be sown as one seed and he split it deftly along its length with his sharp knife. His eldest son, Nwoye, and Ikemefuna helped him by fetching the yams in long baskets from the barn and in counting the prepared seeds in groups of four hundred. Sometimes Okonkwo gave them a few yams each to prepare. But he always found fault with their effort, and he said so with much threatening.

"Do you think you are cutting up yams for cooking?" he asked Nwoye. "If you split another yam of this size, I shall break your jaw. You think you are still a child. I began to own a farm at your age. And you," he said to Ikemefuna, "do you not grow yams where you come from?"

Inwardly Okonkwo knew that the boys were still too young to understand fully the difficult art of preparing seed-yams. But he thought that one could not begin too early. Yam stood for manliness, and he who could feed his family on yams from one harvest to another was a very great man indeed. Okonkwo wanted his son to be a great farmer and a great man. He would stamp out the disquieting signs of laziness which he thought he already saw in him.

"I will not have a son who cannot hold up his head in the gathering of the clan. I would sooner strangle him with my own hands. And if you stand staring at me like that," he swore, "Amadiora will break your head for you!"

Some days later, when the land had been moistened by two or three heavy rains, Okonkwo and his family went to the farm with baskets of seed-yams, their hoes and matchets, and the planting began. They made single mounds of earth in straight lines all over the field and sowed the yams in them.

Yam, the king of crops, was a very exacting king. For three or four moons it demanded hard work and constant attention from cockcrow till the chickens went back to roost. The young tendrils were protected from earth-heat with rings of sisal leaves. As the rains became heavier the women planted maize, melons and beans between the yam mounds. The yams were then staked, first with little sticks and later with tall and big tree branches. The women weeded the farm three times at definite periods in the life of the yams, neither early nor late.

And now the rains had really come, so heavy and persistent that even the village rain-maker no longer claimed to be able to intervene. He could not stop the rain now, just as he would not attempt to start it in the heart of the dry season, without serious danger to his own health. The personal dynamism required to counter the forces of these extremes of weather would be far too great for the human frame.

And so nature was not interfered with in the middle of the rainy season. Sometimes it poured down in such thick sheets of water that earth and sky seemed merged in one grey wetness. It was then uncertain whether the low rumbling of Amadiora's thunder came from above or below. At such times, in each of the countless thatched huts of Umuofia, children sat around their mother's cooking fire telling stories, or with their father in his *obi* warming themselves from a log fire, roasting and eating maize. It was a brief resting period between the exacting and arduous planting season and the equally exacting but light-hearted month of harvests.

Ikemefuna had begun to feel like a member of Okonkwo's family. He still thought about his mother and his three-year-old sister, and he had moments of sadness and depression. But he and Nwoye had become so deeply attached to each other that such moments became less frequent and less poignant. Ikemefuna had an endless stock of folk tales. Even those which Nwoye knew already were told with a new freshness and the local flavour of a different clan. Nwoye remembered this period very vividly till the end of his life. He even remembered how he had laughed when Ikemefuna told him that the proper name for a corn-cob with only a few scattered grains was *ezeagadi-nwayi,* or the teeth of an old woman. Nwoye's mind had gone immediately to Nwayieke, who lived near the udala tree. She had about three teeth and was always smoking her pipe.

Gradually the rains became lighter and less frequent, and earth and sky once again became separate. The rain fell in thin, slanting showers through sunshine and quiet breeze. Children no longer stayed indoors but ran about singing:

> *"The rain is falling, the sun is shining,*
> *Alone Nnadi is cooking and eating."*

Nwoye always wondered who Nnadi was and why he should live all by himself, cooking and eating. In the end he decided that Nnadi must live in that land of Ikemefuna's favourite story where the ant holds his court in splendour and the sands dance for ever.

Chapter 5

The Feast of the New Yam was approaching and Umuofia was in a festival mood. It was an occasion for giving thanks to Ani, the earth goddess and the source of all fertility. Ani played a greater part in the life of the people than any other deity. She was the ultimate judge of morality and conduct. And what was more, she was in close communion with the departed fathers of the clan whose bodies had been committed to earth.

The Feast of the New Yam was held every year before the harvest began, to honour the earth goddess and the ancestral spirits of the clan. New yams could not be eaten until some had first been offered to these powers. Men and women, young and old, looked forward to the New Yam Festival because it began the season of plenty—the new year. On the last night before the festival, yams of the old year were all disposed of by those who still had them. The new year must begin with tasty, fresh yams and not the shrivelled and fibrous crop of the previous year. All cooking-pots, calabashes and wooden bowls were thoroughly washed, especially the wooden mortar in which yam was pounded. Yam foo-foo and vegetable soup was the chief food in the celebration. So much of it was cooked that, no matter how heavily the family ate or how many friends and relations they invited from neighbouring villages, there was always a huge quantity of food left over at the end of the day. The story was always told of a wealthy man who set before his guests a mount of foo-foo so high that those who sat on one side could not see what was happening on the other, and it was not until late in the evening that one of them saw for the first time his in-law who had arrived during the course of the meal and had fallen to on the opposite side. It was only then that they exchanged greetings and shook hands over what was left of the food.

The New Yam Festival was thus an occasion for joy throughout Umuofia. And every man whose arm was strong, as the Ibo people say, was expected to invite large numbers of guests from far and wide. Okonkwo always asked his wives' relations, and since he now had three wives his guests would make a fairly big crowd.

But somehow Okonkwo could never become as enthusiastic over feasts as most people. He was a good eater and he could drink one or two fairly big gourds of palm-wine. But he was always uncomfortable sitting around for days waiting for a feast or getting over it. He would be very much happier working on his farm.

The festival was now only three days away. Okonkwo's wives had scrubbed the walls and the huts with red earth until they reflected light. They had then drawn patterns on them in white, yellow and dark green. They then set about painting themselves with cam wood and drawing beautiful black patterns on their stomachs and on their backs. The children were also decorated, especially their hair, which was shaved in beautiful patterns. The three women talked excitedly about the relations who had been invited, and the children revelled in the thought of being spoilt by these visitors from mother-land. Ikemefuna was equally excited. The New Yam Festival seemed to him to be a much bigger event here than in his own village, a place which was already becoming remote and vague in his imagination.

And then the storm burst. Okonkwo, who had been walking about aimlessly in his compound in suppressed anger, suddenly found an outlet.

"Who killed this banana tree?" he asked.

A hush fell on the compound immediately.

"Who killed this tree? Or are you all deaf and dumb?"

As a matter of fact the tree was very much alive. Okonkwo's second wife had merely cut a few leaves off it to wrap some food, and she said so. Without further argument Okonkwo gave her a sound beating and left her and her only daughter weeping. Neither of the other wives dared to interfere beyond an occasional and tentative, "It is enough, Okonkwo," pleaded from a reasonable distance.

His anger thus satisfied, Okonkwo decided to go out hunting. He had an old rusty gun made by a clever blacksmith who had come to live in Umuofia long ago. But although Okonkwo was a great man whose prowess was universally acknowledged, he was not a hunter. In fact he had not killed a rat with his gun. And so when he called Ikemefuna to fetch his gun, the wife who had just been beaten murmured something about guns that never shot. Unfortunately for her, Okonkwo heard it and ran madly into his room for the loaded gun, ran out again and aimed at her as she clambered over the dwarf wall of the barn. He pressed the trigger and there was a loud report accompanied by the wail of his wives and children. He threw down the gun and jumped into the barn, and there lay the woman, very much shaken and frightened but quite unhurt. He heaved a heavy sigh and went away with the gun.

In spite of this incident the New Yam Festival was celebrated with great joy in Okonkwo's household. Early that morning as he offered a sacrifice of new yam and palm-oil to his ancestors he asked them to protect him, his children and their mothers in the new year.

As the day wore on his in-laws arrived from three surrounding villages, and each party brought with them a huge pot of palm-wine. And there was eating and drinking till night, when Okonkwo's in-laws began to leave for their homes.

The second day of the new year was the day of the great wrestling match between Okonkwo's village and their neighbours. It was difficult to say which the people enjoyed more—the feasting and fellowship of the first day or the wrestling contest of the second. But there was one woman who had no doubt whatever in her mind. She was Okonkwo's second wife, Ekwefi, whom he nearly shot. There was no festival in all the seasons of the year which gave her as much pleasure as the wrestling match. Many years ago when she was the village beauty Okonkwo had won her heart by throwing the Cat in the greatest contest within living memory. She did not marry him because he was too poor to pay her bride-price. But a few years later she ran away from her husband and came to live with Okonkwo. All this happened many years ago. Now Ekwefi was a woman of forty-five who had suffered a great deal in her time. But her love of wrestling contests was still as strong as it was thirty years ago.

It was not yet noon on the second day of the New Yam Festival. Ekwefi and her only daughter, Ezinma, sat near the fireplace waiting for the water in the pot to boil. The fowl Ekwefi had just killed was in the wooden mortar. The water began to boil, and in one deft movement she lifted the pot from the fire and poured the boiling water on to the fowl. She put back the empty pot on the circular pad in the corner, and looked at her palms, which were black with soot. Ezinma was always surprised that her mother could lift a pot from the fire with her bare hands.

"Ekwefi," she said, "is it true that when people are grown up, fire does not burn them?" Ezinma, unlike most children, called her mother by her name.

"Yes," replied Ekwefi, too busy to argue. Her daughter was only ten years old but she was wiser than her years.

"But Nwoye's mother dropped her pot of hot soup the other day and it broke on the floor."

Ekwefi turned the hen over in the mortar and began to pluck the feathers.

"Ekwefi," said Ezinma, who had joined in plucking the feathers, "my eyelid is twitching."

"It means you are going to cry," said her mother.

"No," Ezinma said, "it is this eyelid, the top one."

"That means you will see something."

"What will I see?" she asked.

"How can I know?" Ekwefi wanted her to work it out herself.

"Oho," said Ezinma at last. "I know what it is—the wrestling match."

At last the hen was plucked clean. Ekwefi tried to pull out the horny beak but it was too hard. She turned round on her low stool and put the beak in the fire for a few moments. She pulled again and it came off.

"Ekwefi!" a voice called from one of the other huts. It was Nwoye's mother, Okonkwo's first wife.

"Is that me?" Ekwefi called back. That was the way people answered calls from outside. They never answered yes for fear it might be an evil spirit calling.

"Will you give Ezinma some fire to bring to me?" Her own children and Ikemefuna had gone to the stream.

Ekwefi put a few live coals into a piece of broken pot and Ezinma carried it across the clean-swept compound to Nwoye's mother.

"Thank you, Nma," she said. She was peeling new yams, and in a basket beside her were green vegetables and beans.

"Let me make the fire for you," Ezinma offered.

"Thank you, Ezigbo," she said. She often called her Ezigbo, which means "the good one."

Ezinma went outside and brought some sticks from a huge bundle of firewood. She broke them into little pieces across the sole of her foot and began to build a fire, blowing it with her breath.

"You will blow your eyes out," said Nwoye's mother, looking up from the yams she was peeling. "Use the fan." She stood up and pulled out the fan which was fastened into one of the rafters. As soon as she got up, the troublesome nanny-goat, which had been dutifully eating yam peelings, dug her teeth into the real thing, scooped out two mouthfuls and fled from the hut to chew the cud in the goats' shed. Nwoye's mother swore at her and settled down again to her peeling. Ezinma's fire was now sending up thick clouds of smoke. She went on fanning it until it burst into flames. Nwoye's mother thanked her and she went back to her mother's hut.

Just then the distant beating of drums began to reach them. It came from the direction of the *ilo,* the village playground. Every village had its own *ilo* which was as old as the village itself and where all the great ceremonies and dances took place. The drums beat the unmistakable wrestling dance—quick, light and gay, and it came floating on the wind.

Okonkwo cleared his throat and moved his feet to the beat of the drums. It filled him with fire as it had always done from his youth. He trembled with the desire to conquer and subdue. It was like the desire for woman.

"We shall be late for the wrestling," said Ezinma to her mother.

"They will not begin until the sun goes down."

"But they are beating the drums."

"Yes. The drums begin at noon but the wrestling waits until the sun begins to sink. Go and see if your father has brought out yams for the afternoon."

"He has. Nwoye's mother is already cooking."

"Go and bring our own, then. We must cook quickly or we shall be late for the wrestling."

Ezinma ran in the direction of the barn and brought back two yams from the dwarf wall.

Ekwefi peeled the yams quickly. The troublesome nanny-goat sniffed about, eating the peelings. She cut the yams into small pieces and began to prepare a pottage, using some of the chicken.

At that moment they heard someone crying just outside their compound. It was very much like Obiageli, Nwoye's sister.

"Is that not Obiageli weeping?" Ekwefi called across the yard to Nwoye's mother.

"Yes," she replied. "She must have broken her water-pot."

The weeping was now quite close and soon the children filed in, carrying on their heads various sizes of pots suitable to their years. Ikemefuna came first with the biggest pot, closely followed by Nwoye and his two younger brothers. Obiageli brought up the rear, her face streaming with tears. In her hand was the cloth pad on which the pot should have rested on her head.

"What happened?" her mother asked, and Obiageli told her mournful story. Her mother consoled her and promised to buy her another pot.

Nwoye's younger brothers were about to tell their mother the true story of the accident when Ikemefuna looked at them sternly and they held their peace. The fact was that Obiageli had been making *inyanga* with her pot. She had balanced it on her head, folded her arms in front of her and began to sway her waist like a grown-up young lady. When the pot fell down and broke she burst out laughing. She only began to weep when they got near the iroko tree outside their compound.

The drums were still beating, persistent and unchanging. Their sound was no longer a separate thing from the living village. It was like the pulsation of its heart. It throbbed in the air, in the sunshine, and even in the trees, and filled the village with excitement.

Ekwefi ladled her husband's share of the pottage into a bowl and covered it. Ezinma took it to him in his *obi.*

Okonkwo was sitting on a goatskin already eating his first wife's meal. Obiageli, who had brought it from her mother's hut, sat on the floor waiting for him to finish. Ezinma placed her mother's dish before him and sat with Obiageli.

"Sit like a woman!" Okonkwo shouted at her. Ezinma brought her two legs together and stretched them in front of her.

"Father, will you go to see the wrestling?" Ezinma asked after a suitable interval.

"Yes," he answered. "Will you go?"

"Yes." And after a pause she said: "Can I bring your chair for you?"

"No, that is a boy's job." Okonkwo was specially fond of Ezinma. She looked very much like her mother, who was once the village beauty. But his fondness only showed on very rare occasions.

"Obiageli broke her pot today," Ezinma said.

"Yes, she has told me about it," Okonkwo said between mouthfuls.

"Father," said Obiageli, "people should not talk when they are eating or pepper may go down the wrong way."

"That is very true. Do you hear that, Ezinma? You are older than Obiageli but she has more sense."

He uncovered his second wife's dish and began to eat from it. Obiageli took the first dish and returned to her mother's hut. And then Nkechi came in, bringing the third dish. Nkechi was the daughter of Okonkwo's third wife.

In the distance the drums continued to beat.

Chapter 6

The whole village turned out on the *ilo,* men, women and children. They stood round in a huge circle leaving the centre of the playground free. The elders and grandees of the village sat on their own stools brought there by their young sons or slaves. Okonkwo was among them. All others stood except those who came early enough to secure places on the few stands which had been built by placing smooth logs on forked pillars.

The wrestlers were not there yet and the drummers held the field. They too sat just in front of the huge circle of spectators, facing the elders. Behind them was the big and ancient silk-cotton tree which was sacred. Spirits of good children lived in that tree waiting to be born. On ordinary days young women who desired children came to sit under its shade.

There were seven drums and they were arranged according to their sizes in a long wooden basket. Three men beat them with sticks, working feverishly from one drum to another. They were possessed by the spirit of the drums.

The young men who kept order on these occasions dashed about, consulting among themselves and with the leaders of the two wrestling teams, who were still outside the circle, behind the crowd. Once in a while two young men carrying palm fronds ran round the circle and kept the crowd back by beating the ground in front of them or, if they were stubborn, their legs and feet.

At last the two teams danced into the circle and the crowd roared and clapped. The drums rose to a frenzy. The people surged forwards. The young men who kept order flew around, waving their palm fronds. Old men nodded to the beat of the drums and remembered the days when they wrestled to its intoxicating rhythm.

The contest began with boys of fifteen or sixteen. There were only three such boys in each team. They were not the real wrestlers; they merely set the scene. Within a short time the first two bouts were over. But the third created a big sensation even among the elders who did not usually show their excitement so openly. It was as quick as the other two, perhaps even quicker. But very few people had ever seen that kind of wrestling before. As soon as the two boys closed in, one of them did something which no one could describe because it had been as quick as a flash. And the other boy was flat on his back. The crowd roared and clapped and for a while drowned the frenzied drums. Okonkwo sprang to his feet and quickly sat down again. Three young men from the victorious boy's team ran forward, carried him shoulder-high and danced through the cheering crowd. Everybody soon knew who the boy was. His name was Maduka, the son of Obierika.

The drummers stopped for a brief rest before the real matches. Their bodies shone with sweat, and they took up fans and began to fan themselves. They also drank water from small pots and ate kola nuts. They became ordinary human beings again, talking and laughing among themselves and with others who stood near them. The air, which had been stretched taut with excitement, relaxed again. It was as if water had been poured on the tightened skin of a drum. Many people looked around, perhaps for the first time, and saw those who stood or sat next to them.

"I did not know it was you," Ekwefi said to the woman who had stood shoulder to shoulder with her since the beginning of the matches.

"I do not blame you," said the woman. "I have never seen such a large crowd of people. Is it true that Okonkwo nearly killed you with his gun?"

"It is true indeed, my dear friend. I cannot yet find a mouth with which to tell the story."

"Your *chi* is very much awake, my friend. And how is my daughter, Ezinma?"

"She has been very well for some time now. Perhaps she has come to stay."

"I think she has. How old is she now?"

"She is about ten years old."

"I think she will stay. They usually stay if they do not die before the age of six."

"I pray she stays," said Ekwefi with a heavy sigh.

The woman with whom she talked was called Chielo. She was the priestess of Agbala, the Oracle of the Hills and the Caves. In ordinary life Chielo was a widow with two children. She was very friendly with Ekwefi and they shared a common shed in the market. She was particularly fond of Ekwefi's only daughter, Ezinma, whom she called "my daughter." Quite often she bought bean-cakes and gave Ekwefi some to take home to Ezinma. Anyone seeing Chielo in ordinary life would hardly believe she was the same person who prophesied when the spirit of Agbala was upon her.

The drummers took up their sticks again and the air shivered and grew tense like a tightened bow.

The two teams were ranged facing each other across the clear space. A young man from one team danced across the centre to the other side and pointed at whomever he wanted to fight. They danced back to the centre together and then closed in.

There were twelve men on each side and the challenge went from one side to the other. Two judges walked around the wrestlers and when they thought they were equally matched, stopped them. Five matches ended in this way. But the really exciting moments were when a man was thrown. The huge voice of the crowd then rose to the sky and in every direction. It was even heard in the surrounding villages.

The last match was between the leaders of the teams. They were among the best wrestlers in all the nine villages. The crowd wondered who would throw the other this year. Some said Okafo was the better man; others said he was not the equal of Ikezue. Last year neither of them had thrown the other even though the judges had allowed the contest to go on longer than was the custom. They had the same style and one saw the other's plans beforehand. It might happen again this year.

Dusk was already approaching when their contest began. The drums went mad and the crowds also. They surged forward as the two young men danced into the circle. The palm fronds were helpless in keeping them back.

Ikezue held out his right hand. Okafo seized it, and they closed in. It was a fierce contest. Ikezue strove to dig in his right heel behind Okafo so as to pitch him backwards in the clever *ege* style. But the one knew what the other was thinking. The crowd had surrounded and swallowed up the drummers, whose frantic rhythm was no longer a mere disembodied sound but the very heart-beat of the people.

The wrestlers were now almost still in each other's grip. The muscles on their arms and their thighs and on their backs stood out and twitched. It looked like an equal match. The two judges were already moving forward to separate them when Ikezue, now desperate, went down quickly on one knee in an attempt to fling his man backwards over his head. It was a sad miscalculation. Quick as the lightning of Amadiora, Okafo raised his right leg and swung it over his rival's head. The crowd burst into a thunderous roar. Okafo was swept off his feet by his supporters and carried home shoulder-high. They sang his praise and the young women clapped their hands:

Who will wrestle for our village?
Okafo will wrestle for our village.
Has he thrown a hundred men?
He has thrown four hundred men.
Has he thrown a hundred Cats?
He has thrown four hundred Cats.
Then send him word to fight for us.

Chapter 7

For three years Ikemefuna lived in Okonkwo's household and the elders of Umuofia seemed to have forgotten about him. He grew rapidly like a yam tendril in the rainy season, and was full of the sap of life. He had become wholly absorbed into his new family. He was like an elder brother to Nwoye, and from the very first seemed to have kindled a new fire in the younger boy. He made him feel grown-up; and they no longer spent the evenings in mother's hut while she cooked, but now sat with Okonkwo in his *obi,* or watched him as he tapped his palm tree for the evening wine. Nothing pleased Nwoye now more than to be sent for by his mother or another of his father's wives to do one of those difficult and masculine tasks in the home, like splitting wood, or pounding food. On receiving such a message through a younger brother or sister, Nwoye would feign annoyance and grumble aloud about women and their troubles.

Okonkwo was inwardly pleased at his son's development, and he knew it was due to Ikemefuna. He wanted Nwoye to grow into a tough young man capable of ruling his father's household when he was dead and gone to join the ancestors. He wanted him to be a prosperous man, having enough in his barn to feed the ancestors with regular sacrifices. And so he was always happy when he heard him grumbling about women. That showed that in time he would be able to control his women-folk. No matter how prosperous a man was, if he was unable to rule his women and his children (and especially his women) he was not really a man. He was like the man in the song who had ten and one wives and not enough soup for his foo-foo.

So Okonkwo encouraged the boys to sit with him in his *obi,* and he told them stories of the land—masculine stories of violence and bloodshed. Nwoye knew that it was right to be masculine and to be violent, but somehow he still preferred the stories that his mother used to tell, and which she no doubt still told to her younger children—stories of the tortoise and his wily ways, and of the bird *eneke-nti-oba* who challenged the whole world to a wrestling contest and was finally thrown by the cat. He remembered the story she often told of the quarrel between Earth and Sky long ago, and how Sky withheld rain for seven years, until crops withered and the dead could not be buried because the hoes broke on the stony Earth. At last Vulture was sent to plead with Sky, and to soften his heart with a song of the suffering of the sons of men. Whenever Nwoye's mother sang this song he felt carried away to the distant scene in the sky where Vulture, Earth's emissary, sang for mercy. At last Sky was moved to pity, and he gave to Vulture rain wrapped in leaves of coco-yam. But as he flew home his long talon pierced the leaves and the rain fell as it had never fallen before. And so heavily did it rain on Vulture that he did not return to deliver his message but flew to a distant land, from where he had espied a fire. And when he got there he found it was a man making a sacrifice. He warmed himself in the fire and ate the entrails.

That was the kind of story that Nwoye loved. But he now knew that they were for foolish women and children, and he knew that his father wanted him to be a man. And so he feigned that he no longer cared for women's stories. And when he did this he saw that his father was pleased, and no longer rebuked him or beat him. So Nwoye and Ikemefuna would listen to Okonkwo's stories about tribal wars or how, years ago, he had stalked his victim, overpowered him and obtained his first human head. And as he told them of the past they sat in darkness or the dim glow of logs, waiting for the women to finish their cooking. When they finished, each brought her bowl of foo-foo and bowl of soup to her husband. An oil lamp was lit and Okonkwo tasted from each bowl, and then passed two shares to Nwoye and Ikemefuna.

In this way the moons and the seasons passed. And then the locusts came. It had not happened for many a long year. The elders said locusts came once in a generation, reappeared every year for seven years and then disappeared for another lifetime. They went back to their caves in a distant land, where they were guarded by a race of stunted men. And then after another lifetime these men opened the caves again and the locusts came to Umuofia.

They came in the cold harmattan season after the harvests had been gathered, and ate up all the wild grass in the fields.

Okonkwo and the two boys were working on the red outer walls of the compound. This was one of the lighter tasks of the after-harvest season. A new cover of thick palm branches and palm leaves was set on the walls to protect them from the next rainy season. Okonkwo worked on the outside of the wall and the boys worked from within. There were little holes from one side to the other in the upper levels of the wall, and through these Okonkwo passed the rope, or *tie-tie,* to the boys and they passed it round the wooden stays and then back to him; and in this way the cover was strengthened on the wall.

The women had gone to the bush to collect firewood, and the little children to visit their playmates in the neighbouring compounds. The harmattan was in the air and seemed to distil a hazy feeling of sleep on the world. Okonkwo and the boys worked in complete silence, which was only broken when a new palm frond was lifted on to the wall or when a busy hen moved dry leaves about in her ceaseless search for food.

And then quite suddenly a shadow fell on the world, and the sun seemed hidden behind a thick cloud. Okonkwo looked up from his work and wondered if it was going to rain at such an unlikely time of the year. But almost immediately a shout of joy broke out in all directions, and Umuofia, which had dozed in the noon-day haze, broke into life and activity.

"Locusts are descending," was joyfully chanted everywhere, and men, women and children left their work or their play and ran into the open to see the unfamiliar sight. The locusts had not come for many, many years, and only the old people had seen them before.

At first, a fairly small swarm came. They were the harbingers sent to survey the land. And then appeared on the horizon a slowly-moving mass like a boundless sheet of black cloud drifting towards Umuofia. Soon it covered half the sky, and the solid mass was now broken by tiny eyes of light like shining star-dust. It was a tremendous sight, full of power and beauty.

Everyone was now about, talking excitedly and praying that the locusts should camp in Umuofia for the night. For although locusts had not visited Umuofia for many years, everybody knew by instinct that they were very good to eat. And at last the locusts did descend. They settled on every tree and on every blade of grass; they settled on the roofs and covered the bare ground. Mighty tree branches broke away under them, and the whole country became the brown-earth colour of the vast, hungry swarm.

Many people went out with baskets trying to catch them, but the elders counselled patience till nightfall. And they were right. The locusts settled in the bushes for the night and their wings became wet with dew. Then all Umuofia turned out in spite of the cold harmattan, and everyone filled his bags and pots with locusts. The next morning they were roasted in clay pots and then spread in the sun until they became dry and brittle. And for many days this rare food was eaten with solid palm-oil.

Okonkwo sat in his *obi* crunching happily with Ikemefuna and Nwoye, and drinking palm-wine copiously, when Ogbuefi Ezeudu came in. Ezeudu was the oldest man in this quarter of Umuofia. He had been a great and fearless warrior in his time, and was now accorded great respect in all the clan. He refused to join in the meal, and asked Okonkwo to have a word with him outside. And so they walked out together, the old man supporting himself with his stick. When they were out of ear-shot, he said to Okonkwo:

"That boy calls you father. Do not bear a hand in his death." Okonkwo was surprised, and was about to say something when the old man continued:

"Yes, Umuofia has decided to kill him. The Oracle of the Hills and the Caves has pronounced it. They will take him outside Umuofia as is the custom, and kill him there. But I want you to have nothing to do with it. He calls you his father."

The next day a group of elders from all the nine villages of Umuofia came to Okonkwo's house early in the morning, and before they began to speak in low tones Nwoye and Ikemefuna were sent out. They did not stay very long, but when they went away Okonkwo sat still for a very long time supporting his chin in his palms. Later in the day he called Ikemefuna and told him that he was to be taken home the next day. Nwoye overheard it and burst into tears, whereupon his father beat him heavily. As for Ikemefuna, he was at a loss. His own home had gradually become very faint and distant. He still missed his mother and his sister and would be very glad to see them. But somehow he knew he was not going to see them. He remembered once when men had talked in low tones with his father; and it seemed now as if it was happening all over again.

Later, Nwoye went to his mother's hut and told her that Ikemufuna was going home. She immediately dropped the pestle with which she was grinding pepper, folded her arms across her breast and sighed, "Poor child."

The next day, the men returned with a pot of wine. They were all fully dressed as if they were going to a big clan meeting or to pay a visit to a neighbouring village. They passed their cloths under the right arm-pit, and hung their goatskin bags and sheathed matchets over their left shoulders. Okonkwo got ready quickly and the party set out with Ikemefuna carrying the pot of wine. A deathly silence descended on Okonkwo's compound. Even the very little children seemed to know. Throughout that day Nwoye sat in his mother's hut and tears stood in his eyes.

At the beginning of their journey the men of Umuofia talked and laughed about the locusts, about their women, and about some effeminate men who had refused to come with them. But as they drew near to the outskirts of Umuofia silence fell upon them too.

The sun rose slowly to the centre of the sky, and the dry, sandy footway began to throw up the heat that lay buried in it. Some birds chirruped in the forests around. The men trod dry leaves on the sand. All else was silent. Then from the distance came the faint beating of the *ekwe.* It rose and faded with the wind—a peaceful dance from a distant clan.

"It is an *ozo* dance," the men said among themselves. But no one was sure where it was coming from. Some said Ezimili, others Abame or Aninta. They argued for a short while and fell into silence again, and the elusive dance rose and fell with the wind. Somewhere a man was taking one of the titles of his clan, with music and dancing and a great feast.

The footway had now become a narrow line in the heart of the forest. The short trees and sparse undergrowth which surrounded the men's village began to give way to giant trees and climbers which perhaps had stood from the beginning of things, untouched by the axe and the bush-fire. The sun breaking through their leaves and branches threw a pattern of light and shade on the sandy footway.

Ikemefuna heard a whisper close behind him and turned round sharply. The man who had whispered now called out aloud, urging the others to hurry up.

"We still have a long way to go," he said. Then he and another man went before Ikemefuna and set a faster pace.

Thus the men of Umuofia pursued their way, armed with sheathed matchets, and Ikemefuna, carrying a pot of palm-wine on his head, walked in their midst. Although he had felt uneasy at first, he was not afraid now. Okonkwo walked behind him. He could hardly imagine that Okonkwo was not his real father. He had never been fond of his real father, and at the end of three years he had become very distant indeed. But his mother and his three-year-old sister . . . of course she would not be three now, but six. Would he recognize her now? She must have grown quite big. How his mother would weep for joy, and thank Okonkwo for having looked after him so well and for bringing him back. She would want to hear everything that had happened to him in all these years. Could he remember them all? He would tell her about Nwoye and his mother, and about the locusts . . . Then quite suddenly a thought came upon him. His mother might be dead. He tried in vain to force the thought out of his mind. Then he tried to settle the matter the way he used to settle such matters when he was a little boy. He still remembered the song:

Eze elina, elina!
Sala
Eze ilikwa ya
Ikwaba akwa oligholi
Ebe Danda nechi eze

Ebe Uzuzu nete egwu
Sala

He sang it in his mind, and walked to its beat. If the song ended on his right foot, his mother was alive. If it ended on his left, she was dead. No, not dead, but ill. It ended on the right. She was alive and well. He sang the song again, and it ended on the left. But the second time did not count. The first voice gets to Chukwu, or God's house. That was a favourite saying of children. Ikemefuna felt like a child once more. It must be the thought of going home to his mother.

One of the men behind him cleared his throat. Ikemefuna looked back, and the man growled at him to go on and not stand looking back. The way he said it sent cold fear down Ikemefuna's back. His hands trembled vaguely on the black pot he carried. Why had Okonkwo withdrawn to the rear? Ikemefuna felt his legs melting under him. And he was afraid to look back.

As the man who had cleared his throat drew up and raised his matchet, Okonkwo looked away. He heard the blow. The pot fell and broke in the sand. He heard Ikemefuna cry, "My father, they have killed me!" as he ran towards him. Dazed with fear, Okonkwo drew his matchet and cut him down. He was afraid of being thought weak.

As soon as his father walked in, that night, Nwoye knew that Ikemefuna had been killed, and something seemed to give way inside him, like the snapping of a tightened bow. He did not cry. He just hung limp. He had had the same kind of feeling not long ago, during the last harvest season. Every child loved the harvest season. Those who were big enough to carry even a few yams in a tiny basket went with grown-ups to the farm. And if they could not help in digging up the yams, they could gather firewood together for roasting the ones that would be eaten there on the farm. This roasted yam soaked in red palm-oil and eaten in the open farm was sweeter than any meal at home. It was after such a day at the farm during the last harvest that Nwoye had felt for the first time a snapping inside him like the one he now felt. They were returning home with baskets of yams from a distant farm across the stream when they had heard the voice of an infant crying in the thick forest. A sudden hush had fallen on the women, who had been talking, and they had quickened their steps. Nwoye had heard that twins were put in earthenware pots and thrown away in the forest, but he had never yet come across them. A vague chill had descended on him and his head had seemed to swell, like a solitary walker at night who passes an evil spirit on the way. Then something had given way inside him. It descended on him again, this feeling, when his father walked in, that night after killing Ikemefuna.

Chapter 8

Okonkwo did not taste any food for two days after the death of Ikemefuna. He drank palm-wine from morning till night, and his eyes were red and fierce like the eyes of a rat when it was caught by the tail and dashed against the floor. He called his son, Nwoye, to sit with him in his *obi.* But the boy was afraid of him and slipped out of the hut as soon as he noticed him dozing.

He did not sleep at night. He tried not to think about Ikemefuna, but the more he tried the more he thought about him. Once he got up from bed and walked about his compound. But he was so weak that his legs could hardly carry him. He felt like a drunken giant walking with the limbs of a mosquito. Now and then a cold shiver descended on his head and spread down his body.

On the third day he asked his second wife, Ekwefi, to roast some plantains for him. She prepared them the way he liked—with slices of oil-bean and fish.

"You have not eaten for two days," said his daughter Ezinma when she brought the food to him. "So you must finish this." She sat down and stretched her legs in front of her. Okonkwo ate the food absentmindedly. "She should have been a boy," he thought as he looked at his ten-year-old daughter. He passed her a piece of fish.

"Go and bring me some cold water," he said. Ezinma rushed out of the hut, chewing the fish, and soon returned with a bowl of cool water from the earthen pot in her mother's hut.

Okonkwo took the bowl from her and gulped the water down. He ate a few more pieces of plantain and pushed the dish aside.

"Bring me my bag," he asked, and Ezinma brought his goatskin bag from the far end of the hut. He searched in it for his snuff-bottle. It was a deep bag and took almost the whole length of his arm. It contained other things apart from his snuff-bottle. There was a drinking horn in it, and also a drinking gourd, and they knocked against each other as he searched. When he brought out the snuff-bottle he tapped it a few times against his knee-cap before taking out some snuff on the palm of his left hand. Then he remembered that he had not taken out his snuff-spoon. He searched his bag again and brought out a small, flat, ivory spoon, with which he carried the brown snuff to his nostrils.

Ezinma took the dish in one hand and the empty water bowl in the other and went back to her mother's hut. "She should have been a boy," Okonkwo said to himself again. His mind went back to Ikemefuna and he shivered. If only he could find some work to do he would be able to forget. But it was the season of rest between the harvest and the next planting season. The only work that men did at this time was covering the walls of their compound with new palm fronds. And Okonkwo had already done that. He had finished it on the very day the locusts came, when he had worked on one side of the wall and Ikemefuna and Nwoye on the other.

"When did you become a shivering old woman," Okonkwo asked himself, "you are known in all the nine villages for your valour in war. How can a man who has killed five men in battle fall to pieces because he has added a boy to their number? Okonkwo, you have become a woman indeed."

He sprang to his feet, hung his goatskin bag on his shoulder and went to visit his friend, Obierika.

Obierika was sitting outside under the shade of an orange tree making thatches from leaves of the raffia-palm. He exchanged greetings with Okonkwo and led the way into his *obi.*

"I was coming over to see you as soon as I finished that thatch," he said, rubbing off the grains of sand that clung to his thighs.

"Is it well?" Okonkwo asked.

"Yes," replied Obierika. "My daughter's suitor is coming today and I hope we will clinch the matter of the bride-price. I want you to be there."

Just then Obierika's son, Maduka, came into the *obi* from outside, greeted Okonkwo and turned towards the compound.

"Come and shake hands with me," Okonkwo said to the lad. "Your wrestling the other day gave me much happiness." The boy smiled, shock hands with Okonkwo and went into the compound.

"He will do great things," Okonkwo said. "If I had a son like him I should be happy. I am worried about Nwoye. A bowl of pounded yams can throw him in a wrestling match. His two younger brothers are more promising. But I can tell you, Obierika, that my children do not resemble me. Where are the young suckers that will grow when the old banana tree dies? If Ezinma had been a boy I would have been happier. She has the right spirit."

"You worry yourself for nothing," said Obierika. "The children are still very young."

"Nwoye is old enough to impregnate a woman. At his age I was already fending for myself. No, my friend, he is not too young. A chick that will grow into a cock can be spotted the very day it hatches. I have done my best to make Nwoye grow into a man, but there is too much of his mother in him."

"Too much of his grandfather," Obierika thought, but he did not say it. The same thought also came to Okonkwo's mind. But he had long learnt how to lay that ghost. Whenever the thought of his father's weakness and failure troubled him he expelled it by thinking about his own strength and success. And so he did now. His mind went to his latest show of manliness.

"I cannot understand why you refused to come with us to kill that boy," he asked Obierika.

"Because I did not want to," Obierika replied sharply. "I had something better to do."

"You sound as if you question the authority and the decision of the Oracle, who said he should die."

"I do not. Why should I? But the Oracle did not ask me to carry out its decision."

"But someone had to do it. If we were all afraid of blood, it would not be done. And what do you think the Oracle would do then?"

"You know very well, Okonkwo, that I am not afraid of blood; and if anyone tells you that I am, he is telling a lie. And let me tell you one thing, my friend. If I were you I would have stayed at home. What you have done will not please the Earth. It is the kind of action for which the goddess wipes out whole families."

"The Earth cannot punish me for obeying her messenger," Okonkwo said. "A child's fingers are not scalded by a piece of hot yam which its mother puts into its palm."

"That is true," Obierika agreed. "But if the Oracle said that my son should be killed I would neither dispute it nor be the one to do it."

They would have gone on arguing had Ofoedu not come in just then. It was clear from his twinkling eyes that he had important news. But it would be impolite to rush him. Obierika offered him a lobe of the kola nut he had broken with Okonkwo. Ofoedu ate slowly and talked about the locusts. When he finished his kola nut he said:

"The things that happen these days are very strange."

"What has happened?" asked Okonkwo.

"Do you know Ogbuefi Ndulue?" Ofoedu asked.

"Ogbuefi Ndulue of Ire village," Okonkwo and Obierika said together.

"He died this morning," said Ofoedu.

"That is not strange. He was the oldest man in Ire," said Obierika.

"You are right," Ofoedu agreed. "But you ought to ask why the drum has not been beaten to tell Umuofia of his death."

"Why?" asked Obierika and Okonkwo together.

"That is the strange part of it. You know his first wife who walks with a stick?"

"Yes. She is called Ozoemena."

"That is so," said Ofoedu. "Ozoemena was, as you know, too old to attend Ndulue during his illness. His younger wives did that. When he died this morning, one of these women went to Ozoemena's hut and told her. She rose from her mat, took her stick and walked over to the *obi.* She knelt on her knees and hands at the threshold and called her husband, who was laid on a mat. "Ogbuefi Ndulue," she called, three times, and went back to her hut. When the youngest wife went to call her again to be present at the washing of the body, she found her lying on the mat, dead."

"That is very strange indeed," said Okonkwo. "They will put off Ndulue's funeral until his wife has been buried."

"That is why the drum has not been beaten to tell Umuofia."

"It was always said that Ndulue and Ozoemena had one mind," said Obierika. "I remember when I was a young boy there was a song about them. He could not do anything without telling her."

"I did not know that," said Okonkwo. "I thought he was a strong man in his youth."

"He was indeed," said Ofoedu.

Okonkwo shook his head doubtfully.

"He led Umuofia to war in those days," said Obierika.

Okonkwo was beginning to feel like his old self again. All that he required was something to occupy his mind. If he had killed Ikemefuna during the busy planting season or harvesting it would not have been so bad; his mind would have been centred on his work. Okonkwo was not a man of thought but of action. But in the absence of work, talking was the next best.

Soon after Ofoedu left, Okonkwo took up his goatskin bag to go.

"I must go home to tap my palm trees for the afternoon," he said.

"Who taps your tall trees for you?" asked Obierika.

"Umezulike," replied Okonkwo.

"Sometimes I wish I had not taken the *ozo* title," said Obierika. "It wounds my heart to see these young men killing palm trees in the name of tapping."

"It is so indeed," Okonkwo agreed. "But the law of the land must be obeyed."

"I don't know how we got that law," said Obierika. "In many other clans a man of title is not forbidden to climb the palm tree. Here we say he cannot climb the tall tree but he can tap the short ones standing on the ground. It is like Dimaragana, who would not lend his knife for cutting up dog-meat because the dog was taboo to him, but offered to use his teeth."

"I think it is good that our clan holds the *ozo* title in high esteem," said Okonkwo. "In those other clans you speak of, *ozo* is so low that every beggar takes it."

"I was only speaking in jest," said Obierika. "In Abame and Aninta the title is worth less than two cowries. Every man wears the thread of title on his ankle, and does not lose it even if he steals."

"They have indeed soiled the name of *ozo,*" said Okonkwo as he rose to go.

"It will not be very long now before my in-laws come," said Obierika.

"I shall return very soon," said Okonkwo, looking at the position of the sun.

There were seven men in Obierika's hut when Okonkwo returned. The suitor was a young man of about twenty-five, and with him were his father and uncle. On Obierika's side were his two elder brothers and Maduka, his sixteen-year-old son.

"Ask Akueke's mother to send us some kola nuts," said Obierika to his son. Maduka vanished into the compound like lightning. The conversation at once centred on him, and everybody agreed that he was as sharp as a razor.

"I sometimes think he is too sharp," said Obierika, somewhat indulgently. "He hardly ever walks. He is always in a hurry. If you are sending him on an errand he flies away before he has heard half of the message."

"You were very much like that yourself," said his eldest brother. "As our people say, 'When mother-cow is chewing grass its young ones watch its mouth.' Maduka has been watching your mouth."

As he was speaking the boy returned, followed by Akueke, his half-sister, carrying a wooden dish with three kola nuts and alligator pepper. She gave the dish to her father's eldest brother and then shook hands, very shyly, with her suitor and his relatives. She was about sixteen and just ripe for marriage. Her suitor and his relatives surveyed her young body with expert eyes as if to assure themselves that she was beautiful and ripe.

She wore a coiffure which was done up into a crest in the middle of the head. Cam wood was rubbed lightly into her skin, and all over her body were black patterns drawn with *uli.* She wore a black necklace which hung down in three coils just above her full, succulent breasts. On her arms were red and yellow bangles, and on her waist four or five rows of *jigida,* or waist-beads.

When she had shaken hands, or rather held out her hand to be shaken, she returned to her mother's hut to help with the cooking.

"Remove your *jigida* first," her mother warned as she moved near the fireplace to bring the pestle resting against the wall. "Every day I tell you that *jigida* and fire are not friends. But you will never hear. You grew your ears for decoration, not for hearing. One of these days your *jigida* will catch fire on your waist, and then you will know."

Akueke moved to the other end of the hut and began to remove the waist-beads. It had to be done slowly and carefully, taking each string separately, else it would break and the thousand tiny rings would have to be strung together again. She rubbed each string downwards with her palms until it passed the buttocks and slipped down to the floor around her feet.

The men in the *obi* had already begun to drink the palm-wine which Akueke's suitor had brought. It was a very good wine and powerful, for in spite of the palm fruit hung across the mouth of the pot to restrain the lively liquor, white foam rose and spilled over.

"That wine is the work of a good tapper," said Okonkwo.

The young suitor, whose name was Ibe, smiled broadly and said to his father: "Do you hear that?" He then said to the others: "He will never admit that I am a good tapper."

"He tapped three of my best palm trees to death," said his father, Ukegbu.

"That was about five years ago," said Ibe, who had begun to pour out the wine, "before I learnt how to tap." He filled the first horn and gave it to his father. Then he poured out for the others. Okonkwo brought out his big horn from the goatskin bag, blew into it to remove any dust that might be there, and gave it to Ibe to fill.

As the men drank, they talked about everything except the thing for which they had gathered. It was only after the pot had been emptied that the suitor's father cleared his voice and announced the object of their visit.

Obierika then presented to him a small bundle of short broomsticks. Ukegbu counted them.

"They are thirty?" he asked.

Obierika nodded in agreement.

"We are at last getting somewhere," Ukegbu said, and then turning to his brother and his son he said: "Let us go out and whisper together." The three rose and went outside. When they returned Ukegbu handed the bundle of sticks back to Obierika. He counted them; instead of thirty there were now only fifteen. He passed them over to his eldest brother, Machi, who also counted them and said:

"We had not thought to go below thirty. But as the dog said, 'If I fall down for you and you fall down for me, it is play.' Marriage should be a play and not a fight; so we are falling down again." He then added ten sticks to the fifteen and gave the bundle to Ukegbu.

In this way Akueke's bride-price was finally settled at twenty bags of cowries. It was already dusk when the two parties came to this agreement.

"Go and tell Akueke's mother that we have finished," Obierika said to his son, Maduka. Almost immediately the woman came in with a big bowl of foo-foo. Obierika's second wife followed with a pot of soup, and Maduka brought in a pot of palm-wine.

As the men ate and drank palm-wine they talked about the customs of their neighbours.

"It was only this morning," said Obierika, "that Okonkwo and I were talking about Abame and Aninta, where titled men climb trees and pound foo-foo for their wives."

"All their customs are upside-down. They do not decide bride-price as we do, with sticks. They haggle and bargain as if they were buying a goat or a cow in the market."

"That is very bad," said Obierika's eldest brother. "But what is good in one place is bad in another place. In Umunso they do not bargain at all, not even with broomsticks. The suitor just goes on bringing bags of cowries until his in-laws tell him to stop. It is a bad custom because it always leads to a quarrel."

"The world is large," said Okonkwo. "I have even heard that in some tribes a man's children belong to his wife and her family."

"That cannot be," said Machi. "You might as well say that the woman lies on top of the man when they are making the children."

"It is like the story of white men who, they say, are white like this piece of chalk," said Obierika. He held up a piece of chalk, which every man kept in his *obi* and with which his guests drew lines on the floor before they ate kola nuts. "And these white men, they say, have no toes."[2]

"And have you never seen them?" asked Machi.

"Have you?" asked Obierika.

"One of them passes here frequently," said Machi. "His name is Amadi."

Those who knew Amadi laughed. He was a leper, and the polite name for leprosy was "the white skin."

Chapter 9

For the first time in three nights, Okonkwo slept. He woke up once in the middle of the night and his mind went back to the past three days without making him feel uneasy. He began to wonder why he had felt uneasy at all. It was like a man wondering in broad day-light why a dream had appeared so terrible to him at night. He stretched himself and scratched his thigh where a mosquito had bitten him as he slept. Another one was wailing near his right ear. He slapped the ear and hoped he had killed it. Why do they always go for one's ears? When he was a child his mother had told him a story about it. But it was as silly as all women's stories. Mosquito, she had said, had asked Ear to marry him, whereupon Ear fell on the floor in uncontrollable laughter. "How much longer do you think you will live?" she asked. "You are already a skeleton." Mosquito went away humiliated, and any time he passed her way he told Ear that he was still alive.

2. Their feet are hidden in shoes.

Okonkwo turned on his side and went back to sleep. He was roused in the morning by someone banging on his door.

"Who is that?" he growled. He knew it must be Ekwefi. Of his three wives Ekwefi was the only one who would have the audacity to bang on his door.

"Ezinma is dying," came her voice, and all the tragedy and sorrow of her life were packed in those words.

Okonkwo sprang from his bed, pushed back the bolt on his door and ran into Ekwefi's hut.

Ezinma lay shivering on a mat beside a huge fire that her mother had kept burning all night.

"It is *iba,*" said Okonkwo as he took his matchet and went into the bush to collect the leaves and grasses and barks of trees that went into making the medicine for *iba.*

Ekwefi knelt beside the sick child, occasionally feeling with her palm the wet, burning forehead.

Ezinma was an only child and the centre of her mother's world. Very often it was Ezinma who had decided what food her mother should prepare. Ekwefi even gave her such delicacies as eggs, which children were rarely allowed to eat because such food tempted them to steal. One day as Ezinma was eating an egg Okonkwo had come in unexpectedly from his hut. He was greatly shocked and swore to beat Ekwefi if she dared to give the child eggs again. But it was impossible to refuse Ezinma anything. After her father's rebuke she developed an even keener appetite for eggs. And she enjoyed above all the secrecy in which she now ate them. Her mother always took her into their bedroom and shut the door.

Ezinma did not call her mother *Nne* like all children. She called her by her name, Ekwefi, as her father and other grown-up people did. The relationship between them was not only that of mother and child. There was something in it like the companionship of equals, which was strengthened by such little conspiracies as eating eggs in the bedroom.

Ekwefi had suffered a good deal in her life. She had borne ten children and nine of them had died in infancy; usually before the age of three. As she buried one child after another her sorrow gave way to despair and then to grim resignation. The birth of her children, which should be a woman's crowning glory, became for Ekwefi mere physical agony devoid of promise. The naming ceremony after seven market weeks became an empty ritual. Her deepening despair found expression in the names she gave her children. One of them was a pathetic cry, Onwumbiko—"Death, I implore you." But Death took no notice; Onwumbiko died in his fifteenth month. The next child was a girl, Ozoemena—"May it not happen again." She died in her eleventh month, and two others after her. Ekwefi then became defiant and called her next child Onwuma—"Death may please himself." And he did.

After the death of Ekwefi's second child, Okonkwo had gone to a medicine-man, who was also a diviner of the Afa Oracle, to inquire what was amiss. This man told him that the child was an *ogbanje,* one of those wicked children who, when they died, entered their mother's wombs to be born again.

"When your wife becomes pregnant again," he said, "let her not sleep in her hut. Let her go and stay with her people. In that way she will elude her wicked tormentor and break its evil cycle of birth and death."

Ekwefi did as she was asked. As soon as she became pregnant she went to live with her old mother in another village. It was there that her third child was born and circumcised on the eighth day. She did not return to Okonkwo's compound until three days before the naming ceremony. The child was called Onwumbiko.

Onwumbiko was not given proper burial when he died. Onkonkwo had called in another medicine-man who was famous in the clan for his great knowledge about *ogbanje* children. His name was Okagbue Uyanwa. Okagbue was a very striking figure, tall, with a full beard and a bald head. He was light in complexion and his eyes were red and fiery. He always gnashed his teeth as he listened to those who came to consult him. He asked Okonkwo a few questions about the dead child. All the neighbours and relations who had come to mourn gathered round them.

"On what market-day was it born?" he asked.

"*Oye,*" replied Okonkwo.

"And it died this morning?"

Okonkwo said yes, and only then realised for the first time that the child had died on the same market-day as it had been born. The neighbours and relations also saw the coincidence and said among themselves that it was very significant.

"Where do you sleep with your wife, in your *obi* or in her own hut?" asked the medicine-man.

"In her hut."

"In future call her into your *obi.*"

The medicine-man then ordered that there should be no mourning for the dead child. He brought out a sharp razor from the goatskin bag slung from his left shoulder and began to mutilate the child. Then he took it away to bury in the Evil Forest, holding it by the ankle and dragging it on the ground behind him. After such treatment it would think twice before coming again, unless it was one of the stubborn ones who returned, carrying the stamp of their mutilation—a missing finger or perhaps a dark line where the medicine-man's razor had cut them.

By the time Onwumbiko died Ekwefi had become a very bitter woman. Her husband's first wife had already had three sons, all strong and healthy. When she had borne her third son in succession, Okonkwo had slaughtered a goat for her, as was the custom. Ekwefi had nothing but good wishes for her. But she had grown so bitter about her own *chi* that she could not rejoice with others over their good fortune. And so, on the day that Nwoye's mother celebrated the birth of her three sons with feasting and music, Ekwefi was the only person in the happy company who went about with a cloud on her brow. Her husband's wife took this for malevolence, as husbands' wives were wont to. How could she know that Ekwefi's bitterness did not flow outwards to others but inwards into her own soul; that she did not blame others for their good fortune but her own evil *chi* who denied her any?

At last Ezinma was born, and although ailing she seemed determined to live. At first Ekwefi accepted her, as she had accepted others—with listless resignation. But when she lived on to her fourth, fifth and sixth years, love returned once more to her mother, and, with love, anxiety. She determined to nurse her child to health, and she put all her being into it. She was rewarded by occasional spells of health during which Ezinma bubbled with energy like fresh palm-wine. At such times she seemed beyond danger. But all of a sudden she would go down again. Everybody knew she was an *ogbanje.* These sudden bouts of sickness and health were typical of her kind. But she had lived so long that perhaps she had decided to stay. Some of them did become tired of their evil rounds of birth and death, or took pity on their mothers, and stayed. Ekwefi believed deep inside her that Ezinma had come to stay. She believed because it was that faith alone that gave her own life any kind of meaning. And this faith had been strengthened when a year or so ago a medicine-man had dug up Ezinma's *iyi-uwa.* Everyone knew then that she would live because her bond with the world of *ogbanje* had been broken. Ekwefi was reassured. But such was her anxiety for her daughter that she could not rid herself completely of her fear. And although she believed that the *iyi-uwa* which had been dug up was genuine, she could not ignore the fact that some really evil children sometimes misled people into digging up a specious one.

But Ezinma's *iyi-uwa* had looked real enough. It was a smooth pebble wrapped in a dirty rag. The man who dug it up was the same Okagbue who was famous in all the clan for his knowledge in these matters. Ezinma had not wanted to co-operate with him at first. But that was only to be expected. No *ogbanje* would yield her secrets easily, and most of them never did because they died too young—before they could be asked questions.

"Where did you bury your *iyi-uwa?*" she asked in return.

"You know where it is. You buried it in the ground somewhere so that you can die and return again to torment your mother."

Ezinma looked at her mother, whose eyes, sad and pleading, were fixed on her.

"Answer the question at once," roared Okonkwo, who stood beside her. All the family were there and some of the neighbours too.

"Leave her to me," the medicine-man told Okonkwo in a cool, confident voice. He turned again to Ezinma. "Where did you bury your *iyi-uwa?*"

"Where they bury children," she replied, and the quiet spectators murmured to themselves.

"Come along then and show me the spot," said the medicine-man.

The crowd set out with Ezinma leading the way and Okagbue following closely behind her. Okonkwo came next and Ekwefi followed him. When she came to the main road, Ezinma turned left as if she was going to the stream.

"But you said it was where they bury children?" asked the medicine-man.

"No," said Ezinma, whose feeling of importance was manifest in her sprightly walk. She sometimes broke into a run and stopped again suddenly. The crowd followed her silently. Women and children returning from the stream with pots of water on their heads wondered what was happening until they saw Okagbue and guessed that it must be something to do with *ogbanje.* And they all knew Ekwefi and her daughter very well.

When she got to the big udala tree Ezinma turned left into the bush, and the crowd followed her. Because of her size she made her way through trees and creepers more quickly than her followers. The bush was alive with the tread of feet on dry leaves and sticks and the moving aside of tree branches. Ezinma went deeper and deeper and the crowd went with her. Then she suddenly turned round and began to walk back to the road. Everybody stood to let her pass and then filed after her.

"If you bring us all this way for nothing I shall beat sense into you," Okonkwo threatened.

"I have told you to let her alone. I know how to deal with them," said Okagbue.

Ezinma led the way back to the road, looked left and right and turned right. And so they arrived home again.

"Where did you bury your *iyi-uwa?*" asked Okagbue when Ezinma finally stopped outside her father's *obi.* Okagbue's voice was unchanged. It was quiet and confident.

"It is near that orange tree," Ezinma said.

"And why did you not say so, you wicked daughter of Akalogoli?" Okonkwo swore furiously. The medicine-man ignored him.

"Come and show me the exact spot," he said quietly to Ezinma.

"It is here," she said when they got to the tree.

"Point at the spot with your finger," said Okagbue.

"It is here," said Ezinma touching the ground with her finger. Okonkwo stood by, rumbling like thunder in the rainy season.

"Bring me a hoe," said Okagbue.

When Ekwefi brought the hoe, he had already put aside his goatskin bag and his big cloth and was in his underwear, a long and thin strip of cloth wound round the waist like a belt and then passed between the legs to be fastened to the belt behind. He immediately set to work digging a pit where Ezinma had indicated. The neighbours sat around watching the pit becoming deeper and deeper. The dark top-soil soon gave way to the bright-red earth with which women scrubbed the floor and walls of huts. Okagbue worked tirelessly and in silence, his back shining with perspiration. Okonkwo stood by the pit. He asked Okagbue to come up and rest while he took a hand. But Okagbue said he was not tired yet.

Ekwefi went into her hut to cook yams. Her husband had brought out more yams than usual because the medicine-man had to be fed. Ezinma went with her and helped in preparing the vegetables.

"There is too much green vegetable," she said.

"Don't you see the pot is full of yams?" Ekwefi asked. "And you know how leaves become smaller after cooking."

"Yes," said Ezinma, "that was why the snake-lizard killed his mother."

"Very true," said Ekwefi.

"He gave his mother seven baskets of vegetables to cook and in the end there were only three. And so he killed her," said Ezinma.

"That is not the end of the story."

"Oho," said Ezinma, "I remember now. He brought another seven baskets and cooked them himself. And there were again only three. So he killed himself too."

Outside the *obi* Okagbue and Okonkwo were digging the pit to find where Ezinma had buried her *iyi-uwa.* Neighbours sat around, watching. The pit was now so deep that they no longer saw the digger. They only saw the red earth he threw up mounting higher and higher. Okonkwo's son, Nwoye, stood near the edge of the pit because he wanted to take in all that happened.

Okagbue had again taken over the digging from Okonkwo. He worked, as usual, in silence. The neigbours and Okonkwo's wives were now talking. The children had lost interest and were playing.

Suddenly Okagbue sprang to the surface with the agility of a leopard.

"It is very near now," he said. "I have felt it."

There was immediate excitement and those who were sitting jumped to their feet.

"Call your wife and child," he said to Okonkwo. But Ekwefi and Ezinma had heard the noise and run out to see what it was.

Okagbue went back into the pit, which was now surrounded by spectators. After a few more hoe-fuls of earth he struck the *iyi-uwa.* He raised it carefully with the hoe and threw it to the surface. Some women ran away in fear when it was thrown. But they soon returned and everyone was gazing at the rag from a reasonable distance. Okagbue emerged and without saying a word or even looking at the spectators he went to his goatskin bag, took out two leaves and began to chew them. When he had swallowed them, he took up the rag with his left hand and began to untie it. And then the smooth, shiny pebble fell out. He picked it up.

"Is this yours?" he asked Ezinma.

"Yes," she replied. All the women shouted with joy because Ekwefi's troubles were at last ended.

All this had happened more than a year ago and Ezinma had not been ill since. And then suddenly she had begun to shiver in the night. Ekwefi brought her to the fireplace, spread her mat on the floor and built a fire. But she had got worse and worse. As she knelt by her, feeling with her palm the wet, burning forehead, she prayed a thousand times. Although her husband's wives were saying that it was nothing more than *iba,* she did not hear them.

Okonkwo returned from the bush carrying on his left shoulder a large bundle of grasses and leaves, roots and barks of medicinal trees and shrubs. He went into Ekwefi's hut, put down his load and sat down.

"Get me a pot," he said, "and leave the child alone."

Ekwefi went to bring the pot and Okonkwo selected the best from his bundle, in their due proportion, and cut them up. He put them in the pot and Ekwefi poured in some water.

"Is that enough?" she asked when she had poured in about half of the water in the bowl.

"A little more . . . I said a *little*. Are you deaf?" Okonkwo roared at her.

She set the pot on the fire and Okonkwo took up his matchet to return to his *obi.*

"You must watch the pot carefully," he said as he went, "and don't allow it to boil over. If it does its power will be gone." He went away to his hut and Ekwefi began to tend the medicine pot almost as if it was itself a sick child. Her eyes went constantly from Ezinma to the boiling pot and back to Ezinma.

Okonkwo returned when he felt the medicine had cooked long enough. He looked it over and said it was done.

"Bring a low stool for Ezinma," he said, "and a thick mat."

He took down the pot from the fire and placed it in front of the stool. He then roused Ezinma and placed her on the stool, astride the steaming pot. The thick mat was thrown over both. Ezinma struggled to escape from the choking and overpowering steam, but she was held down. She started to cry.

When the mat was at last removed she was drenched in perspiration. Ekwefi mopped her with a piece of cloth and she lay down on a dry mat and was soon asleep.

Chapter 10

Large crowds began to gather on the village *ilo* as soon as the edge had worn off the sun's heat and it was no longer painful on the body. Most communal ceremonies took place at that time of the day, so that even when it was said that a ceremony would begin "after the midday meal" everyone understood that it would begin a long time later, when the sun's heat had softened.

It was clear from the way the crowd stood or sat that the ceremony was for men. There were many women, but they looked on from the fringe like outsiders. The titled men and elders sat on their stools waiting for the trials to begin. In front of them was a row of stools on which nobody sat. There were nine of them. Two little groups of people stood at a respectable distance beyond the stools. They faced the elders. There were three men in one group and three men and one woman in the other. The woman was Mgbafo and the three men with her were her brothers. In the other group were her husband, Uzowulu, and his relatives. Mgbafo and her brothers were as still as statues into whose faces the artist has moulded defiance. Uzowulu and his relatives, on the other hand, were whispering together. It looked like whispering, but they were really talking at the top of their voices. Everybody in the crowd was talking. It was like the market. From a distance the noise was a deep rumble carried by the wind.

An iron gong sounded, setting up a wave of expectation in the crowd. Everyone looked in the direction of the *egwugwu* house. *Gome, gome, gome, gome* went the gong, and a powerful flute blew a high-pitched blast. Then came the voices of the *egwugwu,* gutteral and awesome. The wave struck the women and children and there was a backward stampede. But it was momentary. They were already far enough where they stood and there was room for running away if any of the *egwugwu* should go towards them.

The drum sounded again and the flute blew. The *egwugwu* house was now a pandemonium of quavering voices: *Aru oyim de de de de dei!*[3] filled the air as the spirits of the ancestors, just emerged from the earth, greeted themselves in their esoteric language. The *egwugwu* house into which they emerged faced the forest, away from the crowd, who saw only its back with the many-coloured patterns and drawings done by specially chosen women at regular intervals. These women never saw the inside of the hut. No woman ever did. They scrubbed and painted the outside walls under the supervision of men. If they imagined what was inside, they kept their imagination to themselves. No woman ever asked questions about the most powerful and the most secret cult in the clan.

Aru oyim de de de dei! flew around the dark, closed hut like tongues of fire. The ancestral spirits of the clan were abroad. The metal gong beat continuously now and the flute, shrill and powerful, floated on the chaos.

And then the *egwugwu* appeared. The women and children sent up a great shout and took to their heels. It was instinctive. A woman fled as soon as an *egwugwu* came in sight. And when, as on that day, nine of the greatest masked spirits in the clan came out together it was a terrifying spectacle. Even Mgbafo took to her heels and had to be restrained by her brothers.

Each of the nine *egwugwu* represented a village of the clan. Their leader was called Evil Forest. Smoke poured out of his head.

The nine villages of Umuofia had grown out of the nine sons of the first father of the clan. Evil Forest represented the village of Umeru, or the children of Eru, who was the eldest of the nine sons.

"*Umuofia kwenu!*" shouted the leading *egwugwu,* pushing the air with his raffia arms. The elders of the clan replied, "*Yao!*"

"*Umuofia kwenu!*"

"*Yaa!*"

"*Umuofia kwenu!*"

"*Yaa!*"

Evil Forest then thrust the pointed end of his rattling staff into the earth. And it began to shake and rattle, like something agitating with a metallic life. He took the first of the empty stools and the eight other *egwugwu* began to sit in order of seniority after him.

Okonkwo's wives, and perhaps other women as well, might have noticed that the second *egwugwu* had the springy walk of Okonkwo. And they might also have noticed that Okonkwo was not among the titled men and elders who sat behind the row of *egwugwu.* But if they thought these things they kept them within themselves. The *egwugwu* with the springy walk was one of the dead fathers of the clan. He looked

3. Greetings, body of my friend.

terrible with the smoked raffia body, a huge wooden face painted white except for the round hollow eyes and the charred teeth that were as big as a man's fingers. On his head were two powerful horns.

When all the *egwugwu* had sat down and the sound of the many tiny bells and rattles on their bodies had subsided, Evil Forest addressed the two groups of people facing them.

"Uzowulu's body, I salute you," he said. Spirits always addressed humans as "bodies." Uzowulu bent down and touched the earth with his right hand as a sign of submission.

"Our father, my hand has touched the ground," he said.

"Uzowulu's body, do you know me?" asked the spirit.

"How can I know you, father? You are beyond our knowledge."

Evil Forest then turned to the other group and addressed the eldest of the three brothers.

"The body of Odukwe, I greet you," he said, and Odukwe bent down and touched the earth. The hearing then began.

Uzowulu stepped forward and presented his case.

"That woman standing there is my wife, Mgbafo. I married her with my money and my yams. I do not owe my in-laws anything. I owe them no yams. I owe them no cocoyams. One morning three of them came to my house, beat me up and took my wife and children away. This happened in the rainy season. I have waited in vain for my wife to return. At last I went to my in-laws and said to them, 'You have taken back your sister. I did not send her away. You yourselves took her. The law of the clan is that you should return her bride-price.' But my wife's brother said they had nothing to tell me. So I have brought the matter to the fathers of the clan. My case is finished. I salute you."

"Your words are good," said the leader of the *egwugwu.* "Let us hear Odukwe. His words may also be good."

Odukwe was short and thick-set. He stepped forward, saluted the spirits and began his story.

"My in-law has told you that we went to his house, beat him up and took our sister and her children away. All that is true. He told you that he came to take back her bride-price and we refused to give it him. That is also true. My in-law, Uzowulu, is a beast. My sister lived with him for nine years. During those years no single day passed in the sky without his beating the woman. We have tried to settle their quarrels time without number and on each occasion Uzowulu was guilty—"

"It is a lie!" Uzowulu shouted.

"Two years ago," continued Odukwe, "when she was pregnant, he beat her until she miscarried."

"It is a lie. She miscarried after she had gone to sleep with her lover."

"Uzowulu's body, I salute you," said Evil Forest, silencing him. "What kind of lover sleeps with a pregnant woman?" There was a loud murmur of approbation from the crowd. Odukwe continued:

"Last year when my sister was recovering from an illness, he beat her again so that if the neighbours had not gone in to save her she would have been killed. We heard of it, and did as you have been told. The law of Umuofia is that if a woman runs away from her husband her bride-price is returned. But in this case she ran away to save her life. Her two children belong to Uzowulu. We do not dispute it, but they are too young to leave their mother. If, on the other hand, Uzowulu should recover from his madness and come in the proper way to beg his wife to return she will do so on the understanding that if he ever beats her again we shall cut off his genitals for him."

The crowd roared with laughter. Evil Forest rose to his feet and order was immediately restored. A steady cloud of smoke rose from his head. He sat down again and called two witnesses. They were both Uzowulu's neighbours, and they agreed about the beating. Evil Forest then stood up, pulled out his staff and thrust it into the earth again. He ran a few steps in the direction of the women; they all fled in terror, only to return to their places almost immediately. The nine *egwugwu* then went away to consult together in their house. They were silent for a long time. Then the metal gong sounded and the flute was blown. The *egwugwu* had emerged once again from their underground home. They saluted one another and then reappeared on the *ilo.*

"*Umuofia kwenu!*" roared Evil Forest, facing the elders and grandees of the clan.

"*Yaa!*" replied the thunderous crowd, then silence descended from the sky and swallowed the noise.

Evil Forest began to speak and all the while he spoke everyone was silent. The eight other *egwugwu* were as still as statues.

"We have heard both sides of the case," said Evil Forest. "Our duty is not to blame this man or to praise that, but to settle the dispute." He turned to Uzowulu's group and allowed a short pause.

"Uzowulu's body, do you know me?"

"How can I know you, father? You are beyond our knowledge," Uzowulu replied.

"I am Evil Forest. I kill a man on the day that his life is sweetest to him."

"That is true," replied Uzowulu.

"Go to your in-laws with a pot of wine and beg your wife to return to you. It is not bravery when a man fights with a woman." He turned to Odukwe, and allowed a brief pause.

"Odukwe's body, I greet you," he said.

"My hand is on the ground," replied Odukwe.

"Do you know me?"

"No man can know you," replied Odukwe.

"I am Evil Forest, I am Dry-meat-that-fills-the-mouth, I am Fire-that-burns-without-faggots. If your in-law brings wine to you, let your sister go with him. I salute you." He pulled his staff from the hard earth and thrust it back.

"*Umuofia kwenu!*" he roared, and the crowd answered.

"I don't know why such a trifle should come before the *egwugwu,*" said one elder to another.

"Don't you know what kind of man Uzowulu is? He will not listen to any other decision," replied the other.

As they spoke two other groups of people had replaced the first before the *egwugwu,* and a great land case began.

Chapter 11

The night was impenetrably dark. The moon had been rising later and later every night until now it was seen only at dawn. And whenever the moon forsook evening and rose at cock-crow the nights were as black as charcoal.

Ezinma and her mother sat on a mat on the floor after their supper of yam foo-foo and bitter leaf soup. A palm-oil lamp gave out yellowish light. Without it, it would have been impossible to eat; one could not have known where one's mouth was in the darkness of that night. There was an oil lamp in all four huts on Okonkwo's compound, and each hut seen from the others looked like a soft eye of yellow half-light set in the solid massiveness of night.

The world was silent except for the shrill cry of insects, which was part of the night, and the sound of wooden mortar and pestle as Nwayieke pounded her foo-foo. Nwayieke lived four compounds away, and she was notorious for her late cooking. Every woman in the neighbourhood knew the sound of Nwayieke's mortar and pestle. It was also part of the night.

Okonkwo had eaten from his wives' dishes and was now reclining with his back against the wall. He searched his bag and brought out his snuff-bottle. He turned it on to his left palm, but nothing came out. He hit the bottle against his knee to shake up the tobacco. That was always the trouble with Okeke's snuff. It very quickly went damp, and there was too much saltpetre in it. Okonkwo had not brought snuff from him for a long time. Idigo was the man who knew how to grind good snuff. But he had recently fallen ill.

Low voices, broken now and again by singing, reached Okonkwo from his wives' huts as each woman and her children told folk stories. Ekwefi and her daughter, Ezinma, sat on a mat on the floor. It was Ekwefi's turn to tell a story.

"Once upon a time," she began, "all the birds were invited to a feast in the sky. They were very happy and began to prepare themselves for the great day. They painted their bodies with red cam wood and drew beautiful patterns on them with *uli.*

"Tortoise saw all these preparations and soon discovered what it all meant. Nothing that happened in the world of the animals ever escaped his notice; he was full of cunning. As soon as he heard of the great feast in the sky his throat began to itch at the very thought. There was a famine in those days and Tortoise had not eaten a good meal for two moons. His body rattled like a piece of dry stick in his empty shell. So he began to plan how he would go to the sky."

"But he had no wings," said Ezinma.

"Be patient," replied her mother. "That is the story. Tortoise had no wings, but he went to the birds and asked to be allowed to go with them.

"'We know you too well,' said the birds when they had heard him. 'You are full of cunning and you are ungrateful. If we allow you to come with us you will soon begin your mischief.'"

"'You do not know me,' said Tortoise. 'I am a changed man. I have learnt that a man who makes trouble for others is also making it for himself.'

"Tortoise had a sweet tongue, and within a short time all the birds agreed that he was a changed man, and they each gave him a feather, with which he made two wings.

"At last the great day came and Tortoise was the first to arrive at the meeting-place. When all the birds had gathered together, they set off in a body. Tortoise was very happy and voluble as he flew among the birds, and he was soon chosen as the man to speak for the party because he was a great orator.

"'There is one important thing which we must not forget,' he said as they flew on their way. 'When people are invited to a great feast like this, they take new names for the occasion. Our hosts in the sky will expect us to honour this age-old custom.'

"None of the birds had heard of this custom but they knew that Tortoise, in spite of his failings in other directions, was a widely-travelled man who knew the customs of different people. And so they each took a new name. When they had all taken, Tortoise also took one. He was to be called *All of you.*

"At last the party arrived in the sky and their hosts were very happy to see them. Tortoise stood up in his many-coloured plumage and thanked them for their invitation.

His speech was so eloquent that all the birds were glad they had brought him, and nodded their heads in approval of all he said. Their hosts took him as the king of the birds, especially as he looked somewhat different from the others.

"After kola nuts had been presented and eaten, the people of the sky set before their guests the most delectable dishes Tortoise had ever seen or dreamt of. The soup was brought out hot from the fire and in the very pot in which it had been cooked. It was full of meat and fish. Tortoise began to sniff aloud. There was pounded yam and also yam pottage cooked with palm-oil and fresh fish. There were also pots of palm-wine. When everything had been set before the guests, one of the people of the sky came forward and tasted a little from each pot. He then invited the birds to eat. But Tortoise jumped to his feet and asked: 'For whom have you prepared this feast?'

"'For all of you,' replied the man.

"Tortoise turned to the birds and said: 'You remember that my name is *All of you.* The custom here is to serve the spokesman first and the others later. They will serve you when I have eaten.'

"He began to eat and the birds grumbled angrily. The people of the sky thought it must be their custom to leave all the food for their king. And so Tortoise ate the best part of the food and then drank two pots of palm-wine, so that he was full of food and drink and his body filled out in his shell.

"The birds gathered round to eat what was left and to peck at the bones he had thrown all about the floor. Some of them were too angry to eat. They chose to fly home on an empty stomach. But before they left each took back the feather he had lent to Tortoise. And there he stood in his hard shell full of food and wine but without any wings to fly home. He asked the birds to take a message for his wife, but they all refused. In the end Parrot, who had felt more angry than the others, suddenly changed his mind and agreed to take the message.

"'Tell my wife,' said Tortoise, 'to bring out all the soft things in my house and cover the compound with them so that I can jump down from the sky without very great danger.'

"Parrot promised to deliver the message, and then flew away. But when he reached Tortoise's house he told his wife to bring out all the hard things in the house. And so she brought out her husband's hoes, matchets, spears, guns and even his cannon. Tortoise looked down from the sky and saw his wife bringing things out, but it was too far to see what they were. When all seemed ready he let himself go. He fell and fell and fell until he began to fear that he would never stop falling. And then like the sound of his cannon he crashed on the compound."

"Did he die?" asked Ezinma.

"No," replied Ekwefi. "His shell broke into pieces. But there was a great medicine-man in the neigbourhood. Tortoise's wife sent for him and he gathered all the bits of shell and stuck them together. That is why Tortoise's shell is not smooth."

"There is no song in the story," Ezinma pointed out.

"No," said Ekwefi. "I shall think of another one with a song. But it is your turn now."

"Once upon a time," Ezinma began, "Tortoise and Cat went to wrestle against Yams—no, that is not the beginning. Once upon a time there was a great famine in the land of animals. Everybody was lean except Cat, who was fat and whose body shone as if oil was rubbed on it . . ."

She broke off because at that very moment a loud and high-pitched voice broke the outer silence of the night. It was Chielo, the priestess of Agbala, prophesying.

There was nothing new in that. Once in a while Chielo was possessed by the spirit of her god and she began to prophesy. But tonight she was addressing her prophecy and greetings to Okonkwo, and so everyone in his family listened. The folk stories stopped.

"*Agbala do-o-o-o! Agbala ekeneo-o-o-o-o,*"[4] came the voice like a sharp knife cutting through the night. "*Okonkwo! Agbala ekene gio-o-o-o! Agbala cholu ifu ada ya Ezinmao-o-o-o!*"[5]

At the mention of Ezinma's name Ekwefi jerked her head sharply like a animal that had sniffed death in the air. Her heart jumped painfully within her.

The priestess had now reached Okonkwo's compound and was talking with him outside his hut. She was saying again and again that Agbala wanted to see his daughter, Ezinma. Okonkwo pleaded with her to come back in the morning because Ezinma was now asleep. But Chielo ignored what he was trying to say and went on shouting that Agbala wanted to see his daughter. Her voice was as clear as metal, and Okonkwo's women and children heard from their huts all that she said. Okonkwo was still pleading that the girl had been ill of late and was asleep. Ekwefi quickly took her to their bedroom and placed her on their high bamboo bed.

The priestess suddenly screamed. "Beware, Okonkwo!" she warned. "Beware of exchanging words with Agbala. Does a man speak when a god speaks? Beware!"

She walked through Okonkwo's hut into the circular compound and went straight towards Ekwefi's hut. Okonkwo came after her.

"Ekwefi," she called, "Agbala greets you. Where is my daughter, Ezinma? Agbala wants to see her."

Ekwefi came out from her hut carrying her oil lamp in her left hand. There was a light wind blowing, so she cupped her right hand to shelter the flame. Nwoye's mother, also carrying an oil lamp, emerged from her hut. Her children stood in the darkness outside their hut watching the strange event. Okonkwo's youngest wife also came out and joined the others.

"Where does Agbala want to see her?" Ekwefi asked.

"Where else but in his house in the hills and the caves?" replied the priestess.

"I will come with you, too," Ekwefi said firmly.

"*Tufia-a!*"[6] the priestess cursed, her voice cracking like the angry bark of thunder in the dry season. "How dare you, woman, to go before the mighty Agbala of your own accord? Beware, woman, lest he strike you in his anger. Bring me my daughter."

Ekwefi went into her hut and came out again with Ezinma.

"Come, my daughter," said the priestess. "I shall carry you on my back. A baby on its mother's back does not know that the way is long."

Ezinma began to cry. She was used to Chielo calling her "my daughter." But it was a different Chielo she now saw in the yellow half-light.

"Don't cry, my daughter," said the priestess, "lest Agbala be angry with you."

"Don't cry," said Ekwefi, "she will bring you back very soon. I shall give you some fish to eat." She went into the hut again and brought down the smoke-black basket in which she kept her dried fish and other ingredients for cooking soup. She broke a piece in two and gave it to Ezinma, who clung to her.

"Don't be afraid," said Ekwefi, stroking her head, which was shaved in places, leaving a regular pattern of hair. They went outside again. The priestess bent down on one knee and Ezinma climbed on her back, her left palm closed on her fish and her eyes gleaming with tears.

4. Agbala greets you. Agbala wants something.
5. Agbala greets you. Agbala wants to see his daughter, Ezinma.
6. Spit!

"*Agbala do-o-o-o! Agbala ekeneo-o-o-o-o!* . . ." Chielo began once again to chant greetings to her god. She turned round sharply and walked through Okonkwo's hut, bending very low at the eaves. Ezinma was crying loudly now, calling on her mother. The two voices disappeared into the thick darkness.

A strange and sudden weakness descended on Ekwefi as she stood gazing in the direction of the voices like a hen whose only chick has been carried away by a kite. Ezinma's voice soon faded away and only Chielo was heard moving farther and farther into the distance.

"Why do you stand there as though she had been kidnapped?" asked Okonkwo as he went back to his hut.

"She will bring her back soon," Nwoye's mother said.

But Ekwefi did not hear these consolations. She stood for a while, and then, all of a sudden, made up her mind. She hurried through Okonkwo's hut and went outside.

"Where are you going?" he asked.

"I am following Chielo," she replied and disappeared in the darkness. Okonkwo cleared his throat, and brought out his snuff-bottle from the goatskin bag by his side.

The priestess's voice was already growing faint in the distance. Ekwefi hurried to the main footpath and turned left in the direction of the voice. Her eyes were useless to her in the darkness. But she picked her way easily on the sandy footpath hedged on either side by branches and damp leaves. She began to run, holding her breasts with her hands to stop them flapping noisily against her body. She hit her left foot against an outcropped root, and terror seized her. It was an ill omen. She ran faster. But Chielo's voice was still a long way away. Had she been running too? How could she go so fast with Ezinma on her back? Although the night was cool, Ekwefi was beginning to feel hot from her running. She continually ran into the luxuriant weeds and creepers that walled in the path. Once she tripped up and fell. Only then did she realise, with a start, that Chielo had stopped her chanting. Her heart beat violently and she stood still. Then Chielo's renewed outburst came from only a few paces ahead. But Ekwefi could not see her. She shut her eyes for a while and opened them again in an effort to see. But it was useless. She could not see beyond her nose.

There were no stars in the sky because there was a rain-cloud. Fireflies went about with their tiny green lamps, which only made the darkness more profound. Between Chielo's outbursts the night was alive with the shrill tremor of forest insects woven into the darkness.

"*Agbala do-o-o-o! . . . Agbala ekeneo-o-o-o!* . . ." Ekwefi trudged behind, neither getting too near nor keeping too far back. She thought they must be going towards the sacred cave. Now that she walked slowly she had time to think. What would she do when they got to the cave? She would not dare to enter. She would wait at the mouth, all alone in that fearful place. She thought of all the terrors of the night. She remembered the night, long ago, when she had seen *Ogbuagali-odu,* one of those evil essences loosed upon the world by the potent "medicines" which the tribe had made in the distant past against its enemies but had now forgotten how to control. Ekwefi had been returning from the stream with her mother on a dark night like this when they saw its glow as it flew in their direction. They had thrown their water-pots and lain by the roadside expecting the sinister light to descend on them and kill them. That was the only time Ekwefi ever saw *Ogbuagali-odu.* But although it had happened so long ago, her blood still ran cold whenever she remembered that night.

The priestess's voice came at longer intervals now, but its vigour was undiminished. The air was cool and damp with dew. Ezinma sneezed. Ekwefi muttered, "Life to you." At the same time the priestess also said, "Life to you, my daughter." Ezinma's voice from the darkness warmed her mother's heart. She trudged slowly along.

And then the priestess screamed. "Somebody is walking behind me!" she said. "Whether you are spirit or man, may Agbala shave your head with a blunt razor! May he twist your neck until you see your heels!"

Ekwefi stood rooted to the spot. One mind said to her: "Woman, go home before Agbala does you harm." But she could not. She stood until Chielo had increased the distance between them and she began to follow again. She had already walked so long that she began to feel a slight numbness in the limbs and in the head. Then it occurred to her that they could not have been heading for the cave. They must have by-passed it long ago; they must be going towards Umuachi, the farthest village in the clan. Chielo's voice now came after long intervals.

It seemed to Ekwefi that the night had become a little lighter. The cloud had lifted and a few stars were out. The moon must be preparing to rise, its sullenness over. When the moon rose later in the night, people said it was refusing food, as a sullen husband refuses his wife's food when they have quarrelled.

"*Agbala do-o-o-o! Umuachi! Agbala ekene unuo-o-o!*" It was just as Ekwefi had thought. The priestess was now saluting the village of Umuachi. It was unbelievable, the distance they had covered. As they emerged into the open village from the narrow forest track the darkness was softened and it became possible to see the vague shape of trees. Ekwefi screwed her eyes up in an effort to see her daughter and the priestess, but whenever she thought she saw their shape it immediately dissolved like a melting lump of darkness. She walked numbly along.

Chielo's voice was now rising continuously, as when she first set out. Ekwefi had a feeling of spacious openness, and she guessed they must be on the village *ilo,* or playground. And she realised too with something like a jerk that Chielo was no longer moving forward. She was, in fact, returning. Ekwefi quickly moved away from her line of retreat. Chielo passed by, and they began to go back the way they had come.

It was a long and weary journey and Ekwefi felt like a sleepwalker most of the way. The moon was definitely rising, and although it had not yet appeared on the sky its light had already melted down the darkness. Ekwefi could now discern the figure of the priestess and her burden. She slowed down her pace so as to increase the distance between them. She was afraid of what might happen if Chielo suddenly turned round and saw her.

She had prayed for the moon to rise. But now she found the half-light of the incipient moon more terrifying than the darkness. The world was now peopled with vague, fantastic figures that dissolved under her steady gaze and then formed again in new shapes. At one stage Ekwefi was so afraid that she nearly called out to Chielo for companionship and human sympathy. What she had seen was the shape of a man climbing a palm tree, his head pointing to the earth and his legs skywards. But at that very moment Chielo's voice rose again in her possessed chanting, and Ekwefi recoiled, because there was no humanity there. It was not the same Chielo who sat with her in the market and sometimes bought bean-cakes for Ezinma, whom she called her daughter. It was a different woman—the priestess of Agbala, the Oracle of the Hills and Caves. Ekwefi trudged along between two fears. The sound of her benumbed steps seemed to come from some other person walking behind her. Her arms were folded across her bare breasts. Dew fell heavily and the air was cold. She could no longer think, not even about the terrors of night. She just jogged along in a half-sleep only waking to full life when Chielo sang.

At last they took a turning and began to head for the caves. From then on, Chielo never ceased in her chanting. She greeted her god in a multitude of names—the owner of the future, the messenger of earth, the god who cut a man down when his life was sweetest to him. Ekwefi was also awakened and her benumbed fears revived.

The moon was now up and she could see Chielo and Ezinma clearly. How a woman could carry a child of that size so easily and for so long was a miracle. But Ekwefi was not thinking about that. Chielo was not a woman that night.

"*Agbala do-o-o-o! Agbala ekeneo-o-o! Chi negbu madu ubosi ndu ya nato ya uto daluo-o-o!* . . ."[7]

Ekwefi could already see the hills looming in the moonlight. They formed a circular ring with a break at one point through which the foot-track led to the centre of the circle.

As soon as the priestess stepped into this ring of hills her voice was not only doubled in strength but was thrown back on all sides. It was indeed the shrine of a great god. Ekwefi picked her way carefully and quietly. She was already beginning to doubt the wisdom of her coming. Nothing would happen to Ezinma, she thought. And if anything happened to her could she stop it? She would not dare to enter the underground caves. Her coming was quite useless, she thought.

As these things went through her mind she did not realise how close they were to the cave mouth. And so when the priestess with Ezinma on her back disappeared through a hole hardly big enough to pass a hen, Ekwefi broke into a run as though to stop them. As she stood gazing at the circular darkness which had swallowed them, tears gushed from her eyes, and she swore within her that if she heard Ezinma cry she would rush into the cave to defend her against all the gods in the world. She would die with her.

Having sworn that oath, she sat down on a stony ledge and waited. Her fear had vanished. She could hear the priestess's voice, all its metal taken out of it by the vast emptiness of the cave. She buried her face in her lap and waited.

She did not know how long she waited. It must have been a very long time. Her back was turned on the footpath that led out of the hills. She must have heard a noise behind her and turned round sharply. A man stood there with a matchet in his hand. Ekwefi uttered a scream and sprang to her feet.

"Don't be foolish," said Okonkwo's voice. "I thought you were going into the shrine with Chielo," he mocked.

Ekwefi did not answer. Tears of gratitude filled her eyes. She knew her daughter was safe.

"Go home and sleep," said Okonkwo. "I shall wait here."

"I shall wait too. It is almost dawn. The first cock has crowed."

As they stood there together, Ekwefi's mind went back to the days when they were young. She had married Anene because Okonkwo was too poor then to marry. Two years after her marriage to Anene she could bear it no longer and she ran away to Okonkwo. It had been early in the morning. The moon was shining. She was going to the stream to fetch water. Okonkwo's house was on the way to the stream. She went in and knocked at his door and he came out. Even in those days he was not a man of many words. He just carried her into his bed and in the darkness began to feel around her waist for the loose end of her cloth.

7. Agbala wants! Agbala greets! Spirit who kills one on the day his life is so pleasant he gives thanks!

Chapter 12

On the following morning the entire neighbourhood wore a festive air because Okonkwo's friend, Obierika, was celebrating his daughter's *uri.* It was the day on which her suitor (having already paid the greater part of her bride-price) would bring palm-wine not only to her parents and immediate relatives but to the wide and extensive group of kinsmen called *umunna.* Everybody had been invited—men, women and children. But it was really a woman's ceremony and the central figures were the bride and her mother.

As soon as day broke, breakfast was hastily eaten and women and children began to gather at Obierika's compound to help the bride's mother in her difficult but happy task of cooking for a whole village.

Okonkwo's family was astir like any other family in the neighbourhood. Nwoye's mother and Okonkwo's youngest wife were ready to set out for Obierika's compound with all their children. Nwoye's mother carried a basket of coco-yams, a cake of salt and smoked fish which she would present to Obierika's wife. Okonkwo's youngest wife, Ojiugo, also had a basket of plantains and coco-yams and a small pot of palm-oil. Their children carried pots of water.

Ekwefi was tired and sleepy from the exhausting experiences of the previous night. It was not very long since they had returned. The priestess, with Ezinma sleeping on her back, had crawled out of the shrine on her belly like a snake. She had not as much as looked at Okonkwo and Ekwefi or shown any surprise at finding them at the mouth of the cave. She looked straight ahead of her and walked back to the village. Okonkwo and his wife followed at a respectful distance. They thought the priestess might be going to her house, but she went to Okonkwo's compound, passed through his *obi* and into Ekwefi's hut and walked into her bedroom. She placed Ezinma carefully on the bed and went away without saying a word to anybody.

Ezinma was still sleeping when everyone else was astir, and Ekwefi asked Nwoye's mother and Ojiugo to explain to Obierika's wife that she would be late. She had got ready her basket of coco-yams and fish, but she must wait for Ezinma to wake.

"You need some sleep yourself," said Nwoye's mother. "You look very tired."

As they spoke Ezinma emerged from the hut, rubbing her eyes and stretching her spare frame. She saw the other children with their water-pots and remembered that they were going to fetch water for Obierika's wife. She went back to the hut and brought her pot.

"Have you slept enough?" asked her mother.

"Yes," she replied. "Let us go."

"Not before you have had your breakfast," said Ekwefi. And she went into her hut to warm the vegetable soup she had cooked last night.

"We shall be going," said Nwoye's mother. "I will tell Obierika's wife that you are coming later." And so they all went to help Obierika's wife—Nwoye's mother and her four children and Ojiugo with her two.

As they trooped through Okonkwo's *obi* he asked: "Who will prepare my afternoon meal?"

"I shall return to do it," said Ojiugo.

Okonkwo was also feeling tired and sleepy, for although nobody else knew it, he had not slept at all last night. He had felt very anxious but did not show it. When Ekwefi had followed the priestess, he had allowed what he regarded as a reasonable and manly interval to pass and then gone with his matchet to the shrine, where he thought they must be. It was only when he had got there that it had occurred to him that the priestess might have chosen to go round the villages first. Okonkwo had returned home and sat waiting. When he thought he had waited long enough he again returned to the shrine. But the Hills and the Caves were as silent as death. It was only on his fourth trip that he had found Ekwefi, and by then he had become gravely worried.

Obierika's compound was as busy as an ant-hill. Temporary cooking tripods were erected on every available space by bringing together three blocks of sun-dried earth and making a fire in their midst. Cooking pots went up and down the tripods, and foo-foo was pounded in a hundred wooden mortars. Some of the women cooked the yams and the cassava, the others prepared vegetable soup. Young men pounded the foo-foo or split firewood. The children made endless trips to the stream.

Three young men helped Obierika to slaughter the two goats with which the soup was made. They were very fat goats, but the fattest of all was tethered to a peg near the wall of the compound. It was as big as a small cow. Obierika had sent one of his relatives all the way to Umuike to buy that goat. It was the one he would present alive to his in-laws.

"The market of Umuike is a wonderful place," said the young man who had been sent by Obierika to buy the giant goat. "There are so many people on it that if you threw up a grain of sand it would not find a way to fall to earth again."

"It is the result of a great medicine," said Obierika. "The people of Umuike wanted their market to grow and swallow up the markets of their neighbours. So they made a powerful medicine. Every market-day, before the first cock-crow, this medicine stands on the market-ground in the shape of an old woman with a fan. With this magic fan she beckons to the market all the neighbouring clans. She beckons in front of her and behind her, to her right and to her left."

"And so everybody comes," said another man, "honest men and thieves. They can steal your cloth from off your waist in that market."

"Yes," said Obierika. "I warned Nwankwo to keep a sharp eye and a sharp ear. There was once a man who went to sell a goat. He led it on a thick rope which he tied round his wrist. But as he walked through the market he realised that people were pointing at him as they do to a madman. He could not understand it until he looked back and saw that what he led at the end of the tether was not a goat but a heavy log of wood."

"Do you think a thief can do that kind of thing single-handed?" asked Nwankwo.

"No," said Obierika. "They use medicine."

When they had cut the goats' throats and collected the blood in a bowl, they held them over an open fire to burn off the hair, and the smell of burning hair blended with the smell of cooking. Then they washed them and cut them up for the women who prepared the soup.

All this ant-hill activity was going smoothly when a sudden interruption came. It was a cry in the distance: *Oji odu achu iiiji-o-o!* (*The one that uses its tail to drive flies away!*) Every woman immediately abandoned whatever she was doing and rushed out in the direction of the cry.

"We cannot all rush out like that, leaving what we are cooking to burn in the fire," shouted Chielo, the priestess. "Three or four of us should stay behind."

"It is true," said another woman. "We will allow three or four women to stay behind."

Five women stayed behind to look after the cooking-pots, and all the rest rushed away to see the cow that had been let loose. When they saw it they drove it back to its owner, who at once paid the heavy fine which the village imposed on anyone whose cow was let loose on his neighbours' crops. When the women had exacted the penalty they checked among themselves to see if any woman had failed to come out when the cry had been raised.

"Where is Mgbogo?" asked one of them.

"She is ill in bed," said Mgbogo's next-door neighbour. "She has *iba.*"

"The only other person is Udenkwo," said another woman, "and her child is not twenty-eight days yet."

Those women whom Obierika's wife had not asked to help her with the cooking returned to their homes, and the rest went back, in a body, to Obierika's compound.

"Whose cow is it?" asked the women who had been allowed to stay behind.

"It was my husband's," said Ezelagbo. "One of the young children had opened the gate of the cow-shed."

Early in the afternoon the first two pots of palm-wine arrived from Obierika's in-laws. They were duly presented to the women, who drank a cup or two each, to help them in their cooking. Some of it also went to the bride and her attendant maidens, who were putting the last delicate touches of razor to her coiffure and cam wood on her smooth skin.

When the heat of the sun began to soften, Obierika's son, Maduka, took a long broom and swept the ground in front of his father's *obi.* And as if they had been waiting for that, Obierika's relatives and friends began to arrive, every man with his goatskin bag hung on one shoulder and a rolled goatskin mat under his arm. Some of them were accompanied by their sons bearing carved wooden stools. Okonkwo was one of them. They sat in a half circle and began to talk of many things. It would not be long before the suitors came.

Okonkwo brought out his snuff-bottle and offered it to Ogbuefi Ezenwa, who sat next to him. Ezenwa took it, tapped it on his knee-cap, rubbed his left palm on his body to dry it before tipping a little snuff into it. His actions were deliberate, and he spoke as he performed them.

"I hope our in-laws will bring many pots of wine. Although they come from a village that is known for being close-fisted, they ought to know that Akueke is the bride for a king."

"They dare not bring fewer than thirty pots," said Okonkwo. "I shall tell them my mind if they do."

At that moment Obierika's son, Maduka, led out the giant goat from the inner compound, for his father's relatives to see. They all admired it and said that that was the way things should be done. The goat was then led back to the inner compound.

Very soon after, the in-laws began to arrive. Young men and boys in single file, each carrying a pot of wine, came first. Obierika's relatives counted the pots as they came. Twenty, twenty-five. There was a long break, and the hosts looked at each other as if to say, "I told you." Then more pots came. Thirty, thirty-five, forty, forty-five. The hosts nodded in approval and seemed to say, "Now they are behaving like men." Altogether there were fifty pots of wine. After the pot-bearers came Ibe, the suitor, and the elders of his family. They sat in a half-moon, thus completing a circle with their hosts. The pots of wine stood in their midst. Then the bride, her mother and half a dozen other women and girls emerged from the inner compound, and went round the circle shaking hands with all. The bride's mother led the way, followed by the bride and the other women. The married women wore their best cloths and the girls wore red and black waist-beads and anklets of brass.

When the women retired. Obierika presented kola nuts to his in-laws. His eldest brother broke the first one. "Life to all of us," he said as he broke it. "And let there be friendship between your family and ours."

The crowd answered: "*Ee-e-e!*"

"We are giving you our daughter today. She will be a good wife to you. She will bear you nine sons like the mother of our town."

"*Ee-e-e!*"

The oldest man in the camp of the visitors replied: "It will be good for you and it will be good for us."

"*Ee-e-e!*"

"This is not the first time my people have come to marry your daughter. My mother was one of you."

"*Ee-e-e!*"

"And this will not be the last, because you understand us and we understand you. You are a great family."

"*Ee-e-e!*"

"Prosperous men and great warriors." He looked in the direction of Okonkwo. "Your daughter will bear us sons like you."

"*Ee-e-e!*"

The kola was eaten and the drinking of palm-wine began. Groups of four or five men sat round with a pot in their midst. As the evening wore on, food was presented to the guests. There were huge bowls of foo-foo and steaming pots of soup. There were also pots of yam pottage. It was a great feast.

As night fell, burning torches were set on wooden tripods and the young men raised a song. The elders sat in a circle and the singers went round singing each man's praise as they came before him. They had something to say for every man. Some were great farmers, some were orators who spoke for the clan; Okonkwo was the greatest wrestler and warrior alive. When they had gone round the circle they settled down in the centre, and girls came from the inner compound to dance. At first the bride was not among them. But when she finally appeared holding a cock in her right hand, a loud cheer rose from the crowd. All the other dancers made way for her. She presented the cock to the musicians and began to dance. Her brass anklets rattled as she danced and her body gleamed with cam wood in the soft yellow light. The musicians with their wood, clay and metal instruments went from song to song. And they were all gay. They sang the latest song in the village:

If I hold her hand
She says, "Don't touch!"
If I hold her foot
She says, "Don't touch!"
But when I hold her waist-beads
She pretends not to know.

The night was already far spent when the guests rose to go, taking their bride home to spend seven market weeks with her suitor's family. They sang songs as they went, and on their way they paid short courtesy visits to prominent men like Okonkwo, before they finally left for their village. Okonkwo made a present of two cocks to them.

Chapter 13

Go-di-di-go-go-di-go. Di-go-go-di-go. It was the *ekwe* talking to the clan. One of the things every man learned was the language of the hollowed-out instrument. Diim! Diim! Diim! boomed the cannon at intervals.

The first cock had not crowed, and Umuofia was still swallowed up in sleep and silence when the *ekwe* began to talk, and the cannon shattered the silence. Men stirred on their bamboo beds and listened anxiously. Somebody was dead. The cannon seemed to rend the sky. Di-go-go-di-go-di-di-go-go floated in the message-laden night air. The faint and distant wailing of women settled like a sediment of sorrow on the earth. Now and again a full-chested lamentation rose above the wailing whenever a man came into the place of death. He raised his voice once or twice in manly sorrow and then sat down with the other men listening to the endless wailing of the women and the esoteric language of the *ekwe*. Now and again the cannon boomed. The wailing of the women would not be heard beyond the village, but the *ekwe* carried the news to all the nine villages and even beyond. It began by naming the clan: *Umuofia obodo dike* "the land of the brave." *Umuofia obodo dike! Umuofia obodo dike!* It said this over and over again, and as it dwelt on it, anxiety mounted in every heart that heaved on a bamboo bed that night. Then it went nearer and named the village: *Iguedo of the yellow grinding-stone!* It was Okonkwo's village. Again and again Iguedo was called and men waited breathlessly in all the nine villages. At last the man was named and people sighed "E-u-u, Ezeudu is dead." A cold shiver ran down Okonkwo's back as he remembered the last time the old man had visited him. "That boy calls you father," he had said. "Bear no hand in his death."

Ezeudu was a great man, and so all the clan was at his funeral. The ancient drums of death beat, guns and cannon were fired, and men dashed about in frenzy, cutting down every tree or animal they saw, jumping over walls and dancing on the roof. It was a warrior's funeral, and from morning till night warriors came and went in their age-groups. They all wore smoked raffia skirts and their bodies were painted with chalk and charcoal. Now and again an ancestral spirit or *egwugwu* appeared from the underworld, speaking in a tremulous, unearthly voice and completely covered in raffia. Some of them were very violent, and there had been a mad rush for shelter earlier in the day when one appeared with a sharp matchet and was only prevented from doing serious harm by two men who restrained him with the help of a strong rope tied round his waist. Sometimes he turned round and chased those men, and they ran for their lives. But they always returned to the long rope he trailed behind. He sang, in a terrifying voice, that Ekwenzu, or Evil Spirit, had entered his eye.

But the most dreaded of all was yet to come. He was always alone and was shaped like a coffin. A sickly odour hung in the air wherever he went, and flies went with him. Even the greatest medicine-men took shelter when he was near. Many years ago another *egwugwu* had dared to stand his ground before him and had been transfixed to the spot for two days. This one had only one hand and with it carried a basket full of water.

But some of the *egwugwu* were quite harmless. One of them was so old and infirm that he leaned heavily on a stick. He walked unsteadily to the place where the corpse was laid, gazed at it a while and went away again—to the underworld.

The land of the living was not far removed from the domain of the ancestors. There was coming and going between them, especially at festivals and also when an old man died, because an old man was very close to the ancestors. A man's life from birth to death was a series of transition rites which brought him nearer and nearer to his ancestors.

Ezeudu had been the oldest man in the village, and at his death there were only three men in the whole clan who were older, and four or five others in his own age-group. Whenever one of these ancient men appeared in the crowd to dance unsteadily the funeral steps of the tribe, younger men gave way and the tumult subsided.

It was a great funeral, such as befitted a noble warrior. As the evening drew near, the shouting and the firing of guns, the beating of drums and the brandishing and clanging of matchets increased.

Ezeudu had taken three titles in his life. It was a rare achievement. There were only four titles in the clan, and only one or two men in any generation ever achieved the fourth and highest. When they did, they became the lords of the land. Because he had taken titles, Ezeudu was to be buried after dark with only a glowing brand to light the sacred ceremony.

But before this quiet and final rite, the tumult increased tenfold. Drums beat violently and men leaped up and down in a frenzy. Guns were fired on all sides and sparks flew out as matchets clanged together in warriors' salutes. The air was full of dust and the smell of gunpowder. It was then that the one-handed spirit came, carrying a basket full of water. People made way for him on all sides and the noise subsided. Even the smell of gunpowder was swallowed in the sickly smell that now filled the air. He danced a few steps to the funeral drums and then went to see the corpse.

"Ezeudu!" he called in his gutteral voice. "If you had been poor in your last life I would have asked you to be rich when you come again. But you were rich. If you had been a coward, I would have asked you to bring courage. But you were a fearless warrior. If you had died young, I would have asked you to get life. But you lived long. So I shall ask you to come again the way you came before. If your death was the death of nature, go in peace. But if a man caused it, do not allow him a moment's rest." He danced a few more steps and went away.

The drums and the dancing began again and reached fever-heat. Darkness was around the corner, and the burial was near. Guns fired the last salute and the cannon rent the sky. And then from the centre of the delirious fury came a cry of agony and shouts of horror. It was as if a spell had been cast. All was silent. In the centre of the crowd a boy lay in a pool of blood. It was the dead man's sixteen-year-old son, who with his brothers and half-brothers had been dancing the traditional farewell to their father. Okonkwo's gun had exploded and a piece of iron had pierced the boy's heart.

The confusion that followed was without parallel in the tradition of Umuofia. Violent deaths were frequent, but nothing like this had ever happened.

The only course open to Okonkwo was to flee from the clan. It was a crime against the earth goddess to kill a clansman, and a man who committed it must flee from the land. The crime was of two kinds, male and female. Okonkwo had committed the female, because it had been inadvertent. He could return to the clan after seven years.

That night he collected his most valuable belongings into headloads. His wives wept bitterly and their children wept with them without knowing why. Obierika and half a dozen other friends came to help and to console him. They each made nine or ten trips carrying Okonkwo's yams to store in Obierika's barn. And before the cock crowed Okonkwo and his family were fleeing to his motherland. It was a little village called Mbanta, just beyond the borders of Mbaino.

As soon as the day broke, a large crowd of men from Ezeudu's quarter stormed Okonkwo's compound, dressed in garbs of war. They set fire to his houses, demolished his red walls, killed his animals and destroyed his barn. It was the justice of the earth goddess, and they were merely her messengers. They had no hatred in their hearts against Okonkwo. His greatest friend, Obierika, was among them. They were merely cleansing the land which Okonkwo had polluted with the blood of a clansman.

Obierika was a man who thought about things. When the will of the goddess had been done, he sat down in his *obi* and mourned his friend's calamity. Why should a man suffer so greviously for an offence he had committed inadvertently? But although he thought for a long time he found no answer. He was merely led into greater complexities. He remembered his wife's twin children, whom he had thrown away. What crime had they committed? The Earth had decreed that they were an offence on the land and must be destroyed. And if the clan did not exact punishment for an offence against the great goddess, her wrath was loosed on all the land and not just on the offender. As the elders said, if one finger brought oil it soiled the others.

Part 2

Chapter 14

Okonkwo was well received by his mother's kinsmen in Mbanta. The old man who received him was his mother's younger brother, who was now the eldest surviving member of that family. His name was Uchendu, and it was he who had received Okonkwo's mother twenty and ten years before when she had been brought home from Umuofia to be buried with her people. Okonkwo was only a boy then and Uchendu still remembered him crying the traditional farewell: "Mother, mother, mother is going."

That was many years ago. Today Okonkwo was not bringing his mother home to be buried with her people. He was taking his family of three wives and eleven children to seek refuge in his motherland. As soon as Uchendu saw him with his sad and weary company he guessed what had happened, and asked no questions. It was not until the following day that Okonkwo told him the full story. The old man listened silently to the end and then said with some relief: "It is a female *ochu*." And he arranged the requisite rites and sacrifices.

Okonkwo was given a plot of ground on which to build his compound, and two or three pieces of land on which to farm during the coming planting season. With the help of his mother's kinsmen he built himself an *obi* and three huts for his wives. He then installed his personal god and the symbols of his departed fathers. Each of Uchendu's five sons contributed three hundred seed-yams to enable their cousin to plant a farm, for as soon as the first rain came farming would begin.

At last the rain came. It was sudden and tremendous. For two or three moons the sun had been gathering strength till it seemed to breathe a breath of fire on the earth. All the grass had long been scorched brown, and the sand felt like live coals to the feet. Evergreen trees wore a dusty coat of brown. The birds were silenced in the forests, and the world lay panting under the live, vibrating heat. And then came the clap of thunder. It was an angry, metallic and thirsty clap, unlike the deep and liquid rumbling of the rainy season. A mighty wind arose and filled the air with dust. Palm trees swayed as the wind combed their leaves into flying crests like strange and fantastic coiffure.

When the rain finally came, it was in large, solid drops of frozen water which the people called "the nuts of the water of heaven." They were hard and painful on the body as they fell, yet young people ran about happily picking up the cold nuts and throwing them into their mouths to melt.

The earth quickly came to life and the birds in the forests fluttered around and chirped merrily. A vague scent of life and green vegetation was diffused in the air. As the rain began to fall more soberly and in smaller liquid drops, children sought for shelter, and all were happy, refreshed and thankful.

Okonkwo and his family worked very hard to plant a new farm. But it was like beginning life anew without the vigour and enthusiasm of youth, like learning to become left-handed in old age. Work no longer had for him the pleasure it used to have, and when there was no work to do he sat in a silent half-sleep.

His life had been ruled by a great passion—to become one of the lords of the clan. That had been his life-spring. And he had all but achieved it. Then everything had been broken. He had been cast out of his clan like a fish on to a dry, sandy beach, panting. Clearly his personal god or *chi* was not made for great things. A man could not rise beyond the destiny of his *chi.* The saying of the elders was not true—that if a man said yea his *chi* also affirmed. Here was a man whose *chi* said nay despite his own affirmation.

The old man, Uchendu, saw clearly that Okonkwo had yielded to despair and he was greatly troubled. He would speak to him after the *isa-ifi* ceremony.

The youngest of Uchendu's five sons, Amikwu, was marrying a new wife. The bride-price had been paid and all but the last ceremony had been performed. Amikwu and his people had taken palm-wine to the bride's kinsmen about two moons before Okonkwo's arrival in Mbanta. And so it was time for the final ceremony of confession.

The daughters of the family were all there, some of them having come a long way from their homes in distant villages. Uchendu's eldest daughter had come from Obodo, nearly half a day's journey away. The daughters of Uchendu's brothers were also there. It was a full gathering of *umuada,* in the same way as they would meet if a death occurred in the family. There were twenty-two of them.

They sat in a big circle on the ground and the bride sat in the centre with a hen in her right hand. Uchendu sat by her, holding the ancestral staff of the family. All the other men stood outside the circle, watching. Their wives watched also. It was evening and the sun was setting.

Uchendu's eldest daughter, Njide, asked the questions.

"Remember that if you do not answer truthfully you will suffer or even die at child-birth," she began. "How many men have lain with you since my brother first expressed the desire to marry you?"

"None," she replied simply.

"Answer truthfully," urged the other women.

"None?" asked Njide.

"None," she answered.

"Swear on this staff of my fathers," said Uchendu.

"I swear," said the bride.

Uchendu took the hen from her, slit its throat with a sharp knife and allowed some of the blood to fall on his ancestral staff.

From that day Amikwu took the young bride to his hut and she became his wife. The daughters of the family did not return to their homes immediately but spent two or three days with their kinsmen.

On the second day Uchendu called together his sons and daughters and his nephew, Okonkwo. The men brought their goatskin mats, with which they sat on the floor, and the women sat on a sisal mat spread on a raised bank of earth. Uchendu pulled gently at his grey beard and gnashed his teeth. Then he began to speak, quietly and deliberately, picking his words with great care:

"It is Okonkwo that I primarily wish to speak to," he began. "But I want all of you to note what I am going to say. I am an old man and you are all children. I know more about the world than any of you. If there is any one among you who thinks he knows more let him speak up." He paused, but no one spoke.

"Why is Okonkwo with us today? This is not his clan. We are only his mother's kinsmen. He does not belong here. He is an exile, condemned for seven years to live in a strange land. And so he is bowed with grief. But there is just one question I would like to ask him. Can you tell me, Okonkwo, why it is that one of the commonest names we give our children is Nneka, or 'Mother is Supreme?' We all know that a man is the head of the family and his wives do his bidding. A child belongs to its father and his family and not to its mother and her family. A man belongs to his fatherland and not to his motherland. And yet we say Nneka—'Mother is Supreme.' Why is that?"

There was silence. "I want Okonkwo to answer me," said Uchendu.

"I do not know the answer," Okonkwo replied.

"You do not know the answer? So you see that you are a child. You have many wives and many children—more children than I have. You are a great man in your clan. But you are still a child, *my* child. Listen to me and I shall tell you. But there is one more question I shall ask. Why is it that when a woman dies she is taken home to be buried with her own kinsmen? She is not buried with her husband's kinsmen. Why is that? Your mother was brought home to me and buried with my people. Why was that?"

Okonkwo shook his head.

"He does not know that either," said Uchendu, "and yet he is full of sorrow because he has come to live in his motherland for a few years." He laughed a mirthless laughter, and turned to his sons and daughters. "What about you? Can you answer my question?"

They all shook their heads.

"Then listen to me," he said and cleared his throat. "It's true that a child belongs to its father. But when a father beats his child, it seeks sympathy in its mother's hut. A man belongs to his fatherland when things are good and life is sweet. But when there is sorrow and bitterness he finds refuge in his motherland. Your mother is there to protect you. She is buried there. And that is why we say that mother is supreme. Is it right that you, Okonkwo, should bring your mother a heavy face and refuse to be comforted? Be careful or you may displease the dead. Your duty is to comfort your wives and children and take them back to your fatherland after seven years. But if you allow sorrow to weigh you down and kill you, they will all die in exile." He paused for a long while. "These are now your kinsmen." He waved at his sons and daughters. "You think you are the greatest sufferer in the world. Do you know that men are sometimes banished for life? Do you know that men sometimes lose all their yams and even their children? I had six wives once. I have none now except that young girl who knows not her right from her left. Do you know how many children I have buried—children I begot in my youth and strength? Twenty-two. I did not hang myself, and I am still alive. If you think you are the greatest sufferer in the world ask my daughter, Akeuni, how many twins she has borne and thrown away. Have you not heard the song they sing when a woman dies?

For whom is it well, for whom is it well?
There is no one for whom it is well.

"I have no more to say to you."

Chapter 15

It was in the second year of Okonkwo's exile that his friend, Obierika, came to visit him. He brought with him two young men, each of them carrying a heavy bag on his head. Okonkwo helped them put down their loads. It was clear that the bags were full of cowries.

Okonkwo was very happy to receive his friend. His wives and children were very happy too, and so were his cousins and their wives when he sent for them and told them who his guest was.

"You must take him to salute our father," said one of the cousins.

"Yes," replied Okonkwo. "We are going directly." But before they went he whispered something to his first wife. She nodded, and soon the children were chasing one of their cocks.

Uchendu had been told by one of his grandchildren that three strangers had come to Okonkwo's house. He was therefore waiting to receive them. He held out his hands to them when they came into his *obi,* and after they had shaken hands he asked Okonkwo who they were.

"This is Obierika, my great friend. I have already spoken to you about him."

"Yes," said the old man, turning to Obierika. "My son has told me about you, and I am happy you have come to see us. I knew your father, Iweka. He was a great man. He had many friends here and came to see them quite often. Those were good days when a man had friends in distant clans. Your generation does not know that. You stay at home, afraid of your next-door neighbour. Even a man's motherland is strange to him nowadays." He looked at Okonkwo. "I am an old man and I like to talk. That is all I am good for now." He got up painfully, went into an inner room and came back with a kola nut.

"Who are the young men with you?" he asked as he sat down again on his goatskin. Okonkwo told him.

"Ah," he said. "Welcome, my sons." He presented the kola nut to them, and when they had seen it and thanked him, he broke it and they ate.

"Go into that room," he aid to Okonkwo, pointing with his finger. "You will find a pot of wine there."

Okonkwo brought the wine and they began to drink. It was a day old, and very strong.

"Yes," said Uchendu after a long silence. "People travelled more in those days. There is not a single clan in these parts that I do not know very well. Aninta, Umuazu, Ikeocha, Elumelu, Abame—I know them all."

"Have you heard," asked Obierika, "that Abame is no more?"

"How is that?" asked Uchendu and Okonkwo together.

"Abame has been wiped out," said Obierika. "It is a strange and terrible story. If I had not seen the few survivors with my own eyes and heard their story with my own ears, I would not have believed. Was it not on an Eke day that they fled into Umuofia?" he asked his two companions, and they nodded their heads.

"Three moons ago," said Obierika, "on an Eke market-day a little band of fugitives came into our town. Most of them were sons of our land whose mothers had been buried with us. But there were some too who came because they had friends in our town, and others who could think of nowhere else open to escape. And so they fled into Umuofia with a woeful story." He drank his palm-wine, and Okonkwo filled his horn again. He continued:

"During the last planting season a white man had appeared in their clan."

"An albino," suggested Okonkwo.

"He was not an albino. He was quite different." He sipped his wine. "And he was riding an iron horse.[1] The first people who saw him ran away, but he stood beckoning to them. In the end the fearless ones were near and even touched him. The elders consulted their Oracle and it told them that the strange man would break their clan and spread destruction among them." Obierika again drank a little of his wine. "And so they killed the white man and tied his iron horse to their sacred tree because it looked as if it would run away to call the man's friends. I forgot to tell you another thing which the Oracle said. It said that other white men were on their way. They were locusts, it said, and that first man was their harbinger sent to explore the terrain. And so they killed him."

"What did the white man say before they killed him?" asked Uchendu.

"He said nothing," answered one of Obierika's companions.

"He said something, only they did not understand him," said Obierika. "He seemed to speak through his nose."

"One of the men told me," said Obierika's other companion, "that he repeated over and over again a word that resembled Mbaino. Perhaps he had been going to Mbaino and had lost his way."

"Anyway," resumed Obierika, "they killed him and tied up his iron horse. This was before the planting season began. For a long time nothing happened. The rains had come and yams had been sown. The iron horse was still tied to the sacred silk-cotton tree. And then one morning three white men led by a band of ordinary men like us came to the clan. They saw the iron horse and went away again. Most of the men and women of Abame had gone to their farms. Only a few of them saw these white men and their followers. For many market weeks nothing else happened. They have a big market in Abame on every other Afo day and, as you know, the whole clan gathers there. That was the day it happened. The three white men and a very large number of other men surrounded the market. They must have used a powerful medicine to make themselves invisible until the market was full. And they began to shoot. Everybody was killed, except the old and the sick who were at home and a handful of men and women whose *chi* were wide awake and brought them out of that market." He paused.

"Their clan is now completely empty. Even the sacred fish in their mysterious lake have fled and the lake has turned the colour of blood. A great evil has come upon their land as the Oracle had warned."

There was a long silence. Uchendu ground his teeth audibly. Then he burst out: "Never kill a man who says nothing. Those men of Abame were fools. What did they know about the man?" He ground his teeth again and told a story to illustrate his point. "Mother Kite once sent her daughter to bring food. She went, and brought back a duckling. 'You have done very well,' said Mother Kite to her daughter, 'but tell me, what did the mother of this duckling say when you swooped and carried its child away?' 'It said nothing,' replied the young kite. 'It just walked away.' 'You must return the duckling,' said the Mother Kite. 'There is something ominous behind the silence.' And so Daughter Kite returned the duckling and took a chick instead. 'What did the mother of this chick do?' asked the old kite. 'It cried and raved and cursed me,' said the young kite. 'Then we can eat the chick,' said her mother. 'There is nothing to fear from someone who shouts.' Those men of Abame were fools."

1. Bicycle.

"They were fools," said Okonkwo after a pause. "They had been warned that danger was ahead. They should have armed themselves with their guns and their matchets even when they went to market."

"They have paid for their foolishness," said Obierika. "But I am greatly afraid. We have heard stories about white men who made the powerful guns and the strong drinks and took slaves away across the seas, but no one thought the stories were true."

"There is no story that is not true," said Uchendu. "The world has no end, and what is good among one people is an abomination with others. We have albinos among us. Do you not think that they came to our clan by mistake, that they have strayed from their ways to a land where everybody is like them?"

Okonkwo's first wife soon finished her cooking and set before their guests a big meal of pounded yams and bitter-leaf soup. Okonkwo's son, Nwoye, brought in a pot of sweet wine tapped from the raffia palm.

"You are a big man now," Obierika said to Nwoye. "Your friend Anene asked me to greet you."

"Is he well?" asked Nwoye.

"We are all well," said Obierika.

Ezinma brought them a bowl of water with which to wash their hands. After that they began to eat and to drink the wine.

"When did you set out from home?" asked Okonkwo.

"We had meant to set out from my house before cock-crow," said Obierika. "But Nweke did not appear until it was quite light. Never make an early morning appointment with a man who has just married a new wife." They all laughed.

"Has Nweke married a wife?" asked Okonkwo.

"He has married Okadigbo's second daughter," said Obierika.

"That is very good," said Okonkwo. "I do not blame you for not hearing the cock crow."

When they had eaten, Obierika pointed at the two heavy bags.

"That is the money from your yams," he said. "I sold the big ones as soon as you left. Later on I sold some of the seed-yams and gave out others to share-croppers. I shall do that every year until you return. But I thought you would need the money now and so I brought it. Who knows what may happen tomorrow? Perhaps green men will come to our clan and shoot us."

"God will not permit it," said Okonkwo. "I do not know how to thank you."

"I can tell you," said Obierika. "Kill one of your sons for me."

"That will not be enough," said Okonkwo.

"Then kill yourself," said Obierika.

"Forgive me," said Okonkwo, smiling. "I shall not talk about thanking you any more."

Chapter 16

When nearly two years later Obierika paid another visit to his friend in exile the circumstances were less happy. The missionaries had come to Umuofia. They had built their church there, won a handful of converts and were already sending evangelists to the surrounding towns and villages. That was a source of great sorrow to the leaders of the clan; but many of them believed that the strange faith and the white man's god would not last. None of his converts was a man whose word was heeded in the assembly of the people. None of them was a man of title. They were mostly the kind of people that were called *efulefu,* worthless, empty men. The imagery of an *efulefu* in the language of the clan was a man who sold his matchet and wore the sheath to battle. Chielo, the priestess of Agbala, called the converts the excrement of the clan, and the new faith was a mad dog that had come to eat it up.

What moved Obierika to visit Okonkwo was the sudden appearance of the latter's son, Nwoye, among the missionaries in Umuofia.

"What are you doing here?" Obierika had asked when after many difficulties the missionaries had allowed him to speak to the boy.

"I am one of them," replied Nwoye.

"How is your father?" Obierika asked, not knowing what else to say.

"I don't know. He is not my father," said Nwoye, unhappily.

And so Obierika went to Mbanta to see his friend. And he found that Okonkwo did not wish to speak about Nwoye. It was only from Nwoye's mother that he heard scraps of the story.

The arrival of the missionaries had caused a considerable stir in the village of Mbanta. There were six of them and one was a white man. Every man and woman came out to see the white man. Stories about these strange men had grown since one of them had been killed in Abame and his iron horse tied to the sacred silk-cotton tree. And so everybody came to see the white man. It was the time of the year when everybody was at home. The harvest was over.

When they had all gathered, the white man began to speak to them. He spoke through an interpreter who was an Ibo man, though his dialect was different and harsh to the ears of Mbanta. Many people laughed at his dialect and the way he used words strangely. Instead of saying "myself" he always said "my buttocks." But he was a man of commanding presence and the clansmen listened to him. He said he was one of them, as they could see from his colour and his language. The other four black men were also their brothers, although one of them did not speak Ibo. The white man was also their brother because they were all sons of God. And he told them about this new God, the Creator of all the world and all the men and women. He told them that they worshipped false gods, gods of wood and stone. A deep murmur went through the crowd when he said this. He told them that the true God lived on high and that all men when they died went before Him for judgment. Evil men and all the heathen who in their blindness bowed to wood and stone were thrown into a fire that burned like palm-oil. But good men who worshipped the true God lived for ever in His happy kingdom. "We have been sent by this great God to ask you to leave your wicked ways and false gods and turn to Him so that you may be saved when you die," he said.

"Your buttocks understand our language," said someone lightheartedly and the crowd laughed.

"What did he say?" the white man asked his interpreter. But before he could answer, another man asked a question: "Where is the white man's horse?" he asked. The Ibo evangelists consulted among themselves and decided that the man probably meant bicycle. They told the white man and he smiled benevolently.

"Tell them," he said, "that I shall bring many iron horses when we have settled down among them. Some of them will even ride the iron horse themselves." This was interpreted to them but very few of them heard. They were talking excitedly among themselves because the white man had said he was going to live among them. They had not thought about that.

At this point an old man said he had a question. "Which is this god of yours," he asked, "the goddess of the earth, the god of the sky, Amadiora of the thunderbolt, or what?"

The interpreter spoke to the white man and he immediately gave his answer. "All the gods you have named are not gods at all. They are gods of deceit who will tell you to kill your fellows and destroy innocent children. There is only one true God and He has made the earth, the sky, you and me and all of us."

"If we leave our gods and follow your god," asked another man, "who will protect us from the anger of our neglected gods and ancestors?"

"Your gods are not alive and cannot do you any harm," replied the white man. "They are pieces of wood and stone."

When this was interpreted to the men of Mbanta they broke into derisive laughter. These men must be mad, they said to themselves. How else could they say that Ani and Amadior were harmless? And Idemili and Ogwugwu too? And some of them began to go away.

Then the missionaries burst into song. It was one of those gay and rollicking tunes of evangelism which had the power of plucking at silent and dusty chords in the heart of an Ibo man. The interpreter explained each verse to the audience, some of whom now stood enthralled. It was a story of brothers who lived in darkness and in fear, ignorant of the love of God. It told of one sheep out on the hills, away from the gates of God and from the tender shepherd's care.

After the singing the interpreter spoke about the Son of God whose name was Jesu Kristi. Okonkwo, who only stayed in the hope that it might come to chasing the men out of the village or whipping them, now said:

"You told us with your own mouth that there was only one god. Now you talk about his son. He must have a wife, then." The crowd agreed.

"I did not say He had a wife," said the interpreter, somewhat lamely.

"Your buttocks said he had a son," said the joker. "So he must have a wife and all of them must have buttocks."

The missionary ignored him and went on to talk about the Holy Trinity. At the end of it Okonkwo was fully convinced that the man was mad. Hs shrugged his shoulders and went away to tap his afternoon palm-wine.

But there was a young lad who had been captivated. His name was Nwoye, Okonkwo's first son. It was not the mad logic of the Trinity that captivated him. He did not understand it. It was the poetry of the new religion, something felt in the marrow. The hymn about brothers who sat in darkness and in fear seemed to answer a vague and persistent question that haunted his young soul—the question of the twins crying in the bush and the question of Ikemefuna who was killed. He felt a relief within as the hymn poured into his parched soul. The words of the hymn were like the drops of frozen rain melting on the dry plate of the panting earth. Nwoye's callow mind was greatly puzzled.

Chapter 17

The missionaries spent their first four or five nights in the market-place, and went into the village in the morning to preach the gospel. They asked who the king of the village was, but the villagers told them that there was no king. "We have men of high title and the chief priests and the elders," they said.

It was not very easy getting the men of high title and the elders together after the excitement of the first day. But the missionaries persevered, and in the end they were received by the rulers of Mbanta. They asked for a plot of land to build their church.

Every clan and village had its "evil forest." In it were buried all those who died of the really evil diseases, like leprosy and smallpox. It was also the dumping ground for the potent fetishes of great medicine-men when they died. An "evil forest" was, therefore, alive with sinister forces and powers of darkness. It was such a forest that the rulers of Mbanta gave to the missionaries. They did not really want them in their clan, and so they made them that offer which nobody in his right senses would accept.

"They want a piece of land to build their shrine," said Uchendu to his peers when they consulted among themselves. "We shall give them a piece of land." He paused, and there was a murmur of surprise and disagreement. "Let us give them a portion of the Evil Forest. They boast about victory over death. Let us give them a real battlefield in which to show their victory." They laughed and agreed, and sent for the missionaries, whom they had asked to leave them for a while so that they might "whisper together." They offered them as much of the Evil Forest as they cared to take. And to their greatest amazement the missionaries thanked them and burst into song.

"They do not understand," said some of the elders. "But they will understand when they go to their plot of land tomorrow morning." And they dispersed.

The next morning the crazy men actually began to clear a part of the forest and to build their house. The inhabitants of Mbanta expected them all to be dead within four days. The first day passed and the second and third and fourth, and none of them died. Everyone was puzzled. And then it became known that the white man's fetish had unbelievable power. It was said that he wore glasses on his eyes so that he could see and talk to evil spirits. Not long after, he won his first three converts.

Although Nwoye had been attracted to the new faith from the very first day, he kept it secret. He dared not go too near the missionaries for fear of his father. But whenever they came to preach in the open market-place or the village playground, Nwoye was there. And he was already beginning to know some of the simple stories they told.

"We have now built a church," said Mr. Kiaga, the interpreter, who was now in charge of the infant congregation. The white man had gone back to Umuofia, where he built his headquarters and from where he paid regular visits to Mr. Kiaga's congregation at Mbanta.

"We have now built a church," said Mr. Kiaga, "and we want you all to come in every seventh day to worship the true God."

On the following Sunday, Nwoye passed and re-passed the little red-earth and thatch building without summoning enough courage to enter. He heard the voice of singing and although it came from a handful of men it was loud and confident. Their church stood on a circular clearing that looked like the open mouth of the Evil Forest. Was it waiting to snap its teeth together? After passing and re-passing by the church, Nwoye returned home.

It was well known among the people of Mbanta that their gods and ancestors were sometimes long-suffering and would deliberately allow a man to go on defying them. But even in such cases they set their limit at seven market weeks or twenty-eight days. Beyond that limit no man was suffered to go. And so excitement mounted in the village as the seventh week approached since the impudent missionaries built their church in the Evil Forest. The villagers were so certain about the doom that awaited these men that one or two converts thought it wise to suspend their allegiance to the new faith.

At last the day came by which all the missionaries should have died. But they were still alive, building a new red-earth and thatch house for their teacher, Mr. Kiaga. That week they won a handful more converts. And for the first time they had a woman. Her name was Nneka, the wife of Amadi, who was a prosperous farmer. She was very heavy with child.

Nneka had had four previous pregnancies and childbirths. But each time she had borne twins, and they had been immediately thrown away. Her husband and his family were already becoming highly critical of such a woman and were not unduly perturbed when they found she had fled to join the Christians. It was a good riddance.

One morning Okonkwo's cousin, Amikwu, was passing by the church on his way from the neighbouring village, when he saw Nwoye among the Christians. He was greatly surprised, and when he got home he went straight to Okonkwo's hut and told him what he had seen. The women began to talk excitedly, but Okonkwo sat unmoved.

It was late afternoon before Nwoye returned. He went into the *obi* and saluted his father, but he did not answer. Nwoye turned round to walk into the inner compound when his father, suddenly overcome with fury, sprang to his feet and gripped him by the neck.

"Where have you been?" he stammered.

Nwoye struggled to free himself from the choking grip.

"Answer me," roared Okonkwo, "before I kill you!" He seized a heavy stick that lay on the dwarf wall and hit him two or three savage blows.

"Answer me!" he roared again. Nwoye stood looking at him and did not say a word. The women were screaming outside, afraid to go in.

"Leave that boy at once!" said a voice in the outer compound. It was Okonkwo's uncle Uchendu. "Are you mad?"

Okonkwo did not answer. But he left hold of Nwoye, who walked away and never returned.

He went back to the church and told Mr. Kiaga that he had decided to go to Umuofia, where the white missionary had set up a school to teach young Christians to read and write.

Mr. Kiaga's joy was very great. "Blessed is he who forsakes his father and his mother for my sake," he intoned. "Those that hear my words are my father and my mother."

Nwoye did not fully understand. But he was happy to leave his father. He would return later to his mother and his brothers and sisters and convert them to the new faith.

As Okonkwo sat in his hut that night, gazing into a log fire, he thought over the matter. A sudden fury rose within him and he felt a strong desire to take up his matchet, go to the church and wipe out the entire vile and miscreant gang. But on further thought he told himself that Nwoye was not worth fighting for. Why, he cried in his heart, should he, Okonkwo, of all people be cursed with such a son? He saw clearly in it the finger of his personal god or *chi.* For how else could he explain his great misfortune and exile and now his despicable son's behaviour? Now that he had time to think of it, his son's crime stood out in stark enormity. To abandon the gods of one's father and go about with a lot of effeminate men clucking like old hens was the very depth of abomination. Suppose when he died all his male children decided to follow Nwoye's steps and abandon their ancestors? Okonkwo felt a cold shudder run through him at the terrible prospect, like the prospect of annihilation. He saw himself and his father crowding round their ancestral shrine waiting in vain for worship and sacrifice and finding nothing but ashes of bygone days, and his children the while praying to the white man's god. If such a thing were ever to happen, he, Okonkwo, would wipe them off the face of the earth.

Okonkwo was popularly called the "Roaring Flame." As he looked into the log fire he recalled the name. He was a flaming fire. How then could he have begotten a son like Nwoye, degenerate and effeminate? Perhaps he was not his son. No! he could not be. His wife had played him false. He would teach her! But Nwoye resembled his grandfather, Unoka, who was Okonkwo's father. He pushed the thought out of his mind. He, Okonkwo, was called a flaming fire. How could he have begotten a woman for a son? At Nwoye's age Okonkwo had already become famous throughout Umuofia for his wrestling and his fearlessness.

He sighed heavily, and as if in sympathy the smouldering log also sighed. And immediately Okonkwo's eyes were opened and he saw the whole matter clearly. Living fire begets cold, impotent ash. He sighed again, deeply.

Chapter 18

The young church in Mbanta had a few crises early in its life. At first the clan had assumed that it would not survive. But it had gone on living and gradually becoming stronger. The clan was worried, but not overmuch. If a gang of *efulefu* decided to live in the Evil Forest it was their own affair. When one came to think of it, the Evil Forest was a fit home for such undesirable people. It was true they were rescuing twins from the bush, but they never brought them into the village. As far as the villagers were concerned, the twins still remained where they had been thrown away. Surely the earth goddess would not visit the sins of the missionaries on the innocent villagers?

But on one occasion the missionaries had tried to overstep the bounds. Three converts had gone into the village and boasted openly that all the gods were dead and impotent and that they were prepared to defy them by burning all their shrines.

"Go and burn your mothers' genitals," said one of the priests. The men were seized and beaten until they streamed with blood. After that nothing happened for a long time between the church and the clan.

But stories were already gaining ground that the white man had not only brought a religion but also a government. It was said that they had built a place of judgement in Umuofia to protect the followers of their religion. It was even said that they had hanged one man who killed a missionary.

Although such stories were now often told they looked like fairy-tales in Mbanta and did not as yet affect the relationship between the new church and the clan. There was no question of killing a missionary here, for Mr. Kiaga, despite his madness, was quite harmless. As for his converts, no one could kill them without having to flee from the clan, for in spite of their worthlessness they still belonged to the clan. And so nobody gave serious thought to the stories about the white man's government or the consequences of killing the Christians. If they became more troublesome than they already were they would simply be driven out of the clan.

And the little church was at that moment too deeply absorbed in its own troubles to annoy the clan. It all began over the question of admitting outcasts.

These outcasts, or *osu,* seeing that the new religion welcomed twins and such abominations, thought that it was possible that they would also be received. And so one Sunday two of them went into the church. There was an immediate stir; but so great was the work the new religion had done among the converts that they did not immediately leave the church when the outcasts came in. Those who found themselves nearest to them merely moved to another seat. It was a miracle. But it only lasted till the end of the service. The whole church raised a protest and were about to drive these people out, when Mr. Kiaga stopped them and began to explain.

"Before God," he said, "there is no slave or free. We are all children of God and we must receive these our brothers."

"You do not understand," said one of the converts. "What will the heathen say of us when they hear that we receive *osu* into our midst? They will laugh."

"Let them laugh," said Mr. Kiaga. "God will laugh at them on the judgment day. Why do the nations rage and the peoples imagine a vain thing? He that sitteth in the heavens shall laugh. The Lord shall have them in derision."

"You do not understand," the convert maintained. "You are our teacher, and you can teach us the things of the new faith. But this is a matter which we know." And he told him what an *osu* was.

He was a person dedicated to a god, a thing set apart—a taboo for ever, and his children after him. He could neither marry nor be married by the free-born. He was in fact an outcast, living in a special area of the village, close to the Great Shrine. Wherever he went he carried with him the mark of his forbidden caste—long, tangled and dirty hair. A razor was taboo to him. An *osu* could not attend an assembly of the free-born, and they, in turn, could not shelter under his roof. He could not take any of the four titles of the clan, and when he died he was buried by his kind in the Evil Forest. How could such a man be a follower of Christ?

"He needs Christ more than you and I," said Mr. Kiaga.

"Then I shall go back to the clan," said the convert. And he went. Mr. Kiaga stood firm, and it was his firmness that saved the young church. The wavering converts drew inspiration and confidence from his unshakable faith. He ordered the outcasts to shave off their long, tangled hair. At first they were afraid they might die.

"Unless you shave off the mark of your heathen belief I will not admit you into the church," said Mr. Kiaga. "You fear that you will die. Why should that be? How are you different from other men who shave their hair? The same God created you and them. But they have cast you out like lepers. It is against the will of God, who has promised everlasting life to all who believe in His holy name. The heathen say you will die if you do this or that, and you are afraid. They also said I would die if I built my church on this ground. Am I dead? They said I would die if I took care of twins. I am still alive. The heathen speak nothing but falsehood. Only the word of our God is true."

The two outcasts shaved off their hair, and soon they were among the strongest adherents of the new faith. And what was more, nearly all the *osu* in Mbanta followed their example. It was in fact one of them who in his zeal brought the church into serious conflict with the clan a year later by killing the sacred python, the emanation of the god of water.

The royal python was the most revered animal in Mbanta and all the surrounding clans. It was addressed as "Our Father," and was allowed to go wherever it chose, even into people's beds. It ate rats in the house and sometimes swallowed hens' eggs. If a clansman killed a royal python accidentally, he made sacrifices of atonement and performed an expensive burial ceremony such as was done for a great man. No punishment was prescribed for a man who killed the python knowingly. Nobody thought that such a thing could ever happen.

Perhaps it never did happen. That was the way the clan at first looked at it. No one had actually seen the man do it. The story had arisen among the Christians themselves.

But, all the same, the rulers and elders of Mbanta assembled to decide on their action. Many of them spoke at great length and in fury. The spirit of war was upon them. Okonkwo, who had begun to play a part in the affairs of his motherland, said that until the abominable gang was chased out of the village with whips there would be no peace.

But there were many others who saw the situation differently, and it was their counsel that prevailed in the end.

"It is not our custom to fight for our gods," said one of them. "Let us not presume to do so now. If a man kills the sacred python in the secrecy of his hut, the matter lies between him and the god. We did not see it. If we put ourselves between the god and his victim we may receive blows intended for the offender. When a man blasphemes what do we do? Do we go and stop his mouth? No. We put our fingers into our ears to stop us hearing. That is a wise action."

"Let us not reason like cowards," said Okonkwo. "If a man comes into my hut and defaecates on the floor, what do I do? Do I shut my eyes? No! I take a stick and break his head. That is what a man does. These people are daily pouring filth over us, and Okeke says we should pretend not to see." Okonkwo made a sound full of disgust. This was a womanly clan, he thought. Such a thing could never happen in his fatherland, Umuofia.

"Okonkwo has spoken the truth," said another man. "We should do something. But let us ostracise these men. We would then not be held accountable for their abominations."

Everybody in the assembly spoke, and in the end it was decided to ostracise the Christians. Okonkwo ground his teeth in disgust.

That night a bell-man went through the length and breadth of Mbanta proclaiming that the adherents of the new faith were thenceforth excluded from the life and privileges of the clan.

The Christians had grown in number and were now a small community of men, women and children, self-assured and confident. Mr. Brown, the white missionary, paid regular visits to them. "When I think that it is only eighteen months since the Seed was first sown among you," he said, "I marvel at what the Lord hath wrought."

It was Wednesday in Holy week and Mr. Kiaga had asked the women to bring red earth and white chalk and water to scrub the church for Easter, and the women had formed themselves into three groups for this purpose. They set out early that morning, some of them with their water-pots to the stream, another group with hoes and baskets to the village red-earth pit, and the others to the chalk quarry.

Mr. Kiaga was praying in the church when he heard the women talking excitedly. He rounded off his prayer and went to see what it was all about. The women had come to the church with empty water-pots. They said that some young men had chased them away from the stream with whips. Soon after, the women who had gone for red earth returned with empty baskets. Some of them had been heavily whipped. The chalk women also returned to tell a similar story.

"What does it all mean?" asked Mr. Kiaga, who was greatly perplexed.

"The village has outlawed us," said one of the women. "The bell-man announced it last night. But it is not our custom to debar anyone from the stream or the quarry."

Another woman said, "They want to ruin us. They will not allow us into the markets. They have said so."

Mr. Kiaga was going to send into the village for his men-converts when he saw them coming on their own. Of course they had all heard the bell-man, but they had never in all their lives heard of women being debarred from the stream.

"Come along," they said to the women. "We will go with you to meet those cowards." Some of them had big sticks and some even matchets.

But Mr. Kiaga restrained them. He wanted first to know why they had been outlawed.

"They say that Okoli killed the sacred python," said one man.

"It is false," said another. "Okoli told me himself that it was false."

Okoli was not there to answer. He had fallen ill on the previous night. Before the day was over he was dead. His death showed that the gods were still able to fight their own battles. The clan saw no reason then for molesting the Christians.

Chapter 19

The last big rains of the year were falling. It was the time for treading red earth with which to build walls. It was not done earlier because the rains were too heavy and would have washed away the heap of trodden earth; and it could not be done later because harvesting would soon set in, and after that the dry season.

It was going to be Okonkwo's last harvest in Mbanta. The seven wasted and weary years were at last dragging to a close. Although he had prospered in his motherland Okonkwo knew that he would have prospered even more in Umuofia, in the land of his fathers where men were bold and warlike. In these seven years he would have climbed to the utmost heights. And so he regretted every day of his exile. His mother's kinsmen had been very kind to him, and he was grateful. But that did not alter the facts. He had called the first child born to him in exile Nneka—"Mother is Supreme"—out of politeness to his mother's kinsmen. But two years later when a son was born he called him Nwofia—"Begotten in the Wilderness."

As soon as he entered his last year in exile Okonkwo sent money to Obierika to build him two huts in his old compound where he and his family would live until he built more huts and the outside wall of his compound. He could not ask another man to build his own *obi* for him, nor the walls of his compound. Those things a man built for himself or inherited from his father.

As the last heavy rains of the year began to fall, Obierika sent word that the two huts had been built and Okonkwo began to prepare for his return, after the rains. He would have liked to return earlier and build his compound that year before the rains stopped, but in doing so he would have taken something from the full penalty of seven years. And that could not be. So he waited impatiently for the dry season to come.

It came slowly. The rain became lighter and lighter until it fell in slanting showers. Sometimes the sun shone through the rain and a light breeze blew. It was a gay and airy kind of rain. The rainbow began to appear, and sometimes two rainbows, like a mother and her daughter, the one young and beautiful, and the other an old and faint shadow. The rainbow was called the python of the sky.

Okonkwo called his three wives and told them to get things together for a great feast. "I must thank my mother's kinsmen before I go," he said.

Ekwefi still had some cassava left on her farm from the previous year. Neither of the other wives had. It was not that they had been lazy, but that they had many children to feed. It was therefore understood that Ekwefi would provide cassava for the feast. Nwoye's mother and Ojiugo would provide the other things like smoked fish, palm-oil and pepper for the soup. Okonkwo would take care of meat and yams.

Ekwefi rose early on the following morning and went to her farm with her daughter, Ezinma, and Ojiugo's daughter, Obiageli, to harvest cassava tubers. Each of them carried a long cane basket, a matchet for cutting down the soft cassava stem, and a little hoe for digging out the tuber. Fortunately, a light rain had fallen during the night and the soil would not be very hard.

"It will not take us long to harvest as much as we like," said Ekwefi.

"But the leaves will be wet," said Ezinma. Her basket was balanced on her head, and her arms folded across her breasts. She felt cold. "I dislike cold water dropping on my back. We should have waited for the sun to rise and dry the leaves."

Obiageli called her 'Salt' because she said that she disliked water. "Are you afraid you may dissolve?"

The harvesting was easy, as Ekwefi had said. Ezinma shook every tree violently with a long stick before she bent down to cut the stem and dig out the tuber. Sometimes it was not necessary to dig. They just pulled the stump and earth rose, roots snapped below, and the tuber was pulled out.

When they had harvested a sizeable heap they carried it down in two trips to the steam, where every woman had a shallow well for fermenting her cassava.

"It should be ready in four days or even three," said Obiageli. "They are young tubers."

"They are not all that young," said Ekwefi. "I planted the farm nearly two years ago. It is a poor soil and that is why the tubers are so small."

Okonkwo never did things by halves. When his wife Ekwefi protested that two goats were sufficient for the feast he told her that it was not her affair.

"I am calling a feast because I have the wherewithal. I cannot live on the bank of a river and wash my hands with spittle. My mother's people have been good to me and I must show my gratitude."

And so three goats were slaughtered and a number of fowls. It was like a wedding feast. There was foo-foo and yam pottage, egusi[2] soup and bitter-leaf soup and pots and pots of palm-wine.

All the *umunna* were invited to the feast, all the descendants of Okolo, who had lived about two hundred years before. The oldest member of this extensive family was Okonkwo's uncle, Uchendu. The kola nut was given to him to break, and he prayed to the ancestors. He asked them for health and children. "We do not ask for wealth because he that has health and children will also have wealth. We do not pray to have more money but to have more kinsmen. We are better than animals because we have kinsmen. An animal rubs its aching flank against a tree, a man asks his kinsman to scratch him." He prayed especially for Okonkwo and his family. He then broke the kola nut and threw one of the lobes on the ground for the ancestors.

As the broken kola nuts were passed round, Okonkwo's wives and children and those who came to help them with the cooking began to bring out the food. His sons brought out the pots of palm-wine. There was so much food and drink that many kinsmen whistled in surprise. When all was laid out, Okonkwo rose to speak.

"I beg you to accept this little kola," he said. "It is not to pay you back for all you did for me in these seven years. A child cannot pay for its mother's milk. I have only called you together because it is good for kinsmen to meet."

Yam pottage was served first because it was lighter than foo-foo and because yam always came first. Then the foo-foo was served. Some kinsmen ate it with egusi soup

2. Melon seed.

and others with bitter-leaf soup. The meat was then shared so that every member of the *umunna* had a portion. Every man rose in order of years and took a share. Even the few kinsmen who had not been able to come had their shares taken out for them in due turn.

As the palm-wine was drunk one of the oldest members of the *umunna* rose to thank Okonkwo:

"If I say that we did not expect such a big feast I will be suggesting that we did not know how open-handed our son, Okonkwo is. We all know him, and we expected a big feast. But it turned out to be even bigger than we expected. Thank you. May all you took out return again tenfold. It is good in these days when the younger generation consider themselves wiser than their sires to see a man doing things in the grand, old way. A man who calls his kinsmen to a feast does not do so to save them from starving. They all have food in their own homes. When we gather together in the moonlit village ground it is not because of the moon. Every man can see it in his own compound. We come together because it is good for kinsmen to do so. You may ask why I am saying all this. I say it because I fear for the younger generation, for you people." He waved his arm where most of the young men sat. "As for me, I have only a short while to live, and so have Uchendu and Unachukwu and Emefo. But I fear for you young people because you do not understand how strong is the bond of kinship. You do not know what it is to speak with one voice. And what is the result? An abominable religion has settled among you. A man can now leave his father and his brothers. He can curse the gods of his fathers and his ancestors, like a hunter's dog that suddenly goes mad and turns on his master. I fear for you; I fear for the clan." He turned again to Okonkwo and said, "Thank you for calling us together."

Part 3

Chapter 20

Seven years was a long time to be away from one's clan. A man's place was not always there, waiting for him. As soon as he left, someone else rose and filled it. The clan was like a lizard; if it lost its tail it soon grew another.

Okonkwo knew these things. He knew that he had lost his place among the nine masked spirits who administered justice in the clan. He had lost the chance to lead his warlike clan against the new religion, which, he was told, had gained ground. He had lost the years in which he might have taken the highest titles in the clan. But some of these losses were not irreparable. He was determined that his return should be marked by his people. He would return with a flourish, and regain the seven wasted years.

Even in his first year in exile he had begun to plan for his return. The first thing he would do would be to rebuild his compound on a more magnificent scale. He would build a bigger barn than he had before and he would build huts for two new wives. Then he would show his wealth by initiating his sons in the *ozo* society. Only the really great men in the clan were able to do this. Okonkwo saw clearly the high esteem in which he would be held, and he saw himself taking the highest title in the land.

As the years of exile passed one by one it seemed to him that his *chi* might now be making amends for the past disaster. His yams grew abundantly, not only in his motherland but also in Umuofia, where his friend gave them out year by year to share-croppers.

Then the tragedy of his first son had occurred. At first it appeared as if it might prove too great for his spirit. But it was a resilient spirit, and in the end Okonkwo overcame his sorrow. He had five other sons and he would bring them up in the way of the clan.

He sent for the five sons and they came and sat in his *obi*. The youngest of them was four years old.

"You have all seen the great abomination of your brother. Now he is no longer my son or your brother. I will only have a son who is a man, who will hold his head up among my people. If any one of you prefers to be a woman, let him follow Nwoye now while I am alive so that I can curse him. If you turn against me when I am dead I will visit you and break your neck."

Okonkwo was very lucky in his daughters. He never stopped regretting that Ezinma was a girl. Of all his children she alone understood his every mood. A bond of sympathy had grown between them as the years had passed.

Ezinma grew up in her father's exile and became one of the most beautiful girls in Mbanta. She was called Crystal of Beauty, as her mother had been called in her youth. The young ailing girl who had caused her mother so much heartache had been transformed, almost overnight, into a healthy, buoyant maiden. She had, it was true, her moments of depression when she would snap at everybody like an angry dog. These moods descended on her suddenly and for no apparent reason. But they were very rare and short-lived. As long as they lasted, she could bear no other person but her father.

Many young men and prosperous middle-aged men of Mbanta came to marry her. But she refused them all, because her father had called her one evening and said to her: "There are many good and prosperous people here, but I shall be happy if you marry in Umuofia when we return home."

That was all he had said. But Ezinma had seen clearly all the thought and hidden meaning behind the few words. And she had agreed.

"Your half-sister, Obiageli, will not understand me," Okonkwo said. "But you can explain to her."

Although they were almost the same age. Ezinma wielded a strong influence over her half-sister. She explained to her why they should not marry yet, and she agreed also. And so the two of them refused every offer of marriage in Mbanta.

"I wish she were a boy," Okonkwo thought within himself. She understood things so perfectly. Who else among his children could have read his thought so well? With two beautiful grown-up daughters his return to Umuofia would attract considerable attention. His future sons-in-law would be men of authority in the clan. The poor and unknown would not dare to come forth.

Umuofia had indeed changed during the seven years Okonkwo had been in exile. The church had come and led many astray. Not only the low-born and the outcast but sometimes a worthy man had joined it. Such a man was Ogbuefi Ugonna,[1] who had taken two titles, and who like a madman had cut the anklet of his titles and cast it away to join the Christians. The white missionary was very proud of him and he was one of the first men in Umuofia to receive the sacrament of Holy Communion, or Holy Feast as it was called in Ibo. Ogbuefi Ugonna had thought of the Feast in terms of eating and drinking, only more holy than the village variety. He had therefore put his drinking-horn into his goatskin bag for the occasion.

But apart from the church, the white men had also brought a government. They had built a court where the District Commissioner judged cases in ignorance. He had

1. Father's honor, lit. "with an eagle feather."

court messengers who brought men to him for trial. Many of these messengers came from Umuru on the bank of the Great River, where the white men first came many years before and where they had built the centre of their religion and trade and government. These court messengers were greatly hated in Umuofia because they were foreigners and also arrogant and high-handed. They were called *kotma,* and because of their ash-coloured shorts they earned the additional name of Ashy-Buttocks. They guarded the prison, which was full of men who had offended against the white man's law. Some of these prisoners had thrown away their twins and some had molested the Christians. They were beaten in the prison by the *kotma* and made to work every morning clearing the government compound and fetching wood for the white Commissioner and the court messengers. Some of these prisoners were men of title who should be above such mean occupation. They were grieved by the indignity and mourned for their neglected farms. As they cut grass in the morning the younger men sang in time with the strokes of their matchets:

> Kotma *of the ash buttocks,*
> *He is fit to be a slave*
> *The white man has no sense,*
> *He is fit to be a slave*

The court messengers did not like to be called Ashy-Buttocks, and they beat the men. But the song spread in Umuofia.

Okonkwo's head was bowed in sadness as Obierika told him these things.

"Perhaps I have been away too long," Okonkwo said, almost to himself. "But I cannot understand these things you tell me. What is it that has happened to our people? Why have they lost the power to fight?"

"Have you not heard how the white man wiped out Abame?" asked Obierika.

"I have heard," said Okonkwo. "But I have also heard that Abame people were weak and foolish. Why did they not fight back? Had they no guns and matchets? We would be cowards to compare ourselves with the men of Abame. Their fathers had never dared to stand before our ancestors. We must fight these men and drive them from the land."

"It is already too late," said Obierika sadly. "Our own men and our sons have joined the ranks of the stranger. They have joined his religion and they help to uphold his government. If we should try to drive out the white men in Umuofia we should find it easy. There are only two of them. But what of our own people who are following their way and have been given power? They would go to Umuru and bring the soldiers, and we would be like Abame." He paused for a long time and then said: "I told you on my last visit to Mbanta how they hanged Aneto."

"What has happened to that piece of land in dispute?" asked Okonkwo.

"The white man's court has decided that it should belong to Nnama's family, who had given much money to the white man's messengers and interpreter."

"Does the white man understand our custom about land?"

"How can he when he does not even speak our tongue? But he says that our customs are bad; and our own brothers who have taken up his religion also say that our customs are bad. How do you think we can fight when our own brothers have turned against us? The white man is very clever. He came quietly and peaceably with his religion. We were amused at his foolishness and allowed him to stay. Now he has won our brothers, and our clan can no longer act like one. He has put a knife on the things that held us together and we have fallen apart."

"How did they get hold of Aneto to hang him?" asked Okonkwo.

"When he killed Oduche in the fight over the land, he fled to Aninta to escape the wrath of the earth. This was about eight days after the fight, because Oduche had not died immediately from his wounds. It was on the seventh day that he died. But everybody knew that he was going to die and Aneto got his belongings together in readiness to flee. But the Christians had told the white man about the accident, and he sent his *kotma* to catch Aneto. He was imprisoned with all the leaders of his family. In the end Oduche died and Aneto was taken to Umuru and hanged. The other people were released, but even now they have not found the mouth with which to tell of their suffering."

The two men sat in silence for a long while afterwards.

Chapter 21

There were many men and women in Umuofia who did not feel as strongly as Okonkwo about the new dispensation. The white man had indeed brought a lunatic religion, but he had also built a trading store and for the first time palm-oil and kernel became things of great price, and much money flowed into Umuofia.

And even in the matter of religion there was a growing feeling that there might be something in it after all, something vaguely akin to method in the overwhelming madness.

This growing feeling was due to Mr. Brown, the white missionary, who was very firm in restraining his flock from provoking the wrath of the clan. One member in particular was very difficult to restrain. His name was Enoch and his father was the priest of the snake cult. The story went around that Enoch had killed and eaten the sacred python, and that his father had cursed him.

Mr. Brown preached against such excess of zeal. Everything was possible, he told his energetic flock, but everything was not expedient. And so Mr. Brown came to be respected even by the clan, because he trod softly on its faith. He made friends with some of the great men of the clan and on one of his frequent visits to the neighbouring villages he had been presented with a carved elephant tusk, which was a sign of dignity and rank. One of the great men in that village was called Akunna and he had given one of his sons to be taught the white man's knowledge in Mr. Brown's school.

Whenever Mr. Brown went to that village he spent long hours with Akunna in his *obi* talking through an interpreter about religion. Neither of them succeeded in converting the other but they learnt more about their different beliefs.

"You say that there is one supreme God who made heaven and earth," said Akunna on one of Mr. Brown's visits. "We also believe in Him and call Him Chukwu. He made all the world and the other gods."

"There are no other gods," said Mr. Brown. "Chukwu is the only God and all others are false. You carve a piece of wood—like that one" (he pointed at the rafters from which Akunna's carved *Ikenga* hung), "and you call it a god. But it is still a piece of wood."

"Yes," said Akunna. "It is indeed a piece of wood. The tree from which it came was made by Chukwu, as indeed all minor gods were. But He made them for His messengers so that we could approach Him through them. It is like yourself. You are the head of your church."

"No," protested Mr. Brown. "The head of my church is God Himself."

"I know," said Akunna, "but there must be a head in this world among men. Somebody like yourself must be the head here."

"The head of my church in that sense is in England."

"That is exactly what I am saying. The head of your church is in your country. He has sent you here as his messenger. And you have also appointed your own messengers and servants. Or let me take another example, the District Commissioner. He is sent by your king."

"They have a queen," said the interpreter on his own account.

"Your queen sends her messenger, the District Commissioner. He finds that he cannot do the work alone and so he appoints *kotma* to help him. It is the same with God, or Chukwu. He appoints the smaller gods to help Him because His work is too great for one person."

"You should not think of him as a person," said Mr. Brown. "It is because you do so that you imagine He must need helpers. And the worst thing about it is that you give all the worship to the false gods you have created."

"That is not so. We make sacrifices to the little gods, but when they fail and there is no one else to turn to we go to Chukwu. It is right to do so. We approach a great man through his servants. But when his servants fail to help us, then we go to the last source of hope. We appear to pay greater attention to the little gods but that is not so. We worry them more because we are afraid to worry their Master. Our fathers knew that Chukwu was the Overlord and that is why many of them gave their children the name Chukwuka—'Chukwu is Supreme.'"

"You said one interesting thing," said Mr. Brown. "You are afraid of Chukwu. In my religion Chukwu is a loving Father and need not be feared by those who do His will."

"But we must fear Him when we are not doing His will," said Akunna. "And who is to tell His will? It is too great to be known."

In this way Mr. Brown learnt a good deal about the religion of the clan and he came to the conclusion that a frontal attack on it would not succeed. And so he built a school and a little hospital in Umuofia. He went from family to family begging people to send their children to his school. But at first they only sent their slaves or sometimes their lazy children. Mr. Brown begged and argued and prophesied. He said that the leaders of the land in the future would be men and women who had learnt to read and write. If Umuofia failed to send her children to the school, strangers would come from other places to rule them. They could already see that happening in the Native Court, where the D. C. was surrounded by strangers who spoke his tongue. Most of these strangers came from the distant town of Umuru on the bank of the Great River where the white man first went.

In the end Mr. Brown's arguments began to have an effect. More people came to learn in his school, and he encouraged them with gifts of singlets[2] and towels. They were not all young, these people who came to learn. Some of them were thirty years old or more. They worked on their farms in the morning and went to school in the afternoon. And it was not long before the people began to say that the white man's medicine was quick in working. Mr. Brown's school produced quick results. A few months in it were enough to make one a court messenger or even a court clerk. Those who stayed longer became teachers; and from Umuofia labourers went forth into the Lord's vineyard. New churches were established in the surrounding villages and a few schools with them. From the very beginning religion and education went hand in hand.

Mr. Brown's mission grew from strength to strength, and because of its link with the new administration it earned a new social prestige. But Mr. Brown himself was breaking down in health. At first he ignored the warning signs. But in the end he had to leave his flock, sad and broken.

2. T-shirts.

It was in the first rainy season after Okonkwo's return to Umuofia that Mr. Brown left for home. As soon as he had learnt of Okonkwo's return five months earlier, the missionary had immediately paid him a visit. He had just sent Okonkwo's son, Nwoye, who was now called Isaac,[3] to the new training college for teachers in Umuru. And he had hoped that Okonkwo would be happy to hear of it. But Okonkwo had driven him away with the threat that if he came into his compound again, he would be carried out of it.

Okonkwo's return to his native land was not as memorable as he had wished. It was true his two beautiful daughters aroused great interest among suitors and marriage negotiations were soon in progress, but, beyond that, Umuofia did not appear to have taken any special notice of the warrior's return. The clan had undergone such profound change during his exile that it was barely recognizable. The new religion and government and the trading stores were very much in the people's eyes and minds. There were still many who saw these new institutions as evil, but even they talked and thought about little else, and certainly not about Okonkwo's return.

And it was the wrong year too. If Okonkwo had immediately initiated his two sons into the *ozo* society as he had planned he would have caused a stir. But the initiation rite was performed once in three years in Umuofia, and he had to wait for nearly two years for the next round of ceremonies.

Okonkwo was deeply grieved. And it was not just a personal grief. He mourned for the clan, which he saw breaking up and falling apart, and he mourned for the warlike men of Umuofia, who had so unaccountably become soft like women.

Chapter 22

Mr. Brown's successor was the Reverend James Smith, and he was a different kind of man. He condemned openly Mr. Brown's policy of compromise and accommodation. He saw things as black and white. And black was evil. He saw the world as a battlefield in which the children of light were locked in mortal conflict with the sons of darkness. He spoke in his sermons about sheep and goats and about wheat and tares. He believed in slaying the prophets of Baal.

Mr. Smith was greatly distressed by the ignorance which many of his flock showed even in such things as the Trinity and the Sacraments. It only showed that they were seeds sown on a rocky soil. Mr. Brown had thought of nothing but numbers. He should have known that the kingdom of God did not depend on large crowds. Our Lord Himself stressed the importance of fewness. Narrow is the way and few the number. To fill the Lord's holy temple with an idolatrous crowd clamouring for signs was a folly of everlasting consequence. Our Lord used the whip only once in His Life—to drive the crowd away from His church.

Within a few weeks of his arrival in Umuofia Mr. Smith suspended a young woman from the church for pouring new wine into old bottles. This woman had allowed her heathen husband to mutilate her dead child. The child had been declared an *ogbanje,* plaguing its mother by dying and entering her womb to be born again. Four times this child had run its evil round. And so it was mutilated to discourage it from returning.

Mr. Smith was filled with wrath when he heard of this. He disbelieved the story which even some of the most faithful confirmed, the story of really evil children who were not deterred by mutilation, but came back with all the scars. He replied that such stories were spread in the world by the Devil to lead men astray. Those who believed such stories were unworthy of the Lord's table.

3. Son of Abraham, Genesis 22.

There was a saying in Umuofia that as a man danced so the drums were beaten for him. Mr. Smith danced a furious step and so the drums went mad. The over-zealous converts who had smarted under Mr. Brown's restraining hand now flourished in full favour. One of them was Enoch, the son of the snake-priest who was believed to have killed and eaten the sacred python. Enoch's devotion to the new faith had seemed so much greater than Mr. Brown's that the villagers called him The Outsider who wept louder than the bereaved.

Enoch was short and slight of build, and always seemed in great haste. His feet were short and broad, and when he stood or walked his heels came together and his feet opened outwards as if they had quarrelled and meant to go in different directions. Such was the excessive energy bottled up in Enoch's small body that it was always erupting in quarrels and fights. On Sundays he always imagined that the sermon was preached for the benefit of his enemies. And if he happened to sit near one of them he would occasionally turn to give him a meaningful look, as if to say, "I told you so." It was Enoch who touched off the great conflict between church and clan in Umuofia which had been gathering since Mr. Brown left.

It happened during the annual ceremony which was held in honour of the earth deity. At such times the ancestors of the clan who had been committed to Mother Earth at their death emerged again as *egwugwu* through tiny ant-holes.

One of the greatest crimes a man could commit was to unmask an *egwugwu* in public, or to say or do anything which might reduce its immortal prestige in the eyes of the uninitiated. And this was what Enoch did.

The annual worship of the earth goddess fell on a Sunday, and the masked spirits were abroad. The Christian women who had been to church could not therefore go home. Some of their men had gone out to beg the *egwugwu* to retire for a short while for the women to pass. They agreed and were already retiring, when Enoch boasted aloud that they would not dare to touch a Christian. Whereupon they all came back and one of them gave Enoch a good stroke of the cane, which was always carried. Enoch fell on him and tore off his mask. The other *egwugwu* immediately surrounded their desecrated companion, to shield him from the profane gaze of women and children, and led him away. Enoch had killed an ancestral spirit, and Umuofia was thrown into confusion.

That night the Mother of the Spirits walked the length and breadth of the clan, weeping for her murdered son. It was a terrible night. Not even the oldest man in Umuofia had ever heard such a strange and fearful sound, and it was never to be heard again. It seemed as if the very soul of the tribe wept for a great evil that was coming—its own death.

On the next day all the masked *egwugwu* of Umuofia assembled in the market-place. They came from all the quarters of the clan and even from the neighbouring villages. The dreadful Otakagu came from Imo, and Ekwensu, dangling a white cock, arrived from Uli. It was a terrible gathering. The eerie voices of countless spirits, the bells that clattered behind some of them, and the clash of matchets as they ran forwards and backwards and saluted one another, sent tremors of fear into every heart. For the first time in living memory the sacred bullroarer was heard in broad daylight.

From the market-place the furious band made for Enoch's compound. Some of the elders of the clan went with them, wearing heavy protections of charms and amulets. These were men whose arms were strong in *ogwu,* or medicine. As for the ordinary men and women, they listened from the safety of their huts.

The leaders of the Christians had met together at Mr. Smith's parsonage on the previous night. As they deliberated they could hear the Mother of Spirits wailing for her son. The chilling sound affected Mr. Smith, and for the first time he seemed to be afraid.

"What are they planning to do?" he asked. No one knew, because such a thing had never happened before. Mr. Smith would have sent for the District Commissioner and his court messengers, but they had gone on tour on the previous day.

"One thing is clear," said Mr. Smith. "We cannot offer physical resistance to them. Our strength lies in the Lord." They knelt down together and prayed to God for delivery.

"O Lord save Thy people," cried Mr. Smith.

"And bless Thine inheritance," replied the men.

They decided that Enoch should be hidden in the parsonage for a day or two. Enoch himself was greatly disappointed when he heard this, for he had hoped that a holy war was imminent; and there were a few other Christians who thought like him. But wisdom prevailed in the camp of the faithful and many lives were thus saved.

The band of *egwugwu* moved like a furious whirlwind to Enoch's compound and with matchet and fire reduced it to a desolate heap. And from there they made for the church, intoxicated with destruction.

Mr. Smith was in his church when he heard the masked spirits coming. He walked quietly to the door which commanded the approach to the church compound, and stood there. But when the first three or four *egwugwu* appeared on the church compound he nearly bolted. He overcame this impulse and instead of running away he went down the two steps that led up to the church and walked towards the approaching spirits.

They surged forward, and a long stretch of the bamboo fence with which the church compound was surrounded gave way before them. Discordant bells clanged, matchets clashed and the air was full of dust and weird sounds. Mr. Smith heard a sound of footsteps behind him. He turned round and saw Okeke, his interpreter. Okeke had not been on the best of terms with his master since he had strongly condemned Enoch's behaviour at the meeting of the leaders of the church during the night. Okeke had gone as far as to say that Enoch should not be hidden in the parsonage, because he would only draw the wrath of the clan on the pastor. Mr. Smith had rebuked him in very strong language, and had not sought his advice that morning. But now, as he came up and stood by him confronting the angry spirits, Mr. Smith looked at him and smiled. It was a wan smile, but there was deep gratitude there.

For a brief moment the onrush of the *egwugwu* was checked by the unexpected composure of the two men. But it was only a momentary check, like the tense silence between blasts of thunder. The second onrush was greater than the first. It swallowed up the two men. Then an unmistakable voice rose above the tumult and there was immediate silence. Space was made around the two men, and Ajofia began to speak.

Ajofia was the leading *egwugwu* of Umuofia. He was the head and spokesman of the nine ancestors who administered justice in the clan. His voice was unmistakable and so he was able to bring immediate peace to the agitated spirits. He then addressed Mr. Smith, and as he spoke clouds of smoke rose from his head.

"The body of the white man, I salute you," he said, using the language in which immortals spoke to men.

"The body of the white man, do you know me?" he asked.

Mr. Smith looked at his interpreter, but Okeke, who was a native of distant Umuru, was also at a loss.

Ajofia laughed in his gutteral voice. It was like the laugh of rusty metal. "They are strangers," he said, "and they are ignorant. But let that pass." He turned round to his comrades and saluted them, calling them the fathers of Umuofia. He dug his rattling spear into the ground and it shook with metallic life. Then he turned once more to the missionary and his interpreter.

"Tell the white man that we will not do him any harm," he said to the interpreter. "Tell him to go back to his house and leave us alone. We liked his brother who was with us before. He was foolish, but we liked him, and for his sake we shall not harm his brother. But this shrine which he built must be destroyed. We shall no longer allow it in our midst. It has bred untold abominations and we have come to put an end to it." He turned to his comrades, "Fathers of Umuofia, I salute you;" and they replied with one gutteral voice. He turned again to the missionary. "You can stay with us if you like our ways. You can worship your own god. It is good that a man should worship the gods and the spirits of his fathers. Go back to your house so that you may not be hurt. Our anger is great but we have held it down so that we can talk to you."

Mr. Smith said to his interpreter: "Tell them to go away from here. This is the house of God and I will not live to see it desecrated."

Okeke interpreted wisely to the spirits and leaders of Umuofia: "The white man says he is happy you have come to him with your grievances, like friends. He will be happy if you leave the matter in his hands."

"We cannot leave the matter in his hands because he does not understand our customs, just as we do not understand his. We say he is foolish because he does not know our ways, and perhaps he says we are foolish because we do not know his. Let him go away."

Mr. Smith stood his ground. But he could not save his church. When the *egwugwu* went away the red-earth church which Mr. Brown had built was a pile of earth and ashes. And for the moment the spirit of the clan was pacified.

Chapter 23

For the first time in many years Okonkwo had a feeling that was akin to happiness. The times which had altered so unaccountably during his exile seemed to be coming round again. The clan which had turned false on him appeared to be making amends.

He had spoken violently to his clansmen when they had met in the market-place to decide on their action. And they had listened to him with respect. It was like the good old days again, when a warrior was a warrior. Although they had not agreed to kill the missionary or drive away the Christians, they had agreed to do something substantial. And they had done it. Okonkwo was almost happy again.

For two days after the destruction of the church, nothing happened. Every man in Umuofia went about armed with a gun or a matchet. They would not be caught unawares, like the men of Abame.

Then the District Commissioner returned from his tour. Mr. Smith went immediately to him and they had a long discussion. The men of Umuofia did not take any notice of this, and if they did, they thought it was not important. The missionary often went to see his brother white man. There was nothing strange in that.

Three days later the District Commissioner sent his sweet-tongued messenger to the leaders of Umuofia asking them to meet him in his headquarters. That also was not strange. He often asked them to hold such palavers, as he called them. Okonkwo was among the six leaders he invited.

Okonkwo warned the others to be fully armed. "An Umuofia man does not refuse a call," he said. "He may refuse to do what he is asked; he does not refuse to be asked. But the times have changed, and we must be fully prepared."

And so the six men went to see the District Commissioner, armed with their matchets. They did not carry guns, for that would be unseemly. They were led into the court-house where the District Commissioner sat. He received them politely. They unslung their goatskin bags and their sheathed matchets, put them on the floor, and sat down.

"I have asked you to come," began the Commissioner, "because of what happened during my absence. I have been told a few things but I cannot believe them until I have heard your own side. Let us talk about it like friends and find a way of ensuring that it does not happen again."

Ogbuefi Ekwueme rose to his feet and began to tell the story.

"Wait a minute," said the Commissioner. "I want to bring in my men so that they too can hear your grievances and take warning. Many of them come from distant places and although they speak your tongue they are ignorant of your customs. James! Go and bring in the men." His interpreter left the court-room and soon returned with twelve men. They sat together with the men of Umuofia, and Ogbuefi Ekwueme began again to tell the story of how Enoch murdered an *egwugwu.*

It happened so quickly that the six men did not see it coming. There was only a brief scuffle, too brief even to allow the drawing of a sheathed matchet. The six men were handcuffed and led into the guardroom.

"We shall not do you any harm," said the District Commissioner to them later, "if only you agree to co-operate with us. We have brought a peaceful administration to you and your people so that you may be happy. If any man ill-treats you we shall come to your rescue. But we will not allow you to ill-treat others. We have a court of law where we judge cases and administer justice just as it is done in my own country under a great queen. I have brought you here because you joined together to molest others, to burn people's houses and their place of worship. That must not happen in the dominion of our queen, the most powerful ruler in the world. I have decided that you will pay a fine of two hundred bags of cowries. You will be released as soon as you agree to this and undertake to collect that fine from your people. What do you say to that?"

The six men remained sullen and silent and the Commissioner left them for a while. He told the court messengers, when he left the guardroom, to treat the men with respect because they were the leaders of Umuofia. They said, "Yes, sir," and saluted.

As soon as the District Commissioner left, the head messenger, who was also the prisoners' barber, took down his razor and shaved off all the hair on the men's heads. They were still handcuffed, and they just sat and moped.

"Who is the chief among you?" the court messenger asked in jest. "We see that every pauper wears the anklet of title in Umuofia. Does it cost as much as ten cowries?"

The six men ate nothing throughout that day and the next. They were not even given any water to drink, and they could not go out to urinate or go into the bush when they were pressed. At night the messengers came in to taunt them and to knock their shaven heads together.

Even when the men were left alone they found no words to speak to one another. It was only on the third day, when they could no longer bear the hunger and the insults, that they began to talk about giving in.

"We should have killed the white man if you had listened to me," Okonkwo snarled.

"We could have been in Umuru now waiting to be hanged," someone said to him.

"Who wants to kill the white man?" asked a messenger who had just rushed in. Nobody spoke.

"You are not satisfied with your crime, but you must kill the white man on top of it." He carried a strong stick, and he hit each man a few blows on the head and back. Okonkwo was choked with hate.

As soon as the six men were locked up, court messengers went into Umuofia to tell the people that their leaders would not be released unless they paid a fine of two hundred and fifty bags of cowries.

"Unless you pay the fine immediately," said their headman, "we will take your leaders to Umuru before the big white man, and hang them."

This story spread quickly through the villages, and was added to as it went. Some said that the men had already been taken to Umuru and would be hanged on the following day. Some said that their families would also be hanged. Others said that soldiers were already on their way to shoot the people of Umuofia as they had done in Abame.

It was the time of the full moon. But that night the voice of children was not heard. The village *ilo* where they always gathered for a moon-play was empty. The women of Iguedo did not meet in their secret enclosure to learn a new dance to be displayed later to the village. Young men who were always abroad in the moonlight kept their huts that night. Their manly voices were not heard on the village paths as they went to visit their friends and lovers. Umuofia was like a startled animal with ears erect, sniffing the silent, ominous air and not knowing which way to run.

The silence was broken by the village crier beating his sonorous *ogene*. He called every man in Umuofia, from the Akakanma age-group upwards, to a meeting in the market-place after the morning meal. He went from one end of the village to the other and walked all its breadth. He did not leave out any of the main footpaths.

Okonkwo's compound was like a deserted homestead. It was as if cold water had been poured on it. His family was all there, but everyone spoke in whispers. His daughter Ezinma had broken her twenty-eight day visit to the family of her future husband, and returned home when she heard that her father had been imprisoned, and was going to be hanged. As soon as she got home she went to Obierika to ask what the men of Umuofia were going to do about it. But Obierika had not been home since morning. His wives thought he had gone to a secret meeting. Ezinma was satisfied that something was being done.

On the morning after the village crier's appeal the men of Umuofia met in the market-place and decided to collect without delay two hundred and fifty bags of cowries to appease the white man. They did not know that fifty bags would go to the court messengers, who had increased the fine for that purpose.

Chapter 24

Okonkwo and his fellow prisoners were set free as soon as the fine was paid. The District Commissioner spoke to them again about the great queen, and about peace and good government. But the men did not listen. They just sat and looked at him and at his interpreter. In the end they were given back their bags and sheathed matchets and told to go home. They rose and left the court-house. They neither spoke to anyone nor among themselves.

The court-house, like the church, was built a little way outside the village. The footpath that linked them was a very busy one because it also led to the stream, beyond the court. It was open and sandy. Footpaths were open and sandy in the dry season. But when the rains came the bush grew thick on either side and closed in on the path. It was now dry season.

As they made their way to the village the six men met women and children going to the stream with their waterpots. But the men wore such heavy and fearsome looks that the women and children did not say "*nno*" or "welcome" to them, but edged out of the way to let them pass. In the village little groups of men joined them until they became a sizeable company. They walked silently. As each of the six men got to his compound, he turned in, taking some of the crowd with him. The village was astir in a silent, suppressed way.

Ezinma had prepared some food for her father as soon as news spread that the six men would be released. She took it to him in his *obi.* He ate absent-mindedly. He had no appetite; he only ate to please her. His male relations and friends had gathered in his *obi,* and Obierika was urging him to eat. Nobody else spoke, but they noticed the long stripes on Okonkwo's back where the warder's whip had cut into his flesh.

The village crier was abroad again in the night. He beat his iron gong and announced that another meeting would be held in the morning. Everyone knew that Umuofia was at last going to speak its mind about the things that were happening.

Okonkwo slept very little that night. The bitterness in his heart was now mixed with a kind of child-like excitement. Before he had gone to bed he had brought down his war dress, which he had not touched since his return from exile. He had shaken out his smoked raffia skirt and examined his tall feather head-gear and his shield. They were all satisfactory, he had thought.

As he lay on his bamboo bed he thought about the treatment he had received in the white man's court, and he swore vengeance. If Umuofia decided on war, all would be well. But if they chose to be cowards he would go out and avenge himself. He thought about wars in the past. The noblest, he thought, was the war against Isike. In those days Okudo was still alive. Okudo sang a war song in a way that no other man could. He was not a fighter, but his voice turned every man into a lion.

"Worthy men are no more," Okonkwo sighed as he remembered those days. "Isike will never forget how we slaughtered them in that war. We killed twelve of their men and they killed only two of ours. Before the end of the fourth market week they were suing for peace. Those were days when men were men."

As he thought of these things he heard the sound of the iron gong in the distance. He listened carefully, and could just hear the crier's voice. But it was very faint. He turned on his bed and his back hurt him. He ground his teeth. The crier was drawing nearer and nearer until he passed by Okonkwo's compound.

"The greatest obstacle in Umuofia," Okonkwo thought bitterly, "is that coward, Egonwanne. His sweet tongue can change fire into cold ash. When he speaks he moves our men to impotence. If they had ignored his womanish wisdom five years ago, we would not have come to this." He ground his teeth. "Tomorrow he will tell them that our fathers never fought a 'war of blame.' If they listen to him I shall leave them and plan my own revenge."

The crier's voice had once more become faint, and the distance had taken the harsh edge off his iron gong. Okonkwo turned from one side to the other and derived a kind of pleasure from the pain his back gave him. "Let Egonwanne talk about a 'war of blame' tomorrow and I shall show him my back and head." He ground his teeth.

The market-place began to fill as soon as the sun rose. Obierika was waiting in his *obi* when Okonkwo came along and called him. He hung his goatskin bag and his sheathed matchet on his shoulder and went out to join him. Obierika's hut was close to the road and he saw every man who passed to the market-place. He had exchanged greetings with many who had already passed that morning.

When Okonkwo and Obierika got to the meeting-place there were already so many people that if one threw up a grain of sand it would not find its way to the earth again. And many more people were coming from every quarter of the nine villages. It warmed Okonkwo's heart to see such strength of numbers. But he was looking for one man in particular, the man whose tongue he dreaded and despised so much.

"Can you see him?" he asked Obierika.

"Who?"

"Egonwanne," he said, his eyes roving from one corner of the huge market-place to the other. Most of the men were seated on goatskins on the ground. A few of them sat on wooden stools they had brought with them.

"No," said Obierika, casting his eyes over the crowd. "Yes, there he is, under the silk-cotton tree. Are you afraid he would convince us not to fight?"

"Afraid? I do not care what he does to *you*. I despise him and those who listen to him. I shall fight alone if I choose."

They spoke at the top of their voices because everybody was talking, and it was like the sound of a great market.

"I shall wait till he has spoken," Okonkwo thought. "Then I shall speak."

"But how do you know he will speak against war?" Obierika asked after a while.

"Because I know he is a coward," said Okonkwo. Obierika did not hear the rest of what he said because at that moment somebody touched his shoulder from behind and he turned round to shake hands and exchange greetings with five or six friends. Okonkwo did not turn around even though he knew the voices. He was in no mood to exchange greetings. But one of the men touched him and asked about the people of his compound.

"They are well," he replied without interest.

The first man to speak to Umuofia that morning was Okika, one of the six who had been imprisoned. Okika was a great man and an orator. But he did not have the booming voice which a first speaker must use to establish silence in the assembly of the clan. Onyeka had such a voice; and so he was asked to salute Umuofia before Okika began to speak.

"*Umuofia kwenu!*" he bellowed, raising his left arm and pushing the air with his open hand.

"*Yaa!*" roared Umuofia.

"*Umuofia kwenu!*" he bellowed again, and again and again, facing a new direction each time. And the crowd answered, "*Yaa!*"

There was immediate silence as though cold water had been poured on a roaring flame.

Okika sprang to his feet and also saluted his clansmen four times. Then he began to speak:

"You all know why we are here, when we ought to be building our barns or mending our huts, when we should be putting our compounds in order. My father used to say to me: 'Whenever you see a toad jumping in broad daylight, then know that something is after its life.' When I saw you all pouring into this meeting from all the quarters of our clan so early in the morning, I knew that something was after our life." He paused for a brief moment and then began again:

"All our gods are weeping. Idemili is weeping. Ogwugwu is weeping. Agbala is weeping, and all the others. Our dead fathers are weeping because of the shameful sacrilege they are suffering and the abomination we have all seen with our eyes." He stopped again to steady his trembling voice.

"This is a great gathering. No clan can boast of greater numbers or greater valour. But are we all here? I ask you: Are all the sons of Umuofia with us here?" A deep murmur swept through the crowd.

"They are not," he said. "They have broken the clan and gone their several ways. We who are here this morning have remained true to our fathers, but our brothers have deserted us and joined a stranger to soil their fatherland. If we fight the stranger we shall hit our brothers and perhaps shed the blood of a clansman. But we must do it. Our fathers never dreamt of such a thing, they never killed their brothers. But a white man never came to them. So we must do what our fathers would never have done. Eneke the bird was asked why he was always on the wing and he replied: 'Men have learnt to shoot without missing their mark and I have learnt to fly without perching on a twig.' We must root out this evil. And if our brothers take the side of evil we must root them out too. And we must do it *now.* We must bale this water now that it is only ankle-deep . . ."

At this point here was a sudden stir in the crowd and every eye was turned in one direction. There was a sharp bend in the road that led from the market-place to the white man's court, and to the stream beyond it. And so no one had seen the approach of the five court messengers until they had come round the bend, a few paces from the edge of the crowd. Okonkwo was sitting at the edge.

He sprang to his feet as soon as he saw who it was. He confronted the head messenger, trembling with hate, unable to utter a word. The man was fearless and stood his ground, his four men lined up behind him.

In that brief moment the world seemed to stand still, waiting. There was utter silence. The men of Umuofia were merged into the mute backcloth of trees and giant creepers, waiting.

The spell was broken by the head messenger. "Let me pass!" he ordered.

"What do you want here?"

"The white man whose power you know too well has ordered this meeting to stop."

In a flash Okonkwo drew his matchet. The messenger crouched to avoid the blow. It was useless. Okonkwo's matchet descended twice and the man's head lay beside his uniformed body.

The waiting backcloth jumped into tumultuous life and the meeting was stopped. Okonkwo stood looking at the dead man. He knew that Umuofia would not go to war. He knew because they had let the other messengers escape. They had broken into tumult instead of action. He discerned fright in that tumult. He heard voices asking: "Why did he do it?"

He wiped his matchet on the sand and went away.

Chapter 25

When the District Commissioner arrived at Okonkwo's compound at the head of an armed band of soldiers and court messengers he found a small crowd of men sitting wearily in the *obi*. He commanded them to come outside, and they obeyed without a murmur.

"Which among you is called Okonkwo?" he asked through his interpreter.

"He is not here," replied Obierika.

"Where is he?"

"He is not here!"

The Commissioner became angry and red in the face. He warned the men that unless they produced Okonkwo forthwith he would lock them all up. The men murmured among themselves, and Obierika spoke again.

"We can take you where he is, and perhaps your men will help us."

The Commissioner did not understand what Obierika meant when he said, "Perhaps your men will help us." One of the most infuriating habits of these people was their love of superfluous words, he thought.

Obierika with five or six others led the way. The Commissioner and his men followed, their firearms held at the ready. He had warned Obierika that if he and his men played any monkey tricks they would be shot. And so they went.

There was a small bush behind Okonkwo's compound. The only opening into this bush from the compound was a little round hole in the red-earth wall through which fowls went in and out in their endless search for food. The hole would not let a man through. It was to this bush that Obierika led the Commissioner and his men. They skirted round the compound, keeping close to the wall. The only sound they made was with their feet as they crushed dry leaves.

Then they came to the tree from which Okonkwo's body was dangling, and they stopped dead.

"Perhaps your men can help us bring him down and bury him," said Obierika. "We have sent for strangers from another village to do it for us, but they may be a long time coming."

The District Commissioner changed instantaneously. The resolute administrator in him gave way to the student of primitive customs.

"Why can't you take him down yourselves?" he asked.

"It is against our custom," said one of the men. "It is an abomination for a man to take his own life. It is an offence against the Earth, and a man who commits it will not be buried by his clansmen. His body is evil, and only strangers may touch it. That is why we ask your people to bring him down, because you are strangers."

"Will you bury him like any other man?" asked the Commissioner.

"We cannot bury him. Only strangers can. We shall pay your men to do it. When he has been buried we will then do our duty by him. We shall make sacrifices to cleanse the desecrated land."

Obierika, who had been gazing steadily at his friend's dangling body, turned suddenly to the District Commissioner and said ferociously: "That man was one of the greatest men in Umuofia. You drove him to kill himself; and now he will be buried like a dog . . ." He could not say any more. His voice trembled and choked his words.

"Shut up!" shouted one of the messengers, quite unnecessarily.

"Take down the body," the Commissioner ordered his chief messenger, "and bring it and all these people to court."

"Yes, sah," the messenger said, saluting.

The Commissioner went away, taking three or four of the soldiers with him. In the many years in which he had toiled to bring civilization to different parts of Africa he had learnt a number of things. One of them was that a District Commissioner must never attend to such undignified details as cutting down a dead man from the tree. Such attention would give the natives a poor opinion of him. In the book which he planned to write he would stress that point. As he walked back to the court he thought about that book. Every day brought him some new material. The story of this man who had killed a messenger and hanged himself would make interesting reading. One could almost write a whole chapter on him. Perhaps not a whole chapter but a reasonable paragraph, at any rate. There was so much else to include, and one must be firm in cutting out details. He had already chosen the title of the book, after much thought: *The Pacification of the Primitive Tribes of the Lower Niger.*

from The African Writer and the English Language

In June 1962, there was a writers' gathering at Makerere, impressively styled: "A Conference of African Writers of English Expression."[1] Despite this sonorous and rather solemn title, it turned out to be a very lively affair and a very exciting and useful experience for many of us. But there was something which we tried to do and failed—that was to define "African literature" satisfactorily.

Was it literature produced *in* Africa or *about* Africa? Could African literature be on any subject, or must it have an African theme? Should it embrace the whole continent or south of the Sahara, or just *Black* Africa? And then the question of language. Should it be in indigenous African languages or should it include Arabic, English, French, Portuguese, Afrikaans, et cetera?

In the end we gave up trying to find an answer, partly—I should admit—on my own instigation. Perhaps we should not have given up so easily. It seems to me from some of the things I have since heard and read that we may have given the impression of not knowing what we were doing, or worse, not daring to look too closely at it.

A Nigerian critic, Obi Wali, writing in *Transition 10,* said: "Perhaps the most important achievement of the conference . . . is that African literature as now defined and understood leads nowhere."

I am sure that Obi Wali must have felt triumphantly vindicated when he saw the report of a different kind of conference held later at Fourah Bay to discuss African literature and the University curriculum. This conference produced a tentative definition of African literature as follows: "Creative writing in which an African setting is authentically handled or to which experiences originating in Africa are integral." We are told specifically that Conrad's *Heart of Darkness* qualifies as African literature while Graham Greene's *Heart of the Matter* fails because it could have been set anywhere outside Africa.

A number of interesting speculations issue from this definition which admittedly is only an interim formulation designed to produce an indisputably desirable end, namely, to introduce African students to literature set in their environment. But I could not help being amused by the curious circumstance in which Conrad, a Pole, writing in English could produce African literature while Peter Abrahams would be ineligible should he write a novel based on his experiences in the West Indies.

1. The conference took place at Makarere University College, in Kampala, Uganda, a colonial overseas extension of the University of London. The many African writers referred to by Achebe in this essay formed the first wave of African intellectuals and authors in postcolonial Africa.

What all this suggests to me is that you cannot cram African literature into a small, neat definition. I do not see African literature as one unit but as a group of associated units—in fact the sum total of all the *national* and *ethnic* literatures of Africa.

A national literature is one that takes the whole nation for its province and has a realized or potential audience throughout its territory. In other words a literature that is written in the *national* language. An ethnic literature is one which is available only to one ethnic group within the nation. If you take Nigeria as an example, the national literature, as I see it, is the literature written in English; and the ethnic literatures are in Hausa, Ibo, Yoruba, Efik, Edo, Ijaw, etc., etc.

Any attempt to define African literature in terms which overlook the complexities of the African scene at the material time is doomed to failure. After the elimination of white rule shall have been completed, the single most important fact in Africa in the second half of the twentieth century will appear to be the rise of individual nation-states. I believe that African literature will follow the same pattern.

What we tend to do today is to think of African literature as a newborn infant. But in fact what we have is a whole generation of newborn infants. Of course, if you only look cursorily, one infant is pretty much like another; but in reality each is already set on its own separate journey. Of course, you may group them together on the basis of anything you choose—the color of their hair, for instance. Or you may group them together on the basis of the language they will speak or the religion of their fathers. Those would all be valid distinctions; but they could not begin to account fully for each individual person carrying, as it were, his own little, unique lodestar of genes.

Those who in talking about African literature want to exclude North Africa because it belongs to a different tradition surely do not suggest that Black Africa is anything like homogeneous. What does Shabaan Robert have in common with Christopher Okigbo or Awoonor-Williams? Or Mongo Beti of Cameroun and Paris with Nzekwu of Nigeria? What does the champagne-drinking upper-class Creole society described by Easmon of Sierra Leone have in common with the rural folk and fishermen of J. P. Clark's plays? Of course, some of these differences could be accounted for on individual rather than national grounds, but a good deal of it is also environmental.

I have indicated somewhat offhandedly that the national literature of Nigeria and of many other countries of Africa is, or will be, written in English. This may sound like a controversial statement, but it isn't. All I have done has been to look at the reality of present-day Africa. This "reality" may change as a result of deliberate, e.g., political, action. If it does, an entirely new situation will arise, and there will be plenty of time to examine it. At present it may be more profitable to look at the scene as it is.

What are the factors which have conspired to place English in the position of national language in many parts of Africa? Quite simply the reason is that these nations were created in the first place by the intervention of the British which, I hasten to add, is not saying that the peoples comprising these nations were invented by the British.

The country which we know as Nigeria today began not so very long ago as the arbitrary creation of the British. It is true, as William Fagg says in his excellent new book, *Nigerian Images,* that this arbitrary action has proved as lucky in terms of African art history as any enterprise of the fortunate Princes of Serendip.[2] And I believe that in political and economic terms too this arbitrary

2. A name for Ceylon, used in a Persian fairy tale about three constantly lucky princes there.

creation called Nigeria holds out great prospects. Yet the fact remains that Nigeria was created by the British—for their own ends. Let us give the devil his due: colonialism in Africa disrupted many things, but it did create big political units where there were small, scattered ones before. Nigeria had hundreds of autonomous communities ranging in size from the vast Fulani Empire founded by Usman dan Fodio in the north to tiny village entities in the east. Today it is one country.

Of course there are areas of Africa where colonialism divided up a single ethnic group among two or even three powers. But on the whole it did bring together many peoples that had hitherto gone their several ways. And it gave them a language with which to talk to one another. If it failed to give them a song, it at least gave them a tongue, for sighing. There are not many countries in Africa today where you could abolish the language of the erstwhile colonial powers and still retain the facility for mutual communication. Therefore those African writers who have chosen to write in English or French are not unpatriotic smart alecks with an eye on the main chance—outside their own countries. They are by-products of the same process that made the new nation-states of Africa.

You can take this argument a stage further to include other countries of Africa. The only reason why we can even talk about African unity is that when we get together we can have a manageable number of languages to talk in—English, French, Arabic.

The other day I had a visit from Joseph Kariuki of Kenya. Although I had read some of his poems and he had read my novels, we had not met before. But it didn't seem to matter. In fact I had met him through his poems, especially through his love poem, *Come Away My Love,* in which he captures in so few words the trials and tensions of an African in love with a white girl in Britain:

> Come away, my love, from streets
> Where unkind eyes divide
> And shop windows reflect our difference.

By contrast, when in 1960 I was traveling in East Africa and went to the home of the late Shabaan Robert, the Swahili poet of Tanganyika, things had been different. We spent some time talking about writing, but there was no real contact. I knew from all accounts that I was talking to an important writer, but of the nature of his work I had no idea. He gave me two books of his poems which I treasure but cannot read—until I have learned Swahili.

And there are scores of languages I would want to learn if it were possible. Where am I to find the time to learn the half dozen or so Nigerian languages, each of which can sustain a literature? I am afraid it cannot be done. These languages will just have to develop as tributaries to feed the one central language enjoying nationwide currency. Today, for good or ill, that language is English. Tomorrow it may be something else, although I very much doubt it.

Those of us who have inherited the English language may not be in a position to appreciate the value of the inheritance. Or we may go on resenting it because it came as part of a package deal which included many other items of doubtful value and the positive atrocity of racial arrogance and prejudice which may yet set the world on fire. But let us not in rejecting the evil throw out the good with it.

Some time last year I was traveling in Brazil meeting Brazilian writers and artists. A number of the writers I spoke to were concerned about the restrictions imposed on them by their use of the Portuguese language. I remember a woman poet saying she had given serious thought to writing in French! And yet their problem is not half as difficult as ours. Portuguese may not have the universal currency of English or French but at least it is the national language of Brazil with her eighty million or so people, to say nothing of the people of Portugal, Angola, Mozambique, etc.

Of Brazilian authors I have only read, in translation, one novel by Jorge Amado, who is not only Brazil's leading novelist but one of the most important writers in the world. From that one novel, *Gabriella,* I was able to glimpse something of the exciting Afro-Latin culture which is the pride of Brazil and is quite unlike any other culture. Jorge Amado is only one of the many writers Brazil has produced. At their national writers' festival there were literally hundreds of them. But the work of the vast majority will be closed to the rest of the world forever, including no doubt the work of some excellent writers. There is certainly a great advantage to writing in a world language.

I think I have said enough to give an indication of my thinking on the importance of the world language which history has forced down our throats. Now let us look at some of the most serious handicaps. And let me say straightaway that one of the most serious handicaps is *not* the one people talk about most often, namely, that it is impossible for anyone ever to use a second language as effectively as his first. This assertion is compounded of half truth and half bogus mystique. Of course, it is true that the vast majority of people are happier with their first language than with any other. But then the majority of people are not writers. We do have enough examples of writers who have performed the feat of writing effectively in a second language. And I am not thinking of the obvious names like Conrad. It would be more germane to our subject to choose African examples.

The first name that comes to my mind is Olauda Equiano, better known as Gustavus Vassa, the African. Equiano was an Ibo, I believe from the village of Iseke in the Orlu division of Eastern Nigeria. He was sold as a slave at a very early age and transported to America. Later he bought his freedom and lived in England. In 1789 he published his life story, a beautifully written document which, among other things, set down for the Europe of his time something of the life and habit of his people in Africa, in an attempt to counteract the lies and slander invented by some Europeans to justify the slave trade.

Coming nearer to our times, we may recall the attempts in the first quarter of this century by West African nationalists to come together and press for a greater say in the management of their own affairs. One of the most eloquent of that band was the Honorable Casely Hayford of the Gold Coast. His presidential address to the National Congress of British West Africa in 1925 was memorable not only for its sound common sense but as a fine example of elegant prose. The governor of Nigeria at the time was compelled to take notice and he did so in characteristic style: he called Hayford's Congress "a self-selected and self-appointed congregation of educated African gentlemen." We may derive some amusement from the fact that British colonial administrators learned very little in the following quarter of a century. But at least they *did* learn in the end—which is more than one can say for some others.

It is when we come to what is commonly called creative literature that most doubt seems to arise. Obi Wali, whose article "Dead End of African Literature" I referred to, has this to say: ". . . until these writers and their Western midwives accept the fact that any true African literature must be written in African languages, they would be merely pursuing a dead end, which can only lead to sterility, uncreativity and frustration."

But far from leading to sterility, the work of many new African writers is full of the most exciting possibilities.

Take this from Christopher Okigbo's *Limits:*

> Suddenly becoming talkative like weaverbird
> Summoned at offside of dream remembered
> Between sleep and waking
> I hand up my egg-shells
> To you of palm grove,
> Upon whose bamboo towers hang
> Dripping with yesterupwine
> A tiger mask and nude spear. . . .
>
> Queen of the damp half light,
> I have had my cleansing.
> Emigrant with air-borne nose,
> The he-goat-on-heat.

Or take the poem, *Night Rain,* in which J. P. Clark captures so well the fear and wonder felt by a child as rain clamors on the thatch roof at night and his mother, walking about in the dark, moves her simple belongings

> Out of the run of water
> That like ants filing out of the wood
> Will scatter and gain possession
> Of the floor. . . .

I think that the picture of water spreading on the floor "like ants filing out of the wood" is beautiful. Of course if you had never made fire with faggots, you may miss it. But Clark's inspiration derives from the same source which gave birth to the saying that a man who brings home ant-ridden faggots must be ready for the visit of lizards.

I do not see any signs of sterility anywhere here. What I do see is a new voice coming out of Africa, speaking of African experience in a world-wide language. So my answer to the question *Can an African ever learn English well enough to be able to use it effectively in creative writing?* is certainly yes. If on the other hand you ask: *Can he ever learn to use it like a native speaker?* I should say, I hope not. It is neither necessary nor desirable for him to be able to do so. The price a world language must be prepared to pay is submission to many different kinds of use. The African writer should aim to use English in a way that brings out his message best without altering the language to the extent that its value as a medium of international exchange will be lost. He should aim at fashioning out an English which is at once universal and able to carry his peculiar experience. I have in mind here the writer who has something new, something different to say. The nondescript writer has little to tell us, anyway, so he might as well tell it in conventional language and get it over with. If I may use an extravagant simile, he is like a man offering a small, nondescript routine sacrifice for which a chick, or less, will do. A serious writer must look for an animal whose blood can match the power of his offering.

In this respect Amos Tutola is a natural. A good instinct has turned his apparent limitation in language into a weapon of great strength—a half-strange dialect that serves him perfectly in the evocation of his bizarre world. His last book, and to my mind, his finest, is proof enough that one can make even an imperfectly learned second language do amazing things. In this book, *The Feather Woman of the Jungle,* Tutola's superb storytelling is at last cast in the episodic form which he handles best instead of being painfully stretched on the rack of the novel.

From a natural to a conscious artist: myself, in fact. Allow me to quote a small example from *Arrow of God,* which may give some idea of how I approach the use of English. The Chief Priest in the story is telling one of his sons why it is necessary to send him to church:

> I want one of my sons to join these people and be my eyes there. If there is nothing in it you will come back. But if there is something there you will bring home my share. The world is like a Mask, dancing. If you want to see it well you do not stand in one place. My spirit tells me that those who do not befriend the white man today will be saying *had we known* tomorrow.

Now supposing I had put it another way. Like this for instance:

> I am sending you as my representative among these people—just to be on the safe side in case the new religion develops. One has to move with the times or else one is left behind. I have a hunch that those who fail to come to terms with the white man may well regret their lack of foresight.

The material is the same. But the form of the one is *in character* and the other is not. It is largely a matter of instinct, but judgment comes into it too.

You read quite often nowadays of the problems of the African writer having first to think in his mother tongue and then to translate what he has thought into English. If it were such a simple, mechanical process, I would agree that it was pointless—the kind of eccentric pursuit you might expect to see in a modern Academy of Lagado;[3] and such a process could not possibly produce some of the exciting poetry and prose which is already appearing.

One final point remains for me to make. The real question is not whether Africans *could* write in English but whether they *ought to.* Is it right that a man should abandon his mother tongue for someone else's? It looks like a dreadful betrayal and produces a guilty feeling.

But for me there is no other choice. I have been given this language and I intend to use it. I hope, though, that there always will be men, like the late Chief Fagunwa, who will choose to write in their native tongue and insure that our ethnic literature will flourish side by side with the national ones. For those of us who opt for English, there is much work ahead and much excitement.

Writing in the London *Observer* recently, James Baldwin said:

> My quarrel with the English language has been that the language reflected none of my experience. But now I began to see the matter another way. . . . Perhaps the language was not my own because I had never attempted to use it, had only learned to imitate it. If this were so, then it might be made to bear the burden of my experience if I could find the stamina to challenge it, and me, to such a test.

I recognize, of course, that Baldwin's problem is not exactly mine, but I feel that the English language will be able to carry the weight of my African experience. But it will have to be a new English, still in full communion with its ancestral home but altered to suit its new African surroundings.

3. A group of scientists producing pointless, trivial experiments in Jonathan Swift's *Gulliver's Travles.*

RESONANCES

Ngugi wa Thiong'o: from *The Language of African Literature*[1]

The language of African literature cannot be discussed meaningfully outside the context of those social forces which have made it both an issue demanding our attention and a problem calling for a resolution.

On the one hand is imperialism in its colonial and neo-colonial phases continuously press-ganging the African hand to the plough to turn the soil over, and putting blinkers on him to make him view the path ahead only as determined for him by the master armed with the bible and the sword. In other words, imperialism continues to control the economy, politics, and cultures of Africa. But on the other, and pitted against it, are the ceaseless struggles of African people to liberate their economy, politics and culture from that Euro-American-based stranglehold to usher a new era of true communal self-regulation and self-determination. It is an ever-continuing struggle to seize back their creative initiative in history through a real control of all the means of communal self-definition in time and space. The choice of language and the use to which language is put is central to a people's definition of themselves in relation to their natural and social environment, indeed in relation to the entire universe. Hence language has always been at the heart of the two contending social forces in the Africa of the twentieth century.

* * *

In 1962 I was invited to that historic meeting of African writers at Makerere University College, Kampala, Uganda. The list of participants contained most of the names which have now become the subject of scholarly dissertations in universities all over the world. The title? "A Conference of *African Writers of English Expression.*"

I was then a student of *English* at Makerere, an overseas college of the University of London. The main attraction for me was the certain possibility of meeting Chinua Achebe. I had with me a rough typescript of a novel in progress, *Weep Not, Child,* and I wanted him to read it. In the previous year, 1961, I had completed *The River Between,* my first-ever attempt at a novel, and entered it for a writing competition organised by the East African Literature Bureau. I was keeping in step with the tradition of Peter Abrahams with his output of novels and autobiographies from *Path of Thunder* to *Tell Freedom* and followed by Chinua Achebe with his publication of *Things Fall Apart* in 1959. Or there were their counterparts in French colonies, the generation of Sédar Senghor and David Diop included in the 1947/48 Paris edition of *Anthologie de la nouvelle poésie nègre et malgache de langue française.*[2] They all wrote in European languages as was the case with all the participants in that momentous encounter on Makerere hill in Kampala in 1962.

1. The Kenyan novelist, playwright, and essayist Ngugi wa Thiong'o (b. 1938) began his career writing novels of disillusionment and family conflict and then turned increasingly to political themes, dramatizing Kenya's struggle for independence from Britain in his novel *A Grain of Wheat.* Following independence in 1963, Kenya's leaders suppressed opposition parties and established dictatorial rule. Ngugi was jailed for a year after publishing *Petals of Blood* (1977), a satirical indictment of Kenya's post-independence leadership; he subsequently took up teaching positions in the United States. The 1986 essay excerpted here, published in book form in *Decolonizing the Mind,* discusses the politics of language and his own decision to begin writing in his native Gĩkũyũ after many years of writing fiction in English.

2. *Anthology of the New and Madagascan Poetry in French,* edited by the poet (and future president of Senegal) Leopold Sédar Senghor (see page 638). With an introduction by Jean-Paul Sartre, the anthology was intended to put Francophone African poetry on the French literary map. Senghor's friend and collaborator Birago (David) Diop (1906-1992) wrote vivid stories in French based on West-African folktale traditions.

The title, "A Conference of African Writers of English Expression," automatically excluded those who wrote in African languages. Now on looking back from the self-questioning heights of 1986, I can see this contained absurd anomalies. I, a student, could qualify for the meeting on the basis of only two published short stories, "The Fig Tree (Mũgumo)" in a student journal, *Penpoint,* and "The Return" in a new journal, *Transition.* But neither Shabaan Robert, then the greatest living East African poet with several works of poetry and prose to his credit in Kiswahili, nor Chief Fagunwa, the great Nigerian writer with several published titles in Yoruba, could possibly qualify.

The discussions on the novel, the short story, poetry, and drama were based on extracts from works in English and hence they excluded the main body of work in Swahili, Zulu, Yoruba, Arabic, Amharic and other African languages. Yet, despite this exclusion of writers and literature in African languages, no sooner were the introductory preliminaries over than this Conference of "African Writers of English Expression' sat down to the first item on the agenda: "What is African Literature?"

The debate which followed was animated: Was it literature about Africa or about the African experience? Was it literature written by Africans? What about a non-African who wrote about Africa: did his work qualify as African literature? What if an African set his work in Greenland: did that qualify as African literature? Or were African languages the criteria? OK: what about Arabic, was it not foreign to Africa? What about French and English, which had become African languages? What if an European wrote about Europe in an African language? If . . . if . . . if . . . this or that, except the issue: the domination of our languages and cultures by those of imperialist Europe: in any case there was no Fagunwa or Shabaan Robert or any writer in African languages to bring the conference down from the realms of evasive abstractions. The question was never seriously asked: did what we wrote qualify as African literature? The whole area of literature and audience, and hence of language as a determinant of both the national and class audience, did not really figure: the debate was more about the subject matter and the racial origins and geographical habitation of the writer.

English, like French and Portuguese, was assumed to be the natural language of literary and even political mediation between African people in the same nation and between nations in Africa and other continents. In some instances these European languages were seen as having a capacity to unite African peoples against divisive tendencies inherent in the multiplicity of African languages within the same geographic state. Thus Ezekiel Mphahlele[3] later could write, in a letter to *Transition* number 11, that English and French have become the common language with which to present a nationalist front against white oppressors, and even "where the whiteman has already retreated, as in the independent states, these two languages are still a unifying force." In the literary sphere they were often seen as coming to save African languages against themselves. Writing a foreword to Birago Diop's book *Contes d'Amadou Koumba* Sédar Senghor commends him for using French to rescue the spirit and style of old African fables and tales. "However while rendering them into French he renews them with an art which, while it respects the genius of the French language, that language of gentleness and honesty, preserves at the same time all the virtues of the negro-african languages." English, French and Portuguese had come to our rescue and we accepted the unsolicited gift with gratitude. Thus in

3. Black South African novelist and opponent of apartheid, who settled in Kenya after emigrating from South Africa in 1957.

1964, Chinua Achebe, in a speech entitled "The African Writer and the English Language," said:

> Is it right that a man should abandon his mother tongue for someone else's? It looks like a dreadful betrayal and produces a guilty feeling. But for me there is no other choice. I have been given the language and I intend to use it.

See the paradox: the possibility of using mother-tongues provokes a tone of levity in phrases like "a dreadful betrayal" and "a guilty feeling;" but that of foreign languages produces a categorical positive embrace, what Achebe himself, ten years later, was to describe as this "fatalistic logic of the unassailable position of English in our literature."

The fact is that all of us who opted for European languages—the conference participants and the generation that followed them—accepted that fatalistic logic to a greater or lesser degree. * * *

How did we arrive at this acceptance of "the fatalistic logic of the unassailable position of English in our literature," in our culture and in our politics? What was the route from the Berlin of 1884 via the Makerere of 1962 to what is still the prevailing and dominant logic a hundred years later? How did we, as African writers, come to be so feeble towards the claims of our languages on us and so aggressive in our claims on other languages, particularly the languages of our colonization?

Berlin of 1884 was effected through the sword and the bullet.[4] But the night of the sword and the bullet was followed by the morning of the chalk and the blackboard. The physical violence of the battlefield was followed by the psychological violence of the classroom. But where the former was visibly brutal, the latter was visibly gentle, a process best described in Cheikh Hamidou Kane's novel *Ambiguous Adventure* where he talks of the methods of the colonial phase of imperialism as consisting of knowing how to kill with efficiency and to heal with the same art.

> On the Black Continent, one began to understand that their real power resided not at all in the cannons of the first morning but in what followed the cannons. Therefore behind the cannons was the new school. The new school had the nature of both the cannon and the magnet. From the cannon it took the efficiency of a fighting weapon. But better than the cannon it made the conquest permanent. The cannon forces the body and the school fascinates the soul.

In my view language was the most important vehicle through which that power fascinated and held the soul prisoner. The bullet was the means of the physical subjugation. Language was the means of the spiritual subjugation. Let me illustrate this by drawing upon experiences in my own education, particularly in language and literature.

I was born into a large peasant family: father, four wives and about twenty-eight children. I also belonged, as we all did in those days, to a wider extended family and to the community as a whole.

We spoke Gĩkũyũ as we worked in the fields. We spoke Gĩkũyũ in and outside the home. I can vividly recall those evenings of storytelling around the fireside. It was mostly the grown-ups telling the children but everybody was interested and involved. We children would re-tell the stories the following day to other children who worked in the fields picking the pyrethrum flowers, tea-leaves or coffee beans of our European and African landlords.

4. At the Berlin Conference of 1884–1885, the major European powers ratified the colonial division of Africa, including Britain's hold on Kenya and Belgium's claim to the Congo.

The stories, with mostly animals as the main characters, were all told in Gĩkũyũ. Hare, being small, weak but full of innovative wit and cunning, was our hero. We identified with him as he struggled against the brutes of prey like lion, leopard, hyena. His victories were our victories and we learnt that the apparently weak can outwit the strong. We followed the animals in their struggle against hostile nature—drought, rain, sun, wind—a confrontation often forcing them to search for forms of co-operation. But we were also interested in their struggles amongst themselves, and particularly between the beasts and the victims of prey. These twin struggles, against nature and other animals, reflected real-life struggles in the human world.

Not that we neglected stories with human beings as the main characters. There were two types of characters in such human-centred narratives: the species of truly human beings with qualities of courage, kindness, mercy, hatred of evil, concern for others; and a man-eat-man two-mouthed species with qualities of greed, selfishness, individualism and hatred of what was good for the larger co-operative community. Co-operation as the ultimate good in a community was a constant theme. It could unite human beings with animals against ogres and beasts of prey, as in the story of how dove, after being fed with castor-oil seeds, was sent to fetch a smith working far away from home and whose pregnant wife was being threatened by these man-eating two-mouthed ogres.

There were good and bad story-tellers. A good one could tell the same story over and over again, and it would always be fresh to us, the listeners. He or she could tell a story told by someone else and make it more alive and dramatic. The differences really were in the use of words and images and the inflexion of voices to effect different tones.

We therefore learnt to value words for their meaning and nuances. Language was not a mere string of words. It had a suggestive power well beyond the immediate and lexical meaning. Our appreciation of the suggestive magical power of language was reinforced by the games we played with words through riddles, proverbs, transpositions of syllables, or through nonsensical but musically arranged words. So we learnt the music of our language on top of the content. The language, through images and symbols, gave us a view of the world, but it had a beauty of its own. The home and the field were then our pre-primary school but what is important, for this discussion, is that the language of our evening teach-ins, and the language of our immediate and wider community, and the language of our work in the fields were one.

And then I went to school, a colonial school, and this harmony was broken. The language of my education was no longer the language of my culture. I first went to Kamaandura, missionary run, and then to another called Maanguuũ run by nationalists grouped around the Gĩkũyũ Independent and Karinga Schools Association. Our language of education was still Gĩkũyũ. The very first time I was ever given an ovation for my writing was over a composition in Gĩkũyũ. So for my first four years there was still harmony between the language of my formal education and that of the Limuru peasant community.

It was after the declaration of a state of emergency over Kenya in 1952[5] that all the schools run by patriotic nationalists were taken over by the colonial regime and were placed under District Education Boards chaired by Englishmen. English became the language of my formal education. In Kenya, English became more than a language: it was *the* language, and all the others had to bow before it in deference.

5. The start of armed struggle against British rule.

Thus one of the most humiliating experiences was to be caught speaking Gĩkũyũ in the vicinity of the school. The culprit was given corporal punishment—three to five strokes of the cane on bare buttocks—or was made to carry a metal plate around the neck with inscriptions such as I AM STUPID or I AM A DONKEY. Sometimes the culprits were fined money they could hardly afford. And how did the teachers catch the culprits? A button was initially given to one pupil who was supposed to hand it over to whoever was caught speaking his mother tongue. Whoever had the button at the end of the day would sing who had given it to him and the ensuing process would bring out all the culprits of the day. Thus children were turned into witch-hunters and in the process were being taught the lucrative value of being a traitor to one's immediate community.

The attitude to English was the exact opposite: any achievement in spoken or written English was highly rewarded; prizes, prestige, applause; the ticket to higher realms. English became the measure of intelligence and ability in the arts, the sciences, and all the other branches of learning. English became *the* main determinant of a child's progress up the ladder of formal education.

As you may know, the colonial system of education in addition to its apartheid racial demarcation had the structure of a pyramid: a broad primary base, a narrowing secondary middle, and an even narrower university apex. Selections from primary into secondary were through an examination, in my time called Kenya African Preliminary Examination, in which one had to pass six subjects ranging from Maths to Nature Study and Kiswahili. All the papers were written in English. Nobody could pass the exam who failed the English language paper no matter how brilliantly he had done in the other subjects. I remember one boy in my class of 1954 who had distinctions in all subjects except English, which he had failed. He was made to fail the entire exam. He went on to become a turn boy in a bus company. I who had only passes but a credit in English got a place at the Alliance High School, one of the most elitist institutions for Africans in colonial Kenya. The requirements for a place at the University, Makerere University College, were broadly the same: nobody could go on to wear the undergraduate red gown, no matter how brilliantly they had performed in all the other subjects unless they had a credit—not even a simple pass!—in English. Thus the most coveted place in the pyramid and in the system was only available to the holder of an English language credit card. English was the official vehicle and the magic formula to colonial elitedom.

Literary education was now determined by the dominant language while also reinforcing that dominance. Orature (oral literature) in Kenyan languages stopped. In primary school I now read simplified Dickens and Stevenson alongside Rider Haggard.[6] Jim Hawkins, Oliver Twist, Tom Brown—not Hare, Leopard and Lion—were now my daily companions in the world of imagination. In secondary school, Scott and G. B. Shaw vied with more Rider Haggard, John Buchan, Alan Paton, Captain W. E. Johns. At Makerere I read English: from Chaucer to T. S. Eliot with a touch of Graham Greene.

Thus language and literature were taking us further and further from ourselves to other selves, from our world to other worlds.

* * *

But African languages refused to die. They would not simply go the way of Latin to become the fossils for linguistic archaeology to dig up, classify, and argue about the international conferences.

6. All Victorian novelists. H. Rider Haggard was particularly known for *She* (1887) and other novels of colonial adventure in "the Dark Continent."

These languages, these national heritages of Africa, were kept alive by the peasantry. The peasantry saw no contradiction between speaking their own mother-tongues and belonging to a larger national or continental geography. They saw no necessary antagonistic contradiction between belonging to their immediate nationality, to their multinational state along the Berlin-drawn boundaries, and to Africa as a whole. These people happily spoke Wolof, Hausa, Yoruba, Ibo, Arabic, Amharic, Kiswahili, Gĩkũyũ, Luo, Luhya, Shona, Ndebele, Kimbundu, Zulu or Lingala without this fact tearing the multinational states apart. During the anti-colonial struggle they showed an unlimited capacity to unite around whatever leader or party best and most consistently articulated an anti-imperialist position. If anything it was the petty-bourgeoisie, particularly the compradors,[7] with their French and English and Portuguese, with their petty rivalries, their ethnic chauvinism, which encouraged these vertical divisions to the point of war at times. No, the peasantry had no complexes about their languages and the cultures they carried!

In fact when the peasantry and the working class were compelled by necessity or history to adopt the language of the master, they Africanised it without any of the respect for its ancestry shown by Senghor and Achebe, so totally as to have created new African languages, like Krio in Sierra Leone or Pidgin in Nigeria, that owed their identities to the syntax and rhythms of African languages. All these languages were kept alive in the daily speech, in the ceremonies, in political struggles, above all in the rich store of orature—proverbs, stories, poems, and riddles.

The peasantry and the urban working class threw up singers. These sang the old songs or composed new ones incorporating the new experiences in industries and urban life and in working-class struggle and organisations. These singers pushed the languages to new limits, renewing and reinvigorating them by coining new words and new expressions, and in generally expanding their capacity to incorporate new happenings in Africa and the world. * * *

The question is this: we as African writers have always complained about the neo-colonial economic and political relationship to Euro-America. Right. But by our continuing to write in foreign languages, paying homage to them, are we not on the cultural level continuing that neo-colonial slavish and cringing spirit? What is the difference between a politician who says Africa cannot do without imperialism and the writer who says Africa cannot do without European languages?

While we were busy haranguing the ruling circles in a language which automatically excluded the participation of the peasantry and the working class in the debate, imperialist culture and African reactionary forces had a field day: the Christian bible is available in unlimited quantities in even the tiniest African language. The comprador ruling cliques are also quite happy to have the peasantry and the working class all to themselves: distortions, dictatorial directives, decrees, museum-type fossils paraded as African culture, feudalistic ideologies, superstitions, lies, all these backward elements and more are communicated to the African masses in their own languages without any challenges from those with alternative visions of tomorrow who have deliberately cocooned themselves in English, French, and Portuguese. It is ironic that the most reactionary African politician, the one who believes in selling Africa to Europe, is often a master of African languages; that the most zealous of European missionaries who believed in rescuing Africa from itself, even from the paganism of its languages, were nevertheless masters of African languages, which they often reduced to writing. The European missionary believed too much in his mission

7. Buyers (Portuguese), native agents for foreign powers, in charge of local workers.

of conquest not to communicate it in the languages most readily available to the people: the African writer believes too much in "African literature" to write it in those ethnic, divisive and under-developed languages of the peasantry!

The added irony is that what they have produced, despite any claims to the contrary, is not African literature. The editors of the Pelican Guides to English literature in their latest volume were right to include a discussion of this literature as part of twentieth-century English literature, just as the French Academy was right to honour Senghor for his genuine and talented contribution to French literature and language. What we have created is another hybrid tradition, a tradition in transition, a minority tradition that can only be termed as Afro-European literature; that is, the literature written by Africans in European languages. It has produced many writers and works of genuine talent: Chinua Achebe, Wole Soyinka, Ayi Kwei Armah, Sembene Ousmane, Agostino Neto, Sédar Senghor and many others. Who can deny their talent? The light in the products of their fertile imaginations has certainly illuminated important aspects of the African being in its continuous struggle against the political and economic consequences of Berlin and after. However we cannot have our cake and eat it! Their work belongs to an Afro-European literary tradition which is likely to last for as long as Africa is under this rule of European capital in a neo-colonial set-up. So Afro-European literature can be defined as literature written by Africans in European languages in the era of imperialism.

But some are coming round to the inescapable conclusion articulated by Obi Wali with such polemical vigour twenty years ago: African literature can only be written in African languages, that is, the languages of the African peasantry and working class, the major alliance of classes in each of our nationalities and the agency for the coming inevitable revolutionary break with neo-colonialism.

I started writing in Gĩkũyũ language in 1977 after seventeen years of involvement in Afro-European literature, in my case Afro-English literature. It was then that I collaborated with Ngũgĩ wa Mĩriĩ in the drafting of the playscript, *Ngaahika Ndeenda* (the English translation was *I Will Marry When I Want*). I have since published a novel in Gĩkũyũ, *Caitaani Mũtharabainĩ* (English translation: *Devil on the Cross*) and completed a musical drama, *Maitũ Njugĩra,* (English translation: *Mother Sing for Me*); three books for children, *Njamba Nene na Mbaathi i Mathagu, Bathitoora ya Njamba Nene, Njamba Nene na Cibũ Kĩng'ang'i,* as well as another novel manuscript: *Matigari Ma Njirũũngi.* Wherever I have gone, particularly in Europe, I have been confronted with the question: why are you now writing in Gĩkũyũ? Why do you now write in an African language? In some academic quarters I have been confronted with the rebuke, "Why have you abandoned us?" It was almost as if, in choosing to write in Gĩkũyũ, I was doing something abnormal. But Gĩkũyũ is my mother tongue! The very fact that what common sense dictates in the literary practice of other cultures is being questioned in an African writer is a measure of how far imperialism has distorted the view of African realities. It has turned reality upside down: the abnormal is viewed as normal and the normal is viewed as abnormal. * * *

We African writers are bound by our calling to do for our languages what Spencer, Milton and Shakespeare did for English; what Pushkin and Tolstoy did for Russian; indeed what all writers in world history have done for their languages by meeting the challenge of creating a literature in them, which process later opens the languages for philosophy, science, technology and all the other areas of human creative endeavours.

But writing in our languages per se—although a necessary first step in the correct direction—will not itself bring about the renaissance in African cultures if that literature does not carry the content of our people's anti-imperialist struggles to liberate their productive forces from foreign control; the content of the need for unity among the workers and peasants of all the nationalities in their struggle to control the wealth they produce and to free it from internal and external parasites.

In other words writers in African languages should reconnect themselves to the revolutionary traditions of an organised peasantry and working class in Africa in their struggle to defeat imperialism and create a higher system of democracy and socialism in alliance with all the other peoples of the world. Unity in that struggle would ensure unity in our multi-lingual diversity. It would also reveal the real links that bind the people of Africa to the peoples of Asia, South America, Europe, Australia and New Zealand, Canada and the U.S.A.

But it is precisely when writers open out African languages to the real links in the struggles of peasants and workers that they will meet their biggest challenge. For to the comprador-ruling regimes, their real enemy is an awakened peasantry and working class. A writer who tries to communicate the message of revolutionary unity and hope in the languages of the people becomes a subversive character. It is then that writing in African languages becomes a subversive or treasonable offence with such a writer facing possibilities of prison, exile or even death. For him there are no "national" accolades, no new year honours, only abuse and slander and innumerable lies from the mouths of the armed power of a ruling minority—ruling, that is, on behalf of U.S.-led imperialism—and who see in democracy a real threat. A democratic participation of the people in the shaping of their own lives or in discussing their own lives in languages that allow for mutual comprehension is seen as being dangerous to the good government of a country and its institutions. African languages addressing themselves to the lives of the people become the enemy of a neo-colonial state.

Mbwil a M. Ngal: from *Giambatista Viko: or, The Rape of African Discourse*[1]

[*Giambatista Viko, essayist and professor at an unnamed institute of African studies, has been struggling to write a major novel so that he can become "the Napoleon of African letters" and be invited to conferences in Europe. In the following passage, he shares with his disciple Niaiseux ("Simpleton") his difficulties and his ambitions for his novel.*]

"Giving birth to any kind of literature has become painful for me. My fame as some kind of black sun spreads around the planet, but my reputation as a writer isn't building up. Only a discourse internal to Africa can liberate my own, enmeshed as it is in one of those sophisms that only the Westerners can master. A subterranean life exists within us. Freudianism taught this to the West; but the primitives themselves have never forgotten it. From time immemorial, the interior life of individuals, as of society, has been ruled by this entreaty from below that Europe is only now beginning to rediscover."

1. Translated by David Damrosch. Born in Zaire (now the Democratic People's Republic of the Congo), Ngal studied at a Jesuit college there before obtaining a doctorate in Fribourg, Switzerland, with a thesis on the Francophone Caribbean poet Aimé Césaire (see page 1721). He then taught in Europe, Africa, and Canada. His 1975 novel *Giambatista Viko* concerns an ambitious, irascible, Paris-oriented Central African intellectual who is arrested and put on trial after he tries to steal the secrets of African oral culture for use in a novel. Viko's name recalls that of the Italian philosopher Giambattista Vico, whose *Scienza Nuova* ("New Science," 1725), argued that all language began in poetry, the natural medium of primitive people's speech.

"Master, I've always said you were born too soon, a century ahead of our times. To tame our African discourse in order to liberate the West's paralyzed, repressed discourse—that seems truly inspired!"

"But consider! No ambiguity! I am of a race that cannot be assimilated to ordinary African writers. We have nothing in common but biology. My place is in Paris, in Geneva. It's only an accident of history that had me born in Africa. To use a resource is not to assimilate. Picasso, Juan Gris, Lipchitz surrounded themselves with Negro masks solely in order to define their own aesthetic intentions;[2] an Apollinaire exerted his own will by turning to fetishes from Guinea and Africa.[3] Let those misunderstand who wish. A means is a means. Don't lose sight of that.

"To give birth to a novel! In effect that means to take up a Western discourse. To develop a story within a visual space. In the spatial-temporal dimension. A yoke that strangely limits the writer's freedom: the possibilities of the discourse itself. 'The power of these diminished words loses the efficacity it enjoys in the magic universe of orality. A spoken word gives power over the thing named; the clay image represents the enemy you kill by piercing it with a needle.' It would take a *Scienza Nuova* to rediscover the spiritual forces that our technological universe has lost, and which have been preserved by the oral societies dismissively called primitive. The power, the ability to decipher the language buried in the depths of symbolism; to decode the enemy's malevolent intentions. The secrets discovered constitute the great epiphanies of the divine beneath the veil of their surroundings—the viewer's essential domain."

"Your childhood was immersed in this universe!"

"Yet we've been torn away far too soon, plunged into the world of the written. We need to rediscover what we've lost. An acoustic space, or rather, an audio-visual one. That of the storyteller! What undefined riches! What freedom in the story's unfolding! None of the novel's rigidity! Novelistic space? Veritable circle of hell! I dream of a novel on the model of the folktale. * * * As far as I'm concerned, my choice is clear. More precisely, I don't have one at all. A humanist culture—Greco-Roman—seasoned with the erudition that everyone grants me! Where would you have me find a place for it? I believe neither in cross-breeding nor in the integration of cultures. Juxtaposition? Perhaps! But who could marry Cartesian logic to Bantu logic? * * * I need a style that will combine many contradictory tendencies: the incantatory, the learned, the moving, the oracular. Sometimes flashing out, glittering, sometimes taken apart. Abrupt opacities here, profound transparencies there. An internal, obsessional discourse, dissolved in an indescribable jumble of times and confusion of perspectives. Punctuation? Don't even mention it!"

[*Viko's plans are interrupted when militant Africanists take over the institute where he works, accusing him of plagiarism, of sexual indiscretions with a visiting Italian structuralist, and above all of trying to forcibly violate native oral culture by reducing it to French prose. Viko and Niaiseux are put in a dungeon cell, where they are visited by a tribal elder.*]

A key grates in the lock. The door opens. A man enters, dressed in a goat skin, biceps ringed with silver bracelets. Pearl headdress, crowned with parrot feathers. He is

2. The Cubist artists Publo Picasso, Juan Gris, and Jacques Lipchitz all used African images in their art, see Color Plate 15 for an example by Picasso.

3. Guillaume Apollinaire (1880–1918) introduced Cubist techniques and African themes into his poetry.

followed by a young man in an elegant suit. The door closes behind them. Yet the room remains light, even though the door is closed; the source of the light is invisible.

In a flash of insight I perceive the reason for our confinement. My audacities at the office are now having their effects. But I don't breathe a word to Niaiseux.

The man turns to the youth and speaks at length. The young man translates:

"Dogs and sons of dogs! My dignity, my honor forbid me to address you directly. Your crime is immeasurable. You will pay for it with the last drop of your blood. But do not dream of being thought of as martyrs; you won't have that honor. The fundamental reason that keeps me from addressing you directly is that our universes—speech and writing—have nothing in common. You have impiously set an abyss between yourselves and us. You have chosen the universe of the book—the space of inscription—abandoning that which nourished your childhood, fed your dreams, and furnished your subconscious. You have tried to drain away this lake of symbols, images, the core that welds together our community's cultural cohesion. For you we are total strangers.

"We have followed your alienation with heavy heart. But we knew that you would never go too far, that a nostalgia would bring you back to our shores. The sacred riches of the orality you have so disdainfully rejected always leave the guilty ones with an odor that pursues them like a gnawing remorse. The gravity of your impiety resides in your attempt to desacralize orality. You have wanted to reappropriate the freedom, the space, the time of the storyteller; to introduce them into novelistic discourse. An atheist's attempt, destitute of faith! Not even stopping at this degree of criminality, you have had the presumption to become initiated in our rites, hoping thus to arrive at your goal. In so doing, you plan to subvert orality and Western discourse alike. You would give birth to hybrid characters, heros, texts! This is why this sacrilege cannot go unpunished."

[*A show trial follows, in which a series of prosecutors harangue Viko and Niaiseux, urging the death penalty, not allowing them to reply. Then "the youngest counselor present" speaks up, urging a degree of clemency.*]

"In undertaking this trial, our intention has not been to construct a Great Wall of China around our continent, to prevent our intellectuals from engaging in dialogue with colleagues elsewhere. The greatest malady that Africa suffers today is the new ideology—found almost everywhere—that seeks a pronounced unanimity. 'Idem velle, idem nolle.'[4] Pluralism has become a crime. I ask myself this question: Progress, or regression? *** Let me make myself clear. Far be it from me to approve what this young man has done. But I would like to draw our attention to a current ideology, the Africanist ideology that wants African realities to be unique, original. What one of our comrades has just called 'an assault on our security' is nothing more than 'an assault on our specificity,' on our withdrawal within ourselves. But let us not forget that a 'specificity' prepares its own asphyxiation to the degree that it receives no oxygen from outside. Cultures survive only by opening up to other cultures that can liberate them from their tendency to collective narcissism."

[*At the close of this speech, the judge renders his verdict, stopping short of a sentence of death.*]

4. Wanting the same things, and not wanting the same things.

"You are in our hands today, and we will not simply let you leave. You are condemned to perform the Return to the Native Land.[5] Will you pass the remainder of your days among us? You will come to know, one by one, the joys of living one place today, another the next, until you have made the rounds of our villages eighty-seven times eighty-seven times."

Sustained applause. Everyone cries out, "Wisdom has spoken!"

* * *

So I've been condemned. Rejected. Torn away from one society and hurled into another! What fate is this? Reintegration, or eternal banishment? Isn't every condemnation a rejection of human society? They meant to get me back, but haven't they lost me for good? * * * Condemned to wandering—me, GIAMBATISTA! Why did they even bother to mitigate their criminal plan? Wouldn't an outright execution have been better? From village to village—that's to say, from oblivion to oblivion! No sooner will I leave one village behind than another will loom up on the horizon of oblivion. . . . I have been condemned to the Gulag Archipelago of oblivion.[6] * * *

Instinctively I rub my eyes, adjust my glasses, take a deep breath. I look around. I am alone. Alone. The Assembly has dispersed, and I didn't notice. Alone on center stage!

5. Unwittingly, the judge echoes the title of Aimé Césaire's long poem, composed in Paris, *Notebook of a Return to the Native Land.*

6. The Gulag Archipelago was the nickname of a chain of Siberian prisons used in Soviet Russia for political prisoners.

PERSPECTIVES
Postcolonial Conditions

One of the developments that most significantly changed the political face of the globe in the twentieth century was decolonization, that is, the transition of large areas of the world from colonies of mostly European powers to independent nation-states. While this transition occurred gradually in some cases, it was abrupt in others; it took place peacefully at times and at others was achieved by means of violent and sometimes protracted conflict with the colonial power. But the achievement of political independence didn't mean that the economic, social, and cultural forms of domination that accompanied colonialism simply came to an end, some of them left profound marks on the colonized society, while others perpetuated themselves in different guises. "Postcolonial" conditions, then, aren't simply the social and cultural configurations that followed chronologically after the end of colonialism but those that are directly or indirectly shaped by the colonial past and that extend or resist its legacies.

These legacies can take a wide range of forms. Materially, they can manifest themselves in economic and financial dependencies on the former metropolis that limit the autonomy political independence seemed to promise. The government can be controlled by elites from among the former colonized whose economic interests are tied up with those of the colonizers. Politically, the end of colonialism sometimes leaves behind structures of social, ethnic, and racial discrimination that persist even when the authorities who originally enforced them have been displaced. At other times, the presence of a colonial power helped to suppress latent conflicts between different social groups in the colonized country that violently erupt when that power wanes. Poets, playwrights, and novelists who write in the aftermath of colonialism explore these and related conflicts, often focusing on the problems of identity and community that arise from colonial domination and its aftermath.

The most prominent of these identity conflicts arises with the question of how to negotiate the balance between the cultural heritage the colonized claim as originally their own and the one that was brought to them by the colonizer. For those whose lives are shaped by colonialism and postcolonialism, these legacies often don't form two distinct blocks that can be easily separated from each other but instead present themselves as an interwoven spectrum of possibilities and conflicts. At the simplest level, the desire to emulate or appropriate what is admirable about the colonizer's culture may conflict with the wish to give pride of place to one's own cultural heritage. Each of these tendencies can be put to very complex uses. For example, one might want to lay claim to certain aspects of the colonizers' culture (such as an emphasis on scientific rationality or freedom of expression) precisely to turn them against the colonizer's own oppression of the colonized; or, inversely, appropriating certain aspects of the colonizer's culture (for instance, certain conceptions of femininity and the role of women) might become a way of pointing out injustices in one's own culture.

Claiming one's own cultural heritage can be an equally complex undertaking since that heritage may turn out to consist not just of one but of several different and possibly conflicting traditions. "Claiming one's own," in this context, may well imply privileging some of these traditions and silencing others—much as the colonizer had done before—or realizing that the cultural unity by means of which one wanted to resist the colonizer is itself a construct rather than a natural given. Yet again, laying claim to one's own culture in a colonial or postcolonial context may turn out to be problematic because some of the colonized themselves no longer wholeheartedly embrace all of its values. Confronting these problems leads the writers in this section again and again to question who they are, what the nature of their homeland and their native culture is, and how the relationship of an individual to his or her culture should be defined in a context of uneven power distribution.

How can women resist colonial oppression and at the same time the gender discrimination their own culture may impose on them? How could whites living in apartheid South Africa resist the racial discrimination that benefited them socially and economically? Does a Western education undermine non-Western cultural identities? These are some of the questions that postcolonial writers ask. Some of the issues they raise, however, are of a more specifically linguistic and literary nature. What language should the postcolonial writer use? Using the colonizer's language may open up a wide audience, but it may also reinforce its dominance; on the other hand, using the language of the colonized may prevent wide public recognition, but it may also help to show its literary powers of expression. What audience is the postcolonial literary text aimed at? How can mostly oral literary traditions be translated into print? What literary forms and conventions are best suited to express the predicaments of the postcolonial situation? How can a non-Western writer appropriate the Western literary tradition and yet resist its claims of superiority over native traditions? In their wrestling with questions such as these, postcolonial writers turn literary texts into a battleground for cultural struggles that are deeply entangled with conflicts over political power and autonomy; they offer the reader literary insights and formal innovations that these very struggles make possible.

Jeremy Cronin
b. 1949

South African poet and activist politician Jeremy Cronin is the son of an officer in the South African navy and an office worker. He studied philosophy at the University of Cape Town and then in Paris. He became a lecturer at Cape Town until he was arrested in 1976 by the Apartheid government, charged with planning terrorist activities with fellow members of the African National Congress. He began writing poetry during his seven-year jail term, and received wide acclaim for his collection *Inside,* published after his release in 1983. Cronin has continued to write poetry while serving as a leader of the South African Communist Party and a member of the post-Apartheid South African parliament.

To learn how to speak

To learn how to speak
With the voices of the land,
To parse the speech in its rivers,
To catch in the inarticulate grunt,
Stammer, call, cry, babble, tongue's knot
A sense of the stoneness of these stones
From which all words are cut.
To trace with the tongue wagon-trails
Saying the suffix of their aches in -kuil, -pan, -fontein,[1]
In watery names that confirm
The dryness of their ways.
To visit the places of occlusion, or the lick
in a vlei-bank dawn.
To bury my mouth in the pit of your arm,
In that planetarium,

1. Endings for place-names, all indicating the presence of water.

Pectoral beginning to the nub of time
Down there close to the water-table, to feel
The full moon as it drums
At the back of my throat
Its cow-skinned vowel.
To write a poem with words like:
I'm telling you,
Stompie, stickfast, golovan,
Songololo, just boombang, just
To understand the least inflections,
To voice without swallowing
Syllables born in tin shacks, or catch
The 5.15 ikwata bust fife° *quarter past five*
Chwannisberg° train, to reach *Johannesburg*
The low chant of the mine gang's
Mineral glow of our people's unbreakable resolve.

To learn how to speak
With the voices of this land.

Derek Walcott
b. 1930

Born and raised on the Caribbean island of Saint Lucia, a British colony until 1967, Derek Walcott has both experienced and written about the often-troubled transition from colonial to postcolonial conditions. Imperial colonial trade in human labor had brought some of his ancestors to the island: Both of his grandmothers were descended from slaves. Walcott's heritage, like that of many, was mixed: His father, Warwick Walcott, was of English descent on his father's side, and Walcott has written of the irony that his father should have been named after Warwickshire, Shakespeare's home county.

Walcott's education in colonial Saint Lucia was thoroughly British. "The writers of my generation were natural assimilators," Walcott has written in his introduction to *Dream on Monkey Mountain and Other Plays.* "We knew the literatures of Empires, Greek, Roman, British, through their essential classics; and both the patois of the street and the language of the classroom had the elation of discovery." Walcott won a British government scholarship to a college in Jamaica, where he earned a degree in English in 1953. After several years as a schoolteacher, he won a fellowship to study theater in New York, then moved to Trinidad and founded the Little Carib Theater Workshop. From that time on, he has written plays fusing Caribbean and European elements while also developing skills as a watercolorist and an extraordinary lyric and narrative poet. He has continued to cross physical borders over the years, dividing his time between his home in Trinidad and a teaching post at Boston University.

Walcott's poems create a landscape of historical and personal memory, overlaying empires, centuries, continents, and stages of his own life, most notably in his 1990 verse novel *Omeros,* which rewrites Homer's epics—and James Joyce's *Ulysses*—as a Caribbean story of imperial and romantic conflict and a multiple search for the past. (A selection from *Omeros* appears on page 491 as a Resonance for Homer's *Odyssey.*) He was awarded the Nobel Prize in literature two years after its publication. The first two poems given here illustrate two major sides of Walcott's response to colonial and postcolonial conditions. His important early poem

"A Far Cry from Africa" (1962) expresses the divisions of history and self that arise from so mixed a heritage, while in "Volcano" (1976) he pays affectionate, ironic homage to his modernist predecessors Conrad and Joyce—artistic exiles both and prime models for the transmutation of colonial experience into lasting art. These poems are followed by "The Fortunate Traveller," a harrowing account of postcolonial border-crossing, self-seeking charity work, and moral corruption.

A Far Cry from Africa

A wind is ruffling the tawny pelt
Of Africa. Kikuyu,[1] quick as flies,
Batten° upon the bloodstreams of the veldt.° *fasten / open country*
Corpses are scattered through a paradise.
Only the worm, colonel of carrion, cries:
"Waste no compassion on these separate dead!"
Statistics justify and scholars seize
The salients of colonial policy.
What is that to the white child hacked in bed?
To savages, expendable as Jews?

Threshed out by beaters, the long rushes break
In a white dust of ibises[2] whose cries
Have wheeled since civilization's dawn
From the parched river or beast-teeming plain.
The violence of beast on beast is read
As natural law, but upright man
Seeks his divinity by inflicting pain.
Delirious as these worried beasts, his wars
Dance to the tightened carcass of a drum,
While he calls courage still that native dread
Of the white peace contracted by the dead.

Again brutish necessity wipes its hands
Upon the napkin of a dirty cause, again
A waste of our compassion, as with Spain,[3]
The gorilla wrestles with the superman.
I who am poisoned with the blood of both,
Where shall I turn, divided to the vein?
I who have cursed
The drunken officer of British rule, how choose
Between this Africa and the English tongue I love?
Betray them both, or give back what they give?
How can I face such slaughter and be cool?
How can I turn from Africa and live?

1. Indigenous people of Kenya.
2. Wading birds resembling storks.
3. In 1936–1939, many in the international community supported the constitutional government of Spain against a coup led by fascist General Francisco Franco. Franco's forces won, and he ruled as a dictator until his death in 1975.

Volcano

Joyce was afraid of thunder,
but lions roared at his funeral
from the Zurich zoo.
Was it Zurich or Trieste?[1]
No matter. These are legends, as much
As the death of Joyce is a legend,
or the strong rumor that Conrad
is dead, and that *Victory* is ironic.[2]
On the edge of the night-horizon
from this beach house on the cliffs
there are now, till dawn,
two glares from the miles-out-
at-sea derricks; they are like
the glow of the cigar
and the glow of the volcano
at *Victory*'s end.
One could abandon writing
for the slow-burning signals
of the great, to be, instead,
their ideal reader, ruminative,
voracious, making the love of masterpieces
superior to attempting
to repeat or outdo them,
and be the greatest reader in the world.
At least it requires awe,
which has been lost to our time;
so many people have seen everything,
so many people can predict,
so many refuse to enter the silence
of victory, the indolence
that burns at the core,
so many are no more than
erect ash, like the cigar,
so many take thunder for granted.
How common is the lightning,
how lost the leviathans
we no longer look for!
There were giants in those days.
In those days they made good cigars.
I must read more carefully.

1. Early in his career James Joyce lived in Trieste, where he began *Ulysses*; he died in Zurich in 1941.
2. *Victory* is a 1915 novel by Joseph Conrad concerning a European man's unsuccessful attempt to flee from the corruption of modern civilization by settling on a deserted island in Malaysia.

The Fortunate Traveller[1]

for Susan Sontag

And I heard a voice in the midst of the four beasts say,
A measure of wheat for a penny,
and three measures of barley for a penny;
and see thou hurt not the oil and the wine.
Revelation 6:6[2]

1

It was in winter. Steeples, spires
congealed like holy candles. Rotting snow
flaked from Europe's ceiling. A compact man,
I crossed the canal in a grey overcoat,
on one lapel a crimson buttonhole
for the cold ecstasy of the assassin.
In the square coffin manacled to my wrist:
small countries pleaded through the mesh of graphs,
in treble-spaced, Xeroxed forms to the World Bank
on which I had scrawled the one word, MERCY;

I sat on a cold bench
under some skeletal lindens.
Two other gentlemen, black skins gone grey
as their identical, belted overcoats,
crossed the white river.
They spoke the stilted French
of their dark river,
whose hooked worm, multiplying its pale sickle,
could thin the harvest of the winter streets.
"Then we can depend on you to get us those tractors?"
"I gave my word."
"May my country ask you why you are doing this, sir?"
Silence.
"You know if you betray us, you cannot hide?"
A tug. Smoke trailing its dark cry.

At the window in Haiti, I remember
a gecko° pressed against the hotel glass, *lizard*
with white palms, concentrating head.
With a child's hands. Mercy, monsieur. Mercy.
Famine sighs like a scythe
across the field of statistics and the desert
is a moving mouth. In the hold of this earth
10,000,000 shoreless souls are drifting.
Somalia: 765,000, their skeletons will go under the tidal sand.
"We'll meet you in Bristol to conclude the agreement?"

1. Walcott's title invokes Thomas Nashe's tale *The Unfortunate Traveller* (1594). Susan Sontag (1933–2004) was an American cultural critic and novelist.

2. One of the Four Horsemen of the Apocalypse is decreeing the famine and inflation that accompany wars as the end of the world approaches.

Steeples like tribal lances, through congealing fog
the cries of wounded church bells wrapped in cotton,
grey mist enfolding the conspirator
like a sealed envelope next to its heart.

No one will look up now to see the jet
fade like a weevil through a cloud of flour.
One flies first-class, one is so fortunate.
Like a telescope reversed, the traveller's eye
swiftly screws down the individual sorrow
to an oval nest of antic numerals,
and the iris, interlocking with this globe,
condenses it to zero, then a cloud.
Beetle-black taxi from Heathrow[3] to my flat.
We are roaches,
riddling the state cabinets, entering the dark holes
of power, carapaced in topcoats,
scuttling around columns, signalling for taxis,
with frantic antennae, to other huddles with roaches;
we infect with optimism, and when
the cabinets crack, we are the first
to scuttle, radiating separately
back to Geneva, Bonn, Washington, London.

Under the dripping planes of Hampstead Heath,
I read her letter again, watching the drizzle
disfigure its pleading like mascara. Margo,
I cannot bear to watch the nations cry.
Then the phone: "We will pay you in Bristol."
Days in fetid bedclothes swallowing cold tea,
the phone stifled by the pillow. The telly
a blue storm with soundless snow.
I'd light the gas and see a tiger's tongue.
I was rehearsing the ecstasies of starvation
for what I had to do. *And have not charity.*[4]

I found my pity, desperately researching
the origins of history, from reed-built communes
by sacred lakes, turning with the first sprocketed
water-driven wheels. I smelled imagination
among bestial hides by the gleam of fat,
seeking in all races a common ingenuity.
I envisaged an Africa flooded with such light
as alchemized the first fields of emmer wheat and barley,
when we savages dyed our pale dead with ochre,
and bordered our temples
with the ceremonial vulva of the conch
in the grey epoch of the obsidian adze.

3. London's primary airport.
4. Quoting St. Paul: "Though I speak with the tongues of men and of angels, and have not charity, I am become as sounding brass, or a tinkling cymbal" (1 Corinthians 13:1).

I sowed the Sahara with rippling cereals,
my charity fertilized these aridities.

What was my field? Late sixteenth century.
My field was a dank acre. A Sussex don,
I taught the Jacobean anxieties: *The White Devil.*[5]
Flamineo's torch startles the brooding yews.
The drawn end comes in strides. I loved my Duchess,
the white flame of her soul blown out between
the smoking cypresses. Then I saw children pounce
on green meat with a rat's ferocity.

I called them up and took the train to Bristol,
my blood the Severn's[6] dregs and silver.
On Severn's estuary the pieces flash,
Iscariot's salary,[7] patron saint of spies.
I thought, who cares how many million starve?
Their rising souls will lighten the world's weight
and level its gull-glittering waterline;
we left at sunset down the estuary.

England recedes. The forked white gull
screeches, circling back.
Even the birds are pulled back by their orbit,
even mercy has its magnetic field.
Back in the cabin,
I uncap the whisky, the porthole
mists with glaucoma. By the time I'm pissed,° *drunk*
England, England will be
that pale serrated indigo on the sea-line.
"You are so fortunate, you get to see the world—"
Indeed, indeed, sirs, I have seen the world.
Spray splashes the portholes and vision blurs.

Leaning on the hot rail, watching the hot sea,
I saw them far off, kneeling on hot sand
in the pious genuflections of the locust,
as Ponce's armoured knees crush Florida
to the funereal fragrance of white lilies.

2

Now I have come to where the phantoms live,
I have no fear of phantoms, but of the real.
The Sabbath benedictions of the islands.
Treble clef of the snail on the scored leaf,
the Tantum Ergo[8] of black choristers
soars through the organ pipes of coconuts.
Across the dirty beach surpliced with lace,
they pass a brown lagoon behind the priest,

5. Revenge tragedy (c. 1612) by John Webster.
6. A river running through Wales and England.
7. For betraying Jesus Christ, Judas Iscariot was paid 30 pieces of silver by the Roman authorities.
8. A hymn sung after the Blessed Sacrament has been exposed in the mass.

pale and unshaven in his frayed soutane,° *black robe*
into the concrete church at Canaries;
as Albert Schweitzer[9] moves to the harmonium
of morning, and to the pluming chimneys,
the groundswell lifts *Lebensraum, Lebensraum.*[1]

Black faces sprinkled with continual dew—
dew on the speckled croton,[2] dew
on the hard leaf of the knotted plum tree,
dew on the elephant ears of the dasheen.[3]
Through Kurtz's teeth, white skull in elephant grass,
the imperial fiction sings. Sunday
wrinkles downriver from the Heart of Darkness.
The heart of darkness is not Africa.
The heart of darkness is the core of fire
in the white center of the holocaust.
The heart of darkness is the rubber claw
selecting a scalpel in antiseptic light,
the hills of children's shoes outside the chimneys,
the tinkling nickel instruments on the white altar;
Jacob, in his last card, sent me these verses:
"Think of a God who doesn't lose His sleep
if trees burst into tears or glaciers weep.
So, aping His indifference, I write now,
not Anno Domini: After Dachau."[4]

3

The night maid brings a lamp and draws the blinds.
I stay out on the verandah with the stars.
Breakfast congealed to supper on its plate.

There is no sea as restless as my mind.
The promontories snore. They snore like whales.
Cetus, the whale, was Christ.
The ember dies, the sky smokes like an ash heap.
Reeds wash their hands of guilt and the lagoon
is stained. Louder, since it rained,
a gauze of sand flies hisses from the marsh.

Since God is dead,[5] and these are not His stars,
but man-lit, sulphurous, sanctuary lamps,
it's in the heart of darkness of this earth
that backward tribes keep vigil of His Body,
in deya, lampion,[6] and this bedside lamp.
Keep the news from their blissful ignorance.
Like lice, like lice, the hungry of this earth
swarm to the tree of life. If those who starve

9. German physician, missionary, and musician in Africa; winner of the Nobel Peace Prize in 1952.

1. Space to live in; the term is especially associated with Nazi Germany's territorial expansion.

2. A tropical plant.

3. The taro plant of tropical Asia.

4. Site of the notorious Nazi concentration camp.

5. So the German philosopher Friedrich Nietzsche declared in his 1882 text *The Gay Science.*

6. A small oil lamp with tinted glass.

like these rain-flies who shed glazed wings in light
grew from sharp shoulder blades their brittle vans
and soared towards that tree, how it would seethe—
ah, Justice! But fires
drench them like vermin, quotas
prevent them, and they remain
compassionate fodder for the travel book,
its paragraphs like windows from a train,
for everywhere that earth shows its rib cage
and the moon goggles with the eyes of children,
we turn away to read. Rimbaud[7] learned that.
Rimbaud, at dusk,
idling his wrist in water past temples
the plumed dates still protect in Roman file,
knew that we cared less for one human face
than for the scrolls in Alexandria's ashes,
that the bright water could not dye his hand
any more than poetry. The dhow's[8] silhouette
moved through the blinding coinage of the river
that, endlessly, until we pay one debt,
shrouds, every night, an ordinary secret.

4

The drawn sword comes in strides.
It stretches for the length of the empty beach;
the fishermen's huts shut their eyes tight.
A frisson° shakes the palm trees. *excited shiver*
and sweats on the traveller's tree.
They've found out my sanctuary. Philippe, last night:
"It had two gentlemen in the village yesterday, sir,
asking for you while you was in town.
I tell them you was in town. They send to tell you,
there is no hurry. They will be coming back."

In loaves of cloud, *and have not charity,*
the weevil will make a sahara of Kansas,
the ant shall eat Russia.
Their soft teeth shall make, *and have not charity,*
the harvest's desolation,
and the brown globe crack like a begging bowl,
and though you fire oceans of surplus grain,
and have not charity,
still, through thin stalks,
the smoking stubble, stalks
grasshopper: third horseman,
the leather-helmed locust.[9]

7. Arthur Rimbaud (1854-1891), French poet. After abandoning poetry at the age of 20, he traveled in Egypt and the Sudan, later settling in Ethiopia as a trader and arms dealer.

8. A sailing vessel used by Arabs.

9. The locust, eater of crops, is here identified with the horseman of the Apocalypse quoted in the poem's epigraph.

Mahmoud Darwish

b. 1941

Mahmoud Darwish is arguably the most important Arab poet writing today. He has succeeded in achieving wide popularity throughout the Arab world while showing constant concern for innovation and poetic experimentation in language and form. From the early years of his poetic career, Darwish was destined to devote his poetic talent to the cause of Palestine. Indeed, Darwish's childhood in an Israeli-controlled area of Palestine enhanced his sense of being an Arab and a Palestinian despite his Hebrew-language education. He was born in the village of al-Birwa in Palestine in 1941 and educated in his village's primary school and then in Nazareth Secondary School. He was seven when the state of Israel was created and his village was completely destroyed. His father, a wealthy farmer and landowner, was dispossessed and forced to work as a laborer in a quarry to sustain his family of eight children. In 1961 when his village became part of the newly created Israel and, like most Palestinians, he lost his civil rights, he joined the Rakah Israeli Communist Party, the only Israeli political party that accepted Arabs at the time. He worked for the Arabic newspaper of the party and its literary journal, where he published his early poems.

Darwish's first poem, which he read at his school's annual party when he was only fourteen, put him in direct confrontation with Israeli military rule. It was a heartfelt cry from an Arab child to his Jewish peer at school about the simple things denied to an Arab boy and allowed to his Jewish counterpart. The following day, he was summoned to the office of the military ruler of the area and threatened that if he persisted in writing poetry, his father would be prevented from working at the local quarry. At the age of nineteen, he published his first collection of poetry, *Sparrows without Wings* (1960). The following year he was arrested for writing poetry and given his first taste of Israeli prison.

The conflict between the poet and his jailers continued. In 1965 he published his second collection, *Olive Branches,* and was arrested for the second time. In 1966 he published his third collection, *A Lover from Palestine,* and was imprisoned once again. In 1967 he published his fourth collection, *The End of Night,* and was jailed for yet a fourth time. His life became a series of poems and cells, and when he was out of prison his freedom of movement and expression were curtailed, and he was subjected to long periods of house arrest. In his *Diaries of Ordinary Grief* (1973), he talks about life under house arrest as a pattern in which he has his days and "they" have control over his nights, for he wasn't allowed to leave his house between sunset and sunrise. The more the Israeli authorities feared his words, the more he became aware of the power of poetry and of the importance of the Arabic language as an expression of his identity.

In 1970 the pattern of poems and prison was broken when he published his collection *Sparrows Die in Galilee* and left immediately for Moscow to complete his education, which was denied him in Israel. Having completed his one-year course in Moscow, he dreaded going back to the old pattern of poetry and prison and decided to join other Palestinians who left their homeland. In 1971 he moved to Egypt and a year later to Beirut, where he stayed until the Israeli invasion of Lebanon in 1982. In his words, he "joined Ulysses in his search for Ithaca," and developed his poetry as the voice of the Palestinian consciousness on the one hand and as the expression of the aspirations of the oppressed on the other. In his *Diaries,* he states, "He who turned me into a refugee changed me into a bomb," and he has continued to explode in strong poetry ever since. Since 1971 he has published twenty more collections of poetry and two prose works, *Something about Home* (1971) and *A Memory for Oblivion* (1986).

Darwish's rich output of poetry can be divided into three different phases. In the Israeli phase (1960–1971), his poetry is marked by its lyrical iconography of simple Palestinian objects redolent with significance and symbolism. The Beirut phase (1972–1982) witnessed the cynical maturity of the poet and the dissipation of the simple optimism of revolutionary innocence, for this is the phase of inter-Arab conflicts, with more Palestinians being killed by Arabs than by Israelis. Like Eliot's "Unreal city" of *The Waste Land,* Darwish's Beirut amalgamates the spirit of the Arab city and the ethos of hell and is entangled in mythological and intertextual allusions. The third, post-Beirut phase (since 1982) oscillates between long dramatic poems and tense short ones in which he invokes the biblical lyric of lament and turns it against itself so that it ceases to sound euphonious and lyrical. The psalmlike poems depict an abandoned people in Babylonian exile and captivity, and pierce like shrapnel. His long poems, with their epic quality, crystallize the sense of physical dislocation, political chaos, and failure of Arab politics, especially since the Israeli invasion of Lebanon in 1982 and the ongoing, unresolved uprisings that have followed. These poems renew some fundamental aspects of literary modernism's pervasive negativity and pessimism; toward the end of this phase, the poet becomes increasingly aware of the apathy of his reader in a world of endless conflict. The poems selected here are from the last two phases.

PRONUNCIATION:

Mahmoud Darwish: mah-MOOD dahr-WEESH

A Poem Which Is Not Green, from My Country[1]

In my country
where Sinbad's sail never swayed in the wind
dreamingly bearing its basket of *jihad*° yarns *holy war*
& tales of the heroes
    & of that sun beyond the gorges
where it wandered through no single night of the nights of Scheherazade
where no dawn broke over it
    nor stretched to it white bountiful hands . . .
In my country
are the graveyards of light & of luminous flowers,
the well-spring of grief.
The colours of our letter are persecuted.
Trussed it cries out.
They stifled it.
They squeezed its spark from it.
They robbed it of the borders of kindness.
They crushed it till it began to burn
& then burst.
Our letter became a wound where dusk is swimming.
In silence it is breaking into bud the flowers & bunches of basil!
& in my country appointments with dawn are calling out
to the swallows lost behind the horizons of my country
where they cast off neglected their poems
    when the long night of lovers' separation lost them.

1. Translated by Ian Wedde and Fawwaz Tuqan.

The swallow may be silent but never forgets its song.
    It will sing it will cry out
when my country's olive trees blossom
when the sky's rains wash away
the spots of consumption the thorns of fate!
In my country
they opened the wound & then said: It must be sutured!
They silenced it anaesthetized it
wrapped it with fog
taught it silence & the early autumn of torture.
& it was awakened by silence & said:
In my country: in the country of mankind: in every country
the wound grows silent but never heals.
The wound believed in its future.
    Is there anything without future?
Where the wound is watered by the blood of songs
in gardens where the colour of life is dry
& the larks sing
& the swallows which returned sing
having come back to life . . .

Diary of a Palestinian Wound[1]

Rubaiyat° for Fadwa Tuqan — quatrains

1

We're free not to remember because Carmel's within us
& on our eyelashes grows the grass of the Province of Galilee.[2]
Don't say: I wish we were running to it like the river /
don't say this.
We exist in the flesh of our country & it in us.

2

Before June we weren't like little doves
which is why our love wasn't crushed among the chains.
O Sister we've *existed* for twenty years.
We haven't been writing poetry but struggling.

3

That shadow cast in your eyes
is a devil / a god:
it came with the month of June to bandage
foreheads with the sun /
it's the colour of a martyr
it's the taste of a prayer.
It can kill or resurrect
    & in either case: ah!

1. Translated by Ian Wedde and Fawwaz Tuqan.

2. Carmel and Galilee are famously beautiful areas now under Israeli control.

4

Night falling in your eyes
was a drop of the long night's end in my heart
& what gathers us at this hour in this place
is the way back from an age of wilting.

5

Your voice tonight's a knife & a wound & a bandage
& torpor which crept from the victims' silence /
Where are my people? They quit the tent of exile & returned
yet again as captives.

6

Love-words didn't rust but the beloved
collapses into captivity /   O Beloved you loaded me
with balconies torn loose by wind / porches of houses & guilts.
Once my heart could hold nothing but your eyes
& now it's enriched with the homeland.

7

& we knew what makes the lark's voice
a dagger flashing in the invader's face
& we knew what makes the silence of the cemetery
a festival & gardens of life!

8

While you sang I saw balconies
migrating from the walls & the square /
    falling back to the mountain's waist.
We weren't listening to music nor peering at the colours of words.
There were a million heroes in the room.

9

Because of his face
    a summer & an unnatural pulse have broken into my blood.
I came home abashed /
    the house collapsed upon a martyr's gash.
It was the Christmas manger
    it was hope
& I was gleaning a festival from the memory of it.

10

His eyes were dew & fire
    & if I drew near his face it sang
& I evaporated on its arm: a moment of silence & a prayer.
Oh call it "a martyr" if you wish.
It's more beautiful than we are.
It left its hovel a youth then returned in its own time
the face of a god!

11

This land which sucks the skin of martyrs
promises wheat & stars to the Summer
so worship it: we are salt & water in its bowels
& in its embrace a wound which is fighting!

12

I was created tearful O Sister & now fire's in my eye
& I shook myself loose of complaints at the Caliph's door.
All those who died & those who will die at the day's gate
embraced me   made a bomb of me.

13

The loved ones' house is deserted & Jaffa[3]
has been translated to its very marrow
& whoever was searching for me
    found nothing but its forehead!
Leave all this death to me O Sister
    leave this vagrancy.
Look! I'm braiding it into a star above its catastrophe.

14

O brave-faced wound
my homeland isn't a suitcase
& I'm not a traveller.
I am the lover & the land is the beloved.

15

If I lingered over memories there would grow
on my forehead the grass of regret
& I'd grieve for something distant
& if I surrendered to desire
I'd adopt the legends of slaves
but I prefer to make a pebble of my voice
& a melody of the rock.

16

My forehead doesn't carry the shadow
    & I can't see my own
& I spit in the wound which fails
to set fire to the night with foreheads.
Save your tears for the festival: we'll cry
from nothing but joy.
Come   let's call sudden death in the square
a wedding & a life!

17

& I was reared on the wound & never told my mother
what makes her a tent in the night.
I preserved my well-spring & my address & my name
& so observed a million stars in her names.

18

My banner is black & the harbour is a coffin & my back is a bridge.
O Autumn of the age crumbling within us
O Spring of the world reborn within us
my rose is red & the harbour is open & my heart is a tree.

3. Palestinian city absorbed into the new Israeli city of Tel Aviv.

19

My language is the sound of rippling water in the river of storms.
The sun's & the grain's mirrors are in a battlefield.
No doubt my verse was sometimes askew
but (why deny it?) I was terrific
when I traded the dictionary for my heart!

20

There had to be enemies for us to find we were twins.
There had to be wind for us to live in the trunks of oaks.
& if the crucified lord hadn't come of age on the throne of the cross
he'd have remained a child whose wound was forfeit: a coward.

21

I have a word for you /
I haven't said it yet
  because the shadow on the balcony occupies the moon.
My country's an epic /
I was a musician in that epic
  & I've become a chord!

22

The archaeologist's busy analysing stones.
He's looking for his eyes in the rubble of legends
to prove I'm a transient on the road /
lacking eyes & language in civilization's book!
Meanwhile I slowly plant my trees & sing about my love.

23

The summer cloud which is carried on the back of defeat
pegged out the offspring of Sultans on the lines of mirages.
I am dead & newborn in the night of the crime.
See! see how I cleave to the soil!

24

It's time for me to trade word for deed.
It's time for me to prove my love to earth & lark
because in this age bludgeon devours guitar
& the mirror shows me diminished
since there came this tree in my eye.

Sirhan Drinks His Coffee in the Cafeteria[1]

They arrive.
Our doors are the sea.
The rain surprised us.
No God but God.
The rain surprised us, and the bullets.
The earth here is a carpet,
And they continue to arrive.

1. Translated by Rana Kabbani.

You do not know the day.
You cannot tell the colour,
Nor the taste. Nor the voice.
You do not know the shape.
Sirhan is born, and Sirhan grows.
He drinks the wine and raves,
He draws his killer and he tears the picture,
He kills him when he sees his final shape.

Sirhan writes upon his jacket's sleeve
And memory takes a bird's beak
And eats the wheat of Galilee.

What was love?
Hands that were expressive,
Chains and prisons being formed,
Exiles being born.
We wrap around your name.
We were a people now we are of stone.
You were a country now you are of smoke.
Old chains are bracelets of blown roses
Old chains are maidenhead and passion
In this new exile.

Sirhan lies when he says he drank your milk.
Sirhan grew up in the kitchens of a ship
Which never touched your shores.

What is your name?
I've forgotten.
What is your father's name?
I've forgotten.
And your mother's?
I've forgotten.
Did you sleep last night?
I slept for an eternity.
Did you dream?
I dreamt.
He cried suddenly:
Why did you drink the oil you smuggled
From the wounds of Christ?

We saw his fingers begging.
We saw him measuring the sky with chains.
Lands that change their people,
Stars that spread like pebbles.
He sang:
Our generation passed and died.
The killers bred in us the victims grew in us
Blood like water.
Mothers who married enemies.

We called out, "wheat!"
The echo came back "war"
We called out, "home!"
The echo came back "war"
We called out, "Jaffa!"
The echo came back "war"
From that day on we measured skies with chains.

Sirhan laughs in the kitchens of the ship.
He holds a tourist and is lost.
All lands are far that lead to Nazareth.
All lands are far except for Nazareth.

Songs speak to him, and holidays make him lonely.
The smell of coffee is geography.
They exiled you.
They murdered you.
Your father hid behind the texts
And watched them come.
The smell of coffee is a tender hand.
The smell of coffee is a voice that takes you.
The smell of coffee is a sound that gurgles
Like the water in the alleys when it rains.

Sirhan knows more than one language
Or one woman. He has a pass to leave the ocean
He has another pass to enter it.
He is a drop of blood looking for its wound.
The smell of coffee is geography.
He drinks his coffee and he dreams.

You were born here. Yet you live there.
Your city does not sleep. It has no lasting names.
Houses change inhabitants,
Windows leave their places as they enter memory.
Sirhan draws a shape then cancels it.
He does not read the papers, so how does sorrow
Reach him?

What is Jerusalem but a stance for speeches,
But a step to hungry power?
What is Jerusalem but cigarettes and liquor?
Yet it is my country.
You would not find a difference
Between its curved fields
And my palm.
You could not find the difference
Between the night that sleeps in memory
And the night upon the Carmel.

He tears the clouds apart
And throws them at the winds.

I ate. I drank. I slept. I dreamt.
I learnt a vowel.
He writes: ص ط ض ع ظ
And they disappear before him,
The dins of oceans in them,
The din of silence in them.
Letters to distinguish us from others.
We stone them with our diphthongs.
Shall we fight?
What matter,
Since the Arab revolution
Remains preserved in anthems,
In flags and at the bank.
In your wounds' name they speak their speech.
Christ becomes a dealer
Who signs away his merchandise of cloth.
No sky for you except this tent:
It burns, you burn.

We come to you as prisoners or corpses.
Sirhan a prisoner of the peace and war.
He reads the details of his fate
On the wall behind the stripper's legs:
Your war is two wars,
Your war is two wars.

Sirhan!
Did you kill?
Sirhan is silent.
He drinks his coffee and he dreams.
He draws a map without a border in it.
He measures earth with chains.
He draws a picture of his killer,
He rips it up,
Then kills it when it takes a final shape.

Birds Die in Galilee[1]

We will meet in a while,
In a year,
In two years,
In sixteen.
She threw into her camera
Twenty gardens
And the birds of Galilee.

She could not know that we gave her,
Death and I, the secrets of love

1. Translated by Rana Kabbani.

At the custom's gate.
So she must leave what makes wheat
The lashes of the earth,
What makes volcanoes
Another name for jasmine.

Nothing tired me at night
Except her silence
When it spread out like a street.
Be what you must, Rita,
Make the silence an axe
Or a frame for stars
Or a place for a tree in labour.

Flocks of birds fell like paper
Into the wells
And when I lifted the blue wings
I saw a growing grave.
I am the man on whose skin
Chains have carved a country.

Salman Rushdie

b. 1947

Born in Bombay on the day India achieved independence from Britain, Salman Rushdie was raised in largely Muslim Pakistan after the subcontinent was divided later that year. He later settled in England and achieved international fame with his 1981 novel *Midnight's Children,* a sprawling, fantasy-filled comedy of Indian history and individual romance, drawing upon both a multitude of Indian tales and the heritage of British novelists from Laurence Sterne to E. M. Forster. *Midnight's Children* won England's prestigious Booker Prize that year and was later judged the best novel of all the winners in the award's first twenty-five years.

Rushdie's fortunes took a very different turn after he published his 1988 novel *Satanic Verses,* which treated the history of Islam with sometimes sardonic irony. The book was taken by many Muslims as a blasphemous affront, and in 1989 Iran's religious and political leader, the Ayatollah Khomeini, issued a *fatwa,* or religious decree, ordering Rushdie's death. Rushdie had to go into hiding, somewhat reluctantly protected by the government of Britain's Margaret Thatcher, whose policies he had satirized as well. Following Khomeini's death, subsequent Iranian leaders have suggested that the decree would not be enforced; Rushdie eventually settled in the United States and resumed making public appearances.

Rushdie has continued to cross borders in his work as well as in his life; the story given here, "Chekov and Zulu," comes from his 1994 collection *East, West.* At first sight, the title may seem to link a classic European writer with an African tribalist, but in fact the names derive from two of the supporting characters in the television and movie series *Star Trek.* The story plays throughout on the overlays and the gaps between visual and verbal media, popular and classical culture, high tech and low humor. Rushdie's unheroic heroes fancy themselves characters aboard the starship *Enterprise,* blasted somehow into a conflict in the Middle Earth of J. R. R. Tolkien. They use this doubled frame of reference to try and make sense of the cultural dislocations and the growing political violence they experience as they move between England and India. Told in a riot of Indian-inflected English and using a wide array of cultural references, Rushdie's story moves from social comedy to a surprising and chilling conclusion.

Chekov and Zulu

1

On 4th November, 1984, Zulu disappeared in Birmingham, and India House sent his old schoolfriend Chekov to Wembley[1] to see the wife.

"Adaabarz, Mrs. Zulu. Permission to enter?"

"Of course come in, Dipty sahib, why such formality?"

"Sorry to disturb you on a Sunday, Mrs. Zulu, but Zulu-tho hasn't been in touch this morning?"

"With me? Since when he contacts me on official trip? Why to hit a telephone call when he is probably enjoying?"

"Whoops, sore point, excuse *me.* Always been the foot-in-it blunderbuss type."

"At least sit, take tea-shee."

"Fixed the place up damn fine, Mrs. Zulu, wah-wah.[2] Tasteful decor, in spades, I must say. So much cut-glass! That bounder Zulu must be getting too much pay, more than yours truly, clever dog."

"No, how is it possible? Acting Dipty's tankha[3] must be far in excess of Security Chief."

"No suspicion intended, ji.[4] Only to say what a bargain-hunter you must be."

"Some problem but there is, na?"

"Beg pardon?"

"Arré,[5] Jaisingh! Where have you been sleeping? Acting Dipty Sahib is thirsting for his tea. And biscuits and jalebis, can you not keep two things in your head? Jump, now, guest is waiting."

"Truly, Mrs. Zulu, please go to no trouble."

"No trouble is there, Diptyji, only this chap has become lazy since coming from home. Days off, TV in room, even pay in pounds sterling, he expects all. So far we brought him but no gratitude, what to tell you, noth-*thing.*"

"Ah, Jaisingh; why not? Excellent jalebi, Mrs. Z. Thanking you."

Assembled on top of the television and on shelf units around it was the missing man's collection of *Star Trek* memorabilia: Captain Kirk and Spock dolls, spaceship models—a Klingon Bird of Prey, a Romulan vessel, a space station, and of course the Starship *Enterprise.* In pride of place were large figurines of two of the series's supporting cast.

"These old Doon School nicknames," Chekov exclaimed heartily. "They stay put like stuck records. Dumpy, Stumpy, Grumpy, Humpy. They take over from our names. As in our case our intrepid cosmonaut aliases."

"I don't like. This 'Mrs. Zulu' I am landed with! It sounds like a blackie."

"Wear the name with pride, begum[6] sahib. We're old comrades-in-arms, your husband and I; since boyhood days, perhaps he was good enough to mention? Intrepid

1. Birmingham is a city in West Midlands, central England; Wembley is a London suburb.
2. Excellent.
3. Wages.
4. Term of respect added to ends of sentences or words.
5. Exclamation of surprise.
6. High-ranking Muslim woman.

diplonauts. Our umpteen-year mission to explore new worlds and new civilisations. See there, our alter egos standing on your TV, the Asiatic-looking Russky and the Chink. Not the leaders, as you'll appreciate, but the ultimate professional servants. 'Course laid in!' 'Hailing frequencies open!' 'Warp factor three!' What would that strutting Captain have been without his top-level staffers? Likewise with the good ship Hindustan.[7] We are servants also, you see, just like your fierce Jaisingh here. Never more important than in a moment like the present sad crisis, when an even keel must be maintained, jalebis must be served and tea poured, no matter what. We do not lead, but we enable. Without us, no course can be laid, no hailing frequency opened. No factors can be warped."

"Is he in difficulties, then, your Zulu? As if it wasn't bad enough, this terrible time."

On the wall behind the TV was a framed photograph of Indira Gandhi,[8] with a garland hung around it. She had been dead since Wednesday. Pictures of her cremation had been on the TV for hours. The flower-petals, the garish, unbearable flames.

"Hard to believe it. Indiraji! Words fail one. She was our mother. Hai, hai! Cut down in her prime."

"And on radio-TV, such-such stories are coming about Delhi goings-on. So many killings, Dipty Sahib. So many of our decent Sikh[9] people done to death, as if all were guilty for the crimes of one-two badmash guards."

"The Sikh community has always been thought loyal to the nation," Chekov reflected. "Backbone of the Army, to say nothing of the Delhi taxi service. Super-citizens, one might say, seemingly wedded to the national idea. But such ideas are being questioned now, you must admit; there are those who would point to the comb, bangle, dagger et cetera as signs of the enemy within."

"Who would dare say such a thing about us? Such an evil thing."

"I know. I know. But you take Zulu. The ticklish thing is, he's not on any official business that we know of. He's dropped off the map, begum sahib. AWOL[1] ever since the assassination. No contact for two days plus."

"O God."

"There is a view forming back at HQ that he may have been associated with the gang. Who have in all probability long-established links with the community over here."

"O God."

"Naturally I am fighting strenuously against the proponents of this view. But his absence is damning, you must see. We have no fear of these tinpot Khalistan wallahs.[2] But they have a ruthless streak. And with Zulu's inside knowledge and security background . . . They have threatened further attacks, as you know. As you must know. As some would say you must know all too well."

"O God."

"It is possible," Chekov said, eating his jalebi, "that Zulu has boldly gone where no Indian diplonaut has gone before."

The wife wept. "Even the stupid name you could never get right. It was with S. 'Sulu.' So-so many episodes I have been made to see, you think I don't know? Kirk Spock McCoy Scott Uhura Chekov *Sulu.*"

7. Persian name for India.
8. Indian prime minister between 1966–1977 and 1980–1984; assassinated in 1984.
9. Community in the Punjab whose religion attempts to combine Hinduism and Islam.
1. Absent without leave.
2. Sikh military who call for a separate Sikh state called Khalistan; *wallah* means boy or man.

"But Zulu is a better name for what some might allege to be a wild man," Chekov said. "For a suspected savage. For a putative traitor. Thank you for excellent tea."

2

In August, Zulu, a shy, burly giant, had met Chekov off the plane from Delhi. Chekov at thirty-three was a small, slim, dapper man in grey flannels, stiff-collared shirt and a double-breasted navy blue blazer with brass buttons. He had bat's-wing eyebrows and a prominent and pugnacious jaw, so that his cultivated tones and habitual soft-spokenness came as something of a surprise, disarming those who had been led by the eyebrows and chin to expect an altogether more aggressive personality. He was a high flyer, with one small embassy already notched up. The Acting Number Two job in London, while strictly temporary, was his latest plum.

"What-ho, Zools! Years, yaar,[3] years," Chekov said, thumping his palm into the other man's chest. "So," he added, "I see you've become a hairy fairy." The young Zulu had been a modern Sikh in the matter of hair—sporting a fine moustache at eighteen, but beardless, with a haircut instead of long tresses wound tightly under a turban. Now, however, he had reverted to tradition.

"Hullo, ji," Zulu greeted him cautiously. "So then is it OK to utilise the old modes of address?"

"Utilise away! Wouldn't hear of anything else," Chekov said, handing Zulu his bags and baggage tags. "Spirit of the *Enterprise* and all that jazz."

In his public life the most urbane of men, Chekov when letting his hair down in private enjoyed getting interculturally hot under the collar. Soon after his taking up his new post he sat with Zulu one lunchtime on a bench in Embankment Gardens and jerked his head in the direction of various passers-by.

"Crooks," he said, *sotto voce*.[4]

"Where?" shouted Zulu, leaping athletically to his feet. "Should I pursue?"

Heads turned. Chekov grabbed the hem of Zulu's jacket and pulled him back on to the bench. "Don't be such a hero," he admonished fondly. "I meant all of them, generally; thieves, every last one. God, I love London! Theatre, ballet, opera, restaurants! The Pavilion at Lord's on the Saturday of the Test Match![5] The royal ducks on the royal pond in royal St. James's Park! Decent tailors, a decent mixed grill when you want it, decent magazines to read! I see the remnants of greatness and I don't mind telling you I am impressed. The Athenaeum, Buck House, the lions in Trafalgar Square. *Damn* impressive. I went to a meeting with the junior Minister at the F. & C.O. and realised I was in the old India Office. All that John Company black teak, those tuskers rampant on the old bookcases. Gave me quite a turn. I applaud them for their success: hurrah! But then I look at my own home, and I see that it has been plundered by burglars. I can't deny there is a residue of distress."

"I am sorry to hear of your loss," Zulu said, knitting his brows. "But surely the culpables are not in the vicinity."

"Zulu, Zulu, a figure of speech, my simpleton warrior prince. Their museums are full of our treasures, I meant. Their fortunes and cities, built on the loot they

3. Friend, buddy.
4. Softly.
5. A cricket match played between international all-star teams.

took. So on, so forth. One forgives, of course; that is our national nature. One need not forget."

Zulu pointed at a tramp, sleeping on the next bench in a ragged hat and coat. "Did he steal from us, too?" he asked.

"Never forget," said Chekov, wagging a finger, "that the British working class collaborated for its own gain in the colonial project. Manchester cotton workers, for instance, supported the destruction of our cotton industry. As diplomats we must never draw attention to such facts; but facts, nevertheless, they remain."

"But a beggarman is not in the working class," objected Zulu, reasonably. "Surely this fellow at least is not our oppressor."

"Zulu," Chekov said in exasperation, "don't be so bleddy difficult."

Chekov and Zulu went boating on the Serpentine, and Chekov got back on his hobby-horse. "They have stolen us," he said, reclining boatered and champagned on striped cushions while mighty Zulu rowed. "And now we are stealing ourselves back. It is an Elgin marbles[6] situation."

"You should be more content," said Zulu, shipping oars and gulping cola. "You should be less hungry, less cross. See how much you have! It is enough. Sit back and enjoy. I have less, and it suffices for me. The sun is shining. The colonial period is a closed book."

"If you don't want that sandwich, hand it over," said Chekov. "With my natural radicalism I should not have been a diplomat. I should have been a terrorist."

"But then we would have been enemies, on opposite sides," protested Zulu, and suddenly there were real tears in his eyes. "Do you care nothing for our friendship? For my responsibilities in life?"

Chekov was abashed. "Quite right, Zools old boy. Too bleddy true. You can't imagine how delighted I was when I learned we would be able to join forces like this in London. Nothing like the friendships of one's boyhood, eh? Nothing in the world can take their place. Now listen, you great lummox, no more of that long face. I won't permit it. Great big chap like you shouldn't look like he's about to blub. Blood brothers, old friend, what do you say? All for one and one for all."

"Blood brothers," said Zulu, smiling a shy smile.

"Onward, then," nodded Chekov, settling back on his cushions. "Impulse power only."

The day Mrs. Gandhi was murdered by her Sikh bodyguards, Zulu and Chekov played squash in a private court in St. John's Wood. In the locker-room after showering, prematurely-greying Chekov still panted heavily with a towel round his softening waist, reluctant to expose his exhaustion-shrivelled purple penis to view; Zulu stood proudly naked, thick-cocked, tossing his fine head of long black hair, caressing and combing it with womanly sensuality, and at last twisting it swiftly into a knot.

"Too good, Zulu yaar. Fataakh! Fataakh! What shots! Too bleddy good for me."

"You desk-pilots, ji. You lose your edge. Once you were ready for anything."

"Yeah, yeah, I'm over the hill. But you were only one year junior."

"I have led a purer life, ji—action, not words."

"You understand we will have to blacken your name," Chekov said softly.

6. A group of sculptures removed from the Acropolis in Athens by Lord Elgin in 1801–1803 and purchased by the British Museum in 1816. Recent opinion polls have suggested that over 90 percent of the British public support the return of the marbles to Greece, though a 1996 resolution in the Parliament was tabled.

Zulu turned slowly in Charles Atlas pose in front of a full-length mirror.

"It has to look like a maverick stunt. If anything goes wrong, deniability is essential. Even your wife must not suspect the truth."

Spreading his arms and legs, Zulu made his body a giant X, stretching himself to the limit. Then he came to attention. Chekov sounded a little frayed.

"Zools? What do you say?"

"Is the transporter ready?"

"Come on, yaar, don't arse around."

"Respectfully, Mister Chekov, sir, it's my arse. Now then: is the transporter ready?"

"Transporter ready. Aye."

"Then, energise."

Chekov's memorandum, classified top-secret, eyes-only, and addressed to "JTK" (James T. Kirk):

> *My strong recommendation is that Operation Startrek be aborted. To send a Federation employee of Klingon origin unarmed into a Klingon cell to spy is the crudest form of loyalty test. The operative in question has never shown ideological deviation of any sort and deserves better, even in the present climate of mayhem, hysteria and fear. If he fails to persuade the Klingons of his* bona fides *he can expect to be treated with extreme prejudice. These are not hostage takers.*
>
> *The entire undertaking is misconceived. The locally settled Klingon population is not the central problem. Even should we succeed, such intelligence as can be gleaned about more important principals back home will no doubt be of dubious accuracy and limited value. We should advise Star Fleet Headquarters to engage urgently with the grievances and aspirations of the Klingon people. Unless these are dealt with fair and square there cannot be a lasting peace.*

The reply from JTK:

> *Your closeness to the relevant individual excuses what is otherwise an explosively communalist document. It is not for you to define the national interest nor to determine what undercover operations are to be undertaken. It is for you to enable such operations to occur and to provide back-up as and when required to do so. As a personal favour to you and in the name of my long friendship with your eminent Papaji I have destroyed your last without keeping a copy and suggest you do the same. Also destroy this.*

Chekov asked Zulu to drive him up to Stratford for a performance of *Coriolanus.*[7]

"How many kiddiwinks by now? Three?"

"Four," said Zulu. "All boys."

"By the grace of God. She must be a good woman."

"I have a full heart," said Zulu, with sudden feeling. "A full house, a full belly, a full bed."

"Lucky so and so," said Chekov. "Always were warm-blooded. I, by contrast, am not. Reptiles, certain species of dinosaur, and me. I am in the wife market, by the way, if you know any suitable candidates. Bachelordom being, after a certain point, an obstacle on the career path."

7. Shakespeare's bloodiest tragedy; its themes are civil unrest and revolt.

Zulu was driving strangely. In the slow lane of the motorway, as they approached an exit lane, he accelerated towards a hundred miles an hour. Once the exit was behind them, he slowed. Chekov noticed that he varied his speed and lane constantly. "Doesn't the old rattletrap have cruise control?" he asked. "Because, sport, this kind of performance would not do on the bridge of the flagship of the United Federation of Planets."

"Anti-surveillance," said Zulu. "Dry-cleaning." Chekov, alarmed, looked out of the back window.

"Have we been rumbled, then?"

"Nothing to worry about," grinned Zulu. "Better safe than sorry is all. Always anticipate the worst-case scenario."

Chekov settled back in his seat. "You liked toys and games," he said. Zulu had been a crack rifle shot, the school's champion wrestler, and an expert fencer. "Every Speech Day," Zulu said, "I would sit in the hall and clap, while you went up for all the work prizes. English Prize, History Prize, Latin Prize, Form Prize. Clap, clap, clap, term after term, year after year. But on Sports Day I got my cups. And now also I have my area of expertise."

"Quite a reputation you're building up, if what I hear is anything to go by."

There was a silence. England passed by at speed.

"Do you like Tolkien?" Zulu asked.

"I wouldn't have put you down as a big reader," said Chekov, startled. "No offence."

"J. R. R. Tolkien," said Zulu. "*The Lord of the Rings*."[8]

"Can't say I've read the gentleman. Heard of him, of course. Elves and pixies. Not your sort of thing at all, I'd have thought."

"It is about a war to the finish between Good and Evil," said Zulu intently. "And while this great war is being fought there is one part of the world, the Shire, in which nobody even knows it's going on. The hobbits who live there work and squabble and make merry and they have no fucking clue about the forces that threaten them, and those that save their tiny skins." His face was red with vehemence.

"Meaning me, I suppose," Chekov said.

"I am a soldier in that war," said Zulu. "If you sit in an office you don't have one small idea of what the real world is like. The world of action, ji. The world of deeds, of things that are done and maybe undone too. The world of life and death."

"Only in the worst case," Chekov demurred.

"Do I tell you how to apply your smooth-tongued musca-polish to people's behinds?" stormed Zulu. "Then do not tell me how to ply my trade."

Soldiers going into battle pump themselves up, Chekov knew. This chest-beating was to be expected, it must not be misunderstood. "When will you vamoose?" he quietly asked.

"Chekov ji, you won't see me go."

Stratford approached. "Did you know, ji," Zulu offered, "that the map of Tolkien's Middle-earth fits quite well over central England and Wales? Maybe all fairylands are right here, in our midst."

"You're a deep one, old Zools," said Chekov. "Full of revelations today."

8. Tolkien's trilogy (1954–1955), written during and just after World War II, concerns a war for control of Middle Earth, in which men, elves, dwarves, and a few British-like hobbits band together to defeat the evil eastern empire of Sauron.

Chekov had a few people over for dinner at his modern-style official residence in a private road in Hampstead: a Very Big Businessman he was wooing, journalists he liked, prominent India-lovers, noted Non-Resident Indians. The policy was business as usual. The dreadful event must not be seen to have derailed the ship of State: whose new captain, Chekov mused, was a former pilot himself. As if a Sulu, a Chekov had been suddenly promoted to the skipper's seat.

Damned difficult doing all this without a lady wife to act as hostess, he grumbled inwardly. The best golden plates with the many-headed lion at the centre, the finest crystal, the menu, the wines. Personnel had been seconded from India House to help him out, but it wasn't the same. The secrets of good evenings, like God, were in the details. Chekov meddled and fretted.

The evening went off well. Over brandy, Chekov even dared to introduce a blacker note. "England has always been a breeding ground for our revolutionists," he said. "What would Pandit Nehru[9] have been without Harrow?[1] Or Gandhiji without his formative experiences here? Even the Pakistan idea was dreamt up by young radicals at college in what we then were asked to think of as the Mother Country. Now that England's status has declined, I suppose it is logical that the quality of the revolutionists she breeds has likewise fallen. The Kashmiris![2] Not a hope in hell. And as for these Khalistan types, let them not think that their evil deed has brought their dream a day closer. On the contrary. On the contrary. We will root them out and smash them to—what's the right word?—to *smithereens*."

To his surprise he had begun speaking loudly and had risen to his feet. He sat down hard and laughed. The moment passed.

"The funny thing about this blasted nickname of mine," he said quickly to his dinner-table neighbour, the septuagenarian Very Big Businessman's improbably young and attractive wife, "is that back then we never saw one episode of the TV series. No TV to see it on, you see. The whole thing was just a legend wafting its way from the US and UK to our lovely hill-station of Dehra Dun.

"After a while we got a couple of cheap paperback novelisations and passed them round as if they were naughty books like *Lady C* or some such. Lots of us tried the names on for size but only two of them stuck; probably because they seemed to go together, and the two of us got on pretty well, even though he was younger. A lovely boy. So just like Laurel and Hardy we were Chekov and Zulu."

"Love and marriage," said the woman.

"Beg pardon?"

"*You* know," she said. "Go together like is it milk and porridge. Or a car and garage, that's right. I love old songs. La-la-la-something-brother, you can't have fun without I think it's your mother."[3]

"Yes, now I do recall," said Chekov.

3

Three months later Zulu telephoned his wife.

"O my God where have you vanished are you dead?"

9. Jawaharlal Nehru, first prime minister of the Republic of India (1947–1964), father of Indira Gandhi.

1. An exclusive English preparatory school.

2. Residents of Kashmir, a territory in dispute between India and Pakistan since 1947.

3. She is mangling the lyrics of Sammy Cahn's 1955 song *Love and Marriage:* "Love and marriage, love and marriage / Go together like a horse and carriage / This I tell you brother / You can't have one without the other."

"Listen please my bivi. Listen carefully my wife, my only love."

"Yes. OK. I am calm. Line is bad, but."

"Call Chekov and say condition red."

"Arré! What is wrong with your condition?"

"Please. Condition red."

"Yes. OK. Red."

"Say the Klingons may be smelling things."

"Clingers-on may be smelly things. Means what?"

"My darling, I beg you."

"I have it all right here only. With this pencil I have written it, both."

"Tell him, get Scotty to lock on to my signal and beam me up at once."

"What rubbish! Even now you can't leave off that stupid game."

"Bivi. It is urgent. *Beam me up.*"

Chekov dropped everything and drove. He went via the dry-cleaners as instructed; he drove round roundabouts twice, jumped red lights, deliberately took a wrong turning, stopped and turned round, made as many right turns as possible to see if anything followed him across the stream of traffic, and, on the motorway, mimicked Zulu's techniques. When he was as certain as he could be that he was clean, he headed for the rendezvous point. "Roll over Len Deighton," he thought, "and tell le Carré the news."[4]

He turned off the motorway and pulled into a lay-by. A man stepped out of the trees, looking newly bathed and smartly dressed, with a sheepish smile on his face. It was Zulu.

Chekov jumped out of the car and embraced his friend, kissing him on both cheeks. Zulu's bristly beard pricked his lips. "I expected you'd have an arm missing, or blood pouring from a gunshot wound, or some black eyes at least," he said. "Instead here you are dressed for the theatre, minus only an opera cloak and cane."

"Mission accomplished," said Zulu, patting his breast pocket. "All present and correct."

"Then what was that 'condition red' bakvaas?"

"The worst-case scenario," said Zulu, "does not always materialise."

In the car, Chekov scanned the names, places, dates in Zulu's brown envelope. The information was better than anyone had expected. From this anonymous Midlands lay-by a light was shining on certain remote villages and urban back-alleys in Punjab.[5] There would be a round-up, and, for some big badmashes at least, there would no longer be shadows in which to hide.

He gave a little, impressed whistle.

Zulu in the passenger seat inclined his head. "Better move off now," he said. "Don't tempt fate."

They drove south through Middle-earth.

Not long after they came off the motorway, Zulu said, "By the way, I quit."

Chekov stopped the car. The two towers of Wembley Stadium were visible through a gap in the houses to the left.

"What's this? Did those extremists manage to turn your head or what?"

"Chekov, ji, don't be a fool. Who needs extremists when there are the killings in Delhi? Hundreds, maybe thousands. Sikh men scalped and burned alive in front of their families. Boy-children, too."

4. Len Deighton and John le Carré are two writers of spy novels. The line refers to the popular song lyric, "Roll over, Beethoven."

5. Province divided between India and Pakistan.

"We know this."

"Then, ji, we also know who was behind it."

"There is not a shred of evidence," Chekov repeated the policy line.

"There are eyewitnesses and photographs," said Zulu. "We know this."

"There are those who think," said Chekov slowly, "that after Indiraji the Sikhs deserved what they got."

Zulu stiffened.

"You know me better than that, I hope," said Chekov. "Zulu, for God's sake, come on. All our bleddy lives."

"No Congress workers have been indicted," said Zulu. "In spite of all the evidence of complicity. Therefore, I resign. You should quit, too."

"If you have gone so damn radical," cried Chekov, "why hand over these lists at all? Why go only half the bleddy hog?"

"I am a security wallah," said Zulu, opening the car door. "Terrorists of all sorts are my foes. But not, apparently, in certain circumstances, yours."

"Zulu, get in, damn it," Chekov shouted. "Don't you care for your career? A wife and four kiddiwinks to support. What about your old chums? Are you going to turn your back on me?"

But Zulu was already too far away.

Chekov and Zulu never met again. Zulu settled in Bombay and as the demand for private-sector protection increased in that cash-rich boom-town, so his Zulu Shield and Zulu Spear companies prospered and grew. He had three more children, all of them boys, and remains happily married to this day.

As for Chekov, he never did take a wife. In spite of this supposed handicap, however, he did well in his chosen profession. His rapid rise continued. But one day in May 1991 he was, by chance, a member of the entourage accompanying Mr. Rajiv Gandhi[6] to the South Indian village of Sriperumbudur, where Rajiv was to address an election rally. Security was lax, intentionally so. In the previous election, Rajivji felt, the demands of security had placed an alienating barrier between himself and the electorate. On this occasion, he decreed, the voters must be allowed to feel close.

After the speeches, the Rajiv group descended from the podium. Chekov, who was just a few feet behind Rajiv, saw a small Tamil[7] woman come forward, smiling. She shook Rajiv's hand and did not let go. Chekov understood what she was smiling about, and the knowledge was so powerful that it stopped time itself.

Because time had stopped, Chekov was able to make a number of private observations. "These Tamil revolutionists are not England-returned," he noted. "So, finally, we have learned to produce the goods at home, and no longer need to import. Bang goes that old dinner-party standby; so to speak." And, less dryly: "The tragedy is not how one dies," he thought. "It is how one has lived."

The scene around him vanished, dissolving in a pool of light, and was replaced by the bridge of the Starship *Enterprise*. All the leading figures were in their appointed places. Zulu sat beside Chekov at the front.

"Shields no longer operative," Zulu was saying. On the main screen, they could see the Klingon Bird of Prey uncloaking, preparing to strike.

"One direct hit and we're done for," cried Dr. McCoy. "For God's sake, Jim, get us out of here!"

6. Indian prime minister 1984–1989, assassinated in May 1991, son of Indira Gandhi.

7. A people of South India and Sri Lanka. The government of India had been aiding the Sri Lankan government in suppressing violent protests by Tamil separatists in Sri Lanka.

"Illogical," said First Officer Spock. "The degradation of our dilithium crystal drive means that warp speed is unavailable. At impulse power only, we would make a poor attempt indeed to flee the Bird of Prey. Our only logical course is unconditional surrender."

"Surrender to a Klingon!" shouted McCoy. "Damn it, you cold-blooded, pointy-eared adding-machine, don't you know how they treat their prisoners?"

"Phaser banks completely depleted," said Zulu. "Offensive capability nil."

"Should I attempt to contact the Klingon captain, sir?" Chekov inquired. "They could fire at any moment."

"Thank you, Mr. Chekov," said Captain Kirk. "I'm afraid that won't be necessary. On this occasion, the worst-case scenario is the one we are obliged to play out. Hold your position. Steady as she goes."

"The Bird of Prey has fired, sir," said Zulu.

Chekov took Zulu's hand and held it firmly, victoriously, as the speeding balls of deadly light approached.

END OF PERSPECTIVES: POSTCOLONIAL CONDITIONS

Murakami Haruki

b. 1949

The novels and short stories of Murakami Haruki—whose name is here given in the usual Japanese order, with the family name preceding the given name—are enormously popular among young readers in Japan and have won the author numerous literary prizes. Increasingly, his works are also becoming best-sellers around the globe among readers who find themselves attracted to Murakami's mix of reflections on specifically Japanese situations and his abundant references to a popular culture of mostly American origin that is shared by young people today across a wide variety of regions, languages, and nations. Murakami himself forms part of the generation of Japanese growing up after World War II who first experienced the full impact of this imported pop culture. Born near Kobe, Japan, in 1949, he studied screenwriting and Greek drama in Tokyo from 1968 until the completion of his bachelor's degree in 1975 and witnessed the upheaval of violent student protests firsthand during this time. From 1974 to 1981 he ran a Tokyo jazz bar together with his wife, thereby establishing another conduit between American and Japanese culture. His first novel, *Hear the Wind Sing,* was published in 1979, and since 1981 he has dedicated himself full time to writing.

The insistently, almost aggressively contemporary idiom of Murakami's fiction has sometimes alienated older Japanese readers, who prefer the more timeless topics and formal diction of a Tanizaki Junichiro or Kawabata Yasunari. Murakami captures elements of late-twentieth-century culture in his themes as well as his language; references to recent technology, Western pop music, and brand-name consumer products come up frequently in his texts, as do changing sexual relations, divorce, and alienation from the professional and social worlds. Some of Murakami's novels are quite realistic, such as *Norwegian Wood* (1987), an account of student life in the 1960s (its title is taken from a Beatles' song), or the parts of *The Wind-up Bird Chronicle* (1994), that deal with the violent confrontations between Chinese and Japanese in World War II. But many others combine late-twentieth-century realism, the hard-boiled detective novel (Raymond Chandler being one of Murakami's models), and science fiction: *A Wild Sheep Chase* (1982) and *Hard-Boiled Wonderland and the End of the World* (1985) are good examples of this signature style. The short story "TV People" also belongs to this kind of writing. As is often the case in Murakami's idiosyncratic narrative worlds, it is difficult to know which of the strange incidents the protagonist experiences are part of an objective reality and which ones are figments of his private imagination; neither is it easy to decide just where the boundary between these two realms lies in a world of television and glossy magazines. In this universe that seems part Kafka and part cyberpunk, what is clearly at stake is the protagonist's encounter with television—a medium that has fundamentally transformed late-twentieth-century culture.

TV People[1]

It was Sunday evening when the TV People showed up.

The season, spring. At least, I think it was spring. In any case, it wasn't particularly hot as seasons go, not particularly chilly.

To be honest, the season's not so important. What matters is that it's a Sunday evening.

I don't like Sunday evenings. Or, rather, I don't like everything that goes with them—that Sunday-evening state of affairs. Without fail, come Sunday evening my head starts to ache. In varying intensity each time. Maybe a third to a half of an inch into my temples, the soft flesh throbs—as if invisible threads lead out and someone far off is yanking at the other ends. Not that it hurts so much. It ought to hurt, but strangely, it doesn't—it's like long needles probing anesthetized areas.

And I hear things. Not sounds, but thick slabs of silence being dragged through the dark. *KRZSHAAAL KKRZSHAAAAAL KKKKRMMMS.* Those are the initial indications. First, the aching. Then, a slight distortion of my vision. Tides of confusion wash through, premonitions tugging at memories, memories tugging at premonitions. A finely honed razor moon floats white in the sky, roots of doubt burrow into the earth. People walk extra loud down the hall just to get me. *KRRSPUMK DUWB KRRSPUMK DUWB KRRSPUMK DUWB.*

All the more reason for the TV People to single out Sunday evening as the time to come around. Like melancholy moods, or the secretive, quiet fall of rain, they steal into the gloom of that appointed time.

Let me explain how the TV People look.

The TV People are slightly smaller than you or me. Not obviously smaller—*slightly* smaller. About, say, 20 or 30%. Every part of their bodies is uniformly smaller. So rather than "small," the more terminologically correct expression might be "reduced."

In fact, if you see TV People somewhere, you might not notice at first that they're small. But even if you don't, they'll probably strike you as somehow strange. Unsettling, maybe. You're sure to think something's odd, and then you'll take another look. There's nothing unnatural about them at first glance, but that's what's so unnatural. Their smallness is completely different from that of children and dwarfs. When we see children, we *feel* they're small, but this sense of recognition comes mostly from the misproportioned awkwardness of their bodies. They are small, granted, but not uniformly so. The hands are small, but the head is big. Typically, that is. No, the smallness of TV People is something else entirely. TV People look as if

1. Translated by Ian Wedde and Fawwaz Tuqan.

Nam June Paik, *Global Encoder,* 1994 (video sculpture, 122 × 84 × 55 inches).

they were reduced by photocopy, everything mechanically calibrated. Say their height has been reduced by a factor of 0.7, then their shoulder width is also in 0.7 reduction; ditto (0.7 reduction) for the feet, head, ears, and fingers. Like plastic models, only a little smaller than the real thing.

Or like perspective demos. Figures that look far away even close up. Something out of a trompe-l'oeil painting where the surface warps and buckles. An illusion where the hand fails to touch objects close by, yet brushes what is out of reach.

That's TV People.

That's TV People.

That's TV People.

There were three of them altogether.

They don't knock or ring the doorbell. Don't say hello. They just sneak right in. I don't even hear a footstep. One opens the door, the other two carry in a TV. Not a very big TV. Your ordinary Sony color TV. The door was locked, I think, but I can't be certain. Maybe I forgot to lock it. It really wasn't foremost in my thoughts at the time, so who knows? Still, I think the door was locked.

When they come in, I'm lying on the sofa, gazing up at the ceiling. Nobody at home but me. That afternoon, the wife has gone out with the girls—some close friends from her high-school days—getting together to talk, then eating dinner out. "Can you grab your own supper?" the wife said before leaving. "There's vegetables in the fridge and all sorts of frozen foods. That much you can handle for yourself, can't you? And before the sun goes down, remember to take in the laundry, okay?"

"Sure thing," I said. Doesn't faze me a bit. Rice, right? Laundry, right? Nothing to it. Take care of it, simple as *SLUPPP KRRRTZ!*

"Did you say something, dear?" she asked.

"No, nothing," I said.

All afternoon I take it easy and loll around on the sofa. I have nothing better to do. I read a bit—that new novel by García Márquez[2]—and listen to some music. I have myself a beer. Still, I'm unable to give my mind to any of this. I consider going back to bed, but I can't even pull myself together enough to do that. So I wind up lying on the sofa, staring at the ceiling.

The way my Sunday afternoons go, I end up doing a little bit of various things, none very well. It's a struggle to concentrate on any one thing. This particular day, everything seems to be going right. I think, Today I'll read this book, listen to these records, answer these letters. Today, for sure, I'll clean out my desk drawers, run errands, wash the car for once. But two o'clock rolls around, three o'clock rolls around, gradually dusk comes on, and all my plans are blown. I haven't done a thing; I've been lying around on the sofa the whole day, same as always. The clock ticks in my ears. *TRPP Q SCHAOUS TRPP Q SCHAOUS.* The sound erodes everything around me, little by little, like dripping rain. *TRPP Q SCHAOUS TRPP Q SCHAOUS.* Little by little, Sunday afternoon wears down, shrinking in scale. Just like the TV People themselves.

The TV people ignore me from the very outset. All three of them have this look that says the likes of me don't exist. They open the door and carry in their TV. The two put the set on the sideboard, the other one plugs it in. There's a mantel clock and a stack of magazines on the sideboard. The clock was a wedding gift, big and heavy—big and heavy as time itself—with a loud sound, too. *TRPP Q SCHAOUS TRPP Q SCHAOUS.* All through the house you can hear it. The TV People move it off the sideboard, down onto the floor. The wife's going to raise hell, I think. She hates it when things get randomly shifted about. If everything isn't in its proper place, she gets really sore. What's worse, with the clock there on the floor, I'm bound to trip over it in the middle of the night. I'm forever getting up to go to the toilet at two in the morning, bleary-eyed and stumbling over something.

Next, the TV People move the magazines to the table. All of them women's magazines. (I hardly ever read magazines; I read books—personally, I wouldn't mind if every last magazine in the world went out of business.) *Elle* and *Marie Claire* and *Home Ideas,* magazines of that ilk. Neatly stacked on the sideboard. The wife doesn't like me touching her magazines—change the order of the stack, and I never hear the end of it—so I don't go near them. Never once flipped through them. But the TV People couldn't care less: They move them right out of the way, they show no concern, they sweep the whole lot off the sideboard, they mix up the order. *Marie Claire* is on

2. Colombian novelist who won the Nobel Prize in literature in 1982.

top of *Croissant; Home Ideas* is underneath *An-An.* Unforgivable. And worse, they're scattering the bookmarks onto the floor. They've lost her place, pages with important information. I have no idea what information or how important—might have been for work, might have been personal—but whatever, it was important to the wife, and she'll let me know about it. "What's the meaning of this? I go out for a nice time with friends, and when I come back, the house is a shambles!" I can just hear it, line for line. Oh, great, I think, shaking my head.

Everything gets removed from the sideboard to make room for the television. The TV People plug it into a wall socket, then switch it on. Then there is a tinkling noise, and the screen lights up. A moment later, the picture floats into view. They change the channels by remote control. But all the channels are blank—probably, I think, because they haven't connected the set to an antenna. There has to be an antenna outlet somewhere in the apartment. I seem to remember the superintendent telling us where it was when we moved into this condominium. All you had to do was connect it. But I can't remember where it is. We don't own a television, so I've completely forgotten.

Yet somehow the TV People don't seem bothered that they aren't picking up any broadcast. They give no sign of looking for the antenna outlet. Blank screen, no image—makes no difference to them. Having pushed the button and had the power come on, they've completed what they came to do.

The TV is brand-new. It's not in its box, but one look tells you it's new. The instruction manual and guarantee are in a plastic bag taped to the side; the power cable shines, sleek as a freshly caught fish.

All three TV People look at the blank screen from here and there around the room. One of them comes over next to me and verifies that you can see the TV screen from where I'm sitting. The TV is facing straight toward me, at an optimum viewing distance. They seem satisfied. One operation down, says their air of accomplishment. One of the TV People (the one who'd come over next to me) places the remote control on the table.

The TV People speak not a word. Their movements come off in perfect order, hence they don't need to speak. Each of the three executes his prescribed function with maximum efficiency. A professional job. Neat and clean. Their work is done in no time. As an afterthought, one of the TV People picks the clock up from the floor and casts a quick glance around the room to see if there isn't a more appropriate place to put it, but he doesn't find any and sets it back down. *TRPP Q SCHAOUS TRPP Q SCHAOUS.* It goes on ticking weightily on the floor. Our apartment is rather small, and a lot of floor space tends to be taken up with my books and the wife's reference materials. I am bound to trip on that clock. I heave a sigh. No mistake, stub my toes for sure. You can bet on it.

All three TV People wear dark-blue jackets. Of who-knows-what fabric, but slick. Under them, they wear jeans and tennis shoes. Clothes and shoes all proportionately reduced in size. I watch their activities for the longest time, until I start to think maybe it's *my* proportions that are off. Almost as if I were riding backward on a roller coaster, wearing strong prescription glasses. The view is dizzying, the scale all screwed up. I'm thrown off balance, my customary world is no longer absolute. That's the way the TV People make you feel.

Up to the very last, the TV People don't say a word. The three of them check the screen one more time, confirm that there are no problems, then switch it off by remote control. The glow contracts to a point and flickers off with a tinkling noise. The screen returns to its expressionless, gray, natural state. The world outside is getting dark. I hear someone calling out to someone else. Anonymous footsteps pass by down the hall, intentionally loud as ever. *KRRSPUMK DUWB KRRSPUMK DUWB.* A Sunday evening.

The TV People give the room another whirlwind inspection, open the door, and leave. Once again, they pay no attention to me whatsoever. They act as if I don't exist.

From the time the TV People come into the apartment to the moment they leave, I don't budge. Don't say a word. I remain motionless, stretched out on the sofa, surveying the whole operation. I know what you're going to say: That's unnatural. Total strangers—not one but three—walk unannounced right into your apartment, plunk down a TV set, and you just sit there staring at them, dumbfounded. Kind of odd, don't you think?

I know, I know. But for whatever reason, I don't speak up, I simply observe the proceedings. Because they ignore me so totally. And if you were in my position, I imagine you'd do the same. Not to excuse myself, but *you* have people right in front of you denying your very presence like that, then see if you don't doubt whether you actually exist. I look at my hands half expecting to see clear through them. I'm devastated, powerless, in a trance. My body, my mind are vanishing fast. I can't bring myself to move. It's all I can do to watch the three TV People deposit their television in my apartment and leave. I can't open my mouth for fear of what my voice might sound like.

The TV People exit and leave me alone. My sense of reality comes back to me. These hands are once again my hands. It's only then I notice that the dusk has been swallowed by darkness. I turn on the light. Then I close my eyes. Yes, that's a TV set sitting there. Meanwhile, the clock keeps ticking away the minutes. *TRPP Q SCHAOUS TRPP Q SCHAOUS.*

Curiously, the wife makes no mention of the appearance of the television set in the apartment. No reaction at all. Zero. It's as if she doesn't even see it. Creepy. Because, as I said before, she's extremely fussy about the order and arrangement of furniture and other things. If someone dares to move anything in the apartment, even by a hair, she'll jump on it in an instant. That's her ascendancy. She knits her brows, then gets things back the way they were.

Not me. If an issue of *Home Ideas* gets put under an *An-An,* or a ballpoint pen finds its way into the pencil stand, you don't see me go to pieces. I don't even notice. This is her problem; I'd wear myself out living like her. Sometimes she flies into a rage. She tells me she can't abide my carelessness. Yes, I say, and sometimes I can't stand carelessness about universal gravitation and π and $E = mc^2$, either. I mean it. But when I say things like this, she clams up, taking them as a personal insult. I never mean it that way; I just say what I feel.

That night, when she comes home, first thing she does is look around the apartment. I've readied a full explanation—how the TV People came and mixed everything up. It'll be difficult to convince her, but I intend to tell her the whole truth.

She doesn't say a thing, just gives the place the once-over. There's a TV on the sideboard, the magazines are out of order on the table, the mantel clock is on the floor, and the wife doesn't even comment. There's nothing for me to explain.

"You get your own supper okay?" she asks me, undressing.

"No, I didn't eat," I tell her.

"Why not?"

"I wasn't really hungry," I say.

The wife pauses, half-undressed, and thinks this over. She gives me a long look. Should she press the subject or not? The clock breaks up the protracted, ponderous silence. *TRPP Q SCHAOUS TRPP Q SCHAOUS.* I pretend not to hear; I won't let it in my ears. But the sound is simply too heavy, too loud to shut out. She, too, seems to be listening to it. Then she shakes her head and says, "Shall I whip up something quick?"

"Well, maybe," I say. I don't really feel much like eating, but I won't turn down the offer.

The wife changes into around-the-house wear and goes to the kitchen to fix zosui and tamago-yaki[3] while filling me in on her friends. Who'd done what, who'd said what, who'd changed her hairstyle and looked so much younger, who'd broken up with her boyfriend. I know most of her friends, so I pour myself a beer and follow along, inserting attentive uh-huhs at proper intervals. Though, in fact, I hardly hear a thing she says. I'm thinking about the TV People. That, and why she didn't remark on the sudden appearance of the television. No way she couldn't have noticed. Very odd. Weird, even. Something is wrong here. But what to do about it?

The food is ready, so I sit at the dining-room table and eat. Rice, egg, salt plum. When I've finished, the wife clears away the dishes. I have another beer, and she has a beer, too. I glance at the sideboard, and there's the TV set, with the power off, the remote-control unit sitting on the table. I get up from the table, reach for the remote control, and switch it on. The screen glows and I hear it tinkling. Still no picture. Only the same blank tube. I press the button to raise the volume, but all that does is increase the white-noise roar. I watch the snowstorm for twenty, thirty seconds, then switch it off. Light and sound vanish in an instant. Meanwhile, the wife has seated herself on the carpet and is flipping through *Elle,* oblivious of the fact that the TV has just been turned on and off.

I replace the remote control on the table and sit down on the sofa again, thinking I'll go on reading that long García Márquez novel. I always read after dinner. I might set the book down after thirty minutes, or I might read for two hours, but the thing is to read every day. Today, though, I can't get myself to read more than a page and a half. I can't concentrate; my thoughts keep returning to the TV set. I look up and see it, right in front of me.

I wake at half past two in the morning to find the TV still there. I get out of bed half hoping the thing has disappeared. No such luck. I go to the toilet, then plop down on the sofa and put my feet up on the table. I take the remote control in hand and try turning on the TV. No new developments in that department, either; only a rerun of the same glow and noise. Nothing else. I look at it a while, then switch it off.

I go back to bed and try to sleep. I'm dead tired, but sleep isn't coming. I shut my eyes and I see them. The TV People carrying the TV set, the TV People moving the clock out of the way, the TV People transferring magazines to the table, the TV People plugging the power cable into the wall socket, the TV People checking the screen, the TV People opening the door and silently exiting. They've stayed on in my head. They're in there walking around. I get back out of bed, go to the kitchen, and pour a double brandy into a coffee cup. I down the brandy and head over to the sofa for

3. A rice stew cooked with a thick broth and a rolled omelette.

another session with Márquez. I open the pages, yet somehow the words won't sink in. The writing is opaque.

Very well, then, I throw García Márquez aside and pick up *Elle*. Reading *Elle* from time to time can't hurt anyone. But there isn't anything in *Elle* that catches my fancy. New hairstyles and elegant white silk blouses and eateries that serve good beef stew and what to wear to the opera, articles like that. Do I care? I throw *Elle* aside. Which leaves me the television on the sideboard to look at.

I end up staying awake until dawn, not doing a thing. At six o'clock, I make myself some coffee. I don't have anything else to do, so I go ahead and fix ham sandwiches before the wife gets up.

"You're up awful early," she says drowsily.

"Mmm," I mumble.

After a nearly wordless breakfast, we leave home together and go our separate ways to our respective offices. The wife works at a small publishing house. Edits a natural-food and life-style magazine. "Shiitake Mushrooms Prevent Gout," "The Future of Organic Farming," you know the kind of magazine. Never sells very well, but hardly costs anything to produce; kept afloat by a handful of zealots. Me, I work in the advertising department of an electrical-appliance manufacturer. I dream up ads for toasters and washing machines and microwave ovens.

In my office building, I pass one of the TV People on the stairs. If I'm not mistaken, it's one of the three who brought the TV the day before—probably the one who first opened the door, who didn't actually carry the set. Their singular lack of distinguishing features makes it next to impossible to tell them apart, so I can't swear to it, but I'd say I'm eight to nine out of ten on the mark. He's wearing the same blue jacket he had on the previous day, and he's not carrying anything in his hands. He's merely walking down the stairs. I'm walking up. I dislike elevators, so I generally take the stairs. My office is on the ninth floor, so this is no mean feat. When I'm in a rush, I get all sweaty by the time I reach the top. Even so, getting sweaty has got to be better than taking the elevator, as far as I'm concerned. Everyone jokes about it: doesn't own a TV or a VCR, doesn't take elevators, must be a modern-day Luddite.[4] Maybe a childhood trauma leading to arrested development. Let them think what they like. They're the ones who are screwed up, if you ask me.

In any case, there I am, climbing the stairs as always; I'm the only one on the stairs—almost nobody else uses them—when between the fourth and fifth floors I pass one of the TV People coming down. It happens so suddenly I don't know what to do. Maybe I should say something?

But I don't say anything. I don't know what to say, and he's unapproachable. He leaves no opening; he descends the stairs so functionally, at one set tempo, with such regulated precision. Plus, he utterly ignores my presence, same as the day before. I don't even enter his field of vision. He slips by before I can think what to do. In that instant, the field of gravity warps.

At work, the day is solid with meetings from the morning on. Important meetings on sales campaigns for a new product line. Several employees read reports. Blackboards fill with figures, bar graphs proliferate on computer screens. Heated discussions. I participate, although my contribution to the meetings is not that critical

4. An opponent of modern technology.

because I'm not directly involved with the project. So between meetings I keep puzzling things over. I voice an opinion only once. Isn't much of an opinion, either—something perfectly obvious to any observer—but I couldn't very well go without saying anything, after all. I may not be terribly ambitious when it comes to work, but so long as I'm receiving a salary I have to demonstrate responsibility. I summarize the various opinions up to that point and even make a joke to lighten the atmosphere. Half covering for my daydreaming about the TV People. Several people laugh. After that one utterance, however, I only pretend to review the materials; I'm thinking about the TV People. If they talk up a name for the new microwave oven, I certainly am not aware of it. My mind is all TV People. What the hell was the meaning of that TV set? And why haul the TV all the way to my apartment in the first place? Why hasn't the wife remarked on its appearance? Why have the TV People made inroads into my company?

The meetings are endless. At noon, there's a short break for lunch. Too short to go out and eat. Instead, everyone gets sandwiches and coffee. The conference room is a haze of cigarette smoke, so I eat at my own desk. While I'm eating, the section chief comes around. To be perfectly frank, I don't like the guy. For no reason I can put my finger on: There's nothing you can fault him on, no single target for attack. He has an air of breeding. Moreover, he's not stupid. He has good taste in neckties, he doesn't wave his own flag or lord it over his inferiors. He even looks out for me, invites me out for the occasional meal. But there's just something about the guy that doesn't sit well with me. Maybe it's his habit of coming into body contact with people he's talking to. Men or women, at some point in the course of the conversation he'll reach out a hand and touch. Not in any suggestive way, mind you. No, his manner is brisk, his bearing perfectly casual. I wouldn't be surprised if some people don't even notice, it's so natural. Still—I don't know why—it does bother me. So whenever I see him, almost instinctively I brace myself. Call it petty, it gets to me.

He leans over, placing a hand on my shoulder. "About your statement at the meeting just now. Very nice," says the section chief warmly. "Very simply put, very pivotal. I was impressed. Points well taken. The whole room buzzed at that statement of yours. The timing was perfect, too. Yessir, you keep 'em coming like that."

And he glides off. Probably to lunch. I thank him straight out, but the honest truth is I'm taken aback. I mean, I don't remember a thing of what I said at the meeting. Why does the section chief have to come all the way over to my desk to praise me for *that?* There have to be more brilliant examples of *Homo loquens*[5] around here. Strange. I go on eating my lunch, uncomprehending. Then I think about the wife. Wonder what she's up to right now. Out to lunch? Maybe I ought to give her a call, exchange a few words, anything. I dial the first three digits, have second thoughts, hang up. I have no reason to be calling her. My world may be crumbling, out of balance, but is that a reason to ring up her office? What can I say about all this, anyway? Besides, I hate calling her at work. I set down the receiver, let out a sigh, and finish off my coffee. Then I toss the Styrofoam cup into the wastebasket.

At one of the afternoon meetings, I see TV People again. This time, their number has increased by two. Just as on the previous day, they come traipsing across the conference room, carrying a Sony color TV. A model one size bigger. Uh-oh. Sony's the rival

5. The speaking human (Latin).

camp. If, for whatever reason, any competitor's product gets brought into our offices, there's hell to pay, barring when other manufacturers' products are brought in for test comparisons, of course. But then we take pains to remove the company logo—just to make sure no outside eyes happen upon it. Little do the TV People care: The Sony mark is emblazoned for all to see. They open the door and march right into the conference room, flashing it in our direction. Then they parade the thing around the room, scanning the place for somewhere to set it down, until at last, not finding any location, they carry it backward out the door. The others in the room show no reaction to the TV People. And they can't have missed them. No, they've definitely seen them. And the proof is they even got out of the way, clearing a path for the TV People to carry their television through. Still, that's as far as it went: a reaction no more alarmed than when the nearby coffee shop delivered. They'd made it a ground rule not to acknowledge the presence of the TV People. The others all knew they were there; they just acted as if they weren't.

None of it makes any sense. Does everybody know about the TV People? Am I alone in the dark? Maybe the wife knew about the TV People all along, too. Probably. I'll bet that's why she wasn't surprised by the television and why she didn't mention it. That's the only possible explanation. Yet this confuses me even more. Who or what, then, are the TV People? And why are they always carrying around TV sets?

One colleague leaves his seat to go to the toilet, and I get up to follow. This is a guy who entered the company around the same time I did. We're on good terms. Sometimes we go out for a drink together after work. I don't do that with most people. I'm standing next to him at the urinals. He's the first to complain. "Oh, joy! Looks like we're in for more of the same, straight through to evening. I swear! Meetings, meetings, meetings, going to drag on forever."

"You can say that again," I say. We wash our hands. He compliments me on the morning meeting's statement. I thank him.

"Oh, by the way, those guys who came in with the TV just now . . ." I launch forth, then cut off.

He doesn't say anything. He turns off the faucet, pulls two paper towels from the dispenser, and wipes his hands. He doesn't even shoot a glance in my direction. How long can he keep drying his hands? Eventually, he crumples up his towels and throws them away. Maybe he didn't hear me. Or maybe he's pretending not to hear. I can't tell. But from the sudden strain in the atmosphere, I know enough not to ask. I shut up, wipe my hands, and walk down the corridor to the conference room. The rest of the afternoon's meetings, he avoids my eyes.

When I get home from work, the apartment is dark. Outside, dark clouds have swept in. It's beginning to rain. The apartment smells like rain. Night is coming on. No sign of the wife. I loosen my tie, smooth out the wrinkles, and hang it up. I brush off my suit. I toss my shirt into the washing machine. My hair smells like cigarette smoke, so I take a shower and shave. Story of my life: I go to endless meetings, get smoked to death, then the wife gets on my case about it. The very first thing she did after we were married was make me stop smoking. Four years ago, that was.

Out of the shower, I sit on the sofa with a beer, drying my hair with a towel. The TV People's television is still sitting on the sideboard. I pick up the remote control from the table and push the "on" switch. Again and again I press, but nothing happens. The screen stays dark. I check the plug; it's in the socket, all right. I unplug it, then plug it back in. Still no go. No matter how often I press the "on" switch, the screen does not glow. Just to be sure, I pry open the back cover of the remote-control unit, remove the batteries, and check them with my handy electrical-contact tester. The batteries are fine. At this point, I give up, throw the remote control aside, and slosh down more beer.

Why should it upset me? Supposing the TV did come on, what then? It would glow and crackle with white noise. Who cares, if that's all that'd come on?

I care. Last night it worked. And I haven't laid a finger on it since. Doesn't make sense.

I try the remote control one more time. I press slowly with my finger. But the result is the same. No response whatsoever. The screen is dead. Cold.

Dead cold.

I pull another beer out of the fridge and eat some potato salad from a plastic tub. It's past six o'clock. I read the whole evening paper. If anything, it's more boring than usual. Almost no article worth reading, nothing but inconsequential news items. But I keep reading, for lack of anything better to do. Until I finish the paper. What next? To avoid pursuing that thought any further, I dally over the newspaper. Hmm, how about answering letters? A cousin of mine has sent us a wedding invitation, which I have to turn down. The day of the wedding, the wife and I are going to be off on a trip. To Okinawa.[6] We've been planning it for ages; we're both taking time off from work. We can't very well go changing our plans now. God only knows when we'll get the next chance to spend a long holiday together. And to clinch it all, I'm not even that close to my cousin; haven't seen her in almost ten years. Still, I can't leave replying to the last minute. She has to know how many people are coming, how many settings to plan for the banquet. Oh, forget it. I can't bring myself to write, not now. My heart isn't in it.

I pick up the newspaper again and read the same articles over again. Maybe I ought to start preparing dinner. But the wife might be working late and could come home having eaten. Which would mean wasting one portion. And if I am going to eat alone, I can make do with leftovers; no reason to make something up special. If she hasn't eaten, we can go out and eat together.

Odd, though. Whenever either of us knows he or she is going to be later than six, we always call in. That's the rule. Leave a message on the answering machine if necessary. That way, the other can coordinate: go ahead and eat alone, or set something out for the late arriver, or hit the sack. The nature of my work sometimes keeps me out late, and she often has meetings, or proofs to dispatch, before coming home. Neither of us has a regular nine-to-five job. When both of us are busy, we can go three days without a word to each other. Those are the breaks—just one of those things that nobody planned. Hence we always keep certain rules, so as not to place unrealistic burdens on each other. If it looks as though we're going to be late, we call in and let the other one know. I sometimes forget, but she, never once.

Still, there's no message on the answering machine.

I toss the newspaper, stretch out on the sofa, and shut my eyes.

I dream about a meeting. I'm standing up, delivering a statement I myself don't understand. I open my mouth and talk. If I don't, I'm a dead man. I have to keep talking. Have to keep coming out with endless blah-blah-blah. Everyone around me is dead. Dead and turned to stone. A roomful of stone statues. A wind is blowing. The windows are all broken; gusts of air are coming in. And the TV People are here. Three of them. Like the first time. They're carrying a Sony color TV. And on the screen are the

6. One of the islands that make up the nation of Japan.

TV People. I'm running out of words; little by little I can feel my fingertips growing stiffer. Gradually turning to stone.

I open my eyes to find the room aglow. The color of corridors at the Aquarium. The television is on. Outside, everything is dark. The TV screen is flickering in the gloom, static crackling. I sit up on the sofa, and press my temples with my fingertips. The flesh of my fingers is still soft; my mouth tastes like beer. I swallow. I'm dried out; the saliva catches in my throat. As always, the waking world pales after an all-too-real dream. But no, this is real. Nobody's turned to stone. What time is it getting to be? I look for the clock on the floor. *TRPP Q SCHAOUS TRPP Q SCHAOUS.* A little before eight.

Yet, just as in the dream, one of the TV People is on the television screen. The same guy I passed on the stairs to the office. No mistake. The one who first opened the door to the apartment. I'm 100% sure. He stands there—against a bright, fluorescent white background, the tail end of a dream infiltrating my conscious reality—staring at me. I shut, then reopen my eyes, hoping he'll have slipped back to never-never land. But he doesn't disappear. Far from it. He gets bigger. His face fills the whole screen, getting closer and closer.

The next thing I know, he's stepping through the screen. Hands gripping the frame, lifting himself up and over, one foot after the other, like climbing out of a window, leaving a white TV screen glowing behind him.

He rubs his left hand in the palm of his right, slowly acclimating himself to the world outside the television. On and on, reduced right-hand fingers rubbing reduced left-hand fingers, no hurry. He has that all-the-time-in-the-world nonchalance. Like a veteran TV-show host. Then he looks me in the face.

"We're making an airplane," says my TV People visitant. His voice has no perspective to it. A curious, paper-thin voice.

He speaks, and the screen is all machinery. Very professional fade-in. Just like on the news. First, there's an opening shot of a large factory interior, then it cuts to a close-up of the work space, camera center. Two TV People are hard at work on some machine, tightening bolts with wrenches, adjusting gauges. The picture of concentration. The machine, however, is unlike anything I've ever seen: an upright cylinder except that it narrows toward the top, with streamlined protrusions along its surface. Looks more like some kind of gigantic orange juicer than an airplane. No wings, no seats.

"Doesn't look like an airplane," I say. Doesn't sound like my voice, either. Strangely brittle, as if the nutrients had been strained out through a thick filter. Have I grown so old all of a sudden?

"That's probably because we haven't painted it yet," he says. "Tomorrow we'll have it the right color. Then you'll see it's an airplane."

"The color's not the problem. It's the shape. That's not an airplane."

"Well, if it's not an airplane, what is it?" he asks me. If he doesn't know, and I don't know, then what *is* it? "So, that's why it's got to be the color." The TV People rep puts it to me gently. "Paint it the right color, and it'll be an airplane."

I don't feel like arguing. What difference does it make? Orange juicer or airplane—flying orange juicer?—what do I care? Still, where's the wife while all this is happening? Why doesn't she come home? I massage my temples again. The clock ticks on. *TRPP Q SCHAOUS TRPP Q SCHAOUS.* The remote control lies on the table, and next to it the stack of women's magazines. The telephone is silent, the room illuminated by the dim glow of the television.

The two TV People on the screen keep working away. The image is much clearer than before. You can read the numbers on the dials, hear the faint rumble of machinery.

TAABZHRAYBGG TAABZHRAYBGG ARP ARRP TAABZHRAYBGG. This bass line is punctuated periodically by a sharp, metallic grating. *AREEEENBT AREEEENBT.* And various other noises are interspersed through the remaining aural space; I can't hear anything clearly over them. Still, the two TV People labor on for all they're worth. That, apparently, is the subject of this program. I go on watching the two of them as they work on and on. Their colleague outside the TV set also looks on in silence. At them. At that *thing*—for the life of me, it does not look like an airplane—that insane machine all black and grimy, floating in a field of white light.

The TV People rep speaks up. "Shame about your wife."

I look him in the face. Maybe I didn't hear him right. Staring at him is like peering into the glowing tube itself.

"Shame about your wife," the TV People rep repeats in exactly the same absent tone.

"How's that?" I ask.

"How's that? It's gone too far," says the TV People rep in a voice like a plastic-card hotel key. Flat, uninflected, it slices into me as if it were sliding through a thin slit. "It's gone too far: She's out there."

"It's gone too far: She's out there," I repeat in my head. Very plain, and without reality. I can't grasp the context. Cause has effect by the tail and is about to swallow it whole. I get up and go to the kitchen. I open the refrigerator, take a deep breath, reach for a can of beer, and go back to the sofa. The TV People rep stands in place in front of the television, right elbow resting on the set, and watches me extract the pull-tab. I don't really want to drink beer at this moment; I just need to do something. I drink one sip, but the beer doesn't taste good. I hold the can in my hand dumbly until it becomes so heavy I have to set it down on the table.

Then I think about the TV People rep's revelation, about the wife's failure to materialize. He's saying she's gone. That she isn't coming home. I can't bring myself to believe it's over. Sure, we're not the perfect couple. In four years, we've had our spats; we have our little problems. But we always talk them out. There are things we've resolved and things we haven't. Most of what we couldn't resolve we let ride. Okay, so we have our ups and downs as a couple. I admit it. But is this cause for despair? C'mon, show me a couple who don't have problems. Besides, it's only a little past eight. There must be some reason she can't get to a phone. Any number of possible reasons. For instance . . . I can't think of a single one. I'm hopelessly confused.

I fall back deep into the sofa.

How on earth is that airplane—if it is an airplane—supposed to fly? What propels it? Where are the windows? Which is the front, which is the back?

I'm dead tired. Exhausted. I still have to write that letter, though, to beg off from my cousin's invitation. My work schedule does not afford me the pleasure of attending. Regrettable. Congratulations, all the same.

The two TV People in the television continue building their airplane, oblivious of me. They toil away; they don't stop for anything. They have an infinite amount of work to get through before the machine is complete. No sooner have they finished one operation than they're busy with another. They have no assembly instructions, no plans, but they know precisely what to do and what comes next. The camera ably follows their deft motions. Clear-cut, easy-to-follow camera work. Highly credible, convincing images. No doubt other TV People (Nos. 4 and 5?) are manning the camera and control panel.

Strange as it may sound, the more I watch the flawless form of the TV People as they go about their work, the more the thing starts to look like an airplane. At least, it'd no longer surprise me if it actually flew. What does it matter which is front or back? With all the exacting detail work they're putting in, it *has* to be an airplane. Even if it doesn't appear so—to them, it's an airplane. Just as the little guy said, "If it's not an airplane, then what is it?"

The TV People rep hasn't so much as twitched in all this time. Right elbow still propped up on the TV set, he's watching me. I'm being watched. The TV People factory crew keeps working. Busy, busy, busy. The clock ticks on. *TRPP Q SCHAOUS TRPP Q SCHAOUS.* The room has grown dark, stifling. Someone's footsteps echo down the hall.

Well, it suddenly occurs to me, maybe so. Maybe the wife *is* out there. She's gone somewhere far away. By whatever means of transport, she's gone somewhere far out of my reach. Maybe our relationship has suffered irreversible damage. Maybe it's a total loss. Only I haven't noticed. All sorts of thoughts unravel inside me, then the frayed ends come together again. "Maybe so," I say out loud. My voice echoes, hollow.

"Tomorrow, when we paint it, you'll see better," he resumes. "All it needs is a touch of color to make it an airplane."

I look at the palms of my hands. They have shrunk slightly. Ever so slightly. Power of suggestion? Maybe the light's playing tricks on me. Maybe my sense of perspective has been thrown off. Yet, my palms really do look shriveled. Hey now, wait just a minute! Let me speak. There's something I should say. I must say. I'll dry up and turn to stone if I don't. Like the others.

"The phone will ring soon," the TV People rep says. Then, after a measured pause, he adds, "In another five minutes."

I look at the telephone; I think about the telephone cord. Endless lengths of phone cable linking one telephone to another. Maybe somewhere, at some terminal of that awesome megacircuit, is my wife. Far, far away, out of my reach. I can feel her pulse. Another five minutes, I tell myself. *Which way is front, which way is back?* I stand up and try to say something, but no sooner have I got to my feet than the words slip away.

BIBLIOGRAPHY

The Ancient World

Perspectives: Creation Myths and Social Concerns • Claude Lévi-Strauss, *Structural Anthropology,* 1967. • Donald H. Mills, *The Hero and the Sea: Patterns of Chaos in Ancient Myth,* 2002. • Robert A. Segal, ed., *Myth and Ritual Theory: An Anthology,* 1998.

Enuma Elish • Stephanie Dalley, *Myths from Mesopotamia,* 1989. • Alexander Heidel, *The Babylonian Genesis: The Story of the Creation,* 1951. • Edward Hugh Henderson, "Archaic Experience and Philosophical Anthropology: The 'Enuma Elish' and the Exodus," in *Philosophy and Archaic Experience,* ed. John Sallis, 1982.

Hesiod • Richard Gotshalk, *Homer and Hesiod: Myth and Philosophy,* 2000. • Bernard M.W. Knox, *Work and Justice in Archaic Greece,* 1982. • Robert Lamberton, *Hesiod,* 1988.

Genesis • Bernard W. Anderson, ed., *Creation in the Old Testament,* 1984. • Eugene Combs, *The Foundations of Political Order in Genesis and the Chondogya Upanishad,* 1987. • R. Gilboa, *Intercourses in the Book of Genesis: Mythic Motifs in Creator-Created Relationships,* 1998. • Dorothy Irvin, *Mytharion: The Comparison of Tales from the Old Testament and the Ancient Near East,* 1978. • Jon D. Levenson, *Creation and the Persistence of Evil: The Jewish Drama of Divine Omnipotence,* 1988. • Terry J. Prewitt, *The Elusive Covenant: A Structural-Semiotic Reading of Genesis,* 1990. • Ellen van Wolde, *Stories of the Beginning: Genesis 1–11 and Other Creation Stories,* 1997. • Claus Westermann, *Genesis: An Introduction,* 1992.

The Rig Veda • F. Raymond Allchin, *The Archaeology of Early Historic South Asia: The Emergence of Cities and States,* 1991. • Steven Collins, *Nirvana and other Buddhist Felicities,* 1998. • Franklin Edgerton, *The Beginnings of Indian Philosophy,* 1965. • George Erdosy, *Urbanization in Early Historic India,* 1988. • Richard Gombrich, *How Buddhism Began,* 1996. • Jan Gonda, *Vedic Literature,* 1975. • Charles Malamoud, *Cooking the World: Ritual and Thought in Ancient India,* 1996. • Michael Witzel, "Vedas and Upanishads," in *The Blackwell Companion to Hinduism,* ed. Gavin Flood, 2003.

The Ancient Near East

General • Bertil Albrektson, *History and the Gods,* 1967. • Cyril Aldred, *Akhenaten, Pharaoh of Egypt: A New Study,* 1968. • Robert Alter, *The Art of Biblical Narrative,* 1981. • Robert Alter, *The Art of Biblical Poetry,* 1985. • Robert Alter and Frank Kermode, eds., *The Literary Guide to the Bible,* 1987. • Jan Assmann, *The Mind of Egypt: History and Meaning in the Time of the Pharaohs,* 2002. • Jan Assmann, *The Search for God in Ancient Egypt,* 2001. • John Barton, *Reading the Old Testament: Method in Biblical Study,* 1984. • Jean Bottéro, *Mesopotamia: Writing, Reasoning and the Gods,* 1992. • Brevard Childs, *Introduction to the Old Testament as Scripture,* 1979. • Frank M. Cross, *Canaanite Myth and Hebrew Epic,* 1973. • Stephanie Dalley, *Myths from Mesopotamia,* 1989. • David Damrosch, *The Narrative Covenant: Transformations of Genre in the Growth of Biblical Literature,* 1987. • Michael Fishbane, *Biblical Interpretation in Ancient Israel,* 1985. • Benjamin Foster, *From Distant Days: Myths, Tales and Poetry of Ancient Mesopotamia,* 1995. • Henri Frankfort et al., *Before Philosophy,* 1954. • Northrop Frye, *The Great Code: The Bible and Literature,* 1982. • Norman Gottwald, *The Hebrew Bible: A Socio-Literary Introduction,* 1985. • James Kugel, *The Bible as It Was,* 1997. • James Kugel, *The Idea of Biblical Poetry,* 1981. • Amélie Kuhrt, *The Ancient Near East c. 3000–300 BC,* 1995. • Miriam Lichtheim, *Ancient Egyptian Literature,* 3 vols., 1975–1980. • Ilana Pardes, *The Biography of Ancient Israel: National Narratives in the Bible,* 2000. • J. N. Postgate, *Early Mesopotamia: Society and Economy at the Dawn of History,* 1992. • James B. Pritchard, *Ancient Near Eastern Texts Relating to the Old Testament,* 1976. • Paul Ricoeur, *The Symbolism of Evil,* 1969. • Herbert Schneidau, *Sacred Discontent: The Bible and Western Tradition,*

1976. • William K. Simpson, ed., *The Literature of Ancient Egypt,* 1973. • Daniel Snell, *Life in the Ancient Near East,* 1997. • Meir Sternberg, *The Poetics of Biblical Narrative,* 1985. • Joyce Tyldesley, *Daughters of Iris: Women of Ancient Egypt,* 1995. • John Van Seters, *In Search of History: Historiography in the Ancient World and the Origins of Biblical History,* 1983.

Perspectives: Death and Immortality • Bendt Alster, *Death in Mesopotamia,* 1980. • James G. Frazer, *The Golden Bough,* 1945. • Thorkild Jacobsen, *The Treasures of Darkness,* 1976. • Dimitri Meeks and Christine Favard-Meeks, *Daily Life of the Egyptian Gods,* 1996.

The Book of the Dead • Robert A. Armour, *Gods and Myths of Ancient Egypt,* 1986. • R.T. Rundle Clark, *Myth and Symbol in Ancient Egypt,* 1959. • A.H. Gardiner and K. Sethe, *Egyptian Letters to the Dead: Mainly from the Old and Middle Kingdom,* 1928. • Paul Hamlyn, *Egyptian Mythology,* 1965. • George Hart, *Egyptian Myths,* 1990.

The Descent of Ishtar to the Underworld • Rivkah Harris, "Inanna-Ishtar and Paradox and a Coincidence of Opposites," *History of Religions* 30:3 (1991), 261–78. • Gwendolyn Leick, *The Babylonians: An Introduction,* 2003. • Hugh R. Page, *The Myth of Cosmic Rebellion: A Study of Its Reflexes in Ugaritic and Biblical Literature,* 1996. • Alice Lenore Perlman, *Aherah and Astarte in the Old Testament and Ugaritic Literatures,* 1978. • Diana White, trans. *The Descent of Ishtar,* 1993.

The Epic of Gilgamesh • David Damrosch, "Gilgamesh and Genesis," in *The Narrative Covenant,* 1987. • Andrew George, ed., *The Epic of Gilgamesh,* 1999. • Rivkah Harris, *Gender and Aging in Mesopotamia: The Gilgamesh Epic and Other Ancient Literature,* 2000. • Alexander Heidel, *The Gilgamesh Epic and Old Testament Parallels,* 1949. • Derrek Hines, *Gilgamesh,* 2002. • John Maier, ed., *Gilgamesh: A Reader,* 1997. • Benjamin Caleb Ray, "The Gilgamesh Epic: Myth and Meaning," in *Myth and Method,* eds. Laurie L. Patton and Wendy Doniger, 1996. • Jeffrey H. Tigay, *The Evolution of the Gilgamesh Epic,* 2002.

The Song of Songs • Blaise Arminjon, *Cantata of Love: A Verse-by-Verse Reading of the Song of Songs,* 1988. • Ariel Bloch and Chana Bloch, *The Song of Songs: A New Translation with an Introduction and Commentary,* 1994. • Athalva Brenner and Carole R. Fontaine, eds., *The Song of Songs: A Feminist Companion to the Bible,* 2000. • Marvin Pope, *The Song of Songs,* 1977. • Luis Stadelmann, *Love and Politics: A New Commentary on the Song of Songs,* 1992.

Classical Greece

General • John Boardman, Jasper Griffin, and Oswyn Murray, eds., *The Oxford History of the Classical World,* 1986. • Paul Cartledge, *The Greeks,* 2002. • J.N. Davidson, *Courtesans and Fishcakes,* 1998. • Thomas R. Martin, *Ancient Greece*, 1996. • Robin Osborne, *Greece in the Making: 1200–479 BC*, 1996. • *Perseus* (database on ancient Greek civilization): www.perseus.tufts.edu • Jean-Pierre Vernant, ed., *The Greeks*, 1995.

Perspectives: Tyranny and Democracy • Michael Gagarin and Paul Woodruff, eds., *Early Greek Political Thought,* 1995. • Thomas Harrison, *Divinity and History,* 2000. • Joseph Mail, *Mythistory: The Making of a Modern Historiography,* 2003. • Arlene W. Saxonhouse, *Athenian Democracy,* 1996. • Norma Thompson, *Herodotus and the Origins of the Political Community,* 1996.

Herodotus • *Herodoti Historiae*, ed. K. Hude, 1926–1927. • *Herodotus: The Histories*, trans. A. de Selincourt, 1972. • F. Hartog, *The Mirror of Herodotus,* 1988. • Henry R. Immerwahr, *Form and Thought in Herodotus*, 1986. • Kenneth H. Waters, *Herodotus the Historian,* 1985.

Plato • W. K. C. Guthrie, *A History of Greek Philosophy,* vol. 3, 1969. • A. Nightingale, *Genres in Dialogue,* 1995. • R. B. Rutherford, *The Art of Plato,* 1995.

Solon • I. M. Linforth, *Solon the Athenian,* 1919. • P. B. Manville, *The Origins of Citizenship in Ancient Athens,* 1990.

Thucydides • George Cawkwell, *Thucydides and the Peloponnesian War,* 1997. • W. R. Connor,

Thucydides, 1984. • John H. Finley, *Thucydides,* 1947. • Nicole Loraux, *The Invention of Athens,* 1986. • Thucydides, *The Peloponnesian War,* trans. Lattimore, 1998. • John E. Ziolkowski, *Thucydides and the Tradition of Funeral Speeches at Athens,* 1981.

Aristotle • J. Barnes, *Aristotle,* 1982. • S. H. Halliwell, *Aristotle's Poetics,* 1986. • G. E. R. Lloyd, *Aristotle,* 1968. • A. Rorty, ed., *Essays on Aristotle's Poetics,* 1992.

Euripides • Page duBois, *Centaurs and Amazons,* 1982. • E. Segal, ed., *Euripides: A Collection of Critical Essays,* 1968.

Homer • George Dimock, *The Unity of the Odyssey,* 1989. • Nancy Felson-Rubin, *Regarding Penelope: From Character to Poetics,* 1994. • Ralph Hexter, *A Guide to the Odyssey,* 1993. • A. B. Lord, *The Singer of Tales,* 1960. • Gregory Nagy, *The Best of the Achaeans,* 1979. • Seth Schein, *The Mortal Hero: An Introduction to Homer's Iliad,* 1987. • Seth Schein, *Reading the Odyssey,* 1991. • W. G. Thalmann, *The Odyssey: An Epic of Return,* 1997.

Sappho • Paqe duBois, *Sappho Is Burning,* 1995. • Denys Page, *Sappho and Alcaeus,* 1955. • E. M. Voigt, *Sappho et Alcaeus,* 1971. • *Sappho's Lyre: Archaic Lyric and Women Poets of Ancient Greece,* 1991. • *If Not, Winter: Fragments of Sappho,* trans. Anne Carson, 2002.

Sophocles • Harold Bloom, ed., *Sophocles's Oedipus Rex,* 1988. • B. M. W. Knox, *Oedipus at Thebes,* 1957. • Charles Segal, *Oedipus Tyrannus: Tragic Heroism and the Limits of Knowledge,* 1993. • J.-P. Vernant and P. Vidal-Naquet, *Myth and Tragedy in Ancient Greece,* trans. J. Lloyd, 1988.

Early South Asia

General • Edward C. Dimock et al., eds. *Literatures of India: An Introduction,* 1974. • Ainslie Embree, ed., *Sources of Indian Tradition,* 1988. • David Ludden, *India and South Asia: A Short History,* 2002. • Sheldon Pollock, ed., *Literary Cultures in History: Reconstructions from South Asia,* 2003. • Sheldon Pollock, "Introduction," and "Sanskrit Literature from the Inside Out," in *Literary Cultures in History,* ed. S. Pollock, 2003. • Joseph Schwartzberg, ed., *A Historical Atlas of South Asia,* 1992. • Romila Thapar, *Early India,* 2002. • Susie Tharu and K. Lalitha, eds., *Women Writing in India, 600 B.C. to the Present,* 1991–1993. • Herman Tieken, *Kavya in South India,* 2001.

Ramayana of Valmiki • John Brockington, *The Sanskrit Epics,* 1998. • Robert Goldman et al., trans., *The Ramayana of Valmiki: An Epic of Ancient India,* 1984–. • Robert P. Goldman and Sally Sutherland, eds., *The Epic Tradition,* 2004. • Sheldon Pollock, "Ramayana and Political Imagination in India," *Journal of Asian Studies* 52.2 (1993), 261–97. • A. K. Ramanujan, "Three Hundred Ramayanas: Five Examples and Three Thoughts on Translation," In *Many Ramayanas,* ed. Paula Richman, 1994.• Paula Richman, ed. *Many Ramayanas: The Diversity of a Narrative Tradition in South Asia,* 1991. • Paula Richman, ed. *Questioning Ramayanas: A South Asian Tradition,* 2000.

China: The Classical Tradition

General • Cyril Birch, *Anthology of Chinese Literature,* vol. I, 1965. • Anne Birrell, *Chinese Mythology,* 1993. • Wing-tsit Chan, *A Sourcebook in Chinese Philosophy,* 1963. • Raymond Dawson, ed., *The Legacy of China,* 1964. • William Theodore de Bary, ed., *Sources of Chinese Tradition,* 1999. • Patricia B. Ebrey, ed., *Chinese Civilization and Society: A Sourcebook,* 1981. • C. P. Fitzgerald, *China: A Short Cultural History,* 1967. • Yu-lan Fung, *A History of Chinese Philosophy,* 1953. • Jacques Gernet, *A History of Chinese Civilization,* 1982. • James Legge, trans., *The Chinese Classics,* 1892. • Michael Loewe and Edward Shaughnessy, eds., *The Cambridge History of Ancient China,* 1999. • Frederick Mote, *Intellectual Foundations of China,* 1971. • William Nienhauser, ed., *The Indiana*

Companion to Traditional Chinese Literature, 1986. • Stephen Owen, *An Anthology of Chinese Literature, Beginnings to 1911,* 1996. • Paul Ropp, ed., *The Heritage of China,* 1990. • Benjamin Schwartz, *The World of Thought in Ancient China,* 1985. • Burton Watson, *Early Chinese Literature,* 1962. • Arthur Waley, *Three Ways of Thought in Ancient China,* 1939. • Pauline Yu et al., eds., *Ways With Words: Writing About Reading Texts from Early China,* 2000.

The Book of Songs • Joseph R. Allen, ed., *The Book of Songs*, trans. Arthur Waley, 1996. • Marcel Granet, *Festivals and Songs of Ancient China,* 1932. • Bernhard Karlgren, trans., *The Book of Odes,* 1950. • William McNaughton, *The Book of Songs,* 1971. • Ezra Pound, trans., *The Confucian Odes,* 1954. • Haun Saussy, *The Problem of a Chinese Aesthetic,* 1993. • Steven Van Zoeren, *Poetry and Personality: Reading, Exegesis and Hermeneutics in Traditional China,* 1991. • Arthur Waley, trans., *The Book of Songs,* 1937. • C. H. Wang, *The Bell and the Drum,* 1974.

Confucius • Roger T. Ames and Henry Rosemont, trans., *The Analects of Confucius: A Philosophical Translation,* 1998. • Herrlee Creel, *Confucius: The Man and the Myth,* 1949. • Raymond Dawson, trans., *The Analects,* 1993. • Herbert Fingarette, *Confucius, the Secular as Sacred,* 1972. • David L. Hall and Roger T. Ames, *Thinking through Confucius,* 1987. • D. C. Lau, trans., *Confucius: The Analects,* 1979. • Simon Leys, trans., *The Analects of Confucius,* 1997. • Pertti Nikkilä, *Preference and Choice in the Confucian Analects,* 1997. • Yuri Pines, *Foundations of Confucian Thought,* 2002. • Edward L. Shaughnessy, *Before Confucius: Studies in the Creation of the Confucius Classics,* 1997. • Bryan W. Van Norden, ed., *Confucius and the Analects: New Essays,* 2002. • Arthur Waley, *The Analects of Confucius,* 1938.

Rome and the Roman Empire

General • Michael von Albrecht, *Roman Epic: An Interpretive Introduction,* Boston: Brill, 1999. • Alessandro Barchiesi, *The Poet and the Prince: Ovid and Augustan Discourse,* 1997. • Anthony A. Barrett, *Livia: First Lady of Imperial Rome,* 2002. • Mary Beard, John North, and Simon Price, *Religions of Rome,* vol. 1: *A History*; vol. 2: *A Sourcebook,* 1998. • John Boardman, Jasper Griffin, and Oswyn Murray, *The Oxford History of the Roman World,* 2001. • Anthony J. Boyle, ed., *Roman Epic.* New York: Routledge, 1993. • Caesar, *The Conquest of Gaul,* trans. S. A. Handford, 1982. • Jérôme Carcopino, *Daily Life in Ancient Rome,* 1968. • Kitty Chisholm and John Ferguson, eds., *Rome, the Augustan Age: A Source Book,* 1981. • Peter Connolly and Hazel Dodge, *The Ancient City: Life in Classical Athens and Rome,* 1998. • Gian Biagio Conte, *Latin Literature: A History,* trans. Joseph B. Solodow, 1994. • Werner Eck, *The Age of Augustus,* trans. Deborah Lucas Schneider, 2003. • Catherine Edwards, *Writing Rome: Textual Approaches to the City.* New York: Cambridge University Press, 1996. • Elaine Fantham, Helene Peet Foley, Natalie Boymel Kampen, and H. A. Shapiro. *Women in the Classical World: Image and Text,* 1995. • Diane Favro, *The Urban Image of Imperial Rome,* 1998. • Dennis Feeney, *Literature and Religion at Rome: Cultures, Contexts, and Beliefs,* 1998. • M. I. Finley, *The Ancient Economy,* 1999. • Karl Galinsky, *Augustan Culture,* 1996. • Edward Gibbon, *The History of the Decline and Fall of the Roman Empire,* 1776–1788. • Thomas Habinek and Alessandro Schiesaro, eds., *The Roman Cultural Revolution,* 1997. • Judith P. Hallett and Marilyn B. Skinner, eds., *Roman Sexualities,* 1998. • Philip R. Hardie, *The Epic Successors of Virgil: A Study in the Dynamics of a Tradition.* New York: Cambridge University Press, 1993. • Fritz Heichelheim et al., *A History of the Roman People,* 2002. • Finley Allison Hooper, *Roman Realities,* 1979. • Peter V. Jones and Keith C. Sidwell, *The World of Rome: An Introduction to Roman Culture,* 1997. • Josephus, *The Jewish War,* 1970. • Livy, *History of Rome,* 14 vols. Loeb Classical Library, 1964–1970. • Livy, *History of Rome from Its Foundation,* 4 vols., 1960–1982. • R. O. A. M. Lyne, *The Latin Love Poets: From Catullus to Horace.* Oxford: Clarendon, 1980. • Ramsay MacMullen, *Romanization in the Time of Augustus,* 2000. • Pliny the Elder, *Natural History,* 10 vols., Loeb Classical Library, 1938–1963. • Plutarch, *The Parallel Lives,* 11 vols., trans. Bernadotte Perrin, Loeb Classical Library, 1967. • Plutarch, *Fall of the Roman Republic,* trans. Rex Warner, 1972. • Plutarch, *Makers of Rome: Nine Lives,* trans., Ian Scott-Kilvert, 1965. • David Quint, *Epic and Empire: Politics and Generic Form from Virgil to Milton.* Princeton: Princeton University Press, 1993.

• Nancy H. Ramage and Andrew Ramage, *Roman Art: From Romulus to Constantine,* 1991. • Howard H. Scullard, *From the Gracchi to Nero: A History of Rome 133 B.C. to A.D. 68,* 1990. • Ronald Syme, *The Roman Revolution*, 2002. • Robert Turcan, *The Gods of Ancient Rome: Religion in Everyday Life from Archaic to Imperial Times,* 2001. • Paul Veyne, ed., *A History of Private Life: I. From Pagan Rome to Byzantium,* 1987. • J. M. Wallace-Hadrill, *Augustan Rome,* 1993. • Peter White, *Promised Verse: Poets in the Society of Augustan Rome,* 1993. • Timothy Peter Wiseman, *Remus: A Roman Myth,* 1995. • Paul Zanker, *The Power of Images in the Age of Augustus,* 1988.

Perspectives: The Culture of Rome and the Beginnings of Christianity • Peter Brown, *The Body and Society: Men, Women, and Sexual Renunciation in Early Chritistianity,* 1988. • Peter Brown, *The World of Late Antiquity,* 1971. • John B. Bury, *History of the Later Roman Empire,* 2 vols., 1958. • Everett Ferguson, *Backgrounds of Early Christianity,* 1993. • Robin Lane Fox, *Pagans and Christians,* 1987. • Richard A. Horsley and John S. Hanson, *Bandits, Prophets, and Messiahs: Popular Movements in the Time of Jesus,* 1985. • A. H. M. Jones, *The Later Roman Empire 284-602: A Social, Economic and Administrative Survey,* 3 vols., 1986. • Santo Mazzarino, *The End of the Ancient World,* 1966.

Augustine • R. H. Barrow, *Introduction to St. Augustine "City of God,"* 1970. • Gerald Bonner, *St. Augustine: His Life and Controversies,* 1986. • Peter Brown, *Augustine of Hippo,* 1967. • Peter Brown, *Religion and Society in the Age of St. Augustine,* 1972. • Kenneth Burke, *The Rhetoric of Religion: Studies in Logology,* 1970. • Henry Chadwick, *Augustine,* 1986. • Gillian Clark, *Saint Augustine: The Confessions,* 1993. • Elizabeth De Mijolla, *Autobiographical Quests: Augustine, Montaigne, Rousseau, and Wordsworth,* 1994. • Allan D. Fitzgerald, ed., *Augustine Through the Ages: An Encyclopedia,* 1999. • Harald Hagendahl, *Augustine and the Latin Classics,* 2 vols. 1967. • Ann Hartle, *The Modern Self in Rousseau's Confessions: A Reply to St. Augustine,* 1983. • Christopher Kirwan, *Augustine,* 1989. • Sabine MacCormack, *The Shadows of Poetry: Vergil in the Mind of Augustine,* 1998. • Robert A. Markus, *Saeculum: History and Society in the Theology of St. Augustine,* 1988. • Robert McMahon, *Augustine's Prayerful Ascent: An Essay on the Literary Form of the Confessions,* 1989. • Robert J. O'Connell, *Soundings in St. Augustine's Imagination,* 1994. • Gerard P. O'Daly, *Augustine's City of God: A Reader's Guide,* 1999. • James J. O'Donnell, *Augustine,* 1985. • John J. O'Meara, *The Young Augustine: The Growth of St. Augustine's Mind up to his Conversion,* 1954. • John J. O'Meara, *Understanding Augustine,* 1997. • Sarah Spence, *Rhetorics of Reason and Desire: Vergil, Augustine, and the Troubadours,* 1988. • Eleonore Stump and Norman Katzmann, eds. *Cambridge Companion to Augustine,* 2001.

Catullus • William Fitzgerald, *Catullan Provocations: Lyric Poetry and the Drama of Position,* 1995. • Richard Jenkyns, *Three Classical Poets—Sappho, Catullus, and Juvenal,* 1982. • Charles Martin, *Catullus,* 1992. • Kenneth Quinn, *The Catullan Revolution,* 1959. • Arthur Leslie Wheeler, *Catullus and the Traditions of Ancient Poetry,* 1934. • T. P. Wiseman, *Catullus and His World: A Reappraisal*, 1985.

Horace • David Armstrong, *Horace,* 1989. • Steele Commager, *The Odes of Horace,* 1962. • Eduard Fraenkel, *Horace,* 1957. • Niall Rudd, ed., *Horace 2000: A Celebration. Essays for the Bimillennium,* 1993. • Niall Rudd, ed., *The Satires of Horace,* 1966. • David Alexander West, *Reading Horace,* 1967. • L. P. Wilkinson, *Horace and His Lyric Poetry,* 1951.

Luke • Robert Alter and Frank Kermode, eds., *The Literary Guide to the Bible,* 1987. • C. K. Barrett, *The Acts of the Apostles: A Shorter Commentary,* 2002. • H. J. Cadbury, *The Making of Luke—Acts,* 1958. • Hans Conzelmann, *The Theology of St. Luke,* 1961. • John Drury, *Tradition and Design in Luke's Gospel,* 1976. • Joel B. Green et al., eds. *Dictionary of Jesus and the Gospels,* 1992. • Ernst Haenchen, *The Acts of the Apostles: A Commentary,* 1971. • Leander G. Keck and J. Louis Martyn, eds., *Studies in Luke—Acts: Studies Presented in Honor of Paul Schubert,* 1966. • E. P. Sanders, *The Historical Figure of Jesus,* 1993. • Charles H. Talbert, ed., *Luke—Acts: New Perspectives from the Society of Biblical Literature Seminar,* 1984. • Robert C. Tannehill, *The Narrative Unity of Luke—Acts: A Literary Interpretation,* 2 vols., 1986.

Ovid • Karl Galinsky, *Ovid's Metamorphoses: An Introduction to the Basic Aspects,* 1975. • Philip Hardie, *Ovid's Poetics of Illusion,* 2002. • Philip Hardie, ed., *The Cambridge Companion to Ovid,* 2002. • P. E. Knox, *Ovid's Metamorphoses and the Traditions of Augustan Poetry,* 1986. • Sara Mack, *Ovid,* 1988. • Brooks Otis, *Ovid as an Epic Poet,* 1966. • Joseph B. Solodow, *The World of Ovid's Metamorphoses,* 1988. • Garth Tissol, *The Face of Nature: Wit, Narrative, and Cosmic Origins in Ovid's Metamorphoses,* 1997.

Paul • Michael Goulder, "The Pauline Epistles," in *The Literary Guide to the Bible,* eds. Robert Alter and Frank Kermode, 1987. • Anthony Tyrell Hanson, *Studies in Paul's Technique and Theology,* 1974. • Gerald Hawthorne et al., eds. *Dictionary of Paul and His Letters,* 1993. • Martin Hengel, with Roland Deines, *The Pre-Christian Paul,* trans. John Bowden, 1991. • Martin Hengel, with Anna Maria Schwemer, *Paul Between Damascus and Antioch,* trans., John Bowden, 1997. • Leander Keck, *Paul and His Letters,* 1988. • Wayne A. Meeks, *The First Urban Christians: The Social World of the Apostle Paul,* 1983. • E. P. Sanders, *Paul,* 1991. • E. P. Sanders, *Paul and Palestinian Judaism: A Comparison of Patterns of Religion,* 1977. • Marion L. Soards, *The Apostle Paul: An Introduction to His Writings and Teaching,* 1987. • Krister Stendahl, *Paul Among Jews and Gentiles: And Other Essays,* 1976. • Stanley K. Stowers, *A Rereading of Romans: Justice, Jews, and Gentiles,* 1994.

Petronius • Gian Biagio Conte, *The Hidden Author: An Interpretation of Petronius' "Satyricon,"* 1996. • Niall W. Slater, *Reading Petronius,* 1990. • J. P. Sullivan, *The "Satyricon" of Petronius: A Literary Study,* 1968. • P. G. Walsh, *The Roman Novel: The "Satyricon" of Petronius and the "Metamorphoses" of Apuleius,* 1970.

Roman Reactions to Christianity • Barry Baldwin, *Suetonius,* 1983. • Julian Bennett, *Trajan, Optimum Princeps: A Life and Times,* 1997. • Donald R. Dudley, *The World of Tacitus,* 1969. • Ronald H. Martin, *Tacitus,* 1981. • Ronald Symes, *Tacitus,* 2 vols., 1958. • Andrew Wallace-Hadrill, *Suetonius, The Scholar and His Caesars,* 1983.

Virgil • Francis Cairns, *Virgil's Augustan Epic,* 1989. • Wendell Clausen, *Virgil's "Aeneid" and the Tradition of Hellenistic Poetry,* 1987. • Steele Commager, ed., *Virgil: A Collection of Critical Essays,* 1966. • Domenico Comparetti, *Vergil in the Middle Ages,* 1966. • K. W. Gransden, *Virgil's "Iliad": An Essay on Epic Narrative,* 1984. • Jasper Griffin, *Virgil,* 1986. • P. R. Hardie, *Virgil's "Aeneid": Cosmos and Imperium,* 1986. • S. J. Harrison, *Oxford Readings in Vergil's "Aeneid,"* 1990. • W. R. Johnson, *Darkness Visible: A Study of Vergil's "Aeneid,"* 1976. • Charles Martindale, ed., *The Cambridge Companion to Virgil,* 1997. • Charles Martindale, ed., *Virgil and His Influence,* 1984. • Michael C. J. Putnam, *Virgil's "Aeneid": Interpretation and Influence,* 1995. • Kenneth Quinn, *Virgil's "Aeneid": A Critical Description,* 1968. • David Slavitt, *Virgil,* 1992. • Theodore Ziolkowski, *Virgil and the Moderns,* 1993.

The Medieval Era

Medieval China

General • Cyril Birch, ed., *Studies in Chinese Literary Genres,* 1974. • Tse-tsung Chow, ed., *Wen-lin: Studies in Chinese Humanities,* 1968. • Christopher Leigh Connery, *The Empire of the Text: Writing and Authority in Early Imperial China,* 1998. • A. R. Davis, *The Penguin Book of Chinese Verse,* 1971. • Hans Frankel, *The Flowering Plum and the Palace Lady: Interpretations of Chinese Poetry,* 1976. • Donald Holzman, *Chinese Literature in Transition from Antiquity to the Middle Ages,* 1998. • Wu-chi Liu, *An Introduction to Chinese Literature,* 1966. • Wu-chi Liu and Irving Lo, eds., *Sunflower Splendor: Three Thousand Years of Chinese Poetry,* 1976. • Michael Loewe, *Everyday Life in Early Imperial China,* 1968. • Stephen Owen, *Traditional Chinese Poetry and Poetics: Omen of the World,* 1984. • Stephen Owen, *Remembrances: The Experience of the Past in Classical Chinese Literature,* 1986. • Scott Pearce, Audrey Spiro and Patricia Ebrey, eds., *Culture and Power in the Reconstitution of the Chinese Realm, 200–600,* 2001. • Burton Watson, *Chinese Lyricism,* 1970. • Burton Watson, *The Columbia Book of Chinese Poetry,* 1984. • Pauline Yu, *The Reading of Imagery in the Chinese Poetic Tradition,* 1987.

Poetry of the Tang Dynasty • Witter Bynner, *The Jade Mountain,* 1964. • François Cheng, *Chinese Poetic Writing,* 1982. • Arthur Cooper, *Li Po and Tu Fu,* 1973. • David Gordon, *Equinox: A Gathering of T'ang Poets,* 1975. • A. C. Graham, *Poems of the Late T'ang,* 1965. • Shuen-fu Lin and S. Owen, eds. *The Vitality of the Lyric Voice,* 1986. • James J. Y. Liu, *The Art of Chinese Poetry,* 1962. • Stephen Owen, *The Poetry of the Early T'ang,* 1977. • Stephen Owen, *The Great Age of Chinese Poetry: The High T'ang,* 1981. • Stephen Owen, *The End of the Chinese "Middle Ages": Essays* *in Mid-Tang Literary Culture,* 1996. • Vikram Seth, *Three Chinese Poets,* 1992. • Hugh Stimson, *Fifty-five T'ang Poems,* 1976. • Arthur Wright and Denis Twitchett, *Perspectives on the T'ang,* 1973. • David Young, trans., *Five T'ang Poets,* 1990.

The Song Lyric • Kang-i Sun Chang, *The Evolution of Chinese Tz'u Poetry,* 1980. • Ronald Egan, *Word, Image, and Deed in the Life of Su Shi,* 1994. • Lois Fusek, *Among the Flowers: The "Hua-chien Chi,"* 1982. • James J. Y. Liu, *Major Lyricists of the Northern Sung,* 1974. • Stephen Soong, ed., *Song Without Music: Chinese Tz'u Poetry,* 1980. • Marsha Wagner, *The Lotus Boat: The Origins of Chinese Tz'u Poetry in T'ang Popular Culture,* 1984. • Pauline Yu, ed., *Voices of the Song Lyric in China,* 1994.

Bo Juyi • Howard S. Levy, *Translations from Po Chü-i's Collected Works,* 1978. • Arthur Waley, *The Life and Times of Po Chü-i,* 1949.

Du Fu • Rewi Alley, trans., *Tu Fu: Selected Poems,* 1962. • Eva Shan Chou, *Reconsidering Tu Fu: Literary Greatness and Cultural Context,* 1995. • A. R. Davis, *Tu Fu,* 1971. • Sam Hamill, trans., *Facing the Snow: Visions of Tu Fu,* 1988. • David Hawkes, *A Little Primer of Tu Fu,* 1967. • William Hung, *Tu Fu: China's Greatest Poet,* 1952. • David McCraw, *Du Fu's Laments from the South,* 1992.

Li Bo • Rewi Alley, trans., *Li Pai: 200 Selected Poems,* 1980. • Shigeyoshi Obata, *The Works of Li Po,* 1922. • J. P. Seaton and James Cryer, trans., *Bright Moon, Perching Bird: Poems,* 1987. • Arthur Waley, *The Poetry and Career of Li Po,* 1950. • Siu-kit Wong, *The Genius of Li Po,* 1984.

Li Qingzhao • James Cryer, trans., *Plum Blossom: Poems of Li Qingzhao,* 1984. • Sam Hamill, trans., *The Lotus Lovers: Poems and Songs,* by Zi Ye and Li Qingzhao, 1985. • Kenneth Rexroth and Ling Chung, trans. and ed., *Li Ch'ing-chao, Complete Poems,* 1979.

Li Yu • Daniel Bryant, ed. and trans., *Lyric Poets of the Southern T'ang: Feng Yen-ssu, 903–960, and Li Yu, 937–978,* 1982.

Wang Wei • Tony Barnstone et al., *Laughing Lost in the Mountains—Selected Poems of Wang Wei,* 1989. • Yin-nan Chang and Lewis C. Walmsley, *Poems by Wang Wei,* 1958. • G. W. Robinson, *Poems of Wang Wei,* 1973. • Marsha L. Wagner, *Wang Wei,* 1981. • Lewis C. Walmsley and Dorothy B. Walmsley, *Wang Wei: The Painter-Poet,* 1968. • Eliot Weinberger and Octavio Paz, *Nineteen Ways of Looking at Wang Wei,* 1987. • Wai-lim Yip, *Hiding the Universe: Poems by Wang Wei,* 1972. • Pauline Yu, *The Poetry of Wang Wei: New Translations and Commentary,* 1980.

Japan

General • Geoffrey Bownas and Anthony Thwaite, trans. and ed. *The Penguin Book of Japanese Verse,* 1964. • Robert Brower and Earl Miner, *Japanese Court Poetry,* 1961. • Steven D. Carter, trans. and ed. *Traditional Japanese Poetry: An Anthology,* 1991. • William T. de Bary, ed. *Sources of Japanese Tradition,* 1958. • John Whitney Hall, *Japan: From Prehistory to Modern Times,* 1970. • Haruo Shirane, *Early Modern Japanese Literature, An Anthology,* 2001. • Donald Keene, *Japanese Literature: An Introduction for Western Readers,* 1953. • Donald Keene, ed. *Anthology of Japanese Literature: From the Earliest Era to the Mid-Nineteenth Century,* 1955. • Donald Keene, *Seeds in the Heart: Japanese Literature from Earliest Times to the late 16th Century,* 1993. • Donald Keene, *World Within Walls: Japanese Literature of the Pre-Modern Era, 1600–1867,* 1976. • Jin'ichi Konishi, *A History of Japanese Literature,* Vols. 1–3, 1984, 1986 and 1991. • Helen Craig McCullough, ed. *Classical Japanese Prose: An Anthology,* 1990. • Helen Craig McCullough, trans. and ed., *Genji and Heike: Selections from "The Tale of Genji" and "The Tale of the Heike,"* 1994. • Earl Miner, *An Introduction to Japanese Court Poetry,* 1968. • Earl Miner, Hiroko Odagiri, and Robert E. Morrell, *The Princeton Companion to Classical Japanese Literature,* 1985. • Ivan Morris, *The World of the Shining Prince: Court Life in Ancient Japan,* 1964. • Edward Putzar, *Japanese Literature: An Historical*

Outline, 1973. • J. Thomas Rimer, *A Reader's Guide to Japanese Literature,* 1988. • George Sansom, *Japan: A Short Cultural History,* 1948. • Conrad Totman, *Japan before Perry: A Short History,* 1981. • Makoto Ueda, *Literary and Art Theories in Japan,* 1967. • H. Paul Varley, *Japanese Culture,* 1984.

Perspectives: Courtly Women • Richard Bowring, *Murasaki Shikibu: Her Diary and Poetic Memoirs,* 1982. • Earl Miner, trans., *Japanese Poetic Diaries,* 1969. • Ivan Morris, trans., *As I Crossed a Bridge of Dreams: Recollections of a Woman in Eleventh-Century Japan,* 1971. • Edith Sarra, *Fictions of Femininity: Literary Conventions of Gender in Japanese Court Women's Memoirs,* 1999.

Murasaki Shikibu • Norma Field, *The Splendor of Longing in the Tale of Genji,* 1987. • Edward Kamens, ed. *Approaches to Teaching Murasaki Shikibu's The Tale of Genji,* 1993. • Ivan Morris, *The Tale of Genji Scroll,* 1971. • H. Richard Okada, *Figures of Resistance: Language, Poetry, and Narrating in The Tale of Genji and Other Mid-Heian Texts,* 1991. • Edward Seidensticker, trans., *The Tale of Genji,* 1981. • Haruo Shirane, *The Bridge of Dreams: A Poetics of "The Tale of Genji,"* 1987. • Amanda Mayer Stinchecum, "Who Tells the Tale? 'Ukifune': A Study in Narrative Voice." *Monumenta Nipponica* 35 (1980): 375–403. • Royall Tyler, trans., *The Tale of Genji,* 2001. • Arthur Waley, trans., *The Tale of Genji,* 1957.

Classical Arabic and Islamic Literatures

General • *The Encyclopaedia of Islam,* 1986. • *The Cambridge History of Iran,* 1968. • T. J. Andrae, *Muhammad: the Man and His Faith,* 1936. • J. Ashtiani et al., eds., *Abbasid Belles-Lettres,* 1988. • J. Bacharach, *A Middle Eastern Studies Handbook,* 1984. • A. F. Beeston et al., eds., *Arabic Literature to the End of the Ummayad Period,* 1983. • R. Blachère, *Histoire de la Littérature Arabe,* 3 vols., 1952–1966. • C. E. Bosworth, *The Islamic Dynasties,* 1967. • Peter Brown, *The World of Late Antiquity,* 1971. • A. J. Butler, *The Arab Conquest of Egypt,* 1902. • J. M. Cook, *The Persian Empire,* 1983. • D. Eikelman, *The Middle East: An Anthropological Approach,* 1981. • H. A. R. Gibb, *Arabic Literature,* 1963. • H. A. R. Gibb, *Islam,* 1969. • H. A. R. Gibb, *Muhammadansim,* 1949. • H. A. R. Gibb, *Studies on the Civilisation of Islam,* 1962. • G. E. von Grunebaum, *Medieval Islam: A Study in Cultural Orientation,* 1953. • Sabry Hafez, *The Genesis of Arabic Narrative Discourse,* 1993. • H. W. Hazard, *Atlas of the Islamic History,* 1957. • P. M. Holts et al., eds., *The Cambridge History of Islam,* 1970. • Albert Hourani, *A History of the Arab Peoples,* 1991. • Albert Hourani, *Syria and Lebanon,* 1946. • G. F. Hourani, *Arab Seafaring in the Indian Ocean in Ancient and Medieval Times,* 1951. • T. Khalidi, *Classical Arab Islam,* 1985. • S. Lane-Poole, *The Muhammadan Dynasties,* 1925. • I. M. Lapidus, *A History of Muslim Societies,* 1988. • Bernard Lewis, *Istanbul and the Civilisation of the Ottoman Empire,* 1963. • Bernard Lewis, ed. *The World of Islam,* 1976. • S. Moscati, *The Semites in Ancient History,* 1959. • J. D. Pearson et al., eds., *Index Islamicus,* 1958. • F. Rahman, *Islam,* 1979. • R. Roolvink, *Historical Atlas of the Muslim Peoples,* 1957. • M. Ruthven, *Islam in the World,* 1984. • Jean Sargent, *Introduction to the History of the Muslim East,* 1965. • J. Sauvaget, *Introduction à l'histoire de l'orient musulman,* 1961. • I. Shahid, *Rome and the Arabs,* 1984. • L. Udovitch, ed., *The Islamic Middle East 700–1900: Studies in Economic and Social History,* 1981. • W. M. Watt, *Muhammad: Prophet and Statesman,* 1961. • W. M. Watt, *Muhammad at Mecca,* 1953. • W. M. Watt, *Muhammad at Medina,* 1956.

The Qur'an • A. J. Arberry, *The Qur'an Interpreted,* 1955. • H. Berkeland, *Old Muslim Opposition against Interpretation of the Qur'an,* 1955. • J. Bowker, *Jesus in the Qur'an,* 1965. • J. Burton, *The Collection of the Qur'an,* 1977. • K. Cragg, *The Event of the Qur'an,* 1971. • K. Cragg, *The Mind of the Qur'an,* 1973. • Ali Dashti, *Twenty-Three Years: A Study of the Prophetic Career of Muhammad,* 1985. • F. Gabrieli, *Muhammad and the Conquests of Islam,* 1968. • H. Gätje, *Qur'an and Its Exegeses,* 1976. • J. B. Glubb, *The Life and Times of Muhammad,* 1979. • M. H. Haykal, *The Life of*

Muhammad, 1976. • R. G. Hovannisian, ed., *Islam's Understanding of Itself,* 1983. • T. Isutsu, *Ethico-Religious Concepts in the Qur'an,* 1966. • T. Isutsu, *God and Man in the Qur'an,* 1964. • J Jansen, *The Interpretation of the Qur'an in Modern Egypt,* 1974. • A. Jeffery, *Reader on Islam,* 1962. • J. Jomier, *The Bible and the Qur'an,* 1964. • M. Lings, *Muhammad: His Life Based on the Earliest Sources,* 1983. • Henry Mercier and Lucien Tremlett, *The Qur'an,* 1973. • A. Abul Qaswm, *The Recitation and Interpretation of the Qur'an,* 1979. • D. Rahbar, *God of Justice: A Study in the Ethical Doctine of the Qur'an,* 1960. • Fazlur Rahman, *Islam,* 1966. • M. Rodinson, *Mohammed,* 1971. • M. S. Seale, *Qur'an and Bible,* 1978. • S. H. Shamma, *The Ethical System underlying the Qur'an,* 1959. • W. Montgomery Watt, *Muhammad at Mecca,* 1953. • W. Montgomery Watt, *Muhammad at Medina,* 1966. • A. J. Wensinck, *Muhammad and the Jews of Mecca,* 1975.

The Thousand and One Nights • Daniel E. Beaumont, *Slave of Desire: Sex, Love, and Death in The 1001 Nights,* 2002. • Sir Richard F. Burton, trans., *The Arabian Nights: Tales from a Thousand and One Nights,* introduction by A. S. Byatt, 2001. • Peter L. Caracciolo, ed., *The "Arabian Nights" in English Literature,* 1988. • André Clot, *Harun al-Rashid and the World of the Thousand and One Nights,* 1989. • Ferial J. Ghazoul, *Nocturnal Poetics: The Arabian Nights in Comparative Perspective,* 1996. • Husain Haddawy, trans., *The Arabian Nights,* 1990. • Husain Haddawy, trans., *The Arabian Nights II: Sinbad and Other Popular Stories,* 1995. • Robert Irwin, *The Arabian Nights: A Companion,* 1995. • Muhsin Mahdi, ed., *The Thousand and One Nights (Alf Layla wa-Layla) from the earliest known sources,* 3 vols., 1984–1994. • Powys Mathers, trans., *The Book of the Thousand Nights and One Night,* 4 vols., from the French translation of J. C. Mardrus, 1964. • David Pinault, *Story-Telling Techniques in the Arabian Nights,* 1992. • Iqbal 'Ali Shah, *Alone in Arabian Nights,* 1933. • Douglas Brooke Wheelton Sladen, *Oriental Cairo: The City of the "Arabian Nights,"* 1987.

Abu Nuwas • W. H. Ingrams, *Abu Nuwas in Life and in Legend,* 1933. • Philip F. Kennedy, *The Wine Song in Classical Arabic Poetry: Abu Nuwas and the Literary Tradition,* 1997. • Arthur Wormhoudt, *The Diwan of Abu Nuwas al-Hasan ibn Hani al-Hakami,* 1974.

Assia Djebar • Gordon Bigelow, "Revolution and Modernity: Assia Djébar's *Les Enfants du Nouveau Monde,*" *Research in African Literatures,* vol. 34, 2003, 13–27. • Miriam Cooke, *Women Claim Islam: Creating Islamic Feminism Through Literature,* 2001. • Anne Donadey, *Recasting Postcolonialism: Women Writing Between Worlds,* 2001. • Ann Donadey, *Polyphonic and Palimpsestic Discourse in the Works of Assia Djebar and Leila Sebbar,* 1993. • Rafika Merini, *Two Major Francophone Women Writers: Assia Djébar and Leila Sebba: A Thematic Study of Their Works,* 1999. • Nada Elia, *Trances, Dances, and Vociferations: Agency and Resistance in Africana Women's Narratives,* 2001. • Elizabeth Warnock, ed., *Remembering Childhood in the Middle East: Memoirs from a Century of Change,* 2002.

Medieval Europe

General • *The New Cambridge Medieval History,* 7 vols., 1995–2003. • Judson Boyce Allen. *The Friar as Critic: Literary Attitudes in the Later Middle Ages,* 1971. • Emily Amt, ed. *Medieval England 1000–1500: A Reader,* 2000. • Erich Auerbach. *Mimesis: The Representation of Reality in Western Literature,* 1968. • R. Howard Bloch, and Stephen G. Nichols, eds. *Medievalism and the Modernist Temper,* 1996. • William Calin. *The French Tradition and the Literature of Medieval England,* 1994. • Norman F. Cantor. *The Medieval World: 300–1300,* 1968. • H. J. Chaytor. *From Script to Print: An Introduction to Medieval Vernacular Literature,* 1966. • H. J. Chaytor, *A History of Aragon and Catalonia,* 1969. • Susan Crane. *Insular Romance: Politics, Faith, and Culture in Anglo-Norman and Middle English Literature,* 1986. • Ernst Robert Curtius. *European Literature and the Latin Middle Ages,* 1973. • Charles Dahlberg. *The Literature of Unlikeness,* 1988. • Marilynn Desmond. *Reading Dido: Gender, Textuality, and the Medieval Aeneid,* 1994. • Carolly Erickson, ed. *The Records of Medieval Europe,* 1971. • Boris Ford, ed. *Medieval Literature: The European Inheritance,* 1983. • C. Warren Hollister, *Medieval Europe: A Short History,* 1982. • George Holmes, ed., *The Oxford Illustrated History of Medieval Europe,* 1988.

• Jackson, W. T. H. *The Literature of the Middle Ages,* 1960. • Jackson, W. T. H. *Medieval Literature: A History and a Guide,* 1966. • Jackson, W. T. H. *The Challenge of the Medieval Text: Studies in Genre and Interpretation,* 1985. • W. P. Ker. *Epic and Romance,* 1908. • Robin Kirkpatrick. *English and Italian Literature from Dante to Shakespeare: A Study of Source, Analogue, and Divergence,* 1995. • H. G. Koenigsberger, *Medieval Europe, 400–1500,* 1987. • C. S. Lewis. *The Discarded Image: An Introduction to Medieval and Renaissance Literature,* 1964. • David L. Pike. *Passage Through Hell: Modernist Descents, Medieval Underworlds,* 1997. • Ezra Pound. *The Spirit of Romance,* 1957. • Barbara H. Rosenwein. *A Short History of the Middle Ages,* 2001. • James Bruce Ross, and Mary Martin McLaughlin. *The Portable Medieval Reader,* 1949. • R. A. Shoaf. Dante. *Chaucer and the Currency of the Word: Money, Images, and Reference in Late Medieval Poetry,* 1983. • Thomas C. Stillenger. *The Song of Troilus: Lyric Authority in the Medieval Book,* 1993 • Brian Tierney, ed. *The Middle Ages,* Volume 1: *Sources of Medieval History,* 1998. • Barbara Tuchman, *A Distant Mirror: The Calamitous Fourteenth Century,* 1978. • Hugh White. *Nature, Sex, and Goodness in a Medieval Literary Tradition,* 2000.

Perspectives: Iberia, The Meeting of Three Worlds • Samuel Armistead, Mishael M. Caspi, et al., eds., *Jewish Culture and the Hispanic World,* 2001. • Eliahu Ashtor, *The Jews of Moslem Spain,* 1992. • Yitzhak Baer, *A History of the Jews in Christian Spain,* 1992. • Stacy N. Beckwith, *Charting Memory: Recalling Medieval Spain,* 1999. • Gilbert Chase, *The Music of Spain,* 1941. • Richard Fletcher, *Moorish Spain,* 1993. • Daniel Frank, ed., *The Jews of Medieval Islam: Community, Society, and Identity,* 1995. • Jane S. Gerber, *The Jews of Spain: A History of the Sephardic Experience,* 1994. • L. P. Harvey, *Islamic Spain 1250–1500,* 1992. • Salma Khadra Jayyusi, *The Legacy of Muslim Spain,* 2 vols. 1992. • John Esten Keller, and Annette Grant Cash, *Daily Life Depicted in the Cantigas de Santa Maria,* 1998. • Hugh Kennedy, *Muslim Spain and Portugal: A Political History of Al-Andalus,* 1997. • Vivian B. Mann, Thomas F. Glick, and Jerrilynn D. Dodds, *Convivencia: Jews, Muslims, and Christians in Medieval Spain,* 1992. • Manuela Marin, Julio Samsó, and Maribel Fierro, *The Formation of Al-Andalus,* 2 vols., 1998. • María Rosa Menocal, *The Arabic Role in Medieval Literary History: A Forgotten Heritage,* 1987. • María Rosa Menocal, *Shards of Love: Exile and the Origins of the Lyric,* 1994. • María Rosa Menocal and Harold Bloom, *The Ornament of the World: How Muslims, Jews, and Christians Created a Culture of Tolerance in Medieval Spain,* 2002. • María Rosa Menocal, Raymond Scheindlin, and Michael Sells, eds., *The Literature of Al-Andalus,* 2000. • Louise Mirrer, *Women, Jews, and Muslims in the Texts of Reconquest Castile,* 1996. • A. R. Nykl, *Hispano-Arabic Poetry and Its Relation to the Old Provençal Troubadours,* 1946. • Bernard F. Reilly, *The Medieval Spains,* 1993. • Julian Ribera, *Music in Ancient Arabia and Spain,* 1929. • Lucy A. Sponsler, *Women in the Medieval Spanish Epic and Lyric Traditions,* 1975. • David Wasserstein, *The Rise and Fall of the Party-Kings: Politics and Society in Islamic Spain 1002–1086,* 1985.

Beowulf • Adrien Bonjour, *The Digressions in Beowulf,* 1950. • R. W. Chambers and C. L. Wrenn, *Beowulf: An Introduction to the Study of the Poem,* 1959. • Craig R. Davis, *Beowulf and the Demise of Germanic Legend in England,* 1996. • Susan E. Deskis, *Beowulf and the Medieval Proverb Tradition,* 1996. • James W. Earl, *Thinking About Beowulf,* 1994. • John Miles Foley, *Traditional Oral Epic: The Odyssey, Beowulf, and the Serbo-Croatian Return Song,* 1990. • Ritchie Girvan and Rupert Bruce-Mitford, *Beowulf and the Seventh Century,* 1971. • John M. Hill, *The Anglo-Saxon Warrior Ethic,* 2000. • Edward B. Irving, *A Reading of Beowulf,* 1968. • J. D. A. Ogilvy, and Donald C. Baker, *Reading Beowulf: An Introduction to the Poem, Its Background, and Its Style,* 1983. • Gillian R. Overing, *Language, Sign, and Gender in Beowulf,* 1990. • Fred C. Robinson, *Beowulf and the Appositive Style,* 1985. • Kenneth Sisam, *The Structure of Beowulf,* 1965. • J. Michael Stitt, *Beowulf and the Bear's Son: Epic, Saga, and Fairytale in Northern Germanic Tradition,* 1992. • J. R. R. Tolkien, *Beowulf and the Critics,* ed. Michael D.C. Drout, 2002. • Dorothy Whitelock, *The Audience of Beowulf,* 1951.

Castilian Ballads and Traditional Songs • Ingrid Bahler and Katherine Gyékényesi Gatto, *Of Kings and Poets: Cancionero Poetry of the Trastámara Courts,* 1992. • Robert Stevenson, *Spanish Music in the Age of Columbus,* 1960. • Ruth H. Webber, ed., *Hispanic Balladry Today,* 1989.

Geoffrey Chaucer • Malcolm Andrew, *Critical Essays on Chaucer's Canterbury Tales,* 1991. • Peter Beidler, ed., *The Wife of Bath,* 1996. • C. David Benson, *Chaucer's Drama of Style: Poetic Variety and Contrast in The Canterbury Tales,* 1986. • Piero Boitano, *Chaucer* *and the Italian Trecento,* 1983. • Piero Boitano and Jill Mann, eds., *The Cambridge Chaucer Companion,* 1986. • Muriel Bowden, *A Commentary on the General Prologue to "The Canterbury Tales,"* 1967. • Susan Crane, *Gender and Romance in Chaucer's "Canterbury Tales,"* 1994. • W. A. Davenport, *Chaucer and His English Contemporaries: Prologue and Tale in "The Canterbury Tales,"* 1998. • Alfred David, *The Strumpet Muse: Art and Morals in Chaucer's Poetry,* 1976. • Carolyn Dinshaw, *Chaucer's Sexual Poetics,* 1989. • E. Talbot Donaldson, *Speaking of Chaucer,* 1970. • Sigmund Eisner, *A Tale of Wonder: A Source Study of The Wife of Bath's Tale,* 1969. • John M. Fyler, *Chaucer and Ovid,* 1979. • Jodi-Anne George, ed. *Geoffrey Chaucer: The General Prologue to the "Canterbury Tales,"* 2000. • Warren Ginsberg, *Chaucer's Italian Tradition,* 2002. • John C. Hirsch, *Chaucer and the Canterbury Tales: A Short Introduction,* 2003. • Donald R. Howard, *Chaucer: His Life, His Works, His World,* 1987. • Donald R. Howard, *The Idea of the Canterbury Tales,* 1976. • Peggy Knapp, *Chaucer and the Social Contest,* 1990. • Stephen Knight, *Geoffrey Chaucer,* 1986. • V. A. Kolve, *Chaucer and the Imagery of Narrative.* Stanford: Stanford University Press, 1984. • H. Marshall Leicester Jr., *The Disenchanted Self: Representing the Subject in the Canterbury Tales,* 1990. • Kathryn L. Lynch, ed. *Chaucer's Cultural Geography,* 2002. • Jill Mann, *Chaucer and Medieval Estates Satire: The Literature of Social Classes and the General Prologue to the "Canterbury Tales,"* 1973. • Robert P. Miller, ed. *Chaucer: Sources and Backgrounds,* 1977. • A. J. Minnis, *Chaucer and Pagan Antiquity,* 1982. • A. J. Minnis, ed., *Chaucer's Boece and the Medieval Tradition of Boethius,* 1993. • Charles Muscatine, *Chaucer and the French Tradition,* 1957. • Richard Neuse, *Chaucer's Dante: Allegory and Epic Theater in The Canterbury Tales,* 1991. • Paul A. Olson, *The Canterbury Tales and the Good Society,* 1986. • Lee Patterson, *Chaucer and the Subject of History,* 1991. • S. H. Rigby, *Chaucer in Context: Society, Allegory, and Gender,* 1996. • D. W. Robertson, *Chaucer's London,* 1968. • D. W. Robertson, *A Preface to Chaucer,* 1962. • Beryl Rowland, ed., *Companion to Chaucer Studies,* 1979. • Brenda Deen Schildgen, *Pagans, Tartars, Moslems, and Jews in Chaucer's "Canterbury Tales,"* 2001. • Paul Strohm, *Social Chaucer,* 1989. • David Wallace, *Chaucerian Polity: Absolutist Lineages and Associational Forms in England and Italy,* 1997. • Winthrop Wetherbee, *Geoffrey Chaucer: "The Canterbury Tales,"* 1989.

Dante Alighieri • William Anderson, *Dante the Maker,* 1980. • Peter Armour, *Dante's Griffin and the History of the World,* 1989. • Peter Armour, *The Door of Purgatory: A Study of Multiple Symbolism in Dante's Purgatorio,* 1983. • Erich Auerbach, *Dante Poet of the Secular World,* 1961. • Erich Auerbach, "Figura," in *Scenes from the Drama of European Literature,* 1984. • Michele Barbi, *Life of Dante,* 1954. • Teodolinda Barolini, *Dante's Poets: Textuality and Truth in the Comedy,* 1983. • Teodolinda Barolini, *The Undivine Comedy: Detheologizing Dante,* 1992. • Steven Botterill, *Dante and the Mystical Tradition: Bernard of Clairvaux in the Commedia,* 1994. • Patrick Boyde, *Dante, Philomythes and Philosopher: Man in the Cosmos,* 1981. • Patrick Boyde, *Human Vices and Human Worth in Dante's Comedy,* 2000. • Anthony K. Cassell, *Inferno I,* 1989. • A. C. Charity, *Events and Their Afterlife: The Dialectics of Christian Typology in the Bible and Dante,* 1966. • Marc Cogan, *The Design in the Wax: The Structure of the Divine Comedy and Its Meaning,* 1999. • Alison Cornish, *Reading Dante's Stars,* 2000. • Charles Davis, *Dante and the Idea of Rome,* 1957. • Charles Davis, *Dante's Italy and Other Essays,* 1984. • Alessandro Passerin d'Entrèves, *Dante as a Political Thinker,* 1952. • Peter Dronke, *Dante and Medieval Latin Traditions,* 1986. • Robert M. Durling and Ronald L. Martinez, *Time and the Crystal: Studies in Dante's Rime Petrose,* 1990. • Francis Fergusson, *Dante,* 1966. • Frances Fergusson, *Dante's Drama of the Mind: A Modern Reading of Purgatorio,* 1953. • Joan M. Ferrante, *The Political Vision of the Divine Comedy,* 1984. • Kenelm Foster, *The Two Dantes and Other Studies,* 1977. • Wallace Fowlie, *A Reading of Dante's Inferno,* 1981. • William Franke, *Dante's Interpretive Journey,* 1996. • John Freccero, ed., *Dante: A Collection of Critical Essays,* 1965. • John Freccero, *Dante: The Poetics of Conversion,* ed. Rachel Jacoff, 1986. • Eileen Gardiner, trans., *Visions of Heaven and Hell Before Dante,* 1989. • Etienne Gilson, *Dante and Philosophy,* trans. David Moore, 1963. • Cecil Grayson, ed., *The World of Dante,* 1980. • Robert Pogue Harrison, *The Body of Beatrice,* 1988. • Robert Hollander, *Allegory* *in Dante's Commedia,* 1969. • Robert Hollander, *Dante: A Life in Works,* 2001. • George Holmes, *Dante,* 1980. • Rachel Jacoff, ed., *The Cambridge Companion to Dante,* 1993. • Rachel Jacoff and Jeffrey Schnapp, ed., *The Poetry of Allusion: Virgil and Ovid in Dante's Commedia,* 1991. • Rachel Jacoff and William A. Stephany, *Inferno II,* 1989. • Robin Kirkpatrick, *Dante's Inferno: Difficulty and Dead Poetry,* 1987. • John Kleiner, *Mismapping the Underworld: Daring and Error in Dante's Comedy,* 1994. • Richard Lansing, ed., *Dante: The Critical Complex,* 8 vols., 2003. • Jacques Le Goff, *The Birth of Purgatory,* 1984. • Ronald Macdonald, *The Burial Places of Memory: Epic Underworlds in Vergil, Dante and Milton,* 1987. • Allen Mandelbaum, et al., eds., *Lectura Dantis: Inferno,* 1998. • Antonio C. Mastrobuono, *Dante's Journey of Sanctification,* 1990. • Jerome Mazzaro, *The Figure of Beatrice,* 1981. • Joseph Anthony Mazzeo, *Structure and Thought in the Paradiso,* 1958. • Giuseppe Mazzotta, ed., *Critical Essays on Dante,* 1991. • Giuseppe Mazzotta, *Dante, Poet of the Desert: History and Allegory in the Divine Comedy,* 1979. • Giuseppe Mazzotta, *Dante's Vision and the Circle of Knowledge,* 1993. • María Rosa Menocal, *The Arabic Role in Medieval Literary History,* 1987. • Edward G. Miller, *Sense Perception in Dante's Commedia,* 1996. • Alison Morgan, *Dante and the Medieval Other World,* 1990. • Mary A. Orr, *Dante and the Early Astronomers,* 1961. • Shirley J. Paolini, *Confessions of Sin and Love in the Middle Ages: Dante's Commedia and St. Augustine's Confessions,* 1982. • Ricardo Quinones, *Dante Alighieri,* 1979. • Brenda Deen Schildgen, *Dante and the Orient,* 2002. • Jeffrey Schnapp, *The Transfiguration of History at the Center of Dante's Paradise,* 1986. • John A. Scott, *Dante's Political Purgatory,* 1996. • J. E. Shaw, *Essays on the Vita Nuova,* 1929. • Maria Picchio Simonelli, *Inferno III,* 1993. • Charles S. Singleton, *Dante's Commedia: Elements of Structure,* 1977. • Charles S. Singleton, *An Essay on the Vita Nuova,* 1949. • Charles S. Singleton, *Journey to Beatrice,* 1958. • Madison U. Sowell, ed., *Dante and Ovid: Essays in Intertextuality,* 1991. • Jeremy Tambling, ed., *Dante,* 1999. • Miguel Tasín Palacios, *Islam and the Divine Comedy,* 1968. • J. F. Took, *Dante, Lyric Poet and Philosopher: An Introduction to the Minor Works,* 1990. • Paget Toynbee, *Dante Alighieri, His Life and Works,* 1965.

Dom Dinis and Martin Codax • Sheila R. Ackerlind, *King Dinis of Portugal and the Alfonsine Heritage,* 1990. • Frede Jensen, *The Earliest Portuguese Lyrics,* 1978.

Sir Gawain and the Green Knight • Ross Arthur, *Medieval Sign Theory and Sir Gawain and the Green Knight,* 1987. • W. R. J. Barron, *English Medieval Romance,* 1987. • Larry D. Benson, *Art and Tradition in Sir Gawain and the Green Knight,* 1965. • Robert J. Blanch and Julian Wasserman, *From Pearl to Gawain,* 1995. • Robert J. Blanch, et al., eds., *Text and Matter: New Critical Perspectives of the Pearl-Poet,* 1991. • Marie Borroff, *Sir Gawain and the Green Knight: A Stylistic and Metrical Study,* 1962. • Derek Brewer, ed., *Studies in Medieval English Romance,* 1988. • Derek Brewer and Jonathan Gibson, eds. *A Companion to the Gawain-Poet,* 1997. • Elisabeth Brewer, ed., *Sir Gawain and the Green Knight: Sources and Analogues,* 1992. • J. A. Burrow, *A Reading of "Sir Gawain and the Green Knight,"* 1966. • Wendy Clein, *Concepts of Chivalry in "Sir Gawain and the Green Knight,"* 1987. • Lynn Staley Johnson, *The Voice of the Gawain-poet,* 1984. • Maldwyn Mills, et al., eds., *Romance in Medieval England,* 1991. • Sandra Pearson Prior, *The Pearl Poet Revisited,* 1994. • Ad Putter, *An Introduction to the Gawain-Poet,* 1996. • Lee C. Ramsey, *Chivalric Romances,* 1983. • A. C. Spearing, *The Gawain-Poet: A Critical Study,* 1970.

Ibn al-'Arabi • A. E. Affifi, *The Mystical Philosophy of Muhyid din-Ibnul 'Arabi,* 1939. • Henri Corbin, *Creative Imagination in the Sufism of Ibn 'Arabi,* trans. Ralph Manheim, 1958. • Seyyed Hossain Nasr, *Three Muslim Sages,* 1969.

Ramon Llull • J. N. Hillgarth, *Raymond Llull and Llullism in Fourteenth-Century France,* 1971. • Mark D. Johnston, *The Evangelical Rhetoric of Ramon Llull: Lay Learning and Piety in the Christian West Around 1300,* 1996. • Mark D. Johnston, *The Spiritual Logic of Ramon Llull,* 1987. • E. Allison Peers, *Ramon Llull: A Biography,* 1969. • Frances A. Yates, *Llull and Bruno: Collected Essays,* Vol. 1, 1982.

Marie de France • R. Howard Bloch, *The Anonymous Marie de France,* 2003. • Margaret M. Boland, *Architectural Structure in the Lais of Marie de France,* 1995. • Glyn S. Burgess, *The Lais of Marie de France: Text and*

Context, 1987. • Caroline Walker Bynum, *Metamorphosis and Identity,* 2001. • Paula Clifford, *Marie de France: Lais,* 1982. • Mortimer J. Donovan, *The Breton Lay: A Guide to Varieties,* 1969. • Chantal Maréchal, ed., *In Quest of Marie de France: A Twelfth-Century Poet,* 1992. • Emanuel J. Mickel, Jr., *Marie de France,* 1974.

Mozarabic Kharjas • Samuel G. Armistead, "A Brief History of *Kharja* Studies." *Hispania* 70: 8–15, 1987 • Richard Hitchcock, *The Kharjas: A Critical Bibliography,* 1977. • Alan Jones, *Romance 'Kharjas' in Andalusian Arabic Muwassah Poetry: A Paleographical Analysis,* 1988. • Samuel Stern, *Hispano-Arabic Strophic Poetry: Studies,* 1974. • Otto Zwartjes, *Love Songs from al-Andalus: History, Structure, and Meaning of the Kharja,* 1997.

Troubadours and Trobairitz • F. R. P. Akehurst and Judith M. Davis, *A Handbook of the Troubadours,* 1995. • Elizabeth Aubrey, *The Music of the Troubadours,* 1996. • Frank M. Chambers, *An Introduction to Old Provençal Versification,* 1985. • Simon Gaunt, *Troubadours and Irony,* 1989. • Simon Gaunt and Sarah Kay, ed., *The Troubadours: An Introduction,* 1999. • Frederick Goldin, *The Mirror of Narcissus in the Courtly Love Lyric,* 1967. • C. Stephen Jaeger, *The Origins of Courtliness: Civilizing Trends and the Formation of Courtly Ideals, 939–1210,* 1987. • Sarah Kay, *Subjectivity in Troubadour Poetry,* 1990. • Laura Kendrick, *The Game of Love: Troubadour Wordplay,* 1988. • Karen Wilk Klein, *The Partisan Voice: A Study of the Political Lyric in France and Germany, 1180–1230,* 1971. • Malcolm Lambert, *The Cathars,* 1998. • William D. Paden, ed., *The Voice of the Trobairitz: Perspectives on the Women Troubadours,* 1989. • Linda Paterson, *The World of the Troubadours: Medieval Occitan Society c. 1100–c. 1300,* 1993. • Sarah Spence, *Rhetorics of Reason and Desire: Vergil, Augustine, and the Troubadours,* 1988. • Jonathan Sumption, *The Albigensian Crusade,* 2000. • Leslie T. Topsfield, *Troubadours and Love,* 1975. • Amelia E. Van Vleck, *Memory and Re-Creation in Troubadour Lyric,* 1991. • Walter L. Wakefield, *Heresy, Crusade and Inquisition in Southern France, 1100–1250,* 1974. • Peter Whigham, ed. *The Music of the Troubadours,* 3 vols., 1979.

Yehudah ha-Levi and Solomon Ibn Gabirol • Ross Brann, *The Compunctious Poet: Cultural Ambiguity and Hebrew Poetry in Muslim Spain,* 1991. • David Hartman, *Israelis and the Jewish Tradition: An Ancient People Debating Its Future,* 2000. • Rudolf Kayser, *The Life and Time of Jehudah Halevi,* trans. Frank Gaynor, 1949. • Raphael Loewe, *Ibn Gabirol,* 1990. • Arie Schippers, *Spanish Hebrew Poetry and the Arabic Literary Tradition: Arabic Themes in Hebrew Andalusian Poetry,* 1994.

THE EARLY MODERN PERIOD

Early Modern Europe

General • Erich Auerbach, *Mimesis: The Representation of Reality in Western Literature,* 1953. • Leonard Barkan, *Unearthing the Past: Archaeology and Aesthetics in the Making of Renaissance Culture,* 2000. • Hans Baron, *The Crisis of the Early Italian Renaissance,* 1966. • Harry Berger, Jr., *Second World and Green World: Studies in Renaissance Fiction-Making,* 1988. • John Bossy, *Christianity in the West, 1400–1700,* 1985. • Karl Brandi. *The Emperor Charles V,* 1980. • Fernand Braudel, *The Mediterranean and the Mediterranean World in the Age of Philip II,* 2 vols., 1972. • Jerry Brotton, *Trading Territories: Mapping the Early Modern World,* 1997. • Peter Burke, *Popular Culture in Early Modern Europe,* 1978. • Douglas Bush, *Classical Influences in Renaissance Literature,* 1952. • Stanley Chojnacki, *Women and Men in Renaissance Venice,* 2000. • Louise Clubb, *Italian Drama in Shakespeare's Time,* 1989. • Marcia L. Colish, *Medieval Foundations of the Western Intellectual Tradition,* 1998. • Natalie Davis, *Society and Culture in Early Modern France,* 1976. • Robert M. Durling, *The Figure of the Poet in Renaissance Epic,* 1965. • J. H. Elliott, *The Old World and the New, 1492–1650,* 1970. • Eugenio Garin, *Italian Humanism: Philosophy and Civic Life in the Renaissance,* 1965. • Deno Geanakoplos, *Greek Scholars in Venice,* 1962. • Richard Goldthwaite, *The Building of Renaissance Florence,* 1981. • Thomas Greene, *The Light in Troy: Imitation and Discovery in Renaissance Poetry,* 1982. • Thomas Greene, *The*

Descent from Heaven: A Study in Epic Continuity, 1963. • Timothy Hampton, *Writing from History: The Rhetoric of Exemplarity in Renaissance Literature,* 1990. • Francis Haskell, *Patrons and Painters,* 1963. • Henry Kamen, *Philip of Spain,* 1997. • Dale Kent, *The Rise of the Medici,* 1978. • Nannerl O. Keohane, *Philosophy and the State in France,* 1980. • Christiane Klapisch-Züber, *Women, Religion and Ritual in Early Modern Italy,* trans. Lydia G. Cochrane, 1985. • Jill Kraye, *The Cambridge Companion to Renaissance Humanism,* 1989. • Paul Oskar Kristeller, *Renaissance Thought and its Sources,* 1979. • Frederic C. Lane, *Venice: A Maritime Republic,* 1973. • Frank Lestringant, *Mapping the Renaissance World: The Geographical Imagination in the Age of Discovery,* 1994. • Garrett Mattingly, *The Armada,* 1959. • Samuel Eliot Morison, *The European Discovery of America,* 1974. • Edward Muir, *Ritual in Early Modern Europe,* 1997. • David Norbrook, *Poetry and Politics in the English Renaissance,* 1984. • Erwin Panofsky, *Renaissance and Renascences in Western Art,* 1969. • Patricia Parker, *Inescapable Romance,* 1979. • Boies Penrose, *Travel and Discovery in the Renaissance, 1420–1620,* 1952. • Mary Elizabeth Perry, *Gender and Disorder in Early Modern Seville,* 1990. • J. G. A. Pocock, *The Machiavellian Moment,* 1975. • David Quint, *Epic and Empire,* 1993. • Albert Rabil, Jr., ed., *Renaissance Humanism: Foundations, Forms, and Legacy,* 3 vols., 1988. • Edward Rosen, *Copernicus and the Scientific Revolution,* 1984. • David B. Ruderman, *Jewish Thought and Scientific Discovery in Early Modern Europe,* 1995. • Londa Schiebinger, *The Mind Has No Sex? Women in the Origins of Modern Science,* 1989. • Charles B. Schmitt, *Studies in Renaissance Philosophy and Science,* 1981. • Robert Schwoebel, *The Shadow of the Crescent: The Renaissance Image of the Turks, 1453–1517,* 1973. • Robert W. Scribner, *Popular Culture and Popular Movements in Reformation Germany,* 1987. • Nancy Siraisi, *Medieval and Early Renaissance Medicine,* 1990. • Dava Sobel, *Galileo's Daughter,* 2000. • Jonathan D. Spence, *The Memory Palace of Matteo Ricci,* 1985. • Dora Thornton, *The Scholar in his Study: Ownership and Experience in Renaissance Italy,* 1998. • Richard Trexler, *Public Life in Renaissance Florence,* 1980. • Charles Trinkaus, *In Our Image and Likeness,* 1970. • Jane Tylus, *Writing and Vulnerablity in the Late Renaissance,* 1993. • William Wallace, *Galileo and His Sources,* 1984. • Merry Wiesner-Hanks, *Women and Gender in Early Modern Europe,* 1993. • Edgar Wind, *Pagan Mysteries in the Renaissance,* 1968. • Frances Yates, *The French Academies of the Sixteenth Century,* 1947.

Perspectives: Lyric Sequences and Self-Definition • Glauco Cambon, *Michelangelo's Poetry: Fury of Form,* 1985. • Heather Dubrow, *Echoes of Desire: English Petrarchism and Its Counterdiscourses,* 1995. • Anne Ferry, *The Inward Language: Sonnets of Wyatt, Sidney, Shakespeare, and Donne,* 1983. • Samuel Fiszman, ed., *The Polish Renaissance in Its European Context,* 1988. • Joseph Gibaldi, "Vittoria Colonna: Child, Woman, and Poet," in *Women Writers of the Renaissance and Reformation,* ed. Katharina Wilson, 1987. • Roland Greene, *Post-Petrarchism: Origins and Innovations of the Western Lyric Sequence,* 1991. • Ann Rosalind Jones, *The Currency of Eros: Women's Love Lyric in Europe, 1540–1620,* 1990. • William Kennedy, *Authorizing Petrarch,* 1994. • Stephen Minta, ed., *Petrarch and Petrarchism: The English and French Traditions,* 1980. • Anne Lake Prescott, *French Poets and the English Renaissance,* 1978. • Ernest Hatch Wilkins, *The Invention of the Sonnet and Other Studies in Italian Literature,* 1959.

Giovanni Boccaccio • Thomas Bergin, *Boccaccio,* 1982. • Vittore Branca, *Boccaccio: The Man and His Works,* 1976. • Pier Massimo Forni, *Adventures in Speech: Rhetoric and Narration in Boccaccio's Decameron,* 1996. • Victoria Kirkham, *The Sign of Reason in Boccaccio's Fiction,* 1993. • Millicent Marcus, *An Allegory of Form: Literary Self-Consciousness in the Decameron,* 1979. • Giuseppe Mazzotta, *The World at Play in Boccaccio's "Decameron,"* 1986. • Aldo Scaglione, *Nature and Love in the Middle Ages,* 1963. • Daniel Williman, ed., *The Black Death: The Impact of the Fourteenth-Century Plague,* 1982.

Miguel de Cervantes • Jean Canavaggio, *Cervantes,* 1990. • Anne J. Cruz, *Discourses of Poverty: Social Reform and the Picaresque Novel in Early Modern Spain,* 1999. • Ruth El Saffar, *Critical Essays on Cervantes,* 1986. • Alban Forcione, *Cervantes and the Humanist Vision,* 1982. • Maria Antonia Garcés, *Cervantes in Algiers: A Captive's Tale,* 2002. • Timothy Hampton, *Writing from History,* 1990. • Steven D. Hutchinson, *Cervantine Journeys,* 1992. • Carroll B. Johnson, *Don Quixote: The Quest for Modern Fiction,* 1990. • Carroll B.

Johnson, *Cervantes and the Material World,* 2000. • Walter Kaiser, *Praisers of Folly,* 1963. • Georg Lukács, *Theory of the Novel,* 1971. • Melveena McKendrick, *Cervantes,* 1980. • Lowry Nelson, Jr., *Cervantes: A Collection of Critical Essays,* 1969. • Edwin Williamson, *The Half-Way House of Fiction: Don Quixote and Arthurian Romance,* 1984.

Niccolò Machiavelli • Albert Ascoli and Victoria Kahn, eds., *Machiavelli and the Discourse of Literature,* 1993. • Sebastian de Grazia, *Machiavelli in Hell,* 1989. • Felix Gilbert, *Machiavelli and Guicciardini: Politics and History in Sixteenth-Century Florence,* 1965. • Thomas Greene, "The End of Discourse in Machiavelli's *Prince,*" in *Literary Theory/Renaissance Texts,* eds. Patricia Parker and David Quint, 1986. • J. R. Hale, *Machiavelli and Renaissance Italy,* 1972. • John Najemy, "Machiavelli and the Medici," *Renaissance Quarterly,* 1982: 551–76. • Hannah Pitkin, *Fortune Is a Woman: Gender and Politics in the Thought of Niccolò Machiavelli,* 1984. • J. G. A. Pocock, *The Machiavellian Moment,* 1975. • Wayne Rebhorn, *Foxes and Lions: Machiavelli's Confidence Men,* 1988. • Roberto Ridolfi, *The Life of Niccolò Machiavelli,* trans. Cecil Grayson, 1963. • Quentin Skinner, *Machiavelli,* 1981.

John Milton • Arthur Barker, *Milton and the Puritan Dilemma, 1641–1660,* 1942. • Cedric C. Brown, *John Milton: A Literary Life,* 1995. • Dennis Danielson, ed., *The Cambridge Companion to Milton,* 1989. • William Empson, *Milton's God,* 1961. • Stanley Fish, *Surprised by Sin: The Reader in Paradise Lost,* 1967. • Christopher Hill, *Milton and the English Revolution,* 1977. • C. S. Lewis, *A Preface to Paradise Lost,* 1942. • Mary Nyquist and Margaret Ferguson, eds., *Re-membering Milton: Essays on the Texts and Traditions,* 1988. • William Riley Parker, *Milton: A Biography,* 2 vols., 1968. • C. A. Patrides, *Milton and the Christian Tradition,* 1966. • B. Rajan, *Paradise Lost and the Seventeenth-Century Reader,* 1962. • Stella Revard, *The War in Heaven,* 1980. • James Turner, *One Flesh: Paradisal Marriage and Sexual Relations in the Age of Milton,* 1987.• Joan Webber, *Milton and his Epic Tradition,* 1979.

Michel de Montaigne • Harold Bloom, ed., *Montaigne's "Essays,"* 1987. • Donald Frame, *Montaigne: A Biography,* 1965. • Hugo Friedrich, *Montaigne,* 1968. • Fredi Chiappelli, ed., *First Images of America: The Impact of the New World on the Old,* 2 vols., 1976. • George Hoffmann, *Montaigne's Career,* 1998. • Glyn Norton, *Montaigne and the Introspective Mind,* 1975. • David Quint, *Montaigne and the Quality of Mercy,* 1998. • R. A. Sayce, *Essays of Montaigne,* 1972. • Jean Starobinski, *Montaigne in Motion,* 1985.

Francis Petrarch • Hans Baron, *From Petrarch to Leonardo Bruni,* 1968. • Thomas Bergin, *Petrarch,* 1970. • Morris Bishop, *Petrarch and his World,* 1963. • Robert M. Durling, "The Ascent of Mount Ventoux and the Crisis of Allegory," *Italian Quarterly* 18, 1974: 7–28. • John Freccero, "The Fig Tree and the Laurel," *Diacritics* 5, 1975: 34–40. • Giuseppe Mazzotta, *The Worlds of Petrarch,* 1993. • Sara Sturm-Maddox, *Petrarch's Laurels,* 1992. • Charles Trinkaus, *The Poet as Philosopher,* 1979. • Marguerite Waller, *Petrarch's Poetics and Literary History,* 1980. • E. H. Wilkins, *Life of Petrarch,* 1961. • E. H. Wilkins, *The Making of the "Canzoniere,"* 1951.

William Shakespeare • Jean Wilson, *The Shakespeare Legacy,* 1995. • Leslie Fiedler, *The Stranger in Shakespeare,* 1972. • Charles Frey, "*The Tempest* and the New World," *Shakespeare Quarterly* 30, 1979. • Northrop Frye, *A Natural Perspective,* 1965. • Stephen Greenblatt, *Marvellous Possessions: The Wonder of the New World,* 1991. • Stephen Greenblatt, "Learning to Curse," in *First Images of America,* ed. Fredi Chiappelli, 1976. • Donna Hamilton, *Virgil and The Tempest: The Politics of Imitation,* 1990. • D. G. James, *The Dream of Prospero,* 1967. • Jeffrey Knapp, *An Empire Nowhere: England, America, and Literature from "Utopia" to "The Tempest,"* 1994. • James Schiffer, ed., *Shakespeare's Sonnets: Critical Essays,* 1999. • Murray M. Schwartz and Coppélia Kahn, eds., *Representing Shakespeare,* 1980. • Bruce Smith, *Homosexual Desire in Shakespeare's England,* 1991. • Stephen Orgel, "Prospero's Wife," in *Representing the English Renaissance,* ed. Stephen Greenblatt, 1988. • Alden T. and Virginia Vaughan, *Shakespeare's Caliban: A Cultural History,* 1991. • Helen Vendler, *The Art of Shakespeare's Sonnets,* 1997.

Mesoamerica: Before Columbus and After Cortés

General • Joan D. Barghusen, *The Aztecs,* 2000. • Robert Carmack, *The Legacy of Mesoamerica,* 1996. • Davíd Carrasco, *Quetzalcoatl and the Irony of Empire*, 1982. • Inga Clendinen, *Aztecs: An Interpretation,* 1991. • Michael D. Coe, *The Maya,* 1987. • Michael D. Coe, *The Maya Scribe and His World,* 1973. • David Damrosch. "The Pope's Blowgun," in *What Is World Literature?,* 2003. • Nancy M. Farriss, *Maya Society Under Colonial Rule: The Collective Enterprise of Survival,* 1984. • Enrique Florescano, *Memory, Myth, and Time in Mexico*, 1994. • Gary H. Gossen and Miguel León-Portilla, eds., *South and Meso-American Native Spirituality,* 1993. • Ross Hassig, *Time, History, and Belief in Aztec and Colonial Mexico,* 2001. • Alvin M. Josephy, ed., *America in 1492: The World of the Indian Peoples Before the Arrival of Columbus,* 1993. • Charles A. F. P. Maza, *Pre-Columbian Socio-Political Structure in the Valley of Mexico*, 1997. • Anthony Pagden, *European Encounters with the New World,* 1994. • Miguel León-Portilla, *The Aztec Image of Self and Society,* 1992. • Miguel León-Portilla, *The Broken Spears: The Aztec Account of the Conquest of Mexico,* 1992. • Miguel León-Portilla, ed., *Native Mesoamerican Spirituality,* 1980. • Bernardino de Sahagún, *The Florentine Codex: General History of the Things of New Spain,* Arthur J.O. Anderson and C.E. Dibble, eds., 1950–1982. • Mary Miller and Karl Taube, *The Gods and Symbols of Ancient Mexico and the Maya,* 1993.

Perspectives: The Conquest and Its Aftermath • Marvin Lunenfield, ed., *1492, Discovery, Invasion, Encounter: Sources and Interpretation,* 1991. • Stuart B. Schwartz, ed., *Victors and Vanquished: Spanish and Nahua Views of the Conquest of Mexico,* 2000. • Patricia Seed, *Ceremonies of Possession in Europe's Conquest of the New World, 1492–1640,* 1995. • Tzvetan Todorov, *The Conquest of America,* 1983. • David M. Traboulay, *Columbus and Las Casas: The Conquest and Christianization of America, 1492–1566,* 1994. • Michael Wood, *Conquistadors,* 2000.

Sor Juana Inéz de la Cruz • Electa Arenal and Stacey Schlau, eds., *Untold Sisters: Hispanic Nuns in their Own Works*, 1989. • Jean Franco, *Plotting Women: Gender and Representation in Mexico,* 1989. • James Henderson, *Ten Notable Women of Latin America,* 1978. • Juana Inéz de la Cruz, *A Woman of Genius: The Intellectual Autobiography of Sor Juana Inés de la Cruz,* 1982. • Pamela Kirk, *Sor Juana Inéz de la Cruz: Religion, Art, and Feminism,* 1998. • Irving Leonard, *Baroque Times in Old Mexico,* 1966. • Stephanie Merrim, ed., *Feminist Perspectives on Sor Juana Inéz de la Cruz,* 1999. • Stephanie Merrim, *Early Modern Women's Writing and Sor Juana Inéz de la Cruz,* 1999. • Octavio Paz, *Sor Juana, or, The Traps of Faith,* 1988. • Ruth S. El Saffar, *Rapture Encaged: The Suppression of the Feminine in Western Culture,* 1994. • George Tavard, *Juana Inés de la Cruz and the Theology of Beauty,* 1991.

Bernal Díaz del Castillo • Herbert Cerwin, *Bernal Díaz: Historian of the Conquest,* 1963. • Charles Gibson, *The Black Legend: Anti-Spanish Attitudes in the Old World and the New,* 1971. • Lewis Hanke, *All Mankind* is One, 1970. • Bernal Díaz del Castillo, *The Discovery and Conquest of Mexico,* 1956.

Songs of the Aztec Nobility • John Bierhorst, ed., *Cantares Mexicanos, Songs of the Aztecs,* 1985. • David Damrosch, "The Aesthetics of Conquest: Aztec Poetry Before and After Cortés," *Representations* 33, 1991. • T. J. Knab, ed., *Scattering of Jades: Stories, Poems, and Prayers of the Aztecs,* 1994. • Miguel León-Portilla, *Fifteen Poets of the Aztec World,* 1992. • Irene Nicholson, *Firefly in the Night: A Study of Ancient Mexican Poetry and Symbolism,* 1959.

The Seventeenth and Eighteenth Centuries

General Background • Linda Colley, *Britons: Forging the Nation, 1707–1837,* 1992. • Christine Guth, *Art of Edo Japan: The Artist and the City, 1615–1868,* 1996. • John Whitney Hall, ed. *The Cambridge History of Japan.* Vol. 4, *Early Modern Japan,* 1988. • Julie C. Hayes, *Reading the French Enlightenment: System and Subversion,* 1999. • Donald Keene, *World Within Walls: Japanese Literature of the Pre-Modern Era,*

1600–1868, 1976. • Chie Nakane and Shinzaburō Ōishi, eds. *Tokugawa Japan: The Social and Economic Antecedents of Modern Japan,* 1991. • Matsunosuke Nishiyama, *Edo Culture: Daily Life and Diversions in Urban Japan, 1600–1868,* 1997. • Felicity Nussbaum and Laura Brown, eds., *The New Eighteenth Century,* 1987. • James Sambrook, *The Eighteenth Century: The Intellectual and Cultural Context of English Literature, 1700–1789,* 1986. • Conrad Totman, *Early Modern Japan,* 1993. • Steven N. Zwicker, *The Cambridge Companion to English Literature, 1650–1740,* 1998.

Chikamatsu Mon'zaemon • Barbara Curtis Adachi, *Backstage at Bunraku: A Behind the Scenes Look at Japan's Traditional Puppet Theater,* 1985. • Barbara Curtis Adachi, *The Voices and Hands of Bunraku,* 1978. • C. U. Dunn, *The Early Japanese Puppet Drama,* 1966. • C. Andrew Gerstle, trans. *Chikamatsu: Five Late Plays,* 2001. • C. Andrew Gerstle, *Circles of Fantasy: Convention in the Plays of Chikamatsu,* 1986. • C. Andrew Gerstle, "Hero as Murderer in Chikamatsu," *Monumenta Nipponica,* vol. 51, 1996, 317–356. • C. Andrew Gerstle, "Heroic Honor: Chikamatsu and the Samurai Ideal," *Harvard Journal of Asiatic Studies,* vol. 57, 1997, 307–382. • Donald Keene, *Bunraku: The Art of the Japanese Puppet Theatre,* 1965. • Donald Keene, trans. *Four Major Plays of Chikamatsu,* 1969. • Donald Keene, trans. *Major Plays of Chikamatsu,* 1961. • Adolphe Clarence Scott, *The Puppet Theater of Japan,* 1963. • Donald H. Shively, trans. *The Love Suicides at Amijima,* 1953.

The Age of the Enlightenment • John Bender, *Imagining the Penitentiary: Fiction and the Architecture of Mind in Eighteenth-Century England,* 1987. • Linda Colley, *Britons: Forging the Nation, 1707–1837,* 1992. • Robert Darnton, *George Washington's False Teeth: An Unconventional Guide to the Eighteenth Century,* 2003. • Joan DeJean, *Ancients Against Moderns: Culture Wars and the Making of a Fin de Siècle,* 1997. • Catherine Gallagher, *Nobody's Story: The Vanishing Acts of Women Writers in the Marketplace, 1670–1820,* 1994. • Julie C. Hayes, *Reading the French Enlightenment: System and Subversion,* 1999. • David Marshall, *The Surprising Effects of Sympathy: Marivaux, Diderot, Rousseau, and Mary Shelley,* 1988. • Michael McKeon, *The Origins of the English Novel, 1600–1740,* 1987. • Nancy K. Miller, *The Heroine's Text: Readings in the French and English Novel, 1722–1782,* 1980. • Dorothea E. von Mücke, *Virtue and the Veil of Illusion: Generic Innovation and the Pedagogical Project in Eighteenth-Century Literature,* 1991. • Felicity Nussbaum and Laura Brown, eds. *The New Eighteenth Century,* 1987. • William Ray, *Story and History: Narrative Authority and Social Identity in the Eighteenth-Century French and English Novel,* 1990. • James Sambrook, *The Eighteenth Century: The Intellectual and Cultural Context of English Literature, 1700–1789,* 1986. • Londa Schiebinger, *Nature's Body: Gender in the Making of Modern Science,* 1993. • Stuart Sherman, *Telling Time: Clocks, Diaries, and English Diurnal Form, 1660–1785,* 1996. • Julia Simon, *Mass Enlightenment: Critical Studies in Rousseau and Diderot,* 1995. • Aram Vartanian, *Science and Humanism in the French Enlightenment,* 1999. • Anne C. Vila, *Enlightenment and Pathology: Sensibility in the Literature and Medicine of Eighteenth-Century France,* 1998. • Ian Watt, *The Rise of the Novel: Studies in Defoe, Richardson, and Fielding,* 1957. • Steven N. Zwicker, *The Cambridge Companion to English Literature, 1650–1740,* 1998.

Eliza Haywood • Ros Ballaster, *Seductive Forms: Women's Amatory Fiction from 1684 to 1740,* 1992. • Christine Blouch, "Eliza Haywood and the Romance of Obscurity," *Studies in English Literature,* vol. 31, 1991, 535–552. • Catherine Craft-Fairchild, *Masquerade and Gender: Disguise and Female Identity in Eighteenth-Century Fictions by Women,* 1993. • Eliza Haywood, *Selections from "The Female Spectator,"* ed. Gabrielle M. Firmager, 1993. • Eliza Haywood, *The Plays of Eliza Haywood,* ed. Valerie C. Rudolph, 1983. • Kirsten T. Saxton and Rebecca P. Bocchicchio, eds. *The Passionate Fictions of Eliza Haywood,* 2000. • Mary Anne Schofield, *Eliza Haywood,* 1985. • Eliza Haywood, *The Masquerade Novels of Eliza Haywood,* ed. Mary Anne Schofield, 1986. • Mary Ann Schofield, *Masking and Unmasking the Female Mind: Disguising Romances in Feminine Fiction, 1713–1799,* 1990. • Jane Spencer, *The Rise of the Woman Novelist: From Aphra Behn to Jane Austen,* 1986. • William B. Warner, *Licensing Entertainment: The Elevation of Novel Reading in Britain, 1684–1750,* 1957. • George Frisbie

Whicher, *The Life and Romances of Mrs. Eliza Haywood,* 1915.

Matsuo Bashō • Dorothy Britton, trans. *A Haiku Journey: Bashō's "Narrow Road to a Far Province,"* 1980. • Cid Corman and Susumu Kamaike, trans. *Back Roads to Far Towns,* 1968. • Koji Kawamoto, *The Poetics of Japanese Verse: Imagery, Structure, Meter,* 2000. • Donald Keene, "Bashō's Diaries," *Japan Quarterly,* vol. 32, 1985, 374–383. • Donald Keene, "Bashō's Journey of 1684," *Asia Major,* vol. 7, 1959, 131–144. • Donald Keene, trans. *The Narrow Road to Oku,* 1996. • Helen McCullough, trans. "The Narrow Road of the Interior," in *Classical Japanese Prose: An Anthology,* ed. Helen McCullough, 1990. • Hiroaki Sato, trans. *Bashō's "Narrow Road": Spring and Autumn Passages: Two Works,* 1996. • Haruo Shirane, *Traces of Dreams: Landscape, Cultural Memory, and the Poetry of Bashō,* 1997. • Makoto Ueda, trans. *Bashō and His Interpreters: Selected Hokku with Commentary,* 1992. • Makoto Ueda, *Matsuo Bashō: The Master Haiku Poet,* 1982. • Nobuyuki Yuasa, trans. *Bashō: The Narrow Road to the Deep North and Other Travel Sketches,* 1968.

Jean Baptiste Poquelin (Molière) • Thomas P. Finn, "Dueling Capitalism in Molière: Cornering the Corner Markets," *Papers on French Seventeenth Century Literature* 29 (2002): 23–32. • J. F. Gaines, *Social Structures in Molière's Theater,* 1984. • Lionel Gossman, *Men and Masks: A Study of Molière,* 1963. • N. Gross, *From Gesture to Idea: Esthetics and Ethics in Molière's Comedy,* 1982. • Jacques Guicharnaud, ed. *Molière: A Collection of Critical Essays,* 1964. • Martha M. Houle, "The Marriage Question, or the Querélle des hommes in Rabelais, Molière, and Boileau," *Dalhousie French Studies,* vol. 56, 2001, 46–54. • W. D. Howarth, *Molière: A Playwright and His Audience,* 1984. • Harold C. Knutson, *The Triumph of Wit,* 1988. • Molière, *The School for Wives,* trans. Ranjit Bolt, 1997. • Molière, *The Miser and Other Plays,* ed. and trans. David Coward, trans. John Wood, 2000. • Molière, *The School for Wives; and The Learned Ladies,* trans. Richard Wilbur, 1991. • L. F. Norman, *The Public Mirror: Molière and the Social Commerce of Depiction,* 1999. • Molière, *The Misanthrope, Tartuffe, and Other Plays,* trans. Maya Slater, 2001. • Martin Turnell, *The Classical Moment: Studies of Corneille, Molière, and Racine,* 1975. • H. Walker, *Molière,* 1990.

Lady Mary Wortley Montagu • Elizabeth A. Bohls, "Aesthetics and Orientalism in Lady Mary Wortley Montagu's Letters," *Studies in Eighteenth-Century Culture,* vol. 23, 1994, 179–205. • Isobel Grundy, *Lady Mary Wortley Montagu,* 1999. • Robert Halsband, *The Life of Lady Mary Wortley Montagu,* 1956. • Donna Landry, "Alexander Pope, Lady Mary Wortley Montagu, and the Literature of Social Comment," in *English Literature 1650–1740,* ed. Steven N. Zwicker, 1998. • Cynthia Lowenthal, *Lady Mary Wortley Montagu and the Eighteenth-Century Familiar Letter,* 1994. • Lady Mary Wortley Montagu, *Selected Letters of Mary Wortley Montagu,* ed. Isobel Grundy, 1997. • Lady Mary Wortley Montagu, *The Complete Letters of Lady Mary Wortley Montagu,* ed. Robert Halsband, 3 vols., 1965–1967. • Lady Mary Wortley Montagu, *The Selected Letters of Lady Mary Wortley Montagu,* ed. Robert Halsband, 1970. • Lady Mary Wortley Montagu, *Turkish Embassy Letters,* eds. Malcolm Jack and Anita Desai, 1993. • Lady Mary Wortley Montagu, *Embassy to Constantinople: The Travels of Lady Mary Wortley Montagu,* eds. Christopher Pick and Dervla Murphy, 1988. • George Paston, *Lady Mary Wortley Montagu and Her Times,* 1907.

Alexander Pope • Rueben Brower, *Alexander Pope: The Poetry of Allusion,* 1959. • Laura Brown, *Alexander Pope,* 1985. • Morris Brownell, *Alexander Pope and the Arts of Georgian England,* 1978. • Alexander Pope, *The Poems of Alexander Pope,* ed. John Butt, 1963. • Alexander Pope, *The Twickenham Edition of the Poems of Alexander Pope,* eds. John Butt et al., 11 vols., 1940–1969. • Helen Deutsch, *Resemblance and Disgrace: Alexander Pope and the Deformation of Culture,* 1996. • Margaret Anne Doody, *The Daring Muse: Augustan Poetry Reconsidered,* 1985. • H. H. Erskine-Hill, *The Social Milieu of Alexander Pope,* 1978. • David Fairer, ed. *Pope: New Contexts,* 1990. • David Fairer, *Pope's Imagination,* 1984. • David F. Foxon, *Pope and the Eighteenth-Century Book Trade,* 1991. • Bertrand A. Goldgar, *Literary Criticism of Alexander Pope,* 1965. • Dustin Griffin, *Alexander Pope: The Poet in the Poems,* 1978. • Brean Hammond, ed.

Longman Critical Readers: Pope, 1966. • J. Paul Hunter, "Pope and the Ideology of the Couplet," *Ideas,* vol. 4, 1996. • Maynard Mack, *Alexander Pope: A Life,* 1985. • Maynard Mack, *The Garden and the City: Retirement and Politics in the Later Poetry of Pope,* 1969. • David B. Morris, *Alexander Pope: The Genius of Sense,* 1984. • Marjorie Hope Nicolson and G. S. Rousseau, *"This Long Disease, My Life": Alexander Pope and the Sciences,* 1968. • Valerie Rumbold, *Women's Place in Pope's World,* 1989. • Alexander Pope, *The Correspondence of Alexander Pope,* ed. George Sherburn, 5 vols., 1956. • George Sherburn, *The Early Career of Alexander Pope,* 1934. • Patricia Meyer Spacks, *An Argument of Images; the Poetry of Alexander Pope,* 1971. • Joseph Spence, *Observations, Anecdotes, and Characters of Books and Men,* ed. James M. Osborn, 2 vols., 1966. • Geoffrey Tillotson, *On the Poetry of Pope,* 1950. • Alexander Pope, *The Rape of the Lock,* ed. Cynthia Wall, 1998. • Howard Weinbrot, *Alexander Pope and the Tradition of the Formal Verse Satire,* 1982. • Alexander Pope, *Poetry and Prose of Alexander Pope,* ed. Aubrey Williams, 1969.

Jonathan Swift • Frank Boyle, *Swift as Nemesis: Modernity and Its Satirist,* 2000. • J. A. Downie, *Jonathan Swift: Political Writer,* 1985. • Irvin Ehrenpreis, *Swift: The Man, His Works, and the Age,* 3 vols., 1962–1983. • Robert C. Elliott, *The Power of Satire: Magic, Ritual, Art,* 1960. • Oliver W. Ferguson, *Jonathan Swift and Ireland,* 1962. • H. J. Real Fischer and J. Wooley, eds. *Swift and His Contexts,* 1989. • John Irwin Fischer and Donald C. Mell Jr., eds. *Contemporary Studies of Swift's Poetry,* 1980. • Victoria Glendinning, *Jonathan Swift: A Portrait,* 1999. • Carol Houlihan Flynn, *The Body in Swift and Defoe,* 1990. • Christopher Fox, ed. *Walking Naboth's Vineyard: New Studies of Swift,* 1995. • Nora Crow Jaffe, *The Poet Swift,* 1977. • David Nokes, *Jonathan Swift, A Hypocrite Reversed: A Critical Biography,* 1985. • Ellen Pollak, *The Poetics of Sexual Myth: Gender and Ideology in the Verse of Swift and Pope,* 1985. • Martin Price, *Swift's Rhetorical Art: A Study in Structure and Meaning,* 1953. • C. J. Rawson, ed. *The Character of Swift's Satire,* 1983. • Richard H. Rodino, *Swift Studies, 1965–1980: An Annotated Bibliography,* 1984. • Edward W. Rosenheim, *Swift and the Satirist's Art,* 1963. • Edward W. Said, "Swift as Intellectual" and "Swift's Tory Anarchy," *The World, the Text, and the Critic,* 1983. • Brian Vickers, ed. *The World of Jonathan Swift: Essays for the Tercentenary,* 1968. • David M. Vieth, *Swift's Poetry 1900–1980: An Annotated Bibliography of Studies,* 1982. • Kathleen Williams, ed. *Swift: The Critical Heritage,* 1970.

François Marie Arouet (Voltaire) • T. Besterman, *Voltaire,* 1969. • William Bottiglia, *Voltaire's Candide: Analysis of a Classic,* 1964. • William Bottiglia, ed. *Voltaire: A Collection of Critical Essays,* 1968. • Maxine G. Cutler, ed. *Voltaire, the Enlightenment, and the Comic Mode: Essays in Honor of Jean Sareil,* 1990. • Diane Fourny, "Literature of Violence or Literature on Violence? The French Enlightenment on Trial," *SubStance: A Review of Theory and Literary Criticism,* vol. 27, 1998, 43–60. • Voltaire, *Candide,* ed. D. Gordon, 1999. • M. Hayden, *Voltaire: A Biography,* 1981. • F. M. Keener, *The Chain of Becoming,* 1983. • Susan Klute, "The Admirable Cunegonde," *Eighteenth-Century Women: Studies in Their Lives, Work, and Culture,* vol. 2, 2002, 95–107. • Bettina L. Knapp, *Voltaire Revisited,* 2000. • Haydn Mason, *Candide: Optimism Demolished,* 1992. • Voltaire, *Candide and Other Stories,* ed. and trans. Roger Pearson, 1998. • P. E. Richter and Ilona Ricardo, *Voltaire,* 1980. • R. S. Ridgway, *Voltaire and Sensibility,* 1973. • I. O. Wade, *Voltaire and "Candide,"* 1959. • Voltaire, *The Complete Tales of Voltaire,* trans. William Walton, 1990. • D. Williams, *Candide,* 1997. • Voltaire, *Candide and Related Texts,* ed. and trans. David Wooton, 2000.

Maria de Zayas y Sotomayor • Marina S. Brownlee, *The Cultural Labyrinth of María de Zayas,* 2000. • Margaret Rich Greer, *María de Zayas Tells Baroque Tales of Love and the Cruelty of Men,* 2000. • Irma V. Vasileski, *María de Zayas y Sotomayor, su Época y su Obra,* 1973. • Lisa Vollendorf, *Reclaiming the Body: María de Zayas's Early Modern Feminism,* 2001. • Amy R. Williamsen and Judith A. Whitenack, eds. *María de Zayas: The Dynamics of Discourse,* 1995. • Maria de Zayas y Sotomayor, *The Enchantments of Love: Amorous and Exemplary Novels,* trans. H. Patsy Boyer, 1990. • Maria de Zayas y Sotomayor, *A Shameful Revenge, and Other Stories,* trans. John Sturrock, 1963.

The Nineteenth Century

General Background • Meyer H. Abrams, *The Mirror and the Lamp: Romantic Theory and the Critical Tradition,* 1953. • Meyer H. Abrams, *Natural Supernaturalism: Tradition and Revolution in Romantic Literature,* 1971. • Nancy Armstrong, *Desire and Domestic Fiction: A Political History of the Novel,* 1987. • Marshall Brown, *The Shape of German Romanticism,* 1979. • J. W. Burrow, *Evolution and Social Theory,* 1970. • Marilyn Butler, *Romantics, Rebels, and Reactionaries: English Literature and Its Background, 1760–1830,* 1981. • Linda Colley, *Britons: Forging the Nation, 1707–1837,* 1992. • Albert Cook, *Thresholds: Studies in the Romantic Experience,* 1985. • Stuart Curran, *Poetic Form and British Romanticism,* 1986. • Sandra M. Gilbert and Susan Gubar, *The Madwoman in the Attic: The Woman Writer and the Nineteenth-Century Imagination,* 1979. • Vesna Goldsworthy, *Inventing Ruritania: The Imperialism of the Imagination* 1998. • Catherine Hall, *Civilising Subjects: Metropole and Colony in the English Imagination 1830–1867,* 2002. • E. J. Hobsbawm, *The Age of Capital, 1848–1875,* 1975. • E. J. Hobsbawm, *The Age of Empire, 1875–1914,* 1987. • Everett Knight, *A Theory of the Classical Novel,* 1970. • Georges Lefebvre, *The Coming of the French Revolution 1789,* trans. R. R. Palmer, 1947. • Jerome J. McGann, *The Romantic Ideology: A Critical Investigation,* 1983. • Ellen Moers, *Literary Women,* 1976. • Franco Moretti, *Atlas of the European Novel, 1800–1900,* 1998. • Karl Polányi, *The Great Transformation: The Political and Economic Origins of Our Time,* 1944. • Charles Rosen, *The Romantic Generation,* 1995. • Kristin Ross, *The Emergence of Social Space: Rimbaud and the Paris Commune,* 1988. • Wolfgang Schivelbusch, *Disenchanted Night: The Industrialization of Light in the Nineteenth Century,* 1983. • Wolfgang Schivelbusch, *The Railway Journey: The Industrialization of Time and Space in the Nineteenth Century,* 1977. • Malini Schueller, *U.S. Orientalisms: Race, Nation, and Gender in Literature 1790–1890,* 1998. • Jean Starobinski, *1789: The Emblems of Reason,* trans. Barbara Bray, 1982. • Alan Trachtenberg, *The Incorporation of America: Culture and Society in the Gilded Age,* 1982. • Gauri Viswanathan, *Masks of Conquest: Literary Study and British Rule in India,* 1989. • Susan J. Wolfson, *Formal Charges: The Shaping of Poetry in British Romanticism,* 1997.

Perspectives: Romantic Nature • John Barrell, *The Idea of Landscape and the Sense of Place, 1730–1840: An Approach to the Poetry of John Clare,* 1972. • Jonathan Bate, *Romantic Ecology: Wordsworth and the Environmental Tradition,* 1991. • Lawrence Buell, *The Environmental Imagination: Thoreau, Nature Writing, and the Formation of American Culture,* 1995. • Stanley Cavell, *The Senses of Walden,* 1981. • F. O. Matthiessen, *American Renaissance: Art and Expression in the Age of Emerson and Whitman,* 1941. • James McIntosh, *Thoreau as Romantic Naturalist: His Shifting Stance Toward Nature,* 1974. • Perry Miller, *Errand into the Wilderness,* 1956. • Raimonda Modiano, *Coleridge and the Concept of Nature,* 1985. • Jean Starobinski, *Jean-Jacques Rousseau: Transparency and Obstruction,* trans. Arthur Goldhammer, 1988. • Raymond Williams, *The Country and the City,* 1973.

Charles Baudelaire • Robert Baldick, trans., *Pages from the Goncourt Journals,* 1962. • Charles Baudelaire: *Les fleurs du mal: The Complete Text of "The Flowers of Evil,"* Richard Howard, trans., 1982. • Charles Baudelaire: *Selected Writings on Art and Literature,* trans. P. E. Charvet, 1992. • Walter Benjamin, *Charles Baudelaire: A Lyric Poet in the Era of High Capitalism,* trans. Harry Zohn, 1973. • Leo Bersani, *Baudelaire and Freud,* 1977. • Keith Bosley, trans., *Mallarmé: The Poems: A Bilingual Edition.* New York: Penguin, 1977. • David Carrier, *High Art: Charles Baudelaire and the Origins of Modernist Painting,* 1996. • A. E. Carter, *Charles Baudelaire,* 1977. • Carol Clark and Robert Sykes, eds. *Baudelaire in English,* 1997. • T. J. Clark, *The Absolute Bourgeois: Artists and Politics in France, 1848–1851,* 1999. • T. J. Clark, *The Painting of Modern Life: Paris in the Art of Manet and His Followers,* 1999. • Arthur Rimbaud, *Complete Works, Selected Letters,* trans., Wallace Fowlie, 1966. • J. A. Hiddleston, *Baudelaire and the Art of Memory,* 1999. • J. A. Hiddleston, *Baudelaire and Le spleen de Paris,* 1987. • Louise Boe Hyslop, *Charles Baudelaire Revisited,* 1992. • Edward K. Kaplan, *Baudelaire's Prose Poems: The Esthetic, the Ethical, and the Religious in "The Parisian Prowler,"* 1990. • Edward K.

Kaplan, trans., *The Parisian Prowler: Le spleen de Paris: petits poèmes en prose,* 1997. • F. W. Leakey, *Baudelaire and Nature,* 1969. • F. W. Leakey, *Baudelaire, Les fleurs du mal,* 1992. • Rosemary Lloyd, *Baudelaire's World,* 2002. • Elissa Marder, *Dead Time: Temporal Disorders in the Wake of Modernity (Baudelaire and Flaubert),* 2001. • Derek Joseph Mossop, *Baudelaire's Tragic Hero: A Study of the Architecture of "Les fleurs du mal,"* 1961. • Henri Peyre, *Baudelaire: A Collection of Critical Essays,* 1962. • Claude Pichois, *Baudelaire,* trans. Graham Robb, 1989. • *Approaches to Teaching Baudelaire's "Flowers of Evil,"* 2000. *Correspondence/Charles Baudelaire,* 2 vols. 1973. • Claude Pichois, ed. Charles Baudelaire *Oeuvres complètes,* 2 vols., 1993. • Laurence M. Porter, *The Crisis of French Symbolism,* 1990. • Georges Poulet, *Exploding Poetry: Baudelaire/Rimbaud,* Trans. Francoise Meltzer, 1984. • Sonya Stephens, *Baudelaire's Prose Poems: The Practice and Politics of Irony,* 1999. • William J. Thompson, *Understanding "Les fleurs du mal": Critical Readings,* 1997. • Nathaniel Wing, *The Limits of Narrative: Essays on Baudelaire, Flaubert, Rimbaud, and Mallarmé,* 1986.

Anton Chekhov • Harold Bloom, ed., *Anton Chekhov: Modern Critical Views,* 1999. • John Coope, *Doctor Chekhov: A Study in Literature and Medicine,* 1997. • Vera Gottlieb and Paul Allain, eds., *The Cambridge Companion to Chekhov,* 2000. • Ronald Hingley, *Chekhov: A Biographical and Critical Study,* 1966. • V.B. Kataev, *If Only We Could Know: An Interpretation of Anton Chekhov,* 2002. • Virginia Llewellyn Smith, *Anton Chekhov and "The Lady with the Dog,"* 1973. • Janet Malcolm, *Reading Chekhov: A Critical Journey,* 2001. • Donald Rayfield, *Anton Chekhov: A Life,* 1998. • Donald Rayfield, *Understanding Chekhov,* 1999.

Fyodor Dostoevsky • Mikhail Bakhtin, *Problems of Dostoevky's Poetics* • Donald Fanger, *Dostoevsky and Romantic Realism,* 1965. • Joseph Frank, *Dostoevsky,* 5 vols., 1983–2002. • Joseph Frank, ed., *Selected Letters of Fyodor Dostoevsky,* 1987. • René Girard, *Resurrection from the Underground: Fyodor Dostoevsky,* 1997. • Frederick Griffiths, *Novel Epics: Gogol, Dostoevsky, and National Narrative,* 1990. • Michael Holquist, *Dostoevsky and the Novel,* 1977. • Michael R. Katz, *Notes from Underground: An Authoritative Translation, Backgrounds, and Sources,* 2001. • Gary Saul Morson, *Narrative Freedom: The Shadows of Time,* 1994. • Victor Terras, *Reading Dostoevsky,* 1998. • Andrew Wachtel, *An Obsession with History,* 1994.

Gustave Flaubert • Julian Barnes, *Flaubert's Parrot,* 1990. • Jonathan Culler, *Flaubert: The Uses of Uncertainty,* 1974. • Peter Eyre, *Chere Maître: The Correspondence of Gustave Flaubert and George Sand,* 2002. • Harry Levin, *The Gates of Horn: A Study of Five French Realists,* 1963. • Herbert Lottman, *Flaubert: A Biography,* 1989. • Franco Moretti, *The Way of the World.* • Laurence Porter, *A Gustave Flaubert Encyclopedia,* 2001. • Francis Steegmuller, *Flaubert in Egypt: A Sensibility on Tour,* 1972. • Richard Terdiman, *Discourse/Counter-Discourse: The Theory and Practice of Symbolic Resistance in Nineteenth-Century France,* 1985. • Geoffrey Wall, *Flaubert: A Life,* 2001.

Ghalib • Aga Shahid Ali, *Call Me Ishmael Tonight: A Book of Ghazals,* 2003. • R. K. Kuldip, *Mirza Ghalib; A Critical Appreciation of Ghalib's Thought and Verse,* 1967. • Daud Rahbar, ed., *Urdu Letters of Mirza Asadu'llah Khan Ghalib,* 1987. • Ralph Russell, Khurshidul Islam, eds., *Ghalib (1787–1869): Life and Letters,* 1994. • Ralph Russell, ed., *Ghalib: The Poet and His Age,* 1972. • Ralph Russell, ed., *The Famous Ghalib,* 2000. • Christopher Shackle, "Classics and the Comparison of Adjacent Literatures: Some Pakistani Perspectives," *Comparative Criticism: An Annual Journal* 21–38 vol. 22, 2000. • Pavan K. Varma, *Ghalib, the Man, the Times,* 1989.

Charlotte Perkins Gilman • Catherine Golden, *The Captive Imagination: A Casebook on "The Yellow Wallpaper,"* 1992. • Joanne Karpinski, ed., *Critical Essays on Charlotte Perkins Gilman,* 1992. • Catherine Golden and Joanna Zangrando, eds., *The Mixed Legacy of Charlotte Perkins Gilman,* 2000. • Jill Rudd and Val Gough, *A Very Different Story: Studies on the Fiction of Charlotte Perkins Gilman,* 1998. • Charlotte Perkins Gilman, *The Living of Charlotte Perkins Gilman: An Autobiography,* 1990. • Ann Lane, *To Herland and Beyond: The Life and Work of Charlotte Perkins Gilman,* 1990.

Johann Wolfgang Goethe • Stuart Atkins, *Goethe's Faust: A Literary Analysis,* 1958.

• Marshall Berman, *All That Is Solid Melts into Air: The Experience of Modernity,* 1982. • Nicholas Boyle, *Goethe: The Poet and the Age,* 2 vols., 1991. • Jane K. Brown, *Faust: Theater of the World,* 1992. • Jane K. Brown, *Goethe's Faust: The German Tragedy,* 1986. • Richard Friedenthal, *Goethe: His Life and Times,* 3 vols., 1963. • Ilse Graham, *Goethe: A Portrait of the Artist,* 1977. • Harry G. Haile, *Invitation to Goethe's "Faust,"* 1978. • *Faust,* Cyrus Hamlin, ed., 2001. • Victor Lange, Eric A. Blackall, and Cyrus Hamlin, eds. *Goethe's Collected Works,* 12 vols., 1983–1989. • Franco Moretti, *Modern Epic: The World-System from Goethe to García Marquez,* trans. Quintin Hoare, 1996. • Lesley Sharpe, ed., *The Cambridge Companion to Goethe,* 2002. • Elizabeth M. Wilkinson and Leonard A. Willoughby, *Goethe: Poet and Thinker,* 1962.

Henrik Ibsen • Robert Ferguson, *Ibsen: A New Biography,* 1996. • Michael Goldman, *Ibsen: The Dramaturgy of Fear,* 1999. • C. D. Innes, *A Sourcebook on Naturalist Theater,* 2000. • Charles Lyons, *Critical Essays on Henrik Ibsen,* 1987. • Frederick Marker, *Ibsen's Lively Art,* 1989. • James McFarlane, *The Cambridge Companion to Ibsen,* 1994. • Yvonne Shafer, *Approaches to Teaching Ibsen's "A Doll's House,"* 1985. • George Bernard Shaw, *The Quintessence of Ibsenism,* 1994. • Joan Templeton "The Doll House Backlash: Criticism, Feminism, and Ibsen," *PMLA,* vol. 104 (1989), pp. 28–40. • Joan Templeton, *Ibsen's Women,* 1997.

Alexander Pushkin • John Bayley, *Pushkin: A Comparative Commentary,* 1971. • J. Douglas Clayton, *Ice and Flame: Pushkin's "Eugene Onegin,"* 1985. • D. S. Mirsky, *Pushkin,* 1926. • Alexander Pushkin, *Eugene Onegin,* trans. Vladimir Nabokov, 4 vols., 1964. • Gary Rosenshield, *Pushkin and the Genres of Madness: The Masterpieces of 1833,* 2003.

Rabindranath Tagore • Ayuiba Abu Sayida, *Modernism and Tagore,* 1995. • Carol A. Breckenridge and Peter van der Veer, eds., *Orientalism and the Postcolonial Predicament: Perspectives on South Asia,* 1993. • K. Chandrasekharan, *Tagore: A Master Spirit,* 1961. • Bhabatosh Chatterjee, *Rabindranath Tagore and Modern Sensibility,* 1996. • Rimi B. Chatterjee, "Canon Without Consensus: Rabindranath Tagore and *The Oxford Book of Bengali Verse,*" *Book History,* vol. 4, 2001. • Shyamal Chattopadhyaya, *Art and the Abyss: Six Essays in Interpretation of Tagore,* 1977. • Krishna Dutta, *Rabindranath Tagore: The Myriad-Minded Man,* 1995. • Krishna Dutta and Andrew Robinson, ed., *Purabi: A Miscellany Memory of Rabindranath Tagore 1941–1991,* 1991. • Rabindranath Tagore: *Selected Letters of Rabindranath Tagore,* Krishna Dutta and Andrew Robinson, eds., 1997. • Rabindranath Tagore: *Rabindranath Tagore: An Anthology,* Krishna Dutta and Andrew Robinson, eds., 1997. • Mahatma Gandhi, *The Mahatma and the Poet: Letters and Debates Between Gandhi and Tagore, 1915–1941,* 1997. • Krishna Kripalani, *Tagore: A Life,* 1971. • Sudhirkumara Nandi, *Art and Aesthetics of Rabindranath Tagore,* 1999. • Ashis Nandy, *The Illegitimacy of Nationalism: Rabindranath Tagore and the Politics of Self,* 1994. • Rabindranath Tagore, *Selected Writings on Literature and Language,* 2001.

Leo Tolst.oy • John Bayley, *Leo Tolstoy,* 1997. • Italo Calvino, *Why Read the Classics?* 1999. • Henry Gifford, *Tolstoy,* 1982. • Georg Lukács, *Studies in European Realism,* 1964. • Donna Orwin, ed., *The Cambridge Companion to Tolstoy,* 2002. • William Rowe, *Leo Tolstoy,* 1986. • George Steiner, *Tolstoy or Dostoevsky?* 1996 • Raymond Williams, *Modern Tragedy,* 2001. • A. N. Wilson, *Tolstoy,* 1988.

William Wordsworth • James Averill, *Wordsworth and the Poetry of Human Suffering,* 1979. • Alan Bewell, *Wordsworth and the Enlightenment,* 1989. • David Bromwich, *Disowned by Memory,* 1998. • Marshall Brown, *Preromanticism,* 1991. • James Chandler, *Wordsworth's Second Nature: A Study of the Poetry and Politics,* 1984. • Steven Gill, *Wordsworth: A Life,* 1989. • Geoffrey Hartman, *The Unremarkable Wordsworth,* 1987. • Geoffrey Hartman, *Wordsworth's Poetry: 1787–1814,* 1971. • Mary Jacobus, *Romanticism, Writing, and Sexual Difference: Essays on The Prelude,* 1989. • Kenneth Johnston, *Wordsworth and "The Recluse,"* 1984. • Marjorie Levinson, *Wordsworth's Great Period Poems,* 1986. • Herbert Lindenberger, *On Wordsworth's "Prelude,"* 1963. • Alan Liu, *Wordsworth: The Sense of History,* 1989. • Gene W. Ruoff, *Wordsworth and Coleridge,* 1989. • David Simpson, *Wordsworth and the Figurings of the Real,* 1982. • David Simpson, *Wordsworth's Historical Imagination: The Poetry of Displacement,* 1987.

The Twentieth Century

General Background • Benedict Anderson, *Imagined Communities: Reflections on the Origin and Spread of Nationalism,* 1991. • Michael Bell, *Myth and the Making of Modernity: The Problem of Grounding in Early Twentieth-Century Literature,* 1998. • Hans Bertens, *The Idea of the Postmodern: A History,* 1995. • James Clifford, *The Predicament of Culture: Twentieth-Century Ethnography, Literature, and Art,* 1988. • Fredric Jameson, *Postmodernism, or, The Cultural Logic of Late Capitalism,* 1991. • Brian McHale, *Postmodernist Fiction,* 1993. • Michael North, *The Dialect of Modernism: Race, Language, and Twentieth-Century Literature,* 1994. • Kenneth Richardson, *Twentieth Century Writing: A Reader's Guide to Contemporary Literature,* 1971. • Steven Serafin, *Encyclopedia of World Literature in the 20th Century,* 1999. • Randall Stevenson, *Modernist Fiction: An Introduction,* 1992. • Philip Malcolm Waller Thody, *Twentieth-Century Literature: Critical Issues and Themes,* 1996. • Tzvetan Todorov, *Literature and Its Theorists: A Personal View of Twentieth-Century Criticism,* 1987.

Perspectives: Postcolonial Conditions • Fawzia Afzal-Khan, *Cultural Imperialism and the Indo-English Novel: Genre and Ideology in R. K. Narayan, Anita Desai, Kamala Markandaya, and Salman Rushdie,* 1993. • Munir Akash, ed., • *Mahmoud Darwish: The Adam of Two Edens,* 2002. • Bill Ashcroft, Gareth Griffiths, and Helen Tiffin, eds., *The Post-Colonial Studies Reader,* 1995. • Bill Ashcroft, ed., *The Empire Writes Back: Theory and Practice in Post-Colonial Literatures,* 1989. • Mita Banerjee, *Chutneyfication of History: Salman Rushdie, Michael Ondaatje, Bharati Mukherjee and the Postcolonial Debate,* 2002. • Mahmoud Darwish: *Unfortunately, It Was Paradise: Selected Poems,* ed., Munir Akash, 2003. • Frantz Fanon, *Black Skin, White Masks,* 1991. • Frantz Fanon, *The Wretched of the Earth,* 1991. • Nadine Gordimer, *The Essential Gesture: Writing, Politics, and Places,* 1989. • Gareth Griffiths, *African Literatures in English: East and West,* 2000. • Dominic Head, *Nadine Gordimer,* 1994. • Michael C. Hillmann, *Forugh Farrokhzad: A Quarter-Century Later,* 1988. • Michael C. Hillmann, *A Lonely Woman: Forugh Farrokhzad and Her Poetry,* 1987. • Nico Israel, *Outlandish: Writing Between Exile and Diaspora,* 2000. • Bruce Alvin King, ed., *New National and Post-Colonial Literatures: An Introduction,* 1996. • Aneete Mansson, *Passage to a New Wor(l)d: Exile and Restoration in Mahmoud Darwish's Writings,* 2003. • Anne McClintock, Aamir Mufti, Ella Shohat, and Social Text Collective, eds., *Dangerous Liaisons: Gender, Nations, and Postcolonial Perspectives,* 1997. • Albert Memmi, *The Colonizer and the Colonized,* 1991. • Padmini Mongia, *Contemporary Postcolonial Theory: A Reader,* 1996. • Ngugi wa Thiong'o, *Decolonising the Mind: The Politics of Language in African Literature,* 1986. • Lulu Norman, trans., "Mahmoud Darwish on Translating Poetry: The Place of the Universal," *Banipal: Magazine of Modern Arab Literature,* vol. 8, 2000, 25–27. • Edward Said, *Orientalism,* 1979. • Edward Said, *Culture and Imperialism,* 1998. • Barbara Temple-Thurston, *Nadine Gordimer Revisited,* 1999.

Chinua Achebe • Benedict-Chiaka Njoki, *The Four Novels of Chinua Achebe: A Critical Study,* 1984. • Ezenwa-Ohaeto, *Chinua Achebe: A Biography,* 1997. • Simon Gikandi, *Reading Chinua Achebe: Language and Ideology in Fiction,* 1991. • Ode Ogede, *Achebe and the Politics of Representation: Form Against Itself, From Colonial Conquest and Occupation to Post-independence Disillusionment,* 2001. • Umelo-Pjinmah, *Chinua Achebe: New Perspectives,* 1991.

Samuel Beckett • Arthur N. Athanason, *Endgame: The Ashbin Play,* 1993. • Deirdre Bair, *Samuel Beckett: A Biography,* 1978. • Harold Bloom, ed., *Samuel Beckett's "Endgame,"* 1988. • Anthony Cronin, *Samuel Beckett: The Last Modernist,* 1996. • Bell Gale Chevigny, ed., *Twentieth-Century Interpretations of "Endgame": A Collection of Critical Essays,* 1969. • Martin Esslin, *The Theatre of the Absurd,* 2001. • Sean Golden, "Familiars in a Ruinstrewn Land: *Endgame* as Political Allegory," *Contemporary Literature,* vol. 22, 1981, 425–455. • James Knowlson, *Damned to Fame: The Life of Samuel Beckett,* 1996. • Patrick A. McCarthy, ed., *Critical Essays on Samuel Beckett,* 1986. • John Pilling, ed., *The Cambridge Companion to Beckett,* 1994. • Richard Keller Simon, "Dialectical Laughter: A Study of *Endgame,*" *Modern Drama,* vol. 25, 1982, 505–513.

Jorge Luis Borges • Lisa Block de Behar, *Borges, the Passion of an Endless Quotation,* 2003. • Gene H. Bell-Villada, *Borges and His Fiction: A Guide to His Mind and Art,* 1999. • Norman Thomas Di Giovanni, *Lesson of the Master: Borges and His Work,* 2003. • Djelal Kadir, *Questing Fictions: Latin America's Family Romance,* 1986. • Martín Lafforgue,

AntiBorges, 1999. • Selden Rodman and Jorge Luis Borges, *Tongues of Fallen Angels: Conversations with Jorge Luis Borges (and Others),* 1974. • Florence L. Yudin, *Nightglow: Borges' Poetics of Blindness,* 1997.

Aimé Césaire • A. James Arnold, *Modernism and Négritude: The Poetry and Poetics of Aimé Césaire,* 1981. • Maryse Condé, *Cahier d'un retour au pays natal: Césaire: analyse critique,* 1978. • Gregson Davis, *Aimé Césaire,* 1997. • Lilyan Kesteloot, *Aimé Césaire: L'homme et l'oeuvre.* 1993. • Janis L. Pallister, *Aimé Césaire,* 1991. • Michael Richardson, ed., *Refusal of the Shadow: Surrealism and the Caribbean,* trans. Krzysztof Fijalkowski and Michael Richardson, 1996. • Ronnie Leah Scharfman, *Engagement and the Language of the Subject in the Poetry of Aimé Césaire,* 1987.

Joseph Conrad • John Batchelor, *The Life of Joseph Conrad: A Critical Biography,* 1993. • Ted Billy ed., *Critical Essays on Joseph Conrad,* 1987. • Harold Bloom, ed., *Joseph Conrad's "Heart of Darkness,"* 1987. • Keith Carabine, ed., *Joseph Conrad: Critical Assessments,* 4 vols., 1992. • Ford Madox Ford, *Joseph Conrad: A Personal Remembrance,* 1989. • Christopher L. GoGwilt, *The Invention of the West: Joseph Conrad and the Double-Mapping of Europe and Empire,* 1995. • Nico Israel, *Outlandish: Writing Between Exile and Diaspora,* 2000. • Fredric Jameson, *The Political Unconscious: Narrative as a Socially Symbolic Act,* 1981. • Fredric R. Karl and Laurence Davies, eds., *The Collected Letters of Joseph Conrad,* 1983. • Owen Knowles and Gene Moore, eds., *The Oxford Reader's Companion to Conrad,* 2000. • Martin Ray, ed., *Joseph Conrad: Interviews and Recollections,* 1990. • Edward W. Said, *The World, the Text, and the Critic,* 1966. • Norman Sherry, ed., *Conrad: The Critical Heritage,* 1973. • Ian Watt, *Joseph Conrad: A Critical Biography,* 1979. • Mark A. Wollaeger, *Joseph Conrad and the Fictions of Skepticism,* 1990.

T. S. Eliot • Peter Ackroyd, *T. S. Eliot: A Life,* 1984. • Harold Bloom, ed., *T. S. Eliot's "The Waste Land,"* 1986. • Jewel Spears Brooker and Joseph Bentley, *Reading "The Wasteland": Modernism and the Limits of Interpretation,* 1990. • Valerie Eliot, ed., *"The Waste Land": Fascimile and Transcript of the Original Drafts Including the Annotations of Ezra Pound,* 1971. • Maud Ellman, *The Poetics of Impersonality: T. S. Eliot and Ezra Pound,* 1987. • Nancy K. Gish, *"The Waste Land": A Poem of Memory and Desire,* 1988. • Louis Menand, *Discovering Modernism: T. S. Eliot and His Context,* 1986. • Anthony David Moody, ed., *The Cambridge Companion to T. S. Eliot,* 1994. • Jeffrey M. Perl, *Skepticism and Modern Enmity: Before and After Eliot,* 1989. • John Paul Riquelme, *Harmony of Dissonances: T. S. Eliot, Romanticism and Imagination,* 1990. • Stanley Sultan, *Eliot, Joyce, and Company,* 1987.

James Joyce • Derek Attridge, ed., *The Cambridge Companion to James Joyce,* 1990. • Vincent Cheng, *Joyce, Race and Empire,* 1995. • Kevin J. H. Dettmar, *The Illicit Joyce of Postmodernism: Reading Against the Grain,* 1996. • Richard Ellman, *James Joyce,* 1982. • Herbert S. Gorman, *James Joyce,* 1948. • Clive Hart and David Hayman, eds., *James Joyce's "Ulysses": Critical Essays,* 1974. • Hugh Kenner, *Joyce's Voices,* 1978. • R. B. Kershner, *Joyce, Bakhtin, and Popular Literature: Chronicles of Disorder,* 1989. • Patrick McGee, *Joyce Beyond Marx,* 2001. • Dominic Manganiello, *Joyce's Politics,* 1980. • E. H. Mikhail, *James Joyce: Interviews and Recollections,* 1990. • Margot Norris, *Joyce's Web: The Social Unraveling of Modernism,* 1992. • Marty T. Reynolds, ed., *James Joyce: A Collection of Critical Essays,* 1993. • Fritz Senn, *Joyce's Dislocutions,* 1984. • Joseph Valente, ed., *Quare Joyce,* 1998.

Franz Kafka • Theodor W. Adorno, "Notes on Kafka," in *Prisms,* trans. Samuel and Shierry Weber, 1967. • Harold Bloom, ed., *Franz Kafka's "The Metamorphosis",* 1988. • Max Brod, *Franz Kafka: A Biography,* 1960. • Stanley Corngold, "Kafka's *The Metamorphosis*: Metamorphosis of the Metaphor," in *Franz Kafka: The Metamorphosis: Translation, Backgrounds and Contexts, Criticism,* trans. and ed. Stanley Corngold, 1996. • Stanley Corngold, *The Commentators' Despair: The Interpretation of Kafka's "Metamorphosis,"* 1971. • Gilles Deleuze and Félix Guattari, *Kafka: Toward a Minor Literature,* trans. Dana Polan, 1986. • Vladimir Nabokov, "Franz Kafka (1883–1924): 'The Metamorphosis (1915),' " in *Lectures on Literature,* ed. Fredson Bowers, 1980. • Johannes Pfeiffer, "The Metamorphosis," trans. Ronald Gray, in *Kafka: A Collection of Critical Essays,* ed. Ronald Gray, 1962. • Heinz Politzer, *Franz Kafka: Parable and Paradox,* 1962. • Allen Thiher, *Franz Kafka: A Study of the Short Fiction,* 1990. • Klaus Wagenbach, *Franz Kafka: Pictures of a Life,* 1984.

Primo Levi • Carole Angier, *The Double Bond: The Life of Primo Levi,* 2002. • Gillian Banner, *Holocaust Literature: Schulz, Levi, Spiegelman and the Memory of the Offence,* 1999. • Robert S. C. Gordon, *Primo Levi's Ordinary Virtues: From Testimony to Ethics,* 2002.

• Frederic D. Homer, *Primo Levi and the Politics of Survival,* 2001. • Paolo Momigliano Levi, *Primo Levi: testimone e scrittore di storia,* 1999.

Lu Xun • Lee Ou-Fan Lee, ed., *Lu Xun and His Legacy,* 1985. • Kang Liu and Xiaobing Tang, eds., *Politics, Ideology, and Literary Discourse in Modern China: Theoretical Interventions and Cultural Critique,* 1993. • Wolfgang Kubin, ed., *Symbols of Anguish: In Search of Melancholy in China,* 2001. • Hua Meng and Sukehiro Hirakawa, eds., *Images of Westerners in Chinese and Japanese Literature,* 2000. • Barbara Stoler Miller, ed., *Masterworks of Asian Literature in Comparative Perspective: A Guide for Teaching,* 1994.

Salman Rushdie • M. Keith Booker, ed., *Critical Essays on Salman Rushdie,* 1999. • Timothy Brennan, *Salman Rushdie and the Third World: Myths of the Nation,* 1989. • Roger Y. Clark, *Stranger Gods: Salman Rushdie's Other Worlds,* 2001. • Catherine Cundy, *Salman Rushdie,* 1996. • Damian Grant, *Salman Rushdie,* 1999. • James Harrison, *Salman Rushdie,* 1992. • Sabrina Hassumani, *Salman Rushdie: A Postmodern Reading of His Major Works,* 2002. • Jaina C. Sanga, *Salman Rushdie's Postcolonial Metaphors: Migration, Translation, Hybridity, Blasphemy, and Globalization,* 2001.

Derek Walcott • Robert D. Hamner, ed., *Critical Perspectives on Derek Walcott,* 1993. • Bruce King, *Derek Walcott: A Caribbean Life,* 2000. • José Luis Martínez-Dueñas Espejo and José María Pérez Fernández, eds., *Approaches to the Poetics of Derek Walcott,* 2001. • Michael Parker and Roger Starkey, eds., *Postcolonial Literatures: Achebe, Ngugi, Desai, Walcott,* 1995. • Rei Terada, *Derek Walcott's Poetry: American Mimicry,* 1992.

Virginia Woolf • Quentin Bell, *Virginia Woolf: A Biography,* 1972. • Alison Booth, *Greatness Engendered: George Eliot and Virginia Woolf,* 1992. • Thomas C. Carmagno, *The Flight of the Mind: Virginia Woolf's Art and Manic-Depressive Illness,* 1992. • Pamela L. Caughie, *Virginia Woolf and the Postmodern Tradition: Literature in Quest and Question of Itself,* 1991. • Margaret Homans, ed., *Virginia Woolf: A Collection of Critical Essays (Twentieth Century Views),* 1992. • Mark Hussey, *Virginia Woolf, A to Z: A Comprehensive Reference for Students, Teachers, and Common Readers to Her Work, and Critical Reception,* 1996. • Douglas Mao, *Solid Objects: Modernism and the Test of Production,* 1998. • John Mepham, *Virginia Woolf: A Literary Life,* 1991. • Panthea Reid, *Archives and Art and Affection: A Life of Virginia Woolf,* 1988. • S. P. Rosenbaum, ed., *Virginia Woolf / Women and Fiction: The Manuscript Versions of A Room of One's Own,* 1992. • Sue Roe and Susan Sellers, eds., *The Cambridge Companion to Virginia Woolf,* 2000. • Bonnie Kime Scott, *Refiguring Modernism,* 2 vols., 1995. • Peter Stansky, *On or About December 1910: Early Bloomsbury and Its Intimate World,* 1996. • J. H. Stape, ed., *Virginia Woolf: Interviews and Recollections,* 1995. • Alex Zwerdling, *Virginia Woolf and Real Life,* 1987.

CREDITS

THE ANCIENT WORLD

From *The Discourse on What Is Primary,* Agganna Sutta, translated by Steven Collins. Reprinted by permission of Steven Collins.

Aristotle: "On the Art of Poetry," from *Classical Literary Criticism of Aristotle, Horace, and Longinus,* translated by T. S. Dorsch. Copyright © 1965 by T. S. Dorsch. Reproduced by permission of Penguin Books, Ltd.

Augustine: From *St. Augustine: The Confessions,* translated with an Introduction and Notes by Henry Chadwick. Translation, Copyright © 1991 by Henry Chadwick. Reprinted by permission of Oxford University Press.

"A New Babylonian Theogony and Hesiod," by Wilfred G. Lambert and Peter Walcot, from *Kadmos Zeitschrift für Vor-und Frühgriechische Epigraphik,* Ernst Grumach, Band IV. Reprinted by permission of Walter de Gruyter GmbH & Co.

The Book of Songs: translated by Arthur Waley. Copyright © 1937 by Arthur Waley. Used by permission of Grove/Atlantic, Inc.

The Book of Songs: "In the Wilds there is a dead deer," "In the open grounds there is the creeping grass," and "Heaven protects and secures you," from *The Book of Odes,* translated by Bernhard Karlgren. Reprinted by permission of the Museum of Far Eastern Antiquities, Stockholm, Sweden.

From *The Book of the Dead,* from *Ancient Egyptian Literature: A Book of Readings, Volume II: The New Kingdom* by Miriam Lichtheim. Copyright © 1976 by the Regents of the University of California. Reprinted by permission of the Regents of the University of California and the University of California Press.

Catullus: From *The Poems of Catullus,* translated by Charles Martin. Copyright © 1989 Charles Martin. Reprinted with permission of the Johns Hopkins University Press.

Confucius: From *The Analects of Confucius,* translated by Simon Leys. Copyright © 1997 by Pierre Ryckmans. Used by permission of W. W. Norton & Company, Inc.

The Descent of Ishtar to the Underworld, reprinted from *Myths from Mesopotamia: Creation, The Flood, Gilgamesh and Others,* translated with an introduction by Stephanie Dalley. Copyright © 1989 Stephanie Dalley. Reprinted by permission of Oxford University Press.

Enuma Elish: The Babylonian Creation Epic, reprinted from *Myths from Mesopotamia: Creation, The Flood, Gilgamesh and Others,* translated with an introduction by Stephanie Dalley. Copyright © 1989 Stephanie Dalley. Reprinted by permission of Oxford University Press.

The Epic of Gilgamesh: translated, with an introduction, by Maureen Gallery Kovacs, with the permission of the publishers, Stanford University Press. Copyright © 1985, 1989 by the Board of Trustees of the Leland Stanford Junior University.

Euripides: From *Medea* by Euripides, translated by Rex Warner published by Bodley Head. Used by permission of The Random House Group Limited.

From *Genesis,* Translation and Commentary by Robert Alter. Copyright © 1996 by Robert Alter. Used by permission of W. W. Norton & Company, Inc.

"The Great Hymn to the Aten," from *Ancient Egyptian Literature: A Book of Readings, Volume II: The New Kingdom* by Miriam Lichtheim. Copyright © 1976 by the Regents of the University of California. Reprinted by permission of the Regents of the University of California and the University of California Press.

Herodotus: From *The Histories* by Herodotus, translated by Aubrey De Selincourt, revised by John Marincola. Translation copyright © 1954 by Aubrey De Selincourt. Revised edition copyright © 1996 by John Marincola. Reproduced by permission of Penguin Books, Ltd.

Homer: From *The Odyssey* by Homer, translated by Robert Fagles. Copyright © 1996 by Robert Fagles. Used by permission of Viking Penguin, a division of Penguin Putnam, Inc.

Homer: From *The Iliad* by Homer, translated by Richmond Lattimore. Copyright © 1951 by the University of Chicago. All rights reserved. Reprinted by permission of the University of Chicago Press.

Horace: Reprinted from *Horace: The Complete Odes and Epodes,* translated by David West. Translation copyright © 1997 by David West. Reprinted by permission of Oxford University Press.

Hymns from the Rig Veda: "The Sacrifice of Primal Man" and "In the Beginning," from *Hindu Scripture,* edited by Dominic Goodall. Copyright © 1996 by Dominic Goodall. Reprinted by permission of The Orion Publishing Group, Ltd.

Kafka, Franz: "The Silence of the Sirens" from *Franz Kafka: The Complete Stories,* by Franz Kafka, edited by Nahum N. Glatzer. Copyright © 1946, 1947, 1948, 1949, 1954, 1958, 1971 by Schocken Books. Reprinted by permission of Schocken Books, a division of Random House, Inc.

Letters to the Dead: From *Egyptian Letters to the Dead Mainly From the Old and Middle Kingdoms,* translated by Alan H. Gardiner and Kurt Sethe (London: The Egypt Exploration Society, 1928).

Luke: *The Gospel According to Luke* and *The Acts of the Apostles* from *The Revised Standard Version of the Bible.* Copyright © 1946, 1952, and 1971 by the Division of Christian Education of the National Council of the Churches of Christ in the USA. Used by permission. All rights reserved.

Montaigne, Michel de: Essays, reprinted from *Montaigne: Essays, Travel Journal, Letters,* translated by Donald M. Frame, with permission of the publishers, Stanford University Press. Copyright © 1943 Donald M. Frame. Copyright © 1948, 1957 by the Board of Trustees of the Leland Stanford Junior University.

Ovid: Reprinted from *The Metamorphoses of Ovid,* translated by A. D. Melville. Translation copyright © 1986 by A. D. Melville. Reprinted by permission of Oxford University Press.

Paul: *Epistle to the Romans* from *The Revised Standard Version of the Bible.* Copyright © 1946, 1952, and 1971 by the Division of Christian Education of the National Council of the Churches of Christ in the USA. Used by permission. All rights reserved.

Pawar, Daya: "We are not your Monkeys," by Daya Pawar, Sambhaji Bhagat, and Anand Patwardhan. Reprinted by permission of the authors.

Petronius: From *Petronius: The Satyricon and Seneca: The Apocolocyntoses,* translated by J. P. Sullivan. Copyright © J. P. Sullivan, 1965, 1969, 1974, 1977, 1986. Reproduced by permission of Penguin Books Ltd.

Pizarnik, Alejandra: "Poem," "Lovers," "Recognition," "Meaning of His Absence," "Dawn," and "Falling," translated by Frank Graziano, Maria Rosa Fort, from *Alejandra Pizarnik: A Profile,* edited by Frank Graziano (Logbridge-Rhodes, 1987). Reprinted by permission of Frank Graziano.

Pliny: Reprinted by permission of the publishers and the Trustees of the Loeb Classical Library, from *Pliny: Volume II:* Loeb Classical Library Volume # L059, translated by Betty Radice, pages 285–293, Cambridge, MA: Harvard University Press, 1969. The Loeb Classical Library ® is a registered trademark of the President and the Fellows of Harvard College.

Pound, Ezra: Reprinted by permission of the publisher from *The Confucian Odes: The Classic Anthology Defined by Confucius* by Ezra Pound, Cambridge, MA: Harvard University Press. Copyright © 1954, 1982 by the President and Fellows of Harvard College.

From *Public Address, Varanasi* [The Birthplace of God Cannot be Moved] by Anonymous, translated by Allison Busch. Reprinted by permission of Allison Busch.

Rousseau, Jean-Jacques: From *The Confessions of Jean-Jacques Rousseau,* translated by J. M. Cohen. Copyright © 1954 by J. M. Cohen. Reproduced by permission of Penguin Books Ltd.

Sappho: "Rich-throned immortal Aphrodite," "Come, goddess," "Some think a fleet," "He looks to me to be in heaven," "Love shakes my heart," "Honestly, I wish I were dead," ". . .she worshipped you," "Like a sweet-apple," and "The doorman's feet," by Sappho. Reprinted from *Greek Lyric Poetry,* translated with an introduction and notes by M. L. West. Copyright © 1993 by M. L. West. Reprinted by permission of Oxford University Press.

Seferis, George: "Upon a Foreign Verse," from *George Seferis: Collected Poems 1924–1955*, translated by Edmund Keeley and Philip Sherrard. Copyright © 1967 Princeton University Press. Reprinted by permission of Princeton University Press.

Solon: "Our state will never fall," "The commons I have granted," and "Those aims for which I called the public meeting," by Solon. Reprinted from *Greek Lyric Poetry* translated with an introduction and notes by M. L. West. Copyright © 1993 by M. L. West. Reprinted by permission of Oxford University Press.

The Song of Songs, from *The Jerusalem Bible,* edited by Alexander Jones. Copyright © 1966 by Darton, Longman & Todd, Ltd. and Doubleday, a division of Random House, Inc. Used by permission of Doubleday, a division of Random House, Inc.

Sophocles: *Oedipus the King,* translated by David Grene, from *The Complete Greek Tragedies,* edited by David Grene and Richmond Lattimore. *Oedipus the King* Copyright © 1942 by the University of Chicago. Copyright © 1954 by the University of Chicago. All rights reserved. Reprinted by permission of the University of Chicago Press.

Suetonius: From *Gaius Suetonius Tranquillus, The Twelve Caesars,* translated by Robert Graves. Reprinted by permission of A. P. Watt on behalf of The Trustees of the Robert Graves Copyright Trust.

Tacitus: From *The Annals of Imperial Rome* by Tacitus, translated by Michael Grant. Copyright © 1956, 1959, 1971, 1989 by Michael Grant Publications Ltd. Reproduced by permission of Penguin Books Ltd.

Thucydides: From *The Peloponnesian War,* by Thucydides, translated by Steven Lattimore. Copyright © 1998 Hackett Publishing Company, Inc. Reprinted by permission of Hackett Publishing Company, Inc. All rights reserved.

Valmiki: "The Exile of Rama" from *The Ramayana of Valmiki: An Ancient Epic of India, Vol. II, Ayodhyakanda,* edited by Robert P. Goldman, translated by Sheldon Pollock. Copyright © 1986 Princeton University Press. Reprinted by permission of Princeton University Press.

Valmiki: "The Abduction of Sita" from *The Ramayana of Valmiki: An Ancient Epic of India, Vol. III, Aranyakanda,* edited by Robert P. Goldman, translated by Sheldon Pollock. Copyright © 1991 Princeton University Press. Reprinted by permission of Princeton University Press.

Valmiki: "The Death of Ravana" and "The Fire Ordeal of Sita," from *The Ramayana of Valmiki: An Ancient Epic of India, Vol. VI,* translated by Robert Goldman and Sally Sutherland Goldman, Sarga 96, 97, 103, 104, and 106. Reprinted by permission of Robert Goldman and Sally Sutherland Goldman.

Virgil: From *The Aeneid* by Virgil, translated by Robert Fitzgerald. Copyright © 1980, 1982, 1983 by Robert Fitzgerald. Used by permission of Random House, Inc.

Walcott, Derek: From *Omeros* by Derek Walcott. Copyright © 1990 by Derek Walcott. Reprinted by permission of Farrar, Straus, and Giroux, LLC.

Wei Hong: From "The Preface to the Book of Songs, attributed to Wei Hong," translated by Pauline Yu. Reprinted by permission of Pauline Yu.

THE MEDIEVAL ERA

"Abenámar," translated by William M. Davis, from *An Anthology of Medieval Lyrics,* edited by Angel Flores (New York: The Modern Library, 1962). Reprinted by permission of Barbara Dederick c/o The Permissions Company.

Abu-Nuwas: "My Body is racked with sickness, worn out by exhaustion," *Journal of Arabic Literature,* Vol. XXVII, (Leiden: E. J. Brill, 1996) p. 9. Reprinted by permission of Brill Academic Publishers.

Abu-Nuwas: "Splendid young blades, like lamps in the darkness," as appeared in *Journal of Arabic Literature,* Vol. XXV, (Leiden: E. J. Brill, 1994) pp. 117–119. Reprinted by permission of Brill Academic Publishers.

Abu-Nuwas: "Praise wine in its sweetness," "O censor, I satisfied the Imam," "Bringing the cup of oblivion for sadness," "What's between me and the censurers," "He spoke these verses about a girl named Sammaja," and "One possessed with a rosy cheek," translated by Arthur Wormhoudt, from *The Diwan of Abu Nuwas al Hasan ibn Hani al Hakami,* diss., William Penn College, 1974. Reprinted by permission of Arthur Wormhoudt.

"Ballad of Juliana," translated by Edwin Honig, from *An Anthology of Medieval Lyrics,* edited by Angel Flores (New York: The Modern Library, 1962). Reprinted by permission of Barbara Dederick c/o The Permissions Company.

Beatriz, Comtessa de Dia: "To sing of what I would not want I must," translated by David L. Pike. Reprinted by permission of David L. Pike.

Beowulf, translated by Andrew Sullivan and Timothy Murphy.

Bernart de Ventadorn: "When I see the skylark moving," translated by David L. Pike. Reprinted by permission of David L. Pike.

Bertran de Born: "I love the glad time of Easter," translated by David L. Pike. Reprinted by permission of David L. Pike.

Bo Juyi: "A Song of Unending Sorrow," translated by Witter Bynner, from *Anthology of Chinese Literature,* edited by Cyril Birch. Copyright © 1965 by Grove Press, Inc. Used by permission of Grove/Atlantic, Inc.

Borges, Jorge Luis: "Poem Written in a Copy of Beowulf," translated by Alastair Reid, *Selected Poems: Jorge Luis Borges,* edited by Alexander Coleman. Copyright © 1999 by Alastair Reid. Reprinted by permission of Alastair Reid.

Dante Alighieri: From *The Divine Comedy of Dante Alighieri—Inferno,* by Allen Mandelbaum. Copyright © 1980 by Allen Mandelbaum. Used by permission of Bantam Books, a division of Random House, Inc.

Dom Dinis: From *Songs of a Friend: Love Lyrics of Medieval Portugal,* translated by Barbara Hughes Fowler. Copyright © 1996 by the University of North Carolina Press. Used by permission of the publisher.

Dom Dinis: "Provençals right well may versify," translated by William M. Davis, from *An Anthology of Medieval Lyrics,* edited by Angel Flores (New York: The Modern Library, 1962). Reprinted by permission of Barbara Dederick c/o The Permissions Company.

Du Fu: "Autumn Meditations" and "Yangtse and Han" from *Poems of The Late T'ang,* translated by A. C. Graham. Copyright © 1965 by A. C. Graham. Reproduced with permission of Penguin Books Ltd.

Du Fu: "Spring Prospect" and "Traveling at Night" from *The Reading of Imagery in the Chinese Poetic Tradition,* translated by Pauline Yu. Copyright © 1999 by Pauline Yu. Reprinted by permission of Pauline Yu.

Du Fu: "Moonlit Night" and "Ballad of the Army Carts" from *Three Chinese Poets, Translations of Poems by Wang Wei, Li Bai, and Du Fu* by Vikram Seth. Translation copyright © 1992 by Vikram Seth. Reprinted by permission of HarperCollins Publishers, Inc.

Sir Gawain and the Green Knight, from *Sir Gawain and the Green Knight, Pearl,* J. R. R. Tolkien. Reprinted by permission of Houghton Mifflin Company. All rights

Guillem de Peiteus: "I'll write a verse about nothing," and "In the sweet time of ren Pike. Reprinted by permission of David L. Pike.

Ibn Ishaq: "The Biography of the Prophet," from *The Life of Muhammad: A Transla lah,* translated by A. Guillaume (London: Oxford University Press, 1955).

Li Bo: "The Jewel Stairs' Grievance," by Li Po, translated by Ezra Pound, from *The* copyright © 1963 by Ezra Pound. Reprinted by permission of New Directions Publis

Li Bo: "Sitting Alone by Jiangting Mountain," *The Great Age of Chinese Poetry,* tra published by Yale University Press. Copyright © 1981 Yale University. Reprinted b

Li Bo: "The Road to Shu Is Hard," "In the Quiet Night," "Question and Answer in t Wine," "Listening to a Monk from Shu Playing the Lute," and "Drinking Alone with *nese Poets: Translations of Poems by Wang Wei, Li Bai, and Du Fu* by Vikram S 1992 by Vikram Seth. Reprinted by permission of HarperCollins Publishers, Inc.

Li Bo: "Farewell to a Friend" from *The Reading of Imagery in the Chinese Poetic Trad* Copyright © 1999 by Pauline Yu. Reprinted by permission of Pauline Yu.

Li Bo: "The River Merchant's Wife: A Letter," translated by Ezra Pound, from *Pe* Ezra Pound. Reprinted by permission of New Directions Publishing Corp.

Li Bo: "Fighting South of the Ramparts," translated by Arthur Waley, from *Anth* edited by Cyril Birch. Copyright © 1965 by Grove Press, Inc. Used by permission of

Li Qingzhao: "The wind has ceased" and "Seeking, seeking," from "Li Ch'ing-ch Shattered Worlds," translated by Pauline Yu, from *Comparative Literature Studies,* Copyright © 1983 by The Board of Trustees of the University of Illinois. Repro Pennsylvania State University Press.

Li Qingzhao: "The scent of red lotus fades" translated by Eugene Eoyang, from *W China: An Anthology of Poetry and Criticism,* edited by Kang-i Sun Chang and Hau by the Board of Trustees of the Leland Stanford Junior University. Reprinted by pe sity Press.

Li Yu: From *Lyric Poets of The Southern T'ang: Feng Yen-ssu, 903–960, and Li Yu, 937* right © 1982 The University of British Columbia Press. All rights reserved. Reprinted wi

Llull, Ramon: From *Blanquerna: The Book of the Lover and the Beloved,* transla Dedalus Ltd).

Marie de France: "Prologue," "Bisclavret," and "Chevrefoil," from *The Lais of M* Robert Hanning and Joan Ferrante. Copyright © 1982. Reprinted by permission of the

Martin Codax: "Ah God, if only my love could know" from *The Medieval Lyric,* by Rochester, NY: D.S. Brewer, 1996). Reprinted by permission of Boydell & Brewer,

Martin Codax: From *Songs of a Friend: Love Lyrics of Medieval Portugal* translate Copyright © 1996 by the University of North Carolina Press. Used by permission of

Mozarabic Kharjas: "As if you were a stranger," "Ah tell me, little sisters," "My lord love," and "Take me out of this plight," from *The Medieval Lyric,* by Peter Dronk NY: D. S. Brewer, 1996). Reprinted by permission of Boydell & Brewer, Ltd.

Mozarabic Kharjas: "Mother, I shall not sleep," translated by William M. Davis, fro *Lyrics,* edited by Angel Flores (New York: The Modern Library, 1962). Reprinte Dederick c/o The Permissions Company.

Murasaki Shikibu: From *Murasaki Shikibu: Her Diary and Poetic Memoirs,* tra Copyright © 1995 by Richard Bowring. Reprinted by permission of Richard Bowrin

Murasaki Shikibu: From *The Tale of Genji, Vol I. & Vol. II* by Lady Murasaki Shik Seidensticker, copyright © 1976, copyright renewed 2004 by Edward O. Seidensticke A. Knopf, a division of Random House, Inc.

From *The Saga of King Hrolf Kraki,* translated by Jesse Byock. Copyright © 1998 with permission of Penguin Books Ltd.

Solomon Ibn Gabirol: "Behold the sun at evening," "The mind is flawed," and "Wi rain and showers" from *Wine, Women, and Death: Medieval Hebrew Poems on the* lated by Raymond Scheindlin. Copyright 1986 by The Jewish Publications Society.

Soloman Ibn Gabirol: "She looked at me and her eyelids burned," translated by Wi *thology of Medieval Lyrics,* edited by Angel Flores (New York: The Modern Library, sion of Barbara Dederick c/o The Permissions Company.

"These mountains, mother" and "I will not pick verbena," translated by James Duffy, from *An Anthology of Medieval Lyrics,* edited by Angel Flores (New York: The Modern Library, 1962). Reprinted by permission of Barbara Dederick c/o The Permissions Company.

From *The Thousand and One Nights,* "Prologue: The Story of King Shahrayer and Shahrazad, His Vizier's Daughter," "The Tale of the Ox and the Donkey," and "The Tale of the Merchant and his Wife," from *The Arabian Nights,* translated by Husain Haddawy. Copyright © 1990 by W. W. Norton & Company, Inc. Used by permission of W. W. Norton & Company, Inc.

From *The Book of the Thousand Nights and One Night, Vol. IV,* "The End of Ja'far and the Barmakids," and "Conclusion," translated by J. C. Mardrus and Powys Mathers (St. Martin's Press, 1972). Reprinted by permission of Routledge and Kegan Paul.

From *The Book of the Thousand Nights and One Night, Vol. I,* "The Tale of the Porter and the Young Girls," "The Tale of Zubaidah, the First of the Girls," translated by J.C. Mardrus and Powys Mathers (London: Routledge & Kegan Paul Ltd., 1964). Reprinted by permission of Routledge and Kegan Paul.

From *The Book of the Thousand Nights and One Night, Vol. II,* "The Tale of Sympathy the Learned" and "An Adventure of the Poet Abu Nuwas," translated by J. C. Mardrus and Powys Mathers (London: Routledge & Kegan Paul Ltd., 1964). Reprinted by permission of Routledge and Kegan Paul.

"Three Pretty Moorish Lasses" [Tres Morillas], Anonymous, English translation by Angela Buxton.

Wang Wei: "Meng Wall Cove," "Deer Enclosure," "Sophora Path," "Lake Yi," "Bamboo Lodge," "Bird Call Valley," "Farewell," "Farewell to Yuan," "Visiting the Temple," "Zhongnan Retreat," "In Response ...," from *The Poetry of Wang Wei: New Translations and Commentary,* translated by Pauline Yu. Copyright © 1980 Indiana University Press. Reprinted by permission of the publisher.

Yehuda ha-Levi: "Cups without wine are lowly," translated by William M. Davis, from *An Anthology of Medieval Lyrics,* edited by Angel Flores (New York: The Modern Library, 1962). Reprinted by permission of Barbara Dederick c/o The Permissions Company.

Yehuda ha-Levi: "Your breeze, Western shore, is perfumed" and "My Heart is in the East," from *Hebrew Poems from Spain,* edited and translated by David Goldstein. Copyright © 1965 by David Goldstein. Used by permission of Schocken Books, a division of Random House.

Yehuda ha-Levi: "From time's beginning, You were love's abode," from *The Gazelle: Medieval Hebrew Poems on God, Israel, and the Soul,* edited and translated by Raymond Scheindlin. Copyright 1991 by Ramond P. Scheindlin. Reprinted by permission of The Jewish Publication Society.

Yehuda ha-Levi: "Ofra does her laundry with my tears" and "Once when I fondled him upon my thighs," from *Wine, Women, and Death: Medieval Hebrew Poems on the Good Life,* edited and translated by Raymond Scheindlin. Copyright 1986 by The Jewish Publications Society. Reprinted by permission.

THE EARLY MODERN PERIOD

"The Aztec-Spanish Dialogues of 1524," translated by J. Jorge Klor de Alva, in *Alcheringa/Ethnopoetics* New Series Vol. 4, No. 2. Reprinted by permission of the editor, Dennis Tedlock.

Boccaccio, Giovanni: From *The Decameron* by Giovanni Boccaccio, translated by G. H. McWilliam. Copyright © 1986 G. H. McWilliam. Reproduced by permission of Penguin Books, Ltd.

Borges, Jorge Luis: "Pierre Menard, Author of the *Quixote*" from *Collected Fictions by Jorge Luis Borges*, translated by Andrew Hurley. Copyright © 1998 by Maria Kodama; translation copyright © 1998 by Penguin Putnam Inc. Used by permission of Viking Penguin, a division of Penguin Putnam Inc.

Castiglione, Baldessar: Sonnets, From *The Book of the Courtier* by Baldessar Castiglione, edited by Edgar de N. Mayhew, translated by Charles S. Singleton. Copyright © 1959 by Charles S. Singleton and Edgar de N. Mayhew. Used by permission of Doubleday, a division of Random House, Inc.

Cervantes Saavedra, Miguel de: From *The Adventures of Don Quixote* by Miguel de Cervantes Saavedra, translated by John Rutherford. Translation copyright © 2000 by John Rutherford. Reproduced by permission of Penguin Books, Ltd.

Colonna, Vittoria: From *Women Poets of the Italian Renaissance,* edited by Laura Anna Stortoni, translated by Laura Anna Stortoni and Mary Prentice Lillie (New York: Italica Press, 1997). Copyright © 1997 by Laura Anna Stortoni. Reprinted by permission of Italica Press.

Cruz, Sor Juana Inés de la: From *The Divine Narcissus,* translated by Patricia A. Peters and Renée Domeier. Copyright © 1988 by the University of New Mexico Press. Reprinted by permission of the University of New Mexico Press.

Labé, Louise: From *Three Women Poets: Renaissance and Baroque,* translated by Frank J. Warnke. Copyright © 1987 by Associated University Presses, Inc. Reprinted by permission of the publisher.

Machiavelli, Niccolò: From *Machiavelli's The Prince,* edited and translated by Mark Musa. Copyright © 1969 by Bedford/St. Martin's. Reprinted with permission of Bedford/St. Martin's.

Montaigne, Michel de: From *The Complete Essays of Montaigne,* translated by Donald M. Frame. Copyright © 1958 by the Board of Trustees of the Leland Stanford Junior University. Reprinted with the permission of Stanford University Press, www.sup.org.

Petrarch, Francis: From *Petrarch, The Canzoniere or Rerum Vulgarium Fragmenta,* translated by Mark Musa with Barbara Manfredi. Copyright © 1996 by Mark Musa. Reprinted by permission of the publisher, Indiana University Press.

Shakespeare, William: Sonnets, From *William Shakespeare: The Complete Works by William Shakespeare,* edited by Alfred Harbage. Copyright © 1969 by Penguin Books, Inc. Used by permission of Viking Penguin, a division of Penguin Putnam Inc.

Shakespeare, William: Text and Footnotes for "The Tempest" from *The Complete Works of Shakespeare* 4th ed. by David Bevington. Copyright © 1992 by HarperCollins Publishers. Reprinted by permission of Pearson Education, Inc.

Valmiki: "Hanuman searches for Sita" from *The Ramayana of Valmiki: An Epic of Ancient India, Vol. V, Sundarakanda,* translated by Robert P. Goldman and Sally J. Sutherland Goldman. Copyright © 1996 by Princeton University Press. Reprinted by permission of Princeton University Press.

THE AGE OF ENLIGHTENMENT

Chikamatsu Mon'zaemon: *Love Suicides at Amijima* from *Four Major Plays of Chikamatsu,* translated by Donald Keene. Copyright © 1961 by Columbia University Press. Reprinted with the permission of the publisher.

Matsuo Bashō: Selected Haiku and selections from *The Narrow Road to the Deep North* translated by Haruo Shirane, from *Early Modern Japanese Literature: An Anthology,* edited by Haruo Shirane. Copyright © 2002 by Columbia University Press. Reprinted with the permission of the publisher.

Molière: "The School for Wives" from *Molière, The School for Wives,* translated by Ranjit Bolt. Translation copyright © 1997 by Ranjit Bolt. Reprinted by permission of Oberon Books Ltd.

Montagu, Lady Mary Wortley: "Letter to Alexander Pope," "Letter to Sarah Chiswell," and "Letter to Lady Mar" from *The Complete Letters of Lady Mary Wortley Montagu, Vol. I, 1708–1720* edited by Robert Halsband. Copyright © 1965 by Oxford University Press. Reprinted by permission of Oxford University Press.

Voltaire: *Candide* from *Voltaire: Candide and Other Stories,* translated by Roger Pearson. Translation and editorial material copyright © 1990 by Roger Pearson. Reprinted by permission of Oxford University Press.

Zayas, Maria de: "Forewarned But Not Forearmed," from *The Enchantments of Love, Amorous and Exemplary Novels,* translated by H. Patsy Boyer. Copyright © 1990 The Regents of the University of California. Reprinted by permission of University of California Press.

THE NINETEENTH CENTURY

Ali, Agha Shahid: "Of Snow" from *Call Me Ishmel Tonight* by Agha Shahid Ali. Copyright © 2003 by Agha Shahid Ali Literary Trust. Used by permission of W. W. Norton & Company, Inc., and The Agha Shahid Ali Literary Trust.

Baudelaire, Charles: "To the Reader," "The Albatross," "Correspondences," "The Head of Hair," "Carrion," "Invitation to the Voyage," "Spleen," "The Swan," "In Passing," "Twighlight: Daybreak," "Ragpickers' Wine," "A Martyr," from *Les Fleurs Du Mal* by Charles Baudelaire, translated from the French by Richard Howard. Translation copyright © 1982 by Richard Howard. Reprinted by permission of David R. Godine Publisher, Inc.

Dostoevsky, Fyodor: *Notes from Underground,* from *Notes from Underground & The Grand Inquisitor* by Fyodor Dostoevsky, translated by Ralph E. Matlaw. Copyright © 1960, 1988 by E. P. Dutton. Used by permission of Dutton, a division of Penguin Putnam Inc.

Droste-Hülshoff, Annette Von: "The Man on the Heath" and "In the Grass," translated by Jane K. Brown. Copyright © Jane K. Brown. Printed by permission of Jane K. Brown.

Effendi, Mustafa Sami: From *Avrupa Risalesi* [On the general conditions of Europe], translated by Laurent Magon. Reprinted by permission of Laurent Magon.

Flaubert, Gustave: "A Simple Heart" by Gustave Flaubert, translated by Arthur McDowal, from *Three Stories.* Copyright © 1924 by Alfred A. Knopf, Inc. Reprinted by permission of New Directions Publishing Corporation.

Ghalib: "Ghazal XII" and "Ghazal XVIII," translated by Adrienne Rich, originally appeared in *The Hudson Review,* Volume 22, Number 4, Winter, 1969-70.

Ghalib: Selected poems from *The Lightning Should Have Fallen on Ghalib, Selected Poems of Ghalib,* translated by Robert Bly and Sunil Dutta. Translation copyright © 1999 by Robert Bly and Sunil Dutta. Reprinted by permission of Georges Borchardt, Inc.

Goethe, Johann Wolfgang: From *Faust Part One,* by Johann Wolfgang von Goethe, translated with an introduction by David Luke. Copyright © 1987 by David Luke. Reprinted by permission of Oxford University Press.

Goethe, Johann Wolfgang: From *Faust Part Two,* by Johann Wolfgang von Goethe, translated with an introduction by David Luke. Copyright © 1994 by David Luke. Reprinted by permission of Oxford University Press.

Ishikawa Takuboku: Excerpts from "The Romaji Diary" by Ishikawa Takuboku, from *Modern Japanese Literature,* edited by Donald Keene. Copyright © 1956 by Grove Press, Inc. Reprinted by permission.

Nietzsche, Friedrich: From *Daybreak: Thoughts on the Prejudices of Morality,* translated by R. J. Hollingdale, with introduction by Michael Tanner. Copyright © 1982 by Cambridge University Press. Reprinted by permission of the publisher.

Pushkin, Alexander: "The Bronze Horseman," from *Narrative Poems by Alexander Pushkin and Michael Lermontov,* translated by Charles Johnston. Copyright © 1984 by Charles Johnston. Reprinted by permission of the Charles Johnston Estate.

Tagore, Rabindranath: "Conclusion" from *Rabindranath Tagore An Anthology,* edited by Krishna Dutta and Andrew Robinson. Copyright © 1997 by Krishna Dutta and Andrew Robinson. Reprinted by permission of St. Martin's Press, LLC.

THE TWENTIETH CENTURY

Achebe, Chinua: *Things Fall Apart* by Chinua Achebe. Copyright © 1958 by Chinua Achebe. Reprinted by permission of Heinemann Educational Publishers.

Achebe, Chinua: "The African Writer and the English Language" from *Morning Yet on Creation Day.* Copyright © 1975 by Chinua Achebe. Reprinted by permission of the author.

Ali, Agha Shahid: "The Country Without a Post Office," Copyright © 1997 by Agha Shahid Ali. Used permission of W. W. Norton & Company, Inc.

Beckett, Samuel: *Endgame* by Samuel Beckett. Copyright © 1958 by Grove Press, Inc.; copyright renewed © 1986 by Samuel Beckett. Used by permission of Grove/Atlantic, Inc.

Borges, Jorge Luis: "The Garden of Forking Paths," "The Library of Babel," and "Borges and I," from *Collected Fictions* by Jorge Luis Borges, translated by Andrew Hurley. Copyright © 1998 by Maria Kodama; translation copyright © 1998 by Penguin Putnam Inc. Used by permission of Viking Penguin, a division of Penguin Putnam Inc.

Borges, Jorge Luis: "The Web" by Jorge Luis Borges, from *Selected Poems* by Jorge Luis Borges, translated by Alastair Reid. Copyright © 1999 by Alastair Reid. Reprinted by permission of Alastair Reid.

Cronin, Jeremy: "To learn how to speak ..." from *Inside and Out* by Jeremy Cronin. Copyright © 1999 by Jeremy Cronin. Reprinted by permission of the author.

Darwish, Mahmoud: "A Poem Which Is Not Green, From My Country" and "Diary of a Palestinian Wound" from *Selected Poems* by Mahmoud Darwish, translated by Ian Wedde and Fawwaz Tuqan. Copyright © 1973 by Ian Wedde. Reprinted by permission of Carcanet Press, Ltd.

Darwish, Mahmoud: "Sirhan drinks his coffee ...," and "Birds die in Galilee," from *Sand and Other Poems,* translated by Rana Kabbani. Reprinted by permission of Paul Kegan International, Ltd.

Djebar, Assia: "The Sister" and "Nuptials on a Straw Mat" from *A Sister to Scheherazade,* by Assia Djebar, translated by Dorothy S. Blair. (Portsmouth, NH: Heinemann, 1993).

Eliot, T. S.: "The Love Song of J. Alfred Prufrock" from *Collected Poems 1909–1962* by T. S. Eliot. Reprinted by permission of the publisher, Faber & Faber, Ltd.

Eliot, T. S.: "The Waste Land" from *Collected Poems 1909–1962* by T. S. Eliot. Reprinted by permission of the publisher, Faber & Faber, Ltd.

Kafka, Franz: *The Metamorphosis* by Franz Kafka, translated by Stanley Corngold. Copyright © 1972 by Stanley Corngold. Used by permission of Bantam Books, a division of Random House, Inc.

Kafka, Franz: "Trees" from *Stories 1904–1924,* by Franz Kafka, translated by J. A. Underwood and published by Abacus, a division of Little, Brown & Co. Reprinted by permission of the publisher.

Kafka, Franz: "The Next Village," "The Cares of a Family Man," "On Parables," translated Willa and Edwin Muir, and "Give it Up!," from *The Complete Stories,* edited by Nahum N. Glatzer, copyright © 1946, 1947, 1948, 1949, 1954, 1958, 1971, by Schocken Books. Used by permission of Schocken Books, a division of Random House, Inc.

Levi, Primo: "Two Flags" from *The Mirror Maker: Stories & Essays* by Primo Levi, translated by Raymond Rosenthal, translation copyright © 1989 by Schocken Books. Used by permission of Schocken Books, a division of Random House, Inc.

Levi, Primo: "The Journey" and "The Canto of Ulysses" from *If This Is a Man (Survival in Auschwitz),* by Primo Levi, translated by Stuart Woolf, copyright © 1959 by Orion Press, Inc., ©1958 by Giulio Einaudi editore S.P.A. Used by permission of Viking Penguin, a division of Penguin Putnam, Inc.

Lu Xun: "A Madman's Diary," from *The Complete Stories of Lu Xun,* translated by Yang Xianyi and Gladys Yang. Copyright © 1981 Indiana University Press. Reprinted by permission of the publisher.

Ngal, Mbwil a M.: from *Giambatista Viko,* translated by David Damrosch, (Paris: Hatier, 1984).

Ngugi wa Thiong'o: "The Language of African Literature" from *Decolonising the Mind: The Politics of Language in African Literature.* (Portsmouth, NH: Heinemann, 1986).

ILLUSTRATION CREDITS

Cover image: Seventeenth century world map by Henricus Hondius. Digital Vision/Getty Images. Inside front cover image: AKG, London. Page xxxiv: Musée du Louvre, Paris. Page 9: National Archeological Museum. Photo: akg-images/John Hios. Page 18: Erich Lessing/Art Resource, New York. Page 28: The British Museum. Page 73: The British Museum. Page 119: The British Museum. Page 339: The British Museum. Page 495: Staatliche Antikensammlungen und Glyptothek, Munich. Page 576: Staatliche, Antikensammlungen, Munich. Erich Lessing/Art Resource, New York. Page 610: Amar Chitra/Katha, Bombay. Page 804: Museo della Civilta Romana, Rome, Italy/Bridgeman Art Library. Page 882: Yale University, Beinecke Rare Book and Manuscript Library. Page 891: The Nasser D. Khalili Collection of Islamic Art (CAL 70). Copyright © Nour Foundation. Page 894: Musée de la Tapisserie, Bayeux. Copyright © Giraudon/Art Resource, New York. Page 984: Tokyo National Museum. Page 1162: Institut Amatller D'Art Hispanic. Page 1436: Bibliothèque Nationale de France. Page 1441: Bodleian Library, University of Oxford. Page 1447: Liverpool City Museum/Werner Forman/Art Resource, New York. Page 1490: Scala/Art Resource, New York. Page 1548: Public domain. Page 1731: The Art Archive. Page 1800: Snark/Art Resource, New York. Page 1891: Courtesy of Idemitsu Museum of Arts. Page 2020: Public domain. Page 2030 (top left): The Granger Collection, New York. Page 2030 (top right): Title page from *Sense and Sensibility* by Jane Austen, 1856 edition. Private collection. Page 2030 (bottom left): S. P. Avery Collection. Miriam and Ira D. Wallach Division of Art, Prints, and Photographs. The New York Public Library. Astor, Lenox, and Tilden Foundations. Page 2030 (bottom right): Fair Street Pictures. Page 2065: Leeds Museums and Galleries (City Art Gallery) U.K./The Bridgeman Art Library. Page 2152: Hamburg Kunsthalle, Hamburg, Germany/The Bridgeman Art Library. Page 2229: Public domain. Page 2428: Digital Image © The Museum of Modern Art/ Licensed by SCALA/Art Resource, New York. The Museum of Modern Art, New York. Acquired through the Lillie P. Bliss Bequest (231.1948). Page 2430: David Alfaro Siqueiros (1896–1974) © VAGA, NY. *Echo of a Scream*, 1937. Gift of Edward M. Warburg. Digital Image © The Museum of Modern Art/Licensed by SCALA/Art Resource, New York. The Museum of Modern Art, New York. Page 2435: Figure, "Global shrinkage: the effect of changing transport technologies on real distance," from *The Future of the Future* by John McHale. (New York: Braziller, 1969). Page 2824: Nam June Paik, *Global Encoder*. Photo courtesy Nam June Paik and Carl Solway Gallery, Cincinnati, Ohio. Photo by Chris Gomien and Tom Allison. Inside back cover image: Staatsbibliothek zu Berlin – Preussischer Kulturbesitz, Kartenabteilung; Photo: Ruth Schacht / bpk, Berlin.

FONTS CREDIT

The EuroSlavic, AfroRoman, Macron, TransIndic, Semitic Transliterator, and ANSEL fonts used to publish this work are available from Linguist's Software, Inc., P.O. Box 580, Edmonds, WA 98020-0580 USA, tel (425) 775-1130, www.linguistsoftware.com.

INDEX